Stanley Gibbons
SIMPLIFIED CATALOGUE

Stamps of the World

2006 Edition

IN COLOUR

An illustrated and priced five-volume guide to the postage stamps of the whole world, excluding changes of paper, perforation, shade and watermark

VOLUME 3

COUNTRIES I–M

STANLEY GIBBONS LTD
London and Ringwood

By Appointment to
Her Majesty the Queen
Stanley Gibbons Limited
London
Philatelists

71st Edition

Published in Great Britain by
Stanley Gibbons Ltd
Publications Editorial, Sales Offices and Distribution Centre
Parkside, Christchurch Road,
Ringwood, Hampshire BH24 3SH
Telephone 01425 472363

ISBN: 085259-606-5

Published as Stanley Gibbons Simplified Stamp Catalogue from 1934 to 1970, renamed Stamps of the World in 1971, and produced in two (1982-88), three (1989-2001), four (2002-2005) or five (from 2006) volumes as Stanley Gibbons Simplified Catalogue of Stamps of the World.
This volume published October 2005

S.G. Item No. 2883 (06)

Printed in Great Britain by CPI Bath Press, Somerset

Stanley Gibbons SIMPLIFIED CATALOGUE

Stamps of the World

This popular catalogue is a straightforward listing of the stamps that have been issued everywhere in the world since the very first–Great Britain's famous Penny Black in 1840.

This edition, in which both the text and the illustrations have been captured electronically, is arranged completely alphabetically in a five-volume format. Volume 1 (Countries A–C), Volume 2 (Countries D–H), Volume 3 (Countries I–M), Volume 4 (Countries N–R) and Volume 5 (Countries S-Z).

Readers are reminded that the Catalogue Supplements, published in each issue of **Gibbons Stamp Monthly**, can be used to update the listings in **Stamps of the World** as well as our 22-part standard catalogue. To make the supplement even more useful the Type numbers given to the illustrations are the same in the Stamps of the World as in the standard catalogues. The first Catalogue Supplement to this Volume appeared in the September 2005 issue of **Gibbons Stamp Monthly**.

Gibbons Stamp Monthly can be obtained through newsagents or on postal subscription from Stanley Gibbons Publications, Parkside, Christchurch Road, Ringwood, Hants BH24 3SH.

The catalogue has many important features:

- The vast majority of illustrations are now in full colour to aid stamp identification.
- All Commonwealth and all Europe and Asia miniature sheets are now included.
- As an indication of current values virtually every stamp is priced. Thousands of alterations have been made since the last edition.
- By being set out on a simplified basis that excludes changes of paper, perforation, shade, watermark, gum or printer's and date imprints it is particularly easy to use. (For its exact scope see "Information for users" pages following.)
- The thousands of colour illustrations and helpful descriptions of stamp designs make it of maximum appeal to collectors with thematic interests.
- Its catalogue numbers are the world-recognised Stanley Gibbons numbers throughout.
- Helpful introductory notes for the collector are included, backed by much historical, geographical and currency information.
- A very detailed index gives instant location of countries in this volume, and a cross-reference to those included in the other volumes.

Over 4,500 stamps and miniature sheets and 490 new illustrations have been added to the listings in this volume.

The listings in this edition are based on the standard catalogues: Part 1, Commonwealth & British Empire Stamps 1840–1952, Part 2 (Austria & Hungary) (6th edition), Part 3 (Balkans) (4th edition), Part 4 (Benelux) (5th edition), Part 5 (Czechoslovakia & Poland) (6th edition), Part 6 (France) (5th edition), Part 7 (Germany) (6th edition), Part 8 (Italy & Switzerland) (6th edition), Part 9 (Portugal & Spain) (5th edition), Part 10 (Russia) (5th edition), Part 11 (Scandinavia) (5th edition), Part 12 (Africa since Independence A-E) (2nd edition), Part 13 (Africa since Independence F-M) (1st edition), Part 14 (Africa since Independence N-Z) (1st edition), Part 15 (Central America) (2nd edition), Part 16 (Central Asia) (3rd edition), Part 17 (China) (6th edition), Part 18 (Japan & Korea) (4th edition), Part 19 (Middle East) (6th edition), Part 20 (South America) (3rd edition), Part 21 (South-East Asia) (4th edition) and Part 22 (United States) (5th edition).

This edition includes major repricing for some Europe countries in addition to the changes for Germany Part 7, Portugal and Spain Part 9 and Middle East Part 19.

Acknowledgements

A wide-ranging revision of prices for European countries has been undertaken for this edition with the intention that the catalogue should be more accurate to reflect the market for foreign issues.

Many dealers in both Great Britain and overseas have participated in this scheme by supplying copies of their retail price lists on which the research has been based.

We would like to acknowledge the assistance of the following for this edition:

ALMAZ CO
of Brooklyn, U.S.A.

AMATEUR COLLECTOR LTD, THE
of London, England

AVION THEMATICS
of Nottingham, England

J BAREFOOT LTD
of York, England

Sir CHARLES BLOMEFIELD
of Chipping Camden, England

T. BRAY
of Shipley, West Yorks, England

CENTRAL PHILATELIQUE
of Brussels, Belgium

EUROPEAN & FOREIGN STAMPS
of Pontypridd, Wales

FILATELIA LLACH SL
of Barcelona, Spain

FILATELIA RIVA RENO
of Bologna, Italy

FILATELIA TORI
of Barcelona, Spain

FORMOSA STAMP COMPANY, THE
of Koahsiung, Taiwan

HOLMGREN STAMPS
of Bollnas, Sweden

INDIGO
of Orewa, New Zealand

ALEC JACQUES
of Selby, England

M. JANKOWSKI
of Warsaw, Poland

D.J.M. KERR
of Earlston, England

LEO BARESCH LTD
of Hassocks, England

LORIEN STAMPS
of Chesterfield, England

MANDARIN TRADING CO
of Alhambra, U.S.A.

MICHAEL ROGERS INC
of Winter Park, U.S.A.

NORAYR AGOPIAN
of Lymassol, Cyprus

PHIL-INDEX
of Eastbourne, England

PHILTRADE A/S
of Copenhagen, Denmark

PITTERI SA
of Chiasso, Switzerland

KEVIN RIGLER
of Shifnal, England

ROLF GUMMESSON AB
of Stockholm, Sweden

R. D. TOLSON
of Undercliffe, England

R. SCHNEIDER
of Belleville, U.S.A.

ROBSTINE STAMPS
of Hampshire, England

ROWAN S BAKER
of London, England

REX WHITE
of Winchester, England

Where foreign countries have been repriced this year in Stamps of the World and where there is no up-to-date specialised foreign volume in a country these will be the new Stanley Gibbons prices.

It is hoped that this improved pricing scheme will be extended to other foreign countries and thematic issues as information is consolidated.

Information for users

Aim

The aim of this catalogue is to provide a straightforward illustrated and priced guide to the postage stamps of the whole world to help you to enjoy the greatest hobby of the present day.

Arrangement

The catalogue lists countries in alphabetical order and there is a complete index at the end of each volume. For ease of reference country names are also printed at the head of each page.

Within each country, postage stamps are listed first. They are followed by separate sections for such other categories as postage due stamps, parcel post stamps, express stamps, official stamps, etc.

All catalogue lists are set out according to dates of issue of the stamps, starting from the earliest and working through to the most recent.

Scope of the Catalogue

The *Simplified Catalogue of Stamps of the World* contains listings of postage stamps only. Apart from the ordinary definitive, commemorative and airmail stamps of each country – which appear first in each list – there are sections for the following where appropriate:

- postage due stamps
- parcel post stamps
- official stamps
- express and special delivery stamps
- charity and compulsory tax stamps
- newspaper and journal stamps
- printed matter stamps
- registration stamps
- acknowledgement of receipt stamps
- late fee and too late stamps
- military post stamps
- recorded message stamps
- personal delivery stamps

We receive numerous enquiries from collectors about other items which do not fall within the categories set out above and which consequently do not appear in the catalogue lists. It may be helpful, therefore, to summarise the other kinds of stamp that exist but which we deliberately exclude from this postage stamp catalogue.

We do *not* list the following:

Fiscal or revenue stamps: stamps used solely in collecting taxes or fees for non-postal purposes. Examples would be stamps which pay a tax on a receipt, represent the stamp duty on a contract or frank a customs document. Common inscriptions found include: Documentary, Proprietary, Inter. Revenue, Contract Note.

Local stamps: postage stamps whose validity and use are limited in area, say to a single town or city, though in some cases they provided, with official sanction, services in parts of countries not covered by the respective government.

Local carriage labels and Private local issues: many labels exist ostensibly to cover the cost of ferrying mail from one of Great Britain's offshore islands to the nearest mainland post office. They are not recognised as valid for national or international mail. Examples: Calf of Man, Davaar, Herm, Lundy, Pabay, Stroma. Items from some other places have only the status of tourist souvenir labels.

Telegraph stamps: stamps intended solely for the prepayment of telegraphic communication.

Bogus or "phantom" stamps: labels from mythical places or non-existent administrations. Examples in the classical period were Sedang, Counani, Clipperton Island and in modern times Thomond and Monte Bello Islands. Numerous labels have also appeared since the War from dissident groups as propaganda for their claims and without authority from the home governments. Common examples are labels for "Free Albania", "Free Rumania" and "Free Croatia" and numerous issues for Nagaland, Indonesia and the South Moluccas ("Republik Maluku Selatan").

Railway letter fee stamps: special stamps issued by railway companies for the conveyance of letters by rail. Example: Talyllyn Railway. Similar services are now offered by some bus companies and the labels they issue likewise do not qualify for inclusion in the catalogue.

Perfins ("perforated initials"): numerous postage stamps may be found with initial letters or designs punctured through them by tiny holes. These are applied by private and public concerns as a precaution against theft and do not qualify for separate mention.

Information for users

Labels: innumerable items exist resembling stamps but – as they do not prepay postage – they are classified as labels. The commonest categories are:

- propaganda and publicity labels: designed to further a cause or campaign;
- exhibition labels: particularly souvenirs from philatelic events;
- testing labels: stamp-size labels used in testing stamp-vending machines;
- Post Office training school stamps: British stamps overprinted with two thick vertical bars or SCHOOL SPECIMEN are produced by the Post Office for training purposes;
- seals and stickers: numerous charities produce stamp-like labels, particularly at Christmas and Easter, as a means of raising funds and these have no postal validity.

Cut-outs: items of postal stationery, such as envelopes, cards and wrappers, often have stamps impressed or imprinted on them. They may usually be cut out and affixed to envelopes, etc., for postal use if desired, but such items are not listed in this catalogue.

Collectors wanting further information about exact definitions are referred to *Philatelic Terms Illustrated,* published by Stanley Gibbons and containing many illustrations in colour.

There is also a priced listing of the postal fiscals of Great Britain in our *Commonwealth & British Empire Stamps 1840–1952* Catalogue and in Volume 1 of the *Great Britain Specialised* Catalogue (5th and later editions).

Prices are shown as follows:

10 means 10p (10 pence);
1.50 means £1.50 (1 pound and 50 pence);
For £100 and above, prices are in whole pounds.

Our prices are for stamps in fine condition, and in issues where condition varies we may ask more for the superb and less for the sub-standard.

The minimum catalogue price quoted is 10p. For individual stamps prices between 10p and 45p are provided as a guide for catalogue users. The lowest price charged for individual stamps purchased from Stanley Gibbons is £1.00.

The prices quoted are generally for the cheapest variety of stamps but it is worth noting that differences of watermark, perforation, or other details, outside the scope of this catalogue, may often increase the value of the stamp.

Prices quoted for mint issues are for single examples. Those in se-tenant pairs, strips, blocks or sheets may be worth more.

Where prices are not given in either column it is either because the stamps are not known to exist in that particular condition, or, more usually, because there is no reliable information as to value.

All prices are subject to change without prior notice and we give no guarantee to supply all stamps priced. Prices quoted for albums, publications, etc. advertised in this catalogue are also subject to change without prior notice.

Due to different production methods it is sometimes possible for new editions of Parts 2 to 22 to appear showing revised prices which are not included in that year's *Stamps of the World.*

Catalogue Numbers

Stanley Gibbons catalogue numbers are recognised universally and any individual stamp can be identified by quoting the catalogue number (the one at the left of the column) prefixed by the name of the country and the letters "S.G.". Do not confuse the catalogue number with the type numbers which refer to illustrations.

Prices

Prices in the left-hand column are for unused stamps and those in the right-hand column for used. Prices are given in pence and pounds:

100 pence (p) 1 pound (£1).

Unused Stamps

In the case of stamps from *Great Britain* and the *Commonwealth*, prices for unused stamps of Queen Victoria to King George V are for lightly hinged examples; unused prices of King Edward VIII to Queen Elizabeth II issues are for unmounted mint. The prices of unused Foreign stamps are for lightly hinged examples for those issued before 1946, thereafter for examples unmounted mint.

Used Stamps

Prices for used stamps generally refer to fine postally used examples, though for certain issues they are for cancelled-to-order.

Information for users

Guarantee

All stamps supplied by us are guaranteed originals in the following terms:

If not as described, and returned by the purchaser, we undertake to refund the price paid to us in the original transaction. If any stamp is certified as genuine by the Expert Committee of the Royal Philatelic Society, London, or by B.P.A. Expertising Ltd., the purchaser shall not be entitled to make any claim against us for any error, omission or mistake in such certificate.

Consumers' statutory rights are not affected by the above guarantee.

Currency

At the beginning of each country brief details give the currencies in which the values of the stamps are expressed. The dates, where given, are those of the earliest stamp issues in the particular currency. Where the currency is obvious, e.g. where the colony has the same currency as the mother country, no details are given.

Illustrations

Illustrations of any surcharges and overprints which are shown and not described are actual size; stamp illustrations are reduced to $\frac{3}{4}$ linear, *unless otherwise stated.*

"Key-Types"

A number of standard designs occur so frequently in the stamps of the French, German, Portuguese and Spanish colonies that it would be a waste of space to repeat them. Instead these are all illustrated on page xiv together with the descriptive names and letters by which they are referred to in the lists.

Type Numbers

These are the bold figures found below each illustration. References to "Type **6**", for example, in the lists of a country should therefore be understood to refer to the illustration below which the number **"6"** appears. These type numbers are also given in the second column of figures alongside each list of stamps, thus indicating clearly the design of each stamp. In the case of Key-Types – see above – letters take the place of the type numbers.

Where an issue comprises stamps of similar design, represented in this catalogue by one illustration, the corresponding type numbers should be taken as indicating this general design.

Where there are blanks in the type number column it means that the type of the corresponding stamps is that shown by the last number above in the type column of the same issue.

A dash (–) in the type column means that no illustration of the stamp is shown.

Where type numbers refer to stamps of another country, e.g. where stamps of one country are overprinted for use in another, this is always made clear in the text.

Stamp Designs

Brief descriptions of the subjects of the stamp designs are given either below or beside the illustrations, at the foot of the list of the issue concerned, or in the actual lists. Where a particular subject, e.g. the portrait of a well-known monarch, recurs frequently the description is not repeated, nor are obvious designs described.

Generally, the unillustrated designs are in the same shape and size as the one illustrated, except where otherwise indicated.

Surcharges and Overprints

Surcharges and overprints are usually described in the headings to the issues concerned. Where the actual wording of a surcharge or overprint is given it is shown in bold type.

Some stamps are described as being "Surcharged in words", e.g. **TWO CENTS**, and others "Surcharged in figures and words", e.g. **20 CENTS**, although of course many surcharges are in foreign languages and combinations of words and figures are numerous. There are often bars, etc., obliterating old values or inscriptions but in general these are only mentioned where it is necessary to avoid confusion.

No attention is paid in this catalogue to colours of overprints and surcharges so that stamps with the same overprints in different colours are not listed separately.

Numbers in brackets after the descriptions of overprinted or surcharged stamps are the catalogue numbers of the unoverprinted stamps.

Note – the words "inscribed" or "inscription" always refer to wording incorporated in the design of a stamp and not surcharges or overprints.

Coloured Papers

Where stamps are printed on coloured paper the description is given as e.g. "4 c. black on blue" – a stamp printed in black on blue paper. No attention is paid in this catalogue to difference in the texture of paper, e.g. laid, wove.

Information for users

Watermarks

Stamps having different watermarks, but otherwise the same, are not listed separately. No reference is therefore made to watermarks in this volume.

Stamp Colours

Colour names are only required for the identification of stamps, therefore they have been made as simple as possible. Thus "scarlet", "vermilion", "carmine" are all usually called red. Qualifying colour names have been introduced only where necessary for the sake of clearness.

Where stamps are printed in two or more colours the central portion of the design is in the first colour given, unless otherwise stated.

Perforations

All stamps are perforated unless otherwise stated. No distinction is made between the various gauges of perforation but early stamp issues which exist both imperforate and perforated are usually listed separately.

Where a heading states "Imperf. or perf". or "Perf. or rouletted" this does not necessarily mean that all values of the issue are found in both conditions.

Dates of Issue

The date given at the head of each issue is that of the appearance of the earliest stamp in the series. As stamps of the same design or issue are usually grouped together a list of King George VI stamps, for example, headed "1938" may include stamps issued from 1938 to the end of the reign.

Se-tenant Pairs

Many modern issues are printed in sheets containing different designs or face values. Such pairs, blocks, strips or sheets are described as being "se-tenant" and they are outside the scope of this catalogue, although reference to them may occur in instances where they form a composite design.

Miniature Sheets

As an increasing number of stamps are now only found in miniature sheets, Stamps of the World will, in future, list these items. This edition lists all Commonwealth, European and Asian countries' miniature sheets, plus those of all other countries which have appeared in the catalogue supplement during the past three years. Earlier miniature sheets of non-Commonwealth countries will be listed in future editions.

"Appendix" Countries

We regret that, since 1968, it has been necessary to establish an Appendix (at the end of each country as appropriate) to which numerous stamps have had to be consigned. Several countries imagine that by issuing huge quantities of unnecessary stamps they will have a ready source of income from stamp collectors – and particularly from the less-experienced ones. Stanley Gibbons refuse to encourage this exploitation of the hobby and we do not stock the stamps concerned.

Two kinds of stamp are therefore given the briefest of mentions in the Appendix, purely for the sake of record. Administrations issuing stamps greatly in excess of true postal needs have the offending issues placed there. Likewise it contains stamps which have not fulfilled all the normal conditions for full catalogue listing.

These conditions are that the stamps must be issued by a legitimate postal authority, recognised by the government concerned, and are adhesives, valid for proper postal use in the class of service for which they are inscribed. Stamps, with the exception of such categories as postage dues and officials, must be available to the general public at face value with no artificial restrictions being imposed on their distribution.

The publishers of this catalogue have observed, with concern, the proliferation of 'artificial' stamp-issuing territories. On several occasions this has resulted in separately inscribed issues for various component parts of otherwise united states or territories.

Stanley Gibbons Publications have decided that where such circumstances occur, they will not, in the future, list these items in the SG catalogue without first satisfying themselves that the stamps represent a genuine political, historical or postal division within the country concerned. Any such issues which do not fulfil this stipulation will be recorded in the Catalogue Appendix only.

Stamps in the Appendix are kept under review in the light of any newly acquired information about them. If we are satisfied that a stamp qualifies for proper listing in the body of the catalogue it is moved there.

Information for users

"Undesirable Issues"

The rules governing many competitive exhibitions are set by the Federation Internationale de Philatelie and stipulate a downgrading of marks for stamps classed as "undesirable issues".

This catalogue can be taken as a guide to status. All stamps in the main listings and Addenda are acceptable. Stamps in the Appendix should not be entered for competition as these are the "undesirable issues".

Particular care is advised with Aden Protectorate States, Ajman, Bhutan, Chad, Fujeira, Khor Fakkan, Manama, Ras al Khaima, Sharjah, Umm al Qiwain and Yemen. Totally bogus stamps exist (as explained in Appendix notes) and these are to be avoided also for competition. As distinct from "undesirable stamps" certain categories are not covered in this catalogue purely by reason of its scope (see page viii). Consult the particular competition rules to see if such are admissable even though not listed by us.

Where to Look for More Detailed Listings

The present work deliberately omits details of paper, perforation, shade and watermark. But as you become more absorbed in stamp collecting and wish to get greater enjoyment from the hobby you may well want to study these matters.

All the information you require about any particular postage stamp will be found in the main Stanley Gibbons Catalogues.

Commonwealth countries before 1952 are covered by the Commonwealth & British Empire Stamps 1840–1952 published annually.

For foreign countries you can easily find which catalogue to consult by looking at the country headings in the present book.

To the right of each country name are code letters specifying which volume of our main catalogues contains that country's listing.

The code letters are as follows:

Pt. 2 Part 2

Pt. 3 Part 3 etc.

(See page xiii for complete list of Parts.)

So, for example, if you want to know more about Chinese stamps than is contained in the *Simplified Catalogue of Stamps of the World* the reference to

CHINA Pt. 17

guides you to the Gibbons Part 17 *(China)* Catalogue listing for the details you require.

New editions of Parts 2 to 22 appear at irregular intervals.

Correspondence

Whilst we welcome information and suggestions we must ask correspondents to include the cost of postage for the return of any stamps submitted plus registration where appropriate. Letters should be addressed to The Catalogue Editor at Ringwood.

Where information is solicited purely for the benefit of the enquirer we regret we cannot undertake to reply.

Identification of Stamps

We regret we do not give opinions as to the genuineness of stamps, nor do we identify stamps or number them by our Catalogue.

Users of this catalogue are referred to our companion booklet entitled *Stamp Collecting – How to Identify Stamps.* It explains how to look up stamps in this catalogue, contains a full checklist of stamp inscriptions and gives help in dealing with unfamiliar scripts.

Stanley Gibbons would like to complement your collection

At Stanley Gibbons we offer a range of services which are designed to complement your collection.

Our modern stamp shop, the largest in Europe, together with our rare stamp department has one of the most comprehensive stocks of Great Britain in the world, so whether you are a beginner or an experienced philatelist you are certain to find something to suit your special requirements.

Alternatively, through our Mail Order services you can control the growth of your collection from the comfort of your own home. Our Postal Sales Department regularly sends out mailings of Special Offers. We can also help with your wants list—so why not ask us for those elusive items?

Why not take advantage of the many services we have to offer? Visit our premises in the Strand or, for more information, write to the appropriate address on page x.

The Stanley Gibbons Group Addresses

Stanley Gibbons Limited,
Stanley Gibbons Auctions

339 Strand, London WC2R 0LX
Telephone 020 7836 8444, Fax 020 7836 7342,
E-mail: enquiries@stanleygibbons.co.uk
Website: www.stanleygibbons.com for all departments.

Auction Room and Specialist Stamp Departments.
Open Monday–Friday 9.30 a.m. to 5 p.m.

Shop. Open Monday–Friday 9 a.m. to 5.30 p.m. and Saturday 9.30 a.m. to 5.30 p.m.

Stanley Gibbons Publications

Parkside, Christchurch Road, Ringwood, Hants BH24 3SH.
Telephone 01425 472363 (24 hour answer phone service), Fax 01425 470247,
E-mail: info@stanleygibbons.co.uk
Website: www.stanleygibbons.com

Publications Mail Order. FREEPHONE 0800 611622
Monday–Friday 8.30 a.m. to 5 p.m.

Fraser's Autographs, photographs, letters, documents

399 Strand, London WC2R 0LX
Autographs, photographs, letters and documents

Telephone 020 7836 8444, Fax 020 7836 7342,
E-mail: info@frasersautographs.co.uk
Website: www.frasersautographs.com

Monday–Friday 9 a.m. to 5.30 p.m. and Saturday 10 a.m. to 4 p.m.

Stanley Gibbons Publications Overseas Representation

Stanley Gibbons Publications are represented overseas by the following sole distributors (*), distributors (**) or licensees (***).

Australia
Lighthouse Philatelic (Aust.) Pty. Ltd.*
Locked Bag 5900 Botany DC, New South Wales, 2019 Australia.

Stanley Gibbons (Australia) Pty. Ltd.***
Level 6, 36 Clarence Street, Sydney, New South Wales 2000, Australia.

Belgium and Luxembourg**
Davo c/o Philac, Rue du Midi 48, Bruxelles, 1000 Belgium.

Canada*
Lighthouse Publications (Canada) Ltd., 255 Duke Street, Montreal Quebec, Canada H3C 2M2.

Denmark**
Samlerforum/Davo, Ostergade 3, DK 7470 Karup, Denmark.

Finland**
Davo c/o Kapylan Merkkiky Pohjolankatu 1 00610 Helsinki, Finland.

France*
Davo France (Casteilla), 10, Rue Leon Foucault, 78184 St. Quentin Yvelines Cesex, France.

Hong Kong**
Po-on Stamp Service, GPO Box 2498, Hong Kong.

Israel**
Capital Stamps, P.O. Box 3769, Jerusalem 91036, Israel.

Italy*
Ernesto Marini Srl, Via Struppa 300, I-16165, Genova GE, Italy.

Japan**
Japan Philatelic Co. Ltd., P.O. Box 2, Suginami-Minami, Tokyo, Japan.

Netherlands*
Davo Publications, P.O. Box 411, 7400 AK Deventer, Netherlands.

New Zealand***
Mowbray Collectables.
P.O. Box 80, Wellington, New Zealand.

Norway**
Davo Norge A/S, P.O. Box 738 Sentrum, N-0105, Oslo, Norway.

Singapore**
Stamp Inc Collectibles Pte Ltd., 10 Ubi Cresent, #01-43 Ubi Tech Park, Singapore 408564.

Sweden*
Chr Winther Soerensen AB, Box 43, S-310 Knaered, Sweden.

Abbreviations

Anniv.	denotes	Anniversary
Assn.	"	Association
Bis.	"	Bistre
Bl.	"	Blue
Bldg.	"	Building
Blk.	"	Black
Br.	"	British or Bridge
Brn.	"	Brown
B.W.I.	"	British West Indies
C.A.R.I.F.T.A.	"	Caribbean Free Trade Area
Cent.	"	Centenary
Chest.	"	Chestnut
Choc.	"	Chocolate
Clar.	"	Claret
Coll.	"	College
Commem.	"	Commemoration
Conf.	"	Conference
Diag.	"	Diagonally
E.C.A.F.E.	"	Economic Commission for Asia and Far East
Emer.	"	Emerald
E.P.T. Conference	"	European Postal and Telecommunications Conference
Exn.		Exhibition
F.A.O.	"	Food and Agriculture Organization
Fig.	"	Figure
G.A.T.T.	"	General Agreement on Tariffs and Trade
G.B.	"	Great Britain
Gen.	"	General
Govt.	"	Government
Grn.	"	Green
Horiz.	"	Horizontal
H.Q.	"	Headquarters
Imperf.	"	Imperforate
Inaug.	"	Inauguration
Ind.	"	Indigo
Inscr.	"	Inscribed or inscription
Int.	"	International
I.A.T.A.	"	International Air Transport Association
I.C.A.O.	"	International Civil Aviation Organization
I.C.Y.	"	International Co-operation Year
I.G.Y.	"	International Geophysical Year
I.L.O.	"	International Labour Office (or later, Organization)
I.M.C.O.	"	Inter-Governmental Maritime Consultative Organization
I.T.U.	"	International Telecommunication Union
Is.	"	Islands
Lav.	"	Lavender
Mar.	"	Maroon
mm.	"	Millimetres
Mult.	"	Multicoloured
Mve.	denotes	Mauve
Nat.	"	National
N.A.T.O.	"	North Atlantic Treaty Organization
O.D.E.C.A.	"	Organization of Central American States
Ol.	"	Olive
Optd.	"	Overprinted
Orge. or oran.	"	Orange
P.A.T.A.	"	Pacific Area Travel Association
Perf.	"	Perforated
Post.	"	Postage
Pres.	"	President
P.U.	"	Postal Union
Pur.	"	Purple
R.	"	River
R.S.A.	"	Republic of South Africa
Roul.	"	Rouletted
Sep.	"	Sepia
S.E.A.T.O.	"	South East Asia Treaty Organization
Surch.	"	Surcharged
T.	"	Type
T.U.C.	"	Trades Union Congress
Turq.	"	Turquoise
Ultram.	"	Ultramarine
U.N.E.S.C.O.	"	United Nations Educational, Scientific Cultural Organization
U.N.I.C.E.F.	"	United Nations Children's Fund
U.N.O.	"	United Nations Organization
U.N.R.W.A.	"	United Nations Relief and Works Agency for Palestine Refugees in the Near East
U.N.T.E.A.	"	United Nations Temporary Executive Authority
U.N.R.R.A.	"	United Nations Relief and Rehabilitation Administration
U.P.U.	"	Universal Postal Union
Verm.	"	Vermilion
Vert.	"	Vertical
Vio.	"	Violet
W.F.T.U.	"	World Federation of Trade Unions
W.H.O.	"	World Health Organization
Yell.	"	Yellow

Arabic Numerals

As in the case of European figures, the details of the Arabic numerals vary in different stamp designs, but they should be readily recognised with the aid of this illustration:

٠	١	٢	٣	٤
0	1	2	3	4
٥	٦	٧	٨	٩
5	6	7	8	9

Stanley Gibbons Stamp Catalogue
Complete List of Parts

1 Commonwealth & British Empire Stamps 1840–1952 (Annual)

Foreign Countries

2 Austria & Hungary (6th edition, 2002)
Austria · U.N. (Vienna) · Hungary

3 Balkans (4th edition, 1998)
Albania · Bosnia & Herzegovina · Bulgaria · Croatia · Greece & Islands · Macedonia · Rumania · Slovenia · Yugoslavia

4 Benelux (5th edition, 2003)
Belgium & Colonies · Luxembourg · Netherlands & Colonies

5 Czechoslovakia & Poland (6th edition, 2002)
Czechoslovakia · Czech Republic · Slovakia · Poland

6 France (5th edition, 2001)
France · Colonies · Post Offices · Andorra · Monaco

7 Germany (6th edition, 2002)
Germany · States · Colonies · Post Offices

8 Italy & Switzerland (6th edition, 2003)
Italy & Colonies · Liechtenstein · San Marino · Switzerland · U.N. (Geneva) · Vatican City

9 Portugal & Spain (5th edition, 2004)
Andorra · Portugal & Colonies · Spain & Colonies

10 Russia (5th edition, 1999)
Russia · Armenia · Azerbaijan · Belarus · Estonia · Georgia · Kazakhstan · Kyrgyzstan · Latvia · Lithuania · Moldova · Tajikistan · Turkmenistan · Ukraine · Uzbekistan · Mongolia

11 Scandinavia (5th edition, 2001)
Aland Islands · Denmark · Faroe Islands · Finland · Greenland · Iceland · Norway · Sweden

12 Africa since Independence A-E (2nd edition, 1983)
Algeria · Angola · Benin · Burundi · Cameroun · Cape Verdi · Central African Republic · Chad · Comoro Islands · Congo · Djibouti · Equatorial Guinea · Ethiopia

13 Africa since Independence F-M (1st edition, 1981)
Gabon · Guinea · Guinea-Bissau · Ivory Coast · Liberia · Libya · Malagasy Republic · Mali · Mauritania · Morocco · Mozambique

14 Africa since Independence N-Z (1st edition, 1981)
Niger Republic · Rwanda · St. Thomas & Prince · Senegal · Somalia · Sudan · Togo · Tunisia · Upper Volta · Zaire

15 Central America (2nd edition, 1984)
Costa Rica · Cuba · Dominican Republic · El Salvador · Guatemala · Haiti · Honduras · Mexico · Nicaragua · Panama

16 Central Asia (3rd edition, 1992)
Afghanistan · Iran · Turkey

17 China (6th edition,1998)
China · Taiwan · Tibet · Foreign P.O.s · Hong Kong · Macao

18 Japan & Korea (4th edition, 1997)
Japan · Korean Empire · South Korea · North Korea

19 Middle East (6th edition, 2005)
Bahrain · Egypt · Iraq · Israel · Jordan · Kuwait · Lebanon · Oman · Qatar · Saudi Arabia · Syria · U.A.E. · Yemen

20 South America (3rd edition, 1989)
Argentina · Bolivia · Brazil · Chile · Colombia · Ecuador · Paraguay · Peru · Surinam · Uruguay · Venezuela

21 South-East Asia (4th edition, 2004)
Bhutan · Burma · Indonesia · Kampuchea · Laos · Nepal · Philippines · Thailand · Vietnam

22 United States (5th edition, 2000)
U.S. & Possessions · Marshall Islands · Micronesia · Palau · U.N. (New York, Geneva, Vienna)

Thematic Catalogues

Stanley Gibbons Catalogues for use with **Stamps of the World.**
Collect Aircraft on Stamps (out of print)
Collect Birds on Stamps (5th edition, 2003)
Collect Chess on Stamps (2nd edition, 1999)
Collect Fish on Stamps (1st edition, 1999)
Collect Fungi on Stamps (2nd edition, 1997)
Collect Motor Vehicles on Stamps (1st edition, 2004)
Collect Railways on Stamps (3rd edition, 1999)
Collect Shells on Stamps (1st edition, 1995)
Collect Ships on Stamps (3rd edition, 2001)

Key-Types

(see note on page vii)

French Group

A. "Blanc."

B. "Mouchon."

C "Merson."

D. "Tablet."

E.

F.

G.

H.

"International Colonial Exhibition."

I. "Faidherbe."

J. "Palms."

K. "Balay."

L. "Natives."

M. "Figure."

German Group

N. "Yacht."

O. "Yacht."

Spanish Group

X. "Alfonso XII."

Y. "Baby."

Z. "Curly Head"

Portuguese Group

P. "Crown."

Q. "Embossed."

R. "Figures."

S. "Carlos."

T. "Manoel."

U. "Ceres."

V. "Newspaper."

W. "Due."

STANLEY GIBBONS SIMPLIFIED CATALOGUE OF STAMPS OF THE WORLD—VOLUME 3 COUNTRIES I–M

ICELAND Pt. 11

An island lying S.E. of Greenland. An independent state formerly under the Danish sovereign, now a republic.

1873. 96 skilling = 1 riksdaler.
1876. 100 aurar (singular: eyrir) = 1 krona.

1

þrír
(6)

1873.

1 1 2s. blue £600 £1300
5 3s. grey £225 £950
2 4s. red £110 £550
3 8s. brown £225 £800
7 16s. yellow 75·00 £425

1876.

42 1 3a. yellow 3·25 11·50
27 4a. grey and red 16·00 11·00
13 5a. blue £350 £700
28 5a. green 2·75 1·80
29a 6a. grey 16·00 9·50
30 10a. red 9·00 1·70
31 16a. brown 65·00 55·00
18a 20a. mauve 32·00 £300
32a 20a. blue 36·00 18·00
33 25a. blue and brown 19·00 15·00
19 40a. green 85·00 £100
23b 40a. mauve 26·00 25·00
24 50a. red and blue 65·00 50·00
25 100a. purple and brown 55·00 60·00

1897. Surch as T **6** with figure **3** under word.
38 1 3 on 5a. green £400 £325

1897. Surch as T **6**.
40 1 3 on 5a. green £400 £325

10 King Christian IX

12 Kings Christian IX and Frederik VIII

13 Jon Sigurdsson

1902.

43 10 3a. orange 6·50 1·60
44 4a. red and grey 4·00 80
45 5a. green 20·00 50
46 6a. brown 18·00 4·25
47 10a. red 5·00 45
48 16a. brown 4·75 4·50
49 20a. blue 1·80 1·70
50 25a. green and brown 2·75 3·00
51 40a. mauve 3·75 2·75
52 50a. black and grey 5·50 14·50
53 1k. brown and blue 6·00 7·25
54 2k. blue and brown 23·00 44·00
55 5k. grey and brown £150 £130

1902. Optd **I GILDI '02–'03**.
67 1 3a. yellow 85 1·50
68 4a. grey and red 29·00 34·00
69 5a. green 65 3·50
71 6a. grey 75 4·00
73 10a. red 90 4·75
74 16a. brown 23·00 26·00
75 20a. blue 60 5·75
77 25a. blue and brown 70 8·00
79 40a. mauve 60 26·00
80 50a. red and blue 2·75 55·00
65 100a. purple and brown 45·00 45·00

1907.

81 12 1e. red and green 1·50 55
82 3a. brown 3·50 70
83 4a. red and grey 1·50 80
84 5a. green 65·00 65
85 6a. grey 35·00 1·90
114 10a. red 2·50 1·30
87 15a. green and red 5·25 70
88 16a. brown 7·50 18·00
89 20a. blue 8·00 2·20
90 25a. green and brown 6·25 5·75
91 40a. red 5·75 7·75
92 50a. red and grey 7·00 6·50
93 1k. brown and blue 19·00 36·00
94 2k. green and brown 26·00 44·00
95 5k. blue and brown £170 £225

1911. Birth Centenary of Jon Sigurdsson (historian and Althing member).
96 13 1e. green 2·00 80
97 3a. brown 3·25 6·25
98 4a. blue 1·10 95
99 6a. grey 8·75 12·00
100 15a. violet 9·25 1·00
101 25a. orange 20·00 22·00

1912. As T **13**, but portrait of King Frederik VIII and "JON SIGURDSSON" omitted.
102 5a. green 25·00 6·00
103 10a. red 20·00 6·50
104 20a. blue 35·00 8·50
105 50a. red 6·50 18·00
106 1k. yellow 26·00 36·00
107 2k. red 15·00 33·00
108 5k. brown £120 £140

15 King Christian X

22 Landing Mails at Vik

1920.

116 15 1e. red and green 55 55
117 3a. brown 3·50 6·50
184 4a. red and grey 1·60 1·20
119 5a. green 2·00 1·10
185 6a. grey 2·10 2·50
186 7a. green 50 1·00
121 8a. brown 6·00 1·20
122 10a. red 2·40 4·75
133 10a. green 3·50 75
187 10a. brown £100 50
123 15a. violet 31·00 65
124 20a. blue 2·50 7·50
134 20a. brown 65·00 70
125 25a. green and brown 15·00 90
135 25a. red 14·00 22·00
189 30a. green and red 28·00 3·00
127 40a. red 48·00 1·90
136 40a. blue 60·00 7·25
128 50a. red and grey £170 5·75
191 1k. brown and blue 40·00 3·25
130 2k. green and brown £250 17·00
131 5k. blue and brown 60·00 8·25
193 10k. black and green £300 £140

1921. Various types surch.
137 10 5a. on 16a. brown 3·00 17·00
138 12 5a. on 16a. brown 1·60 4·25
139 15 10a. on 5a. green 8·50 2·50
140 10 20a. on 25a. green & brn 5·00 4·00
141 12 20a. on 25a. green & brn 4·50 4·25
142 10 20a. on 40a. mauve 7·50 12·00
143 12 20a. on 40a. red 7·75 10·50
144 10 30a. on 50a. grey 35·00 14·50
145 50a. on 5k. grey & brown 46·00 28·00
146 15 1k. on 40a. blue £120 30·00
147 13 2k. on 25a. orange £100 80·00
148 – 10k. on 50a. red (No. 105) £250 £275
149 – 10k. on 1k. yell (No. 106) £275 £400
150 10 10k. on 2k. black & brn 50·00 17·00
150a 12 10k. on 5k. black & brn £325 £425

1925.

151 22 7a. green 38·00 3·75
152 – 10a. brown and blue 42·00 45
153 – 20a. red 41·00 45
154 – 35a. blue 65·00 4·00
155 22 50a. brown and green 60·00 85
DESIGNS: 10a., 35a. Reykjavik and Esjaberg (mountain); 20a. National Museum, Reykjavik.

1928. Air. Optd with airplane.
156 15 10a. red 90 7·25
157 12 50a. purple and grey 41·00 85·00

24 Discovery of Iceland

25 Gyrfalcon

1930. Parliament Millenary Celebration.
158 – 3a. violet and lilac (postage) 1·90 4·50
159 24 5a. blue and grey 2·00 4·50
160 – 7a. green and dp green 2·00 4·75
161 – 10a. purple and mauve 6·50 7·50
162 – 15a. dp blue & blue 1·80 4·75
163 – 20a. red and pink 31·00 42·00
164 – 25a. brown and lt brown 5·75 7·25
165 – 30a. green and grey 4·75 6·50
166 – 35a. blue & ultramarine 6·00 8·00
167 – 40a. red, blue and grey 4·75 6·00
168 – 50a. dp brown and brown 60·00 70·00
169 – 1k. green and grey 48·00 65·00
170 – 2k. blue and green 65·00 80·00
171 – 5k. orange and yellow 35·00 60·00
172 – 10k. lake and red 34·00 60·00

173 25 10a. blue & dp blue (air) 17·00 30·00
DESIGNS—HORIZ: 3a. Parliament House, Reykjavik; 7a. Encampment at Thingvellir; 10a. Arrival of Ingolf Arnarsson; 15a. Naming the Island; 20a. Chieftains riding to the "Althing" (Parliament); 25a. Discovery of Arnarsson's pillar; 30a. View of Thingvellir; 35a. Queen Aud; 40a. National flag; 50a. Proclamation at Thingvellir; 1k. Map of Iceland; 2k. Winter-bound farmstead; 5k. Woman spinning; 10k. Viking sacrifice to Thor.

26 Snaefellsjokull

1930. Air. Parliamentary Millenary Celebration.
174 26 15a. blue and brown 23·00 30·00
175 – 20a. blue and brown 22·00 28·00
176 – 35a. brown and green 46·00 50·00
177 – 50a. blue and green 46·00 50·00
178 – 1k. red and green 46·00 50·00
DESIGNS: 20a. Old Icelandic fishing boat; 35a. Icelandic pony; 50a. The Gullfoss Falls; 1k. Statue of Arnarsson, Reykjavik.

1931. Air. Optd **Zeppelin 1931**.
179 15 30a. green and red 28·00 85·00
180 1k. brown and blue 8·75 85·00
181 2k. green and brown 50·00 85·00

29 Gullfoss Falls

30 Shipwreck and Breeches-buoy

1931.

195 29 5a. grey 10·50 40
196 20a. red 9·00 20
197 35a. blue 16·00 5·50
198 60a. mauve 9·75 60
199 65a. brown 1·60 60
200 75a. blue 80·00 20·00

1933. Philanthropic Associations.
201 30 10a.+10a. brown 1·20 3·25
202 – 20a.+20a. red 1·20 3·25
203 30 35a.+25a. blue 1·20 3·25
204 – 50a.+25a. green 1·20 3·25
DESIGNS: 20a. Children gathering flowers; 50a. Aged fisherman and rowing boat.

1933. Air. Balbo Transatlantic Mass Formation Flight. Optd **Hopflug Itala 1933**.
205 15 1k. brown and blue £180 £325
206 5k. blue and brown £425 £1100
207 10k. black and green £1100 £2200

32 Avro 504K Biplane over Thingvellir

1934. Air.
208 32 10a. blue 2·00 1·40
209 20a. green 3·75 4·25
210a – 25a. violet 17·00 12·00
211 – 50a. purple 3·25 3·75
212 – 1k. brown 18·00 18·00
213 – 2k. red 8·00 7·50
DESIGNS: 25a., 50a. Monoplane and Aurora Borealis; 1k., 2k. Monoplane over map of Iceland.

33 Dynjandi Falls

35 Matthias Jochumsson

36 King Christian X

1935.

214 33 10a. blue 23·00 20
215 – 1k. green 36·00 20
DESIGN—HORIZ: 1k. Mt. Hekla.

1935. Birth Centenary of M. Jochumsson (poet).
216 35 3a. green 60 2·10
217 5a. grey 15·00 70
218 7a. green 24·00 1·10
219 35a. blue 50 80

1937. Silver Jubilee of King Christian X.
220 36 10a. green 1·30 11·50
221 30a. brown 1·30 4·75
222 40a. red 1·30 4·75
MS223 128½ × 112 mm. 36 15a. violet; 25a. red; 50a. blue (sold at 2k.) 38·00 £200

37 The Great Geyser

37b Leif Eiriksson's Statue, Reykjavik

1938.

226 37 15a. purple 3·75 5·50
227 20a. red 21·00 25
228 35a. blue 60 45
229 – 40a. brown 10·00 15·00
230 – 45a. blue 70 40
231 – 50a. green 20·00 50
232a – 60a. blue 3·00 5·00
233 – 1k. blue 2·75 25
The frames of the 40a. to 1k. differ from Type **37**.

1938. Leif Eiriksson's Day. Sheet 140 × 100 mm.
MS233b 30a. red (T **37b**), 40a. violet; 60a. green (sold at 2k.) 3·25 21·00
DESIGNS: 40a. Figure from statue; 60a. Part of globe showing Iceland and Vinland (larger).

38 Reykjavik University

1938. 20th Anniv of Independence.
234 38 25a. green 4·50 9·25
235 30a. brown 4·50 8·25
236 40a. purple 4·50 8·25

1939. Surch **5**.
237 35 5 on 35a. blue 45 70

40 Trylon and Perisphere

1939. New York World's Fair.
238 40 20a. red 3·25 4·25
239 – 35a. blue 3·25 6·00
240 – 45a. green 4·00 6·75
241 – 2k. black 45·00 £110
DESIGNS: 35a. Viking longship and route to America; 45a., 2k. Statue of Thorfinn Karlsefni, Reykjavik.

41 Atlantic Cod

42 Icelandic Flag

1939.

242a 41 1e. blue 45 2·75
243a – 3a. violet 35 55
244a 41 5a. brown 45 30
245 – 7a. green 3·75 5·25
246 42 10a. red and blue 2·00 65
247a – 10a. green 43·00 35
248 – 10a. black 25 15
249 – 12a. green 30 50
250a 41 25a. red 30·00 30
251 25a. brown 35 30
252 – 35a. red 40 25
253 41 50a. green 55 20
DESIGN: 3, 7, 10a. (Nos. 247a/8), 12, 35a. Atlantic herring.

43 Statue of Thorfinn Karlsefni

46 Statue of Snorri Sturluson (O. Vigeland)

1939.
254 **43** 2k. grey . . . . 2·50 25
255 5k. brown . . . . 20·00 30
256 10k. brown . . . . 9·00 1·30

1940. New York World's Fair. Optd **1940.**
257 **40** 20a. red . . . . 9·50 16·00
258 – 35a. blue (No. 239) . . . 10·00 16·00
259 – 45a. green (No. 240) . . . 9·50 16·00
260 – 2k. black (No. 241) . . . 85·00 £225

1941. Surch **25.**
261 **35** 25a. on 3a. olive 50 75

1941. 700th Death Anniv of Snorri Sturluson (historian).
262 **46** 25a. red . . . . 75 1·30
263 50a. blue . . . . 1·80 3·50
264 1k. olive . . . . 1·80 3·25

47 Jon Sigurdsson (historian and Althing member)

48 Grumman G-21 Goose Amphibian over Thingvellir

1944. Proclamation of Republic.
265 **47** 10a. grey 35 60
266 25a. brown 35 60
267 50a. green 35 60
268 1k. black 60 60
269 5k. brown . . . . 3·00 9·50
270 10k. brown . . . . 43·00 65·00

1947. Air.
271 **48** 15a. orange 65 85
272 – 30a. black . . . . 65 1·00
273 – 75a. red 50 75
274 – 1k. blue 50 75
275 – 1k.80 blue . . . . 11·00 10·50
276 – 2k. brown . . . . 1·30 1·50
277 – 2k.50 green . . . . . . 22·00 75
278 – 3k. green . . . . 1·20 1·50
279 – 3k.30 blue . . . . 9·25 4·25
DESIGNS—HORIZ: 30a. Consolidated PBY-5 Catalina flying boat over Isafjordur; 75a. Douglas DC-3 over Eyjafjord; 1k.80, Douglas DC-3 over Snaefellsjokull; 2k.50, Consolidated PBY-5 Catalina over Eiriksjokull; 3k. Douglas DC-4 over Reykjavik; 3k.30, Douglas DC-4 over Oraefajokull. VERT: 1k. Grumman G-21 Goose over Sethisfjordur, Strandatindur; 2k. Consolidated PBY-5 Catalina over Hvalfjordur, Thyrill.
For stamps as Type **48** but without airplane, see Nos. 346/8.

50 Mt. Hekla in Eruption

53 Hospital and Child

1948. Inscr "HEKLA 1947".
280 **50** 12a. purple 20 15
281 – 25a. green . . . . 1·40 15
282 – 35a. red 45 15
283 **50** 50a. brown . . . . 1·80 15
284 – 60a. blue . . . . 5·50 2·50
285 – 1k. brown . . . . 13·50 15
286 – 10k. violet . . . . 43·00 90
DESIGNS—VERT: 35a., 60a. Mt. Hekla in Eruption (different view). HORIZ: 25a., 1k., 10k. Mt. Hekla.

1949. Red Cross Fund.
287 **53** 10a.+10a. green 35 55
288 – 35a.+15a. red 35 65
289 – 50a.+25a. brown 40 65
290 – 60a.+25a. blue 50 70
291 – 75a.+25a. blue . . . . . 1·10 95
DESIGNS: 35a. Nurse and patient; 50a. Nurse arranging patient's bed; 60a. Aged couple; 75a. Freighter and ship's lifeboat.

54 Pony Pack-train

1949. 75th Anniv of U.P.U.
292 **54** 25a. green 25 45
293 – 35a. red 25 50
294 – 60a. blue 25 90
295 – 2k. orange . . . . 1·00 95
DESIGNS: 35a. Reykjavik; 60a. Map of Iceland; 2k. Almannagja Gorge.

55 "Ingolfur Arnarson" (trawler)

56 Bishop Jon Arason

1950.
296 – 5a. brown 15 15
297 **55** 10a. grey 30 30
298 – 20a. brown 30 25
299 **55** 25a. red 30 20
300 – 60a. green . . . . 10·00 14·50
301 – 75a. orange 45 25
302 – 90a. red 45 30
303 – 1k. brown . . . . 4·00 25
304 **55** 1k.25 purple . . . . 16·00 25
305 1k.50 blue . . . . 12·00 30
306 – 2k. violet . . . . 14·50 30
307 – 5k. green . . . . 25·00 55
308 – 25k. black . . . . £120 13·00
DESIGNS—As T **55**: 5, 90a., 2k. Vestmannaeyjar harbour; 20, 75a., 1k. Tractor; 60a., 5k. Flock of sheep; 25k. Parliament Building, Reykjavik ($29\frac{1}{2} \times 23\frac{1}{2}$ mm).

1950. 400th Death Anniv of Bishop Arason.
309 **56** 1k.80 red . . . . 2·30 2·50
310 3k.30 green . . . . 1·30 2·40

57 Postman, 1776

58 President Bjornsson

1951. 175th Anniv of Icelandic Postal Service.
311 **57** 2k. blue . . . . 1·90 1·70
312 – 3k. purple . . . . 1·90 2·40
DESIGN: 3k. as 2k. but Saab 90 Scandia aeroplane replaces man.

1952. Death of S. Bjornsson (first President of Iceland).
313 **58** 1k.25 blue . . . . 2·00 20
314 2k.20 green . . . . 50 3·00
315 5k. blue . . . . 6·25 1·00
316 10k. brown . . . . 30·00 21·00

1953. Netherlands Flood Relief Fund. Surch **Hollandshjalp 1953 + 25.**
317 – 75a.+25a. orange (No. 301) 65 2·40
318 **55** 1k.25+25a. purple . . . . 1·40 3·50

60 "Reykjabok" (Saga of Burnt Njal)

62 Hannes Hafstein

1953.
319 **60** 10a. black 15 15
320 – 70a. green 20 20
321 – 1k. red 35 15
322 – 1k.75 blue . . . . 23·00 1·10
323 – 10k. brown . . . . 11·00 70
DESIGNS: 70a. Hand writing on manuscript; 1k. "Stjorn" (15th century manuscript); 1k.75, Books and candle; 10k. Page from "Skardsbok" (14th century law manuscript).

1954. No. 282 surch **5 AURAR** and bars.
324 5a. on 35a. red 20 15

1954. 50th Anniv of Appointment of Hannes Hafstein as First Native Minister of Iceland. Portraits of Hafstein.
325 **62** 1k.25 blue . . . . 2·20 35
326 – 2k.45 green . . . . 19·00 27·00
327 – 5k. red . . . . 13·50 3·25

63 Icelandic Wrestling

64 St. Thorlacas

1955. Icelandic National Sports.
328 **63** 75a. brown 20 25
329 – 1k.25 blue (Diving) 30 25
330 **63** 1k.50 red 60 25
331 – 1k.75 blue (Diving) 30 25

1956. 9th Centenary of Consecration of First Icelandic Bishop and Skalholt Rebuilding Fund. Inscr as in T **64**.
332 **64** 75a.+25a. red 15 30
333 – 1k.25+75a. brown 15 35
334 – 1k.75+1k.25 black . . . . 90 1·10
DESIGNS—HORIZ: 1k.25, Skalholt Cathedral, 1772. VERT: 1k.75, J. P. Vidalin, Bishop of Skalholt, 1698–1720.

65 Skogafoss

67 Map of Iceland

1956. Power Plants and Waterfalls.
335 **65** 15a. blue 15 20
336 – 50a. green 15 20
337 – 60a. brown . . . . 2·20 2·75
338 – 1k.50 violet . . . . 22·00 60
339 – 2k. brown . . . . 1·70 35
340 – 2k.45 black . . . . 5·50 5·50
341 – 3k. blue . . . . 3·00 55
342 – 5k. green . . . . 8·00 1·20
DESIGNS—HORIZ: 50a. Ellidaarvirkjun; 60a. Godafoss; 1k.50, Sogsvirkjun; 2k. Dettifoss; 2k.45, Andakilsarvirkjun; 3k. Laxarvirkjun. VERT: 5k. Gullfoss.

1956. 50th Anniv of Icelandic Telegraph System.
343 **67** 2k.30 blue 30 65

67a Whooper Swans

1956. Northern Countries' Day.
344 **67a** 1k.50 red 70 80
345 1k.75 blue . . . . 8·50 8·75

1957. Designs as T **48** but airplane omitted.
346 2k. green . . . . 2·50 20
347 3k. blue . . . . 2·50 20
348 10k. brown . . . . 5·25 45
DESIGNS—HORIZ: 2k. Snaefellsjokull; 3k. Eiriksjokull; 10k. Oraefajokull.

68 Presidential Residence, Bessastadir

69 Norwegian Spruce

1957.
349 **68** 25k. black . . . . 13·50 3·25

1957. Reafforestation Campaign.
350 **69** 35a. green 20 20
351 – 70a. green 20 20
DESIGN: 70a. Icelandic birch and saplings.

70 Jonas Hallgrimsson

71 River Beauty

72 Icelandic Pony

1957. 150th Birth Anniv of Hallgrimsson (poet).
352 **70** 5k. black and green . . . 1·10 40

1958. Flowers. Multicoloured.
353 1k. Type **71** 20 20
354 2k.50 Wild pansy 30 45

1958.
355 **72** 10a. black 40 15
356 1k. red 50 25
357 2k.25 brown 40 25

73 Icelandic Flag

74 Old Government House

1958. 40th Anniv of Icelandic Flag.
358 **73** 3k.50 red and blue . . . . 1·10 50
359 50k. red and blue . . . . 5·00 4·50
No. 359 is $23\frac{1}{2} \times 26\frac{1}{2}$ mm.

1958.
360 **74** 1k.50 blue 20 25
361 2k. green 40 40
362 3k. red 20 25
363 4k. brown 40 40

75 Jon Thorkelsson with Children

76 Vickers Viscount 700 and 1919 Avro 504K Biplane

1959. Death Bicentenary of Jon Thorkelsson (Johannes Thorkillius, Rector of Skalholt).
364 **75** 2k. green 45 50
365 3k. purple 45 50

1959. Air. 40th Anniv of Iceland Civil Aviation.
366 **76** 3k.50 blue 65 55
367 – 4k.05 green 50 80
DESIGN: 4k.05, Douglas DC-4 and Avro 504K aircraft.

77 Atlantic Salmon

78 "The Outcast" (after Jonsson)

1959.
368 **77** 25a. blue 20 25
369 – 90a. black and brown . . . 30 30
370 – 2k. black 45 10
371 **77** 5k. green . . . . 4·00 75
372 – 25k. violet and yellow . . 10·00 10·00
DESIGNS—VERT: 90a., 2k. Eiders; 25k. Gyr falcon.

1960. World Refugee Year.
373 **78** 2k.50 brown 15 20
374 4k.50 blue 90 90

78a Conference Emblem

1960. Europa.
375 **78a** 3k. green 90 40
376 5k.50 blue . . . . 65 1·30

79 Dandelions

80 Sigurdsson

1960. Wild Flowers.
377 – 50a. violet, green and myrtle (Campanulas) . . 15 15
378 – 1k.20 violet, green and brown (Geraniums) . . . 15 25
379 **79** 2k.50 yellow, green & brn 20 20
380 – 3k.50 yellow, green and blue (Buttercup) 65 15
See also Nos. 412/15 and 446/7.

1961. 150th Birth Anniv of Jon Sigurdsson (historian and Althing member).
381 **80** 50a. red 15 20
382 3k. blue . . . . 1·20 1·00
383 5k. purple 55 55

81 Reykjavik Harbour

1961. 175th Anniv of Reykjavik.

384	**81**	2k.50 blue and green . . .	55	25
385		4k.50 blue and violet . . .	70	30

82 Doves

1961. Europa.

386	**82**	5k.50 multicoloured . . .	40	60
387		6k. multicoloured	40	60

83 B. Sveinsson

84 Productivity Institute

1961. 50th Anniv of Iceland University.

388	**83**	1k. brown	15	20
389	–	1k.40 blue	15	20
390	–	10k. green	90	80
MS391		99 × 50 mm. Nos. 388/90. Imperf	45	1·00

DESIGNS—VERT: 1k.40, B. M. Olsen (first Vice-chancellor). HORIZ: 10k. University building.

1962. Icelandic Buildings.

392	**84**	2k.50 blue	25	20
393	–	4k. green	35	25
394	–	6k. brown	50	20

DESIGNS: 4k. Fishing Research Institute; 6k. Agricultural Society's Headquarters.

85 Europa "Tree"

1962. Europa.

395	**85**	5k.50 brown, green & yell	25	20
396		6k.50 brown, green & yell	50	60

86 Cable Map

1962. Opening of North Atlantic Submarine Telephone Communications.

397	**86**	5k. green, red and lavender	95	45
398		7k. green, red and blue . .	40	25

87 S. Gudmundsson (scholar and curator)

88 Herring Catch

1963. Centenary of National Museum.

399	**87**	4k. brown and bistre . . .	50	25
400	–	5k.50 brown and olive . .	45	25

DESIGN: 5k.50, Detail from carving on church door, Valthjofsstad.

1963. Freedom from Hunger.

401	**88**	5k. multicoloured	75	20
402		7k.50 multicoloured . . .	25	25

89 View of Akureyri

1963.

403	**89**	3k. green	20	25

90 "Co-operation"

1963. Europa.

404	**90**	6k. yellow, ochre and brown	40	40
405		7k. yellow, green and blue	40	40

91 Ambulance

1963. Red Cross Centenary.

406	**91**	3k.+50a. multicoloured . .	25	70
407		3k.50+50a. mult	25	50

92 "Gullfoss" (cargo liner)

93 Scout Emblem

1964. 50th Anniv of Iceland Steamship Co.

408	**92**	10k. black, purple and blue	1·50	1·10

1964. Icelandic Boy Scouts Commemoration.

409	**93**	3k.50 multicoloured . . .	40	15
410		4k.50 multicoloured . . .	40	30

94 Arms of Iceland

95 Europa "Flower"

1964. 20th Anniv of Icelandic Republic.

411	**94**	25k. multicoloured	1·50	1·30

1964. Wild Flowers. As T **79**. Multicoloured.

412	50a. Mountain avens	15	15
413	1k. Glacier buttercup	10	10
414	1k.50 Bogbean	25	20
415	2k. White clover	30	15

1964. Europa.

416	**95**	4k.50 turquoise, cream and brown	50	30
417		9k. sepia, cream and blue	70	50

96 Running

97 Rock Ptarmigan (summer plumage)

1964. Olympic Games, Tokyo.

418	**96**	10k. black and green . . .	70	60

1965. Charity stamps.

419	**97**	3k.50+50a. mult	70	1·20
420	–	4k.50+50a. mult	75	1·20

DESIGN: 4k.50, Rock ptarmigan in winter plumage.

98 "Sound Waves"

99 Eruption, November 1963

1965. Centenary of I.T.U.

421	**98**	4k.50 green	75	65
422		7k.50 blue	25	20

1965. Birth of Surtsey Island. Multicoloured.

423	1k.50 Type **99**	50	50
424	2k. Surtsey in April 1964 (horiz)	50	50
425	3k.50 Surtsey in September 1964 (horiz)	75	55

100 Europa "Sprig"

1965. Europa.

426	**100**	5k. green, brown and ochre	95	95
427		8k. green, brown & turq	90	65

101 E. Benediktsson

1965. 25th Death Anniv of Einar Benediktsson (poet).

428	**101**	10k. brown, black and blue	2·25	3·00

102 Girl in National Costume

103 White-tailed Sea Eagle

1965.

429	**102**	100k. multicoloured . . .	4·75	5·00

1966. Multicoloured.

430	20k. Great northern diver . .	3·00	3·25
431	50k. Type **103**	6·50	7·00

104 Londrangar

105 Europa "Ship"

1966. Landscapes (1st series). Multicoloured.

432	2k.50 Type **104**	20	30
433	4k. Myvatn	40	30
434	5k. Bulandstindur	50	30
435	6k.50 Dyrholaey	60	30

See also Nos. 465/8.

1966. Europa.

436	**105**	7k. turquoise blue and red	1·30	1·30
437		8k. brown, cream and red	1·30	1·30

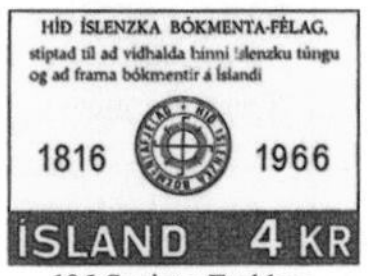
106 Society Emblem

107 Cogwheels

1966. 150th Anniv of Icelandic Literary Society.

438	**106**	4k. blue	30	20
439		10k. red	65	60

1967. Europa.

440	**107**	7k. blue, brown and yellow	1·40	1·10
441		8k. blue, grey and green	1·40	1·00

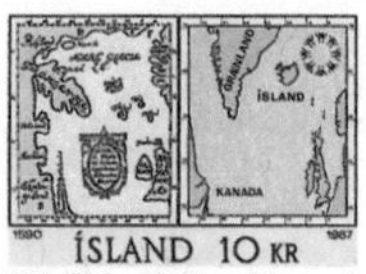
108 Old and New Maps of Iceland

1967. World Fair, Montreal.

442	**108**	10k. multicoloured . . .	30	40

109 Trade Symbols

1967. 50th Anniv of Icelandic Chamber of Commerce.

443	**109**	5k. multicoloured	25	25

110 Nest and Eggs of Ringed Plover

1967. Charity stamps.

444	**110**	4k.+50a. multicoloured	65	1·30
445	–	5k.+50a. multicoloured	65	1·30

DESIGN: 5k. Nest and eggs of rock ptarmigan.

1968. Wild Flowers. As T **79**. Multicoloured.

446	50a. Saxifrage	20	15
447	2k.50 Orchid	20	20

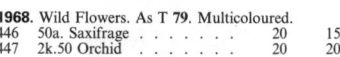

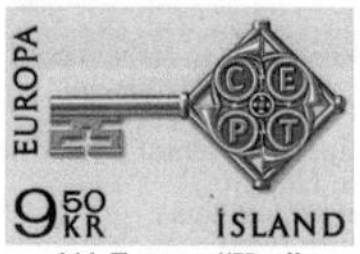
111 Europa "Key"

1968. Europa.

448	**111**	9k.50 mauve, black & yell	1·30	90
449		10k. yellow, sepia & green	1·30	95

112 Right-hand Traffic

1968. Adoption of Changed Rule of the Road.

450	**112**	4k. brown and yellow . .	15	20
451		5k. brown	15	20

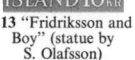

113 "Fridriksson and Boy" (statue by S. Olafsson)

114 Library Interior

1968. Birth Cent of Pastor Fridrik Fridriksson (founder of Icelandic Y.M.C.A. and Y.W.C.A.).

452	**113**	10k. black and blue . . .	35	30

1968. 150th Anniv of National Library.

453	**114**	5k. brown and buff . . .	10	15
454		20k. ultramarine and blue	95	90

115 Jon Magnusson (former Prime Minister)

116 Viking Ships

1968. 50th Anniv of Independence.

455	**115**	4k. lake	25	20
456		50k. sepia	4·00	3·75

1969. 50th Anniv of Northern Countries' Union.

457	**116**	6k.50 red	45	45
458		10k. blue	45	45

117 Colonnade

1969. Europa.

459	**117**	13k. multicoloured . . .	2·50	2·10
460		14k.50 multicoloured . .	75	65

118 Republican Emblem (after S. Jonsson) **119** Boeing 727 Airliner

1969. 25th Anniv of Republic.
461 **118** 25k. multicoloured . . . 95 65
462 100k. multicoloured . . . 4·75 5·75

1969. 50th Anniv of Icelandic Aviation.
463 **119** 9k.50 ultramarine & blue 45 50
464 – 12k. ultramarine and blue 45 50
DESIGN: 12k. Canadair CL-44-D4 (inscr "Rolls-Royce 400").

120 Snaefellsjokull

1970. Landscapes (2nd series). Multicoloured.
465 1k. Type **120** 15 20
466 4k. Laxfoss and Baula . . . 15 20
467 5k. Hattver (vert) 15 20
468 20k. Fjardagil (vert) . . . . 1·20 45

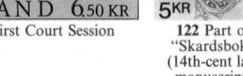

121 First Court Session **122** Part of "Skardsbok" (14th-cent law manuscript)

1970. 50th Anniv of Icelandic Supreme Court.
469 **121** 6k.50 multicoloured . . . 20 20

1970. Icelandic Manuscripts. Multicoloured.
470 5k. Type **122** 15 20
471 15k. Part of preface to "Flateyjarbok" 50 60
472 30k. Illuminated initial from "Flateyjarbok" . . . . . 1·00 1·00

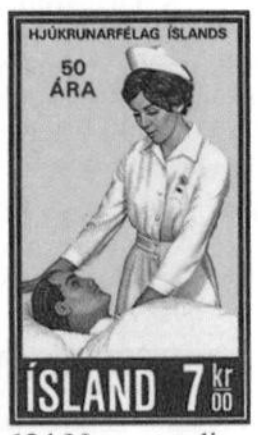

123 "Flaming Sun" **124** Nurse tending Patient

1970. Europa.
473 **123** 9k. yellow and brown . . 2·50 1·70
474 25k. brown and green . . 2·50 1·80

1970. 50th Anniv of Icelandic Nurses Assn.
475 **124** 7k. ultramarine and blue 25 25

125 G. Thomsen **126** "The Halt" (T. B. Thorlaksson)

1970. 150th Birth Anniv of Grimur Thomsen (poet).
476 **125** 10k. indigo and blue . . . 30 30

1970. International Arts Festival, Reykjavik.
477 **126** 50k. multicoloured . . . 1·20 1·10

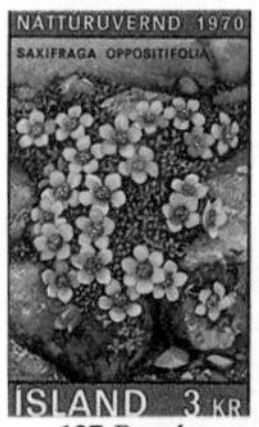

127 Purple Saxifrage **128** U.N. Emblem and Map

1970. Nature Conservation Year. Mult.
478 3k. Type **127** 25 25
479 15k. Lakagigar (view) 85 80

1970. 25th Anniv of United Nations.
480 **128** 12k. multicoloured . . . 30 45

129 "Flight" (A. Jonsson)

1971. "Help for Refugees".
481 **129** 10k. multicoloured . . . 40 45

130 Europa Chain

1971. Europa.
482 **130** 7k. yellow, red and black 2·00 1·30
483 15k. yellow, blue and black . . . . 1·90 1·10

131 Postgiro Emblem **132** Society Emblem

1971. Inauguration of Postal Giro Service.
484 **131** 5k. blue and light blue . . 15 25
485 7k. green and light green 15 25

1971. Centenary of Icelandic Patriotic Society.
486 **132** 30k. lilac and blue . . . . 1·00 70
487 – 100k. black and grey . . 5·50 5·50
DESIGN: 100k. T. Gunnarsson (president and editor).

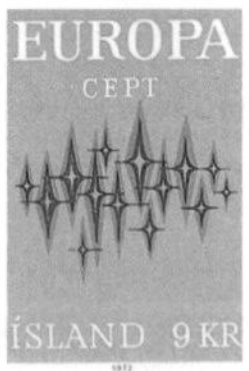

133 Freezing Plant and Haddock ("Melanogrammus aeglefinus") **135** "Communications"

134 Mt. Herdubreid

1971. Icelandic Fishing Industry. Mult.
488 5k. Type **133** 15 20
489 7k. Landing catch and Atlantic cod ("Gadus morhua") 15 20
490 20k. Canning shrimps and "Pandalus borealis" . . . 70 65

1972.
491 **134** 250k. multicoloured . . . 45 25

1972. Europa.
492 **135** 9k. multicoloured . . . . 1·30 70
493 13k. multicoloured . . . . 1·30 1·50

136 "Municipalities"

1972. Centenary of Icelandic Municipal Laws.
494 **136** 16k. multicoloured . . . 20 20

137 World Map on Chessboard

1972. World Chess Championship, Reykjavik.
495 **137** 15k. multicoloured . . . 25 25

138 Tomatoes

1972. Hot-house Plant Cultivation. Mult.
496 8k. Type **138** 15 20
497 12k. Steam source and valve 15 20
498 40k. Rose cultivation . . . . 1·00 85

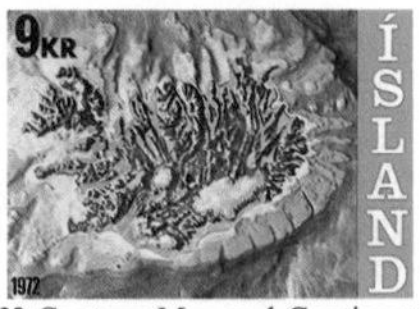

139 Contour Map and Continental Shelf

1972. Iceland's Offshore Claims.
499 **139** 9k. multicoloured 20 20

140 Arctic Tern feeding Young **141** Europa "Posthorn"

1972. Charity Stamps.
500 **140** 7k.+1k. multicoloured . . 45 55
501 9k.+1k. multicoloured . . 50 60

1973. Europa.
502 **141** 13k. multicoloured . . . 2·50 2·10
503 25k. multicoloured . . . 35 35

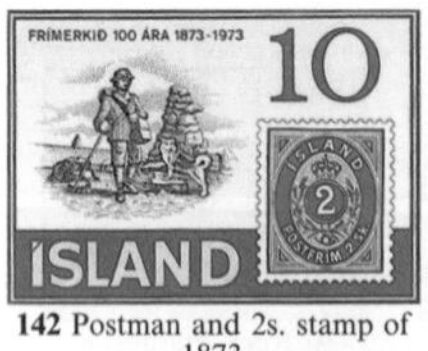

142 Postman and 2s. stamp of 1873 **144** Pres. Asgeirsson

143 "The Nordic House", Reykjavik

1973. Stamp Centenary. Multicoloured.
504 10k. Type **142** 45 30
505 15k. Pony train 15 20
506 20k. "Esja" (mail steamer) 15 20
507 40k. Mail van 15 20
508 80k. Beech Model 18 mail plane . . . . 1·70 90

1973. Nordic Countries' Postal Co-operation.
509 **143** 9k. multicoloured 45 15
510 10k. multicoloured . . . 1·30 1·20

1973. 5th Death Anniv of Asgeir Asgeirsson (politician).
511 **144** 13k. red 30 25
512 15k. blue 30 20

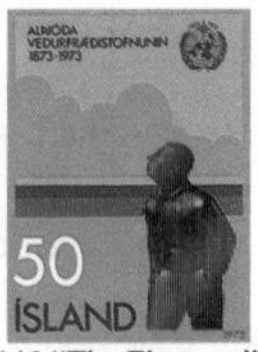

145 Exhibition Emblem **146** "The Elements"

1973. "Islandia 73" Stamp Exhibition. Mult.
513 17k. Type **145** 35 30
514 20k. Exhibition emblem (different) 35 25

1973. Centenary of I.M.O.
515 **146** 50k. multicoloured . . . 45 40

147 "Ingolfur and High-Seat Pillar" (tapestry, J. Briem) **148** "Horseman" (17th-century wood-carving)

1974. 1100th Anniv of Icelandic Settlement. Multicoloured.
516 10k. Type **147** 15 20
517 13k. "Grimur Geitskor at Thingvellir" (painting) (horiz) 15 15
518 15k. Bishop G. Thorlaksson of Holar 15 20
519 17k. "Snorri Sturluson slaying the King's messenger" (T. Skulason) 25 20
520 20k. Stained glass window from Hallgrimskirkja, Saurbaer 25 20
521 25k. Illuminated "I", from "Flateyjarbok" (manuscript) 10 15
522 30k. "Christ the King" (mosaic altar-piece, Skalholt Cathedral) 50 60
523 40k. 18th-century wood-carving 55 70
524 60k. "Curing the Catch" (concrete relief by S. Olafsson) . . . . 85 1·00
525 70k. "Saemunder smiting the Devil Seal" (bronze) . . . 85 1·10
526 100k. Altar-cloth, Church of Stafafell (horiz) . . . . . 1·20 75

1974. Europa. Sculptures. Multicoloured.
527 13k. Type **148** 15 30
528 20k. "Through the Sound Barrier" (bronze, A. Sveinsson) . . . . . . 1·20 80

149 Purchasing Stamps **150** Village with Erupting Volcano in distance

1974. Centenary of Universal Postal Union.
529 **149** 17k. brown, blue & yellow 25 20
530 – 20k. brown, blue & green 30 25
DESIGN: 20k. Postman sorting mail.

1975. Volcanic Eruption, Heimaey (1973).
531 **150** 20k. multicoloured . . . 35 40
532 25k. multicoloured . . . 20 30

151 "Autumn Bird" (T. Skullason) **152** Stephan G. Stephansson (poet)

1975. Europa. Paintings. Multicoloured.
533 18k. Type **151** 25 15
534 23k. "Sun Queen" (J. S. Kjarval) (vert.) 95 55

1975. Centenary of Icelandic Settlements in North America.
535 **152** 27k. brown and green . . 35 25

153 Hallgrimur Petursson (religious poet)

154 Red Cross Flag on Map of Iceland

1975. Celebrities.
536 **153** 18k. black and green . . 15 20
537 – 23k. blue 15 20
538 – 30k. red 15 25
539 – 50k. blue 35 25
PORTRAITS: 23k. Arni Magnusson (historian); 30k. Jon Eiriksson (statesman); 50k. Einar Jonsson (painter and sculptor).

1975. 50th Anniv of Icelandic Red Cross.
540 **154** 23k. multicoloured . . . 25 25

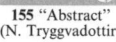

155 "Abstract" (N. Tryggvadottir)

156 "Bertel Thorvaldsen" (self-statue)

1975. International Women's Year.
541 **155** 100k. multicoloured . . . 80 50

1975. Centenary of Thorvaldsen Society (Charity organization).
542 **156** 27k. multicoloured . . . 45 35

157 "Forestry"

158 "Landscape" (Asgrimur Jonsson)

1975. Reafforestation.
543 **157** 35k. multicoloured . . . 45 25

1976. Birth Cent of Asgrimur Jonsson (painter).
544 **158** 150k. multicoloured . . . 95 1·10

159 Wooden Bowl

1976. Europa. Old Wooden Crafts. Mult.
545 35k. Type **159** 90 90
546 45k. Spinning-wheel (vert) . . 90 85

160 Title page of Postal Services Order

161 Iceland 5a. Stamp with Reykjavik Postmark, 1876

1976. Bicent of Icelandic Postal Services.
547 **160** 35k. brown 35 30
548 – 45k. blue 30 30
DESIGN: 45k. Signature appended to Postal Services Order.

1976. Cent of Icelandic Aurar Currency Stamps.
549 **161** 30k. multicoloured . . . 20 35

162 "Workers" and Federation Emblem

1976. 60th Anniv of Icelandic Labour Federation.
550 **162** 100k. multicoloured . . . 70 50

163 Water-lilies

164 Ofaerufoss, Eldgja

1977. Nordic Countries' Co-operation in Nature Conservation and Environment Protection.
551 **163** 35k. multicoloured . . . 60 40
552 45k. multicoloured . . . 65 40

1977. Europa. Multicoloured.
553 45k. Type **164** . . . . . . 1·90 70
554 85k. Kirkufell from Grundarfjord 55 40

165 Harlequin Duck

166 Co-operative Emblem

1977. European Wetlands Campaign.
555 **165** 40k. multicoloured . . . 25 25

1977. 75th Anniv of Federation of Icelandic Co-operative Societies.
556 **166** 60k. blue and light blue 60 40

167 Thermal Spring and Rheumatic Treatment

1977. World Rheumatism Year.
557 **167** 90k. multicoloured . . . 50 40

168 Cairn and Glacier

169 Thorvaldur Thoroddsen (geologist)

1977. 50th Anniv of Icelandic Touring Club.
558 **168** 45k. blue 35 50

1978. Famous Icelanders.
559 **169** 50k. green and brown . . 15 20
560 – 60k. brown and green . . 50 60
DESIGN: 60k. Briet Bjarnhedinsdottir (suffragette).

170 Videy Mansion

1978. Europa. Multicoloured.
561 80k. Type **170** 65 55
562 120k. Husavik Church (vert.) 85 45

171 Dr. A. Johannesson, Junkers W.34 "Island 1" and Junkers F-13 "Island 2"

1978. 50th Anniv of Domestic Flights.
563 **171** 60k. black and blue . . . 30 30
564 – 100k. multicoloured . . . 45 25
DESIGN: 100k. Fokker F.27 Friendship TF-F1K.

172 Skeidara Bridge

1978. Skeidara Bridge.
565 **172** 70k. multicoloured . . . 15 15

173 "Lava Scene near Mt. Hekla" (J. Stefansson)

1978.
566 **173** 1000k. multicoloured . . 3·00 2·75

174 Wreck of "Sargon" and Breeches-buoy

1978. 50th Anniv of National Life-Saving Association of Iceland.
567 **174** 60k. black 15 20

175 "Reykjanesviti" Lighthouse

176 Halldor Hermannsson

1978. Centenary of Lighthouses in Iceland.
568 **175** 90k. multicoloured . . . 35 35

1978. Birth Centenary of Halldor Hermannsson (scholar and librarian).
569 **176** 150k. blue 35 35

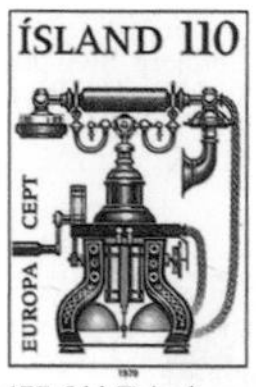

177 Old Telephone

178 Bjarni Thorsteinsson (clergyman and composer)

1979. Europa. Multicoloured.
570 110k. Type **177** 95 35
571 190k. Posthorn and mailbag 1·00 80

1979. Famous Icelanders.
572 – 80k. purple 15 20
573 **178** 100k. black 15 20
574 – 120k. red 15 20
575 – 130k. brown 30 40
576 – 170k. red 50 45
DESIGNS: 80k. Ingibjorg H. Bjarnason (headmistress and first female member of Althing); 120k. Petur Gudjohnsen (organist); 130k. Sveinbjorn Sveinbjornson (composer); 170k. Torfhildur Holm (poetess and novelist).

179 Children with Flowers

180 Icelandic Arms to 1904 and 1904–19

1979. International Year of the Child.
577 **179** 140k. multicoloured . . . 45 40

1979. 75th Anniv of Ministry of Iceland.
578 **180** 500k. multicoloured . . . 1·10 75

181 Sigurdsson and I. Einarsdottir

1979. Death Centenaries of Jon Sigurdsson (historian and Althing member) and of his wife, Ingibjorg Einarsdottir.
579 **181** 150k. black 25 35

182 Part of Kringla Leaf (MS of "Heimskringla")

183 Icelandic Dog

1979. 800th Birth Anniv of Snorri Sturluson (saga writer).
580 **182** 200k. multicoloured . . . 30 40

1980. Fauna.
581 **183** 10k. black 15 15
582 – 90k. brown 15 20
583 – 160k. purple 50 20
584 – 170k. black 40 60
585 – 190k. brown 30 40
DESIGNS: 90k. Arctic fox; 160k. Greater redfish; 170k. Atlantic puffins; 190k. Common seal.

184 Jon Sveinsson alias Nonni (writer)

185 Rowan Berries

1980. Europa.
586 **184** 140k. pink and black . . 50 35
587 – 250k. pink and black . . 80 60
DESIGN: 250k. Gunnar Gunnarsson (writer).

1980. Year of the Tree.
588 **185** 120k. multicoloured . . . 15 40

186 Sports Complex, Reykjavik

187 Embroidered Cushion

1980. Olympic Games, Moscow.
589 **186** 300k. turquoise 50 50

1980. Nordic Countries' Postal Co-operation. Multicoloured.
590 150k. Carved and painted cabinet door 60 45
591 180k. Type **187** 80 55

188 University Hospital

189 Loudspeaker

1980. 50th Anniv of University Hospital.
592 **188** 200k. multicoloured . . . 40 30

1980. 50th Anniv of State Broadcasting Service.
593 **189** 400k. multicoloured . . . 70 35

(New currency. 100 (old) Kronur = 1 (new) Krona).

190 Magnus Stephensen (Chief Justice and publisher)

191 Loftur the Sorcerer

1981. Famous Icelanders.
594 **190** 170a. blue 30 20
595 – 190a. green 30 25
DESIGN: 190a. Finnur Magnusson (writer and Keeper of Privy Archives).

1981. Europa. Illustrations of Icelandic legends. Multicoloured.
596 180a. Type **191** . . . . . . 1·10 65
597 220a. Witch wading the deeps off Iceland . . . . 1·10 75

192 Winter Wren

193 Human Jigsaw

1981. Birds.
598 **192** 50a. brown 10 15
599 – 100a. blue 10 15
600 – 200a. black 45 30
DESIGNS: 100a. Golden plover; 200a. Common raven.

1981. International Year for Disabled Persons.
601 **193** 200a. multicoloured . . . 20 25

194 Skyggnir Dish Aerial

195 "Hauling the Line" (Gunnlaugur Scheving)

1981. 75th Anniv of Icelandic Telephone Service.
602 **194** 500a. multicoloured . . . 45 45

1981.
603 **195** 5000a. multicoloured . . 3·00 3·25

196 Medieval Driftwood crucifix from Alftamyri

197 Leaf-bread (star pattern)

1981. Millenary of Missionary Work in Iceland.
604 **196** 200a. lilac 20 20

1981. Christmas. Multicoloured.
605 200a. Type **197** 60 50
606 250a. Leaf-bread (tree pattern) 60 45

198 Common Northern Whelk

199 Casting Dais Post into Sea (first Iceland settlement, 874)

1982. Shells.
607 **198** 20a. red 10 15
608 – 600a. brown 70 25
DESIGN: 600a. Iceland scallop.

1982. Europa. Multicoloured.
609 350a. Type **199** . . . . . . 1·80 65
610 450a. Discovery of Vinland (America), 1000 . . . . . 1·80 80

200 Sheep

201 Co-operative Trading House, Husavik

1982. Domestic Animals.
611 **200** 300a. brown 85 45
612 – 400a. red 35 25
613 – 500a. grey 35 25
DESIGNS: 400a. Cow; 500a. Cat.

1982. Centenary of Thingeyjar Co-operative Society.
614 **201** 1000a. black and brown 55 35

202 Horseman

1982. Iceland Ponies and Horsemanship.
615 **202** 700a. multicoloured . . . 40 30

203 Holar

1982. Cent of Holar Agricultural College.
616 **203** 1500a. multicoloured . . 70 60

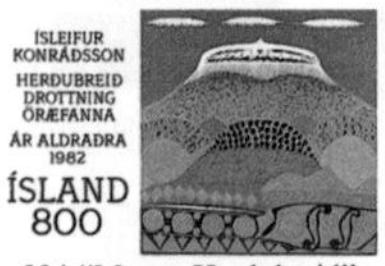
204 "Mount Herdubreid" (Isleifur Konradsson)

205 T. Sveinsdottir

1982. Year of the Aged.
617 **204** 800a. multicoloured . . . 45 35

1982. Famous Icelanders. Thorbjorg Sveindsdottir (midwife and founder of Icelandic Women's Association).
618 **205** 900a. brown 35 35

206 Reynistadur Monastery Seal

1982. "Nordia 84" Stamp Exhibition, Reykjavik (1st issue). Sheet 82 × 80 mm containing T **206** and similar vert design.
MS619 400a. brown and black; 800a. brown and black (sold at 18k.) 4·00 4·25
DESIGN:—800a. Thingeyrar Monastery seal.
See also Nos. **MS**636 and **MS**645.

207 Doves and Opening of "The Night was such a Splendid One"

1982. Christmas. Multicoloured.
620 300a. Type **207** 45 35
621 350a. Bells and close of "The Night was such a Splendid One" (composed by Sigvaldi Kaldalons from poem by E. Sigurdsson) . . 55 55

208 Marsh Marigold

209 Mount Sulur

1983. Flowers. Multicoloured.
622 7k.50 Type **208** 35 20
623 8k. Alpine catchfly 50 25
624 10k. Marsh cinquefoil . . . 1·00 25
625 20k. Water forgetmenot . . . 2·10 1·10

1983. Nordic Countries' Postal Co-operation. "Visit the North". Multicoloured.
626 4k.50 Type **209** 75 65
627 5k. Urridafossar Falls . . . 75 65

210 Thermal Area and Heat-exchange Plant

211 Stern Trawler

1983. Europa. Multicoloured.
628 5k. Type **210** . . . . 3·50 90
629 5k.50 Thermal area heating houses . . . . 11·00 1·30

1983. Fishing Industry.
630 **211** 11k. blue 65 65
631 – 13k. blue 90 50
DESIGN: 13k. Line fishing.

212 "Laki Craters" (Finnur Jonsson)

1983. Bicentenary of Skafta Eruption.
632 **212** 15k. multicoloured . . . 55 45

213 Skiing

1983. Outdoor Sports. Multicoloured.
633 12k. Type **213** 90 45
634 14k. Jogging 90 45

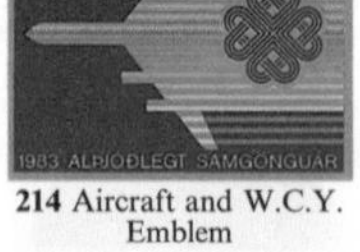
214 Aircraft and W.C.Y. Emblem

1983. World Communications Year.
635 **214** 30k. multicoloured . . . 1·40 1·00

215 Seal of Bishop Magnus Eyjolfsson

1983. "Nordia 84" Stamp Exhibition, Reykjavik (2nd issue). Sheet 82 × 80 mm containing T **215** and similar vert design.
MS636 8k. blue and black; 12k. green and black (sold at 30k.) 5·75 5·75
DESIGN: 12k. seal of Bishop Ogmundur Palsson.

216 Virgin Mary and Child

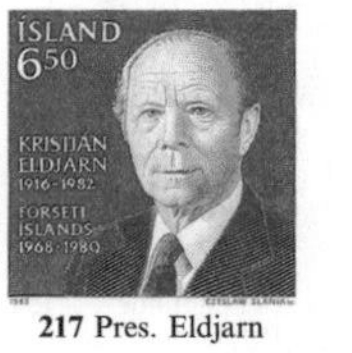
217 Pres. Eldjarn

1983. Christmas. Multicoloured.
637 600a. Type **216** 65 45
638 650a. Visitation of the Angel 65 45

1983. 1st Death Anniv (September) of Kristjan Eldjarn (President, 1968–80).
639 **217** 6k.50 red 75 65
640 7k. blue 40 25

218 Burnet Rose

219 Bridge

1984. Flowers. Multicoloured.
641 6k. Type **218** 70 40
642 25k. Silverweed 80 35
See also Nos. 648/9, 657/60 and 717/18.

1984. Europa. 25th Anniv of European Post and Telecommunications Conference.
643 **219** 6k.50 deep blue and blue 1·50 55
644 7k.50 dp purple & purple 60 45

220 Map of North Atlantic by Abraham Ortelius, 1570

1984. "Nordia 84" Stamp Exhibition, Reykjavik (3rd issue). Sheet 114 × 76 mm.
MS645 **220** 40k. multicoloured (sold at 60k.) . . . . 9·00 9·00

221 Icelandic Flags

222 I.O.G.T. Lodge, Akureyri

1984. 40th Anniv of Republic.
646 **221** 50k. multicoloured . . . 3·75 2·10

1984. Centenary of International Order of Good Templars in Iceland.
647 **222** 10k. green 65 40

1984. Flowers. As T **218**. Multicoloured.
648 6k.50 Wild azalea 55 40
649 7k.50 Alpine bearberry . . . 55 45

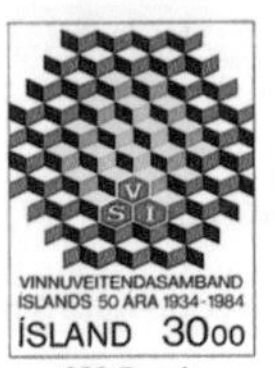
223 Basalt symbolising Industries

224 Bjorn Bjarnarson (founder) (after J. P. Wildenradt)

1984. 50th Anniv of Confederation of Icelandic Employers.
650 **223** 30k. multicoloured . . . 1·40 95

1984. Centenary of National Gallery.
651 **224** 12k. black, brown and green 70 45
652 – 40k. black, green and red 1·80 1·20
DESIGN: 40k. New gallery building.

225 Virgin and Child

226 Text from Bible

1984. Christmas.
653 **225** 600a. blue, lt blue & gold . . . 50 25
654 – 650a. red and gold . . . 60 25
DESIGN: 650a. Angel with Christmas rose.

1984. 400th Anniv of Gudbrand's Bible.
655 **226** 6k.50 red 50 30
656 – 7k.50 purple 40 60
DESIGN: 7k.50, Illustration from Bible.

1985. Flowers. As T **218**. Multicoloured.
657 8k. Stone bramble 40 25
658 9k. Rock speedwell 55 30
659 16k. Sea pea . . . . 1·70 65
660 17k. Alpine whitlow-grass . . 80 50

227 Lady playing Langspil

228 Swedish Whitebeam

1985. Europa. Music Year. Multicoloured.
661 6k.50 Type **227** . . . . . . 1·20 40
662 7k.50 Man playing Icelandic violin . . . . 1·10 1·10

1985. Centenary of Iceland Horticultural Society.
663 **228** 20k. multicoloured . . . 80 55

229 Girl and I.Y.Y. Emblem

230 Common Squid

1985. International Youth Year.
664 **229** 25k. multicoloured . . . 80 65

1985. Marine Life.
665 **230** 7k. purple 30 20
666 – 8k. brown 30 20
667 – 9k. red 50 50
DESIGNS: 8k. Common spider crab; 9k. Sea anemone.

231 Rev. Hannes Stephensen (politician)

1985. Famous Icelanders.
668 **231** 13k. red 45 35
669 – 30k. violet 65 60
DESIGN: 30k. Jon Gudmundsson (editor and politician).

232 "Flight Yearning"

233 Snow Scene

1985. Birth Centenary of Johannes Sveinsson Kjarval (artist).
670 **232** 100k. multicoloured . . . 4·00 3·50

1985. Christmas. Multicoloured.
671 8k. Type **233** 45 25
672 9k. Snow scene (different) . . 70 50

234 Pied Wagtail

1986. Birds. Multicoloured.
673 6k. Type **234** 40 20
674 10k. Pintail . . . . 1·20 50
675 12k. Merlin 95 50
676 15k. Razorbill 90 50
See also Nos. 697/700, 720/1, 726/7, 741/2 and 763/4.

235 Skaftafell National Park

1986. Europa. Multicoloured.
677 10k. Type **235** . . . . . . 5·00 1·20
678 12k. Jokulsargljufur National Park . . . . 2·40 75

236 Stykkisholmur

1986. Nordic Countries' Postal Co-operation. Twinned Towns. Multicoloured.
679 10k. Type **236** 75 65
680 12k. Seydisfjordur 75 40

237 Head Office, Reykjavik

1986. Centenary of National Bank. Mult.
681 **237** 13k. green 55 50
682 – 250k. brown . . . . . . 10·00 5·75
DESIGN: 250k. Reverse of first National Bank 5k. note.

238 First Official Seal

239 Early Telephone Equipment

1986. Bicentenary of Reykjavik.
683 **238** 10k. red 50 30
684 – 12k. brown 60 30
685 – 13k. green 50 45
686 – 40k. blue . . . . 1·80 85
DESIGNS: 12k. "Reykjavik pond, 1856" (illustration from "Journey in the Northern Seas" by Charles Edmond); 13k. Women washing clothes in natural hot water brook, Laugardalur; 40k. City Theatre.

1986. 80th Anniv of Icelandic Telephone and Telegraph Service. Multicoloured.
687 10k. Type **239** 40 20
688 20k. Modern digital telephone system 95 65

240 Hvita River Crossing, 1836 (after Auguste Mayer)

241 "Christmas at Peace"

1986. Stamp Day. Sheet 95 × 67 mm.
MS689 **240** 20k. black (sold at 30k.) 2·75 4·00

1986. Christmas. Multicoloured.
690 10k. Type **241** 60 30
691 12k. "Christmas Night" . . . 45 45

242 "Svanur" (ketch) anchored off Olafsvik

1987. 300th Anniv of Olafsvik Trading Station.
692 **242** 50k. purple . . . . 2·20 1·20

243 Terminal and Boeing 727 Tail

1987. Opening of Leif Eiriksson Terminal, Keflavik Airport.
693 **243** 100k. multicoloured . . . 3·75 1·60

244 Christ carrying Cross

245 Rask

1987. Europa. Stained Glass Windows by Leifur Breidfoerd, Fossvogur Cemetery Chapel. Multicoloured.
694 12k. Type **244** 85 60
695 15k. Soldiers and peace dove 85 50

1987. Birth Bicentenary of Rasmus Kristjan Rask (philologist).
696 **245** 20k. black 80 60

1987. Birds. As T **234**. Multicoloured.
697 13k. Short-eared owl 60 35
698 40k. Redwing . . . . 1·80 1·10
699 70k. Oystercatcher . . . . . 3·00 1·80
700 90k. Mallard . . . . 4·25 2·10

246 Girl Brushing Teeth

247 Vulture

1987. Dental Protection.
701 **246** 12k. multicoloured . . . 55 40

1987. National Guardian Spirits. Each red.
702 13k. Type **247** 60 70
703 13k. Dragon 60 70
704 13k. Bull 60 70
705 13k. Giant 60 70
See also Nos. 713/16, 732 and 743/50.

248 Djupivogur Trading Station, 1836 (after Auguste Mayer)

1987. Stamp Day. Sheet 95 × 67 mm.
MS706 **248** 30k. black (sold at 45k.) 3·25 3·75

249 Christmas Tree

250 Steinn Steinarr (poet)

1987. Christmas. Multicoloured.
707 13k. Type **249** 65 35
708 17k. "Christmas Light" . . . 65 55

1988. Famous Icelanders. Multicoloured.
709 16k. Type **250** 65 30
710 21k. David Stefansson (writer) 65 55

251 Transmission of Messages by Modern Data System

1988. Europa. Communications. Multicoloured.
711 16k. Type **251** 70 40
712 21k. Phone pad and globe within envelope (transmission of letters by facsimile machine) . . . . 1·60 1·50

1988. National Guardian Spirit. As Nos. 702/5 but values and colour changed.
713 16k. black (Type **247**) 75 75
714 16k. black (Dragon) 75 75
715 16k. black (Bull) 75 75
716 16k. black (Giant) 75 75

1988. Flowers. As T **218**. Multicoloured.
717 10k. Tufted vetch 55 25
718 50k. Wild thyme . . . . . . 2·20 75

252 Handball

254 Mother and Baby

253 "Nupsstadur Farm, Fljotshverfi, 1836" (after Auguste Mayer)

1988. Olympic Games, Seoul.
719 **252** 18k. multicoloured . . . 70 45

1988. Birds. As T **234**. Multicoloured.
720 5k. Black-tailed godwit . . . 15 20
721 30k. Long-tailed duck . . . 1·40 65

1988. Stamp Day. Sheet 95 × 67 mm.
MS722 **253** 40k. black (sold at 60k.) 3·75 4·25

1988. 40th Anniv of W.H.O. "Health for All in 2000".
723 **254** 19k. multicoloured . . . 80 35

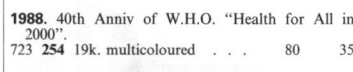

255 Fisherman with Haul of Fish

1988. Christmas. Multicoloured.
724 19k. Type **255** 65 45
725 24k. Trawler and buoy . . . 1·20 1·70

1989. Birds. As T **234**. Multicoloured.
726 19k. Red-necked phalarope 75 45
727 100k. Snow buntings . . . . 4·25 2·30

256 Peysufot (dress costume)

257 Children at Seaside

1989. Nordic Countries' Postal Co-operation. Traditional Costumes. Multicoloured.
728 21k. Type **256** 85 35
729 26k. Upphlutur (everyday wear) 85 50

1989. Europa. Childrens' Toys and Games. Multicoloured.
730 21k. Type **257** . . . . . . 2·20 55
731 26k. Girl with hoop and boy with hobby-horse . . . . 2·20 70

1989. National Guardian Spirits. As No. 703 but colour and value changed.
732 500k. brown (Dragon) . . . 16·00 7·00

258 Mount Skeggi, Arnarfjord

1989. Landscapes. Multicoloured.
733 35k. Type **258** . . . . . . 1·40 50
734 45k. Namaskard thermal spring . . . . 1·60 80
See also Nos. 757/8 and 765/6.

259 College

1989. Cent of Hvanneyri Agricultural College.
735 **259** 50k. multicoloured . . . 1·50 90

260 Seaman throwing Barrels at Whales

1989. Stamp Day. "Nordia 91" Stamp Exhibition, Reykjavik (1st issue). Sheet 114 × 74 mm containing T **260** and similar vert designs, showing details of the 1539 Carta Marina by Olaus Magnus.
MS736 30k. Type **260**; 30k. Ship harpooning whale; 30k. Sea serpent encircling ship (sold at 130k.) . . . . 5·00 6·75
See also Nos. **MS**760 and **MS**771.

261 Stefan Stefansson (co-founder) and Flowers

262 "Virgin and Child"

1989. Centenary of Icelandic Natural History Society. Multicoloured.
737 21k. Type **261** 65 40
738 26k. Bjarni Saemundsson (first Chairman) and Atlantic cod 90 50

1989. Christmas. Multicoloured.
739 21k. Type **262** 65 40
740 26k. "Three Wise Men" . . . 1·00 60

1990. Birds. As T **234**. Multicoloured.
741 21k. European wigeons . . . 70 45
742 80k. Pink-footed goose and goslings . . . . 2·10 1·10

1990. National Guardian Spirits. As Nos. 702/5 but value and colours changed.
743 5k. green (Type **247**) 15 25
744 5k. green (Dragon) 15 25
745 5k. green (Bull) 15 25
746 5k. green (Giant) 15 25
747 21k. blue (Type **247**) 60 70
748 21k. blue (Dragon) 60 70
749 21k. blue (Bull) 60 70
750 21k. blue (Giant) 60 70

263 Gudrun Larusdottir (writer and politician) (after Halldor Petursson)

264 Posthouse Street, Reykjavik, Post Office and Old Scales

1990. 110th Birth Anniversaries. Mult.
751 21k. Type **263** 75 45
752 21k. Ragnhildur Petursdottir (women's educationist) (after Asgrimur Jonsson) 75 45

1990. Europa. Post Office Buildings. Mult.
753 21k. Type **264** . . . . . . 1·00 70
754 40k. Thoenglabakki 4, Reykjavik, Post Office and modern scales . . . . . . 2·20 1·00

265 Archery

1990. Sport. Multicoloured.
755 21k. Type **265** 70 45
756 21k. Football 65 40

1990. Landscapes. As T **258**. Multicoloured.
757 25k. Hvitserkur, Hunafjord 70 45
758 200k. Lomagnupur . . . . . 5·75 3·00

266 Bird, Stars and Map

1990. European Tourism Year.
759 **266** 30k. multicoloured . . . 90 45

267 Denmark

1990. Stamp Day. "Nordia 91" Stamp Exhibition, Reykjavik (2nd issue). Sheet 114 × 74 mm containing T **267** and similar vert designs, showing details of the 1539 Carta Marina by Olaus Magnus.
MS760 40k. Type **267**; 40k. Sweden; 40k. Gotland and sailing ship (sold at 170k.) . . . . 7·00 7·50

268 Children around Christmas Tree

1990. Christmas. Multicoloured.
761 25k. Type **268** . . . . . . 1·20 55
762 30k. Carol singers . . . . . 1·10 65

1991. Birds. As T **234**. Multicoloured.
763 25k. Slavonian grebes . . . . 1·00 35
764 100k. Northern gannets . . . 3·50 1·60

1991. Landscapes. As T **258**. Multicoloured.
765 10k. Mt. Vestrahorn 60 20
766 300k. Kverkfjoll range . . . 9·50 5·00

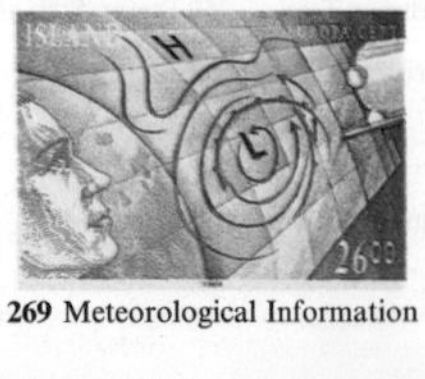

269 Meteorological Information

1991. Europa. Europe in Space. Mult.
767 26k. Type **269** . . . . . . 2·10 60
768 47k. Telecommunications satellite . . . . 2·10 1·10

270 Jokulsarlon

1991. Nordic Countries' Postal Co-operation. Tourism. Multicoloured.
769 26k. Type **270** . . . . . . 1·20 60
770 31k. Strokkur hot spring . . 1·30 75

271 Western Iceland

1991. "Nordia 91" Stamp Exhibition (3rd issue). Sheet 114 × 74 mm containing T **271** and similar vert designs, showing details of the 1539 Carta Marina by Olaus Magnus.
MS771 50k. Type **271**; 50k. Arms and central part of Iceland; 50k. Eastern Iceland, ice floes and compass rose (sold at 215k.) 7·75 8·50

272 Golf

273 Pall Isolfsson (composer) (after Hans Muller)

1991. Sports. Multicoloured.
772 26k. Type **272** 85 45
773 26k. Glima (wrestling) . . . 85 45

1991. Famous Icelanders. Multicoloured.
774 60k. Ragnar Jonsson (founder of Reykjavik College of Music) (after Joannes Kjarval) (horiz) . . 1·80 1·00
775 70k. Type **273** . . . . . . 2·20 1·40

274 College Building and Student using Sextant

1991. Cent of College of Navigation, Reykjavik.
776 **274** 50k. multicoloured . . . 1·60 90

275 "Soloven" (mail brigantine)

276 "Light of Christmas"

1991. Stamp Day. Ships. Multicoloured.
777 30k. Type **275** . . . . . . 2·20 1·40
778 30k. "Arcturus" (cargo liner) 2·20 1·40
779 30k. "Gullfoss I" (cargo liner) . . . . 2·20 1·40
780 30k. "Esja II" (cargo liner) 2·20 1·40

1991. Christmas. Multicoloured.
781 30k. Type **276** . . . . . . 1·00 50
782 35k. Star . . . . 1·20 75

277 Skiing

1992. Sport. Multicoloured.
783 30k. Type **277** . . . . . . 1·10 55
784 30k. Volleyball . . . . 1·10 55

278 Map and "Santa Maria"

1992. Europa. 500th Anniv of Discovery of America by Columbus. Multicoloured.
785 55k. Map and Viking ship (Leif Eriksson) . . . . . . 1·80 1·30
786 55k. Type **278** . . . . . . 1·80 1·30
MS787 85 × 67 mm. Nos. 785/6 3·00 3·50

279 Agricultural and Industrial Symbols

1992. 75th Anniv of Iceland Chamber of Commerce (30k.) and 50th Anniv of Icelandic Freezing Plants Corporation (35k.). Multicoloured.
788 30k. Type **279** 90 60
789 35k. Trawler and Atlantic cod . . . . 1·40 75

280 River Fnjoska Bridge, Skogar

282 Face and Candle reflected in Window

281 Ford "TT", 1920–26

1992. Bridges. Multicoloured.
790 5k. Type **280** 15 20
791 250k. River Olfusa bridge, Selfoss . . . . 8·25 5·50
See also Nos. 804/5.

1992. Postal Vehicles. Multicoloured.
792 30k. Type **281** . . . . . . 1·70 1·30
793 30k. Citroen snowmobile, 1929 . . . . 1·70 1·30
794 30k. Mail/passenger transport car "RE 231", 1933 . . . 1·70 1·30
795 30k. Ford bus, 1946 . . . . 1·70 1·30

1992. Christmas. Multicoloured.
796 30k. Type **282** . . . . . . 1·20 60
797 35k. Full moon . . . . . . 1·40 70

283 Gyr Falcon with Chicks

284 Handball

1992. Endangered Species. The Gyr Falcon. Multicoloured.
798 5k. Type **283** 30 20
799 10k. Beating wings . . . . . 1·20 40
800 20k. Eating . . . . 1·80 80
801 35k. On ground . . . . . . 3·25 1·30

1993. Sport. Multicoloured.
802 30k. Type **284** 85 45
803 30k. Running 85 45

1993. Bridges. As T **280**. Multicoloured.
804 90k. River Hvita bridge, Ferjukot . . . . 3·00 1·60
805 150k. River Jokulsa a Fjollum bridge, Grimsstadir . . . . 5·25 3·00

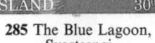

285 The Blue Lagoon, Svartsengi

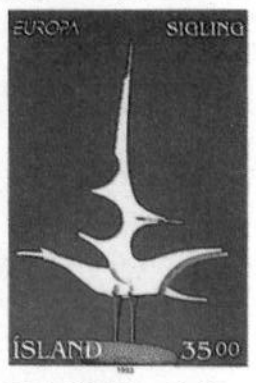

286 "Sailing" (Jon Gunnar Arnason)

1993. Nordic Countries' Postal Co-operation. Tourism. Multicoloured.

806	30k. Type **285**	95	60
807	35k. Perlan (The Pearl), Reykjavik	1·20	85

1993. Europa. Contemporary Art. Mult.

808	35k. Type **286**	1·40	1·10
809	55k. "Hatching of the Jet" (Magnus Tomasson)	2·10	1·70

287 1933 1k. Balbo Flight Stamp

1993. 60th Anniv of Balbo Transatlantic Mass Formation Flight. Sheet 110 × 76 mm containing T **287** and similar vert designs. Multicoloured.

MS810	10k. Type **287**; 50k. 1933 5k. Balbo flight stamp; 100k. 1933 10k. Balbo flight stamp (sold at 200k.)	5·75	6·00

288 Junkers "F-13" Seaplane "Sulan" D-483

1993. 65th Anniv of 1st Icelandic Postal Flight. Multicoloured.

811	30k. Type **288**	1·80	90
812	30k. Waco YKS-7 seaplane TF-0RH	1·80	1·00
813	30k. Grumman G-21 Goose amphibian TF-VK	1·80	1·00
814	30k. Consolidated PBY-5 Catalina flying boat "Old Peter" TF-TSP	1·80	1·00

289 Three Wise Men adoring Child

290 Swimming

1993. Christmas. Multicoloured.

815	30k. Type **289**	95	60
816	35k. Madonna and Child	1·10	85

1994. Sport. Multicoloured.

817	30k. Type **290**	1·00	45
818	30k. Weightlifting	1·00	45

291 Finger Puppets

1994. International Year of the Family.

819	**291** 40k. multicoloured	1·10	65

292 St. Brendan visiting Iceland

1994. Europa. St. Brendan's Voyages. Multicoloured.

820	35k. Type **292**	1·30	80
821	55k. St. Brendan discovering Faroe Islands	1·90	1·30
MS822	81 × 76 mm. Nos. 820/1	2·75	2·50

293 Conductor and Instruments

1994. 50th Anniv of Independence. Art and Culture. Multicoloured.

823	30k. Type **293** (44th anniv of Icelandic Symphony Orchestra)	90	45
824	30k. Pottery (55th anniv of College of Arts and Crafts)	90	45
825	30k. Cameraman and actors (16th anniv of National Film Fund)	90	45
826	30k. Ballerina and modern dancers (21st anniv of Icelandic Dance Company)	90	45
827	30k. Theatre masks (44th anniv of Icelandic National Theatre)	90	45

294 Gisli Sveinsson (President of United Althing, 1944)

1994. 50th Anniv of New Constitution.

828	**294** 30k. multicoloured	95	65

295 Sveinn Bjornsson (1944–52)

1994. 50th Anniv of Republic. Presidents. Sheet 118 × 71 mm containing T **295** and similar vert designs. Multicoloured.

MS829	50k. Type **295**; 50k. Asgeir Asgeirsson (1952–68); 50k. Kristjan Eldjarn (1968–80); 50k. Vigdis Finnbogadottir (1980 onwards)	5·50	5·50

296 Children looking at Stamp Album

1994. Stamp Day. Stamp Collecting. Sheet 120 × 50 mm containing T **296** and similar square designs. Multicoloured.

MS830	30k. Type **296**; 35k. Magnifying glass over stamps; 100k. Girl and elderly man studying globe (sold at 200k.)	6·00	6·25

297 Woman and Stars

1994. Christmas. Multicoloured.

831	30k. Type **297**	1·00	60
832	35k. Man and stars	1·20	85

298 Emblem and Airplane

1994. 50th Anniv of I.C.A.O.

833	**298** 100k. multicoloured	3·25	1·60

299 Flag and Salvation Army Members

300 Geyser

1995. Anniversaries. Multicoloured.

834	35k. Type **299** (centenary of Salvation Army in Iceland)	1·10	70
835	90k. Map of fjord (centenary of Seydisfjordur)	2·75	1·40

1995. 14th World Men's Handball Championship. Multicoloured.

836	35k. Type **300**	1·30	1·70
837	35k. Stadium	1·30	1·70
838	35k. Volcano	1·30	1·70
839	35k. Entrance to fjord	1·30	1·70

301 Laufas

302 "Spell-broken" (sculpture, Einar Jonsson)

1995. Nordic Countries' Postal Co-operation. Tourism. Multicoloured.

840	30k. Type **301**	95	55
841	35k. Fjallsjokull Glacier	1·10	65

1995. Europa. Peace and Freedom.

842	**302** 35k. multicoloured	1·20	1·00
843	55k. multicoloured	1·60	1·40

303 "Laura" (mail ship)

1995. Mail Ships. Multicoloured.

844	30k. Type **303**	1·10	1·00
845	30k. "Dronning Alexandrine"	1·10	1·00
846	30k. "Laxfoss"	1·10	1·00
847	30k. "Godafoss III"	1·10	1·00

304 Redpoll ("Acanthis flammea")

1995. European Nature Conservation Year. Birds. Multicoloured.

848	25k. Type **304**	75	45
849	250k. Common snipe ("Gallinago gallinago")	7·50	5·25

305 Boeing 757

1995. 40th Anniv of Iceland–Luxembourg Air Link.

850	**305** 35k. multicoloured	1·10	75

306 Hraunfossar Waterfalls (left detail)

1995. "Nordia 96" Stamp Exhibition, Reykjavik (1st issue). Sheet 105 × 65 mm containing T **306** and similar horiz design. Multicoloured.

MS851	10k. Type **306**; 150k. Waterfalls (right detail) (sold at 200k.)	5·75	6·00

The stamps form a composite design.
See also No. **MS**871.

307 Snowman and Snowwoman

308 Anniversary Emblem

1995. Christmas. Multicoloured.

852	30k. Type **307**	90	60
853	35k. Coloured fir trees	1·40	65

1995. 50th Anniv of U.N.O.

854	**308** 100k. multicoloured	3·25	1·80

309 Common Cormorant ("Phalacrocorax carbo")

1996. Birds. Multicoloured.

855	20k. Type **309**	55	40
856	40k. Barrow's goldeneye ("Bucephala islandica")	1·30	80

310 "Seamen in a Boat" (Gunnlaugur Scheving)

1996. Paintings. Multicoloured.

857	100k. Type **310**	2·75	1·80
858	200k. "At the Washing Springs" (Kristin Jonsdottir)	6·25	3·50

311 Halldora Bjarnadottir (founder of women's societies)

1996. Europa. Famous Women. Mult.

859	35k. Type **311**	1·20	80
860	55k. Olafia Johannsdottir (women's rights campaigner and temperance worker)	2·10	1·40

312 1931 Buick

1996. Post Buses. Multicoloured.

861	35k. Type **312**	1·10	75
862	35k. 1933 Studebaker	1·10	75
863	35k. 1937 Ford	1·10	75
864	35k. 1946 Reo	1·10	75

313 Running

1996. Olympic Games, Atlanta. Mult.

865	5k. Type **313**	15	15
866	25k. Javelin	75	60
867	45k. Long jumping	1·40	1·00
868	65k. Shot put	2·20	1·60

314 Hospital Ward

1996. Centenary of Order of the Sisters of St. Joseph in Iceland.
869 **314** 65k. black, stone & purple 2·00 1·80

315 School

1996. 150th Anniv of Reykjavik School.
870 **315** 150k. multicoloured . . . 4·25 3·25

316 Godafoss Waterfalls (central detail)

1996. "Nordia 96" Stamp Exhibition, Reykjavik (2nd issue). Sheet 105 × 65 mm containing T **316** and similar square designs. Multicoloured.
MS871 45k. Type **316**; 65k. Waterfalls (right detail); 90k. Waterfalls (left detail) (sold at 300k.) . . . . 7·50 5·50
The stamps form a composite design.

317 Reykjavik Cathedral **318** "Virgin Mary holding Child Jesus" (ivory figurine)

1996. Bicentenary of Reykjavik Cathedral.
872 **317** 45k. multicoloured . . . 1·40 1·00

1996. Christmas. Exhibits from National Museum of Iceland. Multicoloured.
873 35k. Type **318** . . . . . . 1·20 65
874 45k. Pax depicting Nativity 1·80 95

319 Red-breasted Merganser ("Mergus serrator")

1997. Ducks. Multicoloured.
875 10k. Type **319** 35 40
876 500k. Green-winged teal ("Anas crecca") . . . . . 13·50 12·50

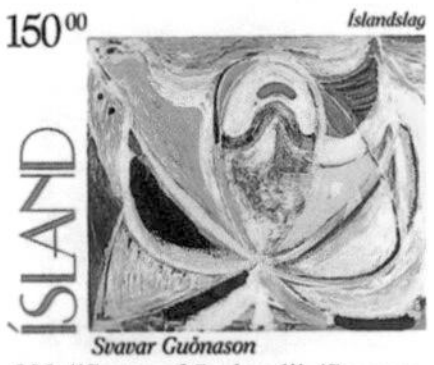

320 "Song of Iceland" (Svavar Gudnason)

1997. Paintings. Multicoloured.
877 150k. Type **320** . . . . . . 5·25 3·75
878 200k. "The Harbour" (Thorvaldur Skulason) . . 6·00 4·25

321 De Havilland D.H.89A Dragon Rapide

1997. Mail Planes. Multicoloured.
879 35k. Type **321** 95 80
880 35k. Stinson S.R. 8B Reliant seaplane 95 80
881 35k. Douglas DC-3 Dakota 95 80
882 35k. De Havilland D.H.C.6 Twin Otter 95 80

322 Hurdling

1997. 7th European Small States' Games. Multicoloured.
883 35k. Type **322** . . . . . . 1·10 1·10
884 45k. Sailing . . . . 1·50 1·00

323 "The Deacon of Myrka"

1997. Europa. Tales and Legends. Paintings by Asgrimur Jonsson. Multicoloured.
885 45k. Type **323** . . . . . . 1·50 1·10
886 65k. "Surtla at Blalandseyjar" . . . . . . 2·20 1·60

324 Printer's Colour Control and Pieces of Type

1997. Centenary of Formation of Icelandic Printers' Association (now part of Union of Icelandic Graphic Workers).
887 **324** 90k. multicoloured . . . 2·75 2·20

325 Stefania Gudmundsdattir and Idno Theatre **326** Western Islands Eight-oared Fishing Boat

1997. Centenary of Reykjavik Theatre.
888 **325** 100k. multicoloured . . . 3·25 2·10
The actress is shown in the role of the Fairy in "New Year's Night" by Indridi Einarsson.

1997. Stamp Day. Icelandic Boats. Sheet 110 × 76 mm containing T **326** and similar square designs. Each black, brown and chestnut.
MS889 35k. Type **326**; 65k. Engey six-oared sailing boat, 1912; 100k. Egil (Breidafjordur boat), 1904 (sold at 250k.) . . . . 5·50 6·00

327 Wise Men

1997. Christmas. Multicoloured.
890 35k. Type **327** . . . . . . 1·20 75
891 45k. Nativity . . . . 1·50 1·00

328 Mounted Mail Carrier

1997. Rural Post.
892 **328** 50k. multicoloured . . . 1·50 1·00

329 Downhill Skiing

1998. Winter Olympic Games, Nagano, Japan. Multicoloured.
893 35k. Type **329** . . . . . . 1·10 70
894 45k. Cross-country skiing . . 1·50 1·00

330 Sailing Dinghies

1998. Nordic Countries' Postal Co-operation. Sailing. Multicoloured.
895 35k. Type **330** . . . . . . 1·20 75
896 45k. Yachts . . . . 1·60 1·10

331 Lumpsucker ("Cyclopterus lumpus")

1998. Fishes (1st series). Multicoloured.
897 5k. Type **331** 20 20
898 10k. Atlantic cod ("Gadus morhua") 20 25
899 60k. Skate ("Raja batis") . . 1·70 1·70
900 300k. Atlantic wolffish ("Anarhichas lupus") . . . 8·00 8·75
MS901 100 × 68 mm. Nos. 897/900 5·50 4·75
See also Nos. 913/14, 972/3 and 983/4.

332 Children waving Flags **333** Scolecite

1998. Europa. National Festivals. National Day. Multicoloured.
902 45k. Type **332** . . . . . . 1·40 1·30
903 65k. Statue of President Jon Sigurdsson and flags . . . 2·20 1·50

1998. Minerals (1st series). Multicoloured.
904 35k. Type **333** 90 70
905 45k. Stilbite . . . . 1·50 1·10
See also Nos. 933/4.

334 Hospital **335** Anniversary Emblem

1998. Centenary of Founding of Leprosy Hospital, Laugarnes.
906 **334** 70k. multicoloured . . . 2·10 1·80

1998. 125th Anniv of First Iceland Stamps.
907 **335** 35k. multicoloured . . . 1·20 90

336 Peat-cutter **337** Cat and Houses (Thelma Ingolfsdottir)

1998. Stamp Day. Agricultural Tools. Sheet 110 × 76 mm containing T **336** and similar square designs.
MS908 35k. green, black and grey; 65k. ochre, black and grey; 100k. blue, black and grey (sold at 250k.) . . . . 5·00 5·75
DESIGNS: 65k. Mower; 100k. Grinder.

1998. Christmas. Multicoloured.
909 35k. Type **337** . . . . . . 1·20 95
910 45k. Two angels (Telma Thrastardottir) . . . . . . 1·50 1·20

338 Writing and Hand forming Fist

1998. 50th Anniv of Universal Declaration of Human Rights.
911 **338** 50k. black, green and red 1·60 1·30

339 Leifs

1999. Birth Centenary of Jon Leifs (composer).
912 **339** 35k. multicoloured . . . 1·10 90

1999. Fishes (2nd series). As T **331**. Multicoloured.
913 35k. Plaice ("Pleuronectes platessa") . . . . 1·00 90
914 55k. Atlantic herring ("Clupea harengus") . . . 1·70 1·10

340 Killer Whale ("Orcinus orca")

1999. Marine Mammals (1st series). Multicoloured.
915 35k. Type **340** . . . . . . 1·10 95
916 45k. Sperm whale ("Physeter macrocephalus") . . . . . 1·40 1·10
917 65k. Blue whale ("Balaenoptera musculus") 2·20 1·70
918 85k. Common porpoise ("Phocoena phocoena") . . 2·75 2·20
MS919 100 × 80 mm. Nos. 915/19 3·75 4·25
See also Nos. 966/9 and 1000/3.

341 Arnold Jung's Steam Locomotive "Minor", 1892

1999. Transport. Multicoloured.
920 25k. Type **341** . . . . . . 1·20 90
921 50k. Type **341** . . . . . . 2·40 1·70
922 75k. "Sigurfari" (fishing cutter) . . . . 3·75 3·00

342 Dates and Doves

1999. 50th Anniv of Council of Europe.
923 **342** 35k. multicoloured . . . 1·10 90

343 Larch Boletes ("Suillus grevillei")

1999. Fungi (1st series). Multicoloured.
924 35k. Type **343** . . . . . . 1·10 1·00
925 75k. Field mushrooms ("Agaricus campestris") . . 2·10 2·00
See also Nos. 954/5.

344 Skutustadagigar, Lake Myvatn

1999. Europa. Parks and Gardens. Multicoloured.
926 50k. Type **344** . . . . . . 1·60 1·40
927 75k. Arnarstapi Point . . . . 2·10 2·10

345 Wheat ("Land Graedsla")

1999. Nature Conservation. Multicoloured.

928	35k. Type **345**	1·10	90
929	35k. Rainbow and tree within sun ("Loft")	1·10	95
930	35k. Nest with eggs ("Vot Lendis")	1·10	95
931	35k. Tree stump ("Skog Raekt")	1·10	95
932	35k. Fish and birds ("Stlendur")	1·10	95

1999. Minerals (2nd series). As T **333**. Mult.

933	40k. Calcite	1·00	95
934	50k. Heulandite	1·60	1·40

346 "Facescape" (Erro)

1999. Reykjavik, European Cultural City. Mult.

935	35k. Type **346**	1·00	95
936	50k. Cultural symbols	1·60	1·40

347 "Danish Sailing Ship off Drangey" (Carl Baagoe)

1999. Stamp Day. Sheet 110 × 65 mm.

MS937	**347** 200k. brown and black (sold at 250k.)	4·00	4·25

348 Man cleaning Globe (Jona Greta Gudmundsdottir)

1999. "Stampin' the Future". Winning Entries in Children's International Painting Competition.

938	**348** 35k. multicoloured	1·20	85

349 Goblin (Stiff-legs)

351 Chanterelle (*Cantharellus cibarius*)

350 Embroidered Altar Frontal, Holar Cathedral

1999. Christmas. Yule Goblins. Multicoloured.

939	35k. Type **349**	1·10	1·00
940	35k. Leaping over rock (Gully-gawk)	1·10	1·00
941	35k. With arm raised (Stubby)	1·10	1·00
942	35k. Licking spoon (Spoon-licker)	1·10	1·00
943	35k. With hand in cooking pot (Pot-scraper)	1·10	1·00
944	35k. With finger in mouth (Bowl-licker)	1·10	1·00
945	35k. Opening door (Door-slammer)	1·10	1·00
946	35k. Drinking from ladle (Skyr-gobbler)	1·10	1·00
947	35k. Carrying sausages (Sausage-swiper)	1·10	1·00
948	35k. Looking through window (Window-peeper)	1·10	1·00
949	50k. With nose raised (Door-sniffer)	1·40	1·40
950	50k. With leg of meat (Meat-hook)	1·40	1·40
951	50k. With candles (Candle-beggar)	1·40	1·40

2000. Millenary of Christianity in Iceland. Mult.

952	40k. Type **350**	45	55
MS953	70 × 46 mm. 40k. Family singing hymns (29 × 39 mm)	45	55

2000. Fungi (2nd series). Multicoloured.

954	40k. Type **351**	1·20	1·20
955	50k. Shaggy ink cap (*Coprinus comatus*)	1·60	1·40

352 Statue of Thorfinn Karlsefni (early settler) and Globe

2000. Millenary of Discovery of the Americas by Leif Eriksson. Multicoloured.

956	40k. Type **352**	1·20	1·30
957	50k. Viking longship under sail	1·50	1·50
958	75k. Longship on shore	2·40	2·20
959	90k. Leif Eriksson and globe	3·00	2·40
MS960	96 × 76 mm. Nos. 956/9	3·25	3·00

353 Quill and Profile

2000. New Millennium. Multicoloured.

961	40k. Type **353**	1·20	1·20
962	50k. Family tree, man and computer chip	1·60	1·40

354 Steam Roller

2000. Transport. Multicoloured.

963	50k. Type **354**	1·30	1·40
964	75k. Fire engine	2·30	2·40

355 "Building Europe"

356 Pansy (*Violea x wittrockiana*)

2000. Europa.

965	**355** 50k. multicoloured	1·70	1·50

2000. Marine Mammals (2nd series). As T **340**. Mult.

966	5k. Bottlenose whale (*Hyperoodon ampullatus*)	20	25
967	40k. Atlantic white-sided dolphin (*Lagenorhynchus actus*)	1·20	1·20
968	50k. Humpback whale (*Megaptera novaeangliae*)	1·40	1·40
969	75k. Minke whale (*Balaenoptera acutorostrata*)	2·20	2·30

2000. Summer Flowers (1st series). Multicoloured.

970	40k. Type **356**	1·30	1·10
971	50k. Petunia (*Petunia x hybrida*)	1·60	1·40

See also Nos. 986/7.

2000. Fishes (3rd series). As T **331**. Multicoloured.

972	10k. Haddock (*Melanogrammus aeglefinus*)	30	30
973	250k. Capelin (*Mallotus villosus*)	6·00	6·75

357 Dark Marbled Carpet (*Chioroclysta citrata*)

2000. Butterflies. Multicoloured.

974	40k. Type **357**	1·10	1·00
975	50k. Antler (*Cerapteryx graminis*)	1·30	1·30

358 "Icelandic settlers on the Shore of Lake Winnipeg" (Arni Sigurdsson)

2000. Stamp Day. Sheet 88 × 73 mm.

MS976	**358** 200k. multicoloured (sold at 250k.)	4·00	4·00

359 Viking Settler's House

2000. Early Dwellings. Multicoloured.

977	45k. Type **359**	1·10	1·10
978	75k. Viking turf houses, Stong Thjorsardal	2·20	2·00

360 Leppaludi

2000. Christmas. Ogres. Multicoloured.

979	40k. Type **360**	1·10	1·00
980	50k. Gryla	1·20	1·20
MS981	105 × 75 mm. As Nos. 979/80, but 21 × 36 mm)	1·50	1·25

361 Super Puma Helicopter, Fokker 27 Airplane and *Tyr* (ship)

363 Marigold (*Calendula officinalis*)

362 Man's Face, Tents and Emblem

2001. 75th Anniv of Coast Guard Service in Iceland.

982	**361** 20k. multicoloured	30	60

2001. Fishes. As T **331**. Multicoloured.

983	55k. Greenland halibut (*Reinhardtius hippogolossides*)	85	1·00
984	80k. Saithe (*Pollachius virens*)	1·30	1·60

2001. 50th Anniv of United Nations Commissioner for Refugees.

985	**362** 50k. black and brown	80	95

2001. Summer Flowers. Multicoloured.

986	55k. Type **363**	85	1·00
987	65k. Livingstone daisy (*Dorotheanthus bellidformis*)	1·00	1·30

364 Dog

2001. Icelandic Sheepdogs. Multicoloured.

988	40k. Type **364**	75	85
989	80k. Black and white dog	1·60	1·10

365 TF-OGN

2001. Airplanes. Multicoloured.

990	55k. Type **365**	1·10	1·00
991	80k. Klemm KL-25E	2·40	1·10

366 Woman's Head and Waterfall

2001. Europa. Water Resources. Multicoloured.

992	55k. Type **366**	1·10	90
993	80k. Cupped hands and wave	1·60	1·10

367 Walking

2001. Horses. Multicoloured.

994	40k. Type **367**	70	75
995	50k. Running walk	75	90
996	55k. Trotting	85	95
997	60k. Pacing	1·00	90
998	80k. Cantering	1·40	1·10

2001. Domestic Letter Rate. No. 915 optd **Bref 50g**.

999	(53k.) multicoloured	1·00	80

2001. Marine Mammals (3rd series). As T **340**. Multicoloured.

1000	5k. Large-beaked dolphin (*Lagenorhynchus albirostris*)	15	20
1001	40k. Fin whale (*Balaenoptera physalus*)	70	75
1002	80k. Sei whale (*Balaenoptera borealis*)	1·40	1·50
1003	100k. Long-finned pilot whale (*Globicephala melas*)	1·70	1·90

369 Grimsey

2001. Islands (1st series). Multicoloured.

1004	40k. Type **369**	70	60
1005	55k. Papey	85	80

See also Nos. 1031/2, 1061/2 and 1094/5.

370 Esja Mountain

2001. Stamp Day. Sheet 105 × 48 mm.

MS1006	**370** 250k. multicoloured	4·25	3·25

371 Brautarholt Church, Kjalarnes

2001. Christmas. Multicoloured.

1007	(42k.) Type **371**	70	55
1008	55k Viomyri Church, Skagafjorour	85	75

372 Northern Wheatear (*Oenanthe oenanthe*)

2001. Birds (1st series). Multicoloured.
1009 42k. Type **372** 65 60
1010 250k. Ringed plover (*Charadrius hiaticula*) . . 4·25 3·25
See also Nos. 1036/7,1055/6 and 1092/3.

373 Brown Birch Bolete (*Leccinum scabrum*)

2002. Fungi. Multicoloured. (a) Inscr "Bref 20g".
1011 (42k.) Type **373** 70 60
(b) With face value.
1012 85k. Hedgehog fungus (*Hydnum repandum*) . . . 1·40 1·20
No. 1011 was for use on domestic mail up to 20 grammes.

374 Stanley and 2 h.p. Mollerup Engine

2002. Centenary of First Motorboat in Iceland.
1013 **374** 60k. multicoloured . . . 1·00 85

375 Mount Snæfell

2002. International Year of the Mountain. Inscr "Bref 20g".
1014 **375** (42k.) multicoloured . . 70 60
No. 1014 was for use on domestic mail up to 20 grammes.

376 Laxness

2002. Birth Centenary of Halldor Laxness (writer and Nobel Prize winner).
1015 **376** 100k. multicoloured . . 1·70 1·40
MS1016 75 × 45 mm. No. 1015 1·70 1·70

377 "Waterfall" (sculpture, Ruri) and Emblem

2002. Nordic Countries' Postal Co-operation. Modern Art. Multicoloured. (a) Inscr "Bref 20g".
1017 (42k.) Type **377** (50th anniv of Nordic Council) . . . 70 60
(b) With face value.
1018 60k. "Tension" (sculpture, Hafsteinn Austmann) and emblem . . . . 1·00 85
No. 1017 was for use on domestic mail up to 20 grammes.

378 Grotta **379** House and Sesselja Sigmundsdottir

2002. Lighthouses. Multicoloured.
1019 60k. Type **378** . . . . . . 1·00 85
1020 85k. Kogur . . . . 1·40 1·20

2002. Birth Centenary of Sesselja H. Sigmundsdottir (mental health pioneer and environmentalist).
1021 **379** 45k. multicoloured . . . 75 65

380 Trapeze Artists and Clown

2002. Europa. Circus. Multicoloured.
1022 60k. Type **380** . . . . . . 1·00 85
1023 85k. Marionette's head and lion leaping through flaming hoop . . . . . . 1·40 1·20

381 Lobelia (*Lobelia erinus*)

2002. Summer Flowers. Multicoloured.
1024 10k. Type **381** 15 15
1025 200k. Cornflower (*Centaurea cyanus*) . . . . 3·50 2·75

382 Arctic Charr (*Salvelinus alpinus*)

2002. Fish from Lake Thingvallavatn. Multicoloured. (a) Inscr "Bref 20g".
1026 (45k.) Type **382** 75 65
(b) Inscr "Bréf 50g".
1027 (55k.) Brown trout (*Salmo trutta*) (vert) 90 80
(c) With face value.
1028 60k. Arctic charr (*Salvelinus alpinus*) . . . . 1·00 85
1029 90k. Arctic charr (*Salvelinus alpinus*) . . . . 1·50 1·30
1030 200k. Arctic charr (*Salvelinus alpinus*) . . . 3·50 2·75
No. 1026 was for use on domestic mail up to 20 grammes.
No. 1027 was for use on domestic mail up to 50 grammes.

2002. Islands (2nd series). As T **369**. Multicoloured.
1031 45k. Vigur 75 65
1032 55k. Flatey 90 80

383 South Street, Reykjavik, and Mount Keilir (volcano) **384** Bauble, Flags and Gift

2002. Stamp Day. Sheet 85 × 55 mm.
MS1033 **383** 250k. multicoloured 4·25 4·25

2002. Christmas. Multicoloured.
1034 45k. Type **384** 75 65
1035 60k. Gifts . . . . 1·00 85

385 Common Redshank (*Tringa totanus*)

2002. Birds (2nd series). Multicoloured.
1036 50k. Type **385** 85 70
1037 85k. Grey phalarope (*Phalaropus fulicarius*) . . 1·40 1·20

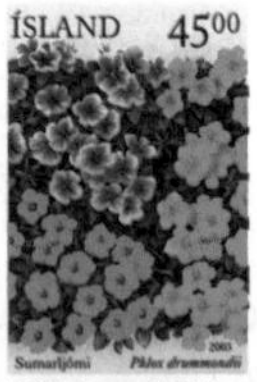

386 Modern Policemen **387** Annual Phlox (*Phlox drummondii*)

2003. Bicentenary of Icelandic Police Force. Multicoloured.
1038 45k. Type **386** 75 65
1039 55k. 1803 policeman 90 75

2002. Summer Flowers. Multicoloured.
1040 45k. Type **387** 75 60
1041 60k. Treasure flower (*Gazania x hybrida*) . . . 95 80

388 Bull and Audhumla (mythological cow)

2003. Icelandic Cattle. Multicoloured.
1042 45k. Type **388** 75 65
1043 85k. Red-mottled cow . . . 1·40 1·20

389 Map, Crow and Sailing Ship

2003. Nordia 2003 International Stamp Exhibition, Rekjavik. Sheet 86 × 76 mm.
MS1044 **389** 250k. multicoloured 4·00 3·50

390 *Saefari*

2003. Ferries. Multicoloured.
1045 45k. Type **390** 70 60
1046 45k. *Saevar* 70 60
1047 60k. *Herjolfur* 95 80
1048 60k. *Baldur* 95 80

391 Church **392** Hen and Cockerel

2003. Centenary of Free Church, Reykjavik.
1049 **391** 200k. multicoloured . . 3·00 2·50

2003. Icelandic Poultry.
1050 **392** 45k. multicoloured . . . 70 60

393 Posters

2003. Europa. Poster Art. Multicoloured.
1051 60k. Type **393** 95 80
1052 60k. Posters (different) . . . 95 80

394 Friendship (Orn Agustsson)

2003. Winning Entry in Children's Stamp Design Competition.
1053 **394** 45k. multicoloured . . . 70 60

395 District Officer and Family

2003. 300th Anniv of First Census.
1054 **395** 60k. multicoloured . . . 95 80

2003. Birds (3rd series). As T **385**. Multicoloured.
1055 70k. Meadow pipit (*Anthus pratensis*) . . . . 1·10 85
1056 250k. Whimbrel (*Numenius phaeopus*) . . . . 4·00 3·50

396 Reindeer (*Rangifer tarandus*)

2003.
1057 **396** 45k. multicoloured . . . 70 60

397 Barrack converted to House

2003. Stamp Day. Sheet 120 × 58 mm.
MS1058 **397** 250k. multicoloured 4·00 3·50

398 Girl hanging Baubles on Tree **399** Marigolds (*Tagetes patula*)

2003. Christmas. Multicoloured.
1059 45k. Type **398** 70 60
1060 60k. Boy lighting candles . . 95 80

2003. Islands (3rd series). As T **369**.
1061 85k. Heimaey . . . . 1·30 1·10
1062 200k. Hrisey . . . . 3·00 1·70

2004. Summer Flowers. Multicoloured.
1063 50k. Type **399** 80 70
1064 55k. Begonias (*begonia x tuberhybrida*) 85 70

400 Hannes Hafstein (first minister)

2004. Centenary of Icelandic Home Rule. Multicoloured.
1065 150k. Type **400** . . . . . . 2·40 2·00
MS1066 79 × 50 mm. No. 1065 2·40 2·00

401 *Coot* (trawler)

2004.
1067 **401** 50k. blue and black . . 80 70

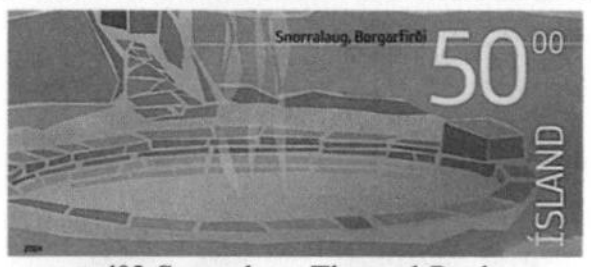

402 Snorralaug Thermal Pool

2004. Geo-thermal Energy. Multicoloured.
1068 50k. Type **402** 80 70
1069 55k. Vent, dome and steam (30 × 48 mm) 85 70
1070 60k. Pipeline 95 80
1071 90k. Turbine . . . . 1·40 1·20
1072 250k. Map of Iceland, mid Atlantic ridge and clouds (30 × 48 mm) . . . . . . 4·00 3·30

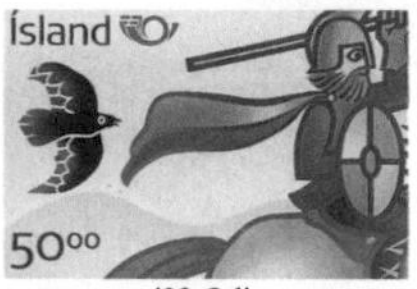

403 Odin

2004. Norse Mythology. Sheet 105 × 70 mm containing T **403** and similar horiz design. Multicoloured.
MS1073 50k. Type **403**; 60k. Sleipnir (Odin's horse) . . . . 1·90 1·90
Stamps of a similar theme were issued by Aland Islands, Denmark, Faroe Islands, Finland, Greenland, Norway and Sweden.

404 Ford Fairlane Victoria, 1956

2004. Cars. Multicoloured.
1074 60k. Type **404** 95 80
1075 60k. Pobeta, 1954 . . . . . 95 80
1076 85k. Chevrolet Bel Air, 1955 1·30 1·10
1077 85k. Volkswagen, 1952 . . . 1·30 1·10

405 Woman reaching into Barrel of Fish

2004. Centenary of Herring Production.
1078 **405** 65k. multicoloured . . . 1·10 85

406 Cyclists

2004. Europa. Holidays. Multicoloured.
1079 65k. Type **406** . . . . . . 1·10 85
1080 90k. Four-wheel drive vehicles in snow . . . . . 1·60 1·40

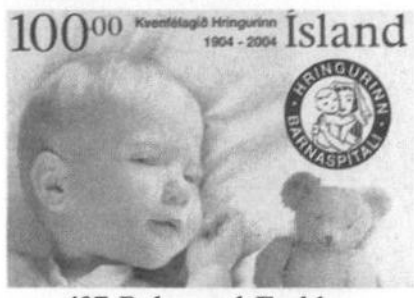

407 Baby and Emblem

2004. Centenary of Hringurinn (women's charitable organization).
1081 **407** 100k. multicoloured . . 1·75 1·50

408 Hand holding Light Bulb

2004. Centenary of Electrification.
1082 **408** 50k. multicoloured . . . 90 75

409 Grisette (*Amanita vaginata*)

2004. Fungi. Multicoloured.
1083 50k. Type **409** 90 75
1084 60k. *Camarophyllus pratensis* 1·10 85

410 Cudell (1901)

2004. Centenary of First Motor Car in Iceland.
1085 **410** 100k. black . . . . . . 1·75 1·50

411 Ground Beetle (*Nebria gyllenhali*)

2004. Insects. Multicoloured.
1086 50k. Type **411** 90 75
1087 70k. White-tailed bumble bee (*Bombus lucorum*) . . 1·20 90

412 Ship and Hospital Building

2004. Centenary of French Hospital, Faskrudsfirdi.
1088 **412** 60k. multicoloured . . . 1·10 85

413 Rock, Hvita River, Bruarhlod

2004. Stamp Day. Sheet 85 × 55 mm.
MS1089 **413** 250k. multicoloured 4·25 4·25

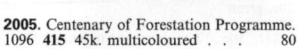

414 Ptarmigan in Winter Plumage

2004. Christmas. Multicoloured.
1090 45k. Type **414** 80 70
1091 65k. Reindeer . . . . 1·10 85

2004. Birds (4th series). As T **385**. Multicoloured.
1092 55k. Sandpiper (*Caladris maritime*) 95 80
1093 75k. Dunlin (*Caladris alpine*) 1·30 1·10

2005. Islands (4th series). As T **369**.
1094 5k. Videy 10 10
1095 90k. Flatey . . . . 1·60 1·40

415 Forest

2005. Centenary of Forestation Programme.
1096 **415** 45k. multicoloured . . . 80 65

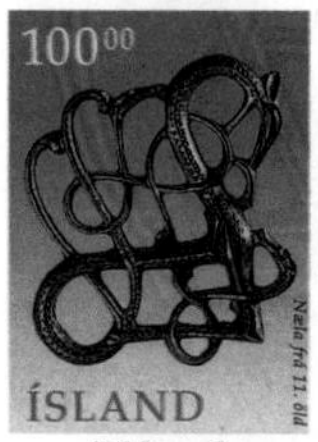

416 Brooch (11th-century)

418 Rose

417 Field Mouse (*Apodemus sylvaticus*)

2005. 60th Anniv of Foundation, and Re-opening (2004) of National Museum. Sheet 105 × 75 mm containing T **416** and similar vert designs. Multicoloured.
MS1097 100k. Type **416**; 150k. Thor (10th-century statue) . . . . . 4·25 4·25

2005. Mice. Multicoloured.
1098 45k. Type **417** 80 65
1099 125k. House mouse (*Mus musculus*) . . . . 2·10 1·70

2005. Greetings Stamps. Flowers. Multicoloured.
1100 50k. Type **418** 90 75
1101 50k. Gerbera 90 75
1102 50k. Zantedeschia 90 75
1103 70k. Tulip . . . . 1·20 90

419 *Araneus diadematus*

2005. Insect and Spider. Multicoloured.
1104 50k. Type **419** 90 75
1105 70k. *Musca domestica* . . . 1·20 90

420 *Vorour PH 4*

2005. Old Fishing Boats. Multicoloured.
1106 70k. Type **420** . . . . . . 1·20 90
1107 70k. *Karl VE 47* . . . . . 1·20 90
1108 95k. *Sædis IS 67* . . . . . 1·60 1·40
1109 95k. *Guobjorg NK 74* . . . 1·60 1·40

OFFICIAL STAMPS

1873. As T 1 but inscr "PJON. FRIM." at foot.
O 8 4s. green . . . . 46·00 £225
O10 8s. mauve £300 £425

O 4

1876.
O36 **O 4** 3a. yellow . . . . . . 9·25 15·00
O37 4a. grey . . . . 19·00 22·00
O21b 5a. brown . . . . . . 5·75 9·25
O22a 10a. blue . . . . 48·00 6·75
O23a 16a. red . . . . 14·00 26·00
O24a 20a. green . . . . . . 10·00 13·00
O25 50a. mauve . . . . . . 46·00 50·00

1902. As T **10**, but inscr "PJONUSTA".
O81 3a. sepia and yellow . . . . 3·00 1·40
O82 4a. sepia and green . . . . 3·50 1·20
O83 5a. sepia and brown . . . . 3·00 1·60
O84 10a. sepia and blue . . . . 3·25 2·25
O85 16a. sepia and red . . . . 2·10 6·75
O86 20a. sepia and green . . . . 12·50 4·25
O87 50a. sepia and mauve . . . 5·75 9·00

1902. Optd **I GILDI '02–'03**.
O94 **O 4** 3a. yellow . . . . . . 75 1·50
O95 4a. grey . . . . 75 1·30
O96 5a. brown . . . . . . 75 4·00
O97 10a. blue . . . . 75 1·75
O91 16a. red . . . . 10·00 34·00
O98 20a. green . . . . 80 12·00
O93 50a. mauve . . . . . . 3·50 33·00

1907. As T **12**, but inscr "PJONUSTU".
O 99 3a. sepia and yellow . . . 6·25 4·00
O100 4a. sepia and green . . . . 2·40 4·50
O101 5a. sepia and brown . . . 6·75 2·50
O102 10a. sepia and blue . . . . 2·00 2·10
O103 15a. sepia and blue . . . . 3·25 10·50
O104 16a. sepia and red . . . . 3·00 15·00
O105 20a. sepia and green . . . 7·50 3·75
O106 50a. sepia and mauve . . . 5·00 7·25

1920. As T **15**, but inscr "PJONUSTU".
O132 3a. black and yellow . . . 1·90 1·70
O133 4a. black and green . . . . 80 1·70
O134 5a. black and orange . . . 60 65
O135 10a. black and blue . . . . 3·75 45
O136 15a. black and blue 45 45
O137 20a. black and green . . . 28·00 2·30
O138 50a. black and violet . . . 31·00 90
O139 1k. black and red . . . . . 31·00 1·30
O140 2k. black and blue . . . . 4·00 10·00
O141 5k. black and brown . . . 26·00 29·00

1922. Optd **Pjonusta**.
O153 **15** 20a. on 10a. red . . . . 15·00 1·20
O151a **13** 2k. red (No. 107) . . . 35·00 38·00
O152 5k. brown (No. 108) . . £180 £130

1930. Parliamentary Commemoratives of 1930 optd **Pjonustumerki**.
O174 **24** 3a. violet and lilac (postage) . . . . . . 7·75 21·00
O175 – 5a. blue and grey . . . . 7·75 21·00
O176 – 7a. green and dp green 7·75 21·00
O177 – 10a. purple and mauve 7·75 21·00
O178 – 15a. dp blue & blue . . . 7·75 21·00
O179 – 20a. red and pink . . . . 7·75 21·00
O180 – 25a. brown & lt brown 7·75 21·00
O181 – 30a. green and grey . . . 7·75 21·00
O182 – 35a. blue & ultramarine 7·75 21·00
O183 – 40a. red, blue and grey 7·75 21·00
O184 – 50a. dp brown & brown £110 £140
O185 – 1k. green and grey . . . £110 £140
O186 – 2k. blue and green . . . £100 £160
O187 – 5k. orange and yellow . . £100 £130
O188 – 10k. lake and red £100 £130
O189 **25** 10a. blue & dp blue (air) 18·00 65·00

1936. Optd **Pjonusta**.
O220 **15** 7a. green . . . . 2·00 18·00
O221 10a. red . . . . 3·75 2·00
O222 **12** 50a. red and grey . . . . 18·00 16·00

IDAR Pt. 1

A state in Western India. Now uses Indian stamps.

12 pies = 1 anna; 16 annas = 1 rupee.

1 Maharaja Singh Himat

2 Maharaja Singh Himat

1939.
1c **1** ½a. green . . . . 14·00 20·00

1944.
3b **2** ½a. green . . . . 3·25 65·00
4 1a. violet . . . . 3·25 55·00
5 2a. blue . . . . 3·50 90·00
6 4a. red . . . . 3·75 95·00

IFNI Pt. 9

Spanish enclave on the Atlantic coast of Northern Morocco ceded in 1860.

By an agreement, made effective on 30 June 1969, Ifni was surrendered by Spain to Morocco.

100 centimos = 1 peseta.

1941. Stamps of Spain optd **TERRITORIO DE IFNI**.
1 **181** 1c. green (imperf) . . . . 6·00 5·25
2 **182** 2c. brown . . . . 6·00 5·25
3 **183** 5c. brown 85 55
4 10c. red . . . . 3·25 1·90
5 15c. green 75 55
6 **196** 20c. violet 75 55
7 25c. red 75 55
8 30c. blue 75 55
9 40c. slate . . . . 1·20 50
10 50c. slate . . . . 6·75 1·70
11 70c. blue . . . . 6·75 4·75
12 1PTA. black . . . . 6·75 4·75
13 2PTAS. brown . . . . . . 80·00 28·00
14 4PTAS. red £250 £140
15 10PTS. brown £800 £375

3 El Santuario

4 Nomad Family

1943.

16	A	1c. mauve & brown (postage)	15	15
17	B	2c. blue and green	15	15
18	C	5c. blue and purple	15	15
19	A	15c. green and deep green	15	15
20	B	20c. brown and violet	15	15
21	A	40c. violet and purple	20	20
22	B	45c. red and brown	25	25
35	4	50c. black and brown	7·50	65
23	C	75c. blue and indigo	25	25
24	A	1p. brown and red	1·50	1·50
25	B	3p. green and blue	1·80	1·80
26	C	10p. black and brown	19·00	19·00
27	3	5c. brown and purple (air)	20	20
28	D	25c. brown and green	20	20
29	3	50c. blue and indigo	25	25
30	D	1p. blue and violet	25	25
31	3	1p.40 blue and green	25	25
32	D	2p. brown and purple	1·10	1·10
33	3	5p. violet and brown	1·50	1·50
34	D	6p. green and blue	21·00	21·00

DESIGNS: A, Nomadic shepherds; B, Arab rifleman; C, La Alcazaba; D, Airplane over oasis.

1947. Air. Autogyro type of Spain optd **IFNI**.

36	195	5c. yellow	2·50	60
37		10c. green	2·50	60

1948. Stamps of Spain optd **Territorio de Ifni**.

45	182	2c. brown (postage)	15	15
46	183	5c. brown	15	15
47		10c. red	15	15
48		15c. green	15	15
39	229	15c. green	3·00	55
49	196	25c. purple	15	15
50		30c. blue	15	15
51	232	40c. brown	15	15
52		45c. red	25	25
53	196	50c. grey	25	15
54	232	75c. blue	40	15
55	201	90c. green	40	25
41	196	1PTA. black	30	15
56	201	1p.35 violet	4·25	2·75
57	196	2PTAS. brown	3·00	1·90
58		4PTAS. pink	11·00	5·25
59		10PTAS. brown	27·00	16·00
60	195	25c. red (air)	45	15
61		50c. brown	55	15
62		1p. blue	55	15
63		2p. green	3·00	60
64		4p. blue	8·50	3·25
65		10p. violet	11·50	6·75

1949. Stamp Day and 75th Anniv of U.P.U. Spanish stamps optd **Territorio de Ifni**.

42	240	50c. brown (postage)	2·00	85
43		75c. blue	2·00	85
44		4p. olive (air)	2·40	85

8 General Franco

9 Lope Sancho de Valenzuela

1950. Child Welfare.

66	8	50c.+10c. sepia	35	25
67		1p.+25c. blue	14·00	5·50
68		6p.50+1p.65 green	4·75	2·50

1950. Air. Colonial Stamp Day.

69	9	5p. green	1·90	60

10 Woman and Dove

11 General Franco

1951. Air. 500th Birth Anniv of Isabella the Catholic.

70	10	5p. red	21·00	6·25

1951. Gen. Franco's Visit to Ifni.

71	11	50c. orange	30	15
72		1p. brown	3·75	90
73		5p. green	30·00	8·75

12 Fennec Fox

13 Mother and Child

1951. Colonial Stamp Day.

74	12	5c.+5c. brown	15	15
75		10c.+5c. orange	15	15
76		60c.+15c. olive	30	15

1952. Child Welfare.

77	13	5c.+5c. brown	15	15
78		50c.+10c. black	15	15
79		2p.+30c. blue	1·10	40

14 Ferdinand the Catholic

15 Shag

1952. Air. 500th Birth Anniv of Ferdinand the Catholic.

80	14	5p. brown	27·00	5·75

1952. Colonial Stamp Day.

81	15	5c.+5c. brown	20	15
82		10c.+5c. red	20	15
83		60c.+15c. green	35	20

16

17 Addra Gazelle and Douglas DC-4 Airliner

1952. 400th Death Anniv of Leo Africanus (geographer).

84	16	5c. orange	15	15
85		35c. green	15	15
86		60c. brown	20	15

1953. Air.

87	17	60c. green	15	15
88		1p.20 lake	20	15
89		1p.60 brown	25	15
90		2p. blue	1·70	20
91		4p. myrtle	95	20
92		10p. purple	5·25	1·20

18 Musician

1953. Child Welfare. Inscr "PRO INFANCIA 1953".

93	18	5c.+5c. lake	15	15
94	–	10c.+5c. purple	15	15
95	18	15c. olive	15	15
96	–	60c. brown	20	15

DESIGN: 10c., 60c. Two native musicians.

19 Fish and Jellyfish

1953. Colonial Stamp Day. Inscr "DIA DEL SELLO COLONIAL 1953".

97	19	5c.+5c. blue	15	15
98	–	10c.+5c. mauve	15	15
99	19	15c. green	15	15
100	–	60c. brown	35	15

DESIGN: 10, 60c. Dusky grouper and seaweed.

20 Mediterranean Gull

21 Asclepiad

1954.

101	20	5c. orange	15	15
102	21	10c. green	15	15
103	–	25c. red	15	15
104	20	35c. green	15	15
105	21	40c. purple	15	15
106	–	60c. brown	15	15
107	20	1p. brown	8·00	55
108	21	1p.25 red	15	15
109	–	2p. blue	15	15
110	21	4p.50 green	20	40
111	–	5p. black	34·00	10·50

DESIGN—VERT: 25, 60c., 2, 5p. Cactus.

22 Woman and Child

23 Lobster

1954. Child Welfare. Inscr "PRO-INFANCIA 1954".

112	22	5c.+5c. orange	15	15
113	–	10c.+5c. mauve	15	15
114	22	15c. green	15	15
115	–	60c. brown	20	15

DESIGN: 10c., 60c. Woman and girl.

1954. Colonial Stamp Day. Inscr "DIA DEL SELLO COLONIAL 1954".

116	23	5c.+5c. brown	15	15
117	–	10c.+5c. violet	15	15
118	23	15c. green	15	15
119	–	60c. lake	20	15

DESIGN: 10, 60c. Smooth hammerhead.

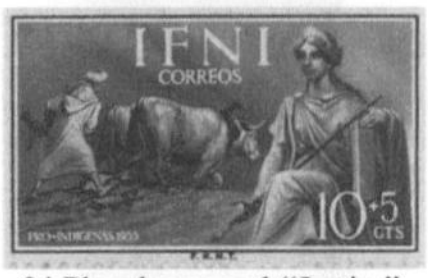
24 Ploughman and "Justice"

1955. Native Welfare. Inscr "PRO-INDIGENAS 1955".

120	24	10c.+5c. purple	15	15
121	–	25c.+10c. lilac	15	15
122	24	50c. olive	20	15

DESIGN: 25c. Camel caravan and "Spain".

25 Eurasian Red Squirrel

1955. Colonial Stamp Day.

123	25	5c.+5c. brown	15	15
124	–	15c.+5c. bistre	15	15
125	25	70c. green	20	15

DESIGN: 15c. Eurasian red squirrel holding nut.

26 "Senecio antheuphorbium"

1956. Child Welfare. Inscr "PRO-INFANCIA 1956".

126	26	5c.+5c. green	15	15
127	–	15c.+5c. brown	15	15
128	26	20c. green	15	15
129	–	50c. sepia	20	15

DESIGN: 15c., 50c., "Limoniastrum ifniensis".

27 Arms of Sidi-Ifni and Drummer

28 Feral Rock Pigeons

1956. Colonial Stamp Day. Inscr "DIA DEL SELLO 1956".

130	–	5c.+5c. sepia	15	15
131	27	15c.+5c. brown	15	15
132	–	70c. green	20	15

DESIGNS—VERT: 5c. Arms of Spain and Bohar reedbucks. HORIZ: 70c. Arms of Sidi-Ifni, shepherd and sheep.

1957. Child Welfare Fund.

133	28	5c.+5c. green and brown	15	15
134	–	15c.+5c. brown & ochre	15	15
135	28	70c. brown and green	20	15

DESIGN: 15c. Stock pigeons in flight.

29 Golden Jackal

1957. Colonial Stamp Day. Inscr "DIA DEL SELLO 1957".

136	29	10c.+5c. brown & purple	15	15
137	–	15c.+5c. green and brown	15	15
138	29	20c. brown and green	20	15
139	–	70c. brown and green	20	15

DESIGN—VERT: 15c., 70c., Head of Golden jackal.

30 Barn Swallows and Arms of Valencia and Sidi-Ifni

1958. "Aid for Valencia".

140	30	10c.+5c. brown	15	15
141	–	15c.+10c. brown	15	15
142	–	50c.+10c. brown	20	15

31 Basketball

1958. Child Welfare Fund.

143	31	10c.+5c. brown	15	15
144	–	15c.+5c. brown	15	15
145	31	20c. green	15	15
146	–	70c. green	20	15

DESIGN: 15, 70c. Cycling.

32 Greater Spotted Dogfish

1958. Colonial Stamp Day.

147	32	10c.+5c. red	15	15
148	–	25c.+10c. purple	15	15
149	–	50c.+10c. brown	20	15

DESIGNS—VERT: 25c. Black-chinned guitar-fish. HORIZ: 50c. Fishing boats.

33 Ewe and Lamb

1959. Child Welfare Fund.

150	33	10c.+5c. brown	15	15
151	–	15c.+5c. brown	15	15
152	–	20c. turquoise	15	15
153	33	70c. green	20	15

DESIGNS—VERT: 15c. Native trader with mule; 20c. Mountain goat.

34 Footballer **35** Dromedaries

1959. Colonial Stamp Day. Inscr "DIA DEL SELLO 1959".

154	**34**	10c.+5c. brown	20	20
155	–	20c.+5c. myrtle	20	20
156	–	50c.+20c. olive	20	20

DESIGNS: 20c. Footballers; 50c. Javelin-thrower.

1960. Child Welfare.

157	**35**	10c.+5c. purple	20	20
158	–	15c.+5c. brown	20	20
159	–	35c. green	20	20
160	**35**	80c. green	20	20

DESIGNS: 15c. Wild boar; 35c. Red-legged partridges.

36 White Stork

1960. Birds.

161	**36**	25c. violet	20	20
162	–	50c. brown	20	20
163	–	75c. purple	20	20
164	**36**	1p. red	20	20
165	–	1p.50 turquoise	20	20
166	–	2p. purple	20	20
167	**36**	3p. blue	45	20
168	–	5p. brown	90	30
169	–	10p. green	3·00	90

BIRDS—HORIZ: 50c., 1p.50, 5p. Eurasian goldfinches. VERT: 75c., 2, 10p. Eurasian skylarks.

37 Church of Santa Cruze del Mar **38** High Jump

1960. Stamp Day. Inscr "DIA DEL SELLO 1960".

170	**37**	10c.+5c. brown	20	20
171	–	20c.+5c. green	20	20
172	**37**	30c.+10c. brown	20	20
173	–	50c.+50c. brown	20	20

DESIGN—HORIZ: 20c., 50c. School building.

1961. Child Welfare. Inscr "PRO-INFANCIA 1961".

174	**38**	10c.+5c. red	20	20
175	–	25c.+10c. violet	20	20
176	**38**	80c.+20c. turquoise	20	20

DESIGN—VERT: 25c. Football.

39

1961. 25th Anniv of General Franco as Head of State.

177	–	25c. grey	20	20
178	**39**	50c. brown	20	20
179	–	70c. green	20	20
180	**39**	1p. red	20	20

DESIGNS—VERT: 25c. Map. HORIZ: 70c. Government Building.

40 Camel and Motor Lorry **41** Admiral Jofre Tenorio

1961. Stamp Day. Inscr "DIA DEL SELLO 1961".

181	**40**	10c.+5c. lake	20	20
182	–	25c.+10c. plum	20	20
183	**40**	30c.+10c. brown	20	20
184	–	1p.+10c. orange	20	20

DESIGN: 25c., 1p. Freighter at wharf.

1962. Child Welfare. Inscr "PRO-INFANCIA 1962".

185	**41**	25c. violet	20	20
186	–	50c. turquoise	20	20
187	**41**	1p. brown	20	20

DESIGN: 50c. C. Fernandez-Duro (historian).

42 Desert Postman **43** "Golden Tower", Seville

1962. Stamp Day.

188	**42**	15c. blue	20	20
189	–	35c. mauve	20	20
190	**42**	1p. purple	20	20

DESIGN: 35c. Winged letter on hands.

1963. Seville Flood Relief.

191	**43**	50c. green	20	20
192	–	1p. brown	20	20

44 Moroccan Copper and Flower

1963. Child Welfare. Inscr "PRO-INFANCIA 1963".

193	–	25c. blue	20	20
194	**44**	50c. green	20	20
195	–	1p. red	20	20

DESIGN: 25c., 1p. Moroccan orange-tips.

45 Child and Flowers

1963. "For Barcelona".

196	**45**	50c. green	20	20
197		1p. brown	20	20

46 Beetle ("Steraspis speciosa") **47** Edmi Gazelle

1964. Stamp Day. Inscr "DIA DEL SELLO 1963".

198	**46**	25c. blue	20	20
199	–	50c. olive	20	20
200	**46**	1p. brown	20	20

DESIGN: 50c. Desert locust.

1964. Child Welfare.

201	**47**	25c. violet	20	20
202	–	50c. grey	20	20
203	**47**	1p. red	20	20

DESIGN: 50c. Head of roe deer.

48 Cyclists Racing

1964. Stamp Day.

204	**48**	50c. brown	20	20
205	–	1p. red	20	20
206	**48**	1p.50 green	20	20

DESIGN: 1p. Motor cycle racing.

49 Port Installation, Sidi Ifni

1965. 25th Anniv of End of Spanish Civil War.

207	–	50c. green	20	20
208	–	1p. red	20	20
209	**49**	1p.50 blue	20	20

DESIGNS—VERT: 50c. Ifnian; 1p. "Education" (children in class).

50 "Eugaster fernandezi"

1965. Child Welfare.

210	**50**	50c. purple	20	20
211	–	1p. red ("Halter halteratus")	20	20
212	**50**	1p.50 blue	20	20

51 Arms of Ifni

1965. Stamp Day.

213	–	50c. brown	20	20
214	**51**	1p. red	20	20
215	–	1p.50 blue	20	20

DESIGN—VERT: 50c., 1p.50, Golden Eagle.

52 De Havilland D.H.9C Biplanes

1966. Child Welfare.

216	–	1p. brown	20	20
217	–	1p.50 blue	20	20
218	**52**	2p.50 violet	1·10	1·10

DESIGN—VERT: 1p., 1p.50, Douglas DC-8 jetliner over Sidi Ifni.

53 Maid Alice Moth **54** Coconut Palm

1966. Stamp Day. Insects.

219	**53**	10c. green and red	20	20
220	–	40c. brown and deep brown	20	20
221	**53**	1p.50 violet and yellow	20	20
222	–	4p. blue and purple	20	20

DESIGN: 40c., 4p. African monarch (butterfly).

1967. Child Welfare.

223	**54**	10c. green and brown	20	20
224	–	40c. green and brown	20	20
225	**54**	1p.50 turquoise and sepia	20	20
226	–	4p. sepia and brown	20	20

DESIGN: 40c., 4p. Cactus.

55 Bulk Carrier and Floating Crane

1967. Inauguration of Port Ifni.

227	**55**	1p.50 brown and green	20	20

56 Skipper

1967. Stamp Day.

228	**56**	1p. green and blue	20	20
229	–	1p.50 purple and yellow	20	20
230	–	3p.50 red and blue	35	35

FISH—VERT: 1p.50, John Dory, HORIZ: 3p.50, Tub gurnard.

1968. Child Welfare. Signs of the Zodiac. As T **47** of Fernando Poo.

231	1p. mauve on yellow	20	20
232	1p.50 brown on pink	20	20
233	2p.50 violet on yellow	35	35

DESIGNS: 1p., Fishes (Pisces); 1p.50, Ram (Aries); 2p.50, Archer (Sagittarius).

57 Posting Letter

1968. Stamp Day.

234	**57**	1p. black and yellow	20	20
235	–	1p.50 black, plum and blue	20	20
236	–	2p.50 black, blue and green	20	20

DESIGNS: 1p.50, Dove with letter; 2p.50, Magnifying-glass and stamp.

EXPRESS LETTER STAMPS

1943. As T **4**, but view of La Alcazaba inscr "URGENTE".

E35	25c. red and green	1·20	1·20

1949. Express Letter stamp of Spain optd **Territorio de Ifni.**

E66	**E 198**	25c. red	20	20

INDIA Pt. 1

A peninsula in the S. of Asia. Formerly consisted of British India and numerous Native States, some of which issued stamps of their own. Divided in 1947 into the Dominion of India and the Dominion of Pakistan. Now a republic within the British Commonwealth.

1852. 12 pies = 1 anna; 16 annas = 1 rupee.
1957. 100 naye paise = 1 rupee.
1964. 100 paisa = 1 rupee.

1 **3**

9 **10**

1852. "Scinde Dawk". Imperf.

S1	**1**	$\frac{1}{2}$a. white	£4750	£850
S2		$\frac{1}{2}$a. blue	£13000	£3750
S3		$\frac{1}{2}$a. red	£70000	£8500

1854. Imperf.

1	**3**	$\frac{1}{2}$a. red	£850	
2		$\frac{1}{2}$a. blue	60·00	16·00
14		1a. red	48·00	38·00
31	**10**	2a. green	85·00	24·00
23	**9**	4a. blue and red	£2500	£225

11 **12**

1855. Perf.

75	**11**	$\frac{1}{2}$a. blue	4·50	50
59		1a. brown	5·50	70
41		2a. pink	£475	29·00
63		2a. orange	22·00	2·00
46		4a. black	£225	4·75
64		4a. green	£325	22·00
73		8a. red	30·00	5·50

1860. Inscr "EAST INDIA POSTAGE". Various frames.

57	**12**	8p. mauve	11·00	9·50
77	–	9p. lilac	14·00	14·00
71	–	4a. green	21·00	2·50
81	–	6a. brown	6·00	1·50
72	–	6a.8p. grey	42·00	21·00
82	–	12a. brown	8·00	21·00
79	–	1r. grey	42·00	24·00

14 23

1866. Optd **POSTAGE**.

66	**14**	6a. purple	£650	£110

1882. Inscr "INDIA POSTAGE". Various frames.

84	**23**	½a. green	3·75	10
86	–	9p. red	1·00	2·00
88	–	1a. purple	4·00	30
90	–	1a.6p. brown	1·00	1·25
91	–	2a. blue	3·75	30
94	–	3a. orange	8·50	1·25
96	–	4a. olive	14·00	1·00
97	–	4a.6p. green	19·00	4·75
99	–	8a. mauve	23·00	2·00
100	–	12a. purple on red	7·50	3·25
101	–	1r. grey	16·00	5·00

1891. No. 97 surch **2½ As.**

102		2½a. on 4½a. green	3·00	60

40 37

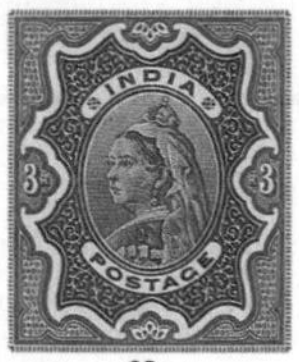

38

1892. As 1882 and some new designs.

111	**40**	3p. red	40	10
112		3p. grey	75	1·10
113	**23**	½a. green	1·60	50
115	–	1a. red	1·90	20
116	–	2a. lilac	3·50	2·00
103	–	2a.6p. green	2·75	40
118	–	2a.6p. blue	3·25	4·00
106	**37**	1r. green and red	11·00	2·00
107	**38**	2r. red and brown	38·00	11·00
108		3r. brown and green	28·00	10·00
109		5r. blue and violet	40·00	26·00

1898. Surch ¼.

110	**23**	¼a. on ½a. green	10	50

41 52

1902. As 1882 and 1892, but portrait of King Edward VII (inscribed "INDIA POSTAGE").

119	**41**	3p. grey	1·00	10
121	–	½a. green	1·50	20
123	–	1a. red	1·50	10
124	–	2a. violet	4·00	40
125	–	2a. mauve	3·50	10
126	–	2a.6p. blue	4·75	60
127	–	3a. orange	4·75	60
128	–	4a. olive	3·00	60
132	–	6a. bistre	10·00	4·50
133	–	8a. purple	8·50	1·00
135	–	12a. purple on red	8·50	2·00
136	–	1r. green and red	6·50	70
139	**52**	2r. red and brown	40·00	4·00
140		3r. brown and green	27·00	19·00
142		5r. blue and violet	60·00	35·00
144		10r. green and red	£110	28·00
146		15r. blue and brown	£140	42·00
147		25r. orange and blue	£750	£800

1905. No. 121 surch ¼.

148		¼a. on ½a. green	55	10

1906. As Nos. 121 and 123, but inscr "INDIA POSTAGE REVENUE".

149		½a. green	3·00	10
150		1a. red	1·75	10

55 56

57 58

59 70

60 61

62 63

71 64

65 66

67

1911. *Two types of 1½a. brown. Type A as illustrated. Type B inscr "1½ As. ONE AND A HALF ANNAS".

201	**55**	3p. grey	30	10
202	**56**	½a. green	1·25	10
161	**57**	1a. red	2·25	15
203		1a. brown	50	10
163	**58**	1½a. brown (A)*	3·00	30
165		1½a. brown (B)*	3·25	4·25
204		1½a. red (B)*	2·25	10
166	**59**	2a. purple	3·25	40
169		2a. violet	6·00	50
206	**70**	2a. purple	1·60	10
170	**60**	2a.6p. blue	2·75	3·00
171	**61**	2a.6p. blue	2·75	20
207		2a.6p. orange	1·90	10
173	**62**	3a. orange	7·00	20
209		3a. blue	9·00	10
210	**63**	4a. olive	1·50	10
211	**71**	4a. green	6·00	10
177	**64**	6a. bistre	4·00	1·25
212	**65**	8a. mauve	4·00	10
213	**66**	12a. red	5·00	30
214	**67**	1r. brown and green	5·00	45
215		2r. red and orange	13·00	80
216		5r. blue and violet	25·00	1·25
217		10r. green and red	50·00	3·00
218w		15r. blue and olive	24·00	30·00
219		25r. orange and blue	95·00	35·00

See also Nos. 232, etc.

1921. Surch **NINE PIES** and bar.

192	**57**	9p. on 1a. red	85	30

1922. Surch ¼.

195	**56**	¼a. on ½a. green	50	35

72 De Havilland Hercules

1929. Air.

220w	**72**	2a. green	1·75	75
221		3a. blue	1·00	2·00
222		4a. olive	2·25	1·25
223		6a. bistre	2·25	1·00
224		8a. purple	2·75	1·00
225		12a. red	13·00	6·00

73 Purana Qila

1931. Inauguration of New Delhi.

226	**73**	¼a. green and orange	2·00	3·50
227	–	½a. violet and green	1·25	40
228	–	1a. mauve and brown	1·25	20
229	–	2a. green and blue	1·50	3·00
230	–	3a. brown and red	3·75	2·75
231	–	1r. violet and green	10·00	27·00

DESIGNS: ½a. War Memorial Arch; 1a. Council House; 2a. Viceroy's House; 3a. Secretariat; 1r. Dominion Columns and Secretariat.

79 80

81 82

83 84 Gateway of India, Bombay

1932.

232	**79**	½a. green	4·50	10
233	**80**	9p. green	2·00	10
234	**81**	1a. brown	4·50	10
235	**82**	1¼a. mauve	60	10
236	**70**	2a. orange	10·00	4·00
236b	**59**	2a. orange	3·75	50
237	**62**	3a. orange	7·00	10
238	**83**	3½a. blue	4·50	20

1935. Silver Jubilee.

240	**84**	½a. black and green	85	20
241	–	9p. black and green	60	20
242w	–	1a. black and brown	75	10
243	–	1¼a. black and violet	50	10
244w	–	2½a. black and orange	1·75	1·00
245	–	3½a. black and blue	3·75	4·00
246	–	8a. black and purple	3·50	3·25

DESIGNS: 9p. Victoria Memorial, Calcutta; 1a. Rameswaram Temple, Madras; 1¼a. Jain Temple, Calcutta; 2½a. Taj Mahal, Agra; 3½a. Golden Temple, Amritsar; 8a. Pagoda in Mandalay.

91 King George VI 93 King George VI

92 Dak Runner

1937.

247	**91**	3p. slate	1·00	10
248		½a. brown	4·50	10
249		9p. green	8·00	30
250		1a. red	1·25	10
251	**92**	2a. orange	5·50	30
252	–	2a.6p. violet	1·25	20
253	–	3a. green	6·50	30
254	–	3a.6p. blue	3·25	50
255	–	4a. brown	13·00	20
256	–	6a. turquoise	14·00	80
257	–	8a. violet	7·50	50
258	–	12a. lake	18·00	1·10
259	**93**	1r. slate and brown	1·25	15
260		2r. purple and brown	4·50	30
261		5r. green and blue	23·00	50
262		10r. purple and red	18·00	80
263		15r. brown and green	75·00	60·00
264		25r. slate and purple	£100	19·00

DESIGNS—As Type **92**: 2a.6p. Dak bullock cart; 3a. Dak tonga; 3a.6p. Dak camel; 4a. Mail train; 6a. "Strathnaver" (liner); 8a. Mail lorry; 12a. Armstrong Whitworth Ensign 1 mail plane (small head).

100a King George VI 101 King George VI

102 King George VI

1940.

265	**100a**	3p. slate	30	10
266		½a. purple	1·00	10
267		9p. green	1·00	10
268		1a. red	1·00	10
269	**101**	1a.3p. brown	1·00	10
269b		1½a. violet	1·25	10
270		2a. orange	1·50	10
271		3a. violet	3·25	10
272		3½a. blue	1·00	75
273	**102**	4a. brown	1·00	10
274		6a. turquoise	3·50	10
275		8a. violet	1·50	30
276		12a. lake	3·50	75
277	–	14a. purple	18·00	1·75

No. 277 is as No. 258, but with large head.

105 "Victory" and King George VI

1946. Victory Commemoration.

278	**105**	9p. green	50	1·25
279		1½a. purple	30	30
280		3½a. blue	85	1·00
281		12a. red	1·50	1·25

1946. Surch **3 PIES** and bars.

282	**101**	3p. on 1a.3p. brown	10	15

DOMINION OF INDIA

303 Douglas DC-4

1947. Independence. Inscr "15TH AUG 1947".

301	–	1½a. green	15	10
302	–	3½a. red, blue and green	1·00	2·25
303	**303**	12a. blue	1·50	2·75

DESIGNS—VERT: 1½a. Asokan capital. HORIZ: 3½a. Indian national flag.

1948. Air. Inauguration of India–U.K. Service. As T **303**, but showing Lockheed Constellation flying in opposite direction and inscr "AIR INDIA INTERNATIONAL FIRST FLIGHT 8TH JUNE 1948".

304		12a. black and blue	1·25	3·00

305 Mahatma Gandhi

1948. 1st Anniv of Independence.

305	**305**	1½a. brown	2·75	50
306		3½a. violet	4·25	2·50
307		12a. green	6·00	1·50
308	–	10r. brown and lake	45·00	40·00

DESIGN—22½ × 37 mm: 10r. Profile portrait of Mahatma Gandhi.

307 Ajanta Panel 308 Konarak Horse

314 Bhuvanesvara

315 Gol Gumbad, Bijapur

319 Red Fort, Delhi

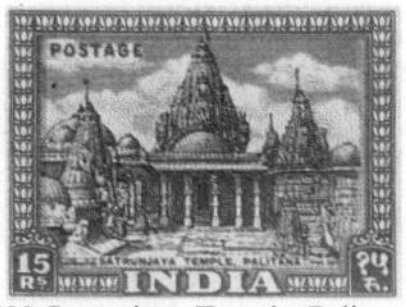

322 Satrunjaya Temple, Palitana

1949.

309	**307**	3p. violet	15	10
310	**308**	6p. brown	25	10
311	–	9p. green	40	10
312	–	1a. blue (A)	60	10
333	–	1a. blue (B)	4·00	10
313	–	2a. red	80	10
333b	–	2½a. lake	3·00	3·25
314	–	3a. orange	1·50	10
315	–	3½a. blue	1·50	3·50
316	**314**	4a. lake	4·00	30
333c		4a. blue	6·00	10
317	**315**	6a. violet	1·50	75
318	–	8a. turquoise	1·50	10
319	–	12a. blue	1·50	30
320	–	1r. violet and green	9·00	10
321	**319**	2r. red and violet	10·00	20
322	–	5r. green and brown	28·00	1·50
323	–	10r. brown and blue	48·00	8·00
324	**322**	15r. brown and red	16·00	20·00

1 anna: (A) Left arm of statue outstretched. (B) Reversed—right arm outstretched.

DESIGNS—As Type **307**: 9p. Trimurti; 1a. Bodhisattva; 2a. Nataraja. As Type **314**: 2½a., 3½a. Bodh Gaya Temple; 3a. Sanchi Stupa, East Gate. As Type **315**: 8a. Kandarya Mahadeva Temple; 12a. Golden Temple, Amritsar. As Type **319**—VERT: 1r. Victory Tower, Chittorgarh; 10r. Qutb Minar, Delhi. HORIZ: 5r. Taj Mahal, Agra.

323 Globe and Asokan Capital

1949. 75th Anniv of U.P.U.

325	**323**	9p. green	1·00	3·00
326		2a. red	1·00	2·50
327		3½a. blue	1·50	2·50
328		12a. purple	2·00	2·50

REPUBLIC OF INDIA

324 Rejoicing Crowds

1950. Inauguration of Republic.

329	**324**	2a. red	1·25	50
330	–	3½a. blue	1·75	3·25
331	–	4a. violet	1·75	1·25
332	–	12a. purple	3·50	2·25

DESIGNS—VERT: 3½a. Quill, ink-well and verse. HORIZ: 4a. Ear of corn and plough; 12a. Spinning-wheel and cloth.

329 "Stegodon ganesa"

1951. Centenary of Geological Survey.

334	**329**	2a. black and red	2·00	1·00

330 Torch

331 Kabir

1951. 1st Asian Games, New Delhi.

335	**330**	2a. purple and orange	1·00	65
336		12a. brown and blue	4·00	1·75

1952. Indian Saints and Poets.

337	**331**	9p. green	30	40
338	–	1a. red (Tulsidas)	30	20
339	–	2a. orange (Meera)	1·25	20
340	–	4a. blue (Surdas)	1·25	50
341	–	4½a. mauve (Ghalib)	30	80
342	–	12a. brown (Tagore)	2·50	1·00

332 Locomotives of 1853 and 1953

1953. Centenary of Indian Railways.

343	**332**	2a. black	1·00	10

333 Mount Everest

1953. Conquest of Mount Everest.

344	**333**	2a. violet	1·25	10
345		14a. brown	3·00	25

334 Telegraph Poles of 1851 and 1951

1953. Centenary of Indian Telegraphs.

346	**334**	2a. green	30	10
347		12a. blue	2·50	40

335 Postal Transport, 1854

1954. Indian Stamp Centenary.

348	**335**	1a. purple	30	20
349	–	2a. mauve	30	10
350	–	4a. brown	2·75	1·50
351	–	14a. blue	1·50	40

DESIGNS: 2, 14a. "Airmail"; 4a. Postal transport, 1954.

338 U.N. Emblem and Lotus

1954. U.N. Day.

352	**338**	2a. turquoise	40	40

339 Forest Research Institute

1954. 4th World Forestry Congress, Dehra Dun.

353	**339**	2a. blue	20	10

340 Tractor

344 Woman Spinning

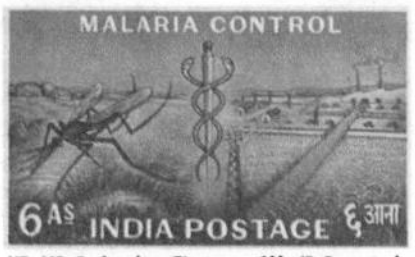

347 "Malaria Control" (Mosquito and Staff of Aesculapius)

1955. Five Year Plan.

354	**340**	3p. mauve	30	10
355	–	6p. violet	30	10
356	–	9p. brown	40	10
357	–	1a. green	45	10
358	**344**	2a. blue	30	10
359	–	3a. green	50	10
360	–	4a. red	50	10
361	**347**	6a. brown	1·50	10
362	–	8a. blue	6·00	10
363	–	10a. turquoise	3·75	2·75
364	–	12a. blue	2·50	10
365	–	14a. green	5·00	60
413	–	1r. myrtle	3·75	10
367	–	1r.2a. grey	2·25	3·50
368	–	1r.8a. purple	8·00	5·00
369	–	2r. mauve	4·25	10
415	–	5r. brown	9·00	40
371	–	10r. orange	14·00	4·75

DESIGNS—As Type **340**: 6p. Power loom; 9p. Bullock-driven well; 1a. Damodar Valley Dam; 4a. Bullocks; 8a. Chittaranjan Locomotive Works; 12a. Hindustan Aircraft Factory, Bangalore; 1r. Telephone engineer; 2r. Rare Earth Factory, Alwaye; 5r. Sindri Fertiliser Factory; 10r. Steel plant. As Type **344**: 3a. Naga woman hand-weaving. As Type **347**: 10a. Marine Drive, Bombay; 14a. Kashmir landscape; 1r.2a. Cape Comorin; 1r.8a. Mt. Kangchenjunga.

358 Bodhi Tree

1956. Buddha Jayanti.

372	**358**	2a. sepia	75	10
373	–	14a. orange	4·00	3·75

DESIGN—HORIZ: 14a. Round parasol and Bodhi tree.

360 Lokmanya Bal Gangadhar Tilak

361 Map of India

1956. Birth Centenary of Tilak (journalist).

374	**360**	2a. brown	10	10

1957. Value in naye paise.

375	**361**	1n.p. green	10	10
376		2n.p. brown	10	10
377		3n.p. brown	10	10
402		5n.p. green	10	10
379		6n.p. grey	10	10
404		8n.p. turquoise	1·00	10
405		10n.p. myrtle	15	10
381		13n.p. red	30	10
407		15n.p. violet	60	10
408		20n.p. blue	30	10
409		25n.p. blue	30	10
410		50n.p. orange	30	10
411		75n.p. purple	40	10
412		90n.p. purple	5·50	10

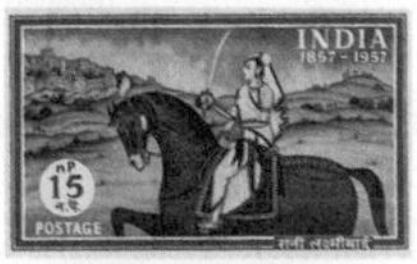

362 The Rani of Jhansi

363 Shrine

1957. Centenary of Indian Mutiny.

386	**362**	15n.p. brown	40	10
387	**363**	90n.p. purple	1·50	1·25

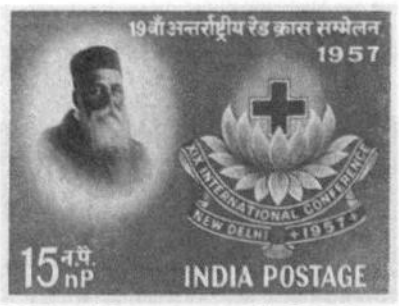

364 Henri Dunant and Conference Emblem

1957. 19th Int Red Cross Conf, New Delhi.

388	**364**	15n.p. grey and red	10	10

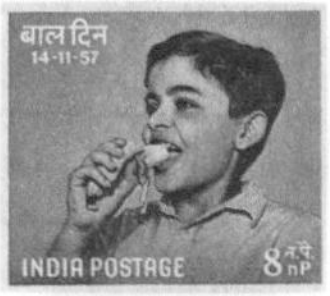

365 "Nutrition"

369 Calcutta University

1957. Children's Day.

389	**365**	8n.p. purple	10	15
390	–	15n.p. turquoise	10	10
391	–	90n.p. brown	25	15

DESIGNS—HORIZ: 15n.p. "Education". VERT: 90n.p. "Recreation".

1957. Centenary of Indian Universities.

392	–	10n.p. violet	15	60
393	**369**	10n.p. grey	15	60
394	–	10n.p. brown	30	60

DESIGNS—21½ × 38 mm: No. 392, Bombay University. As Type **369**: No. 394, Madras University.

371 J. N. Tata (founder) and Steel Plant

1958. 50th Anniv of Steel Industry.

395	**371**	15n.p. red	10	10

372 Dr. D. K. Karve

1958. Birth Centenary of Karve (educationist).

396	**372**	15n.p. brown	10	10

373 Westland Wapiti Biplane and Hawker Hunter

1958. Silver Jubilee of Indian Air Force.

397	**373**	15n.p. blue	1·00	10
398		90n.p. blue	1·25	2·00

375 Bipin Chandra Pal

1958. Birth Centenary of Pal (patriot).

418	**375**	15n.p. green	10	10

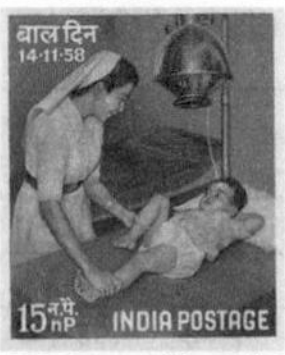

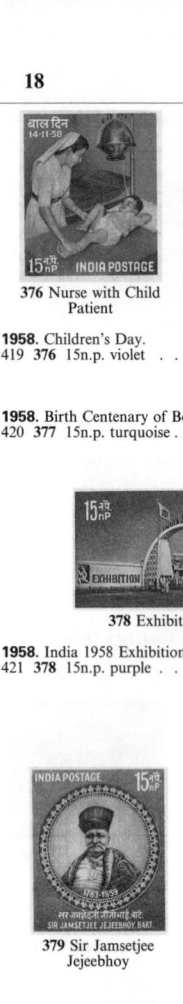

376 Nurse with Child Patient **377** Jagadish Chandra Bose

1958. Children's Day.
419 **376** 15n.p. violet 10 10

1958. Birth Centenary of Bose (botanist).
420 **377** 15n.p. turquoise 20 10

378 Exhibition Gate

1958. India 1958 Exhibition, New Delhi.
421 **378** 15n.p. purple 10 10

379 Sir Jamsetjee Jejeebhoy **381** Boys awaiting admission to Children's Home

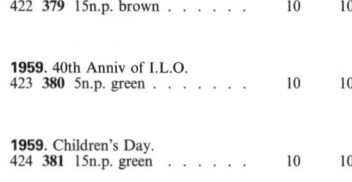

380 "The Triumph of Labour" (after Chowdhury)

1959. Death Centenary of Sir Jamsetjee Jejeebhoy (philanthropist).
422 **379** 15n.p. brown 10 10

1959. 40th Anniv of I.L.O.
423 **380** 5n.p. green 10 10

1959. Children's Day.
424 **381** 15n.p. green 10 10

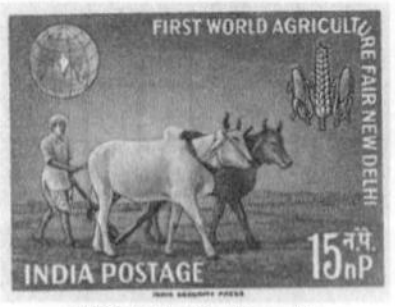

382 "Agriculture" **383** Thiruvalluvar (philosopher)

1959. 1st World Agriculture Fair, New Delhi.
425 **382** 15n.p. grey 30 10

1960. Thiruvalluvar Commemoration.
426 **383** 15n.p. purple 10 10

384 Yaksha pleading with the Cloud (from the "Meghaduta") **385** Shakuntala writing a letter to Dushyanta (from the "Shakuntala")

1960. Kalidasa (poet) Commemoration.
427 **384** 15n.p. grey 30 10
428 **385** 1r.3n.p. yellow and brown 1·60 1·75

386 S. Bharati (poet) **387** Dr. M. Visvesvaraya

1960. Subramania Bharati Commemoration.
429 **386** 15n.p. blue 10 10

1960. Birth Centenary of Dr. M. Visvesvaraya (engineer).
430 **387** 15n.p. brown and red . . 10 10

388 "Children's Health"

1960. Children's Day.
431 **388** 15n.p. green 10 10

389 Children greeting U.N. Emblem

1960. UNICEF Day.
432 **389** 15n.p. brown and drab 10 10

390 Tyagaraja **391** "First Aerial Post" Cancellation

392 Air India Boeing 707 Airliner and Humber Sommer Biplane

1961. 114th Death Anniv of Tyagaraja (musician).
433 **390** 15n.p. blue 10 10

1961. 50th Anniv of 1st Official Airmail Flight, Allahabad–Naini.
434 **391** 5n.p. olive . . . . 1·10 30
435 **392** 15n.p. green and grey . . 1·10 30
436 – 1r. purple and grey . . . 3·75 2·75
DESIGN—As Type **392**: 1r. H. Pecquet flying Humber Sommer plane, and "Aerial Post" cancellation.

394 Shivaji on Horseback **395** Motilal Nehru (politician)

1961. Chatrapati Shivaji (Maratha ruler) Commemoration.
437 **394** 15n.p. brown and green 80 40

1961. Birth Centenary of Pandit Motilal Nehru.
438 **395** 15n.p. brown and orange 30 10

396 Tagore (poet) **397** All India Radio Emblem and Transmitting Aerials

1961. Birth Centenary of Rabindranath Tagore.
439 **396** 15n.p. orange and turquoise 80 40

1961. Silver Jubilee of All India Radio.
440 **397** 15n.p. blue 10 10

398 Ray **399** Bhatkande

1961. Birth Centenary of Prafulla Chandra Ray (social reformer).
441 **398** 15n.p. grey 10 20

1961. Birth Centenary (1960) of V. N Bhatkande (composer).
442 **399** 15n.p. drab 10 10

400 Child at Lathe **401** Fair Emblem and Main Gate

1961. Children's Day.
443 **400** 15n.p. brown 10 20

1961. Indian Industries Fair, New Delhi.
444 **401** 15n.p. blue and red . . . 10 10

402 Indian Forest **403** Pitalkhora: Yaksha

1961. Centenary of Scientific Forestry.
445 **402** 15n.p. green and brown 40 30

1961. Cent of Indian Archaeological Survey.
446 **403** 15n.p. brown 20 10
447 – 90n.p. olive and brown 40 20
DESIGN—HORIZ: 90n.p. Kalibangan seal.

405 M. M. Malaviya **406** Gauhati Refinery

1961. Birth Centenary of Malaviya (educationist).
448 **405** 15n.p. slate 10 20

1962. Inauguration of Gauhati Oil Refinery.
449 **406** 15n.p. blue 40 20

407 Bhikaiji Cama **408** Village Panchayati and Parliament Building

1962. Birth Centenary of Bhikaiji Cama (patriot).
450 **407** 15n.p. purple 10 10

1962. Inauguration of Panchayati System of Local Government.
451 **408** 15n.p. mauve 10 10

409 D. Saraswati (religious reformer) **410** G. S. Vidhyarthi (journalist)

1962. Dayanard Saraswati Commem.
452 **409** 15n.p. brown 10 10

1962. Ganesh Shankar Vidhyarthi Commem.
453 **410** 15n.p. brown 10 10

411 Malaria Eradication Emblem **412** Dr. R. Prasad

1962. Malaria Eradication.
454 **411** 15n.p. yellow and lake . . 10 10

1962. Retirement of President Dr. Rajendra Prasad.
455 **412** 15n.p. purple 30 20

413 Calcutta High Court

1962. Centenary of Indian High Courts.
456 **413** 15n.p. green 50 20
457 – 15n.p. brown (Madras) 50 20
458 – 15n.p. slate (Bombay) . . 50 20

416 Ramabai Ranade **417** Indian Rhinoceros

1962. Birth Centenary of Ramabai Ranade (social reformer).
459 **416** 15n.p. orange 10 20

1962. Wild Life Week.
460 **417** 15n.p. brown and turquoise 40 15

418 "Passing the Flag to Youth"

1962. Children's Day.
461 **418** 15n.p. red and green . . . 15 20

419 Human Eye within Lotus Blossom

1962. 19th Int Ophthalmology Congress, New Delhi.
462 **419** 15n.p. brown 20 10

420 S. Ramanujan

1962. 75th Birth Anniv of Srinivasa Ramanujan (mathematician).
463 **420** 15n.p. brown 70 40

421 S. Vivekananda **423** Hands reaching for F.A.O. Emblem

1963. Birth Cent of Vivekananda (philosopher).
464 **421** 15n.p. brown and olive 40 20

1963. Surch.
465 **385** 1r. on 1r.3n.p. yellow and brown 30 10

1963. Freedom from Hunger.
466 **423** 15n.p. blue . . . . 1·25 30

424 Henri Dunant (founder) and Centenary Emblem **427** D. Naoroji (parliamentarian)

425 Artillery and Mil Mi-4 Helicopter

1963. Centenary of Red Cross.
467 **424** 15n.p. red and grey . . . 2·75 40

1963. Defence Campaign.
468 **425** 15n.p. green 55 10
469 – 1r. brown 70 65
DESIGN: 1r. Sentry and parachutists.

1963. Dadabhai Naoroji Commemoration.
470 **427** 15n.p. grey 10 10

428 Annie Besant (patriot and theosophist) **434** "School Meals"

1963. Annie Besant Commemoration.
471 **428** 15n.p. green 15 10
No. 471 is incorrectly dated "1837". Mrs. Besant was born in 1847.

1963. Wild Life Preservation. Animal designs as T **417**.
472 10n.p. black and orange . . . 75 1·50
473 15n.p. brown and green . . . 1·50 60
474 30n.p. slate and ochre . . . 3·75 1·50
475 50n.p. orange and green . . . 3·50 80
476 1r. brown and blue . . . . . 2·50 50

ANIMALS—As Type **417**: 10n.p. Gaur. 25½ × 35½ mm: 15n.p. Lesser panda; 30n.p. Indian elephant. 35½ × 25½ mm: 50n.p. Tiger; 1r. Lion.

1963. Children's Day.
477 **434** 15n.p. bistre 10 10

435 Eleanor Roosevelt at Spinning-wheel

1963. 15th Anniv of Declaration of Human Rights.
478 **435** 15n.p. purple 10 15

436 Dipalakshmi (bronze) **437** Gopabandhu Das (social reformer)

1964. 26th Int Orientalists Congress, New Delhi.
479 **436** 15n.p. blue 20 15

1964. Gopabandhu Das Commemoration.
480 **437** 15n.p. purple 10 10

438 Purandaradasa **439** S. C. Bose and I.N.A. Badge

1964. 400th Death Anniv of Purandaradasa (composer).
481 **438** 15n.p. brown 15 10

1964. 67th Birth Anniv of Subhas Chandra Bose (nationalist).
482 **439** 15n.p. olive 50 20
483 – 55n.p. black, orange & red 50 45
DESIGN: 35n.p. Bose and Indian National Army.

441 Sarojini Naidu **442** Kasturba Gandhi

1964. 85th Birth Anniv of Sarojini Naidu (poetess).
484 **441** 15n.p. green and purple 10 10

1964. 20th Death Anniv of Kasturba Gandhi.
485 **442** 15n.p. brown 10 10

443 Dr. W. M. Haffkine (immunologist) **444** Jawaharlal Nehru (statesman)

1964. Haffkine Commemoration.
486 **443** 15n.p. brown on buff . . 30 10

1964. Nehru Mourning Issue.
487 **444** 15p. slate 10 10

445 Sir Asutosh Mookerjee

1964. Birth Centenary of Sir Asutosh Mookerjee (education reformer).
488 **445** 15p. brown and olive . . 10 10

446 Sri Aurobindo

1964. 92nd Birth Anniv of Sri Aurobindo (religious teacher).
489 **446** 15p. purple 15 10

447 Raja R. Roy (social reformer)

1964. Raja Rammohun Roy Commemoration.
490 **447** 15n.p. brown 10 10

448 I.S.O. Emblem and Globe

1964. 6th Int Organization for Standardisation General Assembly, Bombay.
491 **448** 15p. red 15 20

449 Jawaharlal Nehru (from 1r. commemorative coin) **450** St. Thomas (after statue, Ortona Cathedral, Italy)

1964. Children's Day.
492 **449** 15p. slate 10 10

1964. St. Thomas Commemoration.
493 **450** 15p. purple 10 30
No. 493 was issued on the occasion of Pope Paul's visit to India.

451 Globe **452** J. Tata (industrialist)

1964. 22nd International Geological Congress.
494 **451** 15p. green 40 30

1965. Jamsetji Tata Commemoration.
495 **452** 15p. dull purple and orange 30 20

453 Lala Lajpat Rai

1965. Birth Centenary of Lala Lajpat Rai (social reformer).
496 **453** 15p. brown 20 10

454 Globe and Congress Emblem

1965. 20th International Chamber of Commerce Congress, New Delhi.
497 **454** 15p. green and red . . . 15 15

455 Freighter "Jalausha" and Visakhapatnam

1965. National Maritime Day.
498 **455** 15p. blue 30 30

456 Abraham Lincoln

1965. Death Centenary of Lincoln.
499 **456** 15p. brown and ochre . . 15 10

457 I.T.U. Emblem and Symbols

1965. Centenary of I.T.U.
500 **457** 15p. purple . . . . 1·00 30

458 "Everlasting Flame" **459** I.C.Y. Emblem

1965. 1st Death Anniv of Nehru.
501 **458** 15p. red and blue 15 10

1965. International Co-operation Year.
502 **459** 15p. green and brown . . 1·25 1·00

460 Climbers on Summit **466** Electric Locomotive

475 Dal Lake, Kashmir

1965. Indian Mount Everest Expedition.
503 **460** 15p. purple 20 10

1965.

504	–	2p. brown	10	50
505	–	3p. olive	30	2·75
505a	–	4p. brown	10	2·75
506	–	5p. red	10	10
507	–	6p. black	10	3·25
508	–	8p. brown	30	4·25
509	**466**	10p. blue	40	10
510	–	15p. green	2·75	10
511	–	20p. purple	6·00	10
512	–	30p. sepia	15	10
513	–	40p. purple	15	10
514	–	50p. green	20	10
515	–	60p. grey	35	10
516	–	70p. blue	60	10
517	–	1r. brown and plum . .	60	10
518	**475**	2r. blue and violet . . .	2·00	10
519	–	5r. violet and brown . .	2·50	90
520	–	10r. black and green . .	17·00	80

DESIGNS—VERT (as Type **466**): 2p. Bidri vase; 3p. Brass lamp; 5p. "Family Planning"; 6p. Konarak elephant; 8p. Spotted deer ("Chital"); 30p. Indian dolls; 50p. Mangoes; 60p. Somnath Temple. (as Type **475**): 1r. Woman writing a letter (medieval sculpture). HORIZ (as Type **466**): 4p. Coffee berries; 15p. Plucking tea; 20p. Hindustan Aircraft Industries Ajeet jet fighter; 40p. Calcutta G.P.O.; 70p. Hampi Chariot (sculpture). (As Type **475**): 5r. Bhakra Dam, Punjab; 10r. Atomic reactor, Trombay.

See also Nos. 721/38c.

479 G. B. Pant (statesman) **480** V. Patel

1965. Govind Ballabh Pant Commemoration.
522 **479** 15p. brown and green . . 10 20

1965. 90th Birth Anniv of Vallabhbhai Patel (statesman).
523 **480** 15p. brown 10 30

481 C. Das **482** Vidyapati (poet)

1965. 95th Birth Anniv of Chittaranjan Das (lawyer and patriot).
524 **481** 15p. brown 10 10

1965. Vidyapati Commemoration.
525 **482** 15p. brown 10 10

483 Sikandra, Agra **484** Soldier, Hindustan Aircraft Industries Ajeet Jet Fighters and Cruiser "Mysore"

1966. Pacific Area Travel Assn Conf, New Delhi.
526 **483** 15p. slate 10 10

1966. Indian Armed Forces.
527 **484** 15p. violet . . . . 1·25 50

485 Lal Bahadur Shastri (statesman) **486** Kambar (poet)

1966. Shastri Mourning Issue.
528 **485** 15p. black 65 10

1966. Kambar Commemoration.
529 **486** 15p. green 10 10

487 B. R. Ambedkar **488** Kunwar Singh (patriot)

1966. 75th Birth Anniv of Dr. Bhim Rao Ambedkar (lawyer).
530 **487** 15p. purple 10 10

1966. Kunwar Singh Commemoration.
531 **488** 15p. brown 10 10

489 G. K. Gokhale

1966. Birth Centenary of Gopal Krishna Gokhale (patriot).
532 **489** 15p. purple and yellow . . 10 10

490 Acharya Dvivedi (poet) **491** Maharaja Ranjit Singh (warrior)

1966. Dvivedi Commemoration.
533 **490** 15p. drab 10 10

1966. Maharaja Ranjit Singh Commemoration.
534 **491** 15p. purple 60 20

492 Homi Bhabha (scientist) and Nuclear Reactor

1966. Dr. Homi Bhabha Commemoration.
535 **492** 15p. purple 15 30

493 A. K. Azad (scholar)

1966. Abul Kalam Azad Commemoration.
536 **493** 15p. blue 15 15

494 Swami Tirtha

1966. 60th Death Anniv of Swami Rama Tirtha (social reformer).
537 **494** 15p. blue 30 30

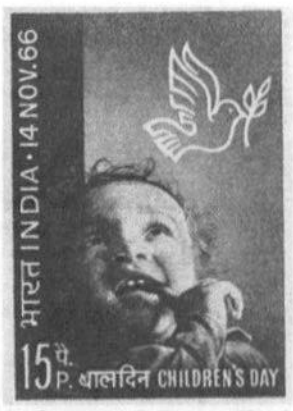

495 Infant and Dove Emblem

1966. Children's Day.
538 **495** 15p. purple 60 20

496 Allahabad High Court

1966. Centenary of Allahabad High Court.
539 **496** 15p. purple 40 30

497 Indian Family

1966. Family Planning.
540 **497** 15p. brown 15 15

498 Hockey Game

1966. India's Hockey Victory in 5th Asian Games.
541 **498** 15p. blue . . . . 1·25 60

499 "Jai Kisan" **500** Voter and Polling Booth

1967. 1st Death Anniv of Shastri.
542 **499** 15p. green 30 30

1967. Indian General Election.
543 **500** 15p. brown 15 15

501 Gurudwara Shrine, Patna **502** Taj Mahal, Agra

1967. 300th Birth Anniv (1966) of Guru Gobind Singh (Sikh religious leader).
544 **501** 15p. violet 50 15

1967. International Tourist Year.
545 **502** 15p. brown and orange 30 15

503 Nandalal Bose and "Garuda"

1967. 1st Death Anniv of Nandalal Bose (painter).
546 **503** 15p. brown 15 15

504 Survey Emblem and Activities

1967. Bicentenary of Survey of India.
547 **504** 15p. lilac 60 40

505 Basaveswara

1967. 800th Anniv of Basaveswara (reformer and statesman).
548 **505** 15p. red 15 15

506 Narsinha Mehta (poet) **507** Maharana Pratap

1967. Narsinha Mehta Commemoration.
549 **506** 15p. sepia 15 15

1967. Maharana Pratap (Rajput leader) Commem.
550 **507** 15p. brown 15 15

508 Narayana Guru **509** Pres. Radhakrishnan

1967. Narayana Guru (philosopher) Commem.
551 **508** 15p. brown 30 20

1967. 75th Birth Anniv of Sarvepalli Radhakrishnan (former President).
552 **509** 15p. red 50 15

510 Martyrs' Memorial, Patna

1967. 25th Anniv of "Quit India" Movement.
553 **510** 15p. lake 15 15

511 Route Map **512** Wrestling

1967. Centenary of Indo-European Telegraph Service.
554 **511** 15p. black and blue . . . 70 20

1967. World Wrestling Championships, New Delhi.
555 **512** 15p. purple and brown . . 50 20

513 Nehru leading Naga Tribesmen **514** Rashbehari Basu (nationalist)

1967. 4th Anniv of Nagaland as a State of India.
556 **513** 15p. blue 15 15

1967. Rashbehari Basu Commemoration.
557 **514** 15p. purple 15 20

515 Bugle, Badge and Scout Salute

1967. 60th Anniv of Scout Movement in India.
558 **515** 15p. brown . . . . 1·00 60

516 Men embracing Universe

517 Globe and Book of Tamil

1968. Human Rights Year.
559 **516** 15p. green 50 30

1968. Int Conf and Seminar of Tamil Studies, Madras.
560 **517** 15p. lilac 60 15

518 U.N. Emblem and Transport

1968. United Nations Conference on Trade and Development, New Delhi.
561 **518** 15p. blue 60 15

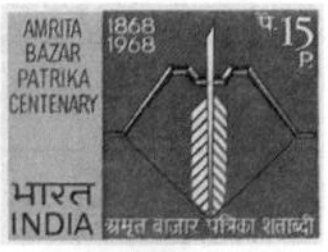

519 Quill and Bow Symbol

520 Maxim Gorky

1968. Centenary of "Amrita Bazar Patrika" (newspaper).
562 **519** 15p. sepia and yellow . . 15 15

1968. Birth Centenary of Maxim Gorky.
563 **520** 15p. plum 15 20

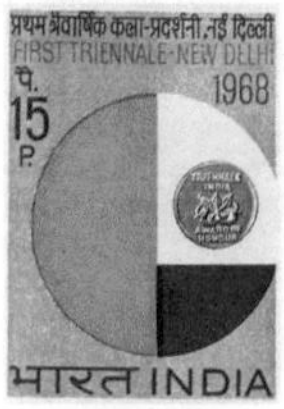

521 Emblem and Medal

522 Letter-box and "100,000"

1968. 1st Triennale Art Exhibition, New Delhi.
564 **521** 15p. orange, blue & lt blue 30 20

1968. Opening of 100,000th Indian Post Office.
565 **522** 20p. red, blue and black 40 15

523 Stalks of Wheat, Agricultural Institute and Production Graph

1968. Wheat Revolution.
566 **523** 20p. green and brown . . 30 15

524 "Self-portrait"

525 Lakshminath Bezbaruah

1968. 30th Death Anniv of Gaganendranath Tagore (painter).
567 **524** 20p. purple and ochre . . 50 15

1968. Birth Cent of Lakshminath Bezbaruah (writer).
568 **525** 20p. brown 30 15

526 Athlete's Legs and Olympic Rings

1968. Olympic Games, Mexico.
569 **526** 20p. brown and grey . . 15 15
570 1r. sepia and olive 50 15

527 Bhagat Singh and Followers

1968. 61st Birth Anniv of Bhagat Singh (patriot).
571 **527** 20p. brown 50 20

528 Azad Hind Flag, Swords and Chandra Bose (founder)

529 Sister Nivedita

1968. 25th Anniv of Azad Hind Government.
572 **528** 20p. blue 30 15

1968. Birth Cent of Sister Nivedita (social reformer).
573 **529** 20p. green 30 30

530 Marie Curie and Radium Treatment

1968. Birth Centenary of Marie Curie.
574 **530** 20p. lilac . . . . 1·40 60

531 Map of the World

532 Cochin Synagogue

1968. 21st Int Geographical Congress, New Delhi.
575 **531** 20p. blue 15 15

1968. 400th Anniv of Cochin Synagogue.
576 **532** 20p. blue and red . . . . 1·00 40

533 I.N.S. "Nilgiri"

1968. Navy Day.
577 **533** 20p. blue . . . . 1·75 40

534 Red-billed Blue Magpie

1968. Birds.
578 **534** 20p. multicoloured . . . 1·25 50
579 – 50p. red, black and green 1·25 1·50
580 – 1r. blue and brown . . . 2·50 1·00
581 – 2r. multicoloured . . . . 1·75 1·50
DESIGNS—HORIZ: 50p. Brown-fronted pied woodpecker; 2r. Yellow-backed sunbird. VERT: 1r. Slaty-headed scimitar babbler.

538 Bankim Chandra Chatterjee

539 Dr. Bhagavan Das

1969. 130th Birth Anniv of Chatterjee (writer).
582 **538** 20p. blue 15 20

1969. Birth Centenary of Das (philosopher).
583 **539** 20p. brown 15 15

540 Dr. Martin Luther King

1969. Martin Luther King Commemoration.
584 **540** 20p. brown 50 20

541 Mirza Ghalib and Letter Seal

1969. Death Centenary of Mirza Ghalib (poet).
585 **541** 20p. sepia, red and flesh 15 15

542 Osmania University

1969. 50th Anniv of Osmania University.
586 **542** 20p. green 15 20

543 Rafi Ahmed Kidwai and Lockheed Constellation Mail Plane

1969. 20th Anniv of "All-up" Airmail Scheme.
587 **543** 20p. blue . . . . 1·00 30

544 I.L.O. Badge and Emblem

1969. 50th Anniv of Int Labour Organization.
588 **544** 20p. brown 15 20

545 Memorial, and Hands dropping Flowers

546 K. Nageswara Rao Pantulu (journalist)

1969. 50th Anniv of Jallianwala Bagh Massacre, Amritsar.
589 **545** 20p. red 15 20

1969. Kasinadhuni Nageswara Rao Pantulu Commemoration.
590 **546** 20p. brown 15 20

547 Ardaseer Cursetjee Wadia, and Ships

1969. Ardaseer Cursetjee Wadia (ship-builder) Commemoration.
591 **547** 20p. turquoise 50 40

548 Serampore College

549 Dr. Zakir Husain

1969. 150th Anniv of Serampore College.
592 **548** 20p. plum 15 20

1969. President Dr. Zakir Husain Commemoration.
593 **549** 20p. sepia 15 20

550 Laxmanrao Kirloskar

1969. Birth Centenary of Laxmanrao Kirloskar (agriculturist).
594 **550** 20p. black 15 15

551 Gandhi and his Wife

1969. Birth Centenary of Mahatma Gandhi.
595 **551** 20p. brown 70 40
596 – 75p. flesh and drab . . . 1·25 90
597 – 1r. blue . . . . 1·25 65
598 – 5r. brown and orange . . 4·50 6·50
DESIGNS AND SIZES—VERT: 75p. Gandhi's head and shoulders (28 × 38 mm); 1r. Gandhi walking (woodcut) (20 × 38 mm). HORIZ: 5r. Gandhi with charkha (36 × 26 mm).

555 "Ajanta" (bulk carrier) and I.M.C.O. Emblem

1969. 10th Anniv of Inter-Governmental Maritime Consultative Organization.
599 **555** 20p. blue . . . . 1·75 40

556 Outline of Parliament Building and Globe

1969. 57th Inter-Parliamentary Conf, New Delhi.
600 **556** 20p. blue 15 20

557 Astronaut walking beside Space Module on Moon

558 Gurudwara Nankana Sahib (birthplace)

1969. 1st Man on the Moon.
601 **557** 20p. brown 50 30

1969. 500th Birth Anniv of Guru Nanak Dev (Sikh religious leader).
602 **558** 20p. violet 30 20

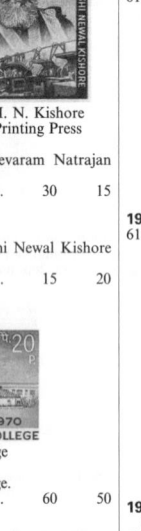

559 Tiger's Head and Hands holding Globe

1969. Int Union for the Conservation of Nature and Natural Resources Conf, New Delhi.
603 **559** 20p. brown and green . . 30 30

560 Sadhu Vaswani **561** Thakkar Bapa

1969. 90th Birth Anniv of Sadhu Vaswani (educationist).
604 **560** 20p. grey 15 15

1969. Birth Centenary of Thakkar Bapa (humanitarian).
605 **561** 20p. brown 15 20

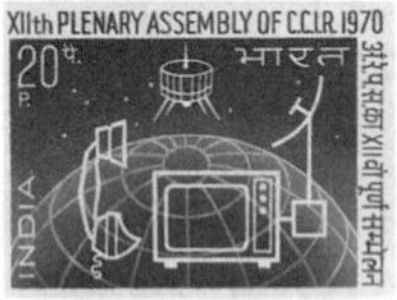

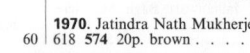

562 Satellite, Television, Telephone and Globe

1970. 12th Plenary Assembly of Int Radio Consultative Committee.
606 **562** 20p. blue 40 20

563 C. N. Annadurai **564** M. N. Kishore and Printing Press

1970. 1st Death Anniv of Conjeevaram Natrajan Annadurai (statesman).
607 **563** 20p. purple and blue . . . 30 15

1970. 75th Death Anniv of Munshi Newal Kishore (publisher).
608 **564** 20p. lake 15 20

565 Nalanda College

1970. Centenary of Nalanda College.
609 **565** 20p. brown 60 50

566 Swami Shraddhanand (social reformer)

1970. Swami Shraddhanand Commemoration.
610 **566** 20p. brown 75 60

567 Lenin

1970. Birth Centenary of Lenin.
611 **567** 20p. brown and sepia . . 40 20

568 New U.P.U. H.Q. Building

1970. New U.P.U. Headquarters Building, Berne.
612 **568** 20p. green, grey and black 15 20

569 Sher Shah Suri (15th century ruler) **571** "U N" and Globe

570 V. D. Savarkar (patriot) and Cellular Jail, Andaman Islands

1970. Sher Shah Suri Commemoration.
613 **569** 20p. green 30 30

1970. Vinayak Damodar Savarkar Commem.
614 **570** 20p. brown 50 30

1970. 25th Anniv of United Nations.
615 **571** 20p. blue 40 20

572 Symbol and Workers

1970. Asian Productivity Year.
616 **572** 20p. violet 20 20

573 Dr. Montessori and I.E.Y. Emblem

1970. Birth Centenary of Dr. Maria Montessori (educationist).
617 **573** 20p. purple 30 30

574 J. N. Mukherjee (revolutionary) and Horse

1970. Jatindra Nath Mukherjee Commem.
618 **574** 20p. brown . . . . 1·50 30

575 V. S. Srinivasa Sastri **576** I. C. Vidyasagar

1970. Srinivasa Sastri (educationist) Commemoration.
619 **575** 20p. yellow and purple . . 30 30

1970. 150th Birth Anniv of Iswar Chandra Vidyasagar (educationist).
620 **576** 20p. brown and purple . . 40 30

577 Maharishi Valmiki

1970. Maharishi Valmiki (ancient author) Commem.
621 **577** 20p. purple 60 30

578 Calcutta Port

1970. Centenary of Calcutta Port Trust.
622 **578** 20p. blue . . . . 1·50 70

579 University Building

1970. 50th Anniv of Jamia Millia Islamia University.
623 **579** 20p. green 60 50

580 Jamnalal Bajaj **581** Nurse and Patient

1970. Jamnalal Bajaj (industrialist) Commemoration.
624 **580** 20p. grey 15 30

1970. 50th Anniv of Indian Red Cross.
625 **581** 20p. red and blue 60 40

582 Sant Namdeo **583** Beethoven

1970. 700th Birth Anniv of Sant Namdeo (mystic).
626 **582** 20p. orange 15 30

1970. Birth Bicentenary of Beethoven.
627 **583** 20p. orange and black . . 2·00 70

584 Children examining Stamps

1970. Indian National Philatelic Exhibition, New Delhi.
628 **584** 20p. orange and green . . 30 10
629 – 1r. brown and ochre . . . 2·50 1·00
DESIGN: 1r. Gandhi commemorative through magnifier.

585 Girl Guide **586** Hands and Lamp (emblem)

1970. Diamond Jubilee of Girl Guide Movement in India.
630 **585** 20p. purple 60 30

1971. Centenary of Indian Life Insurance.
631 **586** 20p. brown and red . . . 20 30

587 Vidyapith Building

1971. 50th Anniv of Kashi Vidyapith University.
632 **587** 20p. brown 20 30

588 Sant Ravidas

1971. Sant Ravidas (15th-century mystic) Commemoration.
633 **588** 20p. red 65 30

589 C. F. Andrews **590** Acharya Narendra Deo (scholar)

1971. Birth Centenary of Charles Freer Andrews (missionary).
634 **589** 20p. brown 35 30

1971. 15th Death Anniv of Acharya Narendra Deo.
635 **590** 20p. green 15 30

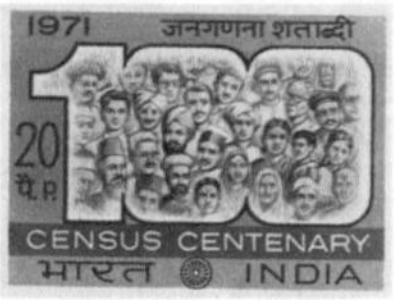

591 Crowd and "100"

1971. Centenary of Decennial Census.
636 **591** 20p. brown and blue . . . 30 30

592 Sri Ramana Maharishi (mystic) **593** Raja Ravi Varma and "Damayanti and the Swan"

1971. 21st Death Anniv of Ramana Maharishi.
637 **592** 20p. orange and brown 20 30

1971. 65th Death Anniv of Ravi Varma (artist).
638 **593** 20p. green 60 50

594 Dadasaheb Phalke and Camera

1971. Birth Centenary of Dadasaheb Phalke (cinematographer).
639 **594** 20p. purple 70 40

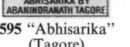

595 "Abhisarika" (Tagore) **596** Swami Virjanand (Vedic scholar)

1971. Birth Centenary of Abanindranath Tagore (painter).
640 **595** 20p. grey, yellow & brown 40 30

1971. Swami Virjanand Commemoration.
641 **596** 20p. brown 30 40

597 Cyrus the Great and Procession

1971. 2500th Anniv of Charter of Cyrus the Great.
642 **597** 20p. brown 75 55

598 Globe and Money Box

1971. World Thrift Day.
643 **598** 20p. grey 20 30

599 Ajanta Caves Painting **600** "Women at Work" (Geeta Gupta)

1971. 25th Anniv of UNESCO.
644 **599** 20p. brown . . . . 1·50 70

1971. Children's Day.
645 **600** 20p. red 20 50

607 Refugees **608** C. V. Raman (scientist) and Light Graph

1971. Obligatory Tax. Refugee Relief. (a) Optd **REFUGEE RELIEF** in Hindi and English.
646 – 5p. red (No. 506) 60 10

(b) Optd **Refugee Relief**.
647 – 5p. red (No. 506) . . . . . 2·50 1·00

(c) Optd **REFUGEE RELIEF**.
649 – 5p. red (No. 506) . . . . . 3·25 1·50

(d) Optd **Refugee relief**.
650c – 5p. red (No. 506). . . . . 17·00 3·75

(e) Optd **Refugee Relief** in Hindi and English.
650d – 5p. red (No. 506) . . . .

(f) Type **607**.
651 **607** 5p. red 40 10

From 15 November 1971 until 31 March 1973 the Indian Government levied a 5p. surcharge on all mail, except postcards and newspapers, for the relief of refugees from the former East Pakistan.

1971. 1st Death Anniv of Chandrasekhara Venkata Raman.
652 **608** 20p. orange and brown 50 40

609 Visva Bharati Building and Rabindranath Tagore (founder)

1971. 50th Anniv of Visva Bharati University.
653 **609** 20p. sepia and brown . . 40 40

610 Cricketers

1971. Indian Cricket Victories.
654 **610** 20p. green, myrtle and sage . . . . 2·00 65

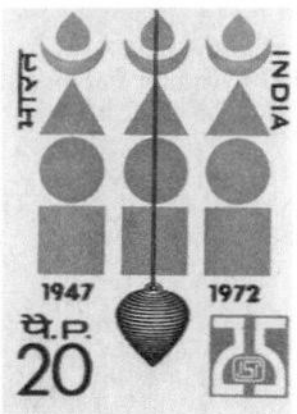

611 Map and Satellite **612** Elemental Symbols and Plumb-line

1972. 1st Anniv of Arvi Satellite Earth Station.
655 **611** 20p. purple 20 30

1972. 25th Anniv of Indian Standards Institution.
656 **612** 20p. grey and black . . . 15 50

613 Signal Box Panel

1972. 50th Anniv of Int Railways Union.
657 **613** 20p. multicoloured . . . 1·00 40

614 Hockey-player

1972. Olympic Games, Munich.
658 **614** 20p. violet . . . . 1·75 25
659 – 1r.45 green and lake . . . 2·50 2·00
DESIGN: 1r.45, Various sports.

615 Symbol of Sri Aurobindo **617** Inter-Services Crest

616 Celebrating Independence Day in front of Parliament

1972. Birth Centenary of Sri Aurobindo (religious teacher).
660 **615** 20p. yellow and blue . . . 20 30

1972. 25th Anniv of Independence. (1st issue).
661 **616** 20p. multicoloured . . . 65 30
See also Nos. 673/4.

1972. Defence Services Commemoration.
662 **617** 20p. multicoloured . . . 30 40

618 V. O. Chidambaran Pillai (trade union leader) and Ship

1972. Birth Cent of V. O. Chidambaran Pillai.
663 **618** 20p. blue and brown . . . 75 40

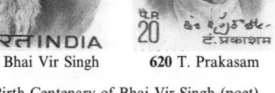

619 Bhai Vir Singh **620** T. Prakasam

1972. Birth Centenary of Bhai Vir Singh (poet).
664 **619** 20p. purple 60 40

1972. Birth Centenary of Tanguturi Prakasam (lawyer).
665 **620** 20p. brown 20 40

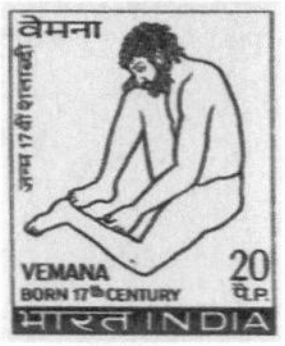

621 Vemana **622** Bertrand Russell

1972. 300th Birth Anniv of Vemana (poet).
666 **621** 20p. black 20 40

1972. Birth Centenary of Bertrand Russell (philosopher).
667 **622** 1r.45 black . . . . 3·25 2·75

623 Symbol of "Asia '72"

1972. "Asia '72" (Third Asian International Trade Fair), New Delhi.
668 **623** 20p. black and orange . . 10 20
669 – 1r.45 orange and black . . 60 1·75
DESIGN: 1r.45, Hand of Buddha.

624 V. A. Sarabhai and Rocket

1972. 1st Death Anniv of Dr. Vikram A. Sarabhai (scientist).
670 **624** 20p. brown and green . . 20 40

625 Flag of U.S.S.R. and Kremlin Tower

1972. 50th Anniv of U.S.S.R.
671 **625** 20p. red and yellow . . . 20 60

626 Exhibition Symbol **627** "Democracy"

1973. "Indipex '73" Stamp Exhibition (1st issue).
672 **626** 1r.45 mauve, gold & black 45 1·25
See also No. 701/**MS**704.

1973. 25th Anniv of Independence (2nd issue). Multicoloured.
673 20p. Type **627** 15 15
674 1r.45 Hindustan Aircraft Industries Ajeet jet fighters over India Gate (38 × 20 mm) . . . . . . 1·40 1·60

628 Sri Ramakrishna Paramahamsa (religious leader) **629** Postal Corps Emblem

1973. Sri Ramakrishna Paramahamsa Commem.
675 **628** 20p. brown 40 60

1973. 1st Anniv of Army Postal Service Corps.
676 **629** 20p. blue and red 40 50

630 Flag and Map of Bangladesh **631** Kumaran Asan

1973. "Jai Bangla" (Inauguration of 1st Bangladesh Parliament).
677 **630** 20p. multicoloured . . . 15 40

1973. Birth Centenary of Kumaran Asan (writer and poet).
678 **631** 20p. brown 20 60

632 Flag and Flames **634** "Radha-Kishangarh" (Nihal Chand)

633 Dr. Bhim Rao Ambedkar (lawyer)

1973. Homage to Martyrs for Independence.
679 **632** 20p. multicoloured . . . 15 40

1973. Ambedkar Commemoration.
680 **633** 20p. green and purple . . 20 1·00

1973. Indian Miniature Paintings. Multicoloured.
681 20p. Type **634** 30 35
682 50p. "Dance Duet" (Aurangzeb's period) . . . 60 1·50
683 1r. "Lovers on a Camel" (Nasir-ud-din) . . . . . 80 1·75
684 2r. "Chained Elephant" (Zain-al-Abidin) . . . . . 1·10 2·50

635 Mount Everest

1973. 15th Anniv of Indian Mountaineering Foundation.
685 **635** 20p. blue 50 50

636 Tail of Boeing 747

1973. 25th Anniv of Air-India's International Services.
686 **636** 1r.45 blue and red . . . . 4·00 4·00

637 Cross, Church of St. Thomas' Mount, Madras

638 Michael Madhusudan Dutt (poet–Death Centenary)

1973. 19th Death Centenary of St. Thomas.
687 **637** 20p. grey and brown . . 20 60

1973. Centenaries.
688 **638** 20p. green and brown . . 1·00 65
689 – 30p. brown . . . . 1·25 2·50
690 – 50p. brown . . . . 1·50 2·50
691 – 1r. violet and red . . . 1·50 1·50
DESIGNS—HORIZ: 30p. Vishnu Digambar Paluskar (musician, birth cent); 50p. Dr. G. A. Hansen (cent of discovery of leprosy bacillus); 1r. Nicolaus Copernicus (astronomer, 5th birth cent).

639 A. O. Hume

641 R. C. Dutt

640 Gandhi and Nehru

1973. Allan Octavian Hume (founder of Indian National Congress) Commemoration.
692 **639** 20p. grey 20 40

1973. Gandhi and Nehru Commemoration.
693 **640** 20p. multicoloured . . . 20 40

1973. Romesh Chandra Dutt (writer) Commem.
694 **641** 20p. brown 20 40

642 K. S. Ranjitsinhji

643 Vithalbhai Patel

1973. K. S. Ranjitsinhji (cricketer) Commemoration.
695 **642** 30p. green . . . . 3·50 3·50

1973. Vithalbhai Patel (lawyer) Commemoration.
696 **643** 50p. brown . . . . 30 1·00

644 Sowar of President's Bodyguard

645 Interpol Emblem

1973. Bicentenary of President's Bodyguard.
697 **644** 20p. multicoloured . . . 1·25 50

1973. 50th Anniv of Interpol.
698 **645** 20p. brown 30 40

646 Syed Ahmad Khan (social reformer)

1973. Syed Ahmad Khan Commemoration.
699 **646** 20p. brown . . . . 20 1·00

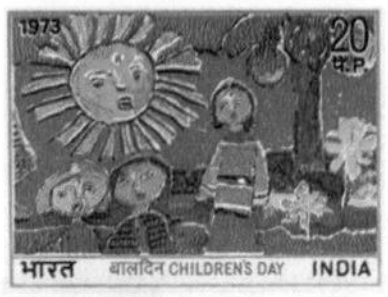

647 "Children at Play" (Bela Raval)

1973. Children's Day.
700 **647** 20p. multicoloured . . . 20 30

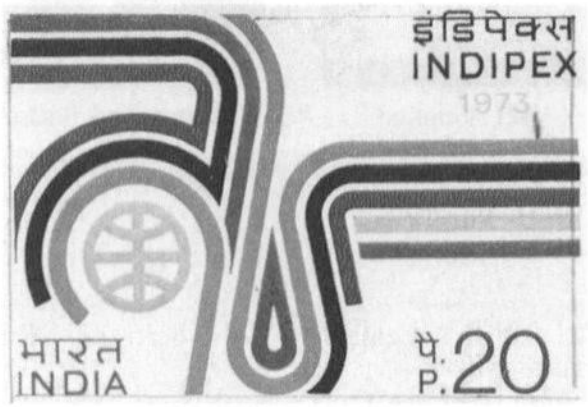

648 Indipex Emblem

1973. "Indipex '73" Philatelic Exhibition, New Delhi (2nd issue). Multicoloured.
701 20p. Type **648** 20 30
702 1r. Ceremonial elephant and $1\frac{1}{2}$a. stamp of 1947 (vert) 1·00 1·50
703 2r. Common peafowl (vert) 1·25 3·00
MS704 127 × 127 mm. Nos. 672 and 701/3. Imperf . . . . 4·00 8·00

649 Emblem of National Cadet Corps

650 C. Rajagopalachari (statesman)

1973. 25th Anniv of National Cadet Corps.
705 **649** 20p. multicoloured . . . 20 30

1973. Chakravarti Rajagopalachari Commemoration.
706 **650** 20p. brown 20 50

651 "Sun" Mask

652 Chhatrapati

1974. Indian Masks. Multicoloured.
707 20p. Type **651** 15 15
708 50p. "Moon" mask 30 60
709 1r. "Narasimha" 55 80
710 2r. "Ravana" (horiz) . . . . 70 1·75
MS711 109 × 135 mm. Nos. 707/10 2·00 2·50

1974. 300th Anniv of Coronation of Chhatrapati Shri Shivaji Maharaj (patriot and ruler).
712 **652** 25p. multicoloured . . . 70 30

653 Maithili Sharan Gupta (poet)

654 Kandukuri Veeresalingam (social reformer)

1974. Indian Personalities (1st series).
713 **653** 25p. brown 15 50
714 – 25p. brown 15 50
715 – 25p. brown 15 50
PORTRAITS: No. 714, Jainarain Vyas (politician and journalist); No. 715, Utkal Gourab Madhusudan Das (social reformer).

1974. Indian Personalities (2nd series).
716 **654** 25p. brown 25 75
717 – 50p. purple . . . . 55 1·75
718 – 1r. brown . . . . 70 1·75
PORTRAITS: 50p. Tipu Sultan; 1r. Max Mueller (Sanskrit scholar).

655 Kamala Nehru

1974. Kamala Nehru Commemoration.
719 **655** 25p. multicoloured . . . 75 75

656 W.P.Y. Emblem

657 Spotted Deer

657a Sitar

1974. World Population Year.
720 **656** 25p. purple and brown . . 20 30

1974. (a) Values expressed with "p" or "Re".
721 – 15p. brown . . . . . . 3·25 1·00
722 **657** 25p. brown . . . . . . 1·00 2·00
723 **657a** 1r. brown and black . . 2·50 30

(b) Values expressed as numerals only.
724 – 2p. brown . . . . . . 1·25 3·00
725 – 5p. red 70 10
729 – 10p. blue 75 15
730 – 15p. brown . . . . . . 1·75 10
731 – 20p. green 15 10
732 – 25p. brown . . . . . . 7·50 2·75
732b – 30p. brown . . . . . . 4·25 55
733 – 50p. violet . . . . . . 6·50 20
734 – 60p. grey . . . . . . 2·75 1·00
735 **657a** 1r. brown and black . . 3·25 10
736 – 2r. violet and brown . . 14·00 40
737 – 5r. violet and brown . . 2·50 1·25
738d – 10r. grey and green . . 1·10 1·25
DESIGNS—VERT (as Type **657**): 2p. Bidri vase; 5p. "Family Planning"; 15p. Tiger; 25p. Gandhi; 30p. Indian dolls; 60p. Somnath Temple. HORIZ (as Type **657a**): 10p. Electric locomotive; 20p. Handicrafts toy; 50p. Great egret in flight. (As Type **657a**): 2r. Himalayas; 5r. Bhakra Dam, Punjab; 10r. Atomic reactor, Trombay.
For 30, 35, 50, 60p. and 1r. values as No. 732 see Nos. 968, 979, 1073, 1320 and 1436.

658 President V. Giri

660 Woman Flute-player (sculpture)

659 U.P.U. Emblem

1974. Retirement of President Giri.
739 **658** 25p. multicoloured . . . 15 30

1974. Centenary of U.P.U.
740 **659** 25p. violet, blue and black 30 10
741 – 1r. multicoloured 50 50
742 – 2r. multicoloured . . . . 75 2·00
MS743 – 108 × 108mm. Nos. 740/2 2·00 6·50
DESIGNS:—1r. Birds and nest, "Madhubani" style. VERT: 2r. Arrows around globe.

1974. Centenary of Mathura Museum.
744 **660** 25p. chestnut and brown 65 80
745 – 25p. chestnut and brown 65 80
DESIGN: No. 745, Vidyadhara with garland.

661 Nicholas Roerich (medallion by H. Dropsy)

1974. Birth Centenary of Professor Roerich (humanitarian).
746 **661** 1r. green and yellow . . . 65 55

662 Pavapuri Temple

1974. 2,500th Anniv of Bhagwan Mahavira's Attainment of Nirvana.
747 **662** 25p. black 60 20

663 "Cat" (Rajesh Bhatia)

665 Territorial Army Badge

664 "Indian Dancers" (Amita Shah)

1974. Children's Day.
748 **663** 25p. multicoloured . . . 1·00 50

1974. 25th Anniv of UNICEF in India.
749 **664** 25p. multicoloured . . . 55 45

1974. 25th Anniv of Indian Territorial Army.
750 **665** 25p. black, yellow & green 60 40

666 Krishna as Gopal Bal with Cows (Rajasthan painting on cloth)

668 Marconi

667 Symbols and Child's Face

1974. 19th International Dairy Congress, New Delhi.
751 **666** 25p. purple and brown . . 40 40

1974. Help for Retarded Children.
752 **667** 25p. red and black . . . 60 60

1974. Birth Centenary of Guglielmo Marconi (radio pioneer).
753 **668** 2r. blue . . . . 2·25 1·25

669 St. Francis Xavier's Shrine, Goa

670 Saraswati (Deity of Language and Learning)

1974. St. Francis Xavier Celebration.
754 **669** 25p. multicoloured . . . 15 40

1975. World Hindi Convention, Nagpur.
755 **670** 25p. grey and red 40 40

671 Parliament House, New Delhi

1975. 25th Anniv of Republic.
756 **671** 25p. black, silver and blue 65 30

672 Table-tennis Bat

1975. World Table-tennis Championships, Calcutta.
757 **672** 25p. black, red and green 85 30

673 "Equality, Development and Peace"

1975. International Women's Year.
758 **673** 25p. multicoloured . . . 85 45

674 Stylized Cannon

676 Saraswati

675 Arya Samaj Emblem

1975. Bicent of Indian Army Ordnance Corps.
759 **674** 25p. multicoloured . . . 1·25 60

1975. Centenary of Arya Samaj Movement.
760 **675** 25p. red and brown . . . 40 40

1975. World Telugu Language Conf, Hyderabad.
761 **676** 25p. black and green . . 45 30

677 Satellite "Aryabhata"

1975. Launch of First Indian Satellite.
762 **677** 25p. lt blue, blue & purple 75 40

678 Blue-winged Pitta

1975. Indian Birds. Multicoloured.
763 25p. Type **678** 75 25
764 50p. Asian black-headed oriole . . . . 1·75 2·25
765 1r. Western tragopan (vert) 2·50 2·75
766 2r. Himalayan monal pheasant (vert) . . . . . . 3·25 5·50

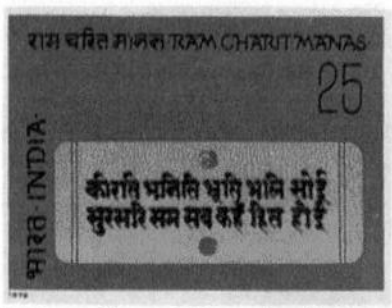

679 Page from "Ramcharitmanas" (manuscript)

1975. 4th Centenary of "Ramcharitmanas" (epic poem by Goswami Tulsidas).
767 **679** 25p. black, yellow and red 75 30

680 Young Women within Y.W.C.A. Badge

681 "The Creation"

1975. Centenary of Indian Y.W.C.A.
768 **680** 25p. multicoloured . . . 40 40

1975. 500th Birth Anniv of Michelangelo. "Creation" Frescoes from Sistine Chapel.
769 **681** 50p. multicoloured . . . 55 90
770 – 50p. multicoloured . . . 55 90
771 – 50p. multicoloured . . . 55 90
772 – 50p. multicoloured . . . 55 90
Nos. 770 and 772 are size 49 × 34 mm. The four stamps form a composite design.

682 Commission Emblem

683 Stylised Ground Antenna

1975. 25th Anniv of Int Commission on Irrigation and Drainage.
773 **682** 25p. multicoloured . . . 50 20

1975. Inauguration of Satellite Instructional Television Experiment.
774 **683** 25p. multicoloured . . . 50 20

684 St. Arunagirinathar

685 Commemorative Text

1975. 600th Birth Anniv of St. Arunagirinathar.
775 **684** 50p. purple and black . . 1·50 1·25

1975. Namibia Day.
776 **685** 25p. black and red . . . 50 50

686 Mir Anees (poet)

687 Memorial Temple to Ahilyabai Holkar (ruler)

1975. Indian Celebrities.
777 **686** 25p. green 30 75
778 **687** 25p. brown 30 75

688 Bharata Natyam

689 Ameer Khusrau

1975. Indian Dances. Multicoloured.
779 25p. Type **688** 65 20
780 50p. Orissi . . . . 1·00 2·00
781 75p. Kathak . . . . 1·25 2·25
782 1r. Kathakali . . . . 1·50 1·25
783 1r.50 Kuchipudi . . . . . . 2·25 3·75
784 2r. Manipuri . . . . 2·25 3·75

1975. 650th Death Anniv of Ameer Khusrau (poet).
785 **689** 50p. brown and bistre . . 1·25 2·00

690 V. K. Krishna Menon

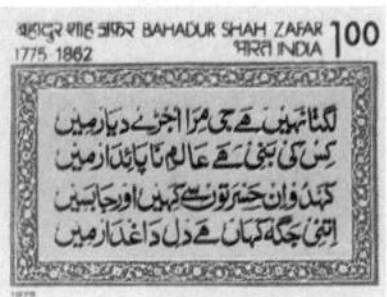

691 Text of Poem

1975. 1st Death Anniv of V. K. Krishna Menon (statesman).
786 **690** 25p. green . . . . 1·00 1·00

1975. Birth Bicentenary of Emperor Bahadur Shah Zafar.
787 **691** 1r. black, buff and brown 1·50 1·00

692 Sansadiya Soudha, New Delhi

1975. 21st Commonwealth Parliamentary Conference, New Delhi.
788 **692** 2r. green . . . . 2·00 2·75

693 V. Patel

694 N. C. Bardoloi

1975. Birth Centenary of Vallabhbhai Patel (statesman).
789 **693** 25p. green 15 50

1975. Birth Centenary of Nabin Chandra Bardoloi (politician).
790 **694** 25p. brown 30 50

695 "Cow" (Sanjay Nathubhai Patel)

1975. Children's Day.
791 **695** 25p. multicoloured . . . 70 70

696 Original Printing Works, Nasik Road

697 Gurdwara Sisganj (site of martyrdom)

1975. 50th Anniv of India Security Press.
792 **696** 25p. multicoloured . . . 40 40

1975. Tercentenary of the Martyrdom of Guru Tegh Bahadur (Sikh leader).
793 **697** 25p. multicoloured . . . 60 60

698 Theosophical Society Emblem

699 Weather Cock

1975. Centenary of Theosophical Society.
794 **698** 25p. multicoloured . . . 40 40

1975. Cent of Indian Meteorological Department.
795 **699** 25p. multicoloured . . . 60 60

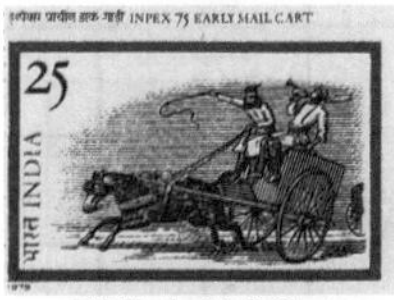

700 Early Mail Cart

1975. "Inpex '75" Nat Philatelic Exn, Calcutta.
796 **700** 25p. black and brown . . 75 30
797 – 2r. brown, purple & black 2·50 3·50
DESIGN: 2r. Indian bishop mark, 1775.

701 L. N. Mishra

702 Tiger

1976. 1st Death Anniv of Lalit Narayan Mishra (politician).
798 **701** 25p. brown 40 40

1976. Birth Cent of Jim Corbett (naturalist).
799 **702** 25p. multicoloured . . . 1·00 70

703 Painted Storks

1976. Keoladeo Ghana Bird Sanctuary, Bharatpur.
800 **703** 25p. multicoloured . . . 1·00 70

704 Vijayanta Tank

1976. Bicent of 16th Light Cavalry Regiment.
801 **704** 25p. green and brown . . 1·75 40

705 Alexander Graham Bell

706 Muthuswami Dikshitar

1976. Alexander Graham Bell Commem.
802 **705** 25p. brown and black . . 1·00 50

1976. Birth Bicentenary of Muthuswami Dikshitar (composer).
803 **706** 25p. violet 70 50

707 Eye and Red Cross

1976. World Health Day. Prevention of Blindness.
804 **707** 25p. brown and red . . . 1·00 60

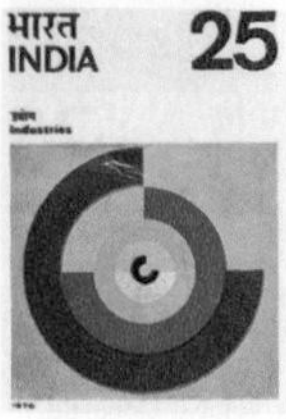

708 "Industries"

710 Nehru

709 Type WDM Diesel Locomotive, 1963

1976. Industrial Development.
805 **708** 25p. multicoloured . . . 30 30

1976. Locomotives. Multicoloured.

806	25p. Type **709**	55	10
807	50p. Rajputara Malwa Railway Class F/1 steam locomotive, 1895	1·50	55
808	1r. Southern Railway Class WP/1 steam locomotive, 1963	2·75	1·25
809	2r. Great Peninsular Railway Class GIP steam locomotive, 1853	3·50	2·50

1976.

810b	**710** 25p. violet	5·00	80
811	– 25p. brown	1·50	30

DESIGN: No. 811, Gandhi.
For these designs in a smaller format see Nos. 732, 968/9, 979/80, 1073/4 and 1320.

713 "Spirit of '76" (Willard)

714 K. Kamaraj (politician)

1976. Bicentenary of American Revolution.
812 **713** 2r.80 multicoloured . . . 1·25 1·25

1976. Kumaraswamy Kamaraj Commemoration.
813 **714** 25p. brown 15 15

715 "Shooting"

716 Subhadra Kumari Chauhan (poetess)

1976. Olympic Games, Montreal.

814	**715** 25p. violet and red . . .	30	10
815	– 1r. multicoloured	1·00	90
816	– 1r.50 mauve and black . .	2·00	3·00
817	– 2r.80 multicoloured . . .	1·75	4·25

DESIGNS: 1r. Shot-put; 1r.50, Hockey; 2r.80, Sprinting.

1976. S. K. Chauhan Commemoration.
818 **716** 25p. blue 15 50

717 Param Vir Chakra Medal

718 University Building, Bombay

1976. Param Vir Chakra Commemoration.
819 **717** 25p. multicoloured . . . 15 50

1976. 60th Anniv of Shreemati Nathibai Damodar Thackersey Women's University.
820 **718** 25p. violet 30 30

719 Bharatendu Harischandra (writer)

720 S. C. Chatterji

1976. Harischandra Commemoration.
821 **719** 25p. brown 15 30

1976. Birth Centenary of Sarat Chandra Chatterji (writer).
822 **720** 25p. black 15 30

721 Planned Family

722 Maharaja Agrasen and Coins

1976. Family Planning.
823 **721** 25p. multicoloured . . . 15 30

1976. Maharaja Agrasen Commemoration.
824 **722** 25p. brown 15 30

723 Swamp Deer

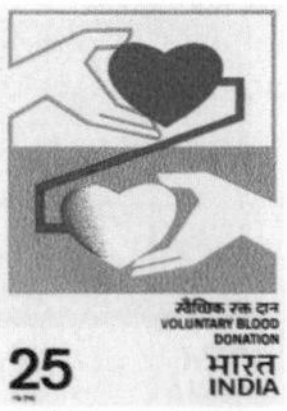

724 Hands holding Hearts

1976. Indian Wildlife. Multicoloured.

825	25p. Type **723**	55	40
826	50p. Lion	1·25	2·25
827	1r. Leopard (horiz)	1·75	2·25
828	2r. Caracal (horiz)	2·00	3·50

1976. Voluntary Blood Donation.
829 **724** 25p. yellow, red and black 1·00 60

725 Suryakant Tripathi ("Nirala")

726 "Loyal Mongoose" (H. D. Bhatia)

1976. 80th Birth Anniv of "Nirala" (poet and novelist).
830 **725** 25p. violet 15 30

1976. Children's Day.
831 **726** 25p. multicoloured . . . 50 50

727 Hiralal Shastri (social reformer)

728 Dr. Hari Singh Gour (lawyer)

1976. Shastri Commemoration.
832 **727** 25p. brown 20 30

1976. Dr. Hari Singh Gour Commemoration.
833 **728** 25p. purple 20 30

729 Airbus Industrie A300B4

1976. Inauguration of Indian Airlines' Airbus Service.
834 **729** 2r. multicoloured . . . . 2·50 2·25

730 Hybrid Coconut Palm

731 First Stanza of "Vande Mataram"

1976. Diamond Jubilee of Coconut Research.
835 **730** 25p. multicoloured . . . 20 30

1976. Centenary of "Vande Mataram" (patriotic song by B. C. Chatterjee).
836 **731** 25p. multicoloured . . . 30 30

732 Globe and Film Strip

1977. 6th International Film Festival of India, New Delhi.
837 **732** 2r. multicoloured . . . . 1·10 2·00

733 Seismograph and Crack in Earth's Crust

734 Tarun Ram Phookun

1977. 6th World Conference on Earthquake Engineering, New Delhi.
838 **733** 2r. lilac . . . . 1·00 2·00

1977. Birth Cent of Tarun Ram Phookun (politician).
839 **734** 25p. grey 15 30

735 Paramahansa Yogananda

736 Asian Regional Red Cross Emblem

1977. Paramahansa Yogananda (religious leader) Commem.
840 **735** 25p. orange . . . . . . 1·00 80

1977. 1st Asian Regional Red Cross Conference, New Delhi.
841 **736** 2r. red, pink and blue . . 2·00 2·50

737 Fakhruddin Ali Ahmed

738 Emblem of Asian-Oceanic Postal Union

1977. Death of President Ahmed.
842 **737** 25p. multicoloured . . . 35 35

1977. 15th Anniv of Asian–Oceanic Postal Union.
843 **738** 2r. multicoloured . . . . 1·10 1·75

739 Narottam Morarjee and "Loyalty" (liner)

740 Makhanlal Chaturvedi (writer and poet)

1977. Birth Cent of Morarjee (ship owner).
844 **739** 25p. blue . . . . 1·00 1·00

1977. Chaturvedi Commemoration.
845 **740** 25p. brown 15 40

741 Mahaprabhu Vallabhacharya (philosopher)

1977. Vallabhacharya Commemoration.
846 **741** 1r. brown 30 40

742 Federation Emblem

1977. 50th Anniv of Federation of Indian Chambers of Commerce and Industry.
847 **742** 25p. purple, brown and yellow 15 40

744 "Environment Protection"

1977. World Environment Day.
848 **744** 2r. multicoloured . . . . 60 1·25

745 Rajya Sabha Chamber

1977. 25th Anniv of Rajya Sabha (Upper House of Parliament).
849 **745** 25p. multicoloured . . . 15 30

746 Lotus

1977. Indian Flowers. Multicoloured.
850 25p. Type **746** 25 15
851 50p. Rhododendron (vert) . . 45 1·25
852 1r. Kadamba (vert) . . . . . 60 1·00
853 2r. Gloriosa lily . . . . . . 90 2·25

747 Berliner Gramophone

1977. Centenary of Sound Recording.
854 **747** 2r. brown and black . . . 1·00 2·00

748 Coomaraswamy and Siva

750 Dr. Samuel Hahnemann (founder of homeopathy)

749 Ganga Ram and Hospital

1977. Birth Centenary of Ananda Kentish Coomaraswamy (art historian).
855 **748** 25p. multicoloured . . . 40 40

1977. 50th Death Anniv of Sir Ganga Ram (social reformer).
856 **749** 25p. purple 30 30

1977. 32nd Int Homeopathic Congress, New Delhi.
857 **750** 2r. black and green . . . 3·50 2·75

751 Ram Manohar Lohia (politician)

752 Early Punjabi Postman

1977. Ram Manohar Lohia Commemoration.
858 **751** 25p. brown 40 30

1977. "Inpex '77" Philatelic Exn, Bangalore.
859 **752** 25p. multicoloured . . . 50 30
860 – 2r. grey and red . . . . . 2·00 2·75
DESIGN: 2r. "Lion and Palm" essay, 1853.

753 Scarlet "Scinde Dawks" of 1852

1977. "Asiana '77" Philatelic Exn, Bangalore.
861 **753** 1r. multicoloured . . . . 1·50 1·00
862 – 3r. blue, orange and black 3·00 3·75
DESIGN: 3r. Foreign mail arriving at Ballard Pier, Bombay, 1927.

754 "Mother and Child" (Khajuraho sculpture)

756 Symbolic Sun

755 Statue of Kittur Rani Channamma, Belgaum

1977. 15th Int Congress of Pediatrics, New Delhi.
863 **754** 2r. blue and brown . . . 2·25 2·75

1977. Kittur Rani Channama (ruler) Commem.
864 **755** 25p. green . . . . 1·00 70

1977. Union Public Service Commission.
865 **756** 25p. multicoloured . . . 35 30

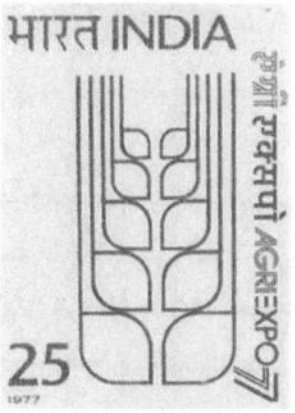
757 Ear of Corn

759 Jotirao Phooley (social reformer)

758 "Cats" (Nikur Dilipbhai Mody)

1977. "Agriexpo '77" Agricultural Exhibition, New Delhi.
866 **757** 25p. green 40 40

1977. Children's Day. Multicoloured.
867 25p. Type **758** 50 30
868 1r. "Friends" (Bhavsar Ashish Ramanlal) . . . . 2·25 3·00

1977. Indian Personalities.
869 **759** 25p. olive 30 75
870 – 25p. brown 30 75
DESIGN: No. 870, Senapti Bapat (patriot).

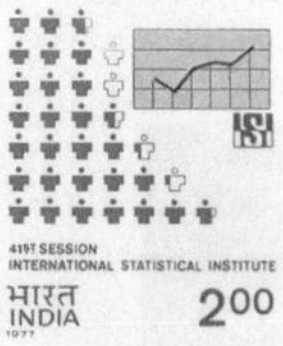
760 Diagram of Population Growth

761 Kamta Prasad Guru and Vyakarna (Hindi Grammar)

1977. 41st Session of International Statistical Institute, New Delhi.
871 **760** 2r. turquoise and red . . 60 1·00

1977. Kamta Prasad Guru (writer) Commem.
872 **761** 25p. brown 20 30

762 Kremlin Tower and Soviet Flag

763 Climber crossing a Crevice

1977. 60th Anniv of October Revolution.
873 **762** 1r. multicoloured 50 75

1978. Conquest of Kanchenjunga (1977). Multicoloured.
874 25p. Type **763** 10 10
875 1r. Indian flag near summit (horiz) 45 90

764 "Shikara" on Lake Dal, Kashmir

1978. 27th Pacific Area Travel Association Conference, New Delhi.
876 **764** 1r. multicoloured . . . . 2·00 1·50

765 Children in Library

1978. 3rd World Book Fair, New Delhi.
877 **765** 1r. brown and slate . . . 50 80

766 Mother-Pondicherry

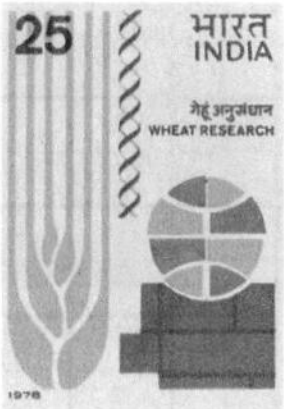
767 Wheat and Globe

1978. Birth Centenary of Mother-Pondicherry (philosopher).
878 **766** 25p. brown and grey . . 20 30

1978. 5th International Wheat Genetics Symposium, New Delhi.
879 **767** 25p. yellow and turquoise 20 30

768 Nanalal Dalpatram Kavi (poet)

769 Surjya Sen (revolutionary)

1978. Nanalal Dalpatram Kavi Commemoration.
880 **768** 25p. brown 20 30

1978. Surjya Sen Commemoration.
881 **769** 25p. bistre and red . . . 20 30

770 "Two Vaishnavas" (Jamini Roy)

1978. Modern Indian Paintings. Multicoloured.
882 25p. Type **770** 20 30
883 50p. "The Mosque" (Sailoz Mookherjea) . . . . . . 40 1·25
884 1r. "Head" (Rabindranath Tagore) . . . . 70 1·50
885 2r. "Hill Women" (Amrita Sher Gil) . . . . 90 2·00

771 "Self-portrait" (Rubens)

772 Charlie Chaplin

1978. 400th Birth Anniv of Peter Paul Rubens.
886 **771** 2r. multicoloured . . . . 2·00 3·00

1978. Charlie Chaplin Commemoration.
887 **772** 25p. blue and gold . . . 1·25 70

773 Deendayal Upadhyaya (politician)

774 Syama Prasad Mookerjee

1978. Deendayal Upadhyaya Commemoration.
888 **773** 25p. brown and orange 20 40

1978. Syama Prasad Mookerjee (politician) Commemoration.
889 **774** 25p. brown 30 50

775 Airavat (mythological elephant), Jain Temple, Gujerat (Kachchh Museum)

776 Krishna and Arjuna in Battle Chariot

1978. Treasures from Indian Museums. Mult.
890 25p. Type **775** 30 30
891 50p. Kalpadruma (magical tree), Besnagar (Indian Museum) . . . . 40 1·25
892 1r. Obverse and reverse of Kushan gold coin (National Museum) . . . . 55 1·50
893 2r. Dagger and knife of Emperor Jehangir, Mughal (Salar Jung Museum) . . . 75 2·00

1978. Bhagawadgeeta (Divine Song of India) Commemoration.
894 **776** 25p. gold and red 20 30

777 Bethune College

1978. Centenary of Bethune College, Calcutta.
895 **777** 25p. brown and green . . 20 30

778 E. V. Ramasami

1978. E. V. Ramasami (social reformer) Commemoration.
896 **778** 25p. black 20 20

779 Uday Shankar

780 Leo Tolstoy

1978. Uday Shankar (dancer) Commem.
897 **779** 25p. brown 20 30

1978. 150th Birth Anniv of Leo Tolstoy (writer).
898 **780** 1r. multicoloured 30 30

781 Vallathol Narayana Menon

783 Machine Operator

782 "Two Friends" (Dinesh Sharma)

1978. Birth Centenary of Vallathol Narayana Menon (poet).
899 **781** 25p. purple and brown . . 15 40

1978. Children's Day.
900 **782** 25p. multicoloured . . . 20 40

1978. National Small Industries Fair, New Delhi.
901 **783** 25p. green 20 30

784 Sowars of Skinner's Horse

785 Mohammad Ali Jauhar

1978. 175th Anniv of Skinner's Horse (cavalry regiment).
902 **784** 25p. multicoloured . . . 1·00 70

1978. Birth Centenary of Mohammad Ali Jauhar (patriot).
903 **785** 25p. olive 20 30

786 Chakravarti Rajagopalachari

787 Wright Brothers and Flyer I

1978. Birth Centenary of Chakravarti Rajagopalachari (first post-independence Governor-General).
904 **786** 25p. brown 20 30

1978. 75th Anniv of Powered Flight.
905 **787** 1r. violet and yellow . . . 1·00 30

788 Ravenshaw College

1978. Centenary of Ravenshaw College, Cuttack.
906 **788** 25p. red and green . . . 20 30

789 Schubert

790 Uniforms of 1799, 1901 and 1979 with Badge

1978. 150th Death Anniv of Franz Schubert (composer).
907 **789** 1r. multicoloured . . . . 1·25 55

1979. 4th Reunion of Punjab Regiment.
908 **790** 25p. multicoloured . . . 1·25 70

791 Bhai Parmanand

792 Gandhi with Young Boy

1979. Bhai Parmanand (scholar) Commemoration.
909 **791** 25p. violet 20 30

1979. International Year of the Child.
910 **792** 25p. brown and red . . . 40 30
911 – 1r. brown and orange . . 60 1·50
DESIGN: 1r. India I.Y.C. emblem.

793 Albert Einstein

794 Rajarshi Shahu Chhatrapati

1979. Birth Centenary of Albert Einstein (physicist).
912 **793** 1r. blue 75 60

1979. Rajarshi Shahu Chhatrapati (ruler of Kolhapur State, and precursor of social reform in India) Commemoration.
913 **794** 25p. purple 20 30

795 Exhibition Logo

1979. "India '80" International Stamp Exhibition (1st issue).
914 **795** 30p. green and orange . . 20 30
See also Nos. 942/5 and 955/8.

796 Postcards under Magnifying Glass

797 Raja Mahendra Pratap

1979. Centenary of Indian Postcards.
915 **796** 50p. multicoloured . . . 20 40

1979. Raja Mahendra Pratap (patriot) Commemoration.
916 **797** 30p. green 20 40

798 Hilsa, Pomfret and Prawn

800 Jatindra Nath Das

1979.

920	–	2p. violet	10	30
921a	**798**	5p. blue	10	10
922a	–	10p. green	70	10
923	–	15p. green	20	10
924a	–	20p. red	70	10
925a	–	25p. brown	70	10
925bb	–	25p. green	75	10
926ab	–	30p. green	1·25	10
927	–	35p. purple	1·50	10
928c	–	50p. violet	1·00	10
929b	–	1r. brown	20	10
932a	–	2r. lilac	20	10
933c	–	2r.25 red and green . .	50	10
934	–	2r.80 red and green . .	2·00	1·00
934ca	–	3r.25 orange and green	25	30
935c	–	5r. red and green . . .	60	40
936b	–	10r. purple and green	30	45

DESIGNS—HORIZ: 2p. Adult education class; 10p. Irrigation canal; 25p. (925a) Chick hatching from egg; 25p. (925bb) Village, wheat and tractor; 30p. Harvesting maize; 50p. Woman dairy farmer, cows and milk bottles. (36 × 19 mm): 10r. Forest on hillside. VERT (17 × 20 mm): 15p. Farmer and agricultural symbols; 20p. Mother feeding child; 35p. "Family Welfare". (17 × 28 mm): 1r. Cotton plant; 2r. Weaving. (20 × 38 mm): 2r.25, Cashew; 2r.80, Apples; 3r.25, Oranges; 5r. Rubber tapping.
For 75p. in same design as No. 927 see No. 1214.

1979. 50th Death Anniv of Jatindra Nath Das (revolutionary).
941 **800** 30p. brown 20 40

801 De Havilland Puss Moth

1979. "Air India 80" International Stamp Exhibition (2nd issue). Mail-carrying Aircraft. Multicoloured.
942 30p. Type **801** 50 25
943 50p. Indian Air Force Hindustan Aircraft Industries Chetak helicopter 70 45
944 1r. Indian Airlines Boeing 737 airliner 85 75
945 2r. Air India Boeing 747 airliner . . . . 1·10 95

802 Early and Modern Lightbulbs

1979. Centenary of Electric Lightbulb.
946 **802** 1r. purple 20 30

803 Gilgit Record

1979. International Archives Week.
947 **803** 30p. yellow and brown . . 20 60

804 Hirakud Dam, Orissa

1979. 50th Anniv and 13th Congress of International Commission on Large Dams.
948 **804** 30p. brown and turquoise 20 30

805 Fair Emblem

806 Child learning to Read

1979. India International Trade Fair, New Delhi.
949 **805** 1r. black and red 20 30

1979. International Children's Book Fair, New Delhi.
950 **806** 30p. multicoloured . . . 20 30

807 Dove with Olive Branch and I.A.E.A. Emblem

1979. 23rd International Atomic Energy Agency Conference, New Delhi.
951 **807** 1r. multicoloured 20 45

808 Hindustan Aircraft Industries HAL-26 Pushpak Light Plane and Rohini-1 Glider

1979. Flying and Gliding.
952 **808** 30p. black, brown and blue . . . . 1·40 1·00

809 Gurdwara Baoli Sahib Temple, Goindwal, Amritsar District

810 Ring of People encircling U.N. Emblem and Cogwheel

1979. 500th Birth Anniv of Guru Amar Das (Sikh leader).
953 **809** 30p. multicoloured . . . 20 40

1980. 3rd United Nations Industrial Development Organization General Conference, New Delhi.
954 **810** 1r. multicoloured 20 30

811 Army Post Office and Postmarks

812 Energy Symbols

1980. "India '80" International Stamp Exhibition (3rd issue).
955 **811** 30p. green 40 30
956 – 50p. brown & deep brown 70 1·00
957 – 1r. red . . . . 80 1·00
958 – 2r. brown . . . . 80 2·00
DESIGNS: 50p. Money order transfer document, 1879; 1r. Copper prepayment ticket, 1774; 2r. Sir Rowland Hill and birthplace at Kidderminster.

1980. Institution of Engineers (India) Commem.
959 **812** 30p. gold and blue . . . 20 30

813 Uniforms of 1780 and 1980, Crest and Ribbon   **814** Books

1980. Bicentenary of Madras Sappers.
960 **813** 30p. multicoloured . . . 1·00 60

1980. 4th World Book Fair, New Delhi.
961 **814** 30p. blue 30 30

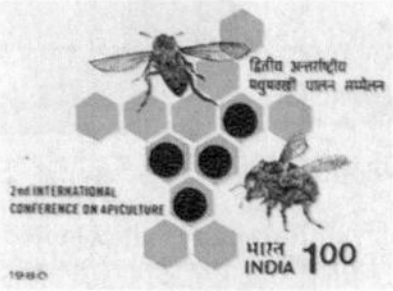

815 Bees and Honey-Comb

1980. 2nd International Conference on Agriculture.
962 **815** 1r. bistre and brown . . . 1·00 55

816 Welthy Fisher and Saksharta Nicketan (Literacy House), Lucknow

1980. Welthy Fisher (teacher) Commemoration.
963 **816** 30p. blue 30 30

817 Darul-Uloom, Deoband   **818** Keshub Chunder Sen

1980. Darul-Uloom College Commemoration.
964 **817** 30p. green 20 30

1980. Keshub Chunder Sen (religious and social reformer) Commemoration.
965 **818** 30p. brown 30 30

819 Chhatrapati Shivaji Maharaj   **820** Table Tennis

1980. 300th Death Anniv of Chhatrapati Shivaji Maharaj (warrior).
966 **819** 30p. multicoloured . . . 20 40

1980. 5th Asian Table Tennis Championships, Calcutta.
967 **820** 30p. purple 30 30

1980. As Nos. 732 and 810, but 17 × 20 mm in size.
968 30p. brown (Gandhi) . . . . 4·50 1·75
969 30p. violet (Nehru) . . . . . 2·00 60

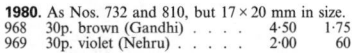

821 N. M. Joshi   **822** Ulloor S. Parameswara Iyer

1980. Narayan Malhar Joshi (trade unionist) Commemoration.
970 **821** 30p. mauve 60 40

1980. Ulloor S. Parameswara Iyer (poet) Commemoration.
971 **822** 30p. purple 60 40

823 S. M. Zamin Ali   **824** Helen Keller

1980. Syed Mohammed Zamin Ali (educationist and poet) Commemoration.
972 **823** 30p. green 20 40

1980. Birth Centenary of Helen Keller (campaigner for the handicapped).
973 **824** 30p. black and orange . . 1·00 40

825 High-jumping   **826** Prem Chand

1980. Olympic Games, Moscow. Multicoloured.
974 1r. Type **825** 40 40
975 2r.80 Horse-riding . . . . . 1·75 3·25

1980. Birth Cent of Prem Chand (novelist).
976 **826** 30p. brown 20 50

827 Mother Teresa and Nobel Peace Prize Medallion

1980. Award of 1979 Nobel Peace Prize to Mother Teresa.
977 **827** 30p. violet . . . . 1·00 60

828 Lord Mountbatten

1980. Lord Mountbatten Commemoration.
978 **828** 2r.80 multicoloured . . . 2·50 2·75

1980. As Nos. 968/9, but new face value.
979 35p. brown . . . . 2·25 50
980 35p. violet 75 20
DESIGNS: No. 979, Gandhi; No. 980, Nehru.

829 Scottish Church College, Calcutta   **830** Rajah Annamalai Chettiar

1980. 150th Anniv of Scottish Church College, Calcutta.
981 **829** 35p. lilac 20 30

1980. Rajah Annamalai Chettiar (banker and educationist) Commemoration.
982 **830** 35p. lilac 20 30

831 Gandhi marching to Dandi   **832** Jayaprakash Narayan

1980. 50th Anniv of "Dandi March" (Gandhi's defiance of Salt Tax Law).
983 **831** 35p. black, blue and gold 80 1·25
984 – 35p. black, mauve and gold . . . . 80 1·25
DESIGN: No. 984, Gandhi picking up handful of salt at Dandi.

1980. Jayaprakash Narayan (socialist) Commemoration.
985 **832** 35p. brown 50 60

833 Great Indian Bustard

1980. International Symposium on Bustards, Juipur.
986 **833** 2r.30 multicoloured . . . 1·00 2·00

834 Arabic Commemorative Inscription

1980. Moslem Year 1400 A.H. Commemoration.
987 **834** 35p. multicoloured . . . 15 30

835 "Girls Dancing" (Pampa Paul)   **836** Dhyan Chand

1980. Children's Day.
988 **835** 35p. multicoloured . . . 1·00 40

1980. Dhyan Chand (hockey player). Commemoration.
989 **836** 35p. brown . . . . 1·25 85

837 Gold Mining   **838** M. A. Ansari

1980. Cent of Kolar Gold Fields, Karnataka.
990 **837** 1r. multicoloured . . . . 1·60 30

1980. Mukhtayar Ahmad Ansari (medical practitioner and politician) Commemoration.
991 **838** 35p. green 40 40

839 India Government Mint, Bombay

1980. 150th Anniv of India Government Mint, Bombay.
992 **839** 35p. black, blue and silver 20 30

840 Bride from Tamil Nadu   **841** Mazharul Haque

1980. Brides in Traditional Costume. Multicoloured.
993 1r. Type **840** 40 75
994 1r. Rajasthan 40 75
995 1r. Kashmir 40 75
996 1r. Bengal 40 75

1981. Mazharul Haque (journalist) Commem.
997 **841** 35p. blue 20 40

842 St. Stephen's College

1981. Centenary of St. Stephen's College, Delhi.
998 **842** 35p. red 20 50

843 Gommateshwara   **844** G. V. Mavalankar

1981. Millenium of Gommateshwara (statue at Shravanabelgola).
999 **843** 1r. multicoloured 20 30

1981. 25th Death Anniv of Ganesh Vasudeo Mavalankar (parliamentarian).
1000 **844** 35p. red 20 40

845 Flame of Martyrdom

1981. "Homage to Martyrs".
1001 **845** 35p. multicoloured . . . 20 30

846 Heinrich von Stephan and U.P.U. Emblem

1981. 150th Birth Anniv of Heinrich von Stephan (founder of U.P.U.).
1002 **846** 1r. brown 20 50

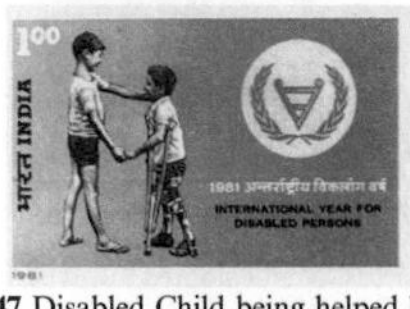

847 Disabled Child being helped by Able-bodied Child

1981. International Year for Disabled Persons.
1003 **847** 1r. black and blue . . . 20 30

848 Bhil

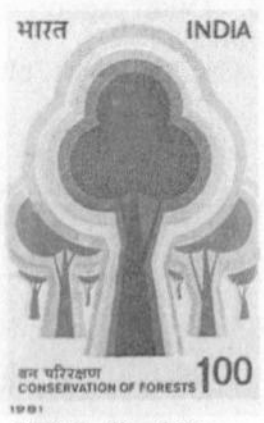

849 Stylized Trees

1981. Tribes of India. Muticoloured.
1004 1r. Type **848** 40 35
1005 1r. Dandami Maria 40 35
1006 1r. Toda 40 35
1007 1r. Khlamngam Naga . . . 40 35

1981. Forests Conservation.
1008 **849** 1r. multicoloured 20 30

850 Nilmoni Phukan

851 Sanjay Gandhi

1981. Nilmoni Phukan (poet) Commemoration.
1009 **850** 35p. brown 20 50

1981. 1st Death Anniv of Sanjay Gandhi (politician).
1010 **851** 35p. multicoloured . . . 40 65

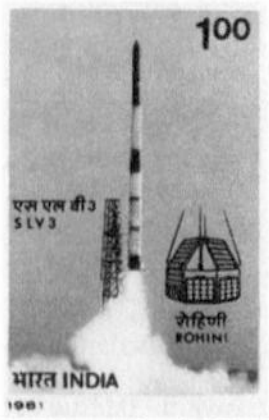

852 Launch of "SLV 3" and Diagram of "Rohini"

853 Games Logo

1981. Launch of "SLV 3" Rocket with "Rohini" Satellite.
1011 **852** 1r. black, pink and blue 30 30

1981. Asian Games, New Delhi (1st issue). Multicoloured.
1012 1r. Type **853** . . . . 1·00 65
1013 1r. Games emblem and stylized hockey players . . 1·00 65

See also Nos. 1026, 1033, 1057, 1059 and 1061/6.

854 Flame of the Forest

855 W. F. D. Emblem and Wheat

1981. Flowering Trees. Multicoloured.
1014 35p. Type **854** 40 15
1015 50p. Crateva 75 75
1016 1r. Golden shower . . . . 1·00 50
1017 2r. Bauhinia . . . . 1·40 2·75

1981. World Food Day.
1018 **855** 1r. yellow and blue . . . 30 20

856 "Stichophthalma camadeva"

1981. Butterflies. Multicoloured.
1019 35p. Type **856** 90 20
1020 50p. "Cethosia biblis" . . . 1·75 1·75
1021 1r. "Cyrestis achates" (vert) 2·25 70
1022 2r. "Teinopalpus imperialis" (vert) . . . . 2·75 6·00

857 Bellary Raghava

1981. Bellary Raghava (actor) Commemoration.
1023 **857** 35p. green 70 30

858 Regimental Colour

859 "Toyseller" (Kumari Ruchita Sharma)

1981. 40th Anniv of Mahar Regiment.
1024 **858** 35p. multicoloured . . . 1·00 30

1981. Children's Day.
1025 **859** 35p. multicoloured . . . 75 30

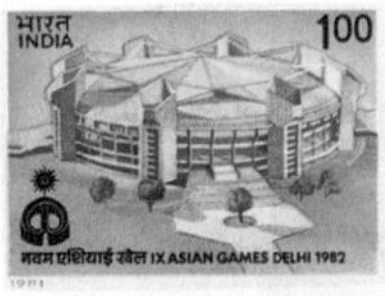

860 Rajghat Stadium

861 Kashi Prasad Jayaswal and Yaudheya Coin

1981. Asian Games, New Delhi (2nd issue).
1026 **860** 1r. multicoloured . . . . 1·75 30

1981. Birth Centenary of Kashi Prasad Jayasawal (lawyer and historian).
1027 **861** 35p. blue 50 30

862 Indian and P.L.O. Flags, and People

1981. Palestinian Solidarity.
1028 **862** 1r. multicoloured . . . . 2·25 40

863 I.N.S. "Taragiri" (frigate)

1981. Indian Navy Day.
1029 **863** 35p. multicoloured . . . 2·25 1·25

864 Henry Heras and Indus Valley Seal

1981. Henry Heras (historian) Commemoration.
1030 **864** 35p. lilac 45 30

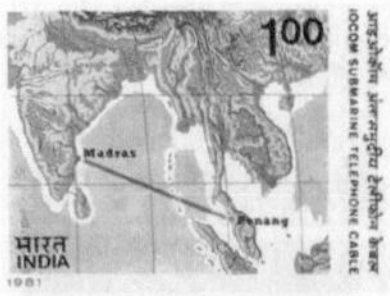

865 Map of South-East Asia showing Cable Route

1981. Inauguration of I.O.C.O.M. (Indian Ocean Commonwealth Cable) Submarine Telephone Cable.
1031 **865** 1r. multicoloured . . . . 2·25 35

866 Stylized Hockey-players and Championship Emblem

1981. World Cup Hockey Championship, Bombay.
1032 **866** 1r. multicoloured . . . . 1·25 30

867 Jawaharlal Nehru Stadium

868 Early and Modern Telephones

1981. Asian Games, New Delhi (3rd issue).
1033 **867** 1r. multicoloured 30 20

1982. Centenary of Telephone Services.
1034 **868** 2r. black, blue and grey 30 30

869 Map of World

870 Sir J. J. School of Art

1982. International Soil Science Congress, New Delhi.
1035 **869** 1r. multicoloured 30 20

1982. 125th Anniv of Sir J. J. School of Art, Bombay.
1036 **870** 35p. multicoloured . . . 20 20

871 "Three Musicians"

872 Deer (stone carving), 5th-century A.D.

1982. Birth Centenary (1981) of Picasso.
1037 **871** 2r.85 multicoloured . . . 1·40 50

1982. Festival of India. Ancient Sculpture. Multicoloured.
1038 2r. Type **872** 20 40
1039 3r.05 Kaliya Mardana (bronze statue), 9th-century A.D 35 60

873 Radio Telescope, Ooty

1982. Festival of India. Science and Technology.
1040 **873** 3r.05 multicoloured . . . 35 40

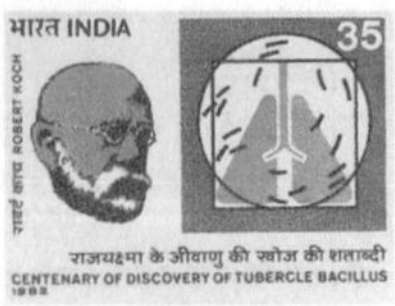

874 Robert Koch and Symbol of Disease

1982. Centenary of Robert Koch's Discovery of Tubercle Bacillus.
1041 **874** 35p. lilac . . . . 1·75 80

875 Durgabai Deshmukh

1982. 1st Death Anniv of Durgabai Deshmukh (social reformer).
1042 **875** 35p. blue 70 80

876 Blue Poppy

877 "Apple" Satellite

1982. Himalayan Flowers. Multicoloured.
1043 35p. Type **876** 70 30
1044 1r. Showy inula . . . . . . 1·75 30
1045 2r. Cobra lily . . . . 2·25 3·00
1046 2r.85 Brahma kamal . . . . 2·75 4·75

1982. 1st Anniv of "Apple" Satellite Launch.
1047 **877** 2r. multicoloured . . . . 50 1·00

878 Bidhan Chandra Roy

1982. Birth Centenary of Bidhan Chandra Roy (doctor and politician).
1048 **878** 50p. brown . . . . . . 1·00 1·50

879 "Sagar Samrat" Oil Rig

1982. 25th Anniv of Oil and Natural Gas Commission.
1049 **879** 1r. multicoloured . . . . 1·50 60

880 "Bindu" (S. H. Raza)

881 Red Deer Stag, Kashmir

1982. Festival of India. Contemporary Paintings. Multicoloured.
1050 2r. Type **880** 50 50
1051 3r.05 "Between the Spider and the Lamp" (M. F. Hussain) . . . . 75 1·25

1982. Wildlife Conservation.
1052 **881** 2r.85 multicoloured . . . 2·50 1·75

882 Westland Wapiti Biplane and Mikoyan Gurevich MiG-25 Aircraft

1982. 50th Anniv of Indian Air Force.
1053 **882** 1r. multicoloured . . . . 5·00 1·25

883 J. Tata with De Havilland Puss Moth

1982. 50th Anniv of Civil Aviation in India.
1054 **883** 3r.25 multicoloured . . . 4·50 1·75

884 Police Patrol

1982. Police Commemoration Day.
1055 **884** 50p. green 60 30

885 Coins and Economic Symbols

1982. Centenary of Post Office Savings Bank.
1056 **885** 50p. brown and light brown 20 20

886 Wrestling Bout

1982. Asian Games, New Delhi (4th issue).
1057 **886** 1r. multicoloured . . . . 1·00 30

887 Troposcatter Communication Link

1982. 1st Anniv of Troposcatter Communication Link between India and U.S.S.R.
1058 **887** 3r.05 multicoloured . . . 30 40

888 Arjuna shooting Arrow at Fish

889 "Mother and Child" (Deepak Sharma)

1982. Asian Games, New Delhi (5th issue).
1059 **888** 1r. multicoloured . . . . 1·75 30

1982. Children's Day.
1060 **889** 50p. multicoloured . . . 30 30

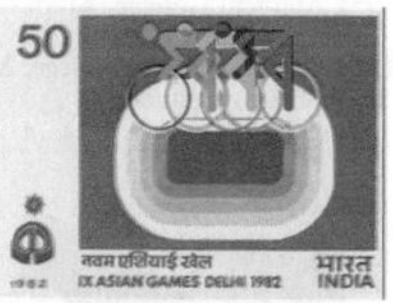

890 Stylized Cyclists

1982. Asian Games, New Delhi (6th issue). Multicoloured.
1061 50p. Type **890** 15 10
1062 2r. Javelin-throwing 25 30
1063 2r.85 Discus-throwing . . . 30 45
1064 3r.25 Football 40 55

891 "Enterprise" Dinghies Race

1982. Asian Games, New Delhi (7th issue). Multicoloured.
1065 2r. Type **891** . . . . 1·25 30
1066 2r.85 Rowing . . . . 1·75 70

892 Chetwode Building

1982. 50th Anniv of Indian Military Academy Dehradun.
1067 **892** 50p. multicoloured . . . 30 50

893 Purushottamdas Tandon

1982. Birth Cent of Purushottamdas Tandon (politician).
1068 **893** 50p. brown 30 80

894 Darjeeling Himalayan Railway

1982. Cent of Darjeeling Himalayan Railway.
1069 **894** 2r.85 multicoloured . . . 5·50 4·75

895 Vintage Rail Coach and Silhouette of Steam Locomotive

1982. "Inpex 82" Stamp Exhibition. Multicoloured.
1070 50p. Type **895** . . . . . . 1·00 1·00
1071 2r. 1854 ½ anna blue stamp and 1947 3½ anna Independence commem (33 × 44 mm) . . . . . . 2·50 3·00

896 Antarctic Camp

1983. 1st Indian Antarctic Expedition.
1072 **896** 1r. multicoloured . . . . 4·25 2·25

1983. As Nos. 968/9, but with new face value.
1073 50p. brown (Gandhi) . . . 4·00 2·25
1074a 50p. blue (Nehru) . . . . 2·50 70

897 Roosevelt with Stamp Collection

1983. Birth Centenary of Franklin D. Roosevelt (American statesman).
1075 **897** 3r.25 brown . . . . . . 55 1·25

898 "Siberian Cranes at Bharatpur" (Diane Pierce)

899 Jat Regiment Uniforms Past and Present

1983. International Crane Workshop, Bharatpur.
1076 **898** 2r.85 multicoloured . . . 3·00 3·00

1983. Presentation of Colours to Battalions of the Jat Regiment.
1077 **899** 50p. multicoloured . . . 2·00 1·75

900 Non-aligned Summit Logo

1983. 7th Non-aligned Summit Conference, New Delhi.
1078 **900** 1r. lt brown, brown & blk 20 30
1079 – 2r. multicoloured 30 95
DESIGN: 2r. Nehru.

901 Shore Temple, Mahabalipuram

1983. Commonwealth Day. Multicoloured.
1080 1r. Type **901** 15 30
1081 2r. Gomukh, Gantgotri Glacier . . . . 30 1·25

902 Acropolis and Olympic Emblems

1983. Int Olympic Committee Session, New Delhi.
1082 **902** 1r. multicoloured 30 50

903 "St. Francis and Brother Falcon" (statue by Giovanni Collina)

904 Karl Marx and "Das Kapital"

1983. 800th Birth Anniv of St. Francis of Assisi.
1083 **903** 1r. brown 65 30

1983. Death Centenary of Karl Marx.
1084 **904** 1r. brown 30 30

905 Darwin and Map of Voyage

1983. Death Centenary (1982) of Charles Darwin (naturalist).
1085 **905** 2r. multicoloured . . . . 3·25 3·25

906 Swamp Deer

907 Globe and Satellite

1983. 50th Anniv of Kanha National Park.
1086 **906** 1r. multicoloured . . . . 2·50 1·00

1983. World Communications Year.
1087 **907** 1r. multicoloured 40 40

908 Simon Bolivar

909 Meera Behn

1983. Birth Bicentenary of Simon Bolivar (South American statesman).
1088 **908** 2r. multicoloured . . . . 2·00 2·00

1983. India's Struggle for Freedom (1st series).
1089 50p. red and green . . . . 1·40 2·25
1090 50p. brown, green and red 1·40 2·25
1091 50p. multicoloured . . . . 1·40 2·00
1092 50p. brown, green and red 15 50
1093 50p. brown, green and orange 15 50
1094 50p. green, yellow and orange 15 50
DESIGNS—VERT: No. 1089, Type **909**; 1090, Mahadev Desai; 1092, Hemu Kalani (revolutionary); 1093, Acharya Vinoba Bhave (social reformer); 1094, Surendranath Banerjee (political reformer). HORIZ (43 × 31 mm): No. 1091, Quit India Resolution.
See also Nos. 1119/24, 1144/9, 1191/4, 1230/5, 1287/96 and 1345/9.

910 Ram Nath Chopra

1983. Ram Nath Chopra (pharmacologist) Commemoration.
1095 **910** 50p. red . . . . 50 1·25

911 Nanda Devi Mountain

1983. 25th Anniv of Indian Mountaineering Federation.
1096 **911** 2r. multicoloured . . . . 2·00 1·25

912 Great Indian Hornbill

913 View of Garden

1983. Centenary of Natural History Society, Bombay.
1097 **912** 1r. multicoloured . . . . 3·25 1·00

1983. Rock Garden, Chandigarh.
1098 **913** 1r. multicoloured . . . . 1·50 1·00

914 Golden Langur

1983. Indian Wildlife. Monkeys. Multicoloured.
1099 1r. Type **914** . . . . 2·00 50
1100 2r. Lion-tailed macaque . . 3·00 4·00

915 Ghats of Varanasi

1983. 5th General Assembly of World Tourism Organization.
1101 **915** 2r. multicoloured 60 60

916 Krishna Kanta Handique

918 Woman and Child (from "Festival" by Kashyap Premsawala)

1983. Krishna Kanta Handique (scholar).
1102 **916** 50p. blue 30 70

1983. Children's Day.
1103 **918** 50p. multicoloured . . . 30 50

920 "Udan Khatola", First Indian Hot Air Balloon

921 Tiger

1983. Bicentenary of Manned Flight.
1104 1r. Type **920** . . . . 1·00 20
1105 2r. Montgolfier balloon . . 1·40 1·25

1983. Ten Years of "Project Tiger".
1106 **921** 2r. multicoloured . . . . 3·50 3·75

922 Commonwealth Logo

923 "Pratiksha"

1983. Commonwealth Heads of Government Meeting, New Delhi. Multicoloured.
1107 1r. Type **922** 40 15
1108 2r. Goanese couple, early 19th century 85 50

1983. Birth Centenary of Nanda Lal Bose (artist).
1109 **923** 1r. multicoloured 30 30

925 Lancer in Ceremonial Uniform

926 Troopers in Ceremonial Uniform and Tank

1984. Bicentenary of 7th Light Cavalry.
1110 **925** 1r. multicoloured . . . . 3·25 1·40

1984. Presentation of Regimental Guidon to the Deccan Horse.
1111 **926** 1r. multicoloured . . . . 3·25 1·40

927 Society Building and Sir William Jones (founder)

1984. Bicentenary of Asiatic Society.
1112 **927** 1r. green and purple . . 30 50

928 Insurance Logo

1984. Centenary of Postal Life Insurance.
1113 **928** 1r. multicoloured 30 30

929 Hawker Siddeley Sea Harrier

1984. President's Review of the Fleet. Multicoloured.
1114 1r. Type **929** . . . . 1·50 2·00
1115 1r. "Vikrant" (aircraft carrier) . . . . 1·50 2·00
1116 1r. "Vela" (submarine) . . . 1·50 2·00
1117 1r. "Kashin" (destroyer) . . 1·50 2·00
Nos. 1114/17 were printed together, se-tenant, forming a composite design.

930 I.L.A. Logo and Hemispheres

1984. 12th International Leprosy Congress.
1118 **930** 1r. multicoloured 65 40

1984. India's Struggle for Freedom (2nd series). As T **909**.
1119 50p. green, lt green & orange 30 70
1120 50p. brown, green and orange 30 70
1121 50p. multicoloured . . . . 75 1·00
1122 50p. multicoloured . . . . 75 1·00
1123 50p. multicoloured . . . . 75 1·00
1124 50p. multicoloured . . . . 75 1·00
DESIGNS: No. 1119, Vasudeo Balvant Phadke (revolutionary); 1120, Baba Kanshi Ram (revolutionary); 1121, Tatya Tope; 1122, Nana Sahib; 1123, Begum Hazrat Mahal; 1124, Mangal Pandey.

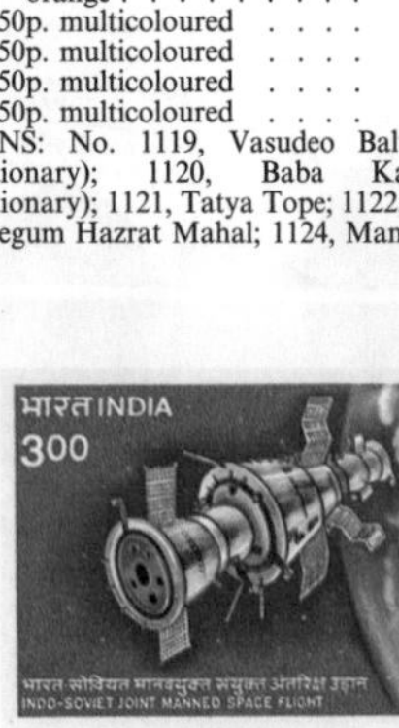

932 "Salyut 7"

1984. Indo-Soviet Manned Space Flight.
1125 **932** 3r. multicoloured . . . . 80 1·00

935 G. D. Birla

1984. 90th Birth Anniv of G. D. Birla (industrialist).
1126 **935** 50p. brown . . . . . . 50 1·00

936 Basketball

937 Gwalior

1984. Olympic Games, Los Angeles. Multicoloured.
1127 50p. Type **936** 90 65
1128 1r. High jumping 75 30
1129 2r. Gymnastics (horiz) . . . 1·00 1·50
1130 2r.50 Weightlifting (horiz) 1·25 2·50

1984. Forts. Multicoloured.
1131 50p. Type **937** 70 55
1132 1r. Vellore (vert) 95 30
1133 1r.50 Simhagad (vert) . . . 1·75 2·75
1134 2r. Jodhpur . . . . 2·00 3·00

938 B. V. Paradkar and Newspaper

939 Dr. D. N. Wadia and Institute of Himalayan Geology, Dehradun

1984. B. V. Paradkar (journalist) Commemoration.
1135 **938** 50p. brown . . . . . . 50 1·00

1984. Birth Centenary (1983) of Dr. D. N. Wadia (geologist).
1136 **939** 1r. multicoloured . . . . 1·50 40

940 "Herdsman and Cattle in Forest" (H. Kassam)

942 Congress Emblem

941 Indira Gandhi

1984. Children's Day.
1137 **940** 50p. multicoloured . . . 75 1·00

1984. Prime Minister Indira Gandhi Commemoration (1st issue).
1138 **941** 50p. black, violet & orange . . . . 2·25 2·25
See also Nos. 1151, 1167 and 1170.

1984. 12th World Mining Congress, New Delhi.
1139 **942** 1r. black and yellow . . 1·50 30

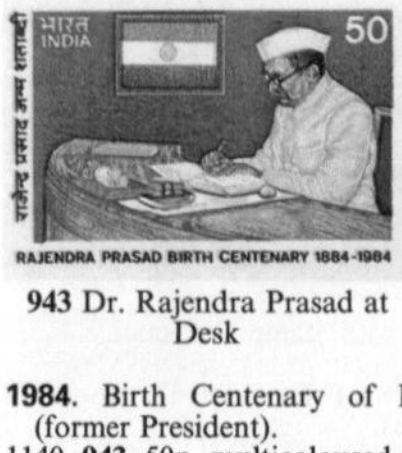

943 Dr. Rajendra Prasad at Desk

944 Mrinalini (rose)

1984. Birth Centenary of Dr. Rajendra Prasad (former President).
1140 **943** 50p. multicoloured . . . 1·00 1·25

1984. Roses. Multicoloured.
1141 1r.50 Type **944** . . . . . . 2·25 2·25
1142 2r. Sugandha . . . . 2·50 2·50

945 "Fergusson College" (Gopal Deuskar)

1985. Centenary of Fergusson College, Pune.
1143 **945** 1r. multicoloured 70 55

1985. India's Struggle for Freedom (3rd series). As T **909**.
1144 50p. brown, green and orange . . . . 70 1·00
1145 50p. brown, green and orange . . . . 70 1·00
1146 50p. brown, green and orange . . . . 70 1·00
1147 50p. brown, green and orange . . . . 70 1·00
1148 50p. blue, green and orange 70 1·00
1149 50p. black, green and orange . . . . 70 1·00
DESIGNS—VERT: No. 1144, Narhar Vishnu Gadgil (politician); 1145, Jairamdas Doulatram (journalist); 1147, Kakasaheb Kalelkar (author); 1148, Master Tara Singh (politician); 1149, Ravishankar Maharaj (politician). HORIZ: No. 1146, Jatindra and Nellie Sengupta (politicians).

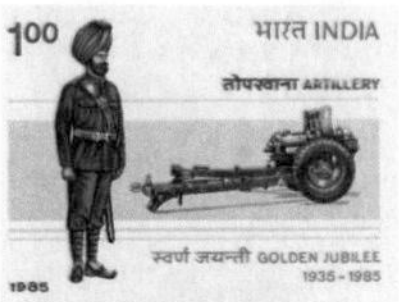

947 Gunner and Howitzer from Mountain Battery

1985. 50th Anniv of Regiment of Artillery.
1150 **947** 1r. multicoloured . . . . 4·25 1·50

948 Indira Gandhi making Speech

1985. Indira Gandhi Commemoration (2nd issue).
1151 **948** 2r. multicoloured . . . . 3·50 3·75

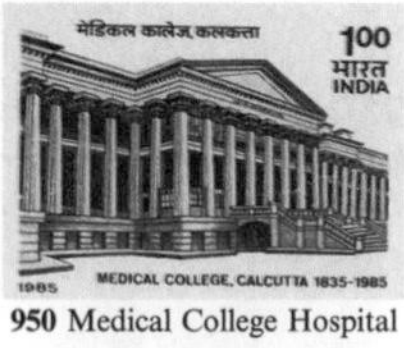

949 Minicoy Lighthouse

950 Medical College Hospital

1985. Centenary of Minicoy Lighthouse.
1152 **949** 1r. multicoloured . . . . 4·50 1·00

1985. 150th Anniv of Medical College, Calcutta.
1153 **950** 1r. yellow, brown & purple . . . . 3·00 70

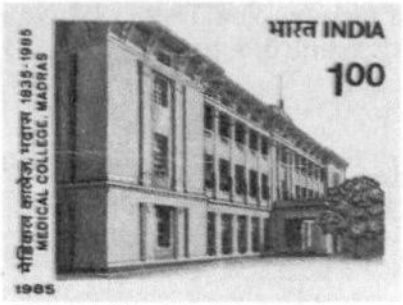

951 Medical College, Madras

1985. 150th Anniv of Medical College, Madras.
1154 **951** 1r. light brown and brown . . . . 3·00 70

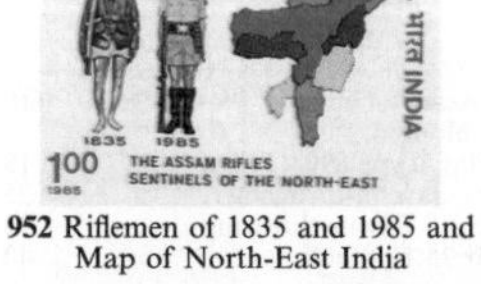

952 Riflemen of 1835 and 1985 and Map of North-East India

1985. 150th Anniv of Assam Rifles.
1155 **952** 1r. multicoloured . . . . 4·25 1·50

953 Potato Plant

1985. 50th Anniv of Potato Research in India.
1156 **953** 50p. deep brown and brown . . . . 1·50 1·60

954 Baba Jassa Singh Ahluwalia **956** White-winged Wood Duck

955 St. Xavier's College

1985. Death Bicentenary (1983) of Baba Jassa Singh Ahluwalia (Sikh leader).
1157 **954** 50p. purple . . . . . . 1·50 1·60

1985. 125th Anniv of St. Xavier's College, Calcutta.
1158 **955** 1r. multicoloured . . . . 1·50 50

1985. Wildlife Conservation. White-winged Wood Duck.
1159 **956** 2r. multicoloured . . . . 6·50 5·50

957 "Mahara" **958** Yaudheya Copper Coin, c. 200 B.C.

1985. Bougainvillea. Multicoloured.
1160 50p. Type **957** . . . . . . 1·75 2·50
1161 1r. "H. B. Singh" . . . . . 2·00 1·50

1985. Festival of India (1st issue).
1162 **958** 2r. multicoloured . . . . 2·75 2·25

959 Statue of Didarganj Yakshi (deity) **962** Swami Haridas

1985. Festival of India (2nd issue).
1163 **959** 1r. multicoloured . . . . 1·50 40

1985. Swami Haridas (philosopher) Commemoration.
1164 **962** 1r. multicoloured . . . . 1·75 1·50

963 Stylized Mountain Road

1985. 25th Anniv of Border Roads Organization.
1165 **963** 2r. red, violet and black 2·00 3·00

964 Nehru addressing General Assembly

1985. 40th Anniv of United Nations Organization.
1166 **964** 2r. multicoloured . . . . 1·10 1·00

965 Indira Gandhi with Crowd

1985. Indira Gandhi Commemoration (3rd issue).
1167 **965** 2r. brown and black . . 2·50 3·00

966 Girl using Home Computer

1985. Children's Day.
1168 **966** 50p. multicoloured . . . 1·00 1·00

967 Halley's Comet **968** Indira Gandhi

1985. 19th General Assembly of International Astronomical Union, New Delhi.
1169 **967** 1r. multicoloured . . . . 2·00 1·50

1985. Indira Gandhi Commemoration (4th issue).
1170 **968** 3r. multicoloured . . . . 2·50 3·00

969 St. Stephen's Hospital

1985. Centenary of St. Stephen's Hospital, Delhi.
1171 **969** 1r. black and brown . . 1·00 40

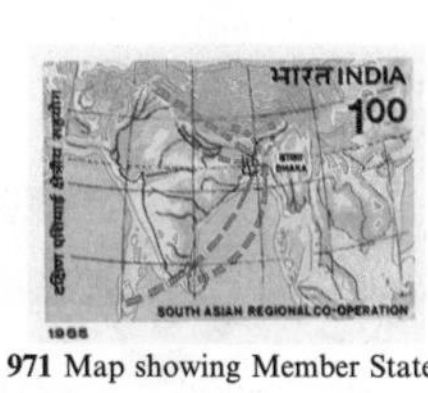
971 Map showing Member States

1985. 1st Summit Meeting of South Asian Association for Regional Co-operation, Dhaka, Bangladesh. Multicoloured.
1172 1r. Type **971** . . . . 1·50 40
1173 3r. Flags of member nations (44 × 32 mm) . . . . . . 2·50 4·00

972 Shyama Shastri **975** Young Runners and Emblem

1985. Shyama Shastri (composer) Commemoration.
1174 **972** 1r. multicoloured . . . . 2·75 1·50

1985. International Youth Year.
1175 **975** 2r. multicoloured . . . . 2·75 1·50

976 Handel and Bach

1985. 300th Birth Annivs of George Frederick Handel and Johann Sebastian Bach (composers).
1176 **976** 5r. multicoloured . . . . 4·50 4·75

977 A. O. Hume (founder) and Early Congress Presidents

1985. Centenary of Indian National Congress. Designs showing miniature portraits of Congress Presidents.
1177 **977** 1r. black, orange, green and grey . . . . . . 2·00 2·50
1178 – 1r. black, orange and green . . . . 2·00 2·50
1179 – 1r. black, orange and green . . . . 2·00 2·50
1180 – 1r. black, orange, green and grey . . . . . . 2·00 2·50

Nos. 1178/80 each show sixteen miniature portraits. The individual stamps can be distinguished by the position of the face value and inscription which are at the top on Nos. 1177/8 and at the foot on Nos. 1179/80. No. 1180 shows a portrait of Prime Minister Rajiv Gandhi in a grey frame at bottom right.

978 Bombay and Duncan Dry Docks, Bombay

1986. 250th Anniv of Naval Dockyard, Bombay.
1181 **978** 2r.50 multicoloured . . . 4·25 4·50

979 Hawa Mahal and Jaipur 1904 2a. Stamp

1986. "INPEX '86" Philatelic Exhibition, Jaipur. Multicoloured.
1182 50p. Type **979** . . . . . . 1·00 1·00
1183 2r. Mobile camel post office, Thar Desert . . . . . . 2·25 3·25

980 I.N.S. "Vikrant" (aircraft carrier) **981** Humber Sommer Biplane and Later Mail Planes

1986. Completion of 25 Years Service by I.N.S. "Vikrant".
1184 **980** 2r. multicoloured . . . . 6·50 6·00

1986. 75th Anniv of First Official Airmail Flight, Allahabad–Naini. Multicoloured.
1185 50p. Type **981** . . . . . . 2·25 2·00
1186 3r. Modern Air India Airbus Industries A300 mail plane and Humber Sommer biplane (37 × 24 mm) . . . . . . 4·75 7·00

982 Triennale Emblem **983** Chaitanya Mahaprabhu

1986. 6th Triennale Art Exhibition, New Delhi.
1187 **982** 1r. purple, yellow & black . . . . 1·50 1·00

1986. 500th Birth Anniv of Chaitanya Mahaprabhu (religious leader).
1188 **983** 2r. multicoloured . . . . 2·75 3·50

984 Main Building, Mayo College

1986. Mayo College (public school), Ajmer, Commemoration.
1189 **984** 1r. multicoloured . . . . 1·50 1·00

985 Two Footballers

1986. World Cup Football Championship, Mexico.
1190 **985** 5r. multicoloured . . . . 4·75 4·75

1986. India's Struggle for Freedom (4th series). As T **909**.
1191 50p. brown, green and red 1·40 2·00
1192 50p. brown, green and red 1·40 2·00
1193 50p. black, green and orange . . . . 1·40 2·00
1194 50p. brown, green and red 1·40 2·00

DESIGNS: No. 1191, Bhim Sen Sachar; 1192, Alluri Seeta Rama Raju; 1193, Sagarmal Gopa; 1194, Veer Surendra Sai.

987 Swami Sivananda **988** Volleyball

1986. Birth Centenary of Swami Sivananda (spiritual leader).
1195 **987** 2r. multicoloured . . . . 3·00 4·00

1986. Asian Games, Seoul, South Korea. Multicoloured.
1196 1r.50 Type **988** . . . . . . 2·50 2·75
1197 3r. Hurdling . . . . 3·00 4·00

989 Madras G.P.O.

1986. Bicentenary of Madras G.P.O.
1198 **989** 5r. black and red . . . . 4·50 5·00

990 Parachutist

991 Early and Modern Policemen

1986. 225th Anniv of 8th Battalion of Coast Sepoys (now 1st Battalion Parachute Regiment).
1199 **990** 3r. multicoloured . . . . 5·00 5·00

1986. 125th Anniv of Indian Police. Designs showing early and modern police.
1200 **991** 1r.50 multicoloured . . . 3·50 4·00
1201 – 2r. multicoloured . . . . 3·50 4·00
Nos. 1200/1 were printed together, se-tenant, forming a composite design.

992 Hand holding Flower and World Map

1986. International Peace Year.
1202 **992** 5r. multicoloured . . . . 3·75 1·75

993 "Girl Rock Climber" (Sujasha Dasgupta)

994 Windmill

1986. Children's Day.
1203 **993** 50p. multicoloured . . . 2·25 2·25

1986. Science and Technology.
1211 – 35p. red 10 10
1212 – 40p. red 10 10
1213 – 60p. green and red . . 10 10
1214a – 75p. red 10 10
1215 – 1r. black and red . . . 20 10
1217 – 5r. brown and orange 30 20
1218 – 20r. brown and blue . . 75 60
1219 **994** 50r. black, blue and mauve . . . . 2·25 2·00
DESIGNS—20 × 17 mm: 35p. Family planning. 37 × 20 mm: 60p. Indian family; 20r. Bio gas. 17 × 20 mm: 40p. Television set, dish aerial and transmitter; 75p. "Family" (as No. 927). 20 × 37 mm: 1r. Petrol pump nozzle (Oil conservation); 5r.Solar energy.

995 Growth Monitoring

1986. 40th Anniv of UNICEF. Multicoloured.
1221 50p. Type **995** . . . . . . 2·00 2·00
1222 5r. Immunization . . . . . 4·25 6·00

996 Tansen

997 Indian Elephant

1986. Tansen (musician and composer) Commem.
1223 **996** 1r. multicoloured . . . . 2·00 60

1986. 50th Anniv of Corbett National Park. Multicoloured.
1224 1r. Type **997** . . . . 3·50 1·00
1225 2r. Gharial . . . . 4·00 6·00

998 St. Martha's Hospital

1986. Centenary of St. Martha's Hospital, Bangalore.
1226 **998** 1r. blue, orange and black . . . . 2·25 1·60

999 Yacht "Trishna" and Route Map

1987. Indian Army Round the World Yacht Voyage, 1985–1987.
1227 **999** 6r.50 multicoloured . . . 4·50 4·00

1000 Map of Southern Africa and Logo

1001 Emblem

1987. Inauguration of AFRICA Fund.
1228 **1000** 6r.50 black . . . . . . 5·00 6·00

1987. 29th Congress of International Chamber of Commerce, New Delhi.
1229 **1001** 5r. violet, blue and red 3·50 2·25

1987. India's Struggle for Freedom (5th series). As T **909**.
1230 60p. brown, green and orange . . . . 2·50 30
1231 60p. violet, green and red 30 30
1232 60p. brown, green and red 30 30
1233 60p. blue, green and orange 30 30
1234 60p. brown, green and red 30 30
1235 60p. brown, green and red 30 30
1236 60p. red, green and orange 30 30
DESIGNS: No. 1230, Hakim Ajmal Khan; No. 1231, Lala Har Dayal; No. 1232, M. N Roy; No. 1233, Tripuraneni Ramaswamy Chowdary; No. 1234, Dr. Kailas Nath Katju; No. 1235, S. Satyamurti; No. 1236, Pandit Hriday Nath Kunzru.

1002 Blast Furnace and Railway Emblem

1003 Kalia Bhomora Bridge, Tezpur, Assam

1987. Cent of South Eastern Railway. Mult.
1237 1r. Type **1002** 40 15
1238 1r.50 Tank locomotive No. 691, 1887 (horiz) . . 45 35
1239 2r. Electric train on viaduct, 1987 . . . . 55 60
1240 4r. Steam locomotive, c. 1900 (horiz) 80 1·25

1987. Inauguration of Brahmaputra Bridge.
1241 **1003** 2r. multicoloured . . . 30 30

1004 Madras Christian College

1987. 150th Anniv of Madras Christian College.
1242 **1004** 1r.50 black and red . . 20 20

1005 Shree Shree Ma Anandamayee

1006 "Rabindranath Tagore" (self-portrait)

1987. Shree Shree Ma Anandamayee (Hindu spiritual leader) Commemoration.
1243 **1005** 1r. brown 65 20

1987. Rabindranath Tagore (poet) Commem.
1244 **1006** 2r. multicoloured . . . 40 30

1007 Garwhal Rifles Uniforms of 1887

1008 J. Krishnamurti

1987. Centenary of Garwhal Rifles Regiment.
1245 **1007** 1r. multicoloured . . . 60 20

1987. J. Krishnamurti (philosopher) Commem.
1246 **1008** 60p. brown . . . . . . 70 1·00

1009 Regimental Uniforms of 1887

1987. Centenary of 37th Dogra Regt (now 7th Battalion) (1 Dogra), Mechanised Infantry Regt.
1247 **1009** 1r. multicoloured . . . 50 20

1010 Hall of Nations, Pragati Maidan, New Delhi

1011 "Sadyah-Snata" Sculpture, Sanghol

1987. "India '89" International Stamp Exhibition, New Delhi (1st issue). Multicoloured.
1248 50p. Exhibition logo 10 15
1249 5r. Type **1010** 45 50
MS1250 156 × 58 mm. Nos. 1248/9 (sold at 8r.) . . . . 70 1·00
See also Nos. 1264/8, 1333/4, 1341/2 and 1358/61.

1987. Festival of India, U.S.S.R.
1251 **1011** 6r.50 multicoloured . . 1·00 75

1012 Flag and Stylized Birds with "40" in English and Hindi

1987. 40th Anniv of Independence.
1252 **1012** 60p. orange, green & bl 20 20

1013 Sant Harchand Singh Longowal

1014 Guru Ghasidas

1987. Sant Harchand Singh Longowal (Sikh leader) Commemoration.
1253 **1013** 1r. multicoloured . . . 75 20

1987. Guru Ghasidas (Hindu leader) Commemoration.
1254 **1014** 60p. red 20 20

1015 Thakur Anukul Chandra

1016 University of Allahabad

1987. Thakur Anukul Chandra (spiritual leader) Commemoration.
1255 **1015** 1r. multicoloured . . . 70 20

1987. Centenary of Allahabad University.
1256 **1016** 2r. multicoloured . . . 30 40

1017 Pankha Offering

1018 Chhatrasal on Horseback

1987. Phoolwalon Ki Sair Festival, Delhi.
1257 **1017** 2r. multicoloured . . . 30 40

1987. Chhatrasal (Bundela ruler) Commemoration.
1258 **1018** 60p. brown 30 20

1019 Family and Stylized Houses

1987. International Year of Shelter for the Homeless.
1259 **1019** 5r. multicoloured . . . 50 60

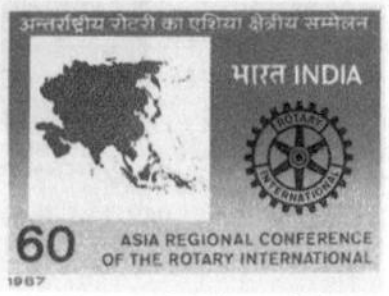
1020 Map of Asia and Logo

1987. Asia Regional Conference of Rotary International.
1260 **1020** 60p. brown and green 15 15
1261 – 6r.50 multicoloured . . 60 80
DESIGN: 6r.50, Oral polio vaccination.

1021 Blind Boy, Braille Books and Computer

1987. Centenary of Service to Blind.
1262 **1021** 1r. multicoloured . . . 15 15
1263 – 2r. deep blue and blue 35 30
DESIGN: 2r. Eye donation.

1022 Iron Pillar, Delhi

1987. "India '89" International Stamp Exhibition, New Delhi (2nd issue). Delhi Landmarks. Mult.
1264 60p. Type **1022** 15 15
1265 1r.50 India Gate 20 20
1266 5r. Dewan-e-Khas, Red Fort 55 50
1267 6r.50 Old Fort 70 65
MS1268 100 × 86 mm. Nos. 1264/7 (sold at 15r.) . . . . 1·40 2·25

1023 Tyagmurti Goswami Ganeshdutt
1024 "My Home" (Siddharth Deshprabha)

1987. Tyagmurti Goswami Ganeshdutt (spiritual leader and social reformer) Commemoration.
1269 **1023** 60p. red 20 20

1987. Children's Day.
1270 **1024** 60p. multicoloured . . 30 20

1025 Chinar
1026 Logo (from sculpture "Worker and Woman Peasant" by V. Mukhina)

1987. Indian Trees. Multicoloured.
1271 **1025** 60p. multicoloured . . 15 15
1272 – 1r.50 multicoloured . . 20 20
1273 – 5r. black, green & brown 55 65
1274 – 6r.50 brown, red & green 80 80
DESIGNS—HORIZ: 1r.50, Pipal; 6r.50, Banyan. VERT: 5r. Sal.

1987. Festival of U.S.S.R., India.
1275 **1026** 5r. multicoloured . . . 50 50

1027 White Tiger
1028 Execution of Veer Narayan Singh

1987. Wildlife. Multicoloured.
1276 1r. Type **1027** 50 15
1277 5r. Snow leopard (horiz) . . 1·25 85

1987. Veer Narayan Singh (patriot) Commemoration.
1278 **1028** 60p. brown 20 20

1029 Rameshwari Nehru
1030 Father Kuriakose Elias Chavara

1987. Rameshwari Nehru (women's rights campaigner) Commemoration.
1279 **1029** 60p. brown 20 20

1987. Father Kuriakose Elias Chavara (founder of Carmelites of Mary Immaculate) Commemoration.
1280 **1030** 60p. brown 20 20

1031 Dr. Rajah Sir Muthiah Chettiar

1987. Dr. Rajah Sir Muthiah Chettiar (politician) Commemoration.
1281 **1031** 60p. grey 20 20

1032 Golden Temple, Amritsar
1033 Rukmini Devi and Dancer

1987. 400th Anniv of Golden Temple, Amritsar.
1282 **1032** 60p. multicoloured . . 40 20

1987. Rukmini Devi (Bharatanatyam dance pioneer) Commemoration.
1283 **1033** 60p. red 30 20

1034 Dr. Hiralal

1987. Dr. Hiralal (historian) Commemoration.
1284 **1034** 60p. blue 20 20

1035 Light Frequency Experiment and Bodhi Tree

1988. 75th Session of Indian Science Congress Association.
1285 **1035** 4r. multicoloured . . . 50 60

1036 Rural Patient
1037 U Tirot Singh

1988. 13th Asian Pacific Dental Congress.
1286 **1036** 4r. multicoloured . . . 50 50

1988. India's Struggle for Freedom (6th series). As T **909**.
1287 60p. black, green and orange 20 40
1288 60p. brown, green and orange 20 40
1289 60p. red, green and orange 20 40
1290 60p. purple, green and orange 20 40
1291 60p. purple, green and red 20 40
1292 60p. black, green and orange 20 40
1293 60p. lilac, green and red . . 20 40
1294 60p. deep green, green and red 20 30
1295 60p. brown, green and green 20 30
1296 60p. mauve, green and orange 20 30
DESIGNS: No. 1287, Mohan Lal Sukhadia; 1288, Dr. S. K. Sinha; 1289, Chandra Shekhar Azad; 1290, G. B. Pant; 1291, Dr. Anugrah Narain Singh; 1292, Kuladhor Chaliha; 1293, Shivprasad Gupta; 1294, Sarat Chandra Bose; 1295, Baba Kharak Singh; 1296, Sheikh Mohammad Abdullah.

1988. U Tirot Singh (Khasis leader) Commem.
1297 **1037** 60p. brown 20 20

1038 Early and Modern Regimental Uniforms
1039 Balgandharva

1988. Bicentenary of 4th Battalion of the Kumaon Regiment.
1298 **1038** 1r. multicoloured . . . 30 20

1988. Birth Centenary of Balgandharva (actor).
1299 **1039** 60p. brown 20 20

1040 Soldiers and Infantry Combat Vehicle
1041 B. N. Rau

1988. Presentation of Colours to Mechanised Infantry Regiment.
1300 **1040** 1r. multicoloured . . . 35 20

1988. B. N. Rau (constitutional lawyer) Commemoration.
1301 **1041** 60p. black 20 20

1042 Mohindra Government College
1043 Dr. D. V. Gundappa

1988. Mohindra Government College, Patiala.
1302 **1042** 1r. mauve 20 20

1988. Dr. D. V. Gundappa (scholar) Commem.
1303 **1043** 60p. grey 20 20

1044 Rani Avantibai
1046 Maharshi Dadhichi

1045 "Malayala Manorama" Office, Kottayam

1988. Rani Avantibai of Ramgarh Commem.
1304 **1044** 60p. mauve 20 20

1988. Centenary of "Malayala Manorama" (newspaper).
1305 **1045** 1r. black and blue . . . 20 20

1988. Maharshi Dadhichi (Hindu saint) Commemoration.
1306 **1046** 60p. red 20 20

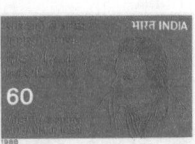

1047 Mohammad Iqbal

1988. 50th Death Anniv of Mohammad Iqbal (poet).
1307 **1047** 60p. gold and red . . . 20 20

1048 Samarth Ramdas
1049 Swati Tirunal Rama Varma

1988. Samarth Ramdas (Hindu spiritual leader) Commemoration.
1308 **1048** 60p. green 20 20

1988. 175th Birth Anniv of Swati Tirunal Rama Varma (composer).
1309 **1049** 60p. mauve 20 20

1050 Bhaurao Patil and Class

1988. Bhaurao Patil (educationist) Commem.
1310 **1050** 60p. brown 20 20

1051 "Rani Lakshmi Bai" (M. F. Husain)

1988. Martyrs from 1st War of Independence.
1311 **1051** 60p. multicoloured . . 20 20

1052 Broad Peak

1988. Himalayan Peaks.
1312 **1052** 1r.50 lilac, violet and blue 35 30
1313 – 4r. multicoloured . . . 70 60
1314 – 5r. multicoloured . . . 80 70
1315 – 6r.50 multicoloured . . 95 85
DESIGNS: 4r. K 2 (Godwin Austen); 5r. Kanchenjunga; 6r.50, Nanda Devi.

1053 Child with Grandparents

1988. "Love and Care for Elders".
1316 **1053** 60p. multicoloured . . 20 20

1054 Victoria Terminus, Bombay

1988. Centenary of Victoria Terminus Station, Bombay.
1317 **1054** 1r. multicoloured . . . 40 20

1055 Lawrence School, Lovedale

1988. 130th Anniv of Lawrence School, Lovedale.
1318 **1055** 1r. brown and green . . 30 20

1056 Khejri Tree

1988. World Environment Day.
1319 **1056** 60p. multicoloured . . 20 15

1988. As No. 732, but new face value.
1320 60p. black (Gandhi) . . . . 1·50 20

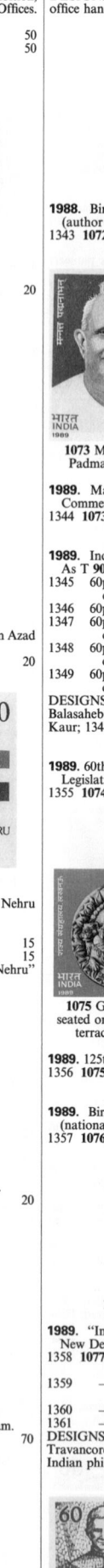

1057 Rani Durgawati

1058 Acharya Shanti Dev

1988. Rani Durgawati (Gondwana ruler) Commemoration.
1322 **1057** 60p. red 20 20

1988. Acharya Shanti Dev (Buddhist scholar) Commemoration.
1323 **1058** 60p. brown 20 20

1059 Y. S. Parmar

1061 Durgadas Rathore

1060 Arm pointing at Proclamation in Marathi

1988. Dr. Yashwant Singh Parmar (former Chief Minister of Himachal Pradesh) Commemoration.
1324 **1059** 60p. violet 20 20

1988. 40th Anniv of Independence. Bal Gangadhar Tilak (patriot) Commemoration. Multicoloured.
1325 60p. Type **1060** 20 20
1326 60p. Battle scene 20 20
Nos. 1325/6 were printed together, se-tenant, forming a composite design showing a painting by M. F. Husain.

1988. 150th Birth Anniv of Durgadas Rathore (Regent of Marwar).
1327 **1061** 60p. brown 20 20

1062 Gopinath Kaviraj

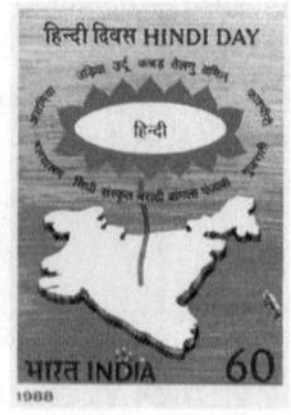

1063 Lotus and Outline Map of India

1988. Gopinath Kaviraj (scholar) Commem.
1328 **1062** 60p. brown 20 20

1988. Hindi Day.
1329 **1063** 60p. red, green & brown 20 20

1064 Indian Olympic Association Logo

1065 Jerdon's Courser

1988. "Sports—1988" and Olympic Games, Seoul.
1330 **1064** 60p. purple 35 15
1331 – 5r. multicoloured . . . 2·50 75
DESIGN—HORIZ: 5r. Various sports.

1988. Wildlife Conservation. Jerdon's Courser.
1332 **1065** 1r. multicoloured . . . 2·50 45

1988. "India '89" International Stamp Exhibition, New Delhi (3rd issue). General Post Offices. As T **1022**. Multicoloured.
1333 4r. Bangalore G.P.O 50 50
1334 5r. Bombay G.P.O 50 50

1066 "Times of India" Front Page

1988. 150th Anniv of "The Times of India".
1335 **1066** 1r.50 black, gold & yell 20 20

1067 "Maulana Abul Kalam Azad" (K. Hebbar)

1988. Birth Centenary of Maulana Abul Kalam Azad (politician).
1336 **1067** 60p. multicoloured . . 20 20

1068 Nehru

1988. Birth Centenary (1989) of Jawaharlal Nehru (1st issue).
1337 **1068** 60p. black, orange and green 30 15
1338 – 1r. multicoloured . . . 35 15
DESIGN—VERT: 1r. "Jawaharlal Nehru" (Svetoslav Roerich).
See also No. 1393.

1069 Birsa Munda

1988. Birsa Munda (Munda leader) Commem.
1339 **1069** 60p. brown 20 20

1070 Bhakra Dam

1988. 25th Anniv of Dedication of Bhakra Dam.
1340 **1070** 60p. red 35 70

1071 Dead Letter Office Cancellations of 1886

1988. "India '89" International Stamp Exhibition, New Delhi (4th series). Postal Cancellations.
1341 **1071** 60p. brown, black & red 40 40
1342 – 6r.50 brown and black 1·40 1·40

DESIGN: 6r.50, Allahabad–Cawnpore travelling post office handstamp of 1864.

1072 K. M. Munshi

1988. Birth Centenary (1987) of K. M. Munshi (author and politician).
1343 **1072** 60p. green 20 20

1073 Mannathu Padmanabhan

1074 Lok Sabha Secretariat

1989. Mannathu Padmanabhan (social reformer) Commemoration.
1344 **1073** 60p. brown 20 20

1989. India's Struggle for Freedom (7th series). As T **909**.
1345 60p. black, green and orange 25 30
1346 60p. orange, green and lilac 25 50
1347 60p. black, green and orange 25 50
1348 60p. brown, green and orange 25 50
1349 60p. brown, green and orange 25 30
DESIGNS: No. 1345, Hare Krishna Mahtab; 1346, Balasaheb Gangadhar Kher; 1347, Raj Kumari Amrit Kaur; 1348, Saifuddin Kitchlew; 1349, Asaf Ali.

1989. 60th Anniv of Lok Sabha Secretariat (formerly Legislative Assembly Department).
1355 **1074** 60p. green 20 20

1075 Goddess Durga seated on Lion (5th-cent terracotta plaque)

1076 Baldev Ramji Mirdha

1989. 125th Anniv of Lucknow Museum.
1356 **1075** 60p. deep blue and blue 20 20

1989. Birth Centenary of Baldev Ramji Mirdha (nationalist).
1357 **1076** 60p. green 20 20

1077 Girl with Stamp Collection

1989. "India'89" International Stamp Exhibition, New Delhi (5th issue). Philately.
1358 **1077** 60p. yellow, red and blue 15 10
1359 – 1r.50 grey, yellow and black 20 15
1360 – 5r. red and blue 60 50
1361 – 6r.50 black, brown & bl 70 60
DESIGNS: 1r.50, Dawk gharry, c. 1842; 5r. Travancore 1888 2ch. conch shell stamp; 6r.50, Early Indian philatelic magazines.

1078 St. John Bosco and Boy

1079 Modern Tank and 19th-century Sowar

1989. St. John Bosco (founder of Salesian Brothers) Commemoration.
1362 **1078** 60p. red 20 20

1989. 3rd Cavalry Regiment.
1363 **1079** 60p. multicoloured . . 30 20

1080 Dargah Sharif, Ajmer

1989. Dargah Sharif (Sufi shrine), Ajmer.
1364 **1080** 1r. multicoloured . . . 20 20

1081 Task Force and Indian Naval Ensign

1989. President's Review of the Fleet.
1365 **1081** 6r.50 multicoloured . . 1·50 1·00

1082 Shaheed Laxman Nayak and Barbed Wire Fence

1989. Shaheed Laxman Nayak Commemoration.
1366 **1082** 60p. brown, grn & orge 20 20

1083 Rao Gopal Singh

1085 Bishnu Ram Medhi

1084 Sydenham College

1989. Rao Gopal Singh Commemoration.
1367 **1083** 60p. brown 20 20

1989. 75th Anniv (1988) of Sydenham College, Bombay.
1368 **1084** 60p. black 30 20

1989. Birth Centenary (1988) of Bishnu Ram Medhi (politician).
1369 **1085** 60p. green, dp grn & red 30 20

1086 Dr. N. S. Hardikar

1087 "Advaita" in Devanagari Script

1989. Birth Centenary of Dr. Narayana Subbarao Hardikar (nationalist).
1370 **1086** 60p. brown 20 20

1989. Sankaracharya (philosopher) Commem.
1371 **1087** 60p. multicoloured . . 20 20

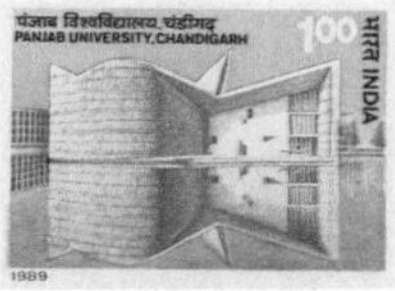
1088 Gandhi Bhavan, Punjab University

1989. Punjab University, Chandigarh.
1372 **1088** 1r. brown and blue . . 20 20

1089 Scene from Film "Raja Harischandra"

1989. 75 Years of Indian Cinema.
1373 **1089** 60p. black and yellow 20 20

1090 Cactus and Cogwheels

1989. Centenary of Kirloskar Brothers Ltd (engineering group).
1374 **1090** 1r. multicoloured . . . 20 20

1091 Early Class and Modern University Students

1989. Centenary of First D.A.V. College.
1375 **1091** 1r. multicoloured . . . 20 20

1092 Post Office, Dakshin Gangotri Base, Antarctica

1989. Opening of Post Office, Dakshin Gangotri Research Station, Antarctica.
1376 **1092** 1r. multicoloured . . . 1·00 20

1093 First Allahabad Bank Building

1989. 125th Anniv (1990) of Allahabad Bank.
1377 **1093** 60p. purple and blue . . 20 20

1094 Nehru inspecting Central Reserve Police, Neemuch, 1954

1989. 50th Anniv of Central Reserve Police Force (formerly Crown Representative's Police).
1378 **1094** 60p. brown . . . . . . 1·00 20

1095 Dairy Cow

1989. Centenary of Military Farms.
1379 **1095** 1r. multicoloured . . . 50 20

1096 Mustafa Kemal Ataturk

1989. 50th Death Anniv (1988) of Mustafa Kemal Ataturk (Turkish statesman).
1380 **1096** 5r. multicoloured . . . 1·25 60

1097 Dr. S. Radhakrishnan

1989. Birth Centenary (1988) of Dr. Sarvepalli Radhakrishnan (former President).
1381 **1097** 60p. black 20 20

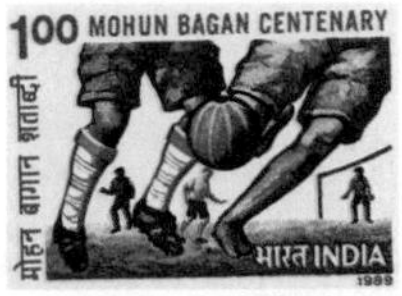
1098 Football Match

1989. Cent of Mohun Bagan Athletic Club.
1382 **1098** 1r. multicoloured . . . 1·25 20

1099 Dr. P. Subbarayan 1100 Shyamji Krishna Varma

1989. Birth Centenary of Dr. P. Subbarayan (politician).
1383 **1099** 60p. brown 20 20

1989. Shyamji Krishna Varma (nationalist) Commemoration.
1384 **1100** 60p. brown, green & red 20 20

1101 Sayajirao Gaekwad III 1103 Namakkal Kavignar

1102 Symbolic Bird with Letter

1989. 50th Death Anniv of Maharaja Sayajirao Gaekwad III of Baroda.
1385 **1101** 60p. grey 20 20

1989. "Use Pincode" Campaign.
1386 **1102** 60p. multicoloured . . 65 20

1989. Namakkal Kavignar (writer) Commem.
1387 **1103** 60p. black 20 20

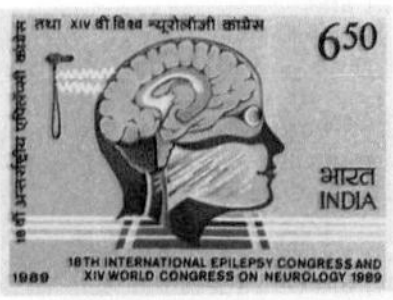
1104 Diagram of Human Brain

1989. 18th International Epilepsy Congress and 14th World Congress on Neurology, New Delhi.
1388 **1104** 6r.50 multicoloured . . 2·25 75

1105 Pandita Ramabai and Original Sharada Sadan Building

1989. Pandita Ramabai (women's education pioneer) Commemoration.
1389 **1105** 60p. brown 30 20

1106 Releasing Homing Pigeons

1989. Orissa Police Pigeon Post.
1390 **1106** 1r. red 50 20

1107 Acharya Narendra Deo 1108 Acharya Kripalani

1989. Birth Centenary of Acharya Narendra Deo (scholar).
1391 **1107** 60p. brown, grn & orge 20 20

1989. Acharya Kripalani (politician) Commemoration.
1392 **1108** 60p. black, green & red 20 20

1109 Nehru

1989. Birth Cent of Jawaharlal Nehru (2nd issue).
1393 **1109** 1r. brown, deep brown and buff 65 20

1110 Meeting Logo 1111 Sir Gurunath Bewoor

1989. 8th Asian Track and Field Meeting, New Delhi.
1394 **1110** 1r. black, orange & grn 30 20

1989. Sir Gurunath Bewoor (former Director-General, Posts and Telegraphs) Commemoration.
1395 **1111** 60p. brown 20 20

1112 Balkrishna Sharma Navin 1113 Abstract Painting of Houses

1989. Balkrishna Sharma Navin (politician and poet) Commemoration.
1396 **1112** 60p. black 20 20

1989. Cent of Bombay Art Society (1988).
1397 **1113** 1r. multicoloured . . . 20 20

1114 Lesser Florican 1115 Centenary Logo

1989. Wildlife Conservation. Lesser Florican.
1398 **1114** 2r. multicoloured . . . 1·50 55

1989. Centenary of Indian Oil Production.
1399 **1115** 60p. brown 30 20

1116 Dr. M. G. Ramachandran 1117 Volunteers working at Sukhna Lake, Chandigarh

1990. Dr. M. G. Ramachandran (former Chief Minister of Tamil Nadu) Commemoration.
1400 **1116** 60p. brown 40 20

1990. Save Sukhna Lake Campaign.
1401 **1117** 1r. multicoloured . . . 20 20

1118 Gallantry Medals

1990. Presentation of New Colours to Bombay Sappers.
1402 **1118** 60p. multicoloured . . 80 1·25

1119 Indian Chank Shell and Logo

1990. 23rd Annual General Meeting of Asian Development Bank, New Delhi.
1403 **1119** 2r. black, orange & yell 75 30

1120 Penny Black and Envelope

1990. 150th Anniv of the Penny Black.
1404 **1120** 6r. multicoloured . . . 1·25 40

1121 Ho Chi-Minh and Vietnamese House **1122** Chaudhary Charan Singh

1990. Birth Centenary of Ho Chi-Minh (Vietnamese leader).
1405 **1121** 2r. brown and green . . 30 30

1990. 3rd Death Anniv of Chaudhary Charan Singh (former Prime Minister).
1406 **1122** 1r. brown 20 20

1123 Armed Forces' Badge and Map of Sri Lanka **1124** Wheat

1990. Indian Peace-keeping Operations in Sri Lanka.
1407 **1123** 2r. multicoloured . . . 30 30

1990. 60th Anniv of Indian Council of Agricultural Research (1989).
1408 **1124** 2r. black, grn & dp grn 30 30

1125 Khudiram Bose **1127** K. Kelappan

1126 "Life in India" (Tanya Vorontsova)

1990. Khudiram Bose (patriot) Commemoration.
1409 **1125** 1r. orange, green and red 20 20

1990. Indo–Soviet Friendship. Children's Paintings. Multicoloured.
1410 1r. Type **1126** . . . . . . 1·50 2·00
1411 6r.50 "St. Basil's Cathedral and Kremlin, Moscow" (Sanjay Adhikari) . . . . 1·50 2·00
Stamps in similar designs were also issued by U.S.S.R.

1990. K. Kelappan (social reformer) Commem.
1412 **1127** 1r. brown 20 20

1128 Girl in Garden

1990. Year of the Girl Child.
1413 **1128** 1r. multicoloured . . . 50 30

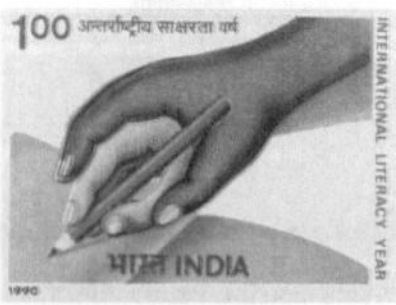

1129 Hand guiding Child's Writing

1990. International Literacy Year.
1414 **1129** 1r. multicoloured . . . 50 30

1130 Woman using Water Pump **1131** Sunder Lal Sharma

1990. Safe Drinking Water Campaign.
1415 **1130** 4r. black, red and green 1·25 1·75

1990. 50th Death Anniv of Sunder Lal Sharma (patriot).
1416 **1131** 60p. red 50 50

1132 Kabbadi **1133** A. K. Gopalan

1990. 11th Asian Games, Peking. Mult.
1417 1r. Type **1132** 40 20
1418 4r. Athletics . . . . 1·50 2·00
1419 4r. Cycling . . . . 1·50 2·00
1420 6r.50 Archery . . . . 1·75 2·50

1990. Ayillyath Kuttiari Gopalan (social reformer) Commemoration.
1421 **1133** 1r. brown 50 30

1134 Gurkha Soldier **1135** Suryamall Mishran

1990. 50th Anniv of 3rd and 5th Battalions, 5th Gurkha Rifles.
1422 **1134** 2r. black and brown . . 1·40 1·60

1990. 75th Birth Anniv of Suryamall Mishran (poet).
1423 **1135** 2r. brown and orange 50 65

1136 "Doll and Cat" (Subhash Kumar Nagarajan)

1990. Children's Day.
1424 **1136** 1r. multicoloured . . . 60 30

1137 Security Post and Border Guard on Camel **1138** Hearts and Flowers

1990. 25th Anniv of Border Security Force.
1425 **1137** 5r. blue, brown & black 1·50 1·75

1990. Greetings Stamps. Multicoloured.
1426 1r. Type **1138** 20 15
1427 4r. Ceremonial elephants (horiz) 50 65

1139 Bikaner

1990. Cities of India. Multicoloured.
1428 4r. Type **1139** 55 60
1429 5r. Hyderabad 65 75
1430 6r.50 Cuttack . . . . 90 1·25

1140 Bhakta Kanakadas and Udipi Temple **1141** Shaheed Minar Monument

1990. Bhakta Kanakadas (mystic and poet) Commemoration.
1431 **1140** 1r. red 55 30

1990. 300th Anniv of Calcutta.
1432 **1141** 1r. multicoloured . . . 30 20
1433 – 6r. black, brown and red . . . . 1·25 1·50
DESIGN—HORIZ (44×36 mm): 6r. 18th-century shipping on the Ganges.

1142 Dnyaneshwari (poet) and Manuscript **1143** Madan Mohan Malaviya (founder) and University

1990. 700th Anniv of Dnyaneshwari (spiritual epic).
1434 **1142** 2r. multicoloured . . . 30 50

1991. 75th Anniv of Banaras Hindu University.
1435 **1143** 1r. red 30 20

1991. As No. 732 but new face value.
1436 1r. brown (Gandhi) 20 10

1144 Road Users **1145** Exhibition Emblem

1991. International Traffic Safety Conference, New Delhi.
1437 **1144** 6r.50 black, blue and red . . . . 75 1·00

1991. 7th Triennale Art Exhibition, New Delhi.
1438 **1145** 6r.50 multicoloured . . 60 75

1146 Jagannath Sunkersett and Central Railways Headquarters **1147** Tata Memorial Centre

1991. 125th Death Anniv (1990) of Jagannath Sunkersett (educationist and railway pioneer).
1439 **1146** 2r. blue and red 50 60

1991. 50th Anniv of Tata Memorial Medical Centre.
1440 **1147** 2r. brown and stone . . 30 40

1148 River Dolphin

1991. Endangered Marine Mammals.
1441 **1148** 4r. brown, blue and green . . . . 1·50 1·50
1442 – 6r.50 multicoloured . . 2·00 2·00
DESIGN: 6r.50, Sea cow.

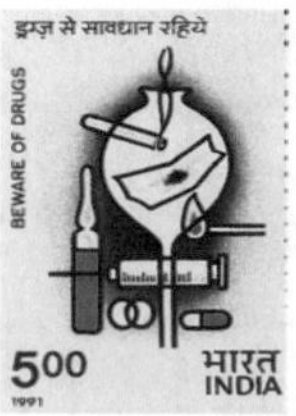

1149 Drugs **1150** Hand, Bomb Explosion and Dove

1991. International Conference on Drug Abuse, Calcutta.
1443 **1149** 5r. violet and red . . . 1·60 1·60

1991. World Peace.
1444 **1150** 6r.50 blk, lt brn & brn 75 1·00

1151 Remote Sensing Satellite "IA"

1991. Launch of Indian Remote Sensing Satellite "IA".
1445 **1151** 6r.50 brown and blue 60 1·00

1152 Babu Jagjivan Ram

1991. Babu Jagjivan Ram (politician) Commemoration.
1446 **1152** 1r. brown 20 20

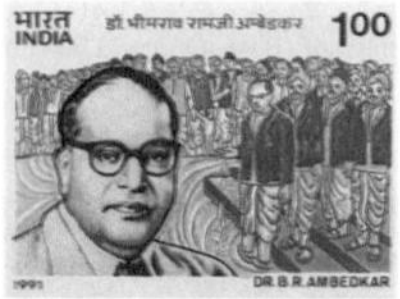

1153 Dr. B. R. Ambedkar and Demonstration

1991. Birth Centenary of Dr. Bhimrao Ramji Ambedkar (social reformer).
1447 **1153** 1r. brown and blue . . 30 20

1154 Valar Dance

1991. Tribal Dances. Multicoloured.
1448 2r.50 Type **1154** 50 40
1449 4r. Kayang 70 80
1450 5r. Hozagiri . . . . 80 1·00
1451 6r.50 Velakali . . . . 1·00 1·60

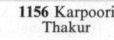

1155 Ariyakudi Ramanuja Iyengar and Temples **1156** Karpoori Thakur

1991. Ariyakudi Ramanuja Iyengar (singer and composer) Commemoration.
1452 **1155** 2r. brown and green . . 50 65

1991. Jan Nayak Karpoori Thakur (politician and social reformer) Commemoration.
1453 **1156** 1r. brown 20 20

1157 Emperor Penguins

1991. 30th Anniv of Antarctic Treaty. Mult.
1454 5r. Type **1157** . . . . . . 1·75 2·00
1455 6r.50 Antarctic map and pair of Adelie penguins 1·75 2·00
Nos. 1454/5 were printed together, se-tenant, forming a composite design.

1158 Rashtrapati Bhavan Building, New Delhi

1991. 60th Anniv of New Delhi. Multicoloured.
1456 5r. Type **1158** . . . . . . 1·00 1·50
1457 6r.50 New Delhi monuments 1·00 1·50
Nos. 1456/7 were printed together, se-tenant, forming a composite design.

1159 Sri Ram Sharma Acharya

1991. Sri Ram Sharma Acharya (social reformer) Commemoration.
1458 **1159** 1r. green and red . . . 20 20

1160 "Shankar awarded Padma Vibhushan" (cartoon)

1991. Keshav Shankar Pillai (cartoonist) Commemoration.
1459 **1160** 4r. brown . . . . . . 1·00 1·50
1460 – 6r.50 lilac . . . . . . 1·40 2·00
DESIGN—VERT: 6r.50, "The Big Show".

1161 Sriprakash and Kashi Vidyapith University — 1162 Gopinath Bardoloi

1991. 20th Death Anniv of Sriprakash (politician).
1461 **1161** 2r. brown & light brown 30 30

1991. Birth Centenary (1990) of Gopinath Bardoloi (Assamese politician).
1462 **1162** 1r. lilac 20 20

1163 Rajiv Gandhi

1991. Rajiv Gandhi (Congress Party leader) Commemoration.
1463 **1163** 1r. multicoloured . . . 65 50

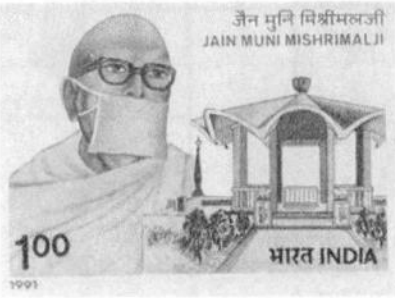

1164 Muni Mishrimalji and Memorial

1991. Birth Centenary of Muni Mishrimalji (Jain religious leader).
1464 **1164** 1r. brown 30 20

1165 Mahadevi Verma (poetess) and "Varsha"

1991. Hindu Writers.
1465 **1165** 2r. black and blue . . . 15 25
1466 – 2r. black and blue . . . 15 25
DESIGN: No. 1466, Jayshankar Prasad (poet and dramatist) and scene from "Kamayani".

1166 Parliament House and C.P.A. Emblem

1991. 37th Commonwealth Parliamentary Association Conference, New Delhi.
1467 **1166** 6r.50 blue and brown 40 60

1167 Frog — 1168 "Cymbidium aloifolium"

1991. Greetings Stamps.
1468 **1167** 1r. green and red . . . 20 45
1469 – 6r.50 red and green . . 35 55
DESIGN: 6r.50, Symbolic bird carrying flower.

1991. Orchids. Multicoloured.
1470 1r. Type **1168** 30 15
1471 2r.50 "Paphiopedilum venustum" 35 35
1472 3r. "Aerides crispum" . . . 40 50
1473 4r. "Cymbidium bicolour" 50 65
1474 5r. "Vanda spathulata" . . 55 70
1475 6r.50 "Cymbidium devonianum" . . . . . . 70 1·00

1169 Gurkha Soldier in Battle Dress — 1170 Couple on Horse (embroidery)

1991. 90th Anniv of 2nd Battalion, Third Gurkha Rifles.
1476 **1169** 4r. multicoloured . . . 1·50 1·75

1991. 3rd Death Anniv of Kamaladevi Chattopadhyaya (founder of All India Handicrafts Board).
1477 **1170** 1r. lake, red and yellow 40 20
1478 – 6r.50 multicoloured . . 1·50 2·00
DESIGN: 6r.50, Traditional puppet.

1171 Chithira Tirunal and Temple Sculpture — 1172 "Children in Traditional Costume" (Arpi Snehalbhai Shah)

1991. Chithira Tirunal Bala Rama Varma (former Maharaja of Travancore) Commemoration.
1479 **1171** 2r. violet 65 75

1991. Children's Day.
1480 **1172** 1r. multicoloured . . . 70 30

1173 Mounted Sowar and Tanks

1991. 70th Anniv (1992) of the 18th Cavalry Regiment.
1481 **1173** 6r.50 multicoloured . . 2·00 2·50

1174 Kites — 1175 Sports on Bricks

1991. India Tourism Year.
1482 **1174** 6r.50 multicoloured . . 60 1·00

1991. International Conference on Youth Tourism, New Delhi.
1483 **1175** 6r.50 multicoloured . . 1·10 1·50

1176 "Mozart at Piano" (unfinished painting, J. Lange) — 1177 Homeless Family

1991. Death Bicentenary of Mozart.
1484 **1176** 6r.50 multicoloured . . 1·50 2·00

1991. South Asian Association for Regional Co-operation Year of Shelter.
1485 **1177** 4r. brown and ochre . . 55 70

1178 People running on Heart

1991. "Run for Your Heart" Marathon, New Delhi.
1486 **1178** 1r. black, grey and red 20 20

1179 "Sidhartha with an Injured Bird" (Asit Kumar Haldar)

1991. Birth Centenary (1990) of Asit Kumar Haldar (artist).
1487 **1179** 2r. yellow, red and black 30 50

1180 Bhujangasana — 1181 Y.M.C.A. Logo

1991. Yoga Exercises. Multicoloured.
1488 2r. Type **1180** 20 25
1489 5r. Dhanurasana 40 55
1490 6r.50 Ustrasana 50 70
1491 10r. Utthita trikonasana . . 85 1·25

1992. Centenary (1991) of National Council of Young Men's Christian Association.
1492 **1181** 1r. red and blue 20 20

1182 Madurai Temple Tower and Hooghly River Bridge — 1183 Goat Seal from Harappa Culture, 2500 to 1500 B.C.

1992. 14th Congress of International Association for Bridge and Structural Engineering, New Delhi.
1493 **1182** 2r. brown, red and blue 75 90
1494 – 2r. brown, red and blue 75 90
DESIGN: No. 1494, Gate, Sanchi Stupa and Hall of Nations, New Delhi.

1992. 5th International Goat Conference, New Delhi.
1495 **1183** 6r. blue and brown . . 2·50 2·75

1184 Early 19th-century Letter with Mail Pouch and National Archives Building, New Delhi — 1185 Krushna Chandra Gajapathi

1992. Centenary (1991) of National Archives.
1496 **1184** 6r. multicoloured . . . 50 75

1992. Krushna Chandra Gajapathi (former Chief Minister of Orissa) Commemoration.
1497 **1185** 1r. lilac 15 15

1186 Vijay Singh Pathik — 1187 Hang-gliding

1992. Vijay Singh Pathik (writer) Commem.
1498 **1186** 1r. brown 15 15

1992. Adventure Sports. Multicoloured.
1499 2r. Type **1187** 25 20
1500 4r. Windsurfing 50 60
1501 5r. River rafting 60 75
1502 11r. Skiing . . . . 1·25 2·25

1188 Henry Gidney and Anglo-Indians

1992. 50th Death Anniv of Sir Henry Gidney (ophthalmologist).
1503 **1188** 1r. black and blue . . . 60 20

1189 Telecommunications Training Centre, Jabalpur

1190 Sardar Udham Singh

1992. 50th Anniv of Telecommunications Training Centre, Jabalpur.
1504 **1189** 1r. bistre 20 15

1992. Sardar Udham Singh (patriot) Commemoration.
1505 **1190** 1r. black and brown . . 20 15

1191 Men's Discus

1992. Olympic Games, Barcelona. Mult.
1506 1r. Type **1191** 30 10
1507 6r. Women's gymnastics . . 90 1·00
1508 8r. Men's hockey . . . . . 2·00 2·50
1509 11r. Boxing . . . . 2·00 2·75

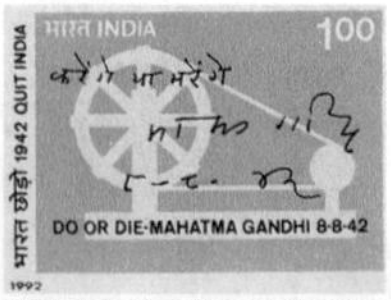

1192 Spinning Wheel Emblem

1992. 50th Anniv of "Quit India" Movement.
1510 **1192** 1r. black and pink . . . 1·50 30
1511 – 2r. black, brown & grey 2·25 2·50
DESIGN: 2r. Mahatma Gandhi and mantra.

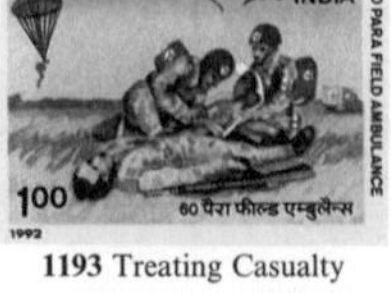

1193 Treating Casualty

1992. 50th Anniv of 60th Parachute Field Ambulance.
1512 **1193** 1r. multicoloured . . . 1·25 40

1194 Dr. S. R. Ranganathan and Madras University

1992. Birth Centenary of Shiyali Ramamrita Ranganathan (librarian).
1513 **1194** 1r. blue . . . . 1·50 30

1195 "Dev Narayan"

1196 Hanuman Prasad Poddar

1992. Phad Scroll Paintings from Rajasthan.
1514 **1195** 5r. multicoloured . . . 60 1·00

1992. Hanuman Prasad Poddar (editor) Commemoration.
1515 **1196** 1r. green 15 15

1197 Mikoyan Guerevich MiG-29 Fighter and Ilyushin Il-76 Transport

1992. 60th Anniv of Indian Air Force. Mult.
1516 1r. Type **1197** . . . . . . 1·00 1·40
1517 10r. MiG-27 fighter and Westland Wapiti biplane 1·75 2·25

1198 Lighting Candle

1992. 150th Anniv of Sisters of Jesus and Mary's Arrival in India.
1518 **1198** 1r. blue and grey . . . 15 15

1199 "Sun" (Harshit Prashant Patel)

1992. Children's Day.
1519 **1199** 1r. multicoloured . . . 20 15

1200 Yogiji Maharaj

1992. Birth Centenary of Yogiji Maharaj (Hindu reformer).
1520 **1200** 1r. blue . . . . 1·50 30

1201 Army Service Corps Transport

1992. Army Service Corps Commemoration.
1521 **1201** 1r. multicoloured . . . 1·75 50

1202 Stephen Smith and Early Rocket Post Covers

1992. Birth Centenary (1991) of Stephen Smith (rocket mail pioneer).
1522 **1202** 11r. multicoloured . . . 1·00 1·50

1203 Electricity Pylons, Farmers and Crops

1992. 25th Anniv of Haryana State.
1523 **1203** 2r. red, dp green & green 15 15

1204 Madanlal Dhingra

1205 Osprey

1992. Madanlal Dhingra (revolutionary) Commemoration.
1524 **1204** 1r. brown, red and green 30 15

1992. Birds of Prey. Multicoloured.
1525 2r. Type **1205** 90 60
1526 6r. Peregrine falcon . . . . 1·25 1·10
1527 8r. Lammergeier . . . . . 1·40 1·75
1528 11r. Golden eagle . . . . . 1·60 2·00

1206 Pandit Ravishankar Shukla

1208 Fakirmohan Senapati

1207 William Carey

1992. Pandit Ravishankar Shukla (social reformer) Commemoration.
1529 **1206** 1r. purple 15 15

1993. Bicent of William Carey's Appointment as Baptist Missionary to India.
1530 **1207** 6r. multicoloured . . . 1·00 1·50

1993. Fakirmohan Senapati Commemoration.
1531 **1208** 1r. red 40 15

1209 Workers and C.S.I.R emblem

1993. 50th Anniv of Council of Scientific and Industrial Research.
1532 **1209** 1r. purple 40 15

1210 Parachute Drop and Field Gun

1993. 50th Anniv of 9th Parachute Field Artillery Regiment.
1533 **1210** 1r. multicoloured . . . 1·25 30

1211 Westland Wapiti Biplane

1993. 60th Anniv of No. 1 Squadron, Indian Air Force.
1534 **1211** 1r. multicoloured . . . 1·25 30

1212 Rahul Sankrityayan

1993. Birth Centenary of Rahul Sankrityayan (politician).
1535 **1212** 1r. black, cinnamon and brown 20 15

1213 Parliament Building and Emblem

1993. 89th Inter-Parliamentary Union Conference, New Delhi.
1536 **1213** 1r. black 20 15

1214 Neral Matheran Railway Tank Locomotive, 1905

1993. Mountain Locomotives. Multicoloured.
1537 1r. Type **1214** 60 20
1538 6r. Darjeeling and Himalayan Railway, Class B, 1889 . . . . 1·25 1·25
1539 8r. Nilgiri Hill Railway, 1914 . . . . 1·40 1·75
1540 11r. Kalka–Simla Railway, 1934 . . . . 1·90 2·50

1215 Students and College Building

1993. Centenary of Meerut College.
1541 **1215** 1r. black and brown . . 20 15

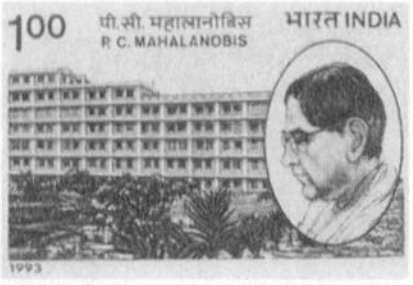

1216 Mahalanobis and Office Block

1993. Prasanta Chandra Mahalanobis Commemoration.
1542 **1216** 1r. brown 60 15

1217 Bombay Town Hall

1993. Centenary of Bombay Municipal Corporation.
1543 **1217** 2r. multicoloured . . . 20 30

1218 Abdul Ghaffar Khan and Mountainside

1993. Abdul Ghaffar Khan Commemoration.
1544 **1218** 1r. multicoloured . . . 15 15

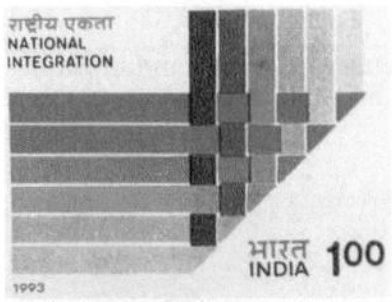

1219 National Integration Emblem

1993. National Integration Campaign.
1545 **1219** 1r. orange and green . . 15 15

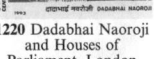

1220 Dadabhai Naoroji and Houses of Parliament, London

1221 Swami Vivekananda and Art Institute, Chicago

1993. Centenary of Dadabhai Naoroji's Election to the House of Commons.
1546 **1220** 6r. multicoloured . . . 50 65

1993. Centenary of Swami Vivekananda's Chicago Address.
1547 **1221** 2r. orange and grey . . 50 50

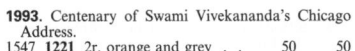

1222 "Lagerstroemia speciosa"

1223 College Building and Emblem

1993. Flowering Trees.
1548 **1222** 1r. red, green and brown 20 15
1549 – 6r. multicoloured . . . 40 55
1550 – 8r. multicoloured . . . 55 80
1551 – 11r. multicoloured . . . 75 1·25
DESIGNS: 6r. "Cochlospermum religiosum"; 8r. "Erythrina variegata"; 11r. "Thespesia populnea".

1993. 50th Anniv of College of Military Engineering, Pune.
1552 **1223** 2r. multicoloured . . . 20 30

1224 Dr. Dwaram Venkataswamy Naidu playing Violin

1225 Children on Elephant

1993. Birth Centenary of Dwaram Venkataswamy Naidu (violinist).
1553 **1224** 1r. red 20 20

1993. Children's Day.
1554 **1225** 1r. multicoloured . . . 20 20

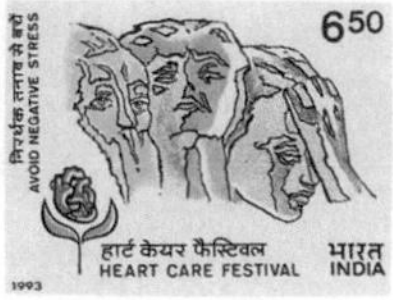

1226 People with Stress

1993. Heart Care Festival.
1555 **1226** 6r.50 multicoloured . . 60 80

1227 Dr. Kotnis performing Operation

1993. Dr. Dwarkanath Kotnis (surgeon) Commemoration.
1556 **1227** 1r. black 20 20

1228 Tea Symbol

1993. Indian Tea Production.
1557 **1228** 6r. green and red . . . 50 75

1229 Papal Seminary Arms and Building

1993. Centenary of Papal Seminary, Pune.
1558 **1229** 6r. multicoloured . . . 50 75

1230 Meghnad Saha and Eclipse of the Sun

1993. Meghnad Saha (astronomer) Commem.
1559 **1230** 1r. blue 30 20

1231 Speedpost Letter and Arrows circling Globe

1993. Inpex '93 National Stamp Exn, Calcutta. Multicoloured.
1560 1r. Type **1231** 20 15
1561 2r. "Custom-house Wharf, Calcutta" (Sir Charles D'Oyly) 55 60

1232 Dinanath Mangeshkar

1233 Nargis Dutt

1993. Dinanath Mangeshkar Commem.
1562 **1232** 1r. red 15 15

1993. Nargis Dutt Commemoration.
1563 **1233** 1r. red 15 15

1234 S. C. Bose inspecting Troops

1993. 50th Anniv of Indian National Army.
1564 **1234** 1r. green, dp grn & red 30 20

1235 Satyendra Nath Bose and Equation

1994. Birth Centenary of Satyendra Nath Bose (scientist).
1565 **1235** 1r. brown 50 15

1236 Dr. Sampurnanand

1994. Dr. Sampurnanand (politician) Commemoration.
1566 **1236** 1r. brown, green and red 15 10

1237 Scene from "Pather Panchali" ($\frac{1}{2}$-size illustration)

1994. Satyajit Ray (film director) Commemoration. Multicoloured.
1567 6r. Type **1237** . . . . . . 1·25 1·75
1568 11r. Satyajit Ray and Oscar (35 × 35 mm) . . . . . . 1·40 1·75

1238 Dr. Bhatnagar and University Building

1994. Dr. Shanti Swarup Bhatnagar (scientist) Commemoration.
1569 **1238** 1r. blue 15 10

1239 Prajapita Brahma and Memorial

1994. 25th Death Anniv of Prajapita Brahma (social reformer).
1570 **1239** 1r. lilac and blue . . . 15 10

1240 "Window" (K. Subramanyan)

1994. 8th Triennale Art Exhibition, New Delhi.
1571 **1240** 6r. orange, red and blue 50 60

1241 Agricultural Products and Tea Garden

1994. Centenary of United Planters' Association of Southern India.
1572 **1241** 2r. multicoloured . . . 20 20

1242 Indian Family

1242a Sanchi Stupa

1994.
1573 **1242** 75p. brown and red 10 10
1574 – 1r. mauve and green 10 10
1575 – 3r. purple 15 10
1576 **1242a** 5r. brown and green 25 20
DESIGNS (as T **1242**)—HORIZ: 1r. Family outside home. VERT: 3r. Baby and drop of polio vaccine.

1243 Rani Rashmoni on River Bank

1994. Birth Bicentenary of Rani Rashmoni.
1589 **1243** 1r. brown 15 10

1244 Indians releasing Peace Doves

1994. 75th Anniv of Jallianwala Bagh Massacre, Amritsar.
1590 **1244** 1r. black and red . . . 15 10

1245 Chandra Singh Garhwali

1994. 15th Death Anniv of Chandra Singh Garhwali (nationalist).
1591 **1245** 1r. green and orange . . 15 10

1246 Emblems and National Flag

1994. 75th Anniv of I.L.O.
1592 **1246** 6r. multicoloured . . . 50 65

1247 Silhouette of Drummer and Logo

1994. 50th Anniv of Indian People's Theatre Association.
1593 **1247** 2r. black, green and gold 15 15

1248 Statue of Sepoy

1249 Institute Building and Emblem

1994. Bicentenary of 4th Battalion, The Madras Regiment.
1594 **1248** 6r.50 multicoloured . . 55 75

1994. Bicentenary of Institute of Mental Health, Madras.
1595 **1249** 2r. red and blue 15 15

1250 Mahatma Gandhi and Indian Flag **1251** Symbols of Cancer

1994. 125th Birth Anniv of Mahatma Gandhi. Multicoloured.
1596 6r. Type **1250** . . . . . . 1·40 1·90
1597 11r. Aspects of Gandhi's life on flag (69 × 34 mm) . . . 1·60 3·25
Nos. 1596/7 were printed together, se-tenant, forming a composite design.

1994. 16th International Cancer Congress, New Delhi.
1598 **1251** 6r. multicoloured . . . 55 75

1252 Human Resources Emblem

1994. Human Resource Development World Conference, New Delhi.
1599 **1252** 6r. blue, red and azure 55 75

1253 "Me and My Pals" (Namarata Amit Shah) **1254** Family and Emblem

1994. Children's Day.
1600 **1253** 1r. multicoloured . . . 10 10

1994. International Year of the Family.
1601 **1254** 2r. multicoloured . . . 20 15

1255 "Taj Mahal" (illustration from Badsha Nama)

1994. Khuda Bakhsh Oriental Public Library, Patna, Commemoration.
1602 **1255** 6r. multicoloured . . . 4·00 1·00

1256 Grey Teal ("Andaman Teal")

1994. Endangered Water Birds. Multicoloured.
1603 1r. Type **1256** . . . . . . 7·00 2·00
1604 6r. Oriental white stork ("Eastern White Stork") 10·00 4·00
1605 8r. Black-necked crane . . . 10·00 4·50
1606 11r. Pink-headed duck . . . 11·00 6·00
It is reported that Nos. 1603/6 were withdrawn shortly after issue.

1257 J. R. D. Tata and Aspects of Industrial Symbols

1994. J. R. D. Tata (industrialist) Commemoration.
1607 **1257** 2r. multicoloured . . . 30 30

1258 School Building and Computer Class

1994. Centenary of Calcutta Blind School.
1608 **1258** 2r. red, brown and cinnamon 20 15

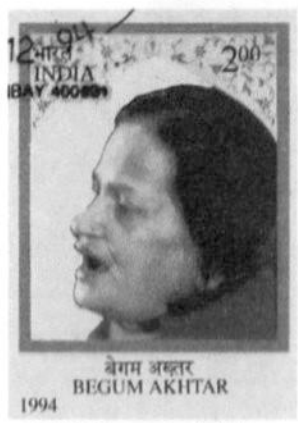

1259 Begum Akhtar **1261** Cavalryman, Infantryman and Dog Handler

1260 College Building

1994. 80th Birth Anniv of Begum Akhtar (singer).
1609 **1259** 2r. multicoloured . . . 4·75 4·50

1994. 125th Anniv of St. Xavier's College, Bombay.
1610 **1260** 2r. brown and blue . . 15 15

1994. 215th Anniv of Remount Veterinary Corps.
1611 **1261** 6r. multicoloured . . . 1·40 1·40

1262 College Building

1994. Bicentenary of College of Engineering, Guindy, Madras.
1612 **1262** 2r. red, brown and black 15 10

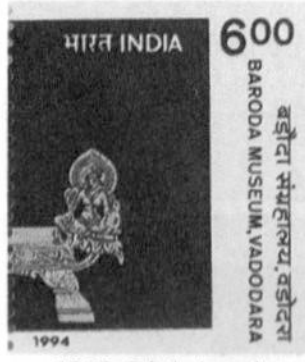

1263 Righthand Ornament of Bronze Stand **1265** Statue of King Rajaraja Chola

1264 "200" and Aspects of Postal Service ($\frac{1}{2}$-size illustration)

1994. Centenary of Baroda Museum.
1613 **1263** 6r. yellow and brown 2·50 1·50
1614 – 11r. yellow and brown 2·50 1·50
DESIGN: 11r. Bronze Rishabhanatha statue of Buddha on stand.

1994. Bicentenary of Bombay General Post Office.
1615 **1264** 6r. multicoloured . . . 5·00 1·75

1995. 8th International Conference-Seminar of Tamil Studies, Thanjavur.
1616 **1265** 2r. blue, ultramarine and black . . . . . 3·50 75

1266 Globe and Emblem **1267** Chhotu Ram

1995. 60th Anniv of National Science Academy.
1617 **1266** 6r. multicoloured . . . 50 80

1995. Chhotu Ram (social reformer) Commem.
1618 **1267** 1r. brown . . . . . . 1·00 25

1268 Film Reel and Globe

1995. Centenary of Cinema. Multicoloured.
1619 6r. Type **1268** . . . . . . 60 1·00
1620 11r. Film reel and early equipment . . . . 80 1·00

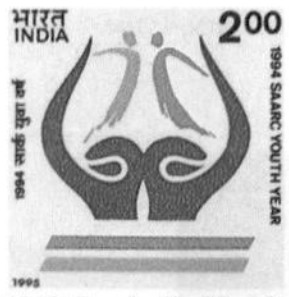

1269 Symbolic Hands and Children **1270** Prithviraj Kapoor and Mask

1995. South Asian Association for Regional Cooperation Youth Year.
1621 **1269** 2r. multicoloured . . . 20 20

1995. 50th Anniv of Prithvi Theatre.
1622 **1270** 2r. multicoloured . . . 3·75 75

1271 Field-Marshal Cariappa **1272** Textile Pattern

1995. Field-Marshal K. Cariappa Commemoration.
1623 **1271** 2r. multicoloured . . . 30 20

1995. "TEX-STYLES INDIA '95" Fair, Bombay.
1624 **1272** 2r. brown, buff and red 20 20

1273 Rafi Ahmed Kidwai **1275** R. S. Ruikar

1274 K. L. Saigal, Film Reel and Gramophone

1995. Birth Centenary (1994) of Rafi Ahmed Kidwai (politician).
1625 **1273** 1r. brown 15 10

1995. 90th Birth Anniv of K. L. Saigal (singer).
1626 **1274** 5r. brown, grey and black . . . . 1·00 1·25

1995. Birth Centenary of R. S. Ruikar (trade unionist).
1627 **1275** 1r. brown 15 10

1276 Radio Tower, Globe and Dish Aerial

1995. Centenary of Telecommunications.
1628 **1276** 5r. multicoloured . . . 1·00 1·25

1277 Leaves and Symbolic Houses

1995. Delhi Development Authority.
1629 **1277** 2r. multicoloured . . . 20 20

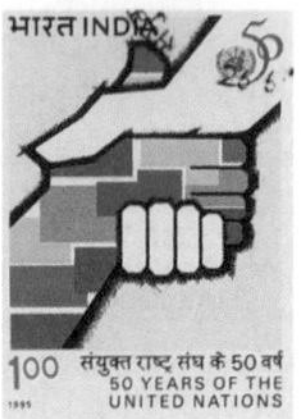
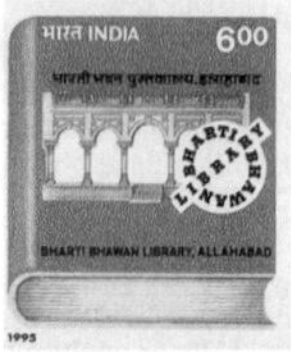

1278 Handshake **1279** Colonnade on Book Cover

1995. 50th Anniv of United Nations. Multicoloured.
1630 1r. Type **1278** 10 10
1631 6r. Work of U.N. Agencies 45 65

1995. Centenary of Bharti Bhawan Library, Allahabad.
1632 **1279** 6r. black, brown and red 55 75

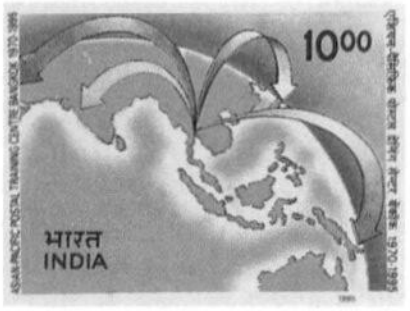

1280 Globe showing South-east Asia

1995. 25th Anniv of Asian-Pacific Postal Training Centre, Bangkok.
1633 **1280** 10r. multicoloured . . . 1·00 1·25

1281 "75" and Taurus Formation Sign **1282** Louis Pasteur in Laboratory (from painting by Edelfelt)

1995. 75th Anniv of Area Army Headquarters, Delhi.
1634 **1281** 2r. multicoloured . . . 50 20

1995. Death Centenary of Louis Pasteur (chemist).
1635 **1282** 5r. black and stone . . 1·75 1·25

1283 La Martiniere College, Lucknow **1284** Gandhi in South Africa

1995. 150th Anniv of La Martiniere College, Lucknow.
1636 **1283** 2r. multicoloured . . . 20 20

1995. India-South Africa Co-operation. 125th Birth Anniv (1994) of Mahatma Gandhi.
1637 **1284** 1r. red 50 65
1638 – 2r. red 50 65
MS1639 68 × 80 mm. Nos. 1637/8 (sold at 8r.) . . . . 1·25 1·75
DESIGN: 2r. Gandhi wearing dhoti.

1285 Ears of Grain, "50" and Emblem on Globe **1286** P. M. Thevar

1995. 50th Anniv of F.A.O.
1640 **1285** 5r. multicoloured . . . 1·00 1·25

1995. Pasumpon Muthuramalingam Thevar (social reformer) Commemoration.
1641 **1286** 1r. red 15 10

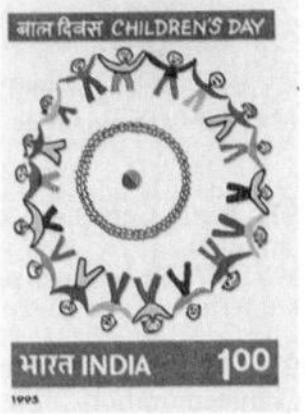

1287 W. C. Rontgen **1288** Children in Circle

1995. 150th Birth Anniv of W. C. Rontgen (discoverer of X-rays).
1642 **1287** 6r. multicoloured . . . 1·50 1·50

1995. Children's Day.
1643 **1288** 1r. multicoloured . . . 20 10

1289 Sitar **1290** Jat War Memorial, Bareilly

1995. Communal Harmony Campaign.
1644 **1289** 2r. multicoloured . . . 1·40 65

1995. Bicentenary of Jat Regiments.
1645 **1290** 5r. multicoloured . . . 1·50 1·25

1291 Men of Rajputana Rifles

1995. 175th Anniv of 5th (Napier's) Battalion, Rajputana Rifles.
1646 **1291** 5r. multicoloured . . . 1·75 1·25

1292 Sant Tukdoji Maharaj and Rural Meeting **1293** Dr. Yellapragada Subbarow

1995. Sant Tukdoji Maharaj Commemoration.
1647 **1292** 1r. brown 20 10
Although dated "1993", No. 1647 was not issued until the date quoted above.

1995. Dr. Yellapragada Subbarow (pharmaceutical scientist) Commemoration.
1648 **1293** 1r. brown 30 10

1294 Pres. Giani Zail Singh **1295** Dargah of Ala Hazrat Barelvi

1995. 1st Death Anniv of Pres. Giani Zail Singhn.
1649 **1294** 1r. multicoloured . . . 20 10

1995. 75th Death Anniv of Ala Hazrat Barelvi (Moslem scholar).
1650 **1295** 1r. multicoloured . . . 20 10

1296 Tata Institute Building

1996. 50th Anniv (1995) of Tata Institute of Fundamental Research.
1651 **1296** 2r. multicoloured . . . 30 20

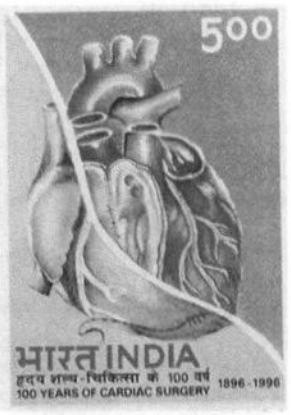

1297 Kasturba Gandhi **1298** Sectioned Heart

1996. 50th Anniv of the Kasturba Trust.
1652 **1297** 1r. grey, green and red 60 20

1996. 100 Years of Cardiac Surgery.
1653 **1298** 5r. multicoloured . . . 1·00 1·00

1299 C. K. Nayudu **1300** "Vasant" (Spring) (Ragini Basanti)

1996. Cricketers. Multicoloured.
1654 2r. Type **1299** 60 60
1655 2r. Vinoo Mankad 60 60
1656 2r. Deodhar 60 60
1657 2r. Vijay Merchant 60 60

1996. Miniature Paintings of the Seasons. Multicoloured.
1658 5r. Type **1300** . . . . . . 1·00 1·25
1659 5r. "Greeshma" (Summer) (Jyestha) . . . . 1·00 1·25
1660 5r. "Varsha" (Monsoon) (Rag Megh Malbar) . . . 1·00 1·25
1661 5r. "Hernant" (Winter) (Pausha) . . . . 1·00 1·25

1301 Kunjilal Dubey **1302** Morarji Desai

1996. Kunjilal Dubey Commemoration.
1662 **1301** 1r. brown & chocolate 20 10

1996. Birth Centenary of Morarji Desai (former Prime Minister) (1st issue).
1663 **1302** 1r. red 30 10
See also No. 1702.

1303 Blood Pheasant

1996. Himalayan Ecology. Multicoloured.
1664 5r. Type **1303** . . . . . . 1·00 1·25
1665 5r. Markhor (goat) . . . . 1·00 1·25
1666 5r. "Meconopsis horridula" (Tsher Gnoin) (plant) . . 1·00 1·25
1667 5r. "Saussurea simpsoniana" (Sunflower) . . . . 1·00 1·25
MS1668 175 × 105 mm. Nos. 1664/7 (sold at 30r.) . . . . 2·50 3·25

1304 S.K.C.G. College Building

1996. Centenary of S.K.C.G. College, Gajapati.
1669 **1304** 1r. brown and cream 20 10

1305 Muhammad Ismail Sahib

1996. Birth Centenary of Muhammad Ismail Sahib (Moslem politician).
1670 **1305** 1r. purple 20 10

1306 Modern Stadium and Ancient Athens **1307** Sister Alphonsa

1996. Olympic Games, Atlanta. Multicoloured.
1671 5r. Type **1306** 35 50
1672 5r. Hand holding Olympic torch 35 50

1996. 50th Death Anniv of Sister Alphonsa.
1673 **1307** 1r. black and blue . . . 20 10

1308 "Communications" **1309** Sir Pherozeshah Mehta

1996. 125th Anniv of Videsh Sanchar Nigam Limited (telecommunications company).
1674 **1308** 5r. multicoloured . . . 1·00 1·00

1996. 150th Birth Anniv of Sir Pherozeshah Mehta (politician).
1675 **1309** 1r. blue 20 10

1310 Ahilyabai **1311** Chembai Vaidyanatha Bhagavathar

1996. Death Bicentenary (1995) of Ahilyabai (ruler of Holkar).
1676 **1310** 2r. brown and deep brown 30 20

1996. Birth Centenary of Chembai Vaidyanatha Bhagavathar (musician).
1677 **1311** 1r. brown and green . . 20 10

1312 Red Junglefowl Cockerel

1996. 20th World Poultry Congress, New Delhi.
1678 **1312** 5r. multicoloured . . . 1·75 1·50

1313 Rani Gaidinliu **1314** Nath Pai

1996. Rani Gaidinliu (Naga leader) Commemoration.
1679 **1313** 1r. blue 20 10

1996. 25th Death Anniv of Nath Pai (politician).
1680 **1314** 1r. blue 20 10

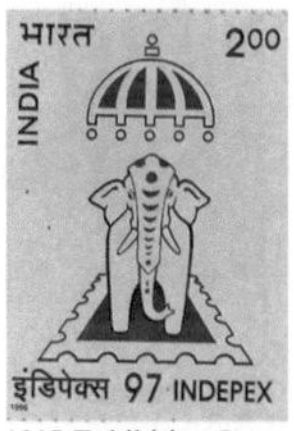

1315 Exhibition Logo **1317** Jananayak Debeswar Sarmah

1316 Historic Steam Locomotives

1996. INDEPEX '97 International Stamp Exhibition, New Delhi (1st issue).
1681 **1315** 2r. gold and purple . . 30 20
See also Nos. 1713/16, 1722/5, 1741/4 and 1758/61.

1996. 25th Anniv of National Rail Museum.
1682 **1316** 5r. multicoloured . . . 1·75 1·50

1996. Birth Centenary of Jananayak Debeswar Sarmah (politician).
1683 **1317** 2r. brown and deep brown 30 20

1318 Monument and Sikh Sentry

1996. 150th Anniv of Sikh Regiment.
1684 **1318** 5r. multicoloured . . . 1·00 1·00

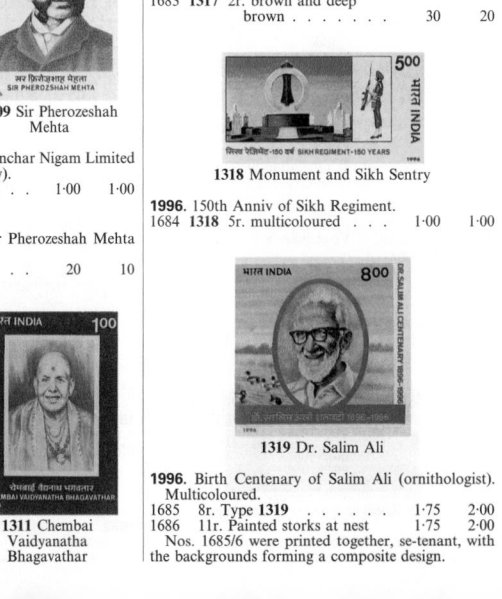

1319 Dr. Salim Ali

1996. Birth Centenary of Salim Ali (ornithologist). Multicoloured.
1685 8r. Type **1319** . . . . . . 1·75 2·00
1686 11r. Painted storks at nest . . 1·75 2·00
Nos. 1685/6 were printed together, se-tenant, with the backgrounds forming a composite design.

1320 "Indian Village" (child's painting)

1996. Children's Day.
1687 **1320** 8r. multicoloured . . . 1·00 1·25

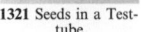

1321 Seeds in a Test-tube

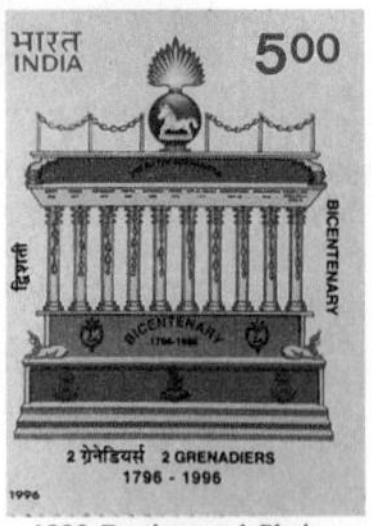

1322 Regimental Shrine

1996. 2nd International Crop Science Congress.
1688 **1321** 2r. multicoloured . . . 40 20

1996. Bicentenary of 2nd Battalion, Grenadiers.
1689 **1322** 5r. multicoloured . . . 1·00 1·00

1323 Woman writing

1324 Abai Konunbaev

1996. 10th Anniv of South Asian Association for Regional Co-operation (S.A.A.R.C.).
1690 **1323** 11r. multicoloured . . . 1·00 1·40

1996. 150th Birth Anniv (1995) of Abai Konunbaev (Kazakh poet).
1691 **1324** 5r. chestnut, brown and lilac . . . . 1·00 1·25

1325 Buglers in front of Memorial

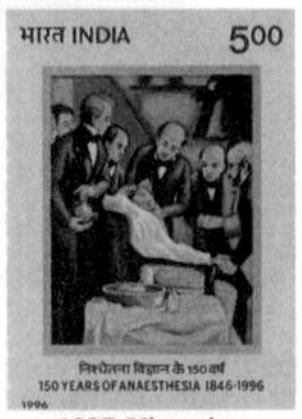

1327 Victorian Doctors performing Operation

1326 Vivekananda Rock Memorial (½-size illustration)

1996. 25th Anniv of the Liberation of Bangladesh.
1692 **1325** 2r. multicoloured . . . 30 20

1996. 25th Anniv of Vivekananda Rock Memorial, Kanyakumari.
1693 **1326** 5r. multicoloured . . . 1·50 1·25

1996. 150th Anniv of Anaesthetics.
1694 **1327** 5r. multicoloured . . . 1·00 1·00

1328 Roorkee University Buildings

1997. 150th Anniv of Roorkee University.
1695 **1328** 8r. multicoloured . . . 80 1·25

1329 Dr. Vrindavanlal Verma

1997. Dr. Vrindavanlal Verma (writer) Commemoration.
1696 **1329** 2r. red 30 20

1330 Field Post Office

1331 Subhas Chandra Bose

1997. 25th Anniv of Army Postal Service Corps.
1697 **1330** 5r. multicoloured . . . 1·25 1·25

1997. Birth Centenary of Subhas Chandra Bose (nationalist).
1698 **1331** 1r. brown 30 10

1332 Jose Marti

1333 Conference Logo

1997. Jose Marti (Cuban writer) Commemoration.
1699 **1332** 11r. black and pink . . 80 1·25

1997. "Towards Partnership between Men and Women in Politics" Inter-Parliamentary Conference, New Delhi.
1700 **1333** 5r. multicoloured . . . 35 45

1334 St. Andrew's Church

1335 Morarji Desai

1997. St. Andrew's Church, Egmore, Madras Commemoration.
1701 **1334** 8r. multicoloured . . . 70 1·00

1997. Birth Centenary of Morarji Desai (former Prime Minister) (2nd issue).
1702 **1335** 1r. brown and deep brown 30 10

1336 Shyam Lal Gupt

1337 Saint Dnyaneshwar

1997. Birth Centenary (1996) of Shyam Lal Gupt (social reformer).
1703 **1336** 1r. cinnamon and brown 20 10

1997. 700th Death Anniv (1996) of Saint Dnyaneshwar.
1704 **1337** 5r. multicoloured . . . 60 60

1338 Parijati Tree

1997. Parijati Tree. Multicoloured.
1705 5r. Type **1338** 65 75
1706 6r. Parijati flower 65 75

1339 Monument, Rashtriya Military College

1997. 75th Anniv of Rashtriya Military College, Dehra Dun.
1707 **1339** 2r. multicoloured . . . 75 30

1340 Ram Manohar Lohia

1341 Society Centenary Emblem

1997. Ram Manohar Lohia Commemoration.
1708 **1340** 1r. multicoloured . . . 20 10

1997. Centenary of the Philatelic Society of India. Multicoloured.
1709 2r. Type **1341** 65 70
1710 2r. Cover of 1st "Philatelic Journal of India", 1897 65 70

1342 Gyandith Award Winners

1343 Madhu Limaye

1997. Gyandith Award Scheme.
1711 **1342** 2r. multicoloured . . . 30 20

1997. Madhu Limaye Commemoration.
1712 **1343** 2r. green 30 20

1344 Nalanda Monastic University

1997. "INDEPEX '97" International Stamp Exhibition, New Delhi (2nd issue). Buddhist Cultural Sites. Multicoloured.
1713 2r. Type **1344** 25 30
1714 6r. The Bodhi Tree, Bodhgaya 45 50
1715 10r. Stupa and Pillar, Vaishali 60 80
1716 11r. Stupa, Kushinagar . . 60 80

1345 Pandit Omkarnath Thakur

1346 Ram Sewak Yadav

1997. Birth Centenary of Pandit Omkarnath Thakur (musician).
1717 **1345** 2r. black and blue . . . 60 20

1997. Ram Sewak Yadav (politician) Commemoration.
1718 **1346** 2r. brown 30 20

1347 Sibnath Banerjee

1348 Rukmini Lakshmipathi

1997. Birth Centenary of Sibnath Banerjee (trade unionist).
1719 **1347** 2r. red and purple . . . 30 20

1997. Rukmini Lakshmipathi (social reformer) Commemoration.
1720 **1348** 2r. brown . . . . . . 1·00 40

1349 Sri Basaveswara

1350 Gopalpur-on-Sea Beach

1997. Sri Basaveswara (reformer and statesman) Commemoration.
1721 **1349** 2r. purple 30 20

1997. "INDEPEX '97" International Stamp Exhibition, New Delhi (3rd issue). Beaches. Multicoloured.
1722 2r. Type **1350** 25 15
1723 6r. Kovalam 65 55
1724 10r. Anjuna . . . . 80 1·00
1725 11r. Bogmalo . . . . 80 1·00

1351 Newspaper Masthead

1997. 50th Anniv of "Swatantra Bharat" (Hindi daily newspaper).
1726 **1351** 2r. multicoloured . . . 30 20

1352 Shah Nawaz Khan, P. K. Sahgal and G. S. Dhillon

1997. I.N.A. Trials Commemoration.
1727 **1352** 2r. multicoloured . . . 30 30

1353 Sir Ronald Ross (bacteriologist)

1354 Firaq Gorakhpuri

1997. Centenary of the Discovery of the Malaria Parasite by Sir Ronald Ross.
1728 **1353** 2r. grey . . . . 1·00 40

1997. Birth Centenary (1996) of Firaq Gorakhpuri (poet).
1729 **1354** 2r. brown 20 20

1355 Bhaktivedanta Swami

1997. Birth Centenary (1996) of Bhaktivedanta Swami (philosopher).
1730 **1355** 5r. brown . . . . . . 1·25 1·25

1356 Parachute Regiment Emblem

1997. Bicentenary of 2nd (Maratha) Battalion, Parachute Regiment.
1731 **1356** 2r. multicoloured . . . 50 30

1357 Fossil of "Birbalsahnia divyadarshanii"
1358 Swami Brahmanand

1997. 50th Anniv of Birbal Sahni Institute of Palaeobotany, Lucknow. Plant Fossils. Multicoloured.
1732 2r. Type **1357** 45 45
1733 2r. "Glossopteris" 45 45
1734 6r. "Pentoxylon" (reconstruction) . . . . . 90 1·00
1735 10r. "Williamsonia sewardiana" (model) . . . 1·40 1·50

1997. Swami Brahmanand (social reformer) Commemoration.
1736 **1358** 2r. grey and stone . . . 30 20

1359 "Sir William Jones"
1361 V. K. Krishna Menon

1360 Lawrence School Building and Crest

1997. 250th Birth Anniv (1996) of Sir William Jones (Sanskrit scholar).
1737 **1359** 4r. multicoloured . . . 35 40

1997. 150th Anniv of Lawrence School, Sanawar.
1738 **1360** 2r. multicoloured . . . 50 30

1997. Birth Centenary (1996) of V. K. Krishna Menon (politician).
1739 **1361** 2r. red 30 30

1362 Policemen and Globe

1997. 66th General Assembly Session of ICPO Interpol.
1740 **1362** 4r. multicoloured . . . 65 75

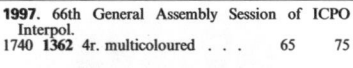

1363 Woman from Arunachal Pradesh
1364 Students in Meditation, Astachai

1997. "INDEPEX '97" International Stamp Exhibition, New Delhi (4th issue). Women's Costumes. Multicoloured.
1741 2r. Type **1363** 30 20
1742 6r. Gujarat costume 60 65
1743 10r. Ladakh costume . . . 80 90
1744 11r. Kerala costume 80 90

1997. Centenary of Scindia School, Gwalior. Multicoloured.
1745 5r. Type **1364** 50 65
1746 5r. Gwalior Fort 50 65

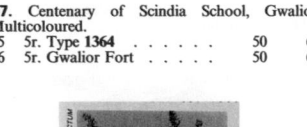

1365 "Ocimum sanctum"

1997. Medicinal Plants. Multicoloured.
1747 2r. Type **1365** 40 20
1748 5r. "Curcuma longa" . . . 60 60
1749 10r. "Rauvolfia serpentina" 85 95
1750 11r. "Aloe barbadensis" . . 85 95

1366 Sant Kavi Sunderdas
1367 K. Rama Rao

1997. 400th Birth Anniv (1996) of Sant Kavi Sunderdas (Hindu theologian).
1751 **1366** 2r. brown 60 30

1997. Birth Centenary of K. Rama Rao (parliamentarian and journalist).
1752 **1367** 2r. bistre and brown . . 75 30

1368 Jawaharlal Nehru and Child

1997. Children's Day.
1753 **1368** 2r. multicoloured . . . 35 30

1369 Animals on Globe
1370 Hazari Prasad Dwivedi

1997. World Convention on Reverence for All Life, Pune.
1754 **1369** 4r. multicoloured . . . 1·00 1·00

1997. 90th Birth Anniv of Hazari Prasad Dwivedi (scholar).
1755 **1370** 2r. grey 30 30

1372 Vallabhbhai Patel and Marchers

1997. 47th Death Anniv of Vallabhbhai Patel (politician).
1757 **1372** 2r. brown 35 30

1373 Head Post Office, Pune

1997. "INDEPEX '97" International Stamp Exhibition, New Delhi (5th issue). Post Office Heritage. Multicoloured.
1758 2r. Type **1373** 20 20
1759 6r. River mail barge 40 50
1760 10r. Jal Cooper (philatelist) and cancellations 70 85
1761 11r. "Hindoostan" (paddle-steamer) 70 85

1374 50th Anniversary Emblem

1997. 50th Anniv of Indian Armed Forces.
1762 **1374** 2r. multicoloured . . . 40 30

1375 Dr. Pattabhi Sitaramayya
1377 Ram Prasad Bismil and Ashfaqullah Khan

1376 Father Jerome d'Souza and Cathedral

1997. Dr. Pattabhi Sitaramayya (politician) Commemoration.
1763 **1375** 2r. brown 65 30

1997. Birth Centenary of Father Jerome d'Souza (academic).
1764 **1376** 2r. brown 30 30

1997. 70th Death Anniv of Ram Prasad Bismil and Ashfaqullah Khan (revolutionaries).
1765 **1377** 2r. brown 30 30

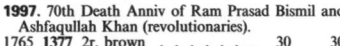

1378 Jail Buildings

1997. Cellular Jail, Port Blair.
1766 **1378** 2r. multicoloured . . . 30 30

1379 Sword and Kukri

1998. 50th Anniv of 11th Gorkha Rifles.
1767 **1379** 4r. multicoloured . . . 1·50 1·00

1380 Nahar Singh
1381 Nanak Singh

1998. 140th Death Anniv of Nahar Singh (Sikh leader).
1768 **1380** 2r. purple 30 30

1998. Birth Centenary (1997) of Nanak Singh (writer).
1769 **1381** 2r. red 30 30

1382 Rotary International Emblem

1998. Meeting of Rotary International Council on Legislation, Delhi.
1770 **1382** 8r. yellow and blue . . 65 80

1383 Maharana Pratap
1384 V. S. Khandekar

1998. 400th Death Anniv of Maharana Pratap (Rajput leader).
1771 **1383** 2r. purple 30 30

1998. Birth Centenary of V. S. Khandekar (writer).
1772 **1384** 2r. red 30 30

1385 Elephant and Dancers

1998. India Tourism Day.
1773 **1385** 10r. multicoloured . . . 1·50 1·50

1386 Jagdish Chandra Jain

1998. Jagdish Chandra Jain (educationist) Commemoration.
1774 **1386** 2r. brown 30 30

1387 Gandhi as a Young Man and Peasants in Fields
1388 A. Vedaratnam

1998. 50th Death Anniv of Mahatma Gandhi. Multicoloured.
1775 2r. Type **1387** 40 45
1776 6r. Woman weaving and Gandhi distributing food 65 75
1777 10r. Gandhi collecting salt 85 90
1778 11r. Gandhi carrying flag . . 85 90
Nos. 1775/8 were printed together, se-tenant, with the backgrounds forming a composite design.

1998. Birth Centenary (1997) of A. Vedaratnam (social reformer).
1779 **1388** 2r. purple 30 30

1389 Anniversary Emblem

1391 Sir Syed Ahmad Khan

1390 Savitribai Phule

1998. 50th Anniv of Universal Declaration of Human Rights.
1780 **1389** 6r. multicoloured . . . 50 60

1998. Death Centenary (1997) of Savitribai Phule (educational reformer).
1781 **1390** 2r. brown 30 30

1998. Death Centenary of Sir Syed Ahmed Khan (social reformer).
1782 **1391** 2r. brown 55 30

1392 Barren Landscape and Living Forest

1998. 1st Assembly Meeting of Global Environment Facility, Delhi.
1783 **1392** 11r. multicoloured . . . 1·00 1·25

1393 Ramana Maharshi

1998. Ramana Maharshi (religious leader) Commemoration.
1784 **1393** 2r. lilac 30 30

1394 College Arms

1998. 50th Anniv of Defence Services Staff College, Wellington.
1785 **1394** 6r. red 80 80

1395 Diesel Train on Viaduct (¾-size illustration)

1998. Completion of Konkan Railway.
1786 **1395** 8r. multicoloured . . . 1·00 1·25

1396 Narayan Ganesh Goray

1397 Dr. Zakir Husain

1998. Narayan Ganesh Goray (social reformer) Commemoration.
1787 **1396** 2r. brown 30 20

1998. Birth Centenary (1997) of Dr. Zakir Husain (former President of India).
1788 **1397** 2r. brown 30 20

1398 Mohammed Abdurahiman Shahib

1399 Lokanayak Omeo Kumar Das

1998. Mohammed Abdurahiman Shahib (nationalist) Commemoration.
1789 **1398** 2r. brown 30 20

1998. Lokanayak Omeo Kumar Das (writer) Commemoration.
1790 **1399** 2r. brown 30 20

1400 Vakkom Abdul Khader, Satyendra Chandra Bardhan and Fouja Singh

1998. Nationalist Martyrs Commemoration.
1791 **1400** 2r. brown and cinnamon 30 20

1401 Bishnu Dey, Tarashankar Bandopadhyay and Ashapurna Devi

1402 Big Ben, London

1998. Bangla Jnanpith Literary Award Winners Commemoration.
1792 **1401** 2r. brown 30 20

1998. 50th Anniv of First Air India International Flight.
1793 5r. Type **1402** 50 65
1794 6r. Lockheed Super Constellation airliner, globe and Gateway of India, Bombay (55 × 35 mm) 50 65
Nos. 1793/4 were printed together, se-tenant, forming a composite design.

1403 Dr. C. Vijiaraghavachariar

1405 Bhagawan Gopinathji

1404 Anniversary Logo and Savings Stream

1998. Dr. C. Vijiaraghavachariar (lawyer and social reformer) Commemoration.
1795 **1403** 2r. brown 60 30

1998. 50th Anniv of National Savings Organization. Multicoloured.
1796 5r. Type **1404** 35 40
1797 6r. Hand dropping coin into jar 35 40
Nos. 1796/7 were printed together, se-tenant, forming a composite design.

1998. Birth Centenary of Bhagawan Gopinathji (spiritual leader).
1798 **1405** 3r. brown 30 30

1406 Ardeshir and Pirojsha Godrej

1998. Centenary of Godrej (industrial conglomerate).
1799 **1406** 3r. green 30 30

1407 Aruna Asaf Ali

1998. Aruna Asaf Ali (nationalist) Commemoration.
1800 **1407** 3r. brown 30 30

1408 Iswar Chandra Vidyasagar (educationist) and College

1998. 125th Anniv of Vidyasagar College, Calcutta.
1801 **1408** 2r. black 20 15

1409 Shivpujan Sahai

1998. Shivpujan Sahai (writer) Commemoration.
1802 **1409** 2r. brown 20 15

1410 Red Fort, Delhi, and Spinning Wheel

1411 Gostha Behari Paul

1998. Homage to Martyrs for Independence. Multicoloured.
1803 3r. Type **1410** 30 30
1804 8r. Industrial and scientific development in modern India 70 90

1998. Gostha Paul (footballer) Commemoration.
1805 **1411** 3r. purple 30 20

1412 Youth Hostel and Logo

1998. 50th Anniv of Youth Hostels Association of India.
1806 **1412** 5r. multicoloured . . . 50 50

1413 Uniforms, Badge and Tank

1998. Bicentenary of 4th Battalion, Guards' Brigade (1 Rajput).
1807 **1413** 6r. multicoloured . . . 60 60

1414 Bhai Kanhaiyaji

1998. Bhai Kanhaiyaji (Sikh social reformer) Commemoration.
1808 **1414** 2r. red 20 15

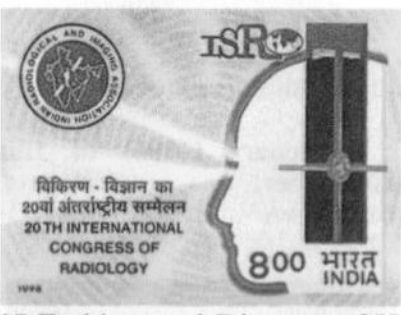

1415 Emblem and Diagram of Head

1998. 20th International Congress of Radiology.
1809 **1415** 8r. multicoloured . . . 1·00 1·10

1416 Dove of Peace and Boy reading Book

1417 Dr. Tristao Braganza Cunha

1998. 26th International Books for Young People Congress.
1810 **1416** 11r. multicoloured . . . 1·00 1·25

1998. Dr. Tristao Braganza Cunha (nationalist) Commemoration.
1811 **1417** 3r. brown 30 30

1418 Jananeta Hijam Irawat Singh

1419 Women Aviators and Bi-plane

1998. Jananeta Hijam Irawat Singh (social reformer) Commemoration.
1812 **1418** 3r. brown 30 30

1998. Indian Women's Participation in Aviation.
1813 **1419** 8r. blue . . . . 1·00 1·10

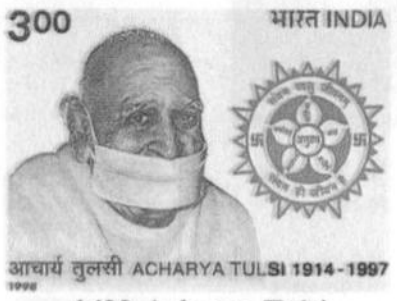

1420 Acharya Tulsi

1998. 1st Death Anniv of Acharya Tulsi (Jain religious leader).
1814 **1420** 3r. brown and orange 30 30

1421 Girl and Bird reading Book

1998. Children's Day.
1815 **1421** 3r. multicoloured . . . 30 30

1422 I.N.S. "Delhi" (destroyer)

1998. Navy Day.
1816 **1422** 3r. multicoloured . . . 50 40

1423 Mounted Trumpeter

1424 Sir David Sassoon and Library, Bombay

1998. 225th Anniv of President's Bodyguard.
1817 **1423** 3r. multicoloured . . . 65 40

1998. David Sassoon Library and Reading Room Commemoration.
1818 **1424** 3r. ultramarine and blue 30 30

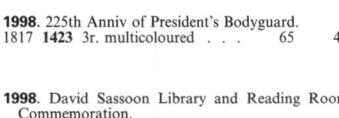

1425 Regimental Arms and Soldier

1998. Bicentenary of 2nd Battalion, Rajput Regiment.
1819 **1425** 3r. multicoloured . . . 75 45

1426 Army Postal Service Centre, Kamptee

1998. 50th Anniv of Army Postal Service Training Centre.
1820 **1426** 3r. multicoloured . . . 65 40

1427 Connemara Public Library, Madras

1998. Centenary (1996) of Connemara Public Library.
1821 **1427** 3r. brown and ochre . . 30 30

1428 Neem Tree and Leaves

1429 Baba Raghav Das

1998. 50th Anniv of The Indian Pharmaceutical Congress Association.
1822 **1428** 3r. multicoloured . . . 65 40

1998. 40th Death Anniv of Baba Raghav Das (social reformer).
1823 **1429** 2r. violet 20 15

1430 Lt. Indra Lal Roy D.F.C.

1998. Birth Centenary of Indra Lal Roy (First World War pilot).
1824 **1430** 3r. multicoloured . . . 65 40

1431 Sant Gadge Baba

1998. Sant Gadge Baba (social reformer) Commemoration.
1825 **1431** 3r. lilac, blue and black 30 30

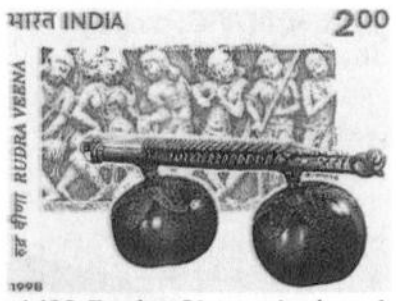

1432 Rudra Veena (stringed instrument)

1998. Musical Instruments. Multicoloured.
1826 2r. Type **1432** 30 15
1827 6r. Flute 55 45
1828 8r. Pakhawaj (wooden barrel drum) 70 80
1829 10r. Sarod (stringed instrument) 75 85

1433 "Chicoreus brunneus" (Murex shell)

1998. Shells. Multicoloured.
1830 3r. Type **1433** 50 50
1831 3r. "Cassis cornuta" (horned helmet) 50 50
1832 3r. "Cypraea staphylaea" (cowrie) 50 50
1833 11r. "Lambis lambis" (common spider conch) 1·40 1·60

1434 Stylized Police Officers

1999. 50th Anniv of Indian Police Service.
1834 **1434** 3r. multicoloured . . . 65 40

1435 Modern Weapon Systems

1999. 40th Anniv of Defence Research and Development Organization.
1835 **1435** 10r. multicoloured . . . 1·00 1·25

1436 Issue of "Orunodoi" (Assamese newspaper) for January, 1846

1999. 150th Anniv of Newspapers in Assam.
1836 **1436** 3r. black, yellow and orange 65 40

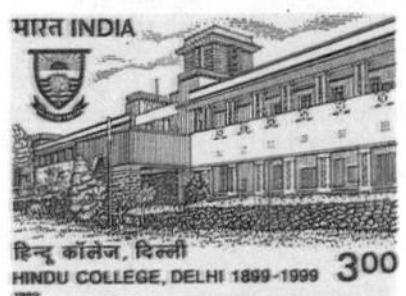

1437 College Building

1999. Centenary of Hindu College, Delhi.
1837 **1437** 3r. blue 30 30

1438 National Defence Academy and Military Equipment

1999. 50th Anniv of National Defence Academy, Khadakwasla.
1838 **1438** 3r. multicoloured . . . 70 45

1439 College Building

1999. 175th Anniv of Sanskrit College, Calcutta.
1839 **1439** 3r. brown and ochre . . 70 45

1440 Patnaik and Tugs

1441 Globe and Satellite Dish

1999. Biju Patnaik (social reformer) Commemoration.
1840 **1440** 3r. brown and green . . 65 40

1999. 50th Anniv of Press Trust of India.
1841 **1441** 15r. multicoloured . . . 1·10 1·50

1442 "Apsara removing a Thorn from her Foot" (temple statue)

1443 Dr. K. B. Hedgewar

1999. Millenary of the Khajuraho Temples.
1842 **1442** 15r. deep brown, light brown and black . . 1·10 1·50

1999. Dr. Keshavrao Hedgewar (founder of Rashtriya Swayamsevak Sangha) Commemoration.
1843 **1443** 3r. multicoloured . . . 30 30

1444 Terracotta Model Boat from Lothal, 2200 B.C., and Seal

1999. Maritime Heritage. Multicoloured.
1844 3r. Type **1444** 40 50
1845 3r. Ghurab (sailing ship) of Kanhoji Angre, 1700 . . 40 50

1445 Anandpur Sahib Temple

1999. 300th Anniv of the Khalsa Panth (Sikh Order).
1846 **1445** 3r. multicoloured . . . 75 45

1446 Bethune College

1999. 150th Anniv of Bethune Collegiate School, Calcutta.
1847 **1446** 3r. green 30 30

1447 Plane, Satellite and Rocket orbiting Globe

1999. Technology Day.
1848 **1447** 3r. multicoloured . . . 30 30

1448 Mumbai Port

1449 Handshake and Airliner

1999. 125th Anniv of Mumbai (Bombay) Port Trust.
1849 **1448** 3r. blue 30 30

1999. Mizoram Accord (peace agreement) Commemoration.
1850 **1449** 3r. multicoloured . . . 30 30

1450 Gulzarilal Nanda

1451 Jijabai and Chatrapati Shivaji

1999. Birth Centenary of Gulzarilal Nanda (former Prime Minster).
1851 **1450** 3r. multicoloured . . . 30 30

1999. Jijabai (mother of Chatrapati Shivaji (Maratha leader)) Commemoration.
1852 **1451** 3r. purple 30 30

1452 P. S. Kumaraswamy Raja

1999. P. S. Kumaraswamy Raja (politician) Commemoration.
1853 **1452** 3r. brown and blue . . 30 30

1453 Balai Chand Mukhopadhyay

1999. Birth Centenary of Balai Chand Mukhopadhyay ("Banaphool") (Bengali writer).
1854 **1453** 3r. blue 30 30

1454 River Sindhu, Ladakh

1999. Sindhu Darshan Festival.
1855 **1454** 3r. multicoloured . . . 30 30

1455 Soldier and Young Girl

1999. 50th Anniv of Geneva Conventions.
1856 **1455** 15r. black and red . . . 1·10 1·50

1456 Sardar Ajit Singh

1457 Kalki Krishnamurthy

1999. Heroes of Struggle for Freedom.
1857 **1456** 3r. brown and red . . . 30 30
1858 – 3r. brown and blue . . 30 30
1859 – 3r. blue and red 30 30
1860 – 3r. purple and drab . . 30 30
DESIGNS: No. 1858, Swami Ramanand Teerth; No. 1859, Vishwambhar Dayalu Tripathi; No. 1860, Swami Keshawanand.

1999. Birth Centenary of Kalki Krishnamurthy (Tamil writer).
1861 **1457** 3r. grey 25 25

1458 Ramdhari Sinha

1999. Ramdhari Sinha "Dinkar" (poet) Commemoration.
1862 **1458** 3r. brown and blue . . 25 25

1459 Jhaverchand Kalidas Meghani and Graves

1999. Jhaverchand Kalidas Meghani (writer) Commemoration.
1863 **1459** 3r. red and green . . . 25 25

1460 Rambrikish Benipuri and Statue of Horse

1999. Rambrikish Benipuri (writer and journalist) Commemoration.
1864 **1460** 3r. brown and light brown 25 25

1461 Kazi Nazrul Islam

1999. Birth Centenary of Kazi Nazrul Islam (Bengali poet).
1865 **1461** 3r. sepia and yellow . . 25 25

1462 Arati Gupta

1999. Arati Gupta (swimmer) Commemoration.
1866 **1462** 3r. multicoloured . . . 25 25

1463 Lionesses

1999. Endangered Species. Asiatic Lion. Mult.
1867 3r. Type **1463** 35 35
1868 3r. Lions and lionesses lying down 35 35
1869 3r. Lioness with cubs . . . 35 35
1870 15r. Two lions . . . . . . 1·10 1·50

1464 A. D. Shroff

1465 A. B. Walawalkar and Map

1999. A. D. Shroff (economist) Commemoration.
1871 **1464** 3r. green and brown . . 25 25

1999. A. B. Walawalkar (railway engineer) Commemoration.
1872 **1465** 3r. purple 30 25

1466 Chhaganlal K. Parekh and Medical Staff with Child

1999. Chhaganlal K. Parekh (social reformer) Commemoration.
1873 **1466** 3r. blue and brown . . 30 25

1467 Dr. T. M. A. Pai and Hospital

1999. 20th Death Anniv of Dr. T. M. A. Pai (educator).
1874 **1467** 3r. chocolate and stone 30 25

1468 Chhau Dance Masks

1999. 125th Anniv of Universal Postal Union. Traditional Arts and Crafts. Multicoloured.
1875 3r. Type **1468** 40 40
1876 3r. Elephant and horseman (Rathva wall painting) (vert) 40 40
1877 3r. Man ploughing (Muria ritual collar) 40 40
1878 15r. Angami ornament (vert) 1·10 1·50

1469 Veerapandia Kattabomman

1470 Ustad Allauddin Khan Saheb (sarod player)

1999. Death Bicentenary of Veerapandia Kattabomman (ruler of Panchalankuruchi).
1879 **1469** 3r. green 25 25

1999. Modern Masters of Indian Classical Music. Multicoloured.
1880 3r. Type **1470** 25 25
1881 3r. Musiri Subramania Iyer (singer) 25 25

1471 Brigadier Rajinder Singh

1472 Elephant and Rhinoceros

1999. Birth Centenary of Brigadier Rajinder Singh (First recipient of M.V.C. medal).
1882 **1471** 3r. purple 30 25

1999. Children's Day.
1883 **1472** 3r. multicoloured . . . 30 25

1473 Dam and Pumping Station

1999. Sri Sathya Sai Water Supply Project.
1884 **1473** 3r. multicoloured . . . 50 30

1474 Supreme Court, New Delhi

1999. 50th Anniv of Supreme Court of India.
1885 **1474** 3r. multicoloured . . . 25 25

1475 A. Vaidyanatha Iyer and Temple Tower

1999. March of Progress.
1886 **1475** 3r. red 30 30
1887 – 3r. brown and green . . 30 30
1888 – 3r. buff and black . . . 30 30
1889 – 3r. brown and green . . 30 30
DESIGNS: No. 1887, Dr. Punjabrao Deshmukh and symbols of agriculture; 1888, Indulal Kanaiyalal Yagnik and newspaper; 1889, Kakkan and machinery.

1476 Aspects of Thermal Power

1999. Centenary of Thermal Power.
1890 **1476** 3r. chocolate and brown 25 25

1477 "Hindustan Times" Front Pages from 1950 and 1999

1999. 75th Anniv of "Hindustan Times" Newspaper.
1891 **1477** 15r. multicoloured . . . 1·10 1·40

1478 Three Faces ("Small Family by Choice")

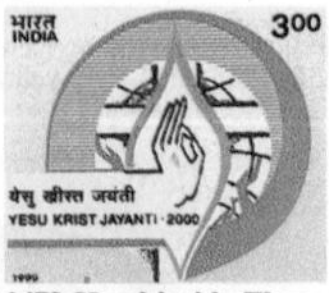

1479 Hand inside Flame in front of Cross

1999. 50th Anniv of Family Planning Association of India.
1892 **1478** 3r. multicoloured . . . 25 25

1999. 2000th Birth Anniv of Jesus Christ.
1893 **1479** 3r. multicoloured . . . 50 25

1480 Tabo Monastery and Mountains

1999. New Millennium. Unity in Diversity. Mult.
1894 5r. Type **1480** 50 60
1895 10r. Traditional scene . . . 60 80

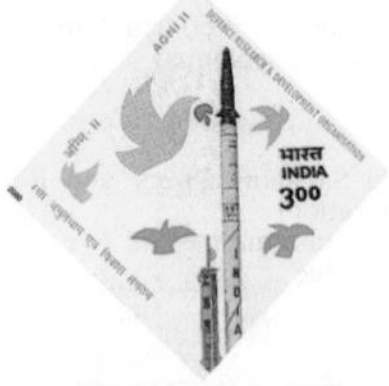

1481 Agni II Rocket and Dove

2000. 41st Anniv of Defence Research and Development Organization.
1896 **1481** 3r. multicoloured . . . 30 25

1482 Sunrise

2000. New Millennium.
1897 **1482** 3r. multicoloured . . . 25 25

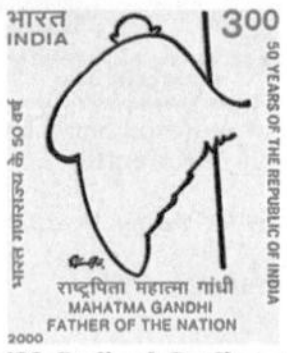

1483 Stylized Outline of Gandhi as Map of India

2000. 50th Anniv of Republic (1st issue).
1898 **1483** 3r. black and red . . . 20 20

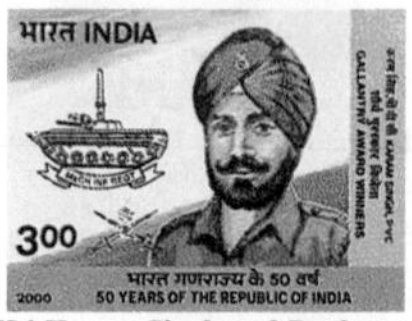

1484 Karam Singh and Regimental Badge

2000. 50th Anniv of Republic (2nd issue). Gallantry Award Winners. Multicoloured.
1899 3r. Type **1484** 25 25
1900 3r. Abdul Hamid and armed jeep 25 25
1901 3r. Albert Ekka, hand grenades and knife . . . 25 25
1902 3r. N. J. S. Sekhon and jet fighter 25 25
1903 3r. M. N. Mulla and warship 25 25

1485 Batagur Terrapin

2000. "Millepex 2000" Stamp Exhibition, Bhubaneshwar. Endangered Species. Multicoloured.
1904 3r. Type **1485** 20 20
1905 3r. Olive Ridley turtle . . . 20 20

1486 Balwantrai Mehta

1487 Dr. Harekrushna Mahatab

2000. Balwantrai Mehta (former Chief Minister of Gujarot) Commemoration.
1906 **1486** 3r. multicoloured . . . 20 20

2000. Dr. Harekrushna Mahatab (former Chief Minister of Orissa) Commemoration.
1907 **1487** 3r. multicoloured . . . 20 20

1488 Arun Kumar Chanda

1490 Dr. Burgula Ramakrishna Rao

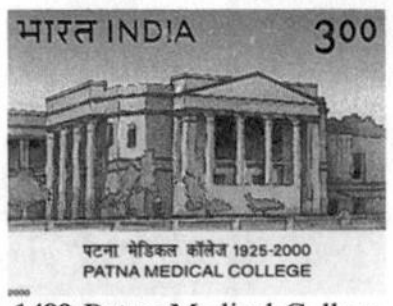

1489 Patna Medical College

2000. Arun Kumar Chanda (trade union leader) Commemoration.
1908 **1488** 3r. multicoloured . . . 20 20

2000. 75th Anniv of Patna Medical College.
1909 **1489** 3r. multicoloured . . . 20 15

2000. Birth Centenary (1999) of Dr. Burgula Ramakrishna Rao (Hyderabad Chief Minister).
1910 **1490** 3r. brown and yellow 20 15

1491 Potti Sriramulu

2000. Potti Sriramulu (Harijan activist) Commemoration.
1911 **1491** 3r. red 20 15

1492 Basawon Sinha

1493 Siroi Lily

2000. Basawon Sinha (politician) Commemoration.
1912 **1492** 3r. multicoloured . . . 20 15

2000. "Indepex Asiana 2000" International Stamp Exhibition, Calcutta (1st issue). Flora and Fauna of Manipur and Tripura. Multicoloured.
1913 3r. Type **1493** 35 35
1914 3r. Sangai deer 35 35
1915 3r. Wild guava 35 35
1916 15r. Slow loris . . . . . . 1·25 1·50
See also Nos. 1934/7 and 1966/71.

1494 Maharshi Dayananda Saraswati, Flame and Pages

2000. 125th Anniv of Arya Samaj (philosophical movement).
1918 **1494** 3r. multicoloured . . . 50 20

1495 Kankrej Breed

2000. Indigenous Breeds of Cattle. Multicoloured.
1919 3r. Type **1495** 40 40
1920 3r. Kangayam 40 40
1921 3r. Gir 40 40
1922 15r. Hallikar . . . . 1·25 1·50

1496 Blackbuck

1497 Leopard Cat

2000. Wildlife.
1923 **1496** 25p. brown 10 10
1924 – 50p. brown 10 10
1925 – 1r. blue 10 10
1925a – 2r. purple 10 10
1926 – 3r. violet 10 10
1927 – 4r. red 10 15
1928 **1497** 5r. brown and green 15 20
1929 – 10r. orange, brn & grn 25 30
1930 – 15r. red, brn & dp brn 40 45
1931 – 20r. yellow and green 50 55
1932 – 50r. red, brown & blue 1·30 1·40
DESIGNS—VERT (as Type **1496**): 50p. Nilgiri tahr; 1r. Saras crane ("Saras Crane"); 2r. Rose. As Type **1497**: 4r. Painted stork. (19 × 37 mm): 20r. Amaltaas (plant); 50r. Asiatic paradise flycatcher (bird) ("Paradise Flycatcher"). HORIZ (as Type **1497**): 3r. Smooth Indian otters. (37 × 19 mm): 10r. Tiger, Sundarban Reserve; 15r. Butterfly.

1498 Railway Locomotive at Dehradoon Station

2000. Centenary of Doon Valley Railway.
1933 **1498** 15r. multicoloured . . . 1·50 1·50

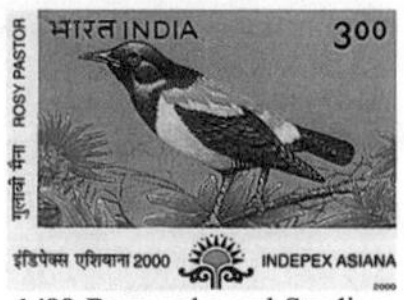

1499 Rose-coloured Starling ("Rosy Pastor")

2000. "Indepex Asiana 2000" International Stamp Exhibition, Calcutta (2nd issue). Migratory Birds. Multicoloured.
1934 3r. Type **1499** 50 50
1935 3r. Garganey ("Garganey Teal") 50 50
1936 3r. Forest wagtail 50 50
1937 3r. White stork 50 50
MS1938 157 × 114 mm. Nos. 1934/7 1·75 1·75

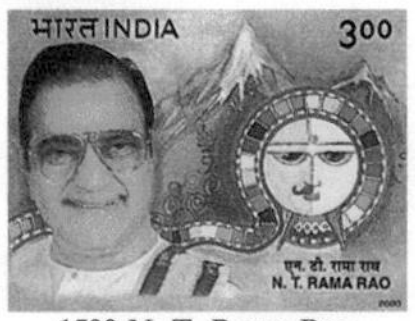

1500 N. T. Rama Rao

2000. Nandamuri Taraka Rama Rao (former Chief Minister of Andhra Pradesh) Commemoration.
1939 **1500** 3r. multicoloured . . . 20 10

1501 Swami Saraswati

1503 Vijaya Lakshmi Pandit (diplomat)

1502 Christian Medical College and Hospital, Vellore

2000. 50th Death Anniv of Swami Sahajanand Saraswati (rural reformer).
1940 **1501** 3r. mauve, brn & stone 20 10

2000. Centenary of Christian Medical College and Hospital, Vellore.
1941 **1502** 3r. multicoloured . . . 20 10

2000. Social and Political Leaders. Each including the Indian flag. Multicoloured.
1942 3r. Type **1503** 30 30
1943 3r. Bahadur R. Srinivasan (social reformer) 30 30
1944 3r. Jaglal Choudhary (social reformer) 30 30
1945 3r. Radha Gobinda Baruah (social reformer) 30 30

1504 Mountain, River and Tree inside Open Book

2000. Centenary of Kodaikanal International School.
1946 **1504** 15r. multicoloured . . . 1·00 1·25

1505 Discus

2000. Olympic Games, Sydney. Multicoloured.
1947 3r. Type **1505** 25 15
1948 6r. Tennis 40 35
1949 10r. Hockey 75 75
1950 15r. Weightlifting . . . . . 1·00 1·25

1506 "Oceansat-1"

2000. India's Space Programme. Multicoloured.
1951 3r. Type **1506** 40 40
1952 3r. "Insat 3B" in orbit . . . 40 40
1953 3r. Astronaut with flag, planets and spacecraft (vert) 40 40
1954 3r. Earth and spacecraft (vert) 40 40
Nos. 1953/4 were printed together, se-tenant, with the backgrounds forming a composite design.

1507 Krishna with Gopies (Anmana Devi)

2000. Madhubani-Mithila Paintings. Multicoloured.
1955 3r. Type **1507** 30 30
1956 3r. "Flower Girls" (Nirmala Devi) 30 30
1957 3r. "Ball and Sugriva" (Sanjula) (vert) 30 30
1958 5r. Geometrical pattern with sedan chair at foot (vert) 50 50
1959 10r. Geometrical pattern with elephant at foot (vert) 75 85

1508 Raj Kumar Shukla

1509 Dr. Shanker Dayal Sharma

2000. 125th Birth Anniv of Raj Kumar Shukla (social reformer).
1960 **1508** 3r. brown and buff . . 30 20

2000. 1st Death Anniv of Dr. Shanker Dayal Sharma (former President of India).
1961 **1509** 3r. multicoloured . . . 30 20

1510 Subhas Chandra Bose

1512 Maharaja Bijli Pasi

1511 "My Best Friend" (Phuhar Uppal)

2000.
1962 **1510** 1r. brown 10 10
1963 – 2r. black 10 10
1963a – 3r. blue 10 10
DESIGNS: 2r. Vallabhbhai Patel. 3r. Dr. B. R. Ambedkar.

2000. Children's Day.
1964 **1511** 3r. multicoloured . . . 40 25

2000. Maharaja Bijli Pasi of Bijnor Commemoration.
1965 **1512** 3r. multicoloured . . . 30 20

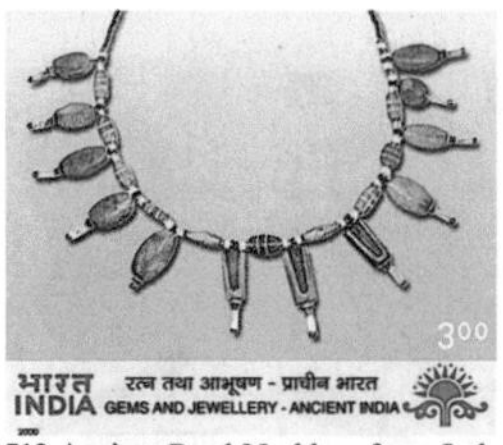

1513 Ancient Bead Necklace from Indus Valley

2000. "Indepex Asiana 2000" International Stamp Exhibition, Calcutta (3rd issue). Gems and Jewellery. Multicoloured.
1966 3r. Type **1513** 30 30
1967 3r. Gold necklace from Taxila 30 30
1968 3r. Turban ornament from Sarpech 30 30
1969 3r. Navaratna necklace . . 30 30
1970 3r. Bridal necklace from South India 30 30
1971 3r. Temple necklace from Rajasthan 30 30
MS1972 162 × 111 mm. Nos. 1966/7 and 1969/70 (sold at 15r.) . . . 1·60 1·75

1514 17th-century Marakkars Galley

2000. 400th Death Anniv of Admiral Kunjali IV Marakkars.
1973 **1514** 3r. multicoloured . . . 60 25

1515 Ustad Hafiz Ali Khan

2000. Ustad Hafiz Ali Khan (musician) Commemoration.
1974 **1515** 3r. multicoloured . . . 40 25

1516 Prithviraj Chauhan, King of Delhi

1518 Sane Guruji (writer)

1517 "St. Aloysius with Children" (painting)

2000. Historical Personalities. Multicoloured.
1975 3r. Type **1516** 35 35
1976 3r. Raja Bhamashah, Dewan of Mewar 35 35
1977 3r. Rajarshi Bhagyachandra, King of Manipur 35 35
1978 3r. General Zorawar Singh of Kashmir (horiz) . . . 35 35

2001. Centenary of Paintings in St. Aloysius College Chapel, Mangalore.
1979 **1517** 15r. multicoloured . . . 1·25 1·40

2001. Personalities. Multicoloured.
1980 3r. Type **1518** 35 35
1981 3r. E. M. S. Namboodiripad (Kerala politician) 35 35
1982 3r. Giani Gurmukh Singh Musafir (Punjab politician) 35 35
1983 3r. Prof. N. G. Ranga (social reformer) 35 35

1519 Sheel Bhadra Yajee
1520 Jubba Sahni

2001. Sheel Bhadra Yajee (patriot) Commemoration.
1984 **1519** 3r. multicoloured . . . 25 20

2001. Personalities. Multicoloured.
1985 3r. Type **1520** 25 25
1986 3r. Yogendra and Baikunth Shukla (patriot) 25 25

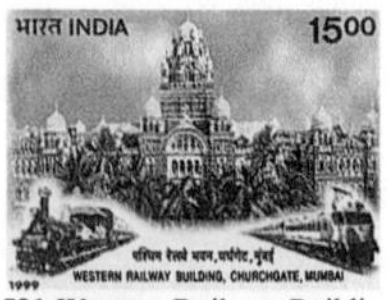

1521 Western Railway Building

2001. Western Railway Building, Churchgate, Mumbai.
1987 **1521** 15r. multicoloured . . . 1·00 1·10

1522 Census Emblem

2001. Census of India.
1988 **1522** 3r. multicoloured . . . 25 20

1523 *Tarangini* (cadet ship)

2001. International Fleet Review. Multicoloured.
1989 3r. Type **1523** 25 25
1990 3r. Maratha pal (sailing ship) 25 25
1991 3r. Maratha galbat (sailing ship) 25 25
1992 15r. Fleet Review logo . . . 1·00 1·10

1524 Rocks and Minerals

2001. 150th Anniv of Geological Survey of India.
1993 **1524** 3r. multicoloured . . . 25 20

1525 Soldier in Ceremonial Uniform and Himalaya Patrol
1526 Symbols of Jain Teaching

2001. Bicentenary of 4th Battalion, Maratha Light Infantry.
1994 **1525** 3r. multicoloured . . . 30 20

2001. 2600th Birth Anniv of Bhagwan Mahavira (Jain teacher).
1995 **1526** 3r. multicoloured . . . 30 20

1527 Yuri Gagarin and Rockets

2001. 40th Anniv of Man's First Space Flight.
1996 **1527** 15r. multicoloured . . . 1·00 1·10

1528 Frederic Chopin

2001. 190th Birth Anniv (2002) of Frederic Chopin (composer).
1997 **1528** 15r. multicoloured . . . 1·25 1·40

1529 Suraj Narain Singh
1530 B. P. Mandal

2001. Suraj Narain Singh (nationalist politician) Commemoration.
1998 **1529** 3r. multicoloured . . . 25 20

2001. B. P. Mandal (former Chief Minister of Bihar) Commemoration.
1999 **1530** 3r. multicoloured . . . 25 20

1531 Samanta Chandra Sekhar, Stars and Gola Yantra (instrument)
1532 "Sant Ravidas" (Phulan Runi)

2001. Samanta Chandra Sekhar (astronomer) Commemoration.
2000 **1531** 3r. black, vio & grn . . 25 20

2001. Sant Ravidas (philosopher-poet) Commem.
2001 **1532** 3r. multicoloured . . . 25 20

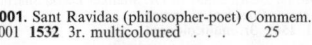

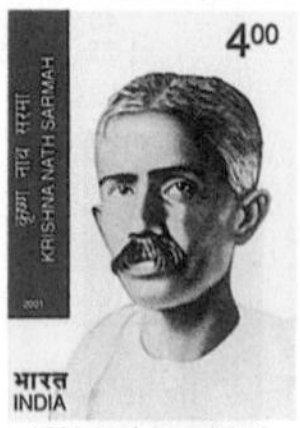

1533 Krishna Nath Sarmah
1535 Jhalkari Bai on Horseback

1534 Chandragupta Maurya

2001. Personalities. Multicoloured.
2002 4r. Type **1533** 40 40
2003 4r. C. Sankaran Nair (lawyer) 40 40
2004 4r. Syama Prasad Mookerjee (politician) 40 40
2005 4r. U Kiang Nongbah (guerilla leader) 40 40

2001. Emperor Chandragupta Maurya Commem.
2006 **1534** 4r. multicoloured . . . 30 30

2001. Jhalkari Bai (female warrior from Jhansi) Commemoration.
2007 **1535** 4r. multicoloured . . . 30 30

1536 *Fungia horrida* (coral)

2001. Corals. Multicoloured.
2008 4r. Type **1536** 20 20
2009 4r. *Acropora digitifera* . . . 20 20
2010 15r. *Montipora acquituberculata* 75 75
2011 45r. *Acropora formosa* . . . 1·75 2·25

1537 Dwarka Prasad Mishra
1538 Chaudhary Brahmparkash

2001. Birth Centenary of Dwarka Prasad Mishra (former Chief Minister of Madhya Pradesh).
2012 **1537** 4r. black and stone . . 25 20

2001. Chaudhary Brahmparkash (former Chief Minister of Delhi) Commemoration.
2013 **1538** 4r. black and blue . . . 25 20

1539 Revolution Monument, Shaheed Park, Ballia
1540 Jagdev Prasad

2001. 60th Anniv (2000) of August Revolution, Ballia.
2014 **1539** 4r. multicoloured . . . 25 20

2001. Jagdev Prasad (journalist and politician) Commemoration.
2015 **1540** 4r. multicoloured . . . 25 20

1541 Rani Avantibai
1542 Rao Tula Ram

2001. Rani Avantibai of Ramgarh Commemoration.
2016 **1541** 4r. multicoloured . . . 25 20

2001. Rao Tula Ram of Rewari (patriot) Commemoration.
2017 **1542** 4r. multicoloured . . . 25 20

1543 Chaudhary Devi Lal
1544 Satis Chandra Samanta

2001. Chaudhary Devi Lal (former Deputy Prime Minister) Commemoration.
2018 **1543** 4r. multicoloured . . . 25 20

2001. Satis Chandra Samanta (West Bengal politician) Commemoration.
2019 **1544** 4r. black and stone . . 25 20

1545 Sivaji Ganesan
1546 Gandhi on Salt March

2001. Sivaji Ganesan (Tamil actor) Commemoration.
2020 **1545** 4r. multicoloured . . . 30 20

2001. "Mahatma Gandhi—Man of the Millennium". Multicoloured.
2021 4r. Type **1546** 30 30
2022 4r. Mahatma Gandhi . . . 30 30

1547 Bharathidsan (Tamil poet)

2001. Cultural Personalities. Each black, red and stone.
2023 4r. Type **1547** 25 25
2024 4r. Lachhu Maharaj (choreographer) 25 25
2025 4r. Master Mitrasen (writer) 25 25

1548 Jayaprakash Narayan

2001. Birth Centenary (2002) of Jayaprakash Narayan (socialist).
2026 **1548** 4r. multicoloured . . . 25 25

1549 Monkey in Tree and Crocodile

2001. Stories from "Panchatantra" (Indian fables). Multicoloured.
2027 4r. Type **1549** 20 25
2028 4r. Monkey on crocodile's back (29 × 39 mm) . . . 20 25

2029 4r. Lion and rabbit 20 25
2030 4r. Lion and rabbit at well (29 × 39 mm) 20 25
2031 4r. Snake attacking crows' eggs 20 25
2032 4r. Snake attacked by villagers (29 × 39 mm) . . 20 25
2033 4r. Geese and tortoise talking 20 25
2034 4r. Tortoise flying with geese (29 × 39 mm) 20 25

1550 Grocer selling Iodized Salt

1551 Thangal Kunju Musaliar

2001. Global Iodine Deficiency Disorders Day.
2035 **1550** 4r. multicoloured . . . 30 25

2001. Thangal Kunju Musaliar (industrialist and philanthropist) Commemoration.
2036 **1551** 4r. black and stone . . 30 25

1552 Woman self-examining for Breast Cancer

1553 Maharajah Ranjit Singh

2001. Cancer Awareness Day.
2037 **1552** 4r. multicoloured . . . 30 25

2001. Bicentenary of Ranjit Singh's Coronation as Maharajah of the Punjab.
2038 **1553** 4r. multicoloured . . . 25 20

1554 Hands clasped around Globe

1556 Sobha Singh

1555 Dr. V. Shantaram and Film Scene

2001. Children's Day.
2039 **1554** 4r. multicoloured . . . 25 20

2001. Birth Centenary of Dr. V. Shantaram (film director).
2040 **1555** 4r. multicoloured . . . 25 20

2001. Birth Centenary of Sobha Singh (painter).
2041 **1556** 4r. multicoloured . . . 25 20

1557 Sun Temple, Konark

2001. Centenary of Conservation at Sun Temple, Konark. Multicoloured.
2042 4r. Type **1557** 25 20
2043 15r. Giant carved wheel, Sun Temple, Konark . . 1·00 1·25

1558 Handshake above Three Symbolic Figures

2001. International Year of Volunteers.
2044 **1558** 4r. multicoloured . . . 25 20

1559 Raj Kapoor and Film Characters

2001. Raj Kapoor (film actor and director) Commemoration.
2045 **1559** 4r. multicoloured . . . 50 25

1560 Digboi Refinery

2001. Centenary of Digboi Oil Refinery, Assam.
2046 **1561** 4r. multicoloured . . . 50 25

1561 Flowers, Fireworks and Christmas Tree

1562 Vijaya Raje Scindia

2001. Greetings. Multicoloured.
2047 3r. Type **1561** 30 20
2048 4r. Butterflies and flowers 40 35

2001. Vijaya Raje Scindia (politician and social reformer) Commemoration.
2049 **1562** 4r. multicoloured . . . 10 15

1563 Kedarnath Temple, Uttaranchal

2001. "Inpex-Empirepex 2001" National Stamp Exhibition. Temple Architecture.
2050 **1563** 4r. brown & lt brn . . 20 20
2051 – 4r. brown & lt brn . . 20 20
2052 – 4r. brown & lt brn . . 20 20
2053 – 15r. brown & lt brn . . 60 75
DESIGNS: No. 2051, Tryambakeshwar Temple, Maharashtra; 2052, Aundha Nagnath Temple, Maharashtra; 2053, Rameswaram Temple.

1564 Mine Winding Gear and Helmet in Hand

1565 Mount Everest and Climber

2002. Centenary of Directorate General of Mines Safety.
2054 **1564** 4r. multicoloured . . . 50 20

2002. Indian Army Expedition to Mt. Everest (2001).
2055 **1565** 4r. multicoloured . . . 50 20

1566 Gridhakuta Hills, Rajgir

2002. Bauddha Mahotsav Festival. Multicoloured.
2056 4r. Type **1566** 25 25
2057 4r. Dhamek Stupa, Sarnath 25 25
2058 8r. Mahaparinirvana Temple, Kushinagar . . . 50 50
2059 15r. Mahabodhi Temple, Bodhgaya . . . . 1·25 1·40

1567 Cartoon of Boy reading

2002. Year of Books.
2060 **1567** 4r. multicoloured . . . 50 20

1568 Swami Ramanand (mystic)

2002. Swami Ramanand (mystic) Commemoration.
2061 **1568** 4r. multicoloured . . . 50 20

1569 Tank and 19th-century Cannon

2002. Bicentenary of Indian Ordnance Factories.
2062 **1569** 4r. multicoloured . . . 50 20

1570 Sido and Kanhu Murmu

2002. Sido and Kanhu Murmu (Santal resistance fighters) Commemoration.
2063 **1570** 4r. multicoloured . . . 50 20

1571 First Railway Train, 1853

2002. 150th Anniv of Indian Railways.
2064 **1571** 15r. multicoloured . . . 1·00 1·10
MS2065 112 × 75 mm. No. 2064 1·00 1·25

1572 Kathakali Dancer (India)

2002. 50th Anniv of Diplomatic Relations between India and Japan. Multicoloured.
2066 15r. Type **1572** . . . . . . 95 1·00
2067 15r. Kabuki actor (Japan) 95 1·00
MS2068 100 × 70 mm. Nos. 2066/7 1·90 2·00

1573 Central Hall of Parliament, New Delhi

2002. 50th Anniv of Indian Parliament.
2069 **1573** 4r. gold 50 20

1574 Prabodhankar Thackeray

2002. Prabodhankar Thackeray (writer) Commemoration.
2070 **1574** 4r. black 50 20

1575 Cotton College, Guwahati

2002. Centenary of Cotton College (2001), Assam.
2071 **1575** 4r. purple and green . . 50 20

1576 P. L. Deshpande

2002. P. L. Deshpande (writer) Commemoration.
2072 **1576** 4r. multicoloured . . . 50 20

1577 Babu Gulabrai

1578 Brajlal Biyani

2002. Indian Literary Figures. Multicoloured.
2073 5r. Type **1577** 50 50
2074 5r. Pandit Vyas 50 50

2002. Brajlal Biyani (journalist and politician) Commemoration.
2075 **1578** 4r. multicoloured . . . 50 20

1579 Sree Thakur Satyananda

1580 Anna Bhau Sathe

2002. Sree Thakur Satyananda Commemoration.
2076 **1579** 5r. multicoloured . . . 55 35

2002. Anna Bhau Sathe (Marathi writer) Commemoration.
2077 **1580** 4r. black and grey . . . 50 20

1581 Anand Rishiji Maharaj

2002. 10th Death Anniv of Anand Rishiji Maharaj (Jain spiritual leader).
2078 **1581** 4r. multicoloured . . . 50 20

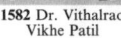

1582 Dr. Vithalrao Vikhe Patil **1583** Sant Tukaram

2002. Dr. Vithalrao Vikhe Patil (co-operative movement pioneer) Commemoration.
2079 **1582** 4r. multicoloured . . . 50 20

2002. Sant Tukaram (Marathi poet) Commemoration.
2080 **1583** 4r. multicoloured . . . 50 20

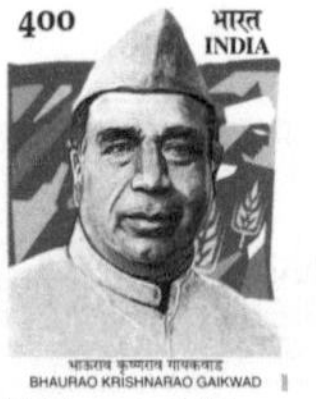

1584 Bhaurao Krishnarao Gaikwad

2002. Birth Centenary of Bhaurao Krishnarao Gaikwad (social reformer).
2081 **1584** 4r. multicoloured . . . 50 20

1585 Ayyan Kali

2002. Social Reformers. Multicoloured.
2082 5r. Type **1585** 40 50
2083 5r. Chandraprabha Saikiani 40 50
2084 5r. Gora 40 50

1586 Ananda Nilayam Vimanam, Tirumala

2002. 700th Anniv of Ananda Nilayam Vimanam Temple Tower, Tirumala.
2085 **1586** 15r. multicoloured . . . 1·00 1·10

1587 Kanika Bandopadhyay

2002. Kanika Bandopadhyay (singer) Commemoration.
2086 **1587** 5r. multicoloured . . . 55 35

1588 Arya Vaidya Sala, Kottakkal, and Vaidyaratnam Varier (founder)

2002. Centenary of Arya Vaidya Kottakkal Sala (Ayurvedic Medicine), Kottakkal.
2087 **1588** 5r. multicoloured . . . 70 70

1589 Bhagwan Baba **1590** Bihar Chamber of Commerce Logo

2002. Bhagwan Baba (mystic and philosopher) Commemoration.
2088 **1589** 5r. multicoloured . . . 70 70

2002. 75th Anniv (2001) of Bihar Chamber of Commerce.
2089 **1590** 4r. multicoloured . . . 60 40

1591 Asiatic Mangrove (*Rhizophora mucronata*)

2002. 8th Session of U.N. Conference on Climate Change, New Delhi. Mangroves. Multicoloured.
2090 5r. Type **1591** 30 30
2091 5r. Mangrove palm (*Nypa fruticans*) 30 30
2092 5r. Burma mangrove (*Bruguiera gymnorrhiza*) 30 30
2093 15r. Mangrove apple (*Sonneratia alba*) . . . . 1·10 1·25
MS2094 192 × 85 mm. Nos. 2090/3 1·75 1·90

1592 Swami Pranavananda

2002. Swami Pranavananda (social reformer) Commemoration.
2095 **159** 5r. multicoloured . . . . 1·00 1·00

1593 Vidhan Bhavan (State Assembly Building) and Samadhi (Buddhist Temple), Nagpur

2002. 300th Anniv of Nagpur.
2096 **1593** 5r. multicoloured . . . 70 70

1594 "Holi Festival" (Aakash Anand)

2002. Children's Day.
2097 **1594** 5r. multicoloured . . . 70 70

1595 Cane and Bamboo Ware

2002. Handicrafts. Multicoloured.
2098 5r. Type **1595** 40 45
2099 5r. Thewa ware (gold leaf work on coloured glass) 40 45
2100 5r. Patola fabric 40 45
2101 5r. Dhokra ornaments (metal casting) 40 45
MS2102 100 × 100 mm. Nos. 2098/101 . . . . 1·40 1·60

1596 Santidev Ghose

2002. Santidev Ghose (classical singer) Commemoration.
2103 **1596** 5r. multicoloured . . . 70 70

1597 Ajoy Kumar Mukherjee (leader) and Newspaper

2002. 60th Anniv of "National Government" of Tamluk (Tamralipta Jatiya Sarkar). Multicoloured.
2104 5r. Type **1597** 65 65
2105 5r. Matangini Hazra and demonstration 65 65

1598 Anglo Bengali Inter College, Allahabad

2002. Anglo-Bengali Inter College, Allahabad.
2106 **1598** 5r. multicoloured . . . 15 20

1599 Gurukula Kangri Vishwavidyalaya University, Hardwar

2002. Gurukula Kangri Vishwavidyalaya University, Hardwar Commemoration.
2107 **1599** 5r. multicoloured . . . 15 20

1600 Dhirubhai H. Ambani

2002. Dhirubhai H. Ambani (industrialist) Commemoration.
2108 **1600** 5r. multicoloured . . . 15 20

1601 T. T. Krishnamachari

2002. T. T. Krishnamachari (Minister of Commerce and Industry, 1952–56, Finance Minister 1963–5) Commemoration.
2109 **1601** 5r. multicoloured . . . 15 20

1602 Golconda Fort

2002. Forts of Andhra Pradesh. Multicoloured.
2110 5r. Type **1602** 15 20
2111 5r. Palace, Chandragiri Fort 15 20

1603 Hindustan Aircraft Industries HT-2 Trainer, 1951

2003. Centenary of Powered Flight. Aero India 2003. Multicoloured.
2112 5r. Type **1603** 15 20
2113 5r. Hindustan Aircraft Industries Marut ground attack aircraft, 1961 . . . 15 20
2114 5r. Hindustan Aircraft Industries LCA light combat aircraft, 2001 . . 15 20
2115 15r. Hindustan Aircraft Industries Dhruv advanced light helicopter 40 45
MS2116 144 × 95 mm. Nos. 2112/15 85 1·00

1604 Ghantasala

2003. Ghantasala (singer and composer) Commemoration.
2117 **1604** 5r. brown and black . . 15 20

1605 S. L. Kirloskar and Cogwheels

2003. Birth Centenary of S. L. Kirloskar (industrialist).
2118 **1605** 5r. multicoloured . . . 15 20

1606 Kusumagraj

2003. Kusumagraj (Marathi poet) Commemoration.
2119 **1606** 5r. multicoloured . . . 15 20

1607 Sant Eknath **1608** Frank Anthony

2003. Sant Eknath (saint and poet) Commemoration.
2120 **1607** 5r. multicoloured . . . 15 20

2003. 10th Death Anniv of Frank Anthony (politician).
2121 **1608** 5r. multicoloured . . . 15 20

1609 Kakaji Maharaj **1610** *Commiphora wightii*

2003. Kakaji Maharaj (Swaminarayan spiritual leader and philosopher) Commemoration.
2122 **1609** 5r. multicoloured . . . 15 20

2003. Medicinal Plants of India. Multicoloured.
2123 5r. Type **1610** 15 20
2124 5r. *Bacopa monnieri* 15 20
2125 5r. *Emblica officinalis* . . . 15 20
2126 5r. *Withania somnifera* . . . 15 20
MS2127 130 × 80 mm. Nos. 2123/6 60 80

1611 Durga Das **1612** Kishore Kumar

2003. Durga Das (journalist and newspaper editor) Commemoration.
2128 **1611** 5r. multicoloured . . . 15 20

2003. "Golden Voices of Yesteryear". Multicoloured.
2129 5r. Type **1612** 15 20
2130 5r. Mukesh 15 20
2131 5r. Mohammed Rafi 15 20
2132 5r. Hemant Kumar 15 20
MS2133 89 × 105 mm. Nos. 2129/32 60 80

1613 Mt. Everest

2003. 50th Anniv of Ascent of Mount Everest by Edmund Hilary and Tenzing Norgay. Multicoloured.
2134 15r. Type **1613** 40 45
MS2135 74 × 97 mm. 15r. As Type **1613** 40 45

1614 Muktabai **1615** Natesa (12th—Century Bronze from Tanjavur)

2003. Muktabai (poet) Commemoration.
2136 **1614** 5r. multicoloured . . . 15 20

2003. Government Museum, Chennai. Multicoloured.
2137 5r. Type **1615** 15 20
2138 5r. Amravati sculpture (medallion) 15 20
2139 15r. Museum Theatre (57 × 28 mm) 40 45
MS2140 161 × 73 mm. Nos. 2137/9 80 85
No. **MS**2140 is also illustrated with other exhibits from the Government Museum.

1616 Vishwanath Kashinath Rajwade **1617** Bade Ghulam Ali Khan

2003. 140th Birth Anniv of Vishwanath Kashinath Rajwade (historian).
2141 **1616** 5r. lilac 15 20

2003. Bade Ghulam Ali Khan (singer) Commemoration.
2142 **1617** 5r. multicoloured . . . 15 20

1618 Three Stylised Children and Rainbow

2003. Autism. Our World of Special Children.
2143 **1618** 5r. multicoloured . . . 15 20

1619 Vishal Badri Temple, Badrinath **1620** Janardan Swami

2003. Temple Architecture. Multicoloured.
2144 5r. Type **1619** 15 20
2145 5r. Mallikarjunaswamy Temple, Srisailam 15 20
2146 5r. Tripureswari Temple, Udaipur 15 20
2147 5r. Jagannath Temple, Puri 15 20

2003. 89th Birth Anniv of Janardan Swami (spiritual leader).
2148 **1620** 5r. brown 15 20

1621 Athirapalli Falls

2003. Waterfalls.Multicoloured.
2149 5r. Type **1622** 15 20
2150 5r. Kempty Falls 15 20
2151 5r. Kakolat Falls 15 20
2152 15r. Jog Falls 15 20
MS2153 134 × 87 mm. Nos. 2149/52 60 80

1622 G. Sankara Kurup

2003. Malayalam Jnanpith Literary Award Winners Commemoration. Each black and cream.
2154 5r. Type **1622** 15 20
2155 5r. S. K. Pottekkatt 15 20
2156 5r. Thakazhi Sivasankara Pillai 15 20

1623 Dr. Kota Shivarama Karanth

2003. Dr. Kota Shivarama Karanth (writer and reformer) Commemoration.
2157 **1623** 5r. multicoloured . . . 15 20

1624 Narendra Mohan

2003. First Death Anniv of Narendra Mohan (writer and editor of Dainik Jagran).
2158 **1624** 5r. brown and flesh . . 15 20

1625 Govindrao Pansare

2003. 90th Birth Anniv of Govindrao Pansare (martyr).
2159 **1625** 5r. multicoloured . . . 15 20

1626 Fish

2003. Greetings Stamps. Multicoloured.
2160 4r. Type **1626** 10 15
2161 4r. Birds 10 15
2162 5r. Butterfly 15 20
2163 5r. Squirrels 15 20

1627 Satellite Dish, Telegraph Key and Mobile Phone

2003. 150th Anniv of Telecommunications.
2164 **1627** 5r. multicoloured . . . 15 20

1628 Bengal Engineer Group memorial, Roorkee and Railroad

2003. Bicentenary of the Benegal Sappers and Miners.
2165 **1628** 5r. multicoloured . . . 15 20

1629 Steam Locomotive on the Kalka-Shimla Railway

2003. Centenary of the Kalka-Shimla Railway.
2166 **1629** 5r. multicoloured . . . 15 20

1630 Python

2003. Snakes. Multicoloured.
2167 5r. Type **630** 15 20
2168 5r. Bamboo pit viper . . . 15 20
2169 5r. King cobra 15 20
2170 5r. Gliding Snake 15 20
MS2171 169 × 123 mm. Nos. 2167/70 . . . . 60 80

1631 Children

2003. Children's Day.
2172 **1631** 5r. multicoloured . . . 15 20

1632 Soldiers of the 2 Guards Battalion

2003. 225th Anniv of the 2 Guards (formerly the 1 Grenadiers).
2173 **1632** 5r. green, vermilion and yellow 15 20

1633 Harivansh Rai Bachchan

2003. Harivansh Rai Bachchan (poet) Commemoration.
2174 **1633** 5r. black and brown . . 15 20

1634 Cockerel

2003. Early French and Indian Art. Multicoloured.
2175 22r. Type **1634** 55 60
2176 22r. Peacock 55 60
MS2177 116 × 95 mm. Nos. 2175/6 1·10 1·20

1635 Yashpal

2003. Birth Centenary of Yashpal (revoluntioanry writer).
2178 **1635** 5r. multicoloured . . . 15 20

1636 Cheomseongdae Astronomical Observatory, Gyeongju

2003. 30th Anniv of Diplomatic Relations with South Korea. Multicoloured.
2179 15r. Type **1636** 40 45
2180 15r. Jantar Mantar astronomical observatory, Jaipur 40 45

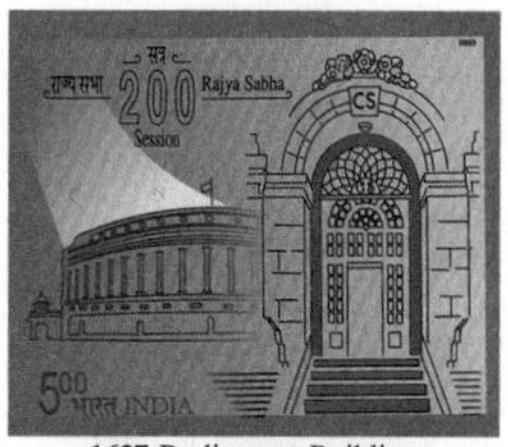

1637 Parliament Building

2003. 200th Session of Rajya Sabha (Council of States).
2181 **1637** 5r. multicoloured . . . 15 20

1638 Mukut Behari Lal Bhargava

2003. Birth Centenary of Mukut Behari Lal Bhargava (politician and lawyer).
2182 **1638** 5r. multicoloured . . . 15 20

1639 Swami Swaroopanandji

2003. Birth Centenary of Swami Swaroopanandji (religious leader).
2183 **1639** 5r. multicoloured . . . 15 20

1640 Actors

2003. 50th Anniv of the Sangeet Natak Akademi. Multicoloured.
2184 5r. Type **1640** 15 20
2185 5r. Dancers 15 20
2186 5r. Musicians 15 20
MS2187 139 × 82 mm. Nos. 2183/5 45 50

1641 Lalan Fakir

2003. Folk Music. Multicoloured.
2188 5r. Type **1641** 15 20
2189 5r. Allah Jilai Bai 15 20

1642 Major Somnath Sharma

2003. 80th Birth Anniv of Major Somnath Sharma.
2190 **1642** 5r. multicoloured . . . 15 20

1643 Siddavanahalli Nijalingappa

2003. Siddavanahalli Nijalingappa Commemoration (politician and lawyer).
2191 **1643** 5r. multicoloured . . . 15 20

1644 Chintaman Dwarkanath Deshmukh

2004. Chintaman Dwarkanath Deshmukh (finance expert) Commemoration.
2192 **1644** 5r. multicoloured . . . 15 20

1645 Nani Ardeshir Palkhivala

2004. 2nd Death Anniv of Nani Ardeshir Palkhivala (jurist).
2193 **1645** 5r. multicoloured . . . 15 20

1646 Dr. Bhalchandra Digamber Garware

2004. Birth Centenary (2003) of Dr. Bhalchandra Digamber Garware (industrialist).
2194 **1646** 5r. multicoloured . . . 15 20

1647 Annamacharya

2004. Annamacharya (saint and composer of devotional songs) Commemoration.
2195 **1647** 5r. multicoloured . . . 15 20

1648 9th Battalion of the Madras Regiment, Travancore

2004. Commemoration of the 9th Battalion of the Madras Regiment, Travancore.
2196 **1648** 5r. multicoloured . . . 15 20

1649 V. L. Akshminarayana

2004. V. L. Akshminarayana (violinist) Commemoration.
2197 **1649** 5r. multicoloured . . . 15 20

1650 INS *Tarangini*

2004. Circumnavigation Voyage of INS *Tarangini* (three masted barque).
2198 **1650** 5r. multicoloured . . . 15 20

1651 Illustrated Blocks, Stylised Stairs and Sheaves of Paper

2004. Indian Institute of Social Welfare and Business Management, Kolkata.
2199 **1651** 5r. multicoloured . . . 15 20

1652 Baji Rao Peshwa

2004. Baji Rao Peshwa Commemoration.
2200 **1652** 5r. multicoloured . . . 15 20

1653 Siddhar Swamigal

2004. Birth Centenary of Siddhar Swamigal (spiritual leader).
2201 **1653** 5r. multicoloured . . . 15 20

1654 Indra Chandra Shastri

2004. 92nd Birth Anniv of Indra Chandra Shastri (philosopher).
2202 **1654** 5r. black, deep green and green 15 20

1655 Woodstock School

2004. Woodstock School.
2203 **1655** 5r. multicoloured . . . 15 20

1656 Jyotiprasad Agarwalla

2004. Birth Centenary of Jyotiprasad Agarwalla (2003) (poet and film maker).
2204 **1656** 5r. multicoloured . . . 15 20

1657 P. N. Panicker

2004. Reading Day. Ninth Death Anniv of P. N. Panicker (education reformer).
2205 **1657** 5r. multicoloured . . . 15 20

1658 Nain Singh

2004. The Great Trigonometrical Survey. Multicoloured.
2206 5r. Type **1658** 15 20
2207 5r. Triangles (40 × 29 mm) 15 20
2208 5r. Radhanath Sikdar . . . 15 20
MS2209 117 × 75 mm. Nos. 2206/7 45 50

1659 Aacharya Bhikshu

2004. Aacharya Bhikshu (philosophical writer and social reformer) Commemoration.
2210 **1659** 5r. multicoloured . . . 15 20

1660 Wrestling

2004. Olympic Games, Athens. Multicoloured.
2211 5r. Type **1660** 15 20
2212 5r. Athletics 15 20
2213 15r. Shooting 40 45
2214 15r. Hockey 40 45

1661 Kabir (Indian)

2004. Iranian and Indian Poets. Sheet 203 × 148 mm containing T **1661** and similar vert designs. Multicoloured.
MS2215 15r. Type **1661**; 15r. Hafiz Shirazi (Iranian) 80 85
Stamps of the same design were issued by Iran.

1662 Murasoli Maran

2004. 70th Birthday Anniv of Murasoli Maran (writer).
2216 **1662** 5r. multicoloured . . . 15 20

1663 Rajiv Gandhi (President, 1984—89)

2004. 60th Birth Anniv of Rajiv Gandhi and Renewable Energy Day.
2217 **1663** 5r. multicoloured . . . 15 20

1664 S. S. *Vasan*

2004. Birth Centenary of S. S. *Vasan* (journalist and film producer).
2218 **1664** 5r. multicoloured . . . 15 20

1666 K. Subrahmanyam

2004. Birth Centenary of K. Subrahmanyam (film maker).
2220 **1666** 5r. multicoloured . . . 15 20

1667 M. C. Chagla

2004. M. C. Chagla (Judge) Commemoration.
2221 **1667** 5r. multicoloured . . . 15 20

1668 Shri N. "Tirupur" Kumaran

2004. Birth Centenary of Tirupur Kumaran (revolutionary).
2222 **1668** 5r. multicoloured . . . 15 20

1669 Early Stamp, Mail Ship and Carriage

2004. 150th Anniv of India Post. Multicoloured.
2223 5r. Type **1669** 15 20
2224 5r. Airmail stamp and postal runner 15 20
2225 5r. General Post Office, Calcutta, stamp and pillar box 15 20
2226 5r. Computer terminal and modern postal services . . 15 20

1670 Neerja Bhanot (Purser, Pan American World Airways)

2004. Winners of the Ashoka Chakra Bravery Award. Multicoloured.
2227 5r. Type **1670** 15 20
2228 5r. Randhir Prasad Verma (Superintendent of Police) 15 20

1671 Guru Dutt

2004. 40th Death Anniv of Guru Dutt (film maker).
2229 **1671** 5r. multicoloured . . . 15 20

1672 Indian Soldiers and Peace Dove

2004. Indian Army in UN Peacekeeping Operations.
2230 **1672** 5r. multicoloured . . .

1673 Marudhu Pandiar Brothers

1674 Kites

2004. Marudhu Pandiar Brothers (anti-colonial leaders and rulers of Sivaganga). Commemoration.
2231 **1673** 5r. multicoloured . . . 15 20

2004. Greetings Stamps. Multicoloured.
2232 4r. Type **1674** 10 10
2233 4r. Dolls 10 10

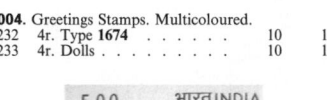

1675 Dr. S. Roerich

2004. Birth Centenary of Dr. S. Roerich (artist).
2234 **1675** 5r. multicoloured . . . 15 20

1676 Tenneti Viswanatham

1677 Schoolgirls and Rural Village

2004. 25th Death Anniv of Tenneti Viswanatham (politician).
2235 **1676** 5r. multicoloured . . . 15 20

2004. Children's Day.
2236 **1677** 5r. multicoloured . . . 15 20

1678 Walchand Hirachand

1679 Dula Bhaya Kag

2004. 121st Birth Anniv of Walchand Hirachand (industrialist).
2237 **1678** 5r. multicoloured . . . 15 20

2004. Birth Centenary (2003) of Dula Bhaya Kag (poet and nationalist).
2238 **1679** 5r. multicoloured . . . 15 20

OFFICIAL STAMPS

1866. Optd **Service**.
O20 **11** ½a. blue . . . . 40·00 50
O 8 **12** 8p. mauve . . . . 21·00 50·00
O23 **11** 1a. brown . . . . 42·00 50
O27 2a. orange . . . . 5·50 2·25
O13 4a. green . . . . £200 80·00
O29 – 4a. green (No. 69) . . . . 3·00 1·50
O30 **11** 8a. red . . . . 3·50 1·50

1866. Fiscal stamp with head of Queen Victoria surch **SERVICE TWO ANNAS**.
O15 2a. purple £275 £225

1866. Fiscal stamps optd **SERVICE POSTAGE**.
O19 ½a. mauve on lilac . . . . . £400 85·00
O16 2a. purple £800 £400
O17 4a. purple £3250 £1100
O18 8a. purple £3750 £3750

1874. Optd **On H. M. S.** (Queen Victoria).
O31 **11** ½a. blue . . . . 12·00 20
O32 1a. brown . . . . 17·00 20
O33a 2a. orange . . . . 48·00 22·00
O34 – 4a. green (No. 69) . . . 17·00 3·00
O35 **11** 8a. red . . . . 8·00 5·50

1883. Queen Victoria stamps of 1882 and 1892 optd **On H. M. S.**
O37a **40** 3p. red 20 10
O39 **23** ½a. green . . . . 1·75 10
O49 ½a. green . . . . 2·25 90
O41 – 1a. purple 75 10
O50 – 1a. red . . . . 3·25 10
O42 – 2a. blue . . . . 6·50 60
O51 – 2a. lilac . . . . 38·00 1·50
O44a – 4a. olive . . . . 20·00 50
O46 – 8a. mauve . . . . 9·50 50
O48 **37** 1r. green and red . . . . 16·00 40

1902. King Edward VII stamps optd **On H. M. S.**
O54 **41** 3p. grey . . . . 2·50 75
O56 – ½a. green (No. 122) . . . 1·25 30
O57 – 1a. red (No. 123) . . . . 1·00 10
O59 – 2a. lilac . . . . 3·25 10
O60 – 4a. olive . . . . 12·00 30
O62 – 6a. bistre . . . . 1·50 15
O63 – 8a. mauve . . . . 6·00 1·00
O65 – 1r. green and red . . . . 4·00 80
O68 **52** 2r. red and orange . . . . 9·00 1·50
O69 5r. blue and violet . . . . 14·00 1·50
O70 10r. green and red . . . . 29·00 16·00
O71 15r. blue and olive . . . . 65·00 40·00
O72 25r. orange and blue . . . £140 60·00

1906. Nos. 149/50 optd **On H. M. S.**
O66 ½a. green . . . . 1·25 10
O67 1a. red . . . . 2·00 10

1912. King George V stamps optd **SERVICE**.
O109 **55** 3p. grey 15 10
O 76 **56** ½a. green 50 10
O 80 **57** 1a. red . . . . 1·00 10
O111 1a. brown 15 10
O 84 **59** 2a. mauve 75 30
O112 **70** 2a. lilac 30 10
O129 2a. red . . . . 1·00 2·50
O132 **63** 4a. olive . . . . 1·50 10
O113 **71** 4a. green 50 20
O 87 **64** 6a. bistre . . . . 1·50 2·50
O115 **65** 8a. mauve . . . . 1·25 10
O116 **66** 12a. red . . . . 70 2·50
O117 **67** 1r. brown and green . . 3·25 1·00
O 92 2r. red and orange . . . 4·00 6·50
O 93 5r. blue and violet . . . 17·00 23·00
O 94 10r. green and red . . . 55·00 50·00
O 95 15r. blue and olive . . . 95·00 £110
O 96 25r. orange and blue . . £200 £170

1921. No. O81 surch **NINE PIES**.
O97 **57** 9p. on 1a. red . . . . . . 1·25 75

1925. Nos. O70/2 surch in words.
O 99 **52** 1r. on 15r. blue and olive 4·25 4·00
O100 1r. on 25r. orange & blue 20·00 70·00
O101 2r. on 10r. green and red 3·75 4·25

1925. Nos. O94/6 surch in words.
O102 **67** 1r. on 15r. blue and olive 19·00 75·00
O103 1r. on 25r. orange & blue 5·00 11·00
O104 2r. on 10r. green and red £850

1926. No. O62 surch **ONE ANNA**.
O105 1a. on 6a. bistre 30 30

1926. Surch **SERVICE ONE ANNA** and two bars.
O106 **58** 1a. on 1½a. brown (A) . . 20 10
O107 1a. on 1½a. brown (B) . . 3·00 4·50
O108 **61** 1a. on 2a.6p. blue . . . 60 80

1932. Optd **SERVICE**.
O126 **79** ½a. green . . . . 1·00 10
O127 **80** 9p. green 30 15
O127b **81** 1a. brown . . . . . . 1·75 15
O128 **82** 1a.3p. mauve 30 10
O130a **59** 2a. orange . . . . . . 1·25 10
O131 **61** 2a.6p. orange 50 10

1937. King George VI stamps optd **SERVICE**.
O135 **91** ½a. brown . . . . 17·00 70
O136 9p. green . . . . 19·00 80
O137 1a. red . . . . 3·50 10
O138 **93** 1r. slate and brown . . . 50 50
O139 2r. purple and brown . . 1·75 2·50
O140 5r. green and blue . . . 4·00 6·50
O141 10r. purple and red . . . 14·00 7·50

1939. King George V stamp surch **SERVICE 1A**.
O142 **82** 1a. on 1¼a. mauve . . . 12·00 20

O 20 King George VI

O 21 Asokan Capital

1939.
O143 **O 20** 3p. slate 60 10
O144 ½a. brown . . . . . . 5·50 10
O144a ½a. purple 30 10
O145 9p. green 30 10
O146 1a. red 30 10
O146a 1a.3p. brown . . . . 3·50 70
O146b 1½a. violet 65 10
O147 2a. orange 60 10
O148 2½a. violet . . . . . . 60 1·25
O149 4a. brown 60 10
O150 8a. violet 90 30

1948. 1st Anniv of Independence. Optd **SERVICE**.
O150a **305** 1½a. brown . . . . . 42·00 35·00
O150b 3½a. violet £800 £500
O150c 12a. green £2250 £1900
O150d – 10r. brown and red (No. 308) £12000

1950.
O151 **O 21** 3p. violet 15 10
O152 6p. brown 30 10
O153 9p. green . . . . . . 1·25 10
O154 1a. blue . . . . 1·25 10
O155 2a. red . . . . 1·75 10
O156 3a. red . . . . 4·00 2·50
O157 4a. purple . . . . . . 5·50 20
O158 4a. blue 50 10
O159 6a. violet . . . . . . 4·00 1·00
O160 8a. brown . . . . . . 2·00 10
O186 – 1r. violet 15 10
O187 – 2r. red 25 10
O188 – 5r. green 40 60
O189 – 10r. brown . . . . . 90 1·00

The rupee values are larger and with a different frame.

1957. Value in naye paise.
O175 **O 21** 1n.p. slate 10 10
O166 2n.p. violet 10 10
O167 3n.p. brown 10 10
O168 5n.p. green 10 10
O169 6n.p. turquoise 20 10
O180 10n.p. green 50 50
O170 13n.p. red 30 10
O182 15n.p. violet 10 10
O183 20n.p. red 70 10
O184 25n.p. blue 10 10
O185 50n.p. brown 70 10

O 23

O 25

O 26

1967.
O200 **O 23** 2p. violet . . . . . . 10 1·00
O201 3p. brown . . . . . . 40 1·25
O202 5p. green 10 10
O203 6p. blue . . . . 1·25 1·50
O204 10p. green 10 30
O205 15p. plum 10 30
O206 20p. red 10 30
O207 25p. red . . . . 11·00 3·75
O208 30p. blue 10 60
O209 50p. brown 10 60
O197 1r. purple 85 10

1971. Obligatory Tax. Refugee Relief. Optd **REFUGEE RELIEF** in English and Devanagari (No. O210) or in English only (No. O211).
O210 **O 23** 5p. green 75 50
O211 5p. green . . . . . . 1·25 80
O213 **O 25** 5p. green 20 20
See note below Nos. 646/51.

1976. Designs redrawn showing face-value in figures only and smaller Capital with Hindi motto beneath as Type **O 26**.
O214 **O 26** 2p. blue . . . . . . 20 1·25
O254 5p. green 10 10
O255 10p. green 10 10
O256 15p. purple 10 10
O257 20p. red 10 10
O258 25p. red 10 10
O259 30p. blue 10 10
O260 35p. violet 10 10
O268 40p. violet (17 × 19½ mm) . . 10 10
O269 50p. brown (17 × 19½ mm) . . 10 10
O263 60p. brown 10 10
O270 1r. purple (17 × 19½ mm) . . 10 10
O225b – 2r. red . . . . 40 1·50
O226b – 5r. green . . . . . . 60 2·25
O227 – 10r. red . . . . 1·25 3·50
The 2, 5 and 10r. values are larger.

O 27

O 28

1982. As 1977 and 1981 issue but with simulated perforations. Imperf.
O231 **O 28** 5p. green . . . . . . 55 1·00
O232 10p. green . . . . . . 70 1·00
O233 15p. purple . . . . . 70 1·00
O234 20p. red . . . . 75 1·00
O235 25p. red . . . . 1·50 2·00
O236 35p. violet 85 65
O237 50p. brown . . . . . 1·50 1·50
O238 1r. brown . . . . . . 1·75 1·50
O239 2r. red . . . . 1·75 4·00
O240 5r. green . . . . . . 2·00 5·00
O241 10r. brown . . . . . 2·50 7·00

1998. Redrawn with face value figures in bottom corners. Size 17 × 19½ mm.
O271 **O 27** 2r. red 10 10
O272 5r. green 15 20
O273 10r. brown 30 35

(b) Size 16½ × 19 mm.
O273b **O 36** 50p. brown 10 10
O274 **O 27** 1r. purple 10 10
O275 2r. red 10 10
O276 3r. orange 10 10
O278 5r. green 15 20
O279 10r. brown 25 30

INDIAN CUSTODIAN FORCES IN KOREA Pt. 1

Stamps used by the Indian Forces on custodian duties in Korea in 1953.

12 pies = 1 anna; 16 annas = 1 rupee.

भारतीय
संरक्षा कटक
कोरिया
(K 1)

1953. Stamps of India (archaeological series) optd with Type K **1**.

K 1	**307**	3p. violet	1·75	4·50
K 2	**308**	6p. brown	1·50	4·50
K 3	–	9p. green	1·75	4·50
K 4	–	1a. blue (B)	1·50	4·50
K 5	–	2a. red	1·50	4·50
K 6	–	$2\frac{1}{2}$a. lake	1·50	4·75
K 7	–	3a. salmon	1·50	4·75
K 8	**314**	4a. blue	1·75	4·75
K 9	**315**	6a. violet	8·50	9·00
K10	–	8a. green	1·75	9·00
K11	–	12a. blue	2·25	17·00
K12	–	1r. violet and green	3·00	17·00

INDIAN EXPEDITIONARY FORCES Pt. 1

Stamps used by Indian Forces during, and after, the War of 1914–18.

12 pies = 1 anna; 16 annas = 1 rupee.

1914. Stamps of India (King George V) optd **I. E. F.**

E 1	**55**	3p. grey	15	30
E 2	**56**	$\frac{1}{2}$a. green	50	30
E 3	**57**	1a. red	1·25	30
E 5	**59**	2a. lilac	1·25	30
E 6	**61**	2a.6p. blue	1·50	3·50
E 7	**62**	3a. orange	1·00	1·50
E 8	**63**	4a. olive	1·00	1·50
E 9	**65**	8a. mauve	1·25	2·50
E11	**66**	12a. red	2·25	6·00
E13	**67**	1r. brown and green	2·50	4·00

INDIAN FORCES IN INDO-CHINA Pt. 1

Stamps used by Indian Forces engaged in the International Commission in Indo-China.

1954. 12 pies = 1 anna; 16 annas = 1 rupee.
1957. 100 naye paise = 1 rupee.
1964. 100 paisa = 1 rupee.

अन्तर्राष्ट्रीय आयोग कम्बोज (N 1) — अन्तर्राष्ट्रीय आयोग लाओस (N 2) — अन्तर्राष्ट्रीय आयोग वियत नाम (N 3)

1954. Stamps of India (archaeological series) overprinted. (a) Optd with Type N **1** for use in Cambodia.

N1	**307**	3p. violet	1·25	9·00
N2	–	1a. blue (B)	90	75
N3	–	2a. red	90	80
N4	–	8a. green	1·50	3·00
N5	–	12a. blue	1·50	3·00

(b) Optd with Type N **2** for use in Laos.

N 6	**307**	3p. violet	1·25	9·00
N 7	–	1a. blue (B)	90	75
N 8	–	2a. red	90	80
N 9	–	8a. green	1·50	3·00
N10	–	12a. blue	1·50	3·00

(c) Optd with Type N **3** for use in Vietnam.

N11	**307**	3p. violet	1·25	9·00
N12	–	1a. blue (B)	90	75
N13	–	2a. red	90	80
N14	–	8a. green	1·50	3·00
N15	–	12a. blue	1·50	3·00

1957. Map type of India overprinted. (a) Optd with Type N **1** for use in Cambodia.

N16	**361**	2n.p. brown	75	30
N17		6n.p. grey	50	30
N18		13n.p. red	70	40
N19		50n.p. orange	2·25	1·25
N20		75n.p. purple	2·25	1·25

(b) Optd with Type N **2** for use in Laos.

N21	**361**	2n.p. brown	75	30
N39		3n.p. brown	10	20
N40		5n.p. green	10	15
N22		6n.p. grey	50	30
N23		13n.p. red	70	40
N24		50n.p. orange	2·25	1·25
N25		75n.p. purple	2·25	1·25

(c) Optd with Type N **3** for use in Vietnam.

N43	**361**	1n.p. turquoise	10	20
N26		2n.p. brown	75	30
N45		3n.p. brown	10	20
N46		5n.p. green	10	15
N27		6n.p. grey	50	30
N28		13n.p. red	70	40
N29		50n.p. orange	2·25	1·25
N30		75n.p. purple	2·25	1·25

1965. Children's Day stamp of India optd **ICC** for use in Laos and Vietnam.

N49	**469**	15p. slate	60	3·25

1968. Nos. 504/6, 509/10, 515 and 517/18, of India optd **ICC** in English and Devanagari, for use in Laos and Vietnam.

N50	–	2p. brown	10	2·75
N51	–	3p. olive	10	2·75
N52	–	5p. red	10	1·00
N53	–	10p. blue	1·75	2·00
N54	**467**	15p. green	60	2·00
N55	–	60p. grey	35	1·25
N56	–	1r. brown and plum	50	2·00
N57	–	2r. blue and violet	1·25	8·50

INDIAN U.N. FORCE IN CONGO Pt. 1

Stamps used by Indian Forces attached to the United Nations Force in Congo.

100 naye paise = 1 rupee.

1962. Map type of India optd **U.N. FORCE (INDIA) CONGO**.

U1	**361**	1n.p. turquoise	1·00	2·75
U2		2n.p. brown	1·00	1·00
U3		5n.p. green	1·00	70
U4		8n.p. turquoise	1·00	40
U5		13n.p. red	1·00	40
U6		50n.p. orange	1·00	70

INDIAN U.N. FORCE IN GAZA (PALESTINE) Pt. 1

Stamps used by Indian Forces attached to the United Nations Force in Gaza.

100 paise = 1 rupee.

1965. Children's Day stamp of India optd **UNEF**.

G1	**449**	15p. slate	1·75	6·50

INDO-CHINA Pt. 6

A French territory in south-east Asia. In 1949 it was split up into the three states of Vietnam, Cambodia and Laos.

1889. 100 centimes = 1 franc.
1918. 100 cents = 1 piastre.

1889. Stamp of French Colonies, "Commerce" type, surch. (a) **INDO-CHINE 1889 5 R-D.**

1	J	5 on 35c. black on orange	70·00	60·00

(b) **INDO-CHINE 89 5 R D.**

2	J	5 on 35c. black on orange	11·00	9·25

1892. "Tablet" key-type inscr "INDO-CHINE" in red (1, 5, 15, 25, 50 (No. 27), 75c., 1f.) or blue (others).

6	D	1c. black on blue	85	30
7		2c. brown on buff	1·75	1·75
8		4c. brown on grey	1·60	2·25
23		5c. green	3·00	80
10		10c. black on lilac	3·00	90
24		10c. red	4·00	35
11		15c. blue	32·00	30
25		15c. grey	8·00	35
12		20c. red on green	8·00	2·25
13		25c. black on pink	13·00	1·10
26		25c. blue	23·00	60
14		30c. brown on drab	19·00	6·00
15		40c. red on yellow	29·00	7·25
16		50c. red on pink	30·00	9·25
27		50c. brown on blue	15·00	2·75
17		75c. brown on orange	23·00	17·00
18		1f. green	42·00	19·00
19		5f. mauve on lilac	£100	85·00

1903. Surch.

28	D	5 on 15c. grey	45	1·25
29		15c. on 25c. blue	95	65

8 "Grasset" type

1904.

30	**8**	1c. green	20	15
31		2c. purple on yellow	30	15
32		4c. mauve on blue	30	15
33		5c. green	1·75	15
34		10c. pink	2·50	15
35		15c. brown on blue	2·50	20
36		20c. red on green	3·25	40
37		25c. blue	17·50	30
38		30c. brown on cream	6·75	2·00
39		35c. black on yellow	18·00	1·10
40		40c. black on grey	5·00	85
41		50c. brown	6·75	1·10
42		75c. red on orange	35·00	19·00
43		1f. green	21·00	3·50
44		2f. brown on yellow	45·00	27·00
45		5f. violet	£180	£140
46		10f. red on green	£160	£140

10 Annamite — 11 Cambodian — 12 Cambodian

1907.

51	**10**	1c. black and sepia	55	15
52		2c. black and brown	15	15
53		4c. black and blue	20	55
54		5c. black and green	2·75	20
55		10c. black and red	2·75	15
56		15c. black and violet	2·75	30
57	**11**	20c. black and violet	3·25	2·00
58		25c. black and blue	7·00	15
59		30c. black and brown	9·25	5·75
60		35c. black and green	3·25	20
61		40c. black and brown	4·00	2·50
62		45c. black and orange	12·00	5·25
63		50c. black and red	17·00	1·75
64	**12**	75c. black and orange	10·00	5·50
65	–	1f. black and red	48·00	9·50
66	–	2f. black and green	16·00	16·00
67	–	5f. black and blue	48·00	28·00
68	–	10f. black and violet	85·00	80·00

DESIGNS—As Type **12**: 1f. Annamites; 2f. Muong; 5f. Laotian; 10f. Cambodian.

1912. Surch in figures.

69	**8**	05 on 4c. mauve on blue	4·25	4·75
70		05 on 15c. brown on blue	50	20
71		05 on 30c. brown on cream	55	2·25
72		10 on 40c. black on grey	1·60	3·00
73		10 on 50c. brown	1·10	2·50
74		10 on 75c. red on orange	4·00	5·50

1914. Red Cross. Surch **5c** and cross.

76	**10**	5c.+5c. black and green	35	2·50
77		10c.+5c. black and red	45	30
78		15c.+5c. black and violet	1·25	3·00

1918. Nos. 75/6 and 78 further surch in figures and words.

79	**10**	4c. on 5c.+5c. blk & grn	3·25	5·50
80		6c. on 10c.+5c. black and red	2·75	5·00
81		8c. on 15c.+5c. blk & vio	10·00	17·00

1919. French stamps of "War Orphans" issue surch **INDOCHINE** and value in figures and words.

82	**23**	10c. on 15c.+10c. grey	2·50	3·50
83		16c. on 25c.+15c. blue	6·00	7·00
84	–	24c. on 35c.+25c. violet and grey	7·00	12·00
85	–	40c. on 50c.+50c. brown	14·00	23·00
86	**26**	80c. on 1f.+1f. red	23·00	35·00
87		4p. on 5f.+5f. blue & blk	£225	£225

1919. Surch in figures and words.

88	**10**	$\frac{2}{5}$c. on 1c. black and sepia	1·75	20
89		$\frac{4}{5}$c. on 2c. black and brown	1·60	35
90		$1\frac{3}{5}$c. on 4c. black and blue	3·50	25
91		2c. on 5c. black and green	2·50	20
92		4c. on 10c. black and red	1·25	15
93		6c. on 15c. black and violet	3·75	20
94	**11**	8c. on 20c. black and violet	4·00	90
95		10c. on 25c. black & blue	4·00	15
96		12c. on 30c. black & brown	6·00	1·00
97		14c. on 35c. black & green	3·25	55
98		16c. on 40c. black & brown	6·00	45
99		18c. on 45c. black & orange	7·50	2·50
100		20c. on 50c. black and red	10·50	1·10
101	**12**	30c. on 75c. black & orange	13·00	1·75
102	–	40c. on 1f. black and red	18·00	95
103	–	80c. on 2f. black and green	16·00	6·50
104	–	2p. on 5f. black and blue	85·00	70·00
105	–	4p. on 10f. black and violet	£120	£120

1922. As T **10** and **11** but value in cents or piastres.

115	**10**	$\frac{1}{10}$c. red and grey	15	90
116		$\frac{1}{5}$c. black and blue	15	15
117		$\frac{2}{5}$c. black and brown	20	1·00
118		$\frac{4}{5}$c. black and mauve	25	30
119		1c. black and brown	75	15
120		2c. black and green	30	15
121		3c. black and violet	40	20
122		4c. black and orange	90	15
123		5c. black and red	35	15
124	**11**	6c. black and red	50	20
125		7c. black and green	1·75	20
126		8c. black on lilac	1·40	65
127		9c. black and yellow	70	85
128		10c. black and blue	1·25	20
129		11c. black and violet	2·00	20
130		12c. black and brown	70	25
131		15c. black and orange	1·25	30
132		20c. black and blue	1·40	1·60
133		40c. black and red	2·25	2·00
134		1p. black and green	6·50	7·25
135		2p. black & purple on pink	10·50	11·00

22 Ploughman and Tower of Confucius

23 Bay of Along

24 Ruins of Angkor

1927.

136	**22**	$\frac{1}{10}$c. olive	15	2·75
137		$\frac{1}{5}$c. yellow	15	2·50
138		$\frac{2}{5}$c. blue	20	2·75
139		$\frac{4}{5}$c. brown	25	2·00
140		1c. orange	45	15
141		2c. green	60	20
142		3c. blue	1·40	20
143		4c. mauve	2·25	3·00
144		5c. violet	95	15
145	**23**	6c. red	1·50	20
146		7c. brown	1·25	1·25
147		8c. olive	1·75	2·75
148		9c. purple	2·25	2·75
149		10c. blue	2·25	40
150		11c. orange	1·75	2·75
151		12c. grey	1·75	2·50
152	**24**	15c. brown and red	10·00	9·00
153		20c. grey and violet	4·50	65
154	–	25c. mauve and brown	5·75	6·00
155	–	30c. olive and blue	3·50	4·00
156	–	40c. blue and red	5·25	4·25
157	–	50c. grey and green	6·25	3·00
158	–	1p. black, yellow and blue	12·00	12·00
159	–	2p. blue, orange and red	22·00	15·00

DESIGNS—As T **24**: 25, 30c. Wood-carver; 40, 50c. Temple, Thuat-Luong; 1, 2p. Founding of Saigon.

1931. "Colonial Exn" key-types inscr "INDOCHINE" and surch with new value.

160	F	4c. on 50c. mauve	3·00	3·50
161	G	6c. on 90c. red	3·25	4·25
162	H	10c. on 1f.50 blue	4·50	3·75

33 Junk

36 "Apsara", or dancing Nymph

1931.

163	**33**	$\frac{1}{10}$c. blue	15	2·00
164		$\frac{1}{5}$c. red	15	90
165		$\frac{2}{5}$c. orange	15	2·75
166		$\frac{1}{2}$c. brown	20	30
167		$\frac{4}{5}$c. violet	20	2·75
168		1c. brown	20	20
169		2c. green	35	20
170	–	3c. brown	20	20
171	–	3c. green	6·25	45
172	–	4c. blue	2·50	20
173	–	4c. green	1·40	2·50
174	–	4c. yellow	15	35
175	–	5c. purple	20	15
176	–	5c. green	45	2·50
177	–	6c. red	20	20
178	–	7c. black	20	20
179	–	8c. red	70	1·50
180	–	9c. black on yellow	20	85
181	–	10c. blue	1·10	20
182	–	10c. blue on pink	35	20
183	–	15c. brown	7·25	1·50
184	–	15c. blue	20	40
185	–	18c. blue	40	2·50
186	–	20c. red	20	15
187	–	21c. green	35	40
188	–	22c. green	50	1·50
189	–	25c. purple	3·00	1·25
190	–	25c. blue	85	1·50
191	–	30c. brown	75	20
192	**36**	50c. brown	90	15
193		60c. purple	50	20
194		70c. blue	85	1·10
195		1p. green	45	40
196		2p. red	55	50

DESIGNS—As Type **33**: 3c. to 9c. Ruins at Angkor; 10c. to 30c. Worker in rice field.

42 Farman F.190 Mail Plane

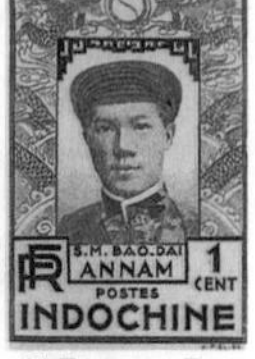

44 Emperor Bao Dai of Annam

1933. Air.

197	**42**	1c. brown	20	1·60
198		2c. green	15	1·25
199		5c. green	70	1·50
200		10c. brown	55	50
201		11c. red	1·60	2·25
202		15c. blue	2·25	1·60
203		16c. mauve	1·10	2·75
204		20c. green	2·50	1·25
205		30c. brown	65	30
206		36c. red	3·00	50
207		37c. green	80	30
208		39c. green	65	3·00
209		60c. purple	1·60	1·40
210		66c. green	2·00	1·75
211		67c. blue	75	2·75
212		69c. blue	65	3·00
213		1p. black	30	15
214		2p. orange	60	20
215		5p. violet	2·75	95

216 10p. red 4·75 2·75
217 20p. green 15·00 6·25
218 30p. brown 17·00 7·25

1936. Issue for Annam.
219 **44** 1c. brown 75 2·50
220 2c. green 1·00 2·75
221 4c. violet 1·25 45
222 5c. lake 1·60 3·00
223 10c. red 2·50 3·25
224 15c. blue 3·00 3·25
225 20c. red 2·75 3·50
226 30c. purple 2·50 3·25
227 50c. green 3·75 3·75
228 1p. mauve 6·00 6·25
229 2p. black 6·25 7·25

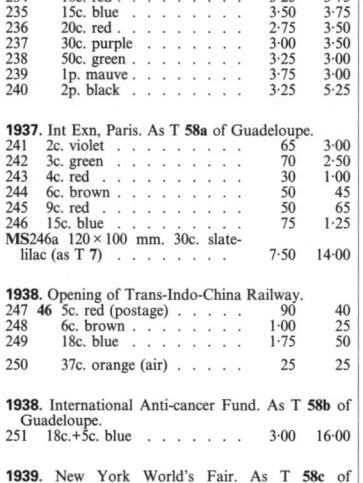

45 King Sisowath Monivong of Cambodia

46 Pres. Doumer

1936. Issue for Cambodia.
230 **45** 1c. brown 1·50 2·25
231 2c. green 1·60 2·25
232 4c. violet 1·60 2·25
233 5c. lake 2·25 3·00
234 10c. red 3·25 3·75
235 15c. blue 3·50 3·75
236 20c. red 2·75 3·50
237 30c. purple 3·00 3·50
238 50c. green 3·25 3·00
239 1p. mauve 3·75 3·00
240 2p. black 3·25 5·25

1937. Int Exn, Paris. As T **58a** of Guadeloupe.
241 2c. violet 65 3·00
242 3c. green 70 2·50
243 4c. red 30 1·00
244 6c. brown 50 45
245 9c. red 50 65
246 15c. blue 75 1·25
MS246a 120×100 mm. 30c. slate-lilac (as T **7**) 7·50 14·00

1938. Opening of Trans-Indo-China Railway.
247 **46** 5c. red (postage) 90 40
248 6c. brown 1·00 25
249 18c. blue 1·75 50
250 37c. orange (air) 25 25

1938. International Anti-cancer Fund. As T **58b** of Guadeloupe.
251 18c.+5c. blue 3·00 16·00

1939. New York World's Fair. As T **58c** of Guadeloupe.
252 13c. red 1·25 2·25
253 23c. blue 1·75 2·75

47 Mot Cot Pagoda, Hanoi

48 King Sihanouk of Cambodia

1939. San Francisco International Exhibition.
254 **47** 6c. sepia 1·50 1·50
255 9c. red 55 50
256 23c. blue 55 1·90
257 39c. purple 1·90 2·25

1939. 150th Anniv of French Revolution. As T **58d** of Guadeloupe.
258 6c.+2c. green & blk (postage) 7·25 14·00
259 7c.+3c. brown and black 7·25 14·00
260 9c.+4c. orange and black 9·50 14·00
261 13c.+10c. red and black 7·75 14·00
262 23c.+20c. blue and black 7·75 14·00
263 39c.+40c. black & orge (air) 18·00 35·00

1941. Coronation of King of Cambodia. No gum.
264 **48** 1c. orange 60 2·75
265 6c. violet 3·25 4·00
266 25c. blue 24·00 29·00

49 Processional Elephant

51 Hanoi University

1942. Fetes of Nam-Giao. No gum.
267 **49** 3c. brown 2·50 3·25
268 6c. red 3·00 3·00

1942. No. 189 surch **10 cents** and bars.
269 10c. on 25c. purple 2·00 2·50

1942. University Fund. No gum.
270 **51** 6c.+2c. red 50 3·00
271 15c.+5c. purple 55 2·50

Surch **10c +2 c.**
272 **51** 10c.+2c. on 6c.+2c. red 40 3·00

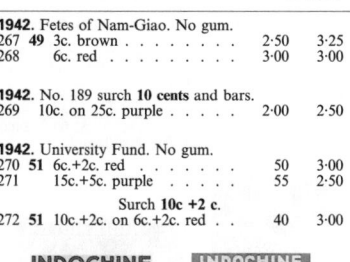

53 Marshal Petain

54 Shield and Sword

1942. No gum.
273 **53** 1c. brown 35 2·25
274 3c. brown 1·25 2·50
275 6c. red 25 1·40
276 10c. green 30 1·60
277 40c. blue 65 2·50
278 40c. grey 55 70

1942. National Relief Fund. No gum.
279 **54** 6c.+2c. red and blue 85 2·50
280 15c.+5c. black, red & bl 45 40

Surch **10c +2 c.**
281 **54** 10c.+2c. on 6c.+2c. red and blue 40 2·75

55 Emperor Bao Dai of Annam

56 King Sihanouk of Cambodia

57 Empress Nam-Phaong of Annam

58 King Sisavang-Vong of Laos

1942. No gum.
282 **55** ½c. purple 30 3·25
283 **56** 1c. purple 35 2·50
284 **58** 1c. brown 40 2·25
285 **55** 6c. red 2·00 2·50
286 **56** 6c. red 45 1·90
287 **57** 6c. red 55 1·10
288 **58** 6c. red 35 2·25

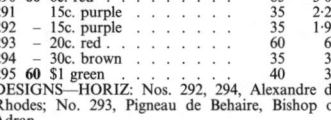

59 Saigon Fair

60 Alexandre Yersin

1942. Saigon Fair. No gum.
289 **59** 6c. red 40 2·75

1943. No gum.
290 **60** 6c. red 65 3·00
291 15c. purple 35 2·25
292 – 15c. purple 35 1·90
293 – 20c. red 60 60
294 – 30c. brown 35 30
295 **60** $1 green 40 30
DESIGNS—HORIZ: Nos. 292, 294, Alexandre de Rhodes; No. 293, Pigneau de Behaire, Bishop of Adran.

63 Do Huu-Vi

1943. Airmen. No gum.
296 **63** 6c.+2c. red 40 2·75
297 – 6c.+2c. red 45 2·50

Surch **10c +2 c.**
298 **63** 10c.+2c. on 6c.+2c. red 20 2·75
299 – 10c.+2c. on 6c.+2c. red 35 2·75
DESIGN—VERT: Nos. 297, 299, Roland Garros.

64 Doudart de Lagree

66 "Family, Homeland and Labour"

1943. Sailors. No gum.
300 **64** 1c. brown 15 40
301 A 1c. brown 45 2·00
302 B 1c. brown 35 2·50
303 5c. brown 25 1·60
304 C 6c. red 1·90 70
305 D 6c. red 75 2·50
306 E 6c. red 35 2·50
307 F 10c. green 25 2·25
308 **64** 15c. purple 35 2·50
309 F 20c. red 35 1·90
310 **64** 40c. blue 25 1·50
311 F 1p. green 40 2·75
DESIGNS—HORIZ: A, Francis Garnier; B, La Grandiere; C, Courbet; D, Rigault de Genouilly. VERT: E, Chasseloup Laubat; F, Charner.

1943. 3rd Anniv of National Revolution. No gum.
312 **66** 6c. red 40 95

67 De Lanessan

1944. Governors. No gum.
313 G 1c. brown 35 2·50
314 **67** 1c. brown 35 2·50
315 H 2c. mauve 25 2·25
316 J 4c. orange 20 60
317 H 4c. brown 25 50
318 K 5c. purple 40 2·25
319 J 10c. green 35 1·10
320 H 10c. green 25 2·00
321 K 10c. green 25 1·90
322 G 10c. green 45 95
323 **67** 15c. purple 60 1·25
DESIGNS—HORIZ: G, Van Vollenhoven; J, Auguste Pavie. VERT: H, Paul Doumer; K, Pierre Pasquier.

69 Athlete

1944. Juvenile Sports. No gum.
324 **69** 10c. purple and yellow 95 1·10
325 50c. red 90 3·25

70 Orleans Cathedral

1944. Martyr Cities. No gum.
326 **70** 15c.+60c. purple 60 3·25
327 40c.+1p.10 blue 70 3·50

1945. As T **149** of France surch **INDOCHINE** and values.
328 50c.+50c. on 2f. olive 50 3·00
329 1p.+1p. on 2f. brown 60 2·75
330 2p.+2p. on 2f. grey 1·00 3·00

1946. Air. Victory. As T **63b** of Guadeloupe.
331 80c. orange 30 1·10

1946. Air. From Chad to the Rhine. As T **63c** of Guadeloupe.
332 50c. green 2·00 3·25
333 1p. mauve 1·75 3·25
334 1p.50 red 1·50 3·25
335 2p. purple 1·90 3·25
336 2p.50 blue 1·90 3·50
337 5p. red 2·25 3·50

1946. Unissued stamps similar to T **24** with portrait of Marshal Petain optd with **R F** monogram.
338 10c. red 40 2·75
339 25c. blue 3·00 3·25

1949. Air. 75th Anniv of U.P.U. As T **39** of French Equatorial Africa.
340 3p. multicoloured 2·75 3·25

OFFICIAL STAMPS

1933. Stamps of 1931 (Nos. 168, etc.) optd **SERVICE.**
O197 1c. sepia 2·50 30
O198 2c. green 2·75 2·75
O199 3c. brown 2·50 2·75
O200 4c. blue 3·00 2·50
O201 5c. purple 2·75 25
O202 6c. red 1·50 2·75
O203 10c. blue 50 40
O204 15c. sepia 2·50 85
O205 20c. red 3·00 45
O206 21c. green 1·60 3·25
O207 25c. purple 1·25 3·50
O208 30c. brown 3·00 2·25
O209 50c. sepia 14·00 4·75
O210 60c. purple 1·25 3·00
O211 1p. green 42·00 12·00
O212 2p. red 10·00 13·00

1934. As T **11** but value in "CENTS" or "PIASTRES" and optd **SERVICE.**
O219 1c. brown 85 1·40
O220 2c. brown 1·00 1·75
O221 3c. green 2·25 2·25
O222 4c. red 3·50 75
O223 5c. orange 1·00 30
O224 6c. red 5·25 7·25
O225 10c. green 3·00 4·50
O226 15c. blue 2·50 3·00
O227 20c. green 3·25 2·50
O228 21c. violet 9·50 11·00
O229 25c. purple 10·00 8·75
O230 30c. violet 3·25 2·75
O231 50c. mauve 8·00 12·00
O232 60c. grey 13·00 13·00
O233 1p. blue 28·00 16·00
O234 2p. red 40·00 35·00

PARCEL POST STAMPS

1891. Stamp of French Colonies, "Commerce" type, optd **INDO-CHINE TIMBRE COLIS POSTAUX.**
P4 J 10c. black on lilac 15·00 4·25

1898. No. 10 optd **Colis Postaux.**
P20 D 10c. black on lilac 17·00 26·00

1899. Nos. 10 and 24 optd **TIMBRE COLIS POSTAUX.**
P21 D 10c. black on lilac 48·00 23·00
P22 10c. red 40·00 17·00

POSTAGE DUE STAMPS

1904. Postage Due stamps of French Colonies optd with value in figures.
D48 U 5 on 40c. black 30·00 11·00
D47 5 on 60c. brown on yellow 8·00 10·00
D49 10 on 60c. black 30·00 16·00
D50 30 on 60c. black 30·00 12·00

D 13 Annamite Dragon

D 28 Mot Cot Pagoda Hanoi

D 29 Annamite Dragon

1908.
D69 **D 13** 2c. black 1·40 45
D70 4c. blue 40 80
D71 5c. green 1·40 25
D72 10c. red 3·00 20
D73 15c. violet 2·75 4·00
D74 20c. brown 1·75 90
D75 30c. olive 2·25 2·75
D76 40c. purple 7·00 8·00
D77 50c. blue 3·50 1·25
D78 60c. yellow 9·00 13·00
D79 1f. grey 19·00 23·00
D80 2f. brown 19·00 19·00
D81 5f. red 35·00 32·00

1919. Surch in figures and words.
D106 **D 13** ⅘c. on 2c. black 1·90 2·75
D107 1⅗c. on 4c. blue 1·90 3·25
D108 2c. on 5c. green 3·25 1·25
D109 4c. on 10c. red 3·00 25
D110 6c. on 15c. violet 6·75 3·25
D111 8c. on 20c. brown 6·50 1·25
D112 12c. on 30c. green 8·25 2·00
D113 16c. on 40c. brown 6·00 1·90
D114 20c. on 50c. blue 13·00 7·50
D115 24c. on 60c. yellow 3·75 65
D116 40c. on 1f. grey 4·00 3·25
D117 80c. on 2f. brown 25·00 23·00
D118 2p. on 5f. red 48·00 28·00

1922. Type D **13**, but values in cents or piastres.
D136 **D 13** ⅖c. black 15 85
D137 ⅘c. black and red 15 2·00
D138 1c. black and yellow 40 50
D139 2c. black and green 1·40 65
D140 3c. black and violet 2·00 1·90
D141 4c. black and orange 1·60 2·00
D142 6c. black and olive 1·75 1·60
D143 8c. black on lilac 1·60 90
D144 10c. black and blue 1·60 1·25
D145 12c. blk & orge on grn 1·75 35
D146 20c. black & bl on yell 1·75 2·25
D147 40c. blk & red on grey 1·75 2·00
D148 1p. black & pur on pk 4·25 3·50

1927.
D160 D **28** ⅕c. orange and purple . . 15 2·25
D161 ⅖c. black and violet . . 15 2·25
D162 1c. grey and red . . . 1·60 1·90
D163 2c. olive and green . . 1·25 40
D164 3c. blue and purple . . 1·00 2·75
D165 4c. brown and blue . . 1·40 40
D166 6c. red and scarlet . . 2·50 3·25
D167 8c. violet and brown 2·50 3·00
D168 D **29** 10c. blue . . . . . . 1·60 2·50
D169 12c. brown . . . . . 4·50 5·00
D170 20c. red . . . . . . 3·50 3·00
D171 40c. green . . . . . 4·00 4·00
D172 1p. red . . . . . . 16·00 19·00

D 37

D 62

1931. All values from ⅕ c. to 50c. are in the same colours.
D197 D **37** ⅕c. black & red on yell 15 2·75
D198 ⅖c. . . . . 15 2·25
D199 ⅗c. . . . . 20 2·25
D200 1c. . . . . 15 1·75
D201 2c. 20 50
D202 2,5c. . . . . 35 3·00
D203 3c. . . . . 35 3·00
D204 4c. . . . . 30 2·50
D205 5c. . . . . 35 3·00
D206 6c. . . . . 50 1·75
D207 10c. . . . . 50 1·50
D208 12c. . . . . 20 2·50
D209 14c. . . . . 20 2·75
D210 18c. . . . . 75 3·00
D211 20c. . . . . 30 2·75
D212 50c. . . . . 70 2·75
D213 1p. blue and red on yell . . . . 2·00 3·50

1943.
D296 D **62** 1c. red on yellow . . . 45 3·00
D297 2c. red on yellow . . . 1·00 3·00
D298 3c. red on yellow . . . 80 3·00
D299 4c. red on yellow . . . 40 3·00
D300 6c. red on yellow . . . 90 3·00
D301 10c. red on yellow . . 1·10 2·75
D302 12c. blue on pink . . 40 3·00
D303 20c. blue on pink . . 40 2·75
D304 30c. blue on pink . . 1·75 3·00

INDO-CHINESE POST OFFICES IN CHINA Pt. 6, Pt. 17

General Issues.

100 centimes = 1 franc.

1902. Stamps of Indo-China, "Tablet" key-type, surch **CHINE** and value in Chinese.
15 D 1c. black on blue . . . . . 1·40 1·60
2 2c. brown on buff . . . . . 4·25 4·25
17 4c. brown on grey . . . . . 2·50 3·75
18 5c. green . . . . 3·00 3·25
5 10c. red . . . . 3·25 4·25
6 15c. grey . . . . 6·50 6·25
20 20c. red on green . . . . . 5·25 6·50
21 25c. black on pink . . . . . 7·00 10·00
22 25c. blue . . . . 7·50 6·75
23 30c. brown on drab . . . . 4·00 5·75
24 40c. red on yellow . . . . 23·00 24·00
11 50c. red on pink . . . . . 65·00 55·00
25 50c. brown on blue . . . . 9·50 10·50
26 75c. brown on orange . . . 24·00 27·00
27 1f. green . . . . 30·00 38·00
28 5f. mauve on lilac . . . . 80·00 70·00

1904. Stamps of Indo-China surch **CHINE** and value in Chinese.
29 **8** 1c. olive . . . . 1·10 1·75
30 2c. red on yellow . . . . . 1·00 1·75
31 4c. brown on grey £650 £525
32 5c. green . . . . 2·75 1·50
33 10c. red . . . . 2·00 2·25
34 15c. brown on blue . . . . 2·25 1·50
36 20c. red on green . . . . . 9·50 13·00
37 25c. blue . . . . 4·25 4·25
38 40c. black on grey . . . . 3·75 3·75
39 1f. green £275 £200
40 2f. brown on yellow . . . . 25·00 25·00
41 10f. red on green £120 £120

INDONESIA Pt. 4, Pt. 21

An independent republic was proclaimed in Java and Sumatra on 17 August 1945 and lasted until the end of 1948. During this period the Dutch controlled the rest of the Netherlands Indies, renamed "Indonesia" in September 1948. On 27 December 1949 all Indonesia except New Guinea became independent as the United States of Indonesia which, during 1950, amalgamated with the original Indonesian Republic (Java and Sumatra), a single state being proclaimed on 15 August 1950 as the Indonesian Republic. This was within the Netherlands-Indonesian Union which was abolished on 10 August 1954.

100 cents (or sen) = 1 gulden (or rupiah).

A. DUTCH ADMINISTRATION

1948. Stamps of Netherlands Indies optd **INDONESIA** and bar or bars.
541 **81** 15c. orange 90 30
533 20c. blue 55 30
543 25c. green 30 30
535 40c. green . . . . 1·10 90
544 45c. mauve 35 30
545 50c. lake . . . . 1·10 30
536 80c. red . . . . 3·75 2·10
537a 1g. violet . . . . 1·25 30
538 – 2½g. orange (No. 479) . . 45·00 9·50
539 **81** 10g. green . . . . 90·00 30·00
540 25g. orange . . . . £125 55·00

86

87 Portal to Tjandi Poentadewa Temple

89 Globe and Arms of Berne

1949. New Currency.
548A **86** 1s. grey 35 20
549A 2s. purple 55 20
550A 2½s. brown 35 20
551A 3s. red 55 20
552A 4s. green 55 55
553A 5s. blue 55 20
554A 7½s. green 55 20
555A 10s. mauve 35 20
556A 12½s. red . . . . 1·75 20
557A **87** 15s. red 35 20
558A 20s. black 35 20
559A 25s. blue 35 20
560A – 30s. red 35 20
561A – 40s. green 55 20
562A – 45s. purple . . . . . . 55 3·50
563A – 50s. brown 55 20
564A – 60s. brown . . . . 75 1·75
565A – 80s. red . . . . 1·10 20
566A – 1r. violet 75 20
567A – 2r. green . . . . 4·50 20
568A – 3r. purple . . . . 90·00 20
569A – 5r. brown . . . . 65·00 35
570A – 10r. black . . . . 80·00 1·75
571A – 25r. brown . . . . 75 1·75
DESIGNS—As Type **87**: 30 to 45s. Sculpture from Temple at Bedjoening, Bali; 50 to 80s. Minangkabau house, Sumatra; 21 × 26 mm: 1 to 3r. Toradja house; 5 to 25r. Detail of Temple of Panahan.

1949. 75th Anniv of U.P.U.
572 **89** 15s. red . . . . 1·10 35
573 25s. blue . . . . 1·10 35

B. REPUBLIC, 1945–48
ISSUES FOR JAVA AND MADURA

1945. Stamps of Netherlands Indies optd **REPOEBLIK INDONESIA**.
J 1 **46** 1c. violet . . . . 1·10 1·70
J 2 2c. purple . . . . 4·50 5·50
J19 – 2c. red (No. 461) . . . . 1·10 2·30
J 4 – 2½c. red (No. 462) . . . 1·40 2·30
J 5 – 3c. green (No. 463) . . . 1·60 2·30
J 3 **46** 3½c. grey . . . . 50·00 55·00
J 6 **71** 4c. olive . . . . 1·60 2·30
J 7 5c. blue (No. 465) . . . 65·00 75·00

1945. Stamps of Japanese Occupation of Netherlands Indies optd as above.
J 8 – 3½s. red (No. 2) £275 £375
J10 – 3½c. red (No. 5) . . . . . 38·00 38·00
J 9 – 5s. green (No. 3) . . . . 14·00 9·50
J11 **2** 5s. green 45 75
J12 – 10c. blue (No. 7) 30 60
J13 – 20c. olive (No. 8) 55 85
J14 – 40c. purple (No. 9) . . . 90 1·20
J15 **4** 60c. orange . . . . 1·20 1·40
J16 – 80s. brown (No. 11) . . . 11·00 15·00

J 5 Bull

1945. Declaration of Independence. Inscr "17 AGOESTOES 1945". Perf or imperf.
J23 **J 5** 10s. (+ 10s.) brown . . . 4·75 6·50
J24 – 20s. (+ 10s.) brown & red 5·75 6·50
DESIGN—VERT: 20s. Bull and Indonesian flag.

J 9 Boat in Storm

J 10 Wayang Puppet

1946.
J49 – 5s. blue 75 85
J50 – 20s. brown . . . . 85 1·10
J51 **J 9** 30s. red . . . . 70 2·75
DESIGNS: 5s. Road and mountains; 20s. Soldier on waterfront.

1946.
J52 **J 10** 50s. blue . . . . 14·00 11·00
J53 – 60s. red . . . . 4·25 £140
J54 – 80s. violet . . . . 52·00 £400
DESIGNS: 60s. Kris and flag; 80s. Temple.

J 13 Buffalo breaking Chains

J 14 Bandung, March, 1946

1946. Perf or imperf.
J55 **J 13** 3s. red 10 50
J56 **J 14** 5s. blue 45 65
J57 – 10s. black . . . . 7·50 10·00
J58 – 15s. purple 90 90
J59 – 30s. green . . . . 1·25 1·50
J60 – 40s. blue . . . . 1·00 1·00
J61a **J 13** 50s. black . . . . . . 1·10 1·00
J62 **J 14** 60s. lilac . . . . 1·50 2·00
J63 – 80s. red . . . . 1·25 8·75
J64 – 100s. red . . . . 1·00 1·00
J65 – 200s. lilac . . . . 1·10 1·90
J66 – 500s. red . . . . 5·00 7·50
J67 – 1000s. green . . . . . . 5·00 7·50
DESIGNS—HORIZ: 10, 15s. Soerabaya, November 1945; 30s. Anti-aircraft gunners; 100s. Ambarawa, November 1945; 200s. Wonokromo Dam, Soerabaya; 1000s. Cavalryman. VERT: 40s. Quay at Tandjong Priok; 80s. Airman; 500s. Mass meeting with flags, Djakarta.

1948. Postage Due Stamps of Netherlands Indies surch **SEGEL 25 sen PORTO**.
J68 D **7** 25s. on 7½c. orange . . . 14·00 28·00
J69 25s. on 15c. orange . . . 9·50 24·00
Although surcharged for use as postage due stamps the above were employed for ordinary postal use.

J 16 "Labour and Transport"

J 18 Flag over Waves

1948. 3rd Anniv of Independence. Imperf.
J70 **J 16** 50s. blue . . . . 5·00 6·00
J71 100s. red . . . . 7·00 7·00

1949. Government's Return to Jogjakarta. Perf. or Imperf.
J77 **J 18** 100s. red . . . . 6·25 18·00
J78 150s. red . . . . 10·00 25·00

POSTAGE DUE STAMPS

1948. Nos. J67 and J70/1 optd **DENDA**, or surch also.
JD72 **J 16** 50s. blue . . . . – 20·00
JD73 – 100s. red . . . . – 20·00
JD74 – 1r. on 50s. blue (A) . . . – 20·00
JD75 1r. on 50s. blue (B) . . . – 20·00
JD76 – 1r. on 1000s. green . . . – 20·00
A. Surcharged "RP 1"; B. Surcharged "1—RP".

ISSUES FOR SUMATRA

1946. Stamps of Netherlands Indies surch **Repoeblik Indonesia** and value.
S 1 – 15s. on 5c. blue (No. 465) 1·50 1·90
S 2 **46** 20s. on 3½c. grey . . . . 7·50 7·50
S 3 30s. on 1c. violet . . . . 7·50 7·50
S 4 40s. on 2c. purple 25 60
S 7 – 50s. on 17½c. orange (No. 431) . . . . 55·00 55·00
S 9 **46** 60s. on 2½c. bistre . . . . 7·50 5·25
S10 80s. on 3c. green . . . . 7·50 7·50
S11 – 1r. on 10c. red (No. 429) 6·00 6·00

S 9 Ploughing

S 10 Pres. Sukarno

S 12

1946. Freedom Fund.
S17 **S 9** 5s. (+25s.) green . . . . 75 2·30
S18 5s. (+25s.) blue . . . . 20 1·50
S19 – 15s. (+35s.) red . . . . 1·90 3·75
S20 – 15s. (+35s.) blue . . . . 20 1·50
S21 – 40s. (+60s.) orange . . . 90 2·30
S22 – 40s. (+60s.) red . . . . 75 4·50
S23 – 40s. (+60s.) purple . . . 7·50 24·00
S24 – 40s. (+60s.) brown . . . 12·50 42·00
DESIGNS—VERT: 15s. Soldier and flag; 40s. Oil well and factories, Palembang.

1946.
S25 **S 10** 40s. (+60s.) red . . . . 75 5·75

1946. "FONDS KEMERDEKAAN" obliterated by one or two bars.
S27 **S 9** 5s. blue . . . . 45·00 £110
S28 – 40s. red (No. S22) . . . . 45·00 45·00

1946. As Type **S 9** but without "FONDS KEMERDEKAAN". Perf or imperf.
S29 2s. red . . . . 1·00 15·00
S30 2s. brown . . . . 6·25 38·00
S31 3s. green . . . . 1·00 15·00
S32 3s. red . . . . 7·50 38·00
S33 3s. blue £180
S34 5s. blue . . . . 85 8·75
S35 15s. blue . . . . 60 4·00
S36 15s. green . . . . 4·00 38·00
S37 40s. brown . . . . 60 6·25
S38 40s. blue . . . . 20·00 60·00
DESIGNS: 2, 3, 5s. As Type **S 9**. 15s. Soldier and flag; 40s. Oil well and factories, Palembang.

1947. Fund for Palembang War Victims. Nos. S18, S20 and S23 optd **BPKPP** over triple circle.
S39 **S 9** 5s. blue . . . . 75·00 90·00
S40 – 15s. blue . . . . 75·00 90·00
S41 – 40s. brown . . . . 75·00 90·00

1947. Fiscal stamps of Japanese Occupation with blank panels optd in black with **prangko N.R.I.** and value as in Type **S 12**.
S42 **S 12** 0f.50 orange . . . . . . 13·50 30·00
S43 1f. orange . . . . 11·50 23·00
S44 2f. orange . . . . 17·00 30·00
S45 2f.50 orange . . . . . . 12·00 15·00

1947. No. S25 surch with new value and bars.
S46 50s. on 40s. red . . . . . . 5·00 5·00
S47 1f. on 40s. red . . . . . . 6·75 6·75
S48 1f.50 on 40s. red . . . . . 4·25 4·25
S49 2f.50 on 40s. red . . . . . 75 2·30
S50 3f.50 on 40s. red . . . . . 75 2·30
S51 5f. on 40s. red . . . . . . 75 2·30

1947. Surch with ornament and new value.
S63 1s. on 15s. (No. S35) . . . . 45 1·90
S64 5s. on 3s. (No. S33) . . . . 40 1·90
S65 10s. on 15s. red (as Nos. S35/6) . . . . 50 1·90
S52 30s. on 40s. (No. S28) . . . 60 1·50
S66 50s. on 3s. (No. S32) . . . . 15·00 38·00
S53 50s. on 5s. (No. S34) . . . . 6·00 4·50
S59 50s. on 40s. (No. S28) . . . 11·50 15·00
S54 1f. on 5s. (No. S34) . . . . 4·50 4·50
S60 1f. on 40s. (No. S28) . . . . 40 1·50
S55 1f.50 on 5s. (No. S34) . . . 6·00 6·00
S61 1f.50 on 40s. (No. S28) . . . 3·00 5·25
S62 2f.50 on 40s. (No. S28) . . . 40 1·50
S56 1r. on 40s. (No. S37) . . . . 40 3·00
S57 2r. on 5s. (No. S34) . . . . 60 3·00

1947. No. S56 surch **50**.
S58 50(r.) on 1r. on 40s. . . . . 45·00 55·00

1947. Air. Surch **Pos Udara** with ornament and new value.
S67 10r. on 40s. (No. S22) . . . 1·90 2·30
S68 20r. on 5s. (No. S34) . . . . 1·10 2·30

1947. Stamps of 1946 (Nos. S 29/37) surch.
S69 10s. on 15s. blue . . . . . . 11·50 11·50
S70 20s. on 15s. blue . . . . . . 11·50 11·50
S71 30s. on 15s. blue . . . . . . 11·50 6·00
S75 50s. on 5s. blue £600 £550
S76 50s. on 15s. blue £600 £600
S77 0f.50 on 15s. blue £550 £550
S78 1f. on 5s. blue £140 £140
S79 1f. on 15s. blue £275 £375
S72 1r. on 2s. red . . . . 47·00 47·00
S88 2r. on 3s. green . . . . . . 33·00 65·00
S80 2f.50 on 5s. blue £750 £650
S73 2f.50 on 15s. blue . . . . . 14·00 14·00
S82 2f.50 on 40s. brown £550 £650
S85 2r.50 on 3s. green . . . . . 19·00 28·00
S83 5f. on 15s. blue £750 £750
S74 5f. on 40s. brown £225 £170
S89 5r. on 15s. blue . . . . . . 7·00 11·50
S87 10r. on 3s. green . . . . . 70·00 70·00
S91 20r. on 2s. red £225 £475
S92 50r. on 15s. blue £325 £475
S93 100r. on 15s. blue £110 £110
S94 150r. on 40s. red £140 £140
No. S94 is surcharged on No. S22 with a pen-stroke through "FONDS KEMERDEKAAN".

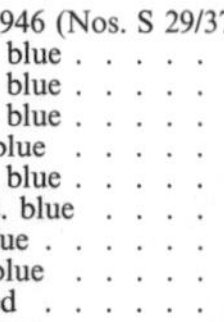
(**S 23**) "O.R.I." = "Oeang Repoeblik Indonesia" (Indonesian Republican Money)

1947. Change of Currency. Various stamps optd with Type **S 23**. (a) On stamps of Netherlands Indies.
S 99 1c. red (No. D226) . . . 8·00 8·50
S 96 **46** 3c. green (No. 338) . . . 4·75 6·00
S 97 **71** 4c. olive (No. 464) . . . 7·25 8·00
S 98 – 5c. blue (No. 465) . . . . 3·50 5·50
S100 15c. red (No. D448) . . . 6·00 7·25

(b) On stamps of Japanese Occupation of Netherlands Indies.
S101 – 1c. green (No. 15) . . . . 1·10 1·50
S102 – 2c. green (No. 16) . . . . 1·10 1·25
S103 – 3c. blue (No. 17) . . . . 1·10 1·25
S104 – 3½c. red (No. 18) . . . . 1·50 1·90
S105 – 4c. blue (No. 19) . . . . 2·50 3·75
S106 – 5c. orange (No. 20) . . . 1·50 1·90
S107 – 10c. blue (No. 21) . . . . 6·00 6·75
S111 – 10c. red (No. 57) . . . . 85 1·10
S108 – 20c. brown (No. 22) . . . 6·00 6·75
S113 – 25c. green (No. 62) . . . 10·00 12·00

S109	6	30c. purple (No. 23)	1·10	1·10
S114	–	30c. brown (No. 63)	8·00	9·00
S110	–	50c. brown (No. 25)	2·20	2·20
S115	–	50c. red (No. 66)	10·50	13·00
S116	–	60c. blue (No. 67)	5·50	6·00
S117	–	80c. red (No. 68)	5·50	7·25
S118	–	1g. violet (No. 69)	11·00	12·50

(c) On stamps of Japan.

S119	–	1s. brown (No. 317)	1·00	1·50
S120	–	3s. green (No. 319)	1·00	1·50
S121	–	4s. green (No. 320)	5·00	5·50
S122	–	6s. orange (No. 322)	1·50	2·00
S123	–	25s. brn & choc (No. 329)	1·00	1·40
S124	–	30s. green (No. 330)	2·40	3·50
S125	–	50s. green & bis (No. 331)	1·00	1·50
S126	–	1y. brown and chocolate (No. 332)	2·40	3·50

(d) On stamps of Indonesia-Sumatra.

S149	–	1s. on 15s. bl (No. S63)	70	1·40
S136	–	2s. red (No. S29)	2·50	3·00
S137	–	3s. green (No. S31)	00	00
S138	–	3s. red (No. S32)	1·00	1·70
S132	S 9	5s. green (No. S17)	2·50	4·00
S133	–	5s. blue (No. S18)	90	1·30
S139	–	5s. blue (No. S34)	75	1·10
S150	–	10s. on 15s. red (No. S65)	2·40	3·75
S134	–	15s. blue (No. S20)	2·40	4·25
S140	–	15s. blue (No. S35)	75	1·10
S141	–	15s. green (No. S36)	3·75	5·50
S127	46	20s. on 3½c. grey (No. S2)	6·50	7·50
S128	–	30s. on 1c. violet (No. S3)	6·50	8·00
S146	–	30s. on 40s. red (No. S52)	80	1·30
S129	46	40s. on 2c. purple (No. S4)	3·00	5·00
S135	–	40s. red (No. S22)	2·75	3·50
S142	–	40s. brown (No. S37)	70	1·00
S151	–	50s. on 5s. blue (No. S53)	1·80	2·40
S143	–	1f.50 on 40s. red (No. S48)	6·50	30·00
S147	–	1f.50 on 40s. red (No. S61)	6·50	7·50
S152	–	1f.50 on 5s. blue (No. S55)	5·50	7·25
S153	–	2r. on 5s. blue (No. S57)	1·60	2·50
S144	–	2f.50 on 40s. red (No. S49)	6·25	7·50
S148	–	2f.50 on 40s. red (No. S62)	6·25	7·50
S145	–	3f.50 on 40s. red (No. S50)	6·25	7·50
S154	–	10r. on 40s. red (No. S67)	7·50	10·00

C. UNITED STATES OF INDONESIA

90 Indonesian Flag

1950. Inauguration of United States of Indonesia.

574	90	15s. red (20½ × 26 mm)	1·10	25
575		15s. red (18 × 23 mm)	6·50	1·10

1950. Stamps of 1949 optd **RIS**.

579	86	1s. grey	80	65
580		2s. purple	1·40	1·80
581		2½s. brown	80	65
582		3s. red	80	40
583		4s. green	80	65
584		5s. blue	80	65
585		7½s. green	80	65
586		10s. mauve	80	60
587		12½s. red	1·00	65
588	87	20s. black	24·00	28·00
589		25s. blue	80	60
590	–	30s. red	8·25	18·00
591	–	40s. green	80	40
592	–	45s. purple	1·60	1·00
593	–	50s. brown	1·40	85
594	–	60s. brown	7·00	10·50
595	–	80s. red	2·75	1·00
596	–	1r. violet	2·10	45
597	–	2r. green	£350	90·00
598	–	3r. purple	£120	55·00
599	–	5r. brown	49·00	16·00
600	–	10r. black	90·00	35·00
601	–	25r. brown	20·00	13·50

D. INDONESIAN REPUBLIC

94 Indonesian Arms

95 Maps and Torch

1950. 5th Anniv of Proclamation of Independence.

602	94	15s. red	2·00	25
603		25s. green	2·75	1·10
604		1r. sepia	9·75	1·70

1951. Asiatic Olympic Games, New Delhi.

605	95	5s.+3s. green	10	10
606		10s.+5s. blue	10	10
607		20s.+5s. red	10	10
608		30s.+10s. brown	25	15
609		35s.+10s. blue	2·75	2·10

96

97 General Post-Office, Bandung

98 "Spirit of Indonesia"

99 President Sukarno

1951.

610	96	1s. grey	40	75
611		2s. mauve	40	60
612		2½s. brown	5·00	15
613		5s. red	40	15
614		7½s. green	40	15
615		10s. blue	40	15
616		15s. violet	40	15
618		20s. red	40	15
619		25s. green	40	15
620	97	30s. red	10	10
621		35s. violet	65	10
622		40s. green	10	10
623		45s. purple	10	25
624		50s. brown	3·00	10
625	98	60s. brown	10	10
626		70s. grey	10	10
627		75s. blue	10	10
628		80s. purple	10	10
629		90s. green	10	10

1951.

630	99	1r. violet	25	10
631		1r.25 orange	1·60	10
632		1r.50 brown	25	10
633		2r. green	25	10
634		2r.50 brown	25	10
635		3r. blue	25	10
636		4r. green	25	10
637		5r. brown	25	10
638		6r. mauve	25	10
639		10r. grey	25	10
640		15r. stone	25	10
641		20r. purple	25	10
642		25r. red	65	10
643		40r. green	80	2·10
644		50r. violet	1·10	15

101 Sports Emblem

102 Doves

1951. National Sports Festival.

655	101	5s.+3s. green	35	40
656		10s.+5s. blue	35	40
657		20s.+5s. orange	35	40
658		30s.+10s. sepia	35	40
659		35s.+10s. blue	35	1·00

1951. U.N. Day.

660	102	7½s. green	2·75	80
661		10s. violet	80	40
662		20s. orange	2·00	80
663		30s. red	2·75	1·00
664		35s. blue	2·75	1·00
665		1r. sepia	21·00	3·25

1953. Natural Disasters Relief Fund. Surch **19 53 BENTJANA ALAM +10s.**

666	97	35s.+10s. violet	25	15

104 Melati Flowers

105 Merapi Volcano in Eruption

1953. Mothers' Day and 25th Anniv of Indonesian Women's Congress.

667	104	50s. green	20·00	55

1954. Natural Disasters Relief Fund.

668	105	15s.+10s. green	1·10	1·40
669		35s.+15s. violet	1·10	1·10
670		50s.+25s. red	1·10	1·10
671		75s.+25s. blue	1·10	1·10
672		1r.+25s. red	1·10	1·10
673		2r.+50s. brown	2·75	1·10
674a		3r.+1r. green	14·00	7·00
675a		5r.+2r.50 brown	16·00	9·75

106 Girls with Musical Instruments

107 Globe and Doves

1954. Child Welfare.

676	106	10s.+10s. purple	10	55
677	–	15s.+10s. green	10	65
678	–	35s.+15s. mauve	15	65
679	–	50s.+15s. purple	50	65
680	–	75s.+25s. blue	25	2·50
681	–	1r.+25s. red	35	4·50

DESIGNS: 15s. Menangkabau boy and girl performing Umbrella Dance; 35s. Girls playing "Tjongkak"; 50s. Boy on bamboo stilts; 75s. Ambonese boys playing flutes; 1r. Srimpi dancing girl.

1955. Asian–African Conference, Bandung.

682	107	15s. black	1·00	65
683		35s. brown	1·00	65
684		50s. red	3·00	65
685		75s. turquoise	1·60	65

108 Semaphore Signaller

109 Proclamation of Independence

1955. National Scout Jamboree.

686	–	15s.+10s. green	15	15
687	108	35s.+15s. blue	15	15
688	–	50s.+25s. red	15	15
689	–	75s.+25s. brown	15	15
690	–	1r.+50s. violet	15	15

DESIGNS: 15s. Indonesian scout badge; 50s. Scouts round campfire; 75s. Scout feeding baby sika deer; 1r. Scout saluting.

1955. 10th Anniv of Independence.

691	109	15s. green	80	65
692		35s. blue	80	65
693		50s. brown	5·25	40
694		75s. purple	1·10	55

110 Postmaster Sukarto

111 Electors

1955. 10th Anniv of Indonesian Post Office.

695	110	15s. brown	80	65
696		35s. red	80	65
697		50s. blue	6·00	1·50
698		75s. green	2·40	65

1955. 1st General Indonesian Elections.

699	111	15s. purple	40	35
700		35s. green	55	65
701		50s. red	2·00	80
702		75s. blue	75	35

112 Memorial Column, Wreath and Helmet

113 Weaving

1955. Heroes' Day.

703	112	25s. green	65	25
704		50s. blue	1·60	55
705		1r. red	12·00	25

1956. Blind Relief Fund.

706	113	15s.+10s. green	55	55
707	–	35s.+15s. brown	55	55
708	–	50s.+25s. red	1·20	1·10
709	–	75s.+50s. blue	55	55

DESIGNS—VERT: 35s. Basketwork; 50s. Map reading; 75s. Reading.

114 Torch and Book

115 Lesser Malay Chevrotain

1956. Asian and African Students' Conf, Bandung.

710	114	25s. blue	1·00	25
711		50s. red	5·00	1·00
712		1r. green	2·10	1·00

1956.

713	115	5s. blue	10	10
714		10s. brown	10	10
715		15s. purple	10	10
716	–	20s. green	10	10
717	–	25s. purple	10	10
718	–	30s. orange	10	10
719	–	35s. blue	10	10
720	–	40s. green	10	10
721	–	45s. purple	1·10	15
722	–	50s. bistre	10	10
723	–	60s. blue	15	10
724	–	70s. red	1·60	25
725	–	75s. sepia	15	10
726	–	80s. red	15	15
727	–	90s. green	15	15

DESIGNS: 20s. to 30s. Hairy-nosed otter; 35s. to 45s. Malayan pangolin; 50s. to 70s. Banteng; 75s. to 90s. Sumatran rhinoceros.

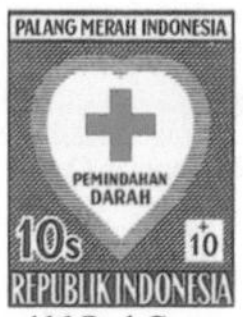

116 Red Cross

117

1956. Red Cross Fund.

728	116	10s.+10s. red and blue	10	10
729		15s.+10s. red & carmine	10	10
730	–	35s.+15s. red and brown	15	15
731	–	50s.+15s. red and green	25	15
732	–	75s.+25s. red & orange	35	25
733	–	1r.+25s. red and violet	50	40

DESIGNS: 35, 50s. Blood transfusion bottle; 75s., 1r. Hands and drop of blood.

1956. Bicentenary of Djokjakarta.

734	117	15s. green	1·60	50
735		35s. brown	1·60	50
736		50s. blue	3·00	80
737		75s. purple	3·00	80

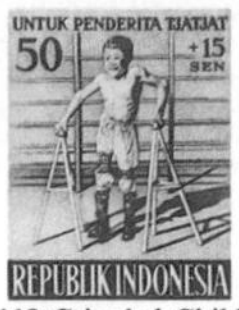

118 Crippled Child

119 Telegraph Key and Tape

1957. Cripples' Rehabilitation Fund. Inscr "UNTUK PENDERITA TJATJAT".

738	–	10s.+10s. blue	10	10
739	–	15s.+10s. brown	10	10
740	–	35s.+15s. red	10	10
741	118	50s.+15s. violet	25	25
742	–	75s.+25s. green	35	35
743	–	1r.+25s. red	50	50

DESIGNS: 10s. One-legged woman painting cloth; 15s. One-handed artist; 35s. One-handed machinist; 75s. Doctor tending cripple; 1r. Man writing with artificial arm.

1957. Centenary of Telegraphs in Indonesia.

744	119	10s. red	2·40	50
745		15s. blue	50	25
746		25s. black	40	15
747		50s. red	50	25
748		75s. green	50	15

120 Two men with Savings-box

1957. Co-operation Day. Inscr "HARI KOOPERASI".

749	120	10s. blue	55	40
750	–	15s. red	55	40
751	120	50s. green	1·00	65
752	–	1r. violet	1·40	15

DESIGN: 15s., 1r. "Co-operative Prosperity" (hands holding ear of rice and cotton).

121 Kembodja ("Plumeria acuminata")

122 Convair CV 340 Airliner

1957. Various Charity Funds. Floral designs. Multicoloured.
753 10s.+10s. Type **121** . . . . 2·10 1·00
754 15s.+10s. Tjempakakuning (michelia) . . . . 1·50 1·00
755 35s.+15s. Matahari (sunflower) . . . . 1·00 80
756 50s.+15s. Melati (jasmine) . . 65 65
757 75s.+50s. Larat (orchid) . . . 65 65

1958. National Aviation Day. Inscr "HARI PENERBANGAN NASIONAL 9-4-1958".
758 **122** 10s. brown 15 10
759 – 15s. blue 15 15
760 – 35s. orange 35 25
761 **122** 50s. turquoise 65 40
762 – 75s. slate . . . . 1·10 55
DESIGNS: 15s. Hiller "Skeeter" helicopter; 35s. Nurtiano Sikumbang trainer; 75s. De Havilland Vampire jet fighter.

123 "Helping Hands"

124 Thomas Cup

1958. Indonesian Orphans Welfare Fund Inscr "ANAK PIATU".
763 **123** 10s.+10s. blue 15 15
764 – 15s.+10s. red 15 15
765 **123** 35s.+15s. green 15 15
766 – 50s.+25s. drab 15 15
767 **123** 75s.+50s. brown 15 15
768 – 1r.+50s. brown 15 15
DESIGN: 15s., 50s., 1r. Girl and boy orphans.

1958. Indonesian Victory in Thomas Cup World Badminton Championships, Singapore.
769 **124** 25s. red 15 15
770 50s. orange 15 15
771 1r. brown 25 15

125 Satellite encircling Globe

126 Racing Cyclist

1958. International Geophysical Year.
785 **125** 10s. pink, green and blue 90 55
786 15s. drab, violet and grey 25 15
787 35s. blue, sepia and pink 25 15
788 50s. brown, blue and drab 25 15
789 75s. lilac, black and yellow 25 15

1958. Tour of Java Cycle Race.
790 **126** 25s. blue 50 25
791 50s. red 80 25
792 1r. grey 50 25

127 "Human Rights"

128 Babirusa

1958. 10th Anniv of Declaration of Human Rights.
793 **127** 10s. sepia 15 15
794 – 15s. brown 15 15
795 – 35s. blue 25 15
796 – 50s. bistre 25 15
797 – 75s. green 25 15
DESIGNS: 15s. Hands grasping "Flame of Freedom"; 35s. Native holding candle; 50s. Family acclaiming "Flame of Freedom"; 75s. "Flame" superimposed on figure "10".

1959. Animal Protection Campaign.
798 **128** 10s. sepia and olive . . . 15 15
799 – 15s. sepia and brown . . 25 25
800 – 20s. sepia and green . . . 35 35
801 – 50s. sepia and brown . . 50 50
802 – 75s. sepia and red . . . 50 50
803 – 1r. black and turquoise 55 55
ANIMALS: 15s. Anoa (buffalo); 20s. Orang-utan; 50s. Javan rhinoceros; 75s. Komodo lizard; 1r. Malayan tapir.

129 Indonesian Scout Badge

130

1959. 10th World Scout Jamboree, Manila. Inscr as in T **129**. Badges in red.
804 **129** 10s.+5s. bistre 15 15
805 – 15s.+10s. green 25 15
806 **129** 20s.+10s. violet 25 25
807 – 50s.+25s. olive 25 40
808 **129** 75s.+35s. brown 25 40
809 – 1r.+50s. slate 35 40
DESIGN: 15s., 50s., 1r. Scout badge within compass.

1959. Re-adoption of 1945 Constitution.
810 **130** 20s. red and blue 15 15
811 50s. black and red 15 15
812 75s. red and brown . . . 15 15
813 1r.50 black and green . . 25 15

131 Factory and Girder

132

1959. 11th Colombo Plan Conference, Djakarta.
814 **131** 15s. black and green . . . 15 10
815 – 20s. black and orange . . 15 10
816 **131** 50s. black and red 15 10
817 – 75s. black and blue . . . 15 10
818 – 1r.15 black and purple . . 15 10
DESIGNS: 20, 75s. Cogwheel and diesel train; 1r.15, Forms of transport and communications.

1960. Indonesian Youth Conference, Bandung. Inscr "1960".
819 **132** 15s.+5s. sepia and bistre 10 25
820 – 20s.+10s. sepia & green 15 25
821 **132** 50s.+25s. purple & blue 15 25
822 – 75s.+35s. green & bis . . 15 25
823 – 1r.15+50s. black & red . . 35 25
DESIGNS: 20s., 75s. Test-tubes in frame; 1r.15, Youth wielding manifesto.

133 Refugee Camp

134 Tea plants

1960. World Refugee Year. Centres in black.
824 **133** 10s. purple 10 15
825 – 15s. ochre 10 15
826 – 20s. brown 10 15
827 **133** 50s. green 15 15
828 – 75s. blue 35 15
829 – 1r.15 red 35 90
DESIGNS: 15s., 75s. Outcast family; 20s., 1r.15, "Care of refugees" (refugee with protecting hands).

1960. Agricultural Products.
830 – 5s. grey 15 10
831 – 10s. brown 15 10
832 – 15s. purple 15 10
833 – 20s. bistre 15 10
834 **134** 25s. green 15 10
835 – 50s. blue 15 10
836 – 75s. red 15 10
837 – 1r.15 red 15 15
DESIGNS: 5s. Oil palm; 10s. Sugar cane; 15s. Coffee plant; 20s. Tobacco plant; 50s. Coconut palm; 75s. Rubber trees; 1r.15, Rice plants.

135 Mosquito

136 Socialist Emblem

1960. World Health Day.
838 **135** 25s. red 10 10
839 50s. brown 15 10
840 75s. green 15 10
841 3r. orange 40 15

1960. 3rd Socialist Day. Inscr as in T **136**.
842 **136** 10s.+10s. brown & blk . . 10 15
843 – 15s.+15s. purple & blk . . 10 15
844 – 20s.+20s. blue and black 15 15
845 – 50s.+25s. black & brn . . 15 25
846 – 75s.+25s. black & green 15 25
847 – 3r.+50s. black and red . . 15 40
DESIGNS: 15s. Emblem similar to Type **136** within plants; 20s. Lotus flower; 50s. Boy and girl; 75s. Ceremonial watering of plant; 3r. Mother with children.

137 Pres. Sukarno and Workers Hoeing

1961. National Development Plan.
848 **137** 75s. black 25 15

1961. Flood Relief Fund. Nos. 832/3 and 836 surch **BENTJANA ALAM 1961** and premium.
849 15s.+10s. purple 10 10
850 20s.+15s. brown 10 10
851 75s.+25s. red 10 10

139 Bull Race

1961. Tourist Publicity.
852 – 10s. purple 50 40
853 – 15s. grey 50 40
854 **139** 20s. orange 50 40
855 – 25s. red 50 40
856 – 50s. lake 50 40
857 – 75s. brown 50 40
858 – 1r. green 90 40
859 – 1r.50 bistre 90 40
860 – 2r. blue . . . . 1·30 40
861 – 3r. grey . . . . 1·30 40
MS862 Three sheets each 140 × 105 mm containing (a) Nos. 852/3, 859; (b) Nos. 854, 856, 860; (c) Nos. 857/8 and a fourth sheet 105 × 140 mm. containing Nos. 855, 861 . . . . 24·00 24·00
DESIGNS: 10s. Ambonese boat; 15s. Tangkuban Perahu crater; 25s. Daja dancer; 50s. Toradja houses; 75s. Balinese temple; 1r. Lake Toba; 1r.50, Bali dancer; 2r. "Buffalo Hole" (gorge); 3r. Borobudur temple.

140 Stadium

1961. Thomas Cup World Badminton Championships.
863 **140** 75s. lilac and blue 10 10
864 1r. olive and green . . . 15 10
865 3r. salmon and blue . . . 25 15

141 "United Efforts"

1961. 16th Anniv of Independence.
866 **141** 75s. violet and blue . . . 10 10
867 1r.50 green and cream . . 10 10
868 3r. red and salmon . . . 35 15

142 Sultan Hasanuddin

1961. National Independence Heroes. Portraits in sepia; inscriptions in black.
869 – 20s. olive 10 35
870 **142** 25s. olive 15 35
871 – 30s. violet 15 35
872 – 40s. brown 15 35
873 – 50s. myrtle 15 35
874 – 60s. turquoise 15 35
875 – 75s. brown 90 35
876 – 1r. blue 90 35
877 – 1r.25 green 75 35
878 – 1r.50 green 90 35
879 – 2r. red 75 35
880 – 2r.50 red 90 35
881 – 3r. slate 75 35
882 – 4r. green 75 35
883 – 4r.50 purple 35 35
884 – 5r. red 80 35
885 – 6r. ochre 90 35
886 – 7r.50 blue . . . . 1·10 35
887 – 10r. green 75 35
888 – 15r. orange 75 35

PORTRAITS: 20s. Abdul Muis; 30s. Surjopranoto; 40s. Tengku Tjhik Di Tiro; 50s. Teuku Umar; 60s. K. H. Samanhudi; 75s. Capt. Pattimura; 1r. Raden Adjeng Kartini; 1r.25, K. H. Achmad Dahlan; 1r.50, Tuanku Imam Bondjol; 2r. Si Singamangaradja XII; 2r.50, Mohammed Husni Thamrin; 3r. Ki Hadjar Dewantoro; 4r. Gen. Sudirman; 4r.50, Dr. G. S. S. J. Ratulangie; 5r. Pangeran Diponegoro; 6r. Dr. Setyabudi; 7r.50, H. O. S. Tjokroaminoto; 10r. K. H. Agus Salim; 15r. Dr. Soetomo.

143 Census Emblems

1961. 1st Indonesian Census.
889 **143** 75s. purple 25 15

144 Nenas (pineapples)

145 Djataju

1961. Charity. Fruits.
890 **144** 20s.+10s. yellow, red and blue 50 40
891 – 75s.+25s. purple, green and slate 75 40
892 – 3r.+1r. red, yell & grn . . 1·20 1·20
FRUITS: 75s. Manggis; 3r. Rambutan.

1962. Ramayana Dancers.
893 **145** 30s. brown and ochre . . 35 40
894 – 40s. violet and purple . . 35 40
895 – 1r. purple and green . . . 50 40
896 – 1r.50 green and pink . . . 50 40
897 – 3r. blue and green . . . . 1·60 40
898 – 5r. brown and buff . . . 1·40 40
DANCERS: 40s. Hanoman; 1r. Dasamuka; 1r.50, Kidang Kentjana; 3r. Dewi Sinta; 5r. Rama.

146 Aerial View of Mosque

1962. Construction of Istiqlal Mosque.
899 **146** 30s.+20s. blue & yellow 35 25
900 – 40s.+20s. red and yellow 35 25
901 **146** 1r.50+50s. brown & yell 35 25
902 – 3r.+1r. green and yellow 35 25
DESIGN: 40s., 3r. Ground-level view of Mosque.

147 Games Emblem

148 Campaign Emblem

1962. 4th Asian Games, Djakarta. Inscr as in T **147**.
903 – 10s. green and yellow . . 15 15
904 – 15s. brown and ochre . . 15 15
905 – 20s. lilac and green . . . 35 25
906 – 25s. red and green 35 25
907 – 30s. green and buff . . . 35 15
908 – 40s. ultramarine and blue 35 15
909 – 50s. brown and drab . . . 35 35
910 – 60s. mauve and grey . . . 35 35
911 – 70s. brown and red . . . 35 35
912 – 75s. brown and orange . . 35 15
913 – 1r. violet and blue 35 35
914 **147** 1r.25 blue and mauve . . 40 40
915 – 1r.50 red and mauve . . . 1·20 40
916 – 1r.75 red and pink . . . 80 40
917 **147** 2r. brown and green . . . 75 40
918 – 2r.50 blue and green . . . 80 40
919 **147** 3r. black and red 75 40
920 – 4r.50 green and red . . . 75 40
921 **147** 5r. green and bistre . . . 55 40
922 – 6r. red and brown 55 40
923 – 7r.50 brown and pink . . 55 25
924 – 10r. ultramarine and blue 1·10 55
925 – 15r. violet and light violet 1·20 1·10
926 – 20r. green and bistre . . . 3·00 1·40

DESIGNS—VERT: 10s. Basketball; 20s. Weightlifting; 40s. Throwing the discus; 50s. Diving; 60s. Football; 70s. Press building; 75s. Boxing; 1r. Volleyball; 1r.50, Badminton; 1r.75, Wrestling; 2r.50, Shooting; 4r.50, Hockey; 6r. Water polo; 7r.50, Tennis; 10r. Table tennis; 15r. Cycling; 20r. "Welcome" monument. HORIZ: 15s. Main stadium; 25s. Hotel Indonesia; 30s. Road improvement.

1962. Malaria Eradication.
927 **148** 40s. blue and violet . . . 10 10
928 1r.50 orange and brown 10 10
929 3r. green and blue 10 10
930 6r. violet and black . . . 25 15
On the 1r.50 and 6r. the inscription is at top.

149 National Monument

150 Atomic Symbol

1962. National Monument.
931 **149** 1r.+50c. brown & black 15 15
932 – 1r.50+50c. green & blue 15 15
933 **149** 3r.+1r. mauve and green 25 15
934 – 6r.+1r.50 blue and red . . 25 15
DESIGN: 1r.50, 6r. Aerial view of Monument.

1962. "Science for Development".
935 **150** 1r.50 blue and yellow . . 15 15
936 4r.50 red and yellow . . . 25 25
937 6r. green and yellow . . . 40 25

151 "Phalaenopis amabilis"

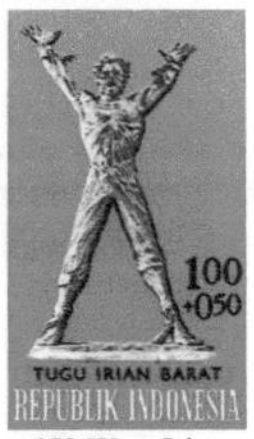
152 West Irian Monument, Djakarta

1962. Charity. Orchids. Multicoloured.
938 1r.+50s. "Vanda tricolor" (horiz) 30 15
939 1r.50+50s. Type **151** 35 15
940 3r.+1r. "Dendrobium phalaenopsis" 35 10
941 6r.+1r.50 "Paphiopedilum praestans" (horiz) 25 10

1963. Construction of West Irian Monument.
942 **152** 1r.+50c. green and red . . 25 10
943 1r.50+50c. sepia, black and mauve 15 10
944 3r.+1r. brown and blue 25 10
945 6r.+1r.50 bistre & grn . . 25 15

153 Conference Emblem

154 Rice Sheaves

1963. 12th Pacific Area Travel Association Conference, Djakarta.
946 **153** 1r. blue and green 15 15
947 – 1r.50 blue and olive . . . 15 15
948 **153** 3r. blue and brown . . . 40 15
949 – 6r. blue and orange . . . 40 15
DESIGNS: 1r.50, Prambanan Temple and Mt. Merapi; 6r. Balinese Meru in Pura Taman Ajun.

1963. Freedom from Hunger.
950 **154** 1r. yellow and blue . . . 10 10
951 – 1r.50 blue and green . . . 15 10
952 **154** 3r. yellow and red 15 15
953 – 6r. orange and black . . . 25 15
DESIGN—HORIZ: 1r.50, 6r. Tractor; Nos. 950/1 are inscr "CONTRE LA FAIM"; Nos. 952/3, "FREEDOM FROM HUNGER".

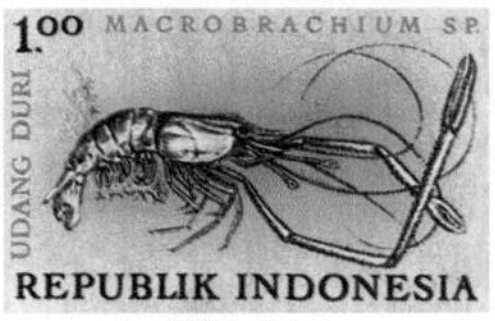
155 Lobster

1963. Marine Life. Multicoloured.
954 1r. Type **155** 35 15
955 1r.50 Kawakawa 35 15
956 3r. River snapper 80 35
957 6r. Chinese pomfret 80 50

156 Conference Emblem

1963. Asian-African Journalists' Conference.
958 **156** 1r. red and blue 15 10
959 – 1r.50 brown and lavender 15 10
960 – 3r. blue, black and olive 40 15
961 – 6r. salmon and black . . 55 25
DESIGNS—HORIZ: 1r.50, Pen, emblem and map. VERT: 3r. Pen. Globe and broken chain; 6r. Pen severing chain around Globe.

157 Indonesia, from Atjeh to Merauke

1963. Acquisition of West Irian (West New Guinea).
962 **157** 1r.50 orange, red & black 15 10
963 – 4r.50 blue, green & purple 15 15
964 – 6r. brown, yellow & green 80 50
DESIGNS: 4r.50, Parachutist; 6r. Greater bird of paradise.

158 Centenary Emblem

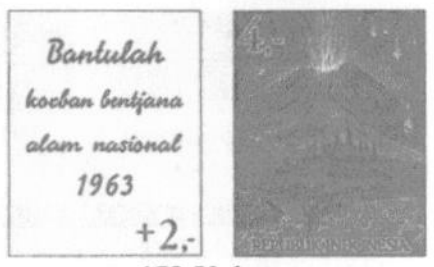
159 Volcano

1963. Centenary of Red Cross.
965 **158** 1r. green and red 25 15
966 – 1r.50 red and blue 25 15
967 **158** 3r. grey and red 25 15
968 – 6r. red and bistre 25 15
DESIGN: 1r.50, 6r. Red Cross (inscr in English).

1963. Bali Volcano Disaster Fund.
969 **159** 4r. (+2r.) red 15 10
970 6r. (+3r.) green 15 15

160 Bank of Indonesia, Djakarta

1963. National Banking Day.
971 **160** 1r.75 purple and blue . . 15 15
972 – 4r. green and yellow . . . 15 15
973 **160** 6r. brown and green . . . 15 10
974 – 12r. purple and orange . . 40 15
DESIGN—VERT: 4r., 12r. Daneswara, God of Prosperity.

161 Athletes with Banners

1963. Games of the New Emerging Forces, Djakarta.
975 **161** 1r.25 sepia and violet . . 10 10
976 – 1r.75 olive and buff . . . 10 10
977 – 4r. sepia and green . . . 10 10
978 – 6r. sepia and brown . . . 25 15
979 – 10r. sepia and green . . . 25 15
980 – 12r. olive and red 35 15
981 – 25r. ultramarine and blue 50 35
982 – 50r. sepia and red 65 40
DESIGNS: 1r.75, "Pendet" dance; 4r. Conference Hall, Djakarta; 6r. Archery; 10r. Badminton; 12r. Throwing the javelin; 25r. Sailing; 50r. "Ganefo" torch.

162 "Papilio blumei"

163 Pres. Sukarno

1963. Social Day. Butterflies. Multicoloured.
983 1r.75+50s. Type **162** 40 15
984 4r.+1r. "Charaxes dehaani" 40 15
985 6r.+1r.50 Purple-spotted swallowtail 40 15
986 12r.+3r. "Troides amphrysus" 80 40

1964.
987 **163** 6r. blue and brown . . . 15 15
988 12r. purple and bistre . . 15 15
989 20r. orange and blue . . . 15 15
990 30r. blue and orange . . . 15 15
991 40r. brown and green . . 15 15
992 50r. green and red 15 15
993 75r. red and violet 15 15
994 100r. brown and grey . . 15 15
995 250r. grey and blue . . . 35 15
996 500r. gold and red . . . 50 35

164 Lorry and Trailer

165 Rameses II, Abu Simbel

1964.
997 – 1r. purple 15 15
998 **164** 1r.25 brown 15 15
999 – 1r.75 blue 15 15
1000 – 2r. red 15 15
1001 – 2r.50 blue 15 15
1002 – 4r. green 15 15
1003 – 5r. brown 15 15
1004 – 7r.50 green 15 15
1005 – 10r. orange 15 15
1006 – 15r. blue 15 15
1007 – 25r. blue 35 15
1008 – 35r. brown 35 15
DESIGNS—HORIZ: 1r. Ox-cart; 1r.75, "Hadju Agus Salim" (freighter); 2r. Lockheed Electra airliner; 4r. Cycle-postman; 5r. Douglas DC-3 airliner; 7r.50, Teletypist; 10r. Diesel train; 15r. "Sam Ratulangi" (freighter); 25r. Convair Coronado airliner; 35r. Telephone operator. VERT: 2r.50, Buginese sailing boat.

1964. Nubian Monuments Preservation. Monuments in brown.
1009 **165** 4r. drab 35 15
1010 – 6r. blue 35 15
1011 **165** 12r. pink 35 15
1012 – 18r. green 35 15
DESIGN: 6r., 18r., Trajan's Kiosk, Philae.

166 Various Stamps of Netherlands Indies and Indonesia

1964. Stamp Centenary.
1013 **166** 10r. multicoloured . . . 1·10 15

167 Indonesian Pavilion at Fair

1964. New York World's Fair.
1014 **167** 25r. red, blue and silver 55 40
1015 50r. red, turquoise & gold . . . . 1·40 40

168 Thomas Cup

170 Pied Fantail

169 "Sandjaja" and "Siliwanghi" (destroyers)

1964. Thomas Cup World Badminton Championships.
1016 **168** 25r. gold, red and green 25 25
1017 50r. gold, red and blue 25 25
1018 75r. gold, red and violet 80 80

1964. Indonesian Navy.
1019 **169** 20r. brown and yellow 40 10
1020 – 30r. black and red . . . 40 10
1021 – 40r. blue and green . . . 80 80
DESIGNS: 30r. "Nanggala" (submarine); 40r. "Matjan Tutul" (torpedo-boat).

1965. Social Day. Birds.
1022 **170** 4r.+1r. black, lilac and yellow 35 25
1023 – 6r.+1r.50 black, buff and green 35 25
1024 – 12r.+3r. black, blue and olive 55 35
1025 – 20r.+5r. yellow, red and purple 55 40
1026 – 30r.+7r.50 black, slate and mauve . . . . . 1·00 40
BIRDS: 6r. Zebra dove; 12r. Black drongo; 20r. Black-naped oriole; 30r. Java sparrow.

171 Map and Mosque

172 Scroll in Hand

1965. Afro-Asian Islamic Conf, Bandung.
1027 **171** 10r. blue and violet . . . 35 10
1028 – 15r. brown and orange 35 10
1029 **171** 25r. green and brown . . 50 15
1030 – 50r. purple and red . . . 50 50
DESIGN: 15r., 50r. Mosque and handclasp.

1965. 10th Anniv of First Afro-Asian Conference, Bandung.
1031 **172** 15r. red and silver . . . 25 10
1032 – 25r. gold, red & turquoise 25 10
1033 **172** 50r. blue and gold . . . 40 15
1034 – 75r. gold, red and lilac 65 65
DESIGN: 25r., 75r. Conference 10th-anniv emblem.

1965. Conf of "New Emerging Forces", Djakarta. T **163** additionally inscr "Conefo". Value, "Conefo" and frame in red; portrait colour given.
1035 1r.+1r. brown 15 10
1036 1r.25+1r.25 red 15 10
1037 1r.75+1r.75 purple 15 10
1038 2r.+2r. green 15 10
1039 2r.50+2r.50 brown 15 10
1040 4r.+3r.50 blue 15 10
1041 6r.+4r. green 15 10
1042 10r.+5r. brown 15 10
1043 12r.+5r.50 orange 15 10
1044 15r.+7r.50 turquoise . . . 15 10
1045 20r.+10r. brown 15 10
1046 25r.+10r. violet 15 10
1047 40r.+15r. purple 15 10
1048 50r.+15r. violet 15 10
1049 100r.+25r. brown 25 15

174 Makara Mask and Rays

175 "Happy Family"

1965. Campaign against Cancer.
1050 **174** 20r.+10r. red and blue 25 15
1051 30r.+15r. blue and red 25 15

1965. The State's Five Principles and 20th Anniv of Republic.
1052 **175** 10r.+5r. yellow, black and brown 40 25
1053 – 20r.+10r. red, black and yellow 25 25
1054 – 25r.+10r. green, black and red 25 25
1055 – 40r.+15r. black, red and blue 50 25
1056 – 50r.+15r. yellow, black and mauve 50 25
DESIGNS: ("State's Principles"): 20r. "Humanitarianism" (globe and clasped hands); 25r. "Nationalism" (map and garland); 40r. "Democracy" (council meeting); 50r. "Belief in God" (churches and mosques).

177 Samudra Beach Hotel

1965. Tourist Hotels.
1060 **177** 10r.+5r. blue & turq . . 25 25
1061 – 25r.+10r. violet, black and green 35 35
1062 **177** 40r.+15r. brown, black and blue 40 35
1063 – 80r.+20r. pur & orge . . 65 35
DESIGN: 25r., 80r. Ambarrukmo Palace Hotel.

178 "Gloriosa superba" **180** Pres. Sukarno

1965. Flowers. Multicoloured, Inscr "1965" and with commas and dashes after figures of value.
1064 30r.+10r. Type **178** . . . . 1·00 1·00
1065 40r.+15r. "Hibiscus tiliaceus" . . . . 1·00 1·00
1066 80r.+20r. "Impatiens balsamina" . . . . 1·00 1·00
1067 100r.+25r. "Lagerstroemia Indica" . . . . 1·00 1·00
See also Nos. 1108/1116.

(Currency revalued. 100 (old) rupiahs = 1 (new) rupiah.)

1965. Revalued Currency. Optd **'65 Sen**. (a) On Nos. 989/94.
1068 **163** (20)s. on 20r. 15 10
1069 (30)s. on 30r. 15 15
1070 (40)s. on 40r. 15 15
1071 (50)s. on 50r. 15 15
1072 (75)s. on 75r. . . . . . 15 2·10
1073 (100)s. on 100r. 50 15
(b) On Nos. 1005/7.
1074 – (10)s. on 10r. 25 10
1075 – (15)s. on 15r. 25 10
1076 – (25)s. on 25r. 25 10

1966. Revalued Currency. Inscr "1967" (12r.) or "1966" (others). Values and frames turquoise (12r., 25r.) or chocolate (others); portrait and country name in colour given.
1077 **180** 1s. blue 15 10
1078 3s. olive 15 10
1079 5s. red 15 10
1080 8s. turquoise 15 10
1081 10s. blue 15 10
1082 15s. black 15 10
1083 20s. green 15 10
1084 25s. brown 15 10
1085 30s. blue 15 10
1086 40s. brown 15 10
1087 50s. violet 15 10
1088 80s. orange 15 10
1089 1r. green 15 10
1090 1r.25 brown 15 10
1091 1r.50 green 15 10
1092 2r. purple 25 10
1093 2r.50 slate 25 15
1094 5r. orange 35 35
1095 10r. olive 35 15
1096 12r. orange 35 15
1097 25r. violet 35 35

1966. Flowers. As T **178** but inscr "1966" and additionally inscr "sen" instead of commas and dashes. Multicoloured.
1108 10s.+5s. "Cassia alata" . . 1·00 1·00
1109 20s.+5s. "Barleria cristata" 1·00 1·00
1110 30s.+10s. "Ixora coccinea" 1·00 1·00
1111 40s.+10s. "Hibiscus rosa sinensis" . . . . 1·00 1·00
MS1112 58 × 78 mm. No. 1111. Imperf . . . . 9·75 2·75

1966. National Disaster Fund. Floral designs as T **178** additionally inscr "BENTJANA ALAM NASIONAL 1966". Multicoloured.
1113 15a.+5s. "Gloriosa superba" 65 65
1114 25a.+5s. "Hibiscus tiliaceus" 65 65
1115 30s.+10s. "Impatiens balsamina" 65 65
1116 80s.+20s. "Lagerstroemia Indica" 65 65

181 Cleaning Ship's Rudder **182** Gen. A. Yani

1966. Maritime Day.
1117 **181** 20s. green and blue . . . 25 10
1118 – 40s. blue and pink . . . 25 10
1119 – 50s. brown and green . . 25 10
1120 – 1r. multicoloured 25 10
1121 – 1r.50 green and lilac . . 25 10
1122 – 2r. red and grey 25 15
1123 – 2r.50 red and mauve . . 25 20
1124 – 3r. black and green . . . 35 15
MS1125 60 × 78 mm. No. 1124. Imperf . . . . 12·00 12·00
DESIGNS: 40s. Anyer Kidul lighthouse; 50s. Fisherman; 1r. Maritime emblem; 1r.50, Madurese sailing boat; 2r. Quayside; 2r.50 Pearl-diving; 3r. Liner in dry-dock.

1966. Victims of Attempted Communist Coup, 1965. Frames and date in blue.
1126 **182** 5r. brown 35 15
1127 A 5r. green 35 15
1128 B 5r. purple 35 15
1129 C 5r. olive 35 15
1130 D 5r. grey 35 15
1131 E 5r. violet 35 15
1132 F 5r. purple 35 15
1133 G 5r. green 35 15
1134 H 5r. purple 35 15
1135 I 5r. orange 35 15
PORTRAITS: A, Lt.-Gen. R. Soeprapto; B, Lt.-Gen. M. Harjono; C, Lt.-Gen. S. Parman; D, Maj.-Gen. D. Pandjaitan; E, Maj.-Gen. S. Siswomihardjo; F, Brig.-Gen. Katamso; G, Col. Soegijono; H, Capt. P. Tendean; I, Insp. K. S. Tubun.

183 Python

1966. Reptiles.
1136 **183** 2r.+25s. brown, green and flesh 15 15
1137 – 3r.+50s. grn, brn & lil 15 15
1138 – 4r.+75s. purple, buff and green 40 15
1139 – 6r.+1r. black, brn & bl 55 15
REPTILES: 3r. Chameleon; 4r. Crocodile; 6r. Green turtle.

184 Tjlempung **185** Pilot and Mikoyan Gurevich MiG-21 Fighter

1967. Musical Instruments.
1140 **184** 50s. red and black . . . 35 35
1141 – 1r. sepia and red 35 35
1142 – 1r.25 lake and blue . . . 35 35
1143 – 1r.50 green and violet . . 35 35
1144 – 2r. blue and ochre . . . 35 35
1145 – 2r.50 green and red . . . 35 35
1146 – 3r. green and purple . . 35 35
1147 – 4r. blue and orange . . . 55 35
1148 – 5r. red and blue 55 35
1149 – 6r. blue and mauve . . . 40 40
1150 – 8r. lake and green . . . 40 40
1151 – 10r. violet and red . . . 40 35
1152 – 12r. green and violet . . 65 55
1153 – 15r. violet and olive . . 50 35
1154 – 20r. black and sepia . . 50 35
1155 – 25r. black and green . . 60 35
INSTRUMENTS: 1r. Sasando; 1r.25, Foi doa; 1r.50, Kultjapi; 2r. Arababu; 2r.50, Genderang; 3r. Katjapi; 4r. Hape; 5r. Gangsa; 6r. Serunai; 8r. Rebab; 10r. Trompet; 12r. Totobuang; 15r. Tamburn; 20r. Kulintang; 25r. Keledi.

1967. Aviation Day. Multicoloured.
1156 2r.50 Type **185** 35 25
1157 4r. Convair Coronado airliner and control tower 35 20
1158 5r. Lockheed C-130 Hercules transport aircraft on tarmac 55 25

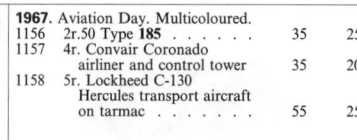

186 Thomas Cup and Silhouettes **187** Balinese Girl

1967. Thomas Cup World Badminton Championships. Multicoloured.
1159 5r. Type **186** 25 15
1160 12r. Thomas Cup on Globe 50 15

1967. International Tourist Year.
1161 **187** 12r. multicoloured . . . 1·10 90
MS1162 85 × 80 mm. No. 1161 (sold at 15r.) . . . . 5·00 5·00

188 Heroes Monument **191** Flood Victims

190 "Forest Fire"

1967. "Heroes of the Revolution". Monument.
1163 **188** 2r.50 brown and green 15 10
1164 – 5r. purple and drab . . 40 25
1165 – 7r.50 green and pink . . 40 25
DESIGNS—HORIZ: 5r. Monument and shrine. VERT: 7r.50, Shrine.

1967. Paintings by Raden Saleh.
1175 **190** 25r. red and green . . . 40 40
1176 – 50r. purple and red . . . 55 40
MS1177 95 × 63 mm. No. 1175 (sold at 30r.) . . . . 6·25 6·25
PAINTING: 50r. "A Fight to the Death".

1967. National Disaster Fund.
1178 **191** 1r.25+10s. blue & yell 35 35
1179 – 2r.50+25s. blue & yell 35 35
1180 – 4r.+40s. black & orge . . 35 35
1181 – 5r.+50s. black & orge . . 35 35
MS1182 95 × 89 mm. Nos. 1180/1 (sold at 12r.50) . . . . 37·00 37·00
DESIGNS: 2r.50, Landslide; 4r. Burning house; 5r. Erupting volcano.

192 Human Rights Emblem **193** Academy Badge

1968. Human Rights Year.
1183 **192** 5r. red, green and blue 20 10
1184 12r. red, green and drab 20 10

1968. Indonesian Military Academy.
1185 **193** 10r. multicoloured . . . 50 25

194/6 "Sudhana and Manohara at Court of Druma" (relief on wall of Borobudur) (⅔-size illustration)

1968. "Save Borobudur Monument".
1186 **194** 2r.50+25s. deep green and green 35 35
1187 **195** 2r.50+25s. deep green and green 35 35
1188 **196** 2r.50+25s. deep green and green 35 35
1189 – 7r.50+75s. green and orange 65 35
MS1190 105 × 64 mm. Nos. 1186/8 (sold at 12r.50) . . . . 37·00 37·00
DESIGN—VERT: 7r.50, Buddhist and statue of Buddha.

197 W.H.O. Emblem and "20"

1968. 20th Anniv of W.H.O.
1191 **197** 2r. purple and yellow . . 35 25
1192 – 20r. black and green . . 35 25
DESIGN: 20r. W.H.O. emblem.

198 Diesel Train (1967) and Steam Train (1867)

1968. Centenary (1967) of Indonesian Railways.
1193 **198** 20r. multicoloured . . . 75 25
1194 30r. multicoloured . . . 1·10 90

199 Scout with Pick **200** Butterfly Dancer

1968. "Wirakarya" Scout Camp.
1195 **199** 5r.+50s. brown & orge 25 15
1196 – 10r.+1r. grey & brown 55 35
1197 – 30r.+3r. brown & grn . . 90 55
DESIGNS—VERT: 10r. Bugler on hillside. HORIZ: (69 × 29 mm); 30r. Scouts in camp.

1968. Tourism.
1198 **200** 30r. multicoloured . . . 1·40 1·40
MS1199 84 × 88 mm. No. 1198 (sold at 35r.) . . . . 6·50 6·50

202 Observatory and Stars

1968. 40th Anniv of Bosscha Observatory.
1207 **202** 15r. blue, yellow & black 40 25
1208 – 30r. violet and orange 65 25
DESIGN—VERT: 30r. Observatory on Globe.

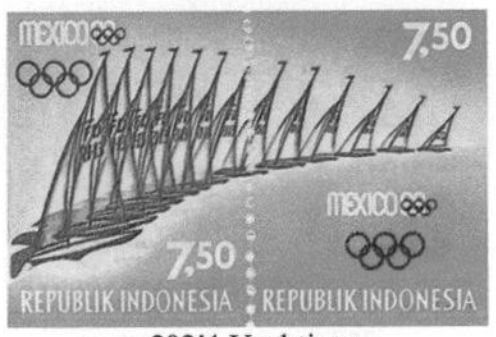

203/4 Yachting

1968. Olympic Games, Mexico.
1209 – 5r. green, brown & black 10 10
1210 **203** 7r.50 blue, yellow & red 25 15
1211 **204** 7r.50 blue, yellow & red 25 15
1212 – 12r. red, blue and yellow 25 10
1213 – 30r. brown, green & orge 50 25
MS1214 95 × 65 mm. Nos. 1210/11 (sold at 20r.) . . . . 7·00 7·00
DESIGNS:—28½ × 44½ mm: 5r. Weightlifting; 12r. Basketball. 44½ × 28½ mm: 30r. Dove and Olympic flame.
Nos. 1210/11 were issued together, se-tenant, forming the composite design illustrated.

205 "Eugenia aquea"

1968. Fruits. Multicoloured.
1215 7r.50 Type **205** 35 15
1216 15r. "Carica papaya" . . . 50 25
1217 30r. "Durio zibethinus" (vert) 80 40
MS1218 Two sheets (a) 96 × 62 mm. No. 1216. (b) 62 × 96 mm. No. 1217 (sold at 55r. the pair) 10·50 10·50

206 I.L.O. Emblem and part of Globe
207 R. Dewi Sartika

1969. 50th Anniv of I.L.O.
1219 **206** 5r. red and green 10 10
1220 – 7r.50 green and orange 15 10
1221 **206** 15r. red and violet . . . 25 15
1222 – 25r. red and turquoise 50 25
DESIGN: 7r.50, 25r. I.L.O. emblem.

1969. National Independence Heroes.
1223 **207** 15r. green and violet . . 35 15
1224 – 15r. purple and green . . 35 15
1225 – 15r. blue and red 35 15
1226 – 15r. ochre and red . . . 35 15
1227 – 15r. sepia and blue . . . 35 15
1228 – 15r. lilac and blue . . . 35 15
PORTRAITS: No. 1224, Tjut Nja Din; 1225, Tjut Nja Meuthia; 1226, Sutan Sjahrir; 1227, Dr. F. L. Tobing; 1228, General G. Subroto.

208 Woman with Flower
209 Red Cross "Mosaic"

1969. Women's Emancipation Campaign.
1229 **208** 20r.+2r. red, yellow and green 65 35

1969. 50th Anniv of League of Red Cross Societies.
1230 **209** 15r. red and green . . . 40 15
1231 – 20r. red and yellow . . . 40 35
DESIGN: 20r. Hands encircling Red Cross.

210 "Planned" Family and Factory

1969. South-East Asia and Oceania Family Planning Conference.
1232 **210** 10r. orange and green . . 35 15
1233 – 20r. mauve and green . . 50 25
DESIGN: 20r. "Planned" family and "National Prosperity".

211 Balinese Mask

1969. Tourism in Ball. Multicoloured.
1234 12r. Type **211** 35 25
1235 15r. Girl with offerings . . . 65 35
1236 30r. Cremation rites 65 35
MS1237 96 × 64 mm. No. 1236 (sold at 35r.) . . . . 5·00 5·00

212 "Agriculture"
213 Dish Aerial

1969. Five-year Development Plan.
1238 – 5r. blue and green . . . 25 10
1239 **212** 7r.50 yellow and purple 25 10
1240 – 10r. red and blue 25 10
1241 – 12r. red and blue . . . . 1·40 65
1242 – 15r. yellow and green . . 25 10
1243 – 20r. yellow and violet . . 25 10
1244 – 25r. red and black . . . 25 15
1245 – 30r. black and red . . . 50 15
1246 – 40r. orange and green . . 55 15
1247 – 50r. brown and orange 1·10 15
DESIGNS: 5r. Religious emblems ("Co-existence"); 10r. Modern family ("Social Welfare"); 12r. Crane and crate ("Overseas Trade"); 15r. Bobbins ("Clothing Industry"); 20r. Children in class ("Education"); 25r. Research worker ("Scientific Research"); 30r. Family and hypodermic syringe ("Health Care"); 40r. Tunas in net ("Fisheries"); 50r. Graph ("Statistics").

1969. Satellite Communications and Inauguration of Djatiluhur Earth Station. Multicoloured.
1248 15r. Type **213** 40 15
1249 30r. Communications satellite 55 50

214 Vickers Vimy Biplane over Borobudur Temple

1969. 50th Anniv of 1st England–Australia Flight by Ross and Keith Smith.
1253 **214** 75r. purple and red . . . 55 50
1254 – 100r. green and yellow 55 55
DESIGNS: 100r. Vickers Vimy and map of Indonesia.

215 Noble Volute

1969. Sea Shells. Multicoloured.
1255 5r.+50c. Type **215** 55 55
1256 7r.50+50c. Common hairy triton 55 55
1257 10r.+1r. Common spider conch 80 80
1258 15r.+1r.50 Bramble murex 80 80

216 Indonesian Pavilion
217 Prisoner's Hands and Scales of Justice

1970. "Expo 70" World Fair, Osaka, Japan.
1259 **216** 5r. yellow, green & brn 55 25
1260 – 15r. red, blue and green 75 35
1261 **216** 30r. yellow, blue and red 1·40 55
DESIGN: 15r. Indonesian "Garuda" symbol.

1970. "Purification of Justice".
1262 **217** 10r. purple and red . . . 55 35
1263 15r. purple and green . . 90 35

218 U.P.U. Monument, Berne
219 Timor Dancers

1970. Inauguration of New U.P.U. Headquarters Building, Berne.
1264 **218** 15r. red and green . . . 65 35
1265 – 30r. blue and ochre . . . 1·40 80
DESIGN: 30r. New Headquarters building.

1970. "Visit Indonesia Year". Traditional Dancers. Multicoloured.
1266 20r. Type **219** . . . . . . 1·10 50
1267 45r. Bali dancers . . . . . 1·60 80
MS1268 63 × 97 mm. No. 1267 (sold at 60r.) . . . . 8·25 8·25

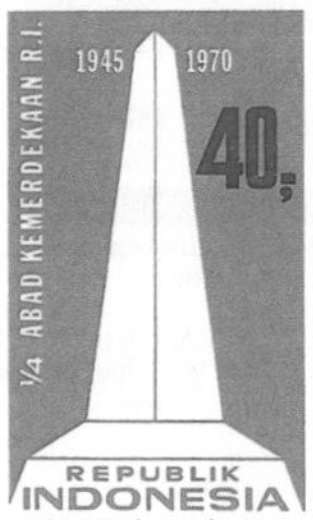

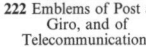

220 "Productivity" Symbol
221 Independence Monument

1970. Asian Productivity Year.
1269 **220** 5r. red, yellow and green 65 15
1270 30r. red, yellow and violet . . . . 1·40 65

1970. 25th Anniv of Independence.
1271 **221** 40r. violet, purple & blue 16·00 5·00

222 Emblems of Post and Giro, and of Telecommunications
223 U.N. Emblem and Doves

1970. 25th Anniv of Indonesian Post and Telecommunications Services.
1272 **222** 10r. brown, yellow & grn 5·00 25
1273 – 25r. black, yellow & pink 10·50 65
DESIGN: 25r. Telephone dial and P.T.T. worker.

1970. 25th Anniv of United Nations.
1274 **223** 40r. multicoloured . . . 16·00 5·00

224 I.E.Y. Emblem on globe
225 "Chrysocoris javanus" (shieldbug)

1970. International Education Year.
1275 **224** 25r. brown, red & yellow 9·75 3·25
1276 – 50r. red, black and blue 20·00 5·00
DESIGNS: 50r. I.E.Y. emblem.

1970. Insects. Multicoloured.
1277 7r.50+50c. Type **225** . . . 7·00 1·60
1278 15r.+1r.50 "Orthetrum testaceum" (darter) . . . 12·00 8·25
1279 20r.+2r. "Xylocopa flavonigrescens" (carpenter bee) . . . . . 24·00 5·75

226 Batik handicrafts

1971. "Visit ASEAN (South East Asian Nations Association) Year". Multicoloured.
1280 20r. Type **226** . . . . . . 3·00 1·40
1281 50r. Javanese girl playing angklung (musical instrument) (vert) . . . . 4·50 3·75
1282 75r. Wedding group, Minangkabau . . . . . 11·50 5·25
MS1283 64 × 97 mm. No. 1281 (sold at 70r.) . . . . 55·00 55·00

227 Restoration of Fatahillah Park

1971. 444th Anniv of Diakarta. Multicoloured.
1284 15r. Type **227** . . . . . . 2·50 1·10
1285 65r. Performance at Lenong Theatre . . . . 4·50 4·00
1286 80r. Ismail Marzuki Cultural Centre . . . . 10·50 3·50
MS1287 121 × 103 mm. 30r. Djakarta City Hall (sold at 60r.) 26·00 26·00

228 Sita and Rama
229 Pigeon with Letter, and Workers

1971. International Ramayana Festival.
1288 **228** 30r. multicoloured . . . 2·75 80
1289 – 100r. black, blue and red 4·00 1·80
DESIGN: 100r. Rama.

1971. 5th Asian Regional Telecommunications Conf.
1290 **229** 50r. chocolate, brown and buff . . . . . . 2·10 1·00

230 U.P.U. Monument, Berne, and Hemispheres

1971. U.P.U. Day.
1291 **230** 40r. purple, black & blue 2·00 1·00

231 Schoolgirl
233 Microwave Tower

232 Clown Surgeonfish

1971. 25th Anniv of UNICEF. Mult.
1292 20r. Type **231** . . . . . . 2·75 55
1293 40r. Boy with rice-stalks . . 4·00 1·10

1971. Fishes (1st series). Multicoloured.
1294 15r. Type **232** . . . . . . 5·25 1·40
1295 30r. Moorish idol . . . . . 10·50 3·75
1296 40r. Emperor angelfish . . . 16·00 5·25
See also Nos. 1318/20, 1343/5, 1390/2 and 1423/5.

1972. 25th Anniv of E.C.A.F.E.
1297 **233** 40r. blue and turquoise 3·50 1·00
1298 – 75r. multicoloured . . . 3·50 1·00
1299 – 100r. multicoloured . . . 5·25 2·10
DESIGNS—VERT: 40r. E.C.A.F.E. emblem. HORIZ: 100r. Irrigation and highways.

234 Human Heart **235** Ancient and Modern Textile Production

1972. World Heart Month.
1300 **234** 50r. multicoloured . . . 2·10 80

1972. 50th Anniv of Textile Technological Institute.
1301 **235** 35r. purple, yellow & orge . . . . 2·10 80

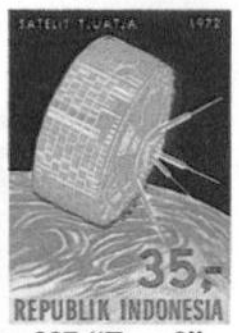

236 Children reading Books **237** "Essa 8" Weather Satellite

1972. International Book Year.
1302 **236** 75r. multicoloured . . . 2·75 1·20

1972. Space Exploration.
1303 **237** 35r. brown, violet & blue 2·00 65
1304 – 50r. blue, black and pink 3·75 3·50
1305 – 60r. black, green & brn 6·50 1·10
DESIGNS: 50r. Astronaut on Moon; 60r. Indonesian "Kartika I" rocket.

238 Hotel Indonesia

1972. 10th Anniv of Hotel Indonesia.
1306 **238** 50r. green, pale grn & red . . . . 2·50 1·10

239 "Silat" (unarmed combat) **240** Family and Religious Buildings

1972. Olympic Games, Munich.
1307 **239** 20r. purple, cobalt & blue . . . . 1·40 15
1308 – 35r. violet, brown & mve 1·40 40
1309 – 50r. emer, dp grn & grn 2·75 75
1310 – 75r. rose, purple and pink . . . . 2·75 1·80
1311 – 100r. brown, blue & green . . . . 5·75 3·00
DESIGNS: 35r. Running; 50r. Diving; 75r. Badminton; 100r. Olympic stadium.

1972. Family Planning Campaign. Mult.
1312 30r. Type **240** . . . . . . 2·00 65
1313 75r. "Healthy family" . . . 3·75 2·40
1314 80r. "Family of workers" 6·00 3·00

241 Moluccas Dancer **242** Thomas Cup and Shuttlecock

1972. "Art and Culture" (1st series).
1315 **241** 30r. brown, pink & green 2·00 65
1316 – 60r. multicoloured . . . 5·00 2·75
1317 – 100r. bl, brn & cinnamon . . . . . . 7·00 2·75
DESIGNS—VERT: 60r. Couple and Toraja traditional house. HORIZ: 100r. West Irian traditional house.
See also 1336/8, 1373/5 and 1401/3.

1972. Fishes (2nd series). As T **232**. Mult.
1318 30r. Triangle butterflyfish 7·00 2·00
1319 50r. Royal angelfish . . . . 12·00 3·00
1320 100r. Clown triggerfish . . . 16·00 5·25

1972. Thomas Cup Badminton Championships, Djakarta.
1321 **242** 30r. blue and green . . . 80 25
1322 – 75r. red and green . . . 1·80 50
1323 – 80r. brown and red . . . 3·50 1·00
DESIGNS: 75r. Thomas Cup and Sports Centre; 80r. Thomas Cup and player.

243 Emblem, Anemometer and "Gatotkaca"

1973. I.M.O. and W.M.O. Weather Organization Centenary.
1324 **243** 80r. multicoloured . . . 2·00 80

244 "Health begins at Home" **245** Java Mask

1973. 25th Anniv of W.H.O.
1325 **244** 80r. blue, orange & green . . . . 1·60 80

1973. Tourism. Indonesian Folk Masks. Mult.
1326 30r. Type **245** . . . . . . 5·25 90
1327 60r. Kalimantan mask . . . 8·25 3·50
1328 100r. Bali mask . . . . . . 13·00 1·80

246 Savings Bank and Thrift Plant **247** Chess

1973. Two-Year National Savings Drive.
1329 **246** 25r. black, yellow & bis 90 50
1330 – 30r. green, gold & yellow 1·60 50
DESIGN—HORIZ: 30r. Hand and "City" savings bank.

1973. National Sports Week. Multicoloured.
1331 30r. Type **247** . . . . . . 1·60 1·10
1332 60r. Karate . . . . 2·75 1·10
1333 75r. Hurdling (horiz) . . . 5·00 90

248 International Policemen

1973. 50th Anniv of Interpol.
1334 **248** 30r. multicoloured . . . 90 35
1335 – 50r. yellow, purple & blk 1·60 65
DESIGN—VERT: 50r. Giant temple guard.

1973. "Art and Culture" (2nd series). Weaving and Fabrics. As T **241**. Multicoloured.
1336 60r. Parang Rusak pattern 2·50 2·00
1337 80r. Pagi Sore pattern . . . 5·00 2·10
1338 100r. Merak Ngigel pattern 9·00 3·75

249 "Food Cultivation"

1973. 10th Anniv of World Food Programme.
1339 **249** 30r. multicoloured . . . 2·10 65

250 "Religion" **252** Bengkulu Costume

251 Admiral Sudarso and Naval Battle of Arafuru

1973. Family Planning.
1340 **250** 20r. blue, light blue & red 80 40
1341 – 30r. black, yellow & brn 1·60 65
1342 – 60r. black, yellow & grn 3·25 55
DESIGNS: 30r. Teacher and class ("Population Education"); 60r. Family and house ("Health").

1973. Fishes (3rd series). As T **232**. Mult.
1343 40r. Powder-blue surgeonfish 1·60 1·10
1344 65r. Melon butterflyfish . . 6·50 2·00
1345 100r. Blue-ringed angelfish 8·25 3·25

1974. Naval Day.
1346 **251** 40r. multicoloured . . . 1·80 80

1974. Pacific Area Travel Association Conference, Djakarta. Provincial Costumes. Multicoloured.
1347 5r. Type **252** . . . . 16·00 1·10
1348 7r.50 Kalimantan. Timor . . 8·25 1·10
1349 10r. Kalimantan, Tengah . . 1·60 80
1350 15r. Jambi . . . . 1·60 80
1351 20r. Sulawesi, Tenggara . . 1·60 80
1352 25r. Nusatenggara, Timor 1·60 80
1353 27r.50 Maluku . . . . . . 1·60 1·60
1354 30r. Lampung . . . . . . 1·60 1·60
1355 35r. Sumatera, Barat . . . 1·60 80
1356 40r. Aceh . . . . 1·60 80
1357 45r. Nusatenggara, Barat . . 4·00 80
1358 50r. Riau . . . . 2·40 2·40
1359 55r. Kalimantan, Barat . . 3·25 80
1360 60r. Sulawesi, Utara . . . 3·25 80
1361 65r. Sulawesi, Tengah . . . 3·25 80
1362 70r. Sumatera, Selatan . . . 3·50 80
1363 75r. Java, Barat . . . . . 3·50 80
1364 80r. Sumatera, Utara . . . 3·50 80
1365 90r. Yogyakarta . . . . . 3·75 3·75
1366 95r. Kalimantan, Selatan . . 3·50 80
1367 100r. Java, Timor . . . . . 3·50 1·60
1368 120r. Irian, Jaya . . . . . 6·50 1·10
1369 130r. Java, Tengah . . . . 6·50 80
1370 135r. Sulawesi, Selatan . . . 7·25 80
1371 150r. Bali . . . . 7·25 80
1372 160r. Djakarta . . . . . . 7·25 1·60

1974. "Art and Culture" (3rd series). Shadow Plays. As T **241**. Multicoloured.
1373 40r. Baladewa . . . . . . 3·00 1·30
1374 80r. Kresna . . . . 5·25 2·50
1375 100r. Bima . . . . 6·50 2·50

254 Pres. Suharto

1974.
1376 **254** 40r. brown, green & blk 80 10
1377 50r. brown, blue & black 2·00 15
1378 65r. brown, mauve & blk 1·10 65
1379 75r. brown, yellow & blk 2·00 15
1380 100r. brown, yellow & blk . . . . 2·00 15
1381 150r. brown, green & blk 2·00 15
See also Nos. 1444/7.

255 "Improvement of Living Standards" **256** "Welfare"

1974. World Population Year.
1382 **255** 65r. multicoloured . . . 1·50 50

1974. Family Planning.
1383 **256** 25r. multicoloured . . . 1·00 40
1384 – 40r. blue, black and green . . . . 1·00 40
1385 – 65r. ochre, brown & yell 3·00 40
DESIGNS: 40r. Young couple ("Development"); 65r. Arrows ("Religion").

257 Bicycle Postmen

1974. Centenary of U.P.U.
1386 **257** 20r. brown, yellow & grn 2·50 50
1387 – 40r. brown, orange & bl 2·50 75
1388 – 65r. brown, yellow & blk 2·50 75
1389 – 100r. black, blue and red 2·50 2·00
DESIGNS: 40r. Mail-cart; 65r. Mounted postman; 100r. East Indies galley.

1974. Fishes (4th series). As T **232**. Mult.
1390 40r. Sail-finned tang . . . . 2·50 50
1391 80r. Blue-girdled angelfish 4·00 2·00
1392 100r. Mandarin fish . . . . 6·50 2·40

258 Drilling for Oil

1974. 17th Anniv of Pertamina Oil Complex. Multicoloured.
1393 40r. Type **258** 55 35
1394 75r. Oil refinery 55 35
1395 95r. Control centre (vert) . . 55 35
1396 100r. Road tanker (vert) . . 55 35
1397 120r. Fokker Fellowship airliner over storage tank farm (vert) 90 35
1398 130r. Pipelines and tanker (vert) 90 35
1399 150r. Petrochemical storage tanks 90 35
1400 200r. Offshore oil rig . . . 90 35

1975. "Art and Culture" (4th series). As T **241**.
1401 50r. silver, red and black . . 1·50 1·30
1402 75r. silver, green and black 2·40 1·30
1403 100r. yellow, blue and black 4·50 1·30
DESIGNS: 50r. Sumatran spittoon; 75r. Sumatran "sirh" dish; 100r. Kalimantan "sirh" dish.

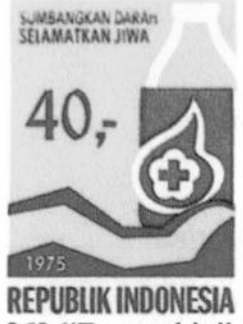

260 "Donorship" **261** Measures and Globe

1975. Blood Donors' Campaign.
1404 **260** 40r. red, yellow and green . . . . 1·10 65

1975. Centenary of Metre Convention.
1405 **261** 65r. blue, red and yellow 2·00 65

262 Women in Public Service

1975. International Women's Year. Mult.
1406 40r. Type **262** . . . . . . 1·60 65
1407 100r. I.W.Y. emblem (21 × 29 mm) . . . . . . 2·10 65

263 "Dendrobium pakarena" **264** Stupas and Damaged Temple

1975. Tourism. Indonesian Orchids. Mult.
1408 40r. Type **263** . . . . . . 5·00 1·10
1409 70r. "Aeridachnis bogor" 5·00 2·10
1410 85r. "Vanda genta" . . . . 9·00 3·25

1975. UNESCO "Save Borobudur Temple" Campaign. Multicoloured.
1411 25r. Type **264** . . . . . . 3·25 80
1412 40r. Buddhist shrines and broken wall . . . . . . 3·75 1·10
1413 65r. Stupas and damaged building (horiz) . . . . . 7·25 4·50
1414 100r. Buddha and stupas (horiz) . . . . 10·50 4·50

265 Battle of Banjarmasin

1975. 30th Anniv of Independence.
1415 **265** 25r. black and yellow . . 80 50
1416 – 40r. black and red . . . 1·10 50
1417 – 75r. black and red . . . 1·60 1·30
1418 – 100r. black and orange 1·60 1·00
DESIGNS: 40r. Battle of Batua; 75r. battle of Margarana; 100r. Battle of Palembang.

266 "Education"

267 Heroes' Monument, Surabaya

1975. Family Planning. Multicoloured.
1419 20r. Type **266** 65 15
1420 25r. "Religion" . . . . . . 1·00 25
1421 40r. "Prosperity" . . . . . 1·60 50

1975. 30th Anniv of Independence War.
1422 **267** 100r. red and green . . . 2·40 50

1975. Fishes (5th series). As T **232**. Mult.
1423 40r. Twin-spotted wrasse . . 1·60 50
1424 75r. Saddleback butterflyfish 5·00 1·50
1425 150r. Dusky batfish (vert) 6·50 3·00

269 Thomas Cup

1976. Indonesian Victory in World Badminton Championships. Multicoloured.
1428 20r. Type **269** . . . . . . 1·00 25
1429 40r. Uber cup . . . . . . 1·00 55
1430 100r. Thomas and Uber cups . . . . 2·10 55

270 Refugees and New Village

1976. World Human Settlements Day. Mult.
1431 30r. Type **270** 80 15
1432 50r. Old and restored villages . . . . 1·50 40
1433 100r. Derelict and rebuilt houses . . . . 1·60 40

271 Early and Modern Telephones

272 Human Eye

1976. Telephone Centenary.
1434 **271** 100r. brown, red & yell 1·30 50

1976. World Health Day. Multicoloured.
1435 20r. Type **272** 40 25
1436 40r. Blind man with stick 90 40

273 Main Stadium, Montreal

1976. Olympic Games, Montreal.
1437 **273** 100r. blue . . . . 1·30 55

274 Lake Tondano, Sulawesi

275 "Light Traffic" Station

1976. Tourism. Multicoloured.
1438 35r. Type **274** 80 40
1439 40r. Lake Kelimutu, Flores 80 40
1440 75r. Lake Maninjau, Sumatra . . . . 1·60 50

1976. Inauguration of Domestic Satellite System.
1441 **275** 20r. multicoloured . . . 80 35
1442 – 50r. black and green . . 80 35
1443 – 100r. turquoise, bl & vio 1·40 65
DESIGNS: 50r. "Master control" station; 100r. "Palapa" satellite.

1976. As T **254** but with background of wavy lines.
1444 200r. brown, blue and green 8·25 15
1445 300r. brown, red and flesh 2·10 15
1446 400r. brown, green and yellow . . . . 4·00 35
1447 500r. brown, red and lilac 5·75 1·00

276 "Vanda Putri Serang"

1976. Orchids. Multicoloured.
1448 25r. "Arachnis flos-aeris" . . 2·40 1·00
1449 40r. Type **276** . . . . . . 2·40 1·00
1450 100r. "Coelogyne pandurata" . . . . 3·50 2·10
MS1451 67 × 90 mm. No. 1448 (sold at 60r.) . . . . 65·00 65·00

277 Stylized Tree

279 Open Book

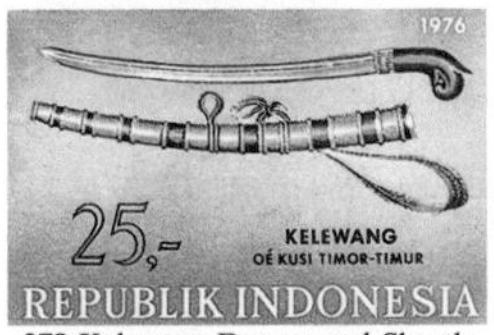

278 Kelewang Dagger and Sheath (Timor)

1976. Reafforestation Week.
1452 **277** 20r. green, blue & brown 80 35

1976. Daggers and Sheaths.
1453 **278** 25r. green, black & brown . . . . 1·10 40
1454 – 40r. brown, yellow & orge . . . . 1·80 75
1455 – 100r. brown, yellow & grn . . . . 2·50 2·10
MS1456 94 × 64 mm. 40r. No. 1454 (sold at 70r.) . . . . 16·00 16·00
DESIGNS: 40r. Mandau dagger and sheath (Borneo); 100r. Rencong dagger and sheath (Aceh).

1976. Books for Children.
1457 **279** 20r. green, orange & blue 65 25
1458 – 40r. violet, red and yellow . . . . 1·30 40
DESIGN: 40r. Children reading book.

280 UNICEF Emblem

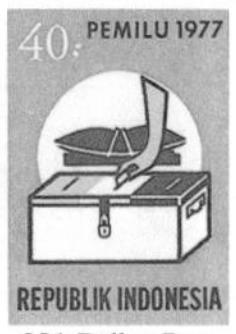

281 Ballot Box

1976. 30th Anniv of UNICEF.
1459 **280** 40r. blue, turquoise & vio . . . . 1·10 50

1977. Elections.
1460 **281** 40r. blue, yellow and grey . . . . 2·10 25
1461 – 75r. blue, yellow and pink . . . . 2·40 40
1462 – 100r. bistre, red and black . . . . 3·75 1·30
DESIGNS: 75r. Ballot box, factory and produce; 100r. Indonesian arrow.

282 Scout Emblems and Camp

283 Letter and A.O.P.U. Emblem

1977. 11th National Scout Jamboree. Mult.
1463 25r. Type **282** 60 35
1464 30r. Emblems, tent and trees 60 35
1465 40r. Emblems, tent and flags 1·40 75

1977. 15th Anniv of Asian–Oceanic Postal Union. Multicoloured.
1466 65r. Type **283** 80 35
1467 100r. Stylized carrier pigeon 1·40 50

284 Anniversary Emblem

285 Rose

1977. 450th Anniv of Jakarta.
1468 **284** 20r. blue and red 80 40
1469 – 40r. green and blue . . . 80 40
1470 – 100r. blue and turquoise 1·60 80
MS1471 72 × 96 mm. No. 1470 (sold at 125r.) . . . . 9·00 9·00
DESIGNS: 40; 100r. Similar to Type **284** but with emblem and arms differently arranged.

1977. "Amphilex 77" International Stamp Exhibition, Amsterdam.
1472 **285** 100r. red, green and black . . . . 1·40 50
1473 – 100r. red, green and black . . . . 1·40 50
MS1474 Two sheets (sold at 550r.). (a) 71 × 95 mm. Nos. 1472/3 each × 2. (b) 72 × 63 mm. **285** 100r. scarlet, blue and black . . . . 20·00 20·00
DESIGN: No. 1473, Envelope.

286 Sports Pictograms

287 Trophy

1977. 9th National Sports Week.
1475 **286** 40r. silver, green and red 2·50 1·60
1476 – 50r. silver, blue and red 3·50 1·60
1477 – 100r. gold, black and red 5·75 3·50
DESIGNS: 50; 100r. Similar to Type **286** but with different pictograms.

1977. 10th National Koran Reading Contest.
1478 **287** 40r. brown, green & yell 2·40 50
1479 – 100r. black, yellow & grn 3·00 90
DESIGN: 100r. Emblem.

288 Carrier Pigeon and Map

289 Government Officer, Djakarta Region

1977. 10th Anniv of Association of South East Asian Nations. Multicoloured.
1480 25r. Type **288** 50 15
1481 35r. Map of ASEAN members . . . . 2·10 65
1482 50r. Transport and flags of ASEAN members . . . . 2·10 80

1977. Economic and Cultural Co-operation with Pakistan.
1483 **289** 25r. brown, gold & green 65 25

290 "Taeniophyllum sp."

291 Child and Mosquito

1977. Orchids. Multicoloured.
1484 25r. Type **290** . . . . . . 2·40 80
1485 40r. "Phalaenopsis violacea" 2·40 1·60
1486 100r. "Dendrobium spectabile" . . . . 5·00 2·40
MS1487 86 × 71 mm. As No. 1486 but with blue background (sold at 125r.) . . . . 11·50 11·50

1977. National Health Campaign.
1488 **291** 40r. red, green and black 65 25

292 Proboscis Monkey

1977. Wildlife (1st series). Multicoloured.
1489 20r. Type **292** 80 40
1490 40r. Indian elephant . . . . 2·00 80
1491 100r. Tiger . . . . 5·25 1·60
MS1492 94 × 64 mm. As No. 1491 but colours of country name and values reversed (sold at 125r.) 9·75 9·75
See also Nos. 1515/**MS**1518 and 1558/**MS**1561.

293 Hands holding U.N. Emblem

294 Mother feeding Baby

1978. U.N. Conference on Technical Co-operation among Developing Countries.
1493 **293** 100r. blue and ultramarine . . . . . 1·40 55

1978. Campaign for the Promotion of Breast Feeding.
1494 **294** 40r. green and blue . . . 50 25
1495 – 75r. brown and red . . . 90 40
DESIGN: 75r. Stylised mother and child.

295 Dome of the Rock

1978. Palestine Welfare.
1496 **295** 100r. multicoloured . . . 1·30 50

296 World Cup Emblem

297 Head and Blood Circulation Diagram

1978. World Cup Football Championship, Argentina.
1497 **296** 40r. green, black and blue 65 25
1498 100r. mauve, black & bl 1·20 65

1978. World Health Day.
1499 **297** 100r. blue, black and red 1·20 50

298 Leather Puppets

1978. Puppets from Wayang Museum, Djakarta. Multicoloured.
1500 40r. Type **298** . . . . . . 2·40 65
1501 75r. Wooden puppets . . . 2·50 1·30
1502 100r. Actors wearing masks 5·00 2·10

300 Congress Emblem

301 I.A.Y. Emblem

1978. 27th Congress of World Confederation of Organizations of the Teaching Profession, Djakarta.
1509 **300** 100r. grey . . . . 1·00 40

1978. International Anti-Apartheid Year.
1510 **301** 100r. blue and red . . . 1·10 40

302 Couple and Tree

303 Anniversary Emblem

1978. 8th World Forestry Congress, Djakarta.
1511 **302** 40r. blue and green . . . 25 15
1512 – 100r. dp green & lt green 1·00 50
DESIGN: 100r. People and trees.

1978. 50th Anniv of Youth Pledge.
1513 **303** 40r. brown and red . . . 65 25
1514 100r. brown, red and pink . . . . 1·00 40

1978. Wildlife (2nd series). As T **292**. Mult.
1515 40r. Long-nosed echidna . . 1·60 40
1516 75r. Sambar . . . . 2·40 80
1517 100r. Clouded leopard . . . 4·00 1·20
MS1518 Two sheets (sold at 700r.). (a) 94 × 63 mm. No. 1517. (b) 115 × 157 mm. No. 1516 and 1517 × 4 but with colours of inscriptions and value reversed 6·00 6·00

304 "Phalaenopsis sri rejeki"

307 Thomas Cup and Badminton Player

306 Douglas DC-3 over Volcano

1978. Orchids. Multicoloured.
1519 40r. Type **304** . . . . . . 1·20 40
1520 75r. "Dendrobium macrophillum" . . . . . 1·60 65
1521 100r. "Cymbidium fynlaysonianum" . . . . 3·25 90
MS1522 63 × 96 mm. As No. 1521 but with some colours changed (sold at 150r.) . . . . 6·00 6·00

1979. 30th Anniv of Garuda Indonesian Airways. Multicoloured.
1531 40r. Type **306** 80 35
1532 75r. Douglas DC-9-30 over village . . . . 1·00 35
1533 100r. Douglas DC-10 over temple . . . . 1·80 1·00

1979. Thomas Cup Badminton Championships, Djakarta.
1534 **307** 40r. pink and turquoise 50 50
1535 – 100r. brown and pink . . 1·00 80
1536 – 100r. brown and pink . . 1·00 80
DESIGNS: No. 1535, Player on left side of net hitting shuttlecock; 1536, Player on right side of net.
Nos. 1535/6 were issued together, se-tenant, forming a composite design.

308 "Paphiopedilum lowii"

309 Family and Houses

1979. Orchids. Multicoloured.
1537 60r. Type **308** . . . . . . 1·10 35
1538 100r. "Vanda limbata" . . . 1·60 50
1539 125r. "Phalaenopsis gigantea" . . . . 2·40 80
MS1540 63 × 96 mm. No. 1539 (sold at 175r.) . . . . 5·00 5·00
See also **MS**1548.

1979. 3rd Five Year Development Plan.
1541 **309** 35r. drab and green . . . 15 10
1542 – 60r. green and blue . . . 25 15
1543 – 100r. brown and blue . . 50 15
1544 – 125r. brown and green 65 25
1545 – 150r. yellow, orge & red 80 25
DESIGNS: 60r. Pylon, dam and fields; 100r. School and clinic; 125r. Loading produce at factory; 150r. Delivering mail.

310/11 Mrs. R. A. Kartini

1979. Birth Centenary of Mrs. R. A. Kartini (pioneer of women's rights).
1546 **310** 100r. brown and green 80 40
1547 **311** 100r. green and brown 80 40

1979. "Asian–Philatelie '79" International Stamp Exhibition, Dortmund. Sheet 96 × 119 mm. Multicoloured.
MS1548 250r. Type **308**; 300r. As No. 1538 (sold at 650r.) . . . 8·25 8·25

312 Bureau Emblem

313 Self Defence

1979. 50th Anniv of International Bureau of Education.
1549 **312** 150r. blue, lt blue & lilac 1·10 40

1979. 10th South East Asia Games, Djakarta.
1550 **313** 60r. yellow, black & grn 55 25
1551 – 125r. orange, grey & blue 90 40
1552 – 150r. yellow, black & red 1·30 65
DESIGNS: 125r. Games emblem; 150r. Main stadium, Senayan.

314 Co-operation Emblem

315 National I.Y.C. Emblem

1979. Co-operation Day.
1553 **314** 150r. multicoloured . . . 1·00 35

1979. International Year of the Child.
1554 **315** 60r. black and green . . 40 15
1555 – 150r. blue and black . . 1·00 40
DESIGN: 150r. International I.Y.C. emblem.

316 Exhibition Emblem

317 Drug Addict

1979. 3rd World Telecommunications Exhibition, Geneva.
1556 **316** 150r. grey, blue & orange . . . . 1·00 50

1979. "End Drug Abuse" Campaign.
1557 **317** 150r. black and pink . . 1·00 50

1979. Wildlife (3rd series). As T **292**. Mult.
1558 60r. Bottle-nosed dolphin . . 1·10 65
1559 125r. Irrawaddy dolphin . . 2·75 90
1560 150r. Leatherback turtle . . 4·50 1·20
MS1561 94 × 64 mm. 200r. As No. 1560 (sold at 250r.) . . . 8·25 8·25

318 Pinisi Sailing Ship

1980. Djakarta–Amsterdam Spice Race.
1562 **318** 60r. blue 40 15
1563 – 125r. brown 65 40
1564 – 150r. purple . . . . . . 1·50 40
MS1565 64 × 120 mm. 300r. brown 4·40 4·50
DESIGNS—HORIZ: 125, 300r. Schooner made of leaves. VERT: 150r. Madurese sailing boat.
See also No. **MS**1578.

319 Riding the Rapids

1980. Adventure Sports. Multicoloured.
1566 60r. Type **319** 50 15
1567 125r. Mountaineering (vert) 90 50
1568 150r. Hang gliding . . . . 1·30 75
MS1569 62 × 76 mm. 300r. Type **319** (sold at 350r.) . . . . 4·50 4·50

320 Cigarettes and Heart

321 Artificial Flowers in Vase

1980. Anti-smoking Campaign.
1570 **320** 150r. flesh, black and pink . . . . 1·00 40

1980. 2nd Flower Festival, Jakarta. Mult.
1571 125r. Type **321** . . . . . . 1·50 40
1572 150r. Artificial bouquet . . 1·80 65
See also No. **MS**1579.

322 Conference Building and Globe

323 Danau Poso Statue

1980. 25th Anniv of First Asian–African Conference, Bandung.
1573 **322** 150r. mauve and gold . . 1·00 40
MS1574 76 × 104 mm. **322** 300r. magenta and gold (sold at 350r.) 4·50 4·50

1980. Prehistoric Monuments. Multicoloured.
1575 60r. Type **323** 65 25
1576 125r. Elephant stone, Pasemah Village, South Sumatra 80 50
1577 150r. Taman Bali sarcophagus . . . . . . 1·30 65

1980. "London 1980" International Stamp Exhibition. Two sheets.
MS1578 120 × 63 mm. 100r. Type **321** 500r. blue . . . . . 16·00 16·00
MS1579 120 × 150 mm. 100r. Type **321**; 100r. As No. 1572; 200r. Type **323**; 200r. As No. 1577, each × 2 (sold at 1300r.) . . . . . 6·50 6·50

324 Discus Thrower

325 Draughtsman in Wheelchair

1980. Olympics for the Disabled, Arnhem.
1580 **324** 75r. brown and orange 90 35

1980. 30th Anniv of Disabled Veterans Corps.
1581 **325** 100r. yellow, blue & blk 90 35

326 President Suharto

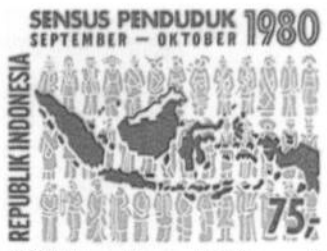

327 People and Map of Indonesia

1980.
1581a **326** 10r. olive and green . . 1·60 10
1582 12r.50 green & lt green 35 10
1582a 25r. brown and orange 50 10
1583 50r. blue and green . . 35 35
1583a 55r. red and vermilion 50 10
1584 75r. brown and yellow 75 15
1585a 100r. blue, violet & mve 1·30 35
1586 200r. brown and orange 2·00 75
1586b 300r. violet, lilac & gold . . . . 2·00 25
1586c 400r. grey, pink and gold . . . . 2·00 25
Nos. 1585a and 1586 exist dated "1980" or "1981", and Nos. 1582a, 1583a and 1586b/c are dated "1983".
See also Nos. 1830/4.

1980. Population Census.
1587 **327** 75r. blue and pink . . . 40 15
1588 200r. blue and yellow . . 1·00 40

328 Ship laying Cable

329 Immigrants

1980. Inauguration of Singapore–Indonesia Submarine Cable.
1589 **328** 75r. green, dp grn & orge 55 15
1590 200r. blue, dp bl & orge 1·00 50

1980. Indonesian Immigration.
1591 **329** 12r.50 red and green . . 35 10

330 1946 50s. Stamp

331 Map of A.O.P.U. Members

1980. 35th Anniv of Independence.
1592 **330** 75r. cream, black & brn 50 35
1593 – 100r. cream, pur & gold 1·10 40
1594 – 200r. cream, pink and silver . . . . 1·50 65
DESIGNS—HORIZ: 100r. 1946 15s. stamp. VERT: 200r. 1946 15s. Freedom Fund stamp.

1980. 10th Anniv of Asian–Oceanic Postal Union Training School, Bangkok.
1595 **331** 200r. blue, lt blue & turq 1·30 25

332 O.P.E.C. Emblem on Globe

1980. 20th Anniv of Organization of Petroleum Exporting Countries.
1596 **332** 200r. turquoise, bl & red 1·30 35

333 Service Members with Linked Arms

1980. 35th Anniv of Armed Forces. Mult.
1597 75r. Indonesians hailing flag 75 25
1598 200r. Type **333** . . . . . . 1·10 40

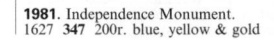

334 Pesquet's Parrot

335 "Dendrobium insigne"

1980. Parrots. Multicoloured.
1599 75r. Type **334** . . . . . . 2·40 75
1600 100r. Chattering lory . . . 2·40 1·50
1601 200r. Rainbow lory . . . . 4·00 2·10
MS1602 95 × 120 mm. 250r. As No. 1601; 350r. Type **334** 400r. As No. 1600 . . . . 24·00 24·00

1980. Orchids. Multicoloured.
1603 75r. Type **335** . . . . . . 1·10 15
1604 100r. "Dendrobium discolor" . . . . 1·80 90
1605 200r. "Dendrobium lasianthera" . . . . . . 3·50 65
MS1606 74 × 104 mm. 250r. As No. 1604; 350r. As No. 1605 16·00 16·00

336 Von Stephan and U.P.U. Emblem

1981. 150th Birth Anniv of Heinrich von Stephan (U.P.U. founder).
1607 **336** 200r. blue and deep blue 1·30 65

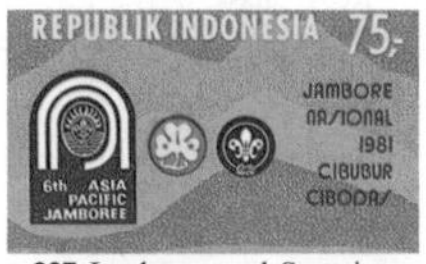
337 Jamboree and Scouting Emblems

1981. 6th Asia–Pacific Scout Jamboree, Cibubur. Multicoloured.
1608 75r. Type **337** 40 35
1609 100r. Scout and Guide map-reading (vert) . . . . . . 1·10 35
1610 200r. Jamboree emblem and tents . . . . 1·30 75
MS1611 77 × 63 mm. 150r. As No. 1609 . . . . 1·60 1·60

338 Ship (relief carving)

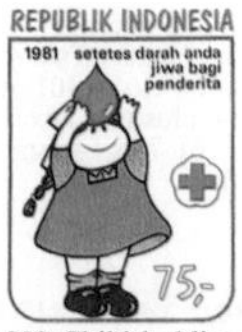
339 Child holding Blood Drop

1981. 5th Asian–Oceanic Postal Union Congress, Yogyakarta.
1612 **338** 200r. blue, black & lt bl 1·50 35

1981. Blood Donors.
1613 **339** 75r. blue, black and red 50 15
1614 – 100r. red and grey . . . 75 35
1615 – 200r. red, dp blue & blue 1·10 65
DESIGNS: 100r. Hands holding blood drop; 200r. Hands and blood drop.

340 Monuments

1981. International Family Planning Conference.
1616 **340** 200r. pale blue, brn & bl 1·00 40

341 "Song of Sritanjung"

1981. Traditional Balinese Paintings. Mult.
1617 100r. Type **341** . . . . . . 1·10 35
1618 200r. "Song of Sritanjung" (different) . . . . 1·60 75
MS1619 96 × 96 mm. 400r. and 600r. "Birth of the Eagle" . . . . . 10·50 10·50
Nos. 1617/18 were issued together, se-tenant, forming a composite design.

342 Secretariat Building and Emblem

343 Uber Cup

1981. Inauguration of A.S.E.A.N. Secretariat, Djakarta.
1620 **342** 200r. yellow, orge & pur 1·50 50

1981. International Ladies' Badminton Championships, Tokyo.
1621 **343** 200r. brown, yell & orge 2·40 50

344 "Tree of Life" (relief from Candi Mendut)

346 Blind Man

345 Students reading Koran, Mosque and Emblem

1981. World Environment Day.
1622 **344** 75r. bistre, grey and black 75 15
1623 – 200r. bistre, grey & black 1·20 35
DESIGN: 200r. "Yaksha Apacaka".

1981. 12th National Koran Reading Contest, Banda Aceh.
1624 **345** 200r. black, red & yellow 1·00 50

1981. International Year of Disabled Persons.
1625 **346** 75r. brown, yellow & bis 40 15
1626 – 200r. blue, brown & grn 1·00 50
DESIGN: 200r. Deaf and dumb person.

347 Soekarno-Hatta Monument, Djakarta

1981. Independence Monument.
1627 **347** 200r. blue, yellow & gold 1·50 40

348 Parachute Jumping

349 Food Produce

1981. National Sports Week, Djakarta.
1628 **348** 75r. red, black and blue 40 15
1629 – 100r. black, blue and red 65 65
1630 – 200r. brown, green & red 1·30 50
DESIGNS—HORIZ: 100r. Scuba diving. VERT: 200r. Horse riding.

1981. World Food Day.
1631 **349** 200r. multicoloured . . . 2·40 75

350 Arms of Aceh Special Territory

351 Salmon-crested Cockatoo

1981. Provincial Arms (1st series).
1632 **350** 100r. yellow, grn & gold 2·40 75
1633 – 100r. multicoloured . . . 2·40 75
1634 – 100r. multicoloured . . . 2·40 75
1635 – 100r. multicoloured . . . 3·25 1·80
1636 – 100r. multicoloured . . . 10·50 90
DESIGNS: No. 1633, Bali; No. 1634, Bengkulu; No. 1635, Irian Jaya; No. 1636, Djakarta.
See also Nos. 1643/62 and 1710.

1981. Cockatoos. Multicoloured.
1637 75r. Type **351** . . . . . . 3·75 80
1638 100r. Sulphur-crested cockatoo . . . . 4·00 80
1639 200r. Palm cockatoo . . . . 6·50 3·00
MS1640 73 × 64 mm. 150r. As No. 1638; 350r. As No. 1639 18·00 18·00

1982. Provincial Arms (2nd series). As T **350**. Multicoloured.
1641 100r. Jambi . . . . 1·10 50
1642 100r. Java Barat (West) . . 1·10 50
1643 100r. Java Tengah (Cent) . . 1·10 50
1644 100r. Java Timur (East) . . 1·10 50
1645 100r. Kalimantan Barat (West) . . . . 1·10 50
1646 100r. Kalimantan Selatan (South) . . . . 1·10 50
1647 100r. Kalimantan Timur (East) . . . . 1·10 50
1648 100r. Kalimantan Tengah (Central) . . . . 1·10 50
1649 100r. Lampung . . . . . . 1·10 50
1650 100r. Moluccas 75 50
1651 100r. Nusa Tengarra Barat (West) 75 15
1652 100r. Nusa Tengarra Timur (East) 75 15
1653 100r. Riau 75 25
1654 100r. Sulawesi Tengah (Central Celebes) 75 15
1655 100r. Sulawesi Tenggara (South-east Celebes) . . . 75 15
1656 100r. Sulawesi Selatan (South Celebes) 75 25
1657 100r. Sumatera Utara (North Celebes) 90 15
1658 100r. Sumatera Barat (West) 90 15
1659 100r. Sumatera Selatan (South) 75 15
1660 100r. Sumatera Utara (North) 75 15
1661 100r. Yogyakarta . . . . . 1·80 15
1662 250r. Republic of Indonesia (45 × 29 mm) . . . . . . 1·00 35

352 Hands enclosing Family

1982. 70th Anniv of Bumiputera Mutual Life Insurance Company.
1663 **352** 75r. yellow, plum & pur 40 15
1664 – 100r. yellow, lt grn & grn 80 35
1665 – 200r. multicoloured . . . 1·10 55
DESIGNS: 100r. Family in countryside; 200r. Hands supporting industrial activities.

353 Helicopter Rescue

354 Houses and Ballot Boxes

1982. 10th Anniv of Search and Rescue Institute.
1666 **353** 250r. multicoloured . . . 1·50 35

1982. General Election. Multicoloured.
1667 75r. Type **354** 40 15
1668 100r. Rural houses and ballot boxes 65 25
1669 200r. Houses and National arms . . . . 1·50 65

355 Human Figures, Satellite and Dove

357 Footballers

356 Thomas Cup

1982. 2nd U.N. Conference on Exploration and Peaceful Uses of Outer Space, Vienna.
1670 **355** 150r. blue, violet & black 75 40
1671 – 250r. green, light green and deep green . . . 1·30 65
DESIGN: 250r. Peace dove and text.

1982. Thomas Cup Badminton Championship, London.
1672 **356** 250r. multicoloured . . . 1·80 50
MS1673 72 × 95 mm. No. 1672 2 45·00 45·00

1982. World Cup Football Championship, Spain.
1674 **357** 250r. multicoloured . . . 1·80 50
MS1675 96 × 72 mm. No. 1674 × 2 70·00 70·00

358 Taman Siswa Emblem

1982. 60th Anniv of Taman Siswa (educational organization).
1676 **358** 250r. yellow, green & red 1·00 35

359 Flags forming "15"

1982. 15th Anniv of Association of South-East Asian Nations.
1677 **359** 150r. orange, red and blue . . . . 1·60 50

360 President Suharto

362 Rothschild's Mynah

1982.
1678 **360** 110r. red and orange . . 40 15
1679 250r. brown and orange 80 15

1680 275r. green and yellow 1·30 15
Nos. 1678 and 1680 are inscribed "1983".

1982. World Cup Football Championship Result. No. **MS**1675 optd **ITALIA WORLD CHAMPION.**
MS1681 96 × 72 mm. 250r. × 2 mult 70·00 70·00

1982. 3rd World National Parks Congress, Bali. Multicoloured.
1682 100r. Type **362** . . . . . . 3·25 40
1683 250r. King bird of paradise 5·00 1·20
MS1684 76 × 104 mm. 500r. Type **362** . . . . 14·00 14·00

363 River Bridge

1982. Five Year Plan.
1685 **363** 17r.50 brown and green 50 10

364 Arfak Parotia

365 Scouts and Anniversary Emblem

1982. Birds of Paradise. Multicoloured.
1686 100r. Type **364** . . . . . . 2·00 40
1687 150r. Twelve-wired bird of paradise . . . . 3·25 80
1688 250r. Red bird of paradise 5·00 1·20
MS1689 76 × 105 mm. 200r. Type **364**; 300r. As No. 1688 20·00 2·00

1983. 75th Anniv of Boy Scout Movement.
1690 **365** 250r. blue, green & violet 1·60 35

366 Temple Restoration and Relief

1983. Borobudur Temple.
1691 **366** 100r. green, blue & lt bl 1·60 50
1692 – 150r. lt green, grn & brn 1·60 50
1693 – 250r. black, dp brn & brn . . . . 5·25 2·75
MS1694 96 × 64 mm. 500r. multicoloured . . . . 16·00 16·00
DESIGNS—VERT: 150r. Temple and statue. HORIZ: 250, 500r. Silhouette of Temple and seated Buddha.

367 President Suharto

368 Gas Storage Tanks

1983.
1695 **367** 500r. brown . . . . . . 1·40 35

1983. 7th International Liquefied Natural Gas Conference, Djarkarta.
1696 **368** 275r. multicoloured . . . 1·40 35

369 Ships and Bird

370 Man and Woman reading Koran

1983. World Communications Year.
1697 **369** 75r. multicoloured . . . 25 15
1698 – 110r. multicoloured . . . 50 25
1699 – 175r. blue and red . . . 80 40
1700 – 275r. blue, dp blue & red 1·20 65
DESIGNS: 110r. Satellite and receiving station; 175r. Aircraft and dish aerial, 275r. Globe and letter.

1983. 13th National Koran Reading Competition.
1701 **370** 275r. yellow, green & blk 1·20 55

371 Eclipse and Map of Indonesia

1983. Total Solar Eclipse.
1702 **371** 110r. brn, dp brn & blk 65 25
1703 – 275r. blue, violet & purple . . . . 2·00 40
MS1704 96 × 64 mm. 500r. blue, violet and purple . . . . . . 14·00 14·00
DESIGN: 275, 500r. Map of Indonesia showing path of eclipse.

372 Satellite transmitting to Indonesia

373 Patient receiving Radiation Treatment

1983. Launching of "Palapa B" Communications Satellite.
1705 **372** 275r. green, blue & silver 1·20 55

1983. Anti-cancer Campaign.
1706 **373** 55r.+20r. multicoloured 65 40
1707 75r.+25r. multicoloured 1·10 40

374 Agricultural Produce

1983. Agricultural Census.
1708 **374** 110r. grey, green & black 65 15
1709 – 275r. red, black and green . . . . 1·10 25
DESIGN: 275r. Farmer with produce.

1983. Provincial Arms (3rd series). As T **350**. Multicoloured.
1710 100r. Timor Timur . . . . 1·80 15

375 Traditional Weaving, Pakistan

1983. Indonesia–Pakistan Economic and Cultural Co-operation. Multicoloured.
1711 275r. Type **375** . . . . . . 1·60 75
1712 275r. Traditional weaving, Indonesia . . . . 1·60 75

376 Eruption of Krakatoa

1983. Centenary of Krakatoa Volcanic Eruption. Multicoloured.
1713 110r. Type **376** 50 25
1714 275r. Map showing position of Krakatoa . . . . . . 1·60 40

377 Casa-Nurtanio CN-235 Short-haul Passenger Aircraft

1983. Indonesian Aircraft.
1715 **377** 275r. multicoloured . . . 1·20 55

1983. World Communications Year. Opening of Philatelic Museum, Djakarta. Sheet 51 × 84 mm.
MS1716 500r. As No. 1700 . . . 7·00 7·00

378 Tiger Barb

1983. Tropical Fishes. Multicoloured.
1717 110r. Type **378** . . . . . . 2·00 65
1718 175r. Brilliant rasbora . . . 2·00 65
1719 275r. Archerfish . . . . . . 6·00 2·00

1983. "Telecom 83" Exhibition, Geneva. Sheet 75 × 83 mm. Multicoloured.
MS1720 400r. As No. 1698 . . . 8·25 8·25

379 Wilson's Bird of Paradise

1983. Birds of Paradise. Multicoloured.
1721 110r. Type **379** . . . . . . 1·60 40
1722 175r. Black sicklebill . . . . 2·40 50
1723 275r. Black-billed sicklebill 3·75 1·10
1724 500r. As No. 1723 . . . . . 5·75 3·00
MS1725 64 × 95 mm. As No. 1724 20·00 20·00

380 Emblems of Peace and Co-operation

1983. Palestinian Solidarity.
1726 **380** 275r. blue, brown & silver . . . . 1·40 35

381 "Stop" Emblem

382 Agriculture

1984. Anti-poliomyelitis Campaign.
1732 **381** 110r. red, purple and blue 40 15
1733 – 275r. purple, orge & red 1·40 35
DESIGN: 275r. Emblem of Save the Children Fund.

1984. 4th Five Year Plan.
1734 **382** 55r. yellow and blue . . 15 10
1735 – 75r. green and brown . . 25 15
1736 – 110r. blue and orange . . 40 25
1737 – 275r. multicoloured . . . 1·10 65
DESIGNS: 75r. Casa-Nurtiano CN-235 airliner (aircraft industry); 110r. Shipbuilding; 275r. Telephone (telecommunications).

383 Manufacturing Plywood

1984. Forestry. Multicoloured.
1738 75r. Type **383** . . . . . . 1·10 15
1739 110r. Seedling . . . . . . 1·10 15
1740 175r. Measuring tree trunk 1·10 40
1741 275r. Transporting trees . . 1·10 55
MS1742 96 × 80 mm. Nos. 1740/1 12·00 12·00

384 Children playing with Toys

1984. Children's Day. Multicoloured.
1743 75r.+25r. Type **384** . . . . 1·10 15
1744 110r.+25r. Scout camp . . . 65 25
1745 175r.+25r. Children on farm 1·60 40
1746 275r.+25r. Scouts and guides in camp . . . . . 1·60 50
See also No. **MS**1760.

385 Flags of Member Nations

1984. Association of South-East Asian Nations Meeting, Djakarta.
1747 **385** 275r. multicoloured . . . 1·80 55

386 Pole Vaulting

387 Horse Dance

1984. Olympic Games, Los Angeles. Multicoloured.
1748 75r. Type **386** 50 15
1749 110r. Archery 50 15
1750 175r. Boxing 50 15
1751 250r. Shooting . . . . . . 1·60 50
1752 275r. Weightlifting . . . . 2·00 50
1753 325r. Swimming . . . . . . 3·50 25

1984. Art and Culture. Multicoloured.
1754 75r. Type **387** 80 15
1755 110r. "Reog" mask . . . . 1·20 25
1756 275r. Lion dance . . . . . 1·20 65
1757 325r. "Barong" mask . . . 2·75 65

388 Thomas Cup (badminton)

1984. National Sports Day. Multicoloured.
1758 110r. Type **388** 80 25
1759 275r. Keep-fit exercise . . . 1·60 40

1984. "Filacento" International Stamp Exhibition, The Hague. Two sheets.
MS1760 101 × 101 mm. No. 1746 × 4 plus two labels . . . . . 18·00 18·00
MS1761 73 × 64 mm. No. 1757 plus label . . . . 45·00 45·00

1984. "Ausipex 84" International Stamp Exhibition, Melbourne. Sheet 101 × 76 mm.
MS1762 Nos. 1745/6 . . . . . . 29·00 29·00

389 Map and Post Code Zones **390** Lauterbach's Bowerbird

1984. Introduction of New Post Code Zones.
1763 **389** 110r. blue, brown & orge . . . 50 25
1764 275r. orange, blue & brn . . . 1·10 65

1984. Birds. Multicoloured.
1765 75r. Type **390** . . . . . . 2·75 35
1766 110r. Flamed bowerbird . . 4·00 65
1767 275r. Arfak bird of paradise 5·25 2·40
1768 325r. Superb bird of paradise . . . . 5·25 1·60
MS1769 76 × 105 mm. Nos. 1765 and 1768 . . . . 26·00 26·00
No. **MS**1769 is inscribed for "Philakorea 1984" International Stamp Exhibition.

391 Flag and Fists **392** Boeing 747-200

1984. Youth Pledge.
1770 **391** 275r. black and red . . . 1·10 75

1984. 40th Anniv of I.C.A.O.
1771 **392** 275r. red, black and blue 1·20 75

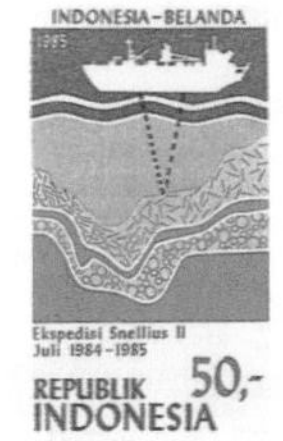

393 "Tyro" and Geological Structure of Seabed **394** Stylized Birds

1985. Indonesia–Belanda Expedition.
1772 **393** 50r. blue and brown . . 65 15
1773 – 100r. blue and purple . . 1·10 15
1774 – 275r. blue and green . . 1·20 35
DESIGNS: 100r. "Tyro" (oceanographic survey ship) and map; 275r. "Tyro" and coral reef.

1985. International Women's Day.
1775 **394** 100r. mauve and red . . 2·00 65
1776 – 275r. red and brown . . 3·00 3·00
DESIGN: 275r. Profile silhouettes.

395 Jet Airliner and workers **396** Pres. Suharto

1985. 4th Five Year Plan.
1777 **395** 75r. red and brown . . . 35 15
1778 – 140r. grey and brown . . 55 40
1779 – 350r. green and brown . . 1·50 1·00
DESIGNS: 140r. Children in classroom; 350r. Industrial equipment and buildings.

1985.
1780 **396** 140r. brown and red . . 65 15
1781 350r. mauve and red . . 1·50 15

397 Conference Building

1985. 30th Anniv of First Asian–African Conference, Bandung.
1786 **397** 350r. multicoloured . . . 1·60 50

398 Globe and Teenagers waving Palm Leaves **399** Profiles

1985. International Youth Year.
1787 **398** 75r. yellow, brown & grn 55 15
1788 – 140r. blue, green & mve 1·40 15
DESIGN: 140r. Flower on globe supported by teenagers.

1985. United Nations Women's Decade.
1789 **399** 55r. brown and green . . 50 25
1790 – 140r. blue, green & brn 80 25
DESIGN: 140r. Globe and decade emblems.

400 Housing and Hydro-electricity **401** Sky Diving

1985. 40th Anniv of Indonesian Republic.
1791 **400** 140r. green and red . . . 55 15
1792 – 350r. blue, mauve & yell 1·50 35
DESIGN: 350r. Tractor and industrial complex.

1985. National Sports Week, Djakarta. Multicoloured.
1793 55r. Type **401** 35 10
1794 100r. Unarmed combat . . 80 15
1795 140r. High jumping 80 25
1796 350r. Sailboards (vert) . . . 1·30 50

402 O.P.E.C. Emblem and Globe **403** Tanker

1985. 25th Anniv of Organization of Petroleum Exporting Countries.
1797 **402** 40r. blue, mauve & orge 1·00 25

1985. Centenary of Indonesian Oil Industry. Multicoloured.
1798 140r. Type **403** 50 25
1799 250r. Refinery 90 40
1800 350r. Derrick and rigs . . . 1·30 80

404 Doves, "40" and U.N. Emblem

1985. 40th Anniv of U.N.O. Multicoloured.
1801 140r. Type **404** 50 15
1802 300r. Bombs and green leaves . . . . 1·10 40

405 Javan Rhinoceros **406** Emblem

1985. Wildlife.
1803 **405** 75r. brown, green & blue 1·00 25
1804 – 150r. brown, orge & grn 1·30 40
1805 – 300r. brown, blue and red . . . . 2·50 65
DESIGNS: 150r. Anoa; 300r. Komodo dragon.

1986. Economic Census. Each orange and violet.
1806 175r. Type **406** 65 25
1807 175r. Symbols of economy 65 25

407 Baby feeding, Powdered Milk, Syringe and Graph **408** Industry

1986. 40th Anniv of UNICEF.
1808 **407** 75r. multicoloured . . . 55 15
1809 – 140r. flesh, brown & pink 90 25
DESIGN: 140r. Vaccinating baby.

1986. 4th Five Year Plan.
1810 **408** 140r. multicoloured . . . 50 15
1811 – 500r. yellow, brown & bl 50 15
DESIGN: 500r. Agriculture.

409 Thomas Cup and Racket **410** Pinisi Sailing Ship

1986. Thomas (men's) and Uber (women's) Cup Badminton Championships, Djakarta.
1812 **409** 55r. black, yellow & blue 65 25
1813 – 150r. red, brown and gold . . . . 1·10 25
DESIGN: 150r. Thomas and Uber Cups and shuttlecock.

1986. "Expo 86" World's Fair, Vancouver.
1814 **410** 75r. black, red and yellow 50 15
1815 – 150r. multicoloured . . . 1·00 25
1816 – 300r. silver, red & purple 1·50 35
DESIGNS: 150r. Kentongan village drum and "Palapa" satellite; 300r. Indonesian pavilion emblem.

411 Guides on Parade

1986. National Jamboree. Multicoloured.
1817 100r. Type **411** 35 15
1818 140r. Guides cooking over fire . . . . 1·30 35
1819 210r. Scouts consulting map (vert) . . . . 1·60 55

412 "86"

1986. Indonesia Air Show.
1820 **412** 350r. multicoloured . . . 1·30 65

413 Tari Legong Kraton

1986. Traditional Dances. Multicoloured.
1821 140r. Type **413** . . . . . . 1·30 15
1822 350r. Tari Barong . . . . . 2·10 50
1823 500r. Tari Kecak . . . . . 3·00 55

414 Woman planting

1986. 19th International Society of Sugar Cane Technologists Congress, Djakarta. Multicoloured.
1824 150r. Type **414** 55 15
1825 300r. Cane and sugar spilled from sack . . . . 1·40 25

415 Route Map of Cable

1986. Opening of Sea-Me-We Communications Cable.
1826 **415** 140r. green, orange & vio 55 25
1827 – 350r. green, yellow & bl 1·40 55
DESIGN: 350r. Route map of cable (different).

416 Doves, Wheat and Globe **417** Party Emblems and Buildings

1986. International Peace Year. Each brown, green and black.
1828 350r. Type **416** . . . . . . 1·10 40
1829 500r. Dove with olive twig flying around globe . . . 1·50 15

1986.
1830 **326** 50r. deep brown & brown 15 10
1831 55r. red and pink . . . 35 10
1833 100r. ultramarine & blue 15 10
1834 300r. turq, grn & gold 1·00 10
1835 400r. green, turq & gold 1·30 15

1987. General Election.
1840 **417** 75r. blue, yellow & brn 50 10
1841 – 140r. green, orange & yell 50 15
1842 – 350r. blue, yellow & blk 1·30 35
DESIGNS: 140r. Party emblems and arms; 350r. Party emblems, map, wheat and ballot box.

418 Satellite and Globe **419** Boy carving Figures

1987. Launch of "Palapa B2" Satellite.
1843 **418** 350r. yellow, green & brn . . . . 1·00 40
1844 – 500r. multicoloured . . . 1·50 25
DESIGN—VERT: 500r. Rocket and satellite.

1987. 4th Five Year Plan.
1845 **419** 140r. brown, yellow & bl 25 15
1846 – 350.r. violet, grn & orge 65 35
DESIGN: 350r. Graph and cattle.

420 Crab and Scanner Unit **421** East Kalimantan Couple

1987. 10th Anniv of Indonesian Cancer Foundation.
1847 **420** 350r.+25r. yellow & bl 1·10 50

1987. Wedding Costumes (1st series). Mult.
1848 140r. Type **421** . . . . . . 1·60 35
1849 350r. Aceh couple . . . . . 9·75 4·50
1850 400r. East Timor couple . . . 11·50 1·00
See also Nos. 1891/6, 1955/60, 1992/7 and 2010/15.

422 Weightlifting **423** Emblems

1987. 14th South-East Asia Games, Djakarta. Designs showing pictograms.
1851 **422** 140r. yellow, red and blue 40 15
1852 – 250r. blue, yellow and red 75 25
1853 – 350r. red, blue and brown . . . . 1·10 40
DESIGNS: 250r. Swimming; 350r. Running.

1987. 460th Anniv of Djakarta and 20th Anniv of Djakarta Fair.
1854 **423** 75r. blue, black & yellow 75 15
1855 – 100r. blue, black & yell 1·40 15
DESIGN—VERT: 100r. Emblems (different).

424 Children reading

425 Headquarters, Djakarta

1987. Children's Day and National Family Planning Co-ordination Board.
1856 **424** 100r. mauve and orange 40 15
1857 – 250r. yellow and blue . . 75 15
DESIGN—VERT: 250r. Globe, baby in cupped hands and dropper.

1987. 20th Anniv of Association of South-East Asian Nations.
1858 **425** 350r. multicoloured . . . 1·30 50

426 Emblem

427 Mount Bromo and Sand Craters

1987. 30th Anniv and 7th National Congress of Association of Specialists in Internal Diseases.
1859 **426** 300r. red and blue . . . 1·00 15

1987. Tourism. Multicoloured.
1860 140r. Type **427** 50 15
1861 350r. Bedugul Lake, Bali . . 1·60 55
1862 500r. Sea gardens, Bunaken Island . . . . 2·10 25

428 Woman with Broken Chains, Helmet and Pennant flying from Pen

429 Giant Gourami

1987. "Woman's Physical Revolution".
1863 **428** 75r. green, red and yellow 35 15
1864 – 100r. green, yellow & red 65 15
DESIGN: 100r. Women with rifles and barbed wire.

1987. Fishes.
1865 **429** 150r. mauve, yellow & bl 1·60 65
1866 – 200r. mauve, yellow & bl 1·60 35
1867 – 500r. black, yellow & bl 5·00 35
DESIGNS: 200r. Goldfish; 300r. Walking catfish.

430 Soldiers

432 Carved Snake and Frog

431 Welder

1988. 31st Anniv of Veterans Legion.
1868 **430** 250r. green and orange 80 15

1988. National Safety and Occupational Health Day.
1869 **431** 350r. blue and green . . 1·10 50

1988. 8th Anniv of National Crafts Council.
1870 **432** 120r. blue and brown . . 65 10
1871 – 350r. blue and brown . . 1·00 50
1872 – 500r. brown and green 1·60 15
DESIGN: 350r. Cane rocking-chair; 500r. Bamboo goods.

433 Industrial Symbols

434 Indonesian Girls

1988. 4th Five Year Plan.
1873 **433** 140r. blue and green . . 25 15
1874 – 400r. purple and red . . 65 35
DESIGN: 400r. Fishing industry.

1988. "Expo 88" World's Fair, Brisbane. Multicoloured.
1875 200r. Type **434** 90 15
1876 300r. Indonesian girl 90 15
1877 350r. Indonesian girl and boy . . . . 1·50 65
MS1878 96 × 95 mm. Nos. 1875/7. Perf or imperf . . . . 9·75 9·75

435 Anniversary Emblem

436 "Dendrobium none betawi"

1988. 125th Anniv of Red Cross.
1879 **435** 350r. grey, black and red 1·00 25

1988. Flowers. Multicoloured.
1880 400r. Type **436** . . . . . . 1·60 50
1881 500r. "Dendrobium abang betawi" . . . . 1·60 35

437 Running

438 Figures around Emblem

1988. Olympic Games, Seoul.
1882 **437** 75r. black, brown & gold 50 15
1883 – 100r. black, red and gold 1·10 15
1884 – 200r. black, mve & gold 1·10 50
1885 – 300r. black, green & gold 50 50
1886 – 400r. black, blue and gold 65 40
1887 – 500r. black, blue and gold . . . . 3·00 40
MS1888 Two sheets, each 72 × 96 mm. Perf or imperf. (a) Nos. 1882, 1885 and 1887; (b) Nos. 1883/4 and 1886 . . . .
DESIGNS: 100r. Weightlifting; 200r. Archery; 300r. Table tennis; 400r. Swimming; 500r. Tennis.

1988. Centenary of International Women's Council.
1889 **438** 140r. black and blue . . 65 15

439 Family, Water and Ear of Wheat

440 President Suharto

1988. National Farmers' and Fishermen's Week.
1890 **439** 350r. stone and red . . . 1·10 50

1988. Wedding Costumes (2nd series). As T **421**. Multicoloured.
1891 55r. Sumatera Barat (West) 25 15
1892 75r. Jambi 15 10
1893 100r. Bengkulu 65 10
1894 120r. Lampung 90 10
1895 200r. Moluccas . . . . . . 1·60 15
1896 250r. Nusa Tenggara Timur (East) . . . . 2·10 1·10

1988.
1897 **440** 200r. blue, pink and red 35 15
1898 700r. mauve, lt grn & grn . . . . 1·10 15
1899 1000r. multicoloured . . 1·10 15

441 Emblem

442 Doves and Envelopes

1988. 13th Non-Aligned News Agencies Co-ordinating Committee Meeting, Djakarta.
1901 **441** 500r. blue and red . . . 1·20 35

1988. International Correspondence Week.
1902 **442** 140r. blue and red . . . 90 15

1988. "Filacept 88" International Stamp Exhibition, The Hague. Two sheets, each 72 × 96 mm, each containing design as no. 1630 but colours changed.
MS1903 Two sheets. (a) 200r. 4, black, emerald and rose. (b) 200r. ultramarine, orange and rose plus label . . . . 29·00 29·00

443 Means of Transport and Communications

1988. Asian–Pacific Transport and Communications Decade.
1904 **443** 350r. blue and black . . 1·10 50

444 Al Mashun Mosque, Medan

445 "Papilio gigon"

1988. Tourism. Multicoloured.
1905 250r. Type **444** 55 40
1906 300r. Pagaruyung Palace, Batusangkar 90 35
1907 500r. Keong Emas Theatre, Djakarta . . . . 2·10 35
MS1908 96 × 57 mm. 1000r. As No. 1906. Perf or imperf . . . 18·00 18·00
See also No. **MS**1954.

1988. Butterflies. Multicoloured.
1909 400r. Type **445** . . . . . . 1·50 40
1910 500r. "Graphium androcles" 2·50 55
MS1911 49 × 93 mm. 1000r. As No 1910 Perf or imperf . . . . . 29·00 29·00

446 "Rafflesia sp."

447 "40" and Boeing 747

1989. Flowers. Multicoloured.
1916 200r. Type **446** 90 40
1917 1000r. "Amorphophallus titanum" . . . . 2·75 40
MS1918 50 × 103 mm. 1000r. As No. 1917 . . . . 49·00 49·00

1989. 40th Anniv of Garuda Airline.
1919 **447** 350r. blue and green . . 2·00 55

448 Mother and Baby

449 Industrial Site

1989. Endangered Animals. The Orang-utan. Multicoloured.
1920 75r. Type **448** . . . . . . 3·75 1·60
1921 100r. Orang-utan in tree . . 3·75 75
1922 140r. Mother and baby in trees . . . . 3·75 75
1923 500r. Orang-utan . . . . . 11·50 6·50
MS1924 Two sheets, each 95 × 125 mm. (a) Nos. 1920/1. (b) Nos. 1922/3 . . . . £200 £200

1989. 5th Five Year Plan.
1925 **449** 55r. violet and green . . 10 10
1926 – 150r. blue and brown . . 25 15
1927 – 350r. green and orange 55 15
DESIGNS: 150r. Cement works; 350r. Gas plant.

450 Stamp and Map

451 Ki Hadjar Dewantara and Graduate

1989. 125th Anniv of First Netherlands Indies Stamp.
1928 **450** 1000r. green, purple & bl 2·00 15

1989. National Education Day.
1929 **451** 140r. red and purple . . 55 15
1930 – 300r. violet and green . . 1·00 35
DESIGN: 300r. Dewantara (founder of Taman Siswa School), pencil and books.

452 Emblem on Map

453 Flag and Cup

1989. 10th Anniv of Asia–Pacific Telecommunity.
1931 **452** 350r. purple and green 1·00 75

1989. Sudirman Cup.
1932 **453** 100r. brown and red . . 1·60 15

454 Students

455 Headquarters

1989. Children's Day.
1933 **454** 100r. brown and orange 50 10
1934 – 250r. blue and green . . 90 25
DESIGN: 250r. Youths exercising.

1989. 10th Anniv of Asia–Pacific Integrated Rural Development Centre.
1935 **455** 140r. brown and blue . . 75 15

456 Skull of "Sangiran 17" and Hunters

457 Globe and People

1989. Centenary of Palaeoanthropology in Indonesia.
1936 **456** 100r. black and brown 65 10
1937 – 150r. green and red . . . 90 15
1938 – 200r. blue and brown . . 1·40 35
1939 – 250r. violet and brown 1·60 25
1940 – 300r. green and red . . . 2·00 40
1941 – 350r. blue and brown . . 2·40 25
DESIGNS—HORIZ: 150r. Skull of "Perning 1" and cavemen; 200r. Skull of "Sangiran 10" and hunter. VERT: 250r. Skull of "Wajak 1"; 300r. Skull of "Sambungmacan 1"; 350r. Skull of "Ngandong 7".

1989. Centenary of Interparliamentary Union.
1942 **457** 350r. green and blue . . 1·00 75

458 Kung Fu

1989. 12th National Games, Djakarta. Mult.
1943 75r. Type **458** 55 15
1944 100r. Tennis 55 15
1945 140r. Judo 55 15
1946 350r. Volleyball . . . . . . 1·60 75
1947 500r. Boxing . . . . 2·75 25
1948 1000r. Archery . . . . . . 3·50 65

459 Taman Burung

460 Trophy

1989. Tourism. Multicoloured.
1949 120r. Type **459** 75 10
1950 350r. Prangko Museum . . 1·10 55
1951 500r. Istana Anak-Anak (vert) . . . . 2·00 35
MS1952 100 × 51 mm. 1500r. As No. 1950 . . . . 11·50 11·50

1989. Film Industry.
1953 **460** 150r. ochre and brown 1·00 15

1989. "World Stamp Expo '89" International Stamp Exhibition, Washington D.C. Sheet 102 × 50 mm. containing designs as Nos. 1905/6. Multicoloured.
MS1954 1500r. Type **444**; 2500r. As No. 1906 . . . . 11·50 11·50

1989. Wedding Costumes (3rd series). As T **421**. Multicoloured.
1955 50r. Sumatera Utara (North) 35 10
1956 75r. Sumatera Selatan (South) 35 10
1957 100r. Djakarta 35 10
1958 140r. Sulawesi Utara (North Celebes) 75 15
1959 350r. Sulawesi Tengah (Central Celebes) . . . . 1·10 1·10
1960 500r. Sulawesi Selatan (South Celebes) . . . . . 1·60 55
MS1961 50 × 102 mm. 1500r. As No 1958 Perf or imperf . . . . 7·00 7·00

461 Worker wearing Safety Belt and Flag

1990. Occupational Safety.
1962 **461** 200r. brown and green 80 15

462 Benteng Marlborough, Bengkulu

1990. Tourism. Multicoloured.
1963 200r. Type **462** . . . . . . 1·00 15
1964 400r. National Museum, Djakarta . . . . 1·50 35
1965 500r. Baiturrahman Mosque, Banda Aceh . . . . . . 1·50 50
MS1966 102 × 51 mm. 1000r. As No. 1964; As No. 1965 . . . . 9·75 9·75

463 "Mammilaria fragilis"

1990. Plants. Multicoloured.
1967 75r. Type **463** 40 10
1968 1000r. Bonsai of "Gmelina elliptica" . . . . 2·00 50
MS1969 105 × 50 mm. 1500r. As No. 1968 . . . . 12·00 12·00

464 Tree-felling Equipment

1990. 5th Five Year Plan.
1970 **464** 200r. brown and blue . . 35 15
1971 – 1000r. black and blue . . 1·60 1·00
DESIGN: 1000r. Lighthouse and freighter.

465 Arrow pointing to Indonesia

466 Battle and Disabled Man using Soldering-iron

1990. Visit Indonesia Year (1991) (1st issue). Multicoloured.
1972 100r. Type **465** 35 10
1973 500r. Temple . . . . 1·30 35
See also Nos. 1998/2000.

1990. "Stamp World London 90" International Stamp exhibition. Sheet 88 × 52 mm.
MS1974 465 5000r. multicoloured 18·00 18·00

1990. 40th Anniv of Disabled Veterans Corp.
1975 **466** 1000r. orange and green 1·50 1·00

467 Player and Goalkeeper

469 U.N. Population Award

1990. World Cup Football Championship, Italy. Multicoloured.
1976 75r. Type **467** . . . . . . 1·60 1·00
1977 150r. Player tackling 55 10
1978 400r. Players competing for high ball 80 15
MS1979 98 × 65 mm. 1500r. As No. 1978 . . . . 9·00 9·00

468 Lampung Bridal Pair

1990. National Stamp exhibition. Sheet 68 × 95 mm.
MS1980 **468** 2000r. multicoloured 7·00 7·00
No. **MS**1980 also bears inscriptions commemorating various stamp exhibition and label for "Stamp World London 90".

1990. 20th Anniv of Family Planning Movement.
1981 **469** 60r. brown and red . . . 40 10

470 Figure with Pencil and Open Book

471 Children

1990. Population Census.
1982 **470** 90r. green and turquoise 55 10

1990. Children's Day.
1983 **471** 500r. purple and red . . 1·10 40

472 Soldier planting Flag

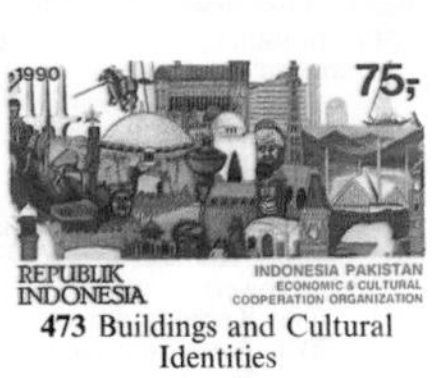
473 Buildings and Cultural Identities

1990. 45th Anniv of Independence. Mult.
1984 200r. Type **472** 65 15
1985 500r. Modern building and roads . . . . 1·10 50
MS1986 50 × 105 mm. 1000r. As No. 1985 . . . . 8·25 8·25

1990. Indonesia–Pakistan Economic and Cultural Co-operation Organization. Multicoloured.
1987 75r. Type **473** 50 15
1988 400r. Dancer (vert) . . . . 1·10 40

474 Emblem

475 Anniversary Emblem

1990. 20th Anniv of Asian–Pacific Postal Training Centre.
1989 **474** 500r. blue & ultramarine 1·00 40

1990. 30th Anniv of Organization of Petroleum Exporting Countries.
1990 **475** 200r. black, grey & orge 80 15

476 Houses

477 Dancer and House

1990. Environmental Health.
1991 **476** 1000r. multicoloured . . 2·00 35

1990. Wedding Costumes (4th series). As T **421**. Multicoloured.
1992 75r. Java Barat (West) . . . 35 10
1993 100r. Java Tengah (Central) 40 10
1994 150r. Yogyakarta 40 10
1995 200r. Java Timur (East) . . 55 15
1996 400r. Bali 80 40
1997 500r. Nusa Tenggara Barat (West) 90 50

1991. Visit Indonesia Year (2nd issue). Dancers and Traditional Houses. Multicoloured.
1998 200r. Type **477** . . . . . . 1·00 15
1999 500r. House and dancer with saucers . . . . . . 1·40 55
2000 1000r. Dancer and house (different) . . . . 2·50 40
MS2001 50 × 100 mm. 1500r. As Type **477** . . . . 14·00 14·00

478 Emblem

479 Palace of Sultan Ternate, Moluccas

1991. 16th National Koran Reading Competition, Yogyakarta.
2002 **478** 200r. green and yellow 80 15

1991. Tourism. Multicoloured.
2003 500r. Type **479** . . . . . . 1·00 25
2004 1000r. Bari House, Palembang . . . . 1·60 35
MS2005 100 × 50 mm. As No. 2004 6·50 6·50
No. **MS**2005 also commemorates Flap Exco Meeting Yogyakarta.

480 Steel Mill

481 Damaged Lungs and Cigarette Smoke forming Skull

1991. 5th Five Year Plan.
2006 **480** 75r. red and blue 10 10
2007 – 200r. blue and black . . 25 15
DESIGN—HORIZ: 200r. Computer technology.

1991. Anti-smoking Campaign.
2008 **481** 90r. red and black . . . 55 10

482 Hands

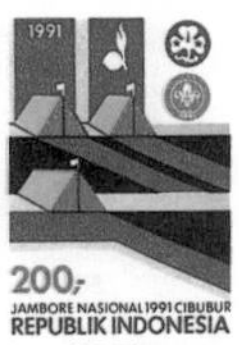
483 Tents

1991. 24th Anniv of National Federation for the Welfare of the Mentally Handicapped.
2009 **482** 200r.+25r. black and red 80 25

1991. Wedding Costumes (5th series). As T **421**. Multicoloured.
2010 100r. Kalimantan Barat (West) 25 10
2011 200r. Kalimantan Tengah (Central) 80 15
2012 300r. Kalimantan Selatan (South) 50 15
2013 400r. Sulawesi Tenggara (South-east Celebes) . . . 55 25
2014 500r. Riau 80 35
2015 1000r. Irian Jaya . . . . . 1·00 55

1991. National Boy Scout Jamboree, Cibubur.
2016 **483** 200r. blue, black and red 1·10 15

484 Monument

485 Temples and Family

1991. 42nd Anniv of Return of Republican Government to Djokjakarta.
2017 **484** 200r. green and brown 80 15

1991. Farmers' Week.
2018 **485** 500r. yellow and blue . . 1·40 15

486 Cells

487 Weightlifters

1991. "chemindo '91" Chemistry Congress, Surabaya.
2019 **486** 400r. red and green . . . 1·00 15

1991. 5th Junior Men's and Fourth Women's Asian Weightlifting Championships, Manado.
2020 **487** 300r. red and black . . . 1·00 15

488 Parachutists

489 Red Cross and Hands

1991. World Parachuting Championships.
2021 **488** 500r. mauve and blue . . 1·00 15

1991. 46th Anniv of Indonesian Red Cross.
2022 **489** 200r. red and green . . . 80 15

490 Radio Mast

491 Script and Mosque

1991. 8th International Amateur Radio Union Region III Conference, Bandung.
2023 **490** 300r. blue and yellow . . 1·00 15

1991. Istiqlal Festival, Djakarta.
2024 **491** 200r. black and red . . . 1·00 15

492 Dancer and Inspectors

1991. International Convention on Quality Control Circles, Bali.
2025 **492** 500r. multicoloured . . . 1·20 50

493 Orang-utan

494 Model of Jakarta Post Office

1991. International Conference on Great Apes of the World. The Orang-utan. Multicoloured.
2026 200r. Type **493** . . . . . . 1·00 15
2027 500r. Orang-utan on forest path . . . . 1·20 25
2028 1000r. Orang-utan sitting on ground . . . . 2·50 55
MS2029 50 × 100 mm. 2500r. As No. 2028 . . . . 8·25 8·25

1992. Automation of Postal Service. Mult.
2030 200r. Type **494** 40 15
2031 500r. Sorting machine . . . 80 35

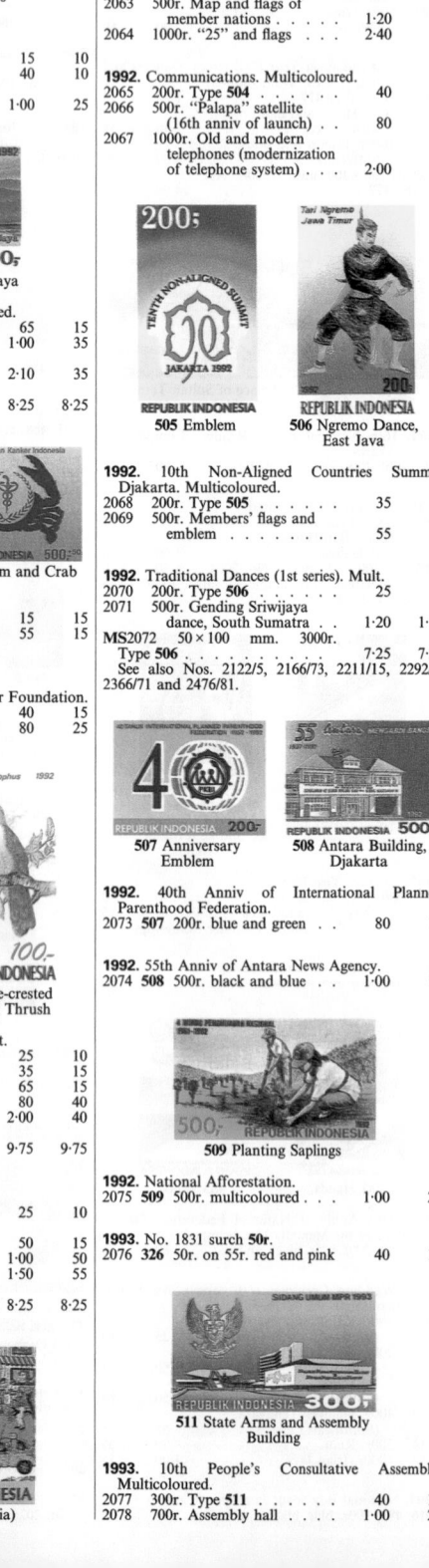

495 "Phalaenopsis ambilis"

1992. Flowers. Multicoloured.
2032 200r. Type **495** 40 15
2033 500r. "Rafflesia arnoldii" . . 80 35
2034 1000r. "Jasminum sambac" 1·80 40
MS2035 106 × 50 mm. 2000r. As No. 2034 . . . . 8·25 8·25

496 Buildings, Ballot Boxes and State Arms

1992. Parliamentary Elections. Mult.
2036 75r. Type **496** 15 10
2037 100r. Ballot boxes and globe 40 10
2038 500r. Ballot boxes and hands holding voting slips 1·00 25

497 Lembah Baliem, Irian Jaya

1992. Visit ASEAN Year. Multicoloured.
2039 300r. Type **497** 65 15
2040 500r. Tanah Lot, Bali . . . 1·00 35
2041 1000r. Lembah Anai, Sumatra Barat . . . . . 2·10 35
MS2042 100 × 50 mm. 3000r. As No. 2040 . . . . 8·25 8·25

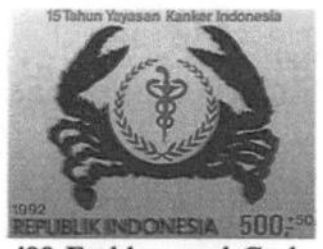

498 Road-building **499** Emblem and Crab

1992. 5th Five Year Plan.
2043 **498** 150r. purple and green 15 15
2044 – 300r. blue and mauve . . 55 15
DESIGN: 300r. Aircraft.

1992. 15th Anniv of Indonesian Cancer Foundation.
2045 **499** 200r.+25r. red & brown 40 15
2046 500r.+50r. red and blue 80 25

500 Weightlifting **501** White-crested Laughing Thrush

1992. Olympic Games, Barcelona. Mult.
2047 75r. Type **500** 25 10
2048 200r. Badminton 35 15
2049 300r. Sports pictograms . . 65 15
2050 500r. Tennis 80 40
2051 1000r. Archery . . . . . . 2·00 40
MS2052 751 × 00 mm. 2000r. As No. 2048; 3000r. As No. 2051 9·75 9·75

1992. Birds. Multicoloured.
2053 100r. Type **501** 25 10
2054 200r. Common golden-backed woodpecker . . . 50 15
2055 400r. Rhinoceros hornbill 1·00 50
2056 500r. Amboina king parrot 1·50 55
MS2057 501 × 00 mm. 3000r. Type **501** . . . . 8·25 8·25

502 Busy Street (Tammy Filia)

1992. National Children's Day. Children's paintings. Multicoloured.
2058 75r. Type **502** 10 10
2059 100r. Children with balloons (Cynthia Widiyana Halim) 25 10
2060 200r. Native boats (Dandy Rahmad Adi Kurniawan) 55 15
2061 500r. Girl and bird (Intan Sari Dewi Saputro) . . . 1·40 80

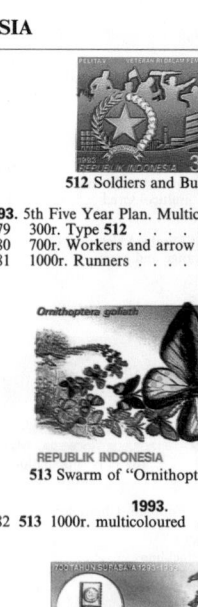

503 Anniversary Emblem **504** Earth and "Palapa B-4" (satellite)

1992. 25th Anniv of Association of South-East Asian Nations. Multicoloured.
2062 200r. Type **503** 40 15
2063 500r. Map and flags of member nations . . . . . 1·20 40
2064 1000r. "25" and flags . . . 2·40 50

1992. Communications. Multicoloured.
2065 200r. Type **504** 40 15
2066 500r. "Palapa" satellite (16th anniv of launch) . . 80 40
2067 1000r. Old and modern telephones (modernization of telephone system) . . . 2·00 50

505 Emblem **506** Ngremo Dance, East Java

1992. 10th Non-Aligned Countries Summit, Djakarta. Multicoloured.
2068 200r. Type **505** 35 10
2069 500r. Members' flags and emblem 55 10

1992. Traditional Dances (1st series). Mult.
2070 200r. Type **506** 25 15
2071 500r. Gending Sriwijaya dance, South Sumatra . . 1·20 1·20
MS2072 50 × 100 mm. 3000r. Type **506** . . . . 7·25 7·25
See also Nos. 2122/5, 2166/73, 2211/15, 2292/6, 2366/71 and 2476/81.

507 Anniversary Emblem **508** Antara Building, Djakarta

1992. 40th Anniv of International Planned Parenthood Federation.
2073 **507** 200r. blue and green . . 80 15

1992. 55th Anniv of Antara News Agency.
2074 **508** 500r. black and blue . . 1·00 15

509 Planting Saplings

1992. National Afforestation.
2075 **509** 500r. multicoloured . . . 1·00 25

1993. No. 1831 surch **50r.**
2076 **326** 50r. on 55r. red and pink 40 10

511 State Arms and Assembly Building

1993. 10th People's Consultative Assembly. Multicoloured.
2077 300r. Type **511** 40 15
2078 700r. Assembly hall . . . . 1·00 25

512 Soldiers and Buildings

1993. 5th Five Year Plan. Multicoloured.
2079 300r. Type **512** 35 35
2080 700r. Workers and arrow . . 75 75
2081 1000r. Runners . . . . . . 1·10 1·10

513 Swarm of "Ornithoptera goliath"

1993.
2082 **513** 1000r. multicoloured . . 1·60 25

514 Peristiwa Hotel, Yamato, and Adipura Kencana Medal

1993. 700th Anniv of Surabaya (300, 700r.) and "indo tourism 93" (1000r.). Multicoloured.
2083 300r. Type **514** 35 35
2084 700r. Modern city and World Habitat Award, 1992 . . . . 75 75
2085 1000r. Candi Bajang Ratu (temple) . . . . 1·10 1·10

516 Mascot

1993. "indopex'93" Asian Stamp Exhibition, Surabaya. Nos. 2082/5 optd **indopex'93 surabaya**.
2086 **514** 300r. multicoloured . . . 35 15
2087 – 700r. multicoloured . . . 75 35
2088 **513** 1000r. mult (No. 2082) 2·00 80
2089 – 1000r. mult (No. 2085) 1·30 50
MS2090 **516** 101 × 50 m. 3500r. multicoloured . . . . 5·25 5·25

517 "Jasminum sambac" **518** Scouts making Road

1993. Environmental Protection. Mult.
2091 300r. Type **517** 35 15
2092 300r. Moth orchid ("Phalaenopsis amabilis") 35 15
2093 300r. "Rafflesia arnoldi" (flower) . . . . 1·30 40
2094 700r. Komodo dragon . . . 1·30 40
2095 700r. Asian bonytongue . . 1·30 40
2096 700r. Java hawk eagle . . . 1·30 40
MS2097 75 × 105 mm. 1500r. Type 517; 1500r. As No. 2094 6·00 6·00
Stamps of the same value were issued together, se-tenant, in strips of three stamps, each strip forming a composite design.

1993. 1st World Community Development Camp, Lebakharjo. Multicoloured.
2098 300r. Type **518** 35 15
2099 700r. Pres. Suharto greeting girl scout . . . . 1·00 15

519 President Suharto **520** "Papilio blumei"

1993.
2100 **519** 150r. multicoloured . . . 15 15
2101 300r. multicoloured . . . 35 15
2102 700r. multicoloured . . . 75 50
On No. 2102 part of the background is a draped flag.

1993. International Butterfly Conference, Ujungpandang.
2103 **520** 700r. multicoloured . . . 1·00 15
MS2104 50 × 100 mm. **520** 3000r. multicoloured . . . . 5·75 5·75
See also **MS**2110.

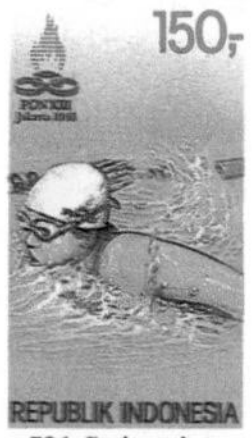

521 Swimming **522** Sigura-Gura Waterfall, North Sumatra

1993. "Pon XIII" Sports Week, Djakarta. Multicoloured.
2105 150r. Type **521** 15 15
2106 300r. Cycling 35 35
2107 700r. Mascot 75 75
2108 1000r. High jumping . . . . 1·10 1·10
MS2109 51 × 101 mm. 3500r. As No. 2018 . . . . 5·25 5·25

1993. "Bangkok 1993" International Stamp Exhibition. Sheet 67 × 75 mm containing design as T **520** but without top inscription.
MS2110 3000r. multicoloured . . 6·00 6·00

1993. World Tourism Organization Meeting, Bali. Multicoloured.
2111 300r. Type **522** 35 35
2112 700r. Goa Petruk (cave), Central Java 75 75
2113 1000r. Danau Segara Anak (cove), West Nusa Tenggara (horiz) . . . . 1·10 1·10
MS2114 71 × 75 mm. 5000r. Similar design to Type **522** . . . . . 4·50 4·50

523 General Soedirman **524** "Michelia champaca"

1993. Armed Forces. Each brown, black and red.
2115 300r. Type **523** 35 15
2116 300r. Lt.-Gen. Oerip Soemohardjo 35 15
Nos. 2115/16 were issued together, se-tenant, forming a composite design.

1993. Flora and Fauna. Multicoloured.
2117 300r. Type **524** 75 15
2118 300r. "Cananga adorata" 75 15
2119 300r. Orange-tailed shama ("Copsychus pyrrhopygus") 75 15
2120 300r. Southern grackle ("Gracula religiosa") . . 75 15

525 Plantation **526** South Sumatran Dancer

1993. Resettlement Programme.
2121 **525** 700r. multicoloured . . . 75 75

1993. Traditional Dances (2nd series). Mult.
2122 300r. Type **526** 55 15
2123 700r. West Kalimantan . . 1·00 15
2124 1000r. Irian Jaya . . . . . 1·30 25
MS2125 50 × 101 mm. 3500r. As No. 2124 . . . . 5·25 5·25

527 Emblems

528 Working Women

1994. International Year of the Family.
2126 **527** 300r. multicoloured . . . 40 15

1994. 6th Five Year Plan. Multicoloured.
2127 100r. Type **528** 10 10
2128 700r. Graduate and school pupils 75 75
2129 2000r. Doctor, nurse and children . . . . 2·10 2·10

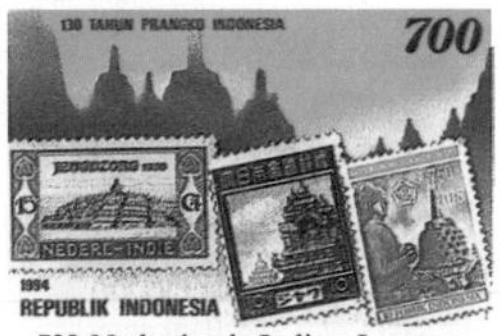

529 Netherlands Indies, Japanese Occupation and Indonesia Stamps

1994. 130th Anniv of 1st Netherlands Indies Stamps.
2130 **529** 700r. multicoloured . . . 80 40

530 Ladige's Rainbowfish

1994. Fishes. Multicoloured.
2131 300r. Type **530** 35 15
2132 700r. Boeseman's rainbow fish 90 35
MS2133 103 × 50 mm. 3500r. As No. 2132 . . . . 5·00 5·00

531 Emblem

532 Figure, Globe, and Anniversary Emblem

1994. National Kidney Foundation.
2134 **531** 300r.+30r. mult 50 25

1994. 75th Anniv of International Red Cross Red Crescent Organization.
2135 **532** 300r. black, red and blue 40 15

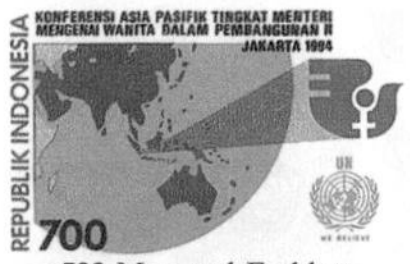

533 Map and Emblem

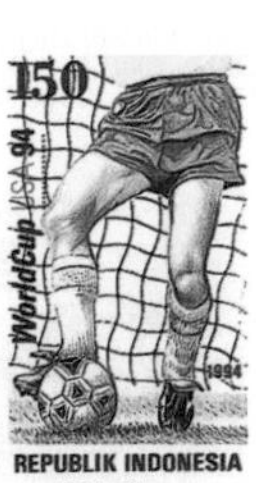

534 Player

1994. Asia–Pacific Ministerial Conference on Women, Djakarta.
2136 **533** 700r. multicoloured . . . 80 35

1994. World Cup Football Championship, U.S.A.
2137 **534** 150r. multicoloured . . . 15 10
2138 – 300r. multicoloured . . . 35 15
2139 – 700r. blue, red and black 75 40
2140 – 1000r. multicoloured . . 1·20 50
MS2141 109 × 50 mm. 3500r. multicoloured . . . . 5·00 5·00
DESIGNS—VERT: 300r. Striker (mascot). HORIZ: 700r. Emblem; 1000, 3500r. Ball in net .

535 Player and Uber Cup (Women's)

536 Hand holding Scales

1994. Indonesian Victories in World Team Badminton Championships. Multicoloured.
2142 300r. Type **535** 40 15
2143 300r. Thomas Cup (Men's) 40 15
MS2144 86 × 92 mm. 1750r. Type **535**; 1750r. As No. 2143 5·00 5·00
Nos. 2142/3 were issued together, se-tenant, forming a composite design.

1994. National Commission on Human Rights.
2145 **536** 700r. multicoloured . . . 80 15

1994. "Philakorea 1994" International Stamp Exhibition, Seoul. Sheet 85 × 91 mm.
MS2146 **529** 3500r. multicoloured 5·00 5·00

537 Vase with Bead Cover

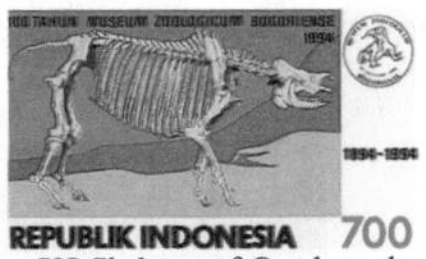

538 Skeleton of Quadruped

1994. Indonesia–Pakistan Economic and Cultural Co-operation Organization. Multicoloured.
2147 300r. Type **537** 25 25
2148 700r. Blue and white vase 65 65

1994. Centenary of Bogoriense Zoological Museum. Multicoloured.
2149 700r. Type **538** 80 50
2150 1000r. Outline and skeleton of whale (80 × 22 mm) . . 1·10 55
MS2151 123 × 48 mm. 3500r. As No. 2150 . . . . 5·00 5·00

539 Mascots

1994. 12th Asian Games, Hiroshima, Japan. Multicoloured.
2152 300r. Type **539** 25 25
2153 700r. Hurdling 65 65

540 Communications and Map

541 "Morus macroura"

1994. 25th Anniv of Bakosurtanal.
2154 **540** 700r. multicoloured . . . 80 35

1994. Flora and Fauna. Multicoloured.
2155 150r. Type **541** 40 15
2156 150r. "Oncosperma tiquillaria" 40 15
2157 150r. "Eucalyptus urophylla" 40 15
2158 150r. Moth orchid ("Phalaenopsis amabilis") 40 15
2159 150r. "Pometia pinnata" . . 40 15
2160 150r. Great argus pheasant ("Argusianus argus") . . 40 15
2161 150r. Blue-crowned hanging parrot ("Loriculus pusillus") 40 15
2162 150r. Timor helmeted friarbird ("Philemon buceroides") 40 15
2163 150r. Amboina king parrot ("Alisterus amboinensis") 40 15
2164 150r. Twelve-wired bird of paradise ("Seleucidis melanoleuca") 40 15
MS2165 48 × 81 mm. 3500r. As No. 2162 . . . . 5·00 5·00
Nos. 2158 and 2161 are incorrectly inscribed, the correct Latin names are "*Dendrobium phalaenopsis*" and "*Loriculus galgulus*" respectively.

542 Venue

1994. Asia–Pacific Economic Co-operation Summit, Bogor.
2166 **542** 700r. multicoloured . . . 80 25

543 Airplane

1994. 50th Anniv of I.C.A.O.
2167 **543** 700r. multicoloured . . . 80 25

1994. Traditional Dances (3rd series). As T **506**. Multicoloured.
2168 150r. Mengaup, Jambi . . . 15 10
2169 300r. Topeng, West Java . . 25 15
2170 700r. Anging Mamiri, South Sulawesi 65 35
2171 1000r. Pisok, North Sulawesi 90 25
2172 2000r. Bidu, East Nusa Tenggara . . . . . . 1·80 1·00
MS2173 47 × 87 mm. 3500r. As No. 2169 . . . . 3·25 3·25

544 Yogyakarta Palace

1995. 20th Anniv of World Tourism Organization. Multicoloured.
2174 300r. Type **544** 25 25
2175 700r. Floating market, Banjarmasin 65 65
2176 1000r. Pasola (equestrian tradition), Sumba 90 90

545 Children, President Suharto and First Lady

1995. "Dedication to the Nation".
2177 **545** 700r. multicoloured . . . 65 65

546 Letter from King of Klungkung, Bali

547 "Schizostachyum brachycladum"

1995. 6th Five Year Plan. National Letter Writing Campaign. Multicoloured.
2178 300r. Type **546** 25 25
2179 700r. Carrier pigeon (campaign mascot) and letters 65 65

1995. 4th International Bamboo Congress, Ubud, Bali. Multicoloured.
2180 300r. Type **547** 25 25
2181 700r. "Dendrocalamus asper" 65 65

548 N250 and National Flag

1995. Inaugural Flight of I.P.T.N. N250 Airliner.
2182 **548** 700r. multicoloured . . . 65 65

549 Anniversary Emblem

1995. 50th Anniv of Indonesian Republic. Multicoloured.
2183 300r. Type **549** 25 25
2184 700r. Boy with national flag 65 65
MS2185 102 × 48 mm. 2500r. As No. 2184 . . . . 4·50 4·50

550 Kota Intan Drawbridge

1995. "Jakarta '95" Asian Stamp Exn. Mult.
2186 300r. Type **550** 25 25
2187 700r. Fatahillah Jakarta History Museum 65 65

551 "Dewarutji" (cadet barquentine), Pinisi Sailing Ship and Flag

1995. "Sail Indonesia '95." Tall Ships Race and Fleet Review.
2188 **551** 700r. multicoloured . . . 65 65
MS2189 91 × 48 mm. 2500r. multicoloured . . . . 4·50 4·50

552 "Mother Love" (Patricia Saerang)

553 Mushaf Istiqlal (illuminated Islamic text)

1995. 10th Asia and Pacific Regional Conference of Rehabilitation International, Indonesia.
2190 **552** 700r.+100r. mult 75 75

1995. Istiqlal Festival.
2191 **553** 700r. multicoloured . . . 65 65

554 P.T.T. Monument

1995. 50th Anniv of Take-over of P.T.T. Headquarters by Republicans.
2192 **554** 700r. multicoloured . . . 65 65

555 Rice

556 Flags and Emblem

1995. 50th Anniv of F.A.O.
2193 **555** 700r. multicoloured . . . 65 65

1995. 50th Anniv of U.N.O. Multicoloured.
2194 300r. Type **556** 25 25
2195 700r. Emblem, Earth and rainbow 65 65

557 "Cyrtostachys renda"

1995. Flora and Fauna. Multicoloured.
2196 150r. Type **557** 15 10
2197 150r. Tiger ("Panthera tigris") 15 10
2198 150r. "Bouea macrophylla" 15 10

2199 150r. Javan rhinoceros ("Rhinoceros sondaicus") 15 10
2200 150r. "Santalum album" . . 15 10
2201 150r. Komodo dragon ("Varanus komodoensis") 15 10
2202 150r. "Diospyros celebica" 15 10
2203 150r. Maleo fowl ("Macrocephalon maleo") 15 10
2204 150r. "Nephelium ramboutan-ake" 15 10
2205 150r. Malay peacock-pheasant ("Polyplectron schleiermacheri") 15 10
MS2206 48 × 95 mm. 2500r. as No. 2197 . . . . 7·75 7·75

558 Yogyakarta Palace

1995. Award of Aga Khan Prize for Architecture to Indonesia. Multicoloured.
2207 300r. Type **558** 25 25
2208 700r. Surakarta Palace . . . 65 65

559 Hill and Postal Carriers **560** Economic Sectors

1995. Birth Bicentenary of Sir Rowland Hill (instigator of postal stamps). Multicoloured.
2209 300r. Type **559** 25 25
2210 700r. Hill and Indonesian Postal Service emblem . . 65 65

1995. Traditional Dances (4th series). As T **506**. Multicoloured.
2211 150r. Nguri dance, West Nusa Tenggara 15 15
2212 300r. Muli Betanggai dance, Lampung 25 25
2213 700r. Mutiara dance, Moluccas 65 65
2214 1000r. Gantar dance, East Kalimantan 90 90
MS2215 48 × 81 mm. 2500r. As No. 2211 . . . . 3·75 3·75

1996. Economic Census.
2216 **560** 300r. orange and blue . . 25 25
2217 – 700r. turquoise & orange 65 65
DESIGN—HORIZ: 700r. Graph of economic activity.

561 Satellite orbiting Earth

1996. Launch of "Palapa-C" Satellite. Mult.
2218 300r. Type **561** 25 25
2219 700r. Satellite orbiting Earth (triangular) 55 55

562 Mixed Flowers **563** Soemanang Soeriowinoto (Association head, 1946–47 and 1949–50)

1996. Greetings Stamps. "Happy Holiday". Inscr "Selamat Hari Raya". Multicoloured.
2220 150r. Type **562** 10 10
2221 300r. Mixed flowers (different) 25 25
2222 700r. Mixed flowers (different) 55 55

1996. 50th Anniv of Indonesian Journalists' Association. Multicoloured.
2223 300r. Type **563** 25 25
2224 700r. Djamaluddin Adinegoro (head of Indonesian Press Bureau Foundation and founder of Academy of Publicity and Publicity Faculty, Padjadjaran University) 55 55

564 Tank firing and Map

1996. 47th Anniv of Return of Republican Government to Djokjakarta. Multicoloured.
2225 700r.+100r. Type **564** . . . 65 65
2226 700r.+100r. Attack on Palace 65 65
Nos. 2225/6 were issued together, se-tenant, forming a composite design.

565 State House, Bandung

1996. "indonesia 96" International Youth Stamp Exhibition, Bandung. Multicoloured.
2227 300r. Type **565** 25 25
2228 700r. Painted parasols . . . 55 55
MS2229 99 × 73 mm. 1250r. Type **565**; 1250r. As No. 2228 4·00 4·00

566 Indonesian Bear Cuscus **567** Roses

1996. Cuscuses. Multicoloured.
2230 300r. Australian spotted cuscus 25 25
2231 300r. Type **566** 25 25
MS2232 98 × 81 mm. 1250r. As No. 2230; 1250r. Type **586** . . . . 2·10 2·10
Nos. 2230/1 were issued together, se-tenant, forming a composite design.

1996. Greetings Stamps. "Congratulations and Best Wishes". Inscr "Selamat dan Sukses". Multicoloured.
2233 150r. Type **567** 10 10
2234 300r. Orchids 25 25
2235 700r. Chrysanthemums . . . 55 55

568 Students (Y. Edwin Purwanto)

1996. Compulsory Nine Year Education Programme. Winning Entries in Children's Stamp Design Competition. Multicoloured.
2236 150r. Type **568** 10 10
2237 300r. Children in playground (Andi Pradhana) 25 25
2238 700r. Teacher and pupils (Intan Sari Dewi) 55 55

569 Archery

1996. Olympic Games, Atlanta. Mult.
2239 300r. Type **569** 25 25
2240 700r. Weightlifting 55 55
2241 1000r. Badminton 90 90
MS2242 81 × 48 mm. 2500r. Type **569** . . . . 2·10 2·20

中国'96——第9届亚洲国际集邮展览
CHINA'96 — 9th Asian International Philatelic Exhibition
(**570**) ($\frac{1}{2}$-size-illustration)

1996. "China '96" International Stamp Exhibition, Peking. No. **MS**2232 optd with T **570** in the margin.
MS2243 98 × 81 mm. 1250r. × 2 multicoloured . . . . 5·75 5·75

571 Pres. Suharto and Procession

1996. National Youth Kirab. Multicoloured.
2244 300r. Type **571** 25 25
2245 700r. Pres. Suharto presenting national flag 55 55

572 Nusantara N-2130 Prototype over Soekarno-Hatta Airport **573** Scouts climbing over Rope Ladders

1996. Aviation and Maritime Year. Mult.
2246 300r. Type **572** 25 25
2247 700r. "Palindo Jaya" (inter-island ferry) 55 55

1996. National Scout Jamboree, Djakarta. Multicoloured.
2248 150r. Type **573** 10 10
2249 150r. Scouts on ladder and death slide 10 10
2250 150r. Scouts at base of rope ladders 10 10
2251 150r. Girl scouts constructing wooden apparatus 10 10
2252 150r. Scouts on unicycle and climbing frame 10 10
2253 150r. Girl scouts building frame on campsite 10 10
2254 150r. Soldering metal . . . 10 10
2255 150r. Girl at radio taking notes 10 10
Nos. 2248/55 were issued together, se-tenant, Nos. 2248/51 and 2252/5 forming composite designs.

574 Pinisi Prows and Wave

1996. 50th Anniv of Bank BNI. Multicoloured.
2256 300r. Type **574** 25 25
2257 700r. Pinisi sailing ship . . . 55 55

575 Mother and Child reading (Salt Iodization Programme)

1996. 50th Anniv of UNICEF. Each brown, green and mauve.
2258 300r. Type **575** 25 25
2259 700r. Giving oral vaccine to children (elimination of polio) 55 55
2260 1000r. Children (Children's Rights Convention) . . . 90 90

576 Ibu Tien Suharto **577** Softball

1996. Ibu Suharto (First Lady) Commem.
2261 **576** 700r. multicoloured . . . 55 55
MS2262 47 × 96 mm. **576** 2500r. multicoloured . . . . 2·10 2·10

1996. National Sports Week. Multicoloured.
2263 300r. Type **577** 25 25
2264 700r. Hockey 55 55
2265 1000r. Basketball 90 90

1996. "Istanbul '96" Stamp Exhibition, Turkey. Two sheets, each 94 × 80 mm. each containing one stamp (62 × 46 mm) featuring composite designs formerly issued in blocks of four.
MS2266 Two sheets (a) 1250r. As Nos. 2248/51; (b) 1250r. As Nos. 2252/5 . . . . 1·60 1·60

578 Head of Sumatran Rhinoceros

1996. The Sumatran Rhinoceros ("Dicerorhinus sumatrensis") and the Javan Rhinoceros ("Rhinoceros sondaicus"). Multicoloured.
2267 300r. Type **578** 40 25
2268 300r. Sumatran rhinoceros 40 25
2269 300r. Javan rhinoceros . . . 40 25
2270 300r. Adult and baby Javan rhinoceros 40 25
MS2271 100 × 47 mm. 1500r. Javan rhinoceros; 1500r. Sumatran rhinoceros . . . . 3·75 3·75

579 Flower Arrangement **581** Sulawesi Hornbill

580 Coins and Banknotes

1996. Greetings Stamps. "Happy New Year". Inscr "Selamat Tahun Baru". Multicoloured.
2272 150r. Type **579** 10 10
2273 300r. Arrangement including red and yellow roses . . . 25 25
2274 700r. Arrangement including white rose and yellow chrysanthemums 55 55

1996. 50th Anniv of Financial Day.
2275 **580** 700r. multicoloured . . . 55 55

1996. National Flora and Fauna Day. Mult.
2276 300r. Type **581** 25 25
2277 300r. Irrawaddy dolphin ("Orcaella brevirostris") 25 25
2278 300r. Black-naped oriole ("Oriolus chinensis") . . 25 25
2279 300r. Sun bear ("Helarctos malayanus") 25 25
2280 300r. Rothschild's mynah ("Leucopsar rothschildi") 25 25
2281 300r. Lontar palms ("Borassus flabellifer") . . 25 25
2282 300r. Black orchid ("Coelogyne pandurata") 25 25
2283 300r. Michelia ("Michelia alba") 25 25
2284 300r. Giant aroid lily ("Amorphophallus titanum") 25 25
2285 300r. Majegau ("Dysoxylum densiflorum") 25 25
MS2286 Two sheets, each 47 × 80 mm. (a) 1250r. As No. 2280; (b) 1250r. As No. 2282 1·20 1·20
See also No. **MS**2287.

1996. "Aseanpex '96" International Stamp Exhibition, Manila, Philippines.
MS2287 **581** 2000r. multicoloured 5·00 5·00

582 Somba Opu Fortress

1996. Eastern Region. Multicoloured.
2288 300r. Divers and sea-bed . . 25 25
2289 700r. Type **582** 55 55

583 School-children at Play **585** Children shaking Hands ("Happy Birthday")

584 Dish Aerial and Control Room

1996. National Movement of Foster Parents. Multicoloured.
2290 150r. Type **583** 15 15
2291 300r. Poor children and photograph of school-child (horiz) 25 25

1996. Traditional Dances (5th series). As T **506**. Multicoloured.
2292 150r. Baksa Kembang dance, South Kalimantan 10 10
2293 300r. Ngarojeng dance, Djakarta 25 25
2294 700r. Rampai dance, Aceh 55 55
2295 1000r. Boituka dance, East Timor 90 90
MS2296 46 × 75 mm. 2000r. As No. 2293 . . . . 2·00 2·00

1997. Telecommunications Year. Mult.
2297 300r. Type **584** 25 25
2298 700r. Key pad, communications satellite orbiting Earth and woman using telephone 55 55

1997. Greetings Stamps.
2299 **585** 600r. multicoloured . . . 50 50
2300 – 600r. black, brn & mve 50 50
DESIGN: No. 2300, Heart and ribbons ("Best Wishes").

586 Transport, Ballot Boxes and National Flag

1997. General Election. Multicoloured.
2301 300r. Type **586** 25 25
2302 700r. State arms, map, ballot boxes and buildings 55 55
2303 1000r. State arms, ballot boxes, map and city skyline 90 90

1997. "Hong Kong '97" Stamp Exhibition. Sheet 81 × 47 mm.
MS2304 2000r. As Type **582** but with addition of postmark . . 2·00 2·00

587 Pres. Suharto and Wahyu Nusantaraaji

1997. Indonesia's 200,000,000th Citizen.
2305 **587** 700r. multicoloured . . . 55 55

588 Children with Stamp Collection

589 Wage Rudolf Soepratman

1997. 75th Anniv of Indonesian Philatelic Association. Multicoloured.
2306 300r. Type **588** 25 25
2307 700r. Magnifying glass on 1994 150r. Flora and Fauna stamp 55 55

1997. Cultural Anniversaries. Multicoloured.
2308 300r. Type **589** (composer of "Indonesia Raya" (national anthem), 60th death anniv (1998)) . . . 25 25
2309 700r. Usmar Ismail (film director, 25th death anniv (1996)) 55 55
2310 1000r. Self-portrait of Affandi (painter, 90th birth anniv) 90 90
MS2311 47 × 97 mm. As No. 2310 2·00 2·00

590 Picture Jasper

1997. "Indonesia 2000" International Stamp Exn, Bandung (1st issue). Minerals. Multicoloured.
2312 300r. Type **590** 25 25
2313 700r. Chrysocolla 55 55
2314 1000r. Geode 90 90
MS2315 80 × 47 mm. 2000r. Banded agate . . . . 2·00 2·00
See also Nos. 2403/**MS**2407, 2529/**MS**2533 and 2593/**MS**2597.

591 Black-naped Oriole

1997. "Pacific 97" International Stamp Exhibition, San Francisco. Sheet 49 × 51 mm.
MS2316 **591** 2000r. multicoloured 2·00 2·00

592 Crowd giving Thumbs Up to "No Smoking" Sign

593 Fishes and Coral Reef

1997. World "No Smoking" Day. Winning Entry in Students' Design Competition.
2317 **592** 1000r. multicoloured . . 90 90

1997. World Environment Day. Mult.
2318 150r. Type **593** 15 15
2319 300r. Rays and other fishes by brain and other corals 25 25
2320 700r. Two coralfishes amongst corals 55 55
MS2321 47 × 79 mm. 2000r. Coral reef . . . . 2·00 2·00

594 Paksi Naga Liman Carriage (built by Pangeran Losari)

1997. 2nd Indonesian Royal Palace Festival, Cirebon. Multicoloured.
2322 300r. Type **594** 25 25
2323 700r. Singa Barong carriage (built by Ki Nataguna), 1549 . . . . 55 55

595 Venue's Main Gateway

1997. 18th National Koran Reading Contest, Jambi. Multicoloured.
2324 300r. Type **595** 25 25
2325 700r. Al Ikhsaniah Mosque, Olak Kemang, Jambi . . 55 55

596 Co-operatives Monument, Tasikmalaya

597 Pres. Suharto and Dr. Mohammad Hatta (first vice-president)

1997. 50th Anniv of Co-operatives Movement. Multicoloured.
2326 150r. Type **596** 10 10
2327 150r. Co-operatives Monument, Djakarta . . . 10 10
2328 300r. Child's hand clasping adult's hand 25 25
2329 300r. Figure before globe . . 25 25
2330 700r. Type **597** 55 55

598 Hands on Globe

1997. 30th Anniv of Association of South-East Asian Nations. Multicoloured.
2331 300r. Type **598** 25 25
2332 700r. Ears of cereals forming "30th" and globe 55 55

599 Games Emblem and Mascot

1997. 19th South-East Asian Games, Djakarta. Multicoloured.
2333 300r. Type **599** 25 25
2334 300r. Torch carrier, flags and emblem 25 25
2335 700r. Running and throwing the discus 55 55
2336 700r. Hurdling and sprinting 55 55

600 Coach, Bus, Java "International Harvester" Bus and Bullock Cart

1997. National Communications Day. Transport Development. Multicoloured.
2337 300r. Type **600** 25 25
2338 300r. Electric, express, diesel and steam railway locomotives 25 25
2339 700r. Container ship, passenger ship, cargo vessel and lette (Madurese sailing boat) 55 55
2340 700r. Seulawah and IPTN CN-235, CN-250 and N-2130 airliners 55 55

601 U.P.U. Monument and Mas Soeharto (first head of Indonesian P.T.T.)

1997. 50th Anniv of Indonesian Membership of U.P.U. Multicoloured.
2341 300r. Type **601** 25 25
2342 700r. Heinrich von Stephan (founder of U.P.U.) and monument 55 55

602 Assembly Emblem and Building

1997. People's Consultative Assembly General Session.
2343 **602** 700r. multicoloured . . . 55 55

603 Village Programme (Army)

1997. Armed Forces Day. Multicoloured.
2344 300r. Type **603** 25 25
2345 300r. Frigates and Jalesveva Jayamahe Monument, Surabaya (Navy) 25 25
2346 300r. "Blue Falcon" acrobatic team (Air Force) 25 25
2347 300r. Rapid Reaction Unit (Police Force) 25 25

604 White Buffalo

1997. "MAKASSAR '97" National Stamp Exhibition, Ujiung Pandeing. Sheet 106 × 49 mm.
MS2348 **604** 2000r. multicoloured 1·30 1·30

605 Duku Fruit ("Lansium domesticum")

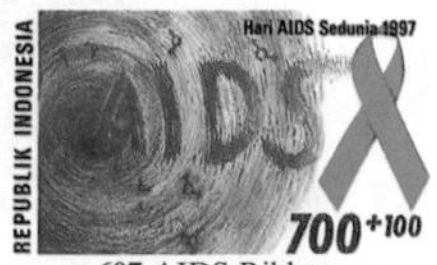

607 AIDS Ribbon

606 Oil Field

1997. National Flora and Fauna Day. Mult.
2349 300r. Type **605** 25 25
2350 300r. Salacca of Condet ("Salacca zalacca") . . . 25 25
2351 300r. Tengawang tungkul ("Shorea stenoptera") . . 25 25
2352 300r. Ebony ("Diospyros macrophylla") 25 25
2353 300r. Fibre orchid ("Diplocaulobium utile") 25 25
2354 300r. Belida fish ("Chitala lopis") 25 25
2355 300r. Brahminy kite ("Haliastur indus") . . . 25 25
2356 300r. Helmeted hornbill ("Rhinoplax vigil") . . . 25 25
2357 300r. Timor deer ("Cervus timorensis") 25 25
2358 300r. Anoa ("Bubalus depressicornis") 25 25
MS2359 98 × 80 mm. 1250r. As No.2351; 1250r. As No. 2355 1·80 1·80

1997. Association of South-east Asian Nations Council on Petroleum Conference, Djakarta. Multicoloured.
2360 300r. Type **606** 25 25
2361 300r. Oil refinery 25 25
2362 300r. "Eka Putra" (oil tanker) 25 25
2363 300r. Petrol tankers 25 25

1997. World AIDS Day.
2364 **607** 700r.+100r. mult 50 50

608 Letter from Foster Son

1997. National Foster Parents Movement.
2365 **608** 700r. multicoloured . . . 50 50

1997. Traditional Dances (6th series). As T **506**. Multicoloured.
2366 150r. Mopuputi Cengke dance, Central Sulawesi 10 10
2367 300r. Mandan Talawang Nyai Balau dance, Central Kalimantan 25 25
2368 600r. Gambyong dance, Central Java 40 40
2369 700r. Cawan dance, North Sumatra 50 50
2370 1000r. Legong Keraton dance, Bali 65 65
MS2371 48 × 79 mm. As No. 2368 1·30 1·30

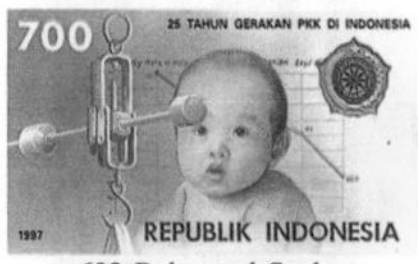

609 Baby and Scales

1997. 25th Anniv of Family Welfare Movement.
2372 **609** 700r. multicoloured . . . 50 50

610 Erau Festival, East Kalimantan

1998. Year of Art and Culture. Festivals. Multicoloured.
2373 300r. Type **610** 10 10
2374 700r. Tabot Festival, Bengkulu 25 25

611 Malin Kundang and his Mother

1998. Folk Tales (1st series). Multicoloured. (a) "Malin Kundung".
2375 300r. Type **611** 10 10
2376 300r. Malin returning home and rejecting mother . . . 10 10
2377 300r. Malin's mother praying to God to curse him 10 10
2378 300r. Malin's ship in storm 10 10
2379 300r. Malin turned to stone 10 10

(b) "Sangkuriang".
2380 300r. Dayang Sumbi weaving 10 10
2381 300r. Dayang Sumbi expelling her son Sanguriang after he killed their dog 10 10
2382 300r. Dayang Sumbi discovering her lover is her son 10 10
2383 300r. Dayang Sumbi creating fake dawn and Sanguriang hurling wooden boat 10 10
2384 300r. Tangkuban Parahu (upturned boat) Mountain 10 10

(c) "Roro Jonggrang".
2385 300r. Pengging people attacking Prambanan people 10 10
2386 300r. Bandung Bondowoso proposing to Roro Jonggrang 10 10
2387 300r. Bandung Bondowoso building temples 10 10
2388 300r. Women banging rice-mothers to prematurely announce dawn 10 10
2389 300r. Prambanan Temple and petrified Roro Jonggrang 10 10

(d) "Tengger".
2390 300r. Roro Anteng and Joko Seger marrying . . . 10 10
2391 300r. Roro and Joko praying to gods for a child 10 10
2392 300r. Volcano erupting . . . 10 10
2393 300r. Raden Kusuma (youngest son) sacrificing himself 10 10
2394 300r. Tengger people giving offerings to volcano . . . 10 10
MS2395 62 × 64 mm. As No. 2394 65 65

Nos. 2375/94 were issued together, se-tenant, forming a composite design.

See also Nos. 2489/**MS**2509, 2572/**MS**2591, 2679/**MS**2699, 2761/**MS**2781/2838/**MS**2858 and 2942/**MS**2962.

612 Djakarta Palace

1997. Presidential Palaces. Multicoloured.
2396 300r. Type **612** 10 10
2397 300r. Bogor Palace 10 10
2398 300r. Cipanas Palace . . . 10 10
2399 300r. Yogyakarta Palace . . 10 10
2400 300r. Tampak Siring Palace, Bali 10 10

613 Man and Pregnant Woman

1998. 50th Anniv of W.H.O. Multicoloured.
2401 300r. Type **613** 10 10
2402 700r. Mother and child (horiz) 10 10

1998. "Indonesia 2000" International Stamp Exhibition, Bandung (2nd issue). Minerals. As T **590**. Multicoloured.
2403 300r. Chrysopal 10 10
2404 700r. Tektite 15 15
2405 1000r. Amethyst 25 25
MS2406 80 × 48 mm. 2500r. Petrified wood 40 40
MS2407 Two sheets. (a) 81 × 48 mm. 2500r. Opal; (b) 118 × 133 mm. Nos. 2403/5, each × 2, plus stamps as in No. **MS**2406 and **MS**2407a (pair of sheets sold at 35000r.) 80 80

614 Boys playing Football

1998. World Cup Football Championship, France. Multicoloured.
2408 300r. Type **614** 10 10
2409 700r. Boys and goal-posts 15 15
2410 1000r. Boys challenging for ball 25 25
MS2411 87 × 57 mm. 2500r. As No. 2411 . . . . 40 40

615 Tropical Rainforest

1998. Environmental Protection. Ecophila Stamp Day. Multicoloured.
2412 700r. Type **615** 15 15
2413 700r. Tropical rainforest (different) 15 15

Nos. 2412/13 were issued together, se-tenant, forming a composite design.

616 Fishing Cat

617 School-children and Drug Addict

1998. "Juvalex 98" Youth Stamp Exhibition, Luxembourg. Sheet 48 × 83 mm.
MS2414 **616** 5000r. multicoloured 65 65

1998. International Day Against Drug Abuse and Illicit Trafficking. Multicoloured.
2415 700r. Type **617** 15 15
2416 700r. Students campaigning against drugs 15 15

618 Besakih Temple (⅔-size illustration)

1998. Tourism. Multicoloured.
2417 700r. Type **618** 15 15
2418 700r. Taman Ayun Temple (31 × 23 mm) 15 15
MS2419 77 × 45 mm. 2500r. Central part of design in Type **618** (41 × 24 mm) 40 40

619 Tiger

1998. "Singpex 98" Asian Stamp Exhibition, Singapore. Sheet 102 × 48 mm.
MS2420 **619** 5000r. multicoloured 2·75 2·75

620 Cattle Wagon and Truck

1998. Railway Rolling Stock. Multicoloured.
2421 300r. Type **620** 10 10
2422 300r. Truck and goods wagon 10 10
2423 300r. Green and yellow passenger carriages . . . 10 10
2424 300r. Passenger carriage and tender 10 10
2425 300r. Class B50 steam locomotive 10 10
2426 300r. Front half of Class D52 steam locomotive . . 10 10
2427 300r. Back half of Class D52 steam locomotive with tender 10 10
2428 300r. Passenger carriage with two doors 10 10
2429 300r. Observation car . . . 10 10
2430 300r. Goods wagon 10 10
MS2431 76 × 48 mm. 2500r. Steam locomotive 50 50

Nos. 2421/30 were issued together, se-tenant, forming a composite design of a train.

621 Pres. Bacharuddin Habibie

1998.
2432 **621** 300r. multicoloured . . . 10 10
2433 700r. multicoloured . . . 15 15
2434 4500r. multicoloured . . 90 90
2435 5000r. multicoloured . . 1·00 1·00

622 Fencing

1998. 13th Asian Games, Bangkok, Thailand. Multicoloured.
2436 300r. Type **622** 10 10
2437 700r. Taekwondo 15 15
2438 4000r. Kung fu 80 80
MS2439 79 × 100 mm. Nos. 2436/8 1·00 1·00

623 "Baruna Jaya IV" (research ship)

1998. International Year of the Ocean.
2440 **623** 700r. multicoloured . . . 15 15

624 Javan Kingfisher

1998. 5th Dutch Stamp Dealers' Association Stamp Exhibition, The Hague, Netherlands. Two sheets containing T **624** or similar multicoloured design.
MS2441 Two sheets. (a) 71 × 46 mm. 5000r. Type **624**; (b) 71 × 60 mm. 35000r. Javanese wattled lapwing (*Vannelus macropterus*) . . . . 9·50 9·50

625 1974 20r. U.P.U. Stamp

1998. World Stamp Day. Multicoloured.
2442 700r. Type **625** 15 15
2443 700r. 1955 15s. Post Office Anniversary stamp . . . 15 15

626 Magpie Goose

1998. Waterfowl (1st series). Multicoloured.
2444 4000r. Type **626** . . . . . 1·00 1·00
2445 5000r. Spotted whistling duck . . . . 1·20 1·20
2446 10000r. Salvadori's duck . . 2·40 2·40
2447 15000r. Radjah shelduck . . 3·50 3·50
2448 20000r. White-winged wood duck . . . . 5·00 5·00
MS2449 206 × 115 mm. Nos. 2444/8 13·00 13·00

See also Nos. 2468/**MS**2475 and 2628/9.

627 Djakarta Cathedral

628 State Flag and Jayawijaya Peak

1998. "Italia 98" International Stamp Exhibition, Milan.
MS2450 55 × 9 mm. **627** 5000r. multicoloured . . . . 1·20 1·20

1998. "The Red and White Flag". Multicoloured.
2451 700r. Type **628** 15 15
2452 700r. State flag and Himalayan peak 15 15

629 State Flag

1998. Political Reforms. Multicoloured.
2453 700r. Type **629** 15 15
2454 700r. Dove and State flag 15 15
2455 1000r. Students in front of Parliament building (82 × 25 mm) 25 25

630 "Stelechocarpus burahol"

631 Monument at Blitar and Museum, Bogor

1998. Flora and Fauna. Multicoloured.
2456 500r. Type **630** 15 15
2457 500r. Tuberose ("Polianthes tuberosa") 15 15
2458 500r. Four o'clock ("Mirabilis jalapa") . . . 15 15
2459 500r. "Mangifera casturi" 15 15
2460 500r. "Ficus minahassae" 15 15
2461 500r. Zebra dove ("Geopelia striata") 15 15
2462 500r. Red and green junglefowl hybrid ("Gallus varius x G. gallus") . . . 15 15
2463 500r. Indian elephant ("Elephas maximus") . . 15 15
2464 500r. Proboscis monkey ("Nasalis larvatus") . . . 15 15
2465 500r. Eastern tarsier ("Tarsius spectrum") . . 15 15
MS2466 Two sheets. (a) 48 × 80 mm. 2500r. As No. 2457; (b) 48 × 92 mm. 2500r. As No. 2464 50 50

1998. 55th Anniv of Formation of Volunteer National Armed Forces (independence fighters).
2467 **631** 700r.+100r. mult 15 15

632 Australian White-eyed Duck

1998. Waterfowl (2nd series). Multicoloured.

2468	250r. Type **632**	10	10
2469	500r. Pacific black duck	10	10
2470	700r. Grey teal	15	15
2471	1000r. Cotton goose	25	25
2472	1500r. Green pygmy goose	35	35
2473	2500r. Indian whistling duck	50	50
2474	3500r. Wandering whistling duck	75	75
MS2475	45 × 83 mm. 5000r. Type **632**	1·00	1·00

1998. Traditional Dances (7th series). As T **506**. Multicoloured.

2476	300r. Oreng oreng gae dance, Sulawesi Tenggara (South-east Celebes)	10	10
2477	500r. Persembahan dance, Bengkulu	10	10
2478	700r. Kipas (fan) dance, Riau	15	15
2479	1000r. Srimpi dance, Yogyakarta	25	25
2480	2000r. Pasambahan, Sumatera Barat (West)	40	40
MS2481	48 × 80 mm. 5000r. As No. 2480	1·00	1·00

633 Water Wheel and Power Lines

1999. Year of Creation and Engineering. Multicoloured.

2482	500r. Type **633**	10	10
2483	700r. Water pipe and pipe network in valley	15	15

634 Throwing the Shot

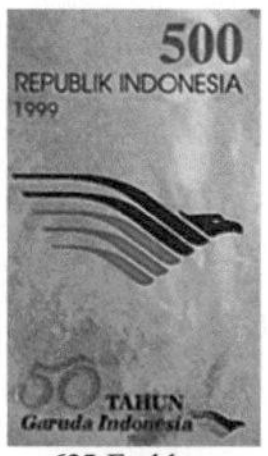

635 Emblem

1999. 7th Far East and South Pacific Games for Disabled Persons, Bangkok. Multicoloured.

2484	500r. Type **634**	10	10
2485	500r. Medal and wheelchair	10	10

1999. 50th Anniv of Garuda Indonesia (state airline). Multicoloured.

2486	500r. Type **635**	10	10
2487	700r. Jet engine	15	15
2488	2000r. Pilot, stewardess and airplane	40	40

1999. Folk Tales (2nd series). As T **611**. Multicoloured. (a) "Lake Toba".

2489	500r. Man and yellow fish	15	15
2490	500r. Man proposing to woman	15	15
2491	500r. Woman giving food for father to son Sam and Sam eating it	15	15
2492	500r. Wife turning back into a fish	15	15
2493	500r. Samosir Island and Lake Toba	15	15
	(b) "Banjarmasin".		
2494	500r. Rebels and contenders to throne	15	15
2495	500r. Local governors crown Prince Samudera	15	15
2496	500r. Tumenggung sends fleet to Samudera's capital, Bandar Masih	15	15
2497	500r. Samudera and Tumenggung meet on board ship	15	15
2498	500r. Ships in Banjarmasin Harbour	15	15
	(c) "Buleleng".		
2499	500r. I Gusti Gede Paseken leaving with guards for Den Bukit	15	15
2500	500r. Forest giant appearing to I Gusti Gede Paseken	15	15
2501	500r. I Gusti Gede Paseken lifting stranded ship	15	15
2502	500r. I Gusti Gede Paseken arriving before King of Den Bukit	15	15
2503	500r. Procession in kingdom of Buleleng	15	15
	(d) "Woiram".		
2504	500r. Woiram teaching archery to Woiwallytmang and with wife Donadebu	15	15
2505	500r. Mesan and Mecy looking for shrimps	15	15
2506	500r. Woiram cursing Demontin village	15	15
2507	500r. Woiwallytmang and Mecy clinging to tree trunk	15	15
2508	500r. Woiram's footprints in rock	15	15
MS2509	75 × 66 mm. 5000r. As No. 2493	1·00	1·00

Nos. 2489/2508 were issued together, se-tenant, forming a composite design.

636 Malang Apple

1999. "Surabaya 99" National Stamp Exhibition. Sheet 78 × 58 mm.
MS2510 **636** 5000r. multicoloured 1·00 1·00

637 Eastern Tarsier

1999. "Australia 99" International Stamp Exhibition, Melbourne. Sheet 60 × 92 mm.
MS2511 **637** 5000r. multicoloured 1·00 1·00

638 "Ascosparassis heinricherii"

1999. Fungi. Multicoloured. (a) T **638** and similar diamond-shaped designs.

2512	500r. Type **638**	10	10
2513	500r. "Mutinus bambusinus"	10	10
2514	500r. "Mycena" sp.	10	10
2515	700r. "Gloephyllum imponens"	15	15
2516	700r. "Microporus xanthopus"	15	15
2517	700r. "Termitomyces eurrhizus"	15	15
2518	1000r. "Boedijnopeziza insititia"	25	25
2519	1000r. "Aseroe rubra"	25	25
2520	1000r. "Calostoma orirubra"	25	25
	(b) As Nos. 2512/14 but rectangular designs, size 31 × 23 mm.		
2521	500r. As No. 2513	15	15
2522	500r. As No. 2512	15	15
2523	500r. As No. 2514	15	15
	(c) Sheet 62 × 92 mm.		
MS2524	5000r. "Termitomyces eurrhizus" (different) (24½ × 41 mm)	1·00	1·00

639 Doctor and Patients outside Surgery

1999. Public Health Care Insurance.
2525 **639** 700r. multicoloured 15 15

640 "Dendrobium abang betawi"

1999. "iBRA 99" International Stamp Exhibition, Nuremberg, Germany. Sheet 63 × 98 mm.
MS2526 **640** 5000r. multicoloured 1·40 1·40

641 Y2K "Bug"

1999. Millennium Bug (computer programming fault). Multicoloured.

2527	500r. Type **641**	15	15
2528	500r. Robot exploding	15	15

Nos. 2527/8 were issued together, se-tenant, forming a composite design.

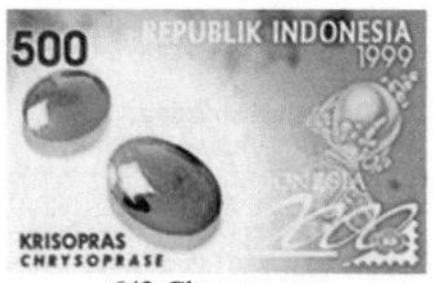

642 Chrysoprase

1999. "Indonesia 2000" International Stamp Exhibition, Bandung (3rd issue). Gemstones. Multicoloured.

2529	500r. Type **642**	15	15
2530	1000r. Smoky quartz	25	25
2531	2000r. Blue opal	55	55
MS2532	80 × 48 mm. 4000r. Silicified coral	1·00	1·00
MS2533	Two sheets. (a) 80 × 48 mm. 4000r. Javan jade; (b) 122 × 160 mm. Nos. 2529 × 4, 2530 × 2, 2531 × 2 plus stamps as in Nos. **MS**2532 and **MS**2533b	3·75	3·75

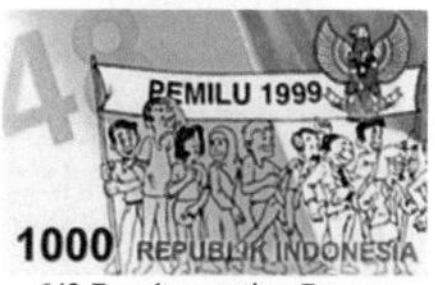

643 People carrying Banner

1999. General Election. Multicoloured.

2534	1000r. Type **643**	15	10
2535	1000r. Ballot box and map of Indonesia	15	10

Nos. 2534/5 were issued together, se-tenant, forming a composite design.

644 Girl in Blanket and People walking through Water

1999. Environmental Protection. Ecophila Stamp Day. Multicoloured.

2536	500r. Type **644**	15	15
2537	1000r. Boy swimming with duck, plant and berry	40	40
2538	2000r. Elderly woman drinking from jug	80	80
MS2539	79 × 46 mm. 3000r. As No. 2537	1·20	1·20

645 Prambanan Temple

1999. "Philexfrance 99" International Stamp Exhibition, Paris. Sheet 59 × 94 mm.
MS2540 **645** 5000r. multicoloured 2·00 2·00

646 Nurses helping Children

1999. Red Cross.
2541 **646** 1000r. multicoloured 35 35

647 Frans Kaisiepo (Governor of Irian Jaya, 1964)

1999. National Heroes and Heroines.

2542	**647**	500r. brown & cinnamon	15	15
2543	–	500r. brown & cinnamon	15	15
2544	–	500r. brown & cinnamon	15	15
2545	–	500r. brown & cinnamon	15	15

DESIGNS: No. 2543, Maria Walanda Maramis (founder of "PIKAT" (women's education organization, 1917)); 2544, Dr. W. Z. Johannes (founder of Indonesian Christian Party, 1942); 2545, Martha Christina Tijahahu (revolutionary).

648 Rabbit

1999. "CHINA 99" International Stamp Exhibition, Beijing. Sheet 81 × 60 mm.
MS2546 **648** 5000r. multicoloured 1·60 1·60

649 University Building, 1949

1999. 50th Anniv of Gadjah Mada University, Yogyakarkta. Multicoloured.

2547	500r. Type **649**	15	15
2548	1000r. University facade, 1999	40	40

650 Woman painting Parasol

1999. International Year of the Elderly Person.
2549 **650** 500r. multicoloured 15 15

651 Batik Design, Cirebon

1999. Batik Designs. Different Batik designs. Mult.

2550	500r. Type **651**	15	15
2551	500r. Madura	15	15
2552	500r. Yogyakarta	15	15
2553	500r. Jambi	15	15

652 Pillar Box, Postman and Kantoon Post Office (½-size illustration)

1999. 125th Anniv of Universal Postal Union. Mult.

2554	500r. Type **652**	15	15
2555	500r. Modern postal building, motorcycle postman and pillar box	15	15

2556 1000r. Pillar box, left-hand side of Kantoon Post Office and postman on horseback (30 × 31 mm) 80 80
2557 1000r. Motorcycle postman, modern postal building and pillar box (30 × 31 mm) 80 80

653 Dog and Puppy

1999. Domestic Animals. Multicoloured.
2558 500r. Type **653** 15 15
2559 500r. Cockerel, hen and chick 15 15
2560 500r. Cat 15 15
2561 500r. Rabbits 15 15
2562 1000r. Feral rock pigeon (20 × 50 mm) 40 40
2563 1000r. Geese and gosling (20 × 50 mm) 40 40
MS2564 79 × 47 mm. 4000r. As No. 2561 . . . . 1·50 1·50
Nos. 2558/9, 2560/1 and 2562/3 respectively were issued together, se-tenant, showing the composite design of a garden.

654 Globe, Diary and Clock Face

1999. New Millennium. Multicoloured.
2565 1000r. Type **654** 40 40
2566 1000r. "2000" and child's face 40 40
MS2567 Two sheets, each 86 × 57 mm. (a) 20000r. As Type **654**; (b) 20000r. As No. 2566 7·75 7·75

From 1 January 2000 stamps are inscribed "Indonesia".

655 Satellite and Fishes

2000. Year of Technology. Multicoloured.
2568 500r. Type **655** 15 15
2569 1000r. Greenhouse and plant 40 40

656 University Campus, Salemba

2000. 50th Anniv of University of Indonesia. Multicoloured.
2570 500r. Type **656** 15 15
2571 1000r. University building, Depok 40 40

2000. Folk Tales (3rd series). As T **611**. Multicoloured. (a) "*Tapak Tuan*".
2572 500r. Dragon finding baby on shore 25 25
2573 500r. Girl meeting other people 25 25
2574 500r. Dragon attacking boat and man 25 25
2575 500r. Man and dragon fighting 25 25
2576 500r. Dead dragon 25 25

(b) "*Batu Ballah*".
2577 500r. Mak Risah and children 25 25
2578 500r. Children playing . . . 25 25
2579 500r. Mak Risah saddened by her children 25 25
2580 500r. Mak Risah being swallowed by stone . . . 25 25
2581 500r. Mak Risah Rock . . . 25 25

(c) "*Sawerigading*".
2582 500r. Sariwegading proposing marriage to twin sister 25 25
2583 500r. We Tanriabeng refusing marriage 25 25
2584 500r. Sariwegdaing in stern of boat 25 25
2585 500r. Bow of boat and wedding 25 25
2586 500r. Bulupoloe Mountain 25 25

(d) "*7 Putri Kahyangan*".
2587 500r. Prince hiding wings and angel weeping 25 25
2588 500r. Prince and angel with their children and angel flying away from Earth 25 25
2589 500r. Prince flying on eagle's back to reclaim wife . . . 25 25
2590 500r. Angel refusing to return to Earth 25 25
2591 500r. Prince wearing magical crown 25 25
MS2592 84 × 61 mm. 5000r. As No. 2576 . . . . 2·00 2·00
Nos. 2572/91 were issued together, se-tenant, forming a composite design.

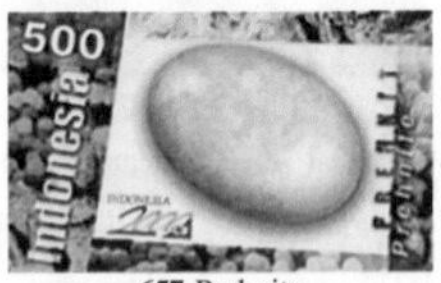

657 Prehnite

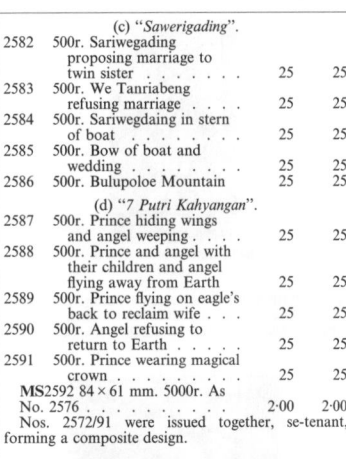

2000. "Indonesia 2000" International Stamp Exhibition, Bandung (4th issue). Gemstones. Multicoloured.
2593 500r. Type **657** 25 25
2594 1000r. Chalcedony 40 40
2595 2000r. Volcanic obsidian . . 75 75
MS2596 80 × 48 mm. 5000r. Jasperized limestone . . . . . 2·00 2·00
MS2597 Two sheets. (a) 80 × 48 mm. 5000r. Copper jasper; (b) 121 × 156 mm. No. 2593 × 4, 2594 × 2, 2595 × 2 plus stamps as in **MS**2596 and **MS**2597a . . . . 3·75 3·75

658 I Brewok (Gun-Gun)

2000. Cartoon Characters. Each black and red.
2598 500r. Type **658** 25 25
2599 500r. "Pak Tuntung" (Basuki) 25 25
2600 500r. "Pak Bei" (Masdi Sunardi) 25 25
2601 500r. "Mang Ohle" (Didin D. Basuni) 25 25
2602 500r. "Panji Koming" (Dwi Koendoro) 25 25

659 Emblem and Weather Chart

2000. 50th Anniv of World Meteorological Organization.
2603 **659** 500r. multicoloured . . . 25 25

660 King Dragon

2000. World Youth Stamp Exhibition and 13th Asian Stamp Exhibition, Bangkok. Sheet 79 × 49 mm.
MS2604 **660** 5000r. multicoloured 1·60 1·60

661 Cycling

2000. 15th National Sports Week. Multicoloured.
2605 500r. Type **661** 50 25
2606 1000r. Canoeing . . . . . 1·10 40
2607 2000r. High-jumping . . . . 2·10 55

662 Coelacanth

2000. "Stamp Show 2000" International Stamp Exhibition, London. Sheet 78 × 54 mm.
MS2608 **662** 5000r. multicoloured 1·60 1·60

663 Red-footed Booby's on Nest

2000. Environmental Protection. Ecophila Stamp Day. Multicoloured.
2609 500r. Type **663** 50 25
2610 1000r. Monkey . . . . . . 1·10 40
2611 2000r. Fishes . . . . 2·10 55
MS2612 68 × 52 mm. 4000r. As No. 2610 . . . . 1·50 1·50

664 Boxing

2000. Olympic Games, Sydney. Multicoloured.
2613 500r. Type **664** 15 15
2614 500r. Judo 15 15
2615 1000r. Badminton 35 35
2616 1000r. Weightlifting 35 35
2617 2000r. Swimming 65 65
2618 2000r. Running 65 65
MS2619 84 × 51 mm. 5000r. As No. 2616 . . . . 1·60 1·60

665 Komodo Dragon

2000. Endangered Species. The Komodo Dragon (*Varanus komodoensis*). Multicoloured.
2620 500r. Type **665** 40 40
2621 500r. Two dragons fighting 40 40
2622 500r. On branch 40 40
2623 500r. Two dragons walking 40 40
MS2624 101 × 56 mm. 2500r. As Type **665**; 2500r. As No. 2621 2·75 2·75

666 President Abdurrahman Wahid

2000. President and Vice-President. Multicoloured.
2625 1000r. Type **666** 40 40
2626 1000r. Vice-President Megawati Soekarnoputri 40 40

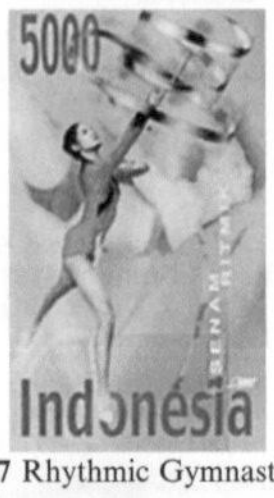

667 Rhythmic Gymnastics

2000. "Olymphilex 2000" Stamp Exhibition, Sydney. Sheet 52 × 79 mm.
MS2627 **667** 5000r. multicoloured 2·50 2·50

2000. Waterfowl (3rd series). As T **632**. Multicoloured.
2628 800r. Indian whistling duck (*Dendrocygna javanica*) . . 80 80
2629 900r. Australian white-eyed duck (*Aythya australis*) . . 1·00 1·00

668 Couple from D. I. Aceh

670 Hand holding 1989 500r. Endangered Species Stamp

669 Chairil Anwar (poet)

2000. Regional Costumes. Showing couples wearing traditional costumes from different regions. Multicoloured.
2630 900r. Type **668** 35 35
2631 900r. Jambi 35 35
2632 900r. Banten 35 35
2633 900r. D. I. Yogyakarta . . . 35 35
2634 900r. Kalimantan Tengah 35 35
2635 900r. Sulawesi Tenggara . . 35 35
2636 900r. Nusa Tenggara Timur 35 35
2637 900r. Sumatera Utara . . . 35 35
2638 900r. Bengkulu 35 35
2639 900r. D. K. I. Jakarta . . . 35 35
2640 900r. Jawa Timur 35 35
2641 900r. Kalimantan Timur . . 35 35
2642 900r. Sulawesi Selatan . . . 35 35
2643 900r. Maluku 35 35
2644 900r. Sumatera Barat . . . 35 35
2645 900r. Sumatera Selatan . . 35 35
2646 900r. Jawa Barat 35 35
2647 900r. Kalimantan Barat . . 35 35
2648 900r. Sulawesi Utara . . . 35 35
2649 900r. Bali 35 35
2650 900r. Maluku Utara 35 35
2651 900r. Riau 35 35
2652 900r. Lampung 35 35
2653 900r. Jawa Tengah 35 35
2654 900r. Kalimantan Selatan 35 35
2655 900r. Sulawesi Tengah . . . 35 35
2656 900r. Nusa Tenggara Barat 35 35
2657 900r. Irian Jaya 35 35

2000. Personalities. Multicoloured.
2658 900r. Type **669** 35 35
2659 900r. Ibu Sud (children's song writer) 35 35
2660 900r. Bing Slamet (entertainer) 35 35
2661 900r. S. Sudjojono (artist) 35 35
2662 900r. I. Ketut Maria (actor) 35 35
MS2663 62 × 2 mm. 4000r. Chairil Anwar (different) (vert) . . . . 1·50 1·50

2000. Communications. Multicoloured.
2664 800r. Type **670** 25 25
2665 900r. Satellite, map, television and letter (horiz) 35 35
2666 1000r. Globe and computer monitor 40 40
2667 4000r. Airplane, globe and computer . . . . 1·50 1·50

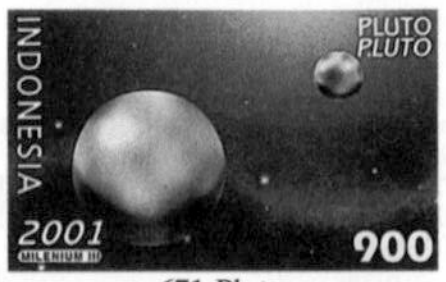

671 Pluto

2001. The Solar System. Multicoloured.
2668 900r. Type **671** 25 25
2669 900r. Neptune 25 25
2670 900r. Uranus 25 25
2671 900r. Saturn 25 25
2672 900r. Jupiter 25 25
2673 900r. Mars 25 25
2674 900r. Earth 25 25
2675 900r. Venus 25 25
2676 900r. Mercury 25 25
2677 900r. Sun 25 25
MS2678 120 × 71 mm. 5000r. Sun (different) . . . . 1·40 1·40

2001. Folk Tales (4th series). As T **611**. Multicoloured. (a) "Batang Tuaka".
2679 900r. Two snakes fighting and Tuaka with stone . . 25 25
2680 900r. Tuaka selling stone to merchant in Tumasik Port 25 25
2681 900r. Tuaka as a successful merchant with his wife . . 25 25
2682 900r. Mother cursing Tuaka and his wife 25 25
2683 900r. Tuaka and his wife become birds 25 25

(b) "Si Pitung".
2684 900r. Si Pitung and gang stealing money from Dutch sympathizers . . . 25 25
2685 900r. Si Pitung's gang leaving money for villagers 25 25
2686 900r. Dutch ruler fighting Si Pitung 25 25
2687 900r. Villagers mourning dead Si Pitung 25 25
2688 900r. Si Pitung Mosque . . 25 25

(c) "Terusan Nusa".
2689 900r. Tambing finding and eating dragon's egg . . . 25 25
2690 900r. Tambing turning into dragon 25 25
2691 900r. Dragon (Tambing) eating all the fish in the river 25 25
2692 900r. Tambing dying after eating his own tail 25 25
2693 900r. Empty river 25 25

(d) "Ile Mauraja".
2694 900r. Raja dreaming 25 25
2695 900r. Raja receiving cotton seeds from bearded man 25 25
2696 900r. Raja and wife 25 25
2697 900r. Snake on bed, burning village and snakes causing upheaval of village . . . 25 25
2698 900r. Mountain formed by village 25 25
MS2699 84 × 61 mm. 5000r. No. 2686 . . . . 1·40 1·40

Nos. 2679/98 were issued together, se-tenant, forming a composite design.

672 Arsa Wijaya, Bali

2001. Traditional Masks. Showing left (a) or right (b) sides of masks. Multicoloured.
2700 500r. Type **672** 15 15
2701 500r. Arsa Wijaya (b) . . . 15 15
2702 800r. Asmat, Irian Jaya (a) 25 25
2703 800r. Asmat (b) 25 25
2704 800r. Cirebon, Jawa Barat (a) 25 25
2705 800r. Cirebon (b) 25 25
2706 900r. Hudoq, Kalimantan Timur (a) 35 35
2707 900r. Hudoq (b) 35 35
2708 900r. Wayang Wong, Yogyakarta (a) 35 35
2709 900r. Wayang Wong (b) . . 35 35
MS2710 61 × 96 mm. 5000r. No. 2706 . . . . 1·60 1·60

Nos. 2700/1, 2702/3, 2704/5, 2706/7 and 2708/9 were issued together, se-tenant, each pair forming a composite design.

673 Beduk

2001. Traditional Instruments. Multicoloured.
2711 900r. Type **673** 15 15
2712 900r. Bende (bronze drum) 15 15
2713 900r. Kentongan (percussion) 15 15
2714 900r. Nafiri (horn) 15 15

674 Bouquet

2001. Greetings Stamps. Multicoloured.
2715 800r. Type **674** 15 15
2716 900r. Rose 25 25
2717 1000r. Bouquet of orange roses and leaves 35 35
2718 1500r. Large white flower and dark green leaf . . . 40 40
2719 2000r. Bouquet of yellow flowers with pink bow . . 55 55
2720 4000r. Amaryllis flower and ribbon . . . . 1·20 1·20
2721 5000r. Table decoration and candles . . . . 1·50 1·50
2722 10000r. White flower with yellow centre . . . . . . 3·00 3·00

675 Children and Fish (Surayadi)

2001. World Environment Day. Winning entries in Stamp Design Competition (Nos. 2723, 2725). Multicoloured.
2723 800r. Type **675** 25 25
2724 900r. Boys feeding deer . . 25 25
2725 1000r. Boy swimming with turtle (Lambok Hutabarat) 35 35
MS2726 82 × 50 mm. 3000r. As No. 2724 . . . . 90 90

676 Youthful Sukarno wearing Turban

2001. Birth Centenary of Dr. Ahmed Sukarno (Bung Karno) (nationalist leader and first president). Multicoloured.
2727 500r. Type **676** 15 15
2728 800r. As young man wearing collar and tie 25 25
2729 900r. Wearing high-necked jacket 25 25
2730 1000r. Wearing uniform with lapel badges 35 35
MS2731 138 × 59 mm. 5000r. Giving speech . . . . 1·50 1·50

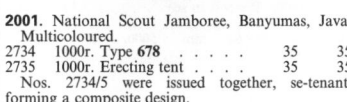

677 Policeman guiding Children across the Road

2001. Indonesian Police Force. Multicoloured.
2732 1000r. Type **677** 35 35
2733 1000r. Helicopter and women police officers giving directions 35 35

678 Scouts raising Flag

2001. National Scout Jamboree, Banyumas, Java. Multicoloured.
2734 1000r. Type **678** 35 35
2735 1000r. Erecting tent 35 35

Nos. 2734/5 were issued together, se-tenant, forming a composite design.

679 Kaki Siapa (blind man's buff)

2001. National Children's Day. Children's Games. Multicoloured.
2736 800r. Type **679** 15 15
2738 900r. Erang Bambu (stilt walking) 25 25
2739 1000r. Dakon (counting game) 25 25
2740 2000r. Kuda Pelepah Pisang (hobby horses) 40 40

680 Sunflower

2001. Philanippon '01 International Stamp Exhibition. Sheet 93 × 46 mm.
MS2741 **680** 10000r. multicoloured 3·25 3·25

681 Dr. R. Soeharso (founder) and Operating Theatre

2001. 50th Anniv of Dr. R. Soeharso Orthopaedic Hospital.
2742 **681** 1000r. multicoloured . . 15 15

682 Makasaar Post Office

2001. Post Office Architecture. Showing Post Office building. Multicoloured.
2743 800r. Type **682** 10 10
2744 900r. Bandung 15 15
2745 1000r. Balikpapan 15 15
2746 2000r. Padang 25 25

683 Perahu (boat)

2001. Traditional Transport. Multicoloured.
2747 1000r. Type **683** 15 15
2748 1000r. Becak Dayung (tricycle rickshaw) 15 15
2749 1000r. Andong (horse-drawn taxi) 15 15

684 Rose Quartz

2001. Gemstones. Multicoloured.
2750 800r. Type **684** 10 10
2751 900r. Brecciated Jasper . . . 15 15
2752 1000r. Malachite 15 15
MS2753 80 × 47 mm. 5000r. Diamond . . . . 1·60 1·60

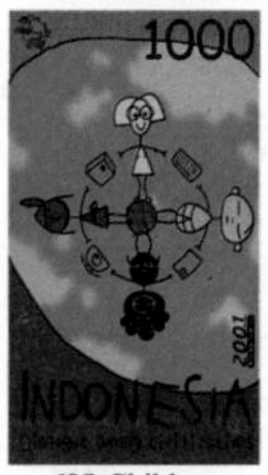

685 Children encircling Globe

686 *Agestrata dehaan*

2001. United Nations Year of Dialogue among Civilizations.
2754 **685** 1000r. multicoloured . . 15 15

2001. Insects. Multicoloured.
2755 800r. Type **686** 10 10
2756 900r. *Mormolyce phyllodes* 15 15
2757 1000r. *Batocera rosenbergi* 15 15
2758 1000r. *Chrysochroa buqueti* 15 15
2759 2000r. *Chalcosoma Caucasus* 15 15
MS2760 61 × 90 mm. 5000r. No. 2759 . . . . 2·10 2·10

2002. Folk Tales (5th series). As T **611**. Multicoloured. (a) Pulau Kembaro, Sumatera Selatan
2761 1000r. Two women 15 15
2762 1000r. Man and woman . . 15 15
2763 1000r. Boat sinking 15 15
2764 1000r. Man and woman standing in boat 15 15
2765 1000r. Serpent, boat and bridge 15 15

(b) Nyi Roro Kidul, Jogjakarta
2766 1000r. Prabu Siliwangi, Dewi Kaita and harem . . 15 15
2767 1000r. Dewi Kaita and mother changing 15 15
2768 1000r. Cast out of palace . . 15 15
2769 1000r. Dewi Kaita changing to Nyi Roro Kidul . . . 15 15
2770 1000r. Sea 15 15

(c) Aji Tatin, Kalimantan Timur
2771 1000r. Palm tree, woman and man with arm outstretched 15 15
2772 1000r. Woman, bird and boat 15 15
2773 1000r. Woman with hand to head 15 15
2774 1000r. Boat breaking . . . 15 15
2775 1000r. Sun and bird 15 15

(d) Danau Tondano, Sulawesi Utara
2776 1000r. Woman seated . . . 15 15
2777 1000r. Man holding spear 15 15
2778 1000r. Man and woman dressed as man 15 15
2779 1000r. Three men under trees 15 15
2780 1000r. Tree and island . . . 15 15
MS2781 108 × 61 mm. 5000r. No. 2765 . . . . 75 75

Nos. 2761/5, 2766/70, 2771/5, 2776/80 respectively were issued together, se-tenant, forming a composite design.

687 Player with Shirt over Head

2002. World Cup Football Championships, Japan and South Korea. Multicoloured.
2782 1000r. Type **687** 15 15
2783 1500r. Players in front of goal 20 20
2784 2000r. Player 25 25
MS2785 52 × 80 mm. 5000r. No. 2784 . . . . 75 75

688 Outline of Two Women

2002. 25th Anniv of Cancer Foundation.
2786 **688** 1000r. multicoloured . . 15 15

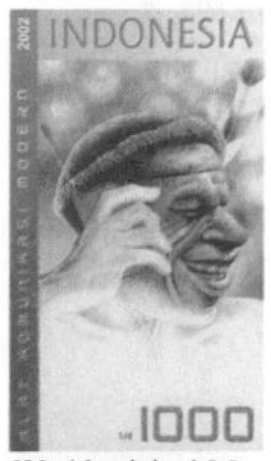

689 Aboriginal Man holding Cell Phone

2002. Communications. Multicoloured.
2787 1000r. Type **689** 15 15
2788 1000r. Woman holding hand set 15 15
2789 1000r. Computer, satellite and disc 15 15
2790 1000r. Satellite above globe 15 15

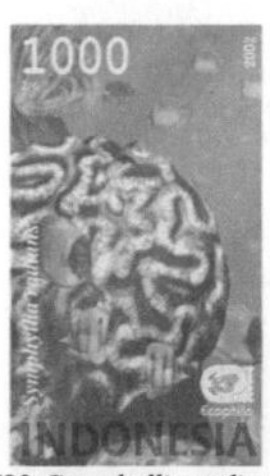

690 *Symphyllia radians*

2002. Marine Life. Ecophila. Multicoloured.
2791 1000r. Type **690** 15 15
2792 1000r. *Charonia tritonis* . . 15 15
2793 1500r. *Acanthaster planci* . . 20 20
2794 1500r. Polka dot grouper (*Cromileptes altivelis*) . . 20 20
2795 2000r. Blue tang (*Paracanthurus hepatus*) 25 25
2796 2000r. *Tridacna gigas* . . . 25 25
MS2797 (a) 97 × 170 mm. Nos. 2791/5; (b) 60 × 91 mm. 5000r. No. 2793 . . . . 1·70 1·70

691 Boy writing and Men dancing

2002. Nanggroe Aceh Province, Darussalam. Multicoloured.

2798 1500r. Type **691** 20 20
2799 3500r. Mosque 45 45

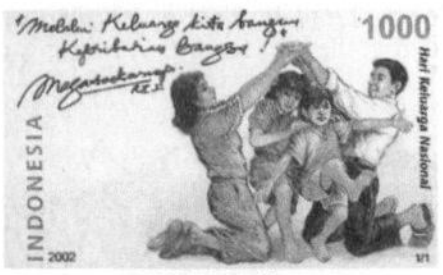

692 Family

2002. National Family Day.

2800 **692** 1000r. multicoloured . . 15 15

693 Solar Eclipse and Olympiad Emblem

2002. 33rd International Physics Olympiad, Bali. Multicoloured.

2801 1000r. Type **693** 15 15
2802 1000r. Colour spectrum and symbols 15 15

694 Bird-shaped Kite

2002. Layang-Layang. Kite Flying. Multicoloured.

2803 1000r. Type **694** 15 15
2804 1000r. Lion 15 15
2805 1000r. Rhomboid 15 15
2806 1000r. Winged kite 15 15
2807 1000r. Box and glider kites 15 15
MS2808 79 × 49 mm. 5000r. No. 2803 . . . . 75 75

Nos. 2803/7 were issued together, se-tenant, forming a composite design.

695 Noni (*Morinda citrifolia*)

2002. Fruit. Multicoloured.

2809 300r. Type **695** 10 10
2810 500r. Mango (*Mangifera indica*) 10 10
2811 1500r. Star fruit (*Averrhoa carambola*) 20 20
2812 3000r. *Durio zibethinus* . . . 40 40

696 Tari Pajaga Dancer, Salawesi Selatan

2002. Philakorea 2002 International Stamp Exhibition, Seoul. Sheet 48 × 80 mm.

MS2813 **696** 7000r. multicoloured 95 95

697 Mohammad Hatta

2002. Birth Centenary of Mohammad Hatta (first vice-president). Multicoloured.

2814 1000r. Type **697** 20 20
2815 1000r. Wearing high-necked jacket 20 20
2816 1500r. Wearing light jacket and dark tie 20 20
2817 1500r. Wearing light jacket and tie 20 20
MS2818 137 × 60 mm. 5000r. Wearing light suit and open neck shirt 75 75

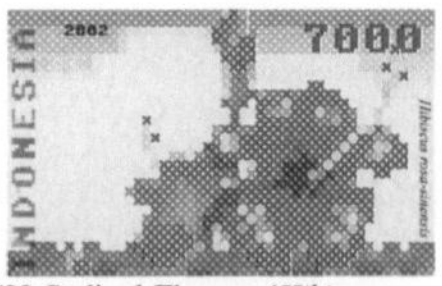

699 Stylised Flowers (*Hibiscus rosa-sinensis*)

2002. Amphilex 2002 International Stamp Exhibition, Amsterdam. Sheet 92 × 47 mm.

MS2821 **699** 7000r. multicoloured 80 80

700 Soldier

702 Hagen's Lanzenotter (*Trimeresurus hageni*)

701 "Cat" (Popo Iskander)

2002. Jogja Panfila 2002 International Stamp Exhibition, Jakarta. Sheet 51 × 85 mm.

MS2822 **700** 6000r. multicoloured 80 80

2002. Art. Multicoloured.

2823 1000r. (1) Type **701** 10 10
2824 1000r. (2) "Guerrilla Sentry, Seko" (S. Sudjojono) . . 10 10
2825 1500r. (3) "Women and child" (Hendra Gunawan) (vert) 15 15
2826 1500r. (4) "Gaututkaca, Prigiwa and Prigiwati" (R. Basoeki Abdullah) (vert) 15 15

2002. Flora and Fauna. Multicoloured.

2827 1000r. Type **702** 10 10
2828 1000r. *Rafflesia micropylora* 10 10
2829 1500r. Leopard (*Panthera pardus*) 15 15
2830 1500r. *Terminalia catappa* 15 15
2831 2000r. *Papilionanthe hookeriana* 20 20
2832 2000r. Water monitor (*Varanus salvator*) 20 20
MS2833 50 × 83 mm. 3500r. No. 2829 Perf and Imperf . . 40 40

Nos. 2827/8, 2829/30 and 2831/2 respectively were issued, together, se-tenant, forming a composite design.

703 Bull

2002. Espana 2002 International Stamp Exhibition, Salamanca. Sheet 83 × 50 mm.

MS2834 **703** 7000r. multicoloured 80 80

704 Buildings, Data Stream and Globe

2002. "LKBN Antara" National News Agency.

2835 **704** 1500r. multicoloured . . 15 15

705 Party Food

2003. Greeting Stamps. "Happy Birthday".

2836 1500r. Type **705** 15 15
2837 1500r. Birthday cake 15 15

2003. Folk Tales (6th series). As T **611**. Multicoloured. (a) "Danau Ranau".

2838 1500r. Man holding golden egg and couple near cooking fire 15 15
2839 1500r. Men, dragon and weeping woman 15 15
2840 1500r. Woman riding dragon 15 15
2841 1500r. Sleeping woman and dragon holding necklace 15 15
2842 1500r. Lake 15 15

Nos. 2838/57 were issued together, se-tenant, forming a composite design.

(b) "Kongga Owose".

2843 1500r. Eagle carrying off cow 15 15
2844 1500r. Eagle attacking villagers 15 15
2845 1500r. Man spearing eagle 15 15
2846 1500r. Eagle, injured man, and villagers 15 15
2847 1500r. Hills, estuary and rocky coastline 15 15

(c) "Putri Gading Cempaku".

2848 1500r. Woman and man wearing tall headdress . . 15 15
2849 1500r. Man looking back at woman 15 15
2850 1500r. Men with raised arms and distressed woman . . 15 15
2851 1500r. Man, couple under thatched roof and woman wearing jewelled headdress 15 15
2852 1500r. Birds and sandy coastline 15 15

(d) "Putri Mandalika Nyale".

2853 1500r. King and Princess . . 15 15
2854 1500r. Princess and suitors bearing gifts 15 15
2855 1500r. Princess and suitors on beach 15 15
2856 1500r. Princess in sea . . . 15 15
2857 1500r. Fishing 15 15
MS2858 106 × 62 mm. 5000r. No. 2842 . . . . 55 55

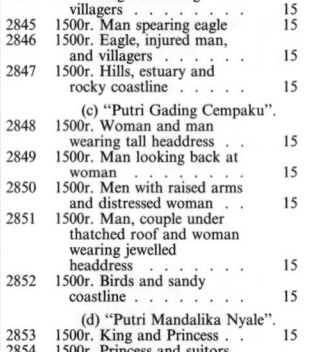

706 Billiard Player

2003. 22nd South East Asian Games, Vietnam. Multicoloured.

2859 1000r. Type **706** 10 10
2860 1500r. Rowers 15 15
2861 2500r. Gymnast 30 30

707 Mount Kerinci

2003. Volcanoes. 50th Anniv of Ascent of Mount Everest (**MS**2867). Volcanoes. Multicoloured.

2862 500r. Type **708** 10 10
2863 1000r. Merapi 10 10
2864 1000r. Krakatau 10 10
2865 1000r. Tambora 10 10
2866 2000r. Ruang 20 20
MS2867 181 × 116 mm. Nos. 2862/6, each × 2 plus 2 labels . . . . . 1·20 1·20

708 Moon

2003. Astronomy. Multicoloured.

2868 1000r. Type **708** 10 10
2869 1000r. Earth and Mars . . . 10 10
2870 1000r. Andromeda galaxy 10 10
2871 1500r. Observatory and telescope 15 15
2872 1500r. Observatory, Lembang, Java 15 15
MS2873 116 × 67 mm. No. 2872 15 15

709 Buildings and Flowers contained in Stylized Banknote (½-size illustration)

2003. 50th Anniv of Bank Indonesia. Multicoloured.

2874 1000r. Type **709** 10 10
2875 1500r. Teacher, pens and open books 15 15

710 Sultan Hamengu Buwono IX and Robert Baden-Powell (½-size illustration)

2003. Pathfinder Scouts.

2876 **710** 1500r. multicoloured . . 15 15

711 Pillow Fighting on Pole over Water

712 Dancers

2003. Traditional Games. Multicoloured.

2877 1000r. Type **711** 10 10
2878 1000r. Pole climbing 10 10
2879 1500r. Sack racing (horiz) 15 15
2880 1500r. Teams of three racing on planks (horiz) 15 15

2003. Emmitan Philex 2003 Stamp Exhibition. Seven sheets containing T **712** and similar vert design showing paintings by Srihadi Soedarsono. Multicoloured.

MS2881 107 × 142 mm. 3000r. × 4, Type **712**; Moonlit landscape, each × 2 (10th Asean Postal Business Meeting, Surabaya) 70 70
MS2882 Six sheets, each 107 × 82 mm. Five sheets (a/e) 3000r. × 2, Type **712**; Moonlit landscape (each with different margin colours). (f) 107 × 82 mm Type **712**; Moonlit landscape. Imperf. Set of 6 sheets . . . . 1·00 1·00

713 Woman leading Procession (Mome'Ati, Gorontalo)

2003. Tourism. Multicoloured.

2883 1000r. Type **713** 10 10
2884 1000r. Man carried in sedan chair (Jou Uci Sabea, Maluku Utara) 10 10
2885 1500r. Boats (Muang Jong, Bangka Belitung) 15 15
2886 1500r. Seated men (Seba Baduy, Banten) 15 15
MS2887 113 × 74 mm. No. 2885 15 15

714 Elephant Football, Lampung

2003. Bangkok 2003 International Stamp Exhibition. Sheet 88 × 25 mm.

MS2888	**714** 8000r. multicoloured	90	90

715 Clasped Hands

716 Anniversary Emblem and Stamps

2003. Greetings Stamps. Multicoloured.

2889	1000r. Type **715**	10	10
2890	1500r. Flag and clasped hands	15	15
2891	1500r. Fish and water lily	15	15
2892	1500r. Sunflower	15	15
2893	1500r. Birds	15	15

2003. 75th Anniv of Youth Pledge.

2894	**716** 1500r. multicoloured . .		

717 *Apis dorsata* (bee)

719 *Styrax benzoin*

718 H. Sutami

2003. Flora and Fauna. Multicoloured.

2895	1500r. Type **717**	15	15
2896	1500r. *Freycinetia pseudoinsignis* (flower) . .	15	15
2897	1500r. *Sia ferox* (grasshopper)	15	15
2898	1500r. *Paphiopedilum mastersianum* (orchid) . .	15	15
2899	1500r. *Platylomia flavida* (insect)	15	15
2900	1500r. *Osmoxylon palmatum* (plant)	15	15
2901	1500r. *Anaphalis javanica* (flower)	15	15
2902	1500r. *Hierodula vitrea* (mantis)	15	15
2903	1500r. *Saraca declinata* (plant)	15	15
2904	1500r. *Aularches miliaris* (insect)	15	15
2905	1500r. *Butea monosperma* (flower)	15	15
2906	1500r. *Orthetrum testaceum*(dragonfly) . . .	15	15
MS2907	119 × 74 mm. 3000r. × 2, Nos. 2901 and 2906	70	70

2003. Personalities. Each sepia and brown.

2908	2000r. Type **718** (engineer)	20	20
2909	2000r. R. Roosseno (engineer)	20	20
2910	2000r. Martinus Putuhena (architect)	20	20
2911	2000r. Nurtanio Pringgoadisuryo (aviation engineer)	20	20

2004. Flowers. Multicoloured.

2912	1500r. Type **719**	15	15
2913	1500r. *Kopsia fruticosa* . . .	15	15
2914	1500r. *Impatiens tujuhensis*	15	15
2915	1500r. *Hoya diversifolia* . .	15	15
2916	1500r. *Etlingera elatior* . . .	15	15
2917	1500r. *Dillenia suffruticosa*	15	15
2918	1500r. *Papilionanthe hookerianum*	15	15
2919	1500r. *Medinilla speciosa* . .	15	15
2920	1500r. *Costus speciosus* . . .	15	15
2921	1500r. *Melastoma sylvaticum*	15	15
2922	1500r. *Nelumbo nucifera* . .	15	15
2923	1500r. *Begonia robusta* . . .	15	15
2924	1500r. *Anaphalis longifolia*	15	15
2925	1500r. *Pisonia grandis* . . .	15	15
2926	1500r. *Ixora javanica* . . .	15	15
2927	1500r. *Plumeria acuminate*	15	15
2928	1500r. *Cassia fistula*	15	15
2929	1500r. *Calotropis gigantean*	15	15
2930	1500r. *Dimorphorchis lowii*	15	15
2931	1500r. *Aeschynanthus radicans*	15	15
2932	1500r. *Sonneratia caseolaris*	15	15
2933	1500r. *Rhododendron orbiculatum*	15	15
2934	1500r. *Passiflora edulis* . . .	15	15
2935	1500r. *Pterospermum celebricum*	15	15
2936	1500r. *Quisqualis indica* . .	15	15
2937	1500r. *Spathiphyllum commutatum*	15	15
2938	1500r. *Lilium longifolium* . .	15	15
2939	1500r. *Clitoria tematea* . . .	15	15
2940	1500r. *Pecteilis susannae* . .	15	15
2941	1500r. *Grammatophyllum speciosum*	15	15

2004. Folk Tales (7th series). As T **611**. Multicoloured. (a) "Putri Selaras Pinang Masak"

2942	1500r. Princess	15	15
2943	1500r. Man striking rocks	15	15
2944	1500r. Couple	15	15
2945	1500r. Crowned couple surrounded by cheering crowd	15	15
2946	1500r. Temple	15	15

Nos. 2942/61 were issued together, se-tenant, forming a composite design.

(b) "Tanjung Lesung".

2947	1500r. Woman and sleeping man	15	15
2948	1500r. Man, horse and dog walking and bathing . . .	15	15
2949	1500r. House, knife, man and turtles	15	15
2950	1500r. Couple and men turning into monkeys . .	15	15
2951	1500r. Monkey in tree . . .	15	15

2004. (c) "Patung Palindo".

2952	1500r. Warrior leading soldiers	15	15
2953	1500r. Battle scene	15	15
2954	1500r. Woman and child, bier, statue and warrior	15	15
2955	1500r. Men toppling statue, fire and battle scene . . .	15	15
2956	1500r. Tilted statue	15	15

(d) "Danae Tolire".

2957	1500r. People carrying plants and seated woman	15	15
2958	1500r. Revelry and drunkenness	15	15
2959	1500r. Woman carrying child running from tidal wave	15	15
2960	1500r. Falling woman . . .	15	15
2961	1500r. Lake and mountain	15	15
MS2962	106 × 62 mm. 6000r. No. 2950	70	70

720 Sail Ship (Maritime Museum, Jakarta)

2004. Museums. Multicoloured.

2963	1500r. Type **720**	15	15
2964	1500r. Dinosaur skeleton (National Geological, Bangdung)	15	15
2965	1500r. Metal artefact (Sri Baduga, Bangdung) . . .	15	15
2966	1500r. Early telephone (Telecommunications, Jakarta)	15	15

721 Voters

722 Gedong Bagoes Oka

2004. Elections. Multicoloured.

2967	1500r. Type **721**	15	15
2968	1500r. Voters placing ballots in ballot box	15	15

2004. Famous Women. Multicoloured.

2969	2500r. Type **722** (teacher and religious reformer) . .	30	30
2970	2500r. Ani Idrus (writer and journalist)	30	30
2971	2500r. Nyonya Meneer (herbal medicine pioneer)	30	30
2972	2500r. Sandiah (Ibu Kasur) (children's campaigner)	30	30

723 Swimming

2004. Olympic Games, Athens 2004. Multicoloured.

2973	2500r. Type **723**	30	30
2974	2500r. High Jump	30	30
2975	2500r. Hurdling	30	30

724 Bird, Porpoise and Boat

2004. Marine Preservation. Multicoloured.

2976	1500r. Type **724**	15	15
2977	1500r. Shark and turtles . .	15	15
MS2978	103 × 74 mm. 2500r. × 2, Nos. 2976/7	60	60

725 Sambal Udang Terung Pipit Kalimantan Barat

2004. Traditional Food. Multicoloured.

2979	1500r. Type **725**	15	15
2980	1500r. Tinotuan Sulawesi Utara	15	15
2981	1500r. Cajebo Sumatera Barat	15	15
2982	1500r. Kare Rajungan Jawa Timur	15	15

726 Kendaraan Presiden R1 Pertama

2004. Presidential Cars. Multicoloured.

2983	2500r. Type **726**	30	30
2984	2500r. Kendaraan Wakil Presiden R1 Pertama . .	30	30
MS2985	105 × 78 mm. Nos. 2983/4	60	60

727 Three Players

2004. Sumsel 2004, Sepaktakraw (ball) Games, Palembang. Multicoloured.

2986	1500r. Type **727**	15	15
2987	1500r. Two players	15	15

EXPRESS LETTER STAMPS

E 189 "Garuda" Bird

1967. Inscr "1967".

E1166	**E 189** 10r. purple and blue	55	15
E1167	15r. purple and orange	1·00	40

1968. As Nos. E1166/7 but dated "1968".

E1202	**E 189** 10r. purple and blue	55	15
E1203	15r. purple & orange	80	25
E1204	20r. purple and yellow	80	25
E1205	30r. purple and green	1·20	50
E1206	40r. purple & lt pur	80	25

1969. As Nos. E1166/7 but dated "1969".

E1250	**E 189** 20r. purple and yellow	40	15
E1251	30r. purple and green	40	15
E1252	40r. purple & lt pur	55	15

POSTAGE DUE STAMPS

1950. Postage Due stamps of Netherlands Indies surch **BAJAR PORTO** and new value.

D576	2½s. on 50c. (No. D499) . .	1·00	65
D577	5s. on 100c. (No. D501) . .	2·75	1·00
D578	10s. on 75c. (No. D500) . .	5·75	1·40

D 100

D 268

D 333a

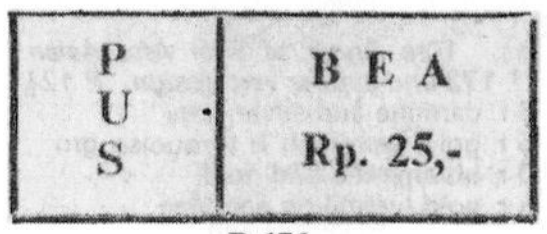

D 176

1951.

D645	**D 100** 2½s. orange	15	55
D646	5s. orange	15	10
D647	10s. orange	15	10
D648	15s. red	15	15
D773	15s. orange	25	55
D649	20s. blue	15	15
D774	20s. orange	25	55
D650	25s. olive	25	15
D775	25s. orange	25	55
D651	30s. brown	25	25
D776	30s. orange	25	50
D652	40s. green	25	25
D777	50s. orange	1·50	55
D778	50s. green	10	10
D779	100s. orange	80	55
D780	100s. brown	10	10
D781	250s. blue	25	10
D782	500s. yellow	10	10
D783	750s. lilac	25	10
D784	1000s. salmon . . .	15	15
D654	1r. green	1·60	1·50

1965. Provisional issue for use on parcels.

D1057	**D 176** 25r. black on yellow	15	

1966.

D1058	**D 100** 50r. red	10	10
D1059	100r. lake	15	15

1966. As Type **D 100**, but with coloured network background incorporating "1966".

D1098	5s. green and yellow . . .	25	25
D1099	10s. red and blue	25	25
D1100	20s. blue and pink	25	25
D1101	30s. sepia and red	25	25
D1102	40s. violet and bistre . . .	25	25
D1103	50s. olive and mauve . . .	25	10
D1104	100s. lake and green . . .	25	10
D1105	200s. green and pink . . .	25	10
D1106	500s. yellow and blue . .	25	10
D1107	1000s. red and yellow . .	25	15

1967. As Nos. 1098/1107 but dated "1967".

D1168	50s. green and lilac . . .	15	15
D1169	100s. red and green . . .	15	15
D1170	200s. green and pink . . .	15	15
D1171	500s. brown and blue . .	50	35
D1172	1000s. mauve and yellow	50	35
D1173	15r. orange and grey . . .	1·00	50
D1174	25r. violet and grey . . .	1·60	1·00

1973. As Type **D 100** but inscr "BAYAR PORTO" and dated "1973".

D1320a	25r. violet and grey . . .	1·10	15

1974. As Type **D 100** but inscr "BAYAR PORTO" and dated "1974".

D1346	65r. green and yellow . .	1·80	40
D1347	125r. purple and pink . .	3·50	1·20

1975. As Type **D 100** but inscr "BAYAR PORTO" and dated "1975".

D1401	25r. violet and drab . . .	1·40	90

1976.

D1426	**D 268** 25r. violet and drab	50	50
D1427	65r. green and stone	1·00	1·00

1978. Various stamps surch **BAYAR PORTO** and value.
D1503 25r. on 1r. sepia and red (No. 1141) 40 40
D1504 50r. on 2r. blue and ochre (No. 1144) 40 40
D1505 100r. on 4r. blue and orange (No. 1147) . . . 80 80
D1506 200r. on 5r. red and blue (No. 1148) . . . . . . 1·60 1·60
D1507 300r. on 10r. violet and red (No. 1151) . . . . 2·30 2·30
D1508 400r. on 15r. violet and olive (No. 1153) . . . . 2·40 2·40

1978. Nos. 1145 and 1152 surch **BAYAR PORTO** and value.
D1523 40r. on 2r.50 green and red . . . . 1·10 1·10
D1524 40r. on 12r. green and violet . . . . 1·10 1·10
D1525 65r. on 2r.50 green and red . . . . 1·30 1·30
D1526 65r. on 12r. green and violet . . . . 2·30 2·30
D1527 125r. on 2r.50 green & red 75 75
D1528 125r. on 12r. green & violet . . . . 1·80 1·80
D1529 150r. on 2r.50 green & red 3·00 3·00
D1530 150r. on 12r. green & violet 75 75

1980. Dated "1980".
D1599 D **268** 25r. mauve and drab 15 15
D1600 D **333a** 50r. green and lilac 40 40
D1601 75r. purple and pink 65 65
D1062 D **268** 125r. mauve & pink . . . . . . 1·00 75

1981. Dated "1981".
D1641 D **333a** 25r. purple & stone 15 15
D1642 50r. green and lilac 35 35
D1643 75r. purple and pink 50 50
D1644 125r. purple & grn 1·00 1·00

1982. Dated "1982".
D1645 D **333a** 125r. purple & pink 25 15

1983. Dated "1983".
D1728 D **333a** 200r. lilac and blue 50 15
D1729 300r. green & yell 50 15
D1730 400r. green & buff 75 35
D1731 500r. brown & pink . . . . . . 1·00 50

1984. Dated "1984".
D1772 D **333a** 25r. purple & stone 75 25
D1773 50r. green and lilac 75 35
D1774 500r. deep brown and brown . . . 7·75 1·00

1988. Dated "1988".
D1912 D **333a** 1000r. pur & grey 75 55
D1913 2000r. red & mauve . . . . . 1·50 1·10
D1914 3000r. red & yellow 2·50 1·60
D1915 5000r. green & blue 4·50 2·10

INDORE (HOLKAR STATE) Pt. 1

A state in C. India. Now uses Indian stamps.

12 pies = 1 anna; 16 annas = 1 rupee.

1 Maharaja Tukoji Rao Holkar II

2

1886.
2 **1** ½a. mauve . . . . 3·00 2·00

1889. No gum. Imperf.
4 **2** ½a. black on pink . . . . . . 3·25 3·75

3 Maharaja Shivaji Rao Holkar

5 Maharaja Tukoji Holkar III

1889.
5 **3** ½a. orange . . . . 1·25 80
6a ½a. purple . . . . 1·75 15
7 1a. green . . . . 2·00 1·00
8 2a. red . . . . 5·00 1·75

1904.
9 **5** ¼a. orange 50 10
10 ½a. red . . . . 8·50 10
11 1a. green . . . . 2·00 10
12 2a. brown . . . . 12·00 75
13 3a. violet . . . . 18·00 7·00
14a 4a. blue . . . . 5·00 1·40

The ½a. is inscr "HOLKAR".

पाव आना.
(6)

1905. No. 6a. surch as T **6**.
15 **3** ¼a. on ½a. purple . . . . . . 5·00 20·00

7 Maharaja Yeshwant Rao Holkar II

9 Maharaja Yeshwant Rao Holkar II

1928.
16 **7** ¼a. orange 50 20
17 ½a. purple . . . . 1·50 10
18 1a. green . . . . 2·25 10
19 1¼a. green . . . . 2·75 60
20 2a. brown . . . . 6·00 1·75
21 2a. green . . . . 13·00 1·75
22 3a. violet . . . . 1·50 9·50
23 3a. blue . . . . 17·00
24 3½a. violet . . . . 7·00 10·00
25 4a. blue . . . . 4·00 4·00
26 4a. yellow . . . . 28·00 1·60
27 8a. grey . . . . 5·50 4·50
28 8a. orange . . . . 23·00 21·00
29 12a. red . . . . 5·00 10·00
30 – 1r. black and blue . . . . . 8·00 14·00
31 – 2r. black and red . . . . . 45·00 48·00
32 – 5r. black and brown . . . . 80·00 80·00

The rupee values are larger, 23 × 28 mm.

1940. Surch diagonally in words.
33 – ¼a. on 5r. (No. 32) . . . . . 13·00 1·75
34 – ½a. on 2r. (No. 31) . . . . . 21·00 2·75
35 **7** 1a. on 1¼a. green (No. 19) . . 20·00 80

1940.
36 **9** ¼a. orange . . . . 2·00 10
37 ½a. red . . . . 2·75 10
38 1a. green . . . . 9·00 10
39 1¼a. green . . . . 15·00 1·50
40 2a. blue . . . . 11·00 1·00
41 4a. yellow . . . . 13·00 12·00
42 – 2r. black and red . . . . . . 12·50 £150
43 – 5r. black and orange . . . . 12·00 £190

The rupee values are larger, 23 × 28 mm.

OFFICIAL STAMPS

1904. Optd **SERVICE**.
S1 **5** ¼a. orange . . . . 40 1·00
S2 ½a. red 25 10
S3 1a. green 20 20
S4 2a. brown 30 30
S5 3a. violet . . . . 2·00 3·00
S6 4a. blue . . . . 4·50 1·50

INHAMBANE Pt. 9

A district of Mozambique, which used its own stamps from 1895 to 1920.

1895. 1000 reis = 1 milreis.
1913. 100 centavos = 1 escudo.

1895. 700th Birth Anniv of St. Anthony. Optd **CENTENARIO DE S. ANTONIO Inhambane MDCCCXCV**. (a) "Embossed" key-type inscr "PROVINCIA DE MOCAMBIQUE".
1 Q 5r. black . . . . 38·00 28·00
2 10r. green . . . . 38·00 28·00
3 20r. red . . . . 55·00 42·00
5 40r. brown . . . . 55·00 42·00
6 50r. blue . . . . 55·00 28·00
8 200r. violet . . . . 75·00 65·00
9 300r. orange . . . . 75·00 65·00

(b) "Figures" key type inscr "MOCAMBIQUE".
12 R 50r. blue . . . . 55·00 42·00
16 75r. red . . . . 90·00 70·00
13 80r. green . . . . 60·00 49·00
14 100r. brown on yellow . . . £200 £200
17 150r. red on rose . . . . . . 90·00 70·00

1903. "King Carlos" key type inscr "INHAMBANE".
18 S 2½r. grey 40 40
19 5r. orange 40 40
20 10r. green 50 45
21 15r. green . . . . 1·30 90
22 20r. lilac . . . . 1·30 90
23 25r. red . . . . 1·30 90
24 50r. brown . . . . 3·00 1·30
25 65r. blue . . . . 14·00 8·00
26 75r. purple . . . . 2·40 1·70
27 100r. blue on blue . . . . . 2·40 1·70
28 115r. brown on pink . . . . 5·50 4·75
29 130r. brown on yellow . . . 5·50 4·75
30 200r. purple on pink . . . . 5·50 4·75
31 400r. blue on yellow . . . . 10·50 6·75
32 500r. black on blue . . . . 15·00 10·00
33 700r. grey on yellow . . . . 24·00 16·00

1905. No. 25 surch **50 REIS** and bar.
34 S 50r. on 65r. blue . . . . . . 4·50 3·25

1911. 1903 issue optd **REPUBLICA**.
35 S 2½r. grey 30 30
36 5r. orange 30 30
37 10r. green 40 30
38 15r. green 40 30
39 20r. lilac 75 55
40 25r. red 75 55
41 50r. brown 40 30
42 75r. purple 55 40
43 100r. blue on blue 55 40
44 115r. brown on pink 75 55
45 130r. brown on yellow . . . 1·80 1·30
46 200r. purple on pink . . . . 1·10 70
47 400r. blue on yellow . . . . 1·80 1·30
48 500r. black on blue . . . . 1·90 1·30
49 700r. black on yellow . . . . 2·50 1·90

1913. Surch **REPUBLICA INHAMBANE** and value on "Vasco da Gama" stamps. (a) Portuguese Colonies.
50 ¼c. on 2½r. green . . . . . . 1·10 70
51 ½c. on 5r. red . . . . 1·10 70
52 1c. on 10r. purple . . . . . 1·10 70
53 2½c. on 25r. green . . . . . 1·10 70
54 5c. on 50r. blue . . . . . . 1·30 70
55 7½c. on 75r. brown . . . . . 2·00 1·40
56 10c. on 100r. brown . . . . . 2·00 1·40
57 15c. on 150r. bistre . . . . . 2·00 1·80

(b) Macao.
58 ¼c. on ½a. green . . . . . . 1·40 1·20
59 ½c. on 1a. red . . . . 1·40 1·20
60 1c. on 2a. purple . . . . . . 1·40 1·20
61 2½c. on 4a. green . . . . . . 1·40 1·20
62 5c. on 8a. blue . . . . 1·40 1·20
63 7½c. on 12a. brown . . . . . 2·40 1·80
64 10c. on 16a. brown . . . . . 2·00 90
65 15c. on 24a. bistre . . . . . 2·00 90

(c) Timor.
66 ¼c. on ½a. green . . . . . . 1·40 1·20
67 ½c. on 1a. red . . . . 1·40 1·20
68 1c. on 2a. purple . . . . . . 1·40 1·20
69 2½c. on 4a. green . . . . . . 1·40 1·20
70 5c. on 8a. blue . . . . 1·40 1·20
71 7½c. on 12a. brown . . . . . 2·40 1·80
72 10c. on 16a. brown . . . . . 2·00 90
73 15c. on 24a. bistre . . . . . 2·00 90

1914. No. 34 optd **REPUBLICA**.
74 S 50r. on 65r. blue . . . . . . 2·50 1·30

1914. "Ceres" key type inscr "INHAMBANE".
75 U ¼c. olive 70 45
76a ½c. black . . . . 2·10 1·60
77 1c. green 80 45
78 1½c. brown 80 45
79 2c. red 80 45
80 2½c. violet 35 30
81 5c. blue 50 45
82 7½c. brown 35 70
83 8c. grey . . . . 1·30 70
84 10c. red . . . . 1·30 90
85 15c. red . . . . 1·70 1·20
86 20c. green . . . . 1·80 1·20
87 30c. brown on green . . . . 2·10 1·30
88 40c. brown on red . . . . . 2·10 1·30
89 50c. orange on pink . . . . 4·50 2·30
90 1e. green on blue . . . . . 4·50 2·30

ININI Pt. 6

A territory in French Guiana, in the N.E. of S. America, separately administered from 1930 but reunited with Fr. Guiana in 1946.

100 centimes = 1 franc.

1931. Stamps of French Guiana optd **TERRITOIRE DE L'ININI** (Type **20**) or **Territoire de l'ININI** (others).
1 **20** 1c. green and lilac . . . . . 30 3·00
2 2c. green and red . . . . . 30 3·25
3 3c. green and violet . . . . 45 3·25
4 4c. mauve and brown . . . . 45 3·00
5 5c. orange and blue . . . . 35 3·25
6 10c. brown and mauve . . . . 20 2·75
7 15c. orange and brown . . . 20 2·75
8 20c. green and blue . . . . 50 3·00
9 25c. brown and red . . . . 95 3·25
10 **21** 30c. green and deep green 3·00 4·00
11 30c. brown and green . . . 55 3·25
12 35c. green and blue . . . . 2·50 3·50
13 40c. grey and brown . . . . 95 3·50
14 45c. green and olive . . . . 1·50 3·75
15 50c. grey and blue . . . . . 65 3·50
16 55c. red and blue . . . . . 2·75 5·00
17 60c. green and red . . . . . 70 3·75
18 65c. green and red . . . . . 2·75 4·50
19 70c. green and blue . . . . 1·60 3·75
20 75c. blue and black . . . . 3·50 4·50
21 80c. blue and black . . . . 2·25 3·75
22 90c. red and carmine . . . . 3·25 4·25
23 90c. brown and mauve . . . 2·25 3·75
24 1f. brown and mauve . . . . 15·00 19·00
25 1f. red . . . . 2·75 3·75
26 1f. blue and black . . . . . 65 3·75
27 **22** 1f.25 green and brown . . . 1·25 4·00
28 1f.25 red . . . . 80 3·75
29 1f.40 mauve and brown . . . 1·25 3·75
30 1f.50 light blue and blue . . 75 3·50
31 1f.60 green and brown . . . 70 3·75
32 1f.75 brown and red . . . . 24·00 30·00
33 1f.75 blue and deep blue . . 1·10 4·00
34 2f. red and green . . . . . 90 3·75
35 2f.25 blue . . . . 65 4·00
36 2f.50 brown and red . . . . 70 4·00
37 3f. mauve and red . . . . . 2·50 3·75
38 5f. green and violet . . . . 1·40 3·75
39 10f. blue and green . . . . 1·10 3·75
40 20f. green and blue . . . . 1·50 4·25

1939. New York World's Fair. As T **58c** of Guadeloupe.
51 1f.25 red . . . . 5·25 7·50
52 2f.25 blue . . . . 5·25 7·50

1939. 150th Anniv of French Revolution. As T **58d** of Guadeloupe.
53 45c.+25c. green and black . . 13·00 19·00
54 70c.+30c. brown and black . . 12·50 19·00
55 90c.+35c. orange and black . . 12·50 19·00
56 1f.25+1f. red and black . . . 12·50 19·00
57 2f.25+2f. blue and black . . . 13·50 19·00

POSTAGE DUE STAMPS

1932. Postage Due Stamps of French Guiana optd **TERRITOIRE DE L'ININI.**
D41 D **23** 5c. blue and deep blue 20 2·50
D42 10c. blue and brown . . 30 3·25
D43 20c. red and green . . . 20 3·25
D44 30c. red and brown . . 20 3·25
D45 50c. brown and mauve 1·25 3·75
D46 60c. brown and red . . 1·60 3·75
D47 D **24** 1f. brown and blue . . 1·75 3·75
D48 2f. green and red . . . 2·00 5·00
D49 3f. grey and mauve . . 5·50 14·00

IONIAN ISLANDS Pt. 1

A group of islands off the W. coast of Greece, placed under the protection of Gt. Britain in 1815 and ceded to Greece in 1864.

12 pence = 1 shilling;
20 shillings = 1 pound.

1

1859. Imperf.
1 **1** (½d.) orange . . . . 85·00 £500
2 (1d.) blue . . . . 22·00 £180
3 (2d.) red . . . . 16·00 £180

IRAN Pt. 16

A State of W. Asia.

1868. 20 shahis (or chahis) = 1 kran;
10 krans = 1 toman.
1932. 100 dinars = 1 rial.

NOTE.—The word "English" in the descriptive headings to various Persian issues is to be taken as referring to the lettering or figures and not to the language which is often French.

1

3 Nasred-Din

4 Nasred-Din

1868. Imperf or roul.
1 **1** 1(sh.) violet . . . . 70·00
1c 1(sh.) grey . . . . 80·00
15 1(sh.) black . . . . 10·00 15·00
2 2(sh.) green . . . . 50·00
16 2(sh.) blue . . . . 80·00 40·00
35 2(sh.) black £250 £3000
3 4(sh.) blue . . . . 70·00
17 4(sh.) red . . . . 70·00 35·00
4 8(sh.) red . . . . 70·00
8a 8(sh.) green . . . . 70·00 70·00
13 1(kr.) yellow £1000
18 1kr. red . . . . £100 45·00
38 1kr. red on yellow . . . . . £1100 50·00
19 4kr. yellow . . . . £300 45·00
36 4kr. blue . . . . £120 70·00
40 5kr. violet £225 £180
41 5kr. gold £750 £200
39 1to. bronze on blue £15000 £2500

1876. Perf.
20 **3** 1(sh.) black and mauve . . . 4·00 2·00
24 2(sh.) black and green . . . 5·00 1·50
25 5(sh.) black and pink . . . . 4·50 75
30 10(sh.) black and blue . . . 6·00 3·00

1879. Perf.
45a **4** 1(sh.) black and red . . . . 11·00 1·00
46a 2(sh.) black and yellow . . . 14·00 1·10
47 5(sh.) black and green . . . 13·00 60
48 10(sh.) black and mauve . . £130 10·00
49 1(kr.) black and brown . . . 40·00 90
50c 5(kr.) black and blue . . . 18·00 50

5

6

1881.
56 5 5c. mauve 5·00 2·00
57a 10c. red 4·50 1·50
61 25c. green £100 1·00
62 6 50c. black, yellow and orange 75·00 6·00
69 50c. black 20·00 3·00
63 1f. black and blue 14·00 1·25
64 5f. black and red 14·00 1·00
65 10f. black, yellow and red (30½ × 36 mm) 15·00 2·75

1882. As T **5** and **6**.
66 – 5s. green 5·00 20
68 – 10s. black, yellow and orange 15·00 90

10

11

13

14

15

16

1885.
70 10 1c. green 5·00 60
71 2c. red 5·00 50
72 5c. blue 5·00 10
73 11 10c. brown 6·50 20
74 1k. grey 7·00 40
75 5k. purple 70·00 5·50

1885. Surch **OFFICIEL** and value in English and Persian.
81a – 3 on 5s. green (No. 66) 18·00 5·50
76 – 6 on 5s. green (No. 66) 40·00 6·00
83 – 6 on 10s. (No. 68) 32·00 5·50
84 6 8 on 50c. black 60·00 9·00
78 12 on 50c. black 70·00 9·00
79 – 18 on 10s. (No. 68) 60·00 7·00
80 6 1t. on 5f. black and red 60·00 4·00

1889.
85 13 1c. pink 25 10
86 2c. blue 20 10
87 5c. mauve 20 10
88 7c. brown 1·00 30
89 14 10c. black 35 10
90 1k. orange 45 10
91 2k. red 3·00 90
92 5k. green 2·25 1·00

1891.
93 15 1c. black 20 10
94 2c. brown 30 10
95 5c. blue 15 10
96 7c. grey 65·00 2·00
97 10c. red 55 10
98 14c. orange 40 20
99 16 1k. green 7·00 15
100 2k. orange £100 5·50
101 5k. orange 80 40

17

18

21 Muzaffered-Din

1894.
102 17 1c. mauve 30 10
103 2c. green 30 10
104 5c. blue 30 10
105 8c. brown 30 10
106 18 10c. yellow 50 15
107 16c. pink 2·50 60
108 1k. pink and yellow 2·00 15
109 2k. brown and blue 2·00 15
110 5k. violet and silver 2·25 30
111 10k. pink and gold 10·00 2·50
112 50k. green and gold 7·00 4·50
See also Nos. 116/24.

1897. Surch in English and Persian in frame.
113 17 5c. on 8c. brown 1·75 20
114 18 1k. on 5k. violet and silver 5·50 1·50
115 2k. on 5k. violet and silver 5·50 2·00

1898. Chahi values on white or green paper.
116 17 1c. grey 20 10
117 2c. brown 30 10
118 3c. purple 30 10
119 4c. red 30 10
120 5c. yellow 30 10
121 8c. orange 1·00 35
154 10c. blue 60 10
123 12c. red 90 10
124 16c. green 1·50 35
125 21 1k. blue 2·00 10
157 1k. red 1·75 20
126 2k. pink 2·00 10
158 2k. green 3·50 60
127 3k. yellow 2·00 20
159 3k. brown 5·00 1·00
128 4k. grey 2·00 50
160 4k. red 5·00 1·00
129 5k. green 2·00 50
161 5k. brown 7·50 1·00
130 10k. orange 3·50 75
162 10k. blue 17·00 3·50
131 50k. mauve 9·50 4·00
163 50k. brown 12·00 2·25

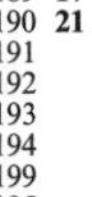
(21a)
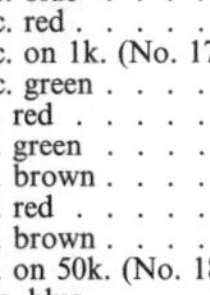
(22)
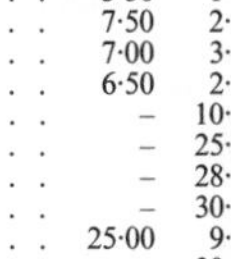

(24)

1899. Optd with control mark of various scroll devices as T **21a**.
132 17 1c. grey 60 10
133 2c. brown 60 10
134 3c. purple 60 10
135 4c. red 60 10
136 5c. yellow 60 10
137 8c. orange 1·50 15
138 10c. blue 60 10
139 12c. red 1·25 10
140 16c. green 1·25 35
141 21 1k. blue 1·50 10
142 2k. pink 2·75 45
143 3k. yellow 8·50 1·50
144 4k. grey 8·50 1·50
145 5k. green 4·50 1·50
146 10k. orange 12·00 1·50
147 50k. mauve 10·00 4·00

1900. Optd with T **22** across two stamps.
164 17 1c. grey 20·00 2·00
165 2c. brown 20·00 2·00
166 3c. purple 28·00 3·00
167 4c. red 65·00 8·50
168 5c. yellow 7·50 1·00
169 10c. blue £275 £110
170 12c. red 28·00 2·00
Prices quoted in this issue are for pairs.

1901. Surch in various ways in English and Persian.
176 17 5 on 8c. brown 2·00 25
179 21 12c. on 1k. red 10·00 4·00
180 5k. on 50k. brown 45·00 12·00

1902. Surch with T **24**.
177 17 5c. on 10c. blue 1·50 60
178 21 5c. on 1k. red 1·50 80

1902. Optd **PROVISOIRE 1319** in ornamental frame.
181 17 1c. grey 2·00 1·00
182 2c. brown 3·50 2·50
183 3c. purple 2·00 1·00
184 4c. red 2·00 1·00
185 5c. yellow 1·75 65
197 5 on 8c. brown (No. 176) 5·00 40
186 8c. orange 2·00 1·50
187 10c. blue 2·00 1·00
188 12c. red 3·50 1·00
198 21 12c. on 1k. (No. 179) 7·50 2·50
189 17 16c. green 7·00 3·00
190 21 1k. red 6·50 2·25
191 2k. green – 10·00
192 3k. brown – 25·00
193 4k. red – 28·00
194 5k. brown – 30·00
199 5k. on 50k. (No. 180) 25·00 9·00
195 10k. blue – 30·00
196 50k. brown – 32·00

28

(29)

1902. Inscr "CHAHIS" or "KRANS" in capital letters. Optd with T **29**.
200 28 1c. grey 1·25 10
201 2c. brown 4·00 20
202 3c. green 7·00 10
203 5c. red 2·00 10
204 10c. yellow 6·00 10
205 12c. blue 9·00 40
206 1k. mauve 22·00 50
207 2k. green 25·00 2·00
208 10k. blue 55·00 13·00
209 50k. red £375 £250

1902. Surch **5 KRANS** in English and Persian.
210 28 5k. on 5k. yellow 60·00 7·00

1902. Optd **PROVISOIRE 1319** in ornamental frame.
211 28 1c. grey 20·00 10·00
212 2c. brown 20·00 10·00
213 3c. green 20·00 10·00
214 5c. red 20·00 10·00
215 12c. blue 20·00 10·00

34

1902. Inscr "Chahis" or "Krans" in lower case letters.
227 34 1c. grey 11·00
228 2c. brown 20·00
229 3c. green 11·00
230 5c. red 11·00 10
231 10c. yellow 13·00 90
232 12c. blue 16·00 1·10
233 1k. mauve
234 2k. green
235 10k. blue
236 50k. red £425

1902. Surch **5 KRANS** without T **29** opt.
237 34 5k. on 5k. yellow 30·00

1903. Optd **PROVISOIRE 1903** and lion in frame, but without Arms opt (T **29**).
239 28 1c. grey – 4·00
240 2c. brown – 4·00
241 5c. red – 4·00
242 10c. yellow – 6·00
243 12c. blue – 10·00
244 1k. mauve – 11·00

38

39 Muzaffered-Din

1903.
246 38 1c. lilac 20 10
247 2c. grey 25 10
248 3c. green 30 10
249 5c. red 40 10
250 10c. brown 40 10
251 12c. blue 40 10
252 39 1k. purple 1·25 15
253 2k. blue 2·00 10
254 5k. brown 3·00 15
255 10k. red 7·50 30
256 20k. orange 12·00 60
257 30k. green 14·00 1·50
258 50k. green 55·00 14·00
See also Nos. 298/303.

1903. Surch in both English and Persian except those marked* which are surch in English only.
272 38 "1 CHAHI" on 3c. green 5·00 1·25
287 "1 CHAI" on 3c. green 3·50 40
288 39 1c. on 1k. purple 12·00 3·50
273 38 2c. on 3c. green 10·00 4·25
289 39 2c. on 5k. brown 17·00 6·00
277 38 3c. on 5c. red 2·50 10
278 6c. on 10c. brown 4·00 10
279 39 9c. on 1k. purple 5·00 15
274 12c. on 10k. red 16·00 3·75
275 2t. on 50k. green* 55·00 25·00
280 2t. on 50k. green 55·00 25·00
276 3t. on 50k. green* 55·00 25·00
281 3t. on 50k. green 55·00 25·00

50

52 Shah Muhammad Ali Mirza

1906. Optd **PROVISOIRE** and lion. Imperf. or perf.
292 50 1c. violet 50 10
293 2c. grey 60 10
294 3c. green 60 10
295 6c. red 1·00 10
296 10c. brown 11·00 50
297 13c. blue 6·00 35

1907.
298 38 1ch. violet on blue 15 10
299 2ch. grey on blue 15 10
300 3ch. green on blue 15 10
301 6ch. red on blue 15 10
302 9ch. yellow on blue 20 10
303 10ch. sepia on blue 20 10
305 52 13c. blue 50 10
306 26c. brown 50 10
307 1k. red 50 10
308 2k. green 50 10
309 3k. blue 50 10
311 4k. brown 1·75 30
312 5k. brown 1·25 15
313 10k. pink 2·00 15
314 20k. brown 4·75 25
315 30k. purple 5·00 40
316 – 50k. red and gold 20·00 17·00
The 50k. is larger with the head facing the other way.

(54)

56

1909. Nos. 298/315 optd as T **54**. Imperf.
320 38 1ch. on 1ch. violet on blue 30·00 20·00
321 1ch. on 2ch. grey on blue 30·00 20·00
322 1ch. on 3ch. green on blue 30·00 20·00
323 1ch. on 6ch. red on blue 30·00 20·00
324 1ch. on 9ch. yellow on blue 30·00 20·00
325 1ch. on 10ch. brown on bl 30·00 20·00
326 52 2ch. on 13ch. blue 32·00 22·00
327 2ch. on 26ch. brown 32·00 22·00
328 2ch. on 1kr. red 32·00 22·00
329 2ch. on 2kr. green 32·00 22·00
330 2ch. on 3kr. blue 32·00 22·00
331 2ch. on 4kr. yellow 32·00 22·00
333 2ch. on 5kr. brown 32·00 22·00
334 2ch. on 10kr. pink 32·00 22·00
335 2ch. on 20kr. black 35·00 24·00
336 2ch. on 30kr. purple 35·00 24·00

1909.
337 56 1c. purple and orange 35 10
338 2c. purple and violet 35 10
339 3c. purple and green 35 10
340 6c. purple and red 35 10
341 9c. purple and grey 40 10
342 10c. maroon and purple 70 10
343 13c. purple and blue 70 10
344 26c. purple and green 3·00 10
345 1k. brown, violet and silver 6·00 10
346 2k. brown, green and silver 6·00 10
347 3k. brown, grey and silver 7·00 15
348 4k. brown, blue and silver 12·00 40
349 5k. sepia, brown and gold 16·00 40
350 10k. brown, orange and gold 30·00 70
351 20k. brown, green and gold 30·00 1·40
352 30k. brown, red and gold 40·00 1·90
Stamps of this issue offered at very low prices are reprints.
For stamps as Type **56** but with curved inscriptions, see Nos. O836 etc.

57 Ahmed Mirza

(65)

1911.
361 57 1c. orange and green 15 10
362 2c. brown and red 15 10
363 3c. green and grey 15 10
364 3c. green and brown 15 10
365 5c. red and brown 15 10
366 6c. red and grey 15 10
367 6c. red and green 15 10
368 9c. lilac and brown 15 10
369 10c. brown and red 15 10
370 12c. blue and green 15 10
371 13c. blue and violet 15 10
372 24c. green and purple 15 10
373 26c. green and blue 4·00 2·00
374 1k. red and blue 10 10
375 2k. purple and green 20 10
376 3k. black and lilac 25 10
377 4k. black and blue 4·00 2·00
378 5k. blue and red 20 10
379 10k. pink and brown 35 10
380 20k. buff and brown 55 10
381 30k. green and red 80 10

1911. Various stamps optd **Relais** in English and Persian.
382 56 2ch. purple and violet 13·00 3·00
383 3ch. purple and green 13·00 3·00
384 6ch. purple and red 13·00 3·00
385 13ch. purple and blue 13·00 3·00
386 57 2ch. brown and red 13·00 3·00
387 3ch. green and grey 13·00 3·00
388 6ch. red and grey 13·00 3·00
388a 13ch. blue and violet 13·00 3·00

1912. Optd **Officiel** in English and Persian.
389 57 1c. orange and green 40 10
390 2c. brown and red 40 10
391 3c. green and grey 40 10
392 6c. red and grey 1·75 10
393 9c. lilac and brown 85 15
394 10c. brown and red 85 15
395 13c. blue and violet 5·00 35
396 26c. green and blue 13·00 70
397 1k. red and blue 10·00 20
398 2k. purple and green 11·00 20
399 3k. black and lilac 15·00 20
400 5k. blue and red 17·00 20
401 10k. pink and brown 30·00 1·25
402 20k. buff and brown 30·00 2·00
403 30k. green and red 30·00 2·75

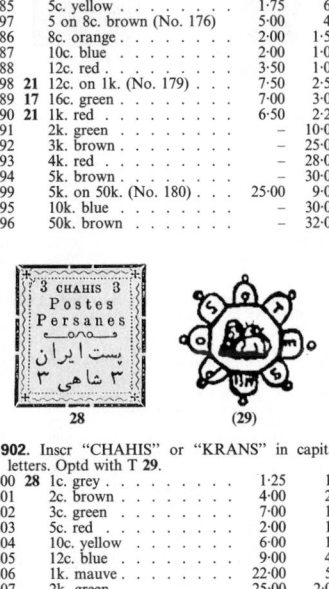

1914. Surch with new value and **1914** in English and Persian.
412 **57** 1c. on 13c. blue and violet . . 2·00 15
413 3c. on 26c. green and blue . . 2·00 15

1915. Surch with new value in frame and **1915** in English and Persian.
414 **57** 1c. on 5c. red and brown . . 1·75 10
415b 2c. on 5c. red and brown . . 1·75 10
416 6c. on 12c. blue and green . . 2·50 10

1915. Surch with new value in English and Persian.
417 **56** 5c. on 1k. (No. 345) . . . 2·50 10
418 12c. on 13c. (No. 343) . . 3·25 10

1915. Optd with T **65** ("1333").
419 **56** 1c. purple and orange . . . 40 10
420 2c. purple and violet . . . 70 10
421 3c. purple and green . . . 1·50 10
422 6c. purple and red . . . . 1·75 10
423 9c. purple and grey . . . . 3·50 10
424 10c. purple and mauve . . 7·00 20
425 1k. brown, violet and silver 7·50 15

66 The Imperial Crown

67 King Darius on his Throne

1915. Coronation of Shah Ahmed.
426 **66** 1c. blue and red 10 10
427 2c. red and blue 10 10
428 3c. green 10 10
429 5c. red 10 10
430 6c. red and green 10 10
431 9c. violet and brown . . . 10 10
432 10c. brown and green . . . 15 10
433 12c. blue 15 10
434 24c. sepia and brown . . . 45 10
435 **67** 1k. black, brown and silver 45 10
436 2k. red, blue and silver . . 45 15
437 3k. brown, lilac and silver 45 15
438 5k. grey, brown and silver 45 15
439 – 1t. black, violet and gold 70 30
440 – 2t. brown, green and gold 70 30
441 – 3t. red, crimson and gold 1·00 30
442 – 5t. grey, blue and gold . . 1·00 30
DESIGNS: 1t. to 5t. Gateway of the Palace of Persepolis.

(69)

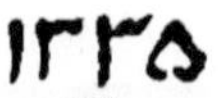
(73)

1915. Optd with T **69** ("1334").
477 **56** 1k. brown, violet and silver 5·50 40
478 10k. brown, orange and gold . . . . 20·00 75
479 20k. brown, green and gold 90·00 8·50
480 30k. brown, red and gold 35·00 2·75

1917. Surch with value in English only.
481 **57** 12c. on 1k. red and blue £225 80·00
482 24c. on 1k. red and blue £100 40·00

1917. Optd with T **73** ("1335") or surch also with new value in English and Persian.
483 **56** 1c. purple and orange . . . 35·00 9·00
484 1c. on 2c. (No. 338) . . . 4·00 10
485 1c. on 9c. (No. 341) . . . 4·00 10
486 1c. on 10c. (No. 342) . . . 4·00 10
490 **57** 1c. on 10c. brown and red 4·00 10
487 **56** 3c. on 9c. purple and grey 4·00 10
491 **57** 3c. on 10c. brown and red 4·00 35
488 **56** 3c. on 26c. (No. 344) . . . 4·50 10
489 5c. on 13c. (No. 343) . . . 4·25 10
492 **57** 5c. on 1k. red and blue . . 6·50 70
493 6c. on 10c. brown and red 4·25 80
494 6c. on 12c. blue and green 4·75 10

(78)

(82)

1918. Optd with T **78** ("1336").
507 **56** 2k. brown, green and silver 12·00 55

1918. Surch as T **78** and new value in English and Persian.
508 **56** 24c. on 4k. (No. 348) . . . 13·00 50
509 10k. on 5k. (No. 349) . . . 14·00 1·25

1918. Coronation issue of 1915 optd **Novembre 1918** (date also in Persian).
510 **67** 2k. red, blue and silver . . 2·00 1·50
511 3k. brown, lilac and silver 2·00 1·50
512 5k. grey, brown and silver 3·00 1·50
513 – 1t. black, violet and gold 3·00 1·50
514 – 2t. brown, green and gold 3·25 1·50
515 – 3t. red, crimson and gold 4·00 1·50
516 – 5t. grey, blue and gold . . 4·50 2·50

1918. Surch as T **82** and new value in English and Persian.
517 **57** 3c. on 12c. blue and green 5·00 10
518 6c. on 10c. brown and red 5·00 10
519 6c. on 1k. red and blue . . 5·00 10

1918. Optd with T **82** ("1337").
520 **56** 2k. brown, green and silver 28·00 1·50
521 3k. brown, grey and silver 12·00 70
522 4k. brown, blue and silver 65·00 2·75
523 5k. sepia, brown and gold 35·00 1·50
524 10k. brown, orange and gold . . . . 28·00 1·50
525 20k. brown, green and gold £150 18·00
526 30k. brown, red and gold 48·00 3·25

84 Ahmed Mirza

92 Ahmed Mirza

1919. Type **84** surch **Provisoire 1919** and value in English and Persian.
527 **84** 1c. yellow 70 10
528 3c. green . . . . 1·00 10
529 5c. purple . . . . 2·00 10
530 6c. violet . . . . 4·00 10
531 12c. blue . . . . 6·00 15

1919. Surch **1919** and value in English and Persian.
532 **13** 2k. on 5c. mauve . . . . . 1·60 70
533 3k. on 5c. mauve . . . . . 1·60 70
534 4k. on 5c. mauve . . . . . 1·60 70
535 5k. on 5c. mauve . . . . . 1·60 70
536 **15** 10k. on 10c. red . . . . . 1·60 70
537 20k. on 10c. red . . . . . 2·25 1·10
538 30k. on 10c. red . . . . . 2·25 1·10
539 50k. on 14c. orange . . . 2·25 1·75

1921. Surch **6-CHAHIS** in English and Persian.
539a **57** 6c. on 12c. blue and green 17·00 15

1921. Coup d'Etat of Reza Khan. Coronation issue of 1915 optd **21. FEV. 1921** in English and Persian.
540 **66** 3c. green . . . . 4·00
541 5c. red . . . . 4·00
542 6c. red and green . . . . 4·00
543 10c. brown and green . . . 4·00
544 12c. blue . . . . 4·00
545 **67** 1k. black, brown and silver 4·00
546 2k. red, blue and silver . . 5·00
547 5k. grey, brown and silver 6·00
548 – 2t. brown, green and gold 6·00
549 – 3t. red, crimson and gold 6·00
550 – 5t. grey, blue and gold . . 6·00

1922. Surch with value in English only.
551 **57** 10c. on 6c. brown & green 22·00 2·25
552 1k. on 12c. blue and green 22·00 3·50

1922. Surcharged with value in English only over **BENADERS.**
553 **57** 10c. on 6c. brown & green 15·00 2·25
554 1k. on 12c. blue and green 15·00 2·75

1922. Optd **CONTROLE 1922** in English and Persian.
555 **57** 1c. orange and green . . . 35 10
556 2c. brown and red 35 10
557 3c. green and grey 35 10
558 3c. green and brown . . . 40 10
559 3c. red and brown . . . . 20·00 3·50
560 6c. brown and green . . . 35 10
561 9c. lilac and brown 70 10
562 10c. brown and red 70 10
563 12c. blue and green . . . . 1·10 10
564 24c. green and purple . . . 3·50 10
565 1k. red and blue . . . . . 9·00 10
566 2k. purple and green . . . 13·00 10
567 3k. black and lilac . . . . 25·00 10
568 4k. blue and black . . . . 60·00 80
569 5k. blue and red . . . . . 30·00 10
570 10k. red and brown . . . 75·00 15
571 20k. yellow and brown . . 75·00 15
572 30k. green and red . . . . 85·00 15

1922. Surch in English and Persian.
573 **57** 3c. on 12c. (No. 563) . . . 2·50 10
574 6c. on 24c. (No. 564) . . . 3·25 10
575 10c. on 20k. (No. 571) . . 5·50 1·50
576 1k. on 30k. (No. 572) . . 14·00 3·00

1924.
577 **92** 1c. orange 20 10
578 2c. red 20 10
579 3c. brown 30 10
580 6c. sepia 30 10
581 9c. green 50 10
582 10c. violet 50 10
583 12c. red 50 10
584 1k. blue . . . . 1·00 10
585 2k. red and blue . . . . . 2·00 10
586 3k. purple and violet . . . 8·00 15
587 5k. sepia and red . . . . 12·00 30
588 10k. violet and sepia . . . 25·00 1·25
589 20k. sepia and green . . . 30·00 1·25
590 30k. black and orange . . . 35·00 1·75

1924. Surch **p. re. 1924** and value in English and Persian.
591 **84** 1c. brown 15 10
592 2c. grey 15 10
593 3c. red 20 10
594 6c. orange 70 10

1925. Surch **p. re. 1925** and value in English and Persian.
595 **84** 2c. green 15 10
596 3c. red 20 10
597 6c. blue 35 10
598 9c. brown . . . . 1·50 10
599 10c. grey . . . . 3·25 15
600 1k. green . . . . 3·25 10
601 2k. mauve . . . . 15·00 20

94

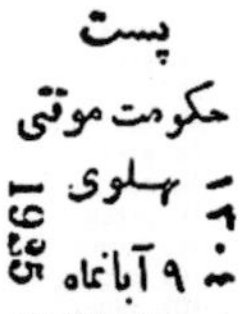
(**95** "Provisional Pahlavi Government, 31 Oct 1925")

1925. Deposition of Shah Ahmed and Provisional Government of Riza Khan Pahlavi. Fiscal stamps as T **94** (various frames) optd with T **95**.
602 **94** 1c. red . . . . 1·50 70
603 2c. yellow . . . . 1·50 70
604 3c. green . . . . 1·50 70
605 5c. grey . . . . 7·00 1·10
606 10c. red . . . . 1·50 1·60
607 1k. blue . . . . 3·00 70

(**96**)

1926. Optd with T **96**.
608 **92** 1c. orange 30 10
609 2c. red 35 10
610 3c. brown 70 15
611 6c. sepia . . . . 20·00 18·00

1926. Optd **Regne de Pahlavi 1926** in English and Persian.
612 **56** 1c. purple and orange . . . 20 10
613 2c. purple and violet . . . 20 10
614 3c. purple and green . . . 20 10
615 6c. purple and red 30 10
616 9c. purple and grey 65 10
617 10c. maroon and purple . . 65 10
618 13c. purple and blue . . . 1·75 10
619 26c. purple and green . . . 5·50 10
620 1k. brown, violet and silver 4·00 10
621 2k. brown, green and silver 4·50 10
622 3k. brown, grey and silver 4·50 15
623 4k. brown, blue and silver 55·00 30
624 5k. sepia, brown and gold 35·00 15
625 10k. brown, orange and gold £200 15
626 20k. brown, green and gold £225 30
627 30k. brown, red and gold £225 1·10

98 Riza Shah Pahlavi

99 Riza Shah Pahlavi

1926.
628 **98** 1c. green 15 10
629 2c. blue 30 10
630 3c. green 55 10
631 6c. red 65 10
632 9c. red . . . . 7·50 10
633 10c. brown . . . . 13·00 10
634 12c. orange . . . . 17·00 10
635 15c. blue . . . . 20·00 10
636 **99** 1k. blue . . . . 32·00 65
637 2k. mauve . . . . 70·00 10·00

1927. Air. Optd with airplane and **POSTE AERIENNE** in English and Persian.
642 **56** 1c. purple and orange . . . 30 20
643 2c. purple and violet . . . 70 35
644 3c. purple and green . . . 40 30
645 6c. purple and red 55 30
646 9c. purple and grey 55 30
647 10c. maroon and purple . . 70 35
648 13c. purple and blue . . . 1·25 70
649 26c. purple and green . . . 1·40 70
650 1k. brown, violet and silver 1·40 70
651 2k. brown, green and silver 3·00 1·50
652 3k. brown, grey and silver 4·50 1·75
653 4k. brown, blue and silver 10·00 4·75
654 5k. sepia, brown and gold 10·00 6·00
655 10k. brown, orange and gold £400 £130
656 20k. brown, green and gold £275 £130
657 30k. brown, red and gold £275 £130

1928. Air. Fiscal stamps surch with Junkers F-13 airplane, **Poste aerien** and new value in French and Persian.
657a **94** 3k. brown . . . . 55·00 16·00
657b 5k. brown . . . . 10·00 2·75
657c 1t. violet . . . . 10·00 4·00
657d 2t. green . . . . 16·00 7·00
657e 3t. green . . . . 23·00 8·00

102

104 Riza Shah Pahlavi

1929. Air. Fiscal stamps as T **102** (various frames) surch with Junkers F-13 airplane, **Poste aerienne** and value in French and Persian.
658 **102** 1c. green 10 10
659 2c. blue 20 10
660 3c. red 10 10
661 5c. brown 10 10
662 10c. green 15 10
663 1k. violet 35 10
664 2k. orange 70 20
665 3k. brown (22 × 30 mm) 50·00 8·00
666 5k. brown (22 × 33 mm) 6·00 3·00
667 10k. violet (21 × 31 mm) 15·00 5·50
668 20k. green (21 × 31 mm) 22·00 4·00
669 30k. green (21 × 31 mm) 27·00 8·00

1929.
670 **104** 1c. red and green 25 10
671 2c. blue and red 25 10
672 3c. green and red 25 10
673 6c. green and brown . . . 25 10
674 9c. red and blue 50 10
675 10c. brown and green . . 85 10
676 12c. violet and black . . . 1·10 10
677 15c. blue and yellow . . . 2·00 10
678 24c. lake and olive . . . 3·50 10
679 1k. black and blue . . . . 4·00 10
680 2k. violet and orange . . 8·00 10
681 3k. red and green . . . . 10·00 15
682 5k. green and brown . . . 9·00 20
683 1t. red and blue . . . . 12·00 45
684 2t. black and red . . . . 25·00 2·00
685 – 3t. violet and gold . . . . 30·00 3·25
DESIGN: 3t. Shah enthroned (28½ × 39 mm).

106 Riza Shah Pahlavi and Elburz Mts

1930. Air.
686 **106** 1c. blue and yellow . . . 10 10
687 2c. black and blue 15 10
688 3c. violet and olive . . . 15 10
689 4c. blue and violet 15 10
690 5c. red and green 15 10
691 6c. green and red 15 10
692 8c. violet and grey 15 10
693 10c. red and blue 20 10
694 12c. orange and grey . . 25 10
695 15c. olive and brown . . 25 10
696 1k. red and blue 55 25
697 2k. blue and black . . . 55 35
698 3k. green and brown . . . 70 45
699 5k. black and red . . . . 1·75 55
700 1t. purple and orange . . 2·50 70
701 2t. brown and green . . . 5·50 2·50
702 3t. green and purple . . . 22·00 16·00

107

1931.
703 **107** 1c. blue and brown . . . 20 10
704 2c. black and red 30 10
705 3c. brown and mauve . . 25 10
706 6c. violet and red 35 10
707 9c. red and blue . . . . 2·00 10
708 10c. grey and red . . . . 5·00 10
709 11c. red and blue . . . . 7·00 10
710 12c. mauve and blue . . . 6·00 10
711 16c. red and black . . . . 5·50 10
712 27c. blue and black . . . 12·00 10
713 1k. blue and red . . . . 12·00 10

108 Riza Shah Pahlavi

109

1933. New Currency.
714 **108** 5d. brown 15 10
715 10d. blue 15 10
716 15d. grey 30 10

717		30d. green	30	10
718		45d. blue	60	10
719		50d. mauve	60	10
720		60d. green	1·75	10
721		75d. brown	1·75	10
722		90d. red	1·75	10
723	109	1r. black and red	2·50	10
724		1r.20 red and black	7·00	15
725		1r.50 blue and yellow	12·00	15
726		2r. brown and blue	10·00	15
727		3r. green and mauve	25·00	35
728		5r. red and brown	32·00	7·00

110 "Justice"

112 Cement Works, Chah-Abdul-Azim

1935. 10th Anniv of Riza Khan's Advent to Power.

729	110	5d. green and brown	20	10
730	–	10d. grey and orange	20	10
731	–	15d. blue and red	20	10
732	–	30d. green and black	55	10
733	–	45d. lake and olive	65	10
734	112	75d. brown and green	2·50	40
735	–	90d. red and blue	4·00	70
736	–	1r. violet and brown	14·00	3·75
737	–	1r.50 blue and purple	6·00	2·00

DESIGNS: 10d. Ruins of Persepolis (40 × 26 mm); 15d. "Education" (23 × 33 mm); 30d. De Havilland Tiger Moth biplanes over Teheran Aerodrome (38 × 25 mm); 45d. Sakhtessar Sanatorium, Mazanderan (40 × 27 mm); 90d. Gunboat "Palang" (38 × 24 mm); 1r. Railway bridge over R. Karun (42 × 29 mm); 1r.50, Post and Customs House, Teheran (42 × 27 mm).

1935. Optd **POSTES IRANIENNES**. (a) Stamps of 1929

738	104	1c. red and green	90·00	25·00
739		2c. blue and red	32·00	12·00
740		3c. green and red	16·00	8·50
741		6c. green and brown	20·00	12·00
742		9c. red and blue	9·00	6·50
743		1t. red and blue	9·00	85
744		2t. black and red	14·00	70
745	–	3t. violet and gold	10·00	3·00

(b) Stamps of 1931.

746	107	1c. blue and brown	90·00	28·00
747		2c. black and red	9·00	3·25
748		3c. brown and mauve	4·50	4·00
749		6c. violet and red	20·00	12·00
750		9c. red and blue	20·00	12·00
751		11c. red and blue	90	10
752		12c. mauve and blue	60·00	22·00
753		16c. red and black	1·60	10
754		27c. blue and black	1·60	10

(c) Stamps of 1933.

755	108	5c. brown	15	10
756		10d. blue	20	10
757		15d. grey	20	10
758		30d. green	1·10	10
759		45d. blue	1·10	30
760		50d. mauve	70	10
761		60d. green	70	10
762		75d. brown	2·50	70
763		90d. red	3·25	3·25
764	109	1r. black and red	10·00	14·00
765		1r.20 red and black	6·00	65
766		1r.50 blue and green	4·00	20
767		2r. brown and blue	6·00	20
768		3r. green and mauve	7·00	20
769		5r. red and brown	45·00	23·00

1935. Air. Air stamps of 1930 optd **Iran**.

770	106	1c. blue and yellow	20	10
771		2c. black and blue	20	10
772		3c. violet and olive	20	10
773		4c. blue and violet	20	10
774		5c. red and green	20	10
775		6c. green and red	20	10
776		8c. violet and grey	20	10
777		10c. red and blue	20	10
778		12c. orange and blue	20	10
779		15c. olive and brown	55	20
780		1k. red and blue	1·75	70
781		2k. blue and black	2·25	70
782		3k. green and brown	2·75	2·25
783		5k. black and red	1·50	70
784		1t. purple and orange	35·00	17·00
785		2t. brown and green	4·50	1·75
786		3t. green and purple	6·50	2·00

116

117 Riza Shah Pahlavi

117a

1935. Rial values are larger, 22 × 31 mm.

787	116	5d. violet	20	10
788		10d. purple	20	10
789		15d. blue	20	10
790		30d. green	35	10
791		45d. orange	75	10
792		50d. brown	1·50	10
793		60d. blue	6·50	10
794		75d. red	4·50	10
795		90d. red	4·50	10
796		1r. purple	7·50	10
797		1r.50 blue	13·00	35
798		2r. green	12·00	15
799		3r. brown	13·00	30
800		5r. grey	22·00	6·00

1936. Rial values are larger, 23 × 31 mm.

801	117	5d. violet	15	10
802		10d. mauve	15	10
803		15d. blue	30	10
804		30d. green	40	10
805		45d. red	55	10
806		50d. brown	80	10
807		60d. brown	55	10
808		75d. red	1·00	10
809		90d. red	1·60	10
810		1r. green	6·00	10
811		1r.50 blue	3·00	10
812		2r. blue	11·00	10
813		3r. purple	15·00	10
814		5r. green	20·00	45
815		10r. blue and brown	35·00	5·50

1938. 60th Birthday of Shah. Perf or imperf.

815a	117a	5d. blue	15	10
815b		10d. red	15	10
815c		30d. blue	15	10
815d		60d. brown	20	10
815e		90d. red	30	15
815f		1r. violet	1·00	
815g		1r.50 blue	35	15
815h		2r. red	1·00	
815i		5r. mauve	1·40	1·00
815j		10r. red	3·25	1·75

118 Riza Shah Pahlavi

119 Princess Fawzieh and Crown Prince

1938. Rial values are larger, 23 × 31 mm.

816	118	5d. violet	15	10
817		10d. mauve	15	10
818		15d. blue	15	10
819		30d. green	20	10
820		45d. red	30	10
821		50d. brown	30	10
822		60d. orange	30	10
823		75d. red	35	10
824		90d. red	70	10
825		1r. green	1·25	10
826		1r.50 blue	7·50	10
827		2r. blue	10·00	10
828		3r. purple	13·00	10
829		5r. green	20·00	25
830		10r. blue and brown	42·00	1·75

1939. Royal Wedding.

831	119	5d. brown	15	10
832		10d. violet	20	10
833		30d. green	70	20
834		90d. red	2·00	30
835		1r.50 blue	3·00	1·10

120 Railway Bridge over Karun River

123 Mohammed Riza Pahlavi

1942.

850	120	5d. violet	1·50	10
851		5d. orange	35	10
852	–	10d. mauve	2·75	20
853	–	10d. green	1·50	10
854	–	20d. violet	30	10
855	–	20d. mauve	30	10
856	–	25d. red	12·50	90
857	–	25d. violet	1·50	10
858	–	35d. green	25	10
859	–	50d. blue	50	10
860	–	50d. green	1·60	10
861	–	70d. brown	50	10
862	–	75d. purple	50	10
863	–	75d. red	7·75	10
864	–	1r. red	2·75	10
865	–	1r. purple	10·00	10
866	–	1r.50 red	1·60	10
867	120	2r. blue	4·00	10
868	–	2r. green	5·25	10
869	–	2r.50 blue	5·25	10
870	–	3r. green	80·00	10
871	–	3r. purple	10·50	10
872	–	5r. green	80·00	20
873	–	5r. blue	5·25	10
874	123	10r. black and orange	20·00	2·00
875		10r. black and brown	12·00	10
876		20r. violet and brown	£600	16·00
877		20r. black and orange	18·00	10
878		30r. green and black	£1400	9·75
879		30r. black and green	18·00	20
880		50r. red and blue	£200	12·00
881		50r. black and purple	32·00	25
882		100r. black and red	£250	28·00
883		200r. black and blue	£275	32·00

DESIGNS—HORIZ: 10d. Vereshk Railway Bridge, N. Iran; 20d. Granary, Ahwaz; 25d. Steam train on Karj Bridge; 50d. Ministry of Justice; 70d. School building. VERT: 35d. Museum; 75d. Side view of museum; 1 to 5r. Full-face portrait of Mohammed Riza Pahlavi.

124 Lion and Bull, Persepolis

1948. Fund to rebuild Avicenna's Tomb at Hamadan (1st issue).

899	124	50d.+25d. green	20	35
900	–	1r.+50d. red	40	50
901	–	2½r.+1¼r. blue	80	70
902	–	5r.+2½r. violet	1·75	1·50
903	–	10r.+5r. purple	3·00	2·00

DESIGNS—VERT: 1r. Persian Warrior, Persepolis. HORIZ: 2½r. Palace of Darius, Persepolis; 5r. Tomb of Cyrus, Pasargades; 10r. King Darius enthroned.

See also Nos. 909/13, 930/4, 939/43 and 1024/28.

126 National Flag

1949. Iran's War Effort.

904	126	25d. multicoloured	50	15
905	–	50d. violet	3·50	70
906	–	1r.50 red	3·50	70
907	–	2r.50 blue	9·00	45
908	–	5r. green	9·00	1·00

DESIGNS: 50d. Bandar Shahpur (port); 1r.50, Lorries on winding road; 2r.50, Vereshk Railway Bridge; 5r. Mohammed Riza Pahlavi and map of Iran.

127 King Ardashir II

128 King Ardashir I and Ahura Mazda

1949. Fund to rebuild Avicenna's Tomb (2nd issue).

909	127	50d.+25d. green	20	20
910	–	1r.+50d. red	30	20
911	–	2½r.+1¼r. blue	60	35
912	–	5r.+2½r. plum	1·10	1·00
913	128	10r.+5r. green	1·90	1·75

DESIGNS—VERT: 1r. King Narses. HORIZ: 2½r. King Shapur I and Emperor Valerian; 5r. Arch of Ctesiphon.

129 Mohammed Riza Pahlavi and Post and Customs House, Teheran

130 Old G.P.O., Teheran

131 Mohammed Riza Pahlavi

1949.

914	–	5d. green and red	10	10
915	–	10d. brown and blue	10	10
916	–	20d. blue and violet	20	10
917	–	25d. blue and brown	25	10
918	–	50d. blue and green	30	10
919	–	75d. red and brown	50	10
920	–	1r. green and violet	60	10
921	–	1r.50 red and green	1·50	10
922	129	2r. brown and red	2·25	10
923	–	2r.50 blue	2·25	10
924	–	3r. orange and blue	4·50	10
925	–	5r. violet and red	6·75	10
926	130	10r. green and red	14·50	15
927		20r. red and black	£225	12·00
928	131	30r. blue and brown	26·00	2·00
929		50r. blue and red	42·00	1·90

DESIGNS—HORIZ: All show buildings. In the dinar values, portrait is to right of stamp, and in rial values, to left; 5d. Ramsar Hotel, Darband, Caspian Sea; 10d. Zayende River Bridge; 20d. Bank Melli Iran building; 25d. Old Royal Palace, Isfahan; 50d. Chaharbagh School, Isfahan; 75d. Railway Square; 1r. Justice Ministry; 1r.50, Shah Mosque, Teheran; 2r.50, Parliament Building; 3r. The Great Gate, Isfahan; 5r. Isfahan.

132 Tomb of Ali Abarquh

134 Allegory

1949. Fund to rebuild Avicenna's Tomb (3rd issue).

930	132	50d.+25d. green	20	20
931	–	1r.+50d. brown	25	20
932	–	2½r.+1¼r. blue	45	35
933	–	5r.+2½r. red	85	85
934	–	10r.+5r. olive	1·75	1·75

DESIGNS—VERT: 1r. Jami Mosque, Isfahan. HORIZ: 2½r. Tomb tower, Hamadan; 5r. Jami Mosque, Ardistan; 10r. Seljuk coin.

1950. 75th Anniv of U.P.U.

935	–	50d. lake	20·00	14·00
936	134	2r.50 blue	28·00	18·00

DESIGN—HORIZ: 50d. Hemispheres and doves.

135 Riza Shah Pahlavi and Mausoleum

1950. Interment of Riza Shah Pahlavi at Shah Abdul Azim.

937	135	50d. brown	6·50	2·50
938		2r. black	13·50	3·50

136 Tomb of Baba Afzal, Kashan

1950. Fund to Rebuild Avicenna's Tomb (4th issue).

939	136	50d.+25d. green	15	15
940	–	1r.+50d. blue	20	20
941	–	2½r.+1¼r. purple	35	30
942	–	5r.+2½r. red	85	75
943	–	10r.+5r. grey	1·90	1·50

DESIGNS—VERT: 1r. Gorgan vase; 2½r. Ghazan Tower, Bistam. HORIZ: 5r. Masjid-i Gawhar Shad Mosque, Meshed; 10r. Niche in wall of Mosque at Rezaieh.

139 Flag and Book

1950. 2nd Economic Conference of Islamic Countries.

944	139	1r.50+1r. multicoloured	12·00	3·25

140 Mohammed Riza Pahlavi in Military School Uniform

1950. Shah's 31st Birthday. Portraits of Shah at different ages, framed as T **140**.

945	**140**	25d. black and red	2·00	20
946	–	50d. black and orange	2·00	30
947	–	75d. black and brown	12·00	1·40
948	–	1r. black and green	8·00	1·60
949	–	2r.50 black and blue	14·00	2·00
950	–	5r. black and red	20·00	2·50

PORTRAITS—Shah in uniform: 50d. Naval cadet; 75d. Boy Scout; 1r. Naval officer; 2r.50, Army officer-cadet; 5r. Army general.

142 Memorial

1950. 4th Anniv of Re-establishment of Control in Azerbaijan.

951	–	10d.+5d. brown	7·00	1·25
952	**142**	50d.+25d. purple	7·50	1·40
953	–	1r.+50d. purple	15·00	1·75
954	–	1r.50+75d. red and green	15·00	3·25
955	–	2r.50+1r.25 blue	16·00	5·00
956	–	3r.+1r.50 blue	22·00	5·00

DESIGNS—VERT: 10d. Shah and map; 1r.50, Map and battle scene; 2r.50, Shah and flags. HORIZ: 1r. Troops marching; 3r. Cavalry parade.

143 Shah and Queen Soraya **144** Farabi

1951. Royal Wedding. T **143** and similar portraits.

959	**143**	5d. purple	1·10	35
960		25d. orange	1·50	45
961		50d. green	3·25	55
962	–	1r. brown	3·75	90
963	–	1r.50 red	5·25	2·10
964	–	2r.50 blue	7·00	2·75

DESIGNS: 1r. to 2r.50, As T **143** but portraits centrally placed.

1951. Millenary of Death of Farabi (philosopher).

965	**144**	50d. red	3·00	60
966		2r.50 blue	11·00	1·75

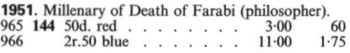

145 Mohammed Riza Pahlavi **146** Mohammed Riza Pahlavi

1951.

967	**145**	5d. red	10	10
968		10d. violet	10	10
969		20d. sepia	10	10
970		25d. blue	10	10
971		50d. green	40	10
972		50d. deep green	5·25	10
973		75d. red	30	10
974	**146**	1r. green	50	10
975		1r. turquoise	50	10
976		1r.50 red	80	10
977		2r. brown	2·75	10
978		2r.50 blue	2·50	10
979		3r. orange	10·00	10
980		5r. green	10·00	10
981		10r. olive	26·00	80
982		20r. brown	13·50	30
983		30r. blue	7·75	40
984		50r. black	26·00	1·25

147 Coran Gate, Shiraz

1951. 600th Death Anniv of Saadi (Muslih-ad-Din) (poet).

985	**147**	25d.+25d. green	1·50	45
986	–	50d.+50d. green	1·50	55
987	–	1r.50+50d. blue	7·00	1·25

DESIGNS—HORIZ: 50d. Tomb of Saadi. VERT: (as T **144**): 1r.50, Saadi.

150 Shah and Lockheed Super Constellation over Mosque

1952. Air.

988	–	50d. green	10	10
989	**150**	1r. red	15	10
990		2r. blue	20	10
991		3r. sepia	30	10
992		5r. lilac	45	10
993		10r. red	65	10
994		20r. violet	1·75	20
995		30r. olive	2·25	30
996		50r. brown	6·00	40
997		100r. sepia	65·00	3·50
998		200r. green	25·00	5·50

DESIGN: 50d. Shah and Lockheed Super Constellation airplane over Mt. Demavend.

151 Oil Well and Mosque

1953. Discovery of Oil at Qum. (a) Postage.

999	**151**	50d. bistre and green	1·00	10
1000	–	1r. bistre and mauve	1·00	10
1001	**151**	2r.50 bistre and blue	1·50	35
1002	–	5r. bistre and brown	2·10	80

(b) Air. With Lockheed Super Constellation airplane.

1003	**151**	3r. bistre and violet	26·00	6·00
1004	–	5r. bistre and brown	35·00	8·00
1005	**151**	10r. bistre and green	45·00	12·00
1006	–	20r. bistre and purple	55·00	14·00

DESIGN: 1r., 5r. (2), 20r. As Type **151** but horiz.

153 Power Station Boiler Plant

1953. 2nd Anniv of Nationalization of Oil Industry.

1007	**153**	50d. green	1·25	15
1008	–	1r. red	1·75	15
1009	–	2r.50 blue	7·00	40
1010	–	5r. orange	7·50	60
1011	–	10r. lilac	8·50	85

DESIGNS—HORIZ: 1r. Crude oil stabilizer; 5r. Pipe-lines; 10r. View of Abadan. VERT: 2r.50, Super fractionaters.

154 Family and U.N. Emblem **155** Gymnast

1953. United Nations Day.

1012	**154**	1r. green and turquoise	50	20
1013		2r.50 blue and light blue	1·00	45

1953. Ancient Persian Sports.

1014	**155**	1r. green	1·40	85
1015	–	2r.50 blue	6·00	1·10
1016	–	3r. grey	18·00	1·40
1017	–	5r. ochre	12·00	3·25
1018	–	10r. violet	24·00	4·50

DESIGNS—HORIZ: 2r.50, Archer; 3r. Mountaineers. VERT: 5r. Polo-player (Persian Sports Club Badge); 10r. Lion-hunter.

156 Iranian Roach **157** Machinery

1954. Nationalization of Fishing Industry.

1019	**156**	1r. multicoloured	2·00	55
1020	–	2r.50 multicoloured	30·00	1·75
1021	–	3r. red	12·00	1·25
1022	**157**	5r. green	11·00	2·25
1023	–	10r. multicoloured	20·00	5·50

DESIGNS—HORIZ: As Type **156**: 2r.50, Clupeid; 10r. Sturgeon. As Type **157**: 3r. Refrigeration machinery.

158 Hamadan **159** Avicenna

1954. Fund to Rebuild Avicenna's Tomb (5th issue).

1024	**158**	50d.+25d. green	15	15
1025	**159**	1r.+½r. brown	20	20
1026	–	2½r.+1¼r. blue	45	30
1027	–	5r.+2½r. red	70	50
1028	–	10r.+5r. olive	1·40	1·25

DESIGNS—VERT: As Type **159**: 2½r. Qabus tower, Gargan. HORIZ: As Type **158**: 5r. Old tomb of Avicenna; 10r. New tomb of Avicenna.

160 Shah in Military Uniform **161** Hands breaking Chain

1954.

1029	**160**	5d. brown	10	10
1062		5d. violet	10	10
1030		10d. violet	10	10
1063		10d. red	10	10
1031		25d. red	10	10
1064		25d. brown	10	10
1032		50d. brown	10	10
1065		50d. red	10	10
1066	–	1r. green	1·25	10
1034	–	1r.50 red	75	10
1067	–	1r.50 brown	20·00	10
1035	–	2r. brown	75	10
1068	–	2r. green	1·90	10
1069	–	2r.50 blue	75	10
1037	–	3r. green	1·25	10
1070	–	3r. brown	5·25	10
1038	–	5r. green	2·50	10
1071	–	5r. purple	2·50	10
1039	–	10r. lilac	6·25	2·00
1072	–	10r. blue	4·25	10
1040	–	20r. blue	50·00	6·00
1073	–	20r. green	26·00	10
1041	–	30r. brown	£110	20·00
1074	–	30r. orange	£130	12·00
1042	–	50r. orange	38·00	2·00
1075	–	50r. brown	£110	16·00
1043	–	100r. violet	£475	38·00
1044	–	200r. yellow	£110	12·00

DESIGN: 1r. to 200r. Shah in naval uniform.

1954. 1st Anniv of Return of Shah. Mult.

1045		2r. Type **161**	3·25	45
1046		3r. Hand holding torch and Iranian flag	5·00	70
1047		5r. Man clasping Iranian flag	9·00	1·25

SIZES: 3r. (19½ × 27½ mm); 5r. (20½ × 28½ mm).

162 Nurse and Child **163** Felling Trees

1954. U.N. Day.

1048	**162**	2r. orange and purple	1·75	50
1049		3r. orange and violet	1·90	1·00

1954. 4th World Forestry Congress. Inscr "4eme congres mondial forestier".

1050	**163**	1r. green and brown	16·00	3·50
1051	–	2r.50 blue and green	25·00	7·00
1052	–	5r. brown and lavender	50·00	15·00
1053	–	10r. lake and blue	60·00	28·00

DESIGNS: 2r.50, Man carrying logs; 5r. Man operating circular saw; 10r. Ancient Persian galley.

164 **165** Parliament Building

1955. National Costumes.

1054	**164**	1r. multicoloured	1·25	45
1055	–	2r. multicoloured	2·25	65
1056	–	2r.50 multicoloured	14·00	1·25
1057	–	3r. multicoloured	6·00	1·25
1058	–	5r. multicoloured	10·00	2·50

DESIGNS—2r. Male costume; 2r.50, 3r., 5r. Female costumes.

1955. 50th Anniv of Constitution.

1059	–	2r. green and purple	1·75	40
1060	–	3r. blue	3·50	60
1061	**165**	5r. orange and green	4·25	95

DESIGNS—HORIZ: 2r. Gateway of Parliament Building. VERT: 3r. Winged Statue.

167 U.N. Emblem and Hemispheres **168** Wrestlers

1955. United Nations Day.

1077	**167**	1r. orange and red	65	30
1078		2r.50 light blue and blue	1·10	35

1955. International Success of Iranian Wrestlers.

1079	**168**	2r.50 multicoloured	3·25	70

169 Hospital Buildings

1956. Opening of Nemazi Hospital, Shiraz. Multicoloured.

1080	–	50d. (24 × 33½ mm)	70	40
1081	**169**	1r. (36 × 24½ mm)	2·75	60
1082	–	2r.50 (24 × 33½ mm)	3·50	1·25
1083	–	5r. (36 × 23 mm)	8·25	2·00
1084	–	10r. (24 × 33½ mm)	13·50	5·00

DESIGNS: 50d. Hospital garden; 2r.50, Spear thrower; 5r. Koran gate, Shiraz; 10r. Poet Hafiz and his tomb.

170 **171** Tusi's Tomb, Maragheh

1956. 10th Anniv of National Olympic Committee.

1085	**170**	5r. lilac	15·00	5·50

1956. 700th Death Anniv of Nasir ed-Din Tusi, 1201–74 (astronomer and scientist).

1086	**171**	1r. orange	2·00	40
1087	–	2r.50 blue (Astrolabe)	4·00	60
1088	–	5r. lilac and sepia (Portrait)	6·50	1·00

172 Reveille

1956. National Scout Jamboree.

1089	**172**	2r.50 blue & ultramarine	7·00	3·50
1090	–	5r. mauve and lilac	13·00	4·00

DESIGN: 5r. Shah in scout's uniform and badge.

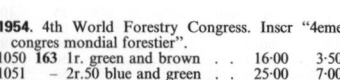

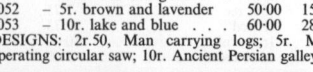

173

174 U.N. Emblem and Young People

1956. World Health Organization.

1091	**173**	6r. mauve	1·60	70

1956. United Nations Day.

1092	**174**	1r. green	50	30
1093	–	2r.50 blue and green	1·25	50

DESIGN: 2r.50, U.N. emblem and scales of justice.

175 Telecommunications Centre, Teheran

1956. Centenary of Persian Telegraphs.

1094	**175**	2r.50 green and blue	2·00	90
1095	–	6r. mauve and pink	6·00	1·40

DESIGN: 6r. Telegraph poles and mosque.

176 Shah and Pres. Mirza

1956. Visit of President of Pakistan.

1096	**176**	1r. multicoloured	1·00	20

177 Mohammed Riza Pahlavi

178 Mohammed Riza Pahlavi

1956.

1097	**177**	5d. red and rose	10	10
1098		10d. violet and blue	10	10
1099		25d. brown and sepia	10	10
1100		50d. olive and sepia	10	10
1101		1r. green and brown	10	10
1102		1r.50 brown and mauve	50	10
1103		2r. red and mauve	50	10
1104		2r.50 blue & ultramarine	55	10
1105		3r. bistre and brown	1·25	10
1106		5r. red	1·50	10
1132		6r. blue and light blue	2·00	10
1133		10r. turquoise and green	2·50	10
1134		20r. olive and green	2·50	10
1135		30r. sepia and blue	15·00	80
1136		50r. brown and sepia	26·00	80
1137		100r. red & bright purple	£160	4·00
1138		200r. bistre and violet	£100	32·00

1956.

1122	**178**	5d. plum and violet	10	10
1123		10d. mauve and purple	10	10
1124		25d. orange and red	10	10
1125		50d. green and grey	10	10
1126		1r. turquoise and green	10	10
1127		1r.50 purple and mauve	50	10
1128		2r. turquoise and blue	55	10
1129		2r.50 turquoise and blue	55	10
1130		3r. red and rose	1·00	10
1131		5r. violet and blue	95	10
1107		6r. mauve and lilac	1·40	10
1108		10r. green and blue	2·50	10
1109		20r. blue and green	3·50	15
1110		30r. orange and red	26·00	8·00
1111		50r. sage and green	13·00	2·00
1112		100r. red and purple	£425	30·00
1113		200r. violet and purple	£225	40·00

179 Lord Baden-Powell

180 Steam Express Train and Mosque

1957. Birth Centenary of Lord Baden-Powell (founder of Boy Scout movement).

1114	**179**	10r. brown and green	4·00	2·00

1957. Inauguration of Teheran–Meshed Railway. Multicoloured.

1115	2r.50 Track and signal	5·00	85
1116	5r. Diesel train and map (horiz)	8·00	1·50
1117	10r. Type **180**	18·00	8·75

181 President Gronchi and Shah

1957. Visit of President of Italy.

1118	**181**	2r. grey, green and red	75	50
1119	–	6r. blue, green and red	2·00	75

DESIGN: 6r. Plaque and flags between ruins of Persepolis and Colosseum.

183 Queen Soraya and Ramsar Hotel

1957. 6th Medical Congress, Ramsar.

1120	**183**	2r. green and blue	1·00	20

184 Shah and King Faisal II of Iraq

1957. Visit of King of Iraq.

1121	**184**	2r. blue, red and green	75	15

185 Globes within Laurel Sprays

1957. Int Cartographical Conf, Teheran.

1140	**185**	10r. multicoloured	4·00	65

186 "Flight"

187 "The Weightlifter"

1957. Air. United Nations Day.

1141	**186**	10r. red and mauve	1·10	60
1142		20r. purple and violet	1·60	1·00

1957. International Weightlifting Championships.

1143	**187**	10r. blue, green and red	1·50	35

188 Radio Mast and Buildings

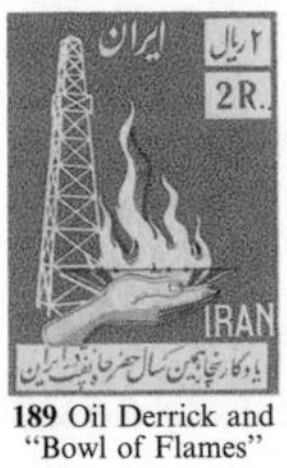
189 Oil Derrick and "Bowl of Flames"

1958. 30th Anniv of Iranian Broadcasting Service.

1144	**188**	10r. sepia, buff and blue	1·75	65

1958. 50th Anniv of Iranian Oil Industry.

1145	**189**	2r. brown, yellow and grey	2·25	30
1146		10r. brown, yellow & blue	5·75	80

190 Exhibition Emblem

1958. Brussels International Exhibition.

1147	**190**	2r.50 red	45	10
1148		6r. red	80	20

191 Steam Train on Viaduct

1958. Inaug of Teheran–Tabriz Railway.

1149	**191**	6r. lilac	12·00	3·00
1150	–	8r. green	16·00	6·50

DESIGN: 8r. Steam express train and route map.

192 Mohammed Riza Pahlavi

193 U.N. Emblem and Map of Persia

1958.

1162	**192**	5d. violet	10	10
1163		5d. brown	10	10
1164		10d. red	10	10
1165		10d. green	10	10
1166		10d. turquoise	10	10
1167		25d. red	10	10
1168		25d. orange	20	10
1169		50d. blue	20	10
1170		50d. red	10	10
1171		1r. green	35	10
1172		1r. violet	35	10
1232		2r. brown	2·50	10
1176		3r. brown	50	10
1177		6r. blue	40	10
1179		8r. purple	1·40	10
1180		8r. brown	50	10
1181		10r. black	50	10
1182		14r. blue	3·00	10
1183		14r. green	50	10
1185		20r. green	2·00	10
1186		30r. red	2·50	20
1187		30r. brown	50	10
1188		50r. purple	26·00	25
1189		50r. blue	1·40	10
1190		100r. orange	2·50	75
1191		100r. green	£100	2·00
1192		200r. green	26·00	1·40
1193		200r. mauve	£225	2·40

1958. United Nations Day.

1194	**193**	6r. blue and light blue	75	60
1195		10r. violet and green	95	80

194 Clasped Hands

195 Rudagi playing Lyre

1958. 10th Anniv of Declaration of Human Rights.

1196	**194**	6r. brown and chocolate	35	20
1197		8r. olive and green	90	35

1958. 1100th Birth Anniv of Rudagi (poet and musician).

1198	**195**	2r.50 blue	2·75	25
1199	–	5r. violet	5·75	45
1200	**195**	10r. sepia	10·00	90

DESIGN: 5r. Rudagi meditating.

196

1959. Red Cross Commemoration.

1201	**196**	1r. multicoloured	85	20
1202		6r. multicoloured	1·40	55

197 Wrestlers

198 Torch of Freedom

1959. World Wrestling Championships.

1203	**197**	6r. multicoloured	4·25	75

1959. United Nations Day.

1204	**198**	6r. red, brown and bistre	65	25

199 Shah and President Khan

1959. Visit of President of Pakistan.

1205	**199**	6r. multicoloured	2·50	45

200 I.L.O. Emblem

1959. 40th Anniv of I.L.O.

1206	**200**	1r. blue and light blue	50	20
1207		5r. brown and light brown	75	35

201 Pahlavi Foundation Bridge, Khorramshahr

1960. Opening of Pahlavi Foundation Bridge, Khorramshahr.

1208	**201**	1r. blue and brown	75	10
1209	–	5r. green and blue	1·00	30

DESIGN: 5r. Close-up view of bridge.

202 "Uprooted Tree and Columns"

203 Insecticide Sprayer

1960. World Refugee Year.

1210	**202**	1r. blue	10	10
1211	–	6r. black and green	35	20

DESIGN: 6r. "Uprooted tree" and columns.

1960. Anti-Malaria Campaign.

1212	–	1r. black & red on yellow	30	15
1213	**203**	2r. blue, black & light bl	80	20
1214	–	3r. black and red on green	1·40	50

DESIGNS (30 × 37 mm): 1r., 3r. Different views of mosquito crossed out in red.

204 Polo Player

206 Scout Emblem within Flower

205 Shah and King Hussein

1960. "Olympic Games Week".
1215 **204** 1r. purple 50 20
1216 – 6r. violet and blue . . . 1·10 50
DESIGN: 6r. Archer.

1960. Visit of King of Jordan.
1217 **205** 6r. multicoloured . . . . 2·50 60

1960. 3rd National Scout Jamboree.
1218 **206** 1r. green 30 10
1219 – 6r. ochre, sepia and blue 60 20
DESIGN: 6r. Scout camp, Persepolis.

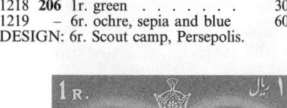

207 Shah and Queen Farah

1960. Royal Wedding.
1220 **207** 1r. green . . . . 1·00 40
1221 5r. blue . . . . 2·75 70

208 UN Emblem

210 Girl playing Pan-pipes

209 Shah and Queen Elizabeth II

1960. 15th Anniv of U.N.O.
1222 **208** 6r. sepia, blue and bistre 55 15

1961. Visit of Queen Elizabeth II.
1223 **209** 1r. brown 65 10
1224 6r. blue . . . . 1·10 20

1961. International Music Congress, Teheran.
1225 **210** 1r. stone and brown . . 50 10
1226 – 6r. slate 90 15
DESIGN—(24 × 39½ mm): 6r. Safiaddin Anmavi (musician).

211 Royal Family

1961. Birth of Crown Prince.
1227 **211** 1r. purple . . . . 1·00 50
1228 6r. blue . . . . 4·50 1·25

212 U.N. Emblem and Birds

213 Tree-planting

1961. United Nations Day.
1236 **212** 2r. red and blue 15 10
1237 6r. violet and blue . . . 45 20

1962. Afforestation Week.
1238 **213** 2r. blue, cream and green 25 10
1239 6r. green, blue & ultram 55 20

214 Worker

215 Family on Map

1962. Workers' Day.
1240 **214** 2r. multicoloured 15 10
1241 6r. multicoloured 45 30

1962. Social Insurance.
1242 **215** 2r. violet, black & yellow 15 10
1243 6r. blue, black & lt blue 45 30

216 Sugar Plantation

1962. Sugar Cane Production.
1244 **216** 2r. green, blue & ultram 25 15
1245 6r. blue, cream & ultram 65 30

217 Karaj Dam

1962. Inauguration of Karaj Dam.
1246 **217** 2r. green and brown . . 1·00 10
1247 6r. blue and ultramarine 1·40 20

218 Sefid Rud Dam

1962. Inauguration of Sefid Rud Dam.
1248 **218** 2r. buff, blue and myrtle 1·00 15
1249 – 6r. black, blue and brown . . . . 1·40 30
DESIGN: 6r. Distant view of dam.

219 U.N. Emblem

1962. 15th Anniv of UNESCO.
1250 **219** 2r. black, green and red 40 15
1251 6r. blue, green and red 85 30

220 Arrow piercing Mosquito

221 Mohammed Riza Pahlavi

222 Shah and Palace of Darius, Persepolis

1962. Malaria Eradication.
1252 **220** 2r. black and green . . . 15 10
1253 – 6r. blue and red 50 20
1254 – 10r. ultramarine and blue 90 25

DESIGNS—VERT (29½ × 34½ mm): 6r. Mosquito and insecticide-sprayer. HORIZ (As Type **220**):10r. Globe and campaign emblem.

1962.
1255 **221** 5d. green 10 10
1256 10d. brown 10 10
1257 25d. blue 10 10
1336 50d. turquoise 10 10
1337 1r. orange 15 10
1338 2r. violet 20 10
1339 5r. brown 65 10
1340 **222** 6r. blue . . . . 1·00 10
1341 8r. green 70 10
1342 10r. blue . . . . 1·00 10
1265a 11r. green 60 10
1266a 14r. violet . . . . . . 1·00 10
1345 20r. brown . . . . . . 1·10 20
1346 50r. red . . . . 1·25 45

223 Oil Pipelines

1962. 2nd Petroleum Symposium of Economic Commission for Asia and the Far East.
1269 **223** 6r. brown and blue . . . 40 15
1270 14r. brown and grey . . 85 35

224 Hippocrates and Avicenna

1962. W.H.O. Medical Congress, Teheran.
1271 **224** 2r. blue, brown and cream . . . . 1·00 15
1272 6r. blue, sage and green 1·50 30

225 New Houses

1962. United Nations Day.
1273 **225** 6r. blue and indigo . . . 45 15
1274 – 14r. green and blue . . . 95 20
DESIGN—HORIZ: 14r. Laying foundation stone.

226 "Bouquet for the Crown Prince"

1962. Crown Prince's Birthday.
1275 **226** 6r. blue . . . . 1·50 30
1276 14r. green . . . . 3·00 70

227 Persian Gulf Map

228 Hilton Hotel, Teheran

1962. Persian Gulf Seminar.
1277 **227** 6r. blue, pink & pale blue 40 15
1278 14r. blue, flesh and pink 85 30

1963. Opening of Royal Teheran Hilton Hotel.
1279 **228** 6r. blue . . . . 1·40 20
1280 14r. brown . . . . 2·25 45

229 Refugees

1963. Earthquake Relief Fund.
1281 **229** 14r.+6r. blue, brn & grn 90 60

230 Mohammed Riza Shah Dam

1963. Inaug of Mohammed Riza Shah Dam.
1282 **230** 6r. multicoloured . . . . 1·75 30
1283 14r. multicoloured . . . 3·75 65

231 Worker with Pickaxe

232 Bird and Globe

1963. Workers' Day.
1283a **231** 2r. black and yellow . . 45 10
1283b 6r. black and blue . . . 60 20

1963. Freedom from Hunger.
1284 **232** 2r. ultramarine, bl & bis 50 10
1285 – 6r. black, bistre and blue 90 20
1286 – 14r. bistre and green . . 2·00 45
DESIGNS: 6r. Globe and ears of wheat (stylized); 14r. Globe encircled by scroll, and campaign emblem.

233 Shah and Scroll

1963. Agrarian Reform Act.
1287 **233** 6r. green and blue . . . 90 20
1288 14r. green and yellow . . 2·00 55

234 Shah and King Frederick

1963. Visit of King of Denmark.
1289 **234** 6r. blue and indigo . . . 1·25 25
1290 14r. brown and sepia . . 3·00 50

235 Flags of Iran and India; Ibn Sina Mosque, Teheran, and Taj Mahal, India

1963. Visit of President Radhakrishnan of India.
1291 **235** 6r. multicoloured . . . . 1·60 25
1292 14r. multicoloured . . . 3·50 50

236 Shahnaz Dam

237 Centenary Emblem

1963. Inauguration of Shahnaz Dam.
1293 **236** 6r. ultramarine, bl & grn . . 1·50 25
1294 14r. green, blue and buff . . 2·25 50

1963. Red Cross Centenary.
1295 **237** 6r. multicoloured . . . . 1·75 30
1296 14r. grey, red and buff . . 3·75 60

238 Shah and Queen Juliana

1963. Visit of Queen of the Netherlands.
1304 **238** 6r. blue and ultramarine . . 2·50 30
1305 14r. green and black . . 3·25 60

240 Students in Class

1963. Formation of Literacy Teaching Corps.
1306 **240** 6r. multicoloured . . . . 1·50 15
1307 14r. multicoloured . . . 2·50 30

241 Pres. De Gaulle and View of Teheran

1963. Visit of President of France.
1308 **241** 6r. ultramarine and blue . . 1·75 30
1309 14r. brown and ochre . . 3·50 60

242 Plant, Route Map and Emblem

1963. Opening of Chemical Fertilizer Plant, Shiraz.
1310 **242** 6r. black, yellow and red . . 1·75 30
1311 – 14r. black, blue & yellow . . 3·50 60
DESIGN—HORIZ: 14r. Fertilizer plant and emblem.

243 Pres. Lubke and Shah Mosque, Isfahan

1963. Visit of President of German Federal Republic.
1312 **243** 6r. blue and violet . . . 1·75 30
1313 14r. brown and grey . . 3·50 55

244 U.N. Emblem

1963. United Nations Day.
1314 **244** 8r. multicoloured . . . . 1·25 20

245 Aircraft crossing U.N. Emblem

246 Crown Prince Riza

1963. Iranian Air Force in Congo.
1315 **245** 6r. multicoloured . . . . 1·25 20

1963. Children's Day.
1316 **246** 2r. brown 75 15
1317 6r. blue . . . . 1·00 25

247 Chairman Brezhnev

1963. Visit of Chairman of Soviet Presidium.
1318 **247** 5r. multicoloured . . . . 1·75 30
1319 11r. multicoloured . . . 2·75 50

248 Ataturk's Mausoleum

1963. 25th Death Anniv of Kemal Ataturk.
1320 **248** 4r. brown, grey and green . . . . 1·50 15
1321 – 5r. black, red and yellow 1·75 20
DESIGN: 5r. Kemal Ataturk.

249 Scales of Justice and Globe

250 Mother and Child

1963. 15th Anniv of Declaration of Human Rights.
1322 **249** 6r. black, blue and green 1·10 20
1323 14r. black, cream & brn 1·75 30

1963. Mothers Day.
1324 **250** 2r. multicoloured . . . . 1·00 15
1325 4r. multicoloured . . . . 2·00 20

251 Cogwheel and Map

252 Hand with Document (Profit-sharing)

1963. Industrial Development.
1326 **251** 8r. blue, cream & turq 1·75 30

1964. Six-Point Reform Law.
1327 **252** 2r. brown, violet and blue 40 10
1328 – 4r. brown and grey . . . 1·10 15
1329 – 6r. multicoloured . . . . 2·00 20
1330 – 8r. multicoloured . . . . 2·25 25
1331 – 10r. red, green & dp grn 2·50 30
1332 – 12r. brown and red . . . 3·25 35
DESIGNS: 4r. Factory and documents on scales (Sale of Shares to Workers); 6r. Worker on Globe (Education Corps); 8r. Tractor (Land reform); 10r. Trees (Nationalization of forests); 12r. Silhouettes within gateway (Votes for Women).

253 U.N. Emblem

254 Blossom

1964. 20th Economic Commission for Asia and the Far East Session, Teheran.
1347 **253** 14r. black and green . . 1·25 30

1964. New Year Greetings.
1348 **254** 50d. orange, sepia & grn 15 10
1349 1r. orange, black and blue 15 10

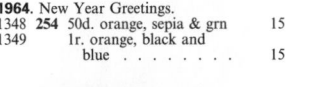

255 Weather Vane

256 "Tourism"

1964. World Meteorological Day.
1350 **255** 6r. violet and blue . . . 75 20

1964. 1st Anniv of Iranian Tourist Organization (INTO).
1351 **256** 6r. green, violet and black 90 20
1352 – 11r. orange, brown & blk . . . . 1·60 45
DESIGN: 11r. Winged beasts, column and INTO emblem.

257 Rudagi (blind poet)

1964. Opening of Blind Institute.
1353 **257** 6r. blue 90 20
1354 8r. brown . . . . 1·60 30

258 Sculptured Head

1964. "7000 Years of Persian Art" Exhibition.
1355 **258** 2r. blue and grey . . . . 1·50 10
1356 – 4r. ultramarine and blue 5·00 20
1357 – 6r. yellow and brown . . 3·00 30
1358 – 10r. green and yellow . . 5·00 50
DESIGNS—HORIZ: 4r. Sumerian war chariot on map. VERT: 6r. Golden cup with lion decorations; 10r. Sculptured head of man.

259 Shah and Emperor Haile Selassie

1964. Visit of Emperor of Ethiopia.
1359 **259** 6r. ultramarine and blue 1·25 20

260 Congress Emblem

1964. 2nd Iranian Dental Assn Congress.
1360 **260** 2r. red, deep blue & blue 40 15
1361 – 4r. multicoloured . . . . 1·00 30
DESIGN: 4r. "2 IDA" in symbolic form.

261 Bark Beetle under Lens

1964. Inauguration of Plant Parasites and Diseases Research Institute.
1362 – 2r. brown, red and buff 1·00 15
1363 **261** 6r. indigo, brown & blue 1·75 30
DESIGN: 2r. Microscope, plants and research centre.

262 Plaque

263 Eleanor Roosevelt

1964. Mehregan Festival.
1364 **262** 8r. red and yellow . . . 1·25 15

1964. Eleanor Roosevelt Commemoration.
1365 **263** 10r. blue and violet . . . 1·50 25

264 Clasped Hands and U.N. Emblem

265 Gymnast

1964. United Nations Day.
1366 **264** 6r. multicoloured 85 15
1367 – 14r. red, blue and orange 1·40 30
DESIGN: 14r. U.N. and "Bird" emblems.

1964. Olympic Games, Tokyo.
1368 **265** 4r. sepia, turquoise & brn 70 15
1369 – 6r. red and blue . . . . 1·00 25
DESIGN—Diamond (39 × 39 mm): 6r. Polo.

266 Crown Prince Riza

1964. Children's Day.
1370 **266** 1r. green and brown . . 50 10
1371 2r. red and blue . . . . 1·25 15
1372 6r. blue and red . . . . 2·25 30

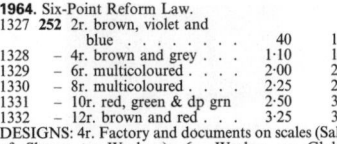

267 Conference and U.N. Emblems

1964. Petro-Chemical Conf and Gas Seminar.
1373 **267** 6r. multicoloured 50 15
1374 8r. multicoloured . . . . 1·00 25

268 Shah and King Baudouin

1964. Visit of King of Belgium.
1375 **268** 6r. black, orange & yell 40 15
1376 8r. black, orange & green 85 15

269 Rhazes

1964. 1100th Birth Anniv of Rhazes (Zakariya Ar-Razi, alchemist).
1377 **269** 2r. multicoloured 60 15
1378 6r. multicoloured 90 20

270 Shah and King Olav

1965. Visit of King of Norway.
1379 **270** 2r. mauve and purple . . 50 15
1380 4r. green and olive . . . 90 20

271 Crown, Map and Star

1965. Six-Point Reform Law.
1381 **271** 2r. orange, black and blue 30 15

272 Woman and U.N. Emblem

1965. 18th Session of United Nations Commission on Status of Women, Teheran.
1382 **272** 6r. black, blue & lt blue 45 10
1383 8r. blue, red and light red 80 15

273 Festival Plant

274 Pres. Bourguiba and Minarets

1965. New Year Festival.
1384 **273** 50d. multicoloured . . . 10 10
1385 1r. multicoloured 20 10

1965. Visit of President of Tunisia.
1386 **274** 4r. multicoloured 75 15

275 Map of Oil Pipelines

1965. 14th Anniv of Nationalization of Oil Industry.
1387 6r. multicoloured 90 20
1388 **275** 14r. multicoloured . . . 1·75 40

276 I.T.U. Emblem and Symbols

1965. Centenary of I.T.U.
1389 **276** 14r. red and grey 90 30

277 I.C.Y. Emblem

1965. International Co-operation Year.
1390 **277** 10r. green and blue . . . 1·40 20

278 Boeing 727-100 and Airline Emblem

1965. Inauguration of Jet Services by Iranian National Airlines.
1391 **278** 14r. multicoloured . . . 1·00 35

279 "Co-operation" (Hands holding Book)

1965. 1st Anniv of Regional Development Co-operation Plan. Multicoloured.
1392 2r. Type **279** 20 10
1393 4r. Globe and flags of Turkey, Iran and Pakistan ($40\frac{1}{2} \times 24\frac{1}{2}$ mm) 30 15

280 Moot Emblem and Arabesque Pattern

1965. Middle East Rover (Scout) Moot.
1394 **280** 2r. multicoloured 40 15

281 Gateway of Parliament Building

1965. 60th Anniv of Iranian Constitution.
1397 **281** 2r. brown and mauve . . 30 10

282 Congress Emblem

283 Teacher and Class

1965. Iranian Dental Congress.
1398 **282** 6r. blue, mauve and silver 35 15

1965. World Eradication of Illiteracy Congress, Teheran. Multicoloured.
1399 2r. Type **283** 10 10
1400 5r. Globe showing alphabets (25×30 mm) 20 10
1401 6r. UNESCO emblem and symbols (diamond, 36×36 mm) 30 15
1402 8r. Various scripts (35×23 mm) 30 15
1403 14r. Shah and multi-lingual inscriptions (41×52 mm) 1·10 30

284 Shah Riza Pahlavi

1965. 25th Anniv (actually 24th) of Shah's Accession.
1404 **284** 1r. red and grey 35 10
1405 2r. red and yellow . . . 70 10

285 Congress Emblem

1965. 14th Medical Congress.
1406 **285** 5r. ultramarine, bl & gold 40 10

286 President Jonas

1965. Visit of President of Austria.
1407 **286** 6r. blue and brown . . . 85 20

287 Plaque

1965. Mehregan Festival.
1408 **287** 4r. multicoloured 30 15
See also No. 1464.

289 U.N. Emblem and "Flowers"

290 Emblem and "Arches"

1965. United Nations Day.
1409 **289** 5r. multicoloured 30 15

1965. Iranian Industrial Exhibition, Teheran.
1410 **290** 3r. multicoloured 20 10

291 Crown Prince Riza

292 "Weightlifting"

1965. Children's Day.
1411 **291** 2r. chocolate, brn & gold 40 10

1965. World Weightlifting Championships, Teheran.
1412 **292** 10r. mauve, violet & blue 45 15

293 Open Book

1965. Book Week.
1416 **293** 8r. multicoloured 40 20

294 Shah and King Faisal

1965. Visit of King of Saudi Arabia.
1417 **294** 4r. brown and bistre . . 70 15

295 Scales of Justice

1966. Human Rights Day.
1418 **295** 14r. multicoloured . . . 45 20

296 Tractor (Land Reform)

1966. 3rd Anniv of Shah's White Revolution (Parliamentary Assent to Shah's Reform Plan).
1419 **296** 1r. brown and yellow . . 10 10
1420 – 2r. green and light green 15 10
1421 – 3r. brown and silver . . 15 10
1422 – 4r. violet and light violet 15 10
1423 – 5r. lake and red 15 10
1424 – 6r. brown and bistre . . 20 10
1425 – 7r. ultramarine and blue 30 15
1426 – 8r. ultramarine and blue 30 15
1427 – 9r. brown & light brown 35 20
DESIGNS: 2r. Trees (Nationalization of Forests); 3r. Cogwheel emblem (Sale of shares to workers); 4r. Cylinders (Profit-sharing); 5r. Parliament gateway (Votes for Women); 6r. Blackboard and pupils (Education Corps); 7r. Staff of Aesculapius (Medical Corps); 8r. Scales (Justice); 9r. Girders (Construction Corps).

297 Mohammed Riza Pahlavi

298 Shah and Ruins of Persepolis

1966.
1428 **297** 5d. green 10 10
1429 10d. brown 10 10
1430 25d. blue 10 10
1431 50d. turquoise 10 10
1432 1r. orange 10 10
1433 2r. violet 10 10
1434 4r. brown . . . . 3·00 10
1435 5r. sepia 15 10
1436 **298** 6r. blue 15 10
1437 8r. green 30 10
1438 10r. blue 20 10
1439 11r. green 70 10
1440 14r. violet . . . . 1·40 10
1441 20r. brown . . . . . . 10·00 10
1442 50r. red . . . . 3·50 10
1443 100r. blue . . . . 9·00 40
1444 200r. brown . . . . . . 7·00 75

299 Nurse taking Oath

300 Narcissus

1966. Nurses' Day.
1445 **299** 5r. blue and deep blue 25 15
1446 5r. mauve and red . . . 25 15

1966. New Year Festival.
1447 **300** 50d. multicoloured . . . 15 10
1448 1r. multicoloured 15 10
See also Nos. 1530/3.

301 Oil Rigs

1966. Inauguration of Six New Oil Companies in Persian Gulf.
1449 **301** 14r. black, purple & blue 70 20

302 Radar Aerial

1966. C.E.N.T.O. (Iran, Pakistan and Turkey) Telecommunications Organization.

1450 **302**	2r. green	15	10
1451 –	4r. orange and blue	15	10
1452 –	6r. grey and purple	25	10
1453 –	8r. indigo and blue	35	10
1454 –	10r. brown and ochre	45	30

DESIGNS—VERT: 4r. Aerial and radio "waves"; 6r. "CENTO" and emblem; 8r. Emblem and "waves"; 10r. Bowl aerial and "waves".

303 W.H.O. Building

1966. Inaug of W.H.O. Headquarters, Geneva.
1455 **303** 10r. black, blue & yellow 35 25

304 Globe Emblem and Motto

1966. Conference of International Women's Council, Teheran.

1456 **304**	6r. multicoloured	20	10
1457	8r. multicoloured	30	15

305 UNESCO Emblem

1966. Air. 20th Anniv of UNESCO.
1458 **305** 14r. multicoloured 75 30

306 Ruins of Persepolis, Map and Globe

1966. Int Iranology Congress, Teheran.
1459 **306** 14r. multicoloured 50 15

307 Medical Emblem

1966. 15th Medical Congress, Teheran.
1460 **307** 4r. gold, blue & ultram 30 10

308 Parliament Gateway

1966. 55th Interparliamentary Union Conference, Teheran.

1461 **308**	6r. green, blue and red	25	10
1462 –	8r. green, blue and mauve	25	15

DESIGN: 8r. Senate Building.

309 President Sunay

1966. Visit of President of Turkey.
1463 **309** 6r. brown and violet 30 10

1966. Mehregan Festival. Plaque design similar to T **287** but vert (30 × 40 mm).
1464 6r. brown and bistre 25 10

310 Farmers

1966. Rural Courts of Justice.
1465 **310** 5r. brown and bistre 35 25

311 U.N. Emblem

1966. U.N. Day and 21st Anniv of U.N.O.
1466 **311** 6r. brown and black 20 10

312 Crown Prince

313 I.W.O. Emblem

1966. Children's Day.

1467 **312**	1r. blue	30	10
1468	2r. violet	30	10

1966. Iranian Women's Organization.
1469 **313** 5r. blue, black and gold 15 10

314 Strip of Film

1966. 1st Children's Film Festival, Teheran.
1470 **314** 4r. black, purple & violet 30 10

315 Counting on the Fingers

316 Cover of Book

1966. National Census.
1471 **315** 6r. brown and grey 30 10

1966. Book Week.
1472 **316** 8r. brown, ochre and blue 20 15

317 Riza Shah Pahlavi

1966. Riza Shah Pahlavi Commemoration.

1473 **317**	1r. brown	60	10
1474	1r. blue	60	10
1475 –	2r. blue	60	10
1476 –	2r. green	60	10

Nos. 1475/6 show Riza Shah Pahlavi bare-headed.

318 E.R.O.P.A. Emblem and Map

1966. 4th General Assembly of Public Administrators Organization (E.R.O.P.A.).
1477 **318** 8r. brown and green 30 15

319 Shah with Farmers

1967. 5th Anniv of Land Reform Laws.
1485 **319** 6r. brown, yellow & bis 30 10

320 Torch and Stars

1967. 4th Anniv of Shah's White Revolution.

1486 **320**	2r. multicoloured	45	10
1487 –	6r. multicoloured	60	15

DESIGN: 6r. Shah acknowledging greetings.

321 Golden "Bull"

1967. Museum Week. Multicoloured.

1488	3r. Type **321**	20	10
1489	5r. Golden "leopard"	25	15
1490	8r. Capital with rams' heads	60	25

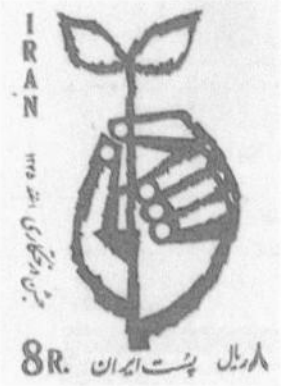

322 Planting a Tree

323 Goldfish

1967. Tree-planting Week.
1491 **322** 8r. green and brown 35 10

1967. New Year Festival.

1492 **323**	1r. blue, red and brown	10	10
1493 –	8r. ultramarine, bl & red	1·25	30

DESIGN—35 × 27 mm: 8r. Barn swallows.

324 Microscope, Horses and Emblem

1967. 2nd Veterinary Congress.
1494 **324** 5r. red, black and grey 20 10

325 Pres. Arif and Mosques

1967. Visit of President of Iraq.
1495 **325** 6r. green and blue 30 10

326 U.N. Emblem and Fireworks

1967. U.N. Stamp Day.
1496 **326** 5r. multicoloured 30 10

327 Map showing Pipeline Routes

1967. Nationalization of Oil Industry.
1497 **327** 6r. multicoloured 60 15

328 Fencing

1967. Int Youth Fencing Championships, Teheran.
1498 **328** 5r. yellow and violet 30 10

329 Shah and King Bhumibol

1967. Visit of King of Thailand.
1499 **329** 6r. brown and light brown 40 20

330 Emblem, Old and Young Couples

1967. 15th Anniv of Social Insurance Scheme.
1500 **330** 5r. blue and bistre 20 10

331 Skiing

1967. Olympic Committee Meeting, Teheran.

1501 **331**	3r. brown and black	15	10
1502 –	6r. multicoloured	15	10
1503 –	8r. brown and blue	25	15

DESIGNS: 6r. Olympic "shield"; 8r. Wrestling.

332 "LIONS" and Lions Head

1967. 50th Anniv of Lions International. Mult.
1504 3r. Type **332** 15 10
1505 7r. Lions emblem (36×42 mm) 40 15

333 President Stoica

1967. Visit of President of Rumania.
1506 **333** 6r. blue and orange . . . 25 10

334 I.T.Y. Emblem

1967. International Tourist Year.
1507 **334** 3r. blue and red 10 10

335 Iranian Pavilion **337** Globe and Schoolchildren

336 First Persian Stamp

1967. World Fair, Montreal.
1508 **335** 4r. red, gold and brown 10 10
1509 10r. brown, gold and red 20 10

1967. Stamp Centenary.
1510 **336** 6r. purple, blue & lt blue 20 10
1511 8r. purple, myrtle & green 25 10

1967. Campaign Against Illiteracy.
1512 **337** 3r. violet and blue . . . 15 10
1513 5r. brown and yellow . . 15 10

338 "Musician" **339** "Helping Hand"

1967. International Musical Education in Oriental Countries Conference, Teheran.
1514 **338** 14r. purple and brown 45 20

1967. 1st "S.O.S." Children's Village in Iran.
1515 **339** 8r. brown and yellow . . 1·60 60

340 Winged Ram **341** U.N. Emblem

1967. 1st Shiraz Arts Festival, Persepolis.
1516 **340** 8r. brown and bistre . . 35 10

1967. United Nations Day.
1517 **341** 6r. blue and bistre . . . 20 10

342 Shah Mohammed Riza Pahlavi and Empress Farah **343** Crown Prince Riza

1967. Coronation of Shah and Empress Farah.
1518 **342** 2r. brown, blue and silver 35 10
1519 10r. violet, blue and silver 70 25
1520 14r. multicoloured . . . 1·10 25

1967. Children's Day.
1521 **343** 2r. violet and silver . . . 15 10
1522 8r. brown and silver . . 40 15

344 Pres. G. Traikov

1967. Visit of President of Bulgaria.
1523 **344** 10r. brown and violet . . 20 10

345 Scout Emblem and Neckerchiefs

1967. Boy Scouts Co-operation Week.
1524 **345** 8r. brown and green . . 40 15

346 "Co-operation" (linked hands)

1967. Co-operation Year.
1525 **346** 6r. multicoloured 20 10

347 Shaikh Sabah

1968. Visit of Shaikh of Kuwait.
1526 **347** 10r. green and blue . . . 25 10

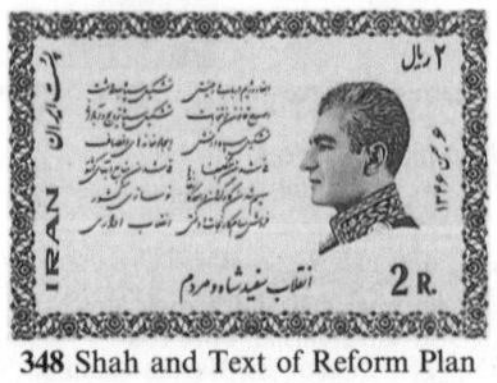

348 Shah and Text of Reform Plan

1968. 5th Anniv of Shah's White Revolution.
1527 **348** 2r. green, sepia and flesh 40 10
1528 8r. violet, green and blue 55 10
1529 14r. brown, blue & mve 80 20

1968. New Year Festival. As T **300**. Mult.
1530 1r. Almond blossom 10 10
1531 2r. Red tulips 10 10
1532 2r. Yellow tulips 15 10
1533 6r. Festival dancer 65 10

349 Oil Technician and Rig **350** W.H.O. Emblem

1968. National Oil Industry.
1534 **349** 14r. black, yellow & green 45 10

1968. 20th Anniv of W.H.O.
1535 **350** 14r. orange, blue & pur 40 10

351 Ancient Chariot (sculpture) **353** Human Rights Emblem

352 Shah and King Hassan

1968. 5th World Congress of Persian Archaeology and Art, Teheran.
1536 **351** 8r. multicoloured 25 10

1968. Visit of King of Morocco.
1537 **352** 6r. violet and flesh . . . 55 15

1968. Human Rights Conference, Teheran.
1538 **353** 8r. red and green 15 10
1539 – 14r. ultramarine and blue 20 15

DESIGN: 14r. As Type **353**, but rearranged, and inscr "INTERNATIONAL CONFERENCE ON HUMAN RIGHTS—TEHERAN 1968".

354 Footballer **355** Oil Refinery

1968. Asian Football Cup Finals, Teheran.
1540 **354** 8r. multicoloured 20 10
1541 10r. multicoloured . . . 40 15

1968. Inauguration of Teheran Oil Refinery.
1542 **355** 14r. multicoloured . . . 55 25

356 Empress Farah in Guides' Uniform **357** Mosquito Emblem

1968. Iranian Girl Guides "Great Camp".
1543 **356** 4r. blue and purple . . . 75 15
1544 6r. brown and red . . . 1·00 25

1968. 8th International Tropical Medicine and Malaria Congresses, Teheran.
1545 **357** 6r. purple and black . . 20 10
1546 14r. green and purple . . 45 15

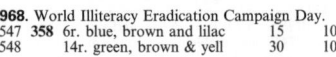

358 Allegory of Literacy **359** "Horseman" and "Flower"

1968. World Illiteracy Eradication Campaign Day.
1547 **358** 6r. blue, brown and lilac 15 10
1548 14r. green, brown & yell 30 10

1968. 2nd Shiraz Arts Festival, Persepolis.
1549 **359** 14r. multicoloured . . . 45 15

360 Police Emblem on Map **361** Interpol Emblem

1968. Police Day.
1550 **360** 14r. multicoloured . . . 90 15

1968. 37th Interpol General Assembly.
1551 **361** 10r. purple, black & blue 50 15

362 U.N. Emblem and Dove

1968. United Nations Day.
1552 **362** 14r. ultramarine and blue 35 15

363 Empress Farah

1968. 1st Anniv of Coronation. Mult.
1553 6r. Type **363** . . . . 2·50 1·00
1554 8r. Shah Mohammed Riza Pahlavi . . . . 2·50 1·00
1555 10r. Family group . . . . . 2·50 1·00

364 Imperial Crown and Bulls' Heads Capital (festival emblem) **365** "Landscape"

1968. National Festival of Art and Culture, Teheran.
1556 **364** 14r. multicoloured . . . 45 15

1968. Children's Day. Children's Paintings. Multicoloured.
1557 2r. Type **365** 10 10
1558 3r. "Boat and House" (35×29 mm) 15 10
1559 5r. "Flowers" (35×29 mm) 20 10

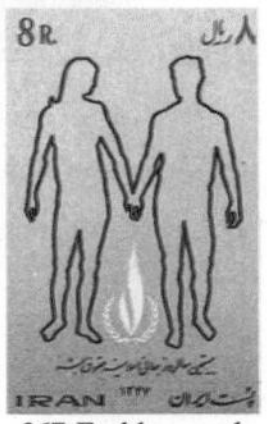

366 Hands supporting Globe — **367** Emblem and Human Figures

1968. Insurance Day.
1560 **366** 4r. blue and grey 10 10
1561 – 5r. multicoloured 20 10
1562 – 8r. multicoloured 15 10
1563 – 10r. multicoloured . . . 75 20
DESIGNS: 5r. Factory aflame ("Fire risk"); 8r. Urban workers ("Life"); 10r. Insurance Institute emblem and transport ("Travel insurance").

1968. 20th Anniv of Declaration of Human Rights.
1564 **367** 8r. purple, ultram & bl 20 10

368 Justice, Construction Corps and Medical Corps

1969. 6th Anniv of Shah's White Revolution. Each green, brown and lilac.
1565 2r. Type **368** 30 10
1566 4r. Working conditions, civil engineering and irrigation 40 15
1567 6r. Land reform, nationalization of forests and sale of shares to workers 50 20
1568 8r. Profit-sharing, votes for women and education corps 80 20
Nos. 1565/8, each showing symbols of three of the reforms, were issued, se-tenant, forming a composite design of a rosette.

369 Shah Mohammed Riza Pahlavi

1969. 10,000th Day of Shah's Reign.
1569 **369** 6r. brown, red and blue 55 15

370 Eurasian Goldfinch

1969. New Year Festival. Multicoloured.
1570 1r. Type **370** 35 10
1571 2r. Common pheasant . . . 55 10
1572 8r. Roses 70 15

371 Scales of Justice and "Blindfold Globe" — **372** Symbols of I.L.O.

1969. 15th FIDA (Female Jurists) Convention, Teheran.
1573 **371** 6r. black and blue . . . 30 10

1969. 50th Anniv of I.L.O.
1574 **372** 10r. violet and blue . . . 30 10

373 Wrestling "Throw"

1969. 3rd Aryamehr Cup International Wrestling Championships.
1575 **373** 10r. multicoloured . . . 40 10

374 "Flower and Birds" — **375** Mask and Cord

1969. World Handicrafts Day.
1576 **374** 10r. multicoloured . . . 40 10

1969. "Philia 1969". Outdoor Course for Scout Patrol Leaders.
1577 **375** 6r. multicoloured 40 15

376 Mughal Miniature (Pakistan)

1969. 5th Anniv of Regional Co-operation for Development. Miniatures. Multicoloured.
1578 25r. Type **376** . . . . . . 1·10 50
1579 25r. "Kneeling Figure" (Safavi, Iran) . . . . . . 1·10 50
1580 25r. "Suleiman the Magnificent and Court" (Ottoman, Turkey) . . . 1·10 50

377 Astronauts on Moon

1969. 1st Man on the Moon.
1581 **377** 24r. brown, blue and buff . . . . 2·50 85

378 "Education" (quotation from Shah's Declaration)

1969. Education Reform Conference.
1582 **378** 10r. red, green and buff 40 20

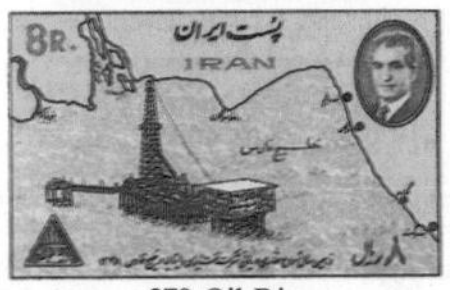

379 Oil Rig

1969. 10th Anniv of Iranian–Italian Marine Drilling Project.
1583 **379** 8r. multicoloured 70 15

380 Festival Emblem — **381** Thumb-print and Cross

1969. 3rd Shiraz Arts Festival.
1584 **380** 6r. multicoloured 15 10
1585 8r. multicoloured 25 10

1969. International Anti-illiteracy Campaign.
1586 **381** 4r. multicoloured 20 10

382 Shah, Persepolis and U.P.U. Emblem (½-size illustration)

1969. 16th U.P.U. Congress, Tokyo.
1587 **382** 10r. multicoloured . . . 65 20
1588 14r. multicoloured . . . 1·60 30

383 Fair Emblem — **384** "Justice"

1969. 2nd International Asian Trade Fair, Teheran. Multicoloured.
1589 8r. Type **383** 15 10
1590 14r. As T **383**, but inscr "ASIA 69" 20 10
1591 20r. Emblem and sections of globe (horiz) 50 20

1969. Rural Courts of Justice Day.
1592 **384** 8r. brown and green . . 30 10

385 U.N. Emblem — **386** Festival Emblem

1969. 25th Anniv of United Nations Day.
1593 **385** 2r. blue and pale blue . . 15 10

1969. National Festival of Art and Culture, Teheran.
1594 **386** 2r. multicoloured 35 10

387 "In the Garden"

1969. Children's Week. Children's Drawings. Multicoloured.
1595 1r. Type **387** 15 10
1596 2r. "Three Children" (horiz) 20 10
1597 5r. "Mealtime" (horiz) . . . 50 15

388 Global Emblem

1969. National Association of Parents and Teachers Congress, Teheran.
1598 **388** 8r. brown and blue . . . 20 10

389 Earth Station — **391** Mahatma Gandhi

(**390**)

1969. Opening of 1st Iranian Satellite Communications Earth Station.
1599 **389** 6r. brown and ochre . . 20 10

1969. Air. 50th Anniv of 1st England–Australia Flight. No. 1281 surch as T **390**.
1600 **229** 4r. on 14r.+6r. . . . . 1·10 45
1601 10r. on 14r.+6r. . . . . 1·10 45
1602 14r. on 14r.+6r. . . . . 1·10 45

1969. Birth Centenary of Mahatma Gandhi.
1603 **391** 14r. brown and grey . . 2·75 70

392 Globe and Flags

1969. 50th Anniv of League of Red Cross Societies. Multicoloured.
1604 2r. Type **392** 30 10
1605 6r. Red Cross emblems on Globe 40 15

393 Shah and Reform Symbols

1970. 7th Anniv of Shah's White Revolution.
1606 **393** 1r. multicoloured 55 15
1607 2r. multicoloured 65 15

394 Pansies — **396** "EXPO" Emblem

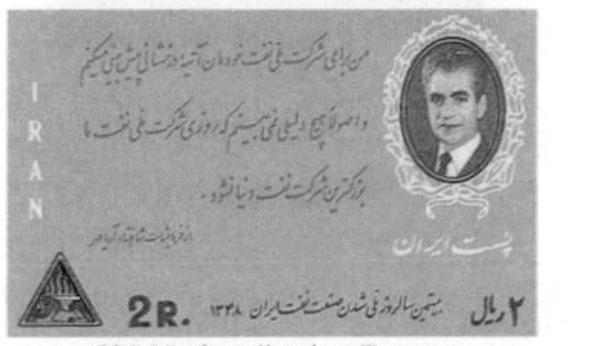

395 Nationalization Decree

1970. New Year Festival. Multicoloured.
1608 1r. Type **394** 15 10
1609 8r. New Year table (40×26 mm) . . . . . . 1·00 20

1970. 20th Anniv of Oil Industry Nationalization. Multicoloured.
1610 2r. Type **395** 50 15
1611 4r. Laying pipeline 70 15
1612 6r. Part of Kharg Island plant 75 15
1613 8r. Ocean terminal, Kharg Island (vert) . . . . . . 1·10 30
1614 10r. Refinery, Teheran . . . 1·10 35

1970. "EXPO 70" World Fair, Osaka, Japan.
1615 **396** 4r. blue and mauve . . . 15 10
1616 10r. violet and blue . . . 35 15

397 Dish Aerial and Satellite

1970. Asian Plan Communications Committee Meeting, Teheran.
1617 **397** 14r. multicoloured . . . 65 20

398 New U.P.U. H.Q.

1970. New U.P.U. Headquarters Building, Berne.
1618 **398** 2r. sepia, mauve & green 20 10
1619 4r. sepia, mauve and lilac 30 10

399 A.P.Y. Emblem **400** Stork carrying Baby

1970. Asian Productivity Year.
1620 **399** 8r. multicoloured 20 10

1970. 50th Anniv of Midwifery School.
1621 **400** 8r. blue and brown . . . 30 15

401 Tomb of Cyrus the Great

1970. 2500th Anniv of Persian Empire (1st issue). Achaemenian Era.
1622 **401** 6r. violet, red and grey 50 15
1623 – 8r. green, black and pink 55 15
1624 – 10r. brown, red & yellow 80 30
1625 – 14r. brown, black & blue 1·40 70
DESIGNS—HORIZ: 10r. Religious ceremony (Median bas-relief); 14r. Achaemenian officers (bas-relief). VERT: 8r. Columns, Palace of Apadana.
See also Nos. 1629/32, 1633/6, 1640/2, 1658/61, 1664/7, 1674/7 and 1679/82.

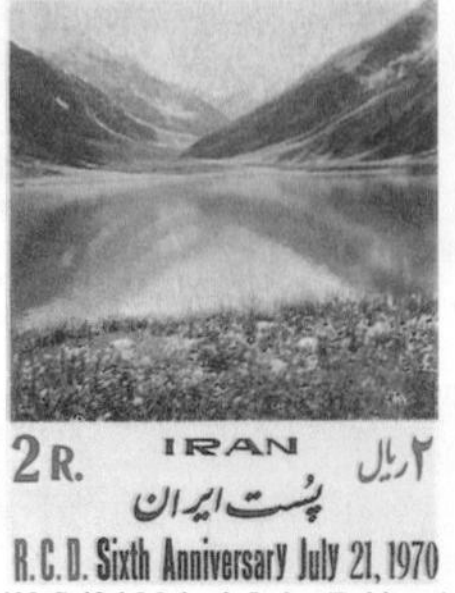

402 Saiful Malook Lake (Pakistan)

1970. 6th Anniv of Regional Co-operation for Development. Multicoloured.
1626 2r. Type **402** 40 15
1627 2r. Seeyo-Se-Pol Bridge, Isfahan (Iran) (62 × 46 mm) 40 15
1628 2r. View from Fethiye (Turkey) 40 15

1970. 2500th Anniv of Persian Empire (2nd issue). Achaemenian Era. Designs as T **401**.
1629 2r. gold, deep green and green 50 15
1630 6r. gold, violet and green . . 50 20
1631 8r. gold, blue and orange . . 1·00 30
1632 14r. red, black and blue . . 1·40 75
DESIGNS—VERT: 2r. Eagle amulet; 6r. "Lion" goblet; 8r. Winged ibex statue. HORIZ: 14r. Tapestry.

1970. 2500th Anniv of Persian Empire (3rd issue). Coins of Sassanid and Parthian Eras. Designs as T **401**. Multicoloured, frames in gold.
1633 1r. Queen Buran dirham . . 50 15
1634 2r. Mithridates I dirham . . 55 15
1635 6r. Shapur I dirham . . . . 1·00 20
1636 8r. Ardeshir I dirham . . . 1·40 55

405 Candle and Globe Emblem

1970. World Literacy Day.
1637 **405** 1r. multicoloured 10 10
1638 2r. multicoloured 15 10

406 Isfahan Tile **408** Councils Emblem

1970. International Architects' Congress, Isfahan.
1639 **406** 6r. multicoloured 20 15

1970. 2500th Anniv of Persian Empire (4th issue). Achaemenian and Sassanid Eras. Designs as T **401**.
1640 2r. multicoloured 50 15
1641 6r. brown, blue and lilac . . 1·00 20
1642 8r. green, red and lilac . . . 1·25 30
DESIGNS—VERT: 2r. Sassanid arch and art. HORIZ: 6r. Archaemenian mounted courier; 8r. Seal of Darius I.

1970. 1st Congress of Provincial Councils.
1643 **408** 2r. violet and blue . . . 10 10

409 Dove and U.N. Emblem **411** Festival Emblem

410 "1970" and I.A.T.A. Emblem

1970. United Nations Day.
1644 **409** 2r. ultramarine, pur & bl 10 10

1970. Air. 26th International Air Transport Association General Meeting, Teheran.
1645 **410** 14r. multicoloured . . . 2·50 40

1970. National Festival of Art and Culture, Teheran.
1646 **411** 2r. multicoloured 15 10

412 "Goatherd and Goats"

1970. Children's Week. Children's Drawings. Multicoloured.
1647 50d. Type **412** 15 10
1648 1r. "Family picnic" 20 10
1649 2r. "Mosque" 40 10

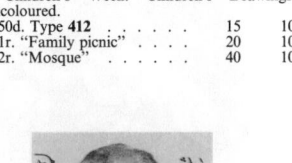

413 Shah Mohammed Riza Pahlavi

1971. 8th Anniv of Shah's White Revolution.
1650 **413** 2r. multicoloured 20 20

414 Common Shelduck

1971. International Wetland and Waterfowl Conference, Ramsar. Multicoloured.
1651 1r. Type **414** . . . . 1·25 25
1652 2r. Ruddy shelduck . . . . 1·25 25
1653 8r. Greater flamingo (vert) 2·75 60

415 Riza Shah Pahlavi

1971. 50th Anniv of Rise of Pahlavi Dynasty.
1654 **415** 6r. multicoloured . . . . 1·40 30

416 Red Junglefowl

1971. New Year Festival. Birds. Multicoloured.
1655 1r. Type **416** 60 15
1656 2r. Barn swallow at nest . . 1·50 20
1657 6r. Hoopoe . . . . 4·00 60

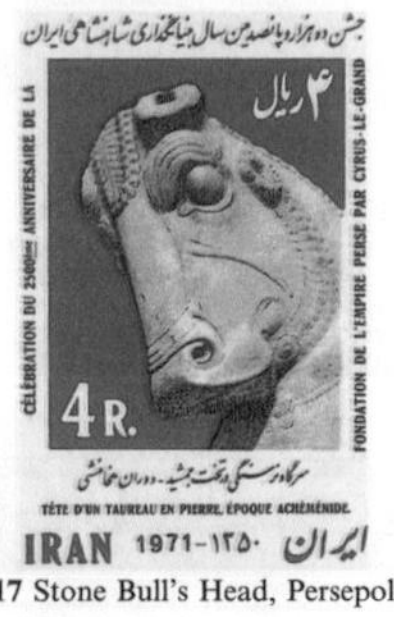

417 Stone Bull's Head, Persepolis

1971. 2500th Anniv of Persian Empire (5th issue). Age of Cyrus the Great. Multicoloured.
1658 4r. Type **417** 90 15
1659 5r. Winged lion ornament 1·25 15
1660 6r. Persian Archer (bas-relief) . . . . 1·25 20
1661 8r. Imperial audience (bas-relief) . . . . 1·50 30

418 Prisoners' Rehabilitation

1971. Rehabilitation Week.
1662 **418** 6r. multicoloured . . . . 1·00 15
1663 8r. multicoloured . . . . 1·50 15

1971. 2500th Anniv of Persian Empire (6th issue). Art of Ancient Persia. As T **417**.
1664 1r. multicoloured 70 15
1665 2r. black and brown 70 15
1666 2r. brown, black and purple 70 15
1667 10r. black, blue and brown 90 30
DESIGNS—VERT: No. 1664, "Harpist" (mosaic); 1667, Bronze head of Parthian prince. HORIZ: No. 1665, "Shapur I hunting" (ornamental plate); 1666, "Investiture of Ardashir I" (bas-relief).

420 Badshahi Mosque, Lahore (Pakistan)

1971. 7th Anniv of Regional Co-operation for Development. Multicoloured.
1668 2r. Type **420** 30 15
1669 2r. Selimiye Mosque, Edirne, Turkey (vert) 30 15
1670 2r. Chaharbagh School, Isfahan (Iran) (vert) . . . 30 15

421 "Shiraz Arts"

1971. 5th Shiraz Arts Festival, Persepolis.
1671 **421** 2r. multicoloured 30 15

422 "Book-reading"

1971. World Literacy Day.
1672 **422** 2r. multicoloured 20 10

423 Kings Abdullah and Hussein II

1971. 50th Anniv of Hashemite Kingdom of Jordan.
1673 **423** 2r. multicoloured 20 10

424 National Steel Foundry

1971. 2500th Anniv of Persian Empire (7th issue). Modern Iran. Multicoloured.
1674 1r. Type **424** 30 15
1675 2r. Shahyad Aryamehr Memorial 65 15
1676 3r. Senate Building, Teheran 65 20
1677 11r. Shah Abbas the Great Dam . . . . 1·25 40

425 Ghatur Railway Bridge

1971. Inaug of Iran–Turkey Railway Link.
1678 **425** 2r. multicoloured . . . . 1·00 10

426 Shah Mohammed Riza Pahlavi

1971. 2500th Anniv of Persian Empire (8th issue). Pahlavi Era. Multicoloured.
1679 1r. Type **426** . . . . 1·40 50
1680 2r. Riza Shah Pahlavi . . . 1·50 50
1681 5r. Proclamation tablet of Cyrus the Great (horiz) 1·60 50
1682 10r. Pahlavi Crown . . . . 3·25 75

427 Racial Equality Year Emblem

428 Shah Mohammed Riza Pahlavi

1971. Racial Equality Year.
1683 **427** 2r. multicoloured 10 10

1971.
1684 **428** 5d. purple 10 10
1685 10d. red 10 10
1686 50d. green 10 10
1687 1r. green 10 10
1688 2r. brown 10 10
1689 6r. green 50 10
1690 8r. violet 90 10
1691 10r. purple 70 10
1692 11r. green . . . . 2·00 10
1693 14r. blue . . . . 7·50 10
1694 20r. mauve . . . . . . 5·50 15
1695 50r. ochre . . . . 3·25 50
Nos. 1689/95 are larger, 27 × 37 mm.
See also Nos. 1715/26b and 1846/50.

429 "Waiters at a Banquet"

1971. Children's Week. Children's Drawings. Multicoloured.
1696 2r. Type **429** 20 15
1697 2r. "Persepolis Ruins" (vert) 20 15
1698 2r. "Persian Archer" (vert) 20 15

430 UNESCO Emblem

1971. 25th Anniv of UNESCO.
1699 **430** 6r. blue and purple . . . 30 15

431 Congress Emblem and Livestock

1971. 4th Iranian Veterinary Congress.
1700 **431** 2r. red, black and grey 30 10

432 I.L.O. Emblem and Globe

1971. 7th Asian International Labour Organization Regional Conference, Teheran.
1701 **432** 2r. orange, blue and black 20 10

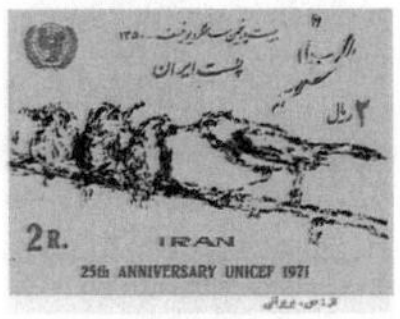
433 Bird feeding Young

1971. 25th Anniv of UNICEF.
1702 **433** 2r. multicoloured 20 10

434 Shah Mohammed Riza Pahlavi

1972. 9th Anniv of Shah's White Revolution.
1703 **434** 2r. multicoloured . . . . 1·00 15
MS1704 80 × 94 mm. **434** 20r. multicoloured. Imperf . . . . 3·00 2·25

435 Chukar Partridge

436 Human Heart

1972. New Year Festival. Birds. Multicoloured.
1705 1r. Type **435** 45 15
1706 1r. Pin-tailed sandgrouse . . 45 15
1707 2r. Swee waxbill and red-cheeked cordon-bleu . . . 2·40 20

1972. World Heart Day.
1708 **436** 10r. multicoloured . . . 80 20

437 Winged Ibex Symbol

438 Scarlet Roses

1972. International Film Festival, Teheran.
1709 **437** 6r. gold and blue 70 15
1710 – 8r. multicoloured . . . . 1·25 20
DESIGN: 8r. Symbolic spectrum.

1972. Roses. Multicoloured.
1711 1r. Type **438** 20 10
1712 2r. Yellow roses 50 10
1713 5r. Red rose 75 15

1972. As Nos. 1684/95, but with bistre frames and inscriptions.
1715 **428** 5d. purple 10 10
1716 10d. brown 10 10
1717 50d. green 10 10
1718 1r. green 10 10
1719 2r. brown 40 10
1720 6r. green 30 10
1721 8r. violet 35 15
1722 10r. purple 55 10
1723 11r. blue 70 15
1724 14r. blue . . . . . . 3·50 20
1725 20r. mauve . . . . . 7·00 30
1726 50r. blue . . . . . . 2·50 65
1726a 110r. violet . . . . . 3·50 75
1726b 200r. black . . . . . 7·50 3·50
Nos. 1720/26b are larger, 27 × 37 mm.

439 "U.I.T." Emblem

1972. World Telecommunications Day.
1726c **439** 14r. multicoloured . . . 1·50 30

440 "Fisherman" (Cevat Dereli, Turkey)

442 Pens

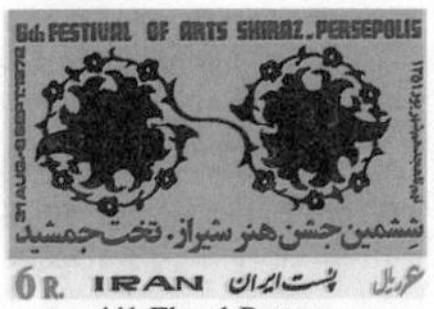
441 Floral Patterns

1972. 8th Anniv of Regional Co-operation for Development. Paintings. Multicoloured.
1727 5r. Type **440** . . . . 1·00 25
1728 5r. "Iranian Woman" (Behzad, Iran) 90 25
1729 5r. "Will and Power" (A. R. Chughtai, Pakistan) . . . 90 25

1972. 6th Shiraz Arts Festival.
1730 **441** 6r. black, red and green 75 15
1731 8r. black and purple . . 1·00 20

1972. World Literacy Day.
1732 **442** 1r. multicoloured 15 10
1733 2r. multicoloured 20 10

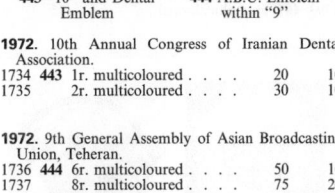

443 "10" and Dental Emblem

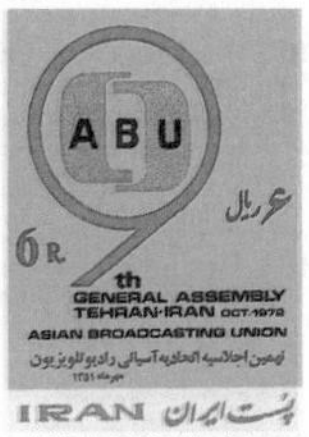
444 A.B.U. Emblem within "9"

1972. 10th Annual Congress of Iranian Dental Association.
1734 **443** 1r. multicoloured 20 10
1735 2r. multicoloured 30 10

1972. 9th General Assembly of Asian Broadcasting Union, Teheran.
1736 **444** 6r. multicoloured 50 10
1737 8r. multicoloured 75 20

445 3ch. stamp of 1910 on Cover

447 Communications Emblem

446 Chess

1972. World Stamp Day.
1738 **445** 10r. multicoloured . . . 1·25 30

1972. Olympic Games, Munich. Iranian Sports. Multicoloured.
1739 1r. Type **446** . . . . 1·25 20
1740 2r. Hunting . . . . 1·25 20
1741 3r. Archery . . . . 1·50 20
1742 5r. Horse-racing . . . . . 1·50 20
1743 6r. Polo . . . . 1·50 20
1744 8r. Wrestling . . . . 1·60 25
MS1745 177 × 106 mm. Nos. 1739/44 . Imperf . . . . 7·50 3·50

1972. United Nations Day.
1746 **447** 10r. multicoloured . . . 1·10 25

448 "Children in Garden"

449 Festival Emblem

1972. Children's Week. Children's Drawings. Multicoloured.
1747 2r. Type **448** 35 10
1748 2r. "At the Theatre" 55 10
1749 6r. "Children at play" (horiz) . . . . 1·25 20

1972. National Festival of Art and Culture, Teheran.
1750 **449** 10r. multicoloured . . . 2·75 30

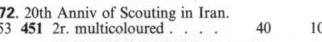

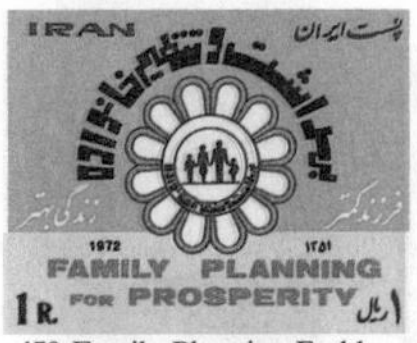
450 Family Planning Emblem

451 Scouting Emblem

1972. Family Planning Campaign.
1751 **450** 1r. multicoloured 15 10
1752 2r. multicoloured 20 10

1972. 20th Anniv of Scouting in Iran.
1753 **451** 2r. multicoloured 40 10

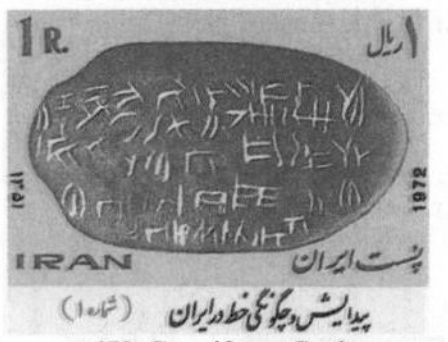
452 Cuneiform Seal

1973. "Origins of Writing" (1st issue). Impressions from ancient seals. Multicoloured. Background colours given.
1754 **452** 1r. blue 40 15
1755 – 1r. yellow 40 15
1756 – 1r. mauve 40 15
1757 – 2r. orange 45 15
1758 – 2r. green 45 15
1759 – 2r. buff 45 15
See also Nos. 1774/9 and 1822/7.

453 Open Books in Space

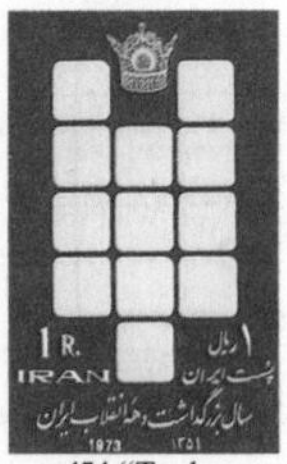
454 "Twelve Reforms"

1973. International Book Year. Multicoloured.
1760 2r. Type **453** 55 10
1761 6r. Illuminated manuscript 85 15

1973. 10th Anniv of Shah's White Revolution. Multicoloured.
1762 1r. Type **454** 15 10
1763 2r. Pyramid of 12 balls . . . 20 10
1764 6r. As Type **454** but size 71 × 92 mm. . . . . 1·00 45
MS1765 71 × 92 mm. 10r. Design as 2r . . . . 1·10 65

455 Long-spined Seabream ("Sparus spinifer")

457 "Footballers"

456 W.H.O. Emblem

1973. New Year Festival. Fishes. Multicoloured.
1766 1r. Type **455** 55 10
1767 1r. Purple tang ("Acanthurus sp.") . . . 55 10
1768 2r. Two-banded seabream ("Anisotremus sp.") . . . 75 15
1769 2r. Sergeant major ("Abdufef") 75 15
1770 2r. Black-spotted snapper ("Lutyanus fulniflamma") 75 15

1973. 25th Anniv of W.H.O.
1771 **456** 10r. multicoloured . . . 80 20

1973. 15th Asian Youth Football Tournament, Teheran.
1772 **457** 14r. multicoloured . . . 1·00 25

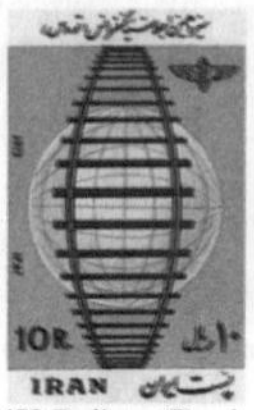

458 Railway Track encircling Globe

459 Ancient Aryan Script

1973. International Railway Conference, Teheran.
1773 **458** 10r. blue, black & mauve 1·25 20

1973. "Origins of Writing". Multicoloured.
1774 1r. Type **459** 25 15
1775 1r. Achaemenian priest and text 25 15
1776 1r. Kharochtani tablet . . . 25 15
1777 2r. Parthian medallion (Arsacid) 45 15
1778 2r. Parthian coin (Mianeh) 45 15
1779 2r. Gachtak inscribed medallion (Dabireh) . . . 45 15

460 Orchid

461 Carved Head, Tomb of Antiochus I (Turkey)

1973. Flowers. Multicoloured.
1780 1r. Type **460** 20 10
1781 2r. Hyacinth 30 10
1782 6r. Wild rose 90 30

1973. 9th Anniv of Regional Co-operation for Development. Multicoloured.
1783 2r. Type **461** 30 15
1784 2r. Statue, Lut excavations (Iran) 30 15
1785 2r. Street in Moenjodaro (Pakistan) 30 15

462 Shah and Oil Installations

463 Soldiers and "Sun"

1973. Full Independence for Iranian Oil Industry.
1786 **462** 5r. black and blue . . . 90 20

1973. 20th Anniv of Gen. Zahedi's Uprising.
1787 **463** 2r. multicoloured 20 10

464 Sportswomen and Globe

1973. 7th International Women's Congress on Physical Education and Sport, Teheran.
1788 **464** 2r. multicoloured (blue background) 20 10
1789 2r. multicoloured (green background) 20 10

465 Festival Poster

467 Wrestling

466 Shahyad Monument and Rainbow

1973. 7th Shiraz Arts Festival.
1790 **465** 1r. multicoloured 15 10
1791 5r. multicoloured 20 15

1973. Cent of World Meteorological Organization.
1792 **466** 5r. multicoloured 60 15

1973. World Wrestling Championships, Teheran.
1793 **467** 6r. multicoloured 55 10

468 Alphabetic "Sun"

469 Globe wearing Earphones

1973. World Literacy Day.
1794 **468** 2r. multicoloured 15 10

1973. Int Audio-visual Exhibition, Teheran.
1795 **469** 10r. multicoloured . . . 45 15

470 Al-Biruni

472 Crown Prince Cup

471 C.I.S.M. Badge and Emblem

1973. Birth Millenary of Abu al-Rayhan al-Biruni (mathematician and philosopher).
1796 **470** 10r. black and brown . . 80 20

1973. 25th Anniv of International Military Sports Council (C.I.S.M.).
1797 **471** 8r. multicoloured 30 15

1973. Crown Prince Cup Football Championship.
1798 **472** 2r. brown, black and lilac 15 10

473 Interpol Emblem

475 U.P.U. Emblem, Post-horn and Letter

474 Curves on Globe

1973. 50th Anniv of International Criminal Police Organization (Interpol).
1799 **473** 2r. multicoloured 30 10

1973. 25th Anniv of World Mental Health Federation.
1800 **474** 10r. multicoloured . . . 50 15

1973. World Post Day.
1801 **475** 6r. orange and blue . . . 30 10

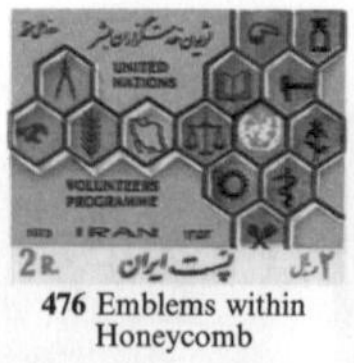

476 Emblems within Honeycomb

477 Festival Emblem and "People"

1973. 5th Anniv of United Nations Volunteers.
1802 **476** 2r. multicoloured (brown background) 10 10
1803 2r. multicoloured (green background) 10 10

1973. National Festival of Art and Culture, Teheran.
1804 **477** 2r. multicoloured 20 10

478 Bosphorus Bridge

1973. 50th Anniv of Turkish Republic. Mult.
1805 2r. Type **478** 50 10
1806 8r. Meeting of Kemal Ataturk and Reza Shah Pahlavi 60 20

479 "House and Garden"

481 Cylinder of Cyrus and Red Cross Emblems

480 Ear of Grain and Cow

1973. Children's Week. Children's Drawings. Multicoloured.
1807 2r. Type **479** 25 15
1808 2r. "Collecting Fruit" . . . 25 15
1809 2r. "Caravan" (horiz) . . . 25 15

1973. 10th Anniv of World Food Programme.
1810 **480** 10r. multicoloured . . . 75 15

1973. 22nd Int Red Cross Conference, Teheran.
1811 **481** 6r. multicoloured 35 10

482 IATA Emblem

483 Emblem, Film and Flags

1973. Tourist Managers Congress, Teheran.
1812 **482** 10r. multicoloured . . . 35 15

1973. International Film Festival, Teheran.
1813 **483** 2r. multicoloured 20 10

484 Flame Emblem

485 Harp Emblem

1973. 25th Anniv of Declaration of Human Rights.
1814 **484** 8r. multicoloured 30 10

1973. "Art of Music" Festival.
1815 **485** 10r. red, green and black 40 15
1816 – 10r. ultram, bl & pur . . 40 15
DESIGN: No. 1816, Musical symbols.

486 Reform Symbols

1974. 11th Anniv of Shah's White Revolution. Multicoloured.
1817 1r. Type **486** 20 15
1818 1r. Tractor, factory in cogwheel, women and parliament gate 20 15
1819 2r. Girders, hose and worker 20 15
1820 2r. Rod of Aesculapius, scales and road passing house 20 15
MS1821 76 × 102 mm. 20r. Symbols from Nos.1817/20 arranged in four panels. Imperf 55 55

487 Pir Amooz Ketabaty Script

1974. "Origins of Writing" (3rd issue). Multicoloured.
1822 1r. Din Dabireh Avesta . . 40 15
1823 1r. Mo Eghely Ketabaty . . 40 15
1824 1r. Type **487** 40 15
1825 2r. Pir Amooz, Naskh style 40 15
1826 2r. Pir Amooz, decorative 40 15
1827 2r. Pir Amooz, decorative and architectural 40 15

488 Chicken, Cow and Syringe

1974. 5th Iranian Veterinary Congress.
1828 **488** 6r. multicoloured 40 15

490 Scarce Swallowtail

491 Mevlana

1974. Nawrooz and Spring Festivals. Butterflies. Multicoloured, background colours given.
1841 **490** 1r. mauve 30 10
1842 – 1r. purple 30 10
1843 – 2r. green 65 10
1844 – 2r. brown 65 10
1845 – 2r. blue 65 10
DESIGNS: No. 1842, Swallowtail; 1843, Peacock; 1844, Painted lady; 1845, Cardinal.

1974. As Nos. 1684/95, but colours changed.
1846 **428** 50d. blue and orange . . 20 10
1847 1r. blue and green . . . 25 10
1848 2r. blue and red . . . 40 10
1849 10r. blue and green . . . 4·50 10
1850 20r. blue and mauve . . 2·75 20
Nos. 1849/50 are larger, 27 × 37 mm.

1974. 700th Death Anniv of Jalal-udin Mevlana (poet).
1851 **491** 2r. multicoloured 20 10

492 Palace of Forty Columns, Isfahan

1974. 9th Near- and Middle-East Medical Congress, Isfahan.
1852 **492** 10r. multicoloured . . . 40 15

493 Asiatic Wild Ass

494 Gymnastics

1974. International Game and Wild Life Protection Congress, Teheran. Multicoloured.
1853 1r. Type **493** 20 15
1854 2r. Great bustard 40 10
1855 6r. Fawn and fallow deer . . 45 20
1856 8r. Caucasian black grouse 1·75 20

1974. 7th Asian Games, Teheran (1st series). Multicoloured.
1857 1r. Type **494** 15 10
1858 1r. Table tennis 20 10
1859 2r. Boxing 50 10
1860 2r. Hurdling 50 10
1861 6r. Weightlifting 70 15
1862 8r. Handball . . . . 1·25 15
See also Nos. 1874/9, 1890/3 and 1909.

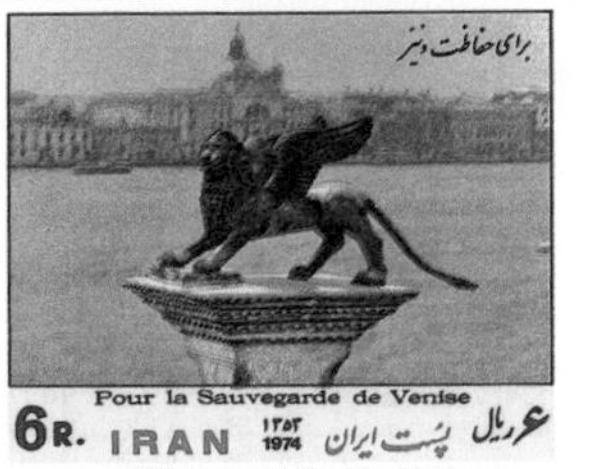
495 Lion of St. Mark's

1974. UNESCO "Save Venice" Campaign. Multicoloured.
1863 6r. Type **495** 30 10
1864 8r. Merchants at the Doge's court 65 15

496 Chain Link

497 Shah and Douglas DC-9-80 Super Eighty

1974. Farm Co-operatives' Day.
1865 **496** 2r. multicoloured 15 10

1974. Air.
1866 **497** 4r. black and orange . . 10 10
1867 10r. black and blue . . . 60 15
1868 12r. black and brown . . 70 20
1869 14r. black and green . . 1·00 20
1870 20r. black and mauve . . 1·25 30
1871 50r. black and blue . . . 5·50 80

498 De Havilland D.H.9A, 1924

1974. 50th Anniv of Imperial Iranian Air Force. Multicoloured.
1872 10r. Type **498** . . . . . . 1·10 15
1873 10r. McDonnell Douglas F-4D Phantom II fighter of 1974 . . . . 1·10 15

499 Tennis (men's doubles)

500 Mazanderan Costume

1974. 7th Asian Games, Teheran (2nd series). Multicoloured.
1874 1r. Type **499** 15 10
1875 1r. Swimming 15 10
1876 2r. Wrestling 20 10
1877 2r. Hockey 20 10
1878 4r. Volleyball 60 15
1879 10r. Tennis (women's singles) . . . . 1·25 15

1974. Regional Costumes. Multicoloured.
1880 2r. Type **500** 70 20
1881 2r. Bakhtiari 70 20
1882 2r. Turkoman 70 20
1883 2r. Ghasgai 70 20
1884 2r. Kirmanshah (Kurdistan) 70 20
1885 2r. Sanandadj (Kurdistan) 70 20

501 Gold Cup

502 Iranian Carpet

1974. Iranian Football Championships.
1886 **501** 2r. yellow, brown & green 20 10

1974. 10th Anniv of Regional Co-operation for Development. Multicoloured.
1887 2r. Pakistani carpet (diamond) centre 35 15
1888 2r. Turkish carpet (striped) 35 15
1889 2r. Type **502** 35 15

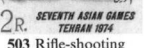

503 Rifle-shooting

504 Persian King

1974. 7th Asian Games, Teheran (3rd series). Multicoloured.
1890 2r. Type **503** 30 15
1891 2r. Fencing 30 15
1892 2r. Football 30 15
1893 2r. Cycling 35 15

1974. 8th Shiraz Arts Festival, Persepolis.
1894 **504** 2r. multicoloured 15 10

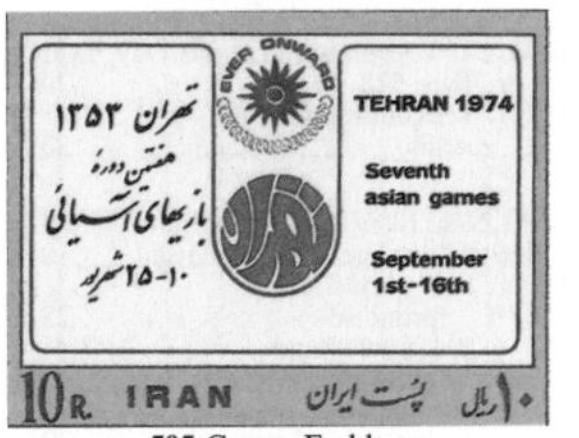
505 Games Emblem

1974. 7th Asian Games, Tehran (4th issue). Two sheets, each 74 × 95 mm, containing single stamps as T **505**. Multicoloured.
MS1895 (a) 10r. Type **505**; (b) 10r. Plan of Games area 70 40

506 Petrochemical Works, Khark

1974.
1896 **506** 5d. green and brown . . 10 10
1897 – 10d. orange and brown 25 10
1898 – 50d. green and brown . . 10 10
1899 – 1r. blue and brown . . . 15 10
1900 – 2r. purple and brown . . 20 10
1901 – 6r. brown and blue . . . 15 10
1902 – 8r. turquoise and blue 20 10
1903 – 10r. purple and blue . . 45 10
1904 – 14r. green and blue . . . 11·00 10
1905 – 20r. red and blue . . . . 1·00 10
1906 – 50r. violet and blue . . . 1·75 20
DESIGNS—As T **506**: 10d. Railway bridge, Ghatur; 50d. Dam, Farahnaz; 1r. Oil Refinery; 2r. Radio telescope. 37 × 27 mm: 6r. Steelworks, Aryamehr; 8r. Tabriz University; 10r. Shah Abbas Kabir Dam; 14r. Teheran Opera House; 20r. Shahyad Square; 50r. Aryamehr Stadium.
See also Nos. 1939/49.

507 Family within Hands

509 Plan of Hasanlu

508 Aryamehr Stadium, Teheran

1974. State Education and Health Services. Multicoloured.
1907 2r. Type **507** 15 10
1908 2r. Children, pen and book within hands 15 10

1974. Seventh Asian Games, Teheran (4th series).
1909 **508** 6r. multicoloured 40 10

1974. 2nd International Architectural Congress, Shiraz.
1910 **509** 8r. multicoloured 30 10

510 Charioteer

1974. Centenary of U.P.U. Multicoloured.
1911 6r. Type **510** 30 10
1912 14r. U.P.U. emblem and letters 50 20

511 Road through Park

1974. Opening of Farahabad Park, Teheran. Multicoloured.
1913 1r. Type **511** 10 10
1914 2r. Recreation pavilion . . . 15 10

512 Festival Emblem

1974. National Festival of Art and Culture, Teheran.
1915 **512** 2r. multicoloured 15 10

513 Crown Prince in Aircraft

1974. Air. Crown Prince's Birthday.
1916 **513** 14r. multicoloured . . . 45 15

514 Destroyer "Palang"

1974. Navy Day.
1917 **514** 10r. multicoloured . . . 80 20

515 Scarecrow

516 Winged Bull Emblem

1974. Children's Week. Children's Drawings. Multicoloured.
1918 2r. Type **515** 15 10
1919 2r. Girl at spinning wheel (horiz) 15 10
1920 2r. New Year picnic (horiz) 15 10

1974. 3rd International Film Festival, Teheran.
1921 **516** 2r. multicoloured 15 10

517 W.P.Y. Emblem

1974. World Population Year.
1922 **517** 8r. multicoloured 30 10

518 Gold Butterfly Brooch

1974. 14th Wedding Anniv of Shah and Empress Farah. Multicoloured.

1923	6r. Type **518**	15	10
1924	8r. Gold diadem	20	10

519 Angel with Banner

1975. International Women's Year.

1925	**519** 2r. orange, blue and red	15	10

520 Emblems of Agriculture, Industry and the Arts

521 Tourism Year Emblem

1975. 12th Anniv of Shah's White Revolution.

1926	**520** 2r. multicoloured	15	10

1975. South Asia Tourism Year.

1927	**521** 6r. multicoloured	15	10

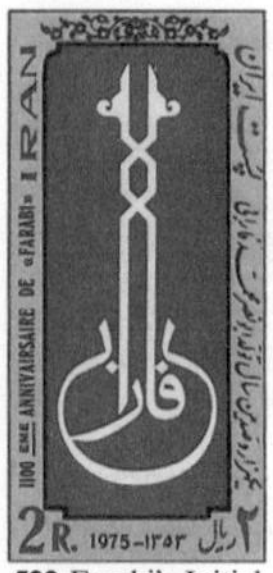

522 Farabi's Initial

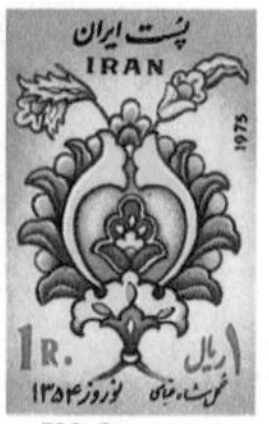

523 Ornament

1975. 1100th Birth Anniv of Abu-Nasr al-Farabi (philosopher).

1928	**522** 2r. multicoloured	15	10

1975. New Year Festival. Multicoloured.

1929	1r. Type **523**	15	10
1930	1r. Blossoms and tree	15	10
1931	1r. Arabesque and patterns	15	10

524 Nasser Khosrov

525 Persian Warriors

1975. Birth Millenary of Nasser Khosrov (poet).

1932	**524** 2r. black, red and bistre	15	10

1975. 70th Anniv of Rotary International. Multicoloured.

1933	2r. Type **525**	55	10
1934	10r. Charioteer (horiz)	1·50	15

526 Biochemical Emblem

527 "Co-operative Peoples"

1975. 5th Biochemical Symposium.

1935	**526** 2r. multicoloured	15	10

1975. Co-operatives Day.

1936	**527** 2r. multicoloured	10	10

528 Ancient Signal-beacons

1975. World Telecommunications Day. Mult.

1937	6r. Type **528**	20	10
1938	8r. Telecommunications satellite	30	15

1975. As Nos. 1896/1906 but colours changed.

1939	**506** 5d. orange and turquoise	10	10
1940	– 10d. purple and turquoise	25	10
1941	– 50d. mauve and turquoise	10	10
1942	– 1r. blue and turquoise	20	10
1943	– 2r. brown and turquoise	20	10
1944	– 6r. violet and brown	50	10
1945	– 8r. red and brown	70	10
1946	– 10r. green and brown	90	15
1947	– 14r. mauve and brown	6·00	25
1948	– 20r. turquoise and brown	1·75	30
1949	– 50r. blue and brown	1·75	70

529 "Iran Air" Boeing 747SP

1975. "Iran Air's" First Teheran–New York Flight.

1950	**529** 10r. multicoloured	35	15

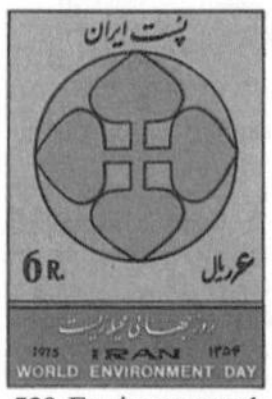

530 Environmental Emblem

532 Party Emblem

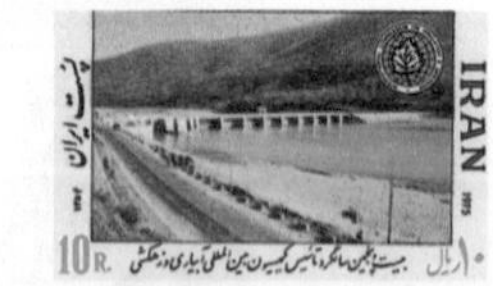

531 Dam and Reservoir

1975. World Environment Day.

1951	**530** 6r. multicoloured	20	10

1975. 25th Anniv of International Commission on Irrigation and Drainage.

1952	**531** 10r. multicoloured	25	15

1975. Formation of Resurgence Party.

1953	**532** 2r. multicoloured	10	10

533 Saluting Hand

1975. 2nd National Girl Scout Camp, Teheran.

1954	**533** 2r. multicoloured	20	10

534 Festival Motif

1975. Festival of Tus (honouring poet Firdausi).

1955	**534** 2r. multicoloured	10	10

535 Iranian Tile

1975. 11th Anniv of Regional Co-operation for Development. Multicoloured.

1956	2r. Type **535**	15	10
1957	2r. Pakistani camel-skin vase (vert)	15	10
1958	2r. Turkish porcelain vase (vert)	15	10

536 Parliament Gateway

1975. 70th Anniv of Iranian Constitution.

1959	**536** 10r. multicoloured	25	15

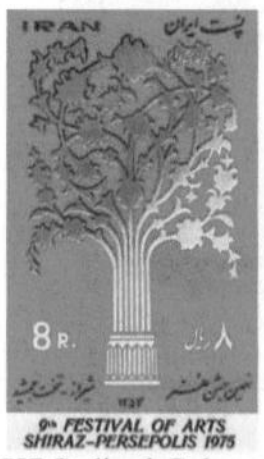

537 Stylized Column

538 Flags over Globe

1975. 9th Shiraz Arts Festival.

1960	**537** 8r. multicoloured	25	15

1975. International Literacy Symposium, Persepolis.

1961	**538** 2r. multicoloured	15	10

539 Stylized Globe

541 Festival Emblem

540 Envelope on World Map

1975. 3rd International Trade Fair, Teheran.

1962	**539** 2r. multicoloured	15	10

1975. World Post Day.

1963	**540** 14r. multicoloured	45	15

1975. National Festival of Art and Culture, Teheran.

1964	**541** 2r. multicoloured	15	10

542 Face within Film

543 "Mother's Face"

1975. International Festival of Children's Films, Teheran.

1965	**542** 6r. multicoloured	15	10

1975. Children's Week. Multicoloured.

1966	2r. Type **543**	15	10
1967	2r. "Young Girl"	15	10
1968	2r. "Our House" (horiz)	15	10

544 "Sound Film"

545 Reform Symbols

1975. 4th International Film Festival, Teheran.

1969	**544** 8r. multicoloured	20	15

1976. 13th Anniv of Shah's White Revolution. Multicoloured.

1970	2r. Type **545**	10	10
1971	2r. Symbols representing "People"	10	10
1972	2r. Five reform symbols	10	10

546 Motor Cycle Patrol

547 Football Cup

1976. Highway Police Day. Multicoloured.

1973	2r. Type **546**	40	15
1974	6r. Bell Model 205 Iroquois police helicopter (horiz)	85	20

1976. 3rd International Football Cup.

1975	**547** 2r. multicoloured	15	10

548 Candlestick

549 Early and Modern Telephones

1976. New Year. Multicoloured.

1976	1r. Type **548**	15	10
1977	1r. Incense burner	15	10
1978	1r. Rosewater jug	15	10

1976. Telephone Centenary.

1979	**549** 10r. multicoloured	25	15

550 Human Eye

1976. World Health Day.

1980	**550** 6r. multicoloured	30	10

551 Nurse holding Child

1976. 30th Anniv of Social Services Organization. Multicoloured.

1981	2r. Type **551**	15	10
1982	2r. Workshop apprentices	15	10
1983	2r. Handclasp (help the aged) (vert)	15	10

552 Linked Men on Map

553 Sound Waves and Headphones

1976. 10th Anniv of Iranian Co-operative Movement.
1984 **552** 2r. multicoloured 15 10

1976. World Telecommunications Day.
1985 **553** 14r. multicoloured . . . 30 15

554 "Patriotism"

555 Nasser-Khosrow and Landmarks on Map

1976. National Resistance Organization.
1986 **554** 2r. multicoloured 15 10

1976. Tourism Day and Birth Anniv of Nasser-Khosrow "The Great Iranian Tourist".
1987 **555** 6r. multicoloured 15 10

556 Riza Shah Pahlavi

557 Olympic Flame and Emblem

1976. 12th Anniv of Regional Co-operation for Development. Multicoloured.
1988 2r. Type **556** 15 10
1989 6r. Mohammed Ali Jinnah (Pakistan) 25 15
1990 8r. Kemal Ataturk (Turkey) 35 15

1976. Olympic Games, Montreal.
1991 **557** 14r. multicoloured . . . 45 20

558 Riza Shah Pahlavi in Coronation Dress

1976. 50th Anniv of Pahlavi Dynasty. Mult.
1992 2r. Riza Shah Pahlavi and Mohammed Riza Pahlavi (horiz) 20 10
1993 6r. Type **558** 75 15
1994 14r. Mohammed Riza Pahlavi in Coronation dress . . . . 1·00 25

559 Festival Emblem

560 Conference Emblem

1976. 10th Shiraz Arts Festival.
1995 **559** 10r. multicoloured . . . 30 15

1976. 10th Asia–Pacific Scout Conference, Teheran.
1996 **560** 2r. multicoloured 15 10

561 Radiation Treatment

562 Target and Presentation to Policewoman

1976. Campaign against Cancer.
1997 **561** 2r. multicoloured 20 10

1976. Police Day.
1998 **562** 2r. multicoloured 30 10

563 Shah in Coronation Dress (⅗-size illustration)

1976. 35th Anniv of Shah's Reign. Sheet 75 × 100 mm.
MS1999 **563** 20r. multicoloured 1·10 65

564 U.P.U. Emblem and Iranian Stamp on Envelope

1976. International Post Day.
2000 **564** 10r. multicoloured . . . 30 15

565 Crown Prince presenting Cup

566 Mohammed Riza Pahlavi, Riza Shah Pahlavi and Steam Train

1976. Society of Village Culture Houses.
2001 **565** 6r. multicoloured 20 10

1976. Railway Day.
2002 **566** 8r. multicoloured . . . . 1·25 50

567 Festival Emblem

568 Census Symbols

1976. National Festival of Art and Culture, Teheran.
2003 **567** 14r. multicoloured . . . 35 15

1976. National Census.
2004 **568** 2r. multicoloured 15 10

569 Flowers and Birds

570 Mohammed Ali Jinnah (Quaid-i-Azam)

1976. Children's Week. Multicoloured.
2005 2r. Type **569** 15 10
2006 2r. Flowers and bird 15 10
2007 2r. Flowers and butterfly . . 15 10

1976. Birth Centenary of Mohammed Ali Jinnah (first Governor-General of Pakistan).
2008 **570** 10r. multicoloured . . . 30 15

571 Tractor (Land reform)

572 Man in Guilan Costume

1977. 14th Anniv of Shah's White Revolution. Shah's head and frame in gold.
2009 **571** 5d. green and pink . . . 10 10
2010 – 10d. green and brown . . 10 10
2011 – 50d. blue and orange . . 10 10
2012 – 1r. blue and mauve . . . 10 10
2013 – 2r. green and orange . . 10 10
2014 – 3r. red and blue 10 10
2015 – 5r. lilac and green . . . 20 10
2016 – 6r. purple, brown & black 30 10
2017 – 8r. purple, blue and black 30 10
2018 – 10r. blue, green and black . . . . 1·40 10
2019 – 12r. brown, lilac & black 70 10
2020 – 14r. red, orange and black . . . . 1·00 10
2021 – 20r. orange, grey & black . . . . 2·00 10
2022 – 30r. green, blue and black . . . . 1·75 10
2023 – 50r. red, yellow and black . . . . 3·50 10
2024 – 100r. blue, mauve & blk 3·25 55
2025 – 200r. violet, green & blk 6·50 1·50

DESIGNS—21 × 28 mm: 10d. Trees (Nationalization of forests); 50d. Banknotes (Profit-sharing); 1r. Factory workers (Sale of shares to workers); 2r. Parliament gate (Votes for women); 3r. Teacher and pupils (Education corps); 5r. Doctor examining patient (Medical corps). 36 × 27 mm: 6r. Bulldozer (Civil engineering); 8r. Scales (Justice); 10r. Dam (Irrigation); 12r. Building site (Construction corps); 14r. Clock and receptionist (Working conditions); 20r. Screen and students (Adult literacy); 30r. Sound waves (Telecommunications); 50r. Students and pupils (Education); 100r. Baby in hands (Child care); 200r. Elderly couple (Care of the aged).

1977. New Year Festival. Multicoloured.
2026 1r. Type **572** 10 10
2027 2r. Women in Guilan costume 15 10

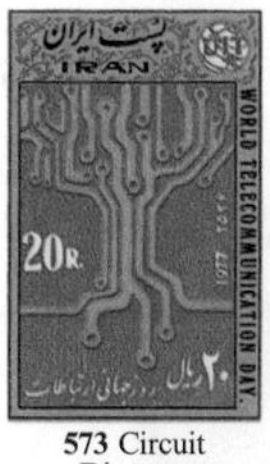

573 Circuit Diagram

574 Riza Shah Dam

1977. World Telecommunications Day.
2028 **573** 20r. multicoloured . . . 55 15

1977. Inauguration of Riza Shah Dam.
2029 **574** 5r. multicoloured 20 10

575 Olympic Rings

1977. Olympic Day.
2030 **575** 14r. multicoloured . . . 35 15

576 Turkish "Human Face" Vase

1977. 13th Anniv of Regional Co-operation for Development. Multicoloured.
2031 5r. Type **576** 20 10
2032 5r. Pakistani toy bullock cart 20 10
2033 5r. Iranian buff earthenware 20 10

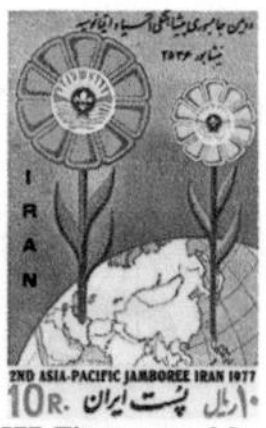

577 Flowers on Map of Asia

578 Map and Emblem

1977. 2nd Asia–Pacific Jamboree, Nishapur.
2034 **577** 10r. multicoloured . . . 25 10

1977. 9th Asian Electronics Conference, Teheran.
2035 **578** 3r. multicoloured 15 10

579 "Tree" in Farsi Script

580 Globe and Envelope

1977. Teachers' Day.
2036 **579** 10r. multicoloured . . . 30 10

1977. Centenary of Iran's Admission to U.P.U.
2037 **580** 14r. multicoloured . . . 30 10

581 "Tree and Lions"

582 Festival Emblem

1977. Popular Arts Festival.
2038 **581** 5r. multicoloured 15 10

1977. National Festival of Art and Culture, Teheran.
2039 **582** 20r. multicoloured . . . 45 20

583 "Two Horsemen" (Persian miniature)

584 Seminar Emblem

1977. Children's Week. Multicoloured.
2040 3r. Type **583** 15 10
2041 3r. "Lover and his mistress" 15 10
2042 3r. "Five people round a bed" 15 10

1977. 1st Regional Seminar on Education and Welfare of the Deaf.
2043 **584** 5r. multicoloured 15 10

585 A. M. Iqbal **586** Bronze Head from Nigeria

1977. Birth Centenary of Allama Mohammad Iqbal (Pakistani poet).
2044 **585** 5r. multicoloured 15 10

1977. "Art of Black Africa" Exhibition, Teheran.
2045 **586** 20r. multicoloured . . . 1·60 30

587 Ruins at Persepolis **588** Mohammed Riza Pahlavi

1978.
2059 **587** 1r. brown and gold . . . 10 10
2060 – 2r. green and gold . . . 20 10
2061 – 3r. purple and gold . . . 30 10
2062 – 5r. green and gold . . . 40 10
2063 – 9r. brown and gold . . . 85 30
2064 – 10r. blue and gold . . . 3·50 35
2065 – 20r. red and gold . . . 1·00 30
2066 – 25r. blue and gold . . . 17·00 2·75
2067 – 30r. red and gold . . . 1·75 35
2068 – 50r. green and gold . . . 2·75 1·75
2069 – 100r. blue and gold . . . 9·00 4·25
2070 – 200r. violet and gold . . 12·00 9·00
DESIGNS: 30 × 23 mm: 2r. Khajou Bridge, Isfahan; 3r. Shah Mosque, Isfahan; 5r. Imam Riza Shrine, Meshed. 35 × 26 mm: 9r. Warrior frieze, Persepolis; 10r. Djameh Mosque, Isfahan; 20r. Bas-relief, Persepolis; 25r. Shaikh Lotfollah Mosque; 30r. Ruins, Persepolis (different); 50r. Ali Ghapou Palace, Isfahan; 100r. Stone relief, Tagh Bastan; 200r. Relief, Naqsh Rostam.

1978. 15th Anniv of Shah's White Revolution.
2071 **588** 20r. multicoloured . . . 1·75 30

589 Animals (carpet) **590** Costume of Mazandera Province

1978. Inauguration of Persian Carpets Museum, Teheran. Multicoloured.
2072 3r. Type **589** 15 10
2073 5r. Court scene 20 10
2074 10r. Floral pattern 30 15

1978. New Year Festival. Multicoloured.
2075 3r. Type **590** 15 10
2076 5r. Woman in costume of Mazandera Province . . . 25 10

591 Riza Shah Pahlavi and Crown Prince inspecting Girls' School

1978. Birth Centenary of Riza Shah Pahlavi. Multicoloured.
2077 3r. Type **591** 15 10
2078 5r. Riza Shah Pahlavi and Crown Prince at inauguration of Trans-Iranian Railway . . . . . 1·25 30
2079 10r. Riza Shah Pahlavi and Crown Prince at Palace of Persepolis 55 15
2080 14r. Shah handing Crown Prince officer's diploma . . 60 20

592 Satellite and Receiving Station

1978. 10th Anniv of Admission to International Telecommunications Union.
2081 **592** 20r. multicoloured . . . 65 20

593 Microwave Antenna

1978. World Telecommunications Day.
2082 **593** 15r. multicoloured . . . 55 20

594 Welfare Legion Emblem **595** Pink Roses

1978. 10th Anniv of Universal Welfare Legion.
2083 **594** 10r. multicoloured . . . 20 10

1978. 14th Anniv of Regional Co-operation for Development. Roses. Multicoloured.
2084 5r. Type **595** 15 10
2085 10r. Salmon rose 35 10
2086 15r. Red roses 60 15

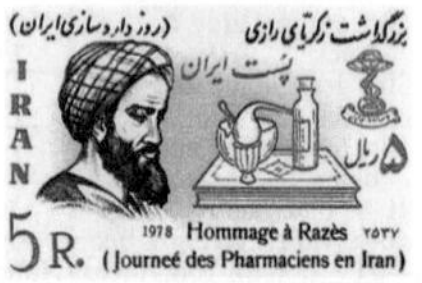

596 Rhazes and Pharmaceutical Equipment

1978. Pharmacists' Day.
2087 **596** 5r. multicoloured 20 10

597 Girl Guides and Aryamehr Arch

1978. 23rd World Girl Guides Conference, Teheran.
2088 **597** 5r. multicoloured 20 10

598 Riza Shah Pahlavi

1978. 50th Anniv of Bank Melli Iran. Mult.
2089 3r. Type **598** 40 15
2090 5r. Mohammed Riza Pahlavi 60 15

599 Young Girl and Bird

1978. Children's Week.
2091 **599** 3r. multicoloured 20 10

600 U.P.U. Emblem over Map of Iran

1978. World Post Day.
2092 **600** 14r. multicoloured . . . 50 10

601 Classroom and Communications Equipment

1978. 50th Anniv of Communications Faculty.
2093 **601** 10r. multicoloured . . . 60 10

602 Human Rights Emblem **603** Rose

1978. 30th Anniv of Human Rights Declaration.
2094 **602** 20r. multicoloured . . . 1·60 15

1979. New Year Festival. Multicoloured.
2095 2r. Type **603** 15 10
2096 3r. Man in Khurdistan costume 60 10
2097 5r. Woman in Khurdistan costume 90 15

604 Revolutionary Crowd

1979. Islamic Revolution. Multicoloured.
2098 3r. Type **604** 80 15
2099 5r. Hands holding flower, gun and torch 60 15
2100 10r. Protest march 70 30
2101 20r. Bloodied hands releasing dove (vert) . . . 1·60 30

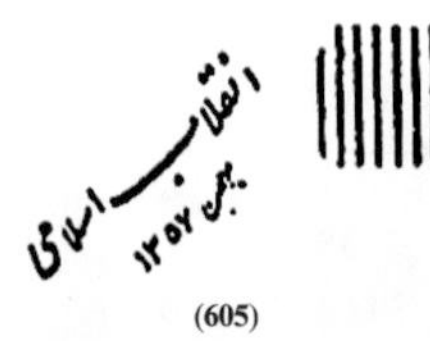

(605)

1979. Designs as T **587** optd with T **605**. (a) Nos. 1945/6.
2102 8r. red and brown . . . . . 1·00 15
2103 10r. green and brown . . . 24·00 85
(b) Nos. 2063/4, 2068/70 and unissued 15r. and 19r. stamps.
2104 9r. brown and gold . . . . 1·00 15
2105 10r. turquoise and gold . . . 30 15
2106 15r. mauve and gold . . . 30 15
2107 19r. green and gold 65 15
2108 50r. green and gold . . . . 2·50 35
2109 100r. blue and gold . . . . 5·00 70
2110 200r. violet and gold . . . . 6·25 1·75
DESIGNS—HORIZ (36 × 26 mm): 15r. Rock carvings, Naqsh Rostam; 19r. Chehel Sotoon Palace, Isfahan.

606 Tulip formed from "Allah" and "Islamic Republic"

1979. Islamic Republic.
2111 **606** 5r. multicoloured 85 15

607 "Iranian Goldsmith" (Kamal el Molk)

1979. 15th Anniv of Regional Co-operation for Development. Paintings. Multicoloured.
2112 5r. Type **607** . . . . 1·50 15
2113 5r. "Turkish Harvest" (Namik Ismail) . . . . . 1·50 15
2114 5r. "Pakistan Village Scene" (Allah Baksh) . . . . . . 1·50 15

608 "Telecom 79"

1979. 3rd World Telecommunications Exhibition, Geneva.
2115 **608** 20r. gold, black and red 3·50 20

609 Tulip rising from Blood of Revolutionary **610** Persian Rug

1979. International Year of the Child. Children's Paintings. Multicoloured.
2116 2r. Type **609** 40 15
2117 3r. Children greeting the rising sun (vert) 50 15
2118 5r. Children with banners 1·00 15

1979.
2119 **610** 50d. brown and orange 10 10
2120 1r. blue and light blue 10 10
2121 2r. red and yellow . . . 10 10
2122 3r. blue and mauve . . . 10 10
2123 5r. olive and green . . . 15 10
2124 10r. black and pink . . . 25 10
2125 20r. brown and grey . . 35 10
2126 50r. violet and grey . . . 85 10
2127 100r. black and green . . 4·00 70
2128 200r. blue and stone . . 3·00 1·50
Nos. 2126/8 are larger, 27 × 37 mm.

611 Globe in Envelope **612** Kashani and Astrolabe

1979. World Post Day.
2134 **611** 10r. multicoloured . . . 1·50 15

1979. 550th Death Anniv of Ghyath-al-din Jamshid Kashani (mathematician and astronomer).
2135 **612** 5r. black and brown . . 85 15

613 Kaaba, Mecca

1980. 1400th Anniv of Hegira (1st issue). Multicoloured.
2136 3r. Type **613** 10 10
2137 5r. Koran and globe (vert) 15 10
2138 10r. Pilgrim and Kaaba . . 30 10
See also Nos. 2148/51.

614 Flag and Revolutionaries

615 Dehkhoda

1980. 1st Anniv of Islamic Revolution. Mult.
2139 1r. Type **614** (28 × 40 mm) 10 10
2432 1r. As No. 2139 but 24 × 35 mm 10 10
2140 3r. Dagger and dripping blood (28 × 40 mm) . . . 10 10
2433 3r. As No. 2140 but 24 × 36 mm 15 15
2141 5r. Open window and rising sun (28 × 40 mm) 15 10
2435 5r. As No. 2141 but 24 × 36 mm 20 20

1980. Birth Centenary of Dehkhoda (compiler, Iranian encyclopedia).
2142 **615** 10r. multicoloured . . . 20 10

616 Female Costume of East Azerbaijan

617 M. Mossadegh

1980. New Year Festival. Multicoloured.
2143 3r. Type **616** 15 10
2144 5r. Male costume of East Azerbaijan 20 10

1980. Birth Centenary of Dr. Mohammed Mossadegh (statesman).
2145 **617** 20r. multicoloured . . . 45 20

618 Morteza Mottahari

619 Telephone

1980. 1st Death Anniv of Prof. Morteza Mottahari.
2146 **618** 10r. black and red . . . 20 10

1980. World Telecommunications Day.
2147 **619** 20r. black, green and red 40 15

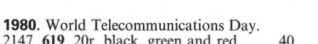

620 Mosque Interior

1980. 1400th Anniv of Hegira (2nd issue). Multicoloured.
2148 50d. Type **620** 10 10
2149 1r. Crowd with banner . . . 10 10
2150 3r. Al-Biruni, Farabi and Avicenna 10 10
2151 5r. Mosque and Kaaba . . 15 10

621 Dr. Ali Shariati

622 Kaaba and Banner

1980. Dr. Ali Shariati (educator) Commemoration.
2152 **621** 5r. multicoloured 20 10

1980. Birth Anniv of Hazrat Mehdi (Shi'ite Imam).
2153 **622** 5r. green, red and black 20 10

623 Ayatollah Teleghani

624 O.P.E.C. Emblem and Globe

1980. Ayatollah Teleghani Commemoration.
2154 **623** 5r. multicoloured 35 10

1980. 20th Anniv of Organization of Petroleum Exporting Countries. Multicoloured.
2155 5r. Type **624** 20 10
2156 10r. Figures supporting O.P.E.C. emblem 35 10

625 Hands breaking Star of David around Dome of the Rock

626 Tulip and Feizieh Theological College

1980. "Let us Liberate Jerusalem".
2157 **625** 5r. multicoloured 20 10
2158 20r. multicoloured . . . 45 20

1981. 2nd Anniv of Islamic Revolution. Mult.
2159 3r. Type **626** (dated "1981" at right) 20 10
2434 3r. As No. 2159 but dated at left 15 15
2160 5r. Tulip (in red), drops of blood and "Martyr" in Persian script 25 10
2436 5r. As No. 2160 but orange tulip 20 20
2161 20r. Open tulip (in red) and crest of Republic 50 20
2441 20r. As No. 2161 but orange tulip 50 50

627 Male Costume of Lorestan

628 I.T.U. and W.H.O. Emblems with Ribbons forming Caduceus

1981. New Year Festival. Multicoloured.
2162 5r. Type **627** 20 10
2163 10r. Female costume, Lorestan 40 10

1981. World Telecommunications Day.
2164 **628** 5r. orange, black & green 20 10

630 Militia Training

631 Ayatollah Kashani

1981.
2165 **630** 50d. black and brown . . 10 10
2166 – 1r. purple and green . . 10 10
2167 – 2r. brown and blue . . . 10 10
2168 – 3r. black and green . . . 10 10
2169 – 5r. blue and brown . . . 15 10
2170 – 10r. ultramarine and blue 20 10
2171 – 20r. black and red . . . 50 20
2172 – 50r. black and mauve . . 80 30
2173 – 100r. black and brown 1·50 55
2174 – 200r. blue and black . . 3·50 75
DESIGNS—As Type **630**: 1r. Man and boy at school desk (Literacy campaign); 2r. Digging irrigation ditch. 37 × 27 mm: 3r. Massed prayers; 20r. Woman with rifle; 50r. Worker at lathe; 100r. Pilgrims around Kaaba. 27 × 37 mm: 5r. Revolutionary Guards emblem and crowd; 10r. Arabic tapestry; 200r. Niche in Mosque illuminated by sun.

1981. Birth Centenary of Ayatollah Kashani.
2175 **631** 15r. purple and green . . 35 15

632 Armed Forces

1981. Islamic Iranian Army.
2176 **632** 5r. multicoloured 20 10

633 Carrier Pigeon flying over Gun Barrels

1981. U.P.U. Day.
2177 **633** 20r. black and blue . . . 55 15

634 Inscription

1981. Millenary of "Nabj al-Blagah" (sacred book).
2178 **634** 25r. green, blue and black 50 15

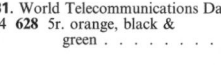

635 Victims of Bomb at Islamic Party's Headquarters

1981. Iranian Bomb and War Victims, Commemoration.
2179 **635** 3r. black and red 15 10
2180 – 5r. brown & deep brown 20 10
2181 – 10r. multicoloured . . . 30 15
DESIGNS: 5r. President Rajai and Prime Minister Bahomar (bomb victims); 10r. Dr. Chamran (killed in Iran–Iraq War).

636 Ayatollah Tabatabaie

637 Hand writing on Board

1981. Death Centenary of Ayatollah Ghazi Tabatabaie.
2182 **636** 5r. brown, green and gold 15 10

1982. Literacy Campaign.
2183 **637** 5r. blue and gold 15 10

638 Text "God is Great" over Map of Iran

639 Banner around Globe

1982. 3rd Anniv of Islamic Revolution. Mult.
2184 5r. Type **638** 15 10
2185 10r. Dove forming tulip . . 25 15
2186 20r. "God is Great" over Globe 45 25

1982. Islamic Unity Week.
2187 **639** 25r. multicoloured . . . 50 15

640 Manacled Hands reaching towards Christ

1982. Glorification of Christ's Birth.
2188 **640** 20r. multicoloured . . . 55 20

641 Male Costume of Khuzestan

642 National Flag

1982. New Year Festival. Multicoloured.
2189 3r. Type **641** 10 10
2190 5r. Female costume of Khuzestan 15 10

1982. 3rd Anniv of Islamic Republic.
2191 **642** 30r. black, red and green 50 20

643 Ayatollah Sadr

1982. 2nd Death Anniv of Ayatollah Sadr.
2192 **643** 50r. multicoloured . . . 60 30

644 Ayatollahs Madani and Dastghib

1982. Ayatollahs Sayed Assadollah Madani and Sayed Abdolhossein Dastghib Commemoration.
2193 **644** 50r. red, black and gold 60 30

645 Hand holding Cogwheels

646 Geometric Pattern

1982. Labour Day.
2194 **645** 100r. multicoloured . . . 1·40 50

1982. World Telecommunications Day.
2195 **646** 100r. multicoloured . . . 1·40 50

647 Symbolic Design

648 Rifles and Clenched Fist

1982. Mab'as Festival.
2196 **647** 32r. multicoloured . . . 60 20

1982. 19th Anniv of 1963 Islamic Rising.
2197 **648** 20r. black, red and silver 60 20

649 Lieutenant Islambuli

650 Ayatollah Beheshti

1982. Lieutenant Khaled Islambuli (assassin of Pres. Sadat of Egypt) Commemoration.
2198 **649** 2r. multicoloured 20 10

1982. 1st Death Anniv of Ayatollah Mohammed Hossein Beheshti.
2199 **650** 10r. multicoloured . . . 30 15

651 Soldiers, Tanks and Hand holding Banner

1982. Victims of War against Iraq Commemoration.
2200 **651** 5r. multicoloured 20 10

652 Dome of the Rock

1982. World Jerusalem Day.
2201 **652** 1r. multicoloured 20 10

653 Pilgrims around Kaaba

654 Globe and Letters

1982. Pilgrimage to Mecca.
2202 **653** 10r. multicoloured . . . 25 10

1982. World U.P.U. Day.
2203 **654** 30r. multicoloured . . . 65 20

655 Bloodied Hand releasing Dove

656 Casting Vote

1983. 4th Anniv of Islamic Revolution.
2204 **655** 30r. multicoloured (crowd in brown) . . 60 15
2445 30r. multicoloured (crowd in orange) . . 75 75

1983. 4th Anniv of Islamic Republic.
2205 **656** 10r. red, black and green 30 10

657 "Enlightenment"

658 Microwave Antenna and "83"

1983. Teachers' Day.
2206 **657** 5r. multicoloured 15 10

1983. World Communications Year.
2207 **658** 20r. blue, mauve & brown 55 10

659 Assembly

660 Doves and Crowd

1983. 1st Session of Islamic Consultative Assembly.
2208 **659** 5r. multicoloured 15 10

1983. 20th Anniv of 1963 Islamic Rising.
2209 **660** 10r. multicoloured . . . 25 10

661 Map of Persian Gulf and burning Oil Wells at Nowruz

1983. Ecology Week.
2210 **661** 5r. black, red and blue 30 10

662 Sadooghi

663 Hands holding Rifle over Dome of the Rock

1983. Ayatollah Mohammad Sadooghi Commem.
2211 **662** 20r. black and red . . . 55 10

1983. World Jerusalem Day.
2212 **663** 5r. yellow, brown & blue 20 10

664 Rajai and Bahomar

1983. Government Week (death anniv of Pres. Rajai and Prime Minister Dr. Bahomar).
2213 **664** 3r. orange and blue . . . 20 10

665 Cartridges and Text

666 Stamps and Map of Iran around Globe

1983. War Week.
2214 **665** 5r. green and red 20 10

1983. World U.P.U. Day.
2215 **666** 10r. multicoloured . . . 30 10

667 Esfahani

668 Mirza Kuchik Khan

1983. 4th Death Anniv of Ayatollah Ashrafi Esfahani.
2216 **667** 5r. multicoloured 15 10

1983. Religious and Political Personalities.
2217 – 1r. black and pink . . . 10 10
2218 **668** 2r. black and orange . . 10 10
2219 – 3r. black and blue . . . 10 10
2220 – 5r. black and red 15 10
2221 – 10r. black and green . . 30 10
2222 – 20r. black and purple . . 55 20
2223 – 30r. black and brown . . 75 30
2224 – 50r. black and blue . . 95 50
2225 – 100r. black and red . . . 2·00 65
2226 – 200r. black and green . . 4·00 1·25

DESIGNS: 1r. Sheikh Mohammed Khiabani; 3r. Seyd Modjtaba Navab Safavi; 5r. Seyd Jamal-ed-Din Assadabadi; 10r. Seyd Hassah Modaress; 20r. Sheikh Fazel Assad Nouri; 30r. Mirza Mohammed Hossein Naieni; 50r. Sheikh Mohammed Hossein Kashef; 100r. Seyd Hassan Shirazi; 200r. Mirza Reza Kermani.

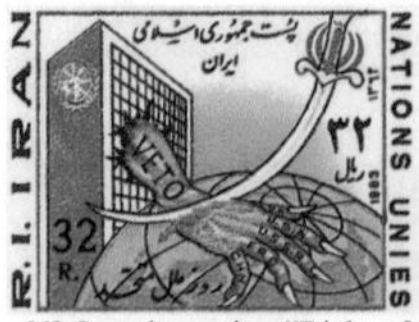
669 Sword severing "Right of Veto" Hand

670 Storming the U.S. Embassy, Hostage and burning American Flag

1983. United Nations Day.
2228 **669** 32r. multicoloured . . . 60 30

1983. 4th Anniv of Storming of United States Embassy.
2229 **670** 28r. multicoloured . . . 40 10

671 Avicenna and Globe

1983. International Medical Seminar, Teheran.
2230 **671** 3r. purple and blue . . . 20 10

672 Young and Old Soldiers

1983. Preparation Day.
2231 **672** 20r. green, black and red 55 20

673 Fist with Gun and Dove

1983. Saddam's Crimes Conference.
2232 **673** 5r. black and mauve . . 20 10

674 Dr. Mohammad Mofatteh

675 Light shining on Globe

1983. 4th Death Anniv of Dr. Mohammed Mofatteh.
2233 **674** 10r. mauve, black & gold 30 10

1983. Mohammed's Birth Anniv.
2234 **675** 5r. blue, brown and green 20 10

676 Tulips and Flag

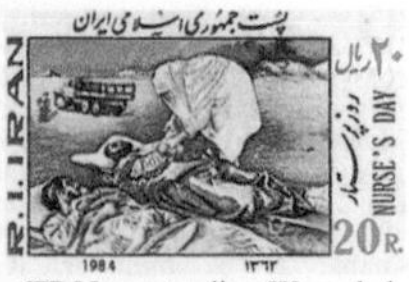
677 Nurse tending Wounded Soldier

1984. 5th Anniv of Islamic Revolution.
2235 **676** 10r. multicoloured . . . 30 10

1984. Nurses' Day.
2240 **677** 20r. multicoloured . . . 55 20

678 Soldier in Wheelchair

679 "Lotus gebelia"

1984. Invalids' Day.
2241 **678** 5r. multicoloured 20 10

1984. New Year Festival. Flowers. Multicoloured.
2242 3r. Type **679** 15 10
2243 5r. "Tulipa chrysantha" . . 25 10
2244 10r. "Glycyrrhiza glabra" 35 15
2245 20r. "Matthiola alyssifolia" 35 25

680 Malcolm Little (founder of Union of Moslem Mosques and Organization for African–American Unity)

1984. Struggle Against Racial Discrimination.
2246 **680** 5r. multicoloured 20 10

681 Flag around Globe

683 Harb

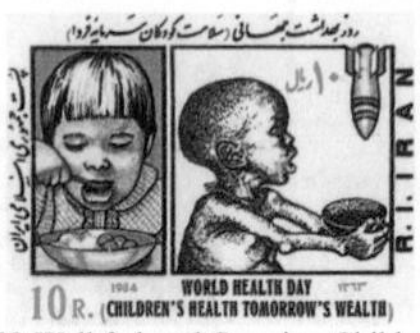
682 Well-fed and Starving Children

1984. 5th Anniv of Islamic Republic.
2247 **681** 5r. multicoloured 20 10

1984. World Health Day.
2248 **682** 10r. multicoloured . . . 30 15

1984. 22nd Death Anniv of Sheikh Ragheb Harb.
2249 **683** 5r. black, red and green 20 10

684 Family holding Red Crescent Banner

685 Transmitter

1984. World Red Cross and Red Crescent Day.
2250 **684** 5r. multicoloured 20 10

1984. World Telecommunications Day.
2251 **685** 20r. black, blue and red 30 10

686 Ghotb

688 Jerusalem, Map of Israel and Koran

687 Kaaba and Destruction of Images

1984. 19th Death Anniv of Seyyed Ghotb.
2252 **686** 10r. black, gold & orange 25 15

1984. Conquest of Mecca.
2253 **687** 5r. multicoloured 20 10

1984. World Jerusalem Day (5r.) and Fetr Feast (10r.). Multicoloured.
2254 5r. Type **688** 20 10
2255 10r. Crowd around mosque 30 20

689 Choga Zanbil, Susa

1984. Preservation of Cultural Heritage. Mult.
2256 5r. Type **689** 20 10
2257 5r. Emamzadeh Hossein shrine, Qazvin (Arabic date at left) 20 10
2258 5r. Imam Mosque, Isfahan 20 10
2259 5r. Ark Fortress, Tabriz . . 20 10
2260 5r. Prophet Daniel's Mausoleum, Susa (with conical tower) 20 10

691 Crowd around Kaaba **692** Spirit Nebula

1984. Feast of Sacrifices.
2261 **691** 10r. multicoloured . . . 25 15

1984. 10th International Trade Fair, Teheran.
2262 **692** 10r. blue and red 25 15

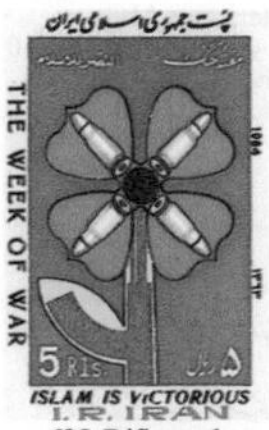

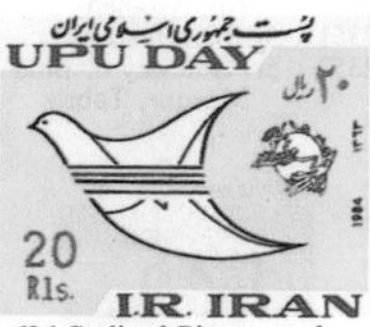

693 Rifle and Cartridges on Flower **694** Stylized Pigeon and U.P.U. Emblem

1984. War Week.
2263 **693** 5r. multicoloured 20 10

1984. World Universal Postal Union Day.
2264 **694** 20r. multicoloured . . . 45 30

695 Khomeini **696** Tabatabaie

1984. 7th Death Anniv of Haj Seyyed Mostafa Khomeini.
2265 **695** 5r. multicoloured 20 10

1984. Ghazi Tabatabaie Commemoration.
2266 **696** 5r. black, gold and red 20 10

697 Saadi **698** Clasped Hands, Mosque and Koran

1984. 800th Birth Anniv of Saadi (poet) Congress.
2267 **697** 10r. multicoloured . . . 25 15

1984. Mohammed's Birth Anniv and Unity Week.
2268 **698** 5r. multicoloured 20 10

699 Doves as Petals **700** Sapling and Forest

1985. 6th Anniv of Islamic Revolution (1st issue).
2269 **699** 40r. multicoloured (tulip emblem in red) . . . 60 35
2446 40r. multicoloured (tulip emblem in mauve) . . 75 45
See also No. 2277.

1985. Tree Planting Day. Multicoloured.
2270 3r. Type **700** 15 10
2271 5r. Sapling growing near forest 20 10

701 Crown Imperial ("Fritillaria imperialis") **702** Procession of Women with Flags

1985. New Year Festival. Multicoloured.
2272 5r. Type **701** 20 10
2273 5r. Pilewort ("Ranunculus ficarioides") 20 10
2274 5r. Saffron crocus ("Crocus sativus") 20 10
2275 5r. "Primula heterochroma" 20 10

1985. Women's Day and Birth Anniv of Fatima.
2276 **702** 10r. multicoloured . . . 25 15

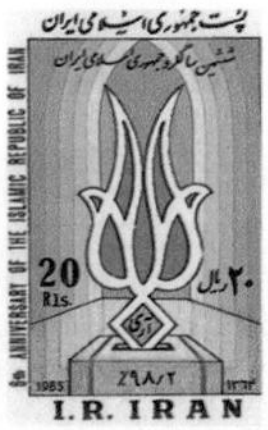

703 Tulip and Ballot Box

1985. 6th Anniv of Islamic Republic (2nd issue).
2277 **703** 20r. multicoloured . . . 50 30

704 Koran

1985. Mab'as Festival.
2278 **704** 10r. multicoloured . . . 25 15

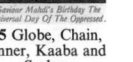

705 Globe, Chain, Banner, Kaaba and Scales **706** I.T.U. Emblem and Telephone Handsets

1985. World Day of the Oppressed.
2279 **705** 5r. multicoloured 20 10

1985. World Telecommunications Day.
2280 **706** 20r. multicoloured . . . 50 30

707 Soldier saluting and Bridge

1985. Liberation of Khorramshahr.
2281 **707** 5r. multicoloured 25 10

708 Fist, Rifles and Qum Theological College

1985. 22nd Anniv of 1963 Islamic Rising.
2282 **708** 10r. multicoloured . . . 25 15

709 Decorated Plates and Vases

1985. World Handicrafts Day.
2283 **709** 20r. multicoloured . . . 50 30

710 Map of Israel and Dome of the Rock **711** Arabic Script

1985. World Jerusalem Day.
2284 **710** 5r. multicoloured 20 10

1985. Fetr Feast.
2285 **711** 5r. blue, red and black 20 10

712 Organization Emblem

1985. 4th Anniv of Islamic Propagation Organization.
2286 **712** 5r. brown, green & black 20 10

713 Abdolhossein Amini and the Koran **714** Pilgrims around Holy Kaaba

1985. Ayatollah Sheikh Abdolhossein Amini (theologian) Commemoration.
2287 **713** 5r. multicoloured 20 10

1985. Pilgrimage to Mecca.
2288 **714** 10r. multicoloured . . . 30 15

715 Two Swords Pattern **716** Revolutionaries and Mosque

1985. Preservation of Cultural History. Ancient Ceramic Plates from Nishabur. Multicoloured.
2289 5r. Type **715** 20 10
2290 5r. Plate with border of Farsi script 20 10
2291 5r. Stylized bird pattern . . 20 10
2292 5r. Four leaves and knot pattern 20 10

1985. 50th Anniv of Rising in Goharshad Mosque, Meshed.
2293 **716** 10r. multicoloured . . . 30 15

717 Health Services **718** Red Tulips dripping Blood

1985. Government and People Week. Multicoloured.
2294 5r. Envelope, crane and mechanical digger 20 10
2295 5r. Factory, cogwheel and ear of wheat 20 10
2296 5r. Type **717** 20 10
2297 5r. Literacy campaign emblem on book 20 10

1985. 7th Anniv of "Bloody Friday" Riots.
2298 **718** 10r. multicoloured . . . 30 15

719 O.P.E.C. Emblem and "25" **720** Dead Iranian

1985. 25th Anniv of Organization of Petroleum Exporting Countries.
2299 **719** 5r. yellow and brown . . 20 10
2300 – 5r. blue and green . . . 20 10
DESIGN: No. 2300, O.P.E.C. emblem and world map.

1985. 5th Anniv of Iran–Iraq War. Multicoloured.
2301 5r. Type **720** 20 10
2302 5r. Dome of mosque and text "Ashura" 20 10
2303 5r. White doves with map of Iran under a hail of bombs 20 10
2304 5r. Oasis and exploding rifle 20 10

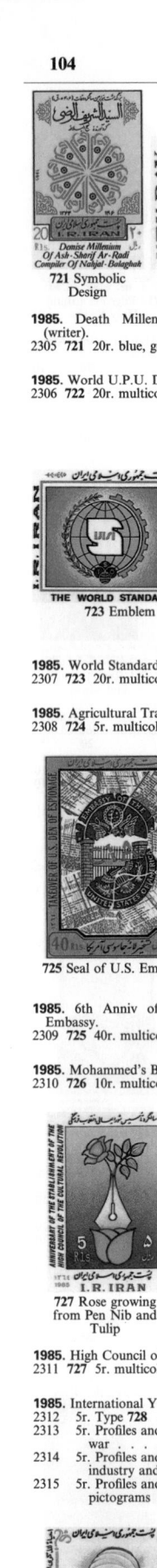

721 Symbolic Design

722 Envelopes and Posthorn

1985. Death Millenary of Ash-Sharif Ar-Radi (writer).
2305 **721** 20r. blue, gold & ultram 50 30

1985. World U.P.U. Day.
2306 **722** 20r. multicoloured . . . 50 30

723 Emblem

724 Seedling and Ear of Wheat in Hand

1985. World Standards Day.
2307 **723** 20r. multicoloured . . . 50 30

1985. Agricultural Training and Extension Year.
2308 **724** 5r. multicoloured 20 10

725 Seal of U.S. Embassy

726 Kaaba, Mosque and Clasped Hands

1985. 6th Anniv of Storming of United States Embassy.
2309 **725** 40r. multicoloured . . . 60 30

1985. Mohammed's Birth Anniv and Unity Week.
2310 **726** 10r. multicoloured . . . 30 15

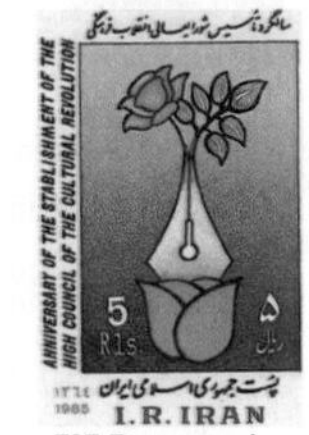
727 Rose growing from Pen Nib and Tulip

728 Profiles and Symbols of Learning

1985. High Council of Cultural Revolution Anniv.
2311 **727** 5r. multicoloured 20 10

1985. International Youth Year. Mult.
2312 5r. Type **728** 20 10
2313 5r. Profiles and symbols of war 20 10
2314 5r. Profiles and symbols of industry and agriculture 20 10
2315 5r. Profiles and sports pictograms 20 10

729 Ezzeddin Al-Qassam

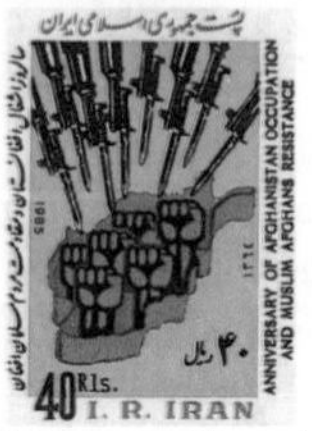
730 Bayonets, Map and Clenched Fists

1985. 50th Death Anniv of Ezzeddin Al-Qassam.
2316 **729** 20r. brown, red and silver 50 30

1985. Afghan Resistance to Occupation.
2317 **730** 40r. multicoloured . . . 75 40

731 Mirza Taqi Khan Amir Kabir

732 Tulips and Crowd destroying Statue

1986. 135th Death Anniv of Mirza Taqi Khan Amir Kabir.
2318 **731** 5r. multicoloured 20 15

1986. 7th Anniv of Islamic Revolution.
2319 **732** 20r. multicoloured . . . 60 35

733 Sulayman Khater and Dome of the Rock

1986. 40th Death Anniv of Sulayman Khater.
2320 **733** 10r. black, blue and red 30 15

734 Woman, Child and Crowd

735 "Papaver orientale"

1986. Women's Day and Birth Anniv of Fatima.
2321 **734** 10r. multicoloured . . . 30 15

1986. New Year Festival. Flowers. Mult.
2322 5r. Type **735** 20 10
2323 5r. "Anemone coronaria" 20 10
2324 5r. "Papaver bracteatum" 20 10
2325 5r. "Anemone biflora" . . . 20 10

736 Fist and Text

737 Rose, Globe and Coloured Bands

1986. "2000th Day of Sacred Defence" (Iran–Iraq war).
2326 **736** 5r. green and red 20 15

1986. Struggle against Racial Discrimination.
2327 **737** 5r. multicoloured 20 15

738 Iranian Flag and Map

1986. 7th Anniv of Islamic Republic.
2328 **738** 10r. multicoloured . . . 30 15

739 Dome

740 Insignia

1986. Mab'as Festival.
2329 **739** 40r. multicoloured . . . 50 25

1986. Army Day.
2330 **740** 5r. multicoloured 25 15

741 Dead Soldier and Wrecked Helicopter

742 Text

1986. 6th Anniv of United States Landing at Tabas.
2331 **741** 40r. orange, green & blk 90 40

1986. World Day of the Oppressed. Birth Anniv of Imam Mahdi.
2332 **742** 10r. black, red and gold 30 20

743 Symbolic Design

744 Antennae and Radio Waves

1986. Teachers' Day.
2333 **743** 5r. multicoloured 20 15

1986. World Communications Day.
2334 **744** 20r. black, silver and blue 60 35

745 Soldier and Tanks

1986. International Children's Day.
2335 **745** 15r. multicoloured . . . 40 30
2336 – 15r. black, blue & mauve 40 30
DESIGN: No. 2336, Boy and text.

746 Qum Theological College and Sun Rays

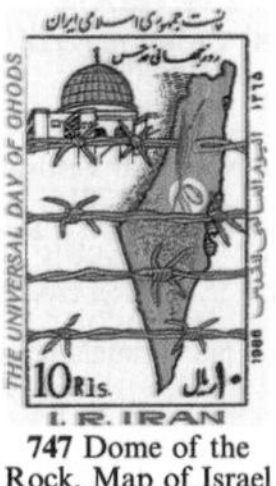
747 Dome of the Rock, Map of Israel and Barbed Wire

1986. 23rd Anniv of 1963 Islamic Rising.
2337 **746** 10r. multicoloured . . . 30 15

1986. World Jerusalem Day.
2338 **747** 10r. multicoloured . . . 40 15

748 Crowd at Prayer

1986. Fetr Festival.
2339 **748** 10r. multicoloured . . . 30 15

749 Baluchi Needle Work

1986. World Handicrafts Day. Multicoloured.
2340 10r. Type **749** 30 20
2341 10r. Master craftswomen at work 30 20
2342 10r. Carpet 30 20
2343 10r. Engraved copper vase 30 20

750 Linked Hands around Map on Globe

751 Dr. Beheshti, Doves and Explosion

1986. Solidarity with South African People.
2344 **750** 10r. multicoloured . . . 30 15

1986. 5th Anniv of Bomb Explosion at Islamic Party Headquarters, Teheran.
2345 **751** 10r. multicoloured . . . 30 15

752 Ayatollah Mohammad Taqi Shirazi and Map

753 Shrine, Meshed

1986. Iraqi Muslim Rising.
2346 **752** 20r. multicoloured . . . 50 30

1986. Birth Anniv of Imam Riza.
2347 **753** 10r. multicoloured . . . 30 15

754 Crowd around Kaaba, Flag and Clenched Fists

755 Soltanieh Mosque

1986. Feast of Sacrifices.
2348 **754** 10r. multicoloured . . . 30 15

1986. Preservation of Cultural Heritage. Mult.
2349 5r. Type **755** 20 10
2350 5r. Mausoleum of Sohel Ben Ali, Astaneh 20 10
2351 5r. Bam fortress 20 10
2352 5r. Gateway of Blue Mosque, Tabriz 20 10

756 "Eid-ul-Ghadir" in Arabic

757 Graph, Roof and People

1986. Ghadir Festival.
2353 **756** 20r. light green, green and black 50 30

1986. Population and Housing Census.
2354 **757** 20r. multicoloured . . . 50 30

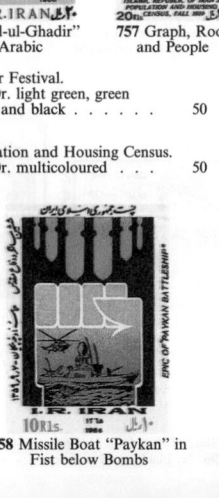

758 Missile Boat "Paykan" in Fist below Bombs

1986. 6th Anniv of Iran–Iraq War. Mult.
2355 **758** 10r. blue, black and red 55 15
2356 – 10r. red and black . . . 30 15
2357 – 10r. yellow, black and red 30 15
2358 – 10r. blue, black and red 30 15
2359 – 10r. green, black and red 30 15
DESIGNS: No. 2356, Khorramshar; 2357, Howeizah; 2358, Siege of Abadan; 2359, Susangard.

759 Wrestling

1986. 10th Asian Games, Seoul. Multicoloured.
2360 15r. Type **759** 35 20
2361 15r. Rifle shooting 35 20

760 Bird with Envelopes as Wings on Globe

1986. World Universal Postal Union Day.
2362 **760** 20r. multicoloured . . . 50 30

761 Emblem

762 Allameh Tabatabaie

1986. 40th Anniv of UNESCO.
2363 **761** 45r. blue, black and red 75 35

1986. 5th Death Anniv of Allameh Tabatabaie.
2364 **762** 10r. green, gold and black 20 15

763 Sun behind Dome and Minaret

764 Militiamen with Flags

1986. Mohammed's Birth Anniv and Unity Week.
2365 **763** 10r. multicoloured . . . 20 15

1986. "Mobilization of the Oppressed" Week.
2366 **764** 5r. multicoloured 20 15

765 Guerrilla Fighters

1986. Afghan Resistance to Occupation.
2367 **765** 40r. multicoloured . . . 65 30

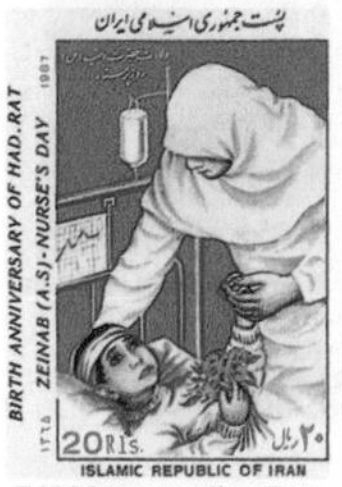
766 Nurse tending Boy

767 Emblem and Tulip on Globe

1987. Nurses' Day.
2368 **766** 20r. multicoloured . . . 50 30

1987. 5th Islamic Theology Conference, Teheran.
2369 **767** 20r. multicoloured . . . 50 30

768 Emblems of Revolution

1987. 8th Anniv of Islamic Revolution.
2370 **768** 20r. multicoloured (38 × 58 mm) 50 30
2444 20r. multicoloured (24 × 37 mm) 50 50

769 Emblem and Crowd

770 Woman and Soldiers

1987. 8th Anniv of Revolutionary Committees.
2371 **769** 10r. yellow, blue and red 30 15

1987. Women's Day and Birth Anniv of Fatima.
2372 **770** 10r. multicoloured . . . 30 15

771 Airbus Industrie A300 Aircraft and Banner around Globe

1987. 25th Anniv of Iranair.
2373 **771** 30r. multicoloured . . . 90 45

772 Ayatollah Naeini

773 Flag Irises

1987. 50th Death Anniv of Ayatollah Mirza Mohammad Hossein Naeini.
2374 **772** 10r. multicoloured . . . 30 15

1987. New Year Festival. Flowers. Mult.
2375 5r. Type **773** 20 10
2376 5r. Tulips 20 10
2377 5r. Dutch irises 20 10
2378 5r. Roses 20 10

774 Arabic Text and Arched Window

775 Flag as Star on Map

1987. Mab'as Festival.
2379 **774** 45r. lt green, grn & gold 70 35

1987. 8th Anniv of Islamic Republic.
2380 **775** 20r. multicoloured . . . 45 30

776 Soldiers with Flag

777 Emblems on Map and Dome of the Rock

1987. Revolutionary Guards' Day. Birth Anniv of Imam Hossein.
2381 **776** 5r. multicoloured 20 15

1987. Commemoration of Lebanese Hizbollah Dead.
2382 **777** 10r. red, green and grey 30 15

778 Child and Vaccination Dropper

779 Stars around Holy Kaaba

1987. World Health Day. Multicoloured.
2383 3r. Syringe and children . . 15 10
2384 5r. Type **778** 20 10

1987. World Day of the Oppressed. Birth Anniv of Imam Mahdi.
2385 **779** 20r. multicoloured . . . 50 30

780 Worker with Rifle and Koran, Factory and Cogwheel

781 Ayatollah Mottahari, Candle and Book

1987. International Labour Day.
2386 **780** 5r. multicoloured 20 15

1987. Teachers' Day.
2387 **781** 5r. red, yellow and blue 20 15

782 Map in Telephone Dial

783 12th-century Ceramic Lidded Pot, Rey

1987. World Telecommunications Day.
2388 **782** 20r. violet and blue . . . 50 30

1987. International Museums Day.
2389 **783** 20r. chestnut, brn & grey 50 30
2390 – 20r. brown, black & grn 50 30
DESIGN: No. 2390, Sassanian silver-gilt flower vase.

784 Dove, Globe and Dome of the Rock dripping Blood onto Star

785 Qum Theological College, Crown and Bayonets

1987. World Jerusalem Day.
2391 **784** 20r. multicoloured . . . 50 30

1987. 24th Anniv of 1963 Islamic Rising.
2392 **785** 20r. multicoloured . . . 50 30

786 Blown Glass

1987. World Crafts Day. Multicoloured.
2393 5r. Type **786** 20 10
2394 5r. Khatam marquetry . . . 20 10
2395 5r. Ceramic ware 20 10
2396 5r. Ceramic master-craftsman 20 10

787 Factory, Freighter and Dam

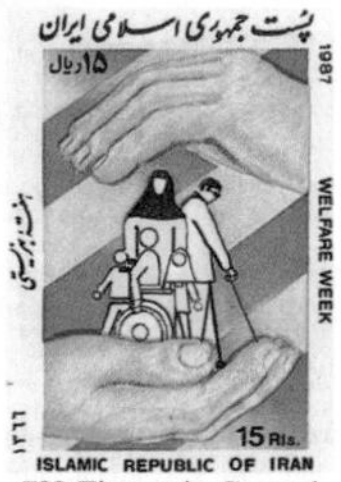
788 Figures in Cupped Hand

1987. Campaign against Tax Evasion.
2397 **787** 10r. gold, black and silver 30 15

1987. Welfare Week.
2398 **788** 15r. multicoloured . . . 35 25

789 Crowd around Mosque

1987. Feast of Sacrifices.
2399 **789** 12r. turquoise, sil & blk 35 20

790 Design from Mosque Tile

791 Hands clasped over National Emblem

1987. Ghadir Festival.
2400 **790** 18r. gold, green and black 45 30

1987. Islamic Banking Week.
2401 **791** 15r. brown, blue and gold 35 25

792 Typical Persian Calligraphy

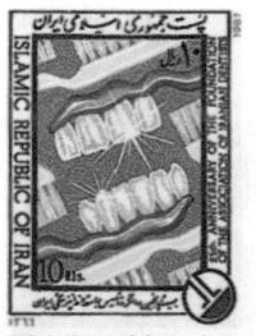
794 Toothbrushes as Mouths

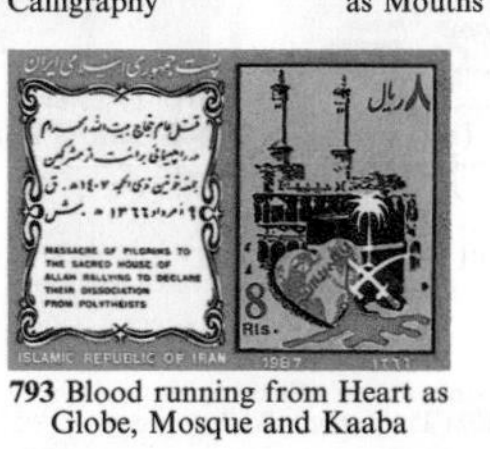
793 Blood running from Heart as Globe, Mosque and Kaaba

1987. 1st Iranian Calligraphers' Cultural and Artistic Congress.
2402 **792** 20r. multicoloured . . . 50 30

1987. Commemoration of Pilgrims killed at Mecca.
2403 **793** 8r. multicoloured 30 15

1987. 25th Anniv of Iranian Dentists Association.
2404 **794** 10r. multicoloured . . . 35 15

795 Dove with Globe as Eye

796 Rifleman and Armed Launch

1987. International Peace Day.
2405 **795** 20r. bronze and blue . . 50 30

1987. 7th Anniv of Iran–Iraq War.
2406 **796** 25r. green, blue and black 60 40
2407 – 25r. red, black and blue 60 40
DESIGN: No. 2407, Rifleman and soldiers.

797 Open Book on Crossed Pistols

798 People in Cupped Hands

1987. Police Day.
2408 **797** 10r. multicoloured . . . 50 20

1987. Int Social Security Co-operation Week.
2409 **798** 15r. black, blue and gold 35 25

799 Dove with Envelopes as Tail on Globe

800 American Flag, Great Seal and Capitol

1987. World Post Day. Multicoloured.
2410 15r. Type **799** 35 25
2411 15r. Dr. M. Ghandi (Postal Minister) commemoration 35 25

1987. 6th Anniv of Storming of United States Embassy.
2412 **800** 40r. multicoloured . . . 75 55

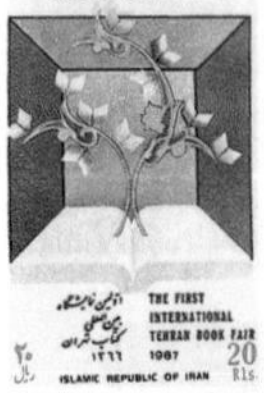

801 Tree growing from Open Book

802 Clasped Hands

1987. 1st Teheran Book Fair.
2413 **801** 20r. multicoloured . . . 50 30

1987. Mohammed's Birth Anniv and Unity Week.
2414 **802** 25r. brown, flesh & green 55 35

803 Ayatollah Modarres

804 Djameh Mosque, Urmia

1987. 50th Death Anniv of Ayatollah Seyyed Hassan Modarres.
2415 **803** 10r. brown and ochre . . 25 15

1987. Mosques.
2415a – 1r. orange and silver . . 10 10
2416 **804** 2r. mauve and silver . . 10 10
2416a – 3r. green and silver . . 10 10
2417 – 5r. red and silver . . . 15 10
2594 – 10r. blue and silver . . 15 10
2419 – 20r. violet and silver . . 35 20
2420 – 30r. red and silver . . . 45 25
2421 – 40r. blue and silver . . 55 30
2422 – 50r. brown and silver 90 40
2423 – 100r. green and silver 1·60 95
2602 – 200r. black and silver 3·00 1·75
2604 – 500r. green and silver 7·25 4·25
DESIGNS—HORIZ: 1r. Djameh Mosque, Schuschter; 3r. Djameh Mosque, Kerman; 5r. Qazvin; 10r. Veramin; 20r. Saveh; 40r. Shiraz; 100r. Hamadan. VERT: 30r. Natanz; 50r. Isfahan; 200r. Dizful; 500r. Yezd.

805 Open Book, Profiles and Ear of Wheat

1987. Agricultural Training and Extension Week.
2426 **805** 10r. multicoloured . . . 25 15

806 Guerrilla Fighters on Map

1987. Afghan Resistance to Occupation.
2427 **806** 40r. multicoloured . . . 75 55

807 Crowd with Banners

1988. 10th Anniv of Qum Uprising.
2428 **807** 20r. multicoloured . . . 50 30

808 Bombs and Pencils

809 Takhti and Mountain

1988. Iranian Schools Victims' Commemoration.
2429 **808** 10r. multicoloured . . . 25 15

1988. Victory of Gholamreza Takhti in World Freestyle Wrestling Championships.
2430 **809** 15r. multicoloured . . . 35 25

810 Woman carrying armed Man

811 Text

1988. Women's Day and Birth Anniv of Fatima.
2431 **810** 20r. multicoloured . . . 50 30

1988. 9th Anniv of Islamic Revolution.
2447 **811** 40r. multicoloured . . . 75 45

812 Crowd burning Statue

1988. 10th Anniv of Tabriz Uprising.
2448 **812** 25r. multicoloured . . . 60 35

813 Tree in Hand

814 "Anthemis hyalina"

1988. Tree Day.
2449 **813** 15r. multicoloured . . . 35 25

1988. New Year Festival. Flowers. Mult.
2450 10r. Type **814** 25 15
2451 10r. Common mallows . . . 25 15
2452 10r. Violets 25 15
2453 10r. "Echium amaenum" . . 25 15

815 Hand putting Ballot Paper into Box

1988. 9th Anniv of Islamic Republic.
2454 **815** 20r. multicoloured . . . 50 30

816 Calligraphy

1988. World Day of the Oppressed. Birth Anniv of Imam Mahdi.
2455 **816** 20r. brown and blue . . 50 30

817 Shahid Mottahari Mosque and Theology School, Teheran

1988. Preservation of Cultural Heritage. Multicoloured.
2456 10r. Type **817** 25 15
2457 10r. Colonnade of Tarikhaneh Mosque, Damghan 25 15
2458 10r. Gateway of Sepahdari Mosque and Theology School, Arak (horiz) . . . 25 15
2459 10r. Agha Bozorg Mosque and Theology School, Kashan (courtyard with pool) (horiz) 25 15

818 Bomb, Gas Cloud and Victims

1988. Halabja Chemical Attack Victims' Commemoration.
2460 **818** 20r. multicoloured . . . 50 30

819 Map, Dome of the Rock and Palestinian

820 Satellite and Telephone Handset

1988. Palestinian "Intifida" Movement. Each brown, red and black.
2461 10r. Type **819** 30 15
2462 10r. Man with rounded beard 30 15
2463 10r. Man wearing crew-necked jumper 30 15
2464 10r. Man with long pointed beard 30 15
2465 10r. Crowd and hand holding stone 30 15

1988. World Telecommunications Day.
2466 **820** 20r. blue and green . . . 50 30

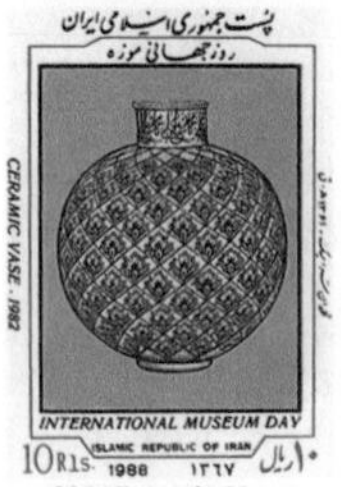

821 Ceramic Vase

822 Miners pushing Coal Truck

1988. International Museum Day. Multicoloured.
2467 10r. Type **821** 25 15
2468 10r. Iran Bastan Museum porch 25 15
2469 10r. 14th-century Tabriz silk rug 25 15
2470 10r. 7th-century B.C. gold ring, Arjan, Behbahan . . 25 15

1988. Mining Day.
2471 **822** 20r. multicoloured . . . 3·25 90

823 Children playing by River

824 Bleeding Dove and Broken Bayonets

1988. International Children's Day.
2472 **823** 10r. multicoloured . . . 30 15

1988. 25th Anniv of 1963 Islamic Rising.
2473 **824** 10r. multicoloured . . . 30 15

825 Glim Weaving

826 Child in Flower

1988. World Handicrafts Day. Multicoloured.

2474	10r. Type **825**	25	15
2475	10r. Miniature of horsemen	25	15
2476	10r. Glim weaver (horiz)	25	15
2477	10r. Straw basket (horiz)	25	15

1988. Child Health Campaign.
2478 **826** 20r. blue, green and black 35 20

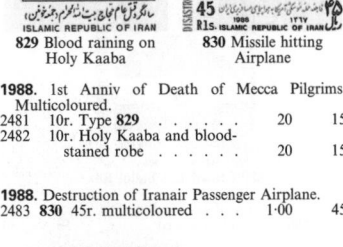

827 Symbols of Industry and Agriculture

828 Balkhi

1988. Campaign Against Tax Evasion.
2479 **827** 20r. gold, blue and silver 35 20

1988. Allameh Balkhi (Afghan revolutionary writer) Commemoration.
2480 **828** 20r. black, red and silver 35 20

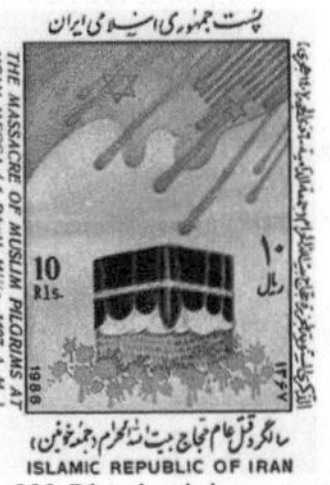
829 Blood raining on Holy Kaaba

830 Missile hitting Airplane

1988. 1st Anniv of Death of Mecca Pilgrims. Multicoloured.

2481	10r. Type **829**	20	15
2482	10r. Holy Kaaba and blood-stained robe	20	15

1988. Destruction of Iranair Passenger Airplane.
2483 **830** 45r. multicoloured . . . 1·00 45

831 Seyyed Ali Andarzgou

832 Central Bank, Teheran

1988. 10th Death Anniv of Seyyed Ali Andarzgou (revolutionary).
2484 **831** 20r. blue, black & brown 35 20

1988. Islamic Banking Week.
2485 **832** 20r. grey, brown and gold 35 20

833 Carrying away Victim

834 Weightlifting

1988. 10th Anniv of "Bloody Friday" Riots.
2486 **833** 25r. green, purple and red 45 25

1988. Olympic Games, Seoul. Multicoloured.

2487	10r. Type **834**	20	15
2488	10r. Men's gymnastics	20	15
2489	10r. Judo	20	15
2490	10r. Football	20	15
2491	10r. Wrestling	20	15

835 Plant

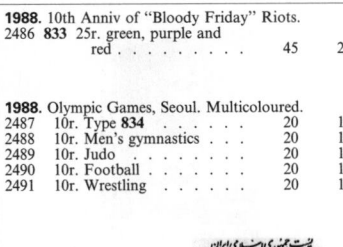

836 Iranians and Rifle

1988. Agricultural Census.
2492 **835** 30r. yellow, black & grn 50 35

1988. 8th Anniv of Iran–Iraq War.
2493 **836** 20r. multicoloured . . . 35 20

837 Envelopes around Globe

1988. World Post Day.
2494 **837** 20r. green, black and blue 35 20

838 Child's Face and Profiles

1988. Parents' and Teachers' Co-operation Week.
2495 **838** 20r. multicoloured . . . 35 20

839 Clasped Hands and Emblem

1988. Mohammed's Birth Anniv and Unity Week.
2496 **839** 10r. multicoloured . . . 20 15

840 Fist and Shattered Eagle

841 Tree as Umbrella

1988. 7th Anniv of Storming of United States Embassy.
2497 **840** 45r. multicoloured . . . 75 45

1988. Insurance Day.
2498 **841** 10r. multicoloured . . . 20 15

842 Tomb of Hafiz

1988. International Hafiz (writer) Congress, Shiraz.
2499 **842** 20r. blue, gold and mauve 35 20

843 Agricultural Symbols on Open Book

1988. Agricultural Training and Extension Week.
2500 **843** 15r. multicoloured . . . 30 15

844 Parvin Etessami (writer)

1988. Iranian Celebrities of Science, Art and Literature. Multicoloured.

2501	10r. Type **844**	20	15
2502	10r. Qaem Maqam Farahani (writer)	20	15
2503	10r. Kamal al-Molk (artist)	20	15
2504	10r. Jalal al-Ahmad (writer)	20	15
2505	10r. Dr. Mohammad Mo'in (writer)	20	15

845 Map and Armed Afghan

1988. Afghan Resistance to Occupation.
2506 **845** 40r. multicoloured . . . 75 45

846 Satellite, Envelopes and Dish Aerial

847 Tulips and Script

1989. Asian and Pacific Transport and Communications Decade. Multicoloured.

2507	20r. Type **846**	45	30
2508	20r. Air transport	45	30
2509	20r. Road and rail transport	1·75	60
2510	20r. Shipping	65	30

1989. Air. 10th Anniv of Islamic Revolution.

2511 **847**	40r. mauve, gold & black	80	55
2512	50r. violet, gold and black	80	55

848 Sun illuminating Koran

1989. Mab'as Festival.
2513 **848** 20r. multicoloured . . . 35 25

849 Hands protecting Tree

1989. Tree Day.
2514 **849** 20r. multicoloured . . . 35 25

850 "Cephalanthera kurdica"

851 Wind Gauge and Wheat

1989. New Year Festival. Flowers. Mult.

2515	10r. Type **850**	20	15
2516	10r. "Dactylorhiza romana"	20	15
2517	10r. "Comperia comperiana"	20	15
2518	10r. "Orchis mascula"	20	15

1989. World Meteorological Day. Mult.

2519	20r. Type **851**	40	25
2520	30r. Wind gauge, airplane and weather ship	80	35

852 State Arms

853 Refinery

1989. 10th Anniv of Islamic Republic.
2521 **852** 20r. multicoloured . . . 35 25

1989. Commissioning of First Phase of Abadan Oil Refinery.
2522 **853** 20r. multicoloured . . . 40 25

854 Mottahari

856 Satellite, Globe and Dish Aerial

855 Dome of the Rock and Barbed Wire

1989. Teachers' Day. 10th Death Anniv of Ayatollah Mottahari.
2523 **854** 20r. multicoloured . . . 35 25

1989. World Jerusalem Day.
2524 **855** 30r. multicoloured . . . 60 35

1989. World Telecommunications Day.
2525 **856** 20r. multicoloured . . . 40 25

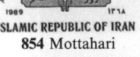

857 Jar

858 Armed Men, Tent and Family with Sheep

1989. International Museums Day. 6th-century Gurgan Artefacts.
2526 **857** 20r. yellow, blue & black 40 25
2527 – 20r. blue, black & mauve 40 25
DESIGN: No. 2527, Flagon.

1989. Nomads' Day.
2528 **858** 20r. multicoloured . . . 35 20

859 Man engraving Vase

1989. World Crafts Day. Multicoloured.
2529 20r. Type **859** 35 25
2530 20r. Engraved copper vase 35 25
2531 20r. Engraved copper plate (vert) 35 25
2532 20r. Engraved copper wall-hanging (vert) 35 25

860 Khomeini and Crowd

861 Pasteur, Avicenna and Hand holding Quill

1989. Ayatollah Khomeini Commemoration.
2533 **860** 20r. orange, black and blue (postage) 40 20
2534 – 70r. blk, vio & gold (air) 1·10 70
DESIGN—HORIZ: 70r. Ayatollah Khomeini.

1989. "Philexfrance 89" International Stamp Exhibition, Paris. Each black, blue and brown, background colour given.
2535 **861** 30r. blue 50 35
2536 50r. brown 75 55

862 Map and Satellite

1989. 10th Anniv of Asia–Pacific Telecommunity.
2537 **862** 30r. orange, black & blue 50 30

863 Araghi

1989. 10th Death Anniv of Mehdi Araghi.
2538 **863** 20r. orange and purple 35 20

864 Shahryar and Monument

1989. Mohammed Hossein Shahryar (poet) Commemoration.
2539 **864** 20r. multicoloured . . . 35 20

865 U.N. Security Council Document

1989. 9th Anniv of Iran–Iraq War.
2540 **865** 20r. multicoloured . . . 35 20

866 Khomeini addressing Crowd

1989. Ayatollah Khomeini.
2541 – 1r. multicoloured 10 10
2542 – 2r. multicoloured 10 10
2543 **866** 3r. multicoloured 10 10
2544 – 5r. multicoloured 25 10
2545 – 10r. multicoloured . . . 60 10
2546 – 20r. multicoloured . . . 35 10
2547 – 30r. multicoloured . . . 50 30
2548 – 40r. multicoloured . . . 65 50
2549 – 50r. multicoloured . . . 80 50
2550 – 70r. multicoloured . . . 1·10 65
2551 – 100r. ultram, bl & grn 1·60 95
2552 – 200r. brown, yell & grn 3·00 1·50
2553 – 500r. multicoloured . . 7·50 4·00
2554 – 1000r. multicoloured . . 15·00 8·25
DESIGNS: 1r. Rose and courtyard; 2r. Khomeini as young man; 5r. Khomeini going into exile; 10r. Khomeini's return from exile; 20r. Khomeini making speech; 30r. Boy kissing Khomeini; 40r. Ayatollahs; 50r. Khomeini; 70r. Meeting in house; 100r. Arabic inscription; 200r. Microphones and chair; 500r. Qum Mosque and roses; 1000r. Sun's rays.

867 Pigeon carrying Letter

1989. World Post Day.
2561 **867** 20r. multicoloured . . . 35 20

868 Multi-pointed Star in Window Arch

869 U.S. Emblem and Crowd in Dove

1989. Mohammed's Birth Anniv and Unity Week.
2562 **868** 10r. multicoloured . . . 15 10

1989. 8th Anniv of Storming of United States Embassy.
2563 **869** 40r. orange, black & blue 65 40

870 Iranian and Launch with Machine Gun

1989. 10th Anniv of People's Militia.
2564 **870** 10r. multicoloured . . . 30 15

871 Mehdi Elahi Ghomshei

1989. Iranian Celebrities of Science, Art and Literature.
2565 **871** 10r. red, black and gold 15 10
2566 – 10r. green, black and gold 15 10
2567 – 10r. yellow, black & gold 15 10
2568 – 10r. green, black and gold 15 10
2569 – 10r. mauve, black & gold 15 10
DESIGNS: No. 2566, Grand Ayatollah Seyyed Hossein Boroujerdi; 2567, Grand Ayatollah Sheikh Abdulkarim Haeri; 2568, Dr. Abdulazim Gharib; 2569, Seyyed Hossein Mirkhani.

872 Guiding Child's Hand

873 Book as Profiles forming Flower

1990. International Literacy Year.
2570 **872** 20r. multicoloured . . . 35 20

1990. Identity Cards.
2571 **873** 10r. multicoloured . . . 15 10

874 Drinking Vessel

1990. Cultural Heritage.
2572 **874** 20r. black and orange . . 35 20
2573 – 20r. black and green . . 35 20
DESIGN: No. 2563, Vase with stem.

875 Crowd

1990. 11th Anniv of Islamic Revolution.
2574 **875** 50r. multicoloured . . . 80 50

876 Emblem

877 Soldier in Wheelchair

1990. Int Koran Recitation Competition.
2575 **876** 10r. black, blue and green 15 10

1990. Invalids' Day.
2576 **877** 10r. multicoloured . . . 15 10

878 Figures encircling Tree

879 "Coronilla varia"

1990. Tree Day.
2577 **878** 20r. multicoloured . . . 35 20

1990. New Year Festival. Flowers. Multicoloured.
2578 10r. Type **879** 15 10
2579 10r. "Astragalus cornucaprae" 15 10
2580 10r. "Astragalus obtusifolius" 15 10
2581 10r. "Astragalus straussii" 15 10

880 Crowd and Ballot Box

1990. 11th Anniv of Islamic Republic.
2582 **880** 30r. multicoloured . . . 50 30

881 Flower growing from Globe

1990. World Health Day.
2583 **881** 40r. multicoloured . . . 65 40

882 Khomeini

1990. 1st Death Anniv of Ayatollah Khomeini.
2584 **882** 50r. multicoloured . . . 80 50

883 Turkoman Jewellery

1990. World Handicrafts Day. Multicoloured.
2585 20r. Type **883** 35 20
2586 50r. Gilded-steel bird . . . 80 50

884 Crayons

885 Seismograph on Map and Red Crescent Camp

1990. International Children's Day.
2587 **884** 20r. multicoloured . . . 35 20

1990. Aid for Earthquake Victims.
2588 **885** 100r. multicoloured . . . 1·60 95

886 P.O.W. and Roses

887 Ayatollah Khomeini and Dome of the Rock

1990. Returned Prisoners of War.
2589 **886** 250r. multicoloured . . . 3·75 2·00

1990. World Jerusalem Day.
2590 **887** 100r. multicoloured . . . 1·60 95

888 Arabic Script

1990. International Congress on Abu-l Kasim Mansur Firdausi (poet). 16 sheets as T **888**, each 60 × 75 mm. Multicoloured (except T**888**).
MS2591 16 sheets. (a) 100r. black, gold and silver (Type **888**); (b) Arabic script in cartouches within floral frame; (c) 100r. Arabic script in rectangles; (d) 100r. Portrait of Firdausi; (e) 100r. Statue of Firdausi, Tehran; (f) 100r. Tomb, Tuss; (g) 200r. Shackled man and miners; (h) 200r. Assault on man; (i) 200r. Hunters in forest; (j) 200r. Horesman riding through flames; (k) 200r. Phoenix, boy and archer; (l) 200r. Domestic scene; (m) 200r. White elephant trampling fallen men; (n) 200r. Archer in cage surrounded by birds; (o) 200r. Sleeping archer, demon and horse; (p) 200r. Horesmen greeting each other . . . . 42·00 42·00
The 200r. values illustrate Firdausi's works.

889 Flowers, Crowd and Khomeini

1991. 12th Anniv of Islamic Revolution.
2605 **889** 100r. multicoloured . . . 1·60 95

890 11th-century Gold Jug

1991. International Museum Day. Multicoloured.
2606 50r. Type **890** 80 50
2607 50r. 14th-century silver-inlaid brass basin 80 50

891 Flowers and Fists

892 Museum

1991. 11th Anniv of Iran–Iraq War.
2608 **891** 100r. multicoloured . . . 1·60 95

1991. Inauguration of Post Museum, Teheran.
2609 **892** 200r. brown and black 3·25 2·00

893 Headset on Globe

894 "Iris spuria"

1991. World Telecommunications Day (1990).
2610 **893** 50r. multicoloured . . . 80 50

1991. New Year Festival. Irises. Multicoloured.
2611 20r. Type **894** 35 20
2612 20r. "Iris lycotis" 35 20
2613 20r. "Iris demawendica" . . 35 20
2614 20r. "Iris meda" 35 20

895 Map, Dome of the Rock and Hosseini

897 Revolutionaries

896 Light Beam on Mountains

1991. 10th Death Anniv of Saleh Hosseini.
2615 **895** 30r. red and black . . . 50 30

1991. Mab'as Festival.
2616 **896** 100r. multicoloured . . . 1·60 95

1991. 25th Death Anniv (1990) of Revolutionaries.
2617 **897** 50r. brown and orange 80 50

898 Arabic Script

1991. World Day of the Oppressed. Birth Anniv of Mahdi.
2618 **898** 50r. multicoloured . . . 80 50

899 Crowd, Flag and Ballot Box

1991. 12th Anniv of Islamic Republic.
2619 **899** 20r. multicoloured . . . 35 20

900 Map and Bayonets

901 Mother and Child

1991. World Jerusalem Day.
2620 **900** 100r. multicoloured . . . 1·60 95

1991. Women's Day and Birth Anniv of Fatima.
2621 **901** 50r. multicoloured . . . 80 50

902 Boroujerdi

903 Disasters

1991. 30th Death Anniv of Ayatollah Boroujerdi.
2622 **902** 200r. black and green . . 3·25 2·00

1991. International Decade for Natural Disaster Reduction.
2623 **903** 100r. multicoloured . . . 2·00 1·10

904 Book, Candle and Dr. Mottahari

1991. Teachers' Day.
2624 **904** 50r. yellow, orange & blk 80 50

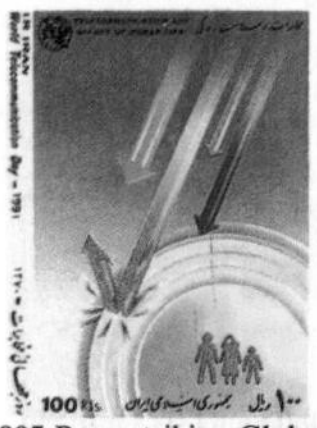
905 Rays striking Globe

906 Mausoleum, Meshed

1991. World Telecommunications Day. "Telecommunications and Safety of Human Life".
2625 **905** 100r. multicoloured . . . 1·60 95

1991. Birth Anniv of Imam Riza. Multicoloured.
2626 10r. Type **906** 15 10
2627 30r. Tombstone 50 30

907 Khomeini

1991. 2nd Death Anniv of Ayatollah Khomeini.
2628 **907** 100r. multicoloured . . . 1·60 95

908 Karbala Shrine

1991. Iraqi Attack on Shi'ite Shrine, Karbala.
2629 **908** 70r. multicoloured . . . 1·10 65

909 Nisami

1991. 900th Birth Anniv of Nisami (writer) International Congress, Tabris.
2630 **909** 50r. multicoloured . . . 80 50

910 Archway

1991. 1330th Death Anniv of Ali ibn Ali Talib (Caliph).
2631 **910** 50r. multicoloured . . . 80 50

911 Hands reaching through Parched Earth to Blood Drop

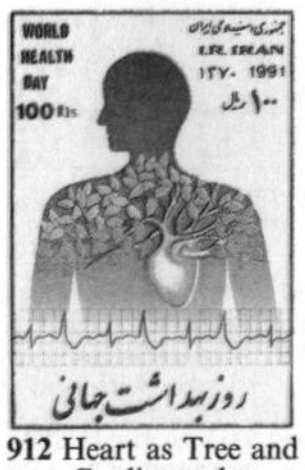
912 Heart as Tree and Cardiograph

1991. Blood Donation.
2632 **911** 50r. multicoloured . . . 80 50

1991. World Health Day.
2633 **912** 100r. multicoloured . . . 1·60 95

913 Nedjefi

1991. Marashi Nedjefi Commemoration.
2634 **913** 30r. multicoloured . . . 50 30

914 Doves flying from Cage

1991. 1st Anniv of Return of Prisoners of War.
2635 **914** 100r. multicoloured . . . 1·60 95

915 Engraved Brassware

1991. World Crafts Day. Multicoloured.
2636 40r. Type **915** 65 40
2637 40r. Gilded samovar 65 40

916 Ayatollah Lari

1991.
2638 **916** 30r. multicoloured . . . 50 30

917 Fist and Roses in Cartouche **918** Islamic Symbols

1991. 11th Anniv of Iran–Iraq War.
2639 **917** 20r. multicoloured . . . 35 20

1991. Islamic Unity Week.
2640 **918** 30r. multicoloured . . . 50 30

919 13th-century Kashan Ewer **920** Gharib

1991. International Museum Day. Multicoloured.
2641 20r. Type **919** 35 20
2642 40r. 13th-century Kashan ewer with bird's head lip 65 40

1991. Dr. Mohammed Gharib.
2643 **920** 100r. black and blue . . 1·60 95

921 Banners **922** Stamped Envelope

1991. Liberation of Khorramshahr.
2644 **921** 30r. multicoloured . . . 50 30

1991. World Post Day.
2645 **922** 70r. multicoloured . . . 1·10 65

923 Khaju-Ye Kermani

1991. International Congress on Khaju-Ye Kermani (writer).
2646 **923** 30r. multicoloured . . . 50 30

924 Globe and Seismograph **925** Cogwheel, Grain, Tree, Figures and Globe

1991. 1st International Seismology and Earthquake Engineering Conference.
2647 **924** 100r. multicoloured . . . 1·60 95

1991. World Food Day.
2648 **925** 80r. multicoloured . . . 1·25 75

926 Conference Emblem **927** Green Woodpecker and Flower Decoration

1991. Palestinian Peoples Conference.
2649 **926** 40r. gold and violet . . . 65 40

1991. 1st Asian Biennial Exhibition of Children's Book Illustrations.
2650 **927** 100r. multicoloured . . . 2·25 80

928 Script and Emblem **929** Festival Award

1991. Children's Book Fair, Teheran.
2651 **928** 20r. multicoloured . . . 35 20

1991. Roshd International Educational Film Festival.
2652 **929** 50r. multicoloured . . . 80 50

930 Meeting Emblem **932** Child throwing Stone at Star of David

931 Militia Members

1991. 7th Ministerial Meeting of Group of 77.
2653 **930** 30r. green and violet . . 50 30

1991. People's Militia Week.
2654 **931** 30r. multicoloured . . . 50 30

1991. World Children's Day.
2655 **932** 50r. multicoloured . . . 80 50

933 Globe and Doves

1991. World Tourism Day.
2656 **933** 200r. black, mauve & bl 3·00 1·60

934 Emblems **935** Trees, Hand, Water and Wheat

1991. World Standards Day.
2657 **934** 100r. multicoloured . . . 1·60 95

1991. Agricultural Training Week.
2658 **935** 70r. multicoloured . . . 1·10 65

936 Araf Hosseini **938** Revolutionary Scenes

937 Sadegh Ghanji

1992.
2659 **936** 50r. multicoloured . . . 55 35

1992.
2660 **937** 50r. multicoloured . . . 55 35

1992. 13th Anniv of Islamic Revolution. Mult.
2661 30r. Type **938** 35 20
2662 50r. Revolutionary scenes (different) 55 35

939 Members' Flags

1992. Economic Co-operation Organization Summit, Teheran.
2663 **939** 200r. multicoloured . . . 2·25 1·40

940 Seyd Abbas Musawi (Hezbollah Secretary-General) and Dome of the Rock **941** Planets, Satellite, Globe and Mobile Dish Aerial

1992. World Jerusalem Day.
2664 **940** 200r. multicoloured . . . 2·25 1·40

1992. World Meteorological Day.
2665 **941** 100r. multicoloured . . . 1·10 75

942 Badshahi Mosque, Lahore, Pakistan **943** Ayatollah Khomeini Voting

1992. South and West Asia Postal Union. Multicoloured.
2666 50r. Type **942** 60 35
2667 50r. Imam's Mosque, Isfahan 60 35
2668 50r. St. Sophia's, Istanbul, Turkey 60 35

1992. 13th Anniv of Islamic Republic.
2669 **943** 50r. multicoloured . . . 60 35

944 Embraer Bandeirante and Crates

1992. Establishment of Postal Air Service.
2670 **944** 60r. multicoloured . . . 80 45

945 Hands holding Trees **946** Tulips

1992. National Resources Week.
2671 **945** 100r. multicoloured . . . 1·10 75

1992. New Year Festival. Flowers. Multicoloured.
2672 20r. Type **946** 40 25
2673 20r. Rose 40 25
2674 40r. Orange blossom 50 30
2675 40r. Yellow jasmine 50 30

947 Members' Flags

1992. Economic Co-operation Organization.
2676 **947** 20r. multicoloured . . . 40 25

948 Morse Apparatus

1992. World Telecommunications Day. Mult.

2677	20r. Type **948**	40	25
2678	20r. Telegraph poles and wires	40	25
2679	20r. Old wall and candlestick telephones . .	40	25
2680	40r. Dish aerials	50	30
2681	40r. Satellite and Earth . .	50	30

Nos. 2677/81 were issued together, se-tenant, forming a composite design.

949 Sabzevari

950 Emblem

1992. Science, Art and Literature. Multicoloured.

2682	50r. Type **949**	60	35
2683	50r. Madjlessi (in turban)	60	35
2684	50r. Arabic script by Mir Emad	60	35
2685	50r. Samani (in fez)	60	35

1992. 21st Near East Regional Conference Session of F.A.O., Teheran.

2686 **950**	40r. green, blue and black	50	25

951 Globe, Equipment and Charts

952 Palm Trees

1992. International Surveying and Mapping Conf.

2687 **951**	40r. multicoloured . . .	50	25

1992. 2nd Anniv of Unification of Yemen.

2688 **952**	50r. multicoloured . . .	60	35

953 Dome of the Rock, Oasis and Child

1992. World Children's Day.

2689 **953**	50r. multicoloured . . .	50	30

954 Khomeini

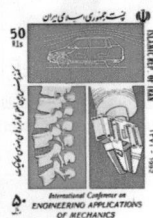

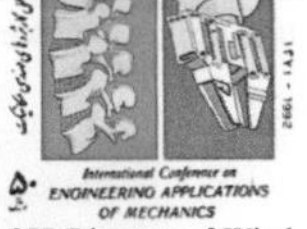
955 Diagram of Wind Tunnel Test, Section of Spine and Robot Hand

1992. 3rd Death Anniv of Ayatollah Khomeini.

2690 **954**	100r. multicoloured . . .	1·10	70

1992. International Engineering Applications of Mechanics Conference, Teheran.

2691 **955**	50r. multicoloured . . .	50	30

956 Building and Books

1992. Hajia Nosrat Baygom Amin Mo'in (lawyer) Commemoration.

2692 **956**	20r. multicoloured . . .	35	20

957 Emblem and Iranian Flag

958 ESCAP Emblem

1992. 6th Non-aligned News Agencies Pool Conference, Teheran.

2693 **957**	100r. multicoloured . . .	1·10	70

1992. Meeting of Economic and Social Commission for Asia and the Pacific Industry and Technology Ministers.

2694 **958**	100r. green, gold & black	1·10	70

959 Drugs in Hand

961 Khomeini winding Turban

960 Ceramic Bowl, Neyshabour City

1992. World Anti-drugs Day.

2695 **959**	100r. multicoloured . . .	1·00	60

1992. International Museum Day. Multicoloured.

2696	40r. Type **960**	45	25
2697	40r. Ceramic vessel, Shahroud City	45	25

1992. Prayers of Ayatollah Khomeini (1st series). Multicoloured.

2698	50r. Type **961**	50	30
2699	50r. Mosque and Khomeini	50	30
2700	50r. Khomeini	50	30

See also Nos. 2701/2 and 2703.

962 Arabic Script

1992. Prayers of Ayatollah Khomeini (2nd series).

2701 **962**	50r. turquoise and blue	50	30
2702 –	50r. yellow and green . .	50	30

DESIGN: No. 2702, Arabic script (different).

963 Kaaba

965 Arabic Script

964 Tanker

1992. Prayers of Ayatollah Khomeini (3rd series).

2703 **963**	50r. multicoloured . . .	50	30

1992. 25th Anniv of Iranian Shipping Lines.

2704 **964**	200r. multicoloured . . .	2·50	1·50

1992. Mohammed's Birth Anniv and Unity Week.

2705 **965**	40r. multicoloured . . .	40	25

966 Soldiers and Sun

968 Foundry and Steel Products

967 Patient and Doctor

1992. 12th Anniv of Iran–Iraq War. Multicoloured.

2706	20r. Type **966**	30	20
2707	40r. Soldier on riverbank (horiz)	40	20

1992. International History of Medicine in Islam and Iran Congress. Multicoloured.

2708	20r. Type **967**	30	20
2709	40r. Medical instruments . .	40	20

Nos. 2708/9 were issued together, se-tenant, forming a composite design.

1992. Steel Industry. Multicoloured.

2710	20r. Type **968**	30	20
2711	70r. Steel products and steel works	70	35

Nos. 2710/11 were issued together, se-tenant, forming a composite design.

969 Isfahan

1992. World Tourism Day. Multicoloured.

2712	20r. Type **969**	30	20
2713	20r. Mazandaran	30	20
2714	30r. Bushehr	45	25
2715	30r. Hormozgan	45	25

970 Map and Flags

1992. International Trade Fair.

2716 **970**	200r. multicoloured . . .	2·00	1·25

971 Early Post Office Service

1992. World Post Day.

2717 **971**	30r. brown and violet . .	50	30

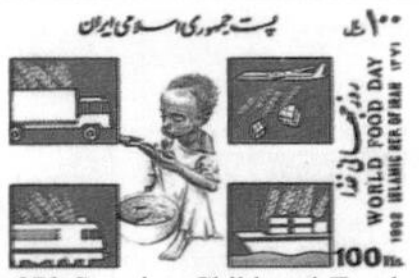
972 Starving Child and Food Distribution

1992. World Food Day.

2718 **972**	100r. multicoloured . . .	3·50	1·25

973 Child drawing

974 Flames and Child's Face

1992. International Children's and Youth Photographic Festival.

2719 **973**	40r. multicoloured . . .	65	35

1992. Bosnia and Herzegovina.

2720 **974**	40r. multicoloured . . .	55	35

975 Storming Embassy, Doves and Crow

976 Emblem

1992. Multicoloured.

2721	100r. Type **975** (11th anniv of storming of U.S. Embassy)	1·00	50
2722	100r. Soldiers, crows and doves (Students' Day) . .	1·00	50
2723	100r. Ayatollah Khomeini, crows and doves (13th anniv of Khomeini's return from exile)	1·00	50

Nos. 2721/3 were issued together, se-tenant, forming a composite design.

1992. 17th Annual Meeting of Islamic Development Bank Board of Governors.

2724 **976**	20r. multicoloured . . .	25	15

977 Flags and Dish Aerials on Maps

1992. Azerbaijan–Iran Telecommunications Co-operation.

2725 **977**	40r. multicoloured . . .	55	35

978 Star

1992. 10th Anniv of Islamic University.

2726 **978**	200r. green & deep green	2·00	1·25

979 Soldiers in Armed Motor Boat

1992. People's Militia Week.

2727 **979**	40r. multicoloured . . .	55	35

980 Shahryar

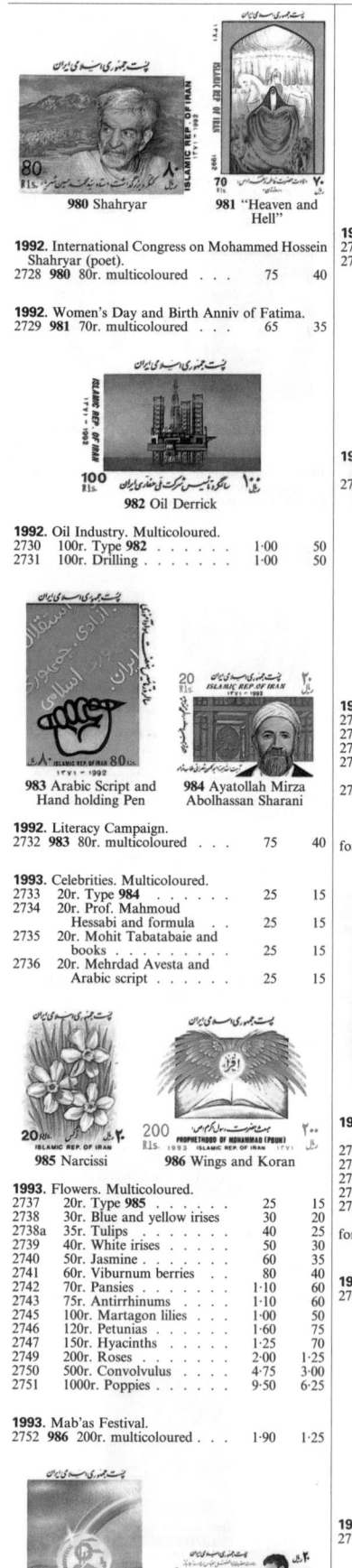

981 "Heaven and Hell"

1992. International Congress on Mohammed Hossein Shahryar (poet).
2728 **980** 80r. multicoloured . . . 75 40

1992. Women's Day and Birth Anniv of Fatima.
2729 **981** 70r. multicoloured . . . 65 35

982 Oil Derrick

1992. Oil Industry. Multicoloured.
2730 100r. Type **982** . . . . . . 1·00 50
2731 100r. Drilling . . . . 1·00 50

983 Arabic Script and Hand holding Pen

984 Ayatollah Mirza Abolhassan Sharani

1992. Literacy Campaign.
2732 **983** 80r. multicoloured . . . 75 40

1993. Celebrities. Multicoloured.
2733 20r. Type **984** 25 15
2734 20r. Prof. Mahmoud Hessabi and formula . . 25 15
2735 20r. Mohit Tabatabaie and books 25 15
2736 20r. Mehrdad Avesta and Arabic script 25 15

985 Narcissi

986 Wings and Koran

1993. Flowers. Multicoloured.
2737 20r. Type **985** 25 15
2738 30r. Blue and yellow irises 30 20
2738a 35r. Tulips 40 25
2739 40r. White irises 50 30
2740 50r. Jasmine 60 35
2741 60r. Viburnum berries . . 80 40
2742 70r. Pansies . . . . 1·10 60
2743 75r. Antirrhinums . . . . 1·10 60
2745 100r. Martagon lilies . . . 1·00 50
2746 120r. Petunias . . . . . . 1·60 75
2747 150r. Hyacinths . . . . . 1·25 70
2749 200r. Roses . . . . 2·00 1·25
2750 500r. Convolvulus . . . . 4·75 3·00
2751 1000r. Poppies . . . . . . 9·50 6·25

1993. Mab'as Festival.
2752 **986** 200r. multicoloured . . . 1·90 1·25

987 Rainbow and Emblem

988 Man in Wheelchair tying Girl's Ribbon

1993. Programming Day.
2753 **987** 100r. multicoloured . . . 90 50

1993. Invalids' Day. Multicoloured.
2754 20r. Type **988** 25 15
2755 40r. Medal winner in wheelchair 50 30
Nos. 2754/5 were issued together, se-tenant, forming a composite design.

989 Fatima Mosque, Qom

1993. Preservation of Cultural Heritage. Mult.
2756 40r. Type **989** 50 30
2757 40r. Interior of mosque . . 50 30

990 Hands reaching towards Sun

1993. World Day of the Oppressed. Birth Anniv of Mahdi.
2758 **990** 60r. multicoloured . . . 50 30

991 National Flag

1993. 14th Anniv of Islamic Revolution. Mult.
2759 20r. Type **991** 25 15
2760 20r. Flag and soldiers . . . 25 15
2761 20r. Guerrillas 25 15
2762 20r. Oil derricks, harvesters and crowd 25 15
2763 20r. Ayatollah Khomeini in motorcade and on arrival in Iran 25 15
Nos. 2759/63 were issued together, se-tenant, forming a composite design.

992 Volleyball

993 Ansari

1993. 1st Islamic Countries Women's Games. Multicoloured.
2764 40r. Type **992** 50 30
2765 40r. Basketball 50 30
2766 40r. Gold medal 50 30
2767 40r. Swimming 50 30
2768 40r. Running 50 30
Nos. 2764/8 were issued together, se-tenant, forming a compostite design.

1993. Congress on Sheikh Morteza Ansari.
2769 **993** 40r. multicoloured . . . 50 30

994 World Map as Tree Foliage and Rainbow

1993. Tree Day.
2770 **994** 70r. multicoloured . . . 90 55

995 Burning Tank and Man with Sling

996 Butterfly and Tulip

1993. World Jerusalem Day.
2771 **995** 20r. multicoloured . . . 25 15

1993. New Year Festival. Flowers and Butterflies. Multicoloured.
2772 20r. Type **996** 25 15
2773 20r. Butterfly and narcissus 25 15
2774 40r. Butterfly, tulips and rose 50 30
2775 40r. Butterfly and roses . . 50 30

997 Grass and Goldfish in Bowl

1993. Fetr Feast.
2776 **997** 100r. multicoloured . . . 2·25 1·25

998 Open Music Book

1993. 14th Anniv of Islamic Republic.
2777 **998** 40r. multicoloured . . . 40 25

999 Door and Landscape

1993. International Birth Millenary of Sheikh Mofeed Congress.
2778 **999** 80r. multicoloured . . . 80 50

1000 Emblem

1001 Globe

1993. 13th Asian and Pacific Labour Ministers' Conference, Teheran.
2779 **1000** 100r. multicoloured . . 1·00 60

1993. Int Congress for Advancement of Science and Technology in Islamic World.
2780 **1001** 50r. multicoloured . . . 50 30

1002 Mirror Box

1993. International Museum Day.
2781 **1002** 40r. multicoloured . . . 40 25

1003 Khomeini

1004 Girl on Swing

1993. 4th Death Anniv of Ayatollah Khomeini.
2782 **1003** 20r. multicoloured . . . 25 10

1993. World Children's Day.
2783 **1004** 50r. multicoloured . . . 50 30

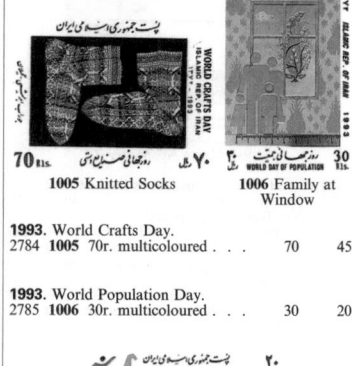

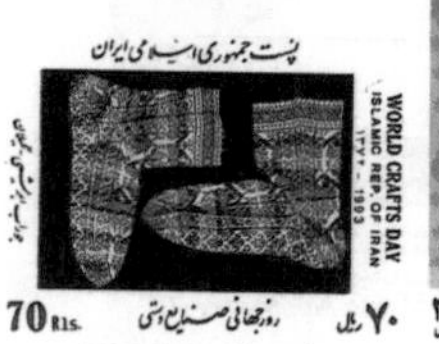
1005 Knitted Socks

1006 Family at Window

1993. World Crafts Day.
2784 **1005** 70r. multicoloured . . . 70 45

1993. World Population Day.
2785 **1006** 30r. multicoloured . . . 30 20

1007 Football

1993. Student Games. Multicoloured.
2786 20r. Type **1007** 20 10
2787 40r. Judo and wrestling . . 40 25
2788 40r. Long jumping, weightlifting, badminton and basketball 40 25

1008 Butterfly and Film Frame

1993. International Children's and Youths' Film Festival, Isfahan.
2789 **1008** 60r. multicoloured . . . 60 30

1009 Postal Messenger

1010 Stars and Birds

1993. World Post Day.
2790 **1009** 60r. multicoloured . . . 60 30

1993. 3rd International Biennial Children's Book Illustrations Exhibition, Teheran. Multicoloured.
2791 30r. Type **1010** 40 25
2792 30r. Moon and girl in boat 85 50
2793 30r. Cherub blowing trumpet 40 25
2794 30r. Trees and clouds . . . 40 25
Nos. 2791/4 were issued together, se-tenant, forming a composite design.

1011 Khaje Nassireddin Tussy

1013 Ayatollah Golpayegani

1012 Militia Member

1993. 719th Death Anniv of Khaje Nassireddin Tussy (scientist).
2795 **1011** 30r. multicoloured . . . 35 20

1993. People's Militia Week. Multicoloured.
2796 50r. Type **1012** 50 25
2797 50r. Woman tying headband for Militia member . . . 50 25

1993. Ayatollah Golpayegani Commem.
2798 **1013** 300r. multicoloured . . 3·00 1·50

1014 Hopscotch Grid drawn in Blood

1015 Flags

1993. Support for Moslems of Bosnia and Herzegovina. Multicoloured.
2799 40r. Type **1014** 45 15
2800 40r. Youth giving "V" sign 45 15
2801 40r. Woman and mosque . . 45 15

1994. Invalids' Day and Birthday of Abalfazil el Abbas.
2802 **1015** 80r. multicoloured . . . 80 50

1016 Trees and Ploughed Field in Book

1994. Agricultural Week.
2803 **1016** 60r. multicoloured . . . 65 40

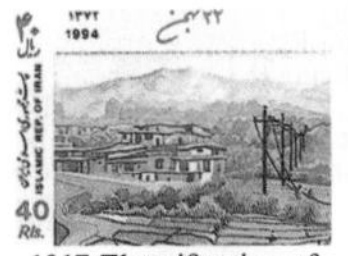
1017 Electrification of Villages

1018 Dome of the Rock

1994. 15th Anniv of Islamic Revolution. Mult.
2804 40r. Type **1017** 65 40
2805 40r. Ayatollah Khomeini and workers with flag . . 65 40
2806 40r. Fishing and new roads 65 40
2807 40r. Harvesting wheat and weaving 65 40
Nos. 2804/7 were issued together, se-tenant, forming a composite design.

1994. Congress on Islamic Law.
2808 **1018** 60r. multicoloured . . . 70 40

1019 Doctor, Gymnast, Camera, Paintbrush, Book and Student

1994. Youth Welfare.
2809 **1019** 30r. multicoloured . . . 50 30

1020 Palestinian and Peaceful Scene

1994. World Jerusalem Day.
2810 **1020** 50r. multicoloured . . . 55 30

1021 Black-crowned Night Heron

1022 Ball and Rectangles

1994. New Year Festival. Birds. Multicoloured.
2811 40r. Type **1021** 75 40
2812 40r. Eurasian bittern 75 40
2813 40r. Chukar partridges (horiz) 75 40
2814 40r. Common pheasants (horiz) 75 40

1994. 25th Annual Mathematics Conference.
2815 **1022** 30r. multicoloured . . . 50 30

1023 Book and Roses

1994. 15th Anniv of Islamic Republic.
2816 **1023** 40r. multicoloured . . . 40 20

1024 Child and Roses

1994. World Health Day.
2817 **1024** 100r. multicoloured . . 1·00 40

1025 Delvari, Cavalrymen and Ship

1994. 80th Death Anniv of Raiss Ali Delvari (revolutionary).
2818 **1025** 50r. multicoloured . . . 50 20

1026 I.Y.F. Emblem

1994. International Year of the Family.
2819 **1026** 50r. multicoloured . . . 50 20

1027 Old Telephone System and Computer Operator

1994. World Telecommunications Day.
2820 **1027** 50r. multicoloured . . . 50 20

1028 Marlik Gold Cup

1029 Kufic Enamelled Pot

1994. International Museum Day.
2821 **1028** 40r. multicoloured . . . 50 20

1994. Cultural Preservation.
2822 **1029** 40r. multicoloured . . . 50 20

1030 Khomeini

1031 Motahhari

1994. 5th Death Anniv of Ayatollah Khomeini.
2823 **1030** 30r. multicoloured . . . 30 15

1994. 15th Death Anniv of Ayatollah Motahhari.
2824 **1031** 30r. multicoloured . . . 30 15

1032 Rose-water Sprinkler

1034 Mosaic and Rose

1033 Games Emblem

1994. World Crafts Day. Multicoloured.
2825 60r. Type **1032** 60 30
2826 60r. Silk weaving, Khorassan 60 30

1994. Islamic Countries' University Student Games.
2827 **1033** 60r. multicoloured . . . 55 30

1994. Mohammed's Birth Anniv and Unity Week.
2828 **1034** 30r. multicoloured . . . 30 15

1035 Cameraman

1994. 14th Anniv of Iran–Iraq War.
2829 **1035** 70r. multicoloured . . . 70 30

1036 Envelope

1994. World Post Day.
2830 **1036** 50r. multicoloured . . . 50 25

1037 Allegory of Woman

1038 Soldier

1994. Women's Day and Birth Anniv of Fatima.
2831 **1037** 70r. multicoloured . . . 70 30

1994. People's Militia Week.
2832 **1038** 30r. multicoloured . . . 35 15

1039 Book

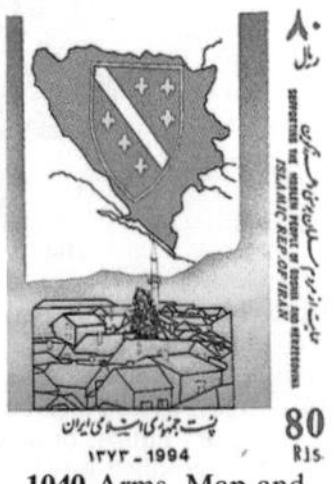
1040 Arms, Map and Town

1994. Book Week.
2833 **1039** 40r. multicoloured . . . 40 20

1994. Support for Moslems of Bosnia and Herzegovina. Multicoloured.
2834 80r. Type **1040** 85 40
2835 80r. Commander Adnan (deceased) and family . . 85 40

1041 Araki

1042 Arabic Script

1995. 2nd Death Anniv of Grand Ayatollah Mohammad Ali Araki (Shia leader).
2836 **1041** 100r. multicoloured . . 1·00 50

1995. World Day of the Oppressed. Birth Anniv of Mahdi.
2837 **1042** 50r. multicoloured . . . 50 25

1043 Flag, Dome and Man

1044 Crowd, National Flag and Ayatollah Khomeini

1995. Revolutionaries (1st series). Multicoloured.
2838 50r. Type **1043** 50 25
2839 50r. Man in patterned shirt 50 25
2840 50r. Man with full beard wearing grey shirt 50 25
2841 50r. Man in jacket and sweater looking to right 50 25
See also Nos. 2874/7, 2909/16, 2953/6, 3029/32 and 3034/7.

1995. 16th Anniv of Islamic Revolution.
2842 **1044** 100r. multicoloured . . 1·00 50

1045 Dome of the Rock

1046 Hand holding Tree

1995. World Jerusalem Day.
2843 **1045** 100r. multicoloured . . 1·00 50

1995. Tree Day.
2844 **1046** 50r. multicoloured . . . 50 25

1047 Hyacinths

1995. New Year Festival. Multicoloured.

2845	50r. Type **1047**	60	30
2846	50r. Pansies	60	30
2847	50r. Grass and bow	60	30
2848	50r. Tulips, bow and goldfish bowl	80	50

1048 Diesel Goods Train on Bridge

1995. Inauguration of Bafq–Bandar Abbas Railway.
2849 **1048** 100r. multicoloured . . 1·50 80

1049 Phoenix rising from Tulips

1050 Shapes

1995. 16th Anniv of Islamic Republic.
2850 **1049** 100r. multicoloured . . 1·00 50

1995. Press Festival.
2851 **1050** 100r. multicoloured . . 1·00 50

1051 Khomeini

1052 Arabic Script

1995. Ayatollah Ahmad Khomeini Commem.
2852 **1051** 50r. multicoloured . . . 50 25

1995. Invalids' Day.
2853 **1052** 80r. multicoloured . . . 80 40

1053 Yezd Mosque and Vaziri

1995. Ayatollah Ali Vaziri Commemoration.
2854 **1053** 100r. multicoloured . . 1·00 50

1054 Telecommunications

1995. World Telecommunications Day.
2855 **1054** 100r. multicoloured . . 1·00 50

1055 Khomeini

1056 Immunizing Baby

1995. 6th Death Anniv of Ayatollah Khomeini.
2856 **1055** 100r. multicoloured . . 1·00 50

1995. 50th Anniv of U.N.O. Multicoloured.

2857	100r. Type **1056**	1·00	50
2858	100r. Child laughing	1·00	50
2859	100r. Cereals and world map	1·00	50
2860	100r. Woman reading	1·00	50

1057 Ashtiany

1059 Man with Gun and Book

1058 Dam Workers

1995. Iqbal Ashtiany (historian) Commem.
2861 **1057** 100r. multicoloured . . 1·00 50

1995. Government Week.
2862 **1058** 100r. multicoloured . . 1·00 50

1995. People's Militia Week.
2863 **1059** 100r. multicoloured . . 1·00 50

1060 Envelopes and Globe forming Flower

1061 Cypher

1995. World Post Day.
2864 **1060** 100r. multicoloured . . 1·00 50

1995. Prophet Mohammed Commemoration.
2865 **1061** 100r. multicoloured . . 1·00 50

1062 Tondgoyan

1063 Shaghaghi

1995. M. J. Tondgoyan (oil minister) Commem.
2866 **1062** 100r. multicoloured . . 1·00 50

1996. Fathi Shaghaghi (Islamic Jihad Secretary-General) Commemoration.
2867 **1063** 100r. multicoloured . . 1·00 50

1064 Crowd, Flowers and Ayatollah Khomeini

1065 Dome of the Rock

1996. 17th Anniv of Islamic Revolution.
2868 **1064** 100r. multicoloured . . 1·00 50

1996. World Jerusalem Day.
2869 **1065** 100r. multicoloured . . 1·00 50

1066 Common Cardinal

1996. New Year Festival. Birds. Multicoloured.

2870	100r. Type **1066**	1·50	80
2871	100r. Budgerigar	1·50	80
2872	100r. Golden oriole	1·50	80
2873	100r. European roller	1·50	80

1996. Revolutionaries (2nd series). As T **1043**. Multicoloured.

2874	100r. Colonel-pilot Abbas Babaiy	1·00	50
2875	100r. Officer-pilot Ali Akbar Sharoudi	1·00	50
2876	100r. Commandant Mohammad Ebrahim Hemmat	1·00	50
2877	100r. Commandant Mohammad Boroudjerdi	1·00	50

1067 Ayatollah Khomeini, Ballot Box and Crowd

1068 Open Book, Flowers and Birds

1996. 17th Anniv of Islamic Republic.
2878 **1067** 200r. multicoloured . . 2·00 1·00

1996. International Book Fair, Teheran.
2879 **1068** 85r. multicoloured . . . 85 40

1069 Diesel Locomotive in Tunnel, Imam Riza's Shrine, Meshed, and Horses

1070 Camel Train and Prisoner tied to Stake

1996. Meshed–Sarakhs–Tajan International Railway.
2880 **1069** 200r. multicoloured . . 1·00 40

1996. Day of Prisoners of War and Missing in Action.
2881 **1070** 200r. multicoloured . . 2·00 1·00

1071 Khomeini

1996. 7th Death Anniv of Ayatollah Khomeini.
2882 **1071** 200r. multicoloured . . 2·00 1·00

1072 Carpet

1996. World Crafts Day.
2883 **1072** 200r. multicoloured . . 2·00 1·00

1073 Emblem

1996. 3rd Posts and Telecommunications Ministerial Conference, Teheran.
2884 **1073** 200r. multicoloured . . 2·00 1·00

1074 Zouqeblateyne Mosque

1996. Mohammed's Birth Anniv and Unity Week. Multicoloured.

2885	200r. Type **1074**	2·00	1·00
2886	200r. Tomb of Imam Hossein (dome with flag flying to right)	2·00	1·00
2887	200r. Prophet's Mosque (dome without flag)	2·00	1·00
2888	200r. Tomb of Imam Riza (dome with flag flying to left)	2·00	1·00
2889	200r. Qaba Mosque (with four corner minarets)	2·00	1·00

1075 Teheran Underground

1996. Government Week. Multicoloured.

2890	200r. Type **1075**	1·00	40
2891	200r. Ispahan iron works	1·00	40
2892	200r. Merchant fleet	1·00	40
2893	200r. Bandar-e-Imam oil refinery	1·00	40
2894	200r. Boumehen Earth Station	1·00	40

1076 Ardabily and Mosque Interior

1996. Allameh Moghaddas Ardabily Commem.
2895 **1076** 200r. multicoloured . . 2·00 1·00

1077 Artillery Position and Soldier praying

1996. 16th Anniv of Iran–Iraq War.
2896 **1077** 200r. multicoloured . . 2·00 1·00

1078 Cogs and Equipment

1996. World Standards Day.
2897 **1078** 200r. multicoloured . . 2·00 1·00

1079 Harvesting and Man working on "Globe" Rick

1996. World Food Summit, Rome.
2898 **1079** 200r. multicoloured . . 2·00 1·00

1080 Men, Houses and Women

1996. National Population and Housing Census.
2899 **1080** 200r. multicoloured . . 2·00 1·00

1081 Wrestlers

1996. 2nd World University Wrestling Championship, Teheran.
2900 **1081** 500r. multicoloured . . 4·75 2·40

1082 Ayatollah Khomeini embracing Youth

1083 Hands holding Tree

1997. 18th Anniv of Islamic Revolution. Mult.
2901 200r. Type **1082** . . . . . 2·25 1·00
2902 200r. Banner of Khomeini above crowd . . . . . . 2·25 1·00
2903 200r. Khomeini waving . . 2·25 1·00
2904 200r. Khomeini returning from exile in France . . . 2·25 1·00
2905 200r. Soldiers . . . . 2·25 1·00

1997. Tree Day.
2906 **1083** 200r. multicoloured . . 2·25 1·00

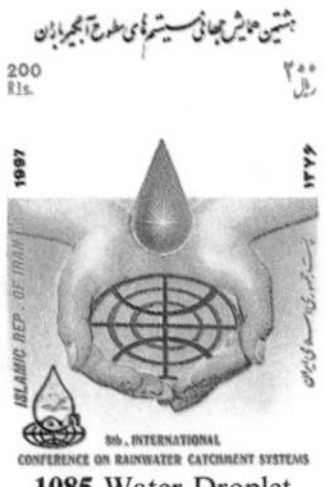

1084 Rainbow and National Flag

1085 Water Droplet falling to "Globe" Pool in Cupped Hands

1997. 18th Anniv of Islamic Republic.
2907 **1084** 200r. multicoloured . . 2·25 1·00

1997. 8th International Rainwater Catchment Systems Conference.
2908 **1085** 200r. multicoloured . . 2·25 1·00

1997. Revolutionaries (3rd series). As T **1043**. Multicoloured.
2909 100r. Alireza Mowahhed Danesh (blue flag, white turban) . . . . 1·25 50
2910 100r. Mohammad Reza Dastwareh (orange flag, white turban) . . . . . . 1·25 50
2911 100r. Abbas Karimi (blue flag, full-face without glasses) . . . . 1·25 50
2912 100r. Nasser Kazemi (orange flag, white vest with red trim) . . . . . 1·25 50
2913 100r. Youssef Kolahdouz (blue flag, three-quarter face) . . . . 1·25 50
2914 100r. Yadollah Kolhar (orange flag, full-face) . . 1·25 50
2915 100r. Fazlollah Mahallati (blue flag, full-face with glasses) . . . . 1·25 50
2916 100r. Abdollah Meyssami (orange flag, green vest and coat) . . . . 1·25 50

1086 Satellite, Letter, Globe and Computer

1087 Khomeini

1997. Post, Telecommunications and Productivity.
2917 **1086** 200r. multicoloured . . 2·25 1·00

1997. 8th Death Anniv of Ayatollah Khomeini.
2918 **1087** 200r. multicoloured . . 2·00 1·00

1088 Teheran Underground Railway Map and Tunnel

1089 Flora and Fauna

1997. National Achievements. Multicoloured.
2919 40r. Type **1088** 15 10
2920 50r. Cornfield and silo . . . 20 10
2921 65r. Medals from Student Scientific Olympiads . . . 25 10
2922 70r. Steelworks, Mobarakeh 30 15
2923 100r. Modern communications systems 40 20
2924 130r. Harbour and tanker 50 25
2925 150r. Oil refinery, Bandar Abbas 60 30
2926 200r. Martyr Radja-ee dam 75 35
2927 350r. Martyr Radja-ee power station . . . . . . 1·40 70
2928 400r. Foreign Ministry building . . . . 1·75 80
2929 500r. Child receiving oral vaccination . . . . 2·10 1·00
2930 650r. Koran Printing House and Koran . . . . 2·75 1·40
2931 1000r. Imam Khomeini International Airport, Teheran . . . . 4·25 2·10
2932 2000r. Tomb of Imam Khomeini, Teheran . . . 8·25 4·00

1997. 10th Anniv of Montreal Protocol (on reduction of use of chlorofluorocarbons).
2933 **1089** 200r. multicoloured . . 2·25 1·00

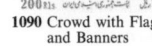

1090 Crowd with Flags and Banners

1091 Allama Mohammad Iqbal (Pakistani poet)

1997. 17th Anniv of Iran–Iraq War.
2934 **1090** 200r. multicoloured . . 2·25 1·00

1997. Iranian–Pakistani Culture. Multicoloured.
2935 200r. Type **1091** . . . . . 2·25 1·00
2936 200r. Jalal-ad-din Moulana Rumi (Persian mystic) . . 2·25 1·00

1092 Airplane, Letters and Computer

1997. World Post Day.
2937 **1092** 200r. multicoloured . . 2·25 1·00

1093 Frasheri and Etehemberg Mosque, Tirana

1997. 150th Birth Anniv (1996) of Naim Frasheri (Albanian writer).
2938 **1093** 200r. multicoloured . . 2·25 1·00

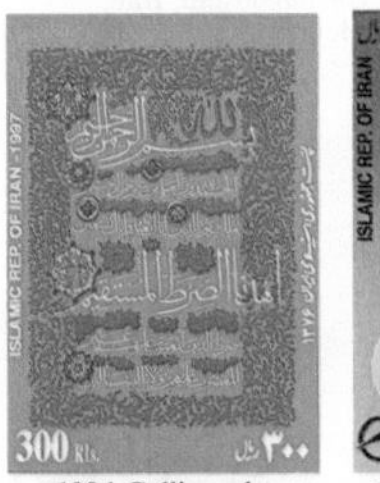

1094 Calligraphy

1095 Games Emblem

1997. 8th Islamic Summit, Teheran. Illustrated pages from the Koran. Each green, gold and red.
2939 300r. Type **1094** . . . . . 3·00 1·50
2940 300r. Page with rose at bottom left . . . . 3·00 1·50
2941 300r. Page with rose on right-hand side . . . . . 3·00 1·50
2942 300r. Page with rose at top left-hand corner . . . . . 3·00 1·50
2943 300r. Summit emblem . . . 3·00 1·50

1997. 2nd Islamic Countries Women's Games, Teheran.
2944 **1095** 200r. multicoloured . . 2·25 1·00

1096 Dome of the Rock

1998. World Jerusalem Day.
2945 **1096** 250r. multicoloured . . 10 10

1097 State Flags and Poppies

1998. 19th Anniv of Islamic Revolution. Mult.
2946 200r. Type **1097** 10 10
2947 200r. Harvesting grain . . . 10 10
2948 200r. Soldiers with flags . . 10 10
2949 200r. Crowd with banner of Khomeini 10 10
2950 200r. Ayatollah Khomeini 10 10
Nos. 2946/50 were issued together, se-tenant, forming a composite design.

1098 Tree and Town

1998. Tree Day.
2951 **1098** 200r. multicoloured . . 10 10

1099 Flower Arrangement and Gifts

1998. New Year Festival.
2952 **1099** 200r. multicoloured . . 10 10

1998. Revolutionaries (4th series). As T **1043**. Multicoloured.
2953 100r. Man in open-necked shirt 10 10
2954 100r. Man in vest and jacket (three-quarter face) . . . 10 10
2955 100r. Man in vest and jacket (profile) 10 10
2956 100r. Man in crew-neck jumper and jacket 10 10

1100 M. Shahryar (poet)

1101 Khomeini

1998.
2957 **1100** 200r. multicoloured . . 10 10

1998. 9th Death Anniv of Ayatollah Khomeini.
2958 **1101** 200r. multicoloured . . 10 10

1102 Map and Emblem

1998. 2nd South and West Asia Postal Union Congress.
2959 **1102** 250r. multicoloured . . 10 10

1103 Player, Ball and Stadium

1998. World Cup Football Championship, France.
2960 **1103** 500r. multicoloured . . 20 10

1104 Globe and Headset   1105 Silver Vessel

1998. World Telecommunications Day.
2961 **1104** 200r. multicoloured . . 10 10

1998. World Handicrafts Day.
2962 **1105** 200r. multicoloured . . 10 10

1106 State Flag as Dove, Birds and Flowers

1998. 1st Anniv of Presidential Election.
2963 **1106** 200r. multicoloured . . 10 10

1107 Khomeini voting

1998. 19th Anniv of Islamic Republic.
2964 **1107** 250r. multicoloured . . 10 10

1108 Handshake, Rainbow and Doves   1109 Arabic Script

1998. Co-operation Day.
2965 **1108** 250r. multicoloured . . 10 10

1998. "1000th Friday of Public Prayer".
2966 **1109** 250r. blue, gold and black 10 10

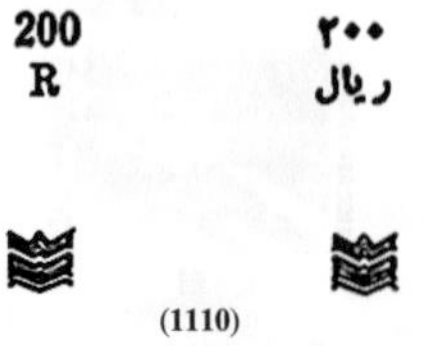

(1110)

1998. Mosques. Nos. 2415a and 2416a surch as T **1110**.
2967 **1110** 200r. on 1r. orange and silver 10 10
2968 200r. on 3r. green and silver 10 10

1111 Globe and Shark's Fin

1998. International Year of the Ocean.
2969 **1111** 250r. multicoloured . . 10 10

1112 Arabic Script

1998. Sacred Defence Week.
2970 **1112** 250r. multicoloured . . 10 10

1113 Envelope and Clouds as World Map

1998. World Post Day.
2971 **1113** 200r. multicoloured . . 10 10

1114 Wrestlers

1998. World Wrestling Championship, Iran.
2972 **1114** 250r. multicoloured . . 10 10

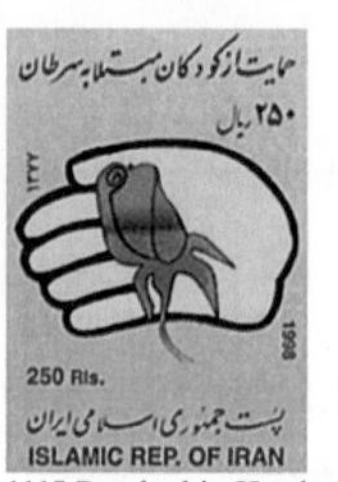

1115 Rosebud in Hand   1116 Navigation Instrument

1998. Children's Cancer Relief.
2973 **1115** 250r. multicoloured . . 10 10

1999. Museum Exhibit.
2974 **1116** 250r. multicoloured . . 10 10

1117 Khomeini

1999. 20th Anniv of Islamic Revolution.
2975 **1117** 250r. multicoloured . . 20 10

(1118)   (1119)

1999. Flowers. Nos. 2738/a surch as T **1118**.
2976 200r. on 35r. multicoloured 15 10
2977 900r. on 30r. multicoloured 70 40

1999. International Book Fair, Teheran. No. 2879 surch as T **1119**.
2978 250r. on 85r. multicoloured 20 10

1120 Flag and Emblem

1999. 20th Anniv of Islamic Republic.
2979 **1120** 250r. multicoloured . . 20 10

1121 Emblem

1999. Ghadir Khom Religious Festival.
2980 **1121** 250r. multicoloured . . 20 10

1122 Harbour

1999. Ayatollah Khomeini Charity Fund. Mult.
2981 250r. Type **1122** 20 10
2982 250r. Houses 20 10

1123 Soldier, Tank, Ship and Aircraft

1999. Army Day.
2983 **1123** 250r. multicoloured . . 20 10

1124 Sadra al-Din Shirazi

1999. Sadra al-Din Shirazi (philosopher) Commem.
2984 **1124** 250r. multicoloured . . 20 10

1125 Khomeini

1999. 10th Death Anniv of Ayatollah Khomeini.
2985 **1125** 250r. multicoloured . . 20 10

1126 Parliament Building and Khomeini

1999. 20th Anniv of Iranian Parliament.
2986 **1126** 250r. multicoloured . . 20 10

1127 Emblem and Map

1999. Organization of Islamic Conference Interparliamentary Union Congress, Tehran.
2987 **1127** 250r. multicoloured . . 20 10

1128 Emblem and Dome

1999. Unity Week.
2988 **1128** 250r. multicoloured . . 20 10

1129 Tapestry   1130 River Kingfisher

1999. World Handicrafts Day.
2989 **1129** 250r. multicoloured . . 20 10

1999. Birds. Multicoloured.
2990 100r. Hoopoe 10 10
2991 150r. Type **1130** 15 10
2992 200r. Robin 15 10
2993 250r. Crested lark 20 10
2994 300r. Red-backed shrike 20 10
2995 350r. Roller 20 10
2996 400r. Blue tit 25 15
2997 500r. Bee eater 35 20
2998 1000r. Redwing 70 40
2999 2000r. Twite . . . . 1·30 60
2999a 3000r. Whitethroat . . . . 1·75 75
2999b 4500r. Collar dove . . . . 2·25 90

1131 Moon partially covering Sun

1999. Solar Eclipse. Multicoloured.

3000	250r. Type **1131**	20	10
3001	250r. Moon passing in front of Sun	20	10
3002	250r. Full solar eclipse	20	10
3003	250r. Sun appearing from right-hand side of Moon	20	10
3004	250r. Sun appearing	20	10

1132 Letters, Globe and Letter Box

1999. 125th Anniv of Universal Postal Union.

3005	**1132** 250r. multicoloured	20	10

1133 Chinese Girl

1999. International Children's Day. Showing children from different cultures. Multicoloured.

3006	150r. Type **1133**	15	10
3007	150r. Indian girl	15	10
3008	150r. Native American girl	15	10
3009	150r. Arabian boy	15	10
3010	150r. Iranian girl	15	10
3011	150r. Mexican boy	15	10
3012	150r. Eskimo boy	15	10
3013	150r. African girl	15	10
3014	150r. Russian boy	15	10
3015	150r. European girl	15	10

1134 Winged Egg

1999. International Children's Book Illustrations Exhibition. Multicoloured.

3016	250r. Type **1134**	20	10
3017	250r. Decorated egg	20	10
3018	250r. Egg decorated with white crescent	20	10
3019	250r. Egg decorated with flowers	20	10

1135 Ayatollah Mohammed Taghi

1999. Ayatollah Mohammed Taghi Commemoration.

3020	**1135** 250r. multicoloured	20	10

1136 Ayatollah Khomeni

2000. 21st Anniv of Islamic Revolution.

3021	**1136** 300r. multicoloured	20	10

2000. Flowers. Nos. 2741, 2743, 2746 surch **250 R.**

3022	250r. on 60r. multicoloured	20	10
3023	250r. on 75r. multicoloured	20	10
3024	250r. on 120r. multicoloured	20	10

1138 Bee Eaters

2000. New Year Festival.

3025	**1138** 300r. multicoloured	20	10

1139 Inscription

2000. National Archives Day.

3026	**1139** 300r. multicoloured	20	10

1140 Books, Cogs, Chimneys and Hand holding Torch

2000. 70th Anniv of Science and Technology University.

3027	**1140** 300r. multicoloured	20	10

1141 Mofatteh and Building

2000. Ayatollah Mofatteh Commemoration.

3028	**1141** 300r. multicoloured	20	10

1142 Khalil Motahar Nia

2000. Revolutionaries (5th series). Multicoloured.

3029	150r. Type **1142**	10	10
3030	150r. Haschem Etemadi (pink shirt)	10	10
3031	150r. Madjid Sepassi (green shirt)	10	10
3032	150r. Mahmud Sotoudeh (blue T-shirt and shirt)	10	10

1143 Mother and Baby

2000. International Breast-feeding Week.

3033	**1143** 300r. multicoloured	20	10

1144 Hadj Reza Habubollahi

2000. Revolutionaries (6th series). Multicoloured.

3034	150r. Type **1144**	10	10
3035	150r. Hassan Agharebparast (shirt with epaulettes)	10	10
3036	150r. Mostafa Ravani Pou (white turban)	10	10
3037	150r. Mohsen Safavi (wearing glasses)	10	10

1145 Books and Educational Symbols

1147 Satellite and Dish

1146 Stylized Bird

2000. University Anniversary.

3038	**1145** 300r. multicoloured	20	10

2000. 8th Asian-Pacific Postal Union Congress, Tehran.

3039	**1146** 300r. blue, mauve and black	20	10

2000. International World Space Week. Multicoloured.

3040	500r. Type **1147**	35	20
3041	500r. Satellite and dish (different)	35	20

1148 Birds, Flowers and Calligraphy

2001. Eid-ul Ghadir.

3042	**1148** 500r. multicoloured	40	25

1149 Flowers, Calligraphy and Sun

2001. Year of Imam Ali.

3043	**1149** 500r. multicoloured	40	25

1150 Red-headed Bunting

2001. New Year Festival. Multicoloured.

3044	300r. Type **1150**	20	10
3045	300r. Hawfinch (vert)	20	10

1151 Mosque and Mohamed Al Dorra and Father

2001. Intifada.

3046	**1151** 350r. multicoloured	25	15

1152 Chaffinch

2001. Belgica 2001 International Stamp Exhibition, Brussels. Multicoloured.

3047	350r. Type **1152**	25	15
3048	350r. Waxwing	25	15
3049	350r. Gate to Melli Bagh National Garden (vert)	25	15

1153 Mount Fuji, Japan

2001. Philanippon '01 International Stamp Exhibition, Tokyo. Multicoloured.

3050	250r. Type **1153**	20	10
3051	250r. Mount Damavand, Iran	20	10

1154 Flag, Globe and Iranian Buildings

2001. World Tourism Day.

3052	**1154** 500r. multicoloured	40	25

1155 Police Helicopters and Vehicles

2001. Police Week. Multicoloured.

3053	250r. Type **1155**	20	10
3054	250r. Flag, boats and Policeman	20	10

Nos. 3053/4 were issued together, se-tenant, forming a composite design.

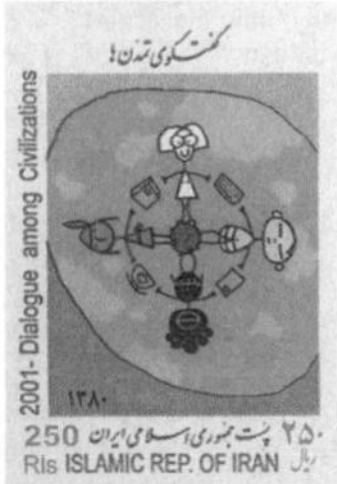

1156 Children encircling Globe

2001. United Nations Year of Dialogue among Civilizations. Multicoloured.

3055	250r. Type **1156**	20	10
3056	250r. European and Asian faces (horiz)	20	10

1157 Ball and Dove

2001. 3rd Islamic Women's Games, Tehran.
3057 **1157** 250r. multicoloured . . 20 10

1158 Koran and Flowers

2001. Koran.
3058 **1158** 500r. multicoloured . . 40 25

1159 P 232 *Tabarza*

2001. Navy Day. Multicoloured.
3059 500r. Type **1159** 40 25
3060 500r. Frigate 40 25
3061 500r. Helicopter and hovercraft 40 25
3062 500r. Submarine 40 25

1160 Bees on Honeycomb

2001. Bee-keeping.
3063 **1160** 500r. multicoloured . . 40 25

1161 Hands enclosing Face

2001. 50th Anniv of United Nations High Commissioner for Refugees.
3064 **1161** 500r. blue, black and mauve 40 25

1162 Vehicle, Roadways and Bridge

2001. Transportation Day. Multicoloured.
3065 350r. Type **1162** 25 15
3066 350r. Bridge, vehicles and buildings 25 15
Nos. 3065/6 were issued together, se-tenant, forming a composite design.

1163 Locomotive

2001. Tehran Subway. Multicoloured.
3067 500r. Type **1163** 40 25
3068 500r. Locomotive right view 40 25

1164 Samand Saloon Car

2002. 1st Iranian Manufactured Car. Multicoloured.
3069 500r. Type **1164** 40 25
3070 500r. Grey car (horiz) . . . 40 25

1165 Globe as Plant Pot containing Tree

2002. Tree Planting Day.
3071 **1165** 500r. multicoloured . . 40 25

1166 Squacco Heron (Ardeola ralloides)

2002. New Year Festival. Multicoloured.
3072 500r. Type **1166** 40 25
3073 500r. Hoopoe (*Upupa epops*) 40 25
3074 500r. Blue tit (*Parus caeruleus*) 40 25
3075 500r. Alexandrine parakeet (*Psittacula eupatria*) . . . 40 25

1167 Imam Hossein's Wounded Horse returning to Kerbala

2002. Death of Imam Hossein (grandson of Mohamed). Sheet 99 × 76 mm. Imperf.
MS3076 **1167** 400r. multicoloured 30 30

1168 Chestnut Tiger (*Danaus sita*)

2002. Butterflies. Multicoloured.
3077 400r. Type **1168** 30 20
3078 400r. Comma (*Polygonia c-album*) 30 20
3079 400r. Blue argus (*Precis orithya*) 30 20
3080 400r. Painted lady (*Vanessa cardui*) 30 20
3081 400r. *Papilio maacki* 30 20

1169 Caspian

2002. Horses. Multicoloured.
3082 400r. Type **1169** 30 20
3083 400r. Kurd 30 20
3084 400r. Turkoman 30 20
3085 400r. Arab 30 20

1170 *Hyoscyamus muticus*

2002. Philakorea 2002 International Stamp Exhibition, Seoul. Flowers. Multicoloured.
3086 400r. Type **1170** 30 20
3087 400r. *Fritillaria* ("Frittillaria") 30 20
3088 400r. *Calotropis procera* . . 30 20
3089 400r. *Ranuculus* 30 20

1171 Ayatollah Khomeini

2002. Birth Centenary of Ayatollah Khomeini.
3090 **1171** 400r. multicoloured . . 40 25

1172 Child and Dome of the Rock

2002. Jerusalem Day.
3091 **1172** 400r. multicoloured . . 30 20

1173 Iranian Decorated Pots

2002. Centenary of Brazil—Iran Diplomatic Relations. Multicoloured.
3092 400r. Type **1173** 30 20
3093 400r. Marajoara pots, Brazil 30 20

1174 Emblem

2002. 2nd Biennial Exhibition of Contemporary Islamic Painting.
3094 **1174** 400r. multicoloured . . 30 20

1175 Smelting Pot and Mill

2003. 31st Anniv of Esfahan Steel Mill.
3095 **1175** 400r. multicoloured . . 90 55

1176 Grumman F-14A Tomcat

2003. Air Force Day. Multicoloured.
3096 300r. Type **1176** 75 45
3097 400r. Northrop F-5E Tiger II 90 55
3098 500r. F-14A Tomcat and missile carrier . . . . . . 1·10 65
3099 600r. Macdonell Douglas F-5E Phantom II . . . . 1·40 85
3100 700r. Mikoyan Mig-29 . . . 1·60 1·00

1177 Urial Sheep (½-size illustration)

2003. New Year Festival. Multicoloured.
3101 1000r. Type **1177** . . . . . 2·20 1·30
3102 1000r. Goitered gazelle male 2·20 1·30
3103 1000r. Goitered gazelle female . . . . 2·20 1·30
3104 1000r. Red deer . . . . . . 2·20 1·30

1178 Mosque, Isfahan

2003. Buildings.
3105 400r. Type **1178** 90 55
3106 400r. Bell Tower, Xi'an . . 90 55
Stamps of the same design were issued by People's Republic of China.

1179 Family enclosed in House of Books

2003. Book, Children and Family.
3107 **1179** 500r. multicoloured . . 75 45

1180 *Zygaena*

2003. Butterflies. Multicoloured.
3108 100r. Type **1180** 10 10
3109 200r. *Issoria lathonia* . . . 40 25
3110 250r. *Utethesia pulchella* . . 40 25
3111 300r. *Argynnis paphia* . . . 75 45
3112 500r. *Polygonia egea* . . . 80 50
3113 600r. *Papilio machaon* . . . 85 50
3113a 650r. *Colias aurorina* . . . 90 55
3114 1000r. *Inachis Io* . . . . . . 1·50 90
3115 2000r. *Papilio demoleus* . . 2·75 1·60
3116 3000r. *Euphyrdryas aurinia* 4·25 2·50

1181 Emblem

2003. 50th Anniv of Social Security.
3125 **1181** 600r. multicoloured . . 75 45

1182 Revolutionaries
(½-size illustration)

2003.
3126 **1182** 600r. multicoloured . . 90 55

1183 Mohammed Ali Rajai and Arabic Script

2003. Government Week.
3127 **1183** 600r. multicoloured . . 90 55

1184 Caspian Seal (*Phoca caspia*)

2003. Preservation of the Caspian Sea. Multicoloured.
3128 600r. Type **1184** 90 55
3129 600r. Beluga (*Huso huso*) . . 90 55
MS3130 130 × 97 mm. Nos. 3128/9 each × 2 . . . . 3·50 2·00
Stamps of a similar design were issued by Russia.

1185 Hand holding Apple

2003.
3131 **1185** 500r. multicoloured . . 75 45

1186 Computer and Satellite

2003. World Post Day. Multicoloured.
3132 600r. Type **1186** 80 50
3133 600r. Post lorries and airplanes 80 50
3134 600r. Seated man holding letter and lorry 80 50
3135 600r. Post rider and statues 80 50

1187 *Asiatic Cheetah*

2003. Endangered Species. Asiatic Cheetah (Acinonyc jubatus). Multicoloured.
3136 500r. Type **1187** 75 45
3137 500r. Adult and cub 75 45
3138 500r. Two adults 75 45
3139 500r. Adult with open mouth 75 45

1188 Minaret

2003. Fetr Feast.
3140 **1188** 600r. multicoloured . . 90 55

1189 City Walls

2004. Bam Earthquake. Sheet 136 × 101 mm containing T **1189** and similar horiz designs. Multicoloured.
MS3141 500r. × 4, Type **1189**; Ruins; Medical staff and patients; Rescue workers . . . . 3·00 3·00

1190 Emblem

2004. 25th Anniv of Republic.
3142 **1190** 600r. multicoloured . . 90 55

1191 Hossein Rezazadeh (⅔-size illustration)

2004. Hossein Rezazadeh, Champion Weightlifter.
3143 **1191** 1200r. multicoloured . . 1·80 1·00

1192 Postman and Customer

2004. Obtaining ISO 9001–2000 Certification (quality control).
3144 **1192** 600r. multicoloured . . 90 55

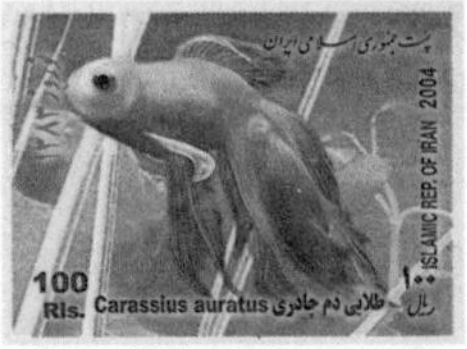

1193 Goldfish (*Carassius auratus*)

2004. New Year. Ornamental Fish. Multicoloured.
3145 100r. Type **1193** 20 10
3146 200r. *Carrasius auratus* with grey tail 35 20
3147 300r. Siamese fighting fish (*Betta splendens*) 40 25
3148 400r. *Carassius auratus* large facing left 50 30
3149 500r. Guppy (*Poecilia reticulate*) 75 45
3150 600r. *Carassius auratus* with raised fin 85 50

1194 Clown Triggerfish (*Balistoides conspicillum*)

2004. Saltwater Fish. Sheet 137 × 166 mm containing T **1194** and similar horiz designs. Multicoloured.
MS3151 250r. Type **1194**; 350r. *Acanthurus glaucopareius*; 450r. Lionfish (*Pterois volitans*); 550r. Sail-finned tang (*Zebrasoma veliferum*); 650r. Regal angelfish (*Pygoplites diacanthus*); 750r. Jigsaw triggerfish (*Pseudobalistes fuscus*) . . . . 4·00 4·00

1195 National Team Members (⅔-size illustration)

2004. Centenary of FIFA (Federation Internationale de Football Association).
3152 **1195** 600r. multicoloured . . 1·20 70

1196 Camera, Hand and Page

2004. Reporters Day.
3153 **1196** 650r. multicoloured . . 50 30

1197 Taekwondo

2004. Olympic Games, Athens. Multicoloured.
3154 650r. Type **1197** 50 30
3155 650r. Weightlifting 50 30
3156 650r. Wrestling 50 30
3157 650r. Judo 50 30

1198 Kabir

2004. Iranian and Indian Poets. Multicoloured.
3158 600r. Type **1198** (Indian) . . 50 30
3159 600r. Khajeh Shamseddin Mohammad Hafez Shirazi (Hafez) (Iranian) 50 30
Stamps of the same design were issued by India.

1199 Memorial, Hamedan

2004. Avicina International Conference, Bu-Ali Sina University, Hamedan. Multicoloured.
3160 650r. Type **1199** 50 30
3161 650r. Abu Ali al-Husain ibn Abdallah ibn Sina (Avicina) (poet) 50 30

1200 Chacma Baboon (*Papio ursinus*)

2004. World Stamp Collecting Championship, Singapore. Sheet 138 × 101 mm containing T **1200** and similar horiz designs. Multicoloured.
MS3162 500r. × 4, Type **1200**; Chimpanzee (*Pan troglodytes*); Two chimpanzees; Mandrill (*Mandrillus sphinx*) . . . . . 2·00 2·00

1201 Tabby Shorthair

2004. Cats. Sheet 168 × 136 mm containing T **1201** and similar vert designs. Multicoloured.
MS3163 500r. × 6, Type **1201**; Silver tabby longhair; Bi-colour longhair; Persian; Silver tabby shorthair; Tabby and white shorthair . . . . 2·40 2·40

1202 Volleyball Players

2004. Paralympics, Athens.
3164 **1202** 650r. multicoloured . . 50 30

1203 Airplanes and Missiles

2004. 24th Anniv of Iran–Iraq War.
3165 **1203** 650r. multicoloured . . 50 30

1204 Emblem

2004. 70th Anniv of Tehran University.
3166 **1204** 650r. multicoloured . . 50 30

1205 Mullah

2004. Multicoloured.
3167 500r. Type **1205** 40 25
3168 500r. Man with moustache 40 25
3169 500r. Man facing right . . . 40 25
3170 500r. Man facing left . . . 40 25

1206 Damavand Mountain, Iran

2004. Mountains. Multicoloured.
3171 650r. Type **1206** 50 30
3172 650r. Bolivar Peak, Venezuela 50 30
Stamps of a similar design were issued by Venezuela.

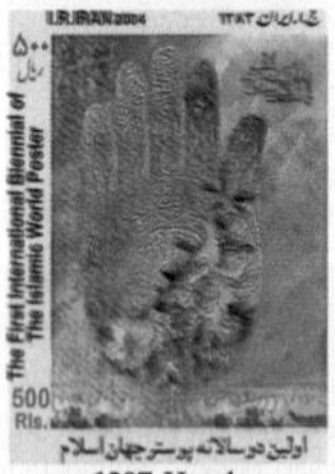

1207 Hand

2004. Biennial International Islamic Poster Exhibition. Multicoloured.
3173 500r. Type **1207** 40 25
3174 500r. Bird on nest 40 25
3175 500r. Slingshot 40 25
3176 500r. Moon 40 25

1208 Tomb

2004. Imam Reza Commemoration. Designs showing parts of shrine. Multicoloured.
3177 500r. Type **1208** 40 25
3178 500r. Roof 40 25
3179 500r. Facade 40 25
3180 500r. Doorway 40 25

NEWSPAPER POSTAGE DUE STAMPS

1909. Optd **Imprimes** in English and Persian.
N319 **38** 2ch. grey on blue . . . . 13·00 2·00

OFFICIAL STAMPS

1902. Stamp of 1898 surch **Service** and value in English and Persian.
O224 **21** 5c. on 1k. red . . . . . 4·00 50
O225 10c. on 1k. red . . . . . 3·00 60
O226 12c. on 1k. red . . . . . 4·25 1·40

1903. Stamps of 1903 optd **Service**.
O259 **38** 1c. lilac 15 10
O260 2c. grey 15 10
O261 3c. green 15 10
O262 5c. red 15 10
O263 10c. brown 15 10
O264 12c. blue 20 10
O265 **39** 1k. purple 40 10
O266 2k. blue 80 10
O267 5k. brown . . . . 6·00 20
O268 10k. red . . . . 6·00 50
O269 20k. orange . . . . . . 9·00 50
O270 30k. green . . . . . . 12·00 1·00
O271 50k. green . . . . 55·00 14·00

1905. Nos. 275/6 and 280/1 optd **Service**.
O283 **39** 2t. on 50k. green (275) 45·00 22·00
O285 2t. on 50k. green (280) 45·00 22·00
O284 3t. on 50k. green (276) 45·00 25·00
O286 3t. on 50k. green (281) 45·00 22·00

(O 57)

O **120**

1911. Stamps of 1909 optd **Service** and with Type O**57**.
O353 **56** 1c. purple and orange . . 3·00 15
O354 2c. purple and violet . . 3·00 15
O355 3c. purple and green . . 3·00 20
O356 6c. purple and red . . . 3·00 20
O357 9c. purple and grey . . . 3·00 50
O358 10c. purple and mauve 6·00 60
O359 1k. brown, violet & silver 7·00 2·00
O360 2k. brown, green & silver 12·00 5·00

1915. Coronation stamps of 1915 optd **SERVICE** in English and Persian.
O460 **66** 1c. blue and red 10 10
O461 2c. red and blue 10 10
O462 3c. green 10 10
O463 5c. red 10 10
O464 6c. red and green 20 10
O465 9c. violet and brown . . 20 10
O466 10c. brown and green . . 20 10
O467 12c. blue 20 10
O468 24c. chocolate and brown 20 10
O469 **67** 1k. black, brown & silver 80 15
O470 2k. red, blue and silver 80 15
O471 – 3k. sepia, lilac and silver 80 20
O472 **67** 5k. grey, sepia and silver 85 20
O473 – 1t. black, violet and gold 85 35
O474 – 2t. brown, green and gold 90 35
O475 – 3t. red, crimson and gold 90 55
O476 – 5t. grey, blue and gold 1·25 60

1941.
O836 O **120** 5d. violet 55 10
O837 10d. mauve 55 10
O838 25d. red 55 10
O839 50d. black 55 10
O840 75d. red 80 10
O841 1r. green . . . . . . 2·00 10
O842 1r.50 blue . . . . . 2·25 10
O843 2r. blue . . . . . . 4·25 10
O844 3r. purple . . . . . 8·50 10
O845 5r. green . . . . . . 12·00 20
O846 10r. blue and brown 35·00 40
O847 20r. mauve and blue £130 1·50
O848 30r. green and violet £250 2·75
O849 50r. brown and blue £300 45·00
The rial values are larger (23 × 30 mm).

O **489** Red Lion and Sun Emblem

1974.
O1829 O **489** 5d. violet and mauve 10 10
O1830 10d. mauve and blue 10 10
O1831 50d. orange & green 10 10
O1832 1r. blue and gold . . 10 10
O2046 1r. black and green 10 10
O1833 2r. green and orange 10 10
O2047 2r. brown and grey 10 10
O2048 3r. blue and orange 10 10
O2049 5r. green and pink 15 15
O1834 6r. green and yellow 35 10
O2050 6r. black and blue 15 15
O1835 8r. blue and yellow 35 15
O2051 8r. red and green . . 20 15
O1836 10r. blue and mauve 2·00 20
O2052 10r. turquoise & grn 35 20
O1837 11r. purple and blue 70 20
O2053 11r. blue and yellow 70 25
O1838 14r. red and blue . . 70 50
O2054 14r. green and grey 75 30
O2055 15r. blue and mauve 1·50 70
O1839 20r. blue and orange 70 55
O2056 20r. purple and yellow . . . . . 1·75 30
O2057 30r. brown & orange 1·75 90
O1840 50r. brown and green . . . . . . 3·50 1·40
O2058 50r. black and gold 3·50 1·00
The 6r. to 50r. are larger, 23 × 37 mm.

PARCEL POST STAMPS

1915. Coronation stamps of 1915 optd **COLIS POSTAUX** in English and Persian.
P443 **66** 1c. blue and red 10 10
P444 2c. red and blue 10 10
P445 3c. green 10 10
P446 5c. red 10 10
P447 6c. red and green 20 10
P448 9c. violet and brown . . 20 10
P449 10c. brown and green . . 20 10
P450 12c. blue 20 10
P451 24c. chocolate and brown 20 10
P452 **67** 1k. black, brown & silver 70 15
P453 2k. red, blue and silver 70 15
P454 3k. sepia, lilac and silver 70 20
P455 5k. grey, sepia and silver 70 20
P456 – 1t. black, violet and gold 75 35
P457 – 2t. brown, green and gold 75 35
P458 – 3t. red, crimson and gold 80 55
P459 – 5t. grey, blue and gold . . 1·25 55

P **192**

1958.
P1151 P **192** 50d. drab 10 10
P1152 1r. red 10 10
P1153 2r. blue 20 10
P1154 3r. myrtle 15 10
P1478 5r. violet 15 10
P1479 10r. brown 30 15
P1480 20r. orange 50 35
P1481 30r. mauve . . . . . 1·00 15
P1482 50r. lake . . . . . . 1·25 85
P1483 100r. yellow . . . . 2·75 1·00
P1484 200r. green . . . . . 6·00 3·75
The word "IRAN" with a black frame is printed in reverse on the back of the above stamps and is intended to show through the stamps when attached to parcels.

POSTAL TAX STAMPS

T **142a** Red Lion and Sun Emblem (8 lines to each ray)

1950. Hospitals Fund.
T1139 T **142a** 50d. red and green 50 15
T1396 2r. red and lilac . . 80 15

1976. As T **142a** but with five lines to each ray.
T2007 T **142a** 50d. red and green 1·25 20
T2008 2r. red and blue . . 1·75 20

IRAQ Pt. 1, Pt. 19

A country W. of Persia, formerly under Turkish dominion, then under British mandate after the 1914–18 War. An independent kingdom since 1932 until 14 July 1958, when the king was assassinated and a republic proclaimed.

1917. 16 annas = 1 rupee.
1931. 1000 fils = 1 dinar.

1918. Stamps of Turkey (Pictorial issue, Nos. 501/514) surch **IRAQ IN BRITISH OCCUPATION** and value in Indian currency.

1		½a. on 5pa. purple	50	1·00
2		½a. on 10pa. green	70	20
3		1a. on 20pa. red	50	10
17		1½a. on 5pa. purple	1·50	1·00
5		2½a. on 1pi. blue	1·25	1·40
6		3a. on 1½pi. grey and red	1·25	25
7		4a. on 1¾pi. brown and grey	1·50	25
8		6a. on 2pi. black and green	1·60	1·50
9		8a. on 2½pi. green and orange	1·25	70
10		12a. on 5pi. lilac	1·75	4·00
11		1r. on 10pi. brown	2·25	1·40
12		2r. on 25pi. green	7·50	2·50
13		5r. on 50pi. red	20·00	22·00
14		10r. on 100pi. blue	55·00	17·00

2 Sunni Mosque, Muadhdham

3 Winged Cherub

4 Allegory of Date Palm

10 King Faisal I

1923.

41	2	½a. green	1·00	10
42	–	1a. brown	2·50	10
43	3	1½a. red	1·00	10
44	–	2a. buff	1·00	15
45	–	3a. blue	1·00	15
46	–	4a. violet	2·75	30
47	–	6a. blue	1·00	30
48	–	8a. bistre	3·00	30
49	4	1r. brown and green	6·00	1·50
50	2	2r. black	14·00	7·00
51		2r. bistre	42·00	3·25
52	–	5r. orange	27·00	13·00
53	–	10r. red	32·00	20·00

DESIGNS—30 × 24 mm: 1a. Gufas on the Tigris; 2a. Bull from Babylonian wall-sculpture; 6a., 10r. Shiah Mosque, Kadhimain. 34 × 24 mm: 3a. Arch of Ctesiphon. 24 × 30 mm: 4, 8a., 5r. Tribal Standard, Dulaim Camel Corps.

1927.

78	10	1r. brown	7·00	50

11 King Faisal I

12

1931.

80	11	½a. green	1·50	30
81		1a. brown	1·50	30
82		1½a. red	1·50	50
83		2a. orange	1·25	10
84		3a. blue	1·25	20
85		4a. purple	1·25	2·25
86		6a. blue	1·50	80
87		8a. green	1·50	2·75
88	12	1r. brown	3·50	2·25
89		2r. brown	6·00	5·50
90		5r. orange	20·00	32·00
91		10r. red	65·00	85·00
92	10	25r. violet	£550	£700

1932. Nos. 80/92 and 46 surch in "Fils" or "Dinar".

106	11	2f. on ½a. green	50	10
107		3f. on ½a. green	50	10
108		4f. on 1a. brown	2·25	25
109		5f. on 1a. brown	75	10
110		8f. on 1½a. red	50	50
111		10f. on 2a. orange	50	10
112		15f. on 3a. blue	1·50	1·00
113		20f. on 4a. purple	1·75	1·75
114	–	25f. on 4a. violet (No. 46)	3·00	4·25
115	11	30f. on 6a. blue	2·25	60
116		40f. on 8a. green	2·50	4·25
117	12	75f. on 1r. brown	2·00	4·25
118		100f. on 2r. brown	5·50	4·00
119		200f. on 5r. orange	15·00	25·00
120		½d. on 10r. red	55·00	80·00
121	10	1d. on 25r. violet	£110	£190

1932. As Types 10/12 but value in FILS or DINAR.

138	11	2f. blue	50	20
139		3f. green	50	10
140		4f. purple	50	10
141		5f. green	50	10
142		8f. red	1·50	10
143		10f. yellow	1·50	10
144		15f. blue	1·50	10
145		20f. orange	1·75	50
146		25f. mauve	1·75	50
147		30f. olive	2·25	15
148		40f. violet	1·50	80
149	12	50f. brown	1·50	20
150		75f. blue	3·25	2·75
151		100f. green	4·50	70
152		200f. red	13·00	3·25
153	10	½d. blue	40·00	35·00
154		1d. purple	80·00	80·00

16 King Ghazi

17

1934.

172	16	1f. violet	35	25
173		2f. blue	25	25
174		3f. green	25	25
175		4f. purple	25	25
176		5f. green	25	25
177		8f. red	40	25
178		10f. yellow	50	25
179		15f. blue	50	25
180		20f. orange	50	25
181		25f. mauve	1·00	35
182		30f. green	75	25
183		40f. violet	85	25
184	17	50f. brown	2·10	25
185		75f. blue	1·70	35
186		100f. green	2·30	40
187		200f. red	4·25	90
188	–	½d. blue	11·00	9·25
189	–	1d. red	50·00	15·00

DESIGN—23 × 27½ mm: ½, 1d. Portrait as in Types 16/17 but different frame.

19 Mausoleum of Sitt Zubaidah

21 Lion of Babylon

22 Spiral Tower of Samarra

1941.

208	19	1f. purple	25	25
209		2f. brown	25	25
210	–	3f. green	25	25
211	–	4f. violet	25	25
212	–	5f. red	25	25
213	21	8f. red	60	25
214		8f. yellow	25	25
215		10f. yellow	11·00	2·50
216		10f. red	60	25
217		15f. blue	1·00	25
218a		15f. black	1·00	40
219		20f. black	3·50	50
220		20f. blue	50	25
221	22	25f. purple	25	25
222		30f. orange	25	25
223b		40f. brown	1·00	40
224b	–	50f. blue	2·10	50
225a	–	75f. mauve	1·30	50
226	–	100f. olive	1·40	90
227	–	200f. orange	5·00	90
228	–	½d. blue	14·50	4·25
229a	–	1d. green	32·00	9·25

DESIGNS—HORIZ: 3f., 4f., 5f. King Faisal's Mausoleum (24 × 20 mm); ½d., 1d. Mosque of the Golden Dome, Samarra (24 × 21 mm). VERT: 50f., 75f. as Type 22, but larger (21 × 24 mm); 100f., 200f. Oil Wells (20 × 22 mm).

26 King Faisal II

27

1942.

255	26	1f. brown and violet	25	25
256		2f. brown and blue	25	25
257		3f. brown and green	25	25
258		4f. sepia and brown	25	25
259		5f. brown and green	25	25
260		6f. brown and red	25	50
261		10f. brown and pink	25	25
262		12f. brown and green	25	25

1948.

271	27	1f. blue	40	10
272		2f. brown	25	10
273		3f. green	25	10
274		3f. red	8·00	1·80
275		4f. lilac	25	10
276		5f. red	25	10
277		5f. green	8·50	3·75
278		6f. mauve	25	10
279		8f. brown	3·75	65
280		10f. red	35	10
281		12f. green	35	10
282		14f. green	2·10	25
283		15f. black	6·25	1·80
284		16f. red	1·80	75
285		20f. blue	65	10
286		25f. purple	75	10
287		28f. blue	2·00	50
288		30f. orange	75	15
289		40f. brown	1·80	65
290		50f. blue	6·25	1·30
291		60f. blue	1·30	65
292		75f. mauve	1·30	65
293		100f. green	5·50	1·30
294		200f. orange	4·25	1·30
295		½d. blue	11·00	4·25
296		1d. green	46·00	16·00
MS297		161 × 179 mm. Nos. 273, 280, 284 and 292/4. Perf or imperf	£100	£150

The 50f. to 1d. are larger (22½ × 27½mm).

29 Vickers Viking "Al Mahfoutha" over Basrah Aerodrome

31 King Faisal I and Equestrian Statue

1949. Air.

330	29	3f. green	25	25
331	–	4f. purple	25	25
332	–	5f. brown	25	25
333	29	10f. red	3·25	1·30
334	–	20f. blue	1·40	60
335	–	35f. orange	1·40	60
336	–	50f. green	2·20	1·00
337	–	100f. violet	5·75	2·10
MS338		235 × 165 mm. Nos. 330/7	65·00	85·00

DESIGNS—As Type **29**: 4, 20f. "Al Mahfoutha" over Kut Barrage; 5, 35f. "Al Mahfoutha" over Faisal II Bridge. 31 × 22½ mm: 50, 100f. "Al Mahfoutha" over Dhiyala Railway Bridge.

1949. 75th Anniv of U.P.U.

339	–	20f. blue	2·10	1·50
340	31	40f. orange	3·00	1·50
341	–	50f. violet	7·25	5·50

DESIGNS: 20f. King Ghazi and mounted postman; 50f. King Faisal II, globe and wreath.

32 King Faisal II

33

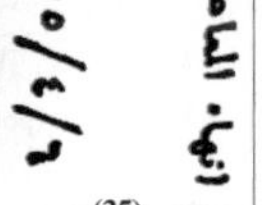
(35)

1953. Coronation of King Faisal II.

342	32	3f. red	1·00	1·00
343		14f. brown	2·10	1·00
344		28f. blue	5·75	1·50
MS345		134 × 138 mm. Nos. 342/4	85·00	£170

1954.

346	33	1f. blue	50	10
347		2f. brown	15	10
348		3f. lake	15	10
349		4f. violet	15	10
350		5f. green	25	10
351		6f. mauve	25	10
352		8f. brown	25	10
353		10f. blue	25	10
354		15f. black	1·30	1·10
355		16f. red	2·10	1·80
356		20f. olive	1·00	25
357		25f. purple	1·00	10
358		30f. red	1·00	10
359		40f. brown	1·20	40
360		50f. blue	1·50	60
361		75f. mauve	2·50	65
362		100f. olive	4·50	65
363		200f. salmon	7·50	1·40

The 50f. to 200f. are larger (22 × 28 mm).

1955. Abrogation of Anglo–Iraqi Treaty. Optd with T **35**.

380	33	3f. lake	90	40
381		10f. blue	1·00	40
382	27	28f. blue	1·70	85

36 King Faisal II

1955. 6th Arab Engineers' Conference, Baghdad.

383	36	3f. red	75	35
384		10f. blue	1·30	50
385		28f. blue	1·80	1·30

37 King Faisal II and Globe

1956. 3rd Arab Postal Union Conference, Baghdad.

386	37	3f. red	1·00	50
387		10f. blue	1·30	50
388		28f. blue	1·80	1·10

38 King Faisal II and Power Loom

39 King Faisal II and Exhibition Emblem

1957. Development Week.

389	38	1f. blue and buff	40	15
390	–	3f. multicoloured	40	15
391	–	5f. multicoloured	50	15
392	–	10f. multicoloured	75	15
393	–	40f. multicoloured	1·50	65

DESIGNS: 3f. Irrigation dam; 5f. Residential road, Baghdad; 10f. Cement kiln; 40f. Tigris Bridge.

1957. Agricultural and Industrial Exn, Baghdad.

394	39	10f. brown and cream	85	85

(40)

1957. Silver Jubilee of Iraqi Red Crescent Society. No. 388 optd with T **40**.

395	37	28f. blue	3·75	1·80

41 King Faisal II

42 King Faisal II and Tanks

1957.

396	41	1f. blue	25	40
397		2f. brown	25	40
398		3f. red	25	40
399		4f. violet	25	40
400		5f. green	60	60
401		6f. red	60	60
402		8f. brown	1·20	90
403		10f. blue	1·20	90

1958. Army Day.

411	42	8f. grey and green	85	85
412	–	10f. black and brown	1·10	1·10
413	–	20f. brown and blue	1·10	1·10
414	–	30f. violet and red	1·60	1·30

DESIGNS—As T **42**: King Faisal II and: 10f. Platoon marching; 20f. Mobile artillery unit and De Havilland D.H.112 Venom jet fighters. 22½ × 27½ mm: 30f. King Faisal II (full-length portrait).

1958. Development Week. As T **38**, inscr "1958".

415		3f. green, drab and violet	35	25
416		5f. multicoloured	50	40
417		10f. multicoloured	1·30	85

DESIGNS—VERT: 3f. Sugar beet and refining plant. HORIZ: 5f. Building and pastoral scene; 10f. Irrigation dam.

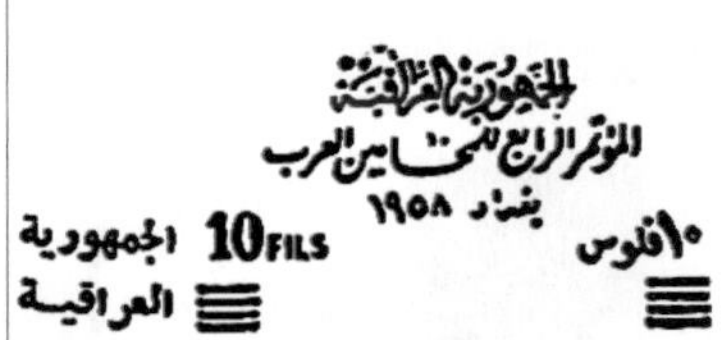
(43 "Iraqi Republic") (44)

1958. Optd with T **43**. (a) On No. 189.

418		1d. purple	23·00	23·00

(b) On T **27**.

418a		1f. blue	30·00	10·00
419		12f. olive	65	25
420		14f. olive	85	25
421		16f. red	11·00	3·25
422		28f. blue	1·10	60
423		60f. blue	3·00	60
424		½d. blue	18·00	4·50
425		1d. green	35·00	17·00

(c) On T **33**.

426 1f. blue 60 25
427 2f. brown 60 25
428 4f. violet 60 25
429 5f. green 60 25
430 6f. mauve 60 25
431 8f. brown 60 25
432 10f. blue 65 25
433 15f. black 85 25
434 16f. red 2·10 50
435 20f. olive 1·00 60
436 25f. purple 65 35
437 30f. red 1·00 35
438 40f. brown 1·00 25
439 50f. blue 4·50 2·75
440 75f. mauve 3·50 85
441 100f. olive 4·25 2·75
442 200f. salmon 12·50 5·50

Nos. 439/42 are larger (22 × 28 mm).

(d) On T **41**.

443 1f. blue 2·75 65
444 2f. brown 60 25
445 3f. red 60 25
446 4f. violet 65 25
447 5f. green 60 25
448 6f. red 60 25
449 8f. brown 60 65
450 10f. blue 60 25
451 20f. green 60 25
452 25f. purple 1·30 75
453 30f. red 1·40 25
454 40f. brown 3·75 1·40
455 50f. purple 2·75 65
456 75f. green 2·75 1·30
457 100f. orange 3·75 1·30
458 200f. blue 10·00 2·20

Nos. 455/8 are larger (22½ × 27½ mm).

1958. Arab Lawyers Conf, Baghdad. Surch with T **44**.
506 **36** 10f. on 28f. blue 1·40 90

45 Republican Soldier and Flag **45a** Orange Tree

1959. Army Day.
507 **45** 3f. blue 35 15
508 10f. olive 65 35
509 40f. violet 1·30 65

1959. Afforestation Day.
510 **45a** 10f. orange and green 65 25

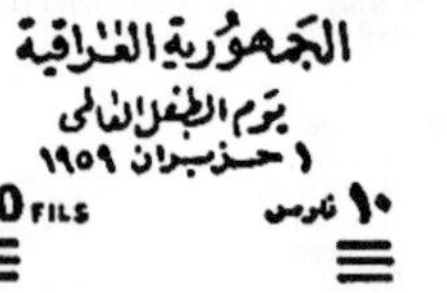

(46)

1959. International Children's Day. Surch with T **46**.
511 **37** 10f. on 28f. blue 1·10 60

47 Worker and Buildings **48** Harvesters

1959. 1st Anniv of Revolution. Inscr "14TH JULY 1958".
512 **47** 10f. blue and ochre 50 40
513 – 30f. green and ochre 1·00 65
DESIGN—HORIZ: 30f. Revolutionaries brandishing weapons.

1959. Agricultural Reform.
514 **48** 10f. black and green 50 15

49 Republican Emblem (50)

1959.
515 **49** 1f. multicoloured 15 15
516 2f. multicoloured 15 15
517 3f. multicoloured 15 15
518 4f. multicoloured 15 15
519 5f. multicoloured 15 15
520 10f. multicoloured 15 15
521 15f. multicoloured 50 15
522 20f. multicoloured 50 15
523 30f. multicoloured 50 25
524 40f. multicoloured 90 35
525 50f. multicoloured 3·50 85
526 75f. multicoloured 1·40 40
527 100f. multicoloured 2·10 85
528 200f. multicoloured 3·75 85
529 500f. multicoloured 6·25 2·75
530 1d. multicoloured 14·50 6·75

1959. "Health and Hygiene". Optd with T **50**.
531 **49** 10f. multicoloured 85 50

51 Gen. Kassem and Military Parade **52** Gen. Kassem

1960. Army Day.
532 **51** 10f. lake and green 50 50
533 – 16f. red and blue 85 65
534 – 30f. olive, brown and buff 85 65
535 – 40f. violet and buff 1·20 85
536 – 60f. buff, chocolate & brn 1·70 1·00
DESIGNS—Gen. Kassem and: HORIZ: 16f. Infantry on manoeuvres; 60f. Partisans. VERT: 30f. Anti-aircraft gun-crew; 40f. Oilfield guards on parade.

1960. Gen. Kassem's Escape from Assassination.
537 **52** 10f. violet 50 35
538 30f. green 90 50

53 Al Rasafi (poet) **54** Gen. Kassem at Tomb of Unknown Soldier

1960. Al Rasafi Commemoration. Optd **1960** in English and Arabic.
539 **53** 10l. red 2·50 1·30
See also No 732.

1960. 2nd Anniv of Revolution.
540 – 6f. gold, olive and orange 60 50
541 **54** 10f. orange, green and blue 60 50
542 16f. orange, violet and blue 75 75
543 – 18f. gold, blue and orange 75 75
544 – 30f. gold, brown and orange 1·00 90
545 **54** 60f. orange, sepia and blue 2·00 1·40
DESIGN—VERT: 6f., 18f., 30f. Symbol of Republic.

55 Gen. Kassem, Flag and Troops **56** Gen. Kassem with Children

1961. Army Day.
546 **55** 3f. multicoloured 25 15
547 6f. multicoloured 25 15
548 10f. multicoloured 50 15
549 – 20f. black, yellow and green 60 25
550 – 30f. black, yellow & brown 60 35
551 – 40f. black, yellow and blue 85 60
DESIGN: 20, 30, 40f. Kassem and triumphal arch.

1961. World Children's Day. Main design brown; background colours given.
558 **56** 3f. yellow 60 40
559 6f. blue 85 40
560 10f. pink 1·20 40
561 30f. lemon 1·20 40
562 50f. green 2·10 65

57 Gen. Kassem saluting **58** Gen. Kassem and Army Emblem

1961. 3rd Anniv of Revolution.
563 – 1f. multicoloured 25 10
564 – 3f. multicoloured 25 10
565 **57** 5f. multicoloured 25 10
566 – 6f. multicoloured 25 10
567 – 10f. multicoloured 35 25
568 **57** 30f. multicoloured 65 50
569 40f. multicoloured 85 50
570 – 50f. multicoloured 1·40 1·00
571 – 100f. multicoloured 4·50 2·50
DESIGN: 1, 3, 6, 10, 50, 100f. Gen. Kassem and Iraqi flag.

1962. Army Day.
572 – 1f. multicoloured 25 25
573 – 3f. multicoloured 25 25
574 – 6f. multicoloured 25 25
575 **58** 10f. black, gold and lilac 40 25
576 30f. black, gold and orange 85 50
577 50f. black, gold and green 1·40 1·00
DESIGN—VERT: 1, 3, 6f. Gen. Kassem saluting and part of speech.

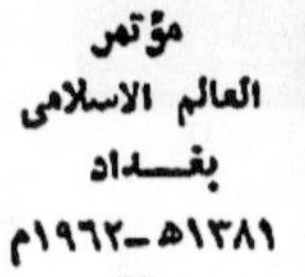

(59) **60** Gen. Kassem, Flag and Handclasp

1962. 5th Islamic Congress. Optd with T **59**.
578 **49** 3f. multicoloured 25 25
579 10f. multicoloured 25 25
580 30f. multicoloured 85 50

1962. 4th Anniv of Revolution. Flag in green and gold.
581 **60** 1f. orange and sepia 10 10
582 3f. green and sepia 10 10
583 6f. brown and black 10 10
584 10f. lilac and sepia 40 40
585 30f. red and sepia 60 40
586 50f. grey and sepia 1·20 75

61 Fanfare **62** Republican Emblem

1962. Millenary of Baghdad. Multicoloured.
603 3f. Type **61** 40 25
604 6f. Al Kindi (philosopher) 40 25
605 10f. Map of old "Round City" of Baghdad 65 35
606 40f. Gen. Kassem and flag 1·80 90

1962. Aerogramme Stamps.
607 **62** 14f. black and green 1·80 65
608 35f. black and red 2·50 1·00
Nos. 607/8 were originally issued only attached to aerogramme forms covering the old imprinted King Faisal II stamps, but later appeared in sheets.

63 Campaign Emblem **64** Gen. Kassem and Tanks

1962. Malaria Eradication.
609 **63** 3f. multicoloured 25 25
610 10f. multicoloured 60 25
611 40f. multicoloured 1·00 50

1963. Army Day.
612 **64** 3f. black and yellow 10 10
613 5f. sepia and purple 10 10
614 6f. black and green 10 10
615 10f. black and blue 25 25
616 10f. black and pink 25 25
617 20f. black and blue 60 35
618 40f. black and mauve 1·00 60
619 50f. sepia and blue 1·40 1·20

65 Gufas on the Tigris **66** Shepherd with Sheep

1963.
620 **65** 1f. green 60 25
621 – 2f. violet 60 25
622 **65** 3f. black 60 25
623 – 4f. black and yellow 60 25
624 – 5f. purple and green 65 25
625 – 10f. red 90 25
626 – 15f. brown and yellow 1·40 25
627 – 20f. violet 1·50 25
628 – 30f. orange 1·00 35
629 – 40f. green 1·70 25
630 – 50f. brown 7·25 60
631 – 75f. black and green 3·50 40
632 – 100f. purple 3·75 50
633 – 200f. brown 7·25 50
634 – 500f. blue 10·00 2·20
635 – 1d. purple 13·50 4·25
DESIGNS: 2f., 500f. Spiral tower of Samarra; 4f., 15f. Sumerian Harp; 5f., 75f. Republican emblem; 10f., 50f. Lion of Babylon; 20f., 40f. Koranic school of Abbasid period; 30f., 200f. Mosque and minarets; 100f., 1d. Winged bull of Kharsabad.

1963. Freedom from Hunger.
636 **66** 3f. black and green 25 25
637 – 10f. mauve and brown 60 25
638 – 20f. brown and blue 1·00 65
MS639 175 × 120 mm. Nos. 636/8 (sold at 50f.) 5·00 5·00
DESIGNS: 10f. Harvester; 20f. Trees.

67 Centenary Emblem **68** Helmet, Rifle and Flag

1963. Red Cross Centenary.
640 **67** 3f. violet and red 25 25
641 10f. blue and red 50 25
642 – 30f. blue and red 90 60
DESIGN—HORIZ: 30f. Hospital.

1964. Army Day.
643 **68** 3f. sepia, green and blue 25 25
644 10f. sepia, green and pink 50 25
645 30f. sepia, green and yellow 90 60

69 Revolutionaries and Flag

1964. 1st Anniv of 14th Ramadan Revolution. Flag in red, green and black.
646 **69** 10f. violet 50 25
647 30f. brown 90 60
MS648 125 × 75 mm. Nos. 646/7 in new colours (sold at 50f.) 5·75 4·25
See also No. **MS**746.

70 Shamash (Sun-God) and Hammurabi **71** Soldier raising Flag on Map of Iraq

1964. 15th Anniv of Declaration of Human Rights.
649 **70** 6f. olive and purple 50 40
650 – 10f. violet and orange 90 40
651 **70** 30f. green and blue 1·40 65
DESIGN: 10f. U.N. Emblem and Scales of Justice.

1964. 6th Anniv of Revolution.
652 – 3f. orange, grey and black 25 25
653 **71** 10f. red, black and green 25 25
654 20f. red, black and green 50 25
655 – 30f. orange, grey and black 1·00 60
DESIGN—HORIZ: 3f., 30f. Soldier "protecting" people and factories with outstretched arm.

72 Soldier, Civilians and Star Emblem **73** Musician

1964. 1st Anniv of 18 November Revolution.

656	**72**	5f. orange and brown . . .	35	25
657		10f. orange and blue . . .	35	25
658		50f. orange and violet . . .	1·00	40

1964. International Arab Music Conf, Baghdad.

659	**73**	3f. multicoloured	90	25
660		10f. multicoloured	90	25
661		30f. multicoloured	1·30	90

74 Conference Emblem and Map

75 A.P.U. Emblem

1964. 9th Arab Engineer's Conf, Baghdad.

662	**74**	10f. green and mauve . . .	60	25

1964. 10th Anniv of Arab Postal Union's Permanent Office.

663	**75**	3f. blue and red	25	15
664		10f. slate and purple . . .	50	15
665		30f. blue and orange . . .	1·10	50

76 Soldier, Civilians and Flag

77 Cogwheel and Factory

1965. Army Day.

666	**76**	5f. multicoloured	25	15
667		15f. multicoloured	35	25
668		30f. multicoloured	1·10	60
MS669		110 × 83 mm. Stamps similar to No. 668 but without value shown together with stamps-size portrait of Pres. Arif. Imperf. (sold at 60f.)	7·25	7·25

1965. 1st Arab Ministers of Labour Conf, Baghdad.

670	**77**	10f. multicoloured	50	25

78 Oil Tanker

79 Armed Soldier with Flag

1965. Inauguration of Deep Sea Terminal for Tankers.

671	**78**	10f. multicoloured	90	40

1965. 2nd Anniv of 14th Ramadan Revolution.

672	**79**	10f. multicoloured	50	15

80 Tree

81 Federation Emblem

1965. Tree Week.

673	**80**	6f. multicoloured	25	25
674		20f. multicoloured	1·10	25

1965. Arab Insurance Federation. Sun in gold.

675	**81**	3f. ultramarine and blue	25	25
676		10f. black and grey	25	25
677		30f. red and pink	90	65

82 Dagger of Deir Yassin, Palestine

1965. Deir Yassin Massacre.

678	**82**	10f. drab and black . . .	90	35
679		20f. brown and blue . . .	1·70	50

83 "Threat of Disease"

1965. World Health Day.

680	**83**	3f. multicoloured	40	25
681		10f. multicoloured	50	25
682		20f. multicoloured	1·20	65

84 I.T.U. Emblem and Symbols

1965. Centenary of I.T.U.

683	**84**	10f. multicoloured	65	15
684		20f. multicoloured	1·40	50
MS685		139 × 95 mm. Nos. 683/4. Imperf or perf	15·00	12·50

85 Flag and Map

86 Revolutionary and Flames

85a Lamp and Burning Library

1965. 1st Anniv of Iraq–U.A.R. Pact.

686	**85**	10f. multicoloured	40	15

1965. Reconstitution of Algiers University Library.

687	**85a**	5f. red, green and black	35	25
688		10f. green, red and black	60	25

1965. 45th Anniv of 1920 Rebellion.

689	**86**	5f. multicoloured	25	15
690		10f. multicoloured	40	15

87 Mosque

1965. Mohammed's Birthday.

691	**87**	10f. multicoloured	60	60
MS692		110 × 75 mm. No. 691 (sold at 50f.)	6·25	6·25

88 Factory and Ear of Wheat

90 Fair Emblem

89 I.C.Y. Emblem

1965. 7th Anniv of 14 July Revolution.

693	**88**	10f. multicoloured	40	40

1965. Air. International Co-operation Year.

694	**89**	5f. black and brown . . .	60	25
695		10f. brown and green . . .	90	25
696		30f. black and blue	2·50	1·00

1965. Baghdad Fair.

697	**90**	10f. multicoloured	35	15

91 Pres. Arif (photo by Studio Jean)

1965. 2nd Anniv of 18 November Revolution.

698	**91**	5f. blue and orange	35	25
699		10f. sepia and blue	40	25
700		50f. blue and mauve . . .	2·00	85

92 Census Graph

1965. National Census.

701	**92**	3f. black and purple . . .	35	15
702		5f. red and brown	35	15
703		15f. bistre and blue	1·50	50

93 Hawker Siddeley Trident 1E Airliner

1965. Air. Inauguration of Hawker Siddeley Trident 1E Aircraft by Iraqi Airways.

704	**93**	5f. multicoloured	35	35
705		10f. multicoloured	35	35
706		40f. multicoloured	3·75	75

94 Date Palms

95 Army Memorial

1965. 2nd F.A.O. Dates Conference, Baghdad.

707	**94**	3f. multicoloured	35	25
708		10f. multicoloured	85	25
709		15f. multicoloured	1·50	75

1966. 45th Anniv of Army Day.

710	**95**	2f. multicoloured	40	25
711		5f. multicoloured	40	25
712		40f. multicoloured	1·70	65

96 "Eagle" and Flag

96a Arab League Emblem

1966. 3rd Anniv of 14th Ramadan Revolution.

713	**96**	5f. multicoloured	25	25
714		10f. multicoloured	60	25

1966. Arab Publicity Week.

715	**96a**	5f. green, brown & orange	40	15
716		15f. blue, purple and olive	40	15

97 Footballers

98 Footballer's Legs, and Iraq Football Union Emblem (½-size illustration)

1966. Arab Football Cup, Baghdad. Mult.

717	2f. Type **97**	20	20
718	5f. Goalkeeper with ball . . .	20	20
719	15f. Type **97**	70	40
MS720	116 × 70 mm. 50f. Type **98**	6·25	8·50

99 Excavator

100 Queen Nefertari

1966. Labour Day.

721	**99**	15f. multicoloured	25	15
722		25f. black, silver and red	40	15

1966. Nubian Monuments Preservation.

723	**100**	5f. yellow, black and olive	35	25
724		15f. yellow, brown & blue	35	25
725	–	40f. brown, chestnut & red	1·80	1·40

DESIGN—HORIZ: (41 × 32 mm): 40f. Rock temples, Abu Simbel.

101 President Arif

1966. 8th Anniv of 14 July Revolution.

726	**101**	5f. multicoloured	35	25
727		15f. multicoloured	50	25
728		50f. multicoloured	1·70	1·00

102

1966. Mohammed's Birthday.

729 **102** 5f. multicoloured 15 10
730 15f. multicoloured 25 10
731 30f. multicoloured . . . . 1·30 75

1966. As No. 539 but without opt.

732 **53** 10f. red . . . . 8·50 8·50

103 Iraqi Museum, Statue and Window 104 Revolutionaries

1966. Inauguration of Iraqi Museum, Baghdad. Multicoloured.

733 15f. Type **103** . . . . 1·20 25
734 50f. Gold headdress . . . . 1·50 75
735 80f. Sumerian head (vert) . . 3·25 1·10

1966. 3rd Anniv of 18 November Revolution.

736 **104** 15f. multicoloured 60 50
737 25f. multicoloured 90 90

105 "Magic Carpet"

1966. Air. Meeting of Arab International Tourist Union, Baghdad. Multicoloured.

738 2f. White stork emblem (27½ × 39 mm) 25 25
739 5f. Type **105** 25 25
740 15f. As 2f. 35 35
741 50f. Type **105** . . . . 1·30 60

106 UNESCO Emblem

1966. 20th Anniv of UNESCO.

742 **106** 5f. brown, black and blue 15 10
743 15f. green, black and red 50 25

107 Soldier and Rocket-launchers

1967. Army Day.

744 **107** 15f. ochre, brown & yellow 40 15
745 20f. ochre, brown and lilac 60 25

1967. 4th Anniv of Revolution of 14th Ramadan. No. MS648 with original inscriptions obliterated "4th" in place of "1st" and sheet value amended to 70fils.

MS746 125 × 75 mm. Nos. 646/7. Imperf (sold at 70f.) . . . . . 6·75 6·75

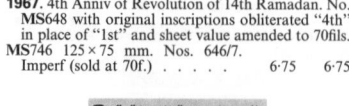

108 Oil Refinery

1967. 6th Arab Petroleum Congress, Baghdad. Multicoloured.

747 5f. Congress emblem (vert) 25 15
748 15f. Type **108** 35 15
749 40f. Congress emblem (vert) 50 65
750 50f. Type **108** . . . . 1·70 90

109 "Spider's Web" Emblem 110 Worker holding Cogwheel

1967. Hajeer Year (1967).

751 **109** 5f. multicoloured 25 15
752 15f. multicoloured 35 25

1967. Labour Day.

753 **110** 10f. multicoloured 25 10
754 15f. multicoloured 35 15

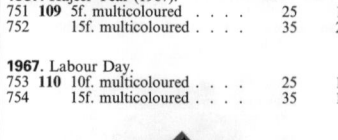

111

1967. Mohammed's Birthday.

755 **111** 5f. multicoloured 35 25
756 15f. multicoloured 40 25

112 Flag and Hands with Clubs

1967. 47th Anniv of 1920 Rebellion.

757 **112** 5f. multicoloured 35 10
758 15f. multicoloured 50 10

113 Um Qasr Port 114 Costume

1967. 9th Anniv of 14 July Revolution and Inaug of Um Qasr Port. Multicoloured.

759 5f. Type **113** 25 15
760 10f. Freighter at quayside . . 60 25
761 15f. As 10f. . . . . 1·00 25
762 40f. Type **113** . . . . 1·80 1·00

1967. Iraqi Costumes.

765 **114** 2f. multicoloured (postage) 25 25
766 – 5f. multicoloured 25 25
767 – 10f. multicoloured 65 25
768 – 15f. multicoloured 85 50
769 – 20f. multicoloured . . . . 1·10 50
770 – 25f. multicoloured . . . . 1·20 60
771 – 30f. multicoloured . . . . 1·40 60
772 – 40f. multicoloured (air) 1·30 65
773 – 50f. multicoloured . . . . 1·80 1·00
774 – 80f. multicoloured . . . . 2·50 1·30

DESIGNS: 5f. to 80f. Different costumes.

115 Pres. Arif and Map

1967. 4th Anniv of 18 November Revolution. Multicoloured.

775 5f. President Arif 35 25
776 15f. Type **115** 75 40

116 Ziggurat of Ur

1967. International Tourist Year. Multicoloured.

777 2f. Type **116** (postage) . . . 25 25
778 5f. Statues of Nimroud . . . 25 25
779 10f. Babylon (arch) 40 25
780 15f. Minaret of Mosul (vert) 50 25
781 25f. Arch of Ctesiphon . . . 60 25
782 50f. Statue, Temple of Hatra (vert) (air) . . . . 2·75 40
783 80f. Spiral Minaret of Samarra (vert) . . . . . . 3·00 60
784 100f. Adam's Tree (vert) . . 2·75 65
785 200f. Aladdin ("Aladdin's Cave") (vert) . . . . . . 6·25 3·00
786 500f. Golden Mosque of Kadhimain . . . . 30·00 18·00

117 Guide Emblem and Saluting Hand

1967. Iraqi Scouts and Guides. Multicoloured.

787 2f. Type **117** . . . . 1·30 35
788 5f. Guides by camp-fire . . . 1·50 40
789 10f. Scout emblem and saluting hand . . . . . . 1·70 60
790 15f. Scouts setting up camp 1·70 75
MS791 120 × 48 mm. Nos. 787/90. Imperf (sold at 50f.) . . . . . 8·50 8·50

118 Soldiers Drilling

1968. Army Day.

792 **118** 5f. brown, green and blue 35 15
793 15f. indigo, olive and blue 65 25

119 White-cheeked Bulbul

1968. Iraqi Birds. Multicoloured.

794 5f. Type **119** 60 25
795 10f. Hoopoe 65 25
796 15f. Jay . . . . 1·10 25
797 25f. Peregrine falcon . . . . 1·70 40
798 30f. White stork . . . . . . 2·20 40
799 40f. Black partridge . . . . 2·75 65
800 50f. Marbled teal . . . . . . 3·75 1·10

120 Battle Scene

1968. 5th Anniv of 14th Ramadan Revolution.

801 **120** 15f. orange, black and blue . . . . 3·00 85

121 Symbols of "Labour"

1968. Labour Day.

802 **121** 15f. multicoloured 35 25
803 25f. multicoloured 60 25

122 Football

1968. 23rd International Military Sports Council Football Championship. Multicoloured.

804 2f. Type **122** 35 25
805 5f. Goalkeeper in mid air . . 35 25
806 15f. Type **122** 40 25
807 25f. As 5f. . . . . 2·30 75
MS808 59 × 61 mm. 70f. Championship shield. Imperf 7·50 8·50

123 Soldier with Iraqi Flag

1968. 10th Anniv of 14 July Revolution.

809 **123** 15f. multicoloured 40 15

124 Anniversary and W.H.O. Emblems

1968. 20th Anniv of W.H.O.

810 – 5f. multicoloured 25 15
811 – 10f. multicoloured 25 15
812 **124** 15f. red, blue and black 50 15
813 – 25f. red, green and black 65 35

DESIGN—VERT: 5, 10f. Combined anniversary and W.H.O. emblems.

125 Human Rights Emblem 126 Mother and children

1968. Human Rights Year.

814 **125** 10f. red, yellow and blue 35 25
815 25f. red, yellow and green 35 25
MS816 55 × 75 mm. **125** 100f. scarlet, lemon and mauve. Imperf. 5·00 5·00

1968. UNICEF Commemoration.

817 **126** 15f. multicoloured 40 25
818 25f. multicoloured . . . . 1·20 35
MS819 56 × 76 mm. **126** 100f. multicoloured. Imperf . . . . 7·50 5·00

127 Army Tanks

1969. Army Day.

820 **127** 25f. multicoloured . . . . 3·00 1·50

128 Agricultural Scene

1969. 6th Anniv of 14th Ramadan Revolution.

821 **128** 15f. multicoloured 50 25

129 Mosque and Worshippers

1969. Hajeer Year.

822 **129** 15f. multicoloured 50 50

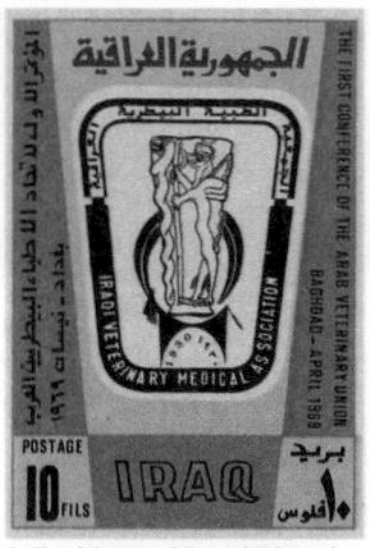

130 Emblem of Iraqi Veterinary Medical Association

1969. 1st Arab Veterinary Union Conf, Baghdad.
823 **130** 10f. multicoloured 60 35
824 15f. multicoloured 90 35

131 Mahseer

1969. Multicoloured. (a) Postage. Fishes.
825 2f. Type **131** . . . . . . 1·40 35
826 3f. Sharpey's barbel . . . . 1·50 35
827 10f. Silver pomfret . . . . 1·70 35
828 100f. Pike barbel . . . . . 5·50 3·00

(b) Air. Fauna.
829 2f. Striped hyena 35 25
830 3f. Leopard 35 25
831 5f. Mountain gazelle 35 25
832 10f. Head of Arab horse . . 40 35
833 200f. Arab horse . . . . . . 10·00 5·50

132 Kaaba, Mecca

1969. Mohammed's Birthday.
834 **132** 15f. multicoloured 60 25

133 I.L.O. Emblem

1969. 50th Anniv of I.L.O.
835 **133** 5f. yellow, blue and black 15 10
836 15f. yellow, green & black 15 10
837 50f. yellow, red and black 1·30 90
MS838 75 × 55 mm. **133** 100f. multicoloured. Imperf . . . . 5·00 5·00

134 Weightlifting

135 Arms of Iraq and "Industry"

1969. Olympic Games, Mexico (1968). Mult.
839 3f. Type **134** 50 25
840 5f. High jumping 50 25
841 10f. As Type **134** 60 35
842 35f. As 5f. . . . . 1·10 85
MS843 91 × 116 mm. Nos. 839/42. Imperf (sold at 100f.) . . . . 9·25 9·25

1969. 11th Anniv of 14 July Revolution.
844 **135** 10f. multicoloured 35 25
845 15f. multicoloured 50 25

136 Rebuilding Roads

1969. Anniv of 17 July Revolution and Inaug of Baghdad International Airport. Mult.
846 10f. Type **136** 50 35
847 15f. Type **136** 50 35
848 20f. Airport building . . . 1·50 40
849 200f. President Bakr (vert) . . 14·50 7·50

137 Ear of Wheat and Fair Emblem

139 Radio Beacon and Outline of Palestine

138 Floating Crane "Antara"

1969. 6th International Baghdad Fair.
850 **137** 10f. brown, gold and green 60 25
851 15f. red, gold and blue . . 75 35

1969. 50th Anniv of Port of Basra. Mult.
852 15f. Type **138** 40 25
853 20f. Harbour tender "Al-Walid" 60 40
854 30f. Pilot boat "Al-Rashid" 90 50
855 35f. Dredger "Hillah" . . . 1·40 85
856 50f. Survey ship "Al-Fao" . . 4·25 2·20

1969. 10th Anniv of Iraqi News Agency.
857 **139** 15f. multicoloured . . . . 1·00 35
858 50f. multicoloured . . . . 2·75 65

140 Emblem, Book and Hands

1969. Campaign Against Illiteracy.
859 **140** 15f. multicoloured 25 15
860 20f. multicoloured 50 35

141 Ross and Keith Smith's Vickers Vimy Biplane

1969. Air. 50th Anniv of 1st England–Australia Flight.
861 **141** 15f. multicoloured . . . . 2·20 1·10
862 35f. multicoloured . . . . 3·50 2·75
MS863 81 × 100 mm. Nos. 861/2 (sold at 100f.). Imperf . . . . 12·00 10·00

142 Newspaper Headline

144 Iraqis supporting Wall

143 Soldier and Map

1969. Centenary of Iraqi Press.
864 **142** 15f. black, orange & yell 50 35

1970. Army Day.
865 **143** 15f. multicoloured 65 35
866 20f. multicoloured . . . . 1·30 65

1970. 7th Anniv of 14th Ramadan Revolution.
867 **144** 10f. multicoloured 15 15
868 15f. multicoloured 40 15

عيد نوروز
1970
(145)

مهرجان الربيع
الموصل
1970
(147)

146 Map of Arab Countries, and Slogans

1970. New Year ("Nawrooz"). Nos. 891/6 optd with T **145**.
869 2f. multicoloured 35 25
870 3f. multicoloured 35 25
871 5f. multicoloured 35 25
872 10f. multicoloured 65 25
873 15f. multicoloured 85 25
874 50f. multicoloured . . . . . 2·20 1·30

1970. 23rd Anniv of Al-Baath Party. Mult.
875 15f. Type **146** 35 25
876 35f. Type **146** 60 50
877 50f. Iraqis acclaiming Party 1·70 65
MS878 115 × 76 mm. 150f. As 50f. Imperf . . . . 10·00 10·00

1970. Mosul Spring Festival. Nos. 891/6 optd with T **147**.
879 2f. multicoloured 50 50
880 3f. multicoloured 50 50
881 5f. multicoloured 50 50
882 10f. multicoloured 50 50
883 15f. multicoloured . . . . . 1·10 85
884 50f. multicoloured . . . . . 2·30 1·00

148 Iraqis celebrating Labour Day

1970. Labour Day.
885 **148** 10f. multicoloured 35 25
886 15f. multicoloured 40 35
887 35f. multicoloured . . . . 1·30 65

149 Kaaba, Mecca, Broken Statues and Koran

1970. Mohammed's Birthday.
888 **149** 15f. multicoloured 35 15
889 20f. multicoloured 35 25

150 Poppies

1970 ١٩٧٠
عيد الصحافة
(151)

1970. Spring Festival. Flowers. Multicoloured.
891 2f. Type **150** 40 25
892 3f. Narcissi 40 25
893 5f. Tulip 40 25
894 10f. Carnations 60 35
895 15f. Roses . . . . 1·00 50
896 50f. As 10f. . . . . 3·00 1·30

1970. Press Day. No. 864 optd with T **151**.
896a **142** 15f. black, orange & yell 50 50

152 Revolutionaries

1970. 50th Anniv of Revolution of 1920.
897 **152** 10f. black and green . . . 15 15
898 15f. black and gold . . . 35 15
899 – 35f. black and orange . . 85 40
MS900 119 × 71 mm. 100f. Designs as Nos. 897 and 899 but without face values. Imperf. . . . . . 5·00 5·00
DESIGN: 35f. Revolutionary and rising sun.

153 Bomb-burst and Broken Chain

1970. 12th Anniv of 14 July Revolution.
901 **153** 15f. multicoloured 25 15
902 20f. multicoloured 40 15

154 Hands and Map of Iraq

1970. 2nd Anniv of 17 July Revolution.
903 **154** 15f. multicoloured 25 15
904 25f. multicoloured 50 25

155 Pomegranates

1970. Fruits. Multicoloured.
905 3f. Type **155** 35 15
906 5f. Grapefruit 35 15
907 10f. Grapes 35 15
908 15f. Oranges . . . . 1·00 35
909 35f. Dates . . . . 3·00 1·70
The Latin inscriptions on Nos. 906/7 are transposed.

156 Kaaba, Mecca

1970. Hajeer Year.
910 **156** 15f. multicoloured 25 15
911 25f. multicoloured 50 25

الدورة السابعة

970 – ٩٧٠
(157)

1970. 7th Int Baghdad Fair. Optd with T **157**.
912 **137** 10f. brown, gold and green . . . . 3·00 1·70
913 15f. red, gold and blue . . 3·00 1·70

158 Arab League Flag and Map

1970. 25th Anniv of Arab League.
914 **158** 15f. purple, green and olive 25 10
915 35f. red, green and grey 50 40

159 Euphrates Bridge

1970. Air. National Development. Multicoloured.
916 10f. Type **159** . . . . 1·70 50
917 15f. Type **159** . . . . 2·50 1·20
918 1d. Pres. Bakr and banknotes (37 × 27 mm) . . . . . . 50·00 18·00

160 I.E.Y. Emblem

1970. International Education Year.
919 **160** 5f. multicoloured 25 15
920 15f. multicoloured 40 25

1970. 25th Anniv of United Nations. No. **MS**639 optd **1945 UNITED NATIONS 1970** together with other inscriptions and with face values of the stamps in the miniature sheet obliterated.
MS921 175 × 120 mm. 50f. . . . 6·25 6·25

161 Baghdad Hospital and Society Emblem

1970. 50th Anniv of Iraq Medical Society.
922 **161** 15f. multicoloured 25 15
923 40f. multicoloured . . . . 1·10 60

162 Union Emblem

163 Sugar Beet

1970. Air. 10th Arab Telecommunications Union Conference, Baghdad.
924 **162** 15f. multicoloured 25 10
925 25f. multicoloured 50 40

1970. 12th Anniv of Mosul Sugar Refinery. Multicoloured.
926 5f. Type **163** 25 10
927 15f. Sugar refinery (horiz) . . 40 15
928 30f. Type **163** . . . . 1·40 65

164 O.P.E.C. Emblem

1970. 10th Anniv of Organization of Petroleum Exporting Countries (O.P.E.C.).
929 **164** 10f. blue, bistre and purple 65 35
930 40f. blue, bistre and green 2·75 1·20

165 Soldiers, Tank and Aircraft

1971. 50th Anniv of Army Day.
931 **165** 15f. black, mauve and gold 50 25
932 – 40f. multicoloured . . . 2·75 1·00
MS933 124 × 91 mm. Nos. 931/2. Imperf (sold at 100f.) . . . . 8·00 8·00
DESIGN—42 × 35 mm: 40f. Soldiers and map of Middle East.

166 "Revolutionary Army"

1971. 8th Anniv of 14th Ramadan Revolution.
934 **166** 15f. multicoloured 40 25
935 40f. multicoloured . . . . 1·30 50

167 Pilgrims and Web

1971. Hajeer Year.
936 **167** 10f. multicoloured 25 15
937 15f. multicoloured 40 25

168 Pres. Bakr with Torch

1971. 1st Anniv of 11th March Manifesto.
938 **168** 15f. multicoloured 65 40
939 100f. multicoloured . . . 2·75 1·40

169 Boatman in Marshland

1971. Tourism Week. Multicoloured.
940 5f. Type **169** 15 25
941 10f. Stork over Baghdad . . 75 25
942 15f. Landscape ("Summer Resorts") 90 40
943 100f. "Return of Sinbad" . . 4·50 2·20

170 Blacksmith taming Serpent

1971. New Year ("Nawrooz").
944 **170** 15f. multicoloured 85 35
945 25f. multicoloured . . . . 1·50 65

1971. World Meteorological Day. Nos. 780 and 783 optd **W.M. DAY 1971** in English and Arabic.
946 15f. multicoloured (postage) 2·75 1·00
947 80f. multicoloured (air) . . . 5·75 4·25

172 Emblem and Workers

1971. 24th Anniv of Al-Baath Party. Mult.
948 15f. Type **172** 75 40
949 35f. Type **172** . . . . 1·30 85
950 250f. As Type **172** but central portion of design only (42 × 42 mm) . . . . . . 10·00 10·00
On No. 950 the circular centre is also perforated.

مهرجان الربيع
1971
(173)

174 Worker and Farm-girl

1971. Mosul Spring Festival. Nos. 765/6 and 770 optd with T **173**.
951 **114** 2f. multicoloured 40 25
952 – 5f. multicoloured 40 25
953 – 25f. multicoloured . . . . 1·80 90

1971. Labour Day.
954 **174** 15f. multicoloured 35 25
955 40f. multicoloured . . . . 1·30 35

175 Muslim at Prayer

1971. Mohammed's Birthday.
956 **175** 15f. multicoloured 60 25
957 100f. multicoloured . . . 2·10 1·40

176 Revolutionaries, and Hands with Broken Chains

1971. 13th Anniv of 14 July Revolution.
958 **176** 25f. multicoloured 50 25
959 50f. multicoloured . . . . 1·60 60

177 Rising Sun and "Prosperity"

1971. 3rd Anniv of 17 July Revolution.
960 **177** 25f. multicoloured 60 35
961 70f. multicoloured . . . . 1·80 75

182 Bank Emblem

1971. 30th Anniv of Rafidain Bank.
989 **182** 10f. multicoloured 50 50
990 15f. multicoloured 85 85
991 25f. multicoloured . . . . 1·60 1·60
992 65f. multicoloured . . . . 8·50 6·75
993 250f. multicoloured . . . 21·00 20·00
Nos. 992/3 are larger, 42 × 42 mm.

التعداد الزراعي العام
١٩٧١/١٠/١٥
(183)

1971. Agricultural Census. Nos. 905, 908/9 optd with T **183**.
994 3f. multicoloured . . . . . 1·80 1·80
995 15f. multicoloured . . . . . 1·80 1·80
996 35f. multicoloured . . . . . 1·80 1·80

184 Football

1971. 4th Pan-Arab Schoolboy Games, Baghdad. Multicoloured.
997 15f. Type **184** 25 25
998 25f. Throwing the discus and running 65 35
999 35f. Table tennis 85 75
1000 70f. Gymnastics . . . . . . 3·50 1·30
1001 95f. Volleyball and basketball . . . . 5·75 2·20
MS1002 195 × 146 mm. Nos. 997/1001. Imperf (sold at 200f.) . . . . 17·00 17·00

70 Fils ●●
يوم الطالب
٢٣ تشرين الثاني
٩٧١ – ٩٦١
٧ فلسا ●●
(185)

186 Society Emblem

1971. Students' Day. Nos. 892/3 surch and 895 optd as T **185**.
1003 15f. multicoloured . . . . . 1·40 35
1004 25f. on 5f. multicoloured . . 2·20 1·10
1005 70f. on 3f. multicoloured . . 8·00 2·75

1971. Air. 20th Anniv of Iraqi Philatelic Society.
1006 **186** 25f. multicoloured . . . 1·20 90
1007 70f. multicoloured . . . 3·50 2·20

1971. 25th Anniv of UNICEF. Nos. 817/18 optd **25th Anniversary 971**.
1008 **126** 15f. multicoloured . . . 2·75 1·10
1009 25f. multicoloured . . . 6·75 3·25

188 Schoolchildren on Zebra Crossing

1971. 2nd Traffic Week.
1010 **188** 15f. multicoloured . . . 1·40 75
1011 25f. multicoloured . . . 2·75 1·40

189 A.P.U. Emblem

190 Racial Equality Year Symbol

1971. 25th Anniv of Founding of Arab Postal Union at Sofar Conference.
1012 **189** 25f. brown, yellow & grn 40 25
1013 70f. red, yellow and blue 1·60 65

1971. Racial Equality Year.
1014 **190** 25f. multicoloured . . . 25 15
1015 70f. multicoloured . . . 1·00 90

191 Soldiers with Flag and Torch

192 Workers

1972. Army Day.
1016 **191** 25f. multicoloured . . . 1·00 60
1017 70f. multicoloured . . . 3·75 2·20

1972. 9th Anniv of 14th Ramadan Revolution.
1018 **192** 25f. multicoloured . . . 2·10 50
1019 95f. multicoloured . . . 3·50 2·20

193 Mosque and Crescent

1972. Hajeer Year.
1020 **193** 25f. multicoloured . . . 35 15
1021 35f. multicoloured . . . 65 40

المؤتمر التاسع للاتحاد الوطني
لطلبة العراق
٢٥ شباط – ٢ آذار / ١٩٧٢

(194)

1972. Air. 9th Iraqi Students' Union Congress. Nos. 916/17 optd with T **194**.
1022 **159** 10f. multicoloured . . . 2·10 2·10
1023 15f. multicoloured . . . 2·10 2·10

195 Dove, Olive Branch and Manifesto

1972. 2nd Anniv of 11 March Manifesto.
1024 **195** 25f. blue, lt blue & black 1·20 25
1025 70f. purple, mauve & blk 3·50 1·40

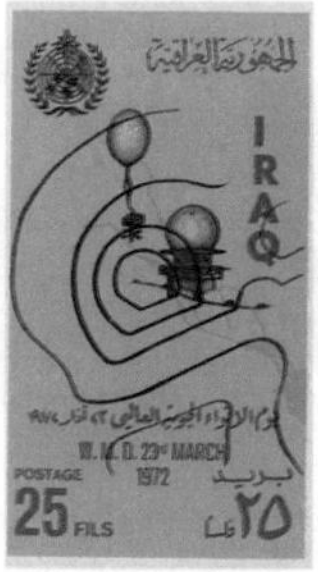

196 Observatory and Weather Balloon on Isobar Map

197 Cogwheel Emblem

1972. World Meteorological Day.
1026 **196** 25f. multicoloured . . . 1·70 50
1027 35f. multicoloured . . . 3·00 1·40

1972. Iraqi Chamber of Commerce.
1028 **197** 25f. multicoloured . . . 50 25
1029 35f. multicoloured . . . 90 40

198 Oil Rig and Flame

1972. Inauguration of North Rumaila Oilfield.
1030 **198** 25f. multicoloured . . . 1·30 25
1031 35f. multicoloured . . . 1·70 90

199 Party Emblem

1972. 25th Anniv of Al Baath Party. Mult.
1032 10f. Type **199** 35 15
1033 25f. Emblem and inscription 75 40
1034 35f. Type **199** 85 50
1035 70f. As 25f. . . . . 2·75 2·10
SIZES—HORIZ: 25f., 70f. 51 × 27 mm.

200 Mountain Scene

1972. New Year ("Nawrooz").
1036 **200** 25f. mauve, yellow & blue . . . . 1·20 25
1037 70f. brown, yellow & blue . . . . 3·75 1·40

201 Congress "Quills" Emblem

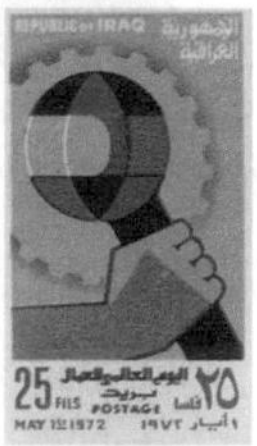

204 Hand holding Spanner

202 Federation Emblem

1972. 3rd Arab Journalists Congress.
1038 **201** 25f. orange, black & grn 50 15
1039 35f. blue, black and green . . . . 1·70 1·10

1972. 4th Anniv of Iraqi Women's Federation.
1040 **202** 25f. multicoloured . . . 50 35
1041 35f. multicoloured . . . 1·70 1·30

1972. Labour Day.
1046 **204** 25f. multicoloured . . . 40 15
1047 35f. multicoloured . . . 75 40

205 Kaaba, Mecca

1972. Mohammed's Birthday.
1048 **205** 25f. black, gold and green 50 15
1049 35f. black, gold and violet . . . . 1·70 1·30

206 Shooting for Goal

1972. Air. 25th International Military Sports Council Football Championship, Baghdad. Multicoloured.
1050 10f. Type **206** 50 25
1051 20f. Players in goalmouth 1·10 25
1052 25f. Type **206** . . . . . . 1·10 25
1053 35f. As 20f. . . . . 3·75 75
MS1054 77 × 64 mm. 100f. Olympic and C.I.S.M. emblems. Imperf 17·00 17·00

207 Soldiers and Artillery

1972. 14th Anniv of 14 July Revolution.
1055 **207** 35f. multicoloured . . . 85 35
1056 70f. multicoloured . . . 2·75 1·10

208 "Spirit of Revolution"

1972. 4th Anniv of 17 July Revolution.
1057 **208** 25f. multicoloured . . . 1·10 60
1058 95f. multicoloured . . . 3·00 2·75

209 Scout Badge and Camp Scene

1972. 10th Jamboree and Conference of Arab Scouts, Mosul.
1059 **209** 20f. multicoloured . . . 2·10 1·10
1060 25f. multicoloured . . . 3·00 1·30

210 Guide Badge and Camp

1972. 4th Conference and Camp of Arab Guides, Mosul.
1061 **210** 10f. multicoloured . . . 1·40 65
1062 45f. multicoloured . . . 4·25 1·30

1972 ١٩٧٢

●● 70 Fils ٧٠ ●●

(211)

1972. 3rd Traffic Week. Nos. 1010/11 surch or optd as T **211**.
1063 **188** 25f. multicoloured . . . 5·50 2·50
1064 70f. on 15f. mult . . . . 7·25 6·25

مهرجان النخيل
وعيد التمور
١٩٧٢
70 Fils ٧٠

(212)

213 "Strong Man" Statuette

1972. Festival of Palm Trees and Feast of Dates. Nos. 707 and 709 surch as T **212**.
1065 **94** 25f. on 3f. multicoloured 3·50 2·20
1066 70f. on 15f. multicoloured 9·25 5·75

1972. Air. World Body-building Championships and Asian Congress, Baghdad. Multicoloured.
1067 25f. Type **213** . . . . . . 1·30 65
1068 70f. Ancient warriors and modern Strong Man . . . 3·25 2·20

214 Bank Building

1972. 25th Anniv of Central Bank of Iraq.
1069 **214** 25f. multicoloured . . . 75 40
1070 70f. multicoloured . . . 2·20 1·00

216 International Railway Union Emblem

1972. 50th Anniv of Int Railway Union.
1073 **216** 25f. multicoloured . . . 1·50 60
1074 45f. multicoloured . . . 4·25 3·00

1973. Various "Faisal" definitives with portrait obliterated with 3 bars. (a) 1954 issue.
1075 **33** 10f. blue . . . . 3·00 1·00
1076 15f. black . . . . 3·00 1·00
1077 25f. purple . . . . 3·00 1·00

(b) 1957 issue.
1078 **41** 10f. blue . . . . 3·00 1·00
1079 15f. black . . . . 3·00 1·00
1080 25f. purple . . . . 3·00 1·00

المؤتمر الدولي
للتاريخ/١٩٧٣

(219)

1973. International History Congress. Nos. 780, 783 and 786 optd with T **219**.
1094 15f. multicoloured (postage) 8·50 3·25
1095 80f. multicoloured (air) . . 17·00 6·25
1096 500f. multicoloured . . . . 55·00 55·00

220 Iraqi Oil Workers

1973. 1st Anniv of Nationalization of Iraqi Oil Industry.
1097 **220** 25f. multicoloured . . . 1·80 75
1098 70f. multicoloured . . . 8·00 2·75

221 Harp

225a Iraqis and Flags

1973.
1099 **221** 5f. black and orange . . 15 10
1100 10f. black and brown . . 15 10
1101 20f. black and mauve . . 25 10
1102 – 25f. black and blue . . . 40 15
1103 – 35f. black and green . . 50 25
1104 – 45f. black and blue . . . 50 25
1105 – 50f. yellow and green . . 75 25
1106 – 70f. yellow and violet . . 1·00 50
1107 – 95f. yellow and brown 1·70 75
DESIGNS: 25, 35, 45f. Minaret of Mosul; 50, 70, 95f. Statue of a Goddess.

1973. July Festivals.
1122 **225a** 25f. multicoloured . . . 65 35
1123 35f. multicoloured . . . 1·30 40

1973. International Journalists' Conference. Nos. 857/8 optd **I.O.J. SEPTEMBER 26-29. 1973.**
1124 **139** 15f. multicoloured . . . 1·80 1·80
1125 50f. multicoloured . . . 2·50 2·50

227 Interpol H.Q., Paris

1973. 50th Anniv of International Criminal Police Organization (Interpol).
1126 **227** 25f. multicoloured . . . 1·00 60
1127 70f. multicoloured . . . 5·00 3·50

228 Flags and Fair Emblems

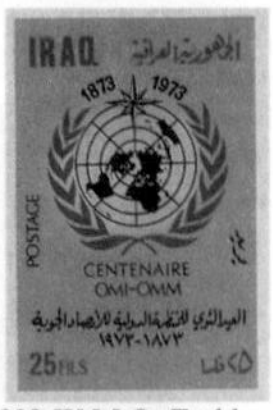

229 W.M.O. Emblem

1973. 10th Baghdad International Fair.
1128 **228** 10f. multicoloured . . . 40 25
1129 20f. multicoloured . . . 75 35
1130 55f. multicoloured . . . 1·70 90

1973. Cent of World Meteorological Organization.
1148 **229** 25f. black, green & orge 65 15
1149 35f. black, green & mve 2·10 1·10

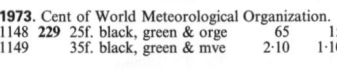

230 Arab Flags and Map

1973. 11th Session of Arab States' Civil Aviation Council, Baghdad.
1150 **230** 20f. multicoloured . . . 40 15
1151 35f. multicoloured . . . 1·30 90

المجلس التنفيذي

بغداد/١٩٧٣

(232)

233 Human Rights Emblem

1973. 6th Executive Council Meeting of Arab Postal Union, Baghdad. No. 665 optd with T **232**.
1153 **75** 30f. blue and orange . . . 4·50 3·00

1973. 25th Anniv of Declaration of Human Rights.
1154 **233** 25f. multicoloured . . . 25 25
1155 70f. multicoloured . . . 85 50

234 Shield and Military Activities

1974. 50th Anniv of Military College.
1156 **234** 25f. multicoloured . . . 40 25
1157 35f. multicoloured . . . 1·40 1·00

236 U.P.U. Emblem

1974. Centenary of Universal Postal Union.
1159 **236** 25f. multicoloured . . . 85 25
1160 35f. multicoloured . . . 85 40
1161 70f. multicoloured . . . 1·50 1·00

237 Allegory of Nationalization

1974. 2nd Anniv of Nationalization of Iraqi Oil Industry.
1162 **237** 10f. multicoloured . . . 40 15
1163 25f. multicoloured . . . 85 25
1164 70f. multicoloured . . . 2·50 2·10

238 Festival Theme

240 Cement Plant

239 National Front Emblem and Heads

1975. July Festivals.
1165 **238** 20f. multicoloured . . . 35 15
1166 35f. multicoloured . . . 1·00 50

1975. 1st Anniv of Progressive National Front.
1167 **239** 20f. multicoloured . . . 60 25
1168 50f. multicoloured . . . 1·40 75

1975. 25th Anniv of Iraqi Cement Industry.
1169 **240** 20f. multicoloured . . . 40 25
1170 25f. multicoloured . . . 60 35
1171 70f. multicoloured . . . 1·30 1·10

1975. Surch.
1172 **155** 10f. on 3f. multicoloured 3·25 2·10
1173 – 25f. on 3f. mult (No. 892) . . . . . . 9·25 6·75

242 W.P.Y. Emblem

1975. World Population Year (1974).
1174 **242** 25f. green and blue . . . 60 15
1175 35f. blue and mauve . . 1·00 60
1176 70f. violet and olive . . 3·00 1·30

243 Festival Emblems

1975. July Festivals.
1177 **243** 5f. multicoloured 25 15
1178 10f. multicoloured . . . 25 25
1179 35f. multicoloured . . . 1·70 65

244 Map and Emblems

1975. 10th Anniv of Arab Labour Organization.
1180 **244** 25f. multicoloured . . . 50 15
1181 35f. multicoloured . . . 85 60
1182 45f. multicoloured . . . 10 65

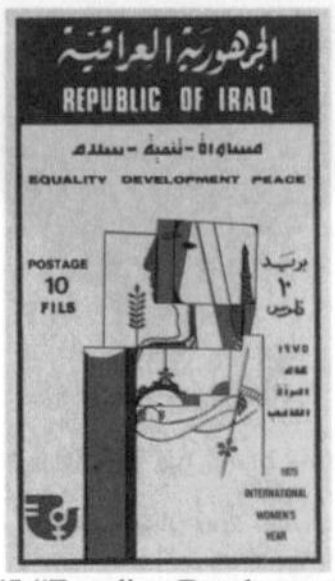

245 "Equality, Development, Peace"

1975. International Women's Year.
1183 **245** 10f. multicoloured . . . 40 25
1184 35f. multicoloured . . . 85 65
1185 70f. multicoloured . . . 3·50 1·30
MS1186 100 × 83 mm. 100f. multicoloured As T **245**, but face value outside design. Imperf . . 8·50 8·50

246 Diyala Barrage

1975. 25th Anniv of International Commission on Irrigation and Drainage.
1187 **246** 3f. multicoloured 15 10
1188 25f. multicoloured . . . 65 25
1189 70f. multicoloured . . . 2·75 1·30

247 Company Seal

1975. 25th Anniv of National Insurance Company, Baghdad.
1190 **247** 20f. multicoloured . . . 65 25
1191 25f. multicoloured . . . 90 40
MS1192 71 × 71 mm. **247** 100f. multicoloured. Imperf . . . 6·25 6·25

248 Court Musicians

1975. International Music Conference, Baghdad.
1193 **248** 25f. multicoloured . . . 60 25
1194 45f. multicoloured . . . 1·40 90

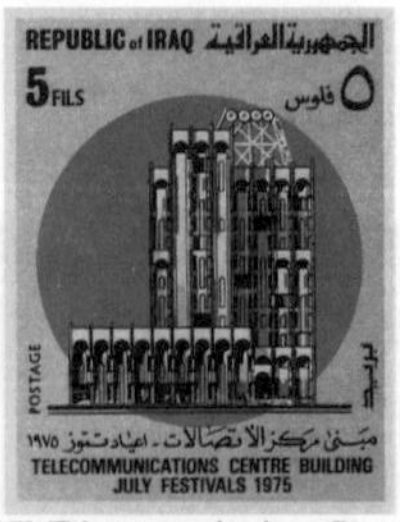

250 Telecommunications Centre

1975. Opening of Telecommunications Centre.
1203 **250** 5f. multicoloured 15 15
1204 10f. multicoloured . . . 25 15
1205 60f. multicoloured . . . 1·70 1·10

251 Diesel Train

252 Goddess (statue)

1975. 15th Taurus Railway Conference, Baghdad. Multicoloured.
1206 25f. Type **251** . . . . . . 4·50 85
1207 30f. Diesel locomotive . . . 7·25 1·70
1208 35f. Tank locomotive and train . . . . 9·25 3·25
1209 50f. Steam locomotive . . . 13·50 8·50

1976.
1210 **252** 5f. multicoloured 10 10
1211 10f. multicoloured . . . 10 10
1212 15f. multicoloured . . . 25 10
1213 – 20f. multicoloured . . . 25 15
1214 – 25f. multicoloured . . . 40 15
1215 – 30f. multicoloured . . . 60 15
1216 – 35f. multicoloured . . . 65 25
1217 – 50f. multicoloured . . . 1·10 25
1218 – 75f. multicoloured . . . 1·50 60
DESIGNS: 20, 25, 30f. Two females forming column; 35, 50, 75f. Head of bearded man.

253 Soldier and Symbols of Industry and Agriculture

254 Crossed-out Thumbprint

1976. Arab Day.
1219 **253** 5f. multicoloured 15 10
1220 25f. multicoloured on silver 50 15
1221 50f. mult on gold . . . 1·40 60

1976. Arab Literacy Day.
1222 **254** 5f. multicoloured 25 25
1223 15f. multicoloured . . . 40 25
1224 35f. multicoloured . . . 1·40 1·00

255 Iraq Earth Station

256 Early and Modern Telephones

1976. 13th Anniv of Revolution of 14th Ramadan.
1225 **255** 10f. multicoloured . . . 35 25
1226 25f. multicoloured on silver . . . . 1·00 40
1227 75f. mult on gold . . . 4·25 1·70

1976. Telephone Centenary.
1228 **256** 35f. multicoloured . . . 1·10 40
1229 50f. multicoloured . . . 2·20 65
1230 75f. multicoloured . . . 3·50 1·00

257 Map and Emblem

258 Iraqi Family on Map

1976. 20th International Arab Trade Unions Conf.
1231 **257** 5f. mult (postage) . . . 35 15
1232 10f. multicoloured . . . 35 15
1233 75f. multicoloured (air) 3·00 1·40

1976. Police Day.
1234 **258** 5f. multicoloured 15 10
1235 15f. multicoloured . . . 40 15
1236 35f. multicoloured . . . 2·10 1·00

259 "Strategy" Pipeline

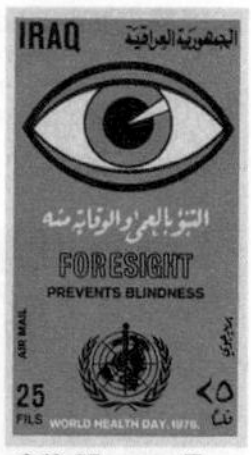
260 Human Eye

1976. 4th Anniv of Oil Nationalization.
1237 **259** 25f. multicoloured . . . 1·40 15
1238 75f. multicoloured . . . 3·25 1·70
MS1239 80×90 mm. 150f. multicoloured. Imperf . . . . 25·00 25·00
DESIGN—35×33 mm.: 150f. President Bakr embracing Prime Minister.

1976. Air. World Health Day. "Foresight Prevents Blindness".
1240 **260** 25f. blue and black . . . 35 15
1241 35f. green and black . . 40 15
1242 50f. orange and brown 1·00 60

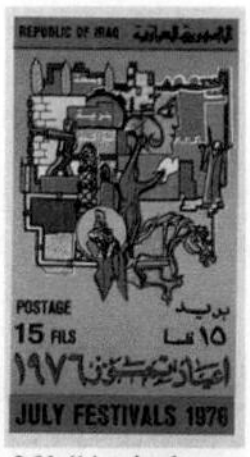
261 "Agriculture, Industry and Construction"

262 Basketball

1976. July Festivals.
1243 **261** 15f. multicoloured . . . 35 25
1244 35f. multicoloured . . . 1·00 65

1976. Olympic Games, Montreal. Mult.
1245 25f. Type **262** 40 15
1246 35f. Volleyball 65 50
1247 50f. Wrestling . . . . . . 1·00 85
1248 75f. Boxing . . . . 1·80 1·50
MS1249 121×91 mm. 100f. Rifle-shooting. Imperf . . . . 5·75 5·75

263 Bishop Capucci, Wounded Dove and Map of Palestine

264 River Kingfisher

1976. 2nd Anniv of Bishop Capucci's Arrest.
1250 **263** 25f. multicoloured . . . 60 15
1251 35f. multicoloured . . . 65 35
1252 75f. multicoloured . . . 2·20 1·30

1976. Birds. Multicoloured.
1253 5f. Type **264** . . . . 2·30 75
1254 10f. Turtle dove . . . . . . 2·30 75
1255 15f. Pin-tailed sandgrouse 3·00 75
1256 25f. Blue rock thrush . . . 5·50 90
1257 50f. Purple heron and grey heron . . . . 8·50 1·30
See also Nos. O1258/62.

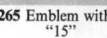

265 Emblem within "15"

266 Children with Banner

1976. 15th Anniv of Iraqi Students' Union.
1263 **265** 30f. multicoloured . . . 60 25
1264 70f. multicoloured . . . 2·10 90

1976. 30th Anniv of UNESCO. "Children's Books". Multicoloured.
1265 10f. Type **266** 25 25
1266 25f. Children in garden . . 1·80 40
1267 75f. Children with Iraqi flag 3·25 1·30

267 Tanker "Rumaila" and Emblem

1976. 4th Anniv of First Iraqi Oil Tanker and 1st Anniv of Basrah Petroleum Co Nationalization. Multicoloured.
1268 10f. Type **267** 60 25
1269 15f. Type **267** 85 35
1270 25f. Oil jetty and installations . . . . . . 1·80 65
1271 50f. As 25f. . . . . 2·75 1·20

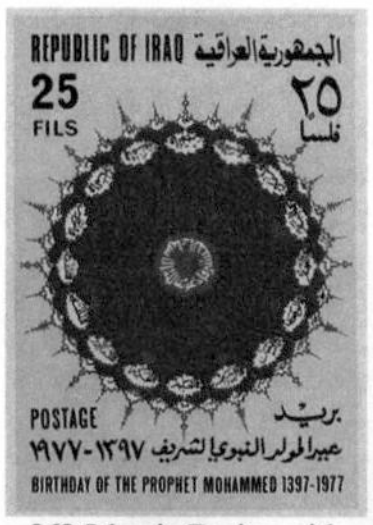
268 Islamic Design with Inscriptions

269 Dove Emblem

1977. Birthday of Prophet Mohammed.
1272 **268** 25f. multicoloured . . . 65 25
1273 35f. multicoloured . . . 1·00 35

1977. Peace Day.
1274 **269** 25f. multicoloured . . . 35 15
1275 30f. multicoloured . . . 60 35

270 Dahlia

1977. Flowers. Multicoloured.
1276 5f. Type **270** 25 25
1277 10f. "Lathyrus odoratus" . . 40 25
1278 35f. "Chrysanthemum coronarium" . . . . . . 1·10 35
1279 50f. "Verbena hybrida" . . 2·10 65

271 "V" Emblem with Doves

1977. 30th Anniv of Al-Baath Party. Mult.
1280 25f. Type **271** 50 15
1281 75f. Human figures as a flame . . . . 1·70 1·00
MS1282 80×60 mm. 100f. Dove with olive-branch. Imperf . . . 5·00 5·00

272 A.P.U. Emblem and Flags

273 1st May Emblem

1977. 25th Anniv of Arab Postal Union.
1283 **272** 25f. multicoloured . . . 35 15
1284 35f. multicoloured . . . 65 40

1977. Labour Day.
1285 **273** 10f. multicoloured . . . 15 10
1286 30f. multicoloured . . . 50 15
1287 35f. multicoloured . . . 65 60

274 First Stage of Lift

275 Dome of the Rock

1977. 8th Asian Weightlifting Championships, Baghdad. Multicoloured.
1288 25f. Type **274** 75 50
1289 75f. Press-up stage of lift . . 2·10 1·20
MS1290 60×80 mm. 100f. Championships emblem. Imperf 7·25 7·25

1977. Palestinian Welfare.
1291 **275** 5f. multicoloured . . . . 2·75 50

276 Arabian Garden

277 Dove and Ear of Wheat

1977. Arab Tourism Year. Multicoloured.
1292 5f. Type **276** 25 25
1293 10f. Town view with minarets (horiz) 25 25
1294 30f. Country stream 85 25
1295 50f. Oasis (horiz) . . . . . 2·30 1·70

1977. July Festivals.
1296 **277** 25f. multicoloured . . . 50 15
1297 30f. multicoloured . . . 65 35

278 Map of Middle East and North Africa

279 Emblem

1977. U.N. Conference on Desertification.
1298 **278** 30f. multicoloured . . . 65 40
1299 70f. multicoloured . . . 2·10 85

1977. Census Day.
1300 **279** 20f. multicoloured . . . 25 15
1301 30f. multicoloured . . . 65 15
1302 70f. multicoloured . . . 1·30 75

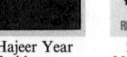

280 Abstract Calligraphic Emblem

281 Kamal Jumblatt and Political Caricatures

1977. Al-Mutanabby Festival.
1303 **280** 25f. multicoloured . . . 25 10
1304 50f. multicoloured . . . 60 40

1977. Kamal Jumblatt (Lebanese socialist) Commemoration.
1305 **281** 20f. multicoloured . . . 35 25
1306 30f. multicoloured . . . 50 25
1307 70f. multicoloured . . . 1·10 60

282 Hajeer Year Emblem

283 Girl, Boy and National Flag Ribbon

1977. Hajeer Year.
1308 **282** 30f. multicoloured . . . 35 15
1309 35f. multicoloured . . . 50 25

1978. Youth Day.
1310 **283** 10f. multicoloured . . . 15 10
1311 15f. multicoloured . . . 15 15
1312 35f. multicoloured . . . 50 35

284 Hand placing Coin in Box

285 Transmitting and Receiving Equipment

1978. 6th Anniv of Postal Savings Bank.
1313 **284** 15f. multicoloured . . . 35 10
1314 25f. multicoloured . . . 50 15
1315 35f. multicoloured . . . 90 40

1978. 10th World Telecommunications Day and 1st Anniv of Iraqi Microwave Network.
1316 **285** 25f. multicoloured . . . 40 15
1317 35f. multicoloured . . . 40 15
1318 75f. multicoloured . . . 90 60

286 Map and Flags

287 Silver Coins

1978. 1st Conference of Arabian Gulf Postal Ministers.
1319 **286** 25f. multicoloured . . . 50 15
1320 35f. multicoloured . . . 85 50

1978. Ancient Iraqi Coins.
1321 **287** 1f. black, silver & yellow 10 10
1322 – 2f. black, gold and blue 10 10
1323 – 3f. black, silver & orange 10 10
1324 – 4f. black, gold and green 15 15
1325 – 5f. black, gold and green 2·10 2·10
DESIGNS—HORIZ: 2f. Two gold coins; 3f. Two silver coins; 4f. Two gold coins. VERT: 75f. Gold coin.

288 Flower Emblem

1978. July Festivals.
1326 **288** 25f. multicoloured . . . 35 15
1327 35f. multicoloured . . . 50 25
MS1328 80×60 mm. 100f. multicoloured (horiz) . . . . . 5·50 5·50
DESIGN: 100f. Flame and emblem.

289 Nurse, Hospital and Sick Child

1978. Global Eradication of Smallpox.
1329 **289** 25f. multicoloured . . . 25 10
1330 35f. multicoloured . . . 60 25
1331 75f. multicoloured . . . 1·70 90

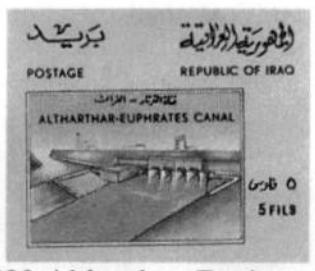
290 Altharthar–Euphrates Canal

1978.
1332 **290** 5f. multicoloured 15 15
1333 10f. multicoloured . . . 15 15
1334 15f. multicoloured . . . 15 15
1335 25f. multicoloured . . . 15 15
1336 35f. multicoloured . . . 35 15
1337 50f. multicoloured . . . 65 35
See also Nos. O1338/41.

291 I.M.C.O. Emblem

1978. World Maritime Day.

1342	**291**	25f. multicoloured . . .	50	25
1343		75f. multicoloured . . .	1·30	50

292 Workers in the Countryside

1978. 10th Anniv of People's Work Groups.

1344	**292**	10f. multicoloured . . .	25	15
1345		25f. multicoloured . . .	50	15
1346		35f. multicoloured . . .	90	60

293 Fair Emblem **294** Map, Rule and Emblem

1978. Baghdad International Fair.

1347	**293**	25f. multicoloured . . .	15	15
1348		35f. multicoloured . . .	25	15
1349		75f. multicoloured . . .	1·50	85

1978. World Standards Day.

1350	**294**	25f. multicoloured . . .	15	10
1351		35f. multicoloured . . .	25	15
1352		75f. multicoloured . . .	1·40	85

295 Conference Chamber **296** Congress Emblem

1978. 9th Arab Summit Conference, Baghdad.

1353	**295**	25f. multicoloured . . .	25	15
1354		35f. multicoloured . . .	35	15
1355		75f. multicoloured . . .	1·10	85

1978. 4th Congress of Association of Thoracic and Cardiovascular Surgeons of Asia.

1356	**296**	25f. multicoloured . . .	35	15
1357		75f. multicoloured . . .	50	25

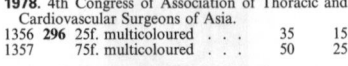

297 Pilgrims and Kaaba

1978. Pilgrimage to Mecca.

1358	**297**	25f. multicoloured . . .	35	15
1359		35f. multicoloured . . .	50	25

298 Map and Symbol

1978. U.N. Conference for Technical Co-operation among Developing Countries.

1360	**298**	25f. multicoloured . . .	25	15
1361		50f. multicoloured . . .	60	25
1362		75f. multicoloured . . .	90	60

299 Hands holding Emblem **300** Globe and Human Rights Emblem

1978. International Year to Combat Racism.

1363	**299**	25f. multicoloured . . .	35	15
1364		50f. multicoloured . . .	65	25
1365		75f. multicoloured . . .	1·80	60

1978. 30th Anniv of Declaration of Human Rights.

1366	**300**	25f. multicoloured . . .	40	15
1367		75f. multicoloured . . .	1·40	1·10

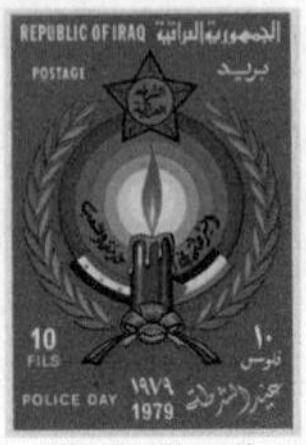

301 Candle and Emblem **302** Open Book, Pencil and Flame

1979. Police Day.

1368	**301**	10f. multicoloured . . .	35	25
1369		25f. multicoloured . . .	35	25
1370		35f. multicoloured . . .	60	25

1979. Anniv of Application of Compulsory Education Law.

1371	**302**	15f. multicoloured . . .	15	15
1372		25f. multicoloured . . .	35	15
1373		35f. multicoloured . . .	85	25

303 School, Teacher and Assyrian Relief **304** Clenched Fist, Pencil and Book

1979. Teachers' Day.

1374	**303**	10f. multicoloured . . .	15	15
1375		15f. multicoloured . . .	15	15
1376		50f. multicoloured . . .	85	50

1979. National Literacy Campaign.

1377	**304**	15f. multicoloured . . .	25	25
1378		25f. multicoloured . . .	40	25
1379		35f. multicoloured . . .	65	25

305 World map, Koran and Symbols of Arab Achievements **306** Girl playing Flute

1979. The Arabs.

1380	**305**	35f. multicoloured . . .	50	15
1381		75f. multicoloured . . .	1·40	65

1979. Mosul Spring Festival.

1382	**306**	15f. multicoloured . . .	35	25
1383		25f. multicoloured . . .	50	25
1384		35f. multicoloured . . .	1·00	40

307 Iraqi Map and Flag with U.P.U. Emblem **308** Championship Emblem with Sea and Sky

1979. 50th Anniv of Admission to Universal Postal Union.

1385	**307**	25f. multicoloured . . .	60	25
1386		35f. multicoloured . . .	60	25
1387		75f. multicoloured . . .	1·40	65

1979. 5th Arabian Gulf Football Championship.

1388	**308**	10f. multicoloured . . .	15	15
1389		15f. multicoloured . . .	35	15
1390		50f. multicoloured . . .	85	50

309 Child with Globe and Candle **310** Flower and Branch

1979. International Year of the Child.

1391	**309**	25f. multicoloured . . .	65	35
1392		75f. multicoloured . . .	1·70	1·10
MS1393		68 × 80 mm. 100f. multicoloured (vert)	22·00	18·00

DESIGN: 100f. Two children and U.N. emblem.

1979. July Festivals.

1394	**310**	15f. multicoloured . . .	15	15
1395		25f. multicoloured . . .	35	15
1396		35f. multicoloured . . .	50	25

311 Children supporting Globe **312** Jawad Selim (sculptor)

1979. 50th Anniv of International Bureau of Education.

1397	**311**	25f. multicoloured . . .	50	25
1398		50f. multicoloured . . .	90	50
1399		100f. multicoloured . . .	1·50	1·00

1979. Writers and Artists. Multicoloured.

1400	25f. Type **312**	40	25
1401	25f. S. al-Hosari (philosopher)	40	25
1402	25f. Mustapha Jawad (historian)	40	25

313 The Kaaba, Mecca **314** Figure "20" and Globe

1979. Pilgrimage to Mecca.

1403	**313**	25f. multicoloured . . .	40	25
1404		50f. multicoloured . . .	75	35

1979. 20th Anniv of Iraqi News Agency.

1405	**314**	25f. multicoloured . . .	40	15
1406		50f. multicoloured . . .	90	25
1407		75f. multicoloured . . .	1·20	40

315 Wave Pattern and Television Screen

1979. World Telecommunications Exhibition and Radio Conference, Geneva.

1408	**315**	25f. multicoloured . . .	40	15
1409		50f. multicoloured . . .	65	35
1410		75f. multicoloured . . .	1·20	60

316 Clenched Fists and Refugee

1979. Palestinian Solidarity Day.

1411	**316**	25f. multicoloured . . .	75	25
1412		50f. multicoloured . . .	1·40	40
1413		75f. multicoloured . . .	2·00	75

317 Ahmed Hassan Al-Bakir **318** Boy with Violin

1979. Inaug of Pres. Saddam Hussain. Mult.

1414	25f. Type **317**	35	25
1415	35f. Pres. Hussain taking the oath	50	25
1416	75f. Type **317**	90	40
1417	100f. As No. 1415	3·50	2·10

1979. Activities of Vanguards (youth organization). Multicoloured.

1418	10f. Type **318**	25	25
1419	15f. Boys on building site	25	25
1420	25f. Boys on assault course and in personal combat	35	25
1421	35f. Vanguards emblem . .	40	25

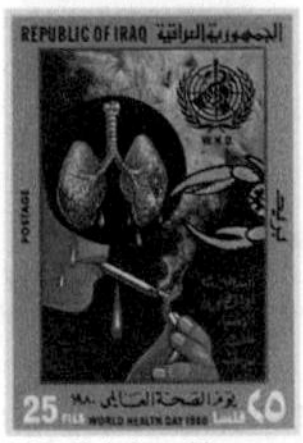

319 Wind-speed Indicator and Thermometer **320** Lighting Cigarette and Cancerous Lungs

1980. World Meteorological Day.

1422	**319**	15f. multicoloured . . .	15	15
1423		25f. multicoloured . . .	25	15
1424		35f. multicoloured . . .	60	25

1980. World Health Day. Anti-smoking Campaign.

1425	**320**	25f. multicoloured . . .	35	25
1426		35f. multicoloured . . .	40	25
1427		75f. multicoloured . . .	1·70	50

321 Festivals Emblem **322** Hurdling

1980. July Festivals.

1428	**321**	25f. multicoloured . . .	35	25
1429		35f. multicoloured . . .	40	25
MS1430		60 × 80 mm. 100f. Pres. Hussain (27 × 44 mm)	5·00	5·00

1980. Olympic Games, Moscow. Multicoloured.

1431	15f. Type **322**	25	25
1432	20f. Weightlifting (vert) . .	40	35
1433	30f. Boxing	75	40
1434	35f. Football (vert)	1·40	65
MS1435	79 × 60 mm. 100f. Wrestling (37 × 29 mm)	8·50	8·50

323 "Rubus sanctus"

1980. Fruit. Multicoloured.

1436	5f. Type **323**	25	15
1437	15f. Peaches	40	15
1438	20f. Pears	60	15
1439	25f. Apples	75	15
1440	35f. Plums	1·00	35

324 Conference Emblem and Arabic Text

325 A.P.U. Emblem Posthorn and Map

1980. World Tourism Conference, Manila.
1441 **324** 25f. multicoloured . . . 35 15
1442 50f. multicoloured . . . 75 25
1443 100f. multicoloured . . . 1·40 85

1980. 11th Congress of Arab Postal Union, Baghdad.
1444 **325** 10f. multicoloured . . . 25 25
1445 30f. multicoloured . . . 40 25
1446 35f. multicoloured . . . 60 25

326 O.P.E.C. Emblem and Globe

1980. 20th Anniv of Organization of Petroleum Exporting Countries.
1447 **326** 30f. multicoloured . . . 65 25
1448 75f. multicoloured . . . 1·40 75

327 African Monarch

1980. Butterflies. Multicoloured.
1449 10f. Swallowtail . . . . . . 1·50 25
1450 15f. Type **327** . . . . . . 1·80 50
1451 20f. Red admiral . . . . . 2·50 65
1452 30f. Clouded yellow . . . . 4·25 1·10

328 Mosque and Ka'aba

1980. 1400th Anniv of Hegira.
1453 **328** 15f. multicoloured . . . 25 15
1454 25f. multicoloured . . . 50 15
1455 35f. multicoloured . . . 60 35

329 Riflemen and Dome of the Rock on Map of Israel

1980. Palestinian Solidarity Day.
1456 **329** 25f. multicoloured . . . 50 15
1457 35f. multicoloured . . . 75 25
1458 75f. multicoloured . . . 1·50 75

330 Soldier and Rocket

331 "8" and Flags forming Torch

1981. 60th Anniv of Army Day.
1459 **330** 5f. multicoloured 25 15
1460 30f. multicoloured . . . 50 15
1461 75f. multicoloured . . . 1·60 65

1981. 18th Anniv of 14th Ramadan Revolution.
1462 **331** 15f. multicoloured . . . 25 15
1463 30f. multicoloured . . . 40 15
1464 35f. multicoloured . . . 60 25

332 Map of Arab States tied with Ribbon

1981. The Arabs.
1465 **332** 5f. multicoloured 15 25
1466 25f. multicoloured . . . 40 25
1467 35f. multicoloured . . . 60 25

333 Pres. Hussain and Modern Military Equipment

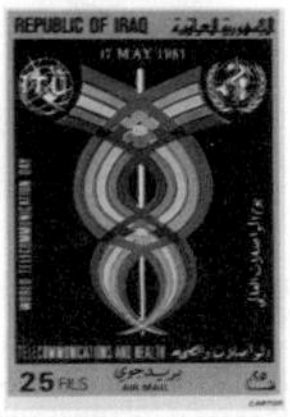

334 I.T.U. and W.H.O. Emblems and Ribbons forming Caduceus

1981. Saddam's Battle of Qadisiya.
1468 **333** 30f. multicoloured . . . 50 25
1469 35f. multicoloured . . . 1·00 40
1470 75f. multicoloured . . . 1·70 85
MS1471 80 × 59 mm. 100f. Pres. Hussain, military equipment and flag (37 × 29 mm) . . . . . . 4·25 4·25

1981. World Telecommunications Day.
1472 **334** 25f. multicoloured . . . 50 25
1473 50f. multicoloured . . . 1·00 40
1474 75f. multicoloured . . . 1·70 85

335 Mil Mi-24 Helicopters attacking Ground Forces

336 Map and Flower enclosing Ballot Box

1981. 50th Anniv of Air Force. Mult.
1475 5f. Type **335** (postage) . . . 15 15
1476 10f. Antonov An-2 biplane trainer 35 15
1477 15f. "SAM-15" missile . . . 40 15
1478 120f. De Havilland Dragon Rapide biplane and Mikoyan Gurevich MiG-21 jet fighters (vert) (air) . . . . 3·50 2·10

1981. 1st Anniv of National Assembly Election.
1479 **336** 30f. multicoloured . . . 40 15
1480 35f. multicoloured . . . 50 15
1481 45f. multicoloured . . . 85 35

337 Festivals Emblem

338 Basket Weaver

1981. July Festivals.
1482 **337** 15f. multicoloured . . . 25 10
1483 25f. multicoloured . . . 35 15
1484 35f. multicoloured . . . 60 15

1981. Popular Industries. Multicoloured.
1485 5f. Type **338** 15 15
1486 30f. Copper worker 50 15
1487 35f. Potter 65 25
1488 50f. Weaver (horiz) 85 35

339 Saddam Hussain Gymnasium

1981. Modern Buildings. Multicoloured.
1489 45f. Type **339** 65 25
1490 50f. Palace of Conferences . . 65 25
1491 120f. As 50f. . . . . 1·80 1·30
1492 150f. Type **339** . . . . . . 2·50 1·50

340 Pilgrims

1981. Pilgrimage to Mecca.
1493 **340** 25f. multicoloured . . . 50 10
1494 45f. multicoloured . . . 90 35
1495 50f. multicoloured . . . 90 35

341 Harvesting

1981. World Food Day.
1496 **341** 30f. multicoloured . . . 50 15
1497 45f. multicoloured . . . 90 40
1498 75f. multicoloured . . . 1·30 75

343 Teacher with Deaf Child

344 Medal and Map

1981. International Year of Disabled Persons.
1501 **343** 30f. multicoloured . . . 40 25
1502 45f. multicoloured . . . 65 35
1503 75f. multicoloured . . . 90 60

1981. Martyr's Day.
1504 **344** 45f. multicoloured . . . 40 35
1505 50f. multicoloured . . . 65 40
1506 120f. multicoloured . . . 1·30 1·00
See also Nos. O1507/9.

345 "Ibn Khaldoon" (freighter)

1981. 5th Anniv of United Arab Shipping Company.
1507 **345** 50f. multicoloured . . . 1·10 50
1508 120f. multicoloured . . . 3·00 1·50

346 Woman and Symbols of Technology

347 President Hussain, "7" and "Flowers"

1982. Iraqi Women's Day.
1509 **346** 25f. multicoloured . . . 50 15
1510 45f. multicoloured . . . 85 40
1511 50f. multicoloured . . . 85 50

1982. 35th Anniv of Al-Baath Party. Mult.
1512 25f. Type **347** 40 15
1513 30f. Rainbow and "7 7 7" . . 40 15
1514 45f. Type **347** 65 40
1515 50f. As 30f. 65 40
MS1516 99 × 53 mm. 150f. Pres. Hussain, globe and Arabic "7" (27 × 39 mm). Imperf . . . . . 3·25 3·25

348 A.P.U. Emblem and Globe

349 White Storks

1982. 30th Anniv of Arab Postal Union.
1517 **348** 25f. multicoloured . . . 50 15
1518 45f. multicoloured . . . 85 35
1519 50f. multicoloured . . . 85 35

1982. Mosul Spring Festival. Multicoloured.
1520 25f. Type **349** . . . . . . 1·00 15
1521 30f. Doll 60 15
1522 45f. Type **349** . . . . . . 1·00 50
1523 50f. As 30f. 90 40

350 World Map, Factories and "1"

1982. Labour Day.
1524 **350** 25f. multicoloured . . . 40 10
1525 45f. multicoloured . . . 60 35
1526 50f. multicoloured . . . 65 40

351 Geometric Figure and I.T.U. Problem

352 Oil Gusher

1982. World Telecommunications Day.
1527 **351** 5f. multicoloured 10 10
1528 45f. multicoloured . . . 65 35
1529 100f. multicoloured . . . 1·50 90

1982. 10th Anniv of Oil Nationalization. Mult.
1530 5f. Type **352** 40 10
1531 25f. Type **352** 50 15
1532 45f. Bronze sculpture of bull and horse flanking couple holding model of oil rig . . . 1·00 40
1533 50f. As 45f. . . . . 1·20 40

353 Nuclear Power Emblem and Lion

354 Footballers

1982. 1st Anniv of Attack on Iraqi Nuclear Reactor. Multicoloured.
1534 30f. Type **353** 50 25
1535 45f. Bomb aimed at egg . . 85 25
1536 50f. Type **353** 90 40
1537 120f. As No. 1535 . . . . . 1·70 1·30

1982. World Cup Football Championship, Spain. Multicoloured.
1538 5f. Type **354** 50 25
1539 45f. Three footballers . . . 85 35
1540 50f. Type **354** 90 40
1541 100f. As 45f. . . . . 1·70 90
MS1542 85 × 60 mm. 150f. Two footballers (horiz) . . . . . . 3·00 3·00

355 President Hussain and Fireworks

356 Green Lizard

1982. July Festivals.
1543 **355** 25f. multicoloured . . . 25 15
1544 45f. multicoloured . . . 60 25
1545 50f. multicoloured . . . 60 35

1982. Reptiles. Multicoloured.
1546 25f. Type **356** . . . . . . 1·80 65
1547 30f. Asp . . . . 1·80 65
1548 45f. Two green lizards . . . 2·50 90
1549 50f. "Natrix tessellata" . . . 2·75 1·30

357 Pandit Nehru (India)

1982. 7th Non-Aligned Countries Conference, Baghdad. Multicoloured.
1550 50f. Type **357** 75 35
1551 50f. Josef Tito (Yugoslavia) 75 35
1552 50f. Abdul Nasser (Egypt) 75 35
1553 50f. Kwame Nkrumah (Ghana) 75 35
1554 100f. President Hussain (Iraq) 1·70 90

358 Microscope and Bacilli

1982. Cent of Discovery of Tubercule Bacillus.
1555 **358** 20f. multicoloured 60 15
1556 50f. multicoloured 1·10 35
1557 100f. multicoloured 1·80 85

359 U.P.U. Building, Berne

1982. U.P.U. Day.
1561 **359** 5f. multicoloured 15 10
1562 45f. multicoloured 60 35
1563 100f. multicoloured 1·50 85

360 Drums

1982. Musical Instruments. Multicoloured.
1564 5f. Type **360** 25 10
1565 10f. Stringed board instrument 25 15
1566 35f. Bowed instruments 75 25
1567 100f. Mandolin 2·50 90

361 Mosque and Minaret, Mecca

362 Flowers

1982. Prophet Mohammed's Birthday. Mult.
1568 25f. Type **361** 15 15
1569 30f. Courtyard of mosque 35 15
1570 45f. Type **361** 50 35
1571 50f. As No. 1569 60 35

1982. Flowers. Multicoloured.
1572 10f. Type **362** 25 15
1573 20f. Flowers (different) 40 15
1574 30f. Type **362** 50 25
1575 40f. As No. 1573 85 40
1576 50f. Type **362** 1·00 50
1577 100f. As No. 1573 2·00 1·00

1983. Nos. 1489/51 surch.
1578 60f. on 50f. Palace of Conferences 1·10 40
1579 70f. on 45f. Type **339** 1·40 50
1580 160f. on 120f. Palace of Conferences 3·50 1·70

364 President Hussain

1983. July Festivals.
1583 **364** 30f. multicoloured 40 25
1584 60f. multicoloured 90 40
1585 70f. multicoloured 1·20 60

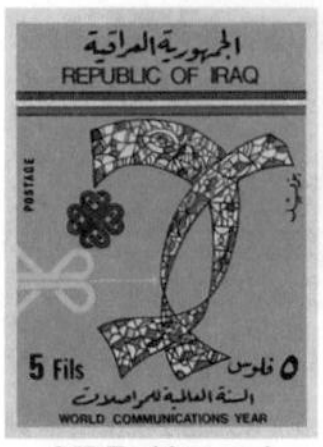

365 Emblem and Interlocked Bands

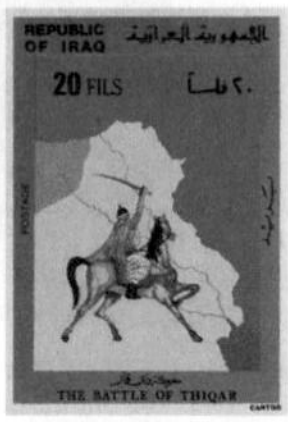

366 Horseman and Map

1983. World Communications Year. Mult.
1586 5f. Type **365** 10 10
1587 25f. Hexagons of primary colours 25 15
1588 60f. Type **365** 90 50
1589 70f. As No. 1587 1·00 60
MS1590 80 × 60 mm. 200f. Emblem. Imperf 3·50 3·50

1983. Battle of Thiqar. Multicoloured.
1591 20f. Type **366** 25 15
1592 50f. Eagle swooping on pyre 65 35
1593 60f. Type **366** 85 40
1594 70f. As No. 1592 90 50

367 Fair Emblem and Silhouette of Baghdad

368 Pres. Hussain within Figure "9"

1983. Baghdad International Fair.
1595 **367** 60f. multicoloured 65 40
1596 70f. multicoloured 85 50
1597 160f. multicoloured 1·00 1·00

1983. 9th Al-Baath Party Congress. Mult.
1598 30f. Type **368** 35 25
1599 60f. Eagle, torch, map and book 65 40
1600 70f. Type **368** 85 50
1601 100f. As No. 1599 1·30 65

369 Fishermen hauling Boat

1983. Paintings. Multicoloured.
1602 60f. Type **369** 1·20 50
1603 60f. Festive crowd 1·20 50
1604 60f. Hanging decorations 1·20 50
1605 70f. Crowd 1·30 75
1606 70f. Bazaar 1·30 75

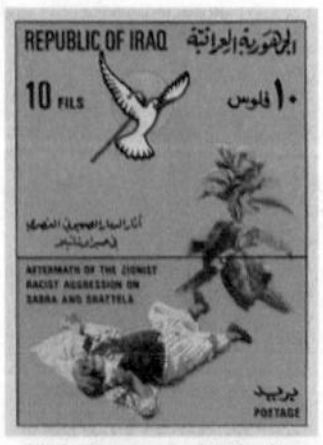

370 Dove and Victim

371 Apartment Building

1983. Massacre of Palestinians in Sabra and Shatila Refugee Camps, Lebanon. Multicoloured.
1607 10f. Type **370** 25 15
1608 60f. Type **370** 90 40
1609 70f. Dove and clasped fist shedding blood and victims 1·10 50
1610 160f. As No. 1609 2·30 1·40

1983. Buildings.
1611 **371** 60f. lt green, black & grn 65 40
1612 – 70f. purple, black & grey 85 50
1613 – 160f. purple, blk & grey 2·10 1·10
1614 **371** 200f. green, black & olive 2·50 1·40
DESIGNS: 70, 160f. Apartment building (different).
See also Nos. O1615/16.

372 President Hussain

1983. 4th Anniv of President Hussain as Party and State Leader.
1617 **372** 60f. multicoloured 65 35
1618 70f. multicoloured 90 50
1619 250f. multicoloured 3·00 1·80

373 Congress Emblem

1984. 25th International Military Medicine and Pharmacy Congress.
1620 **373** 60f. multicoloured 75 40
1621 70f. multicoloured 90 50
1622 200f. multicoloured 2·50 1·40

374 President Hussain and Flowers

1984. Pres. Saddam Hussain's 47th Birthday. Multicoloured.
1623 60f. Type **374** 60 35
1624 70f. Pres. Hussain in army uniform 65 40
1625 160f. As No. 1623 1·80 1·30
1626 200f. Type **374** 2·20 1·60
MS1627 81 × 61 mm. 250f. Pres. Hussain and rose (horiz) 3·50 3·50

375 Boxing

1984. Olympic Games, Los Angeles. Multicoloured.
1628 50f. Type **375** 65 50
1629 60f. Hurdling, weightlifting and wrestling 85 50
1630 70f. Type **375** 1·00 60
1631 100f. As No. 1629 1·40 90
MS1632 80 × 60 mm. 200f. Footballers (30 × 40 mm) 3·25 3·25

376 Pres. Hussain and Horses' Heads

377 Flag as Ribbon and Two Domes

1984. Battle of Qadisiya. Multicoloured.
1633 50f. Type **376** 50 35
1634 60f. President Hussain and symbolic representation of battle 65 40
1635 70f. Type **376** 75 50
1636 100f. As No. 1634 1·20 65
MS1637 80 × 60 mm. 200f. Shield and eagle (30 × 40 mm) 3·25 3·25

1984. Martyr's Day. Multicoloured.
1638 50f. Type **377** 40 35
1639 60f. Woman holding rifle and medal 60 35
1640 70f. Type **377** 65 40
1641 100f. As No. 1639 90 65

378 Text

1985. 5th Anniv of President Hussain's Visit to Al-Mustansiriyah University.
1646 **378** 60f. red and blue 50 35
1647 70f. red and green 60 40
1648 250f. red and black 2·20 1·40

379 Pres. Hussain and Jet Fighters

380 Pres. Hussain within Flower

1985. 54th Anniv of Iraqi Air Force. Mult.
1649 10f. Type **379** 25 10
1650 60f. Fighter airplanes trailing flag and "54" (horiz) 1·20 65
1651 70f. As No. 1650 1·30 65
1652 160f. Type **379** 3·25 1·70
MS1653 80 × 60 mm. 200f. As No. 1650 4·25 4·25

1985. 48th Birthday of President Saddam Hussain. Multicoloured.
1654 30f. Type **380** 35 25
1655 60f. Pres. Hussain, candle and flowers 60 35
1656 70f. Type **380** 65 40
1657 100f. As No. 1655 1·00 60
MS1658 87 × 60 mm. 200f. "28", flowers and text 3·00 3·00

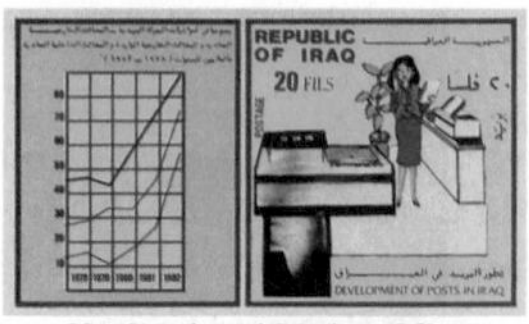

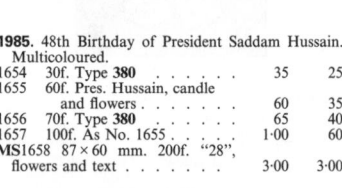

381 Graph and Modern Office

1985. Posts and Telecommunications Development. Multicoloured.
1659 20f. Type **381** 35 15
1660 50f. Dish aerial and graph 65 35
1661 60f. Type **381** 65 35
1662 70f. As No. 1660 85 50

382 Arms at Crossroads, and Building

1985. Saddam's Battle of Qadisiya. Multicoloured.
1663 10f. Type **382** 15 15
1664 20f. Pres. Hussain and emblem of Al-Baath Party 25 15
1665 60f. Type **382** 85 40
1666 70f. As No. 1664 90 65
MS1667 80 × 60 mm. 200f. Peace dove and soldiers (27 × 43 mm) 2·75 2·75

383 Solar Energy Research Centre

1985.
1668 **383** 10f. multicoloured 15 10
1669 50f. multicoloured 85 40
1670 100f. multicoloured 1·70 90

384 Disabled Children

385 Hand holding Quill

1985. UNICEF Child Survival Campaign. Multicoloured.

1671	10f. Type **384**	10	10
1672	15f. Toddler and baby	15	15
1673	50f. Type **384**	65	35
1674	100f. As No. 1672	1·30	85

1985. Death Millenary of Al-Sharif Al-Radhi (poet).

1675	**385**	10f. multicoloured	25	10
1676		50f. multicoloured	50	35
1677		100f. multicoloured	1·10	75

386 U.N. Emblem

1985. 40th Anniv of U.N.O.

1678	**386**	10f. multicoloured	10	10
1679		40f. blue, black & yellow	50	25
1680		100f. multicoloured	1·30	75

387 World Map

1985. Palestinian Solidarity Day.

1681	**387**	10f. multicoloured	25	10
1682		50f. multicoloured	85	40
1683		100f. multicoloured	1·80	90

388 Flag, Man and Blood Vessels as Roots

389 I.Y.Y. Emblem and Soldier with Flag

1985. Martyr's Day.

1684	**388**	10f. multicoloured	15	15
1685		40f. multicoloured	40	25
1686		100f. multicoloured	1·20	75

1985. International Youth Year. Multicoloured.

1687	40f. Type **389**	40	25
1688	50f. Young couple, flag and I.Y.Y. emblem	60	35
1689	100f. Type **389**	1·30	65
1690	200f. As No. 1688	2·30	2·00
MS1691	80 × 60 mm. 250f. Cogwheel, flag, rifle and symbols of agriculture, industry and science (29 × 44 mm)	3·75	3·75

390 Pres. Hussain and Soldier in "6"

391 Pen as Knife in Sheet of Text

1986. Army Day. Multicoloured.

1692	10f. Type **390**	15	15
1693	40f. Pres. Hussain, cogwheel, "6" and missiles (horiz)	60	25
1694	50f. Type **390**	75	35
1695	100f. As No. 1693	1·60	90
MS1696	80 × 60 mm. 200f. Pres. Hussain, "6" in star and rifle (51 × 36 mm)	3·50	3·50

1986. Iraqi Prisoners of War Commemoration. Multicoloured.

1697	30f. Type **391**	35	25
1698	70f. Dove, cherub holding flag and three prisoners	65	40
1699	100f. Type **391**	1·00	65
1700	200f. As No. 1698	2·20	1·30
MS1701	110 × 80 mm. 250f. As Nos. 1699/1700	3·50	3·50

392 Pres. Hussain with Children

393 Worker, Globe and Cogwheel

1986. 49th Birthday of President Saddam Hussain. Multicoloured.

1702	30f. Type **392**	40	25
1703	50f. Pres. Hussain and doves holding flag	65	35
1704	100f. Type **392**	1·30	65
1705	150f. As No. 1703	1·80	90
MS1706	80 × 60 mm. 250f. Pres. Hussain, flag and flowers	3·50	3·50

1986. Labour Day. Multicoloured.

1707	10f. Type **393**	25	25
1708	40f. Candle in cogwheel	65	25
1709	100f. Type **393**	1·30	65
1710	150f. As No. 1708	1·80	90

394 Pres. Hussain and "30 July 17"

1986. July Festivals and 7th Anniv of Pres. Hussain's State Leadership. Multicoloured.

1711	20f. Type **394**	25	15
1712	30f. Pres. Hussain and "17 1986"	35	15
1713	100f. Type **394**	1·30	65
1714	150f. As No. 1712	1·70	1·10
MS1715	80 × 60 mm. 250f. Pres. Hussain within laurel wreath and text	3·50	3·50

395 Pres. Hussain and Jet Fighter

1986. 55th Anniv of Iraqi Air Force. Multicoloured.

1716	30f. Type **395**	65	25
1717	50f. Pres. Hussain and jet fighters	1·30	35
1718	100f. Type **395**	2·50	1·40
1719	150f. As No. 1717	3·75	1·80
MS1720	80 × 60 mm. 250f. Air Force Medal. Imperf	4·50	4·50

396 Refinery

1986. Oil Nationalization Day. Multicoloured.

1721	10f. Type **396**	10	10
1722	40f. Derrick and pipeline within flag (vert)	50	15
1723	100f. Type **396**	1·30	75
1724	150f. As No. 1722	1·80	1·30

397 Arab Warrior

1986. 1st Battle of Qadisiya. Multicoloured.

1725	20f. Type **397**	35	10
1726	60f. Pres. Hussain and battle scene	75	40
1727	70f. Type **397**	85	50
1728	100f. As No. 1726	1·40	65

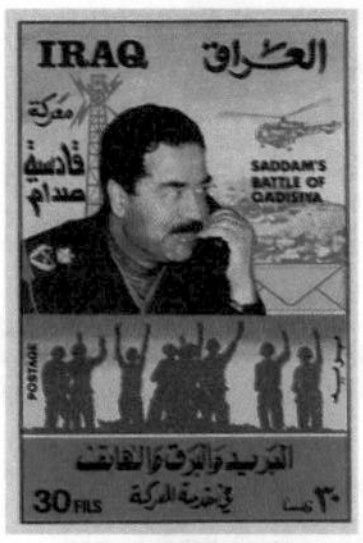
398 Pres. Hussain, Battlefield and Cheering Soldiers

399 Pres. Hussain

1986. Saadam's Battle of Qadisiya. Mult.

1729	30f. Type **398**	85	25
1730	40f. Pres. Hussain within flag "swords" and symbols of ancient and modern warfare (horiz)	1·10	40
1731	100f. Type **398**	2·20	1·20
1732	150f. As No. 1730	3·75	1·70
MS1733	80 × 60 mm. 250f. Pres. Hussain, soldiers and flag "swords". Imperf	4·25	4·25

1986.

1734	**399**	30f. multicoloured	60	15
1735		50f. multicoloured	85	25
1736		100f. multicoloured	1·70	65
1737		150f. multicoloured	2·20	85
1738		250f. multicoloured	4·25	1·40
1739		350f. multicoloured	5·75	1·80

401 Women

402 Flag and Treble Clef forming Dove

1986. Iraqi Women's Day. Multicoloured.

1744	30f. Type **401**	40	25
1745	50f. Woman and battle scenes (horiz)	60	35
1746	100f. Type **401**	1·30	75
1747	150f. As No. 1745	2·00	1·10

1986. International Peace Year. Multicoloured.

1748	50f. Type **402**	60	25
1749	100f. Globe, dove with flag and horns holding rifle and olive branch	1·10	60
1750	150f. Type **402**	1·60	1·10
1751	250f. As No. 1749	2·20	1·40
MS1752	80 × 60 mm. 200f. I.P.Y. emblem, flag and dove and fist on map. Imperf	2·20	2·20

403 Freighter "Al Alwah" and Map

1987. 10th Anniv of United Arab Shipping Company. Multicoloured.

1753	50f. Type **403**	50	25
1754	100f. Container ship "Khaled Ibn Al Waleed"	1·00	60
1755	150f. Type **403**	1·60	85
1756	250f. As No. 1754	2·50	1·40
MS1757	100 × 90 mm. 200f. "Khaled Ibn Al Waleed" at wharf. Imperf	3·00	3·00

404 Activities on Tree

405 Pres. Hussain in "6"

1987. 40th Anniv of UNICEF. Mult.

1758	20f. Type **404**	25	25
1759	40f. Doves and "40" containing children and UNICEF emblem (horiz)	35	35
1760	90f. Type **404**	85	85
1761	100f. As No. 1759	90	90

406 Torch, Cogwheel, Wheat and Map

408 Pres. Hussain, Civilians, Soldiers and buried Soldier

407 Pres. Hussain

1987. Army Day. Multicoloured.

1762	20f. Type **405**	25	25
1763	40f. Pres. Hussain and military scenes	35	35
1764	90f. Type **405**	85	85
1765	100f. As No. 1763	90	90

1987. 40th Anniv of Al-Baath Party. Mult.

1766	20f. Type **406**	25	25
1767	40f. Pres. Hussain, map and flag as "7"	35	35
1768	90f. Type **406**	85	85
1769	100f. As No. 1767	90	90

1987. 50th Birthday of President Saddam Hussain. Multicoloured.

1770	20f. Type **407**	25	25
1771	40f. Anniversary dates, flowers and Pres. Hussain	35	35
1772	90f. Type **407**	85	85
1773	100f. As No. 1771	90	90

1987. July Festivals and 8th Anniv of Pres. Hussain's State Leadership. Multicoloured.

1774	20f. Pres. Hussain and flag (horiz)	25	25
1775	40f. Type **408**	35	35
1776	90f. As No. 1174	85	85
1777	100f. Type **408**	90	90

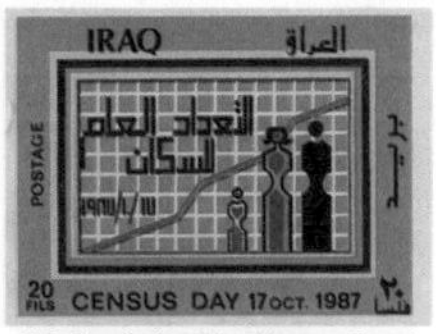
409 Symbolic Family on Graph

1987. Census. Multicoloured.

1778	20f. Type **409**	25	15
1779	30f. People on graph	35	25
1780	50f. As No. 1779	50	25
1781	500f. Type **409**	4·50	3·50

410 Pres. Hussain in "6" and Troops

412 Flag as "V" and Lyre

411 "8" and Pres. Hussain

1988. Army Day. Multicoloured.

1782	20f. Type **410**	25	25
1783	30f. Soldier and medal (horiz)	25	25
1784	50f. Type **410**	50	25
1785	150f. As No. 1783	1·40	60

1988. 18th Anniv of People's Army (1786, 1788) and 25th Anniv of 8th February Revolution (others). Multicoloured.

1786	20f. Type **411**	35	25
1787	30f. Pres. Hussain and eagle on "8" (vert)	40	25
1788	50f. Type **411**	60	35
1789	150f. As No. 1787	1·80	65

1988. Art Day. Multicoloured.
1790 20f. Type **412** 35 25
1791 30f. Pres. Hussain, rifle as torch, clef and dove on film strip 40 35
1792 50f. Type **412** 60 35
1793 100f. As No. 1791 1·20 40
MS1794 60 × 80 mm. 150f. Musical notes, lute and keyboard. Imperf 2·10 2·10

413 Rally and Ears of Wheat

1988. 41st Anniv of Al-Baath Party. Mult.
1795 20f. Type **413** 35 25
1796 30f. Flowers and "7 April 1947–1988" 40 35
1797 50f. Type **413** 60 35
1798 150f. As No. 1796 1·80 60

414 Emblem

415 Pres. Hussain

1988. Regional Marine Environment Day. Multicoloured.
1799 20f. Type **414** 40 25
1800 40f. Fishes (horiz) 40 35
1801 90f. Type **414** 1·10 40
1802 100f. As No. 1800 1·20 40

1988. 51st Birthday of President Saddam Hussain. Multicoloured.
1803 20f. Type **415** 35 25
1804 30f. Pres. Hussain and hands holding flowers 40 35
1805 50f. Type **415** 60 35
1806 100f. As No. 1804 1·20 50
MS1807 90 × 100 mm. 150f. Pres. Hussain and flowers within flag as heart. Imperf 1·80 1·80

416 Emblem

1988. 40th Anniv of W.H.O. Multicoloured.
1808 20f. Type **416** 35 25
1809 40f. Red crescent protecting line of people (vert) 40 35
1810 90f. Type **416** 1·10 35
1811 100f. As No. 1809 1·20 40

417 Bomb and Open Book showing School, Child and Wreath

418 Hand holding Flash of Lightning

1988. Bilat Al-Shuhada School Bomb Victims. Multicoloured.
1812 20f. Type **417** 35 25
1813 40f. Explosion and girl (horiz) 40 35
1814 90f. Type **417** 1·20 40
1815 100f. As No. 1813 1·20 40
MS1816 80 × 60 mm. 150f. Child's severed head in clawed hand (49 × 39 mm) 1·70 1·70

1988. July Festivals and 9th Anniv of President Hussain's State Leadership. Multicoloured.
1817 50f. Type **418** 60 35
1818 90f. Sun, map and Pres. Hussain 1·10 40
1819 100f. Type **418** 1·20 40
1820 150f. As No. 1818 1·70 50
MS1821 90 × 70 mm. 250f. Pres. Hussain and flag. Imperf 3·00 3·00

419 Pres. Hussain and al-Sail al-Kabir Miqat

1988. President Hussain's Pilgrimage to Mecca.
1822 **419** 90f. multicoloured 1·10 40
1823 100f. multicoloured 1·20 60
1824 150f. multicoloured 1·80 60

420 Mosul

1988. Tourism. Multicoloured.
1825 50f. Type **420** 85 25
1826 100f. Basrah 1·30 60
1827 150f. Baghdad (vert) 2·75 1·00

421 Pres. Hussain and Soldiers

1988. "Victorious Iraq".
1828 **421** 50f. multicoloured 4·25 4·25
1829 100f. multicoloured 8·00 8·00
1830 150f. multicoloured 11·50 11·50

422 Emblem

1988. Navy Day. Multicoloured.
1831 50f. Type **422** 90 35
1832 90f. Missile boats 1·70 50
1833 100f. Type **422** 1·80 60
1834 150f. As No. 1832 2·75 90
MS1835 90 × 70 mm. 250f. Emblem and Pres. Hussain decorating officers. Imperf 5·50 5·50

423 Map and Hands holding Flag

1988. Liberation of Fao City.
1836 **423** 100f. multicoloured 1·80 60
1837 150f. multicoloured 2·75 90
MS1838 60 × 80 mm. 500f. multicoloured. Imperf 11·00 11·00
DESIGN: 100f. Pres. Hussain and document.

424 Missile Launch from Winged Map

425 Boxer and Hodori (mascot)

1988. Iraq Missile Research.
1839 **424** 100f. multicoloured 1·20 40
1840 150f. multicoloured 1·80 65
MS1841 80 × 60 mm. 500f. multicoloured. Imperf 5·75 5·75
DESIGN: 500f. President Hussain, map and missiles.

1988. Olympic Games, Seoul. Multicoloured.
1842 100f. Type **425** 1·80 60
1843 150f. Games emblem 2·75 90
MS1844 100 × 90 mm. 500f. Pres. Hussain presenting football trophy. Imperf 11·00 11·00

426 Dancers and Golden Cow

427 Crescent and Camel Train

1988. 2nd Babylon International Festival.
1845 **426** 100f. multicoloured 1·20 40
1846 150f. multicoloured 1·70 60
MS1847 60 × 80 mm. 500f. multicoloured. Imperf 5·75 5·75
DESIGN: 500f. Medallion and laurel wreath.

1988. Mohammed's Birth Anniv.
1848 **427** 100f. multicoloured 1·20 50
1849 150f. multicoloured 1·70 75
1850 1d. multicoloured 11·50 5·00

428 Hand holding Candle

انتصار العراق
١٩٨٨/٨/٨
(**429** "Victory")

1988. Martyr's Day.
1851 **428** 100f. multicoloured 90 40
1852 150f. multicoloured 1·70 75
1853 500f. multicoloured 5·75 2·20

1988. Nos. 1738/9 optd with T **429**.
1854 **399** 250f. multicoloured 4·25 1·40
1855 350f. multicoloured 5·75 2·10

430 Family on Pedestrian Crossing

1989. Police Day.
1856 **430** 50f. multicoloured 60 35
1857 100f. multicoloured 1·20 40
1858 150f. multicoloured 1·70 75

431 Children and Money

1989. Postal Savings Bank. (a) Size 32 × 32 mm.
1859 **431** 50f. multicoloured 1·50 75

(b) Size 24 × 25 mm. With or without Arabic opt.
1860a – 100f. multicoloured 25 25
1861a – 150f. multicoloured 35 35
DESIGN: 100, 150f. Motif as Type **431** but with inscriptions differently arranged and inscr "REPUBLIC OF IRAQ".

432 Members' Flags and Leaders

1989. Formation of Arab Co-operation Council (Egypt, Iraq, Jordan and Yemen Arab Republic). Multicoloured.
1862 100f. Type **432** 1·20 40
1863 150f. Leaders in formal pose 1·70 65

433 Dates

1989. 1st Anniv of Liberation of Fao City.
1864 **433** 100f. multicoloured 1·10 40
1865 150f. multicoloured 1·50 40
MS1866 60 × 80 mm. 250f. multicoloured. Imperf 1·50 1·50
DESIGN: 250f. Calendar.

434 Pres. Hussain

1989. 52nd Birthday of President Saddam Hussain.
1867 **434** 100f. multicoloured 1·10 40
1868 150f. multicoloured 1·50 40
MS1869 60 × 80 mm. 250f. multicoloured. Imperf 2·75 2·75
DESIGN: 250f. Hussain and laurel branches.

435 Khairalla

436 Hussain laying Mortar

1989. General Adnan Khairalla Commem.
1870 **435** 50f. multicoloured 75 35
1871 100f. multicoloured 1·40 40
1872 150f. multicoloured 2·75 75

1989. Completion of Basrah Reconstruction Project.
1873 **436** 100f. multicoloured 1·40 40
1874 150f. multicoloured 2·10 75

437 Crane and Buildings

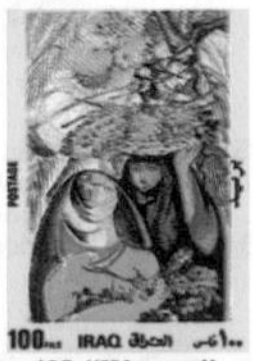
438 "Women"

1989. Start of Reconstruction of Fao City.
1875 **437** 100f. multicoloured 1·40 40
1876 150f. multicoloured 2·10 75

1989.
1877 **438** 100f. multicoloured 85 35
1878 150f. multicoloured 1·30 50
1879 1d. multicoloured 8·50 3·25
1880 5d. multicoloured 42·00 14·50

439 Pres. Hussain

440 Flag and Victory Signs

1989. July Festivals and 10th Anniv of President Hussain's State Leadership.
1881 **439** 50f. multicoloured 60 40
1882 100f. multicoloured 1·20 40
1883 150f. multicoloured 1·80 65

1989. Victory Day.
1884 **440** 100f. multicoloured 1·20 40
1885 150f. multicoloured 1·80 65
MS1886 70 × 90 mm. 250f. multicoloured. Imperf 3·50 3·50
DESIGN: 250f. Hussain, palm, Boeing 737 airliner and container ship "Khawla".

441 Children, Heart and Bride

1989. Iraqi Family.
1887 **441** 50f. multicoloured 90 40
1888 100f. multicoloured 1·70 75
1889 150f. multicoloured 5·75 2·20

442 Najaf

1989. Tourism. Multicoloured.
1890 100f. Type **442** . . . . . . 1·50 50
1891 100f. Arbil . . . . 1·50 50
1892 100f. Marsh Arab punt and Ziggurat of Ur . . . . . 1·50 50

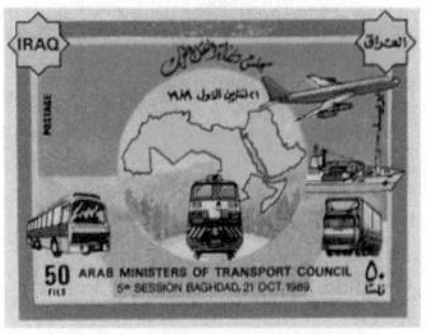

443 Map and Means of Transport

1989. 5th Session of Arab Ministers of Transport Council, Baghdad. Multicoloured.
1893 50f. Type **443** . . . . . . 1·00 50
1894 100f. Sun, means of transport and map . . . 2·10 65
1895 150f. Means of transport and members' flags (vert) 3·25 1·00

444 City and Pres. Hussain placing Final Stone

1989. Completion of Fao City Reconstruction.
1896 **444** 100f. multicoloured . . . 1·30 40
1897 150f. multicoloured . . . 1·80 65

445 Anniversary Emblem

1989. 30th Anniv of Iraqi News Agency.
1898 **445** 50f. multicoloured . . . 50 35
1899 100f. multicoloured . . . 1·00 40
1900 150f. multicoloured . . . 1·50 65

446 Emblem

447 Pansies

1989. 1st Anniv of Declaration of Palestinian State. Multicoloured.
1901 25f. Type **446** 25 25
1902 50f. Crowd of children . . . 60 35
1903 100f. Type **446** . . . . . . 1·20 40
1904 150f. As No. 1902 . . . . . 1·80 60

1989. Flowers. Multicoloured.
1905 25f. Type **447** 35 35
1906 50f. Antirrhinums 65 35
1907 100f. "Hibiscus trionum" . . 1·30 40
1908 150f. Mesembryanthemums 2·00 65
MS1909 90 × 110 mm. As Nos. 1905/8 but larger (26½ × 36 mm) . . . . 7·50 7·50

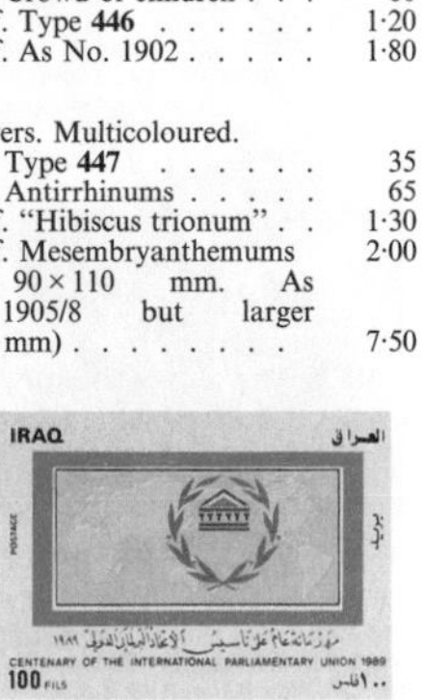

448 Map and Emblem

1989. Centenary of Interparliamentary Union.
1910 **448** 25f. multicoloured . . . 35 25
1911 100f. multicoloured . . . 1·20 40
1912 150f. multicoloured . . . 1·80 85

449 Sun, Flag, Doves and Mosque Domes

450 Dove, Red Crescent and Pres. Hussain

1989. Martyr's Day.
1913 **449** 50f. multicoloured . . . 60 35
1914 100f. multicoloured . . . 1·10 40
1915 150f. multicoloured . . . 1·50 65

1989. Iraqi Red Crescent Society.
1916 **450** 100f. multicoloured . . . 65 35
1917 150f. multicoloured . . . 1·60 65
1918 500f. multicoloured . . . 5·50 2·10

451 Members' Flags on Map

1990. 1st Anniv of Arab Co-operation Council.
1919 **451** 50f. multicoloured . . . 90 50
1920 100f. multicoloured . . . 2·20 90
MS1921 80 × 60 mm. **451** 250f. multicoloured. Imperf . . . . 6·25 6·25

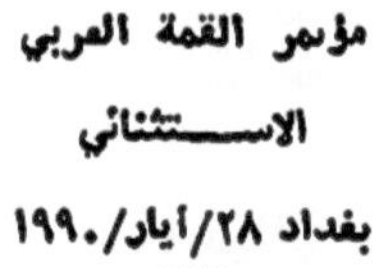

(452)

1990. Arab League Summit Conference, Baghdad. Nos. 1906 and 1908 optd with T **452**.
1922 50f. multicoloured . . . . . 1·00 85
1923 150f. multicoloured . . . . 3·25 2·00

453 Doves and Flag as Flame

1990. 2nd Anniv of Liberation of Fao City.
1924 **453** 50f. multicoloured . . . 50 50
1925 100f. multicoloured . . . 1·10 1·10

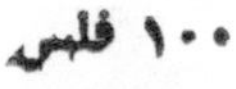

(454)

1992. No. 1291 surch with T **454**.
1927 100f. on 5f. multicoloured 2·50 2·50

455 Children and Currency

1993. Postal Savings.
1928 **455** 100f. multicoloured . . . 25 25
1929 150f. multicoloured . . . 35 35
1930 250f. multicoloured . . . 60 60

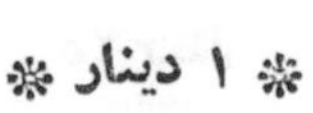

(456)

1993. No. O1742 surch with T **456**.
1931 1d. on 100f. multicoloured 7·25 7·25

(457)

1993. No. 1901 surch with T **457**.
1932 10d. on 25f. multicoloured 25·00 25·00

458 Satellite and Receiver

1993. Re-construction. Multicoloured.
1933 250f. Type **458** 65 65
1934 500f. Bridge over Tigris river . . . . 1·30 1·30
1935 750f. Power transformers . . 1·80 1·80
1936 1d. Damaged and restored buildings . . . . 2·50 2·50

459 *Ibn Khaldoon* (trading vessel)

1993.
1937 **459** 2d. multicoloured . . . 2·10 2·10
1938 5d. multicoloured . . . 5·50 5·50

(460) (461)

(461a) (461b)

(461c) (461d)

(462) (462a)

(463) (463a)

(464) (464a)

(464b) (464c)

(465) (466)

(466a) (467)

1994. No. 1291 surch with T **460/67**.
1939 500f. on 5f. multicoloured (T **460**) . . . . 1·70 1·70
1940 1d. on 5f. multicoloured (T **461**) . . . . 1·70 1·70
1941 1d. on 5f.multicoloured (T **461a**) . . . . 2·50 2·50
1942 1d. on 5f. multicoloured (T **461b**) . . . . 5·00 5·00
1943 1d. on 5f. multicoloured (T **461c**) . . . . 2·50 2·50
1944 1d. on 5f. multicoloured (T **461d**) . . . . 2·50 2·50
1945 2d. on 5f. multicoloured (T **462**) . . . . 3·00 3·00
1946 2d. on 5f. multicoloured (T **462a**) . . . . 3·00 3·00
1947 3d. on 5f. multicoloured (T **463**) . . . . 1·70 1·70
1948 3d. on 5f. multicoloured (T **463a**) . . . . 1·70 1·70
1950 5d. on 5f. multicoloured (T **464**) . . . . 1·70 1·70
1951 5d. on 5f. multicoloured (T **464a**) . . . . 2·50 2·50
1952 5d. on 5f. multicoloured (T **464b**) . . . . 3·75 3·50
1953 5d. on 5f. multicoloured (T **464c**) . . . . 3·75 3·50
1954 10d. on 5f. multicoloured (T **465**) . . . . 3·50 3·50
1955 25d. on 5f. multicoloured (T **466**) . . . . 7·25 7·25
1957 25d. on 5f. multicoloured (T **466a**) . . . . 11·50 11·50
1958 50d. on 5f. multicoloured (T **467**) . . . . 23·00 23·00

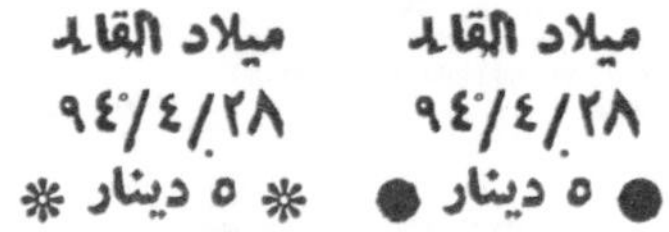

(472) (473)

1994. 57th Birth Anniv of Pres. Hussein. No. 1739 surch with T **472/3**.
1967 5d. on 350f. multicoloured (T **472**) . . . . 5·00 5·00
1968 5d. on 350f. multicoloured (T **473**) . . . . 5·00 5·00

474 Alqaid Bridge

1994.
1969 **474** 1d. multicoloured . . . 1·00 1·00
1970 3d. multicoloured . . . 3·00 3·00

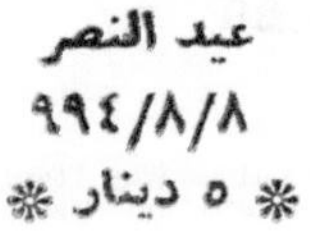

(475)

1994. Victory Day. No. 1739 surch with T **475**.
1971 5d. on 350f. multicoloured 4·00 4·00

(476)

1995. 20th Anniv of World Tourism Organization. No. 1878 surch with T **476**.
1972 5d. on 150f. multicoloured (Arabic inscription) . . . 3·25 3·25
1973 5d. on 150f. multicoloured (English inscription) . . . 3·25 3·25

477 Baghdad Clock

1995. Multicoloured.
1974 **477** 7d. blue and black . . . 2·10 2·10
MS1975 86 × 110 mm. 25d. As No. 1974 but with design enlarged. Imperf . . . . 10·00 10·00

478 Saddam Tower (television transmitter)

1995.
1976 **478** 2d. multicoloured . . . 85 85
1977 5d. multicoloured . . . 1·80 1·80

479 Pres. Hussein

1995. 58th Birth Anniv of Pres. Hussein. Two sheets. Imperf.

MS1978 (a) 60 × 78 mm. 25d. Type **479**; (b) 78 × 60 mm. 25d. President and child (horiz) Set of 2 sheets . . . . 22·00 22·00

480 Woman and River Basin

1995. Completion of "Saddam River" (canal between Iraq and Persian Gulf).

1979 **480** 4d. red and blue . . . . 3·25 3·25

1980 4d. ochre and blue . . . 3·25 3·25

MS1981 106 × 86m. **480** 25d. multicoloured . . . . 11·00 11·00

481 Barbed Wire, Tower, Woman and Child

1995.

1982 **481** 10d. blue and red . . . 2·25 2·50

MS1983 85 × 110 mm. **481** 25d. multicoloured . . . . 11·50 11·50

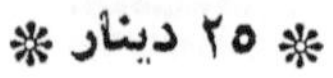

(482)

1995. No. 1739 surch with T **482**.

1984 25d. on 350f. multicoloured 1·00 1·00

1985 250d. on 350f. multicoloured 6·25 6·25

1986 350d. on 350f. multicoloured 15·00 15·00

1987 1000d. on 350f. multicoloured . . . . . . 30·00 30·00

(483) **(484)**

(485) **(486)**

1995. Nos. 1930 surch as T **483/6**.

1988 **483** 50d. on 250f. multicoloured . . . . 2·00 2·00

1989 **484** 500d. on 250f. multicoloured . . . . 20·00 20·00

1990 **485** 2500d. on 250f. multicoloured . . . . 80·00 80·00

1991 **485** 5000d. on 250f. multicoloured £170 £170

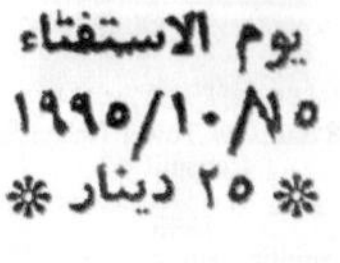

(487)

Referendum
15/10/1995
✻25 Dinars✻

(488)

1995. Referendum Day. No. 1739 surch with T **487/8**.

1992 25d. on 350f. multicoloured 2·50 2·50

1993 25d. on 350f. multicoloured 2·50 2·50

(489)

1996. No. 1297 surch with T **489** (overprint on overprint).

1994 25d. on 100f. on 5f multicoloured . . . . . . 3·75 3·75

(490) **(490a)**

(490b)

1996. Nos. 1859/61 surch with T **490/a/b**.

1995 25d. on 100f. multicoloured (T **490**) . . . . 1·00 1·00

1996 25d. on 150f. multicoloured (T **490a**) . . . . 1·00 1·00

1997 50d. on 50f. multicoloured (T **490b**) (32 × 32 mm) . . 2·00 2·00

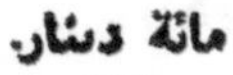

(491)

1996. No. O1616 surch with T **491**.

1998 100d. on 70f. yellow, black and flesh . . . . 4·25 4·25

492 Flag, Doves and Flames

1996. Sheet 86 × 62 mm. Imperf.

MS1999 **492** 100d. multicoloured 9·25 9·25

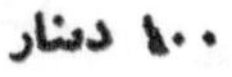

(493)

1996. No. 1878 surch with T **493**.

2000 100d. on 150f. multicoloured 4·25 4·25

(494) **(495)**

1996. Nos. 1989/91 surch with T **494/5** (overprint on overprint).

2001 **494** 25d. on 500d. on 250f.multicoloured . . 3·75 3·75

2002 25d. on 5000d. on 250f. multicoloured . . . 3·75 3·75

2003 **495** 50d. on 2500d. on 250f.multicoloured . . 7·50 7·50

(496) **(497)**

1996. Un-issued stamps surch with T **496/7**.

2004 **496** 25d. on 10f. multicoloured . . . . 29·00 29·00

2005 – 25d. on 25f. multicoloured . . . . 1·70 1·70

2006 **497** 50d. on 10f. multicoloured . . . . 50·00 50·00

2007 – 50d. on 50f. multicoloured . . . . 2·50 2·50

DESIGNS: Nos. 2004/7 School children in classroom.

(498)

1996. No.1906 surch with T **498**.

2008 100d. on 50f. Antirrhinums 4·50 4·50

(499)

1996. No. 1930 surch with T **499**.

2009 25d. on 250f. multicoloured 1·00 1·00

(500)

1996. No. O1645 surch with T **500**.

2010 100d. on 60f. multicoloured 4·25 4·25

(501)

1996. Nos. 1572/7 surch as T **501/a**.

2011 **501** 25d. on 10f. multicoloured . . . . 1·60 1·60

2012 25d. on 30f. multicoloured . . . . 1·60 1·60

2013 25d. on 50f. multicoloured . . . . 1·60 1·60

2014 **501a** 100d. on 20f. multicoloured . . . . 6·75 6·75

2015 100d. on 40f. multicoloured . . . . 6·75 6·75

2016 100d. on 100f. multicoloured . . . . 6·75 6·75

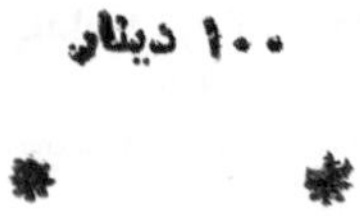

(502)

1996. No. 1924 surch with T **502**.

2017 100d. on 50f. multicoloured 4·25 4·25

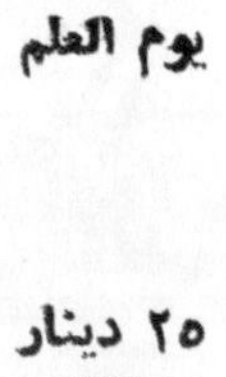

(503)

1997. No. 1933 surch as T **503**.

2018 25d. on 250f. multicoloured 1·00 1·00

504 Geometric Design

1997.

2019 **504** 25d. emerald, black and rosine 85 85

2020 100d. emerald, blue and vermilion . . . . . . 4·25 4·25

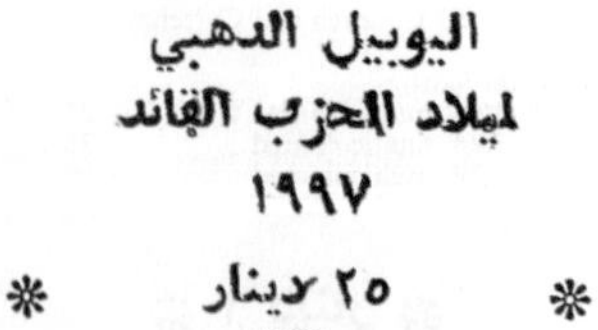

(505)

1997. 50th Anniv of Baath Party. No. 1920 surch with T **505**.

2021 25d. on 100f. multicoloured 1·50 1·50

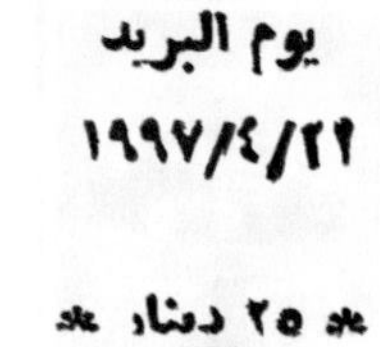

(506)

1997. 45th Anniv of Arab Post Union. No. 1878 surch with T **506**.

2022 25d. on 150f. multicoloured 3·50 3·50

507 Pres. Hussein

1997. 2nd Anniv of Referendum.

2023 **507** 25d. multicoloured . . . 1·30 1·30

2024 100d. multicoloured . . 5·00 5·00

MS2025 96 × 81 mm. 250d. President Saddam Hussein and map. Imperf 8·50 8·50

508 Pres. Hussein, Water and Plants

1997. Completion of Al Qaid Water Project. Multicoloured. (a) Sheet stamps. (i) Ordinary gum

2026 25d. Type **508** 50 50

(ii) Self-adhesive gum.

2027 100d. As No. 2026 . . . . 2·00 2·00

(b) Miniature Sheets. Ordinary gum.

MS2028 Two sheets. (a) 79 × 91 mm. 250d. As No. 2026; (b) 75 × 92 mm. 250d. Pres. Hussein and pipeline Set of 2 sheets . . 10·00 10·00

509 Saladin and Pres. Hussain

1998. Jerusalem Day. Self-adhesive.

2029 **509** 25d. multicoloured . . . 50 50

2030 100d. multicoloured . . 2·00 2·00

MS2031 88 × 75 mm. **509** 250d. multicoloured. Imperf . . . . 5·00 5·00

510 Zinnias

1998. Kurdish New Year. Two sheets containing T **510** and similar vert design. Imperf.

MS2032 (a) 71 × 93 mm. 250d. Type **510**; (b) 68 × 93 mm. 250d. Iris Set of 2 sheets . . . . . . 15·00 15·00

511 Goalkeeper and Players

1998. World Cup Football Championships, France (1st issue). Two sheets containing T **511** and similar multicoloured design. Imperf.
MS2033 (a) 72 × 85 mm. 250d. Type **511**; (b) 84 × 62 mm. 250d. Two players (vert) Set of 2 sheets 11·50 11·50
See also Nos. 2061/2.

512 Emblem

1998. 25th Anniv of Arab Police Security Chiefs' Conference. Sheet 93 × 67 mm. Imperf.
MS2034 **512** 250d. multicoloured 5·00 5·00

513 *Chamomile recuita*

514 Pres. Hussain and Map

1998. Flora. Multicoloured. (a) Ordinary gum.
2035 25d. Type **513** 25 25
2036 50d. *Helianthus annuus* . . . 40 40
2037 1000d. *Carduus nutans* . . . 7·25 7·25

(b) Self-adhesive gum.
2038 25d. Type **513** . . . . . . 1·30 1·30

1998. Arab Languages Day. Multicoloured.
2039 25d. Type **514** 40 40
2040 100d. Map and emblem . . 1·60 1·60

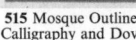

515 Mosque Outline, Calligraphy and Dove

517 Ishtar Gate, Babylon

516 *Precis orithya*

1998. Martyrs Day. Multicoloured.
2041 25d. Type **515** 35 35
2042 100d. Calligraphy and banner . . . . 1·30 1·30
MS2043 94 × 74 mm. 250d. Emblem 3·50 3·50

1998. Butterflies. Multicoloured.
2044 100d. Type **516** . . . . . . 2·50 2·50
2045 150d. *Anthocharis euphome* 3·75 3·75

1999. Tower of Babylon and Borsippa Ziggurat Conference. Multicoloured.
2046 25d. Type **517** 35 35
2047 50d. Ishtar Gate (different) 65 65
MS2048 71 × 90 mm. 250d. Ziggurat, Borsippa . . . . 5·00 5·00

518 Tower and Dam

519 Pres. Hussain

1999. Dams on the Tigris River. Multicoloured.
2049 25d. Type **518** 40 40
2050 100d. Dam, flowers, fruit and pylon . . . . 1·60 1·60
MS2051 71 × 93 mm. 250d. As No. 2050. Imperf . . . . . . 5·00 5·00

1999. 62nd Birthday of Pres. Hussain. Multicoloured.
2052 25d. Type **519** 15 15
2053 50d. With flag in background 35 35
2054 150d. With tree in background 90 90
2055 500d. Wearing uniform facing right . . . . 3·25 3·25
2056 1000d. Wearing uniform facing left . . . . 6·00 6·00
2057 5000d. Seated with clasped hands (horiz) . . . . . . 32·00 32·00

520 Emblem and Pres. Hussain

1999. Saddamiya al Therthar. Multicoloured.
2058 25d. Type **520** 40 40
2059 100d. Flowers, tower and gateway . . . . . . 1·40 1·40
MS2060 93 × 71 mm. 250d. Emblem, tower and Pres. Hussain. Imperf 5·00 5·00

521 Two Players

522 Bees (*Apis mellifica*)

1999. World Cup Football Championships, France (2nd issue). Multicoloured.
2061 25d. Type **521** 65 65
2062 100d. Goalkeeper and players (horiz) . . . . . 2·50 2·50

1999. Apiculture.
2063 **522** 25d. multicoloured . . . 85 85
2064 100d. multicoloured . . 1·80 1·80

523 Dome of the Rock

525 Pres. Hussain and Flowers

524 Flags and Pres. Hussain

1999. Jerusalem Day. Multicoloured.
2065 25d. Type **523** 25 25
2066 50d. Dome and map (horiz) 40 40
2067 100d. Dome, flag and shield 85 85
2068 150d. Dome and Pres. Hussain (horiz) . . . . . 1·30 1·30
MS2069 93 × 71 mm. 250d. As No. 2068. Imperf . . . . . . 3·75 3·75

1999. Victory Day. Multicoloured.
2070 25d. Type **524** 40 40
2071 50d. Pres. Hussain and crowd 75 75
MS2072 93 × 71 mm. 250d. Eagle's head and Pres. Hussain. Imperf 3·75 3·75

2000. 63rd Birthday of Pres. Hussain. Multicoloured.
2073 25d. Type **525** 35 35
2074 100d. Pres. Hussain and "28" (horiz) 65 65
MS2075 93 × 71 mm. 500d. Pres. Hussain wearing coat with fur collar. Imperf . . . . 6·75 6·75

526 Men and Women holding Tools (detail)

2000. Nasb al-Hurriyyah (sculpture by Jawad Salim). Multicoloured.
2076 25d. Type **526** 35 35
2077 25d. Women and child carrying corn 35 35
2078 25d. Men and broken fence 35 35
2079 25d. Grieving women . . . 35 35
2080 25d. Men with raised arms 35 35

527 Pres. Hussain

2000. Victory Day. Multicoloured.
2081 25d. Type **527** 65 65
2082 50d. Flag and guns . . . . 1·30 1·30
MS2083 72 × 92 mm. 255d. As No. 2081. Imperf . . . . . . 3·75 3·75

528 Mallards (*Anas platyrhynchos*)

2000. Birds. Multicoloured.
2084 25d. Type **528** 35 35
2085 50d. House sparrow (*Passer domesticus*) 75 75
2086 100d. Purple swamphen (*Porphyrio porphyrio*) . . 2·30 2·30
MS2087 92 × 71 mm. 500d. Goldfinch (*Carduelis carduelis*). Imperf . . . . 7·50 7·50

529 Emblem

530 Flag, Pres. Hussain and Voting Cards

2000. 430th Birth Anniv of Mohammed. Multicoloured.
2088 25d. Type **529** 60 60
2089 50d. Emblem (different) . . 1·20 1·20

2000. 5th Anniv of Referendum. Multicoloured.
2090 25d. Type **530** 25 25
2091 50d. Pres. Hussain wearing uniform (horiz) 60 60
MS2092 93 × 72 mm. 250d. Pres. Hussain wearing traditional clothes. Imperf . . . . 3·75 3·75

531 Emblem

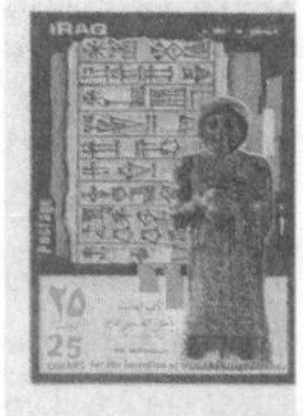

533 Inscribed Tablet and Statuette

532 Woman carrying Child

2000. 1200th Anniv of Baytol Hikma.
2093 **531** 50d. multicoloured . . . 40 40
2094 100d. multicoloured . . 85 85

2001. 10th Anniv of Al-Amiriyah. Multicoloured.
2095 25d. Type **532** 40 40
2096 50d. National colours and doves 85 85
MS2097 93 × 71 mm. 250d. As No. 2095. Imperf . . . . . . 3·00 3·00

2001. 5000th Anniv of Writing in Mesopotamia. Multicoloured.
2098 25d. Type **533** 15 15
2099 50d. Sumerian script and figures 40 40
2100 75d. As No. 2098 . . . . . 60 60
2101 100d. As No. 2099 . . . . 75 75
2102 150d. Figure wearing skirt (statue) . . . . 1·20 1·20
2103 250d. As No. 2102 . . . . 2·00 2·00

534 Arabic Script as Torch Flame and Crowd

2001. 54th Anniv of Al Baath Party. Multicoloured.
2104 25d. Type **534** 25 25
2105 50d. Michael Aflaq (founder) and Pres. Hussain 40 40
2106 100d. Map of Arab states 85 85

535 Pres. Hussain

536 Pres. Hussain

2001. 13th Anniv of Cessation of Hostilities. Multicoloured.
2107 25d. Type **535** 25 25
2108 100d. Pres. Hussain, soldier and map (horiz) 85 85

2001. 64th Birthday of Pres. Hussain. Multicoloured.
2109 25d. Type **536** 15 15
2110 50d. Seated with children (horiz) 35 35
2111 100d. Wearing dark suit (horiz) 65 65
MS2112 90 × 69 mm. 250d. With children carrying flowers. Imperf 3·25 3·25

537 *Barbus sharpeyi*

2001. Fish. Multicoloured.
2113 25d. Type **537** 25 25
2114 50d. *Barbus esocinus* 50 50
2115 100d. *Barbus xanthopterus* 1·00 1·00
2116 150d. *Pampus argenteus* . . 1·60 1·60

538 Gazelle (*Gazella subgutturosa*)

2001. Fauna. Multicoloured.
2117 100d. Type **538** 65 65
2118 250d. Hare (*Lepus europaeus*) (vert) . . . . . 1·70 1·70
2119 500d. Dromedary (*Camelus dromedaries*) . . . . . . 3·25 3·25
MS2120 92 × 70 mm. 1000d. Horse, gazelle, sheep and camel. Imperf 6·75 6·75

539 Hawk and Flags

541 Drilling Rig and Workers

540 National Colours joining Maps of Palestine and Iraq

2001. 10th Anniv of Um Al Marik.
2121 **539** 25d. multicoloured . . . 15 15
2122 100d. multicoloured . . 75 75

2001. Al Asqa Intifada. Multicoloured.
2123 25d. Type **540** 25 25
2124 25d. Dome of the Rock, flag and man carrying gun (vert) 25 25
2125 50d. Dome of the Rock, leaves and man with raised arms (vert) 50 50
MS2126 Two sheets, each 89 × 67 mm. (a) 250d. Mohammed Dorra and father; (b) 250d. Tank and protester. Imperf Set of 2 sheets . . . . 4·25 4·25

2001. 29th Anniv of Nationalization of Oil Industry. Multicoloured.
2127 25d. Type **541** 25 25
2128 50d. Flaming tower, processing plant and oil 50 50

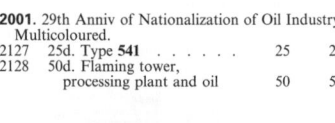

542 World Map and Footballers

2001. Under 20 Junior World Cup Football Championships, Argentina. Multicoloured.
2129 25d. Type **542** 25 25
2130 50d. Player and trophy (vert) 50 50

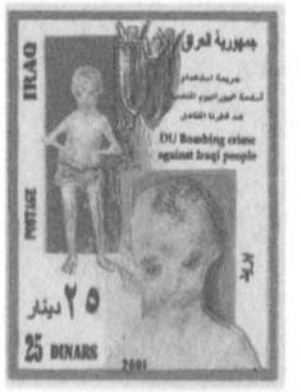

543 Sick Child

545 Aircraft, Flames and Girl

544 Soldiers and Flag

2001. 10th Anniv of Gulf War. Multicoloured.
2131 25d. Type **543** 40 40
2132 25d. Woman and children 40 40
2133 50d. Flag and family (horiz) 80 80
MS2134 70 × 92 mm. 250d. As No. 2131. Imperf . . . . . . 3·00 3·00

2002. Army Day. Multicoloured.
2135 25d. Type **544** 40 40
2136 50d. Statue of soldiers (vert) 85 85
2137 100d. Soldier (vert) . . . .
MS2138 70 × 90 mm. 250d. As No. 2135. Imperf . . . . . . 1·70 1·70

2002. 11th Anniv of Gulf War.
2139 **545** 100d. multicoloured . . 1·30 1·30

546 Pres. Hussain wearing Hat

547 Flags and Fist

2002. Jerusalem Day.
2140 **546** 25d. multicoloured . . . 25 25
2141 50d. multicoloured . . . 40 40
2142 100d. multicoloured . . 85 85

1963. 2002. 39th Anniv of 8 February. Multicoloured.
2143 50d. Type **547** 40 40
2144 100d. Sumerians, Saladin and modern crowd (horiz) 85 85

548 Aircraft Sights

549 Orange Roses

2002. 11th Anniv of Al-Amiriyah.
2145 **548** 25d. multicoloured . . . 25 25
2146 50d. multicoloured . . . 40 40

2002. Flowers. Multicoloured.
2147 25d. Type **549** 25 25
2148 50d. Pink and red roses . . 40 40
2149 150d. Carnations, anemone and narcissi . . . . . . 1·30 1·30
MS2150 73 × 91 mm. 250d. Bouquet. Imperf . . . . 2·50 2·50

550 Web and Mosques

2002. Hajeer New Year. Multicoloured.
2151 25d. Type **550** 25 25
2152 50d. Crescent moon and mosque (vert) 40 40
2153 75d. Web and doves 65 65

551 Envelope

2002. Post Day. Multicoloured.
2154 50d. Type **551** 50 50
2155 100d. Aircraft, ship and train . . . . 1·00 1·00
MS2156 70 × 91 mm. 250d. Envelope and globe. Imperf . . . . . . 3·75 3·75

552 Pres. Hussain as Boy

553 Trophy and Player

2002. 65th Birth Anniv of Pres. Hussain. Multicoloured.
2157 25d. Type **552** 25 25
2158 50d. As young man 40 40
2159 75d. With flag at left . . . 65 65
2160 100d. With flag at right . . . 85 85
MS2161 Two sheets, each 74 × 91 mm. (a) 250d. Wearing traditional clothes; (b) 250d. Surrounded by flowers. Imperf Set of 2 sheets . . . . 5·00 5·00

2002. World Cup Football Championships, Japan and South Korea. Multicoloured.
2162 50d. Type **553** 40 40
2163 100d. Player chasing ball . . 85 85
2164 150d. Player kicking ball . . 1·30 1·30
MS2165 69 × 91 mm. 250d. Championship emblem and trophy enclosing players. Imperf . . . 3·25 3·25

554 Soldier, Child and Woman

555 Sheikh Maruf Mosque

2002. 2nd Anniv of Al Asqa Intifada.
2166 **554** 5000d. multicoloured . . 25·00 25·00

2002. Mosques. Multicoloured.
2167 25d. Type **555** 25 25
2168 50d. Al- Mouiz 50 50
2169 75d. Um Al Marik 75 75

556 Stylized Eagle, Flag and Pres. Hussain

2002. Victory Day. Multicoloured.
2170 25d. Type **556** 25 25
2171 50d. As No. 2149 . . . . . 40 40
MS2172 70 × 91 mm. 150d. Eagle's head. Imperf . . . . 2·50 2·50

557 Reed Boats and Coracle

2002. Traditional Watercraft. Multicoloured.
2173 150d. Type **557** . . . . . . 1·30 1·30
2174 250d. Galley . . . . 2·10 2·10
2175 500d. Sail boat . . . . . . 4·25 4·25

558 Jameel Sidqi Al-Zahawi

559 Hands holding Flowers and Pres. Hussain

2002. Writers. Multicoloured.
2176 25d. Type **558** 25 25
2177 50d. Abdul Musin Al-Qadumi 40 40
2178 75d. Badr Shaker Al-Sayab 65 65
2179 100d. Ma'rouf Al-Rasafi . . 85 85
MS2180 71 × 91 mm. 150d. Badr Shaker Al-Sayab and rose. Imperf 2·50 2·50

2002. Referendum. Multicoloured.
2181 100d. Type **559** 85 85
2182 150d. Fist and ballot box 1·30 1·30
MS2183 70 × 92 mm. 250d. As No. 2181. Imperf . . . . . . 2·20 2·20

560 Woman Spinning

2002. Baghdad Day. Multicoloured.
2184 25d. Type **560** 25 25
2185 50d. Street performer and children 40 40
2186 75d. Two women talking (horiz) 65 65
MS2187 91 × 71 mm. 250d. Musicians. Imperf . . . . 4·25 4·25

561 *Oryx leucoryx*

2003. Fauna. Multicoloured.
2188 25d. Type **561** 25 25
2189 50d. *Acinonyx jubatus* (vert) 40 40
2190 75d. *Panthera leo* (vert) . . 65 65
2191 100d. *Castor fiber* 85 85
2192 150d. *Equus hemionus* . . . 1·30 1·30
MS2193 69 × 93 mm. 250d. As No. 2188. Imperf . . . . . . 4·25 4·25

562 Emblem

2003. 10th Anniv of Saddam University.
2194 **562** 50d. multicoloured . . . 40 40
2195 100d. multicoloured . . 85 85

OBLIGATORY TAX

28a King Faisal II

28b

مالية
فلسان
انقاذ فلسطين

(**28c** "Tax 2 Fils Save Palestine")

مالية
انقاذ فلسطين

(**28d** "Tax Save Palestine")

انقاذ
فلسطين

(**28e** "Save Palestine" (size varies))

١٠ فلوس
انقاذ فلسطين

(**28g** "Tax 10 Fils Save Palestine" (size varies))

مالية
٥ فلوس
انقاذ فلسطين

(**28h** "Tax 5 Fils Save Palestine")

1949. Aid for Palestine. (a) Nos. O300 and 278 surch as T **28**.
T324 **27** 2f. on 3f. green . . . . . 25·00 15·00
T325 2f. on 6f. mauve . . . . 34·00 14·50

(b) Nos. O299 and O303 optd as T **28d** but smaller.
T326 **27** 2f. brown . . . . 20·00 9·25
T327 5f. red . . . . 40·00 22·00

(c) No. O234 optd with T **28d**.
T328 **20** 5f. red . . . . 21·00 5·50

(d) Revenue stamp surch in Arabic (="2 Fils Save Palestine") as bottom two lines of T **28c**.
T329 **28a** 2f. on 5f. blue . . . . . 13·50 7·50

(e) Revenue stamps optd with T **28e**.
T330 **28a** 5f. blue . . . . 6·75 1·20
T335 10f. orange . . . . . . 27·00 16·00
T332 **28b** 10f. orange . . . . . . – 38·00

(f) Revenue stamp surch as T **28g**.
T336 **28b** 10f. on 20f. green . . . . 60·00 27·00

(h) No. 278 surch with T **28h**.
T337 **27** 5f. on 6f. mauve . . . . 42·00 16·00

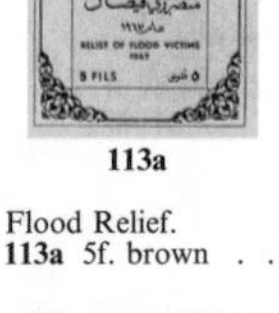

113a

دفـاع
وطـني

(**113b**)

1968. Flood Relief.
T763 **113a** 5f. brown 40 25

1968. Defence Fund. Optd with Type **113b**.
T764 **113a** 5f. brown 40 40

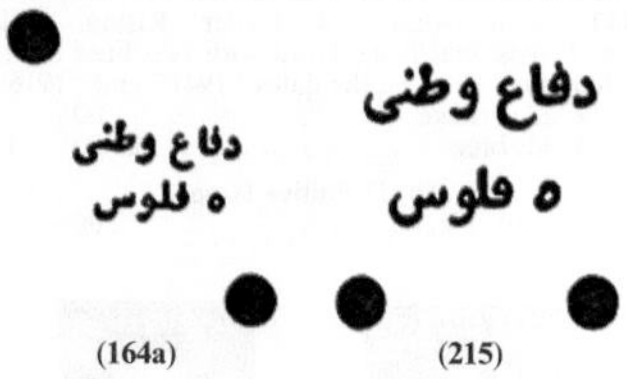

(164a) (215)

1970. Obligatory Tax. Defence Fund. Nos. 620 and 625/9 surch with Type T **164a**.

T931	**65**	5f. on 1f. green	3·75	4·50
T932	–	5f. on 10f. red	3·75	4·50
T933	–	5f. on 15f. brown & yell	3·75	4·50
T934	–	5f. on 20f. violet	3·75	4·50
T935	–	5f. on 30f. orange	3·75	4·50
T936	–	5f. on 40f. green	3·75	4·50

1973. Obligatory Tax. Defence Fund. Nos. 607/8 surch with Type **215**.

T1071	**62**	5f. on 14f. black & grn	6·75	6·75
T1072		5f. on 35f. black and red	6·75	6·75

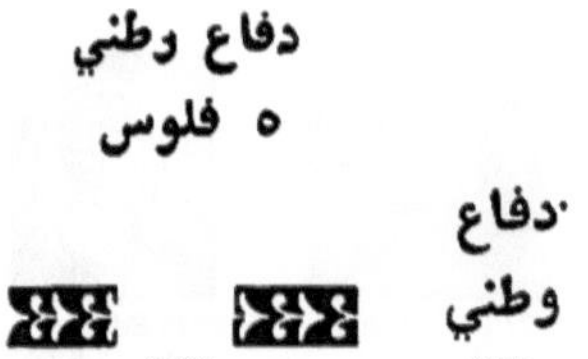

(223) (231)

1973. Nos. 738, 765, 777, 787 and 891 optd similar to Type **215** (No. T1119) or as Type **223** (others).

T1117	–	5f. on 2f. multicoloured	8·50	8·50
T1118	**114**	5f. on 2f. multicoloured	8·50	8·50
T1119	**116**	5f. on 2f. multicoloured	8·50	8·50
T1120	**117**	5f. on 2f. multicoloured	8·50	8·50
T1121	**150**	5f. on 2f. multicoloured	8·50	8·50

1973. No. 1099 optd with Type **231**.

T1152	**221**	5f. black and orange	5·75	4·25

235 Soldier

1974. Defence Fund.

T1158	**235**	5f. black, yellow & brn	2·50	3·00

OFFICIAL STAMPS

1920. Issue of 1918 (surch Turkish stamps) optd **ON STATE SERVICE**.

O33	½a. on 10pa. green	1·00	1·00
O20	1a. on 20pa. red	2·00	60
O35	1½a. on 5pa. brown	2·75	65
O22	2½a. on 1pi. blue	2·25	2·50
O23	3a. on 1½pi. black and pink	17·00	80
O36	4a. on 1¾pi. brown and blue	2·00	1·60
O25	6a. on 2pi. black and green	17·00	4·75
O38	8a. on 2½pi. green and brown	3·25	2·00
O27	12a. on 5pi. purple	10·00	7·00
O28	1r. on 10pi. brown	15·00	7·00
O29	2r. on 25pi. green	15·00	7·00
O30	5r. on 50pi. red	35·00	28·00
O31	10r. on 100pi. blue	50·00	75·00

1923. Nos. 41/50 and 52/3 optd **ON STATE SERVICE** in English only.

O54	**2**	½a. green	1·50	1·00
O55	–	1a. brown	1·75	20
O56	**3**	1½a. red	1·75	1·75
O57	–	2a. buff	2·00	40
O58	–	3a. blue	2·50	1·00
O59	–	4a. violet	4·25	1·00
O60	–	6a. blue	3·75	1·25
O61	–	8a. bistre	4·00	2·50
O62	**4**	1r. brown and green	7·50	1·75
O63	**2**	2r. black	20·00	8·50
O64	–	5r. orange	48·00	30·00
O65	–	10r. red	75·00	48·00

1924. Nos. 41/9 and 51/3 optd **ON STATE SERVICE** in English and Arabic.

O66	**2**	½a. green	1·25	10
O67	–	1a. brown	1·00	10
O68	**3**	1½a. red	1·00	30
O69	–	2a. buff	1·50	10
O70	–	3a. blue	2·00	10
O71	–	4a. violet	4·00	30
O72	–	6a. blue	1·75	20
O73	–	8a. bistre	3·75	35
O74	**4**	1r. brown and green	9·50	1·50
O75	**2**	2r. bistre	35·00	3·75
O76	–	5r. orange	50·00	42·00
O77	–	10r. red	80·00	42·00

1927. Optd **ON STATE SERVICE** in English and Arabic.

O79	**10**	1r. brown	6·00	1·75

1931. Optd **ON STATE SERVICE** in English and Arabic.

O 93	**11**	½a. green	65	2·75
O 94		1a. brown	80	10
O 95		1½a. red	4·50	21·00
O 96		2a. orange	80	10
O 97		3a. blue	85	1·25
O 98		4a. purple	1·00	1·50
O 99		6a. blue	4·50	19·00
O100		8a. green	4·75	19·00
O101	**12**	1r. brown	14·00	18·00
O102		2r. brown	22·00	65·00
O103		5r. orange	42·00	£120
O104		10r. red	80·00	£190
O105	**10**	25r. violet	£600	£700

1932. Official stamps of 1924 and 1931 surch in "Fils" or "Dinar".

O122	**11**	3f. on ½a. green	3·50	3·50
O123		4f. on 1a. brown	2·50	10
O124		5f. on 1a. brown	2·50	10
O125	**4**	8f. on 1½a. red	5·50	50
O126	**11**	10f. on 2a. orange	3·00	10
O127		15f. on 3a. blue	4·25	2·50
O128		20f. on 4a. purple	4·25	2·50
O129		25f. on 4a. purple	4·50	2·00
O130	–	30f. on 6a. bl (No. O72)	4·75	1·75
O131	**11**	40f. on 8a. green	4·00	3·50
O132	**12**	50f. on 1r. brown	5·50	3·50
O133		75f. on 1r. brown	6·00	6·00
O134	**2**	100f. on 2r. bistre	18·00	3·50
O135	–	200f. on 5r. orange (No. O76)	23·00	23·00
O136	–	½d. on 10r. red (No. 77)	65·00	85·00
O137	**10**	1d. on 25r. violet	£120	£190

1932. Issue of 1932 optd **ON STATE SERVICE** in English and Arabic.

O155	**11**	2f. blue	1·50	10
O156		3f. green	1·50	10
O157		4f. purple	1·50	10
O158		5f. green	1·50	10
O159		8f. red	1·50	10
O160		10f. yellow	2·25	10
O161		15f. blue	2·50	10
O162		20f. orange	2·50	15
O163		25f. mauve	2·50	15
O164		30f. olive	3·50	20
O165		40f. violet	4·50	30
O166	**12**	50f. brown	3·25	20
O167		75f. blue	2·50	1·00
O168		100f. green	11·00	2·00
O169		200f. red	20·00	6·50
O170	**10**	½d. blue	12·00	25·00
O171		1d. purple	60·00	90·00

1934. Issue of 1934 optd **ON STATE SERVICE** in English and Arabic.

O190	**16**	1f. violet	1·30	50
O191		2f. blue	1·30	15
O192		3f. green	60	15
O193		4f. purple	1·30	15
O194		5f. green	1·10	15
O195		8f. red	4·25	25
O196		10f. yellow	10	15
O197		15f. blue	9·25	1·50
O198		20f. orange	90	15
O199		25f. mauve	18·00	5·75
O200		30f. green	4·25	25
O201		40f. violet	5·50	40
O202	**17**	50f. brown	90	65
O203		75f. blue	6·25	85
O204		100f. green	1·70	1·00
O205		200f. red	4·50	2·50
O206	–	½d. blue (No. 188)	11·50	18·00
O207	–	1d. red (No. 189)	46·00	55·00

1941. Issue of 1941 optd **ON STATE SERVICE** in English and Arabic.

O230	**19**	1f. purple	25	15
O231		2f. brown	25	15
O232	–	3f. green (No. 210)	25	15
O233	–	4f. violet (No. 211)	25	15
O234	–	5f. red (No. 212)	25	15
O235	**21**	8f. red	85	15
O236		8f. yellow	25	15
O237		10f. yellow	6·25	40
O238		10f. red	65	15
O239		15f. blue	6·25	75
O240		15f. black	1·10	35
O241		20f. black	1·80	35
O242		20f. blue	60	15
O244	**22**	25f. purple	60	35
O246a		30f. orange	40	25
O248a		40f. brown	50	25
O249c	–	50f. blue (No. 224)	1·10	65
O250	–	75f. mauve (No. 225)	1·10	25
O251	–	100f. olive (No. 226)	2·20	25
O252	–	200f. orange (No. 227)	3·00	85
O253	–	½d. blue (No. 228)	11·00	5·00
O254	–	1d. green (No. 229)	18·00	9·25

1942. Issue of 1942 optd **ON STATE SERVICE** in English and Arabic.

O263	**26**	1f. brown and violet	35	35
O264		2f. brown and blue	35	35
O265		3f. brown and green	35	35
O266		4f. sepia and brown	35	35
O267		5f. brown and green	40	40
O268		6f. brown and red	40	40
O269		10f. brown and pink	65	60
O270		12f. brown and green	75	60

1948. Issue of 1948 optd **ON STATE SERVICE** in English and Arabic.

O298	**27**	1f. blue	15	35
O299		2f. brown	15	40
O300		3f. green	15	40
O301		3f. red	3·00	1·00
O302		4f. lilac	15	35
O303		5f. red	15	50
O304		5f. green	3·25	1·00
O305		6f. mauve	15	40
O306		8f. brown	15	40
O307		10f. red	15	35
O308		12f. green	15	35
O309		14f. green	1·70	35
O310		15f. black	3·75	6·25
O311		16f. red	3·00	35
O312		20f. blue	25	15
O313		25f. purple	25	15
O314		28f. blue	90	35
O315		30f. orange	25	25
O316		40f. brown	50	40
O317		50f. blue	75	35
O318		60f. blue	50	25
O319		75f. mauve	1·30	25
O320		100f. green	1·30	1·00
O321		200f. orange	2·10	1·10
O322		½d. blue	18·00	15·00
O323		1d. green	25·00	32·00

1955. Issue of 1954 optd **ON STATE SERVICE** in English and Arabic.

O364	**33**	1f. blue	15	15
O365		2f. brown	15	15
O366		3f. lake	15	15
O367		4f. violet	25	15
O368		5f. green	25	15
O369		6f. mauve	25	15
O370		8f. brown	25	15
O371		10f. blue	25	15
O372		16f. red	22·00	22·00
O373		20f. olive	40	25
O374		25f. purple	2·20	1·10
O375		30f. red	1·00	25
O376		40f. brown	40	25
O377	–	50f. blue	2·20	75
O378	–	60f. purple	14·50	5·50
O379	–	100f. olive	23·00	15·00

No. O378 does not exist without opt.

1958. Issue of 1957 optd **ON STATE SERVICE** in English and Arabic.

O404	**41**	1f. blue	4·25	1·70
O405		2f. brown	5·00	3·75
O406		3f. red	6·25	2·50
O407		4f. violet	7·50	1·70
O408		5f. green	4·25	1·70
O409		6f. red	4·25	2·50
O410		10f. blue	4·25	1·30

1958. Official stamps optd with T **43**. (a) Nos. O251/2.

O459		100f. green		
O459a		200f. orange	9·25	5·50

(b) Nos. O298 etc.

O460	**27**	1f. blue	34·00	34·00
O461		2f. brown	34·00	34·00
O462		3f. green	34·00	34·00
O463		3f. red	34·00	34·00
O464		4f. lilac	34·00	34·00
O465		5f. red	34·00	34·00
O466		5f. green	34·00	34·00
O467		6f. mauve	34·00	34·00
O468		8f. brown	34·00	34·00
O470		12f. green	1·00	75
O471		14f. green	1·20	85
O472		15f. black	85	50
O473		16f. red	3·50	2·10
O474		25f. purple	3·25	2·00
O475		28f. blue	1·80	1·60
O476		40f. brown	1·30	1·00
O477		60f. blue	4·50	2·50
O478		75f. mauve	2·20	1·80
O479		200f. orange	2·75	2·30
O480		½d. blue	16·00	5·75
O481		1d. green	25·00	11·50

(c) Nos. O364 etc.

O482	**33**	1f. blue	60	25
O483		2f. brown	60	25
O484		3f. red	60	25
O485		4f. violet	60	25
O486		5f. green	60	40
O487		6f. mauve	50	25
O488		8f. brown	65	25
O489		10f. blue	65	25
O490		16f. red	7·25	6·75
O491		20f. green	60	25
O492		25f. purple	60	25
O493		30f. red	65	40
O494		40f. brown	90	40
O495	–	50f. blue	90	50
O496	–	60f. purple	90	60
O497	–	100f. green	2·00	60

(d) Nos. O404 etc.

O498	**41**	1f. blue	25	25
O499		2f. brown	25	25
O500		3f. red	40	25
O501		4f. violet	25	25
O502		5f. green	25	25
O503		6f. red	25	25
O504		8f. brown	60	15
O505		10f. blue	65	10

No. O504 does not exist without opt T **43**.

1961. Nos. 515, etc. optd **On State Service** in English and Arabic.

O552	**49**	1f. multicoloured	35	35
O553		2f. multicoloured	35	35
O554		4f. multicoloured	35	35
O555		5f. multicoloured	40	35
O556		10f. multicoloured	75	60
O557		50f. multicoloured	12·50	10·00

1962. Nos. 515, etc. optd **ON STATE SERVICE** in English and Arabic.

O587	**49**	1f. multicoloured	35	35
O588		2f. multicoloured	35	35
O589		3f. multicoloured	35	35
O590		4f. multicoloured	35	35
O591		5f. multicoloured	35	35
O592		10f. multicoloured	35	35
O593		15f. multicoloured	35	35
O594		20f. multicoloured	35	35
O595		30f. multicoloured	40	35
O596		40f. multicoloured	40	35
O597		50f. multicoloured	50	35
O598		75f. multicoloured	85	40
O599		100f. multicoloured	90	65
O600		200f. multicoloured	3·25	1·40
O601		500f. multicoloured	11·50	5·75
O602		1d. multicoloured	23·00	11·50

1971. Various stamps optd or surch **Official** in English and Arabic. (a) Costumes. Nos. 768 and 770/4.

O962		15f. multicoloured (postage)	1·70	65
O963		25f. multicoloured	11·00	2·75
O964		30f. multicoloured	11·00	2·75
O965		40f. multicoloured (air)	4·50	1·40
O966		50f. multicoloured	5·75	1·40
O967		80f. multicoloured	5·50	1·40

(b) International Tourist Year. Nos. 778 and 780/2.

O969		5f. multicoloured (postage)	5·75	35
O970		15f. multicoloured	5·75	60
O971		25f. multicoloured	8·50	1·60
O972		50f. multicoloured (air)	5·50	3·75

(c) Birds. No. 798.

O1178		30f. multicoloured	4·00	3·25

(d) 20th Anniv of W.H.O. Nos. 811/13.

O973	–	10f. multicoloured	6·25	4·25
O974	**124**	15f. red, blue and black	6·25	4·25
O975		25f. red, green and black	6·25	4·25

(e) Human Rights Year. Nos. 814/15.

O976	**125**	10f. red, yellow and blue	5·00	50
O977		25f. red, yellow & green	5·00	90

(f) UNICEF. Nos. 817/18.

O978	**126**	15f. multicoloured	5·00	40
O979		25f. multicoloured	5·00	1·10

(g) Army Day. No. 820.

O980	**127**	25f. multicoloured	11·00	3·25

(h) Fish and Fauna. Nos. 825/7, 829/30 and 832.

O981		10f. multicoloured (postage)	6·25	4·25
O982		15f. on 3f. multicoloured	6·25	4·25
O983		25f. on 2f. multicoloured	6·25	4·25
O984		10f. multicoloured (air)	6·25	4·25
O985		15f.+3f. multicoloured	6·25	4·25
O986		25f.+2f. multicoloured	6·25	4·25

(i) Fruits. Nos. 906/9.

O987		5f. multicoloured	5·00	3·75
O988		10f. multicoloured	5·00	3·75
O989		15f. multicoloured	5·00	3·75
O990		35f. multicoloured	5·00	3·75

(j) Arab Football Cup, Baghdad. No. 717.

O991	**97**	25f. multicoloured	5·75	4·25

(k) 50th Anniv of I.L.O. No. 836.

O992	**133**	15f. yellow, green & blk	5·75	4·25

1972. Nos. 625/8 optd **Official** in English and Arabic.

O1042	10f. red	7·50	7·50
O1043	15f. brown and yellow	7·50	7·50
O1044	20f. violet	7·50	7·50
O1045	30f. orange	7·50	7·50

1973. Various stamps with portrait obliterated by 3 bars. (i) 1948 issue.

O1081	**27**	25f. purple (No. O313)	6·25	1·60
O1082		50f. blue (No. O317)	6·25	5·75

(ii) 1955 issue.

O1083	**33**	25f. purple (No. O374)	6·25	1·60
O1084	–	50f. blue (No. O377)	6·25	5·75

(iii) Similar to 1958 issue (T **41**) but size 22½ × 27½ mm.

O1085	50f. purple	6·25	5·75

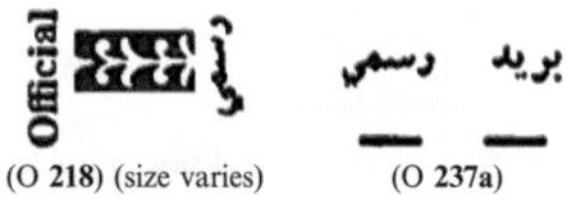

(O **218**) (size varies) (O **237a**)

1973. "Faisal" stamps with portrait obliterated. (a) Optd with 3 bars and Type O **218**.

O1086	**33**	10f. blue	3·75	3·75
O1087	**41**	15f. black	3·75	3·75

(b) Optd with Type O **218** only.

O1090	**33**	15f. black	3·75	85
O1091	**41**	15f. black	3·75	85
O1096	**27**	25f. purple	14·00	5·75
O1092	**33**	25f. purple	3·75	85
O1093	**41**	25f. purple	3·75	85

1973. No. 1097 optd **Official** in English and Arabic.

O1099	**220**	25f. multicoloured	3·75	1·20

1973. Nos. 1099/1107 optd **OFFICIAL** in English and Arabic.

O1108	**221**	5f. black and orange	35	35
O1109		10f. black and brown	35	35
O1110		20f. black and mauve	60	35
O1111	–	25f. black and blue	1·20	1·20
O1112	–	35f. black and green	1·20	50
O1113	–	45f. black and blue	1·20	60
O1114	–	50f. yellow and green	1·60	65
O1115	–	70f. yellow and violet	1·60	90
O1116	–	95f. yellow and brown	2·30	1·20

1973. Various "Faisal" Official stamps optd **ON STATE SERVICE** in English and Arabic, with portrait obliterated by "leaf" motif similar to that used in Type O **218**. (a) 1948 issue.

O1130a	**27**	12f. olive	1·60	35
O1131		14f. olive	1·60	50
O1132		15f. black	1·60	50
O1133		16f. red	3·25	85
O1134		28f. blue	6·25	1·20
O1134a		30f. orange	6·25	90
O1134b		40f. brown	6·25	1·40
O1135		60f. blue	6·25	5·00
O1136		100f. green	21·00	8·00
O1137		½d. blue	55·00	21·00
O1138		1d. green	£110	£110

(b) 1955 issue.

O1139	**33**	3f. lake	1·60	60
O1140		6f. mauve	1·60	60
O1141		8f. brown	1·60	60
O1142		16f. red	16·00	16·00
O1142a		20f. green	1·60	60
O1142b		30f. red	1·60	60
O1142c		40f. brown	1·60	60
O1143	–	60f. purple	1·60	60
O1144	–	100f. green	29·00	8·00

(c) 1958 issue.

O1145	**41**	3f. lake	5·00	1·20
O1146		6f. mauve	5·00	1·20
O1147		8f. brown	5·00	1·20
O1147a		30f. red	5·00	1·20

1974. No. T1168 optd with Type O **237a**.

O1165	**235**	5f. black, yellow & brn	3·00	3·00

O **249** Eagle Emblem

O **342** Entrance to Baghdad University

1975.

O1195	O **249**	5f. multicoloured	35	35
O1196		10f. multicoloured	35	35
O1197		15f. multicoloured	40	40
O1198		20f. multicoloured	60	60
O1199		25f. multicoloured	85	85
O1200		30f. multicoloured	1·00	1·00
O1201		50f. multicoloured	1·60	1·60
O1202		100f. multicoloured	3·25	3·25

1976. Nos. 1253/7 additionally inscr "OFFICIAL" in English and Arabic.

O1258	**264**	5f. multicoloured	1·30	75
O1259	–	10f. multicoloured	1·30	85
O1260	–	15f. multicoloured	1·30	85
O1261	–	25f. multicoloured	3·50	1·30
O1262	–	50f. multicoloured	5·75	2·20

1978. As T **290**, but additionally inscr "OFFICIAL" in English and Arabic.

O1338	5f. multicoloured	35	35
O1339	10f. multicoloured	35	35
O1340	15f. multicoloured	40	35
O1341	25f. multicoloured	85	35

1981.

O1499	O **342**	45f. multicoloured	60	40
O1500		50f. multicoloured	65	50

1982. As Nos. 1504/6, additionally inscr "OFFICIAL" in English and Arabic.

O1507	45f. multicoloured	1·30	40
O1508	50f. multicoloured	1·30	50
O1509	120f. multicoloured	3·25	1·30

1983. Nos. O1499/1500 surch.

O1581	O **342**	60f. on 45f. mult	2·50	50
O1582		70f. on 50f. mult	3·00	75

1983. Design as T **371**.

O1615	60f. yellow, black and pink	85	50
O1616	70f. yellow, black and pink	90	65

DESIGN: Nos. O1615/16, Aerial view of building.

1984. Multicoloured.

O1642	20f. Type **377**	35	35
O1643	30f. Type **377**	35	35
O1644	50f. As No. 1639	50	40
O1645	60f. As No. 1639	65	40

O **400** Pres. Hussain

1986.

O1740	O **400**	30f. multicoloured	60	15
O1741		50f. multicoloured	85	15
O1742		100f. multicoloured	1·70	60
O1743		150f. multicoloured	2·30	1·80

Nos. O1740/3 are inscribed "POSTAGE".

IRELAND (REPUBLIC) Pt. 1

Ireland (Eire) consisting of Ireland less the six counties of Ulster, became the Irish Free State in 1922 and left the British Empire in 1949 when it became an independent republic.

1949. 12 pence = 1 shilling;
20 shillings = 1 pound.
1971. 100 (new) pence = 1 pound (Punt).
2002. 100 cents = 1 euro.

Rialtar Sealadac na hÉireann 1922

(**1**) "Provisional Government of Ireland, 1922"

Rialtar Sealadac na hÉireann 1922.

(**2**)

1922. Stamps of Great Britain optd with T **1** (date in thin figures and no full point).

1	**105**	½d. green	1·75	40
2	**104**	1d. red	1·75	35
4a		2½d. blue	1·25	3·75
5	**106**	3d. violet	4·25	4·25
6		4d. green	4·50	12·00
7	**107**	5d. brown	4·25	8·50
8	**108**	9d. black	12·00	22·00
9		10d. blue	8·50	45·00
17	**109**	2s.6d. brown	42·00	80·00
19		5s. red	70·00	£150
21		10s. blue	£130	£300

On Nos. 17, 19 and 21 the overprint is in four lines instead of five.

1922. Stamps of Great Britain optd with T **2** (date in thick figures followed by full point).

47	**105**	½d. green	1·00	1·75
31	**104**	1d. red	2·50	50
10	**105**	1½d. brown	2·00	1·25
12	**106**	2d. orange	3·50	50
35	**104**	2½d. blue	6·00	22·00
36	**106**	3d. violet	3·00	2·00
37		4d. green	3·25	6·00
38	**107**	5d. brown	5·50	10·00
39		6d. purple	5·50	3·25
40	**108**	9d. black	13·00	17·00
41		9d. green	5·50	38·00
42		10d. blue	27·00	60·00
43		1s. brown	10·00	12·00

Saorstát Éireann 1922

(**5** "Irish Free State, 1922")

1922. Stamps of Great Britain optd with T **5**.

52	**105**	½d. green	1·25	30
53	**104**	1d. red	1·50	50
54	**105**	1½d. brown	3·50	8·50
55	**106**	2d. orange	1·50	1·00
56	**104**	2½d. blue	6·50	8·50
57	**106**	3d. violet	4·00	11·00
58		4d. green	3·25	8·00
59	**107**	5d. brown	4·00	4·75
60		6d. purple	2·00	2·00
61	**108**	9d. green	3·00	5·50
62		10d. blue	18·00	60·00
63		1s. brown	7·00	11·00
86	**109**	2s.6d. brown	48·00	55·00
87		5s. red	70·00	75·00
88		10s. blue	£160	£200

6 "Sword of Light"

7 Map of Ireland

8 Arms of Ireland

9 Celtic Cross

1922.

71	**6**	½d. green	1·50	90
112	**7**	1d. red	30	10
73		1½d. purple	1·60	2·50
114		2d. green	30	10
75	**8**	2½d. brown	4·00	4·25
116	**9**	3d. blue (18½×22½ mm)	70	10
227		3d. blue (17×21 mm)	40	15
117	**8**	4d. blue	55	10
118	**6**	5d. violet (18½×22½ mm)	65	10
228		5d. violet (17×21 mm)	30	15
119b		6d. purple	1·25	20
119c		8d. red	80	80
120	**8**	9d. violet	1·50	80
121	**9**	10d. brown	60	80
121b		11d. red	1·50	2·25
82	**6**	1s. blue	17·00	5·50

12 Daniel O'Connell

13 Shannon Barrage

1929. Centenary of Catholic Emancipation.

89	**12**	2d. green	50	45
90		3d. blue	4·00	8·50
91		9d. violet	4·00	4·00

1930. Completion of Shannon Hydro-electric Scheme.

92	**13**	2d. deep brown	1·00	55

14 Reaper

15 The Cross of Cong

1931. Bicentenary of Royal Dublin Society.

93	**14**	2d. blue	65	30

1932. International Eucharistic Congress.

94	**15**	2d. green	1·50	30
95		3d. blue	2·50	5·00

16 Adoration of the Cross

17 Hurler

1933. "Holy Year".

96	**16**	2d. green	1·25	15
97		3d. blue	2·50	2·00

1934. 50th Anniv of Gaelic Athletic Assn.

98	**17**	2d. green	1·00	55

18 St. Patrick

19 Ireland and New Constitution

1937.

123b	**18**	2s.6d. green	1·50	2·50
124ca		5s. purple	5·00	8·00
125ba		10s. blue	6·00	16·00

1937. Constitution Day.

105	**19**	2d. red	1·50	20
106		3d. blue	4·00	3·75

For similar stamps see Nos. 176/7.

20 Father Mathew

1938. Centenary of Temperance Crusade.

107	**20**	2d. black	2·00	50
108		3d. blue	10·00	6·50

21 George Washington, American Eagle and Irish Harp

1939. 150th Anniv of U.S. Constitution and Installation of First U.S. President.

109	**21**	2d. red	1·75	1·00
110		3d. blue	3·25	4·50

24 Volunteer and G.P.O., Dublin

1941. 25th Anniv of Easter Rising (1916). (a) Provisional issue. Optd with two lines of Irish characters between the dates "1941" and "1916".

126	**7**	2d. orange	1·00	70
127	**9**	3d. blue	24·00	11·00

(b) Definitive Issue.

128	**24**	2½d. black	2·00	80

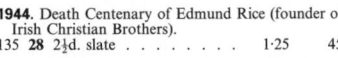

25 Dr. Douglas Hyde

26 Sir William Rowan Hamilton

1943. 50th Anniv of Gaelic League.

129	**25**	½d. green	65	30
130		2½d. purple	1·60	10

1943. Centenary of Announcement of Discovery of Quaternions.

131	**26**	½d. green	40	60
132		2½d. brown	1·75	10

27 Bro. Michael O'Clery

28 Edmund Ignatius Rice

1944. Death Tercentenary of Michael O'Clery (Franciscan historian) (commemorating the "Annals of the Four Masters").

133	**27**	½d. green	10	10
134		1s. brown	80	10

1944. Death Centenary of Edmund Rice (founder of Irish Christian Brothers).

135	**28**	2½d. slate	1·25	45

29 "Youth sowing Seeds of Freedom"

30 "Country and Homestead"

1945. Death Centenary of Thomas Davis (founder of Young Ireland Movement).

136	**29**	2½d. blue	1·00	50
137		6d. purple	6·00	4·50

1946. Birth Centenaries of Michael Davitt and Charles Parnell (land reformers).

138	**30**	2½d. red	2·00	25
139		3d. blue	3·00	3·75

31 Angel Victor over Rock of Cashel

1948. Air. Inscr "VOX HIBERNIAE".

140	**31**	1d. brown	1·75	3·75
141	–	3d. blue	3·00	2·25
142	–	6d. purple	1·00	1·75
142b	–	8d. lake	6·50	8·00
143	–	1s. green	1·00	1·75
143a	**31**	1s.3d. orange	8·00	1·25
143b		1s.5d. blue	3·00	1·25

DESIGNS: 3d., 8d. Angel Victor over Lough Derg; 6d. Over Croagh Patrick; 1s. Over Glendalough.

35 Theobald Wolfe Tone

1948. 150th Anniv of Insurrection.

144	**35**	2½d. purple	1·00	10
145		3d. violet	3·25	3·50

36 Leinster House and Arms of Provinces

37 J. C. Mangan

1949. International Recognition of Republic.

146	**36**	2½d. brown	1·50	10
147		3d. blue	6·00	4·25

1949. Death Centenary of James Clarence Mangan (poet).
148 **37** 1d. green . . . . 1·50 35

38 Statue of St. Peter, Rome

39 Thomas Moore

1950. Holy Year.
149 **38** 2½d. violet . . . . 1·00 40
150 3d. blue . . . . 8·00 11·00
151 9d. brown . . . . 8·00 11·00

1952. Death Centenary of Thomas Moore (poet).
152 **39** 2½d. purple 75 10
153 3½d. olive . . . . 1·60 3·75

40 Irish Harp

1953. "An Tostal" (Ireland at Home) Festival.
154 **40** 2½d. green . . . . 1·75 35
155 1s.4d. blue . . . . 15·00 24·00

41 Robert Emmet

42 Madonna and Child (Della Robbia)

1953. 150th Death Anniv of Emmet (patriot).
156 **41** 3d. green . . . . 3·00 15
157 1s.3d. red . . . . 42·00 10·00

1954. Marian Year.
158 **42** 3d. blue . . . . 1·00 10
159 5d. green . . . . 1·50 3·25

43 Cardinal Newman (first Rector)

44 Statue of Commodore Barry

45 John Redmond

1954. Centenary of Founding of Catholic University of Ireland.
160 **43** 2d. purple . . . . 1·50 10
161 1s.3d. blue . . . . 16·00 6·00

1956. Barry Commemoration.
162 **44** 3d. lilac . . . . 1·50 10
163 1s.3d. blue . . . . 5·50 9·00

1957. Birth Centenary of John Redmond (politician).
164 **45** 3d. blue . . . . 1·00 10
165 1s.3d. purple . . . . . . 8·00 15·00

46 Thomas O'Crohan

47 Admiral Brown

48 "Father Wadding" (Ribera)

1957. Birth Cent of Thomas O'Crohan (author).
166 **46** 2d. purple . . . . 1·00 15
167 5d. violet . . . . 1·00 4·50

1957. Death Cent of Admiral William Brown.
168 **47** 3d. blue . . . . 2·25 20
169 1s.3d. red . . . . 24·00 16·00

1957. Death Tercentenary of Father Luke Wadding (theologian).
170 **48** 3d. blue . . . . 2·00 10
171 1s.3d. lake . . . . 15·00 8·50

49 Tom Clarke

50 Mother Mary Aikenhead

1958. Birth Centenary of Thomas J. ("Tom") Clarke (patriot).
172 **49** 3d. green . . . . 2·00 10
173 1s.3d. brown . . . . . . 3·50 11·00

1958. Death Centenary of Mother Mary Aikenhead (foundress of Irish Sisters of Charity).
174 **50** 3d. blue . . . . 1·75 10
175 1s.3d. red . . . . 11·00 8·00

1958. 21st Anniv of Irish Constitution.
176 **19** 3d. brown . . . . 1·00 10
177 5d. green . . . . 2·00 4·50

51 Arthur Guinness

52 "The Flight of the Holy Family"

1959. Bicentenary of Guinness Brewery.
178 **51** 3d. purple . . . . 3·00 10
179 1s.3d. blue . . . . 11·00 12·00

1960. World Refugee Year.
180 **52** 3d. purple 40 10
181 1s.3d. sepia . . . . 60 3·25

53 Conference Emblem

1960. 1st Anniv of Europa.
182 **53** 6d. brown . . . . 12·00 3·00
183 1s.3d. violet . . . . 26·00 20·00

54 Dublin Airport, De Havilland Dragon Mk 2 "Iolar" and Boeing 720

55 St Patrick

1961. Silver Jubilee of Aer Lingus Airlines.
184 **54** 6d. blue . . . . 1·50 3·50
185 1s.3d. green . . . . 2·00 5·00

1961. 15th Death Centenary of St. Patrick.
186 **55** 3d. blue . . . . 1·00 10
187 8d. purple . . . . 2·75 5·50
188 1s.3d. green . . . . 2·75 1·60

56 John O'Donovan and Edugen O'Curry

1962. Death Centenaries of O'Donovan and O'Curry (scholars).
189 **56** 3d. red 30 10
190 1s.3d. purple . . . . . . 1·25 2·25

57 Europa "Tree"

1962. Europa.
191 **57** 6d. red . . . . 90 1·00
192 1s.3d. turquoise . . . . . 1·00 1·50

58 Campaign Emblem

1963. Freedom from Hunger.
193 **58** 4d. violet 50 10
194 1s.3d. red . . . . 2·50 2·75

59 "Co-operation"

1963. Europa.
195 **59** 6d. red . . . . 1·50 75
196 1s.3d. blue . . . . 4·00 3·75

60 Centenary Emblem

1963. Centenary of Red Cross.
197 **60** 4d. red and grey 50 10
198 1s.3d. red, grey and green 1·50 2·25

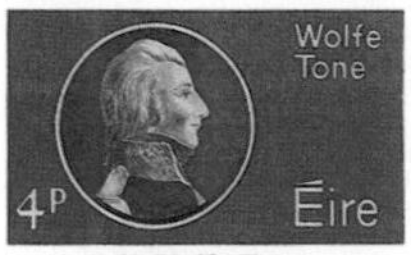

61 Wolfe Tone

1964. Birth Bicentenary of Wolfe Tone (revolutionary).
199 **61** 4d. black 40 10
200 1s.3d. blue . . . . 1·50 2·00

62 Irish Pavilion at Fair

63 Europa "Flower"

1964. New York World's Fair.
201 **62** 5d. multicoloured 35 10
202 1s.5d. multicoloured . . . 1·75 2·00

1964. Europa.
203 **63** 8d. green and blue . . . . 1·75 1·25
204 1s.5d. brown and orange 5·25 2·75

64 "Waves of Communications"

65 W. B. Yeats (poet)

1965. Centenary of I.T.U.
205 **64** 3d. blue and green 30 10
206 8d. black and green . . . 1·25 1·60

1965. Birth Centenary of Yeats.
207 **65** 5d. black, brown and green 30 10
208 1s.5d. black, green & brown . . . . 2·25 1·75

66 I.C.Y. Emblem

1965. International Co-operation Year.
209 **66** 3d. blue 60 10
210 10d. brown . . . . 1·00 3·00

67 Europa "Sprig"

1965. Europa.
211 **67** 8d. black and red . . . . 2·50 1·00
212 1s.5d. purple and turquoise 7·50 3·50

68 James Connolly

76 Roger Casement

1966. 50th Anniv of Easter Rising.
213 **68** 3d. black and blue 50 10
214 – 3d. black and bronze . . . 50 10
215 – 5d. black and olive 50 10
216 – 5d. black, orange and green 50 10
217 – 7d. black and brown . . . 50 2·25
218 – 7d. black and green . . . 50 2·25
219 – 1s.5d. black and turquoise 50 1·50
220 – 1s.5d. black and green . . 50 1·50

DESIGNS: No. 214, Thomas J. Clarke; No. 215, P. H. Pearse; No. 216, "Marching to Freedom"; No. 217, Eamonn Ceannt; No. 218, Sean MacDiarmada; No. 219, Thomas MacDonagh; No. 220, Joseph Plunkett.

1966. 50th Death Anniv of Roger Casement (patriot).
221 **76** 5d. black 15 10
222 1s. brown 30 50

77 Europa "Ship"

78 Interior of Abbey (from lithograph)

1966. Europa.
223 **77** 7d. green and orange . . . 1·00 40
224 1s.5d. green and grey . . . 2·50 1·00

1966. 750th Anniv of Ballintubber Abbey.
225 **78** 5d. brown 10 10
226 1s. black 20 25

79 Cogwheels

80 Maple Leaves

1967. Europa.
229 **79** 7d. green, gold and cream 75 40
230 1s.5d. red, gold and cream 1·75 1·00

1967. Canadian Centennial.
231 **80** 5d. multicoloured 10 10
232 1s.5d. multicoloured . . . 20 75

81 Rock of Cashel (from photo by Edwin Smith)

1967. International Tourist Year.
233 **81** 7d. sepia 15 20
234 10d. blue 15 40

82 1c. Fenian Stamp Essay

84 Jonathan Swift

1967. Centenary of Fenian Rising.
235 **82** 5d. black and green . . . 10 10
236 – 1s. black and pink 20 30
DESIGN: 1s.24c. Fenian Stamp Essay.

1967. 300th Birth Anniv of Jonathan Swift.
237 **84** 3d. black and grey 10 10
238 – 1s.5d. brown and blue . . 20 30
DESIGN: 1s.5d. Gulliver and Lilliputians.

86 Europa Key

1968. Europa.
239 **86** 7d. red, gold and brown 60 50
240 1s.5d. blue, gold and brown . . . . 90 1·00

87 St Mary's Cathedral, Limerick

1968. 800th Anniv of St. Mary's Cathedral, Limerick.
241 **87** 5d. blue 10 10
242 10d. green 20 60

88 Countess Markievicz

89 James Connolly

1968. Birth Centenary of Countess Markievicz (patriot).
243 **88** 3d. black 10 10
244 1s.5d. indigo and blue . . 20 20

1968. Birth Centenary of James Connolly (patriot).
245 **89** 6d. brown and chocolate 20 75
246 1s. green, lt green & myrtle 20 10

90 Stylized Dog (brooch)

92 Winged Ox (Symbol of St. Luke)

1968.
247 **90** ½d. orange 10 30
248 1d. green 15 10
249 2d. ochre 50 10
250 3d. blue 35 10
251 4d. red 30 10
252 5d. green . . . . 1·00 50
253 6d. brown 30 10
254 – 7d. brown and yellow . . . 45 3·50
255 – 8d. brown and chestnut . . 45 1·50
256 – 9d. blue and green 50 10
257 – 10d. brown and violet . . 1·50 2·50
258 – 1s. chocolate and brown 40 10
259 – 1s.9d. black and turquoise 4·00 2·50
260 **92** 2s.6d. multicoloured . . . 1·75 30
261 5s. multicoloured . . . . . 3·00 2·50
262 – 10s. multicoloured . . . . 4·75 3·75
DESIGNS—As Type **90**: 7d., 8d., 9d., 10d., 1s., 1s.9d., Stag. As Type **92**: 10s Eagle (Symbol of St. John The Evangelist).
See also Nos. 287, etc.

94 Human Rights Emblem

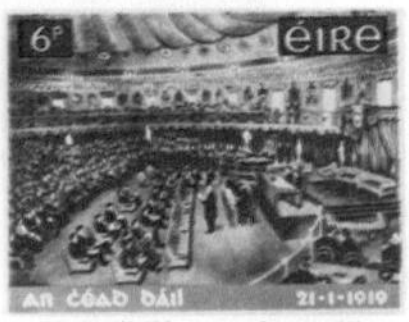

95 Dail Eireann Assembly

1968. Human Rights Year.
263 **94** 5d. yellow, gold and black 15 10
264 7d. yellow, gold and red 15 40

1969. 50th Anniv of Dail Eireann (1st National Parliament).
265 **95** 6d. green 15 10
266 9d. blue 15 30

96 Colonnade

97 Quadruple I.L.O. Emblems

1969. Europa.
267 **96** 9d. grey, ochre and blue 75 1·10
268 1s.9d. grey, gold and red 1·25 1·40

1969. 50th Anniv of I.L.O.
269 **97** 6d. black and grey 20 10
270 9d. black and yellow . . . 20 25

98 "The Last Supper and Crucifixion" (Evie Hone Window, Eton Chapel)

1969. Contemporary Irish Art (1st issue).
271 **98** 1s. multicoloured . . . . . 30 1·50
See also Nos. 280, 306, 317, 329, 362, 375, 398, 408, 452, 470 and 498.

99 Mahatma Gandhi

1969. Birth Centenary of Mahatma Gandhi.
272 **99** 6d. black and green . . . 20 10
273 1s.9d. black and yellow . . . 30 90

100 Symbolic Bird in Tree

1970. European Conservation Year.
274 **100** 6d. bistre and black . . . 20 10
275 9d. violet and black . . . 25 80

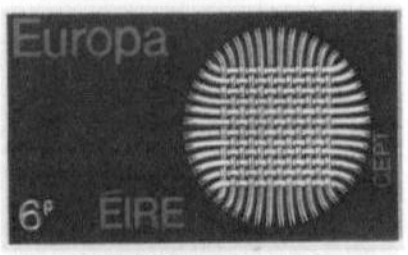

101 "Flaming Sun"

1970. Europa.
276 **101** 6d. violet and silver . . . 70 10
277 9d. brown and silver . . . 1·10 1·25
278 1s.9d. grey and silver . . 2·00 2·00

102 "Sailing Boats" (Peter Monamy)

103 "Madonna of Eire" (Mainie Jellett)

1970. 250th Anniv of Royal Cork Yacht Club.
279 **102** 4d. multicoloured 15 10

1970. Contemporary Irish Art (2nd issue).
280 **103** 1s. multicoloured 15 20

104 Thomas MacCurtain

106 Kevin Barry

1970. 50th Death Annivs of Irish Patriots.
281 **104** 9d. black, violet and grey 50 25
282 – 9d. black, violet and grey 50 25
283 **104** 2s.9d. black, blue and grey . . . . 1·40 1·50
284 – 2s.9d. black, blue and grey . . . . 1·40 1·50
DESIGN: Nos. 282 and 284, Terence MacSwiney.

1970. 50th Death Anniv of Kevin Barry (patriot).
285 **106** 6d. green 30 10
286 1s.2d. blue . . . . 40 1·10

1971. Decimal Currency. As Nos. 247/62 but with face values in new currency, without "p", and some colours changed.
287 **90** ½p. green 10 10
340 1p. blue 10 10
289 1½p. red 15 50
341 2p. green 10 10
291 2½p. brown 15 10
342 3p. brown 10 10
293 3½p. orange 15 10
294 4p. violet 15 10
295 – 5p. brown and olive . . . 1·00 20
344 **90** 5p. green 60 10
296 – 6p. grey and brown . . . 3·50 50
346 **90** 6p. grey 20 10
347 – 7p. blue and green . . . 70 35
348 **90** 7p. green 35 10
297 – 7½p. mauve and brown 50 85
349 – 8p. brown and deep brown 60 50
350 **90** 8p. brown 30 10
351 – 9p. black and green . . . 70 30
352 **90** 9p. green 30 10
352a 9½p. red 35 20
353 **92** 10p. multicoloured . . . 1·00 30
354 – 10p. black and lilac . . . 70 10
354a **90** 10p. mauve 70 10
355 – 11p. black and red . . . 45 30
299b **92** 12p. multicoloured . . . 60 1·25
355a – 12p. black and green . . 55 10
355b **90** 12p. green 30 10
355c – 13p. brown . . . . . . 40 1·50
356 **92** 15p. multicoloured . . . 55 40
356a **90** 15p. blue 40 10
356b – 16p. black and green . . 40 80
356c **92** 17p. multicoloured . . . 50 1·00
478 **90** 18p. red 45 50
479 19p. blue . . . . 55 1·75
357 **92** 20p. multicoloured . . . 50 15
480 **90** 22p. blue 65 10
481 24p. brown . . . . 1·50 1·25
482 26p. green . . . . 1·50 40
483 29p. mauve . . . . 1·75 2·00
358 – 50p. multicoloured . . . 70 30
359 – £1 multicoloured . . . . 1·50 30
DESIGNS—As Type **90**: 5p. (295); 6p. (296); 7p. (347); 7½p., 8p., 9p. (351) 10p. (354), 11p., 12p. (No. 355a), 13p., 16p. Stag. As Type **92**: 50p., £1, Eagle (symbol of St. John the Evangelist).

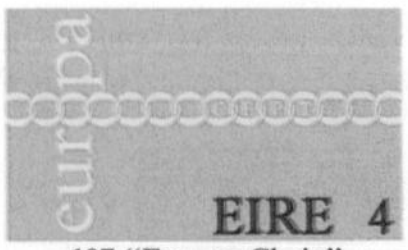

107 "Europa Chain"

108 J. M. Synge

1971. Europa.
302 **107** 4p. brown and green . . . 1·00 10
303 6p. black and blue . . . 3·75 2·50

1971. Birth Centenary of J. M. Synge (playwright).
304 **108** 4p. multicoloured 15 10
305 10p. multicoloured . . . 60 80

109 "An Island Man" (Jack B. Yeats)

110 Racial Harmony Symbol

1971. Contemporary Irish Art (3rd issue). Birth Centenary of J. B. Yeats (artist).
306 **109** 6p. multicoloured 55 55

1971. Racial Equality Year.
307 **110** 4p. red 20 10
308 10p. black 50 75

111 "Madonna and Child" (statue by J. Hughes)

112 Heart

1971. Christmas.
309 **111** 2½p. black, gold and green 10 10
310 6p. black, gold and blue 65 65

1972. World Health Day.
311 **112** 2½p. gold and brown . . 30 15
312 12p. silver and grey . . . 1·10 1·75

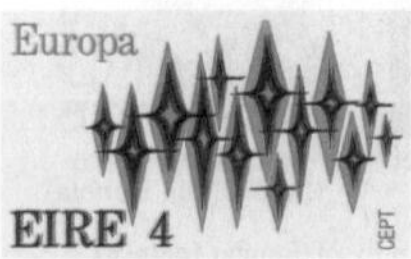

113 "Communications"

114 Dove and Moon

1972. Europa.
313 **113** 4p. orange, black and silver . . . . 1·50 25
314 6p. blue, black and silver 5·00 4·75

1972. Patriot Dead 1922–1923.
315 **114** 4p. multicoloured 10 10
316 6p. yellow, green & dp grn 65 50

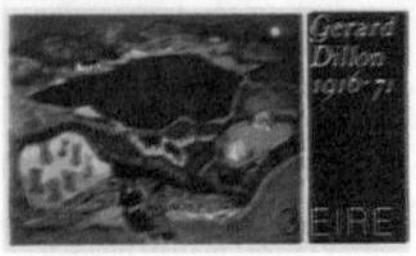

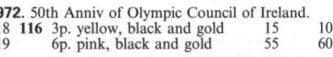

115 "Black Lake" (Gerard Dillon)

116 "Horseman" (Carved Slab)

1972. Contemporary Irish Art (4th issue).
317 **115** 3p. multicoloured 60 35

1972. 50th Anniv of Olympic Council of Ireland.
318 **116** 3p. yellow, black and gold 15 10
319 6p. pink, black and gold 55 60

117 Madonna and Child (from Book of Kells)

118 2d. Stamp of 1922

1972. Christmas.
320 **117** 2½p. multicoloured . . . 10 10
321 4p. multicoloured 25 10
322 12p. multicoloured . . . 80 65

1972. 50th Anniv of 1st Irish Postage Stamp.
323 **118** 6p. grey and green . . . 60 60
MS324 72 × 104 mm. No. 323 × 4 5·50 10·00

119 Celtic Head Motif

1973. Entry into European Communities.
325 **119** 6p. multicoloured 60 90
326 12p. multicoloured . . . 80 1·10

120 Europa "Posthorn"

1973. Europa.
327 **120** 4p. blue . . . . 1·00 10
328 6p. black . . . . 3·00 2·00

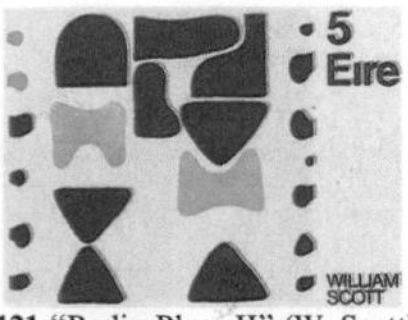

121 "Berlin Blues II" (W. Scott)

1973. Contemporary Irish Art (5th issue).
329 **121** 5p. blue and black . . . 40 30

122 Weather Map

1973. Centenary of I.M.O./W.M.O.
330 **122** 3½p. multicoloured . . . 30 10
331 12p. multicoloured . . . 1·10 2·00

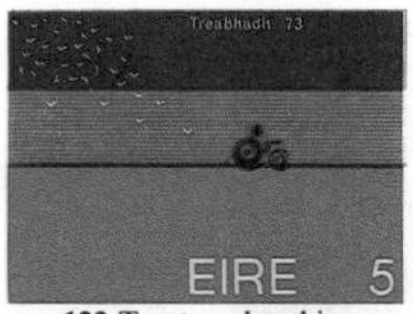

123 Tractor ploughing

1973. World Ploughing Championships, Wellington Bridge.
332 **123** 5p. multicoloured 15 10
333 7p. multicoloured 85 50

124 "Flight into Egypt" (Jan de Cock)

125 Daunt Island Lightship and "Mary Stanford" (Ballycotton Lifeboat), 1936

1973. Christmas.
334 **124** 3½p. multicoloured . . . 15 10
335 12p. multicoloured . . . 1·10 1·50

1974. 150th Anniv of R.N.L.I.
336 **125** 5p. multicoloured 30 30

126 "Edmund Burke" (statue by J. H. Foley)

127 "Oliver Goldsmith" (statue by J. H. Foley)

1974. Europa.
337 **126** 5p. black and blue . . . 1·00 10
338 7p. black and green . . . 4·00 2·50

1974. Death Bicentenary of Oliver Goldsmith (writer).
360 **127** 3½p. black and yellow . . 25 10
361 12p. black and green . . 1·25 1·00

128 "Kitchen Table" (Norah McGuiness)

129 Rugby Players

1974. Contemporary Irish Art (6th issue).
362 **128** 5p. multicoloured 35 30

1974. Centenary of Irish Rugby Football.
363 **129** 3½p. green 50 10
364 12p. multicoloured . . . 2·50 2·75

130 U.P.U. "Postmark"

131 "Madonna and Child" (Bellini)

1974. Centenary of Universal Postal Union.
365 **130** 5p. green and black . . . 25 10
366 7p. blue and black . . . 35 55

1974. Christmas.
367 **131** 5p. multicoloured 15 10
368 15p. multicoloured . . . 60 90

132 "Peace"

1975. International Women's Year.
369 **132** 8p. purple and blue . . . 25 75
370 15p. blue and green . . . 50 1·25

133 "Castletown Hunt" (R. Healy)

1975. Europa.
371 **133** 7p. grey . . . . 1·25 15
372 9p. green . . . . 3·75 2·50

134 Putting

1975. Ninth European Amateur Golf Team Championship, Killarney.
373 **134** 6p. multicoloured 75 45
374 – 9p. multicoloured . . . . 1·50 1·50
No. 374 is similar to Type **134** but shows a different view of the putting green.

135 "Bird of Prey" (sculpture by Oisin Kelly)

1975. Contemporary Irish Art (7th issue).
375 **135** 15p. brown 75 75

136 Nano Nagle (founder) and Waifs

137 Tower of St. Anne's Church, Shandon

1975. Bicentenary of Presentation Order of Nuns.
376 **136** 5p. black and blue . . . 20 10
377 7p. black and brown . . . 30 30

1975. European Architectural Heritage Year.
378 **137** 5p. brown 25 10
379 6p. multicoloured 60 85
380 – 7p. blue 60 10
381 – 9p. multicoloured 65 80
DESIGN: Nos. 380/1, Interior of Holycross Abbey, Co. Tipperary.

138 St. Oliver Plunkett (commemorative medal by Imogen Stuart)

139 "Madonna and Child" (Fra Filippo Lippi)

1975. Canonization of Oliver Plunkett.
382 **138** 7p. black 15 10
383 15p. brown 55 45

1975. Christmas.
384 **139** 5p. multicoloured 15 10
385 7p. multicoloured 15 10
386 10p. multicoloured . . . 45 30

140 James Larkin (from a drawing by Sean O'Sullivan)

141 Alexander Graham Bell

1975. Birth Centenary of James Larkin (Trade Union Leader).
387 **140** 7p. green and grey . . . 20 10
388 11p. brown and yellow . . 40 55

1976. Centenary of Telephone.
389 **141** 9p. multicoloured 20 10
390 15p. multicoloured . . . 45 50

142 1847 Benjamin Franklin Essay

1976. Bicentenary of American Revolution.
391 – 7p. blue, red and silver . . 20 10
392 – 8p. blue, red and silver . . 25 1·10
393 **142** 9p. blue, orange and silver 25 10
394 15p. red, grey and silver 45 75
MS395 95 × 75 mm. Nos. 391/4 2·75 8·00
DESIGNS: 7p. Thirteen Stars; 8p. Fifty Stars.

143 Spirit Barrel

1976. Europa. Irish Delft. Multicoloured.
396 9p. Type **143** 75 20
397 11p. Dish . . . . 2·00 1·60

144 "The Lobster Pots, West of Ireland" (Paul Henry)

1976. Contemporary Irish Art (8th issue).
398 **144** 15p. multicoloured . . . 60 60

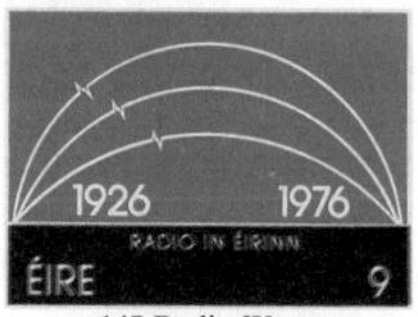

145 Radio Waves

1976. 50th Anniv of Irish Broadcasting Service.
399 **145** 9p. blue and green . . . 20 10
400 – 11p. brown, red and blue 60 1·00
DESIGN—VERT: 11p. Transmitter, radio waves and globe.

146 "The Nativity" (Lorenzo Monaco)

1976. Christmas.
401 **146** 7p. multicoloured 15 10
402 9p. multicoloured 15 10
403 15p. multicoloured . . . 55 55

147 16th Century Manuscript

1977. Centenaries of National Library (8p.) and National Museum (10p.). Multicoloured.
404 8p. Type **147** 30 30
405 10p. Prehistoric stone 40 35

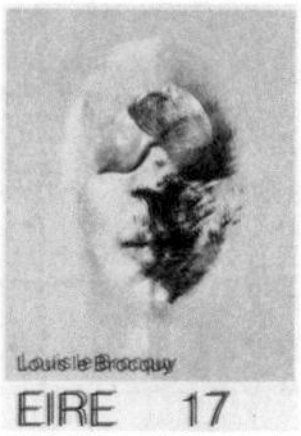

148 Ballynahinch, Galway

149 "Head" (Louis le Brocquy)

1977. Europa. Multicoloured.
406 10p. Type **148** . . . . . . 1·25 25
407 12p. Lough Tay, Wicklow . . 3·25 1·50

1977. Contemporary Irish Art (9th issue).
408 **149** 17p. multicoloured . . . 55 75

150 Guide and Tents

1977. Scouting and Guiding. Multicoloured.
409 8p. Type **150** 45 10
410 17p. Tent and Scout saluting 95 1·75

151 "The Shanachie" (drawing by Jack B. Yeats)

1977. Anniversaries.
411 **151** 10p. black 35 15
412 – 12p. black . . . . 45 1·00
DESIGNS AND EVENTS: 10p. Type **151** (Golden Jubilee of Irish Folklore Society); 12p. The philosopher Eriugena (1100th death anniv).

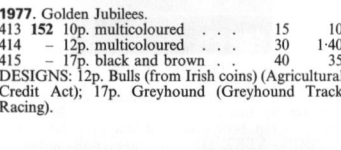

152 "Electricity" (Golden Jubilee of Electricity Supply Board)

1977. Golden Jubilees.
413 **152** 10p. multicoloured . . . 15 10
414 – 12p. multicoloured . . . 30 1·40
415 – 17p. black and brown . . 40 35
DESIGNS: 12p. Bulls (from Irish coins) (Agricultural Credit Act); 17p. Greyhound (Greyhound Track Racing).

153 "The Holy Family" (Giorgione)

154 Junkers W.33 "Bremen" in Flight

1977. Christmas.
416 **153** 8p. multicoloured 20 10
417 10p. multicoloured . . . 20 10
418 17p. multicoloured . . . 75 1·25

1978. 50th Anniv of 1st East–West Transatlantic Flight.
419 **154** 10p. black and blue . . . 20 15
420 17p. black and brown . . 35 1·10

155 Spring Gentian

156 Catherine McAuley

1978. Wild Flowers. Multicoloured.
421 8p. Type **155** 25 40
422 10p. Strawberry tree 25 15
423 11p. Large-flowered Butterwort 25 50
424 17p. St. Dabeoc's Heath . . 45 2·00

1978. Anniversaries and Events. Multicoloured.
425 10p. Type **156** (founder of Sisters of Mercy) (birth bicent) 25 10
426 11p. Doctor performing vaccination (Global Eradication of Smallpox) (horiz) 35 80
427 17p. "Self-portrait" Sir William Orpen (painter) (birth cent) . . . . 55 1·10

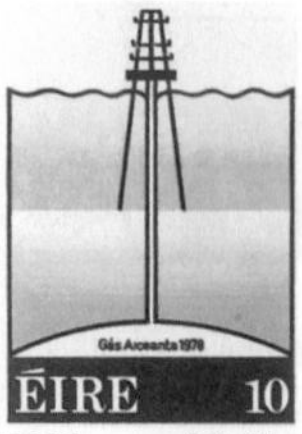

157 Diagram of Drilling Rig

159 "Virgin and Child" (Guercino)

158 Farthing

1978. Arrival Onshore of Natural Gas.
428 **157** 10p. multicoloured . . . 30 30

1978. 50th Anniv of Irish Currency.
429 **158** 8p. black, copper and green 25 20
430 – 10p. black, silver and green 30 10
431 – 11p. black, copper & brn 35 50
432 – 17p. black, silver and blue 65 1·00
DESIGNS: 10p. Florin; 11p. Penny; 17p. Half-crown.

1978. Christmas.
433 **159** 8p. brown, blue and gold 15 10
434 10p. brown, blue & purple 15 10
435 17p. brown, blue and green . . . . 45 1·40

160 Conolly Folly, Castletown

1978. Europa.
436 **160** 10p. brown . . . . 1·40 15
437 – 11p. green . . . . 1·40 1·75
DESIGN: 11p. Dromoland Belvedere.

161 Athletes in Cross-country Race

1979. 7th World Cross-country Championships, Limerick. Multicoloured.
438 **161** 8p. multicoloured 20 30

162 "European Communities" (in languages of member nations)

163 Sir Rowland Hill

1979. 1st Direct Elections to European Assembly.
439 **162** 10p. green 15 15
440 11p. violet 15 35

1979. Death Centenary of Sir Rowland Hill.
441 **163** 17p. black, grey and red 30 60

164 Winter Wren

1979. Birds. Multicoloured.
442 8p. Type **164** 40 80
443 10p. Great crested grebe . . 40 15
444 11p. White-fronted goose . . 45 80
445 17p. Peregrine falcon . . . . 70 2·00

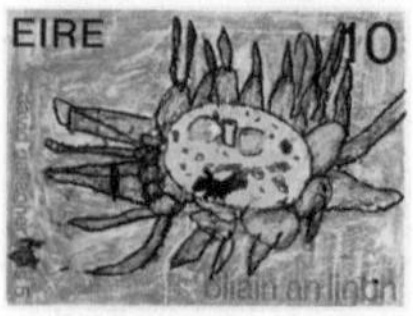

165 "A Happy Flower" (David Gallagher)

1979. International Year of the Child. Paintings by Children. Multicoloured.
446 10p. Type **165** 20 10
447 11p. "Myself and My Skipping Rope" (Lucy Norman) (vert) 25 60
448 17p. "Swans on a Lake" (Nicola O'Dwyer) 35 85

166 Pope John Paul II

1979. Visit of Pope John Paul II.
449 **166** 12p. multicoloured . . . 30 20

167 Brother with Child

1979. Anniversaries and Events.
450 **167** 9½p. brown and mauve . . 20 10
451 – 11p. orange, black and blue 20 70
452 – 20p. multicoloured . . . . 40 1·40
DESIGNS—VERT: 11p. Windmill and sun (Int Energy Conservation Month). HORIZ: 9½p. Type **167** (Cent of Hospitaller Order of St. John of God in Ireland); 20p. "Seated Figure" (sculpture F. E. McWilliam) (Contemporary Irish Art (10th issue)).

168 Patrick Pearse, "Liberty" and G.P.O., Dublin

169 "Madonna and Child" (panel painting from the Domnach Airgid Shrine)

1979. Birth Centenary of Patrick Pearse (patriot).
453 **168** 12p. multicoloured . . . 30 15

1979. Christmas.
454 **169** 9½p. multicoloured . . . 15 10
455 20p. multicoloured . . . 30 55

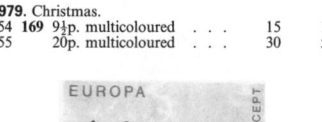

170 Bianconi Long Car, 1836

1979. Europa. Multicoloured.
456 12p. Type **170** . . . . . . 1·00 30
457 13p. Transatlantic cable, Valentia, 1866 . . . . . . 1·10 1·40

171 John Baptist de la Salle (founder)

172 George Bernard Shaw

1980. Cent of Arrival of De La Salle Order.
458 **171** 12p. multicoloured . . . 30 30

1980. Europa. Personalities. Multicoloured.
459 12p. Type **172** . . . . . . 1·00 50
460 13p. Oscar Wilde (28 × 38 mm) . . . . . . 1·00 1·50

173 Stoat

174 Playing Bodhran and Whistle

1980. Wildlife. Multicoloured.
461 12p. Type **173** 25 40
462 15p. Arctic hare 25 15
463 16p. Red fox 25 80
464 25p. Red deer . . . . 35 1·60
MS465 73 × 97 mm. Nos. 461/4 1·00 2·75

1980. Traditional Music and Dance. Mult.
466 12p. Type **174** 15 10
467 15p. Playing Uilleann pipes 20 15
468 25p. Dancing . . . . 35 1·10

175 Sean O'Casey

176 Nativity Scene (painting by Geraldine McNulty)

1980. Commemorations.
469 12p. multicoloured 20 10
470 25p. black, buff and brown 35 55
DESIGNS AND COMMEMORATIONS: 12p. Type **175** (playwright) (birth centenary); 25p. "Gold Painting No. 57" (P. Scott) (Contemporary Irish Art (11th issue)).

1980. Christmas.
471 **176** 12p. multicoloured . . . 15 10
472 15p. multicoloured . . . 20 10
473 25p. multicoloured . . . 40 1·25

177 Boyle Air-pump, 1659

178 "The Legend of the Cock and the Pot"

1981. Irish Science and Technology. Mult.
474 12p. Type **177** 20 10
475 15p. Ferguson tractor, 1936 25 10
476 16p. Parsons turbine, 1884 30 90
477 25p. Holland submarine, 1878 35 1·25

1981. Europa. Folklore. Paintings by Maria Simonds-Gooding.
491 **178** 18p. black, yellow and red 1·00 10
492 – 19p. black, orange & yellow . . . . 1·25 90
DESIGN: 19p. "The Angel with the Scales of Judgement".

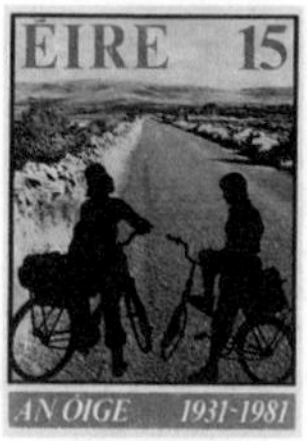

179 Cycling

180 Jeremiah O'Donovan Rossa

1981. 50th Anniv of "An Oige" (Irish Youth Hostel Association). Multicoloured.
493 15p. Type **179** 25 40
494 18p. Hill-walking (horiz) . . 25 10
495 19p. Mountaineering (horiz) 25 95
496 30p. Rock-climbing 40 95

1981. 150th Birth Anniv of Jeremiah O'Donovan Rossa (politician).
497 **180** 15p. multicoloured . . . 60 30

181 "Railway Embankment" (W. J. Leech)

1981. Contemporary Irish Art (12th issue).
498 **181** 30p. multicoloured . . . 1·00 70

182 James Hoban and White House

1981. 150th Death Anniv of James Hoban (White House architect).
499 **182** 18p. multicoloured . . . 50 30

183 "Arkle" (steeplechaser)

1981. Famous Irish Horses. Multicoloured.
500 18p. Type **183** . . . . . . 50 1·00
501 18p. "Boomerang" (show-jumper) . . . . 50 1·00
502 22p. "King of Diamonds" (Draught horse) 50 30
503 24p. "Ballymoss" (flat-racer) 50 70
504 36p. "Coosheen Finn" (Connemara pony) . . . . 60 1·00

184 "Nativity" (F. Barocci)
185 Eviction Scene

1981. Christmas.
505 **184** 18p. multicoloured . . . 25 10
506 22p. multicoloured . . . 30 10
507 36p. multicoloured . . . 80 1·50

1981. Anniversaries. Multicoloured.
508 18p. Type **185** 65 25
509 22p. Royal Dublin Society emblem 75 30
ANNIVERSARIES: 18p. Centenary of Land Law (Ireland) Act. 22p. Royal Dublin Society (organization for the advancement of agriculture, industry, art and science), 250th Anniv.

186 Upper Lake, Killarney National Park

1982. 50th Anniv of Killarney National Park. Multicoloured.
510 18p. Type **186** 40 20
511 36p. Eagle's Nest . . . . . . 85 1·60

187 "The Stigmatization of St. Francis" (Sassetta)
188 The Great Famine, 1845–50

1982. Religious Anniversaries.
512 **187** 22p. multicoloured . . . 50 15
513 – 24p. brown 75 85
DESIGNS AND ANNIVERSARIES: 22p. Type **187** (St. Francis of Assisi (founder of Franciscan order) (500th birth anniv); 24p. Francis Makemie (founder of American Presbyterianism) and old Presbyterian Church, Ramelton, Co. Donegal (300th anniv of ordination).

1982. Europa. Historic Events.
514 **188** 26p. black and stone . . . 3·00 50
515 – 29p. multicoloured . . . 3·50 2·00
DESIGN—HORIZ: 29p. The coming of Christianity to Ireland.

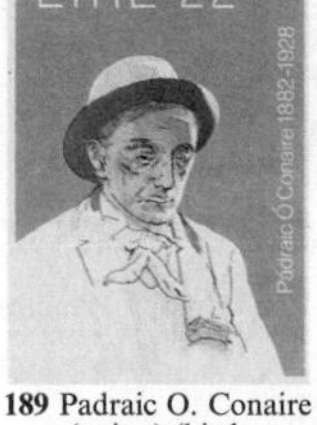

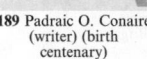

189 Padraic O. Conaire (writer) (birth centenary)
191 "St. Patrick" (Galway hooker)

190 Porbeagle Shark

1982. Anniversaries of Cultural Figures.
516 **189** 22p. black and blue . . . 25 30
517 – 26p. black and brown . . 55 30
518 – 29p. black and blue . . . 65 1·75
519 – 44p. black and grey . . . 65 1·60
DESIGNS AND ANNIVERSARIES: 26p. James Joyce (writer) (birth centenary); 29p. John Field (musician) (birth centenary); 44p. Charles Kickham (writer) (death centenary).

1982. Marine Life. Multicoloured.
520 22p. Type **190** . . . . . . 75 1·25
521 22p. Common European oyster . . . . 75 1·25
522 26p. Atlantic salmon 90 30
523 29p. Dublin Bay prawn . . . 90 2·25

1982. Irish Boats. Multicoloured.
524 22p. Type **191** . . . . . . 75 1·25
525 22p. Currach (horiz) . . . . 75 1·25
526 26p. "Asgard II" (cadet brigantine) (horiz) 90 30
527 29p. Howth 17 foot yacht . . 90 2·25

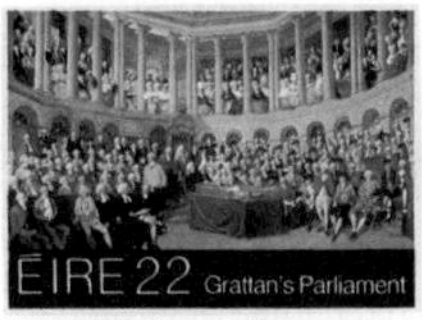

192 "Irish House of Commons" (painting by Francis Wheatley)

1982. Bicentenary of Grattan's Parliament and Birth Centenary of Eamon de Valera. Multicoloured.
528 22p. Type **192** . . . . . . 35 1·25
529 26p. Eamon de Valera (vert) 40 40

193 "Madonna and Child" (sculpture)
194 Aughnanure Castle

1982. Christmas.
530 **193** 22p. multicoloured . . . 30 90
531 26p. multicoloured . . . 30 35

1983. Irish Architecture.
532 – 1p. blue 10 10
533 – 2p. green 20 10
534 – 3p. black 20 10
535 – 4p. red 20 10
536 – 5p. brown 30 10
537 – 6p. blue 30 15
538 – 7p. green 30 75
539 – 10p. black 30 10
540 – 12p. brown . . . . . . 30 1·25
541 **194** 15p. green 45 35
542 20p. purple 50 45
543 22p. blue 50 10
544 – 23p. green . . . . . . 85 1·25
544a – 24p. brown . . . . . . 1·25 35
545 – 26p. black 75 10
545c – 28p. red 75 45
546 – 29p. green 70 65
547 – 30p. black 70 30
547c – 32p. brown . . . . . . 2·50 2·50
547d – 37p. blue . . . . . . 1·00 2·50
547e – 39p. red . . . . . . 2·25 2·75
548 – 44p. black and grey . . 1·00 70
548b – 46p. green and grey . . 6·50 2·00
549 – 50p. blue and grey . . . 1·75 65
550 – £1 brown and grey . . . 4·50 3·50
550b – £1 blue and grey . . . 5·00 1·25
550c – £2 green and black . . . 5·00 4·50
551 – £5 red and grey . . . 12·00 6·00
DESIGNS—HORIZ: (As T **194**): 1 to 5p. Central Pavilion, Dublin Botanic Gardens; 6 to 12p. Dr. Steevens' Hospital, Dublin; 28 to 37p. St. MacDara's Church. (37 × 21 mm); 46p., £1 (No. 550) Cahir Castle; 50p., £2 Casino Marino. £5 Central Bus Station, Dublin. VERT: (As T **194**): 23 to 26p., 39p. Cormac's Chapel. (21 × 37 mm); 44p., £1 (No. 550b) Killarney Cathedral.

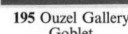

195 Ouzel Gallery Goblet
196 Padraig O. Siochfhradha (writer and teacher)

1983. Bicentenaries of Dublin Chamber of Commerce (22p.) and Bank of Ireland (26p.). Multicoloured.
552 22p. Type **195** 30 65
553 26p. Bank of Ireland building (horiz) 35 35

1983. Anniversaries. Multicoloured.
554 26p. Type **196** (birth cent) . . 50 75
555 29p. Young Boys' Brigade member (centenary) . . . 90 1·50

197 Neolithic Carved Pattern, Newgrange Tomb

1983. Europa.
556 **197** 26p. black and yellow . . 2·75 50
557 – 29p. black, brown & yellow . . . . 5·25 5·00
DESIGN: 29p. Sir William Rowan Hamilton's formulae for the multiplication of quaternions.

198 Kerry Blue Terrier

1983. Irish Dogs. Multicoloured.
558 22p. Type **198** 75 35
559 26p. Irish wolfhound 85 45
560 26p. Irish water spaniel . . . 85 45
561 29p. Irish terrier . . . . . . 1·00 2·25
562 44p. Irish setters . . . . . . 1·40 2·50
MS563 142 × 80 mm. Nos. 558/62 6·00 8·00

199 Animals (Irish Society for the Prevention of Cruelty to Animals)

1983. Anniversaries and Commemorations.
564 **199** 22p. multicoloured . . . 50 1·00
565 – 22p. multicoloured . . . 50 1·00
566 – 26p. multicoloured . . . 50 60
567 – 26p. multicoloured . . . 50 60
568 – 44p. blue and black . . . 75 2·00
DESIGNS—VERT: No. 565, Sean MacDiarmada (patriot) (birth cent); 567, "St. Vincent de Paul in the Streets of Paris" (150th anniv of Society of St. Vincent de Paul); 568, "Andrew Jackson" (Frank McKelvey) (President of the United States). HORIZ: No. 566, "100" (Centenary of Industrial Credit Company).

200 Postman with Bicycle
201 Weaving

1983. World Communications Year. Multicoloured.
569 22p. Type **200** 85 75
570 29p. Dish antenna . . . . . 90 2·00

1983. Irish Handicrafts. Multicoloured.
571 22p. Type **201** 45 50
572 26p. Basket making 45 35
573 29p. Irish crochet . . . . . 50 1·25
574 44p. Harp making . . . . . 80 2·00

202 "La Natividad" (R. van der Weyden)

1983. Christmas.
575 **202** 22p. multicoloured . . . 40 30
576 26p. multicoloured . . . 60 30

203 Dublin and Kingstown Railway Steam Locomotive "Princess"

1984. 150th Anniv of Irish Railways. Mult.
577 23p. Type **203** . . . . . . 75 1·25
578 26p. Great Southern Railways steam locomotive "Macha" 75 35
579 29p. Great Northern Railway steam locomotive No. 87 "Kestrel" . . . . 85 1·75
580 44p. Two-car electric train Coras Iompair Eireann . . 1·10 2·25
MS581 129 × 77 mm. Nos. 577/80 5·50 7·00

204 "Sorbus hibernica"

1984. Irish Trees. Multicoloured.
582 22p. Type **204** 75 70
583 26p. "Taxus baccata fastigiata" 80 30
584 29p. "Salix hibernica" . . . 90 1·75
585 44p. "Betula pubescens" . . 1·50 2·50

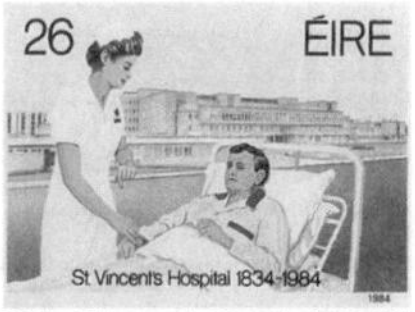

205 St. Vincent's Hospital, Dublin

1984. 150th Anniv of St. Vincent's Hospital and Bicentenary of Royal College of Surgeons. Multicoloured.
586 26p. Type **205** 60 30
587 44p. Royal College and logo 1·00 1·50

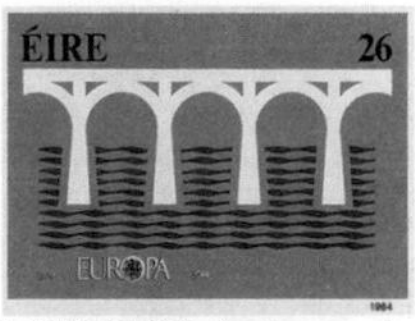

206 C.E.P.T. 25th Anniversary Logo

1984. Europa.
588 **206** 26p. blue, dp blue & black . . . . 2·25 50
589 29p. lt green, green & blk 3·00 3·25

207 Flags on Ballot Box
208 John McCormack

1984. Second Direct Elections to European Assembly.
590 **207** 26p. multicoloured . . . 50 70

1984. Birth Centenary of John McCormack (tenor).
591 **208** 22p. multicoloured . . . 50 70

209 Hammer-throwing

1984. Olympic Games, Los Angeles.

592	**209**	22p. mauve, black and gold	35	80
593	–	26p. violet, black and gold	40	65
594	–	29p. blue, black and gold	60	1·25

DESIGNS: 26p. Hurdling; 29p. Running.

210 Hurling

1984. Cent of Gaelic Athletic Association. Mult.

595	22p. Type **210**	50	90
596	26p. Irish football (vert)	60	90

211 Galway Mayoral Chain

1984. Anniversaries. Multicoloured.

597	26p. Type **211** (500th anniv of mayoral charter)	35	50
598	44p. St. Brendan (from 15th-cent Bodleian manuscript) (1500th birth anniv) (horiz)	75	1·50

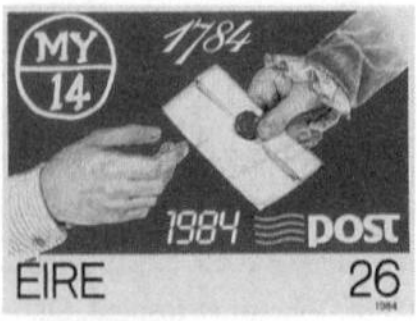

212 Hands passing Letter

1984. Bicentenary of Irish Post Office.

599	**212**	26p. multicoloured	60	70

213 "Virgin and Child" (Sassoferrato)

1984. Christmas. Multicoloured.

600	17p. Christmas star (horiz)	45	80
601	22p. Type **213**	45	1·25
602	26p. Type **213**	65	40

214 "Love" and Heart-shaped Balloon

1985. Greetings Stamps. Multicoloured.

603	22p. Type **214**	50	75
604	26p. Bouquet of hearts and flowers (vert)	60	75

215 Dunsink Observatory (bicentenary)

216 "Polyommatus icarus"

1985. Anniversaries. Multicoloured.

605	22p. Type **215**	50	50
606	26p. "A Landscape at Tivoli, Cork, with Boats" (Nathaniel Grogan) (800th anniv of City of Cork) (horiz)	50	30
607	37p. Royal Irish Academy (bicentenary)	70	1·75
608	44p. Richard Crosbie's balloon flight (bicentenary of first aeronautic flight by an Irishman)	80	1·75

1985. Butterflies. Multicoloured.

609	22p. Type **216**	1·50	1·00
610	26p. "Vanessa atalanta"	1·50	70
611	28p. "Gonepteryx rhamni"	1·75	3·00
612	44p. "Eurabyas aurinia"	2·00	3·25

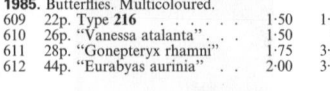

217 Charles Villiers Stanford (composer)

1985. Europa. Irish Composers. Multicoloured.

613	26p. Type **217**	2·50	50
614	37p. Turlough Carolan (composer and lyricist)	6·00	5·50

218 George Frederick Handel

1985. European Music Year. Composers. Mult.

615	22p. Type **218**	1·25	2·50
616	22p. Guiseppe Domenico Scarlatti	1·25	2·50
617	26p. Johann Sebastian Bach	1·50	50

219 U.N. Patrol of Irish Soldiers, Congo, 1960

1985. Anniversaries. Multicoloured.

618	22p. Type **219** (25th anniv of Irish Participation in U.N. Peace-keeping Force)	55	80
619	26p. Thomas Ashe (patriot) (birth cent) (vert)	55	60
620	44p. "Bishop George Berkeley" (James Lathan) (philosopher, 300th birth anniv) (vert)	85	3·00

220 Group of Young People

1985. International Youth Year. Mult.

621	22p. Type **220**	55	50
622	26p. Students and young workers (vert)	55	50

221 Visual Display Unit

1985. Industrial Innovation. Multicoloured.

623	22p. Type **221**	75	75
624	26p. Turf cutting with hand tool and with modern machinery	80	55
625	44p. "The Key Man" (Sean Keating) (150th anniv of Institution of Engineers of Ireland)	1·50	2·50

222 Lighted Candle and Holly

224 Stylized Love Bird with Letter

1985. Christmas. Multicoloured.

626	22p. Type **222**	75	65
627	22p. "Virgin and Child in a Landscape" (Adrian van Ijsenbrandt)	1·25	2·25
628	22p. "The Holy Family" (Murillo)	1·25	2·25
629	26p. "The Adoration of the Shepherds" (Louis le Nain) (horiz)	1·25	25

No. 626 was only issued in sheetlets of 16 sold at £3, providing a discount of 52p. off the face value of the stamps.

1986. Greetings Stamps. Multicoloured.

630	22p. Type **224**	75	90
631	26p. Heart-shaped pillar-box	75	90

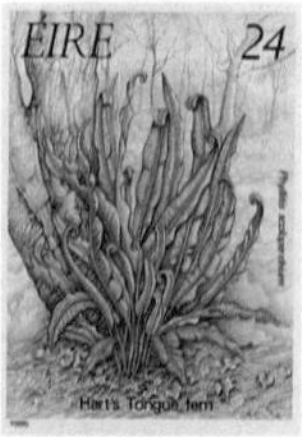

225 Hart's Tongue Fern

226 "Harmony between Industry and Nature"

1986. Ferns. Multicoloured.

632	24p. Type **225**	70	70
633	28p. Rusty-back fern	80	70
634	46p. Killarney fern	1·25	2·10

1986. Europa. Protection of the Environment. Multicoloured.

635	28p. Type **226**	5·00	50
636	39p. "Vanessa atalanta" (butterfly) and tractor in field ("Preserve hedgerows") (horiz)	16·00	5·00

227 Boeing 747-200 over Globe showing Aer Lingus Routes

1986. 50th Anniv of Aer Lingus (airline). Multicoloured.

637	28p. Type **227**	1·40	75
638	46p. De Havilland Dragon Mk 2 "Iolar" (first airplane)	1·90	3·00

228 Grand Canal at Robertstown

1986. Irish Waterways. Multicoloured.

639	24p. Type **228**	1·50	1·00
640	28p. Fishing in County Mayo (vert)	1·60	1·00
641	30p. Motor cruiser on Lough Derg	1·75	2·50

229 "Severn" (19th-century paddlesteamer)

1986. 150th Anniv of British and Irish Steam Packet Company. Multicoloured.

642	24p. Type **229**	75	1·00
643	28p. "Leinster" (modern ferry)	85	60

230 Kish Lighthouse and Bell JetRanger III Helicopter

231 J. P. Nannetti (first president) and Linotype Operator (Dublin Council of Trade Unions centenary)

1986. Irish Lighthouses. Multicoloured.

644	24p. Type **230**	1·25	75
645	30p. Fastnet Lighthouse	2·25	2·75

1986. Anniversaries and Commemorations.

646	**231**	24p. multicoloured	60	90
647	–	28p. black and grey	75	80
648	–	28p. multicoloured	75	80
649	–	30p. multicoloured	85	1·00
650	–	46p. multicoloured	1·00	1·75

DESIGNS:—VERT: No. 647, Arthur Griffith (statesman); 649, Clasped hands (International Peace Year). HORIZ: No. 648, Woman surveyor (Women in Society); 650, Peace dove (International Peace Year).

232 William Mulready and his Design for 1840 Envelope

1986. Birth Bicentenaries of William Mulready (artist) (24p.) and Charles Bianconi (originator of Irish mail coach service) (others). Multicoloured.

651	24p. Type **232**	70	70
652	28p. Bianconi car outside Hearns Hotel, Clonmel (vert)	85	55
653	39p. Bianconi car on the road	1·40	1·75

233 "Adoration of the Shepherds" (Francesco Pascucci)

1986. Christmas. Multicoloured.

654	21p. Type **233**	1·10	1·40
655	28p. "Adoration of the Magi" (Frans Francken III) (vert)	65	60

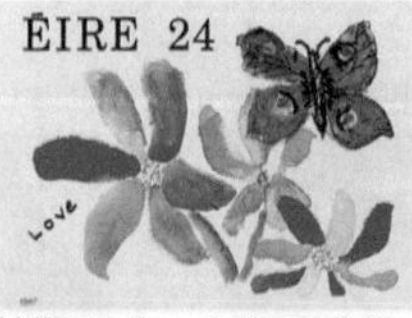

234 "Butterfly and Flowers" (Tara Collins)

1987. Greetings Stamps. Children's Paintings. Multicoloured.

656	24p. Type **234**	70	1·25
657	28p. "Postman on Bicycle delivering Hearts" (Brigid Teehan) (vert)	80	1·25

235 Cork Electric Tram

1987. Irish Trams. Multicoloured.
658 24p. Type **235** 65 65
659 28p. Dublin standard tram No. 29 . . . . 70 85
660 30p. Howth (Great Northern Railway) tram . . . . . . 80 2·00
661 46p. Galway horse tram . . . 1·25 2·25
MS662 131 × 85 mm. Nos. 658/61 4·25 6·50

236 Ships from Crest (Bicentenary of Waterford Chamber of Commerce)

1987. Anniversaries.
663 **236** 24p. black, blue and green 70 60
664 – 28p. multicoloured . . . 70 60
665 – 30p. multicoloured . . . 70 2·00
666 – 39p. multicoloured . . . 75 1·75
DESIGNS—HORIZ: 28p. Canon John Hayes and symbols of agriculture and development (birth centenary and 50th anniv of Muintir na Tire programme); 39p. Mother Mary Martin and International Missionary Training Hospital, Drogheda (50th anniv of Medical Missionaries of Mary). VERT: 30p. "Calceolaria burbidgei" and College crest (300th anniv of Trinity College Botanic Gardens, Dublin).

237 Bord na Mona Headquarters and "The Turf Cutter" (sculpture, John Behan), Dublin

1987. Europa. Modern Architecture. Mult.
667 28p. Type **237** . . . . . . 2·00 60
668 39p. St. Mary's Church, Cong . . . . 5·00 5·00

238 Kerry Cow

1987. Irish Cattle. Multicoloured.
669 24p. Type **238** 80 75
670 28p. Friesian cow and calf . . 95 60
671 30p. Hereford bullock . . . 1·00 2·25
672 39p. Shorthorn bull . . . . 1·10 2·25

239 Fleadh Nua, Ennis

1987. Festivals. Multicoloured.
673 24p. Type **239** 75 70
674 28p. Rose of Tralee International Festival . . . 80 60
675 30p. Wexford Opera Festival (horiz) . . . . 1·10 2·00
676 46p. Ballinasloe Horse Fair (horiz) . . . . 1·25 2·00

240 Flagon (1637), Arms and Anniversary Ornament (1987) (350th anniv of Dublin Goldsmiths' Company)

1987. Anniversaries and Commemorations.
677 **240** 24p. multicoloured . . . 70 80
678 – 24p. grey and black . . . 70 80
679 – 28p. multicoloured . . . 85 60
680 – 46p. multicoloured . . . 1·25 1·10
DESIGNS—VERT: 24p. (No. 678) Cathal Brugha (patriot); 46p. Woman chairing board meeting (Women in Society). HORIZ: 28p. Arms of Ireland and inscription (50th anniv of Constitution).

241 Scenes from "The Twelve Days of Christmas" (carol)

1987. Christmas. Multicoloured.
681 21p. Type **241** . . . . . . 60 1·00
682 24p. The Nativity (detail, late 15th-century Waterford Vestments) (vert) . . . . . 75 1·00
683 28p. Figures from Neapolitan crib, c. 1850 (vert) 75 80

242 Acrobatic Clowns spelling "LOVE"

1988. Greetings Stamps. Multicoloured.
684 24p. Type **242** 75 60
685 28p. Pillar box and hearts (vert) 75 65

243 "Robert Burke" (Sidney Nolan) and Map of Burke and Wills Expedition Route

1988. Bicent of Australian Settlement. Mult.
686 24p. Type **243** . . . . . . 1·00 60
687 46p. "Eureka Stockade" (mural detail, Sidney Nolan) . . . . 1·25 1·75

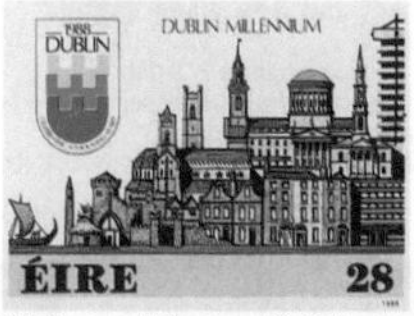

244 Past and Present Buildings of Dublin

1988. Dublin Millennium.
688 **244** 28p. multicoloured . . . 45 55

245 Showjumping

1988. Olympic Games, Seoul. Multicoloured.
689 28p. Type **245** . . . . . . 1·00 1·40
690 28p. Cycling . . . . 1·00 1·40

246 William T. Cosgrave (statesman)

1988. Anniversaries and Events.
691 **246** 24p. grey and black . . . 45 45
692 – 30p. multicoloured . . . 80 1·00
693 – 50p. multicoloured . . . 1·00 1·90
DESIGNS—HORIZ: 30p. Members with casualty and ambulance (50th anniv of Order of Malta Ambulance Corps). VERT: 50p. Barry Fitzgerald (actor) (birth centenary).

247 Air Traffic Controllers and Airbus Industrie A320

1988. Europa. Transport and Communications. Multicoloured.
694 28p. Type **247** . . . . . . 2·00 55
695 39p. Globe with stream of letters from Ireland to Europe . . . . 2·25 3·00

248 "Sirius" (paddle-steamer)

1988. Transatlantic Transport Anniversaries. Multicoloured.
696 24p. Type **248** (150th anniv of regular transatlantic steamship services) . . . . 1·00 50
697 46p. Short S.20 seaplane "Mercury" and Short S.21 flying boat "Maia" (Short Mayo composite aircraft) in Foynes Harbour (50th anniv of first commercial transatlantic flight) . . . . 1·75 2·75

249 Cottonweed

251 Computer and Abacus

250 Garda on Duty

1988. Endangered Flora of Ireland. Mult.
698 24p. Type **249** 85 55
699 28p. Hart's saxifrage 95 55
700 46p. Purple milk-vetch . . . 1·40 2·75

1988. Irish Security Forces. Multicoloured.
701 28p. Type **250** . . . . . . 70 1·10
702 28p. Army unit with personnel carrier . . . . . 70 1·10
703 28p. Navy and Air Corps members with "Eithne" (helicopter patrol vessel) 70 1·10
704 28p. Army and Navy reservists . . . . 70 1·10

1988. Anniversaries. Multicoloured.
705 24p. Type **251** (Institute of Chartered Accountants in Ireland centenary) 40 40
706 46p. "Duquesa Santa Ana" off Donegal (400th anniv of Spanish Armada) (horiz) 1·25 1·25

252 "President Kennedy" (James Wyeth)

253 St. Kevin's Church, Glendalough

1988. 25th Death Anniv of John F. Kennedy (American statesman).
707 **252** 28p. multicoloured . . . 1·00 80

1988. Christmas. Multicoloured.
708 21p. Type **253** . . . . . . 80 1·00
709 24p. The Adoration of the Magi 60 60
710 28p. The Flight into Egypt 70 55
711 46p. The Holy Family . . . 1·25 2·75
The designs of Nos. 709/11 are from a 15th-century French Book of Hours.

254 Spring Flowers spelling "Love" in Gaelic

1989. Greetings Stamps. Multicoloured.
712 24p. Type **254** 60 55
713 28p. "The Sonnet" (William Mulready) (vert) 65 55

255 Italian Garden, Garinish Island

1989. National Parks and Gardens. Multicoloured.
714 24p. Type **255** 90 55
715 28p. Lough Veagh, Glenveagh National Park 1·10 55
716 32p. Barnaderg Bay, Connemara National Park 1·25 1·25
717 50p. St. Stephen's Green, Dublin . . . . 1·75 1·75

256 "Silver Stream", 1908

1989. Classic Irish Cars. Multicoloured.
718 24p Type **256** 50 55
719 28p Benz "Comfortable", 1898 . . . . 50 55
720 39p "Thomond", 1929 . . . 1·25 1·50
721 46p Chambers' 8 h.p. model, 1905 . . . . 1·50 1·50

257 Ring-a-ring-a-roses

1989. Europa. Children's Games. Multicoloured.
722 28p. Type **257** 75 75
723 39p. Hopscotch . . . . . . 1·00 2·25

258 Irish Red Cross Flag (50th anniv)

1989. Anniversaries and Events.
724 **258** 24p. red and black . . . 55 60
725 – 28p. blue, black and yellow . . . . 1·60 1·10
DESIGN: 28p. Circle of twelve stars (third direct elections to European Parliament).

259 Saints Kilian, Totnan and Colman (from 12th-century German manuscript)

1989. 1300th Death Anniv of Saints Kilian, Totnan and Colman.
726 **259** 28p. multicoloured . . . 75 1·10

260 19th-century Mail Coach passing Cashel

1989. Bicentenary of Irish Mail Coach Service.
727 **260** 28p. multicoloured . . . 1·50 75

261 Crest and 19th- century Dividers (150th anniv of Royal Institute of Architects of Ireland)

1989. Anniversaries and Commemorations.
728 – 24p. grey and black . . . 65 55
729 **261** 28p. multicoloured . . . 65 55
730 – 30p. multicoloured . . . 1·75 2·00
731 – 46p. brown . . . . 2·50 2·50
DESIGNS—VERT: 24p. Sean T. O'Kelly (statesman) (drawing by Sean O'Sullivan); 46p. Jawaharlal Nehru (birth centenary). HORIZ: 30p. Margaret Burke-Sheridan (soprano) (portrait by De Gennaro) and scene from "La Boheme" (birth centenary).

262 "NCB Ireland' rounding Cape Horn" (Des Fallon)

1989. First Irish Entry in Whitbread Round the World Yacht Race.
732 **262** 28p. multicoloured . . . 1·25 1·25

263 Willow/Red Grouse

264 "The Annunciation"

1989. Game Birds. Multicoloured.
733 24p. Type **263** . . . . . . 1·10 55
734 28p. Northern lapwing . . . 1·25 55
735 39p. Eurasian woodcock . . 1·50 2·25
736 46p. Common pheasant . . . 1·75 2·25
MS737 128 × 92 mm. Nos. 733/6 4·50 6·50

1989. Christmas. Multicoloured.
738 21p. Children decorating crib 75 75
739 24p. Type **264** 95 60
740 28p. "The Nativity" . . . . 1·00 55
741 46p. "The Adoration of the Magi" . . . . 2·00 2·50

265 Logo (Ireland's Presidency of the European Communities)

1990. European Events. Multicoloured.
742 30p. Type **265** . . . . . . 1·00 60
743 50p. Logo and outline map of Ireland (European Tourism Year) . . . . . . 2·25 3·00

266 Dropping Messages from Balloon

1990. Greetings Stamps.
744 **266** 26p. multicoloured . . . 1·50 1·25
745 – 30p. red, buff and brown 1·50 1·25
DESIGN: 30p. Heart and "Love" drawn in lipstick.

267 Silver Kite Brooch

268 Posy of Flowers

1990. Irish Heritage.
746 **267** 1p. black and blue . . . 10 10
747 2p. black and orange . . 10 10
748 – 4p. black and violet . . 15 10
749 – 5p. black and green . . 20 10
750 – 10p. black and orange 30 25
751 – 20p. black and yellow 50 40
752 – 26p. black and violet . . 1·50 65
809 – 28p. black and orange 80 1·00
754 – 30p. black and blue . . 1·25 90
810 – 32p. black and green . . 50 60
756 – 34p. black and yellow 1·25 1·25
757 – 37p. black and green . . 1·50 1·50
758 – 38p. black and violet . . 1·50 1·50
758b – 40p. black and blue . . 1·50 1·50
759 – 41p. black and orange 1·50 1·50
760 – 44p. brown and yellow 2·50 2·25
760a – 45p. black and violet . . 1·75 2·00
761 – 50p. black and yellow 1·75 1·50
762 – 52p. black and blue . . 2·00 2·00
763 – £1 black and yellow . . 3·00 2·25
764 – £2 black and green . . . 4·50 3·25
765 – £5 black and blue . . . 9·00 8·50
DESIGNS: 4, 5p. Dunamase food vessel; 26, 28p. Lismore crozier; 34, 37, 38, 40p. Gleninsheen collar; 41, 44p. Silver thistle brooch; 45, 50, 52p. Broighter boat. 22 × 38 mm: £5 St. Patrick's Bell Shrine. HORIZ: 10p. Derrinboy armlets; 20p. Gold dress fastener; 30p. Enamelled latchet brooch: 32p. Broighter collar. 38 × 22 mm: £1 Ardagh Chalice; £2 Tara brooch.

For 32p. value as No. 755 but larger, 27 × 20 mm, see No. 823.

1990. Greetings Stamps. Multicoloured.
766 26p. Type **268** . . . . . . 2·00 2·50
767 26p. Birthday presents . . . 2·00 2·50
768 30p. Flowers, ribbon and horseshoe . . . . 2·00 2·50
769 30p. Balloons . . . . 2·00 2·50

269 Player heading Ball

1990. World Cup Football Championship, Italy. Multicoloured.
770 30p. Type **269** . . . . . . 1·75 2·00
771 30p. Tackling . . . . 1·75 2·00

270 Battle of the Boyne, 1690

1990. 300th Anniv of the Williamite Wars (1st issue). Multicoloured.
772 30p. Type **270** . . . . . . 1·75 1·75
773 30p. Siege of Limerick, 1690 1·75 1·75
See also Nos. 806/7.

271 1990 Irish Heritage 30p. Stamp and 1840 Postmark

1990. 150th Anniv of the Penny Black. Mult.
774 30p. Type **271** 90 90
775 50p. Definitive stamps of 1922, 1969, 1982 and 1990 1·25 2·00

272 General Post Office, Dublin

274 Narcissus "Foundling" and Japanese Gardens, Tully

273 Medical Missionary giving Injection

1990. Europa Post Office Buildings. Mult.
776 30p. Type **272** . . . . . . 1·25 60
777 41p. Westport Post Office, County Mayo . . . . . . 2·25 2·75

1990. Anniversaries and Events.
778 **273** 26p. multicoloured . . . 80 40
779 – 30p. black . . . . 1·00 2·75
780 – 50p. multicoloured . . . 1·00 1·75
DESIGNS—VERT: 30p. Michael Collins (statesman) (birth centenary). HORIZ: 50p. Missionaries working at water pump (Irish missionary service).

1990. Garden Flowers. Multicoloured.
781 26p. Type **274** 60 55
782 30p. "Rosa x hibernica" and Mulahide Castle gardens 70 80
783 41p. Primula "Rowallane Rose" and Rowallane garden . . . . 1·40 2·50
784 50p. "Erica erigena" "Irish Dusk" and Palm House, National Botanical Gardens . . . . 1·75 2·75

275 "Playboy of the Western World" (John Synge)

1990. Irish Theatre. Multicoloured.
785 30p. Type **275** . . . . . . 1·25 1·75
786 30p. "Juno and the Paycock" (Sean O'Casey) . . . 1·25 1·75
787 30p. "The Field" (John Keane) . . . . 1·25 1·75
788 30p. "Waiting for Godot" (Samuel Beckett) . . . . . 1·25 1·75

276 Nativity

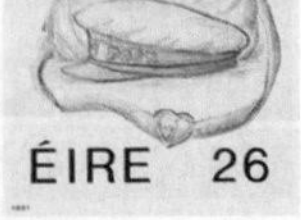

277 Hearts in Mail Sack and Postman's Cap

1990. Christmas. Multicoloured.
789 26p. Child praying by bed . . 75 80
790 26p. Type **276** 75 60
791 30p. Madonna and Child . . 1·25 90
792 50p. Adoration of the Magi 2·25 3·50

1991. Greetings Stamps. Multicoloured.
793 26p. Type **277** . . . . . . 85 1·00
794 30p. Boy and girl kissing . . 90 1·00

278 Starley "Rover" Bicycle, 1886

1991. Early Bicycles. Multicoloured.
795 26p. Type **278** 80 60
796 30p. Child's horse tricycle, 1875 . . . . 90 1·00
797 50p. "Penny Farthing", 1871 1·60 2·50
MS798 113 × 72 mm. Nos. 795/7 3·25 3·75

279 "Cuchulainn" (statue by Oliver Sheppard) and Proclamation

1991. 75th Anniv of Easter Rising.
799 **279** 32p. multicoloured . . . 85 1·40

280 Scene from "La Traviata" (50th anniv of Dublin Grand Opera Society)

1991. "Dublin 1991 European City of Culture". Multicoloured.
800 28p. Type **280** . . . . . . 1·00 1·00
801 32p. City Hall and European Community emblem . . . 1·10 1·60
802 44p. St. Patrick's Cathedral (800th anniv) . . . . . . 90 1·60
803 52p. Custom House (bicent) (41 × 24 mm) . . . . . . 1·00 1·60

281 "Giotto" Spacecraft approaching Halley's Comet

1991. Europa. Europe in Space. Multicoloured.
804 32p. Type **281** . . . . . . 1·00 1·00
805 44p. Hubble Telescope orbiting Earth . . . . . . 1·50 3·00

282 Siege of Athlone

1991. 300th Anniv of the Williamite Wars (2nd issue). Multicoloured.
806 28p. Type **282** . . . . . . 1·25 1·75
807 28p. Generals Ginkel and Sarsfield (signatories of Treaty of Limerick) . . . 1·25 1·75

283 John A. Costello (statesman)

1991. Anniversaries.
811 **283** 28p. black . . . . 1·00 70
812 – 32p. multicoloured . . . 1·25 1·00
813 – 52p. multicoloured . . . 1·75 2·50
DESIGNS—VERT: 28p. Type **283** (birth cent) (drawing by Sean O'Sullivan); 32p. "Charles Stewart Parnell" (Sydney Hall) (death cent); HORIZ: 52p. Meeting of United Irishmen.

284 Player on 15th Green, Portmarnock (Walker Cup)

1991. Golf Commemorations. Multicoloured.
814 28p. Type **284** . . . . . . 1·00 75
815 32p. Logo and golfer of 1900 (cent of Golfing Union of Ireland) (vert) . . . . . . 1·25 1·00

285 Wicklow Cheviot

1991. Irish Sheep. Multicoloured.
816 32p. Type **285** . . . . . . 1·00 80
817 38p. Donegal Blackface . . . 1·40 1·75
818 52p. Galway (horiz) . . . . 2·00 3·50

286 Boatyard

1991. Fishing Fleet. Multicoloured.
819 28p. Type **286** 70 65
820 32p. Traditional inshore trawlers 80 80
821 44p. Inshore lobster pot boat 1·60 2·50
822 52p. "Veronica" (fish factory ship) . . . . 1·90 2·75

1991. As No. 755, but larger, 27 × 20 mm. Self-adhesive.
823a 32p. black and green . . . 75 1·00

287 The Annunciation **289** Healthy Family on Apple

288 Multicoloured Heart

1991. Christmas.
827 – 28p. multicoloured . . . 1·00 1·00
828 **287** 28p. blue, green and black 1·00 65
829 – 32p. red and black . . . 1·10 75
830 – 52p. multicoloured . . . 2·00 3·25
DESIGNS: No. 827, Three Kings; No. 829, The Nativity; No. 830, Adoration of the Kings:

1992. Greetings Stamps. Multicoloured.
831 28p. Type **288** . . . . . . 1·00 95
832 32p. "LOVE" at end of rainbow (vert) . . . . . . 1·10 1·10

1992. "Healthy Living" Campaign.
833 **289** 28p. multicoloured . . . 1·25 85

290 Boxing

1992. Olympic Games, Barcelona. Mult.
834 32p. Type **290** 75 90
835 44p. Sailing . . . . 1·00 2·25
MS836 130 × 85 mm. Nos. 834/5 × 2 4·75 5·00

291 "Mari" (cog) and 14th-century Map

1992. Irish Maritime Heritage. Multicoloured.
837 32p. Type **291** . . . . . . 1·00 90
838 52p. "Ovoca" (trawler) and chart (vert) . . . . 1·50 2·75

292 Chamber Logo and Commercial Symbols

1992. Bicentenary of Galway Chamber of Commerce and Industry.
839 **292** 28p. multicoloured . . . 70 85

293 Cliffs and Cove

1992. Greetings Stamps. Multicoloured.
840 28p. Type **293** . . . . . . 75 1·10
841 28p. Meadow . . . . 75 1·10
842 32p. Fuchsia and honeysuckle 75 1·10
843 32p. Lily pond and dragonfly 75 1·10

294 Fleet of Columbus

1992. Europa. 500th Anniv of Discovery of America by Columbus. Multicoloured.
844 32p. Type **294** . . . . . . 1·00 90
845 44p. Columbus landing in the New World . . . . 1·50 2·50

295 Irish Immigrants

1992. Irish Immigrants in the Americas. Mult.
846 52p. Type **295** . . . . . . 1·75 1·75
847 52p. Irish soldiers, entertainers and politicians 1·75 1·75

296 Pair of Pine Martens

1992. Endangered Species. Pine Marten. Mult.
848 28p. Type **296** . . . . . . 1·00 70
849 32p. Marten on branch . . . 1·00 80
850 44p. Female with kittens . . 1·60 1·50
851 52p. Marten catching great tit 2·00 1·75

297 "The Rotunda and New Rooms" (James Malton)

1992. Dublin Anniversaries. Multicoloured.
852 28p. Type **297** 70 65
853 32p. Trinity College Library (28 × 45 mm) . . . . . . 1·00 1·00
854 44p. "Charlemont House" . . 1·10 2·00
855 52p. Trinity College main gate (28 × 45 mm) . . . . 1·40 2·25
ANNIVERSARIES: 28, 44p. Bicentenary of Publication of Malton's "Views of Dublin"; 32, 52p. 400th anniv of Founding of Trinity College.

298 European Star and Megalithic Dolmen

1992. Single European Market.
856 **298** 32p. multicoloured . . . 70 80

299 Farm Produce **300** "The Annunciation" (from illuminated manuscript)

1992. Irish Agriculture. Multicoloured.
857 32p. Type **299** . . . . . . 1·00 1·25
858 32p. Dairy and beef herds . . 1·00 1·25
859 32p. Harvesting cereals . . . 1·00 1·25
860 32p. Market gardening . . . 1·00 1·25
Nos. 857/60 were printed together, se-tenant, forming a composite design.

1992. Christmas. Multicoloured.
861 28p. Congregation entering church 80 65
862 28p. Type **300** 80 65
863 32p. "Adoration of the Shepherds" (Da Empoli) 1·10 1·00
864 52p. "Adoration of the Magi" (Rottenhammer) . . 1·40 1·50

301 Queen of Hearts **303** Bee Orchid

302 "Evening at Tangier" (Sir John Lavery)

1993. Greetings Stamps. Multicoloured.
865 28p. Type **301** 90 75
866 32p. Hot air balloon trailing hearts (horiz) . . . . . . 1·00 85

1993. Irish Impressionist Painters. Multicoloured.
867 28p. Type **302** 85 60
868 32p. "The Goose Girl" (William Leech) 90 65
869 44p. "La Jeune Bretonne" (Roderic O'Conor) (vert) 1·50 1·60
870 52p. "Lustre Jug" (Walter Osborne) (vert) . . . . . 2·00 2·25

1993. Irish Orchids. Multicoloured.
871 28p. Type **303** 90 60
872 32p. O'Kelly's orchid . . . . 1·10 80
873 38p. Dark red helleborine . . 1·60 2·25
874 52p. Irish lady's tresses . . . 1·90 2·75
MS875 130 × 71 mm. Nos. 871/4 4·75 6·00

304 "Pears in a Copper Pan" (Hilda van Stockum)

1993. Europa. Contemporary Art. Mult.
876 32p. Type **304** 75 75
877 44p. "Arrieta Orzola" (Tony O'Malley) . . . . 1·10 1·10

305 Cultural Activities

1993. Centenary of Conradh Na Gaelige (cultural organization). Multicoloured.
878 32p. Type **305** 85 75
879 52p. Illuminated manuscript cover (vert) . . . . 1·50 1·50

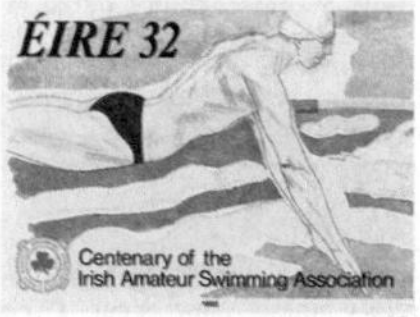

306 Diving

1993. Centenary of Irish Amateur Swimming Association. Multicoloured.
880 32p. Type **306** . . . . . . 1·00 1·50
881 32p. Swimming . . . . . . 1·00 1·50

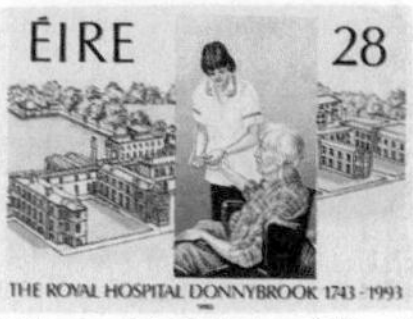

307 Nurse with Patient and Hospital Buildings

1993. Anniversaries and Events. Multicoloured.
882 28p. Type **307** (250th anniv of Royal Hospital, Donnybrook) . . . . . . 1·25 60
883 32p. College building and crest (bicentenary of St. Patrick's College, Carlow) (vert) 80 60
884 44p. Map of Neolithic field system, Ceide (opening of interpretative centre) . . . 1·60 1·40
885 52p. Edward Bunting (musicologist) (150th death anniv) (25 × 42 mm) . . . 1·75 1·60

308 Great Northern Railways Gardner at Drogheda

1993. Irish Buses. Multicoloured.
886 28p. Type **308** 85 70
887 32p. C.I.E. Leyland Titan at College Green, Dublin . . 1·00 70
888 52p. Horse-drawn omnibus at Old Baal's Bridge, Limerick . . . . 1·75 2·50
889 52p. Char-a-banc at Lady's View, Killarney . . . . . 1·75 2·50

309 The Annunciation

1993. Christmas. Multicoloured.
890 28p. The flight into Egypt (vert) 80 80
891 28p. Type **309** 80 55
892 32p. Holy Family 90 70
893 52p. Adoration of the shepherds . . . . 2·00 2·50

310 Biplane skywriting "Love"

1994. Greetings Stamps. Multicoloured.
894 28p. Type **310** 90 75
895 32p. Couple within heart (vert) . . . . 1·00 85

311 Smiling Sun

1994. Greetings Stamps. Multicoloured.
896 32p. Type **311** . . . . . . 1·00 1·00
897 32p. Smiling daisy . . . . . 1·00 1·00
898 32p. Smiling heart . . . . . 1·00 1·00
899 32p. Smiling rose . . . . . . 1·00 1·00

1994. "Hong Kong '94" International Stamp Exhibition. Chinese New Year ("Year of the Dog").
MS900 137 × 74 mm. Nos. 896/8 4·25 5·00

312 Stylized Logo of Macra na Feirme (50th anniv)

1994. Anniversaries and Events.
901 **312** 28p. gold and blue . . . 75 65
902 – 32p. multicoloured . . . 1·25 75
903 – 38p. multicoloured . . . 2·00 1·75
904 – 52p. black, cobalt and blue . . . . 1·90 2·00
DESIGNS—38 × 35 mm: 32p. "The Taking of Christ" (Caravaggio) (loan of painting to National Gallery). 37½ × 27 mm: 38p. Sir Horace Plunkett with 19th-century milk carts and modern tankers (centenary of Irish Co-operative Organization Society); 52p. Congress emblem (centenary of Irish Congress of Trade Unions).

313 St. Brendan visiting Iceland

1994. Europa. St. Brendan's Voyages. Mult.
905 32p. Type **313** 75 70
906 44p. Discovering Faroe Islands . . . . 1·50 2·00
MS907 82 × 76 mm. Nos. 905/6 2·50 3·25

314 First Meeting of Dail, 1919

1994. Parliamentary Anniversaries. Multicoloured.
908 32p. Type **314** (75th anniv) 90 1·00
909 32p. European Parliament (4th direct elections) . . . 90 1·00

315 Irish and Argentine Footballers

317 Statue of Edmund Rice and Class

316 "Arctia caja"

1994. Sporting Anniversaries and Events. Multicoloured.
910 32p. Type **315** . . . . . . 80 1·25
911 32p. Irish and German footballers . . . . 80 1·25
912 32p. Irish and Dutch women's hockey match (horiz) . . . . 1·50 1·25
913 52p. Irish and English women's hockey match (horiz) . . . . 1·75 2·50
ANNIVERSARIES AND EVENTS: Nos. 910/11, World Cup Football Championship, U.S.A.; 912, Women's Hockey World Cup, Dublin; 913, Centenary of Irish Ladies' Hockey Union.

1994. Moths. Mult. (a) Size 37 × 26 mm.
914 28p. Type **316** 65 60
915 32p. "Calamia tridens" . . . 75 70
916 38p. "Saturnia pavonia" . . 90 1·10
917 52p. "Deilephila elpenor" . . 1·50 2·00
MS918 120 × 71 mm. Nos. 914/17 3·50 4·00

(b) Size 34 × 22 mm. Self-adhesive.
919 32p. "Calamia tridens" . . . 1·10 1·40
920 32p. Type **316** . . . . . . 1·10 1·40
921 32p. "Deilephila elpenor" . . 1·10 1·40
922 32p. "Saturnia pavonia" . . 1·10 1·40

1994. Anniversaries and Events. Multicoloured.
923 28p. St. Laurence Gate, Drogheda (41½ × 25 mm) 1·25 1·40
924 32p. Type **317** . . . . . . 1·25 1·40
925 32p. Edmund Burke (politician) . . . . 1·25 1·40
926 52p. Vickers FB-27 Vimy and map (horiz) . . . . 1·25 1·40
927 52p. Eamonn Andrews (broadcaster) . . . . . . 1·50 1·50
ANNIVERSARIES AND EVENTS: No. 923, 800th anniv of Drogheda; 924, 150th death anniv of Edmund Rice (founder of Irish Christian Brothers); 925, 927, The Irish abroad; 926, 75th anniv of Alcock and Brown's first transatlantic flight.

318 George Bernard Shaw (author) and "Pygmalion" Poster

1994. Irish Nobel Prize Winners. Multicoloured.
928 28p. Type **318** 60 90
929 28p. Samuel Beckett (author) and pair of boots 60 90
930 32p. Sean MacBride (human rights campaigner) and peace doves 70 90
931 52p. William Butler Yeats (poet) and poem . . . . . 1·10 2·00

319 "The Annunciation" (ivory plaque)

320 Tree of Hearts

1994. Christmas. Multicoloured.
932 28p. Nativity 70 60
933 28p. Type **319** 70 60
934 32p. "Flight into Egypt" (wood carving) 80 70
935 52p. "Nativity" (ivory plaque) . . . . 1·10 2·00

1995. Greetings Stamps. Multicoloured.
936 32p. Type **320** . . . . . . 95 1·25
937 32p. Teddy bear holding balloon . . . . 95 1·25
938 32p. Clown juggling hearts 95 1·25
939 32p. Bouquet of flowers . . . 95 1·25

1995. Chinese New Year ("Year of the Pig").
MS940 137 × 74 mm. Nos. 936, 938/9 3·00 3·50

321 West Clare Railway Steam Locomotive No. 1 "Kilkee" at Kilrush Station

1995. Transport. Narrow Gauge Railways. Mult.
941 28p. Type **321** 75 60
942 32p. County Donegal Railway tank locomotive No. 2 "Blanche" at Donegal Station 90 90
943 38p. Cork and Muskerry Railway tank locomotive No. 1 "City of Cork" on Western Road, Cork . . . 1·25 1·75
944 52p. Cavan and Leitrim Railway tank locomotive No. 3 "Lady Edith" on Arigna Tramway . . . . . 1·75 2·50
MS945 127 × 83 mm. Nos. 941/4 4·50 5·50

322 English and Irish Rugby Players

1995. World Cup Rugby Championship, South Africa. Multicoloured.
946 32p. Type **322** 75 75
947 52p. Australian and Irish players . . . . 1·25 1·75
MS948 108 × 77 mm. £1 Type **322** 4·25 3·50

323 Peace Dove and Skyscrapers

1995. Europa. Peace and Freedom. Mult. (a) Size 38 × 26 mm. Ordinary gum.
949 32p. Type **323** 85 75
950 44p. Peace dove and map of Europe and North Africa 1·40 2·00

(b) Size 34½ × 23 mm. Self-adhesive.
951 32p. Type **323** 90 90
952 32p. As No. 950 . . . . . . 90 90

324 Soldiers of the Irish Brigade and Memorial Cross

325 Irish Brigade, French Army, 1745

1995. 250th Anniv of Battle of Fontenoy.
953 **324** 32p. multicoloured . . . 80 80

1995. Military Uniforms. Multicoloured.
954 28p. Type **325** 70 60
955 32p. Tercio Irlanda, Spanish army in Flanders, 1605 . . 80 75
956 32p. Royal Dublin Fusiliers, 1914 . . . . 80 75
957 38p. St. Patrick's Battalion, Papal Army, 1860 . . . . 1·10 1·25
958 52p. 69th Regiment, New York State Militia, 1861 1·60 1·75

326 Guglielmo Marconi and Original Radio Transmitter

1995. Centenary of Radio. Multicoloured.
959 32p. Type **326** . . . . . . 1·40 1·50
960 32p. Traditional radio dial 1·40 1·50

327 Bartholomew Mosse (founder) and Hospital Building

1995. Anniversaries. Multicoloured.
961 28p. Type **327** (250th anniv of Rotunda Hospital) . . . 70 70
962 32p. St. Patrick's House, Maynooth College (bicent) (25 × 41 mm) 80 80
963 32p. Laurel wreath and map of Europe (50th anniv of end of Second World War) 80 80
964 52p. Geological map of Ireland (150th anniv of Geological Survey of Ireland) (32½ × 32½ mm) . . 1·25 1·50

328 Natterjack Toad

1995. Reptiles and Amphibians. Multicoloured. (a) Size 40 × 27 mm. Ordinary gum.
965 32p. Type **328** . . . . . . 1·00 1·25
966 32p. Common lizards . . . . 1·00 1·25
967 32p. Smooth newts . . . . . 1·00 1·25
968 32p. Common frog . . . . . 1·00 1·25

(b) Size 34 × 23 mm. Self-adhesive.
969 32p. Type **328** . . . . . . 1·00 1·25
970 32p. Common lizard . . . . 1·00 1·25
971 32p. Smooth newts . . . . . 1·00 1·25
972 32p. Common frog . . . . . 1·00 1·25
Nos. 965/8 were printed together, se-tenant, with the backgrounds forming a composite design.

329 "Crinum moorei"

1995. Bicentenary of National Botanic Gardens, Glasnevin. Flowers. Multicoloured.
973 32p. Type **329** . . . . . . 1·50 70
974 38p. "Sarracenia x moorei" 1·25 1·10
975 44p. "Solanum crispum" "Glasnevin" . . . . 1·50 2·50

330 Anniversary Logo and Irish United Nations Soldier

1995. 50th Anniv of United Nations. Mult.
976 32p. Type **330** 80 70
977 52p. Emblem and "UN" . . 1·25 1·40

331 "Adoration of the Shepherds" (illuminated manuscript) (Benedotto Bardone)

1995. Christmas. Multicoloured.
978 28p. Adoration of the Magi 1·00 65
979 28p. Type **331** . . . . . . 1·00 65
980 32p. "Adoration of the Magi" (illuminated manuscript) (Bardone) . . 1·10 70
981 52p. "The Holy Family" (illuminated manuscript) (Bardone) . . . . 1·90 2·75

332 Zig and Zag on Heart

333 Wheelchair Athlete

1996. Greetings Stamps. Multicoloured.
982 32p. Type **332** . . . . . . 1·25 75
983 32p. Zig and Zag waving . . 2·25 2·50
984 32p. Zig and Zag in space suits . . . . 2·25 2·50
985 32p. Zig and Zag wearing hats . . . . 2·25 2·50

1996. Chinese New Year ("Year of the Rat").
MS986 130 × 74 mm. Nos. 982, 984/5 3·00 3·00

1996. Olympic and Paralympic Games, Atlanta. Multicoloured.
987 28p. Type **333** 70 65
988 32p. Running 80 80
989 32p. Throwing the discus . . 80 80
990 32p. Single kayak 80 80

334 Before the Start, Fairyhouse Race Course

1996. Irish Horse Racing. Multicoloured.
991 28p. Type **334** 70 65
992 32p. Steeplechase, Punchestown 80 80
993 32p. On the Flat, The Curragh 80 80
994 38p. Steeplechase, Galway . . 1·25 1·25
995 52p. After the race, Leopardstown . . . . . . 1·50 1·50

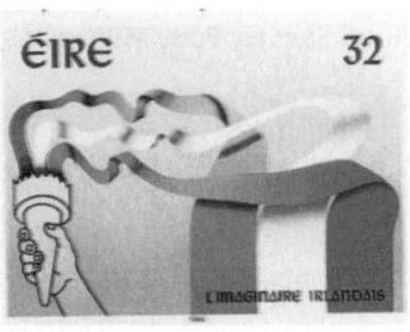

335 Irish and French Coloured Ribbons merging

1996. "L'Imaginaire Irlandais" Festival of Contemporary Irish Arts, France.
996 **335** 32p. multicoloured . . . 80 80

336 Louie Bennett (suffragette)

1996. Europa. Famous Women. (a) Size 40 × 29 mm. Ordinary gum.
997 **336** 32p. violet 80 70
998 – 44p. green . . . . 1·10 1·25

(b) Size 34 × 23 mm. Self-adhesive.
999 **336** 32p. violet . . . . . . 1·10 1·25
1000 – 32p. green . . . . 1·10 1·25
DESIGN: Nos. 998, 1000, Lady Augusta Gregory (playwright).

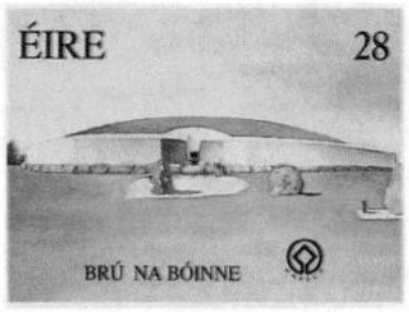

337 Newgrange Passage Tomb (Boyne Valley World Heritage Site)

1996. Anniversaries and Events.
1001 **337** 28p. brown and black . . 1·00 60
1002 – 32p. multicoloured . . . 1·10 90
DESIGN: 32p. Children playing (50th anniv of UNICEF.).

1996. "CHINA '96" 9th Asian International Stamp Exhibition, Peking. Sheet 120 × 95 mm, containing Nos. 992/3.
MS1003 32p. Steeplechase, Punchestown; 32p. On the Flat, The Curragh . . . . 11·00 11·00

338 Stanley Woods

1996. Isle of Man Tourist Trophy Motor Cycle Races. Irish Winners. Multicoloured.
1004 32p. Type **338** 80 70
1005 44p. Artie Bell . . . . . . 1·25 1·50
1006 50p. Alec Bennett . . . . . 1·50 1·75
1007 52p. Joey and Robert Dunlop . . . . 1·50 1·75
MS1008 100 × 70 mm. 50p. As 52p. 1·50 1·75

339 Michael Davitt (founder of The Land League)

1996. Anniversaries and Events. Multicoloured.
1009 28p. Type **339** (150th birth anniv) 80 60
1010 32p. Presidency logo (Ireland's Presidency of European Union) (horiz) 80 70
1011 38p. Thomas McLaughlin (hydro-electric engineer) and Ardnacrusha Power Station (birth centenary) (horiz) . . . . 1·25 1·10
1012 52p. Mechanical peat harvester (50th anniv of Bord na Mona) (horiz) . . 1·75 1·75

340 "Ciara" (coastal patrol vessel)

1996. 50th Anniv of Irish Naval Service. Multicoloured.
1013 32p. Type **340** 80 70
1014 44p. "Cliona" (corvette) . . 1·40 1·50
1015 52p. "M-1" (motor torpedo boat) (vert) . . . . 1·50 1·60

341 Blind Woman with Child

1996. People with Disabilities. Multicoloured.
1016 28p. Type **341** . . . . . . 1·10 1·10
1017 28p. Man in wheelchair playing bowls . . . . . . 1·10 1·10

342 Green-winged Teal

1996. Freshwater Ducks. Multicoloured.
1018 32p. Type **342** . . . . . . 1·00 70
1019 38p. Common shoveler . . . 1·10 1·25
1020 44p. European wigeon . . . 1·25 1·75
1021 52p. Mallard . . . . 1·60 2·00
MS1022 127 × 85 mm. Nos. 1018/21 4·50 5·50

343 "Man of Aran"

1996. Centenary of Irish Cinema. Multicoloured.
1023 32p. Type **343** 85 90
1024 32p. "My Left Foot" . . . 85 90
1025 32p. "The Commitments" 85 90
1026 32p. "The Field" 85 90

344 Visit of the Magi

1996. Christmas. Designs from 16th-century "Book of Hours" (Nos.1028/30). Multicoloured.
1027 28p. The Holy Family . . . 75 60
1028 28p. Type **344** 60 60
1029 32p. The Annunciation . . 80 75
1030 52p. The Shepherds receiving new of Christ's birth . . . . 1·40 1·60

345 Black-billed Magpie ("Magpie")

346 Pair of Doves

1997. Birds. Ordinary gum. Multicoloured. (a) Size 21 × 24 mm or 24 × 21 mm.
1031 1p. Type **345** 10 50
1032 2p. Northern gannet ("Gannet") (vert) 15 50
1033 4p. Corn crake (vert) . . . 20 20
1034 5p. Wood pigeon (horiz) . . 20 50
1035 10p. River kingfisher ("Kingfisher") (vert) . . . 30 70
1036 20p. Northern lapwing ("Lapwing") (vert) . . . 50 45
1037 28p. Blue tit (horiz) . . . . 1·50 50
1038 30p. Blackbird (vert) 70 50
1039 30p. Goldcrest (vert) . . . . 1·25 1·25
1040 30p. Common stonechat ("Stonechat") (vert) . . . 70 75
1041 30p. As No. 1036 . . . . . 70 75
1042 30p. As No. 1032 . . . . . 70 75
1043 30p. As No. 1033 . . . . . 70 75
1044 30p. Type **345** 70 75
1045 30p. As No. 1035 . . . . . 70 75
1046 30p. Peregrine falcon (vert) 70 75
1047 30p. Barn owl (vert) 70 75
1048 30p. European robin ("Robin") (vert) 70 75
1049 30p. Song thrush (vert) . . 70 75
1050 30p. Winter wren ("Wren") (vert) 70 75
1051 30p. Pied wagtail (vert) . . 70 75
1052 30p. Atlantic puffin ("Puffin") (vert) 70 75
1053 32p. As No. 1048 . . . . . 1·10 55
1054 35p. As No. 1040 . . . . . 90 75
1055 40p. Ringed plover (horiz) . 1·00 85
1056 44p. As No. 1052 . . . . . 2·25 85
1057 45p. As No. 1049 . . . . . 2·25 1·75
1058 50p. Northern sparrow hawk ("European Sparrow Hawk") (horiz) 1·50 1·75
1059 52p. As No. 1047 . . . . . 2·00 1·00

(b) Size 24 × 45 mm or 45 × 24 mm.
1060 £1 White-fronted goose ("Greenland White-fronted Goose") (vert) . . 2·00 1·60
1061 £2 Northern pintail ("Pintail") (horiz) . . . . 3·75 3·50
1062 £5 Common shelduck ("Shelduck") (vert) . . . 8·50 9·00

(c) Size 17 × 21 mm or 21 × 17 mm.
1080 4p. Corn crake . . . . . . 65 1·00
1081 5p. Wood pigeon 55 75
1082 30p. Blackbird . . . . . . 1·00 1·00
1083 30p. Goldcrest . . . . . . 1·00 1·00
1084 32p. European robin ("Robin") . . . . 1·00 1·00
1085 32p. Peregrine falcon . . . 1·25 1·25

(d) Size 25 × 30 mm. Self-adhesive.
1086 30p. Goldcrest . . . . . . 1·00 1·10
1087 30p. Blackbird 75 80
1088 32p. Peregrine falcon . . . 2·00 2·50
1089 32p. European robin ("Robin") . . . . 2·00 2·50

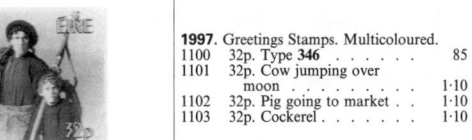

1997. Greetings Stamps. Multicoloured.
1100 32p. Type **346** 85 50
1101 32p. Cow jumping over moon . . . . 1·10 1·10
1102 32p. Pig going to market . . 1·10 1·10
1103 32p. Cockerel . . . . 1·10 1·10

1997. "HONG KONG '97" International Stamp Exhibition. Chinese New Year ("Year of the Ox").
MS1104 124 × 74 mm. Nos. 1101/3 2·40 2·40

347 Troops on Parade

1997. 75th Anniv of Irish Free State. Mult.
1105 28p. Page from the "Annals of the Four Masters", quill and 1944 ½d. O'Clery stamp 55 55
1106 32p. Type **347** 60 65
1107 32p. The Dail, national flag and Constitution 60 65
1108 32p. Athlete, footballer and hurling player 60 65
1109 32p. Singer, violinist and bodhran player 60 65
1110 32p. Stained glass window and 1929 9d. O'Connell stamp 60 60
1111 32p. 1923 2d. map stamp and G.P.O., Dublin . . . 60 60
1112 52p. Police personnel and Garda badge . . . . . . 1·00 1·25
1113 52p. The Four Courts and Scales of Justice . . . . . 1·00 1·25
1114 52p. Currency, blueprint and food-processing plant . . 1·00 1·25
1115 52p. Books, palette and Seamus Heaney manuscript . . . . 1·00 1·25
1116 52p. Air Lingus airliner and 1965 1s.5d. air stamp . . 1·00 1·25
MS1117 174 × 209 mm. As Nos. 1105/16, but each with face value of 32p. . . . . 8·50 9·00

348 Grey Seals

1997. Marine Mammals. Multicoloured.
1118 28p. Type **348** 75 60
1119 32p. Bottle-nosed dolphins 85 80
1120 44p. Harbour porpoises (horiz) . . . . 1·25 1·40
1121 52p. Killer whale (horiz) . . 1·40 1·50
MS1122 150 × 68 mm. As Nos. 1118/21 . . . . 6·00 6·00

349 Dublin Silver Penny of 997

1997. Millenary of Irish Coinage.
1123 **349** 32p. multicoloured . . . 65 65

350 "The Children of Lir"

1997. Europa. Tales and Legends. Multicoloured. (a) Size 38 × 28 mm. Ordinary gum.
1124 32p. Type **350** 75 60
1125 44p. Oisin and Niamh . . . 1·10 2·00

(b) Size 36 × 25 mm. Self-adhesive.
1126 32p. Type **350** 70 70
1127 32p. Oisin and Niamh . . . 70 70

351 Emigrants waiting to board Ship

1997. 150th Anniv of The Great Famine.
1128 **351** 28p. blue, red and stone 1·00 60
1129 – 32p. orange, blue & stone . . . . 1·25 70
1130 – 52p. brown, blue & stone 1·75 1·40
DESIGNS: 32p. Family and dying child; 52p. Irish Society of Friends soup kitchen.

1997. "Pacific '97" International Stamp Exhibition, San Francisco. Sheet 100 × 70 mm, containing No. 1061. Multicoloured.
MS1131 £2 Pintail (48 × 26 mm) 4·50 5·00

352 Kate O'Brien (novelist) (birth centenary)

1997. Anniversaries. Multicoloured.
1132 28p. Type **352** 60 90
1133 28p. St. Columba crossing to Iona (stained glass window) (1400th death anniv) 60 90
1134 32p. "Daniel O'Connell" (J. Haverty) (politician) (150th death anniv) (27 × 49 mm) 70 70
1135 52p. "John Wesley" (N. Hone) (founder of Methodism) (250th anniv of first visit to Ireland) . . 1·25 2·25

353 The Baily Lighthouse

1997. Lighthouses. Multicoloured.
1136 32p. Type **353** . . . . . . 1·00 80
1137 32p. Tarbert . . . . 1·00 80
1138 38p. Hookhead (vert) . . . 1·10 85
1139 50p. The Fastnet (vert) . . . 1·40 1·25

354 Commemorative Cross

355 Dracula and Bat

1997. Ireland–Mexico Joint Issue. 150th Anniv of Mexican St. Patrick's Battalion.
1140 **354** 32p. multicoloured . . . 55 60

1997. Centenary of Publication of Bram Stoker's "Dracula". Multicoloured.
1141 28p. Type **355** 60 55
1142 32p. Dracula and female victim 65 60
1143 38p. Dracula emerging from coffin (horiz) 80 90
1144 52p. Dracula and wolf (horiz) . . . . 1·10 1·50
MS1145 150 × 90 mm. As Nos. 1141/4 . . . . 4·25 4·50

356 "The Nativity" (Kevin Kelly)

357 Christmas Tree

1997. Christmas. Multicoloured. (a) Stained-glass Windows. Ordinary gum.
1146 28p. Type **356** 70 55
1147 32p. The Nativity (Sarah Purser and A. E. Child) 80 65
1148 52p. The Nativity (A. E. Child) . . . . 1·50 1·40

(b) Self-adhesive.
1149 28p. Type **357** 55 65

358 Holding Heart

1998. Greetings Stamps (1st series). Designs based on the "love is ..." cartoon characters of Kim Casali. Multicoloured.
1150 32p. Type **358** 70 50
1151 32p. Receiving letter . . . . 70 1·00
1152 32p. Sitting on log . . . . 70 1·00
1153 32p. With birthday presents 70 1·00
See also Nos. 1173/6.

1998. Chinese New Year ("Year of the Tiger").
MS1154 124 × 73 mm. Nos. 1151/3 2·50 2·75

359 Lady Mary Heath and Avro Avian over Pyramids

1998. Pioneers of Irish Aviation. Multicoloured.
1155 28p. Type **359** 60 55
1156 32p. Col. James Fitzmaurice and Junkers W.33 "Bremen" over Labrador 65 60
1157 44p. Captain J. P. Saul and Fokker F.VIIa/3m "Southern Cross" . . . . 1·25 1·25
1158 52p. Captain Charles Blair and Sikorsky V-s 44 (flying boat) . . . . . . 1·50 1·50

360 Show-jumping

1998. Equestrian Sports. Multicoloured.
1159 30p. Type **360** 80 60
1160 32p. Three-day eventing . . 85 65
1161 40p. Gymkhana . . . . . . 1·00 1·25
1162 45p. Dressage (vert) . . . . 1·00 1·25
MS1163 126 × 84 mm. Nos. 1159/62 3·25 3·25

361 Figure of "Liberty"

1998. Bicentenary of United Irish Rebellion. Mult.
1164 30p. Type **361** . . . . . . 1·00 1·00
1165 30p. United Irishman . . . 1·00 1·00
1166 30p. French soldiers . . . . 1·00 1·00
1167 45p. Wolfe Tone . . . . . 1·00 1·25
1168 45p. Henry Joy McCracken 1·00 1·25

362 Gathering of the Boats, Kinvara

1998. Europa. Festivals. Multicoloured. (a) Size 39 × 27 mm.
1169 30p. Type **362** . . . . . . 1·25 80
1170 40p. Puck Fair, Killorglin 1·50 95

(b) Size 34 × 23 mm. Self-adhesive.
1171 30p. Type **362** 65 90
1172 30p. Puck Fair, Killorglin 65 90

1998. Greetings Stamps (2nd series). As Nos. 1105/8, but with changed face value. Multicoloured.
1173 30p. As No. 1153 . . . . . 70 95
1174 30p. As No. 1152 . . . . . 70 95
1175 30p. As No. 1151 . . . . . 70 95
1176 30p. Type **358** 70 95

363 Cyclists rounding Bend

1998. Visit of "Tour de France" Cycle Race to Ireland. Multicoloured.
1177 30p. Type **363** 75 85
1178 30p. Two cyclists ascending hill 75 85
1179 30p. "Green jersey" cyclist and other competitor . . 75 85
1180 30p. "Yellow jersey" (race leader) 75 85

364 Voter and Local Councillors of 1898

1998. Democracy Anniversaries. Multicoloured.
1181 30p. Type **364** (cent of Local Government (Ireland) Act) 60 60
1182 32p. European Union flag and harp symbol (25th anniv of Ireland's entry into European Community) 65 65
1183 35p. Woman voter and suffragettes, 1898 (cent of women's right to vote in local elections) 75 75
1184 45p. Irish Republic flag (50th anniv of Republic of Ireland Act) . . . . . . 1·00 1·25

365 "Asgard II" (cadet brigantine)

366 Ashworth Pillbox (1856)

1998. "Cutty Sark" International Tall Ships Race, Dublin. Multicoloured. (a) Ordinary gum.
1185 30p. Type **365** (26 × 38 mm) 70 70
1186 30p. U.S.C.G. "Eagle" (cadet barque) (26 × 38 mm) 70 70
1187 45p. "Boa Esperanza" (replica caravel) (38 × 26 mm) . . . . . . 1·00 1·00
1188 £1 "Royalist" (training brigantine) (38 × 26 mm) 1·90 2·50

(b) Self-adhesive.
1189 30p. "Boa Esperanza" (34 × 23 mm) 65 70
1190 30p. Type **365** (23 × 34 mm) 65 70
1191 30p. U.S.C.G. "Eagle" (23 × 34 mm) 65 70
1192 30p. "Royalist" (34 × 23 mm) 65 70

1998. Irish Postboxes. Multicoloured.
1193 30p. Type **366** 75 85
1194 30p. Irish Free State wallbox (1922) 75 85
1195 30p. Double pillarbox (1899) 75 85
1196 30p. Penfold pillarbox (1866) 75 85

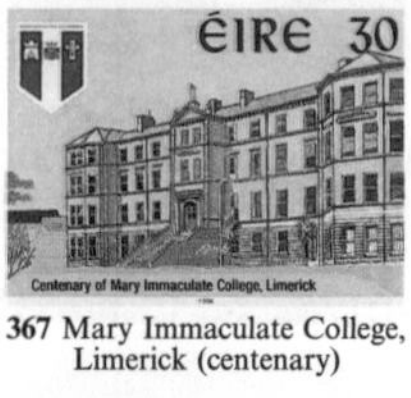

367 Mary Immaculate College, Limerick (centenary)

1998. Anniversaries. Multicoloured.
1197 30p. Type **367** 75 60
1198 40p. Newtown School, Waterford (bicent) (vert) 1·00 1·10
1199 45p. Trumpeters (50th anniv of Universal Declaration of Human Rights) . . . . 1·10 1·25

1998. "Portugal '98" International Stamp Exhibition, Lisbon. Sheet 101 × 71 mm, containing design as No. 1187.
MS1200 £2 "Boa Esperanza" (caravel) (horiz) . . . . 4·50 5·00

368 Cheetah

1998. Endangered Animals. Multicoloured.
1201 30p. Type **368** . . . . . . 1·40 1·00
1202 30p. Scimitar-horned oryx 1·40 1·00
1203 40p. Golden lion tamarin (vert) . . . . 1·40 1·00
1204 45p. Tiger (vert) . . . . . 1·60 1·25
MS1205 150 × 90 mm. As Nos. 1201/4 . . . . 4·25 4·25

369 The Holy Family

370 Choir Boys

1998. Christmas. Mult. (a) Ordinary gum.
1206 30p. Type **369** 70 60
1207 32p. Shepherds 75 65
1208 45p. Three Kings . . . . . 1·00 1·75

(b) Self-adhesive.
1209 30p. Type **370** 65 60

371 Puppy and Heart

372 Micheal Mac Liammoir

1999. Greetings Stamps. Pets. Multicoloured.
1210 30p. Type **371** 65 50
1211 30p. Kitten and ball of wool 65 75
1212 30p. Goldfish 65 75
1213 30p. Rabbit with lettuce leaf 65 75

1999. Chinese New Year ("Year of the Rabbit").
MS1214 124 × 74 mm. Nos. 1211/13 2·25 2·25

1999. Irish Actors and Actresses.
1215 **372** 30p. black and brown . . 65 60
1216 – 45p. black and green . . 1·00 1·10
1217 – 50p. black and blue . . 1·00 1·25
DESIGNS: 45p. Siobhan McKenna, 50p. Noel Purcell.

373 Irish Emigrant Ship

1999. Ireland–U.S.A. Joint Issue. Irish Emigration.
1218 **373** 45p. multicoloured . . . 1·25 1·00

374 "Polly Woodside" (barque)

375 Sean Lemass

1999. Maritime Heritage. Multicoloured.
1219 30p. Type **374** 55 60
1220 35p. "Ilen" (schooner) . . . 65 70
1221 45p. R.N.L.I. Cromer class lifeboat (horiz) 80 85
1222 £1 "Titanic" (liner) (horiz) 2·00 2·00
MS1223 150 × 90 mm. No. 1222 × 2 3·00 3·25

1999. Ireland—Australia Joint Issue. "Polly Woodside" (barque). Sheet 137 × 72 mm. Multicoloured.
MS1224 45c. Type **603** of Australia; 30p. Type **374** (No. **MS**1224 was sold at 52p. in Ireland) . . . . 1·25 1·40
No. **MS**1224 includes the "Australia '99" emblem on the sheet margin and was postally valid in Ireland to the value of 30p.

The same miniature sheet was also available in Australia.

1999. Birth Centenary of Sean Lemass (politician).
1225 **375** 30p. black and green . . 1·00 65

376 European Currency Emblem

1999. Introduction of Single European Currency.
1226 **376** 30p. multicoloured . . . 75 65
The face value of No. 1226 is shown in both Irish and euro currency.

377 European Flags

379 Father James Cullen and St. Francis Xavier Church, Dublin

378 Whooper Swans, Kilcolman Nature Reserve

1999. 50th Anniv of Council of Europe.
1227 **377** 45p. multicoloured . . . 1·00 1·00

1999. Europa. Parks and Gardens. Multicoloured.
(a) Size 36 × 26 mm. Ordinary gum.
1228 30p. Type **378** 90 50
1229 40p. Fallow deer, Phoenix Park . . . . 1·00 1·00
(b) Size 34 × 23 mm. Self-adhesive.
1230 30p. Type **378** 65 65
1231 30p. Fallow deer, Phoenix Park 65 65

1999. Centenary of Pioneer Total Abstinence Association.
1232 **379** 32p. brown, bistre and black 70 65

380 Elderly Man and Child using Computer

1999. International Year of Older Persons.
1233 **380** 30p. multicoloured . . . 70 65

381 Postal Van, 1922

1999. 125th Anniv of Universal Postal Union.
1234 **381** 30p. green and deep green . . . . 1·00 1·00
1235 – 30p. multicoloured . . . 1·00 1·00
DESIGN: No. 1235, Modern postal lorries.

382 Danno Keeffe

1999. Gaelic Athletic Association "Millennium Football Team". Multicoloured. (a) Size 37 × 25 mm. Ordinary gum.
1236 30p. Type **382** 60 70
1237 30p. Enda Colleran 60 70
1238 30p. Joe Keohane 60 70
1239 30p. Sean Flanagan 60 70
1240 30p. Sean Murphy 60 70
1241 30p. John Joe Reilly 60 70
1242 30p. Martin O'Connell . . . 60 70
1243 30p. Mick O'Connell . . . 60 70
1244 30p. Tommy Murphy . . . 60 70
1245 30p. Sean O'Neill 60 70
1246 30p. Sean Purcell 60 70
1247 30p. Pat Spillane 60 70
1248 30p. Mikey Sheehy 60 70
1249 30p. Tom Langan 60 70
1250 30p. Kevin Heffernan . . . 60 70
(b) Size 33 × 23 mm. Self-adhesive.
1251 30p. Type **382** . . . . . . 1·50 2·00
1252 30p. Enda Colleran 65 80
1253 30p. Joe Keohane . . . . . 1·50 2·00
1254 30p. Sean Flanagan 65 80
1255 30p. Sean Murphy . . . . 1·50 2·00
1256 30p. John Joe Reilly 55 60
1257 30p. Martin O'Connell . . . 55 60
1258 30p. Mick O'Connell . . . 1·50 2·00
1259 30p. Tommy Murphy . . . 65 80
1260 30p. Sean O'Neill 55 60
1261 30p. Sean Purcell 65 80
1262 30p. Pat Spillane 65 80
1263 30p. Mikey Sheehy 65 80
1264 30p. Tom Langan 65 80
1265 30p. Kevin Heffernan . . . 55 60

383 Douglas DC-3

1999. Commercial Aviation. Multicoloured.
1266 30p. Type **383** 65 50
1267 32p. Britten Norman Islander 75 55
1268 40p. Boeing 707 . . . . . . 80 85
1269 45p. Lockheed Constellation 90 1·00

384 Mammoth

386 Grace Kelly (American actress)

385 Holy Family

1999. Extinct Irish Animals. Multicoloured. (a) Size 26 × 38 mm (vert) or 38 × 26 mm (horiz). Ordinary gum.
1270 30p. Type **384** 70 60
1271 30p. Giant deer 70 60
1272 45p. Wolves (horiz) . . . . 90 1·00
1273 45p. Brown bear (horiz) . . 90 1·00
MS1274 150 × 63 mm. Nos. 1270/3 2·50 2·75
(b) Size 33 × 23 mm (horiz) or 22 × 34 mm (vert). Self-adhesive.
1275 30p. Brown bear (horiz) . . 70 85
1276 30p. Type **384** 70 85
1277 30p. Wolves (horiz) 70 85
1278 30p. Giant deer 70 85

1999. Christmas. Children's Nativity Plays. Mult. (a) Size 35 × 25 mm. Ordinary gum.
1279 30p. Type **385** 60 50
1280 32p. Visit of the Shepherds 65 55
1281 45p. Adoration of the Magi 1·25 1·25
(b) Size 16 × 26 mm. Self-adhesive.
1282 30p. Angel 55 50

1999. New Millennium (1st issue). Famous People of the 20th Century. Multicoloured.
1283 30p. Type **386** . . . . . . 1·50 1·75
1284 30p. Jesse Owens (American athlete) . . . . 1·50 1·75
1285 30p. John F. Kennedy (former American President) . . . . 1·50 1·75
1286 30p. Mother Teresa (missionary) . . . . . . 1·50 1·75
1287 30p. John McCormack (tenor) . . . . 1·50 1·75
1288 30p. Nelson Mandela (South African statesman) . . . 1·50 1·75
See also Nos. 1289/94, 1300/5, 1315/20, 1377/82 and 1383/88.

387 Ruined Castle (Norman Invasion, 1169)

2000. New Millennium (2nd issue). Irish Historic Events. Multicoloured.
1289 30p. Type **387** . . . . . . 1·00 1·25
1290 30p. Flight of the Earls, 1607 . . . . 1·00 1·25
1291 30p. Opening of Irish Parliament, 1782 . . . . 1·00 1·25
1292 30p. Eviction (formation of the Land League) . . . . 1·00 1·25
1293 30p. First four Irish Prime Ministers (Irish Independence) . . . . . 1·00 1·25
1294 30p. Irish soldier and personnel carrier (U.N. Peace-keeping) . . . . . 1·00 1·25

388 Frog Prince

389 Revd. Nicholas Callan (electrical scientist)

2000. Greetings Stamps. Mythical Creatures. Multicoloured.
1295 30p. Type **388** 55 60
1296 30p. Pegasus 55 60
1297 30p. Unicorn 55 60
1298 30p. Dragon 55 60

2000. Chinese New Year ("Year of the Dragon").
MS1299 124 × 74 mm. Nos. 1296/8 1·75 2·00

2000. New Millennium (3rd issue). Discoveries. Multicoloured.
1300 30p. Type **389** . . . . . . 1·25 1·40
1301 30p. Birr Telescope . . . . 1·25 1·40
1302 30p. Thomas Edison (inventor of light bulb) . . 1·25 1·40
1303 30p. Albert Einstein (mathematical physicist) 1·25 1·40
1304 30p. Marie Curie (physicist) 1·25 1·40
1305 30p. Galileo Galilei (astronomer and mathematician) . . . . . 1·25 1·40

390 "Jeanie Johnston" (emigrant ship)

2000. Completion of "Jeanie Johnston" Replica.
1306 **390** 30p. multicoloured . . . 70 50

391 "Building Europe"

392 Oscar Wilde

2000. Europa. (a) $25\frac{1}{2} \times 36\frac{1}{2}$ mm.
1307 **391** 32p. multicoloured . . . 80 55
(b) 22 × 34 mm. Self-adhesive.
1308 **391** 30p. multicoloured . . . 75 50

DENOMINATION. From No. 1309 to 1465 some Irish stamps are denominated both in Irish pounds and in euros. As no cash for the latter is in circulation, the catalogue continues to use the pound value.

2000. Death Centenary of Oscar Wilde (writer). Multicoloured.
1309 30p. Type **392** . . . . . . 90 1·00
1310 30p. *The Happy Prince* . . . 90 1·00
1311 30p. Lady Bracknell from *The Importance of being Earnest* . . . . 90 1·00
1312 30p. *The Picture of Dorian Gray* . . . . 90 1·00
MS1313 150 × 190 mm. £2 Type **392** 3·75 4·00
A further 30p. exists in a design similar to Type **392**, but 29 × 29 mm, printed in sheets of 20, each stamp having a se-tenant half-stamp size label attached at right inscribed "Oscar". These sheets could be personalized by the addition of a photograph in place of the inscription on the labels. Such stamps are not listed as they were not available at face value, the sheets of 20 containing the "Oscar" labels being sold for £10.

393 Ludwig van Beethoven (German composer)

394 Running

2000. New Millennium (4th issue). The Arts. Mult.
1315 30p. Type **393** . . . . . . 1·00 1·25
1316 30p. Dame Ninette de Valois (ballet director) . . 1·00 1·25
1317 30p. James Joyce (author) 1·00 1·25
1318 30p. "Mona Lisa" (Leonardo da Vinci) . . . 1·00 1·25
1319 30p. "Lady Lavery" (Sir John Lavery) . . . . . . 1·00 1·25
1320 30p. William Shakespeare (playwright) . . . . . . 1·00 1·25

2000. Olympic Games, Sydney. Multicoloured.
1321 30p. Type **394** 70 70
1322 30p. Javelin throwing . . . 70 70
1323 50p. Long jumping . . . . 1·00 1·25
1324 50p. High jumping . . . . 1·00 1·25

395 "Space Rocket over Flowers" (Marguerite Nyhan)

397 Peacock Butterfly

396 Tony Reddin

2000. "Stampin' the Future" (children's stamp design competition). Multicoloured.
1325 30p. Type **395** 60 50
1326 32p. "Tree, rocket and hands holding globe in '2000'" (Kyle Staunton) (horiz) 70 55
1327 45p. "People holding hands on globe" (Jennifer Branagan) (horiz) . . . . 90 1·10
1328 45p. "Colony on Moon" (Diarmuid O'Ceochain) (horiz) . . . . 90 1·10

2000. "Hurling Team of the Millennium". Multicoloured. (a) Size 36 × 27 mm.
1329 30p. Type **396** 60 70
1330 30p. Bobby Rackard 60 70
1331 30p. Nick O'Donnell . . . 60 70
1332 30p. John Doyle 60 70
1333 30p. Brian Whelahan . . . 60 70
1334 30p. John Keane 60 70
1335 30p. Paddy Phelan 60 70
1336 30p. Lory Meagher 60 70
1337 30p. Jack Lynch 60 70
1338 30p. Jim Langton 60 70
1339 30p. Mick Mackey 60 70
1340 30p. Christy Ring 60 70
1341 30p. Jimmy Doyle 60 70
1342 30p. Ray Cummins 60 70
1343 30p. Eddie Keher 60 70
(b) Size 33 × 23 mm. Self-adhesive.
1344 30p. Type **396** . . . . . . 75 1·00
1345 30p. Jimmy Doyle . . . . . 75 1·00
1346 30p. John Doyle . . . . . 75 1·00
1347 30p. Paddy Phelan . . . . 1·25 1·60
1348 30p. Jim Langton . . . . . 1·25 1·60
1349 30p. Lory Meagher . . . . 75 1·00
1350 30p. Eddie Keher . . . . . 75 1·00
1351 30p. Mick Mackey . . . . 75 1·00
1352 30p. Brian Whelahan . . . 75 1·00
1353 30p. John Keane . . . . . 75 1·00
1354 30p. Bobby Rackard . . . . 75 1·00
1355 30p. Nick O'Donnell . . . 75 1·00
1356 30p. Jack Lynch . . . . . 75 1·00
1357 30p. Ray Cummins . . . . 75 1·00
1358 30p. Christy Ring . . . . . 75 1·00

2000. Butterflies. Multicoloured.
1359 30p. Type **397** 80 50
1360 32p. Small tortoiseshell . . 85 55
1361 45p. Silver-washed fritillary 1·25 1·40
1362 50p. Orange-tip . . . . . . 1·40 1·50
MS1363 150 × 90 mm. Nos. 1359/62 3·00 3·00

2000. Military Aviation. Multicoloured. (a) Size 37 × 26 mm.
1364 30p. Hawker Hurricane Mk IIc 80 60
1365 30p. Bristol F.2b Mk II . . 80 60
1366 45p. De Havilland DH.115 Vampire T.55 . . . . . . 1·10 1·25
1367 45p. Sud S.E. 3160 Alouette III (helicopter) . . . . . 1·10 1·25

(b) Size 33 × 22 mm. Self-adhesive.
1368 30p. Bristol F.2b Mk II . . 70 70
1369 30p. Hawker Hurricane Mk IIc 70 70
1370 30p. De Havilland DH.115 Vampire T.55 . . . . . . 70 70
1371 30p. SUD SE. 3160 Alouette III 70 70

398 Tractor ploughing Field

399 The Nativity

2000. Centenary of An Roinn Talmhaiochta (Department of Agriculture).
1372 **398** 50p. multicoloured . . . 1·00 1·10

2000. Christmas. Multicoloured. (a) Size 24 × 27 mm.
1373 30p. Type **399** 65 50
1374 32p. Three Magi 75 55
1375 45p. Shepherds . . . . . . 1·00 1·25

(b) Size 24 × 29 mm. Self-adhesive.
1376 30p. Flight into Egypt . . . 65 50

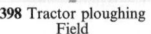

400 Storming the Bastille, Paris, 1789

2000. New Millennium (5th issue). World Events. Multicoloured.
1377 30p. Type **400** . . . . . . 1·10 1·40
1378 30p. Early railway . . . . . 1·10 1·40
1379 30p. Returning troop ship, 1945 . . . . 1·10 1·40
1380 30p. Suffragettes . . . . . 1·10 1·40
1381 30p. Destruction of the Berlin Wall, 1989 . . . . 1·10 1·40
1382 30p. Internet communications . . . . . 1·10 1·40

2001. New Millennuim (6th issue). Epic Journeys. As T **400**. Multicoloured.
1383 30p. Marco Polo . . . . . 1·25 1·40
1384 30p. Captain James Cook 1·25 1·40
1385 30p. Burke and Wills expedition crossing Australia, 1860 . . . . . 1·25 1·40
1386 30p. Ernest Shackleton in Antarctica . . . . 1·25 1·40
1387 30p. Charles Lindbergh and *Spirit of St. Louis* . . . . 1·25 1·40
1388 30p. Astronaut on Moon . . 1·25 1·40

401 Goldfish

2001. Greetings Stamps. Pets. (a) As Type **401**. Mult.
1389 30p. Type **401** 80 50

(b) Designs smaller, 20 × 30 mm. Self-adhesive.
1390 30p. Lizard 80 70
1391 30p. Frog 80 70
1392 30p. Type **401** 80 70
1393 30p. Snake 80 70
1394 30p. Tortoise 80 70

2001. Chinese New Year ("Year of the Snake").
MS1395 124 × 75 mm. As Nos. 1391 and 1393/4, but larger, 28 × 39 mm 1·75 2·00

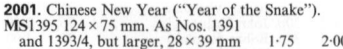

402 Television Presenter and Audience

2001. Irish Broadcasting.
1396 **402** 30p. multicoloured . . . 70 50
1397 – 32p. black, ultramarine and blue 80 55
1398 – 45p. black, brown and orange . . . . 1·00 1·10
1399 – 50p. brown, yellow and green . . . . 1·00 1·25

DESIGNS: 32p. Radio sports commentators; 45p. Family around radio; 50p. Play on television set.

403 Archbishop Narcissus Marsh and Library Interior

404 Bagpipe Player

2001. Literary Anniversaries. Multicoloured.
1400 30p. Type **403** (300th anniv of Marsh's Library) . . . 60 50
1401 32p. Book of Common Prayer, 1551 (450th anniv of first book printed in Ireland) 65 75

2001. 50th Anniv of Comhaltas Ceoltoiri Eireann (cultural organization). Multicoloured.
1402 30p. Type **404** 70 70
1403 30p. Bodhran player 70 70
1404 45p. Young fiddler and Irish dancer (horiz) . . . . . 1·00 1·25
1405 45p. Flautist and singer (horiz) . . . . 1·00 1·25

405 Jordan Formula 1 Racing Car

2001. Irish Motorsport. Multicoloured. (a) As Type **405**.
1406 30p. Type **405** 75 50
1407 32p. Hillman Imp on Tulip Rally 80 55
1408 45p. Mini Cooper S on Monte Carlo Rally . . . 1·25 80
1409 £1 Mercedes SSK, winner of 1930 Irish Grand Prix . . 2·00 2·50
MS1410 150 × 90 mm. £2 Type **405** 3·75 4·25

(b). Designs smaller, 33½ × 22½. Self-adhesive.
1411 30p. Type **405** 90 75
1412 30p. Hillman Imp on Tulip Rally 90 75
1413 30p. Mini Cooper S on Monte Carlo Rally . . . 90 75
1414 30p. Mercedes SSK, winner of 1930 Irish Grand Prix 90 75

406 Peter Lalor (leader at Eureka Stockade) and Gold Licence

2001. Irish Heritage in Australia. Multicoloured.
1415 30p. Type **406** 60 60
1416 30p. Ned Kelly (bush ranger) and "Wanted" poster 60 60
1417 45p. Family leaving for Australia and immigrant ship . . . . 90 1·25
1418 45p. Irish settler and life in gold camp . . . . 90 1·25
MS1419 150 × 90 mm. £1 As No. 1416 . . . . 1·90 2·25

407 Children playing in River

408 Blackbird

2001. Europa; Water Resources. Multicoloured. (a) Size 36½ × 26½ mm.
1420 30p. Type **407** 85 50
1421 32p. Man fishing 90 75

(b) Designs smaller, 33 × 22 mm. Self-adhesive.
1422 30p. Type **407** 65 65
1423 30p. As 32p 65 65

2001. Dual Currency Birds. Vert designs as Nos. 1038, 1050, 1053, 1056/7 and 1060 (some with different face values) showing both Irish currency and euros as in T **408**. Multicoloured. (a) Ordinary gum.
1424 30p./38c. Type **408** 60 60
1425 32p./41c. European robin ("Robin") 70 70
1426 35p./44c. Atlantic puffin ("Puffin") 75 80
1427 40p./51c. Winter wren ("Wren") 85 90
1428 45p./57c. Song thrush . . . 95 1·00
1429 £1/€1.25 White-fronted goose ("Greenland White-fronted Goose") (23 × 44 mm) . . . . . . 2·00 2·25

(b) Designs as Nos. 1038/9, but 25 × 30 mm. Self-adhesive.
1430 30p./38c. Type **408** 65 65
1431 30p./38c. Goldcrest 65 65

409 Irish Pikeman

410 Ruffian 23 Yachts

2001. 400th Anniv of Battle of Kinsale. Nine Years War. Multicoloured.
1432 30p. Type **409** 70 70
1433 30p. English cavalry 70 70
1434 32p. Spanish pikeman . . . 80 80
1435 45p. Town of Kinsale . . . 1·10 1·25

2001. Yachts. Multicoloured. (a) Size 26 × 37½ mm.
1436 30p. Type **410** 70 60
1437 32p. Howth 17 yacht . . . 75 65
1438 45p. 1720 Sportsboat yacht 1·10 1·25
1439 45p. Glen class cruising yacht . . . . 1·10 1·25

(b) Self-adhesive. Size 22 × 34 mm.
1440 30p. Type **410** 70 70
1441 30p. Howth 17 yacht . . . 70 70
1442 30p. Glen class cruising yacht 70 70
1443 30p. 1720 Sportsboat yacht 70 70

411 Padraic Carney (footballer)

2001. Gaelic Athletic Association Hall of Fame 2001 (1st series). Multicoloured. (a) Size 36½ × 27 mm.
1444 30p. Type **411** 70 70
1445 30p. Frank Cummins (hurler) 70 70
1446 30p. Jack O'Shea (footballer) 70 70
1447 30p. Nicky Rackard (hurler) 70 70

(b) Self-adhesive. Size 33½ × 22½ mm.
1448 30p. Type **411** 70 70
1449 30p. Frank Cummins (hurler) 70 70
1450 30p. Jack O'Shea (footballer) 70 70
1451 30p. Nicky Rackard (hurler) 70 70

2001. "Belgica 2001" International Stamp Exhibition, Brussels. No. **MS**1410 with "Belgica 2001" added to the sheet margin.
MS1452 150 × 90 mm. £2 Type **405** 4·00 4·25
See also Nos. 1550/3.

412 Blackbird

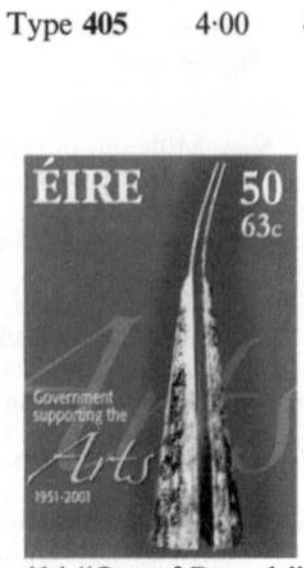

414 "Out of Bounds" (sculpture by Eilis O'Connell)

413 Perch

2001. Birds. Vert designs as Nos. 1038/9, 1048 and 1049, but 23½ × 28½ mm, each showing a letter in place of face values as T **412**. Multicoloured. Self-adhesive.
1453 (N) Type **412** 60 50
1454 (N) Goldcrest 60 50
1455 (E) Robin 70 55
1456 (W) Song thrush 85 90

Nos. 1453/6 were intended to cover the changeover period to euros. Nos. 1453/4 were sold for 30p, No. 1455 for 32p. and No. 1456 for 45p.

2001. Freshwater Fish. Multicoloured.
1457 30p. Type **413** 75 50
1458 32p. Arctic charr 80 85
1459 32p. Pike 80 85
1460 45p. Common bream . . . 1·10 1·25

2001. 50th Anniv of Government Support for Arts.
1461 **414** 50p. multicoloured . . . 1·25 1·40

415 "The Nativity" (Richard King)

416 Black-billed Magpie ("Magpie")

2001. Christmas. Paintings by Richard King. Multicoloured. (a) Size 25½ × 36½ mm.
1462 30p. Type **415** 70 50
1463 32p. "The Annunciation" 75 55
1464 45p. "Presentation in the Temple" . . . . 1·10 1·25

(b) Size 25 × 30 mm. Self-adhesive.
1465 30p. "Madonna and Child" 70 50

2002. New Currency. Birds, as Nos. 1031/62, and new designs, with face values in cents and euros, as T **416**. (i) Size 20 × 22½ mm or 22½ × 20 mm.
1466 1c. Type **416** 10 10
1467 2c. Northern gannet ("Gannet") 10 10
1468 3c. Blue tit (horiz) 10 10
1469 4c. Corn crake 10 10
1470 5c. Woodpigeon (horiz) . . 10 10
1470a 7c. Common stonechat . . 10 10
1471 10c. River kingfisher ("Kingfisher") 10 15
1472 20c. Northern lapwing ("Lapwing") 25 30
1473 38c. Blackbird 50 55
1474 41c. Chaffinch 55 60
1475 41c. Goldcrest 55 60
1476 44c. European robin ("Robin") 60 65
1477 47c. Kestrel (horiz) 65 70
1477a 48c. Peregrine falcon . . . 65 70
1477b 48c. Pied wagtail 65 70
1478 50c. Grey heron (horiz) . . 65 70
1479 51c. Roseate tern (horiz) 70 75
1480 55c. Oystercatcher (horiz) 75 80
1481 57c. Western curlew ("Curlew") 75 80
1482 60c. Jay (horiz) 80 85
1482a 60c. Atlantic puffin 80 85
1482b 65c. Song thrush 85 90
1482c 75c. Ringed plover (horiz) 1·00 1·10
1482d 95c. Sparrowhawk (horiz) 1·30 1·40

(ii) Size 44 × 23 mm or 23 × 44 mm.
1483 €1 Barnacle goose (horiz) 1·30 1·40
1484 €2 White-fronted goose ("Greenland White-fronted Goose") . . . . 2·75 3·00
1485 €5 Northern pintail ("Pintail") (horiz) . . . . 6·75 7·00
1486 €10 Common shelduck ("Shelduck") . . . . . . 13·50 14·00

(b) Size 16 × 20 mm.
1486a 4c. Corncrake 10 10
1487 10c. River kingfisher ("Kingfisher") 10 15
1488 36c. Wren 50 55
1489 38c. Blackbird 50 55
1490 41c. Chaffinch 55 60
1490a 48c. Peregrine falcon . . . 65 70

(c) Self-adhesive. Size 21 × 26 mm.
1491 38c. Blackbird 50 55
1492 38c. Goldcrest 50 55
1493 41c. Chaffinch 55 60
1494 41c. Goldcrest 55 60
1495 44c. Robin 60 65
1495b (–) Peregrine falcon . . . 65 70
1495c (–) Pied wagtail 65 70
1495d 48c. Peregrine falcon . . . 65 70
1495e 48c. Pied wagtail 65 70
1496 50c. Puffin 65 70
1497 57c. Song thrush 75 80
1497b 60c. Atlantic puffin 80 85
1497c 65c. Song thrush 85 90

Nos. 1495b/c were sold for 48c.

417 Reverse of Irish €1 Coin, 2002

2002. Introduction of Euro Currency. Irish Coins.
1506 38c. Type **417** 75 50
1507 41c. Reverse of 50p. coin, 1971–2001 . . . . 80 60
1508 57c. Reverse of 1d. coin, 1928–71 . . . . 1·10 1·25

418 Teddy Bear

2002. Greetings Stamps. Toys. Multicoloured. (a) Design 25 × 37 mm.
1509 38c. Type **418** 70 50

(b) Designs 20 × 27 mm. Self-adhesive.
1510 38c. Type **418** 70 70
1511 38c. Rag doll 70 70
1512 38c. Rocking horse 70 70
1513 38c. Train 70 70
1514 38c. Wooden blocks 70 70

2002. Chinese New Year ("Year of the Horse").
MS1515 124 × 74 mm. As Nos. 1511/13, but 25 × 37 mm 2·00 2·25

419 Around the Camp Fire

2002. 75th Anniv of Scouting Ireland CSI. Multicoloured.
1516 41c. Type **419** 75 75
1517 41c. Setting up camp . . . 75 75
1518 57c. Scouts canoeing . . . . 1·10 1·25
1519 57c. Scouts on hill walk . . 1·10 1·25

420 "Arkle"

2002. 250th Anniv of Steeplechasing in Ireland. Irish Steeplechasers. Multicoloured.
1520 38c. Type **420** 70 70
1521 38c. "L'Escargot" 70 70
1522 38c. "Dawn Run" 70 70
1523 38c. "Istabraq" 70 70

421 Badger

2002. Irish Mammals. Multicoloured.
1524 41c. Type **421** 75 60
1525 50c. Otter 90 70
1526 57c. Red squirell (vert) . . . 1·10 80
1527 €1 Hedgehog (vert) . . . . 1·75 1·90
MS1528 150 × 67 mm. €5 As 50c. 7·00 7·50

422 Roy Keane

2002. World Cup Football Championship, Japan and Korea (2002). Irish Footballers. Multicoloured. (a) Size 26 × 39 mm or 39 × 26 mm.
1529 41c. Packie Bonner (horiz) 75 75
1530 41c. Type **422** 75 75
1531 41c. Paul McGrath 75 75
1532 41c. David O'Leary 75 75

(b) Size 22 × 33 mm or 33 × 22 mm. Self-adhesive.
1533 41c. Packie Bonner (horiz) 75 75
1534 41c. Type **422** 75 75
1535 41c. Paul McGrath 75 75
1536 41c. David O'Leary 75 75

423 Clown

2002. Europa. Circus. Multicoloured. (a) Size 37 × 26 mm. Ordinary gum.
1537 41c. Type **423** 70 70
1538 44c. Girl on horse 70 70

(b) Self-adhesive. Size 34 × 22 mm.
1539 41c. Type **423** 70 70
1540 41c. As No. 1538 . . . . . 70 70

424 Padre Pio

425 Brian Boru leading Army

2002. Canonisation of St. Pio de Pietrelcina (Padre Pio).
1541 **424** 41c. multicoloured . . . 75 70

2002. 1000th Anniv of Declaration of Brian Boru as High King of Ireland. Multicoloured.
1542 41c. Type **425** 75 60
1543 44c. Leading fleet 75 60
1544 57c. Receiving surrender of the O'Neills 90 80
1545 £1 Decreeing primacy of bishopric of Armagh in the Irish Church . . . . 1·75 1·90

426 "Before the Start" (J. B. Yeats)

2002. 140th Anniv of National Gallery of Ireland (2004) (1st series). Paintings. Multicoloured.
1546 41c. Type **426** 70 70
1547 41c. "The Conjuror" (Nathaniel Hone) 70 70
1548 41c. "The Colosseum and Arch of Constantine, Rome" (Giovanni Panini) 70 70
1549 41c. "The Gleaners" (Jules Breton) 70 70
See also Nos. 1606/9 and 1700/3.

2002. Gaelic Athletic Association Hall of Fame 2002 (2nd series). As T **411**.
1550 41c. Peter McDermott (footballer) 70 75
1551 41c. Jimmy Smyth (hurler) 70 75
1552 41c. Matt Connor (footballer) 70 75
1553 41c. Seanie Duggan (hurler) 70 75

427 Archbishop Thomas Croke

429 "Adoration of the Magi"

428 U2

2002. Death Centenary of Archbishop Croke (first patron of Gaelic Athletic Association).
1554 **427** 44c. multicoloured . . . 80 70

2002. Irish Rock Legends. Multicoloured.
1555 41c. Type **428** 75 75
1556 41c. Phil Lynott 75 75
1557 57c. Van Morrison . . . . 1·00 1·10
1558 57c. Rory Gallagher . . . . 1·00 1·10
MS1559 Four sheets, each 150 × 90 mm. (a) €2 Type **428**. (b) €2 No. 1556. (c) €2 No. 1557. (d) €2 No. 1558 . . . . . . 12·00 13·00

2002. Christmas. Illustrations from "Les Tres Riches Heures du Duc de Berry" (medieval book of hours). Multicoloured. (a) Size 30 × 41 mm.
1560 41c. Type **429** 70 60
1561 44c. "The Annunciation to the Virgin Mary" 75 60
1562 57c. "The Annunciation to the Shepherds" . . . . . 1·00 1·10

(b) Size 25 × 30 mm. Self-adhesive.
1563 41c. "The Nativity" 80 60

430 Labrador Puppies

2003. Greetings Stamps. Baby Animals. Multicoloured. (a) 27 × 38 mm.
1564 41c. Type **430** 80 65

(b) Designs 23 × 27 mm. Self-adhesive.
1565 41c. Type **430** 80 80
1566 41c. Chicks 80 80
1567 41c. Kids 80 80
1568 41c. Kittens 80 80
1569 41c. Baby rabbits 80 80

2003. Chinese New Year ("Year of the Goat"). Designs as Nos. 1566/8, but 27 × 38 mm.
MS1570 124 × 74 mm. 50c. Chicks; 50c. Kids; 50c. Kittens . . . . 2·40 2·50

431 St. Patrick

2003. St. Patrick's Day. Multicoloured. Size 25 × 37 mm.
1571 41c. Type **431** 75 60
1572 50c. St. Patrick's Day Parade passing St. Patrick's Cathedral, Dublin 95 90
1573 57c. St. Patrick's Day Parade, New York . . . 1·10 1·25

(b) Size 22 × 30 mm. Self-adhesive.
1574 41c. St. Patrick 75 60
1575 50c. St. Patrick's Day Parade passing St. Patrick's Cathedral, Dublin 90 90
1576 57c. St. Patrick's Day Parade, New York . . . 1·00 1·50

432 Seven-spotted Ladybird

2003. Irish Beetles. Multicoloured.
1577 41c. Type **432** 75 60
1578 50c. Great diving beetle . . 65 90
1579 57c. Leaf beetle . . . . . . 1·10 1·10
1580 €1 Green tiger beetle . . . 1·90 2·25
MS1581 150 × 68 mm. €2 Type **432** 3·50 3·75

433 Dingle Peninsula ("IRELAND for HOLIDAYS")

2003. Europa. Poster Art. Posters by Paul Henry. Multicoloured.
1582 41c. Type **433** 75 65
1583 57c. Connemara ("IRELAND THIS YEAR") . . . . 1·00 1·10

434 "2003" and EYPD Logo

2003. European Year of People with Disabilities.
1584 **434** 41c. multicoloured . . . 75 60

435 Athletes waving to Crowd

2003. 11th Special Olympics World Summer Games, Dublin. Multicoloured.
1585 41c. Type **435** 75 60
1586 50c. Swimmer 90 70
1587 57c. Athlete on starting block . . . . 1·10 1·10
1588 €1 Athlete running . . . . 2·00 2·50

436 Napier

2003. Centenary of Gordon Bennett Race in Ireland. Racing cars of 1903. Multicoloured. (a) Ordinary gum. Size 38 × 28 mm.
1589 41c. Type **436** 80 90
1590 41c. Mercedes 80 90
1591 41c. Mors 80 90
1592 41c. Winton 80 90

(b) Self-adhesive. Size 33 × 22 mm.
1593 41c. As No. 1592 . . . . . 80 90
1594 41c. As No. 1591 . . . . . 80 90
1595 41c. As No. 1590 . . . . . 80 90
1596 41c. Type **436** 80 90

437 Henry Ford and Model T Ford, 1908–28

2003. Centenary of the Ford Motor Company.
1597 **437** 41c. multicoloured . . . 80 60

438 Harry Ferguson flying first Irish Monoplane, 1909

2003. Centenary of Powered Flight. Multicoloured.
1598 41c. Type **438** 80 60
1599 50c. Alcock and Brown's Vickers FB-27 Vimy over Galway after first transatlantic flight, 1919 1·10 1·00
1600 57c. *Wright Flyer I*, 1903 . . 1·25 1·50
1601 57c. Lillian Bland's biplane, 1910 . . . . 1·25 1·50
MS1602 150 × 90 mm. €5 As No. 1600 . . . . 8·00 8·50

439 Robert Emmet

2003. Centenary of Rebellion of 1803. Multicoloured.
1603 41c. Type **439** 85 60
1604 50c. Thomas Russell . . . . 1·10 1·10
1605 57c. Anne Devlin . . . . . 1·40 1·60

2003. 140th Anniv of National Gallery of Ireland (2004) (2nd issue). Paintings. As T **426** but vert. Multicoloured.

1606 48c. "Self-portrait as Timanthes" (James Barry) 1·00 1·10
1607 48c. "Man writing a Letter" (Gabriel Metsu) 1·00 1·10
1608 48c. "Woman reading a Letter" (Gabriel Metsu) 1·00 1·10
1609 48c. "Woman seen from the Back" (Jean-Antoine Watteau) 1·00 1·10

440 Frank O'Connor

441 E. T. S. Walton

2003. Birth Centenary of Frank O'Connor (writer).

1610 **440** 50c. multicoloured 1·00 1·00

2003. Birth Centenary of E. T. S. Walton (Nobel Prize for Physics, 1951).

1611 **441** 57c. cream, black and brown 1·25 1·40

442 Admiral William Brown (founder of the Argentine Navy)

2003. Irish Mariners. Multicoloured. (a) Ordinary gum. Size 40 × 26 mm.

1612 48c. Type **442** 1·00 1·00
1613 48c. Commodore John Barry (Commanding Officer of US Navy, 1794–1803) 1·00 1·00
1614 57c. Captain Robert Halpin (Commander of cable ship *Great Eastern*) 1·10 1·10
1615 57c. Captain Richard Roberts (captain of *Sirius*, first scheduled passenger steamship London to New York voyage) 1·10 1·10

(b) Self-adhesive. Size 32 × 21 mm.

1616 48c. Commodore John Barry 1·00 1·00
1617 48c. Admiral William Brown 1·00 1·00
1618 48c. Captain Robert Halpin 1·00 1·00
1619 48c. Captain Richard Roberts 1·00 1·00
MS1620 150 × 90 mm. €5 Commodore John Barry 8·00 8·50

443 Pope John Paul II

2003. 25th Anniv of the Election of Pope John Paul II. Multicoloured.

1621 48c. Type **443** 1·00 1·00
1622 50c. Pope in St. Peter's Square, Rome 1·10 1·10
1623 57c. Making speech at United Nations 1·25 1·25

444 Angel

2003. Christmas. Multicoloured. (a) Ordinary gum.

1624 48c. Flight into Egypt (32 × 32 mm) 90 70
1625 50c. Type **444** 1·00 75
1626 57c. Three Kings 1·10 1·40

(b) Self-adhesive. Size 26 × 21 mm.

1627 48c. Nativity 1·00 1·00

445 Boyne Bridge

2004. Ireland's Presidency of European Union.

1628 **445** 48c. multicoloured 1·00 1·00

446 "Monkeys in Love"

2004. Greetings Stamps. Animals. Multicoloured. Ordinary gum. Size 26 × 37 mm.

1629 48c. Type **446** 1·00 1·00
MS1630 124 × 74 mm. 60c. Type **446**; 60c. "Jolly Panda"; 60c. "Cute Koalas" 3·25 3·50

(b) Self-adhesive. Size 21 × 26 mm.

1631 48c. Type **446** 1·00 1·00
1632 48c. "Jolly Panda" 1·00 1·00
1633 48c. "Cute Koalas" 1·00 1·00
1634 48c. "Happy Hippo" 1·00 1·00

447 St. Patrick and Stained Glass Window from Church of the Holy and Undivided Trinity, Magheralin, Co. Down

2004. St. Patrick's Day.

1635 **447** 65c. multicoloured 1·50 1·50

448 Abbey Theatre Logo

2004. Centenary of Abbey Theatre, Dublin.

1636 **448** 48c. multicoloured 1·10 1·10

449 Expedition Members, Dogs and *Endurance* trapped in Ice

2004. 90th Anniv of Shackleton's Antarctic Expedition. Multicoloured.

1637 48c. Type **449** 1·25 1·00
1638 48c. Two crew members, huskies and bow of *Endurance* 1·25 1·00
1639 65c. Crew member looking out of tent 1·75 1·75
1640 65c. Crew members and tented camp on ice 1·75 1·75
MS1641 149 × 90 mm. €1 As No. 1639; €1 As No. 1640 4·50 4·50

450 Flags, Football and Globe

2004. Centenary of FIFA (Federation Internationale de Football Association).

1642 **450** 60c. multicoloured 1·40 1·40

451 Map of Europe showing Acceding Countries

2004. Enlargement of the European Union.

1643 **451** 65c. multicoloured 1·40 1·40

452 Tufted Duck

2004. Ducks. Multicoloured.

1644 48c. Type **452** 90 70
1645 60c. Red-breasted merganser 1·25 1·25
1646 65c. Gadwall 1·25 1·25
1647 €1 Garganey 1·90 2·00
MS1648 150 × 90 mm. Nos. 1644/7 4·75 5·00

453 Ross Castle, Co. Kerry

454 Emblem

2004. Europa. Holidays. Multicoloured.

1649 48c. Type **453** 90 70
1650 65c. Cliffs of Moher, Co. Clare 1·25 1·50

2004. 10th Anniv of UN International Year of the Family.

1651 **454** 65c. scarlet, yellow and green 1·25 1·25

455 "Frog" (Daire Lee)

456 "James Joyce" (Tullio Pericoli)

2004. Winning Entries in Children's Painting Competition. Multicoloured.

1652 48c. Type **455** 90 70
1653 60c. "Marmalade Cat" (Cian Colman) 1·25 1·25
1654 65c. "Ralleshin Dipditch" (Daire O'Rourke) 1·25 1·25
1655 €1 "Fish on a Dish" (Ailish Fitzpatrick) (horiz) 1·90 2·00

2004. Centenary of "Leopold Bloom's Adventure" (from *Ulysses* by James Joyce). Multicoloured.

1656 48c. Type **456** 65 70
1657 65c. James Joyce 85 90

457 College Entrance

458 LUAS Tram

2004. 426th Anniv of Irish College, Paris.

1658 **457** 65c. multicoloured 85 90

2004. Introduction of LUAS Tram System, Dublin. Multicoloured.

1659 48c. Type **458** 65 70
1660 48c. People accessing LUAS tram 65 70

459 Javelin Thrower and Olympic Flame

2004. Olympic Games, Athens. Multicoloured.

1661 48c. Type **459** 65 70
1662 60c. Discobolus (sculpture, Myron) and Olympic flame 80 85

460 Two Camogie Players and O'Duffy Cup

461 Common Dog-violet

2004. Centenary of Camogie (Gaelic game for women). Multicoloured.

1663 48c. Type **460** 65 70
1664 48c. Two players and Camogie emblem 65 70

2004. Wild Flowers. Multicoloured. (a) Size 23 × 26 mm. Ordinary gum.

1665 4c. Type **461** 10 10
1666 5c. Dandelion 10 10
1667 48c. Daisy 65 70
1668 48c. Primrose 65 70
1669 60c. Hawthorn 80 85
1670 65c. Bluebell 90 95
1671 €2 Lords-and-ladies (26 × 47 mm) 2·75 3·00
1672 €5 Dog-rose (47 × 26 mm) 6·75 7·00

(b) Size 23 × 29 mm. Self-adhesive.

1673 48c. Daisy 65 70
1674 48c. Primrose 65 70

2004. 140th Anniv of National Gallery of Ireland (3rd issue). As T **426**. Multicoloured.

1700 48c. "The House Builders" (Walter Osborne) 65 70
1701 48c. "Kitchen Maid with the Supper at Emmaus" (Diego Velazquez) 65 70
1702 48c. "The Lamentation over the Dead Christ" (Nicolas Poussin) 65 70
1703 48c. "The Taking of Christ" (Caravaggio) 65 70

462 William Butler Yeats

2004. Irish Winners of Nobel Prize for Literature. Multicoloured.

1704 (N) Type **462** 65 70
1705 (N) George Bernard Shaw 65 70
1706 (N) Samuel Beckett 65 70
1707 (N) Seamus Heaney 65 70

Nos. 1706 were inscribed "N" and sold for 48c.each. Stamps of similar designs were issued by Sweden.

463 George Fox (Founder of The Society of Friends ("Quakers"))

2004. 350th Anniv of Quakers in Ireland.

1708	**463** 60c. multicoloured . . .	65	70

464 Patrick Kavanagh

2004. Birth Centenary of Patrick Kavanagh (poet).

1709	**464** 48c. green and dull green	65	70

465 The Holy Family

2004. Christmas. Multicoloured.

1710	48c. Type **465**	65	70
1711	60c. The flight into Egypt	80	85
1712	65c. The Adoration of the Magi	90	95
	(b) Size 24 × 29 mm. Self-adhesive.		
1713	48c. The Holy Family . . .	65	70

466 Lovebirds

2005. Love, Greetings and Chinese New Year of the Rooster. Multicoloured. (a) Ordinary gum.

1714	48c. Type **466**	65	70
MS1715	130 × 74 mm. 60c. Rooster; 60c. Type **466**; 60c. Owl . . .	2·40	2·50
	(b) Self-adhesive. Designs 30 × 25 mm.		
1716	48c. Rooster	65	70
1717	48c. Stork	65	70
1718	48c. Type **466**	65	70
1719	48c. Owl	65	70

467 St. Patrick

2005. St. Patrick's Day.

1720	**467** 65c. multicoloured . . .	90	95

468 "Landscape, Co. Wicklow" (Evie Hone)

2005. Female Artists. Multicoloured.

1721	48c. Type **468**	65	70
1722	48c. "Seabird and Landmarks" (Nano Reid)	65	70
1723	65c. "Three Graces" (Gabriel Hayes) (vert) . .	90	95
1724	65c. "Threshing" (Mildred Anne Butler) (vert) . . .	90	95

469 Statue, City Hall and Churches

2005. Cork – European Capital of Culture 2005. Multicoloured.

1725	48c. Type **469**	65	70
1726	48c. Court House and Shandon Steeple (clock tower)	65	70

Nos. 1725/6 were printed together, se-tenant, forming a composite design showing Patrick's Bridge and a montage of landmark buildings and monuments of the city of Cork.

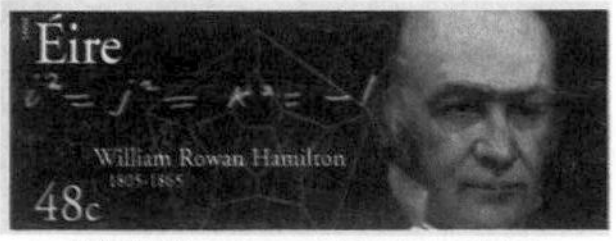

470 William Rowan Hamilton (birth bicentenary)

2005. UNESCO World Year of Physics. Multicoloured.

1727	48c. Type **470**		
1728	60c. UNESCO Headquarters, Paris, trees and reflections of sunlight	80	85
1729	65c. Albert Einstein (50th death anniv)	90	95

POSTAGE DUE STAMPS

D 1

1925.

D 1	D **1**	1½d. green	12·00	16·00
D 6		1d. red	1·50	70
D 7		1½d. orange	2·25	6·50
D 8		2d. green	2·75	70
D 9		3d. blue	2·50	2·75
D10		5d. violet	4·50	3·00
D11a		6d. plum	1·00	1·00
D12		8d. orange	8·50	9·00
D13		10d. purple	8·50	7·50
D14		1s. green	6·00	9·50

1971. Decimal Currency. Colours changed.

D15	D **1**	1p. brown	30	60
D16		1½p. green	40	1·50
D17		3p. stone	60	2·00
D18		4p. orange	60	1·25
D19		5p. blue	60	3·00
D20		7p. yellow	40	3·50
D21		8p. red	40	2·75

D 2

D 3

1980.

D25	D **2**	1p. green	30	70
D26		2p. blue	30	70
D27		4p. green	40	70
D28		6p. flesh	40	80
D29		8p. blue	40	85
D30		18p. green	75	1·25
D31		20p. red	2·25	5·50
D32		24p. green	75	2·00
D33		30p. violet	3·00	6·50
D34		50p. pink	3·75	7·50

1988.

D35	D **3**	1p. black, red and yellow	10	50
D36		2p. black, red and brown	10	50
D37		3p. black, red and purple	15	50
D38		4p. black, red and violet	15	50
D39		5p. black, red and blue	15	50
D40		17p. black, red and green	40	65
D41		20p. black, red and blue	55	80
D42		24p. black, red and green	60	85
D43		30p. black, red and grey	80	1·25
D44		50p. black, red and grey	1·25	1·75
D45		£1 black, red and brown	1·75	2·25

ISLE OF MAN Pt. 1

An island in the Irish Sea to the north-west of England. Man became a possession of the English Crown during the Middle Ages, but retains its own Assembly.

Regional issues from 1958 to 1971 are listed at end of "GREAT BRITAIN".

Isle of Man had an independent postal administration from 1973.

100 pence = 1 pound.

4 Castletown

5 Manx Cat

1973. Multicoloured.

12	½p. Type **4**	10	10
13	1p. Port Erin	10	10
14	1½p. Snaefell	10	10
15	2p. Laxey	10	10
16	2½p. Tynwald Hill	10	10
17	3p. Douglas Promenade . . .	10	10
18	3½p. Port St. Mary	10	10
19	4p. Fairy Bridge	10	10
20	4½p. As 2½p.	20	15
21	5p. Peel	15	10
22	5½p. As 3p.	20	15
23	6p. Cregneish	20	15
24	7p. As 2p.	20	15
25	7½p. Ramsey Bay	20	20
26	8p. As 7½p.	25	25
27	9p. Douglas Bay	20	20
28	10p. Type **5**	35	20
29	11p. Monk's Bridge, Ballasalla	35	30
30	13p. Derbyhaven	40	35
31	20p. Manx loaghtyn ram . . .	50	50
32	50p. Manx shearwater	1·20	1·10
33	£1 Viking longship	2·00	2·00

SIZES: Nos. 13/27 and 29/30 as Type **4**; Nos. 31/3 as Type **5**.

6 Viking Landing on Man, A.D. 938

1973. Inauguration of Postal Independence.

34	**6** 15p. multicoloured	35	30

7 No. 1 "Sutherland", 1873

1973. Cent of Steam Railway. Multicoloured.

35	2½p. Type **7**	15	10
36	3p. No. 4 "Caledonia", 1885	15	15
37	7½p. No. 13 "Kissack", 1910	25	25
38	9p. No. 3 "Pender", 1873 . .	25	25

8 Leonard Randles, First Winner, 1923

1973. Golden Jubilee of Manx Grand Prix. Mult.

39	3p. Type **8**	10	15
40	3½p. Alan Holmes, Double Winner, 1957	15	25

9 Princess Anne and Capt. Mark Phillips

1973. Royal Wedding.

41	**9** 25p. multicoloured	45	50

10 Badge, Citation and Sir William Hillary (founder)

1974. 150th Anniv of Royal National Lifeboat Institution. Multicoloured.

42	3p. Type **10**	10	10
43	3½p. Wreck of "St. George", 1830	15	10
44	8p. R.N.L.B. "Manchester and Salford", 1868–87	25	25
45	10p. R.N.L.B. "Osman Gabriel"	30	25

11 Stanley Woods, 1935

1974. Tourist Trophy Motor-cycle Races (1st issue). Multicoloured.

46	3p. Type **11**	10	10
47	3½p. Freddy Frith, 1937 . . .	10	10
48	8p. Max Deubel and Emil Horner, 1961	25	20
49	10p. Mike Hailwood, 1961 . .	25	20

See also Nos. 63/6.

12 Rushen Abbey and Arms

1974. Historical Anniversaries. Multicoloured.

50	3½p. Type **12**	10	10
51	4½p. Magnus Haraldson rows King Edgar on the Dee . .	10	10
52	8p. King Magnus and Norse fleet	15	15
53	10p. Bridge at Avignon and bishop's mitre	20	20

COMMEMORATIONS: Nos. 50 and 53, William Russell, Bishop of Sodor and Man, 600th death anniv; Nos. 51/2, 1000th anniv of rule of King Magnus Haraldson.

13 Churchill and Bugler Dunne at Colenso, 1899

1974. Birth Centenary of Sir Winston Churchill. Multicoloured.

54	3½p. Type **13**	10	10
55	4½p. Churchill and Government Buildings, Douglas	10	10
56	8p. Churchill and Manx ack-ack crew	15	15
57	20p. Churchill as Freeman of Douglas	30	25
MS58	121 × 91 mm. Nos. 54/7 . .	75	75

14 Cabin School and Names of Pioneers

1975. Manx Pioneers in Cleveland, Ohio. Multicoloured.

59	4½p. Type **14**	10	10
60	5½p. Terminal Tower Building, J. Gill and R. Carran . . .	10	10
61	8p. Clague House Museum, and Robert and Margaret Clague	15	15
62	10p. S.S. "William T. Graves" and Thomas Quayle	25	25

15 Tom Sheard, 1923

1975. Tourist Trophy Motor-cycle Races (2nd issue). Multicoloured.
63 5½p. Type **15** 10 10
64 7p. Walter Handley, 1925 . . 15 15
65 10p. Geoff Duke, 1955 . . . . 15 15
66 12p. Peter Williams, 1973 . . 25 20

16 Sir George Goldie and Birthplace

1975. 50th Death Anniv of Sir George Goldie. Multicoloured.
67 5½p. Type **16** 10 10
68 7p. Goldie and map of Africa (vert) 15 15
69 10p. Goldie as President of Geographical Society (vert) 15 15
70 12p. River scene on the Niger 25 25

17 Title Page of Manx Bible

18 William Christian listening to Patrick Henry

1975. Christmas and Bicentenary of Manx Bible. Multicoloured.
71 5½p. Type **17** 10 10
72 7p. Rev. Philip Moore and Ballaugh Old Church . . . 15 15
73 11p. Bishop Hildesley and Bishops Court 20 20
74 13p. John Kelly saving Bible manuscript 25 25

1976. Bicent of American Independence. Mult.
75 5½p. Type **18** 10 10
76 7p. Conveying the Fincastle Resolutions 15 15
77 13p. Patrick Henry and William Christian 30 30
78 20p. Christian as an Indian fighter 35 35
MS79 153 × 89 mm. Nos. 75/8 . . 80 1·00

19 First Horse Tram, 1876

1976. Cent of Douglas Horse-Trams. Mult.
80 5½p. Type **19** 10 10
81 7p. "Toast-rack" tram, 1890 15 15
82 11p. Horse-bus, 1895 . . . . 20 20
83 13p. Royal tram, 1972 . . . . 25 25

20 Barrose Beaker

21 Diocesan Banner

1976. Europa. Ceramic Art. Multicoloured.
84 5p. Type **20** 20 20
85 5p. Souvenir teapot 20 20
86 5p. Laxey jug 20 20
87 10p. Cronk Aust food vessel (horiz) 20 20
88 10p. Sansbury bowl (horiz) . . 20 20
89 10p. Knox urn (horiz) 20 20

1976. Christmas and Centenary of Mothers' Union. Multicoloured.
90 6p. Type **21** 10 10
91 7p. Onchan banner 15 15
92 11p. Castletown banner . . . 20 20
93 13p. Ramsey banner 25 25

22 Queen Elizabeth II

1977. Silver Jubilee. Multicoloured.
94 6p. Type **22** 10 10
95 7p. Queen Elizabeth and Prince Philip (vert) 20 20
96 25p. Queen Elizabeth (different) 50 50

23 Carrick Bay from "Tom-the-Dipper"

1977. Europa. Landscapes. Multicoloured.
97 6p. Type **23** 15 15
98 10p. View from Ramsey . . . 25 25

24 F. A. Applebee, 1912

1977. Linked Anniversaries. Multicoloured.
99 6p. Type **24** 15 10
100 7p. St. John's Ambulance Brigade at Governor's Bridge, 1938 . . . . 15 15
101 11p. Scouts operating the scoreboard 25 25
102 13p. John Williams, 1976 . . 25 30
The events commemorated are: 70th anniv of Manx TT races; 70th anniv of Boy Scouts; Centenary of St. John's Ambulance Brigade.

25 Old Summer House, Mount Morrison, Peel

27 Watch Tower, Langness

26 Short Type 184 Seaplane and H.M.S. "Ben-My-Chree", 1915

1977. Bicentenary of First Visit of John Wesley. Multicoloured.
103 6p. Type **25** 15 10
104 7p. Wesley preaching in Castletown Square 15 15
105 11p. Wesley preaching outside Braddan Church 25 25
106 13p. New Methodist Church, Douglas 25 25
Nos. 104/5 are larger, 38 × 26 mm.

1978. 60th Anniv of Royal Air Force. Mult.
107 6p. Type **26** 15 10
108 7p. Bristol Scout C and H.M.S. "Vindex", 1915 . . 15 15
109 11p. Boulton Paul Defiant over Douglas Bay, 1941 . . 25 25
110 13p. Sepecat Jaguar over Ramsey, 1977 . . . . . . 25 25

1978. Multicoloured.
111 ½p. Type **27** 10 10
112 1p. Jurby Church (horiz) . . 10 10
113 6p. Government Buildings 30 30
114 7p. Tynwald Hill (horiz) . . 35 35
115 8p. Milner's Tower 25 25
116 9p. Laxey Wheel 35 35
117a 10p. Castle Rushen (horiz) 35 35
118 11p. St. Ninian's Church . . 40 40
119 12p. Tower of Refuge (horiz) 40 25
120a 13p. St. German's Cathedral (horiz) 30 25
121a 14p. Point of Ayre Lighthouse (horiz) 30 25
122a 15p. Corrin's Tower (horiz) 30 25
123 16p. Douglas Head Lighthouse (horiz) 55 30
124 20p. Fuchsia 50 35
125 25p. Manx cat 65 45
126 50p. Red-billed chough ("Chough") 90 75
127 £1 Viking warrior . . . . . 1·90 2·00
128 £2 Queen Elizabeth II . . . 3·50 3·50
Nos. 124/78 are larger, 25 × 31 mm and No. 128, 38 × 48 mm.

28 Queen Elizabeth in Coronation Regalia

29 Wheel-headed Cross-slab

1978. 25th Anniv of Coronation.
132 **28** 25p. multicoloured 50 45

1978. Europa. Celtic and Norse Crosses. Multicoloured.
133 6p. Type **29** 10 10
134 6p. Celtic wheel-cross 10 10
135 6p. Keeil Chiggyrt Stone . . 10 10
136 11p. Olaf Liotulfson Cross 20 20
137 11p. Odd's and Thorleif's Crosses 20 20
138 11p. Thor Cross 20 20

30 J. K. Ward and Ward Library, Peel

1978. Anniversaries and Events. Multicoloured.
139 6p. Type **30** 10 10
140 7p. Swimmer, cyclist and walker (42 × 26 mm) . . . 20 15
141 11p. American bald eagle, Manx arms and maple leaf (42 × 26 mm) 25 25
142 13p. Lumber camp, Three Rivers, Quebec 25 25
ANNIVERSARIES AND EVENTS: 6, 13p. James Kewley Ward (Manx pioneer in Canada) commemoration; 7p. Commonwealth Games, Edmonton; 11p. 50th anniv of North American Manx Association.

31 Hunt the Wren

33 Postman, 1859

32 P. M. C. Kermode and "Nassa kermodei"

1978. Christmas.
143 **31** 5p. multicoloured 20 20

1979. Centenary of Natural History and Antiquarian Society. Multicoloured.
144 6p. Type **32** 10 10
145 7p. Peregrine falcon 20 15
146 11p. Fulmar 25 25
147 13p. "Epitriptus cowini" (fly) 25 25

1979. Europa. Communications. Multicoloured.
148 6p. Type **33** 15 10
149 11p. Postman, 1979 . . . . . 25 25

34 Viking Longship Emblem

35 Viking Raid at Garwick

1979. Millennium of Tynwald. Multicoloured.
150b 3p. Type **34** 10 10
151 4p. "Three Legs of Man" emblem 10 10
152 6p. Type **35** 15 10
153 7p. 10th-century meeting of Tynwald 20 20
154 11p. Tynwald Hill and St. John's Church 25 25
155 13p. Procession to Tynwald Hill 30 25
The 4p. value is as Type **34** and the remainder as Type **35**.

36 Queen and Court on Tynwald Hill

1979. Royal Visit. Multicoloured.
156 7p. Type **36** 15 15
157 13p. Queen and procession from St. John's Church to Tynwald Hill 25 25

37 "Odin's Raven"

1979. Voyage of "Odin's Raven".
158 **37** 15p. multicoloured 35 30

38 John Quilliam seized by the Press Gang

1979. 150th Death Anniv of Captain John Quilliam. Multicoloured.
159 6p. Type **38** 15 15
160 8p. Steering H.M.S. "Victory", Battle of Trafalgar 20 15
161 13p. Captain John Quilliam and H.M.S. "Spencer" . . 25 25
162 15p. Captain John Quilliam (member of the House of Keys) 30 25

39 Young Girl with Teddybear and Cat

1979. Christmas. Int Year of the Child. Mult.
163 5p. Type **39** 10 10
164 7p. Father Christmas with young children 20 20

40 Conglomerate Arch, Langness

1980. 150th Anniv of Royal Geographical Society. Multicoloured.
165 7p. Type **40** 15 15
166 8p. Braaid Circle 20 20
167 12p. Cashtal-yn-Ard 25 25
168 13p. Volcanic rocks at Scarlett 25 25
169 15p. Sugar-loaf Rock 30 25

41 "Mona's Isle I"

1980. 150th Anniv of Isle of Man Steam Packet Company. Multicoloured.
170 7p. Type **41** 15 15
171 8p. "Douglas I" 20 20
172 11½p. H.M.S. "Mona's Queen II" sinking U-boat 20 25

173 12p. H.M.S. "King Orry III" at surrender of German fleet, 1918 . . . . 25 25
174 13p. "Ben-My-Chree IV" . . 25 25
175 15p. "Lady of Mann II" . . 30 25
MS176 180 × 125 mm. Nos. 170/5 1·25 1·25
No. MS176 was issued to commemorate "London 1980" International Stamp Exhibition.

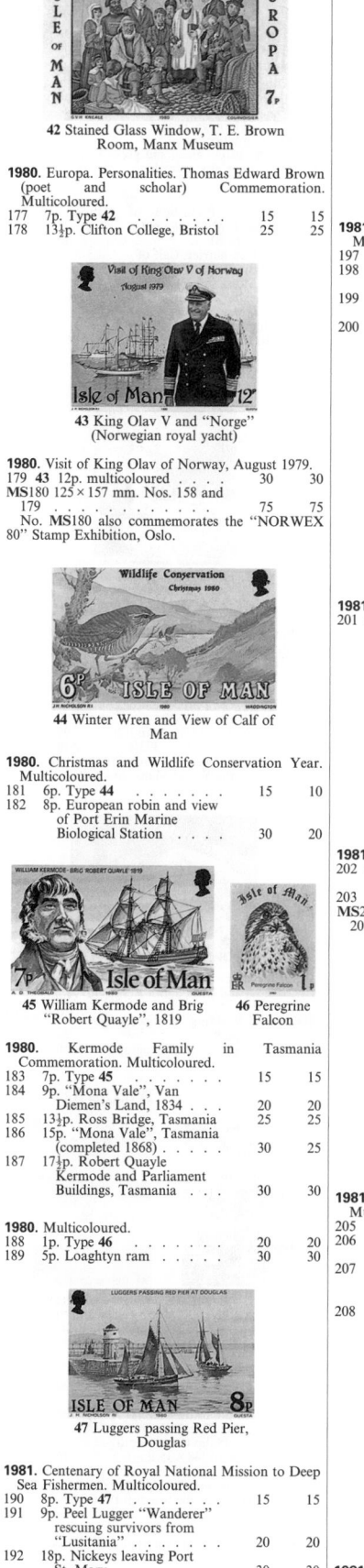

42 Stained Glass Window, T. E. Brown Room, Manx Museum

1980. Europa. Personalities. Thomas Edward Brown (poet and scholar) Commemoration. Multicoloured.
177 7p. Type **42** 15 15
178 13½p. Clifton College, Bristol 25 25

43 King Olav V and "Norge" (Norwegian royal yacht)

1980. Visit of King Olav of Norway, August 1979.
179 **43** 12p. multicoloured 30 30
MS180 125 × 157 mm. Nos. 158 and 179 . . . . 75 75
No. MS180 also commemorates the "NORWEX 80" Stamp Exhibition, Oslo.

44 Winter Wren and View of Calf of Man

1980. Christmas and Wildlife Conservation Year. Multicoloured.
181 6p. Type **44** 15 10
182 8p. European robin and view of Port Erin Marine Biological Station 30 20

45 William Kermode and Brig "Robert Quayle", 1819

46 Peregrine Falcon

1980. Kermode Family in Tasmania Commemoration. Multicoloured.
183 7p. Type **45** 15 15
184 9p. "Mona Vale", Van Diemen's Land, 1834 . . . 20 20
185 13½p. Ross Bridge, Tasmania 25 25
186 15p. "Mona Vale", Tasmania (completed 1868) 30 25
187 17½p. Robert Quayle Kermode and Parliament Buildings, Tasmania . . . 30 30

1980. Multicoloured.
188 1p. Type **46** 20 20
189 5p. Loaghtyn ram 30 30

47 Luggers passing Red Pier, Douglas

1981. Centenary of Royal National Mission to Deep Sea Fishermen. Multicoloured.
190 8p. Type **47** 15 15
191 9p. Peel Lugger "Wanderer" rescuing survivors from "Lusitania" 20 20
192 18p. Nickeys leaving Port St. Mary 30 30
193 20p. Nobby entering Ramsey Harbour 30 30
194 22p. Nickeys "Sunbeam" and "Zebra" at Port Erin . . . 35 35

48 "Crosh Cuirn" Superstition

1981. Europa. Folklore. Multicoloured.
195 8p. Type **48** 15 10
196 18p. "Bollan Cross" superstition 30 30

49 Lt. Mark Wilks (Royal Manx Fencibles) and Peel Castle

1981. 150th Death Anniv of Colonel Mark Wilks. Multicoloured.
197 8p. Type **49** 20 20
198 20p. Ensign Mark Wilks and Fort St. George, Madras 30 30
199 22p. Governor Mark Wilks and Napoleon, St. Helena 40 35
200 25p. Col. Mark Wilks (Speaker of the House of Keys) and estate, Kirby . . 45 35

50 Miss Emmeline Goulden (Mrs. Pankhurst) and Mrs. Sophia Jane Goulden

1981. Centenary of Manx Women's Suffrage.
201 **50** 9p. black, grey and stone 20 20

51 Prince Charles and Lady Diana Spencer

1981. Royal Wedding.
202 **51** 9p. black, blue and light blue 15 20
203 25p. black, blue and pink 75 80
MS204 130 × 183 mm. Nos. 202/3 × 2 . . . . 2·00 2·00

52 Douglas War Memorial, Poppies and Commemorative Inscription

1981. 60th Anniv of The Royal British Legion. Multicoloured.
205 8p. Type **52** 20 20
206 10p. Major Robert Cain (war hero) 25 25
207 18p. Festival of Remembrance, Royal Albert Hall 30 30
208 20p. T.S.S. "Tynwald" at Dunkirk, May 1940 . . . 35 35

53 Nativity Scene (stained glass window, St. George's Church)

1981. Christmas. Multicoloured.
209 7p. Type **53** 15 15
210 9p. Children from Special School performing nativity play (48 × 30 mm) 20 20

54 Joseph and William Cunningham (founders of Isle of Man Boy Scout Movement) and Cunningham House Headquarters

1982. 75th Anniv of Boy Scout Movement and 125th Birth Anniv of Lord Baden-Powell. Multicoloured.
211 9p. Type **54** 20 15
212 10p. Baden-Powell visiting Isle of Man, 1911 . . . . 25 25
213 19½p. Baden-Powell and Scout emblem (40 × 31 mm) 45 40
214 24p. Scouts and Baden-Powell's last message . . . 50 45
215 29p. Scout salute, handshake, emblem and globe 70 60

55 "The Principals and Duties of Christianity" (Bishop T. Wilson) (first book printed in Manx, 1707)

1982. Europa. Historic Events. Multicoloured.
216 9p. Type **55** 15 10
217 19½p. Landing at Derbyhaven (visit of Thomas, 2nd Earl of Derby, 1507) 40 40

56 Charlie Collier (first TT race (single cylinder) winner) and Tourist Trophy Race, 1907

1982. 75th Anniv of Tourist Trophy Motorcycle Racing. Multicoloured.
218 9p. Type **56** 15 15
219 10p. Freddie Dixon (Sidecar and Junior TT winner) and Junior TT Race, 1927 . . . 15 15
220 24p. Jimmie Simpson (TT winner and first to lap at 60, 70 and 80 mph) and Senior TT, 1932 . . . . . 60 50
221 26p. Mike Hailwood (winner of fourteen TT's) and Senior TT, 1961 . . . . . 60 50
222 29p. Jock Taylor (Sidecar TT winner, 1978, 1980 and 1981) and Sidecar TT (with Benga Johansson), 1980 . . 60 55

57 "Mona I"

1982. 150th Anniv of Isle of Man Steam Packet Company Mail Contract. Multicoloured.
223 12p. Type **57** 30 25
224 19½p. "Manx Maid II" . . . 75 70

58 Three Wise Men bearing Gifts

1982. Christmas. Multicoloured.
225 8p. Type **58** 15 15
226 11p. Christmas snow scene (vert) 30 30

59 Princess Diana with Prince William

1982. 21st Birthday of Princess of Wales and Birth of Prince William. Sheet 100 × 83 mm.
MS227 **59** 50p. multicoloured . . 1·50 1·50

60 Opening of Salvation Army Citadel, and T. H. Cannell, J.P.

1983. Centenary of Salvation Army in Isle of Man. Multicoloured.
228 10p. Type **60** 20 15
229 12p. Early meeting place and Gen. William Booth . . . 30 25
230 19½p. Salvation Army band 45 45
231 26p. Treating lepers and Lt.-Col. Thomas Bridson . . . 65 60

61 Atlantic Puffins ("Puffins")

61a "Queen Elizabeth II" (Ricardo Macarron)

1983. Sea Birds. Multicoloured.
232 1p. Type **61** 30 30
233 2p. Northern gannets ("Gannets") 30 30
234 5p. Lesser black-backed gulls 60 40
235 8p. Great cormorants ("Cormorants") 60 40
236 10p. Black-legged kittiwakes ("Kittiwakes") 60 35
237 11p. Shags 60 35
238 12p. Grey herons ("Herons") 70 40
239 13p. Herring gulls 70 40
240 14p. Razorbills 70 40
241 15p. Greater black-backed gulls ("Great Black-backed Gulls") 80 50
242 16p. Common shelducks ("Shelducks") 80 50
243 18p. Oystercatchers 80 50
244 20p. Arctic terns . . . . . . 1·00 70
245 25p. Common guillemots ("Guillemots") . . . . . . 1·25 75
246 50p. Common redshank ("Redshanks") . . . . . . 1·75 1·50
247 £1 Mute swans . . . . . . 3·00 2·25
248 £5 Type **61a** . . . . 9·00 10·00
Nos. 244/7 are larger, 39 × 26 mm.

62 Design Drawings by Roger Casement for the Great Laxey Wheel (½-size illustration)

1983. Europa. The Great Laxey Wheel.
249 **62** 10p. black, blue and buff 25 20
250 – 20½p. multicoloured . . . 50 55
DESIGN: 20½p. Roger Casement and the Great Laxey Wheel.

63 Nick Keig (international yachtsman) and Trimaran "Three Legs of Man III"

1983. 150th Anniv of King William's College. Multicoloured.

251	10p. Type **63**	15	15
252	12p. King William's College, Castletown	20	20
253	28p. Sir William Bragg (winner of Nobel Prize for Physics) and spectrometer	55	55
254	31p. General Sir George White, V.C. and action at Charasiah	65	65

64 New Post Office Headquarters, Douglas

1983. World Communications Year and 10th Anniv of Isle of Man Post Office Authority. Multicoloured.

255	10p. Type **64**	25	25
256	15p. As Type **64** but inscr "POST OFFICE DECENNIUM 1983"	35	40

65 Shepherds

1983. Christmas. Multicoloured.

257	9p. Type **65**	20	20
258	12p. Three Kings	30	30

66 "Manx King" (full-rigged ship)

1984. The Karran Fleet. Multicoloured.

259	10p. Type **66**	20	15
260	13p. "Hope" (barque)	30	20
261	20½p. "Rio Grande" (brig)	45	35
262	28p. "Lady Elizabeth" (barque)	65	50
263	31p. "Sumatra" (barque)	75	65

MS264 103 × 94 mm. 28p. As No. 262; 31p. "Lady Elizabeth" (as shown on Falkland Islands No. 417) (sold at 60p.) . . . . 2·25 1·50

No. **MS**264 was issued to commemorate links between the Isle of Man and the Falkland Islands.

67 C.E.P.T. 25th Anniversary Logo

69 Window from Glencrutchery House, Douglas

68 Railway Air Services De Havilland D.H.84 Dragon Mk 2

1984. Europa.

265	**67**	10p. orange, brown and light orange	30	25
266		20½p. blue, deep blue and light blue	50	50

1984. 50th Anniv of First Official Airmail to the Isle of Man and 40th Anniv of International Civil Aviation Organization. Multicoloured.

267	11p. Type **68**	35	30
268	13p. West Coast Air Services De Havilland D.H. 86A Dragon Express "Ronaldsway"	40	30
269	26p. B.E.A. Douglas DC-3	70	65
270	28p. B.E.A. Vickers Viscount 800	70	65
271	31p. Telair Britten Norman Islander	70	65

1984. Christmas. Stained-glass Windows. Multicoloured.

272	10p. Type **69**	20	20
273	13p. Window from Lonan Old Church	40	40

70 William Cain's Birthplace, Ballasalla

1984. William Cain (civic leader, Victoria) Commemoration. Multicoloured.

274	11p. Type **70**	25	20
275	22p. The "Anna" leaving Liverpool, 1852	50	50
276	28p. Early Australian railway	70	65
277	30p. William Cain as Mayor of Melbourne, and Town Hall	75	65
278	33p. Royal Exhibition Building, Melbourne	70	65

71 Queen Elizabeth II and Commonwealth Parliamentary Association Badge

1984. Links with the Commonwealth. 30th Commonwealth Parliamentary Association Conference. Multicoloured.

279	14p. Type **71**	35	35
280	33p. Queen Elizabeth II and Manx emblem	65	65

72 Cunningham House Headquarters and Mrs. Willie Cunningham and Mrs. Joseph Cunningham (former Commissioners)

1985. 75th Anniv of Girl Guide Movement. Multicoloured.

281	11p. Type **72**	30	25
282	14p. Princess Margaret, Isle of Man standard and guides	35	30
283	29p. Lady Olave Baden-Powell opening Guide Headquarters, 1955	70	60
284	31p. Guide uniforms from 1910 to 1985	75	75
285	34p. Guide handclasp, salute and early badge	90	85

73 Score of Manx National Anthem

1985. Europa. European Music Year.

286	**73**	12p. black, light brown and brown	30	30
287	–	12p. black, light brown & brown	30	30
288	–	22p. black, light blue & blue	80	70
289	–	22p. black, light blue & blue	80	70

DESIGNS: No. 287, William H. Gill (lyricist); 288, Score of hymn "Crofton"; 289, Dr. John Clague (composer).

74 Charles Rolls in 20 h.p. Rolls-Royce (1906 Tourist Trophy Race)

1985. Century of Motoring. Multicoloured.

290	12p. Type **74**	25	25
291	12p. W. Bentley in 3 litre Bentley (1922 Tourist Trophy Race)	25	25
292	14p. F. Gerrard in E.R.A. (1950 British Empire Trophy Race)	30	25
293	14p. Brian Lewis in Alfa Romeo (1934 Mannin Moar Race)	30	25
294	31p. Jaguar "XJ-SC" ("Roads Open" car, 1984 Motor Cycle TT Races)	1·00	80
295	31p. Tony Pond and Mike Nicholson in Vauxhall "Chevette" (1981 Rothmans International Rally)	1·00	80

75 Queen Alexandra and Victorian Sergeant with Wife

1985. Centenary of Soldiers', Sailors' and Airmen's Families Association. Association Presidents. Multicoloured.

296	12p. Type **75**	25	20
297	15p. Queen Mary and Royal Air Force family	35	30
298	29p. Earl Mountbatten and Royal Navy family	65	55
299	34p. Prince Michael of Kent and Royal Marine with parents, 1982	90	85

76 Kirk Maughold (birthplace)

1985. Birth Bicentenary of Lieutenant-General Sir Mark Cubbon (Indian administrator). Mult.

300	12p. Type **76**	30	25
301	22p. Lieutenant-General Sir Mark Cubbon (vert)	70	65
302	45p. Memorial statue, Bangalore, India (vert)	1·00	95

77 St. Peter's Church, Onchan

1985. Christmas. Manx Churches. Multicoloured.

303	11p. Type **77**	30	25
304	14p. Royal Chapel of St. John, Tynwald	40	35
305	31p. Bride Parish Church	1·00	90

78 Swimming

1986. Commonwealth Games, Edinburgh. Mult.

306	12p. Type **78**	20	15
307	15p. Race walking	25	30
308	31p. Rifle-shooting	90	95
309	34p. Cycling	1·00	95

No. 309 also commemorates the 50th anniversary of Manx International Cycling Week.

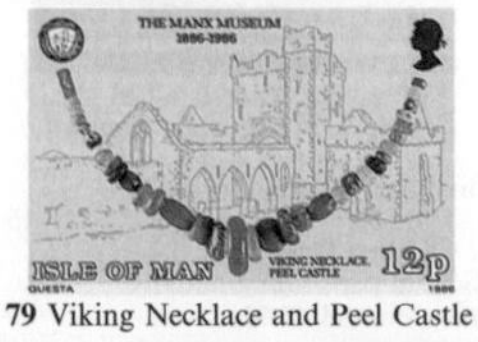

79 Viking Necklace and Peel Castle

1986. Centenary of Manx Museum. Multicoloured.

310	12p. Type **79**	20	15
311	15p. Meayll Circle, Rushen	25	20
312	22p. Skeleton of Great Deer and Manx Museum (vert)	65	50
313	26p. Viking longship model (vert)	80	60
314	29p. Open Air Museum, Cregneash	90	60

80 Viking Longship

81 "Usnea articulata" (lichen) and "Neotinea intacta" (orchid), The Ayres

1986. Manx Heritage Year.

315	**80**	2p. multicoloured	40	40
316	–	10p. black, green and grey	35	35

DESIGN: 10p. Celtic cross logo.

1986. Europa. Protection of Nature and the Environment. Multicoloured.

317	12p. Type **81**	30	30
318	12p. Hen harrier, Calf of Man	30	30
319	22p. Manx stoat, Eary Cushlin	60	60
320	22p. "Stenobothus stigmaticus" (grasshopper), St. Michael's Isle	60	60

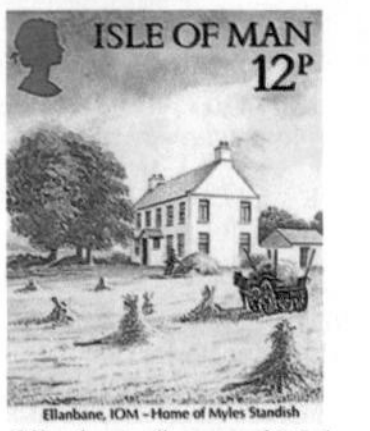

82 Ellanbane (home of Myles Standish)

1986. "Ameripex '86" International Stamp Exhibition, Chicago. Captain Myles Standish of the "Mayflower". Multicoloured.

321	12p. Type **82**	20	20
322	15p. "Mayflower" crossing the Atlantic, 1620	25	25
323	31p. Pilgrim Fathers landing at Plymouth, 1620	90	90
324	34p. Captain Myles Standish	95	95
MS325	100 × 75 mm. Nos. 323/4	2·10	2·10

No. **MS**325 also commemorates the 75th anniversary of the World Manx Association.

83 Prince Andrew in Naval Uniform and Miss Sarah Ferguson

1986. Royal Wedding. Multicoloured.

326	15p. Type **83**	25	25
327	40p. Engagement photograph	1·50	90

84 Prince Philip (from photo by Karsh)

85 European Robins on Globe and "Peace and Goodwill" in Braille

1986. Royal Birthdays. Multicoloured.

328	15p. Type **84**	30	30
329	15p. Queen Elizabeth II (from photo by Karsh)	30	30
330	34p. Queen Elizabeth and Prince Philip (from photo by Karsh) (48 × 35 mm)	1·10	1·10

Nos. 328/30 also commemorate "Stockholmia '86" International Stamp Exhibition, Sweden and the 350th anniversary of the Swedish Post Office.

1986. Christmas and International Peace Year. Multicoloured.

331	11p. Type **85**	30	30
332	14p. Hands releasing peace dove	30	30
333	31p. Clasped hands and "Peace" in sign language	80	80

86 North Quay

1987. Victorian Douglas. Multicoloured.
334 2p. Type **86** 10 10
335 3p. Old Fishmarket 10 10
336 10p. The Breakwater 25 25
337 15p. Jubilee Clock 30 30
338 31p. Loch Promenade . . . 90 80
339 34p. Beach . . . . 1·00 1·90

87 "The Old Fishmarket and Harbour, Douglas"

1987. Paintings by John Miller Nicholson. Multicoloured.
340 12p. Type **87** 20 20
341 26p. "Red Sails at Douglas" 70 60
342 29p. "The Double Corner, Peel" 90 80
343 34p. "Peel Harbour" . . . . 1·00 1·00

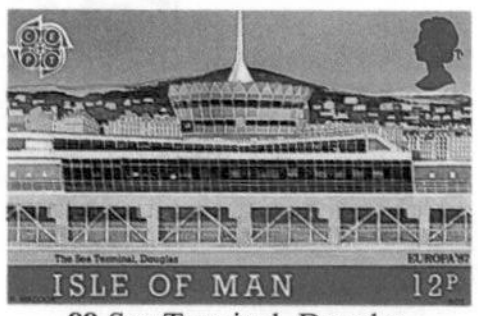

88 Sea Terminal, Douglas

1987. Europa. Architecture. Multicoloured.
344 12p. Type **88** 45 40
345 12p. Tower of Refuge, Douglas 45 40
346 22p. Gaiety Theatre, Douglas 65 50
347 22p. Villa Marina, Douglas 65 50

89 Supercharged "BMW" 500cc Motor Cycle, 1939

1987. 80th Anniv of Tourist Trophy Motor Cycle Races. Multicoloured.
348 12p. Type **89** 45 25
349 15p. Manx "Kneeler" Norton 350cc, 1953 . . . . . . 50 35
350 29p. MV Agusta 500cc 4, 1956 . . . . 90 70
351 31p. Guzzi 500cc V8, 1957 90 75
352 34p. Honda 250cc 6, 1967 . . 1·00 90
MS353 150 × 140 mm. Nos. 348/52 3·50 3·50

Nos. 348/**MS**353 also commemorate the Centenary of the St. John Ambulance Brigade and No. **MS**353 carries the logo of "Capex '87" International Stamp Exhibition, Toronto, on its margin.

90 Fuchsia and Wild Roses

91 Stirring the Christmas Pudding

1987. Wild Flowers. Multicoloured.
354 16p. Type **90** 50 30
355 29p. Field scabious and ragwort 90 80
356 31p. Wood anemone and celandine 90 80
357 34p. Violets and primroses 1·00 80

1987. Christmas. Victorian Scenes. Multicoloured.
358 12p. Type **91** 40 35
359 15p. Bringing home the Christmas tree 50 55
360 31p. Decorating the Christmas tree 90 90

92 Russell Brookes in Vauxhall "Opel" (Manx Rally winner, 1985)

1988. Motor Sport. Multicoloured.
361 13p. Type **92** 75 35
362 26p. Ari Vatanen in Ford "Escort" (Manx Rally winner, 1976) . . . . . . 1·25 80
363 31p. Terry Smith in Repco "March 761" (Hill Climb winner, 1980) . . . . . . 1·40 90
364 34p. Nigel Mansell in Williams/Honda (British Grand Prix winner, 1986 and 1987) . . . . 1·60 1·00

93 Horse Tram Terminus, Douglas Bay Tramway

93a Queen Elizabeth II taking Salute at Trooping the Colour

1988. Manx Railways and Tramways. Mult.
365 1p. Type **93** 10 10
366 2p. Snaefell Mountain Railway 10 10
367 3p. Marine Drive Tramway 10 10
367c 4p. Douglas Cable Tramway 20 10
368 5p. Douglas Head Incline Railway 20 20
369 10p. Douglas & Laxey Coast Electric Tramway car at Maughold Head . . 30 30
370 13p. As 4p. 50 50
371 14p. Manx Northern Railway No. 4, "Caledonia", at Gob-y-Deigan 50 50
372 15p. Laxey Mine Railway Lewin locomotive "Ant" 50 50
373 16p. Port Erin Breakwater Tramway locomotive "Henry B. Loch" 50 50
374 17p. Ramsey Harbour Tramway 50 50
375 18p. Locomotive No. 7, "Tynwald", on Foxdale line 55 55
375a 18p. T.P.O. Special leaving Douglas, 3 July 1991 . . 70 70
376 19p. Baldwin Reservoir Tramway steam locomotive No. 1, "Injebreck" 60 60
377 20p. I.M.R. No. 13, "Kissack", near St. Johns 60 60
377a 21p. As 14p. 60 60
377b 23p. Double-deck horse tram, Douglas 80 80
378 25p. I.M.R. No. 12, "Hutchinson", leaving Douglas 60 60
379 50p. Groudle Glen Railway locomotive "Polar Bear" 1·30 1·20
380 £1 I.M.R. No. 11, "Maitland", pulling Royal Train, 1963 . . . . . . 2·50 2·50
380a £2 Type **93a** . . . . 5·00 5·00

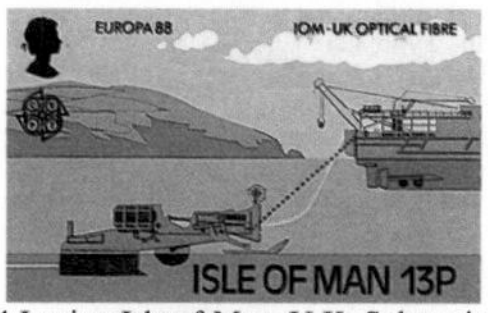

94 Laying Isle of Man–U.K. Submarine Cable

1988. Europa. Transport and Communications. Multicoloured.
381 13p. Type **94** 50 45
382 13p. "Flex Services" (cable ship) 50 45
383 22p. Earth station, Braddan 75 75
384 22p. "INTELSAT 5" satellite 75 75

Nos. 381/2 and 383/4 were each printed together, se-tenant, Nos. 381/2 forming a composite design.

95 "Euterpe" (full-rigged ship) off Ramsey, 1863

1988. Manx Sailing Ships. Multicoloured.
385 16p. Type **95** 45 30
386 29p. "Vixen" (topsail schooner) leaving Peel for Australia, 1853 . . . . . 90 90
387 31p. "Ramsey" (full-rigged ship) off Brisbane, 1870 . . 90 90
388 34p. "Star of India" (formerly "Euterpe") (barque) off San Diego, 1976 . . . . 1·10 1·10
MS389 110 × 85 mm. Nos. 385 and 388 . . . . 1·90 2·00

Nos. 386/7 also commemorate the Bicent of Australian Settlement.

96 "Magellanica"

1988. 50th Anniv of British Fuchsia Society. Multicoloured.
390 13p. Type **96** 40 25
391 16p. "Pink Cloud" 45 35
392 22p. "Leonora" 65 50
393 29p. "Satellite" 90 65
394 31p. "Preston Guild" . . . . 1·00 70
395 34p. "Thalia" . . . . 1·10 70

97 Long-eared Owl

1988. Christmas. Manx Birds. Multicoloured.
396 12p. Type **97** 40 30
397 15p. European robin 60 65
398 31p. Grey partridge . . . . 1·25 1·25

98 Ginger Cat

1989. Manx Cats. Multicoloured.
399 16p. Type **98** 50 25
400 27p. Black and white cat . . 90 85
401 30p. Tortoiseshell and white cat . . . . 1·25 85
402 40p. Tortoiseshell cat . . . . 1·50 1·25

99 Tudric Pewter Clock, c. 1903

1989. 125th Birth Anniv of Archibald Knox (artist and designer). Multicoloured.
403 13p. Type **99** 40 20
404 16p. "Celtic Cross" watercolour 50 25
405 23p. Silver cup and cover 1902–03 . . . . 65 50
406 32p. Gold and silver brooches from Liberty's Cymric range (horiz) . . . . . . 1·25 1·00
407 35p. Silver jewel box, 1900 (horiz) . . . . 1·40 1·00

100 William Bligh and Old Church, Onchan

1989. Bicentenary of the Mutiny on the "Bounty". Multicoloured.
408 13p. Type **100** 40 20
409 16p. Bligh and loyal crew cast adrift 45 30
410 23p. Pitcairn Islands 1989 Settlement Bicentenary 90c., No. 345 . . . . 1·00 1·00
411 27p. Norfolk Island 1989 Bicentenary 39c., No. 461 1·00 1·00
412 30p. Midshipman Peter Heywood and Tahiti . . . 70 60
413 32p. H.M.S. "Bounty" anchored off Pitcairn Island 70 60
414 35p. Fletcher Christian and Pitcairn Island 70 60
MS415 110 × 85 mm. Nos. 410/11 and 414 . . . . 4·00 4·25

101 Skipping and Hopscotch

1989. Europa. Children's Games. Multicoloured.
416 13p. Type **101** 45 50
417 13p. Wheelbarrow, leapfrog and piggyback 45 50
418 23p. Completing model house and blowing bubbles . . . 70 75
419 23p. Girl with doll and doll's house 70 75

Nos. 416/17 and 418/19 were printed together, se-tenant, forming composite designs.

102 Atlantic Puffin

104 Mother with Baby, Jane Crookall Maternity Home

103 Red Cross Cadets learning Resuscitation

1989. Sea Birds. Multicoloured.
420 13p. Type **102** 55 55
421 13p. Black guillemot 55 55
422 13p. Great cormorant ("Cormorant") 55 55
423 13p. Black-legged kittiwake ("Kittiwake") 55 55

1989. 125th Anniv of International Red Cross and Centenary of Noble's Hospital, Isle of Man.
424 **103** 14p. multicoloured . . . 40 30
425 – 17p. grey and red 60 35
426 – 23p. multicoloured . . . 75 85
427 – 30p. multicoloured . . . 1·00 1·10
428 – 35p. multicoloured . . . 1·25 1·25

DESIGNS: 17p. Anniversary logo; 23p. Signing Geneva Convention, 1864; 30p. Red Cross ambulance; 35p. Henri Dunant (founder).

1989. Christmas. 50th Anniv of Jane Crookall Maternity Home and 75th Anniv of St. Ninian's Church, Douglas. Multicoloured.
429 13p. Type **104** 50 45
430 16p. Mother with child . . . 60 60
431 34p. Madonna and Child . . 1·10 1·25
432 37p. Baptism, St. Ninian's Church . . . . 1·25 1·40

105 "The Isle of Man Express going up a Gradient"

1990. Isle of Man Edwardian Postcards. Mult.
433 15p. Type **105** 35 35
434 19p. "A way we have in the Isle of Man" 60 50
435 32p. "Douglas-waiting for the male boat" . . . . . . 1·10 80
436 34p. "The last toast rack home, Douglas Parade" . . 1·50 1·10
437 37p. "The last Isle of Man boat" . . . . 1·60 1·50

106 Modern Postman

107 Penny Black

1990. Europa. Post Office Buildings. Mult.
438 15p. Type **106** 55 55
439 15p. Ramsey Post Office, 1990 (40 × 26 mm) 55 55
440 24p. Postman, 1890 90 90
441 24p. Douglas Post Office, 1890 (40 × 26 mm) 90 90

1990. 150th Anniv of the Penny Black.
442 **107** 1p. black, buff and gold 15 15
443 – 19p. gold, black and buff 60 50
444 – 32p. multicoloured 1·25 1·10
445 – 34p. multicoloured 1·50 1·10
446 – 37p. multicoloured 1·60 1·10
MS447 100 × 71 mm. £1 black, gold and buff (50 × 60 mm) 4·00 3·50
DESIGNS: 19p. Wyon Medal, 1837; 32p. Wyon's stamp essay; 34p. Perkins Bacon engine-turned essay, 1839; 37p. Twopence Blue, 1840; £1 Block of four Penny Black stamps lettered IM-JN.
No. **MS**447 also commemorates "Stamp World London 90" International Stamp Exhibition.

108 Queen Elizabeth the Queen Mother

110 Churchill with Freedom of Douglas Casket

109 Hawker Hurricane Mk 1, Bristol Type 142 Blenheim Mk 1 and Home Defence

1990. 90th Birthday of Queen Elizabeth the Queen Mother.
448 **108** 90p. multicoloured 3·00 3·00

1990. 50th Anniv of Battle of Britain. Mult.
449 15p. Type **109** 35 35
450 15p. Supermarine Spitfire with Westland Lysander Mk I rescue aircraft and launch 35 35
451 24p. Rearming Hawker Hurricanes Mk I fighters 80 80
452 24p. Ops room and scramble 80 80
453 29p. Civil Defence personnel 1·00 1·00
454 29p. Anti-aircraft battery 1·00 1·00

1990. 25th Death Anniv of Sir Winston Churchill. Multicoloured.
455 19p. Type **110** 45 45
456 32p. Churchill and London blitz 1·00 1·00
457 34p. Churchill and searchlights over Westminster 1·25 1·25
458 37p. Churchill with R.A.F. Hawker Hurricane Mk I fighters 1·25 1·25

111 Boy on Toboggan and Girl posting Letter

112 Henry Bloom Noble and Orphans (Marshall Wane)

1990. Christmas. Multicoloured.
459 14p. Type **111** 40 40
460 18p. Girl on toboggan and skaters 50 50
461 34p. Boy with snowman 1·00 1·00
462 37p. Children throwing snowballs 1·25 1·25
MS463 123 × 55 mm. As Nos. 459/62, but face values in black 3·00 3·75

1991. Manx Photography.
464 **112** 17p. brown, grey and black 35 35
465 – 21p. brown and ochre 50 50
466 – 26p. brown, stone and black 65 65
467 – 31p. brown, lt brown & blk 90 90
468 – 40p. multicoloured 1·10 1·10
DESIGNS: 21p. Douglas (Frederick frith); 26p. Studio portrait of three children (Hilda Newby); 31p. Castital yn Ard (Christopher Killip); 40p. Peel Castle (Colleen Corlett).

113 Lifeboat "Sir William Hillary", Douglas

1991. Manx Lifeboats. Multicoloured.
469 17p. Type **113** 45 45
470 21p. "Osman Gabriel", Port Erin 55 55
471 26p. "Ann and James Ritchie", Ramsey 90 90
472 31p. "The Gough Ritchie", Port St. Mary 1·25 1·25
473 37p. "John Batstone", Peel 1·40 1·40
No. 469 is inscribed "HILARY" and No. 471 "JAMES & ANN RITCHIE", both in error.

114 "Intelsat" Communications Satellite

116 Laxey Hand-cart, 1920

115 Oliver Godfrey with Indian 500cc at Start, 1911

1991. Europa. Europe in Space. Multicoloured.
474 17p. Type **114** 70 70
475 17p. "Ariane" rocket launch and fishing boats in Douglas harbour 70 70
476 26p. Weather satellite and space station 1·00 1·00
477 26p. Ronaldsway Airport, Manx Radio transmitter and Space shuttle launch 1·00 1·00
Nos. 474/5 and 476/7 were each printed together, se-tenant, each pair forming a composite design.

1991. 80th Anniv of Tourist Trophy Mountain Course. Multicoloured.
478 17p. Type **115** 50 40
479 21p. Freddie Dixon on Douglas "banking" sidecar, 1923 65 60
480 26p. Bill Ivy on Yamaha 125cc, 1968 80 80
481 31p. Giacomo Agostini on MV Agusta 500cc, 1972 1·25 1·10
482 37p. Joey Dunlop on RVF Honda 750cc, 1985 1·50 1·50
MS483 149 × 144 mm. Nos. 478/82 4·00 4·00

1991. 9th Conference of Commonwealth Postal Administration, Douglas. Sheet 119 × 77 mm. Multicoloured.
MS484 Nos. 367c and 377a, to each × 2 1·90 2·00

1991. Fire Engines. Multicoloured.
485 17p. Type **116** 45 40
486 21p. Horse-drawn steamer, Douglas, 1909 65 65
487 30p. Merryweather "Hatfield" pump, 1936 85 90
488 33p. Dennis "F8" pumping appliance, Peel, 1953 1·25 1·25
489 37p. Volvo turntable ladder, Douglas, 1989 1·40 1·50

117 Mute Swans, Douglas Harbour

1991. Swans. Multicoloured.
490 17p. Type **117** 40 40
491 17p. Black swans, Curraghs Wildlife Park 40 40
492 26p. Whooper swans, Bishop's Dub, Ballaugh 1·10 1·00
493 26p. Tundra ("Bewick's") swans, Eairy Dam, Foxdale 1·10 1·00
494 37p. Coscoroba swans, Curraghs Wildlife Park 1·20 1·25
495 37p. Whooper ("Trumpeter") swans, Curraghs Wildlife Park 1·20 1·25
The two designs of each value were printed together, se-tenant, forming a composite design.

118 The Three Kings

120 Queen Elizabeth II at Coronation, 1953

119 North African and Italian Campaigns, 1942–43

1991. Christmas. Paper Sculptures. Multicoloured.
496 16p. Type **118** 45 35
497 20p. Mary with manger 65 70
498 26p. Shepherds with sheep 85 85
499 37p. Choir of angels 1·10 1·10

1992. 50th Anniv of Parachute Regiment. Mult.
502 23p. Type **119** 70 70
503 23p. D-Day, 1944 70 70
504 28p. Arnhem, 1944 80 80
505 28p. Rhine crossing, 1945 80 80
506 39p. Operations in Near, Middle and Far East, 1945–68 1·25 1·25
507 39p. Liberation of Falkland Islands. 1982 1·25 1·25

1992. 40th Anniv of Accession. Multicoloured.
508 18p. Type **120** 45 40
509 23p. Queen visiting Isle of Man, 1979 60 60
510 28p. Queen in evening dress 70 70
511 33p. Queen visiting Isle of Man, 1989 1·25 1·40
512 39p. Queen arriving for film premiere, 1990 1·40 1·40

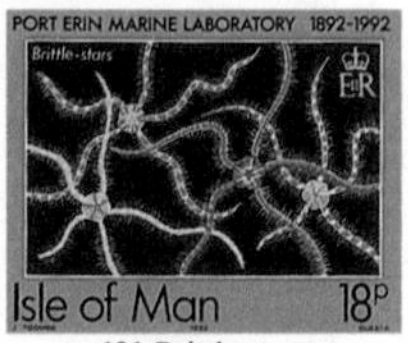

121 Brittle-stars

1992. Centenary of Port Erin Marine Laboratory. Multicoloured.
513 18p. Type **121** 40 35
514 23p. Phytoplankton 60 55
515 28p. Atlantic herring 60 55
516 33p. Great scallop 1·25 1·25
517 39p. Dahlia anemone and delesseria 1·50 1·25

122 The Pilgrim Fathers embarking at Delfshaven

1992. Europa. 500th Anniv of Discovery of America by Columbus. Multicoloured.
518 18p. Type **122** 80 80
519 18p. "Speedwell" leaving Delfshaven 80 80
520 28p. "Mayflower" setting sail for America 1·75 1·75
521 28p. "Speedwell" anchored at Dartmouth 1·75 1·75
The two designs for each value were printed together, se-tenant, in horizontal pairs forming composite designs.

123 Central Pacific Locomotive "Jupiter", 1869

1992. Construction of the Union Pacific Railroad, 1866–69. Multicoloured.
522 33p. Type **123** 90 1·00
523 33p. Union Pacific locomotive No. 119, 1869 90 1·00
524 39p. Union Pacific locomotive No. 844, 1992 1·25 1·50
525 39p. Union Pacific locomotive No. 3985, 1992 1·25 1·50
MS526 105 × 78 mm. £1.50 Golden Spike ceremony, 10 May 1869 (60 × 50 mm) 3·70 4·50

124 "King Orry V" in Douglas Harbour

1992. Manx Harbours. Multicoloured.
527 18p. Type **124** 45 45
528 23p. Castletown 55 55
529 37p. Port St. Mary 1·25 1·25
530 40p. Ramsey 1·25 1·25

125 "Saint Eloi" in 1972

126 Stained Glass Window, St. German's Cathedral, Peel

1992. "Genova '92" International Thematic Stamp Exhibition. Sheet 111 × 68 mm, containing T **125** and similar horiz design. Multicoloured.
MS531 18p. "King Orry V" in 1992 (as in Type **124**); £1 Type **125** 3·25 3·50

1992. Christmas. Manx Churches. Mult.
532 17p. Type **126** 45 40
533 22p. Reredos, St. Matthew the Apostle Church, Douglas 65 65
534 28p. Stained glass window, St. George's Church, Douglas 80 80
535 37p. Reredos, St. Mary of the Isle Catholic Church, Douglas 95 95
536 40p. Stained glass window, Trinity Methodist Church, Douglas 1·00 1·00

127 Mansell on Lap of Honour, British Grand Prix, 1992

1992. Nigel Mansell's Victory in Formula 1 World Motor Racing Championship. Multicoloured.
537 20p. Type **127** 80 80
538 24p. Mansell in French Grand Prix, 1992 1·00 1·00

128 H.M.S. "Amazon" (frigate)

128a Manx Red Ensign

128b Queen Elizabeth II (hologram)

1993. Ships. Multicoloured.

539	1p. Type **128**	10	10
540	2p. "Fingal" (lighthouse tender)	10	10
541	4p. "Sir Winston Churchill" (cadet schooner)	10	10
542	5p. "Dar Mlodziezy" (full-rigged cadet ship)	10	10
543	20p. "Tynwald I" (paddle-steamer)	40	25
544	21p. "Ben Veg" (freighter)	50	50
545	22p. "Waverley" (paddle-steamer)	50	50
546	23p. Royal Yacht "Britannia"	55	55
547	24p. "Francis Drake" (ketch)	50	35
548	25p. "Royal Viking Sky" (liner)	60	60
549	26p. "Lord Nelson" (cadet barque)	65	65
550	27p. "Europa" (liner)	65	65
551	30p. "Snaefell V" (ferry) leaving Ardrossan	75	75
552	35p. "Seacat" (catamaran ferry)	85	85
553	40p. "Lady of Man I" (ferry) off Ramsey	1·00	90
554	50p. "Mona's Queen II" (paddle ferry) leaving Fleetwood	1·25	1·10
555	£1 "Queen Elizabeth 2" (liner) and "Mona's Queen V" (ferry) off Liverpool	2·50	2·40
556	£2 Type **128a**	3·75	4·00
557	£5 Type **128b**	10·00	11·00

For 4, 20 and 24p. in smaller size, 21 × 18 mm, see Nos. 687/93.

129 No. 1 Motor Car and No. 13 Trailer at Groudle Glen Hotel

1993. Cent of Manx Electric Railway. Mult.

559	20p. Type **129**	60	60
560	24p. No. 9 Tunnel Car and No. 19 Trailer at Douglas Bay Hotel	90	90
561	28p. No. 19 Motor Car and No. 59 Royal Trailer Special at Douglas Bay	1·00	1·00
562	39p. No. 33 Motor Car, No. 45 Trailer and No. 13 Van at Derby Castle	1·40	1·40

130 "Sir Hall Caine" (statue) (Bryan Kneale)

1993. Europa. Contemporary Art. Works by Bryan Kneale. Multicoloured.

563	20p. Type **130**	60	60
564	20p. "The Brass Bedstead" (painting)	60	60
565	28p. Abstract bronze sculpture	1·00	1·00
566	28p. "Polar Bear Skeleton" (drawing)	1·00	1·00

131 Graham Oates and Bill Marshall (1933 International Six Day Trial) on Ariel Square Four

1993. Manx Motor Cycling Events. Mult.

567	20p. Type **131**	35	35
568	24p. Sergeant Geoff Duke (1947 Royal Signals Display Team) on Triumph 3T Twin	45	45
569	28p. Denis Parkinson (1953 Senior Manx Grand Prix) on Manx Norton	70	60
570	33p. Richard Swallow (1991 Junior Classic MGP) on Aermacchi	90	90
571	39p. Steve Colley (1992 Scottish Six Day Trial) on Beta Zero	1·00	95
MS572	165 × 120 mm. Nos. 567/71	4·50	4·50

132 "Inachis io" (Peacock) **133** Children decorating Christmas Tree

1993. Butterflies. Multicoloured.

573	24p. Type **132**	75	65
574	24p. "Argynnis aglaja" (Dark green fritillary)	75	65
575	24p. "Cynthia cardui" (Painted lady)	75	65
576	24p. "Celastrina argiolus" (Holly blue)	75	65
577	24p. "Vanessa atalanta" (Red admiral)	75	65

1993. Christmas. Multicoloured.

578	19p. Type **133**	50	50
579	23p. Girl with snowman	60	60
580	28p. Boy opening presents	70	70
581	39p. Girl with teddy bear	1·10	1·10
582	40p. Children with toboggan	1·10	1·10

134 White-throated Robin

1994. Calf of Man Bird Observatory. Mult.

583	20p. Type **134**	50	60
584	20p. Black-eared wheatear	50	60
585	24p. Goldcrest	80	90
586	24p. Northern oriole	80	90
587	30p. River kingfisher ("Kingfisher")	1·00	1·10
588	30p. Hoopoe	1·00	1·10
MS589	100 × 71 mm. £1 Black-billed magpie (51½ × 61 mm)	3·00	3·50

No. **MS**589 also commemorates the "Hong Kong '94" philatelic exhibition.

135 Gaiety Theatre, Douglas

1994. Manx Tourism Centenary. Multicoloured.

590	24p. Type **135**	65	60
591	24p. Sports	65	60
592	24p. Artist at work and yachts racing	65	60
593	24p. TT Races and British Aerospace Hawk T.1s of Red Arrows display team	65	60
594	24p. Musical instruments	65	60
595	24p. Laxey Wheel and Manx cat	65	60
596	24p. Tower of Refuge, Douglas, with bucket and spade	65	60
597	24p. Cyclist	65	60
598	24p. Tynwald Day and classic car	65	60
599	24p. Santa Mince Pie train, Groudle Glen	65	60

136 "Eubranchus tricolor" (sea slug)

1994. Europa. Discoveries of Edward Forbes (marine biologist). Multicoloured.

600	20p. Type **136**	50	50
601	20p. "Loligo forbesii" (common squid)	50	50
602	20p. Edward Forbes and signature	50	50
603	30p. "Solaster moretonis" (fossil starfish)	90	90
604	30p. "Adamsia carciniopados" (anenome) on hermit crab	90	90
605	30p. "Solaster endeca" (starfish)	90	90

137 Maj-Gen. Bedell Smith and Naval Landing Force including "Ben-my-Chree IV" (ferry)

1994. 50th Anniv of D-Day. Multicoloured.

606	4p. Type **137**	15	15
607	4p. Admiral Ramsay and naval ships including "Victoria" and "Lady of Man" (ferries)	15	15
608	20p. Gen. Montgomery and British landings	70	70
609	20p. Lt-Gen. Dempsey and 2nd Army landings	70	70
610	30p. Air Chief Marshal Leigh-Mallory and U.S. paratroops and aircraft	1·00	1·00
611	30p. Air Chief Marshal Tedder and British paratroops and aircraft	1·00	1·00
612	41p. Lt-Gen. Bradley and U.S. 1st Army landings	1·25	1·25
613	41p. Gen. Eisenhower and American landings	1·25	1·25

138 Postman Pat, Jess and Ffinlo at Sea Terminal, Douglas

1994. Postman Pat visits the Isle of Man. Multicoloured.

614	1p. Type **138**	15	15
615	20p. Laxey Wheel	60	60
616	24p. Cregneash	80	80
617	30p. Manx Electric Railway trains	90	90
618	36p. Peel Harbour	1·10	1·10
619	41p. Douglas Promenade	1·25	1·25
MS620	110 × 85 mm. £1 Postman Pat (25 × 39 mm)	2·25	2·25

139 Cycling

1994. Centenary of International Olympic Committee. Multicoloured.

621	10p. Type **139**	35	25
622	20p. Downhill skiing	55	50
623	24p. Swimming	70	65
624	35p. Hurdling	95	90
625	48p. Centenary logo	1·60	1·25

140 Santa Train to Santon

1994. Christmas. Father Christmas in the Isle of Man. Multicoloured.

626	19p. Type **140**	60	60
627	23p. Father Christmas and Postman Pat on mini tractor, Douglas (vert)	80	80
628	60p. Father Christmas and majorettes in sleigh, Port St. Mary	2·00	2·00

141 Foden Steam Wagon, Highway Board Depot, Douglas

1995. Steam Traction Engines. Multicoloured.

629	20p. Type **141**	55	60
630	24p. Clayton & Shuttleworth and Fowler engines pulling dead whale	60	70
631	30p. Wallis and Steevens engine at Ramsey Harbour	80	85
632	35p. Marshall engine with threshing machine, Ballarhenny	1·10	1·10
633	41p. Marshall convertible steam roller	1·10	1·25

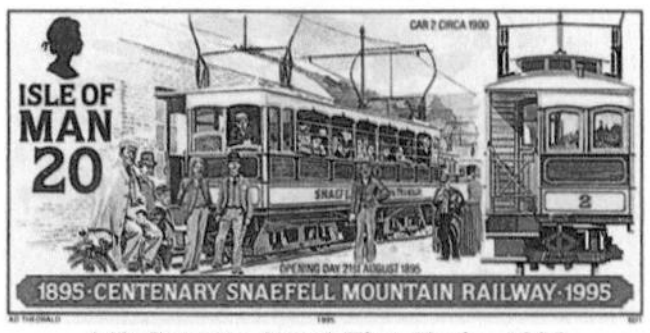

142 Car No. 2 and First Train, 1895

1995. Centenary of Snaefell Mountain Railway. Multicoloured.

634	20p. Type **142**	70	70
635	24p. Car No. 4 in green livery and Car No. 3 in Laxey Valley	80	80
636	35p. Car No. 6 and Car No. 5 in 1971	1·10	1·10
637	42p. Goods Car No. 7 and "Caledonia" steam locomotive pulling construction train	1·25	1·25
MS638	110 × 87 mm. £1 Passenger car and Argus char-a-banc at Bungalow Hotel (60 × 37 mm)	3·25	3·25

143 Peace Doves forming Wave and Tower of Refuge, Douglas Bay

1995. Europa. Peace and Freedom. Multicoloured.

639	20p. Type **143**	60	75
640	30p. Peace dove breaking barbed wire	1·00	1·00

144 Spitfire, Tank and Medals

1995. 50th Anniv of End of Second World War. Multicoloured.

641	10p. Type **144**	30	30
642	10p. Typhoon, anti-aircraft gun and medals	30	30
643	20p. Lancaster, H.M.S. "Biter" (escort carrier) and medals	55	55
644	20p. U.S. Navy aircraft, jungle patrol and medals	55	55
645	24p. Celebrations in Parliament Square	70	70
646	24p. V.E. Day bonfire	70	70
647	40p. Street party	1·10	1·10
648	40p. King George VI and Queen Elizabeth on Isle of Man in July 1945	1·10	1·10

145 Reg Parnell in Maserati "4 CLT", 1951

1995. 90th Anniv of Motor Racing on Isle of Man. Multicoloured.

649	20p. Type **145**	65	60
650	24p. Stirling Moss in Frazer Nash, 1951	80	75
651	30p. Richard Seaman in Delage, 1936	90	85
652	36p. Prince Bira in ERA R2B "Romulus", 1937	1·10	1·00
653	41p. Kenelm Guinness in Sunbeam 1, 1914	1·25	1·10
654	42p. Freddie Dixon in Riley, 1934	1·25	1·10
MS655	103 × 73 mm. £1 John Napier in Arrol Johnston, 1905 (47 × 58 mm)	3·00	3·00

146 Thomas the Tank Engine and Bertie Bus being Unloaded

1995. 50th Anniv of Thomas the Tank Engine Stories by Revd. Awdry. "Thomas the Tank Engine's Dream". Multicoloured.

656	20p. Type **146**	65	60
657	24p. Mail train	80	75
658	30p. Bertie and engines at Ballasalla	90	85
659	36p. "Viking" the diesel engine, Port Erin	1·10	1·00
660	41p. Thomas and railcar at Snaefell summit	1·25	1·10
661	45p. Engines racing past Laxey Wheel	1·50	1·25

147 "Amanita muscaria" **148** St. Catherine's Church, Port Erin

1995. Fungi. Multicoloured.

662	20p. Type **147**	40	40
663	24p. "Boletus edulis"	50	50
664	30p. "Coprinus disseminatus"	60	60
665	35p. "Pleurotus ostreatus"	75	75
666	45p. "Geastrum triplex"	1·25	1·25
MS667	100 × 71 mm. £1 Shaggy ink cap and bee orchid (50 × 59 mm)	3·00	3·50

No. **MS**667 is inscribed "Singapore World Stamp Exhibition 1st–10th September 1995" on the sheet margin.

1995. Christmas. Multicoloured.

668	19p. Type **148**	55	55
669	23p. European robin on holly branch	70	70
670	42p. St. Peter's Church and wild flowers	1·50	1·50
671	50p. Hedgehog hibernating under farm machinery	1·75	1·75

149 Langness Lighthouse **151** Douglas Borough Arms

150 White Manx Cat and Celtic Interlaced Ribbons

1996. Lighthouses. Multicoloured.

672	20p. Type **149**	50	50
673	24p. Point of Ayre lighthouse (horiz)	60	60
674	30p. Chicken Rock lighthouse	90	90
675	36p. Calf of Man lighthouse (horiz)	1·00	1·00
676	41p. Douglas Head lighthouse	1·10	1·10
677	42p. Maughold Head lighthouse (horiz)	1·25	1·25

1996. Manx Cats. Multicoloured.

678	20p. Type **150**	50	50
679	24p. Cat and Union Jack ribbons	60	60
680	36p. Cat on rug in German colours, mouse and Brandenburg Gate	90	90
681	42p. Cat, U.S.A. flag and Statue of Liberty	1·10	1·10
682	48p. Cat, map of Australia and kangaroo	1·25	1·25
MS683	100 × 71 mm. £1.50 Cat with kittens (51 × 61 mm)	3·50	3·50

See also No. **MS**712.

1996. Centenary of Douglas Borough. Self-adhesive.

684	**151** (20p.) multicoloured	70	1·00

1996. Ships. As Nos. 541, 543 and 547, but smaller, 21 × 18 mm. Multicoloured.

687	4p. "Sir Winston Churchill" (cadet schooner)	20	15
689	20p. "Tynwald I" (paddle-steamer), 1846	60	70
693	24p. "Francis Drake" (ketch)	90	90

The 20p. and 24p. show the positions of the face value and Queen's head reversed.

152 Princess Anne (President, Save the Children Fund) and Children

1996. Europa. Famous Women. Multicoloured.

701	24p. Type **152**	70	75
702	30p. Queen Elizabeth II and people of the Commonwealth	90	1·00

153 Alec Bennett

1996. Tourist Trophy Motorcycle Races. Irish Winners. Multicoloured.

703	20p. Type **153**	50	45
704	24p. Stanley Woods	60	60
705	45p. Artie Bell	90	90
706	60p. Joey and Robert Dunlop	1·40	1·40
MS707	100 × 70 mm. £1 R.A.F. Red Arrows display team (vert)	3·00	3·00

154 National Poppy Appeal Trophy

1996. 75th Anniv of Royal British Legion. Mult.

708	20p. Type **154**	65	55
709	24p. Manx War Memoial, Braddan	70	60
710	42p. Poppy appeal collection box	1·10	1·00
711	75p. Royal British Legion badge	2·00	2·00

1996. "Capex '96" International Stamp Exhibition, Toronto. No. **MS**683 additionally inscribed with "CAPEX '96" exhibition logo on sheet margin.

MS712	100 × 71 mm. £1.50 Cat with kittens (51 × 61 mm)	6·00	6·50

155 UNICEF Projects in Mexico

1996. 50th Anniv of UNICEF. Multicoloured.

713	24p. Type **155**	65	60
714	24p. Projects in Sri Lanka	65	60
715	30p. Projects in Colombia	85	75
716	30p. Projects in Zambia	85	75
717	42p. Projects in Afghanistan	1·25	1·10
718	42p. Projects in Vietnam	1·25	1·10

156 Labrador

1996. Dogs. Multicoloured.

719	20p. Type **156**	60	55
720	24p. Border collie	70	65
721	31p. Dalmatian	1·00	90
722	38p. Mongrel	1·10	1·00
723	43p. English setter	1·50	1·25
724	63p. Alsatian	2·00	1·75
MS725	100 × 71 mm. £1.20 Labrador guide dog and working Border collie (38 × 50 mm)	3·75	3·75

157 "Snowman and Pine Trees" (David Bennett) **158** Primroses and Cashtyl ny Ard

1996. Christmas. Children's Paintings. Multicoloured.

726	19p. Type **157**	55	50
727	23p. "Three-legged Father Christmas" (Louis White)	70	65
728	50p. "Family around Christmas Tree" (Robyn Whelan)	1·60	1·40
729	75p. "Father Christmas in Sleigh" (Claire Bradley)	2·10	1·90

1997. Spring in Man. Multicoloured.

730	20p. Type **158**	50	50
731	24p. Lochtan sheep and lambs	70	70
732	43p. Daffodils, mallard and ducklings	1·10	1·10
733	63p. Dabchick with young and frog on lily pad	1·60	1·60

159 Barn Owl

1997. Owls. Multicoloured.

734	20p. Type **159**	65	60
735	24p. Short-eared owl	80	75
736	31p. Long-eared owl	1·00	90
737	36p. Little owl	1·25	1·10
738	43p. Snowy owl	1·40	1·25
739	56p. Eurasian tawny owl	1·60	1·50
MS740	100 × 71 mm. £1.20 Long-eared owl (different) (51 × 60 mm)	4·00	4·25

No. **MS**740 includes the "HONG KONG '97" International Stamp Exhibition logo on the sheet margin.

160 Moddey Dhoo, Peel Castle

1997. Europa. Tales and Legends. Multicoloured.

741	21p. Type **160**	55	55
742	25p. Fairies in tree and cottage	65	65
743	31p. Fairies at Fairy Bridge	85	85
744	36p. Giant Finn Macooil and Calf of Man	1·10	1·10
745	37p. The Buggane of St. Trinian's	1·10	1·10
746	43p. Fynoderee and farm	1·40	1·40

Nos. 742/3 include the "EUROPA" emblem.

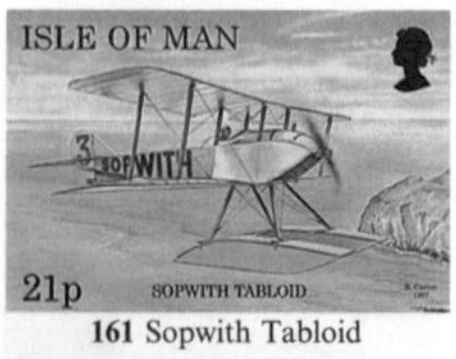

161 Sopwith Tabloid

1997. Manx Aircraft. Multicoloured.

747	21p. Type **161**	45	45
748	21p. Grumman Tiger (1996 Schneider Trophy)	45	45
749	25p. BAe ATP (15th anniv of Manx Airlines)	55	55
750	25p. BAe 146-200 (15th anniv of Manx Airlines)	55	55
751	31p. Boeing 757-200 (largest aircraft to land on Isle of Man)	70	70
752	31p. Farman biplane (1st Manx flight, 1911)	70	70
753	36p. Spitfire	80	80
754	36p. Hawker Hurricane	80	80

Nos. 747/8, 749/50, 751/2 and 753/4 respectively were each printed together, se-tenant, the backgrounds forming composite of Isle of Man.

No. 752 is inscribed "EARMAN BIPLANE" in error.

162 14th Hole, Ramsey Golf Club

1997. Golf. Multicoloured.

755	21p. Type **162**	50	50
756	25p. 15th Hole, King Edward Bay Golf and Country Club	60	60
757	43p. 17th Hole, Rowany Golf Club	1·10	1·10
758	50p. 8th Hole, Castletown Golf Links	1·50	1·50
MS759	100 × 71 mm. £1.30 Golf ball (circular, diameter 39 mm)	3·50	3·50

No. **MS**759 includes the "Pacific '97" International Stamp Exhibition logo on the sheet margin.

1997. Return of Hong Kong to China. Sheet 130 × 90 mm, containing No. 546. Multicoloured.

MS760	23p. Royal Yacht "Britannia"	1·40	1·60

163 Steve Colley

1997. F.I.M. "Trial de Nations" Motorcycle Team Trials. Multicoloured.

761	21p. Type **163**	55	50
762	25p. Steve Saunders (vert)	65	60
763	37p. Sammy Miller (vert)	1·25	1·00
764	44p. Don Smith	1·50	1·25

164 Angel and Shepherd **165** Engagement of Princess Elizabeth and Lieut. Philip Mountbatten, 1947

1997. Christmas. Multicoloured.

765	20p. Type **164**	65	55
766	24p. Angel and King	75	70
767	63p. The Nativity (54 × 39 mm)	1·60	1·50

1997. Golden Wedding of Queen Elizabeth and Prince Philip. Multicoloured (except No. 768).

768	50p. Type **165** (brown and gold)	1·40	1·40
769	50p. Wedding photograph, 1947	1·40	1·40
770	50p. At Ascot, 1952	1·40	1·40
771	50p. Golden Wedding photograph, 1997	1·40	1·40
MS772	100 × 72 mm. £1 Queen Elizabeth and Prince Philip at Peel, 1989 (47 × 58 mm)	3·00	3·00

166 Shamrock **168** Viking Figurehead

167 Queen Elizabeth II and Queen Elizabeth the Queen Mother

1998. Flowers. Multicoloured.

773	1p. Bearded iris	10	10
774	2p. Daisy	10	10
775	4p. Type **166**	10	10
776	5p. Silver Jubilee rose	10	15
777	10p. Oriental poppy	20	25
778	20p. Heath spotted orchid	40	30
779	21p. Cushag	40	45
780	22p. Gorse	45	50

781	25p. Princess of Wales rose	50	40
782	26p. Dog rose	50	40
783	30p. Fuchsia "Lady Thumb"	60	60
784	50p. Daffodil	1·00	1·00
785	£1 Spear thistle	2·00	2·00
790	£2.50 Type **167**	5·00	4·75

1998. Viking Longships. Multicoloured.

793	21p. Type **168**	55	50
794	25p. Viking longship at sea	75	70
795	31p. Viking longship on beach	90	80
796	75p. Stern of ship	2·25	2·00
MS797	100 × 71 mm. £1 Viking ship at Peel Castle	3·00	3·00

169 Bottle-nosed Dolphins

1998. UNESCO International Year of the Ocean. Multicoloured.

798	10p. Type **169**	30	30
799	21p. Basking shark	50	50
800	25p. Front view of basking shark	65	65
801	31p. Minke whale	75	75
802	63p. Killer whale and calf	1·60	1·60

170 Locomotive No. 12 "Hutchinson"

1998. 125th Anniv of Isle of Man Steam Railway. Multicoloured.

803	21p. Type **170**	60	50
804	25p. Locomotive No. 10 "G. H. Wood"	70	60
805	31p. Locomotive No. 11 "Maitland"	90	80
806	63p. Locomotive No. 4 "Loch"	1·60	1·60
MS807	119 × 54 mm. 25p. Pillar box and train at Douglas Station; £1 Locomotive No. 1 "Sutherland"	3·00	3·00

171 Purple Helmets Display Team

1998. Isle of Man T.T. Races and 50th Anniv of Honda (manufacturer). Multicoloured.

808	21p. Type **171**	40	45
809	25p. Joey Dunlop	50	55
810	31p. Dave Molyneux	65	65
811	43p. Naomi Taniguchi	1·00	1·00
812	63p. Mike Hailwood	1·40	1·50

172 Princess Diana wearing Protective Clothing, Angola

1998. Diana, Princess of Wales Commemoration. Multicoloured.

813	25p. Type **172**	55	55
814	25p. Receiving award from United Cerebral Palsy Charity, New York, 1995	55	55
815	25p. With children, South Korea, 1992	55	55
816	25p. Wearing blue jacket, July 1993	55	55

173 Tynwald Day Ceremony

1998. Europa. Festivals. Multicoloured.

817	25p. Type **173**	50	45
818	30p. Traditional dancers, Tynwald Fair	75	65

174 Father Christmas at North Pole

1998. Christmas. "A Very Special Delivery". Multicoloured.

819	20p. Type **174**	40	30
820	24p. Father Christmas checking list	50	45
821	30p. Flying over Spring Valley sorting office	75	60
822	43p. Passing through Baldrine village	95	85
823	63p. Father Christmas delivering presents	1·40	1·25

175 Large Oval Pillar Box, Kirk Onchan   **176** Cottage, Ballaglass Glen

1999. Local Post Boxes. Multicoloured.

824	10p. Type **175**	25	25
825	20p. Wall box, Ballaterson	45	45
826	21p. King Edward VII pillar box, Laxey Station	50	50
827	25p. Wall box, Spaldrick	60	55
828	44p. Small oval pillar box, Derby Road, Douglas	1·00	95
829	63p. Wall box, Baldrine Station	1·50	1·40

1999. Europa. Parks and Gardens. Multicoloured.

830	25p. Type **176**	50	50
831	30p. Glen Maye Waterfall	75	60

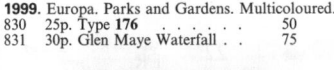

177 "Ann and James Ritchie", Ramsey

1999. 175th Anniv of Royal National Lifeboat Institution. Multicoloured.

832	21p. Type **177**	50	50
833	25p. "Sir William Hillary", Douglas	55	55
834	37p. "Ruby Clery, Peel"	80	80
835	43p. "Herbert and Edith" (inshore lifeboat), Port Erin	90	90
836	43p. 1974 150th Anniv 8p. stamp	2·25	3·00
837	56p. "Gough Ritchie II", Port St. Mary	1·25	1·25
838	56p. 1991 Manx Lifeboats 21p. stamp	2·50	3·00
MS839	100 × 70 mm. £1 Sir William Hillary (founder) (37 × 50 mm)	3·00	3·00

No. **MS**839 includes the "Australia '99" World Stamp Exhibition emblem on the sheet margin.

178 Winter

1999. Centenary of Yn Cheshaght Ghailckagh (Manx Gaelic Society). The Seasons. Multicoloured.

840	22p. Type **178**	60	60
841	26p. Spring	65	65
842	50p. Summer	1·10	1·10
843	63p. Autumn	1·60	1·60

Nos. 840/3 are inscribed "Ellan Vannin", the Manx name for the Isle of Man.

179 Queen Victoria

1999. British Monarchs of the 20th Century. Sheet 170 × 75 mm, containing T **179** and similar horiz designs. Multicoloured.

MS844	26p. Type **179**; 26p. King Edward VII; 26p. King George V; 26p. King Edward VIII; 26p. King George VI; 26p. Queen Elizabeth II	3·25	3·25

180 Tilling-Stevens Double-deck Bus, 1922

1999. Manx Buses. Multicoloured.

845	22p. Type **180**	50	50
846	26p. Thornycroft BC single-deck, 1928	55	55
847	28p. Cumberland ADC 416 single-deck, 1927	65	65
848	37p. Straker-Squire single-deck, 1914	80	80
849	38p. Thornycroft A2 single-deck, 1927	90	90
850	40p. Leyland Lion LT9 single-deck, 1938	1·00	1·00

181 Miss Sophie Rhys-Jones

1999. Royal Wedding. Multicoloured.

851	22p. Type **181**	55	55
852	26p. Leaving St. George's Chapel, Windsor	55	55
853	39p. Prince Edward	80	80
854	44p. Miss Sophie Rhys-Jones and Prince Edward (horiz)	1·10	1·10
855	53p. In landau (horiz)	1·25	1·25

1999. "Philexfrance 99" International Stamp Exhibition, Paris. No. **MS**807 additionally inscribed with "Philexfrance" exhibition logo on sheet margin.

MS856	119 × 54 mm. 25p. Pillar box and train at Douglas Station; £1 Locomotive No. 1 "Sutherland"	3·50	3·75

182 St. Luke's Church, Baldwin

1999. Christmas. Churches. Multicoloured.

857	21p. Type **182**	45	45
858	25p. St. Mark's Chapel, Malew	60	60
859	30p. St. German's Parish Church and Cathedral, Peel	70	70
860	64p. Kirk Christ Church, Rushen	1·50	1·50

183 "Massachusetts", 1967

1999. Legends of Music. The Bee Gees (pop group). Designs showing compact discs. Multicoloured.

861	22p. Type **183**	60	50
862	26p. "Words", 1968	70	65
863	29p. "I've Gotta Get a Message to You", 1968	75	65
864	37p. "Ellan Vannin", 1998	90	85
865	38p. "You Win Again", 1987	90	85
866	66p. "Night Fever", 1978	1·50	1·50
MS867	Two sheets, each 119 × 108 mm. (a) 60p. "Immortality", 1998 (circular, 40 mm diam). (b) 90p. "Stayin' Alive", 1978 (circular, 40 mm diam) Set of 2 sheets	3·00	3·50

184 Sky at Sunset over Calf of Man

1999. New Millennium. Sheet 169 × 74 mm, containing T **184** and similar vert designs. Multicoloured.

MS868	50p. Type **184**; 50p. Sky at dawn over Maughold Head; £2 Constellations over Man at start of new millennium	6·50	6·75

185 Harrison's Chronometer, 1735, and Map   **187** Barn Swallow ("Swallow")

186 Duke and Duchess of York on Wedding Day, 1923

2000. "The Story of Time". Multicoloured.

869	22p. Type **185**	50	55
870	26p. Daniels' chronometer, 2000, and clock face	55	60
871	29p. Harrison's chronometer, 1767, map and clock	65	70
872	34p. Mudge's chronometer, 1769, and steam locomotives	75	80
873	38p. Arnold's chronometer, 1779, and map of Africa	80	85
874	44p. Earnshaw's chronometer, 1780, and map of Caribbean	95	1·00

2000. "Queen Elizabeth the Queen Mother's Century". Multicoloured (except 26p. and 30p).

875	22p. Type **186**	50	55
876	26p. Queen Elizabeth with Princess Elizabeth, 1940 (brown and black)	55	60
877	30p. King George VI and Queen Elizabeth visiting troops, 1944 (brown and black)	65	70
878	44p. Queen Mother and Queen Elizabeth, 1954	95	1·00
879	52p. Queen Mother with Prince Charles, 1985	1·10	1·25
880	64p. Queen Mother, 1988	1·40	1·50
MS881	100 × 70 mm. £1 Queen Mother visiting Isle of Man (74 × 49 mm)	2·25	2·25

2000. Endangered Species. Song Birds. Mult.

882	22p. Type **187**	50	55
883	26p. Spotted flycatcher	55	60
884	64p. Eurasian sky lark ("Sky Lark")	1·50	1·50
885	77p. Yellowhammer	1·75	1·75

2000. "The Stamp Show 2000" International Stamp Exhibition, London. As No. **MS**881, but with "The Stamp Show 2000" multicoloured logo added to the bottom sheet margin.

MS886	100 × 70 mm. £1 Queen Mother visiting Isle of Man (74 × 49 mm)	2·40	2·50

188 Lieut. John Quilliam and Admiral Lord Nelson, Battle of Trafalgar

2000. Isle of Man at War. Multicoloured.

887 22p. Type **188** 50 55
888 26p. Ensign Caster Bacon and Duke of Wellington, Battle of Waterloo 55 60
889 36p. Col. Thomas Leigh Goldie and Earl of Cardigan, Crimea 75 80
890 48p. Bugler John Dunne and Sir Robert Baden Powell, Boer War . . . . 1·00 1·10
891 50p. George Kneale and Viscount Kitchener of Khartoum, First World War . . . . 1·00 1·25
892 77p. First Officer Alan Watterson and Sir Winston Churchill, Second World War . . . . 1·50 1·60
MS893 170×75 mm. 60p. Two Supermarine Spitfires (40×29 mm); 60p. Spitfire on ground (40×29 mm), Battle of Britain . . . . 2·75 2·75

189 Prince William as Child

2000. 18th Birthday of Prince William. Sheet 170×75 mm, containing T **189** and similar vert designs. Multicoloured.

MS894 22p. Type **189**; 26p. With Queen Mother; 45p. Prince William; 52p. With Prince Charles and Prince Harry; 56p. Wearing ski-suit . . . . 4·50 4·50

190 Ballet Shoes and Painted Ceiling

2000. Centenary of Gaiety Theatre, Douglas. Mult.

895 22p. Type **190** 50 55
896 26p. Comedy mask and box decoration 55 60
897 36p. Drama mask and statue 75 80
898 45p. Pantomime dame with wig and mosaic . . . . . . 95 1·00
899 52p. Opera glasses and decoration . . . . 1·10 1·25
900 65p. Top hat with cane and painted ceiling . . . . . . 1·40 1·50

191 Map of Great Britain, Union Jack and Liner

2000. "BT Global Challenge" Round the World Yacht Race. Each showing spinnaker of *Isle of Man*. Multicoloured.

901 22p. Type **191** 50 55
902 26p. Sydney Opera House, Australian flag and map 55 60
903 36p. New Zealand map and flag 75 80
904 40p. Map of Buenos Aires and waterfront 85 90
905 44p. U.S. flag, map of Boston and harbour . . . . . . 95 1·00
906 65p. South African flag, map and Table Mountain . . . 1·40 1·50

192 Sailing and Holiday Tours Poster, 1925

193 Girl with Christingle Candle

2000. 170th Anniv of Steam Packet Company. Tourism posters. Multicoloured.

907 22p. Type **192** 50 55
908 26p. "Isle of Man for Happy Holidays" 55 60
909 36p. Woman in swim suit standing on Isle of Man, 1929 . . . . 75 80
910 45p. Stewardess and ferry . . 95 1·00
911 65p. "Isle of Man for Holidays 1931" and ferry 1·40 1·50

2000. Christmas and Europa. Multicoloured.

912 21p. Type **193** 45 50
913 25p. Children dancing around Christmas tree 55 60
914 36p. "Building Europe" . . . 75 80
915 45p. Girl hugging teddy bear 95 1·00
916 65p. Children with stars . . . 1·40 1·50

194 Wyon Medal, Penny Black and Queen Victoria

2001. Death Centenary of Queen Victoria. Mult.

917 22p. Type **194** 50 55
918 26p. Great Exhibition medal and Albert Tower, Ramsey 55 60
919 34p. Silver coin and *Great Britain* (early steamship) 75 80
920 39p. Manx coin of 1839, *Oliver Twist* and St. Thomas' Church, Douglas 85 90
921 40p. Silver coin of 1887, arrival of first train at Vancouver and Jubilee lamp standard 85 90
922 52p. Silver coin of 1893, Joe Mylchreest at Kimberley diamond mine and Foxdale Clock Tower . . . . . . 1·10 1·25

195 St. Patrick and Snakes (½-size illustration)

2001. Chinese New Year ("Year of the Snake"). Sheet 110×85 mm.

MS923 **195** £1 multicoloured . . . 2·25 2·40

No. **MS**923 includes the "Hong Kong 2001" logo on the sheet margin.

196 White-tailed Bumble Bee

2001. Insects. Multicoloured.

924 22p. Type **196** 50 55
925 26p. Seven-spot ladybird . . 55 60
926 29p. Lesser mottled grasshopper 65 70
927 59p. Manx robber fly . . . . 1·25 1·40
928 66p. Elephant hawkmoth . . 1·40 1·50

197 Letter-carrier, 1805

198 1967–70 Great Britain ½d. Machin

2001. Postal Uniforms. Multicoloured.

929 22p. Type **197** 50 55
930 26p. Postman, 1859 . . . . . 55 60
931 36p. Postman, 1910 . . . . . 75 80
932 39p. Postman, 1933 . . . . . 85 90
933 40p. Postman, 1983 . . . . . 85 90
934 66p. Postman, 2001 . . . . . 1·40 1·50

2001. 75th Birthday of Queen Elizabeth II. Sheet 170×75 mm, containing T **198** and similar vert designs showing stamps. Multicoloured.

MS935 29p. Type **198**; 34p. 1952–54 Great Britain 6d. Wilding; 37p. 1971 Isle of Man 2½p. Regional; 50p. 1958–68 Isle of Man 4d. Regional . . . . 3·50 3·75

199 Joey Dunlop on Rea Yamaha, Parliament Square, 1977 TT Races

2001. Joey Dunlop (motorcycle champion) Commemoration. Each incorporating different portraits. Multicoloured.

936 22p. Type **199** 50 55
937 26p. At Governor's, 1983 TT Races 55 60
938 36p. Leaving Ramsey, 1988 TT Races 75 80
939 45p. On Honda motorbike, 1991 . . . . 95 1·00
940 65p. On 250cc Honda at Ballaspur, 1999 . . . . . 1·40 1·50
941 77p. On the Mountain . . . 1·60 1·75

200 "The Manx Derby, 1627" (Johnny Jonas)

2001. Horse Racing Paintings. Multicoloured.

942 22p. Type **200** 50 55
943 26p. "Post Haste" (Johnny Jonas) 55 60
944 36p. "Red Rum" (Hamilton-Rennick) 85 80
945 52p. "Hyperion" (Sir Alfred Munnings) . . . . 1·20 1·40
946 63p. "Isle of Man" (Johnny Jonas) . . . . 1·50 1·50

201 Beef

203 Royal Refreshments at Glasgow

202 Castletown Police Station

2001. Europa. Local Dishes prepared by Kevin Woodford. Multicoloured.

947 22p. Type **201** 50 55
948 26p. Queenies with salmon caviar 55 60
949 36p. Seafood 75 80
950 45p. Lamb . . . . 95 1·00
951 50p. Kipper tart . . . . . . 1·10 1·25
952 66p. Lemon tart with raspberries . . . . 1·40 1·50

The 26p. and 36p. show the inscription "EUROPA 2001" at bottom right.

2001. The Architecture of Mackay Hugh Bailie Scott. Multicoloured.

953 22p. Type **202** 50 55
954 26p. "Leafield" (semi-detached house) 55 60
955 37p. "The Red House" (Bailie Scott's home) . . . 80 85
956 40p. "Ivydene" (detached house) 85 90
957 80p. Onchan Village Hall . . 1·75 1·90

Nos. 953/7 are inscribed "HUGH MACKAY" in error.

2001. "Hafnia 01" International Stamp Exhibition, Denmark. No. **MS**935 additionally inscr with "Hafnia 01" logo in red on sheet margin.

MS958 170×75 mm. 29p. Type **198**; 34p. 1952–54 Great Britain 6d. Wilding; 37p. 1971 Isle of Man 2½p. Regional; 50p. 1958–68 Isle of Man 4d. Regional . . . . . 3·00 3·25

2001. Golden Jubilee (1st issue). "The Daily Life of the Queen—An Artist's Diary" (paintings by Michael Noakes). Multicoloured.

959 22p. Type **203** 50 55
960 26p. Queen on visit to Lancaster 55 60
961 39p. Queen with labradors, Sandringham 85 90
962 40p. Queen meeting Scottish Korean War veterans . . . 85 90
963 45p. Queen at desk, Sandringham . . . . . . 95 1·00
964 65p. Queen with bouquet, Oxford . . . . 1·40 1·50

See also Nos. 970/4.

204 Christmas Tree Wall Decoration

205 "The Coronation, 1953" (Terence Cuneo)

2001. Christmas. Decorations by Isle of Man Floreat Workshop. Multicoloured.

965 21p. Type **204** 45 50
966 25p. Traditional wreath . . . 55 60
967 37p. Table decoration 80 85
968 45p. Topiary tree . . . . . . 95 1·00
969 65p. Contemporary wreath 1·40 1·50

2002. Golden Jubilee (2nd issue). Royal Paintings. Multicoloured.

970 50p. Type **205** . . . . 1·00 1·10
971 50p. "Queen Elizabeth II as Colonel-in-Chief of Grenadier Guards on Imperial, 1962" (T. Cuneo) 1·00 1·10
972 50p. "Queen Elizabeth II in Evening Dress, 1981" (June Mendoza) . . . . 1·00 1·10
973 50p. "Queen Elizabeth II in Garter Robes, 2000" (Chen Yan Ning) . . . . 1·00 1·10
974 50p. "The Royal Family in the White Drawing Room, Buckingham Palace" (John Wonnacott) . . . . 1·00 1·10
MS975 110×85 mm. £1 Sculpture of Queen Elizabeth II by David Cregeen (40×61 mm) . . . . 2·00 2·10

206 Cycling

2002. 17th Commonwealth Games, Manchester. Each showing photographic montages. Mult.

976 22p. Type **206** 45 50
977 26p. Running 50 55
978 29p. Javelin and high jump 60 65
979 34p. Swimming 70 75
980 40p. Decathlon 80 85
981 45p. Wheelchair racing . . . 90 95

207 "Queen Elizabeth the Queen Mother" (Johnny Jonas)

208 Ireland v Czech Republic

2002. Queen Elizabeth the Queen Mother Commemoration.

982 **207** £3 multicoloured . . . . 6·00 6·25

2002. World Cup Football Championship, Japan and Korea (2002). Multicoloured.

983 22p. Type **208** 45 50
984 26p. England v Greece . . . 50 55
985 39p. Italy v Belgium 80 85
986 40p. France v Portugal . . . 80 85
987 66p. England v Brazil . . . . 1·25 1·40
988 68p. France v Japan . . . . . 1·40 1·50

209 "Monk's Bridge, Ballasalla" (Toni Onley)

2002. Watercolours by Toni Onley. Multicoloured.

989 22p. Type **209** 45 50
990 26p. "Laxey" 50 55
991 37p. "Langness Lighthouse" 75 80
992 45p. "King William's College" 90 95
993 65p. "The Mull Circle and Bradda Head" . . . . . . 1·25 1·40

2002. Golden Jubilee Celebrations. Nos. **MS**975 additionally inscribed "THE ISLE OF MAN CELEBRATES THE JUBILEE 4th JUNE 2002" in purple on the sheet margin.

MS994 110 × 85 mm. £1 Sculpture of Queen Elizabeth II by David Cregeen (40 × 61 mm) . . . . 2·00 2·10

210 Magenta Flower on Yellow Background

2002. Memories of the Isle of Man. Multicoloured.

995 22p. Type **210** 45 50
996 26p. Green flower on pink background 50 55
997 29p. Purple flower on green background 60 65
998 52p. Maroon flower on brown background . . . 1·00 1·10
999 63p. Red flower on blue background . . . . . . 1·25 1·40
1000 77p. Orange flower on yellow background . . . 1·50 1·60

211 Manx Milestone (Mrs. B. Trimble) **212** Father Christmas

2002. Photography – The People's Choice. Designs showing competition winners. Multicoloured. Ordinary or self-adhesive gum.

1001 23p. Type **211** 45 50
1002 23p. Plough horses (Miss D. Flint) 45 50
1003 23p. Manx emblem (Ruth Nicholls) 45 50
1004 23p. Loaghtan sheep (Diana Burford) 45 50
1005 23p. Peel fishing fleet, Port St. Mary (Phil Thomas) 45 50
1006 23p. Peel (Michael Thompson) 45 50
1007 23p. Daffodils (Michael Thompson) 45 50
1008 23p. Millennium sword (Mr. F. K. Smith) 45 50
1009 23p. Peel Castle (Kathy Brown) 45 50
1010 23p. Snaefell Railway (Joan Burgess) 45 50
1011 27p. Laxey Wheel (Kathy Brown) 55 60
1012 27p. Sheep at Druidale (John Hall) 55 60
1013 27p. Carousel at Silverdale (Colin Edwards) 55 60
1014 27p. Grandma (Stephanie Corkhill) 55 60
1015 27p. Manx rock (Ruth Nicholls) 55 60
1016 27p. T.T. riders at Signpost (Neil Brew) 55 60
1017 27p. Groudle Railway (Albert Lowe) 55 60
1018 27p. Royal cascade (Brian Speedie) 55 60
1019 27p. St. Johns (John Hall) 55 60
1020 27p. Niarbyl cottages with poppies (Cathy Galbraith) 55 60

2002. Christmas. Entertainment. Multicoloured.

1041 22p. Type **212** 45 50
1042 26p. Virgin Mary and Jesus 50 55
1043 37p. Clown 75 80
1044 47p. Bandsman playing cymbals . . . . 95 1·00
1045 68p. Fairy . . . . 1·40 1·50

MS1046 123 × 55 mm. £1.30 "CHRISTMAS" and festive characters (103 × 40 mm) . . . 2·50 2·75

The 37p. value includes the "EUROPA" emblem.

213 Dish Aerial and Peel Castle

2003. Isle of Man Involvement in Space Exploration. Multicoloured.

1047 23p. Type **213** 45 50
1048 23p. Dish aerial, Tromode Teleport 45 50
1049 27p. Camp on Moon and lunar vehicle 55 60
1050 27p. Astronaut exploring lunar surface 55 60
1051 37p. *Sea Launch Odyssey* (marine launch platform) 75 80
1052 37p. *Sea Launch Commander* (assembly command ship) 75 80
1053 42p. Loral Telstar 1 satellite 85 90
1054 42p. Loral Telstar 8 satellite 85 90

MS1055 110 × 85 mm. 75p. Phobos and American spaceship (30 × 36 mm); 75p. Mars, astronauts and transfer vehicle (30 × 36 mm) . . . . . . 3·00 3·25

Nos. 1047/8, 1049/50, 1051/2 and 1053/4 were each printed together, as horizontal se-tenant pairs, in sheets of 8 with enlarged illustrated right margins.

214 Delivery Handcart (1900–45)

2003. Post Office Vehicles. Multicoloured.

1056 23p. Type **214** 45 50
1057 27p. Morris Z van (1942) 55 60
1058 37p. Morris L diesel van (1960s) 75 80
1059 42p. DI BSA Bantam telegraph delivery motorbikes 85 90
1060 89p. Ford Escort 55 van . . 1·75 1·90

215 Queen Elizabeth II wearing St. Edward's Crown

2003. 50th Anniv of Coronation. Multicoloured.

1061 50p. Type **215** (26 × 57 mm) 1·00 1·10
1062 50p. The Ring (23 × 28 mm) 1·00 1·10
1063 50p. The Orb (23 × 28 mm)
1064 50p. Royal Sceptre and Rod of Equity and Mercy (23 × 28 mm) . . . . . . 1·00 1·10
1065 50p. Queen Elizabeth II wearing Imperial State Crown (26 × 57 mm) . . . 1·00 1·10
1066 50p. State Coach (81 × 27 mm) . . . . . . 1·00 1·10

216 De Havilland D.H. 83 Fox Moth and Saro Cloud (amphibian)

2003. Centenary of Powered Flight. Each showing two aircraft. Multicoloured.

1067 23p. Type **216** 45 50
1068 27p. De Havilland D.H. 61 Giant Moth and D.H. 80 Puss Moth 55 60
1069 37p. Avro Type 652 and Boeing B-17 Flying Fortress 75 80
1070 40p. Eurofighter Typhoon and Avro Vulcan 80 85
1071 67p. Handley Page Herald and Bristol Wayfarer . . 1·40 1·50
1072 89p. Aerospatiale Concorde and projected Airbus Industrie A380 . . . . . 1·75 1·90

217 Avro Lancaster attacking Mohne Dam (½-size illustration)

2003. 60th Anniv of Attack on German Dams by No. 617 ("Dambusters") Squadron. Sheet 170 × 75 mm.

MS1073 **217** £2 multicoloured . . 4·00 4·25

218 Prince William

2003. 21st Birthday of Prince William of Wales.

1074 **218** 42p. black and grey . . 85 90
1075 – 47p. black and grey . . 95 1·00
1076 – 52p. black and grey . . 1·00 1·10
1077 – 68p. black and grey . . 1·40 1·50

DESIGNS: 47p. to 68p. Showing recent photographs.

2003. Trilaterale Ticino Exhibition, Locarno, Switzerland. No. **MS**1073 additionally inscr with "Ticino 2003" logo in blue on sheet margin.

MS1078 £2 multicoloured . . . . 4·00 4·25

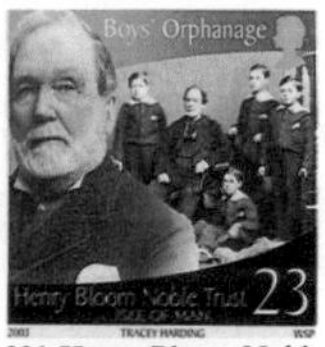

219 *Manx Gold* (Agatha Christie) **221** Henry Bloom Noble and Orphanage Boys

220 King Henry VII and Henry Tudor crowned by Sir Thomas Stanley on Bosworth Battlefield

2003. "The Manx Bookshelf". Book covers. Multicoloured.

1079 23p. Type **219** 45 50
1080 27p. *Quatermass and the Pit* (Nigel Kneale) 55 60
1081 30p. *Flashman at the Charge* (George MacDonald Fraser) 60 65
1082 38p. *The Eternal City* (Hall Caine) 75 80
1083 40p. *Peveril of the Peak* (Sir Walter Scott) 80 85
1084 53p. *Emma's Secret* (Barbara Taylor Bradford) . . . . 1·00 1·10

The 38p. value includes the "EUROPA 2003" emblem.

2003. 400th Anniv of End of the Tudor Reign. Multicoloured.

1085 23p. Type **220** 45 50
1086 27p. King Henry VIII and Manx church (Dissolution of the Monasteries) . . . 55 60
1087 38p. Queen Elizabeth I and globe showing route of Drake's circumnavigation 75 80
1088 40p. King Henry VIII, Cardinal Wolsey and Hampton Court Palace 80 85
1089 47p. Queen Mary I and Tudor rose . . . . 95 1·00
1090 67p. Queen Elizabeth I and ships of Spanish Armada 1·40 1·50

2003. Centenary of Henry Bloom Noble Trust. Multicoloured.

1091 23p. Type **221** 45 50
1092 23p. Nurse and Ramsey Cottage Hospital 45 50
1093 23p. Children and Children's Home 45 50
1094 23p. Bathers at Noble's Baths 45 50
1095 23p. Scout and Headquarters 45 50
1096 27p. Noble's Hospital, c. 1912 . . . . 55 60
1097 27p. Villa Marina 55 60
1098 27p. Noble's Park 55 60
1099 27p. St. Ninian's Church . . 55 60
1100 27p. Noble's Library . . . 55 60

Nos. 1091/1100 also come self-adhesive.

222 Boy tying Scarf on Snowman

2003. Christmas. *The Snowman* by Raymond Briggs. Multicoloured.

1111 22p. Type **222** 45 50
1112 26p. Snowman (wearing black hat and scarf) . . . 50 55
1113 38p. Boy and Snowman holding hands 75 80
1114 47p. Snowman (wearing brown hat and scarf) . . 95 1·00
1115 68p. Boy flying with Snowman . . . . 1·40 1·50

223 Aragorn

2003. Making of *The Lord of the Rings* Film Trilogy: *The Return of the King*. Multicoloured.

1116 23p. Type **223** 45 50
1117 27p. Gimli 55 60
1118 30p. Gandalf 60 65
1119 38p. Legolas on horseback 75 80
1120 42p. Gollum 85 90
1121 47p. Frodo and Sam . . . 95 1·00
1122 68p. Legolas drawing bow 1·40 1·50
1123 85p. Aragorn on horseback 1·75 1·90

MS1124 120 × 78 mm. £2 The Ring (44 × 40 mm) . . . . 4·00 4·25

224 *Maitland* (Simon Hall)

2004. Bicentenary of Running of First Steam Locomotive. Paintings of steam locomotives by named artists. Multicoloured.

1125 23p. Type **224** 75 75
1126 27p. *Evening Star* (Terence Cuneo) 90 90
1127 40p. *Pen-y-Darren* Tramroad Locomotive (Terence Cuneo) . . . . 1·30 1·30
1128 57p. *Duchess of Hamilton* (Craig Tiley) . . . . . . 1·80 1·80
1129 61p. *City of Truro* (B. J. Freeman) . . . . 2·00 2·00
1130 90p. *Mallard* (Terence Cuneo) . . . . 3·00 3·00

225 Troops on Landing Craft and Tanks going Ashore

2004. 60th Anniv of D-Day. Multicoloured.

1131 23p. Type **225** 75 75
1132 23p. Troops leaving landing craft and tanks going ashore 75 75
1133 27p. Troops leaving landing craft 90 90
1134 27p. Landing craft and troops wading ashore . . 90 90
1135 47p. *Lady of Mann* (ferry used as landing craft carrier) . . . . 1·50 1·50
1136 47p. *Ben-my-Chree* (ferry used as landing craft carrier) . . . . 1·50 1·50
1137 68p. Consolidated B-24 Liberators (bombers) and North American P-51 Mustang (fighter) . . . . 2·20 2·20
1138 68p. Airspeed AS51 Horsa gliders (troop carriers) . . 2·20 2·20

MS1139 170 × 75 mm. 50p. Winston Churchill; 50p. Troops and aircraft; 50p. Military vehicles on street; 50p. Soldiers with France guidebook . . . . 6·50 6·50

Nos. 1131/2, 1133/4, 1135/6 and 1137/8 were each printed together, se-tenant, each pair forming a composite design.

226 Lesser Celandine

2004. Bicentenary of Royal Horticultural Society. Wild Flowers. Multicoloured.

1140	25p. Type **226**	85	85
1141	28p. Red campion	95	95
1142	37p. Devil's-bit scabious	1·20	1·20
1143	40p. Northern harebell	1·30	1·30
1144	68p. Wood anemone	2·20	2·20
1145	85p. Common spotted orchid	2·75	2·75

227 In *No Limit*, 1936

2004. Birth Centenary of George Formby (entertainer). Showing scenes from film *No Limit*. Multicoloured.

1146	25p. Type **227**	80	80
1147	28p. Pushing motorcycle	90	90
1148	40p. Riding in TT race	1·30	1·30
1149	43p. With Florence Desmond	1·40	1·40
1150	50p. On motorcycle	1·70	1·70
1151	74p. Goerge Formby in close-up	2·40	2·40

228 Johnny Weismuller (swimmer), Paris, 1924

2004. Olympic Games, Athens. Olympic Legends. Multicoloured.

1152	25p. Type **228**	85	85
1153	28p. Jesse Owens (athlete), Berlin, 1936	95	95
1154	43p. John Mark carrying Olympic Flame, London, 1948	1·40	1·40
1155	55p. Fanny Blankers-Koen (sprinter), London, 1948	1·80	1·80
1156	91p. Steve Redgrave and Coxless Four (Gold Medallists), Sydney, 2000	3·00	3·00

229 Celtic Islanders and Viking Invaders

2004. Manx National Heritage. The Story of Mann. Multicoloured. Ordinary or self-adhesive gum.

1157	(25p.) Type **229**	80	80
1158	(25p.) Fisherman ("Ships and the Sea")	80	80
1159	(25p.) Miner and Laxey Wheel ("Laxey Miners")	80	80
1160	(25p.) Soldier with Longbow and Castle ("Kings and Lords of Mann")	80	80
1161	(25p.) Woman with Spinning Wheel ("Farmers and Crofters")	80	80
1162	(28p.) Calf of Man	80	80
1163	(28p.) Peel Castle	80	80
1164	(28p.) Laxey Wheel	80	80
1165	(28p.) Castle Rushen	80	80
1166	(28p.) Cregneash	80	80

Nos. 1157/61 and 1167/71 are inscribed "IOM" and were initially sold at 25p. Nos. 1162/6 and 1172/6 are inscribed "UK" and were initially sold at 28p.

230 Laxey Wheel (½-size illustration)

2004. 150th Anniv of the Great Laxey Wheel. Sheet 120 × 78 mm.

MS1177	**230** £2 multicoloured	6·50	6·50

231 "Maughold Church"

2004. The Isle of Man Watercolours by Alfred Heaton Cooper. Multicoloured.

1178	25p. Type **231**	80	80
1179	28p. "Port St. Mary"	90	90
1180	40p. "Ballaugh Old Church"	1·30	1·30
1181	41p. "Douglas Bay (A Midsummer's Night)"	1·30	1·30
1182	43p. "Point of Ayre"	1·40	1·40
1183	74p. "Peel Harbour and Castle"	2·40	2·40

The 28p. and 40p. values include the 'EUROPA 2004' emblem.

2004. Sindelfingen International Stamp Exhibition, Sindelfingen, Germany. No. **MS**1177 additionally inscribed with "Sindelfingen" logo on the sheet margin.

MS1184	**230** £2 multicoloured	6·60	6·60

232 Robin on Flower Pot

2004. Robins—Winter's Friends. Multicoloured.

1185	25p. Type **232**	80	80
1186	28p. Robin at foot of tree	90	90
1187	40p. Robin perched on branch	1·30	1·30
1188	47p. Robin on window ledge	1·50	1·50
1189	68p. Robin on snowy logs	2·30	2·30
MS1190	148 × 200 mm. Nos. 1185/9	6·75	6·75

233 Harry Potter (Daniel Radcliffe), Ron Weasley (Rupert Grint) and Hermione Granger (Emma Watson)

2004. "Harry Potter and the Prisoner of Azkaban" (film). Multicoloured.

1191	25p. Type **233**	80	80
1192	28p. Snowy Owl delivering Owl Post	90	90
1193	39p. Harry Potter and White Stag	1·30	1·30
1194	40p. Hogwarts Express	1·30	1·30
1195	49p. Rubeus Hagrid (Robbie Coltrane)	1·60	1·60
1196	55p. Purple Triple-decker Bus	1·80	1·80
1197	57p. Dementor and Harry Potter flying	1·90	1·90
1198	68p. Harry Potter on the Hippogriff Buckbeak	2·20	2·20

234 The Nile Campaign

2005. 200th Anniv of the Battle of Trafalgar. Multicoloured.

1199	25p. Type **234**	50	55
1200	25p. The Battle of Copenhagen	50	55
1201	28p. Emma, Horatia and Nelson	55	60
1202	28p. Band of Brothers	55	60
1203	50p. Prepare for Battle	1·00	1·10
1204	50p. Victory in Sight	1·00	1·10
1205	65p. The Fall of Nelson	1·30	1·40
1206	65p. The Death of Nelson	1·30	1·40
MS1207	170 × 75 mm. £1 Lieut. John Quilliam and Admiral Lord Nelson (No. 887); £1 Steering HMS *Victory* (No. 160)	4·00	4·25

POSTAGE DUE STAMPS

D 1

D 2

1973.

D1	D 1	½p. red, black and yellow	1·50	1·10
D2		1p. red, black and brown	50	60
D3		2p. red, black and green	15	20
D4		3p. red, black and grey	20	20
D5		4p. red, black and pink	30	35
D6		5p. red, black and blue	30	35
D7		10p. red, black and violet	40	40
D8		20p. red, black and green	75	60

1975.

D 9	D 2	½p. yellow, black and red	10	10
D10		1p. brown, black and red	10	10
D11		4p. lilac, black and red	10	15
D12		7p. blue, black and red	15	20
D13		9p. grey, black and red	25	30
D14		10p. mauve, blk & red	25	20
D15		50p. orange, blk & red	90	90
D16		£1 green, black and red	1·50	1·60

D 3

D 4

1982.

D17	D 3	1p. multicoloured	10	10
D18		2p. multicoloured	10	10
D19		5p. multicoloured	10	10
D20		10p. multicoloured	20	25
D21		20p. multicoloured	40	45
D22		50p. multicoloured	90	1·10
D23		£1 multicoloured	1·60	2·10
D24		£2 multicoloured	3·25	4·25

1992.

D25	D 4	£5 multicoloured	8·00	8·50

ISRAEL Pt. 19

The former British Mandate over Palestine was ended by the partition plan approved by the United Nations General Assembly on 29 November 1947, and on 14 May 1948 the new state of Israel was proclaimed.

1948. 1000 prutot (mils) = 1 Israeli pound.
1960. 100 agorot = 1 Israeli pound.
1980. 100 agorot = 1 shekel.

"TABS" All Israeli stamps (except the Postage Dues) exist with descriptive sheet margin attached. These so-called "Tabs" are popular and in some cases scarce. Prices are for stamps without "tab". Separate prices for stamps with "tabs" are given in Stanley Gibbons Catalogue, Part 19 (Middle East).

1 Palm Tree and Baskets with Dates

2 Silver Shekel and Pomegranates

1948. Ancient Jewish Coins. Perf or roul.

1	**1**	3m. orange	65	35
2	–	5m. green	65	35
3a	–	10m. mauve	65	35
4	–	15m. red	1·30	35
5	–	20m. blue	2·50	50
6	–	50m. brown	15·00	1·80
7	**2**	250m. green	34·00	17·00
8		500m. red on buff	£170	75·00
9		1000m. blue on blue (36 × 24 mm)	£300	£150

DESIGNS ON COINS: 5m. Vine leaf; 10m. Ritual jar; 15m. Bunch of grapes; 20m. Ritual cup; 50m. Tied palm branches and lemon.

See also Nos. 21/6, 40/51 and 90/93.

3 "Flying Scroll" Emblem

1948. Jewish New Year.

10	**3**	3m. brown and blue	65	40
11		5m. green and blue	65	40
12		10m. red and blue	85	65
13		20m. blue and light blue	3·25	1·50
14		65m. brown and red	17·00	7·50

4 Road to Jerusalem

5 National Flag

1949. Inauguration of Constituent Assembly.

15	**4**	250pr. brown and grey	2·10	1·80

1949. Adoption of New National Flag.

16	**5**	20pr. blue	1·00	50

1949. 1st Anniv of Israeli Postage Stamps. Sheet containing stamp similar to T **8** in block of four.

MS16a	75 × 95 mm. 10pr. claret	£130	65·00

6 Petah Tiqwa Well

1949. 70th Anniv of Founding of Petah Tiqwa.

17	**6**	40pr. brown and green	12·50	2·10

7 Air Force Badge

1949. Jewish New Year.

18	**7**	5pr. blue	85	40
19	–	10pr. green	85	40
20	–	35pr. brown	6·75	4·25

BADGES: 10pr. Navy; 35pr. Army.

8 Ancient Jewish Coin

10 Stag and Globe

1949. 2nd Jewish Coins issue. Inscr at left of 6 or 8 characters.

21	**8**	3pr. grey	15	15
22	–	5pr. violet (as No. 2)	15	15
23	–	10pr. green (as No. 3)	15	15
24	–	15pr. red (as No. 4)	35	15
25	–	30pr. blue	60	35
26	–	50pr. brown (as No. 6)	2·00	50

DESIGN: 30p.r. Ritual vessel.

For designs with larger inscription at left, see Nos. 40/51 and 90/93.

1950. Israel's Membership and 75th Anniv of U.P.U.

27	**10**	40pr. violet	1·30	65
28		80pr. red	1·50	85

11 Landing of Immigrants

1950. 2nd Anniv of Independence.

29	**11**	20pr. brown	3·25	1·70
30	–	40pr. green	13·50	7·50

DESIGN: 40pr. Line of immigrant ships.

12 Library and Book

1950. 25th Anniv of Founding of Hebrew University, Jerusalem.

31	**12**	100pr. green	50	50

13 Eagle

1950. Air.

32	–	5pr. blue	65	40
33	–	30pr. grey	40	40
34	–	40pr. green	40	40
35	–	50pr. brown	40	40
36	**13**	100pr. red	21·00	13·50
37	–	250pr. blue	2·50	1·70

DESIGNS—VERT: 5pr. Doves pecking grapes; 30pr. Eagle; 40pr. Ostrich; 50pr. Dove. HORIZ: 250pr. Dove with olive branch.

14 Star of David and Fruit

16 Runner and Track

1950. Jewish New Year.

38	**14**	5pr. violet and orange	15	15
39		15pr. brown and green	85	85

1950. 3rd Jewish Coins issue. Inscr at left of 13 characters.

40	3pr. grey	15	15
41	5pr. violet	15	15
42	10pr. green	15	15
43	15pr. red	15	15
44	20pr. orange	15	15
45	30pr. blue	15	15
46	35pr. green	60	35
47	40pr. brown	20	20
48	45pr. mauve	20	20
49	50pr. brown	25	20
50	60pr. red	20	20
51	85pr. blue	60	35

DESIGNS ON COINS: 3, 20pr. Palm tree and baskets with dates; 5, 35pr. Vine leaf; 10, 40pr. Ritual jar; 15, 45pr. Bunch of grapes; 30, 60pr. Ritual vessel; 50, 85pr. Tied palm branches and lemon.

For further designs with value at right, see Nos. 90/93.

1950. 3rd Maccabiah (sports meeting).

52	**16**	80pr. green and olive	4·25	2·10

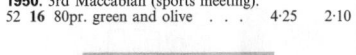

17 "The Negev" (after R. Rubin)

1950. Opening of Post Office at Elat.

53	**17**	500pr. brown & light brown	15·00	10·00

19 Memorial Tablet

1951. 40th Anniv of Founding of Tel Aviv.

54	**19**	40pr. brown	75	50

20 "Supporting Israel"

21 Metsudat Yesha

1951. Independence Bonds Campaign.

55	**20**	80pr. red	50	50

1951. 3rd Anniv of State of Israel.

56	**21**	15pr. red	25	25
57	–	40pr. blue (Hakastel)	75	75

22 Tractor

23 Ploughing and Savings Stamp

1951. 50th Anniv of Jewish National Fund.

58	**22**	15pr. brown	15	15
59	–	25pr. green	15	15
60	**23**	80pr. blue	1·70	1·20

DESIGN—As Type **22**: 25pr. Stylized tree.

24 Dr. T. Herzl

25 Carrier Pigeons

1951. 23rd Zionist Congress.

61	**24**	80pr. green	50	40

1951. Jewish New Year.

62	**25**	5pr. blue	15	10
63	–	15pr. red	15	10
64	–	40pr. violet	25	25

DESIGNS: 15pr. Woman and dove; 40pr. Scroll of the Law.

26 Menora and Emblems

1952.

64a	**26**	1000pr. black and blue	20·00	12·50

26a Haifa Bay, Mt. Carmel and City Seal

1952. Air. National Stamp Exn ("TABA").

64b	–	100pr. blue and black	85	60
64c	**26a**	120pr. purple and black	1·20	85

DESIGN: 100pr. Haifa Bay and City Seal.

27 Thistle and Yad Mordechai

1952. 4th Anniv of Independence.

65	**27**	30pr. brown and mauve	25	15
66	–	60pr. slate and blue	40	25
67	–	110pr. brown and red	85	60

DESIGNS: 60pr. Cornflower and Deganya; 110pr. Anemone and Safed.

28 New York Skyline and Z.O.A. Building

29 Figs

1952. Opening of American Zionist Building, Tel Aviv.

68	**28**	220pr. grey and blue	1·00	50

1952. Jewish New Year.

69	**29**	15pr. yellow and green	35	15
70	–	40pr. yellow, blue and violet	50	35
71	–	110pr. grey and red	75	65
72	–	220pr. green, brown & orge	1·10	85

FLOWERS: 40pr. Lily ("Rose of Sharon"); 110pr. Dove; 220pr. Nuts.

30 Dr. C. Weizmann (from sketch by R. Errell)

1952. Death of First President.

73	**30**	30pr. blue	25	15
74		110pr. black	75	60

31

32 Douglas DC-4 Airliner over Tel Aviv Yafo

1952. 70th Anniv of Bet Yaakov Lechu Venelcha Immigration Organization.

75	**31**	110pr. buff, green and brown	75	50

1953. Air.

76	–	10pr. deep green and green	35	20
77	–	70pr. violet and lilac	35	25
78	–	100pr. deep green and green	35	20
79	–	150pr. brown and orange	35	20
80	–	350pr. red and pink	50	50
81	–	500pr. deep blue and blue	1·10	85
81a	–	750pr. deep brown & brown	15	15
82	**32**	1000pr. deep green & green	4·25	3·25
82a	–	3000pr. purple	40	40

DESIGNS—HORIZ: 10pr. Olive tree; 70pr. Sea of Galilee; 100pr. Shaar Hogay on road to Jerusalem; 150pr. Lion Rock, Negev; 350pr. Bay of Elat. VERT: 500pr. Tanour Falls, near Metoulla; 750pr. Lake Hula; 3000pr. Tomb of Meir Baal Haness.

33 Anemones and Arms

35 Maimonides (philosopher)

1953. 5th Anniv of Independence.

83	**33**	110pr. red, green and blue	40	25

1953. 7th Int Congress of History of Science.

84	**35**	110pr. brown	1·40	60

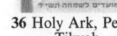

36 Holy Ark, Petah-Tikvah

37 Hand holding Globe/Football

1953. Jewish New Year.

85	–	20pr. blue	10	10
86	**36**	45pr. red	15	15
87	–	200pr. violet	75	50

DESIGNS: 20pr. Holy Ark, Jerusalem; 200pr. Holy Ark, Zefat.

1953. 4th Maccabiah.

88	**37**	110pr. brown and blue	50	25

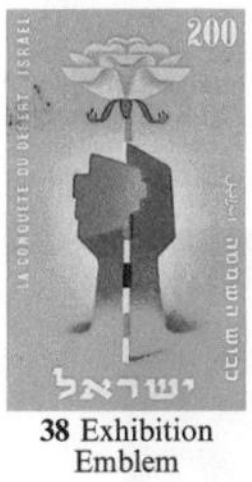
38 Exhibition Emblem

39 Ancient Jewish Coin

1953. "Conquest of the Desert" Exhibition.

89	**38**	200pr. multicoloured	50	25

1954. 4th Jewish Coins issue.

90	**39**	80pr. bistre	10	10
91	–	95pr. green	15	10
92	–	100pr. brown	15	10
93	–	125pr. blue	25	15

DESIGNS ON COINS: 95pr. Wheat; 100pr. Gate; 125pr. Lyre.

40 Gesher and Narcissus

41 Dr. T. Z. Herzl

1954. 6th Anniv of Independence.

94	–	60pr. blue, red and grey	10	10
95	**40**	350pr. brown, yellow & grn	50	35

DESIGN: 60pr. Yehiam and helichrysum.

1954. 50th Death Anniv of Herzl (founder of World Zionist Movement).

96	**41**	160pr. sepia, buff and blue	40	25

43

1954. Jewish New Year.

97	**43**	25pr. sepia	15	15

44 19th century Mail Coach and P.O.

1954. National Stamp Exhibition.

98	**44**	60pr. black, yellow and blue	10	10
99	–	200pr. black, red and green	40	40

DESIGN: 200pr. Mail van and G.P.O., 1954.

45 Baron Edmond de Rothschild

1954. 20th Death Anniv of De Rothschild (financier).

100	**45**	300pr. turquoise	40	25

46 Lamp of Knowledge

1955. 50th Anniv of Teachers' Association.

101	**46**	250pr. blue	35	25

47 Parachutist and Barbed Wire

48 Menora and Olive Branches

1955. Jewish Mobilization during 2nd World War.

102	**47**	120pr. black and turquoise	25	15

1955. 7th Anniv of Independence.

103	**48**	150pr. orange, black & grn	40	25

49 Immigrants and Ship

50 Musicians playing Timbrel and Cymbals

1955. 20th Anniv of Youth Immigration Scheme.

104	**49**	5pr. black and blue	10	10
105	–	10pr. black and red	10	10

106 – 25pr. black and green . . . 10 10
107 – 30pr. black and orange . . 10 10
108 – 60pr. black and violet . . . 10 10
109 – 750pr. black and brown . . 1·00 60
DESIGNS: 10pr. Immigrants and Douglas DC-3 airplane; 25pr. Boy and calf; 30pr. Girl watering flowers; 60pr. Boy making pottery; 750pr. Boy using theodolite.

1955. Jewish New Year.
110 **50** 25pr. green and orange . . 10 10
111 – 60pr. grey and orange . . 10 10
112 – 120pr. blue and yellow . . 10 10
113 – 250pr. brown and orange 35 25
DESIGNS—Musicians playing: 60pr. Ram's horn; 120pr. Tuba; 250pr. Harp.

51 Ambulance

52 "Reuben"

1955. 25th Anniv of Magen David Adom (Jewish Red Cross).
114 **51** 160pr. green, black and red 15 15

1955. Twelve Tribes of Israel.
115A **52** 10pr. green 10 10
116A – 20pr. mauve 10 10
117A – 30pr. blue 10 10
118A – 40pr. brown 10 10
119A – 50pr. blue 10 10
120A – 60pr. bistre 10 10
121A – 80pr. violet 10 10
122A – 100pr. red 10 10
123A – 120pr. olive 15 10
124A – 180pr. mauve 50 25
125A – 200pr. green 25 10
126A – 250pr. grey 35 10
EMBLEMS: 20pr. "Simeon" (castle); 30pr. "Levi" (High Priest's breastplate); 40pr. "Judah" (lion); 50pr. "Dan" (scales); 60pr. "Naphtali" (gazelle); 80pr. "Gad" (tents); 100pr. "Asher" (tree); 120pr. "Issachar" (sun and stars); 180pr. "Zebulun" (ship); 200pr. "Joseph" (sheaf of wheat); 250pr. "Benjamin" (wolf).

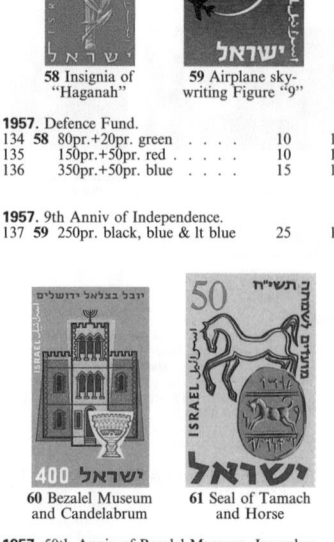

53 Professor Einstein

1956. Einstein Commemoration.
127 **53** 350pr. brown 25 15

54 Technion

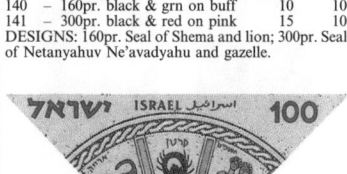

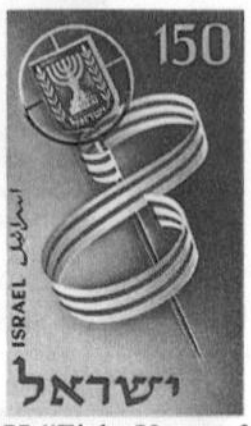
55 "Eight Years of Independence"

1956. 30th Anniv of Israel Institute of Technology, Haifa.
128 **54** 350pr. green and black . . 25 25

1956. 8th Anniv of Independence.
129 **55** 150pr. multicoloured . . . 15 10

56 Oranges

57 Musican playing Lyre

1956. 4th International Congress of Mediterranean Citrus Fruit Growers.
130 **56** 300pr. multicoloured . . . 25 25

1956. Jewish New Year. Musicians playing instruments.
131 **57** 30pr. brown and blue . . . 10 10
132 – 50pr. violet and orange . . 10 10
133 – 150pr. turquoise and orange 15 15
INSTRUMENTS—VERT: 50pr. Sistrum. HORIZ: 150pr. Double oboe.

58 Insignia of "Haganah"

59 Airplane sky-writing Figure "9"

1957. Defence Fund.
134 **58** 80pr.+20pr. green 10 10
135 150pr.+50pr. red 10 10
136 350pr.+50pr. blue 15 15

1957. 9th Anniv of Independence.
137 **59** 250pr. black, blue & lt blue 25 15

60 Bezalel Museum and Candelabrum

61 Seal of Tamach and Horse

1957. 50th Anniv of Bezalel Museum, Jerusalem.
138 **60** 400pr. multicoloured . . . 15 15

1957. Jewish New Year. Ancient Hebrew Seals.
139 **61** 50pr. black & brn on blue 10 10
140 – 160pr. black & grn on buff 10 10
141 – 300pr. black & red on pink 15 10
DESIGNS: 160pr. Seal of Shema and lion; 300pr. Seal of Netanyahuv Ne'avadyahu and gazelle.

61a Part of Ancient "Bet Alpha" Synagogue Floor Mosaic

1957. 1st Israeli International Stamp Exhibition. Sheet containing four triangular stamps, which together form the complete centre-piece of floor mosaic.
MS141a 103 × 105 mm. 100pr. Type **61a**; 200., 300, 400pr. (similar) 50 50

62 Throwing the Hammer

63 Ancient Hebrew Ship

1958. 25th Anniv of Maccabiah Games.
142 **62** 500pr. red and bistre . . . 15 15

1958. Israel Merchant Marine Commemoration.
143 **63** 10pr. red, blue and brown 10 10
144 – 20pr. brown and green . . 10 10
145 – 30pr. grey and red 15 10
146 – 1000pr. green and blue . . 35 35
DESIGNS—As T **63**: 20pr. Immigration ship "Nirit"; 30pr. Freighter "Shomron". 57 × 22 ½ mm: 1000pr. Liner "Zion".

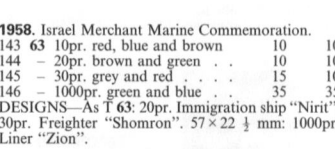

64 Menora and Olive Branch

1958. 10th Anniv of Independence.
147 **64** 400pr. green, black and gold 25 25

65 Dancing Children forming "10"

1958. 1st World Conference of Jewish Youth, Jerusalem.
148 **65** 200pr. green and orange 25 15

66 Convention Centre, Jerusalem, and Exhibition Emblem

1958. 10th Anniv (of Israel) Exn, Jerusalem.
149 **66** 400pr. orange and lilac on cream 25 25

67 Wheat

68 Ancient Stone

1958. Jewish New Year.
150 **67** 50pr. brown and ochre . . 10 10
151 – 60pr. black and yellow . . 10 10
152 – 160pr. purple and violet . . 10 10
153 – 300pr. green and apple . . 25 25
DESIGNS: 60pr. Barley; 160pr. Grapes; 300pr. Figs.
See also Nos. 166/8.

1958. 10th Anniv of Declaration of Human Rights.
154 **68** 750pr. black, yellow & blue 35 25

69 Post Office Emblem

70 Sholem Aleichem

1959. 10th Anniv of Israel Postal Services.
155 **69** 60pr. black, red and olive 10 10
156 – 120pr. black, red and olive 15 15
157 – 250pr. black, red and olive 20 15
158 – 500pr. black, red and olive 25 25
DESIGNS—HORIZ: 120pr. Mail van. VERT: 250pr. Radio-telephone equipment; 500pr. "Telex" dial and keyboard.

1959. Birth Cent of Sholem Aleichem (writer).
159 **70** 250pr. brown and green . . 20 15

71 Tel Aviv

72 Anemone

1959. 50th Anniv of Tel Aviv.
160 **71** 120pr. multicoloured . . . 20 15

1959. 11th Anniv of Independence. Mult.
161 60pr. Type **72** 10 10
162 120pr. Cyclamen 10 10
163 300pr. Narcissus 10 10
See also Nos. 188/9, 211/13 and 257/9.

73 C. N. Bialik

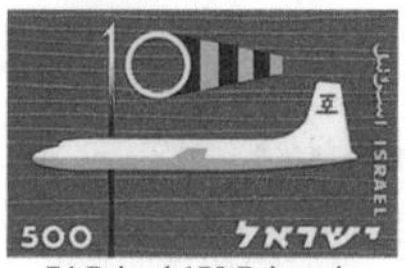
74 Bristol 175 Britannia Airliner and Wind-sock

1959. 25th Anniv of Chaim Bialik (poet).
164 **73** 250pr. olive and orange . . 25 15

1959. 10th Anniv of Civil Aviation in Israel.
165 **74** 500pr. multicoloured . . . 35 25

1959. Jewish New Year. As T **67**.
166 60pr. red and brown 10 10
167 200pr. green and deep green 15 15
168 350pr. orange and brown . . 25 25
DESIGNS: 60pr. Pomegranates; 200pr. Olives; 350pr. Dates.

76 E. Ben-Yehuda

77 Merhavya Settlement

1959. Birth Centenary of Ben-Yehuda (pioneer of Hebrew language).
169 **76** 250pr. deep blue and blue 25 25

1959. 50th Anniv of Merhavya and Deganya Settlements. 75th Anniv of Yesud Ha-Maala Settlement.
170 **77** 60pr. green and yellow . . 10 10
171 – 120pr. brown & light brown 25 15
172 – 180pr. green and blue . . . 40 35
DESIGNS: 120pr. Yesud Ha-Maala; 180pr. Deganya.

78 Ancient Jewish Coin

79 Tiberias

1960. New currency. Values in black.
173 **78** 1a. bistre on pink 10 10
174 3a. red on pink 10 10
175 5a. slate on pink 15 10
176 6a. green on blue 15 10
176a 7a. grey on blue 15 10
177 8a. mauve on blue 15 10
178 12a. blue on blue 15 10
179 18a. orange 15 10
180 25a. blue 20 15
181 30a. red 25 15
182 50a. lilac 35 15

1960. Air.
183 – 15a. black and lilac . . . 25 15
184 – 20a. black and green . . . 35 25
184a – 25a. black and orange . . 50 40
184b – 30a. black and turquoise 85 85
184c – 35a. black and green . . 1·10 85
184d – 40a. black and lilac . . . 2·10 1·70
184e – 50a. black and olive . . . 85 85
185 **79** 65a. black and blue . . . 2·10 2·10
185a – I£1 black and pink . . . 4·50 4·50
DESIGNS—VERT: 15a. Old town, Zefat; 20a. Tower, Ashqelon; 25a. Akko Tower and boats; 30a. View of Haifa from Mt. Carmel. HORIZ: 35a. Ancient synagogue, Capernaum; 40a. Kefar Hittim—Tomb of Jethro; 50a. City walls, Jerusalem. I£1, Old city, Yafo (Jaffa).

80 Operation "Magic Carpet"

1960. World Refugee Year.
186 **80** 25a. brown 25 25
187 – 50a. green 25 25
DESIGN: 50a. Resettled family.

1960. 12th Anniv of Independence. Flowers as T **72**.
188 12a. multicoloured 35 25
189 32a. yellow, green and brown 50 25
DESIGNS: 12a. "Pancratium maritimum"; 32a. "Oenothera drummondi".

81 Atomic Symbol and Reactor Building

83 King Saul

1960. Inauguration of Atomic Reactor.
190 **81** 50a. red, black and blue . . 85 50

1960. Jewish New Year. Centres multicoloured.
191 **83** 7a. green 25 15
192 – 25a. brown 50 35
193 – 40a. blue 65 35
DESIGNS: 25a. King David; 40a. King Solomon.

84 Dr. Theodor Herzl

85 Postal Courier, Prague, 1741

1960. Birth Centenary of Dr. Theodor Herzl (founder of World Zionist Movement).
194 **84** 25a. sepia and cream . . . 40 40

1960. "TAVIV" National Stamp Exhibition, Tel Aviv.
195 **85** 25a. black and grey . . . 1·50 90
MS195a 192 × 135 mm. No. 195 but in brown and green . . . . . 34·00 26·00
No. **MS**195a was only sold at the stamp exhibition.

86 Henrietta Szold

1960. Birth Centenary of Henrietta Szold (founder of Youth Immigration Scheme).
196 **86** 25a. violet and blue . . . 40 25

87 Badges of First Zionist Congress and Jerusalem

1960. 25th Zionist Congress, Jerusalem.
197 **87** 50a. light and deep blue . . 1·30 60

88 Ram (Aries)

89 The Twelve Signs

1961. Signs of the Zodiac.
198 **88** 1a. green 15 10
199 – 2a. red 15 10
200 – 6a. blue 15 10
201 – 7a. brown 15 10
202 – 8a. myrtle 15 10
203 – 10a. orange 15 10
204 – 12a. violet 20 15
205 – 18a. mauve 40 35
206 – 20a. olive 25 20
207 – 25a. purple 35 25
208 – 32a. black 60 50
209 – 50a. turquoise 65 60
210 **89** I£1 blue, gold and indigo 1·70 1·50
DESIGNS—As Type **88**: 2a. Bull (Taurus); 6a. Twins (Gemini); 7a. Crab (Cancer); 8a. Lion (Leo); 10a. Virgin (Virgo); 12a. Scales (Libra); 18a. Scorpion (Scorpio); 20a. Archer (Sagittarius); 25a. Goat (Capricorn); 32a. Waterman (Aquarius); 50a. Fishes (Pisces).

1961. 13th Anniv of Independence. Flowers as T **72**.
211 7a. yellow, brown and green 20 15
212 12a. green, purple and mauve 35 35
213 32a. red, green and blue . . . 50 40
FLOWERS: 7a. Myrtle; 12a. Squill; 32a. Oleander.

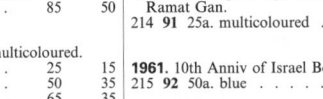

91 Throwing the Javelin

92 "A Decade of Israel Bonds"

1961. 7th "Hapoel" Sports Association Int Congress, Ramat Gan.
214 **91** 25a. multicoloured 50 40

1961. 10th Anniv of Israel Bond Issue.
215 **92** 50a. blue 60 50

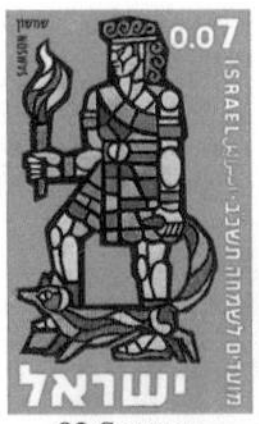
93 Samson

94 Bet Hamidrash (synagogue), Medzibozh (Russia)

1961. Jewish New Year. Heroes of Israel. Centres multicoloured.
216 **93** 7a. red 35 25
217 – 25a. grey 40 35
218 – 40a. lilac 50 40
HEROES: 25a. Yehuda Maceabi; 40a. Bar Kochba.

1961. Death Bicentenary of Rabbi Baal Shem Tov (founder of Hassidism movement).
219 **94** 25a. sepia and yellow . . . 40 35

95 Fir Cone

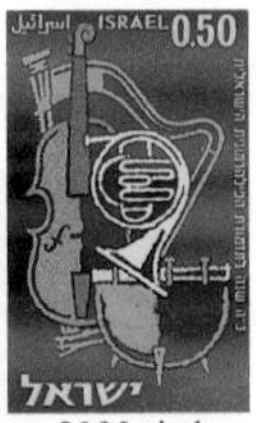
96 Musical Instruments

1961. Afforestation Achievements.
220 **95** 25a. yellow, black and green . . . . 1·00 85
221 – 30a. multicoloured . . . . 1·10 90
DESIGN: 30a. Symbol of afforestation.

1961. 25th Anniv of Israel Philharmonic Orchestra.
222 **96** 50a. multicoloured . . . . 2·00 2·00

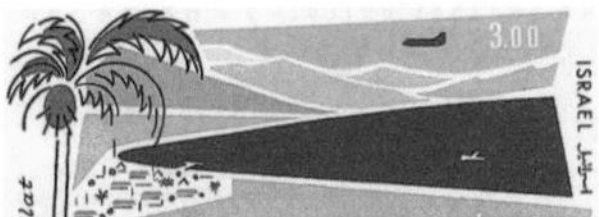
97 Bay of Elat

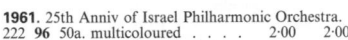

1962. Air.
223 **97** I£3 multicoloured . . . . 14·50 11·00

1962. As Nos. 198, 201 and 208 but colours changed and surch.
224 **88** 3a. on 1a. mauve 15 15
225 – 5a. on 7a. grey 15 15
226 – 30a. on 32a. green 15 15

99 Symbolic Flame

100 Sud Aviation Vatour IIA Bomber

1962. Heroes and Martyrs Day.
227 **99** 12a. yellow, red and black 35 25
228 – 55a. multicoloured . . . . 1·00 85
DESIGN: 55a. Nazi "Yellow Star" and candles.

1962. 14th Anniv of Independence.
229 **100** 12a. blue 65 65
230 – 30a. green . . . . 1·20 1·00
DESIGN: 30a. Flight of Vatour IIA bombers.

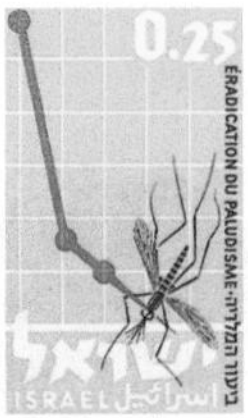
101 Mosquito and Malaria Graph

102 Rosh Pinna

1962. Malaria Eradication.
231 **101** 25a. bistre, red and black 50 40

1962. 80th Anniv of Rosh Pinna.
232 **102** 20a. green and yellow . . 50 40

103 Fair Flags

104 "The wolf also shall dwell with the lamb ..."

1962. Near East International Fair, Tel Aviv.
233 **103** 55a. multicoloured . . . 85 75

1962. Jewish New Year. Illustrating quotations from the Book of Isaiah.
234 **104** 8a. black, red and olive 40 35
235 – 28a. black, purple & olive 85 50
236 – 43a. black, orange & olive 1·30 1·00
DESIGNS: 28a. "And the leopard shall lie down with the kid ..."; 43a. "And the suckling child shall play on the hole of the asp ...".

105 Boeing 707 Jetliner

1962. El Al Airline Commemoration.
237 **105** 55a. indigo, lilac and blue 1·10 1·00
MS237a 195 × 36 mm. **105** 55a. indigo, lilac and blue (sold at I£1) 3·50 3·00

106 Pennant Coralfish

1962. Red Sea Fish (1st series). Multicoloured.
238 3a. Type **106** 15 15
239 6a. Racoon butterflyfish . . . 15 15
240 8a. Indian Ocean lionfish . . 25 20
241 12a. Royal angelfish 35 25
See also Nos. 265/8.

107 Symbolic Cogwheels

1962. 25th Anniv of United Jewish Appeal.
242 **107** 20a. blue, silver and red 60 50

108 J. Korczak (child educator)

109 Houbara Bustard

1962. Janusz Korczak Commemoration.
243 **108** 30a. sepia and grey . . . 60 50

1963. Air. Birds.
244 – 5a. pink, brown and violet 15 15
245 – 20a. turquoise, brn & red 35 25
246 – 28a. black, brown & green 35 25
247 – 30a. multicoloured . . . 35 25
248 – 40a. multicoloured . . . 50 25
249 – 45a. multicoloured . . . 75 60
250 **109** 55a. orange, black & turq 75 60
251 – 70a. bistre, brown & black 85 75
252 – I£1 orange, black and red 1·00 75
253 – I£3 multicoloured . . . . 3·00 3·00
DESIGNS—HORIZ: 5a. Sinai rosefinch; 20a. White-throated kingfisher; 28a. Mourning wheatear. VERT: 30a. European bee eater; 40a. Graceful prinia; 45a. Palestine sunbird; 70a. Eurasian scops owl; I£1 Purple heron; I£3, White-tailed sea eagle.

110 Bird in the Hand

1963. Freedom from Hunger.
254 **110** 55a. grey and black . . . 1·00 1·00

111 Construction at Daybreak

112 Compositor

1963. 25th Anniv of Stockade and Tower Settlements.
255 **111** 12a. brown, black & yell 35 35
256 – 30a. purple, black and blue 65 65
DESIGN: 30a. Settlement at night.

1963. 15th Anniv of Independence. Flowers. As T **72**.
257 8a. multicoloured 35 35
258 30a. yellow, rose and pink . . 1·00 1·00
259 37a. multicoloured . . . . . 1·70 85
FLOWERS: 8a. White lily; 30a. Bristly hollyhock; 37a. Sharon tulip.

1963. Centenary of Hebrew Press.
260 **112** 12a. purple and buff . . . 1·00 85
No. 260 comes in sheets of 16 (4 × 4) with overall background of replica of front page of first issue of Hebrew newspaper "Halbanon".

113 "And the sun beat upon the head of Jonah ..."

114 Hoe clearing Thistles

1963. Jewish New Year. Illustrating quotations from the Book of Jonah. Multicoloured.
261 8a. Type **113** 40 40
262 30a. "And there was a mighty tempest in the sea" (horiz) . . . . 1·10 1·10
263 55a. "And Jonah was in the belly of the fish" (horiz) . . 2·10 2·10

1963. 80th Anniv of Israeli Agricultural Settlements.
264 **114** 37a. multicoloured . . . 1·00 75

1963. Red Sea Fish (2nd series). As T **106**. Multicoloured.
265 2a. Undulate triggerfish . . . 15 15
266 6a. Radial lionfish 25 25
267 8a. Catalufa 35 35
268 12a. Emperor angelfish . . . 50 40

115 "Shalom"

1963. Maiden Voyage of Liner "Shalom".
269 **115** I£1 blue, turquoise & pur 8·50 6·25

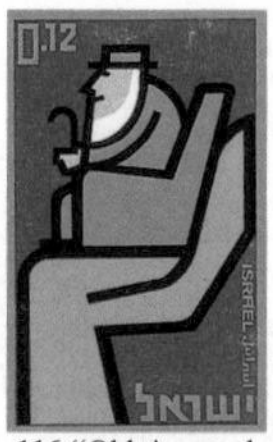

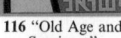

116 "Old Age and Survivors" **117** Pres. Ben-Zvi

1964. 10th Anniv of National Insurance. Multicoloured.
270 12a. Type **116** . . . . 1·30 60
271 25a. Nurse and child within hands ("Maternity") . . . 2·10 1·10
272 37a. Family within hand ("Large families") . . . . 2·50 1·30
273 50a. Hand with arm and crutch ("Employment injuries") . . . . 4·25 2·10

1964. 1st Death Anniv of President Izhak Ben-Zvi.
274 **117** 12a. brown 25 25

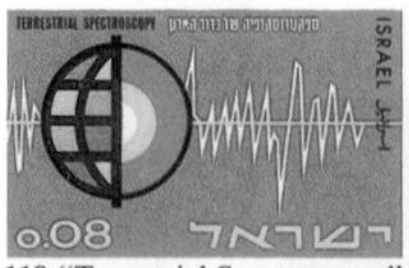

118 "Terrestrial Spectroscopy" **119** Running

1964. 16th Anniv of Independence. Israel's Contribution to Science. Multicoloured.
275 8a. Type **118** 35 35
276 35a. Macromolecules of living cell . . . . 1·00 85
277 70a. Electronic computer . . 2·10 1·80

1964. Olympic Games, Tokyo.
278 **119** 8a. black and red 15 15
279 – 12a. black and mauve . . 20 20
280 – 30a. red, black and blue 25 25
281 – 50a. red, purple and green 40 40
DESIGNS: 12a. Throwing the discus; 30a. Basketball; 50a. Football.

120 3rd Century Glass Vessel **121** Congress Emblem

1964. Jewish New Year. Showing glass vessels in Haaretz Museum, Tel Aviv. Multicoloured.
282 8a. Type **120** 15 15
283 35a. 1st-2nd century vessel 40 35
284 70a. 1st century vessel . . . 60 40

1964. 6th Israel Medical Assn's World Congress.
285 **121** I£1 multicoloured . . . . 1·00 85

122 "Exodus" (immigrant ship) **123** Eleanor Roosevelt

1964. "Year of the Blockade-Runners".
286 **122** 25a. black, blue & turq 40 35

1964. 80th Birth Anniv of Eleanor Roosevelt.
287 **123** 70a. purple 50 50

124 Olympics Symbols and Knight

1964. 16th Chess Olympics.
288 **124** 12a. brown 40 25
289 – 70a. green . . . . 1·80 1·30
DESIGN: 70a. Olympics symbol and rook.

125 "African–Israeli Friendship" **126** Masada

1964. "TABAI" National Stamp Exn, Haifa.
290 **125** 57a. multicoloured . . . 1·80 1·00
MS290a 125 × 81 mm. No. 290 (I£1) 2·30 3·00
No. **MS**290a was only sold at the stamp exhibition.

1965. Masada.
291 **126** 25a. green 40 25
292 – 36a. blue 60 40
293 – I£1 brown 85 65
DESIGNS—HORIZ: 36a. "Northern Palace", lower section. VERT: I£l, "Northern Palace" aerial view.

127 Ashdod **128** Fair Emblem

1965. Civic Arms (1st series).
294 – 1a. brown (Lod) 15 15
295 – 2a. mauve (Qiryat Shmona) 15 15
296 – 5a. black (Petah Tiqwa) 15 15
297 – 6a. violet (Nazareth) . . 15 15
298 – 8a. orange (Beer Sheva) 15 15
299 – 10a. green (Bet Shean) 15 15
300 – 12a. purple (Tiberias) . . 15 15
301 **127** 15a. green 15 15
302 – 20a. red (Elat) 15 15
303 – 25a. blue (Akko) 35 15
304 – 35a. purple (Dimona) . . 35 15
305 – 37a. green (Zefat) . . . 1·20 1·00
305a – 40a. brown (Mizpe Ramon) 50 35
306 – 50a. blue (Rishon Le Zion) 50 35
306a – 55a. red (Ashqelon) . . 50 35
307 – 70a. brown (Jerusalem) 85 65
307a – 80a. red (Rosh Pinna) 1·20 1·00
308 – I£1 green (Tel Aviv-Yafo) . . . . 1·00 85
309 – I£3 mauve (Haifa) . . . 1·30 1·20
Nos. 307, 308/9 are 22½ × 27 mm in size.
See also Nos. 413/24.

1965. 2nd International Book Fair, Jerusalem.
310 **128** 70a. black, blue and green 40 40

129 Hands reaching for barbed wire **130** "National Water Supply"

1965. 20th Anniv of Concentration Camps Liberation.
311 **129** 25a. black, yellow and grey 50 35

1965. 17th Anniv of Independence.
312 **130** 37a. brown, dp blue & bl 35 35

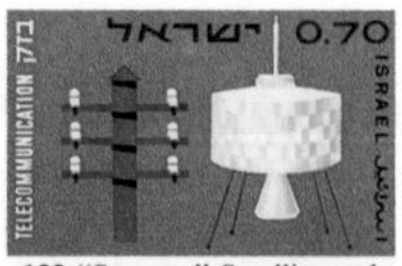

131 Potash Works, Sedom **132** "Syncom" Satellite and Telegraph Pole

1965. Dead Sea Industrial Development. Mult.
313 12a. Potash Works, Sedom 25 10
314 50a. Type **131** 65 35
The two stamps form one composite design when placed side by side.

1965. I.T.U. Centenary.
315 **132** 70a. violet, black and blue 60 40

133 "Co-operation" **134** "Light"

1965. International Co-operation Year.
316 **133** 36a. multicoloured . . . 40 35

1965. Jewish New Year. "The Creation". Multicoloured.
317 6a. Type **134** 15 15
318 8a. "Heaven" 15 15
319 12a. "Earth" 15 15
320 25a. "Stars" 35 35
321 35a. "Birds and Beasts" . . . 50 50
322 70a. "Man" 85 85

135 Foxy Charaxes **136** War of Independence Memorial

1965. Butterflies and Moths. Multicoloured.
323 2a. Type **135** 15 15
324 6a. Southern swallowtail . . 25 25
325 8a. Oleander hawk moth . . 25 25
326 12a. Sooty orange-tip 35 35

1966. Memorial Day.
327 **136** 40a. brown and black . . 35 35

137 Flags

1966. 18th Anniv of Independence. Mult.
328 12a. Type **137** 10 10
329 30a. Fireworks 15 15
330 80a. Dassault Mirage IIICJ jet fighters and warships 25 25

138 Knesset Building

1966. Inaug of Knesset Building, Jerusalem.
331 **138** I£1 blue 75 65

139 Scooter Rider **140** Spice Box

1966. Road Safety. Multicoloured.
332 2a. Type **139** 10 10
333 5a. Cyclist 10 10
334 10a. Pedestrian on crossing 10 10
335 12a. Child with ball 10 10
336 15a. Motorist in car 15 15

1966. Jewish New Year. Religious Ceremonial Objects. Multicoloured.
337 12a. Type **140** 15 15
338 15a. Candlesticks 15 15
339 35a. Kiddush cup 15 15
340 40a. Torah pointer 15 15
341 80a. Hanging lamp 40 40

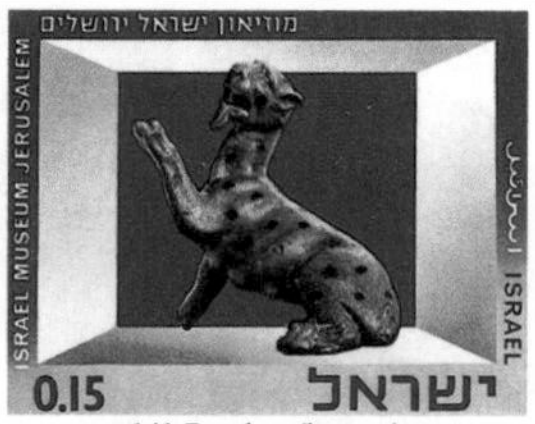

141 Panther (bronze)

1966. Israel Museum Exhibits. Multicoloured.
342 15a. Type **141** . . . . 1·30 1·30
343 30a. Synagogue menora (stone) . . . . 1·70 1·70
344 40a. Phoenician sphinx (ivory) . . . . 2·10 2·10
345 55a. Earring (gold) . . . . . 2·50 2·50
346 80a. Miniature capital (gold) 3·25 3·25
347 I£1.15 Drinking horn (gold) (vert) . . . . 5·75 5·75

142 Levant Postman and Mail Coach **143** "Fight Cancer and Save Life"

1966. Stamp Day.
348 **142** 12a. green and brown . . 10 10
349 – 15a. mauve, brown & grn 15 15
350 – 40a. blue and mauve . . . 25 25
351 – I£1 brown and blue . . . 50 40
DESIGNS: 15a. Turkish postman and camels; 40a. Palestine postman and steam locomotive. I£1, Israeli postman and Boeing 707 jetliner.

1966. Cancer Research.
352 **143** 15a. green and red . . . 25 25

144 Akko (Acre) **145** Book and Crowns

1967. Ancient Israeli Ports.
353 **144** 15a. purple 25 15
354 – 40a. green 40 35
355 – 80a. blue 60 50
PORTS: 40a. Caesarea; 80a. Yafo (Jaffa).

1967. Shulhan Arukh ("Book of Wisdom").
356 **145** 40a. multicoloured . . . 40 40

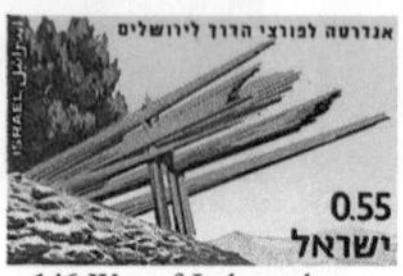

146 War of Independence Memorial

1967. Memorial Day.
357 **146** 55a. silver, blue & turq 50 40

147 Taylorcraft Auster AOP.5 Reconnaissance Plane

1967. Independence Day. Military Aircraft.
358 **147** 15a. blue and green . . . 15 15
359 – 30a. brown and orange 35 35
360 – 80a. violet and turquoise 50 50
AIRCRAFT: 30a. Dassault Mystere IVA jet fighter; 80a. Dassault Mirage IIICJ jet fighters.

148 Freighter "Dolphin" in Straits of Tiran

149 Law Scroll

1967. Victory in Arab–Israeli War.
361 – 15a. black, yellow and red . . . 10 10
362 **148** 40a. green 15 15
363 – 80a. violet 15 15
DESIGNS—VERT: 15a. Sword emblem of "Zahal" (Israeli Defence Forces). HORIZ: 80a. "Wailing Wall", Jerusalem.

1967. Jewish New Year. Scrolls of the Torah (Mosaic Law), and similar designs.
364 **149** 12a. multicoloured . . . 15 15
365 – 15a. multicoloured . . . 15 15
366 – 35a. multicoloured . . . 25 25
367 – 40a. multicoloured . . . 25 25
368 – 80a. multicoloured . . . 25 25

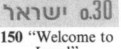

150 "Welcome to Israel"

151 Lord Balfour

1967. International Tourist Year. Each with "Sun" emblem. Multicoloured.
369 30a. Type **150** 15 15
370 40a. "Air hostess" 25 25
371 80a. "Orange" child 25 25

1967. 50th Anniv of Balfour Declaration.
372 – 15a. green 15 15
373 **151** 40a. brown 25 25
DESIGN: 15a. Dr. C. Weizmann.

152 Ibex

1967. Israeli Nature Reserves. Multicoloured.
374 12a. Type **152** 10 10
375 18a. Caracal 20 20
376 60a. Dorcas gazelle 35 35

153 Diamond

1968. Air. Israeli Exports.
377 – 10a. multicoloured . . . 15 15
378 – 30a. multicoloured . . . 15 15
379 – 40a. multicoloured . . . 15 15
380 – 50a. multicoloured . . . 35 35
381 – 55a. multicoloured . . . 35 35
382 – 60a. multicoloured . . . 40 35
383 – 80a. multicoloured . . . 40 35
384 – I£1 multicoloured 60 50
385 – I£1.50 multicoloured . . . 60 50
386 **153** I£3 violet and green . . . 1·00 90
DESIGNS: 10a. Draped curtains ("Textiles"); 30a. "Stamps"; 40a. Jar and necklace ("Arts and Crafts"); 50a. Chick and egg ("Chicks"); 55a. Melon, avocado and strawberries ("Fruits"); 60a. Gladioli ("Flowers"); 80a. Telecommunications equipment ("Electronics"). I£1, Atomic equipment ("Isotopes"). I£1.50, Models ("Fashion").

154 Beflagged Football

155 "Immigration"

1968. Pre-Olympic Football Tournament.
387 **154** 80a. multicoloured . . . 35 35

1968. Independence Day. Multicoloured.
388 15a. Type **155** 10 10
389 80a. "Settlement" 25 25

156 Rifles and Helmet

157 Zahal Emblem

1968. Memorial Day.
390 **156** 55a. multicoloured . . . 25 25

1968. Independence Day (Zahal–Israel Defence Forces).
391 **157** 40a. multicoloured . . . 25 25

158 Resistance Fighter (detail from Warsaw Monument)

159 Moshe Sharett

1968. 25th Anniv of Warsaw Ghetto Rising.
392 **158** 60a. bistre 40 35

1968. 27th Zionist Congress, Jerusalem.
393 **159** I£1 sepia 35 35

160 Candle and Cell Bars

161 Jerusalem

1968. Fallen Freedom Fighters.
394 **160** 80a. black, grey and brown 35 35

1968. Jewish New Year.
395 **161** 12a. multicoloured . . . 15 15
396 – 15a. multicoloured . . . 35 35
397 – 35a. multicoloured . . . 40 40
398 – 40a. multicoloured . . . 50 50
399 – 60a. multicoloured . . . 65 65
DESIGNS: Jerusalem—views of the Old City (12, 15, 35a.) and of the New City (40, 60a.).

162 Scout Badge and Knot

163 "Lions' Gate", Jerusalem (detail)

1968. 50th Anniv of Jewish Scout Movement.
400 **162** 30a. multicoloured . . . 15 15

1968. "Tabira" Stamp Exhibition, Jerusalem.
401 **163** I£1 brown 25 25
MS402 122×75 mm. No. 401 (sold at I£1.50) . . . . 2·10 2·50

164 A. Mapu

165 Paralytics playing Basketball

1968. Death Cent of Abraham Mapu (writer).
403 **164** 30a. olive 25 15

1968. International Games for the Paralysed.
404 **165** 40a. green and light green 25 25

166 Elat

1969. Israeli Ports.
405 **166** 30a. mauve 65 65
406 – 60a. brown (Ashdod) . . 85 85
407 – I£1 green (Haifa) . . . . 1·00 1·00

167 "Worker" and I.L.O. Emblem

168 Israeli Flag at Half-mast

1969. 50th Anniv of I.L.O.
408 **167** 80a. green and lilac . . . 35 35

1969. Memorial Day.
409 **168** 55a. gold, blue and violet 35 25

169 Army Tank

170 Flaming Torch

1969. Independence Day. Multicoloured.
410 15a. Type **169** 15 15
411 80a. "Elat" (destroyer) . . . 35 35

1969. 8th Maccabiah.
412 **170** 60a. multicoloured . . . 50 50

171 Arms of Hadera

172 Building the Ark

1969. Civic Arms (2nd series).
413 2a. green (Type **171**) 25 25
414 3a. purple (Herzliyya) 35 35
415 5a. orange (Holon) 40 40
416 15a. red (Bat Yam) 50 50
417 18a. blue (Ramla) 60 60
418 20a. brown (Kefar Sava) . . 60 60
419 25a. blue (Giv'atayim) . . . 75 75
420 30a. mauve (Rehovot) . . . 35 35
421 40a. violet (Netanya) 90 90
422 50a. blue (Bene Beraq) . . . 1·30 1·30
423 60a. green (Nahariyya) . . . 85 85
424 80a. green (Ramat Gan) . . 1·80 1·80

1969. Jewish New Year, showing scenes from "The Flood". Multicoloured.
425 12a. Type **172** 10 10
426 15a. Animals going aboard 15 15
427 35a. Ark afloat 20 20
428 40a. Dove with olive branch 25 25
429 60a. Ark on Mt. Ararat . . . 25 25

173 "King David" (Chagall)

174 Atomic "Plant"

1969. "King David".
430 **173** I£3 multicoloured . . . . 1·70 1·70

1969. 25th Anniv of Weizmann Institute of Science.
431 **174** I£1.15 multicoloured . . . 1·30 1·30

175 Dum Palms, Emeq He-Arava

176 Immigrant "Aircraft"

1970. Nature Reserves.
432 **175** 2a. olive 10 10
433 – 3a. blue 10 10
434 – 5a. red 10 10
435 – 6a. green 10 10
436 – 30a. violet 15 15
DESIGNS: 3a. Tahana Waterfall, Nahal Iyon; 5a. Nahal Baraq Canyon, Negev; 6a. Ha-Masreq, Judean Hills; 30a. Soreq Cave, Judean Hills.

1970. 20th Anniv of Operation "Magic Carpet" (Immigration of Yemenite Jews).
437 **176** 30a. multicoloured . . . 35 25

177 Joseph Trumpeldor

178 Prime Minister Levi Eshkol

1970. 50th Anniv of Defence of Tel Hay.
438 **177** I£1 violet 85 85

1970. Levi Eshkol Commemoration.
439 **178** 15a. multicoloured . . . 25 25

179 Ze'ev Jabotinsky (commander)

180 Camel and Diesel Train

1970. 50th Anniv of Defence of Jerusalem.
440 **179** 80a. green and cream . . 35 35

1970. Opening of Dimona–Oron Railway.
441 **180** 80a. multicoloured . . . 90 90

181 Mania Schochat (author)

183 Memorial Flame

184 "Orchis laxifloris"

182 Scene from "The Dybbuk"

1970. 60th Anniv of "Ha-Shomer".
442 **181** 40a. purple and cream . . 35 35

1970. 50th Anniv of Habimah National Theatre.
443 **182** I£1 multicoloured 65 65

1970. Memorial Day.
444 **183** 55a. black, red and violet 35 35

1970. Independence Day. Israeli Wild Flowers. Multicoloured.
445 12a. Type **184** 25 25
446 15a. "Iris mariae" 40 35
447 80a. "Lupinus pilosus" . . . 65 60

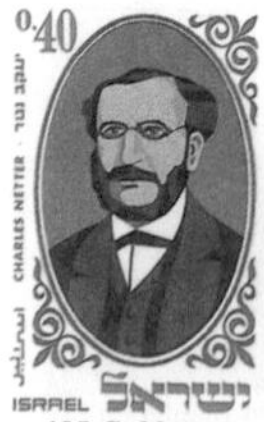
185 C. Netter (founder)

186 I.A.I. Arava Transport Airplane

1970. Centenary of Miqwe Yisrael Agricultural College. Multicoloured.
448 40a. Type **185** 60 40
449 80a. College building and gate . . . . 1·00 65

1970. Israeli Aircraft Industry.
450 **186** I£1 silver, violet and blue 50 40

187 Yachts

188 Keren Hayesod

1970. World "420" Class Sailing Championships. Multicoloured.
451 15a. Type **187** 35 35
452 30a. Yacht with spinnaker . . 40 35
453 80a. Yachts turning around buoy 60 50

1970. 50th Anniv of Keren Hayesod.
454 **188** 40a. multicoloured . . . 35 35

189 Old Synagogue, Cracow

1970. Jewish New Year. Multicoloured.
455 12a. Type **189** 10 10
456 15a. Great Synagogue, Tunis 10 10
457 35a. Portuguese Synagogue, Amsterdam 15 15
458 40a. Great Synagogue, Moscow 15 15
459 60a. Shearith Israel Synagogue, New York . . 25 25

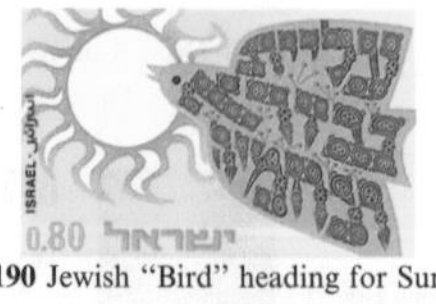
190 Jewish "Bird" heading for Sun

1970. "Operation Ezra and Nehemiah" (Exodus of Iraqi Jews to Israel).
460 **190** 80a. multicoloured . . . 35 35

191 Mother and Child

1970. 50th Anniv of Women's International Zionist Organization (W.I.Z.O).
461 **191** 80a. yellow, green & silver 60 50

192 Tel Aviv Post Office, 1920

193 Histadrut Emblem

1970. "Tabit" Stamp Exhibition, Tel Aviv, and 50th Anniv of Tel Aviv Post Office.
462 **192** I£1 multicoloured 40 40
MS463 115 × 70 mm. No. 462 (sold at I£1.50) . . . . 2·50 2·50

1970. 50th Anniv of "Histadrut" (General Federation of Labour).
464 **193** 35a. multicoloured . . . 25 25

194 "Landscape with Bridge" (C. Pissaro)

1970. Paintings in Tel Aviv Museum. Mult.
465 85a. "Jewish Wedding" (J. Israels) 25 25
466 I£1 Type **194** 40 40
467 I£2 "Flowers in a Vase" (F. Leger) 65 65

195 "Inn of the Ghosts" (Cameri Theatre)

1971. Israeli Theatre. Multicoloured.
468 50a. Type **195** 35 35
469 50a. "Samson and Delilah" (National Opera Company) 35 35
470 50a. "A Psalm of David" (I.N.B.A.L. Dance Theatre) 35 35

196 Fallow Deer

197 "Haganah" Emblem

1971. Nature Reserves. Animals of Biblical Times. Multicoloured.
471 2a. Type **196** 15 15
472 3a. Asiatic wild ass 15 15
473 5a. Arabian oryx 15 15
474 78a. Cheetah 40 15

1971. Memorial Day.
475 **197** 78a. multicoloured . . . 40 40

198 Jaffa Gate

1971. Independence Day. Gates of Jerusalem (1st series). Multicoloured.
476 15a. Type **198** 40 40
477 18a. New Gate 50 50
478 35a. Damascus Gate 65 65
479 85a. Herod's Gate . . . . . 1·10 1·10
MS480 93 × mm. As Nos. 476/9, but each in 28 × 28 mm format (sold for I£2) . . . . 4·50 4·25
See also 527/**MS**531

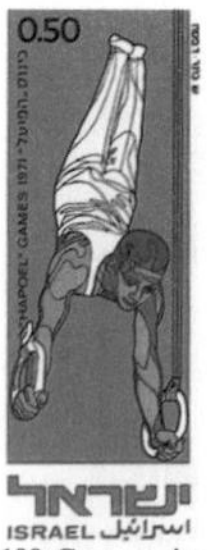
199 Gymnastics

200 "... and he wrote upon the tables ..."

1971. 9th "Hapoel" Games. Multicoloured.
481 50a. Type **199** 25 25
482 50a. Basketball 25 25
483 50a. Running 25 25

1971. Feast of Weeks ("Shavuot"). Illuminated verses from the Bible. Multicoloured.
484 50a. Type **200** 40 40
485 85a. "The first of the firstfruits ..." 60 50
486 I£1. 50 "... and ye shall observe the feast ..." . . . 85 75
See also Nos. 488/92.

201 "Sun over the Emeq"

1971. 50th Anniv of Settlements in the "Emeq" (Yezreel Valley).
487 **201** 40a. multicoloured . . . 25 25

1971. Jewish New Year. Feast of the Tabernacles ("Sukkot"). Illuminated Verses from the Bible. As T **200**. Multicoloured.
488 15a. "You shall rejoice in your feast" 15 15
489 18a. "You shall dwell in booths ..." 15 15
490 20a. "That I made the people ..." 25 25
491 40a. "... gathered in the produce" 25 25
492 65a. "... I will give you your rains ..." 25 25

202 Kinneret

203 "Agricultural Research"

1971. Landscapes (1st series).
493 – 3a. blue 40 40
494 – 5a. green 25 25
495 – 15a. orange 25 25
496 **202** 18a. purple . . . . . 1·50 1·50
497 – 20a. green 85 85
498 – 22a. blue . . . . . . 1·80 1·80
498a – 25a. red 40 40
499 – 30a. mauve 35 35
500 – 35a. purple 85 85
501 – 45a. blue 35 35
502 – 50a. green 50 50
503 – 55a. green 50 50
504 – 65a. brown . . . . . 1·00 1·00
505 – 70a. red 50 50
505apa – 80a. blue . . . . . . 1·70 1·70
506 – 88a. blue . . . . . . 1·90 1·90
507 – 95a. red . . . . 1·90 1·90
508 – I£1.10 brown . . . . 1·50 1·50
508a – I£1.30 blue 85 85
508b – I£1.70 brown 40 40
509pa – I£2 brown . . . . . 2·50 2·50
510pa – I£3 violet . . . . . 8·50 8·50
510a – I£10 blue . . . . . . 2·20 2·10
DESIGNS—As T **202**: 3a. Judean desert; 5a. Gan Ha-Shelosha; 15a. Negev desert; 20a. Tel Dan; 22a. Yafo; 25a. Arava; 30a. En Avedat; 35a. Brekhat Ram; 45a. Mt. Hermon; 50a. Rosh Pinna; 55a. Natanya; 65a. Plain of Zebulun; 70a. Engedi; 80a. Beach at Elat; 88a. Akko (Acre); 95a. Hamifratz Hane'Elam; I£1.10, Aqueduct near Acre; I£1.30, Zefat; I£1.70, Nazerat Illit; I£2, Coral Island; I£3, Haifa. 28 × 27 mm: I£10, Elat.
See also Nos. 682/4a.

1971. 50th Anniv of Volcani Institute of Agricultural Research.
511 **203** I£1 multicoloured 40 40

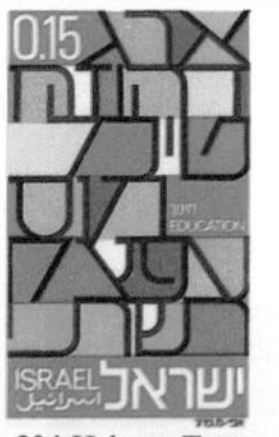
204 Hebrew Text

1971. Educational Development. Multicoloured.
512 15a. Type **204** 15 15
513 18a. Mathematical formulae 15 15
514 20a. Engineering symbols . . 15 15
515 40a. University degree abbreviations 15 15

205 "The Scribe" (sculpture, B. Schatz)

1972. Jewish Art.
516 **205** 40a. brown, copper & blk 25 25
517 – 55a. multicoloured . . . 25 25
518 – 70a. multicoloured . . . 40 40
519 – 85a. black and yellow . . 50 50
520 – I£1 multicoloured . . . 50 50
DESIGNS—VERT: 55a. "Sarah" (A. Pann); 85a. "Old Jerusalem" (woodcut, J. Steinhardt); I£1; "Resurrection" (A. Kahana). HORIZ: 70a. "Zefat" (M. Shemi).

206 The Flight from Egypt

207 "Let My People Go"

1972. Passover Feast ("Pesah"). Multicoloured.
521 18a. Type **206** 35 35
522 45a. Baking unleavened bread 40 40
523 95a. "Seder" table 60 60

1972. Campaign for Jewish Immigration.
524 **207** 55a. multicoloured . . . 2·10 2·10

208 Bouquet

209 Jethro's Tomb

1972. Memorial Day.
525 **208** 55a. multicoloured . . . 35 35

1972. "Nebi Shuaib" (Jethro's Tomb) (Druse shrine).
526 **209** 55a. multicoloured . . . 35 35

1972. Independence Day. Gates of Jerusalem (2nd series). As T **198**. Multicoloured.
527 15a. Lion's Gate 65 50
528 18a. Golden Gate 85 60
529 45a. Dung Gate 85 65
530 55a. Zion Gate . . . . . . 1·00 75
MS531 93 × 93 mm. As Nos. 527/530, but each in format 28 × 28 mm (sold for I£2) . . . 4·25 4·25

210 Ghetto Entrance

211 Book Year Texts

1972. 400th Death Anniv of Rabbi Yizhaq Luria ("Ari").
532 **210** 70a. multicoloured . . . 2·50 2·50

1972. International Book Year.
533 **211** 95a. black, red and blue 50 50

212 Dish Aerial

213 Ancona Ark

1972. Opening of Satellite Earth Station.
534 **212** I£1 multicoloured 35 35

1972. Jewish New Year. Holy Arks from Italy.
535 **213** 15a. brown and yellow . . 15 15
536 – 45a. green, gold & lt green 25 25
537 – 70a. red, blue and yellow 40 40
538 – 95a. purple and gold . . . 60 60
DESIGNS: 45a. Soragna Ark; 70a. Padua Ark; 95a. Reggio Emilia Ark.

214 Menora Emblem

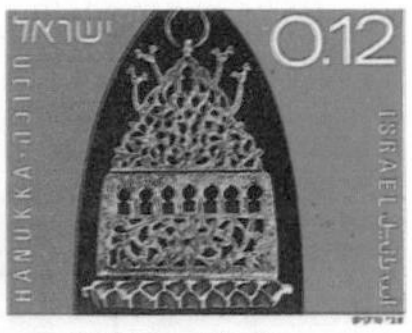
215 Hanukka Lamp (Morocco, 18th–19th century)

1972. 25th Anniv of State of Israel.
539 **214** I£1 blue, purple and silver 25 25

1972. Festival of Lights ("Hanukka"). Ceremonial Lamps. Multicoloured.
540 12a. Type **215** 15 15
541 25a. 18th-century Polish lamp 15 15
542 70a. 17th-century German silver lamp 35 35

216 Pendant

217 "Horse and Rider"

1973. Immigration of North African Jews.
543 **216** 18a. multicoloured . . . 25 25

1973. Children's Drawings. Multicoloured.
544 2a. Type **217** 10 10
545 3a. "Balloon ride" (17 × 48 mm) 10 10
546 55a. "Party-time" 25 25

218 "Reuben" Window

219 Flame of Remembrance

1973. "Tribes of Israel" Stained-glass Windows by Chagall, Hadassah Synagogue, Jerusalem. Multicoloured.
547 I£1 "Levi" 85 85
548 I£1 "Simeon" 85 85
549 I£1 Type **218** 85 85
550 I£1 "Issachar" 85 85
551 I£1 "Zebulun" 85 85
552 I£1 "Judah" 85 85
553 I£1 "Asher" . . . . 1·30 1·30
554 I£1 "Gad" . . . . 1·30 1·30
555 I£1 "Dan" . . . . 1·30 1·30
556 I£1 "Benjamin" . . . . . . 1·30 1·30
557 I£1 "Joseph" . . . . 1·30 1·30
558 I£1 "Naphtali" . . . . . . 1·30 1·30

1973. Memorial Day.
559 **219** 65a. multicoloured . . . 35 35

220 Skeletal Hand

1973. Holocaust (Persecution of European Jews 1933–45) Memorial.
560 **220** 55a. blue 25 25

221 Signatures of Declaration of Independence

1973. Independence Day.
561 **221** I£1 multicoloured 35 35
MS562 65 × 147 mm. No. 561 (sold for I£1.50) . . . . 1·30 1·40

222 Star of David and Runners

223 Isaiah

1973. 9th Maccabiah.
563 **222** I£1.10 multicoloured . . . 25 25

1973. Jewish New Year. Prophets of Israel.
564 18a. Type **223** 10 10
565 65a. Jeremiah 15 15
566 I£1.10 Ezekiel 15 15

224 Jews in Boat, and Danish Flag

225 Institute Emblem and Cogwheel

1973. 30th Anniv of Rescue of Danish Jews.
567 **224** I£5 black, red and brown 1·00 90

1973. 50th Anniv of "Technion" Israel Institute of Technology.
568 **225** I£1.25 multicoloured . . . 25 25

226 Collectors within "Stamp"

227 Soldier with Prayer Shawl

1973. "Jerusalem 73" International Stamp Exhibition. Multicoloured.
569 20a. Type **226** 10 10
570 I£1 Collectors within "Stamp" (different) 15 15
MS571 Three sheets, each 121 × 75 mm. (a) I£1 250m. stamp of 1948; (b) I£2 500m. stamp of 1948; (c) I£3 1000m. stamp of 1948 3·75 3·75

1974. Memorial Day.
572 **227** I£1 black and blue . . . 25 25

228 Quill and Bottle of Ink

229 "Woman in Blue" (M. Kisling)

1974. 50th Anniv of Hebrew Writers' Association.
573 **228** I£2 black and gold . . . 35 35

1974. Jewish Art. Multicoloured.
574 I£1.25 Type **229** 25 25
575 I£2 "Mother and Child" (bronze, C. Orloff) 35 25
576 I£3 "Girl in Blue" (C. Soutine) 35 35
See also Nos. 604/6.

230 Spanner

1974. 50th Anniv of Young Workers' Movement.
577 **230** 25a. multicoloured . . . 15 15

231 Lady Davis Technical Centre, Tel Aviv

1974. "Architecture in Israel" (1st series).
578 **231** 25a. grey 10 10
579 – 60a. blue 10 15
580 – I£1.45 brown 15 15
DESIGNS: 60a. Elias Sourasky Library, Tel Aviv University. I£1.45, Mivtahim Rest-home, Zikhron Yaaqov.
See also Nos. 596/8.

232 Istanbuli Synagogue

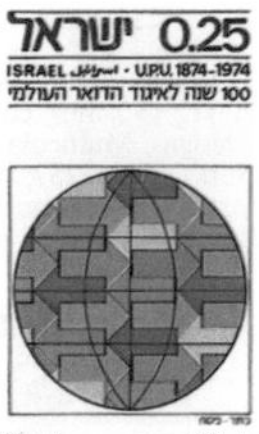
233 Arrows on Globe

1974. Jewish New Year. Rebuilt Synagogues in Jerusalem's Old City. Multicoloured.
581 25a. Type **232** 10 10
582 70a. Emtzai Synagogue . . . 10 10
583 I£1 Raban Yohanan Ben Zakai Synagogue 15 15

1974. Centenary of U.P.U. Multicoloured.
584 25a. Type **233** 10 10
585 I£1.30 Dove "postman" (27 × 27 mm) 25 25

234 David Ben Gurion (statesman)

1974. Ben Gurion Memorial.
586 **234** 25a. brown 10 10
587 I£1.30 green 25 25

236 Child with Plant, and Rainbow

238 Welding

237 Hebrew University, Jerusalem

1975. Arbour Day. Multicoloured.
588 1a. Type **236** 10 10
589 35a. Bird in tree 10 10
590 I£2 Child with plant and sun 20 20

1975. 50th Anniv of Hebrew University, Jerusalem.
591 **237** I£2.50 multicoloured . . . 35 35

1975. "Occupational Safety". Multicoloured.
592 30a. Type **238** 10 10
593 80a. Tractor-driving 10 10
594 I£1.20 Telegraph line maintenance 15 15

239 Harry S. Truman

240 Memorial

1975. Truman Commemoration.
595 **239** I£5 brown 50 50

1975. "Architecture in Israel" (2nd series). As T **231**.
596 80a. brown 15 15
597 I£1.30 green 20 20
598 I£1.70 brown 25 25
DESIGNS: 80a. Hebrew University Synagogue, Jerusalem. I£1.30, Museum, Yad Mordechai. I£1.70, City Hotel, Bat Yam.

1975. Memorial Day.
599 **240** I£1 red, black and mauve 30 30

241 Text and Poppy

242 Hurdling

1975. Fallen Soldiers' Memorial.
600 **241** I£1.45 black, red and grey 30 30

1975. 10th Hapoel Games. Multicoloured.
601 25a. Type **242** 15 15
602 I£1.70 Cycling 20 20
603 I£3 Volleyball 25 25

1975. Jewish Art. As T **229**. Multicoloured.
604 I£1 "Hanukka" (M. D. Oppenheim) 25 25
605 I£1.40 "The Purim Players" (J. Adler) (horiz) 35 35
606 I£4 "Yom Kippur" (M. Gottlieb) 40 40

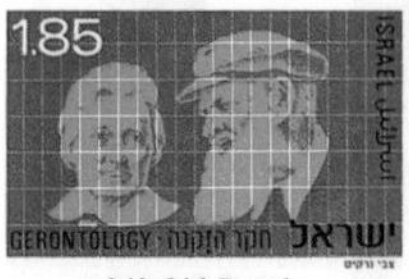

243 Old People **244** Gideon

1975. Gerontology.
607 **243** I£1.85 multicoloured . . . 25 25

1975. Jewish New Year. Judges of Israel. Mult.
608 35a. Type **244** 10 10
609 I£1 Deborah 15 15
610 I£1.40 Jephthah 25 25

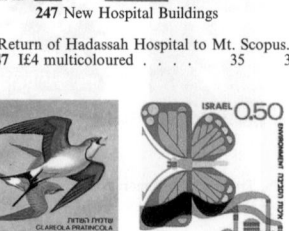

245 Zalman Shazar **246** Emblem of Pioneer Women

1975. 1st Death Anniv of Zalman Shazar (President 1963–73).
611 **245** 35a. black and silver . . . 25 25

1975. 50th Anniv of Pioneer Women's Organization.
612 **246** I£5 multicoloured 30 25

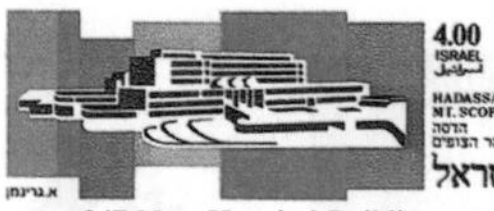

247 New Hospital Buildings

1975. Return of Hadassah Hospital to Mt. Scopus.
613 **247** I£4 multicoloured 35 35

248 Pratincole **249** "Air Pollution"

1975. Protected Wild Birds. Multicoloured.
614 I£1.10 Type **248** 25 25
615 I£1.70 Spur-winged plover . . 35 35
616 I£2 Black-winged stilt 40 40

1975. "Environmental Quality". Multicoloured.
617 50a. Type **249** 15 15
618 80a. "Water pollution" . . . 15 15
619 I£1.70 "Noise pollution" . . 25 25

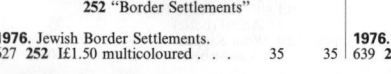

250 Star of David **251** Symbolic "Key"

1975.
620 **250** 75a. blue and red . . . 35 35
621 I£1.80 blue and grey . . 40 40
622 I£1.85 blue and brown 35 35
623 I£2.45 blue and green . . 35 35
623a I£2.70 blue and mauve 50 50
623b I£4.30 blue and red . . 25 25
624 I£5.40 blue and bistre . . 1·00 1·00
625 I£8 blue and turquoise 75 75

1976. 70th Anniv of Bezalel Academy of Arts and Design, Jerusalem.
626 **251** I£1.85 multicoloured . . . 35 35

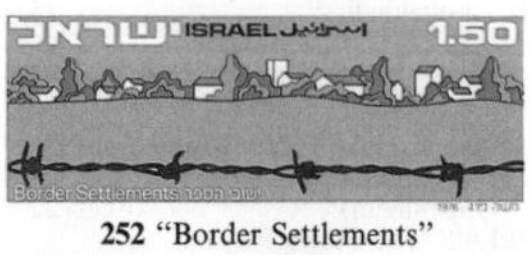

252 "Border Settlements"

1976. Jewish Border Settlements.
627 **252** I£1.50 multicoloured . . . 35 35

253 "In the days of Ahasuerus ..." **254** Monument to the Fallen

1976. "Purim" Festival. Multicoloured.
628 40a. Type **253** 10 10
629 80a. "He set the royal crown ..." 10 10
630 I£1.60 "Thus shall it be done ..." 15 15
MS631 127 × 86 mm. Nos. 628/30 65 65

1976. Memorial Day.
632 **254** I£1.85 multicoloured . . . 35 35

255 "Dancers of Meron" (R. Rubin)

1976. Lag Ba-Omer Festival.
633 **255** I£1.30 multicoloured . . . 50 40

256 "200" Flag

1976. Bicentenary of American Revolution.
634 **256** I£4 multicoloured 50 50

257 Diamond ("Industry")

1976. "Netyanya 76" National Stamp Exhibition. Sheet 112 × 75 mm, containing T **257** and similar vert designs. Multicoloured.
MS635 I£1 Type **257**; I£2 Sailing ("sport"); I£4 Beach umbrella ("tourism") . . . . 1·30 1·30

258 High Jump

1976. Olympic Games, Montreal.
636 **258** I£1.60 black and red . . . 35 35
637 – I£2.40 black and blue . . 35 35
638 – I£4.40 black and mauve 40 40
DESIGNS: I£2.40, Swimming. I£4.40, Gymnastics.

259 Multiple Tent Emblems **260** "Truth"

1976. Camping.
639 **259** I£1.60 multicoloured . . . 25 25

1976. Jewish New Year. Multicoloured.
640 45a. Type **260** 40 40
641 I£1.50 "Judgement" 40 40
642 I£1.90 "Peace" 40 40

261 Excavated Byzantine House

1976. Archaeology in Jerusalem (1st series). Multicoloured.
643 I£1.30 Type **261** 25 25
644 I£2.40 Arch of 2nd Temple 40 40
645 I£2.80 Staircase to 2nd Temple 50 50

262 Pawn **263** Clearing Ground

1976. 22nd Chess Olympiad, Haifa. Mult.
646 I£1.30 Type **262** 50 50
647 I£1.60 Rook 50 50

1976. Archaeology in Jerusalem (2nd series). As T **261**. Multicoloured.
648 70a. City Wall, First Temple period 15 15
649 I£5 Omayyad palace 85 85

1976. Pioneers.
650 **263** 5a. brown and gold . . . 10 10
651 – 10a. lilac and gold 10 10
652 – 60a. red and gold 15 15
653 – I£1.40 blue and gold . . . 15 15
654 – I£1.80 green and gold . . 15 15
DESIGNS—HORIZ: 10a. Building breakwater. I£1.40, Ploughing. I£1.80, Ditch-clearing. VERT: 60a. Road construction.

264 "Grandfather's Carrot"

1977. Voluntary Service.
655 **264** I£2.60 multicoloured . . . 40 40

265 "By the Rivers of Babylon"

1977. Drawings of E. M. Lilien.
656 **265** I£1.70 brown, grey & black 35 30
657 – I£1.80 black, stone & brn 35 30
658 – I£2.10 green, lt green & blk 40 40
PAINTINGS—VERT: I£1.80, "Abraham". HORIZ: I£2.10, "May Our Eyes Behold".

266 Jew and Arab shaking Hands

1977. Children's Drawings on Peace. Mult.
659 50a. Type **266** 15 15
660 I£1.40 Arab and Jew holding hands 25 25
661 I£2.70 Peace dove, Jew and Arab 40 40

267 Parachute Troops Memorial

1977. Memorial Day.
662 **267** I£3.30 multicoloured . . . 55 55

268 Embroidery showing Sabbath Loaves **269** Trumpet

1977. Sabbath.
663 **268** I£3 multicoloured 40 40

1977. Ancient Musical Instruments. Mult.
664 I£1.50 Type **269** 25 25
665 I£2 Lyre 25 25
666 I£5 "Jingle" (cymbals) . . . 30 30

270 Fencing **272** American Zionist Emblem

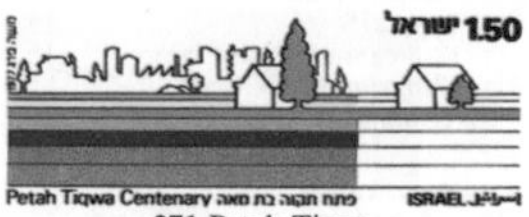

271 Petah Tiqwa

1977. 10th Maccabiah Games.
667 **270** I£1 grey, blue and black 25 25
668 – I£2.50 grey, red and black 30 30
669 – I£3.50 grey, green & black 40 40
DESIGNS: I£2.50, Putting the shot. I£3.50, Judo.

1977. Centenary of Petah Tiqwa.
670 **271** I£1.50 multicoloured . . . 30 30

1977. Zionist Organization of America Convention.
671 **272** I£4 multicoloured 50 50

273 Page of 16th-cent Book "Kohelet Yaakov" **274** Sarah

1977. 400th Anniv of Hebrew Printing at Zefat.
672 **273** I£4 black, gold and red 65 40

1977. Jewish New Year. Matriarchs of Israel. Multicoloured.
673 70a. Type **274** 10 10
674 I£1.50 Rebekah 15 15
675 I£2 Rachel 25 25
676 I£3 Leah 30 30
See also Nos. 728/30.

275 Police **276** Helmet and Model Settlement

1977. National Police Force. Multicoloured.
677 I£1 Type **275** 15 15
678 I£1 Civil Guard 15 15
679 I£1 Frontier Guard 15 15

1977. "Nahal" Pioneering Fighting Youth.
680 **276** I£3.50 multicoloured . . . 40 40

277 Accelerator Building, Weizmann Institute **278** Caesarea

1977. Inauguration of Koffler Accelerator.
681 **277** I£8 blue and black . . . 70 70

1977. Landscapes (2nd series).
682 **278** 10a. blue 80 80
683b – I£1 bistre 95 95
684 – I£20 green and orange 2·00 1·90
684a – I£50 multicoloured . . . 2·40 2·20
DESIGNS—As T **278**: I£1, Arava. 29 × 27 mm: I£20, Rosh Pinna. 27½ × 36½ mm: I£50, Soreq Cave.

279 "Mogul" Steam Locomotive, 1892

1977. Railways in the Holy Land. Mult.
685 65a. Type **279** 25 20
686 I£1.50 Steam locomotive . . 30 30
687 I£2 4-6-0 Class P steam locomotive 30 30
688 I£2.50 Diesel locomotive . . 40 30
MS689 112 × 75 mm. Nos. 685/8 1·70 1·80

280 Blood-stained Scallop ("Gloripallium pallium")

1977. Red Sea Shells. Multicoloured.
690 I£2 Type **280** 20 20
691 I£2 Pacific grinning tun ("Malea pomum") 20 20
692 I£2 Isabelle cowrie ("Cypraea isabella") 20 20
693 I£2 Camp Pitar venus ("Lioconcha castrensis") 20 20

281 "The Marriage Parties" (Dutch Ketubah)

1978. Illuminated Jewish Marriage Contracts (Ketubah). Multicoloured.
694 75a. Type **281** 15 15
695 I£3.90 Moroccan Ketubah . . 30 25
696 I£6 Jerusalem Ketubah . . . 40 35

282 "A Street in Jerusalem" (H. Gliksberg) **283** Eliyahu Golomb (leader of Hagana)

1978. Jewish Art.
697 **282** I£3 multicoloured 25 20
698 – I£3.80 black, yellow & grey 30 30
699 – I£4.40 multicoloured . . . 40 40
DESIGNS: I£3.80, "Thistles" (L. Krakauer).I£4.40, "An Alley in Zefat" (M. Levanon).

1978. Historical Personalities (1st series).
700 **283** I£2 green and yellow . . 30 30
701 – I£2 blue and grey 30 30
702 – I£2 purple and stone . . . 30 30
703 – I£2 brown and stone . . 30 30
704 – I£2 black and grey . . . 30 30
DESIGNS: No. 701, David Raziel (Irgun commander); 702, Yitzhak Sadeh (nationalist and military commander); 703, Dr. Moshe Sneh (Zionist politician); 704, Abraham Stern (underground fighter).
See also Nos. 721/2, 725/6, 732/3, 738/40, 763/5, 809/11 and 831/3.

284 Children's Flower Paintings (from mural, Petah Tikvah Museum)

1978. Memorial Day.
705 **284** I£1.50 multicoloured . . . 10 10
706 – I£1.50 multicoloured . . . 10 10
707 – I£1.50 multicoloured . . . 10 10
708 – I£1.50 multicoloured . . . 10 10
709 – I£1.50 multicoloured . . . 10 10
710 – I£1.50 multicoloured . . . 10 10
711 – I£1.50 multicoloured . . . 10 10
712 – I£1.50 multicoloured . . . 10 10
713 – I£1.50 multicoloured . . . 10 10
714 – I£1.50 multicoloured . . . 10 10
715 – I£1.50 multicoloured . . . 50 40
716 – I£1.50 multicoloured . . . 50 40
717 – I£1.50 multicoloured . . . 50 40
718 – I£1.50 multicoloured . . . 50 40
719 – I£1.50 multicoloured . . . 50 40
Nos. 705/19 issued together form a composite design, each showing a different portion of the Memorial Wall.

1978. Historical Personalities (2nd series). As T **283**.
721 I£2 blue and stone 60 50
722 I£2 brown and grey 60 60
DESIGNS: No. 721, Dr. Chaim Weizmann (first president of Israel); No. 722, Dr. Theodor Herzl (founder of Zionism).

286 Y.M.C.A. Building Jerusalem

1978. Centenary of Jerusalem Y.M.C.A.
723 **286** I£5.40 multicoloured . . . 50 50

287 Verse of National Anthem **288** Family Groups

1978. Centenary of Publication of "Hatiqwa" (Jewish National Anthem).
724 **287** I£8.40 silver, dp blue & bl 65 65

1978. Historical Personalities (3rd series). As T **283**.
725 I£2 purple and cream 60 50
726 I£2 green and cream 60 60
DESIGNS: No. 725, Rabbi Ouziel; No. 726, Rabbi Kook.

1978. Social Welfare.
727 **288** I£5.10 multicoloured . . . 50 50

1978. Jewish New Year, Patriarchs of Israel. As T **274**. Multicoloured.
728 I£1.10 Abraham 25 20
729 I£5.20 Isaac 30 30
730 I£6.60 Jacob 40 40

289 Star of David, Young Tree and Globe showing U.S.A. **291** Indian Silver and Enamelled Vase

290 Shaare Zedek Medical Centre, New and Old Buildings

1978. United Jewish Appeal.
731 **289** I£8.40 multicoloured . . . 65 65

1978. Historical Personalities (4th series). As T **283**.
732 I£2 purple and stone 15 15
733 I£2 blue and grey 15 15
DESIGNS: No. 732, David Ben-Gurion (first Prime Minister); No. 733, Ze'ev Jabotinsky (Zionist leader).

1978. Opening of New Shaare Zedek Medical Centre, Jerusalem.
734 **290** I£5.40 multicoloured . . . 15 10

1978. Institute for Islamic Art, Jerusalem. Multicoloured.
735 I£2.40 Type **291** 15 10
736 I£3 13th-century Persian pottery chess rook (elephant with howdah) . . 25 25
737 I£4 Syrian Mosque lamp . . 30 30

1978. Historical Personalities (5th series). As T **283**.
738 I£2 black and stone 15 15
739 I£2 blue and grey 15 15
740 I£2 black and stone 15 15
DESIGNS: No. 738, Menahem Ussishkin (president of Jewish National Fund); No. 739, Berl Katzenelson (pioneer of Zionist socialism); No. 740, Dr. Max Nordau (journalist).

292 "Iris lortetii" **293** Agricultural Mechanization

1978. Wild Irises. Multicoloured.
741 I£1.10 Type **292** 25 25
742 I£5.40 "Iris haynei" 40 40
743 I£8.40 "Iris nazarena" . . . 50 50

1979. Technological Achievements. Mult.
744 I£1.10 Type **293** 10 10
745 I£2.40 Sea water desalination 20 15
746 I£4.30 Electronics 20 15
747 I£5 Chemical fertilizers . . . 20 15

294 Jewish Brigade Flag **295** "Good from Evil"

1979. Yishuv Volunteers serving in Second World War.
748 **294** I£5.10 yellow, blue & dp bl 50 50

1979. "Salute to the Righteous among Nations".
749 **295** I£5.40 multicoloured . . . 50 50

296 Prayer for Peace in Western Wall **297** Naval Memorial, Ashdod

1979. Signing of Egyptian–Israeli Peace Treaty.
750 **296** I£10 multicoloured . . . 50 50
MS751 119 × 78 mm. No. 750. Imperf 65 65

1979. Memorial Day.
752 **297** I£5.10 multicoloured . . . 40 40

298 Weightlifting **299** "50" and Rotary Emblem

1979. 11th Hapoel Games. Multicoloured.
753 I£1.50 Type **298** 25 20
754 I£6 Tennis 40 40
755 I£11 Gymnastics 65 60

1979. 50th Anniv of Rotary in Israel.
756 **299** I£7 multicoloured 50 50

300 Rabbi Joshua Ben Hananiah (blacksmith) **301** Tiberias Hot Springs

1979. Jewish New Year. The "Hazal" (sages and craftsmen). Multicoloured.
757 I£1.80 Type **300** 20 10
758 I£8.50 Rabbi Meir Ba'al Ha-Nes (scribe) 30 20
759 I£13 Rabbi Johanan the Sandal-maker 40 40

1979. Health Resorts. Multicoloured.
760 I£8 Type **301** 25 20
761 I£12 Dead Sea Hot Spring 50 50

302 "Searchlight Beam" **303** Arab and Jew before Jerusalem

1979. 50th Anniv of Jewish Agency.
762 **302** I£10 blue, grey & turquoise 40 40

1979. Historical Personalities (6th series). As T **283**.
763 I£7 purple and grey 25 20
764 I£9 blue 25 20
765 I£13 black and stone 40 40
DESIGNS: I£7, Dr. Arthur Ruppin ("father of Zionist settlement"). I£9, Joseph Trumpeldor (founder of Zion Mule Corps and Jewish Legion). I£13, Aaron Aaronsohn (botanist).

1979. Children Paint Jerusalem. Multicoloured.
766 I£1.80 Type **303** 10 10
767 I£4 Jewish, Christian and Muslim citizens of Jerusalem (horiz) 20 15
768 I£5 Worshippers at the Western Wall (horiz) . . . 20 15

304 Boy sliding down Rainbow

305 Cog with Star of David

1979. International Year of the Child.

769	**304** I£8.50 multicoloured . . .	40	40

1980. Centenary of Organization for Rehabilitation through Training.

770	**305** I£13 multicoloured . . .	65	65

306 "Scolymus maculatus"

307 "The Road of Courage" Monument

1980. Thistles. Multicoloured.

771	50a. Type **306**	20	10
772	I£5.50 "Echinops viscosus"	35	25
773	I£8.50 "Cynara syriaca" . .	40	30

1980. Memorial Day.

774	**307** I£12 multicoloured . . .	40	40

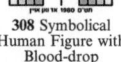

308 Symbolical Human Figure with Blood-drop

309 Sabbath Lamp, Netherlands, 18th-century

1980. 50th Anniv of Magden David Adom (voluntary medical corps).

775	**308** I£2.70 red, grey and black	20	15
776	– I£13 multicoloured . . .	30	30
MS777	124 × 64 mm. Nos. 775/776 × 2	2·40	2·30

DESIGN: I£13, Mobile intensive care unit and graph.

1980. Jewish New Year. Sabbath Lamps. Multicoloured.

778	I£4.30 Type **309**	15	20
779	I£20 Germany, 18th-century	50	40
780	I£30 Morocco, 19th-century	65	50

310 Yizhak Gruenbrum

311 Tree and Flowers

1980. 10th Death Anniv of Yizhak Gruenbaum (Zionist and politician).

781	**310** I£32 brown	95	95

1980. Renewal of Jewish Settlement in Gush Etzion.

782	**311** I£19 multicoloured . . .	55	55

312 Haifa

1980. "Hafia 80" National Stamp Exhibition. Sheet 100 × 84 mm containing T **312** and similar vert design showing details of 17th-century engraving of Hafia. Multicoloured.

MS783	2s. Type **312**; 3s. Hafia (different) (sold at 7s.50) . . .	2·75	3·25

New currency.
1 (new) shekel = 10 (old) Israeli pounds.

313 "Shekel"

314 Golda Meir

1980.

784	**313**	5a. green and emerald	30	30
785		10a. red and mauve . .	30	30
786		20a. turquoise and blue	30	30
787		30a. violet & deep violet	30	30
788		50a. orange and red . .	40	30
789 a		60a. green and purple	40	30
790		70a. blue and black . .	95	95
791		90a. violet and brown	1·20	1·20
792		1s. mauve and green . .	55	55
793		1s.10 green and red . .	50	50
794		1s.20 blue and red . .	50	50
795		2s. green and purple . .	70	70
796		2s.80 brown and green	70	70
797 a		3s. red and blue . . .	2·00	2·00
798		3s.20 grey and red . .	80	70
799 b		4s. purple and mauve	1·50	1·50
800		4s.20 blue and violet . .	80	70
801 a		5s. green and black . .	80	70
802pa		10s. brown & dp brown	11·50	10·50

1981. Golda Meir (former Prime Minister). Commemoration.

803	**314** 2s.60 purple	50	50

315 Landscape (Anna Ticho)

1981. Paintings of Jerusalem. Multicoloured.

804	50a. Type **315**	20	15
805	1s.50 "View of City" (Joseph Zaritsky) (vert)	40	30
806	2s.50 Landscape (Mordechai Ardon)	50	40

316 Hand putting Coin into Light Bulb

317 A. H. Silver (Zionist)

1981. Energy. Multicoloured.

807	2s.60 Type **316**	40	40
808	4s.20 Hand squeezing energy from the sun	55	45

1981. Historical Personalities (7th series).

809	– 2s. blue	50	40
810	– 2s.80 green	50	50
811	**317** 3s.20 ochre and black . .	50	50

DESIGNS—As T **283**: 2s. Shmuel Yosef Agnon (writer); 2s.80, Moses Montefiore (Zionist).

318 Biq'at Ha-yarden Memorial

319 Board Sailing

1981. Memorial Day.

812	**318** 1s. multicoloured	30	30

1981. 11th Maccabiah Games. Multicoloured.

813	80a. Type **319**	30	25
814	4s. Basketball	50	45
815	6s. High jump	65	60

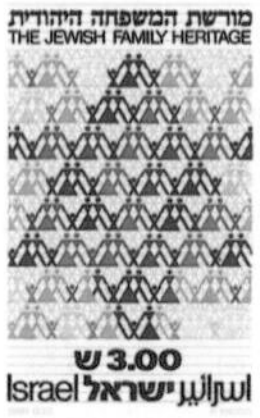

320 "Family Tree"

321 Moses and the Burning Bush

1981. The Jewish Family Heritage.

816	**320** 3s. multicoloured	55	55

1981. Jewish New Year. Moses. Multicoloured.

817	70a. Type **321**	15	15
818	1s. Moses and Aaron petitioning Pharoah for Israelites' freedom	25	20
819	3s. Israelites crossing the Red Sea	50	45
820	4s. Moses with the Tablets	55	50

322 "Rosa damascena"

1981. Roses. Multicoloured.

821	90a. Type **322**	65	60
822	3s.50 "Rosa phoenicia" . . .	65	60
823	4s.50 "Rosa hybrida"	65	60

323 Ha-Shiv'a Interchange

1981. Ha-Shiv'a Motorway Interchange.

824	**323** 8s. multicoloured	70	70

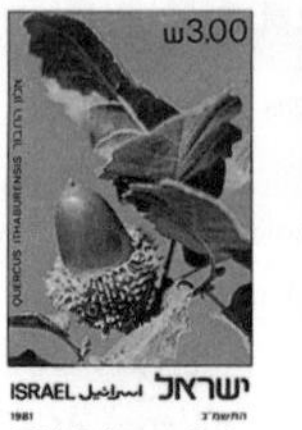

324 Balonea Oak

325 Elat Stone

1981. Trees. Multicoloured.

825	3s. Type **324**	40	35
826	3s. Wild strawberry	40	35
827	3s. Judas tree	40	35

1981. Precious Stones. Multicoloured.

828	2s.50 Type **325**	30	20
829	5s.50 Star sapphire	55	50
830	7s. Emerald	70	60

1982. Historical Personalities (8th series). As T **283**.

831	7s. multicoloured	65	60
832	8s. brown, stone and black	65	60
833	9s. blue and grey	65	60

DESIGNS: 7s. Perez Bernstein (politician); 8s. Rabbi Arye Levin; 9s. Joseph Gedaliah Klausner (writer, editor and President of Hebrew Language Academy).

327 Child crossing Road

1982. Road Safety.

834	**327** 7s. multicoloured	70	70
MS835	127 × 79 mm. No. 834 (sold at 10s.)	2·00	2·20

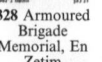

328 Armoured Brigade Memorial, En Zetim

330 Emblem and Flowers

329 Landscape (Aryeh Lubin)

1982. Memorial Day.

836	**328** 1s.50 multicoloured . . .	30	30

1982. Israeli Art. Multicoloured.

837	7s. Type **329**	65	65
838	8s. "Landscape" (Sionah Tagger) (vert)	80	70
839	15s. "Pastorale" (Israel Paldi)	1·40	1·40

1982. 40th Anniv of Gadna (Youth Corps).

840	**330** 5s. multicoloured	95	95

331 Agricultural Products

332 Joshua and Israelites setting out for Canaan

1982.

841	**331**	40a. blue and green . . .	80	80
842		80a. blue and mauve . . .	80	80
843		1s.40 green and red . . .	50	50
844		6s. mauve and red	95	95
845		7s. red and green	40	40
846		8s. green and red	40	40
847		9s. green and brown . . .	1·60	1·60
848		15s. red and green	8·00	8·00
849		30s. purple and red . . .	3·50	3·50
850		50s. bistre and red . . .	2·40	2·40
851		100s. black and green . .	4·75	4·75
852		500s. red and black . . .	6·00	6·00

1982. Jewish New Year. Joshua. Mult.

860	1s.50 Type **332**	25	20
861	5s.50 Priests carrying Ark of the Covenant over River Jordan	30	30
862	7s.50 The fall of the walls of Jericho	40	35
863	9s.50 The suspension of twilight during the battle against the five kings of Amorite	50	40

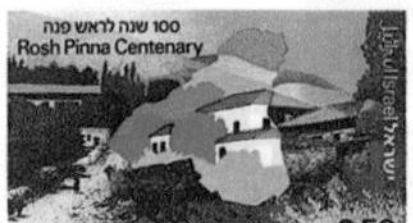

333 Rosh Pinna

334 Symbolic Figures on Star of David

1982. Centenaries of Rosh Pinna and Rishon Le Zion Settlements. Multicoloured.
864 2s.50 Type **333** 40 40
865 3s.50 Rishon Le Zion 40 40
See also Nos. 868/9, 905/6 and 967.

1982. 70th Anniv of Hadassah (Women's Zionist Organization of America).
866 **334** 12s. multicoloured 95 95

335 Branch

336 Flower

1982. No value expressed.
867 **335** (–) brown and orange . . 50 50
No. 867 was initially sold at 1s.70 but this value was subsequently increased several times.

1982. Centenaries of Zikhron Yaaqov and Mazkeret Batya. As T **333**. Multicoloured.
868 6s. Zikhron Yaaqov 65 65
869 9s. Mazkeret Batya 80 80

1982. Council for a Beautiful Israel.
870 **336** 17s. multicoloured . . . . 1·20 1·20

1982. Beer Sheva 82" National Stamp Exhibition. Sheet 130 × 78 mm.
MS871 No. 870 (sold at 25s.) . . 2·00 2·20

337 Eliahu Bet Tzuri

338 Honey Bee, Honeycomb and Flowers

1982. "Martyrs of the Struggle for Israel's Independence".
872 **337** 3s. grey, black and brown 25 25
873 – 3s. grey, black and olive 25 25
874 – 3s. grey, black and blue 25 25
875 – 3s. grey, black and olive 25 25
876 – 3s. grey, black and brown 25 25
877 – 3s. grey, black and blue 25 25
878 – 3s. grey, black and brown 25 25
879 – 3s. grey, black and olive 25 25
880 – 3s. grey, black and blue 25 25
881 – 3s. grey, black and olive 25 25
882 – 3s. grey, black and brown 25 25
883 – 3s. grey, black and olive 25 25
884 – 3s. grey, black and blue 25 25
885 – 3s. grey, black and brown 25 25
886 – 3s. grey, black and blue 25 25
887 – 3s. grey, black and olive 25 25
888 – 3s. grey, black and blue 25 25
889 – 3s. grey, black and brown 25 25
890 – 3s. grey, black and olive 25 25
891 – 3s. grey, black and brown 25 25
DESIGNS: No. 873, Hannah Szenes; 874, Shlomo Ben Yosef; 875, Yosef Lishanski; 876, Naaman Belkind; 877, Eliezer Kashani; 878, Yechiel Dresner; 879, Dov Gruner; 880, Mordechai Alkachi; 881, Eliahu Hakim; 882, Meir Nakar; 883, Avshalom Haviv; 884, Ya'akov Weiss; 885, Meir Feinstein; 886, Moshe Barazani; 887, Eli Cohen; 888, Samuel Azaar; 889, Dr. Moshe Marzouk; 890, Shalom Salih; 891, Yosef Basri.

1983. Bee-keeping.
892 **338** 30s. multicoloured . . . . 2·00 2·00

339 Sweets in Ashtray

1983. Anti-smoking Campaign.
893 **339** 7s. multicoloured 50 50

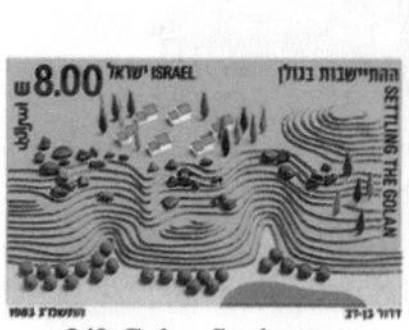

340 Golan Settlement

341 84th Division "of Steel" Memorial, Besor (Israel Godowitz)

1983. Settlements. Multicoloured.
894 8s. Type **340** 65 60
895 15s. Galil settlement 80 80
896 20s. Yehuda and Shomeron settlements 95 90

1983. Memorial Day.
897 **341** 3s. multicoloured 40 40

342 Star of David

1983. 35th Anniv of Independence.
898 **342** 25s. multicoloured . . . . 1·80 1·80
MS899 120 × 84 mm. No. 898. Imperf . . . . 3·50 3·25

343 Running

1983. 12th Hapoel Games.
900 **343** 6s. multicoloured 50 50

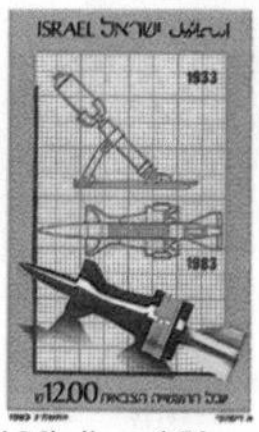

344 Missile and Blueprint

1983. 50th Anniv of Israel Military Industries.
901 **344** 12s. multicoloured 70 70

345 "The Last Way" (Iosef Kuzhovsky)

1983. Babi Yar Massacre.
902 **345** 35s. multicoloured . . . . 1·60 1·60

346 Yosef Giazman

1983. 40th Anniv of Warsaw and Vilna Ghettos Uprising. Sheet 120 × 86 mm containing T **346** and similar square designs. Multicoloured.
MS903 10s. Type **346**; 10s. Commemorative text; 10s. Mordechai Anielewicz (sold at 45s.) . . . . 3·50 3·50

347 Raoul Wallenberg

348 Ohel Moed Synagogue, Tel Aviv

1983. Raoul Wallenberg (Swedish diplomat) Commemoration.
904 **347** 14s. stone and brown . . 1·20 1·20

1983. Centenary of Yesud Ha-Maala and Nes Ziyyona. As T **333**. Multicoloured.
905 11s. Yesud Ha-Maala 65 60
906 13s. Nes Ziyyona 65 60

1983. Jewish New Year. Synagogues. Mult.
907 3s. Type **348** 25 25
908 12s. Yeshurun Synagogue, Jerusalem 40 40
909 16s. Ohel Aharon Synagogue, Haifa 70 70
910 20s. Khalaschi Synagogue, Beer Sheva 80 80

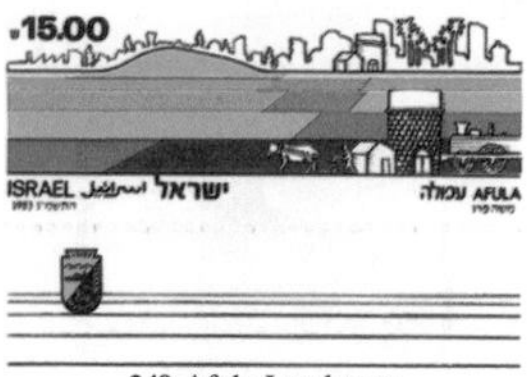

349 Afula Landscape

1983. Afula Urban Centre, Jezreel Valley.
911 **349** 15s. multicoloured 90 90

350 Promenade, Tel Aviv

1983. "Tel Aviv 83" Stamp Exhibition. Sheet 142 × 88 mm containing T **350** and similar vert design. Multicoloured.
MS912 30s. Type **350**; 50s. Promenade (sold at 120s.) . . . 7·25 7·25

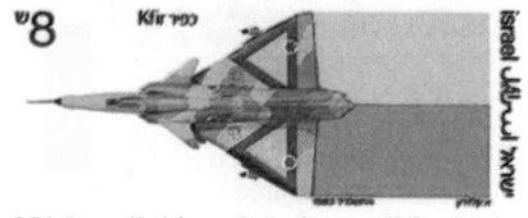

351 Israeli Aircraft Industry Kfir-C2 Jet Fighter

1983. Military Equipment. Multicoloured.
913 8s. Type **351** 25 20
914 18s. "Reshef" (missile vessel) 40 40
915 30s. "Merkava" battle tank 65 60

352 Rabbi Meir Bar-Ilan

353 "Aliya" ("immigration")

1983. 34th Death Anniv of Rabbi Meir Bar-Ilan (Zionist leader).
916 **352** 9s. blue and green 40 40

1983. 50th Anniv of Jewish Immigration from Germany.
917 **353** 14s. red, gold and blue . . 40 40

354 Michael Halperin

355 Yigal Allon

1984. 65th Death Anniv of Michael Halperin (nationalist).
918 **354** 7s. brown, stone & dp brn 30 30

1984. 4th Death Anniv of Yigal Allon (politician).
919 **355** 15s. blue, green and black 30 30

356 Uri Zvi Grinberg

357 Hevel Ha-Besor

1984. 3rd Death Anniv of Uri Zvi Grinberg (poet).
920 **356** 16s. brown and red . . . 30 30

1984. Settlements. Multicoloured.
921 12s. Type **357** 30 30
922 17s. Arava 40 40
923 40s. Hevel Azza 80 80

358 Alexander Zaid Monument (David Polus)

1984. Sculptures.
924 **358** 15s. stone, black and blue 40 40
925 – 15s. stone, black & brown 40 40
926 – 15s. green, black and grey 40 40
DESIGNS: No. 925, Tel Hay Memorial (Abraham Melnikov); 926, Dov Gruner monument (Chana Orloff).

359 Oliphant House, Dalyat Al Karmil (memorial to Druse Community)

360 Worker with Flag

1984. Memorial Day.
927 **359** 10s. multicoloured 25 25

1984. 50th Anniv of National Labour Federation.
928 **360** 35s. multicoloured 50 50

361 Leon Pinsker

362 Stars and Hearts

1984. 93rd Death Anniv of Leon Pinsker (Zionist leader).
929 **361** 20s. lilac and purple . . . 30 30

1984. 70th Anniv of American Jewish Joint Distribution Committee.
930 **362** 30s. red, blue and black 40 40

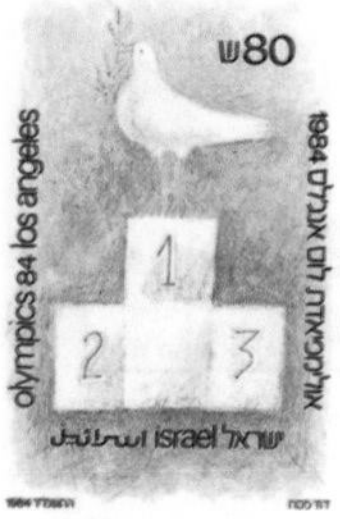

363 Dove on Olympic Podium

364 General Charles Orde Wingate

1984. Olympic Games, Los Angeles.
931 **363** 80s. multicoloured 90 90
MS932 119 × 80 mm. **363** 240s. multicoloured . . . . 6·50 6·50

1984. 40th Death Anniv of Gen. Charles Orde Wingate (military strategist).
933 **364** 20s. grey, black and green 30 30

365 Hannah **366** Nahalal (first Moshav)

1984. Jewish New Year. Women in the Bible. Multicoloured.
934 15s. Type **365** 30 25
935 70s. Ruth 65 60
936 100s. Huldah the prophetess 80 75

1984. Moshavim (Co-operative Workers' Settlements).
937 **366** 80s. multicoloured 70 70

367 David Wolffsohn **368** "Apartment to Let" (Leah Goldberg, illus Shemuel Katz)

1984. 70th Death Anniv of David Wolffsohn (president of Zionist Organization).
938 **367** 150s. brown, blue & black 1·50 1·50

1984. Children's Books. Multicoloured.
939 20s. Type **368** 25 25
940 30s. "Why is the Zebra wearing pyjamas?" (O. Hille, illus Alona Frankel) (28 × 28 mm) . . 30 30
941 50s. "Across the Sea" (Haim Nahman Bialik, illus Nahum Gutman) 40 40

369 Bread and Wheat

1984. World Food Day.
942 **369** 200s. multicoloured . . . 1·20 1·20

370 Isaac Herzog

1984. 25th Death Anniv of Isaac Herzog (Israel's first Chief Rabbi).
943 **370** 400s. multicoloured . . . 2·20 2·20

371 Lappet-faced Vulture

1985. Biblical Birds of Prey (1st series). Multicoloured.
944 100s. Type **371** 80 80
945 200s. Bonelli's eagle . . . . 1·20 1·20
946 300s. Sooty falcon . . . . . 2·00 2·00
947 500s. Griffon vulture . . . . 3·25 3·25
MS948 120 × 82 mm. As Nos. 944/7 but smaller (33 × 23 mm) . . . 9·75 10·50
See also Nos. 1015/**MS**1019

372 Golani Brigade Monument and Museum

1985. Memorial Day.
949 **372** 50s. multicoloured 40 40

373 Bleriot XI

1985. Aviation in the Holy Land. Mult.
950 50s. Type **373** (landing by Jules Vedrines, 1913) . . . 30 30
951 150s. Short S.17 Kent flying boat "Scipio" (Imperial Airways regular flights via Palestine, 1931–42) 65 65
952 250s. De Havilland D.H.82A Tiger Moth (foundation of Palestine Flying Club, 1934) . . . . 1·00 1·00
953 300s. Short S.16 Scion II (international flights by Palestine Airways, 1937–40) 1·20 1·20

374 Zivia and Yitzhak Zuckerman

1985. Zivia and Yitzhak Zuckerman (Polish Jewish freedom fighters) Commemoration.
954 **374** 200s. brown, grey & black 95 95

375 Nurses tending Patients

1985. 18th International Congress of Nurses.
955 **375** 400s. multicoloured . . . 1·50 1·50

376 Dome of the Rock

1985. "Israphil 85" International Stamp Exhibition, Tel Aviv. Three sheets containing various designs.
MS956 Three sheets. (a) 120 × 80 mm. 200s. Type **376**; 200s. Western wall; 200s. Church of the Holy Sepulchre; (b) 120 × 80 mm. 350s. 16th-century relief; 350s. 18th-century relief; 350s. 12–13th century relief (each 25 × 39 mm); (c) 79 × 120 mm. 800s. Adam and Eve with serpent (30 × 30 mm) (sold at 1200s) 17·00 17·00

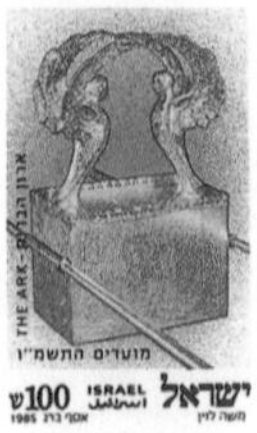

377 Ark of the Covenant **378** "Medals"

1985. Jewish New Year. Tabernacle Furnishings. Multicoloured.
957 100s. Type **377** 40 35
958 150s. The table 40 35
959 200s. Candlestick 50 45
960 300s. Incense altar 70 70

1985. International Youth Year.
961 **378** 150s. multicoloured . . . 40 40

379 Basketball **380** Recanati

1985. 12th Maccabiah Games. Multicoloured.
962 400s. Type **379** 80 80
963 500s. Tennis . . . . 1·20 1·00
964 600s. Windsurfing . . . . . 1·60 1·50

1985. 40th Death Anniv of Leon Yehuda Racanati (founder of Palestine Discount Bank).
965 **380** 200s. brown, grey and blue 50 50

381 Dizengoff (after J. Steinhardt and M. Sima)

1985. 49th Death Anniv of Meir Dizengoff (founder and Mayor of Tel Aviv).
966 **381** 500s. black, brown & silver . . . . 1·50 1·50

1985. Centenary of Gedera. As T **333**. Mult.
967 600s. Gedera . . . . 1·20 1·20

382 Kibbutz Members

1985. The Kibbutz.
968 **382** 900s. multicoloured . . . 1·90 1·90

Currency Reform.
1000 (old) Shekalim = 1 (new) Shekel.

383 Dr. Theodor Herzl **384** Corinthian Capital, 1st Century B.C.

1986.
969 **383** 1a. blue and red 55 55
970 2a. blue and green . . . 65 65
971 3a. blue and bistre . . . 80 80
972 5a. blue and turquoise 95 95
973 10a. blue and orange . . 1·50 1·50
974a 20a. blue and purple . . 6·00 6·00
975a 30a. blue and yellow . . 6·00 6·00
976a 50a. blue and violet . . 3·25 3·25

1986. Jerusalem Archaeology.
977 – 40a. green, orange & blk 2·75 2·75
978 – 60a. brown, violet & blk 6·00 6·00
979 – 70a. green, brown & blk 2·75 2·40
980 – 80a. purple, bistre & blk 3·25 2·75
981 – 90a. yellow, lilac & black 2·50 2·00
982 **384** 1s. brown, green & black 3·25 3·25
983a – 2s. blue, green and black 8·75 8·75
984 – 3s. mauve, blue and black . . . . 4·75 4·75
987 – 10s. green, blue and black . . . . 8·75 8·75
DESIGNS—As T **384**: 40a. Relief, 1st century B.C. (Second Temple); 60a. Byzantine capital, 6th century A.D.; 3s. Archaic Ionic capital, 1st century B.C. (Second Temple). 32 × 23 mm: 70a. Relief from palace of Umayyid Caliphs, 8th century A.D.; 80a. Crusader capital from Church of Ascension, Mount of Olives, 12–13th centuries; 90a. Relief from Suleiman's Wall, 16th century A.D.; 2s. Insignia of Sayif addin Attaz from Mameluke Academy, 14th century A.D.; 10s. Frieze from burial cave entrance, end of Second Temple period.

385 "Balanophyllia coccinea" **387** Microphone and Map

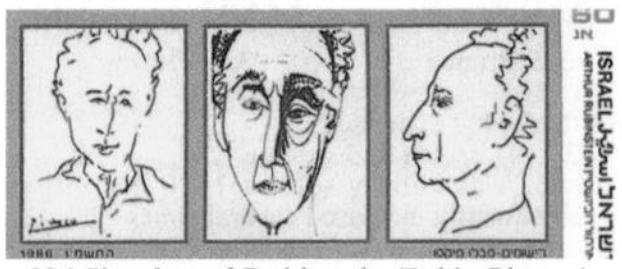

386 Sketches of Rubinstein (Pablo Picasso)

1986. Red Sea Corals. Multicoloured.
991 30a. Type **385** 95 95
992 40a. "Goniopora" . . . . . 1·00 1·00
993 50a. "Dendronephthya" . . . 1·20 1·20

1986. Birth Cent (1987) of Arthur Rubinstein and 5th International Rubinstein Piano Competition.
994 **386** 60a. multicoloured . . . 1·50 1·50

1986. 50th Anniv of Broadcasting from Jerusalem.
995 **387** 70a. multicoloured . . . 1·20 1·20

388 Negev Bridge Monument, Beer Sheva **389** El-Jazzar Mosque, Akko

1986. Memorial Day.
996 **388** 20a. multicoloured . . . 65 65

1986. Id Al-Fitr (end of Ramadan).
997 **389** 30a. emerald, green & ol 65 65

390 Hebrew Union College, Cincinnati

1986. "Ameripex '86" International Stamp Exhibition, Chicago. Jewish Institutes of Higher Learning. Multicoloured.
998 50a. Type **390** . . . . . . 1·10 1·10
999 50a. Yeshiva University, New York . . . . . . 1·10 1·10
1000 50a. Jewish Theology Seminary, New York . . 1·10 1·10
MS1001 100 × 70 mm. 75a. × 3 As Nos. 998/1000 but smaller (35 × 22 mm) (sold at 3s.) . . . 6·50 6·50

391 Nabi Sabalan's Tomb, Hurfeish

1986. Feast of Nabi Sabalan (Druse feast).
1002 **391** 40a. multicoloured . . . 80 80

392 Graffiti on Wall

1986. Anti-racism Campaign.
1003 **392** 60a. multicoloured . . . 1·30 1·30

393 Sprinzak

395 Gates of Heaven, with Jerusalem above, opening to Power of Prayer

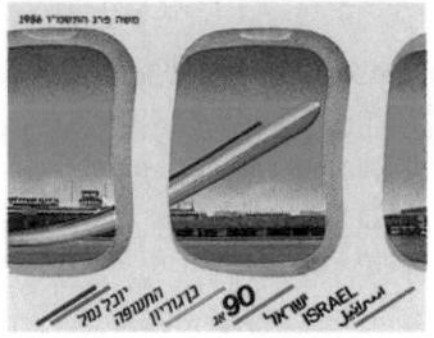

394 Airport through Cabin Windows

1986. Birth Centenary (1985) of Joseph Sprinzak (first Speaker of Knesset).
1004 **393** 80a. blue, green and black . . . . 1·30 1·30

1986. 50th Anniv of Ben Gurion Airport.
1005 **394** 90a. multicoloured . . . 1·60 1·60

1986. Jewish New Year. Pages from Worms Mahzor (prayer book). Multicoloured.
1006 20a. Type **395** (prayers for Yom Kippur) 95 95
1007 40a. Man weighing shekel for Temple (prayer for Sheqalim, first special Sabbath) . . . . 1·00 1·00
1008 90a. Roses (illustration of liturgical poem) . . . . . 1·40 1·40

396 David Ben Gurion

1986. Birth Centenary of David Ben Gurion (Prime Minister, 1948–53 and 1955–63).
1009 **396** 1s. bistre, brown & black 1·70 1·70

397 Map of Holy Land by Gerard de Jode, 1578

1986. "Netanya 86" National Stamp Exhibition. Sheet 126 × 80 mm.
MS1010 **397** 2s. multicoloured (sold at 3s.) . . . . 7·25 7·25

398 Satellite and Isobars over Map

399 Basilica of the Annunciation, Nazareth

1986. 50th Anniv of Meteorological Service.
1011 **398** 50a. multicoloured . . . 1·20 1·20

1986. Christmas.
1012 **399** 70a. multicoloured . . . 1·80 1·80

400 Bronislaw Huberman (violinist and founder)

1986. 50th Anniv of Israel Philharmonic Orchestra.
1013 **400** 1s.50 brown, blk & yell 3·50 3·50
1014 – 1s.50 grey, black & yell 3·50 3·50
DESIGN: No. 1014, Arturo Toscanini (conductor of Orchestra's first concert, 1936).

401 Hume's Owl

1987. Biblical Birds of Prey (2nd series). Owls. Multicoloured.
1015 30a. Desert eagle owl . . . 80 80
1016 40a. Pallid striated scops owl . . . . 1·20 1·20
1017 50a. Barn owl . . . . . . 1·60 1·50
1018 80a. Type **401** . . . . . 2·75 2·50
MS1019 102 × 82 mm. As Nos. 1015/18 but smaller (31 × 23 mm) (sold at 3s.) . . . 7·25 7·25

402 Six-Day War Memorial, Ammunition Hill, Jerusalem

1987. Memorial Day.
1020 **402** 30a. multicoloured . . . 95 95

403 Emblem

1987. 13th Hapoel Games.
1021 **403** 90a. multicoloured . . . 1·90 1·90

404 1952 120pr. "TABA" Stamp

1987. "Hafia 87" National Stamp Exhibition. Sheet 111 × 77 mm.
MS1022 **404** 2s.70 multicoloured (sold at 4s.) . . . . 8·00 8·00

405 Street Cleaner

406 Saluki

1987. "A Clean Environment".
1023 **405** 40a. multicoloured . . . 95 95

1987. World Dog Show. Dogs of Israeli Origin. Multicoloured.
1024 40a. Type **406** . . . . . . 1·50 1·40
1025 50a. Sloughi . . . . 1·50 1·40
1026 2s. Canaan dog . . . . . 3·50 3·50

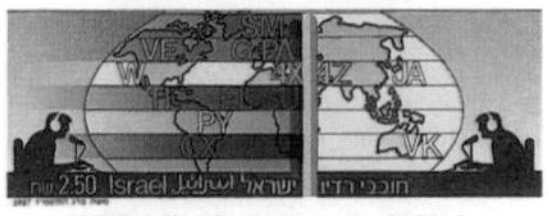

407 Radio Operators and Globe

1987. Israel Radio Amateurs.
1027 **407** 2s.50 multicoloured . . . 5·25 5·25

408 Altneuschul Synagogue, Prague

409 Rabbi Amiel

1987. Jewish New Year. Synagogue Models in Museum of the Diaspora, Tel Aviv (1st issue). Multicoloured.
1028 30a. Type **408** 65 65
1029 50a. Main Synagogue, Aleppo, Syria . . . . . 1·10 1·10
1030 60a. Israelite Temple, Florence . . . . 1·50 1·50
See also Nos. 1054/6.

1987. 104th Birth Anniv of Rabbi Moshe Avigdor Amiel (Chief Rabbi of Tel Aviv).
1031 **409** 1s.40 multicoloured . . . 3·00 3·00

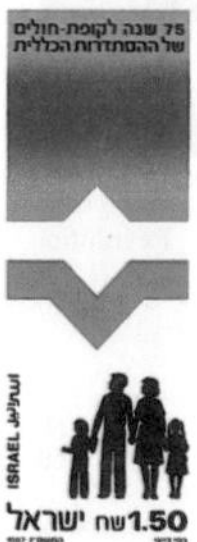

410 Family

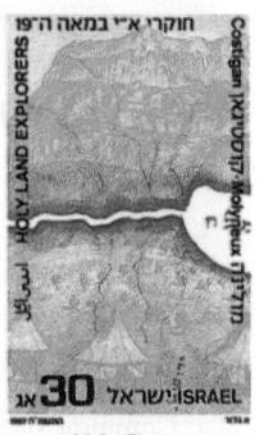

411 Camp (Christopher Costigan, 1835, and Thomas Howard Molyneux, 1847)

1987. 75th Anniv of Kupat Holim Health Insurance Institution.
1032 **410** 1s.50 multicoloured . . . 3·00 3·00

1987. Holy Land Explorers. Multicoloured.
1033 30a. Type **411** 85 80
1034 50a. Map of River Jordan (William Francis Lynch, 1848) . . . . 1·00 90
1035 60a. Men in canoe (John MacGregor, 1868–9) . . . 1·40 1·40
MS1036 106 × 75 mm. 40a. Type **411**; 50a. As No. 1034; 80a. As No. 1035; but each smaller (22 × 35 mm) (sold at 2s.50) . . 4·75 4·75

412 Rosen

413 Computers in Industry

1987. Birth Centenary of Pinhas Rosen (lawyer and politician).
1037 **412** 80a. multicoloured . . . 1·50 1·50

1988. Centenary of Israeli Industry. Mult.
1038 10a. Type **413** 55 40
1039 80a. Genetic engineering . . 2·00 1·50
1040 1s.40 Medical engineering 2·40 1·60

414 Corked Tap

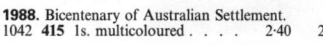

415 Kangaroos holding Birthday Cake

1988. "Save Water".
1041 **414** 40a. multicoloured . . . 95 95

1988. Bicentenary of Australian Settlement.
1042 **415** 1s. multicoloured . . . . 2·40 2·40

416 Sunflower

417 Hebrew Year 5748

1988. No value expressed.
1043 **416** (30a.) green and yellow 95 95

1988. Memorial Day.
1044 **417** 40a. multicoloured . . . 95 95
MS1045 86 × 70 mm. As No. 1044 but smaller (33 × 25 mm) (sold at 60a.) . . . . 3·25 3·25

418 Anne Frank and House, Amsterdam

419 Jerusalem

1988. 43rd Death Anniv of Anne Frank (concentration camp victim).
1046 **418** 60a. multicoloured . . . 1·60 1·60

1988. "Independence 40" National Stamp Exhibition, Jerusalem.
1047 **419** 1s. light brown and brown . . . . 2·00 2·00
MS1048 68 × 85 mm. 2s. cinnamon and brown . . . . 3·25 3·25
DESIGN. 34 × 25 mm. 2s. Jerusalem (detail of No. 1047).

420 1963 37a. Kibbutzim Stamp (Settling)

1988. "40th Anniv of Independence" Exhibition, Tel Aviv. Sheet 118 × 88 mm containing T **420** and similar horiz designs showing stamps. Multicoloured.
MS1049 20a. × 9 Type **420**; 1965 50a. Potash Works (Industry); 1956 300pr. Oranges (Agriculture); 1955 25pr. Youth Immigration (Immigrant absorption); 1981 8s. Ha-Shiv'a motorway interchange (Construction); 1964 Cancer Research (Health); 1972 40a. Educational Development (Education) (sold at 2s.40) . . 8·00 8·00

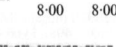

421 Ein Zin Nature Reserve

422 Jerusalem Lodge

1988. Nature Reserves in the Negev. Mult.
1050 40a. Type **421** 90 70
1051 60a. She' zaf . . . . 1·20 1·10
1052 70a. Ramon . . . . 1·40 1·20

1988. Centenary of B'nai B'rith in Jerusalem.
1053 **422** 70a. multicoloured . . . 1·40 1·40

1988. Jewish New Year. Synagogue Models in Museum of the Diaspora, Tel Aviv (2nd issue). As T **408**. Multicoloured.
1054 35a. 12th-century Kai-Feng Fu Synagogue, China . . 90 90
1055 60a. 17th-century Zabludow Synagogue, Poland . . . 95 95
1056 70a. 18th-century Touro Synagogue, Newport, Rhode Island . . . . . . 1·00 1·00

423 Havivah Reik

1988. Jewish World War II Underground Fighters. Multicoloured.
1057 **423** 40a. multicoloured . . . 80 80
1058 – 1s.65 dp blue, blue & blk 3·25 3·25
DESIGN: 1s.65, Enzo Hayyim Sereni.

424 Dayan

425 Burning Illustration of German Synagogue

1988. 7th Death Anniv of Moshe Dayan (soldier and politician).
1059 **424** 40a. multicoloured . . . 3·50 3·50

1988. 50th Anniv of "Kristallnacht" (Nazi pogrom).
1060 **425** 80a. multicoloured . . . 2·00 2·00

426 Menorah and Soldiers

1988. 74th Anniv of Formation of Jewish Legion.
1061 **426** 2s. dp brown, brn & bis 4·00 4·00

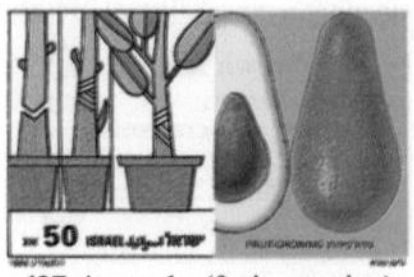
427 Avocado (fruit-growing)

1988. Agricultural Achievements in Israel. Mult.
1062 50a. Type **427** 95 95
1063 60a. Easter lily (plant breeding) . . . . 1·20 1·20
1064 90a. Plants and drip-pipe (irrigation systems) . . . 1·50 1·50

428 Red Sea **429** Rabbi Maimon

1989. Tourism. Multicoloured.
1065 40a. Type **428** 65 65
1066 60a. Dead Sea 80 80
1067 70a. Mediterranean 95 95
1068 1s.70 Sea of Galilee . . . . 2·00 2·00

1989. 114th Birth Anniv of Rabbi Judah Leib Maimon (writer).
1069 **429** 1s.70 multicoloured . . . 3·00 3·00

430 "Rashi" in Rashi Script **431** Airforce Memorial, Har Tayassim

1989. 950th Birth Anniv of Rashi (Rabbi Solomon Ben Isaac of Troyes) (scholar).
1070 **430** 4s. cream and brown . . 6·00 6·00

1989. Memorial Day.
1071 **431** 50a. multicoloured . . . 80 80

432 Child **433** Games Emblem

1989. 20th Anniv of Israel United Nations Children's Fund National Committee.
1072 **432** 90a. multicoloured . . . 1·50 1·50

1989. 13th Maccabiah Games.
1073 **433** 80a. multicoloured . . . 1·20 1·20

434 Smoira **436** Garganey

1989. Birth Centenary (1988) of Moshe Smoira (first President of Israel's Supreme Court).
1074 **434** 90a. blue . . . . 1·90 1·90

435 Tree of Liberty

1989. Bicentenary of French Revolution. Sheet 120 × 80 mm.
MS1075 **435** 3s.50 multicoloured 12·00 12·00

1989. Ducks. Multicoloured.
1076 80a. Type **436** . . . . . . 1·60 1·50
1077 80a. Mallard . . . . 1·60 1·50
1078 80a. Green-winged teal ("Teal") . . . . 1·60 1·50
1079 80a. Common shelduck ("Shelduck") . . . . . . 1·60 1·50

437 Printed Circuit and Pencil **438** Lion Design (Ukraine, 1921)

1989. 13th International Council of Graphic Design Associations Congress.
1080 **437** 1s. multicoloured . . . . 1·80 1·80

1989. Jewish New Year. Paper-cuts. Mult.
1081 50a. Type **438** 65 60
1082 70a. Hand design (Morocco, 1800s) 80 80
1083 80a. Stag design (Germany, 1818) . . . . 1·20 90

439 Founders of Safa Brurah **440** Rabbi Alkalai

1989. Centenaries of Safa Brurah ("Clear Language") and Hebrew Language Committee (precursors of Hebrew Language Council).
1084 **439** 1s. multicoloured . . . . 1·50 1·50

1989. 11th Death Anniv of Rabbi Hai Alkalai (Zionist).
1085 **440** 2s.50 multicoloured . . . 3·50 3·50

441 "Stag" **442** Postal Authority Emblem

1989. "Tevel 89" Youth Stamp Exhibition.
1086 **441** 50a. multicoloured . . . 1·50 1·50

1989. First Stamp Day.
1087 **442** 1s. multicoloured 95 95

443 "See You Again" **444** Rebab and Carpet

1989. Greetings Stamps. No value expressed. Multicoloured.
1088 (–) Type **443** . . . . 3·25 3·00
1089 (–) Patched heart ("With Love") . . . . 3·25 3·00
1090 (–) Flower ("Good Luck") 3·25 3·00
See also Nos. 1111/13 and 1128/30.

1989. "World Stamp Expo 89" International Stamp Exhibition, Washington D.C. Sheet 99 × 64 mm containing design as Nos. 1076/9 but smaller 27 × 22 mm.
MS1091 80a. × 4 multicoloured (sold at 5s.) . . . . 8·00 8·00

1990. The Bedouin in Israel.
1092 **444** 1s.50 multicoloured . . . 1·90 1·90

445 Traditional Dancing **446** Photograph Album and Orange

1990. Circassians in Israel.
1093 **445** 1s.50 multicoloured . . . 2·40 2·40

1990. Centenary of Rehovot Settlement.
1094 **446** 2s. multicoloured . . . . 2·75 2·75

447 Artillery Corps Monument, Zikhron Yaaqov

1990. Memorial Day.
1095 **447** 60a. multicoloured . . . 90 90

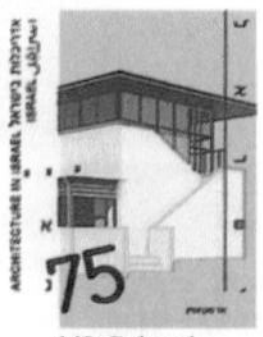
448 Ruins of Gamla, Yehudiyya **449** School, Deganya Kibbutz (Richard Kauffmann)

1990. Nature Reserves (1st series). Mult.
1096 60a. Type **448** 80 60
1097 80a. Huleh . . . . 1·10 70
1098 90a. Mt. Meron . . . . . . 1·30 1·00
See also Nos. 1200/2.

1990. Architecture.
1099b 75a. Type **449** . . . . . 32·00 32·00
1100 1s.10 Dining hall, Tel Yosef Kibbutz (Leopold Krahauer) . . . . 1·20 80
1101 1s.20 Engel House, Tel Aviv (Ze'ev Rechter) . . 1·20 80
1102 1s.40 Weizmann House, Rehovot (Erich Mendelsohn) . . . . . . 1·60 95
1103 1s.60 National Institutions Building, Jerusalem (Yohanan Ratner) . . . 1·50 1·20

450 Roads to Jerusalem

1990. "Stamp World London 90" International Stamp Exhibition. Stained Glass Windows by Mordecai Ardon in National and University Library illustrating Book of Isiah. Sheet 151 × 67 mm containing T **450** and similar vert design. Multicoloured.
MS1110 1s.50 Type **450**; 1s.50 Weapons beaten into ploughshares (sold at 4s.50) . . . . 9·75 9·75

1990. Greetings Stamps. As Nos. 1088/90 but with value.
1111 55a. As No. 1090 . . . . 4·00 4·00
1112a 80a. Type **443** . . . . . . 4·00 4·00
1113a 1s. As No. 1089 . . . . . 4·00 4·00

451 Badges **452** Dancers

1990. 70th Anniv of Formation of Hagana (underground military organization).
1114 **451** 1s.50 multicoloured . . . 2·40 2·40

1990. 8th International Folklore Festival, Haifa. Multicoloured.
1115 1s.90 Type **452** . . . . . . 2·50 2·00
1116 1s.90 Dancers and accordion player . . . . 2·50 2·00
Nos. 1115/16 were printed together, se-tenant, forming a composite design.

453 19th-century Austro-Hungarian Spice Box **454** People forming Star of David

1990. Jewish New Year. Silver Spice Boxes. Multicoloured.
1117 55a. Type **453** 95 70
1118 80a. 19th-century Italian box . . . . 1·00 80
1119 1s. German painted and gilt box by Matheus Wolf, 1700 . . . . 1·20 1·00

1990. Absorption of Immigrants.
1120 **454** 1s.10 multicoloured . . . 1·50 1·50

455 Ancient and Modern Means of Communication **457** Basketball

1990. Electronic Mail.
1121 **455** 1s.20 green, black & yell 1·50 1·50

456 Abraham's well (after 17th-century engraving)

1990. "Beer Sheva 90" National Stamp Exhibition. Sheet 90 × 86 mm.
MS1122 **456** 3s. multicoloured (sold at 4s.) . . . . 6·00 6·00

1990. Computer Games. Multicoloured.
1123 60a. Type **457** 80 60
1124 60a. Chess 80 60
1125 60a. Racing cars 80 60

458 Tel Aviv-Yafo Post Office and 1948 20m. Stamp **459** Jabotinsky

1990. Stamp Day.
1126 **458** 1s.20 multicoloured . . . 2·50 2·50

1990. 50th Death Anniv of Ze'ev Jabotinsky (Zionist leader).
1127 **459** 1s.90 multicoloured . . . 1·90 1·90

1991. Greetings Stamps. No value expressed. As T **443**. Multicoloured.
1128 (–) Birthday cake ("Happy Birthday") . . . . 3·00 2·75
1129 (–) Champagne bottle ("Greetings") . . . . . . 3·00 2·75
1130 (–) Envelopes ("Keep in Touch") . . . . 3·00 2·75
Nos. 1128/30 were sold at the current inland letter rate.

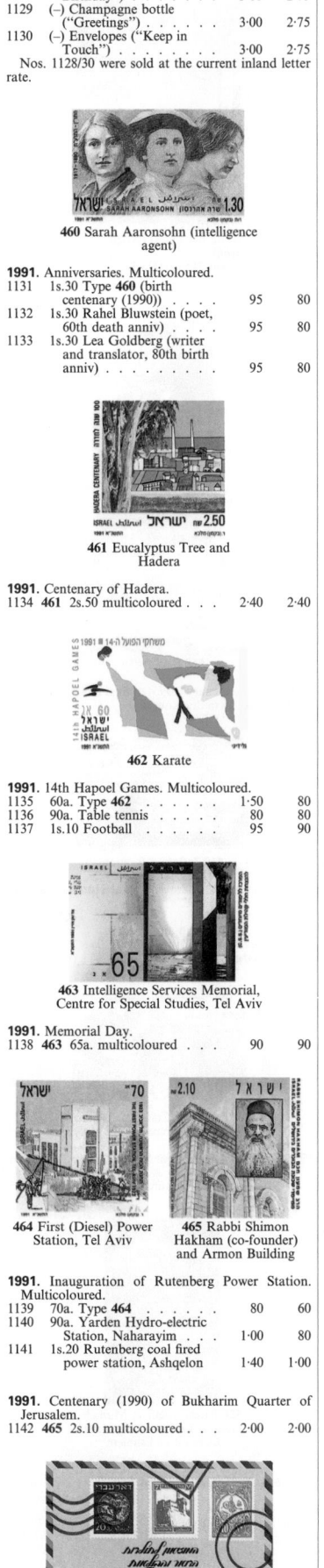

460 Sarah Aaronsohn (intelligence agent)

1991. Anniversaries. Multicoloured.
1131 1s.30 Type **460** (birth centenary (1990)) 95 80
1132 1s.30 Rahel Bluwstein (poet, 60th death anniv) 95 80
1133 1s.30 Lea Goldberg (writer and translator, 80th birth anniv) 95 80

461 Eucalyptus Tree and Hadera

1991. Centenary of Hadera.
1134 **461** 2s.50 multicoloured . . . 2·40 2·40

462 Karate

1991. 14th Hapoel Games. Multicoloured.
1135 60a. Type **462** . . . . . . 1·50 80
1136 90a. Table tennis 80 80
1137 1s.10 Football 95 90

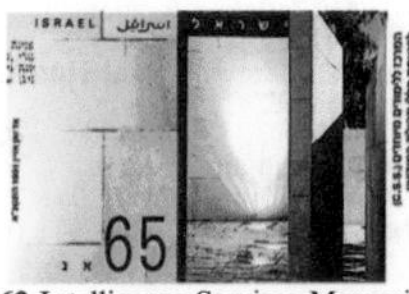

463 Intelligence Services Memorial, Centre for Special Studies, Tel Aviv

1991. Memorial Day.
1138 **463** 65a. multicoloured . . . 90 90

464 First (Diesel) Power Station, Tel Aviv

465 Rabbi Shimon Hakham (co-founder) and Armon Building

1991. Inauguration of Rutenberg Power Station. Multicoloured.
1139 70a. Type **464** 80 60
1140 90a. Yarden Hydro-electric Station, Naharayim . . . 1·00 80
1141 1s.20 Rutenberg coal fired power station, Ashqelon 1·40 1·00

1991. Centenary (1990) of Bukharim Quarter of Jerusalem.
1142 **465** 2s.10 multicoloured . . . 2·00 2·00

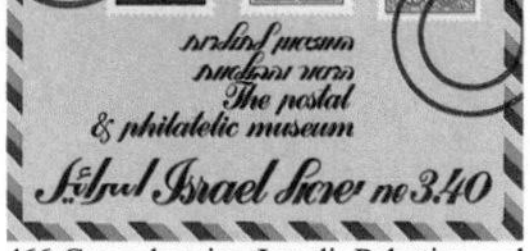

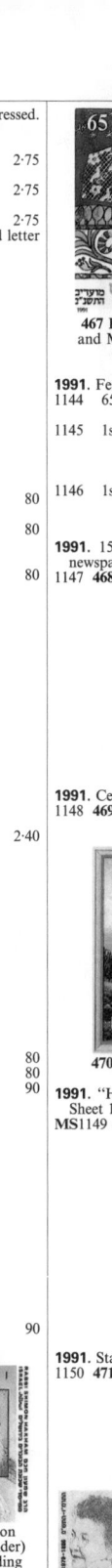

466 Cover bearing Israeli, Palestine and Turkish Stamps

1991. Tel Aviv Postal and Philatelic Museum Project. Sheet 120 × 89 mm.
MS1143 **466** 3s.40 multicoloured 6·50 6·50

467 Ram's Head and Man blowing Shofar

468 Front Page of First Edition

1991. Festivals. Multicoloured.
1144 65a. Type **467** (Jewish New Year) 65 60
1145 1s. "Penitence Cock", father blessing children and men blowing shofars (Day of Atonement) . . . . . . 1·00 90
1146 1s.20 Family in booth (Festival of Tabernacles) 1·10 1·00

1991. 150th Anniv of "Jewish Chronicle" (weekly newspaper).
1147 **468** 1s.50 black, blue and red 1·60 1·60

469 Colonists and Baron Maurice de Hirsch (founder)

1991. Centenary of Jewish Colonization Association.
1148 **469** 1s.60 multicoloured . . . 1·80 1·80

470 "Haifa, 1898" (Gustav Bauernfreind)

1991. "Haifa 91" Israel—Poland Stamp Exhibition. Sheet 104 × 62 mm.
MS1149 **470** 3s. multicoloured . . 6·50 6·50

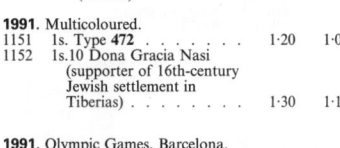

471 Cancelled 1948 5m. Stamp

1991. Stamp Day.
1150 **471** 70a. multicoloured . . . 80 80

472 Rahel Yanait Ben-Zvi (Zionist)

473 Runner

1991. Multicoloured.
1151 1s. Type **472** . . . . 1·20 1·00
1152 1s.10 Dona Gracia Nasi (supporter of 16th-century Jewish settlement in Tiberias) . . . . 1·30 1·10

1991. Olympic Games, Barcelona.
1153 **473** 1s.10 multicoloured . . . 1·30 1·30

474 Flame and Hebrew Script

475 Southern Wing of Acre Prison

1991. 51st Anniv of Lehi (resistance organization).
1154 **474** 1s.50 multicoloured . . . 1·60 1·60

1991. 60th Anniv of Etzel (resistance organization).
1155 **475** 1s.50 black, red and grey 1·60 1·60

476 Mozart and Score of "Don Giovanni"

477 Anemone

1991. Death Bicentenary of Wolfgang Amadeus Mozart (composer).
1156 **476** 2s. multicoloured . . . . 2·40 1·90

1992. No value expressed.
1157 **477** (–) red and green . . . . 2·00 2·00
No. 1157 was sold at the current inland letter rate, initially 75a.

478 Hanna Rovina (actress)

479 Trees

1992. Multicoloured.
1158 80a. Type **478** 95 95
1159 1s.30 Rivka Guber (teacher and writer) . . . . 1·20 1·20

1992. Sea of Galilee. Multicoloured.
1160 85a. Type **479** . . . . . . 2·00 1·60
1161 85a. Sailboard . . . . . . 2·00 1·60
1162 85a. Fishes . . . . 2·00 1·60

480 Palmah Emblem

481 Samaritans praying on Mount Gerizim

1992. 51st Anniv of Palmah (resistance organization).
1163 **480** 1s.50 gold, blue & mauve 1·60 1·60

1992. The Samaritans.
1164 **481** 2s.60 multicoloured . . . 2·75 2·75

482 Border Guard Memorial, Eiron Junction (Yechiel Arad)

1992. Memorial Day.
1165 **482** 85a. multicoloured . . . 95 95

483 Azulai

484 Hayyim

1992. 186th Death Anniv of Rabbi Hayyim Joseph David Azulai (scholar).
1166 **483** 85a. multicoloured . . . 1·60 1·60

1992. 83rd Death Anniv of Rabbi Joseph Hayyim Ben Elijah.
1167 **484** 1s.20 multicoloured . . . 1·60 1·60

485 "Almanach Perpetuum" and Models of Columbus's Ships

1992. 500th Anniv of Discovery of America by Columbus.
1168 **485** 1s.60 multicoloured . . . 1·80 1·80

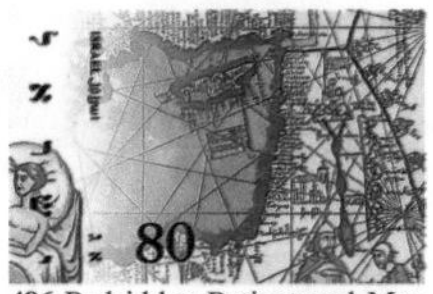

486 Bedridden Patient and Map

1992. 500th Anniv of Expulsion of Jews from Spain. Sheet 140 × 71 mm containing T **486** and similar horiz designs showing details of map by Abraham Cresques. Multicoloured.
MS1169 80a. Type **486**; 1s.10 Doctor and map; 1s.40 Writer-philosopher and map . . . . 5·75 5·75

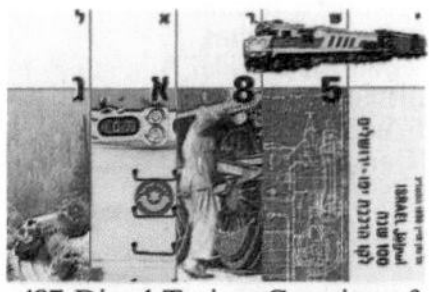

487 Diesel Trains, Greasing of Wheels and Blueprint of Baldwin Engine

1992. Centenary of Jaffa–Jerusalem Railway. Mult.
1170 85a. Type **487** 70 60
1171 1s. Scottish steam locomotive, track plan at Lod, electric signalling board at Tel Aviv, semaphore arms and points at Lod 80 70
1172 1s.30 Diesel locomotive, interior and exterior of passenger carriages, Palestine Railways ticket and 1926 timetable . . . 1·00 90
1173 1s.60 Diesel train, drawing of facade of Jerusalem station, platform at Lod, Jaffa station in 1900 and points at Bar-Giora station . . . . 1·10 1·00
MS1174 140 × 71 mm. 4 × 50a. As Nos. 1170/3 . . . . 5·25 5·25

488 Cover of "Or-HaHayyim" ("Light of Life") (Rabbi Hayyim Benatar, 250th (1993) anniv)

1992. Death Anniversaries.
1175 **488** 1s.30 lilac, green & gold 90 80
1176 – 3s. lilac, green and gold 1·10 1·90
DESIGN: 3s. 19th-century drawing of Bet-El Yeshiva, Jerusalem (Rabbi Shalom Sharabi, 215th anniv).

489 Leopard

1992. Zoo Animals. Multicoloured.
1177 50a. Type **489** 50 40
1178 50a. Indian elephant 50 40
1179 50a. Chimpanzee 50 40
1180 50a. Lion 50 40

490 "Parables" (Yitzhak ben Shlomo ibn Sahula) (1st edition, Brescia, 1491)

1992. Jewish New Year. Centenary of Jewish National and University Library, Jerusalem. Multicoloured.
1181 85a. Type **490** 80 65
1182 1s. Mahzor (prayer book) (15th-century manuscript by Leon ben Yehoshua de Rossi) 90 70
1183 1s.20 Draft of translation by Martin Buber of Leviticus 25: 10-13 . . . . 95 85

491 Court Building

492 Wallcreeper

1992. Inauguration of New Supreme Court Building.
1184 **491** 3s.60 multicoloured . . . 3·25 3·00

1992. Songbirds. Multicoloured.
1185 10a. Type **492** 25 20
1186 20a. Tristram's grackle . . . 25 20
1187 30a. Pied wagtail ("White") 30 25
1188 50a. Palestine sunbird . . . 40 40
1189 85a. Sinai rosefinch . . . . 1·30 45
1190 90a. Barn swallows ("Swallow") 65 35
1191 1s. Trumpeter finches . . . 65 35
1192 1s.30 Graceful prinia ("Graceful Warbler") . . 80 60
1193 1s.50 Black-eared wheatear 95 80
1194 1s.70 White-eyed bulbuls ("Common Bulbul") . . 1·40 1·10

493 "Judah Released"

494 European Community Emblem on Graph

1992. 75th Anniv of First All-Hebrew Film. Scenes from films. Multicoloured.
1195 80a. Type **493** (first Hebrew film) . . . . 1·20 1·10
1196 2s.70 "Oded the Wanderer" (first Hebrew feature film) 1·80 1·65
1197 3s.50 "This is the Land" (first Hebrew talking film) 2·30 2·00

1992. Stamp Day. European Single Market.
1198 **494** 1s.50 multicoloured . . . 1·20 1·00

495 Begin

496 Shrine of the Bab

1993. 1st Death Anniv of Menahem Begin (Prime Minister, 1977–83).
1199 **495** 80a. multicoloured . . . 80 60

1993. Nature Reserves (2nd series). As T **448**. Multicoloured.
1200 1s.20 Hof Dor . . . . . . 1·20 80
1201 1s.50 Nahal Ammud . . . . 1·00 90
1202 1s.70 Nahal Ayun . . . . . 1·20 1·10

1993. Baha'i World Centre, Haifa.
1203 **496** 3s.50 multicoloured . . . 2·20 2·00

497 Medical Corps Memorial, Carmel, Haifa (Akiva Lomnitz)

498 "The Eye's Memory"

1993. Memorial Day.
1204 **497** 80a. multicoloured . . . 70 65

1993. Illustration of Scientific Concepts. Exhibits from the Israel National Museum of Science, Haifa (Nos. 1205/6) or the Bernard M. Bloomfield Science Museum, Jerusalem (others).
1205 80a. Type **498** 65 60
1206 80a. Colour mixing 65 60
1207 80a. Waves 65 60
1208 80a. Floating balls (principle of lift) 65 60

499 Prisoner

500 Hurbat Rabbi Yehuda Hassid Synagogue, Jerusalem

1993. 50th Anniv of Uprisings in the Ghettos and Concentration Camps.
1209 **499** 1s.20 black, yellow & bl 95 80

1993. 45th Anniv of Independence.
1210 **500** 3s.60 multicoloured . . . 2·75 2·20

501 Giulio Racah

502 Family using Crossing (Lior Abohovsky)

1993. Physicists. Multicoloured.
1211 80a. Type **501** 65 60
1212 1s.20 Aharon Katchalsky-Katzir 90 80

1993. Road Safety. Children's Paintings. Mult.
1213 80a. Type **502** 70 65
1214 1s.20 Vehicles and road signs (Elinor Paz) 95 85
1215 1s.50 Road signals on "man" (Moran Dadush) 1·10 95

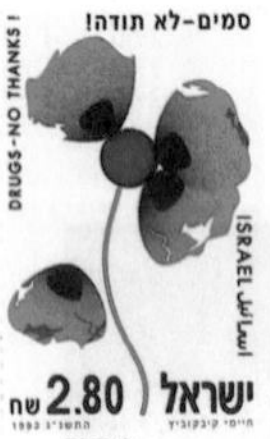

503 Poppy

504 Passing Baton

1993. Anti-drugs Campaign.
1216 **503** 2s.80 multicoloured . . . 1·90 1·70

1993. 14th Maccabiah Games.
1217 **504** 3s.60 multicoloured . . . 2·75 2·20

505 Tree

506 Ear of Wheat

1993. International Day of the Elderly.
1218 **505** 80a. multicoloured . . . 65 55

1993. Jewish New Year. Multicoloured.
1219 80a. Type **506** 65 55
1220 1s.20 Grapes 90 70
1221 1s.50 Olives . . . . 1·30 1·00

507 Environmental Concerns

1993. Environment Year.
1222 **507** 1s.20 multicoloured . . . 90 75

508 Emblems

1993. 150th Anniv of B'nai B'rith (cultural and social organization).
1223 **508** 1s.50 multicoloured . . . 90 75

509 "Immigrant Ship" (Marcel Janco)

1993. "Telafila 93" Israel—Rumania Stamp Exhibition, Tel Aviv. Sheet 60 × 90 mm.
MS1224 **509** 3s.60 multicoloured 4·75 4·75

510 Talmudic Oil Lamp

1993. Festival of Hanukka. Multicoloured.
1225 90a. Type **510** 65 50
1226 1s.30 Hanukka lamp in shape of building 95 75
1227 2s. "Lighting the Hanukka Lamp" (illustration from the "Rothschild Miscellany") . . . . . . 1·40 1·10

511 Cover of First Issue

1993. Stamp Day. Centenary (1992) of "Miniature World" (children's magazine).
1228 **511** 1s.50 multicoloured . . . 1·20 80

512 Yellow-banded Borer ("Chlorophorus varius")

1994. Beetles. Multicoloured.
1229 85a. Type **512** 70 60
1230 85a. Copper beetle ("Potosia cuprea") 70 60
1231 85a. Pied ground beetle ("Graphopterus serrator") 70 60
1232 85a. Seven-spotted ladybird ("Coccinella septempunctata") 70 60

513 Man carrying Car ("Exercise Regularly")

1994. Health and Well-being. Multicoloured.
1233 85a. Type **513** 65 50
1234 1s.30 Blowing soap bubbles ("Don't Smoke") 90 70
1235 1s.60 Inspecting food through magnifying glass ("Eat Sensibly") . . . . 1·10 95

514 Haffkine

515 Communications, Electronics and Computer Corps Memorial, Yehud (Claude Grundman)

1994. 64th Death Anniv of Dr. Mordecai Haffkine (bacteriologist).
1236 **514** 3s.85 multicoloured . . . 2·20 1·90

1994. Memorial Day.
1237 **515** 85a. multicoloured . . . 65 55

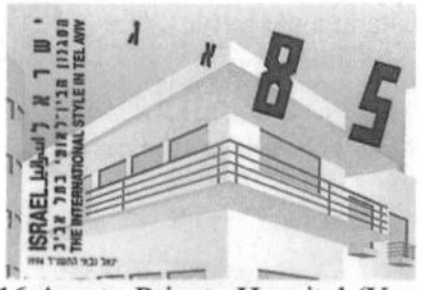
516 Assuta Private Hospital (Yosef Neufeld)

1994. International Style Architecture in Tel Aviv. Each grey, blue and green.
1238 85a. Type **516** 70 60
1239 85a. Co-operative workers' housing (flats with separate balconies) (Arieh Sharon) 70 60
1240 85a. Citrus House (Karl Rubin) 70 60

517 Battered Child

1994. "No to Violence" Campaign.
1241 **517** 3s.85 black and red . . . 2·10 1·80

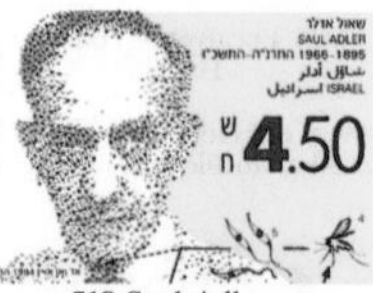

518 Saul Adler

1994. Birth Centenary (1995) of Saul Adler (scientist).
1242 **518** 4s.50 multicoloured . . . 2·40 1·90

519 Inflating Balloon

1994. Ayalon Valley International Hot-Air Balloon Race. Multicoloured.
1243 85a. Type **519** 65 55
1244 85a. Balloons in air 65 55
1245 85a. Balloon hovering over target (cross on ground) 65 55

520 Chemistry Class at Bialystok and Physical Education at Wolyn

1994. 75th Anniv of Tarbut Schools (Hebrew schools in Eastern Europe).
1246 **520** 1s.30 multicoloured . . . 70 55

521 Israeli Team at Munich Games, 1972, and National Committee Emblem

1994. Centenary of Int Olympic Committee.
1247 **521** 2s.25 multicoloured . . . 1·20 1·00

522 The Little Prince (book character) and Saint-Exupery

1994. 50th Death Anniv of Antoine de Saint-Exupery (writer and pilot).
1248 **522** 5s. multicoloured . . . . 2·75 2·40

523 "Adam and Eve" (Itai Cohen)

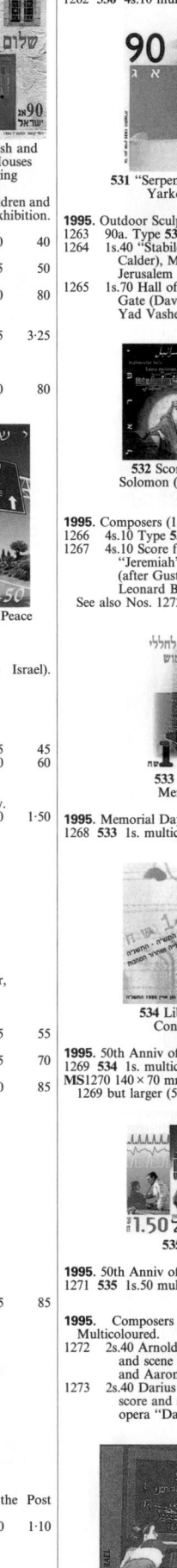

524 Jewish and Arab Houses merging

1994. Jewish New Year. Entries in the "Children and Young People draw the Bible" exhibition. Multicoloured.
1249 85a. Type **523** 50 40
1250 1s.30 "Jacob's Dream" (Moran Sheinberg) . . . 65 50
1251 1s.60 "Moses in the Bulrushes" (Carmit Crspi) 90 80
MS1252 65 × 90 mm. 4s. "Parting of the Red Sea" (Avital Kaisar) (39 × 50 mm) . . . . 3·25 3·25

1994. Israeli–Palestinian Peace Process.
1253 **524** 90a. multicoloured . . . 90 80

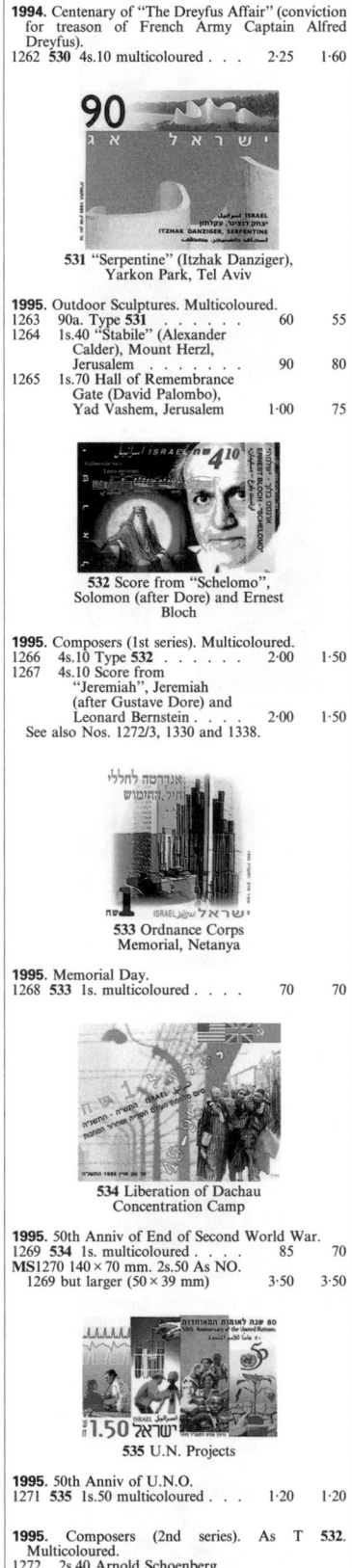

525 Silicat Brick Factory, Tel Aviv (Fourth Aliya, 1924–28)

526 Road to Peace

1994. Aliyot (immigration of Jews to Israel). Multicoloured.
1254 1s.40 Settlers and booklet distributed in Poland to encourage Jews to settle the Valley of Jezreel (Third Aliya, 1919–23) . . 55 45
1255 1s.70 Type **525** 80 60

1994. Signing of Israel–Jordan Peace Treaty.
1256 **526** 3s.50 multicoloured . . . 1·90 1·50

527 Ford Model "T" Converted Car, 1920s

1994. Public Transport. Multicoloured.
1257 90a. Type **527** 65 55
1258 1s.40 "White Super" bus, 1940s 85 70
1259 1s.70 Leyland "Royal Tiger" bus, 1960s . . . . 1·00 85

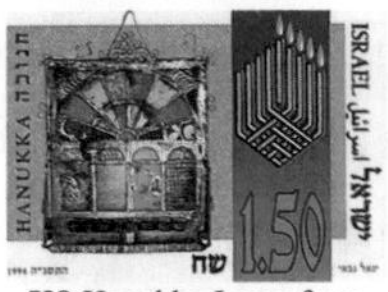
528 Hanukka Lamp from Mazagan, Morocco

1994. Festival of Hanukka.
1260 **528** 1s.50 multicoloured . . . 95 85

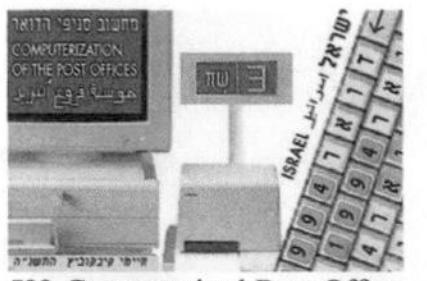
529 Computerized Post Office Counter

1994. Stamp Day. Computerization of the Post Office.
1261 **529** 3s. multicoloured . . . . 1·40 1·10

530 Breaking Dreyfus's Sword

1994. Centenary of "The Dreyfus Affair" (conviction for treason of French Army Captain Alfred Dreyfus).
1262 **530** 4s.10 multicoloured . . . 2·25 1·60

531 "Serpentine" (Itzhak Danziger), Yarkon Park, Tel Aviv

1995. Outdoor Sculptures. Multicoloured.
1263 90a. Type **531** 60 55
1264 1s.40 "Stabile" (Alexander Calder), Mount Herzl, Jerusalem 90 80
1265 1s.70 Hall of Remembrance Gate (David Palombo), Yad Vashem, Jerusalem 1·00 75

532 Score from "Schelomo", Solomon (after Dore) and Ernest Bloch

1995. Composers (1st series). Multicoloured.
1266 4s.10 Type **532** . . . . . . 2·00 1·50
1267 4s.10 Score from "Jeremiah", Jeremiah (after Gustave Dore) and Leonard Bernstein . . . . 2·00 1·50
See also Nos. 1272/3, 1330 and 1338.

533 Ordnance Corps Memorial, Netanya

1995. Memorial Day.
1268 **533** 1s. multicoloured 70 70

534 Liberation of Dachau Concentration Camp

1995. 50th Anniv of End of Second World War.
1269 **534** 1s. multicoloured 85 70
MS1270 140 × 70 mm. 2s.50 As NO. 1269 but larger (50 × 39 mm) 3·50 3·50

535 U.N. Projects

1995. 50th Anniv of U.N.O.
1271 **535** 1s.50 multicoloured . . . 1·20 1·20

1995. Composers (2nd series). As T **532**. Multicoloured.
1272 2s.40 Arnold Schoenberg and scene from "Moses and Aaron" . . . . . . 1·50 1·30
1273 2s.40 Darius Milhaud and score and scene from opera "David" . . . . . 1·50 1·30

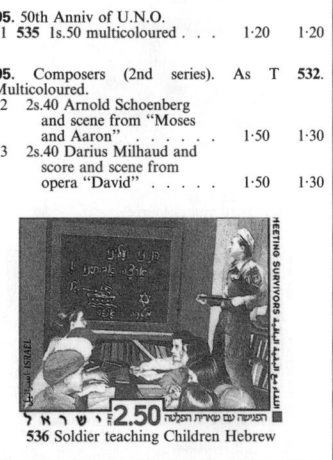

536 Soldier teaching Children Hebrew

1995. Jewish Brigade of Second World War. Sheet 95 × 65 mm.
MS1274 **536** 2s.50 multicoloured 3·50 3·50

537 Canoeist

1995. 15th Hapoel Games.
1275 **537** 1s. multicoloured . . . . 1·60 1·60

538 Box Kite and Cody "War" Kite

1995. Kites. Multicoloured.
1276 1s. Type **538** 50 40
1277 1s. Bird-shaped, hexagonal "Tiara" and rhombic "Eddy" kites 50 40
1278 1s. Multiple rhombic and triangular "Deltic" aerobatic kites 50 40
Nos. 1276/8 were printed together, se-tenant, forming a composite design.

539 "Stars in a Bucket" (Anda Amir-Pinkerfeld, illus. Hava Nathan)

1995. Children's Books. Designs illustrating poems. Multicoloured.
1279 1s. Type **539** 60 40
1280 1s.50 "Hurry, Run, Dwarfs" (Miriam Yallan-Stekelis, illus. Tirzah Tanny) . . . 90 70
1281 1s.80 "Daddy's Big Umbrella" (Levin Kipnis, illus. Pazit Meller-Dushi) 95 70

540 "Zim Israel" (container ship)

1995. 50th Anniv of Zim Navigation Company.
1282 **540** 4s.40 multicoloured . . . 2·40 2·00

541 Elijah's Chair (German, 1768)

1995. Jewish New Year. Multicoloured.
1283 1s. Type **541** (circumcision) 80 50
1284 1s.50 Velvet bag for prayer shawl (Moroccan, 1906) (Bar-Mitzvah) . . . . . 1·20 1·00
1285 1s.80 Marriage stone (from Bingen Synagogue, Germany, 1700) . . . . . 1·10 80

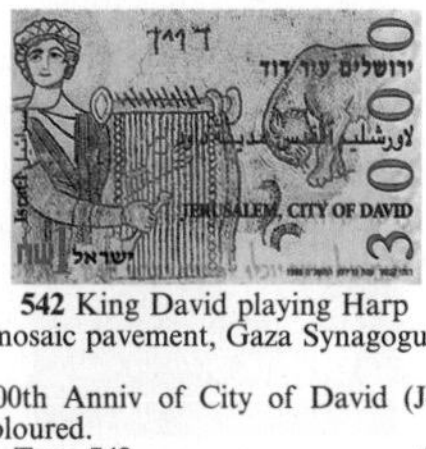
542 King David playing Harp (mosaic pavement, Gaza Synagogue)

1995. 3000th Anniv of City of David (Jerusalem). Multicoloured.
1286 1s. Type **542** 65 55
1287 1s.50 Illustration of Jerusalem from 19th-century map by Rabbi Pinie . . . . . . 1·10 80
1288 1s.80 Aerial view of Knesset (parliament) . . . . . . 90 1·90

543 "Sheep" (Menashe Kadishman)

1995. 75th Anniv of Veterinary Services.
1289 **543** 4s.40 multicoloured . . . 2·40 1·90

544 Rabin

1995. Yitzhak Rabin (Prime Minister) Commem.
1290 **544** 5s. multicoloured . . . . 2·40 2·00

545 Putting out Fire

1995. 70th Anniv of Fire and Rescue Service. Multicoloured.
1291 1s. Type **545** 55 50
1292 1s. Cutting crash victim out of car 55 50

546 Miniature Silver Menorah (Zusia Ejbuszyc)

1995. Festival of Hanukka.
1293 **546** 1s.50 multicoloured . . . 90 80

547 Flying Model Plane

1995. Stamp Day.
1294 **547** 1s.80 multicoloured . . . 1·00 80

548 Film Stars

550 Cycling

1995. Centenary of Motion Pictures.
1295 **548** 4s.40 multicoloured . . . 2·20 1·80
The stars depicted are the Marx Brothers, Simone Signoret, Peter Sellers, Danny Kaye and Al Jolson.

549 Illustration from Jerusalem From 19-century Map of Rabbi Pinie

1995. 3000th Anniv of City of David (Jerusalem) (2nd issue) and "Jerusalem 3000" Israeli—European Stamp Exhibition. Sheet 140 × 70 mm containing T **549** and similar horiz designs. Multicoloured.
MS1296 1s. King David playing Harp (mosaic pavement, Gaza Synagogue); 1s.50 Type **549**; 1s.80 Aerial view of Knesset (Parliament) . . . . 5·25 5·25
The stamps in No. **MS**1296 depict the same motifs as No. 1286/8 but with differences in inscriptions.

1996. Sport. Multicoloured.
1301 1s.05 Type **550** 60 50
1302 1s.10 Show jumping 60 50
1303 1s.80 Water skiing 90 70
1304 1s.90 Paragliding . . . . . 1·10 80
1305 2s. Volleyball . . . . 1·20 80
1306 2s.30 Whitewater rafting . . 90 70
1307 3s. Bat and ball . . . . . . 1·40 90
1308 5s. Archery . . . . 2·10 1·60
1309 10s. Abseiling . . . . 4·00 3·00

551 "Temple and Walls of Jerusalem"

1996. 3000th Anniv of City of David (Jerusalem) (3rd issue). Third-century Murals from Dura-Europos Synagogue, Syria. Sheet 141 × 71 mm containing T **551** and similar vert designs. Multicoloured.
MS1310 1s.05 Type **551**; 1s.60, Torah Ark niche; 1s.90 Prophet Samuel anointing David as King 6·50 6·50

552 Cow and Computer

553 Abraham Shlonsky (poet)

1996. 70th Anniv of Israel Dairy Cattle Breeders' Association.
1311 **552** 4s.65 multicoloured . . . 2·75 2·20

1996. "China 96" International Stamp Exhibition, Peking. Birds. Sheet 128 × 89 mm containing designs as Nos. 1185/94 but face values and colours changed.
MS1312 30a. × 10 multicoloured 9·75 9·00

1996. Modern Hebrew Writers. Multicoloured.
1313 40a. Type **553** 30 30
1314 40a. Joseph Brenner (novelist and essayist) . . 30 30
1315 40a. Judah Gordon (poet) 30 30
1316 40a. Haim Hazaz (novelist) 30 30
1317 40a. Devorah Baron (novelist) 30 30
1318 40a. Yehuda Burla (novelist) 30 30
1319 40a. Micha Berdyczewski (novelist and historian) . . 30 30
1320 40a. Yaakov Shabtai (novelist) 30 30
1321 40a. Isaac Peretz (novelist) 30 30
1322 40a. Nathan Alterman (poet) 30 30
1323 40a. Saul Tchernichowsky (poet) 30 30
1324 40a. Amir Gilboa (poet) . . 30 30
1325 40a. Yokheved Bat-Miriam (poet) 30 30
1326 40a. Mendele Sefarim (novelist) 30 30

554 Fallen Policemen Monument, National Police Academy, Kiryat Ata (Yosef Assa)

1996. Memorial Day.
1327 **554** 1s.05 multicoloured . . . 1·10 1·00

555 Circuit Boards

556 Emblem and Old Photographs

1996. 75th Anniv of Manufacturers' Association.
1328 **555** 1s.05 multicoloured . . . 1·10 1·00

1996. Centenary of Metulla.
1329 **556** 1s.90 multicoloured . . . 1·30 1·10

1996. Composers (3rd series). As T **532**. Multicoloured.
1330 4s.65 Gustav Mahler, score from "Resurrection Symphony" and creation of light . . . . 1·50 1·30

557 Plant growing in Cracked Earth

558 Fencing

1996. 50th Anniv of the 11 Negev Settlements.
1331 **557** 1s.05 multicoloured . . . 70 60

1996. Olympic Games. Atlanta. Multicoloured.
1332 1s.05 Type **558** 90 70
1333 1s.60 Pole vaulting . . . . 1·10 80
1334 1s.90 Wrestling . . . . . . 1·30 1·00

559 Jaffa Orange Tree and Citrus Fruit

1996. Israeli Fruit Production. Multicoloured.
1335 1s.05 Type **559** 90 70
1336 1s.60 Grape vine, avocado, date, sharon fruit and mango . . . . 1·10 80
1337 1s.90 Star fruit plant and exotic fruit . . . . 1·30 1·00

1996. Composers (4th series). As T **532**. Multicoloured.
1338 4s.65 Felix Mendelssohn, Prophet Elijah (after Albrecht Durer) and score from oratorio "Elijah" . . 2·75 2·00

560 Road Systems

1996. 75th Anniv of Public Works Department.
1339 **560** 1s.05 multicoloured . . . 1·10 90

561 New Year

1996. Jewish Festivals. Paintings by Sahar Pick. Multicoloured.
1340 1s.05 Type **561** 90 80
1341 1s.60 Booth decoration (Festival of Tabernacles) 1·20 1·00
1342 1s.90 Pulpit (Simchat Torah Festival) . . . . 1·40 1·20

1996. Centenary of First Zioist Congress, Basel, Switzerland. Multicoloured.
1343 4s.65 Type **562** . . . . . . 3·25 2·30
MS1344 70 × 97 mm. 5s. Casino, Basel (venue) (39 × 50 mm) . . 6·50 6·50

563 Lighted Candles

1996. Festival of Hanukkah. Self-adhesive.
1345 **563** 2s.50 multicoloured . . . 1·70 1·60

564 Bird and Fighter Aircraft

1996. Coexistence between Man and Animals. Multicoloured.
1346 1s.10 Type **564** 85 75
1347 1s.75 Dog, people and cat 1·00 80
1348 2s. Dolphins and diver . . . 1·40 1·20

565 Ahad Ha'am

1996. Centenary of First Edition of "Ha-Shilo'ah" (periodical) and 140th Birth Anniv of Ahad Ha'am (editor and Zionist).
1349 **565** 1s.15 multicoloured . . . 1·00 90

566 Shavit Rocket, Earth and "Ofeq-3" (satellite)

1996. Stamp Day. Space Research.
1350 **566** 2s.05 multicoloured . . . 1·50 1·30

567 Equal Opportunities Emblem

570 Windmills, Don Quixote and Sancho Panza (Ya'acov Farkas (Ze'ev))

568 Woman, Ethiopia

1996. Equal Opportunities for Disabled People.
1351 **567** 5s. multicoloured . . . . 2·75 2·20

1997. Traditional Costumes of Jewish Communities Abroad. Multicoloured.
1352 1s.10 Type **568** 90 80
1353 1s.70 Man, Kurdistan . . . 1·40 1·20
1354 2s. Woman, Salonica . . . 1·80 1·50

569 Alexander Graham Bell demonstrating Telephone

1997. "Hong Kong 97" International Stamp Exhibition. Inventors' 150th Birth Anniversaries. Sheet 90 × 56 mm containing T **569** and similar vert design.
MS1355 1s.50 Type **569**; 2s. Thomas Edison and lightbulb . . . . . 4·50 4·50

1997. 450th Birth Anniv of Miguel de Cervantes (writer).
1356 **570** 3s. multicoloured . . . . 1·90 1·20

571 Logistics Corps Memorial, Hadir

1997. Memorial Day.
1357 **571** 1s.10 multicoloured . . . 80 70

572 Ark of the Torah, Old–New Synagogue (east side)

573 Rabbi Elijah (Mario Sermoneta)

1997. Jewish Monuments in Prague. Mult.
1358 1s.70 Type **572** . . . . . . 1·50 1·20
1359 1s.70 Grave of Rabbi Loew (chief Rabbi of Prague), Old Jewish Cemetery . . 1·50 1·20

1997. Death Bicentenary of Vilna Gaon (Rabbi Elijah ben Solomon).
1360 **573** 2s. multicoloured . . . . 1·20 1·10

574 "Exodus" in Haifa Port

575 Ben Ezra Synagogue, Cairo

1997. Clandestine Immigration, 1934–48.
1361 **574** 5s. multicoloured . . . . 2·50 2·00

1997. "Pacific 97" International Stamp Exhibition, San Francisco. Sheet 90 × 60 mm containing T **575** and similar square design. Multicoloured.
MS1362 2s. Type **575** (centenary of discovery of Cairo Hebrew archives); 3s. Qumran and the Dead Sea, Prof E. Sukenik and Shrine of Dead Sea Scrolls) . . 4·50 4·50

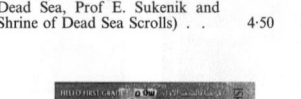

576 Classroom (Navit Mangashsa)

1997. Winning Entry in "Hello First Grade!" Stamp Drawing Competition.
1363 **576** 1s.10 multicoloured . . . 95 85

577 Drunk Driver

1997. Road Safety. Multicoloured.
1364 1s.10 Type **577** ("Don't Drink and Drive") . . . 80 70
1365 1s.10 Car sinking in water ("Keep in Lane") 80 70
1366 1s.10 Car hitting bird ("Keep your Distance") 80 70

578 Ice Skating

1997. 15th Maccabiah Games.
1367 **578** 5s. multicoloured . . . . 3·50 2·30

579 Abraham and Tamarisk Tree

580 Mt. Scopus (Jerusalem) and Choirs

1997. Festival of Sukkot. The Visiting Patriarchs (1st series). Paintings from the Sukkah of Rabbi Loew Immanuel of Szeged, Hungary. Multicoloured.
1368 1s.10 Type **579** 75 60
1369 1s.70 Abraham preparing to sacrifice Isaac 95 70
1370 2s. Jacob dreaming of angels on ladder to heaven . . . 1·30 90
See also Nos. 1453/6.

1997. Music and Dance Festivals. Mult.
1371 1s.10 Type **580** (Zimriya World Assembly of Choirs, Hebrew University) 80 70
1372 2s. Fireworks over Karmiel and dancers (Dance Festival) . . . . 1·10 95
1373 3s. Zefat and klezmers (Hassidic musicians) (Klezmer Festival) . . . . 1·60 1·10

581 "The Night of 29th November" (Ya'acov Eisenscher)

582 Sketch by Pushkin of Himself and Onegin

1997. 50th Anniv of U.N. Resolution on Establishment of State of Israel.
1374 **581** 5s. multicoloured . . . . 2·50 2·10

1997. Translation into Hebrew by Arbraham Shlonsky of Eugene Onegin (poem) by Aleksandr Pushkin. Sheet 75 × 60 mm.
MS1375 **582** 5s. multicoloured . . 2·75 2·75

583 National Flag and Srulik with Flower

584 Norseman Aircraft, Soldier, Missile Corvette and Cannon "Napoleon-Chick"

1997. 50th Anniv (1998) of State of Israel. (1st issue). No value expressed. (a) Size 18 × 23½ mm.
1376 **583** (–) multicoloured 40 35
(b) Size 17½ × 21½ mm.
1377 **583** (–) multicoloured 40 35
See also No. 1395.

1997. 50th Anniv of Arrival in Israel of Machal (overseas volunteers) (1377) and Gachal (overseas recruits) (1378). Multicoloured.
1378 1s.15 Type **584** 65 55
1379 1s.80 Infantry soldier and Holocaust survivors . . . 80 50

585 Bezalel (spinning-top)

1997. Festival of Hanukka. Museum Exhibits. Multicoloured.
1380 1s.80 Type **585** (Eretz Israel Museum, Tel Aviv) . . . 1·00 1·00
1381 2s.10 Coin of Bar-Kokhba during war against the Romans (Israel Museum, Jerusalem) . . . . 1·20 90

586 Children leaving Airliner

1997. Chabad Children of Chernobyl Organization (for evacuation of Jewish children from irradiated areas of Europe to Israel).
1382 **586** 2s.10 multicoloured . . . 1·20 90

587 Julia Set Fractal

588 Photograph of Soldiers of Palmach Battalion and Civilians (Zefat)

1997. Stamp Day.
1383 **587** 2s.50 multicoloured . . . 1·40 1·20

1998. 50th Anniv of War of Independence. Battle Fronts. Multicoloured.
1384 1s.15 Type **588** 60 50
1385 1s.15 "Castel Conquered" (Arieh Navon) superimposed on armoured vehicles (Jerusalem) 60 50
1386 1s.15 Soldiers raising flag (Elat) 60 50
MS1387 140 × 70 mm. 1s.50, 2s.50, 3s. showing enlarged details of Nos. 1383/5 . . . . 5·75 5·75

589 Herzog

1998. 80th Birth Anniv of Chaim Herzog (President 1983–93).
1388 **589** 5s.35 multicoloured . . . 2·20 1·60

590 Franz Kafka (writer)

1998. Jewish Contribution to World Culture (1st series). Multicoloured.
1389 90a. Type **590** 55 40
1390 90a. George Gershwin (composer) 55 40
1391 90a. Lev Davidovich Landau (physicist) 55 40
1392 90a. Albert Einstein (physicist and mathematician) 55 40
1393 90a. Leon Blum (writer) . . 55 40
1394 90a. Elizabeth Rachel Felix (actress) 55 40
See also Nos. 1436/41.

591 Declaration Ceremony, 1948

592 Olive Branch

1998. 50th Anniv of State of Israel (2nd issue).
1395 **591** 1s.15 multicoloured . . . 60 50

1998. Memorial Day.
1396 **592** 1s.15 multicoloured . . . 60 50

593 Swearing In Ceremony in 1948 and Badge entwined with Medal Ribbons

595 Kitten

594 Giorgio Perlasca, Aristides de Sousa Mendes, Charles Lutz, Sempo Sugihara and Selahattin Ulkumen (diplomats) (½-size illustration)

1998. 50th Anniv of Defence Forces.
1397 **593** 5s.35 multicoloured . . . 2·40 1·90

1998. Holocaust Memorial Day. Righteous Among the Nations (non-Jews who risked their lives to save Jews during the Holocaust).
1398 **594** 6s. multicoloured . . . . 3·75 3·75

1998. Children's Pets. Multicoloured.
1399 60a. Type **595** 40 35
1400 60a. Puppy 40 35
1401 60a. Crimson rosella 40 35
1402 60a. Goldfish 40 35
1403 60a. Hamster 40 35
1404 60a. Rabbit 40 35

Nos. 1399/1404 were issued together in se-tenant sheetlets of six stamps and six triangular labels bearing the emblem of "Israel 98" International Stamp Exhibition, each label with an adjacent stamp completing a square. The complete sheetlet forms a composite design.

596 Srulik at Post Office Counter

1998. Inauguration of Postal and Philatelic Museum, Tel Aviv. Sheet 142 × 72 mm containing T **596** and similar horiz designs showing illustrations by K. Gardosh. Multicoloured.
MS1405 1s.50 Type **596**; 2s.50 Srulik viewing stamp through magnifying glass; 3s. Srulik posting letter 4·75 4·75

597 Drawing of Temple Entrance

1998. "Israel 98" International Stamp Exhibition, Tel Aviv (1st issue). King Solomon's Temple. Sheet 92 × 66 mm containing T **597** and similar square design. Multicoloured.
MS1406 2s. Type **597**; 3s. Inscribed ivory pomegranate . . . . . . 3·50 3·50

598 De Havilland D.H.89 Dragon Rapide

1998. Aircraft of War of Independence. Mult.
1407 2s.20 Type **598** 90 70
1408 2s.20 Supermarine Spitfire 90 70
1409 2s.20 Boeing B-17 Flying Fortress 90 70

599 Woman's Head (mosaic from Zippori)

1998. "Israel 98" International Stamp Exhibition, Tel Aviv (2nd issue). Sheet 90 × 60 mm.
MS1410 **599** 5s. multicoloured . . 3·50 3·50

600 "Amos" Satellite, Immigration, Grapes, Dove and Lion's Gate, Jerusalem

1998. "Israel Jubilee" Exhibition, Tel Aviv.
1411 **600** 5s.35 multicoloured . . . 2·20 1·75

601 Holding Hands (Nitzan Shupak)

1998. "Living in a World of Mutual Respect" Elementary Education Programme.
1412 **601** 1s.15 multicoloured . . . 55 45

602 Birds (Hechal Yitshak Synagogue, Moshav Yonatan)

1998. Jewish New Year. Synagogue Curtains. Multicoloured.
1413 1s.15 Type **602** 55 45
1414 1s.80 Lions (Ohal Chanah Synagogue, Neve Tsuf) 80 70
1415 2s.20 Leaves (Hatzvi Israel Synagogue, Jerusalem) . . 1·10 90

603 Hebron

1998. Jewish Life in Eretz Israel (1st series). Showing sections from Holy Cities Wall Plaque. Multicoloured.
1416 1s.80 Type **603** 80 70
1417 2s.20 Jerusalem 95 80
See also Nos. 1430/1.

604 State Flag

1998. Self-adhesive.
1418 **604** 1s.15 blue and deep blue 70 60
1419 2s.15 blue and green . . 1·00 90
1420 3s.25 blue and mauve . . 1·60 1·10
1421 5s.35 blue and yellow . . 2·75 2·00

605 Hanukka Lamp showing Mattathias (Boris Schatz)

606 "Hyacinthus orientalis"

1999. Festival of Hanukka.
1426 **605** 2s.15 multicoloured . . . 95 95

1999. Wild Hyacinths. No value expressed.
1427 **606** (1s.15) green and lilac . . 40 30

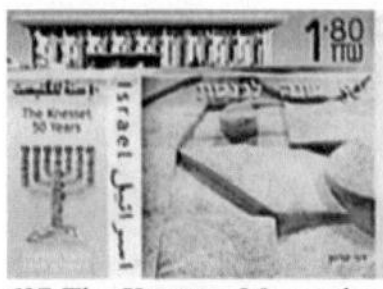

607 The Knesset, Menorah and Knesset Stone Wall (des. Danny Karavan)

1999. 50th Anniv of the Knesset (Parliament).
1428 **607** 1s.80 multicoloured . . . 70 60

608 Manuscript

1999. 380th Birth Anniv of Rabbi Shalem Shabazi (Yemeni poet).
1429 **608** 2s.20 multicoloured . . . 95 80

1999. Jewish Life in Eretz Israel (2nd series). As T **603**, showing sections from Holy Cities Wall Plaque. Multicoloured.
1430 1s.15 Zefat 55 45
1431 5s.35 Tiberias . . . . 2·00 1·75

609 Part of £1 Share Certificate

1999. Centenary of Jewish Colonial Trust.
1432 **609** 1s.80 multicoloured . . . 70 60

610 Yemeni Woman

1999. Traditional Costumes of Jewish Communities (1st series). Multicoloured.
1433 2s.15 Type **610** 90 80
1434 3s.25 Woman wearing sari, India . . . . 1·30 1·10
See also Nos. 1457/8.

611 Reconstruction of Ship

1999. "Australia 99" International Stamp Exhibition, Melbourne. Excavation of Ancient Ship, Sea of Galilee. Sheet 100 × 63 mm containing T **611** and similar square design. Multicoloured.
MS1435 3s. Type **611**; 5s. Remains of ship . . . . 2·40 2·10

1999. Jewish Contribution to World Culture (2nd series). As T **590**. Multicoloured.
1436 90a. Emile Durkheim (sociologist) 40 35
1437 90a. Paul Ehrlich (medical researcher) 40 35
1438 90a. Rosa Luxemburg (revolutionary) 40 35
1439 90a. Norbert Wiener (mathematician) 40 35
1440 90a. Sigmund Freud (psychologist) 40 35
1441 90a. Martin Buber (philosopher) 40 35

612 Memorial to Bedouin Soldiers, Rish Lakish

1999. Memorial Day.
1442 **612** 1s.20 multicoloured . . . 50 40

613 Flags of U.N., Israel and Other States

1999. 50th Anniv of Israel's Admission to United Nations.
1443 **613** 2s.30 multicoloured . . . 85 70

614 Holtzberg

1999. 75th Birth Anniv of Simcha Holtzberg.
1444 **614** 2s.50 multicoloured . . . 1·00 85

615 "My Favourite Room" (detail)

1999. 50th Death Anniv of James Ensor (artist).
1445 **615** 2s.30 multicoloured . . . 90 70

616 Ouza the Goose

1999. Lovely Butterfly (children's television programme). Multicoloured.
1446 1s.20 Type **616** 50 40
1447 1s.20 Nooly the chick and Shabi the snail 50 40
1448 1s.20 Batz the tortoise and Pingi the penguin 50 40

617 "Church of the Holy Sepulchre, Jerusalem" (F. Geyer)

1999. Paintings of Christian Pilgrimage Sites. Multicoloured.
1449 3s. Type **617** . . . . 1·20 1·10
1450 3s. "Mary's Well, Nazareth" (W. H. Bartlett) . . . . . 1·20 1·10
1451 3s. "The River Jordan" (E. Finden after A. W. Callcott) . . . . 1·20 1·10

618 Illustration from Nehemia Emshel's Manuscript of Musa-Nameh by Shahin (poet)

1999. 205th Death Anniv of Rabbi Or Sharga from Persia.
1452 **618** 5s.60 multicoloured . . . 1·90 1·50

1999. Festival of Sukkot. The Visiting Patriarchs (2nd series). As T **579**, showing paintings from the Sukkah of Rabbi Loew Immanuel of Szeged, Hungary. Multicoloured.
1453 1s.20 Joseph interpreting Pharaoh's dreams 55 40
1454 1s.90 Moses and the burning bush 75 60
1455 2s.30 Aaron and Holy Ark 1·00 80
1456 5s.60 David playing harp . . 2·00 1·75

1999. Traditional Costumes of Jewish Communities (2nd series). As T **610**. Multicoloured.
1457 2s.30 Woman from Seus region, Morocco 95 80
1458 3s.40 Man from Bukhara . . 1·50 1·10

619 Family and Part of 1948 250m. Stamp

1999. Stamp Day.
1459 **619** 5s.35 multicoloured . . . 2·00 1·80

620 18th-century Ceramic Urn showing Funeral Procession

622 "The Street of the Jews in Old Jersusalem" (Ludwig Blum)

621 View over Town from Arch of Columns

1999. Jewish Culture in Slovakia. Multicoloured.
1460 1s.90 Type **620** 80 60
1461 1s.90 18th-century urn showing visit to a sick man 80 60

1999. 50th Anniv of Kiryat Shemona.
1462 **621** 1s.20 multicoloured . . . 50 40

1999. 50th Anniv of Proclamation of Jerusalem as Capital.
1463 **622** 3s.40 multicoloured . . . 1·30 1·00

623 Sali

1999. 15th Death Anniv of Admor (Rabbi) Israel Abihssira Sidna "Baba Sali".
1464 **623** 4s.40 multicoloured . . . 1·50 1·20

624 Children and Aliens holding Hands (Renana Barak)

2000. "Stampin' the Future" Children's Painting Competition. Multicoloured.
1465 1s.20 Type **624** 55 45
1466 1s.90 Man and robot (Tal Engelsten) 70 60
1467 2s.30 Futuristic street scene (Asia Aizenshteyn) . . . 90 70
1468 3s.40 Alien's and child's heads (Ortal Hasid) . . . 1·30 1·00

625 Globe, Joggers and Skiers

2000. Year 2000. Multicoloured.
1469 1s.40 Type **625** (quality of life) 60 50
1470 1s.90 Da Vinci's "Proportion of Man", ear of corn and scientist (biotechnology) 75 60
1471 2s.30 Computer, satellite dish and website address (information technology) 90 80
1472 2s.80 Moon's surface, astronaut and globe (space research) . . . . . 1·10 80

626 "The Little Mermaid"

2000. 125th Death Anniv of Hans Christian Andersen (writer). Illustrations by Samuel Katz. Multicoloured.
1473 1s.20 Type **626** 55 45
1474 1s.90 "The Emperor's New Clothes" 85 65
1475 2s.30 "The Ugly Duckling" 1·00 80

627 "All Apostles Church, Capernaum"

2000. Paintings of Christian Pilgrimage Sites (2nd series). Depicting paintings by Zina Roitman. Mult.
1476 1s.40 Type **627** 65 55
1477 1s.90 "St. Andrew's Church, Jerusalem" 80 70
1478 2s.30 "The Church of the Visitation, Ein Kerem" 1·00 80

628 Fort Shuni (Zina Roitman)

629 King Hussein

2000. Buildings and Historical Sites.
1479 **628** 2s.30 multicoloured . . . 95 70

2000. King Hussein of Jordan Commemoration.
1480 **629** 4s.40 multicoloured . . . 1·70 1·30

630 Monument to Jewish Volunteers in British Army, Jerusalem

631 Fox yawning

2000. Memorial Day.
1481 **630** 1s.20 multicoloured . . . 70 60

2000. Endangered Species. Blanford's Fox. Mult.
1482 1s.20 Type **631** 50 40
1483 1s.20 Fox watching mourning wheater (bird) 50 40
1484 1s.20 Fox 50 40
1485 1s.20 Three foxes 50 40

632 Mobile Telephone

633 Cross, Crescent and Menorah

2000. International Communications Day.
1486 **632** 2s.30 multicoloured . . . 90 80

2000. "The Holy Land".
1487 **633** 3s.40 multicoloured . . . 1·50 1·20

634 Bach (bust) and Manuscript of Juara Chaconne for Violin Solo

635 Fortified Stone Building (Zina Roitman)

2000. 250th Death Anniv of Johann Sebastian Bach (composer).
1488 **634** 5s.60 multicoloured . . . 2·00 1·60

2000. Buildings and Historical Sites.
1489 **635** 1s.20 multicoloured . . . 30 25

636 Couscous

637 Olympic Rings and Koala

2000. Traditional Foods. Multicoloured.
1490 1s.40 Type **636** 65 50
1491 1s.90 Stuffed carp 80 65
1492 2s.30 Falafel . . . . 1·00 80

2000. Olympic Games, Sydney.
1493 **637** 2s.80 multicoloured . . . 1·30 95

638 King Hassan II

639 Young Boy and Girl

2000. 1st Death Anniv of King Hassan II of Morocco.
1494 **638** 4s.40 multicoloured . . . 1·80 1·40

2000. Festivals. New Year Cards. Multicoloured.
1495 1s.20 Type **639** 50 40
1496 1s.90 Young woman holding Zionist flag 70 65
1497 2s.30 Man presenting flowers to woman 90 70

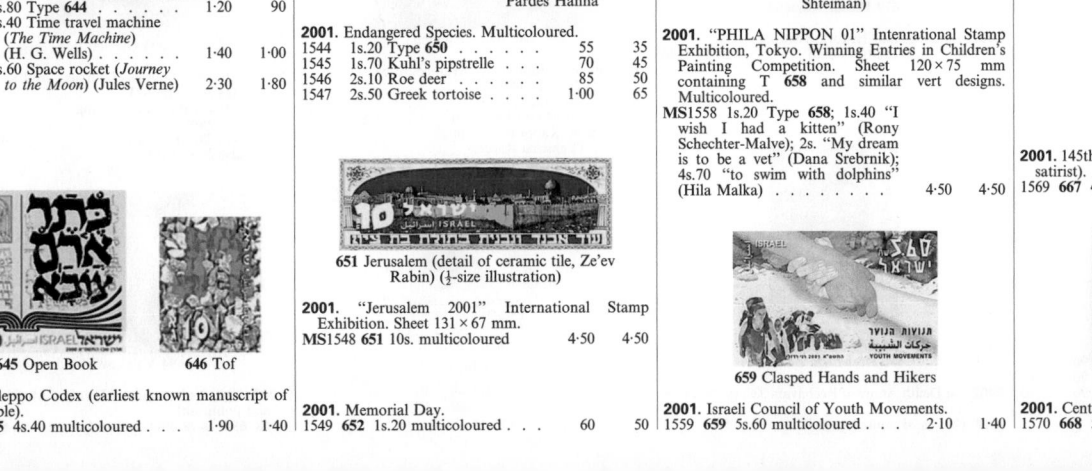

640 Adam and Eve

2000. Dental Health Campaign.
1498 **640** 2s.20 multicoloured . . . 60 60

641 Menorah and Interior of Synagogue

642 Revivim Observatory, Negev (Zina Roitman)

2000. Dohany Synagogue, Budapest.
1499 **641** 5s.60 multicoloured . . . 2·20 1·70

2000. Buildings and Historical Sites.
1500 **642** 2s.20 multicoloured . . . 90 70

643 Struthiomymus running

2000. Dinosaurs. Multicoloured.
1501 2s.20 Type **643** 90 70
1502 2s.20 Head of Struthiomymus 90 70
1503 2s.20 Struthiomymus standing by tree 90 70

644 Robot (*I, Robot*) (Isaac Asimov)

2000. Science Fiction Novels. Multicoloured.
1504 2s.80 Type **644** . . . . . . 1·20 90
1505 3s.40 Time travel machine (*The Time Machine*) (H. G. Wells) . . . . . . 1·40 1·00
1506 5s.60 Space rocket (*Journey to the Moon*) (Jules Verne) 2·30 1·80

645 Open Book

646 Tof

2000. Aleppo Codex (earliest known manuscript of the Bible).
1507 **645** 4s.40 multicoloured . . . 1·90 1·40

2001. Hebrew Alphabet. Designs each showing a different Hebrew letter. Multicoloured.
1508 10a. Type **646** 10 10
1509 10a. Shin 10 10
1510 10a. Reish 10 10
1511 10a. Kuf 10 10
1512 10a. Tzadi Kekufa 10 10
1513 10a. Pay Kekufah 10 10
1514 10a. Ayin 10 10
1515 10a. Samech 10 10
1516 10a. Nun 10 10
1517 10a. Mem 10 10
1518 10a. Lamed 10 10
1519 10a. Chof Kefufa 10 10
1520 10a. Yud 10 10
1521 10a. Tes 10 10
1522 10a. Ches 10 10
1523 10a. Zayin 10 10
1524 10a. Vov 10 10
1525 10a. Heh 10 10
1526 10a. Daled 10 10
1527 10a. Gimel 10 10
1528 10a. Beis 10 10
1529 10a. Aleph 10 10
1530 10a. Tzade Peshuta 10 10
1531 10a. Pay Peshuta 10 10
1532 10a. Chof Peshuta 10 10
1533 10a. Mem Stumah 10 10
1534 10a. Vov 10 10
1535 1s. Aleph and Beis 50 35

647 Pupils in front of School (Yavne'el)

2001. Village Centenaries. Multicoloured.
1536 2s.50 Type **647** . . . . . . 1·00 80
1537 4s.70 Farmers, horses and cart (Kefar Tavor) . . . 1·70 1·30
1538 5s.90 Cart full of flowers (Menahamiya) . . . . . 2·20 1·40

648 Segera Spring, Ilaniyya

649 Prairie Gentian

2001. Buildings and Historical Sites.
1539 **648** 3s.40 multicoloured . . . 1·40 90

2001. Flowers. Multicoloured.
1540 1s.20 Type **649** 55 35
1541 1s.20 Barberton daisy . . . 55 35
1542 1s.20 Star of Bethlehem . . 55 35
1543 1s.20 Florists calla 55 35

650 Lesser Kestrel

652 Monument for the Fallen Nahal Soldiers, Pardes Hanna

2001. Endangered Species. Multicoloured.
1544 1s.20 Type **650** 55 35
1545 1s.70 Kuhl's pipstrelle . . . 70 45
1546 2s.10 Roe deer 85 50
1547 2s.50 Greek tortoise . . . . 1·00 65

651 Jerusalem (detail of ceramic tile, Ze'ev Rabin) (½-size illustration)

2001. "Jerusalem 2001" International Stamp Exhibition. Sheet 131 × 67 mm.
MS1548 **651** 10s. multicoloured 4·50 4·50

2001. Memorial Day.
1549 **652** 1s.20 multicoloured . . . 60 50

653 Marquise Diamonds

2001. "Belgica 2001" International Stamp Exhibition, Brussels. Diamonds. Sheet 117 × 70 mm containing T **653** and similar vert designs. Multicoloured.
MS1550 1s.40 Type **653**; 1s.70 Round diamond; 4s.70 Square diamond . . . . 4·50 4·50

654 Sha'ar HaGay Inn

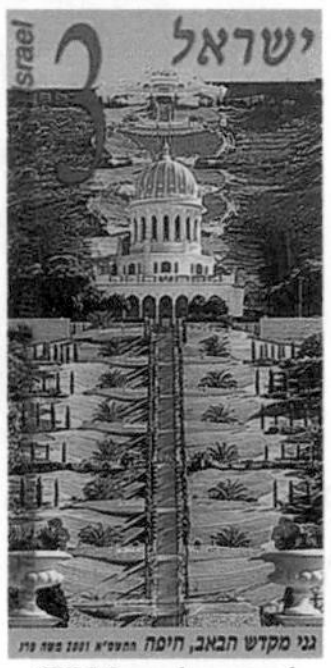

655 Mausoleum and Terraces

2001. Buildings and Historical Sites.
1551 **654** 2s. multicoloured 90 55

2001. Shrine of the Bab, Haifa.
1552 **655** 3s. multicoloured . . . . 1·20 75

656 Prayer Shawl and Tassel

657 Hebron

2001. Karaite Jews.
1553 **656** 5s.60 multicoloured . . . 2·10 1·30

2001. Ceramic Tiles. Showing tiles from facade of Ahad Ha'am Municipal Boys School, Tel Aviv. Multicoloured.
1554 1s.20 Type **657** 55 35
1555 1s.40 Jaffa 65 45
1556 1s.90 Haifa 95 50
1557 2s.30 Tiberias . . . . 1·00 60

658 "and me? I want to ride in a hot air balloon" (Eyar Shteiman)

2001. "PHILA NIPPON 01" Intenrational Stamp Exhibition, Tokyo. Winning Entries in Children's Painting Competition. Sheet 120 × 75 mm containing T **658** and similar vert designs. Multicoloured.
MS1558 1s.20 Type **658**; 1s.40 "I wish I had a kitten" (Rony Schechter-Malve); 2s. "My dream is to be a vet" (Dana Srebrnik); 4s.70 "to swim with dolphins" (Hila Malka) . . . . 4·50 4·50

659 Clasped Hands and Hikers

2001. Israeli Council of Youth Movements.
1559 **659** 5s.60 multicoloured . . . 2·10 1·40

660 Soldier and Peace Dove

661 Rustaveli

2001. Festivals. New Year Cards. Multicoloured.
1560 1s.20 Type **660** 55 35
1561 1s.90 Two women 90 55
1562 2s.30 Boy carrying flowers 1·00 70

2001. 32nd Anniv of the Translation into Hebrew of *The Knight in a Tiger's Skin* (poem by Shota Rustaveli).
1563 **661** 3s.40 multicoloured . . . 1·20 90

662 Field, Leaves and Sky

2001. Centenary of Jewish National Fund.
1564 **662** 5s.60 multicoloured . . . 2·10 1·30

663 Amichai

664 Sunshade on Beach

2001. 1st Death Anniv of Yehuda Amichai (poet).
1565 **663** 5s.60 multicoloured . . . 2·10 1·30

2001. Coastal Conservation.
1566 **664** 10s. multicoloured . . . 4·00 2·75

665 Flags reflected in Helmet Visor

666 Child Painting (Yaffa Dahan)

2001. 1st Israeli Astronaut.
1567 **665** 1s.20 multicoloured . . . 50 40

2001. 50th Anniv of Association for Rehabilitation of the Handicapped (AKIM).
1568 **666** 2s.20 multicoloured . . . 95 60

667 "Heinrich Heine"

2001. 145th Death Anniv of Heinrich Heine (poet and satirist).
1569 **667** 4s.40 multicoloured . . . 1·70 1·10

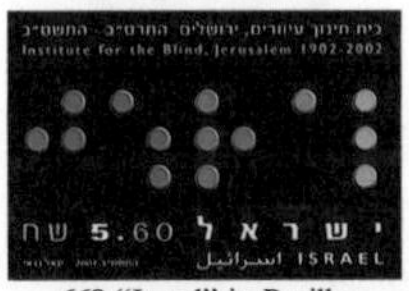

668 "Israel" in Braille

2001. Centenary of Institute for the Blind, Jerusalem.
1570 **668** 5s.60 multicoloured . . . 2·00 1·40

669 Lily

670 Hat and Rattle (Adar)

2002.

1571 **669** 1s.20 multicoloured . . . 50 35

2002. Months of the Year. Multicoloured. Ordinary or self-adhesive gum.

1572	1s.20 Type **670**	50	40
1573	1s.20 Almond twig, flowers and fruit (Shevat)	50	40
1574	1s.20 Grapefruit and anemones (Tevet)	50	40
1575	1s.20 Spinning top and candles (Kislev)	50	40
1576	1s.20 Autumn leaves (Heshvan)	50	40
1577	1s.20 Ram's horn and pomegranates (Tishrei) . .	50	40
1578	1s.20 Cup, unleavened bread and flowers (Nisan) . . .	50	40
1579	1s.20 Bow, arrows and oleanders (Iyyar)	50	40
1580	1s.20 Sickle and grains (Sivian)	50	40
1581	1s.20 Sunflower and shells (Tammuz)	50	40
1582	1s.20 Couple wearing wedding dress and grapes (Av)	50	40
1583	1s.20 Torah, cotton and figs (Elul)	50	40

671 Field Mushroom

2002. Fungi. Multicoloured.

1596	1s.90 Type **671** (*Agaricus campestri*) (inscr "campester")	80	55
1597	2s.20 Fly agaric (*Amanita muscaria*)	90	60
1598	2s.80 Granulated boletus (*Suillus granulatus*) . . .	1·00	80

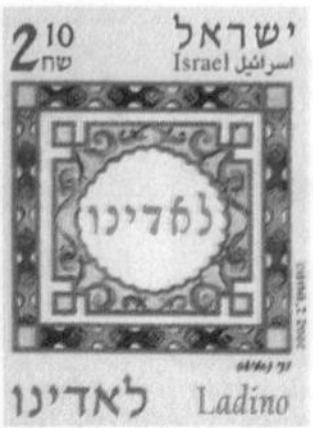

672 "Ladino" in Rashi Script

2002. Judaic Languages. Multicoloured.

1599	2s.10 Type **671** (Ladino (Judeo-Spanish))	90	65
1600	2s.10 Peacock (Yiddish) . .	90	65

673 Military Police Memorial And Eternal Flame, Bet Lid

2002. Memorial Day.

1601 **673** 1s.20 multicoloured . . . 50 40

674 Heinrich Graetz

2002. Historians. Multicoloured.

1602	2s.20 Type **674**	90	65
1603	2s.20 Simon Dubnow . . .	90	65
1604	2s.20 Benzion Dinur	90	65
1605	2s.20 Yitzhak Baer	90	65

See also No. 1686/8.

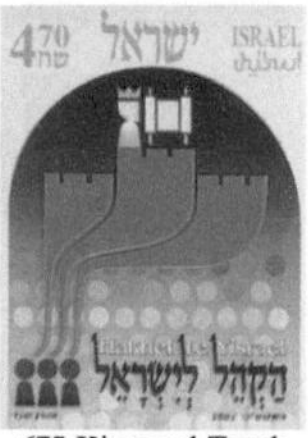

675 King and Torah

2002. Hakel Ceremony.

1606 **675** 4s.70 multicoloured . . . 1·80 1·10

676 "50" and Wheels

2002. 50th Anniv of ILAN (Israel foundation for handicapped children).

1607 **676** 5s.90 multicoloured . . . 2·20 1·40

677 Cable Cars, Menara

2002. Tourism. Cable Cars. Multicoloured.

1608	2s.20 Type **677**	80	55
1609	2s.20 Rosh Haniqra	80	55
1610	2s.20 Haifa	80	55
1611	2s.20 Massada	80	55

678 Fish Fossil

2002. Geology. Sheet 115 × 70 mm containing T **678** and similar vert designs. Multicoloured.

MS1612 2s.20 Type **678**; 3s.40, Copper mineral; 4s.40 Ammonite 3·50 3·50

679 Hatsar Kinneret

2002. Buildings and Historical Sites.

1613 **679** 3s.30 multicoloured . . . 1·20 80

680 Rechavam Ze'evy

2002. 1st Death Anniv of Rechavam Ze'evy (Minister for tourism).

1614 **680** 1s.20 multicoloured . . . 50 40

681 Grape Scissors and Grapes

2002. Festivals. Wine. Multicoloured.

1615	1s.20 Type **681**	60	30
1616	1s.90 Cork screw and cork	80	50
1617	2s.30 Wine glass and bottle	90	60

682 Golden Eagle

2002. Birds of Jordan Valley. Multicoloured.

1618	2s.20 Type **682**	90	60
1619	2s.20 Black stork	90	60
1620	2s.20 Crane	90	60

683 Kadoorie School

2002. Buildings and Historical Sites.

1621 **683** 4s.60 multicoloured . . . 1·70 1·10

684 Baruch Spinoza

2002. 370th Birth Anniv of Baruch (Benedictus) Spinoza.

1622 **684** 5s.90 multicoloured . . . 2·20 1·70

685 Menorah Candlestick

2002.

1623	**685**	20a. red	15	10
1624		30a. brown	15	10
1625		40a. green	15	10
1626		50a. olive	15	15
1647		1s. violet	50	40
1628		1s.30 blue	40	40

686 Abba Ahimeir

2002. Political Journalists. Multicoloured.

1630	1s.20 Type **686**	50	35
1631	3s.30 Israel Eldad	1·20	80
1632	4s.70 Moshe Beilinson . . .	1·80	1·20
1633	5s.90 Rabbi Binyamin (Yehshua Radler-Feldman)	2·20	1·50

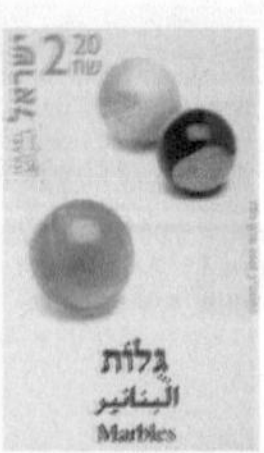

687 Marbles

2002. Stamp Day. Children's Toys. Multicoloured.

1634	2s.20 Type **687**	80	55
1635	2s.20 Top	80	55
1636	2s.20 Five stones	80	55
1637	2s.20 Yo-yo	80	55

688 Students

2003. Yeshivot Hahesder (college).

1638 **688** 1s.20 multicoloured . . . 40 30

689 "11 September 2001" (Michael Gross)

2003.

1639 **689** 2s.30 multicoloured . . . 80 55

690 Glider (1902)

2003. Centenary of Powered Flight. Multicoloured.

1640	2s.30 Type **690**	80	50
1641	3s.30 Engine and Wright brothers	1·10	70
1642	5s.90 Orville Wright flying *Wright Flier*	1·90	1·30

691 Memorial Monument, Mount Herzl

2003.

1643 **691** 4s.70 multicoloured . . . 1·60 1·10

692 Burnt-out Vehicle

2003. Memorial Day.

1644 **692** 1s.20 multicoloured . . . 40 30

693 Opened Box

2003. Greetings Stamps (1st issue). Multicoloured.

1645	(1s.20) Type **693**	50	40
1646	(1s.20) Boy and growing heart	50	40
1647	(1s.20) Married couple . . .	40	25

See also Nos. 1655/7.

694 Ya'akov Meridor

2003. 90th Birth Anniv of Ya'akov Meridor (soldier and politician).

1648 **694** 1s.90 multicoloured . . . 65 50

695 Star of David

2003. Holocaust Memorial Day.
1649 **695** 2s.20 multicoloured . . . 80 65

696 Ya'akov Dori

2003. 30th Death Anniv of Ya'akov Dori (Chief of Staff 1948—50).
1650 **696** 2s.20 multicoloured . . . 80 65

697 Sheikh Ameen Tarif

2003. 10th Death Anniv of Sheikh Ameen Tarif (Druze (religious sect) leader).
1651 **697** 2s.80 multicoloured . . . 70 40

698 Soldier

2003. Jewish Immigration from Yemen, 1881.
1652 **698** 3s.30 multicoloured . . . 1·10 80

699 Paper Airplane and Computer Circuit Board

2003. 50th Anniv of Israel Aircraft Industries.
1653 **699** 3s.30 multicoloured . . . 1·10 80

700 "55"

2003. 55th Anniv of Israel.
1654 **700** 5s.90 multicoloured . . . 2·00 1·20

2003. Greetings Stamps (2nd issue). As T **693**. Multicoloured.
1655 (1s.20) Flowers 50 50
1656 (1s.20) Air balloon 50 50
1657 (1s.20) Boy holding teddy bear 50 50

701 Prague Jewish Community Flag (15th-century)

2003. Development of Israel State Flag. Multicoloured.
1658 1s.90 Type **701** 70 55
1659 2s.30 Ness Ziona (Jewish settlement) (1891) 80 65
1660 4s.70 Draft design from *Der Judenstaat* (Theodor Herzl) (1896) . . . . . . 1·60 1·00
1661 5s.90 State flag (1948) . . . 2·10 1·50

702 Coast, Ruined Castle and Houses (Atlit)

2003. Village Centenaries. Multicoloured.
1662 3s.30 Type **702** . . . . . . 1·30 70
1663 3s.30 Tractor, crops and houses (Givat-Ada) . . . 1·30 70
1664 3s.30 Houses and bungalow amongst trees (Kfar-Saba) 1·30 70

703 Olives

2003. Olive Oil Production. Multicoloured.
1665 1s.30 Type **703** 50 40
1666 1s.90 Mill stone and wheel 65 50
1667 2s.30 Oil 90 50

704 Teddy Bear and Page of Testimony

2003. 50th Anniv of Vad Yashem (Holocaust remembrance organization). Multicoloured.
1668 2s.20 Type **704** 90 50
1669 2s.20 Rail tracks and list of forced labourers 90 50

705 Deer and flowers (Karakashian-Balian studio, c.1940)

2003. Armenian Ceramics in Jerusalem. Sheet 120 × 65 mm containing T **705** and similar circular designs showing ceramic patterns. Multicoloured.
MS1670 2s.30 Type **705**; 3s.30 Bird (Stepan Karakshian, c. 1980); 4s.70 Tree of life (Marie Balian, c. 1990) . . . . 3·50 3·50

2003. No value expressed. As T **600**. Self-adhesive.
1671 **600** (1s.30) green and lilac . . 50 35

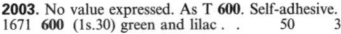

706 Yehoshua Hankin

2003. 58th Death Anniv of Yehoshua Hankin (Zionist pioneer).
1672 **706** 6s.20 multicoloured . . . 2·30 1·40

707 Boy riding Bicycle

2003. Philately Day. Children and Wheels. Multicoloured.
1673 1s.30 Type **707** 60 40
1674 1s.30 Girl on roller skates 60 40
1675 1s.30 Girl pushing scooter 60 40
1676 1s.30 Boy on skateboard . . 60 40

708 Leibowitch Family and Administrative Building, Zikhron Ya'akov

2003. 1st and 2nd Aliya (immigration to Eretz Yisrael). Multicoloured.
1677 2s.10 Type **708** (1st Aliya) 1·10 55
1678 6s.20 Young men (2nd Aliya) . . . . 2·30 1·40

709 Aharon David Gordon

2003. Personalities. Multicoloured.
1679 3s.30 Type **709** (land purchase pioneer) (81st death anniv) . . . . . . 1·10 65
1680 4s.90 Emile Habiby (writer) (82nd death anniv) . . . 1·70 1·10

710 Two-banded Anemonefish (*Amphirion Bicinctus*)

2003. Fish. Multicoloured.
1681 1s.30 Type **710** 60 40
1682 1s.30 Butterfly perch (*Pseudanthias squamipinnis*) 60 40
1683 1s.30 *Pseudochromis fridmani* 60 40
1684 1s.30 Crown butterflyfish (*Chaetodon paucifasciatus*) 60 40
MS1685 118 × 77 mm. Nos. 1681/4 1·90 1·90

2004. Historians. As T **674**. Multicoloured.
1686 2s.40 Emanuel Ringelblum 90 60
1687 3s.70 Jacob Talmon . . . . 1·40 95
1688 6s.20 Jacob Herzog . . . . 2·30 1·50

711 Menachem Begin and Building

2004. Menachem Begin Heritage Centre, Jerusalem.
1689 **711** 2s.50 multicoloured . . . 95 65

712 Ilan Ramon

2004. 1st Death Anniv of Ilan Ramon (astronaut on *Columbia* Space Shuttle).
1690 **712** 2s.60 multicoloured . . . 95 65

713 Memorial Garden, Mount Herzl

2004. Memorial Day.
1691 **713** 1s.30 multicoloured . . . 30 20

714 Saraya Clock Tower, Safed

715 Football and Israel—USA Match, 1948

2004. Ottoman Clock Towers.
1692 1s.30 Type **714** 35 20
1693 1s.30 Khan El-Umdan, Acre 35 20
1694 1s.30 El-Jarina Mosque, Haifa 35 20
1695 1s.30 Jaffa Gate, Jerusalem 35 20
1696 1s.30 Clock Square, Jaffa 35 20
1697 3s.10 No. 1692 . . . . . . 80 50
1698 3s.70 No. 1693 . . . . . . 95 55
1699 5s.20 No. 1694 . . . . . . 1·30 80
1700 5s.50 No. 1695 . . . . . . 1·40 85
1701 7s. No. 1696 . . . . 1·75 1·10

2004. Centenary of FIFA (Federation Internationale de Football Association).
1702 **715** 2s.10 multicoloured . . . 50 30

716 Football

2004. 50th Anniv of UEFA (Union of European Football Associations).
1703 **716** 6s.20 multicoloured . . . 1·60 95

717 Candlestick, Ornamental Panel and Synagogue Facade

2004. Centenary of the Great Synagogue, Rome. Multicoloured.
1704 2s.10 Type **717** 55 35
1705 2s.10 Synagogue (different) 55 35
Stamps of the same design were issued by Italy.

718 Judo and Israeli Silver Medal (Barcelona, 1992)

2004. Olympic Games 2004, Athens. Multicoloured.
1706 1s.50 Type **718** 40 25
1707 2s.40 Wind surfing and Israeli bronze medal (Atlanta, 1996) 60 35
1708 6s.90 Kayaking and Israeli bronze medal (Sydney, 2000) . . . . 1·75 1·10

719 Theodor Herzl

720 Anniversary Emblem

2004. Death Centenary of Theodor Herzl (writer and Zionist pioneer).
1709 **719** 2s.50 multicoloured . . . 60 40
A stamp of the same design was issued by Austria.

2004. 50th Anniv of National Insurance Institute.
1710 **720** 7s. multicoloured . . . . 1·75 1·10

721 Ear of Corn

2004. Bread. Multicoloured.

1711		1s.50 Type **721**	40	25
1712		2s.40 Grinding stones	60	35
1713		2s.70 Bread in oven	70	45

722 Building Facade and Test Tubes

723 Parachutist

2004. Centenary (2005) of Herzliya Hebrew High School.

1714	**722**	2s.20 multicoloured	50	30

2004. Children's Adventure Stories. Illustrations from book covers. Multicoloured.

1715		2s.20 Type **723** ("Eight on the Trail of One" by Yemima Avidar-Tchernovitz)	50	30
1716		2s.50 Children and donkey ("Hasamba" by Igal Mossinsohn)	60	40
1717		2s.60 Faces ("Our Gang" by Pucho)	65	40

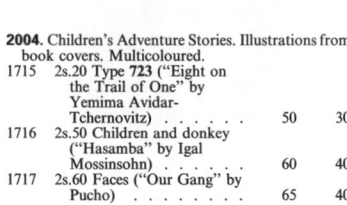

724 Building and David Ben-Gurion

2004. Ben-Gurion Heritage Institute.

1718	**724**	2s.50 multicoloured	60	40

725 Airport Buildings

2004. Ben Gurion Airport.

1719	**725**	2s.70 multicoloured	75	45

726 Post Woman and Envelope

2004. Telabul 2004 International Stamp Exhibition, Tel Aviv. Design a Stamp Competition Winner.

1720	**726**	1s.30 multicoloured	35	25

727 Ottoman Period Austrian Mailbox

2004. Stamp Day. Mailboxes. Multicoloured.

1721		2s.10 Type **727**	55	30
1722		2s.20 British Mandate period	55	30
1723		3s.30 Modern	1·90	1·20

728 "20, 50, 100, 200"

2004. 50th Anniv of Bank of Israel.

1724	**728**	6s.20 multicoloured	1·60	90

729 Brown Bear

2005. Biblical Animals. Multicoloured.

1725		1s.30 Type **729**	35	25
1726		1s.30 Ostrich	35	25
1727		2s.20 Nile crocodile	55	30
1728		2s.20 Wolf	55	50
MS1729		110 × 72 mm. 1s.30 No. 1726; 2s.10 Type **729**; 2s.30 No. 1728; 2s.80 No. 1727	2·20	2·20

730 Tunnel and Spoon

2005. Ancient Water Systems. Multicoloured.

1730		2s.10 Type **730** (Hazor) (9th—8th century BC)	55	30
1731		2s.20 Top of shaft (Megiddo) (10th century)	55	30
1732		3s.30 Aqueduct (Caesarea) (BC)	1·90	1·20
1733		6s.20 Tunnel and pool (Hezekiah's Tunnel) (8th century)	1·60	95

OFFICIAL STAMPS

בול שרות

(O 18)

1951. As Nos. 41 etc, but colours changed. Optd with Type O **18**.

O54		5pr. mauve	15	10
O55		15pr. red	15	10
O56		30pr. blue	30	25
O57		40pr. brown	35	25

POSTAGE DUE STAMPS

דמי דאר

(D 3)

1948. As T **1**, optd with Type D **3**.

D10	**1**	3m. orange on yellow	2·40	1·60
D11		5m. green on yellow	3·25	2·40
D12		10m. mauve on yellow	8·00	5·75
D13		20m. blue on yellow	24·00	20·00
D14		50m. brown on yellow	95·00	75·00

D 9

D 30

1949.

D27	D **9**	2pr. orange	25	15
D28		5pr. violet	40	25
D29		10pr. green	40	15
D30		20pr. red	50	15
D31		30pr. blue	65	30
D32		50pr. brown	1·10	95

1952.

D73	D **30**	5pr. brown	10	10
D74		10pr. blue	10	10
D75		20pr. purple	20	15
D76		30pr. black	10	10
D77		40pr. green	10	10
D78		50pr. sepia	10	10
D79		60pr. violet	10	10
D80		100pr. red	20	15
D81		250pr. blue	30	15

ITALIAN COLONIES Pt. 8

GENERAL ISSUES

100 centesimi = 1 lira.

1932. As Garibaldi stamps of Italy, but inscr "POSTE COLONIALI ITALIANE".

1	–	10c. green (postage)	2·30	5·75
2	**128**	20c. red	2·30	3·75
3	–	25c. green	2·30	3·75
4	**128**	30c. green	2·30	5·75
5	–	50c. red	2·30	3·75
6	–	75c. red	2·30	6·25
7	–	1l.25 blue	2·30	6·25
8	–	1l.75 +25c. blue	4·00	11·50
9	–	2l.55 +50c. sepia	4·00	18·00
10	–	5l.+1l. blue	4·00	21·00
11	**130**	50c. red (air)	2·30	5·75
12	–	80c. green	2·30	5·75
13	**130**	1l.+25c. sepia	4·75	13·50
14	–	2l.+50c. sepia	4·75	13·50
15	–	5l.+1l. sepia	4·75	13·50

1932. Dante stamps of Italy (colours changed) optd **COLONIE ITALIANE**.

18	–	10c. slate (postage)	55	1·20
19	–	15c. sepia	55	1·20
20	–	20c. green	55	55
21	–	25c. green	55	55
22	–	30c. brown	55	70
23	–	50c. blue	55	40
24	–	75c. red	90	1·60
25	–	1l.25 blue	90	2·10
26	–	1l.75 violet	1·10	4·25
27	–	2l.75 orange	1·10	10·50
28	–	5l.+2l. olive	1·10	13·00
29	**124**	10l.+2l.50 blue	1·10	17·00
30	**125**	50c. slate (air)	70	3·00
31	–	1l. blue	70	3·00
32	–	3l. green	1·40	4·00
33	–	5l. sepia	1·40	6·25
34	**125**	7l.70 +2l. red	1·40	10·50
35	–	10l.+2l.50 orange	1·40	16·00
36	**127**	100l. sepia and green	10·50	45·00

No. 36 is inscribed instead of overprinted.

9 Ploughing

10 Savoia Marchetti S-55X Flying Boat

1933. 50th Anniv of Foundation of Colony of Eritrea.

37	**9**	10c. brown (postage)	4·50	5·75
38	–	20c. purple	4·50	5·75
39	–	25c. green	4·50	5·75
40	**9**	50c. violet	4·50	5·75
41	–	75c. red	4·50	7·75
42	–	1l.25 blue	4·50	7·75
43	**9**	2l.75 red	7·00	13·00
44	–	5l.+2l. green	11·50	28·00
45	–	10l.+2l. brown	11·50	35·00
46	–	50c. brown (air)	4·00	5·75
47	–	1l. black	4·00	5·75
48	**10**	3l. red	7·75	11·50
49		5l. brown	7·75	11·50
50	–	7l.70+2l. green	11·50	28·00
51	**10**	10l.+2l.50 blue	11·50	28·00
52	–	50l. violet	11·50	28·00

DESIGNS—VERT: (Postage): 20, 75c., 5l. Camel transport; 25c., 1l.25, 10l. Lioness with star on left shoulder (Arms). HORIZ: (Air): 50c., 1l., 7l. 70, Eagle; 50l. Savoia Marchetti S-55X flying boat over map of Eritrea.

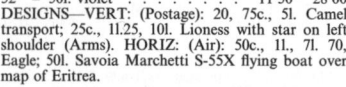

11 Agricultural Implements

13 Macchi Castoldi MC-72 Seaplane

1933. 10th Anniv of Fascist March on Rome. (a) Postage.

53	**11**	5c. orange	4·75	5·25
54	–	25c. green	4·75	5·25
55	–	50c. violet	4·75	3·75
56	**11**	75c. red	4·75	7·75
57	–	1l.25 blue	4·75	7·75
58	–	1l.75 red	4·75	7·75
59	**11**	2l.75 blue	4·75	13·50
60	–	5l. black	7·75	17·00
61	–	10l. blue	7·75	20·00
62	–	25l. olive	11·50	28·00

DESIGNS—HORIZ: 50c., 1l.75, 10l. Tractor. VERT: 25c., 1l.25, 5l. Arab and camel; 25l. Soldier.

(b) Air.

63	**13**	50c. brown	5·25	6·00
64	–	75c. purple	5·25	6·00
65	**13**	1l. sepia	5·25	6·00
66	–	3l. green	5·25	15·00
67	**13**	10l. violet	5·25	16·00
68	–	12l. blue	5·25	20·00
69	–	20l. green	10·00	23·00
70	–	50l. blue	17·00	23·00

DESIGNS—HORIZ: 75c., 3, 12l. Savoia Marchetti S-71 airplane. VERT: 20l. Pilot swinging propeller; 50l. Propeller.

15

16 Hailing Marina Fiat MF.5 Flying Boat

1934. 15th Milan Exhibition.

71	**15**	20c. red	70	3·50
72		30c. green	70	3·50
73		50c. black	70	3·50
74		1l.25 blue	70	7·00

1934. Air. Honouring the Duke of the Abruzzi (explorer).

75	**16**	25l. black	23·00	80·00

17 Scoring a Goal

18 Marina Fiat MF.5 Flying Boat over Stadium

1934. World Football Championship.

76	**17**	10c. green (postage)	18·00	22·00
77		50c. violet	35·00	14·00
78		1l.25 blue	35·00	55·00
79	–	5l. brown	44·00	£130
80	–	10l. blue	44·00	£130

DESIGN—VERT: 5, 10l. Fascist salute before kick-off.

81	**18**	50c. brown (air)	8·75	22·00
82		75c. purple	8·75	22·00
83	–	5l. black	32·00	44·00
84	–	10l. red	32·00	44·00
85	**18**	15l. red	32·00	44·00
86	–	25l. green	32·00	90·00
87	–	50l. green	32·00	90·00

DESIGNS—VERT: 5, 10, 25l. "Saving a goal". HORIZ: 50l. Giant football and Marina Fiat MF.5 flying boat.

EXPRESS STAMPS

1932. Air. As Garibaldi stamps of Italy.

E16	E **131**	2l.25+1l. blk & vio	4·75	13·50
E17		4l.50+1l.50 grn & brn	4·75	17·00

ITALIAN EAST AFRICA Pt. 8

Italian Empire in East Africa comprising Eritrea, Ethiopia and Italian Somaliland, constituted by Royal Decree of 1 June 1936. Occupied by British Forces 1942–43 (see BRITISH OCCUPATION OF ITALIAN COLONIES (MIDDLE EAST FORCES) in Volume 1).

100 centesimi = 1 lira.

1 Grant's Gazelle

2 R. Nile Statue and Lake Tsana

1938.

1	**1**	2c. red	15	90
2	A	5c. brown	35	10
3	B	7½c. violet	55	2·30
4	**2**	10c. brown	1·60	10
5	C	15c. green	35	35

6 B 20c. red 35 10
7 D 25c. green . . . . 1·40 10
8 1 30c. brown 55 70
9 A 35c. blue . . . . 1·20 3·50
10 B 50c. violet 35 10
11 C 75c. red . . . . 1·40 35
12 D 1l. green 90 10
13 B 1l.25 blue . . . . 1·20 35
14 2 1l.75 orange . . . . 18·00 10
15 A 2l. red . . . . 1·10 35
16 D 2l.55 brown . . . . 7·75 14·00
17 1 3l.70 violet . . . . 23·00 23·00
18 C 5l. blue . . . . 6·25 2·30
19 A 10l. red . . . . 7·75 7·00
20 2 20l. green . . . . 14·00 14·00
DESIGN—VERT: A, Italian eagle and Lion of Judah; B, Profile of King Emmanuel III; C, Soldier implanting Fascist emblem. HORIZ: D, Shadows on road.

5 Mussolini Monument and Mt. Amba Aradam

1938. Air.
21 E 25c. green . . . . 1·80 2·30
22 5 50c. brown . . . . 39·00 10
23 F 60c. red . . . . 1·10 6·25
24 E 75c. brown . . . . 1·80 1·60
25 G 1l. blue 10 10
26 5 1l.50 violet 70 35
27 F 2l. blue 70 90
28 E 3l. red . . . . 1·10 3·50
29 G 5l. brown . . . . 2·40 2·40
30 5 10l. purple . . . . 6·00 5·25
31 E 25l. blue . . . . 12·00 12·50
DESIGNS—HORIZ: E, Savoia Marchetti S-73 airplane, rock sculpture of eagle and Mt. Amba Aradam; F, Savoia Marchetti S-73 airplane over Lake Tsana. VERT: G, Bateleur.

9 Statue of Augustus

10 Eagle and Serpent

1938. Birth Bimillenary of Augustus the Great.
36 9 5c. brown (postage) . . . . 10 1·10
37 – 10c. red 10 90
38 9 25c. green 80 90
39 – 50c. violet 80 70
40 9 75c. red . . . . 80 1·80
41 – 1l.25 blue . . . . 80 3·50
DESIGN: 10c., 50c., 1l.25, Statue of Goddess of Abundance.

42 10 50c. brown (air) . . . . . . 35 1·80
43 1l. violet . . . . 55 2·75

11 Ethiopian Canoe

1940. Naples Exhibition.
44 11 5c. brown (postage) 10 70
45 – 10c. orange 10 70
46 – 25c. green . . . . 80 1·20
47 11 50c. violet 80 70
48 – 75c. red . . . . 80 2·10
49 – 1l.25 blue . . . . 80 1·60
50 – 2l.+75c. red . . . . 80 8·75
DESIGNS—VERT: 10c., 75c., 2l. Soldier; 25c., 1l.25, Allegory of Italian Conquest of Ethiopia.

51 – 50c. grey (air) . . . . . . 65 2·75
52 – 1l. violet . . . . 65 2·75
53 – 2l.+75c. blue . . . . 80 2·25
54 – 5l.+2l. brown . . . . 80 2·25
DESIGNS—VERT: 50c., 2l. Savoia Marchetti S-66 flying boat over tractor. HORIZ: 1l., 5l. Savoia Marchetti S.M.83 airplane over city.

15 Hitler and Mussolini

1941. Axis Commemoration.
55 15 5c. yellow (postage) 10
56 10c. brown 10
57 20c. black . . . . 1·10
58 25c. green . . . . 1·10
59 50c. purple . . . . 1·10
60 75c. red . . . . 1·10
61 1l.25 blue . . . . 1·10
62 1l. blue (air) . . . . 26·00
63 1l. blue . . . . 1·80
In No. 62 the "l lira" tablet is in the centre; in No. 63 it is in the lower left corner.

EXPRESS LETTER STAMPS

E 7 Plough and Native Huts

1938. Air.
E32 E 7 2l. blue . . . . 90 2·75
E33 2l.50 brown . . . . 90 4·50

E 8 King Victor Emmanuel III

1938.
E34 E 8 1l.25 green . . . . 90 2·75
E35 2l.50 red (inscr "EXPRESS") . . . . 90 8·00

POSTAGE DUE STAMPS

1941. Nos. D395/407 of Italy optd **A.O.I.**
D64 D 141 5c. brown 55
D65 10c. blue 55
D66 20c. red . . . . 1·60
D67 25c. green . . . . . . 1·60
D68 30c. orange . . . . . . 4·00
D69 40c. brown . . . . . . 4·00
D70 50c. violet . . . . . . 4·00
D71 60c. blue . . . . . . 7·00
D72 D 142 1l. orange . . . . . . 15·00
D73 2l. green . . . . . . 15·00
D74 5l. violet . . . . . . 15·00
D75 10l. blue . . . . . . 15·00
D76 20l. red . . . . 15·00

ITALIAN OCCUPATION OF CEPHALONIA AND ITHACA Pt. 3

Two of the Greek Ionian Islands off the W. coast of Greece, under Italian occupation in 1941.

100 lepta = 1 drachma.

PRICES. Prices are for unsevered pairs. Single stamps from severed pairs are worth $\frac{1}{3}$ unused and $\frac{1}{2}$ used prices.

1941. Stamps of Greece optd **ITALIA Occupazione Militare Italiana isole Cefalonia e Itaca** across a pair of stamps. (a) On postage stamps of 1937.
1 86 5l. blue and brown . . . . 2·75 12·00
2 – 10l. brown and blue . . . 2·75 12·00
3 – 20l. green and black . . . 2·75 12·00
4 – 40l. black and green . . . 2·75 12·00
5 – 50l. black and brown . . . 2·75 12·00
6 – 80l. brown and violet . . . 8·50 23·00
7 89 1d. green . . . . 60·00 £160
8 89a 1d.50 green . . . . 40·00 £100
9 – 2d. blue . . . . 4·00 16·00
10 – 5d. red . . . . 17·00 70·00
11 – 6d. brown . . . . 17·00 70·00
12 – 7d. brown . . . . 17·00 70·00
13 89 8d. blue . . . . 45·00 £120
14 – 10d. brown . . . . 22·00 70·00
15 – 15d. green . . . . 35·00 £110
16 – 25d. blue . . . . 45·00 £140
17 89a 30d. red £140 £475

(b) On air stamps of 1938 and 1935.
18 D 20 50l. brown (No. 521) . . 60·00 75·00
19 79 1d. red . . . . 19·00 65·00
20 – 2d. blue . . . . 11·00 26·00
21 – 5d. mauve . . . . . . 19·00 50·00
22 – 7d. blue . . . . 29·00 65·00
23 – 25d. red . . . . 85·00 £300
24 – 30d. green £110 £325
25 – 50d. mauve £700 £1900
26 – 100d. brown £300 £900

(c) On Charity Tax stamps.
27 D 20 10l. red (No. C498) . . . 6·50 12·00
28 C 96 10l. red . . . . 8·50 20·00
29 50l. green (No. C525) . . 2·75 12·00
30 50l. green (No. C554) . . £140
31 1d. blue (No. C526) . . . 14·00 40·00

ITALIAN OCCUPATION OF CORFU Pt. 3

One of the Greek Ionian Islands situated off the coast of Albania temporarily occupied by Italy during a dispute with Greece in 1923. For later Occupation Issues see ITALIAN OCCUPATION OF CORFU AND PAXOS below.

100 centesimi = 1 lira.
100 lepta = 1 drachma.

1923. Stamps of Italy optd **CORFU.**
1 37 5c. green . . . . 4·25 4·25
2 10c. red . . . . 4·25 4·25
3 15c. grey . . . . 4·25 4·25
4 41 20c. orange . . . . 4·25 4·25
5 39 30c. brown . . . . 4·25 4·25
6 50c. mauve . . . . 4·25 4·25
7 60c. blue . . . . 4·25 4·25
8 34 1l. brown and green . . . . 4·25 4·25

1923. Stamps of Italy surch **CORFU** and value.
9 37 25l. on 10c. red . . . . . . 43·00 18·00
10 39 60l. on 25c. blue . . . . . 6·50
11 70l. on 30c. brown . . . . 6·50
12 1d.20 on 50c. mauve . . . . 24·00 18·00
13 34 2d.40 on 1l. brown & green 24·00 18·00
14 4d.75 on 2l. green & orange 9·25

ITALIAN OCCUPATION OF CORFU AND PAXOS Pt. 3

Greek Ionian Islands occupied by Italy in 1941.

100 lepta = 1 drachma.

1941. Stamps of Greece optd **CORFU.** (a) On postage stamps of 1937.
1 86 5l. blue and brown . . . . 3·25 2·30
2 – 10l. brown and blue . . . 1·30 1·40
4 – 20l. green and black . . . 1·30 1·40
5 – 40l. black and green . . . 1·60 2·10
6 – 50l. black and brown . . . 1·30 1·40
7 – 80l. brown and violet . . . 1·60 2·10
8 89 1d. green . . . . 7·25 4·75
9 89a 1d.50 green . . . . 6·25 3·25
10 – 2d. blue . . . . 4·00 2·75
11 89 3d. brown . . . . 7·25 4·75
12 – 5d. red . . . . 4·00 3·25
13 – 6d. olive . . . . 4·00 3·50
14 – 7d. brown . . . . 6·00 4·00
15 89 8d. blue . . . . 11·50 9·25
16 – 10d. brown £400 £130
17 – 15d. green . . . . 19·00 11·00
18 – 25d. blue . . . . 13·00 11·50
19 89a 30d. red . . . . 65·00 48·00
20 89 100d. red £225 £110

(b) On air stamps of 1938 and 1935.
22 D 20 50l. brown (No. 521) . . 4·50 2·40
23 79 1d. red £475 £160
24 2d. blue . . . . 7·00 2·40
25 5d. mauve . . . . . . 8·25 3·75
26 7d. blue . . . . 8·25 3·75
27 10d. brown £600 £250
28 10d. orange . . . . . . 40·00 25·00
29 25d. red . . . . 65·00 28·00
30 30d. green . . . . . . 80·00 40·00
31 50d. mauve . . . . . . 70·00 38·00
32 100d. brown £800 £425

(c) On Charity Tax stamps of 1939.
33 C 96 10l. red . . . . 1·70 1·30
34 50l. green . . . . 2·00 1·30
35 1d. blue . . . . 21·00 14·00

(d) On Postage Due stamps of 1902 and 1913.
D36 D 20 10l. red . . . . 1·60 1·60
D37 25l. blue . . . . 2·10 1·60
D38 80l. purple £700 £200
D39 1d. blue £1200 £450
D40 2d. red . . . . 4·25 4·50
D41 5d. blue . . . . 14·00 11·00
D42 10d. green . . . . . . 11·00 7·25
D43 15d. brown . . . . . . 11·50 7·25
D44 25d. red . . . . 11·50 7·25
D45 50d. orange . . . . . . 11·50 7·25
D46 100d. green £450 £275

ITALIAN OCCUPATION OF IONIAN ISLANDS Pt. 3

A group of islands off the W. coast of Greece, placed under the protection of Gt. Britain in 1815 and ceded to Greece in 1864. Under Italian occupation in 1941.

For use in all islands except Kithyra.

100 lepta = 1 drachma.

1941. Stamps of Italy optd **ISOLE JONIE.** (a) On postage stamps of 1929.
1 98 5c. brown . . . . 45 1·70
2 – 10c. brown . . . . 45 1·70
3 99 20c. red . . . . 45 1·70
4 – 25c. green . . . . 45 1·70
5 103 30c. brown . . . . 45 1·70
6 50c. violet . . . . 45 1·70
7 – 75c. red . . . . 45 1·70
8 – 1l.25 blue . . . . 45 1·70

(b) On air stamp of 1930.
9 110 50c. brown . . . . 70 2·10

(c) On Postage Due stamps of 1934.
D10 D 141 10c. blue . . . . 1·00 2·75
D11 20c. red . . . . 1·00 2·75
D12 30c. orange . . . . . . 1·00 2·75
D13 D 142 1l. orange . . . . . . 1·00 2·75

ITALIAN POST OFFICES IN CHINA Pt. 8

Italian Military Posts in China, including Peking and Tientsin, now closed.

100 centesimi = 1 lira. 100 cents = 1 dollar.

Stamps of Italy overprinted or surcharged.

A. PEKING

1917. Surch **PECHINO** and value.
1 37 2c. on 5c. green . . . . . . £120 70·00
3 4c. on 10c. pink £225 £120
4 41 6c. on 15c. grey £475 £250
5 8c. on 20c. on 15c. grey . . . £2250 £1100
6 8c. on 20c. orange £3750 £1200
7 39 20c. on 50c. violet £22000 £14000
8 34 40c. on 1l. brown and green £140000 £19000

1917. Optd **Pechino.**
9 30 1c. brown . . . . 9·50 15·00
10 31 2c. brown . . . . 9·50 15·00
11 37 5c. green . . . . 3·00 4·00
12 10c. pink . . . . 3·00 4·00
13 41 20c. orange . . . . 90·00 75·00
14 39 25c. blue . . . . 3·00 6·75
15 50c. violet . . . . 3·00 8·25
16 34 1l. brown and green . . . . 6·75 13·50
17 5l. blue and pink . . . . 11·00 24·00
18 10l. green and pink . . . . 90·00 £225

1918. Surch **Pechino** and value.
19 30 $\frac{1}{2}$c. on 1c. brown . . . . . 80·00 80·00
20 31 1c. on 2c. brown . . . . . 3·00 5·25
21 37 2c. on 5c. green . . . . . . 3·00 5·25
22 4c. on 10c. pink . . . . . . 3·00 5·25
23 41 8c. on 20c. orange . . . . . 13·50 11·00
28 39 10c. on 25c. blue . . . . . 3·50 9·50
25 20c. on 50c. violet . . . . . 8·25 11·00
26 34 40c. on 1l. brown and green £100 £130
27 2 dollari. on 5l. blue and pink £190 £325
30 2 DOLLARI. on 5l. blue and pink £45000 £35000

EXPRESS LETTER STAMPS

1917. Express Letter stamp optd **Pechino** or surch **12 CENTS** also.
E28 E 41 12c. on 30c. bl & pink 45·00 £140
E19 30c. blue and pink . . . 6·75 19·00

POSTAGE DUE STAMPS

1917. Postage Due stamps optd **Pechino.**
D19 D 12 10c. mauve and orange 2·75 6·75
D20 20c. mauve and orange 2·75 6·75
D21 30c. mauve and orange 2·75 6·75
D22 40c. mauve and orange 5·50 6·75

1918. Surch **Pechino** and value.
D28 D 12 4c. on 10c. mve & orge £45000 £35000
D29 8c. on 20c. mve & orge £6000 £4500
D30 12c. on 30c. mve & orge . . . . 41·00 60·00
D31 16c. on 40c. mve & orge £200 £300

B. TIENTSIN

1917. Surch **TIENTSIN** and value.
31 37 2c. on 5c. green £225 £190
32 4c. on 10c. pink £400 £225
33 41 6c. on 15c. grey £950 £300
Prices for the above are for stamps with surcharge inverted.

1917. Optd **Tientsin.**
34 30 1c. brown . . . . 9·50 15·00
35 31 2c. brown . . . . 9·50 15·00
36 37 5c. green . . . . 3·00 4·00
37 10c. pink . . . . 3·00 4·00
38 41 20c. orange . . . . 90·00 75·00
39 39 25c. blue . . . . 3·00 6·75
40 50c. violet . . . . 3·00 8·25
41 34 1l. brown and green . . . . 6·50 13·50
42 5l. blue and pink . . . . 11·00 24·00
43 10l. green and pink . . . . 90·00 £225

1918. Surch **Tientsin** and value.
44 30 $\frac{1}{2}$c. on 1c. brown . . . . . 80·00 80·00
45 31 1c. on 2c. brown . . . . . 3·00 5·25
46 37 2c. on 5c. green . . . . . . 3·00 5·25
47 4c. on 10c. pink . . . . . . 3·00 5·25
48 41 8c. on 20c. orange . . . . . 13·50 11·00
49 39 10c. on 25c. blue . . . . . 6·75 11·00
50 20c. on 50c. violet . . . . . 8·25 11·00
51 34 40c. on 1l. brown and green £100 £130
52 2 Dollari. on 5l. blue and pink £190 £325
54 2 dollari. on 5l. blue and pink £6000 £4500

EXPRESS LETTER STAMPS

1917. Express Letter stamp optd **Tientsin** or surch **12 CENTS** also.
E53 E 41 12c. on 30c. blue & pink 45·00 £140
E44 30c. blue and pink . . . 6·75 19·00

POSTAGE DUE STAMPS

1917. Postage Due stamps optd **Tientsin**.
D44 D **12** 10c. mauve and orange 2·75 6·75
D45 20c. mauve and orange 2·75 6·75
D46 30c. mauve and orange 2·75 6·75
D47 40c. mauve and orange 5·50 6·75

1918. Surch **Tientsin** and value.
D53 D **12** 4c. on 10c. mve & orge £1900 £2250
D54 8c. on 20c. mve & orge 13·50 21·00
D55 12c. on 30c. mve & orge . . . . 41·00 60·00
D56 16c. on 40c. mve & orge £200 £300

ITALIAN POST OFFICES IN CRETE Pt. 8

Italian P.O.s in Crete, now closed.

1900. 40 paras = 1 piastre.
1906. 100 centesimi = 1 lira.

Stamps of Italy surcharged or overprinted.

1900. Surch **1 PIASTRA 1**.
1 **27** 1pi. on 25c. blue . . . . . . 5·50 34·00

1901. Surch **LA CANEA 1 PIASTRA 1**.
2 **33** 1pi. on 25c. blue . . . . . . 3·00 6·25

1906. 1901 stamps optd **LA CANEA**.
3 **30** 1c. brown . . . . 50 1·20
4 **31** 2c. brown . . . . 50 1·20
5 5c. green . . . . 1·00 1·50
6 **33** 10c. red . . . . £100 75·00
7 15c. on 20c. orange . . . . 1·20 1·70
8 25c. blue . . . . 5·75 5·75
9 40c. brown . . . . 5·25 5·75
10 45c. green . . . . 4·50 5·75
11 50c. mauve . . . . 5·75 8·25
12 **34** 1l. brown and green . . . . 31·00 34·00
13 5l. blue and pink £150 £150

1907. 1906 stamps optd **LA CANEA**.
14 **37** 5c. green . . . . 85 1·20
15 10c. red . . . . 85 1·20
16 **41** 15c. black . . . . 1·70 3·00
17 **39** 25c. blue . . . . 1·70 4·00
18 40c. brown . . . . 17·00 21·00
19 50c. violet . . . . 1·70 4·00

EXPRESS LETTER STAMP

1906. Express Letter stamp optd **LA CANEA**.
E1 E **35** 25c. red . . . . 4·25 8·50

ITALIAN POST OFFICES IN THE TURKISH EMPIRE Pt. 8

Currency: Italian and Turkish.

Stamps of Italy overprinted and surcharged.

A. GENERAL ISSUES.

The following were in use in P.O.s in Alexandria, Assab, La Goletta, Massawa, Susa, Tripoli and Tunis and also at Consular post offices at Buenos Aires and Montevideo.

1874. 1863 type, slightly altered, optd **ESTERO**.
1 **4** 1c. green . . . . 6·75 15·00
2 **5** 2c. brown . . . . 8·25 19·00
3 **6** 5c. grey . . . . £450 19·00
4 10c. orange . . . . £1100 34·00
10 10c. blue . . . . £225 12·50
5 **10** 20c. blue . . . . £1000 19·00
11 20c. orange . . . . £3750 9·50
6 **6** 30c. brown . . . . 1·40 10·50
7 40c. red . . . . 1·40 9·50
8 60c. mauve . . . . 3·50 75·00
9 **7** 2l. red . . . . 90·00 £400

1881. 1879 type, slightly altered, optd **ESTERO**.
12 **12** 5c. green . . . . 5·50 8·25
13 10c. red . . . . 4·00 5·50
14 20c. orange . . . . 4·00 4·75
15 25c. blue . . . . 4·00 8·25
16 50c. mauve . . . . 8·25 41·00

B. OFFICES IN TURKISH EMPIRE.

(a) **Albania.**

1902. Surch **ALBANIA** and value.
18 **31** 10pa. on 5c. green . . . . 2·20 1·00
24 **37** 10pa. on 5c. green . . . . 27·00 34·00
25 20pa. on 10c. red . . . . 16·00 14·50
19 **33** 35pa. on 20c. orange . . . 3·75 3·00
20 40pa. on 25c. blue . . . . 7·75 3·00
26 80pa. on 50c. mauve . . . . 16·00 14·50

1902. Surch with figures of value repeated twice and currency in words thus, **20 Para 20**.
21 **31** 10pa. on 5c. green . . . . . 4·50 1·50
27 **37** 10pa. on 5c. green . . . . . 1·00 1·00
28 20pa. on 10c. red . . . . . 1·00 1·00
22 **33** 35pa. on 20c. orange . . . . 3·00 1·90
23 40pa. on 25c. blue . . . . 21·00 4·25
29 80pa. on 50c. mauve . . . . 38·00 29·00

(b) **General Offices in Europe and Asia.**

1908. Surch with figures of value repeated twice and currency in words thus, **30 Para 30**.
32 **41** 30pa. on 15c. grey . . . . . 1·40 1·70
30 **39** 40pa. on 25c. blue . . . . . 2·10 1·70
31 80pa. on 50c. mauve . . . . 3·00 2·40

EXPRESS LETTER STAMPS

1908. Express Letter stamps surch **LEVANTE** and new value.
E33 E **35** 1pi. on 25c. red . . . . 2·10 2·40
E34 E **41** 60pa. on 30c. blue & red 3·00 3·75

C. INDIVIDUAL OFFICES IN EUROPE AND ASIA.

(a) **Constantinople.**

1908. Surch in one line with figure of value and currency in words.
40 **37** 10pa. on 5c. green . . . . . 4·75 6·75
41 20pa. on 10c. pink . . . . . 4·75 6·75
47 **41** 30pa. on 15c. grey . . . . . 2·10 2·10
43 **39** 1pi. on 25c. blue . . . . . 4·75 6·75
44 2pi. on 50c. mauve . . . . 41·00 41·00
45 **34** 4pi. on 1l. brown and green £600 £475
46 20pi. on 5l. blue and pink £2500 £1500

1908. Surch in two lines with figures of value repeated twice and currency in words.
48 **34** 4pi. on 1l. brown and green 34·00 41·00
51 20pi. on 5l. blue and pink 34·00 41·00

1909. Surch **Costantinopoli** (10pa. to 2pi.) or **COSTANTINOPOLI** (4 to 40pi.) and value in figures twice repeated and currency in words.
52 **37** 10pa. on 5c. green . . . . . 1·00 1·50
53 20pa. on 10c. pink . . . . 1·00 1·50
54 **41** 30pa. on 15c. grey . . . . 1·00 1·50
55 **39** 1pi. on 25c. blue . . . . 1·00 1·50
56 2pi. on 50c. mauve . . . . 1·40 1·80
57 **34** 4pi. on 1l. brown and green 1·70 2·20
58 20pi. on 5l. blue and pink 41·00 39·00
59 40pi. on 10l. green and pink 3·00 19·00

1921. Surch with value in figures and currency in words thus, **4 PIASTRE**.
60 **37** 1pi. on 5c. green £110 £200
61 2pi. on 15c. grey . . . . . 4·00 6·75
62 **41** 4pi. on 20c. orange . . . . 46·00 46·00
63 **39** 5pi. on 25c. blue . . . . 46·00 46·00
64 10pi. on 60c. red . . . . . 2·10 3·50

1921. Surch with value in figures and currency in words thus, **PARA 20**.
65 **30** 10pa. on 1c. brown . . . . 1·40 2·10
66 **31** 20pa. on 2c. brown . . . . 1·40 2·10
67 **37** 30pa. on 5c. green . . . . 3·00 3·75
68 1pi. 20 on 15c. grey . . . . 4·75 2·10
69 **41** 3pi. on 20c. orange . . . . 5·50 10·50
70 **39** 3pi. 30 on 25c. blue . . . . 2·40 2·10
71 7pi. 20 on 60c. red . . . . 4·75 3·75
72 **34** 15pi. on 1l. brown and green . . . . 19·00 29·00

1922. Surch **COSTANTINOPOLI** and value in figures once only after currency in words.
73 **37** 20pa. on 5c. green . . . . . 12·50 17·00
74 1pi. 20 on 15c. grey . . . . 1·20 1·70
75 **39** 3pi. on 30c. brown . . . . 1·20 1·70
76 3pi. 30 on 40c. brown . . . . 1·20 1·70
77 **34** 7pi. 20 on 1l. brown & green . . . . 1·20 1·70

1922. Surch **Piastre 3,75** in two lines.
78 **39** 3,75pi. on 25c. blue . . . . 1·70 2·10

1922. Para values surch in one line thus **30 PARA** and piastre values with **PIASTRE** over new value except Nos. 81, 86, 98 and 99 where the figures of value are above.
79 **31** 30pa. on 2c. brown . . . . 1·50 2·75
80 **37** 30pa. on 5c. green . . . . 3·50 8·25
81 **41** 1,50pi. on 20c. orange . . . 1·50 2·10
82 **39** 1,50pi. on 25c. blue . . . . 1·50 4·00
83 3,75pi. on 40c. brown . . . . 2·20 5·25
84 4,50pi. on 50c. mauve . . . 6·75 12·50
85 7,50pi. on 60c. red . . . . 5·50 9·50
86 15pi. on 85c. brown . . . . 10·50 19·00
87 **34** 18,75pi. on 1l. brown & grn 4·75 15·00
98 45pi. on 5l. blue and red . . 85·00 60·00
99 90pi. on 10l. olive and red 60·00 £110

1922. Para values surch in two lines and piastre values with **PIASTRE** under new value.
90 **37** 30pa. on 5c. green . . . . . 1·00 2·10
91 1½pi. on 10c. red . . . . . 1·40 2·10
92 **39** 3pi. on 25c. blue . . . . . 12·00 5·25
93 3¾pi. on 40c. brown . . . . 1·90 2·10
94 4½pi. on 50c. mauve . . . . 31·00 26·00
95 7½pi. on 85c. brown . . . . 5·25 6·00
96 **34** 7½pi. on 1l. brown and green . . . . 6·00 8·50
97 15pi. on 1l. brown and red green . . . . 50·00 £100

1923. Surch **COSTANTINOPOLI** and value in figures once only after currency in words.
100 **37** 30pa. on 5c. green . . . . 1·70 1·90
101 **39** 1pi. 20 on 25c. blue . . . . 1·70 1·90
103 4pi. 20 on 50c. mauve . . . 1·70 1·50
104 7pi. 20 on 60c. red . . . . 1·70 1·50
105 15pi. on 85c. brown . . . 1·70 2·75
106 **34** 18pi. 30 on 1l. brown and green . . . . 1·70 2·75
107 45pi. on 5l. blue and pink 2·50 5·50
108 90pi. on 10l. green & pink 2·50 6·25

EXPRESS LETTER STAMPS

1922. Express Letter stamps surch **15 PIASTRE**.
E 90 E **41** 15pi. on 1l.20 on 30c. blue and red . . . . 17·00 34·00
E100 15pi. on 30c. blue and red £225 £375

1923. Express Letter stamp surch **COSTANTINOPOLI 15 PIASTRE**.
E109 E **41** 15pi. on 1l.20 blue and red . . . . 4·25 17·00

POSTAGE DUE STAMPS

1922. Postage Due stamps optd **Costantinopoli**.
D100 E **12** 10c. mauve and orange 34·00 48·00
D101 30c. mauve and orange 34·00 48·00
D102 60c. mauve and orange 1·70 1·50
D103 1l. mauve and blue . . 34·00 48·00
D104 2l. mauve and blue . . £700 £1100
D105 5l. mauve and blue . . £250 £350

Nos. D100/5 bear a control cachet applied over blocks of four so that a quarter of the circle falls in a corner of each stamp.

(b) **Durazzo.**

1909. Surch **Durazzo** (10pa. to 2pi.) or **DURAZZO** (4 to 40pi.) and value.
109 **37** 10pa. on 5c. green . . . . 70 1·20
110 20pa. on 10c. pink . . . . 70 1·20
111 **41** 30pa. on 15c. grey . . . . 31·00 2·10
112 **39** 1pi. on 25c. blue . . . . . 1·40 1·70
113 2pi. on 50c. mauve . . . . 1·40 1·70
114 **34** 4pi. on 1l. brown and green . . . . 2·75 2·40
115 20pi. on 5l. blue and pink £140 £140
116 40pi. on 10l. green & pink 6·75 60·00

1915. No. 111 of Durazzo surch **CENT. 20**.
116a **41** 20c. on 30pa. on 15c. grey 2·75 13·00

(c) **Janina.**

1909. Surch **Janina** (10pa. to 2pi.) or **JANINA** (4 to 40pi.) and value.
117 **37** 10pa. on 5c. green 85 85
118 20pa. on 10c. pink 85 85
119 **41** 30pa. on 15c. grey . . . . 1·20 1·20
120 **39** 1pi. on 25c. blue . . . . . 1·20 1·20
121 2pi. on 50c. mauve . . . . 1·20 1·40
122 **34** 4pi. on 1l. brown and green . . . . 2·40 1·70
123 20pi. on 5l. blue and pink £170 £190
124 40pi. on 10l. green & pink 10·50 50·00

(d) **Jerusalem.**

1909. Surch **Gerusalemme** (10pa. to 2pi.) or **GERUSALEMME** (4 to 40pi.) and value.
125 **37** 10pa. on 5c. green . . . . 2·20 4·75
126 20pa. on 10c. pink . . . . 2·20 4·75
127 **41** 30pa. on 15c. grey . . . . 2·20 6·75
128 **39** 1pi. on 25c. blue . . . . . 2·20 4·75
129 2pi. on 50c. mauve . . . . 10·50 13·50
130 **34** 4pi. on 1l. brown and green . . . . 13·50 27·00
131 20pi. on 5l. blue and pink £650 £425
132 40pi. on 10l. green & pink 21·00 £200

(e) **Salonica.**

1909. Surch **Salonicco** (10pa. to 2pi.) or **SALONICCO** (4 to 40pi.) and value.
133 **37** 10pa. on 5c. green 50 70
134 20pa. on 10c. pink 50 70
135 **41** 30pa. on 15c. grey . . . . 85 1·20
136 **39** 1pi. on 25c. blue . . . . . 85 1·20
137 2pi. on 50c. mauve . . . . 1·00 1·40
138 **34** 4pi. on 1l. brown and green . . . . 1·40 1·70
139 20pi. on 5l. blue and pink £250 £250
140 40pi. on 10l. green & pink 6·75 45·00

(f) **Scutari.**

1909. Surch **Scutari di Albania** (4pa. to 2pi.) or **SCUTARI DI ALBANIA** (4 to 40pi.) and value.
141 **31** 4pa. on 2c. brown . . . . 1·70 3·50
142 **37** 10pa. on 5c. green 35 85
143 20pa. on 10c. pink 35 85
144 **41** 30pa. on 15c. grey . . . . 17·00 3·50
145 **39** 1pi. on 25c. blue . . . . . 35 1·40
146 2pi. on 50c. mauve . . . . 70 1·70
147 **34** 4pi. on 1l. brown and green . . . . 85 2·10
148 20pi. on 5l. blue and pink 19·00 27·00
149 40pi. on 10l. green & pink 45·00 90·00

1916. No. 144 of Scutari surch **CENT. 20**.
150 **41** 20c. on 30pa. on 15c. grey 4·00 15·00

(g) **Smyrna.**

1909. Surch **Smirne** (10pa. to 2pi.) or **SMIRNE** (4 to 40pi.) and value.
151 **37** 10pa. on 5c. green 35 60
152 20pa. on 10c. pink 35 60
153 **41** 30pa. on 15c. grey . . . . 1·20 1·40
154 **39** 1pi. on 25c. blue . . . . . 1·20 1·40
155 2pi. on 50c. mauve . . . . 1·70 2·10
156 **34** 4pi. on 1l. brown and green . . . . 2·40 2·50
157 20pi. on 5l. blue and pink £100 £110
158 40pi. on 10l. green & pink 12·00 65·00

(h) **Valona.**

1909. Surch **Valona** (10pa. to 2pi.) or **VALONA** (4 to 40pi.) and value.
159 **37** 10pa. on 5c. green . . . . 25 1·00
160 20pa. on 10c. pink . . . . 25 1·00
161 **41** 30pa. on 15c. grey† . . . . 12·00 3·50
167 30pa. on 15c. grey† . . . . 3·50 8·50
162 **39** 1pi. on 25c. blue . . . . . 85 1·20
163 2pi. on 50c. mauve . . . . 85 1·50
164 **34** 4pi. on 1l. brown and green . . . . 1·20 2·10
165 20pi. on 5l. blue and pink 33·00 38·00
166 40pi. on 10l. green & pink 38·00 90·00

†On No. 161 the surcharge is **Para**, on No. 167 **PARA**.

1916. No. 167 of Valona surch **CENT. 20**.
168 **41** 20c. on 30pa. on 15c. grey 1·40 10·00

D. OFFICES IN AFRICA.

(a) **Benghazi.**

1901. Surch **BENGASI 1 PIASTRA 1**.
169 **33** 1pi. on 25c. blue . . . . . 27·00 80·00
170 **39** 1pi. on 25c. blue . . . . . 31·00 80·00

(b) **Tripoli.**

1909. Optd **Tripoli di Barberia** (1 to 50c.) or **TRIPOLI DI BARBERIA** (1, 2l.).
171 **30** 1c. brown . . . . 3·00 2·75
173 **31** 2c. brown . . . . 1·00 1·70
174 **37** 5c. green . . . . 70·00 6·25
175 10c. red . . . . 2·10 1·70
176 **41** 15c. grey . . . . 2·50 3·00
177 **39** 25c. blue . . . . 1·70 1·70
178 40c. brown . . . . 4·25 3·75
179 50c. violet . . . . 6·00 5·25
180 **34** 1l. brown and green . . . 75·00 50·00
181 5l. blue and pink . . . . . 24·00 £130

EXPRESS LETTER STAMPS

1909. Express Letter stamps optd **TRIPOLI DI BARBERIA**.
E182 E **35** 25c. pink . . . . . . 10·50 6·75
E183 E **41** 30c. blue and pink . . 3·50 10·50

ITALY Pt. 8

A Republic in S. Europe on the Mediterranean and Adriatic Seas. Originally a kingdom formed by the union of various smaller kingdoms and duchies that issued their own stamps.

1862. 100 centesimi = 1 lira.
2002. 100 cents = 1 euro.

1 King Victor Emmanuel II

3

1862. Head embossed. Imperf (15c.) or perf (others).
1 **1** 10c. bistre £4500 £100
5 15c. blue . . . . 50·00 22·00
2a 20c. blue £600 £550
3 40c. red . . . . £200 60·00
4a 80c. yellow . . . . 50·00 £1200

For stamps of this type imperf, see Sardinia Nos. 27 etc.

1863. Imperf.
7 **3** 15c. blue . . . . 3·50 1·90

4

5

6

7

10

1863. Perf.
8 **4** 1c. green . . . . 3·50 50
9 **5** 2c. brown . . . . 7·50 35
10 **6** 5c. grey £1600 60
11 10c. brown £2000 65
21 10c. blue . . . . £4500 1·00
12 15c. blue £2000 85
20a **10** 20c. blue . . . . £1300 3·00
22 20c. orange £3500 80
13 **6** 30c. brown . . . . 10·00 1·40
14 40c. red . . . . £4000 1·30
15 60c. mauve . . . . 10·00 6·25
16 **7** 2l. red . . . . 16·00 30·00

1865. Surch **C 20 20 C** and curved bar.
17 **6** 20c. on 15c. blue £600 75

1878. Official stamps surch **2 C** and wavy bars.
23 O **11** 2c. on 2c. red . . . . . £160 4·25
24 2c. on 5c. red . . . . . £160 5·75
25 2c. on 20c. red . . . . . £300 1·60
26 2c. on 30c. red . . . . . £200 2·30
27 2c. on 1l. red . . . . . £250 1·70
28 2c. on 2l. red . . . . . £250 2·75
29 2c. on 5l. red . . . . . £300 3·75
30 2c. on 10l. red . . . . . £200 4·50

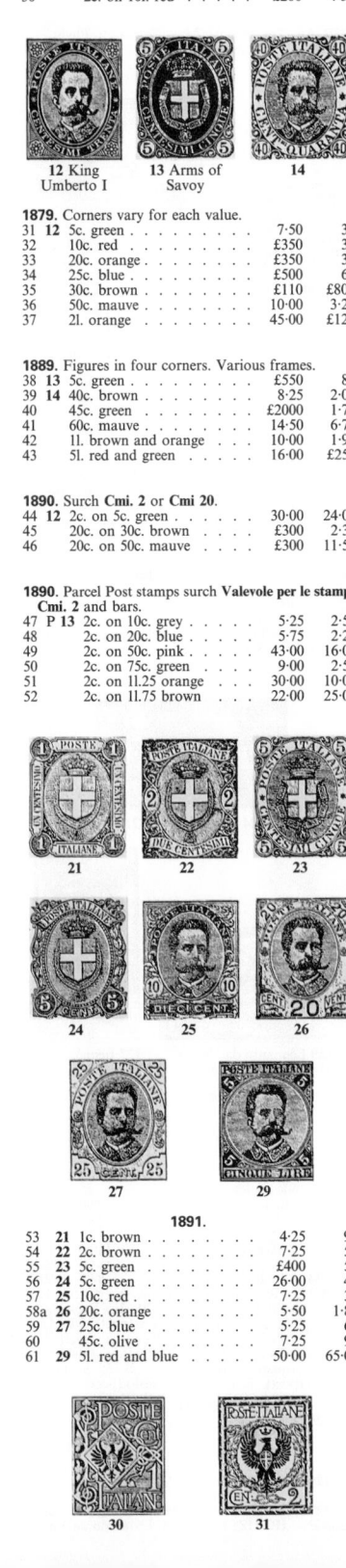

12 King Umberto I

13 Arms of Savoy

14

1879. Corners vary for each value.
31 **12** 5c. green . . . . 7·50 30
32 10c. red £350 35
33 20c. orange £350 30
34 25c. blue £500 65
35 30c. brown £110 £800
36 50c. mauve . . . . 10·00 3·25
37 2l. orange . . . . 45·00 £120

1889. Figures in four corners. Various frames.
38 **13** 5c. green £550 80
39 **14** 40c. brown . . . . 8·25 2·00
40 45c. green . . . . £2000 1·70
41 60c. mauve . . . . 14·50 6·75
42 1l. brown and orange . . . 10·00 1·90
43 5l. red and green . . . . . 16·00 £250

1890. Surch **Cmi. 2** or **Cmi 20**.
44 **12** 2c. on 5c. green . . . . . . 30·00 24·00
45 20c. on 30c. brown . . . . £300 2·30
46 20c. on 50c. mauve . . . . £300 11·50

1890. Parcel Post stamps surch **Valevole per le stampe Cmi. 2** and bars.
47 P **13** 2c. on 10c. grey . . . . . 5·25 2·50
48 2c. on 20c. blue . . . . . 5·75 2·20
49 2c. on 50c. pink . . . . . 43·00 16·00
50 2c. on 75c. green . . . . 9·00 2·50
51 2c. on 1l.25 orange . . . 30·00 10·00
52 2c. on 1l.75 brown . . . 22·00 25·00

21

22

23

24

25

26

27

29

1891.
53 **21** 1c. brown . . . . 4·25 95
54 **22** 2c. brown . . . . 7·25 50
55 **23** 5c. green £400 55
56 **24** 5c. green . . . . 26·00 45
57 **25** 10c. red . . . . 7·25 35
58a **26** 20c. orange . . . . 5·50 1·80
59 **27** 25c. blue . . . . 5·25 60
60 45c. olive . . . . 7·25 90
61 **29** 5l. red and blue . . . . . 50·00 65·00

30

31

33 King Victor Emmanuel III

34 King Victor Emmanuel III

1901. Designs vary.
62 **30** 1c. brown 25 10
63 **31** 2c. brown 25 10
64 5c. green . . . . 47·00 15
65 **33** 10c. red . . . . 60·00 25
66 20c. orange . . . . 9·00 25
67 25c. blue . . . . 90·00 35
68 40c. brown . . . . £400 1·90
69 45c. green . . . . 7·75 10
70 50c. violet . . . . £500 3·25
71 **34** 1l. brown and green . . . . 3·00 10
72 5l. blue and pink . . . . . 17·00 50
85 10l. green and pink . . . . 60·00 3·00
See also Nos. 171s, 181, 185 and 186/7.

1905. Surch **C. 15**.
73 **33** 15c. on 20c. orange . . . . 60·00 40

37

39

41

1906.
75 **37** 5c. green 45 30
76 10c. red 45 10
90 **41** 15c. grey . . . . 27·00 35
77 **39** 25c. blue . . . . 2·00 10
78 40c. brown . . . . 2·50 10
79 50c. violet . . . . 2·50 10
See also Nos. 104 etc, 171d/h and 171j/r.

42 Garibaldi

43

1910. 50th Anniv of Plebiscite in Naples and Sicily.
81 **42** 5c.(+5c.) green . . . . . . 25·00 11·00
82 15c.(+5c.) red . . . . 50·00 34·00

1910. National Plebiscite of Southern States, 1860.
83 **43** 5c.(+5c.) pink . . . . £120 43·00
84 15c.(+5c.) green . . . . . . £200 60·00

45

46

1911. Jubilee of Italian Kingdom.
86 **45** 2c.(+3c.) brown . . . . . . 8·50 1·30
87 **46** 5c.(+5c.) green . . . . . . 11·00 8·00
88 – 10c.(+5c.) red . . . . 14·00 14·00
89 – 15c.(+5c.) grey . . . . . . 14·00 14·00
DESIGNS: Symbolic of the Genius of Italy (10c.) and the Glory of Rome (15c.).

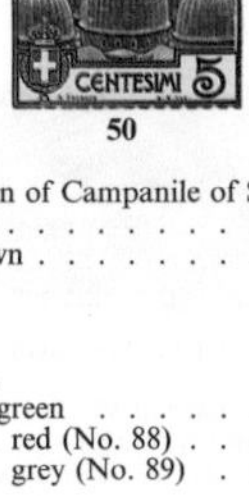
50

1912. Re-erection of Campanile of St. Mark, Venice.
91 **50** 5c. black . . . . 6·50 3·25
92 15c. brown . . . . 17·00 13·00

1913. Surch **2 2**.
93 **46** 2 on 5c. green . . . . . . 1·10 1·30
94 – 2 on 10c. red (No. 88) . . . 1·60 1·20
95 – 2 on 15c. grey (No. 89) . . 1·20 1·20

53 Banner of United Italy

54 Italian Eagle and Arms of Savoy

1915. Red Cross Society. No. 98 is surch **20**.
96 **53** 10c.+5c. red . . . . 2·50 2·50
97 **54** 15c.+5c. grey . . . . 5·00 3·50
98 20 on 15c.+5c. grey . . . . 7·00 10·50
99 20c.+5c. orange . . . . . . 7·25 9·25

1916. Surch **CENT. 20**.
100 **41** 20c. on 15c. grey . . . . . 14·00 35

1917. Air. Express Letter stamp optd **ESPERIMENTO POSTA AEREA MAGGIO 1917 TORINO = ROMA = ROMA = TORINO**.
102 E **35** 25c. red . . . . 11·00 8·50

1917. Air. Express Letter stamp surch **IDROVOLANTE NAPOLI-PALERMO NAPOLI 25 CENT 25**.
103 E **59** 25c. on 40c. violet . . . 11·50 9·00

1917.
104 **37** 15c. grey . . . . 2·75 15
105 **41** 20c. orange . . . . 7·50 15
178 **39** 20c. orange 75 80
179 20c. green 35 10
180 20c. purple . . . . 2·30 15
181 **34** 25c. green and light green 1·70 10
182 **39** 25c. green . . . . 7·75 3·50
106 30c. brown . . . . 2·30 20
183 30c. grey . . . . 1·90 10
107 55c. purple . . . . 11·00 2·75
108 60c. red . . . . 2·40 15
109 60c. blue . . . . 5·50 11·00
184 60c. orange . . . . 7·00 15
185 **34** 75c. red and carmine . . . 1·50 10
110 **39** 85c. brown . . . . 6·75 70
186 **34** 1l.25 blue and ultramarine 5·50 10
111 2l. green and orange . . . 15·00 1·00
187 2l.50 green and orange . . 40·00 1·30
See also Nos. 171a/c and 171i.

59 Ancient Seal of Republic of Trieste

60

1921. Union of Venezia Giulia with Italy.
112 **59** 15c. red and black . . . . 3·00 12·50
113 25c. red and blue . . . . 3·00 12·50
114 40c. red and brown . . . . 3·00 12·50

1921. 600th Death Anniv of Dante.
115 **60** 15c. red . . . . 3·75 6·25
116 – 25c. green . . . . 3·75 6·25
117 – 40c. brown . . . . 3·75 6·25
DESIGNS: 25c. Woman with book; 40c. Dante.

62 "Victory"

64

1921. Victory of 1918.
118 **62** 5c. green 50 70
119 10c. red 75 85
120 15c. grey . . . . 1·80 3·25
121 25c. blue . . . . 90 1·90

1922. 9th Italian Philatelic Congress. Trieste. Optd **IX CONGRESSO FILATELICO ITALIANO TRIESTE 1922**.
122 **37** 10c. red £250 £130
123 15c. grey £180 £130
124 **39** 25c. blue £180 £130
125 40c. brown £275 £130

1922. 50th Death Anniv of Mazzini.
126 **64** 25c. purple . . . . 5·00 10·00
127 – 40c. purple . . . . 7·00 10·50
128 – 80c. blue . . . . 5·00 13·00
DESIGNS—VERT: 40c. Mazzini. HORIZ: 80c. Tomb of Mazzini.

66

1923. Tercentenary of Propagation of the Faith.
129 **66** 20c. orange and green . . 1·80 23·00
130 30c. orange and red . . . 1·80 23·00
131 50c. orange and violet . . 1·80 23·00
132 1l. orange and blue . . . . 2·50 23·00
The portraits and arms in the corners at right vary for each value.

1923. Surch in words and figures. (15c. surch **DIECI** only).
133 **39** 7½c. on 85c. brown 10 80
135 **30** 10c. on 1c. brown 35 15
136 **31** 10c. on 2c. brown 35 15
137 **37** 10c. on 15c. grey 10 15
138 **39** 20c. on 25c. blue 10 25
139 **33** 25c. on 45c. olive . . . . 10 6·50
140 **39** 25c. on 60c. blue 70 40
141 30c. on 50c. mauve 10 15
142 30c. on 55c. purple 10 25
143 50c. on 40c. brown 75 15
144 50c. on 55c. purple . . . 27·00 2·50
145 **34** 1l.75 on 10l. olive and red 10·00 8·25

73

74

75

1923. 1st Anniv of Fascist March on Rome.
146 **73** 10c. green . . . . 3·25 1·60
147 30c. violet . . . . 3·50 1·60
148 50c. red . . . . 4·50 2·50
149 **74** 1l. blue . . . . 4·25 1·70
150 2l. brown . . . . 4·25 4·00
151 **75** 5l. black and blue . . . . 6·50 14·00

76

1923. Fascist "Black Shirt" Fund.
152 **76** 30c.+30c. brown . . . . . 23·00 33·00
153 50c.+50c. mauve . . . . . 27·00 33·00
154 1l.+1l. grey . . . . 23·00 33·00

77

1923. 50th Death Anniv of A. Manzoni (writer).
155 **77** 10c. black and red . . . . 2·40 24·00
156 – 15c. black and green . . . 2·40 24·00
157 – 30c. black . . . . 2·40 24·00
158 – 50c. black and brown . . . 2·40 24·00
159 – 1l. black and blue . . . . 25·00 95·00
160 – 5l. black and purple . . . £350 £650
DESIGNS: 10c. to 50c. Scenes from Manzoni's "I Promessi Sposi"; 1l. Manzoni's home, Milan; 5l. Portrait of Manzoni.

1924. Victory stamps surch **LIRE UNA** between stars.
161 **62** 1l. on 5c. green . . . . . 19·00 38·00
162 1l. on 10c. red . . . . . . 12·00 38·00
163 1l. on 15c. grey . . . . . 19·00 38·00
164 1l. on 25c. blue . . . . . 12·00 38·00

1924. Trade Propaganda. Optd **CROCIERA ITALIANA 1924**.
165 **37** 10c. red . . . . 2·30 5·50
166 **39** 30c. brown . . . . 2·30 5·50
167 50c. violet . . . . 2·30 5·50
168 60c. blue . . . . 12·00 23·00

169 85c. brown . . . . 8·25 23·00
170 **34** 1l. brown and green . . . 35·00 95·00
171 2l. green and orange . . . 55·00 95·00
Used on an Italian cruiser which visited South America for trade propaganda.

1924. Previous issues with attached advertising labels (imperf between stamp and label). Colour of label given.
171a 15c. (104) + Columbia (blue) . . . . 29·00 24·00
171b 15c. (104) + Bitter Campari (blue) . . . . 2·40 9·00
171c 15c. (104) + Cordial Campari (black) . . . . 2·40 9·00
171d 25c. (77) + Coen (green) . . £180 24·00
171e 25c. (77) + Piperno (brown) £1200 £375
171f 25c. (77) + Tagliacozzo (brown) £600 £375
171g 25c. (77) + Abrador (blue) 75·00 60·00
171h 25c. (77) + Reinach (green) 75·00 45·00
171i 30c. (106) + Columbia (green) . . . . 24·00 23·00
171j 50c. (79) + Coen (blue) . . £1200 45·00
171k 50c. (79) + Columbia (red) 16·00 2·50
171l 50c. (79) + De Montel (blue) . . . . 2·75 8·00
171m 50c. (79) + Piperno (green) £1300 £140
171n 50c. (79) + Reinach (blue) £180 13·00
171o 50c. (79) + Singer (red) . . 2·75 95
171p 50c. (79) + Tagliacozzo (green) £1800 £275
171q 50c. (79) + Siero Casali (blue) . . . . 16·00 9·75
171r 50c. (79) + Tantal (red) . . £225 65·00
171s 1l. (71) + Columbia (blue) £550 £450

81 Church of St. John Lateran

1924. Holy Year (1925).
172 – 20c.+10c. brown & green 2·50 3·25
173 **81** 30c.+15c. brown & choc 2·50 3·25
174 – 50c.+25c. brown & violet 2·50 3·25
175 – 60c.+30c. brown and red 2·50 10·00
176 – 1l.+50c. purple and blue 2·50 9·75
177 – 5l.+2l.50 purple and red . . 2·75 22·00
DESIGNS: 20c. Church of St. Maria Maggiore; 50c. Church of St. Paul; 60c. St. Peter's; 1l. Pope opening Holy Door; 5l. Pope shutting Holy Door.

82

83 Vision of St. Francis

1925. Royal Jubilee.
188B **82** 60c. red 55 20
189B 1l. blue 55 20
190A 1l.25 blue . . . . 4·25 50

1926. 700th Death Anniv of St. Francis of Assisi.
191 **83** 20c. green 35 25
194B – 30c. black 35 25
192 – 40c. violet 35 25
193 – 60c. red 35 25
195B – 1l.25 blue 35 25
196 – 5l.+2l.50 brown . . . . . 3·00 34·00
DESIGNS—HORIZ: 40c. St. Damian's Church and Monastery, Assisi; 60c. St. Francis's Monastery, Assisi; 1l.25, Death of St. Francis, from fresco in Church of the Holy Cross, Florence. VERT: 30c., 5l. St. Francis (after Luca della Robbia).

88

1926. Air.
197 **88** 50c. red . . . . 5·25 2·00
198 60c. grey . . . . 2·50 1·90
199 80c. brown and purple . . 29·00 17·00
200 1l. blue . . . . 1·70 3·00
201 1l.20 brown . . . . 10·50 28·00
202 1l.50 orange . . . . 9·50 7·50
203 5l. green . . . . 23·00 21·00

89 Castle of St. Angelo

1926. 1st National Defence issue.
204 **89** 40c.+20c. black & brown 2·00 3·25
205 – 60c.+30c. brown and red 2·00 3·25
206 – 1l.25+60c. black & grn . . 2·00 8·75
207 – 5l.+2l.50 black and blue . . 3·25 32·00
DESIGNS: 60c. Aqueduct of Claudius; 1l.25, Capitol; 5l. Porta del Popolo.
See also Nos. 219/22 and 278/81.

90 Volta

91

92

1927. Death Centenary of Volta.
208 **90** 20c. red 55 30
209 50c. green . . . . 1·50 15
210 60c. purple . . . . 2·75 85
211 1l.25 blue . . . . 3·25 1·20

1927.
216 **91** 50c. grey and brown . . . 2·50 10
212 1l.75 brown . . . . 3·75 15
213 1l.85 black 80 30
214 2l.55 red . . . . 5·25 3·00
215 2l.65 purple . . . . 5·25 23·00
No. 216 is smaller (17½ × 21½ mm).

1927. Air. Surch.
217 **88** 50c. on 60c. grey . . . . . 6·25 11·00
218 80c. on 1l. blue . . . . . 19·00 60·00

1928. 2nd National Defence issue. As Nos. 204/7.
219 **89** 30c.+10c. black and violet 5·25 6·25
220 – 50c.+20c. black and olive 5·25 6·00
221 – 1l.25+50c. black & blue . . 10·50 17·00
222 – 5l.+2l. black and red . . 20·00 50·00

1928.
223 **92** 7½c. brown . . . . 3·50 2·00
224 15c. orange . . . . 3·00 15
225 35c. grey . . . . 7·00 1·00
226 50c. mauve . . . . 11·00 10

93 Emmanuele Filiberto

94 Soldier of First World War and Statue

95 Statue, Turin (Maroghetti)

96 King Victor Emmanuel II

1928. 400th Birth Anniv of Emmanuele Filiberto, Duke of Savoy, and 10th Anniv of Victory in World War.
227a **93** 20c. blue and brown . . . 60 55
228a 25c. green and red . . . 60 55
229a 30c. brown and green . . 85 75
230 **94** 50c. red and blue . . . 50 20
231 75c. red and pink . . . 65 30
232 **95** 1l.25 black and blue . . . 90 40
233 **94** 1l.75 green and blue . . . 1·90 2·00
234 **93** 5l. green and mauve . . . 8·75 25·00
235 **94** 10l. black and pink . . . 22·00 60·00
236 **95** 20l. green and mauve . . 35·00 £325

1929. 50th Death Anniv of King Victor Emmanuel II. Veterans' Fund.
237 **96** 50c.+10c. green . . . . . 2·75 2·20

97 Fascist Arms of Italy

98 Romulus, Remus and Wolf

99 Julius Caesar

103 King Victor Emmanuel III

1929. Imperial Series.
238 **97** 2c. orange 10 20
239 **98** 5c. brown 20 10
240 **99** 7½c. violet 20 10
241 – 10c. brown 20 10
242 – 15c. green 20 10
243 **99** 20c. red 20 10
244 – 25c. green 20 10
245 **103** 30c. brown 20 10
246 – 35c. blue 20 10
247 **103** 50c. violet 20 10
248 – 75c. red 20 10
249 **99** 1l. violet 20 15
250 – 1l.25 blue 20 10
251 – 1l.75 orange 20 10
252 – 2l. red 20 10
253 **98** 2l.55 green 20 15
254 3l.70 violet 10 10
255 5l. red 25 10
256 – 10l. violet . . . . 1·60 35
257 **99** 20l. green . . . . 3·75 2·75
258 – 25l. black . . . . 8·00 11·00
259 – 50l. violet . . . . 10·00 20·00
DESIGNS—As Type **99**: 10c., 1l.75, 25l. Augustus the Great; 15c., 35c., 2l., 10l. Italia (Woman with castle on her head); 25c., 75c., 1l.25, 50l. Profile of King Victor Emmanuel III.
For stamps as above but without Fascist emblems, see Nos. 633 etc, and for stamps with integral label for armed forces see Nos. 563/74.

104 Bramante Courtyard

1929. 1400th Anniv of Abbey of Montecassino.
260 **104** 20c. orange 80 25
261 – 25c. green 80 25
262 – 50c.+10c. brown . . . . 3·25 4·00
263 – 75c.+15c. red . . . . . 4·25 6·00
264 **104** 1l.25+25c. blue . . . . . 4·50 7·00
265 – 5l.+1l. purple . . . . . 4·75 24·00
266 – 10l.+2l. green . . . . . 7·75 48·00
DESIGNS—HORIZ: 25c. "Death of St. Benedict" (fresco); 50c. Monks building Abbey; 75c., 5l. Abbey of Montecassino. VERT: 10l. St. Benedict.

109

1930. Marriage of Prince Umberto and Princess Marie Jose.
267 **109** 20c. orange 50 15
268 50c.+10c. brown . . . . 1·20 1·10
269 1l.25+25c. blue . . . . . 1·90 4·50

110 Pegasus

113

1930. Air.
270 – 25c. green 10 10
271 **110** 50c. brown 10 10
272 – 75c. brown 10 10
273 – 80c. orange 10 20
274 – 1l. violet 10 10
275 **113** 2l. blue 10 15
276 **110** 5l. green 10 25
277 10l. red 10 80
DESIGNS—As Type **110**: 25c., 80c. Wings; 75c., 1l. Angel.

1930. 3rd National Defence issue. Designs as Nos. 204/7.
278 **89** 30c.+10c. violet & green . . 1·10 4·50
279 – 50c.+10c. blue and green 1·60 3·00
280 – 1l.25+30c. green & blue . . 4·50 8·75
281 – 5l.+1l.50 choc & brn . . . 7·50 31·00

114 Ferrucci on Horseback

117 Francesco Ferrucci

1930. 400th Death Anniv of Francesco Ferrucci.
282 **114** 20c. red (postage) 35 30
283 – 25c. green 45 30
284 – 50c. violet 30 15
285 – 1l.25 blue . . . . 2·00 90
286 – 5l.+2l. orange . . . . . 6·00 39·00
287 **117** 50c. violet (air) . . . . . 85 3·50
288 1l. brown . . . . 85 4·00
289 5l.+2l. purple . . . . . . 2·10 31·00
DESIGNS—HORIZ: 25c., 50c., 1l.25, Ferrucci assassinated by Maramaldo. VERT: 5l. Ferrucci in helmet.

119 Jupiter sending forth Eagle

1930. Birth Bimillenary of Virgil.
290 – 15c. brown (postage) . . 70 35
291 – 20c. orange 70 20
292 – 25c. green 85 20
293 – 30c. purple . . . . 1·00 40
294 – 50c. violet 70 15
295 – 75c. red . . . . 1·40 70
296 – 1l.25 blue . . . . 1·40 65
297 – 5l.+1l.50 brown . . . . . 28·00 48·00
298 – 10l.+2l.50 olive . . . . . 28·00 60·00
299 **119** 50c. brown (air) . . . . . 5·00 3·25
300 1l. orange . . . . 7·50 5·00
301 7l.70+1l.30 purple . . . . 26·00 55·00
302 9l.+2l. blue . . . . 28·00 55·00
DESIGNS (scenes from "Aeneid" or "Georgics"): 15c. Helenus and Anchises; 20c. The passing legions; 25c. Landing of Aeneas; 30c. Earth's bounties; 50c. Harvesting; 75c. Rural life; 1l.25, Aeneas sights Italy; 5l. A shepherd's hut; 10l. Turnus, King of the Rutuli.

120 Savoia Marchetti S-55A Flying Boats

1930. Air. Transatlantic Mass Formation Flight.
303 **120** 7l.70 blue and brown . . £300 £850

121 St. Antony's Installation as a Franciscan

123 Tower of the Marzocco

1931. 700th Death Anniv of St. Antony of Padua.
304 **121** 20c. purple 70 25
305 – 25c. green 80 20
306 – 30c. brown . . . . 1·40 30
307 – 50c. violet 70 15
308 – 75c. lake . . . . 8·00 1·20
309 – 1l.25 blue . . . . 6·25 95
310 – 5l.+2l.50 olive . . . . . 36·00 46·00
DESIGNS—HORIZ: 25c. Sermon to the Fishes; 30c. Hermitage of Olivares; 50c. Basilica of the Saint at Padua; 75c. Death of St. Antony; 1l.25, St. Antony liberating prisoners. VERT: 5l. Vision of St. Antony.

1931. 50th Anniv of Naval Academy, Leghorn.
311 **123** 20c. red . . . . 2·50 25
312 – 50c. violet . . . . 2·50 15
313 – 1l.25 blue . . . . 8·00 55
DESIGNS—HORIZ: 50c. Cadet ship "Amerigo Vespucci"; 1l.25, Cruiser "Trento".

124 Dante (1265–1321)

125 Leonardo da Vinci's Drawing "Flying Man"

127 Leonardo da Vinci

1932. Dante Alighieri Society. (a) Postage.
314 – 10c. brown 65 25
315 – 15c. green 70 20
316 – 20c. red 70 20
317 – 25c. green 70 20
318 – 30c. brown . . . . 1·30 25
319 – 50c. violet 55 15
320 – 75c. red . . . . 2·00 95
321 – 1l.25 blue . . . . 1·40 65
322 – 1l.75 orange . . . . . . 1·50 95
323 – 2l.75 green . . . . 11·50 6·75
324 – 5l.+2l. red . . . . 18·00 48·00
325 **124** 10l.+2l.50 olive . . . . . 18·00 60·00
DESIGNS: 10c. Giovanni Boccaccio (writer); 15c. Niccolo Machiavelli (statesman); 20c. Fra Paolo Sarpi (philosopher); 25c. Vittorio Alfieri (poet); 30c. Ugo Foscolo (writer); 50c. Giacomo Leopardi (poet); 75c. Giosue Carducci (poet); 1l.25, Carlo Botta (historian); 1l.75, Torquato Tasso (poet); 2l.75, Francesco Petrarch (poet); 5l. Ludovico Ariosto (poet).

(b) Air.
326 **125** 50c. brown . . . . 1·40 1·50
327 – 1l. violet . . . . 2·10 1·80
328 – 3l. red . . . . 3·75 5·25
329 – 5l. green . . . . 4·25 7·50
330 **125** 7l.70+2l. blue . . . . . . 8·00 27·00
331 – 10l.+2l.50 grey . . . . . 9·25 36·00
332 **127** 100l. green and blue . . . 33·00 £130
DESIGN—HORIZ: 1, 3, 5, 10l. Leonardo da Vinci.

128 Garibaldi and Victor Emmanuel   **130** Caprera

1932. 50th Death Anniv of Garibaldi.

333	–	10c. blue (postage)	85	35
334	**128**	20c. brown	95	20
335	–	25c. green	1·30	30
336	**128**	30c. orange	1·50	35
337	–	50c. violet	85	20
338	–	75c. red	3·00	1·10
339	–	1l.25 blue	2·30	70
340	–	1l.75+25c. blue	12·00	30·00
341	–	2l.55+50c. brown	20·00	40·00
342	–	5l.+1l. lake	20·00	45·00

DESIGNS—HORIZ: 10c. Garibaldi's birthplace, Nice; 25c., 50c. "Here we make Italy or die"; 75c. Death of Anita (Garibaldi's wife); 1l.25, Garibaldi's tomb; 1l.75, Quarto Rock. VERT: 2l.55, Garibaldi's statue in Rome; 5l. Garibaldi.

343	**130**	50c. lake (air)	1·50	1·60
344	–	80c. green	2·75	3·00
345	**130**	1l.+25c. brown	5·50	8·00
346	–	2l.+50c. blue	7·25	13·00
347	–	5l.+1l. green	9·00	15·00

DESIGNS—VERT: 80c. The Ravenna hut; 2l. Anita; 5l. Garibaldi.

132 Agriculture

1932. 10th Anniv of Fascist March on Rome. (a) Postage.

350	**132**	5c. sepia	60	15
351	–	10c. sepia	60	15
352	–	15c. green	85	30
353	–	20c. red	75	15
354	–	25c. green	85	15
355	–	30c. sepia	90	45
356	–	35c. blue	3·00	1·90
357	–	50c. violet	60	15
358	–	60c. brown	3·00	1·20
359	–	75c. red	1·40	50
360	–	1l. violet	3·00	75
361	–	1l.25 blue	1·40	40
362	–	1l.75 orange	2·10	40
363	–	2l.55 green	18·00	11·50
364	–	2l.75 green	18·00	11·50
365	–	5l.+2l.50 red	30·00	85·00

DESIGNS: 10c. Fascist soldier; 15c. Fascist coastguard; 20c. Italian youth; 25c. Tools forming a shadow of the Fasces; 30c. Religion; 35c. Imperial highways; 50c. Equestrian statue of Mussolini; 60c. Land reclamation; 75c. Colonial expansion; 1l. Marine development; 1l.25, Italians abroad; 1l.75, Sport, 2l.55, Child Welfare; 2l.75. "O.N.D." Recreation; 5l. Caesar's statue.

(b) Air.

366	–	50c. brown	3·50	3·00
367	–	75c. brown	9·25	7·25

DESIGNS: 50c. Eagle (front of Air Ministry Building, Rome); 75c. Aerial view of Italian cathedrals.

134 Airship "Graf Zeppelin"

1933. Air. "Graf Zeppelin" issue.

372	**134**	3l. green and black	6·50	14·00
373	–	5l. brown and green	9·75	14·00
374	–	10l. blue and red	9·75	35·00
375	–	12l. orange and blue	13·50	55·00
376	–	15l. black and brown	13·50	65·00
377	–	20l. blue and brown	18·00	70·00

DESIGNS (all with airship): 3l. S. Paola Gate and tomb of Consul Caius Cestius; 5l. Appian Way and tomb of Cecilia Metella; 10l. Portion of Mussolini Stadium; 12l. S. Angelo Castle; 15l. Forum Romanum; 20l. Empire Way, Colosseum and Baths of Domitian.

135 Italian Flag / King Victor Emmanuel III / "Flight" (½-size illustration)

136 Italian Flag / King Victor Emmanuel III / Rome–Chicago (½-size illustration)

1933. Air. Balbo Transatlantic Mass Formation Flight by Savoia Marchetti S-55X Flying Boats.

378	**135**	5l.25+19l.75 red, green and blue	85·00	£1300
379	**136**	5l.25+44l.75 red, green and blue	85·00	£1300

The first part of the illustration in each group is of the Registered Air Express label and has an abbreviation of one of the pilots' names overprinted on it; the second part is the stamp for Ordinary Postage and the third is the actual Air Mail stamp.

137 Athlete

1933. International University Games, Turin.

380	**137**	10c. brown	20	20
381		20c. red	20	25
382		50c. violet	35	15
383		1l.25 blue	1·70	1·40

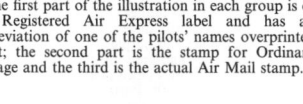

138 Dome of St. Peter's   **139** St. Peter's and Church of the Holy Sepulchre

1933. "Holy Year". (a) Postage.

384	**138**	20c. red	1·60	15
385	–	25c. green	2·30	25
386	–	50c. violet	1·90	10
387	**138**	1l. 25 blue	2·40	55
388	–	2l.55+2l.50 black	6·75	32·00

DESIGNS: 25, 50c. Angel with Cross; 2l.55, Cross with Doves of Peace.

(b) Air.

389	**139**	50c.+25c. brown	85	6·75
390		75c.+50c. purple	1·60	8·75

1934. Air. Rome-Buenos Aires Flight. Surch with airplane, **1934 XII PRIMO VOLO DIRETTO ROMA = BUENOS-AYRES TRIMOTORE "LOMBARDI MAZZOTTI"**, value and fasces.

391	**113**	2l. on 2l. yellow	3·25	32·00
392		3l. on 2l. green	3·25	38·00
393		5l. on 2l. red	3·25	50·00
394		10l. on 2l. violet	3·25	60·00

141 Anchor of the "Emmanuele Filiberto"   **142** Antonio Pacinotti

1934. 10th Anniv of Annexation of Fiume.

395	**141**	10c. brown (postage)	3·50	30
396		20c. red	40	20
397	–	50c. violet	40	15
398	–	1l.25 blue	45	1·10
399	–	1l.75+1l. blue	70	15·00
400	–	2l.55+2l. purple	90	20·00
401	–	2l.75+2l.50 olive	90	20·00

DESIGNS: 50c. Gabriele d'Annunzio; 1l.25, St. Vito's Tower barricaded; 1l.75, Hands supporting crown of historical monuments; 2l.55, Victor Emmanuel III's arrival in the "Brindisi" (cruiser); 2l.75, Galley, gondola and battleship.

402	–	25c. green (air)	55	80
403	–	50c. brown	55	50
404	–	75c. brown	55	1·90
405	–	1l.+50c. purple	55	5·25
406	–	2l.+1l.50 blue	55	7·50
407	–	3l.+2l. black	55	7·50

DESIGNS—Marina Fiat MF.5 flying boat over: 25, 75c. Fiume Harbour; 50c., 1l. War Memorial; 2l. Three Venetian lions; 3l. Roman Wall.

1934. 75th Anniv of Invention of Pacinotti's Dynamo.

411	**142**	50c. violet	70	15
412		1l.25 blue	1·00	85

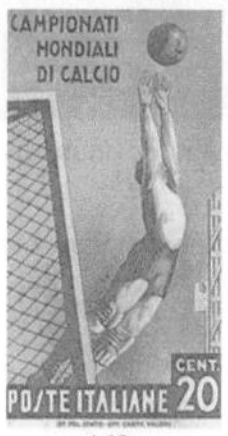

143   **145** Luigi Galvani

1934. World Cup Football Championship, Italy.

413	**143**	20c. red (postage)	9·50	1·90
414	–	25c. green	8·00	80
415	–	50c. violet	9·50	30
416	–	1l.25 blue	21·00	3·75
417	–	5l.+2l.50 brown	55·00	£120

DESIGNS—VERT: 5l. Players heading the ball. HORIZ: 25c., 50c., 1l.25, Two footballers.

418	–	50c. red (air)	6·00	5·25
419	–	75c. blue	6·25	6·25
420	–	5l.+2l.50 olive	26·00	65·00
421	–	10l.+5l. brown	31·00	75·00

DESIGNS—HORIZ: 50c. Marina Fiat MF.5 flying boat over Mussolini Stadium, Turin; 5l. Marina Fiat MF.5 flying boat over Stadium, Rome. VERT: 75c. Savoia Marchetti S-55X flying boat over footballer; 10l. Marina Fiat MF.5 flying boat over Littoral Stadium, Bologna.

1934. 1st Int Congress of Electro-radio-biology.

422	**145**	30c. brown on buff	85	25
423		75c. red on pink	1·20	1·40

146 Military Symbol   **148** King Victor Emmanuel III

1934. Military Medal Centenary.

424	**146**	10c. brown (postage)	1·00	40
425	–	15c. green	1·10	80
426	–	20c. red	1·00	30
427	–	25c. green	1·30	30
428	–	30c. brown	1·80	90
429	–	50c. violet	1·40	20
430	–	75c. red	5·50	1·60
431	–	1l.25 blue	4·25	1·00
432	–	1l.75+1l. red	10·00	20·00
433	–	2l.55+2l. purple	16·00	19·00
434	–	2l.75+2l. violet	18·00	22·00

DESIGNS—VERT: 25c. Mountaineers; 1l.75, Cavalry. HORIZ: 15c., 50c. Barbed-wire cutter; 20c. Throwing hand-grenade; 30c. Cripple wielding crutch; 75c. Artillery; 1l.25, Soldiers cheering; 2l.55, Sapper; 2l.75, First Aid.

435	–	25c. green (air)	1·30	1·40
436	–	50c. grey	1·30	1·60
437	–	75c. brown	1·30	2·30
438	–	80c. blue	2·40	2·75
439	–	1l.+50c. brown	4·25	9·00
440	–	2l.+1l. blue	5·50	15·00
441	–	3l.+2l. black	8·75	15·00

DESIGNS—HORIZ: 25, 80c. Italian "P" Type airship under fire; 50, 75c. Naval launch; 1l. Caproni Ca 101 airplane and troops in desert; 2l. Pomilio PC type biplane and troops. VERT: 3l. Unknown soldier's tomb.

1934. Air. Rome–Mogadiscio Flight and King's visit to Italian Somaliland.

444	**148**	1l. violet	1·40	6·75
445		2l. blue	1·40	8·50
446		4l. brown	2·50	35·00
447		5l. green	2·50	55·00
448		8l. red	11·50	65·00
449		10l. brown	12·50	70·00

149 Man with Fasces   **150**

1935. University Contests. Inscr "LITTORIALI".

450	**149**	20c. red	30	15
451	–	30c. brown	2·20	1·20
452	–	50c. violet	30	15

DESIGNS: 30c. Eagle and soldier. 50c. Standard-bearer and bayonet attack.

1935. National Militia. Inscr "PRO OPERA PREVID. MILIZIA".

453	**150**	20c.+10c. red (postage)	5·75	3·75
454	–	25c.+15c. green	5·75	5·00
455	–	50c.+30c. violet	5·75	6·00
456	–	1l.25+75c. blue	5·75	9·50
457	–	50c.+50c. brown (air)	9·25	11·00

DESIGNS: 25c. Roman standards; 50c. Soldier and cross; 50c.+50c. Wing over Globe; 1l.25, Soldiers and arch.

152 Symbol of Flight   **153** Leonardo da Vinci

1935. International Aeronautical Exn, Milan.

458	**152**	20c. red	5·75	45
459		30c. brown	15·00	1·30
460	**153**	50c. violet	22·00	25
461		1l.25 blue	20·00	90

154 Vincenzo Bellini   **155** "Music"

1935. Death Centenary of Bellini (composer).

462	**154**	20c. red (postage)	3·50	40
463		30c. brown	5·75	60
464		50c. violet	5·25	25
465		1l.25 blue	7·25	1·60
466	–	1l.75+1l. orange	25·00	32·00
467	–	2l.75+2l. olive	41·00	40·00

DESIGNS—VERT: 2l.75, Bellini's villa. HORIZ: 1l.75, Hands at piano.

468	**155**	25c. brown (air)	1·70	1·20
469		50c. brown	1·70	1·20
470		60c. red	4·25	1·60
471	–	1l.+1l. violet	9·75	28·00
472	–	5l.+2l. green	14·50	40·00

DESIGNS: 1l. Angelic musicians; 5l. Mountain landscape (Bellini's birthplace).

156 "Commerce" and Industrial Map of Italy

1936. 17th Milan Fair. Inscr as in T **156**.

473	**156**	20c. red	45	25
474	–	30c. brown	45	40
475	–	50c. violet	55	20
476	**156**	1l.25 blue	80	65

DESIGN—HORIZ: 30c., 50c. Cog-wheel and plough.

157 "Fertility"

1936. 2000th Birth Anniv of Horace.

477	**157**	10c. green (postage)	2·10	25
478	–	20c. red	1·60	25
479	–	30c. brown	4·25	65
480	–	50c. violet	4·25	15
481	–	75c. red	7·25	80
482	–	1l.25+1l. blue	17·00	30·00
483	–	1l.75+1l. red	24·00	42·00
484	–	2l.55+1l. blue	27·00	46·00

DESIGNS—HORIZ: 20c., 1l.25, Landscape; 75c. Capitol; 2l.55, Dying gladiator. VERT: 30c. Ajax defying lightning; 50c. Horace; 1l.75, Pan.

485	–	25c. green (air)	1·80	1·40
486	–	50c. brown	2·50	1·40
487	–	60c. red	3·00	2·30
488	–	1l.+1l. violet	9·00	30·00
489	–	5l.+2l. green	12·00	55·00

DESIGNS—HORIZ: 25c. Savoia Marchetti S-55A flying boat; 50c., 1l. Caproni Ca 101 airplane over lake; 60c. Eagle and oak tree; 5l. Rome.

159

160

1937. Child Welfare. Inscr as in T **159/60**.

490	**159**	10c. brown (postage)	1·70	50
491	**160**	20c. red	1·70	40
492	**159**	25c. green	1·70	50
493	–	30c. sepia	1·90	1·20
494	**160**	50c. violet	1·80	20
495	–	75c. red	5·25	1·60
496	**160**	1l.25 blue	6·25	1·70
497	–	1l.75+75c. orange	29·00	42·00
498	–	2l.75+1l.25 green	23·00	45·00
499	**160**	5l.+3l. blue	25·00	50·00

DESIGNS—As Type **159**: 30c., 1l.75, Boy between Fasces; 75c., 2l.75, "Bambino" (after della Robbia).

500	–	25c. green (air)	5·00	2·00
501	–	50c. brown	5·25	1·40
502	–	1l. violet	5·00	3·00
503	–	2l.+1l. blue	7·50	30·00
504	–	3l.+2l. orange	10·50	34·00
505	–	5l.+3l. red	16·00	38·00

DESIGNS—As Type **160**: 25c., 1l., 3l. Little child with rifle. As Type **159**: 50c., 2l., 5l. Children's heads.

163 Naval Memorial

164 Augustus the Great

1937. 2000th Birth Anniv of Augustus the Great.

506	**163**	10c. green (postage)	80	20
507	–	15c. brown	80	25
508	–	20c. red	80	25
509	–	25c. green	80	25
510	–	30c. brown	1·00	25
511	–	50c. violet	90	10
512	–	75c. red	1·10	70
513	–	1l.25 blue	1·80	75
514	–	1l.75+1l. purple	29·00	30·00
515	–	2l.55+2l. black	32·00	35·00

DESIGNS—VERT: 15c. Military trophies; 20c. Reconstructing temples of Rome; 25c. Census (with reference to birth of Jesus Christ); 30c. Statue of Julius Caesar; 50c. Election of Augustus as Emperor; 75c. Head of Augustus (conquest of Ethiopia); 1l.25, Constructing new fleet; 1l.75, Building Altar of Peace; 2l.55, The Capitol.

516	–	25c. purple (air)	3·50	2·20
517	–	50c. brown	3·50	2·40
518	–	80c. brown	6·25	3·75
519	–	1l.+1l. blue	24·00	25·00
520	**164**	5l.+1l. violet	30·00	40·00

DESIGNS—HORIZ: 25c. "Agriculture"; 50c. Prosperity of the Romans; 80c. Horses of the Sun Chariot; 1l. Staff and map of ancient Roman Empire.

165 Gasparo Spontini (composer)

166 Marconi

1937. Famous Italians.

521	**165**	10c. sepia	35	35
522	–	20c. red	35	35
523	–	25c. green	35	30
524	–	30c. brown	35	40
525	–	50c. violet	35	15
526	–	75c. red	95	1·00
527	–	1l.25 blue	1·20	1·00
528	**165**	1l.75 orange	1·20	1·00
529	–	2l.55+2l. green	11·00	35·00
530	–	2l.75+2l. brown	11·00	38·00

DESIGNS: 20c., 2l.55, Antonio Stradivarius (violin maker); 25, 50c. Giacomo Leopardi (poet); 30, 75c., Giovanni Battista Pergolesi (composer); 1l.25, 2l.75, Giotto di Bondone (painter and architect).

1938. Guglielmo Marconi (telegraphy pioneer) Commemoration.

531	**166**	20c. red	1·60	20
532		50c. violet	45	15
533		1l.25 blue	60	1·50

167 Founding of Rome

168 Victor Emmanuel III

1938. 2nd Anniv of Proclamation of Italian Empire.

534	**167**	10c. brown (postage)	70	15
535	–	20c. red	1·00	15
536	–	25c. green	1·00	15
537	–	30c. brown	85	15
538	–	50c. violet	1·50	15
539	–	75c. red	2·30	30
540	–	1l.25 blue	3·00	25
541	–	1l.75 violet	3·50	55
542	–	2l.75 green	12·50	8·75
543	–	5l. red	23·00	11·00

DESIGNS—VERT: 20c. Emperor Augustus; 25c. Dante; 30c. Columbus; 50c. Leonardo da Vinci; 75c. Garibaldi and Victor Emmanuel II; 1l.25, Italian Unknown Warrior's Tomb; 1l.75, "March on Rome"; 2l.75, Wedding ring on map of Ethiopia; 5l. Victor Emmanuel III.

544	**168**	25c. green (air)	85	1·00
545	–	50c. brown	1·40	1·00
546	–	1l. violet	1·70	3·25
547	–	2l. blue	2·30	6·00
548	**168**	3l. red	4·50	10·00
549	–	5l. green	4·75	15·00

DESIGNS—HORIZ: 50c., 1l. Dante: 2, 5l. Leonardo da Vinci.

169 Steam Locomotive and ETR 200 Express Train

1939. Centenary of Italian Railways.

550	**169**	20c. red	50	20
551		50c. violet	65	20
552		1l.25 blue	1·10	1·50

170 Hitler and Mussolini

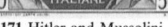

171 Hitler and Mussolini

172 Roman Cavalry

1941. Italo-German Friendship.

553	**170**	10c. brown	1·40	45
554		20c. orange	1·40	35
555		25c. green	1·40	40
556	**171**	50c. violet	1·90	35
557		75c. red	2·30	80
558		1l.25 blue	2·30	1·20

1941. 2000th Birth Anniv of Livy (Latin historian).

559	**172**	20c.+10c. red	35	55
560		30c.+15c. brown	35	70
561	–	50c.+25c. violet	40	75
562	–	1l.25+1l. blue	40	90

DESIGN: 50c., 1l.25, Roman legionary.

1942. War Propaganda. Nos. 244/5 and 247 with attached labels (imperf between stamp and label) to encourage war effort.

563		25c. green (Navy)	20	40
564		25c. green (Army)	20	40
565		25c. green (Air Force)	20	40
566		25c. green (Militia)	20	40
567		30c. brown (Navy)	20	1·20
568		30c. brown (Army)	20	1·20
569		30c. brown (Air Force)	20	1·20
570		30c. brown (Militia)	20	1·20
571		50c. violet (Navy)	20	40
572		50c. violet (Army)	20	40
573		50c. violet (Air Force)	20	40
574		50c. violet (Militia)	20	40

173 Galileo teaching at Padua

174 Rossini

1942. Death Tercentenary of Galileo.

575	**173**	10c. red and orange	35	25
576	–	25c. green and olive	35	25
577	–	50c. violet and purple	35	25
578	–	1l.25 blue and grey	50	1·30

DESIGNS: Galileo at Venice (25c.) and at Arcetri, near Florence (1l.25), 50c. Portrait of Galileo.

1942. 150th Birth Anniv of Rossini (composer).

579	–	25c. green	20	25
580	–	30c. brown	20	25
581	**174**	50c. violet	20	25
582		1l. blue	20	40

DESIGN: 25c., 30c. Rossini Monument, Pescaro.

175

187 Romulus, Remus and Wolf (after Pollaiuolo)

1943. Allied Military Government issue.

583	**175**	15c. orange	35	50
584		25c. bistre	35	50
585		30c. grey	35	50
586		50c. violet	35	50
587		60c. yellow	35	65
588		1l. green	35	50
589		2l. red	35	65
590		5l. blue	35	1·20
591		10l. brown	35	1·50

1943. Allied Military Government issue. Stamps of 1929 optd **GOVERNO MILITARE ALLEATO**.

592	**99**	20c. red	45	1·20
593		35c. blue	5·00	7·25
594	**103**	50c. violet	30	1·10

1944.

619	**187**	50c. purple	10	65

1944. As issue of 1929, but with Fascist emblems removed.

633	–	10c. brown (Augustus the Great)	00	00
640	**99**	20c. red	10	30
620	**103**	30c. brown	20	25
635	–	50c. violet (Italia)	00	00
621	**103**	50c. violet	20	1·80
636	–	60c. orange (Italia)	00	00
641	**103**	60c. green	10	35
637	**99**	1l. violet	00	00
643	–	1l.20 brown (Italia)	10	30
638	–	2l. red (Italia)	00	00
645	**98**	5l. red	10	30
646	–	10l. violet (Italia)	2·10	5·00

1945. Stamps of Italy surch **L. 2,50** (No. 629) and stamps of Italian Social Republic surch **POSTE ITALIANE** and new value (Nos. 627/8).

627		1l.20 on 20c. red (No. 102)	10	15
628		2l. on 25c. green (No. 103)	10	15
629		2l.50 on 1l.75 orange (No. 251)	10	25

193 "Work, Justice and Family"

195 Planting a Sapling

196 "Peace"

197 "Work, Justice and Family"

1945.

647	–	10c. brown	15	10
648	**193**	20c. brown	15	10
649	–	25c. blue	15	10
650	**195**	40c. grey	15	10
651	–	50c. violet	15	10
652	–	60c. green	15	15
653	–	80c. red	15	10
654	**195**	1l. green	15	10
655	–	1l.20 brown	15	25
656	–	2l. brown	15	10
657	–	3l. red	15	10
658	–	4l. red	20	10
659	**193**	5l. blue	45	10
660	**195**	6l. violet	6·75	10
661	–	8l. green	3·25	10
662	–	10l. grey	1·50	10
663	**193**	10l. red	32·00	10
664	**195**	15l. blue	7·00	10
665	–	20l. purple	3·25	10
666	**196**	25l. green	19·00	10
667	–	30l. blue	£275	25
668	**196**	50l. purple	7·75	10
669	**197**	100l. red	£275	95

DESIGNS: 10, 50, 80c., 8, 10l. (662) Hammer breaking chain ("Freedom"); 25c., 1l.20, 3, 4, 20, 30l. Flaming torch ("Enlightenment"); 60c., 2l. Gardener tying sapling to stake.

198 Clasped Hands and Caproni Campini N-1 Jet

200 Amalfi

1945. Air.

670	**198**	1l. grey	20	20
671	–	2l. blue	20	20
672	**198**	3l.20 red	20	20
673	–	5l. green	20	20
674	**198**	10l. red	20	10
675	–	25l. blue	10·00	5·25
676	–	25l. brown	15	10
677	**198**	50l. green	18·00	9·25
678		50l. violet	15	10

DESIGN: 2, 5, 25l. Barn swallows in flight.

1946. Mediaeval Italian Republics.

679	**200**	1l. sepia	15	10
680	–	2l. blue	15	10
681	–	3l. green	15	10
682	–	4l. orange	15	10
683	–	5l. violet	15	10
684	–	10l. red	20	20
685	–	15l. blue	65	60
686	–	20l. brown	25	10

DESIGNS—VERT: 2l. Lucca; 3l. Siena; 4l. Florence. HORIZ: 5l. Pisa; 10l. Genoa; 15l. Venice; 20l. "The Oath of Pontida".

1947. Air. Surch **LIRE 6-**.

687	**198**	6l. on 3l.20 orange	20	15

202 Wireless Mast

204 Douglas DC-2 over Rome

1947. Air. 50th Anniv of Radio.

688	**202**	6l. violet	20	15
689	–	10l. red	20	15
690	–	20l. orange	85	55
691	**202**	25l. blue	90	65
692	–	35l. blue	1·30	75
693	–	50l. purple	2·50	1·40

DESIGNS: 10, 35l. Ship's aerial; 20, 50l. Heinkel He 70 Blitz wireless-equipped airplane.

1948. Air.

911	**204**	100l. green	3·00	10
912		300l. mauve	40	30
913		500l. blue	90	55
914		1000l. brown	1·60	1·30

For No. 911 in smaller size see No. 1297.

205 St. Catherine giving her Cloak to a Beggar

206 St. Catherine carrying the Cross

1948. 600th Birth Anniv of St. Catherine of Siena.

698	**205**	3l. blue and green (postage)	15	30
699	–	5l. blue and violet	15	40
700	–	10l. violet and brown	3·25	2·75
701	–	30l. grey and bistre	20·00	10·00

702	206	100l. violet and brown (air)	55·00	32·00
703	–	200l. blue and bistre	30·00	13·00

DESIGNS—All show St. Catherine. VERT: 5l. Carrying the Cross; 10l. Extending her arms to Italy; 30l. Dictating "The Dialogue" to a Disciple. HORIZ: 200l. Extending her arms to Italy.

207 "Proclamation of New Constitution"

1948. Proclamation of New Constitution.

704	207	10l. violet	95	70
705		30l. blue	2·40	1·50

208 Rising at Palermo

1948. Centenary of Revolution of 1848.

706	208	3l. brown	35	35
707	–	4l. purple	35	35
708	–	5l. blue	85	50
709	–	6l. green	55	60
710	–	8l. brown	55	45
711	–	10l. red	1·20	25
712	–	12l. green	3·00	1·70
713	–	15l. black	7·25	85
714	–	20l. red	21·00	5·25
715	–	30l. blue	6·25	50
716	–	50l. violet	75·00	2·75
717	–	100l. blue	£140	11·50

DESIGNS: 4l. Rising at Padua; 5l. Concession of Statute, Turin; 6l. Storming Porta Tosa, Milan; 8l. Proclamation of Venetian Republic; 10l. Defence of Vicenza; 12l. Hero of Curtatone; 15l. Hero of Goito; 20l. Austrian retreat from Bologna; 30l. Fighting at Brescia; 50l. Garibaldi; 100l. Goffredo Mameli (party patriot) on death bed, July 1849.

209 Alpinist and Bassano Bridge

210 Gaetano Donizetti

1948. Rebuilding of Bassano Bridge.

718	209	15l. green	1·10	1·10

1948. Death Centenary of Donizetti (composer).

719	210	15l. brown	80	2·10

211 Exhibition Grounds

212

1949. 27th Milan Fair.

720	211	20l. sepia	7·00	2·50

1949. 25th Biennial Art Exhibition. Venice.

721	212	5l. red and flesh	65	20
722	–	15l. green and cream	3·50	95
723	–	20l. brown and buff	9·00	1·40
724	–	50l. blue and yellow	40·00	1·20

DESIGNS: 15l. Clock bell-ringers, St. Mark's Column and Campanile; 20l. Emblem of Venice and "Bucentaur" (state gallery); 50l. Winged lion on St. Mark's Column.

213 Globes and Forms of Transport

1949. 75th Anniv of U.P.U.

725	213	50l. blue	50·00	4·25

214 Vascello Castle

215 Worker and Ship

1949. Centenary of Roman Republic.

726	214	100l. brown	£160	60·00

1949. European Recovery Plan.

727	215	5l. green	7·00	2·50
728		15l. violet	19·00	10·00
729		20l. brown	55·00	11·00

216 Statue of Mazzini

217 V. Alfieri

1949. Honouring Giuseppe Mazzini (founder of "Young Italy").

730	216	20l. black	7·00	1·50

1949. Birth Bicentenary of Vittorio Alfieri (poet).

731	217	20l. brown	6·00	1·50

218 San Giusto Cathedral

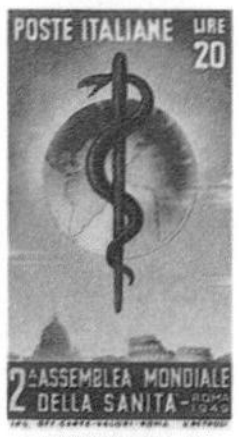

219 Staff of Aesculapius and Globe

1949. 1st Trieste Free Election.

732	218	20l. lake	10·50	10·00

1949. 2nd World Health Congress, Rome.

733	219	20l. violet	30·00	6·25

220 A. Palladio and Vicenza Basilica

221 Lorenzo de Medici

1949. 400th Anniv of Completion of Palladio's Basilica at Vicenza.

734	220	20l. violet	9·00	4·50

1949. 500th Birth Anniv of Lorenzo de Medici "The Magnificent".

735	221	20l. blue	6·75	1·50

222 Galleon and Exhibition Buildings

1949. 13th Levant Fair, Bari.

736	222	20l. red	3·50	1·70

223 Voltaic Pile

224 Count Alessandro Volta

1949. 150th Anniv of Volta's Discovery of the Electric Cell.

737	223	20l. red	6·50	1·50
738	224	50l. blue	75·00	23·00

225 Holy Trinity Bridge, Florence

226 Caius Valerius Catullus

1949. Rebuilding of Holy Trinity Bridge, Florence.

739	225	20l. green	10·00	1·30

1949. Death Bimillenary of Catullus (poet).

740	226	20l. blue	10·00	1·30

227 Domenico Cimarosa

228 Entrance to Exhibition

1949. Birth Bicentenary of Cimarosa (composer).

741	227	20l. violet	8·50	1·00

1950. 28th Milan Fair.

742	228	20l. brown	3·00	1·00

229 Car and Flags

1950. 32nd Int Automobile Exhibition, Turin.

743	229	20l. violet	9·00	1·00

230 Statue of Perseus

231 St. Peter's Basilica

1950. 5th General UNESCO Conference, Florence.

744	–	20l. green	7·00	1·20
745	230	55l. blue	45·00	4·75

DESIGN—HORIZ: 20l. Pitti Palace, Florence.

1950. Holy Year.

746	231	20l. violet	6·00	45
747		55l. blue	45·00	1·70

232 Gaudenzio Ferrari

233 Town Hall, Florence, Statue of Columbus and Wireless Mast

1950. Honouring Gaudenzio Ferrari (painter).

748	232	20l. green	10·00	1·50

1950. International Radio Conf, Florence.

749	233	20l. violet	10·50	5·50
750		55l. blue	£160	95·00

234 L. Muratori

1950. Death Bicentenary of Ludovico Muratori (historian).

751	234	20l. brown	4·75	1·20

235 Guido D'Arezzo

236 Galleon

1950. 9th Death Cent of D'Arezzo (musician).

752	235	20l. green	15·00	2·10

1950. 14th Levant Fair, Bari.

753	236	20l. brown	6·75	1·10

237 Marzotto and Rossi

238 Tobacco Plant and Factory

1950. Pioneers of Wool Industry.

754	237	20l. blue	1·80	65

1950. European Tobacco Conference, Rome.

755	238	5l. green and mauve	3·00	1·20
756	–	20l. green and brown	5·00	50
757	–	55l. brown and blue	46·00	12·50

DESIGNS: 20l. Plant; 55l. Girl and plant.

239 Seal of Academy

240 A. Righi

1950. Bicentenary of Academy of Fine Arts, Venice.

758	239	20l. lt brown and brown	2·20	1·10

1950. Birth Centenary of Augusto Righi (physicist).

759	240	20l. black and buff	2·30	1·10

241 Blacksmith

242 First Tuscan Stamp

1950. Provincial Occupations. As T **241**.

760	241	50c. blue	20	30
881	–	1l. violet	10	10
762	–	2l. brown	20	15
763	–	5l. black	40	15
764	–	6l. brown	20	15
765	–	10l. green	3·25	15
766	–	12l. green	2·00	15
883	–	15l. blue	50	10
768	–	20l. violet	10·50	15
769	–	25l. brown	3·50	15
770	–	30l. purple	1·30	15
771	–	35l. red	8·50	30
772	–	40l. brown	75	15
773	–	50l. violet	10·00	15
774	–	55l. blue	50	30
775	–	60l. red	4·00	30
776	–	65l. green	1·10	30
777	–	100l. brown	65·00	30
778	–	200l. brown	13·00	1·40

DESIGNS: 1l. Motor mechanic; 2l. Stonemason; 5l. Potter; 6l. Girls embroidering and water-carrying; 10l. Weaver; 12l. Fisherman at tiller; 15l. Boat builder; 20l. Fisherman trawling; 25l. Girl packing oranges; 30l. Girl carrying grapes; 35l. Gathering olives; 40l. Carter and wagon; 50l. Shepherd; 55l. Ploughman; 60l. Ox-cart; 65l. Girl harvester; 100l. Women handling maize; 200l. Woodcutter.

243 Car and Flags

1951. Centenary of First Tuscan Stamp.
779 **242** 20l. red and purple . . . 1·40 85
780 55l. blue and ultramarine 27·00 25·00

1951. 33rd International Motor Show, Turin.
781 **243** 20l. green . . . . 9·00 1·40

244 Peace Hall, Rome

1951. Consecration of Hall of Peace, Rome.
782 **244** 20l. violet . . . . 6·25 1·60

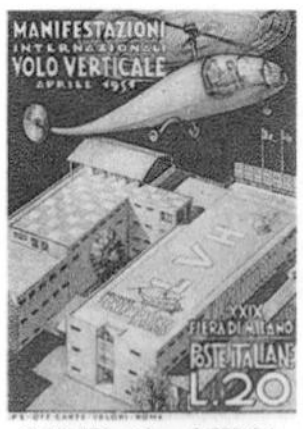

245 Westland W.81 Helicopter over Fair

246 Fair Building

1951. 29th Milan Fair.
783 **245** 20l. brown . . . . 7·50 1·00
784 **246** 55l. blue . . . . 60·00 31·00

247 Allegory

248 Columbus disembarking

1951. 10th International Textile Art and Fashion Exhibition, Turin.
785 **247** 20l. violet . . . . 20·00 2·10

1951. 500th Birth Anniv of Columbus.
786 **248** 20l. green . . . . 15·00 1·80

249 Gymnastics Symbols

250 Montecassino Abbey restored

1951. Int Gymnastic Festival, Florence.
787 **249** 5l. red and brown . . . . 33·00 £120
788 10l. red and green . . . . 33·00 £120
789 15l. red and blue . . . . 33·00 £120

1951. Restoration of Montecassino Abbey.
790 **250** 20l. violet . . . . 4·50 1·40
791 – 55l. blue . . . . 55·00 28·00
DESIGN: 55l. Abbey in ruins, 1944.

251 Perugino

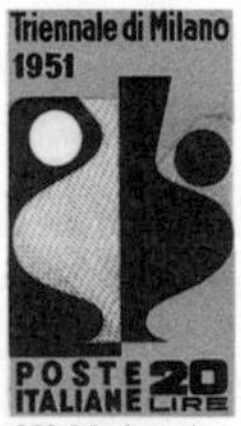

252 Modern Art

1951. 500th Birth Anniv of Perugino (painter).
792 **251** 20l. brown and sepia . . 2·50 1·70

1951. Triennial Art Exhibition, Milan.
793 **252** 20l. black and green . . . 7·75 1·30
794 – 55l. pink and blue . . . . 35·00 26·00
DESIGN—HORIZ: 55l. Jug and symbols.

253 Cyclist and Globe

254 Galleon and Hemispheres

1951. World Cycling Championship.
795 **253** 25l. black . . . . 6·00 2·10

1951. 15th Levant Fair, Bari.
796 **254** 25l. blue . . . . 5·50 1·40

255 "Jorio's Daughter"

1951. Birth Centenary of Francesco Paolo Michetti (painter).
797 **255** 25l. brown . . . . 6·00 2·10

256 T 1 of Sardinia and Arms of Cagliari

1951. Sardinian Postage Stamp Centenary.
798 **256** 10l. black and sepia . . . 1·40 1·60
799 – 25l. green and red . . . . 2·00 1·30
800 – 60l. red and blue . . . . 10·00 10·50
DESIGNS: 25l. 20c. stamp and arms of Genoa; 60l. 40c. stamp and arms of Turin.

257 "Industry and Commerce"

1951. 3rd Industrial and Commercial Census.
801 **257** 10l. green . . . . 1·00 80

258 Census in Ancient Rome

1951. 9th National Census.
802 **258** 25l. black . . . . 2·50 1·10

259 G. Verdi and Roncole Church

260 Mountain Forest

1951. 50th Death Anniv of Giuseppe Verdi (composer).
803 – 10l. green and purple . . 1·40 2·10
804 **259** 25l. brown and chocolate 6·00 2·00
805 – 60l. blue and green . . . 25·00 8·00
DESIGNS: 10l. Verdi, Theatre Royal and Cathedral, Parma; 60l. Verdi, La Scala Opera House and Cathedral, Milan.

1951. Forestry Festival. Inscr "FESTA DEGLI ALBERI".
806 **260** 10l. green and olive . . . 1·50 2·10
807 – 25l. green . . . . 3·75 1·30
DESIGN—HORIZ: 25l. Tree and wooded hills.

261 V. Bellini

262 Royal Palace, Caserta

1952. 150th Birth Anniv of Bellini (composer).
808 **261** 25l. black . . . . 2·50 60

1952. Bicentenary of Construction of Caserta Palace by Vanvitelli.
809 **262** 25l. bistre and green . . . 2·50 80

263

264 Motor-boat Pavilion

1952. 1st Int Sports Stamps Exhibition, Rome.
810 **263** 25l. brown and black . . 85 60

1952. 30th Milan Fair.
811 **264** 60l. blue . . . . 25·00 7·00

265 Leonardo da Vinci

267 Campaniles and First Stamps

1952. 500th Birth Anniv of Leonardo da Vinci.
812 **265** 25l. orange 40 20
813 – 60l. blue . . . . 3·75 3·75
814 **265** 80l. red . . . . 18·00 30
DESIGN—(inscr "LEONARDO DA VINCI 1452–1952"): 60l. "The Virgin of the Rocks".

1952. Modena and Parma Stamp Centenary.
815 **267** 25l. black and brown . . 1·00 65
816 60l. indigo and blue . . . 6·50 6·50

268 Hand, Torch and Globe

269 Lion of St. Mark

1952. Overseas Fair, Naples.
817 **268** 25l. blue . . . . 1·30 65

1952. 26th Biennial Art Exhibition, Venice.
818 **269** 25l. black and cream . . 1·40 60

270 Emblem of Fair

271 San Giusto Cathedral and Flag

1952. 30th Padua Fair.
819 **270** 25l. red and blue . . . . 2·00 65

1952. 4th Trieste Fair.
820 **271** 25l. green, red and brown 1·50 65

272 Caravel and Bari Fair

273 Girolamo Savonarola

1952. 16th Levant Fair, Bari.
821 **272** 25l. green . . . . 1·20 65

1952. 5th Birth Cent of Savonarola (reformer).
822 **273** 25l. violet . . . . 2·75 65

274 Savoia Marchetti S.M.95C over Colosseum

275 Alpine Climbing Equipment

1952. 1st Civil Aeronautics Law Conf, Rome.
823 **274** 60l. blue and ultramarine 12·00 11·50

1952. Alpine Troops National Exhibition.
824 **275** 25l. black 45 40

276 Army, Navy and Air Force Symbols

277 Sailor, Soldier and Airman

1952. Armed Forces Day.
825 **276** 10l. green 25 10
826 **277** 25l. sepia and brown . . 60 10
827 – 60l. black and blue . . . 5·00 1·80
DESIGN—As Type **277**: 60l. Airplane, motor torpedo boat and tank.

278 Cardinal Massaia and Map

279 V. Gemito

1952. Centenary of Mission to Ethiopia.
828 **278** 25l. deep brown & brown 85 1·20

1952. Birth Centenary of Gemito (sculptor).
829 **279** 25l. brown 40 50

280 A. Mancini

281

1952. Birth Centenary of Mancini (painter).
830 **280** 25l. myrtle 40 45

1952. Centenary of Martyrdom of Belfiore.
831 **281** 25l. blue and black . . . 1·40 45

282 Antonello da Messina

283 Cars Racing

1953. Antonello Exhibition, Messina.
832 **282** 25l. red . . . . 1·20 70

1953. 20th "Mille Miglia" Car Race.
833 **283** 25l. violet 45 60

284 Bee and Medals **285** Arcangelo Corelli

1953. Creation of Orders of Meritorious Labour.
834 **284** 25l. violet 45 45

1953. Birth Tercentenary of Corelli (composer).
835 **285** 25l. brown 50 85

286 Coin of Syracuse **287** St. Clare of Assisi

1953. (a) Size 17 × 21 mm.
887 **286** 1l. black 10 20
888 5l. grey 10 10
889 6l. brown 10 20
890 10l. red 10 10
891 12l. green 10 10
892 13l. purple 10 10
893 15l. grey 10 10
894 20l. brown 10 10
895 25l. violet 30 10
896 30l. brown 15 10
897 35l. red 10 10
898 40l. mauve 60 10
899 50l. green 50 10
900 60l. blue 10 10
901 70l. green 20 10
902 80l. brown 10 10
903 90l. brown 20 10
1008 100l. brown 25 10
905 130l. red and grey . . . 10 20
1009 200l. blue 25 10
(b) Size 22½ × 28 mm.
904 **286** 100l. brown . . . . . . 15·00 10
846 200l. blue . . . . 4·75 60
See also Nos. 1202/19b.

1953. 700th Death Anniv of St. Clare.
847 **287** 25l. red and brown . . . 40 55

288 Mountains and Reservoirs **289** "Agriculture"

1953. Mountains Festival.
848 **288** 25l. green . . . . 1·00 40

1953. International Agricultural Exn, Rome.
849 **289** 25l. brown 70 30
850 60l. blue . . . . 2·75 1·30

290 Rainbow over Atlantic **291** L. Signorelli

1953. 4th Anniv of Atlantic Pact.
851 **290** 25l. turquoise and orange 3·50 20
852 60l. blue and mauve . . . 7·00 2·00

1953. 500th Birth Anniv of Signorelli (painter).
853 **291** 25l. green and brown . . 45 20

292 A. Bassi **293** Capri

1953. 6th Int Microbiological Congress, Rome.
854 **292** 25l. brown and black . . 40 20

1953. Tourist Series.
855 – 10l. brown and sepia . . 35 10
856 – 12l. black and blue . . . 35 10
857 – 20l. brown and orange . . 75 10
858 – 25l. green and blue . . . 75 10
859 – 35l. brown and buff . . . 1·20 20
860 **293** 60l. blue and green . . . 1·60 40
DESIGNS—VERT: 10l. Siena; 25l. Cortina d'Ampezzo. HORIZ: 12l. Rapallo; 20l. Gardone; 35l. Taormina.

294 Lateran Palace **295** Television Aerial and Screen

1954. 25th Anniv of Lateran Treaty.
861 **294** 25l. brown and sepia . . 45 20
862 60l. blue and bright blue 1·80 1·40

1954. Introduction of Television in Italy.
863 **295** 25l. violet . . . . 1·30 20
864 60l. turquoise . . . . . . 3·75 1·80

296 "Everyone Must Contribute to the Public Expense" **297** Vertical Flight Trophy

1954. "Encouragement to Taxpayers".
865 **296** 25l. violet . . . . 1·00 10

1954. 1st Experimental Helicopter Mail Flight, Milan–Turin.
866 **297** 25l. green 30 35

298 Golden Eagle and Campanile **299** A. Catalani

1954. 10th Anniv of Resistance Movement.
867 **298** 25l. black and brown . . 25 20

1954. Birth Centenary of Catalani (composer).
868 **299** 25l. green 25 30

300 Marco Polo, Lion of St. Mark, Venice, and Dragon Pillar, Peking

1954. 7th Birth Centenary of Marco Polo.
869 **300** 25l. brown 30 20
870 60l. green . . . . 2·75 2·50

301 Cyclist, Car and Landscape **302** "St. Michael the Archangel" (after Guido Reni)

1954. 60th Anniv of Italian Touring Club.
871 **301** 25l. green and red 30 30

1954. International Police Congress, Rome.
872 **302** 25l. red 15 20
873 60l. blue . . . . 80 1·20

303 "Pinocchio" **304** Amerigo Vespucci

1954. 64th Death Anniv of Carlo Lorenzini (Collodi) (writer).
874 **303** 25l. red 35 30

1954. 5th Birth Cent of Vespucci (explorer).
875 **304** 25l. purple 25 25
876 60l. blue . . . . 1·20 1·50

305 "Madonna" (Perugino) **306** Silvio Pellico

1954. Termination of Marian Year.
877 **305** 25l. brown and buff . . . 20 20
878 – 60l. black and cream . . 85 1·30
DESIGN: 60l. Madonna's head (Michelangelo).

1955. Death Centenary of Pellico (dramatist).
879 **306** 25l. blue and violet . . . 25 20

308 "The Nation Expects a Faithful Declaration of Your Income"

1955. "Encouragement to Taxpayers".
907 **308** 25l. lilac . . . . 1·10 10

309 **310** A. Rosmini

1955. 4th World Petroleum Congress.
908 **309** 25l. green 20 20
909 – 60l. red . . . . 60 1·10
DESIGN: 60l. Oil derricks and globe.

1955. Death Cent of Rosmini (theologian).
910 **310** 25l. brown 50 20

311 Girolamo Fracastoro (physician) and Roman Arena, Verona

1955. International Medical Conf, Verona.
915 **311** 25l. brown and black . . 35 20

312 Basilica of St. Francis

1955. Bicentenary of Elevation of Basilica of St. Francis of Assisi to Papal Chapel.
916 **312** 25l. black and cream . . 20 20

313 Scholar and Drawing-board

1955. Centenary of "Montani" Institute, Fermo.
917 **313** 25l. green 20 30

314 "The Harvester" **315** F.A.O. Building, Rome

1955. 50th Anniv of Int Agricultural Institute.
918 **314** 25l. brown and red . . . 15 20

1955. 10th Anniv of F.A.O.
919 **315** 60l. violet and black . . . 60 60

316 G. Matteotti **317** B. Grassi

1955. 70th Birth Anniv of Giacomo Matteotti (politician).
920 **316** 25l. red 55 20

1955. 30th Death Anniv of Grassi (biologist).
921 **317** 25l. green 20 20

318 "St. Stephen giving Alms to the Poor"

1955. 5th Death Cent of Fra Angelico (painter).
922 **318** 10l. black and cream . . 10 30
923 – 25l. blue and cream . . . 15 30
DESIGN—HORIZ: 25l. "St. Lawrence giving goods of the Church to the poor".

319 G. Pascoli

1955. Birth Centenary of Pascoli (poet).
924 **319** 25l. black 15 20

320 G. Mazzini

321 "Italia" Ski-jump

1955. Air. 150th Birth Anniv of Mazzini (founder of "Young Italy").
925 **320** 100l. green . . . . 1·40 85

1956. 7th Winter Olympic Games, Cortina d'Ampezzo.
926 **321** 10l. green and orange . . 10 20
927 – 12l. black and yellow . . 10 20
928 – 25l. purple and orange . . 10 20
929 – 60l. blue and orange . . . 95 1·50
DESIGNS: 12l. Snow Stadium; 25l. Ice Stadium; 60l. Skating Arena, Misurina.

1956. Air. Italian President's Visit to U.S.A. and Canada. Surch **1956 Visita del Presidente della Repubblica negli U.S.A. e nel Canada L. 120.**
930 **198** 120l. on 50l. mauve . . . 65 1·60

323 Coach and Steam Train

1956. 50th Anniv of Simplon Tunnel.
931 **323** 25l. green . . . . 3·50 55

324

1956. 10th Anniv of Republic.
932 **324** 10l. grey and blue 15 20
933 25l. carmine and red . . . 20 20
934 60l. light blue and blue 2·10 1·80
935 80l. orange and brown . . 3·25 20

325 Count Avogadro

326

1956. Death Centenary of Avogadro (physicist).
936 **325** 25l. black 15 20

1956. Europa.
937 **326** 25l. deep green and green 65 10
938 60l. deep blue and blue 6·00 35

327

1956. Int Astronautical Congress, Rome.
939 **327** 25l. blue 15 20

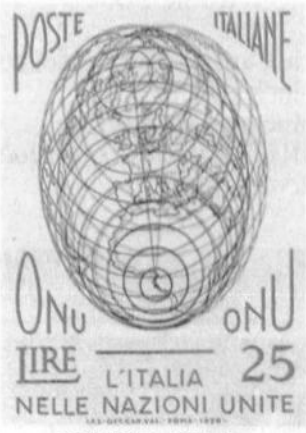

328 The Globe

1956. 1st Anniv of Admission to U.N.
940 **328** 25l. red and green on pink 15 20
941 60l. green and red on green 20 20

329 Savings Bank, Books and Certificates

330 Ovid

1956. 80th Anniv of Post Office Savings Bank.
942 **329** 25l. blue and slate 10 20

1957. Birth Bimillenary of Ovid (poet).
943 **330** 25l. black and olive . . . 10 20

331 St. George (after Donatello)

332 Antonio Canova

1957.
944a **331** 500l. green . . . . . . 1·50 10
945a 1000l. red . . . . 5·00 55

1957. Birth Bicentenary of Canova (sculptor).
946 **332** 25l. brown 10 20
947 – 60l. slate 10 40
948 – 80l. blue 10 20
DESIGNS—VERT: 60l. Hercules and Lica. HORIZ: 80l. Pauline Borghese (bust).

333 Traffic Lights at Crossroads

334 "Europa" Flags

1957. Road Safety Campaign.
949 **333** 25l. red, black and green 15 10

1957. Europa. Flags in national colours.
950 **334** 25l. blue 20 10
951 60l. blue . . . . 1·70 35

335 Giosue Carducci

336 Filippino Lippi (after self-portrait)

1957. 50th Death Anniv of Carducci (poet).
954 **335** 25l. sepia 15 20

1957. 500th Birth Anniv of Filippino Lippi (painter).
955 **336** 25l. brown 10 20

337 Cicero (bust)

338 Garibaldi (after M. Lorusso)

1957. Death Bimillenary of Cicero (statesman).
956 **337** 25l. red 10 20

1957. 150th Birth Anniv of Garibaldi.
957 **338** 15l. grey 10 20
958 – 110l. lilac 15 20
DESIGN—HORIZ: 110l. Statue of Garibaldi on horseback (after Romanelli).

339 St. Domenico Savio and Youths

340 St. Francis of Paola

1957. Death Centenary of St. Domenico Savio.
959 **339** 15l. black and violet . . . 10 20

1957. 450th Death Anniv of St. Francis of Paola.
960 **340** 25l. black 10 20

341 Dams, Peasant and Map of Sardinia

342 Statue of the Holy Virgin and Lourdes Basilica

1958. Inaug of Flumendosa–Mulargia Irrigation Scheme, Sardinia.
961 **341** 25l. turquoise 10 20

1958. Centenary of Apparition of Virgin Mary at Lourdes.
962 **342** 15l. purple 10 15
963 60l. blue 10 20

343 "The Constitution"

344 Exhibition Emblem and Ancient Roman Road

1958. 10th Anniv of Constitution.
964 **343** 25l. green and brown . . 10 10
965 – 60l. sepia and blue . . . 10 10
966 – 110l. sepia and brown . . 10 10
DESIGNS—VERT: 60l. Oak tree with new growth. HORIZ: 110l. Montecitorio Palace, Rome.

1958. Brussels International Exhibition.
967 **344** 60l. yellow and blue . . . 10 20

345 Rodolfo's Attic ("La Boheme")

346 The Prologue ("I Pagliacci")

1958. Birth Centenary of Puccini (operatic composer).
968 **345** 25l. blue 10 20

1958. Birth Centenary of Leoncavallo (operatic composer).
969 **346** 25l. red and indigo . . . 10 20

347 "Ave Maria" (after Segantini)

348 "Fattori in his Studio" (self-portrait)

1958. Birth Centenary of Giovanni Segantini (painter).
970 **347** 110l. green on cream . . 20 20

1958. 50th Death Anniv of Giovanni Fattori (painter).
971 **348** 110l. brown 20 20

349 Federal Palace, Brasilia and Arch of Titus, Rome

349a "Europa"

1958. Visit of Pres. Gronchi to Brazil.
972 **349** 175l. green 40 70

1958. Europa.
973 **349a** 25l. blue and red 10 10
974 60l. red and blue 20 20

350 Naples ½ grano stamp of 1858

351 "Winged Horse" (sculpture in Sorrento Cathedral)

1958. 1st Naples Postage Stamps Centenary.
975 **350** 25l. brown 10 10
976 – 60l. brown and sepia . . 10 20
DESIGN: 60l. Naples 1 grano stamp of 1858.

1958. Visit of Shah of Iran.
977 **351** 25l. sepia and lavender . . 10 20
978 60l. blue and pale blue . . 25 50

352 E. Torricelli

353 "Triumphs of Julius Caesar" (after fresco by Mantegna)

1958. 350th Birth Anniv of Evangelista Torricelli (physicist).
979 **352** 25l. red 35 45

1958. 40th Anniv of Victory in World War I.
980 **353** 15l. green 10 10
981 – 25l. slate 10 10
982 – 60l. red 10 25
DESIGNS—HORIZ: 25l. Arms of Trieste, Rome and Trento. VERT: 60l. Memorial bell of Rovereto.

354 Eleonora Duse

355 "Drama"

1958. Birth Centenary of Eleonora Duse (actress).
983 **354** 25l. blue 10 20

1958. 10th Anniv of "Premio Italia" (international contest for radio and television plays).
984 **355** 25l. black, blue and red 10 20
985 – 60l. black and blue . . . 10 20
DESIGN: 60l. "Music" (radio mast and grand piano).

356 Sicily 5gr. stamp of 1859

357 Capitol, Quirinal Square Obelisk and Dome of St. Peter's

1959. 1st Sicilian Postage Stamps Centenary.
986 – 25l. turquoise 10 10
987 **356** 60l. orange 10 20
DESIGN: 25l. Sicily 2gr. stamp of 1859.

1959. 30th Anniv of Lateran Treaty.
988 **357** 25l. blue 10 10

358 N.A.T.O. Emblem and Map

1959. 10th Anniv of N.A.T.O.

989	**358**	25l. blue and yellow	10	20
990		60l. blue and green	10	20

359 Arms of Paris and Rome **360** Olive Branch growing from shattered Tree

1959. Rome-Paris Friendship.

991	**359**	15l. red, brown and blue	10	10
992		25l. red, brown and blue	10	10

1959. Int War Veterans' Assn Convention, Rome.

993	**360**	25l. green	10	10

361 Lord Byron Monument **362** C. Prampolini

1959. Unveiling of Lord Byron Monument, Rome.

994	**361**	15l. green	10	20

1959. Birth Centenary of Camillo Prampolini (politician).

995	**362**	15l. red	1·60	25

363 Quirinal Square Obelisk, Rome **364** Victor Emmanuel II, Garibaldi, Cavour and Mazzini

1959. Olympic Games Propaganda. Roman Monuments and Ruins. Inscr "ROMA MCMLX".

996	**363**	15l. sepia and orange	10	10
997	–	25l. sepia and blue	10	10
998	–	35l. sepia and buff	10	20
999	–	60l. sepia and mauve	10	20
1000	–	110l. sepia and yellow	15	10

DESIGNS—VERT: 25l. Tower of City Hall, Quirinal Hill. HORIZ: 35l. Baths of Caracalla; 60l. Arch of Constantine (Colosseum); 110l. Basilica of Massentius.

1959. Centenary of 2nd War of Independence.

1001	**364**	15l. black	10	10
1002	–	25l. red and brown	10	10
1003	–	35l. violet	10	10
1004	–	60l. blue	10	20
1005	–	110l. lake	10	20

DESIGNS—VERT: 25l. Italian camp after the Battle of Magenta (after painting by Fattori); 110l. Battle of Magenta (after painting by Induno). HORIZ: 35l. Battle of San Fermo (after painting by Trezzini); 60l. Battle of Palestro.

The 25l. is also a Red Cross commemorative.

365 Workers' Monument and I.L.O. Building, Geneva **366** Romagna 8b. Stamp of 1859

1959. 40th Anniv of I.L.O.

1006	**365**	25l. violet	10	10
1007		60l. brown	10	20

1959. Romagna Postage Stamps Centenary.

1010	**366**	25l. brown and black	10	10
1011	–	60l. green and black	10	10

DESIGN: 60l. Romagna 20b. stamp of 1859.

366a "Europa" **367**

1959. Europa.

1012	**366a**	25l. green	25	10
1013		60l. blue	25	10

1959. Stamp Day.

1014	**367**	15l. red, black and grey	10	10

368 "The Fire of Borgo" (after Raphael) **369** Garibaldi's Message to Sicilians

1960. World Refugee Year.

1015	**368**	25l. red	10	10
1016		60l. purple	10	20

1960. Cent of Garibaldi's Expedition to Sicily.

1017	**369**	15l. brown	10	10
1018	–	25l. red	10	10
1019	–	60l. blue	10	25

DESIGNS—VERT: 25l. Garibaldi meeting King Victor Emmanuel II near Naples (after Matania). HORIZ: 60l. Embarkation of volunteers at Quarto, near Genoa (after T. van Elven).

370 "The Discus Thrower" (after Miron) **371** Vittorio Bottego (after Ettore Ximenes)

1960. Olympic Games. Inscr as in T **370**.

1020	–	5l. brown	10	10
1021	–	10l. blue and orange	10	10
1022	–	15l. blue	10	10
1023	–	25l. sepia and lilac	10	10
1024	**370**	35l. red	10	10
1025	–	60l. sepia and green	10	20
1026	–	110l. purple	10	10
1027	–	150l. brown and blue	65	1·00
1028	–	200l. green	35	20

DESIGNS—VERT: 5l. Games emblem; 15l. "Starting the Race" (statue); 110l. "Pugilist at rest" (after Apollonius); 200l. "The Apoxiomenos" (after Lisippos). HORIZ: 10l. Olympic Stadium, Rome; 25l. Cycling Stadium, Rome; 60l. Sports Palace, Rome; 150l. Little Sports Palace.

1960. Birth Centenary of Vittorio Bottego (explorer).

1029	**371**	30l. brown	10	20

371a Conference Emblem

1960. Europa.

1030	**371a**	30l. brown and green	20	10
1031		70l. orange and blue	20	10

372 Caravaggio

1960. 350th Death Anniv of Caravaggio (painter).

1032	**372**	25l. brown	10	10

373 Coach and Posthorn

1960. Stamp Day.

1033	**373**	15l. sepia and red	10	10

374 Michelangelo **375** Douglas DC-8 Jetliner crossing Atlantic Ocean

1961. Works of Michelangelo. Frescoes on ceiling of Sistine Chapel. (a) Size 17 × 20½ mm.

1034	–	1l. black	10	20
1035	–	5l. orange	10	10
1036	–	10l. red	10	10
1037	–	15l. purple	10	10
1038	–	20l. green	10	10
1039	–	25l. brown	20	10
1040	–	30l. purple	10	10
1041	–	40l. red	10	10
1042	–	50l. green	15	10
1043	–	55l. brown	10	10
1044	–	70l. blue	15	10
1045	–	85l. green	15	20
1046	–	90l. mauve	20	20
1047	–	100l. violet	30	10
1048	–	115l. blue	15	20
1049	–	150l. brown	65	20
1050	**374**	200l. blue	1·10	20

(b) Size 22 × 26½ mm.

1051	–	500l. green	3·50	25
1052	–	1000l. red	2·40	4·00

DESIGNS: 1, 5, 10, 115, 150l. Ignudo (different versions); 15l. Joel; 20l. Libyan Sibyl; 25l. Isaiah; 30l. Erythraean Sibyl; 40l. Daniel; 50l. Delphic Sibyl; 55l. Cumaean Sibyl; 70l. Zachariah; 85l. Jonah; 90l. Jeremiah; 100l. Ezekiel; 500l. Adam; 1000l. Eve.

1961. Visit of President Gronchi to S. America.

1053	**375**	170l. blue (Argentina)	2·30	4·25
1054		185l. green (Uruguay)	2·30	5·25
1055		205l. violet (Peru)	8·50	13·00

The countries indicated are shown in deep colours on the map.

376 Pliny the Younger **377** Ippolito Nievo

1961. 19th Birth Cent of Pliny the Younger.

1056	**376**	30l. brown and buff	10	20

1961. Birth Centenary of Ippolito Nievo (poet).

1057	**377**	30l. blue and red	10	20

378 St. Paul in Ship (from 15th-century Bible of Borso d'Este)

1961. 19th Cent of St. Paul's Arrival in Rome.

1058	**378**	30l. multicoloured	10	30
1059		70l. multicoloured	15	55

379 Cannon and Gaeta Fortress

1961. Cent of Italian Unification and Independence.

1060	**379**	15l. brown and blue	10	20
1061	–	30l. brown and blue	10	10
1062	–	40l. brown and blue	15	20
1063	–	70l. mauve and brown	20	20
1064	–	115l. blue and brown	85	20
1065	–	300l. red, brown & green	4·25	8·00

DESIGNS: 30l. Carignano Palace, Turin; 40l. Montecitorio Palace, Rome; 70l. Vecchio Palace, Florence; 115l. Madama Palace, Rome; 300l. Capitals, "Palace of Work", Int. Exn. of Work, Turin.

380 Doves **381** G. Romagnosi

1961. Europa.

1066	**380**	30l. red	15	10
1067		70l. green	15	20

1961. Birth Bicent of Romagnosi (philosopher).

1068	**381**	30l. green	10	30

382 Imprint of 50c. Provisional Postal Franked Paper of Sardinia, 1819

1961. Stamp Day.

1069	**382**	15l. mauve and black	10	10

383 "The Sweet-burning Lamp" from Pascoli's "La Poesia" (after wood-eng by P. Morbiducci)

1962. 50th Death Anniv of G. Pascoli (poet).

1070	**383**	30l. red	10	10
1071		70l. blue	10	30

384 Pacinotti's Dynamo (diagram) **385** St. Catherine (after 15th-century woodcut)

1962. 50th Death Anniv of Antonio Pacinotti (physicist).

1072	**384**	30l. black and red	10	10
1073		70l. black and blue	10	30

1962. 5th Centenary of Canonization of St. Catherine of Siena.

1074	–	30l. violet	10	10
1075	**385**	70l. black and red	10	45

DESIGN: 30l. St. Catherine (after A. Vanni).

386 Camera Lens

1962. 30th Anniv of International Cinematograph Art Fair. Venice.

1076	**386**	30l. black and blue	10	20
1077	–	70l. black and red	10	30

DESIGN: 70l. Lion of St. Mark.

387 Cyclist being paced

1962. World Cycling Championships.
1078 **387** 30l. black and green . . 10 10
1079 – 70l. blue and black . . . 10 10
1080 – 300l. black and red . . . 1·90 6·25
DESIGNS: 70l. Cyclists road-racing; 300l. Cyclists on track.

388 Europa "Tree"

1962. Europa.
1081 **388** 30l. red and carmine . . 30 10
1082 70l. ultramarine and blue 30 25

389 Balzan Medal **390** Campaign Emblem

1962. International Balzan Foundation.
1083 **389** 70l. red and green . . . 25 30

1962. Malaria Eradication.
1084 **390** 30l. violet 10 30
1085 70l. blue 10 40

391 10c. Stamp of 1862 and 30l. Stamp of 1961 **392** "The Pentecost" (from "Codex Syriacus")

1962. Stamp Day.
1086 **391** 15l. multicoloured . . . 10 10

1962. Ecumenical Council, Vatican City.
1087 **392** 30l. orange & bl on cream 10 10
1088 70l. blue & orge on cream 10 10

393 Statue of Cavour (statesman) **394** Pico della Mirandola (scholar)

1962. Centenary of Court of Accounts.
1089 **393** 30l. green 10 30

1963. 5th Birth Cent of G. Pico della Mirandola.
1090 **394** 30l. violet 10 10

395 D'Annunzio

1963. Birth Centenary of Gabriele D'Annunzio (author and soldier).
1091 **395** 30l. green 10 30

396 "Sowing" (bas-relief after G. and N. Pisano) **397** Monviso, Italian Alps, Ice-axe and Rope

1963. Freedom from Hunger.
1092 **396** 30l. sepia and red . . . 10 30
1093 – 70l. sepia and blue . . . 15 40
DESIGN: 70l. "Harvesting" (bas-relief after G. and N. Pisano).

1963. Italian Alpine Club Centenary.
1094 **397** 115l. sepia and blue . . 10 30

398 "I.N.A." Lighthouse

1963. 50th Anniv of Italian National Insurance Corporation.
1095 **398** 30l. black and green . . 10 30

399 Posthorn and Globe

1963. Paris Postal Conference Centenary.
1096 **399** 70l. blue and green . . . 10 30

400 Three-dimensional Emblem

1963. Red Cross Centenary.
1097 **400** 30l. red and purple . . . 10 30
1098 70l. red and blue 10 40

401 "World Tourism"

1963. U.N. Tourism Conference, Rome.
1099 **401** 15l. blue and olive . . . 10 30
1100 70l. brown and blue . . 10 30

402 "Co-operation" **403** "Naples"

1963. Europa.
1101 **402** 30l. brown and red . . . 15 10
1102 70l. green and brown . . 15 10

1963. 4th Mediterranean Games, Naples. Inscr "NAPOLI 1963".
1103 **403** 15l. ochre and blue . . . 10 10
1104 – 70l. orange and green . . 10 30
DESIGN: 70l. Greek "Olympic" vase.

404 Mascagni and Costanzi Theatre **405** G. Belli

1963. 150th Birth Anniv of Verdi (1105) and Birth Centenary of Mascagni (1106) (composers).
1105 – 30l. brown and green . . 10 30
1106 **404** 30l. green and brown . . 10 30
DESIGN: No. 1105, Verdi and La Scala Opera House.

1963. Death Centenary of Giuseppe Belli (poet).
1107 **405** 30l. brown 10 30

406 Stamp "Flower" **407** Galileo Galilei

1963. Stamp Day.
1108 **406** 15l. red and blue 10 10

1964. 400th Birth Anniv of Galileo Galilei.
1109 **407** 30l. brown 10 30
1110 70l. black 10 30

408 Nicodemus (from Michelangelo's "Pieta") **410** Carabinieri on Parade

1964. 400th Death Anniv of Michelangelo.
1111 **408** 30l. sepia (postage) . . . 10 30
1112 – 185l. black (air) 10 55
DESIGN: 185l. Michelangelo's "Madonna of Bruges".

1964. 150th Anniv of Carabinieri (military police).
1113 **410** 30l. red and blue 10 10
1114 – 70l. brown 10 30
DESIGN: 70l. "The Charge at Pastrengo (1848)" (De Albertis).

411 G. Bodoni **412** Europa "Flower"

1964. 150th Death Anniv (1963) of Giambattista Bodoni (type-designer and printer).
1115 **411** 30l. red 10 30

1964. Europa.
1116 **412** 30l. purple 15 10
1117 70l. blue 15 10

413 European Buildings **414** Victor Emannuel Monument, Rome

1964. 7th European Municipalities' Assembly.
1118 **413** 30l. brown and green . . 10 10
1119 70l. brown and blue . . 10 10
1120 500l. red . . . . 40 1·70

1964. War Veterans' Pilgrimage to Rome.
1121 **414** 30l. brown 10 10
1122 70l. blue 10 10

415 G. da Verrazzano and Verrazano Narrows Bridge

1964. Opening of Verrazano Narrows Bridge, New York.
1123 **415** 30l. black and brown (postage) 10 10
1124 130l. black and green (air) 10 30
This American bridge is designated "Verrazano" with one "z".

416 Italian Stamps **417** Prisoners of War

1964. Stamp Day.
1125 **416** 15l. brown and bistre . . 10 10

1965. 20th Anniv of Resistance.
1126 **417** 10l. black 10 10
1127 – 15l. black, red and green 10 10
1128 – 30l. purple 10 15
1129 – 70l. blue 10 15
1130 – 115l. red 10 15
1131 – 130l. brown, green & red 10 15
DESIGNS—VERT: 15l. Servicemen and casualty ("Liberation Army"); 70l. Alpine soldiers ("Resistance in the mountains"). HORIZ: 30l. Gaunt hands and arms on swastika ("Political and Racial Persecution"); 115l. Patriots with banners ("Resistance in the Towns"); 130l. Ruined building and torn flags ("Martyred Cities").

418 I.T.U. Emblem, Meucci and Marconi

1965. I.T.U. Centenary.
1132 **418** 70l. red and green . . . 10 30

419 "Flying Dutchman" Dinghies

1965. World Sailing Championships, Alassio and Naples.
1133 **419** 30l. black and red . . . 10 10
1134 – 70l. black and blue . . . 10 30
1135 – 500l. black and blue . . 20 70
DESIGNS—VERT: 70l. "5.5 S.1" class yachts. HORIZ: 500l. "Lightning" dinghies.

420 Mont Blanc and Tunnel **421** A. Tassoni and Episode from his "Secchia Rapita"

1965. Opening of Mont Blanc Road Tunnel.
1136 **420** 30l. black 10 30

1965. 400th Birth Anniv of Alessandro Tassoni (poet).
1137 **421** 40l. multicoloured . . . 10 10

422 Europa "Sprig"

1965. Europa.
1138 **422** 40l. green and orange . . 15 10
1139 90l. green and blue . . . 15 10

423 "Hell" (Codex, Vatican Library)

1965. 700th Birth Anniv of Dante.
1140 **423** 40l. multicoloured . . . 10 10
1141 – 90l. multicoloured . . . 10 10
1142 – 130l. multicoloured . . . 10 20
1143 – 500l. green 20 70
DESIGNS—VERT: 90l. "Purgatory" (codex, Marciana Library, Venice); 500l. Head of Dante (bronze, Naples Museum). HORIZ: 130l. "Paradise" (codex, British Museum).

424 House and Savings-bank
425 Douglas DC-6B Airliner passing Control-tower

1965. Savings Day.
1144 **424** 40l. multicoloured . . . 10 10

1965. Night Airmail Service.
1145 **425** 40l. red and blue 10 10
1146 – 90l. multicoloured . . . 10 30
DESIGN: 90l. Sud Aviation Caravelle jetliner within airmail envelope "border".

426 Map of "Highway to the Sun"
427 Two-man Bobsleigh

1965. Stamp Day.
1147 **426** 20l. multicoloured . . . 10 10

1966. World Bobsleigh Championships, Cortina d'Ampezzo.
1148 **427** 40l. red, blue and grey 10 10
1149 – 90l. violet and blue . . . 10 30
DESIGN: 90l. Four-man bobsleigh.

428 Skier carrying Torch
429 B. Croce

1966. University Winter Games, Turin.
1150 **428** 40l. black and red . . . 10 10
1151 – 90l. violet and red . . . 10 10
1152 – 500l. brown and red . . 20 45
DESIGNS—VERT: 90l. Ice skating; 500l. Ice hockey.

1966. Birth Centenary of Benedetto Croce (philosopher).
1153 **429** 40l. sepia 10 15

430 Arms of Cities of Venezia

1966. Centenary of Union of Venezia and Italy.
1154 **430** 40l. multicoloured . . . 10 15

431 Pine, Palatine Hill, Rome
432 "Visit Italy"

1966. "Trees and Flowers". Multicoloured.
1155 20l. Type **431** 10 10
1156 25l. Apples 10 10
1157 40l. Carnations 10 10
1158 50l. Irises 10 10
1241 55l. Cypresses (26 × 35½ mm) 10 10
1159 90l. Anthemis (Golden Marguerite) 10 10
1160 170l. Olive tree, Villa Adriana, Tivoli 10 10
1242 180l. Broom (26 × 35½ mm) 10 10

1966. Tourist Propaganda.
1161 **432** 20l. multicoloured . . . 10 15

433 Capital "I"
434 Battle Scene

1966. 20th Anniv of Republic.
1162 **433** 40l. multicoloured . . . 10 15
1163 90l. multicoloured . . . 10 20

1966. Centenary of Battle of Bezzecca.
1164 **434** 90l. olive 10 15

435 "Singing Angels" (from copper panel on altar of St. Antony's Basilica, Padua)

1966. 5th Death Centenary of Donatello.
1165 **435** 40l. multicoloured . . . 10 15

436 Europa "Ship"
437 "Madonna in Maesta" (after Giotto)

1966. Europa.
1166 **436** 40l. violet 15 15
1167 90l. blue 15 15

1966. Giotto's 700th Birth Anniv.
1168 **437** 40l. multicoloured . . . 10 10

438 Filzi, Battisti, Chiesa and Sauro

1966. 50th Death Annivs of World War I Heroes.
1169 **438** 40l. green and slate . . . 10 10

439 Postal Emblem
440 Compass and Globe

1966. Stamp Day.
1170 **439** 20l. multicoloured . . . 10 10

1967. Centenary of Italian Geographical Society.
1171 **440** 40l. blue and black . . . 10 10

441 Toscanini

1967. Birth Centenary of Arturo Toscanini (orchestral conductor).
1172 **441** 40l. buff and blue . . . 10 10

442 Campidoglio, Rome

1967. 10th Anniv of Rome Treaties.
1173 **442** 40l. brown and black . . 10 15
1174 90l. purple and black . . 10 20

443 Cogwheels
444 Brown Bear (Abruzzo Park)

1967. Europa.
1175 **443** 40l. purple and pink . . 10 10
1176 90l. blue and cream . . 10 20

1967. Italian National Parks. Multicoloured.
1177 20l. Ibex (Gran Paradiso Park) (vert) 10 10
1178 40l. Type **444** 10 10
1179 90l. Red deer stag (Stelvio Park) 10 10
1180 170l. Tree (Circeo Park) (vert) 10 20

445 Monteverdi

1967. 400th Death Anniv of Claudio Monteverdi (composer).
1181 **445** 40l. brown and chestnut 10 10

446 Racing Cyclists

1967. 50th Tour of Italy Cycle Race. Designs showing cyclists.
1182 **446** 40l. multicoloured . . . 10 10
1183 – 90l. multicoloured . . . 10 10
1184 – 500l. multicoloured . . . 45 80

447 Pirandello and Stage

1967. Birth Centenary of Luigi Pirandello (dramatist).
1185 **447** 40l. multicoloured . . . 10 10

448 Stylized Mask

1967. Two Worlds Festival, Spoleto.
1186 **448** 20l. black and green . . 10 10
1187 40l. black and red . . . 10 10

449 Coded Addresses

1967. Introduction of Postal Codes.
1188 **449** 20l. black, blue & yellow 10 10
1189 25l. black, red and yellow 10 10
1190 40l. black, purple & yell 10 10
1191 50l. black, green & yellow 10 10

450 Pomilio PE Type Biplane and Postmark
451 St. Ivo's Church, Rome

1967. 50th Anniv of 1st Airmail Stamp.
1192 **450** 40l. black and blue . . . 10 10

1967. 300th Death Anniv of Francesco Borromini (architect).
1193 **451** 90l. multicoloured . . . 10 10

452 U. Giordano and Music from "Andrea Chenier"
453 "The Oath of Pontida" (from painting by Adolfo Cao)

1967. Birth Centenary of Umberto Giordano (composer).
1194 **452** 20l. brown and black . . 10 10

1967. 800th Anniv of Oath of Pontida.
1195 **453** 20l. brown 10 10

454 I.T.Y. Emblem
455 Lions Emblem

1967. International Tourist Year.
1196 **454** 20l. black, blue and yellow 10 10
1197 50l. black, blue & orange 10 10

1967. 50th Anniv of Lions International.
1198 **455** 50l. multicoloured . . . 10 10

456 Sentry
457 E. Fermi (scientist) and Reactor

1967. 50th Anniv of Stand on the Piave.
1199 **456** 50l. multicoloured . . . 10 10

1967. 25th Anniv of 1st Nuclear Chain Reaction.
1200 **457** 50l. black and brown . . 10 10

458 Stamp and Dove

1967. Stamp Day.
1201 **458** 25l. multicoloured . . . 10 10

1968. As Nos. 887, etc (1952), size 16 × 20 mm.

1202	**286**	1l. black	10	30
1203		5l. slate	10	10
1204		6l. brown	10	30
1205		10l. red	10	10
1206		15l. violet	10	10
1207		20l. sepia	10	10
1208		25l. violet	10	10
1209		30l. brown	10	10
1210		40l. purple	10	10
1211		50l. olive	10	10
1212		55l. violet	10	10
1213		60l. blue	10	10
1214		70l. green	10	10
1215		80l. brown	10	10
1215a		90l. brown	10	10
1216		100l. brown	10	10
1216a		120l. blue and green	10	10
1216b		125l. purple and brown	10	20
1217		130l. red and grey	10	10
1217a		150l. violet	10	10
1217b		170l. green and brown	15	10
1218		180l. purple and grey	10	10
1218a		200l. blue	10	10
1219		300l. green	10	10
1219a		350l. orange, red & yell	20	20
1219b		400l. red	15	10

459 Scouts around Campfire

1968. Italian Boy Scouts.
1220 **459** 50l. multicoloured . . . 15 10

460 Europa "Key"

1968. Europa.
1221 **460** 50l. green and pink . . . 15 10
1222 90l. brown and blue . . 15 20

461 "Tending the Sick" **462** Boito and "Mephistopheles"

1968. 400th Birth Anniv of Luigi Gonzaga (St. Aloysius).
1223 **461** 25l. violet and brown . . 10 30

1968. 50th Death Anniv of Arrigo Boito (composer and librettist).
1224 **462** 50l. multicoloured . . . 10 10

463 F. Baracca and "Aerial Combat" (abstract by G. Balla) **464** Giambattista Vico (300th Birth Anniv)

1968. 500th Death Anniv of Francesco Baracca (airman of World War I).
1225 **463** 25l. multicoloured . . . 10 10

1968. Italian Philosophers' Birth Annivs.
1226 **464** 50l. blue 10 10
1227 – 50l. black 10 20
DESIGN: No. 1227, Tommaso Campanella (400th birth anniv).

465 Cycle Wheel and Stadium **467** Rossini

466 "St. Mark's Square, Venice" (Canaletto)

1968. World Road Cycling Championships.
1228 **465** 25l. blue, pink and brown 10 10
1229 – 90l. indigo, red and blue 10 20
DESIGN: 90l. Cyclists and Imola Castle.

1968. Death Bicentenary of Canaletto (painter).
1230 **466** 50l. multicoloured . . . 10 20

1968. Death Centenary of Gioacchino Rossini (composer).
1231 **467** 50l. red 10 20

468 Mobilization **469** "Conti Correnti Postali"

1968. 50th Anniv of Victory in World War I. Multicoloured.
1232 20l. Type **468** 10 10
1233 25l. Trench warfare 10 10
1234 40l. Naval forces 10 10
1235 50l. Air Force 10 10
1236 90l. Battle of Vittorio Veneto 10 10
1237 180l. Tomb of Unknown Soldier 10 15

1968. 50th Anniv of Postal Cheque Service.
1238 **469** 50l. multicoloured . . . 10 10

470 Tracking Equipment and Buildings **471** "Postal Development"

1968. Space Telecommunications Centre, Fucino.
1239 **470** 50l. multicoloured . . . 10 10

1968. Stamp Day.
1240 **471** 25l. red and yellow . . . 10 10

472 Commemorative Medal **473** Colonnade

1969. Centenary of State Audit Department.
1243 **472** 50l. black and pink . . . 10 10

1969. Europa.
1244 **473** 50l. multicoloured . . . 15 10
1245 90l. multicoloured . . . 15 20

474 Machiavelli **475** I.L.O. Emblem

1969. 500th Birth Anniv of Niccolo Machiavelli (statesman).
1246 **474** 50l. multicoloured . . . 10 10

1969. 50th Anniv of I.L.O.
1247 **475** 50l. black and green . . 10 10
1248 90l. black and red . . . 10 10

476 Postal Emblem

1969. 50th Anniv of Italian Philatelic Federation.
1249 **476** 50l. multicoloured . . . 10 30

477 Sondrio-Tirano Mailcoach of 1903

1969. Stamp Day.
1250 **477** 25l. blue 10 10

478 Skiing

1970. World Skiing Championships, Val Gardena. Multicoloured.
1251 50l. Type **478** 10 20
1252 90l. Dolomites 10 10

479 "Galatea" (detail of fresco by Raphael)

1970. 450th Death Anniv of Raphael. Mult.
1253 20l. Type **479** 10 10
1254 50l. "Madonna of the Goldfinch" 10 10

480 Symbols of Flight

1970. 50th Anniv of Rome–Tokyo Flight by A. Ferrarin.
1255 **480** 50l. multicoloured . . . 10 10
1256 90l. multicoloured . . . 10 10

481 "Flaming Sun" **482** Erasmo da Narni (from statue by Donatello)

1970. Europa.
1257 **481** 50l. yellow and red . . . 15 10
1258 90l. yellow and green . . 15 20

1970. 600th Birth Anniv of Erasmo da Narni "Il Gattamelata" (condottiere).
1259 **482** 50l. green 10 10

483 Running

1970. World University Games, Turin. Mult.
1260 20l. Type **483** 10 10
1261 180l. Swimming 10 20

484 Dr. Montessori and children

1970. Birth Centenary of Dr. Maria Montessori (educationist).
1262 **484** 50l. multicoloured . . . 10 10

485 Map and Cavour's Declaration

1970. Centenary of Union of Rome and Papal States with Italy.
1263 **485** 50l. multicoloured . . . 10 10

486 Loggia of Campanile, St. Mark's Square, Venice

1970. 400th Death Anniv of Jacopo Tatti, "Il Sansovino" (architect).
1264 **486** 50l. brown 10 10

487 "Garibaldi at Dijon" (engraving)

1970. Centenary of Garibaldi's Participation in Franco-Prussian War.
1265 **487** 20l. grey and blue . . . 10 10
1266 50l. purple and blue . . 10 20

488 U.N. Emblem within Tree **489** Rotary Emblem

1970. 25th Anniv of United Nations.
1267 **488** 25l. green, black & brown 10 20
1268 90l. yellow, black and blue 10 20

1970. 65th Anniv of Rotary International.
1269 **489** 25l. ultramarine, yell & bl 10 10
1270 90l. ultramarine, yell & bl 10 20

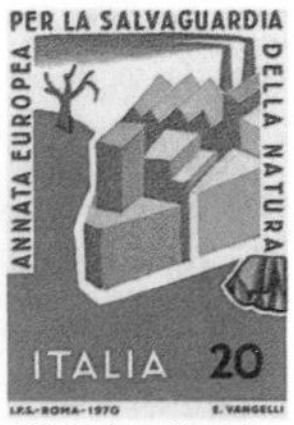

490 Telephone Dial and "Network"   **491** Urban Complex and Tree

1970. Completion of Telephone Trunk-dialling System.
1271 **490** 25l. green and red . . . 10 10
1272 90l. blue and red 10 10

1970. Nature Conservation Year.
1273 **491** 20l. red and green . . . 10 10
1274 25l. grey and green . . . 10 10

492 Electric Locomotive "Tartaruga"   **493** "The Adoration" (F. Lippi)

1970. Stamp Day.
1275 **492** 25l. black 10 20

1970. Christmas. Multicoloured.
1276 25l. Type **493** (postage) . . 10 10
1277 150l. "The Adoration of the Magi" (Gentile da Fabriano) (44 × 35 mm) (air) 10 30

494 Saverio Mercadante

1970. Death Centenary of Saverio Mercadante (composer).
1278 **494** 25l. violet and grey . . . 10 10

495 "Mercury" (part of Cellini's "Perseus with the Head of Medusa")   **496** Bramante's "Little Temple", St. Peter's Montorio, Rome

1971. 400th Death Anniv of Benvenuto Cellini (goldsmith and sculptor).
1279 **495** 50l. blue 10 10

1971.
1280 **496** 50l. black and brown . . 10 10

497 Adenauer, Schuman and De Gasperi

1971. 20th Anniv of European Coal and Steel Community.
1281 **497** 50l. brown, black & grn 10 20
1282 90l. brown, black and red 10 10

498 Europa Chain   **499** Mazzini

1971. Europa.
1283 **498** 50l. red 15 10
1284 90l. purple 15 10

1971. 25th Anniv of Republic.
1285 **499** 50l. multicoloured . . . 10 30
1286 90l. multicoloured . . . 10 10

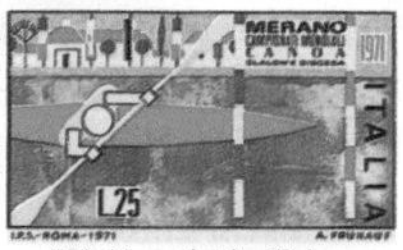

500 Canoeist in Slalom

1971. World Canoeing Slalom and Free Descent Championships, Merano. Multicoloured.
1287 25l. Type **500** 10 10
1288 90l. Canoeist making free descent 10 10

501 Three Sports

1971. Youth Games.
1289 **501** 20l. black, green & brn 10 10
1290 – 50l. black, violet & orge 10 10
DESIGN: 50l. Four other sports.

502 Alitalia Emblem

1971. 25th Anniv of Alitalia State Airline. Multicoloured.
1291 50l. Type **502** 10 10
1292 90l. Emblem and Globe . . 10 10
1293 150l. Tailplane of Boeing 747 . . . . 10 20

503 Grazia Deledda   **504** Boy in "Savings" Barrel

1971. Birth Cent of Grazia Deledda (writer).
1294 **503** 50l. black and brown . . 10 10

1971. Postal Savings Bank.
1295 **504** 25l. multicoloured . . . 10 20
1296 50l. multicoloured . . . 10 10

1971. Air. As No. 911 but smaller, 20 × 36 mm.
1297 **204** 100l. green 15 25

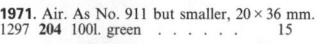

505 UNICEF Emblem and Paper Dolls

1971. 25th Anniv of UNICEF. Multicoloured.
1301 25l. Type **505** 10 10
1302 90l. Children acclaiming UNICEF emblem 10 20

506 Liner "Tirrenia"

1971. Stamp Day.
1303 **506** 25l. green 10 20

507 "The Nativity"

1971. Christmas. Miniatures from "Matilda's Evangelarium", Nonantola Abbey, Modena. Multicoloured.
1304 25l. Type **507** 10 20
1305 90l. "The Adoration of the Magi" 10 10

508 G. Verga and Sicilian Cart

1972. 50th Death Anniv of Giovanni Verga (writer).
1306 **508** 25l. multicoloured . . . 10 10
1307 50l. multicoloured . . . 10 10

509 G. Mazzini   **510** Stylized Flags

1972. Death Cent of Giuseppe Mazzini (statesman).
1308 **509** 25l. green and black . . 10 20
1309 90l. grey and black . . . 10 10
1310 150l. red and black . . . 10 10

1972. 50th International Fair, Milan.
1311 **510** 25l. green and black . . 10 20
1312 – 50l. red and black . . . 10 10
1313 – 90l. blue and black . . . 10 10
DESIGNS: 50l. "Windows, stand and pavilions" (abstract); 90l. Abstract general view of Fair.

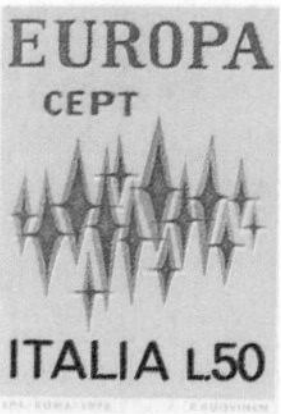

511 "Communications"   **512** Alpine Soldier

1972. Europa.
1314 **511** 50l. multicoloured . . . 15 30
1315 90l. multicoloured . . . 15 30

1972. Centenary of Alpine Corps. Multicoloured.
1316 25l. Type **512** 10 10
1317 50l. Soldier's hat 10 30
1318 90l. Soldier and mountains 10 10

513 Brenta Mountains

1972. Centenary of Tridentine Alpinists Society. Multicoloured.
1319 25l. Type **513** 10 30
1320 50l. Alpinist 10 10
1321 180l. Mt. Crozzon 10 30

514 Diagram of Conference Hall

1972. 60th Interparliamentary Union Conference, Rome.
1322 **514** 50l. multicoloured . . . 10 10
1323 90l. multicoloured . . . 10 10

515 "St. Peter Damiani" (miniature, after G. di Paolo)   **516** "The Three Graces" (Canova)

1972. 900th Death Anniv of St. Peter Damiani.
1324 **515** 50l. multicoloured . . . 10 10

1972. 150th Death Anniv of Antonio Canova (sculptor).
1325 **516** 50l. green 10 10

517 Initial and First Verse (Foligno edition)

1972. 500th Anniv of "The Divine Comedy". Multicoloured.
1326 50l. Type **517** 10 10
1327 90l. Initial and first verse (Mantua edition) (vert) . . 10 10
1328 180l. Initial and first verse ("Jesino" edition) 10 20

518 "Angel"

1972. Christmas. Multicoloured.
1329 20l. Type **518** 10 10
1330 25l. "Holy Child in Crib" (horiz) 10 10
1331 150l. "Angel" (looking to left) 10 30

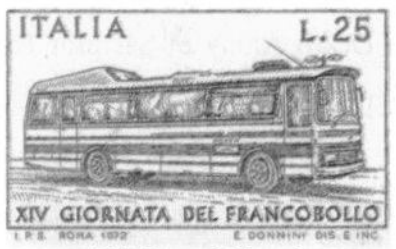

519 Postal Coach

1972. Stamp Day.
1332 **519** 25l. red 10 30

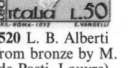

520 L. B. Alberti (from bronze by M. de Pasti, Louvre)   **521** L. Perosi

1972. 500th Death Anniv of Leon B. Alberti (writer and savant).
1333 **520** 50l. blue and yellow . . 10 30

1972. Birth Centenary of Lorenzo Perosi (composer and priest).
1334 **521** 50l. brown and yellow 10 10
1335 90l. black and green . . 10 10

522 Don Orione   **523** Oceanic Survey

1972. Birth Centenary of Don Orione (child-welfare pioneer).
1336 **522** 50l. blue and turquoise 10 10
1337 90l. green and yellow . . 10 10

1973. Centenary of Military Marine Institute of Hydrography.
1338 **523** 50l. multicoloured . . . 10 10

524 Grand Staircase, Royal Palace, Caserta

1973. Death Bicentenary of Luigi Vanvitelli (architect).
1339 **524** 25l. green 10 30

525 Schiavoni Shore

1973. "Save Venice" Campaign. Multicoloured.
1340 20l. Type **525** 10 10
1341 25l. "The Tetrarchs" (sculpture) (vert) 10 10
1342 50l. "The Triumph of Venice" (V. Carpaccio) 10 10
1343 90l. Bronze horses, St. Mark's Basilica (vert) 10 10
1344 300l. Piazetta S. Marco . . 20 45

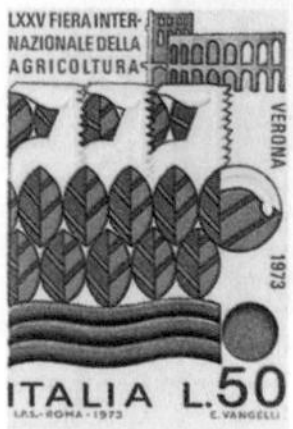

526 Fair Theme

527 Title-page of "Diverse Figure"

1973. 75th Int Agricultural Fair, Verona.
1345 **526** 50l. multicoloured . . . 10 10

1973. 300th Death Anniv of Salvator Rosa (painter and poet).
1346 **527** 25l. black and orange . . 10 10

528 Formation of Fiat PAN Acrobatic Jet Aircraft

1973. 50th Anniv of Military Aviation. Mult.
1349 20l. Type **528** (postage) . . 10 10
1350 25l. Formation of Savoia Marchetti S-55X flying boats 10 10
1351 50l. Fiat G-91Y jet fighters on patrol 10 10
1352 90l. Fiat CR-32 biplanes performing aerobatics . . 10 30
1353 180l. Caproni Campini N-1 jet airplane 10 30
1354 150l. Lockheed F-104S Starfighter over Aeronautical Academy, Pozzuoli (air) 10 30

529 Football and Pitch

530 A. Manzoni (after F. Hayez)

1973. 75th Anniv of Italian Football Association. Multicoloured.
1355 25l. Type **529** 10 30
1356 90l. Players in goalmouth 35 40

1973. Death Centenary of Alessandro Manzoni (writer and politician).
1357 **530** 25l. brown and black . . 10 30

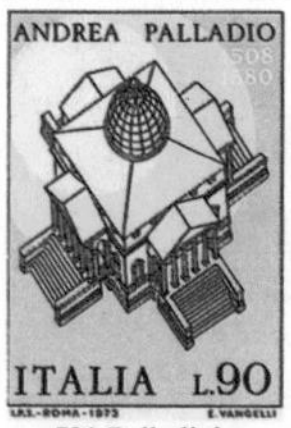

531 Palladio's "Rotunda", Vicenza

532 Spring and Cogwheels

1973. Andrea Palladio Commemoration.
1358 **531** 90l. multicoloured . . . 10 10

1973. 50th Anniv of Italian State Supplies Office.
1359 **532** 50l. multicoloured . . . 10 10

533 Europa "Posthorn"

1973. Europa.
1360 **533** 50l. gold, lilac and yellow 15 10
1361 90l. gold, green & yellow 15 10

534 "Catcher" and Baseball Field

1973. 1st Intercontinental Baseball Cup. Mult.
1362 25l. Type **534** 10 30
1363 90l. "Striker" and baseball field 10 10

535 Carnival Setting

536 "Argenta Episode"

1973. Viareggio Carnival.
1364 **535** 25l. multicoloured . . . 10 10

1973. 50th Death Anniv of Don Giovanni Minzoni (military chaplain).
1365 **536** 50l. multicoloured . . . 10 10

537 G. Salvemini

538 Farnese Palace, Caprorola

1973. Birth Centenary of Gaetano Salvemini (political historian).
1366 **537** 50l. multicoloured . . . 10 10

1973. 400th Birth Anniv of "Vignola" (Jacopa Barozzi—architect).
1367 **538** 90l. purple and yellow 10 10

539 "St. John the Baptist"

540 Leaning Tower of Pisa

1973. 400th Birth Anniv of Caravaggio (painter).
1368 **539** 25l. black and yellow . . 10 10

1973. Tourism.
1369 **540** 50l. multicoloured . . . 10 10

541 Botticelli

542 Immacolatella Fountain, Naples

1973. Italian Painters (1st series).
1370 **541** 50l. brown and red . . . 10 10
1371 – 50l. blue and brown . . 10 10
1372 – 50l. green and emerald 10 10
1373 – 50l. black and red . . . 10 10
1374 – 50l. brown and blue . . 10 10
PAINTERS: No. 1371, Piranesi; No. 1372, Veronese; No. 1373, Verrocchio; No. 1374, Tiepolo.
See also Nos. 1392/6, 1456/61, 1495/9 and 1518/22.

1973. Italian Fountains (1st series). Mult.
1375 25l. Type **542** 10 20
1376 25l. Trevi Fountain, Rome 10 20
1377 25l. Pretoria Fountain, Palermo 10 20
See also Nos. 1418/20, 1453/5, 1503/5, 1529/31, 1570/2 and 1618/20.

543 "Angels"

544 Map and Emblems

1973. Christmas. Sculptures by A. di Duccio.
1378 **543** 20l. black and green . . 10 10
1379 – 25l. black and blue . . . 10 10
1380 – 150l. black and yellow 10 30
DESIGNS: 25l. "Virgin and Child"; 150l. "Angels" (different).

1973. 50th Anniv of Italian Rotary.
1381 **544** 50l. blue, green and red 10 10

545 Sud Aviation Super Caravelle 12

546 Military Medal for Valour

1973. Stamp Day.
1382 **545** 25l. blue 10 30

1973. 150th Anniv of Holders of the Gold Medal for Military Valour Organisation.
1383 **546** 50l. multicoloured . . . 10 10

547 Caruso as Duke of Mantua in Verdi's "Rigoletto"

548 "Christ crowning King Roger" (Martorana Church, Palermo)

1973. Birth Centenary of Enrico Caruso (operatic tenor).
1384 **547** 50l. red 10 20

1974. Norman Art in Sicily. Mosaics.
1385 **548** 20l. blue and yellow . . 10 20
1386 – 50l. red and green . . 10 10
DESIGN: 50l. "King William offering Church to the Virgin Mary" (Monreale Cathedral).

549 Pres. L. Einaudi

550 G. Marconi in Headphones

1974. Birth Centenary of Luigi Einaudi (President 1948–55).
1387 **549** 50l. green 10 10

1974. Birth Centenary of Guglielmo Marconi (radio pioneer).
1388 **550** 50l. brown and green . . 10 10
1389 – 90l. multicoloured . . . 10 30
DESIGN: 90l. Marconi and world map.

551 "David" (Bernini)

552 Guards from Lombardy-Venetia (1848), Sardinian Marines (1815) and Tebro Battalion (1849)

1974. Europa. Sculptures. Multicoloured.
1390 50l. Type **551** 15 10
1391 90l. "Spirit of Victory" (Michelangelo) 15 20

1974. Italian Painters (2nd series). As T **541**.
1392 50l. blue and green 10 15
1393 50l. brown and blue 10 15
1394 50l. black and red 10 15
1395 50l. brown and yellow . . . 10 15
1396 50l. blue and brown 10 15
PORTRAITS: No. 1392, Borromini; No. 1393, Carriera; No. 1394, Giambellino (Giovanni Bellini); No. 1395, Mantegna; No. 1396, Raphael.

1974. Bicentenary of Italian Excise Guards. Uniforms. Multicoloured.
1397 40l. Sardinian chasseurs, 1774 and 1795, and Royal Fusilier of 1817 . . . . . 10 20
1398 50l. Type **552** 10 10
1399 90l. Lieutenant (1866), Sergeant-major of Marines (1892) and guard (1880) 10 20
1400 180l. Helicopter pilot, naval and alpine guards of 1974 10 20

553 Feather Headdress

1974. 50th Anniv of National Bersaglieri Association. Multicoloured.
1401 40l. Type **553** 10 10
1402 50l. Bersaglieri emblem on rosette 10 10

554 Running

1974. European Athletics Championships, Rome. Multicoloured.
1403 40l. Type **554** 10 10
1404 50l. Pole vaulting 10 10

555 Francesco Petrarch

1974. 600th Death Anniv of Francesco Petrarch (poet and scholar).
1405 **555** 40l. multicoloured . . . 10 20
1406 – 50l. blue, yellow & brown 10 20
DESIGN: 50l. Petrarch at work in his study.

556 Portofino

1974. Tourist Publicity (1st series). Mult.
1407 40l. Type **556** 10 20
1408 40l. Gradara 10 20
See also Nos. 1442/4, 1473/5, 1513/14, 1515/17, 1543/5, 1596/9, 1642/5, 1722/5, 1762/5, 1806/9, 1845/8, 1877/80, 1917/20, 1963/6, 1992/5, 2031/4, 2088/91, 2115/18, 2165/8, 2212/15, 2248/51, 2315/16, 2365/8, 2425/8, 2486/9, 2550/3, 2661/4, 2752/5 and 2872/4.

557 Tommaseo's Statue, Sebenico

558 Giacomo Puccini

1974. Death Centenary of Niccolo Tommaseo (writer).
1409 **557** 50l. green and pink . . . 10 10

1974. 50th Death Anniv of Giacomo Puccini (composer).
1410 **558** 40l. multicoloured . . . 10 10

559 Cover Engraving of Ariosto's "Orlando Furioso"

560 Commemoration Tablet (Quotation from Varrone's "Menippean Satire")

1974. 500th Birth Anniv of Ludovico Ariosto (poet).
1411 **559** 50l. blue and red 10 10

1974. 2000th Death Anniv of Marco Varrone (Varrone Reatino) (author).
1412 **560** 50l. lake, red and yellow 10 10

561 "The Month of October" (detail from 15th-century mural)

1974. 14th International Wine Congress.
1413 **561** 50l. multicoloured . . . 10 10

562 "U.P.U." and Emblem

1974. Centenary of Universal Postal Union. Mult.
1414 50l. Type **562** 10 10
1415 90l. "U.P.U." emblem and letters 10 10

563 "The Triumph of St. Thomas Aquinas" (detail—F. Traini)

564 Detail of Bas-relief, Ara Pacis

1974. 700th Death Anniv of St. Thomas Aquinas.
1416 **563** 50l. multicoloured . . . 10 10

1974. Centenary of Italian Order of Advocates.
1417 **564** 50l. black, green & brown 10 10

1974. Italian Fountains (2nd series). As T **542** Multicoloured.
1418 40l. Oceanus Fountain, Florence 10 20
1419 40l. Neptune Fountain, Bologna 10 20
1420 40l. Maggiore Fountain, Perugia 10 20

565 "The Adoration" (Presepe di Greccio)

1974. Christmas.
1421 **565** 40l. multicoloured . . . 10 10

566 Pulcinella

567 "God admonishing Adam" (Jacopo della Quercia (sculptor) (1374–1438))

1974. Children's Comic Characters. Mult.
1422 40l. Type **566** 10 10
1423 50l. Clowns 10 10
1424 90l. Pantaloon from Bisognosi 10 10

1974. Italian Artists' Anniversaries (1st series).
1425 **567** 90l. violet 10 20
1426 – 90l. multicoloured . . . 10 20
DESIGN: No. 1426, Uffizi Gallery, Florence (Giorgio Vasari (architect and painter) (1511–1574)).
See also Nos. 1445/6, 1480/2, 1523/4, 1564/5, 1593/4, 1699/1700, 1731/2, 1774/5, 1824/5, 1885/6, 1949/50 and 1987.

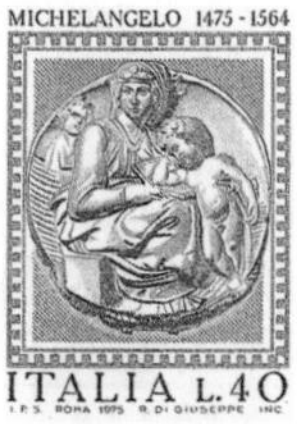

568 "Angel with Tablet"

569 "Pitti Madonna"

1975. Holy Year. Multicoloured.
1427 40l. Type **568** 10 10
1428 50l. Angel with column . . 10 10
1429 90l. Bridge of the Holy Angels, Rome (49 × 40 mm) 10 20
1430 150l. Angel with crown of thorns 10 10
1431 180l. Angel with cross . . . 10 20

1975. 500th Birth Anniv of Michelangelo.
1432 **569** 40l. green 10 10
1433 – 50l. brown 10 10
1434 – 90l. red 10 20
DESIGNS: 50l. Sculptured niche, Vatican Palace; 90l. Detail from fresco "Flood of the Universe" (Sistine Chapel).

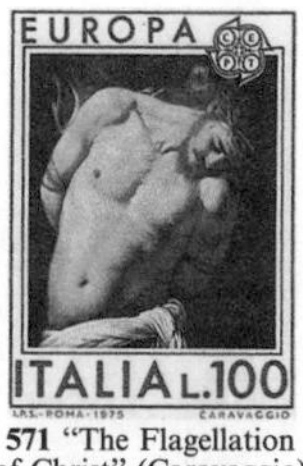

570 "The Four Days of Naples" (M. Mazzacurati)

571 "The Flagellation of Christ" (Caravaggio)

1975. 30th Anniv of Italian Resistance Movement. Resistance Monuments. Multicoloured.
1435 70l. Type **570** 10 20
1436 100l. "Martyrs of the Ardeatine Caves" (F. Coccia) 10 10
1437 150l. "The Resistance Fighters of Cuneo" (U. Mastroianni) 10 20

1975. Europa. Paintings. Multicoloured.
1438 100l. Type **571** 20 10
1439 150l. "The Appearance of the Angel to Agar and Ishmael in the Desert" (Tiepolo) 20 10

572 Globe and Emblems

1975. International Women's Year.
1440 **572** 70l. multicoloured . . . 10 10

573 "San Marco III" (satellite) and "Santa Rita" (marine launching pad)

574 Cover Engraving from Palestrina's "Primo Libro delle Messe"

1975. Italian Space Project.
1441 **573** 70l. multicoloured . . . 10 10

1975. Tourist Publicity (2nd series). As T **556**. Multicoloured.
1442 150l. Cefalu 10 20
1443 150l. Isola Bella 10 20
1444 150l. Montecatini Terme . . 10 20

1975. Italian Artists' Annivs (2nd series). As T **567**. Multicoloured.
1445 90l. "Flora" (Guido Reni (1575–1642)) 10 20
1446 90l. "Artist and Model" (Armando Spadini (1883–1925)) 10 20

1975. 450th Birth Anniv of Giovanni Pierluigi da Palestrina (composer).
1447 **574** 100l. purple and brown 10 20

575 Boat in Harbour

1975. Italian Emigration.
1448 **575** 70l. multicoloured . . . 10 20

576 Notoriat Emblem

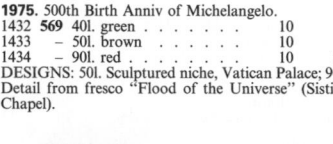

1975. Centenary of Unification of Italian Laws.
1449 **576** 100l. mauve, stone & blue 10 10

577 Railway Steam Locomotive Driving-wheels

1975. 21st International Railway Congress, Bologna.
1450 **577** 70l. multicoloured . . . 10 10

578 "D'Acquisto's Sacrifice" (Vittorio Pisani)

1975. 32nd Death Anniv of Salvo d'Acquisto (carabiniere who sacrificed himself to save 22 hostages).
1451 **578** 100l. multicoloured . . . 10 10

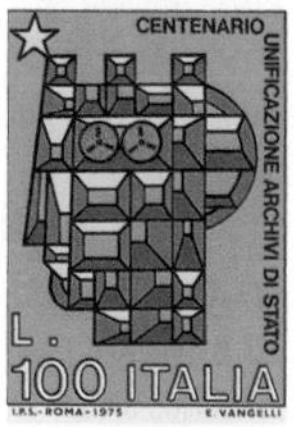

579 Symbolised Head representing Files

581 "Annunciation to the Shepherds"

1975. Centenary of State Archives Unification.
1452 **579** 100l. multicoloured . . . 10 10

1975. Italian Fountains (3rd series). As T **542**. Multicoloured.
1453 70l. Rosello Fountain, Sassari 10 20
1454 70l. 99 Channel Fountain, L'Aquila 10 20
1455 70l. Piazza Fountain, Milan 10 20

1975. Italian Composers. As T **541**.
1456 100l. blue, pink and red . . 10 10
1457 100l. blue, green & deep green 10 10
1458 100l. green, brown & dp brn 10 10
1459 100l. brown, red and lake 10 10
1460 100l. purple, grey and green 10 10
1461 100l. black, lt yellow & yellow 10 10
DESIGNS: No. 1456, Ferruccio Busoni; 1457, Alessandro Scarlatti; 1458, Francesco Cilea; 1459, Antonio Vivaldi; 1460, Franco Alfa; No. 1461, Gaspare Spontini.

1975. Christmas. Alatri Cathedral Carvings. Multicoloured.
1462 70l. Type **581** 10 20
1463 100l. "The Nativity" 10 10
1464 150l. "Annunciation to the Kings" 10 20

582 "Children on Horseback"

1975. Stamp Day. Children's Stories. Mult.
1465 70l. Type **582** 10 10
1466 100l. "The Magic Orchard" (vert) 10 10
1467 150l. "Church Procession" 10 20

583 "Boccaccio" (from fresco by A. del Castagno)

1975. 600th Death Anniv of Giovanni Boccaccio. Multicoloured.
1468 100l. Type **583** 10 10
1469 150l. Cover engraving from Boccaccio's "Fiammetta" 10 20

584 Entrance to State Advocate's Office

585 "Italia 1976" Emblem

1976. Centenary of State Advocate's Office.
1470 **584** 150l. multicoloured . . . 10 10

1976. "Italia 76" International Stamp Exhibition, Milan (1st issue).
1471 **585** 150l. red, green and black 10 20
1472 – 180l. multicoloured . . . 10 20
DESIGN: 180l. Exhibition Hall, Milan.
See also Nos. 1487/91.

1976. Tourist Publicity (3rd series). As T **556**. Multicoloured.
1473 150l. Fenis Castle, Aosta . . 10 20
1474 150l. Forio Ischia 10 20
1475 150l. Itria Valley 10 20

586 Majolica Plate

587 Republican Flags

1976. Europa. Italian Crafts. Multicoloured.
1476 150l. Type **586** 20 10
1477 180l. Vase in form of woman's head 20 20

1976. 30th Anniv of Republic. Multicoloured.
1478 100l. Type **587** 10 10
1479 150l. Statesmen 10 10

588 "Fortitude" (Giacomo Serpotta) (1656–1732)

1976. Italian Artists' Annivs (3rd series).
1480 **588** 150l. blue 10 10
1481 – 150l. multicoloured . . . 10 20
1482 – 150l. black and red . . . 10 10
DESIGNS: No. 1481, "Woman at Table" (Umberto Boccioni (1882–1916)); 1482, "Gunner's Letter from the Front" (Filippo Tommaso Marinetti (1876–1944)).

589 "The Dragon"

1976. 450th Death Anniv of Vittore Carpaccio (painter).
1483 **589** 150l. red 15 20
1484 – 150l. red 15 20
DESIGN: No. 1484, "St. George".
Nos. 1483/4 form Carpaccio's "St. George and the Dragon".

590 "Flora" (Titian)

1976. 400th Death Anniv of Titian.
1485 **590** 150l. red 10 20

591 St. Francis (13th-century fresco)

592 "Cursus Publicus" Post Cart

1976. 750th Death Anniv of St. Francis of Assisi.
1486 **591** 150l. brown & lt brown 10 10

1976. "Italia 76" International Stamp Exhibition, Milan (2nd issue).
1487 **592** 70l. black, grey and blue 10 20
1488 – 100l. black, grey & yellow 10 10
1489 – 150l. black, grey & brown 10 20
1490 – 200l. multicoloured . . . 10 10
1491 – 400l. multicoloured . . . 15 40
DESIGNS: 100l. Emblem of Royal Sardinian Posts; 150l. 19th-century "Lion's head" letterbox; 200l. Early cancelling machine; 400l. Modern letter-coding machine.

593 Girl with "Protective Umbrella" and Animals

1976. Stamp Day. Nature Protection. Multicoloured.
1492 40l. Type **593** 10 10
1493 100l. "Protective scarf" . . 10 10
1494 150l. Doctor with bandaged tree 10 10

1976. Italian Painters (3rd series). As T **541**.
1495 170l. green, yellow and red 10 10
1496 170l. black, turquoise & green 10 10
1497 170l. black, purple and mauve 10 10
1498 170l. brown, lavender & violet 10 10
1499 170l. black and brown . . . 10 10
DESIGNS: No. 1495, Carlo Dolci; 1496, Lorenzo Ghiberti (sculptor); 1497, Domenico Ghirlandaio; 1498, Giovanni Piazzetta; 1499, "Sassoferrato" (Giovanni Salvi).

594 "The Visit" (S. Lega)

1976. 150th Birth Anniv of Silvestro Lega (painter).
1500 **594** 170l. multicoloured . . . 10 10

595 "Adoration of the Magi" (Bartolo di Fredi)

596 Net of Serpents obscuring the Sun

1976. Christmas. Multicoloured.
1501 70l. Type **595** 10 20
1502 120l. "The Nativity" (Taddao Gaddi) 10 20

1976. Italian Fountains (4th series). As T **542** Multicoloured.
1503 170l. Antique Fountain, Gallipoli 10 20
1504 170l. Erbe Madonna Fountain, Verona 10 20
1505 170l. Fountain of Palazzo Doria, Gerona 10 20

1977. Campaign against Drug Abuse. Mult.
1506 120l. Type **596** 10 10
1507 170l. "Addict" and poppy 10 10

597 Igniting Explosives

1977. 300th Birth Anniv of Pietro Micca (national hero).
1508 **597** 170l. multicoloured . . . 10 10

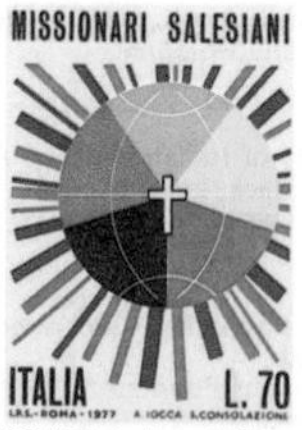

598 "Globe" and Cross

1977. Salesian Missionaries. Multicoloured.
1509 70l. Type **598** 10 20
1510 120l. St. John Bosco and "United people" 10 20

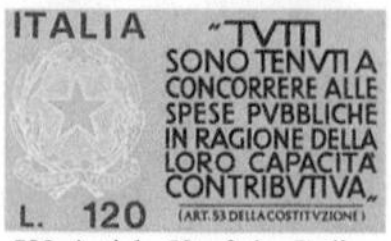

599 Article 53 of the Italian Constitution

1977. "Encouragement to Taxpayers".
1511 **599** 120l. black, brn & stone 10 10
1512 170l. black, olive & green 10 10

1977. Europa. As T **556** but with C.E.P.T. emblem. Multicoloured.
1513 170l. Mount Etna 25 20
1514 200l. Castel del Monte . . . 25 20

1977. Tourist Publicity (4th series). As T **556**. Multicoloured.
1515 170l. Canossa Castle 10 20
1516 170l. Castellana Grotto . . 10 20
1517 170l. Fermo 10 20

1977. Famous Italians. As T **541**.
1518 70l. brown, green & dp green 10 20
1519 70l. black, blue and green 10 20
1520 70l. brown, yellow & lt brown 10 20
1521 70l. blue, pink and red . . . 10 20
1522 70l. black, brown & dp brown 10 20
DESIGNS: No. 1518, Filippo Brunelleschi (architect); 1519, Pietro Aretino (satirist); 1520, Carlo Goldoni (dramatist); 1521, Luigi Cherubini (composer); 1522, Edoardo Bassini (surgeon).

1977. Italian Artists' Anniversaries (4th series). As T **567** Multicoloured.
1523 170l. "Winter" (G. Arcimboldi (c. 1527–93)) 10 10
1524 170l. "Justice" (Andrea Delitio (15th century)) . . 10 20

601 Paddle-steamer "Ferdinando Primo"

1977. Italian Ship-building (1st series). Multicoloured.
1525 170l. Type **601** 15 30
1526 170l. Sail corvette "Carracciolo" 15 30
1527 170l. Liner "Saturnia" . . . 15 30
1528 170l. Hydrofoil missile boat "Sparviero" 15 30
See also Nos. 1552/5, 1621/4 and 1691/4.

1977. Italian Fountains (5th series). As T **542**. Multicoloured.
1529 120l. Pacassi Fountain, Gorizia 10 20
1530 120l. Fraterna Fountain, Isernia 10 20
1531 120l. Palma Fountain, Palmi 10 20

602 Handball

604 Quintino Sella and 1863 1l. Stamps

603 "Pulse"

1977. Stamp Day. "Leisure Time". Multicoloured.
1532 120l. Type **602** 10 10
1533 120l. Catching butterflies . . 10 10
1534 120l. Kites 10 10

1977. "Give Blood". Multicoloured.
1535 70l. Type **603** 10 20
1536 120l. "Transfusion" 10 10

1977. 150th Birth Anniv of Quintino Sella (statesman).
1537 **604** 170l. green and brown 10 10

605 Dina Galli

607 La Scala Opera House

606 "Adoration of the Shepherds" (P. Testa)

1977. Birth Centenary of Dina Galli (actress).
1538 **605** 170l. multicoloured . . . 10 10

1977. Christmas.
1539 **606** 70l. black and green . . 10 20
1540 – 120l. black and green . . 10 20
DESIGN: 120l. "The Adoration of the Shepherds" (J. Caraglio).

1978. Bicentenary of La Scala Opera House.
1541 170l. Type **607** 15 20
1542 200l. Theatre interior . . . 20 20

1978. Tourist Publicity (5th series). As T **556**. Multicoloured.
1543 70l. Gubbio 10 30
1544 200l. Udine 10 20
1545 600l. Paestum 35 40

608 Dusky Grouper

1978. Environmental Protection. Mediterranean Fauna. Multicoloured.
1546 170l. Type **608** 25 20
1547 170l. Leathery turtle 25 20
1548 170l. Mediterranean monk seal 25 20
1549 170l. Audouin's gull 25 20

609 Maschio Angioino Castle, Naples

1978. Europa. Multicoloured.
1550 170l. Type **609** 20 20
1551 200l. Pantheon, Rome . . . 30 20

1978. Italian Ship-building (2nd series). As T **601**. Multicoloured.
1552 170l. Brigantine "Fortuna" 30 30
1553 170l. Cruiser "Benedetto Brin" 30 30
1554 170l. Frigate "Lupo" . . . 30 30
1555 170l. Container ship "Africa" 30 30

610 Matilde Serao (writer)

611 First and Last Paragraphs of Constitution

1978. Famous Italians.
1556 **610** 170l. black and red . . . 15 20
1557 – 170l. brown and blue . . 15 20
1558 – 170l. blue and pale blue 15 20
1559 – 170l. black and green . . 15 20
1560 – 170l. brown and green 15 20
1561 – 170l. blue and red . . . 15 20
DESIGNS: No. 1557, Vittorino da Feltre (scientist); No. 1558, Victor Emmanuel II; No. 1559, Pope Pius IX; No. 1560, Marcello Malpighi (biologist); No. 1561, Antonio Meucci (telephone pioneer).
See also Nos. 1600/4.

1978. 30th Anniv of Constitution.
1562 **611** 170l. multicoloured . . . 15 20

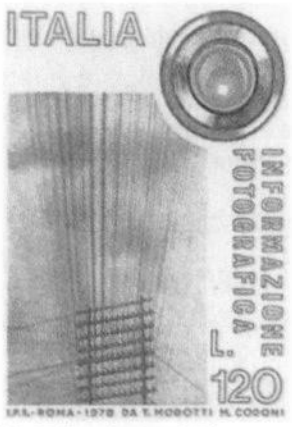

612 Telephone Wires and Lens

1978. Photographic Information.
1563 **612** 120l. grey, blue and green 10 20

1978. Italian Artists' Annivs (5th series). As T **567**. Multicoloured.
1564 170l. "The Ivy" (Tranquillo Cremona, 1837–78) . . . 25 20
1565 520l. "The Cook" (Bernardo Strozzi, 1581–1644) . . . 70 90

613 The Holy Shroud of Turin

1978. 400th Anniv of Translation of the Holy Shroud from Savoy to Turin.
1566 **613** 220l. yellow, black & red 20 20

614 Volleyball Players

615 Detail from "St. Peter distributing Ananias's Silver"

1978. World Volleyball Championships.
1567 **614** 80l. black, red and blue 15 20
1568 – 120l. black, blue & orge 15 20
DESIGN: 120l. Players with ball.

1978. 550th Death Anniv of Tommaso Guidi (Masaccio).
1569 **615** 170l. blue 10 10

1978. Italian Fountains (6th series). As T **542**. Multicoloured.
1570 120l. Neptune Fountain, Trento 10 20
1571 120l. Fountain of Fortune, Fano 10 20
1572 120l. Cavallina Fountain, Genzano di Lucania . . . 10 20

616 "Madonna and Child" (Giorgione)

617 "Flowers"

1978. Christmas.
1573 **616** 80l. red and brown . . . 10 20
1574 – 120l. multicoloured . . . 10 20
DESIGN—HORIZ (48 × 27 mm): 120l. "Adoration of the Magi" (Giorgione).

1978. Stamp Day. United Europe. Mult.
1575 120l. Type **617** 10 20
1576 120l. Flags and ribbon . . . 10 20
1577 120l. Figures raising globe inscribed "E" 10 20

618

619 State Polygraphic Institute

1978.
1578 **618** 1500l. multicoloured . . 35 10
1579 2000l. multicoloured . . 45 10
1580 3000l. multicoloured . . 1·20 10
1581 4000l. multicoloured . . 1·50 20
1582 5000l. multicoloured . . 2·10 25
1583 10000l. multicoloured . . 3·50 1·20
1584 20000l. multicoloured . . 7·50 6·00

1979. 50th Anniv of State Polygraphic Institute. Multicoloured.
1588 170l. Type **619** 20 20
1589 220l. Printing press 10 15

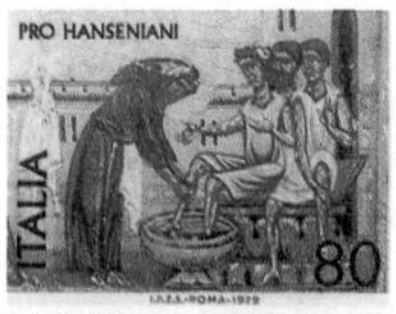

620 "St. Francis washing the Feet of a Leper" (Maestro di Francesco Bardi)

1979. Leprosy Relief.
1590 **620** 80l. multicoloured . . . 10 15

621 Cyclist carrying Bicycle

622 Albert Einstein

1979. World Cyclo-cross Championships.
1591 **621** 170l. multicoloured . . . 10 15
1592 220l. multicoloured . . . 15 15

1979. Italian Artists' Annivs (6th series). As T **567**. Multicoloured.
1593 170l. "Annunciation" (Antonella da Messina c. 1430–79) . . . 20 15
1594 520l. "Field with Haystack" (Ardengo Soffici 1879–1964) . . . . 75 1·10

1979. Birth Centenary of Albert Einstein (physicist).
1595 **622** 120l. purple, grey & bl 10 15

1979. Tourist Publicity (6th series). As T **556**. Multicoloured.
1596 70l. Asiago 10 30
1597 90l. Castelsardo, Sardinia 10 20
1598 170l. Orvieto 15 15
1599 220l. Scilla 20 15

1979. Famous Italians. As T **610**.
1600 170l. brown, blue and black 10 15
1601 170l. green, yellow and violet 10 15
1602 170l. blue and pink 10 15
1603 170l. brown and ochre . . . 10 15
1604 170l. mauve, brown and green 10 15
DESIGNS: No. 1600, Carlo Maderno (architect); No. 1601, Lazzaro Spallanzani (biologist); No. 1602, Ugo Foscolo (author); No. 1603, Massimo Bontempelli (writer); No. 1604, Francesco Severi (mathematician).

623 Morse Telegraph Apparatus

1979. Europa. Multicoloured.
1605 170l. Type **623** 30 15
1606 220l. Carrier pigeon with message tube 45 15

624 Flags of Member States forming "E"

1979. First Direct Elections to European Parliament.
1607 **624** 170l. multicoloured . . . 15 15
1608 220l. multicoloured . . . 20 15

625 Head of Aeneas (bas-relief, Ara Pacis, Rome)

626 Ball in Basket (poster)

1979. 70th World Rotary Congress, Rome.
1609 **625** 220l. multicoloured . . . 15 15

1979. 21st European Basketball Championships.
1610 **626** 80l. multicoloured . . . 10 15
1611 – 120l. lake, black & yellow 15 15
DESIGN: 120l. Two players.

627 "Doctor examining Patient with Stomach Ailment" (woodcut from Giovanni da Cuba's "Hortus Sanitatus")

629 Ottorino Respighi and Appian Way, Rome

628 Emblem, Ribbon "3" and Milan Cathedral

1979. Prevention of Digestive Illnesses.
1612 **627** 120l. multicoloured . . . 10 15

1979. Third World Machine Tool Exhibition, Milan.
1613 **628** 170l. multicoloured . . . 15 15
1614 220l. multicoloured . . . 20 15

1979. Birth Centenary of Ottorino Respighi (composer).
1615 **629** 120l. multicoloured . . . 10 15

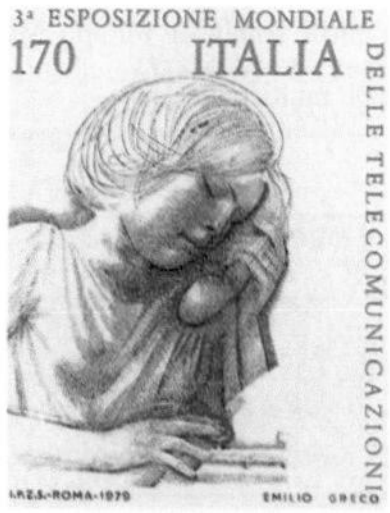

630 Woman with Telephone and Morse Key

1979. 3rd World Telecommunications Exhibition, Geneva.
1616 **630** 170l. black and red . . . 10 15
1617 – 220l. grey and green . . 15 15
DESIGN: 220l. Woman with early telephone and communications satellite.

1979. Italian Fountains (7th series). As T **542**. Multicoloured.
1618 120l. Melograno Fountain, Issogne 15 15
1619 120l. Bollente Fountain, Acqui Terme 15 15
1620 120l. Grand Fountain, Viterbo 15 15

1979. Italian Ship-building (3rd series). As T **601**. Multicoloured.
1621 170l. Full-rigged ship "Cosmos" 25 15
1622 170l. Cruiser "Dandolo" . . 25 15
1623 170l. Ferry "Deledda" . . . 25 15
1624 170l. Submarine "Carlo Fecia di Cossato" 25 15

631 Sir Rowland Hill and Penny Black

1979. Death Centenary of Sir Rowland Hill.
1625 **631** 220l. multicoloured . . . 20 15

632 Christmas Landscape

1979. Christmas.
1626 **632** 120l. multicoloured . . . 10 15

633 Children under Umbrella (Group IIB, Varapodio School)

1979. Stamp Day. International Year of the Child. Drawings by Schoolchildren. Multicoloured.
1627 70l. Children of different races holding hands (L. Carra) (horiz) 10 15
1628 120l. Type **633** 10 15
1629 150l. Children with balloons (V. Fedon) (horiz) 10 15

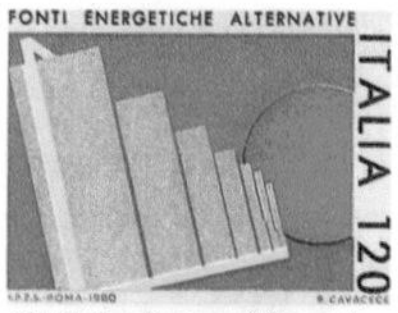

634 Solar Energy (alternative sources)

1980. Energy Conservation. Multicoloured.
1630 120l. Type **634** 15 15
1631 170l. Oil well (reduction of consumption) 15 15

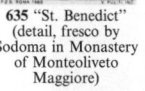

635 "St. Benedict" (detail, fresco by Sodoma in Monastery of Monteoliveto Maggiore)

636 Royal Palace, Naples

1980. 1500th Birth Anniv of St. Benedict of Nursia (founder of Benedictine Order).
1632 **635** 220l. blue 15 15

1980. "Europa 80" International Stamp Exhibition, Naples.
1633 **636** 220l. multicoloured . . . 15 15

637 Antonio Pigafetta (navigator) and "Vitoria"

638 St. Catherine (reliquary bust)

1980. Europa. Multicoloured.
1634 170l. Type **637** 35 15
1635 220l. Antonio lo Surdo (geophysicist) 50 15

1980. 600th Death Anniv of St. Catherine of Siena.
1636 **638** 170l. multicoloured . . . 15 15

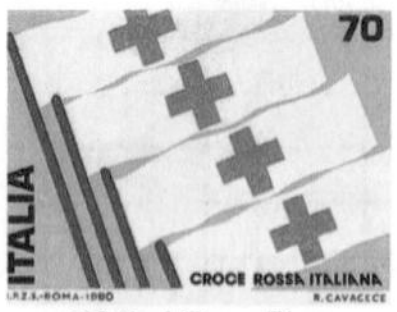

639 Red Cross Flags

1980. 1st International Exhibition of Red Cross Stamps in Italy.
1637 **639** 70l. multicoloured . . . 15 15
1638 80l. multicoloured . . . 15 15

640 Philae Temples

1980. Italian Work for the World (1st series). Preservation of Philae Temples, Egypt. Multicoloured.
1639 220l. Type **640** 15 15
1640 220l. Right hand view of temples 15 15
Nos. 1639/40 were issued together se-tenant, forming a composite design.
See also Nos. 1720/1, 1758/9, 1780/1, 1830/1, 1865/6 and 1937/40.

641 Footballer

1980. European Football Championship, Italy.
1641 **641** 80l. multicoloured . . . 1·10 95

1980. Tourist Publicity (7th series). As T **556**. Multicoloured.
1642 80l. Erice 10 30
1643 150l. Ravello 15 15
1644 200l. Roseto degli Abruzzi 20 30
1645 670l. Salsomaggiore Terme 45 90

642 "Cosimo I with his Artists" (Vasari)

1980. "Florence and Tuscany of the Medicis in 16th Century Europe" Exhibition. Multicoloured.
1646 170l. Type **642** (ceiling medallion, Palazzo Vecchio, Florence) . . . 15 15
1647 170l. Armillary sphere . . . 15 15

643 Fonte Avellana Monastery

1980. Millenary of Fonte Avellana Monastery.
1648 **643** 200l. dp green, grn & brn 20 15

644 Castel Sant' Angelo, Rome

645 Filippo Mazzei

1980. Castles. (a) Size 22 × 27 mm.
1649 **644** 5l. blue and red 20 10
1650 – 10l. brown and ochre 20 10
1651 – 20l. brown and blue 20 10
1652 – 30l. orange and blue 20 10
1653 – 40l. brown and blue 20 10
1654 – 50l. multicoloured 20 10
1655 – 60l. green and mauve 20 15
1656 – 70l. multicoloured 10 10
1657 – 80l. multicoloured 10 10
1658 – 90l. multicoloured 20 15
1659 – 100l. multicoloured 20 10
1660 – 120l. blue and pink 20 10
1661 – 150l. violet and brown 20 10
1662 – 170l. black and yellow 20 15
1663 – 180l. blue and pink 55 80
1664 – 200l. multicoloured 20 10
1665 – 250l. multicoloured 25 10
1666a – 300l. multicoloured 30 10
1667 – 350l. brown, blue & grn 30 10
1667a – 380l. multicoloured 30 10
1668 – 400l. blue, green & brn 35 10
1669 – 450l. multicoloured 40 10
1670 – 500l. blue, brown & grn 45 10
1670a – 550l. multicoloured 40 10
1671 – 600l. black and green 55 10
1671a – 650l. multicoloured 45 10
1672 – 700l. multicoloured 65 10
1673 – 750l. brown, green & bl 65 10
1674 – 800l. brown, grn & mve 75 15
1675 – 850l. multicoloured 80 15
1676 – 900l. multicoloured 80 15
1677 – 1000l. multicoloured 85 15
1678 – 1400l. brown, blue & vio 1·10 15

(b) Size 16 × 21 mm.
1679 – 30l. mauve 20 15
1680b – 50l. blue 25 15
1680c – 100l. brown 15 15
1681 – 120l. brown 25 15
1682 – 170l. violet 40 40
1683 – 200l. violet and blue 3·00 5·50
1684 – 300l. light green and green 55 65
1685 – 400l. brown and green 85 1·10
1686a – 450l. green 25 80
1687 – 500l. blue 45 1·10
1687a – 600l. green 60 80
1688 – 650l. mauve 50 80
1689 – 750l. violet 60 95
1690 – 800l. red 85 95

DESIGNS: 10l. Sforzesco Castle, Milan; 20l. Castel del Monte, Andria; 30l. (1652), L'Aquila Castle; 30l. (1679), 100l. (1680c), Santa Severa Castle; 40l. Ursino Castle, Catania; 50l. (1654), Rocca di Calascio, L'Aquila; 50l. (1680b), Scilla; 60l. Norman Tower, San Mauro; 70l. Aragonese Castle, Reggio Calabria; 80l. Sabbionara, Avio; 90l. Isola Capo Rizzuto; 100l. (1659), Aragonese Castle, Ischia; 120l. (1660), Estense Castle, Ferrara; 120l. (1681), Lombardia Enna; 150l. Miramare, Trieste; 170l. (1662), Ostia; 170l. (1682), 650l. (1688), Serralunga d'Alba; 180l. Castel Gavone, Finale Ligure; 200l. (1664), Cerro al Volturno; 200l. (1683), Svevo Angioina Fortress, Lucera; 250l. Rocca di Mondavio, Pesaro; 300l. (1666a), Norman Castle, Svevo, Bari; 300l. (1684), 500l. (1687), Norman Castle, Melfi; 350l. Mussomeli; 380l. Rocca di Vignola, Modena; 400l. (1668), Emperor's Castle, Prato; 400l. (1685), 750l. (1689), Venafro; 450l. (1669), Bosa; 450l. (1686a) Piobbico Castle, Pesaro; 500l. (1670), Rovereto; 550l. Rocca Sinibalda; 600l. Scaligero Castle, Sirmione; 650l. (1671a), Montecchio; 700l. Ivrea; 750l. (1673), Rocca di Urbisaglia; 800l. Rocca Maggiore, Assisi; 850l. Castello di Arechi, Salerno; 900l. Castello di Saint-Pierre, Aosta; 1000l. Montagnana, Padua; 1400l. Caldoresco Castle, Vasto.

1980. Italian Ship-building (4th series). As T **601**. Multicoloured.
1691 200l. Corvette "Gabbiano" 65 50
1692 200l. Destroyer "Audace" 65 50
1693 200l. Barque "Italia" 65 50
1694 200l. Pipe-layer "Castoro Sei" 65 50

1980. 250th Birth Anniv of Filippo Mazzei (writer and American revolutionary).
1695 **645** 320l. multicoloured . . . 25 15

646 Villa Foscari Malcontenta, Venice

1980. Italian Villas (1st series). Multicoloured.
1696 80l. Type **646** 20 30
1697 150l. Barbaro Maser, Treviso 25 15
1698 170l. Godi Valmarana, Vicenza 35 45
See also Nos. 1737/9, 1770/2, 1811/14, 1853/6, 1893/6 and 1943/7.

1980. Italian Artists Anniversaries (7th series). As T **567**. Multicoloured.
1699 520l. "Saint Barbara" (Jacopo Palma, the Elder (1480–1528)) 40 55
1700 520l. "Apollo and Daphne" (Gian Lorenzo Bernini (1598–1680)) 40 55

647 "Nativity" (Federico Brandani)

1980. Christmas.
1701 **647** 120l. green and brown 10 15

648 "My Town" (Treviso)

1980. Stamp Day. Paintings by Schoolchildren entitled "My Town". Multicoloured.
1702 70l. Type **648** 10 15
1703 120l. Sansepolcro 10 15
1704 170l. Sansepolcro (different) 15 15

649 Daniele Comboni and African Village

1981. 150th Birth Anniv and Death Centenary of Daniele Comboni (missionary).
1705 **649** 80l. brown, indigo and blue 10 15

650 Alcide de Gasperi

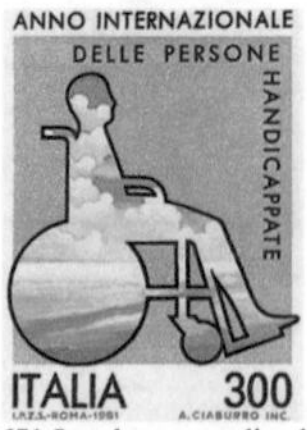

651 Landscape outlined by Person in Wheelchair

1981. Birth Centenary of Alcide de Gasperi (politician).
1706 **650** 200l. green 15 15

1981. International Year of Disabled Persons.
1707 **651** 300l. multicoloured . . . 25 15

652 Anemone

653 Human Chess Game, Marostica

1981. Flowers (1st series). Multicoloured.
1708 200l. Type **652** 15 15
1709 200l. Oleander 15 15
1710 200l. Rose 15 15
See also Nos. 1753/5 and 1797/9.

1981. Europa. Multicoloured.
1711 300l. Type **653** 65 15
1712 300l. "Il Palio" horse race, Siena 65 15

654 St. Rita of Cascia

655 Ciro Menotti

1981. 600th Birth Anniv of St. Rita of Cascia.
1713 **654** 600l. multicoloured . . . 40 40

1981. 150th Death Anniv of Ciro Menotti (patriot).
1714 **655** 80l. black and brown . . 10 10

656 Agusta A.109 Helicopter

1981. Italian Aircraft (1st series). Multicoloured.
1715 200l. Type **656** 15 15
1716 200l. Partenavia P.68B Victor airplane 15 15
1717 200l. Aeritalia G.222 transport 15 15
1718 200l. Aermacchi MB 339 jet trainer 15 15
See also Nos. 1748/51 and 1792/5.

657 Fertile and Barren Soil

1981. Water Conservation.
1719 **657** 80l. multicoloured . . . 10 15

1981. Italian Work for the World (2nd series). As T **640**.
1720 300l. blue 25 15
1721 300l. red 25 15
DESIGNS: No. 1720, Sao Simao, Brazil; No. 1721, High Island, Hong Kong.

1981. Tourist Publicity (8th series). As T **556**. Multicoloured.
1722 80l. Matera 15 15
1723 150l. Riva del Garda 20 80
1724 300l. Santa Teresa di Gallura 40 30
1725 900l. Tarquinia 1·30 55

658 Naval Academy and Badge

1981. Centenary of Naval Academy, Livorno. Multicoloured.
1726 80l. Type **658** 10 15
1727 150l. Aerial view of Academy 10 30
1728 200l. "Amerigo Vespucci" (cadet ship) and sailor using sextant 15 15

659 Spada Palace, Rome, and Decorative Motif from Grand Hall

1981. 150th Anniv of Council of State.
1729 **659** 200l. brown, green & blue 10 15

660 Running

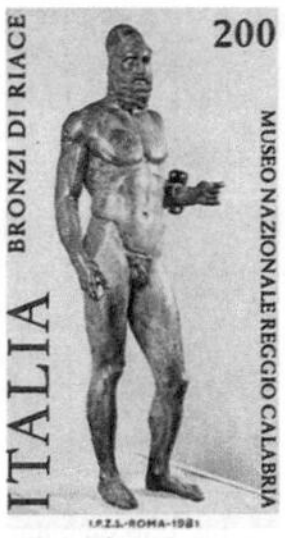

661 Riace Bronze

1981. World Cup Light Athletics Championships, Rome.
1730 **660** 300l. multicoloured . . . 25 30

1981. Italian Artists' Annivs (8th series). As T **567**. Multicoloured.
1731 200l. "Harbour" (Carlo Carra (1881–1966)) . . . 10 15
1732 200l. "Nightfall" (Giuseppe Ugonia (1881–1944)) . . . 10 15

1981. Riace Bronzes (ancient Greek statues). Multicoloured.
1733 200l. Type **661** 20 15
1734 200l. Riace bronze (different) 20 15

662 Virgil (Treviri mosaic)

1981. Death Bimillenary of Virgil (poet).
1735 **662** 600l. multicoloured . . . 40 45

663 "Still-life" (Gregorio Sciltian)

1981. World Food Day.
1736 **663** 150l. multicoloured . . . 25 20

1981. Italian Villas (2nd series). As T **646**. Multicoloured.
1737 100l. Villa Campolieto, Ercolano 10 25
1738 200l. Villa Cimbrone, Ravello 20 25
1739 300l. Villa Pignatelli, Naples 30 30

664 "Adoration of the Magi" (Giovanni da Campione d'Italia)

1981. Christmas.
1740 **664** 200l. dp blue, brown & bl 15 15

665 Pope John XXIII

1981. Birth Centenary of Pope John XXIII.
1741 **665** 200l. multicoloured . . . 20 15

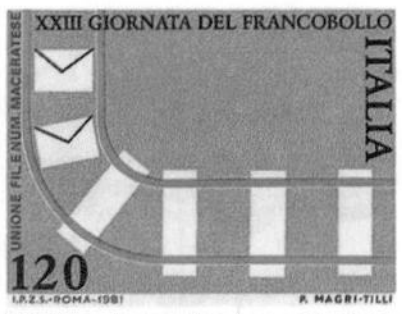

666 Envelopes forming Railway Track

1981. Stamp Day.
1742 **666** 120l. green, red and black 10 15
1743 – 200l. multicoloured . . . 20 30
1744 – 300l. multicoloured . . . 30 15
DESIGNS—VERT: 200l. Caduceus, chest, envelopes and cherub blowing posthorn. HORIZ: 300l. Letter seal.

667 "St. Francis receiving the Stigmata" (Pietro Cavaro)

668 Paganini (after Ingres)

1982. 800th Birth Anniv of St. Francis of Assisi.
1745 **667** 300l. brown and blue . . 20 30

1982. Birth Bicentenary of Niccolo Paganini (composer and violinist).
1746 **668** 900l. multicoloured . . . 70 1·90

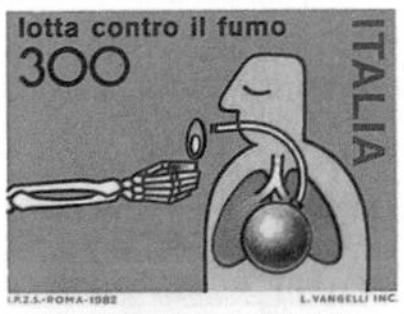

669 Skeletal Hand lighting Cigarette "Bomb"

1982. Anti-smoking Campaign.
1747 **669** 300l. multicoloured . . . 25 15

1982. Italian Aircraft (2nd series). As T **656**. Multicoloured.
1748 300l. Panavia (inscr "Aeritalia") MRCA Tornado jet fighter . . . 45 65
1749 300l. Savoia SIAI 260 Turbo trainer 45 65
1750 300l. Piaggio P-166 DL-3 Turbo 45 65
1751 300l. Nardi NH 500 helicopter 45 65

670 Church of Santo Spirito o del Vespro, Palermo

671 Coronation of Charlemagne, 799

1982. 700th Anniv of Sicilian Vespers (uprising).
1752 **670** 120l. red, blue and purple 10 30

1982. Flowers (2nd series). As T **652**. Mult.
1753 300l. Camellias 30 80
1754 300l. Carnations 30 80
1755 300l. Cyclamen 30 80

1982. Europa.
1756 **671** 200l. brown, black & blue 40 80
1757 – 450l. multicoloured . . . 75 50
DESIGN: 450l. Stars and signatures to Treaty of Rome, 1957.

1982. Italian Work for the World (3rd series). As T **640**. Multicoloured.
1758 450l. Radio communication across Red Sea 35 15
1759 450l. Automatic letter sorting 35 15

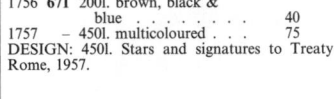

672 Garibaldi

673 Bridge Game, Pisa

1982. Death Centenary of Giuseppe Garibaldi.
1760 **672** 200l. multicoloured . . . 35 65

1982. Folk Customs (1st series).
1761 **673** 200l. multicoloured . . . 20 65
See also Nos. 1804, 1850, 1875/6, 1914, 1972, 2004, 2028 and 2092.

1982. Tourist Publicity (9th series). As T **556**. Multicoloured.
1762 200l. Frasassi Grotto . . . 25 95
1763 200l. Fai della Paganella . . 25 80
1764 450l. Rodi Garganico . . . 40 50
1765 450l. Temples of Agrigento 40 50

674 Coxless Four

1982. World Junior Rowing Championships.
1766 **674** 200l. multicoloured . . . 20 50

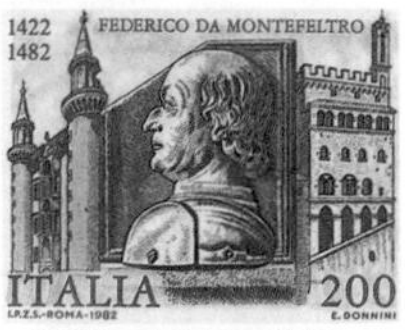

675 Ducal Palace, Urbino, Montefeltro and Palazzo dei Consoli, Gubbio

1982. 500th Death Anniv of Federico da Montefeltro, Duke of Urbino.
1767 **675** 200l. multicoloured . . . 15 15

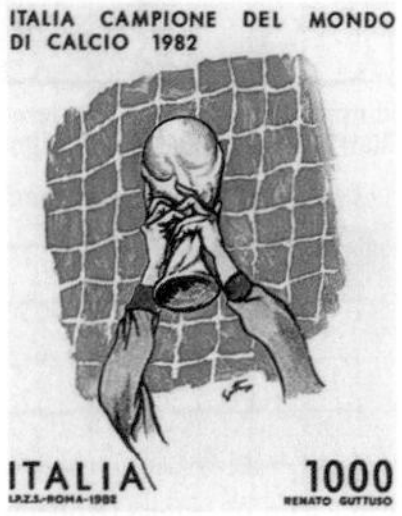

676 Footballer holding aloft World Cup

1982. Italy's World Cup Football Victory.
1768 **676** 1000l. multicoloured . . 1·40 3·00

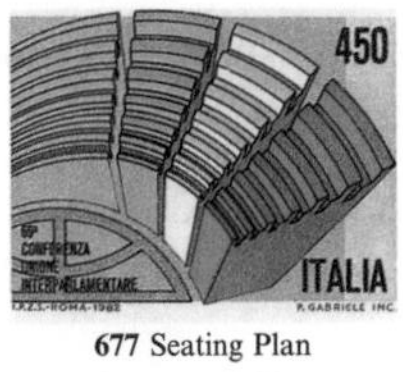

677 Seating Plan

1982. 69th Interparliamentary Union Conference.
1769 **677** 450l. multicoloured . . . 35 15

1982. Italian Villas (3rd series). As T **646**. Multicoloured.
1770 150l. Temple of Aesculapius, Villa Borghese, Rome . . 20 50
1771 250l. Villa D'Este, Tivoli . . 35 15
1772 350l. Villa Lante, Bagnaia, Viterbo . . . . 95 1·40

678 Francis of Taxis

1982. Commemoration of Establishment of First Public Postal System in Europe.
1773 **678** 300l. red, blue & verm 25 15

1982. Italian Artists' Annivs (9th series). As T **567**. Multicoloured.
1774 300l. "Portrait of Antonietta Negroni Prati Morosini as a Child" (Francesco Hayez (1791–1882)) . . . 30 50
1775 300l. "The Fortuneteller" (Giovanni Piazzetta (1682–1754)) 30 50

679 Tree, Chair and Bed (Maria di Pastena)

1983. Stamp Day. Timber in Human Life. Drawings by Schoolchildren. Multicoloured.
1776 150l. Type **679** 15 15
1777 250l. Tree with timber products in branches (Lucia Andreoli) 20 50
1778 350l. Forest (Marco Gallea) 80 65

680 Microscope

1983. Cancer Control.
1779 **680** 400l. multicoloured . . . 35 50

1983. Italian Work for the World (4th series). Automobile Industry. As T **640**. Multicoloured.
1780 400l. Factories on globe . . 35 50
1781 400l. Assembly line 35 50

681 Academy Emblem

682 Shooting

1983. 400th Anniv of Accademia della Crusca (Florentine Academy of Letters).
1782 **681** 400l. red, brown and blue 35 50

1983. World Biathlon Championships, Antholz.
1783 **682** 200l. multicoloured . . . 20 65

683 Gabriele Rossetti

684 Guicciardini (after G. Bugiardini)

1983. Birth Centenary of Gabriele Rossetti (poet).
1784 **683** 300l. blue and brown . . 25 50

1983. 500th Birth Anniv of Francesco Guicciardini (lawyer and diplomat).
1785 **684** 450l. brown 35 15

685 Saba and Trieste

1983. Birth Centenary of Umberto Saba (poet).
1786 **685** 600l. multicoloured . . . 45 50

686 Pope Pius XII

1983. 25th Death Anniv of Pope Pius XII.
1787 **686** 1400l. blue . . . . . . 1·00 80

687 Pope and St. Paul's Basilica
688 Launch of Ship

1983. Holy Year. Multicoloured.
1788 250l. Type **687** 45 30
1789 300l. Pope John Paul II and Basilica of Santa Maria Maggiore 25 15
1790 400l. Pope and St. John's Basilica 30 15
1791 500l. Pope and St. Peter's Cathedral. 90 15

1983. Italian Aircraft (3rd series). As T **656**. Multicoloured.
1792 400l. Savoia SIAI 211 . . . 40 65
1793 400l. Agusta A.129 Mangusta helicopter . . . 40 65
1794 400l. Caproni C22J glider 40 65
1795 400l. Aeritalia/Aermacchi AM-X jet fighter 40 65

1983. Labour Day.
1796 **688** 1200l. blue . . . . . . 1·20 95

1983. Flowers (3rd series). As T **652**. Mult.
1797 200l. Gladiolus . . . . . . 60 1·30
1798 200l. Mimosa . . . . 60 1·30
1799 200l. Rhododendron . . . . 60 1·30

689 Galileo (after O. Leoni) and Telescope

1983. Europa. Multicoloured.
1800 400l. Type **689** . . . . . . 4·50 1·10
1801 500l. Archimedes (marble bust) and screw . . . . . 4·50 80

690 Moneta and Doves

1983. 150th Birth Anniv of Ernesto Teodoro Moneta (Nobel Peace Prize winner).
1802 **690** 500l. multicoloured . . . 35 30

691 Quadriga, Globe and V.D.U.

1983. 3rd International Juridical Information Congress, Rome.
1803 **691** 500l. multicoloured . . . 35 30

1983. Folk Customs (2nd series). As T **673**. Multicoloured.
1804 300l. Ceri procession, Gubbio 35 50

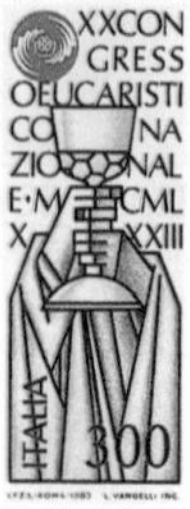

692 Elevation of Host
693 Frescobaldi

1983. 20th National Eucharistic Congress, Milan.
1805 **692** 300l. multicoloured . . . 25 15

1983. Tourist Publicity (10th series). As T **556**. Multicoloured.
1806 250l. Alghero . . . . 40 1·60
1807 300l. Bardonecchia 50 80
1808 400l. Riccione 75 65
1809 500l. Taranto . . . . 1·50 15

1983. 400th Birth Anniv of Girolamo Frescobaldi (composer).
1810 **693** 400l. green, blue & brn 35 50

1983. Italian Villas (4th series). As T **646**. Multicoloured.
1811 250l. Villa Fidelia, Spello . . 50 1·20
1812 300l. Villa Imperiale, Pesaro 40 65
1813 400l. Michetti Convent, Francavilla al Mare . . . 65 65
1814 500l. Villa di Riccia 80 15

694 Francesco de Sanctis

1983. Death Centenary of Francesco de Sanctis (writer).
1815 **694** 300l. multicoloured . . . 25 15

695 "Madonna of the Chair"
697 Battered Road Sign

696 Chain of Letters (Roberta Rizzi)

1983. Christmas. 500th Birth Anniv of Raphael (artist). Multicoloured.
1816 250l. Type **695** 20 15
1817 400l. "Sistine Madonna" . . 25 15
1818 500l. "Madonna of the Candles" 60 15

1983. Stamp Day. Drawings by school-children. Multicoloured.
1819 200l. Type **696** 15 50
1820 300l. Space postman delivering letter (Maria Grazia Federico) (vert) . . 35 20
1821 400l. Steam train leaving envelope and globe (Paolo Bucciarelli) 50 20

1984. Road Safety. Multicoloured.
1822 300l. Type **697** 20 50
1823 400l. Crashed car and policeman 30 50

1984. Italian Artists Anniversaries (10th series). As T **567**. Multicoloured.
1824 300l. "Races at Bois de Boulogne" (Giuseppe de Nittis (1846–84)) 35 15
1825 400l. "Paul Guillaume" (Amedeo Modigliani (1884–1920)) 45 50

698 Maserati "Biturbo"

1984. Italian Motor Industry (1st series). Multicoloured.
1826 450l. Type **698** 75 65
1827 450l. Iveco "190.38 Special" lorry 75 65
1828 450l. Same Trattori "Galaxy" tractor 75 65
1829 450l. Alfa "33" 75 65
See also Nos. 1867/70 and 1933/6.

699 Glassblower, Glasses and Jug

1984. Italian Work for the World (5th series). Ceramic and Glass Industries. Multicoloured.
1830 300l. Ceramic plaque and furnace 25 15
1831 300l. Type **699** 25 15

700 European Parliament Building, Strasbourg

1984. Second European Parliament Direct Elections.
1832 **700** 400l. multicoloured . . . 35 65

701 State Forest Corps Helicopter

1984. Nature Protection. Forests. Multicoloured.
1833 450l. Type **701** . . . . . . 1·20 65
1834 450l. Forest animals and burning cigarette . . . . 1·20 65
1835 450l. River and litter . . . 1·20 65
1836 450l. Wildlife and building construction . . . . . . 1·20 65

702 Ministry of Posts and Telecommunications, Rome

1984. "Italia '85" International Stamp Exhibition, Rome (1st issue). Multicoloured.
1837 450l. Type **702** 45 25
1838 550l. Appian Way 55 30
See also Nos. 1857/9, 1862/4, 1871/3 and 1898/1911.

703 G. di Vittorio, B. Buozzi and A. Grandi

1984. 40th Anniv of Rome Pact (foundation of Italian Trade Unions).
1839 **703** 450l. multicoloured . . . 70 50

704 Bridge

1984. Europa. 25th Anniv of European Post and Telecommunications Conference.
1840 **704** 450l. multicoloured . . . 2·00 1·10
1841 550l. multicoloured . . . 3·75 4·75

705 Symposium Emblem
706 Horse-race

1984. Int Telecommunications Symposium, Florence.
1842 **705** 550l. multicoloured . . . 50 65

1984. Centenary of Italian Derby. Multicoloured.
1843 250l. Type **706** . . . . . . 70 3·25
1844 400l. Horse-race (different) 1·10 1·10

1984. Tourist Publicity (11th series). As T **556**. Multicoloured.
1845 350l. Campione d'Italia . . 80 3·00
1846 400l. Chianciano Terme . . 60 1·10
1847 450l. Padula 85 95
1848 550l. Syracuse . . . . . . 85 1·40

1984. Folk Customs (3rd series). As T **673**. Multicoloured.
1850 400l. Procession of Shrine of Santa Rosa, Viterbo . . . 40 50

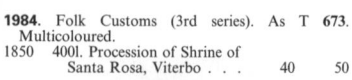

708 Harvester, Thresher and Medieval Fields Map

1984. Peasant Farming. Multicoloured.
1851 250l. Type **708** . . . . . . 25 1·40
1852 350l. Hand oil press, cart and medieval fields map 30 50

1984. Italian Villas (5th series). As T **646**. Multicoloured.
1853 250l. Villa Caristo, Stignano 60 2·10
1854 350l. Villa Doria Pamphili, Genoa . . . . 60 1·90
1855 400l. Villa Reale, Stupinigi 80 65
1856 450l. Villa Mellone, Lecce 80 50

709 Etruscan Bronze of Warrior
710 Dish Aerial, Globe and Punched Tape

1984. "Italia '85" International Stamp Exhibition, Rome (2nd issue). Multicoloured.
1857 550l. Type **709** 60 50
1858 550l. Exhibition emblem . . 60 50
1859 550l. Etruscan silver-backed mirror 60 50

1985. Information Technology.
1860 **710** 350l. multicoloured . . . 25 50

711 Man helping Old Woman
712 "Venus in her Chariot" (fresco, Raphael)

1985. Problems of Elderly People.
1861 **711** 250l. multicoloured . . . 25 65

1985. "Italia '85" International Stamp Exhibition, Rome (3rd issue). Multicoloured.
1862 600l. Type **712** 60 15
1863 600l. Exhibition emblem . . 60 15
1864 600l. Warriors (detail of fresco, Baldassare Peruzzi) 60 15

713 Plate, Vase and Pot

1985. Italian Work for the World (6th series). Ceramics. Multicoloured.
1865 600l. Type **713** 60 15
1866 600l. Decorated plate 60 15

1985. Italian Motor Industry (2nd series). As T **698**. Multicoloured.
1867 450l. Fiat "Uno" 1·20 50
1868 450l. Lamborghini "Countach LP500" 1·20 50
1869 450l. Lancia "Thema" 1·20 50
1870 450l. Fiat Abarth "100 Bialbero" 1·20 50

714 St. Mary of Peace Church, Rome **715** Pope Sixtus V

1985. "Italia '85" International Stamp Exhibition, Rome (4th issue). Baroque Art. Multicoloured.
1871 250l. Type **714** 25 50
1872 250l. Exhibition emblem 25 50
1873 250l. Fountain obelisk and Saint Agnes's Church, Rome 25 50

1985. 400th Anniv of Election of Pope Sixtus V.
1874 **715** 1500l. multicoloured 1·60 95

1985. Folk Customs (4th series). As T **673**. Multicoloured.
1875 250l. March of the Turks, Potenza 45 65
1876 350l. Republican regatta, Amalfi 65 65

1985. Tourist Publicity (12th series). As T **556**. Multicoloured.
1877 350l. Bormio 35 1·90
1878 400l. Castellammare di Stabia 50 65
1879 450l. Stromboli 60 65
1880 600l. Termoli 1·60 25

716 European Otter **717** Aureliano Pertile and Giovanni Martinelli (singers)

1985. Nature Protection. Multicoloured.
1881 500l. Type **716** 55 50
1882 500l. Primulas 55 50
1883 500l. Fir tree 55 50
1884 500l. Black-winged stilts 55 50

1985. Anniversaries of Italian Artists (11th series). As T **567**. Multicoloured.
1885 350l. "Madonna" (Giambattista Salvi (1609–85)) 55 95
1886 400l. "The Pride of Work" (Mario Sironi (1885–1961)) 70 95

1985. Europa. Music Year. Multicoloured.
1887 500l. Type **717** 2·75 95
1888 600l. Vicenzo Bellini and Johann Sebastian Bach (composers) 4·75 1·30

718 San Salvatore Abbey

1985. 950th Anniv of San Salvatore Abbey, Mt. Amiata.
1889 **718** 450l. multicoloured 40 15

719 Cyclists

1985. World Cycling Championships, Bassano del Grappa.
1890 **719** 400l. multicoloured 70 50

720 U.N. and Congress Emblems and Globe

1985. 7th United Nations Crime Prevention Congress, Milan.
1891 **720** 600l. multicoloured 55 15

721 Profile and Emblem

1985. International Youth Year.
1892 **721** 600l. multicoloured 60 15

1985. Villas (6th series). As T **646**. Multicoloured.
1893 300l. Villa Nitti, Maratea 65 50
1894 400l. Villa Aldrovandi Mazzacorati, Bologna 85 15
1895 500l. Villa Santa Maria, Pula 1·10 15
1896 600l. Villa de Mersi, Villazzano 1·40 15

722 State Emblems of Italy and Vatican City and Medallion (Mario Soccorsi)

1985. Ratification of the Modification of 1929 Lateran Concordat.
1897 **722** 400l. multicoloured 70 50

723 Parma Town Hall and 1857 25c. Stamp

724 Basel 1845 2$\frac{1}{2}$r. Stamp

1985. "Italia '85" International Stamp Exhibition. Rome (5th issue). Multicoloured. (a) As T **723**.
1898 300l. Type **723** 25 65
1899 300l. Naples New Castle and 1858 2g. stamp 25 65
1900 300l. Palermo Cathedral and Sicily 1859 $\frac{1}{2}$g. stamp 25 65
1901 300l. Modena Cathedral and 1852 15c. stamp 25 65
1902 300l. Piazzo Navona, Rome, and Papal States 1852 7b. stamp 25 65
1903 300l. Palazzo Vecchio, Florence, and Tuscany 1851 2c. stamp 25 65
1904 300l. Turin and Sardinia 1861 3l. stamp 25 65
1905 300l. Bologna and Romagna 1859 6b. stamp 25 65
1906 300l. Palazzo Litta, Milan, and Lombardy and Venetia 1850 15c. stamp 25 65

(b) As T **724**.
1907 500l. Type **724** 50 80
1908 500l. Japan 1871 48m. stamp 50 80
1909 500l. United States 1847 10c. stamp 50 80
1910 500l. Western Australia 1854 1d. stamp 50 80
1911 500l. Mauritius 1848 2d. stamp 50 80

(c) Sheet 86 × 56 mm. Imperf
MS1912 4000l. Sardinia 1851 5c. stamp and Great Britain "Penny Black" 3·00 5·50

725 Skiers

1986. Cross-country Skiing.
1913 **725** 450l. multicoloured 35 50

1986. Folk Customs (5th series). As T **673**. Multicoloured.
1914 450l. Le Candelore, Catania 40 50

726 Amilcare Ponchielli and Scene from "La Gioconda"

1986. Composers. Multicoloured.
1915 2000l. Type **726** (death centenary) 2·10 65
1916 2000l. Giovan Battista Pergolesi (250th death anniv) 2·30 80

727 Acitrezza

1986. Tourist Publicity (13th series). Mult.
1917 350l. Type **727** 45 50
1918 450l. Capri 55 80
1919 550l. Merano 70 50
1920 650l. San Benedetto del Tronto 85 15

728 Heart-shaped Tree (life)

1986. Europa. Multicoloured.
1921 650l. Type **728** 1·80 50
1922 650l. Star-shaped tree (poetry) 1·80 50
1923 650l. Butterfly-shaped tree (colour) 1·80 50
1924 650l. Sun-shaped tree (energy) 1·80 50

729 "Eyes"

1986. 25th International Ophthalmology Congress, Rome.
1925 **729** 550l. multicoloured 45 15

730 Italian Police

1986. European Police Meeting, Chianciano Terme.
1926 **730** 550l. multicoloured 95 50
1927 650l. multicoloured 1·20 95

731 Battle Scene

1986. 120th Anniv of Battle of Bezzecca.
1928 **731** 550l. multicoloured 50 50

732 Figure with Flag

1986. National Independence Martyrs' Day.
1929 **732** 2000l. multicoloured 2·40 65

733 Bersagliere and Helmets

1986. 150th Anniv of Turin Bersaglieri Corps (alpine troops).
1930 **733** 450l. multicoloured 85 50

734 Dish Aerial, Transmitter and "Messages"

1986. Telecommunications.
1931 **734** 350l. multicoloured 50 15

735 Varallo

1986. Holy Mountain of Varallo.
1932 **735** 2000l. green and blue 1·90 65

1986. Italian Motor Industry (3rd series). As T **698**. Multicoloured.
1933 450l. Alfa Romeo "AR 8 Turbo" 90 50
1934 450l. Innocenti "650 SE" 90 50
1935 450l. Ferrari "Testarossa" 90 50
1936 450l. Fiatallis "FR 10B" 90 50

736 Clothes and Woman (fashion)

1986. Italian Work for the World (7th series). Mult.
1937 450l. Type **736** 75 15
1938 450l. Man and clothes (fashion) 75 15

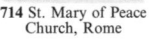

1939 650l. Olivetti personal computer, keyboard and screen . . . . 2·10 50
1940 650l. Breda steam turbine 2·10 50

737 Airplane flying through "40"

738 "Madonna and Child" (bronze sculpture by Donatello)

1986. 40th Anniv of Alitalia (national airline). Multicoloured.
1941 550l. Type **737** 55 15
1942 650l. Airplane and landing lights 70 15

1986. Italian Villas (7th series). As T **646**. Mult.
1943 350l. Villa Necker, Trieste 40 50
1944 350l. Villa Borromeo, Cassana d'Adda 40 50
1945 450l. Villa Palagonia, Bagheria 60 15
1946 550l. Villa Medicea, Poggio a Caiano 65 15
1947 650l. Issogne Castle 80 15

1986. Christmas.
1948 **738** 450l. bistre 45 15

1986. Anniversaries of Italian Artists (12th series). As T **567**.
1949 450l. black and orange . . . 1·00 15
1950 550l. multicoloured . . . . 1·20 15
DESIGNS: 450l. Drawing of woman (Andrea del Sarto (1486–1531)); 550l. "Daphne at Pavarola" (Felice Casorati (1883–1963)).

739 Lockheed Hercules Transport dropping Squares in National Colours onto Globe

740 Engraving 1862 Stamp

1986. International Peace Year. Multicoloured.
1951 550l. Type **739** 50 15
1952 650l. Airplane, Cross and people (commemoration of Italian airmen killed on mission to Kindu, Congo) 60 15

1986. Stamp Day. Francesco Maria Matraire (engraver).
1953 **740** 550l. multicoloured . . . 85 15

741 Woven Threads (Marzotto Textile Industry)

1987. Italian Industry.
1954 **741** 700l. multicoloured . . . 65 15
1955 – 700l. blue and turquoise 65 15
DESIGN: No. 1955, Clouds and flame (Italgas Gas Corporation).

742 River Volturno

743 Gramsci

1987. Nature Protection. Rivers and Lakes. Multicoloured.
1956 500l. Type **742** 75 15
1957 500l. Lake Garda 75 15
1958 500l. Lake Trasimeno . . . 75 15
1959 500l. River Tirso 75 15

1987. 50th Death Anniv of Antonio Gramsci (politician).
1960 **743** 600l. grey, black and red 70 50

744 Church of the Motorway of the Sun, Florence (Giovanni Michelucci)

745 View of Naples on Football

1987. Europa. Architecture. Multicoloured.
1961 600l. Type **744** . . . . . . 1·20 65
1962 700l. Termini station, Rome (Nervi) . . . . 1·50 65

1987. Tourist Publicity (14th series). As T **556**. Multicoloured.
1963 380l. Verbania Pallanza . . 50 1·40
1964 400l. Palmi 55 80
1965 500l. Vasto 70 50
1966 600l. Villacidro 80 80

1987. S.S.C. Naples, National Football Champion, 1986–87.
1967 **745** 500l. multicoloured . . . 1·10 1·10

746 "The Absinthe Drinker" (Edgar Degas)

1987. Anti-alcoholism Campaign.
1968 **746** 380l. multicoloured . . . 55 50

747 Liguori and Gulf of Naples

1987. Death Bicentenary of St. Alfonso Maria de Liguori (co-founder of Redemptorists).
1969 **747** 400l. multicoloured . . . 35 50

748 Emblem and Olympic Stadium, Rome

1987. World Light Athletics Championships, Rome (1970) and "Olymphilex '87" Stamp Exhibition, Rome (1971).
1970 700l. Type **748** 55 15
1971 700l. International Olympic Committee building, Foro Italico, Rome 55 15

1987. Folk Customs (6th series). As T **673**. Multicoloured.
1972 380l. Joust, Foligno 45 50

749 Piazza del Popolo, Ascoli Piceno

750 "The Adoration in the Manger" (St. Francis's Basilica, Assisi)

1987. Piazzas (1st series). Multicoloured.
1973 380l. Type **749** 45 50
1974 500l. Piazza Giuseppe Verdi, Palermo 60 15
1975 600l. Piazza San Carlo, Turin 75 15
1976 700l. Piazza dei Signori, Verona 85 65
See also Nos. 2002/3 and 2023/4.

1987. Christmas. Frescoes by Giotto. Mult.
1977 500l. Type **750** 65 15
1978 600l. "Epiphany" (Scrovegni Chapel, Padua) 75 15

751 Battle Scene

1987. 120th Anniv of Battle of Mentana.
1979 **751** 380l. multicoloured . . . 50 50

752 "Christ Pantocrator" (mosaic, Monreale Cathedral)

1987. Artistic Heritage. Multicoloured.
1980 500l. Type **752** 85 50
1981 500l. San Carlo Theatre, Naples (18th-century engraving) 85 50

753 College and 1787 and 1987 Uniforms

754 Marco de Marchi (philatelist) and Milan Cathedral

1987. Bicentenary of Nunziatella Military Academy, Naples.
1982 **753** 600l. multicoloured . . . 60 50

1987. Stamp Day.
1983 **754** 500l. multicoloured . . . 90 50

755 Man chipping Flints

756 Lyceum

1988. "Homo aeserniensis".
1984 **755** 500l. multicoloured . . . 40 65

1988. E.Q. Visconti Lyceum, Rome.
1985 **756** 500l. multicoloured . . . 45 30
See also Nos. 2019, 2109 and 2127.

757 Statue, Bosco and Boy

758 15th-Century Soncino Bible

1988. Death Centenary of St. John Bosco (founder of Salesian Brothers).
1986 **757** 500l. multicoloured . . . 40 50

1988. Anniversaries of Italian Artists (13th series). As T **567**. Multicoloured.
1987 650l. "Archaeologists" (Giorgio de Chirico (1888–1978)) . . . . . . 1·00 65

1988. 500th Anniv of First Printing of Bible in Hebrew.
1988 **758** 550l. multicoloured . . . 60 30

759 St. Valentine, Epileptics and Wave Patterns

1988. Anti-epilepsy Campaign.
1989 **759** 500l. multicoloured . . . 60 65

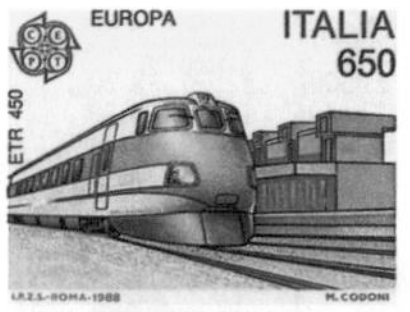

760 ETR 450 High Speed Train in Station

761 Golfer on Ball

1988. Europa. Transport and Communications. Multicoloured.
1990 650l. Type **760** . . . . . . 1·20 95
1991 750l. Map and keyboard operator (electronic postal systems) . . . . 1·40 1·40

1988. Tourist Publicity (15th series). As T **556**. Multicoloured.
1992 400l. Castiglione della Pescaia 35 65
1993 500l. Lignano Sabbiadoro 50 50
1994 650l. St. Domenico's Church, Noto 60 50
1995 750l. Vieste 70 80

1988. Golf.
1996 **761** 500l. multicoloured . . . 45 65

762 Stadium and Mascot

763 Milan Cathedral on Football

1988. World Cup Football Championship, Italy (1990) (1st issue).
1997 **762** 3150l. multicoloured . . 2·30 4·75
See also Nos. 2049 and 2052/87.

1988. A. C. Milan. National Football Champion, 1987–88.
1998 **763** 650l. multicoloured . . . 55 1·10

764 Horse's Head

1988. Artistic Heritage. Pergola Bronzes. Multicoloured.
1999 500l. Type **764** 40 95
2000 650l. Bust of woman 55 95

765 Student (bas-relief)

766 Emblem and Appian Way

1988. 900th Anniv of Bologna University.
2001 **765** 500l. violet 40 65

1988. Piazzas (2nd series). As T **749**. Mult.
2002 400l. Piazza del Duomo, Pistoia 50 50
2003 550l. Piazza del Unita d'Italia, Trieste 65 50

1988. Folk Customs (7th series). As T **673**. Multicoloured.
2004 500l. Candle procession, Sassari 90 50

1988. "Roma 88" Int Gastroenterology and Digestive Endoscopy Congress.
2005 **766** 750l. multicoloured . . . 80 50

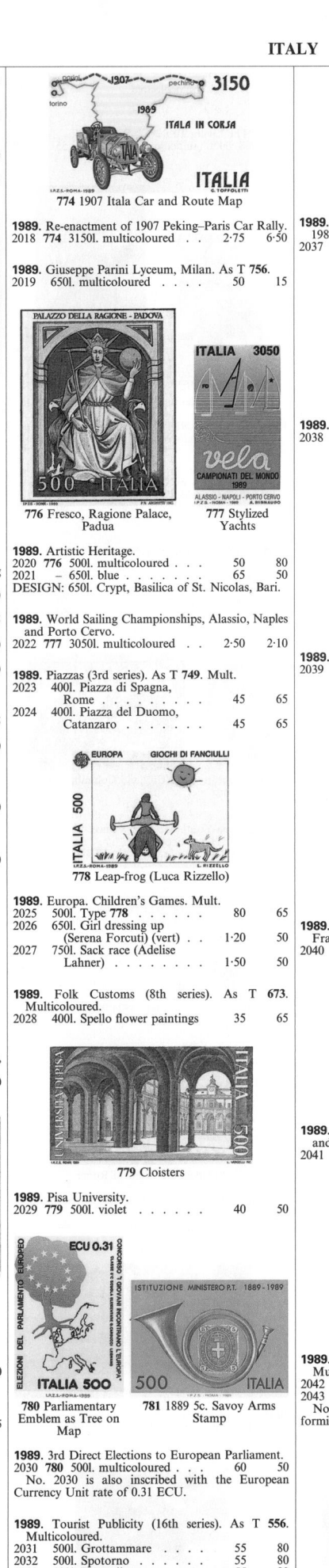

767 "Ossessione" (Luchino Visconti, 1942)

769 "Holy Family" (Pasquale Celommi)

768 Bird (aluminium)

1988. Italian Films. Scenes from and Advertising Posters of named Films. Multicoloured.
2006 500l. Type **767** . . . . . . 90 1·10
2007 650l. "Ladri di Biciclette" (Vittorio de Sica, 1948) 90 95
2008 2400l. "Roma Citta Aperta" (Roberto Rossellini, 1945) 3·25 1·30
2009 3050l. "Riso Amaro" (Giuseppe de Santis, 1949) 3·50 2·20

1988. Italian Industry. Multicoloured.
2010 750l. Type **768** 50 15
2011 750l. Oscilloscope display (electronics) 50 50
2012 750l. Banknote engraving, 1986 tourism stamp and medals (60th anniv of State Polygraphic Institute) 50 50

1988. Christmas (1st issue).
2013 **769** 650l. multicoloured . . . 85 30
See also No. 2015.

770 Borromeo and Plague Victims

1988. 450th Birth Anniv of St. Carlo Borromeo, Archbishop of Milan.
2014 **770** 2400l. multicoloured . . 1·90 1·30

771 "Nativity" (bas-relief)

772 Edoardo Chiossone (stamp designer) and Japanese 1879 2s. "Koban" Stamp

1988. Christmas (2nd issue).
2015 **771** 500l. green and brown 90 50

1988. Stamp Day.
2016 **772** 500l. multicoloured . . . 50 15

773 AIDS Virus

1989. Anti-AIDS Campaign.
2017 **773** 650l. multicoloured . . . 55 15

774 1907 Itala Car and Route Map

1989. Re-enactment of 1907 Peking–Paris Car Rally.
2018 **774** 3150l. multicoloured . . 2·75 6·50

1989. Giuseppe Parini Lyceum, Milan. As T **756**.
2019 650l. multicoloured 50 15

776 Fresco, Ragione Palace, Padua

777 Stylized Yachts

1989. Artistic Heritage.
2020 **776** 500l. multicoloured . . . 50 80
2021 – 650l. blue 65 50
DESIGN: 650l. Crypt, Basilica of St. Nicolas, Bari.

1989. World Sailing Championships, Alassio, Naples and Porto Cervo.
2022 **777** 3050l. multicoloured . . 2·50 2·10

1989. Piazzas (3rd series). As T **749**. Mult.
2023 400l. Piazza di Spagna, Rome 45 65
2024 400l. Piazza del Duomo, Catanzaro 45 65

778 Leap-frog (Luca Rizzello)

1989. Europa. Children's Games. Mult.
2025 500l. Type **778** 80 65
2026 650l. Girl dressing up (Serena Forcuti) (vert) . . 1·20 50
2027 750l. Sack race (Adelise Lahner) . . . . 1·50 50

1989. Folk Customs (8th series). As T **673**. Multicoloured.
2028 400l. Spello flower paintings 35 65

779 Cloisters

1989. Pisa University.
2029 **779** 500l. violet 40 50

780 Parliamentary Emblem as Tree on Map

781 1889 5c. Savoy Arms Stamp

1989. 3rd Direct Elections to European Parliament.
2030 **780** 500l. multicoloured . . . 60 50
No. 2030 is also inscribed with the European Currency Unit rate of 0.31 ECU.

1989. Tourist Publicity (16th series). As T **556**. Multicoloured.
2031 500l. Grottammare 55 80
2032 500l. Spotorno 55 80
2033 500l. Pompeii 55 80
2034 500l. Giardini Naxos . . . 55 80

1989. Centenary of Ministry of Posts and Telecommunications. Multicoloured.
2035 500l. Type **781** . . . . . . 50 1·60
2036 2400l. Globe within posthorn . . . . 1·80 1·60

782 Ball and Club Emblem

1989. Inter Milan, National Football Champion, 1988–89.
2037 **782** 650l. multicoloured . . . 50 65

783 Stylized Chamber

1989. Centenary of Interparliamentary Union.
2038 **783** 750l. multicoloured . . . 55 50

784 Phrygian Cap

1989. Bicentenary of French Revolution.
2039 **784** 3150l. multicoloured . . 2·75 6·50

785 Corinaldo Wall

1989. Artistic Heritage. 550th Birth Anniv of Francesco di Giorgio Martini (architect).
2040 **785** 500l. multicoloured . . . 55 50

786 Chaplin in Film Scenes

1989. Birth Centenary of Charlie Chaplin (film actor and director).
2041 **786** 750l. black and brown 70 50

787 "Inauguration of Naples–Portici Line" (left-hand detail, S Fergola)

1989. 150th Anniv of Naples–Portici Railway. Multicoloured.
2042 550l. Type **787** 45 50
2043 550l. Right-hand detail . . . 45 50
Nos. 2042/3 were printed together, se-tenant, forming a composite design.

788 Castelfidardo, Accordion and Stradella

1989. Italian Industry. Multicoloured.
2044 450l. Type **788** 40 50
2045 450l. Books (Arnoldo Mondadori Publishing House) 40 50

789 Madonna and Child

790 Emilio Diena (stamp dealer)

1989. Christmas. Details of "Adoration of the Magi" (Correggio). Multicoloured.
2046 500l. Type **789** 55 50
2047 500l. Magi 55 50
Nos. 2046/7 were printed together, se-tenant, forming a composite design.

1989. Stamp Day.
2048 **790** 500l. black, brown & blue 60 50

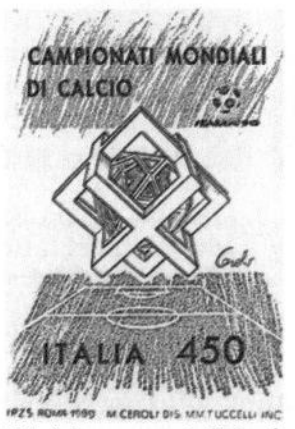

791 Monument (Mario Ceroli) and Football Pitch

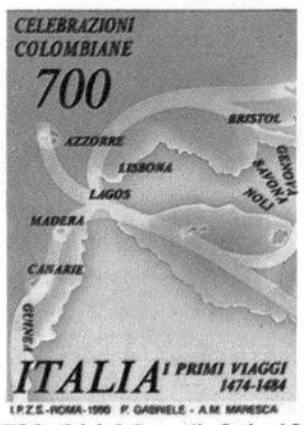

792 Old Map (left half) with Route superimposed

1989. World Cup Football Championship, Italy (1990) (2nd issue).
2049 **791** 450l. multicoloured . . . 40 65

1990. Columbus's First Voyages, 1474–84, Multicoloured.
2050 700l. Type **792** 60 50
2051 700l. Right half of map . . 60 50
Nos. 2050/1 were printed together, se-tenant, forming a composite design.

793 Italy

1990. World Cup Football Championship, Italy (3rd issue). Designs showing finalists' emblems or playing venues. Multicoloured.
2052 450l. Type **793** 30 65
2053 450l. U.S.A. 30 65
2054 450l. Olympic Stadium, Rome 30 65
2055 450l. Comunale Stadium, Florence 30 65
2056 450l. Austria 30 65
2057 450l. Czechoslovakia 30 65
2058 600l. Argentina 40 65
2059 600l. U.S.S.R. 40 65
2060 600l. San Paolo Stadium, Naples 40 65
2061 600l. New Stadium, Bari . . 40 65
2062 600l. Cameroun 40 65
2063 600l. Rumania 40 65
2064 650l. Brazil 50 65
2065 650l. Costa Rica 50 65
2066 650l. Delle Alpi Stadium, Turin 50 65
2067 650l. Ferraris Stadium, Genoa 50 65
2068 650l. Sweden 50 65
2069 650l. Scotland 50 65
2070 700l. United Arab Emirates 50 65
2071 700l. West Germany 50 65
2072 700l. Dall'Ara Stadium, Bologna 50 65
2073 700l. Meazza Stadium, Milan 50 65
2074 700l. Colombia 50 65
2075 700l. Yugoslavia 50 65
2076 800l. Belgium . . . . 60 1·30
2077 800l. Uruguay . . . . 60 1·30
2078 800l. Bentegodi Stadium, Verona . . . . 60 1·30
2079 800l. Friuli Stadium, Udine 60 1·30
2080 800l. South Korea . . . . . 60 1·30
2081 800l. Spain . . . . 60 1·30
2082 1200l. England . . . . . . 85 1·60
2083 1200l. Netherlands . . . . 85 1·60
2084 1200l. Sant'Elia Stadium, Cagliari . . . . 85 1·60
2085 1200l. La Favorita Stadium, Palermo . . . . 85 1·60
2086 1200l. Ireland . . . . 85 1·60
2087 1200l. Egypt . . . . 85 1·60
See also No. 2104.

1990. Tourist Publicity (17th series). As T **556**. Multicoloured.
2088 600l. San Felice Circeo . . . 55 50
2089 600l. Castellammare del Golfo 55 50
2090 600l. Montepulciano 55 50
2091 600l. Sabbioneta 55 50

1990. Folk Customs (9th series). As T **673**. Multicoloured.
2092 600l. Avelignesi horse race, Merano 45 50

794 National Colours

1990. Death Centenary of Aurelio Saffi.
2093 **794** 700l. multicoloured . . . 50 40

795 Giovanni Giorgi (inventor)
796 Flags, Globe and Workers (after "The Four States" (Pellizza da Volpedo))

1990. 55th Anniv of Invention of Giorgi/MKSA System of Electrotechnical Units.
2094 **795** 600l. multicoloured . . . 40 50

1990. Centenary of Labour Day.
2095 **796** 600l. multicoloured . . . 40 50

797 Ball on Map

1990. S. S. C. Naples, National Football Champion, 1989–90.
2096 **797** 700l. multicoloured . . . 50 50

798 Piazza San Silvestro Post Office, Rome

1990. Europa. Post Office Buildings. Mult.
2097 700l. Type **798** . . . . . . 1·00 50
2098 800l. Fondaco Tedeschi post office, Venice . . . . . . 1·50 65

799 Paisiello

1990. 250th Birth Anniv of Giovanni Paisiello (composer).
2099 **799** 450l. multicoloured . . . 30 50

800 Globe, Open Book and Bust of Dante

1990. Centenary of Dante Alighieri Society.
2100 **800** 700l. multicoloured . . . 45 80

801 Byzantine Mosaic, Ravenna
802 Malatestiana Temple, Rimini

1990. Artistic Heritage. Multicoloured.
2101 450l. Type **801** 30 50
2102 700l. "Christ and Angels" (detail of Rachis altar, Friuli) (Lombard art) . . 50 50

1990. 40th Anniv of Malatestiana Religious Music Festival.
2103 **802** 600l. multicoloured . . . 45 50

1990. West Germany, Winner of World Cup Football Championship. As No. 2071 but value changed and additionally inscr "CAMPIONE DEL MONDO".
2104 600l. multicoloured . . . . 2·00 1·90

803 "Still Life"

1990. Birth Cent of Giorgio Morandi (painter).
2105 **803** 750l. black 60 50

804 Ancient and Modern Wrestlers

1990. World Greco-Roman Wrestling Championships, Rome.
2106 **804** 3200l. multicoloured . . 2·75 2·40

805 "New Life" (Emidio Vangelli)

1990. Christmas. Multicoloured.
2107 600l. Type **805** 45 50
2108 750l. "Adoration of the Shepherds" (fresco by Pellegrino in St. Daniel's Church, Friuli) 60 50

806 Catania University

1990.
2109 – 600l. multicoloured . . . 45 50
2110 **806** 750l. blue and ultramarine 60 50
DESIGN—As T **756**: 600l. Bernardino Telesio High School, Cosenza.

807 Corrado Mezzana (stamp designer, self-portrait)
808 Holy Family

1990. Stamp Day.
2111 **807** 600l. multicoloured . . . 55 50

1991. "The Living Tableau", Rivisondoli.
2112 **808** 600l. multicoloured . . . 55 50

809 Fair Emblem
810 Emblem

1991. "EuroFlora '91" Fair, Genoa.
2113 **809** 750l. multicoloured . . . 60 50

1991. 750th Anniv of Siena University.
2114 **810** 750l. gold, black and blue 60 50

1991. Tourist Publicity (18th series). As T **556**. Multicoloured.
2115 600l. Cagli 50 50
2116 600l. La Maddalena 50 50
2117 600l. Roccaraso 50 50
2118 600l. Sanremo 50 50

811 European Community Flag
812 City and Columbus's Fleet

1991. Europa Youth Meeting, Venice.
2119 **811** 750l. multicoloured . . . 65 15
No. 2119 is also valued in ECUs (European Currency Unit).

1991. 500th Anniv (1992) of Discovery of America by Christopher Columbus (1st issue). Multicoloured.
2120 750l. Type **812** 60 50
2121 750l. Map, Columbus, seal and King and Queen of Spain 60 50
Nos. 2120/1 were printed together, se-tenant, forming a composite design.
See also Nos. 2151/4 and **MS**2158.

813 Belli and View of Rome

1991. Birth Bicentenary of Giuseppe Gioachino Belli (poet).
2122 **813** 600l. brown and blue . . 45 50

814 St Gregory's Church, Rome

1991. Artistic Heritage.
2123 **814** 3200l. multicoloured . . 2·30 1·30

815 "DRS" Satellite

1991. Europa. Europe in Space. Multicoloured.
2124 750l. Type **815** . . . . . . 1·30 50
2125 800l. "Hermes" spaceship and "Columbus" space station . . . . 1·30 50

816 Sta Maria Maggiore Church, Lanciano
817 Football and Genoa Lantern

1991. Artistic Heritage.
2126 **816** 600l. brown 50 50

1991. D. A. Azuni Lyceum, Sassari. As T **756**.
2127 600l. multicoloured 50 50

1991. Sampdoria, National Football Champion, 1990–91.
2128 **817** 3000l. multicoloured . . 2·30 4·00

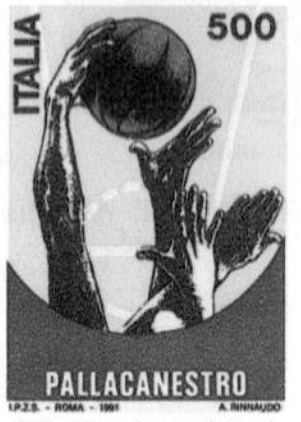

818 Hands and Ball
819 Children and Butterflies

1991. Centenary of Basketball.
2129 **818** 500l. multicoloured . . . 40 50

1991. United Nations Conference on Rights of the Child. Multicoloured.
2130 600l. Type **819** 50 50
2131 750l. Child with balloon on man's shoulders 65 50

820 "Youth and Gulls" (sculpture, Pericle Fazzini)

1991. Artistic Heritage. Multicoloured.
2132 **820** 600l. yellow, blue & black 45 65
2133 – 3200l. multicoloured . . 2·50 2·40
DESIGN: 3200l. Palazzo Esposizioni, Turin (Pier Luigi Nervi (birth centenary)).

821 Winged Sphinx

1991. Egyptian Museum, Turin.
2134 **821** 750l. gold, green & yellow 65 50

822 Luigi Galvani (physiologist) and Experimental Equipment

1991. 100 Years of Radio (1st issue).
2135 **822** 750l. multicoloured . . . 65 50
Galvani carried out experiments in electricity.
See also Nos. 2148, 2203, 2241 and 2321/2.

823 Mozart at Spinet

825 "The Angel of Life" (Giovanni Segantini)

824 Bear

1991. Death Bicentenary of Wolfgang Amadeus Mozart (composer).
2136 **823** 800l. multicoloured . . . 70 65

1991. Nature Protection. Multicoloured.
2137 500l. Type **824** 50 65
2138 500l. Peregrine falcon . . . 50 65
2139 500l. Deer 50 65
2140 500l. Marine life 50 65

1991. Christmas.
2141 **825** 600l. multicoloured . . . 50 50

826 Giulio and Alberto Bolaffi (stamp catalogue publishers)

1991. Stamp Day.
2142 **826** 750l. multicoloured . . . 60 50

827 Signature and National Flag

1991. Birth Cent of Pietro Nenni (politician).
2143 **827** 750l. multicoloured . . . 60 65

828 Runners

1992. 22nd European Indoor Light Athletics Championships, Genoa.
2144 **828** 600l. multicoloured . . . 55 50

829 Neptune Fountain, Florence

830 Statue of Marchese Alberto V of Este (founder) and University

1992. 400th Death Anniv of Bartolomeo Ammannati (architect and sculptor).
2145 **829** 750l. multicoloured . . . 60 50

1992. 600th Anniv (1991) of Ferrara University.
2146 **830** 750l. multicoloured . . . 60 50

831 Pediment

1992. Naples University.
2147 **831** 750l. multicoloured . . . 60 50

1992. 100 Years of Radio (2nd issue). As T **822**. Multicoloured.
2148 750l. Alessandro Volta (physicist) and Voltaic pile 75 65
Volta formulated the theory of current electricity and invented an electric battery.

832 Emblem and Venue **833** Medal of Lorenzo (Renato Beradi)

1992. "Genova '92" International Thematic Stamp Exhibition (1st issue).
2149 **832** 750l. multicoloured . . . 60 15
See also Nos. 2170/5.

1992. 500th Death Anniv of Lorenzo de Medici, "The Magnificent".
2150 **833** 750l. multicoloured . . . 60 50

834 Columbus before Queen Isabella **835** Scenes from Life of St. Maria Filippini (altar, Montefiascone Cathedral)

1992. 500th Anniv of Discovery of America by Columbus (2nd issue). Multicoloured.
2151 500l. Type **834** 50 80
2152 500l. Columbus's fleet . . . 50 80
2153 500l. Sighting land 50 80
2154 500l. Landing in the New World 50 80

1992. 300th Anniv of Maestre Pie Filippini Institute.
2155 **835** 750l. multicoloured . . . 60 50

836 Columbus Monument, Genoa (G. Giannetti)

1992. Europa. 500th Anniv of Discovery of America by Columbus. Multicoloured.
2156 750l. Type **836** . . . . . . 1·10 50
2157 850l. Emblem of "Colombo '92" exhibition, Genoa . . 1·40 50

837 Columbus presenting Natives

1992. 500th Anniv of Discovery of America by Columbus (3rd issue). Six sheets each 113 × 93 mm containing horiz designs as T **837** reproducing scenes from United States 1893 Columbian Exposition issue.
MS2158 Six sheets (a) 50l. green (Type **837**); 300l. blue (Columbus announcing discovery); 4000l. mauve (Columbus in chains). (b) 100l. lilac (Columbus welcomed at Barcelona); 800l. red (Columbus restored to favour); 3000l. green (Columbus describing third voyage). (c) 200l. blue (Columbus sighting land); 900l. blue (Columbus's fleet); 1500l. red (Queen Isabella pledging jewels). (d) 400l. brown (Columbus soliciting aid of Queen Isabella); 700l. red (Columbus at La Rabida); 1000l. blue (Recall of Columbus). (e) 500l. brown (Landing of Columbus); 600l. green ("Santa Maria"); 2000l. red (Portraits of Queen Isabella and Columbus). (f) 5000l. green ("America", Columbus and "Liberty") Set of 6 sheets . . 22·00 27·00

838 Seascape and Cyclists

1992. 75th "Tour of Italy" Cycle Race. Mult.
2159 750l. Type **838** 75 65
2160 750l. Mountains and cyclists 75 65
Nos. 2159/60 were issued together, se-tenant, forming a composite design.

839 Ball, Team Badge and Stylization of Milan Cathedral

1992. A.C. Milan, National Football Champion, 1991–92.
2161 **839** 750l. green, red and black 75 50

840 Viareggio

1992. Seaside Resorts. Multicoloured.
2162 750l. Type **840** 60 50
2163 750l. Rimini 60 50

841 Nuvolari

1992. Birth Centenary of Tazio Nuvolari (racing driver).
2164 **841** 3200l. multicoloured . . 2·75 2·10

1992. Tourist Publicity (19th series). As T **556**. Multicoloured.
2165 600l. Arcevia 50 65
2166 600l. Braies 50 65
2167 600l. Maratea 50 65
2168 600l. Pantelleria 50 65

842 "Adoration of the Shepherds" (detail)

1992. 400th Death Anniv of Jacopo da Ponte (painter).
2169 **842** 750l. multicoloured . . . 60 50

843 Columbus's House, Genoa **844** Woman's Eyes and Mouth

1992. "Genova '92" International Thematic Stamp Exhibition (2nd issue). Multicoloured.
2170 500l. Type **843** 40 50
2171 600l. Departure of Columbus's fleet from Palos, 1492 . . . . 50 50
2172 750l. Route map of Columbus's first voyage 60 50
2173 850l. Columbus sighting land 65 50
2174 1200l. Columbus landing on San Salvador . . . . . . 1·00 1·40
2175 3200l. Columbus, "Man" (Leonardo da Vinci), "Fury" (Michelangelo) and Raphael's portrait of Michelangelo . . . . . . 2·50 1·40

1992. Stamp Day. Ordinary or self-adhesive gum.
2176 **844** 750l. multicoloured . . . 75 50

845 Map of Europe and Lions Emblem

1992. 75th Anniv of Lions International and 38th Europa Forum, Genoa.
2178 **845** 3000l. multicoloured . . 2·30 50

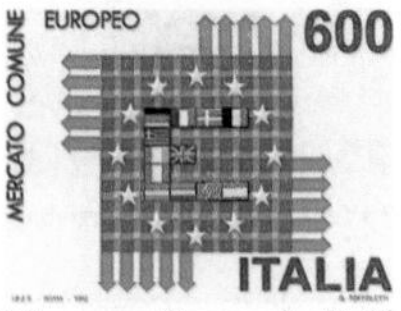

846 European Community Emblem and Members' Flags

1992. European Single Market (1st issue).
2179 **846** 600l. multicoloured . . . 50 1·60
See also Nos. 2182/93.

847 Woman with Food Bowl

1992. International Nutrition Conference, Rome.
2180 **847** 500l. multicoloured . . . 45 50

848 Caltagirone Crib **849** Buildings on Flag of Italy

1992. Christmas.
2181 **848** 600l. multicoloured . . . 55 50

1993. European Single Market (2nd issue). Designs differing in flag of country and language of inscription. Multicoloured.
2182 750l. Type **849** 55 50
2183 750l. Belgium 55 50
2184 750l. Denmark 55 50
2185 750l. France 55 50
2186 750l. Germany 55 50
2187 750l. Greece 55 50
2188 750l. Ireland 55 50
2189 750l. Luxembourg 55 50
2190 750l. Netherlands 55 50
2191 750l. Portugal 55 50
2192 750l. United Kingdom . . . 55 50
2193 750l. Spain 55 50

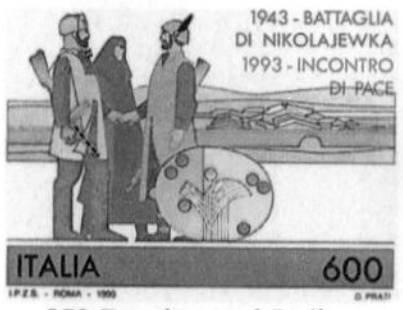

850 Russian and Italian Alpine Veterans
851 Mezzettino, Colombina and Arlecchino

1993. 50th Anniv Meeting of Veterans of Battle of Nikolayevka.
2194 **850** 600l. multicoloured . . . 50 50

1993. Death Bicentenary of Carlo Goldoni (dramatist). Multicoloured.
2195 500l. Type **851** 45 50
2196 500l. Arlecchino and portrait of Goldoni . . . 45 65

852 "Africa" (mosaic, Roman villa, Piazza Armerina)

1993. Artistic Heritage.
2197 **852** 750l. multicoloured . . . 65 50

853 Wedge stopping Heart-shaped Cog

1993. National Health Day. Campaign against Heart Disease.
2198 **853** 750l. multicoloured . . . 65 50

854 Tabby

1993. Domestic Cats. Multicoloured.
2199 600l. Type **854** 45 50
2200 600l. White Persian 45 50
2201 600l. Devon rex (vert) . . . 45 50
2202 600l. Maine coon (vert) . . 45 50

1993. 100 Years of Radio (3rd issue). As T **822**. Multicoloured.
2203 750l. Temistocle Calzecchi Onesti (physicist) and apparatus for detecting electromagnetic waves . . 65 50

855 "The Piazza"
856 Horace

1993. Death Bicentenary of Francesco Guardi (artist).
2204 **855** 3200l. multicoloured . . 2·50 2·75

1993. 2000th Death Anniv of Horace (Quintus Horatius Flaccus) (poet).
2205 **856** 600l. multicoloured . . . 50 50

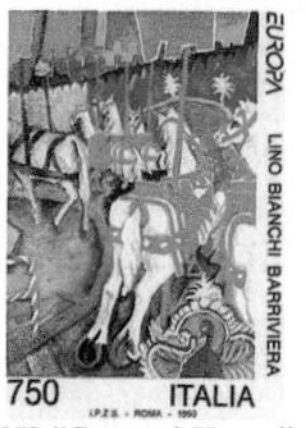

857 Cottolengo and Small House of the Divine Providence, Turin
858 "Carousel Horses" (Lino Bianchi Barriviera)

1993. St. Giuseppe Benedetto Cottolengo Commemoration.
2206 **857** 750l. multicoloured . . . 65 50

1993. Europa. Contemporary Art. Mult.
2207 750l. Type **858** 70 50
2208 850l. "Dynamism of Coloured Shapes" (Gino Severini) 80 50

859 Medal (Giuseppe Romagnoli)
860 Emblem

1993. 400th Anniv of San Luca National Academy.
2209 **859** 750l. multicoloured . . . 65 50

1993. "Family Fest '93" International Conference, Rome.
2210 **860** 750l. multicoloured . . . 65 50

861 Player and Club Badge
863 Canoeing

862 Carloforte

1993. Milan, National Football Champion, 1992–93.
2211 **861** 750l. multicoloured . . . 65 50

1993. Tourist Publicity (20th series). Mult.
2212 600l. Type **862** 50 50
2213 600l. Palmanova 50 50
2214 600l. Senigallia 50 50
2215 600l. Sorrento 50 50
See also Nos. 2248/51 and 2315/18.

1993. World Canoeing Championships, Trentino.
2216 **863** 750l. multicoloured . . . 65 50

864 Observatory

1993. Centenary of Regina Margherita Observatory.
2217 **864** 500l. multicoloured . . . 45 50

865 Staircase, St. Salome's Cathedral, Veroli
866 Soldier, Boy with Rifle and German Helmet

1993. Artistic Heritage.
2218 **865** 750l. multicoloured . . . 65 50

1993. Second World War 50th Anniversaries (1st issue). Multicoloured.
2219 750l. Type **866** (the Four Days of Naples) 75 50
2220 750l. Menorah, people in railway truck and Star of David (deportation of Roman Jews) 75 50
2221 750l. Seven Cervi brothers (execution) 75 50
See also Nos. 2259/61.

867 Carriage

1993. The Taxis Family in Postal History. Multicoloured.
2222 750l. Type **867** 60 50
2223 750l. Taxis arms 60 50
2224 750l. Gig 60 50
2225 750l. 17th-century postal messenger 60 50
2226 750l. 18th-century postal messenger 60 50

868 Head Office, Rome

1993. Centenary of Bank of Italy. Mult.
2227 750l. Type **868** . . . . . . 1·10 50
2228 1000l. 1000 lire banknote (first note issued by Bank) 1·50 80

869 Colonies Express Letter Stamp Design

1993. Stamp Day. Centenary of First Italian Colonies Stamps.
2229 **869** 600l. red and blue . . . 50 50

870 Tableau Vivant, Corchiano

1993. Christmas. Multicoloured.
2230 600l. Type **870** 50 50
2231 750l. "The Annunciation" (Piero della Francesca) . . 60 50

871 17th-century Map of Foggia

1993. Treasures from State Archives and Museums (1st series). Multicoloured.
2232 600l. Type **871** (Foggia Archives) 50 50
2233 600l. "Concert" (Bartolomeo Manfredi) (Uffizi Gallery, Florence) 50 50
2234 750l. View of Siena from 15th-century illuminated manuscript (Siena Archives) (vert) 55 50
2235 850l. "The Death of Adonis" (Sebastiano del Piombo) (Uffizi Gallery) 65 50
See also Nos. 2266/9, 2306/9 and 2346/9.

872 Ringmaster and Bareback Riders
873 Mother and Child inside House

1994. The Circus. Multicoloured.
2236 600l. Type **872** 45 50
2237 750l. Clowns 55 50

1994. "The Housewife, a Presence that Counts".
2238 **873** 750l. multicoloured . . . 60 50

874 "Bread" (Dario Piazza)
876 "The Risen Christ" (statue)

875 Boxer

1994. Paintings of Italian Food. Multicoloured.
2239 500l. Type **874** 45 50
2240 600l. "Italian Pasta in the World" (Erminia Scaglione) 60 50

1994. 100 Years of Radio (4th issue). As T **822**. Multicoloured.
2241 750l. Augusto Righi (physicist) and his Hertzian oscillator 65 50

1994. Dogs. Multicoloured.
2242 600l. Type **875** 45 50
2243 600l. Dalmatian 45 50
2244 600l. Maremma sheepdog 45 50
2245 600l. German shepherd . . 45 50

1994. Procession of "The Risen Christ", Tarquinia.
2246 **876** 750l. multicoloured . . . 60 50

877 Pacioli in Study

1994. 500th Anniv of Publication of "Summary of Arithmetic, Geometry, Proportion and Proportionality" by Fra' Luca Pacioli.
2247 **877** 750l. multicoloured . . . 60 50

1994. Tourist Publicity (21st series). As T **862**. Multicoloured.
2248 600l. Odescalchi Castle, Santa Marinella 45 50
2249 600l. St. Michael's Abbey, Monticchio 45 50
2250 600l. Orta San Giulio . . . 45 50
2251 600l. Cathedral, Messina . . 45 50

878 Kossuth
879 Women's High-diving

1994. Death Centenary of Lajos Kossuth (Hungarian statesman).
2252 **878** 3750l. multicoloured . . 2·75 1·60

1994. World Water Sports Championships. Multicoloured.
2253 600l. Type **879** 50 50
2254 750l. Water polo 60 50

880 Club Badge, Football and Colours

1994. Milan, National Football Champion, 1993–94.
2255 **880** 750l. multicoloured . . . 70 50

881 Camillo Golgi (cytologist) and Golgi Cells
882 "Goddess of Caldevigo" (bronze statuette, 5th century B.C.)

1994. Europa. Discoveries. Italian Nobel Prize winners. Multicoloured.
2256 750l. Type **881** (medicine, 1906) 65 50
2257 850l. Giulio Natta (chemist) and diagram of polymer structure (chemistry, 1963) 75 50

1994. "Ancient Peoples of Italy" Archaeological Exhibition, Rimini.
2258 **882** 750l. multicoloured . . . 60 50

883 Destruction of Montecassino
884 Washing of Feet

1994. Second World War 50th Anniversaries (2nd issue). Multicoloured.
2259 750l. Type **883** 45 50
2260 750l. Bound prisoners (Ardeatine Caves Massacre) 45 50
2261 750l. Family (Marzabotto Massacre) 45 50

1994. 22nd National Eucharistic Congress, Siena.
2262 **884** 600l. multicoloured . . . 45 50

885 "Ariadne, Venus and Bacchus"

1994. Artistic Heritage. 400th Death Anniv of Tintoretto (artist).
2263 **885** 750l. multicoloured . . . 60 50

886 "Piazza del Duomo during the Plague, 1630" (attr Cigoli)

1994. 750th Anniv of Arciconfraternita della Misericordia, Florence.
2264 **886** 750l. multicoloured . . . 50 50

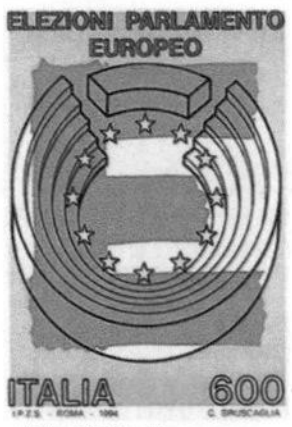

887 "E", European Union Emblem and Parliament
888 Olympic Rings and Pierre de Coubertin (founder)

1994. European Parliament Elections.
2265 **887** 600l. multicoloured . . . 50 50

1994. Treasures from State Archives and Museums (2nd series). As T **871**. Multicoloured.
2266 600l. Frontispiece of notary's register, 1623–24 (Catania Archives) (vert) 45 50
2267 600l. "Death of Patroclus" (Attic vase, 5th century B.C.) (Agrigento Archaeological Museum) (vert) 50 50
2268 750l. "Galata and his Wife" (statue) (National Roman Museum) (vert) 50 50
2269 850l. Civic seal, 1745 (Campobasso Archives) (vert) 60 50

1994. Centenary of Int Olympic Committee.
2270 **888** 850l. multicoloured . . . 70 50

889 Vesuvius and "G 7"
890 Church of the Holy House and "Madonna and Child"

1994. Group of Seven (industrialized countries) Summit, Naples.
2271 **889** 600l. blue, ultram & grn 50 50

1994. 700th Anniv of Shrine of the Nativity of the Virgin, Loreto.
2272 **890** 500l. multicoloured . . . 50 50

891 Pietro Miliani (papermaker) (after Francesco Rosaspina)
892 Frederick II (sculpture, Bitonto Cathedral)

1994. Stamp Day. Multicoloured.
2273 600l. Type **891** 45 50
2274 750l. Paper and Watermark Museum (former St. Dominic's Monastery), Fabriano 60 50

1994. 800th Birth Anniv of Frederick II, Holy Roman Emperor.
2275 **892** 750l. multicoloured . . . 65 50

893 St. Mark's Basilica

1994. 900th Anniv of Dedication of St. Mark's Basilica, Venice.
2276 **893** 750l. multicoloured . . . 70 65
MS2277 80 × 115 mm. No. 2276 together with No. 1491 of San Marino . . . . 1·30 2·75

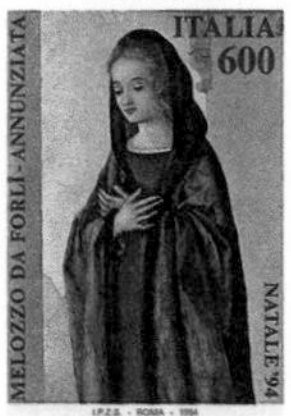

894 "The Annunciation" (Melozzo da Forlì)
895 Club Emblem on Globe

1994. Christmas. Multicoloured.
2278 600l. Type **894** 50 50
2279 750l. "Sacred Conversation" (detail, Lattanzio da Rimini) 65 50

1994. Centenary of Italian Touring Club.
2280 **895** 600l. multicoloured . . . 45 50

896 Headquarters, Rome

1994. 75th Anniv of Credit for Businesses and Public Works.
2281 **896** 750l. multicoloured . . . 70 50

897 New Emblem

1994. Incorporation of Italian Post. Size 34 × 26 mm.
2282 – 600l. red and silver . . . 60 50
2283 **897** 750l. black, green and red 85 50
2284 750l. red 85 50
DESIGN—VERT: 600l. Palazzo Querini Dubois, Venice (restored with Post Office help).
For 750 and 850l. values, size 26 × 17 mm, see Nos. 2343/4.

898 Gentile
899 Rainbow, Dove, Olive Tree and Flood

1994. 50th Death Anniv of Giovanni Gentile (philosopher).
2285 **898** 750l. multicoloured . . . 65 50

1995. For Flood Victims.
2286 **899** 750l.+2250l. mult . . . 3·25 5·50

900 Skater

1995. World Speed Skating Championships, Baselga di Pine.
2287 **900** 750l. multicoloured . . . 65 50

901 First Issue of "La Domenica del Corriere"
902 Rice

1995. 50th Death Anniv of Achille Beltrame (painter).
2288 **901** 500l. multicoloured . . . 55 50

1995. Italian Food. Multicoloured.
2289 500l. Type **902** 50 50
2290 750l. Olives and olive oil . . 65 50

903 Grey Herons

1995. Birds, Multicoloured.
2291 600l. Type **903** 45 50
2292 600l. Griffon vultures ("Grifone") 45 50
2293 600l. Golden eagles ("Aquila Reale") 45 50
2294 600l. White-winged snow finches ("Fringuello Alpino") 45 50

904 Anniversary Emblem

1995. 50th Anniv of U.N.O.
2295 **904** 850l. black, blue and gold 65 50

905 Detail of Monument (Giuseppe Grande)

1995. Centenary of Monument to the Fallen of the Five Days of Milan (1848 uprising).
2296 **905** 750l. multicoloured . . . 60 50

906 Princess Mafalda of Savoy and Concentration Camp

1995. 50th Anniv of End of Second World War. Multicoloured.
2297 750l. Type **906** 55 65
2298 750l. DUKW at Anzio . . . 55 65
2299 750l. Teresa Gullace and scene of her death 55 65
2300 750l. Florence Town Hall and Military Medal . . . 55 65
2301 750l. Vittorio Veneto Town Hall and Military Medal 55 65
2302 750l. Cagliari Town Hall and Military Medal . . . 55 65
2303 750l. Battle of Mount Lungo 55 65
2304 750l. Parachuting supplies in the Balkans 55 65
2305 750l. Light cruisers of the Eighth Division in Atlantic 55 65

1995. Treasures from State Archives and Museums (3rd series). As T **871**. Multicoloured.
2306 500l. Illuminated letter "P" from statute of Pope Innocent III (Rome Archives) (vert) 35 50
2307 500l. "Port of Naples" (detail, Bernardo Strozzi) (St. Martin National Museum, Naples) 45 50
2308 750l. Illuminated letter "I" showing the Risen Christ from 1481 document (Mantua Archives) (vert) 50 50
2309 850l. "Sacred Love and Profane Love" (Titian) (Borghese Museum and Gallery, Rome) 60 50

907 Emblem

908 Santa Croce Basilica, Florence

1995. Centenary of Venice Biennale.
2310 **907** 750l. blue, gold & yellow 60 50

1995. Artistic Heritage.
2311 **908** 750l. brown 60 50

909 Soldiers and Civilians celebrating

910 Players

1995. Europa. Peace and Freedom. Mult.
2312 750l. Type **909** (50th anniv of end of Second World War in Europe) 65 50
2313 850l. Mostar Bridge, (Bosnia) and Council of Europe emblem 75 50

1995. Centenary of Volleyball.
2314 **910** 750l. blue, orange & grn 60 50

1995. Tourist Publicity (22nd series). As T **862**. Multicoloured.
2315 750l. Alatri 55 50
2316 750l. Nuoro 55 50
2317 750l. Susa 55 50
2318 750l. Venosa 55 50

911 Experiment demonstrating X-rays

1995. Centenary of Discovery of X-rays by Wilhelm Rontgen.
2319 **911** 750l. multicoloured . . . 60 50

912 Player and Club Badge

1995. Juventus, National Football Champion, 1994–95.
2320 **912** 750l. multicoloured . . . 60 50

913 Villa Griffone (site of Marconi's early experiments)

1995. 100 Years of Radio (5th issue). Centenary of First Radio Transmission. Multicoloured.
2321 750l. Type **913** 60 50
2322 850l. Guglielmo Marconi and transmitter (36 × 21 mm) 70 50

914 St. Antony, Holy Basilica (Padua) and Page of Gospel

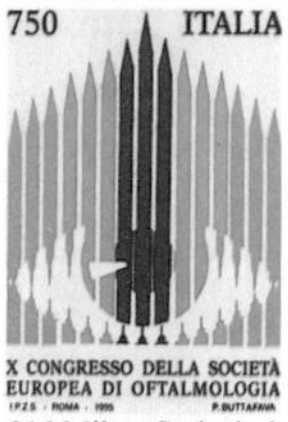

916 Milan Cathedral and Eye (congress emblem)

915 Durazzo Pallavicini, Pegli

1995. 800th Birth Anniv of St. Antony of Padua. Multicoloured.
2323 750l. Type **914** 60 50
2324 850l. St. Antony holding Child Jesus (painting, Vieira Lusitano) (horiz) 70 50

1995. Public Gardens (1st series). Multicoloured.
2325 750l. Type **915** 60 50
2326 750l. Boboli, Florence . . . 60 50
2327 750l. Ninfa, Cisterna di Latina 60 50
2328 750l. Parco della Reggia, Caserta 60 50
See also Nos. 2439/42.

1995. 10th European Ophthalmological Society Congress, Milan.
2329 **916** 750l. multicoloured . . . 60 50

917 "Sailors' Wives"

1995. Birth Centenary of Massimo Campigli (painter).
2330 **917** 750l. multicoloured . . . 75 50

918 Dome of Santa Maria del Fiore (Florence), Galileo and Albert Einstein

1995. 14th World Relative Physics Conference, Florence.
2331 **918** 750l. blue, brown & black 60 50

919 Rudolph Valentino in "The Son of the Sheik"

1995. Centenary of Motion Pictures.
2332 **919** 750l. black, blue and red 55 50
2333 – 750l. multicoloured . . . 55 50
2334 – 750l. multicoloured . . . 55 50
2335 – 750l. multicoloured . . . 55 50
DESIGNS: No. 2333, Toto in "The Gold of Naples"; 2334, Frederico Fellini's "Cabiria Nights"; 2335, Poster (by Massimo Geleng) for "Cinecitta 95" film festival.

920 Wheatfield and Anniversary Emblem

1995. 50th Anniv of F.A.O.
2336 **920** 850l. multicoloured . . . 70 65

921 St. Albert's Stone Coffin (detail) and Basilica

1995. 900th Anniversaries of Pontida Basilica and Death of St. Albert of Prezzate.
2337 **921** 1000l. brown and blue 80 80

922 Athletes

1995. 1st World Military Games, Rome.
2338 **922** 850l. multicoloured . . . 75 65

923 Globe and Means of Communication

1995. 50th Anniv of Ansa News Agency.
2339 **923** 750l. multicoloured . . . 60 50

924 Crib (Stefano da Putignano), Polignano Cathedral

1995. Christmas. Multicoloured.
2340 750l. Type **924** 85 50
2341 850l. "Adoration of the Wise Men" (detail, Fra Angelico) . . . . 1·00 65

925 Renato Mondolfo (philatelist) and Trieste 1949 20l. Stamp

1995. Stamp Day.
2342 **925** 750l. multicoloured . . . 55 50

1995. 1st Anniv of Incorporation of Italian Post. Size 26 × 17 mm.
2343 **897** 750l. red 55 50
2344 850l. black, green and red 70 65

926 Collage representing Marinetti's Works

1996. 120th Birth Anniv of Filippo Marinetti (writer and founder of Futurist movement).
2345 **926** 750l. multicoloured . . . 55 50

1996. Treasures from State Archives and Museums (4th series). As T **871**. Multicoloured.
2346 750l. Arms (Georgofili Academy, Florence) . . . 55 50
2347 750l. Illuminated letter showing St. Luke and his ox from Constitution of 1372 (Lucca Archives) (vert) 55 50
2348 850l. Inkwells, pen and manuscript of Gabriele d'Annunzio (writer) (Il Vittoriale, Gardone Riviera) 60 50
2349 850l. "Life of King Modus and Queen Racio" from 1486 miniature (Turin Archives) 60 50

927 "Sarah and the Angel" (fresco, Archbishop's Palace, Udine)

1996. 300th Birth Anniv of Giambattista Tiepolo (painter).
2350 **927** 1000l. multicoloured . . 90 80

928 White Wine

1996. Italian Wine Production. Multicoloured.
2351 500l. Type **928** 30 50
2352 750l. Red wine 45 50

929 Marco Polo and Palace in the Forbidden City

1996. 700th Anniv (1995) of Marco Polo's Return from Asia and "China '96" International Stamp Exhibition, Peking.
2353 **929** 1250l. multicoloured . . 1·10 1·10

930 Milan Cathedral (left detail)

931 Quill pen and Satellite (50th Anniv of National Federation of Italian Press)

1996. "Italia 98" International Stamp Exhibition, Milan (1st issue). Multicoloured.
2354 750l. Type **930** . . . . . . 1·90 50
2355 750l. Cathedral (right detail) 1·90 50
Nos. 2354/5 were issued together, se-tenant, forming a composite design of the Cathedral.
See also Nos. **MS**2412, 2518, 2523, 2528/30 and 2531.

1996. Anniversaries.
2356 **931** 750l. multicoloured . . . 65 50
2357 – 750l. blue, pink and black 65 50
DESIGN—HORIZ: No. 2357, Globe (centenary of "La Gazetta dello Sport" (newspaper)).

932 Postman and Emblem

933 Uniforms of Different Periods

1996. International Museum of Postal Images, Belvedere Ostrense.
2358 **932** 500l. multicoloured . . . 50 50

1996. Centenary of Academy of Excise Guards.
2359 **933** 750l. multicoloured . . . 70 50

934 Truck and Route Map

935 Carina Negrone (pilot)

1996. Trans-continental Drive, Rome–New York.
2360 **934** 4650l. multicoloured . . 4·25 3·25

1996. Europa. Famous Women. Multicoloured.
2361 750l. Type **935** 60 50
2362 850l. Adelaide Ristori (actress) 75 50

936 Fishes, Sea and Coastline from St. Raphael to Genoa

1996. 20th Anniv of Ramoge Agreement on Environmental Protection of the Mediterranean.
2363 **936** 750l. multicoloured . . . 65 50

937 Celestino V and Town of Fumone

1996. 700th Death Anniv of Pope Celestino V.
2364 **937** 750l. multicoloured . . . 70 50

938 St Anthony's Church, Diano Marina

1996. Tourist Publicity (23rd series). Mult.
2365 750l. Type **938** 60 50
2366 750l. Pienza Cathedral . . . 60 50
2367 750l. Belltower of St. Michael the Archangel's Church, Monte Sant'Angelo . . . 60 50
2368 750l. Prehistoric stone dwelling, Lampedusa . . 60 50

939 Abbey and Relief from 12th-century Ivory Reliquary

1996. 500th Anniv of Reconsecration of Farfa Abbey.
2369 **939** 1000l. black, yell & orge 90 80

940 Fair Entrance and Mt. Pellegrino

1996. Mediterranean Fair, Palermo.
2370 **940** 750l. multicoloured . . . 65 50

941 State Arms

942 Rider and Emblem

1996. 50th Anniv of Italian Republic.
2371 **941** 750l. multicoloured . . . 60 50

1996. 50th Anniv of Production of Vespa Motor Scooters.
2372 **942** 750l. multicoloured . . . 60 50

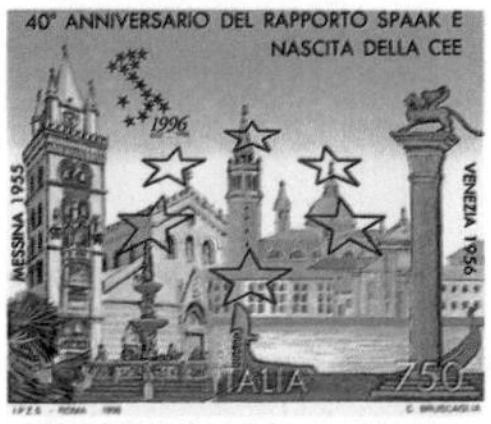

943 Views of Messina and Venice

1996. 40th Anniv of Founding Meetings of European Economic Community, Messina and Venice.
2373 **943** 750l. multicoloured . . . 60 50

944 Athlete on Starting Block and 1896 Athletes

1996. Centenary of Modern Olympic Games and Olympic Games, Atlanta. Multicoloured.
2374 500l. Type **944** 45 50
2375 750l. Putting the shot and view of Atlanta (vert) . . 65 50
2376 850l. Gymnast, stadium and basketball player 75 50
2377 1250l. 1896 stadium, Athens, and 1996 stadium, Atlanta (vert) . . . . 1·00 1·10

945 "Acanthobrahmaea europaea"

1996. Butterflies. Multicoloured.
2378 750l. Type **945** 55 50
2379 750l. "Melanargia arge" . . 55 50
2380 750l. "Papilio hospiton" . . 55 50
2381 750l. "Zygaena rubicundus" 55 50

946 "Prima Comunione"

1996. Italian Films (1st series).
2382 **946** 750l. black, red and blue 60 50
2383 – 750l. multicoloured . . . 60 50
2384 – 750l. multicoloured . . . 60 50
DESIGNS: No. 2383, Poster for "Cabiria"; 2384, "Scusate il Ritardo".

See also Nos. 2453/5 and 2528/30.

947 Santa Maria del Fiore

1996. 700th Anniv of Cathedral of Santa Maria del Fiore, Florence.
2385 **947** 750l. blue 70 50

948 Player, Shield and Club Badge

949 Choppy (congress mascot)

1996. Milan, National Football Champion, 1995–96.
2386 **948** 750l. multicoloured . . . 85 50

1996. 13th International Prehistoric and Protohistoric Sciences Congress.
2387 **949** 850l. multicoloured . . . 75 50

950 Games Emblem and Pictograms

952 Rejoicing Crowd and Club Badge

951 Fair Entrance

1996. Mediterranean Games, Bari (1997).
2388 **950** 750l. multicoloured . . . 70 50

1996. Levant Fair, Bari.
2389 **951** 750l. multicoloured . . . 70 50

1996. Juventus, European Football Champion, 1995–96.
2390 **952** 750l. multicoloured . . . 70 50

953 Pertini

954 Montale and Hoopoe

1996. Birth Centenary of Alessandro Pertini (President 1978–85).
2391 **953** 750l. multicoloured . . . 65 50

1996. Birth Centenary of Eugenio Montale (poet).
2392 **954** 750l. brown and blue . . 65 50

955 "The Annunciation"

1996. 400th Birth Anniv of Pietro Berrettini da Cortona (artist).
2393 **955** 500l. multicoloured . . . 55 50

956 Tex Willer (Galep)

1996. Stamp Collecting. Strip Cartoons. Mult.
2394 750l. Type **956** 65 50
2395 850l. Corto Maltese (Hugo Pratt) 75 50

957 Vortex and "Stamps"

958 Bell Tower and Former Benedictine Abbey (seat of faculty)

1996. Stamp Day.
2396 **957** 750l. multicoloured . . . 60 50

1996. Universities.
2397 **958** 750l. brown 60 50
2398 – 750l. blue 60 50
2399 – 750l. green 60 50
DESIGNS—VERT: No. 2397. Type **958** (centenary of Faculty of Agriculture, Perugia University); 2398, Former St. Matthew's Cathedral (seat of Medical School), Salerno University. HORIZ: No. 2399, Athenaeum, Sassari University.

959 Emblem

960 "Madonna of the Quail" (Antonio Pisanello)

1996. World Food Summit, Rome.
2400 **959** 850l. green and black . . 65 50

1996. Christmas. Multicoloured.
2401 750l. Type **960** 60 50
2402 850l. Father Christmas and toys (horiz) 75 50

961 "UNESCO" and Globe

962 Headquarters, Rome

1996. 50th Anniversaries of UNESCO and UNICEF.
2403 750l. Type **961** 55 50
2404 850l. UNICEF emblem on kite, baby and globe . . . 70 50

1996. 70th Anniv of National Statistics Institute.
2405 **962** 750l. multicoloured . . . 60 50

963 Bookcase

964 Hall of the Tricolour, Reggio Emilia

1996. 50th Anniv of Strega Prize.
2406 **963** 3400l. multicoloured . . 2·30 2·40

1997. Bicentenary of First Tricolour (now national flag), Cisalpine Republic.
2407 **964** 750l. multicoloured . . . 60 50

965 Tower Blocks and Skier

1997. World Alpine Skiiing Championships, Sestriere. Multicoloured.

2408	750l. Type **965**	60	50
2409	850l. Olympic colours forming ski run and ski	60	50

966 Ferraris, Early Motor and Ferraris National Electrotechnology Institute, Turin

1997. Death Centenary of Galileo Ferraris (physicist).
2410 **966** 750l. multicoloured . . . 60 50

967 Loi

1997. 5th Death Anniv of Emanuela Loi (bodyguard killed in Mafia car bombing).
2411 **967** 750l. multicoloured . . . 60 50

1997. "Italia 98" International Stamp Exhibition, Milan (2nd issue). Sheet 150 × 80 mm containing T **968** and similar vert designs. Multicoloured.
MS2412 750l. Bologna 1910 cancellation aerogramme from Balboa flight and postcard with 1917 25c. airmail stamp (Aerophilately); 750l. Cancellations used for the signing of the Rome Treaty (forming European Economic Community), Rome Olympic Games and Holy Year, 1952 Leonardo da Vinci 80l. stamp and 1931 inauguration of Milan railway station postcard (Thematic Philately); 750l. Type **968** (Postal History); 750l. "Democratica", Italian stamp catalogue and L'Italia Filatelica (stamp review) (Philatelic Literature) . . . . 5·25 4·00

969 Statue of Marcus Aurelius

970 St. Germiniano (after Bartolomeo Schedoni) holding Modena Cathedral

1997. 40th Anniv of Treaty of Rome (foundation of European Economic Community).
2413 **969** 750l. multicoloured . . . 50 50

1997. 1600th Death Anniv of St. Germiniano (patron saint of Modena).
2414 **970** 750l. multicoloured . . . 60 50

971 "Baptism of St. Ambrose" and "Hand of God recalling him to City"

972 Statue of Minerva, Central Square, Rome University

1997. 1600th Death Anniv of St. Ambrose, Bishop of Milan.
2415 **971** 1000l. multicoloured . . 75 50

The illustrations are taken from reliefs by Volvinio on the Golden Altar in St. Ambrose's Cathedral, Milan.

1997. Universities.

2416	**972**	750l. red	60	50
2417	–	750l. blue	60	50

DESIGN: No. 2417, Palace of Bo, Padua University.

973 St. Peter's Cathedral and Colosseum within "Wolf suckling Romulus and Remus"

1997. 2750th Anniv of Foundation of Rome.
2418 **973** 850l. multicoloured . . . 70 50

974 Pre-Roman Walls, Gela

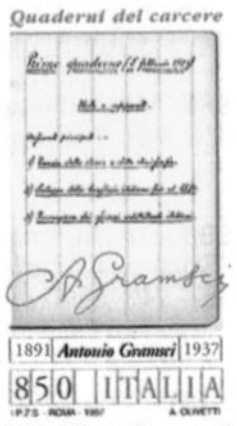

975 First Page of Prison Notebook and Signature

1997.
2419 **974** 750l. multicoloured . . . 60 50

1997. 60th Death Anniv of Antonio Gramsci (politician).
2420 **975** 850l. multicoloured . . . 60 50

976 Teracotta Relief and Cloisters

978 Detail of 1901 Poster for "Tosca" and Theatre

977 Shoemaker's Workshop

1997. 500th Anniv of Consecration of Pavia Church.
2421 **976** 1000l. multicoloured . . 85 50

1997. Europa. Tales and Legends. Mult.

2422	800l. Type **977** ("He who becomes the Property of Others works for his Soup")	55	50
2423	900l. Street singer (19th-century copper etching)	65	50

1997. Centenary of Teatro Massimo, Palermo.
2424 **978** 800l. multicoloured . . . 65 50

979 St. Sebastian's Church, Acireale

1997. Tourist Publicity (24th series). Mult.

2425	800l. Type **979**	65	50
2426	800l. Cicero and his tomb, Formia	65	50
2427	800l. St. Mary of the Assumption, Positano	65	50
2428	800l. St. Vitale's Basilica, Ravenna	65	50

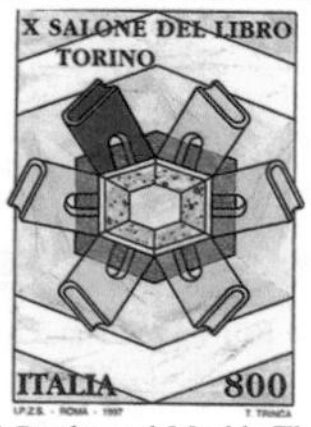

980 Books and Marble Floor

1997. 10th Book Salon, Turin.
2429 **980** 800l. multicoloured . . . 70 50

981 Queen Paola and Castel Sant'Angelo, Rome

1997. 60th Birthday of Queen Paola of Belgium.
2430 **981** 750l. multicoloured . . . 70 50

982 Palazzo della Civilta del Lavoro and Fair Pavilions

1997. Rome Fair.
2431 **982** 800l. multicoloured . . . 70 50

983 Orvieto Cathedral

984 Morosini in Via Tasso Prison, 1944

1997.
2432 **983** 450l. violet 40 50

1997. 53rd Death Anniv of Father Giuseppe Morosini.
2433 **984** 800l. multicoloured . . . 65 50

985 Player, Club Emblem and Football

986 Chamois and "Iris marsica"

1997. Juventus, National Football Champion, 1996–97.
2434 **985** 800l. multicoloured . . . 65 50

1997. 75th Anniv of Abruzzo National Park.
2435 **986** 800l. multicoloured . . . 55 50

987 Towers and Fair Complex

1997. Bologna Fair.
2436 **987** 800l. multicoloured . . . 65 50

988 Pennant and Ships' Bows

990 Cogwheel and Robot Arm (industry)

989 Runner, High Jumper and Gymnast

1997. Centenary of Italian Naval League.
2437 **988** 800l. multicoloured . . . 70 50

1997. 13th Mediterranean Games, Bari.
2438 **989** 900l. multicoloured . . . 75 50

1997. Public Gardens (2nd series). As T **915**. Multicoloured.

2439	800l. Orto Botanico, Palermo	60	50
2440	800l. Villa Sciarra, Rome	60	50
2441	800l. Cavour, Santena	60	50
2442	800l. Miramare, Trieste	60	50

1997. Italian Work. Multicoloured.

2443	800l. Type **990**	55	50
2444	900l. Cereals, fruit trees, grapes and sun (agriculture) (horiz)	60	50

991 Globe and the "Matthew"

1997. 500th Anniv of John Cabot's Discovery of North America.
2445 **991** 1300l. multicoloured . . 1·10 80

992 Verri

993 "Madonna of the Rosary" (Pomarancio il Vecchio)

1997. Death Bicentenary of Pietro Verri (illuminist).
2446 **992** 3600l. multicoloured . . 3·75 2·40

1997. Painters' Anniversaries. Multicoloured.

2447	450l. Type **993** (400th death anniv)	55	50
2448	650l. "The Miracle of Ostia" ((detail, Paolo Uccello) (600th birth anniv)) (26 × 37 mm)	45	50

994 Procession

1997. Varia Festival, Palmi.
2449 **994** 800l. multicoloured . . . 70 50

995 Basketball

1997. University Games, Sicily. Multicoloured.

2450	450l. Type **995**	35	50
2451	800l. High jumping	65	50

996 Rosmini

1997. Birth Bicentenary of Antonio Rosmini (philosopher).

2452 **996** 800l. multicoloured . . . 70 50

1997. Italian Films (2nd series). As T **946**.

2453 800l. multicoloured 55 50

2454 800l. black, blue and red . . 55 50

2455 800l. multicoloured 55 50

DESIGNS: No. 2453, Pietro Germi in "Il Ferroviere"; 2454, Anna Magnani in "Mamma Roma"; 2455, Ugo Tognazzi in "Amici Miei".

997 Open Book and Beach, Viareggio

1997. Viareggio-Repaci Prize.

2456 **997** 4000l. multicoloured . . 3·25 2·40

998 Venue and Bell Tower

1997. International Trade Fair, Bolzano.

2457 **998** 800l. multicoloured . . . 70 50

999 Bronze Head (500 BC)

1000 Pope Paul VI and Door of Death, St. Peter's Cathedral, Rome

1997. Museum Exhibits. Multicoloured.

2458 450l. Type **999** (National Museum, Reggio Calabria) 40 50

2459 650l. "Madonna and Child with Two Vases of Roses" (Ercole de Roberti) (National Picture Gallery, Ferrara) 45 50

2460 800l. Miniature of poet Sordello da Goito (Arco Palace Museum, Mantua) 50 50

2461 900l. "St. George and the Dragon" (Vitale di Bologna) (National Picture Gallery, Bologna) 55 50

1997. Birth Centenary of Pope Paul VI.

2462 **1000** 4000l. blue . . . . . . 3·25 2·10

1001 Portello Pavilion (venue) and Milan Cathedral

1002 War-ravaged and Reconstructed Cities

1997. Milan Fair.

2463 **1001** 800l. multicoloured . . 65 50

1997. 50th Anniv of European Recovery Programme ("Marshall Plan").

2464 **1002** 800l. multicoloured . . 65 50

1003 Nativity (crib, St Francis's Church, Leonessa)

1997. Christmas. Multicoloured.

2465 800l. Type **1003** 65 50

2466 900l. "Nativity" (painting, Sta. Maria Maggiore, Spelo) 85 50

1004 Production Plant and Merloni

1005 Cavalcaselle and Drawings

1997. Birth Centenary of Aristide Merloni (entrepreneur).

2467 **1004** 800l. multicoloured . . 65 50

1997. Death Centenary of Giovanni Battista Cavalcaselle (art historian).

2468 **1005** 800l. multicoloured . . 70 50

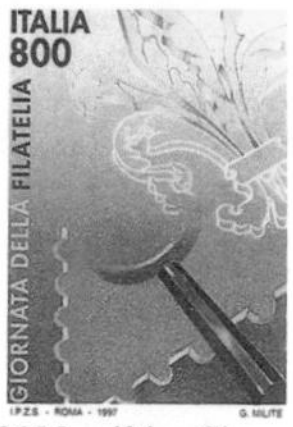

1006 Magnifying Glass and Fleur-de-lis

1997. Stamp Day.

2469 **1006** 800l. multicoloured . . 70 50

1007 Refugees aboard "Toscana" (steamer)

1997. 50th Anniv of Exodus of Italian Inhabitants from Istria, Fiume and Dalmatia.

2470 **1007** 800l. multicoloured . . 70 50

1008 Arms of State Police and Badge of Traffic Police

1997. 50th Anniv of Traffic Police.

2471 **1008** 800l. multicoloured . . 70 50

1009 Map of Italy in Column and Flag

1998. 50th Anniv of Constitution.

2472 **1009** 800l. black, red & green 65 50

1010 "Hercules and the Hydra"

1998. 500th Death Anniv of Antonio del Pollaiolo (painter).

2473 **1010** 800l. multicoloured . . 65 50

1011 Bertolt Brecht

1998. Writers' Birth Centenaries.

2474 **1011** 450l. multicoloured . . 40 50

2475 – 650l. multicoloured . . 55 50

2476 – 800l. multicoloured . . 65 65

2477 – 900l. blue, green & black 75 50

DESIGNS—HORIZ: 650l. Federico Garcia Lorca (poet); 800l. Curzio Malaparte. VERT: 900l. Leonida Repaci.

1012 Fair Complex

1998. Verona Fair.

2478 **1012** 800l. multicoloured . . 65 50

1013 Memorial Tablet in Casale Montferrato Synagogue

1998. 150th Anniv of Granting of Full Citizen Rights to Italian Jews.

2479 **1013** 800l. multicoloured . . 55 50

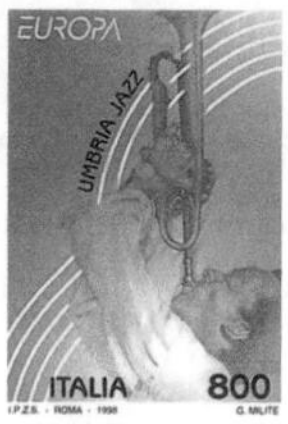

1014 Trombonist

1998. Europa. National Festivals. Mult.

2480 800l. Type **1014** (Umbria Jazz Festival) 60 50

2481 900l. Boy holding animal (Giffoni Film Festival) . . 65 50

1015 "The Last Supper"

1998. 500th Anniv of Completion of "The Last Supper" (mural) by Leonardo da Vinci.

2482 **1015** 800l. brown 65 50

1016 Costumes designed by Bernardo Buontalenti for First Opera in Florence

1017 Turin Cathedral and Holy Shroud

1998. Italian Theatre. Multicoloured.

2483 800l. Type **1016** (400th anniv of opera) 55 50

2484 800l. Gaetano Donizetti (composer, 150th death anniv) (horiz) 55 50

1998. 500th Anniv of Turin Cathedral. Display of the Holy Shroud.

2485 **1017** 800l. multicoloured . . 65 50

1018 Otranto Castle

1998. Tourist Publicity (25th series). Mult.

2486 800l. Type **1018** 65 50

2487 800l. Mori Fountain and Orsini Tower. Marino . . 65 50

2488 800l. Valfederia Chapel, Livigno 65 50

2489 800l. Marciana Marina, Elba 65 50

1019 Cagliari Cathedral, Drummer and Fair Building

1998. International Sardinia Fair, Cagliari.

2490 **1019** 800l. multicoloured . . 65 50

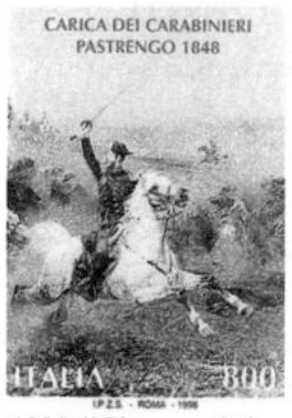

1020 "Charge of the Carabinieri at Pastrengo" (Sebastiano de Albertis)

1021 Flags

1998. 150th Anniv of Battle of Pastrengo.

2491 **1020** 800l. multicoloured . . 65 50

1998. Padua Fair.

2492 **1021** 800l. multicoloured . . 60 50

1022 Player and Club Badge

1998. Juventus, National Football Champion, 1997–98.

2493 **1022** 800l. multicoloured . . 65 50

1023 Turin Polytechnic

1024 Emblem

1998. Universities.

2494 **1023** 800l. blue 60 50

1998. World Food Programme.

2495 **1024** 900l. multicoloured . . 85 50

1025 Santa Maria de Pesio Carthusian Monastery

1998. Artistic Heritage.

2496 **1025** 800l. multicoloured . . 60 50

1026 Ammonites and Pergola

1998. 4th International "Fossils, Evolution, Ambience" Congress, Pergola.
2497 **1026** 800l. multicoloured . . 60 50

1027 Flag at Half-mast

1028 Endoscope and Globe

1998. "The Forces of Order, the Fallen".
2498 **1027** 800l. multicoloured . . 60 50

1998. 6th World General Endoscopic Surgery Congress, Rome.
2499 **1028** 900l. multicoloured . . 85 50

1029 First Parliamentary Chamber

1998. National Museums. Multicoloured.
2500 800l. Type **1029** (Italian Risorgimento Museum, Turin) 60 50
2501 800l. Statue of an ephebus (Athenian youth), Temple of Concord and column of Temple of Vulcan (Regional Archaeology Museum, Agrigento) (vert) 60 50
2502 800l. Sculpture by Umberto Boccioni and Palazzo Venier dei Leoni (venue) (Peggy Guggenheim Collection, Venice) . . . 60 50

1030 Fair Complex and Basilica

1998. Vicenza Trade Fair.
2503 **1030** 800l. multicoloured . . 65 50

1031 Leopardi (after Luigi Lolli) and Palazzo Leopardi, Recanati

1998. Birth Bicentenary of Giacomo Leopardi (poet).
2504 **1031** 800l. brown and black 55 50

1032 Young Etruscan Girl (detail of tomb painting)

1033 Pitch, Pitcher and Batter

1998. Women in Art.
2505 **1032** 100l. black, green & sil 15 15
2506 – 450l. multicoloured . . 40 15
2507 – 650l. multicoloured . . 60 15
2508 – 800l. brown and black 70 15
2509 – 1000l. blue, brn & blk 90 65
DESIGNS: 450l. Detail of "Herod's Banquet and the Dance of Salome" (fresco by Filippo Lippi in Prato Cathedral); 650l. "Profile of a Woman" (Antonio del Pollaiuolo); 800l. "Lady with a Unicorn" (detail, Raphael); 1000l. "Constanza Buonarelli" (bust by Gian Lorenzo Bernini).
For these designs but with face values in euros added, see Nos. 2537/41.

1998. 33rd World Cup Baseball Championship, Florence.
2510 **1033** 900l. multicoloured . . 75 50

1034 Columbus and Vespucci

1998. 500th Anniversaries of Landing of Christopher Columbus in Venezuela and of Amerigo Vespucci's Explorations.
2511 **1034** 1300l. multicoloured . . 1·00 80

1035 Emblem

1998. 50th International Stamp Fair, Riccione.
2512 **1035** 800l. multicoloured . . 65 50

1036 Mother Teresa and Child

1998. 1st Death Anniv of Mother Teresa (founder of Missionaries of Charity). Multicoloured.
2513 800l. Type **1036** 65 50
2514 900l. Mother Teresa (vert) 75 50

1037 Father Pio and Monastery Church, San Giovanni Rotondo

1998. 30th Death Anniv of Father Pio da Pietrelcina (Capuchin friar who bore the stigmata).
2515 **1037** 800l. blue 65 50

1038 Titus Arch, Rome, and Sicilian Mosaic of Rider

1998. World Equestrian Championships, Rome.
2516 **1038** 4000l. multicoloured . . 3·25 1·90

1039 Telecommunications College, Rome

1998. Universities.
2517 **1039** 800l. blue 65 50

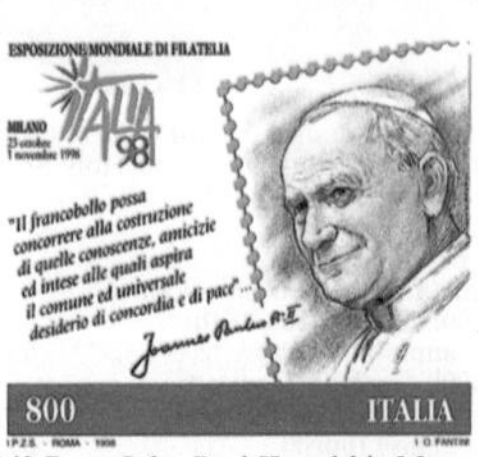

1040 Pope John Paul II and his Message

1998. "Italia 98" International Stamp Exhibition, Milan (3rd issue). Stamp Day.
2518 **1040** 800l. multicoloured . . 75 50

1041 "Giuseppe Garibaldi" (aircraft carrier)

1998. Armed Forces Day. Multicoloured.
2519 800l. Type **1041** (Navy) . . 65 50
2520 800l. Eurofighter 2000 (75th anniv of Air Force) . . . 65 50
2521 800l. Carabiniere (vert) . . . 65 50
2522 800l. Battle of El-Alamein at night (Army) (vert) . . . 65 50

1042 "Dionysus" (bronze statue)

1998. "Italia 98" International Stamp Exhibition, Milan (4th issue). Art Day.
2523 **1042** 800l. multicoloured . . 65 50

1043 Ferrari competing in Race, 1931

1998. "Italia 98" International Stamp Exhibition, Milan (5th issue). Birth Centenary of Enzo Ferrari (car designer). Sheet 160 × 110 mm containing T **1043** and similar horiz designs. Multicoloured.
MS2524 800l. Type **1043**; 800l. Formula 1 Ferrari, 1952; 800l. Ferrari GTO, 1963; 800l. Formula 1 Ferrari, 1998 . . . . 3·50 4·00

1044 Hand releasing Birds

1998. 50th Anniv of Universal Declaration of Human Rights.
2525 **1044** 1400l. multicoloured . . 1·10 80

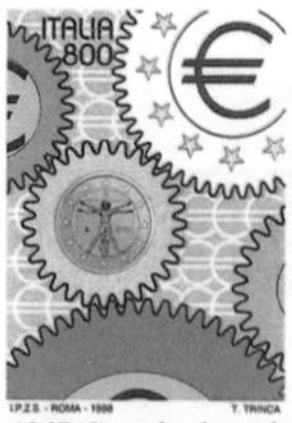

1045 Cogwheels and "Proportions of Man" (Leonardo da Vinci)

1046 Satellite Dish, Type, Book and "Internet"

1998. Europa Day. Ordinary or self-adhesive gum.
2526 **1045** 800l. multicoloured . . 65 50

1998. "Italia 98" International Stamp Exhibition, Milan (6th issue). Cinema Day. As T **946**. Multicoloured.
2528 450l. "Ti Conosco Mascherino" (dir. Eduardo de Filippo) . . . 40 50
2529 800l. "Fantasmia a Roma" (Antonio Pietrangeli) . . 65 50
2530 900l. "Il Signor Max" (Mario Camerini) 75 50

1998. "Italia 98" International Stamp Exhibition, Milan (7th issue). Communications Day.
2531 **1046** 800l. multicoloured . . 55 50

1047 Arrows circling Letter

1048 "Epiphany" (sculpture, St. Mark's Church, Seminara)

1998. "Italia 98" International Stamp Exhibition, Milan (8th issue). Post Day. Sheet 130 × 90 mm.
MS2532 **1047** 4000l. multicoloured 3·00 5·50

1998. Christmas.
2533 **1048** 800l. blue 60 50
2534 – 900l. brown 65 50
DESIGN—HORIZ: 900l. "Adoration of the Shepherds" (drawing, Giulio Romano).

1049 "Ecstasy of St. Teresa"

1998. 400th Birth Anniv of Gian Lorenzo Bernini (sculptor).
2535 **1049** 900l. multicoloured . . 65 50

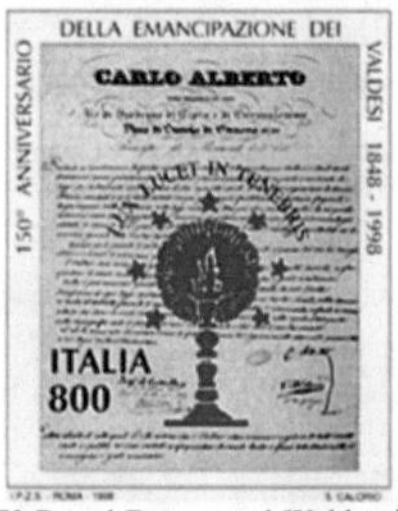

1050 Royal Decree and Waldensian Emblem

1998. 150th Anniv of Toleration of the Waldenses (religious sect).
2536 **1050** 800l. multicoloured . . 55 50

DENOMINATION. From No. 2537 Italian stamps are denominated both in lira and in euros. As no coins or notes for the latter were in circulation until 2002, the catalogue continues to use the lira value.

1999. As Nos. 2505/9, but with face value in euros added.
2537 100l. black, green and silver 10 15
2538 450l. multicoloured 35 15
2539 650l. multicoloured 50 15
2540 800l. brown and black . . . 65 50
2541 1000l. blue, brown and black 75 65

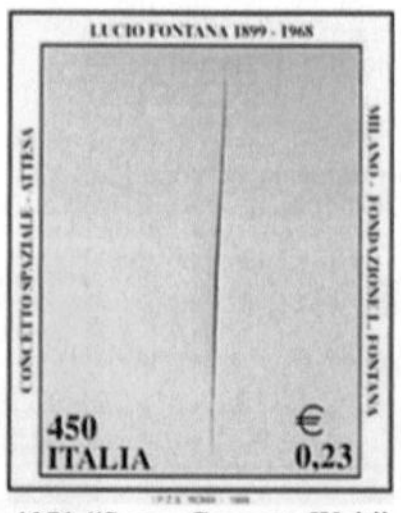

1051 "Space Concept–Wait"

1999. Birth Centenary of Lucio Fontana (artist).
2542 **1051** 450l. blue and black . . 35 50

1052 La Sila National Park, Calabria

1053 Holy Door, St. Peter's Cathedral

1999. Europa. Parks and Gardens. Multicoloured.
2543 800l. Type **1052** 60 50
2544 900l. Tuscan Archipelago National Park (horiz) . . 70 50

1999. Holy Year 2000.
2545 **1053** 1400l. multicoloured . . 1·00 95

1054 St. Egidius's Church, Cellere

1999. Artistic Heritage.
2546 **1054** 800l. brown 55 50

1055 Holy Year 2000 and 11th-century Bells

1999. Museums. Multicoloured.
2547 800l. Type **1055** (History of Campanology Museum, Agnone) 55 50
2548 800l. "Lake with Swan" (stained glass) (Casina delle Civette Museum, Rome) 55 50
2549 800l. Renaissance majolica dish (International Ceramics Museum, Faenza) (vert) 55 50

1056 Earth Pyramids, Segonzano

1999. Tourist Publicity (26th series). Multicoloured.
2550 800l. Type **1056** 55 50
2551 800l. Marmore Waterfall, Terni 55 50
2552 800l. Cathedral, Lecce . . . 55 50
2553 800l. Lipari 55 50

1057 Audience Chamber

1999. Constitutional Court.
2554 **1057** 800l. multicoloured . . 55 50

1058 Fire Engine at Fire

1999. Fire Brigade.
2555 **1058** 800l. multicoloured . . 55 50

1059 Cadet and Academy

1999. Modena Military Academy.
2556 **1059** 800l. multicoloured . . 55 50

1060 Players and Airplane

1999. 50th Anniv of Death in Aircrash of Grand Turin Football Team. Multicoloured.
2557 800l. Type **1060** 65 50
2558 900l. Superga Basilica, club arms and names of victims 75 50

1061 Council Seat, Strasbourg

1999. 50th Anniv of Council of Europe.
2559 **1061** 800l. multicoloured . . 55 50

1062 Players and Club Emblem

1999. Milan, National Football Champion, 1998–99.
2560 **1062** 800l. multicoloured . . 70 50

1063 Ballot Box and Parliament Chamber, Strasbourg

1999. 20th Anniv of First Direct Elections to European Parliament.
2561 **1063** 800l. multicoloured . . 55 50

1064 Coppi

1999. 80th Birth Anniv of Fausto Coppi (racing cyclist).
2562 **1064** 800l. multicoloured . . 55 50

1065 "P"

1999. Priority Mail stamp. Self-adhesive.
2563 **1065** 1200l. black and gold 85 1·40
See also Nos. 2591 and 2660.

1066 First Fiat Car (advertising poster)

1067 "Our Lady of the Snow"

1999. Centenary of Fiat (motor manufacturer).
2564 **1066** 4800l. multicoloured . . 3·25 1·60

1999. Centenary of Erection of Statue of "Our Lady of the Snow" on Mt. Rocciamelone.
2565 **1067** 800l. multicoloured . . 55 50

1068 Pimentel and St. Elmo Castle, Naples

1999. Death Bicentenary of Eleonora de Fonseca Pimentel (writer and revolutionary).
2566 **1068** 800l. multicoloured . . 55 50

1069 Canoes

1999. 30th World Speed Canoeing Championships.
2567 **1069** 900l. multicoloured . . 60 50

1070 "Goethe in the Rome Countryside" (Johann Tischbein)

1999. 250th Birth Anniv of Johann Wolfgang Goethe (poet and playwright).
2568 **1070** 4000l. multicoloured . . 2·75 1·80

1071 Cyclist and Stopwatch

1072 Child with Rucksack

1999. World Cycling Championships, Treviso and Verona.
2569 **1071** 1400l. multicoloured . . 1·00 80

1999. Stamp Day.
2570 **1072** 800l. multicoloured . . 55 50

1073 Architectural Drawing of Basilica

1999. Re-opening of Upper Basilica of St. Francis of Assisi.
2571 **1073** 800l. multicoloured . . 55 50

1074 Parini (after Francesco Rosaspina)

1075 Volta (bust by Giovan Commolli) and Voltaic Pile

1999. Death Bicentenary of Giuseppe Parini (poet).
2572 **1074** 800l. blue 55 50

1999. Bicentenary of Invention of Electrochemical Battery by Alessandro Volta.
2573 **1075** 3000l. multicoloured . . 2·10 1·60

1076 Forms and U.P.U. Emblem

1999. 125th Anniv of Universal Postal Union.
2574 **1076** 900l. multicoloured . . 65 50

1077 Mameli with 1948 and 1949 100l. Stamps

1999. 150th Death Anniv of Goffredo Mameli (poet and patriot) and 150th Anniv of Roman Republic.
2575 **1077** 1500l. multicoloured . . 1·10 1·30

1078 Man and Town

1079 First World War Soldiers (after postcard)

1999. "The Stamp Our Friend". Multicoloured.
2576 450l. Type **1078** 35 80
2577 650l. Campaign emblem . . 50 95
2578 800l. Schoolchildren . . . . 60 1·10
2579 1000l. Windmill (toy) . . . 70 1·10

1999. Centenary of Generation of '99.
2580 **1079** 900l. multicoloured . . 65 50

1080 Santa Claus

1999. Christmas. Multicoloured.
2581 800l. Type **1080** 60 50
2582 1000l. "Nativity" (Dosso Dossi) 75 50

1081 Peutinger Tablet (medieval map showing pilgrim route by C. Celtes and Conrad Peutinger)

1999. Holy Year 2000. Multicoloured.
2583 1000l. Type **1081** 70 50
2584 1000l. 18th-century pilgrim's stamp 70 50
2585 1000l. 13th-century bas-relief of pilgrims (facade of Fidenza Cathedral) . . . 70 50

1082 Urbino State Art Institute

1999. Schools and Universities.
2586 **1082** 450l. black 35 50
2587 – 650l. brown 45 50
DESIGN: 650l. Pisa High School.

1083 "Leopard bitten by Tarantula"

1999. Birth Centenary of Antonio Ligabue (artist).
2588 **1083** 1000l. multicoloured . . 70 50

1084 Robot's Hand meeting Man's Hand (after Michelangelo)

1999. Year 2000.
2589 **1084** 4800l. multicoloured . . 3·25 2·40

1085 Child looking at Aspects of Earth

2000. New Millennium. "The Past and the Future". Sheet 110 × 80 mm containing T **1085** and similar horiz design. Multicoloured.
MS2590 2000l. Type **1085**; 2000l. Astronaut looking at Moon . . 3·00 4·75

2000. Priority Mail Stamp. As T **1065** but different colour. Self-adhesive.
2591 1200l. black, yellow and gold 85 65

1086 Tosca and Scenery

2000. Centenary of the First Performance of *Tosca* (opera).
2592 **1086** 800l. multicoloured . . 55 50

1087 St. Paul (statue) and Holy Door, St. Peter's Basilica, Rome

2000. Holy Year 2000.
2593 **1087** 1000l. multicoloured . . 70 50

1088 Players

2000. Six Nations Rugby Championship.
2594 **1088** 800l. multicoloured . . 55 50

1089 Painting

1091 Skier and Trophy

1090 "Enigma of an Autumn Afternoon"

2000. 5th Conference on Breast Diseases. Mult.
2595 800l. Type **1089** 55 50
2596 1000l. Painting (different) 70 50

2000. New Millennium (1st issue). Art and Science. Sheet 111 × 80 mm containing T **1090** and similar horiz design showing paintings by Giorgio de Chirico. Multicoloured.
MS2597 800l. Type **1090** (art); 800l. "The Inevitable Temple" (science) 2·00 2·40
See also Nos. **MS**2613 and 2623.

2000. World Cup Skiing Championships.
2598 **1091** 4800l. multicoloured . . 3·25 2·40

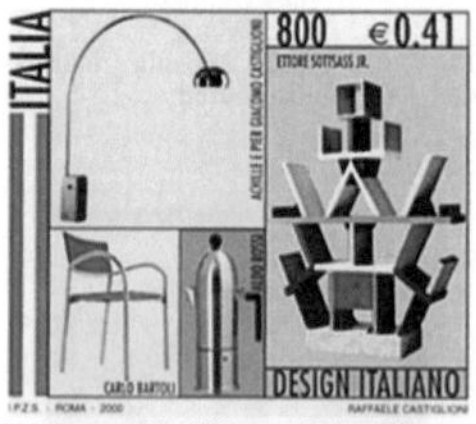

1092 Lamp (Achillle and Pier Giacomo Castiglioni), Chair (Carlo Batroli), Coffee Pot (Aldo Rossi) and Bookcase (Ettore Softsass Jr.)

2000. Italian Design. Sheet 154 × 138 mm containing T **1092** and similar horiz designs. Multicoloured.
MS2599 800l. Type **1092**; 800l. Armchair (Mario Bellini), corkscrew (Alessandro Mendini), table lamp (Vico Magistretti) and suspended lamp (Alberto Meda and Paolo Rizzatto); 800l. Chair (Gio Ponti), bean bag (Gatti Paolini Teodoro), pasta set (Massimo Morozzi) and standard uplighter (Tobia Scarpa); 800l. White standard uplighter (Pietro Chiesa), hostess trolley (Joe Columbo), chair (Cini Boeri and Tomu Katayanagi) and sideboard (Lodovico Acerbis and Giotto Stoppino); 800l. Easy chairs (Gaetano Pesce), chair (Enzo Mari), clothes horse (De Pas d'Urbino Lomazzi) and mobile filing cabinet (Antonio Citterio and Oliver Loew); 800l. Chair (Marco Zanuso), anglepoise lamp (Michele de Lucchi and Giancarlo Fassina), ice bucket (Bruno Munari) and stool (Anna Castelli Ferrieri) . . . . 3·50 6·50

1093 "Adoration of the Magi" (Domenico Ghirlandaio)

2000. Holy Year 2000. Multicoloured.
2600 450l. Type **1093** 40 50
2601 650l. "Baptism of Christ" (Paolo Caliari Veronese) (vert) 55 50
2602 800l. "The Last Supper" (Ghirlandaio) (vert) . . . 70 50
2603 1000l. "Regret of Christ's Death" (Giotto di Bondone) 85 50
2604 1200l. "The Resurrection" (Piero della Francesca) (vert) . . . . 1·00 80

1094 Library and Emblem

2000. 150th Anniv of La Civilta Cattolica Foundation (collection of Church publications).
2605 **1094** 800l. multicoloured . . 55 50

1095 Courtyard

2000. 150th Anniv of St. Joseph's College, Rome.
2606 **1095** 800l. multicoloured . . 55 50

1096 Terre di Franciacorta, Erbrusco

2000. Tourist Publicity (27th series). Multicoloured.
2607 800l. Type **1096** 55 50
2608 800l. Dunarobba fossil forest, Avigliano Umbro 55 50
2609 800l. View of Ercolano . . . 55 50
2610 800l. Beauty Island, Taormina 55 50

1097 Cyclist

2000. Centenary of International Cycling Union.
2611 **1097** 1500l. multicoloured . . 1·10 80

1098 Christ carrying Cross

2000. Papier-mache Figurines, Caltanisetta.
2612 **1098** 800l. multicoloured . . 55 50

1099 Landscape (Gilorgione)

2000. New Millennium (2nd issue). Countryside and City. Sheet 110 × 80 mm containing T **1099** and similar horiz design. Multicoloured.
MS2613 800l. Type **1099**; 800l. "Perspective of an Ideal Town" (Piero della Francesca) . . . . 2·30 1·20

1100 Piccinni

1101 "Building Europe"

2000. Death Bicentenary of Niccolo Piccinni (composer).
2614 **1100** 4000l. multicoloured . . 2·75 2·40

2000. Europa.
2615 **1101** 800l. multicoloured . . 55 50

1102 Sardinia 1851 5, 20 and 40c. Stamps

2000. Museum of Posts and Telecommunications. Multicoloured.
2616 800l. Type **1102** 60 50
2617 800l. Reconstruction of radio and telegraph cabin aboard Elettra (Marconi's steam yacht) 60 50

1103 Footballer and Pitch

1104 Cathedral Facade

2000. Lazio, National Football Champion, 1999–2000.
2618 **1103** 800l. multicoloured . . 55 50

2000. 700th Anniv of Monza Cathedral.
2619 **1104** 800l. multicoloured . . 55 50

1105 Globe and Ears of Corn

1106 Statue

2000. United Nations World Food Programme.
2620 **1105** 1000l. multicoloured . . 70 50

2000. Centenary of the Jesus the Redeemer Monument, Nuoro.
2621 **1106** 800l. multicoloured . . 55 50

1107 Bridge, Parana River, Argentina

2000. 120th Anniv of Italian Water Board.
2622 **1107** 800l. multicoloured . . 55 50

1108 Profiles

2000. New Millennium (3rd issue). Technology and Space. Sheet 110 × 80 mm containing T **1108** and similar horiz design. Multicoloured.
MS2623 800l. Type **1108**; 800l. Symbolic man . . . . 2·30 1·20

1109 Child with Ladder to Moon (Giacomo Chiesa)

1110 Archer

2000. "Stampin the Future". Winning Entry in Children's International Painting Competition.
2624 **1109** 1000l. multicoloured . . 70 50

2000. World Archery Championship, Campagna.
2625 **1110** 1500l. multicoloured . . 1·10 80

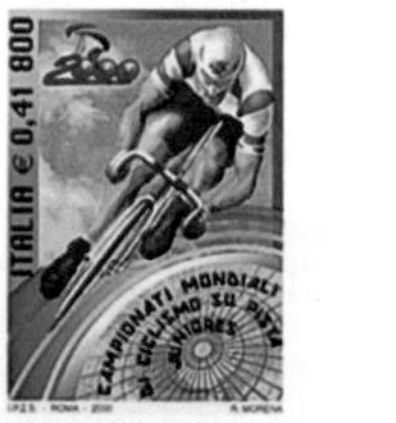

1111 Cyclist and Globe

2000. World Junior Cycling Championships.
2626 **1111** 800l. multicoloured . . 55 50

1112 Fair Attractions

2000. Millenary of St. Orso.
2627 **1112** 1000l. multicoloured . . 70 50

1113 "Madonna and Child" (Crivelli)

2000. 570th Birth Anniv of Carlo Crivelli (artist).
2628 **1113** 800l. multicoloured . . 55 50

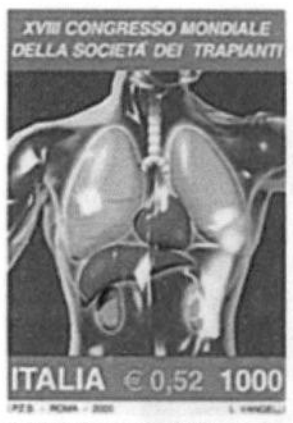

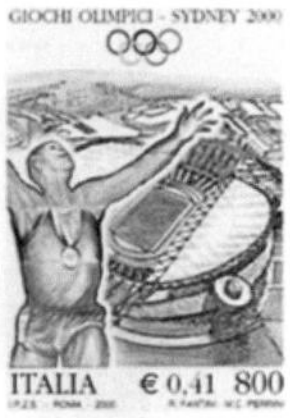

1114 Internal Organs **1115** Athlete and Stadium

2000. 18th International Transplantation Society Congress, Rome.
2629 **1114** 1000l. multicoloured . . 70 80

2000. Olympic Games, Sydney. Multicoloured.
2630 800l. Type **1115** 55 50
2631 1000l. "Discus Thrower" (statue) and Sydney Harbour 70 80

1116 "War"

2000. New Millennium (4th issue). War and Peace. Frescoes by Taddeo Zuccan. Sheet 110 × 80 mm containing T **1116** and similar vert design. Multicoloured.
MS2632 800l. Type **1116**; 800l. "Peace" . . . . 2·30 1·20

1117 Battle Scene (Jacques Debreville) **1118** Figures in Evening Dress and City Skyline

2000. Bicentenary of Marengo.
2633 **1117** 800l. multicoloured . . 55 50

2000. New Year.
2634 **1118** 800l. multicoloured . . 55 50

1119 Child holding Magnifying Glass

2000. Stamp Day.
2635 **1119** 800l. multicoloured . . 55 50

1120 Monti and Sick Child

2000. Death Centenary of Father Luigi Monti.
2636 **1120** 800l. multicoloured . . 55 50

1121 Salieri **1122** Disabled Athletes

2000. 250th Birth Anniv of Antonio Salieri (composer).
2637 **1121** 4800l. multicoloured . . 3·25 2·40

2000. Paralympic Games, Sydney.
2638 **1122** 1500l. multicoloured . . 1·10 1·30

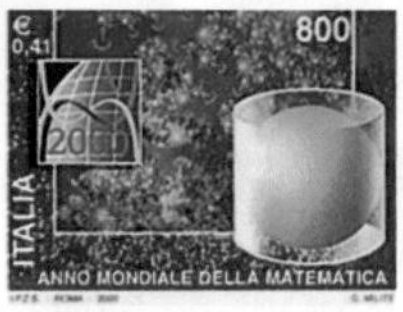

1123 Emblem, Chaos Model and Globe in Container

2000. World Mathematics Year.
2639 **1123** 800l. multicoloured . . 55 50

1124 Couple and Globe

2000. Volunteers.
2640 **1124** 800l. multicoloured . . 55 50

1125 Quill, Text and Bust of Bruno (Pietro Masulli)

2000. 400th Death Anniv of Giordano Bruno (writer and philosopher).
2641 **1125** 800l. multicoloured . . 55 50

1126 "Madonna of the Rose Garden"

2000. 600th Birth Anniv of Luca della Robbia (artist).
2642 **1126** 800l. multicoloured . . 55 50

1127 Arms of Academy

2000. 250th Anniv of Roveretana degli Agiati Academy.
2643 **1127** 800l. multicoloured . . 55 50

1128 Martino and Map of Europe

2000. Birth Centenary of Gaetano Martino (politician).
2644 **1128** 800l. multicoloured . . 55 50

1129 "Perseus with the Head of Medusa" (bronze statue)

2000. 500th Birth Anniv of Benvenuto Cellini (goldsmith and sculptor).
2645 **1129** 1200l. multicoloured . . 85 95

1130 Young Woman

2000. New Millennium (5th series). Meditation and Expression. Sheet 110 × 80 mm containing T **1130** and similar horiz design. Multicoloured.
MS2646 800l. Type **1130**; 800l. Dancing figures . . . . 2·30 1·20

1131 Camerino University

2000. Universities. Each blue.
2647 800l. Type **1131** 55 50
2648 1000l. Calabria University 70 65

1132 Snowflakes and Globe **1133** Snowboarding

2000. Christmas. Multicoloured.
2649 800l. Type **1132** 55 50
2650 1000l. Crib, Matera Cathedral 70 80

2001. World Snowboarding Championships, Madonna di Campiglio.
2651 **1133** 1000l. multicoloured . . 70 50

1134 "The Annunciation" (detail, Botticelli)

2001. "Italy in Japan 2001" (cultural and scientific event).
2652 **1134** 1000l. multicoloured . . 70 50

1135 Vincenzo Bellini (composer, birth bicentenary)

2001. Composers' Anniversaries. Sheet 87 × 180 mm containing T **1135** and similar vert designs. Multicoloured.
MS2653 800l. Type **1135**; 800l. Domenico Cimarosa (death bicentenary); 800l. Gasparo Luigi Pacifico Spontini (150th death anniv); 800l. Giuseppe Verdi (death centenary) . . . . . . 2·40 4·00

1136 St. Rose and Angels (Francesco Podesti di Ancona) **1137** Racing Car

2001. 750th Death Anniv of St. Rose of Viterbo.
2654 **1136** 800l. multicoloured . . 55 50

2001. Ferrari, Formula One Constructor's Championship Winner (2000). Sheet 110 × 81 mm.
MS2655 **1137** 5000l. multicoloured 3·50 6·50

1138 Abbey of Santa Maria in Sylvis, Sesto al Reghena

2001.
2656 **1138** 800l. blue 55 50

1139 Lombardy and Venetia 1850 5c. Stamp (151st anniv)

2001. Stamp Anniversaries. Multicoloured.
2657 800l. Type **1139** 55 50
2658 800l. Sardinia 1851 5c. stamp (150th anniv) . . . 55 50
2659 800l. Tuscany 1851 1q. stamp (150th anniv) . . . 55 50

2001. Priority Mail Stamp. As T **1065** but central "P" larger, 12 × 12 mm. Self-adhesive.
2660 1200l. black, yellow and gold 85 50

1140 Bridge, Comacchio

2001. Tourist Publicity (28th series). Multicoloured.
2661 800l. Type **1140** 55 50
2662 800l. Diamante 55 50
2663 800l. Pioraco 55 50
2664 800l. Stintino 55 50

1141 Campanula

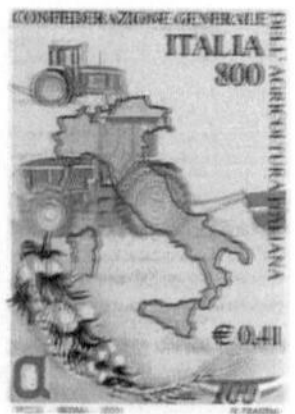

1142 Map of Italy and Tractors

2001. World Day to Combat Desertification and Drought. Multicoloured.

2665	450l. Type **1141**	30	15
2666	650l. Marmosets	45	50
2667	800l. White storks	50	50
2668	1000l. Desert and emblem	65	65

2001. Confederation General of Italian Agriculture.

2669 **1142**	800l. multicoloured . .	55	50

1143 Castle and Emblem

2001. Millenary of Gorzia City.

2670 **1143**	800l. multicoloured . .	55	50

1144 Water pouring from Vase

2001. Europa. Water Resources.

2671 **1144**	800l. multicoloured . .	65	50

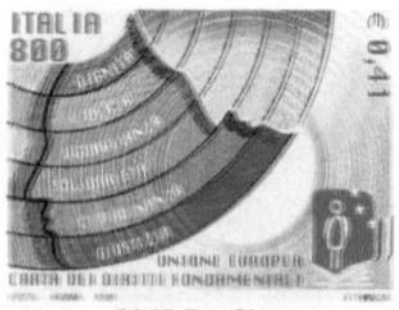

1145 Profiles

2001. European Union.

2672 **1145**	800l. multicoloured . .	55	50

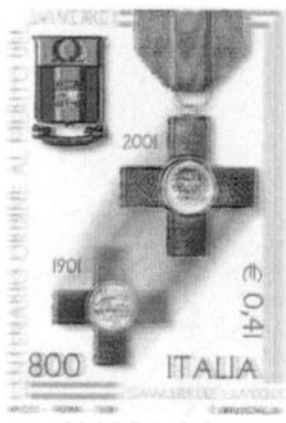

1146 Medals

1147 Rose and Workers' Silhouettes

2001. Centenary of Order of Merit for Labour.

2673 **1146**	800l. multicoloured . .	55	50

2001. National Day for Victims of Industrial Accidents.

2674 **1147**	800l. multicoloured . .	55	50

1148 Child with Stamp and Magnifying Glass (Rita Vergari)

1149 "St. Peter healing with his Shadow"

2001. Day for Art and Student Creativity. Multicoloured.

2675	800l. Type **1148**	55	50
2676	800l. People standing on rainbow (Lucia Catena)	55	50
2677	800l. Painting with eye (Luigi di Cristo)	55	50
2678	800l. Colours and profile (Barbara Grilli)	55	50

2001. 600th Birth Anniv of Tommaso de Giovanni di Simone Guidi "Masaccio" (painter).

2679 **1149**	800l. multicoloured . .	55	50

1150 "Madonna and Child" (Piero della Francesca)

2001. 500th Death Anniv of Giovanni della Rovere.

2680 **1150**	800l. multicoloured . .	55	50

1151 Emblem

1152 Guaita Tower, Mt. Titano

2001. 50th Anniv of Panathlon International (sports organization).

2681 **1151**	800l. multicoloured . .	55	50

2001. 1700th Anniv of San Marino.

2682 **1152**	800l. multicoloured . .	55	50

1153 Footballer and Net

1155 Quasimodo

1154 Motorboat and Helicopter

2001. A S Roma, National Football Champion, 2000–1.

2683 **1153**	800l. multicoloured . .	55	50

2001. Harbour Master's Office.

2684 **1154**	800l. multicoloured . .	55	50

2001. Birth Centenary of Salvatore Quasimodo (writer).

2685 **1155**	1500l. multicoloured . .	1·10	1·30

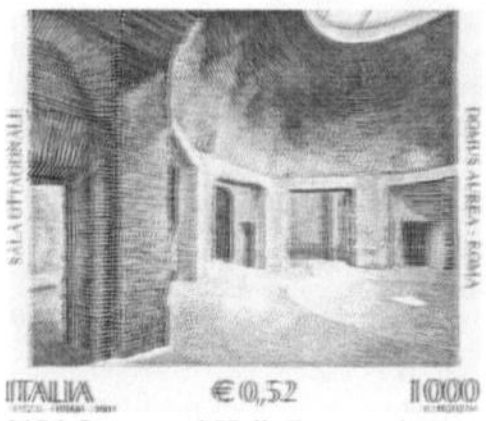

1156 Octagonal Hall, Domus Aurea, Rome

2001.

2686 **1156**	1000l. brown	70	50

1157 Bookcase (Piero Lissoni and Patricia Urquiola) and Chair (Anna Bartolli)

2001. Italian Design. Sheet 155 × 137 mm containing T **1157** and similar horiz designs. Multicoloured.

MS2687 800l. Type **1157**; 800l. Chair (Monica Graffeo) and table lamp (Rodolfo Dordoni); 800l. Lamp (Ferruccio Laviani) and sofa (Massimo Iosa Ghini); 800l. Armchair (Anna Gili) and side table (Miki Astori); 800l. Vertical storage unit (Marco Ferreri) and double seat (M. Cananzi and R. Semprini); 800l. Stool (Stefano Giovannoni) and flexible-necked lamp (Massimiliano Datti) . . 3·00 3·00

1158 "The Fourth State" (detail, Guiseppe Pellizza da Volpedo)

2001.

2688 **1158**	1000l. brown	70	50

1159 Stone Age Man and Pick

1161 Fermi

1160 Schoolchildren

2001. Archaeological Museum, Alto Adige.

2689 **1159**	800l. multicoloured . .	55	50

2001. Youth Philately.

2690 **1160**	800l. multicoloured . .	55	50

2001. Birth Centenary of Enrico Fermi (physicist).

2691 **1161**	800l. multicoloured . .	55	50

1162 Pavia University

2001. Universities.

2692 **1162**	800l. blue	55	50
2693 –	800l. brown	55	50
2694 –	800l. turquoise	55	50

DESIGNS—VERT: No. 2693 Bari, University. HORIZ: 2694, School of Science, Rome.

1163 Latinas and Messanger

2001. Unione Latina (Romance language speaking countries).

2695 **1163**	800l. black, yellow and blue	55	50

1164 Exhibits

2001. National Archaeological Museum, Taranto.

2696 **1164**	1000l. multicoloured . .	70	50

1165 International Fund for Agricultural Development Emblem

1166 "Enthroned Christ with Angels" (painting on wood)

2001. World Food Day. Each stamp featuring "The Seed" (sculpture) by Roberto Joppolo. Multicoloured.

2697	800l. Type **1165**	50	25
2698	800l. Plants and woman hoeing (50th anniv of Food and Agriculture Organization Summit Conference, Rome) (50 × 29 mm)	50	25
2699	800l. World Food Programme emblem . . .	50	25

2001.

2700 **1166**	800l. multicoloured . .	50	25

1167 "Madonna and Child" (painting from triptych)

2001. 500th Anniv of "Madonna and Child, Angels, St. Francis, St. Thomas Aquinas and two Donors" (triptych, Macrino d'Alba).

2701 **1167**	800l. multicoloured . .	50	25

1168 "Dawn of Peace" (collage, San Vito dei Normani Primary School)

2001. Christmas. Multicoloured.

2702	800l. Type **1168**	50	25
2703	1000l. "Nativity" (painting, St. Mary Major Basilica)	65	30

1169 Fabric

2001. Italian Silk Industry. Sheet 140 × 92 mm. Self-adhesive gum. Imperf.

MS2704 **1169** 5000l. multicoloured 3·25 3·25

No. **MS**2704 was printed on fabric mounted on silk jacquard. A peel-off plastic backing featured instructions for use. If required, the address could be written in the blank area at the bottom right of the sheet.

New Currency. 100 cents = 1 euro.

2002. Women in Art. As T **1032** but with values expressed in euros.

2705	1c. multicoloured	10	10
2706	2c. multicoloured	10	10
2707	3c. multicoloured	10	10
2708	5c. multicoloured	10	10
2709	10c. multicoloured	15	10
2710	20c. multicoloured	30	15
2711	23c. multicoloured	30	15
2715	41c. brown, grey and black	60	30
2716	45c. purple, blue and black	65	30
2716b	65c. blue and red	90	45
2716c	70c. violet and green . . .	95	45
2717	50c. turquoise, red and black	70	35
2717	77c. brown, green and black	1·10	55
2718	85c. purple and black . . .	1·20	60
2719	90c. green and red	1·30	65

DESIGNS: 1c. "Ebe" (detail, painting, Antonia Canova); 2c. Profile (5th-century B.C. coin, Syracuse); 3c. Woman's head (detail from mural, Piero della Francesca); 5c. As No. 2505; 10c. Head (3rd-century B.C. sculpture, "G. Fiorelli" civic museum, Lucera); 20c. Portrait of a Lady (Correggio); 23c. As No. 2506; 41c. As No. 2508; 45c. "Venere di Urbino" (Tiziano Vecellio); 50c. "Portrait of a young girl" (detail, painting, Francesco Mazzola); 65c. "San Giorgio e la Principessa di Trebisonda"(detail by Antonis Pisano); 70c." Wettuno a Venezia" (detail by Giambattista Foggini, sculpture); 77c. "Spring" (detail, painting, Botticelli); 85c."Costigiana" (detail, by Vittore (arpaccio), 90c."Venere e Marte legati de Amore" (detail, by Paolo Calieri).

1170 "Ducato" (Venetian coin), 1285

2002. European Coins. Multicoloured.
2725 41c. Type **1170** 60 30
2726 41c. "Genovino" (Genoa) and "Fiorino" (Florence), 1252 . . . . 60 30
2727 41c. Flags of E.U. forming Euro symbol 60 30
2728 41c. 1946 lira coin transforming into euro coin 60 30

2002. Priority Mail Stamps. Designs as No. 2660 but with face values in euros only. Multicoloured, background colour given. Self-adhesive gum.
2729 62c. yellow 90 45
2730 77c. blue . . . . 1·10 55
2731 €1 lavender . . . . 1·40 70
2732 €1.24 green . . . . 1·80 90
2733 €1.86 pink . . . . 2·75 1·30
2734 €4.13 lilac . . . . 6·00 3·00

1171 Woman's Head and State Arms

1173 Luigi Bocconi and University Building

1172 Escriva

2002.
2735 **1171** €1 multicoloured . . 1·40 70
2736 €1.24 multicoloured 1·80 90
2737 €1.55 multicoloured 2·20 1·10
2738 €2.17 multicoloured 2·10 1·50
2738a €2.35 multicoloured 3·25 1·50
2739 €2.58 multicoloured 3·75 1·80
2739a €2.80 multicoloured 3·75 1·80
2739b €3 multicoloured . . 4·00 2·00
2740 €3.62 multicoloured 5·25 2·75
2741 €6.20 multicoloured 9·00 4·75

2002. Birth Centenary of Josemaria Escriva de Balaguer (founder of Opus Dei (religious organization)).
2745 **1172** 41c. multicoloured . . . 60 30

2002. Centenary of Bocconi University.
2746 **1173** 41c. brown and stone 60 30
The University was established with an endowment from Ferinando Bocconi in memory of his son Luigi.

1174 1852 5c. Stamp

1175 Mountain Peak

2002. 150th Anniv of First Stamp of Parma. Fluorescent paper.
2747 **1174** 41c. multicoloured . . . 60 30

2002. International Year of Mountains.
2748 **1175** 41c. multicoloured . . . 60 30

1176 Emblem and Olympic Rings

1177 Queen Elena

2002. Winter Olympic Games, Turin (2006).
2749 **1176** 41c. multicoloured . . . 60 30

2002. 50th Death Anniv of Queen Elena of Savoy.
2750 **1177** 41c. + 21c. multicoloured 90 45

1178 Sculpture (Arnolfo di Cambio)

2002. 700th Death Anniv of Arnolfo di Cambio (sculptor).
2751 **1178** 41c. mauve 60 30

1179 Venaria Reale

2002. Tourist Publicity (29th series). Multicoloured.
2752 41c. Type **1179** 60 30
2753 41c. Capo d'Orlando . . . 60 30
2754 41c. San Gimignano 60 30
2755 41c. Sannicandro di Bari . . 60 30

1180 Santa Maria delle Grazie Sanctuary

2002.
2756 **1180** 41c. brown 60 30

1181 Police Officers, Computer Screen and Patrol Car

2002. 150th Anniv of State Police Force.
2757 **1181** 41c. multicoloured . . . 60 30

1182 Ricci and World Map

2002. 450th Birth Anniv of Matteo Rici (missionary).
2758 **1182** 41c. multicoloured . . . 60 30

1183 Circus Performers

2002. Europa. Circus.
2759 **1183** 41c. multicoloured . . . 60 30

1184 Sailing Ship and Student

2002. Francesco Morosini Naval Military School, Venice.
2760 **1184** 41c. multicoloured . . . 60 30

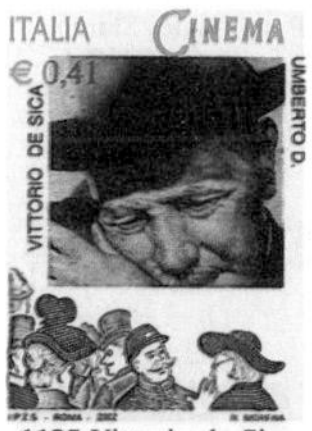

1185 Vittorio de Sica (film director, birth centenary)

1186 Football Player and Emblem

2002. Cinema Anniversaries. Multicoloured.
2761 41c. Type **1185** 60 30
2762 41c. Text and clouds (birth centenary (1901) of Cesare Zavattini (screen writer)) 60 30

2002. Juventus, National Football Champions, 2001–2002.
2763 **1186** 41c. multicoloured . . . 60 30

1187 Falcone and Boresellino

2002. 10th Death Annivs of Giovanni Falcone and Paolo Borsellino (judges).
2764 **1187** 62c. multicoloured . . . 90 45

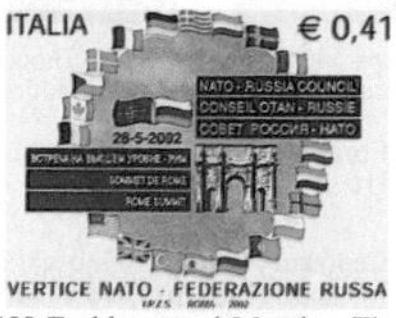

1188 Emblems and Member Flags

2002. Russia's Membership of North Atlantic Treaty Organization (N.A.T.O.).
2765 **1188** 41c. multicoloured . . . 60 30

1189 Kayaking

1190 Modena 1853 1 lira Arms of Este Stamp

2002. World Kayaking Championship, Valsesia.
2766 **1189** 52c. multicoloured . . . 75 35

2002. 150th Anniv of Modena (Italian State) Stamps.
2767 **1190** 41c. multicoloured . . . 60 30

1191 Arms

1192 Binda

2002. Italian Military Involvement in Peace Missions.
2768 **1191** 41c. multicoloured . . . 60 30

2002. Birth Centenary of Alfrodo Binda (cyclist).
2769 **1192** 41c. multicoloured . . . 60 30

1193 Santo

2002. Canonization of Father Padre Pio Santo.
2770 **1193** 41c. multicoloured . . . 60 30

1194 Divisione Acqui (monument, Mario Salazzari)

2002. "Divisione Acqui" (World War II resistance group on Cephalonia).
2771 **1194** 41c. multicoloured . . . 60 30

1195 Crucifixion (Arezzo Basilica)

2002.
2772 **1195** €2.58 multicoloured 3·75 1·90

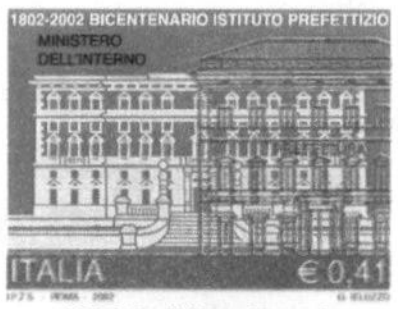

1196 Building Facade

2002. Bicentenary of Ministry of Interior.
2773 **1196** 41c. multicoloured . . . 60 30

1197 Maria Goretti

2002. Death Centenary of Saint Maria Goretti.
2774 **1197** 41c. multicoloured . . . 60 30

1198 Mazarin

2002. 400th Birth Anniv of Cardinal Jules Mazarin (minister to Louis XIV of France).
2775 **1198** 41c. multicoloured . . . 60 30

1199 National Colours encircling Globe

1200 Monument (Vincenzo Gasperetti)

2002. "Italians in the World".
2776 **1199** 52c. multicoloured . . . 75 35

2002. Monument to the Victims of Massacre at Sant' Anna di Stazzema.
2777 **1200** 41c. multicoloured . . . 60 30

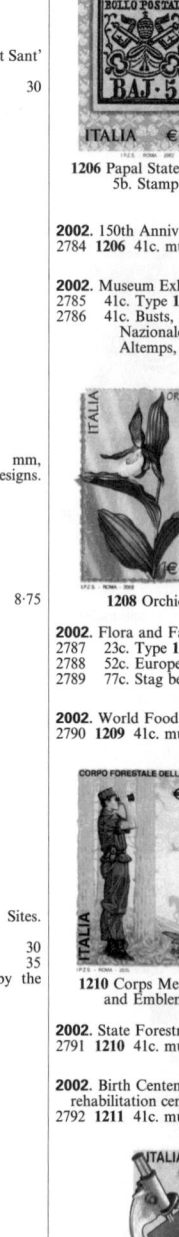

1201 Jacket (Krizia)

2002. Italian Design. Sheet 157×137 mm, containing T **1201** and similar vert designs. Multicoloured.
MS2778 41c. Type **1201**; 41c. Brassiere (Dolce & Gabbana); 41c. Drawing of dress (Gianfranco Ferre); 41c. Drawing of suit (Giorgio Armani); 41c. Dress (Laura Biagiotti); 41c. Shoes (Prada) . . . . 8·75 8·75

1202 Cathedral and Tower, Pisa

2002. UNESCO World Heritage Sites. Multicoloured.
2779 41c. Type **1202** 60 30
2780 52c. Aeolian Islands 75 35
Stamps of a similar design were issued by the United Nations.

1203 Dalla Chiesa

2002. 20th Anniv of Assassination of Carlo Alberto Dalla Chiesa (police chief and prefect of Palermo).
2781 **1203** 41c. multicoloured . . . 60 30

1204 Teatro della Concordia, Monte Castello di Vibio, Perugia

2002.
2782 **1204** 41c. multicoloured . . . 60 30

1205 Yacht

2002. 12th Prada Classic Yacht Challenge, Imperia.
2783 **1205** 41c. multicoloured . . . 60 30

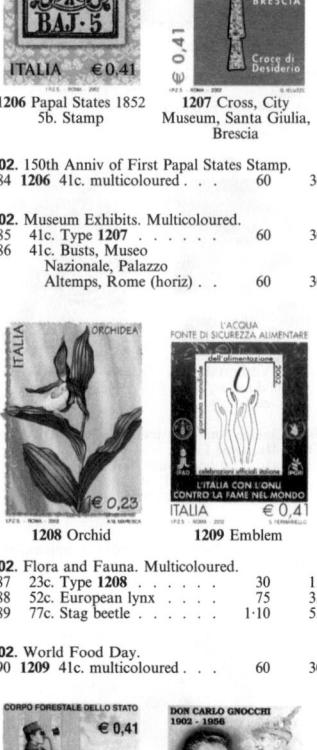

1206 Papal States 1852 5b. Stamp

1207 Cross, City Museum, Santa Giulia, Brescia

2002. 150th Anniv of First Papal States Stamp.
2784 **1206** 41c. multicoloured . . . 60 30

2002. Museum Exhibits. Multicoloured.
2785 41c. Type **1207** 60 30
2786 41c. Busts, Museo Nazionale, Palazzo Altemps, Rome (horiz) . . 60 30

1208 Orchid

1209 Emblem

2002. Flora and Fauna. Multicoloured.
2787 23c. Type **1208** 30 15
2788 52c. European lynx 75 35
2789 77c. Stag beetle . . . . . . 1·10 55

2002. World Food Day.
2790 **1209** 41c. multicoloured . . . 60 30

1210 Corps Member and Emblem

1211 Gnocchi and Children

2002. State Forestry Corps.
2791 **1210** 41c. multicoloured . . . 60 30

2002. Birth Centenary of Carlo Gnocchi (founder of rehabilitation centres for disabled children).
2792 **1211** 41c. multicoloured . . . 60 30

1212 Microscope and Emblem

2002. "Telethon 2002" (campaign to combat muscular dystrophy and genetic disease).
2793 **1212** 41c. multicoloured . . . 60 30

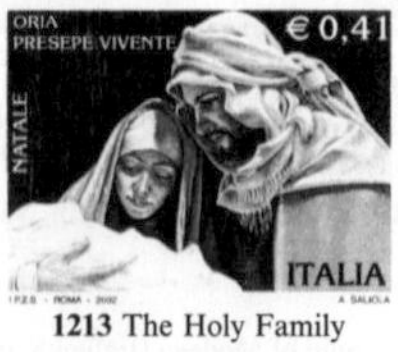
1213 The Holy Family

2002. Christmas. Multicoloured.
2794 41c. Type **1213** 60 30
2795 62c. Child and Christmas tree 90 45

1214 "Nike di Samotracia" (statue) and Athlete

1215 Flags of Championship Winners and Football

2002. Women in Sport.
2796 **1214** 41c. multicoloured . . . 60 30

2002. 20th-century World Cup Football Champions. Multicoloured.
2797 52c. Type **1215** 70 35
2798 52c. Italian footballer . . . 70 35

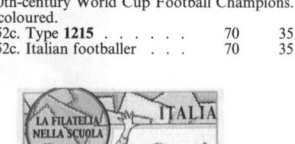

1216 Magnifying Glass, Stamps and Children

2002. Stamp Day. Philately in Schools.
2799 **1216** 62c. multicoloured . . . 85 40

1217 Vittorio Orlando

1218 Event Emblem

2002. 50th Death Anniv of Vittorio Emanuele Orlando (politician).
2800 **1217** 41c. multicoloured . . . 60 30

2003. "Tarvisio 2003" (winter sports competition).
2801 **1218** 52c. multicoloured . . . 70 35

1219 Family and Scales

2003. The Italian Republic on Stamps.
2802 **1219** 62c. multicoloured . . . 85 40

1220 Cyclist carrying Cycle

2003. World Cyclo-cross Championship, Monopoli.
2803 **1220** 41c. multicoloured . . . 60 30

1221 Building and Tandem

2003. 150th Anniv (2002) of Fratelli Alinari (photographic company).
2804 **1221** 77c. multicoloured . . . 1·00 50

1222 Jigsaw Puzzle

2003. European Year of the Disabled.
2805 **1222** 41c. multicoloured . . . 60 30

1223 Skiers

2003. World Nordic Skiing Championship, Val di Fiemme.
2806 **1223** 41c. multicoloured . . . 60 30

1224 Couple, Flower and Emblem

2003. National Civil Service.
2807 **1224** 62c. multicoloured . . . 85 40

1225 Knights on Horseback

2003. 500th Anniv of the Barletta Challenge (battle between 13 French and 13 Italian knights).
2808 **1225** 41c. multicoloured . . . 60 30

1226 Building Facade

2003. Torquato Tasso Grammar School (gymnasium).
2809 **1226** 41c. multicoloured . . . 60 30

1227 "Encounter by the Golden Door" (Giotto)

2003.
2810 **1227** 41c. multicoloured . . . 60 30

1228 Gian Rinaldo Carli and Building

2003. Gian Rinaldo Carli Grammar School (gymnasium).
2811 **1228** 41c. multicoloured . . . 60 30

1229 Academy Emblem

2003. 400th Anniv of "Accademia dei Lincei" (academy of lynxes) (scientific society).
2812 **1229** 41c. multicoloured . . . 60 30

1230 Foils and Fencers

2003. World Junior Fencing Championships, Trapani.
2813 **1230** 41c. multicoloured . . . 60 30

1231 Sestri Levante

2003. Tourist Publicity (30th series). Multicoloured.
2814 41c. Type **1231** 60 30
2815 41c. Lanciano 60 30
2816 41c. Procida 60 30

1232 Golfer

2003. Centenary of Roma Acquasanta Golf Course.
2817 **1232** 77c. multicoloured . . . 1·00 50

1233 Minerva (statue) and Building Facade

2003. 700th Anniv of La Sapienza University, Rome.
2818 **1233** 41c. multicoloured . . . 60 30

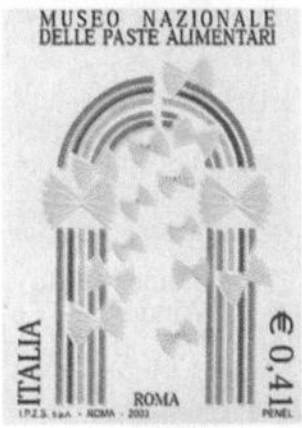

1234 Pasta

1236 Woman in Blue Dress

1235 Guido Carli and University Building

2003. National Pasta Museum, Rome.
2819 **1234** 41c. multicoloured . . . 60 30

2003. Guido Carli-LUISS (international liberal social studies) University.
2820 **1235** €2.58 multicoloured 3·50 1·75

2003. Europa. Poster Art. Posters by Marcello Dudovich. Multicoloured.
2821 41c. Type **1236** 60 30
2822 52c. Woman in white dress 70 35

1237 Buildings and Text

2003. 50th Anniv of State Archives.
2823 **1237** 41c. multicoloured . . . 60 30

1238 Logo and St. Peter of Verona

2003. Centenary of Veronafil Exhibition.
2824 **1238** 41c. multicoloured . . . 60 30

1239 Aldo Moro

1240 Antonio Meucci

2003. 25th Death Anniv of Aldo Moro (politician).
2825 **1239** 62c. multicoloured . . . 85 40

2003. Antonio Meucci (telephone pioneer) Commemoration. Sheet 90 × 70 mm.
MS2826 **1240** 52c. multicoloured 70 70

1241 Padre E. Barsanti and F. Matteucci (motor pioneers)

2003. 150th Anniv of Invention of Internal Combustion Engine.
2827 **1241** 52c. multicoloured . . . 70 35

1242 Post and Telegraph Building (Angiolo Mazzoni)

2003.
2828 **1242** 41c. blue 60 30

1243 Flags of Italy and European Union

2003. Italian Presidency of the European Union.
2829 **1243** 41c. multicoloured . . . 60 30

1244 Ezio Vanoni

2003. Birth Centenary of Ezio Vanoni (politician).
2830 **1244** €2.58 multicoloured 3·75 1·90

1245 "The Ascension of Mary"

2003. 300th Birth Anniv of Corrado Giaquinto (artist).
2831 **1245** 77c. multicoloured . . . 1·00 50

1246 Eugenio Balzan

2003. 50th Death Anniv of Eugenio Balzan (journalist).
2832 **1246** 41c. multicoloured . . . 60 30

1247 "Diana and Atteone"

2003. 500th Birth Anniv of Francesco Mazzola (Parmigianino) (artist).
2833 **1247** 41c. multicoloured . . . 60 30

1248 Player and Club Emblem

2003. Juventus, National Football Champions, 2002–3.
2834 **1248** 41c. multicoloured . . . 60 30

1249 San Silvestro Abbey, Nonantola

2003.
2835 **1249** 41c. multicoloured . . . 60 30

1250 Mario Calderara

2003. Centenary of First Powered Flight. Italian Aviation. Multicoloured.
2836 52c. Type **1250** (first Italian pilot) . . . . 2·10 1·00
2837 52c. Mario Cobianchi (pilot) 2·10 1·00
2838 52c. Gianni Caproni (aircraft designer) . . . . 2·10 1·00
2839 52c. Alessandro Marchetti (aircraft designer) . . . . 2·10 1·00
MS2840 105 × 146 mm. Nos. 2836/9 8·50 4·00

1251 Giovanni Giolitti

2003. 75th Death Anniv of Giovanni Giolitti (prime minister 1892–3 and 1903–14).
2841 **1251** 41c. multicoloured . . . 60 30

1252 "Still Life" (Giorgio Morandi)

2003. Europhalia 2003 Italy Festival. Italian Presidency of European Union. Multicoloured.
2842 41c. Type **1252** 60 30
2843 52c. Cistalia 202 (1947) . . 70 35
Stamps of the same design were issued by Belgium.

1253 Attilio Vallecchi (founder) and "Leonardo"

2003. Centenary of First Publication of "Leonardo". Centenary of Vallecchi Publishing House.
2844 **1253** 41c. multicoloured . . . 60 30

1254 Family enclosed in Atom Model

2003. The Family.
2845 **1254** 77c. multicoloured . . . 1·00 50

1255 "Maesta" (detail) (Duccio di Buoninsegna)

2003. Extension to Metropolitan Opera House, Sienna.
2846 **1255** 41c. multicoloured . . . 60 30

1256 Vittorio Alfieri

2003. Death Bicentenary of Vittorio Alfieri (writer).
2847 **1256** 41c. multicoloured . . . 60 30

1257 Ugo La Malfa and Chamber of Deputies Assembly Hall

2003. Birth Centenary of Ugo La Malfa (politician).
2848 **1257** 62c. multicoloured . . . 80 40

1258 Bernando Ramazzini and Frontispiece of "De morbis aertifcum diatriba"

2003. 370th Birth Anniv of Bernando Ramazzini (medical pioneer).
2849 **1258** 41c. multicoloured . . . 60 30

1259 Building Facade

2003. 120th Anniv of Confediliizia Institute, Rome.
2850 **1259** $2.58 multicoloured . . 3·75 1·90

1260 "Nativity" (Gian Paolo Cavagna)

2003. Christmas. Multicoloured.
2851 41c. Type **1260** 60 30
2852 62c. Poinsettia 80 40

1261 "Forme Grido Viva l'Italia"

2003. 40th Death Anniv of Giacomo Balla (artist). Multicoloured.
2853 41c. Type **1261** . . . . . .
2854 62c. "Linee—Forza del Pugno di Boccioni" . . .

1262 Pencil and Sharpener

2003. Stamp Day.
2855 **1262** 41c. multicoloured . . .

2004. Priority Mail Stamps. Designs as No. 2660. Multicoloured, background colour given. Self-adhesive gum.
2856 60c. orange 80 40
2856a 80c. red . . . . 1·10 55
2857 €1.40 green . . . . . . 2·00 1·00
2857a €1.50 grey . . . . . . 2·00 1·00
2858 €2 green . . . . 2·75 1·40
2859 €2.20 cannine . . . . . 3·00 1·50
No. 2856/9 were issued with an attached label inscribed "postaprioritaria Priority Mail".

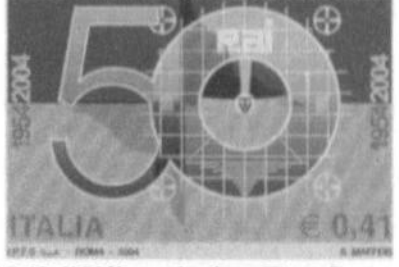

1263 "50" enclosing Test Screen

2004. 50th Anniv of Television.
2860 **1263** 41c. blue and grey . . . 60 30
2861 – 62c. multicoloured . . . 80 40
DESIGN: 62c. "50" enclosed in colour blocks.

1264 Giorgio La Pira and Script

2004. Birth Centenary of Giorgio La Pira (politician).
2862 **1264** 41c. cinnamon, blue and red 60 30

1265 Tower, Map and Compass

1266 Santa Maria Assunta Church, Pragelato

2004. Genoa–European Capital of Culture, 2004.
2863 **1265** 45c. multicoloured . . . 60 30

2004. Winter Olympic Games, Turin (2006). Multicoloured.
2864 23c. Type **1266** 30 15
2865 45c. San Pietro Apostolo church, Bardonecchia . . 60 30
2866 62c. 28th-century fountain, Sauze d'Oulx 85 40
2867 65c. Mole Antonelliana, Turin 90 45

1267 Petrarch

1269 Heart-shaped Seat Belt Buckle and Map covered with Traffic Signs

1268 Mortar, Pestle, Museum Building and Liquorice Sticks

2004. 700th Birth Anniv of Francesco Petrarca (Petrarch) (poet).
2868 **1267** 45c. multicoloured . . . 60 30

2004. Giorgio Amarelli Liquorice Museum.
2869 **1268** 45c. multicoloured . . . 60 30

2004. Road Safety. Multicoloured.
2870 60c. Type **1269** 80 40
2871 62c. Dashboard and traffic signs (horiz) 85 40

1270 Vignola

2004. Tourist Publicity (31st series). Multicoloured.
2872 45c. Type **1270** 60 30
2873 45c. Viterbo 60 30
2874 45c. Egadi Islands 60 30

1271 Casa del Fascio

2004. Birth Centenary of Guiseppe Terragni (architect).
2875 **1271** 85c. multicolored . . . 1·20 60

1272 Sakate Temple, Bangkok

2004. Bangkok and Rome. Sheet 140 × 70 mm containing T **1272** and similar horiz design. Multicoloured.
MS2876 65c. × 2, Type **1272**; Colosseum, Rome . . . . . . 1·75 1·75
Stamps of a similar design were issued by Thailand.

1273 St. George and Crowd

2004. 1700th Anniv of Martyrdom of St. George.
2877 **1273** €2.80 multicoloured 4·00 2·00

1274 Case

2004. Europa. Holidays. Multicoloured.
2878 45c. Type **1274** 60 30
2879 62c. Open case 85 40

1275 Sheep and Castle, Bologna

2004. Tratturo Magno (drovers' way). Sheet 90 × 70 mm.
MS2880 **1275** 45c. multicoloured 60 60

1276 Synagogue Facade

1278 Giacomo Puccini

1277 Football, Player and Emblem

2004. Centenary of the Great Synagogue, Rome. Multicoloured.
2881 60c. Type **1276** 80 40
2882 62c. Candlestick, ornamental panel and synagogue . . 85 40
Stamps of the same design were issued by Israel.

2004. A. C. Milan, National Football Champions, 2004.
2883 **1277** 45c. multicoloured . . . 60 30

2004. 50th Anniv of Puccini Festival, Torre del Lago.
2884 **1278** 60c. multicoloured . . . 80 40

1279 Courtyard and Emblem

2004. 600th Anniv of Turin University.
2885 **1279** 45c. brown 60 30

1280 Achille Varzi, Motorcycle and Racing Cars

2004. Birth Centenary of Achille Varzi (motorcyclist and racing driver).
2886 **1280** 45c. multicoloured . . . 60 30

1281 Arms and Policemen

2004. Prison Police.
2887 **1281** 45c. multicoloured . . . 60 30

1282 Ice Pick and Mountain Peak

1284 Stained Glass Window

1283 Statuette and Map

2004. 50th Anniv of First Assent of K2 (mountain).
2888 **1282** 65c. blue, black and ultramarine 90 45

2004. Regions. Multicoloured.
2889 45c. Type **1283** (Abruzzo) 60 30
2890 45c. Troglodyte settlement and map (Basilicata) . . . 60 30
2891 45c. Medieval map (Liguria) 60 30
2892 45c. Roman mosaic (Emilia Romagna) 60 30

2004. 500th Anniv of the Apparition of Madonna di Tirano.
2893 **1284** 45c. multicoloured . . . 60 30

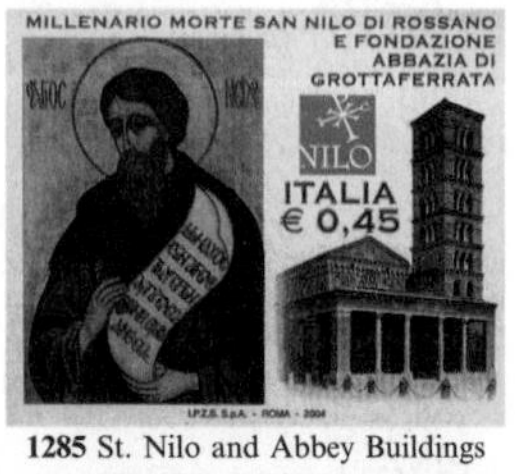

1285 St. Nilo and Abbey Buildings

2004. Death Millenary Nilo di Rossano and Millenary of Foundation of Grottaferrata Abbey.
2894 **1285** 45c. multicoloured . . . 60 30

1286 Map and Stylized Building Faade

2004. Florence State Archive.
2895 **1286** 45c. multicoloured . . . 60 30

1287 Flower

2004. Lace Making. Self-adhesive. Textile. Imperf.
2896 **1287** €2.80 blue and cream 4·00 2·00

1288 Hands **1290** Luigi Guanella

1289 Institute Buildings

2004. 40th Anniv of "Lega del Filo d'Oro" (humanitarian organization for deaf blind people).
2897 **1288** 45c. multicoloured . . . 60 30

2004. Vittorio Emanuele III Technical Institute.
2898 **1289** 45c. multicoloured . . . 60 30

2004. Luigi Guanella Commemoration (priest and humanitarian).
2899 **1290** 45c. multicoloured . . . 60 30

1291 Piazza dell'Unita, Trieste

2004. 50th Anniv of Return of Trieste to Italy.
2900 **1291** 45c. multicoloured . . . 60 30

1292 Emblem

2004. Information and Military Emergency Service.
2901 **1292** 60c. multicoloured . . . 80 40

1293 Stars and Map of Europe

2004. Constitution of Europe Treaty.
2902 **1293** 62c. multicoloured . . . 80 40

1294 Nativity

2004. Christmas. Multicoloured.
2903 45c. Type **1294** 60 30
2904 62c. Decorated tree (vert) 80 40

1295 Map of Arsenal

2004. 900th Anniv of Venice Arsenal.
2905 **1295** €2.80 multicoloured 4·00 2·00

1296 St. Lucia

2004. 1700th Anniv of Martyrdom of St. Lucia.
2906 **1296** 45c. multicoloured . . . 60 30

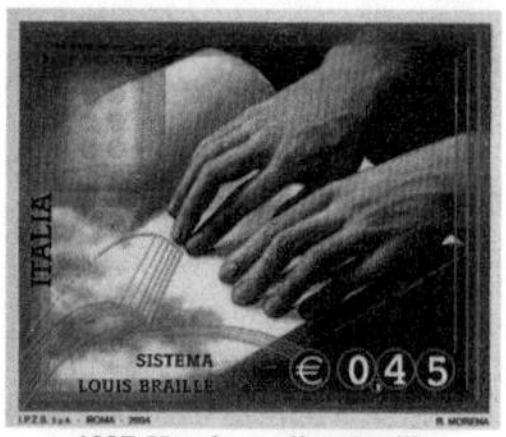

1297 Hands reading Braille

2004. Louis Braille System of Reading and Writing for the Blind.
2907 **1297** 45c. multicoloured . . . 60 30
No. 2907 was embossed with Braille letters.

1298 Boy holding Stamp **1299** Emblem and Water

2004. Stamp Day.
2908 **1298** 45c. multicoloured . . . 60 30

2004. 10th "Sport for All" Congress.
2909 **1299** 65c. multicoloured . . . 90 45

1300 University Building

2004. Libera Universita Maria SS. Assunta (LUMSA) (university), Rome.
2910 **1300** 45c. multicoloured . . . 60 30

1301 Woman's High-heeled Shoe **1302** Club Emblem and Italy

2004. Made in Italy. Shoes. Sheet 90×114 mm containing T **1301** and similar vert designs. Multicoloured.
2911/14 45c.×4 Type **1301**; Man's laced shoe; Man's loafer; Trainers 2·40 2·40

2005. Centenary of Automobile Club d'Italia (ACI).
2915 **1302** 45c. multicoloured . . . 60 30

2005.
2916 **1171** €1 multicoloured . . . 1·30 65

1303 Luigi Calabresi

2005. Luigi Calabresi (Milanese police officer) Commemoration.
2917 **1303** 45c. multicoloured . . . 60 30

CONCESSIONAL LETTER POST

CL **93** Arms of Savoy and Fasces CL **109** Arms and Fasces

1928.
CL227 CL **93** 10c. blue . . . . . 3·00 15

1930.
CL267 CL **109** 10c. brown 10 15

1945. No. CL267, surch with Royal Arms (obliterating fasces) and new value.
CL647 CL **109** 40c. on 10c. brown 10 1·30

1945. As Type CL **109**, but Arms redrawn without fasces.
CL648 10c. brown . . . . 10 1·00
CL649 1l. brown . . . . 2·10 2·10

CL **201** Italia CL **220** Italia

1947.
CL687 CL **201** 1l. green 60 30
CL688 8l. red . . . . . . 18·00 15

1948.
CL734 CL **220** 15l. violet . . . . 50·00 15
CL916 20l. violet 10 15
CL917 30l. green 10 15
CL918 35l. brown 10 15
CL919 110l. blue 10 15
CL920 270l. mauve . . . 50 40
CL921 300l. green & pink 35 55
CL922 370l. brown & orge 35 55

CONCESSIONAL PARCEL POST

CP **288**

1953.
CP918 CP **288** 40l. orange 45 40
CP919 50l. blue 00 40
CP920 60l. violet . . . . 00 6·00
CP921 70l. green . . . . 00 12·00
CP850 75l. sepia . . . . . 00 12·00
CP923 80l. brown 00 10
CP924 90l. lilac 00 10
CP851 110l. red . . . . . 00 12·00
CP926 110l. yellow 00 10
CP927 120l. green 00 10
CP928 140l. black 00 10
CP929 150l. red 00 10
CP930 180l. red 00 10
CP931 240l. slate 00 10
CP932 500l. brown . . . 00 15
CP933 600l. turquoise . . 00 15
CP934 900l. blue 00 15

Unused prices are for the complete pair. Used prices are for the left half; right halves are worth more.

CP **707**

1984.
CP1849 CP **707** 3000l. blue and red . . . . . . 3·25 2·10

EXPRESS LETTER STAMPS

E **35**

1903. For inland letters.
E 73 E **35** 25c. red . . . . 26·00 25
E113 50c. red . . . . 1·70 45
E129 60c. red . . . . 3·25 40
E178 70c. red 25 15
E179 1l.25 blue 15 10

E **41** King Victor Emmanuel III

1908. For foreign letters.
E 80 E **41** 30c. blue and pink . . 1·00 85
E180 2l. blue and pink . . . 2·30 15·00
E181 2l.50 blue and pink . . 65 1·30

E **59**

1917. Surch **25** and bars.
E112 E **59** 25c. on 40c. violet . . 20·00 17·00

1921. Surch with new value.
E118 E **41** L.1.20 on 30c. blue and pink . . . . 2·50 10·00
E173 L.1.60 on 1l.20 blue and pink . . . . . 70 11·00

1922. Surch in words and figures.
E122 E **35** 60c. on 50c. red . . . 34·00 25
E172 70c. on 60c. red . . . 30 25

E **131** "Garibaldi" (statue), Savoia Marchetti S-55A Flying Boat and "Anita Garibaldi" (statue)

1932. Air. 50th Death Anniv of Garibaldi.
E348 E **131** 2l.25+1l. violet and red . . . . 6·00 15·00
E349 4l.50+1l.50 brown and green . . . . 6·25 15·00

E **132** King Victor Emmanuel III

1932.
E350 E **132** 1l.25 green 25 10
E351 2l.50 orange 25 95

1932. 10th Anniv of March on Rome. As T **132**.
(a) For inland letters. Inscribed "ESPRESSO".
E368 1l.25 green 75 70

(b) For foreign letters. Inscribed "EXPRES".
E369 2l.50 orange . . . . 2·75 55·00
DESIGNS: 1l.25, Roman road; 2l.50, Flags and head of Mussolini.

E 133 Savoia Marchetti S-55A Flying Boat

1933. Air.

E370	E 133	2l. black	10	80
E371		2l.25 black	3·25	55·00

1934. Air. 10th Anniv of Annexation of Fiume. Inscr as in T **141**.

E408	2l.+1l.25 blue	1·40	10·00
E409	2l.25+1l.25 green	55	9·50
E410	4l.50+2l. red	55	9·50

DESIGN: Foundation of Fiume.

1934. Air. Military Medal Centenary. Inscr as in T **146**.

E442	2l.+1l.25 brown	5·25	14·00
E443	4l.50+2l. red	7·25	14·00

DESIGN—HORIZ: 2l., 4l.50, Caproni Ca 101 airplane over triumphal arch.

E 192 Italia

1945.

E647	E 192	5l. red	10	1·00

E 200 Winged Foot of Mercury

1945.

E679	E 200	5l. red	10	10
E680	–	10l. blue	10	30
E681	–	15l. red	1·90	15
E682	E 200	25l. orange	27·00	10
E683		30l. violet	2·75	75
E915		50l. purple	23·00	15
E685	–	60l. red	40·00	15

DESIGN: 10, 15, 60l. Horse and torch bearer.

E 209 Rising at Naples

1948. Centenary of 1848 Revolution.

E718	E 209	35l. violet	85·00	11·00

E 341 Etruscan Horses

1958.

E 961	E 341	75l. purple	10	10
E1220		150l. green	10	10
E1221		250l. blue & light blue	15	15
E1222		300l. brown & lt brn	20	15

MILITARY POST STAMPS

1943. Stamps of Italy optd **P.M.** (a) Postage stamps of 1929 (Nos. 239/56).

M583	5c. brown	25	35
M584	10c. brown	25	70
M585	15c. green	25	70
M586	20c. red	25	70
M587	25c. green	25	70
M588	30c. brown	25	70
M589	50c. violet	25	70
M590	1l. violet	1·40	11·00
M591	1l.25 blue	25	85
M592	1l.75 orange	25	70
M593	2l. red	25	85
M594	5l. red	25	2·40
M595	10l. violet	25	17·00

(b) Air stamps of 1930 (Nos. 271/7).

M596	50c. brown	20	70
M597	1l. violet	20	70
M598	2l. blue	30	8·50
M599	5l. green	1·40	15·00
M600	10l. red	1·40	21·00

(c) Air Express stamp of 1933 (No. E370).

M601	2l. black	1·40	17·00

(d) Express Letter stamp of 1932 (No. E350).

M602	1l.25 green	20	1·40

NEWSPAPER STAMPS

N 2

1862. Imperf.

N5	N 2	2c. yellow	40·00	85·00

For similar stamps in black, see Sardinia.

OFFICIAL STAMPS

O 11

1875.

O21	O 11	2c. red	75	65
O22		5c. red	75	65
O23		20c. red	15	15
O24		30c. red	25	20
O25		1l. red	1·60	3·00
O26		2l. red	10·50	8·00
O27		5l. red	55·00	60·00
O28		10l. red	60·00	28·00

1934. Air. Optd **SERVIZIO DI STATO**.

O450	148	10l. grey	£650	£7500

PARCEL POST STAMPS

P 13 King Umberto I

1884. Various frames.

P38	P 13	10c. grey	70·00	16·00
P39		20c. blue	£110	26·00
P40		50c. pink	11·50	3·75
P41		75c. green	10·50	3·75
P42		1l.25 orange	15·00	9·75
P43		1l.75 brown	20·00	29·00

The left-hand portion of the following parcel post stamps is affixed to the packet-card, the right-hand portion to the receipt. Unused prices are for the complete pair and used prices for the half-stamp. Unsevered stamps in used condition are usually from cancelled-to-order material and are worth more than the half-stamp.

P 53

1914.

P 96	P 53	5c. brown	40	60
P 97		10c. blue	40	60
P 98		20c. black	60	60
P 99		25c. red	70	60
P100		50c. orange	95	70
P101		1l. violet	1·20	80
P102		2l. green	1·60	60
P103		3l. yellow	3·25	70
P104		4l. grey	4·75	70
P105		10l. purple	27·00	3·50
P106		12l. brown	£100	£140
P107		15l. olive	£100	£140
P108		20l. purple	£100	£140

1923. Surch with figures on left half and words and figures on right half.

P146	P 53	30c. on 5c. brown	1·20	38·00
P147		60c. on 5c. brown	2·10	38·00
P148		1l.50 on 5c. brown	6·75	£100
P149		3l. on 10l. purple	4·25	£100

P 92

1927.

P217	P 92	5c. brown	25	30
P218		10c. blue	25	30
P219		25c. red	25	30
P220		30c. blue	25	40
P221		50c. orange	25	30
P222	–	60c. red	25	40
P223	P 92	1l. violet	25	30
P224		2l. green	25	40
P225		3l. bistre	25	80
P226		4l. black	25	80
P227		10l. purple	1·10	13·50
P228		20l. purple	1·60	22·00

The value in the right-hand portion of the 60c. is in figures.

1945. Optd with ornamental device obliterating Fascist emblems in centre.

P647	P 92	5c. brown	55	1·25
P648		10c. blue	55	1·25
P649		25c. red	55	1·25
P650		30c. blue	10·50	13·00
P651		50c. orange	55	80
P652	–	60c. red	55	80
P653	P 92	1l. violet	55	80
P654		2l. green	55	80
P655		3l. bistre	55	80
P656		4l. black	55	80
P657		10l. purple	12·50	27·00
P658		20l. purple	18·00	60·00

1946. As Type P **92**, but without fasces between stamps.

P679	P 92	1l. mauve	1·20	45
P680		2l. green	85	45
P681		3l. orange	1·50	45
P682		4l. black	2·10	45
P683		10l. purple	36·00	34·00
P684		20l. purple	48·00	65·00

P 201

1946.

P 687a	P 201	25c. blue	10	10
P 688		50c. brown	35	10
P 689		1l. brown	35	10
P 690		2l. blue	80	10
P 691		3l. orange	40	50
P 692		4l. grey	7·00	75
P 910		5l. purple	10	10
P 911		10l. violet	10	10
P 912		20l. purple	10	10
P1348		30l. purple	10	10
P 914		40l. violet	10	10
P 915		50l. red	10	10
P 916		60l. violet	10	10
P 917		100l. blue	10	10
P 918		140l. red	10	10
P 919		150l. brown	10	10
P 920		200l. green	10	10
P 921		280l. yellow	10	10
P 922		300l. purple	10	10
P 923		400l. black	20	10
P 924		500l. brown	35	10
P 925		600l. brown	30	10
P 926		700l. blue	70	15
P 927		800l. orange	1·20	15

P 298

1954.

P928a	P 298	1000l. blue	50	50
P929		2000l. red and brown	2·40	20

PNEUMATIC POST LETTERS

PE 53

1913.

PE 96	PE 53	10c. brown	1·60	5·50
PE 97		15c. lilac	1·70	8·75
PE191		15c. pink	5·00	5·50
PE192		15c. purple	1·70	8·00
PE193		20c. purple	11·50	14·00
PE 98		30c. blue	4·75	42·00
PE194		35c. red	9·50	55·00
PE195		40c. red	16·00	60·00

1924. Surch.

PE165	PE 53	15c. on 10c. brown	4·50	10·50
PE166		15c. on 20c. purple	6·25	12·00
PE167		20c. on 10c. brown	3·50	12·00
PE168		20c. on 15c. lilac	5·75	8·75
PE169		35c. on 40c. red	10·50	60·00
PE170		40c. on 30c. blue	4·00	55·00

PE 134 Galileo Galilei

PE 204 Minerva

1933.

PE372	–	15c. purple	20	50
PE373	PE 134	35c. red	20	85

DESIGN: 15c. Dante Alighieri.

1945. As Type PE **134**, but inscr "ITALIA" instead of "REGNO D'ITALIA".

PE679	–	60c. brown (Dante)	25	1·10
PE680	PE 134	1l.40 blue	25	1·10

1947.

PE694	PE 204	3l. purple	4·00	5·50
PE695		5l. blue	10	15
PE961		10l. red	10	30
PE962		20l. blue	10	30

POSTAGE DUE STAMPS

D 3

D 11

1863. Imperf.

D6B	D 3	10c. yellow	35·00	80·00

FOOTNOTE: Our price for mint stamps is for stamps without gum. Stamps with gum are worth considerably more.

1869. Perf.

D21	D 11	10c. brown	£4000	12·50

D 12

D 13

1870.

D22	D 12	1c. mauve and orange	4·25	2·20
D23		2c. mauve and orange	9·00	7·25
D24		5c. mauve and orange	35	10
D25		10c. mauve and orange	35	10
D26		20c. mauve and orange	1·50	10
D27		30c. mauve and orange	3·50	30
D28		40c. mauve and orange	3·00	40
D29		50c. mauve and orange	3·50	20
D30		60c. mauve and orange	£750	95
D31		60c. brown and orange	20·00	3·00
D32		1l. brown and blue	£5500	4·50
D33		1l. mauve and blue	6·50	20
D34		2l. brown and blue	£5500	7·50
D35		2l. mauve and blue	55·00	55
D36		5l. brown and blue	£375	10·00
D37		5l. mauve and blue	85·00	3·50
D38		10l. brown and blue	£8000	9·25
D39		10l. mauve and blue	£225	1·10

1884.

D40	D 13	50l. green	90·00	15·00
D73		50l. yellow	45·00	10·00
D41		100l. red	95·00	4·75
D74		100l. blue	60·00	4·50

(D 20)

1890. Surch over numeral as Type D **20**.

D47	D 12	10(c.) on 2c. (D23)	60·00	14·00
D48		20(c.) on 1c. (D22)	£250	7·50
D49		30(c.) on 2c. (D23)	£950	3·50

D 141

D 142

1934. With Fascist emblems.

D395	D 141	5c. brown	25	15
D396		10c. blue	25	15
D397		20c. red	40	15
D398		25c. green	40	15
D399		30c. orange	40	15
D400		40c. brown	40	45
D401		50c. violet	25	10
D402		60c. blue	35	1·90
D403	D 142	1l. orange	40	15
D404		2l. green	40	20
D405		5l. violet	95	35
D406		10l. blue	3·00	70
D407		20l. red	7·50	3·75

D 191

D 192

D 201

1945. Fascist emblems removed.

D630	D 191	5c. brown	45	70
D631		10c. blue	10	10
D632		20c. red	45	45
D633		25c. green	10	10
D634		30c. orange	10	10
D635		40c. black	10	10
D636		50c. violet	10	10
D637		60c. blue	10	30
D685	D 192	1l. orange	10	10
D639		2l. green	10	10
D640		5l. violet	10	10
D641		10l. blue	10	10
D642		20l. red	10	1·20

1947.

D690	D **201**	1l. orange	30	10
D691		2l. green	30	10
D692		3l. red	60	85
D693		4l. brown	65	50
D924		5l. violet	10	10
D695		6l. blue	2·20	80
D696		8l. mauve	7·25	1·10
D926		10l. blue	10	10
D698		12l. brown	3·00	1·00
D927		20l. purple	10	10
D928		25l. red	10	10
D929		30l. purple	20	10
D930		40l. brown	10	10
D931		50l. green	25	10
D932		100l. orange	15	10
D935		500l. red and blue	2·30	10
D936		500l. purple and blue	45	10
D937		900l. mve, blk & grn	55	40
D938		1500l. orange & brown	1·30	45

PUBLICITY ENVELOPE STAMPS

1921. Optd **B.L.P.**

B129	**37**	10c. red	75·00	55·00
B137		15c. grey	£250	£250
B138	**41**	20c. orange	£250	£250
B132	**39**	25c. blue	£100	£225
B140		30c. brown	£170	£100
B115		40c. brown	60·00	11·00
B134		50c. violet	£550	£375
B135		60c. red	£1600	£1400
B141		85c. brown	£250	£250
B136	**34**	1l. brown and green	£2750	£1500

ITALIAN SOCIAL REPUBLIC

Following the surrender of Italy on 3 September 1943, and his rescue from imprisonment on 12 September, Mussolini proclaimed the Italian Social Republic at Salo on 23 September 1943. From this town on Lake Garda the Republican government administered those parts of Italy, north of the Gustav Line, which were under German occupation.

1944. Stamps of Italy optd **G. N. R.** (a) Postage. (i) Nos. 239 and 241/59.

1	**98**	5c. brown	2·20	5·50
2	–	10c. brown	2·20	5·50
3	–	15c. green	2·20	5·50
4	**99**	20c. red	2·20	5·50
5	–	25c. green	2·20	5·50
6	**103**	30c. brown	1·80	3·75
7	–	35c. blue	1·80	3·75
8	**103**	50c. violet	1·80	3·75
9	–	75c. red	1·80	3·75
10	**99**	1l. violet	2·75	5·75
11	–	1l.25 blue	3·50	7·25
12	–	1l.75 red	5·00	10·00
13	–	2l. red	13·00	30·00
14	**98**	2l.55 green	£190	£180
15		3l.70 violet	£100	£140
16		5l. red	26·00	50·00
17	–	10l. violet	65·00	£140
18	**99**	20l. green	£225	£450
19	–	25l. black	£650	£1400
20	–	50l. violet	£500	£1400

(ii) War Propaganda issue. Nos. 563/74.

21	25c. green (Navy)	5·00	16·00
22	25c. green (Army)	5·00	16·00
23	25c. green (Air Force)	5·00	16·00
24	25c. green (Militia)	5·00	16·00
25	30c. brown (Navy)	6·50	21·00
26	30c. brown (Army)	6·50	21·00
27	30c. brown (Air Force)	6·50	21·00
28	30c. brown (Militia)	6·50	21·00
29	50c. violet (Navy)	4·50	16·00
30	50c. violet (Army)	4·50	16·00
31	50c. violet (Air Force)	4·50	16·00
32	50c. violet (Militia)	4·50	16·00

(b) Air. Nos. 270/7.

33	–	25c. green	25·00	45·00
34	**110**	50c. brown	3·50	9·00
35	–	75c. brown	33·00	45·00
36	–	80c. red	95·00	£140
37	–	1l. violet	3·50	9·00
38	**113**	2l. blue	£275	£160
39	**110**	5l. green	£130	£225
40		10l. red	£1100	£1800

(4)

(5)

1944. Stamps of Italy. (a) Optd with T **4**.

57	–	25c. green (No. 244)	30	1·80
60	–	75c. red (No. 248)	75	1·80

(b) Optd with T **5**.

58	**103**	30c. brown	35	1·80
61	–	1l.25 blue (No. 250)	35	1·80
77	–	50l. violet (No. 259)	£200	£1800

(c) Optd **REPUBBLICA SOCIALE ITALIANA**.

59	**103**	50c. violet	30	1·80

1944. War Propaganda stamps. Nos. 563/74 optd with T **4** (25c.), T **5** (30c.) or **REPUBBLICA SOCIALE ITALIANA** (50c.).

64	25c. green (Navy)	30	2·10
65	25c. green (Army)	30	2·10
66	25c. green (Air Force)	30	2·10
67	25c. green (Militia)	30	2·10
68	30c. brown (Navy)	60	6·50
69	30c. brown (Army)	60	6·50
70	30c. brown (Air Force)	60	6·50
71	30c. brown (Militia)	60	6·50
72	50c. violet (Navy)	35	4·00
73	50c. violet (Army)	35	4·00
74	50c. violet (Air Force)	35	4·00
75	50c. violet (Militia)	35	4·00

Prices are for examples overprinted on the stamp part only; items overprinted twice (on stamp and label) are worth more.

10 Loggia dei Mercanti, Bologna

11 Loggia dei Mercanti, Bologna

12 Basilica de St. Lorenzo, Rome

13 Basilica de St. Lorenzo, Rome

1944. Inscr "REPUBBLICA SOCIALE ITALIANA".

106	–	5c. brown	10	50
107	–	10c. brown	10	20
102	**10**	20c. red	20	55
108	**11**	20c. red	10	20
103	**12**	25c. green	20	55
109	**13**	25c. green	10	20
110	–	30c. brown	10	20
111	–	50c. violet	10	20
112	–	75c. red	10	5·00
113	–	1l. violet	10	20
114	–	1l.25 blue	45	9·00
115	–	3l. green	60	33·00

DESIGN: 5c. St. Ciriaco's Church, Ancona; 10c., 1l. Montecassino Abbey; 30c., 75c. Drummer; 50c. Fascist allegory; 1l.25, 3l. St. Mary of Grace, Milan.

17 Bandiera Brothers

1944. Death Centenary of Attilio and Emilio Bandiera (revolutionaries).

117	**17**	25c. green	15	50
118		1l. violet	15	50
119		2l.50 red	15	4·50

CONCESSIONAL LETTER POST

1944. Concessional Letter Post stamp of Italy optd as T **5** but smaller.

CL76	CL **109**	10c. brown	15	1·00

EXPRESS LETTER STAMPS

1944. Express stamps of Italy optd **G. N. R.**

E41	E **132**	1l.25 green (postage)	31·00	45·00
E42		2l.50 red	£190	£400
E43	E **133**	2l. black (air)	£700	£1100

(E 7)

1944. Express stamps of Italy optd with Type E **7**.

E62	E **132**	1l.25 green	25	1·90
E63		2l.50 orange	25	12·50

E **16** Palermo Cathedral

1944.

E116	E **16**	1l.25 green	10	90

PARCEL POST STAMPS

1944. Parcel Post stamps of Italy optd **REP. SOC. ITALIANA** on left-hand side and Fascist Emblem on right.

P77	P **92**	5c. brown	9·00	10·50
P78		10c. blue	9·00	10·50
P79		25c. red	9·00	10·50
P80		30c. blue	9·00	10·50
P81		50c. orange	9·00	10·50
P82		60c. red	9·00	10·50
P83		1l. violet	9·00	10·50
P84		2l. green	£350	£550
P85		3l. bistre	15·00	35·00
P86		4l. black	28·00	55·00
P87		10l. purple	£180	
P88		20l. purple	£425	

The unused and used prices are for unsevered stamps.

POSTAGE DUE STAMPS

1944. Postage Due stamps of Italy optd **G. N. R.**

D44	D **141**	5c. brown	16·00	42·00
D45		10c. blue	12·50	42·00
D46		20c. red	16·00	24·00
D47		25c. green	9·75	24·00
D48		30c. orange	16·00	42·00
D49		40c. brown	25·00	24·00
D50		50c. violet	50·00	£200
D51		60c. blue	£250	£800
D52	D **142**	1l. orange	12·50	32·00
D53		2l. green	80·00	85·00
D54		5l. violet	£190	£325
D55		10l. blue	65·00	£225
D56		20l. red	65·00	£225

1944. Postage Due stamps of Italy optd with small Fascist emblems.

D 89	D **141**	5c. brown	1·70	4·50
D 90		10c. blue	1·70	3·75
D 91		20c. red	1·70	3·75
D 92		25c. green	1·70	3·75
D 93		30c. orange	1·70	5·25
D 94		40c. brown	1·70	8·75
D 95		50c. violet	1·70	3·00
D 96		60c. blue	3·75	18·00
D 97	D **142**	1l. orange	1·70	3·00
D 98		2l. green	5·50	12·50
D 99		5l. violet	55·00	£110
D100		10l. blue	95·00	£170
D101		20l. red	95·00	£170

IVORY COAST Pt. 6; Pt. 13

A French colony in W. Africa on the Gulf of Guinea, incorporated in French West Africa in 1944. In 1958 it became an autonomous republic within the French Community, and in 1960 it became fully independent.

100 centimes = 1 franc.

1892. "Tablet" key-type inscr "COTE D'IVOIRE" in blue (Nos. 2, 3, 5, 14, 7, 9/11) or red (others).
1 D 1c. black on blue 1·90 2·50
2 2c. brown on buff 1·75 2·25
3 4c. brown on grey 2·25 3·50
4a 5c. green on green 9·50 4·75
5 10c. black on lilac 8·75 8·75
14 10c. red 85·00 75·00
6 15c. blue 22·00 9·00
15 15c. grey 5·00 2·00
7 20c. red on green 10·00 22·00
8 25c. black on pink 10·00 2·25
16 25c. blue 27·00 25·00
9 30c. brown on drab 32·00 24·00
10 40c. red on yellow 17·00 10·50
11 50c. red on pink 55·00 60·00
17 50c. brown on blue 16·00 8·00
12 75c. brown on yellow 7·50 23·00
13 1f. green 42·00 24·00

1904. Surch in figures and bars.
18 D 0.05 on 30c. brown 55·00 65·00
19 0.10 on 75c. brown on yellow 10·00 13·50
20 0.15 on 1f. olive 11·50 14·50

1906. "Faidherbe", "Palms" and "Balay" key-types inscr "COTE D'IVOIRE" in blue (10c., 5f.) or red (others).
22 I 1c. grey 1·25 25
23 2c. brown 60 50
24 4c. brown on blue 50 40
25 5c. green 50 80
26 10c. pink 4·50 60
27 J 20c. black on blue 4·50 4·25
28 25c. blue 3·00 1·25
29 30c. brown on pink 7·00 8·50
30 35c. black on yellow 4·50 1·75
32 45c. brown on green 8·50 9·50
33 50c. violet 10·50 11·00
34 75c. green on orange 12·00 14·50
35 K 1f. black on blue 32·00 38·00
36 2f. blue on pink 35·00 50·00
37 5f. red on yellow 65·00 80·00

1912. Surch in figures.
38 D 05 on 15c. grey 45 1·60
39 05 on 30c. brown on drab 1·00 3·50
40 10 on 40c. red on yellow 40 3·25
41 10 on 50c. brown on blue 1·00 3·00
42 10 on 75c. brown on orange 2·25 7·25

7 River Scene

1913.
43 7 1c. violet and purple 10 10
44 2c. black and brown 10 1·50
45 4c. purple and violet 10 1·75
46 5c. green and light green 2·50 1·50
61 5c. brown and chocolate 35 90
47 10c. pink and red 90 1·25
62 10c. green and light green 45 2·50
63 10c. pink on blue 25 1·00
48 15c. red and orange 20 1·25
49 20c. grey and black 1·40 1·10
50 25c. blue and ultramarine 8·00 4·25
64 25c. violet and black 1·25 15
51 30c. brown and chocolate 1·75 2·50
65 30c. pink and red 2·75 3·00
66 30c. red and blue 15 75
67 30c. green and olive 1·00 2·25
52 35c. orange and violet 1·75 3·00
53 40c. green and grey 2·00 1·75
54 45c. brown and red 1·25 1·90
68 45c. purple and red 4·75 8·50
55 50c. violet and black 3·50 3·75
69 50c. blue and ultramarine 50 1·75
70 50c. blue and green 1·00 25
71 60c. violet on pink 35 3·00
72 65c. green and red 2·50 3·75
56 75c. pink and brown 1·00 45
73 75c. ultramarine and blue 4·00 4·75
74 85c. black and purple 1·25 3·75
75 90c. carmine and red 8·00 18·00
57 1f. black and yellow 1·75 35
76 1f.10 brown and green 5·50 10·00
77 1f.50 blue and light blue 5·50 6·75
78 1f.75 mauve and blue 11·50 11·50
58 2f. blue and brown 2·00 1·10
79 3f. mauve on pink 4·25 3·50
59 5f. brown and blue 5·50 3·75

1915. Surch **5c** and red cross.
60 7 10c.+5c. pink and red 80 2·00

1934. Surch with new value twice.
80 7 50 on 45c. purple and red 3·50 3·50
81 50 on 75c. ultramarine & blue 1·75 2·25
82 50 on 90c. pink and red 2·25 2·50
83 60 on 75c. violet on pink 35 95
84 65 on 15c. red and orange 40 3·00
85 85 on 75c. pink and brown 50 3·25

1922. Surch in figures and bars.
86 7 25c. on 2f. blue and brown 90 3·25
87 25c. on 5f. brown and blue 55 3·25
88 90c. on 75c. pink and red 35 3·00
89 1f.25 on 1f. ultram & blue 15 2·75
90 1f.50 on 1f. blue & light blue 80 1·50
91 3f. on 5f. green and red 1·90 4·50
92 10f. on 5f. mauve and red 6·75 19·00
93 20f. on 5f. red and green 13·00 24·00

1931. "Colonial Exhibition" key-types inscr "COTE D'IVOIRE".
94 E 40c. black and green 2·50 4·00
95 F 50c. black and mauve 4·25 7·00
96 G 90c. black and red 1·75 3·50
97 H 1f.50 black and blue 5·50 8·75

1933. Stamps of Upper Volta optd **Cote d'Ivoire** or surch also.
98 3 2c. brown and violet 10 2·25
99 4c. black and yellow 20 2·50
100 5c. indigo and blue 95 3·00
101 10c. blue and pink 65 1·60
102 15c. brown and blue 40 3·00
103 20c. brown and green 1·75 2·50
104 – 25c. brown and yellow 1·50 2·75
105 – 30c. deep green and green 1·25 3·50
106 – 45c. brown and blue 7·00 8·25
107 – 65c. indigo and blue 2·50 4·75
108 – 75c. black and violet 1·90 2·75
109 – 90c. red and mauve 1·25 3·25
110 6 1f. brown and green 1·25 3·00
111 – 1f.25 on 40c. black and pink 40 65
112 6 1f.50 ultramarine and blue 85 1·40
113 – 1f.75 on 50c. black & green 2·75 95

12 Baoule Woman

16 General Binger

1936.
114 12 1c. red 10 2·00
115 2c. blue 40 2·25
116 3c. green 70 2·50
117 4c. brown 40 2·25
118 5c. violet 40 1·75
119 10c. blue 10 1·40
120 15c. red 10 50
121 – 20c. blue 50 85
122 – 25c. red 10 75
123 – 30c. green 6·50 2·00
124 – 30c. brown 10 2·50
125 12 35c. green 1·00 2·50
126 – 40c. red 20 60
127 – 45c. brown 1·10 2·00
128 – 45c. green 1·60 3·00
129 – 50c. purple 10 10
130 – 55c. violet 1·75 2·00
131 – 60c. red 1·40 3·00
132 – 65c. brown 90 2·00
133 – 70c. brown 75 2·75
134 – 75c. violet 50 1·60
135 – 80c. brown 45 1·75
136 – 90c. red 3·50 7·25
137 – 90c. green 60 2·75
138 – 1f. green 1·60 45
139 – 1f. red 1·50 1·60
140 – 1f. violet 65 1·75
141 – 1f.25 red 75 75
142 – 1f.40 blue 85 2·75
143 – 1f.50 blue 80 75
144 – 1f.50 grey 1·75 3·00
145 – 1f.60 brown 85 3·00
146 – 1f.75 red 85 1·75
147 – 1f.75 blue 1·60 3·25
148 – 2f. blue 50 15
149 – 2f.50 blue 1·50 3·25
150 – 2f.50 red 1·40 1·75
151 – 3f. green 60 20
152 – 5f. brown 45 50
153 – 10f. violet 80 60
154 – 20f. red 2·75 2·25
DESIGNS—HORIZ: 20c. to 30c. and 40c. to 55c. Mosque at Bobo-Dioulasso; 60c. to 1f.60, Coastal scene. VERT: 1f.75, to 20f. Comoe Rapids.

1937. International Exhibition, Paris. As **T16** of Mauritania.
155 20c. violet 40 2·50
156 30c. green 45 1·75
157 40c. red 55 1·90
158 50c. brown and blue 35 2·75
159 90c. red 45 1·75
160 1f.50 blue 85 1·90
MS160a 120 × 100 mm. 3f. brown (as T **4**) 4·75 20·00

1937. 50th Anniv of Gen. Binger's Exploration.
161 **16** 65c. brown 20 15

1938. International Anti-cancer Fund. As T **22** of Mauritania.
162 1f.75+50c. blue 2·00 9·75

1939. Death Centenary of Rene Caillie (explorer). As T **27** of Mauritania.
163 90c. orange 55 1·00
164 2f. violet 90 85
165 2f.25 blue 60 1·25

1939. New York World's Fair. As T **28** of Mauritania.
166 1f.25 red 1·40 3·00
167 2f.25 blue 1·10 1·25

1939. 150th Anniv of French Revolution. As T **29** of Mauritania.
168 45c.+25c. green and black 3·75 9·50
169 70c.+30c. brown and black 4·25 9·25
170 90c.+35c. orange and black 3·75 9·25
171 1f.25+1f. red and black 3·50 5·25
172 2f.25+2f. blue and black 4·00 5·25

1940. Air. As T **6a** of Mauritania.
173 1f.90 blue 50 1·40
174 2f.90 red 60 1·75
175 4f.50 green 50 80
176 4f.90 olive 60 2·00
177 6f.90 orange 60 1·25

1941. National Defence Fund. Surch **SECOURS NATIONAL** and value.
178 +1f. on 50c. (No. 129) 2·25 4·00
178a +2f. on 80c. (No. 135) 10·00 17·00
178b +2f. on 1f.50 (No. 143) 10·00 17·00
178c +3f. on 2f. (No. 148) 11·00 16·00

16a Pirogue

1942. Marshal Petain issue.
178d **16a** 1f. green 20 2·00
178e 2f.50 blue 20 2·00

1942. Air. Colonial Child Welfare Fund. As T **16c** of Mauritania.
178f 1f.50+3f.50 green 20 1·90
178g 2f.+6f. brown 15 1·90
178h 3f.+9f. red 25 1·90

1942. Air Imperial Fortnight. As T **16d** of Mauritania.
178i 1f.20+1f.80 blue and red 20 1·90

1942. Air. As T **27** of French Sudan, but inscr "COTE D'IVOIRE".
179 50f. olive and green 2·25 3·00

REPUBLIC

17 African Elephant

19 Pres. Houphouet-Boigny

18 Place Lapalud, Abidjan

1959.
180 **17** 10f. black and green 1·75 1·25
181 25f. brown and bistre 1·10 40
182 30f. olive and turquoise 1·60 1·60

1959. Air.
183 **18** 100f. brown, green & choc 4·50 1·60
184 – 200f. brown, myrtle & turq 9·00 3·50
185 – 500f. turquoise, brn & grn 11·00 5·00
DESIGNS: 200f. Houphouet-Boigny railway bridge, Abidjan; 500f. Ayame Barrage.

1959. 1st Anniv of Republic.
186 **19** 25f. brown 2·00 2·00

20 Bete Mask

21 Conseil de l'Entente Emblem

1960. Native Masks.
187 **20** 50c. chocolate and brown 35 1·75
188 – 1f. violet and red 1·10 1·75
189 – 2f. green and blue 1·10 1·75
190 – 4f. red and green 1·60 1·25
191 – 5f. brown and red 1·60 1·25
192 – 6f. blue and purple 1·75 1·75
193 – 45f. purple and green 3·25 1·50
194 – 50f. blue and brown 3·75 1·25
195 – 85f. green and red 6·00 3·25

DESIGNS—VERT: MASKS OF: 1f. Guere; 2f. Guere (different type); 45f. Bete (different type); 50f. Gouro; 85f. Gouro (different type). HORIZ: 4f. Baole; 5f. Senoufo; 6f. Senoufo (different type).

1960. 10th Anniv of African Technical Co-operation Commission. As T **14** of Malagasy.
196 25f. violet and turquoise 2·00 1·50

1960. 1st Anniv of Conseil de l'Entente.
197 **21** 25f. multicoloured 2·00 2·50

21a "World Peace"

1961. 1st Anniv of Independence.
198 **21a** 25f. black, green & brown 55 35

22 "Thoningia sanguinea"

1961.
199 – 5f. red, yellow and green 55 15
200 – 10f. yellow, red and blue 30 20
201 – 15f. purple, green & orange 1·10 30
202 **22** 20f. yellow, red and brown 60 30
203 – 25f. yellow, red and green 70 30
204 – 30f. red, green and black 90 50
205 – 70f. yellow, red and green 2·50 1·00
206 – 85f. multicoloured 3·25 1·40
FLOWERS: 5f. "Plumeria rubra"; 10f. "Haemanthus cinnabarinus"; 15f. "Bougainvillea spectabilis"; 25f. "Eulophia cucullata"; 30f. "Newbouldia laevis"; 70f. "Mussaenda erythrophylla"; 85f. "Strophanthus sarmentosus".

23 Mail-carriers

1961. Stamp Day.
207 **23** 25f. brown, blue and green 55 40

24 Ayame Dam

26 Palms

25 Swimming

1961.
208 **24** 25f. sepia, blue and green 55 30

1961. Abidjan Games. Inscr as in T **25**.
209 **25** 5f. sepia, green and blue (postage) 20 10
210 – 20f. brown, green and grey 35 20
211 – 25f. brown, green and blue 55 25
211a – 100f. blk, red & bl (air) 2·75 1·60
DESIGNS: 20f. Basketball; 25f. Football; 100f. High-jumping.

1962. 17th Session of African Technical Co-operation Commission, Abidjan.
212 **26** 25f. multicoloured 55 35

1962. Air. "Air Afrique" Airline. As T **32** of Mauritania.
213 50f. blue, brown and chestnut 1·25 65

1962. Malaria Eradication. As T **43** of Mauritania.
214 25f.+5f. green 65 65

27 Fort Assinie

1962. Postal Centenary.
215 **27** 85f. multicoloured . . . . 1·90 1·10

28 Village, Man Region

1962. Air.
216 – 200f. sepia, purple & green 5·00 1·90
217 **28** 500f. green, purple & black 8·50 4·00
DESIGN—VERT: 200f. Street Scene, Odienne.

1962. 1st Anniv of Union of African and Malagasy States. As T **45** of Mauritania.
218 30f. red . . . . 1·00 55

29 U.N. Headquarters and Emblem

1962. Air. 2nd Anniv of Admission to U.N.
219 **29** 100f. multicoloured . . . . 1·90 85

30 Bouake Arms and Cotton Exhibit

1963. Bouake Fair.
220 **30** 50f. sepia, brown and green 65 35

1963. Freedom from Hunger. As T **51** of Mauritania.
221 25f.+5f. violet, brown & pur 85 85

31 Map of Africa

1963. Conference of African Heads of State, Addis Ababa.
222 **31** 30f. green and blue 60 60

32 Sassandra Bay

1963. Air.
223 – 50f. green, brown and blue 1·25 45
224 **32** 100f. brown, blue & myrtle 1·90 95
225 – 200f. turquoise, grn & brn 3·50 1·60
DESIGNS: 50f. Moosou Bridge; 200f. River Comoe.

1963. Air. African and Malagasian Posts and Telecommunications Union. As T **59** of Mauritania.
226 85f. multicoloured . . . . . 1·40 85

33 Hartebeest

34 Scales of Justice, Globe and UNESCO Emblem

1963. "Tourism and Hunting".
227 – 1f. multicoloured 30 10
228 – 2f. multicoloured 30 15
229 – 4f. multicoloured 25 15
230 – 5f. multicoloured 25 10
247 – 5f. green, yellow and brown 45 20
231 **33** 10f. brown, green and grey 45 20
248 – 10f. brown, green & purple 1·00 20
232 – 15f. black, green and brown 60 30
249 – 15f. brown, green & purple 1·60 30
233 – 20f. brown, green and red 85 30
234 – 25f. brown, green & yellow 1·40 50
235 – 45f. purple, green & turq 2·75 1·00
236 – 50f. black, green and brown . . . . 3·75 1·40
DESIGNS—HORIZ: 1f. Yellow-backed duiker; 4f. Beecroft's hyrax; 5f. (No. 247) African manatee; 10f. (No. 248) Pygmy hippopotamus; 15f. (No. 232) Giant forest hog; 20f. Warthog; 45f. Hunting dogs. VERT: 2f. Potto; 5f. (No. 230) Water chevrotain; 15f. (No. 249) Royal antelope; 25f. Bongo; 50f. Western black and white colobus.

1963. Air. 1st Anniv of "Air Afrique" and "DC-8" Service Inauguration. As T **87** of Mauritania.
237 25f. multicoloured 55 25

1963. 15th Anniv of Declaration of Human Rights.
238 **34** 85f. black, blue and orange 1·25 70

35 Rameses II and Nefertari, Abu Simbel

36 Map of Africa

1964. Air. Nubian Monuments Preservation.
239 **35** 60f. black, brown and red 1·60 85

1964. Inter-African National Education Ministers' Conference, Abidjan.
240 **36** 30f. red, green and blue . . 60 35

37 Weather Balloon

38 Doctor tending Child

1964. World Meteorological Day.
241 **37** 25f. multicoloured 60 40

1964. National Red Cross Society.
242 **38** 50f. multicoloured 95 50

39 Arms of the Ivory Coast

1964. Air.
243 **39** 200f. gold, blue and green 3·00 1·40

40 Globe and Athletes

41 Symbolic Tree

1964. Olympic Games, Tokyo.
244 **40** 35f. brown, green and violet 95 45
245 – 65f. ochre, brown and blue 1·90 95
DESIGN—HORIZ: 65f. Wrestling and Globe.

1964. 1st Anniv of European–African Convention.
246 **41** 30f. multicoloured 65 35

1964. French, African and Malagasy Co-operation. As T **57** of Gabon.
250 25f. brown, red and green . . 55 35

42 Pres. Kennedy

43 Korhogo Mail-carriers, 1914

1964. Air. Pres. Kennedy Commemoration.
251 **42** 100f. brown and grey . . . 1·90 1·40

1964. Stamp Day.
252 **43** 85f. sepia, brown and blue 1·60 95

44 Pottery

1965. Native Handicrafts.
253 **44** 5f. black, red and green . . 20 15
254 – 10f. black, purple and green 25 15
255 – 20f. blue, chocolate & brn 50 20
256 – 25f. brown, red and olive 55 30
DESIGNS: 10f. Wood-carving; 20f. Ivory-carving; 25f. Weaving.

45 Mail coming ashore

1965. Stamp Day.
257 **45** 30f. multicoloured 60 45

46 I.T.U. Emblem and Symbols

1965. I.T.U. Centenary.
258 **46** 85f. blue, red and green . . 1·40 85

47 Abidjan Railway Station

1965.
259 **47** 30f. multicoloured . . . . 1·25 45

48 Pres. Houphouet-Boigny and Map

49 Hammerkop

1965. 5th Anniv of Independence.
260 **48** 30f. multicoloured 55 35

1965. Birds.
261 – 1f. green, yellow and violet 65 35
262 – 2f. multicoloured 65 40
263 – 5f. purple, red and olive . . 75 45
264 **49** 10f. brown, black & purple 1·00 40
265 – 15f. red, grey and green . . 90 45
266 – 30f. brown, green and lake 1·25 45
267 – 50f. blue, black and brown 2·40 85
268 – 75f. red, green and orange 2·40 1·00
269 – 90f. multicoloured . . . . 3·75 2·10
BIRDS—HORIZ: 1f. Yellow-bellied green pigeon; 2f. Spur-winged goose; 30f. Namaqua dove; 50f. Lizard buzzard. VERT: 5f. Stone partridge; 15f. White-breasted guineafowl; 75f. Yellow-billed stork; 90f. Latham's francolin.

50 Lieupleu Rope-bridge

1965. Air.
270 **50** 100f. brown, green & lt grn 1·90 1·10
271 – 300f. purple, flesh and blue 5·50 2·75
DESIGN: 300f. Street in Kong.

51 Steam Mail Train, 1906

52 "Maternity"

1966. Stamp Day.
272 **51** 30f. green, black and purple . . . . 3·25 1·60

1966. World Festival of Negro Arts, Dakar.
273 **52** 5f. black and green 20 15
274 – 10f. black and violet . . . 30 20
275 – 20f. black and orange . . . 90 45
276 – 30f. black and red . . . . 1·10 65
DESIGNS—CARVED WORK: 10f. Pomade box; 20f. Drums; 30f. "Ancestor".

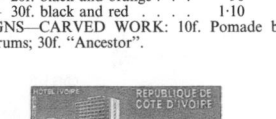

53 Ivory Hotel

1966. Inauguration of Ivory Hotel.
277 **53** 15f. multicoloured 45 25

54 Tractor Cultivation

1966. 6th Anniv of Independence.
278 **54** 30f. multicoloured 50 35

1966. Air. Inauguration of Douglas DC-8F Air Services. As T **84** of Gabon.
279 30f. grey, black and green . . 55 30

55 Open-air Class

1966. National School of Administration.
280 **55** 30f. black, blue and lake 55 35

56 Inoculating Cattle

57 UNESCO. "Waves" enveloping "Man"

1966. Campaign for Prevention of Cattle Plague.
281 **56** 30f. brown, green and blue 65 40

1966. 20th Anniv of UNESCO.
282 **57** 30f. violet and blue 60 40
283 – 30f. black, brown and blue 55 35
DESIGN: No. 283, Distributing food parcels to children.

58 Bouake Hospital

1966.
284 **58** 30f. multicoloured 55 35

59 "Air Afrique" Headquarters

1966. Air.
285 **59** 500f. blue, ochre and green 8·25 3·25

60 Sikorsky S-43 Amphibian (30th anniv)

1967. Stamp Day.
286 **60** 30f. blue, brown & turq . . 1·25 80

61 Cutting Pineapples

62 "African Mythology"

1967. Fruits.
287 **61** 20f. purple, brown & green 35 15
288 – 30f. red, brown and green 45 30
289 – 100f. brown, olive and blue 1·90 85
DESIGNS: 30f. Cutting palm-nuts; 100f. Cutting bananas.

1967. 35th Pen Club Int Congress, Abidjan.
290 **62** 30f. black, green and lake 60 40

63 "Improvement of Rural Housing"

1967. 7th Anniv of Independence.
291 **63** 30f. multicoloured 50 30

64 Lions Emblems

65 African Man and Woman

1967. 50th Anniv of Lions International.
292 **64** 30f. multicoloured 80 45

1967. Air. 5th Anniv of U.A.M.P.T. As T **139a** of Mauritania.
293 100f. red, blue and violet . . 1·60 85

1967. 5th Anniv of West African Monetary Union. As T **103** of Mauritania.
294 30f. black, green and mauve 50 30

1967. 20th Anniv of Recognition Days.
295 **65** 90f. multicoloured . . . . 1·10 65
See also No. 342.

66 Senoufo Village

1968. Air.
296 **66** 100f. brown, yellow & green . . . . 1·90 90
297 – 500f. brown, blue and green . . . . 8·25 3·25
DESIGN: 500f. Tiegba lake village.

67 Tabou Radio Station, 1912

1968. Stamp Day.
298 **67** 30f. green, brown & turq 60 35

68 Cotton Loom

1968. Industries.
299 – 5f. black, red and green . . 20 10
300 **68** 10f. brown, green and slate 30 15
301 – 15f. black, blue and red . . 70 45
302 – 20f. blue and purple . . . 50 30
303 – 30f. brown, green and blue 65 35
304 – 50f. black, green and mauve 95 45
305 – 70f. chocolate, blue & brn 1·40 70
306 – 90f. black, purple and blue 1·60 1·10
DESIGNS—HORIZ: 5f. Palm-oil works; 30f. Flour mills; 50f. Cocoa-butter extraction machine; 90f. Timber sawmill and logs. VERT: 15f. Oil refinery, Abidjan; 20f. Raw cotton and reeling machine; 70f. Soluble-coffee plant.
See also Nos. 335/7.

69 Canoeing

1968. Olympic Games, Mexico.
307 **69** 30f. brown, blue and green 60 30
308 – 100f. purple, ultram & blue 1·60 65
DESIGN: 100f. 100 m sprint.

70 Sacrificial Offering

1968. 8th Anniv of Independence.
309 **70** 30f. multicoloured 55 30

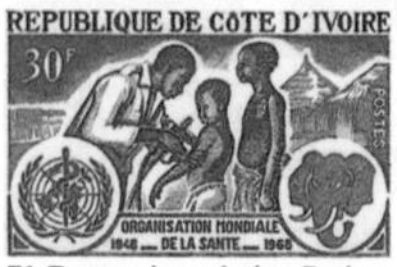

71 Doctor inoculating Patient

72 Impala in Forest

1968. 20th Anniv of W.H.O.
310 **71** 30f. chocolate, brown & bl 55 30

1968. Fauna and Flora Protection.
311 **72** 30f. brown, green and blue 1·10 55

73 Museum and Carved Screen

1968. Opening of Abidjan Museum.
312 **73** 30f. brown, red and blue 55 30

74 Human Rights Emblem and "Justice" Totems

1968. Human Rights Year.
313 **74** 30f. orange, purple and blue 55 30

1969. Air. "Philexafrique" Stamp Exhibition, Abidjan, Ivory Coast (1st issue). As T **113a** of Mauritania. Multicoloured.
314 100f. "Grand Bassam" (Achalme) . . . . 3·25 3·25

1969. Air. "Philexafrique" Stamp Exn, Abidjan, Ivory Coast (2nd issue). As T **114a** of Mauritania.
315 50f. red, blue and green . . . 1·90 1·90
316 100f. blue, brown and orange 3·00 3·00
317 200f. slate, blue and brown 4·50 4·50
DESIGNS—HORIZ: 50f. Aerial view of San Pedro village and stamp of 1936; 200f. Chambers of Agriculture and Industry building, Abidjan, and 5f. stamp of 1913. VERT: 100f. Chief's costume and 5f. stamp of 1936.

75 "Ville de Maranhao" (mail steamer) at Grand-Bassam

1969. Stamp Day.
319 **75** 30f. purple, blue and green 65 30

76 Ivory Hotel

1969. Opening of Ivory Hotel.
320 **76** 30f. blue, red and green . . 65 30

77 "Man on Horseback" (statuette)

78 Hertzian-wave Radio Station, Man

1969. Ivory Coast Art Exn, Vevey, Switzerland.
321 **77** 30f. black, purple and red 65 45

1969. 9th Anniv of Independence.
322 **78** 30f. green, brown and blue 60 35

79 Bank Emblem

1969. 5th Anniv of African Development Bank.
323 **79** 30f. brown, green and lake 50 30

80 Arms of Bouake

81 Game Fishing

1969. Coats of Arms.
324 **80** 10f. multicoloured 20 10
325 – 15f. multicoloured 30 15
326 – 30f. black, gold and green 45 15
ARMS: 15f. Abidjan; 30f. Ivory Coast Republic.
See also Nos. 402/3 and 432/6.

1969. Int SKAL Tourist Assn Congress, Abidjan.
327 **81** 30f. blue, purple and violet 2·00 50
328 – 100f. multicoloured . . . . 3·00 1·50
DESIGN: 100f. Assinie Holiday Village.

1969. 10th Anniv of Aerial Navigation Security Agency for Africa and Madagascar (A.S.E.C.N.A.). As T **147** of Gabon.
329 30f. red 55 35

82 Man Waterfall

1970. Air.
330 **82** 100f. blue, green and brown . . . . 1·90 1·00
331 – 200f. red, green and emerald . . . . 2·75 1·10
DESIGN: 200f. Mt. Niangbo.

83 University Hospital Centre, Abidjan

1970. "10 Years of Higher Education".
332 **83** 30f. indigo, green and blue 55 35

84 Telegraphist and Gabriel Dadie (Postal administrator)

1970. Stamp Day.
333 **84** 30f. black, green and red 50 30

85 Abidjan University

1970. 3rd A.U.P.E.L.F. (Association of French Speaking Universities). General Assembly, Abidjan.
334 **85** 30f. purple, green and blue 55 35

86 Safety-match Manufacture

88 Wild Life

87 Dish Aerial and Television Class

1970. Industrial Expansion.
335 **86** 5f. brown, blue & chocolate 20 15
336 – 20f. red, green and grey . . 40 15
337 – 50f. brown, blue and green 90 35
DESIGNS: 20f. Textile-printing; 50f. Ship-building.

1970. World Telecommunications Day.
338 **87** 40f. green, drab and red . . 65 40

1970. New U.P.U. Headquarters Building, Berne. As T **80a** of Malagasy.
339 30f. brown, green and purple 65 35

1970. 25th Anniv of United Nations.
340 **88** 30f. brown, green and blue 90 55

89 Coffee Plant

90 African Man and Woman

1970. 10th Anniv of Independence (1st issue).
341 **89** 30f. green, brown & orange 55 35
See also Nos. 344/9.

1970. 5th P.D.C.I. (Ivory Coast Democratic Party) Congress.
342 **90** 40f. multicoloured 65 35

91 Power Station

1970. Thermal Power Plant, Vridi.
343 **91** 40f. brown, blue and green 60 20

92 Pres. Houphouet-Boigny and De Gaulle

1970. 10th Anniv of Independence (2nd issue). Embossed on silver (300f. values) or gold foil.
344 300f. Type **92** (postage) . . . 9·00
345 300f. Ivory Coast Arms . . . 7·75
346 1000f. Type **92** . . . . . . 32·00
347 1000f. As No. 345 . . . . . 29·00
348 300f. Pres. Houphouet-Boigny and African elephants (air) . . . . . . 7·25
349 1200f. As No. 348 . . . . . 29·00

93 Mail Bus, 1925

1971. Stamp Day.
350 **93** 40f. purple, green & brown 70 30

94 Port of San Pedro

1971. Air.
351 **94** 100f. red, blue and green 1·50 55
352 – 500f. green, blue and brown . . . . 7·75 3·50
DESIGN: 500f. African Riviera coastline.

95 Desjardin's Marginella

1971. Marine Life.
353 – 1f. brown, blue and green 15 10
354 – 5f. red, lilac and blue . . . 20 15
355 – 10f. red, blue and green . . 45 20
356 **95** 15f. brown, purple and blue 50 25
357 – 15f. brown, violet and red 75 25
358 – 20f. red and yellow . . . . 1·10 40
359 – 20f. lake, purple and red 1·25 45
360 – 25f. brown, black and lake 75 25
361 – 35f. red, yellow and green 1·40 55
362 – 40f. brown, blue and green 3·00 1·25
363 – 40f. red, turquoise & brown . . . . 2·25 90
364 – 45f. brown, green & emer 2·75 1·25
365 – 50f. green, red and violet 2·75 1·10
366 – 65f. blue, green and brown 3·25 2·25
DESIGNS—HORIZ: 1f. African pelican's-foot; 5f. "Neptunus validus"; 20f. (No. 359) Digitate carrier shell; 25f. Butterfly cone; 40f. (No. 362) Garter cone; 45f. Bubonion conch; 65f. Rat cowrie. VERT: 10f. "Hermodice carunculata"; 15f. (No. 357) Fanel moon; 20f. (No. 358) "Goniaster cuspidatus"; 35f. "Polycheles typhiops"; 40f. (No. 363) African fan scallop; 50f. "Enoplometopus callistas".

96 Telegraph Station, Grand Bassam, 1891

1971. World Telecommunications Day.
367 **96** 100f. brown, green and blue . . . . 1·10 65

97 Treichville Swimming Pool

1971. Air.
368 **97** 100f. multicoloured . . . . 1·90 70

98 Tool-making

99 African Telecommunications Map

1971. Technical Training and Instruction.
369 **98** 35f. blue, red and green . . 60 30

1971. Pan-African Telecommunications Network.
370 **99** 45f. yellow, red and purple 60 30

100 Bondoukou Market

1971. 11th Anniv of Independence.
371 **100** 35f. brown, blue and grey (postage) 60 35
372 – 200f. black and blue on gold (air) . . . . . 2·50 1·60
No. 372 has a similar design to Type **100** but in smaller format, size 38 × 27 mm.

101 Children of Three Races

1971. Racial Equality Year. Multicoloured.
373 40f. Type **101** 55 20
374 45f. Children around Globe 55 20

1971. 10th Anniv of U.A.M.P.T. As T **139a** of Mauritania.
375 100f. H.Q. and Ivory Coast Arms . . . . 1·40 65
U.A.M.P.T. = African and Malagasy Posts and Telecommunications Union.

102 Gaming Table

1971. National Lottery.
376 **102** 35f. multicoloured 50 20

103 Technicians working on Power Cables

105 Cogwheel and Students

104 Lion of St. Mark's

1971. Electricity Works Centre, Akovai-Santai.
377 **103** 35f. multicoloured 70 35

1972. Air. UNESCO. "Save Venice" Campaign. Multicoloured.
378 100f. Type **104** . . . . . . 1·60 85
379 200f. St. Mark's Square . . . 3·25 1·60

1972. Technical Instruction Week.
380 **105** 35f. blue, brown and red 50 35

106 Heart Emblem

107 Child learning to write

1972. World Heart Month.
381 **106** 40f. blue, red and green 60 35

1972. International Book Year.
382 – 35f. brown, orange & grn 40 20
383 **107** 40f. black, orange & green 55 30
DESIGN—HORIZ: 35f. Students and open book.

108 Gouessesso Tourist Village

1972. Air.
384 **108** 100f. brown, green & blue 1·90 85
385 – 200f. green, brown & blue 2·75 1·10
386 – 500f. brown, bistre & blue 7·75 3·50
DESIGNS: 200f. Jacqueville Lake; 500f. Mosque of Kawara.

109 Regional Postal Training Centre, Abidjan

110 Aerial Mast, Abobo Hertzian Centre

1972. Stamp Day.
387 **109** 40f. bistre, green & purple 60 35

1972. World Telecommunications Day.
388 **110** 40f. red, blue and green 70 35

112 Computer Operator

1972. Development of Information Services.
393 **112** 40f. blue, brown and green 70 35

113 Odienne

1972. 12th Anniv of Independence.
394 **113** 35f. brown, green and blue 55 35

114 Africans and 500f. Coin

1972. 10th Anniv of West African Monetary Union.
395 **114** 40f. grey, purple and brown 60 35

115 Diamond and Mine

1972. Development of the Diamond Industry.
396 **115** 40f. blue, grey and brown 1·60 85

116 Lake-dwellings, Bletankoro

1972. Air.
397 **116** 200f. purple, green & blue 2·50 1·10
398 – 500f. brown, green & blue 7·75 3·50
DESIGN: 500f. Kossou Dam.

117 Louis Pasteur and Institute

1972. Inauguration of Pasteur Institute, Abidjan.
399 **117** 35f. blue, green and brown 60 35

118 Satellite Earth Station

1972. Air. Opening of Satellite Earth Station, Akakro.
400 **118** 200f. brown, green & blue 2·75 1·10

119 Child pumping Water 120 Dr. G. A. Hansen

1972. "Conserve Water" Campaign.
401 **119** 35f. black, green and red 60 30
See also No. 414.

1973. Coats of Arms. As T **80**. Multicoloured.
402 5f. Arms of Daloa 15 10
403 10f. Arms of Gagnoa 20 10
See also Nos. 432/6.

1973. Centenary of Hansen's Identification of Leprosy Bacillus.
404 **120** 35f. brown, blue & purple 60 30

121 Pearly Razorfish

1973. Fishes.
405 – 15f. blue and green . . . 60 40
406 – 20f. red and brown . . . 1·00 55
406a – 25f. red and green . . . 1·50 40
406b – 35f. red and green . . . 1·90 85
407 **121** 50f. red, blue and black 2·75 1·40
FISHES: 15f. Grey triggerfish; 20f. West African goatfish; 25f. African hind; 35f. Bigeye.

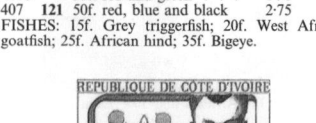

122 Child and Emblem

1973. Establishment of first S.O.S. Children's Village in Africa.
408 **122** 40f. black, red and green 55 30

123 National Assembly Building

1973. 112th Interparliamentary Council Session, Abidjan.
409 **123** 100f. multicoloured . . . 85 35

124 Classroom and Shop

1973. "Commercial Action" Programme.
410 **124** 40f. multicoloured 45 15

125 "Women's Work"

1973. Technical Instruction for Women.
411 **125** 35f. multicoloured 50 30

126 Scouts helping with Food Cultivation

1973. 24th World Scouting Congress, Nairobi, Kenya.
412 **126** 40f. multicoloured 65 35

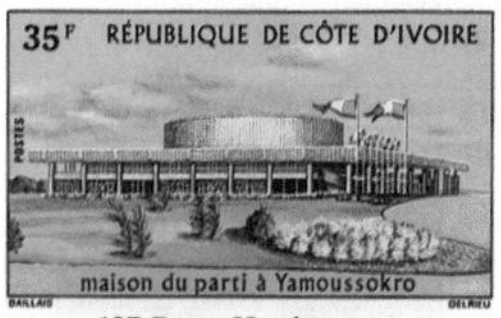

127 Party Headquarters

1973. New Party Headquarters Building, Yamoussokro.
413 **127** 35f. multicoloured 45 25

128 Children at Dry Pump

1973. Pan-African Drought Relief.
414 **128** 40f. sepia, brown and red 60 30

129 "The Judgment of Solomon" (Nandjui Legue)

1973. Air. 6th World Peace and Justice Conf.
415 **129** 500f. multicoloured . . . 9·00 4·00

1973. U.A.M.P.T. As T **155a** of Mauritania.
416 100f. black, red and violet . . 1·10 60

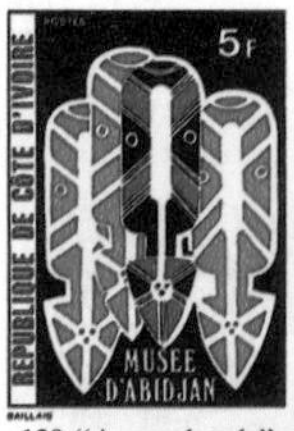

130 "Arrow-heads" 132 Motorway Junction

131 Ivory Coast 1c. Stamp of 1892

1973. Abidjan Museum.
417 **130** 5f. black, red and brown 15 10

1973. Stamp and Post Day.
418 **131** 40f. black, orange & green 65 35

1973. Motorway Projects. Indenie Interchange, Abidjan.
419 **132** 35f. black, green and blue 55 30

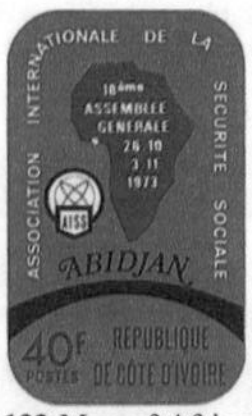

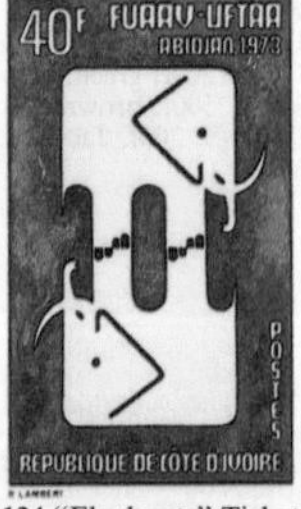

133 Map of Africa and Emblem 134 "Elephants" Ticket

1973. 18th General Assembly of International Social Security Association.
420 **133** 40f. brown, ultram & bl 50 20

1973. Travel-Agents Assns' 7th World Congress.
421 **134** 40f. multicoloured 50 20

136 Kong Mosque

1974.
426 **136** 35f. brown, blue and green 55 35

137 Grand-Lahou Post Office

1974. Stamp Day.
427 **137** 35f. brown, green and blue 55 20

138 Converging Columns

1974. "Formation Permanente".
428 **138** 35f. multicoloured 40 20

139 Sassandra Bridge

1974. Air.
429 **139** 100f. brown and green . . 1·10 50
430 500f. black and green . . 7·25 2·50

140 Map of Member Countries 141 Arms of Ivory Coast

1974. 15th Anniv of Conseil de l'Entente.
431 **140** 40f. multicoloured 45 20

1974.
432 **141** 35f. gold, green and brown 35 10
433 40f. gold, green and blue 40 10
434 60f. gold, green and red 50 20
435 65f. gold, lt green & green 55 20
436 70f. gold, green and blue 60 30

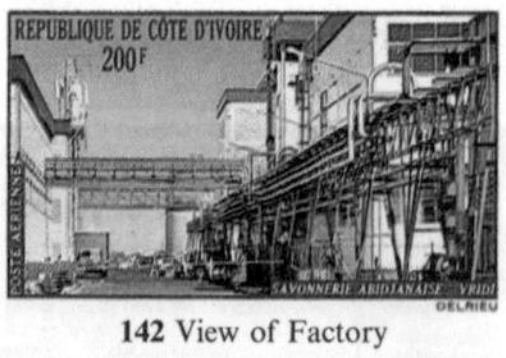

142 View of Factory

1974. Air. Vridi Soap Factory, Abidjan.
437 **142** 200f. multicoloured . . . 2·25 1·10

143 Pres. Houphouet-Boigny 144 W.P.Y. Emblem

1974.
438 **143** 25f. brown, orange & grn 35 15

1974. World Population Year.
439 **144** 40f. blue and green . . . 55 20

145 Cotton-picking 146 Pres. Houphouet-Boigny

1974. Cotton Production (1st series).
440 **145** 50f. multicoloured 60 30
See also Nos. 456/7.

1974.
889 **146** 5f. brown, mauve and red 10 10
890 10f. brown, blue and green 10 10
891 20f. lt brown, brown & red 15 10
892 25f. brown, mauve & blue 15 10
893 30f. lt brown, brown & red 20 10
441 35f. brown, green & orge 30 10
894 40f. brown, orange & grn 25 10
895 50f. brown, purple and red 30 15
443 60f. brown, red and blue 55 15
444 65f. brown, blue and red 55 10
896 90f. brown, red and purple 55 15
897 125f. brown, red & purple 65 20
898 155f. brown, blue and lilac 85 35

147 U.P.U. Emblem

148 Flag and U.P.U. Emblems

1974. Centenary of U.P.U.
445 **147** 40f. green, blue and brown (postage) 60 30
446 **148** 200f. multicoloured (air) 3·00 1·60
447 300f. multicoloured . . . 4·00 2·25

149 Raoul Follereau

1974. Follereau (leprosy pioneer) Commem.
448 **149** 35f. red, yellow and green 50 30

150 Civic Service Emblem

1974. 14th Anniv of Independence.
449 **150** 35f. multicoloured 50 20

151 Library Building and Students

1975. 1st Anniv of Inauguration of National Library.
450 **151** 40f. multicoloured 50 20

152 Congress Emblem

153 Coffee Flower

1975. 52nd International Seedcrushers Association Congress, Abidjan.
451 **152** 40f. black and green . . . 45 20

1975. Coffee Production. Multicoloured.
452 5f. Type **153** 20 10
453 10f. Coffee-berries 30 15

154 Sassandra Wharf

1975.
454 **154** 100f. brown, green & blue 1·10 65

155 Postal Sorters

1975. Stamp Day.
455 **155** 40f. multicoloured 60 30

156 Cotton Flower

1975. Cotton Production (2nd series). Multicoloured.
456 5f. Type **156** 20 15
457 10f. Cotton bolls 35 15

157 Marie Kore and I.W.Y. Emblem

1975. International Women's Year.
458 **157** 45f. brown, blue and green 55 30

158 Dabou Fort

1975.
459 **158** 50f. violet, blue and green 55 30

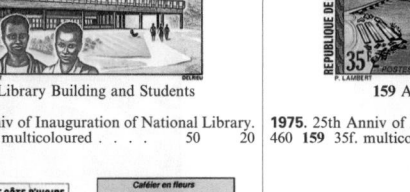

159 Abidjan Harbour

1975. 25th Anniv of Abidjan Port.
460 **159** 35f. multicoloured . . . . 1·25 40

160 Cocoa Tree

1975.
462 **160** 35f. multicoloured 80 35

161 Rural Activities

1975. Promotion of Rural Development.
463 **161** 50f. mauve, violet & black 55 35

162 Railway Bridge over the N'Zi, Dimbokro

1975. 15th Anniv of Independence.
464 **162** 60f. multicoloured . . . . 1·25 45

163 "Mother" (statue)

165 Early and Modern Telephones

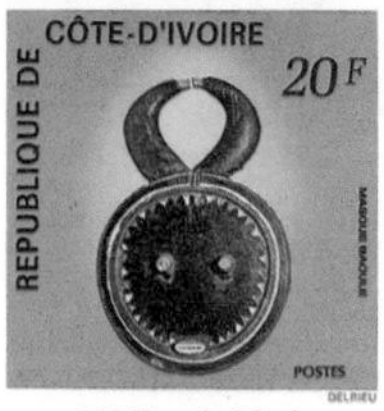

164 Baoule Mask

1976. Mothers' Day.
465 **163** 65f. multicoloured 85 45

1976. Ivory Coast Art. Multicoloured.
466 20f. Type **164** (postage) . . . 30 15
467 25f. Senoufo statuette 35 20
468 150f. Chief Abron's chair . . 1·75 85
469 200f. Akans royal symbols: fly swatter and panga (air) 3·25 1·40

1976. Telephone Centenary.
470 **165** 70f. blue, brown and black 65 40

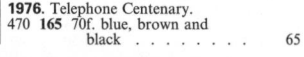

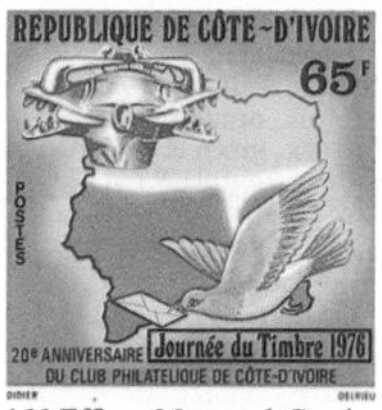

166 Effigy, Map and Carrier Pigeon

1976. 20th Anniv of Stamp Day and Ivory Coast Philatelic Club.
471 **166** 65f. multicoloured 55 35

167 "Smiling Trees" and Cat

168 Children Reading

1976. Nature Protection.
472 **167** 65f. multicoloured 65 35

1976. Literature for Children.
473 **168** 65f. multicoloured 60 35

169 Throwing the Javelin

1976. Olympic Games, Montreal. Multicoloured.
474 60f. Type **169** 55 30
475 65f. Running (horiz) 55 30

170 Mohammed Ali Jinnah

1976. Birth Centenary of Mohammed Ali Jinnah (first Governor-General of Pakistan).
476 **170** 50f. multicoloured . . . . 28·00 5·50

171 Cashew-nut

1976.
477 **171** 65f. multicoloured . . . . 1·10 45

172 Houphouet-Boigny Bridge, Abidjan

1976. 3rd African Roads Conference, Abidjan.
478 **172** 60f. multicoloured . . . . 2·50 60

173 John Paul Jones (after Peale) and detail of "First Salute to the Stars and Stripes" (E. Moran)

1976. Bicentenary of American Revolution. Multicoloured.
479 100f. Type **173** 90 35
480 125f. Comte de Rochambeau, grenadier and flag . . . . 1·10 30
481 150f. Admiral D'Estaing, French marine and French warships . . . . 1·40 55
482 175f. Marquis de Lafayette (after Peale), grenadier and flag . . . . 1·40 40
483 200f. Thomas Jefferson (after Peale), militiaman and Declaration of Independence . . . . . . 1·60 45

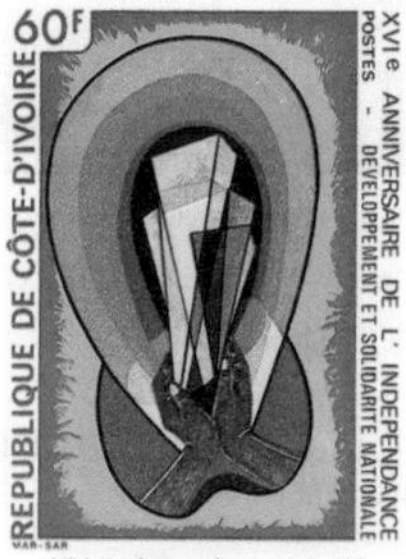

174 Independence Motif

1976. 16th Anniv of Independence.
485 **174** 60f. multicoloured 60 35

175 Ife Bronze Mask

1977. 2nd World Festival of Negro Arts, Lagos.
486 **175** 65f. multicoloured 65 45

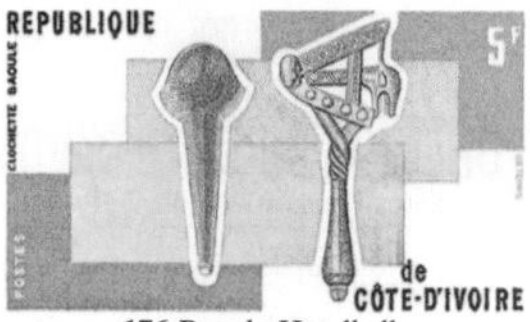

176 Baoule Handbells

1977. Musical Instruments (1st series).
487 **176** 5f. brown and green . . . 15 15
488 – 10f. black and red 20 15
489 – 20f. black and violet . . . 35 15
DESIGNS: 10f. Senoufo xylophone; 20f. Dida tom-tom.
See also Nos. 603/4.

177 Unloading Mail from Douglas DC-8

1977. Stamp Day.
490 **177** 60f. multicoloured 60 30

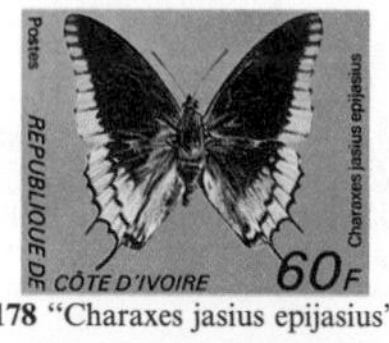

178 "Charaxes jasius epijasius"

1977. Butterflies (1st series). Multicoloured.
491 30f. "Epiphora rectifascia boolana" . . . . 1·60 55
492 60f. Type **178** . . . . 10·00 5·00
493 65f. "Imbrasia arata" . . . . 2·75 1·10
494 100f. "Palla decius" . . . . 3·25 1·60
See also Nos. 546/9 and 585/7.

179 Tingrela Mosque

1977. Air.
495 **179** 500f. brown, green & blue 5·00 2·75

180 Chateau Sassenage, Grenoble

1977. 10th Anniv of International French Language Council.
496 **180** 100f. multicoloured . . . 80 40

181 Wright Brothers and Wright Type A Biplane

1977. History of Flying. Multicoloured.
497 60f. Type **181** 45 15
498 75f. Louis Bleriot crossing English Channel 65 20
499 100f. Ross Smith and Vickers Vimy aircraft 90 20
500 200f. Charles Lindbergh and "Spirit of St. Louis" . . . 1·75 45
501 300f. Concorde . . . . . . 2·75 85

182 Santos Dumont's "Ville de Paris"

1977. History of the Airship. Multicoloured.
503 60f. Type **182** 55 15
504 65f. Launch of LZ-1 . . . . 55 15
505 150f. "Schwaben" . . . . . 1·25 35
506 200f. "Bodensee" . . . . . . 1·90 55
507 300f. "Graf Zeppelin" over Egypt . . . . 2·50 85

183 Congress Emblem

1977. 17th International Congress of Administrative Sciences in Africa.
509 **183** 60f. green and emerald . . 50 30

184 Pres. Houphouet-Boigny

185 Container Ship "Yamoussoukro"

1977.
510 **184** 35f. black, mauve & brown 20 10
511 40f. black, orange & green 90 30
512 45f. black, green & orange 1·10 30
513 60f. black, purple & brown . . . . 1·25 35
514 65f. black, orange & green 1·40 45

1977. Yamoussoukro Container Port.
515 **185** 65f. multicoloured 85 45

186 Hand holding Symbols of Development

187 "Strophantus hispidus"

1977. 17th Anniv of Independence.
516 **186** 60f. black, orange & green 55 30

1977. Flowers (1st series). Multicoloured.
517 5f. Type **187** 15 10
518 20f. "Anthurium cultorum" 30 20
519 60f. "Arachnis flos-aeris" . . 50 30
520 65f. "Renanthera storiei" . . 55 35
See also Nos. 571/3, 622/5, 678/80, 791c/e, 827a/b and 873e/f.

188 Presidents Giscard d'Estaing and Houphouet-Boigny

1978. Visit of President Giscard d'Estaing of France.
521 **188** 60f. multicoloured 70 30
522 65f. multicoloured 70 30
523 100f. multicoloured . . . 1·10 55

189 "St. George and the Dragon"

1978. 400th Birth Anniv of Peter Paul Rubens (artist). Multicoloured.
525 65f. Type **189** 50 15
526 150f. "Head of a Child" . . 1·25 45
527 250f. "The Annunciation" . . 1·90 65
528 300f. "The Birth of Louis XIII" . . . . 2·75 95

190 Members of the Royal Guard

1978. Images of History.
530 **190** 60f. red, black and blue 80 35
531 – 65f. black, blue and red 80 35
DESIGN: 65f. Figures of traditional cosmology.

191 Rural Post Office

1978. Stamp Day.
532 **191** 60f. multicoloured 55 30

192 Microwave Antenna

1978. Telecommunications Day.
533 **192** 60f. multicoloured 60 35

193 S. A. Arrhenius and Equipment (Chemistry, 1903)

1978. Nobel Prize Winners. Multicoloured.
534 60f. Type **193** 45 10
535 75f. Jules Bordet (Medicine, 1920) 55 15
536 100f. Andre Gide (Literature, 1947) 80 20
537 200f. John Steinbeck (Literature, 1962) . . . . 1·40 45
538 300f. UNICEF. (Peace, 1965) 2·40 70

194 Player kicking Ball

1978. World Cup Football Championship, Argentina. Multicoloured.
540 60f. Football and player (horiz) 45 15
541 65f. Type **194** 50 20
542 100f. Football and player (different) (horiz) 70 35
543 150f. Goalkeeper (horiz) . . 1·10 35
544 300f. Football "sun" and player . . . . 2·25 65

1978. Butterflies (2nd series). As T **178**. Multicoloured.
546 60f. "Miniodes discolor" . . 90 45
547 65f. "Charaxes lactetinctus" 90 45
548 100f. "Papilio zalmoxis" . . 1·40 80
549 200f. "Papilio antimachus" 3·00 1·60

195 Banded Cricket

1978. Insects (1st series). Multicoloured.
550 10f. Type **195** 20 15
551 20f. "Nepa cinerea" (water scorpion) 30 15
552 60f. Horned tree-hopper . . . 70 35
553 65f. "Goliathus cassicus" (beetle) . . . . 1·00 45
See also Nos. 600/2.

196 Passengers in Train

1978. Educational Television. Multicoloured.
554 60f. Figures emerging from television screen 45 20
555 65f. Type **196** . . . . 1·50 60

197 "Astragale" (oil exploration ship)

1978. 1st Anniv of Discovery of Oil in Ivory Coast. Multicoloured.
556 60f. Type **197** . . . . 1·10 35
557 65f. Ram, map of Ivory Coast and gold goblets . . 85 35

1978. Air. "Philexafrique" Stamp Exhibition, Gabon (1st issue) and International Stamp Fair, Essen, West Germany. As T **203a** of Mauritania. Multicoloured.
559 100f. Common pheasant and Bavaria 1849 1k. stamp . . 2·25 1·75
560 100f. African elephant and Ivory Coast 1965 90f. stamp . . . . 2·25 1·75
See also Nos. 588/9.

198 National Assembly Building, Paris

1978. Centenary of Paris U.P.U. Congress.
561 **198** 200f. multicoloured . . . 1·40 55

199 African with Ballot Box

200 Ribbon of Flags

1978. 18th Anniv of Independence.
562 **199** 60f. multicoloured 55 30

1978. Technical Co-operation among Developing Countries. Multicoloured.
563 60f. Type **200** 50 20
564 65f. Ribbon of flags forming arrows 50 20

201 Ploughing

1979. Agriculture.
565 **201** 100f. multicoloured . . . 90 35

202 King Hassan and Pres Houphouet-Boigny

1979. Visit of King Hassan of Morocco.
566 **202** 60f. multicoloured . . . . 1·60 35
567 65f. multicoloured . . . . 2·25 35
568 500f. multicoloured . . . 10·00 2·50

203 Isis

1979. UNESCO. Campaign for Preservation of Nubian Monuments.

569 **203**	200f. silver, green & turq	1·60	85
570 –	500f. gold, brown & orge	4·00	2·25

DESIGN: 500f. Gold medal.

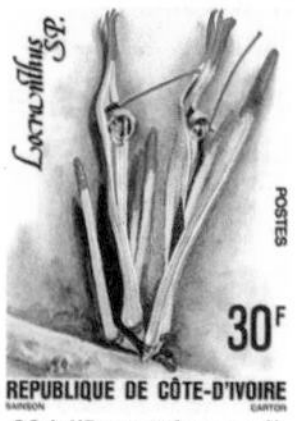

204 "Loranthus sp."

206 Children and Globe

205 Sable Antelopes

1979. Flowers (2nd series). Mult.

571	30f. Type **204**	45	35
572	60f. "Vanda josephine"	90	45
573	65f. "Renanthera storiei"	90	55

1979. Endangered Animals (1st series). Mult.

574	5f. Type **205**	20	15
575	20f. Yellow-backed duiker	35	20
576	50f. Pygmy hippopotamus	55	20
577	60f. Aardvark	1·10	55

See also Nos. 613/18.

1979. International Year of the Child. Mult.

578	60f. Type **206**	45	30
579	65f. Child on dove	50	30
580	100f. Type **206**	95	55
581	500f. As 65f.	3·75	2·25

207 Travelling Post Office

1979. Stamp Day.

582 **207**	60f. multicoloured	55	20

208 Korhogo Cathedral

1979. 75th Anniv of Arrival of Holy Fathers.

583 **208**	60f. multicoloured	55	30

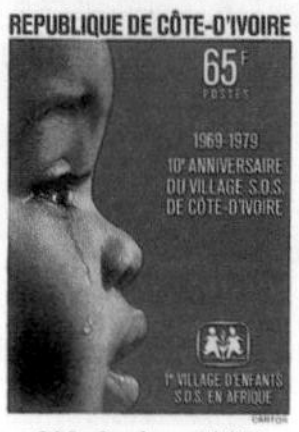

209 Crying Child

1979. 10th Anniv of S.O.S. Children's Village.

584 **209**	65f. multicoloured	55	30

210 "Euphaedra xypete"

1979. Butterflies (3rd series). Multicoloured.

585	60f. Type **210**	80	35
586	65f. "Pseudacraea bois duvali"	90	35
587	70f. "Auchenisa schausi"	1·40	55

211 Carved Figure and Antelope

212 Astronaut Greeting Boy

1979. "Philexafrique", Stamp Exhibition, Gabon (2nd issue).

588 **211**	70f. multicoloured	1·40	1·10
589 –	70f. green, turquoise & red	1·40	1·10

DESIGN: No. 589, U.P.U. emblem, antenna, ship and truck.

1979. 10th Anniv of Moon Landing. Mult.

590	60f. Type **212**	65	45
591	65f. Trajectory between Earth and Moon (horiz)	65	45
592	70f. Type **212**	1·10	55
593	150f. As 65f.	2·00	1·40

213 "Flying Scotsman" and Great Britain £1 stamp, 1878

1979. Death Centenary of Sir Rowland Hill. Multicoloured.

594	60f. Type **213**	30	10
595	75f. Steam locomotive and Ivory Coast 45c. stamp, 1936	45	15
596	100f. Diesel locomotive No. 105, U.S.A. and Hawaiian 13c. "missionary" stamp, 1852	70	20
597	150f. Steam locomotive No. 1, Japan and Japanese 20s. stamp, 1872	1·00	30
598	300f. Class BB 15000 electric locomotive, France and French 15c. stamp, 1850	2·00	60

214 "Delta sp."

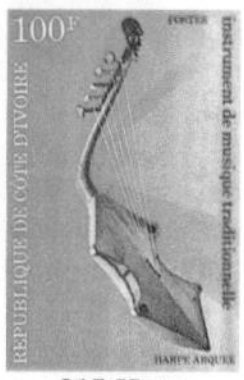

215 Harp

1979. Insects (2nd series). Mult.

600	30f. Type **214**	2·25	1·10
601	60f. "Mantis religiosa" (vert)	4·00	1·60
602	65f. "Locusta migratorius"	4·50	1·60

1979. Musical Instruments (2nd series). Mult.

603	100f. Type **215**	11·00	4·50
604	150f. Senoufo funeral horns	17·00	6·75

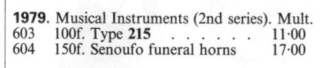

216 "Telecom 79"

217 Carved Head

1979. 3rd World Telecommunications Exhibition, Geneva.

605 **216**	60f. grey, orange and blue	55	30

1979. Culture Days.

606 **217**	65f. multicoloured	55	20

218 Boxing

1979. Pre-Olympic Year. Multicoloured.

607	60f. Type **218**	45	15
608	65f. Running	45	15
609	100f. Football	70	30
610	150f. Cycling	1·10	45
611	300f. Wrestling	2·25	80

See also Nos. 642/5.

219 Jentink's Duiker

1979. Endangered Animals (2nd series). Multicoloured.

613	40f. Type **219**	45	20
614	60f. Olive colobus	50	20
615	75f. African manatees	70	25
616	100f. Temminck's giant squirrel	1·00	35
617	150f. Pygmy hippopotamus	1·40	45
618	300f. Chimpanzee	2·75	90

220 Raoul Follereau and Institute

1979. Raoul Follereau d'Adzope Institute.

619 **220**	60f. multicoloured	60	35

221 Post, Adze and Plant

222a Coelancanth

222 Concorde and Map of Africa

1979. 19th Anniv of Independence.

620 **221**	60f. multicoloured	55	15

1979. 20th Anniv of ASECNA (African Air Safety Organization).

621 **222**	60f. multicoloured	75	30

1979. Fishes (1st series). Multicoloured.

621a	60f. Lionfish		
621b	65f. Type **222a**		

See also Nos. 629/31 and 666/8

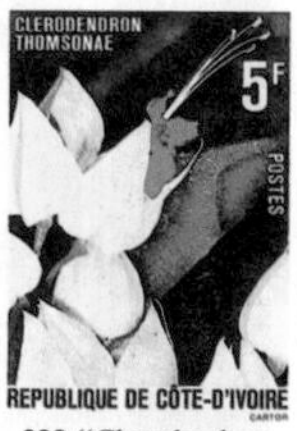

223 "Clerodendron thomsonae"

224 Elephant, Map and Rotary Emblem

1980. Flowers (3rd series). Multicoloured.

622	5f. Type **223**	10	10
623	10f. "La Boule de Feu" (horiz)	15	10
624	50f. "Costus incanusiamus"	55	15
625	60f. "Ficus elastica"	55	20

1980. 75th Anniv of Rotary International.

626 **224**	65f. multicoloured	55	30

225 Seal

1980. International Archives Day.

627 **225**	65f. multicoloured	55	35

226 Boys with Stamp Album

1980. Stamp Day.

628 **226**	65f. brown and turquoise	60	20

1980. Fishes (2nd series). As T **222a**. Multicoloured.

629	60f. Emperor snapper	90	40
630	65f. Guinean fingerfish (vert)	90	40
631	100f. Banded gourami	1·50	75

228 Missionary and Church, Aboisso

1980. 75th Anniv of Settlement of Holy Fathers at Aboisso.

632 **228**	60f. multicoloured	60	35

229 Hands protecting Child from Cigarettes

1980. Anti-Smoking Campaign.

633 **229**	60f. multicoloured	60	20

230 Pope John-Paul II and President Houphouet-Boigny

1980. Papal Visit.

634 **230**	65f. yellow, brn & dp brn	1·00	45

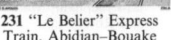

231 "Le Belier" Express Train, Abidjan–Bouake

232 Headquarters Building, Dakar

1980. Railways. Multicoloured.
635 60f. Type **231** 60 35
636 65f. Abidjan Station, 1904 . . 60 35
637 100f. Steam train, 1908 . . . 1·10 45
638 150f. Steam goods train, 1940 1·75 80

1980. 1st Anniv of West African Central Bank.
639 **232** 60f. multicoloured 60 35

233 Cobra

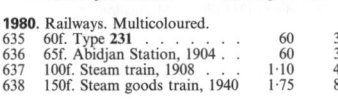

1980. Animals. Multicoloured.
640 60f. Type **233** 55 20
641 150f. Toad . . . . 1·50 65

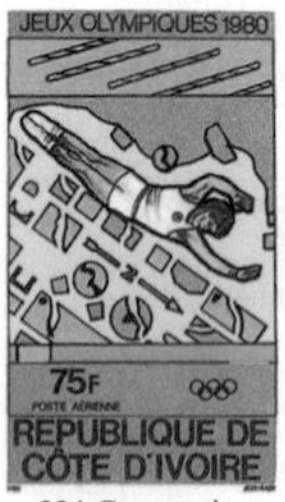

234 Gymnastics

235 World Tourism Conference Emblem

1980. Air. Olympic Games, Moscow. Multicoloured.
642 75f. Type **234** 65 15
643 150f. Ring exercise . . . . . 1·10 30
644 250f. Vaulting horse (horiz) 2·00 55
645 350f. Bar exercise . . . . . 3·00 85

1980. Tourism. Multicoloured.
647 60f. Village scene 45 15
648 65f. Type **235** 45 15

1980. Insects (3rd series). As T **214**. Mult.
649 60f. "Ugada limbata" (25 × 35 mm) 85 55
650 60f. "Forticula auricularia" (36 × 26 mm) . . . . . . 1·60 95
651 65f. "Mantis religiosa" (26 × 32 mm) . . . . . . 1·60 85
652 200f. Grasshopper (35 × 25 mm) . . . . . . 2·25 1·40

236 Hands breaking Chains, Map and President

1980. President Houphouet-Boigny's 75th Birthday.
653 **236** 60f. mult (postage) . . . 55 30
654 – 65f. multicoloured . . . 55 30
655 – 70f. multicoloured . . . 70 45
656 **236** 150f. multicoloured . . . 1·75 1·10
657 – 300f. multicoloured . . . 3·25 1·75

658 – 2000f. silver (air) . . . . 15·00 15·00
659 – 3000f. gold . . . . 22·00 22·00

DESIGNS—SQUARE: 70f. Presidential speech on map in national colours. HORIZ (44 × 29 mm): 65f., 300f. President and symbols of progress. VERT (35 × 45 mm): 2000f., 3000f. President Houphouet-Boigny.

237 Map of Ivory Coast

1980. 7th P.D.C.I.–R.D.A. Congress.
660 **237** 60f. green, orange & black 45 15
661 65f. green, orange & black 45 15

238 "Sotra" (ferry)

1980. New Lagoon Transport.
662 **238** 60f. multicoloured 55 30

239 Abidjan

1980. 20th Anniv of Independence.
663 **239** 60f. multicoloured . . . . 1·50 45

240 Conference Emblem

241 Map of Africa and Posthorn

1980. 5th General Conference of African Universities Association, Yamoussoukro.
664 **240** 60f. multicoloured 55 30

1980. 5th Anniv of African Posts and Telecommunications Union.
665 **241** 150f. multicoloured . . . 1·10 35

241a Red-billed Dwarf Hornbill

1980. Birds. Multicoloured.
665a 60f. Superb starling . . . . 45·00 4·25
665b 65f. Type **241a** . . . . . . 45·00 4·25
665c 65f. South African crowned crane . . . . 45·00 4·50
665d 100f. Saddle-bill stork . . . £140 12·00

242 Rio Grande Cichlid

1981. Fishes (3rd series). Multicoloured.
666 60f. Type **242** 80 50
667 65f. Red-tailed black shark 80 50
668 200f. Green pufferfish . . . . 2·25 1·25

243 Post Office, Grand Lahou

1981. Stamp Day.
669 **243** 60f. multicoloured 55 20

244 Mask

1981. 25th Anniv of Ivory Coast Philatelic Club.
670 **244** 65f. black, lt brown & brn 45 20

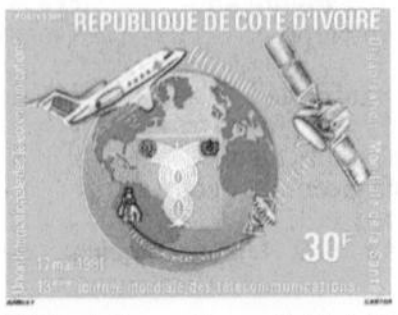

245 Red Cross Aircraft, Satellite and Globe (Telecommunications and Health)

1981. World Telecommunications Day.
671 **245** 30f. multicoloured 20 10
672 60f. multicoloured 45 20

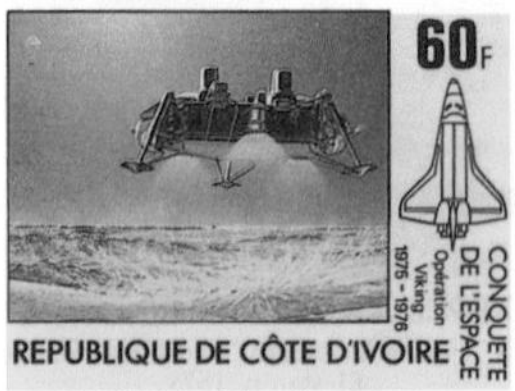

246 "Viking" landing on Mars

1981. Conquest of Space. Multicoloured.
673 60f. Type **246** 45 15
674 75f. Space Shuttle on launch pad 55 20
675 125f. Space Shuttle erecting experiment 85 40
676 300f. Space Shuttle performing experiment . . 2·10 90

247 "Amorphophallus sp."

249 Map formed of Flag

248 Prince Charles, Lady Diana Spencer and Coach

1981. Flowers (4th series). Multicoloured.
678 50f. Type **247** 55 20
679 60f. Sugar cane flowers . . . 65 35
680 100f. "Heliconia ivoirea" . . 1·25 55
See also Nos. 791c/e, 827a/b and 873e/f.

1981. Royal Wedding.
681 **248** 80f. multicoloured 55 20
682 – 100f. multicoloured . . . 65 35
683 – 125f. multicoloured . . . 85 40

DESIGNS: 100f., 125f. Similar designs showing portraits and coaches.

1981.
684a **249** 5f. multicoloured . . . 10 10
684aa 10f. multicoloured . . . 15 10
684ab 20f. multicoloured . . . 15 10
684b 25f. multicoloured . . . 15 10
684c 30f. multicoloured . . . 20 10
684ca 35f. multicoloured . . . 20 10
684d 40f. multicoloured . . . 30 10
684e 50f. multicoloured . . . 35 10
685 80f. multicoloured . . . 50 20
686 100f. multicoloured . . 60 35
687 125f. multicoloured . . 85 40

250 Goalkeeper

1981. World Cup Football Championship, Spain (1982). Multicoloured.
688 70f. Type **250** 45 30
689 80f. Saving a goal 55 35
690 100f. Diving for ball (vert) 65 40
691 150f. Goalmouth scene . . . 1·00 60
692 350f. Fighting for ball (vert) 2·40 1·10

251 Association Emblem

1981. West Africa Rice Development Association.
694 **251** 80f. multicoloured 60 30

252 Post Office

1981. Stamp Day.
695 **252** 70f. multicoloured 45 20
696 80f. multicoloured 55 35
697 100f. multicoloured . . . 65 35

253 Hands with and without Fruit, and F.A.O. Emblem

1981. World Food Day.
698 **253** 100f. multicoloured . . . 65 35

254 Felice Nazarro

1981. 75th Anniv of French Grand Prix Motor Race. Multicoloured.
699 15f. Type **254** 15 10
700 40f. Jim Clark 35 15
701 80f. Fiat, 1907 . . . . 65 40
702 100f. Auto Union, 1936 . . . 80 45
703 125f. Ferrari, 1961 . . . . . 1·10 55

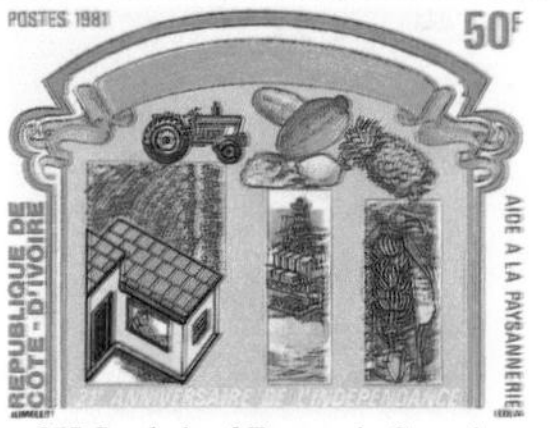

255 Symbols of Economic Growth

1981. 21st Anniv of Independence.
705 **255** 50f. multicoloured 35 15
706 80f. multicoloured 55 30

256 "Queue de Cheval" **258** Rotary Emblem on Map of Africa

257 Bingerville Post Office, 1902

1982. Hairstyles. Multicoloured.
707 80f. Type **256** 55 30
708 100f. "Belier" . . . . 1·10 45
709 125f. "Cheri regarde mon visage" . . . . 1·40 55

1982. Stamp Day.
710 **257** 100f. multicoloured . . . 65 35

1982. Rotary International Conference, Abidjan.
711 **258** 100f. blue and gold . . . 70 40

259 George Washington

1982. Celebrities' Anniversaries. Multicoloured.
712 80f. Type **259** (250th birth anniv) 55 20
713 100f. Auguste Piccard (20th death anniv) 65 30
714 350f. Goethe (150th death anniv) . . . . 2·25 85
715 450f. Princess of Wales (21st birthday) . . . . 3·00 1·25

260 Hexagonal Pattern and Telephone

1982. World Telecommunications Day.
717 **260** 80f. multicoloured 55 20

261 Presidents Mitterand and Houphouet-Boigny

1982. Visit of President Mitterand of France.
718 **261** 100f. multicoloured . . . 90 45

262 Dr. Koch, Bacillus and Microscope **263** Scouts in Dinghy

1982. Cent of Discovery of Tubercle Bacillus.
719 **262** 30f. multicoloured 30 20
720 80f. multicoloured 85 45

1982. 75th Anniv of Boy Scout Movement. Multicoloured.
721 80f. Type **263** 60 40
722 100f. Dinghy (horiz) 70 50
723 150f. Leaning into wind . . . 1·00 65
724 350f. Hauling sail . . . . . 2·50 80

264 Aerial View of Coastline **265** Congress Emblem

1982. 10th Anniv of U.N. Environmental Programme.
726 **264** 40f. multicoloured 35 15
727 80f. multicoloured 55 30

1982. First League of Ivory Coast Secretaries Congress, Abidjan.
728 **265** 80f. multicoloured 55 20
729 100f. multicoloured . . . 65 35

1982. Birth of Prince William of Wales. Nos. 681/3 optd **NAISSANCE ROYALE 1982.**
730 **247** 80f. multicoloured 55 30
731 – 100f. multicoloured . . . 65 35
732 – 125f. multicoloured . . . 85 40

267 "Child with Dove"

1982. Picasso Paintings. Multicoloured.
734 80f. Type **267** 55 20
735 100f. "Self-portrait" 65 20
736 185f. "Les Demoiselles d'Avignon" . . . . 1·60 40
737 350f. "The Dream" . . . . . 2·75 85
738 500f. "La Colombe de l'Avenir" (horiz) . . . . . 4·00 1·10

268 Post Office Counter, Abidjan 17

1982. World U.P.U. Day. Multicoloured.
739 80f. Type **268** 55 30
740 100f. Postel 2001 Building, Abidjan (vert) 85 35
741 350f. Counter clerks at Abidjan 17 Post Office . . 2·50 95
742 500f. Exterior and interior views of Postel 2001 (48 × 36 mm) . . . . . . 3·50 1·50

1982. World Cup Football Championship Results. Nos. 688/92 optd.
743 70f. Type **249** 45 25
744 80f. Saving a goal 55 25
745 100f. Diving for ball (vert) 60 35
746 150f. Goalmouth scene . . . 90 55
747 350f. Fighting for ball (vert) 2·25 1·10
OVERPRINTS: 70f. **1966 VAINQUEUR GRANDE-BRETAGNE**; 80f. **1970 VAINQUEUR BRESIL**; 100f. **1974 VAINQUEUR ALLEMAGNE (RFA)**; 150f. **1978 VAINQUEUR ARGENTINE**; 350f. **1982 VAINQUEUR ITALIE.**

270 President Houphouet-Boigny with Farming Implements and Agricultural Produce

1982. 22nd Anniv of Independence.
749 **270** 100f. multicoloured . . . 70 35

271 Emblem and Map of Member Countries

1982. 20th Anniv of West African Monetary Union.
750 **271** 100f. brown, blue & dp bl 65 35

272 Man Waterfall

1982. Landscapes. Multicoloured.
751 80f. Type **272** . . . . 2·25 55
752 80f. Wooded savanna 70 35
753 500f. Type **272** . . . . . . 9·00 2·75

273 Child and S.O.S. Village **274** Long-tailed Pangolin

1983. S.O.S. Children's Village.
754 **273** 125f. multicoloured . . . 90 40

1983. Animals. Multicoloured.
755 35f. Type **274** 30 15
756 90f. Bush pig (horiz) 65 35
757 100f. Eastern black-and-white colobus 70 40
758 125f. African buffalo (horiz) 95 50

275 Post Office, Grand Bassam, 1903

1983. Stamp Day.
759 **275** 100f. multicoloured . . . 2·00 60

276 Montgolfier Balloon, 1783

1983. Bicentenary of Manned Flight. Mult.
760 100f. Type **276** 70 25
761 125f. Charles's hydrogen balloon, 1783 . . . . . . 95 30
762 150f. Balloon "Armand Barbes" (Paris siege post, 1870) (horiz) . . . . . . 1·10 35
763 350f. Balloon "Double Eagle II" over Atlantic . . . . . 2·50 80
764 500f. Advertising airship (horiz) . . . . 4·00 1·10

277 "Descent from the Cross"

1983. Easter. Multicoloured.
765 100f. Type **277** 65 20
766 125f. "The Resurrection of Christ" (horiz) 85 30
767 350f. "The Raising of the Cross" (horiz) . . . . . . 2·25 85
768 400f. "The Piercing of the Lance" . . . . 2·75 90
769 500f. "Descent from the Cross" . . . . 3·25 1·10

278 Safe containing U.N. Emblem

1983. 25th Anniv of U.N. Economic Commission for Africa.
770 **278** 100f. multicoloured . . . 65 30

279 African Fish Eagle

1983. Birds. Multicoloured.
771 100f. Type **279** . . . . . . 1·75 40
772 125f. Grey parrot (horiz) . . 2·25 30
773 150f. Violet turaco (horiz) . . 3·50 65

280 Swimming

1983. Air. Pre-Olympic Year. Multicoloured.
774 100f. Type **280** 65 20
775 125f. Diving 90 30
776 350f. Backstroke . . . . . . 2·40 80
777 400f. Butterfly stroke . . . . 2·75 95

281 Forest destroyed by Fire

1983. Ecology in Action. Multicoloured.
779 25f. Type **281** 35 20
780 100f. Animals running from fire . . . . 1·10 45
781 125f. Protected animals . . . 1·40 65

282 Flali Dance

1983. Traditional Dances. Multicoloured.
782 50f. Type **282** 35 15
783 100f. Mask dance 65 30
784 125f. Stilt dance 95 40

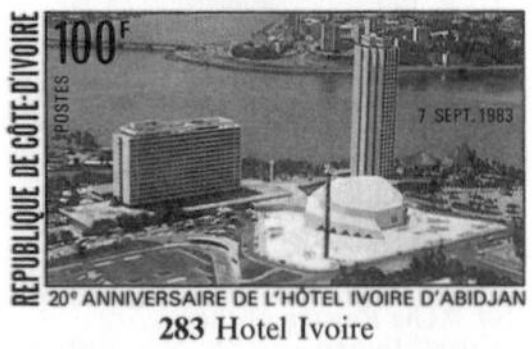

283 Hotel Ivoire

1983. 20th Anniv of Hotel Ivoire, Abidjan.
785 **283** 100f. multicoloured . . . 65 35

284 Rally Car and Route

1983. World and African Car Rally Championships.
786 **284** 100f. multicoloured . . . 90 45

285 "Christ and St. Peter"

1983. Christmas. Paintings by Raphael. Mult.
787 100f. Type **285** 65 30
788 125f. Study for St. Joseph . . 90 35
789 350f. "Virgin of the House of Orleans" . . . . 2·40 80
790 500f. "Virgin of the Blue Diadem" . . . . 3·25 1·10

286 President Houphouet-Boigny

1983. 23rd Anniv of Independence.
791 **286** 100f. multicoloured . . . 65 30

286a Telegraphist, Dish Aerial and National Postal Sorting Centre

1983. World Communications Year. Mult.
791a 100f. Cable-laying, Postel 2001 building, Abidjan, and telephonists . . . .
791b 125f. Type **286a** . . . . .

1983. Flowers (5th series). As T **247**. Multicoloured.
791c 100f. Pineapple flowers . . . 40 35
791d 125f. "Heliconia rostrata" . . 2·25 85
791e 150f. "Rose de Porcelaine" . . 2·75 1·40

287 Arrow piercing Television Screen

1984. First Audio-Visual Forum.
792 **287** 100f. black and green . . 65 30

288 Competition Emblem

289 Spider

1984. Africa Cup Football Competition.
793 **288** 100f. multicoloured . . . 65 30
794 – 200f. orange, green & blk 1·40 55
DESIGN: 200f. Maps of Africa and Ivory Coast shaking hands.

1984. Multicoloured.
795 100f. Type **289** . . . . . . 1·00 55
796 125f. "Polistes gallicus" (wasp) . . . . 1·25 65

290 Abidjan Post Office, 1934

1984. Stamp Day.
797 **290** 100f. multicoloured . . . 65 30

291 Swimming

1984. Air. Olympic Games, Los Angeles. Multicoloured.
798 100f. Type **291** 65 30
799 125f. Cross-country 80 30
800 185f. Pistol shooting . . . . 1·25 45
801 350f. Fencing . . . . 2·40 65

292 Lions Club Badge

1984. 3rd Lions Multi District 403 Convention. Multicoloured.
803 100f. Type **292** 85 35
804 125f. As Type **292** but with badge at right . . . . . . 1·00 55

293 Telecommunications Stations on Map of Ivory Coast

1984. World Telecommunications Day.
805 **293** 100f. multicoloured . . . 65 30

294 Flags, Agriculture and Symbols of Unity and Growth

1984. 25th Anniv of Council of Unity.
806 **294** 100f. multicoloured . . . 65 30
807 125f. multicoloured . . . 85 35

295 First Government House, Grand-Bassam

1984. Old Buildings (1st series). Multicoloured.
808 100f. Type **295** 65 30
809 125f. Palace of Justice, Grand-Bassam 85 35
See also Nos. 873a/c.

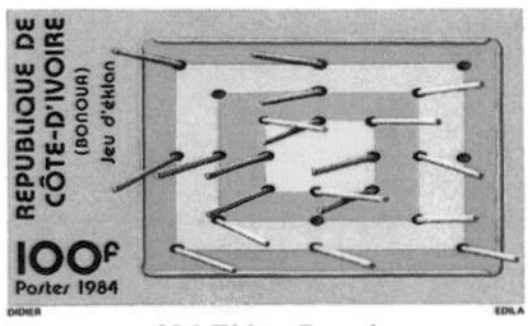

296 Eklan Board

1984. Eklan. Multicoloured.
810 100f. Type **296** 65 35
811 125f. Two Eklan players . . 85 45

297 "La Gazelle" Express Train, Abidjan–Ouagadougou

1984. Transport. Multicoloured. (a) Locomotives.
812 100f. Type **297** 75 30
813 125f. Steam locomotive, 1931, France . . . . 1·00 40
814 350f. Type 10 steam locomotive, Belgium . . . 3·00 70
815 500f. Class GT2 Mallet steam locomotive . . . . 5·25 1·10

(b) Ships.
816 100f. Container Ship 65 40
817 125f. Cargo liner 90 50
818 350f. "Queen Mary" (liner) 2·40 1·60
819 500f. "France" (liner) . . . . 4·25 2·50

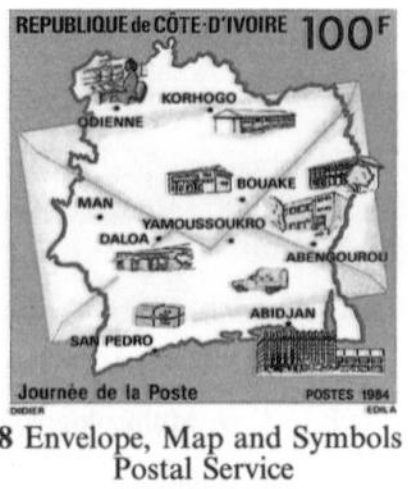

298 Envelope, Map and Symbols of Postal Service

1984. Stamp Day.
820 **298** 100f. multicoloured . . . 85 45

299 Emblem

1984. 10th Anniv of West African Economic Community.
821 **299** 100f. multicoloured . . . 65 30

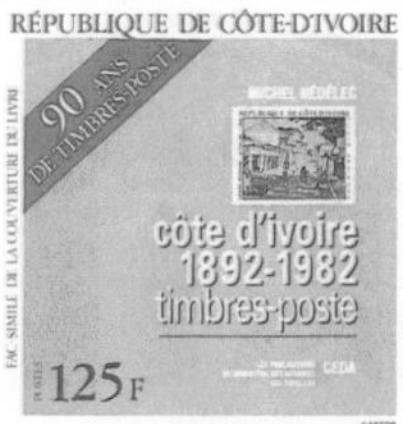

300 Book Cover

1984. 90th Anniv (1982) of Ivory Coast Postage Stamps.
822 **300** 125f. multicoloured . . . 95 65

301 Map Outline, People and Flag

1984. 24th Anniv of Independence.
823 **301** 100f. multicoloured . . . 65 30

302 G. Tiacoh (400 m silver)

1984. Air. Olympic Games Medallists. Mult.
824 100f. Type **302** 65 20
825 150f. C. Lewis (100 and 200 m gold) . . . . 1·00 35
826 200f. A. Babers (400 m gold) 1·40 45
827 500f. J. Cruz (800 m gold) . . 3·25 1·00

1984. Flowers (6th series). As T **247**. Mult.
827a 100f. "Allamanda cathartica" . . . . 22·00 8·25
827b 125f. Baobab flowers . . . 22·00 8·25

302a Serval

1984. Animals. Multicoloured.
827c 100f. Bushbuck . . . . . . 22·00 8·25
827d 150f. Type **302a** . . . . . 22·00 8·25

302b Valtur Club, Assouinde

1984.
827e 50f. Type **302b** . . . . . . 19·00 3·25
827f 100f. Azagni Canal . . . . 19·00 5·00

303 "Virgin and Child" (Correggio)

1985. Air. Christmas. Multicoloured.
828 100f. Type **303** 80 30
829 200f. "Virgin and Child" (Andrea del Sarto) . . . . 1·40 55
830 400f. "Virgin and Child" (Jacopo Bellini) . . . . . 2·75 1·10
Nos. 829/30 are wrongly inscribed "Le Correge" (Correggio).

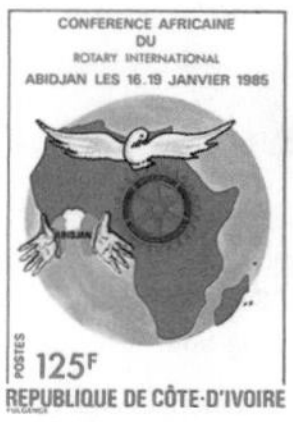

304 Map, Hands, Emblem and Dove

305 "Le Babou" (Dan costume)

1985. African Conference of Rotary International, Abidjan.
831 **304** 100f. multicoloured . . . 65 30
832 125f. multicoloured . . . 85 35

1985. Traditional Costumes. Multicoloured.
833 90f. Type **305** 70 35
834 100f. Avikam post-natal dress 95 45

305a Hadada Ibis

1985. Birds. Multicoloured.
834a 25f. Marabou stork . . . .
834b 100f. African jacana . . . .
834c 350f. Type **305a** . . . . .

306 River Steamer "Adjame"

1985. Stamp Day.
835 **306** 100f. multicoloured . . . 1·00 55

308 Emblem

1985. 7th Conference of District 18 of Zonta International, Abidjan.
836 **308** 125f. multicoloured . . . 85 30

309 Airplane, Van and Industrial Landscape

1985. "Philexafrique" Stamp Exhibition, Lome, Togo (1st issue). Multicoloured.
837 200f. Type **309** . . . . . . 1·60 1·25
838 200f. Sports and agriculture 1·60 1·25
See also Nos. 864/5.

310 Red-breasted Mergansers

1985. Air. Birth Bicentenary of John J. Audubon (ornithologist). Multicoloured.
839 100f. Type **310** 95 45
840 150f. American white pelican (vert) . . . . 1·50 50
841 200f. American wood stork (vert) . . . . 3·00 55
842 350f. Velvet scoters . . . . . 4·50 90

311 Chemical Plant, Senegal

1985. 20th Anniv of African Development Bank.
843 100f. Type **311** 65 20
844 125f. Tree seedlings, Gambia 85 35

312 Profiles within Map and IYY Emblem

1985. International Youth Year.
845 **312** 125f. multicoloured . . . 85 35

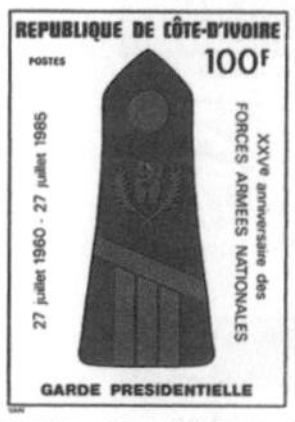

313 Presidential Guard Shoulder Flash **314** Ivory Coast Arms

1985. 25th Anniv of National Armed Forces.
846 **313** 100f. gold and purple . . 65 20
847 – 100f. gold and blue . . . 65 20
848 – 125f. gold and black . . . 95 30
849 – 200f. gold and brown . . 1·50 45
850 – 350f. silver and blue . . . 2·40 80
DESIGNS: Shoulder flashes of—No. 847, F.A.N.C.I. (army); 848, Air Force; 849, Navy; 850, Gendarmerie.

1985. Postal Convention with Sovereign Military Order of Malta. Multicoloured.
851 125f. Type **314** 85 35
852 350f. Sovereign Military Order of Malta arms . . . 2·50 1·40

315 Footballers

1985. World Cup Football Championship, Mexico. Multicoloured.
853 100f. Type **315** 65 20
854 150f. Footballers (different) 1·00 35
855 200f. Footballers (different) 1·40 40
856 350f. Footballers (different) 2·50 70

316 Pope and Abidjan Cathedral

1985. Visit of Pope John Paul II.
858 **316** 100f. multicoloured . . . 1·00 55

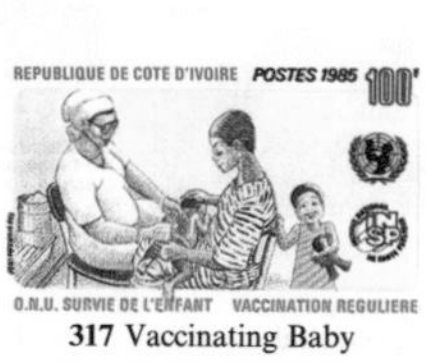

317 Vaccinating Baby

1985. UNICEF Child Survival Campaign. Multicoloured.
859 100f. Type **317** 65 30
860 100f. Mother breast-feeding baby while child plays . . 65 30
861 100f. Mother spoon-feeding child 65 30
862 100f. Mother giving child a drink (oral rehydration) . . 65 30

318 Rainbow, U.N. Emblem and Joined Hands

1985. 40th Anniv of U.N.O. and 25th Anniv of Ivory Coast Membership.
863 **318** 100f. multicoloured . . . 65 20

319 Footballers and Children with Injured Animal

1985. Air. "Philexafrique" International Stamp Exhibition, Lome, Togo (2nd issue). Mult.
864 250f. Type **319** . . . . . . 2·00 1·40
865 250f. Dish aerial, rocket and container ship . . . . . . 2·00 1·40

320 City Skyline

1985. "Expo 85" World's Fair, Tsukuba, Japan.
866 **320** 125f. multicoloured . . . 85 30

321 Young Duiker

1985. World Wildlife Fund. Banded Duiker. Multicoloured.
867 50f. Type **321** 45 20
868 60f. Duiker in front of bushes 55 20
869 75f. Two duikers . . . . . . 1·10 35
870 100f. Duiker (different) . . . 1·60 45

322 Children on Open Ground **323** Woman spinning Cotton

1985. "Return to the Earth".
871 **322** 125f. multicoloured . . . 85 35

1985. Rural Handicrafts. Multicoloured.
872 125f. Type **323** 85 35
873 155f. Man painting on cotton cloth . . . . 1·10 45

323a Samatiguila Mosque

1985. Old Buildings (2nd series). Multicoloured.
873a 100f. Bondoukou Market 17·00 5·50
873b 125f. Type **323a** . . . . . 17·00 5·50
873c 200f. Samory House, Bondoukou . . . . . . 17·00 5·50

1985. Flowers (7th series). As T **247**. Mult.
873d 100f. "Amorphophallus staudtii" . . . . 22·00 5·50
873e 125f. Crinum . . . . 22·00 5·50
873f 200f. "Triphyophyllum peltotum" . . . . 22·00 5·50

324 Edmond Halley and Computer Picture of Comet

1986. Air. Appearance of Halley's Comet. Multicoloured.
874 125f. Type **324** 85 25
875 155f. Sir William Herschel and Uranus . . . . 1·00 30
876 190f. Space telescope and comet . . . . 1·25 40
877 350f. "MS T-5" space probe and comet . . . . 2·50 85
878 440f. "Skylab" and Kohoutek's comet . . . . 2·75 1·00

325 "Millettia takou"

1986. Plants. Multicoloured.
879 40f. "Omphalocarpum elatum" 30 15
880 50f. "Momordica charantia" 35 15
881 125f. Type **325** 85 40
882 200f. "Costus afer" . . . . . 1·40 65

326 Vase from We

1986. Traditional Kitchenware and Tools. Multicoloured.
883 20f. Type **326** 15 10
884 30f. Baoule vase 20 10
885 90f. Baoule dish 60 20
886 125f. Dan knife (vert) 90 30
887 440f. Baoule pottery jug (vert) . . . . 3·25 1·25

327 Institute Building

1986. 10th Anniv of Institute for Higher Technical and Professional Education.
888 **327** 125f. multicoloured . . . 85 30

329 Cable Ship "Stephan", 1910

1986. Stamp Day.

899	329	125f. multicoloured	1·50	65

330 Footballers

1986. Air. World Cup Football Championship, Mexico.

900	330	90f. multicoloured	60	20
901	–	125f. multicoloured	85	25
902	–	155f. multicoloured	1·10	35
903	–	440f. multicoloured	3·00	90
904	–	500f. multicoloured	3·25	1·10

DESIGNS: 125f. to 500f. Different football scenes.

331 Emblem 333 Sacred Tom-tom

332 Endlicher's Bichir

1986. 25th Anniv of National Youth and Sports Institute.

906	331	125f. green and orange	85	30

1986. Fishes. Multicoloured.

907	5f. Type 332	10	10
908	125f. Daget's squeaker	1·10	70
909	150f. West African lung-fish	1·40	90
910	155f. Ivory Coast squeaker	1·75	90
911	440f. Electric catfish	4·50	2·50

1986. Enthronement of King of the Agni. Multicoloured.

912	50f. Type 333	35	20
913	350f. King being carried	2·50	1·40
914	440f. King and his Court	3·25	1·90

334 Baoule Village, Aoulo

1986. Rural Dwellings (1st series). Multicoloured.

915	125f. Type 334	85	45
916	155f. Avikam village, Eva	1·10	65
917	350f. Lobi village, Soukala	2·50	1·40

See also Nos. 938/9, 990 and 1012.

335 Ivory Coast Arms 336 Rocky Coastline

1986.

921	335	50f. red	30	10
924		125f. green	70	15
926		155f. red	95	20
927		195f. blue	1·10	30

1986. Coastal Landscapes. Multicoloured.

930	125f. Type 336	1·00	55
931	155f. Sandy beach	1·40	85

337 Fishery Lake

1986. Oceanographic Research Centre. Mult.

932	125f. Type 337	85	45
933	155f. Fishermen hauling in net	1·75	80

338 Pres. Houphouet-Boigny, Rainbow and Dove

1986. International Peace Year.

934	338	155f. multicoloured	1·00	55

339 Bull

1986. Research and Development. Mult.

935	125f. Type 339	1·10	65
936	155f. Rice (IDSA 6)	1·10	65

340 Pres. Houphouet-Boigny and Symbols of Development

1986. 26th Anniv of Independence.

937	340	155f. multicoloured	1·10	55

341 Guesseple Dan Village

1987. Rural Dwellings (2nd series). Mult.

938	190f. Type 341	1·40	90
939	550f. M'Bagui Senoufo village	4·00	2·25

342 Postman, 1918 343 Elephant and Cockerel

1987. Stamp Day.

940	342	155f. multicoloured	1·10	65

1987. 25th Anniv of French–Ivory Coast Cultural Friendship. Jean Mermoz College. Multicoloured.

941	40f. Type 343	30	15
942	155f. Children's faces in dove	1·10	55

344 Child running to Adult

1987. World Red Cross Day.

943	344	195f.+5f. multicoloured	1·50	1·40

345 "Soling" Class Yachts

1987. Air. Olympic Games, Seoul (1988) (1st issue). Sailing. Multicoloured.

944	155f. Type 345	1·10	85
945	195f. Windsurfers	1·40	80
946	250f. "470" class dinghies	1·90	90
947	550f. Windsurfer	4·00	1·60

See also Nos. 959/62.

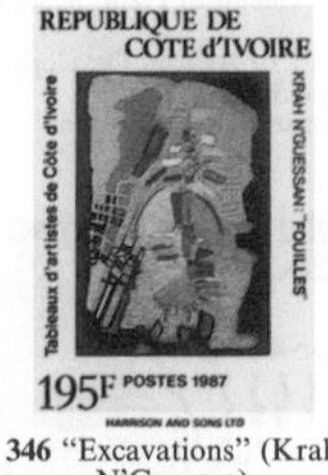

346 "Excavations" (Krah N'Guessan)

1987. Paintings. Multicoloured.

949	195f. Type 346	1·40	90
950	500f. "Ceremonial Cortege" (Santoni Gerard)	3·25	2·25

347 Airplane and Van

1987. World Post Day. International Express Post.

951	347	155f. multicoloured	1·10	80
952		195f. multicoloured	1·40	90

348 Map and Forms of Communication

1987. 100 Years of International Mail and Communications Exchanges.

953	348	155f. multicoloured	1·10	65

349 Tower Block reflecting Symbols of Progress 350 Baby in Aloe Plant on Map

1987. 27th Anniv of Independence.

954	349	155f. multicoloured	1·10	65

1988. Lions International. "For the Life of a Child".

955	350	155f. multicoloured	1·10	65

351 Bereby Post Office, 1900 352 Heart

1988. Stamp Day.

956	351	155f. multicoloured	1·00	55

1988. 15th Francophone Cardiological Congress, Abidjan.

957	352	195f. red and black	1·60	1·10

353 Man working Soil

1988. 10th Anniv of International Agricultural Development Fund.

958	353	195f. multicoloured	1·40	80

354 Gymnastics (rings)

1988. Air. Olympic Games, Seoul (2nd issue). Multicoloured.

959	100f. Type 354	65	35
960	155f. Women's handball	1·00	45
961	195f. Boxing	1·40	45
962	500f. Gymnastics (parallel bar)	3·25	1·25

355 Stone Sculpture with Deep Nostrils 356 Healthy Youth and Drug Addict

1988. Archaeological Research. Stone Sculptures from Niangoran-Bouah Collection.

964	355	5f. brown and flesh	10	10
965	–	10f. brown and green	10	10
966	–	30f. brown and green	20	10
967	–	155f. brown and yellow	1·00	55
968	–	195f. brown and green	1·40	80

DESIGNS: 10f. Sculpture with full lips; 30f. Sculpture with large nose; 155f. Sculpture with triangular mouth; 195f. Sculpture with sunken eyes.

1988. 1st International Drug Abuse and Illegal Trafficking Day.

969	356	155f. multicoloured	1·10	80

357 "The Couple" (K. J. Houra)

1988. Paintings by Local Artists. Multicoloured.

970	20f. Type 357	15	10
971	30f. "The Canary of Gentleness" (Monne Bou) (horiz)	20	10
972	150f. "The Eternal Dancer" (Monne Bou)	1·00	55
973	155f. "The Termite Hill" (Mathilde Moro)	1·00	55
974	195f. "The Sun of Independence" (Michel Kodjo)	1·25	70

358 Emblem

1988. 25th Anniv of Organization of African Unity.

975	358	195f.+5f. multicoloured	1·40	1·25

359 Collector with Album

1988. World Post Day.
976 **359** 155f. multicoloured . . . 1·00 65

360 Emblem

1988. 28th Anniv of Independence. Forestry Year. Multicoloured.
977 40f. Type **360** 30 20
978 155f. "To each his tree" . . . 1·10 65
979 155f. "Stop fires" . . . . . 1·10 65

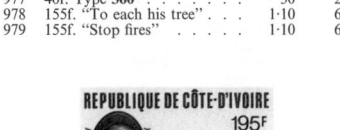

361 Marie Therese Houphouet-Boigny and Emblem

1988. 1st Anniv of N'Daya International.
980 **361** 195f.+5f. multicoloured 1·40 1·25

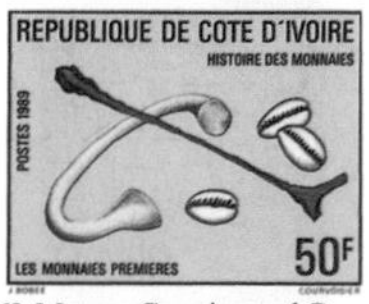

362 Money Cowries and Bones

1989. History of Money (1st series).
981 **362** 50f. multicoloured 70 30
982 – 195f. black, grey and blue 1·50 90
DESIGN: 195f. Bank of Senegal notes.
See also Nos. 1004/5, 1019/21 and 1053.

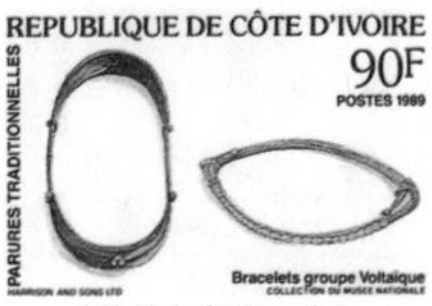

363 Voltaic Bracelets

1989. Traditional Jewellery. Multicoloured.
983 90f. Type **363** 70 45
984 155f. Dan ankle bracelets . . 1·25 90

364 Stamp used as Money

365 "Old Man and Child"

1989. Stamp Day.
985 **364** 155f. multicoloured . . . 1·25 85

1989. Carvings by Christian Lattier. Mult.
986 40f. Type **365** 30 20
987 155f. "Saxophone Player" . . 1·10 55
988 550f. "Panther" (horiz) . . . 3·50 2·00

366 Map and Tractor

1989. 30th Anniv of Council of Unity.
989 **366** 75f. multicoloured 50 30

367 Sirikukube Dan

1989. Rural Dwellings (3rd series).
990 **367** 155f. multicoloured . . . 1·10 65

368 Congress Venue and Pres. Houphouet-Boigny

1989. International Peace Congress, Yamoussoukro.
991 **368** 195f. multicoloured . . . 1·40 80

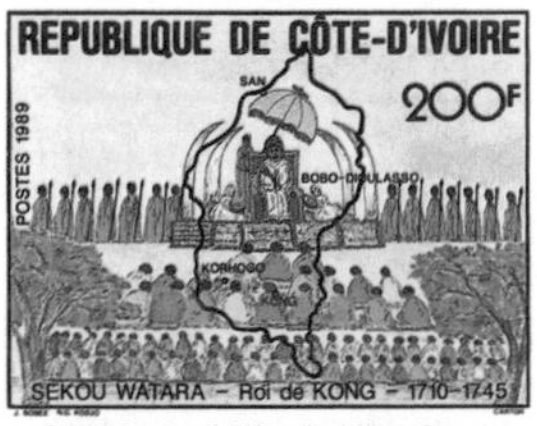

369 Map and King holding Court

1989. Anniversaries. Multicoloured.
992 200f. Type **369** (279th anniv of accession of King Sekou Watara of Kong) . . . . . 1·50 1·00
993 200f. Bastille and detail of Declaration of Rights of Man (bicentenary of French Revolution) . . . . 1·50 1·00

370 Nile Monitor

1989. Reptiles. Multicoloured.
994 25f. Type **370** 15 10
995 100f. Nile crocodile 70 50

371 Globe and Emblem

1989. World Post Day.
996 **371** 195f. multicoloured . . . 1·40 65

372 Telephone Kiosks and Mail Boxes

1989. 30th Anniv of West African Posts and Telecommunications Association.
997 **372** 155f. multicoloured . . . 1·10 65

373 Milan

374 Crowd and Handclasp

1989. Air. World Cup Football Championship (1990) Preliminary Rounds. Multicoloured.
998 195f. Type **373** . . . . . . 1·40 45
999 300f. Genoa . . . . 2·00 65
1000 450f. Turin . . . . 2·75 1·00
1001 550f. Bologna . . . . . . 4·00 1·25

1989. 29th Anniv of Independence.
1002 **374** 155f. multicoloured . . . 1·00 55

375 Emblem

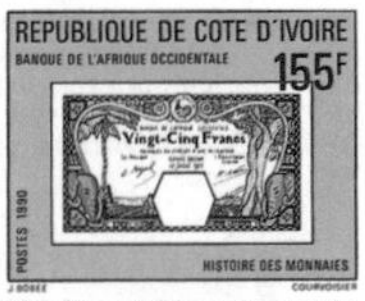

376 West African Bank 25f. Banknote

1990. 10th Anniv of Pan-African Postal Union.
1003 **375** 155f. multicoloured . . . 1·00 55

1990. History of Money (2nd series).
1004 **376** 155f. black and green . . 1·00 55
1005 – 195f. black and orange 1·50 85
DESIGN: 195f. Banknotes, 1917–44.
See also Nos. 1019/21 and 1053.

377 "Afrique" (steam packet)

1990. Stamp Day.
1006 **377** 155f. multicoloured . . . 2·00 85

378 Envelopes on Map

1990. 20th Anniv of Multinational Postal Training School, Abidjan.
1007 **378** 155f. multicoloured . . . 1·10 55

379 Footballers

1990. Air. World Cup Football Championship, Italy. Designs showing match scenes. Multicoloured.
1008 155f. Type **379** . . . . . . 1·00 35
1009 195f. Brazil v. West Germany . . . . 1·25 45
1010 500f. England v. Russia . . 3·25 1·10
1011 600f. England v. Netherlands . . . . . . 4·25 1·40

1990. Rural Dwellings (4th series). As T **367**. Multicoloured.
1012 155f. Malinke village . . . 1·00 45

380 Teacher writing Letters on Blackboard

1990. International Literacy Year.
1013 **380** 195f. multicoloured . . . 1·40 65

381 Cathedral

1990. Consecration of Our Lady of Peace Cathedral, Yamoussoukro. Multicoloured.
1014 155f. Type **381** . . . . . . 1·00 55
1015 195f. Aerial view . . . . . 1·40 80

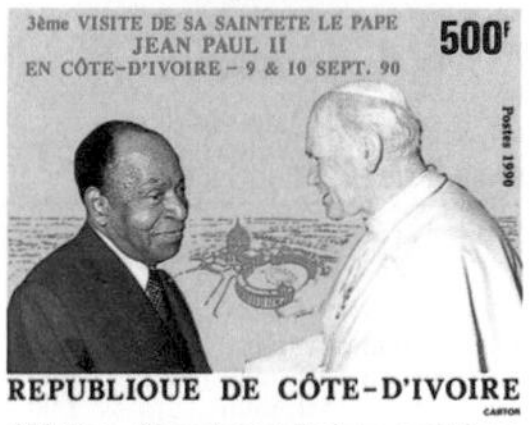

382 Pres. Houphouet-Boigny and Pope

1990. 3rd Visit of Pope John Paul II.
1016 **382** 500f. multicoloured . . . 3·50 1·90

383 Postman delivering to Village

1990. World Stamp Day.
1017 **383** 195f. multicoloured . . . 1·40 80

384 Modern Building and Road Network

1990. 30th Anniv of Independence.
1018 **384** 155f. multicoloured . . . 1·00 55

1991. History of Money (3rd series). As T **376**.
1019 40f. black and yellow . . . 30 15
1020 155f. black and green . . . 1·00 65
1021 195f. black and mauve . . . 1·25 85
DESIGNS: 40, 155f. West African Bank 100f. and 5f. notes, 1942; 195f. Issuing Institute for French West Africa and Togo 50f. and 500f. notes.

385 Communications

1991. Stamp Day.
1022 **385** 150f. multicoloured . . . 1·00 35

386 Suzanne Lenglen

1991. Centenary of French Open Tennis Championships. Tennis players. Multicoloured.

1023 200f. Type **386** . . . . . . 1·40 1·10
1024 200f. Helen Wills Moody . . 1·40 1·10
1025 200f. Simone Mathieu . . . 1·40 1·10
1026 200f. Maureen Connolly . . 1·40 1·10
1027 200f. Francoise Durr . . . 1·40 1·10
1028 200f. Margaret Court . . . 1·40 1·10
1029 200f. Chris Evert . . . . . 1·40 1·10
1030 200f. Martina Navratilova 1·40 1·10
1031 200f. Steffi Graf . . . . . . 1·40 1·10
1032 200f. Henri Cochet . . . . 1·40 1·10
1033 200f. Rene Lacoste . . . . 1·40 1·10
1034 200f. Jean Borotra . . . . 1·40 1·10
1035 200f. Donald Budge . . . . 1·40 1·10
1036 200f. Marcel Bernard . . . 1·40 1·10
1037 200f. Ken Rosewall . . . . 1·40 1·10
1038 200f. Rod Laver . . . . . 1·40 1·10
1039 200f. Bjorn Borg . . . . . 1·40 1·10
1040 200f. Yannick Noah . . . . 1·40 1·10

387 "Europe"

1991. Steam Packets. Multicoloured.

1041 50f. Type **387** 35 20
1042 550f. "Asie" . . . . 3·50 2·25

1991. Various stamps surch.

1043 – 150f. on 155f. mult (987) 1·00 35
1044 **367** 150f. on 155f. mult . . . 1·00 35
1045 – 150f. on 155f. black and green (1020) . . . . . 1·10 45
1046 – 200f. on 195f. black and mauve (1021) . . . . 1·40 55

389 Post and Savings Society's Emblem and Letter-box

1991. World Post Day. Multicoloured.

1047 50f. Type **389** 35 20
1048 100f. S.I.P.E. emblem and globe 65 35

390 We Drum

1991. Drums.

1049 **390** 5f. purple and lilac . . . 10 10
1050 – 25f. red and pink . . . 15 10
1051 – 150f. green and turquoise 1·10 80
1052 – 200f. green and brown 1·40 1·00

DESIGNS: 25f. Krou drum, Soubre; 150f. Nafana drum, Sinematiau; 200f. Akye drum, Alepe.

1991. History of Money (4th series). As T **376**.

1053 100f. black and mauve . . . 65 45

DESIGN: 100f. French West Africa and Togo banknotes.

391 Government Buildings

1991. 31st Anniv of Independence.

1054 **391** 150f. multicoloured . . . 1·00 45

392 Orchid

394 African Civet

393 Footballer and Cup

1991. Orchids.

1055 **392** 150f. mauve, green & blk 1·00 35
1056 – 200f. red, emerald & grn 1·25 45

DESIGNS—HORIZ: 200f. Different orchid.

1992. Ivory Coast Victory in African Nations Football Cup Championship, Senegal. Mult.

1057 20f. Type **393** 20 15
1058 150f. Elephants supporting cup with their trunks (vert) . . . . 1·10 95

1992. Animals in Abidjan Zoo.

1059 **394** 5f. brown, red and green 10 10
1060 – 40f. brown, green & orge 30 15
1061 – 150f. brown, green & red 1·00 55
1062 – 500f. brown, grn & ochre 3·25 2·25

DESIGNS: 40f. African palm civet; 150f. Bongo; 500f. Leopard.

395 World Map

1992. World Post Day.

1063 **395** 150f. blue and black . . 1·00 55

396 1892 "Tablet" and 1962 Postal Centenary Stamps

1992. Stamp Day. Centenary of First Ivory Coast Stamps. Multicoloured.

1064 150f. Type **396** . . . . . . 1·00 65
1065 150f. 1961 Independence and 1991 World Post Day stamps . . . . 1·00 65

397 Tomb Entrance

1992. Tourism, Funerary Monuments.

1067 **397** 5f. red, green and blue 10 10
1068 – 50f. brown, green & blue 50 15
1069 – 150f. brown, blue & green . . . . 1·10 35
1070 – 400f. green, blue and red 2·75 1·40

DESIGNS (tombs): 50f. Angels, lions and figures; 150f. Drummer, angel, sentry and animals; 400f. Angels, figures and tree.

398 Dove, Flag and Head of Statue of Liberty

400 Emblem and Map

399 Runners and Flags

1992. 32nd Anniv of Independence. Mult.

1071 30f. Type **398** 20 10
1072 150f. Crowd waving flags, Statue of Liberty and map 70 35

1992. International Marathon. Multicoloured.

1073 150f. Type **399** 70 35
1074 200f. Runners and landmarks . . . . 1·40 50

1992. 1st Anniv of Ity Gold Mine.

1075 **400** 200f. multicoloured . . . 1·40 50

400a Dent de Man

1992. Tourist Sites. Multicoloured.

1075a 10f. Hotel complex . . . .
1075b 25f. Type **400a** . . . . .
1075c 100f. Holiday village (horiz) . . . .
1075d 200f. Tourist map . . . .

400b Building and Emblem

1992. 1st World Conference on Environmental Protection. Multicoloured.

1075e 150f. Tree (vert) . . . . .
1075f 200f. Type **400b** . . . . .

401 Girl with Stockbook and Collectors swapping Stamp

402 "Argemone mexicana"

1993. Stamp Day. Youth Philately. Multicoloured.

1076 50f. Type **401** 25 15
1077 50f. Girl pointing at stamps 25 15
1078 150f. Boy perusing album and girls viewing exhibition display . . . . 1·00 35

1993. Medicinal Plants. Multicoloured.

1079 5f. Type **402** 10 10
1080 20f. "Hibiscus esculentus" 35 10
1081 200f. "Cassia alata" . . . . 1·40 90

403 Presidential Decree establishing Colony

404 "Calyptrochilum emarginatum"

1993. Centenary of Ivory Coast.

1082 **403** 25f. black and green . . 10 10
1083 – 100f. blue and black . . 70 50
1084 – 500f. black and brown 3·25 2·25

DESIGNS: 100f. Louis Binger (first Governor) and Felix Houphouet-Boigny (President); 500f. Factory.

1993. Orchids. Multicoloured.

1085 10f. Type **404** 10 10
1086 50f. "Plectrelminthus caudathus" 25 15
1087 150f. "Eulophia guineensis" 1·00 65

405 Heading Ball

407 Abstract Design

406 19th-century Map of Ivory Coast

1993. World Cup Football Championship, U.S.A. (1994). Multicoloured.

1088 150f. Type **405** 70 35
1089 200f. Players jumping . . . 1·40 50
1090 300f. Player dribbling ball past opponent . . . . . 2·00 1·40
1091 400f. Ball ricocheting off players . . . . 2·75 1·60

1993. World Post Day.

1092 **406** 30f. red, black and blue 15 10
1093 – 200f. multicoloured . . . 1·40 90

DESIGN: 200f. Bouake post office.

1993. African Plastic Arts Biennale, Abidjan.

1094 **407** 200f. multicoloured . . . 90 45

408 Map of Mining Centre

1993. 33rd Anniv of Independence.

1095 **408** 200f. multicoloured . . . 1·40 70

409 Boigny and Modern Developments

1994. Felix Houphouet-Boigny (President, 1960–93) Commemoration. Multicoloured.

1096 150f. Type **409** 35 20
1097 150f. Boigny, tractor, ploughing with oxen and container ship 35 20
1098 150f. Boigny and Our Lady of the Peace Cathedral, Yamoussoukro 35 20
1099 200f. Type **409** 50 25
1100 200f. As No. 1097 . . . . . 50 25
1101 200f. As No. 1098 . . . . . 50 25

410 Raoul Follereau and Globe

1994. 50th Anniv (1992) of World Anti-leprosy Campaign.

1103 **410** 150f. multicoloured . . . 35 20

411 Globe, Satellites and Flags

412 Country-woman with Basket on Back

1994. 1st Meeting of Regional African Satellite Communications Organization Board of Directors, Abidjan.

1104 **411** 150f. multicoloured . . . 35 20

1994. Multicoloured, colour of frame given.

1105 **412**	5f. orange	10	10
1106	25f. blue	10	10
1107	30f. bistre	10	10
1108	40f. green	10	10
1109	50f. brown	15	10
1110	75f. purple	20	10
1111	150f. green	40	20
1112	180f. purple	45	25
1115	280f. grey	75	40
1116	300f. violet	80	40

413 "Christ"

414 Modern Developments

1994. Stained Glass Windows by Pierre Fakhoury from Our Lady of Peace Cathedral, Yamoussoukro. Multicoloured.

1120	25f. Type **413**	10	10
1121	150f. "The Fisher of Men"	40	20
1122	200f. "Madonna and Child"	50	25

1994. 34th Anniv of Independence. The Family.

1124 **414** 150f. multicoloured . . . 40 20

415 Green Mamba

1995. Snakes. Multicoloured.

1125	10f. Royal python	10	10
1126	20f. Green bush snake . . .	10	10
1127	100f. Type **415**	25	15
1128	180f. Common puff adder	70	50
1129	500f. Rhinoceros viper . . .	1·50	1·10

416 Women collecting Water

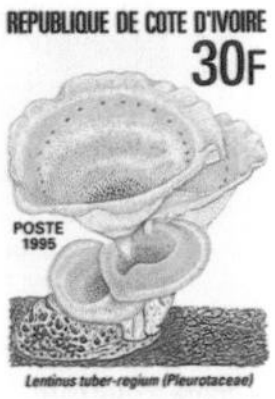

417 "Lentinus tuberregium"

1995. 50th Anniversaries. Multicoloured.

1130	100f. Type **416** (F.A.O.) . .	25	15
1131	280f. Dove on globe (U.N.O.)	75	40

1995. Fungi. Multicoloured.

1132	30f. Type **417**	20	10
1133	50f. Chinese mushroom . .	30	15
1134	180f. "Dictyophora indusiata"	90	45
1135	250f. Termite mushroom . .	1·25	60

418 Laboratory Worker and Pasteur

1995. Death Centenary of Louis Pasteur (chemist).

1136 **418** 280f. multicoloured . . . 1·00 60

419 GSR Emblem on Butterfly Wing

1995. School Philatelic Clubs. Multicoloured.

1137	50f. Type **419**	10	10
1138	180f. LBP emblem on butterfly wing	70	50

420 Palla

1995. Butterflies. Multicoloured.

1139	180f. Type **420**	70	50
1140	280f. Mocker swallowtail . .	1·00	65
1141	550f. Emperor swallowtail	1·75	1·10

421 Motor Vehicles and Handcart

1996. Abidjan Transport. Multicoloured.

1142	180f. Type **421**	45	25
1143	280f. Catching bus	70	35

422 African Bonytongue

1996. Fishes. Multicoloured.

1144	50f. Type **422**	10	10
1145	180f. Western grunter . . .	55	30
1146	700f. Guinean butter catfish	2·10	1·25

423 "Cyrtorchis arcuata"

424 Boxing

1996. Flowers. Multicoloured.

1147	40f. Type **423**	10	10
1148	100f. "Eulophia horsfalii"	25	15
1149	180f. "Eulophidium maculatum"	45	25
1150	200f. "Ansellia africana" . .	50	25

1996. Centenary of Modern Olympic Games and Olympic Games, Atlanta. Multicoloured.

1151	200f. Type **424**	50	25
1152	280f. Running	70	35
1153	400f. Long jumping	95	50
1154	500f. National Olympic Committee arms and pictograms	1·25	65

425 Huntsmens' Sticks, Birifor

1996. Ceremonial Sticks.

1155 **425**	180f. black and green . .	45	25
1156 –	200f. black and orange	50	25
1157 –	280f. black and lilac . .	70	35

DESIGNS: 200f. Lobi chief's stick from Bindam; 280f. Lobi chief's stick from Gboberi.

426 Sacred Lotus

1997. Water Plants. Multicoloured.

1158	50f. Type **426**	10	10
1159	180f. White lotus	40	20
1160	280f. Cape Blue water-lily	60	30
1161	700f. White water-lily . . .	1·50	75

427 Pres. Houphouet-Boigny and Cathedral

1997. Our Lady of Peace Cathedral, Yamoussoukro. Multicoloured.

1162	180f. Type **427**	40	20
1163	200f. Interior of church . .	45	25
1164	280f. Pope John Paul II and elevated view of cathedral	60	30

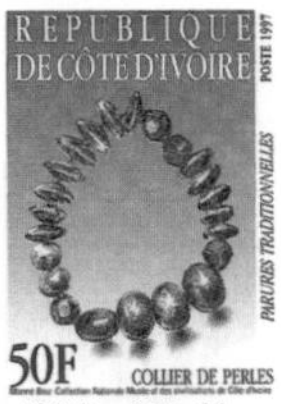

428 Pearl Necklace

429 Stone Head

1997. Traditional Necklaces. Each lilac and black.

1165	50f. Type **428**	10	10
1166	100f. Necklace of small pearls	20	10
1167	180f. Broken necklace of pearls	40	20

1997. Stone Heads from Gohitafla. Multicoloured.

1168	100f. Type **429**	20	10
1169	180f. Stone head (full-face)	40	20
1170	500f. Stone head (side-view)	1·10	55

430 Pulley

431 Manatees

1997. Wooden Weaving Tools.

1171 **430**	180f. multicoloured . . .	40	20
1172 –	280f. black, grn & dp grn	60	30
1173 –	300f. black, bl & ultram	65	35

DESIGNS—VERT: 280f. Combing frame. HORIZ: 300f. Shuttle.

1997. Endangered Species. Multicoloured.

1174	180f. Type **431**	40	20
1175	280f. Jentink's duiker . . .	60	30
1176	400f. Waterbuck	85	45

432 Goalkeeper

1998. World Cup Football Championship, France. Multicoloured.

1177	180f. Type **432**	40	20
1178	280f. Player composed of flags of competing nations (vert)	60	30
1179	400f. Match scene showing trajectory of ball	85	45
1180	500f. Players and ball as mascot (vert)	1·10	55

433 "Agaricus bingensis"

434 "Hutchinsonia barbata"

1998. Fungi. Multicoloured.

1181	50f. Type **433**	10	10
1182	180f. "Lactarius gymnocarpus"	40	20
1183	280f. "Termitomyces letestui"	60	30

1998. Plants. Multicoloured.

1184	40f. Type **434**	10	10
1185	100f. "Synsepalum aubrevillei"	20	10
1186	180f. "Cola lorougnonis" . .	40	20

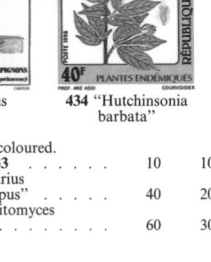

435 Tapa Woman

1998. Traditional Costumes. Multicoloured.

1187	180f. Type **435**	35	20
1188	280f. Raphia woman . . .	55	30

436 Steam Locomotive, South Africa, 1918

1999. Railways of Africa. Multicoloured.

1189	180f. Type **436**	35	20
1190	280f. Beyer Peacock 15th Class Garratt type steam locomotive, 1925 (wrongly inscr "Garret")	55	30

437 Man carrying Parcel

1999. 40th Anniv of Rural Development Council.

1192 **437** 180f.+20f. mult 35 25

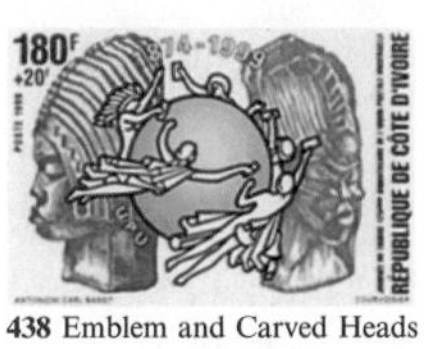

438 Emblem and Carved Heads

1999. 125th Anniv of Universal Postal Union. Multicoloured.

1193	180f.+20f. Type **438** . . .	35	20
1194	280f. Emblem and forms of transport	50	25

439 African Elephants

1999. "PHILEX FRANCE '99" International Stamp Exhibition, Paris. Animals in Abidjan Zoo. Mult.

1195	180f.+20f. Type **439** . . .	35	20
1196	250f. African buffaloes . . .	45	25
1197	280f. Chimpanzees	50	25
1198	400f. Savanna monkey . . .	70	35

440 *Ancistrochilus rothschildianus*

1999. Flowers. Multicoloured.
1199 100f. Type **440** 20 10
1200 180f.+20f. *Brachycorythis pubescens* 35 20
1201 200f. *Bulbophyllum barbigerum* 35 20
1202 280f. *Habenaria macrandra* 50 25

441 Rock and Trees

1999. Rock Formations, Ahouakro. Multicoloured.
1203 180f.+20f. Type **441** 35 25
1204 280f. Two rocks 50 30
1205 400f. Large rock (vert) . . . 70 45

442 France 1849 20c. Ceres Stamp

1999. 150th Anniv of First French Stamp.
1206 **442** 280f. multicoloured . . . 50 25

443 African Golden Oriole (*Oriolus auratus*)

1999. Birds. Multicoloured.
1207 50f. Type **443** 10 10
1208 180f.+20f. Variable sunbird (*Nectarinia venusta*) . . . 35 25
1209 280f. Madagascar green pigeon (*Treron australis*) 50 30
1210 300f. Grey parrot (*Psittacus erithacus*) 55 35

444 Wahrindi (*Synodontis schall*)

1999. Fishes. Multicoloured.
1211 100f. Type **444** 20 15
1212 180f.+20f. Gunther's krib (*Chromidotilapia guntheri*) 35 25
1213 280f. Grass-eater perch (*Distichodus rostratus*) . . 50 30

445 School Children and "EDUCATION"

1999. New Millennium. Multicoloured.
1214 100f. Type **445** 20 15
1215 180f.+20f. Fruit and "AGRICULTURE" . . . 35 25
1216 200f. Factory and "INDUSTRIE" 35 25
1217 250f. Computer and "INFORMATIQUE" . . 45 30
1218 280f. Dove and "PAIX" . . 50 30
1219 400f. Mask and "CULTURE" 70 45

446 Wambele

2000. Traditional Masks. Multicoloured.
1220 50f. Type **446** 10 10
1221 180f.+20f. Dje 35 25
1222 400f. Korobla (vert) 70 45

447 *Blighia sapida*

2000. Native Plants. Multicoloured.
1223 30f. Type **447** 10 10
1224 180f.+20f. *Ricinodendron heudelotti* 35 25
1225 300f. *Telfaira occidentalis* . . 55 35
1226 400f. *Napoleonaea vogelii* . . 70 45

448 Pres. Robert Guei, Map, Elephant and Dove

449 Cacao

2000. 40th Anniv of Independence.
1227 **448** 180f.+20f. mult 35 25
1228 400f. multicoloured . . . 70 45

2000.
1229 **449** 5f. multicoloured 10 10
1230 10f. multicoloured . . . 10 10
1231 20f. multicoloured . . . 10 10
1232 25f. multicoloured . . . 10 10
1233 30f. multicoloured . . . 10 10
1234 40f. multicoloured . . . 10 10
1235 50f. multicoloured . . . 10 15
1236 100f. multicoloured . . . 20 15
1237 180f.+20f. mult 35 25
1238 300f. multicoloured . . . 55 35
1239 350f. multicoloured . . . 60 40
1240 400f. multicoloured . . . 70 45
1241 600f. multicoloured . . . 1·10 70

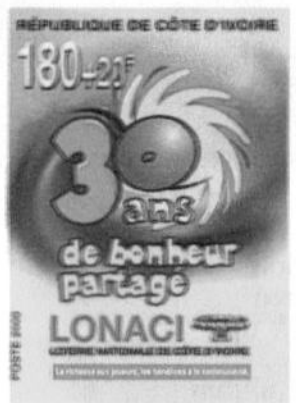

450 Emblem

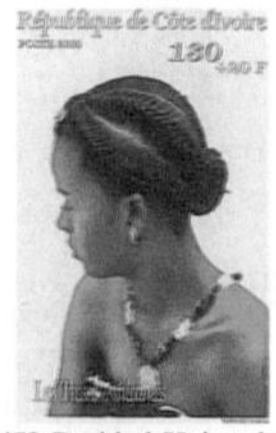

452 Braided Hairstyle

451 Football

2000. 30th Anniv of National Lottery.
1242 **450** 180f.+20f. mult 35 25
1243 400f. multicoloured . . . 70 45

2000. Olympic Games, Sydney. Multicoloured.
1244 180f.+20f. Type **451** 35 25
1245 400f. Kangaroo holding rugby ball and Sydney Opera House 70 45
1246 600f. Athletics . . . . . . 1·10 70
1247 750f. Olympic stadium and bird . . . . 1·40 85

2000. Hairstyles. Multicoloured.
1248 180f.+20f. Type **452** 35 25
1249 300f. Braid in hair 55 35
1250 400f. Twisted hair on head 70 35
1251 500f. Braided into loops . . 90 55

453 Mandela

454 "Queen Pokou"

2000. 10th Anniv of Release of Nelson Mandela.
1252 **453** 300f. multicoloured . . . 55 35

2000. Statues. Multicoloured.
1253 180f.+20f. Type **454** 35 25
1254 400f. "Akwaba" 70 45
1255 600f. "Invocation of the Spirits" . . . . 1·10 70

455 Refugees

2000. 50th Anniv of United Nations Commissioner for Refugees.
1256 **455** 400f. multicoloured . . . 70 35

456 Buffalo

2001. Abokouamekro National Park. Multicoloured.
1257 50f. Type **456** 10 10
1258 100f. Rhinoceros and calf 20 15
1259 180f.+20f. Rhinoceros . . . 35 25
1260 400f.+20f. Buffalo under trees 75 45

457 Carved Wooden Poles

458 Maps and Flag

2001. Exhibits in National Museum, Abidjan. Multicoloured.
1261 100f. Type **457** 20 15
1262 180f.+20f. Blolo Bian . . . 35 25
1263 300f.+20f. Botoumo 55 35
1264 400f.+20f. Odi Oka 75 45

2001. 41st Anniv of Independence.
1265 **458** 180f.+20f. multicoloured 40 25

459 Player heading Ball

2001. World Cup Football Championship (2002), Japan and South Korea. Multicoloured.
1266 180f.+20f. Type **459** 55 25
1267 400f.+20f. Players legs . . . 75 45
1268 600f.+20f. Players tackling 1·10 70
1269 700f. Players tackling . . . 1·25 75

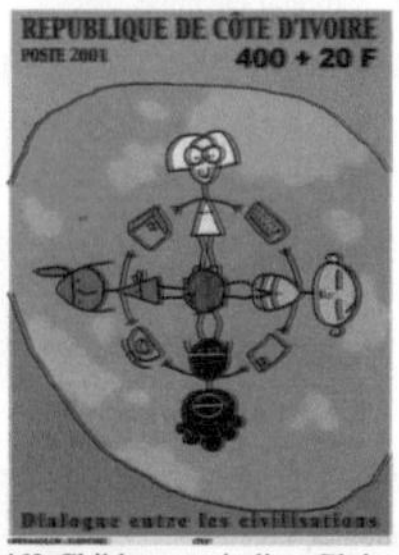

460 Children encircling Globe

2001. United Nations Year of Dialogue among Civilisations.
1270 **460** 400f.+20f. multicoloured 85 50

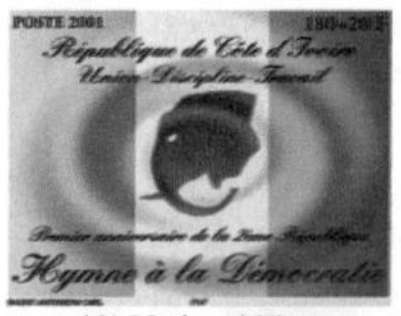

461 National Flag

2001. 1st Anniv of Second Republic.
1271 **461** 180f.+20f. multicoloured 40 25

462 Cloth

2001. Traditional Crafts. Korhogo Cloth. Multicoloured.
1272 100f. Type **462** 20 10
1273 180f.+20f. Animals and birds 40 25
1274 400f.+20f. Man decorating cloth (vert) 85 50

463 Emblem, Map of Africa and Dancers

2001. 23rd UPU Congress (2004), Abidjan.
1275 **463** 180f.+20f. multicoloured 40 25
1276 400f.+20f. multicoloured (26 × 37 mm) 85 50
1277 600f.+20f. multicoloured (36 × 49 mm) . . . . 1·30 80

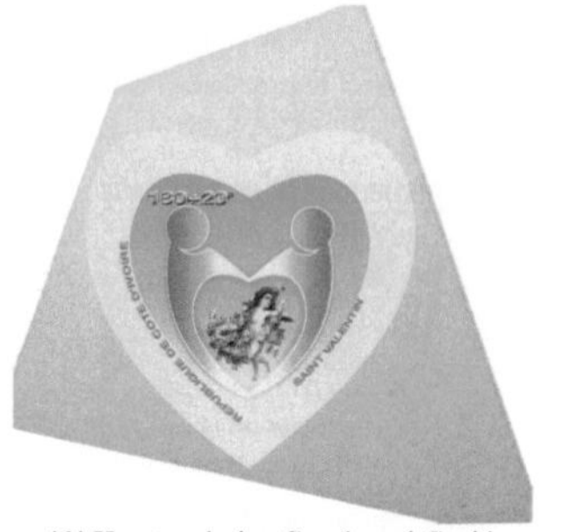

464 Heart enclosing Couple and Cupid

2002. St. Valentine's Day. Self-adhesive.
1278 **464** 180f.+20f. multicoloured 40 25

465 Airplane, Flags and Globe

2002. 40th Anniv of Jean Mermoz International College. Multicoloured.
1279 180f.+20f. Type **465** 40 25
1280 400f.+20f. As No. 1279 but with title banner changed 80 50

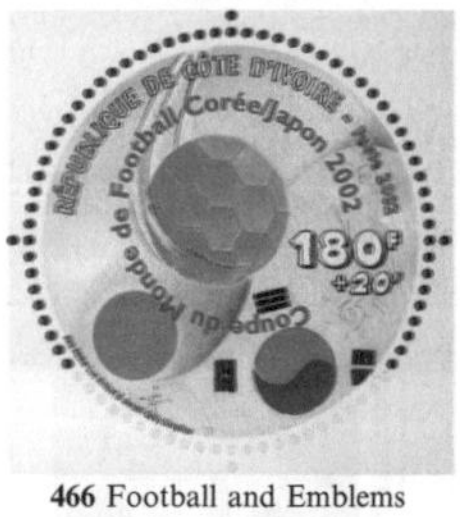

466 Football and Emblems

2002. World Cup Football Championships, Japan and South Korea. Multicoloured.
1281 180f.+20f. Type **466** 40 25
1282 300f.+20f. Players tackling (36 × 28 mm) 60 35

1283	400f.+20f. As No.1281 but with colours changed	80	50
1284	600f.+20f. Trophy enclosing two players (28 × 36 mm)	1·20	70
MS1285	96 × 96 mm (circular) 500f. No. 1283	95	95

467 Elephants

2002. Decentralization.

1286 **467**	400f.+20f. multicoloured	80	50

MILITARY FRANK STAMP

MF **59**

1967. No value indicated.

MF1 MF **59**	(–) multicoloured	1·90	1·90

OFFICIAL STAMPS

O **135** Arms of Ivory Coast

1973. No value indicated. Multicoloured. Background colours given.

O422 O **135**	(–) green and turquoise	45	20
O423	(–) yellow and orange	75	35
O424	(–) pink and mauve	1·00	55
O425	(–) violet and blue	2·75	1·10

Nos. O422/5 represent the following face values. No. O422, 35f. No. O423, 75f. No. O424, 100f. No. O425, 250f.

PARCEL POST STAMPS

1903. Postage Due stamps of French Colonies optd.

(a) **Cote d'Ivoire COLIS Postaux**.

P18 U	50c. purple	27·00	35·00
P20	1f. pink on buff	32·00	28·00

(b) **Colis Postaux**.

P19 U	50c. purple	£3000	£3000
P21	1f. pink on buff	£2750	£3000

(c) **Cote d'Ivoire Colis Postaux**.

P22 U	50c. purple	£100	£120
P23	1f. pink on buff	65·00	70·00

1903. Postage Due stamps of French Colonies surch.

(a) **Cote d'Ivoire Colis Postaux** and new value.

P24 U	50c. on 15c. green	13·50	11·00
P25	50c. on 60c. brown on buff	35·00	35·00
P26	1f. on 5c. blue	12·50	12·50
P27	1f. on 10c. brown	15·00	20·00
P30	4f. on 60c. brown on buff	£120	90·00

(b) **Colis Postaux Cote d'Ivoire** and new value.

P35 U	4f. on 5c. blue	£225	£225
P28	4f. on 15c. green	£120	90·00
P29	4f. on 30c. pink	£110	90·00
P36	8f. on 15c. green	£225	£225

1904. Postage Due stamps of French Colonies optd.

(a) **C. P. Cote d'Ivoire**.

P31 U	50c. purple	25·00	38·00
P32	1f. pink on buff	25·00	35·00

(b) **Cote d'Ivoire C.P.**

P33 U	50c. purple	26·00	27·00
P34	1f. pink on buff	35·00	35·00

1905. Postage Due stamps of French Colonies surch **Cote d'Ivoire C. P.** and new value.

P39 U	2f. on 1f. pink on buff	£200	£200
P40	4f. on 1f. pink on buff	£200	£225
P41	8f. on 1f. pink on buff	£500	£500

POSTAGE DUE STAMPS

1906. "Natives" key-type inscr "COTE D'IVOIRE".

D38 L	5c. green	55	75
D39	10c. purple	55	1·40
D40	15c. blue on blue	2·00	1·50
D41	20c. black on yellow	75	90
D42	30c. red on cream	3·50	4·75
D43	50c. violet	1·75	5·25
D44	60c. black on buff	5·50	27·00
D45	1f. black on pink	17·00	42·00

1915. "Figure" key-type inscr "COTE D'IVOIRE".

D60 M	5c. green	10	1·60
D61	10c. red	10	65
D62	15c. grey	10	1·25
D63	20c. brown	15	2·00
D64	30c. blue	20	2·00
D65	50c. black	20	2·50
D66	60c. orange	35	2·75
D67	1f. violet	50	3·00

1927. Surch in figures.

D94 M	"2 F." on 1f. purple	20	2·75
D95	"3 F." on 1f. brown	25	3·25

D **21** Guere Mask

D **30** Mask

D **70** Baoule Weight

1960. Values in black.

D196 D **21**	1f. violet	1·25	2·00
D197	2f. green	1·25	2·00
D198	5f. yellow	1·40	2·00
D199	10f. blue	1·75	2·50
D200	20f. mauve	2·25	5·25

1962.

D220 D **30**	1f. blue and orange	15	15
D221	– 2f. red and black	20	20
D222	– 5f. green and red	30	30
D223	– 10f. purple and green	55	55
D224	– 20f. black and violet	90	90

DESIGNS: 2f. to 20f. Various native masks from Bingerville Art School.

1968. Designs showing different types of weights.

D309 D **70**	5f. multicoloured	15	15
D310	– 10f. multicoloured	20	20
D311	– 15f. multicoloured	50	50
D312	– 20f. multicoloured	80	80
D313	– 30f. multicoloured	1·10	1·10

D **111** "Animal" Weight

1972. Gold Weights and Measures.

D389 D **111**	20f. brown and violet	65	65
D390	– 40f. brown and red	1·00	1·00
D391	– 50f. purple and orange	1·50	1·50
D392	– 100f. brown and green	3·00	3·00

DESIGNS: 40f. "Dagger"; 50f. "Bird"; 100f. "Triangle".

JAIPUR Pt. 1

A state of Rajasthan, India. Now uses Indian stamps.

12 pies = 1 anna; 16 annas = 1 rupee.

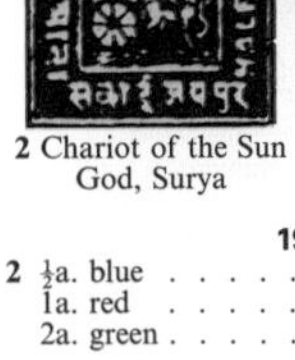

2 Chariot of the Sun God, Surya

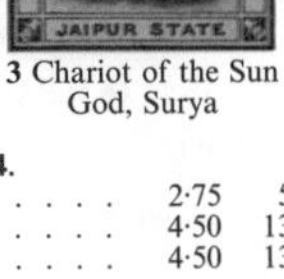

3 Chariot of the Sun God, Surya

1904.

3 **2**	½a. blue	2·75	5·50
4	1a. red	4·50	13·00
5	2a. green	4·50	13·00

1904.

9 **3**	¼a. olive	75	1·00
10a	½a. blue	1·25	50
11	1a. red	3·00	50
12	2a. green	2·25	90
13	4a. brown	6·00	2·00
14	8a. violet	3·00	2·75
15a	1r. yellow	19·00	18·00

This set was issued engraved in 1904 and surface-printed in 1913.

4 Chariot of the Sun God, Surya

३ आना

(**5**)

1911. No gum.

17 **4**	¼a. olive	30	70
18	¼a. blue	30	70
20	1a. red	50	90
21a	2a. green	2·00	6·00

1926. Surch with T **5**.

32 **3**	3a. on 8a. violet	1·50	2·75
33	3a. on 1r. yellow	2·25	5·00

6 Chariot of the Sun God, Surya

7 Maharaja Sawai Man Singh II

1931. Investiture of Maharaja. Centres in black.

40 **6**	¼a. red	2·25	2·25
58 **7**	¼a. red	40	30
41	½a. violet	40	20
59	¾a. red	6·50	3·50
42	– 1a. blue	7·50	8·00
60 **7**	1a. blue	8·00	3·00
43	– 2a. orange	7·00	8·00
61 **7**	2a. orange	7·50	4·00
44	– 2½a. red	30·00	55·00
62 **7**	2½a. red	3·25	2·50
45	– 3a. green	15·00	55·00
63 **7**	3a. green	2·75	60
46	– 4a. green	15·00	55·00
64 **7**	4a. green	35·00	£120
47	– 6a. blue	6·00	48·00
65 **7**	6a. blue	4·25	25·00
48	– 8a. brown	15·00	80·00
66 **7**	8a. brown	22·00	£100
49	– 1r. olive	32·00	£250
67 **7**	1r. bistre	20·00	£150
50	– 2r. green	30·00	£300
51	– 5r. purple	45·00	£325

DESIGNS—VERT: 1a. (No. 42), Elephant and banner; 2a. (No. 43), Sowar in armour; 2½a. (No. 44), Common peafowl; 8a. (No. 48), Sireh-Deorhi Gate. HORIZ: 3a. (No. 45), Bullock carriage; 4a. (No. 46), Elephant carriage; 6a. (No. 47), Albert Museum; 1r. (No. 49), Chandra Mahal; 2r. Amber Palace; 5r. Maharajas Sawai Jai Singh and Man Singh.

1932. As T **7**, but inscr "POSTAGE & REVENUE". Portrait in black.

52	1a. blue	2·00	1·00
53	2a. brown	3·00	2·00
54	4a. green	4·50	9·00
55	8a. brown	6·00	12·00
56	1r. bistre	22·00	95·00
57	2r. green	85·00	40·00

1936. Nos. 57 and 51 surch **One Rupee**.

68	1r. on 2r. green	8·50	90·00
69	1r. on 5r. purple	8·50	75·00

1938. No. 41 surch in native characters.

70 **7**	¼a. on ½a. violet	12·00	16·00

13 Maharaja and Amber Palace

1947. Silver Jubilee of Maharaja's Accession to the Throne. Inscr as in T **13**.

71	– ¼a. brown and green	1·25	3·75
72 **13**	½a. green and violet	40	3·50
73	– ¾a. black and red	1·25	4·50
74	– 1a. brown and blue	75	3·75
75	– 2a. violet and red	75	4·00
76	– 3a. green and black	1·40	5·00
77	– 4a. blue and brown	60	3·75
78	– 8a. red and brown	70	4·75
79	– 1r. purple and green	2·25	35·00

DESIGNS: ¼a. Palace Gate; ¾a. Map of Jaipur; 1a. Observatory; 2a. Wind Palace; 3a. Coat of Arms; 4a. Amber Fort Gate; 8a. Chariot of the Sun; 1r. Maharaja's portrait between State flags.

1947. No. 41 surch **3 PIES** and bars.

80 **7**	3p. on ½a. violet	15·00	25·00

OFFICIAL STAMPS

1929. Optd **SERVICE**. No gum (except for No. O6a).

O1 **3**	¼a. bistre	1·50	2·25
O2	½a. blue	75	30
O3c	1a. red	90	30
O5	2a. green	85	40
O6a	4a. brown (with gum)	2·00	1·75
O7	8a. violet	17·00	55·00
O8	1r. orange	35·00	£300

1931. Stamps of 1931–32 optd **SERVICE**.

O23 **7**	¼a. red	40	10
O13	½a. violet	30	10
O24	¾a. red	1·50	50
O25	1a. blue	4·00	30
O14	– 1a. blue (No. 42)	£250	2·25
O18	– 1a. blue (No. 52)	3·50	15
O15	– 2a. orange (No. 43)	3·00	5·50
O19	– 2a. brown (No. 53)	4·00	15
O26 **7**	2a. orange	4·00	2·50
O27	2½a. red	9·50	95·00
O16	– 4a. green (No. 46)	38·00	30·00
O20	– 4a. green (No. 54)	£300	8·50
O28 **7**	4a. green	4·50	5·50
O21	– 8a. brown (No. 55)	8·50	1·10
O29 **7**	8a. brown	4·00	7·00
O22	– 1r. bistre (No. 56)	22·00	22·00
O30 **7**	1r. bistre	40·00	

1932. No. O5 surch in native characters.

O17 **3**	½a. on 2a. green	£150	1·50

1947. Official stamps surch.

O33 **7**	3p. on ½a. violet	5·00	12·00
O32	9p. on 1a. blue	3·75	3·00

1948. No. O13 surch in native characters.

O34 **7**	¾a. on ½a. violet	16·00	17·00

For later issues see **RAJASTHAN**.

JAMAICA Pt. 1

An island in the W. Indies. Part of the Br. Caribbean Federation from 3 January 1958, until 6 August 1962 when Jamaica became an independent state within the Commonwealth.

1860. 12 pence = 1 shilling;
20 shillings = 1 pound.
1969. 100 cents = 1 dollar.

8

11

1860. Portrait as T **8**. Various frames.

7 **8**	½d. red	14·00	3·50
16a	½d. green	1·00	10
8	1d. blue	60·00	75
18a	1d. red	35·00	60
9	2d. red	65·00	70
20a	2d. grey	75·00	50
21a	3d. green	2·50	1·25
11	4d. orange	£190	11·00
22b	4d. brown	2·00	35
52a	6d. lilac	10·00	18·00
23a	6d. yellow	4·00	3·50
24	1s. brown	5·00	6·00
25	2s. red	27·00	21·00
26	5s. lilac	50·00	75·00

See also Nos. 47a etc.

1889.

27 **11**	1d. purple and mauve	4·00	20
28a	2d. green	6·50	6·00
29	2½d. purple and blue	5·50	50

1890. No. 22a surch **TWO PENCE HALF-PENNY**.

30 **8**	2½d. on 4d. orange	27·00	9·00

13 Llandovery Falls, Jamaica

1900.

31 **13**	1d. red	3·50	20
32	1d. black and red	3·25	20

14 Arms of Jamaica

16

1903.

33 **14**	½d. grey and green	1·50	30
34	1d. grey and red	1·75	10
35	2½d. grey and blue	3·00	30
42	2½d. blue	2·50	1·25
36	5d. grey and yellow	15·00	23·00
44	6d. purple	13·00	12·00
45	5s. grey and violet	45·00	38·00

1906.

38b **16**	½d. green	3·75	20
40	1d. red	1·50	10

1908. Queen Victoria portraits as 1860.

47a	3d. purple on yellow	2·00	1·50
49	4d. black on yellow	7·50	40·00
50	4d. red on yellow	1·50	8·00
54	1s. black on green	8·50	8·50
56	2s. purple on blue	6·50	3·50

17

1911.

57	17	2d. grey	3·00	13·00

1912. As T 17, but King George V.

89a	½d. green	1·75	10
58	1d. red	1·50	10
59	1½d. orange	1·00	60
60	2d. grey	2·00	1·75
61	2½d. blue	1·50	15
62	3d. purple on yellow	50	45
63	4d. black and red on yellow	50	3·50
64a	6d. purple and mauve	75	1·00
65	1s. black on green	2·25	2·00
66	2s. purple and blue on blue	13·00	25·00
67	5s. green and red on yellow	65·00	90·00

1916. Optd **WAR STAMP.** in one line (with full point).

68	16	½d. green	10	35
69a	–	3d. purple on yellow (62)	13·00	28·00

See also Nos. 76/77a.

1916. Optd **WAR STAMP.** in two lines.

73	16	½d. green	50	30
74	–	1½d. orange (No. 59)	20	10
75	–	3d. purple on yellow (No. 62)	50	1·40

1919. Optd **WAR STAMP** in one line (no full point).

76	15	½d. green	20	15
77a	–	3d. purple on yell (No. 62)	3·25	1·25

23 Jamaica Exhibition, 1891

24 Arawak Woman preparing Cassava

27 Return of War Contingent, 1919

34

1919.

91a	23	½d. green and olive	30	50
79	24	1d. red and orange (A)*	1·75	1·75
92		1d. red and orange (B)*	1·50	10
93	–	1½d. green	1·00	45
81	–	2d. blue and green	1·00	4·00
82a	27	2½d. blue	1·50	1·75
96a	–	3d. green and blue	1·25	15
97	–	4d. brown and green	1·00	30
98a	–	6d. black and blue	12·00	1·50
99a	–	1s. orange	1·75	65
100	–	2s. blue and brown	3·25	65
101	–	3s. violet and orange	11·00	9·00
102c	–	5s. blue and bistre	27·00	22·00
103	34	10s. green	50·00	70·00

*Two types of the 1d. (A) Without and (B) with "POSTAGE & REVENUE" at foot.

DESIGNS—HORIZ (41½×26 mm): 1½d. War Contingent embarking, 1915; 6d. Port Royal, 1853. (27×22 mm): 3d. Landing of Columbus, 1494. VERT (22×29 mm): 2d. King's House, Spanish Town; 4d. Cathedral, Spanish Town. (25×30 mm): 1s. Statue of Queen Victoria, Kingston; 2s. Admiral Rodney Memorial, Spanish Town; 3s. Sir Charles Metcalfe Monument; 5s. Jamaican scenery.

37

41

1923. Child Welfare. Designs as T 37.

104	37	½d.+½d. black and green	60	5·50
105	–	1d.+½d. black and red	1·75	10·00
106	–	2½d.+½d. black and blue	8·50	18·00

1929. Various frames.

108	41	1d. red	3·00	20
109		1½d. brown	2·25	15
110		9d. red	3·50	1·00

43 Coco Palms at Don Christopher's Cove

45 Priestman's River, Portland

1932.

111	43	2d. black and green	16·00	2·75
112	–	2½d. turquoise and blue	3·75	1·50
113	45	6d. black and purple	15·00	1·75

DESIGN—As T **43**: 2½d. Wag Water River, St. Andrew.

1935. Silver Jubilee. As T **14a** of Kenya, Uganda and Tanganyika.

114	1d. blue and red	40	15
115	1½d. blue and black	60	1·50
116	6d. green and blue	6·00	16·00
117	1s. grey and purple	5·00	9·00

1937. Coronation. As T **14b** of Kenya, Uganda and Tanganyika.

118	1d. red	30	15
119	1½d. grey	65	30
120	2½d. blue	1·00	70

48 King George VI

49 Coco Palms at Don Christopher's Cove

50 Bananas

54 Bamboo Walk

1938.

121	48	½d. green	1·75	10
121b		½d. orange	1·00	30
122		1d. red	1·25	10
122a		1d. green	1·50	10
123		1½d. brown	1·25	10
124b	49	2d. black and green	1·25	10
125	–	2½d. green and blue	3·00	1·75
126	50	3d. blue and green	75	1·50
126b		3d. green and blue	1·25	1·25
126c		3d. green and red	2·75	30
127	–	4d. brown and green	50	10
128a	–	6d. black and purple	2·25	10
129	–	9d. red	50	50
130	–	1s. green and brown	6·00	20
131	54	2s. blue and brown	22·00	1·00
132ba	–	5s. blue and brown	7·00	3·00
133aa	–	10s. green	11·00	7·00
133a	–	£1 brown and violet	30·00	26·00

DESIGNS—As Type **49**: 2½d. Wag Water River, St. Andrew. As Type **50**: 4d. Citrus grove; 9d. Kingston Harbour; 1s. Sugar industry; £1 Tobacco growing and cigar making. As previous issues, but with portrait of King George VI: 6d. As Type **45**; 5s. As No. 102c; 10s. As Type **34**.

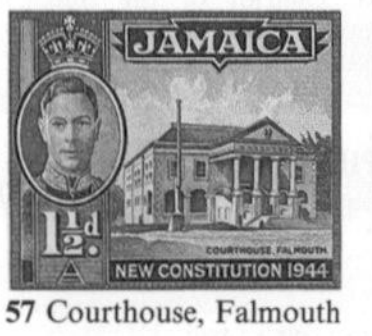

57 Courthouse, Falmouth

59 Institute of Jamaica

1945. New Constitution.

134	57	1½d. brown	20	30
135a	–	2d. green	30	50
136	59	3d. blue	20	50
137	–	4½d. black	30	30
138	–	2s. brown	30	50
139	–	5s. blue	1·25	1·00
140	59	10s. green	85	2·25

DESIGNS—VERT (as Type **57**): 2s. "Labour and Learning". HORIZ (as Type **57**): 2d. Kings Charles II and George VI. (As Type **59**): 4½d. House of Assembly; 5s. Scroll, flag and King George VI.

60 Houses of Parliament, London

1946. Victory.

141a	60	1½d. brown	30	1·75
142a		3d. blue	30	4·75

61 King George VI and Queen Elizabeth

62

1948. Silver Wedding.

143	61	1½d. brown	30	10
144	62	£1 red	25·00	50·00

63 Hermes, Globe and forms of Transport

64 Hemispheres, Jet-powered Vickers Viking Airliner and Steamer

65 Hermes and Globe

66 U.P.U. Monument

1949. U.P.U.

145	63	1½d. brown	20	15
146	64	2d. green	1·25	2·75
147	65	3d. blue	35	1·25
148	66	6d. purple	40	2·50

67 University Arms

68 Princess Alice

1951. Inauguration of B.W.I. University College.

149	67	2d. black and brown	30	50
150	68	6d. black and purple	35	30

69 Scout Badge and Map of Caribbean

70 Scout Badge and Map of Jamaica

1952. 1st Caribbean Scout Jamboree.

151	69	2d. blue, green and black	15	10
152	70	6d. green, red and black	30	50

71 Queen Elizabeth II

1953. Coronation.

153	71	2d. black and green	70	10

1953. Royal Visit. As T **49** but with portrait of Queen Elizabeth II and inscr "ROYAL VISIT 1953".

154	2d. black and green	40	10

73 H.M.S. "Britannia" (ship of the line) at Port Royal

1955. Tercentenary Issue.

155	73	2d. black and green	35	10
156	–	2½d. black and blue	15	35
157	–	3d. black and claret	15	30
158	–	6d. black and red	20	20

DESIGNS: 2½d. Old Montego Bay; 3d. Old Kingston; 6d. Proclamation of Abolition of Slavery, 1838.

74 Coconut Palms

76 Blue Mountain Peak

75 Mahoe

77 Arms of Jamaica

1956.

159	74	½d. black and red	10	10
160	–	1d. black and green	10	10
161	–	2d. black and red	10	10
162	–	2½d. black and blue	65	50
163	75	3d. green and brown	20	10
164	–	4d. green and blue	20	10
165	–	5d. red and green	20	1·50
166	–	6d. black and red	2·25	10
167	76	8d. blue and orange	30	10
168	–	1s. green and blue	1·00	10
169	–	1s.6d. blue and purple	80	10
170	–	2s. blue and green	7·00	2·00
171	77	3s. black and blue	1·50	2·00
172	–	5s. black and red	3·75	4·75
173	–	10s. black and green	29·00	18·00
174	–	£1 black and purple	29·00	18·00

DESIGNS—As Type **74**: 1d. Sugar cane; 2d. Pineapples; 2½d. Bananas. As Type **75**: 4d. Breadfruit; 5d. Ackee; 6d. Streamertail. As Type **76**: 1s. Royal Botanic Gardens, Hope; 1s.6d. Rafting on the Rio Grande; 2s. Fort Charles. As Type **77** but vert: 10s., £1 Arms without portrait.

79 Federation Map

1958. British Caribbean Federation.

175	79	2d. green	50	10
176		5d. blue	95	3·50
177		6d. red	95	40

81 Bristol Britannia 312 flying over "City of Berlin", 1860

83 1s. Stamps of 1860 and 1956

1960. Centenary of Jamaica Postage Stamps.

178	**81**	2d. blue and purple	45	10
179	–	6d. red and olive	45	50
180	**83**	1s. brown, green and blue	45	55

DESIGN—As Type **81**: 6d. Postal mule-cart and motor-van.

1962. Independence. (a) Nos. 159/74 optd **INDEPENDENCE** and **1962** (3d. to 2s.) or **1962 1962** (others).

205	**74**	½d. black and red	10	15
182	–	1d. black and green	10	10
183	–	2½d. black and blue	10	1·00
184	**75**	3d. green and brown	10	10
185	–	5d. red and olive	20	60
186	–	6d. black and red	2·50	10
187	**76**	8d. blue and orange	20	10
188	–	1s. green and blue	20	10
189	–	2s. blue and olive	80	1·50
190	**77**	3s. black and blue	90	1·50
191	–	10s. black and green	2·75	4·25
192	–	£1 black and purple	2·75	5·50

86 Military Bugler and Map

(b) As T **86** inscr "INDEPENDENCE".

193	**86**	2d. multicoloured	1·00	10
194		4d. multicoloured	1·00	10
195	–	1s.6d. black and red	3·50	85
196	–	5s. multicoloured	4·50	4·00

DESIGNS: 1s.6d. Gordon House and banner; 5s. Map, factories and fruit.

89 Kingston Seal, Weightlifting, Boxing, Football and Cycling

1962. 9th Central American and Caribbean Games, Kingston.

197	**89**	1d. sepia and red	20	10
198	–	6d. sepia and blue	20	10
199	–	8d. sepia and bistre	20	10
200	–	2s. multicoloured	30	90

DESIGNS: 6d. Diver, sailing, swimming and water polo; 8d. Javelin, discus, pole-vault, hurdles and relay-racing; 2s. Kingston coat of arms and athlete.

93 Farmer and Crops

1963. Freedom from Hunger.

201	**93**	1d. multicoloured	20	10
202		8d. multicoloured	60	60

94 Red Cross Emblem

1963. Cent of Red Cross.

203	**94**	2d. red and black	15	10
204		1s.6d. red and blue	50	1·50

95 Carole Joan Crawford ("Miss World 1963")

1964. "Miss World 1963" Commem.

214	**95**	3d. multicoloured	10	10
215		1s. multicoloured	15	10
216		1s.6d. multicoloured	20	50
MS216a		153 × 101 mm. Nos. 214/16. Imperf	1·10	2·75

96 "Lignum vitae"

103 Gypsum Industry

1964.

217	**96**	1d. blue, green and brown	10	10
218	–	1½d. multicoloured	15	10
219	–	2d. red, yellow and green	15	10
220	–	2½d. multicoloured	1·00	60
221	–	3d. yellow, black & green	15	10
222	–	4d. ochre and violet	50	10
223	–	6d. multicoloured	2·25	10
224	–	8d. multicoloured	2·50	1·50
225	**103**	9d. blue and bistre	1·50	10
226	–	1s. black and brown	20	10
227	–	1s.6d. black, blue & buff	4·00	15
228	–	2s. brown, black and blue	2·75	15
229b	–	3s. blue and green	35	65
230	–	5s. black, ochre and blue	1·25	1·00
231	–	10s. multicoloured	1·25	1·25
232	–	£1 multicoloured	1·75	1·00

DESIGNS—HORIZ (As T **96**): 1½d. Ackee (fruit); 2½d. Land shells; 3d. National flag over Jamaica; 4d. Antillean murex (sea shell); 6d. "Papilio homerus" (butterfly); 8d. Streamertail. VERT (As T **96**): 2d. Blue Mahoe (tree). HORIZ (As T **103**): 1s. National Stadium; 1s.6d. Palisadoes International Airport; 2s. Bauxite mining; 3s. Blue marlin (sport fishing); 5s. Exploration of sunken city, Port Royal; £1 Queen Elizabeth II and national flag. VERT (As T **96**): 10s. Arms of Jamaica.

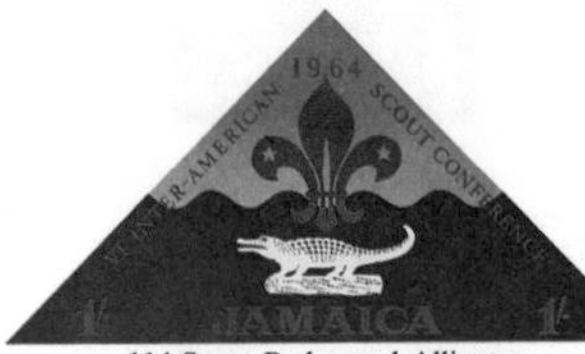

114 Scout Badge and Alligator

1964. 6th Inter-American Scout Conf, Kingston.

233	–	3d. red, black and pink	10	10
234	–	8d. blue, olive and black	15	25
235	**114**	1s. gold, blue and light blue	20	45

DESIGNS—VERT (25½ × 30 mm): 3d. Scout belt; 8d. Globe, scout hat and scarf.

115 Gordon House, Kingston

1964. 10th Commonwealth Parliamentary Conference, Kingston.

236	**115**	3d. black and green	10	10
237	–	6d. black and red	30	10
238	–	1s.6d. black and blue	50	30

DESIGNS: 6d. Headquarters House, Kingston; 1s.6d. House of Assembly, Spanish Town.

118 Eleanor Roosevelt

1964. 16th Anniv of Declaration of Human Rights.

239	**118**	1s. black, red and green	10	10

119 Guides' Emblem on Map

121 Uniform Cap

1965. Golden Jubilee of Jamaica Girl Guides' Association. Inscr "1915–1965".

240	**119**	3d. yellow, green and black	10	10
241	–	1s. yellow, black and green	20	40

DESIGN—TRIANGULAR (61½ × 30½ mm): 1s. Guide emblems.

1965. Centenary of Salvation Army. Mult.

242		3d. Type **121**	25	10
243		1s.6d. Flag-bearer and drummer (vert)	50	50

123 Paul Bogle, William Gordon and Morant Bay Court House

1965. Centenary of Morant Bay Rebellion.

244	**123**	3d. brown, blue and black	10	10
245		1s.6d. brown, green & blk	20	10
246		3s. brown, red and black	30	75

124 Abeng-blower, "Telstar", Morse Key and I.T.U. Emblem

1965. Centenary of I.T.U.

247	**124**	1s. black, slate and red	40	20

1966. Royal Visit. Nos. 221, 223, 226/7 optd **ROYAL VISIT MARCH 1966**.

248		3d. yellow, black and green	15	10
249		6d. multicoloured	1·75	30
250		1s. black and brown	55	10
251		1s.6d. black, blue and buff	2·00	2·00

126 Sir Winston Churchill

1966. Churchill Commemoration.

252	**126**	6d. black and green	50	30
253		1s. brown and blue	75	80

127 Statue of Athlete and Flags

1966. 8th British Empire and Commonwealth Games.

254	**127**	3d. multicoloured	10	10
255	–	6d. multicoloured	40	10
256	–	1s. multicoloured	10	10
257	–	3s. gold and blue	35	45
MS258		128 × 103 mm. Nos. 254/7. Imperf	4·00	8·00

DESIGNS: 6d. Racing cyclists; 1s. National Stadium, Kingston; 3s. Games emblem.

131 Bolivar's Statue and Flags of Jamaica and Venezuela

133 Sir Donald Sangster (Prime Minister)

132 Jamaican Pavilion

1966. 150th Anniv of "Jamaica Letter".

259	**131**	8d. multicoloured	20	10

1967. World Fair, Montreal.

260	**132**	6d. multicoloured	10	15
261		1s. multicoloured	10	15

1967. Sangster Memorial Issue.

262	**133**	3d. multicoloured	10	10
263		1s.6d. multicoloured	20	20

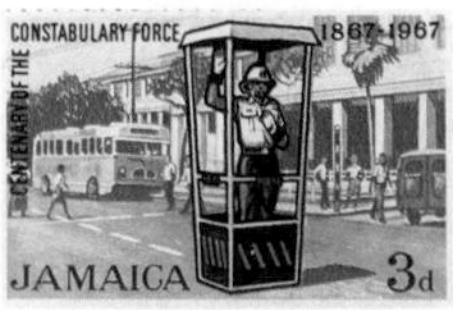

134 Traffic Duty

1967. Centenary of Constabulary Force. Mult.

264		3d. Type **134**	40	10
265		1s. Personnel of the Force (56½ × 20½ mm)	40	10
266		1s.6d. Badge and Constables of 1867 and 1967	50	75

1968. M.C.C.'s West Indies Tour. As Nos. 445/7 of Guyana.

267		6d. multicoloured	50	65
268		6d. multicoloured	50	65
269		6d. multicoloured	50	65

137 Sir Alexander and Lady Bustamante

1968. Labour Day.

270	**137**	3d. red and black	10	15
271		1s. olive and black	10	15

138 Human Rights Emblem over Map of Jamaica

1968. Human Rights Year. Multicoloured.

272		3d. Type **138**	10	10
273		1s. Hands cupping Human Rights emblem	10	10
274		3s. Jamaican holding "Human Rights"	30	90

141 I.L.O. Emblem

1969. 50th Anniv of I.L.O.

275	**141**	6d. yellow and brown	10	10
276		3s. green and brown	30	30

142 Nurse and Children being Weighed and Measured

146 "The Adoration of the Kings" (detail, Foppa)

1969. 20th Anniv of W.H.O. Multicoloured.

277		6d. Type **142**	10	10
278		1s. Malaria eradication (horiz)	10	10
279		3s. Trainee nurse	20	1·00

1969. Decimal Currency. Nos. 217, 219, 221/3 and 225/32 surch **C-DAY 8th September 1969** and value.

280	**95**	1c. on 1d. blue, grn & brn	10	10
281	–	2c. on 2d. red, yellow & grn	10	10
282	–	3c. on 3d. yellow, black and green	10	10
283	–	4c. on 4d. ochre and violet	1·25	10
284	–	5c. on 6d. multicoloured	1·25	10
285	**103**	8c. on 9d. blue and bistre	10	10
286	–	10c. on 1s. black & brown	10	10
287	–	15c. on 1s.6d. black, blue and buff	50	90
288	–	20c. on 2s. brown, blk & bl	1·50	1·50
289	–	30c. on 3s. blue & green	2·00	2·75
290	–	50c. on 5s. black, ochre and blue	1·25	3·00
291	–	$1 on 10s. multicoloured	1·25	6·50
292	–	$2 on £1 multicoloured	1·25	6·50

1969. Christmas. Paintings. Multicoloured.

293		2c. Type **146**	20	40
294		5c. "Madonna, Child and St. John" (Raphael)	25	40
295		8c. "The Adoration of the Kings" (detail, Dosso Dossi)	25	40

149 Half Penny, 1869

1969. Centenary of 1st Jamaican Coins.

296	**149**	3c. silver, black and mauve	15	25
297	–	15c. silver, black and green	10	10

DESIGN: 15c. One penny, 1869.

151 George William Gordon

156 "Christ appearing to St. Peter" (Carracci)

1970. National Heroes. Multicoloured; background colours given.

298	**151**	1c. mauve	10	10
299	–	3c. blue	10	10
300	–	5c. grey	10	10
301	–	10c. red	15	10
302	–	15c. green	30	25

PORTRAITS: 3c. Sir Alexander Bustamante; 5c. Norman Manley; 10c. Marcus Garvey; 15c. Paul Bogle.

1970. Easter. Centres multicoloured; frame colours given.

303	**156**	3c. red	10	10
304	–	10c. green	10	10
305	–	20c. grey	20	60

DESIGNS: 10c. "Christ Crucified" (Antonello); 20c. Easter lily.

1970. No. 219 surch **2c**.

306		2c. on 2d. red, yellow & green	20	20

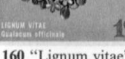

160 "Lignum vitae"

164 Bananas, Citrus, Sugar-Cane and Tobacco

161 Cable Ship "Dacia"

1970. Decimal Currency. Designs as Nos. 217, 219, 221/23, 225/32, but with values inscr as T **160** in new currency.

307	**160**	1c. blue, green and brown	75	2·00
308	–	2c. red, yell & grn (as 2d.)	30	10
309	–	3c. yell, blk & grn (as 3d.)	50	1·00
310	–	4c. ochre and violet (as 4d.)	2·75	30
311	–	5c. multicoloured (as 6d.)	3·00	65
312	**103**	8c. blue and yellow	2·25	10
313	–	10c. black & brown (as 1s.)	60	20
314	–	15c. black, blue and buff (as 1s.6d.)	2·75	3·00
315	–	20c. brown, black and blue (as 2s.)	1·25	3·00
316	–	30c. blue and green (as 3s.)	4·00	6·50
317	–	50c. black, ochre and blue (as 5s.)	1·25	4·50
318	–	$1 multicoloured (as 10s.)	1·00	3·75
319	–	$2 multicoloured (as £1)	1·25	4·00

1970. Centenary of Telegraph Service.

320	**161**	3c. yellow, black and red	15	10
321	–	10c. black and green	20	10
322	–	50c. multicoloured	50	1·00

DESIGNS: 10c. Bright's cable gear aboard "Dacia"; 50c. Morse key and chart.

1970. 75th Anniv of Jamaican Agricultural Society.

323	**164**	2c. multicoloured	25	60
324		10c. multicoloured	45	10

165 Locomotive "Projector" (1845)

168 Church of St. Jago de la Vega

1970. 125th Anniv of Jamaican Railways.

325		3c. Type **165**	30	10
326		15c. Steam locomotive No. 54 (1944)	65	30
327		50c. Steam locomotive No. 102 (1967)	1·25	1·75

1971. Centenary of Disestablishment of Church of England in Jamaica.

328	**168**	3c. multicoloured	10	10
329		10c. multicoloured	10	10
330		20c. multicoloured	30	30
331	–	30c. multicoloured	30	1·25

DESIGN: 30c. Emblem of Church of England in Jamaica.

169 Henry Morgan and Ships

1971. Pirates and Buccaneers. Multicoloured.

332		3c. Type **169**	75	10
333		15c. Mary Read, Anne Bonny and trial pamphlet	1·00	15
334		30c. Pirate schooner attacking merchantman	1·75	1·25

170 1s. Stamp of 1919 with Frame Inverted

1971. Tercentenary of Post Office.

335	–	3c. black and brown	15	20
336	–	5c. black and green	20	20
337	–	8c. black and violet	20	10
338	–	10c. brown, black and blue	20	10
339	–	20c. multicoloured	35	45
340	**170**	50c. brown, black and grey	50	2·00

DESIGNS—HORIZ: 3c. Drummer packet letter, 1705; 5c. Pre-stamp inland letter, 1793; 8c. Harbour St. P.O., Kingston, 1820; 10c. Modern stamp and cancellation; 20c. British stamps used in Jamaica, 1859.

171 Satellite and Dish Aerial

172 Causeway, Kingston Harbour

1972. Opening of Jamaican Earth Satellite Station.

341	**171**	3c. multicoloured	15	10
342		15c. multicoloured	20	15
343		50c. multicoloured	65	1·25

1972. Multicoloured.

344		1c. Pimento (vert)	10	10
345		2c. Red ginger (vert)	10	10
346		3c. Bauxite Industry	10	10
347		4c. Type **172**	10	10
348		5c. Oil refinery	10	10
349		6c. Senate Building, University of the West Indies	10	10
350		8c. National Stadium	30	10
351		9c. Devon House	10	10
352		10c. Air Jamaica Hostess and Vickers VC-10	20	10
353		15c. Old Iron Bridge, Spanish Town (vert)	2·00	10
354		20c. College of Arts, Science and Technology	30	15
355		30c. Dunn's River Falls (vert)	65	15
356		50c. River rafting	1·75	40
357		$1 Jamaica House	75	1·50
358		$2 Kings House	1·00	1·50

Designs for 8c. to $2 are larger, 35 × 27 or 27 × 35 mm.

1972. 10th Anniv of Independence Nos. 346, 352 and 356 optd **TENTH ANNIVERSARY INDEPENDENCE 1962–1972**.

359		3c. multicoloured	30	30
360		10c. multicoloured	30	10
361		50c. multicoloured	75	2·25

175 Arms of Kingston

1972. Centenary of Kingston as Capital.

362	**175**	5c. multicoloured	15	10
363		30c. multicoloured	35	35
364	–	50c. multicoloured	60	2·25

DESIGN—HORIZ: 50c. design similar to Type **175**.

176 Mongoose on Map

1973. Centenary of Introduction of the Small Indian Mongoose.

365	**176**	8c. green, yellow and black	15	10
366	–	40c. dp blue, blue & black	35	75
367	–	60c. pink, salmon & black	60	1·40
MS368		165 × 95 mm. Nos. 365/7	1·10	4·00

DESIGNS: 40c. Mongoose and rat; 60c. Mongoose and chicken.

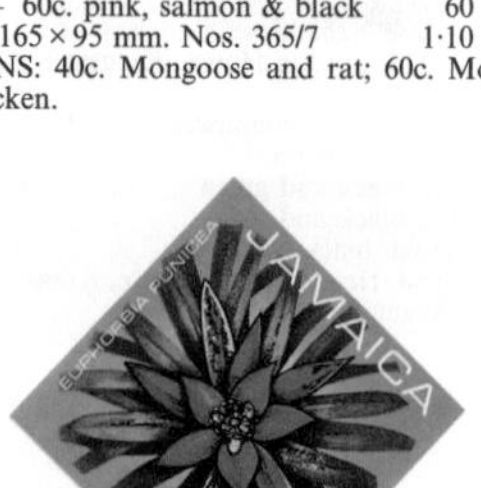

177 "Euphorbia punicea"

1973. Flora. Multicoloured.

369		1c. Type **177**	10	30
370		6c. "Hylocereus triangularis"	15	20
371		9c. "Columnea argentea"	15	20
372		15c. "Portlandia grandiflora"	25	20
373		30c. "Samyda pubescens"	40	60
374		50c. "Cordia sebestena"	60	1·40

178 "Broughtonia sanguinea"

1973. Orchids. Multicoloured.

375		5c. Type **178**	40	10
376		10c. "Arpophyllum jamaicense" (vert)	50	10
377		20c. "Oncidium pulchellum" (vert)	1·00	25
378		$1 "Brassia maculata"	2·50	3·25
MS379		161 × 95 mm. Nos. 375/8	4·50	6·00

179 "Mary", 1808–15

1974. Mail Packet Boats. Multicoloured.

380		5c. Type **179**	75	10
381		10c. "Queensbury", 1814–27	75	10
382		15c. "Sheldrake", 1829–34	1·00	40
383		50c. "Thames I", 1842	2·00	2·50
MS384		133 × 159 mm. Nos. 380/3 (sold at 90c.)	2·75	5·00

180 "Journeys"

1974. National Dance Theatre Company. Mult.

385		5c. Type **180**	10	10
386		10c. "Jamaican Promenade"	10	10
387		30c. "Jamaican Promenade" (different)	30	30
388		50c. "Misa Criolla"	50	80
MS389		161 × 102 mm. Nos. 385/8 (sold at $1)	1·50	2·50

181 U.P.U. Emblem and Globe

1974. Centenary of U.P.U.

390	**181**	5c. multicoloured	10	10
391		9c. multicoloured	10	10
392		50c. multicoloured	35	80

182 Senate Building and Sir Hugh Wooding

1975. 25th Anniv of University of West Indies. Mult.

393		5c. Type **182**	10	10
394		10c. University Chapel and Princess Alice	10	10
395		30c. Type **182**	20	25
396		50c. As 10c.	35	60

183 Commonwealth Symbol

1975. Heads of Commonwealth Conf. Mult.

397		5c. Type **183**	10	10
398		10c. Jamaican coat of arms	10	10
399		30c. Dove of Peace	15	30
400		50c. Jamaican flag	30	2·25

184 Jamaican Kite Swallowtail

185 Koo Koo or Actor Boy

1975. Butterflies (1st series), showing the family "Papilionidae". Multicoloured.
401 10c. Type **184** 55 20
402 20c. Orange swallowtail ("Papilo thoas") . . . . . 1·10 1·10
403 25c. False androyeus swallowtail ("Papilo thersites") . . . . 1·25 2·00
404 30c. Homerus swallowtail ("Papilo homerus") . . . . 1·40 2·75
MS405 134 × 179 mm. Nos. 401/4 (sold at 95c.) . . . . 5·50 7·50
See also Nos. 429/32 and 443/6.

1975. Christmas. Belisario prints of "John Canoe" Festival (1st series). Multicoloured.
406 8c. Type **185** 15 10
407 10c. Red Set-girls 15 10
408 20c. French Set-girls 50 20
409 50c. Jaw-bone or House John Canoe . . . . 95 2·50
MS410 138 × 141 mm. Nos. 406/9 (sold at $1) . . . . 1·75 3·25
See also Nos. 421/3.

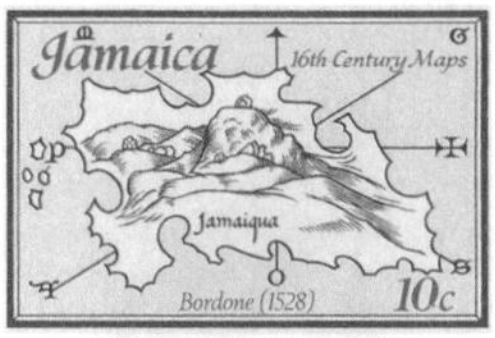

186 Bordone Map, 1528

1976. 16th Century Maps of Jamaica.
411 **186** 10c. brown, lt brown & red 25 10
412 – 20c. multicoloured 45 25
413 – 30c. multicoloured 70 85
414 – 50c. multicoloured . . . . 95 2·75
DESIGNS: 20c. Porcacchi map, 1576; 30c. De Bry map, 1594; 50c. Langenes map, 1598.
See also Nos. 425/8.

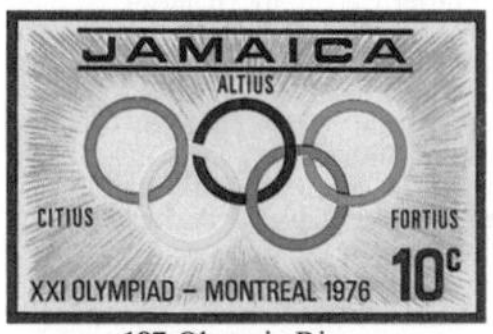

187 Olympic Rings

1976. Olympic Games, Montreal.
415 **187** 10c. multicoloured . . . 15 10
416 20c. multicoloured . . . 30 20
417 **187a** 25c. multicoloured . . . 30 25
418 50c. multicoloured . . . 45 2·25

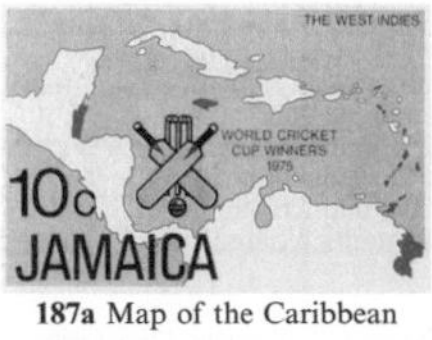

187a Map of the Caribbean

1976. West Indian Victory in World Cricket Cup.
419 10c. Type **187a** 50 50
420 25c. Prudential Cup . . . . 75 1·75

1976. Christmas. Belisario Prints (2nd series). As T **185**. Multicoloured.
421 10c. Queen of the Set-girls . . 10 10
422 20c. Band of the Jaw-bone John Canoe 25 10
423 50c. Koo Koo (actor-boy) . . 45 2·00
MS424 110 × 140 mm. Nos. 421/3 (sold at 90c.) . . . . 70 2·00

1977. 17th Cent Maps of Jamaica. As T **186**.
425 9c. multicoloured 30 40
426 10c. red, brown and buff . . 30 10
427 25c. black, blue and light blue 70 60
428 40c. black, blue and green . . 80 2·25
DESIGNS: 9c. Hickeringill map, 1661; 10c. Ogilby map, 1671; 25c. Visscher map, 1680; 40c. Thornton map, 1689.

1977. Butterflies (2nd series). As T **184**. Mult.
429 10c. False barred sulphur ("Eurema elathea") 35 10
430 20c. Bronze wing ("Dynamine egaea") . . . 75 55
431 25c. Jamaican harlequin ("Chlosyne pantoni") . . . 1·00 1·50
432 40c. Mimic ("Hypolimnas misippus") . . . . 1·50 4·50
MS433 139 × 120 mm. Nos. 429/32 (sold at $1.05) . . . . 4·50 7·00

188 Map, Scout Emblem and Streamertail

190 Half-figure with Canopy

189 Trumpeter

1977. Sixth Caribbean Scout Jamboree, Jamaica.
434 **188** 10c. multicoloured 65 10
435 20c. multicoloured . . . . 1·00 25
436 25c. multicoloured . . . . 1·00 35
437 50c. multicoloured . . . . 1·50 1·75

1977. 50th Anniv of Jamaica Military Band. Mult.
438 9c. Type **189** 15 10
439 10c. Clarinet players 15 10
440 20c. Two kettle drummers (vert) 40 35
441 25c. Double-bass player and trumpeter (vert) 55 65
MS442 120 × 137 mm. Nos. 438/41 (sold at 75c.) . . . . 2·50 4·50

1978. Butterflies (3rd series). As T **184**. Multicoloured.
443 10c. Jamaican hairstreak ("Callophrys crethona") . . 50 10
444 20c. Malachite ("Siproeta stelenes") 85 20
445 25c. Common long-tailed skipper ("Urbanus proteus") 95 65
446 50c. Troglodyte ("Anaea troglodyta") . . . . 2·00 3·25
MS447 100 × 125 mm. Nos. 443/6 (sold at $1.15) . . . . 4·50 6·50

1978. Arawak Artefacts (1st series).
448 **190** 10c. brown, yellow & black 10 10
449 – 20c. brown, mauve & black 15 10
450 – 50c. brown, green & black 35 35
MS451 135 × 90 mm. Nos. 448/50 (sold at 90c.) . . . . 60 1·25
DESIGNS: 20c. Standing figure; 50c. Birdman.
See also Nos. 479/83.

191 Norman Manley (statue)

193 "Negro Aroused" (sculpture by Edna Manley)

192 Band and Banner

1978. 24th Commonwealth Parliamentary Conference. Multicoloured.
452 10c. Type **191** 15 10
453 20c. Sir Alexander Bustamante (statue) . . . 25 15
454 25c. City of Kingston Crest 35 20
455 40c. Gordon House Chamber, House of Representatives 35 65

1978. Christmas. Centenary of Salvation Army. Multicoloured.
456 10c. Type **192** 30 10
457 20c. Trumpeter 35 20
458 25c. Banner 35 30
459 50c. William Booth (founder) 60 2·00

1978. International Anti-Apartheid Year.
460 **193** 10c. multicoloured 30 20

194 Tennis, Montego Bay

197 Grinding Stone, c. 400 B.C.

1979. Multicoloured.
461 1c. Type **194** 70 75
462 2c. Golf, Tryall, Hanover . . 2·25 2·75
463 4c. Horse riding, Negril Beach . . . . 50 2·25
464 5c. Old waterwheel, Tryall, Hanover . . . . 1·25 30
465 6c. Fern Gully, Ocho Rios 1·50 2·50
466 7c. Dunn's River Falls, Ocho Rios 50 30
467 8c. Jamaican tody . . . . . 1·00 1·25
468 10c. Jamaican mango . . . . 1·00 20
469 12c. Yellow-billed amazon . . 1·00 2·00
470 15c. Streamertail . . . . . . 1·00 30
471 35c. White-chinned thrush . . 1·50 30
472 50c. Jamaican woodpecker 1·75 30
473 65c. Rafting, Martha Brae Trelawny . . . . 1·75 2·75
474 75c. Blue Marlin fleet, Port Antonio . . . . 2·00 2·25
475 $1 Scuba diving, Ocho Rios 2·00 2·25
476 $2 Sailing boats, Montego Bay . . . . 2·00 65
477 $5 Arms and map of Jamaica (37 × 27 mm) . . . . . . 1·00 1·75

1979. 10th Anniv of Air Jamaica. No. 352 optd **TENTH ANNIVERSARY AIR JAMAICA 1st APRIL 1979.**
478 10c. multicoloured 75 75

1979. Arawak Artefacts (2nd series). Multicoloured.
479 5c. Type **197** 10 10
480 10c. Stone implements, c. 500 B.C. (horiz) 10 10
481 20c. Cooking pot, c. 300 A.D. (horiz) 10 15
482 25c. Serving boat, c. 300 A.D. (horiz) 10 20
483 50c. Storage jar fragment, c. 300 A.D. . . . 25 60

198 1962 1s.6d. Independence Commemorative Stamp

1979. Death Centenary of Sir Rowland Hill.
484 **198** 10c. black, brown and red 15 10
485 – 20c. yellow and brown . . 15 15
486 – 25c. mauve and blue . . . 20 20
487 – 50c. multicoloured 25 70
MS488 146 × 94 mm. No. 485 (sold at 30c.) 30 85
DESIGNS: 20c. 1920 1s. with frame inverted; 25c. 1860 6d. stamp; 50c. 1968 3d. Human Rights Year commemorative.

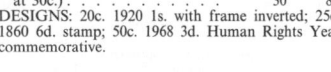

199 Group of Children

1979. Christmas. International Year of the Child. Multicoloured.
489 10c. Type **199** 10 10
490 20c. Doll (vert) 10 10
491 25c. "The Family" (painting by child) 15 15
492 50c. "House on the Hill" (painting by child) 25 40

200 Date Tree Hall, 1886 (original home of Institute)

1980. Centenary of Institute of Jamaica. Mult.
493 5c. Type **200** 10 10
494 15c. Institute building, 1980 15 10
495 35c. Microfilm reader (vert) 25 20
496 50c. Hawksbill turtle and green turtle 45 85
497 75c. Jamaican owl (vert) . . 1·75 3·00

201 Don Quarrie (200 m, 1976)

1980. Olympic Games, Moscow. Jamaican Olympic Gold Medal Winners. Multicoloured.
498 15c. Type **201** 40 15
499 35c. Arthur Wint (4 × 400 m Relay, 1952) . . 45 80
500 35c. Leslie Laing (4 × 400 m Relay, 1952) . . 45 80
501 35c. Herbert McKenley (4 × 400 m Relay, 1952) . . 45 80
502 35c. George Rhoden (4 × 400 m, 1952) 45 80

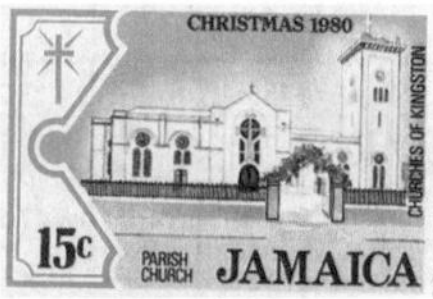

202 Parish Church

1980. Christmas. Churches (1st series). Multicoloured.
503 15c. Type **202** 10 10
504 20c. Coke Memorial Church 10 10
505 25c. Church of the Redeemer 15 10
506 $5 Holy Trinity Cathedral . . 1·00 2·00
MS507 120 × 139 mm. Nos. 503/6 (sold at $5.70) . . . . 1·25 3·00
See also No. 537/9 and 570/2.

203 Blood Cup Sponge

205 White Orchid

204 Brown's Hutia (or Indian Coney)

1981. Marine Life (1st series). Multicoloured.
508 20c. Type **203** 15 10
509 45c. Tube sponge (horiz) . . 25 35
510 60c. Black coral 35 45
511 75c. Tyre reef (horiz) 40 75
See also Nos. 541/5.

1981. Brown's Hutia (or Indian Coney).
512 20c. Hutia facing right . . . 15 20
513 20c. Type **204** 15 20
514 20c. Hutia facing left and eating 15 20
515 20c. Hutia family 15 20

1981. Royal Wedding. Multicoloured.
516 20c. Type **205** 10 10
517 45c. Royal Coach 15 10
518 60c. Prince Charles and Lady Diana Spencer 25 20
519 $5 St. James' Palace 70 85
MS520 98 × 85 mm. No. 519 . . 75 1·75

206 Blind Man at Work

1981. International Year for Disabled Persons. Multicoloured.
521 20c. Type **206** 20 15
522 45c. Painting with the mouth 40 40
523 60c. Deaf student communicating with sign language 50 75
524 $1.50 Basketball players . . . 2·25 2·00

207 W.F.D. Emblem on 1964 1½d. Definitive   **208** "Survival" (song title)

1981. World Food Day. Stamps on Stamps.

525 **207** 20c. multicoloured 45 15
526 – 45c. black, red and orange 80 40
527 – $2 black, blue and green 2·25 1·40
528 – $4 black, green and brown 3·25 2·50

DESIGNS—VERT (As T **207**): 45c. 1922 1d. value. HORIZ (40 × 26 mm): $2 As 1938 3d. but with W.F.D. emblem replacing King's head; $4 As 1938 1s. but with W.F.D. emblem replacing King's head.

1981. Bob Marley (musician) Commemoration. Song Titles. Multicoloured.

529 1c. Type **208** 70 1·10
530 2c. "Exodus" 70 1·10
531 3c. "Is this Love" 70 1·10
532 15c. "Coming in from the Cold" 3·25 30
533 20c. "Positive Vibration" 3·25 30
534 60c. "War" 4·00 3·00
535 $3 "Could you be Loved" 6·50 12·00
MS536 134 × 110 mm. $5.25 Bob Marley 7·50 4·75

No. 533 is incorrectly inscribed "OSITIVE VIBRATION".

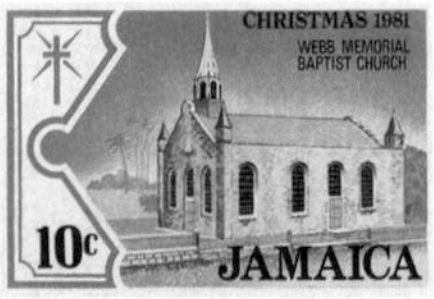

209 Webb Memorial Baptist Church

1981. Christmas. Churches (2nd series). Multicoloured.

537 10c. Type **209** 10 10
538 45c. Church of God in Jamaica 30 15
539 $5 Bryce United Church 1·75 2·50
MS540 120 × 168 mm. Nos. 537/9 3·50 3·50

210 Gorgonian Coral   **211** Cub Scout

1982. Marine Life (2nd series). Multicoloured.

541 20c. Type **210** 45 10
542 45c. Hard sponge and diver (horiz) 65 25
543 60c. American manatee (horiz) 90 55
544 75c. Plume worm (horiz) 1·00 65
545 $3 Coral banded shrimp (horiz) 2·50 1·75

1982. 75th Anniv of Boy Scout Movement. Mult.

546 20c. Type **211** 50 15
547 45c. Scout camp 85 40
548 60c. "Out of Many, One People" 1·10 90
549 $2 Lord Baden-Powell 1·75 2·50
MS550 80 × 130 mm. Nos. 546/9 5·00 6·00

212 "Lignum vitae" (national flower)   **213** Prey Captured

1982. 21st Birthday of Princess of Wales.

551 20c. Type **212** 35 20
552 45c. Carriage ride 50 35
553 60c. Wedding 70 60
554 75c. "Saxifraga longifolia" 1·25 2·75
555 $2 Princess of Wales 1·60 3·00
556 $3 "Viola gracilis major" 1·60 3·50
MS557 106 × 75 mm. $5 Honeymoon photograph 1·40 2·50

1982. Birth of Prince William of Wales. Nos. 551/6 optd **ROYAL BABY 21.6.82.**

558 20c. Type **212** 20 20
559 45c. Carriage ride 30 35
560 60c. Wedding 40 60
561 75c. "Saxifraga longifolia" 70 2·25
562 $2 Princess of Wales 75 2·75
563 $3 "Viola gracilis major" 1·00 3·25
MS564 106 × 75 mm. $5 Honeymoon photograph 1·50 3·50

1982. Jamaican Birds (1st series). Jamaican Lizard Cuckoo. Multicoloured.

565 $1 Type **213** 1·40 1·60
566 $1 Searching for prey 1·40 1·60
567 $1 Calling prior to prey search 1·40 1·60
568 $1 Adult landing 1·40 1·60
569 $1 Adult flying in 1·40 1·60

See also Nos. 642/5 and 707/10.

1982. Christmas. Churches (3rd series). As T **209**. Multicoloured.

570 20c. United Pentecostal Church 70 10
571 45c. Disciples of Christ Church 1·25 25
572 75c. Open Bible Church 2·00 3·75

214 Queen Elizabeth II

1983. Royal Visit. Multicoloured.

573 $2 Type **214** 3·00 3·50
574 $3 Coat of arms 4·00 6·00

215 Folk Dancing

1983. Commonwealth Day. Multicoloured.

575 20c. Type **215** 15 15
576 45c. Bauxite mining 35 35
577 75c. World map showing position of Jamaica 45 45
578 $2 Coat of arms and family 60 1·40

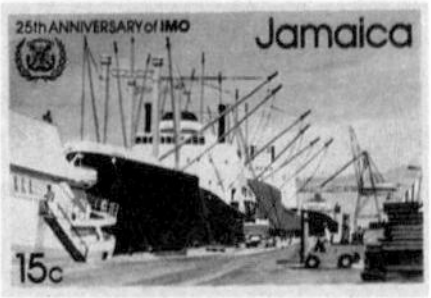

216 General Cargo Ship at Wharf

1983. 25th Anniv of International Maritime Organization. Multicoloured.

579 15c. Type **216** 75 30
580 20c. "Veendam" (cruise liner) at Kingston 1·00 40
581 45c. "Astronomer" (container ship) entering port 1·75 85
582 $1 Tanker passing International Seabed Headquarters Building 2·75 5·00

217 Norman Manley and Sir Alexander Bustamante   **218** Ship-to-Shore Radio

1983. 21st Anniv of Independence.

583 **217** 15c. multicoloured 15 50
584 20c. multicoloured 15 60
585 45c. multicoloured 30 85

1983. World Communications Year. Multicoloured.

586 20c. Type **218** 90 15
587 45c. Postal services 1·40 40
588 75c. Telephone communications 1·75 3·25
589 $1 T.V. via satellite 1·90 3·75

219 "Racing at Caymanas" (Sidney McLaren)

1983. Christmas. Paintings. Multicoloured.

590 15c. Type **219** 15 10
591 20c. "Seated Figures" (Karl Parboosingh) 15 10
592 75c. "The Petitioner" (Henry Daley) (vert) 50 65
593 $2 "Banana Plantation" (John Dunkley) (vert) 1·25 4·00

220 Sir Alexander Bustamante

1984. Birth Centenary of Sir Alexander Bustamante. Multicoloured.

594 20c. Type **220** 90 1·60
595 20c. Birthplace, Blenheim 90 1·60

221 De Havilland Gipsy Moth Seaplane

1984. Seaplanes and Flying Boats. Multicoloured.

596 25c. Type **221** 1·50 20
597 55c. Consolidated Commodore flying boat 2·00 85
598 $1.50 Sikorsky S-38A flying boat 3·25 4·00
599 $3 Sikorsky S-40 flying boat "American Clipper" 4·00 6·00

222 Cycling

1984. Olympic Games, Los Angeles. Multicoloured.

600 25c. Type **222** 2·00 50
601 55c. Relay running 60 30
602 $1.50 Start of race 2·00 5·00
603 $3 Finish of race 1·75 4·50
MS604 135 × 105 mm. Nos. 600/3 (sold at $5.40) 5·50 8·00

1984. Nos. 465 and 469 surch.

605 5c. on 6c. Fern Gully, Ocho Rios 15 40
606 10c. on 12c. Yellow-billed amazon 1·10 60

224 Head of Jamaican Boa Snake

1984. Endangered Species. Jamaican Boa Snake. Multicoloured.

607 25c. Type **224** 6·00 40
608 55c. Boa snake on branch over tree 7·00 80
609 70c. Snake with young 8·00 4·75
610 $1 Snake on log 9·00 5·00
MS611 133 × 97 mm. As Nos. 607/10 but without W.W.F. emblem (sold at $2.60) 6·00 7·00

225 Locomotive "Enterprise" (1845)

1984. Railway Locomotives (1st series). Mult.

612 25c. Type **225** 1·50 30
613 55c. Tank locomotive (1880) 1·75 70
614 $1.50 Kitson-Meyer tank locomotive (1904) 2·75 3·50
615 $3 Super-heated locomotive No. 40 (1916) 4·00 5·50

See also Nos. 634/7.

226 "Accompong Madonna" (Namba Roy)   **227** Brown Pelicans flying

1984. Christmas. Sculptures. Multicoloured.

616 20c. Type **226** 30 10
617 25c. "Head" (Alvin Marriott) 35 10
618 55c. "Moon" (Edna Manley) 80 65
619 $1.50 "All Women are Five Women" (Mallica Reynolds (Kapo)) 1·90 4·00

1985. Birth Bicentenary of John J. Audubon (ornithologist). Brown Pelican. Multicoloured.

620 20c. Type **227** 1·00 20
621 55c. Diving for fish 1·50 40
622 $2 Young pelican taking food from adult 2·50 3·25
623 $5 "Brown Pelican" (John J. Audubon) 3·75 6·50
MS624 100 × 100 mm. Nos. 620/3 (sold at $7.85) 6·00 8·00

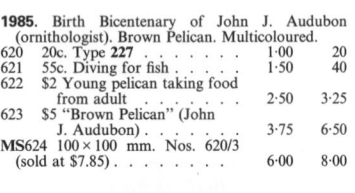

228 The Queen Mother at Belfast University

1985. Life and Times of Queen Elizabeth the Queen Mother. Multicoloured.

625 25c. With photograph album, 1963 50 10
626 55c. With Prince Charles at Garter Ceremony, Windsor Castle, 1983 70 15
627 $1.50 Type **228** 1·00 1·50
628 $3 With Prince Henry at his christening (from photo by Lord Snowdon) 1·90 3·00
MS629 91 × 74 mm. $5 With the Queen, Prince Philip and Princess Anne at Ascot 2·75 1·75

229 Maps and Emblems

1985. International Youth Year and 5th Pan-American Scout Jamboree.

630 **229** 25c. multicoloured 1·25 10
631 55c. multicoloured 1·50 25
632 70c. multicoloured 1·75 1·40
633 $4 multicoloured 3·50 8·00

1985. Railway Locomotives (2nd series). As T **225**. Multicoloured.

634 25c. Baldwin steam locomotive No. 16 1·25 30
635 55c. Rogers locomotive 1·75 35
636 $1.50 Locomotive "Projector", 1845 2·75 3·50
637 $4 Diesel locomotive No. 102 3·75 6·50

230 "The Old Settlement" (Ralph Campbell)

1985. Christmas. Jamaican Paintings. Mult.

638 20c. Type **230** 10 10
639 55c. "The Vendor" (Albert Huie) (vert) 15 15

640 75c. "Road Menders" (Gaston Tabois) 20 35
641 $4 "Woman, must I not be about my Father's business?" (Carl Abrahams) (vert) . . . . . 1·10 3·25

1986. Jamaican Birds (2nd series). As T **213**. Multicoloured.
642 25c. Chestnut-bellied cuckoo 50 10
643 55c. Jamaican becard 65 30
644 $1.50 White-eyed thrush . . . 85 2·00
645 $5 Rufous-tailed flycatcher 1·75 4·75

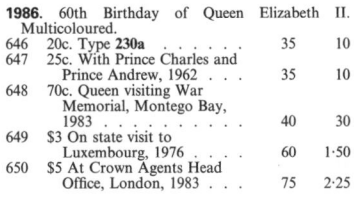

230a Princess Elizabeth and Princess Margaret, 1939

1986. 60th Birthday of Queen Elizabeth II. Multicoloured.
646 20c. Type **230a** 35 10
647 25c. With Prince Charles and Prince Andrew, 1962 . . . 35 10
648 70c. Queen visiting War Memorial, Montego Bay, 1983 . . . . 40 30
649 $3 On state visit to Luxembourg, 1976 . . . . 60 1·50
650 $5 At Crown Agents Head Office, London, 1983 . . . 75 2·25

231 Bustamante Children's Hospital

231a Prince Andrew and Miss Sarah Ferguson, Ascot, 1985

1986. "Ameripex '86" International Stamp Exhibition, Chicago. Multicoloured.
651 25c. Type **231** 70 15
652 55c. Air Jamaica Boeing 737 airliner and map of holiday resorts . . . . 2·25 40
653 $3 Norman Manley Law School . . . . 1·25 4·00
654 $5 Bauxite and agricultural exports . . . . 7·50 9·50
MS655 85 × 106 mm. Nos. 651/4 (sold at $8.90) . . . . 10·00 12·00

1986. Royal Wedding. Multicoloured.
656 20c. Type **231a** 15 10
657 $5 Prince Andrew making speech, Fredericton, Canada, 1985 . . . . . . 1·00 1·90

232 Richard "Shrimpy" Clarke

1986. Jamaican Boxing Champions. Multicoloured.
658 45c. Type **232** 20 15
659 70c. Michael McCallum . . . 30 30
660 $2 Trevor Berbick . . . . . 70 1·75
661 $4 Richard "Shrimpy" Clarke, Michael McCallum and Trevor Berbick . . . . 1·25 3·00

1986. Nos. 472/3 surch.
662 5c. on 50c. Jamaican woodpecker . . . . 3·00 3·00
663 10c. on 65c. Rafting, Martha Brae Trelawny . . . . . . 1·75 2·50

234 "Heliconia wagneriana"

235 Crown Cone

1986. Christmas. Flowers (1st series). Mult.
664 20c. Type **234** 10 10
665 25c. "Heliconia psittacorum" (horiz) 10 10
666 55c. "Heliconia rostrata" . . 20 30
667 $5 "Strelitzia reginae" (horiz) 1·60 4·50
See also Nos. 703/6 and 739/42.

1987. Sea Shells. Multicoloured.
668 35c. Type **235** 45 15
669 75c. Measled cowrie 65 60
670 $1 Atlantic trumpet triton . . 75 90
671 $5 Rooster-tail conch . . . . 1·50 4·50

236 Norman Manley

237 Arms of Jamaica

1987. Portraits.
672A **236** 1c. red and pink . . . 10 75
673A 2c. red and pink . . . 10 75
674A 3c. green and stone . . 10 75
675A 4c. green & light green 10 75
676B 5c. blue and grey . . . 50 75
677A 6c. blue and grey . . . 20 75
678A 7c. violet and mauve 50 75
679A 8c. mauve and pink . . 20 10
680A 9c. sepia and brown . . 50 10
681B – 10c. red and pink . . . 70 10
682B – 20c. orange and flesh 50 10
683A – 30c. green & light green 40 10
684B – 40c. deep green & green 30 20
685B – 50c. green and grey . . 55 20
685cB – 55c. bistre and cream 75 10
686A – 60c. blue and light blue 30 20
687A – 70c. violet & light violet 30 20
688A – 80c. violet and lilac . . 50 30
689B – 90c. brown & lt brown 1·25 30
690A **237** $1 brown and cream 50 30
690cB $1.10 brown and cream 70 40
691aB $2 orange and cream 70 70
692A $5 green and stone . . 60 1·00
693A $10 blue and azure . . 70 1·50
693cB $25 violet and lilac . . 1·50 1·75
693dB $50 mauve and lilac . . 2·50 3·00
DESIGN: 10c. to 90c. Sir Alexander Bustamante.
The 5, 20, 40, 50, 90c. and $1 exist with or without imprint date at foot.

238 Jamaican Flag and Coast at Sunset

239 Marcus Garvey

1987. 25th Anniv of Independence. Multicoloured.
694 55c. Type **238** . . . . 1·50 60
695 70c. Jamaican flag and inscription (horiz) . . . . 1·50 2·75

1987. Birth Centenary of Marcus Garvey (founder of Universal Negro Improvement Association). Each black, green and yellow.
696 25c. Type **239** . . . . 1·25 2·00
697 25c. Statue of Marcus Garvey 1·25 2·00

240 Salvation Army School for the Blind

1987. Cent of Salvation Army in Jamaica. Mult.
698 25c. Type **240** . . . . 1·50 30
699 55c. Col. Mary Booth and Bramwell Booth Memorial Hall . . . . 1·50 30
700 $3 Welfare Service lorry, 1929 . . . . 4·75 5·50
701 $5 Col. Abram Davey and S.S. "Alene", 1887 . . . 6·00 8·50
MS702 100 × 80 mm. Nos. 698/701 (sold at $8.90) . . . . 13·00 14·00

1987. Christmas. Flowers (2nd series). As T **234**. Multicoloured.
703 20c. Hibiscus hybrid 15 10
704 25c. "Hibiscus elatus" . . . 15 10
705 $4 "Hibiscus cannabinus" . . 2·00 3·75
706 $5 "Hibiscus rosasinensis" . . 2·25 3·75

1988. Jamaican Birds (3rd series). As T **213**. Multicoloured.
707 45c. Chestnut-bellied cuckoo, black-billed amazon and Jamaican euphonia . . . . 1·75 2·50
708 45c. Black-billed amazon, jamaican white-eyed vireo, rufous-throated solitaire and yellow elaenia . . . . 1·75 2·50
709 $5 Snowy plover, little blue heron and great blue heron (white phase) . . . . . . 4·25 5·50
710 $5 Black-necked stilt, snowy egret, snowy plover and black-crowned night heron 4·25 5·50
The two designs of each value were printed together, se-tenant, each pair forming a composite design.

243 Blue Whales

1988. Marine Mammals. Multicoloured.
711 20c. Type **243** . . . . 2·00 70
712 25c. Gervais's whales . . . . 2·00 70
713 55c. Killer whales . . . . . 3·00 80
714 $5 Common dolphins . . . . 5·00 10·00

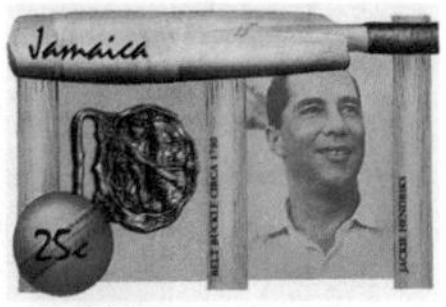

243a Jackie Hendriks

1988. West Indian Cricket. Each showing portrait, cricket equipment and early belt buckle. Multicoloured.
715 25c. Type **243a** . . . . . . 1·75 40
716 55c. George Headley . . . . 1·75 40
717 $2 Michael Holding . . . . 3·50 3·00
718 $3 R. K. Nunes . . . . . . 3·75 4·75
719 $4 Allan Rae . . . . 4·00 5·00

244 Jamaican Red Cross Workers with Ambulance

1988. 125th Anniv of Int Red Cross. Mult.
720 55c. Type **244** 50 30
721 $5 Henri Dunant (founder) in field hospital . . . . . . 2·00 4·00

245 Boxing

1988. Olympic Games, Seoul. Multicoloured.
722 25c. Type **245** 30 10
723 45c. Cycling . . . . 2·00 70
724 $4 Athletics . . . . 2·25 3·25
725 $5 Hurdling . . . . 2·25 3·25
MS726 127 × 87 mm. Nos. 722/5 (sold at $9.90) . . . . 4·50 5·50

246 Bobsled Team Members and Logo

1988. Jamaican Olympic Bobsled Team. Mult.
727 25c. Type **246** . . . . 50 1·25
728 25c. Two-man bobsled . . . 50 1·25
729 $5 Bobsled team members (different) and logo . . . . 2·25 3·25
730 $5 Four-man bobsled . . . . 2·25 3·25

1988. Hurricane Gilbert Relief Fund. Nos. 722/5 surch **+ 25c HURRICANE GILBERT RELIEF FUND**.
731 25c.+25c. Type **245** 10 20
732 45c.+45c. Cycling 20 30
733 $4+$4 Athletics . . . . . . 1·10 2·25
734 $5+$5 Hurdling . . . . . . 1·10 2·50

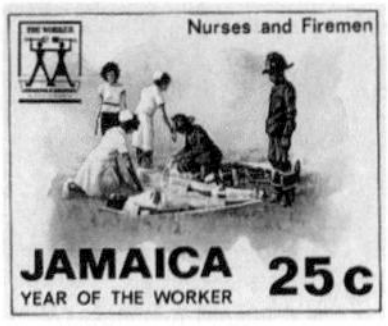

248 Nurses and Firemen

1988. Year of the Worker. Multicoloured.
735 25c. Type **248** . . . . 1·25 30
736 55c. Woodcarver 45 30
737 $3 Textile workers . . . . . 1·00 3·00
738 $5 Workers on fish farm . . 1·25 3·50

1988. Christmas. Flowers (3rd series). As T **234**. Multicoloured.
739 25c. "Euphorbia pulcherrima" 70 10
740 55c. "Spathodea campanulata" (horiz) . . . 85 15
741 $3 "Hylocereus triangularis" 2·00 1·60
742 $4 "Broughtonia sanguinea" (horiz) . . . . 2·00 1·75

249 Old York Castle School

1989. Bicent of Methodist Church in Jamaica.
743 **249** 25c. black and blue . . . 30 10
744 – 45c. black and red 35 10
745 – $5 black and green . . . 3·00 5·00
DESIGNS: 45c. Revd. Thomas Coke and Parade Chapel, Kingston; $5 Father Hugh Sherlock and St. John's Church.

250 "Syntomidopsis variegata"

251 Arawak Fisherman with Catch

1989. Jamaican Moths (1st series). Multicoloured.
746 25c. Type **250** 50 10
747 55c. "Himantoides perkinsae" 80 30
748 $3 "Arctia nigriplaga" . . . 1·50 3·50
749 $5 "Sthenognatha toddi" . . 1·90 4·25
See also Nos. 758/61 and 790/3.

1989. 500th Anniv (1992) of Discovery of America by Columbus (1st issue). Multicoloured.
750 25c. Type **251** 20 10
751 70c. Arawak man smoking 45 30
752 $5 King Ferdinand and Queen Isabella inspecting caravels . . . . 3·00 4·00
753 $10 Columbus with chart . . 5·50 8·50
MS754 150 × 200 mm. Nos. 750/3 (sold at $16.15) . . . . 15·00 15·00
See also Nos. 774/7 and 802/7.

252 Girl Guide

1990. 75th Anniv of Girl Guide Movement in Jamaica. Multicoloured.
755 45c. Type **252** . . . . 1·50 30
756 55c. Guide leader . . . . . 1·50 30
757 $5 Brownie, guide and ranger 6·00 9·00

1990. Jamaican Moths (2nd series). As T **250**. Multicoloured.
758 25c. "Eunomia rubripunctata" 85 35
759 55c. "Perigonia jamaicensis" 1·25 35
760 $4 "Uraga haemorrhoa" . . 2·50 4·50
761 $5 "Empyreuma pugione" . . 2·50 4·50

1990. "EXPO '90" International Garden and Greenery Exhibition, Osaka. Nos. 758/61 optd **EXPO '90** and logo.
762 25c. "Eunomia rubripunctata" 85 35
763 55c. "Perigonia jamaicensis" 1·25 35
764 $4 "Uraga haemorrhoa" . . 2·50 4·50
765 $5 "Empyreuma pugione" . . 2·50 4·50

254 Teaching English

1990. International Literacy Year. Mult.
766 55c. Type **254** 40 25
767 $5 Teaching maths . . . . . 3·00 5·00

255 "To the Market"

1990. Christmas. Children's Paintings. Mult.
768 20c. Type **255** 35 10
769 25c. "House and Garden" . . 35 10
770 55c. "Jack and Jill" 50 15
771 70c. "Market" 65 40
772 $1.50 "Lonely" . . . . . . 1·50 3·50
773 $5 "Market Woman" (vert) 3·00 6·00

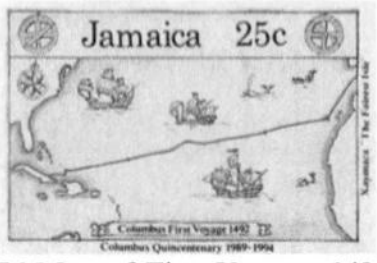

256 Map of First Voyage, 1492

1990. 500th Anniv (1992) of Discovery of America by Columbus (2nd issue). Multicoloured.
774 25c. Type **256** . . . . 1·25 40
775 45c. Map of second voyage, 1493 . . . . 1·40 40
776 $5 Map of third voyage, 1498 4·50 5·50
777 $10 Map of fourth voyage, 1502 . . . . 7·00 9·00
MS778 126 × 99 mm. 25, 45c., $5, $10 Composite map of Caribbean showing routes of voyages . . 14·00 15·00
MS779 148 × 207 mm. Nos. 774/7. Imperf . . . . 14·00 15·00

257 Weather Balloon, Dish Aerial and Map of Jamaica

1991. 11th World Meteorological Congress, Kingston.
780 **257** 50c. multicoloured 50 20
781 $10 multicoloured . . . . 6·50 8·50

258 Bust of Mary Seacole

1991. International Council of Nurses Meeting of National Representatives.
782 **258** 50c. multicoloured 85 30
783 – $1.10 multicoloured . . . 1·75 2·25
MS784 89 × 60 mm. $8 agate, brown and ochre (sold at $8.20) . . . 3·75 6·00
DESIGNS: $1.10 Mary Seacole House; $8 Hospital at Scutari, 1854.

259 Jamaican Iguana

1991. 50th Anniv of Natural History Society of Jamaica. Jamaican Iguana. Multicoloured.
785 $1.10 Type **259** 65 85
786 $1.10 Head of iguana looking right 65 85
787 $1.10 Iguana climbing . . . 65 85
788 $1.10 Iguana on rock looking left 65 85
789 $1.10 Close-up of iguana's head 65 85

1991. Jamaican Moths (3rd series). As T **250**. Multicoloured.
790 50c. "Urania sloanus" . . . 65 20
791 $1.10 "Phoenicoprocta jamaicensis" 90 60
792 $1.40 "Horama grotei" . . . 1·10 90
793 $8 "Amplypterus gannascus" 3·25 6·00

1991. "Phila Nippon '91" International Stamp Exhibition, Tokyo. Nos. 790/3 optd **PHILA NIPPON 91** and emblem.
794 50c. "Urania sloanus" . . . 80 20
795 $1.10 "Phoenicoprocta jamaicensis" . . . . 1·10 60
796 $1.40 "Horama grotei" . . . 1·25 90
797 $8 "Amplypterus gannascus" 4·25 7·00

261 "Doctor Bird"

1991. Christmas. Children's Paintings. Mult.
798 50c. Type **261** 70 10
799 $1.10 "Road scene" . . . . 1·10 25
800 $5 "Children and house" . . 3·50 3·75
801 $10 "Cows grazing" . . . . 5·00 8·00

262 Indians threatening Ships

263 Compasses and Square Symbol

1991. 500th Anniv (1992) of Discovery of America by Columbus (3rd issue). Multicoloured.
802 50c. Type **262** 55 15
803 $1.10 Spaniards setting dog on Indians 65 30
804 $1.40 Indian with gift of pineapple 65 30
805 $25 Columbus describes Jamaica with crumpled paper . . . . 7·00 11·00
MS806 125 × 102 mm. Nos. 802/5 (sold at $28.20) . . . . 8·00 11·00
MS807 210 × 150 mm. Nos. 802/5. Imperf . . . . 9·00 11·00

1992. 250th Anniv of First Provisional Grand Master of English Freemasonry in Jamaica. Multicoloured.
808 50c. Type **263** 70 30
809 $1.10 Symbol in stained glass window 90 40
810 $1.40 Compasses and square on book 90 40
811 $25 Eye in triangle symbol 8·00 9·00
MS812 140 × 80 mm. Nos. 808/11 (sold at $28.50) . . . . 11·00 12·00

264 Ship in Flooded Street

1992. 300th Anniv of Destruction of Port Royal. Multicoloured.
813 50c. Type **264** 55 40
814 $1.10 Church tower falling 70 45
815 $1.40 Houses collapsing . . . 70 45
816 $25 Inhabitants falling into fissure . . . . 7·00 9·50
MS817 116 × 75 mm. $5 Contemporary broadsheet of earthquake . . . . 4·75 5·50

265 Credit Union Symbol

1992. 50th Anniv of Credit Union Movement.
818 **265** 50c. blue, emerald & green . . . . 1·00 50
819 – $1.40 multicoloured . . . 1·75 1·75
DESIGN: $1.40, O'Hare Hall.

266 Jamaican Flag and Beach Scene

1992. 30th Anniv of Independence.
820 **266** 50c. multicoloured 10 10
821 $1.10 multicoloured . . . 20 20
822 $25 multicoloured . . . . 2·75 5·50

267 "Rainbow" (Cecil Baugh)

269 Cadet, Armoured Car and Emblem

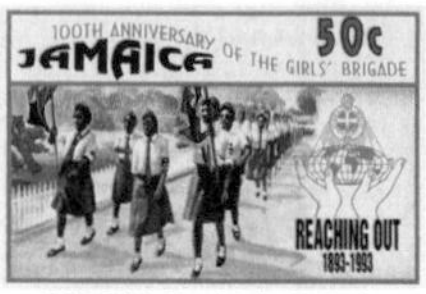

268 Girls' Brigade Parade

1993. Art Ceramics and Pottery. Multicoloured.
823 50c. Type **267** 20 10
824 $1.10 "Yabba Pot" (Louisa Jones) 30 20
825 $1.40 "Sculptured Vase" (Gene Pearson) 30 20
826 $25 "Lidded Form" (Norma Harrack) . . . . 4·50 6·50

1993. Centenary of Girls' Brigade. Mult.
827 50c. Type **268** 90 50
828 $1.10 Brigade members . . . 1·00 1·10

1993. 50th Anniv of Jamaica Combined Cadet Force. Multicoloured.
829 50c. Type **269** 40 20
830 $1.10 Cadet and Britten Norman Islander aircraft (horiz) 60 40
831 $1.40 Cadet and patrol boats 60 40
832 $3 Cadet and emblem (horiz) 80 2·00

270 Constant Spring Golf Course

1993. Golf Courses. Multicoloured.
833 50c. Type **270** 45 10
834 $1.10 Type **270** 65 20
835 $1.40 Half Moon 70 20
836 $2 As $1.40 . . . . 1·00 90
837 $3 Jamaica Jamaica . . . . 1·10 1·25
838 $10 As $3 . . . . 2·50 3·50
MS839 66 × 71 mm. $25 Tryall (vert) (sold at $28) . . . . 4·50 6·50

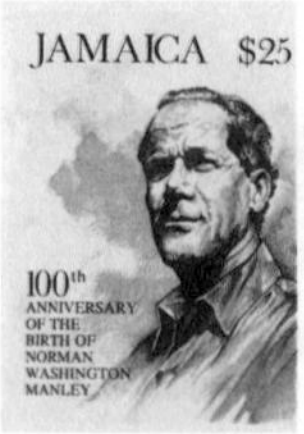

271 Norman Manley

273 Flags of Great Britain and Jamaica

1994. Birth Centenary of Norman Manley.
840 **271** $25 multicoloured . . . . 2·00 2·75
841 $50 multicoloured . . . . 2·50 4·25

1994. "Hong Kong '94" International Stamp Exhibition. No. **MS**839 optd **HONG KONG '94** and emblem.
MS842 66 × 71 mm. $25 Tryall 6·00 6·50

1994. Royal Visit. Multicoloured.
843 $1.10 Type **273** 55 10
844 $1.40 Royal Yacht "Britannia" . . . . 1·25 30
845 $25 Queen Elizabeth II . . . 2·75 3·50
846 $50 Queen Elizabeth and Prince Philip . . . . . . 4·50 7·00

274 Douglas DC-9

1994. 25th Anniv of Air Jamaica. Mult.
847 50c. Type **274** 35 25
848 $1.10 Douglas DC-8 . . . . 35 25
849 $5 Boeing 727 . . . . 75 75
850 $50 Airbus A300 . . . . . . 3·50 6·00

275 Giant Swallowtail

1994. Giant Swallowtail Butterfly Conservation. Multicoloured.
851 50c. Type **275** 40 25
852 $1.10 With wings closed . . . 40 25
853 $10 On flower . . . . 1·60 2·25
854 $25 With wings spread . . . 2·75 4·50
MS855 56 × 61 mm. $50 Pair of butterflies . . . . 6·00 7·50

276 "Royal Botanical Gardens" (Sidney McLaren)

1994. Tourism. Multicoloured.
856 50c. Type **276** 55 20
857 $1.10 Blue Mountains . . . 85 30
858 $5 Tourist in hammock and water sports . . . . 3·00 3·75
MS859 105 × 80 mm. $25 Carolina parakeets; $25 Silhouetted scuba diver; $25 Carolina parakeet and foliage; $25 Tourist raft . . . 5·50 7·50

277 Jamaican Red Poll Calf

1994. Jamaican Red Poll Cattle. Multicoloured.
860 50c. Type **277** 10 10
861 $1.10 Red Poll heifer 10 10
862 $25 Red Poll cow . . . . . 1·25 2·25
863 $50 Red Poll bull . . . . . 2·50 4·50

278 Refuse Collectors

1994. Christmas. Children's Paintings. Multicoloured.
864 50c. Type **278** 10 10
865 90c. Hospital ward 10 10
866 $1.10 House 10 10
867 $50 Landscape . . . . 2·75 5·00

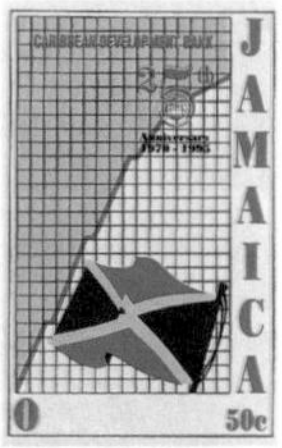

279 Jamaican Band-tailed Pigeon ("Ring-tailed Pigeon")

280 Graph, National Flag and Logo

1995. Jamaican Wild Birds. Multicoloured.
868 50c. Type **279** 65 30
869 90c. Yellow-billed amazon ("Yellow-billed parrot") . . 80 30

870 $1.10 Black-billed amazon (“Black-billed parrot”) . . 80 30
871 $50 Jamaican owl (“Brown owl”) . . . . 5·50 7·00
MS872 47 × 62 mm. $50 Streamertail 4·75 6·50
For No. **MS**872 additionally inscribed for “Singapore ’95” see No. **MS**888.

1995. 25th Anniv of Caribbean Development Bank.
873 **280** 50c. green, black and yellow 10 10
874 $1 green, black and yellow 10 10
875 – $1.10 multicoloured . . . 10 10
876 – $50 multicoloured . . . . 2·75 5·00
DESIGNS—HORIZ: $1.10, Industry, agriculture and commerce; $50 Jamaican currency.

281 “Song of Freedom”

282 Queen Elizabeth the Queen Mother

1995. 50th Birth Anniv of Bob Marley (reggae singer). Record covers. Multicoloured.
877 50c. Type **281** 20 10
878 $1.10 “Fire” 30 15
879 $1.40 “Time will Tell” . . . 30 15
880 $3 “Natural Mystic” 40 45
881 $10 “Live at Lyceum” . . . 1·10 2·25
MS882 105 × 57 mm. $100 “Legend” . . . . 8·00 8·00

1995. 95th Birthday of Queen Elizabeth the Queen Mother. Sheet 81 × 95 mm.
MS883 **282** $75 multicoloured . . 4·50 5·50

283 Michael Manley

1995. Recipients of the Order of the Caribbean Community. Multicoloured.
884 50c. Type **283** 15 15
885 $1.10 Sir Alister McIntyre . . 20 15
886 $1.40 Justice P. Telford Georges 20 15
887 $50 Dame Nita Barrow . . . 4·75 7·00

1995. “Singapore ’95” International Stamp Exhibition. No. **MS**872 additionally inscr with exhibition emblem on sheet margin.
MS888 47 × 62 mm. $50 Streamertail 3·75 5·00

284 Dish Aerial and Landrover, Balkans

1995. 50th Anniv of United Nations. Multicoloured.
889 50c. Type **284** 30 20
890 $1.10 Antonov An-32 aircraft, Balkans 55 25
891 $3 Bedford articulated road tanker, Balkans 70 90
892 $5 Fairchild C-119 Flying Boxcar, Korea . . . . . . 80 1·40
MS893 100 × 70 mm. $50 U.N.T.A.G. vehicles, Namibia 2·25 3·50

285 Landing of Indian Immigrants

1996. 150th Anniv of Indian Immigration to Jamaica. Multicoloured.
894 $2.50 Type **285** 25 15
895 $10 Indian musicians and traditional dancers . . . . 75 1·25

286 Jamaican Flag and UNICEF Emblem

1996. 50th Anniv of UNICEF.
896 **286** $2.50 multicoloured . . . 50 15
897 $8 multicoloured . . . . 1·00 90
898 $10 multicoloured . . . . 1·00 1·00

287 Brown’s Hutia

1996. Endangered Species. Brown’s Hutia (“Jamaican Hutia”). Multicoloured.
899 $2.50 Type **287** 15 10
900 $10 Hutia on rock 50 65
901 $12.50 Female with young . . 60 1·00
902 $25 Head of hutia . . . . . 1·25 2·25

288 High Altar, Church of St. Thomas the Apostle

1997. 300th Anniv of Kingston Parish Church. Multicoloured.
903 $2 Type **288** 30 10
904 $8 Church of St. Thomas the Apostle 90 80
905 $12.50 “The Angel” (wood carving by Edna Manley) (vert) . . . . 1·40 1·75
MS906 106 × 76 mm. $60 St. Thomas the Apostle at sunset (42 × 56 mm) . . . . 3·50 4·50
No. 903 is inscribed “ALTER” in error.

289 Child’s Face and UNESCO Emblem

1998. 10th Anniv of Chernobyl Nuclear Disaster.
907 **289** $55 multicoloured . . . . 2·00 3·00

289a Map of Caribbean

1997. 50th Anniv of Caribbean Integration Movement and 18th CARICOM Heads of Government Conference. Multicoloured.
907a $2.50 Type **289a** . . . . . 4·00 3·75
907b $8 Coastal scenery . . . . 5·00 2·00
907c $10 As $8 . . . . 5·50 2·00

290 “Coelia triptera”

291 Diana, Princess of Wales

1997. Orchids. Multicoloured.
908A $1 Type **290** 10 10
909A $2 “Oncidium pulchellum” (horiz) 10 10
910A $2.50 “Oncidium triquetium” 10 10
911A $3 “Broughtonia negrilensis” 10 10
912A $4.50 “Oncidium gauntlettii” (horiz) . . . 10 10
913A $5 “Encyclia fragans” (horiz) 10 15
914A $8 “Broughtonia sanguinea” (horiz) . . . 15 20
915A $12 “Phaius tankervilleae” 20 25
916B $25 “Cochleanthes flabelliformis” (horiz) . . 40 45
917A $50 “Broughtonia sanguinea” (three varieties) (horiz) 85 90

1998. Diana, Princess of Wales Commemoration. Multicoloured.
918 $20 Type **291** . . . . 1·00 1·25
MS919 70 × 100 mm. $80 Princess Diana and Mother Teresa (42 × 55 mm) . . . . 4·50 5·50

292 University Chapel, Mona

1998. 50th Anniv of University of West Indies. Multicoloured.
920 $8 Type **292** 40 40
921 $10 Philip Sherlock Centre for Creative Arts, Mona 40 40
922 $50 University arms (vert) . . 2·25 3·50

293 Flags of Jamaica and CARICOM

1998. 25th Anniv of Caribbean Community.
923 **293** $30 multicoloured . . . . 1·75 2·25

294 Jamaican Footballer

295 Coral Reef

1998. World Cup Football Championship, France. Multicoloured.
924 $10 Type **294** 55 40
925 $25 Jamaican team (horiz) . . 1·25 1·25
926 $100 As $25 . . . . 4·50 6·50

1998. Christmas. International Year of the Ocean. Multicoloured.
927 $10 Type **295** 90 40
928 $30 Fishing boats, Negril . . 2·25 1·25
929 $50 Black spiny sea urchin 3·25 3·50
930 $100 Composite design as Nos. 927/9 (22 × 41 mm) 6·50 9·00

296 Michael Collins (astronaut)

1999. 30th Anniv of First Manned Landing on Moon. Multicoloured.
931 $7 Type **296** 40 25
932 $10 Service module docking with lunar module 50 40
933 $25 Buzz Aldrin on Moon’s surface . . . . 1·00 1·40
934 $30 Command module in Earth orbit . . . . 1·10 1·50
MS935 90 × 80 mm. $100 Earth as seen from Moon (circular, 40 mm diam) . . . . 3·50 4·75

297 Lesley Ann Masterton and Fong-Yee (polo)

1999. Jamaican Sporting Personalities. Mult.
936 $5 Type **297** 60 20
937 $10 Lawrence Rowe, Collie Smith and Alfred Valentine (cricket) . . . . 1·00 55
938 $20 Vivalyn Latty-Scott (women’s cricket) (vert) . . 1·40 1·25
939 $25 Lindy Delapenha (football) (vert) . . . . . 1·40 1·25
940 $30 Joy Grant-Charles (netball) (vert) . . . . . . 1·40 1·60
941 $50 Percy Hayles, Gerald Gray and Bunny Grant (boxing) . . . . 1·60 2·50
MS942 110 × 90 mm. $100 Lindy Delapenha and Joy Grant-Charles (56 × 42 mm) . . . . 4·00 6·00

298 “Spey” (mail ship), 1891

1999. 125th Anniv of Universal Postal Union. Multicoloured.
943 $7 Type **298** 85 25
944 $10 “Jamaica Planter” (mail ship), 1936 . . . . 1·00 45
945 $25 Lockheed Constellation (aircraft), 1950 . . . . . . 2·00 2·00
946 $30 Airbus A-310 (aircraft), 1999 . . . . 2·00 2·25

299 Airbus A-310

1999. 30th Anniv of Air Jamaica. Multicoloured.
947 $10 Type **299** 60 40
948 $25 A-320 . . . . 1·25 1·50
949 $30 A-340 . . . . 1·40 1·75

300 Shih Tzu

1999. Dogs. Multicoloured.
950 $7 Type **300** . . . . 1·00 50
951 $10 German shepherd . . . 1·25 50
952 $30 Doberman pinscher . . . 2·75 3·25

301 Nelson Mandela Park

1999. Parks and Gardens. Multicoloured.
953 $7 Type **301** 25 25
954 $10 St. William Grant Park 35 35
955 $25 Seaview Park . . . . . 95 1·10
956 $30 Holruth Park . . . . . 1·25 1·60

302 “The Prophet” (sculpture)

2000. Birth Centenary of Edna Manley (artist). Multicoloured.
957 $10 Type **302** 35 35
958 $25 “Horse of the Morning” 85 90
959 $30 “The Angel” . . . . . . 1·10 1·25
960 $100 Edna Manley . . . . . 3·75 6·50
MS961 128 × 159 mm. Nos. 957/60 5·50 8·00

303 Lennox Lewis

2000. Lennox Lewis, World Heavyweight Boxing Champion. Multicoloured.
962 $10 Holding W.B.C. Championship belt 30 45
963 $10 In ring with right arm raised 30 45
964 $10 Holding W.B.C. belt above head 30 45
965 $25 Taking punch on chin . . 75 1·00
966 $25 Type **303** . . . . 75 1·00
967 $25 In corner . . . . 75 1·00
968 $30 With W.B.C. belt after fight . . . . 95 1·10
969 $30 Holding all four belts . . 95 1·10
970 $30 With belts in front of skyscraper . . . . 95 1·10

304 Ferrari Racing Car 125 S, 1947

2000. Birth Centenary (1998) of Enzo Ferrari (car designer). Racing cars. Multicoloured.
971 $10 Type **304** 60 70
972 $10 375 F1, 1950 . . . . . . 60 70
973 $10 312 F1, 1966 . . . . . . 60 70
974 $25 DINO 166 P, 1965 . . . 1·10 1·50
975 $25 312 P, 1971 . . . . . . 1·10 1·50
976 $25 F1 90, 1990 . . . . . . 1·10 1·50

305 Queen Elizabeth the Queen Mother **307** Bull Thatch Palm

306 "The Runner", Jamaican Flag and Olympic Rings

2000. Queen Elizabeth the Queen Mother's 100th Birthday. Multicoloured, background colours given.
977 **305** $10 lavender 60 35
978 – $25 green . . . . 1·10 90
979 – $30 mauve . . . . 1·40 1·25
980 – $50 blue . . . . 2·25 2·75
DESIGNS: $25 to $50, Various recent photographs.

2000. Olympic Games, Sydney. Each showing "The Runner" (sculpture by Alvin Marriot), Jamaican flag and Olympic Rings. Multicoloured.
981 $10 Type **306** 60 35
982 $25 Head and shoulders . . . 1·10 80
983 $30 With flag at top (vert) . . 1·40 1·10
984 $50 With flag in centre (vert) 2·25 2·75

2000. Native Trees. Multicoloured.
985 $10 Type **307** 80 35
986 $25 Blue mahoe . . . . . . 1·75 1·00
987 $30 Silk cotton . . . . . . 2·00 1·50
988 $50 Yellow poui . . . . . . 3·00 3·75
MS989 112 × 70 mm. $100 Lignum Vitae (horiz) . . . . 6·50 7·50

308 "Madonna and Child" (Osmond Watson)

2000. Christmas. Jamaican Religious Paintings. Multicoloured.
990 $10 Type **308** 60 35
991 $20 "Boy in the Temple" (Carl Abrahams) (horiz) . . 1·10 75
992 $25 "Ascension" (Carl Abrahams) . . . . 1·25 90
993 $30 "Jah Lives" (Osmond Watson) . . . . 1·40 1·40

309 Children of the Commonwealth

2001. 25th Anniv of Commonwealth Day.
994 **309** $30 multicoloured . . . . 1·50 1·50

310 Andrew Mowatt (founder)

2001. Centenary of Jamaica Burial Scheme Society.
995 **310** $15 multicoloured . . . . 1·00 1·00

311 "Falmouth Market" (lithograph)

2001. Birth Bicentenary of Adolphe Duperly (pioneer photographer). Multicoloured.
996 $15 Type **311** 85 50
997 $40 "Ferry Inn, Spanish Town Road" (lithograph) 2·00 2·00
998 $45 "Coke Chapel, Kingston" (lithograph) . . 2·25 2·25
999 $60 "King Street, Kingston" (lithograph) . . . . . . 2·75 3·00
MS1000 103 × 170 mm. Nos. 996/9 7·00 7·50

312 Poinsettia in Church Window

2001. Christmas.
1001 **312** $15 multicoloured . . . 85 50
1002 $30 multicoloured . . . 1·75 1·25
1003 $40 multicoloured . . . 2·00 2·00

2002. Golden Jubilee. As T **219** of Falkland Islands.
1004 $15 agate, blue and gold . . 85 50
1005 $40 multicoloured . . . . . 2·00 2·00
1006 $45 black, blue and gold . . 2·25 2·25
1007 $60 multicoloured . . . . . 2·75 3·00
MS1008 162 × 95 mm. Nos. 1004/7 and $30 multicoloured . . . . 7·50 7·50
DESIGNS—HORIZ: $15 Princess Elizabeth in orchard, 1941; $40 Queen Elizabeth wearing pearls and striped dress; $45 Queen Elizabeth in evening dress, 1953; $60 Queen Elizabeth visiting Gloucester, 1995. VERT (38 × 51 mm): $30 Queen Elizabeth after Annigoni.
Designs as Nos. 1004/7 in No. **MS**1008 omit the gold frame around each stamp and the "Golden Jubilee 1952–2002" inscription.

313 Queen Elizabeth and Jamaican Royal Standard

2002. Royal Visit. Multicoloured.
1009 $15 Type **313** 75 50
1010 $45 Queen Elizabeth in evening dress and Jamaican coat of arms . . 2·25 2·50

314 Sir Philip Sherlock **315** Female Dancers

2002. Birth Centenary of Sir Philip Sherlock (historian).
1011 **314** $40 mauve, magenta and blue . . . . 1·50 1·60

2002. 40th Anniv of National Dance Theatre Company.
1012 **315** $15 multicoloured . . . 1·25 1·00

316 P.A.H.O. Centenary Logo

2002. Centenary of Pan American Health Organization.
1013 **316** $40 multicoloured . . . 2·00 1·75

317 "Masquerade" (Osmond Watson)

2002. Christmas. Local Works of Art. Multicoloured.
1014 $15 Type **317** 70 45
1015 $40 "John Canoe in Guanaboa Vale" (Gaston Tabois) (horiz) . . . . . 1·50 1·40
1016 $45 "Mother and Child" (carving by Kapo) . . . . 1·60 1·60
1017 $60 "Hills of Papine" (carving by Edna Manley) (horiz) . . . . 1·90 2·25

318 Dancers

2002. 40th Anniv of Independence. Multicoloured.
1018 $15 Type **318** 80 45
1019 $40 Independence Day celebrations . . . . . . 1·75 1·25
1020 $60 Welder and fish processing worker . . . . 2·25 2·50

319 Kingston in Early 1800s

2002. Bicentenary of Kingston. Multicoloured.
1021 $15 Type **319** 75 80
1022 $15 Wharf and statue of Queen Victoria, early 1900s 75 80
1023 $15 Horse-drawn cab, early 1900s, and modern street scene 75 80
Nos. 1021/3 were printed together, se-tenant, as horizontal strips of 3 throughout the sheet, forming a montage.

320 Queen Elizabeth II in St. Edward's Chair flanked by Bishops of Durham and Bath & Wells

2003. 50th Anniv of Coronation. Multicoloured.
1024 $15 Type **320** 75 40
1025 $45 Coronation Coach in procession . . . . 1·50 1·60
MS1026 95 × 115 mm. $50 As $45; $100 As Type **320** . . . . . . 5·00 6·00
Nos. 1024/5 have scarlet frame; stamps from **MS**1026 have no frame and country name in mauve panel.

321 "30" as Key

2003. 30th Anniv of CARICOM.
1027 **321** $40 multicoloured . . . 1·40 1·40

322 Jamaican Stripe-headed Tanager

2003. Bird Life International. (1st series). Jamaican Birds. Multicoloured.
1028 $15 Type **322** 75 50
1029 $40 Crested quail dove (horiz) . . . . 1·50 1·25
1030 $45 Jamaican tody (horiz) 1·60 1·25
1031 $60 Blue mountain vireo . . 2·00 2·50
MS1032 175 × 80 mm. $30 Jamaican blackbird nestlings (34 × 30 mm); $30 Searching for food in bromeliad (30 × 34 mm); $30 Singing from perch (30 × 34 mm); $30 Singing from perch (34 × 30 mm); $30 With insect in beak (34 × 30 mm) . . . . . . 5·50 6·00
See also Nos. 1040/9.

323 Sailing ships and Map of Kingston Harbour

2003. Maritime History. Multicoloured.
1033 $40 Type **323** . . . . 1·50 1·50
1034 $40 Passengers on cruise ship and sailing ships . . 1·50 1·50
1035 $40 *Sugar Refiner* (cargo ship) . . . . 1·50 1·50
Nos. 1033/5 were printed together, se-tenant, forming a composite design.

324 Baby Jesus

2003. Christmas. Multicoloured.

1036	$15 Type **324**	60	35
1037	$30 Close-up of Baby Jesus	1·10	60
1038	$60 Holy Family	1·90	2·00

325 Toussaint L'Ouverture

2004. Bicentenary of Haitian Revolution.

1039	**325** $40 multicoloured . . .	70	75

326 Yellow-billed Amazon

2004. Bird Life International (2nd series). Caribbean Endemic Birds Festival. Multicoloured.

1040	$10 Type **326**	15	20
1041	$10 Jamaican oriole	15	20
1042	$10 Orangequit	15	20
1043	$10 Yellow-shouldered grassquit	15	20
1044	$10 Jamaican woodpecker	15	20
1045	$10 Streamertail ("Red-billed Streamertail") . . .	15	20
1046	$10 Jamaican mango . . .	15	20
1047	$10 White-eyed thrush . . .	15	20
1048	$10 Jamaican lizard cuckoo	15	20
1049	$10 Arrow-headed warbler	15	20

327 Water Lilies

2004. World Environment Day. Sheet 195 × 85 mm containing T **327** and similar horiz designs. Multicoloured.

MS1050	$10 Type **327**; $10 Hawksbill turtle; $10 Tube sponge; $10 Man in canoe, Parottee pond; $40 Vase sponge and Star coral; $40 Sea fan and black and white crinoid; $40 Glassy sweeper; $40 Giant sea anemone	3·50	3·50

328 Hurdling

2004. Olympic Games, Athens. Multicoloured.

1051	$30 Type **328**	50	55
1052	$60 Running	1·00	1·10
1053	$70 Swimming	1·20	1·30
1054	$90 Badminton and shooting	1·50	1·60

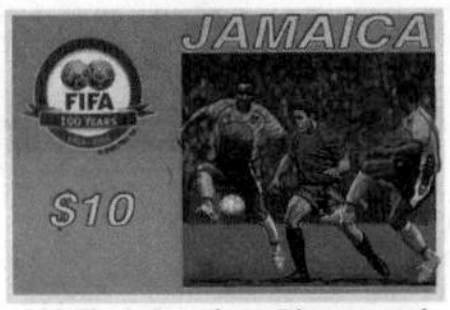

329 Two Jamaican Players and Opponent (blue strip)

2004. Centenary of FIFA (Federation Internationale de Football Association). Multicoloured.

1055	$10 Type **329**	15	20
1056	$30 Two Jamaican players and opponent (white top)	50	55
1057	$45 Two Jamaican players and opponent (blue top)	75	80
1058	$50 Two Jamaican players and opponent (white strip)	85	90

330 Ambassador John Pringle and Round Hill Hotel

2004. Centenary of the Jamaica Hotel Law. Multicoloured.

MS1059	152 × 114 mm. $40 Type **330** (bottom left panel in pink or blue, three of each) . .	1·40	1·50
MS1060	152 × 114 mm. $40 Abe Issa and Tower Isle Hotel; $40 John Issa and Tower Isle Hotel (both with bottom right panels in green, light green or carmine, two of each)	1·40	1·50
MS1061	152 × 114 mm. $40 Ralph Lauren and Doctors Cave Beach, Montego Bay (with left-hand panel in dark blue, blue or azure, two of each)	1·40	1·50

331 White Sorrel

2004. Christmas.

1062	**331** $10 multicoloured . . .	15	20
1063	– $20 multicoloured . . .	30	40
1064	– $50 multicoloured (horiz)	85	90
1065	– $60 multicoloured (horiz)	1·00	1·10

DESIGNS: $20 to $60 All showing white sorrel.

332 Mary Morris Knibb and Mizpah Moravian Church

2004. 250th Anniv of the Moravian Church in Jamaica. Multicoloured.

1066	90c. Type **332**	10	15
1067	$10 Reverend W. O'Meally and Mizpah Moravian Church	15	20
1068	$50 Bishop S. U. Hastings and Redeemer Moravian Church	85	90

OFFICIAL STAMPS

1890. Optd **OFFICIAL**.

O3	**8** ½d. green	10·00	1·00
O4	**11** 1d. red	5·00	1·25
O5	2d. grey	12·00	1·25

JAMMU AND KASHMIR — Pt. 1

A state in the extreme N. of India.

12 pies = 1 anna; 16 annas = 1 rupee.

1

Gum. The stamps of Jammu and Kashmir were issued without gum.

1866. Imperf.

41	**1** ½a. black	28·00	55·00
26	½a. red	35·00	55·00
44	½a. blue	45·00	£250
20	½a. green	£100	£250
48	½a. yellow	£140	
15	1a. black	£250	
27	1a. red	40·00	£170
34	1a. blue	30·00	£250
21	1a. green	£110	£250
24	1a. yellow	£850	
16	4a. black	£250	
8	4a. red	85·00	£120
19	4a. blue	£190	
37	4a. green	£130	
25	4a. yellow	£500	

Prices for the circular stamps (Nos. 5/48) are for cut-square examples. Cut-to-shape examples are worth from 10% to 20% of these prices, according to condition.

4

1867.

69a	**4** ½a. black	£140	£170
58	½a. blue	£180	95·00
60	½a. red	7·50	3·75
64	½a. orange	£110	£120
68	½a. green	£2000	£1100
69b	1a. black	£2000	£1600
55	1a. blue	£800	£375
61	1a. red	17·00	11·00
65	1a. orange	£2500	£1500
69	1a. green	£3000	£1800

The characters denoting the value are in the upper part of the inner circle and contains three ½a. and one 1a. values.

8 (¼a.)

12 (¼a.)

1867. Imperf.

90	**8** ¼a. black	3·50	4·00
91	½a. blue	4·00	1·50
93	1a. blue	£3750	£1500
94	1a. orange	12·00	10·00
97	2a. yellow	16·00	18·00
99	4a. green	42·00	42·00
101	8a. red	45·00	42·00

1878. Imperf or perf.

139	**12** ⅛a. yellow	1·25	1·75
125	¼a. red	3·25	4·00
131	¼a. orange	9·00	13·00
130a	¼a. blue	£800	£500
142	¼a. brown	1·10	75
105	½a. violet	16·00	14·00
126	½a. red	85	85
132	½a. orange	21·00	15·00
143	½a. blue	6·50	
127	1a. red	2·50	3·25
106	1a. mauve	25·00	26·00
133	1a. orange	21·00	12·00
148	1a. grey	85	85
150	1a. green	85	85
108	2a. violet	26·00	26·00
110	2a. blue	55·00	55·00
128	2a. red	3·25	4·50
134	2a. orange	16·00	12·00
152	2a. red on yellow	2·25	1·25
153	2a. red on green	3·25	3·50
129	4a. red	9·50	9·50
135	4a. orange	38·00	48·00
156	4a. green	3·75	3·50
130	8a. red	10·00	11·00
136	8a. orange	65·00	70·00
159	8a. blue	7·50	9·00
161a	8a. lilac	10·00	20·00

OFFICIAL STAMPS

1878. Imperf or perf.

O 6	**12** ¼a. black	1·25	1·50
O 7	½a. black	15	50
O 8	1a. black	20	80
O 9	2a. black	30	45
O10	4a. black	75	1·25
O11	8a. black	2·00	1·10

JAPAN — Pt. 18

An empire of E. Asia, consisting of numerous islands.

1871. 100 mon = 1 sen.
1872. 10 rin = 1 sen; 100 sen = 1 yen.

1 (48 mon)

1871. Imperf.

1	**1** 48m. brown	£180	£225
3	100m. blue	£200	£180
5	200m. red	£350	£225
15b	500m. green	£400	£400

1872. Perf.

17	**1** ½s. brown	80·00	£125
19	1s. blue	£170	£160
21	2s. red	£350	£275
22	5s. green	£375	£425

5

12

13 Bean Goose

1872. Various sizes. Design details differ.

34	**5** ½s. brown	18·00	24·00
66	½s. grey	16·00	15·00
35	1s. blue	70·00	28·00
67	1s. brown	30·00	13·00
36	2s. red	£110	30·00
74	2s. yellow	70·00	12·00
46	4s. red	£100	30·00
68	4s. green	£110	18·00
75	**12** 5s. green	£200	85·00
57	6s. brown	£110	40·00
69	6s. orange	75·00	15·00
58	**5** 10s. green	£110	45·00
70	10s. blue	£125	17·00
59	20s. violet	£200	70·00
71	20s. red	£100	12·00
60	30s. black	£250	70·00
72	30s. violet	£125	35·00

1875.

61	**13** 12s. red	£550	£225
62	– 15s. lilac (Pied Wagtail) . .	£450	£190
63	– 45s. red (Northern Goshawk)	£650	£300

20

21

22

23

24

1876.

116	**20** 5r. grey	3·50	30
77	1s. black	25·00	3·00
78	1s. brown	12·00	1·00
113	1s. green	5·50	25
79	2s. grey	50·00	2·00
102	2s. violet	24·00	1·50
114	2s. red	7·50	10
95	3s. orange	50·00	24·00
117	3s. red	12·00	25
82a	4s. blue	32·00	2·75
103	4s. green	40·00	1·75
118	4s. bistre	8·50	30
83	**21** 5s. brown	50·00	18·00
115	5s. blue	14·00	15
104	6s. orange	£150	70·00
105	8s. brown	45·00	2·75
119	8s. violet	15·00	90
86	10s. blue	40·00	1·50
120	10s. brown	16·00	30
87	12s. red	£200	£160
88	**22** 15s. green	£125	6·50
121	15s. violet	45·00	40
89	20s. blue	£150	12·00
122	20s. orange	55·00	1·40
123	**23** 25s. green	90·00	1·25
90	**22** 30s. mauve	£200	75·00
111	45s. red	£500	£500
112	50s. red	£160	10·00
124	50s. brown	85·00	3·00
125	**24** 1y. red	£120	2·50

25 Imperial Crest and Cranes

1894. Emperor's Silver Wedding.

126	**25**	2s. red	20·00	30
127		5s. blue	25·00	4·00

26 Prince Kitashirakawa — **27** Prince Arisugawa

1896. China War.

128	**26**	2s. red	14·00	75
129	**27**	2s. red	14·00	75
130	**26**	5s. blue	35·00	2·00
131	**27**	5s. blue	35·00	2·00

Both 2s. have an oval medallion, and both 5s. a circular one.

28 — **29** — **30**

31 — **32** Empress Jingu

1899.

132	**28**	5r. grey	5·50	1·00
133		½s. grey	3·50	10
134		1s. brown	4·50	10
135		1½s. blue	15·00	85
136		1½s. violet	8·00	15
137		2s. green	6·00	10
138		3s. purple	6·50	10
139		3s. red	6·00	10
140		4s. red	6·00	1·00
141		5s. yellow	14·00	10
142	**29**	6s. red	30·00	3·00
143		8s. olive	35·00	4·00
144		10s. blue	10·00	15
145		15s. violet	40·00	1·00
146		20s. orange	32·00	10
147	**30**	25s. green	70·00	75
148		50s. brown	65·00	80
149	**31**	1y. red	80·00	1·00
183	**32**	5y. green	£475	4·50
184		10y. violet	£650	6·50

33 Rice Cakes used at Japanese Weddings

1900. Prince Imperial Wedding.

152	**33**	3s. red	25·00	30

34 Symbols of Korea and Japan — **35** Gun and Japanese Flag

1905. Amalgamation of Japanese and Korean Postal Services.

153	**34**	3s. red	90·00	20·00

1906. Triumphal Military Review of Russo-Japanese War.

154	**35**	1½s. blue	40·00	3·50
155		3s. red	70·00	14·00

36 — **37** — **38**

1914.

167	**36**	½s. brown	2·25	10
168		1s. orange	3·25	10
232		1½s. blue	3·00	10
170		2s. green	5·50	10
298		3s. red	1·50	20
172	**37**	4s. red	16·00	1·50
300		5s. violet	7·50	10
174		6s. brown	24·00	4·00
302		7s. orange	12·00	15
175		8s. grey	18·00	15·00
176		10s. blue	12·00	10
236		13s. brown	10·00	10
178		20s. red	60·00	15
179		25s. olive	18·00	50
180	**38**	30s. brown	22·00	45
238		30s. orange and green	25·00	25
181		50s. brown	30·00	25
239		50s. brown and blue	15·00	30
309		1y. green and brown	80·00	75

40 Ceremonial Cap — **42** Hall of Ceremony

1915. Emperor's Coronation.

185	**40**	1½s. grey and red	3·00	50
186	–	3s. violet and brown	3·50	65
187	**42**	4s. red	16·00	7·50
188		10s. blue	38·00	15·00

DESIGN—As T **40**: 3s. Imperial throne.

43 Mandarin Duck — **44** "Kammuri" (ceremonial headband)

1916. Investiture of Prince Hirohito as Heir Apparent.

189	**43**	1½s. green, red and yellow	4·00	85
190		3s. red and yellow	5·00	1·00
191	**44**	10s. blue	£800	£300

45 Dove of Peace — **46** Dove of Peace

1919. Restoration of Peace.

192	**45**	1½s. brown	2·50	1·00
193	**46**	3s. green	3·50	1·25
194	**45**	4s. red	7·00	3·50
195	**46**	10s. blue	22·00	8·00

1919. Air. 1st Tokyo–Osaka Airmail Service. Optd with airplane.

196	**36**	1½s. blue	£275	£100
197		3s. red	£425	£250

48 7th-century Censor — **49** Meiji Shrine

1920. First Census.

198	**48**	1½s. purple	8·00	4·25
199		3s. red	9·00	4·25

1920. Dedication of Meiji (Emperor Mutsuhito) Shrine.

200	**49**	1½s. violet	3·00	1·50
201		3s. red	3·00	1·50

50 Postal and National Flags — **51** Dept. of Communications, Tokyo

1921. 50th Anniv of Japanese Post.

202	**50**	1½s. red and green	3·00	1·50
203	**51**	3s. brown	3·50	1·75
204	**50**	4s. red and pink	50·00	25·00
205	**51**	10s. blue	£250	90·00

52 Warships "Katori" and "Kashima" — **53** Mt. Fuji and Sika Deer

1921. Return of Crown Prince from European Tour.

206	**52**	1½s. violet	3·00	2·10
207		3s. olive	3·50	2·25
208		4s. red	42·00	35·00
209		10s. blue	60·00	35·00

1922.

293	**53**	4s. green	3·25	20
266		4s. orange	12·00	30
211		8s. red	20·00	8·00
267		8s. green	20·00	15
303		8s. bistre	14·00	75
305		20s. blue	16·00	60
268		20s. purple	65·00	30

54 Mt. Niitaka — **55**

56 — **58** Empress Jingu

1923. Crown Prince's visit to Taiwan.

213	**54**	1½s. yellow	20·00	18·00
214		3s. violet	25·00	8·00

1923. Imperf.

215	**55**	½s. grey	3·00	2·75
216		1½s. blue	5·00	60
217		2s. brown	5·00	60
218		3s. red	2·50	50
219		4s. green	30·00	15·00
220		5s. violet	14·00	60
221		8s. red	45·00	35·00
222	**56**	10s. brown	24·00	50
223		20s. blue	30·00	1·00

1924.

224	**58**	5y. green	£225	3·50
225		10y. violet	£425	2·75

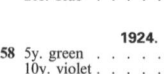

59 Cranes — **60** Phoenix

1925. Imperial Silver Wedding.

226	**59**	1½s. purple	2·25	1·40
227a	**60**	3s. brown and silver	3·00	3·00
228	**59**	8s. red	25·00	15·00
229b	**60**	20s. green and silver	65·00	50·00

61a Yomei Gate, Tosho Shrine, Nikko

1926.

241	–	2s. green	2·40	10
242	**61a**	6s. red	12·00	25
243	–	10s. blue	10·00	10
304	–	10s. red	10·00	15

DESIGNS: 2s. Mt. Fuji; 10s. Nagoya Castle.

62 Baron Maeshima — **63** Globe

1927. 50th Anniv of Membership of U.P.U.

244	**62**	1½s. purple	2·75	1·75
245		3s. olive	2·75	1·75
246	**63**	6s. red	85·00	60·00
247		10s. blue	95·00	50·00

64 Phoenix — **65** Ceremonial Shrines

1928. Emperor's Enthronement.

248	**64**	1½s. green on yellow	1·00	50
249	**65**	3s. purple on yellow	1·00	50
250	**64**	6s. red on yellow	3·75	3·00
251	**65**	10s. blue on yellow	5·00	3·75

66 Shrine of Ise — **67** Nakajima-built Fokker F.VIIb/3m over Lake Ashi, Hakone

1929. 58th Vicennial Removal of Shrine of Ise.

255	**66**	1½s. violet	2·00	1·50
256		3s. red	2·75	1·50

1929. Air.

257	**67**	8½s. brown	50·00	40·00
258		9½s. red	15·00	12·00
259		16½s. green	15·00	14·00
260		18s. blue	16·00	8·00
261		33s. black	35·00	5·00

68 Map of Japan — **69** Meiji Shrine

1930. 3rd Census.

262	**68**	1½s. purple	2·75	1·25
263		3s. red	3·00	1·25

Although Type **68** is inscr "Second Census", this was actually the third census.

1930. 10th Anniv of Meiji Shrine Dedication.

264	**69**	1½s. green	2·00	1·50
265		3s. orange	2·75	1·50

1934. Air. Establishment of Communications Commemoration Day. Sheet containing Nos. 258/61.

MS271	**67**	110 × 100 mm	£1100	£1100

70 Insignia of Red Cross Society

1934. 15th Int Red Cross Conference, Tokyo.

272	**70**	1½s. green	2·50	1·40
273	–	3s. violet	2·75	1·90
274	**70**	6s. red	10·00	7·00
275	–	10s. blue	14·00	10·00

DESIGN—HORIZ: 3s.; 10s. Red Cross Society Buildings, Tokyo.

72 Cruiser "Hiyei" and Pagoda, Liaoyang — **73** Akasaka Palace, Tokyo

1935. Visit of Emperor of Manchukuo.

276	**72**	1½s. green	2·50	1·60
277	**73**	3s. brown	2·00	1·00
278	**72**	6s. red	14·00	7·50
279	**73**	10s. blue	10·00	7·00

74 Mt. Fuji (after Kazan Watanabe) — **75c** Mt. Fuji from Mishima

1935. New Year's Greetings.

280	**74**	1½s. red	15·00	10

1936. Fuji-Hakone National Park.

281	–	1½s. brown	5·00	4·00
282	–	3s. green	7·00	6·00
283	–	6s. red	16·00	14·00
284	**75c**	10s. blue	22·00	15·00

DESIGNS: Mt. Fuji (1½s.); from Lake Ashi (3s.); from Lake Kawaguchi (6s.).

76 Dove of Peace

77 Shinto Shrine Port Arthur

1936. 30 Years of Occupation of Kwantung.

285	**76**	1½s. violet	12·00	12·00
286	**77**	3s. brown	15·00	16·00
287	–	10s. green	£180	£225

DESIGN—HORIZ: 10s. Govt. House, Kwantung.

78 Imperial Diet

80 Wedded Rocks, Futami Bay

1936. Inauguration of New Houses of the Imperial Diet, Tokyo.

288	**78**	1½s. green	1·50	1·25
289	–	3s. purple	1·50	1·50
290	–	6s. red	5·50	5·00
291	**78**	10s. blue	12·00	4·50

DESIGN: 3, 6s. Grand Staircase.

1936. New Year's Greetings.

292	**80**	1½s. red	6·00	10

82 Goshuinsen (16th-cent trading ship)

83 General Nogi

84 Lake Taisho, Kamikochi

85 Mitsubishi B5N1 and Map

86 Kamatari Fujiwara

87 Plum Tree

1937. Imperf or perf (424), perf (others). Without gum (424), with or without gum (392, 394, 396), with gum (others).

313	**82**	½s. violet	1·50	80
314	–	1s. brown	2·00	50
392b	**83**	2s. red	15	10
316	–	3s. green	75	10
394	**83**	3s. brown	75	20
317	–	4s. green	1·00	10
318	**84**	5s. blue	2·00	10
396	–	5s. purple	30	10
319	–	6s. orange	4·00	2·00
320	–	7s. green	75	20
398	–	7s. red	25	15
321	–	8s. violet	1·00	50
322	–	10s. red	6·00	10
323	**85**	12s. blue	60	60
324	–	14s. red and brown	1·00	30
325	–	20s. blue	1·00	10
326	–	25s. light brown and brown	80	10
327	–	30s. blue	3·00	10
328	–	50s. green and bistre	2·00	10
329	–	1y. light brown and brown	6·00	75
424	**86**	5y. green	5·50	60
331	**87**	10y. purple	20·00	1·50

DESIGNS: 1s. Rice harvesting; 3s. Hydro-electric Power Station; 4, 5s. (No. 396), 7s. (No. 398), Admiral Togo; 6s. Garambi Lighthouse, Taiwan; 7s. (No. 320), Diamond Mountains, Korea; 8s. Meiji Shrine; 10s. Yomei Gate, Tosho Shrine, Nikko; 14s. Inner Gate, Kasuga Shrine; 20s. Mt. Fuji and cherry blossom; 25s. Horyu Temple; 30s. Torii, Itsukushima Shrine at Miyajima; 50s. Temple of Golden Pavilion, Kyoto; 1y. Great Buddha, Kamakura.

88 Nakajima-built Douglas DC-2 Airliner

89 New Year's Emblem

1937. Aerodrome Fund.

336	**88**	2s.+2s. red	2·25	1·25
337		3s.+2s. violet	2·25	1·50
338		4s.+2s. green	3·25	1·25

1937. New Year's Greetings.

339	**89**	2s. red	12·00	10

90 Nantai Volcano

92 Shinkyo Bridge

91 Kegon Falls

93 Hiuchi Volcano

1938. Nikko National Park.

340	**90**	2s. orange	75	55
341	**91**	4s. green	75	55
342	**92**	10s. red	7·00	4·00
343	**93**	20s. blue	8·00	5·00
MS344		128×182 mm. Nos. 340/3 (sold at 50s.)	50·00	60·00

94 Daisen Volcano and Meadow

95 Yashima Plateau and Estuary

96 Abuto Kwannon Shrine

97 Tomo Bay

1939. Daisen and Setonaikai National Parks.

345	**94**	2s. brown	50	60
346	**95**	4s. green	2·25	2·00
347	**96**	10s. red	8·00	7·00
348	**97**	20s. blue	8·00	6·00
MS349		127×180 mm. Nos. 345/8 (sold at 50s.)	26·00	40·00

98 Mt. Kuju and Village

99 Naka Volcano

100 Naka Crater

101 Volcanic Cones of Mt. Aso

1939. Aso National Park.

350	**98**	2s. brown	60	70
351	**99**	4s. green	3·25	3·25
352	**100**	10s. red	26·00	18·00
353	**101**	20s. blue	30·00	20·00
MS354		127×181 mm. Nos. 350/3 (sold at 50s.)	85·00	£120

102 Globe

1939. 75th Anniv of Membership of International Red Cross Union.

355	**102**	2s. brown	2·00	1·25
356	–	4s. green	2·25	1·40
357	**102**	10s. red	12·00	8·50
358	–	20s. blue	14·00	8·50

DESIGN: 4s., 20s. Count Tsunetami Sano.

104 Golden Bird

105 Mt. Takachiho

106 Sake Jar and Ayu

107 Kashiwara Shrine

1940. 2600th Anniv of Japanese Empire.

359	**104**	2s. orange	90	85
360	**105**	4s. green	45	40
361	**106**	10s. red	4·00	4·25
362	**107**	20s. blue	1·00	75

108 Mt. Hokuchin

109 Mt. Asahi

110 Sounkyo Gorge, Kobako

111 Tokachi Range

1940. Daisetsu-zan National Park.

363	**108**	2s. brown	60	60
364	**109**	4s. green	2·50	2·50
365	**110**	10s. red	8·50	6·50
366	**111**	20s. blue	11·00	5·00
MS367		127×181 mm. Nos. 363/6 (sold at 50s.)	£180	£225

112 Mt. Shimmoe

113 Takachiho Peak

114 Kirishima Shrine

115 Lake Roku-Kwannon

1940. Kirishima National Park, Kyushu.

368	**112**	2s. brown	60	60
369	**113**	4s. green	1·00	1·00
370	**114**	10s. red	7·50	5·00
371	**115**	20s. blue	10·00	5·00
MS372		127×181 mm. Nos. 368/71 (sold at 50s.)	£200	£275

116 Ceremonial Shrine (after Y. Araka)

117 "Loyalty and Filial Piety"

1940. 50th Anniv of Promulgation of Imperial Rescript on Education.

373	**116**	2s. violet	85	1·00
374	**117**	4s. green	1·25	1·40

118 Mt. Daiton

119 Central Peak, Mt. Niitaka

120 Buddhist Temple, Mt. Kwannon

121 View of Mt. Niitaka

1941. Daiton and Niitaka-Arisan National Parks.

375	**118**	2s. brown	80	60
376	**119**	4s. green	1·25	1·00
377	**120**	10s. red	5·00	3·00
378	**121**	20s. blue	6·00	2·75
MS379		128×182 mm. Nos. 375/8 (sold at 90s. together with No. **MS**384)	70·00	50·00

122 Seisui Precipice, East Taiwan Coast

124 Taroko Gorge, Taiwan

123 Mt. Tsugitaka

125 Mt. Taroko, Source of R. Takkiri

1941. Tsugitaka and Taroko National Parks.
380 **122** 2s. brown 75 60
381 **123** 4s. green . . . . 1·25 1·00
382 **124** 10s. red . . . . 4·00 4·25
383 **125** 20s. blue . . . . 5·50 4·00
MS384 128 × 182 mm. Nos. 380/3 (sold at 90s. together with No. **MS**379) . . . . 75·00 65·00

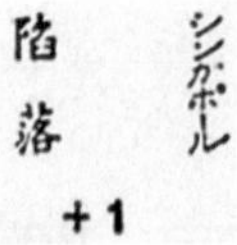

(126)

1942. Surrender of Singapore. Surch as T **126**.
385 **83** 2s.+1s. red . . . . 1·00 1·25
386 – 4s.+2s. green (No. 317) . . 1·00 1·25

127 Kenkoku Shrine

129 Orchids and Crest of Manchukuo

1942. 10th Anniv of Establishment of Manchukuo.
387 **127** 2s. brown 40 50
388 – 5s. olive 60 90
389 **127** 10s. red . . . . 85 1·25
390 **129** 20s. blue . . . . 3·00 2·75
DESIGN—VERT: 5s. Boys of Japan and Manchukuo.

130 Girl War-worker

135 "The Enemy will Surrender"

140 Garambi Lighthouse, Taiwan

141 Garambi Lighthouse, Taiwan

1942. Imperf (418/19, 421), imperf or perf (400, 420), perf (others). With or without gum (398, 420), without gum (400, 418/19, 421), with gum (others).
391 **130** 1s. brown 10 10
393 – 2s. green 80 45
395 – 4s. green 20 10
397 – 6s. blue 60 60
399 – 10s. red and pink 85 10
400 **135** 10s. grey . . . . 7·50 8·00
418 10s. blue . . . . 25·00
419 – 10s. orange 30 10
401 – 15s. blue . . . . 2·00 50
402 – 17s. violet 60 25
420 – 20s. blue 30 10
404 – 27s. red 65 80
405 – 30s. green . . . . 3·00 1·00
421 – 30s. blue . . . . 2·00 40
406 **140** 40s. purple 90 10
407 **141** 40s. purple . . . . 2·00 1·00

DESIGNS: 2s. Shipbuilding; 4s. Hyuga Monument and Mt. Fuji; 6s. War-worker; 10s. (No. 399) Palms and map of Greater East Asia; 10s. (No. 419); 20s. Mt. Fuji; 15s. Airman; 17s., 27s. Yasukuni Shrine; 30s. (2) Myajima Shrine.

142 Class C59 Steam Locomotive No. 28

143 Tanks in action at Bataan

1942. 70th Anniv of First National Railway.
408 **142** 5s. green . . . . 4·00 6·00

1942. 1st Anniv of Declaration of War.
409 **143** 2s.+1s. brown . . . . . 2·00 2·75
410 – 5s.+2s. blue . . . . . . 2·50 3·25
DESIGN: 5s. Attack on Pearl Harbor.

144 Yasukuni Shrine

145 Kwantung Shrine and Map of Kwantung Peninsula

1944. 75th Anniv of Yasukuni Shrine.
411 **144** 7s. green . . . . 85 1·00

1944. Dedication of Kwantung Shrine.
412 **145** 3s. brown . . . . 3·00 10·00
413 7s. grey . . . . 3·00 10·00

146 Sun and Cherry Blossom

149 Torii of Yasukuni Shrine

1945. Imperf or perf and with or without gum (422), imperf without gum (others).
415 **146** 3s. red 35 40
416 – 5s. green 40 20
422 – 50s. brown 60 10
423 **149** 1y. olive . . . . 1·50 85
DESIGNS: 5s. Sunrise and Kawasaki Ki-61 Hien fighter; 50s. Coal miners.

150 Pagoda of Horyu Temple, Nara

153 Kiyomizu Temple, Kyoto

154 Noh Mask

1946. Imperf or perf (30s., 50, 100y.), imperf (others). With or without gum (30s., 5, 50, 100y.), without gum (others).
426 – 15s. green 45 45
427 **150** 30s. violet 75 10
428a – 1y. blue . . . . 1·00 10
429 – 1y.30 bistre . . . . . . 5·00 1·60
430 – 1y.50 grey . . . . 3·00 50
431 **153** 2y. red . . . . 2·50 10
432 – 5y. mauve . . . . 7·50 25
433b **154** 50y. brown . . . . . . 80·00 30
434a – 100y. purple . . . . . . 80·00 40
DESIGNS: 15s. Baron H. Maeshima; 1y. Mt. Fuji, after Hokusai; 1y.30, Snow and white-fronted geese (after Hokusai); 1y.50, Kintai Bridge, Iwakuni; 5y. Veil-tailed goldfish; 100y. Plum tree.
For 30s., 1y.20, 4y. and 10y. as Nos. 427, 429 and 434a but with Japanese characters reading in reverse order, see Nos. 441, 445/6 and 449.

156 Mediaeval Postman's Bell

157 Baron Maeshima

1946. 75th Anniv of Government Postal Service.
436 **156** 15s. orange . . . . 4·00 3·00
437 **157** 30s. green . . . . 6·00 5·00
438 – 50s. red . . . . 3·25 2·50
439 – 1y. blue . . . . 4·75 4·75
MS440 183 × 125 mm. Nos. 436/9 (sold at 3y.). Imperf. No gum. £100 £120
DESIGNS—As Type **156**: 50s. First Japanese Postage Stamp; 1y. Symbols of communication.

160

161 Baron Maeshima

163 National Art

1947. As issues of 1946 but with Japanese characters in reverse order and new designs. Imperf without gum (449), perf with gum (others).
441 **150** 30s. violet . . . . 3·00 2·00
442 **160** 35s. green 75 30
443 – 45s. mauve 85 50
444 **161** 1y. brown . . . . 3·25 40
445 **150** 1y.20 green . . . . 2·00 30
446 – 4y. blue (as No. 429) . . 7·25 35
447 – 5y. blue . . . . 8·00 10
448 **163** 10y. violet . . . . 14·00 10
449 – 10y. purple (as No. 434a) 28·00 70
DESIGNS—VERT: 45s. Numeral; 5y. Whaling.
For similar designs, but without the chrysanthemum emblem, see Nos. 467/70.

164 Mother and Child

165 Roses and Wisteria

1947. Inauguration of New Constitution.
451 **164** 50s. red 60 40
452 **165** 1y. blue 70 40
MS453 128 × 180 mm. Nos. 451/2 (sold at 3y.). Imperf. No gum 8·50 9·00

1947. "Know Your Stamps" Exhibition, Tokyo, 1947. May Sheet containing No. 445 in block of fifteen.
MS454 237 × 76 mm (sold at 18y.) 25·00 25·00

166 National Products

167 Lily of the Valley

1947. Re-opening of Private Foreign Trade.
455 **166** 1y.20 brown . . . . . . 3·00 1·25
456 4y. blue . . . . 5·00 1·50

1947. "Know Your Stamps" Exhibition, Kyoto, August 1947. Sheet containing No. 431 in block of five. Imperf. No gum.
MS457 115 × 69 mm (sold at 10y.) 25·00 25·00

1947. Relief of Ex-convicts Day.
458 **167** 2y. green . . . . 4·00 1·75

1947. 75th Anniv of Japanese Railway Service. Imperf. No gum.
MS459 115 × 72 mm. **168** 4y. blue (sold at 5y.) . . . . 18·00 15·00

169 Hurdling

170

1947. 2nd National Athletic Meeting. Kanazawa. Each mauve.
460 1y.20 Type **169** . . . . . . 10·00 6·00
461 1y.20 Diving . . . . 10·00 6·00
462 1y.20 Throwing the discus . . 10·00 6·00
463 1y.20 Volleyball . . . . . . 10·00 6·00

1947. Philatelic Week. Sheet containing No. 428a in strip of five. No gum.
MS464 114 × 71 mm . . . . . . 4·00 5·00

1947. Community Chest.
465 **170** 1y.20+80s. red 75 85

1947. Philatelic Exhibition, Sapporo, November 1947. Sheet containing No. 422 in block of five. Imperf. No gum.
MS466 114 × 71 mm. (sold at 2y.50) 12·00 15·00

172 Kiyomizu Temple, Kyoto

173 National Art

1948. Designs without chrysanthemum.
467 – 1y.50 blue . . . . 2·50 50
468 **172** 2y. red . . . . 8·00 10
469 – 3y.80 brown . . . . . . 8·00 6·50
470 **173** 10y. violet . . . . 12·00 10
DESIGNS: 1y.50, 3y.80, Numeral types.

1948. Philatelic Exhibition, Osaka. Sheet containing No. 432 twice with two Japanese characters in centre below stamps. Imperf. No gum.
MS472 114 × 71 mm . . . . . . 14·00 16·00

1948. Philatelic Exhibition, Nagoya. Sheet as last but three Japanese characters in centre below stamps.
MS473 114 × 71 mm . . . . . . 16·00 18·00

174 Stylized Tree

176 Boy and Girl reading

1948. Encouragement of Afforestation.
474 **174** 1y.20 green 80 60

1948. Philatelic Exhibition, Mishima, April, 1948. Sheet No. **MS**473 optd at top, bottom and sides with Japanese characters and flowers in green.
MS475 114 × 71 mm . . . . . . 65·00 40·00

1948. Death Centenary of Hokusai Katsushika (painter). Sheet No. **MS**464 optd at top and bottom with Japanese characters in purple.
MS476 114 × 71 mm . . . . . . 20·00 20·00

175 Sampans, Seto Inland Sea

1948. Sheets Commemorating Various Exhibitions. Each sheet contains two stamps as T **175** (2y. red), with coloured borders and inscriptions. Imperf. No gum. (a) Communications Exhibition, Tokyo, April 27 to May 4 1948
MS477 113 × 71 mm. Green border 12·00 6·00
(b) Newspaper and Postage Stamp Exhibition, Aomori City
MS478 113 × 71 mm. Blue border 14·00 10·00
(c) Communications Exhibition, Fukushima
MS479 113 × 71 mm. Turquoise 14·00 10·00

1948. Re-organization of Educational System.
480 **176** 1y.20 red 65 65

177 Horse Race

178 Swimmer

1948. 25th Anniv of Japanese Horse Racing Laws.
481 **177** 5y. brown . . . . 2·25 85

1948. 3rd National Athletic Meeting, Yawata.
482 **178** 5y. blue . . . . 3·00 1·25

179 Distillery Towers

1948. 10th Anniv of Govt. Alcohol Monopoly.
483 **179** 5y. brown . . . . 3·75 2·25

1948. Philatelic Exhibition, Kumamoto. Sheet containing two copies of Nos. 467 and 469. Imperf. Nogum. Imperf. No gum.
MS484 114 × 71 mm . . . . . . 30·00 35·00

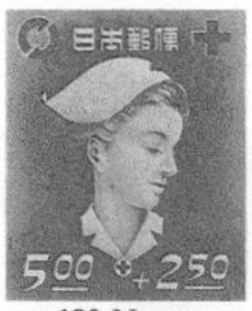

180 Nurse

181 Varied Tit Feeding Young

1948. Red Cross and Community Chest.
485 **180** 5y.+2y.50 red . . . . 8·00 5·00
486 **181** 5y.+2y.50 green . . . . . 17·00 15·00
MS487 128 × 90 mm. T **181** (both 5y.+5y.). Imperf. No gum . . . 50·00 50·00

182 Farm Girl **183** Harpooning **184** Miner

185 Girl plucking Tea **186** Girl Printer **187** Mill Girl

188 Mt. Hodaka

189 Tree Planting

190 Postman

191 Blast-Furnace

192 Constructing Class C62 Steam Locomotive

1948.
488 **182** 2y. green and light green 2·00 10
489 **183** 3y. turquoise . . . . . . 5·00 10
490 **184** 5y. bistre . . . . 16·00 10
491 **185** 5y. green . . . . 40·00 7·00
492 **186** 6y. orange . . . . 7·00 10
493 **184** 8y. brown . . . . 8·00 10
494 **187** 15y. blue . . . . 3·00 10
495 **188** 16y. blue . . . . 8·00 5·00
496 **189** 20y. green . . . . 32·00 10
497 **190** 30y. blue . . . . 36·00 10
506 **191** 100y. red £400 40
507 **192** 500y. blue . . . . £375 2·50

1948. Philatelic Exhibition, Nagano. Sheet comprising No. 494. Imperf. No gum.
MS508 114 × 71 mm . . . . . . 40·00 40·00

193 Baseball

1948. 3rd National Athletic Meeting, Fukuoke.
509 **193** 5y. green . . . . 12·00 5·00
510 – 5y. green (bicycle race) . . 12·00 5·00
511 – 5y. green (sprinter) . . . 12·00 5·00
512 – 5y. green (high jumper) 12·00 5·00

1948. Commemorating the Shikoku Travelling Philatelic Exhibition, November 1948. Sheet containing two copies of No. 490. Imperf. No gum.
MS513 115 × 72 mm . . . . . . 45·00 45·00

194 "Beauty Looking Back" (Moronobu Hishikawa)

195 Girl playing with Shuttlecock

1948. Philatelic Week.
514 **194** 5y. brown . . . . 60·00 40·00

1948. Postal Service Exhibition, Kanazawa and Takaoka. Sheet containing No. 514. Imperf. No gum.
MS515 71 × 115 mm. . . . . . . 40·00 30·00

1948. New Year's Greetings.
516 **195** 2y. red . . . . 3·75 2·25

196 Skater

197 Ski Jumper

1949. 4th National Athletic Meeting. (a) Suwa City.
517 **196** 5y. violet . . . . 3·50 2·00
(b) Sapporo, Hokkaido.
518 **197** 5y. blue . . . . 4·00 2·00

198 "Koan Maru" (ferry) in Beppu Harbour

199 Exhibition Grounds

1949.
519 **198** 2y. blue and red . . . . 2·00 1·25
520 5y. blue and green . . . . 5·50 1·50

1949. Foreign Trade Fair, Yokohama. Perf or imperf.
521 **199** 5y. red . . . . 2·50 1·00

200 Seto Inland Sea

201 Stylized Trees

1949. Matsuyama, Okayama and Takamatsu Exhibitions.
522 **200** 10y. red (Matsuyama) . . 30·00 15·00
523 10y. pink (Okayama) . . 35·00 20·00
524 10y. claret (Takamatsu) 50·00 25·00

1949. Encouragement of Afforestation.
525 **201** 5y. green . . . . 5·00 2·00

202 Shishi-Iwa (Lion Rock)

203 Mt. Omine

204 Doro-Hatcho River Pool

205 Hashikui-Iwa

1949. Yoshino-Kumano National Park.
526 **202** 2y. brown . . . . 1·00 60
527 **203** 5y. green . . . . 3·25 1·00
528 **204** 10y. red . . . . 14·00 8·00
529 **205** 16y. blue . . . . 7·50 2·25

MS530 126 × 182 mm. Nos. 526/9. No gum. (sold at 40y.) . . . . 22·00 22·00

206 Boy

1949. Children's Day.
531 **206** 5y. purple and buff . . . 5·00 1·50

1949. Children's Exhibition, Inuyama. Sheet containing No. 531 in block of ten. Imperf.
MS532 143 × 90 mm. £300 £300

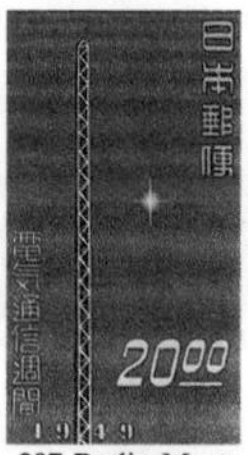

207 Radio Mast

1949. Electrical Communications Week. Sheet containing T **207**.
MS533 71 × 108 mm. 20y. blue £100 90·00

208 Observatory Tower

209 Radio Mast, Pigeon and Globe

1949. 75th Anniv of Central Meteorological Observatory, Tokyo.
534 **208** 8y. green . . . . 3·50 1·40

1949. Establishment of Joint Ministries of Postal and Electrical Communications.
535 **209** 8y. blue . . . . 3·50 1·25

210 Park in Autumn

211 Park in Spring

212 Park in Summer

213 Park in Winter

1949. Fuji-Hakone National Park.
536 **210** 2y. brown . . . . 2·50 60
537 **211** 8y. green . . . . 3·00 1·00
538 **212** 14y. red . . . . 1·75 30
539 **213** 24y. blue . . . . 3·25 40
MS540 127 × 180 mm. Nos. 536/9 (sold at 55y.) . . . . 30·00 20·00

214 Woman holding Rose

1949. Establishment of Memorial City at Hiroshima.
541 **214** 8y. brown . . . . 6·00 2·00

215 Doves

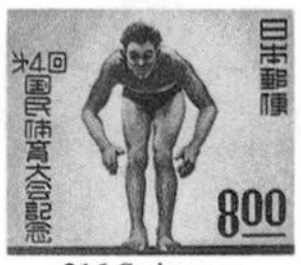

216 Swimmer

1949. Establishment of International Cultural City at Nagasaki.
542 **215** 8y. green . . . . 5·00 2·00

1949. 4th National Athletic Meeting, Yokohama.
543 **216** 8y. blue . . . . 4·00 1·25

217 Boy Scout

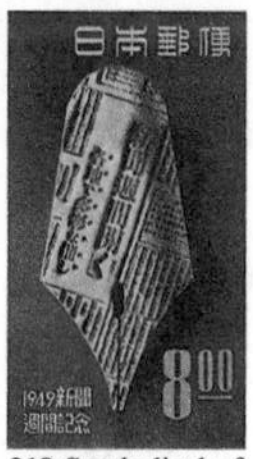

218 Symbolical of Writing and Printing

1949. 1st National Scout Jamboree, Tokyo.
544 **217** 8y. brown . . . . 7·50 2·00

1949. Press Week.
545 **218** 8y. blue . . . . 4·50 2·00

219 Map of Japan and Letters

220 Globe and Forms of Transport

1949. 75th Anniv of U.P.U.
546 **219** 2y. green . . . . 2·75 1·50
547 **220** 8y. red . . . . 4·75 1·60
548 **219** 14y. red . . . . 9·50 4·00
549 **220** 24y. blue . . . . 17·00 9·25
MS550 115 × 70 mm. Nos. 546/7. Imperf. No gum . . . . 4·50 5·50

221 Throwing the Javelin

222 Telescope

1949. 4th National Athletic Meeting, Tokyo. Each brown.
551 8y. Type **221** . . . . 4·00 1·50
552 8y. Dinghy sailing . . . . . 4·00 1·50
553 8y. Relay racing . . . . . . 4·00 1·50
554 8y. Tennis . . . . 4·00 1·50

1949. 50th Anniv of Establishment of Latitude Observatory, Mizusawa.
555 **222** 8y. green . . . . 3·50 2·00

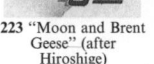

223 "Moon and Brent Geese" (after Hiroshige)

224 Dr. H. Noguchi

A B C D

E F G H I

J K L M N

O P Q R

1949. Postal Week.

556	**223**	8y. violet	£150	65·00

1949. Various portraits as illustrated, in frame as T **224**.

557	A	8y. green	10·00	1·00
558	B	8y. green	4·00	1·00
559	C	8y. green	4·00	1·00
560	D	8y. green	3·50	1·00
561	E	8y. violet	10·00	4·00
562	F	8y. purple	3·50	1·00
563	G	8y. green	8·00	2·00
564	H	8y. violet	8·00	2·00
565	I	8y. red	16·00	2·00
566	J	8y. red	30·00	2·50
567	K	8y. brown	15·00	2·25
568	L	8y. blue	9·00	2·25
569	M	10y. green	60·00	4·50
570	N	10y. purple	9·00	1·50
571	O	10y. red	4·00	1·40
572	P	10y. grey	7·00	1·40
573	Q	10y. brown	6·00	1·40
574	R	10y. blue	6·00	1·40

PORTRAITS: A, Hideyo Noguchi (bacteriologist); B, Y. Fukuzawa (educationist); C, Soseki Natsume (novelist); D, Shoyo Tsubouchi (dramatist); E, Danjuro Ichikawa (actor); F, Jo Niijima (religious leader); G, Hogai Kano (painter); H, Kanzo Uchimura (religious leader); I, Mme. Higuchi (author); J, Ogai Mori (doctor); K, S. Masaoka (poet); L, S. Hishida (painter); M, A. Nishi (scholar); N, K. Ume (lawyer); O, H. Kimura (astrophysicist); P, I. Nitobe (statesman); Q, T. Torada (physicist); R, Tenshin Okakura (writer).

225 Green Pheasant and Pampas Grass

1950. Air.

575	**225**	16y. grey	40·00	20·00
576		34y. purple	80·00	25·00
577		59y. red	£120	20·00
578		103y. orange	90·00	35·00
579		144y. olive	90·00	35·00

226 Tiger (after Maruyama Okyo)

1950. New Year's Greetings.

580	**226**	2y. red	8·00	1·00

227 Microphones of 1925 and 1950

228 Dove

1950. 25th Anniv of Japanese Broadcasting System.

582	**227**	8y. blue	4·00	1·50

1950. 1st Anniv of Joint Ministries of Postal and Electrical Communications.

583	**228**	8y. green	3·75	1·25

229 Lake Akan and Mt. O-Akani

230 Lake Kutcharo

231 Mt. Akan-Fuji

232 Lake Mashu

1950. Akan National Park.

584	**229**	2y. brown	1·10	50
585	**230**	8y. green	1·75	75
586	**231**	14y. red	8·50	2·25
587	**232**	24y. blue	10·00	2·25
MS588		127×181 mm. Nos. 584/7 (sold at 55y.)	28·00	30·00

233 Gymnast on Rings

1950. 5th National Athletic Meeting.

589	**233**	8y. red	30·00	12·00
590	–	8y. red (Pole vaulting)	30·00	12·00
591	–	8y. red (Football)	30·00	12·00
592	–	8y. red (Horse jumping)	30·00	12·00

234 Tahoto Pagoda, Ishiyama Temple

235 Baron Maeshima

236 Long-tailed Cock

237 Kannon Bosatsu (detail of wall painting, Horyu Temple)

238 Himeji Castle

239 Phoenix Temple, Uji

240 Buddhisattva Statue, Chugu Temple

1950. With noughts for sen after value.

593	**234**	80s. red	2·00	1·75
594	**235**	1y. brown	4·75	30
595	**236**	5y. green and brown	8·00	30
596	**237**	10y. lake and mauve	18·00	10
597	**238**	14y. brown	50·00	35·00
598	**239**	24y. blue	40·00	16·00
599	**240**	50y. brown	£140	1·00

For designs without noughts see Nos. 653 etc and for designs additionally inscr "NIPPON" see Nos. 1041/59.

1950. Miniature sheets, each 76×50 mm and each containing one of stamps from the above issue.

MS600	**234**	80s. carmine	10·00	10·00
MS601	**238**	14y. brown	65·00	60·00
MS602	**239**	24y. blue	45·00	45·00
MS603	**240**	50y. brown	£250	£300

241 Girl and Rabbit

242 Skiing, Mt. Zao

1951. New Year's Greetings.

604	**241**	2y. red	7·00	1·00

For 50y. in this design dated "1999" see No. 2565.

1951. Tourist Issue. Mt. Zao.

606	**242**	8y. olive	14·00	3·00
607	–	24y. blue	15·00	5·00

DESIGN—HORIZ: 24y. Two skiers on Mt. Zao.

243 Nihon-Daira

244 Mt. Fuji from Nihon Daira

1951. Tourist Issue. Nihon-Daira.

608	**243**	8y. green	14·00	3·00
609	**244**	24y. blue	70·00	18·00

1951. 80th Anniv of Japanese Postal Service. Sheet containing No. 594 in block of four.

MS610	86×64 mm	15·00	15·00

245 Child's Head

1951. Children's Charter.

611	**245**	8y. brown	25·00	3·00

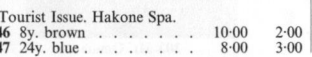

246 Hot Springs, Owaki Valley

247 Lake Ashi

1951. Tourist Issue. Hakone Spa.

612	**246**	8y. brown	10·00	2·00
613	**247**	24y. blue	8·00	3·00

248 Senju Waterfall

249 Ninai Waterfall

1951. Tourist Issue. Akame Waterfalls.

614	**248**	8y. green	10·00	2·00
615	**249**	24y. blue	10·00	3·00

250 Waka-no-Ura

251 Tomo-ga-Shima

1951. Tourist Issue. Coastal Resorts.

616	**250**	8y. brown	8·00	2·00
617	**251**	24y. blue	8·00	3·00

252 Oirase River

253 Lake Towada

254 View from Kankodai

255 Hakkoda Mountains

1951. Towada National Park.

618	**252**	2y. brown	1·25	30
619	**253**	8y. green	6·50	70
620	**254**	14y. red	5·50	4·00
621	**255**	24y. blue	7·50	4·00
MS622		128×182 mm. Nos. 618/21 (sold at 55y.)	27·00	28·00

256 Uji River

257 Uji Bridge

1951. Tourist Issue. Uji River.

623	**256**	8y. brown	9·00	2·00
624	**257**	24y. blue	8·00	3·00

258 Douglas DC-4 Airliner over Horyuji Pagoda
259 Douglas DC-4 Airliner and Mt. Tate

1951. Air. With noughts for sen after numerals of value.

625	**258**	15y. violet	4·00	3·25
626		20y. blue	32·00	1·00
627		25y. green	35·00	15
628		30y. red	26·00	15
629		40y. black	7·00	30
630	**259**	55y. blue	£225	45·00
631		75y. red	£175	28·00
632		80y. mauve	30·00	3·50
633		85y. black	22·00	12·00

634 125y. brown 18·00 3·25
635 160y. green 40·00 5·50
For similar designs, but without noughts after numerals of value, see Nos. 671/81.

260 Chrysanthemum **261** Japanese Flag

1951. Peace Treaty.
636 **260** 2y. brown 2·50 1·00
637 **261** 8y. red and blue 7·00 2·00
638 **260** 24y. green 18·00 6·00

262 Oura Catholic Church, Nagasaki **263** Gateway, Sofuku Temple

1951. Tourist Issue. Nagasaki.
639 **262** 8y. red 10·00 2·00
640 **263** 24y. blue 8·00 3·00

264 Lake Marunuma **265** Lake Sugenuma

1951. Tourist Issue.
641 **264** 8y. purple 10·00 2·00
642 **265** 24y. green 8·00 3·00

266 Shosenkyo Valley **267** Nagatoro Bridge

1951. Tourist Issue. Shosenkyo.
643 **266** 8y. red 9·50 2·00
644 **267** 24y. blue 9·00 3·00

268 Putting the Shot **269** Noh Mask

1951. 6th National Athletic Meeting.
645 **268** 2y. brown 3·50 1·00
646 – 2y. blue (Hockey) 3·50 1·00

1952. New Year's Greetings.
647 **269** 5y. red 10·00 90

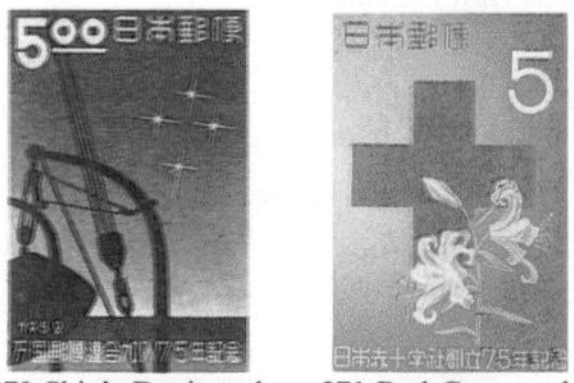
270 Ship's Davit and Southern Cross **271** Red Cross and Lily

1952. 75th Anniv of U.P.U. Membership.
649 **270** 5y. violet 5·00 1·25
650 – 10y. green 16·00 3·00
DESIGN: 10y. Earth and Ursa Major. Inscr "1952".

1952. 75th Anniv of Japanese Red Cross.
651 **271** 5y. red 5·00 1·00
652 – 10y. green and red (Nurse) 11·00 2·00

272 Akita Dog **273** Small Cuckoo **274** Tahoto Pagoda, Ishiyama Temple

275 Mandarins **276** Japanese Serow **277** Chuson Temple

278 Veil-tailed Goldfish **279** Yomei Gate, Tosho Shrine, Nikko **280** "Marimo" (water plant) and Sockeye Salmon

281 Great Purple **282** Fishing with Japanese Cormorants **283** "Bridge and Irises" (from lacquered box)

1952. Without noughts after numerals of value.
653 **235** 1y. brown 30 10
654 **272** 2y. black 40 10
655 **273** 3y. turquoise 20 20
656 **274** 4y. purple and red 2·50 10
657 **275** 5y. brown and blue 65 20
658 **276** 8y. brown and light brown 30 10
659 **237** 10y. red and mauve 6·00 10
660 **238** 14y. green 7·50 1·25
661 **277** 20y. green 1·00 10
662 **239** 24y. violet 16·00 2·00
663 30y. purple 35·00 40
664 **278** 35y. orange 10·00 10
665 **279** 45y. blue 4·50 10
666 **240** 50y. brown 4·50 10
667 **280** 55y. green, black and blue 16·00 30
668 **281** 75y. multicoloured 14·00 90
669 **282** 100y. red 40·00 20
670 **283** 500y. purple 85·00 10
For 1, 2, 3, 50, 55 and 75y. in same designs, but inscr "NIPPON", see Nos. 1041, 1582a, 1226, 1058/60, 1232 and 1064.

1952. Air. As Nos. 625/35 but without noughts after numerals of value.
671 **258** 15y. violet 2·00 1·10
672 20y. blue 50·00 70
673 25y. green 1·00 10
674 30y. red 3·50 10
675 40y. black 4·00 10
676 **259** 55y. blue 75·00 4·50
677 75y. red £140 10·00
678 80y. mauve 95·00 3·00
679 85y. black 5·00 1·25
680 125y. brown 10·00 1·40
681 160y. green 40·00 1·75

284 Mt. Yari **285** Kurobe Valley

286 Mt. Shirouma

287 Mt. Norikura

1952. Chubu-Sangaku National Park.
682 **284** 5y. brown 2·75 40
683 **285** 10y. green 18·00 2·00
684 **286** 14y. red 5·50 2·00
685 **287** 24y. blue 8·00 2·75
MS686 129 × 182 mm. Nos. 682/5 but imperf. No gum (sold at 60y.) 55·00 55·00

288 Central Hall **289** Wrestlers

1952. 75th Anniv of Tokyo University.
687 **288** 10y. green 11·00 2·00

1952. 7th National Athletic Meeting.
688 – 5y. blue (Mountaineer) 6·00 1·00
689 **289** 5y. brown 6·00 1·00

290 Mt. Azuma-Kofuji

291 Mt. Asahi

292 Mt. Bandai

293 Mt. Gessan

1952. Bandai-Asahi National Park.
690 **290** 5y. brown 2·00 40
691 **291** 10y. olive 11·00 1·75
692 **292** 14y. red 4·25 2·75
693 **293** 24y. blue 8·00 4·00
MS694 128 × 181 mm. Nos. 690/3 but imperf. No gum (sold at 60y.) 55·00 55·00

294 "Kirin" and Chrysanthemums **295** Flag of Crown Prince

1952. Investiture of Crown Prince Akihito.
695 **294** 5y. orange and brown 2·75 50
696 10y. orange and green 3·00 75
697 **295** 24y. blue 15·00 4·25
MS698 130 × 130 mm. Nos. 695/7. Imperf. No gum (sold at 50y.) 80·00 £200

296 Dancing Doll **297** First Japanese Electric Lamp

1953. New Year's Greetings.
699 **296** 5y. red 7·00 1·00

1953. 75th Anniv of Electric Lamp in Japan.
701 **297** 10y. brown 7·50 2·00

299 Kintai Bridge **302** Great Buddha, Kamakura

300 Lake Shikotsu (½-size illustration) **301** Mt. Yotei (½-size illustration)

1953. Tourist Issue. Kintai Bridge.
702 – 10y. brown 7·50 2·00
703 **299** 24y. blue 7·50 3·00
DESIGN—VERT: 10y. Kintai Bridge (after Hiroshige).

1953. Shikotsu-Toya National Park.
704 **300** 5y. blue 1·75 35
705 **301** 10y. green 5·50 75
MS706 148 × 105 mm. Nos. 704/5 but imperf. No gum (sold at 20y.) 28·00 30·00

1953. Air.
707 **302** 70y. brown 3·50 10
708 80y. blue 5·00 10
709 115y. olive 2·75 30
710 145y. turquoise 18·00 2·00

303 Wedded Rocks, Futami Bay (½-size illustration) **304** Nakiri Coast (½-size illustration)

1953. Ise Shima National Park.
711 **303** 5y. red 1·75 30
712 **304** 10y. blue 4·00 70
MS713 148 × 105 mm. Nos. 711/2 but imperf. No gum (sold at 2y.) 15·00 15·00

305 "Ho-o" (Happy Phoenix)

1953. Return of Crown Prince from Overseas Tour.
714 **305** 5y. lake 3·00 1·50
715 – 10y. blue 9·25 3·50
DESIGN: 10y. Manchurian crane in flight.

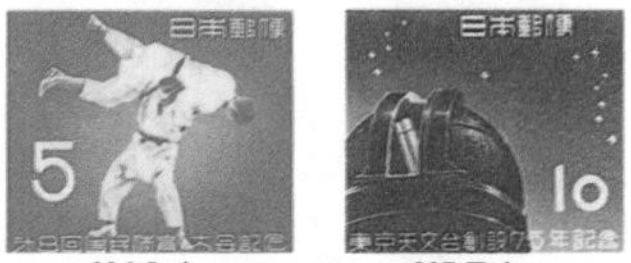
306 Judo **307** Tokyo Observatory

1953. 8th National Athletic Meeting, Matsuyama.
716 **306** 5y. green 8·00 2·00
717 – 5y. black 8·00 2·00
DESIGN: 5y. Rugby footballers.

1953. 75th Anniv of Tokyo Observatory.
718 **307** 10y. blue 10·00 2·00

308 Mt. Unzen (½-size illustration) **309** Mt. Unzen (½-size illustration)

1953. Unzen National Park.
719 **308** 5y. red 1·50 25
720 **309** 10y. blue 4·00 65
MS721 148 × 105 mm. Nos. 719/20 but imperf. No gum (sold at 20y.) 15·00 15·00

310 Wooden Horse **311** Ice Skaters

1953. New Year's Greetings.
722 **310** 5y. red 5·50 25

1954. World Speed Skating Championships, Sapporo.
724 **311** 10y. blue 4·00 1·10

312 **313** Wrestlers

1954. International Trade Fair, Osaka.
725 **312** 10y. red . . . . 4·25 1·10

1954. Int Free-style Wrestling Championship.
726 **313** 10y. green . . . . 4·00 1·00

314 Mt. Asama (½-size illustration)

315 Mt. Tanigawa (½-size illustration)

1954. Jo-Shin-Etsu Kogen National Park.
727 **314** 5y. sepia . . . . 1·50 25
728 **315** 10y. turquoise . . . . . 3·75 65
MS729 148 × 108 mm. Nos. 727/8 but imperf. No gum (sold at 20y.) 15·00 15·00

316 Archery

317 Telegraph Table

1954. 9th National Athletic Meeting, Sapporo.
730 **316** 5y. green . . . . 5·00 1·50
731 – 5y. brown (Table tennis) 5·00 1·50

1954. 75th Anniv of Japan's Membership of I.T.U.
732 **317** 5y. purple . . . . 2·25 75
733 – 10y. blue . . . . 6·00 1·00
DESIGN—HORIZ: 10y. I.T.U. Monument.

1954. Philatelic Week. Sheet 150 × 50 mm containing ten of No. 659 (arranged as one row of 6 and one row of 4 (with printed label at each end).
MS734 **237** 10y. lake and mauve £150 £120

318 Tumbler

319 Tama Gorge

320 Chichibu Mountains

1954. New Year's Greetings.
735 **318** 5y. red and black . . . . 7·00 80

1955. Chichibu-Tama National Park.
737 **319** 5y. blue . . . . 1·25 25
738 **320** 10y. lake . . . . 1·50 40
MS739 148 × 105 mm. Nos. 737/8 but imperf. No gum (sold at 20y.) 14·00 14·00

321 Paper Carp

1955. 15th International Chamber of Commerce Congress, Tokyo.
740 **321** 10y. multicoloured . . . 6·00 1·50

322 Bentenzaki Peninsula

323 Jodoga Beach

1955. Rikuchu-Kaigan National Park.
741 **322** 5y. green . . . . 1·50 25
742 **323** 10y. red . . . . 2·00 40
MS743 147 × 104 mm. Nos. 741/2 but imperf. No gum (sold a20y.) 13·00 13·00

324 Gymnastics

325 "Girl Playing Glass Flute" (Utamaro)

1955. 10th National Athletic Meeting, Kanagawa.
744 **324** 5y. red . . . . 3·00 1·00
745 – 5y. blue (Running) . . . 3·00 1·00

1955. Philatelic Week.
746 **325** 10y. multicoloured . . . 12·00 8·00

326 "Kokeshi" Dolls

327 Table Tennis

1955. New Year's Greetings.
747 **326** 5y. green and red . . . . 3·00 20

1956. World Table Tennis Championships.
749 **327** 10y. brown . . . . 1·10 35

328 Judo

1956. World Judo Championships.
750 **328** 10y. purple and green . . 1·40 40

329 Children and Paper Carps

1956. International Children's Day.
751 **329** 5y. black and blue . . . . 1·00 30

330 Osezaki Lighthouse (½-size illustration)

331 Kujuku Island (½-size illustration)

1956. 25th Anniv of National Park Law. Saikai National Park.
752 **330** 5y. brown . . . . 1·25 50
753 **331** 10y. indigo and blue . . . 1·75 85
MS754 147 × 104 mm. Nos. 752/3 but imperf. No gum (sold at 20y.) 14·00 14·00

332 Imperial Palace, and Modern Buildings

1956. 5th Centenary of Tokyo.
755 **332** 10y. purple . . . . 3·25 50

333 Sakuma Dam

334 Basketball

1956. Completion of Sakuma Dam.
756 **333** 10y. blue . . . . 2·50 50

1956. 11th National Athletic Meeting, Kobe.
757 **334** 5y. green . . . . 1·50 30
758 – 5y. purple (Long jumping) 1·50 30

335 Ebizo Ichikawa (actor) (after Sharaku)

1956. Philatelic Week.
759 **335** 10y. black, orange and grey . . . . 13·00 4·75

336 Mt. Manaslu and Mountaineer

1956. Conquest of Mt. Manaslu.
760 **336** 10y. multicoloured . . . 4·50 1·25

337 View of Yui (after Hiroshige) and Type EF 58 Electric Locomotive No. 4

1956. Electrification of Tokaido Railway Line.
761 **337** 10y. black, green & brown 10·00 3·00

338 Cogwheel, Valve and Freighter "Nissyo Maru"

339 Whale (float)

1956. Floating Machinery Fair.
762 **338** 10y. blue . . . . 1·60 70

1956. New Year's Greetings.
763 **339** 5y. multicoloured . . . . 2·00 15

340 U.N.O. Emblem

341 I.G.Y. Emblem, Emperor Penguin and Antarctic Research Vessel "Soya"

1957. 1st Anniv of Japan's Admission into U.N.
765 **340** 10y. red and blue . . . . 1·00 95

1957. International Geophysical Year.
766 **341** 10y. blue, yellow and black . . . . 2·25 85

342 Atomic Reactor

343 Gymnast

1957. Completion of Atomic Reactor at Tokai-Mura.
767 **342** 10y. violet 50 15

1957. 12th National Athletic Meeting, Shizuoka.
768 **343** 5y. blue 60 15
769 – 5y. red (Boxing) 60 15

344 "Girl Bouncing Ball" (after Harunobu)

345 Ogochi Dam

1957. Philatelic Week.
770 **344** 10y. multicoloured . . . 4·00 1·50

1957. Completion of Ogochi Dam.
771 **345** 10y. blue 45 15

346 Japan's First Blast Furnace and Modern Plant

347 "Inu-hariko" (toy dog)

1957. Centenary of Japanese Iron Industry.
772 **346** 10y. purple and orange 35 15

1957. New Year's Greetings.
773 **347** 5y. multicoloured 30 15

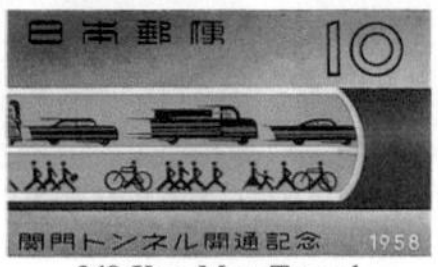
348 Kan-Mon Tunnel

1958. Opening of Kan-Mon Undersea Tunnel.
775 **348** 10y. multicoloured . . . 50 10

349 "Lady returning from Bath-house" (after Kiyonaga)

1958. Philatelic Week.
776 **349** 10y. multicoloured . . . 1·00 15

350 Statue of Ii Naosuke, "Powhattan" (1858 paddle-steamer) and Modern Liner

351 National Stadium, Tokyo

1958. Centenary of Opening of Ports to Traders.
777 **350** 10y. red and blue 30 10

1958. 3rd Asian Games, Tokyo. Inscr as in T **351**. Multicoloured.
778 5y. Type **351** 30 10
779 10y. Flame and Games emblem 45 50
780 14y. Runner breasting tape 35 15
781 24y. High-diver 40 50

352 Emigration Ship "Kasato Maru" and South American Map

1958. 50th Anniv of Japanese Emigration to Brazil.
782 **352** 10y. multicoloured . . . 50 10

353 Dado-Okesa Dancer on Sado Island

354 Mt. Yahiko and Echigo Plain

1958. Sado-Yahiko Quasi-National Park.
783 **353** 10y. multicoloured . . . 70 10
784 **354** 10y. multicoloured . . . 40 10

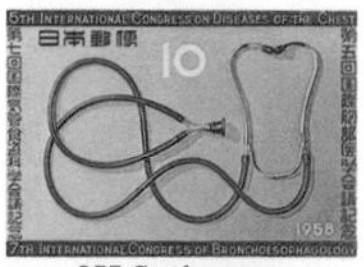
355 Stethoscope

1958. International Congresses of Chest Diseases and Bronchoesophagology, Tokyo.
785 **355** 10y. turquoise 60 10

356 "Old Kyoto Bridge" (after Hiroshige)

357 Badminton Player

1958. International Correspondence Week.
786 **356** 24y. multicoloured . . . 4·50 50
The design is taken from the series of 53 woodcuts, showing stages of the Tokaido Road. Others from this series are shown on Nos. 810, 836, 878 and 908.

1958. 13th National Athletic Meeting, Toyama.
787 **357** 5y. purple 75 10
788 – 5y. blue (Weightlifting) . . 75 10

358 Yukichi Fukuzawa (founder) and Keio University

359 Children Skipping across Globe

1958. Centenary of Keio University.
789 **358** 10y. red 30 10

1958. International Child and Social Welfare Conferences, Tokyo.
790 **359** 10y. green 30 10

360 "Flame of Freedom"

361 Ebisu with Madai Seabream (toy)

1958. 10th Anniv of Declaration of Human Rights.
791 **360** 10y. multicoloured . . . 30 10

1958. New Year's Greetings.
792 **361** 5y. multicoloured 50 10

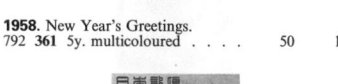

362 Map of Kojima Bay and Tractor

1959. Completion of Kojima Bay Reclamation Project.
794 **362** 10y. purple and ochre . . 50 15

363 Karst Plateau

364 Akiyoshi Cavern

1959. Akiyoshidai Quasi-National Parks.
795 **363** 10y. multicoloured . . . 1·75 10
796 **364** 10y. multicoloured . . . 2·25 10

365 Map of Asia

366 Crown Prince Akihito and Princess Michiko

1959. Asian Congress Commemorating 2500th Anniv of Buddha's Death.
797 **365** 10y. red 40 10

1959. Imperial Wedding.
798 – 5y. violet and purple . . . 35 10
799 **366** 10y. purple and brown . . 85 10
800 – 20y. sepia and brown . . 1·00 15
801 **366** 30y. deep green and green 2·00 15
MS802 127 × 88 mm. Nos. 798/9 but imperf. No gum (sold at 20y.) 4·50 4·50
DESIGN: 5, 20y. Ceremonial fan.

367 "Ladies reading poems" (from "Ukiyo Genji" after Eishi)

368 Graduated Glass and Scales

1959. Philatelic Week.
803 **367** 10y. multicoloured . . . 2·50 1·25

1959. Ratification of Adoption of Metric System in Japan.
804 **368** 10y. sepia and blue . . . 30 10

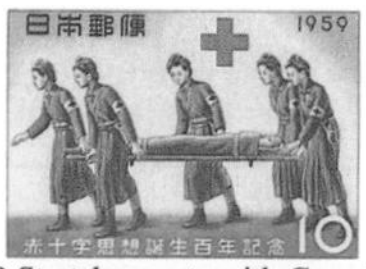
369 Stretcher-party with Casualty

1959. Red Cross.
805 **369** 10y. red and green . . . 40 10

370 Mt. Fuji from Lake Motosu

1959. National Parks Day.
806 **370** 10y. green, purple and blue 60 10

371 Ao Caves, Yabakei

372 Japanese Cormorant with Hita and Mt. Hiko background

1959. Yaba-Hita-Hikosan Quasi-National Parks.
807 **371** 10y. multicoloured . . . 2·00 30
808 **372** 10y. multicoloured . . . 1·40 50

373 Nagoya and Golden Dolphin

374 "Kuwana" (after Hiroshige)

1959. 350th Anniv of Nagoya.
809 **373** 10y. gold, black and blue 60 10

1959. International Correspondence Week.
810 **374** 30y. multicoloured . . . 10·00 2·00

375 Flying Manchurian Crane and I.A.T.A. Emblem

376 Throwing the Hammer

1959. 15th International Air Transport Association Meeting, Tokyo.
811 **375** 10y. blue . . . . 1·10 35

1959. 14th National Athletic Meeting, Tokyo.
812 **376** 5y. blue . . . . 1·00 10
813 – 5y. brown (Fencer) . . . 1·00 10

377 Open Book showing portrait of Shoin Yoshida

378 Halves of Globe

1959. Death Centenary of Shoin Yoshida (educator) and National Parents/Teachers Assn Convention.
814 **377** 10y. brown 40 10

1959. 15th Session of Contracting Parties to G.A.T.T.
815 **378** 10y. brown 60 10

379 Rice-eating Rat of Kanazawa (toy)

380 Yukio Ozaki and Clock Tower Memorial Hall

1959. New Year's Greetings.
816 **379** 5y. multicoloured . . . . 1·00 10

1960. Completion of Ozaki Memorial Hall, Tokyo.
818 **380** 10y. purple and brown . . 40 10

381 Deer

1960. 1250th Anniv of Transfer of Capital to Nara.
819 **381** 10y. olive 70 10

382 Godaido Temple, Matsushima

383 Bridge of Heaven (sandbank), Miyazu Bay

384 Miyajima from the Sea

1960. "Scenic Trio".
820 **382** 10y. turquoise and brown 2·50 25
821 **383** 10y. green and blue . . . 3·00 25
822 **384** 10y. green and violet . . 3·00 25

385 Takeshima-Gamagori Causeway

1960. Mikawa Bay Quasi-National Park.
823 **385** 10y. multicoloured . . . 1·25 20

386 "Ise" (from Satake picture scroll "Thirty-six Immortal Poets")

1960. Philatelic Week.
824 **386** 10y. black, red and brown 3·75 2·00

387 "Kanrin Maru" (barque) crossing the Pacific

388 Japanese Crested Ibis

1960. Centenary of Japanese–American Treaty.
825 **387** 10y. sepia and green . . . 2·25 30
826 – 30y. black and red . . . 1·60 20
DESIGN: 30y. Pres. Buchanan receiving Japanese mission.

1960. 12th Int Bird Preservation Congress, Tokyo.
827 **388** 10y. red, pink and grey 1·40 55

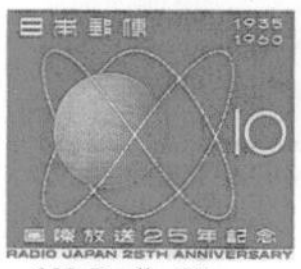
389 Radio Waves around Globe

390 Abashiri Flower Gardens

1960. 25th Anniv of Japanese Overseas Broadcasting Service, "Radio Japan".
828 **389** 10y. red 40 10

1960. Abashiri Quasi-National Park.
829 **390** 10y. multicoloured . . . 1·50 25

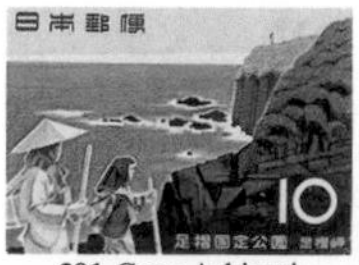
391 Cape Ashizuri

392 Rainbow linking Hawaii and Japan

1960. Ashizuri Quasi-National Park.
830 **391** 10y. multicoloured . . . 1·00 25

1960. 75th Anniv of Japanese Emigration to Hawaii.
831 **392** 10y. multicoloured . . . 1·00 20

393 Douglas DC-8 Jetliner and Farman H.F.III Biplane

394 Seat Plan of the Diet

1960. 50th Anniv of Japanese Aviation.
832 **393** 10y. brown and grey . . . 1·25 25

1960. 49th Inter-Parliamentary Union Conference. Inscr "49TH INTER-PARLIAMENTARY CONFERENCE TOKYO 1960".
833 **394** 5y. orange and blue . . . 70 10
834 – 10y. brown and blue . . . 1·60 20
DESIGN: 10y. "Clear Day with Southern Breeze" (from "36 Views of Mt. Fuji" by Hokusai Katsushika).

1960. Visit of Crown Prince Akihito and Princess Michiko to the United States. Sheet containing Nos. 825/6.
MS835 120 × 76 mm . . . . . . 30·00 25·00

395 "Kambara" (after Hiroshige)

1960. International Correspondence Week.
836 **395** 30y. multicoloured . . . 18·00 4·00

396 Okayama Observatory

1960. Opening of Okayama Astrophysical Observatory.
837 **396** 10y. violet 90 25

397 "Kendo" (Japanese fencing)

398 Lieut. Shirase and Map of Antarctica

1960. 15th National Athletic Meeting, Kumamoto.
838 **397** 5y. blue . . . . 1·00 15
839 – 5y. purple (Vaulting) . . 1·00 15

1960. 50th Anniv of 1st Japanese Antarctic Expedition.
840 **398** 10y. black and brown . . 1·00 15

399 Red Beko and Golden Bekokko (Japanese toys)

400 Diet Building and Stars

1960. New Year's Greetings.
841 **399** 5y. multicoloured 50 10

1960. 70th Anniv of Diet.
843 **400** 5y. violet and black . . . 60 10
844 – 10y. red 75 15
DESIGN: 10y. Opening ceremony of first session of Diet.

401 Narcissus

402 Pearl-divers at Shirahama

1961. Japanese Flowers. Flowers in natural colours. Background colours given.
845 10y. purple (T **401**) . . . . . 5·00 80
846 10y. brown (Plum blossom) 3·00 80
847 10y. bistre (Camellia) . . . . 2·00 70
848 10y. grey (Cherry blossom) 2·00 70
849 10y. sepia (Peony) . . . . . 1·90 55
850 10y. grey (Iris) . . . . 1·50 55
851 10y. turquoise (Lily) . . . . 1·00 30
852 10y. blue (Morning glory) . . 1·00 30
853 10y. sage (Bellflower) . . . . 1·00 30
854 10y. orange (Gentian) . . . . 1·00 30
855 10y. blue (Chrysanthemum) 1·25 30
856 10y. slate (Camellia) . . . . 1·00 30

1961. Minami-Boso Quasi-National Park.
857 **402** 10y. multicoloured . . . 1·00 10

403 Hirase's Slit Shell **404** Nanten **405** Cherry Blossoms

406 Engaku Temple **407** Yomei Gate, Tosho Shrine, Nikko **408** Noh Mask

409 Copper Pheasant **410** "The Wind God" **411** Manchurian Cranes

412 "Kalavinka" (legendary bird)

1961.
858 **403** 4y. red and brown . . . 35 10
859 **404** 6y. red and green 20 10
860 **405** 10y. mauve and purple . . 45 10
861 **406** 30y. violet . . . . 5·00 10
862 **407** 40y. red . . . . 6·00 10
863 **408** 70y. black and ochre . . 3·00 10
864 **409** 80y. brown and red . . . 3·25 20
865 **410** 90y. green . . . . 35·00 15
866 **411** 100y. grey, black and pink 30·00 20
867 **412** 120y. violet . . . . 12·00 30
For 70, 80, 90, 100, and 120y. in different colours and additionally inscr "NIPPON" see Nos. 1065/6, 1068, 1234/6 and 1238.

413 Baron Maeshima

414 "Dancing Girl" (from 17th-century screen)

1961. 90th Anniv of Japanese Postal Service.
868 **413** 10y. green and black . . . 1·00 15

1961. Philatelic Week.
869 **414** 10y. multicoloured . . . 1·75 90

415 Lake Biwa

416 Rotary Emblem and "Peoples of the World"

1961. Lake Biwa Quasi-National Park.
870 **415** 10y. multicoloured . . . 1·10 20

1961. 52nd Rotary International Convention.
871 **416** 10y. orange and black . . 45 10

417 "Benefits Irrigation"

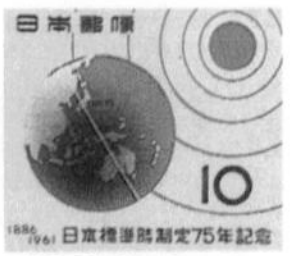
418 Globe showing Longitude 135° E. and Sun

1961. Inauguration of Aichi Irrigation Scheme.
872 **417** 10y. blue and purple . . . 50 15

1961. 75th Anniv of Japanese Standard Time.
873 **418** 10y. red, black and ochre 50 15

419 Parasol Dancer, Tottori Beach

1961. San'in Kaigan Quasi-National Park.
874 **419** 10y. multicoloured . . . 80 20

420 Komagatake Volcano

1961. Onuma Quasi-National Park.
875 **420** 10y. multicoloured . . . 80 20

421 Gymnast

422 "Hakone" (after Hiroshige)

1961. 16th National Athletic Meeting, Akita.
876 **421** 5y. green . . . . 1·00 10
877 – 5y. blue (Rowing) . . . . 1·00 10

1961. International Correspondence Week.
878 **422** 30y. multicoloured . . . 9·00 4·00

423 Throwing the Javelin

1961. Olympic Games, Tokyo, 1964 (1st issue).
879 **423** 5y.+5y. brown . . . . . 1·50 70
880 – 5y.+5y. green . . . . . . 1·50 70
881 – 5y.+5y. red . . . . 1·50 70
DESIGNS: No. 880, Wrestling; 881, Diver (Woman).
See also Nos. 899/901, 909/11, 935/7, 949/52, 969/72 and 981/5.

424 Library and Book

425 Tiger (Izumo toy)

1961. Opening of National Diet Library.
882 **424** 10y. blue and gold . . . 60 15

1961. New Year's Greetings.
883 **425** 5y. multicoloured 75 10

426 Mt. Fuji from Lake Aishi

427 Minokake-Iwa, Irozaki

428 Mt. Fuji from Mitsutoge

429 Mt. Fuji from Osezaki

1962. Fuji-Hakone-Izu National Park.
885 **426** 5y. green . . . . 1·00 10
886 **427** 5y. blue . . . . 1·00 10
887 **428** 10y. brown . . . . 1·75 25
888 **429** 10y. black . . . . 1·25 25

430 Omishima Island

431 Doll Festival

1962. Kitanagato-Kaigan Quasi-National Park.
889 **430** 10y. multicoloured . . . 60 20

1962. National Festivals. Multicoloured.
890 10y. Type **431** . . . . 1·75 25
891 10y. Children and decorated tree ("Star Festival") . . . 75 20
892 10y. Three children ("Seven-Five-Three Festival") . . . 65 20
893 10y. Children throwing beans ("Spring Festival") 55 15

432 "Dancer" (after N. Kano)

1962. Philatelic Week.
894 **432** 10y. multicoloured . . . 1·50 1·00

433 Sakurajima Volcano

1962. Kinkowan Quasi-National Park.
895 **433** 10y. multicoloured . . . 60 20

434 Mount Kongo

1962. Kongo-Ikoma Quasi-National Park.
896 **434** 10y. multicoloured . . . 60 20

435 Suigo View

436 "Hakucho" (swan) Express Train emerging from Tunnel

1962. Suigo Quasi-National Park.
897 **435** 10y. multicoloured . . . 80 20

1962. Opening of Hokuriku Railway Tunnel.
898 **436** 10y. brown . . . . 2·50 45

1962. Olympic Games, Tokyo, 1964 (2nd issue). Sports. As T **423**.
899 5y.+5y. red 75 35
900 5y.+5y. green 75 35
901 5y.+5y. purple 75 35
SPORTS: No. 899 Judo; 900, Water-polo; 901, Gymnastics (female).

437 Scout's Hat on Map

1962. Asian Scout Jamboree, Mt. Fuji.
902 **437** 10y. black, bistre and red 40 10

438 Mt. Shibutsu and Ozegahara Swamp

439 Smoking Summit of Mt. Chausu, Nasu

440 Lake Chuzenji and Mt. Nantai

441 Senryu-kyo Narrows, Shiobara

1962. Nikko National Park.
903 **438** 5y. turquoise 60 10
904 **439** 5y. lake 60 10
905 **440** 10y. purple 80 10
906 **441** 10y. olive 80 10

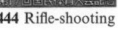

442 Wakato Suspension Bridge
443 "Nihonbashi" (after Hiroshige)

1962. Opening of Wakato Suspension Bridge.
907 **442** 10y. red . . . . 1·50 35

1962. International Correspondence Week.
908 **443** 40y. multicoloured . . . 7·50 3·00

1962. Olympic Games, Tokyo, 1964 (3rd issue). Sports. As T **423**.
909 5y.+5y. green 65 25
910 5y.+5y. lilac 65 25
911 5y.+5y. red 65 25
SPORTS: No. 909, Basketball; 910, Rowing; 911, Fencing.

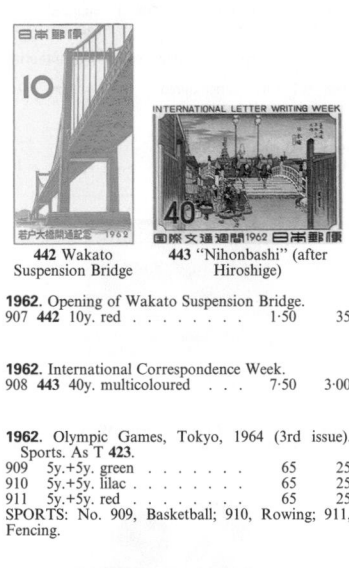

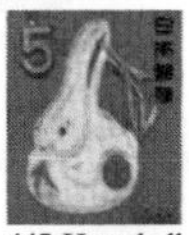
444 Rifle-shooting
445 Hare-bell (Nogomi toy)

1962. 17th National Athletic Meeting, Okayama.
912 **444** 5y. purple 40 10
913 – 5y. blue 40 10
DESIGN: No. 913, Softball.

1962. New Year's Greetings.
914 **445** 5y. multicoloured 40 10
For 50y. in this design dated "1999" see No. 2566.

446 Mt. Ishizuchi and Kamega Forest
447 "Five Towns"

1963. Ishizuchi Quasi-National Park.
916 **446** 10y. multicoloured . . . 30 10

1963. Amalgamation of Five Towns as Kita-Kyushu.
917 **447** 10y. brown 25 10

448 Frosted Foliage, Fugen Peak

449 Amakusa Islands and Mt. Unzen

1963. Unzen-Amakusa National Park.
918 **448** 5y. blue 35 10
919 **449** 10y. red 65 10

450 Midorigaike (Green Pond)

451 Hakusan Mountains

1963. Hakusan National Park.
920 **450** 5y. brown 45 10
921 **451** 10y. green 75 10

452 Great Rocks, Keya

1963. Genkai Quasi-National Park.
922 **452** 10y. multicoloured . . . 25 10

453 Globe and Emblem

1963. Freedom from Hunger.
923 **453** 10y. green 40 10

454 "Portrait of Heihachiro Honda" (anon-Yedo period)

1963. Philatelic Week.
924 **454** 10y. multicoloured . . . 85 45

455 Centenary Emblem and World Map
456 Globe and Leaf

1963. Centenary of Red Cross.
925 **455** 10y. multicoloured . . . 35 10

1963. 5th International Irrigation and Drainage Commission Congress, Toyko.
926 **456** 10y. blue 15 10

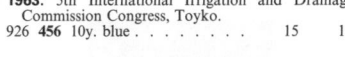

457 Mt. Ito, Asahi Range

458 Mt. Bandai across Lake Hibara

1963. Bandai-Asahi National Park.
927 **457** 5y. green 45 10
928 **458** 10y. brown 75 10

459 Purple Jay

1963. Japanese Birds. Multicoloured.
929 10y. Type **459** . . . . 2·00 1·25
930 10y. Rock ptarmigan 65 20
931 10y. Eastern turtle dove . . . 65 20
932 10y. White stork 65 20
933 10y. Japanese bush warbler 65 20
934 10y. Siberian meadow bunting 65 20

1963. Olympic Games, Tokyo, 1964 (4th issue). Sports. As T **423**.
935 5y.+5y. blue 75 25
936 5y.+5y. brown 75 25
937 5y.+5y. brown 75 25
SPORTS: No. 935, Dinghy sailing; 936, Boxing; 937, Volleyball.

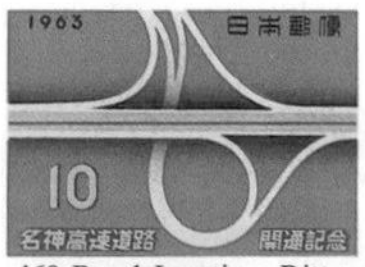

460 Road Junction, Ritto, Shiga
461 Girl Scout and Flag

1963. Opening of Nagoya–Kobe Expressway.
938 **460** 10y. green, black & orange 35 10

1963. Asian Girl Scout Camp, Nagano.
939 **461** 10y. multicoloured . . . 35 10

462 Mt. Washiu

463 Whirlpool at Naruto

1963. Seto Inland Sea National Park.
940 **462** 5y. brown 25 10
941 **463** 10y. green 35 10

464 Lake Shikaribetsu

465 Mt. Kurodake

1963. Daisetsuzan National Park.
942 **464** 5y. blue 25 10
943 **465** 10y. purple 35 10

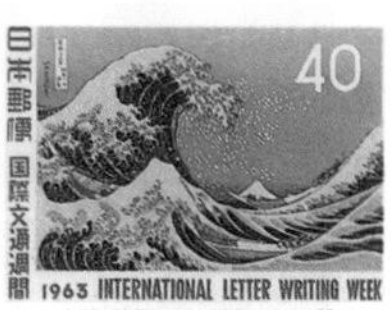

466 Antenna
467 "Great Wave off Kanagawa" (from "36 Views of Mt. Fuji" by Hokusai Katsushika)

1963. 14th International Scientific Radio Union Conference, Tokyo.
944 **466** 10y. multicoloured . . . 25 10

1963. International Correspondence Week.
945 **467** 40y. multicoloured . . . 4·25 50
The design is taken from the series of 36 woodcuts showing Mt. Fuji. Others from this series are shown as Nos. 989, 1010, 1075, 1100, 1140 and 1185.

468 Athletes
469 Wrestling

1963. "Pre-Olympic" Athletic Meeting, Tokyo.
946 **468** 10y. multicoloured . . . 15 10

1963. 18th National Athletic Meeting, Yamaguchi.
947 **469** 5y. brown 20 10
948 – 5y. green 20 10
DESIGN: No. 948, Free-style gymnastics.

1963. Olympic Games, Tokyo, 1964 (5th issue). Sports. As T **423**.
949 5y.+5y. blue 35 10
950 5y.+5y. olive 35 10
951 5y.+5y. black 35 10
952 5y.+5y. purple 35 10
SPORTS: No. 949, Cycling; 950, Show jumping; 951, Hockey; 952, Pistol-shooting.

470 Hachijo Island
471 Kai and Iwai Dragon Toys

1963. Izu Islands Quasi-National Park.
953 **470** 10y. multicoloured . . . 25 10

1963. New Year's Greetings.
954 **471** 5y. multicoloured 35 10

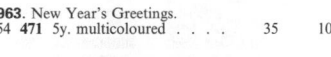

472 Wakasa Bay

1964. Wakasa Bay Quasi-National Park.
956 **472** 10y. multicoloured . . . 35 10

473 View from Horikiri Pass and Agave Plant

1964. Nichinan-Kaigan Quasi-National Park.
957 **473** 10y. multicoloured . . . 15 10

474 Uji Bridge

475 View of Toba

1964. Ise-Shima National Park.
958 **474** 5y. brown 15 10
959 **475** 10y. purple 20 10

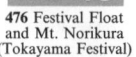

476 Festival Float and Mt. Norikura (Tokayama Festival) **477** "Yamaboko" Shrine (Gion Festival)

478 Warriors on Horseback (Soma Horse Festival)

479 Festival Scene (Chichibu Festival)

1964. Regional Festivals.
960 **476** 10y. multicoloured . . . 35 10
961 **477** 10y. multicoloured . . . 35 10
962 **478** 10y. multicoloured . . . 35 10
963 **479** 10y. multicoloured . . . 35 10

480 Prince Niou playing for Lady Nakanokimi (detail of Takayoshi "Yadorigi" scroll illustrating "Tale of Genji" by Lady Murasaki)

1964. Philatelic Week.
964 **480** 10y. multicoloured . . . 40 15

481 Himeji Castle **482** Handball

1964. Rebuilding of Himeji Castle.
965 **481** 10y. brown 15 10

1964. 19th National Athletic Meeting, Niigata.
966 **482** 5y. green 10 10
967 – 5y. red (Gymnastics) . . . 10 10

483 Cross-section of Cable

1964. Opening of Japan–U.S. Submarine Telephone Cable.
968 **483** 10y. multicoloured . . . 15 10

1964. Olympic Games, Tokyo (6th issue). Sports. As T **423**.
969 5y.+5y. violet 45 10
970 5y.+5y. blue 45 10
971 5y.+5y. lake 45 10
972 5y.+5y. olive 45 10
SPORTS: No. 969, Modern pentathlon; 970, Canoeing; 971, Football; 972, Weightlifting.

484 Nihonbashi Bridge **485** "Coins"

1964. Opening of Tokyo Expressway.
973 **484** 10y. green, silver and black 25 10

1964. Olympic Games, Tokyo (12th issue). Set of six miniature sheets each 135×60 mm containing stamps as indicated below.
MS974 Nos. 879/81 . . . . . . 4·25 4·25
MS975 Nos. 899/901 . . . . . 3·25 3·25
MS976 Nos. 909/11 . . . . . . 2·50 2·50
MS977 Nos. 935/7 . . . . 4·50 4·50
MS978 Nos. 949/52 . . . . . . 4·50 4·50
MS979 Nos. 969/72 . . . . . . 4·50 4·50

1964. Int Monetary Fund Convention, Tokyo.
980 **485** 10y. gold and red 25 10

486 Olympic Flame **487** "Agriculture"

1964. Olympic Games, Tokyo (7th issue). Inscr "1964". Multicoloured.
981 5y. Type **486** 20 15
982 10y. Main stadium (horiz) . . 30 20
983 30y. Fencing hall (horiz) . . 50 30
984 40y. Indoor stadium (horiz) 70 30
985 50y. Komazawa hall (horiz) 90 30
MS986 93×144 mm. Nos. 981/5 8·00 6·50

1964. Reclamation of Hachirogata Lagoon.
987 **487** 10y. gold and purple . . . 15 10

488 "Hikari" (light) Express Train

1964. Inauguration of Tokyo–Osaka Shinkansen Railway Line.
988 **488** 10y. blue and black . . . 1·00 20

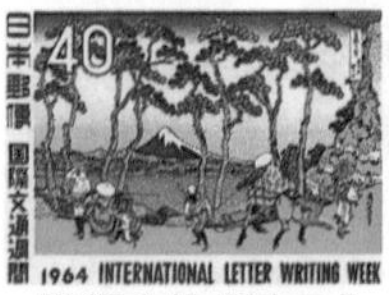

489 "Tokaido Highway" (from "36 Views of Mt. Fuji" by Hokusai Katsushika) **490** Straw Snake

1964. International Correspondence Week.
989 **489** 40y. multicoloured . . . 1·75 10

1964. New Year's Greetings.
990 **490** 5y. multicoloured 15 10

491 Mt. Daisen and Akamatsu Pond

492 Jodo-ga-Ura (Paradise Islands) of Oki

1965. Daisen-Oki National Park.
992 **491** 5y. blue 25 10
993 **492** 10y. brown 35 10

493 Niseko-Annupuri Mountains

1965. Niseko Shakotan Otaru Quasi-National Park.
994 **493** 10y. multicoloured . . . 30 10

494 Radar Station

1965. Completion of Meteorological Radar Station, Mt. Fuji.
995 **494** 10y. multicoloured . . . 25 10

495 Kiyotsu Gorge **496** Mt. Myoko across Lake Nojiri

1965. Jo-Shin-Etsu Kogen National Park.
996 **495** 5y. brown 20 10
997 **496** 10y. purple 35 10

497 Postal Museum

1965. Inauguration of Postal Museum, Ote-machi, Tokyo, and Stamp Exhibition.
998 **497** 10y. green 15 10

498 "The Prelude" (after Shoen Uyemura) **499** Children at Play

1965. Philatelic Week.
999 **498** 10y. multicoloured . . . 50 10

1965. Inaug of National Children's Gardens.
1000 **499** 10y. multicoloured . . . 20 10

500 Tree within "Leaf" **501** Globe and Symbols

1965. Reafforestation.
1001 **500** 10y. multicoloured . . . 20 10

1965. Centenary of I.T.U.
1002 **501** 10y. multicoloured . . . 35 10

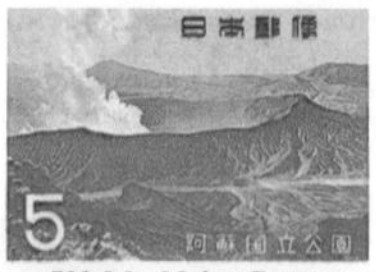

502 Mt. Naka Crater

503 Aso Peaks

1965. Aso National Park.
1003 **502** 5y. red 25 10
1004 **503** 10y. green 35 10

504 I.C.Y. Emblem and Doves

1965. International Co-operation Year.
1005 **504** 40y. multicoloured . . . 75 10

505 "Meiji Maru" (cadet ship) and Japanese Gulls

1965. 25th Maritime Day.
1006 **505** 10y. multicoloured . . . 60 20

506 "Blood Donation"

1965. Campaign for Blood Donors.
1007 **506** 10y. multicoloured . . . 25 10

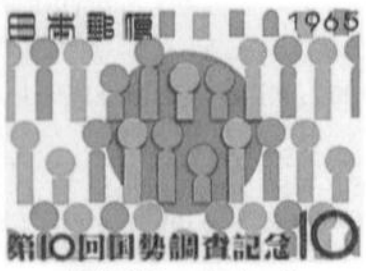

507 Atomic Power Station, Tokyo **508** "Population"

1965. 9th International Atomic Energy Authority Conference, Tokyo.
1008 **507** 10y. multicoloured . . . 35 10

1965. 10th National Census.
1009 **508** 10y. multicoloured . . . 20 10

509 "Water at Misaka" (from "36 Views of Mt. Fuji" by Hokusai Katsushika)

1965. International Correspondence Week.
1010 **509** 40y. multicoloured . . . 80 60

510 Emblems and Plan of Diet

1965. 75th Anniv of National Suffrage.
1011 **510** 10y. multicoloured . . . 20 10

511 Walking **512** Outline of Face, and Baby

1965. 20th National Athletic Meeting, Gifu.
1012 **511** 5y. green 15 10
1013 – 5y. brown (Gymnastics) 15 10

1965. International Conferences of Otology, Rhinology and Laryngology (ICORL) and Pediatrics (ICP), Tokyo.
1014 **512** 30y. multicoloured . . . 40 10

513 Mt. Iwo **514** Mt. Rausu

1965. Shiretoko National Park.
1015 **513** 5y. turquoise 25 10
1016 **514** 10y. blue 35 10

515 Antarctic Map, Research Vessel "Fuji" and Aurora Australis

516 "Straw Horse"

1965. Antarctic Expedition of 1965.
1017 **515** 10y. multicoloured . . . 1·40 15

1965. New Year's Greetings.
1018 **516** 5y. multicoloured . . . 15 10

517 Telephone Switchboard (1890) and Modern Dial

518 Spiny Lobster

1965. 75th Anniv of Japanese Telephone Service.
1020 **517** 10y. multicoloured . . . 15 10

NIPPON. From this point onwards all stamps are additionally inscribed "NIPPON".

1966. Fishery Products. Multicoloured.
1021 10y. Type **518** 30 15
1022 10y. Golden carp 30 15
1023 10y. Madai seabream . . . 30 15
1024 10y. Skipjack tuna 30 15
1025 10y. Ayu 30 15
1026 15y. Japanese eel 40 15
1027 15y. Chub mackerel 40 15
1028 15y. Chum salmon 40 15
1029 15y. Buri 60 15
1030 15y. Tiger pufferfish 60 20
1031 15y. Japanese common squid 75 30
1032 15y. Horned turban (shellfish) 85 30

519 Pleasure Garden, Mito

519a Pleasure Garden and Manchurian Cranes, Okayama

519b Kerokuen Garden, Kanazawa

1966. Famous Japanese Gardens.
1033 **519** 10y. green, black & gold 25 10
1034 **519a** 15y. black, red and blue 80 30
1035 **519b** 15y. black, green & sil 35 10

520 Crater of Mt. Zao

1966. Zao Quasi-National Park.
1036 **520** 10y. multicoloured . . . 35 10

521 Muroto Cape

522 Senba Cliffs, Anan

1966. Muroto-Anan Kaigan Quasi-National Park.
1037 **521** 10y. multicoloured . . . 25 10
1038 **522** 10y. multicoloured . . . 30 10

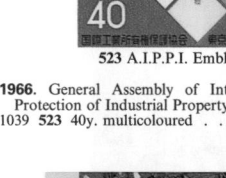

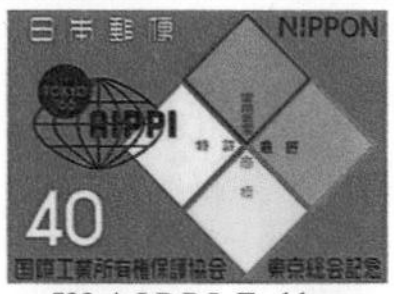
523 A.I.P.P.I. Emblem

1966. General Assembly of Int Association for Protection of Industrial Property (A.I.P.P.I.).
1039 **523** 40y. multicoloured . . . 35 10

524 "Butterflies" (after T. Fujishima)

1966. Philatelic Week.
1040 **524** 10y. multicoloured . . . 35 10

525 Goldfish 526 Chrysanthemums 527 Fuji (wisteria)

528 Hydrangea 529 Golden Hall, Chuson Temple 530 "Watasenia scintillans" (squid)

531 Yomei Gate, Tosho Shrine, Nikko 532 Mizubasho 533 Konponchudo Hall, Enryaku Temple

534 Ancient Clay Horse

535 Garden of Katsura Palace

536 Onjo Bosatsu (relief from bronze lantern, Todai Temple)

537 Kongo-Rikishi Statue, Todai Temple Nara

1966. Inscr "NIPPON".
1041 **235** 1y. bistre 10 10
1047 **525** 7y. orange and green . . 40 10
1049 **526** 15y. yellow and blue . . 1·25 10
1050 15y. yellow and blue . . 25 10
1052 **527** 20y. green and violet . . 1·25 10
1053 **528** 25y. blue and green . . . 60 10
1054 **529** 30y. gold and blue . . . 40 10
1055 **530** 35y. black, brown & blue 3·25 10
1056 **531** 40y. green and brown . . 60 10
1057 **532** 45y. multicoloured . . . 50 10
1058 **240** 50y. red . . . . 11·00 10
1059 50y. mauve 80 10
1060 **280** 55y. green, black and blue 75 10
1061 **533** 60y. green . . . . 1·00 10
1062 **534** 65y. brown . . . . . . 16·00 10
1063 65y. orange . . . . . . 1·00 10
1064 **281** 75y. multicoloured . . . 1·40 10
1065 **410** 90y. brown and gold . . 2·00 10
1066 **411** 100y. grey, black and red 2·25 20
1067 **535** 110y. brown . . . . . . 1·50 10
1068 **412** 120y. red . . . . 3·50 10
1069 **536** 200y. green . . . . . . 7·50 10
1070 **537** 500y. purple . . . . . . 8·50 10
No. 1050 is as T **526** but with white figures of value.
See also Nos. 1226/49.

538 U.N. and UNESCO Emblems

539 Pacific Ocean

1966. 20th Anniv of UNESCO.
1071 **538** 15y. multicoloured . . . 15 10

1966. 11th Pacific Science Congress, Tokyo.
1072 **539** 15y. multicoloured . . . 20 10

540 Amakusa Bridges

1966. Completion of Amakusa Bridges.
1073 **540** 15y. multicoloured . . . 20 10

541 Family and Emblem

542 "Sekiya on the Sumida" (from "36 Views of Mt. Fuji" by Hokusai Katsushika)

1966. 50th Anniv of Post Office Life Insurance Office.
1074 **541** 15y. multicoloured . . . 15 10

1966. International Correspondence Week.
1075 **542** 50y. multicoloured . . . 1·75 15

543 Rotary Cobalt Radiator

544 Triple Jump

1966. 9th. International Cancer Congress, Tokyo.
1076 **543** 7y.+3y. black & orge . . 25 15
1077 – 15y.+5y. multicoloured 35 15
DESIGN—VERT: 15y. Detection by X-rays.

1966. 21st National Athletic Meeting, Oita.
1078 **544** 7y. red 30 10
1079 – 7y. blue (Clay-pigeon shooting) 30 10

545 National Theatre Building

546 Rice Year Emblem

1966. Inauguration of Japanese National Theatre. Multicoloured.
1080 15y. Type **545** 25 10
1081 25y. "Kabuki" performance (48 × 33½ mm) 90 10
1082 50y. "Bunraku" puppet act (33½ × 48 mm) . . . . . 1·00 10

1966. International Rice Year.
1083 **546** 15y. black, ochre and red 15 10

547 Ittobori Sheep (sculpture)

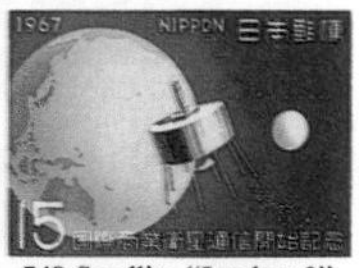
548 Satellite "Intelsat 2", Earth and Moon

1966. New Year's Greetings.
1084 **547** 7y. multicoloured . . . 15 10

1967. Inauguration of International Commercial Satellite Communications in Japan.
1086 **548** 15y. brown and blue . . 15 10

549 Douglas DC-8 and Flight Route

1967. Inauguration of Round-the-World Air Service.
1087 **549** 15y. multicoloured . . . 50 10

550 Literature Museum

1967. Opening of Japanese Modern Literature Museum, Meguro-ku, Tokyo.
1088 **550** 15y. multicoloured . . . 15 10

551 "Lakeside" (after S. Kuroda)

1967. Philatelic Week.
1089 **551** 15y. multicoloured . . . 60 10

552 Port of Kobe

553 Emblem of Welfare Service

1967. 5th International Association of Ports and Harbours Congress, Tokyo.
1090 **552** 50y. multicoloured . . . 80 10

1967. 50th Anniv of Welfare Commissioner Service.
1091 **553** 15y. gold and agate . . 25 10

554 Pedestrian Road Crossing

555 Mts. Kita and Koma

556 Mts. Akashi, Hijiri and Higashi

1967. 20th Anniv of Road Safety Campaign.
1092 **554** 15y. multicoloured . . . 15 10

1967. Southern Alps National Park.
1093 **555** 7y. blue 25 10
1094 **556** 15y. purple 35 10

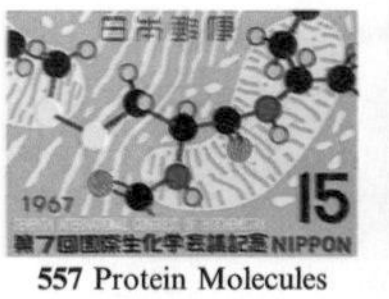
557 Protein Molecules

558 Gymnast

1967. 7th Int Biochemistry Congress, Tokyo.
1095 **557** 15y. multicoloured . . . 15 10

1967. "Universiade 1967" (Sports Meeting), Tokyo. Multicoloured.
1096 15y. Type **558** 20 10
1097 50y. Universiade "U" emblem (25 × 35½ mm) . . 90 10

559 Paper Lantern

560 Mt. Fuji (after T. Yokoyama)

1967. International Tourist Year.
1098 **559** 15y. multicoloured . . . 25 10
1099 **560** 50y. multicoloured . . . 1·40 1·75

561 "Kajikazawa in Kai Province" (from "36 Views of Mt. Fuji" by Hokusai Katsushika)

562 Athlete

1967. International Correspondence Week.
1100 **561** 50y. multicoloured . . . 2·75 15

1967. 22nd National Athletic Meeting, Saitama.
1101 **562** 15y. multicoloured . . . 50 10

563 Buddha, Koryu Temple, Kyoto

564 Kudara Kannon (Budda), Horyu Temple, Nara

565 Horyu Temple, Nara

1967. National Treasures. Asuka Period.
1102 **563** 15y. multicoloured . . . 40 10
1103 **564** 15y. multicoloured . . . 60 10
1104 **565** 50y. multicoloured . . . 2·50 20
See also Nos. 1113/15, 1120/2, 1134/6, 1152/4, 1170/2 and 1177/80.

566 Motor Expressway

569 "Noborizaru" (Miyazaki toy)

567 Mt. Kumotori

568 Lake Chichibu

1967. 13th World Road Congress, Tokyo.
1105 **566** 50y. multicoloured . . . 75 10

1967. Chichibu-Tama National Park.
1106 **567** 7y. olive 35 10
1107 **568** 15y. violet 45 10

1967. New Year's Greetings.
1108 **569** 7y. multicoloured . . . 35 10

570 Mt. Sobo

571 Takachiho Gorge

1967. Sobo-Katamuki Quasi-National Park.
1110 **570** 15y. multicoloured . . . 35 10
1111 **571** 15y. multicoloured . . . 35 10

572 Boy and Girl and Cruise Liner "Sakura Maru"

573 Asura Statue, Kofuku Temple, Nara

574 Gakko Bosatsu, Todai Temple, Nara

575 Srimaha devi (painting), Yakushi Temple, Nara

1968. Youth Goodwill Cruise to mark Meiji Centenary.
1112 **572** 15y. violet, yellow & blue 15 10

1968. National Treasures. Nara Period (710–784).
1113 **573** 15y. multicoloured . . . 45 10
1114 **574** 15y. multicoloured . . . 70 10
1115 **575** 50y. multicoloured . . . 2·50 20

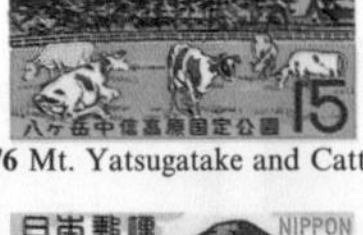
576 Mt. Yatsugatake and Cattle

577 Mt. Tateshina and Lake

1968. Yatsugatake-Chushin Kogen Quasi-National Park.
1116 **576** 15y. multicoloured . . . 30 10
1117 **577** 15y. multicoloured . . . 30 10

578 "Dancer in a Garden" (after Bakusen Tsuchida)

1968. Philatelic Week.
1118 **578** 15y. multicoloured . . . 40 10

579 View of Rishiri Island from Rebun Island

1968. Rishiri-Rebun Quasi-National Park.
1119 **579** 15y. multicoloured . . . 15 10

580 Lacquer Casket

582 "Fugen Bosatsu" (painting of Bodishattva Samantabhadva)

581 "The Origin of Shigisan" (painting in Chogo-sonshi Temple)

1968. National Treasures. Heinan Period (794–1185).
1120 **580** 15y. multicoloured . . . 30 10
1121 **581** 15y. multicoloured . . . 60 10
1122 **582** 50y. multicoloured . . . 4·25 35

583 Centenary Tower and Star

584 Biro Trees and Pacific Sunrise

1968. Hokkaido Centenary.
1123 **583** 15y. multicoloured . . . 15 10

1968. Return of Ogasawara Islands to Japan.
1124 **584** 15y. multicoloured . . . 15 10

585 "Map of Japan" in Figures

1968. Postal Codes Campaign.
1125 **585** 7y. red, brown & grn (I) 2·75 10
1126 – 7y. red, brown & grn (II) 2·75 10
1127 **585** 15y. mauve, vio & bl (I) 1·00 10
1128 – 15y. mauve, vio & bl (II) 1·00 10
(I) Inscr as in Type **585** reading "Don't omit postal code on the address" measures 11 mm.
(II) Inscr reading "Postal code also on your address" measures 12 mm.

586 River Kiso

587 Inuyama Castle and View

1968. Hida-Kisogawa Quasi-National Park.
1129 **586** 15y. multicoloured . . . 25 10
1130 **587** 15y. multicoloured . . . 25 10

588 Federation Emblem and "Sun"

1968. Int Youth Hostel Conference, Tokyo.
1131 **588** 15y. multicoloured . . . 20 10

589 Humans forming Emblem

590 Baseball "Pitcher"

1968. 50th All-Japan High School Baseball Championships, Koshi-en, Tokyo.
1132 **589** 15y. multicoloured . . . 60 10
1133 **590** 15y. multicoloured . . . 60 10

591 "Minamoto Yoritomo" (Jingo Temple Collection)

593 Red-braided Armour (Kasuga Grand Shrine Collection)

592 Emperor Nijo escaping from Black Palace (from "Tale of Heiji" picture scroll)

1968. National Treasures. Kamakura Period (1185–1334).
1134 **591** 15y. multicoloured . . . 40 10
1135 **592** 15y. multicoloured . . . 40 10
1136 **593** 50y. multicoloured . . . 3·00 30

594 Mt. Iwate

595 Lake Towada

1968. Towada-Hachimantai National Park.
1137 **594** 7y. brown 25 10
1138 **595** 15y. green 45 10

596 Gymnastics

597 "Fujimihara in Owari Province" (from "36 Views of Mt. Fuji" by Hokusai Katsushika)

1968. 23rd National Athletic Meeting.
1139 **596** 15y. multicoloured . . . 40 10

1968. International Correspondence Week.
1140 **597** 50y. multicoloured . . . 2·00 25

598 Centenary Emblem and Sail Warship "Shohei Maru", 1868

599 "Arrival of the Imperial Carriage in Tokyo" (after Tomone Kobori)

1968. Centenary of Meiji Era.
1141 **598** 15y. multicoloured . . . 15 10
1142 **599** 15y. multicoloured . . . 15 10

600 Old and New Kannonzaki Lighthouses

1968. Centenary of Japanese Lighthouses.
1143 **600** 15y. multicoloured . . . 30 10

601 Ryo's Dancer and State Hall

1968. Completion of Imperial Palace.
1144 **601** 15y. multicoloured . . . 20 10

602 Mt. Takachiho

603 Mt. Motobu, Yaku Island

1968. Kirishima-Yaku National Park.
1145 **602** 7y. violet 20 10
1146 **603** 15y. orange 25 10

604 "Niwatori" (Yamagata toy)

605 Human Rights Emblem and Dancers

1968. New Year's Greetings.
1147 **604** 7y. multicoloured . . . 25 10

1968. Human Rights Year.
1149 **605** 50y. multicoloured . . . 25 15

606 Siberian Chipmunk with Nuts

607 Coastal Scenery

1968. Savings Promotion.
1150 **606** 15y. sepia and green . . 70 10

1969. Echizen-Kaga-Kaigan Quasi-National Park.
1151 **607** 15y. multicoloured . . . 15 10

608 Silver Pavilion, Jisho Temple, Kyoto

609 Pagoda, Anraku Temple, Nagano

610 "Winter Landscape" (Sesshu)

1969. National Treasures. Muromachi Period.
1152 **608** 15y. multicoloured . . . 40 10
1153 **609** 15y. multicoloured . . . 40 10
1154 **610** 50y. multicoloured . . . 2·00 30

611 Mt. Chokai, from Tobishima

1969. Chokai Quasi-National Park.
1155 **611** 15y. multicoloured . . . 35 20

612 "Expo" Emblem and Globe

613 "Cherry Blossom" (from mural Chichakuin Temple, Kyoto)

1969. "EXPO 70" World Fair, Osaka (1st issue).
1156 **612** 15y.+5y. mult 35 15
1157 **613** 50y.+10y. mult 85 50
See also Nos. 1193/5 and 1200/2.

614 Mt. Koya from Jinnogamine

615 Mt. Gomadan and Rhododendrons

1969. Koya-Ryujin Quasi-National Park.
1158 **614** 15y. multicoloured . . . 15 10
1159 **615** 15y. multicoloured . . . 15 10

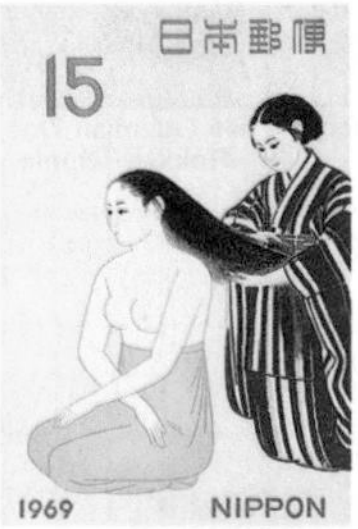

616 "Hair" (Kokei Kobayashi)

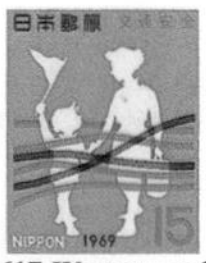

617 Woman and Child crossing "Roads"

1969. Philatelic Week.
1160 **616** 15y. multicoloured . . . 40 10

1969. Road Safety Campaign.
1161 **617** 15y. green, blue and red 15 10

618 Sakawagawa Bridge

1969. Completion of Tokyo–Nagoya Expressway.
1162 **618** 15y. multicoloured . . . 30 10

619 Museum Building

1969. Opening of National Museum of Modern Art, Tokyo.
1163 **619** 15y. multicoloured . . . 15 10

620 Nuclear-powered Freighter "Mutsu" and Atomic Symbol

1969. Launching of Japan's 1st Nuclear Ship "Mutsu".
1164 **620** 15y. multicoloured . . . 30 10

621 Cable Ship "KDD Maru" and Map

622 Symbol and Cards

1969. Opening of Japanese Ocean Cable.
1165 **621** 15y. multicoloured . . . 15 10

1969. Postal Codes Campaign.
1166 **622** 7y. red and green . . . 15 10
1167 – 15y. red and blue . . . 20 10
DESIGN: 15y. Symbol, postbox and code numbers.

624 Lions Emblem and Rose

625 Hotoke-ga-ura (coast)

1969. 52nd Lions Int Convention, Tokyo.
1168 **624** 15y. multicoloured . . . 20 10

1969. Shimokita-Hanto Quasi-National Park.
1169 **625** 15y. multicoloured . . . 15 10

626 Himeji Castle, Hyogo Prefecture

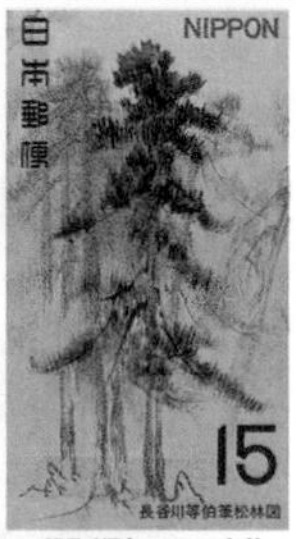

627 "Pinewoods" (T. Hasegawa)

628 "The Japanese Cypress" (artist unknown)

1969. National Treasures. Momoyama Period.
1170 **626** 15y. multicoloured . . . 50 10
1171 **627** 15y. black and drab . . 50 10
1172 **628** 50y. multicoloured . . . 1·00 10

629 Harano-fudo Waterfalls

630 Mt. Nagisan

1969. Hyonosen-Ushiroyama-Nagisan Quasi-National Park.
1173 **629** 15y. multicoloured . . . 25 10
1174 **630** 15y. multicoloured . . . 25 10

631 Mt. O-akan

632 Mt. Iwo

1969. Akan National Park.
1175 **631** 7y. blue 25 10
1176 **632** 15y. sepia 25 10

633 "Choben" (T. Ikeno)

634 "The Red-plum Tree" (K. Ogata)

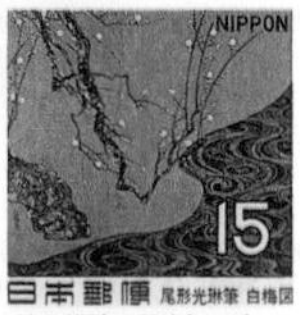

635 "The White-plum Tree" (K. Ogata)

636 "Japanese Pheasant" Incense-burner (after Ninsei)

1969. National Treasures. Edo Period.
1177 **633** 15y. multicoloured . . . 40 10
1178 **634** 15y. multicoloured . . . 50 10
1179 **635** 15y. multicoloured . . . 50 10
1180 **636** 50y. multicoloured . . . 1·00 65

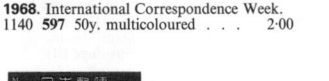

637 Globe and Doves

638 "Woman Reading a Letter" (Utamaro Kitagawa)

639 "Reading a Letter" (Harunobu Suzuki)

640 "Miyako Dennai" (Sharaku Toshusai)

1969. 16th U.P.U. Congress, Tokyo.
1181 **637** 15y. multicoloured . . . 30 10
1182 **638** 30y. multicoloured . . . 65 10
1183 **639** 50y. multicoloured . . . 1·25 10
1184 **640** 60y. multicoloured . . . 1·40 10

641 "Mishima Pass" (from "36 Views of Mt. Fuji" by Hokusai Katsushika)

642 Rugby Football

1969. International Correspondence Week.
1185 **641** 50y. multicoloured . . . 1·00 10

1969. 24th National Athletic Meeting.
1186 **642** 15y. multicoloured . . . 50 10

643 Cape Kitayama

644 Goishi Coast

1969. Rikuchu-Kaigan National Park.
1187 **643** 7y. blue 15 10
1188 **644** 15y. red and salmon . . 20 10

645 Worker in Safety Helmet

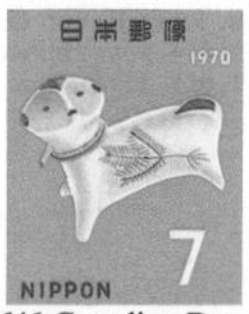
646 Guardian Dog, Hokkeji Temple

1969. 50th Anniv of I.L.O.
1189 **645** 15y. multicoloured . . . 15 10

1969. New Year's Greetings.
1190 **646** 7y. multicoloured . . . 35 10

647 Peasants, Tsushima Island

1970. Iki-Tsushima Quasi-National Park.
1192 **647** 15y. multicoloured . . . 20 10

648 View of Fair and Firework Display

651 "Woman with Drum" (Saburosuke Okada)

1970. "EXPO 70" World Fair, Osaka (2nd issue). Multicoloured.
1193 7y. Type **648** 15 10
1194 15y. Earth and cherry blossom garland 25 10
1195 50y. "Irises" (Korin Ogata) (48 × 33 mm) 45 10
MS1196 144 × 93 mm. Nos. 1193/5 2·25 2·25

1970. Philatelic Week.
1197 **651** 15y. multicoloured . . . 40 10

652 Cherry Blossom, Mt. Yoshino

653 Waterfall, Nachi

1970. Yoshino-Kumano National Park.
1198 **652** 7y. black and pink . . . 30 10
1199 **653** 15y. dp green, green & bl 45 10

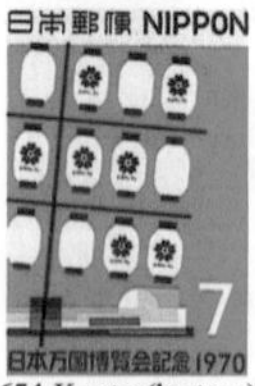
654 Kanto (lantern) Festival

655 Japanese Pavilions

656 "Flowers of Autumn" (detail, Hoitsu Sakai)

1970. "EXPO 70" World Fair, Osaka (3rd issue).
1200 **654** 7y. multicoloured . . . 20 10
1201 **655** 15y. multicoloured . . . 30 10
1202 **656** 50y. multicoloured . . . 45 10
MS1203 144 × 93 mm. Nos. 1200/2 1·25 1·25

657 Houses and Code Symbol

658 Utaemon Nakamura VI as Hanako in "Musume Dojoji"

659 Danjuro Ichikawa XI as Sukeroku in "Sukeroku"

661 Girl Scout saluting

660 "Kanjincho"

1970. Postal Codes Campaign.
1204 **657** 7y. violet and green . . 25 10
1205 15y. purple and blue . . 35 10

1970. Japanese Theatre "Kabuki".
1206 **658** 15y. multicoloured . . . 25 10
1207 **659** 15y. multicoloured . . . 25 10
1208 **660** 50y. multicoloured . . . 75 10
See also Nos. 1250/2, 1284/6 and 1300/2.

1970. 50th Anniv of Japanese Girl Scouts.
1209 **661** 15y. multicoloured . . . 35 10

662 Festival Drummer and Kinoura Coastline

663 Mt. Tate from Himi Shore

1970. Noto-Hanto Quasi-National Park.
1210 **662** 15y. multicoloured . . . 25 10
1211 **663** 15y. multicoloured . . . 25 10

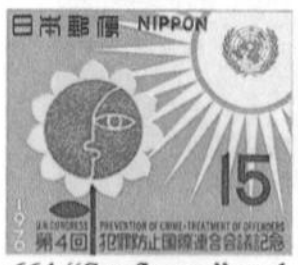
664 "Sunflower" and U.N. Emblem

667 "Tokyo Post Office" (woodcut, Hiroshige III)

665 Mt. Myogi

666 Mt. Arafune

1970. 4th U.N. Congress on Prevention of Crime and Treatment of Offenders, Kyoto.
1212 **664** 15y. multicoloured . . . 25 10

1970. Myogi-Arafune-Sakukuogen Quasi-National Park.
1213 **665** 15y. multicoloured . . . 20 10
1214 **666** 15y. multicoloured . . . 20 10

1970. International Correspondence Week.
1215 **667** 50y. multicoloured . . . 85 10

668 Show Jumping, Mt. Iwate and Paulownia Flowers

669 "Hodogaya Stage" (print, Hiroshige III)

1970. 25th National Athletic Meeting, Iwate.
1216 **668** 15y. multicoloured . . . 50 10

1970. Centenary of Telegraph Service.
1217 **669** 15y. multicoloured . . . 45 10

670 U.N. Emblem within "Tree"

672 Competition Emblem

1970. 25th Anniv of U.N.O. Multicoloured.
1218 15y. Type **670** 15 10
1219 50y. U.N. emblem, New York H.Q. and flags . . . 40 10

1970. 19th International Vocational Training Competition, Chiba City.
1220 **672** 15y. multicoloured . . . 15 10

673 Diet Building and Doves

674 "Wild Boar" (folk-handicraft)

1970. 80th Anniv of Japanese Diet.
1221 **673** 15y. multicoloured . . . 15 10

1970. New Year's Greetings.
1222 **674** 7y. multicoloured . . . 20 10

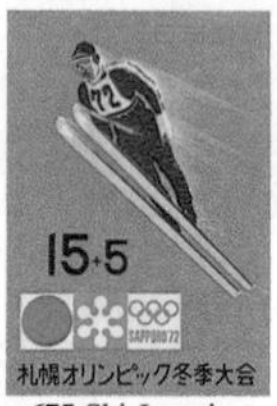
675 Ski Jumping

1971. Winter Olympic Games, Sapporo (1972) (1st issue). Multicoloured.
1224 15y.+5y. Type **675** 30 10
1225 15y.+5y. Ice-hockey (horiz) 30 10
See also Nos. 1280/82.

677 Mute Swan **678** Sika Deer **679** "Allomyrina dichotomus"

680 "Pine Tree" (T. Kano) **682** Golden Eagle **684** "Ho-o" (Phoenix), Byodoin Temple, Uji

692 Statue of Kissho, Joruri Temple

1971. Inscr "NIPPON".
1226 **273** 3y. green 20 20
1227 **677** 5y. blue 20 20
1228 **678** 10y. brown and green 25 10
1229 **679** 12y. brown 20 10
1230 **680** 20y. brown and green 20 10
1231 **528** 25y. blue and green . . 35 10
1232 **240** 50y. green 35 10
1233 – 60y. green and yellow 40 10
1234 **408** 70y. black and orange 95 10
1235 **409** 80y. brown and red . . 1·40 20
1236 **410** 90y. brown and orange 1·40 10
1237 **682** 90y. black and red . . 2·00 20
1238 **412** 120y. brown and green 55 10
1239 – 140y. purple and mauve 75 10
1240 **684** 150y. turquoise & green 1·75 10
1240a 150y. brown and red 60 10
1241 – 200y. red . . . . 3·00 10
1242 – 200y. brown . . . . . 3·50 10
1243 – 200y. red . . . . . . 1·25 10
1244 – 250y. blue . . . . . . 1·25 10
1245 – 300y. blue . . . . . . 3·50 10
1246 – 350y. brown . . . . . 2·00 10
1247 – 400y. red . . . . 2·40 10
1248 – 500y. green . . . . . . 3·00 10
1249 **692** 1000y. multicoloured 5·50 60
MS1249a 51 × 102 mm. No. 1249 10·00 9·00
DESIGNS: 60y. Narcissi; 140y. Noh mask of aged man; 200y. (No. 1241), Onjo Bosatsu (relief), Todai Temple; 200y. (Nos. 1242/3), Warrior (statuette); 250y. Komainu (guardian dog), Katori Shrine; 300y. Buddha, Kofuku Temple; 350y. Goddess of Mercy, Yaluski Temple, Nara; 400y. Tentoki (demon); 500y. Buddhist deity.

No. 1231 is Type **528**, redrawn. The inscription and face value are smaller, but the main difference is in the position of the leaves. On No. 1053 they touch the left edge of the design, but on No. 1231 they are completely clear of it.

No. 1241 is as Type **536** but smaller, 18 × 22 mm.

For 210y. as Nos. 1242/3 and 360y. as No. 1246, see Nos. 1600 and 1604.

693 "Gen-jo-raku"

694 "Ko-cho"

695 "Tai-hei-raku"

1971. Japanese Theatre "Gagaku".
1250 **693** 15y. multicoloured . . . 30 10
1251 **694** 15y. multicoloured . . . 30 10
1252 **695** 50y. multicoloured . . . 85 10

696 Voter and Diet Building

697 Pine Trees and Maple Leaves

1971. 25th Anniv of Women's Suffrage.
1253 **696** 15y. multicoloured . . . 15 10

1971. National Afforestation Campaign.
1254 **697** 7y. black, violet & green 40 10

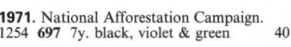

698 "Tsukiji-akashicho" (K. Kaburagi)

699 "Posting a Letter" (K. Dogishi)

700 "Postman" (K. Kasai)

701 "Railway Post Office" (S. Onozaki)

1971. Philatelic Week.
1255 **698** 15y. multicoloured . . . 40 10

1971. Centenary of Japanese Postal Services.
1256 **699** 15y. multicoloured . . . 20 10
1257 **700** 15y. black and brown . . 20 10
1258 **701** 15y. multicoloured . . . 40 10

702 Great Tit

703 Adelie Penguins

1971. 25th Bird Week.
1259 **702** 15y. multicoloured . . . 85 20

1971. 10th Anniv of Antarctic Treaty.
1260 **703** 15y. multicoloured . . . 1·10 20

704 Goto-Wakamatsu-Seto

705 Kuzyuku-shima

1971. Saikai National Park.
1261 **704** 7y. green 25 10
1262 **705** 15y. brown 35 10

706 Postal Code Numerals

707 Scout Bugler

1971. Postal Code Campaign.
1263 **706** 7y. red and green . . . 20 10
1264 15y. red and blue . . . 30 10

1971. 13th World Scout Jamboree, Asagiri.
1265 **707** 15y. multicoloured . . . 40 10

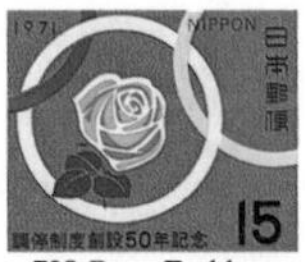
708 Rose Emblem

1971. 50th Anniv of Family Conciliation System.
1266 **708** 15y. multicoloured . . . 25 10

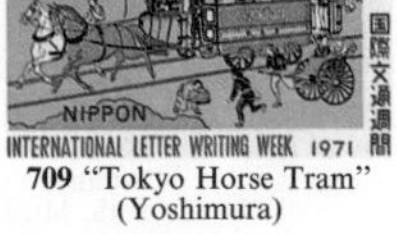
709 "Tokyo Horse Tram" (Yoshimura)

1971. International Correspondence Week.
1267 **709** 50y. multicoloured . . . 60 25

710 Emperor's Standard

712 Tennis

1971. European Tour by Emperor Hirohito and Empress Nagako. Multicoloured.
1268 15y. Type **710** 15 10
1269 15y. "Beyond the Sea" (drawing by Empress Nagako) 15 10
MS1270 141 × 111 mm. Nos. 1268/9. Imperf 35 30

1971. 26th National Athletic Meeting.
1271 **712** 15y. multicoloured . . . 30 10

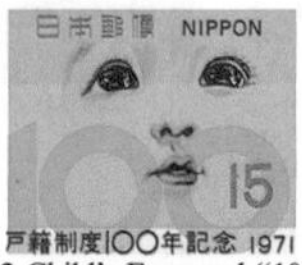
713 Child's Face and "100"

1971. Centenary of National Family Registration System.
1272 **713** 15y. multicoloured . . . 15 10

714 "Dragon" (G. Hashimoto)

1971. Centenary of Government Printing Works, Tokyo. Multicoloured.
1273 15y. Type **714** 20 10
1274 15y. "Tiger" (from same drawing as above) 20 10

716 Mt. Yotei from Lake Toya

718 Takarabune ("Treasure Ship")

717 Mt. Showa-Shinzan

1971. Shikotsu-Toya National Park.
1275 **716** 7y. green and olive . . . 25 10
1276 **717** 15y. blue and brown . . 40 10

1971. New Year's Greetings.
1277 **718** 7y. multicoloured . . . 25 10
1278 10y. multicoloured . . . 35 10

719 Skiing

1972. Winter Olympic Games, Sapporo (2nd issue). Multicoloured.
1280 20y. Type **719** 15 10
1281 20y. Bobsleighing 15 10
1282 50y. Figure skating (pair) (52 × 36 mm) 45 10
MS1283 145 × 94 mm. Nos. 1280/2 1·50 35

722 "Kumagai-jinya"

723 "Nozaki-mura"

724 "Awa-no-Naruto"

1972. Japanese Theatre. "Banraku" Puppet Theatre.
1284 **722** 20y. multicoloured . . . 30 10
1285 **723** 20y. multicoloured . . . 30 10
1286 **724** 50y. multicoloured . . . 70 10

725 "Hikari" Express Train

727 Fishing, Taishakukyo Valley

726 Hiba Mountains

1972. Centenary of Japanese Railways (1st issue) and Opening of Sanyo Shinkansen Line.
1287 **725** 20y. multicoloured . . . 25 10
See also Nos. 1305/6.

1972. Hiba-Dogo-Taishaku Quasi-National Park.
1288 **726** 20y. multicoloured . . . 15 10
1289 **727** 20y. multicoloured . . . 20 10

728 Adult with Human Heart

729 "Rising Balloon" (Gakuryo Nakamura)

1972. World Heart Month.
1290 **728** 20y. multicoloured . . . 15 10

1972. Philatelic Week.
1291 **729** 20y. multicoloured . . . 15 10

730 Courtesy Gate, Shuri

731 Japanese Camellia

1972. Return of Ryukyu Islands to Japan.
1292 **730** 20y. multicoloured . . . 15 10

1972. National Afforrestation Campaign.
1293 **731** 20y. yellow blue & green 35 10

732 Mt. Kurikoma and Kokeshi Doll

733 Naruko-kyo Gorge and Kokeshi Doll

1972. Kurikoma Quasi-National Park.

1294	**732**	20y. multicoloured	15	10
1295	**733**	20y. multicoloured	15	10

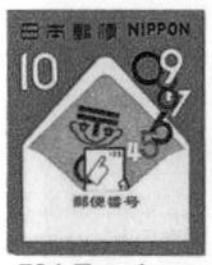

734 Envelope and Code Symbol

736 Mt. Hodaka

737 Mt. Tate

1972. Postal Codes Campaign (5th issue).

1296	**734**	10y. black, purple & blue	10	10
1297	–	20y. red and green	15	10

DESIGN: 20y. Mail-box and code symbol.

1972. Chubu Sangaku National Park.

1298	**736**	10y. violet and mauve	20	10
1299	**737**	20y. blue and brown	30	10

738 "Tamura"

739 "Aoi-no-ue"

740 "Hagoromo"

1972. Japanese Theatre. "Noh".

1300	**738**	20y. multicoloured	20	10
1301	**739**	20y. multicoloured	20	10
1302	**740**	50y. multicoloured	45	15

741 "Profiles of Schoolchildren"

742 "Eitai Bridge" (Hiroshige III)

1972. Centenary of Japanese Educational System.

1303	**741**	20y. multicoloured	15	10

1972. International Correspondence Week.

1304	**742**	50y. multicoloured	60	10

743 "Inauguration of Railway Service" (Hiroshige III)

745 Kendo (Japanese Fencing)

1972. Centenary of Japanese Railways (2nd issue). Multicoloured.

1305	20y. Type **743**	50	10
1306	20y. Class C-62 steam locomotive No. 2	50	10

1972. 27th National Athletic Meeting, Kagoshima.

1307	**745**	10y. multicoloured	35	10

746 Scout and Cub

747 "Harbour and Bund, Yokohama" (Hiroshige III)

1972. 50th Anniv of Japanese Boy Scouts.

1308	**746**	20y. multicoloured	35	10

1972. Centenary of Japanese Customs Service.

1309	**747**	20y. multicoloured	55	10

748 "Plum Blossoms" Plate (K. Ogata)

749 Mt. Tsurugi

750 River Yoshino, Oboke Valley

1972. New Year's Greetings.

1310	**748**	10y. multicoloured	15	10

1973. Tsurugi-San Quasi-National Park.

1312	**749**	20y. multicoloured	30	10
1313	**750**	20y. multicoloured	30	10

751 Mt. Takao

752 Minoo Falls and Japanese Macaques

1973. Meiji-no-mori Quasi-National Park.

1314	**751**	20y. multicoloured	20	10
1315	**752**	20y. multicoloured	20	10

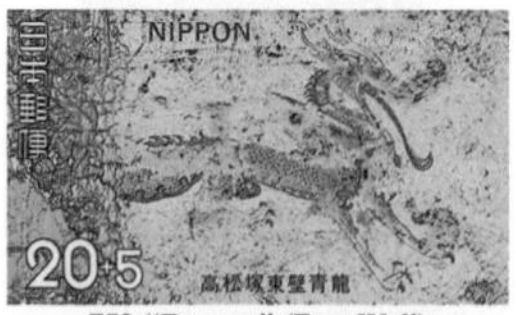

753 "Dragon" (East Wall)

754 "Male Figures" (East Wall)

755 "Female Figures" (West Wall)

1973. Asuka Archaeological Conservation Fund. Takamatsuzuka Kofun Tomb Murals.

1316	**753**	20y.+5y. multicoloured	30	10
1317	**754**	20y.+5y. multicoloured	30	10
1318	**755**	50y.+10y. multicoloured	80	35

756 Phoenix Tree

757 "Sumiyoshimode" (R. Kishida)

1973. National Afforestation Campaign.

1319	**756**	20y. multicoloured	35	10

1973. Philatelic Week.

1320	**757**	20y. multicoloured	15	10

758 Mt. Kama

759 Rock Outcrops, Mt. Haguro

1973. Suzuka Quasi-National Park.

1321	**758**	20y. multicoloured	25	10
1322	**759**	20y. multicoloured	25	10

760 Chichi-jima Island Beach

761 Coral Reef, Minami-jimi Island

1973. Ogasawara Islands National Park.

1323	**760**	10y. blue	25	10
1324	**761**	20y. purple	35	10

762 Postal Code Symbol and Tree

765 Waterfall, Sandan-kyo Gorge

764 Mt. Shinnyu

1973. Postal Codes Campaign.

1325	**762**	10y. gold and green	10	10
1326	–	20y. lilac, red and blue	15	10

DESIGN: 20y. Postman and symbol.

1973. Nishi-Chugoku-Sanchi Quasi-National Park.

1327	**764**	20y. multicoloured	30	10
1328	**765**	20y. multicoloured	30	10

766 Valley of River Tenryu

767 Oriental Scops Owl and Woodland Path, Mt. Horaiji

1973. Tenryu-Okumikowa Quasi-National Park.

1329	**766**	20y. multicoloured	25	10
1330	**767**	20y. blue, green and silver	45	20

768 "Cock" (J. Ito)

769 Sprinting

1973. International Correspondence Week.

1331	**768**	50y. multicoloured	65	10

1973. 28th National Athletic Meeting. Chiba.

1332	**769**	10y. multicoloured	20	10

770 Kan-Mon Bridge

1973. Opening of Kan-Mon Suspension Bridge.

1333	**770**	20y. multicoloured	40	10

771 Hanasaka-jijii and his Dog

772 Hanasaka-jijii finds the Gold

773 Hanasaka-jijii and Tree in Blossom

1973. Japanese Folk Tales (1st series). "Hanasaki-jijii".

1334	**771**	20y. multicoloured	15	10
1335	**772**	20y. multicoloured	15	10
1336	**773**	20y. multicoloured	15	10

See also Nos. 1342/4, 1352/4, 1358/60, 1362/4, 1378/80 and 1387/9.

774 Lantern

775 Niju-bashi Bridge

1973. New Year's Greetings.

1337	**774**	10y. multicoloured	10	10

1974. Imperial Golden Wedding. Mult.

1339	20y. Type **775**	15	10
1340	20y. Imperial Palace	15	10
MS1341	145 × 89 mm. Nos. 1339/40	85	60

777 "The Crane Damsel"

1974. Japanese Folk Tales (2nd series). "Tsuru-Nyobo". Multicoloured.

1342	20y. Type **777**	15	10
1343	20y. Manchurian Crane "weaving"	45	20
1344	20y. Manchurian Cranes in flight	45	20

780 "A Reefy Coast" (Hyakusui Hirafuku)

1974. International Ocean Exposition, Okinawa (1975) (1st issue).
1345 **780** 20y.+5y. multicoloured 15 10
See also Nos. 1401/3.

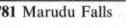

781 Marudu Falls

782 Seascape

1974. Iriomote National Park.
1346 **781** 20y. multicoloured . . . 25 10
1347 **782** 20y. multicoloured . . . 25 10

783 Iriomote Cat

1974. Nature Conservation (1st series).
1348 **783** 20y. multicoloured 25 10
See also Nos. 1356, 1361, 1372, 1377, 1381, 1405, 1419, 1422, 1430, 1433/4, 1449, 1457, 1469, 1470, 1475, 1490, 1497 and 1502.

784 "Finger" (Shinsui Ito)

1974. Philatelic Week.
1349 **784** 20y. multicoloured . . . 40 10

785 Nambu Red Pine

786 Supreme Court Building

1974. National Afforestation Campaign.
1350 **785** 20y. multicoloured . . . 20 10

1974. Completion of Supreme Court Building, Tokyo.
1351 **786** 20y. brown 15 10

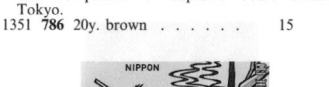

787 "Sailing in a Wooden Bowl"

788 "Conquering the Goblins"

789 "Wielding the Little Magic Mallet"

1974. Japanese Folk Tales (3rd series). "The Dwarf".
1352 **787** 20y. multicoloured . . . 15 10
1353 **788** 20y. multicoloured . . . 15 10
1354 **789** 20y. multicoloured . . . 15 10

790 "Uniform Rivalry" (detail after Kunimasa Baido)

792 World Blood Donation

1974. Centenary of Japanese Police System.
1355 **790** 20y. multicoloured . . . 15 10

1974. Nature Conservation (2nd series). As T **783**. Multicoloured.
1356 20y. European otter ("Lutra lutra") 25 10

1974. International Red Cross Day.
1357 **792** 20y. multicoloured . . . 15 10

793 "Discovery of Kaguya Hime"

794 "Kaguya Hime as Young Woman"

795 "The Ascent to Heaven"

1974. Japanese Folk Tales (4th series). "Kaguya Hime".
1358 **793** 20y. multicoloured . . . 25 10
1359 **794** 20y. multicoloured . . . 25 10
1360 **795** 20y. multicoloured . . . 25 10

1974. Nature Conservation (3rd series). As T **783**. Multicoloured.
1361 20y. Ryukyu rabbit ("Pentalagus furnessi") . . 25 10

797 Old Men in front of Yahata Shrine

798 Old Man dancing with Demons

799 Old Man with Two Warts

1974. Japanese Folk Tales (5th series). "Kobutori-Jiisan".
1362 **797** 20y. multicoloured . . . 15 10
1363 **798** 20y. multicoloured . . . 15 10
1364 **799** 20y. multicoloured . . . 15 10

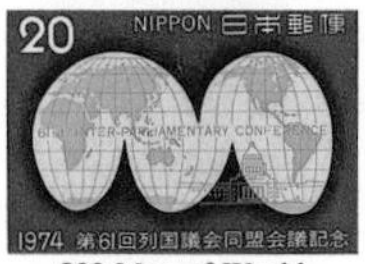

800 Map of World

802 "Pine and Northern Goshawk" (detail, Sesson)

1974. 61st Inter-Parliamentary Union Congress, Tokyo. Multicoloured.
1365 20y. Type **800** 25 10
1366 50y. "Aizen"—Mandarins in pond (Kawabata) (48 × 33 mm) 70 30

1974. International Correspondence Week.
1367 **802** 50y. brown and purple 70 30

803 U.P.U. Emblem

805 Footballers

1974. Centenary of U.P.U. Multicoloured.
1368 20y. Type **803** 10 10
1369 50y. "Tending a Cow" (fan-painting—Sotatsu Tawaraya) (50 × 29 mm) 30 10

1974. 29th National Athletic Meeting.
1370 **805** 10y. multicoloured . . . 15 10

806 Shii-take Mushrooms

808 Class D51 Locomotive

809 Class C57 Locomotive

1974. 9th International Scientific Congress on Cultivation of Edible Fungi.
1371 **806** 20y. multicoloured . . . 40 10

1974. Nature Conservation (4th series). As T **783**. Multicoloured.
1372 20y. Bonin Islands flying fox ("Pteropus pselaphon") 15 10

1974. Railway Steam Locomotives (1st series).
1373 **808** 20y. multicoloured . . . 65 15
1374 **809** 20y. multicoloured . . . 65 15
See also Nos. 1382/3, 1385/6, 1395/6 and 1398/9.

810 "Kugikakushi" (ornamental nail-covering) in the form of a daffodil

1974. New Year's Greetings.
1375 **810** 10y. multicoloured . . . 15 10

1975. Nature Conservation (5th series). As T **783**. Multicoloured.
1377 20y. Short-tailed albatrosses ("Diomedea albatrus") (vert) 70 20

812 Taro releasing Tortoise

813 Sea-God's Palace

814 Taro and Pandora's Box

1975. Japanese Folk Tales (6th series). "Urashima Taro".
1378 **812** 20y. multicoloured . . . 25 10
1379 **813** 20y. multicoloured . . . 25 10
1380 **814** 20y. multicoloured . . . 25 10

1975. Nature Conservation (6th series). As T **783**. Multicoloured.
1381 20y. Manchurian cranes ("Grus japonensis") (vert) 70 20

816 Class C58 Locomotive

817 Class D52 Locomotive

1975. Railway Steam Locomotives (2nd series).
1382 **816** 20y. multicoloured . . . 65 10
1383 **817** 20y. multicoloured . . . 65 10

818 "Sight and Hearing" (Shiko Munakata)

1975. 50th Anniv of Japanese Broadcasting Corporation.
1384 **818** 20y. multicoloured . . . 15 10

819 Class 8620 Locomotive No. 68622

820 Class C11 Locomotive

1975. Railway Steam Locomotives (3rd series).
1385 **819** 20y. multicoloured . . . 65 10
1386 **820** 20y. multicoloured . . . 65 10

821 Old Man feeding Mouse

822 Old Man holding Mouse's Tail

823 Mice giving Feast to Old Man

1975. Japanese Folk Tales (7th series). "Nezumi No Jodo".
1387 **821** 20y. multicoloured . . . 25 10
1388 **822** 20y. multicoloured . . . 25 10
1389 **823** 20y. multicoloured . . . 25 10

824/5 Matsuura Screen

1975. Philatelic Week.
1390 **824** 20y. multicoloured . . . 30 10
1391 **825** 20y. multicoloured . . . 30 10
Nos. 1390/1 were issued together, se-tenant, forming the composite design shown.

827 Oil Rigs

1975. 9th World Petroleum Congress, Tokyo.
1394 **827** 20y. multicoloured . . . 15 10

828 Class 9600 Locomotive No. 69820

829 Class C51 Locomotive No. 225

830 Plantation

1975. Railway Steam Locomotives (4th series).
1395 **828** 20y. multicoloured . . . 65 10
1396 **829** 20y. multicoloured . . . 65 10

1975. National Land Afforestation Campaign.
1397 **830** 20y. multicoloured . . . 15 10

831 Class 7100 Locomotive "Benkei", 1880

832 Class 150 Locomotive, 1872

1975. Railway Steam Locomotives (5th series).
1398 **831** 20y. black and buff . . . 65 10
1399 **832** 20y. black and yellow . . 65 10

833 Woman's Head and I.W.Y. Emblem

834 Okinawa Dance

1975. International Women's Year.
1400 **833** 20y. multicoloured . . . 15 10

1975. International Ocean Exposition, Okinawa (2nd issue). Multicoloured.
1401 20y. Type **834** 25 10
1402 30y. Bingata textile pattern 40 10
1403 50y. "Aquapolis and Globe" emblem (48 × 34 mm) . . 55 10
MS1404 144 × 94 mm. Nos. 1401/3 1·25 75

1975. Nature Conservation (7th series). As T **783**. Multicoloured.
1405 20y. Bonin Island honey-eater ("Apalopteron familiare") 70 10

838 Kentoshisen (7th–9th centuries)

839 Kenminsen (7th–9th centuries)

1975. Japanese Ships (1st series).
1406 **838** 20y. red 45 15
1407 **839** 20y. brown 45 15
See also Nos. 1409/10, 1420/1, 1423/4, 1428/9 and 1431/2.

840 Apple

843 "Green Peafowl" (after K. Ogata)

841 Goshuin-sen (16th-century trading ship)

842 "Tenchi-maru" (state barge), 1630

1975. Centenary of Apple Cultivation in Japan.
1408 **840** 20y. multicoloured . . . 15 10

1975. Japanese Ships (2nd series).
1409 **841** 20y. green 45 15
1410 **842** 20y. blue 45 15

1975. International Correspondence Week.
1411 **843** 50y. multicoloured . . . 1·00 15

844 United States Flag

1975. American Tour by Emperor Hirohito and Empress Nagako. Multicoloured.
1412 20y. Type **844** 25 10
1413 20y. Japanese flag 25 10
MS1414 146 × 93 mm. Nos. 1412/3 75 25

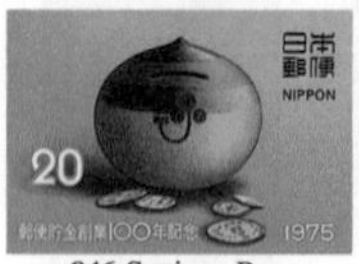
846 Savings Box

847 Weightlifting

1975. Centenary of Japanese Post Office Savings Bank.
1415 **846** 20y. multicoloured . . . 15 10

1975. 30th National Athletic Meeting.
1416 **847** 10y. multicoloured . . . 20 10

848 "Tatsu-guruma" (toy)

850 Sengoku-bune (fishing boat)

851 "Shohei Maru" (sail warship)

1975. New Year's Greetings.
1417 **848** 10y. multicoloured . . . 35 10

1976. Nature Conservation (8th series). As T **783**. Multicoloured.
1419 50y. Ryukyu robin ("Erithacus komadori") 60 20

1976. Japanese Ships (3rd series).
1420 **850** 50y. blue 65 15
1421 **851** 50y. violet 65 15

1976. Nature Conservation (9th series). As T **783**. Multicoloured.
1422 50y. Tortoise ("Goemyda spengleri") 60 15

853 "Taisei Maru" (cadet ship)

854 "Tenyo Maru" (liner)

1976. Japanese Ships (4th series).
1423 **853** 50y. black 65 15
1424 **854** 50y. brown 65 15

855 Section of Hikone Folding Screen

857 Cedar Forest, Plum Blossom, and Mt. Tsukuba

1976. Philatelic Week. Multicoloured.
1425 50y. Type **855** 45 10
1426 50y. Similar to Type **855** 45 10
NOTE: The two stamps form a composite design of the "Hikone Folding Screen".

1976. National Land Afforestation Campaign.
1427 **857** 50y. multicoloured . . . 30 10

858 "Asama Maru" (liner)

859 "Kinai Maru" (cargo liner)

1976. Japanese Ships (5th series).
1428 **858** 50y. green 65 15
1429 **859** 50y. brown 65 15

1976. Nature Conservation (10th series). As T **783**. Multicoloured.
1430 50y. Green tree frog ("Racophorus arboreus") (vert) 50 10

861 "Kamakura Maru" (container ship)

862 "Nissei Maru" (oil tanker)

1976. Japanese Ships (6th series).
1431 **861** 50y. blue 65 15
1432 **862** 50y. blue 65 15

1976. Nature Conservation (11th and 12th series). As T **783**. Multicoloured.
1433 50y. Tokyo bitterling ("Tanakia tanago") . . . 95 10
1434 50y. Three-spined sticklebacks ("Gasterosteus aculeatus") 95 10

865 "Kite and Rooks" (detail, Yosa Buson)

866 Gymnastics

1976. International Correspondence Week.
1435 **865** 100y. multicoloured . . 1·25 20

1976. 31st National Athletic Meeting.
1436 **866** 20y. multicoloured . . . 35 10

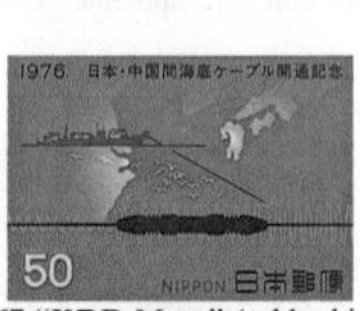
867 "KDD Maru" (cable ship) laying cable

1976. Opening of Sino-Japanese Cable.
1437 **867** 50y. multicoloured . . . 60 10

868 Man-zai-raku (classical dance)

870 Children at First Kindergarten

1976. Golden Jubilee of Emperor's Accession.
1438 **868** 50y. multicoloured . . . 40 10
1439 – 50y. red, gold and black 40 10
MS1440 144 × 93 mm. Nos. 1438/9 1·00 30
DESIGN: No. 2439, Coronation coach.

1976. Centenary of First Kindergarten. Tokyo.
1441 **870** 50y. multicoloured . . . 50 10

871 Family Group

872 Bamboo Snake

1976. 50th Anniv (1977) of Health Insurance System.
1442 **871** 50y. multicoloured . . . 40 10

1976. New Year's Greetings.
1443 **872** 20y. multicoloured . . . 20 10

873 East Pagoda, Yakushi Temple

1976. National Treasures (1st series). Mult.
1445 50y. Type **873** 50 10
1446 100y. Deva King, Todai Temple (33 × 48 mm) . . 1·25 10
See also Nos. 1447/8, 1452/3, 1463/4, 1471/2, 1480/1 and 1486/9.

875 Golden Pavilion, Toshodai Temple

1977. National Treasures (2nd series). Mult.
1447 50y. Type **875** 50 10
1448 100y. Illustration from "Heike Nokyo Sutra" (33 × 48 mm) . . . . . . 1·25 10

1977. Nature Conservation (13th series). As T **783**. Multicoloured.
1449 50y. Horseshoe crabs ("Tachypleus tridentatus") 45 10

878 Figure Skating

879 Figure Skating

1977. World Figure Skating Championships, Tokyo.
1450 **878** 50y. multicoloured . . . 55 10
1451 **879** 50y. multicoloured . . . 55 10

880 Detail of Picture Scroll (attr. Toba Sojo Kakuyu)

881 Wood Carving of Buddhist Saint (attr. Jocho) Byodoin Temple, Uji

1977. National Treasures (3rd series).
1452 **880** 50y. multicoloured . . . 50 10
1453 **881** 100y. dp brn, brn & grn 1·25 10

882 Forest in Sunshine

1977. National Land Afforestation Campaign.
1454 **882** 50y. multicoloured . . . 40 10

883/4 "Women" Weavers (part)

1977. Philatelic Week.
1455 **883** 50y. multicoloured . . . 50 10
1456 **884** 50y. multicoloured . . . 50 10
Nos. 1455/6 were issued in se-tenant pairs, forming a composite design.

1977. Nature Conservation (14th series). As T **783**. Multicoloured.
1457 50y. Mikado swallowtail ("Graphium doson") (vert) 60 10

886 Nurses

887 Central Part of Nuclear Reactor

1977. 16th Congress of the International Council of Nurses.
1458 **886** 50y. multicoloured . . . 40 10

1977. Reaching of Critical Mass by Joyo Fast-Breeder Reactor, Oarai Town.
1459 **887** 50y. multicoloured . . . 40 10

888 Carrier Pigeons and Mail Box with U.P.U. Emblem

889 U.P.U. Emblem and World Map

1977. Centenary of Japan's Admission to U.P.U.
1460 **888** 50y. multicoloured . . . 40 10
1461 **889** 100y. multicoloured . . 1·40 10
MS1462 144 × 93 mm. Nos. 1460/1 1·75 85

890 Illustration from "Picture Scroll of Lady Murasaki's Diary"

891 Statue of Seitaka Doji

892 Green Cross (safety emblem) and Workmen

1977. National Treasures (4th series).
1463 **890** 50y. multicoloured . . . 55 10
1464 **891** 100y. brown, deep brown and light brown . . . 1·40 10

1977. National Safety Week. Multicoloured.
1465 50y. Type **892** 80 10
1466 50y. Worker and high-rise building 80 10
1467 50y. Unloading freight . . . 80 10
1468 50y. Machine-worker . . . 80 10

1977. Nature Conservation (15th series). As T **783**. Multicoloured.
1469 50y. Firefly ("Luciola cruciata") 50 10

1977. Nature Conservation (16th series). As T **783**. Multicoloured.
1470 50y. Cicada ("Euterpnosia chibensis") 60 10

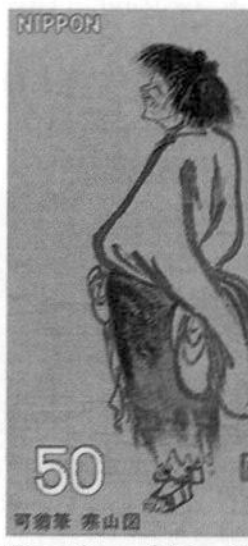

898 Drawing of Han Shan by Kao

899 Matsumoto Castle

1977. National Treasures (5th series).
1471 **898** 50y. multicoloured . . . 60 10
1472 **899** 100y. multicoloured . . 1·40 10

900 Map and Child on Telephone

1977. Opening of Okinawa–Luzon–Hong Kong Submarine Cable.
1473 **900** 50y. multicoloured . . . 40 10

901 Surgeon

1977. 27th Congress of International Society of Surgeons.
1474 **901** 50y. multicoloured . . . 50 10

1977. Nature Conservation (17th series). As T **783**. Multicoloured.
1475 50y. Dragonfly ("Boninthemis insularis") (vert) 60 10

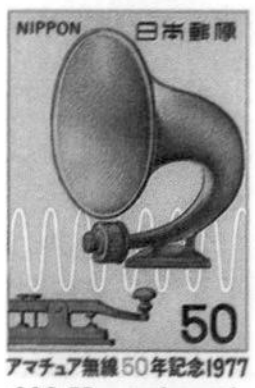

903 Horn-shaped Speaker and Telegraph Key

904 Racing Cyclist and Mt. Iwaki

1977. 50th Anniv of Amateur Radio League.
1476 **903** 50y. multicoloured . . . 40 10

1977. 32nd National Athletic Meeting.
1477 **904** 20y. multicoloured . . . 40 10

905 "Kacho-zu" (Nobuharu Hasegawa)

906 Long-necked Dinosaur and Museum

1977. International Correspondence Week.
1478 **905** 100y. multicoloured . . 1·25 30

1977. Centenary of National Science Museum.
1479 **906** 50y. multicoloured . . . 75 10

907 Detail, Folding Screen, Chishakuin Temple, Kyoto

908 Kiyomizu-dera Temple

1977. National Treasures (6th series).
1480 **907** 50y. multicoloured . . . 50 10
1481 **908** 100y. brown, green & bl 1·25 10

909 Toy Horse

1977. New Year's Greetings.
1482 **909** 20y. multicoloured . . . 25 10

910 Underground Train, 1927

911 Underground Train No. 1101, 1977

1977. 50th Anniv of Japanese Underground Railway.
1484 **910** 50y. multicoloured . . . 90 10
1485 **911** 50y. multicoloured . . . 90 10

912 Genji's Carriage at Sumiyoshi Shrine (scene on folding screen (Sotatsu Tawaraya) from "Tale of Genji" by Lady Murasaki)

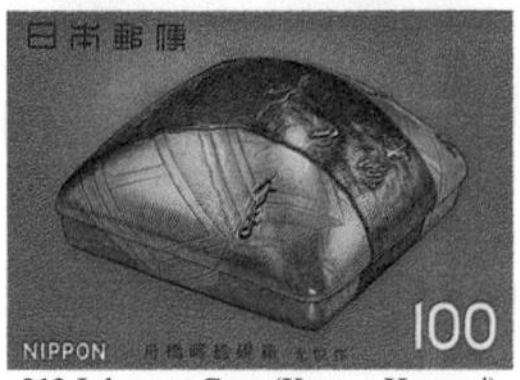

913 Inkstone Case (Koetsu Honami)

1978. National Treasures (7th series).
1486 **912** 50y. multicoloured . . . 50 10
1487 **913** 100y. multicoloured . . 1·40 10

914 "Noryozu" (Morikage Kusumi)

915 Yomei Gate, Tosho Shrine, Nikko

1978. National Treasures (8th series).
1488 **914** 50y. multicoloured . . . 50 10
1489 **915** 100y. multicoloured . . 1·40 10

916 "Primula sieboldi"

1978. Nature Conservation (18th series).
1490 **916** 50y. multicoloured . . . 50 10

917 Seated Woman With Flower (hanging scroll)

918 Dancing Woman (hanging scroll)

1978. Philatelic Week. "Kanbun Bijinzu" Genre Paintings.
1491 **917** 50y. multicoloured . . . 40 10
1492 **918** 50y. multicoloured . . . 40 10

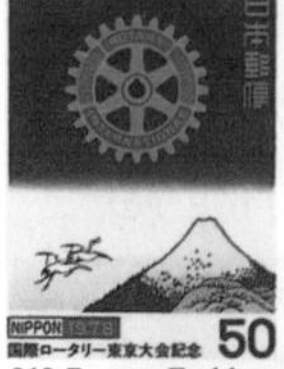

919 Rotary Emblem and Mt. Fuji (from "36 Views of Mt. Fuji" by Hokusai Katsushita)

920 Congress Emblem

1978. Rotary International Convention, Tokyo.
1493 **919** 50y. multicoloured . . . 55 20

1978. 23rd Int Ophthalmological Congress.
1494 **920** 50y. multicoloured . . . 45 10

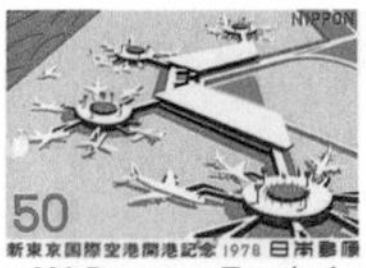

921 Passenger Terminal Buildings

922 Cape Ashizuri, Rainbow and Cedar Trees

1978. Opening of Narita Airport, Tokyo.
1495 **921** 50y. multicoloured . . . 60 10

1978. National Afforestation Campaign.
1496 **922** 50y. multicoloured . . . 50 10

923 "Pinguicula ramosa"

924 "Karashishi" (attr. Sotatsu Tawaraya) and Lions Emblem

1978. Nature Conservation (19th series).
1497 **923** 50y. multicoloured . . . 50 10

1978. 61st Lions International Convention, Tokyo.
1498 **924** 50y. multicoloured . . . 55 10

925/6 "Grand Champion Raigoyo Hidenoyama in the Ring" (Toyokuni III)

927 "Drum Tower of Ekoin Temple, Ryogoku" (Hiroshige)

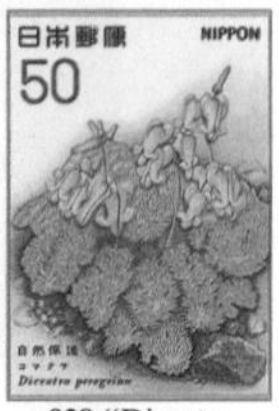

928 "Dicentra peregrina"

1978. Sumo (Japanese Wrestling) Pictures (1st series).
1499 **925** 50y. multicoloured . . . 50 10
1500 **926** 50y. multicoloured . . . 50 10
1501 **927** 50y. multicoloured . . . 60 10
Nos. 1499/500 were issued together, se-tenant, forming the composite design illustrated.
See also Nos. 1505/7, 1513/15, 1519/21 and 1523/5.

1978. Nature Conservation (20th series).
1502 **928** 50y. multicoloured . . . 35 10

929 Keep Fit Exercise

930 Chamber of Commerce and Industry Building and Centenary Emblem

1978. 50th Anniv of Radio Gymnastic Exercises.
1503 **929** 50y. multicoloured . . . 1·25 10

1978. Centenary of 1st Chambers of Commerce, Tokyo and Osaka.
1504 **930** 50y. multicoloured . . . 40 10

931/2 "Dohyoiri" wrestlers Tanikaze and Onogawa (Shunsho Katsukawa)

933 "Jinmaku versus Raiden" (Shunnei Katsukawa)

934 Statues on Tokyo Securities Exchange Building

1978. Sumo Pictures (2nd series).
1505 **931** 50y. multicoloured . . . 50 10
1506 **932** 50y. multicoloured . . . 50 10
1507 **933** 50y. multicoloured . . . 60 10
Nos. 1505/6 were issued together se-tenant, forming the composite design illustrated.

1978. Centenary of Tokyo and Osaka Stock Exchanges.
1508 **934** 50y. brown, purple & grn 50 10

935 Copper Pheasant (detail of door painting attr. Sanraku Kano)

936 Mt. Yari and Softball Players

1978. International Correspondence Week.
1509 **935** 100y. multicoloured . . 1·25 30

1978. 33rd National Athletic Meeting.
1510 **936** 20y. multicoloured . . . 40 10

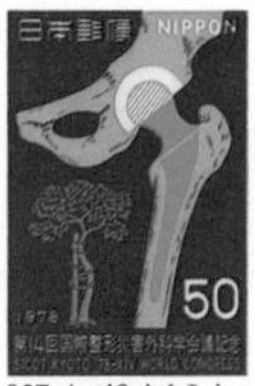

937 Artificial Joint

938 Refracting Telescope and Stars

1978. 14th Congress of International Society of Orthopaedic and Traumatic Surgeons, Kyoto.
1511 **937** 50y. blue, ultram & silver 55 10

1978. Centenary of Tokyo Astronomical Observatory.
1512 **938** 50y. multicoloured . . . 55 10

939/40 "The then Heroic Champion's Sumo Wrestling" (detail, Toyokuni III)

941 "Children's Charming Sumo Play" (Utamaro Kitagawa)

942 Sheep Bell (folk toy)

1978. Sumo Pictures (3rd series).
1513 **939** 50y. multicoloured . . . 50 10
1514 **940** 50y. multicoloured . . . 50 10
1515 **941** 50y. multicoloured . . . 60 10
Nos. 1513/14 were issued together se-tenant, forming the composite design illustrated.

1978. New Year's Greetings.
1516 **942** 20y. multicoloured . . . 35 10

943 Family and Human Rights Emblem

1978. 30th Anniv of Declaration of Human Rights.
1518 **943** 50y. multicoloured . . . 45 10

944/5 "Great Sumo Wrestlers crossing Ryogoku Bridge" (Toyokuni III)

946 "Yumitori Ceremony at Grand Fund-raising Tournament" (Kunisada II)

947 Hands protecting Children

1979. Sumo Pictures. (4th series).
1519 **944** 50y. multicoloured . . . 50 10
1520 **945** 50y. multicoloured . . . 50 10
1521 **946** 50y. multicoloured . . . 60 10
Nos. 1519/20 were issued together se-tenant, forming the composite design illustrated.

1979. Education for the Handicapped.
1522 **947** 50y. multicoloured . . . 45 10

948/9 "Takekuma versus Iwamigata" (Kuniyoshi Utagawa)

950 "Daidozan's Dohyoiri" (Sharaku Toshusai)

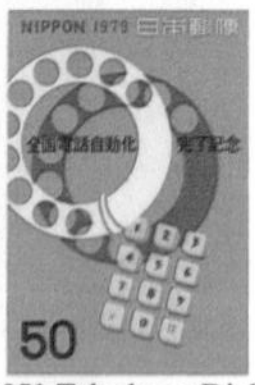

951 Telephone Dial and Pushbuttons

1979. Sumo Pictures (5th series).
1523 **948** 50y. multicoloured . . . 50 10
1524 **949** 50y. multicoloured . . . 50 10
1525 **950** 50y. multicoloured . . . 60 10
Nos. 1523/4 were issued together se-tenant, forming the composite design illustrated.

1979. Telephone Automation Completion.
1526 **951** 50y. multicoloured . . . 50 10

952 Drawing by Leonardo da Vinci

1979. Centenary of Western Medicine in Japan.
1527 **952** 50y. multicoloured . . . 55 10

953 "Standing Beauties" (Kaigetsudo School)

954 "Standing Beauties" (Kaigetsudo School)

1979. Philatelic Week.

1528	**953**	50y. multicoloured . . .	50	10
1529	**954**	50y. multicoloured . . .	50	10

955 Mt. Horaiji and Maple Leaves

1979. National Afforestation Campaign.

1530	**955**	50y. multicoloured . . .	50	10

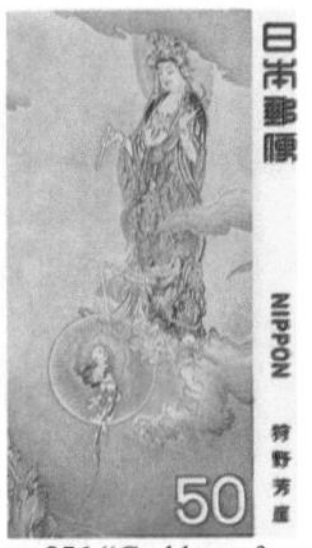
956 "Goddess of Maternal Mercy" (Kano Hogai)

957 "The Princess of the Sea God" (Aoki Shigeru)

1979. Modern Japanese Art (1st series).

1531	**956**	50y. multicoloured . . .	60	10
1532	**957**	50y. multicoloured . . .	60	10

See also Nos. 1533/4. 1544/5, 1550/1, 1558/9, 1567/8, 1574/5, 1610/11, 1618/19, 1628/9, 1650/1, 1656/7, 1675/6, 1689/90, 1693/4 and 1697/8.

958 "Fire Dance" (Gyosha Hayami)

959 "Leaning Figure" (Tetsugoro Yorozu)

1979. Modern Japanese Art (2nd series).

1533	**958**	50y. multicoloured . . .	60	10
1534	**959**	50y. multicoloured . . .	60	10

960 Quarantine Officers

1979. Centenary of Quarantine System.

1535	**960**	50y. multicoloured . . .	75	10

961 Girl with Letter

962 Hakata Doll

1979. Letter writing Day.

1536	**961**	20y. multicoloured . . .	30	10
1537	**962**	50y. multicoloured . . .	45	10

963 Baseball Pitcher and Ball

1979. 50th National Inter-City Amateur Baseball Tournament.

1538	**963**	50y. multicoloured . . .	70	10

964 Girl collecting Stars

965 Boy catching Toy Insects

1979. International Year of the Child.

1539	**964**	50y. multicoloured . . .	50	10
1540	**965**	50y. multicoloured . . .	50	10
MS1541		144×93 mm. Nos. 1539/40	1·25	1·00

966 "The Moon over the Castle Ruins" (Bansui Doi and Rentaro Taki)

967 "Evening Glow" (Uko Nakamura and Shin Kusakawa)

1979. Japanese Songs (1st series).

1542	**966**	50y. multicoloured . . .	70	10
1543	**967**	50y. multicoloured . . .	70	10

See also Nos. 1552/3, 1556/7, 1561/2, 1565/6, 1572/3, 1580/1, 1616/17 and 1620/1.

968 "Black Cat" (Shunso Hishida)

969 "Kinyo" (Sotaro Yasui)

1979. Modern Japanese Art (3rd series).

1544	**968**	50y. multicoloured . . .	70	10
1545	**969**	50y. multicoloured . . .	70	10

970 "Steep Mountains and the Dark Dale" (Okyo Maruyama)

971 Long Distance Runner

1979. International Correspondence Week.

1546	**970**	100y. multicoloured . .	1·60	30

1979. 34th National Athletic Meeting, Miyazaki.

1547	**971**	20y. multicoloured . . .	60	10

972 "ITU" and Globe

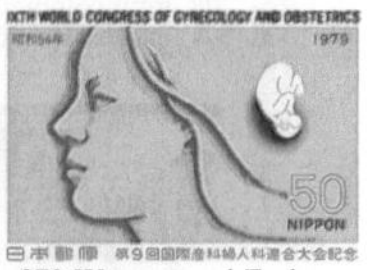
973 Woman and Embryo

1979. Centenary of Admission to International Telecommunications Union.

1548	**972**	50y. multicoloured . . .	60	10

1979. 9th International Obstetrics and Gynaecology Convention, Tokyo.

1549	**973**	50y. multicoloured . . .	60	10

974 "Nude" (Kagaku Murakami)

975 "Harvest" (Asai Chu)

1979. Modern Japanese Art (4th series).

1550	**974**	50y. multicoloured . . .	50	10
1551	**975**	50y. multicoloured . . .	50	10

976 "Maple Leaves" (Tatsuyuki Takano and Teiichi Okano)

977 "Birthplace" (Tatsuyuki Takano and Teiichi Okano)

1979. Japanese Songs (2nd series).

1552	**976**	50y. multicoloured . . .	50	10
1553	**977**	50y. multicoloured . . .	50	10

978 "Happy Monkeys" (folk toy)

979 "Winter Scene" (anon)

980 "Mount Fuji" (anon)

1979. New Year's Greeting.

1554	**978**	20y. multicoloured . . .	30	10

1980. Japanese Songs (3rd series).

1556	**979**	50y. multicoloured . . .	50	20
1557	**980**	50y. multicoloured . . .	50	10

981 "Salmon" (Yuichi Takahashi)

982 "Hall of the Supreme Buddha" (Kokei Kobayashi)

1980. Modern Japanese Art (5th series).

1558	**981**	50y. multicoloured . . .	55	10
1559	**982**	50y. multicoloured . . .	55	10

983 Scales

1980. Centenary of Government Auditing Bureau.

1560	**983**	50y. multicoloured . . .	50	10

984 "Spring Brook" (Tatsuyuki Takano and Teiichi Okano)

985 "Cherry Blossoms" (anon)

1980. Japanese Songs (4th series).

1561	**984**	50y. multicoloured . . .	55	10
1562	**985**	50y. multicoloured . . .	55	10

986 "Scenes of Outdoor Play in Spring" (Sukenobu Nishikawa)

987 "Scenes of Outdoor Play in Spring" (Sukenobu Nishikawa)

1980. Philatelic Week.

1563	**986**	50y. multicoloured . . .	30	10
1564	**987**	50y. multicoloured . . .	50	10

988 "Sea" (Ryuha Hayashi and Takeshi Inoue)

989 "Misty Moonlight Night" (Tatsuyuki Takano and Teiichi Okano)

1980. Japanese Songs (5th series).

1565	**988**	50y. multicoloured . . .	55	10
1566	**989**	50y. multicoloured . . .	55	10

990 "Maiko Girls" (Seiki Kuroda) **991** "Mother and Child" (Shoen Uemura)

1980. Modern Japanese Art (6th series).

1567	**990**	50y. multicoloured . . .	55	10
1568	**991**	50y. multicoloured . . .	55	10

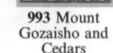

992 "Nippon Maru I" **993** Mount Gozaisho and Cedars

1980. 50th Anniv of Training Cadet Ships "Nippon Maru I" and "Kaio Maru".

1569	**992**	50y. multicoloured . . .	75	20

1980. National Afforestation Campaign.

1570	**993**	50y. multicoloured . . .	60	10

994 "Acrobatic Performances on a Ladder at New Year's Parade of Yayosu Fire Brigades" (Hiroshige III)

1980. Centenary of Fire Fighting System.

1571	**994**	50y. multicoloured . . .	60	10

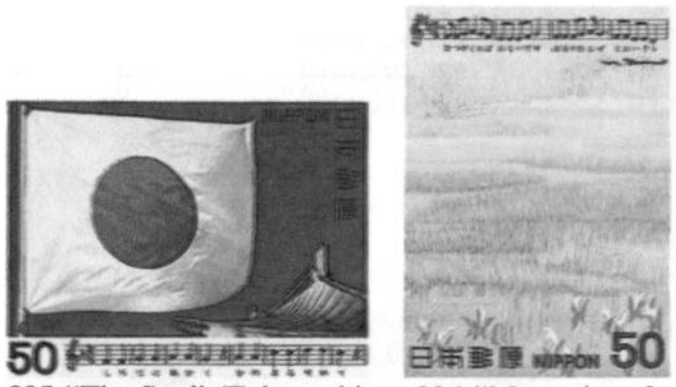

995 "The Sun" (Taksuyuki Takano and Teiichi Okano) **996** "Memories of Summer" (Shoko Ema and Yoshinao Nakata)

1980. Japanese Songs (6th series).

1572	**995**	50y. multicoloured . . .	60	10
1573	**996**	50y. multicoloured . . .	60	10

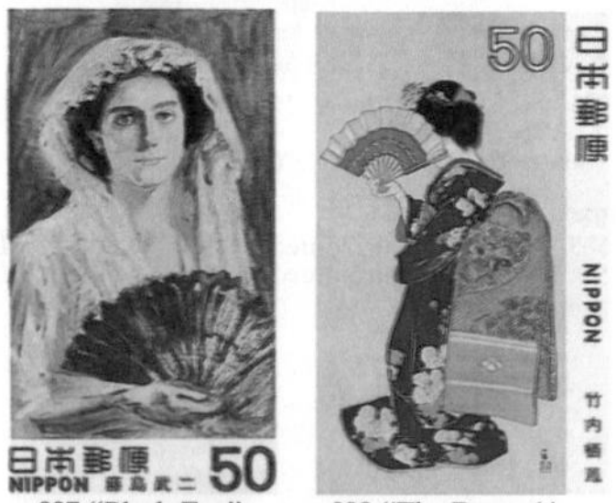

997 "Black Fan" (Takeji Fujishima) **998** "The Dance 'Are Yudachi ni'" (Seiho Takeuchi)

1980. Modern Japanese Art (7th series).

1574	**997**	50y. multicoloured . . .	65	10
1575	**998**	50y. multicoloured . . .	65	10

999 Teddy Bear holding Letter **1000** Knotted Letter

1980. Letter Writing Day.

1576	**999**	20y. multicoloured . .	30	10
1577	**1000**	50y. multicoloured . .	50	10

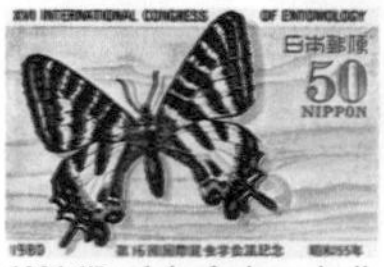

1001 "Luehdorfia japonica"

1980. 16th International Congress of Entomology, Kyoto.

1578	**1001**	50y. multicoloured . .	90	10

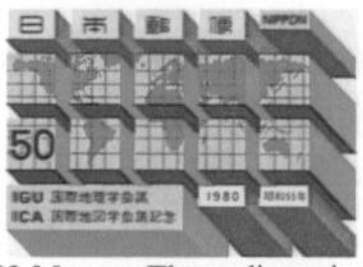

1002 Map on Three- dimensional Graph

1980. 24th International Geographical Congress and 10th International Cartographic Conference, Tokyo.

1579	**1002**	50y. multicoloured . .	40	10

1003 "Red Dragonfly" (Rofu Miki and Kosaku Yamada) **1004** "Song by the Sea" (Kokui Hayashi and Tamezo Narita)

1980. Japanese Songs (7th series).

1580	**1003**	50y. multicoloured . .	70	10
1581	**1004**	50y. multicoloured . .	70	10

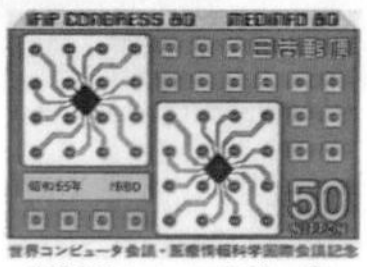

1005 Integrated Circuit

1980. 8th World Computer Congress and Third World Conference on Medical Informatics, Tokyo.

1582	**1005**	50y. multicoloured . .	60	10

1006 Akita Dog **1007** Adonis **1008** Lily

1009 Camellia **1010** Small Cabbage Whites on Rape Blossom **1011** Japanese Babylonia

1012 Noble Scallops **1013** Flowering Cherry **1014** Hanging Bell, Byodoin Temple, Uji

1015 Yoka Star Shell **1016** Precious Wentletrap **1017** Flautist, Horyu Temple

1018 Deer (from lacquer writing box) **1019** Mirror with Figures **1020** Heart-shaped Earthen Figurine

1021 Silver Crane, Kasuga Taisha Shrine, Nara **1022** Miroku Bosatsu, Horyu Temple **1023** Dainichi Buddha, Chuson Temple

1024 Keiki Doji, Kongobu Temple **1025** Komoku Ten, Todai Temple, Nara **1026** Lady Maya, Horyu Temple

1027 Tea Jar with Wisteria Decoration (Ninsei Nonomura) **1028** Miroku Bosatsu

1980. 41y. and 62y. perf or imperf (self-adhesive), others perf.

1582a	**1006**	2y. blue	10	10
1583	**1007**	10y. yellow, grn & brn	10	10
1584	**1008**	20y. yellow, blue & grn	15	10
1585	**1009**	30y. multicoloured . .	20	25
1586	**1010**	40y. multicoloured . .	40	10
1587	**1011**	40y. multicoloured . .	35	10
1588	**1012**	41y. multicoloured . .	35	10
1589	**1013**	50y. multicoloured . .	60	10
1590	**1014**	60y. green and black	70	10
1591	**1015**	60y. multicoloured . .	50	10
1592	**1016**	62y. multicoloured . .	50	10
1593	**1017**	70y. blue and yellow	90	10
1594	**1018**	70y. yellow, black & bl	60	10
1594a		72y. yellow, black & bl	60	10
1595	**1019**	80y. green and black	1·25	10
1596	**1020**	90y. yellow, blk & grn	1·25	10
1597	**1021**	100y. black, blue and ultramarine	85	10
1598	**1022**	170y. purple and bistre	65	10
1599		175y. brown, grn & bis	1·25	10
1600	–	210y. orange and lilac (as No. 1242) . . .	1·25	10
1601	**1023**	260y. brown and red	2·00	10
1602	**1024**	300y. brown	2·00	10
1603	**1025**	310y. brown and violet	2·00	10
1604	–	360y. purple and pink (as No. 1246) . . .	2·25	10
1605	**1026**	410y. orange and blue	5·50	10
1606	**1027**	410y. multicoloured	1·50	10
1607	**1028**	600y. yellow, purple and lilac	4·00	10

1031 "Manchurian Cranes" (door painting, Motooki Watanabe) **1032** Archery and Mt. Nantai

1980. International Correspondence Week.

1608	**1031**	100y. multicoloured . .	1·40	20

1980. 35th National Athletic Meeting, Tochigi.

1609	**1032**	20y. multicoloured . .	40	10

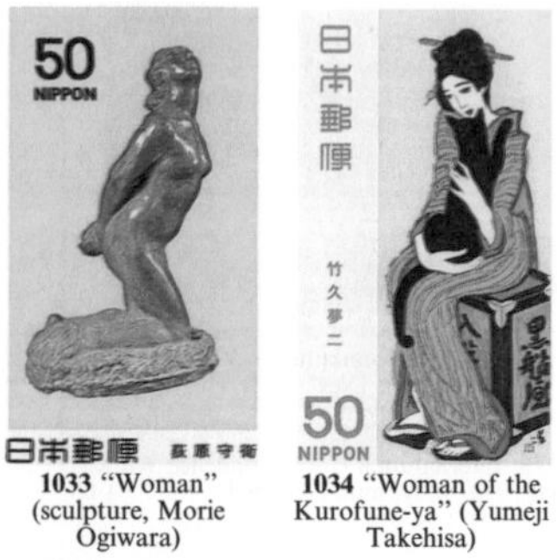

1033 "Woman" (sculpture, Morie Ogiwara) **1034** "Woman of the Kurofune-ya" (Yumeji Takehisa)

1980. Modern Japanese Art (8th series).

1610	**1033**	50y. multicoloured . .	65	10
1611	**1034**	50y. multicoloured . .	65	10

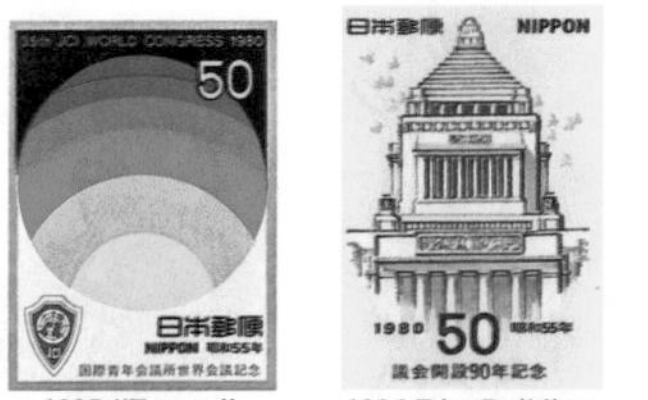

1035 "Energy" **1036** Diet Building and Doves

1980. 35th World Congress of Junior Chambers of Commerce, Osaka.

1612	**1035**	50y. multicoloured . .	45	10

1980. 90th Anniv of Japanese Diet.

1613	**1036**	50y. multicoloured . .	35	10

1037 Toy Rooster

1980. New Year's Greetings.

1614	**1037**	20y. multicoloured . .	40	10

1038 "Komori-Uta" (nursery song) **1039** "Coconut" (Toson Shimazaki and Toraji Ohaka)

1981. Japanese Songs (8th series).

1616	**1038**	60y. multicoloured . .	55	10
1617	**1039**	60y. multicoloured . .	55	10

1040 "Power Station in the Snow" (Shiskanosuke Oka)

1041 "Nukada-no-Okimi of Asuka in Spring" (Yukihiko Yasuda)

1981. Modern Japanese Art (9th series).

1618	**1040**	60y. multicoloured . .	60	10
1619	**1041**	60y. multicoloured . .	60	10

1042 "Spring has Come" (Tatsuyuki Takano and Teiichi Okano) **1043** "Cherry Blossoms" (Hagoromo Takeshima and Rentaro Taki)

1981. Japanese Songs (9th series).

1620	**1042**	60y. multicoloured . .	60	10
1621	**1043**	60y. multicoloured . .	60	10

1044 Port Island and Exposition Emblem

1981. Kobe Port Island Exposition, Kobe City.
1622 **1044** 60y. multicoloured . . 35 10

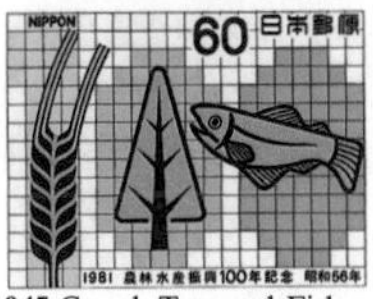

1045 Cereal, Tree and Fish on "100"

1981. Centenary of Agricultural, Forestry and Fishery Promotion.
1623 **1045** 60y. multicoloured . . 50 10

1046/7 "Yugao" (Lady of the Evening Roses) and Genji

1981. Philatelic Week. Details of Harunobu Suzuki's Illustrations of "Tale of Genji" by Lady Murasaki.
1624 **1046** 60y. multicoloured . . 50 10
1625 **1047** 60y. multicoloured . . 50 10
Nos. 1624/5 were issued together, se-tenant, forming a composite design.

1048 Pagodas at Nara and Double Cherry Blossom

1049 Container Ship and Crane

1981. National Afforestation Campaign.
1626 **1048** 60y. multicoloured . . 55 10

1981. 12th International Port and Harbour Association Conference.
1627 **1049** 60y. multicoloured . . 75 10

1050 "N's Family" (Narashinge Koide)

1051 "Bamboo Shoots" (Heihachiro Fukuda)

1981. Modern Japanese Art (10th series).
1628 **1050** 60y. multicoloured . . 65 10
1629 **1051** 60y. multicoloured . . 65 10

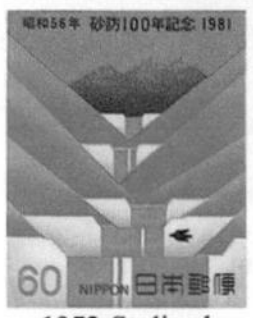

1052 Stylized Debris Barriers

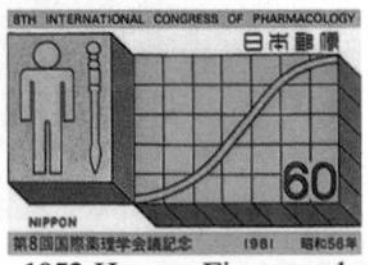

1053 Human Figure and Dose Response Chart

1981. Centenary of Land Erosion Control.
1630 **1052** 60y. multicoloured . . 40 10

1981. 8th International Congress of Pharmacology, Tokyo.
1631 **1053** 60y. multicoloured . . 40 10

1054 Girl writing Letter

1055 Boy with Pencil and Stamp

1981. Letter Writing Day.
1632 **1054** 40y. multicoloured . . 40 10
1633 **1055** 60y. multicoloured . . 55 10

1056 Japanese Crested Ibis

1981. 50th Anniv of National Parks.
1634 **1056** 60y. multicoloured . . 1·10 20

1057 Electric Plug and dripping Tap

1058 Energy Recycling

1981. Energy Conservation.
1635 **1057** 40y. dp blue, lilac & bl 40 10
1636 **1058** 60y. multicoloured . . 50 10

1059 Oura Cathedral, Nagasaki

1060 Hyokei Hall, Tokyo

1981. Modern Western-style Architecture (1st series).
1637 **1059** 60y. multicoloured . . 55 10
1638 **1060** 60y. multicoloured . . 55 10
See also Nos. 1648/9, 1654/5, 1658/9, 1669/70, 1680/1, 1695/6, 1705/6, 1710/11 and 1732/3.

1061 Bluebird and I.Y.D.P. Emblem

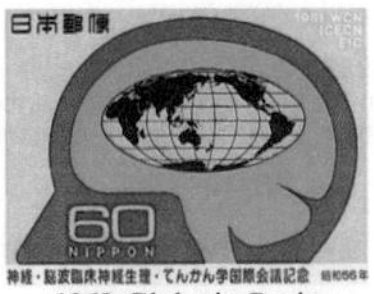

1062 Globe in Brain

1981. International Year of Disabled Persons.
1639 **1061** 60y.+10y. mult 45 10

1981. International Neurological Conferences, Kyoto.
1640 **1062** 60y. multicoloured . . 35 10

1063 Convention Emblem

1064 "Eastern Turtle Doves" (Sanraku Kano)

1981. International Federation of Postal, Telegram and Telephone Workers' Unions World Convention, Tokyo.
1641 **1063** 60y. multicoloured . . 45 10

1981. International Correspondence Week.
1642 **1064** 130y. multicoloured . . 2·00 30

1065 48m. Stamp 1871

1069 Badminton and Lake Biwa

1981. "Philatokyo '81" International Stamp Exhibition, Tokyo. Multicoloured, frame colour of stamp within design given.
1643 **1065** 60y. brown 60 10
1644 – 60y. blue 60 10
1645 – 60y. red 60 10
1646 – 60y. green 60 10
DESIGNS: No. 1644, 100m. stamp, 1871; 1645, 200m. stamp, 1871; 1646, 500m. stamp, 1871.

1981. 36th National Athletic Meeting, Shiga.
1647 **1069** 40y. multicoloured . . 50 10

1070 Former Kaichi School Matsumoto

1071 Doshisha Chapel, Kyoto

1981. Modern Western-style Architecture (2nd series).
1648 **1070** 60y. multicoloured . . 50 10
1649 **1071** 60y. multicoloured . . 50 10

1072 "Portrait of Reiko" (Ryusei Kishida)

1073 "Ichiyo" (Kiyokata Kaburagi)

1981. Modern Japanese Art (11th series).
1650 **1072** 60y. multicoloured . . 55 10
1651 **1073** 60y. multicoloured . . 55 10

1074 Clay Dog (folk toy)

1981. New Year's Greetings.
1652 **1074** 40y. multicoloured . . 45 10

1075 St John's Church, Inuyama

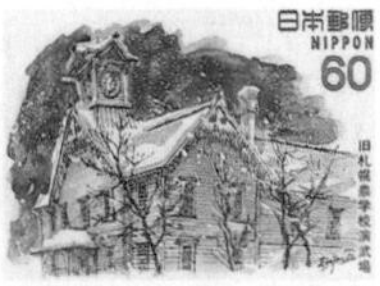

1076 Military Exercise Hall, Sapporo Agricultural School

1982. Modern Western-style Architecture (3rd series).
1654 **1075** 60y. multicoloured . . 55 10
1655 **1076** 60y. multicoloured . . 55 10

1077 "Yoritomo in a Cave" (Seison Maeda)

1078 "Posters on a Terrace" (Yuzo Saeki)

1982. Modern Japanese Art (12th series).
1656 **1077** 60y. multicoloured . . 55 10
1657 **1078** 60y. multicoloured . . 55 10

1079 Bank of Japan, Kyoto Branch (now museum)

1080 Saiseikan Hospital, Yamagata

1982. Modern Western-style Architecture (4th series).
1658 **1079** 60y. multicoloured . . 50 10
1659 **1080** 60y. multicoloured . . 50 10

1081 Gorilla and Greater Flamingo

1982. Ueno Zoo. Centenary. Multicoloured.
1660 60y. Type **1081** 65 20
1661 60y. Lion and king penguins 65 20
1662 60y. Giant panda and Indian elephants . . . . 1·00 55
1663 60y. Giraffe and common zebras . . . . 1·00 55

1085/6 "Enjoying Snow Landscape of Matsuchi-yama" (Torii Kiyonaga)

1982. Philatelic Week.
1664 **1085** 60y. multicoloured . . 50 10
1665 **1086** 60y. multicoloured . . 50 10
Nos. 1664/5 were issued together se-tenant forming the composite design illustrated.

1087 Lion

1088 Arbor Festival Emblem and Blue and White Fly-catcher

1982. 10th Anniv of Return of Okinawa (Ryukyu Islands).
1666 **1087** 60y. multicoloured . . 60 10

1982. National Afforestation Campaign.
1667 **1088** 60y. multicoloured . . 65 20

1089 Noh Mask

1982. 16th World Dermatology Congress, Tokyo.
1668 **1089** 60y. multicoloured . . 65 10

1090 Divine Gate of Oyama Shrine, Kanazawa

1091 Former Iwasaki Mansion, Taito-ku, Tokyo (now Training Institute)

1982. Modern Western-style Architecture (5th series).
1669 **1090** 60y. multicoloured . . 50 10
1670 **1091** 60y. multicoloured . . 50 10

1092 Class 1290 Locomotive "Zenko", 1881

1093 "Yamabiko" (echo) Express Train

1982. Opening of Tohoku–Shinkansen Railway Line.
1671 **1092** 60y. multicoloured . . 1·00 30
1672 **1093** 60y. multicoloured . . 1·00 30

1094 Gull and Balloon with Letter

1095 Bird carrying Letter to Fairy

1982. Letter Writing Day.
1673 **1094** 40y. multicoloured . . 40 10
1674 **1095** 60y. multicoloured . . 55 10

1096 "Garment Patterned with Irises" (Saburosuke Okada)

1097 "Buddhisattva Kannon on Potalaka Island" (Tessai Tomioka)

1982. Modern Japanese Art (13th series).
1675 **1096** 40y. multicoloured . . 65 10
1676 **1097** 60y. multicoloured . . 65 10

1098 Wreath (condolences)

1099 Folded Paper Crane (congratulations)

1100 Pine, Plum and Bamboo Blossom (congratulations)

1982. Special Correspondence Stamps.
1677 **1098** 60y. multicoloured . . 75 10
1678 **1099** 60y. multicoloured . . 75 10
1679 **1100** 70y. multicoloured . . 95 10

For other values see Nos. 1722/3, 2013/16 and 2289/92.

1101 Hokkaido Prefectural Building, Sapporo

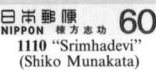

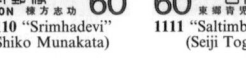

1102 Saigo Tsugumichi Mansion, Meguro (now in Inuyama)

1982. Modern Western-style Architecture (6th series).
1680 **1101** 60y. multicoloured . . 75 10
1681 **1102** 60y. multicoloured . . 75 10

1103 16th-century Portuguese Galleon and World Map

1982. 400th Anniv of Christian Boys' Delegation to Europe.
1682 **1103** 60y. multicoloured . . 70 10

1104 "T'ien T'an in the Clouds" (Ryuzaburo Umehara)

1982. 10th Anniv of Restoration of Diplomatic Relations with China.
1683 **1104** 60y. multicoloured . . 55 10

1105 Table Tennis and Monument of the Meet

1106 "Amusement" (wooden doll by Goyo Hirata)

1982. 37th National Athletic Meeting, Matsue.
1684 **1105** 40y. multicoloured . . 60 10

1982. International Correspondence Week.
1685 **1106** 130y. multicoloured . . 2·00 10

1107 "Bank of Japan near Eitaibashi in Snow" (Yasuji Inoue)

1982. Centenary of Central Bank System.
1686 **1107** 60y. multicoloured . . 45 10

1108 "Asahi" (rising sun) Express Train

1109 ED 16 Electric Locomotive No. 8

1982. Opening of Joetsu–Shinkansen Railway Line.
1687 **1108** 60y. multicoloured . . 1·00 30
1688 **1109** 60y. multicoloured . . 1·00 30

1110 "Srimhadevi" (Shiko Munakata)

1111 "Saltimbanque" (Seiji Togo)

1982. Modern Japanese Art (14th series).
1689 **1110** 60y. multicoloured . . 65 10
1690 **1111** 60y. multicoloured . . 65 10

1112 "Kintaro on a Wild Boar" (clay Tsutsumi doll)

1982. New Year Greetings.
1691 **1112** 40y. multicoloured . . 45 10

1113 "Snowstorm" (Shinsui Ito)

1114 "Spiraea and Calla in a Perrian Vase" (Zenzaburo Kojima)

1983. Modern Japanese Art (15th series).
1692 **1113** 60y. multicoloured . . 75 10
1693 **1114** 60y. multicoloured . . 75 10

1115 Fujimura Memorial Hall, Kofu (formerly Mutsuzawa School)

1116 Porch of Sakuranomiya Public Hall, Osaka

1983. Modern Western-style Architecture (7th series).
1695 **1115** 60y. multicoloured . . 75 10
1696 **1116** 60y. multicoloured . . 75 10

1117 "Selflessness" (Taikan Yokoyama)

1118 "Aged Monkey" (wood carving, Koun Takamura)

1983. Modern Japanese Art (16th series).
1697 **1117** 60y. multicoloured . . 75 10
1698 **1118** 60y. multicoloured . . 75 10

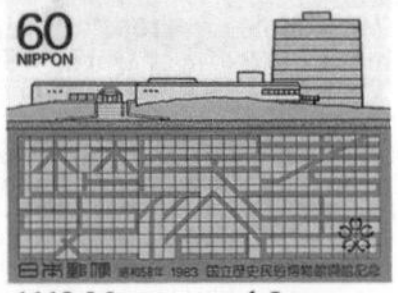
1119 Museum and Japanese Characters representing History, Folklore and Antiquity

1983. Opening of National Museum of History and Folklore.
1699 **1119** 60y. multicoloured . . 40 10

1120/1 "Women working in the Kitchen" (Utamaro Kitagawa)

1983. Philatelic Week.
1700 **1120** 60y. multicoloured . . 75 10
1701 **1121** 60y. multicoloured . . 75 10

Nos. 1695/6 were issued together, se-tenant, forming the composite design illustrated.

1122 "Hiba arborvitae", Japanese Black Fritillary and Hakusan Mountains

1123 Colt and Racehorse

1983. National Afforestation Campaign.
1702 **1122** 60y. multicoloured . . 75 10

1983. 50th Nippon Derby.
1703 **1123** 60y. multicoloured . . 85 10

1124 Rabbit and Empty Can

1983. Islands Clean-up Campaign.
1704 **1124** 60y. multicoloured . . 70 10

1125 Hohei-kan House (Wedding Hall), Sapporo

1126 Glover House, Nagasaki

1983. Modern Western-style Architecture (8th series).
1705 **1125** 60y. multicoloured . . 75 10
1706 **1126** 60y. multicoloured . . 75 10

1127 First Issue and Nihonbashi Bulletin Board

1983. Centenary of "Government Journal".
1707 **1127** 60y. multicoloured . . 75 10

1128 Boy with Letter

1129 Fairy with Letter

1983. Letter Writing Day.
1708 **1128** 40y. multicoloured . . 35 10
1709 **1129** 60y. multicoloured . . 65 10

1130 59th Bank, Hirosaki

1131 Auditorium of Gakushuin Elementary School (now in Narita)

1983. Modern Western-style Architecture (9th series).
1710 **1130** 60y. multicoloured . . 75 10
1711 **1131** 60y. multicoloured . . 75 10

1132 Theatre and Noh Player

1983. Opening of National Noh Theatre. Tokyo.
1712 **1132** 60y. multicoloured . . 75 10

1133 Okinawa Rail

1983. Endangered Birds (1st series). Multicoloured.
1713 60y. Type **1133** . . . . . . 1·00 20
1714 60y. Blakiston's fish owl ("Ketupa blakistoni") (horiz) . . . . 1·00 20
See also Nos. 1724/5, 1729/30, 1735/6 and 1742/3.

1135 "Chi-kyu" (paper doll by Juzo Kagoshima)

1136 Naginata Player and Myogi Mountains

1983. International Correspondence Week.
1715 **1135** 130y. multicoloured . . 1·75 25

1983. 38th National Athletic Meeting, Gumman.
1716 **1136** 40y. multicoloured . . 40 10

1137 Ferris Wheel

1138 Children supporting Globe

1983. World Communications Year.
1717 **1137** 60y. multicoloured . . 50 10
1718 **1138** 60y. multicoloured . . 50 10

1139 Park and Monument

1140 Congress Emblem and Mouth Mirror

1983. Opening of Showa Memorial National Park.
1719 **1139** 60y. multicoloured . . 60 10

1983. 71st World Dental Congress, Tokyo.
1720 **1140** 60y. multicoloured . . 60 10

1141 "Shirase"

1983. Maiden Voyage of Antarctic Research Ship "Shirase".
1721 **1141** 60y. multicoloured . . 65 20

1983. Special Correspondence Stamps.
1722 **1098** 40y. multicoloured . . 45 10
1723 **1099** 40y. multicoloured . . 45 10

1983. Endangered Birds (2nd series). As T **1133**. Multicoloured.
1724 60y. Pryer's woodpecker ("Sapheopipo noguchii") 1·10 20
1725 60y. Canada goose ("Branta canadensis leucopareia") (horiz) . . . . 1·10 20

1144 "Mouse riding a Small Hammer" (folk toy)

1145 Human Rights Emblem

1983. New Year's Greetings.
1726 **1144** 40y. multicoloured . . 60 10

1983. 35th Anniv of Declaration of Human Rights.
1728 **1145** 60y. multicoloured . . 45 10

1984. Endangered Birds (3rd series). As T **1133**. Multicoloured.
1729 60y. Japanese marsh warbler ("Megalurus pryeri pryeri") (horiz) . . . . . 1·10 20
1730 60y. Crested serpent eagle ("Spilornis cheela perplexus") . . . . 1·10 20

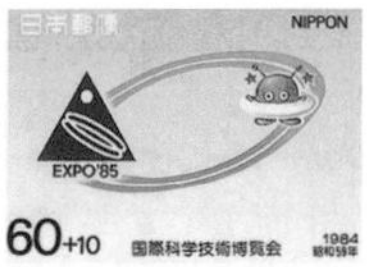
1148 Exhibition Emblem and Mascot

1984. "Expo '85" International Science and Technology Exhibition, Tsukuba (1985).
1731 **1148** 60y.+10y. mult 80 15

1149 Bank of Japan Head Office

1150 Hunter House, Kobe

1984. Modern Western-style Architecture (10th series).
1732 **1149** 60y. multicoloured . . 75 10
1733 **1150** 60y. multicoloured . . 75 10

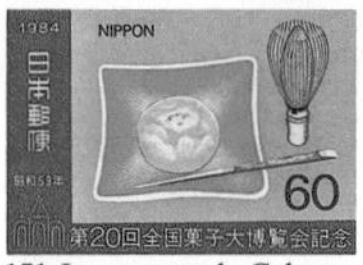
1151 Japanese-style Cake and Bamboo Tea Whisk

1984. 20th Confectionery Fair, Tokyo.
1734 **1151** 60y. multicoloured . . 55 10

1984. Endangered Birds (4th series). As T **1133**. Multicoloured.
1735 60y. Black wood pigeon ("Columba janthina nitens") . . . . 1·10 20
1736 60y. Spotted greenshank ("Tringa guttifer") (horiz) 1·10 20

1154 Bunraku Puppet and Theatre

1984. Opening of National Bunraku Theatre, Osaka.
1737 **1154** 60y. multicoloured . . 75 10

1155 "Otani Oniji as Edobeh" (Toshusai Sharaku)

1156 "Iwai Hanshiro IV as Shigenoi" (Toshusai Sharaku)

1984. Philatelic Week.
1738 **1155** 60y. multicoloured . . 75 10
1739 **1156** 60y. multicoloured . . 75 10

1157 Kaikozu Tree and Sakura Volcano

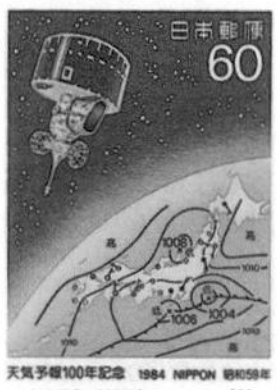
1158 "Himawari" Weather Satellite and Chart

1984. National Afforestation Campaign.
1740 **1157** 60y. multicoloured . . 75 10

1984. Centenary of National Weather Forecasts.
1741 **1158** 60y. multicoloured . . 75 10

1984. Endangered Birds (5th series). As T **1133**. Multicoloured.
1742 60y. White-backed woodpecker ("Dendrocopos leucotos owstoni") (horiz) . . . . 1·10 20
1743 60y. Peregrine falcon ("Falco peregrinus fruitii") . . . . 1·10 20

1161 Doves

1984. Federation of UNESCO Clubs and Associations World Congress, Sendai.
1744 **1161** 60y. multicoloured . . 45 10

1162 Birds in Tree

1163 Bird and Flowers

1984. Letter Writing Day.
1745 **1162** 40y. multicoloured . . 35 10
1746 **1163** 60y. multicoloured . . 60 10

1164 "Fire and Wind" (Motomi Hagimoto)

1165 "Bonds" (Noboru Kanda)

1984. Disaster Prevention Week.
1747 **1164** 40y. multicoloured . . 35 10
1748 **1165** 60y. black and yellow 60 10

1166 "Leontopodium fauriei"

1168 Basho's Crossroads, Sendai

1984. Alpine Plants (1st series). Multicoloured.
1749 60y. Type **1166** 70 10
1750 60y. "Lagotis glauca" (horiz) 70 10
See also Nos. 1752/3, 1769/70, 1775/6, 1802/3, 1813/14 and 1827/8.

1984. 6th International Virology Congress, Sendai.
1751 **1168** 60y. multicoloured . . 55 10

1984. Alpine Plants (2nd series). As T **1166**. Multicoloured.
1752 60y. Globe flower ("Trollius riederianus") 75 10
1753 60y. "Primula cuneifolia" 75 10

1171 Logo

1172 "Serenity" (doll by Ryujo Hori)

1984. Electronic Mail.
1754 **1171** 500y. multicoloured . . 8·00 3·00

1984. International Correspondence Week.
1755 **1172** 130y. multicoloured . . 2·00 15

1173 Silver Pavilion, Jisho Temple

1174 Hockey and East Pagoda of Yakushi Temple

1984. 17th International Internal Medicine Congress, Kyoto City.
1756 **1173** 60y. multicoloured . . 55 10

1984. 39th National Athletic Meeting, Nara.
1757 **1174** 40y. multicoloured . . 70 10

1175 Birds in Tree

1176 Flowers

1177 Chrysanthemums Design

1178 Leaf and Bird Design

1984. Traditional Crafts (1st series). Kutani Porcelain Plates and Nishijin Silk Weavings.
1758 **1175** 60y. multicoloured . . 80 10
1759 **1176** 60y. multicoloured . . 80 10
1760 **1177** 60y. multicoloured . . 80 10
1761 **1178** 60y. multicoloured . . 80 10
See also Nos. 1771/4, 1787/90, 1795/8, 1805/8, 1820/3 and 1829/32.

1179 Eiji Sawamura (pitcher)

1984. 50th Anniv of Japan Tokyo Baseball Club. Multicoloured.
1762 60y. Type **1179** 60 10
1763 60y. Masaru Kageura (striker) 60 10
1764 60y. Ball, birds and Matsutaro Shoriki (founder) 60 10

1182 Workers' Profiles and Symbols

1183 Bamboo Ox (Sakushu folk toy)

1984. Centenary of Technical Education.
1765 **1182** 60y. multicoloured . . 45 10

1984. New Year's Greetings.
1766 **1183** 40y. multicoloured . . 40 10

1984. Endangered Birds (6th series). Sheet 93 × 120 mm. As Nos. 1714 and 1743.
MS1768 60y. blue (as No. 1714); 60y. purple (as No. 1730); 60y. black (as No. 1743) . . . . . 3·00 2·00

1984. Alpine Plants (3rd series). As T **1166**. Multicoloured.
1769 60y. "Rhododendron aureum" 70 10
1770 60y. "Oxytropis nigrescens" (horiz) 70 10

1186 Dolls

1187 Doll with Cat

1188 Bird and Flower Design

1189 Birds and Chrysanthemums Design

1985. Traditional Crafts (2nd series). Edo Kimekomi Dolls and Okinawa Bingata Cloth.
1771 **1186** 60y. multicoloured . . 75 10
1772 **1187** 60y. multicoloured . . 75 10
1773 **1188** 60y. multicoloured . . 75 10
1774 **1189** 60y. multicoloured . . 75 10

1985. Alpine Plants (4th series). As T **1166**. Multicoloured.
1775 60y. "Dryas octopetala" (horiz) 75 10
1776 60y. "Draba japonica" . . . 75 10

1192 Theme Pavilion and Symbol Tower

1194 University Buildings, Chiba City, and Transmitter

1985. "EXPO '85" World Fair, Tsukuba. Multicoloured.
1777 40y. Type **1192** 40 10
1778 60y. Geometric city 60 10
MS1779 144 × 93 mm. Nos. 1777/8 2·25 75

1985. Inauguration of University of the Air.
1780 **1194** 60y. multicoloured . . 45 10

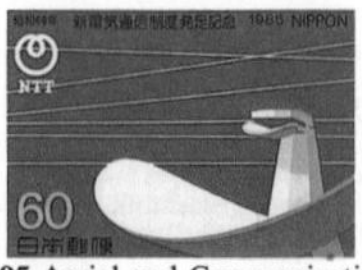
1195 Aerial and Communication Lines

1985. Privatization of Nippon Telegraph and Telephone Corporation.
1781 **1195** 60y. multicoloured . . 45 10

1196 Map of Japan (after Teixeira's Map in Ortelius's "Atlas", 1595)

1197 Korekiyo Takahashi (proposer of Patent Laws)

1985. World Import Fair, Nagoya.
1782 **1196** 60y. multicoloured . . 60 10

1985. Centenary of Industrial Patents System.
1783 **1197** 60y. multicoloured . . 45 10

1198 "Winter in the North" (Yumeji Takehisa)

1199 "Toward the Morning Light" (Yumeji Takehisa)

1985. Philatelic Week.
1784 **1198** 60y. multicoloured . . 75 10
1785 **1199** 60y. multicoloured . . 75 10

1200 Mt. Aso and Gentian

1985. National Afforestation Campaign.
1786 **1200** 60y. multicoloured . . 50 10

1201 Hawk

1202 Ducks

1203 Bowl

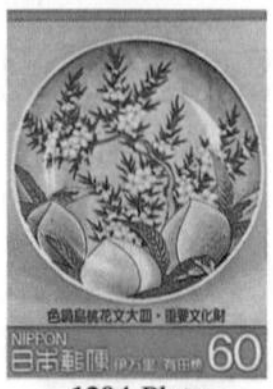
1204 Plate

1985. Traditional Crafts (3rd series). Yew Wood Carvings and Arita Porcelain.
1787 **1201** 60y. multicoloured . . 60 10
1788 **1202** 60y. multicoloured . . 60 10
1789 **1203** 60y. multicoloured . . 50 10
1790 **1204** 60y. multicoloured . . 50 10

1205/6 "Cherry Trees at Night" (Taikan Yokoyama)

1985. 50th Anniv of Radio Japan (overseas broadcasting station).
1791 **1205** 60y. multicoloured . . 60 10
1792 **1206** 60y. multicoloured . . 60 10
Nos. 1791/2 were issued together, se-tenant, forming the composite design illustrated.

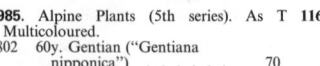

1207 Maeshima and "Tokyo Post Office" (Hiroshige III)

1208 Bridge

1985. 150th Birth Anniv of Baron Hisoka Maeshima (first Postmaster-General).
1793 **1207** 60y. multicoloured . . 55 10

1985. Opening of Great Naruto Bridge.
1794 **1208** 60y. multicoloured . . 70 10

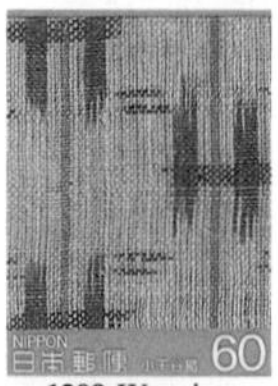
1209 Weaving

1210 Weaving

1211 Dish

1212 Panel

1985. Traditional Crafts (4th series). Ojiya Linen Weavings and Kamakura Lacquered Wood Carvings.
1795 **1209** 60y. multicoloured . . 50 10
1796 **1210** 60y. multicoloured . . 50 10
1797 **1211** 60y. multicoloured . . 50 10
1798 **1212** 60y. multicoloured . . 50 10

1213 Silhouette of Laurel and Couple

1985. International Youth Year.
1799 **1213** 60y. multicoloured . . 50 10

1214 Owl with Letter

1215 Girl holding Bird, Letter and Cat

1985. Letter Writing Day.
1800 **1214** 40y. multicoloured . . 60 10
1801 **1215** 60y. multicoloured . . 60 10

1985. Alpine Plants (5th series). As T **1166**. Multicoloured.
1802 60y. Gentian ("Gentiana nipponica") 70 10
1803 60y. "Callianthemum insigne" 70 10

1218 Logo

1985. Electronic Mail.
1804 **1218** 500y. multicoloured . . 5·00 30

1219 Noh Theatre Actor

1220 Mother with Child

1221 Tea Kettle with Fish Design

1222 Tea Kettle

1985. Traditional Crafts (5th series). Hakata Clay Figurines and Nambu Iron Ware.
1805 **1219** 60y. multicoloured . . 75 10
1806 **1220** 60y. multicoloured . . 75 10
1807 **1221** 60y. multicoloured . . 75 10
1808 **1222** 60y. multicoloured . . 75 10

1223 Hideki Yukawa (physicist) and Meson Field

1224 Gymnasts

1985. 50th Anniv of Yukawa's Meson Theory.
1809 **1223** 60y. multicoloured . . 55 10

1985. University Games, Kobe.
1810 **1224** 60y. multicoloured . . 70 10

1225 Competitor filing Test Piece

1226 "Hibiscus syriacus" (national flower of S. Korea)

1985. 28th International Vocational Training Competition, Osaka.
1811 **1225** 40y. multicoloured . . 40 10

1985. 20th Anniv of Japan–South Korea Diplomatic Relations.
1812 **1226** 60y. multicoloured . . 75 10

1985. Alpine Plants (6th series). As T **1166**. Multicoloured.
1813 60y. "Viola crassa" (horiz) 1·00 10
1814 60y. "Campanula chamissonis" . . . . . . 1·00 10

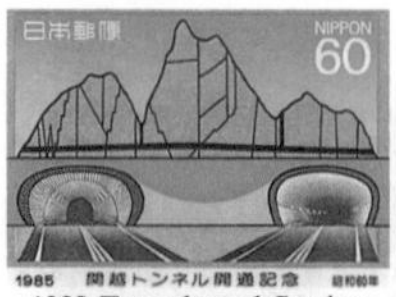
1229 Tunnels and Section through Mt. Tanigawa

1230 "Seisen" (doll by Goyo Hirata)

1985. Opening of North-bound Kan-Etsu Tunnel.
1815 **1229** 60y. multicoloured . . 70 10

1985. International Correspondence Week.
1816 **1230** 130y. multicoloured . . 1·50 10

1231 Youth helping African Farmer

1985. 20th Anniv of Japanese Overseas Co-operation Volunteers.
1817 **1231** 60y. multicoloured . . 50 10

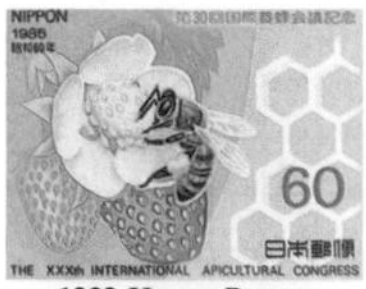
1232 Honey Bee on Strawberry Blossom

1233 Handball Player and Mt. Daisen

1985. 30th International Bee-keeping Congress, Nagoya.
1818 **1232** 60y. multicoloured . . 80 10

1985. 40th Int Athletic Meeting, Tottori.
1819 **1233** 40y. multicoloured . . 70 10

1234 Table

1235 Bowl

1236 Lantern on Column

1237 Lantern

1985. Traditional Crafts (6th series). Wajima Lacquerware and Izumo Sandstone Lanterns.
1820 **1234** 60y. multicoloured . . 60 10
1821 **1235** 60y. multicoloured . . 60 10
1822 **1236** 60y. multicoloured . . 60 10
1823 **1237** 60y. multicoloured . . 60 10

1238 Osaka Papier-mache Tiger

1239 Cabinet Emblem and Official Seal

1985. New Year's Greetings.
1824 **1238** 40y. multicoloured . . 50 10

1985. Cent of Cabinet System of Government.
1826 **1239** 60y. multicoloured . . 55 10

1986. Alpine Plants (7th series). As T **1166**. Multicoloured.
1827 60y. "Diapensia lapponica" 55 10
1828 60y. "Pedicularis apodochila" 55 10

1242 Fan with Tree Design

1243 Fan with Flower Design

1244 Flask with Fish Pattern

1245 Tea Caddy

1986. Traditional Craft (7th series). Kyoto Fans and Tobe Porcelain.
1829 **1242** 60y. multicoloured . . 75 10
1830 **1243** 60y. multicoloured . . 75 10
1831 **1244** 60y. multicoloured . . 75 10
1832 **1245** 60y. multicoloured . . 75 10

1246 Gothic Style Finial and "Golden Norm"

1986. Centenary of Architecture Institute, Shiba, Tokyo.
1833 **1246** 60y. multicoloured . . 60 10

1247 Standing Lady

1248 Seated Lady

1986. Philatelic Week. Details of "South of Hateruma" by Kaigetsu Kikuchi.
1834 **1247** 60y. multicoloured . . 80 10
1835 **1248** 60y. multicoloured . . 80 10

1249 Phoenix and Enthronement Hall, Kyoto Palace

1250 Imperial Palace Ridge Decoration

1986. 60th Anniv of Emperor Hirohito's Accession.
1836 **1249** 60y. multicoloured . . 70 10
1837 **1250** 60y. multicoloured . . 70 10
MS1838 144 × 93 mm. Nos. 1836/7 1·50 1·25

1251 "Mt. Fuji in Early Morning" (Yukihiko Yasuda)

1252 Bull-headed Shrike in Reeds

1986. 12th Economic Summit of Industrialized Countries, Tokyo.
1839 **1251** 60y. multicoloured . . 75 10

1986. National Afforestation Campaign.
1840 **1252** 60y. multicoloured . . 1·25 20

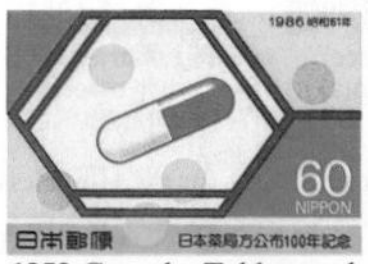
1253 Capsule, Tablets and Structure of Toluene

1254 Map and Clock

1986. Centenary of Japanese Pharmacopoeia.
1841 **1253** 60y. multicoloured . . 85 10

1986. Centenary of Japanese Standard Time.
1842 **1254** 60y. multicoloured . . 65 10

1255 Bird on Chair and Letter on Table

1257 Yataro Iwasaki, Makoto Kondo and Cadet Ship "Nippon Maru II"

1986. Letter Writing Day. Multicoloured.
1843 40y. Type **1255** 40 10
1844 60y. Girl holding rabbit and letter 70 10

1986. 110th Anniv of Merchant Navy Education.
1846 **1257** 60y. multicoloured . . 1·75 35

1258 Asian Apollo ("Parnassius eversmanni")

1262 "Folkways in Twelve Months" (detail, Shunsho Katsukawa)

1986. Insects (1st series). Multicoloured.
1847 60y. Type **1258** . . . . . . 1·00 10
1848 60y. Shieldbug ("Poecilocoris lewisi") . . 1·00 10
1849 60y. Longhorn beetle ("Rosalia batesi") . . . . 1·00 10
1850 60y. "Epiophlebia superstes" 1·00 10
See also Nos. 1854/7, 1861/4, 1869/72, 1878/81 and 1911/12.

1986. 52nd International Federation of Library Associations General Conference, Tokyo.
1851 **1262** 60y. multicoloured . . 75 10

1263 Electron Microscope

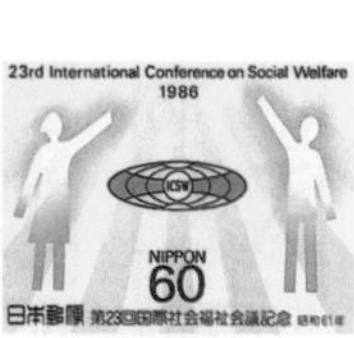
1264 Couple and Conference Emblem

1986. 11th International Electron Microscopy Congress, Kyoto.
1852 **1263** 60y. multicoloured . . 85 10

1986. 23rd International Social Welfare Conference, Tokyo.
1853 **1264** 60y. multicoloured . . 60 10

1986. Insects (2nd series). As T **1258**. Mult.
1854 60y. Dragonflies ("Sympetrum pedemonatanum") . . . . 1·00 10
1855 60y. Weevil ("Damaster blaptoides") . . . . . . 1·00 10
1856 60y. Stag beetle ("Dorcus hopei") . . . . 1·00 10
1857 60y. Wonderful hair-streak ("Thermozephyrus ataxus") . . . . . . 1·00 10

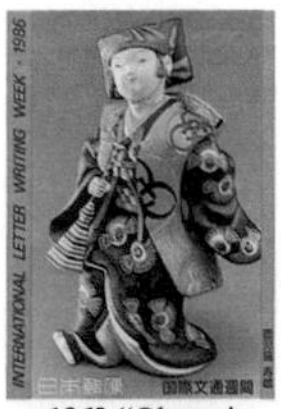
1269 "Ohmori Miyage" (shiso doll, Juzoh Kagoshima)

1270 Gymnast and Mt. Fuji

1986. International Correspondence Week.
1858 **1269** 130y. multicoloured . . 1·50 15

1986. 41st National Athletic Meeting, Yamanashi.
1859 **1270** 40y. multicoloured . . 70 10

1271 "Flowers in Autumn and Girl in Rakuhoku"

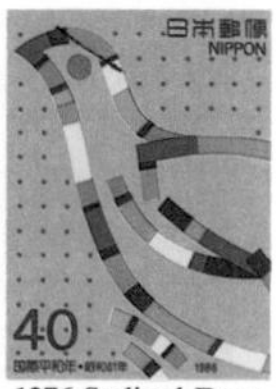
1276 Stylized Dove

1986. 5th World Ikebana Convention, Kyoto.
1860 **1271** 60y. multicoloured . . 85 10

1986. Insects (3rd series). As T **1258**. Mult.
1861 60y. "Elcysma westwoodii" (moth) . . . . 1·00 10
1862 60y. "Rhyothemis variegata" . . . . 1·00 10
1863 60y. Cicada ("Tibicen japonicus") . . . . 1·00 10
1864 60y. "Chrysochroa holstii" 1·00 10

1986. International Peace Year. Mult.
1865 40y. Type **1276** 40 10
1866 60y. Circle of children (horiz) 60 10

1278 "Rabbits making Rice Cake" (Nagoya clay model)

1283 Characters for "Toki" (Registry) and Map

1986. New Year's Greetings.
1867 **1278** 40y. multicoloured . . 75 10
For 50y. in this design dated "1999" see No. 2567.

1987. Insects (4th series). As T **1258**. Mult.
1869 60y. "Cheirotonus jambar" 1·00 10
1870 60y. Chestnut tiger ("Parantica sita") . . . . 1·00 10
1871 60y. "Anotogaster sieboldii" 1·00 10
1872 60y. Stag beetle ("Lucanus maculifemoratus") . . . . 1·00 10

1987. Centenary of Land Registration.
1873 **1283** 60y. multicoloured . . 65 10

1284 Basho Matsuo (after Haritsu Ogawa)

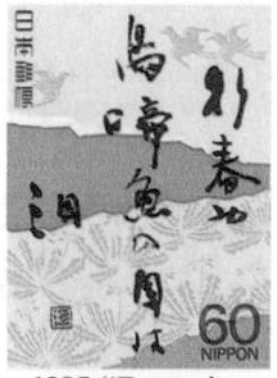
1285 "Departing Spring" (Senju)

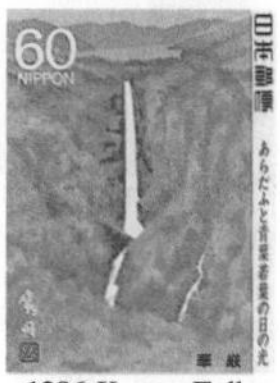
1286 Kegon Falls

1287 "Sunlight" (Toshu Shrine)

1987. "Narrow Road to a Far Province" (travel diary) by Basho Matsuo (1st series).
1874 **1284** 60y. multicoloured . . 75 10
1875 **1285** 60y. multicoloured . . 75 10
1876 **1286** 60y. multicoloured . . 75 10
1877 **1287** 60y. multicoloured . . 75 10
In this series, each pair of stamps (except Nos. 1874/5) illustrates one "haiku" (17-syllable poem) from the diary. The full text of the "haiku" is printed on one stamp and given in calligraphy on the other with appropriate illustrations. Each "haiku" was written at a particular point in the journey (given in brackets in the caption to the second stamp of each pair).
See also Nos. 1896/9, 1906/9, 1925/8, 1932/5, 1945/8, 1962/5, 1973/6, 1982/5 and 2000/3.

1987. Insects (5th series). As T **1258**. Mult.
1878 60y. Owl-fly ("Ascaraphus ramburi") . . . . 1·00 10
1879 60y. Cockchafer ("Polyphylla laticollis") 1·00 10
1880 60y. Leaf butterfly ("Kallima inachus") . . . 1·00 10
1881 60y. "Calopteryx cornelia" 1·00 10
MS1882 143 × 93 mm. multicoloured. 40y. Orange-tip ("Anthocaris cardamines"); 40y. Great purple ("Sasakia charonda"); 60y. Asian apollo ("Parnassius eversmanni"); 60y. Chestnut tiger ("Parantica sita") 4·00 2·00

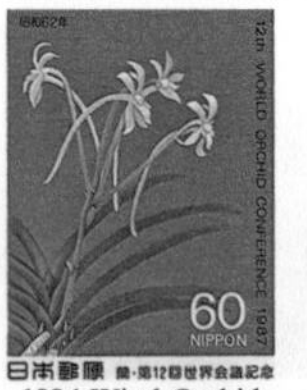

1294 Wind Orchid **1295** Lobster-root

1987. 12th International Orchid Conference, Tokyo.
1883 **1294** 60y. multicoloured . . 70 10
1884 **1295** 60y. multicoloured . . 70 10

1296 Early Mail Sorting Carriage

1987. Ending of Railway Mail Carriage Contracts.
1885 60y. Type **1296** . . . . . . 1·00 30
1886 60y. Loading mail sacks (detail of scroll painting by Beisen Kubota) . . . 1·00 30

1298 Class 860 Tank Locomotive No. 137, 1893

1987. Privatization of Japan Railways. Mult.
1887 60y. Type **1298** . . . . . . 1·00 30
1888 60y. Maglev MLU 002 . . . 1·00 30

1300 Nudibranchs **1301** "Woman with a Comb"

1987. Centenary of Marine Biology Studies in Japan.
1889 **1300** 60y. multicoloured . . 85 15

1987. Philatelic Week. Paintings by Goyo Hashiguchi. Multicoloured.
1890 60y. Type **1301** 85 10
1891 60y. "Woman putting on make-up" 85 10

1303 Map and Emblem **1304** Black-billed Magpie and Forested Coastline

1987. 20th Annual General Meeting of Asian Development Bank.
1892 **1303** 60y. multicoloured . . 60 10

1987. National Afforestation Campaign.
1893 **1304** 60y. multicoloured . . 1·25 20

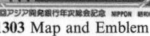

1305 Yatsuhashi Gold Lacquer and Nacre Inkstone Case (Kohrin Ogata)

1306 Hikone Castle

1987. National Treasures (1st series).
1894 **1305** 60y. multicoloured . . 75 10
1895 **1306** 110y. multicoloured . . 1·50 15
See also Nos. 1900/1, 1929/30, 1949/50, 1968/9, 1980/1, 2006/7 and 2017/18.

1307 European Cuckoo **1308** Horse and River (Nasu)

1309 "In the Shade of the Willow" **1310** Paddy Field (Ashino)

1987. "Narrow Road to a Far Province" by Basho Matsuo (2nd series).
1896 **1307** 60y. multicoloured . . 1·25 20
1897 **1308** 60y. multicoloured . . 60 10
1898 **1309** 60y. multicoloured . . 60 10
1899 **1310** 60y. multicoloured . . 60 10

1311 Golden Turtle Reliquary for Buddha's Ashes (Tashodai Temple) **1312** Inuyama Castle

1987. National Treasures (2nd series). Multicoloured.
1900 **1311** 60y. multicoloured . . 85 10
1901 **1312** 110y. multicoloured . . 1·40 15

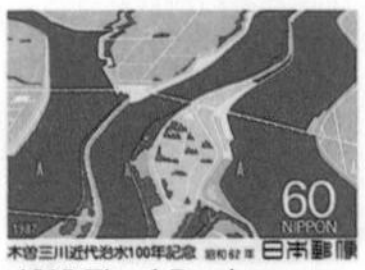

1313 Flowers in Envelope **1315** Flood Barrier across Rivers

1987. Letter Writing Day. Multicoloured.
1902 40y. Type **1313** 35 10
1903 60y. Elephant holding letter in trunk 45 10

1987. Centenary of Modern Flood Control of Rivers Kiso, Nagara and Ibi.
1905 **1315** 60y. multicoloured . . 60 10

1316 Chestnut Blossoms **1317** Chestnut Leaves (Sukagawa)

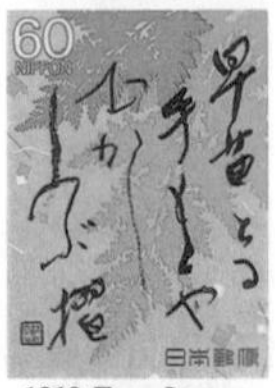

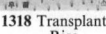

1318 Transplanting Rice **1319** Fern Leaves ("Dyeing Stone", Shinobu)

1987. "Narrow Road to a Far Province" by Basho Matsuo (3rd series).
1906 **1316** 60y. multicoloured . . 60 10
1907 **1317** 60y. multicoloured . . 60 10
1908 **1318** 60y. multicoloured . . 60 10
1909 **1319** 60y. multicoloured . . 60 10

1320 Temple of Emerald Buddha and Cherry Blossom **1321** "Gensho Kanto" (Ryujo Hori)

1987. Centenary of Japan–Thailand Friendship Treaty.
1910 **1320** 60y. multicoloured . . 65 10

1987. Insects (6th series). As T **1258**. Mult.
1911 40y. Orange-tip ("Anthocaris cardamines") 75 10
1912 40y. Great purple ("Sasakia charonda") 75 10

1987. International Correspondence Week. Multicoloured.
1913 130y. Type **1321** . . . . . 1·40 10
1914 150y. "Utage-no-Hana" (Goyo Hirata) . . . . . 1·60 10

1323 "Three Beauties" (detail, Toyokuni Utagawa) **1324** Lion's Head Public Water Tap

1987. 13th International Certified Public Accountants Congress, Tokyo.
1915 **1323** 60y. multicoloured . . 55 10

1987. Centenary of Yokohama Waterworks.
1916 **1324** 60y. multicoloured . . 55 10

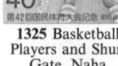

1325 Basketball Players and Shuri Gate, Naha **1326** Playing Card with Queen holding Bird and King smoking

1987. 42nd National Athletic Meeting, Okinawa.
1917 **1325** 40y. multicoloured . . 45 10

1987. 6th International Smoking and Health Conference, Tokyo.
1918 **1326** 60y. multicoloured . . 70 10

1327 Dish Aerial, Kashima Station **1328** Nijo Castle

1987. International Telecommunications Conference, Tokyo.
1919 **1327** 60y. multicoloured . . 65 10

1987. World Historic Cities Conference, Kyoto.
1920 **1328** 60y. multicoloured . . 65 10

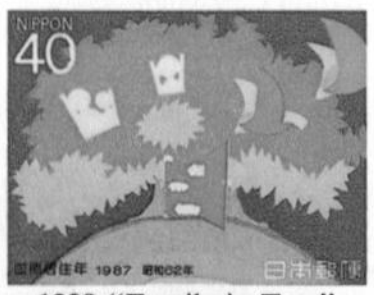

1329 "Family in Tree" (Takahiro Nagahama) **1331** Kurashiki Papier-mache Dragon

1987. International Year of Shelter for the Homeless. Multicoloured.
1921 40y. Type **1329** 40 10
1922 60y. "Houses" (Yoko Sasaki) 60 10

1987. New Year's Greetings.
1923 **1331** 40y. multicoloured . . 50 10

1332 Sweet Flags **1333** Sweet Flags and Birds (Sendai)

1334 "Recollecting the Past" **1335** "Summer Grasses" (Hiraizumi)

1988. "Narrow Road to a Far Province" by Basho Matsuo (4th series).
1925 **1332** 60y. multicoloured . . 60 10
1926 **1333** 60y. multicoloured . . 60 10
1927 **1334** 60y. multicoloured . . 60 10
1928 **1335** 60y. multicoloured . . 60 10

1336 Kongo Samma-in Pagoda, Mt. Koya **1337** Ekoh-Doji, Kongobu Temple

1988. National Treasures (3rd series).
1929 **1336** 60y. multicoloured . . 60 10
1930 **1337** 110y. multicoloured . . 1·25 10

1338 Class ED 79 Locomotive "Sea of Japan" leaving Tunnel and Map

1988. Opening of Seikan (Aomori–Hakodate) Railway Tunnel.
1931 **1338** 60y. multicoloured . . 70 30

1339 Safflower **1340** Willow Trees (Obanazawa)

1341 Risshaku (or Mountain) Temple **1342** Pine Trees (Risshaku Temple)

1988. "Narrow Road to a Far Province" by Basho Matsuo (5th series).
1932 **1339** 60y. multicoloured . . 60 10
1933 **1340** 60y. multicoloured . . 60 10
1934 **1341** 60y. multicoloured . . 60 10
1935 **1342** 60y. multicoloured . . 60 10

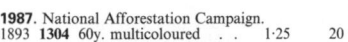

1343/4 South Bisan Section from Kagawa Side

1345/6 Shimotsui Section from Okayama Side

1988. Opening of Seto Great Road and Rail Bridge.
1936 **1343** 60y. multicoloured . . 85 30
1937 **1344** 60y. multicoloured . . 85 30
1938 **1345** 60y. multicoloured . . 85 30
1939 **1346** 60y. multicoloured . . 85 30

Nos. 1936/7 and 1938/9 were printed together, se-tenant, each pair forming the composite design illustrated.

1347 "Long Undergarment" (Kotondo Torii)

1349 Detail of Biwa Plectrum Guard

1988. Philatelic Week. Multicoloured.
1940 60y. Type **1347** 60 10
1941 60y. "Kimono Sash" (Kotondo Torii) 60 10

1988. "Silk Road" Exhibition. Nara.
1943 **1349** 60y. multicoloured . . 60 10

1350 Yashima, Small Cuckoo and Olive Tree

1988. National Afforestation Campaign.
1944 **1350** 60y. multicoloured . . 1·10 20

1351 River Mogami

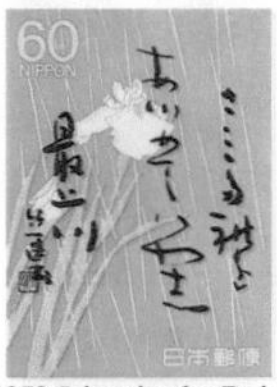

1352 Irises in the Rain (Oishida)

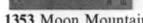

1353 Moon Mountain

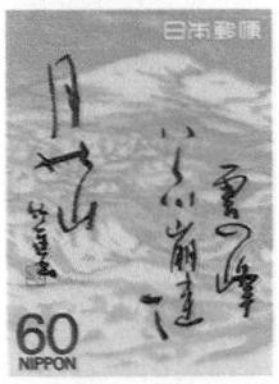

1354 Moon Mountain (Gassan)

1988. "Narrow Road to a Far Province" by Basho Matsuo (6th series).
1945 **1351** 60y. multicoloured . . 80 15
1946 **1352** 60y. multicoloured . . 60 10
1947 **1353** 60y. multicoloured . . 60 10
1948 **1354** 60y. multicoloured . . 60 10

1355 Morodo Shrine, Itsukushima

1356 Kozakura-gawa Braided Armour

1988. National Treasures (4th series).
1949 **1355** 60y. multicoloured . . 60 10
1950 **1356** 100y. multicoloured . . 95 20

1357 Mt. Sakura

1358 Cat with Letter

1988. International Conference on Volcanoes, Kagoshima.
1951 **1357** 60y. multicoloured . . 60 10

1988. Letter Writing Day. Multicoloured.
1952 40y. Type **1358** 45 10
1953 40y. Crab with letter (34 × 25 mm) 45 10
1954 60y. Fairy with letter . . . 60 10
1955 60y. Girl and letter (25 × 32 mm) 60 10

Nos. 1952 and 1954 exist both perforated with ordinary gum and imperforate with self-adhesive gum.

1362 Ohana (Kinosuke puppet, Japan)

1366 Peonies

1988. International Puppetry Festival, Nagoya, Iida and Tokyo. Multicoloured.
1956 60y. Type **1362** 60 10
1957 60y. Stick puppet of girl (Czechoslovakia) . . . 60 10
1958 60y. Shadow puppet (China) 60 10
1959 60y. Knight (Italy) 60 10

1988. 10th Anniv of Japanese–Chinese Treaty of Peace and Friendship. Multicoloured.
1960 60y. Type **1366** 60 10
1961 60y. Ton-ton (giant panda) 75 10

1368 Mimosa Flowers

1369 Lagoon and Grass (Kisagata)

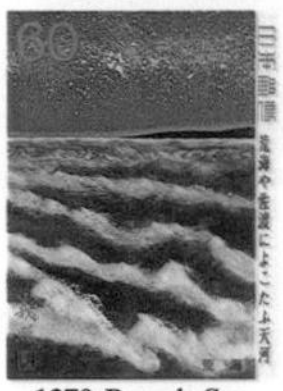

1370 Rough Sea

1371 Waves (Ichiburi)

1988. "Narrow Road to a Far Province" by Basho Matsuo (7th series).
1962 **1368** 60y. multicoloured . . 60 10
1963 **1369** 60y. multicoloured . . 60 10
1964 **1370** 60y. multicoloured . . 60 10
1965 **1371** 60y. multicoloured . . 60 10

1372 Nagoya and Egg

1373 Globe and "Rehabilitation" in Braille

1988. 18th International Poultry Congress, Nagoya.
1966 **1372** 60y. multicoloured . . 70 10

1988. 16th Rehabilitation International World Congress, Tokyo.
1967 **1373** 60y. multicoloured . . 60 10

1374 Nakatsuhime-no-mikoto, Yakushi Temple

1375 Murou Temple

1988. National Treasures (5th series).
1968 **1374** 60y. multicoloured . . 60 10
1969 **1375** 100y. multicoloured . . 95 20

1376 "Kimesaburo Iwai as Chiyo" (Kunimasa Utagawa)

1378 Gymnast and Temple of the Golden Pavilion

1988. International Correspondence Week. Mult.
1970 80y. Type **1376** 85 10
1971 120y. "Komazo Ichikawa III as Ganryu Sasaki" (Toyokuni Utagawa) . . 1·25 20

1988. 43rd National Athletic Meeting, Kyoto.
1972 **1378** 40y. multicoloured . . 45 10

1379 Rice

1380 Ariso Sea (Kurikara Pass)

1381 Sun

1382 "Autumn Wind and Sun" (Kanazawa)

1988. "Narrow Road to a Far Province" by Basho Matsuo (8th series).
1973 **1379** 60y. multicoloured . . 60 10
1974 **1380** 60y. multicoloured . . 60 10
1975 **1381** 60y. multicoloured . . 60 10
1976 **1382** 60y. multicoloured . . 60 10

1383 Mexican State Arms

1384 Snake (Shimotsuke clay bell)

1988. Centenary of Japan–Mexico Friendship and Trade Treaty.
1977 **1383** 60y. multicoloured . . 60 10

1988. New Year's Greetings.
1978 **1384** 40y. multicoloured . . 45 10

1385 Figures on Globe

1988. 40th Anniv of Declaration of Human Rights.
1979 **1385** 60y. multicoloured . . 60 10

1386 Gold-plated Silver Pot with Hunting Design, Todai Temple

1387 Bronze Figure of Yakushi (Buddha of Medicine), Horyu Temple

1989. National Treasures (6th series).
1980 **1386** 60y. multicoloured . . 60 10
1981 **1387** 100y. multicoloured . . 95 20

1388 Nata Temple

1389 Pampas Grass (Natadera)

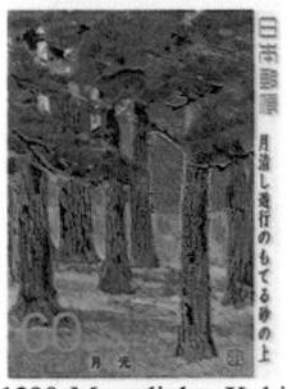

1390 Moonlight, Kehi Shrine

1391 Moon and Pine Trees (Tsuruga)

1989. "Narrow Road to a Far Province" by Basho Matsuo (9th series).
1982 **1388** 60y. multicoloured . . 60 10
1983 **1389** 60y. multicoloured . . 60 10
1984 **1390** 60y. multicoloured . . 60 10
1985 **1391** 60y. multicoloured . . 60 10

1989. Letter Writing Day (1988).
1986 40y. As Type **1354** 45 10
1987 60y. As No. 1954 . . . . . 60 10

1989. Narrow Road to a Far Province by Basho Matsuo (10th series). Ten sheets, each 112 × 72 mm.
MS1988 10 sheets. (a) Nos. 1874/5; (b) Nos. 1876/7; (c) Nos. 1896/7; (d) Nos. 1898/9; (e) Nos. 1906/7; (f) Nos. 1908/9; (g) Nos. 1925/6; (h) Nos. 1927/8; (i) Nos. 1932/3; (j) Nos. 1934/5 . . . . 12·50 12·50

1392 Globe and Exhibition Site

1989. "Fukuoka '89" Asian–Pacific Exhibition, Fukuoka.
1989 **1392** 60y. multicoloured . . 60 10
1996 62y. multicoloured . . 60 10

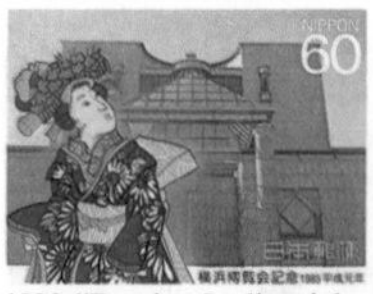
1393 "Russian Ladies sight-seeing at Port" (detail, Yoshitora) and Art Gallery

1394 Bonsai Japanese White Pine

1989. "Space and Children" Exhibition, Yokohama.
1990 **1393** 60y. multicoloured . . 60 10
1997 62y. multicoloured . . 60 10

1989. World Bonsai Convention, Omiya.
1993 **1394** 62y. multicoloured . . 60 10

1395 Lute-player

1397 "Dutch East Indiaman entering Harbour" (Nagasaki woodblock print)

1989. Philatelic Week. Details of "Awa Dance" (painting) by Tsunetomi Kitano. Multicoloured.
1994 62y. Type **1395** 60 10
1995 62y. Dancer 60 10

1989. "Holland Festival '89".
1998 **1397** 62y. multicoloured . . 1·00 15

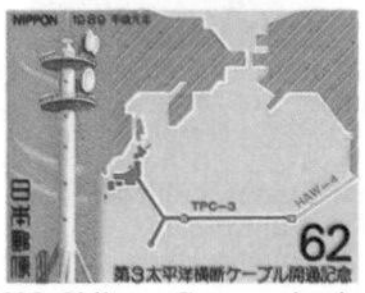
1398 Chikura Communication Tower and Cable Route

1989. Opening of 3rd Trans-Pacific Submarine Telephone Cable (Japan–Hawaii).
1999 **1398** 62y. multicoloured . . 60 10

1399 Beach in Autumn

1400 Bush Clover (Ironohama)

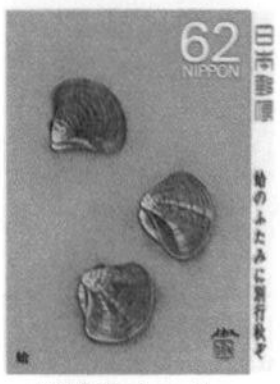
1401 Poker-drop Venuses

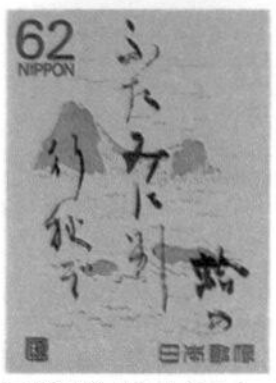
1402 Wedded Rocks, Futami Bay (Ohgaki)

1989. "Narrow Road to a Far Province" by Basho Matsuo (11th series).
2000 **1399** 62y. multicoloured . . 60 10
2001 **1400** 62y. multicoloured . . 60 10
2002 **1401** 62y. multicoloured . . 70 15
2003 **1402** 62y. multicoloured . . 60 10

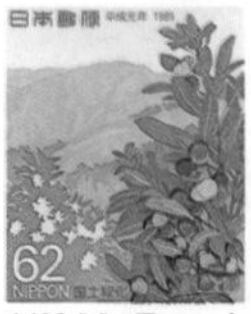
1403 Mt. Tsurugi, Lime and Bay Trees

1404 Children in Bird and Flower "Balloon"

1989. National Afforestation Campaign.
2004 **1403** 62y. multicoloured . . 60 10

1989. International Garden and Greenery Exposition, Osaka (1990) (1st issue).
2005 **1404** 62y.+10y. mult 70 10
See also Nos. 2035/6.

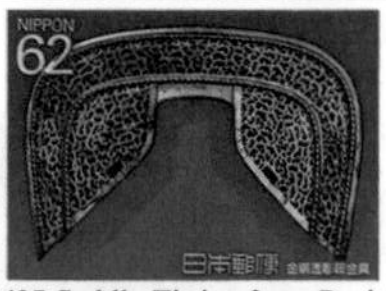
1405 Saddle Fitting from Burial Mound, Konda

1406 "Beetle Wings" Zushi, Horyu Temple

1989. National Treasures (7th series).
2006 **1405** 62y. multicoloured . . 60 10
2007 **1406** 100y. multicoloured . . 95 20

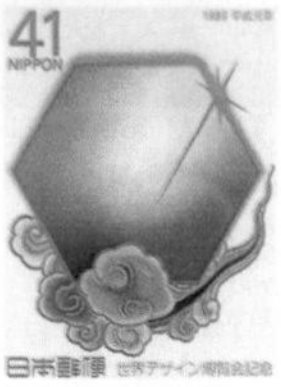
1407 "Crystal of Light and Auspicious Clouds"

1409 Bird as Vase holding Envelope

1989. World Design Exposition, Nagoya. Multicoloured.
2008 41y. Type **1407** 45 10
2009 62y. "design" 60 10

1989. Letter Writing Day. Multicoloured.
2010 41y. Type **1409** 45 10
2011 62y. Mother Rabbit reading letter 60 10

1989. Narrow Road to a Far Province by Basho Matsuo (12th series). Ten sheets, each 112 × 72 mm.
MS2012 10 sheets. (a) Nos. 1945/6; (b) Nos. 1947/8; (c) Nos. 1963/4; (d) Nos. 1965/6; (e) Nos. 1973/4; (f) Nos. 1975/6; (g) Nos. 1982/3; (h) Nos. 1984/5; (i) Nos. 2000/2001; (j) Nos. 2002/3 12·50 12·50

1989. Special Correspondence Stamps.
2013 **1098** 41y. multicoloured . . 40 10
2014 **1099** 41y. multicoloured . . 40 10
2015 62y. multicoloured . . 55 10
2016 **1100** 72y. multicoloured . . 65 10

1411 Gold Stamp

1412 Bronze Mirror

1989. National Treasures (8th series).
2017 **1411** 62y. multicoloured . . 60 10
2018 **1412** 100y. multicoloured . . 95 20

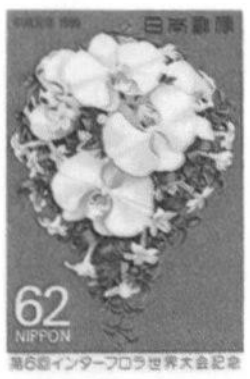
1413 Bouquet of Orchids and Stephanotis

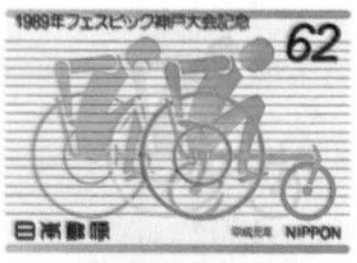
1414 Wheelchair Race

1989. 6th Interflora World Congress, Tokyo.
2019 **1413** 62y. multicoloured . . 60 10

1989. Far East and South Pacific Games for the Disabled, Kobe.
2020 **1414** 62y. multicoloured . . 60 10

1415 Narrators and Drummers

1419 Ear of Rice and Paddy Field

1417 New Emperor and Kaoru playing Go ("Yadorigi" scroll)

1989. "Europalia 89 Japan" Festival, Belgium. Details of "Okuni Theatre" (painting on folding screen). Multicoloured.
2021 62y. Type **1415** 60 10
2022 70y. Okuni (actress) 60 10

1989. International Correspondence Week. Details of Takayoshi Picture Scrolls illustrating "Tale of Genji" by Lady Murasaki. Multicoloured.
2023 80y. Type **1417** 75 10
2024 120y. Yugao's granddaughters playing Go ("Takekawa scroll") 1·25 20

1989. 7th Asian/African Conference of Int Irrigation and Drainage Commission.
2025 **1419** 62y. multicoloured . . 60 10

1420 Shinzan (first winner of all five major races)

1421 Hot-air Balloons

1989. 100th Tenno Sho Horse Race.
2026 **1420** 62y. multicoloured . . 70 10

1989. 9th Hot Air Balloon World Championship, Saga City.
2027 **1421** 62y. multicoloured . . 60 10

1422 Conductor

1423 Yawata Wooden Horse

1989. 50th Anniv of Japanese Copyright Control Act.
2028 **1422** 62y. multicoloured . . 60 10

1989. New Year's Greetings.
2029 **1423** 41y. multicoloured . . 45 10

1424 Hamamatsu Papier-mache Horse

1425 Type 10000

1989. New Year Lottery Stamp.
2030 **1424** 62y. multicoloured . . 60 10
Each stamp carries a lottery number.

1990. Electric Railway Locomotives (1st series).
2031 **1425** 62y. purple, lilac & grn 1·25 25
2032 – 62y. multicoloured . . 1·25 25
DESIGN: No. 2032, Type EF 58 No. 38, 1946.
See also Nos. 2033/4, 2039/40, 2089/90 and 2101/2.

1990. Electric Railway Locomotives (2nd series). As T **1425**. Multicoloured.
2033 62y. Type ED 40 No. 12, 1919 . . . . 1·25 25
2034 62y. Type EH 10 No. 8, 1954 . . . . 1·25 25

1429 Fairies on Flower

1431 "Women gazing at the Stars" (Chou Ohta)

1990. "Expo 90" International Garden and Greenery Exposition, Osaka. Multicoloured.
2035 41y.+4y. Type **1429** 45 10
2036 62y. Bicycle under tree . . . 55 10

1990. Philatelic Week.
2037 **1431** 62y. multicoloured . . 55 10
MS2038 60 × 77 mm. No. 2037 55 35

1990. Electric Railway Locomotives (3rd series). As T **1425.** Multicoloured.
2039 62y. Type EF 53, 1932 . . . 1·25 25
2040 62y. Type ED 70, 1957 . . 1·25 25

1434 Sweet Briar (Hokkaido)
1435 Apple Blossom (Aomori)

1436 "Paulownia tomentosa" (Iwate)
1437 Japanese Bush Clover (Miyagi)

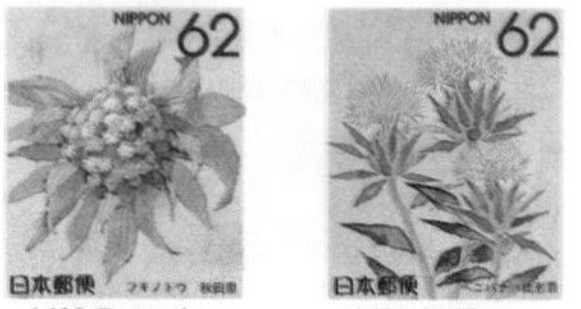
1438 Butterbur Flower (Akita)
1439 Safflower (Yamagata)

1440 Rhododendron (Fukushima)
1441 Rose (Ibaraki)

1442 Yashio Azalea (Tochigi)
1443 Japanese Azalea (Gunma)

1444 Primrose (Saitama)
1445 Rape (Chiba)

1446 Cherry Blossom (Yamanashi)
1447 Gold-banded Lily (Kanagawa)

1448 Cherry Blossom (Tokyo) **1449** Gentian (Nagano)

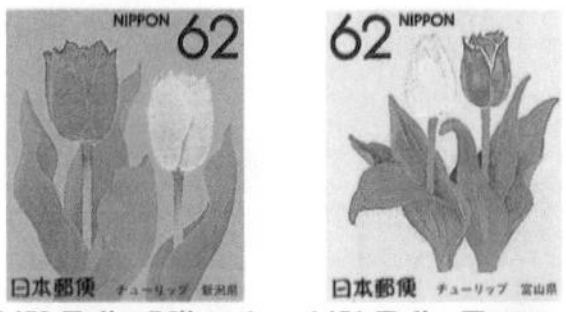
1450 Tulip (Niigata) **1451** Tulip (Toyama)

1452 Fritillaria (Ishikawa) **1453** Narcissi (Fukui)

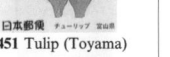

1454 Chinese Milk Vetch (Gifu) **1455** Azalea (Shizuoka)

1456 Rabbit-ear Iris (Aichi) **1457** Iris (Mie)

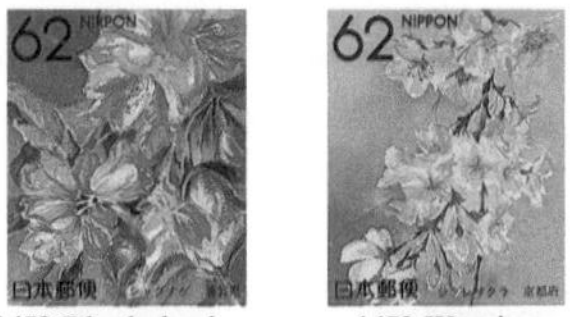
1458 Rhododendron (Shiga) **1459** Weeping Cherry Blossom (Kyoto)

1460 Japanese Apricot and Primrose (Osaka) **1461** Marguerites (Hyogo)

1462 Double Cherry Blossom (Nara) **1463** Japanese Apricot (Wakayama)

1464 Pear Blossom (Tottori) **1465** Peony (Shimane)

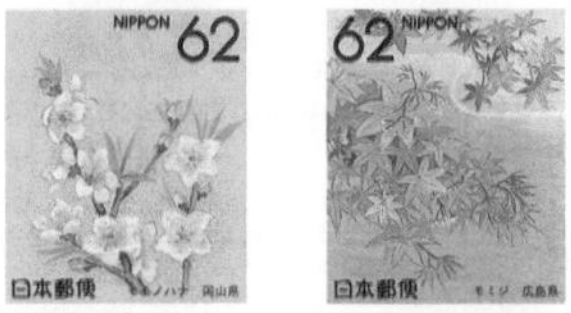
1466 Peach Blossom (Okayama) **1467** Japanese Maple (Hiroshima)

1468 Summer Orange Blossom (Yamaguchi) **1469** Sudachi Orange Blossom (Tokushima)

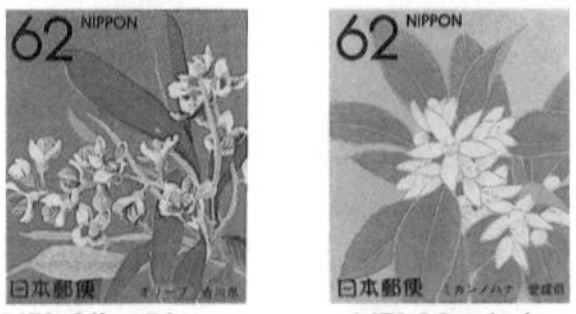
1470 Olive Blossom (Kagawa) **1471** Mandarin Orange Blossom (Ehime)

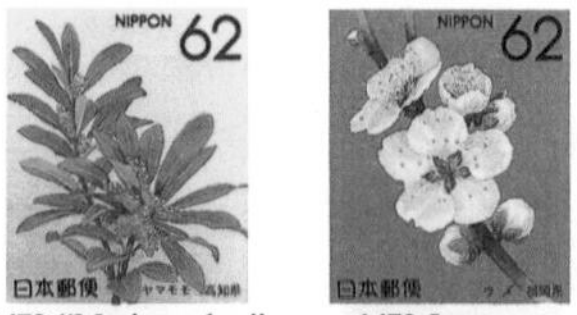
1472 "Myrica rubra" (Kochi) **1473** Japanese Apricot (Fukuoka)

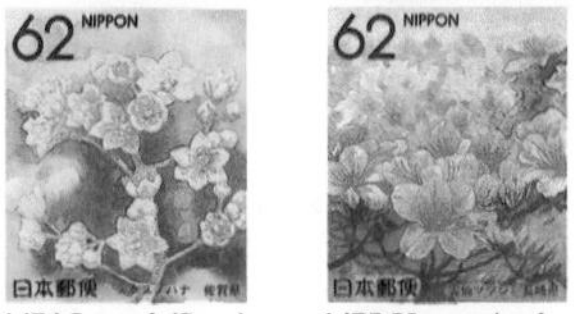
1474 Laurel (Saga) **1475** Unzen Azalea (Nagasaki)

1476 Gentian (Kumamoto) **1477** Japanese Apricot (Oita)

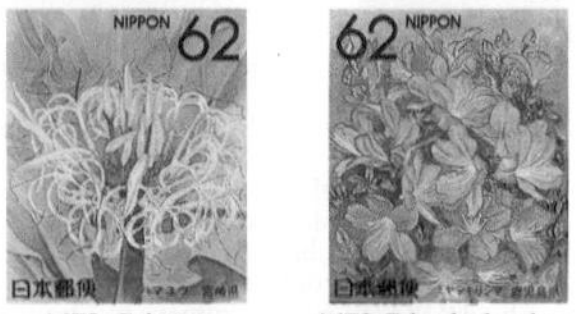
1478 Crinum (Miyazaki) **1479** Rhododendron (Kagoshima)

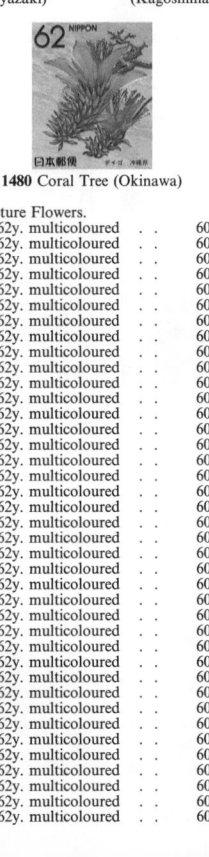

1480 Coral Tree (Okinawa)

1990. Prefecture Flowers.

2041 **1434** 62y. multicoloured . . 60 10
2042 **1435** 62y. multicoloured . . 60 10
2043 **1436** 62y. multicoloured . . 60 10
2044 **1437** 62y. multicoloured . . 60 10
2045 **1438** 62y. multicoloured . . 60 10
2046 **1439** 62y. multicoloured . . 60 10
2047 **1440** 62y. multicoloured . . 60 10
2048 **1441** 62y. multicoloured . . 60 10
2049 **1442** 62y. multicoloured . . 60 10
2050 **1443** 62y. multicoloured . . 60 10
2051 **1444** 62y. multicoloured . . 60 10
2052 **1445** 62y. multicoloured . . 60 10
2053 **1446** 62y. multicoloured . . 60 10
2054 **1447** 62y. multicoloured . . 60 10
2055 **1448** 62y. multicoloured . . 60 10
2056 **1449** 62y. multicoloured . . 60 10
2057 **1450** 62y. multicoloured . . 60 10
2058 **1451** 62y. multicoloured . . 60 10
2059 **1452** 62y. multicoloured . . 60 10
2060 **1453** 62y. multicoloured . . 60 10
2061 **1454** 62y. multicoloured . . 60 10
2062 **1455** 62y. multicoloured . . 60 10
2063 **1456** 62y. multicoloured . . 60 10
2064 **1457** 62y. multicoloured . . 60 10
2065 **1458** 62y. multicoloured . . 60 10
2066 **1459** 62y. multicoloured . . 60 10
2067 **1460** 62y. multicoloured . . 60 10
2068 **1461** 62y. multicoloured . . 60 10
2069 **1462** 62y. multicoloured . . 60 10
2070 **1463** 62y. multicoloured . . 60 10
2071 **1464** 62y. multicoloured . . 60 10
2072 **1465** 62y. multicoloured . . 60 10
2073 **1466** 62y. multicoloured . . 60 10
2074 **1467** 62y. multicoloured . . 60 10
2075 **1468** 62y. multicoloured . . 60 10
2076 **1469** 62y. multicoloured . . 60 10
2077 **1470** 62y. multicoloured . . 60 10
2078 **1471** 62y. multicoloured . . 60 10
2079 **1472** 62y. multicoloured . . 60 10
2080 **1473** 62y. multicoloured . . 60 10
2081 **1474** 62y. multicoloured . . 60 10
2082 **1475** 62y. multicoloured . . 60 10
2083 **1476** 62y. multicoloured . . 60 10
2084 **1477** 62y. multicoloured . . 60 10
2085 **1478** 62y. multicoloured . . 60 10
2086 **1479** 62y. multicoloured . . 60 10
2087 **1480** 62y. multicoloured . . 60 10

1481 Mt. Unzen and Unzen Azalea

1484 Fritillary on Thistle

1990. National Afforestation Campaign.

2088 **1481** 62y. multicoloured . . 55 10

1990. Electric Railway Locomotives (4th series). As T **1425**. Multicoloured.

2089 62y. Type EF 55, 1936 . . . 1·25 25
2090 62y. Type ED 61 No. 13, 1958 . . . . 1·25 25

1990. Winning Entries in Postage Stamp Design Contest. Multicoloured.

2091 62y. Type **1484** 55 25
2092 70y. "Communication" . . 65 20

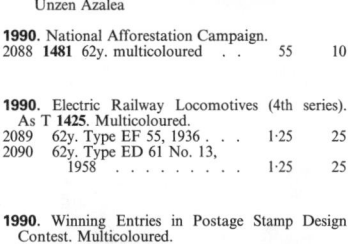

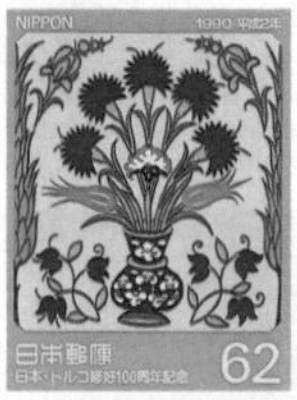
1486 17th-century Ottoman Tile

1990. Century of Japan–Turkey Friendship.

2093 **1486** 62y. multicoloured . . 55 10

1487/91 Folding Screen (½-size illustration)

1492 "Ponies" (Kayo Yamaguchi)

1493 Emblem and Landscape

1990. The Horse in Culture (1st series).

2094 **1487** 62y. multicoloured . . 65 10
2095 **1488** 62y. multicoloured . . 65 10
2096 **1489** 62y. multicoloured . . 65 10
2097 **1490** 62y. multicoloured . . 65 10
2098 **1491** 62y. multicoloured . . 65 10
2099 **1492** 62y. multicoloured . . 65 10

Nos. 2094/8 were printed together, se-tenant, forming a composite design showing a 17th-century folding screen painting.

See also Nos. 2106/8, 2113/14, 2132/4 and 2135/6.

1990. 38th International Youth Hostel Federation Congress. Muikamachi and Kashiwazaki.

2100 **1493** 62y. multicoloured . . 55 10

1990. Electric Railway Locomotives (5th series). As T **1425**. Multicoloured.

2101 62y. Type ED 57, 1941 . . 1·25 25
2102 62y. Type EF 30 Nos. 3 and 6, 1961 . . . . 1·25 25

1496 Bluebird and Heart

1497 Fairy on Horse

1990. Letter Writing Day.

2103 **1496** 41y. multicoloured . . 40 10
2104 **1497** 62y. multicoloured . . 55 10
MS2105 72 × 93 mm. No. 2104 55 35

For similar design to No. 2104, see No. 2157.

1500 "A Horse" (Suisho Nishiyama)

1990. The Horse in Culture (2nd series). Multicoloured.

2106 62y. 16th-century lacquered saddle 65 10
2107 62y. 16th-century lacquered stirrups 65 10
2108 62y. Type **1500** 65 10

1501 Origami Polyhedron

1502 Track Race

1990. Int Mathematicians Congress, Kyoto.

2109 **1501** 62y. multicoloured . . 60 10

1990. World Cycling Championships. Maebashi and Tochigi Prefecture.

2110 **1502** 62y. multicoloured . . 60 10

1503 Ogai Mori (translator) and Passage from Goethe's "Faust"

1504 "Ji" (character) and Rosetta Stone

1990. 8th International Association for Germanic Studies Congress, Tokyo.

2111 **1503** 62y. blue, yellow & brn 55 10

1990. International Literacy Year.

2112 **1504** 62y. multicoloured . . 55 10

1505 "Kurabeuma Race" (detail of Kimono)

1506 "Kettei" (Shodo Sasaki)

1990. The Horse in Culture (3rd series).

2113 **1505** 62y. multicoloured . . 65 10
2114 **1506** 62y. multicoloured . . 65 10

1507 Peaceful Landscape

1990. International Decade for Natural Disaster Reduction Conference, Yokohama.

2115 **1507** 62y. multicoloured . . 55 10

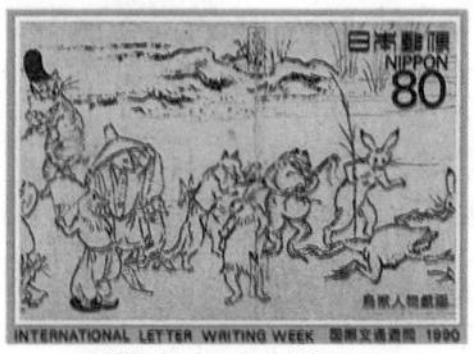
1508 Animals at Dance

1990. International Correspondence Week. Details from "Choju-jinbutsu-giga" Picture Scroll. Multicoloured.

2116 80y. Type **1508** 75 10
2117 120y. Dancing frogs . . . . 1·10 20

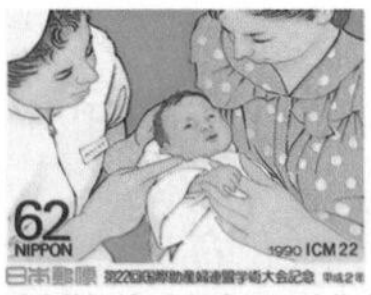

1510 Midwife, Mother and Baby

1990. 22nd International Confederation of Midwives Congress, Kobe City.
2118 **1510** 62y. multicoloured . . 55 10

1511 "Letter Bearer" (detail, Harunobu Suiendo)

1990. "Phila Nippon '91" International Stamp Exhibition, Tokyo (1st issue).
2119 **1511** 100y. multicoloured . . 1·00 20
MS2120 94 × 90 mm. No. 2119 1·10 45
See also. Nos. 2170/**MS**2171.

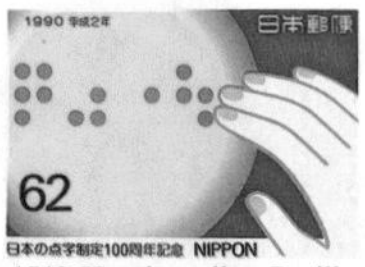

1512 Hand reading Braille

1513 "Justice" (Supreme Court bronze statue, Katsuzo Entsuba)

1990. Centenary of Japanese Braille.
2121 **1512** 62y. multicoloured . . 55 10

1990. Centenary of Modern Judiciary System.
2122 **1513** 62y. multicoloured . . 55 10

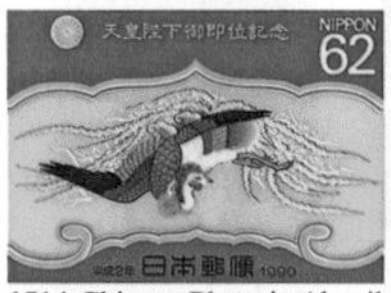

1514 Chinese Phoenix (detail from dais of Emperor's enthronement seat)

1516 Stained Glass Window (Diet building)

1990. Enthronement of Emperor. Multicoloured.
2123 62y. Type **1514** 55 10
2124 62y. Pattern from robe of Manzai Raku dancers . . 55 10
MS2125 144 × 93 mm. Nos. 2123/4 1·10 1·10

1990. Centenary of Diet.
2126 **1516** 62y. multicoloured . . 55 10

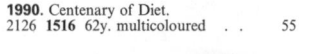

1517 Sheep (Nogomi ceramic bell)

1519 Tsuneishi-Hariko Papier-mache Ram

1990. New Year's Greetings.
2127 **1517** 41y. multicoloured . . 40 10

1990. New Year Lottery Stamps. Multicoloured.
2128 41y. Sheep (Tosa ceramic bell) 40 10
2129 62y. Type **1519** 55 10
Each stamp carries a lottery number.

1520 Dr. Nishina and Radio Isotope

1521 "Lady using Telephone" (Senseki Nakamura)

1990. Birth Centenary of Dr. Yoshio Nishina (physicist) and 50th Anniv of First Japanese Cyclotron (radio isotope generator).
2130 **1520** 62y. multicoloured . . 55 10

1990. Centenary of Telephone Service in Japan.
2131 **1521** 62y. multicoloured . . 55 10

1522/3 Horse-drawn Post Carriages (details of scroll painting by Beisen Kubota)

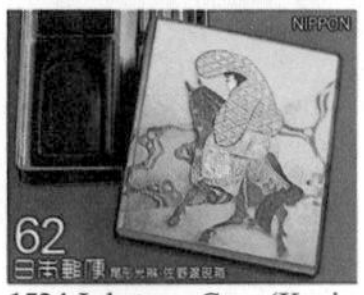

1524 Inkstone Case (Korin Ogata)

1991. The Horse in Culture (4th series).
2132 **1522** 62y. multicoloured . . 60 10
2133 **1523** 62y. multicoloured . . 60 10
2134 **1524** 62y. multicoloured . . 60 10
Nos. 2132/3 were issued together, se-tenant, forming the composite design illustrated.

1525 "Spring Warmth" (Kogetsu Saigo)

1526 "Senju in Musashi Province" (from "36 Views of Mt. Fuji" by Hokusai Katsushika)

1991. The Horse in Culture (5th series).
2135 **1525** 62y. multicoloured . . 65 10
2136 **1526** 62y. multicoloured . . 65 10

1527 Figure Skating

1529 Bouquet

1991. Winter Universiade, Sapporo and Furano. Multicoloured.
2137 41y. Type **1527** 45 10
2138 62y. Short-track speed skating (horiz) 60 10

1991. New Postal Life Insurance System.
2139 **1529** 62y. multicoloured . . 55 10

1530 "Glory of the Earth" (Komei Bekki)

1531 "Beauty looking Back" (Moronobu Hishikawa)

1991. "Ceramic World Shigaraki '91" Exn.
2140 **1530** 62y. multicoloured . . 55 10

1991. Philatelic Week. 120th Anniv of First Japanese Stamps.
2141 62y. Type **1531** 60 10
2142 62y. "The Prelude" (Shuho Yamakawa) 60 10
MS2143 93 × 77 mm. Nos. 2141/2 1·50 1·10

1533 Weeping Cherry Blossom and Phoenix Hall, Byodoin Temple

1534 Early Leveller and Standard Datum Repository, Tokyo

1991. National Afforestation Campaign.
2144 **1533** 41y. multicoloured . . 40 10

1991. Centenary of Standard Datum of Levelling.
2145 **1534** 62y. multicoloured . . 55 10

1535 Flowers

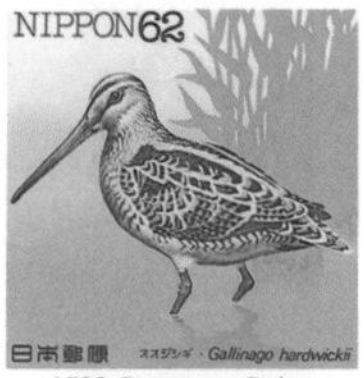

1539 Japanese Snipe ("Gallinago hardwickii")

1991. Winning Entries in Postage Stamp Design Contest.
2146 **1535** 41y. multicoloured . . 40 10
2147 – 62y. multicoloured . . 55 10
2148 – 70y. brown, blue & blk 65 10
2149 – 100y. multicoloured . . 90 20
DESIGNS—HORIZ: 62y. Couple in traditional dress; 100y. Butterfly. VERT: 70y. "World Peace".

1991. Water Birds (1st series). Multicoloured.
2150 62y. Type **1539** . . . . . . 1·25 20
2151 62y. Brown booby ("Sula leucogaster") . . . . . . 1·25 20
See also Nos. 2162/3, 2179/80, 2184/5, 2198/9, 2241/2, 2247/8 and 2251/2.

1541 Kikugoro Onoe VI in Title Role of "Spirit of the Lion"

1542 Utaemon Nakamura VI as Princess Yaegaki in "24 Examples of Filial Piety"

1991. Kabuki Theatre (1st series).
2152 **1541** 62y. green, gold & black 55 10
2153 **1542** 100y. multicoloured . . 90 20
See also Nos. 2164/5, 2172/3, 2181/2, 2186/7 and 2190/1.

1543 "Solidarity" in Sign Language and Congress Emblem

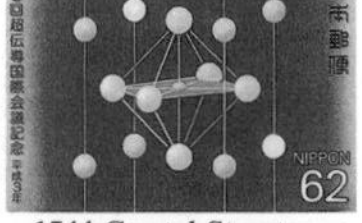

1544 Crystal Structure

1991. 11th World Federation of the Deaf International Congress, Tokyo.
2154 **1543** 62y.+10y. mult 65 10
The premium was assigned to programmes for helping the deaf.

1991. International Conf on Materials and Mechanism of Superconductivity, Kanazawa.
2155 **1544** 62y. multicoloured . . 55 10

1545 Girl sitting on Morning Glory

1546 Fairy on Horse

1991. Letter Writing Day.
2156 **1545** 41y. multicoloured . . 40 10
2157 **1546** 62y. multicoloured . . 55 10
MS2158 72 × 93 mm. No. 2157 55 55
For design similar to No. 2157 but with central motif drawn larger, see No. 2104.

1547 High Jumping

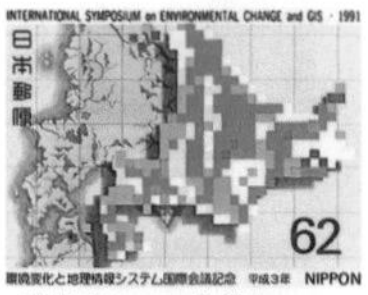

1549 Map and Computer Image of Hokkaido

1991. 3rd World Athletics Championships, Tokyo. Multicoloured.
2159 41y. Type **1547** 50 10
2160 62y. Putting the shot . . . 70 15

1991. International Symposium on Environmental Change and Geographic Information Systems, Asahikawa, Hokkaido.
2161 **1549** 62y. multicoloured . . 70 15

1991. Water Birds (2nd series). As T **1539**. Multicoloured.
2162 62y. Japanese gull ("Larus crassirostris") . . . . . . 1·25 20
2163 62y. Little grebe ("Podiceps ruficollis") . . . . 1·25 20

1552 Koshiro Matsumoto VII as Benkei in "The Subscription List"

1553 Danjuro Ichikawa XI as Danjo in "Tweezers"

1991. Kabuki Theatre (2nd series).
2164 **1552** 62y. black, grey & gold 70 15
2165 **1553** 100y. multicoloured . . 1·25 30

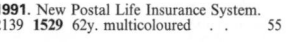

1554 Nobles watching burning Oten Gate

1991. International Correspondence Week. Details from Ban Dainagon Picture Scrolls by Mitsunaga Tokiwa. Multicoloured.
2166 80y. Type **1554** 95 20
2167 120y. Arrest of Yoshio Tomo (arsonist) . . . . . 1·40 30

1556 "Clear Day with Southern Breeze" (from "36 Views of Mt. Fuji" by Hokusai Katsushika) and Seismographic Wave

1557 Tea Utensils and Flower

1991. Earthquake and Natural Disaster Countermeasures Conference. Tokyo.
2168 **1556** 62y. multicoloured . . 70 15

1991. 800th Anniv of Introduction of Green Tea into Japan.
2169 **1557** 62y. multicoloured . . 70 15

1558 "Saucy Girl" (from "A Selection of Beautiful Women" by Kunisada Utagawa)

1991. "Phila Nippon '91" International Stamp Exhibition, Tokyo (2nd issue).
2170 **1558** 62y. multicoloured . . 70 15
MS2171 93 × 77 mm. No. 2170 × 2 1·50 1·50

1559 Baigyoku Nakamura III as the Ogiya Courtesan Yugiri in "Yoshida-ya"

1560 Ganjiro Nakamura III as Jihei Kamiya in "Shinju-Ten no Amijima"

1991. Kabuki Theatre (3rd series). Works by Chikamatsu Monzaemon.
2172 **1559** 62y. black, pur & gold 70 15
2173 **1560** 100y. multicoloured . . 1·25 30

1561 Boy building Toy Town

1562 Ishikawa Papier-mache Monkey

1991. 30th Anniv of Administrative Councillors System.
2174 **1561** 62y. multicoloured . . 70 15

1991. New Year's Greetings. Multicoloured.
2175 41y. Type **1562** 50 10
2176 62y. Obata monkey 70 15

1565 Obata Monkey

1991. New Year Lottery Stamps. Multicoloured.
2177 41y.+3y. Ishikawa papier-mache monkey 50 10
2178 62y.+3y. Type **1565** 75 15
Each stamp carries a lottery number.

1992. Water Birds (3rd series). As T **1539**. Multicoloured.
2179 62y. Tufted puffin ("Lunda cirrhata") . . . . 1·25 20
2180 62y. Hooded cranes ("Grus monacha") . . . . 1·25 20

1568 Kichiemon Nakamura I as Jiro Naozane Kumagai in "Chronicle of Two Boys in Battle of Ichinotani" by Munesuke Namiki

1569 Nizaemon Kataoka XIII as Old Man in "Kotobuki Shiki Sambaso"

1992. Kabuki Theatre (4th series).
2181 **1568** 62y. multicoloured . . 70 15
2182 **1569** 100y. multicoloured . . 1·25 30

1570 Orchid and Chimpanzees

1992. 8th Conference of Parties to Convention on International Trade in Endangered Species, Kyoto City.
2183 **1570** 62y. multicoloured . . 70 15

1992. Water Birds (4th series). As T **1539**. Multicoloured.
2184 62y. Whooper swan ("Cygnus cygnus") . . . 1·25 20
2185 62y. Painted-snipe ("Rostratula benghalensis") . . . . . 1·25 20

1573 Enjaku Jitsukawa II as Ishikawa-Geomon in "Two-Storey Gate—Pawlonia" by Gohei Namiki

1574 Hakuo Matsumoto I as Oishi-Kuranosuke in "Loyal Retainers in Genroku" by Seika Mayama

1992. Kabuki Theatre (5th series).
2186 **1573** 62y. multicoloured . . 70 15
2187 **1574** 100y. multicoloured . . 1·25 30

1575 "Flowers on Chair" (Hoshun Yamaguchi)

1576 Shuri Castle

1992. Philatelic Week.
2188 **1575** 62y. multicoloured . . 70 15

1992. 20th Anniv of Return of Okinawa (Ryukyu Islands).
2189 **1576** 62y. multicoloured . . 70 15

1577 Baiko Onoe VII as the Wisteria Maiden

1578 Shoroku Onoe II as Goro Soga and Kanzaburo Nakamura XVII as Juro Soga in "Kotobuki-Soga-taimen"

1992. Kabuki Theatre (6th series).
2190 **1577** 62y. multicoloured . . 70 15
2191 **1578** 100y. multicoloured . . 1·25 30

1579 "ADEOS" Observation Satellite

1581 Bird delivering Letter to Flower

1992. International Space Year. Multicoloured.
2192 62y. Type **1579** 70 15
2193 62y. "BS-3" broadcasting satellite and space station 70 15
Nos. 2192/3 were printed together, se-tenant, forming a composite design.

1992. Letter Writing Day. Multicoloured.
2194 41y. Type **1581** 50 10
2195 62y. Bird delivering letter to dog 70 15
MS2196 76 × 93 mm. No. 2195 70 70

1583 Ammonite, Map and Stratigraphic Plan

1586 Canoeing

1992. 29th Int Geological Congress, Kyoto.
2197 **1583** 62y. multicoloured . . 75 15

1992. Water Birds (5th series). As T **1539**. Multicoloured.
2198 62y. White-faced shearwater ("Calonectris leucomelas") 1·25 40
2199 62y. Ruddy kingfisher ("Halcyon coromanda") 1·25 40

1992. 47th National Athletic Meeting, Yamagata.
2200 **1586** 41y. multicoloured . . 50 10

1587 Japanese Jar (Ninsei Nonomura)

1588 Chinese Vase (Tang dynasty)

1992. 20th Anniv of Restoration of Diplomatic Relations with China.
2201 **1587** 62y. multicoloured . . 70 15
2202 **1588** 62y. multicoloured . . 70 15

1589 Nobles arriving at Taiken Gate

1590 Fujiwarano Nobuyori giving Audience

1992. International Correspondence Week. Details from "Tale of Heiji" Shinzei Picture Scroll.
2203 **1589** 80y. multicoloured . . 95 20
2204 **1590** 120y. multicoloured . . 1·40 30

1591 "Friends" (Tomoko Komoto)

1593 "Kyo" Ideograph, Mt. Fuji, Sun and Waves

1992. 3rd Stamp Design Competition Winners. Multicoloured.
2205 62y. Type **1591** 70 15
2206 70y. "Gaiety on Christmas Night" (Brat Anca) . . . 80 20

1992. 30th International Co-operative Alliance Congress, Tokyo.
2207 **1593** 62y. multicoloured . . 70 15

1594 Takakazu Seki (mathematician, 350th birth)

1595 Akiko Yosano (poet, 50th death)

1992. Anniversaries.
2208 **1594** 62y. multicoloured . . 70 15
2209 **1595** 62y. multicoloured . . 70 15

1596 Certified Public Tax Accountants' Assn Emblem

1992. 50th Anniv of Tax Accountants Law.
2210 **1596** 62y. multicoloured . . 70 15

1597 Papier-mache and Clay Cock

1600 Tsuyazaki Clay Cock on Drum

1992. New Year's Greetings. Multicoloured.
2211 41y. Type **1597** 50 10
2212 62y. Tsuyazaki clay cock on drum 70 15

1992. New Year Lottery Stamps. Multicoloured.
2213 41y.+3y. Papier-mache and clay cock 50 10
2214 62y.+3y. Type **1600** 75 15
Each stamp carries a lottery number.

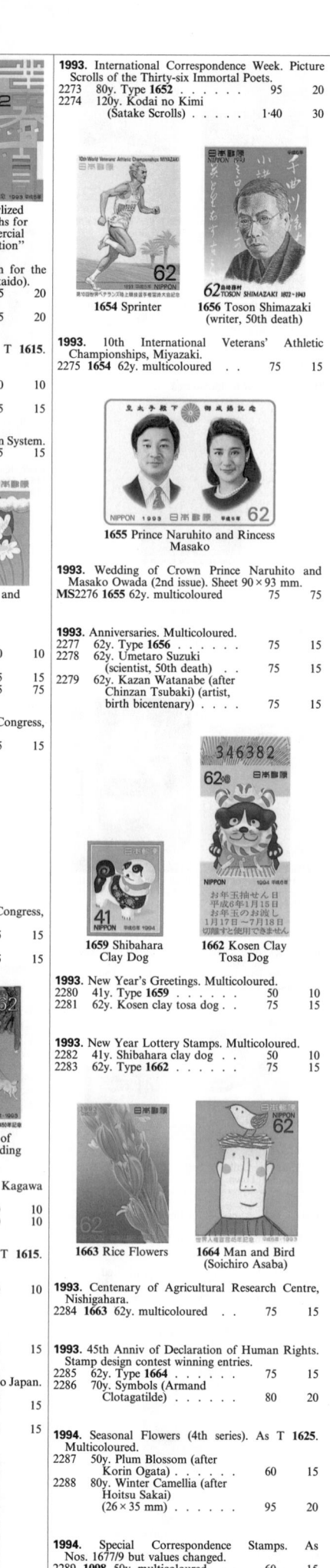

1601 "Orthetrum albistylum" (dragonfly) · 1601a "Oxycetonia jucunda" (beetle) · 1602 Mikado Swallowtail

1603 Ladybirds · 1603a Honey Bee · 1603b "Lycaena phleas" (copper butterfly)

1604 Mandarin · 1605 Japanese White-Eye · 1606 Eastern Turtle Dove

1606a Great Tit · 1607 Varied Tit · 1608 Greater Pied Kingfisher

1609 Pacific Black Duck · 1609a Little Ringed Plover · 1609b Bull-headed Shrike

1610 Northern Bullfinch · 1610a Masked Hawfinch · 1610b Jay

1611 Orchids · 1612 Wild Pink · 1613 Adder's Tongue Lily

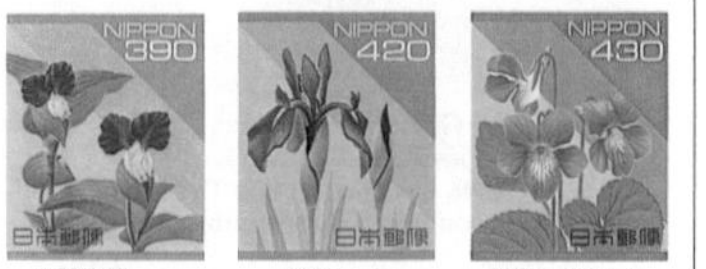

1614 Day-flowers · 1615 Iris · 1616 Violets

1617 Praying Mantis, Chrysanthemums and Hibiscus (after Hatsu Sakai) · 1618 "Pine and Hawk" (Sesson Shukei)

1992.

2215	**1601**	9y. yellow, black & bl	10	10
2215a	**1601a**	10y. multicoloured	10	10
2216	**1602**	15y. brown, light green and green	20	10
2217	**1603**	18y. green, grey and red	20	10
2217a	**1603a**	20y. multicoloured	20	10
2217b	**1603b**	30y. multicoloured	30	10
2218	**1604**	41y. orge, dp bl & bl	55	20
2219	**1605**	50y. yellow, bl & blk	55	20
2220	**1606**	62y. orge, dp bl & bl	75	20
2220a	**1606a**	70y. multicoloured	70	15
2221	**1607**	72y. orange, bl & grn	85	20
2222	**1608**	80y. blue, stone and green	85	20
2223	**1609**	90y. brown, yell & bl	85	20
2223a	**1609a**	110y. multicoloured	1·10	25
2223b	**1609b**	120y. multicoloured	1·10	25
2224	**1610**	130y. multicoloured	85	20
2224a	**1610a**	140y. multicoloured	1·40	25
2224b	**1610b**	160y. multicoloured	1·60	35
2225	**1611**	190y. multicoloured	2·25	45
2226	**1612**	270y. multicoloured	3·25	65
2227	**1613**	350y. mauve, lilac and green	4·00	80
2228	**1614**	390y. multicoloured	4·50	90
2229	**1615**	420y. violet, light green and green	5·00	1·00
2230	**1616**	430y. multicoloured	5·00	1·00
2231	**1617**	700y. multicoloured	8·25	1·60
2232	**1618**	1000y. multicoloured	12·00	2·40

The 41, 50, 62 and 80y. also exist imperforate with self-adhesive gum.

1993. Water Birds (6th series). As T **1539**. Multicoloured.

2241 62y. River kingfisher ("Alcedo atthis") 1·25 40
2242 62y. Cattle egret ("Bubulcus ibis") 1·25 40

1623 Super Giant Slalom

1625 Poppies (after Hochu Nakamura)

1993. World Alpine Skiing Championships, Shizukuishi (nr. Morioka). Multicoloured.

2243 41y. Type **1623** 50 10
2244 62y. Downhill 75 15

1993. Seasonal Flowers (1st series). Multicoloured.

2245 41y. Type **1625** 50 10
2246 62y. Cherry Blossoms (after Haitsu Sakai) (25 × 35 mm) 75 15

See also Nos. 2258/9, 2269/70 and 2287/8.

1993. Water Birds (7th series). As T **1539**. Multicoloured.

2247 62y. White-fronted geese ("Anser albifrons") 1·25 20
2248 62y. Japanese white-naped cranes ("Grus vipio") 1·25 20

No. 2247 is wrongly inscribed "Ansner".

1629 "In the Studio" (Nanpu Katayama)

1630 Coral Trees and Reef, Minnajima Island

1993. Philatelic Week.

2249 **1629** 62y. multicoloured 75 15

1993. National Afforestation Campaign.

2250 **1630** 41y. multicoloured 50 10

1993. Water Birds (8th series). As T **1539**. Multicoloured.

2251 62y. Baikal teal ("Anas formosa") 1·25 20
2252 62y. White-tailed sea eagle ("Haliaeetus albicilla") 1·25 20

1635 "Mandarin Duck in Nest" and "Gardenia in Nest"

1993. Wedding of Crown Prince Naruhito and Masako Owada. Multicoloured.

2253 62y. "Mandarin Duck in Nest" (pattern of groom's jacket) (vert) 75 15
2254 62y. "Gardenia in Nest" (pattern of bride's robe) (vert) 75 15
2255 70y. Type **1635** 80 20

1636 Manchurian Crane with Chicks

1640 Stylized Ideographs for "Commercial Registration"

1993. 5th Meeting of Ramsar Convention for the Preservation of Wetlands, Kushiro (Hokkaido).

2256 62y. Type **1636** 1·25 20
2257 62y. Head of Manchurian crane 1·25 20

1993. Seasonal Flowers (2nd series) As T **1615**. Multicoloured.

2258 41y. Lily (after Kiitsu Suzuki) 50 10
2259 62y. Thistle (after Shiko Watanabe) (25 × 35 mm) 75 15

1993. Centenary of Commercial Registration System.

2260 **1640** 62y. multicoloured 75 15

1641 Puppy reading Letter under Tree

1643 Heart, Clouds and Flowers

1993. Letter Writing Day. Multicoloured.

2261 41y. Type **1641** 50 10
2262 62y. Man pointing at flying letter (23 × 27 mm) 75 15
MS2263 72 × 93 mm. No. 2262 75 75

1993. World Federation for Mental Health Congress, Chiba City.

2264 **1643** 62y. multicoloured 75 15

1644 "Glaucidium palmatum"

1993. 15th International Botanical Congress, Yokohama. Multicoloured.

2265 62y. Type **1644** 75 15
2266 62y. "Sciadopitys verticillata" 75 15

1646 Swimming

1650 "Arrival of Portuguese" (folding screen)

1993. 48th National Athletic Meeting, Kagawa Prefecture. Multicoloured.

2267 41y. Type **1646** 50 10
2268 41y. Karate 50 10

1993. Seasonal Flowers (3rd series). As T **1615**. Multicoloured.

2269 41y. "Chinese Bell-flowers" (Korin Ogata) 50 10
2270 62y. Chrysanthemums (detail of "Cranes and Plants in Spring and Autumn", Kiitsu Suzuki) (25 × 35 mm) 75 15

1993. 450th Anniv of First Portuguese Visit to Japan. Multicoloured.

2271 62y. Type **1650** 75 15
2272 62y. Jesuit mother-of-pearl inlaid host box 75 15

1652 Ki no Tsurayuki (Agetatami Scrolls)

1993. International Correspondence Week. Picture Scrolls of the Thirty-six Immortal Poets.

2273 80y. Type **1652** 95 20
2274 120y. Kodai no Kimi (Satake Scrolls) 1·40 30

1654 Sprinter

1656 Toson Shimazaki (writer, 50th death)

1993. 10th International Veterans' Athletic Championships, Miyazaki.

2275 **1654** 62y. multicoloured 75 15

1655 Prince Naruhito and Rincess Masako

1993. Wedding of Crown Prince Naruhito and Masako Owada (2nd issue). Sheet 90 × 93 mm.

MS2276 **1655** 62y. multicoloured 75 75

1993. Anniversaries. Multicoloured.

2277 62y. Type **1656** 75 15
2278 62y. Umetaro Suzuki (scientist, 50th death) 75 15
2279 62y. Kazan Watanabe (after Chinzan Tsubaki) (artist, birth bicentenary) 75 15

1659 Shibahara Clay Dog

1662 Kosen Clay Tosa Dog

1993. New Year's Greetings. Multicoloured.

2280 41y. Type **1659** 50 10
2281 62y. Kosen clay tosa dog 75 15

1993. New Year Lottery Stamps. Multicoloured.

2282 41y. Shibahara clay dog 50 10
2283 62y. Type **1662** 75 15

1663 Rice Flowers

1664 Man and Bird (Soichiro Asaba)

1993. Centenary of Agricultural Research Centre, Nishigahara.

2284 **1663** 62y. multicoloured 75 15

1993. 45th Anniv of Declaration of Human Rights. Stamp design contest winning entries.

2285 62y. Type **1664** 75 15
2286 70y. Symbols (Armand Clotagatilde) 80 20

1994. Seasonal Flowers (4th series). As T **1625**. Multicoloured.

2287 50y. Plum Blossom (after Korin Ogata) 60 15
2288 80y. Winter Camellia (after Hoitsu Sakai) (26 × 35 mm) 95 20

1994. Special Correspondence Stamps. As Nos. 1677/9 but values changed.

2289 **1098** 50y. multicoloured 60 15
2290 **1099** 50y. multicoloured 60 15
2291 80y. multicoloured 95 20
2292 **1100** 90y. multicoloured 1·10 25

1668 Ladies' Figure Skating

1672 "Irises" (Heihachiro Fukuda)

1994. World Figure Skating Championships, Chiba City. Multicoloured.
2293 50y. Type **1668** 60 15
2294 50y. Ice dancing 60 15
2295 80y. Men's figure skating . . 95 20
2296 80y. Pairs figure skating . . 95 20

1994. Philatelic Week.
2297 **1672** 80y. multicoloured . . 95 20

1673 "Love" (Chieko Kitajima)

1677 White Stork, Marguerites and Camphor Tree

1994. International Year of the Family. Winning Entries in Stamp Design Contest. Multicoloured.
2298 50y. Type **1673** 60 15
2299 50y. "Happiness Flower" (Shigenobu Nagaishi) . . 60 15
2300 80y. "Family flowering at Home" (Junichi Mineta) 95 20
2301 80y. "Family in Flight" (Soichiro Asaba) 95 20

1994. National Afforestation Campaign.
2302 **1677** 50y. multicoloured . . 1·10 20

1678 Houses by the Waterside

1679 Pylon and Monju Building

1994. International Conference on Reduction of Natural Disasters, Yokohama.
2303 **1678** 80y. multicoloured . . 95 20

1994. Achievement of Initial Criticality (self-sustaining reaction) in Monju Nuclear Fast Breeder Reactor, Tsuruga.
2304 **1679** 80y. multicoloured . . 95 20

1680 Wildlife

1681 Envelope "Ship" and Man

1994. Environment Day.
2305 **1680** 80y. multicoloured . . 95 20

1994. Letter Writing Day. Multicoloured.
2306 50y. Type **1681** 60 15
2307 80y. Giraffe carrying envelope 95 20
MS2308 72 × 93 mm. No. 2307 95 95

1683 Emblem in Eye

1684 Baron Maeshima (Postal Minister) and 1871 48 mon "Dragon" Stamp

1994. 10th Int AIDS Conference, Yokohama.
2309 **1683** 80y. multicoloured . . 95 20

1994. History of Stamps (1st series). First Japanese Issue. Multicoloured, frame colour of "Dragon" stamp given.
2310 **1684** 80y. brown 95 20
2311 – 80y. blue 95 20
2312 – 80y. red 95 20
2313 – 80y. green 95 20
DESIGNS: No. 2311, 100mon "Dragon" stamp; 2312, 200mon "Dragon" stamp; 2313, 500mon "Dragon" stamp.

The central portion of the stamp portrayed varies according to value.

See also Nos. 2339/42, 2345/6, 2363/4, 2382/5 and 2416/19.

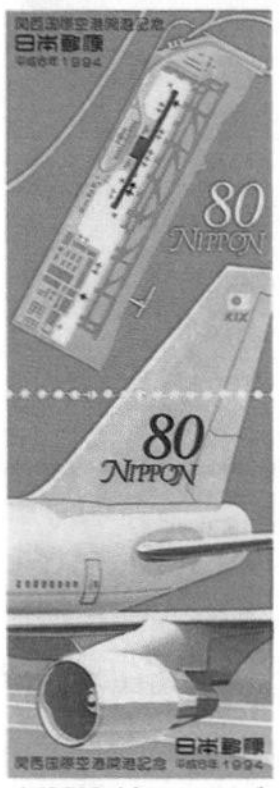

1685/6 Airport and Airplane bearing Airport Code

1688 Dish Aerial and Satellite

1994. Opening of Kansai International Airport, Osaka. Multicoloured.
2314 80y. Type **1685** 95 20
2315 80y. Type **1686** 95 20
2316 80y. Airplane approaching Airport 95 20

Nos. 2314/15 form the composite design shown.

1994. I.T.U. Plenipotentiary Conference, Kyoto.
2317 **1688** 80y. multicoloured . . 95 20

1689 Kickball

1695 Handball

1692 Sugoroku

1994. 12th Asian Games, Hiroshima. Mult.
2318 50y. Type **1689** 60 15
2319 80y. Steeplechase 95 20
2320 80y. Synchronized swimming 95 20

1994. International Correspondence Week. Details of "House of Entertainment" (folding screen). Multicoloured.
2321 90y. Type **1692** . . . . . . 1·10 25
2322 110y. Shogi . . . . 1·25 25
2323 130y. Go . . . . 1·50 30

1994. 49th National Athletic Meeting, Aichi.
2324 **1695** 50y. multicoloured . . 60 15

1696 Michio Miyagi (composer)

1698 Fujiwara no Michinaga and Insulin Crystals

1994. Birth Anniversaries. Multicoloured.
2325 80y. Type **1696** 95 20
2326 80y. Gyosho Hayami (painter) and "Moths" . . 95 20

1994. 15th International Diabetes Federation Congress, Kobe.
2327 **1698** 80y. multicoloured . . 95 20

Fujiwara no Michinaga (966–1028) was the earliest known Japanese diabetic.

1699/1703 "Viewing Maple Leaves at Takao" (folding screen, Hideyori Kano) (⅔-size illustration)

1704 "Yokuryuchi Pool, Shugakuin Imperial Villa" (Kenji Kawai)

1705 "Rock Garden, Ryoan Temple" (Eizo Kato)

1994. 1200th Anniv of Kyoto. Paintings.
2328 **1699** 80y. multicoloured . . 95 20
2329 **1700** 80y. multicoloured . . 95 20
2330 **1701** 80y. multicoloured . . 95 20
2331 **1702** 80y. multicoloured . . 95 20
2332 **1703** 80y. multicoloured . . 95 20
2333 **1704** 80y. multicoloured . . 95 20
2334 **1705** 80y. multicoloured . . 95 20

Nos. 2328/32 were issued together, se-tenant, forming the composite design illustrated.

1706 Izumo Papier-mache Boar

1709 Boar (Takayama soft toy)

1994. New Year's Greetings. Multicoloured.
2335 50y. Type **1706** 60 15
2336 80y. Boar (Takayama soft toy) 95 20

1994. New Year's Greetings. Lottery Stamps. Multicoloured.
2337 50y.+3y. Izumo Papier-mache boar 60 15
2338 80y.+3y. Type **1709** . . . . . 1·00 20

Each stamp carries a lottery number.

1710 5r. Stamp and Eduardo Chiossone (designer)

1994. History of Stamps (2nd series). "Koban" issue of 1876–88. Multicoloured, colour of featured stamp given.
2339 **1710** 80y. grey 95 20
2340 – 80y. brown 95 20
2341 – 80y. red 95 20
2342 – 80y. blue 95 20
FEATURED STAMPS: No. 2340, 1s. stamp (Type **20**); 2341, 12s. stamp (Type **21**); 2342, 20s. stamp (Type **22**).

1711 Himeji Castle Tower

1712 "Himeji Castle" (Masami Takahashi)

1994. World Heritage Sites (1st series).
2343 **1711** 80y. multicoloured . . 95 20
2344 **1712** 80y. multicoloured . . 95 20

See also Nos. 2347/8, 2373/4 and 2400/1.

1713 2s. Stamp and Postal Delivery by Hand-drawn Cart

1715 "Kannon Bosatsu" (wall painting, Kondo Hall)

1716 Kondo Hall, Horyu Temple

1995. History of Stamps (3rd series). 1894 Emperor's Silver Wedding issue and paintings by Shinsai Shibata. Multicoloured.
2345 80y. Type **1713** 95 20
2346 80y. 5s. stamp and postal delivery by horse-drawn carriage 95 20

1995. World Heritage Sites (2nd series). Multicoloured.
2347 **1715** 80y. multicoloured . . 95 20
2348 **1716** 110y. multicoloured . . 1·25 25

1717 Emblem and National Flowers

1995. Centenary of Japan–Brazil Treaty of Friendship. Multicoloured.
2349 80y. Type **1717** 95 20
2350 80y. Emblem and sports . . 95 20

1719 Unebi and Nijo Mountains and Tile from Palace

1720 "Remembering Times Past" (Saburosuke Okada)

1995. 1300th Anniv of Fujiwara Palace, Kashihara.
2351 **1719** 50y. multicoloured . . 60 15
2352 **1720** 80y. multicoloured . . 95 20

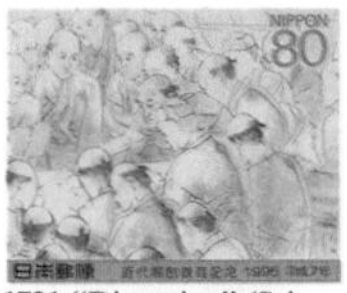
1721 "Dissection" (Seison Maeda)

1722 "National Census" and "16"

1995. Modern Anatomy Education.
2353 **1721** 80y. multicoloured . . 95 20

1995. 16th National Census.
2354 **1722** 80y. multicoloured . . 95 20

1723 Volunteer teaching Bangladeshi Woman to Read

1724 "Visitor to Art Studio" (Keika Kanashima)

1995. 30th Anniv of Japanese Overseas Co-operation Volunteers Service.
2355 **1723** 80y. multicoloured . . 95 20

1995. Philatelic Week.
2356 **1724** 80y.+20y. mult . . . . 1·25 25

The premium was for the Osaka/Kobe and Awaji earthquake victims' fund.

1725 Auspicious Clouds

1726 Reeds (mourning)

1727 Water Lily (mourning)

1728 Cloud, "Wind" and Pine Bark Pattern

1729 "Daphniphyllum macropodum"

1730 Maple and Shrine Island, Akiteline

1995. Special Correspondence Stamps.
2357 **1725** 50y. multicoloured . . 60 15
2358 **1726** 50y. multicoloured . . 60 15
2359 **1727** 80y. multicoloured . . 95 20
2360 **1728** 80y. multicoloured . . 95 20
2361 **1729** 90y. multicoloured . . 1·10 25

1995. National Afforestation Campaign.
2362 **1730** 50y. multicoloured . . 60 15

1731 8½s. Stamp and First Airmail Flight from Osaka to Tokyo

1733 Hearts forming Flower

1995. History of Stamps (4th series). 1929 First Airmail issue. Multicoloured.
2363 110y. Type **1731** . . . . 1·25 25
2364 110y. 18s. stamp and loading freight onto airplane . . . . 1·25 25

1995. Greetings Stamps. Mult. Self-adhesive.
2365 80y. Type **1733** 95 20
2366 80y. Child with balloon . . 95 20
2367 80y. Flower and pencil . . 95 20
2368 80y. Star, sun and moon . . 95 20
2369 80y. Child with dog 95 20

1738 Postman

1740 Cedar

1995. Letter Writing Day. Multicoloured.
2370 50y. Type **1738** 60 15
2371 80y. Ostrich 95 20
MS2372 72 × 93 mm. No. 2371 95 95

1995. World Heritage Sites (3rd series). Yaku Island. Multicoloured.
2373 80y. Type **1740** 95 20
2374 80y. Sika deer 95 20

1742 "Friends, One and All" (Yuki Ogawa)

1743 Atomic Bomb Dome, Hiroshima (Nobuya Nagata)

1744 "Light of Peace" (Nobuo Suenaga)

1745 Marathon Runners

1995. 50th Anniv of End of Second World War. Stamp Design Contest Winners.
2375 **1742** 50y. multicoloured . . 60 15
2376 **1743** 80y. multicoloured . . 95 20
2377 **1744** 80y. multicoloured . . 95 20

1995. 18th International University Games, Fukuoka.
2378 **1745** 80y. multicoloured . . 95 20

1746 Radio-controlled Plane

1748 Horse, Cow and Labrador

1995. World Aeromodel Championships, Kasaoka. Multicoloured.
2379 50y. Type **1746** 60 15
2380 80y. Radio-controlled helicopter 95 20

1995. World Veterinary Congress, Yokohama.
2381 **1748** 80y. multicoloured . . . 95 20

1749 5y. Stamp and Cherub and Tokyo Mailbox

1753 Judo (Makuhari, Chiba)

1995. History of Stamps (5th series). Industries issue of 1948–49. Multicoloured.
2382 80y. Type **1749** 95 20
2383 80y. 50y. stamp and mail van . . . . 1·60 25
2384 80y. 90y. stamp and mail van 95 20
2385 80y. 10y. stamp and cherub on Tokyo mailbox . . . 95 20

1995. World Sports Championships. Mult.
2386 80y. Type **1753** 95 20
2387 80y. Gymnastics (Sabae, Fukui) 95 20

1755 Shell Matching Game (from "New Year's Amusements")

1995. International Correspondence Week. Details of paintings on folding screens. Multicoloured.
2388 90y. Type **1755** . . . . . . 1·10 25
2389 110y. Battledore and Shuttlecock (from "Twelve Months") . . . 1·25 25
2390 130y. Playing Cards (from "Matsuura Folding Screen") . . . . 1·50 30

1758 Cyclists

1759 Patchwortk Hearts (Tomoko Suzuki)

1995. 50th Anniv of National Athletic Meeting, Fukushima.
2391 **1758** 50y. multicoloured . . 60 15

1995. 50th Anniversaries of U.N.O. (2392) and UNESCO (2393). Multicoloured.
2392 80y. Type **1759** 95 20
2393 80y. Children with Heart Balloon (Yukino Ikeda) 95 20

1761 Tadataka Ino (cartographer, 250th birth)

1995. Anniversaries. Multicoloured.
2394 80y. Type **1761** 95 20
2395 80y. Kitaro Nishida (philosopher, 50th death) 95 20

1763 Tsutsumi Clay Rat on Cayenne Pepper

1766 Satsuma Papier-mache Rat in Rice Store

1995. New Year's Greetings. Multicoloured.
2396 50y. Type **1763** 60 15
2397 80y. Satsuma papier-mache rat in rice store 95 20

1995. New Year's Lottery Stamps. Multicoloured.
2398 50y.+3y. Tsutsumi clay rat on turnip 60 15
2399 80y.+3y. Type **1766** . . . . 1·00 20

Each stamp carries a lottery number.

1767 Beech Forest

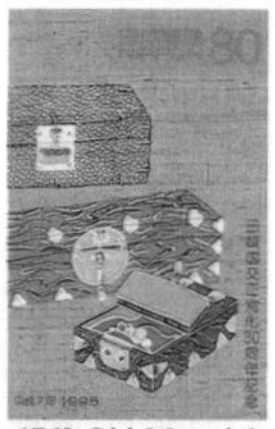
1769 Obi Material showing Choson Dynasty Boxes (Keisuke Serizawa)

1995. World Heritage Sites (4th series). Shirakami Mountains. Multicoloured.
2400 80y. Type **1767** 95 20
2401 80y. Black woodpecker . . 95 20

1995. 30th Anniv of Resumption of Japan–Korea Diplomatic Relations.
2402 **1769** 80y. multicoloured . . 95 20

1770 Siebold

1771 Twined Ropes

1996. Birth Bicentenary of Philipp Franz von Siebold (physician and Japanologist).
2403 **1770** 80y. multicoloured . . 95 20

1996. 50th Anniv of Labour Relations Commissions.
2404 **1771** 80y. multicoloured . . 95 20

1772 Turtle and Crane

1996. Senior Citizens.
2405 **1772** 80y. multicoloured . . 95 20

1773 Driving to Diet for Promulgation of Constitution, 1946

1774 Signing San Francisco Peace Treaty, 1951

1775 Return of Okinawa, 1972

1776 Woman and Diet Building

1996. 50 Post-war Years (1st series).
2406 **1773** 80y. mauve, lilac & gold 95 20
2407 **1774** 80y. dp grn, grn & gold 95 20
2408 **1775** 80y. indigo, blue and gold 95 20

See also Nos. 2420/1, 2429/30, 2443/4 and 2449/54.

1996. 50th Anniv of Women's Suffrage.
2409 **1776** 80y. multicoloured . . 95 20

1777 "Window" (Yukihiko Yasuda)

1778 Mother and Child

1996. Philatelic Week.
2410 **1777** 80y. multicoloured . . 95 20

1996. 50th Anniv of UNICEF.
2411 **1778** 80y. multicoloured . . 95 20

1779 Children and Sun

1780 Narcissus Flycatcher

1996. Child Welfare Week.
2412 **1779** 80y. multicoloured . . 95 20

1996. Bird Week. Multicoloured.
2413 80y. Type **1780** 95 20
2414 80y. Binoculars and bird feeding nestlings 95 20

1782 Cherry Blossom and Tokyo Buildings

1996. National Afforestation Campaign.
2415 **1782** 50y. multicoloured . . 60 15

1783 1991 Design

1784 1949 Design

1996. History of Stamps (6th series). Philatelic Week Issues.
2416 **1783** 80y. brown, ochre and lilac 95 20
2417 80y. multicoloured . . 95 20
2418 **1784** 80y. deep lilac and lilac 95 20
2419 80y. multicoloured . . 95 20

1785 Olympic Flame (Olympic Games, Tokyo, 1964)

1786 Sun Tower ("EXPO 70" World Fair, Osaka)

1996. 50 Post-war Years (2nd series).
2420 **1785** 80y. multicoloured . . 95 20
2421 **1786** 80y. multicoloured . . 95 20

1787/8 "Oirase no Keiryu" (Chikkyo Ono)

1996. Centenary of Modern River Control Systems.
2422 **1787** 80y. multicoloured . . 95 20
2423 **1788** 80y. multicoloured . . 95 20
Nos. 2422/3 were issued together, se-tenant, forming the composite design illustrated.

1789 Emblem

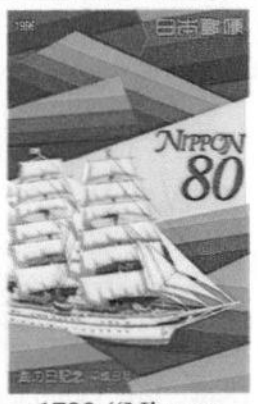
1790 "Nippon Maru II" (cadet ship)

1996. Marine Day.
2424 **1789** 50y. multicoloured . . 60 15
2425 **1790** 80y. multicoloured . . 95 20

1791 Cat

1996. Letter Writing Day. Multicoloured.
2426 50y. Type **1791** 60 15
2427 80y. Toy horse 95 20
MS2428 72 × 93 mm. No. 2427 95 95

1793 "Hikari" Express Train and Motorway

1794 Woman and Modern Appliances

1996. 50 Post-war Years (3rd series). Modern Life.
2429 **1793** 80y. multicoloured . . 95 20
2430 **1794** 80y. multicoloured . . 95 20

1795 Kenji Miyazawa (writer, centenary)

1797 Archer

1996. Birth Anniversaries. Multicoloured.
2431 80y. Type **1795** 95 20
2432 80y. Hokiichi Hanawa (scholar and editor, 250th) 95 20

1996. 51st National Athletic Meeting, Hiroshima.
2433 **1797** 50y. multicoloured . . 95 20

1798 Paper-chain People around Red Feather (donor pin)

1799 Piano Keys and Double Clef

1996. 50th Anniv of Community Chest.
2434 **1798** 80y. multicoloured . . 95 20

1996. International Music Day.
2435 **1799** 80y. multicoloured . . 95 20

1800 "Water Mill in Onden"

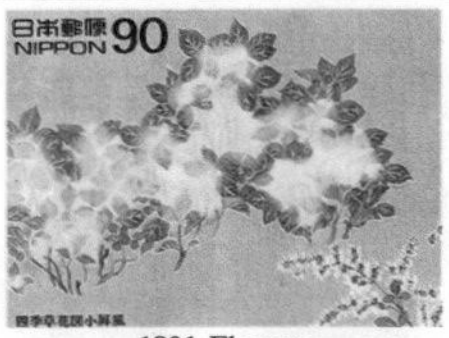
1801 Flowers

1803 Flowers

1805 Flowers

1996. International Correspondence Week. Paintings from "36 Views of Mt. Fuji" by Hokusai Katsushika (2436, 2438, 2440) and details of paintings on folding screen by Kohrin Ogata (others).
2436 **1800** 90y. multicoloured . . 95 20
2437 **1801** 90y. multicoloured . . 95 20
2438 – 110y. multicoloured . . 1·10 25
2439 **1803** 110y. multicoloured . . 1·10 25
2440 – 130y. multicoloured . . 1·40 30
2441 **1805** 130y. multicoloured . . 1·40 30
DESIGNS—As T **1800**: No. 2438; "Fine Day with a South Wind"; 2440, "Lake in Sosyu Hakone".

1806 Congress Emblem and Squirrel

1996. 18th Int Savings Banks Congress, Tokyo.
2442 **1806** 80y. multicoloured . . 85 20

1807 Mobile Telephone, Fibre-optic Cable and Communications Satellite

1808 Satellite Photograph of Earth

1996. 50 Post-war Years (4th series). Telecommunications and Environmental Protection.
2443 **1807** 80y. multicoloured . . 85 20
2444 **1808** 80y. multicoloured . . 85 20

1809 Okinawa Papier-mache Fighting Bull

1812 Child on Bull (Takamatus Wedding Doll)

1996. New Year's Greetings. Multicoloured.
2445 50y. Type **1809** 55 15
2446 80y. Child on bull (Takamatsu wedding doll) 85 20

1996. New Year Lottery Stamps. Multicoloured.
2447 50y.+3y. Okinawa papier-mache fighting bull . . . 55 15
2448 80y.+3y. Type **1812** 85 20
Each stamp carries a lottery number.

1813 Yujiro Ishihara (actor) as Youth

1814 Ishihara smoking Pipe

1815 Hibari Misora (actress' and singer) in "Kanashiki Kuchibue"

1816 Misora singing

1817 Osamu Tezuka (cartoonist) and Cartoon Characters

1818 Self-portrait and Astroboy

1997. 50 Post-war Years (5th series). Entertainers.
2449 **1813** 80y. black, brn & gold 80 20
2450 **1814** 80y. multicoloured . . 80 20
2451 **1815** 80y. black, blue & gold 80 20
2452 **1816** 80y. multicoloured . . 80 20
2453 **1817** 80y. multicoloured . . 80 20
2454 **1818** 80y. multicoloured . . 80 20

1819 Emblem

1821 "Daigo" (Togyu Okumura)

1997. Winter Olympic Games, Nagano (1998). Multicoloured.
2455 80y.+10y. Type **1819** . . . 90 20
2456 80y.+10y. Snowlets (mascots) 90 20

1997. Philatelic Week.
2457 **1821** 80y. multicoloured . . 75 15

1822 Main Court Room

1997. 50th Anniv of Supreme Court.
2458 **1822** 80y. multicoloured . . 80 20

1823 Parachutist

1824 Waving to Mechanical Doll

1825 Stamp Lover

1826 Helicopter Postman

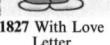

1827 With Love Letter

1828 Mexican Mythological Figures (Luis Nishizawa)

1997. Greetings Stamps. Doraemon (cartoon character). Self-adhesive gum.
2459 **1823** 80y. multicoloured . . 80 20
2460 **1824** 80y. multicoloured . . 80 20
2461 **1825** 80y. multicoloured . . 80 20
2462 **1826** 80y. multicoloured . . 80 20
2463 **1827** 80y. multicoloured . . 80 20

1997. Centenary of Japanese Emigration to Mexico.
2464 **1828** 80y. multicoloured . . 80 20

1829 Zao Crater Lake and Bush Clover

1830 House's Seal and Diet Building

1997. National Afforestation Campaign.
2465 **1829** 50y. multicoloured . . 50 10

1997. 50th Anniv of House of Councillors.
2466 **1830** 80y. multicoloured . . 80 20

1831 "Happy Balloon" (Orville Isaac)

1832 "Bird Friends" (Haruka Kumiya)

1833 "Message from Rainbow Forest" (Anna Romanovskaya)

1834 "Greetings" (Yumi Kiryu)

1997. Letter Writing Day.
2467 **1831** 50y. multicoloured . . 50 10
2468 **1832** 70y. multicoloured . . 70 15
2469 **1833** 80y. multicoloured . . 80 20
2470 **1834** 90y. multicoloured . . 90 20
MS2471 72 × 93 mm. No. 2469 80 80

1835 Bird with Letter and Owl on Blackboard

1836 Stylized Worker

1997. 50th Anniv of High School Part-time and Correspondence Courses.
2472 **1835** 50y. multicoloured . . 50 10

1997. 50th Anniv of Labour Standards Law.
2473 **1836** 80y. multicoloured . . 80 20

1837 Pacific Ocean and Mt. Osorno (after Hokusai Katsushika)

1838 Mopi (mascot) and Synchronized Swimmers

1997. Centenary of Japan–Chile Relations.
2474 **1837** 80y. multicoloured . . 80 20

1997. 52nd National Athletic Meeting, Osaka.
2475 **1838** 80y. multicoloured . . 80 20

1839 "Hodogaya" (from "53 Stations of Tokaido")

1840 Woodpecker and Flower

1842 Foliage

1844 Snow-covered Tree

1997. International Correspondence Week. Paintings by Hiroshige Ando (Nos. 2476, 2478, 2480) and details from "The Four Seasons" by Hoitsu Sakai (others). Multicoloured.
2476 90y. Type **1839** 90 20
2477 90y. Type **1840** 90 20
2478 110y. "Kameyama" (from "53 Stations of Tokaido") 1·10 25
2479 110y. Type **1842** . . . . . . 1·10 25
2480 130y. "Snow View from Sumida River Revetment" (from "Edo Scenic Sites: Snow, Moon and Flower") . . . . 1·25 25
2481 130y. Type **1844** . . . . . 1·25 25

1845 Auditorium, Takeru (opera character) and Ballerina

1997. Inaug of New National Theatre, Tokyo.
2482 **1845** 80y. multicoloured . . 80 20

1846 "Iihi Tabidachi" (Shinji Tanimura)

1847 "Tsuki no Sabaku" (Masao Kato and Suguru Sasaki)

1997. Favourite Songs (1st series).
2483 **1846** 50y. multicoloured . . 50 10
2484 **1847** 80y. multicoloured . . 80 20

See also Nos. 2497/8, 2499/2500, 2522/3, 2527/8, 2531/2, 2558/9, 2568/9 and 2578/9.

1848 Rohan Kouda (writer, 130th anniv)

1997. Birth Anniversaries. Multicoloured.
2485 80y. Type **1848** 80 20
2486 80y. Hiroshige Ando (after Toyo Kuni III) (painter, bicentenary) 80 20

1850 Miharu Hariko Paper Tiger

1853 Hakata Hariko Paper Tiger

1997. New Year's Greetings. Multicoloured.
2487 50y. Type **1850** 50 10
2488 80y. Hakata Hariko paper tiger 80 20

1997. New Year Lottery Stamps. Multicoloured.
2489 50y.+3y. Miharu Hariko paper tiger 55 15
2490 80y.+3y. Type **1853** 85 20

Each stamp carries a lottery number.

1854 "Yotsutake, Ryukyu Dance" (Taiji Hamada)

1997. 25th Anniv of Return of Okinawa (Ryukyu Islands).
2491 **1854** 80y. multicoloured . . 80 20

1855 Former Shibuya House, Yamagata

1856 Tomizawa House

1997. Traditional Houses (1st series).
2492 **1855** 80y. multicoloured . . 80 20
2493 **1856** 80y. multicoloured . . 80 20

See also Nos. 2513/14, 2529/30, 2539/40 and 2570/2.

1857 "Mother Sea" (Bokunen Naka)

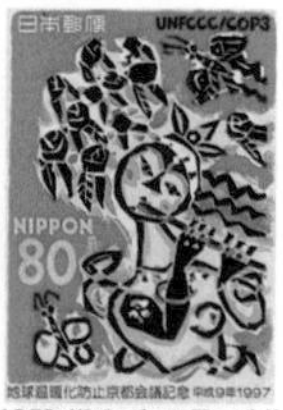

1858 "Mother Earth" (Bokunen Naka)

1997. United Nations Framework Convention on Climate Change, Kyoto.
2494 **1857** 80y. multicoloured . . 80 20
2495 **1858** 80y. multicoloured . . 80 20

1859 Drying Harvested Rice

1997. 50th Anniv of Agricultural Insurance System.
2496 **1859** 80y. multicoloured . . 80 20

1860 "Sunayama" (Hakushu Kitahara and Shinpei Nakayama)

1861 "Jingle Bells" (Shoji Miyazawa and J. Pierpont)

1997. Favourite Songs (2nd series).
2497 **1860** 50y. multicoloured . . 50 10
2498 **1861** 80y. multicoloured . . 80 20

1862 "Shabondama" (Ujo Noguchi and Shinpei Nakayama)

1863 "Kitaguni no Haru" (Haku Ide and Minoru Endo)

1998. Favourite Songs (3rd series).
2499 **1862** 50y. multicoloured . . 50 10
2500 **1863** 80y. multicoloured . . 80 20

1864 Hollyhock

1998. Winter Paralympics, Nagano. Mult.
2501 50y. Type **1864** 50 10
2502 80y. Ice sledge hockey . . . 80 20

1866 Miyama Gentian ("Gentiana nipponica")

1871 Snow-boarding

1998. Winter Olympic Games, Nagano. Mult.
2503 50y. Type **1866** 50 10
2504 50y. Marsh marigold ("Caltha palustris") . . . 50 10
2505 50y. Black lily ("Fritillaria camtschaensis") 50 10

2506 50y. Peony ("Paeonia japonica") 50 10
2507 50y. Adder's tongue lily ("Erythronium japonicum") 50 10
2508 80y. Type **1871** 80 20
2509 80y. Curling 80 20
2510 80y. Speed skating 80 20
2511 80y. Cross-country skiing 80 20
2512 80y. Alpine skiing 80 20

1876 Former Baba House, Nagano

1877 Naka House

1998. Traditional Houses (2nd series).
2513 **1876** 80y. multicoloured . . 80 20
2514 **1877** 80y. multicoloured . . 80 20

1878 Fireman and Ambulance
1879 Fireman and Fire Engine

1998. 50th Anniv of Japanese Fire Service.
2515 **1878** 80y. multicoloured . . 80 20
2516 **1879** 80y. multicoloured . . 80 20

The firemen in the designs are taken from paintings of actors by Kunichika Toyohara.

1880 Puppy

1998. Greetings Stamps. Self-adhesive. Mult.
2517 80y. Type **1880** 80 20
2518 80y. Kitten 80 20
2519 80y. Budgerigars 80 20
2520 80y. Pansies 80 20
2521 80y. Rabbit 80 20

1885 "Medaka-no-Gakko" (Shigeru Chaki and Yoshinao Nakada)
1886 "Aoi Sanmyaku" (Yaso Saijo and Ryoichi Hattori)

1998. Favourite Songs (4th series).
2522 **1885** 50y. multicoloured . . 50 10
2523 **1886** 80y. multicoloured . . 80 20

1887 "Poppies" (Kokei Kobayashi)
1889 Trout and Japanese Azalea

1888 "Liberty Leading the People" (Eugene Delacroix)

1998. Philatelic Week.
2524 **1887** 80y. multicoloured . . 80 20

1998. Year of France in Japan.
2525 **1888** 110y. multicoloured . . 1·10 25

1998. National Afforestation Campaign.
2526 **1889** 50y. multicoloured . . 50 10

1890 "Wild Roses" (Sakufu Kondo and Franz Schubert)
1891 "Hill abloom with Tangerine Flowers" (Minoru Uminuma and Shogo Kato)

1998. Favourite Songs (5th series).
2527 **1890** 50y. multicoloured . . 50 10
2528 **1891** 80y. multicoloured . . 80 20

1892 Kowata Residence, Shinji

1893 Kamihaga Residence, Uchiko

1998. Traditional Houses (3rd series).
2529 **1892** 80y. multicoloured . . 80 20
2530 **1893** 80y. multicoloured . . 80 20

1894 "This Road" (Hakusyu Kitahara and Kousaku Yamada)
1895 "I'm a Boy of the Sea" (anon)

1998. Favourite Songs (6th series).
2531 **1894** 50y. multicoloured . . 50 10
2532 **1895** 80y. multicoloured . . 80 20

1896 Boy writing

1998. Letter Writing Day. Multicoloured.
2533 50y. Type **1896** 80 20
2534 50y. Girl with letter 80 20
2535 80y. Girl holding pen . . . 80 20
2536 80y. Boy holding pen . . . 80 20
2537 80y. Boy and girl reading letters (horiz) 80 20
MS2538 93 × 72 mm. No. 2537 80 80

1901 Kamio Residence, Oita

1902 Nakamura Residence, Okinawa

1998. Traditional Houses (4th series).
2539 **1901** 80y. multicoloured . . 80 20
2540 **1902** 80y. multicoloured . . 80 20

1903 FJ Class Dinghy Racing

1998. 53rd National Athletic Meeting, Kanagawa.
2541 **1903** 50y. multicoloured . . 50 10

1904 "Sketch of Maple Leaf" (detail)

1905 "Parakeet in Oak Tree"

1907 "Coloured Chicken in Snow-laden Bamboo"

1909 "Parakeet in Rose Bush"

1998. International Correspondence Week. Paintings by Shakuchu Ito. Multicoloured.
2542 90y. Type **1904** 90 20
2543 90y. Type **1905** 90 20
2544 110y. "Drake and Duck in Snow" (detail) . . . . . 1·25 25
2545 110y. Type **1907** . . . . . 1·10 25
2546 130y. "Butterfly in the Peonies" (detail) . . . . 1·25 25
2547 130y. Type **1909** . . . . . 1·25 25

1910 Serving
1911 Receiving

1912 Set and Attack
1913 Blocking

1998. World Volleyball Championships, Japan.
2548 **1910** 80y. multicoloured . . 80 20
2549 **1911** 80y. multicoloured . . 80 20
2550 **1912** 80y. multicoloured . . 80 20
2551 **1913** 80y. multicoloured . . 80 20

1914 Bakin Takizawa (writer, 150th death anniv)
1915 Yoshie Fujiwara (opera singer, birth centenary)

1998. Anniversaries.
2552 **1914** 80y. multicoloured . . 80 20
2553 **1915** 80y. multicoloured . . 80 20

1916 Sahara Papier-mache Rabbit making Rice Cake
1919 Yamagata Papier-mache Rabbit on Ball

1998. New Year's Greetings. Multicoloured.
2554 50y. Type **1916** 50 10
2555 80y. Yamagata papier-mache rabbit on ball . . 80 20

1998. New Year's Lottery Stamps. Multicoloured.
2556 50y.+3y. Sahara papier-mache rabbit making rice cake 55 15
2557 50y.+3y. Type **1919** 55 15

Each stamp carries a lottery number.

1920 "The Apple Song" (Hachiro Sato and Tadashi Manjome)
1921 "The Toy Cha-Cha-Cha" (Akiyuki Nasaka and Osamu Yoshioka)

1998. Favourite Songs (7th series).
2558 **1920** 50y. multicoloured . . 50 10
2559 **1921** 80y. multicoloured . . 80 20

1922 Tango Dancers (Goro Sasaki)

1998. Centenary of Friendship Treaty between Japan and Argentina.

2560	**1922**	80y. multicoloured . .	80	20

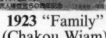

1923 "Family" (Chakou Wiam)

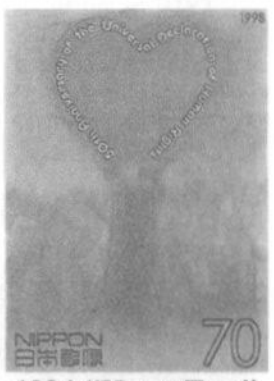
1924 "Heart Tree" (Atsuko Niizato)

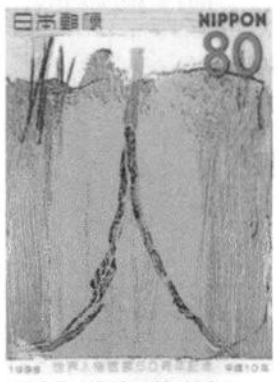
1925 "Hito" (Shozo Somekawa)

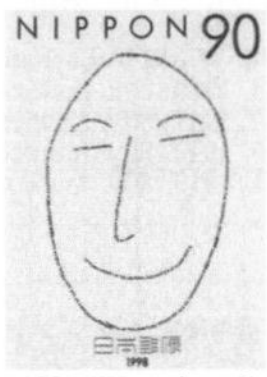
1926 "Happiness" (Mary Carmel Mulloor)

1998. 50th Anniv of Universal Declaration of Human Rights.

2561	**1923**	50y. multicoloured . .	50	10
2562	**1924**	70y. multicoloured . .	50	10
2563	**1925**	80y. multicoloured . .	80	20
2564	**1926**	90y. multicoloured . .	90	20

1998. 50th Anniv of New Year's Greetings Stamps. Previous issues now dated "1999".

2565	**241**	50y. mauve	50	10
2566	**445**	50y. multicoloured . .	50	10
2567	**1278**	50y. multicoloured . .	50	10

1927 "Flowing like a River" (Yasushi Akimoto and Akira Mitake)

1928 "Song of the Four Seasons" (Toyohisa Araki)

1999. Favourite Songs (8th series).

2568	**1927**	50y. multicoloured . .	60	15
2569	**1928**	80y. multicoloured . .	95	20

1929 Iwase Residence, Nishi-Akao

1930/1 Ogimachi Houses, Shirakawa (½-size illustration)

1999. Traditional Houses (5th series).

2570	**1929**	80y. multicoloured . .	95	20
2571	**1930**	80y. multicoloured . .	95	20
2572	**1931**	80y. multicoloured . .	95	20

Nos. 2571/2 were issued together, se-tenant, forming the composite design illustrated.

1932 "The Kaen-daiko Drum" (Shinsho Kokontei V)

1933 "Toku the Boatman" (Bunraku Katsura VIII)

1934 "Mr. Kobee, the Faultfinder" (Ensho Sanyutei VI)

1935 "Time Noodles" (Kosan Yanagiya V)

1936 "Once in a Hundred Years" (Beicho Katsura III)

1999. Comic Stories.

2573	**1932**	80y. multicoloured . .	95	20
2574	**1933**	80y. multicoloured . .	95	20
2575	**1934**	80y. multicoloured . .	95	20
2576	**1935**	80y. multicoloured . .	95	20
2577	**1936**	80y. multicoloured . .	95	20

1937 "Sukiyaki" (Rokusuke Ei and Hachidai Nakamura)

1938 "Early Spring" (Kazumasa Yoshimaru and Akira Nakada)

1999. Favourite Songs (9th series).

2578	**1937**	50y. multicoloured . .	60	15
2579	**1938**	80y. multicoloured . .	95	20

1939 Kitten

1999. Greetings Stamps. Mult. Self-adhesive.

2580	80y. Type **1939**	95	20
2581	80y. Roses	95	20
2582	80y. Puppy (47 × 37 mm) . .	95	20
2583	80y. Brown rabbit	95	20
2584	80y. Grey and white rabbit (41 × 38 mm)	95	20

1944 Body Parts and Staff of Asclepius

1999. 25th General Assembly of Japan Medical Congress.

2585	**1944**	80y. multicoloured . .	95	20

1945/6 "Hare playing on the field in Spring" (Insho Domoto)

1999. Philatelic Week.

2586	**1945**	80y. multicoloured . .	95	20
2587	**1946**	80y. multicoloured . .	95	20

Nos. 2586/7 were issued together, se-tenant, forming the composite design illustrated.

1947 Nazca Lines, Llama and Machu Picchu Ruins

1948 Amagi Alpine Rose and Mount Fuji

1999. 100 Years of Japanese Emigration to Peru.

2588	**1947**	80y. multicoloured . .	95	20

1999. National Afforestation Campaign.

2589	**1948**	50y. multicoloured . .	60	15

1949 Tholos, Delphi

1950 Demon Dancer (Ouro Carnival), Lake Titicaca and Andean Condor

1999. Centenary of Japan–Greece Treaty of Commerce and Navigation.

2590	**1949**	80y. multicoloured . .	95	20

1999. 100 Years of Japanese Emigration to Bolivia.

2591	**1950**	80y. multicoloured . .	95	20

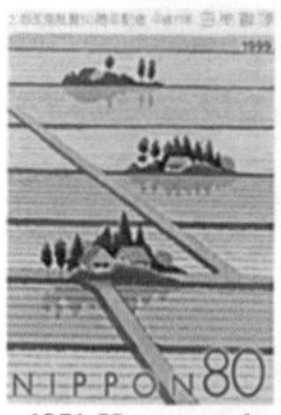
1951 Houses and Paddy Fields

1952 "Hill where Camellias Bloom" (detail of statue, Naoki Tominaga) and "Hope" (detail of stained glass window, Louis Fransen)

1999. 50th Anniv of Land Improvement Law.

2592	**1951**	80y. multicoloured . .	95	20

1999. 50th Anniv of Family Court.

2593	**1952**	80y. multicoloured . .	95	20

1953 Primroses

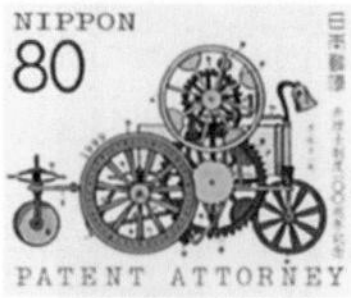
1954 Rickshaw, 1899

1999. 50th Anniv of Rehabilitation Support Programme.

2594	**1953**	80y. multicoloured . .	95	20

1999. Centenary of Patent Attorney System.

2595	**1954**	80y. multicoloured . .	95	20

1955 Masaakira Tomii, Kenjiro Ume and Nobushige Hozumi (drafters)

1956 Sayo-chan, Saku-chan and Ken-chan (originator, developer and inspector) (Takashi Yanase)

1999. Centenaries of Civil (1998) and Commercial (1999) Laws.

2596	**1955**	80y. multicoloured . .	95	20

1999. Centenary of Japanese Copyright System.

2597	**1956**	80y. multicoloured . .	95	20

1957 Children and Envelope

1971 Doves and Hearts

1999. Letter Writing Day. 50th Anniv of Japanese Association of Pen Friend Clubs.

2598	**1957**	50y. multicoloured . .	60	15
2599	–	50y. multicoloured . .	60	15
2600	–	50y. multicoloured . . .	60	15
2601	–	50y. multicoloured . .	60	15
2602	–	80y. blue, black & yell	95	20
2603	–	80y. multicoloured . .	95	20
2604	–	80y. black, blue & yell	95	20
2605	–	80y. black, red & yellow	95	20
2606	–	80y. multicoloured . .	95	20
2607	–	80y. black, yellow & bl	95	20
2608	–	80y. multicoloured . .	95	20
2609	–	80y. black and red . .	95	20
2610	–	80y. black, yellow & grn	95	20
2611	–	80y. green, black & yell	95	20

DESIGNS: As T **1957**—No. 2599, Bear and crayon; 2600, Girl with pen; 2601, Clown jumping from envelope; 2604, Boy and star; 2606, Miffie and Barbara; 2610, Girl with letter. 52 × 27 mm—2602, Giraffes. 35 × 27 mm—2603, Kite. 29 × 29 mm—2605, Girl with pencil; 2609, Girl; 2611, Ducklings. 38 × 38 mm—2607, Boy playing trumpet. 27 × 36 mm—2608, Girl playing cello.

1999. Greetings Stamps.

2613	50y. Type **1971**	60	15
2614	80y. Japanese character . .	95	20
2615	90y. Manchurian crane and leaves	1·10	20

1974 "Wagahai wa Neko de Aru" (novel by Natsume Soseki)

1976 Yosano Akiko (poet)

1978 Tram, Tokyo, 1903

1980 "Haikara" (western-style fashion)

1982 Moving Casualties, Russo–Japanese War, 1904–05

1984 Golfer and Gentian

1999. The Twentieth Century (1st series). The 1900s. Multicoloured.

2616	50y. Type **1974**	60	15
2617	50y. "Bochan" (novel by Natsume Soseki)	60	15
2618	80y. Type **1976**	95	20
2619	80y. Denkikan Cinema, Asakusa	95	20
2620	80y. Type **1978**	95	20
2621	80y. Kawakami Otojirou and Sadayakko (actor couple)	95	20
2622	80y. Type **1980**	95	20
2623	80y. Sumo wrestlers (opening of Sumo Ring, Ryogoku, Tokyo, 1909)	95	20
2624	80y. Type **1982**	95	20
2625	80y. Military hospital, Russo–Japanese War	95	20

See also Nos. 2627/36, 2664/53, 2677/86, 2687/96, 2697/2706, 2707/16, 2717/26, 2739/48, 2759/68, 2771/80, 2798/807, 2808/17, 2819/28, 2832/41, 2850/59 and 2861/70.

1999. 54th National Sports Festival, Kumamoto.

2626	**1984** 50y. multicoloured	60	15

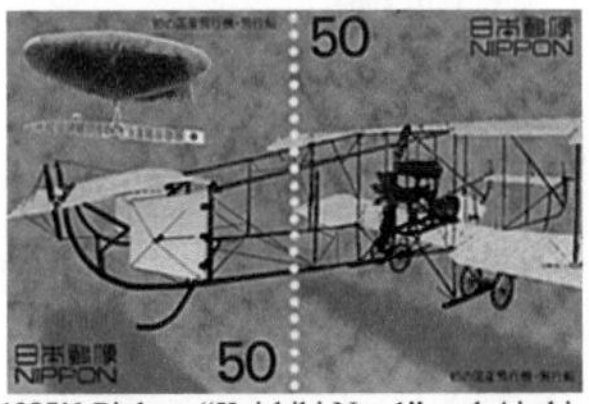

1985/6 Biplane "Kaishiki No. 1" and Airship "Yamadashiki No. 1" (first Japanese built aircraft)

1987 Children singing (School Song Book, 1910)

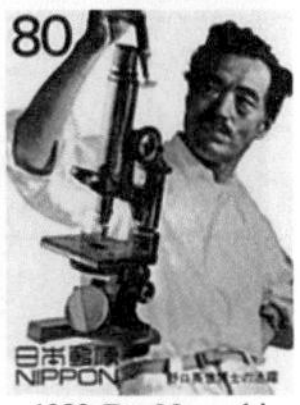

1989 Dr. Noguchi Hideyo (discovery of Oroya Fever germ, 1926)

1991 Kanaguri Shizo and Mishima Yahiko at Opening Parade, Olympic Games, Stockholm, 1912

1993 Matsui Sumako as Kachucha in "Resurrection" (play by Shimamura Hogetsu), 1914

1999. The Twentieth Century (2nd series). Multicoloured.

2627	50y. Type **1985**	60	15
2628	50y. Type **1986**	60	15
2629	80y. Type **1987**	95	20
2630	80y. Explorer and dog (Shirase Antarctic Expedition, 1910)	95	20
2631	80y. Type **1989**	95	20
2632	80y. Wolf (extinction of indigenous wolves, 1905)	95	20
2633	80y. Type **1991**	95	20
2634	80y. Dancers (formation of Takarazuka Musical Company, 1913)	95	20
2635	80y. Type **1993**	95	20
2636	80y. Mother and children (first sale of milk caramel in Japan, 1913)	95	20

Nos. 2627/8 were issued together, se-tenant forming the composite design illustrated.

1995 Stork on Elephant

1999. International Year of the Elderly.

2637	**1995** 80y. multicoloured	95	20

1996 "Sea Route in Kazusa Area" (from "36 Views of Mt. Fuji" by Hokusai Katsushika)

1998 "Rain beneath the Mountain Top" (from "36 Views of Mt. Fuji")

1999 "Chrysanthemums and a Horsefly"

2000 "Under the Fukagawa Mannen Bridge" (from "36 Views of Mt. Fuji")

1999. International Correspondence Week. 125th Anniv of Universal Postal Union. Multicoloured.

2638	90y. Type **1996**	1·10	20
2639	90y. "Confederate Roses and a Sparrow"	1·10	20
2640	110y. Type **1998**	1·30	25
2641	110y. Type **1999**	1·30	25
2642	130y. Type **2000**	1·50	30
2643	130y. "Peonies and a Butterfly"	1·50	30

2002 Couple in Junk (Takehisa Yumeji)

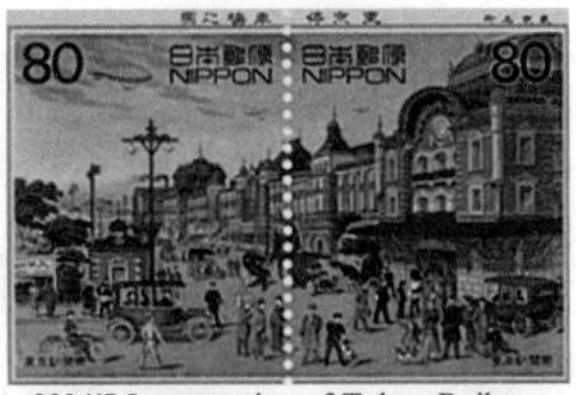

2004/5 Inauguration of Tokyo Railway Station, 1914

2006 Navy Cadets (Start of First World War, 1914)

2008 Akutagawa Ryunosuke and Title Page of Rashomon (first book of poetry, published 1915)

2010 Yoshino Sakuzo (political scientist) (Taisho Democracy)

1999. The Twentieth Century (3rd series). Mult.

2644	50y. Type **2002**	65	15
2645	50y. Takehisa Yumeji (artist)	65	15
2646	80y. Type **2004**	1·00	20
2647	80y. Type **2005**	1·00	20
2648	80y. Type **2006**	1·00	20
2649	80y. "Yohatsu" (western-style hair)	1·00	20
2650	80y. Type **2008**	1·00	20
2651	80y. Princess and Clouds (postal life assurance, 1916)	1·00	20
2652	80y. Type **2010**	1·00	20
2653	80y. Farmers (rice riots, 1918)	1·00	20

Nos. 2646/7 were issued together, se-tenant, forming the composite design illustrated.

2012 Yokohama Bay Stars Mascot (Central League)

2013 Chunichi Dragon Mascot (Central League)

2014 Seibu Lions Mascot (Pacific League)

2015 Nippon Ham Fighters Mascot (Pacific League)

2016 Yomiuri Giants Mascot (Central League)

2017 Yakult Swallows Mascot (Central League)

2018 Orix Blue Wave Mascot (Pacific League)

2019 Fukuoka Daiei Hawks Mascot (Pacific League)

2020 Hiroshima Toyo Carp Mascot (Central League)

2021 Hanshin Tigers Mascot (Central League)

2022 Kintetsu Buffaloes Mascot (Pacific League)

2023 Chiba Lotte Marines Mascot (Pacific League)

1999. Professional Japanese Baseball Clubs. Self-adhesive.

2654	**2012** 80y. multicoloured	1·00	20
2655	**2013** 80y. multicoloured	1·00	20
2656	**2014** 80y. multicoloured	1·00	20
2657	**2015** 80y. multicoloured	1·00	20
2658	**2016** 80y. multicoloured	1·00	20
2659	**2017** 80y. multicoloured	1·00	20
2660	**2018** 80y. multicoloured	1·00	20
2661	**2019** 80y. multicoloured	1·00	20
2662	**2020** 80y. multicoloured	1·00	20
2663	**2021** 80y. multicoloured	1·00	20
2664	**2022** 80y. multicoloured	1·00	20
2665	**2023** 80y. multicoloured	1·00	20

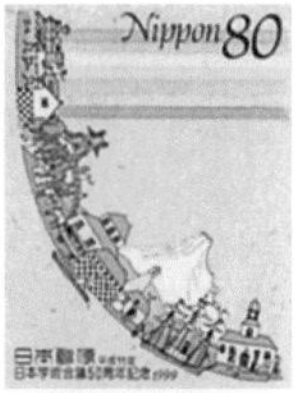

2024 Rainbow, Buildings and Mt. Fuji

2025 Katsushika Hokusai (artist, 150th death anniv)

2026 Uemera Shoen (artist, 50th death anniv)

2027 Kawabata Yasunari (author, birth centenary)

1999. 50th Anniv of Japanese Science Council.

2666	**2024** 80y. multicoloured	1·00	80

1999. Anniversaries.

2667	**2025** 80y. multicoloured	1·00	20
2668	**2026** 80y. multicoloured	1·00	20
2669	**2027** 80y. multicoloured	1·00	20

2028 Paulownia and Bamboo Embroidery (Manzairaku costume)

1999. 10th Anniv of Accession of Emperor Akihito. Multicoloured.

2670	80y. Type **2028**	1·00	20
2671	80y. Chinese phoenix embroidery (Engiraku costume)	1·00	20
MS2672	144×93 mm. As Nos. 2670/1	2·00	2·00

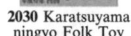

2030 Karatsuyama ningyo Folk Toy

2033 Tsuneishihariko Doll

1999. New Year's Greetings. Multicoloured.
2673 50y. Type **2030** 65 15
2674 80y. Tsuneishihariko doll . . 1·00 20

1999. New Year's Lottery Stamps. Multicoloured.
2675 50y.+3y. Karatsuyama ningyo folk toy 70 15
2676 80y.+3y. Type **2033** . . . . 1·10 25

Each stamp carries a lottery number.

2034 Onoe Matsunosuke (silent film star, 1925)

2035 Bandoh Tsumasaburo (silent film star, 1925)

2036 Runners (first Hakone relay marathon, 1920)

2038 Ruined Building (Great Kanto earthquake, 1923)

2040 Adventures of Sho-chan (comic illustrated by Katsuichi Kabashima, 1923)

2042 Baseball Players (opening of Koshien Stadium, 1924)

1999. The Twentieth Century (4th series). Mult.
2677 50y. Type **2034** 65 15
2678 50y. Type **2035** 65 15
2679 80y. Type **2036** . . . . . . 1·00 20
2680 80y. Gramophone (*Gondola Song*, 1920) . . . . . . 1·00 20
2681 80y. Type **2038** . . . . . . 1·00 20
2682 80y. Easygoing Dad (comic strip character by Yutaka Aso, 1923) . . . . 1·00 20
2683 80y. Type **2040** . . . . . . 1·00 20
2684 80y. Manchurian crane (protected species, 1924) 1·00 20
2685 80y. Type **2042** . . . . . . 1·00 20
2686 80y. Couple wearing western-style clothes . . . 1·00 20

2044 Underground Train (opening of Tokyo Underground, 1927)

2046 Arashi Chozaburo in Title Role (*Kurama Tengu* (film), 1927)

2048 Tsuruta Yoshiyuki (swimmer) (Gold Medal winner, Olympic Games, Amsterdam, 1928)

2050 2nd August Track and Field Programme (Olympic Games, Amsterdam)

2052 Man (emergence of cafes for social gatherings)

2000. The Twentieth Century (5th series). Mult.
2687 50y. Type **2044** 65 15
2688 50y. Platform (opening of Tokyo Underground) . . 65 15
2689 80y. Type **2046** . . . . . . 1·00 20
2690 80y. Man doing gymnastics (first radio broadcast of gymnastic exercises, 1928) 1·00 20
2691 80y. Type **2048** . . . . . . 1·00 20
2692 80y. Oda Mikio (athlete) (Gold medal winner, Olympic Games, Amsterdam) . . . . . . 1·00 20
2693 80y. Type **2050** . . . . . . 1·00 20
2694 80y. Hitomi Kinue (athlete) (Silver medal winner, Olympic Games, Amsterdam) . . . . . . 1·00 20
2695 80y. Type **2052** . . . . . . 1·00 20
2696 80y. Cover of Horoki (novel by Hayashi Fumiko) . . . 1·00 20

2054/5 Datsun Model 10, 1932 and Toyota Model AA, 1936 (mass production of domestic cars)

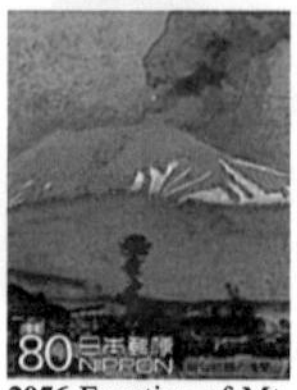

2056 Eruption of Mt. Asama, 1929

2058 Couple wearing Western Clothes (importing of western fashion)

2060 Kabutoyama (winner of first Japanese Derby, 1932)

2062 Woman (release of *Longing for Your Shadow* (song by Koga Masao), 1931)

2000. The Twentieth Century (6th series). Mult.
2697 50y. Type **2054** 65 15
2698 50y. Type **2055** 65 15
2699 80y. Type **2056** . . . . . . 1·00 20
2700 80y. Kobayashi Takiji (author) (*Crab Cannery Ship* published in *War Banner* paper) (25 × 32 mm) . . . . . . 1·00 20
2701 80y. Type **2058** . . . . . . 1·00 20
2702 80y. Kuro (comic strip character by Tagawa Suiha, 1931) (27 × 33 mm) 1·00 20
2703 80y. Type **2060** . . . . . . 1·00 20
2704 80y. Matsumidori (winner of 14th Derby) (27 × 33 mm) 1·00 20
2705 80y. Type **2062** . . . . . . 1·00 20
2706 80y. Prime Minister's Residence (assassinations of Prime Minister Tsuyoshi Inukai, 1932, and of Finance Minister Takahashi Korekiyo and Lord Keeper of the Privy Seal Saito Makoto, 1936) (25 × 35 mm) . . . . . . 1·00 20

Nos. 2697/8 were issued together, se-tenant, forming the composite design illustrated.

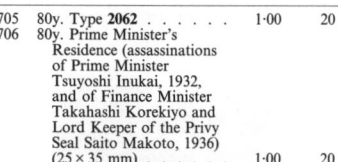

2064/5 D51 Steam Locomotive, 1936

2066 Otsuki Fumihiko (first edition of Daigenkai (dictionary compiled by Otsuki Fumihiko and Otsuki Joden), 1932)

2071 Chuken Hachiko and Statue (erection of statue of Chuken Hachiko, Shikuya Station, 1934)

2069/70 Players (formation of Tokyo Baseball Club, 1934)

2000. The Twentieth Century (7th series). Mult.
2707 50y. Type **2064** 65 15
2708 50y. Type **2065** 65 15
2709 80y. Type **2066** . . . . . . 1·00 20
2710 80y. Woman (release of *Tokyo Ondo* (song by Nakayama Shimpei), 1933) (25 × 33 mm) . . . 1·00 20
2711 80y. Enomoto Kenichi (actor) (25 × 33 mm) . . . 1·00 20
2712 80y. Type **2069** . . . . . . 1·00 20
2713 80y. Type **2070** . . . . . . 1·00 20
2714 80y. Type **2071** . . . . . . 1·00 20
2715 80y. Yoshikawa Eiji (author) (*Miyamoto* (story) first published in 1935) (27 × 33 mm) . . . 1·00 20
2716 80y. Silver-banded black pigeon (declared extinct, 1936) (27 × 33 mm) . . . 1·00 20

Nos. 2707/8 and 2712/13 respectively were issued together, se-tenant, forming the composite design illustrated.

2074/5 Mitsubishi Twin-engined Transport and Ki-15 Prototype Type 97 *Kamikaze* Airplanes

2076 Helen Keller's First Visit to Japan, 1937

2078 Yamamoto Yuzo (author) (*Robo No Ishi* (novel) first published in 1937)

2080 Yokozuna Futabayama (sumo wrestler) (victory in 69 consecutive matches, 1936–39)

2082 Birds (release of *Dareka Kokyo wo Omowazaru* (song by Koga Masao))

2000. The Twentieth Century (8th series). Mult.
2717 50y. Type **2074** 65 15
2718 50y. Type **2075** 65 15
2719 80y. Type **2076** . . . . . . 1·00 20
2720 80y. Woman with bag and civilian in national uniform (wartime clothing, 1937–40) (25 × 33 mm) . . . . . . 1·00 20
2721 80y. Type **2078** . . . . . . 1·00 20
2722 80y. Tanaka Kinuyo and Uehara Ken (actors) in *Aizenkatsura* (film), 1938 (25 × 33 mm) . . . . . . 1·00 20
2723 80y. Type **2080** . . . . . . 1·00 20
2724 80y. Sawamura Eiji (baseball player) (27 × 33 mm) . . . . . . 1·00 20
2725 80y. Type **2082** . . . . . . 1·00 20
2726 80y. Woodblock carving (Munakata Shiko) (25 × 34 mm) . . . . . . 1·00 20

Nos. 2717/18 were issued together, se-tenant, forming the composite design illustrated.

2084/5 Children and Flowers

2086/7 Faces and Building

2088 Girl as Butterfly with Book

2089 Two Faces and Building

2000. Children's Book Day.
2727 **2084** 80y. multicoloured . . 1·00 20
2728 **2085** 80y. multicoloured . . 1·00 20
2729 **2086** 80y. multicoloured . . 1·00 20
2730 **2087** 80y. multicoloured . . 1·00 20
2731 **2088** 80y. multicoloured . . 1·00 20
2732 **2089** 80y. multicoloured . . 1·00 20

Nos. 2727/8 and 2929/30 respectively were issued together, se-tenant, forming the composite designs illustrated.

2090 Hanaoka Seisyu (surgeon) and Korean Morning Glory

2000. Cent of Japanese Surgical Society Congress.
2733 **2090** 80y. multicoloured . . 1·00 20

2091/2 *Liefde* (17th-century merchant ship), Dutchman and Nagasaki

2000. 400th Anniv of Japan–Netherlands Cultural Relations.

2734 **2091** 80y. multicoloured . . 1·00 20
2735 **2092** 80y. multicoloured . . 1·00 20

Nos. 2734/5 were issued together, se-tenant, forming a composite design.

2093/4 "Ryukozu" (Hashimoto Gaho)

2000. Philatelic Week.

2736 **2093** 80y. multicoloured . . 1·00 20
2737 **2094** 80y. multicoloured . . 1·00 20

Nos. 2736/7 were issued together, se-tenant, forming the composite design illustrated.

2095 Japanese White-eye, Plum Tree and Kuju Mountain Range

2000. National Afforestation Campaign.

2738 **2095** 50y. multicoloured . . 65 15

2096 Golden Bat (comic strip character by Suzuki Ichiro)

2098 Vice-Consul Sugihara Chiune (issued visas to Jews from Consulate in Lithuania), 1940

2100 Airplane over Pearl Harbor (outbreak of Second World War in the Pacific, 1941)

2102 Mt. Showashinzan (formed by volcanic activity of Mt. Usu, 1944)

2104 Statue (atomic bomb on Nagasaki, 9 August 1945)

2000. The Twentieth Century (9th series). Mult.

2739 50y. Type **2096** 65 15
2740 50y. Golden Bat (27 × 36 mm) 65 15
2741 80y. Type **2098** . . . . . . 1·00 20
2742 80y. Children (Kokumin Gakko school system, 1941) (25 × 33 mm) . . . 1·00 20
2743 80y. Type **2100** . . . . . . 1·00 20
2744 80y. Takamura Kotaro (poet) (*Dotei* (collected poems) awarded First Imperial Art Academy Prize, 1942) (26 × 35 mm) 1·00 20
2745 80y. Type **2102** . . . . . . 1·00 20
2746 80y. Damaged buildings (atomic bomb on Hiroshima, 6 August 1945) (27 × 33 mm) . . . 1·00 20
2747 80y. Type **2104** . . . . . . 1·00 20
2748 80y. Lieut-General Umezu, Chief of the Imperial General Staff signing Surrender (end of Second World War, 1945) . . . . 1·00 20

2106 Bean Goose

2109 "Girl playing Glass Flute" (Kitagawa Utamaro)

2111 Roses and Pansies

2113 Girl with Pen and Boy with Letter

2000. "Phila Nippon '01" International Stamp Exhibition, Tokyo. Multicoloured. Self-adhesive.

2749 80y. Type **2106** . . . . . . 1·00 20
2750 80y. White wagtail (25 × 34 mm) . . . . . . 1·00 20
2751 80y. Northern goshawk (25 × 35 mm) . . . . . . 1·00 20
2752 80y. Type **2109** . . . . . . 1·00 20
2753 80y. Ichikawa Ebizo (actor) (Toshusai Sharaku) (25 × 48 mm) . . . . . . 1·00 20
2754 80y. Type **2111** . . . . . . 1·00 20
2755 80y. Puppy and kitten (24 × 42 mm) . . . . . . 1·00 20
2756 80y. Type **2113** . . . . . . 1·00 20
2757 80y. Children and letter (31 × 43 mm) . . . . . . 1·00 20
2758 80y. Girl with letter and boy with pen (31 × 40 mm) . . 1·00 20

2116 Astro Boy (comic strip character by Tezuka Osamu, 1951) on cover of *Shonen* (magazine), July, 1951

2118 Cover of Music Score and Apples (release of *Song of Apples* (song by Sato Hachiro and Manjoume Tadashi), 1945)

2120 Mother and Child (promulgation of new constitution, 1947)

2122 Dr. Yukawa Hideki and Atoms (winner of Nobel Prize for Physics, 1949)

2124 Kishi Keiko and Sata Keiji (actors) in *Kimino Na Wa* (film), 1953

2000. The Twentieth Century (10th series). Mult.

2759 50y. Type **2116** 65 15
2760 50y. Astro Boy from cover of *Shonen*, August, 1961 (26 × 36 mm) 65 15
2761 80y. Type **2118** . . . . . . 1·00 20
2762 80y. Sazae San (comic strip by Hasegawa Machiko) (25 × 34 mm) . . . . . . 1·00 20
2763 80y. Type **2120** . . . . . . 1·00 20
2764 80y. Trophy (new world records set by Furuhashi Hironoshin (swimmer), 1949) (25 × 34 mm) . . . 1·00 20
2765 80y. Type **2122** . . . . . . 1·00 20
2766 80y. Championship flag (first radio broadcast of Kohaku Uta Gassen (singing competition), 1951) (25 × 34 mm) . . . 1·00 20
2767 80y. Type **2124** . . . . . . 1·00 20
2768 80y. Tsuboi Sakae (author) and cover illustration by Morita Motoko from first edition of *Nijyu-Yon No Hitomi* (novel) (25 × 34 mm) . . . . . . 1·00 20

2126 Flowers

2127 Flowers and Sea

2000. Kyushu–Okinawa Summit.

2769 **2126** 80y. multicoloured . . 1·00 20
2770 **2127** 80y. multicoloured . . 1·00 20

2128 Tokyo Tower Entrance Ticket, 1958

2131/2 Kurosawa Akira (film director) and Scene from *Seven Samurai*, 1954

2133 Rikidozan (wrestler) and Championship Belt

2136 Prince Shotoku (issue of 10,000 yen banknote, 1958)

2000. The Twentieth Century (11th series).

2771 **2128** 50y. multicoloured . . 65 15
2772 – 50y. multicoloured (27 × 35 mm) 65 15
2773 – 80y. multicoloured (25 × 35 mm) . . . . 1·00 20
2774 **2131** 80y. multicoloured . . 1·00 20
2775 **2132** 80y. multicoloured . . 1·00 20
2776 **2133** 80y. multicoloured . . 1·00 20
2777 – 80y. multicoloured (28 × 36 mm) . . . . 1·00 20
2778 – 80y. multicoloured (25 × 33 mm) . . . . 1·00 20
2779 **2136** 80y. brown and stone 1·00 20
2780 – 80y. multicoloured (25 × 33 mm) . . . . 1·00 20

DESIGNS: No. 2772, Tokyo Tower (construction completed in 1958); 2773, Early radio and television sets (regular television broadcasts, 1953); 2777, Rikidozan; 2778, *Godzilla* (release of film, 1954); 2780, Influence of Taiyozoku Fashion on Youth Culture (release of *Taiyo No Kisetsu* (film), 1956).

Nos. 2774/5 were issued together, se-tenant, forming the composite design illustrated.

2138/9 Sunflowers

2000. 50th Anniv of Crime Prevention Campaign.

2781 **2138** 80y. multicoloured . . 1·00 20
2782 **2139** 80y. multicoloured . . 1·00 20

Nos. 2781/2 were issued together, se-tenant, forming the composite design.

2140 Girl with Pen

2000. Letter Writing Day. Multicoloured.

2783 50y. Type **2140** 65 15
2784 50y. House and birds (25 × 33 mm) 65 15
2785 50y. Clown and envelope (25 × 33 mm) 65 15
2786 50y. Boy with dog (25 × 33 mm) 65 15
2787 80y. Girl and dog in balloon basket (27 × 36 mm) . . . 1·00 20
2788 80y. Apple tree (30 × 30 mm) . . . . . . 1·00 20
2789 80y. Parrots holding letter (22 × 34 mm) . . . . . . 1·00 20
2790 80y. Bicycle (28 × 40 mm) 1·00 20
2791 80y. Girl and boy holding dove (29 × 35 mm) . . . 1·00 20
2792 80y. Girl, letter and hedgehog (27 × 40 mm) 1·00 20
2793 80y. Girl playing harp (28 × 35 mm) . . . . . . 1·00 20
2794 80y. Boy playing recorder (27 × 35 mm) . . . . . . 1·00 20
2795 80y. Boy playing cello (23 × 39 mm) . . . . . . 1·00 20
2796 80y. Boy carrying pen (27 × 36 mm) . . . . . . 1·00 20
MS2797 72 × 93 mm. Nos. 2784 and 2791 . . . . 1·60 1·60

2154/5 Taro and Giro (left at Showa Base, 1958)

2156 Commemorative Cake Box (marriage of Prince Akihito, 1959)

2158 Stars and Music Score (release of *Sukiyaki* (song by Ei Rokusuke and Nakamura Hachidai), 1960)

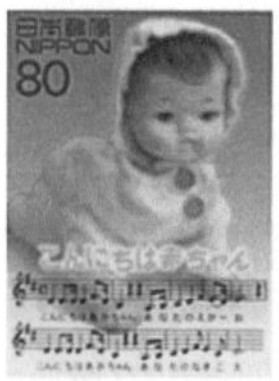

2160 Doll and Music Score (release of *Hello, My Baby* (song by Ei Rokusuke and Nakamura Hachidai)), 1963

2162 Official Poster of Olympic Games, Tokyo, 1964

2000. The Twentieth Century (12th series). Mult.

2798	50y. Type **2154**	65	15
2799	50y. Type **2155**	65	15
2800	80y. Type **2156**	1·00	20
2801	80y. Meteorological chart showing the Isewan typhoon, 1959 (25 × 33 mm)	1·00	20
2802	80y. Type **2158**	1·00	20
2803	80y. Shiba Ryotaro (author) (serialization of *Ryomaga Yuku* (novel)), 1962 (25 × 33 mm)	1·00	20
2804	80y. Type **2160**	1·00	20
2805	80y. Tokyo–Osaka High Speed Bullet Train Service, 1964 (25 × 33 mm)	1·00	20
2806	80y. Type **2162**	1·00	20
2807	80y. Official poster of Olympic Games, Tokyo (28 × 36 mm)	1·00	20

Nos. 2798/9 were issuesd together, se-tenant, forming the composite design illustrated.

2164/5 Characters from *Hyokkori Hyotan-jima* (launch of children's television programme, 1964)

2166 Television, Car and Air Conditioning Unit, 1960

2168 Baltan (character from *Ultraman*)

2170 Kawabata Yasunari and Oe Kenzaburo (winners of the Nobel Prize for Literature)

2172 Tower of the Sun (sculpture, Okamoto Taro) (World's Fair, Osaka, 1970)

2000. The Twentieth Century (13th series). Mult.

2808	50y. Type **2164**	65	15
2809	50y. Type **2165**	65	15
2810	80y. Type **2166**	1·00	20
2811	80y. Ultraman (launch of *Ultraman* (television series), 1966) (27 × 33 mm)	1·00	20
2812	80y. Type **2168**	1·00	20
2813	80y. Guitars (formation of pop bands following 1966 tour by The Beatles) (25 × 33 mm)	1·00	20
2814	80y. Type **2170**	1·00	20
2815	80y. Atsumi Taro (actor) in *Otokowa Tsuraiyo* (film) (25 × 34 mm)	1·00	20
2816	80y. Type **2172**	1·00	20
2817	80y. Youths and music score (release of *Children Who Didn't Know the War* (song), by Kitayama Osamu and Sugita Jiro, 1971) (25 × 33 mm)	1·00	20

Nos. 2808/9 were issued together, se-tenant, forming the composite design illustrated.

2174 Naruse Jinzo (founder of Women's University), Yoshioka Yayoi (founder of Women's Medical College, Tokyo) and Tsuda Umeko (founder of Tsuda College)

2175 Oh Sadaharu (baseball player) swinging Bat, 1964

2177 Wall Painting (discovery of wall paintings at Takamatsu Zuka, 1972)

2179 Pandas (gift from China to Japan, 1972)

2181 Lady Oscar (character from *Belubara*, 1972) (cartoon by Ikeda Riyoko)

2183 Cliffs and Music Score (release of *Erimo Misaki* (song) by Okamoto Osami and Yoshida Takuro, 1974)

2000. Centenary of Private Higher Education for Women.

2818	**2174** 80y. multicoloured	85	20

2000. The Twentieth Century (14th series). Multicoloured.

2819	50y. Type **2175**	50	10
2820	50y. Nagashima Shigeo (baseball player) running, 1962	50	10
2821	80y. Type **2177**	85	20
2822	80y. Wall painting (from Takamatsu Zuka)	85	20
2823	80y. Type **2179**	85	20
2824	80y. Shureimon Gate (return to Japan of administrative rights over Okinawa, 1972)	85	20
2825	80y. Type **2181**	85	20
2826	80y. Ozawa Seiji (conductor)	85	20
2827	80y. Type **2183**	85	20
2828	80y. Futuristic space shuttle (cartoon series *Uchu Senkan Yamato* by Matsumoto Reiji, 1974)	85	20

2185 "Okabe"

2000. International Correspondence Week. Paintings from "53 Stations of the Tokaido" by Ando Hiroshige. Multicoloured.

2829	90y. Type **2185**	95	20
2830	110y. "Maisaka"	1·10	25
2831	130y. "Okazaki"	1·25	25

2188 Gundam (cartoon character) (launch of *Kidosenshi Gundam*, television programme, 1979)

2190 Guitar and Music Score (release of *Jidai* (song by Nakajima Miyuki), 1975)

2192 Microphones and Musical Notes (introduction of Karaoke, 1977)

2194 Alien Space Ship and Music Score (release of *UFO* (song by Aku Yu and Tokura Shunichi), 1979)

2196 Keyboard and Musical Notes (popularity of synthesizer music, 1970s)

2000. The Twentieth Century (15th series). Multicoloured.

2832	50y. Type **2188**	50	10
2833	50y. Amuro (cartoon character from *Kidosenshi Gundam*)	50	10
2834	80y. Type **2190**	85	20
2835	80y. Fish and music score (release of *Oyoge! Taiyaki-kun* (song by Takada Hiroo and Sase Juichi), 1975)	85	20
2836	80y. Type **2192**	85	20
2837	80y. Flowers and music score (release of *Cosmos* (song by Sada Masashi), 1977)	85	20
2838	80y. Type **2194**	85	20
2839	80y. People crossing field (launch of *San Nen B Gumi Kinpachi Sensi* (television series), 1979)	85	20
2840	80y. Type **2196**	85	20
2841	80y. Woman and snow-covered house (launch of *Oshine* (television drama), 1983)	85	20

2198 Nagaoka Hantaro (physicist, 50th death anniv) and Atomic Models

2199 Nakaya Ukichiro (physicist, birth centenary) and Snow Crystal

2200 Nakamura Teijo (haiku poet, birth centenary) and Text

2000. Anniversaries.

2842	**2198** 80y. multicoloured	85	20
2843	**2199** 80y. multicoloured	85	20
2844	**2200** 80y. multicoloured	85	20

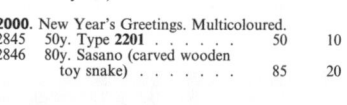

2201 Jindaiji (snake-shaped clay bell)

2204 Sasano (carved wooden toy snake)

2000. New Year's Greetings. Multicoloured.

2845	50y. Type **2201**	50	10
2846	80y. Sasano (carved wooden toy snake)	85	20

2000. New Year's Lottery Stamps. Multicoloured.

2847	50y.+3y. Jindaiji (snake-shaped clay bell)	55	10
2848	80y.+3y. Type **2204**	85	20

Each stamp carries a lottery number.

2205/6 Characters from *Go! Anpanman* (launch of children's television programme, 1988)

2207 Trains on Trial and Inaugural Runs (opening of Seikan Tunnel, 1988)

2209 Rebuilt Watchtower (excavation of ruins at Yoshinogari Iseki, 1989)

2211/12 "J-Boy" (mascot) and Football (Inception of J-League Football, 1993)

2213 "Tonkomeisya" (detail of painting, Hirayama Ikuo) (World Heritage Site, 1987)

2000. The Twentieth Century (16th series). Multicoloured.

2849	50y. Type **2205**	50	10
2850	50y. Type **2206**	50	10
2851	80y. Type **2207**	85	20
2852	80y Halley's Comet (first appearance for 76 years, 1986)	85	20
2853	80y. Type **2209**	85	20
2854	80y. Misora Hibari (singer) (recipient of National Medal of Honor, 1989)	85	20
2855	80y. Type **2211**	85	20
2856	80y. Type **2212**	85	20
2857	80y. Type **2213**	85	20
2858	80y. "Ikarugano Sato Cyoyo Horyuji" (detail of painting, Hirayama Ikuo) (World Heritage Site, 1998)	85	20

Nos. 2849/50 and 2855/6 were respectively issued together, se-tenant, forming the composite design illustrated.

2215 Central Tower and Mosaic Marble Floors (detail)

2216 Emblem, Nagano Olympic Games, 1998

2218 Crown Prince Noruhito and Princess Masako (wedding, 1993)

2220 Lap-top Computer and Mobile Phone (increased use of wireless telecommunications)

2222 Doi Takao (Japanese astronaut) outside Spaceship

2224 "Mother Earth" (Bokunan Naka) (United Nations Framework Convention on Climate Change, Kyoto, 1997)

2000. 110th Anniv of Diet (Japanese Parliament).
2859 **2215** 80y. multicoloured . .

2000. The Twentieth Century (17th series). Multicoloured.

2860	50y. Type **2216**	50	10
2861	50y. "Snowlets" (Nagano Olympic mascots)	50	10
2862	80y. Type **2218**	85	20
2863	80y. Phoenix, map of Hanshin-Awaji and collapsed bridge (Hanshin-Awaji earthquake, 1995)	85	20
2864	80y. Type **2220**	85	20
2865	80y. Launch of space shuttle *Endeavor* (inclusion of first Japanese astronaut on N.A.S.A. mission, 1992)	85	20
2866	80y. Type **2222**	85	20
2867	80y. Footballer (Japanese participation in World Cup Football Championship, France, 1998)	85	20
2868	80y. Type **2224**	85	20
2869	80y. Official poster of Nagano Olympic Games	85	20

2226/7 Manchurian Cranes (*"Grus japonensis"*, Matazo Kayama)

2001. "Internet Expo 2001 Japan" (virtual Internet fair).

2870	**2226**	80y. multicoloured . .	85	20
2871	**2227**	80y. multicoloured . .	85	20

Nos. 2870/1 were issued together, se-tenant, forming a composite design.

2228 Heliotrope, Flax and Emblem

2229 "Gyoseishoshi" (Japanese calligraphy) and Computer

2001. United Nations Year of Volunteers.
2872 **2228** 80y. multicoloured . . 85 20

2001. 50th Anniv of Gyoseishoshi Lawyer System (specialist administrative lawyers).
2873 **2229** 80y. multicoloured . . 85 20

2230 Shinkyo Bridge, Futarasan Shrine

2231 Main Sanctuary, Futarasan Shrine

2232 Karamon Gate, Toshugu Shrine

2233 Kirin (mythical winged horse) (painting), Toshugu Shrine

2234 Wind God (statue), Rinnoji Temple

2235 Thunder God (statue), Rinnoji Temple

2236 Peacock, Toshugu Shrine

2237 Sleeping Cat, Toshugu Shrine

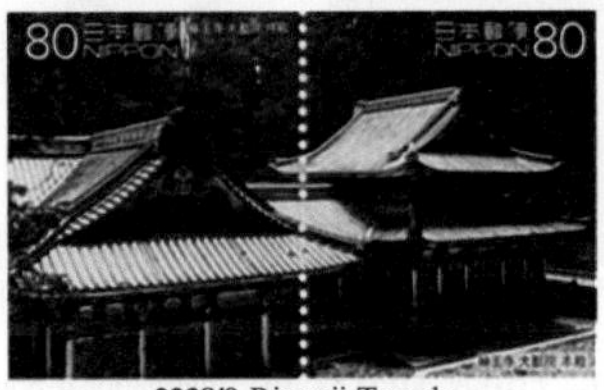

2238/9 Rinnoji Temple

2001. World Heritage Sites (1st series). Shrines and Temples, Nikko.

2874	**2230**	80y. multicoloured . .	85	20
2875	**2231**	80y. multicoloured . .	85	20
2876	**2232**	80y. multicoloured . .	85	20
2877	**2233**	80y. multicoloured . .	85	20
2878	**2234**	80y. multicoloured . .	85	20
2879	**2235**	80y. multicoloured . .	85	20
2880	**2236**	80y. multicoloured . .	85	20
2881	**2237**	80y. multicoloured . .	85	20
2882	**2238**	80y. multicoloured . .	85	20
2883	**2239**	80y. multicoloured . .	85	20

Nos. 2883/4 were issued together, se-tenant, forming the composite design illustrated.

See also Nos. 2887/96, 2906/15, 2960/9, 2985/94, 2997/3006, 3020/9, 3045/54, 3060/9, 3083/92 and 3107/16.

2240 Emblem

2241 "The Annunciation" (detail, Botticelli)

2242 "The Annunciation" (detail, Botticelli)

2001. "Italy in Japan 2001" (cultural and scientific event).

2884	**2240**	80y. multicoloured . .	85	20
2885	**2241**	110y. multicoloured . .	1·25	25
2886	**2242**	110y. multicoloured . .	1·25	25

Nos. 2885/6 were issued together in se-tenant pairs featuring two separate panels of the painting.

2243/4 Marodo Shrine

2245 Main Sanctuary

2246 Lion Dog (statue)

2247 Marodo Shrine and Pagoda

2248 Traditional Dance Mask

2249 Horse (statue)

2250 Buildings

2251 Treasure Pagoda

2252 Oomoto Shrine

2001. World Heritage Sites (2nd series). Itsukushima Shrine.

2887	**2243**	80y. multicoloured . .	85	20
2888	**2244**	80y. multicoloured . .	85	20
2889	**2245**	80y. multicoloured . .	85	20
2890	**2246**	80y. multicoloured . .	85	20
2891	**2247**	80y. multicoloured . .	85	20
2892	**2248**	80y. multicoloured . .	85	20
2893	**2249**	80y. multicoloured . .	85	20
2894	**2250**	80y. multicoloured . .	85	20
2895	**2251**	80y. multicoloured . .	85	20
2896	**2252**	80y. multicoloured . .	85	20

Nos. 2888/9 were issued together, se-tenant, forming the composite design illustrated.

2253 Emblem

2254 Woman posting Letter (Nakamura Senseki)

2001. Centenary of Japanese Dermatological Association. Multicoloured, colour of triangle beneath face value given.

2897	**2253**	80y. pink	85	20
2898		80y. flesh	85	20
2899		80y. yellow	85	20
2900		80y. green	85	20
2901		80y. blue	85	20

2001. Philatelic Week. Centenary of Red Cylindrical Letter Boxes (designed by Taraya Takashhichi and Nakamura Koji).
2902 **2254** 80y. multicoloured . . 85 20

2255 "Ato, Nik and Kaz" (mascots)

2256 "Kaz"

2257 "Nik"

2001. World Cup Football Championship, Japan and South Korea (2002).

2903	**2255**	80y.+10y. mult	95	20
2904	**2256**	80y.+10y. mult	95	20
2905	**2257**	80y.+10y. mult	95	20

2258 Hosodono, Maidono and Tsuchinoya Halls, Kamowakeikazuchi Shrine

2259 Roman Gate, Kamowakeikazuchi Shrine

2260 East Main Hall, Kamomioya Shrine

2261 Guardian Dog (statue), Kamomioya Shrine

2262 Pagoda and South Great Gate, Toji Temple

2263 Fukuu Joju Nyorai (statue), Toji Temple

2264 Pagoda and West Gate, Kiyomizudera Temple

2265 Main Hall, Kiyomizudera Temple

2266 "Nyorin Kannon" (painting), Toji Temple

2267 Daiitoku Myoo (statue), Toji Temple

2001. World Heritage (3rd series). Temples and Shrines, Kyoto.

2906 **2258** 80y. multicoloured . . 85 20
2907 **2259** 80y. multicoloured . . 85 20
2908 **2260** 80y. multicoloured . . 85 20
2909 **2261** 80y. multicoloured . . 85 20
2910 **2262** 80y. multicoloured . . 85 20
2911 **2263** 80y. multicoloured . . 85 20
2912 **2264** 80y. multicoloured . . 85 20
2913 **2265** 80y. multicoloured . . 85 20
2914 **2266** 80y. multicoloured . . 85 20
2915 **2267** 80y. multicoloured . . 85 20

2268 Flowers and Pigeons **2269** Swimming

2001. 50th Anniv of Membership of United Nations Educational, Scientific and Cultural Organization.

2916 **2268** 80y. multicoloured . . 85 20

2001. 9th International Swimming Federation Championships, Fukuoka. Multicoloured.

2917 **2269** 80y. Type **2269** 85 20
2918 **2270** 80y. Synchronized swimming 85 20
2919 **2271** 80y. Diving 85 20
2920 **2272** 80y. Water polo 85 20

Nos. 2917/20 were issued together, se-tenant, the backgrounds forming a composite design.

2273 Rabbits

2001. Letter Writing Day. Multicoloured.

2921 50y. Type **2273** 85 20
2922 50y. Girl and pencil (28 × 36 mm) 85 20
2923 50y. Boy holding envelope (28 × 36 mm) 85 20
2924 50y. Girl with ribbons (28 × 36 mm) 85 20
2925 80y. Bird in tree (30 × 30 mm) 85 20
2926 80y. Girl holding rabbit (27 × 36 mm) 85 20
2927 80y. Boy holding pen (27 × 36 mm) 85 20
2928 80y. Girl with envelope and dog (27 × 26 mm) 85 20
2929 80y. Girl and flowers (27 × 36 mm) 85 20
2930 80y. Flowers and bird with envelope (30 × 30 mm) . . 85 20
2931 80y. Birds and roof (27 × 36 mm) 85 20
2932 80y. Rabbit and flowers (22 × 33 mm) 85 20
2933 80y. Boy and rabbit (27 × 33 mm) 85 20
2934 80y. Chicks, hen and pig (27 × 39 mm) 85 20

MS2935 72 × 93 mm Nos. 2923 and 2932 . . . . 1·75 1·75

2287 "Ootani Oniji as Edobei" (Toshusai Sharaku)

2288 "Iwai Hanshiro IV as Shigenoi" (Toshusai Shakuru)

2289 "Sakata Hangoro as Fujikwa Mizuemon" (Toshusai Shakuru)

2290 "Segawa Kikunojo as Oshizu, Tanabe Bunzo's Wife" (Toshusai Shakuru)

2291 "Ichikawa Omezo as Yakko Ippei" (Toshusai Shakuru)

2292 "Beauty looking Back" (Hishikawa Moronobu)

2293 "Girl playing Glass Flute" (Kitagawa Utamaro)

2294 "Fuzoku Higashino Nishiki, returning from the Bath-house in the Rain" (Torii Kiyonaga)

2295 "Iwai Kumesaburo as Chiyo" (Utagawa Kunimasa)

2296 "Ichikawa Komazo III as Sasaki Ganryu" (Utagawa Toyokuni)

2297 "Iwai Hanshiro IV as Shigenoi" (Toshusai Shakuru)

2298 "Ootani Oniji as Edobei" (Toshusai Shakuru)

2299 Mandarin Duck

2300 Japanese White-Eye

2301 Girl and Boy holding Envelopes

2302 "Iwai Kumesaburo as Chiyo" (Utagawa Kunimasa)

2303 "Ichikawa Komazo III as Sasaki Ganryu" (Utagawa Toyokuni)

2304 Eastern Turtle Dove **2305** Greater Pied Kingfisher

2306 1871 48m. Stamp

2307 Fly Casting and Discus

2001. "PHILA NIPPON '01" International Stamp Exhibition, Tokyo. (a) Ordinary gum.

2936 **2287** 50y. multicoloured . . 85 20
2937 **2288** 50y. multicoloured . . 85 20
2938 **2289** 50y. multicoloured . . 85 20
2939 **2290** 50y. multicoloured . . 85 20
2940 **2291** 50y. multicoloured . . 85 20
2941 **2292** 80y. multicoloured . . 85 20
2942 **2293** 80y. multicoloured . . 85 20
2943 **2294** 80y. multicoloured . . 85 20
2944 **2295** 80y. multicoloured . . 85 20
2945 **2296** 80y. multicoloured . . 85 20

(b) Self-adhesive gum.

2946 **2297** 50y. multicoloured . . 85 20
2947 **2298** 50y. multicoloured . . 85 20
2948 **2299** 50y. multicoloured . . 85 20
2949 **2300** 50y. multicoloured . . 85 20
2950 **2301** 50y. multicoloured . . 85 20
2951 **2302** 80y. multicoloured . . 85 20
2952 **2303** 80y. multicoloured . . 85 20
2953 **2304** 80y. multicoloured . . 85 20
2954 **2305** 80y. multicoloured . . 85 20
2955 **2306** 80y. multicoloured . . 85 20

2001. 6th World Games, Akita. Multicoloured.

2956 50y. Type **2307** 50 10
2957 50y. Aerobics and billiards 50 10
2958 80y. Water skiing and life saving 85 20
2959 80y. Tug of war and body building 85 20

2311 Konpon Chudo Hall, Enryakuji Temple

2312 Eternal Flame, Enryakuji Temple

2313 Ninai-do Hall, Enryakuji Temple

2316 Pagoda, Daigoji Temple

2314/15 Sanbo-in Temple Garden, Daigoji Temple

2317 Palace, Ninnaji Temple

2318 Pagoda, Ninnaji Temple

2319 Phoenix Hall, Byodoin Temple

2320 Bodhisattva floating on Clouds (statue), Byodoin Temple

2001. World Heritage (4th series). Temples, Kyoto.

2960 **2311** 80y. multicoloured . . 85 20
2961 **2312** 80y. multicoloured . . 85 20
2962 **2313** 80y. multicoloured . . 85 20
2963 **2314** 80y. multicoloured . . 85 20
2964 **2315** 80y. multicoloured . . 85 20
2965 **2316** 80y. multicoloured . . 85 20
2966 **2317** 80y, multicoloured . . 85 20
2967 **2318** 80y. multicoloured . . 85 20
2968 **2319** 80y. multicoloured . . 85 20
2969 **2320** 80y. multicoloured . . 85 20

Nos. 2963/4 were issued together, se-tenant, forming the composite design illustrated.

2321 War Memorial Opera House and Flowers

2001. 50th Anniv of San Francisco Peace Treaty.

2970 **2321** 80y. multicoloured . . 85 20

2322 "Hara"

2001. International Correspondence Week. Paintings from "53 Stations of Tokaido" by Ando Hiroshige. Multicoloured.
2971 90y. Type **2322** 95 20
2972 110y. "Oiso" . . . . 1·25 25
2973 130y. "Sakanoshita" . . . . 1·40 30

2325 Boy with Birds and Insects

2327 Man catching Disc

2001. "Let's Keep our Towns Safe" (national community safety campaign). Multicoloured.
2974 80y. Type **2325** 85 20
2975 80y. Girl with bird and animals 85 20

2001. 1st National Sports Games for the Disabled, Sendai City and Miyagi-gun. Multicoloured.
2976 80y. Type **2327** 85 20
2977 80y. Wheelchair race 85 20

2329 Norinaga Motoori (writer and scholar, death bicentenary)

2330 Gidayu Takemoto (jojuri chanter and puppeteer, 350th birth) and Illustration from "Sonezaki Shinju"

2001. Anniversaries.
2978 **2329** 80y. multicoloured . . 85 20
2979 **2330** 80y. multicoloured . . 85 20

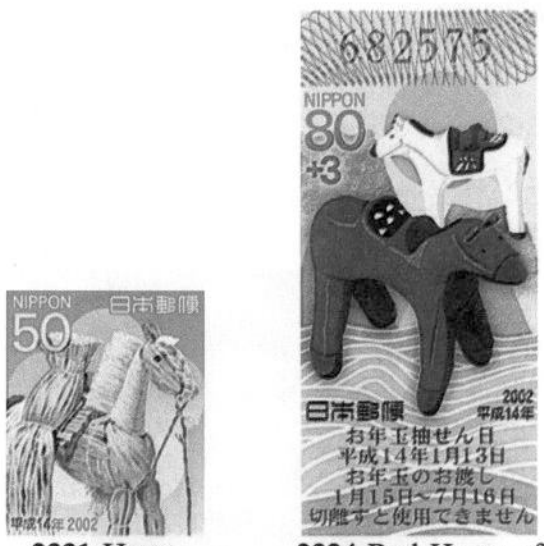

2331 Horse carrying Rice

2334 Red Horse of Kira (sedge handicraft)

2001. New Years Greeting's. Multicoloured.
2980 50y. Type **2331** 55 10
2981 80y. Red horse of Kira . . 85 20

2001. New Year's Lottery Stamps. Multicoloured.
2982 50y. + 3y. Horse carrying rice 55 10
2983 80y. + 3y. Type **2334** . . . 85 20

Each stamp carries a lottery number.

2335 Television Camera, Television Set and Radio Microphone

2001. 50th Anniv of Commercial Broadcasting.
2984 **2335** 80y. multicoloured . . 85 20

2336 Ujikami Shrine

2337 Kaeru Mata (main shrine), Ujikami Shrine

2338 Path to Kozanji Temple

2339 Sekisuiin, Kozanji Temple

2340 Kasumijima Garden, Saihoji Temple

2341 Kojokan Garden, Saihoji Temple

2342/3 Garden, Tenryuji Temple

2344 Golden Temple, Rokuonji Temple

2345 Golden Temple in Winter

2001. World Heritage (5th series). Temples and Shrines, Kyoto.
2985 **2336** 80y. multicoloured . . 85 20
2986 **2337** 80y. multicoloured . . 85 20
2987 **2338** 80y. multicoloured . . 85 20
2988 **2339** 80y. multicoloured . . 85 20
2989 **2340** 80y. multicoloured . . 85 20
2990 **2341** 80y. multicoloured . . 85 20
2991 **2342** 80y. multicoloured . . 85 20
2992 **2343** 80y. multicoloured . . 85 20
2993 **2344** 80y. multicoloured . . 85 20
2994 **2345** 80y. multicoloured . . 85 20

Nos. 2985/94 were issued together in sheetlets of ten stamps, Nos. 2991/2 forming the composite design illustrated, with descriptions of each stamp in Japanese in the illustrated margin.

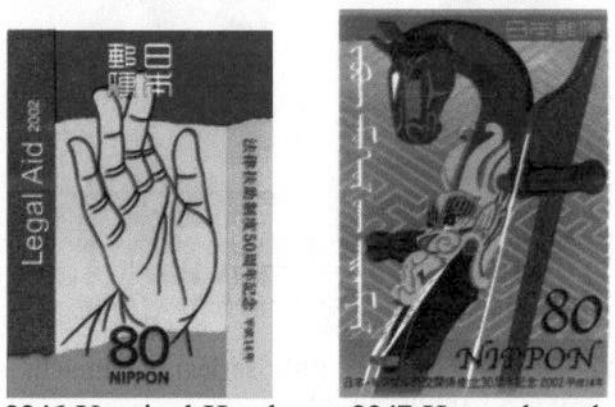

2346 Upraised Hand

2347 Horse-shaped Fiddle Head

2002. 50th Anniv of Legal Aid System.
2995 **2346** 80y. multicoloured . . 85 20

2002. 30th Anniv of Japan—Mongolia Diplomatic Relations.
2996 **2347** 80y. multicoloured . . 85 20

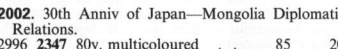

2348 Silver Pavilion in Snow, Jishoji Temple

2349 Silver Pavilion

2350 Hojo Garden, Ryoanji Temple

2351 Hojo Garden in Winter

2352 Karamon Gate, Honganji Temple

2353 Hiunkaku, Honganji Temple

2354 Shoin, Honganji Temple

2355 Ninomaru Palace, Nijo Castle

2356 Hawk on Pine (detail, painting), Nijo Castle

2357 Hawk on Pine (detail)

2002. World Heritage (6th series). Temples, Kyoto.
2997 **2348** 80y. multicoloured . . 85 20
2998 **2349** 80y. multicoloured . . 85 20
2999 **2350** 80y. multicoloured . . 85 20
3000 **2351** 80y. multicoloured . . 85 20
3001 **2352** 80y. multicoloured . . 85 20
3002 **2353** 80y. multicoloured . . 85 20
3003 **2354** 80y. multicoloured . . 85 20
3004 **2355** 80y. multicoloured . . 85 20
3005 **2356** 80y. multicoloured . . 85 20
3006 **2357** 80y. multicoloured . . 85 20

2358 Bell and Mythical Lion-dog

2359 Men's Singles Skater

2002. 50th Anniv of Japan Lions (charitable organization).
3007 **2358** 80y. multicoloured . . 80 15

2002. World Figure Skating Championships, Nagano. Multicoloured.
3008 80y. Type **2359** 80 15
3009 80y. Pairs skaters 80 15

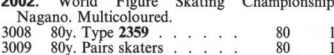

2361 Taj Mahal, India

2362 Artefact and Ruins, Moenjodaro, Pakistan

2363 Sigiriya, Sri Lanka

2364 Terracotta Panel and Ruins, Paharpur, Bangladesh

2002. 50th Anniv of Japan–South East Asia Diplomatic Relations.
3010 **2361** 80y. multicoloured . . 80 15
3011 **2362** 80y. multicoloured . . 80 15
3012 **2363** 80y. multicoloured . . 80 15
3013 **2364** 80y. multicoloured . . 80 15

2365 Two Horsemen

2367 *Hikawa-Maru* (passenger ship)

2002. Philately Week. (Kamo folding screen). Multicoloured.
3014 80y. Type **2365** 80 15
3015 80y. Horseman and spectator 80 15

2002. 50th Anniv of Japan–U.S.A. Fulbright Exchange Programme.
3016 **2367** 80y. multicoloured . . 80 15

2368 Ship and Irises

2369 Stylized Football Pitch

2002. 30th Anniv of Return of Okinawa.
3017 **2368** 80y. multicoloured . . 80 15

2002. World Cup Football Championships, Japan and South Korea. Multicoloured.
3018 80y. Type **2369** 80 15
3019 80y. FIFA World Cup Trophy 80 15

2371 Great Buddha Hall, Todaiji Temple

2372 Southern Gate, Todaiji Temple

2373 Great Buddha (detail), Todaiji Temple

2374 Virupaksu (statue), Todaiji Temple

2375 Lotus Hall, Todaiji Temple

2376 Five-storied Pagoda, Kofukuji Temple

2377 Northern Octagonal Hall, Kofukuji Temple

2378 Ashura (statue), Kofukuji Temple

2379 Buddha Head, Kofukuji Temple

2380 Ryutoki Demon (statue), Kofukuji Temple

2002. World Heritage (7th series). Temples, Nara.

3020	**2371**	80y. multicoloured . .	80	15
3021	**2372**	80y. multicoloured . .	80	15
3022	**2373**	80y. multicoloured . .	80	15
3023	**2374**	80y. multicoloured . .	80	15
3024	**2375**	80y. multicoloured . .	80	15
3025	**2376**	80y. multicoloured . .	80	15
3026	**2377**	80y. multicoloured . .	80	15
3027	**2378**	80y. multicoloured . .	80	15
3028	**2379**	80y. multicoloured . .	80	15
3029	**2380**	80y. multicoloured . .	80	15

Nos. 3020/9 were issued in sheetlets of ten stamps, with descriptions of each stamp in Japanese in the illustrated margin.

2381 Girl carrying Envelope

2002. National Letter Writing Day.

3030	**2381**	50y. multicoloured . .	50	10
3031	–	50y. multicoloured . .	50	10
3032	–	50y. multicoloured . .	50	10
3033	–	50y. multicoloured . .	50	10
3034	–	80y. multicoloured . .	80	15
3035	–	80y. lemon, black and blue	80	15
3036	–	80y. multicoloured . .	80	15
3037	–	80y. multicoloured . .	80	15
3038	–	80y. multicoloured . .	80	15
3039	–	80y. multicoloured . .	80	15
3040	–	80y. multicoloured . .	80	15
3041	–	80y. multicoloured . .	80	15
3042	–	80y. multicoloured . .	80	15
3043	–	80y. multicoloured . .	80	15
MS3044		72 × 94 mm. Nos. 3031 and 3040	1·30	25

DESIGNS: No. 2383, House and flowers (28 × 34 mm); 2384, Young boy and fence (25 × 34 mm); 2385, Ladybird and caterpillar (28 × 25 mm); 2386, Farmer and sheep (30 × 25 mm); 2387, Cow (32 × 25 mm); 2388, Girl and flowers (30 × 41 mm); 2389, Boy with football (22 × 35 mm); 2390, Girl carrying Tennis racquet (22 × 35 mm); 2391, Mother and child (28 × 36 mm); 2392, Man riding bicycle (28 × 36 mm); 2393, Girl and vase (27 × 27 mm); 2394, Van and car (27 × 27 mm).

2395 Covered Passageway, Kasuga Taisha Shrine

2396 Middle Gate, Kasuga Taisha Shrine

2397 Deer, Kasuga-yama Forest

2398 Zen Meditation Hall, Gango-ji Temple

2399 Pagoda, Gango-ji Temple

2400 East and West Pagodas, Yakushi-ji Temple

2401 Buddha of Healing, Yakushi-ji Temple

2402 Golden Hall, Toshodai-ji Temple

2403 Standing Image of the Thousand Handed Goddess of Mercy, Toshodai-ji Temple

2404 Suzakumon Gate, Heijo Imperial Palace

2002. World Heritage (8th series). Temples.

3045	**2395**	80y. multicoloured . .	80	15
3046	**2396**	80y. multicoloured . .	80	15
3047	**2397**	80y. multicoloured . .	80	15
3048	**2398**	80y. multicoloured . .	80	15
3049	**2399**	80y. multicoloured . .	80	15
3050	**2400**	80y. multicoloured . .	80	15
3051	**2401**	80y. multicoloured . .	80	15
3052	**2402**	80y. multicoloured . .	80	15
3053	**2403**	80y. multicoloured . .	80	15
3054	**2404**	80y. multicoloured . .	80	15

Nos. 3045/54 were issued in sheetlets of ten stamps, with descriptions of each stamp in Japanese in the illustrated margin.

2405 Stylized Human and Flowers

2406 Basketball Players

2002. 12th World Psychiatry Congress.

3055	**2405**	80y. multicoloured . .	80	15

2002. World Wheelchair Basketball Championship, Japan.

3056	**2406**	80y. multicoloured . .	80	15

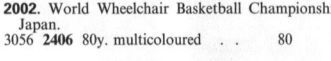

2407 Twin-engined and Four-propeller Aircrafts

2002. 50th Anniv of Japanese Civil Aviation.

3057	**2407**	80y. multicoloured . .	80	15

2408 "Shitoka" (Denj Lin)

2409 "Generyucho" (Wang Chuan Feng)

2002. 30th Anniv of Japan–China Diplomatic Relations.

3058	**2408**	80y. multicoloured . .	80	15
3059	**2409**	80y. multicoloured . .	80	15

2410/11 Houses, Ogimachi, Shirakawa-Mura

2412 House and Flowers, Ogimachi

2413 Houses, Ogimachi

2414 Houses covered in Snow, Ogimachi

2415 Aerial View, Ainokura, Taira-Mura

2416 House, Ainokura

2417 Houses, Ainokura

2418 House, Ainokura

2419 House covered in Snow, Ainokura

2002. World Heritage (9th series). Ogimachi and Ainokura Communitites.

3060	**2410**	80y. multicoloured . .	80	15
3061	**2411**	80y. multicoloured . .	80	15
3062	**2412**	80y. multicoloured . .	80	15
3063	**2413**	80y. multicoloured . .	80	15
3064	**2414**	80y. multicoloured . .	80	15
3065	**2415**	80y. multicoloured . .	80	15
3066	**2416**	80y. multicoloured . .	80	15
3067	**2417**	80y. multicoloured . .	80	15
3068	**2418**	80y. multicoloured . .	80	15
3069	**2419**	80y. multicoloured . .	80	15

Nos. 3060/9 were issued in sheetlets of ten stamps, Nos. 3060/1 forming the composite design illustrated, with descriptions of each stamp in Japanese in the illustrated margin.

2420 Naval Ships and Flags

2002. Fleet Review.

3070	**2420**	80y. multicoloured . .	80	15

2421 "Yui"

2002. International Correspondence Week. Paintings from "53 Stations of Tokaido" by Ando Hiroshige. Multicoloured.

3071	90y. Type **2421**	90	20
3072	110y. "Shono"	1·10	25
3073	130y. "Tozuka"	1·30	30

2424 Stylized People

2002. Asian and Pacific Decade of Disabled Persons Conference.

3074	**2424**	80y. multicoloured . .	80	15

2425 Masaoka Shiki (writer, death centenary)

2426 "Three Women" (Torii Kiyonaga (artist, 250th birth))

2427 Tanakadate Aikitu (geophysicist, 50th death)

2002. Anniversaries.

3075	**2425**	80y. multicoloured . .	80	15
3076	**2426**	80y. multicoloured . .	80	15
3077	**2427**	80y. multicoloured . .	80	15

2428 Sheep (earthenware Dorei figure)

2430 Sheep holding Fan (Aizunakayugawa doll)

2002. New Year's Greetings. Multicoloured.

3078	50y. Type **2428**	50	10
3079	80y. Sheep with Gem (Edo folk toy)	80	15
MS3080	94 × 72 mm. Nos. 3078/9	1·30	1·30

2002. New Year Lottery Stamps. Multicoloured.

3081	50y.+3y. Type **2430**	50	10
3082	80y.+3y. Sheep (Oku Hariko doll)	80	15

Each stamp carries a lottery number.

2432 Stone Lion, Shou Dynasty Royal Mausoleum

2433 Stone Gate, Sonohyan'utaki Sanctuary

2434 Cherry Blossom, Nakijinjou castle

2435 Stone Gate, Zakimijou Castle

2436 Katsurenjou Castle Walls

2437 Second Citadel, Nakagusukujou Castle

2438 "Kankaimon", Shurijou Castle Gate

2439 Main Hall, Shurijou Castle

2440 "Shikina'en" (royal garden)

2441 Seifautaki Sanctuary

2002. World Heritage (10th series).

3083	**2432**	80y. multicoloured . .	80	15
3084	**2433**	80y. multicoloured . .	80	15
3085	**2434**	80y. multicoloured . .	80	15
3086	**2435**	80y. multicoloured . .	80	15
3087	**2436**	80y. multicoloured . .	80	15
3088	**2437**	80y. multicoloured . .	80	15
3089	**2438**	80y. multicoloured . .	80	15
3090	**2439**	80y. multicoloured . .	80	15
3091	**2440**	80y. multicoloured . .	80	15
3092	**2441**	80y. multicoloured . .	80	15

2442 Kabuki Screen showing Izumo no Okuni in Costume

2443 Actors from "Shibaraku" and "Tsuchigumo"

2003. 400th Anniv of First Kabuki Theatre Performance.

3093	**2442**	80y. multicoloured . .	80	15
3094	**2443**	80y. multicoloured . .	80	15

2444 Television Company Emblem and Street Television Set

2446 Heart

2003. 50th Anniv of Japanese Television. Multicoloured.

3095	80y. Type **2444**	80	50
3096	80y. "Hyokkori Hyotan-Jima" (puppet) and early television set	80	15

2003. Greetings Stamps. Multicoloured. Self-adhesive.

3097	80y. Type **2446**	80	15
3098	80y. Dog wearing party clothes	80	15
3099	80y. Snowman	80	15
3100	80y. Bird on cake	80	15
3101	80y. Cranes and turtle . . .	80	15
3102	80y. Roses	80	15
3103	80y. Reindeer	80	15
3104	80y. Cat	80	15
3105	80y. Cats in car	80	15
3106	80y. Cherry blossom	80	15

2456 Genbaku Dome (atomic bomb memorial)

2466 Posuton

2003. World Heritage (11th series). Peace Stamp Design Competition Winners. Multicoloured.

3107	80y. Type **2456**	80	15
3108	80y. Hiroshima Prefectural Hall	80	15
3109	80y. "La Paix" (Jean-Paul Veret LeMarinier)	80	15
3110	80y. "Taika" (peace) (Pakalkaite Joskaude) . .	80	15
3111	80y. "Universal Shrine of Peace" (Issac M. Oriville)	80	15
3112	80y. "A Prayer for Peace" (Keiji Sugita)	80	15
3113	80y. "The Radiance of Life" (Shigenobu Nagaishi) . .	80	15
3114	80y. "An Encounter" (Natsuki Nakatani) . . .	80	15
3115	80y. Rainbow-coloured Dove" (Makoto Oooka)	80	15
3116	80y. "Rabbit" (Shiho Kobayashi)	80	15

2003. Postal Services Mascots. Self-adhesive. Multicoloured.

3117	50y. Aichan	50	10
3118	50y. Kanchan boy	50	10
3118a	50y. Posuton	50	10
3118b	50y. Yuchan	50	10
3119	50y. Kanchan girl	50	10
3120	50y. Posuton	50	10
3121	80y. Type **2466**	80	15
3122	80y. Aichan	80	15
3123	80y. Kanchan girl	80	15
3124	80y. Posuton	80	15
3125	80y. Yuchan	80	15
3126	80y. Kanchan boy	80	15

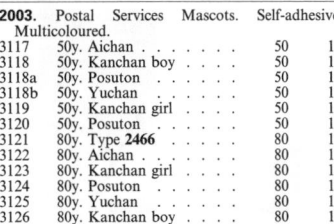

2476 Yellow Flower

2486 Tree and Sheep

2003. Inauguration of Japan Post (public postal corporation). Designs from "Birds and Flowers of the Four Seasons" (folding screen by Sakai Hoitsu). Multicoloured. Self-adhesive.

3127	80y. Type **2476**	80	15
3128	80y. Primula	80	15
3129	80y. Violets and quince . .	80	15
3130	80y. Horsetail	80	15
3131	80y. White wisteria	80	15
3132	80y. Flowering cherry and swallow	80	15
3133	80y. Hydrangea	80	15
3134	80y. Magnolia	80	15
3135	80y. Water lily and moorhen	80	15
3136	80y. Peonies and butterfly	80	15

2003. Philately Week. (Batik folding screen).

3137	**2486**	80y. multicoloured . .	80	15

2487 Map of Edo (folding screen)

2492 "Nihonbashi Bridge" ("53 Stations of Tokaido")

2003. 400th Anniv of Edo Shogunate (1st issue). Multicoloured.

3138	80y. Type **2487**	80	15
3139	80y. Hon-maru (fresco, Edo Castle)	80	15
3140	80y. Domarugusoku Helmet and Armour	80	15
3141	80y. Hatsune maki-e Lacquer Box(detail) . . .	80	15
3142	80y. 24 91 "Chujo" (Noh mask)	80	15

See also Nos. 3143/8 and 3159/64.

2003. 400th Anniv of Edo Shogunate (2nd issue). Multicoloured.

3143	80y. Type **2492**	80	15
3144	80y. Fireman's Haori (coat)	80	15
3145	80y. "Beauty Spots in Edo" (folding screen)	80	15
3146	80y. Kyoho-Bina Girl Doll	80	15
3147	80y. Kyoho-Bina Boy Doll	80	15
3148	80y. Danjuro Ichikawa (actor) as Goro Takenuki	80	15

2498 Omar Ali Saifuddien Mosque,

2499 Angkor Wat, Cambodia Brunei Darussalam

2500 Borobudur Temple, Indonesia

2501 That Luang, Laos

2502 Sultan Abdul Samad Building, Malaysia

2503 Shwedagon Pagoda, Myanmar

2504 Rice Terraces, Cordilleras, Philippines

2505 Merlion (legendary beast), Singapore

2506 Wat Phra Kaeo, Thailand

2507 Van Mieu, Vietnam

2003. ASEAN—Japan Exchange Year (Association of Southeast Asian Nations and Japan co-operation).

3149	**2498**	80y. multicoloured . .	80	15
3150	**2499**	80y. multicoloured . .	80	15
3151	**2500**	80y. multicoloured . .	80	15
3152	**2501**	80y. multicoloured . .	80	15
3153	**2502**	80y. multicoloured . .	80	15
3154	**2503**	80y. multicoloured . .	80	15
3155	**2504**	80y. multicoloured . .	80	15
3156	**2505**	80y. multicoloured . .	80	15
3157	**2506**	80y. multicoloured . .	80	15
3158	**2507**	80y. multicoloured . .	80	15

2508/9 *Powhatan*

2003. 400th Anniv of Edo Shogunate (3rd issue). Multicoloured.

3159	80y. Type **2508**	80	15
3160	80y. Type **2509**	80	15
3161	80y. Bakumatsu Fusoku Zukan (detail, screen) . .	80	15
3162	80y. Dutch East India Company plate	80	15
3163	80y. European Woman (detail, painting)	80	15
3164	80y. Wind-up Clock (Hisahige Tanaka)	80	15

2514 Bear playing Guitar ($28\frac{1}{2} \times 36$ mm)

2003. Letter Writing Day. Multicoloured.

3165	50y. Type **2514**	50	10
3166	50y. Monkey ($28\frac{1}{2} \times 36$ mm)	50	10
3167	50y. Crocodile playing Accordion ($28\frac{1}{2} \times 36$) . . .	50	10
3168	50y. Cat holding Camera and Envelope ($28\frac{1}{2} \times 36$ mm)	50	10
3169	80y. Hippo holding Flowers (29 × 40 mm)	80	15
3170	80y. Parrot (28 × 37 mm) . .	80	15
3171	80y. Owl (30 × 30 mm) . . .	80	15
3172	80y. Seated Bear holding Envelope (28 × 40 mm) . .	80	15
3173	80y. Elephant (28 × 37 mm)	80	15
3174	80y. Giraffe (29 × 40 mm)	80	15
3175	80y. Rabbit holding Envelope and Flowers (41 × 24 mm)	80	15
3176	80y. Lion carrying Lantern (28 × 37 mm)	80	15

3177 80y. Goat holding Envelope (28 × 37 mm) 80 15
3178 80y. Gorilla (28 × 37) . . . 80 15
MS3179 72 × 94 mm. Nos. 3170 and 3165 . . . . 1·60 1·60

2528 "Kawaski"

2529 "Miya"

2530 "Otsu"

2003. International Correspondence Week. Paintings from "53 Stations of Tokaido" by Ando Hiroshige.
3180 **2528** 90y. multicoloured . . 90 20
3181 **2529** 110y. multicoloured . . 1·10 25
3182 **2530** 130y. multicoloured . . 1·30 30

2531 Byakko (White Tiger of the West)

2003. Cultural Heritage. Wall Paintings, Kitora Tumulus, Nara Prefecture. Multicoloured.
3183 80y.+10y. Type **2532** . . . 90 20
3184 80y.+10y. Suzaku (Red Bird of the South) 90 20

2533 Mokichi Saito (writer, 150th death)

2534 Shibasaburo Kitasato (scientist, 150th birth)

2003. Anniversaries.
3185 **2533** 80y. multicoloured . . 80 15
3186 **2534** 80y. multicoloured . . 80 15

2535 Flowers and Butterflies, Amami Forest (painting, Isson Tanaka)

2003. 50th Anniv of Return of Amami Islands to Japan.
3187 **2535** 80y. multicoloured . . 80 15

2536 Monkey (Iyo Ittobori wood carving)

2539 The Successful Monkey (Edo folk toy)

2003. New Year's Greetings. Multicoloured.
3188 50y. Type **2536** 50 10
3189 80y. The Successful Monkey (Edo folk toy) 80 15
MS3190 93 × 72 mm. Nos. 3188/9 1·30 1·30

2003. New Year Lottery Stamps. Multicoloured.
3191 50y.+3y. Monkey (Iyo Ittobori wood carving) . . 50 10
3192 80y.+3y. Type **2539** 80 15
Each stamp carries a lottery number.

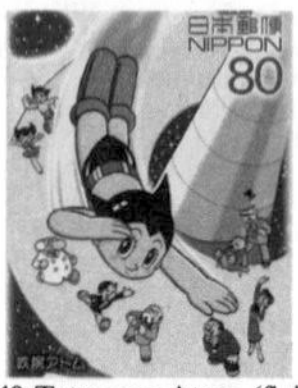

2540 Tetsuwan Atom (flying down)

2003. Science, Technology and Animation (1st issue). Multicoloured.
3193 80y. Type **2540** 80 15
3194 80y. Tetsuwan Atom (with raised arm) 80 15
3195 80y. Tetsuwan Atom (upside down) 80 15
3196 80y. Yumihiki Doji (Edo mechanical doll) 80 15
3197 80y. Nagaoka Hantaro (physicist) 80 15
3198 80y. H-II Rocket 80 15
3199 80y. Morph 3 Robot . . . 80 15
3200 80y. Tetsuwan Atom (flying up) 80 15
See also Nos. 3202/8; 3224/31; 3232/9, 3264/71 and 3286/93.

2548 Super Jetter 1

2549 Wadokei (clock)

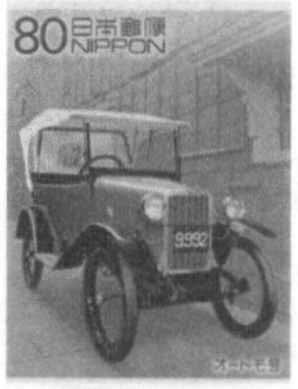

2550 Otomo-go (vintage car)

2551 KAZ (modern car)

2552 Stratospheric Balloon

2553 Super Jetter

2554 Super Jetter 3

2555 Super Jetter 4

2004. Science, Technology and Animation (2nd issue).
3201 **2548** 80y. multicoloured . . 80 15
3202 **2549** 80y. multicoloured . . 80 15
3203 **2550** 80y. multicoloured . . 80 15
3204 **2551** 80y. multicoloured . . 80 15
3205 **2552** 80y. multicoloured . . 80 15
3206 **2553** 80y. multicoloured . . 80 15
3207 **2554** 80y. multicoloured . . 80 15
3208 **2555** 80y. multicoloured . . 80 15

2556 Hello Kitty
2557 Hello Kitty

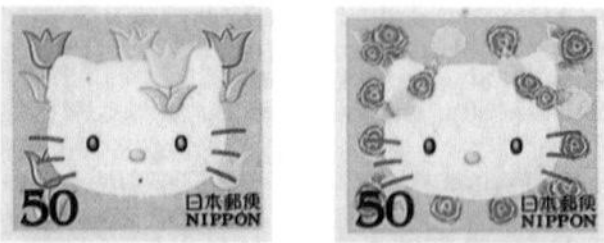

2558 Hello Kitty
2559 Hello Kitty

2560 Hello Kitty
2561 Hello Kitty

2562 Hello Kitty
2563 Hello Kitty

2564 Hello Kitty
2565 Hello Kitty

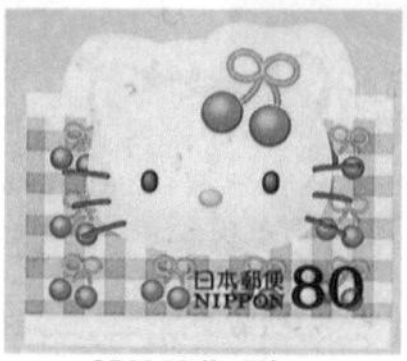

2566 Hello Kitty

2567 Hello Kitty

2568 Hello Kitty

2569 Hello Kitty

2570 Hello Kitty

2004. Greetings Stamps. Hello Kitty. Self-adhesive.
3209 **2556** 50y. multicoloured . . 50 10
3210 **2557** 50y. multicoloured . . 50 10
3211 **2558** 50y. multicoloured . . 50 10
3212 **2559** 50y. multicoloured . . 50 10
3213 **2560** 50y. multicoloured . . 50 10
3214 **2561** 50y. multicoloured . . 50 10
3215 **2562** 50y. multicoloured . . 50 10
3216 **2563** 50y. multicoloured . . 50 10
3217 **2564** 50y. multicoloured . . 50 10
3218 **2565** 50y. multicoloured . . 50 10
3219 **2566** 70y. multicoloured . . 70 10
3220 **2567** 70y. multicoloured . . 70 10
3221 **2568** 70y. multicoloured . . 70 10
3222 **2569** 70y. multicoloured . . 70 10
3223 **2570** 70y. multicoloured . . 70 10

2571 Marvellous Melmo 1

2572 Hanaoka Seishu

2573 Wooden Microscope

2574 Takamine Jokichi

2575 Drug Delivery System

2576 Marvellous Melmo 2

2577 Marvellous Melmo 3

2578 Marvellous Melmo 4

2004. Science, Technology and Animation (3rd issue).
3224 **2571** 80y. multicoloured . . 80 15
3225 **2572** 80y. multicoloured . . 80 15
3226 **2573** 80y. multicoloured . . 80 15
3227 **2574** 80y. multicoloured . . 80 15
3228 **2575** 80y. multicoloured . . 80 15
3229 **2576** 80y. multicoloured . . 80 15
3230 **2577** 80y. multicoloured . . 80 15
3231 **2578** 80y. multicoloured . . 80 15

2579 Kagaku Ninja-Tai Gatchman 1

2580 Perpetual Motion Machine

2581 OHSUMI (satellite) 2502 Conducting Polymer

2583 Eye (Tissue/Organ Reproductive Medicine)

2584 Kagaku Ninja-Tai Gatchman 2

2585 Kagaku Ninja-Tai Gatchman 3

2586 Kagaku Ninja-Tai Gatchman 4

2004. Science, Technology and Animation (4th issue).

3232	**2579**	80y. multicoloured . .	80	15
3233	**2580**	80y. multicoloured . .	80	15
3234	**2581**	80y. multicoloured . .	80	15
3235	**2582**	80y. multicoloured . .	80	15
3236	**2583**	80y. multicoloured . .	80	15
3237	**2584**	80y. multicoloured . .	80	15
3238	**2585**	80y. multicoloured . .	80	15
3239	**2586**	80y. multicoloured . .	80	15

2587 Morizo and Kiccoro (official mascots) in Orbit

2589 "Uchuno sakura gohiki no saru zu" (Mori Sosen)

2005. EXPO 2005 World Exhibition, Aichi, Japan. Multicoloured.

3240	80y.+10y. Type **2587** . . .	85	20
3241	80y.+10y. Morizo and Kiccoro holding hands . .	85	20

2004. Philately Week.

3242	**2589** 80y. multicoloured . .	80	15

2590 *Ten Point* and *Tosho Boy* (22nd Arima Memorial Stakes)

2592 Police Car

2004. 50th of Japan Racing Association. Multicoloured.

3243	80y. Type **2590**	80	15
3244	80y. *Narita Brian* (61st Tokyo Yushun (Japanese Derby))	80	15

2004. 50th Anniv of Police Law. Multicoloured.

3245	80y. Type **2592**	80	15
3246	80y. Police motorcyclist . .	80	15

Nos. 3245/6 were issued together, se-tenant, forming a composite design.

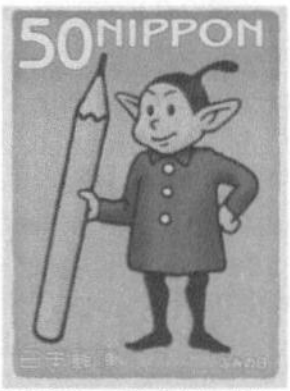

2594 Donkichi holding Pencil

2608 Athens 2004 Emblem

2003. Letter Writing Day. Multicoloured.

3247	50y. Type **2594**	50	10
3248	50y. Hime (25 × 33 mm) . .	50	10
3249	50y. Shochan (25 × 33 mm)	50	10
3250	50y. Owl (33 × 36 mm) . . .	50	10
3251	80y. Pigeon carrying envelope (33 × 34 mm) . .	80	15
3252	80y. Squirrel with wings (33 × 36 mm)	80	15
3253	80y. Stork (30 × 30 mm) . .	80	15
3254	80y. Hime with wings (27 × 36 mm)	80	15
3255	80y. Donkichi (27 × 37 mm)	80	15
3256	80y. Kuriko (27 × 37 mm)	80	15
3257	80y. Goddess (28 × 40 mm)	80	15
3258	80y. Shochan with wings (28 × 36 mm)	80	15
3259	80y. Squirrel holding envelope and flowers (28 × 29 mm)	80	15
3260	80y. Rabbit (30 × 30 mm)	80	15
MS3261	72 × 94 mm. Nos. 3247 and 3256	90	90

2004. Olympic Games, Athens. Multicoloured.

3262	80y. Type **2608**	80	15
3263	80y. Olympic Rings, Flame and Olympia Ruins . . .	80	15

2610 Majinga Z 4

2611 Model Steam Engine

2612 KS Steel

2613 Shinkai 6500

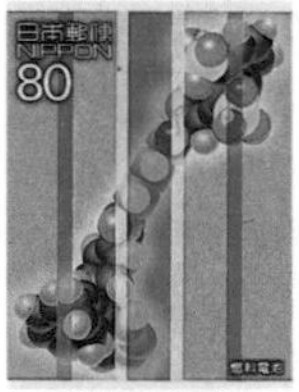

2614 Fuel Cell

2615 Majinga Z 1

2616 Majinga Z 2

2617 Majinga Z 3

2004. Science, Technology and Animation (5th issue).

3264	**2610**	80y. multicoloured . .	80	15
3265	**2611**	80y. multicoloured . .	80	15
3266	**2612**	80y. multicoloured . .	80	15
3267	**2613**	80y. multicoloured . .	80	15
3268	**2614**	80y. multicoloured . .	80	15
3269	**2615**	80y. multicoloured . .	80	15
3270	**2616**	80y. multicoloured . .	80	15
3271	**2617**	80y. multicoloured . .	80	15

2618 *Mount Fuji* (Frederic Harris)

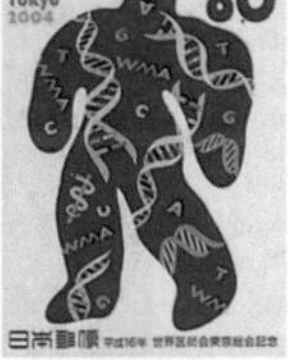

2620 Medical Symbols as Figure

2004. 150th Anniv of America—Japan Relations. Multicoloured.

3272	80y. Type **2618**	80	15
3273	80y. Cafe (Yasuo Kuniyoshi)	80	15

2004. World Medical Association (WMA) General Assembly, Tokyo.

3274	**2620** 80y. multicoloured . .	80	15

2621 "Hirarsukai"

2004. International Correspondence Week. Paintings from "53 Stations of Tokaido" by Utagawa Hiroshige. Multicoloured.

3275	90y. Type **2621**	90	20
3276	110y. "Yokkaichi"	1·10	25
3277	130y. "Tsuchiyama"	1·30	30

2624 Lafcadio Hearn (Koizumi Yakumo) (writer) (death centenary)

2004. Anniversaries. Multicoloured.

3278	80y. Type **2624**	80	15
3279	80y. Isamu Noguchi (sculptor) (birth centenary)	80	15
3280	80y. Koga Masao (composer) (birth centenary)	80	15

2627 Rooster (Hita-Dorei (clay bell))

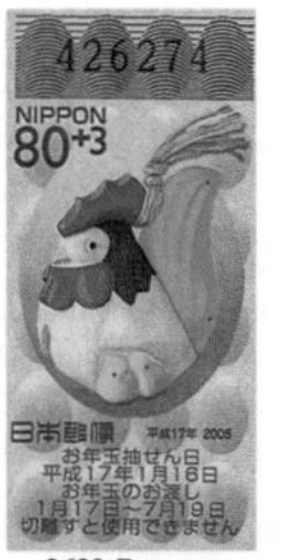

2630 Rooster (Shimotsuke-Dorei (clay bell))

2004. New Year's Greetings.

3281	50y. Type **2627**	50	10
3282	80y. Rooster (Shimotsuke-Dorei (clay bell))	80	15
MS3283	94 × 72 mm. Nos. 3281/2	1·30	1·30

2004. New Year Lottery Stamps. Multicoloured.

3284	50y.+3y. Rooster (Hita-Dorei (clay bell))	50	10
3285	80y.+3y. Type **2630**	80	15

Each stamp carries a lottery number.

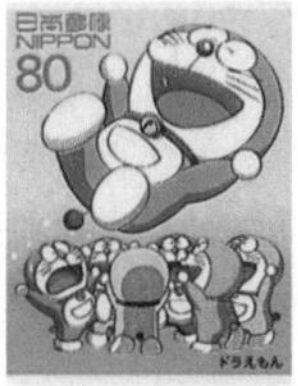

2631 Doraemon 4

2632 Hiraga Gennai

2633 Mechanical "netsuke"

2634 Television Set

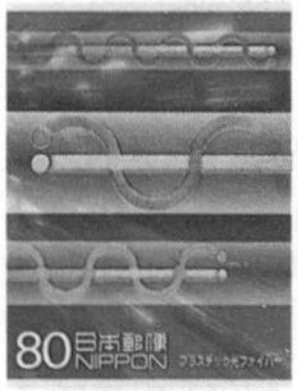

2635 Plastic Optical Fibre (POF)

2636 Doraemon 1

2637 Doraemon 2

2638 Doraemon 3

2004. Science, Technology and Animation (6th issue). Multicoloured.

3286	**2631**	80y. multicoloured . .	80	15
3287	**2632**	80y. multicoloured . .	80	15
3288	**2633**	80y. multicoloured . .	80	15
3289	**2634**	80y. multicoloured . .	80	15
3290	**2635**	80y. multicoloured . .	80	15
3291	**2636**	80y. multicoloured . .	80	15
3292	**2637**	80y. multicoloured . .	80	15
3293	**2638**	80y. multicoloured . .	80	15

2639 "tori" (Tensho style) (Toda Teizan)

2640 "tori" (Kinbun style) (Seki Masato)

2641 "tori" (Kinbun style) (Onchi Shunyou)

2642 "tori" (Tensho style) (Funamoto Hou'un)

2643 "tori" (Kana style) (Koyama Yasuko)

2644 "tori" (Sousho style) (Watanabe Kan'ou)

2645 "tori" (Kobun style) (Inamuru un'dou)

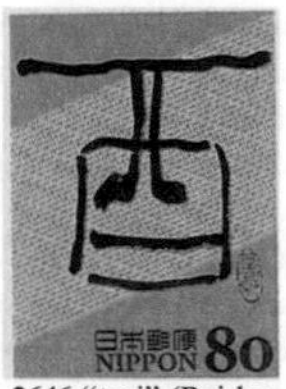

2646 "tori" (Reisho style) (Oono Kouken)

2647 "tori" (Kokotsumoji style) (Oohira Santou)

2648 "tori" (Kobun style) (Noguchi Hakutei)

2004. Greetings Stamps. Eto Calligraphy.

3294	**2639**	80y. multicoloured . .	80	15
3295	**2640**	80y. multicoloured . .	80	15
3296	**2641**	80y. multicoloured . .	80	15
3297	**2642**	80y. multicoloured . .	80	15
3298	**2643**	80y. multicoloured . .	80	15
3299	**2644**	80y. multicoloured . .	80	15
3300	**2645**	80y. multicoloured . .	80	15
3301	**2646**	80y. multicoloured . .	80	15
3302	**2647**	80y. multicoloured . .	80	15
3303	**2648**	80y. multicoloured . .	80	15

MILITARY FRANK STAMPS

(M 36)

1910. No. 139 optd with Type M **36**.
M156 **28** 3s. red . . . . £225 35·00

1913. No. 298 optd with Type M **36**.
M185 **36** 3s. red . . . . 30·00 11·00

1921. No. 37 of Japanese Post Offices in China optd with Type M **36**.
M202 **36** 3s. red £7000 £3250

PREFECTURE STAMPS

Since 1 April 1989 the Japanese Ministry of Posts and Telecommunications has issued stamps, some apparently commemorative, inscribed for various prefectures.

The Japanese local government system contains 47 prefectures which vary from Tokyo, Osaka, Kyoto, Hokkaido and Okinawa to rural areas; the powers of the prefectures are similar to those of English or Welsh counties. Each prefecture issue is sold within the area for which it is inscribed and also in other prefectures grouped with it in one of 11 postal regions; the stamps are also available from the Tokyo Central Post Office. All issues are valid for postal purposes throughout Japan.

These issues do not fulfil the published criteria for full listing in the Stanley Gibbons catalogue and, in consequence, are recorded in abbreviated form below.

The sheet of 47 prefecture flowers was sold throughout Japan and is given full listing as Nos. 2041/87.

1989.

Nagano. Monkeys in hot spring. 62y.

Yamagata. Cherries. 62y.

Okinawa. Courtesy Gate, Shuri. 62y.

Ehime. Dogo Hot Spa buildings. 62y.

Kanagawa. Doll and gas lamps. 62y.

Hiroshima. Seto Inland Sea. 62y. × 2.

Niigata. Memorial Hall and Bandai Bridge. 62y.

Aichi. Nagoya Castle and golden dolphin. 62y.

Oita. Monkey and Mt. Takasaki. 62y.

Hokkaido. Old Prefectural Building, Sapporo. 62y.

Hokkaido. Runner and wild rose (athletic meeting). 62y.

Kumamoto. Kumamoto Castle. 62y.

Ishikawa. Stone lantern, Kenroku Park. 62y.

Aomori. Apples. 62y.

Osaka. Bunraku puppets and Nakanoshima Theatre. 62y.

Shiga. Lake Biwa and racoon-dog. 62y.

Chiba. Racoon-dogs dancing. 62y.

Tokyo. Railway station. 62y.

Yamaguchi. Blowfish lanterns. 62y.

1990.

Hokkaido. Ice hockey (Asian Winter Olympics). 62y.

Toyama. Mt. Tate and Shomyo Falls. 62y.

Ibaraki. "Seven Baby Crows" (nursery rhyme). 62y.

Nagano. Old inns of Tsumago and Magome. 62y. × 2.

Shizuoka. Mt. Fuji and tea picker. 62y.

Fukushima. Peaches. 62y.

Akita. Omagari Fireworks Festival. 62y.

Kagoshima. Mt. Sakura. 62y.

Nagasaki. Sailing ship. 62y.

Okinawa. Ryukyu dancer. 62y.

Tokyo. New post office and logger. 62y.

Shimane. Male dancer with basket. 62y.

Fukuoka. High jumping and Fukuoka Tower (athletic meeting). 62y.

Kyoto. Dancing girl crossing bridge. 62y.

Wakayama. Three pilgrims on old path to Kumano. 62y.

Miyagi. Izunuma Swamp and five whistling swans. 62y.

Gifu. Four seasons in Hida. 62y. × 4.

Saitama. Tenjin Shrine and children playing song game. 62y.

Hokkaido. Two Manchurian cranes. 62y.

1991.

Kagawa. Mounted archer at Battle of Yashima. 62y.

Okayama. Water jars (Bizen ware). 62y. × 2.

Saga. Watchtower, Yoshinogari. 62y.

Yamanashi. "Bride under Cherry Blossoms" (nursery rhyme). 62y.

Niigata. Two fancy carps. 62y.

Hokkaido. Lily of the valley, lilac, lily, rowanberries. 62y. × 4.

Tochigi. Mt. Nikkou and ramblers. 62y.

Iwate. Mt. Iwate. 62y.

Kochi. Sakamoto Ryoma and child standing on whale. 62y.

Tokushima. Wooden puppet. 62y.

Tokyo. Fringed orchid. 41y.

Miyazaki. Cape Toi and wild horses. 62y.

Kumamoto. Tsu-jun Aqueduct releasing water into river. 62y.

Okinawa. Black pearls in oyster and Kabira Bay. 41y.

Tottori. Pears. 62y.

Ishikawa. Genki (mascot) and sunrise (46th National Athletic Meeting). 41y.

Mie. Ninja holding shuriken (throwing weapon), rainbow, Iga Ueno Castle and Ninja house. 62y.

Fukui. Woman wearing spectacles. 62y.

Gunma. "Hare and Tortoise" (fable). 62y.

Hyogo. Weathercock and Kobe City lights. 62y.

Nara. Mt. Yoshino in spring and autumn. 62y. × 2.

1992.

Niigata. Ryokan's Hermitage, Bunsui. 41y.

Fukuoka. Mt. Togami, Japanese bush warbler and azaleas (National Afforestation Campaign). 41y.

Hokkaido. Arctic foxes. 62y.

Toyama. Mt. Tate and tulips. 62y.

Ehime. Islets in Kurushima Strait. 62y.

Iwate. Cape Kitayama, Rikuchu, in winter. 62y.

Ohita. Three Tsurusaki dancers. 62y.

Yamaguchi. Tanabata lantern festival. 62y.

Kanagawa. Shasui waterfall. 62y.

Fukuoka. Mari Tahei with spear and sake dish (Kuroda samurai folk song). 62y.

Okinawa. Naha regatta. 62y.

Osaka. Osaka Business Park and Castle. 41y.

Aichi. Scops owl. 62y.

1993.

Akita. Rocks at Oga Peninsula. 41y.

Ibaraki. Fukuroda waterfall. 62y.

Ishikawa. Nanao Bay and Notojima Bridge. 62y.

Tokyo. Cherry blossom and Tama District mountain ranges. 62y.

Hokkaido. Harbour seals. 62y.

Kagawa. Peace statue. 62y.

Hiroshima. Drummer (rice transplanting ritual). 62y.

Shizuoka. Black paradise flycatcher and Mt. Fuji. 41y.

Shiga. Yachts on Lake Biwa. 62y.

Nagano. Matsumoto Castle and mountains. 62y.

Kagoshima. Drummer and dancer (Ohara Festival) and Mt. Sakura. 41y.

Aomori. Oirase mountain stream. 62y.

Chiba. Waterfall in Yoro Gorge. 41y.

1994.

Tokyo. Rainbow Bridge. 50y.

Toyama. Kurobe Dam and Gorge. 80y.

Shimane. Izumo no Okuni (Kabuki dancer) and Izumo Shrine. 80y.

Nagano. Home at Kashiwabara of Issa Kobayushi (poet). 80y.

Gunma. Fukiwari Waterfalls. 80y.

Hokkaido. Sika deer. 50y.

Hyogo. White stork and Drum Tower, Izushi. 50y.

Wakayama. Yachts off Wakaura Coast and Marina City. 80y.

Mie. Kentish plovers and Wedded Rocks, Futami Bay. 80y.

Tokushima. Awa dance. 50y.

Okinawa. Tug-of-war. 50y.

Fukui. Pine grove in Kehi. 50y.

Miyagi. Junks and Godaido Temple, Matsushima. 80y.

Nagasaki. Dragon Festival. 80y.

1995.

Hokkaido. Chipmunks. 80y.

Kyoto, Ushiwaka and Benkei on bridge. 80y.

Gifu. Flowers (Rose, cyclamen, African violets etc). 80y.

Niigata. Jade and Gyofu Soma (poet). 80y.

Kochi. Cape Ashizuri-Misaki Lighthouse. 80y.

Ishikawa. Kanizawa Castle. 80y.

Hokkaido. Lady's slipper orchid. 80y.

Saitama. Kuroyama Waterfall. 80y.

Tokyo. Red Gate, Tokyo University. 50y.

Okinawa. Procession of drummers (folk festival dance). 80y.

Miyagi. Avenue of zelkova trees. 50y.

Osaka. Float in Kishiwada Danjiri Festival. 80y.

Yamagata. Yamadera (or Risshaku) Temple, Mt. Houju, in autumn. 80y.

Hida. Four seasons in Hida. 80y. × 4 se-tenant.

Saga Boy and fish (Karatsu Kunchi Festival). 80y.

Okayama. Woman writing (Niimi Estate festival). 80y.

Tochigi. Kirihuri Waterfall. 50y.

Nara. Yoshino in autumn and spring. 80y. × 2.

Chiba. Cows in field ("Farmpia '95" dairy farming exhibition). 80y.

1996.

Hokkaido. Sea butterflies. 80y.

Kumamoto. Boy dancing, bridge and ships (Ushibuka Haiya festival). 80y.

Fukushima. Pink peony. 80y.

Mie. Wild crinums (flowers). 80y. and Women collecting shells. 80y. se-tenant.

Saga. Jar, flames and pavilion (ceramics exhibition). 80y.

Yamanashi. Waterfall in Shosenkyo Gorge. 50y.

Fukui. Murasaki Shikibu (author of "Tale of Genji") and Mt. Hino. 80y.

Shiga. Enryaku Temple and ancient trees, Mt. Hiei. 80y.

Ehime. Nishiumi Marine Park. 80y.

Hokkaido. Wild rose. 80y.

Aomori. Kabuki characters (Nebuta festival). 80y.

1997.

Miyazaki. Dancers with drums (Shimozuru Usudaiko Odori folk dance). 80y.

Okinawa. Main Palace of Shuri Castle and stone dragon's head. 80y.

Tokyo. Kaminari Gate, Asakusa. 80y.

Tottori. Umbrella Dance, Shanshan Festival. 80y.

Nagano. Orchestra (Saito Memorial Festival, Matsumoto). 80y.

Nagano. Gentians. 80y.

Kanagawa. Mountains and flowers, Sengokubara Marsh. 80y.

Aichi. Floats, Nagoya Festival. 80y. × 2 se-tenant.

Nara. Pagodas on Mt. Wakakusa (grassburning rite). 50y.

Kumamoto. Ball in air above temple (Men's World Handball Championship). 80y.

Hokkaido. Dahurian rhododendron. 80y.

Shizuoka. Tea picking. 50y.

Shizuoka. Mt. Fuji in summer (cows and daisies) and autumn (dry grass). 80y. × 2 se-tenant.

Kagawa. Visitors at foot of Marugame Castle. 80y.

Hokkaido. Ermine. 50y.

Okayama. Castle. 80y.

Okinawa. Pineapples and mangoes. 50y. × 2 se-tenant.

Nagasaki, Saga and Fukuoka. Nagasaki Kaido Highway route map. 80y. × 4 se-tenant.

Kyoto. University clock tower. 80y.

Niigata. "Bride" by Fukiya Koji. 50y.

Akita. Lanterns on bamboo poles (Kanto Festival). 80y.

Tottori. Ship, flower, dolphin and buildings (Expo Tottori 97). 80y.

Saitama. Waterwheel plant at Hozoji-numa Pond, Hanyu. 50y.

Toyama. Street dancers (Good Wind Festival). 80y. × 2 se-tenant.

Ibaraki. Sailing dinghies on Lake Kasumigaura. 80y.

Tokyo. Tokyo Big Site (exhibition buildings overlooking lake), Telecom Centre (monorail), Rainbow Bridge, Tokyo International Forum (glass building), Edo Tokyo Museum (steps leading to building). 80y. × 5 se-tenant.

Saitama. Collared doves on tree and three walkers (First World Walking Festival). 80y.

Chiba and Kanagawa. Kanagawa-Chiba Bridge and Tunnel. 80y. × 2 se-tenant.

1998.

Hokkaido. Rowanberries in snow and pink moss in spring. 80y. × 2 se-tenant.

Kyoto. Hiyoshi Dam. 80y.

Okinawa. Sanshin (musical instrument), towel and banana plant cloth. 80y.

Gifu. Crowd surrounding float (Okoshi Daiko drum festival). 80y.

Hyogo and Tokushima. Ko–Awaj–Naruto Motorway. Ohnaruto Bridge (with whirlpool), Akashi Kaikyo Bridge (with spring blossom). 80y. × 2 se-tenant.

Nagano. "Jomon's Venus" (figurine from Chino). 80y.

Iwate. Procession of caparisoned horses. 80y.

Tokyo. Towers as hand (Business Show). 80y.

Nagasaki. Mt. Heisei Shinzan. 80y.

Gunma. 80y. Oze Moor in spring and autumn. 80y. × 2 se-tenant.

Yamagata. Two dancers carrying hats (Flower Hat Dance). 50y.

Shizuoka. Women's World Softball Championship. 80y.

Ishikawo. Mt. Hakusan (with woods in foreground). 50y.

Oita. Decorated cart (Gion Festival). 50y.

Nagano. World Puppet Festival. 50y. × 2 se-tenant.

Hiroshima. Views of Seto Inland Sea. Itsukushima Shrine with torii gate; bridge over Ondo Strait. 80y. × 2 se-tenant.

Okinawa. First and last Ryukyu Islands stamps. 80y. × 2 se-tenant.

Kagoshima. Ceramic teabowl and vase (400th anniv of Satsuma-yoki Pottery). 80y. × 2 se-tenant.

Kagawa. Seto Great Road and Rail Bridge. 80y.

Hyogo. Kobe Lights. 80y.

Aomori. Apples. 80y. (as 1989 issue but face value changed).

Wakayama. Three pilgrims on old path to Kumano. 80y. (as 1990 issue).

Tokyo. Tama intercity monorail. 80y.

1999.

Okayama and Hiroshima. Train (Thera Railway). 80y.

Oita. Mt. Kyoshu and R. Yamkunigawa and Blue Tunnel in Spring. 80y. × 2 se-tenant.

Ehime. Bath house, Dogo Spa. 80y.

Hokkaido. Icefloes and Manchurian cranes. 50y. × 2 se-tenant. Ice crystal and snowman. 80y. × 2 se-tenant.

Niigata. Building (Tokamachi Snow Festival). 80y.

Tokyo. White and purple orchids. 80y. × 2 se-tenant.

Fukui. Green and brown dinosaurs. 80y. × 2 se-tenant.

Tochigi. Lake Chuzenji in spring (flowers) and autumn (brown leaves). 80y. × 2 se-tenant.

Gifu. Tree in blossom (Renewed cherry tree). 80y.

Okinawa. Woman and two masks (125th anniv of Universal Postal Union). 80y. × 2 se-tenant.

Nagano. Kiso Observatory, Mt. Ontaki. 80y.

Mie. Hills, coast, paved path and terraces (Old path for Kuimani). 80y. × 4 se-tenant.

Nagano. Taiko Mon Gate, Matsumoto Castle. 80y.

Toyama. Firefly Squid. 80y.

Yamagata. Sweet Cherries. 80y.

Ishikawa. Four Seasons in Kenrokuen Garden. 80y. × 4 se-tenant.

Hiroshima and Ehime. Opening of Shimanami Seaside Highway. 80y. × 10 se-tenant.

Hokkaidou. Plants and flowers. 80y. × 4 se-tenant.

Wakayama. Waterfall and seascape. 80y. × 2 se-tenant.

Okinawa. Ryuku Dancers. 80y.

Miyagi and Fukushima. Banners and flags (summer festivals). 80y. × 2 se-tenant.

Hokkaido. Lavender and wheat fields. 50y. and 80y.

Okayama. Kurashiki District. 80y.

Niigata. Kites over river (Shirane Big Kite Battle). 80y. × 2 se-tenant.

Ishikawa. Carnival procession (Noto Kirko Festival). 80y.

Hokkaido. Foxes and seals. 80y. × 2.

Yamanashi. Lakes around Mt. Fuji. 80y. × 5 se-tenant.

Fukouka. Summer Festival. 80y.

Tokyo. Lotus flower. 80y., and firework display at Sumida River. 80y. × 2 se-tenant.

Kyoto. Flowers and Amano Hashidate (sand bar). 80y.

Niigata. Birds (Japanese crested ibis). 80y. × 2 se-tenant.

Chiba. Lotus flower and building. 80y.

Nagano. Tsumago and Magome Post Stations. 80y. × 2 se-tenant.

Hokkaido. Birds (steller's sea eagle, tufted puffin, blakiston's fish owl and manchurian crane). 50y. × 4 se-tenant.

Okinawa. Fishermen and boat. 80y.

Wakayama. Landscape and statue. 80y. × 2 se-tenant.

Iwate. Autumn bellflowers. 50y.

Shizuoka. View over port (Centenary of Shimizu Port). 80y.

Kagawa. Bridge, Ritsurin Park. 80y.

Kumamoto. Sailing boat. 80y.

Nagasaki. Dejima (artificial island). 80y.

Kanagawa. Minamotono (Yoritomo horseman). 80y.

Aomori. Shirakami Mountains. 80y.

Toyama. Kokiriko dancer and farmhouses. 80y.

Gunma. Archaeological finds (50th anniv of Excavations of Iwajuku Paleolithic Site). 80y.

Hokkaidou. Farmers and foods. 50y. × 4 se-tenant.

Osaka. Rhythmic gymnast (23rd World Rhythmic Sports Gymnastics Championship). 80y.

Fukushima. Chrysanthemum Figure of Nihonmatsu. 80y.

Miyazaki. Old Town of Obi. 80y. × 2 se-tenant.

Aichi. Paintings. 80y. × 2 se-tenant.

Nagano. Monkeys in hot spring. 80y.

Shimane and Yamaguchi. Hagi and Tsuwano Cities. 80y. × 2 se-tenant.

Nara. Birds over Asuka Bay and Tomb of Ishibutai. 80y. × 2 se-tenant.

Okinawa. Stone bridge and teahouse (Shikina-en Garden). 50y. × 2 se-tenant.

Fukui. Crab and Rock Formation. 80y. × 2 se-tenant.

Saga. Yoshinogari (archaeological site). 80y.

Hokkaidou. Christmas elves in sleigh. 80y.

Kouchi. Moonlit night, Katsura Beach and whale's tail flukes. 80y. × 2 se-tenant.

Akita. Snow-covered Samurai Houses, Kakunodate. 80y.

2000.

Tokyo. Whale, mother and child, procession, family and floodlit bridge (New Millennium). 50y. × 5 se-tenant.

Hokkaido. Bridge, canal, clock tower and church. 80y. × 4 se-tenant.

Hyogo. Bee and flowers, fairy and flowers ("Japan Flora 2000" gardening exhibition). 50y. and 80y.

Okayama. Courting manchurian cranes, bridge, pagoda and cranes in flight (300th anniv of Korakuen Garden). 80y. × 4 se-tenant.

Nagano. Cherry Blossom. 80y.

Okinawa. Dragon. 50y.

Nagano. Azumino. 80y.

Akita, Aomori, Fukushima, Iwate, Miyagi, Yamagata. Cherry Blossom. 80y. × 6

Toyama. Tateyama Mountain Range and tulips. 50y. and 80y. se-tenant.

Ehime. Uwajima Castle. 80y.

Saitama. New Urban Centre. 50y. × 2 se-tenant.

Hiroshima, Okayama, Shimane, Tottori, Yamaguchi. Flowers and cornfield, flower and roof ridge, flowers and roof, maple leaves, flowers and sea. 50y. × 5 se-tenant.

Tokyo. Pink flowers, red roses, orange flowers, snow-covered pink flowers, yellow flowers. 50y. × 5 se-tenant.

Kanagawa. Tassels and woman with girl (Shonan Hiratsuku Tanabata Festival). 50y. × 2 se-tenant.

Okinawa. Bankoku shinryokan. 80y.

Osaka. World Performing Arts Festival. 80y.

Akita. Kujuku Islands. 80y.

Hokkaido. Flowering Potato Field. 50y. × 2 se-tenant.

Hokkaido. Pasture. (premium for victims of Mt. Usu eruption). 80y.+20y. × 2 se-tenant.

Tokushima. Awaodori Dance. 80y.

Iwate. Golden Hall, Chusonji Temple. 80y.

Fukuoka. Hakata Doll. 80y.

Toyama. Badminton Player (55th National Athletics Meeting). 50y.

Mie. Parachutists (25th World Championships). 80y. × 2 se-tenant.

Tokyo. Two Children. 80y.

Yamaguchi. Iwakuni Kintaikyo Bridge. 80y.

Oita. Disabled Athletes (International Wheelchair Marathon) 80y.

Aichi. Man with parasol. 80y.

Kyoto. Four Seasons. 80y. × 4 se-tenant.

Kanagawa. Odawara Castle. 50y. × 2 se-tenant.

Saitama. Fireworks and illuminated float (Chichibu Night Festival). 80y. × 2 se-tenant.

Saga. Child and Balloons (International Balloon Festival) 80y.

Tokyo. Tower blocks and view of city (premium for victims of the disaster). 80y.+20y. × 2 se-tenant.

Shizuoka. Blossoms and waterfall. 50y. × 2 se-tenant.

Fukushima. Hata Festival, Kohata. 80y.

Miyazaki. Sekino'o Falls and Kirishima Mountain Range. 80y. × 2 se-tenant.

Gunma. Megane-bashi Bridge and Maruyama Hendensho Transformer Station. 50y. × 2 se-tenant.

Nagano. Chikumagawa River and Kamikochi Highland (centenary of *Shinano-no kuni* (song by Asai Retsu and Kitamura Suehara)) 50y. × 2 se-tenant.

2001.

Hyogo. Giant Panda. 50y. and Millennium celebrations, Kobe. 80y. se-tenant.

Fukuoka. Oe Kowakamai Dancer. 80y.

Ibaraki. Four seasons in Kairakuen Garden. 50y. × 4 se-tenant and miniature sheet.

Hokkaido. Ermine. 80y.

Kochi. Castle and Sunday Market, Kochi. 80y. × 2 se-tenant.

Hyogo. Takarazuka Revue dancer and Violets. 80y. × 2 se-tenant.

Shimane. Matsue Castle and Teahouse. 80y. × 2 se-tenant.

Yamanashi. Grapes and jewellery. 80y.

Osaka. Thunder God playing table tennis, Wind God playing table tennis, Bowler, Kick boxers. 50y. × 4 se-tenant.

Fukushima. Bee (Beautiful Fukushima Future Expo). 80y.

Niigata. Cherry blossoms, Takada Castle. 80y.

Shizuoka. Decorated palace float and kites (Hamamatsu Festival). 80y. × 2 se-tenant.

Tochigi. Ashikaga School buildings. 50y. and Gate. 80y.

Yamanashi. Mt. Mizugakisan, Azuma-Shakunage (National Afforestation Campaign). 50y.

Miyagi. Runners (400th Anniversary of Sendai City). 80y.

Nagano. Zenkoji Temple and Mt. Iizunayama. 80y. × 2 se-tenant.

Yamaguchi. Animal band. 50y. and Wild ducks. 80y. (Japan Expo Yamaguchi 2001) se-tenant.

Hokkaido. Pink flowers and Yellow flowers. 50y. × 2 se-tenant.

Tokyo. Cherry blossoms, hydrangea, salvias, chrysanthemums, camellias. 50y. × 5 se-tenant.

Tottori. Snow crab and coastline (Uradome). 50y. Dunes (Tottori). 50y. Flowers and dolls in basket on river. 50y. Mt. Daisen. 50y. Nageiredo Hall. 80y. Mukibanda Paleolithic Site. 80y. se-tenant.

Ishikawa. Samurai warrior on horseback (Kanazawa Hyakumangoku Matsuri Festival). 80y.

Okinawa. Memorial and flowers. 80y.

Yamanashi. Scenery. Mountains and blossom (Kyoto), Mt. Kitadake and irises(Kyochu), Mt. Yatsugatake and horses (Kyohoku), Mountain, building and water (Gunnnai), Cherry blossoms (Kyonan). 50y. × 5 se-tenant.

Aichi. Cars on Toyota-oohashi Bridge and Toyota stadium. 50y. × 2 se-tenant.

Fukuoka. Fireworks over buildings and sunflowers (Kitakyushu Expo-Festival 2001). 80y.

Osaka. Namdaemun (building), Seoul and Doton-bori (buildings), Osaka. 80y. Bunraku (Japan) and Nong-ak drummers (Korea) (14th General Assembly of World Trade Organization). 80y. se-tenant.

Niigata. Fireworks, Nagaoka. 50y. × 2 se-tenant.

Hokkaido. Poplar trees and Statue of Dr. Clark, Hitsujigaoka. 80y. × 2 se-tenant.

Miyagi. Volleyball players (56th National Athletic Meeting). 50y.

Ehime. Masaoka Shiki (Haiku poet) and Matsuyama Castle. 50y. Locomotive SL "Bocchasn" and Dogo Spa. 50y. se-tenant.

Shiga. Trout and rhododendron flowers (Ninth International Conference on the Conservation and Management of Lakes). 50y.

Gifu. Tanigumi-Odori dancers. 50y. Fruit, train and children. 50y. × 2 se-tenant.

Akita. Igloo, children and dog. 80y.

Kagoshima. Stylized cyclist (World Indoor Cycling Championships). 80y.

Tokyo. Okuma Auditorium, Waseda University. 80y.

Fukui. Narcissi. 50y. Coastline, Echizen. 80y. se-tenant.

Tokyo. Illuminations (Third Tokyo Millenario). 80y.

2002.

Hokkaido. Ezo Flying Squirrels. 80y.

Hiroshima. Nukui Dam and On-bashi Bridge. 80y. × 2 se-tenant.

Wakayama. Azaleas, Wakayama Marina City and Wakaura Bay. 80y.

Nagasaki. Houses, T. B. Glover's mansion. 50y. × 2 se-tenant.

Shimane, Okayama. Cherry blossoms, Hiikawa and Bicchu Pagoda, Kokubunji Temple. 80y. × 2 se-tenant.

Ehime, Tokushima, Kouchi, Kagawa. Mandarin orange, Citrus fruit, Bayberry and Olive and Shodoshima island. 50y. × 5 se-tenant.

Hokkaido. Tulips and Sunflowers. 80y. × 2 se-tenant.

Yamagguchi. Kaikyo-Messe tower, Shimonoseki and blue whale (54th International Whaling Commission (IWG)). 80y.

Saitama. Bonsai tree. 80y.

Kanagawa. Sail ship, Yokohama and Woman, modern boat, and skyline. 80y. × 2 se-tenant.

Niigata. Camellia, Daylily, Iris and pink flower. 50y. × 4 se-tenant.

Yamagata. Flowers, river and hills (National Re-afforestation Campaign). 80y.

Fukushima. Path, arums and trees and Lilies. 50y. × 2 se-tenant.

Gunma. Rhododendron and Tanigawa Mountain range and Autumn colours. 80y. × 2 se-tenant.

Tokyo. Morning glory and Chines lanterns (pot plants). 80y. × 2 se-tenant.

Ishikawa. Campanula, Fritillaria, Pink geranium and Anemone. 50y. × 4 se-tenant.

Gifu. Gujou-odori dance. 50y.

Osaka. Lion and Osaka Dome (85th Lions Clubs International Convention). 80y.

Osaka. Scouts and Osakajo Castle (23rd Asia-Pacific Scout Jamboree). 80y.

Kumamoto. Yachiyoza Theatre. 80y.

Okinawa. Cherry blossom, Hibiscus, Purple flowers, White lilies and Pink flowers. 50y. × 5 se-tenant.

Tokyo. Azalea, Lily, Myrtle and Gingko tree 50y. × 4 se-tenant.

Kouchi. Runners (57th National Athletic Meet). 50y.

Mie. Matsuo Basho and Iga-Ueno castle and Haisei-den hall. 80y. × 2 se-tenant.Aomori. Blossom, apple and mountains. 80y.

2003.

Aomori. Speed Skater and Skier. (Fifth Winter Asian Games Aomori 2003) 50y.

Miyazaki. Noh play. Tengaichi Tkigi-Noh (actor) (Nobeoka, the City of Noh). 80y. × 2 se-tenant.

Hokkaido. Ainu design. Lake Mashuko. 80y.

Nagano. Dogtooth violet and Hakuba mountains. Skunk cabbage and Okususobana-shizen'en. Nikkoday lily and Mt. Kirigamine. Cosmos and Cosmos highway 50y. × 4 se-tenant.

Okayama. Kibitsu-jinja Shrine main hall and gate. 80y.

Kagawa. Kompira-Ohshibai Theater and Mt. Zouzusan. 80y.

Saga. Iroe Komainu (lion dog). 80y.

Yamagguchi. Kaneko Misuzu (write). "Tairyo" (poem) 80y. × 2 se-tenant.

Gifu. Cormorant fishing. Gifu Castle 50y. × 2 se-tenant.

Kyoto. Aoi-matsuri (carriage decorated with Japanese wisteria). Gion-masturi (festival float). Okuribi (fire to send off spirits at Mt. Nyoigatake). Jidai-matsuri (royal carriage) 50y. × 4 se-tenant.

Chiba. Flower, tree and bubbles. (National Re-afforestation Campaign). 50y.

Ibaraki. Mt. Tsukuba, woman in boat and iris. 80y.

Fukushima. Tsurugajou Castle and persimmons. 80y.

Ishikawa. Fukada Kyuya and Mt. Hakusan. (birth centenary of Fukada Kyuya (writer and mountaineer). 80y.

Okinawa. Monorail, Shurijo Castle and coral tree. Monorail, Naha Airport, and hibiscus. 80y. se-tenant

Shizuoka. Football players, Mt. Fuji and azaleas. (58th National Athletic Meets). 50y

Tokyo. Ume blossom. Fuji (wisteria). Hanashobu (irises). Chanohana (tea blossom). 50y. × 2 se-tenant

Ishikawa. Morning glories. Chiyojo (poet). 80y. × 2 se-tenant.

Mie. Ozu Yasujiro and Mitchel camera. (Birth Centenary of Ozu Yasujiro (film director)). 80y.

JAPANESE TAIWAN (FORMOSA)

From 1895 to 1945 Taiwan was part of the Japanese Empire, using the stamps of Japan. During 1945 American naval and air forces disrupted communications between Taiwan and Japan. The following were issued when supplies of Japanese stamps ran short.

1 Numeral and Chrysanthemum

1945. Imperf.

J1	**1**	3s. red	25·00	28·00
J2		5s. green	25·00	23·00
J3		10s. blue	35·00	35·00

JAPANESE OCCUPATION OF CHINA Pt. 17

100 cents = 1 dollar.

I. KWANGTUNG

Japanese troops occupied Canton in 1938 and by 1945 had overrun much of Kwangtung province. Unoverprinted stamps of China were used until the following stamps were issued.

(**1** "Special for Kwangtung")

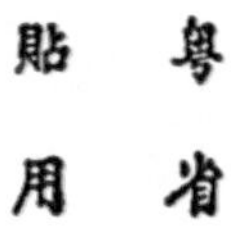

(**2**)

1942. Stamps of China optd with T **1**.

1	–	1c. orange (411)	70	1·25
2	**77**	1c. orange	90	1·50
3	**58**	2c. green	7·50	4·25
4	**72**	3c. red	50	1·25
5	**77**	5c. green	95	1·00
7	**72**	8c. olive	1·25	60
8	**77**	8c. green	1·40	1·25
9	**72**	10c. green	1·25	1·10
11	**77**	10c. emerald	2·00	2·00
12	**72**	16c. brown	2·50	2·75
13		17c. green	2·75	3·25
14	–	20c. blue (519)	2·75	2·50
15	**72**	30c. red	2·50	2·50
16	**77**	30c. red	3·00	3·50
17	**72**	50c. blue	3·75	3·00
18	**77**	50c. blue	3·00	2·25
19	**72**	$1 sepia and brown	6·00	5·00
20		$2 brown and blue	6·00	5·00
21		$5 green and red	7·00	4·50
22		$10 violet and green	12·00	7·50
23		$20 blue and purple	8·00	5·50

1942. Stamps of China optd with T **2**. (a) On 1938 issue.

24	**72**	2c. green	30	1·00
25		3c. red	30	1·00
26		5c. green	35	25
28		8c. green	30	30
29		10c. green	55	75
30		16c. brown	60	1·50
31		25c. blue	1·25	2·25
32		30c. red	1·50	2·25
33		50c. blue	1·25	1·25
35		$1 brown and red	5·00	5·50
37		$2 brown and blue	5·00	6·00
39		$5 green and red	6·50	6·50
40		$10 violet and green	12·00	9·00
42		$20 blue and purple	7·00	10·00

(b) On 1941 issue.

44	**77**	2c. blue	25	1·50
45		5c. green	25	1·25
46		8c. orange	90	2·25
47		8c. green	70	2·25
48		10c. green	75	2·25
49		17c. green	75	3·00
50		25c. purple	1·00	2·75
51		30c. red	1·00	2·25
52		50c. blue	1·25	2·25
53		$1 black and brown	6·00	4·50
54		$2 black and blue	6·00	4·25
55		$5 black and red	9·00	7·00
56		$10 black and green	10·00	8·00
57		$20 black and purple	7·00	6·00

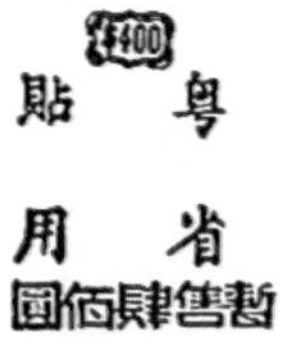

(**3**)

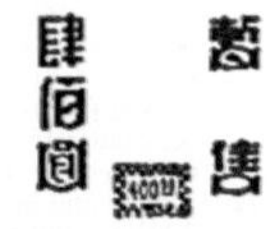

(**4**)

1945. Canton provisionals. Surch as T **3**.

58	**72**	$200 on 10c. green (No. 29)	55·00	45·00
59		$400 on 8c. olive (No. 28)	55·00	45·00

1945. Swatow provisional. No. 508 of China surch with T **4**.

60	$400 on 1c. orange	£375	£300

POSTAGE DUE STAMP

(D **3**)

1945. Postage Due stamp of China surch with Type D **3**.

D58	D **62**	$100 on $2 orange	£400	£400

II. MENGKIANG (INNER MONGOLIA)

The autonomous area of Mengkiang ("the Mongolian Borderlands"), consisting of Suiyuan, South Chahar and North Shansi, was established by the Japanese in November, 1937.

For the first issue in 1941 see the note at the beginning of III North China.

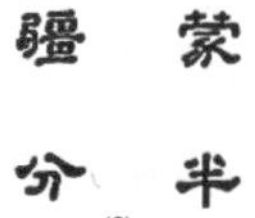

(**3**)

1942. Stamps of China optd "Mengkiang" and surch half original value at T **3**.

86	–	½c. on 1c. orange (411)	1·00	1·00
93	**58**	1c. on 2c. green	1·00	1·00
69	**72**	1c. on 2c. green	75	75
94	**58**	2c. on 4c. green	10	50
87	**60**	2c. on 4c. lilac	3·25	2·25
72	**72**	4c. on 8c. green	1·50	75
73		5c. on 10c. green	1·50	1·50
99	–	5c. on 10c. purple (515)	75	1·75
95	**72**	8c. on 16c. brown	1·25	40
68	**58**	10c. on 20c. blue	28·00	23·00
100	–	10c. on 20c. red (418)	75	1·75
88	–	10c. on 20c. blue (519)	2·50	2·25
101	–	15c. on 30c. purple (542)	2·25	2·00
75	**72**	15c. on 30c. red	3·00	3·25
102	–	20c. on 40c. orange (524)	3·25	2·25
103	–	25c. on 50c. green (525)	2·75	2·25
77	**72**	25c. on 50c. blue	5·00	5·50
96		50c. on $1 sepia and brown	6·00	6·00
82		$1 on $2 brown and blue	9·00	9·00
98		$5 on $10 violet and green	30·00	30·00
84		$10 on $20 blue and purple	75·00	65·00

4 Dragon Pillar, Peking

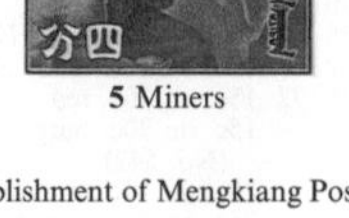

5 Miners

1943. 5th Anniv of Establishment of Mengkiang Post and Telegraph Service.

104	**4**	4c. orange	2·00	2·50
105		8c. blue	2·00	2·50

1943. 2nd Anniv of War in East Asia.

106	5	4c. green	2·00	2·75
107		8c. red	2·00	2·75

6 Stylized Horse

7 Prince Yun

8 Blast Furnace

1943. 1st Anniv of Federation of Autonomous Governments of Mongolian Provinces.

108	6	3c. red	1·50	2·75
109	7	8c. blue	1·50	2·75

1944. Productivity Campaign.

110	8	8c. brown	2·00	3·50

1945. Stamps of China optd "Mengkiang" as top characters in T **3**.

117	–	1c. orange (411)	50	50
111	58	2c. green	1·25	1·00
112		4c. green	4·50	3·00
113		5c. green	1·75	1·00
118	–	8c. orange (514)	10	35
119	–	10c. purple (515)	10	40
120	–	20c. red (418)	15	40
121	–	30c. red (542)	15	50
122	–	40c. orange (524)	10	50
123	–	50c. green (525)	70	80
114	72	$1 sepia and brown	2·75	2·25
115		$2 brown and blue	7·00	5·50
116		$5 green and red	24·00	17·00

(10)

1945. Stamps of China optd "Mengkiang" (as T **3** of North China) and surch as T **10**.

124B	60	10c. on ½c. sepia	50	2·00
126B	–	10c. on 1c. orange (411)	25	2·00
135	58	50c. on 2c. olive	55	2·25
130	72	50c. on 2c. olive	35	2·50
136	58	50c. on 4c. green	2·00	3·75
131	60	50c. on 4c. lilac	85	3·25
137	58	50c. on 5c. green	50	2·50
132B	72	50c. on 5c. olive	50	2·00
138	–	$1 on 8c. orange (514)	15	3·25

III. NORTH CHINA

The Japanese conquered North China in 1937 and formed a puppet Government in Peking.

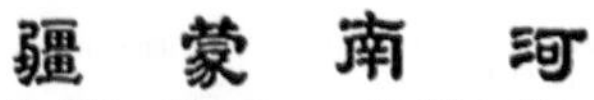
(2 of Meng Kiang "Mengkiang") (B. "Honan")

(D. "Hopeh") (E. "Shansi")

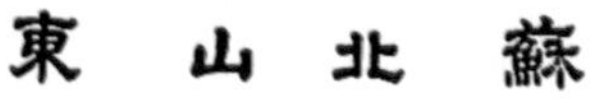
(H. "Shantung") (J. "Supeh")

Type **2** of Meng Kiang and **B** to **J** are the six "district" overprints comprising North China (including Mengkiang) and a detailed list of the overprints on the stamps of China is given in the Stanley Gibbons' Catalogue, Part 17 (China).

(1) (2)

In 1942 stamps of China overprinted with Types **B** to **J** were further overprinted with Type **1** (to commemorate the Fall of Singapore) or with Type **2** (to commemorate the tenth Anniversary of Manchukuo). These stamps are also listed in the Stanley Gibbons' Catalogue Part 17 (China).

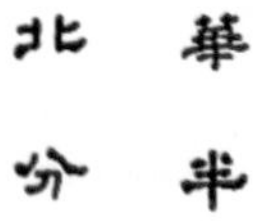
(3)

1942. Stamps of China optd "Hwa Pei" (= North China) and surch half original value at T **3**.

111	–	½c. on 1c. orange (No. 411)	45	45
128	58	1c. on 2c. olive	75	20
114	–	1c. on 2c. blue (No. 509)	1·50	1·00
88	72	1c. on 2c. olive	50	40
129	58	2c. on 4c. green	10	10
116	60	2c. on 4c. lilac	1·10	1·10
134	–	4c. on 8c. orange (No. 514)	10	10
91	72	4c. on 8c. olive	60	25
120	–	5c. on 10c. pur (No. 515)	2·25	2·25
92	72	5c. on 10c. green	80	25
130		8c. on 16c. olive	75	20
135	–	10c. on 20c. lake (No. 418)	40	10
122	–	10c. on 20c. blue (No. 519)	75	1·10
96	72	15c. on 30c. red	1·50	1·10
136	–	15c. on 30c. purple (No. 542)	45	10
137	–	20c. on 40c. orge (No. 542)	1·00	15
138	–	25c. on 50c. grn (No. 525)	1·25	25
98	72	25c. on 50c. blue	1·10	85
131		50c. on $1 brown and red	3·00	1·25
132		$1 on $2 brown and blue	6·00	5·50
133		$5 on $10 violet and green	20·00	15·00
109		$10 on $20 blue and purple	60·00	40·00

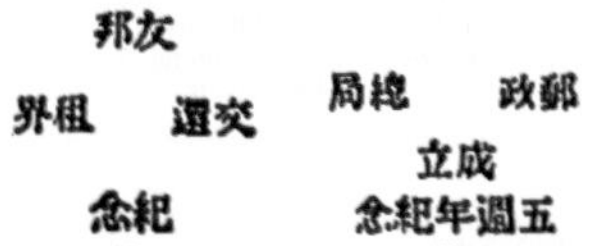
(4) (5)

1943. Return to China of Foreign Concessions. Optd with T **4**.

139	58	2c. on 4c. green (No. 129)	2·00	2·00
140	72	4c. on 8c. olive (No. 91)	2·00	2·00
141		8c. on 16c. olive (No. 130)	2·00	2·00

1943. 5th Anniv of Directorate-General of Posts for North China. Optd with T **5**.

142	58	2c. on 4c. green (No. 129)	2·00	2·00
143	72	4c. on 8c. olive (No. 91)	2·00	2·00
144		8c. on 16c. olive (No. 130)	2·00	2·00

1943. Stamps of China optd "Hwa Pei" as top characters in T **3**.

164	–	1c. orange (No. 411)	20	25
153	58	2c. olive	10	15
154		4c. green	10	10
155		5c. green	10	10
156	72	9c. olive	15	25
165	–	10c. purple (No. 515)	10	15
145	72	10c. green	3·00	1·50
157		16c. olive	15	15
158		18c. olive	20	25
166	–	20c. lake (No. 418)	15	15
167	–	30c. red (as No. 542)	10	15
168	–	40c. orange (No. 524)	15	15
169	–	50c. green (No. 525)	20	15
159	72	$1 brown and red	5·00	1·00
160		$2 brown and blue	2·75	75
161		$5 green and red	4·00	2·25
162		$10 violet and green	7·00	5·50
163		$20 blue and purple	8·00	6·50

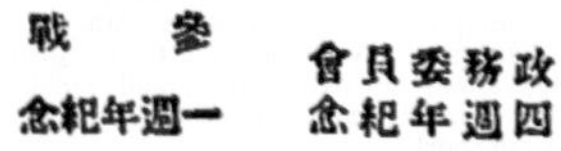
(6) (7)

1944. 1st Anniv of Declaration of War on Allies by Japanese-controlled Nanking Govt. Optd with T **6**.

170	58	4c. green (No. 154)	3·00	3·00
171	72	10c. green (No. 149)	3·00	3·00

1944. 4th Anniv of North China Political Council. Optd with T **7**.

172	72	9c. olive (No. 156)	2·00	2·00
173		18c. olive (No. 158)	2·00	2·25
174	–	50c. green (No. 169)	2·00	2·25
175	72	$1 brown and red (No. 159)	4·00	3·00

(8) (9)

1944. Stamps of Japanese Occupation of Shanghai and Nanking optd "Hwa Pei" and surch as T **8**.

176	5	9c. on 50c. orange	2·00	2·25
177		18c. on $1 green	2·25	2·25
178	6	36c. on $2 blue	3·00	2·75
179		90c. on $5 red	3·25	3·00

1944. 6th Anniv of Directorate-General of Posts for North China. Optd with T **9**.

180	72	9c. olive (No. 156)	2·00	2·25
181		18c. olive (No. 158)	2·00	2·25
182	–	50c. green (No. 169)	2·50	2·25
183	72	$1 brown and red (No. 159)	5·00	3·25

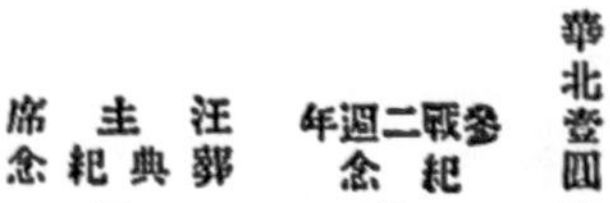
(10) (11) (12)

1944. Death of Wang Ching-wei. Optd with T **10**.

184	–	20c. lake (No. 166)	2·25	2·25
185	–	50c. green (No. 169)	2·25	2·25
186	72	$1 brown and red (No. 159)	3·00	2·50
187		$2 brown and blue (No. 160)	3·00	2·75

1945. 2nd Anniv of Declaration of War on Allies by Nanking Govt. Optd with T **11**.

188	–	20c. lake (No. 166)	2·25	2·25
189	–	50c. green (No. 169)	2·25	2·25
190	72	$1 brown and red (No. 159)	3·00	2·50
191		$2 brown and blue (No. 160)	3·00	2·75

1945. Stamps of Japanese Occupation of Shanghai and Nanking surch as T **12**.

192	7	50c. on $3 orange	4·50	6·25
193		$1 on $6 blue	4·50	6·25

13 Dragon Pillar

14 Long Bridge

15 Imperial City Tower

16 Marble Boat, Summer Palace

17

1945. 5th Anniv of Establishment of North China Political Council. Views of Peking.

194	13	$1 yellow	1·25	1·50
195	14	$2 blue	1·50	1·50
196	15	$5 red	1·50	1·25
197	16	$10 green	2·00	1·75

1945. Optd "Hwa Pei" as top characters in T **3**.

198	17	$1 brown	1·25	25
199		$2 blue	1·40	15
200		$5 red	1·50	45
201		$10 green	1·75	1·00
202		$20 purple	3·25	1·10
203		$50 brown	15·00	8·50

18 Wutai Mountain, Shansi

19 Kaifeng Iron Pagoda, Honan

20 International Bridge, Tientsin

21 Taishan Mountain, Shantung

22 G.P.O., Peking

1945. 7th Anniv of Directorate-General of Posts for North China.

204	18	$5 green	60	1·25
205	19	$10 brown	65	1·10
206	20	$20 purple	75	1·10
207	21	$30 grey	1·00	1·00
208	22	$50 red	1·10	1·00

IV. NANKING AND SHANGHAI

The Japanese captured Shanghai and Nanking in 1937 and Hankow in 1938. During the same year Nanking was made the seat of Japanese-controlled administration for the Yangtse Basin. The stamps listed below were used in parts of Anhwei, Southern Kiangsu, Chekiang, Hupeh, Kiangsi, Hunan and Fukien.

N.B. With the exception of Nos. 114 to 119 the following are all surcharged on stamps of China.

(1)

1941. Air. Surch as T **1**.

1	61	10s. on 50c. brown	25	2·50
2		18s. on 90c. olive	60	3·50
4		20s. on $1 green	1·00	4·00
5		25s. on 90c. olive	25	2·75
6		35s. on $2 brown	25	2·50
7		60s. on 35s. on $2 brn (No. 6)	25	3·50

(2)

1943. Return to China of Shanghai Concessions. Surch as T **2**.

8	72	25c. on 5c. green	2·00	1·75
9	77	50c. on 8c. orange	2·00	1·75
10	72	$1 on 16c. olive	2·00	1·75
11	77	$2 on 50c. blue	2·00	1·75

1943. As No. 422 but colour changed. Issued at Shanghai.

12	72	15c. brown	15·00	16·00

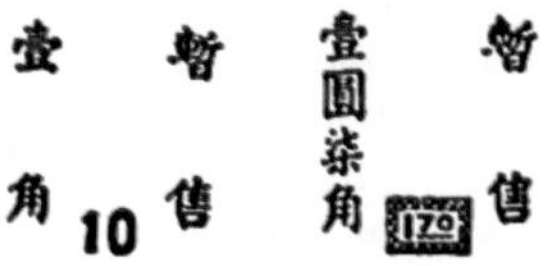
(3) (4)

1943. Stamps of China and No. 12 above surch as T **3** (cent values) or T **4** (dollar values).

(a) On T **58**.

13	58	$6 on 5c. green	1·50	2·50
14		$20 on 15c. red	1·50	1·75
15		$500 on 15c. green	1·50	1·75
17		$1000 on 20c. blue	2·75	3·25
18		$1000 on 25c. blue	3·00	3·25

(b) On Martyrs issue (as T **60**).

88	60	$7.50 on ½c. sepia	35	4·50
89	–	$15 on 1c. orange	25	1·50
91	–	$30 on 2c. blue	45	1·50
93	–	$200 on 1c. orange	40	1·00
94	–	$200 on 8c. orange	45	1·25

(c) On T **72**.

19	72	25c. on 5c. green	50	2·25
20		30c. on 2c. green	1·00	2·50
21		50c. on 3c. red	10	45
22		50c. on 5c. green	20	40
23		50c. on 8c. green	1·00	1·75
24		$1 on 8c. green	10	15
26		$1 on 15c. brown	70	1·00
27		$1.30 on 16c. brown	10	1·00
28		$1.50 on 3c. red	10	50
54		$1.70 on 30c. red	1·40	2·75
55		$2 on 5c. green	15	45
30		$2 on 10c. green	10	40
56		$2 on $1 sepia and brown	4·00	3·50
59		$3 on 8c. green	10	15
31		$3 on 15c. brown	25	50
32		$4 on 16c. brown	30	50
33		$5 on 15c. brown	75	60
61		$6 on 5c. green	50	75
62		$6 on 8c. green	15	35
38		$6 on 10c. green	50	70
39		$10 on 10c. green	10	30
40		$10 on 16c. brown	10	20
41		$20 on 3c. red	10	40
42		$20 on 15c. red	2·00	4·00
43		$20 on 15c. brown	35	1·00
64		$20 on $2 brown and blue	1·75	2·25
65		$50 on 30c. red	75	1·90
66		$50 on 50c. blue	75	2·00
67		$50 on $5 green and red	1·25	2·00
68		$50 on $20 blue and purple	2·25	3·00
45		$100 on 3c. red	1·00	1·00
83		$100 on $10 violet and green	45	75
84		$200 on $20 blue and purple	45	75
46		$500 on 8c. green	1·75	2·25
47		$500 on 10c. green	1·50	2·25
48		$500 on 15c. red	4·00	3·50
49		$500 on 15c. brown	3·50	3·25
50		$500 on 16c. brown	2·50	3·25
51		$1000 on 25c. blue	3·00	4·25
86		$1000 on 30c. red	2·00	3·50
75		$1000 on 50c. blue	2·50	3·50
76		$1000 on $2 brown and blue	2·25	4·75
77		$2000 on $5 green and red	2·50	3·75
87a		$5000 on $10 violet & green	15·00	18·00

(d) On T **77**.

95	77	5c. on ½c. sepia	10	1·50
96		10c. on 1c. orange	10	1·25
97		20c. on 1c. orange	15	1·00
98		40c. on 5c. green	10	1·10
99		$5 on 5c. green	15	35
100		$10 on 10c. green	35	70
101		$50 on ½c. sepia	25	50
102		$50 on 1c. orange	35	50
103		$50 on 17c. olive	75	1·00
104		$200 on 5c. green	50	1·00
105		$200 on 8c. green	60	1·10
106		$200 on 8c. orange	1·25	2·00
107		$500 on $5 black and red	1·75	3·00
108		$1000 on 1c. orange	1·50	2·75
109		$1000 on 25c. purple	1·75	2·50
110		$1000 on 30c. red	2·00	2·75
111		$1000 on $2 black and blue	2·25	3·00
112		$1000 on $10 black & green	2·75	2·75
113		$2000 on $5 black and red	3·25	3·00

5 Wheat and Cotton Flower

6 Purple Mountain, Nanking

1944. 4th Anniv of Establishment of Chinese Puppet Government at Nanking.

114	5	50c. orange	10	50
115		$1 green	10	50
116	6	$2 blue	10	50
117		$5 red	10	50

7 Map of Shanghai and Foreign Concessions

1944. 1st Anniv of Return to China of Shanghai Foreign Concessions.

118	7	$3 orange	35	1·50
119		$6 blue	35	1·50

1945. 5th Anniv of Establishment of Chinese Puppet Government at Nanking. Surch as T 4.

124	5	$15 on 50c. orange	10	1·50
125		$30 on $1 green	10	1·50
126	6	$60 on $2 blue	10	1·50
127		$200 on $5 red	10	1·25

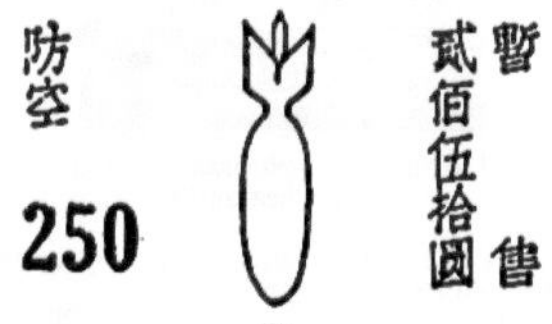

(9)

1945. Air Raid Precautions Propaganda. Air stamps surch as T 9.

128	61	$150 on 15c. green	75	1·25
129		$250 on 25c. orange	75	1·25
130		$600 on 60c. blue	75	1·25
131		$1000 on $1 green	75	1·25

POSTAGE DUE STAMPS

(D 8)

1945. Postage Due stamps surch as Type D 8.

D120	D 62	$1 on 2c. orange	35	2·75
D121		$2 on 5c. orange	35	2·50
D122		$5 on 10c. orange	35	2·50
D123		$10 on 20c. orange	35	2·25

JAPANESE OCCUPATION OF NETHERLANDS INDIES Pt. 4

The Japanese occupied the Netherlands Indies from March 1942 to 1945.

100 sen (cents) = 1 rupee (gulden).

I. JAVA

1 Eastern Asia

1943. 1st Anniv of Japanese Occupation of Java.

1	1	2s. brown	4·00	3·25
2	–	3½s. red	4·00	3·25
3	–	5s. green	5·50	3·25
4	–	10s. blue	15·00	4·00

DESIGNS: 3½s. Farmer ploughing ricefield; 5s. Mt. Soemer; 10s. Bantam Bay.

2 Native soldier

3 Wayang puppet

5 Bird of Vishnu and Mt. Soemer

1943. Savings Campaign.

5	2	3½c. red	13·00	6·00
6		10c. blue	15·00	2·25

1943. Designs with rectangular panel of characters as at foot of T 3 and 5.

7	–	3½c. red	2·75	1·75
8	3	5c. green	2·75	1·75
9	–	10c. blue	3·00	1·75
10	–	20c. olive	4·00	3·00
11	–	40c. purple	7·25	4·00
12	5	60c. orange	19·00	4·75
13	–	80c. brown	22·00	8·00
14	–	1r. violet	50·00	5·50

DESIGNS—As Type 3: 3½c. Native head; 10c. Boroboudur Temple; 20c. Map of Java; 40c. Seated dancer and Temple. As Type 5: 80c. Ploughing with oxen; 1r. Terraced ricefields.

II. SUMATRA

6 Lake Toba

1943. Designs with rectangular panel characters as at foot of T 6.

15	–	1c. olive	1·90	1·50
16	–	2c. green	1·90	1·50
17	–	3c. blue	1·90	1·50
18	–	3½c. red	3·50	1·50
19	–	4c. blue	2·50	1·50
20	–	5c. orange	1·90	1·10
21	–	10c. blue	5·00	1·10
22	–	20c. brown	2·50	1·10
23	6	30c. purple	2·75	1·90
24		40c. brown	3·25	2·10
25	–	50c. bistre	7·75	3·25
26	–	1r. violet	40·00	5·25

DESIGNS: 1c. to 3c. Batak house; 3½c. to 5c. Minangkabau house; 10c., 20c. Ploughing with oxen; 50c., 1r. Carabao Canyon (20 × 28 mm).

(7)

1944. Various stamps optd with T 7. (a) On Netherlands Indies stamps of 1933.

37A	46	1c. violet	60	1·60
38A		2c. purple	60	1·60
39A		2½c. bistre	60	1·60
40A		3c. green	27·00	38·00
27A		3½c. grey	80	1·90
50B	67	10c. red	1·00	1·60
42B	47	15c. blue	1·75	5·25
43B		20c. purple	90	1·60
44B		25c. green	1·75	2·75
45A		30c. blue	20·00	27·00
46B		35c. violet	1·75	2·75
47B		40c. green	2·75	2·75
34A		42½c. yellow	45·00	50·00
35A		50c. blue	20·00	27·00
48A		2g. green	£400	£550
36A		2g.50 purple	£250	£325
49B		5g. bistre	18·00	27·00

(b) On Nos. 429/44 of Netherlands Indies.

28A	–	10c. red	10·00	13·50
52B	–	15c. blue	1·90	2·75
53B	–	17½c. orange	1·75	2·75
43A	–	20c. mauve	15·00	27·00
44A	–	25c. green	3·75	6·50
56B	–	30c. brown	1·25	2·75
57A	–	35c. purple	18·00	9·00
58B	–	40c. green	1·90	4·00
59B	–	50c. red	2·75	3·25
60B	–	60c. blue	2·50	3·25
61B	–	80c. red	3·25	4·25
62B	–	1g. violet	4·00	5·50
63B	–	2g. green	3·50	5·50
64A	–	5g. brown	£170	£225
65A	–	10g. green	35·00	55·00
66A	68	25g. orange	£325	£450

(c) On Nos. 463/6 of Netherlands Indies.

66	–	3c. green	80	2·00
67	71	4c. green	80	2·00
68	–	5c. blue	80	2·00
69	–	7½c. violet	80	2·00

(d) On Nos. 506 and 509 of Netherlands.

70	94	5c. green	9·75	12·25
71		12½c. blue	4·75	10·50

III. JAPANESE NAVAL CONTROL AREA

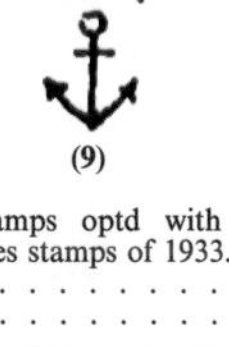

(9)

1942. Various stamps optd with T 9. (a) On Netherlands Indies stamps of 1933.

89	46	1c. violet	4·00	16·00
90		2c. purple	90	3·50
91		2½c. bistre	75	3·50
92		3c. green	70	3·50
83		4c. green	25·00	40·00
84		5c. blue	10·00	15·00
95	47	10c. red	50·00	65·00
96		15c. blue	9·00	14·00
97		20c. purple	95	3·50
98		25c. green	4·25	8·00
86		30c. blue	40·00	40·00
100		35c. violet	95	3·50
101		40c. green	95	3·50
88		50c. blue	55·00	75·00
102		80c. red	£200	£300
103		1g. violet		
104		2g. green		
105		5g. bistre		

(b) On Nos. 270 and 360 of Netherlands Indies.

107	–	5c. blue	1·00	3·25
106	48	30c. blue	£225	£325

(c) On Nos. 429/44 of Netherlands Indies.

108	–	10c. red	3·00	4·00
110	–	15c. blue	3·75	15·00
111	–	17½c. orange	1·10	4·00
112	–	20c. mauve	22·00	32·00
113	–	25c. green	27·00	42·00
114	–	30c. brown	4·00	10·00
115	–	35c. purple	45·00	55·00
116	–	40c. green	18·00	26·00
117	–	50c. red	9·50	11·00
118	–	60c. blue	4·50	8·50
119	–	80c. red	8·00	14·00
120	–	1g. violet	6·00	11·00
121	–	2g. green	40·00	65·00
122	–	5g. brown		
123	68	25g. orange		

(d) On Nos. 462/6 of Netherlands Indies.

124	–	2½c. purple	4·50	7·50
125	–	3c. green	2·00	3·75
126	71	4c. green	2·75	8·50
127	–	5c. blue	6·00	14·00
128	–	7½c. violet	90	4·00

(e) On Nos. 506 and 509 of Netherlands.

129	94	5c. green		
130		12½c. blue		

1943. Air. Nos. 89 and 91 surch.

148	46	"f. 2" on 1c. violet	12·50	20·00
151		"f. 8.50" on 2½c. bistre	12·00	18·00

10 Japanese Flag and Palms

11 Mt. Fuji, Flag and Bird

1943.

152	10	2c. brown	80	16·00
153		3c. green	80	16·00
154		3½c. orange	1·40	15·00
155		5c. blue	80	12·00
156		10c. red	80	12·00
157		15c. blue	90	12·00
158		20c. violet	90	12·00
159	11	25c. orange	3·00	14·00
160		30c. blue	3·00	15·00
161		50c. green	6·00	23·00
162		1g. purple	27·00	30·00

POSTAGE DUE STAMPS

1942. Netherlands Indies Postage Due stamps of 1913 and 1937 optd with T 9.

D142	1c. orange	6·75	13·50
D132	2½c. orange	1·50	3·50
D133	3½c. orange	3·25	6·75
D134	5c. orange	1·75	3·50
D135	7½c. orange	1·75	3·50
D136	10c. orange	1·25	3·50
D144	15c. orange	1·75	3·50
D137	20c. orange	1·75	3·50
D138	20c. on 37½c. orange	50·00	80·00
D139	25c. orange	1·50	3·50
D140	30c. orange	3·75	8·25
D146	40c. orange	2·00	4·00
D147	1g. blue	5·75	10·00

JAPANESE OCCUPATION OF PHILIPPINES Pt. 22

100 centavos or sentimos = 1 peso.

1942. Stamps of Philippines optd with bars or surch also.

J1	104	2c. green	10	10
J4a	–	5c. on 6c. brn (No. 526)	10	10
J2	–	12c. black (No. 529)	10	15
J3	–	16c. blue (No. 530)	3·50	2·50
J5	–	16c. on 30c. red (No. 505)	20	20
J6	–	50c. on 1p. black and orange (No. 534)	50	55
J7	–	1p. on 4p. black and blue (No. 508)	75·00	85·00

1942. No. 460 of Philippines surch **CONGRATULATIONS FALL OF BATAAN AND CORREGIDOR 1942 2.**

J8	2c. on 4c. green	4·00	4·00

J 4 Agricultural Produce

1942. Red Cross Fund.

J 9	J 4	2c.+1c. violet	15	15
J10		5c.+1c. green	15	15
J11		16c.+2c. orange	17·00	16·00

1942. 1st Anniv of "Greater East Asia War". No. 460 of Philippines surch with native characters, **12-8-1942** and **5.**

J12	5c. on 4c. green	40	35

1943. 1st Anniv of Philippine Executive Commission. Nos. 566 and 569 of Philippines surch with native characters, **1-23-43** and value.

J13	105	2c. on 8c. red	30	30
J14		5c. on 1p. sepia	45	45

J 7 Nipa Hut

J 9 Mt. Mayon and Mt. Fuji

1943.

J15	J 7	1c. orange	10	10
J16	–	2c. green	10	10
J17	J 7	4c. green	10	10
J18	J 9	5c. brown	10	10
J19	–	6c. red	10	10
J20	J 9	10c. blue	10	10
J21	–	12c. blue	80	80
J22	–	16c. brown	10	10
J23	J 7	20c. purple	95	95
J24	J 9	21c. violet	30	30
J25	–	25c. brown	10	10
J26	J 9	1p. red	55	55
J27	–	2p. purple	3·75	3·75
J28	–	5p. olive	6·50	6·00

DESIGNS—VERT: 2, 6, 25c. Rice planter; 12, 16c., 2, 5p. Morro vinta (sailing canoe).

J 11 Map of Manila Bay

1943. 1st Anniv of Fall of Bataan and Corregidor.

J29	J 11	2c. red	20	20
J30		5c. green	20	20

1943. 350th Anniv of Printing in the Philippines. No. 531 of Philippines surch **Limbagan 1593–1943** and value.

J31	12c. on 20c. bistre	25	25

J 13 Filipino Girl

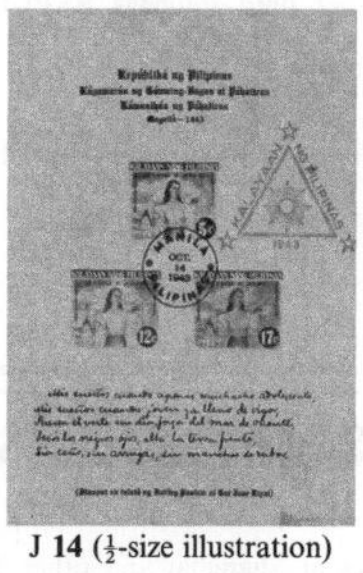

J 14 (½-size illustration)

1943. Japanese Declaration of the "Independence of the Philippines". Imperf or perf. (a)

J32	J 13	5c. blue	15	15
J33		12c. orange	15	15
J34		17c. red	15	15

(b) Miniature sheet, 127 × 177 mm containing Nos. J32/4.

MSJ35	J 14	(sold at 2p.50)	75·00	14·50

1943. Luzon Flood Relief. Surch **BAHA 1943** + and premium.

J36	–	12c.+21c. blue (No. J21)	15	15
J37	J 7	20c.+36c. purple	10	10
J38	J 9	21c.+40c. violet	10	10

J 17 Rev. Jose Burgos

J 24 Jose P. Laurel

J 19 (½-size illustration)

1944. National Heroes. Imperf or perf. (a)

J39	–	5c. blue (Rizal)	20	20
J40	J 17	12c. red	10	10
J41	–	17c. orange (Mabini)	15	15

(b) Miniature sheet 101 × 143 mm containing Nos. J39/41. Without gum.

MSJ42	J 19	(sold at 1p.)	3·25	5·25

1944. 2nd Anniv of Fall of Bataan and Corregidor. Nos. 567/8 of Philippines surch **REPUBLIKA NG PILIPINAS 5-7-44** and value.

J43	105	5c. on 20c. blue	45	45
J44		12c. on 60c. green	95	95

1945. 1st Anniv of Republican Government. Imperf.

J45	J 24	5s. brown	10	10
J46		7s. green	10	10
J47		20s. blue	10	10

POSTAGE DUE STAMP

1942. Postage Due stamp of Philippines surch **3 CVOS. 3** and bar.

JD9	D 51	3c. on 4c. red	23·00	13·00

OFFICIAL STAMPS

1943. Stamps of Philippines optd variously with bars, **(K.P.)** and Japanese characters or surch also.

JO29	104	2c. green (No. 563)	10	10
JO30	–	5c. on 6c. brown (No. 526)	15	15
JO32	–	16c. on 30c. red (No. 505)	40	40

1944. No. 526 of Philippines surch **5 REPUBLIKA NG PILIPINAS (K.P.)** and four bars.

JO45		5c. on 6c. brown	10	10

1944. Official stamp of Philippines (No. 531 optd **O.B.**), further optd **Pilipinas REPUBLIKA K.P.** and bars.

JO46		20c. bistre	30	30

1944. Air stamp of Philippines optd **REPUBLIKA NG PILIPINAS (K.P.)** and two bars.

JO47	105	1p. sepia	55	60

JAPANESE POST OFFICES IN CHINA Pt. 17

Post Offices at Shanghai and other Treaty Ports operated between 1876 and 1922.

10 rin = 1 sen; 100 sen = 1 yen.

(1)

1900. Stamps of Japan, 1899, optd with T **1**.

1	28	5r. grey	4·50	5·00
2		½s. grey	3·25	1·75
3		1s. brown	3·50	1·25
4		1½s. blue	10·00	4·00
5		1½s. violet	5·50	1·50
6		2s. green	6·00	1·50
7		3s. purple	7·00	1·00
8		3s. red	4·50	1·00
9		4s. red	7·00	2·25
10		5s. yellow	16·00	2·25
11	29	6s. red	20·00	16·00
12		8s. green	13·00	15·00
13		10s. blue	11·00	1·00
14		15s. purple	20·00	2·00
15		20s. orange	20·00	1·25
16	30	25s. green	40·00	10·00
17		50s. brown	45·00	2·00
18	31	1y. red	75·00	3·00
19	32	5y. green	£475	75·00
20		10y. violet	£750	£130

1900. Imperial Wedding issue of Japan optd with T **1**.

21	33	3s. red	50·00	35·00

1913. Stamps of Japan, 1913, optd with T **1**.

33	36	½s. brown	3·00	2·00
34		1s. orange	3·00	2·00
35		1½s. blue	3·25	2·00
36		2s. green	4·25	2·00
37		3s. red	3·00	1·00
38	37	4s. red	12·00	10·00
39		5s. violet	16·00	3·00
40		6s. brown	30·00	30·00
41		8s. grey	40·00	40·00
42		10s. blue	15·00	2·00
43		20s. red	35·00	6·00
44		25s. olive	45·00	8·00
45	38	30s. brown	75·00	50·00
46		50s. brown	£100	50·00
47		1y. green and brown	£140	10·00
48		5y. green	£1500	£600
49		10y. violet	£2500	£1500

JAPANESE POST OFFICES IN KOREA Pt. 18

10 rin = 1 sen; 100 sen = 1 yen.

(1)

1900. Stamps of Japan, 1899, optd with T **1**.

1	28	5r. grey	12·00	10·00
2		1s. brown	18·00	6·50
3a		1½s. blue	£225	£140
4		2s. green	24·00	16·00
5		3s. purple	16·00	6·00
6		4s. red	70·00	30·00
7		5s. yellow	60·00	30·00
8	29	8s. green	£225	£160
9		10s. blue	30·00	3·00
10		15s. purple	75·00	6·00
11		20s. orange	75·00	5·00
12	30	25s. green	£200	50·00
13		50s. brown	£150	18·00
14	31	1y. red	£400	14·00

1900. Wedding of Prince Imperial. No. 152 of Japan optd with T **1**.

15	33	3s. red	90·00	22·00

JASDAN Pt. 1

A state of India. Now uses Indian Stamps.

12 pies = 1 anna; 16 annas = 1 rupee.

1 Sun

1942.

4	1	1a. green	16·00	£130

JERSEY Pt. 1

Island in the English Channel off N.W. coast of France. Occupied by German forces from June 1940 to May 1945 with separate stamp issues.

The general issue of 1948 for Channel Islands and the regional issues of 1958 are listed at end of GREAT BRITAIN.

Jersey had its own postal administration from 1969.

1941. 12 pence = 1 shilling; 20 shillings = 1 pound.
1971. 100 (new) pence = 1 pound sterling.

(a) War Occupation Issues.

1

2 Old Jersey Farm

1941.

1	1	½d. green	5·25	3·75
2		1d. red	6·25	3·50

1943.

3a	2	½d. green	9·00	6·50
4	–	1d. red	2·25	50
5	–	1½d. brown	7·00	5·25
6	–	2d. yellow	6·50	2·00
7a	–	2½d. blue	1·00	1·75
8	–	3d. violet	1·25	2·75

DESIGNS: 1d. Portelet Bay; 1½d. Corbiere Lighthouse; 2d. Elizabeth Castle; 2½d. Mont Orgueil Castle; 3d. Gathering vraic (seaweed).

(b) Independent Postal Administration.

10 Elizabeth Castle

1969. Multicoloured.

15	½d. Type **10**	10	60
16	1d. La Hougue Bie (prehistoric tomb)	10	10
17	2d. Portelet Bay	10	10
18	3d. La Corbiere Lighthouse	10	10
19	4d. Mont Orgueil Castle by night	10	10
20	5d. Arms and Royal Mace	10	10
21	6d. Jersey cow	10	10
22	9d. Chart of the English Channel	10	20
23	1s. Mont Orgueil Castle by day	25	25
24	1s.6d. Chart of the English Channel	80	75
25	1s.9d. Queen Elizabeth II (after Cecil Beaton) (vert)	80	75
26	2s.6d. Jersey Airport	1·25	1·00
27	5s. Legislative Chamber	4·75	3·50
28	10s. The Royal Court	12·00	9·00
29	£1 Queen Elizabeth II (after Cecil Beaton) (vert)	1·75	1·50

24 First Day Cover

1969. Inauguration of Post Office.

30	24	4d. multicoloured	10	10
31		5d. multicoloured	20	10
32		1s.6d. multicoloured	50	75
33		1s.9d. multicoloured	80	1·00

25 Lord Coutanche, former Bailiff of Jersey

1970. 25th Anniv of Liberation. Multicoloured.

34	4d. Type **25**	20	20
35	5d. Sir Winston Churchill	20	20
36	1s.6d. "Liberation" (Edmund Blampied) (horiz)	90	1·00
37	1s.9d. S.S. "Vega" (horiz)	90	1·00

29 "A Tribute to Enid Blyton"

1970. "Battle of Flowers" Parade. Multicoloured.

38	4d. Type **29**	20	10
39	5d. "Rags to Riches" (Cinderella and pumpkin)	20	20
40	1s.6d. "Gourmet's Delight" (lobster and cornucopia)	2·75	2·25
41	1s.9d. "We're the Greatest" (ostriches)	2·75	2·25

33 Jersey Airport

1970. Decimal Currency. Nos. 15, etc, but with new colours, new design (6p.) and decimal values, as T **33**.

42	½p. multicoloured (as No. 15)	10	10
43	1p. multicoloured (as No. 18)	10	10
44	1½p. multicoloured (as No. 21)	10	10
45	2p. multicoloured (as No. 19)	10	10
46	2½p. multicoloured (as No. 20)	10	10
47	3p. multicoloured (as No. 16)	10	10
48	3½p. multicoloured (as No. 17)	10	10
49	4p. multicoloured (as No. 22)	10	10
49a	4½p. multicoloured (as No. 20)	20	20
50	5p. multicoloured (as No. 23)	10	10
50a	5½p. multicoloured (as No. 21)	40	30
51	6p. multicoloured (Martello Tower, Archirondel, 23 × 22 mm)	20	10
52	7½p. multicoloured (as No. 24)	20	15
52a	8p. multicoloured (as No. 19)	15	15
53	9p. multicoloured (as No. 25)	25	20
54	10p. multicoloured (as No. 26)	40	30
55	20p. multicoloured (as No. 27)	90	80
56	50p. multicoloured (as No. 28)	1·50	1·25

34 White Eared-pheasant ("White-eared Pheasant")

1971. Wildlife Preservation Trust (1st series). Multicoloured.

57	2p. Type **34**	20	10
58	2½p. Thick-billed parrot (vert)	20	15
59	7½p. Western black-and-white colobus monkey (vert)	2·20	1·50
60	9p. Ring-tailed lemur	3·00	1·50

See also Nos. 73/6, 217/21, 324/9, 447/51 and 824/9.

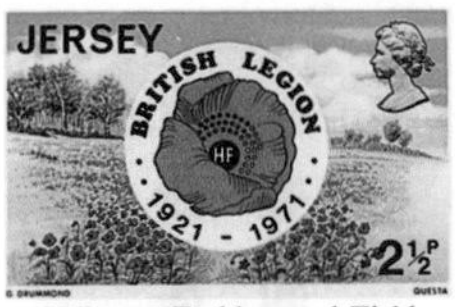

35 Poppy Emblem and Field

1971. 50th Anniv of Royal British Legion. Mult.

61	2p. Royal British Legion Badge	20	10
62	2½p. Type **35**	20	10
63	7½p. Jack Counter and Victoria Cross	1·00	1·10
64	9p. Crossed Tricolour and Union Jack	1·00	1·10

36 "Tante Elizabeth" (E. Blampied)

37 Jersey Fern

1971. Paintings (1st series). Multicoloured.

65	2p. Type **36**	15	10
66	2½p. "English Fleet in the Channel" (P. Monamy) (horiz)	20	10
67	7½p. "The Boyhood of Raleigh" (Millais) (horiz)	1·25	1·40
68	9p. "The Blind Beggar" (W. W. Ouless)	1·40	1·50

See also Nos. 115/118.

1972. Wild Flowers of Jersey. Multicoloured.

69	3p. Type **37**	20	10
70	5p. Jersey thrift	30	20
71	7½p. Jersey orchid	1·25	1·40
72	9p. Jersey viper's bugloss	1·25	1·40

1972. Wildlife Preservation Trust (2nd series). As T **34**. Multicoloured.

73	2½p. Cheetah	30	10
74	3p. Rothschild's mynah (vert)	25	20
75	7½p. Spectacled bear	50	70
76	9p. Tuatara	80	90

38 Artillery Shako

39 Princess Anne

1972. Royal Jersey Militia. Multicoloured.

77	2½p. Type **38**	10	10
78	3p. Shako (2nd North Regt.)	10	10
79	7½p. Shako (5th South-West Regt.)	30	20
80	9p. Helmet (3rd Jersey Light Infantry)	50	60

1972. Royal Silver Wedding. Multicoloured.

81	2½p. Type **39**	10	10
82	3p. Queen Elizabeth and Prince Philip (horiz)	10	10
83	7½p. Prince Charles	35	35
84	20p. The Royal Family (horiz)	35	35

40 Armorican Bronze Coins

1973. Centenary of La Societe Jersiaise. Mult.

85	2½p. Silver cups	10	10
86	3p. Gold torque (vert)	10	10
87	7½p. Royal Seal of Charles II (vert)	25	20
88	9p. Type **40**	30	30

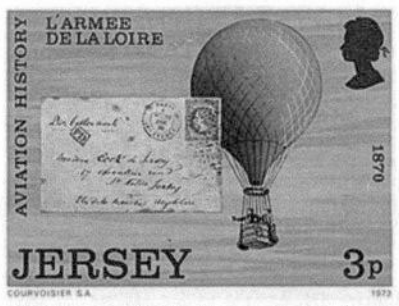

41 Balloon "L'Armee de la Loire" and Letter, Paris, 1870

1973. Jersey Aviation History. Multicoloured.

89	3p. Type **41**	10	10
90	5p. Astra seaplane, 1912	10	10
91	7½p. Supermarine Sea Eagle	35	35
92	9p. De Havilland Dragon Express "Giffard Bay"	45	45

42 "North Western", 1870

1973. Centenary of Jersey Eastern Railway. Early Locomotives. Multicoloured.

93	2½p. Type **42**	10	10
94	3p. "Calvados", 1873	10	10
95	7½p. "Carteret" at Grouville station, 1893	25	35
96	9p. "Caesarea", 1873, and route map	35	45

43 Princess Anne and Capt. Mark Phillips

1973. Royal Wedding.

97 **43**	3p. multicoloured	10	10
98	20p. multicoloured	50	50

44 Spider Crab

1973. Marine Life. Multicoloured.

99	2½p. Type **44**	10	10
100	3p. Conger eel	10	10
101	7½p. Lobster	30	35
102	20p. Tuberculate ormer	40	45

45 Freesias

47 John Wesley

46 First Letter Box and Contemporary Cover

1974. Spring Flowers. Multicoloured.

103	3p. Type **45**	10	10
104	5½p. Anemones	15	15
105	8p. Carnations and Gladioli	25	30
106	10p. Daffodils and Iris	30	35

1974. Centenary of U.P.U. Multicoloured.

107	2½p. Type **46**	10	10
108	3p. Postmen, 1862 and 1969	10	15
109	5½p. Letter-box and letter, 1974	25	20
110	20p. R.M.S. "Aquila" (1874) and B.A.C. One Eleven 200 (1974)	35	40

1974. Anniversaries.

111 **47**	3p. black and brown	10	10
112 –	3½p. violet and blue	10	10
113 –	8p. black and lilac	20	20
114 –	20p. black and stone	45	45

PORTRAITS AND EVENTS: 3p. (Bicentenary of Methodism in Jersey); 3½p. Sir William Hillary, founder (150th anniv of R.N.L.I.); 8p. Canon Wace (poet and historian) (800th death anniv; 20p. Sir Winston Churchill (Birth cent).

48 "Catherine" and "Mary" (Royal yachts)

1974. Marine Paintings by Peter Monamy. Mult.

115	3½p. Type **48**	10	10
116	5½p. French two-decker	15	10
117	8p. Dutch vessel (horiz)	25	20
118	25p. Battle of Cap La Hague, 1692 (55 × 27 mm)	55	55

49 Potato Digger

1975. 19th-century Farming. Multicoloured.

119	3p. Type **49**	10	10
120	3½p. Cider crusher	10	10
121	8p. Six-horse plough	20	20
122	10p. Hay cart	35	30

50 H.M. Queen Elizabeth, the Queen Mother (photograph by Cecil Beaton)

51 Nautilus Shell

1975. Royal Visit.

123 **50**	20p. multicoloured	50	45

1975. Jersey Tourism. Multicoloured.

124	5p. Type **51**	10	10
125	8p. Parasol	10	10
126	10p. Deckchair	30	25
127	12p. Sandcastle with flags of Jersey and the U.K.	40	35
MS128	146 × 68 mm. Nos. 124/7	90	1·10

52 Common Tern

53 Armstrong Whitworth Siskin IIIA

1975. Sea Birds. Multicoloured.

129	4p. Type **52**	10	10
130	5p. British storm petrel ("Storm-Petrel")	15	10
131	8p. Brent geese	40	25
132	25p. Shag	70	50

1975. 50th Anniv of Royal Air Force Association, Jersey Branch. Multicoloured.

133	4p. Type **53**	10	10
134	5p. Supermarine Southampton I flying boat	15	10
135	10p. Supermarine Spitfire Mk 1	40	25
136	25p. Folland Gnat T.1	70	50

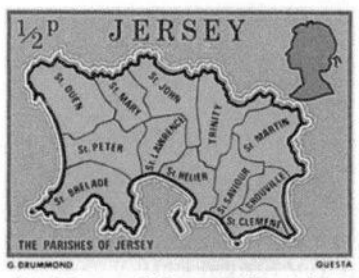

54 Map of Jersey Parishes

55 Parish Arms and Island Scene

1976. Multicoloured. (a) Parish Arms and Views.

137	½p. Type **54**	10	10
138	1p. Zoological Park	10	10
139	5p. St. Mary's Church	10	10
140	6p. Seymour Tower	10	10
141	7p. La Corbiere Lighthouse	10	10
142	8p. St. Saviour's Church	15	10
143	9p. Elizabeth Castle	15	10
144	10p. Gorey Harbour	20	10
145	11p. Jersey Airport	25	25
146	12p. Grosnez Castle	25	20
147	13p. Bonne Nuit Harbour	25	20
148	14p. Le Hocq Tower	30	20
149	15p. Morel Farm	30	25
	(b) Emblems.		
150	20p. Type **55**	45	35
151	30p. Flag and map	55	40
152	40p. Postal H.Q. and badge	80	50
153	50p. Parliament, Royal Court and arms	1·00	70
154	£1 Lieutenant-Governor's flag and Government House	3·00	1·50
155	£2 Queen Elizabeth II (vert)	4·00	2·50

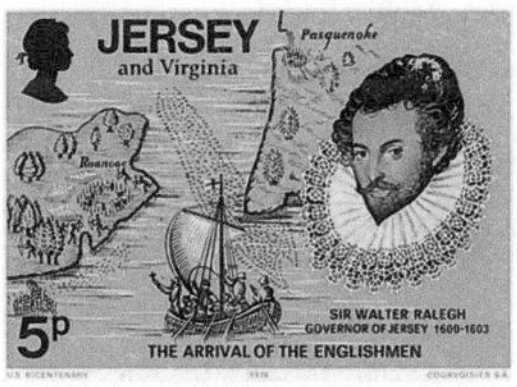

56 Sir Walter Raleigh and Map of Virginia

1976. Bicentenary of American Independence. Multicoloured.

160	5p. Type **56**	10	10
161	7p. Sir George Carteret and map of New Jersey	15	10
162	11p. Philippe Dauvergne and Long Island landing	40	25
163	13p. John Copley and sketch	50	40

57 Dr. Grandin and Map of China

1976. Birth Centenary of Dr. Lilian Grandin (medical missionary).

164 **57**	5p. multicoloured	10	10
165 –	7p. yellow, brown and black	10	10
166 –	11p. multicoloured	35	25
167 –	13p. multicoloured	50	40

DESIGNS: 7p. Sampan on the Yangtze; 11p. Overland trek; 13p. Dr. Grandin at work.

58 Coronation, 1953 (photographed by Cecil Beaton)

1977. Silver Jubilee. Multicoloured.

168	5p. Type **58**	15	10
169	7p. Visit to Jersey, 1957	20	15
170	25p. Queen Elizabeth II (photo by Peter Grugeon)	40	35

59 Coins of 1871 and 1877

1977. Centenary of Currency Reform. Mult.

171	5p. Type **59**	10	10
172	7p. One-twelfth shilling, 1949	15	10
173	11p. Silver crown, 1966	30	30
174	13p. £2 piece, 1972	35	35

60 Sir William Weston and "Santa Anna", 1530

1977. Centenary of St. John Ambulance. Mult.

175	5p. Type **60**	10	10
176	7p. Sir William Drogo and ambulance, 1877	10	10
177	11p. Duke of Connaught and ambulance, 1917	25	20
178	13p. Duke of Gloucester and stretcher-team, 1977	30	25

61 Arrival of Queen Victoria, 1846

1977. 125th Anniv of Victoria College. Mult.

179	7p. Type **61**	15	10
180	10½p. Victoria College, 1852	20	15
181	11p. Sir Galahad Statue, 1924 (vert)	25	25
182	13p. College Hall (vert)	30	25

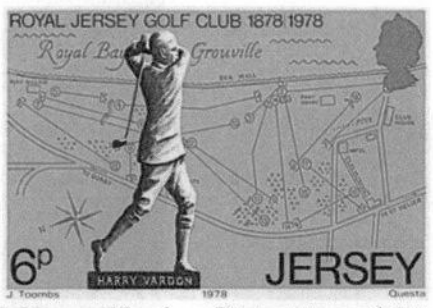

62 Harry Vardon Statuette and Map of Royal Jersey Course

1978. Cent of Royal Jersey Golf Club. Mult.

183	6p. Type **62**	10	10
184	8p. Harry Vardon's grip and swing	15	10
185	11p. Harry Vardon's putt	35	25
186	13p. Golf trophies and book by Harry Vardon	40	35

63 Mont Orgueil Castle

1978. Europa. Castles from Paintings by Thomas Phillips. Multicoloured.

187	6p. Type **63**	10	10
188	8p. St. Aubin's Fort	15	15
189	10½p. Elizabeth Castle	35	25

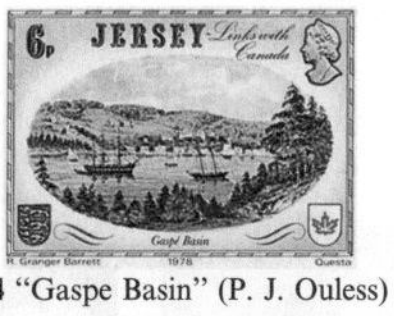

64 "Gaspe Basin" (P. J. Ouless)

1978. Links with Canada. Multicoloured.

190	6p. Type **64**	10	10
191	8p. Map of Gaspe Peninsula	15	10
192	10½p. "Century" (brigantine)	20	15
193	11p. Early map of Jersey	40	25
194	13p. St. Aubin's Bay, town and harbour	45	40

65 Queen Elizabeth and Prince Philip

66 Mail Cutter, 1778–1827

1978. 25th Anniv of Coronation.

195	65	8p. silver, black and red . .	20	10
196	–	25p. silver, black and blue	50	45

DESIGN: 25p. Hallmarks of 1953 and 1977.

1978. Bicentenary of England–Jersey Government Mail Packet Service.

197	66	6p. black, brown and yellow	10	10
198	–	8p. black, green and yellow	15	10
199	–	10½p. black, ultram & bl	30	20
200	–	11p. black, purple and lilac	35	30
201	–	13p. black, red and pink	40	40

DESGNS—SHIPS: 8p. "Flamer", 1831–7; 10½p. "Diana", 1877–90; 11p. "Ibex", 1891–1925; 13p. "Caesarea", 1960–75.

67 Jersey Calf

68 Jersey Pillar Box, c. 1860

1979. 9th Conference of World Jersey Cattle Bureau. Multicoloured.

202		6p. Type **67**	10	10
203		25p. "Ansom Designette" (calf presented to the Queen, 1978) (46 × 29 mm)	50	45

1979. Europa. Multicoloured.

204		8p. Type **68**	25	25
205		8p. Clearing modern post box	25	25
206		10½p. Telephone switchboard, c. 1900 . . .	25	25
207		10½p. Modern SPC telephone system	25	25

69 Percival Mew Gull "Golden City"

70 "My First Sermon"

1979. 25th International Air Rally. Mult.

208		6p. Type **69**	10	10
209		8p. De Havilland Chipmunk	25	15
210		10½p. Druine Turbulent . . .	25	20
211		11p. De Havilland Tiger Moth	30	25
212		13p. North American Harvard	40	35

1979. International Year of the Child and 150th Birth Anniversary of Sir John Millais (painter). Paintings. Multicoloured.

213		8p. Type **70**	20	15
214		10½p. "Orphans"	30	20
215		11p. "The Princes in the Tower"	30	30
216		25p. "Christ in the House of his Parents" (50 × 32 mm)	50	40

1979. Wildlife Preservation Trust (3rd series). As T **34**. Multicoloured.

217		6p. Pink pigeon (vert)	10	10
218		8p. Orang-utan (vert)	20	15
219		11½p. Waldrapp ("Waldrapp Ibis")	30	30
220		13p. Lowland gorilla (vert)	45	35
221		15p. Rodriguez flying fox (vert)	45	35

71 Plan of Mont Orgueil

72 Sir Walter Raleigh

1980. Jersey Fortresses. Drawings by Thomas Phillips. Multicoloured.

222		8p. Type **71**	20	15
223		11½p. Plan of La Tour de St. Aubin	30	30
224		13p. Plan of Elizabeth Castle	30	30
225		25p. Map of Jersey (38 × 27 mm)	50	45

1980. Europa. Links with Britain. Multicoloured.

226		9p. Type **72**	15	15
227		9p. Paul Ivy (engineer) discussing Elizabeth Castle	15	15
228		13½p. Sir George Carteret receiving deeds to Smith's Island, Virginia from Charles II	30	30
229		13½p. Lady Carteret, maid and Jean Chevalier	30	30

Nos. 226/7 and 228/9 were issued together, se-tenant, forming composite designs.

73 Planting

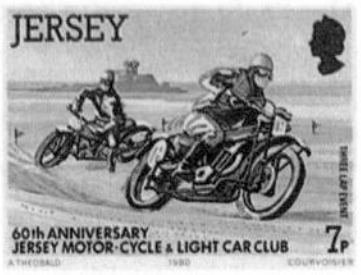

74 Three Lap Event

1980. Cent of Jersey Royal Potato. Mult.

230		7p. Type **73**	15	10
231		15p. Digging	30	25
232		17½p. Weighbridge	30	35

1980. 60th Anniv of Jersey Motor Cycle and Light Car Club. Multicoloured.

233		7p. Type **74**	15	15
234		9p. Jersey International Road Race	20	15
235		13½p. Scrambling	30	25
236		15p. Sand racing (saloon cars)	30	30
237		17½p. National Hill Climb . .	35	35

75 "Eye of the Wind"

1980. "Operation Drake" and 150th Anniv of Royal Geographical Society (14p). Multicoloured.

238		7p. Type **75**	15	15
239		9p. Inflatable raft	20	20
240		13½p. Shooting rapids	30	25
241		14p. "Discovery"	30	30
242		15p. Aerial walkway	35	35
243		17½p. Goodyear Aerospace airship "Europa"	40	40

76 Detail of "The Death of Major Peirson"

1981. Bicentenary of Battle of Jersey. Details of J. S. Copley's painting.

244	76	7p. multicoloured	15	15
245	–	10p. multicoloured	25	20
246	–	15p. multicoloured	35	30
247	–	17½p. multicoloured . . .	40	35
MS248		144 × 97 mm. Nos. 244/7	1·40	1·60

Stamps from No. **MS**248 are without white margins.

77 De Bagot

78a "Queen Elizabeth II" (Norman Hepple)

1981. Crests of Jersey Families.

249	77	½p. black, silver and green	20	20
250	–	1p. multicoloured . . .	10	10
251	–	2p. multicoloured . . .	10	10
252	–	3p. multicoloured . . .	10	15
253	–	4p. silver, black and mauve	15	15
254	–	5p. multicoloured . . .	15	15
255	–	6p. multicoloured . . .	20	20
256	–	7p. multicoloured . . .	25	25
257	–	8p. multicoloured . . .	30	30
258	–	9p. multicoloured . . .	30	25
259	–	10p. multicoloured . . .	25	25
260	–	11p. multicoloured . . .	30	30
261	–	12p. multicoloured . . .	35	30
262	–	13p. multicoloured . . .	35	35
263	–	14p. multicoloured . . .	40	40
264	–	15p. multicoloured . . .	40	40
265	–	16p. multicoloured . . .	35	35
266	–	17p. multicoloured . . .	45	45
266a	–	18p. multicoloured . . .	50	50
266b	–	19p. multicoloured . . .	60	60
267	–	20p. black, silver & yellow	50	50
268	–	25p. black and blue . .	45	45
268a	77	26p. black, silver and red	50	50
269	–	30p. multicoloured . . .	50	50
270	–	40p. multicoloured . . .	80	80
271	–	50p. multicoloured . . .	1·00	1·00
272	–	75p. multicoloured . . .	1·50	1·50
273	–	£1 multicoloured . . .	2·00	2·00
274	78a	£5 multicoloured	10·00	10·00

DESIGNS—As T **77**: 1p. De Carteret; 2p. La Cloche; 3p. Dumaresq; 4p. Payn; 5p. Janvrin; 6p. Poingdestre; 7p. Pipon; 8p. Marett; 9p. Le Breton; 10p. Le Maistre; 11p. Bisson; 12p. Robin; 13p. Herault; 14p. Messervy; 15p. Fiott; 16p. Malet; 17p. Mabon; 18p. De St. Martin; 19p. Hamptonne; 20p. Badier; 25p. L'Arbalestier; 30p. Journeaux; 40p. Lempriere; 50p. Auvergne; 75p. Remon. 38 × 22 mm: £1 Jersey crest and map of Channel.

79 Knight of Hambye slaying Dragon

1981. Europa. Folklore. Multicoloured.

275		10p. Type **79**	25	25
276		10p. Servant slaying Knight of Hambye and awaiting execution	25	25
277		18p. St. Brelade celebrating Easter on island	50	45
278		18p. Island revealing itself as a huge fish	50	45

LEGENDS: 10p. (both) Slaying of the Dragon of Lawrence by the Knight of Hambye; 18p. (both) Voyages of St. Brelade.

80 The Harbour by Gaslight

1981. 150th Anniv of Gas in Jersey. Multicoloured.

279		7p. Type **80**	20	15
280		10p. The Quay	25	25
281		18p. Royal Square	40	40
282		22p. Halkett Place	45	45
283		25p. Central Market	55	55

81 Prince Charles and Lady Diana Spencer

1981. Royal Wedding.

284	81	10p. multicoloured	20	20
285		25p. multicoloured	75	90

82 Christmas Tree in Royal Square

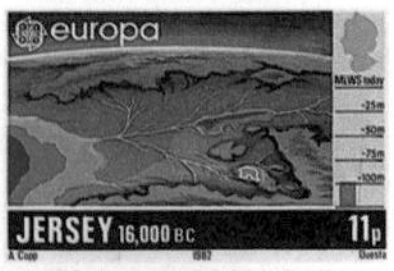

83 Jersey, 16,000 B.C.

1981. Christmas. Multicoloured.

286		7p. Type **82**	15	10
287		10p. East window, Parish Church, St. Helier	25	25
288		18p. Boxing Day meet of Jersey Drag Hunt	30	30

1982. Europa. Formation of Jersey. Mult.

289		11p. Type **83**	20	20
290		11p. In 10,000 B.C. (vert) . .	20	20
291		19½p. In 7,000 B.C. (vert) . .	45	45
292		19½p. In 4,000 B.C.	45	45

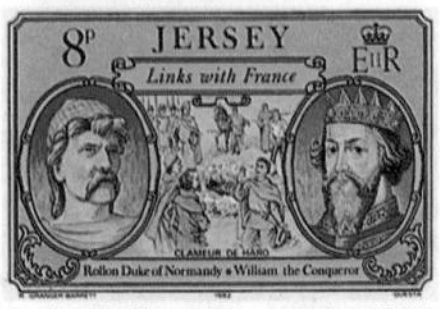

84 Duke Rollo of Normandy, William the Conqueror and "Clameur de Haro" (traditional procedure for obtaining justice)

1982. Links with France. Multicoloured.

293		8p. Type **84**	20	15
294		8p. John of England, Philippe Auguste of France, and Siege of Rouen	20	15
295		11p. Jean Martell (brandy merchant), early still and view of Cognac	30	30
296		11p. Victor Hugo, "Le Rocher des Proscrits" (rock where he used to meditate) and Marine Terrace . . .	30	30
297		19½p. Pierre Teilhard de Chardin (philosopher) and "Maison Saint Louis" (science institute)	45	45
298		19½p. Pere Charles Rey (scientist), anemotachymeter and The Observatory, St. Louis . .	45	45

85 Sir William Smith, Founder of Boys' Brigade

1982. Youth Organizations. Multicoloured.

299		8p. Type **85**	20	15
300		11p. Boys' Brigade "Old Boys" band, Liberation Parade, 1945 (vert)	20	15
301		24p. William Smith and Lord Baden-Powell at Royal Albert Hall, 1903	45	40
302		26p. Lord and Lady Baden-Powell, St. Helier, 1924 (vert)	60	50
303		29p. Scouts at "Westward Ho" campsite, St. Ouen's Bay	75	60

Nos. 299/301 commemorate the centenary of the Boys' Brigade and Nos. 302/3 the 75th anniversary of the Boy Scout Movement.

86 H.M.S. "Tamar" and H.M.S. "Dolphin" at Port Egmont

1983. Jersey Adventurers (1st series). Mult.

304		8p. Type **86**	20	15
305		11p. H.M.S. "Dolphin" and H.M.S. "Swallow" off Magellan Strait	25	15
306		19½p. Discovering Pitcairn Island	40	35
307		24p. Carteret taking possession of English Cove, New Ireland	45	45
308		26p. H.M.S. "Swallow" sinking a pirate, Macassar Strait	50	50
309		29p. H.M.S. "Endymion" leading convoy from West Indies	65	60

See also Nos. 417/21 and 573/8.

87 1969 5s. Legislative Chamber Definitive

1983. Europa. Multicoloured.

310	11p. Type **87**	35	30
311	11p. Royal Mace (23 × 32 mm)	35	30
312	19½p. 1969 10s. Royal Court definitive showing green border error	45	40
313	19½p. Bailiff's Seal (23 × 32 mm)	45	40

88 Charles Le Geyt and Battle of Minden (1759)

1983. World Communications Year and 250th Birth Anniv of Charles Le Geyt (1st Jersey postmaster). Multicoloured.

314	8p. Type **88**	20	20
315	11p. London to Weymouth mail coach	30	30
316	24p. P.O. Mail Packet "Chesterfield" attacked by French privateer	55	55
317	26p. Mary Godfray and the Hue Street Post Office	65	65
318	29p. Mail steamer leaving St. Helier harbour	80	80

89 Assembly Emblem

1983. 13th General Assembly of the A.I.P.L.F. (Association Internationale des Parlementaires de Langue Francaise) Jersey.

319 **89**	19½p. multicoloured	50	50

90 "Cardinal Newman"

91 Golden Lion Tamarin

1983. 50th Death Anniv of Walter Ouless (artist). Multicoloured.

320	8p. Type **90**	20	20
321	11p. "Incident in the French Revolution"	30	30
322	20½p. "Thomas Hardy"	50	50
323	31p. "David with the head of Goliath" (38 × 32 mm)	80	80

1984. Wildlife Preservation Trust (4th series). Multicoloured.

324	9p. Type **91**	25	10
325	12p. Snow leopard	25	15
326	20½p. Jamaican boa	45	40
327	26p. Round island gecko	75	65
328	28p. Coscoroba swan	80	70
329	31p. St. Lucia amazon ("St Lucia Parrot")	1·00	90

92 C.E.P.T. 25th Anniversary Logo

1984. Europa.

330 **92**	9p. light blue, blue and black	20	15
331	12p. lt green, green and black	30	25
332	20½p. lilac, purple and black	60	50

93 Map showing Commonwealth

1984. Links with the Commonwealth. Sheet 108 × 74 mm.

MS333 **93**	75p. multicoloured	2·00	2·00

94 "Sarah Bloomshoft" at Demie de Pas Light, 1906

1984. Centenary of Jersey R.N.L.I. Lifeboat Station. Multicoloured.

334	9p. Type **94**	25	15
335	9p. "Hearts of Oak" and "Maurice Georges", 1949	25	15
336	12p. "Elizabeth Rippon" and "Hanna", 1949	35	30
337	12p. "Elizabeth Rippon" and "Santa Maria", 1951	35	30
338	20½p. "Elizabeth Rippon" and "Bacchus", 1973	60	60
339	20½p. "Thomas James King" and "Cythara", 1983	60	60

95 Bristol Type 170 Freighter Mk 32

1984. 40th Anniv of I.C.A.O. Multicoloured.

340	9p. Type **95**	20	15
341	12p. Airspeed A.S.57 Ambassador 2	35	35
342	26p. De Havilland D.H.114 Heron 1B	75	75
343	31p. De Havilland D.H.89A Dragon Rapide	1·00	1·00

96 "Robinson Crusoe leaves the Wreck"

1984. Links with Australia. Paintings by John Alexander Gilfillan. Multicoloured.

344	9p. Type **96**	25	20
345	12p. "Edinburgh Castle"	30	20
346	20½p. "Maori Village"	60	50
347	26p. "Australian Landscape"	70	60
348	28p. "Waterhouse's Corner, Adelaide"	80	80
349	31p. "Captain Cook at Botany Bay"	80	80

97 "B.L.C. St. Helier" Orchid

1984. Christmas. Jersey Orchids (1st series). Multicoloured.

350	9p. Type **97**	25	20
351	12p. "Oda Mt. Bingham"	50	50

See also Nos. 433/7, 613/17, 892/7 and 1143/**MS**1149.

98 "'Hebe' off Corbiere, 1874"

1984. Death Centenary of Philip John Ouless (artist). Multicoloured.

352	9p. Type **98**	25	20
353	12p. "The 'Gaspe' engaging the 'Diomede'"	30	30
354	22p. "The Paddle-steamer 'London' entering Naples, 1856"	65	60
355	31p. "'The Rambler' entering Cape Town, 1840"	1·00	90
356	34p. "St. Aubin's Bay from Mount Bingham, 1871"	1·25	1·00

99 John Ireland (composer) and Faldouet Dolmen

1985. Europa. European Music Year. Mult.

357	10p. Type **99**	30	30
358	13p. Ivy St. Helier (actress) and His Majesty's Theatre, London	45	45
359	22p. Claude Debussy (composer) and Elizabeth Castle	80	80

100 Girls' Brigade

1985. International Youth Year. Mult.

360	10p. Type **100**	30	30
361	13p. Girl Guides (75th anniversary)	40	40
362	29p. Prince Charles and Jersey Youth Service Activities Base	70	70
363	31p. Sea Cadet Corps	75	75
364	34p. Air Training Corps	90	90

101 "Duke of Normandy" at Cheapside

1985. The Jersey Western Railway. Mult.

365	10p. Type **101**	45	45
366	13p. Saddletank at First Tower	50	50
367	22p. "La Moye" at Millbrook	90	90
368	29p. "St. Heliers" at St. Aubin	95	95
369	34p. "St. Aubyns" at Corbiere	1·00	1·00

102 Memorial Window to Revd. James Hemery (former Dean) and St. Helier Parish Church

1985. 300th Anniv of Huguenot Immigration. Multicoloured.

370	10p. Type **102**	30	30
371	10p. Judge Francis Jeune, Baron St. Helier, and Houses of Parliament	30	30
372	13p. Silverware by Pierre Amiraux	40	40
373	13p. Francis Voisin (merchant) and Russian port	40	40
374	22p. Robert Brohier, Schweppes carbonation plant and bottles	55	50
375	22p. George Ingouville, V.C., R.N. and attack on Viborg	55	40

103 Howard Davis Hall, Victoria College

1985. Thomas Benjamin Davis (philanthropist) Commemoration. Multicoloured.

376	10p. Type **103**	35	35
377	13p. Racing schooner "Westward"	50	50
378	31p. Howard Davis Park, St. Helier	70	70
379	34p. Howard Davis Experimental Farm, Trinity	85	85

104 "Amaryllis belladonna" (Pandora Sellars)

1986. Jersey Lilies. Multicoloured.

380	13p. Type **104**	45	45
381	34p. "A Jersey Lily" (Lily Langtry) (Sir John Millais) (30 × 48 mm)	1·00	1·10
MS382	140 × 96 mm. Nos. 380 × 4 and 381	2·75	3·00

105 King Harold, William of Normandy and Halley's Comet, 1066 (from Bayeux Tapestry)

1986. Appearance of Halley's Comet. Multicoloured.

383	10p. Type **105**	35	35
384	22p. Lady Carteret, Edmond Halley, map and Comet	80	85
385	31p. Aspects of communications in 1910 and 1986 on TV screen	1·00	1·10

106 Dwarf Pansy

107 Queen Elizabeth II (from photo by Karsh)

1986. Europa. Environmental Conservation. Multicoloured.

386	10p. Type **106**	35	35
387	14p. Sea stock	45	45
388	22p. Sand crocus	70	70

1986. 60th Birthday of Queen Elizabeth II.

389 **107**	£1 multicoloured	2·50	1·50

See also No. 491b.

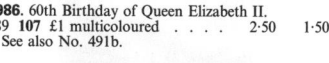

108 Le Rat Cottage

1986. 50th Anniv of National Trust for Jersey. Multicoloured.

390	10p. Type **108**	25	20
391	14p. The Elms (Trust headquarters)	35	30
392	22p. Morel Farm	65	65
393	29p. Quetivel Mill	70	70
394	31p. La Vallette	75	75

109 Prince Andrew and Miss Sarah Ferguson

1986. Royal Wedding.

395 **109**	14p. multicoloured	35	35
396	40p. multicoloured	1·25	1·25

110 "Gathering Vraic"

1986. Birth Centenary of Edmund Blampied (artist).

397 110	10p. multicoloured	25	25
398 –	14p. black, blue and grey	40	40
399 –	29p. multicoloured	75	75
400 –	31p. black, orange and grey	90	90
401 –	34p. multicoloured	95	95

DESIGNS: 14p. "Driving Home in the Rain"; 29p. "The Miller"; 31p. "The Joy Ride"; 34p. "Tante Elizabeth".

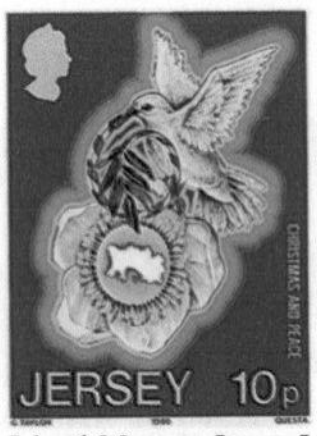

111 Island Map on Jersey Lily, and Dove holding Olive Branch

1986. Christmas. Int Peace Year. Mult.

402	10p. Type **111**	20	20
403	14p. Mistletoe wreath encircling European robin and dove	40	40
404	34p. Christmas cracker releasing dove	95	95

112 "Westward" under Full Sail

1987. Racing Schooner "Westward". Mult.

405	10p. Type **112**	40	35
406	14p. T. B. Davis at the helm	50	55
407	31p. "Westward" overhauling "Britannia"	95	95
408	34p. "Westward" fitting-out at St. Helier	95	95

113 De Havilland Dragon Express "Belcroute Bay"

1987. 50th Anniv of Jersey Airport. Multicoloured.

409	10p. Type **113**	25	25
410	14p. Boeing 757 and Douglas DC-9-15	40	45
411	22p. Britten Norman "long nose" Trislander and Islander aircraft	55	50
412	29p. Short 330 and Vickers Viscount 800	90	90
413	31p. B.A.C. One Eleven 500 and Handley Page Dart Herald	95	95

114 St. Mary and St. Peter's Roman Catholic Church

1987. Europa. Modern Architecture. Mult.

414	11p. Type **114**	40	40
415	15p. Villa Devereux, St. Brelade	50	45
416	22p. Fort Regent Leisure Centre, St. Helier (57 × 29 mm)	75	75

115 H.M.S. "Racehorse" and H.M.S. "Carcass" (bomb ketches) trapped in Arctic

1987. Jersey Adventurers (2nd series). Philippe D'Auvergne. Multicoloured.

417	11p. Type **115**	30	35
418	15p. H.M.S. "Alarm" on fire, Rhode Island	40	35
419	29p. H.M.S. "Arethusa" wrecked off Ushant	70	75
420	31p. H.M.S. "Rattlesnake" stranded on Isle de Trinidad	80	90
421	34p. Mont Orgueil Castle and fishing boats	85	95

See also Nos. 501/6 and 539/44.

116 Grant of Lands to Normandy, 911 and 933

1987. 900th Death Anniv of William the Conqueror. Multicoloured.

422	11p. Type **116**	30	30
423	15p. Edward the Confessor and Duke Robert I of Normandy landing on Jersey, 1030	35	35
424	22p. King William's coronation, 1066 and fatal fall, 1087	70	65
425	29p. Death of William Rufus, 1100 and Battle of Tinchebrai, 1106	75	65
426	31p. Civil war between Matilda and Stephen, 1135–41	85	75
427	34p. Henry inherits Normandy, 1151; John asserts ducal rights in Jersey, 1213	95	90

117 "Grosnez Castle"

1987. Christmas. Paintings by John Le Capelain. Multicoloured.

428	11p. Type **117**	35	30
429	15p. "St. Aubin's Bay"	50	50
430	22p. "Mont Orgueil Castle"	65	65
431	31p. "Town Fort and Harbour, St. Helier"	90	80
432	34p. "The Hermitage"	1·00	1·00

118 "Cymbidium pontac"

1988. Jersey Orchids (2nd series). Multicoloured.

433	11p. Type **118**	40	35
434	15p. "Odontioda" "Eric Young" (vert)	45	45
435	29p. "Lycaste auburn", "Seaford" and "Ditchling"	70	70
436	31p. "Odontoglossum" "St. Brelade" (vert)	80	80
437	34p. "Cymbidium mavourneen" "Jester"	95	95

119 Labrador Retriever

1988. Centenary of Jersey Dog Club. Mult.

438	11p. Type **119**	40	30
439	15p. Wire-haired dachshund	60	30
440	22p. Pekingese	80	75
441	31p. Cavalier King Charles spaniel	90	95
442	34p. Dalmatian	1·00	1·00

120 De Havilland D.H.C.7 Dash Seven, London Landmarks and Jersey Control Tower

1988. Europa. Transport and Communications. Multicoloured.

443	16p. Type **120**	40	45
444	16p. Weather radar and Jersey airport landing system (vert)	40	45
445	22p. Hydrofoil, St. Malo and Elizabeth Castle, St. Helier	75	75
446	22p. Port control tower and Jersey Radio maritime communication centre, La Moye (vert)	75	75

121 Rodriguez Fody ("Rodrigues Fody")

1988. Wildlife Preservation Trust (5th series). Multicoloured.

447	12p. Type **121**	45	45
448	16p. Volcano rabbit (horiz)	55	50
449	29p. White-faced marmoset	90	1·00
450	31p. Ploughshare tortoise (horiz)	1·10	1·10
451	34p. Mauritius kestrel	1·25	1·25

122 Rain Forest Leaf Frog, Costa Rica

1988. Operation Raleigh. Multicoloured.

452	12p. Type **122**	35	25
453	16p. Archaeological survey, Peru	40	40
454	22p. Climbing glacier, Chile	60	60
455	29p. Red Cross Centre, Solomon Islands	70	70
456	31p. Underwater exploration, Australia	80	80
457	34p. "Zebu" (brigantine) returning to St. Helier	90	90

123 St. Clement Parish Church

1988. Christmas. Jersey Parish Churches (1st series). Multicoloured.

458	12p. Type **123**	30	15
459	16p. St. Ouen	45	30
460	31p. St. Brelade	90	80
461	34p. St. Lawrence	85	85

See also Nos. 535/8 and 597/600.

124 Talbot "Type 4 CT Tourer", 1912

1989. Vintage Cars (1st series). Multicoloured.

462	12p. Type **124**	35	30
463	16p. De Dion "Bouton Type 1-D", 1920	50	45
464	23p. Austin 7 "Chummy", 1926	60	55
465	30p. Ford "Model T", 1926	80	80
466	32p. Bentley 8 litre, 1930	1·00	1·00
467	35p. Cadillac "452A–V16 Fleetwood Sports Phaeton", 1931	1·00	1·00

See also Nos. 591/6 and 905/10.

125 Belcroute Bay

125a Arms of King George VI

1989. Jersey Scenes. Multicoloured.

468	1p. Type **125**	10	10
469	2p. High Street, St. Aubin	10	10
470	4p. Royal Jersey Golf Course	10	10
471	5p. Portelet Bay	10	15
472	10p. Les Charrieres D'Anneport	30	30
473	13p. St. Helier Marina	40	45
474	14p. Sand yacht racing, St. Ouen's Bay	40	45
475	15p. Rozel Harbour	45	50
476	16p. St. Aubin's Harbour	50	55
477	17p. Jersey Airport	50	55
478	18p. Corbiere Lighthouse	55	60
479	19p. Val de la Mare	55	60
480	20p. Elizabeth Castle	45	45
481	21p. Greve de Lecq	50	55
482	22p. Samares Manor	45	50
483	23p. Bonne Nuit Harbour	75	55
484	24p. Grosnez Castle	60	60
485	25p. Augres Manor	70	75
486	26p. Central Market	75	80
487	27p. St. Brelade's Bay	80	90
488	30p. St. Ouen's Manor	85	90
489	40p. La Hougue Bie	1·00	1·00
490	50p. Mont Orgueil Castle	1·25	1·40
491	75p. Royal Square, St. Helier	2·00	1·50
491b	£2 Type **107**	4·00	3·25
491c	£4 Type **125a**	7·00	6·75

Nos. 469/91 are as Type **125**.

126 Agile Frog

1989. Endangered Jersey Fauna. Multicoloured.

492	13p. Type **126**	80	85
493	13p. "Heteropterus morpheus" (butterfly) (vert)	80	85
494	17p. Barn owl (vert)	80	85
495	17p. Green lizard	80	85

127 Toddlers' Toys

1989. Europa. Children's Toys and Games. Designs showing clay plaques. Multicoloured.

496	17p. Type **127**	45	45
497	17p. Playground games	45	45
498	23p. Party games	80	80
499	23p. Teenage sports	80	80

128 Queen Elizabeth II and Royal Yacht "Britannia" in Elizabeth Harbour

1989. Royal Visit.

500 128	£1 multicoloured	2·50	2·00

129 Philippe D'Auvergne presented to Louis XVI, 1786

1989. Bicentenary of the French Revolution. Philippe D'Auvergne. Multicoloured.

501	13p. Type **129**	40	30
502	17p. Storming the Bastille, 1789	50	40
503	23p. Marie de Bouillon and revolutionaries, 1790	60	50
504	30p. Auvergne's headquarters at Mont Orgueil, 1795	95	90

505 32p. Landing arms for Chouan rebels, 1796 . . . 1·00 90
506 35p. The last Chouan revolt, 1799 . . . . 1·25 1·00
See also Nos. 539/44.

130 "St. Helier" off Elizabeth Castle

1989. Centenary of Great Western Railway Steamer Service to Channel Islands. Multicoloured.
507 13p. Type **130** 30 30
508 17p. "Caesarea II" off Corbiere Lighthouse . . . 35 35
509 27p. "Reindeer" in St. Helier harbour 80 75
510 32p. "Ibex" racing "Frederica" off Portelet . . 95 95
511 35p. "Lynx" off Noirmont 1·10 1·00

131 "Gorey Harbour"

1989. 150th Birth Anniv of Sarah Louisa Kilpack (artist). Multicoloured.
512 13p. Type **131** 25 25
513 17p. "La Corbiere" 30 30
514 23p. "Greve de Lecq" . . . 80 75
515 32p. "Bouley Bay" 85 85
516 35p. "Mont Orgueil" . . . . 90 1·00

132 Head Post Office, Broad Street, 1969 **133** "Battle of Flowers" Parade

1990. Europa. Post Office Buildings. Mult.
517 18p. Type **132** 50 40
518 18p. Postal Headquarters, Mont Millais, 1990 . . . 50 50
519 24p. Hue Street Post Office, 1815 (horiz) 65 65
520 24p. Head Post Office, Halkett Place, 1890 (horiz) 65 65

1990. Festival of Tourism. Multicoloured.
521 18p. Type **133** 55 55
522 24p. Sports 70 70
523 29p. Mont Orgueil Castle and German Underground Hospital Museum 85 85
524 32p. Salon Culinaire 90 90
MS525 151 × 100 mm. Nos. 521/4 2·75 3·00

134 Early Printing Press and Jersey Newspaper Mastheads

1990. International Literacy Year. Jersey News Media. Multicoloured.
526 14p. Type **134** 45 45
527 18p. Modern press, and offices of "Jersey Evening Post" in 1890 and 1990 . . 45 45
528 34p. Radio Jersey broadcaster 90 90
529 37p. Channel Television studio cameraman 95 95

135 British Aerospace Hawk T.1

1990. 50th Anniv of Battle of Britain. Multicoloured.
530 14p. Type **135** 40 45
531 18p. Supermarine Spitfire . . 55 60
532 24p. Hawker Hurricane Mk I 85 85
533 34p. Vickers-Armstrong Wellington . . . . 1·50 1·60
534 37p. Avro Lancaster . . . . 1·60 1·60

1990. Christmas. Jersey Parish Churches (2nd series). As T **123**. Multicoloured.
535 14p. St. Helier 45 40
536 18p. Grouville 45 40
537 34p. St. Saviour . . . . . . 1·00 1·10
538 37p. St. John . . . . 1·25 1·40

1991. 175th Death Anniv of Philippe d'Auvergne. As T **129**. Multicoloured.
539 15p. Prince's Tower, La Hougue Bie 45 40
540 20p. Auvergne's arrest in Paris 55 55
541 26p. Auvergne plotting against Napoleon 70 75
542 31p. Execution of George Cadoudal 90 90
543 37p. H.M.S. "Surly" (cutter) attacking French convoy 1·10 1·10
544 44p. Auvergne's last days in London . . . . 1·25 1·25

136 "Landsat 5" and Thematic Mapper Image over Jersey **137** 1941 1d. Stamp (50th anniv of first Jersey postage stamp)

1991. Europa. Europe in Space. Multicoloured.
545 20p. Type **136** 50 50
546 20p. "ERS-1" earth resources remote sensing satellite . . 50 50
547 26p. "Meteosat" weather satellite 80 85
548 26p. "Olympus" direct broadcasting satellite . . . 80 85

1991. Anniversaries. Multicoloured.
549 15p. Type **137** 30 30
550 20p. Steam train (centenary of Jersey Eastern Railway extension to Gorey Pier) 50 55
551 26p. Jersey cow and Herd Book (125th anniv of Jersey Herd Book) 60 70
552 31p. Stone-laying ceremony (from painting by P. J. Ouless) (150th anniv of Victoria Harbour) 75 80
553 53p. Marie Bartlett and hospital (250th anniv of Marie Bartlett's hospital bequest) . . . . 1·75 1·75

138 "Melitaea cinxia"

1991. Butterflies and Moths. Multicoloured.
554 15p. Type **138** 35 35
555 20p. "Euplagia quadripunctaria" 45 30
556 37p. "Deilephila porcellus" 1·40 1·50
557 57p. "Inachis io" . . . . . . 1·75 1·90

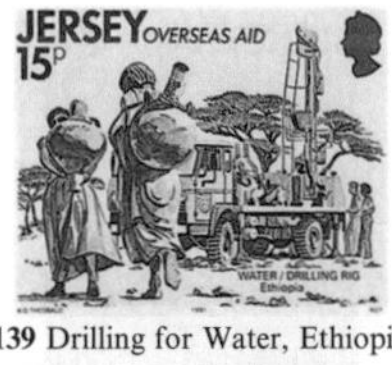

139 Drilling for Water, Ethiopia

1991. Overseas Aid. Multicoloured.
558 15p. Type **139** 45 40
559 20p. Building construction, Rwanda 50 45
560 26p. Village polytechnic, Kenya 70 70
561 31p. Treating leprosy, Tanzania 85 90
562 37p. Ploughing, Zambia . . . 1·10 1·10
563 44p. Immunization clinic, Lesotho . . . . 1·25 1·40

140 "This is the Place for Me" **141** Pied Wagtail

1991. Christmas. Illustrations by Edmund Blampied for J. M. Barrie's "Peter Pan". Multicoloured.
564 15p. Type **140** 40 40
565 20p. "The Island Come True" 65 65
566 37p. "The Never Bird" . . . 1·25 1·25
567 53p. "The Great White Father" . . . . 1·60 1·60

1992. Winter Birds. Multicoloured.
568 16p. Type **141** 50 25
569 22p. Firecrest 70 55
570 28p. Common snipe ("Snipe") 80 85
571 39p. Northern lapwing ("Lapwing") . . . . 1·25 1·25
572 57p. Fieldfare . . . . 1·75 1·75
See also Nos. 635/9.

142 Shipping at Shanghai, 1860

1992. Jersey Adventurers (3rd series). 150th Birth Anniv of William Mesny. Multicoloured.
573 16p. Type **142** 40 45
574 16p. Mesny's junk running Taiping blockade, 1862 . . 40 45
575 22p. General Mesny outside river gate, 1874 . . . . 65 65
576 22p. Mesny in Burma, 1877 65 65
577 33p. Mesny and Governor Chang, 1882 . . . . . . 90 95
578 33p. Mesny in mandarin's sedan chair, 1886 . . . . 90 95

143 "Tickler" (brigantine)

1992. Jersey Shipbuilding. Multicoloured.
579 16p. Type **143** 45 40
580 22p. "Hebe" (brig) 70 75
581 50p. "Gemini" (barque) . . . 1·40 1·50
582 57p. "Percy Douglas" (full-rigged ship) . . . . 1·60 1·75
MS583 148 × 98 mm. Nos. 579/82 4·00 4·25

144 John Bertram (ship owner) and Columbus

1992. Europa. 500th Anniv of Discovery of America by Columbus. Multicoloured.
584 22p. Type **144** 65 50
585 28p. Sir George Carteret (founder of New Jersey) . . 75 80
586 39p. Sir Walter Raleigh (founder of Virginia) . . . 1·10 1·40

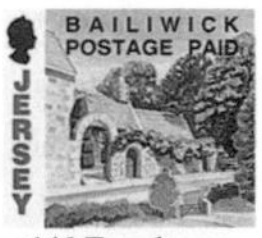

145 "Snow Leopards" (Allison Griffiths) **146** Farmhouse

1992. Batik Designs. Multicoloured.
587 16p. Type **145** 45 40
588 22p. "Three Elements" (Nataly Miorin) 65 45
589 39p. "Three Men in a Tub" (Amanda Crocker) . . . . 1·10 1·25
590 57p. "Cockatoos" (Michelle Millard) . . . . 1·50 1·75

1992. Vintage Cars (2nd series). As T **124**. Multicoloured.
591 16p. Morris Cowley "Bullnose", 1925 . . . . . 30 30
592 22p. Rolls Royce "20/25", 1932 . . . . 45 45
593 28p. Chenard and Walcker "T5", 1924 . . . . 70 75
594 33p. Packard 900 series "Light Eight", 1932 . . . 90 95
595 39p. Lanchester "21", 1927 1·00 1·10
596 50p. Buick "30 Roadster", 1913 . . . . 1·50 1·75

1992. Christmas. Jersey Parish Churches (3rd series). As T **123**. Multicoloured.
597 16p. Trinity 40 30
598 22p. St. Mary 55 50
599 39p. St. Martin . . . . . . 1·10 1·00
600 57p. St. Peter . . . . 1·50 1·40

1993. Multicoloured.
601 (–) Type **146** 60 70
602 (–) Trinity Church 60 70
603 (–) Daffodils and cows . . . 60 70
604 (–) Jersey cows 60 70
605 (–) Sunbathing 70 60
606 (–) Windsurfing 70 60
607 (–) Crab (Queen's head at left) 70 60
608 (–) Crab (Queen's head at right) 70 60
609 (–) "Singin' in the Rain" float 85 80
610 (–) "Dragon Dance" float . . 85 80
611 (–) "Bali, Morning of the World" float 85 80
612 (–) "Zulu Fantasy" float . . 85 80
The above do not show face values, but are inscribed "BAILIWICK POSTAGE PAID" (Nos. 601/4), "U.K. MINIMUM POSTAGE PAID" (Nos. 605/8) or "EUROPE POSTAGE PAID" (Nos. 609/12). They were initially sold at 17p., 23p. or 28p., but it is intended that these face values will be increased to reflect postage rate changes in the future.

147 "Phragmipedium" Eric Young "Jersey" **149** "Jersey's Opera House" (Ian Rolls)

148 Douglas DC-3 Dakota

1993. Jersey Orchids (3rd series). Multicoloured.
613 17p. Type **147** 45 35
614 23p. "Odontoglossum" Augres "Trinity" 70 65
615 28p. "Miltonia" St. Helier "Colomberie" 80 75
616 39p. "Phragmipedium pearcei" . . . . 1·25 1·40
617 57p. "Calanthe" Grouville "Grey" . . . . 1·75 1·90

1993. 75th Anniv of Royal Air Force. Mult.
618 17p. Type **148** 45 30
619 23p. Wight seaplane 60 65
620 28p. Avro Shackleton A.E.W.2 . . . . 70 70
621 33p. Gloster Meteor Mk III and De Havilland Vampire FB.5 . . . . 80 85
622 39p. Hawker Siddeley Harrier GR.IA . . . . 1·00 1·10
623 57p. Panavia Tornado F Mk 3 . . . . 1·50 1·60
MS624 147 × 98 mm. Nos. 619 and 623 . . . . 4·50 4·75
Nos. 618/23 also commemorate the 50th anniv of the Royal Air Force Association and the 40th anniv of the first air display on Jersey.

1993. Europa. Contemporary Art. Multicoloured.
625 23p. Type **149** 60 60
626 28p. "The Ham and Tomato Bap" (Jonathan Hubbard) 70 70
627 39p. "Vase of Flowers" (Neil MacKenzie) . . . . 1·10 1·10

150 1943 ½d. Occupation Stamp

1993. 50th Anniv of Edmund Blampied's Occupation Stamps. Designs showing stamps from the 1943 issue.

628 **150** 17p. green, lt green & blk . . 35 35
629 – 23p. red, pink and black . . 50 50
630 – 28p. brown, cinnamon and black 70 70
631 – 33p. orange, salmon & blk 85 85
632 – 39p. blue, cobalt and black . . . . 1·25 1·25
633 – 50p. mauve, lt mauve & blk . . . . 1·40 1·40

DESIGNS: 23p. 1d. value; 28p. 1½d. value; 33p. 2d. value; 39p. 2½d. value; 50p. 3d. value.

151 Queen Elizabeth II (from painting by Marca McGregor)

1993. 40th Anniv of Coronation.

634 **151** £1 multicoloured . . . . 2·75 2·75

152 Short-toed Treecreeper

153 Two Angels holding "Hark the Herald Angels Sing" Banner

1993. Summer Birds. Multicoloured.

635 17p. Type **152** 45 50
636 23p. Dartford warbler . . . 70 75
637 28p. Northern wheatear ("Wheatear") 80 85
638 39p. Cirl bunting . . . . . . 1·25 1·25
639 57p. Jay . . . . 1·75 1·75

1993. Christmas. Stained Glass Windows by Henry Bosdet from St. Aubin on the Hill Church. Multicoloured.

640 17p. Type **153** 40 35
641 23p. Two angels playing harps 60 60
642 39p. Two angels playing violins . . . . 1·10 1·25
643 57p. Two angels holding "Once in Royal David's City" banner . . . . . . 1·75 1·90

154 "Coprinus comatus"

156 Maine Coon

155 Pekingese

1994. Fungi. Multicoloured.

644 18p. Type **154** 45 40
645 23p. "Amanita muscaria" . . 65 70
646 30p. "Cantharellus cibarius" . 80 85
647 41p. "Macrolepiota procera" 1·25 1·25
648 60p. "Clathrus ruber" . . . 1·60 1·60

1994. "Hong Kong '94" International Stamp Exhibition. "Chinese Year of the Dog". Sheet 110 × 75 mm.

MS649 **155** £1 multicoloured . . 2·50 2·75

1994. 21st Anniv of Jersey Cat Club. Mult.

650 18p. Type **156** 40 30
651 23p. British shorthair (horiz) 60 50
652 35p. Persian 80 80
653 41p. Siamese (horiz) . . . . 1·10 1·25
654 60p. Non-pedigree . . . . . 1·60 1·75

157 Mammoth Hunt, La Cotte de St. Brelade

1994. Europa. Archaeological Discoveries. Multicoloured.

655 23p. Type **157** 50 55
656 23p. Stone Age hunters pulling mammoth into cave 50 55
657 30p. Chambered passage, La Hougue Bie 75 85
658 30p. Transporting stones . . 75 85

158 Gliders and Towing Aircraft approaching France

1994. 50th Anniv of D-Day. Multicoloured.

659 18p. Type **158** 55 50
660 18p. Landing craft approaching beaches . . . 55 50
661 23p. Disembarking from landing craft on Gold Beach 75 70
662 23p. British troops on Sword Beach 75 70
663 30p. Spitfires over beaches . . 80 75
664 30p. Invasion map 80 75

159 Sailing

1994. Centenary of International Olympic Committee. Multicoloured.

665 18p. Type **159** 40 35
666 23p. Rifle-shooting 55 55
667 30p. Hurdling 75 75
668 41p. Swimming . . . . . . 1·10 1·10
669 60p. Hockey . . . . 1·50 1·60

160 Strawberry Anemone

1994. Marine Life. Multicoloured.

670 18p. Type **160** 40 45
671 23p. Hermit crab and parasitic anemone 60 65
672 41p. Velvet swimming crab 1·25 1·40
673 60p. Common jellyfish . . . 1·60 1·60

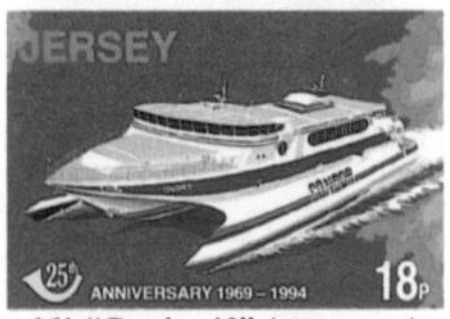

161 "Condor 10" (catamaran)

1994. 25th Anniv of Jersey Postal Administration. Multicoloured.

674 18p. Type **161** 50 45
675 23p. Map of Jersey and pillar box 60 50
676 35p. Vickers Type 953 Vanguard of B.E.A. . . . 85 85
677 41p. Shorts 360 of Aurigny Air Services . . . . 1·10 1·00
678 60p. "Caesarea" (Sealink ferry) . . . . 1·60 1·50
MS679 150 × 100 mm. Nos. 674/8 4·50 4·50

162 "Away in a Manger"

1994. Christmas. Carols. Multicoloured.

680 18p. Type **162** 40 40
681 23p. "Hark! the Herald Angels Sing" 50 50
682 41p. "While Shepherds Watched" . . . . 1·25 1·25
683 60p. "We Three Kings of Orient Are" . . . . 1·50 1·50

163 Dog and "GOOD LUCK"

164 Camellia "Captain Rawes"

1995. Greetings Stamps. Multicoloured.

684 18p. Type **163** 50 40
685 18p. Rose and "WITH LOVE" 50 40
686 18p. Chick and "CONGRATULATIONS" 50 40
687 18p. Bouquet of flowers and "THANK YOU" 50 40
688 23p. Dove with letter and "WITH LOVE" 60 55
689 23p. Cat and "GOOD LUCK" 60 55
690 23p. Carnations and "THANK YOU" 60 55
691 23p. Parrot and "CONGRATULATIONS" 60 55
692 60p. Pig and "HAPPY NEW YEAR" (25 × 63 mm) . . . 1·50 1·50

No. 692 commemorates the Chinese New Year of the Pig.

1994. Camellias. Multicoloured.

693 18p. Type **164** 55 50
694 23p. "Brigadoon" 80 70
695 30p. "Elsie Jury" 90 85
696 35p. "Augusto L'Gouveia Pinto" . . . . 1·10 1·00
697 41p. "Bella Romana" . . . . 1·25 1·10

165 "Liberation" (sculpture, Philip Jackson)

1995. Europa. Peace and Freedom.

698 **165** 23p. black and blue . . . 55 55
699 30p. black and pink . . . 70 95

166 Bailiff and Crown Officers in Launch

1995. 50th Anniv of Liberation. Multicoloured.

700 18p. Type **166** 40 40
701 18p. "Vega" (Red Cross supply ship) 40 40
702 23p. H.M.S. "Beagle" (destroyer) 60 60
703 23p. British troops in Ordnance Yard, St. Helier 60 60
704 60p. King George VI and Queen Elizabeth in Jersey 1·50 1·50
705 60p. Unloading supplies from landing craft, St. Aubin's 1·50 1·50
MS706 110 × 75 mm. £1 Royal Family with Winston Churchill on Buckingham Palace balcony, V.E. Day (80 × 39 mm) . . . . . . 2·75 2·75

167 Bell Heather

1995. European Nature Conservation Year. Wild Flowers. Multicoloured.

707 19p. Type **167** 60 55
708 19p. Sea campion 60 55
709 19p. Spotted rock-rose . . . 60 55
710 19p. Thrift 60 55
711 19p. Sheep's-bit scabious . . 60 55
712 23p. Field bind-weed 70 65
713 23p. Common bird's-foot trefoil 70 65
714 23p. Sea-holly 70 65
715 23p. Common centaury . . . 70 65
716 23p. Dwarf pansy 70 65

Nos. 707/11 and 712/16 respectively were printed together, se-tenant, forming composite designs.

168 "Precis almana"

1995. Butterflies. Multicoloured.

717 19p. Type **168** 50 55
718 23p. "Papilio palinurus" . . 55 60
719 30p. "Catopsilia scylla" . . . 80 85
720 41p. "Papilio rumanzovia" . . 1·00 1·10
721 60p. "Troides helena" . . . 1·60 1·75
MS722 150 × 100 mm. Nos. 720/1 2·40 2·50

No. MS722 includes the "Singapore '95" International Stamp Exhibition logo on the sheet margin and shows the two stamp designs without frames.

169 Peace Doves and United Nations Anniversary Emblem

1995. 50th Anniv of United Nations.

723 **169** 19p. cobalt and blue . . . 60 50
724 – 23p. turquoise and green 70 70
725 – 41p. green and turquoise 1·25 1·25
726 **169** 60p. blue and cobalt . . . 1·50 1·50

DESIGN: 23p., 41p. Symbolic wheat and anniversary emblem.

170 "Puss in Boots"

1995. Christmas. Pantomimes. Multicoloured.

727 19p. Type **170** 50 40
728 23p. "Cinderella" 55 45
729 41p. "Sleeping Beauty" . . . 1·00 1·00
730 60p. "Aladdin" . . . . . . 1·60 1·50

171 Rat with Top Hat

1996. Chinese New Year ("Year of the Rat"). Sheet 110 × 75 mm.

MS731 **171** £1 multicoloured . . 2·50 2·50

172 African Child and Map

1996. 50th Anniv of UNICEF. Multicoloured.

732 19p. Type **172** 45 40
733 23p. Children and globe . . . 55 45
734 30p. European child and map 70 65
735 35p. South American child and map 90 80
736 41p. Asian child and map . . 1·00 1·00
737 60p. South Pacific child and map . . . . 1·50 1·40

173 Queen Elizabeth II (from photo by T. O'Neill)

1996. 70th Birthday of Queen Elizabeth II.
738 **173** £5 multicoloured . . . . 10·00 9·00

174 Elizabeth Garrett (first British woman doctor)

1996. Europa. Famous Women. Multicoloured.
739 23p. Type **174** 60 60
740 30p. Emmeline Pankhurst (suffragette) 90 90

175 Player shooting at Goal

1996. European Football Championship, England. Multicoloured.
741 19p. Type **175** 50 40
742 23p. Two players chasing ball 60 50
743 35p. Player avoiding tackle 95 90
744 41p. Two players competing for ball . . . . 1·00 1·00
745 60p. Players heading ball . . 1·60 1·60

176 Rowing

1996. Sporting Anniversaries. Multicoloured.
746 19p. Type **176** 50 40
747 23p. Judo 60 50
748 35p. Fencing 95 95
749 41p. Boxing . . . . 1·00 1·00
750 60p. Basketball . . . . . . 1·60 1·60
MS751 150 × 100 mm. £1 Olympic torch (50 × 37 mm) . . . . . 2·50 2·50
ANNIVERSARIES: Nos. 746/8, 750/1, Centenary of modern Olympic Games; 749, 50th anniv of International Amateur Boxing Association.
No. **MS**751 also includes the "CAPEX '96" International Stamp Exhibition logo.

177 Bay on North Coast

1996. Tourism. Beaches. Multicoloured.
752 19p. Type **177** 50 50
753 23p. Portelet Bay 60 60
754 30p. Greve de Lecq Bay . . . 80 80
755 35p. Beauport Beach 95 95
756 41p. Plemont Bay . . . . . 1·10 1·10
757 60p. St. Brelade's Bay . . . 1·60 1·60

178 Drag Hunt

1996. Horses. Multicoloured.
758 19p. Type **178** 50 50
759 23p. Pony and trap 60 60
760 30p. Training racehorses on beach 80 80
761 35p. Show jumping 95 95
762 41p. Pony Club event . . . . 1·10 1·10
763 60p. Shire mare and foal . . 1·60 1·60

179 The Journey to Bethlehem

1996. Christmas. Multicoloured.
764 19p. Type **179** 50 50
765 23p. The Shepherds 60 70
766 30p. The Nativity 90 95
767 60p. The Three Kings . . . . 1·40 1·50

180 Jersey Cow wearing Scarf

1997. Chinese New Year ("Year of the Ox"). Sheet 110 × 74 mm.
MS768 **180** £1 multicoloured . . 3·25 3·75

1997. "HONG KONG '97" International Stamp Exhibition. No. **MS**768 optd with exhibition emblem in black and "JERSEY AT HONG KONG '97" in red, both on sheet margin.
MS769 **180** £1 multicoloured . . 3·25 3·75

181 Lillie the Cow on the Beach

182 Red-breasted Merganser

1997. Tourism. "Lillie the Cow". Multicoloured. Self-adhesive.
770 (23p.) Type **181** 80 85
771 (23p.) Lillie taking photograph 80 85
772 (23p.) Carrying bucket and spade 80 85
773 (23p.) Eating meal at Mont Orgueil 80 85

1997. Seabirds and Waders. Multicoloured.
774 1p. Type **182** 10 10
775 2p. Sanderling 10 10
776 4p. Northern gannet ("Gannet") 10 10
777 5p. Great crested grebe . . 10 15
778 10p. Common tern 20 25
779 15p. Black-headed gull . . . 30 35
780a 20p. Dunlin 40 45
781 21p. Sandwich tern 40 45
782 22p. Ringed plover 45 50
783 23p. Bar-tailed godwit . . . 45 50
784a 24p. Atlantic puffin ("Puffin") 45 50
785 25p. Brent goose 50 55
786 26p. Grey plover 50 55
787 27p. Black scoter ("Common Scoter") . . . 55 60
788 28p. Lesser black-backed gull 60 65
789 29p. Little egret 60 65
790 30p. Fulmar 60 65
791 31p. Golden plover 60 65
792 32p. Common greenshank ("Greenshank") 65 70
793 33p. Little grebe 65 70
794 34p. Great cormorant ("Common Cormorant") 70 75
795 35p. Western curlew ("Curlew") 70 75
796 37p. Oystercatcher 75 80
797 40p. Ruddy turnstone ("Turnstone") 80 85
798 44p. Herring gull 90 95
799 45p. Rock pipit 90 95
800 50p. Great black-backed gull 1·00 1·10
801 60p. Pied avocet ("Avocet") 1·25 1·40
802 65p. Grey heron . . . . . 1·25 1·40
803 75p. Common redshank ("Redshank") . . . . . . 1·50 1·60
804 £1 Razorbill . . . . 2·00 2·10
805 £2 Shag . . . . 4·00 4·25
MS806 Four sheets, each 136 × 130 mm. (a) Nos. 774, 778/80, 784, 796, 803 and 805. (b) Nos. 775, 777, 781, 785, 790, 797, 801 and 804. (c) Nos. 776, 782, 786, 791/2, 795, 798 and 800. (d) Nos. 783, 787/9, 793/4, 799 and 802 Set of 4 sheets . . . . . 24·00 24·00

183 De Havilland D.H.95 Flamingo

1997. 60th Anniv of Jersey Airport. Multicoloured.
807 20p. Type **183** 45 40
808 24p. Handley Page H.P.R. Marathon 55 40
809 31p. De Havilland D.H.114 Heron 65 65
810 37p. Boeing 737-236 . . . . 95 90
811 43p. Britten Norman Trislander . . . . 1·10 1·00
812 63p. BAe 146-200 . . . . . 1·75 1·60

184 The Bull of St. Clement

1997. Europa. Tales and Legends. Multicoloured.
813 20p. Type **184** 65 60
814 24p. The Black Horse of St. Ouen 75 70
815 31p. The Black Dog of Bouley Bay . . . . 1·10 1·00
816 63p. Les Fontaines des Mittes 1·75 1·60
Nos. 814/15 include the "EUROPA" emblem.

1997. "Pacific 97" International Stamp Exhibition, San Francisco. No. **MS**806a optd with exhibition emblem on sheet margin.
MS817 136 × 130 mm. Nos. 774, 778/80, 784, 796, 803 and 805 7·50 8·00

185 Cycling

1997. 7th Island Games, Jersey. Multicoloured.
818 20p. Type **185** 55 55
819 24p. Archery 65 65
820 31p. Windsurfing 80 80
821 37p. Gymnastics . . . . . . 1·00 1·00
822 43p. Volleyball . . . . 1·10 1·10
823 63p. Running . . . . 1·75 1·75

186 Mallorcan Midwife Toad

1997. Wildlife Preservation Trust (6th series). Multicoloured.
824 20p. Type **186** 50 45
825 24p. Aye-aye 60 50
826 31p. Mauritius parakeet ("Echo Parakeet") 90 80
827 37p. Pigmy hog . . . . . . 1·00 1·00
828 43p. St. Lucia whip-tail . . . 1·10 1·10
829 63p. Madagascar teal . . . . 1·75 1·75

187 Ash

1997. Trees. Multicoloured.
830 20p. Type **187** 50 45
831 24p. Elder 60 50
832 31p. Beech 90 80
833 37p. Sweet chestnut . . . . 1·00 1·00
834 43p. Hawthorn . . . . . . 1·10 1·10
835 63p. Common oak . . . . . 1·75 1·75

188 Father Christmas and Reindeer outside Jersey Airport

1997. Christmas. Multicoloured.
836 20p. Type **188** 60 60
837 24p. Father Christmas with presents, St. Aubin's Harbour 70 70
838 31p. Father Christmas in sleigh, Mont Orgueil Castle 1·00 1·00
839 63p. Father Christmas with children, Royal Square, St. Helier . . . . 1·90 1·90

189 Wedding Photograph, 1947

1997. Golden Wedding of Queen Elizabeth and Prince Philip. Multicoloured.
840 50p. Type **189** . . . . . . 1·50 1·50
841 50p. Queen Elizabeth and Prince Philip, 1997 . . . . 1·50 1·50
MS842 150 × 100 mm. £1.50 Full-length Wedding photograph, 1947 (38 × 50 mm) . . . . 4·50 4·50

190 Tiger wearing Scarf

1998. Chinese New Year ("Year of the Tiger"). Sheet 110 × 75 mm.
MS843 **190** £1 multicoloured . . 2·50 2·75

191 J.M.T. Bristol 4 Tonner, 1923

1998. 75th Anniv of Jersey Motor Transport Company. Buses. Multicoloured.
844 20p. Type **191** 55 50
845 24p. Safety Coach Service Regent double decker, 1934 65 50
846 31p. Slade's Dennis Lancet, c. 1936 . . . . . 75 70
847 37p. Tantivy Leyland PLSC Lion, 1947 . . . . 1·00 1·00
848 43p. J.B.S. Morris, c. 1958 . . 1·10 1·10
849 63p. J.M.T. Titan TD4 double decker, c. 1961 . . 1·50 1·40

192 Creative Arts Festival

193 Hobie Cat and "Duke of Normandy" (launch)

1998. Europa. National Festivals. Multicoloured.
850 20p. Type **192** 65 45
851 24p. Jazz Festival 70 55
852 31p. Good Food Festival . . 90 90
853 63p. Floral Festival . . . . . 1·75 1·75
Nos. 851/2 include the "EUROPA" emblem.

1998. Opening of Elizabeth Marina, St. Helier. Multicoloured.
854 20p. Type **193** 50 50
855 20p. Hobie Cat with white, yellow, red and green sails 50 50
856 20p. Hobie Cats with pink, purple and orange sails . . 50 50
857 20p. Bow of Hobie Cat with yellow, blue and purple sail 50 50
858 20p. Hobie Cat heeling . . . 50 50
859 24p. Yacht with red, white and blue spinnaker 60 55
860 24p. Yacht with pink spinnaker 60 55
861 24p. Yacht with two white sails 60 55
862 24p. Trimaran 60 55
863 24p. Yacht with blue, white and yellow spinnaker in foreground 60 55
Nos. 854/8 and 859/63 respectively were printed together, se-tenant, forming composite designs of yacht races.

194 Bass

1998. International Year of the Ocean. Fishes. Multicoloured.

864	20p. Type **194**	50	50
865	24p. Red gurnard	65	65
866	31p. Skate	80	80
867	37p. Mackerel	1·00	1·00
868	43p. Tope	1·10	1·10
869	63p. Cuckoo wrasse	1·50	1·50

195 Cider-making

196 Irises

1998. Days Gone By. Multicoloured. Self-adhesive.

870	(20p.) Type **195**	90	90
871	(20p.) Potato barrels on cart	90	90
872	(20p.) Collecting seaweed for fertilizer	90	90
873	(20p.) Milking Jersey cows	90	90

1998. Flowers. Multicoloured.

874	20p. Type **196**	50	40
875	24p. Carnations	60	50
876	31p. Chrysanthemums	75	70
877	37p. Pinks	90	90
878	43p. Roses	1·00	1·00
879	63p. Lilies	1·40	1·40
MS880	150 × 100 mm. £1.50 Lilium "Star Gazer" (50 × 37 mm)	3·00	3·75

No. **MS**880 includes the "ITALIA '98" stamp exhibition emblem on the margin.

197 Central Market Crib

1998. Christmas. Cribs. Multicoloured.

881	20p. Type **197**	40	40
882	24p. St. Thomas's Church crib	50	55
883	31p. Trinity Parish Church crib	65	65
884	63p. Royal Square crib	1·50	1·60

198 Rabbit

1999. Chinese New Year ("Year of the Rabbit"). Sheet 110 × 75 mm.

MS885	**198** £1 multicoloured	2·50	2·75

199 Jersey Eastern Railway Mail Train

1999. 125th Anniv of U.P.U. Multicoloured.

886	20p. Type **199**	55	50
887	24p. "Brighton" (paddle-steamer)	65	60
888	43p. De Havilland D.H.86 Dragon Express at Jersey Airport	95	90
889	63p. Jersey Postal Service Morris Minor van	1·40	1·40

200 "Jessie Eliza", St. Catherine

1999. 175th Anniv of Royal National Lifeboat Institution. Multicoloured.

890	75p. Type **200**	2·00	2·00
891	£1 "Alexander Coutanche", St. Helier	2·50	2·50

201 "Cymbidium" Maufant "Jersey"

1999. Jersey Orchids (4th series). Multicoloured.

892	21p. Type **201**	55	50
893	25p. "Miltonia" Millbrook "Jersey"	55	50
894	31p. "Paphiopedilum" "Transvaal"	75	70
895	37p. "Paphiopedilum" "Elizabeth Castle"	85	80
896	43p. "Calanthe" "Five Oaks"	90	90
897	63p. "Cymbidium" Icho Tower "Trinity"	2·00	2·00
MS898	150 × 100 mm. £1.50 "Miltonia" Portelet	4·00	4·50

No. **MS**898 also includes the "Australia '99" World Stamp Exhibition, Melbourne, emblem on the margin at top left.

202 Howard Davis Park

1999. Europa. Parks and Gardens. Multicoloured.

899	21p. Type **202**	50	50
900	25p. Sir Winston Churchill Memorial Park	70	70
901	31p. Coronation Park	1·00	1·00
902	63p. La Collette Gardens	2·00	2·00

Nos. 900/1 include the "EUROPA" logo at top left and all four values show the "iBRA '99" International Stamp Exhibition, Nuremberg, emblem at top right.

203 Prince Edward and Miss Sophie Rhys-Jones

1999. Royal Wedding.

903	**203** 35p. multicoloured (yellow background)	1·00	1·00
904	35p. multicoloured (blue background)	1·00	1·00

204 Jersey-built Benz, 1899

1999. Vintage Cars (3rd series). Centenary of Motoring in Jersey. Multicoloured.

905	21p. Type **204**	45	45
906	25p. Star Tourer, 1910	55	55
907	31p. Citroen "Traction Avant", 1938	65	65
908	37p. Talbot BG110 Tourer, 1937	80	80
909	43p. Morris Cowley Six Special Coupe, 1934	90	90
910	63p. Ford Anglia Saloon, 1946	1·50	1·50

205 West European Hedgehog

1999. Small Mammals. Multicoloured.

911	21p. Type **205**	45	45
912	25p. Eurasian red squirrel	55	55
913	31p. Nathusius pipistrelle	65	65
914	37p. Jersey bank vole	80	80
915	43p. Lesser white-toothed shrew	90	90
916	63p. Common mole	1·50	1·50

206 Gorey Pierhead Light

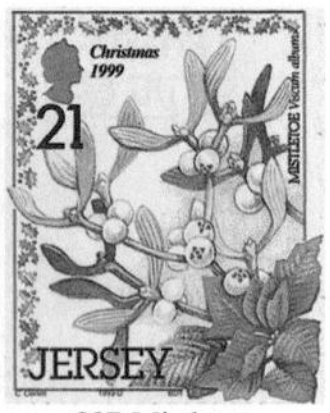

207 Mistletoe

1999. 150th Anniv of First Lighthouse on Jersey (1st series). Multicoloured.

917	21p. Type **206**	45	45
918	25p. La Corbiere	75	55
919	34p. Noirmont Point	55	75
920	38p. Demie de Pas	1·00	1·00
921	44p. Greve d'Azette	1·25	1·25
922	64p. Sorel Point	2·00	2·00

See also Nos. 1086/91.

1999. Christmas. Festive Foliage. Multicoloured.

923	21p. Type **207**	45	45
924	25p. Holly	55	55
925	34p. Ivy	1·10	75
926	64p. Christmas Rose	1·50	1·50

208 Jersey Crest

2000. New Millennium.

927	**208** £10 gold, red and carmine	20·00	20·00

209 Dragon

2000. Chinese New Year ("Year of the Dragon"). Sheet 110 × 75 mm.

MS928	**209** £1 multicoloured	2·50	2·50

210 "Ocean Adventure" (Gemma Care)

2000. "Stampin' the Future" (children's stamp design competition) Winners. Multicoloured.

929	22p. Type **210**	55	55
930	22p. "Solar Power" (Chantal Varley-Best)	55	55
931	22p. "Floating City and Space Cars" (Nicola Singleton)	55	55
932	22p. "Conservation" (Carly Logan)	55	55
MS933	150 × 100 mm. Nos. 929/32	3·00	3·50

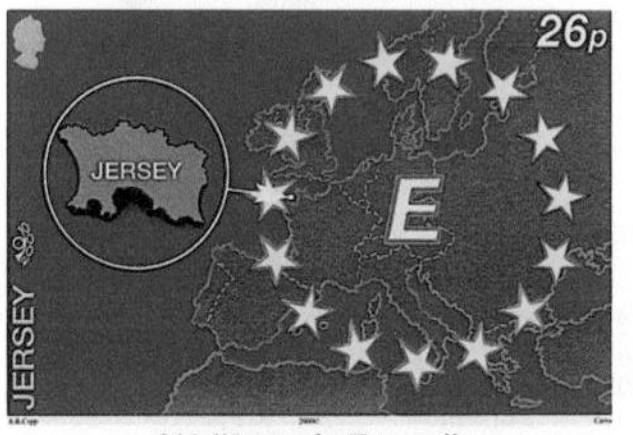

211 "Jersey in Europe"

2000. Europa. Multicoloured.

934	26p. Type **211**	90	90
935	34p. "Building Europe" (29 × 39 mm)	1·25	1·25

212 Roman Merchant Ship

2000. "The Stamp Show 2000" International Stamp Exhibition, London. Maritime Heritage. Mult.

936	22p. Type **212**	60	60
937	22p. Viking longship	60	60
938	22p. 13th-century warship	60	60
939	22p. 14th–15th-century merchant ship	60	60
940	22p. Tudor warship	60	60
941	26p. 17th-century warship	65	65
942	26p. 18th-century naval cutter	65	65
943	26p. 19th-century barque	65	65
944	26p. 19th-century oyster cutter	65	65
945	26p. 20th-century ketch	65	65
MS946	174 × 104 mm. Nos. 936/45	6·00	6·00

213 Bottle-nosed Dolphins

2000. World Environment Day. Marine Mammals. Multicoloured.

947	22p. Type **213**	50	55
948	26p. Long-finned pilot whales	55	60
949	34p. Common porpoises	80	85
950	38p. Grey seals	1·00	1·10
951	44p. Risso's dolphins	1·10	1·25
952	64p. White-beaked dolphin	1·50	1·75
MS953	150 × 100 mm. £1.50 Common dolphins (80 × 29 mm)	4·00	4·50

214 Prince William and Alps

2000. 18th Birthday of Prince William. Multicoloured.

954	75p. Type **214**	1·50	1·50
955	75p. Prince William and polo player	1·50	1·50
956	75p. Prince William and Beaumaris Castle	1·50	1·50
957	75p. Prince William and fireworks	1·50	1·50

2000. "World Stamp Expo 2000", Anaheim, U.S.A. As No. **MS**953, but with multicoloured exhibition logo added to top left corner of sheet margin.

MS958	150 × 100 mm. £1.50 Common dolphins (80 × 29 mm)	3·50	4·00

215 Queen Elizabeth the Queen Mother with Roses

2000. Queen Elizabeth the Queen Mother's 100th Birthday. Multicoloured.

959	50p. Type **215**	1·25	1·25
960	50p. Queen Elizabeth the Queen Mother with daisies	1·25	1·25
MS961	150 × 100 mm. Nos. 959/60	2·25	3·00

216 Supermarine Spitfire Mk Ia

2000. 60th Anniv of Battle of Britain. Multicoloured.

962	22p. Type **216**	50	55
963	26p. Hawker Hurricane Mk I	60	65
964	36p. Bristol Blenheim Mk IV	80	85
965	40p. Vickers Wellington Mk Ic	90	95
966	45p. Boulton Paul Defiant Mk I	1·00	1·10
967	65p. Short Sunderland Mk I	1·50	1·60

217 Virgin Mary

2000. Christmas. Children's Nativity Play. Multicoloured.
968 22p. Type **217** 55 55
969 26p. Shepherd 65 65
970 36p. Angel 90 90
971 65p. Magi with gift . . . . . 1·50 1·50

218 Snake

2001. Chinese New Year ("Year of the Snake"). Sheet 110 × 75 mm.
MS972 **218** £1 multicoloured . . 2·25 2·50

219 *Rose* (1851–61)

2001. Maritime Links with France. Mail Packet Ships. Multicoloured.
973 22p. Type **219** 50 55
974 26p. *Comete* (1856–67) . . . 60 65
975 36p. *Cygne* (1894–1912) . . . 80 85
976 40p. *Victoria* (1896–1918) . . . 90 95
977 45p. *Attala* (1920–25) . . . . 1·00 1·10
978 65p. *Brittany* (1933–62) . . . 1·50 1·60

220 H.M.S. *Jersey* (4th Rate), 1654–91

2001. Royal Navy Ships named after Jersey. Multicoloured.
979 23p. Type **220** 50 55
980 26p. H.M.S. *Jersey* (6th Rate), 1694–98 . . . . . . 60 65
981 37p. H.M.S. *Jersey* (4th Rate), 1698–1731 . . . . . 80 85
982 41p. H.M.S. *Jersey* (4th Rate), 1736–83 . . . . . . 1·00 95
983 46p. H.M.S. *Jersey* (cutter), 1860–73 . . . . 1·20 1·10
984 66p. H.M.S. *Jersey* (destroyer), 1938–41 . . . 1·50 1·60

221 Jersey Cows

2001. Jersey Agriculture. Multicoloured. Self-adhesive.
985 (26p.) Type **221** 65 70
986 (26p.) Potatoes 65 70
987 (26p.) Tomatoes 65 70
988 (26p.) Cauliflower and purple-sprouting broccoli 65 70
989 (26p.) Peppers and courgettes 65 70
Nos. 985/9, which are inscribed "UK MINIMUM POSTAGE PAID", were initially sold at 26p each.

222 Queen Elizabeth II

2001. 75th Birthday of Queen Elizabeth II.
990 **222** £3 multicoloured . . . . 6·00 6·50

223 Agile Frog

2001. Europa. Pond Life. Multicoloured.
991 23p. Type **223** 60 65
992 26p. Trout 70 75
993 37p. White water-lily . . . . 1·00 1·10
994 41p. Common blue damselfly . 1·00 1·25
995 46p. Palmate newt . . . . . 1·25 1·40
996 66p. Tufted duck . . . . . . 5·00 5·50
MS997 150 × 100 mm. £1.50 Common kingfisher (36 × 50 mm) 5·00 5·50
The 26 and 37p. values include "EUROPA" emblem.

2001. "Belgica 2001" International Stamp Exhibition, Brussels. No. MS997 optd "JERSEY AT BELGICA 2001" on sheet margin.
MS998 150 × 100 mm. £1.50 Common kingfisher (36 × 50 mm) 5·00 4·50

224 Long-eared Owl

2001. Birds of Prey. Multicoloured.
999 23p. Type **224** 50 55
1000 26p. Peregrine falcon . . . 60 65
1001 37p. Short-eared owl . . . 80 85
1002 41p. Western marsh harrier ("Marsh Harrier") . . . 1·00 95
1003 46p. Northern sparrow hawk ("Sparrowhawk") 1·20 1·10
1004 66p. Tawny owl . . . . . . 1·50 1·60
MS1005 110 × 75 mm. £1.50 Barn owl (30 × 47 mm) . . . . . . 5·00 5·00

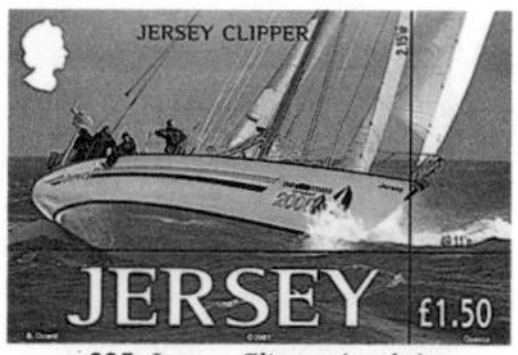

225 *Jersey Clipper* (yacht)

2001. The Times Clipper 2000 Round the World Yacht Race. Sheet 150 × 100 mm.
MS1006 **225** £1.50 multicoloured 4·00 5·00

226 Tilley 26 Manual Fire Engine, c. 1845

2001. Centenary of Jersey Fire and Rescue Service. Fire Engines. Multicoloured.
1007 23p. Type **226** 50 55
1008 26p. Albion Merryweather, c. 1935 . . 60 65
1009 37p. Dennis Ace, c. 1940 . . 80 85
1010 41p. Dennis F8 Pump Escape, c. 1952 . . . . . 90 95
1011 46p. Land Rover Merryweather, c. 1968 . . 1·00 1·10
1012 66p. Dennis Carmichael, c. 1989 . . . 1·50 1·60

2001. "Hafnia 01" International Stamp Exhibition, Copenhagen. As No. **MS**1005, but with brown-red exhibition logo added to bottom left corner of sheet margin and additionally inscr "Jersey visits Hafnia 01 Denmark".
MS1013 £1.50 Barn owl (30 × 47 mm) . . . . 3·75 3·50

227 Nativity

2001. Christmas. Bells. Multicoloured. Self-adhesive.
1014 (23p.) Type **227** 45 50
1015 (23p.) Street decorations . . 45 50
1016 (23p.) Carol singers with hand bells 45 50
1017 (23p.) Father Christmas . . 45 50
1018 (23p.) Christmas tree decorations 45 50
1019 (26p.) Adoration of the shepherds 50 55
1020 (26p.) Carol singers and Father Christmas in sleigh 50 55
1021 (26p.) Paper bell, chains and Christmas tree 50 55
1022 (26p.) Church bells ringing 50 55
1023 (26p.) Christmas cracker . . 50 55
Nos. 1014/18, which are inscribed "JERSEY MINIMUM POSTAGE PAID", were initially sold for 23p., and Nos. 1019/23, inscribed "U.K. MINIMUM POSTAGE PAID", were sold for 26p.

228 *Duchess of Normandy* (launch)

2002. States Vessels. Multicoloured.
1024 23p. Type **228** 50 55
1025 29p. *Duke of Normandy* (tug) 65 70
1026 38p. *Challenger* (customs patrol boat) 80 85
1027 47p. *Le Fret* (pilot boat) . . 1·00 1·10
1028 68p. *Norman le Brocq* (fisheries protection vessel) 1·50 1·60

229 Queen Elizabeth in Coronation Robes (after Cecil Beaton)

2002. Golden Jubilee.
1029 **229** £3 multicoloured . . . . 6·25 6·50

230 Horse

2002. Chinese New Year ("Year of the Horse"). Sheet 110 × 75 mm.
MS1030 **230** £1 multicoloured . . 2·25 2·50

231 Elephant Float, Parish of St. John, 1980

2002. Europa. Circus. Designs showing carnival floats. Multicoloured.
1031 23p. Type **231** 50 55
1032 29p. Clown with red hair, Grouville, 1996 . . . . . 65 70
1033 38p. Clown with white hat, Optimists, 1988 . . . . . 80 85
1034 68p. Performing seal, Grouville, 1996 . . . . . 3·00 3·50
The 29p. and 38p. values include the "EUROPA" emblem.

232 Aubrey Boomer

2002. Centenary of La Moye Golf Club. Multicoloured.
1035 23p. Type **232** 50 55
1036 29p. Harry Vardon 65 70
1037 38p. Sir Henry Cotton . . . 80 85
1038 47p. Diagram of golf swing 1·00 1·10
1039 68p. Putting . . . . 1·50 1·75

233 Vauxhall 12, 1952

2002. 50th Anniv of States of Jersey Police. Patrol Vehicles. Multicoloured.
1040 23p. Type **233** 50 55
1041 29p. Jaguar 2.4 MkII, 1959–60 . . . . 65 70
1042 38p. Austin 1800, 1972–73 80 85
1043 40p. Ford Cortina MkIV, 1978 . . . . 85 90
1044 47p. Honda ST 1100 motorcycle, 1995–2000 . . 1·00 1·10
1045 68p. Vauxhall Vectra, 1998–2000 . . . . 1·50 1·75

234 Honey Bee

2002. Insects. Multicoloured.
1046 23p. Type **234** 50 55
1047 29p. Seven-spot ladybird . . 65 70
1048 38p. Great green bush-cricket 80 45
1049 40p. Greater horn-tail . . . 85 90
1050 47p. Emperor dragonfly . . 1·10 1·25
1051 68p. Hawthorn shield bug 1·50 1·75

235 Queen Elizabeth the Queen Mother in 1910, 1923 and 2002

2002. Queen Elizabeth the Queen Mother Commemoration.
1052 **235** £2 multicoloured . . . . 4·25 4·50

236 Hydrangeas

2002. Centenary of "Battle of Flowers" Parade. Multicoloured.
1053 23p. Type **236** 50 55
1054 29p. Chrysanthemums . . . 65 70
1055 38p. Hare's tails and pampas grasses 80 85
1056 40p. Asters 85 90
1057 47p. Carnations . . . . . . 1·00 1·10
1058 68p. Gladioli . . . . 1·50 1·75
MS1059 150 × 100 mm. £2 "Zanzibar" float (winner of Prix d'Honneur, 1999) (75 × 38 mm) 4·25 4·50

237 British Dilute Tortoiseshell

2002. 25th Anniv of Caesarea Cat Club. Multicoloured.
1060 23p. Type **237** 50 55
1061 29p. Cream Persian 75 70
1062 38p. Blue exotic shorthair 80 85
1063 40p. Black smoke Devon rex 85 90
1064 47p. British silver tabby . . 1·00 1·10
1065 68p. Usual Abyssinian . . . 1·50 1·75
MS1066 110 × 75 mm. £2 British cream/white bi-colour cross (38 × 51 mm) . . . . 4·25 4·50

238 Victorian Pillar Box

2002. 150th Anniv of the First Pillar Box. Multicoloured.

1067	23p. Type **238**	50	55
1068	29p. Edward VII wall box	65	70
1069	38p. George V wall box	80	85
1070	40p. George V ship box	85	90
1071	47p. Elizabeth II pillar box (1952)	1·00	1·10
1072	68p. Elizabeth II pillar boxes (2000)	1·50	1·60
MS1073	150 × 100 mm. £2 Posting letter in Victorian pillar box (40 × 77 mm)	4·25	4·50

239 Sanchez-Besa Hydroplane

2003. Centenary of Powered Flight. Multicoloured.

1074	23p. Type **239**	50	55
1075	29p. Supermarine S.6B seaplane	65	70
1076	38p. De Havilland DH84 Dragon	80	85
1077	40p. De Havilland DH89a Rapide	85	90
1078	47p. Vickers 701 Viscount	1·00	1·10
1079	68p. BAC One Eleven	1·50	1·60
MS1080	112 × 76 mm. £2 Jacob Ellehammer's Biplane, 1906 (60 × 40 mm)	4·25	4·50

240 Ram

2003. Chinese New Year ("Year of the Ram"). Sheet 110 × 75 mm.

MS1081	**240** £1 multicoloured	2·25	2·40

241 "Portelet" (Adrian Allinson)

2003. Europa. Travel Posters. Multicoloured.

1082	23p. Type **241**	50	55
1083	29p. "Jersey" (Lander) (vert)	65	70
1084	38p. "Channel Islands Map" (vert)	80	85
1085	68p. "Jersey, the Sunny Channel Island" (A. Allinson)	1·50	1·60

The 29p. and 38p. values include the "EUROPA" emblem.

2003. Jersey Lighthouses (2nd series). T **206**. Multicoloured.

1086	29p. Violet Channel light buoy	65	70
1087	29p. St. Catherine's Breakwater Light	65	70
1088	30p. Frouquie Aubert light buoy	65	70
1089	30p. Mont Ube Lighthouse	65	70
1090	48p. Banc des Ormes light buoy	1·00	1·10
1091	48p. Gronez Point Lighthouse	1·00	1·10

242 Southern-marsh Orchid

2003. Wild Orchids. Multicoloured.

1092	29p. Type **242**	60	65
1093	30p. Loose-flowered orchid	60	65
1094	39p. Spotted orchid	80	85
1095	50p. Autumn ladies tresses	1·00	1·10
1096	53p. Green-winged orchid	1·10	1·25
1097	69p. Pyramidal orchid	1·40	1·50
MS1098	110 × 75 mm. £2 Loose-flowered orchid (different)	4·00	4·25

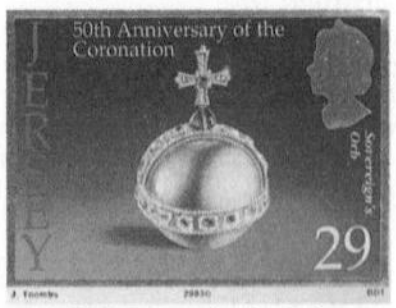

243 Sovereign's Orb

2003. 50th Anniv of Coronation. Coronation Regalia. Multicoloured.

1099	29p. Type **243**	60	65
1100	30p. St. Edward's Crown	60	65
1101	39p. Sceptre with Cross	80	85
1102	50p. Ampulla and Spoon	1·00	1·10
1103	53p. Sovereign's Ring	1·00	1·10
1104	69p. Armills	1·40	1·50
MS1105	150 × 100 mm. Nos. 1099/1104	5·25	5·75

244 Prince William, Prince Charles and Queen Elizabeth

2003. Royal Links. Sheet 110 × 75 mm.

MS1106	**244** £2 multicoloured	4·00	4·25

245 Rock Samphire and Paternosters **246** Albino Rex Rabbit

2003. Offshore Reefs. Multicoloured. Self-adhesive.

1107	(29p.) Type **245**	60	65
1108	(29p.) Bluebells and Les Ecrehous	60	65
1109	(29p.) Tree-mallow and Les Ecrehous	60	65
1110	(29p.) Smooth Sow-thistle and Les Minquiers	60	65
1111	(29p.) Thrift and Les Minquiers	60	65

Nos. 1107/11 are inscribed "JERSEY MINIMUM POSTAGE PAID" and were initially sold at 29p.

2003. Pets. Multicoloured.

1112	29p. Type **246**	95	95
1113	30p. Black labrador	95	95
1114	38p. Canary and budgerigar	1·20	1·20
1115	53p. Hamster	1·70	1·70
1116	69p. Guinea pig	2·20	2·20
MS1117	150 × 100 mm. £2 Border collie (39 × 51 mm)	6·50	6·50

2003. "Bangkok 2003" International Stamp Exhibition. No. **MS**1098 optd **Jersey at Bangkok 2003** and emblem on sheet margin.

MS1118	110 × 75 mm. £2 Loose-flowered orchid	6·50	6·50

2003. Winter Flowers. As T **196**. Multicoloured.

1119	29p. Japanese quince	60	65
1120	30p. Winter jasmine	60	65
1121	39p. Snowdrop	80	85
1122	48p. Winter heath	95	1·00
1123	53p. Chinese witch-hazel	1·00	1·10
1124	69p. Winter daphne	1·40	1·50

247 Rook

2004. Jersey Festivals (1st issue). Festival of Chess. Multicoloured.

1125	29p. Type **247**	95	95
1126	30p. Knight	1·00	1·00
1127	39p. Bishop	1·30	1·30
1128	48p. Pawn	1·60	1·60
1129	53p. Queen	1·70	1·70
1130	69p. King	2·20	2·20

248 Monkey

2004. Chinese New Year ("Year of the Monkey"). Sheet 110 × 75 mm.

MS1131	**248** £1 multicoloured	3·25	3·25

249 St. Aubin's Harbour

2004. Europa. Holidays. Multicoloured.

1132	29p. Type **249**	95	95
1133	30p. Mont Orgueil Castle	95	95
1134	39p. Corbiere Lighthouse	1·30	1·30
1135	69p. Rozel Harbour	2·30	2·30

The 30p. and 39p. values include the "EUROPA" emblem.

250 Green-winged Teal ("Eurasian Teal")

2004. Ducks and Swans. Multicoloured.

1136	32p. Type **250**	1·00	1·00
1137	33p. Mute swan	1·10	1·10
1138	40p. Northern shoveler	1·30	1·30
1139	49p. Common pochard	1·60	1·60
1140	62p. Black swan	2·00	2·00
1141	70p. European Wigeon ("Eurasian Wigeon")	2·30	2·30
MS1142	150 × 100 mm. £2 Mallard (38 × 50 mm)	6·50	6·50

251 *Cymbidium lowianum* "Concolor"

2004. Jersey Orchids (5th series). Multicoloured.

1143	32p. Type **251**	1·00	1·00
1144	33p. *Phragmipedium besseae var. flavum*	1·10	1·10
1145	40p. *Peristeria elata*	1·30	1·30
1146	54p. *Cymbidium tracyanum*	1·80	1·80
1147	62p. *Paphiopedilum Victoria* Village "Isle of Jersey"	2·00	2·00
1148	70p. *Paphiopedilum hirsutissimum*	2·30	2·30
MS1149	110 × 75 mm. £2 *Phragmipedium* "Jason Fischer"	6·50	6·50

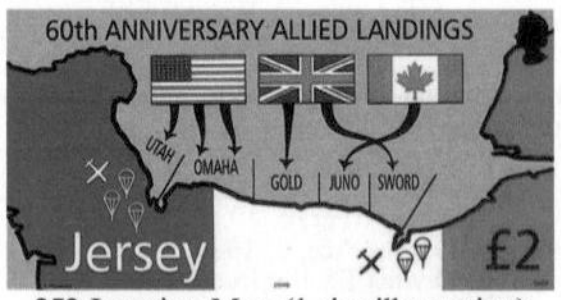

252 Invasion Map (½-size illustration)

2004. 60th Anniv of D-Day. Sheet 110 × 75 mm.

MS1150	**252** £2 multicoloured	6·50	6·50

253 Mont Orgueil Castle in 13th Century

2004. Jersey–"A Peculiar of the Crown". Multicoloured.

1151	32p. Type **253**	1·00	1·00
1152	32p. King John, c. 1204 (23 × 31 mm)	1·00	1·00
1153	33p. Mont Orgueil Castle in 17th century	1·00	1·00
1154	33p. King Charles II, c. 1684 (23 × 31 mm)	1·00	1·00
1155	40p. Mont Orgueil Castle, 2004	1·30	1·30
1156	40p. Queen Elizabeth II, 2002 (23 × 31 mm)	1·30	1·30

2004. Salon du Timbre Stamp Exhibition, Paris. As No. **MS**1149, but optd **Jersey at Le Salon du Timbre 2004** at top left corner of sheet margin.

MS1157	110 × 75 mm. £2 *Phragmipedium* (Jason Fischer)	6·50	6·50

254 Wall Lizard

2004. Endangered Species. Multicoloured.

1158	32p. Type **254**	1·00	1·00
1159	33p. Ant lion	1·10	1·10
1160	49p. Field cricket	1·60	1·60
1161	70p. Dartford warbler	2·30	2·30
MS1162	141 × 174 mm. Nos. 1158/61 each × 2	12·00	12·00

255 Dead Man's Fingers

2004. Corals. Multicoloured.

1163	32p. Type **255**	1·00	1·00
1164	33p. Devonshire cup	1·10	1·10
1165	40p. White sea fan	1·30	1·30
1166	54p. Pink sea fan	1·80	1·80
1167	62p. Sunset cup	2·00	2·00
1168	70p. Red fingers	2·30	2·30
MS1169	150 × 100 mm. Nos. 1166/8	6·00	6·00

256 Nativity Scene

2004. Christmas. Illuminations. Multicoloured. Self-adhesive.

1170	(32p.) Type **256**	1·00	1·00
1171	(32p.) Fairy lights over busy street	1·00	1·00
1172	(32p.) Santa Claus, children and Christmas tree	1·00	1·00
1173	(32p.) Candles in church	1·00	1·00
1174	(32p.) Three candles and holly	1·00	1·00
1175	(33p.) Mary and Jesus	1·00	1·00
1176	(33p.) Stockings and candle on mantelpiece	1·00	1·00
1177	(33p.) Five candles	1·00	1·00
1178	(33p.) Angel and candle	1·00	1·00
1179	(33p.) Candles in window	1·00	1·00

Nos. 1170/4 are inscribed "JERSEY MINIMUM POSTAGE PAID" and were sold for 32p., and Nos. 1175/9 are inscribed "U.K. MINIMUM POSTAGE PAID" and were sold for 33p.

2004. Designs as Nos. 1107/11. Self-adhesive.

1180	(32p.) Type **245**	65	70
1181	(32p). Bluebells and Les Ecrehous	65	70
1182	(32p.) Tree-mallow and Les Ecrehous	65	70
1183	(32p.) Smooth Sow-thistle and Les Minquiers	65	70
1184	(32p.) Thrift and Les Minquiers	65	70

Nos. 1180/4, which are inscribed "JERSEY MINIMUM POSTAGE PAID" and were initially sold at 32p each. Nos. 1180/4 are inscribed "2004" with copyright symbol after date.

257 C 1 Air Search Aircraft

2005. Rescue Craft. Multicoloured.

1185	32p. Type **257**	65	70
1186	33p. Burby helicopter	65	70
1187	40p. Beach lifeguard service	80	85
1188	49p. Fire rescue inflatable	1·00	1·10
1189	70p. R.A.F. Sea King helicopter	1·40	1·50

POSTAGE DUE STAMPS

D 1

D 3 Arms of St. Clement and Dovecote at Samares

1969.
D1 D 1 1d. violet 65 1·10
D2 2d. sepia 90 1·10
D3 3d. mauve 1·00 1·10
D4 – 1s. green 5·50 5·00
D5 – 2s.6d. grey 13·00 14·00
D6 – 5s. red 15·00 16·00
DESIGNS: 1s., 2s.6d., 5s. Map.

1971. Decimal Currency. Design as Nos. D4/6, but values in new currency.
D 7 ½p. black 10 10
D 8 1p. blue 10 10
D 9 2p. brown 10 10
D10 3p. purple 10 10
D11 4p. red 10 10
D12 5p. green 10 10
D13 6p. orange 10 10
D14 7p. yellow 10 10
D15 8p. blue 15 20
D16 10p. green 15 20
D17 11p. brown 20 20
D18 14p. violet 30 30
D19 25p. green 35 40
D20 50p. purple 90 90

1978. Parish Arms and Views.
D21 D 3 1p. black and green 10 10
D22 – 2p. black and yellow 10 10
D23 – 3p. black and brown 10 10
D24 – 4p. black and red 10 10
D25 – 5p. black and blue 10 10
D26 – 10p. black and olive 10 10
D27 – 12p. black and blue 15 10
D28 – 14p. black and orange 20 15
D29 – 15p. black and mauve 25 25
D30 – 20p. black and green 30 30
D31 – 50p. black and brown 90 55
D32 – £1 black and blue 1·40 1·00
DESIGNS: 2p. Arms of St. Lawrence and Handois Reservoir; 3p. Arms of St. John and Sorel Point; 4p. Arms of St. Ouen and Pinnacle Rock; 5p. Arms of St. Peter and Quetivel Mill; 10p. Arms of St. Martin and St. Catherine's Breakwater; 12p. Arms of St. Helier and Harbour; 14p. Arms of St. Saviour and Highlands College; 15p. Arms of St. Brelade and Beauport Bay; 20p. Arms of Grouville and La Hougue Bie; 50p. Arms of St. Mary and Perry Farm; £1 Arms of Trinity and Bouley Bay.

D 4 St. Brelade

1982. Jersey Harbours.
D33 D 4 1p. green 10 10
D34 – 2p. yellow 10 10
D35 – 3p. brown 10 10
D36 – 4p. red 10 10
D37 – 5p. blue 10 10
D38 – 6p. green 10 15
D39 – 7p. mauve 15 20
D40 – 8p. red 15 20
D41 – 9p. green 20 20
D42 – 10p. blue 20 15
D43 – 20p. green 40 30
D44 – 30p. purple 60 40
D45 – 40p. orange 80 45
D46 – £1 violet 2·00 75
DESIGNS: 2p. St. Aubin; 3p. Rozel; 4p. Greve de Lecq; 5p. Bouley Bay; 6p. St. Catherine; 7p. Gorey; 8p. Bonne Nuit; 9p. La Roque; 10p. St. Helier; 20p. Ronez; 30p. La Collette; 40p. Elizabeth Castle; £1 Upper Harbour Marina.

JHALAWAR Pt. 1

A state of Rajasthan, India. Now uses Indian stamps.

4 paisa = 1 anna.

1 Apsara (dancing nymph of Hindu Paradise)

1886. Imperf.
1 1 1p. green 45·00 12·00
2 – ½a. green 1·10 1·25
The ½a. is larger and has a different frame.

JIND Pt. 1

A "convention" state of the Punjab, India, which now uses Indian stamps.

12 pies = 1 anna; 16 annas = 1 rupee.

J 1 (½a.)

J 6 (½a.)

1874. Imperf.
J 8 J 1 ½a. blue 75 4·00
J 9 1a. purple 1·75 9·00
J 3 2a. bistre 1·00 4·00
J11 4a. green 2·50 12·00
J12 8a. purple 7·00 11·00

1882. Various designs and sizes. Imperf or perf.
J16 J 6 ½a. brown 30 1·50
J19 ½a. bistre 80 60
J20 1a. brown 1·75 3·25
J22 2a. blue 2·50 1·00
J23 4a. green 1·50 90
J25 8a. red 5·50 4·50

Stamps of India (Queen Victoria) overprinted.

1885. Optd **JHIND STATE** vert (curved).
1 23 ½a. turquoise 3·25 4·00
2 – 1a. purple 32·00 42·00
3 – 2a. blue 14·00 16·00
4 – 4a. green (No. 71) 55·00 75·00
5 – 8a. mauve £425
6 – 1r. grey (No. 101) £475

1885. Optd **JEEND STATE.**
7 23 ½a. turquoise £110
8 – 1a. purple £110
9 – 2a. blue £110
10 – 4a. green (No. 71) £150
11 – 8a. mauve £190
12 – 1r. grey (No. 101) £170

1886. Optd **JHIND STATE** horiz.
17 23 ½a. turquoise 80 10
18 – 1a. purple 1·50 20
20 – 1a.6p. brown 1·75 3·00
21 – 2a. blue 2·00 40
23 – 3a. orange 2·00 50
15 – 4a. green (No. 71) 50·00
24 – 4a. green (No. 96) 3·00 2·00
27 – 6a. brown 2·50 11·00
28 – 8a. mauve 5·50 16·00
30 – 12a. purple on red 5·50 22·00
31 – 1r. grey (No. 101) 11·00 45·00
32 37 1r. green and red 9·50 50·00
33 38 2r. red and orange £275 £800
34 3r. brown and green £475 £750
35 5r. blue and violet £500 £750

1900. Optd **JHIND STATE** horiz.
36 40 3p. red 1·10 1·10
37 3p. grey 40 3·25
38 23 ½a. green 3·50 5·50
40 – 1a. red 60 5·50

Stamps of India optd **JHIND STATE.**

1903. King Edward VII.
41 41 3p. grey 25 10
43 – ½a. green (No. 122) 1·25 1·50
44 – 1a. red (No. 123) 2·25 1·40
46 – 2a. lilac 2·25 80
47 – 2½a. blue 60 5·50
48 – 3a. orange 1·25 40
50 – 4a. olive 7·00 9·00
51 – 6a. bistre 6·50 19·00
52 – 8a. mauve 2·75 19·00
54 – 12a. purple on red 2·75 12·00
55 – 1r. green and red 2·75 17·00

1907. King Edward VII (inscr "INDIA POSTAGE and REVENUE").
56 ½a. green (No. 149) 20 20
57 1a. red (No. 150) 70 70

1913. King George V.
58 55 3p. grey 10 2·00
59 56 ½a. green 10 75
60 57 1a. red 10 45
61 59 2a. purple 15 4·00
62 62 3a. orange 1·50 11·00
63 64 6a. bistre 6·50 25·00

1914. Stamps of India (King George V) optd **JIND STATE** in two lines.
64a 55 3p. grey 85 20
65b 56 ½a. green 2·25 15
66 57 1a. red 1·50 15
80 1a. brown 4·75 2·25
67 58 1½a. brown (A. No. 163) 2·25 4·50
68 1½a. brown (B. No. 165) 50 1·50
81 1½a. red (B.) 20 1·50
69 59 2a. purple 3·00 60
70 61 2a.6p. blue 35 4·00
82 2a.6p. orange 60 6·50
71 62 3a. orange 50 3·25
83 3a. blue 1·75 4·00
72 63 4a. olive 1·75 8·00
73a 64 6a. brown 2·75 13·00
74 65 8a. mauve 4·00 11·00
75 66 12a. red 3·50 15·00
76 67 1r. brown and green 8·50 18·00
77 2r. red and brown 6·00 £120
78 5r. blue and violet 40·00 £225

1922. No. 192 of India optd **JIND.**
79 57 9p. on 1a. red 1·25 13·00

Stamps of India optd **JIND STATE** in one line.

1927. King George V.
84 55 3p. grey 10 10
85 56 ½a. green 10 35
86 80 9p. green 1·75 40
87 57 1a. brown 15 10
88 82 1a.3p. mauve 25 30
89 58 1½a. red 60 2·75
90 70 2a. lilac 2·25 40
91w 61 2a.6p. orange 1·10 9·00
92 62 3a. blue 4·50 13·00
93w 83 3a.6p. blue 60 17·00
94w 71 4a. green 1·50 2·75
95 64 6a. bistre 65 18·00
96 65 8a. mauve 4·50 2·00
97w 66 12a. red 6·00 19·00
98 67 1r. brown and green 4·00 4·50
99 2r. red and orange 35·00 £130
100 5r. blue and violet 13·00 40·00
101 10r. green and red 14·00 18·00
102 15r. blue and olive 75·00 £550
103 25r. orange and blue £120 £700

1934. King George V.
104 79 ½a. green 30 25
105 81 1a. brown 1·75 30
106 59 2a. orange 2·25 60
107 62 3a. red 3·00 40
108 63 4a. olive 3·25 1·50

1937. King George VI.
109 91 3p. slate 12·00 1·75
110 ½a. brown 75 3·50
111 9p. green 75 3·25
112 1a. red 75 60
113 92 2a. red 1·75 16·00
114 – 2a.6p. violet 1·25 18·00
115 – 3a. green 6·50 15·00
116 – 3a.6p. blue 3·25 18·00
117 – 4a. brown 9·50 16·00
118 – 6a. green 6·00 23·00
119 – 8a. violet 5·00 20·00
120 – 12a. red 2·75 25·00
121 93 1r. slate and brown 12·00 35·00
122 2r. purple and brown 15·00 £100
123 5r. green and blue 25·00 75·00
124 10r. purple and red 45·00 70·00
125 15r. brown and green £100 £700
126 25r. slate and purple £475 £800

1941. Stamps of India (King George VI) optd **JIND.**
(a) On issue of 1937.
127 91 3p. slate 14·00 18·00
128 ½a. brown 1·00 1·50
129 9p. green 13·00 15·00
130 1a. red 1·00 4·50
131 93 1r. slate and brown 9·00 23·00
132 2r. purple and brown 18·00 30·00
133 5r. green and blue 40·00 90·00
134 10r. purple and red 55·00 85·00
135 15r. brown and green £130 £150
136 25r. slate and purple 60·00 £350
(b) On issue of 1940.
137 100a 3p. slate 50 85
138 ½a. mauve 50 1·50
139 9p. green 60 3·50
140 1a. red 65 1·40
141 101 1a.3p. yellow-brown 1·00 4·00
142 1½a. violet 8·00 4·25
143 2a. red 1·75 3·75
144 3a. violet 23·00 4·50
145 3½a. blue 9·00 9·00
146 102 4a. brown 4·75 4·75
147 6a. green 5·50 14·00
148 8a. violet 2·75 12·00
149 12a. purple 14·00 15·00

OFFICIAL STAMPS
Postage stamps of Jind optd **SERVICE.**

1885. Nos. 1/3 (Queen Victoria).
O1 O 23 ½a. green 1·10 30
O2 – 1a. purple 70 10
O3 – 2a. blue 35·00 42·00

1886. Nos. 17/32 and No. 38 (Queen Victoria).
O12 23 ½a. turquoise 1·25 10
O22 – ½a. green (No. 38) 2·00 30
O14 – 1a. purple 10·00 80
O16 – 2a. blue 1·25 30
O17 – 4a. green (No. 24) 2·50 1·25
O19 – 8a. mauve 4·50 3·50
O21 37 1r. green and red 6·00 40·00

1903. Nos. 42/55 (King Edward VII).
O23 41 3p. grey 60 10
O25 – ½a. green (No. 43) 2·50 10
O26 – 1a. red (No. 44) 2·00 10
O28 – 2a. lilac 1·25 10
O29 – 4a. olive 1·00 45
O31 – 8a. mauve 4·50 1·50
O32 – 1r. green and red 2·50 2·25

1907. Nos. 56/7 (King Edward VII).
O33 ½a. green 60 10
O34 1a. red 1·00 10

1914. Official stamps of India. Nos. O75/96 (King George V) optd **JIND STATE.**
O35 55 3p. grey 10 10
O36 56 ½a. green 10 10
O37 57 1a. red 60 10
O46 1a. brown 60 10
O39 59 2a. purple 25 15
O40 63 4a. olive 1·00 20
O41 64 6a. bistre 1·50 2·25
O42 65 8a. mauve 70 1·00
O43 67 1r. brown and green 1·75 1·75
O44 2r. red and brown 14·00 70·00
O45 5r. blue and violet 20·00 £190

Stamps of India optd **JIND STATE SERVICE.**

1927. King George V.
O47 55 3p. grey 10 20
O48 56 ½a. green 10 90
O49 80 9p. green 60 15
O50 57 1a. brown 10 10
O51 82 1a.3p. mauve 40 15
O52 70 2a. lilac 25 15
O64 59 2a. orange 30 15
O53 61 2a.6p. orange 1·00 20·00
O54 71 4a. green 35 25
O55w 64 6a. bistre 3·25 15·00
O56w 65 8a. mauve 60 1·75
O57 66 12a. red 17·50 15·00
O58 67 1r. brown and green 4·25 4·25
O59 2r. red and orange 42·00 35·00
O60 5r. blue and purple 13·00 £200
O61 10r. green and red 35·00 £120

1934. King George V.
O62 79 ½a. green 20 15
O63 81 1a. brown 20 15
O65 63 4a. olive 5·00 30

1937. King George VI.
O66 91 ½a. brown 55·00 30
O67 9p. green 85 10·00
O68 1a. red 55 30
O69 93 1r. slate and brown 28·00 45·00
O70 2r. purple and brown 42·00 £190
O71 5r. green and blue 70·00 £325
O72 10r. purple and red £275 £900

1939. Official stamps of India optd **JIND.**
O73 O 20 3p. slate 50 1·25
O74 ½a. brown 1·50 70
O75 ½a. purple 60 30
O76 9p. green 2·50 10·00
O77 1a. red 3·25 15
O78 1½a. violet 8·50 1·50
O79 2a. orange 5·00 30
O80 2½a. violet 4·00 8·50
O81 4a. brown 7·00 3·25
O82 8a. violet 6·50 6·00

1943. Stamps of India (King George VI) optd **JIND SERVICE.**
O83 93 1r. slate and brown 18·00 45·00
O84 2r. purple and brown 32·00 £140
O85 5r. green and blue 70·00 £350
O86 10r. purple and red £120 £450

JOHORE Pt. 1

A state of the Federation of Malaya, incorporated in Malaysia in 1963.

100 cents = 1 dollar (Straits or Malayan).

Queen Victoria stamps of Straits Settlements overprinted.

1876. Optd with Crescent and Star.
1 1 2c. brown £13000 £4500

1882. Optd **JOHORE.**
8 1 2c. pink (no full point) 90·00 £100
6 2c. pink (with full point) £170 £180

1884. Optd **JOHOR.**
10 1 2c. pink (no full point) 12·00 8·00
14 2c. pink (with full point) £140 60·00

1891. Surch **JOHOR Two CENTS.**
17 1 2c. on 24c. green 26·00 38·00

21 Sultan Aboubakar

24 Sultan Ibrahim

1891.
21 21 1c. purple 50 50
22 2c. purple and yellow 50 1·50

23		3c. purple and red	55	50
24		4c. purple and black	2·75	17·00
25		5c. purple and green	7·00	21·00
26		6c. purple and blue	8·00	21·00
27		$1 green and red	75·00	£160

1892. Surch **3 cents.**

28	**21**	3c. on 4c. purple and black	2·25	50
29		3c. on 5c. purple and green	1·75	3·25
30		3c. on 6c. purple and blue	3·00	3·75
31		3c. on $1 green and red	11·00	70·00

1896. Sultan's Coronation. Optd **KEMAHKOTAAN.**

32	**21**	1c. purple	50	85
33		2c. purple and yellow	50	1·00
34		3c. purple and red	55	1·00
35		4c. purple and black	80	2·25
36		5c. purple and green	5·50	7·50
37		6c. purple and blue	3·50	6·50
38		$1 green and red	50·00	£110

1896.

39	**24**	1c. green	80	1·00
40		2c. green and blue	50	30
41		3c. green and purple	4·00	2·50
42		4c. green and red	1·00	1·25
43		4c. yellow and red	1·50	1·00
44		5c. green and brown	2·00	2·50
45		6c. green and yellow	2·00	3·50
46		10c. green and black	7·00	48·00
47		25c. green and mauve	9·00	42·00
48		50c. green and red	16·00	45·00
49		$1 purple and green	32·00	75·00
50		$2 purple and red	35·00	80·00
51		$3 purple and blue	35·00	£110
52		$4 purple and brown	35·00	85·00
53		$5 purple and yellow	75·00	£130

1903. Surch in figures and words.

54	**24**	3c. on 4c. yellow and red	60	1·10
55		10c. on 4c. green & red (A)	2·50	9·00
59		10c. on 4c. green & red (B)	9·50	48·00
58		10c. on 4c. yellow & red (B)	20·00	40·00
56		50c. on $3 purple and blue	30·00	80·00
60		50c. on $5 purple and yellow	70·00	£160
57		$1 on $2 purple and red	60·00	£110

10c. on 4c. Type A, "cents" in small letters. Type B, "CENTS" in capitals.

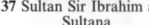

33 Sultan Sir Ibrahim

1904.

78	**33**	1c. purple and green	1·25	15
90		2c. purple and orange	1·00	4·00
63		3c. purple and black	4·75	60
91		4c. purple and red	1·75	70
109		5c. purple and green	50	30
83		8c. purple and blue	4·00	7·00
84		10c. purple and black	50·00	3·00
116		25c. purple and green	3·75	1·00
119		50c. purple and red	3·75	1·60
120		$1 green and mauve	3·75	1·25
121		$2 green and red	7·50	4·00
72		$3 green and blue	27·00	75·00
73		$4 green and brown	27·00	£100
124		$5 green and orange	55·00	50·00
75		$10 green and black	65·00	£160
76		$50 green and blue	£225	£350
77		$100 green and red	£400	£600
128		$500 blue and red	£18000	

1912. Surch **3 CENTS.** and bars.

88	**33**	3c. on 8c. purple and blue	3·50	8·00

1918.

103	**33**	1c. purple and black	30	20
89		2c. purple and green	50	1·00
104		2c. purple and sepia	1·25	4·00
105		2c. green	50	40
106		3c. green	2·00	4·50
107		3c. purple and sepia	1·40	1·50
110		6c. purple and red	50	50
93		10c. purple and blue	2·00	1·40
112		10c. purple and yellow	50	25
113		12c. purple and blue	1·00	1·25
114		12c. blue	42·00	3·25
115		21c. purple and orange	2·00	3·00
117		30c. purple and orange	8·00	7·00
118		40c. purple and brown	8·00	7·50

37 Sultan Sir Ibrahim and Sultana

38 Sultan Sir Ibrahim

1935.

129	**37**	8c. violet and grey	3·50	2·00

1940.

130	**38**	8c. black and blue	18·00	1·00

1948. Silver Wedding. As T **61/2** of Jamaica.

131		10c. violet	20	75
132		$5 green	25·00	40·00

39 Sultan Sir Ibrahim

40 Sultan Sir Ibrahim

1949.

133	**39**	1c. black	50	10
134		2c. orange	20	20
135		3c. green	50	1·00
136		4c. brown	60	10
136a		5c. purple	30	30
137		6c. grey	60	20
138		8c. red	3·25	1·25
138a		8c. green	4·00	2·25
139		10c. mauve	70	10
139a		12c. red	4·00	4·50
140		15c. blue	2·75	10
141		20c. black and green	50	1·00
141a		20c. blue	1·00	10
142		25c. purple and orange	1·75	10
142a		30c. red and purple	1·75	2·75
142b		35c. red and purple	4·50	1·25
143		40c. red and purple	10·00	9·50
144		50c. black and blue	2·50	10
145		$1 blue and purple	5·00	2·00
146		$2 green and red	14·00	6·00
147		$5 green and brown	40·00	11·00

1949. U.P.U. As T **63/6** of Jamaica.

148		10c. purple	30	40
149		15c. blue	1·75	1·00
150		25c. orange	65	3·00
151		50c. black	1·25	3·50

1953. Coronation. As T **71** of Jamaica.

152		10c. black and purple	1·25	10

1955. Diamond Jubilee of Sultan.

153	**40**	10c. red	10	10

41 Sultan Sir Ismail and Johore Coat of Arms

1960. Coronation of Sultan.

154	**41**	10c. multicoloured	20	20

1960. As Nos. 92/102 of Kedah but with inset portrait of Sultan Sir Ismail.

155		1c. black	10	40
156		2c. red	10	1·25
157		4c. sepia	10	10
158		5c. lake	10	10
159		8c. green	1·50	3·00
160		10c. purple	30	10
161		20c. blue	2·00	1·00
162		50c. black and blue	50	20
163		$1 blue and purple	1·50	3·50
164		$2 green and red	9·00	15·00
165		$5 brown and green	29·00	35·00

42 "Vanda hookeriana"

1965. Inset portrait of Sultan Ismail. Multicoloured.

166		1c. Type **42**	10	30
167		2c. "Arundina graminifolia"	10	1·00
168		5c. "Paphiopedilum niveum"	10	10
169		6c. "Spathoglottis plicata"	40	30
170		10c. "Arachnis flos-aeris"	40	20
171		15c. "Rhyncostylis retusa"	1·50	10
172		20c. "Phalaenopsis violacea"	1·50	75

The higher values used in Johore were Nos. 20/7 of Malaysia (National Issues).

44 "Delias ninus"

1971. Butterflies. Inset portrait of Sultan Ismail. Multicoloured.

175		1c. Type **44**	50	2·00
176		2c. "Danaus melanippus"	1·50	2·25
177		5c. "Parthenos sylvia"	1·50	30
178		6c. "Papilio demoleus"	1·50	2·25
179		10c. "Hebomoia glaucippe"	1·50	20
180		15c. "Precis orithya"	1·75	10
181		20c. "Valeria valeria"	1·75	50

The higher values in use with this issue were Nos. 64/71 of Malaysia (National Issues).

45 "Rafflesia hasseltii" (inset portrait of Sultan Ismail)

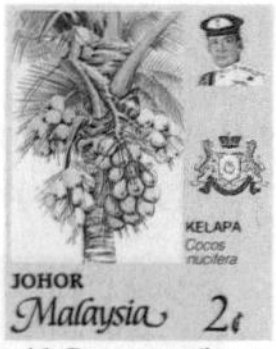

46 Coconuts (inset portrait of Sultan Mahmood)

1979. Flowers. Multicoloured.

188		1c. Type **45**	10	1·00
189		2c. "Pterocarpus indicus"	10	1·00
190		5c. "Lagerstroemia speciosa"	10	60
191		10c. "Durio zibethinus"	15	10
192		15c. "Hibiscus rosa-sinensis"	15	10
193		20c. "Rhododendron scortechinii"	20	25
194		25c. "Etlingera elatior" (inscr "Phaeomeria speciosa")	40	25

1986. Agricultural Products of Malaysia. Mult.

202		1c. Coffee	10	10
203		2c. Type **46**	10	10
204		5c. Cocoa	10	10
205		10c. Black pepper	10	10
206		15c. Rubber	10	10
207		20c. Oil palm	10	10
208		30c. Rice	10	15

POSTAGE DUE STAMPS

D 1

1938.

D1	**D 1**	1c. red	14·00	40·00
D2		4c. green	40·00	40·00
D3		8c. orange	48·00	£140
D4		10c. brown	48·00	48·00
D5		12c. purple	55·00	£130

JORDAN — Pt. 1, Pt. 19

A territory to the E. of Israel, formerly called Transjordan; under British mandate from 1918 to 1946. Independent kingdom since 1946.

1920. 1000 milliemes = 100 piastres = £1 Egyptian.
1927. 1000 milliemes = £1 Palestinian.
1950. 1000 fils = 1 Jordan dinar.

شرق الاردن

(**1** "East of Jordan")

1920. Stamps of Palestine optd with T **1**.

1	**3**	1m. brown	1·00	2·00
10		2m. green	60	1·25
3		3m. brown	1·25	1·50
4		4m. red	1·50	1·50
5		5m. orange	2·75	1·50
14		1p. blue	1·50	2·00
15		2p. olive	4·00	4·00
16		5p. purple	2·50	7·00
17		9p. ochre	3·50	24·00
18		10p. blue	7·00	24·00
19		20p. grey	9·00	42·00

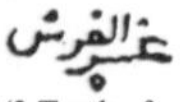

(**2** Tenth of a piastre)

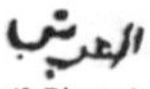

(**3** Piastre)

1922. Handstamped with T **2** or **3** (piastre values). (a) 1920 issue of Jordan (No. 1 etc).

28	**2**	$\frac{1}{10}$p. on 1m. brown	20·00	25·00
29		$\frac{2}{10}$p. on 2m. green	25·00	25·00
22		$\frac{3}{10}$p. on 3m. brown	10·00	10·00
23		$\frac{4}{10}$p. on 4m. red	50·00	50·00
24		$\frac{5}{10}$p. on 5m. orange	£180	£100
31	**3**	1p. on 1p. blue	£200	60·00
25		2p. on 2p. olive	£250	75·00
26		5p. on 5p. purple	50·00	70·00
27a		9p. on 9p. ochre	£130	£140
33		10p. on 10p. blue	£850	£1000
34		20p. on 20p. grey	£650	£850

(b) Type **3** of Palestine.

35	**3**	10p. on 10p. blue	£1800	£2500
36		20p. on 20p. grey	£2500	£3000

(**4** "Arab Government of the East, April, 1921")

1922. Stamps of Jordan handstamped with T **4**.

45	**3**	1m. brown	12·00	15·00
46a		2m. green	8·00	8·00
39b		3m. brown	7·00	7·00
40		4m. red	45·00	50·00
41a		5m. orange	15·00	10·00
48a		1p. blue	15·00	9·00
42c		2p. olive	12·00	10·00
43b		5p. purple	60·00	80·00
44b		9p. ochre	65·00	80·00
52a		10p. blue	£1100	£1600
53a		20p. grey	£1100	£1800

حكومة الشرق
العربية
نيسان سنة ٩٢١

(**5** "Arab Government of the East, April, 1921")

1923. Stamps of Jordan optd with T **5**.

62	**3**	1m. brown	16·00	24·00
63		2m. green	14·00	18·00
56		3m. brown	12·00	15·00
57		4m. red	10·00	12·00
64		5m. orange	10·00	12·00
65		1p. blue	10·00	14·00
59		2p. olive	15·00	15·00
60		5p. purple	60·00	80·00
66		9p. ochre	75·00	£100
67		10p. blue	70·00	£100
68		20p. grey	70·00	£100

(**6**)

(**7**)

(**8**)

(**9**)

1923. Various stamps surch as T **6/9**. (a) 1920 issue of Jordan (No. 1 etc).

70	–	$2\frac{1}{2}$/10thsp. on 5m.	£160	£160
70c	**6**	$\frac{1}{10}$p. on 3m.	†	£5000
70d		$\frac{1}{10}$p. on 5m.		
70e	**9**	2p. on 20p.		

(b) No. 7 of Palestine.

71	**6**	$\frac{1}{10}$p. on 3m.	£3000	

(c) 1922 issue of Jordan (Nos. 22 etc).

72	**6**	$\frac{1}{10}$p. on 3m.	£7000	
73		$\frac{1}{10}$p. on 5p.	70·00	80·00
73b		$\frac{1}{10}$p. on 9p.	£1200	
74	**7**	$\frac{1}{2}$p. on 5p.	70·00	80·00
75a		$\frac{1}{2}$p. on 9p.	£350	£400
77	**8**	1p. on 5p.	80·00	£100

(d) 1922 issue of Jordan (Nos. 396 etc).

78b	**6**	$\frac{1}{10}$p. on 3m.	40·00	50·00
79		$\frac{1}{10}$p. on 5p.	8·00	14·00
79d		$\frac{1}{10}$p. on 9p.	–	£1200
80c	**7**	$\frac{1}{2}$p. on 2p.	60·00	£110
81a		$\frac{1}{2}$p. on 5p.	£1000	
83b	**8**	1p. on 5p.	£2000	£2250

(e) 1923 issue of Jordan (Nos. 56 etc).

84	**6**	$\frac{1}{10}$p. on 3m.	25·00	30·00
85	**7**	$\frac{1}{2}$p. on 9p.	90·00	£150
87	**9**	1p. on 10p.	£2250	£2500
88		2p. on 20p.	60·00	80·00

حكومة

الشرق العربية

٩ شعبان ١٣٤١

(**10** "Arab Government of the East, 9 Sha'ban, 1341")

1923. Stamps of Saudi Arabia optd with T **10**.

89	**11**	$\frac{1}{8}$p. brown	2·50	2·25
96		$\frac{1}{4}$ on $\frac{1}{8}$p. brown (47)	5·00	6·00
90		$\frac{1}{2}$p. red	2·50	2·25
91		1p. blue	2·00	1·00
92		$1\frac{1}{2}$p. lilac	2·00	2·00
93		2p. orange	2·50	6·50
94		3p. brown	3·75	10·00
95		5p. green	7·50	15·00
97		10 on 5p. green (49)	16·00	25·00

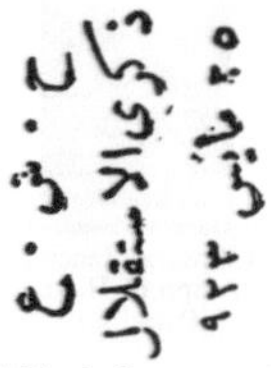

(**11** "Arab Government of the East, Commemoration of Independence, 25 May, 1923")

1923. Stamps of Palestine optd with T **11**.

98A	**3**	1m. brown	17·00	17·00
99A		2m. green	29·00	35·00
100A		3m. brown	10·00	12·00
101A		4m. red	10·00	12·00
102A		5m. orange	50·00	60·00
103B		1p. blue	50·00	60·00
104A		2p. olive	50·00	70·00
105A		5p. purple	60·00	70·00
106B		9p. ochre	50·00	60·00
107A		10p. blue	60·00	80·00
108B		20p. grey	70·00	90·00

1923. No. 107 surch with T **9**.

109	1p. on 10p. blue	£6000	

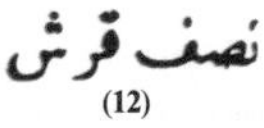

(**12**)

1923. No. 92 surch with T **12**.

110	½p. on 1½p. lilac	7·50	8·00

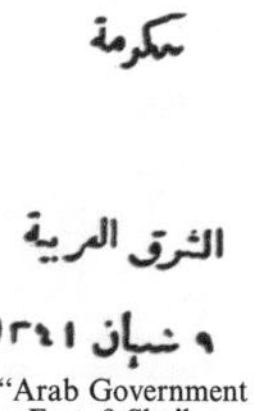

(**13a** "Arab Government of the East, 9 Sha'ban, 1341")

1923. Stamp of Saudi Arabia handstamped as T **13**.

112	**11**	½p. red	7·50	9·00

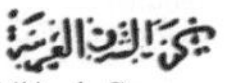

(**15** "Arab Government of the East")

1924. Stamps of Saudi Arabia optd with T **15**.

114	**11**	½p. red	8·50	10·00
115		1p. blue	£300	£200
116		1½p. violet	£350	

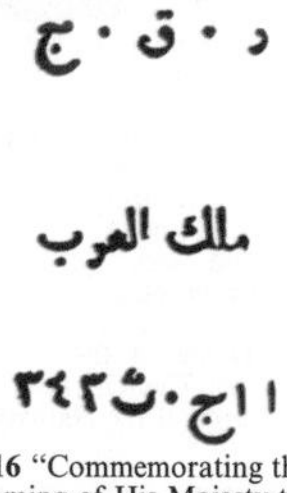

(**16** "Commemorating the coming of His Majesty the King of the Arabs" and date)

1924. Stamps of Saudi Arabia optd with T **15** and **16**.

117	**11**	½p. red	1·25	2·00
118		1p. blue	1·50	2·50
119		1½p. violet	2·25	3·25
120		2p. orange	4·25	5·50

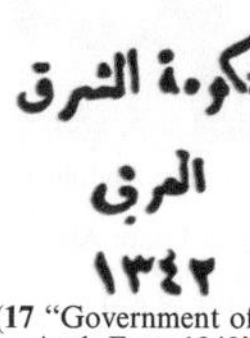

(**17** "Government of the Arab East, 1342")

1924. Stamps of Saudi Arabia optd with T **17**.

125	**11**	⅛p. brown	50	50
126		¼p. green	50	50
127		½p. red	50	50
129		1p. blue	3·50	1·50
130		1½p. lilac	3·00	3·50
131		2p. orange	2·50	2·50
132		3p. red	2·00	2·25
133		5p. green	2·50	3·25
134		10p. purple and mauve	5·50	7·50

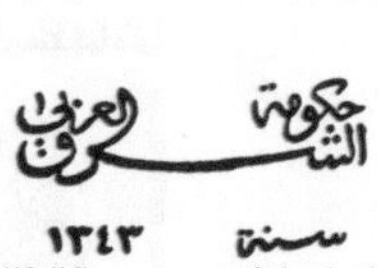

(**18** "Government of the Arab East, 1343")

1925. Stamps of Saudi Arabia optd with T **18**.

135	⅛p. brown	40	1·25
136	¼p. blue	50	1·50
137	½p. red	50	40
138	1p. green	50	1·00
139	1½p. orange	1·25	2·50
140	2p. blue	1·75	3·00
141	3p. green	2·25	4·00
142	5p. brown	2·75	8·50

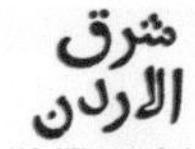

(**19** "East of the Jordan")

1925. Stamps of Palestine (without Palestine opt) optd with T **19**.

143	**3**	1m. brown	20	1·75
144		2m. yellow	20	40
145		3m. blue	70	80
146		4m. red	60	1·75
147		5m. orange	1·25	50
148		6m. green	70	1·25
149		7m. brown	70	1·25
150		8m. red	70	70
151		1p. grey	70	50
152		13m. blue	1·00	1·25
153		2p. olive	2·00	2·25
154		5p. purple	3·25	5·50
155		9p. ochre	6·50	11·00
156		10p. blue	15·00	19·00
157		20p. violet	22·00	35·00

22 Emir Abdullah

23 Emir Abdullah

1927. Figures at left and right.

159	**22**	2m. blue	20	30
160		3m. red	1·75	1·50
161		4m. green	2·50	2·25
162		5m. orange	65	30
163		10m. red	1·50	2·00
164		15m. blue	1·00	30
165		20m. olive	1·00	1·75
166	**23**	50m. purple	2·50	6·00
167		90m. brown	7·00	17·00
168		100m. blue	8·00	13·00
169		200m. violet	17·00	28·00
170		500m. brown	60·00	85·00
171		1000m. grey	£100	£140

(**24** "Constitution")

1928. Optd with T **24**.

172	**22**	2m. blue	1·75	3·00
173		3m. red	1·75	4·25
174		4m. green	2·00	5·50
175		5m. orange	2·00	2·75
176		10m. red	2·25	5·50
177		15m. blue	2·25	2·75
178		20m. olive	4·50	11·00
179	**23**	50m. purple	7·00	11·00
180		90m. brown	18·00	60·00
181		100m. blue	22·00	60·00
182		200m. violet	65·00	£140

1930. "Locust campaign". Optd **LOCUST CAMPAIGN** in English and Arabic.

183	**22**	2m. blue	2·00	5·50
184		3m. red	2·00	6·50
185		4m. green	2·25	8·50
186		5m. orange	18·00	14·00
187		10m. red	2·00	4·00
188		15m. blue	2·00	2·25
189		20m. olive	2·50	4·00
190	**23**	50m. purple	5·00	11·00
191		90m. brown	10·00	45·00
192		100m. blue	12·00	45·00
193		200m. violet	30·00	85·00
194		500m. brown	75·00	£200

28 Emir

29 Emir

1930.

230	**28**	1m. brown	20	75
195		2m. green	50	50
258		3m. pink	15	15
196a		3m. green	2·50	85
259		4m. green	15	15
233		4m. pink	1·75	1·25
198		5m. orange	50	40
199		10m. red	1·25	15
260		10m. violet	15	15
261		12m. red	35	30
200		15m. blue	1·25	20
262		15m. green	40	40
201		20m. green	1·50	35
263		20m. blue	45	45
202	**29**	50m. purple	2·25	1·25
203		90m. bistre	2·50	4·25
240		100m. blue	5·00	1·75
241		200m. violet	9·50	7·00
242		500m. brown	13·00	12·00
243		£P1 grey	24·00	22·00

30 Mushetta

32 The Khasneh at Petra

1933.

208	**30**	1m. black and purple	1·00	1·40
209	–	2m. black and red	1·75	1·00
210	–	3m. green	2·25	1·60
211	–	4m. black and brown	2·50	2·50
212	–	5m. black and orange	3·00	1·25
213	–	10m. red	3·75	3·25
214	**32**	15m. blue	3·00	1·25
215	–	20m. black and olive	4·00	5·00
216	–	50m. black and purple	15·00	13·00
217	**30**	90m. black and yellow	17·00	32·00
218	–	100m. black and blue	17·00	32·00
219	–	200m. black and violet	48·00	75·00
220	**32**	500m. red and brown	£150	£190
221	–	$P1 black and green	£375	£600

DESIGNS—HORIZ: 2m. Nymphaeum, Jerash; 3, 90m. Kasr Kharana; 4m. Kerak Castle; 5, 100m. Temple of Artemis, Jerash; 10, 200m. Ajlun Castle; 20m. Allenby Bridge over Jordan; 50m. Threshing. VERT: £P1, Emir Abdullah.

Nos. 216 to 221 are larger (33½ × 24 mm or 24 × 33½ mm).

35 Map of Jordan

39 Parliament Building

1946. Installation of King Abdullah and National Independence.

249	**35**	1m. purple	15	15
250		2m. orange	15	15
251		3m. green	15	15
252		4m. violet	15	15
253		10m. brown	15	15
254		12m. red	15	15
255		20m. blue	25	25
256		50m. blue	60	60
257		200m. green	2·50	2·50

1947. Inauguration of 1st National Parliament.

276	**39**	1m. violet	15	15
277		3m. red	15	15
278		4m. green	15	15
279		10m. purple	15	15
280		12m. red	15	15
281		20m. blue	15	15
282		50m. red	25	25
283		100m. pink	50	50
284		200m. green	1·10	1·10

40 Globe and Forms of Transport

44 Lockheed Constellation Airliner and Globe

1949. 75th Anniv of U.P.U.

285	**40**	1m. brown	25	25
286		4m. green	45	45
287		10m. red	60	60
288		20m. blue	1·00	1·00
289	–	50m. green	1·70	1·70

DESIGN: 50m. King Abdullah.

1950. Air.

295	**44**	5f. purple and yellow	70	50
296		10f. brown and violet	70	50
297		15f. red and olive	70	50
298		20f. black and blue	95	80
299		50f. green and mauve	1·60	80
300		100f. brown and blue	2·75	1·90
301		150f. orange and black	4·00	2·75

1952. Optd **FILS** and bars or **J.D.** (on 1d.).

313	**28**	1f. on 1m. brown	35	35
314		2f. on 2m. green	35	35
315		3f. on 3m. green	25·00	
316		3f. on 3m. pink	35	35
310		4f. on 4m. pink	6·75	3·25
318		4f. on 4m. green	35	35
319		5f. on 5m. orange	45	45
320		10f. on 10m. red	28·00	
321		10f. on 10m. violet	60	60
322		12f. on 12m. red	60	60
312		15f. on 15m. blue	22·00	11·50
325		15f. on 15m. green	80	45
326		20f. on 20m. green	29·00	
327		20f. on 20m. blue	1·50	70
328	**29**	50f. on 50m. purple	1·50	1·10
329		90f. on 90m. bistre	11·00	7·25
330		100f. on 100m. blue	7·00	2·50
331		200f. on 200m. violet	9·50	3·00
332		500f. on 500m. brown	22·00	9·50
333		1d. on £P1 grey	50·00	12·00

48 Dome of the Rock and Khazneh at Petra

49 King Abdullah

1952. Unification of Jordan and Palestine.

355	**48**	1f. green and brown	25	25
356		2f. red and green	25	25
357		3f. black and red	25	25
358		4f. orange and green	25	25
359		5f. purple and brown	35	35
360		10f. brown and violet	35	35
361		20f. black and blue	85	45
362		100f. sepia and brown	3·00	2·20
363		200f. orange and violet	7·25	4·25

1952. (a) Size 18 × 21½ mm.

364	**49**	5f. orange	25	25
365		10f. lilac	25	25
366		12f. red	1·10	80
367		15f. olive	70	25
368		20f. blue	70	35

(b) Size 20 × 24½ mm.

369	**49**	50f. purple	1·70	70
370		90f. brown	4·75	2·50
371		100f. blue	5·25	1·60

1953. Optd with two horiz bars across Arabic commemorative inscription.

378A	**48**	1f. green and brown	25	25
379A		2f. red and green	25	25
380A		3f. black and red	25	25
381A		4f. orange and green	25	25
382A		5f. purple and brown	25	25
383A		10f. brown and violet	85	45
384A		20f. black and blue	85	60
385A		100f. brown and blue	4·75	1·30
386A		200f. orange and violet	6·50	4·25

(**51**)

51a King Hussein

1953. Obligatory Tax stamps optd for postal use as in T **51**. (a) Inscr "MILS".

387	T **36**	1m. blue	25	25
388		3m. green	25	25
389		5m. purple	95·00	95·00
390	–	10m. red	38·00	31·00
391	–	15m. black	2·40	1·30
392	–	20m. brown	85·00	60·00
393	–	50m. violet	70	60
394	–	100m. red	7·75	6·00

(b) Inscr "MILS" and optd **PALESTINE**.

395	T **36**	1m. blue	50·00	31·00
396		3m. green	50·00	31·00
397		5m. purple	50·00	31·00
398	–	10m. red	50·00	31·00
399	–	15m. black	50·00	31·00
400	–	20m. brown	50·00	31·00
400a	–	50m. violet		
401	–	100m. red	55·00	47·00

(c) Inscr "MILS", optd **FILS** (T334, etc).

402	T **36**	1f. on 1m. blue	43·00	39·00
403		3f. on 3m. green	43·00	39·00
404	–	10f. on 10m. red	43·00	39·00
405	–	15f. on 15m. black	43·00	39·00
406	–	20f. on 20m. brown	43·00	39·00
407	–	100f. on 100m. red	47·00	47·00

(d) Inscr "FILS".

408	T **36**	5f. purple	25	15
409	–	10f. red	35	15
410	–	15f. black	85	70
411	–	20f. brown	1·60	1·10
412	–	100f. orange	4·00	2·20

1953. Enthronement of King Hussein.

413	**51a**	1f. black and green	15	15
414		4f. black and red	15	10
415		15f. black and blue	1·30	25
416		20f. black and lilac	2·20	25
417		50f. black and green	4·75	2·20
418		100f. black and blue	9·50	6·50

52 El-Deir Temple, Petra

54a Temple of Artemis Jerash

1954.

445	**52**	1f. brown & grn (postage)	15	15
446	–	2f. black and red	15	15
447	**52**	3f. violet and purple	15	15
448	–	4f. green and brown	15	15
449	**52**	5f. green and violet	25	15
450	–	10f. green and purple	2·50	1·70

451	–	12f. sepia and red	1·00	15
452	–	15f. red and brown	60	15
453	–	20f. green and blue	45	15
454	–	50f. red and blue	1·00	15
428	–	100f. blue and green	2·50	80
456	–	200f. blue and lake	6·00	1·70
457	–	500f. purple and brown	22·00	8·50
458	–	1d. lake and olive	36·00	13·00
470	54a	5f. orange and blue (air)	25	15
433		10f. red and brown	50	50
434		25f. blue and green	70	50
435		35f. blue and mauve	85	50
436		40f. slate and red	1·00	50
437		50f. orange and blue	1·40	70
438		100f. brown and blue	1·60	1·20
439		150f. lake and turquoise	2·75	1·60

DESIGNS—VERT: 2f., 4f., 500f., 1d. King Hussein. HORIZ: 10f., 15f., 20f. Dome of the Rock, Jerusalem; 12f., 50f., 100f., 200f. Facade of Mosque of El Aqsa.

1955. Arab Postal Union. As Nos. 502/4 of Egypt but inscr "H. K. JORDAN" at top and "ARAB POSTAL UNION" at foot.

440	15f. green	45	25
441	20f. violet	45	25
442	25f. brown	60	45

56 King Hussein and Queen Dina

1955. Royal Wedding.

443	56	15f. blue	1·50	60
444		100f. lake	5·50	2·50

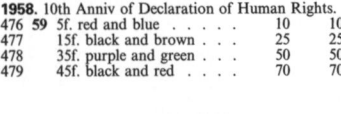

58 Envelope with Postmarks in English and Arabic

59 "Flame of Freedom"

1956. 1st Arab Postal Congress, Amman.

459	58	1f. brown and black	25	25
460		4f. red and black	25	25
461		15f. blue and black	25	25
462		20f. bistre and black	25	25
463		50f. blue and black	60	25
464		100f. orange and black	95	60

1958. 10th Anniv of Declaration of Human Rights.

476	59	5f. red and blue	10	10
477		15f. black and brown	25	25
478		35f. purple and green	50	50
479		45f. black and red	70	70

60 King Hussein

1959. Centres in black.

480	60	1f. green	10	10
481		2f. violet	10	10
482		3f. red	25	10
483		4f. purple	25	10
484		7f. green	35	10
485		12f. red	50	10
486		15f. red	50	10
487		21f. green	50	15
488		25f. brown	70	15
489		35f. blue	1·00	15
490		40f. green	1·50	15
491		50f. red	1·90	15
492		100f. green	2·50	50
493		200f. purple	6·50	1·90
494		500f. blue	17·00	7·25
495		1d. purple	31·00	19·00

61 Arab League Centre, Cairo

1960. Inaug of Arab League Centre, Cairo.

496	61	15f. black and green	25	15

62 "Care of Refugees"

1960. World Refugee Year.

497	62	15f. red and blue	25	15
498		35f. blue and bistre	50	45

63 Shah of Iran and King Hussein

1960. Visit of Shah of Iran.

499	63	15f. multicoloured	45	45
500		35f. multicoloured	60	60
501		50f. multicoloured	85	85

64 Petroleum Refinery, Zarka

1961. Inaug of Jordanian Petroleum Refinery.

502	64	15f. blue and violet	25	15
503		35f. brown and violet	45	35

65 Jordanian Families and Graph

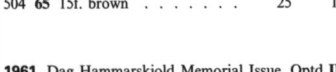

67 Campaign Emblem

1961. 1st Jordanian Census Commemoration.

504	65	15f. brown	25	15

1961. Dag Hammarskjold Memorial Issue. Optd **IN MEMORIAL OF DAG HAMMARSKJOELD 1904–1961** in English and Arabic and laurel leaves at top and bottom.

505	62	15f. red and blue	4·00	4·00
506		35f. blue and bistre	4·00	4·00

1962. Malaria Eradication.

507	67	15f. mauve	25	25
508		35f. blue	50	35
MS509		75 × 76 mm. Nos. 507/8	5·25	5·25

68 Telephone Exchange, Amman

1962. Inauguration of Amman's Automatic Telephone Exchange.

510	68	15f. blue and purple	15	25
511		35f. purple and green	50	50

69 Aqaba Port and King Hussein

1962. Opening of Aqaba Port.

512	69	15f. black and purple	35	15
513		35f. black and blue	70	35
MS514		80 × 93 mm. Nos. 512/13	3·50	3·50

70 Dag Hammarskjold and U.N. Headquarters

1963. 17th Anniv of U.N.

515	70	15f. red, olive and blue	35	15
516		35f. blue, red and olive	85	45
517		50f. olive, blue and red	1·40	85
MS518		135 × 95 mm. Nos. 515/17. Imperf	8·55	8·50

71 Church of Holy Virgin's Tomb, Jerusalem

72 League Centre, Cairo and Emblem

1963. "Holy Places". Multicoloured.

519	50f. Type **71**	1·10	1·10
520	50f. Basilica of the Agony, Gethsemane	1·10	1·10
521	50f. Holy Sepulchre, Jerusalem	1·10	1·10
522	50f. Nativity Church, Bethlehem	1·10	1·10
523	50f. Haram of Ibrahim, Hebron	1·10	1·10
524	50f. Dome of the Rock, Jerusalem	1·10	1·10
525	50f. Omer-el-Khetab Mosque, Jerusalem	1·10	1·10
526	50f. El-Aqsa Mosque, Jerusalem	1·10	1·10

1963. Arab League.

527	72	15f. blue	25	15
528		35f. red	85	35

73 Wheat and F.A.O. Emblem

74 Canal and Symbols

1963. Freedom from Hunger.

529	73	15f. green, black and blue	25	15
530		35f. green, black and apple	45	25
MS531		98 × 85 mm. Nos. 529/30	1·70	1·50

1963. East Ghor Canal Project.

532	74	1f. black and bistre	15	10
533		4f. black and blue	15	10
534		5f. black and purple	15	10
535		10f. black and green	35	10
536		35f. black and orange	1·90	1·40

75 Scales of Justice and Globe

1963. 15th Anniv of Declaration of Human Rights.

537	75	50f. red and blue	70	70
538		50f. blue and red	70	70

1963. Surch in English and Arabic.

539	60	1f. on 21f. black and green	25	25
540		2f. on 21f. black and green	25	25
541		4f. on 12f. black and red	16·00	14·50
542	–	4f. on 12f. sepia and red (No. 451)	35	35
543	60	5f. on 21f. black and green	70	50
544		25f. on 35f. blue	2·50	1·10

77 King Hussein and Red Crescent

1963. Red Crescent Commemoration.

545	77	1f. purple and red	15	15
546		2f. turquoise and red	15	15
547		3f. blue and red	15	15
548		4f. turquoise and red	15	15
549		5f. sepia and red	15	15
550		85f. green and red	1·90	1·90
MS551		90 × 65 mm. 100f. purple and red (larger). Imperf	17·00	17·00

78 Red Cross Emblem

1963. Centenary of Red Cross.

552	78	1f. purple and red	25	25
553		2f. turquoise and red	25	25
554		3f. blue and red	25	25
555		4f. turquoise and red	25	25
556		5f. sepia and red	25	25
557		85f. green and red	3·50	2·50
MS558		90 × 65 mm. 100f. purple and red (larger). Imperf	22·00	22·00

79 Kings Hussein of Hejaz and Hussein of Jordan

1963. Arab Renaissance Day.

559	79	15f. multicoloured	60	25
560		25f. multicoloured	80	45
561		35f. multicoloured	1·40	95
562		50f. multicoloured	3·00	2·50
MS563		112 × 93 mm. Nos. 559/62	6·50	6·50

80 Al Aqsa Mosque, Pope Paul and King Hussein

1964. Pope Paul's Visit to the Holy Land.

564	80	15f. green and black	35	25
565	–	35f. mauve and black	50	35
566	–	50f. brown and black	1·00	80
567	–	80f. blue and black	1·90	1·40
MS567a		138 × 108 mm. Nos. 564/7. Imperf	22·00	22·00

DESIGNS: 35f. Dome of the Rock (Mosque of Omar), Jerusalem; 50f. Church of the Holy Sepulchre, Jerusalem; 80f. Church of the Nativity, Bethlehem.

81 Prince Abdullah

1964. 2nd Birthday of Prince Abdullah. Mult.

568	5f. Prince standing by wall	35	10
569	10f. Head of Prince and roses	45	35
570	35f. Type **81**	95	70

SIZES: 5f. as Type **81** but vert; 10f. diamond (63 × 63 mm).

NOTE.—A set of ten triangular 20f. stamps showing astronauts and rockets was issued, but very few were put on sale at the Post Office and we are not listing them unless we receive satisfactory evidence as to their status.

82 Basketball

83 Woman and Child

1964. Olympic Games, Tokyo (1st issue).

571	82	1f. red	15	15
572	–	2f. blue	15	15
573	–	3f. green	15	15

574 – 4f. buff 15 15
575 – 5f. violet 15 15
576 – 35f. red 1·90 85
577 – 50f. green 3·50 1·70
578 – 100f. brown 5·25 3·00
MS579 88 × 64 mm. 200f. blue (as 100f. but larger). Imperf 30·00 28·00

DESIGNS—VERT: 2f. Volleyball; 3f. Football; 5f. Running. HORIZ: 4f. Table tennis; 35f. Cycling; 50f. Fencing; 100f. Pole vaulting.

See also Nos. 610/**MS**618 and 641/**MS**647.

1964. 4th Session of Social Studies Seminar, Amman.
580 **83** 5f. multicoloured 35 35
581 10f. multicoloured 35 35
582 25f. multicoloured 35 35

84 King Hussein Sports Stadium, Amman

1964. Air. Inaug of "Hussein Sports City".
583 **84** 1f. multicoloured 25 25
584 4f. multicoloured 25 25
585 10f. multicoloured 25 25
586 35f. multicoloured 50 50
MS587 120 × 94 mm. Nos. 583/6 2·20 2·20

85 President Kennedy

1964. Pres. Kennedy Memorial Issue.
588 **85** 1f. violet 35 35
589 2f. red 35 35
590 3f. blue 35 35
591 4f. brown 35 35
592 5f. green 35 35
593 85f. red 17·00 10·50
MS594 110 × 77 mm. **85** 100f. sepia (larger). Imperf 12·00 12·00

86 Statues at Abu Simbel

1964. Nubian Monuments Preservation.
595 **86** 4f. black and blue 35 35
596 15f. violet and yellow 35 35
597 25f. red and green 35 35

87 King Hussein and Map of Palestine in 1920

1964. Arab Summit Conference.
598 **87** 10f. multicoloured 15 10
599 15f. multicoloured 25 15
600 25f. multicoloured 35 15
601 50f. multicoloured 80 25
602 80f. multicoloured 1·50 1·20
MS603 110 × 90 mm. Nos. 598/602. Imperf. No gum 4·00 4·00

88 Pope Paul VI, King Hussein and Ecumenical Patriarch

1964. Meeting of Pope, King and Patriarch, Jerusalem. Multicoloured, background colour given.
604 **88** 10f. green 15 15
605 15f. purple 25 25
606 25f. brown 35 15
607 50f. blue 80 80
608 80f. green 1·50 1·50
MS609 130 × 100 mm. Nos. 604/8. Imperf. No gum 6·50 6·50

89 Olympic Flame

1964. Olympic Games, Tokyo (2nd issue).
610 **89** 1f. red 10 10
611 2f. violet 15 15
612 3f. green 15 15
613 4f. brown 15 15
614 5f. red 25 25
615 35f. blue 85 85
616 50f. olive 1·30 1·30
617 100f. blue 3·00 3·00
MS618 108 × 76 mm. **89** 100f. rose (larger). Imperf 16·00 16·00

90 Scouts crossing River

1964. Jordanian Scouts.
619 **90** 1f. brown 15 15
620 – 2f. violet 15 15
621 – 3f. ochre 15 15
622 – 4f. lake 15 15
623 – 5f. green 15 15
624 – 35f. blue 4·00 1·50
625 – 50f. green 4·25 2·40
MS626 108 × 76 mm. 100f. blue (as 50f. but larger). Imperf 19·00 9·50

DESIGNS: 2f. First aid; 3f. Exercising; 4f. Practising knots; 5f. Cooking meal; 35f. Sailing; 50f. Around camp-fire.

91 Four-coloured Bush Shrike

1964. Air. Birds. Multicoloured.
627 150f. Type **91** 19·00 8·50
628 500f. Ornate hawk eagle (vert) 55·00 26·00
629 1000f. Grey-headed kingfisher (vert) 95·00 47·00

92 Bykovsky

1965. Russian Astronauts.
630 40f. brown and green (Type **92**) 1·00 70
631 40f. violet & brown (Gagarin) 1·00 70
632 40f. maroon & bl (Nikolaev) 1·00 70
633 40f. lilac and bistre (Popovich) 1·00 70
634 40f. sepia & blue (Tereshkova) 1·00 70
635 40f. green and pink (Titov) 1·00 70
MS636 115 × 83 mm. 100f. blue and black (space ship and the six cosmonauts). Imperf 16·00 16·00
MS637 As above opt **VOSKHOD 12/10/64/VLADIMIR KOMATOV/KONSTANTIN FEOKTISTOV/BORIS YEGEROV** 16·00 16·00

93 U.N. Headquarters and Emblem

1965. 19th Anniv (1964) of U.N.
638 **93** 30f. violet, turquoise & brn 50 45
639 70f. brown, blue and violet 1·00 60
MS640 76 × 102 mm. Nos. 638/9. Imperf 14·00 14·00

94 Olympic Flame

1965. Air. Olympic Games, Tokyo (3rd issue).
641 **94** 10f. red 35 35
642 15f. violet 35 35
643 20f. blue 35 35
644 30f. green 35 35
645 40f. brown 50 50
646 60f. mauve 70 70
MS647 102 × 102 mm. **94** 100f. blue (larger). Imperf 13·00 13·00

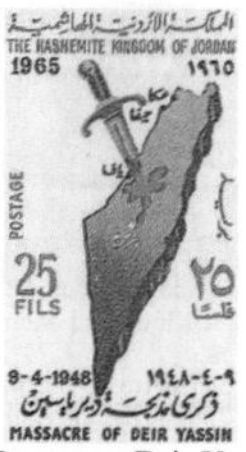

95 Dagger on Deir Yassin, Palestine

1965. Deir Yassin Massacre.
648 **95** 25f. red and olive 2·50 1·40

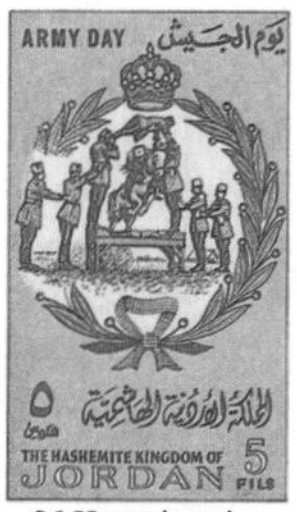

96 Horse-jumping **97** Volleyball Player and Cup

1965. Army Day.
649 **96** 5f. green 15 10
650 – 10f. blue 35 15
651 – 35f. brown 1·10 45

DESIGNS: 10f. Tank; 35f. King Hussein making inspection in army car.

1965. Arab Volleyball Championships.
652 **97** 15f. olive 80 25
653 35f. lake 1·50 70
654 50f. blue 2·50 1·50
MS655 63 × 89 mm. **97** 100f. brown (larger). Imperf 19·00 19·00

98 President J. F. Kennedy

1965. 1st Death Anniv of Pres. Kennedy.
656 **98** 10f. black and green 35 35
657 15f. violet and orange 50 35
658 25f. brown and blue 80 50
659 50f. purple and green 1·60 95
MS660 114 × 90 mm. **98** 50f. salmon and blue. Imperf 13·00 13·00

99 Pope Paul, King Hussein and Dome of the Rock

1965. 1st Anniv of Pope Paul's Visit to the Holy Land.
661 **99** 5f. brown and mauve 45 10
662 10f. lake and green 85 35
663 15f. blue and flesh 1·20 45
664 50f. grey and pink 3·00 1·50
MS665 102 × 76 mm. **99** 50f. blue and violet. Imperf 19·00 19·00

100 Cathedral Steps

1965. Air. Jerash Antiquities. Multicoloured.
666 55f. Type **100** 1·20 1·20
667 55f. Artemis Temple Gate 1·20 1·20
668 55f. Street of Columns 1·20 1·20
669 55f. Columns of South Theatre 1·20 1·20
670 55f. Forum (horiz) 1·20 1·20
671 55f. South Theatre (horiz) 1·20 1·20
672 55f. Triumphal Arch (horiz) 1·20 1·20
673 55f. Temple of Artemis (horiz) 1·20 1·20

101 Jordan Pavilion at Fair

1965. New York World's Fair.
674 **101** 15f. multicoloured 15 15
675 25f. multicoloured 45 25
676 50f. multicoloured 95 60
MS677 113 × 75 mm. **101** 100f. multicoloured 2·75 2·75

102 Lamp and Burning Library

1965. Burning of Algiers Library.
678 **102** 25f. green, red and black 35 15

103 I.T.U. Emblem and Symbols

1965. Centenary of I.T.U.
679 **103** 25f. blue and light blue 35 15
680 45f. black and green 60 35
MS681 40 × 32 mm. **103** 100f. lake and red (larger). Imperf 2·50 2·50

104 "Syncom" Satellite and Pagoda

1965. Space Achievements. Multicoloured.
682 5f. Type **104** 35 35
683 10f. North American X-15 rocket airplane 35 35
684 15f. Astronauts 50 45
685 20f. As 10f. 70 50
686 50f. Type **104** . . . . 1·60 1·20
MS687 101 × 76 mm. 50f. Syncom Satellite and Earth's sphere. Imperf . . . . 13·00 13·00

105 Dead Sea

1985. Dead Sea. Multicoloured.
688 35f. Type **105** 80 50
689 35f. Boats and palms 80 50
690 35f. Qumran Caves 80 50
691 35f. Dead Sea Scrolls 80 50

1965. Air. Space Flight of McDivitt and White. Nos. 641/6 optd **James McDivitt Edward White 2-6-1965** in English and Arabic and rocket.
692 **94** 10f. red . . . . 1·30 1·30
693 15f. violet . . . . 1·70 1·70
694 20f. blue . . . . 2·40 2·40
695 30f. green . . . . 3·50 3·50
696 40f. brown . . . . 4·75 4·75
697 60f. mauve . . . . 7·00 7·00
MS698 102 × 102 mm. **94** 100f. blue (larger). Imperf . . . . 21·00 21·00

107 King Hussein, U.N. Emblem and Headquarters

1965. King Hussein's Visit to France and the U.S.A.
699 **107** 5f. sepia, blue and pink 35 35
700 – 10f. sepia, green and grey 35 35
701 – 20f. agate, brown and blue 60 60
702 **107** 50f. lilac, brown and blue 1·50 1·50
MS703 102 × 102 mm. **107** 50f. lilac, brown and blue. Imperf . . . 8·50 8·50
DESIGNS: 10f. King Hussein, Pres. de Gaulle and Eiffel Tower; 20f. King Hussein, Pres. Johnson and Statue of Liberty.

108 I.C.Y. Emblem

109 A.P.U. Emblem

1965. International Co-operation Year.
704 **108** 5f. red and orange . . . 25 15
705 10f. violet and blue . . . 60 25
706 45f. purple and green . . 2·20 1·70

1965. 10th Anniv (1964) of Arab Postal Union's Permanent Office at Cairo.
707 **109** 15f. black and blue . . . 15 15
708 25f. black and green . . . 60 25

110 Dome of the Rock

1965. Inaug (1964) of "Dome of the Rock".
709 **110** 15f. multicoloured 95 35
710 25f. multicoloured . . . . 1·60 1·00

111 King Hussein

115 First Station of the Cross

114 Agricultural Symbols

1966. (a) Postage. Portraits in blue (1f. to 15f.) or purple (21f. to 150f.); background colours given.
711 **111** 1f. orange 10 10
712 2f. blue 10 10
713 3f. violet 10 10
714 4f. purple 10 10
715 7f. brown 25 10
716 12f. mauve 25 10
717 15f. brown 35 10
718 21f. green 50 10
719 25f. blue 60 10
720 35f. stone 80 15
721 40f. yellow 85 25
722 50f. green 95 45
723 100f. green . . . . 1·60 95
724 150f. violet . . . . 3·50 1·50

(b) Air. Portraits in brown; background colours given.
725 **111** 200f. turquoise . . . . . 5·50 1·60
726 500f. green . . . . 9·50 6·50
727 1d. blue . . . . 16·00 10·50

1966. Space Flights of Belyaev and Leonov. Nos. 630/5 optd **Alexei Leonov Pavel Belyaev 18 3-1965** in English and Arabic and spacecraft motif.
728 **92** 40f. brown and green . . . 4·25 4·25
729 – 40f. violet and brown . . . 4·25 4·25
730 – 40f. purple and blue . . . 4·25 4·25
731 – 40f. lilac and bistre . . . 4·25 4·25
732 – 40f. sepia and blue . . . . 4·25 4·25
733 – 40f. green and pink . . . . 4·25 4·25
MS734 115 × 83 mm. 100f. blue and black (No. **MS**636) . . . . . 43·00 43·00
MS735 115 × 83 mm. 100f. blue and black (No. **MS**637) . . . . . 43·00 43·00

1966. Pope Paul's Visit to U.N. (1965). Nos. 604/8 optd **PAPA PAULUS VI WORLD PEACE VISIT TO UNITED NATIONS 1965** in English and Arabic.
736 **88** 10f. green 15 10
737 15f. purple 60 25
738 25f. brown 60 35
739 50f. blue . . . . 1·10 60
740 80f. green . . . . 1·90 95
MS740a 130 × 100 mm. Nos. 736/40. Imperf. No gum . . . . 11·00 11·00

1966. Anti-T.B. Campaign. (a) Unissued "Freedom from Hunger" stamps optd as in T **114**.
741 **114** 15f. multicoloured 45 35
742 35f. multicoloured . . . . 1·10 80
743 50f. multicoloured . . . . 1·70 1·60
MS744 108 × 76 mm. Nos. 741/3. Gold background . . . . 13·00 13·00
MS744a 108 × 76 mm. Nos. 741/2. White background. Imperf . . . 13·00 13·00

(b) As Nos. 741/3 but with additional premium obliterated by bars.
745 – 15f. multicoloured 45 35
746 – 35f. multicoloured . . . . . 1·10 80
747 – 50f. multicoloured . . . . . 1·70 1·60

1966. Christ's Passion. The Stations of the Cross.
749 **115** 1f. multicoloured 15 10
750 – 2f. multicoloured 15 10
751 – 3f. multicoloured 25 15
752 – 4f. multicoloured 25 15
753 – 5f. multicoloured 45 25
754 – 6f. multicoloured 60 35
755 – 7f. multicoloured 85 50
756 – 8f. multicoloured 85 50
757 – 9f. multicoloured . . . . 1·10 60
758 – 10f. multicoloured . . . . 1·20 70
759 – 11f. multicoloured . . . . 1·50 95
760 – 12f. multicoloured . . . . 1·50 95
761 – 13f. multicoloured . . . . 1·60 95
762 – 14f. multicoloured . . . . 1·60 1·10
MS763 101 × 76 mm. **115**100f. multicoloured . . . . 17·00 17·00
DESIGNS: The 14 Stations. The denominations, expressed in Roman numerals, correspond to the numbers of the stations.

116 Schirra and "Gemini 6"

118 Dag Hammarskjold

117 The Three Kings

1966. Space Achievements.
764 **116** 1f. blue, violet and green 15 15
765 – 2f. green, violet and blue 15 15
766 – 3f. violet, blue and green 15 15
767 – 4f. violet, green and ochre 25 15
768 – 30f. turquoise, brn & vio 1·70 1·20
769 – 60f. brown, turq & vio . . 2·20 1·70
MS770 114 × 88 mm. 100f. multicoloured (The six astronauts etc). Imperf . . . . 17·00 17·00
DESIGNS: 2f. Stafford and "Gemini 6"; 3f. Borman and "Gemini 7"; 4f. Lovell and "Gemini 7"; 30f. Armstrong and "Gemini 8"; 60f. Scott and "Gemini 8".

1966. Christmas. Multicoloured.
771 5f. Type **117** 15 10
772 10f. The Magi presenting gifts to the infant Christ 35 15
773 35f. The flight to Egypt (vert) 3·25 1·10
MS774 115 × 90 mm. 50f. As 10f. Imperf . . . . 19·00 19·00

1967. "Builders of World Peace". Multicoloured. (a) (1st issue).
775 5f. Type **118** 10 10
776 10f. Pandit Nehru 25 15
777 35f. President Kennedy . . . 80 45
778 50f. Pope John XXIII . . . 1·90 60
779 100f. King Abdullah (of Jordan) . . . . 2·20 1·70
MS780 99 × 64 mm. 100f. The above five portraits. Imperf . . . . 18·00 18·00

(b) (2nd issue).
781 5f. U. Thant 10 10
782 10f. President De Gaulle . . 25 15
783 35f. President Johnson . . . 80 45
784 50f. Pope Paul VI . . . . . 1·90 60
785 100f. King Hussein . . . . . 2·20 1·70
MS786 99 × 64 mm. 100f. The above five portraits . . . . 17·00 17·00

119 King Hussein

1967. "Gold Coins". Circular designs, centre and rim embossed on gold foil. Imperf. (a) As T **119**. (i) Diameter 41 mm.
787 **119** 5f. orange and blue . . . 50 50
788 10f. orange and violet . . 50 50

(ii) Diameter 47 mm.
789 **119** 50f. lilac and brown . . . 2·75 2·75
790 100f. pink and green . . . 3·50 3·50

(iii) Diameter 54 mm.
791 **119** 200f. blue and deep blue 7·75 7·75

(b) Crown Prince Hassan of Jordan. (i) Diameter 41 mm.
792 – 5f. black and green 50 50
793 – 10f. black and lilac 50 50

(ii) Diameter 47 mm.
794 – 50f. black and blue . . . . 2·75 2·75
795 – 100f. black and brown . . . . 3·50 3·50

(iii) Diameter 54 mm.
796 – 200f. black and mauve . . . 7·75 7·75
A similar set was also issued in the same values and sizes but different colours with portrait of John F. Kennedy.

120 University City, Statue and Olympic Torch

1967. Preparation for Olympic Games in Mexico (1968).
797 **120** 1f. red, black and violet 25 25
798 – 2f. black, violet and red 25 25
799 – 3f. violet, red and black 25 25
800 – 4f. blue, brown and green 25 25
801 – 30f. green, blue and brown 60 60
802 – 60f. brown, green and blue . . . . 1·20 1·20
MS803 115 × 90 mm. 100f. brown, green and ultramarine (as 60f.). Imperf . . . . 17·00 17·00
DESIGNS (each with Olympic torch): 2f. Fishermen on Lake Patzcuaro; 3f. University City and skyscraper, Mexico City; 4f. Avenida de la Reforma, Mexico City; 30f. Guadalajara Cathedral; 60f. Fine Arts Theatre, Mexico City.

121 Decade Emblem

1967. International Hydrological Decade.
804 **121** 10f. black and red 25 10
805 15f. black and turquoise 50 25
806 25f. black and purple . . 95 60

122 UNESCO Emblem

1967. 20th Anniv of UNESCO.
807 **122** 100f. multicoloured . . . 1·10 1·10

123 Dromedary

1967. Animals. Multicoloured.
808 1f. Type **123** (postage) . . . 1·10 25
809 2f. Karakul sheep . . . . . 1·10 25
810 3f. Angora goat . . . . . . 1·10 25
811 4f. Striped hyena (air) . . . 1·10 25
812 30f. Arab horses . . . . . . 1·50 50
813 60f. Goitred gazelle . . . . . 2·50 1·10
MS814 115 × 89 mm. 100f. (as 30f.). Imperf . . . . 24·00 24·00

124 W.H.O. Building

1967. Inaug of W.H.O. Headquarters, Geneva.
815 **124** 5f. black and green . . . 15 15
816 45f. black and orange . . 70 35

125 Arab League Emblem, Open Book and Reaching Hands

1968. Literacy Campaign.

817	125	20f. green and orange	60	25
818		20f. blue and mauve	45	25

126 W.H.O. Emblem and "20"

1968. 20th Anniv of W.H.O.

819	126	30f. multicoloured	60	25
820		100f. multicoloured	1·70	95

127 Eurasian Goldfinch ("Goldfinch")

1968. Game Protection. Multicoloured.

821	5f. Type **127** (postage)	2·40	1·10
822	10f. Chukar partridge ("Rock Partridge") (vert)	4·25	1·10
823	15f. Ostriches (vert)	6·00	1·40
824	20f. Sand partridge	6·00	1·60
825	30f. Mountain gazelle	4·00	1·20
826	40f. Arabian oryx	5·50	1·40
827	50f. Houbara bustard ("Bustard")	8·50	3·00
828	60f. Ibex (vert) (air)	7·00	3·75
829	100f. Flock of mallard ("Duck")	11·00	7·00

128 Human Rights Emblem

129 I.L.O. Emblem

1968. Human Rights Year.

830	128	20f. black, buff and brown	25	15
831		60f. black, blue and green	85	70

1969. 50th Anniv of I.L.O.

832	129	10f. black and blue	25	10
833		20f. black and brown	25	15
834		25f. black and green	35	25
835		45f. black and mauve	60	45
836		60f. black and orange	85	60

130 Horses in Pasture

1969. Arab Horses. Multicoloured.

837	10f. Type **130**	1·10	25
838	20f. White horse	3·00	80
839	45f. Black mare and foal	5·50	2·40

131 Kaaba, Mecca, and Dome of the Rock, Jerusalem

1969. Multicoloured.

840	5f. As Type **131**	35	10
841	10f. Dome of the Rock (30 × 36 mm)	60	45
842	20f. As 10f.	1·10	60
843	45f. As 5f.	2·75	70

132 Oranges

133 Prince Hassan and Bride

1969. Fruits. Multicoloured.

844	10f. Type **132**	25	10
845	20f. Gooseberry	45	25
846	30f. Lemons	95	25
847	40f. Grapes	1·40	35
848	50f. Olives	1·90	95
849	100f. Apples	3·00	1·70

1969. Wedding of Prince Hassan (1968).

850	–	20f. multicoloured	45	45
851	–	60f. multicoloured	1·00	85
852	133	100f. multicoloured	1·70	1·70

Nos. 850/1 show a similar design to Type **133**.

134 Wrecked Houses

1970. "Tragedy of the Refugees". Various vert designs as T **134**. Multicoloured.

853/82	1f. to 30f. inclusive Set of 30	28·00	19·00

135 Bombed Mosque

1970. "Tragedy in the Holy Lands". Various vert designs as T **135**. Multicoloured.

883/912	1f. to 30f. inclusive Set of 30	28·00	19·00

136 Pomegranate

137 Football

1970. Flowers. Multicoloured.

913	5f. Type **136**	35	10
914	15f. Wattle	60	10
915	25f. Caper	95	15
916	35f. Convolvulus	1·40	25
917	45f. Desert scabious	1·90	70
918	75f. Black iris	3·00	2·50

Nos. 913/15 and 917 are wrongly inscribed on the stamps.

1970. Sports. Multicoloured.

919	5f. Type **137**	15	10
920	10f. Diving	25	15
921	15f. Boxing	45	15
922	50f. Running	1·30	60
923	100f. Cycling (vert)	3·00	1·10
924	150f. Basketball (vert)	4·75	2·50

138 Arab Children

1970. Children's Day. Multicoloured.

925	5f. Type **138**	25	10
926	10f. Refugee boy with kettle (vert)	25	15
927	15f. Refugee girl in camp (vert)	60	15
928	20f. Refugee child in tent (vert)	85	25

139 White-crowned Black Wheatear ("Black Chat")

1970. Birds.

929	139	120f. black and orange	10·50	2·20
930	–	180f. brown, black & lilac	13·00	4·75
931	–	200f. multicoloured	16·00	7·00

DESIGNS: 180f. Masked shrike; 200f. Palestine sunbird.

140 Grotto of the Nativity, Bethlehem

1970. Christmas. Church of the Nativity, Bethlehem. Multicoloured.

932	5f. Type **140**	25	15
933	10f. Christmas crib	35	15
934	20f. Crypt Altar	60	25
935	25f. Nave, Church of the Nativity	80	25

141 Arab League Flag, Emblem and Map

1971. 25th Anniv (1970) of Arab League.

936	141	10f. green, violet & orange	15	15
937		20f. green, brown and blue	45	15
938		30f. green, blue and olive	60	25

142 Heads of Four Races and Emblem

144 Ibn Sinai (Avicenna)

143 Shore of the Dead Sea

1971. Racial Equality Year. Multicoloured.

939	5f. Type **142**	25	25
940	10f. "Plant" and emblem	25	25
941	15f. Doves and emblem (horiz)	35	25

No. 939 is inscribed "KINIGDOM" in error.

1971. Tourism. Multicoloured.

942	5f. Type **143**	25	15
943	30f. Ed Deir, Petra	80	35
944	45f. Via Dolorosa, Jerusalem (vert)	1·20	45
945	60f. River Jordan	1·90	1·00
946	100f. Christmas Bell, Bethlehem (vert)	2·75	1·90

1971. Famous Arab Scholars, Multicoloured.

947	5f. Type **144**	15	10
948	10f. Ibn Rushd	25	10
949	20f. Ibn Khaldun	45	15
950	25f. Ibn Tufail	80	15
951	30f. Ibn El Haytham	1·10	60

145 New U.P.U. H.Q. Building

1971. Inauguration of New U.P.U. Headquarters Building, Berne.

952	145	10f. brown, green & yellow	45	25
953		20f. purple, green & yellow	60	25

146 Young Pupil

147 Mothers and Children

1972. International Education Year.

954	146	5f. multicoloured	10	10
955		15f. multicoloured	25	10
956		20f. multicoloured	45	15
957		30f. multicoloured	95	50

1972. Mothers Day. Multicoloured.

958	10f. Type **147**	50	25
959	20f. Mother and child (vert)	50	1·10
960	30f. Bedouin mother and child (vert)	60	2·20

148 Pope Paul VI leaving Holy Sepulchre, Jerusalem

1972. Easter. Multicoloured.

961	30f. Type **148** (postage)	50	15
962	60f. The Calvary, Church of the Holy Sepulchre (air)	1·00	45
963	100f. "Washing of the Feet", Jerusalem	1·90	85

149 Children and UNICEF Emblem

1972. 25th Anniv of UNICEF.

964	149	10f. turquoise, blue & brn	45	25
965	–	20f. brown, green & pur	45	25
966	–	30f. brown, mauve & blue	50	25

DESIGNS—VERT: 20f. Child with toy bricks. HORIZ: 30f. Nurse holding baby.

150 Dove of Peace

152 Arab with Kestrel

151 Al Aqsa Mosque and Pilgrims

1972. 25th Anniv (1970) of United Nations.

967	150	5f. green, violet and yellow	10	10
968		10f. green, red and yellow	25	10
969		15f. blue, black and yellow	50	15
970		20f. blue, green and yellow	70	25
971		30f. green, brown & yell	1·30	60

1972. Burning of Al Aqsa Mosque (1970). Mult.

972	30f. Type **151**	1·70	25
973	60f. Mosque in flames	4·00	1·10
974	100f. Mosque interior	5·50	2·20

1972. Jordanian Desert Life. Multicoloured.

975	5f. Type **152**	50	25
976	10f. Desert bungalow (horiz)	50	25
977	15f. Camel trooper, Arab Legion (horiz)	50	25
978	20f. Boring operations (horiz)	80	25
979	25f. Shepherd (horiz)	80	25
980	30f. Dromedaries at water-trough (horiz)	1·40	45
981	35f. Chicken farm (horiz)	1·50	80
982	45f. Irrigation scheme (horiz)	2·20	1·40

153 Wasfi el Tell and Dome of the Rock, Jerusalem

1972. Wasfi el Tell (assassinated statesman) Memorial Issue. Multicoloured.

983	5f. Type **153**	25	10
984	10f. Wasfi el Tell, map and flag	35	15
985	20f. Type **153**	80	15
986	30f. As 10f.	85	70

154 Clay-pigeon shooting

1972. World Clay-pigeon Shooting Championships. Multicoloured.

987	25f. Type **154**	35	25
988	75f. Marksman on range (horiz)	1·20	1·00
989	120f. Marksman taking aim (horiz)	2·20	1·60

155 Aero Club Emblem

1973. Royal Jordanian Aero Club.

990	155	5f. blk, bl & yell (postage)	60	25
991		10f. black, blue and yellow	60	25
992	–	15f. multicoloured (air)	60	25
993	–	20f. multicoloured	70	25
994	–	40f. multicoloured	1·40	60

DESIGNS: 15f. Piper Cherokee 140 aircraft; 20f. Beech B55 Baron airplane; 40f. Winged horse emblem.

156 Dove and Flag

1973. 50th Anniv of Hashemite Kingdom of Jordan. Multicoloured.

995	5f. Type **156**	10	10
996	10f. Anniversary emblem	25	10
997	15f. King Hussein	60	15
998	30f. Map and emblems	1·30	1·10

157 Map and Jordanian Advance

1973. 5th Anniv of Battle of Karama. Mult.

999	5f. Type **157**	25	15
1000	10f. Jordanian attack, and map	50	25
1001	15f. Map, and King Hussein on tank	1·30	85

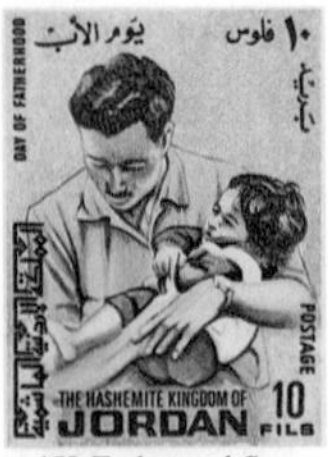

158 Father and Son

1973. Fathers' Day. Multicoloured.

1002	10f. Type **158**	15	15
1003	20f. Father and daughter	60	15
1004	30f. Family group	95	45

159 Phosphate Mines

1973. Development Projects. Multicoloured.

1005	5f. Type **159**	25	10
1006	10f. Cement factories	35	15
1007	15f. Sharhabil Dam	60	15
1008	20f. Kafrein Dam	85	45

160 Racing Camel

1973. Camel Racing. Multicoloured.

1009	5f. Type **160**	80	25
1010	10f. Camels in "paddock"	80	25
1011	15f. Start of race	80	25
1012	20f. Camel racing	80	35

161 Book Year Emblem

1973. International Book Year (1972).

1013	161	30f. multicoloured	50	25
1014		60f. multicoloured	1·20	35

162 Family Group

1973. Family Day.

1015	162	20f. multicoloured	50	25
1016	–	30f. multicoloured	50	25
1017	–	60f. multicoloured	95	35

DESIGNS: 30, 60f. Different family groups.

163 Shah of Iran, King Hussein, Cyrus's Tomb and Mosque of Omar

1973. 2500th Anniv of Iranian Monarchy.

1018	163	5f. multicoloured	45	10
1019		10f. multicoloured	60	10
1020		15f. multicoloured	70	15
1021		30f. multicoloured	1·60	45

164 Emblem of Palestine Week

1973. Palestine Week. Multicoloured.

1022	5f. Type **164**	45	25
1023	10f. Torch and emblem	60	25
1024	15f. Refugees (26 × 47 mm)	70	35
1025	30f. Children and map on Globe	1·60	50

165 Traditional Harvesting

1973. Ancient and Modern Agriculture. Multicoloured.

1026	5f. Type **165** (postage)	15	15
1027	10f. Modern harvesting	25	15
1028	15f. Traditional seeding	50	15
1029	20f. Modern seeding	80	15
1030	30f. Traditional ploughing	85	25
1031	35f. Modern ploughing	1·00	25
1032	45f. Pest control	1·30	25
1033	60f. Horticulture	2·20	1·10
1034	100f. Agricultural landscape (air)	2·50	1·30

166 Long-nosed Butterflyfish

168 "The Club-footed Boy" (Murillo)

167 Battle of Muta

1974. Red Sea Fishes. Multicoloured.

1035	5f. Type **166**	35	15
1036	10f. Monocle bream	45	15
1037	15f. As No. 1036	80	15
1038	20f. Slender-spined mojarra	95	15
1039	25f. As No. 1038	1·40	45
1040	30f. Russell's snapper	1·40	45
1041	35f. As No. 1040	2·20	70
1042	40f. Blue-barred orange parrotfish	2·20	80
1043	45f. As No. 1042	2·75	85
1044	50f. Type **166**	3·00	95
1045	60f. Yellow-edged lyretail	3·50	1·20

1974. Islamic Battles against the Crusaders. Multicoloured.

1046	10f. Type **167**	45	15
1047	20f. Battle of Yarmouk	1·10	25
1048	30f. Battle of Hattin	1·90	80

1974. Famous Paintings. Multicoloured.

1049	5f. Type **168**	1·10	35
1050	10f. "Praying Hands" (Durer)	1·10	35
1051	15f. "St. George and the Dragon" (Uccello)	1·10	35
1052	20f. "The Mona Lisa" (L. da Vinci)	1·10	35
1053	30f. "Hope" (F. Watts)	1·10	35
1054	40f. "The Angelus" (Jean Millet) (horiz)	1·40	35
1055	50f. "The Artist and her Daughter" (Angelica Kauffmann)	1·70	45
1056	60f. "Whistler's Mother" (J. Whistler) (horiz)	2·50	85
1057	100f. "Master Hare" (Sir J. Reynolds)	3·50	1·60

المؤتمر الدولي لتاريخ بلاد الشام

٢٠ – ١٩٧٤/٤/٢٥

الجامعة الاردنية

(169)

1974. International Conference for Damascus History. Nos. 1013/14 optd with T **169**.

1058	161	30f. multicoloured	50	35
1059		60f. multicoloured	1·20	80

170 U.P.U. Emblem

171 Camel Caravan

1974. Centenary of Universal Postal Union.

1060	170	10f. multicoloured	35	35
1061		30f. multicoloured	50	35
1062		60f. multicoloured	95	45

1974. The Dead Sea. Multicoloured.

1063	2f. Type **171**	15	10
1064	3f. Palm and shore	15	10
1065	4f. Hotel on coast	15	10
1066	5f. Jars from Qumram Caves	80	35
1067	6f. Copper scrolls (vert)	80	35
1068	10f. Cistern steps, Qumram (vert)	80	35
1069	20f. Type **171**	70	15
1070	30f. As 3f.	1·00	15
1071	40f. As 4f.	1·00	50
1072	50f. As 5f.	1·70	45
1073	60f. As 6f.	2·20	50
1074	100f. As 10f.	3·50	80

172 W.P.Y. Emblem

173 Water-skier

1974. World Population Year.

1075	172	5f. purple, green & black	15	10
1076		10f. red, green and black	25	15
1077		20f. orange, green & blk	60	25

1974. Water-skiing. Multicoloured.

1078	5f. Type **173**	35	35
1079	10f. Water-skier (side view) (horiz)	35	35
1080	20f. Skier turning (horiz)	35	35
1081	50f. Type **173**	70	35
1082	100f. As 10f.	1·20	60
1083	200f. As 20f.	2·50	1·20

174 Ka'aba, Mecca, and Pilgrims

1974. "Pilgrimage Season".

1084	174	10f. multicoloured	25	15
1085		20f. multicoloured	80	50

175 Amrah Palace

176 King Hussein at Wheel of Car

1974. Desert Ruins. Multicoloured.

1086	10f. Type **175**	25	15
1087	20f. Hisham Palace	60	50
1088	30f. Kharana Castle	1·60	80

1975. Air. Royal Jordanian Automobile Club.

1089	176	30f. multicoloured	50	15
1090		60f. multicoloured	1·60	85

177 Woman in Costume   178 Treasury, Petra

1975. Jordanian Women's Costumes.
1091 **177** 5f. multicoloured 15 10
1092 – 10f. multicoloured . . . 25 15
1093 – 15f. multicoloured . . . 50 15
1094 – 20f. multicoloured . . . 80 25
1095 – 25f. multicoloured . . . 1·00 60
DESIGNS: 10f. to 25f. Various costumes as T **177**.

1975. Tourism. Multicoloured.
1096 15f. Type **178** (postage) . . 85 35
1097 20f. Ommayyad Palace, Amman (horiz) 85 35
1098 30f. Dome of the Rock, Jerusalem (horiz) . . . . 1·20 35
1099 40f. Forum columns, Jerash (horiz) . . . . 1·60 35
1100 50f. Palms, Aqaba (air) . . 1·20 45
1101 60f. Obelisk Tomb, Petra (horiz) . . . . 1·70 50
1102 80f. Fort of Wadi Rum (horiz) . . . . 2·10 50

179 King Hussein   180 Globe and "Desert"

1975.
1103 **179** 5f. blue and green . . . 25 10
1104 – 10f. blue and violet . . . 25 10
1105 – 15f. blue and pink . . . 10 10
1106 – 20f. blue and brown . . . 50 15
1107 – 25f. blue and ultramarine 50 15
1108 – 30f. blue and brown . . 15 15
1109 – 35f. blue and violet . . . 25 15
1110 – 40f. blue and red 60 25
1111 – 45f. blue and mauve . . 35 25
1112 – 50f. blue and green . . . 35 25
1113 – 60f. brown and green . . 1·10 45
1114 – 100f. brown & lt brown 1·90 50
1115 – 120f. brown and blue . . 95 80
1116 – 180f. brown and mauve 1·60 1·10
1117 – 200f. brown and blue . . 1·90 1·60
1118 – 400f. brown and purple 3·00 2·50
1119 – 500f. brown and red . . 4·00 4·00
Nos. 1113/19 are larger, 22 × 27 mm.

1975. 10th Anniv of ALIA (Royal Jordanian Airlines). Multicoloured.
1120 10f. Type **180** 15 15
1121 30f. Boeing 707 linking globe and map of Jordan (horiz) 35 15
1122 60f. Globe and "ALIA" logo 50 35

181 Satellite and Earth Station

1975. Satellite Earth Station Opening.
1123 **181** 20f. multicoloured . . . 70 15
1124 30f. multicoloured . . . 1·20 60

182 Emblem of Chamber of Commerce

1975. 50th Anniv of Amman Chamber of Commerce.
1125 **182** 10f. multicoloured . . . 15 15
1126 15f. multicoloured . . . 35 15
1127 20f. multicoloured . . . 50 35

183 Emblem and Hand with Spanner

1975. Completion of Three Year Development Plan.
1128 **183** 5f. black, red and green 15 15
1129 10f. black, red and green 25 25
1130 20f. black, red and green 60 35

184 Jordanian Family   185 A.L.O. Emblem and Salt Mine

1976. International Women's Year (1975). Mult.
1131 5f. Type **184** 10 10
1132 25f. Woman scientist . . . 50 25
1133 60f. Woman graduate . . . 1·40 80

1976. Arab Labour Organization. Multicoloured.
1134 10f. Type **185** 45 35
1135 30f. Welding 45 35
1136 60f. Quayside, Aqaba . . . 85 45

1976. Nos. 853/82 surch in English and Arabic.
1137/46 25f. on 1f. to 10f. . . .
1147/51 40f. on 11f. to 15f. . . .
1152/56 50f. on 16f. to 20f. . . .
1157/61 75f. on 21f. to 25f. . . .
1162/66 125f. on 26f. to 30f. . .
Set of 30 . . . . £100 70·00

1976. Nos. 883/912 surch in English and Arabic.
1167/76 25f. on 1f. to 10f. . . .
1178/82 40f. on 11f. to 15f. . . .
1183/87 50f. on 16f. to 20f. . . .
1188/92 75f. on 21f. to 25f. . . .
1192/96 125f. on 26f. to 30f. . .
Set of 30 . . . . £100 70·00

187 Tennis   188 Schu'aib Dam

1976. Sports and Youth. Multicoloured.
1197 5f. Type **187** 15 10
1198 10f. Body-building 25 10
1199 15f. Football 35 15
1200 20f. Show jumping 50 15
1201 30f. Weightlifting 85 35
1202 100f. Stadium, Amman . . 3·50 1·90

1976. Dams. Multicoloured.
1203 30f. Type **188** 70 35
1204 60f. Al-Kafrein Dam . . . 1·40 45
1205 100f. Ziqlab Dam . . . . . 2·20 80

189 Early and Modern Telephones   190 Road Crossing and Traffic Lights

1977. Telephone Centenary. Multicoloured.
1206 75f. Type **189** . . . . . . 1·30 80
1207 125f. Early telephone and modern receiver . . . . . 2·20 1·30

1977. International Traffic Day. Multicoloured.
1208 5f. Type **190** 50 25
1209 75f. Roundabout and traffic lights . . . . 1·60 80
1210 125f. Motorcycle policemen, road signs and traffic lights . . . . 2·50 1·10

191 Airliner over Ship   192 Child, Toys and Money-box

1977. Silver Jubilee of King Hussein. Mult.
1211 10f. Type **191** 15 10
1212 25f. Pylons and factories . . 35 15
1213 40f. Fertilizer plant 50 15
1214 50f. Ground-to-air missile 70 35
1215 75f. Mosque . . . . 1·20 60
1216 125f. Ground satellite receiving aerial . . . . . 1·90 1·20
MS1217 100 × 70 mm. 100f. Silver Jubilee emblem. Imperf . . . . 8·50 8·50

1977. Postal Savings Bank. Multicoloured.
1218 10f. Type **192** 10 10
1219 25f. Child with piggy bank 35 15
1220 50f. Savings Bank emblem 80 35
1221 75f. Boy and bank teller . . 1·60 80

193 King Hussein and Queen Alia   194 Queen Alia

1977.
1222 **193** 10f. multicoloured . . . 15 15
1223 25f. multicoloured . . . 35 15
1224 40f. multicoloured . . . 60 25
1225 50f. multicoloured . . . 80 50

1977. Queen Alia Commemoration.
1226 **194** 10f. multicoloured . . . 15 15
1227 25f. multicoloured . . . 35 15
1228 40f. multicoloured . . . 60 25
1229 50f. multicoloured . . . 80 50

195 Mohammed Ali Jinnah   196 A.P.U. Emblem and Flags

1977. Birth Centenary of Mohammed Ali Jinnah (1st Governor-General of Pakistan).
1230 **195** 25f. multicoloured . . . 50 25
1231 75f. multicoloured . . . 1·50 60

1978. 25th Anniv (1977) of Arab Postal Union.
1232 **196** 25f. multicoloured . . . 70 45
1233 40f. multicoloured . . . 1·10 80

197 Coffee Pots and Cups   198 Roman Amphitheatre, Jerash

1978. Handicrafts. Multicoloured.
1234 25f. Type **197** 35 15
1235 40f. Porcelain plate and ashtray 50 15
1236 75f. Vase, necklace and chains . . . . 1·20 50
1237 125f. Containers holding pipes . . . . 2·20 1·30

1978. Tourism. Multicoloured.
1238 5f. Type **198** 50 25
1239 20f. Roman columns, Jerash 50 25
1240 40f. Roman mosaic, Madaba 70 35
1241 75f. Rock formations, Rum 1·60 70

199 King Hussein and Pres. Sadat of Egypt   200 Cement Works

1978. Visits of Arab Leaders to Jordan. Mult.
1242 40f. Type **199** 50 15
1243 40f. King Hussein and Pres. Assad (horiz) 50 15
1244 40f. King Hussein and King Khalid (horiz) 50 15

1978. Industrial Development. Multicoloured.
1245 5f. Type **200** 10 10
1246 10f. Science laboratory . . . 35 15
1247 25f. Printing press 85 25
1248 75f. Fertilizer plant . . . . 2·20 85

201 UNESCO Emblem   202 King Hussein

1978. 30th Anniv of UNESCO.
1249 **201** 40f. multicoloured . . . 60 45
1250 75f. multicoloured . . . 1·40 95

1979. Dated "1979".
1251 **202** 25f. brown, flesh and blue 50 15
1252 40f. brown, flesh & pur 85 15
See also Nos. 1265/72 for values dated "1980" and Nos. 1309/13 for those dated "1981".

203 Emblems within Cogwheels   204 I.Y.C. Emblem and Flag of Jordan

1979. Five Year Development Plan.
1253 **203** 25f. multicoloured . . . 45 15
1254 40f. multicoloured . . . 60 15
1255 50f. multicoloured . . . 70 45

1979. International Year of the Child.
1256 **204** 25f. multicoloured . . . 50 25
1257 40f. multicoloured . . . 80 25
1258 50f. multicoloured . . . 1·20 35

205 Census Emblem   206 Nurse holding Baby

1979. Population and Housing Census.
1259 **205** 25f. multicoloured . . . 35 15
1260 40f. multicoloured . . . 60 15
1261 50f. multicoloured . . . 85 45

1980. International Nursing Day.
1262 **206** 25f. multicoloured . . . 50 15
1263 40f. multicoloured . . . 85 35
1264 50f. multicoloured . . . 1·00 60

1980.
1265 **202** 5f. brown, pink and green 10 10
1266 10f. brown, pink & violet 15 10
1267 20f. brown and pink . . 15 10
1268 25f. brown, pink and blue 25 25
1269 40f. brown and mauve 50 25
1270 50f. brown, pink & green 60 50
1271 75f. brown, pink and grey 60 35
1272 125f. brown, pink and red . . . . 1·90 60
Nos. 1265/72 are similar to Nos. 1251/2 but are inscr "1980".

207 El Deir Temple, Petra   208 Mosque and Kaaba, Mecca

1980. World Tourism Conference, Manila.
1273 **207** 25f. black, grey and green 50 25
1274 40f. black, grey and blue 95 35
1275 50f. black, grey & purple 1·20 45

1980. 1400th Anniv of Hegira.
1276 **208** 25f. multicoloured . . . 25 25
1277 40f. multicoloured . . . 60 35
1278 50f. multicoloured . . . 80 45
1279 75f. multicoloured . . . 1·40 70
1280 100f. multicoloured . . . 1·40 95
MS1281 127 × 89 mm. Nos. 1276/80. Imperf . . . . 6·50 6·50

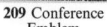

209 Conference Emblem

210 Picking Crops, examining Patients and Flag-raising Ceremony

1980. 11th Arab Summit Conference, Amman.
1282 **209** 25f. multicoloured . . . 25 25
1283 40f. multicoloured . . . 50 35
1284 50f. multicoloured . . . 70 45
1285 75f. multicoloured . . . 1·10 70
1286 100f. multicoloured . . . 1·40 95
MS1287 100 × 100 mm. Nos. 1282/6. Imperf . . . . 6·50 6·50

1981. Red Crescent.
1288 **210** 25f. multicoloured . . . 60 25
1289 40f. multicoloured . . . 80 45
1290 50f. multicoloured . . . 85 50

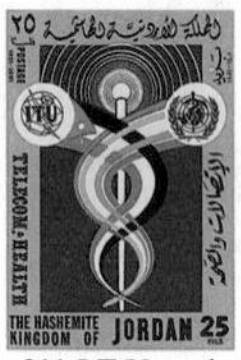

211 I.T.U. and W.H.O. Emblems and Ribbons forming Caduceus

212 Jordan Stamps of 1930 and 1975

1981. World Telecommunications Day.
1291 **211** 25f. multicoloured . . . 60 25
1292 40f. multicoloured . . . 1·00 45
1293 50f. multicoloured . . . 1·40 80

1981. Opening of Postal Museum. Multicoloured.
1294 25f. Type **212** 60 15
1295 40f. Jordan stamps of 1933 and 1954 (vert) 85 35
1296 50f. Jordan stamps of 1946 and 1952 . . . . 1·20 60

213 Khawla Bint el-Azwar

214 F.A.O. Emblem and Olive Branches

1981. Arab Women in History. Multicoloured.
1297 25f. Type **213** 85 25
1298 40f. El-Khansa (writer) . . . 1·50 45
1299 50f. Rabia el-Adawiyeh (Sufi religious leader) . . . . . 2·40 1·20

1981. World Food Day.
1300 **214** 25f. multicoloured . . . 45 25
1301 40f. multicoloured . . . 80 45
1302 50f. multicoloured . . . 95 45

215 I.Y.D.P. Emblem

216 Hands reading Braille

1981. International Year of Disabled Persons.
1303 **215** 25f. multicoloured . . . 45 25
1304 40f. multicoloured . . . 95 35
1305 50f. multicoloured . . . 1·20 45

1981. The Blind.
1306 **216** 25f. multicoloured . . . 45 25
1307 40f. multicoloured . . . 95 35
1308 50f. multicoloured . . . 1·20 45

1982.
1309 **202** 5f. brown, pink and green 25 15
1310 10f. brown, pink & violet 25 15
1311 20f. brown and pink . . 25 15
1312 25f. brown, pink and blue 25 15
1313 40f. brown, pink & pur 45 25
Nos. 1309/13 are similar to Nos. 1251/2, but are inscr "1981".

217 Hand holding Jug and Stone Tablets

218 A.P.U. Emblem

1982. Jordan Monuments.
1314 **217** 25f. multicoloured . . . 60 15
1315 40f. multicoloured . . . 95 25
1316 50f. multicoloured . . . 1·20 60

1982. 30th Anniv of Arab Postal Union.
1317 **218** 10f. multicoloured . . . 50 25
1318 25f. multicoloured . . . 80 25
1319 40f. multicoloured . . . 95 35
1320 50f. multicoloured . . . 1·20 45
1321 100f. multicoloured . . . 2·40 85

219 King Hussein and Jet Fighter

1982. Independence, Army Day and 30th Anniv of King's Accession to Throne. Multicoloured.
1322 10f. King Hussein and rockets 25 15
1323 25f. King Hussein and tanks 50 15
1324 40f. Type **219** 95 35
1325 50f. King Hussein and tanks (different) . . . . 1·20 60
1326 100f. King Hussein and flag being hoisted by armed forces . . . . 2·40 1·70

220 Salt Secondary School

1982. Salt Secondary School.
1327 **220** 10f. multicoloured . . . 45 25
1328 25f. multicoloured . . . 60 25
1329 40f. multicoloured . . . 95 35
1330 50f. multicoloured . . . 1·00 50
1331 100f. multicoloured . . . 2·10 85

221 City Gate, Jerusalem

222 Soldiers, Flags and Badge

1982. Jerusalem. Multicoloured.
1332 10f. Type **221** 25 10
1333 25f. Minaret 50 15
1334 40f. Mosque 85 35
1335 50f. Mosque (different) . . . 1·00 60
1336 100f. Dome of the Rock . . . 1·90 1·40

1982. Yarmouk Forces.
1337 **222** 10f. multicoloured . . . 25 10
1338 25f. multicoloured . . . 50 15
1339 40f. multicoloured . . . 85 35
1340 50f. multicoloured . . . 1·00 60
1341 100f. multicoloured . . . 1·90 1·60
MS1342 71 × 51 mm. 100f. multicoloured (Forces badge). Imperf . . . . 14·50 14·50

223 Dish Aerial, Earth and U.N. Emblem

224 King Abdullah and Dome of the Rock

1982. 2nd U.N. Conference on the Exploration and Peaceful Uses of Outer Space, Vienna.
1343 **223** 10f. multicoloured . . . 25 10
1344 25f. multicoloured . . . 50 15
1345 40f. multicoloured . . . 85 35
1346 50f. multicoloured . . . 1·00 60
1347 100f. multicoloured . . . 1·90 1·60

1982. Birth Centenary of King Abdullah.
1348 **224** 10f. multicoloured . . . 25 10
1349 25f. multicoloured . . . 50 15
1350 40f. multicoloured . . . 85 35
1351 50f. multicoloured . . . 1·00 60
1352 100f. multicoloured . . . 1·90 1·60

225 King Hussein and Temple Colonnade

226 King Hussein

1982. Roman Ruins at Jerash. Multicoloured.
1353 10f. Type **225** 70 35
1354 25f. Archway 85 35
1355 40f. Temple of Artemis . . 1·20 45
1356 50f. Amphitheatre . . . . . 1·60 45
1357 100f. Hippodrome . . . . . 2·75 95

1983.
1358 **226** 10f. multicoloured . . . 25 25
1359 25f. multicoloured . . . 25 25
1360 40f. multicoloured . . . 45 35
1361 60f. multicoloured . . . 70 45
1362 100f. multicoloured . . . 1·00 70
1363 125f. multicoloured . . . 1·40 80

227 Massacre Victims

1983. Massacre of Palestinian Refugees in Sabra and Shatila Camps. Multicoloured.
1364 10f. Type **227** 25 15
1365 25f. Covered bodies 80 15
1366 40f. Orphans . . . . 1·10 35
1367 50f. Massacre victims in street . . . . 1·60 70
1368 100f. Massacre victims (different) . . . . 2·50 1·60
MS1369 80 × 59 mm. 100f. Wounded child in hospital (sold at 1500f.) . . . . 17·00 17·00

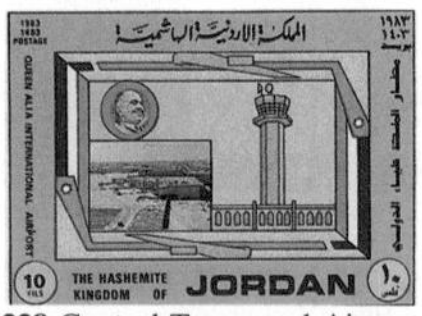

228 Control Tower and Airport Buildings

1983. Opening of Queen Alia International Airport. Multicoloured.
1370 10f. Type **228** 25 10
1371 25f. Tower and terminal building 70 15
1372 40f. Tower and hangar . . . 1·10 35
1373 50f. Tower and aerial view of airport . . . . 1·40 70
1374 100f. Tower and embarkation bridge . . . 2·50 1·70

229 King Hussein with Radio Equipment

1983. Royal Jordanian Radio Amateurs Society.
1375 **229** 10f. multicoloured . . . 25 10
1376 25f. multicoloured . . . 70 15
1377 40f. multicoloured . . . 1·00 35
1378 50f. multicoloured . . . 1·10 70
1379 100f. multicoloured . . . 2·20 1·70

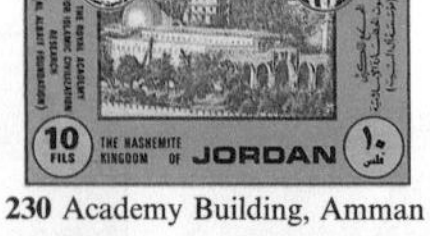

230 Academy Building, Amman

1983. Establishment of Royal Academy for Islamic Civilization Research. Multicoloured.
1380 10f. Type **230** 35 35
1381 25f. Silk rug 70 45
1382 40f. View of Amman . . . 1·00 70
1383 50f. Panorama of Jerusalem 1·20 85
1384 100f. Holy sites of Islam . . 2·75 1·70
MS1385 80 × 60 mm. 100f. Letter from Mohammed to Heraclius. Imperf . . . . 14·50 14·50

231 Irrigation Canal

1983. Food Security. Multicoloured.
1386 10f. Type **231** 25 15
1387 25f. Growing crops under glass 70 15
1388 40f. Battery hens . . . . . 1·10 35
1389 50f. Harvesting . . . . . . 1·30 60
1390 100f. Flock of sheep . . . . 2·20 1·70

232 Switchboard and Emblem

1983. World Communications Year. Mult.
1391 10f. Type **232** 50 35
1392 25f. Aerial view of satellite receiving station 80 35
1393 40f. Microwave antenna and emblems of communication . . . . . 1·10 45
1394 50f. W.C.Y. emblems . . . 1·50 45
1395 100f. Airmail letter . . . . 2·20 1·00

233 Dome of the Rock, Jerusalem

1983. Palestinian Solidarity.
1396 **233** 5f. multicoloured 50 35
1397 10f. multicoloured . . . 1·00 45

234 Human Rights Emblems

1983. 35th Anniv of Declaration of Human Rights.
1398 **234** 10f. multicoloured . . . 25 10
1399 25f. multicoloured . . . 70 15
1400 40f. multicoloured . . . 1·00 35
1401 50f. multicoloured . . . 1·10 70
1402 100f. multicoloured . . . 2·20 1·70

235 "Stop Polio Campaign" Emblem

1984. Anti-poliomyelitis Campaign.
1403 **235** 40f. orange, black & blue 95 25
1404 60f. silver, black and red 1·60 70
1405 100f. green, black & yell 2·50 1·50

236 Bomb and Cogwheel

1984. Israel's Attack on Iraqi Nuclear Reactor. Multicoloured.
1406 40f. Type **236** . . . . . . 1·30 45
1407 60f. Hand with dagger attacking nuclear symbol 1·70 50
1408 100f. Aircraft bombing nuclear symbol . . . . . 2·50 95

237 King Hussein and Tanks

1984. Independence and Army Day. Mult.
1409 10f. Type **237** 25 15
1410 25f. King Hussein and naval patrol boat 70 15
1411 40f. King Hussein and Camel Corps . . . . . . 1·10 35
1412 60f. King Hussein and soldiers at Independence Monument . . . . 1·70 70
1413 100f. Parading soldiers . . . 2·20 1·60

238 Sports Pictogram

1984. Olympic Games. Los Angeles. Mult.
1414 25f. Type **238** 60 15
1415 40f. Swimming . . . . . . 1·00 35
1416 60f. Shooting and archery pictograms . . . . 1·60 80
1417 100f. Gymnastics (floor exercises) . . . . 2·75 1·20
MS1418 90 × 70 mm. 100f. Pole vaulting. Imperf . . . . . . 13·00 13·00

239 Amman Power Station

1984. Water and Electricity Year. Multicoloured.
1419 25f. Power lines and factories 45 15
1420 40f. Type **239** 80 25
1421 60f. Reservoirs and water pipe . . . . 1·10 70
1422 100f. Telephone lines, street light, water tap and pipeline . . . . 1·70 1·10

240 Omayyid Coins

1984. Coins. Multicoloured.
1423 40f. Type **240** 95 45
1424 60f. Abbasid coins . . . . 1·40 60
1425 125f. Hashemite coins . . . 3·00 1·50

241 Shield and Antelope

1984. Release of Antelope in Jordan. Multicoloured.
1426 25f. Type **241** 60 15
1427 40f. Four antelope . . . . 1·00 35
1428 60f. Three antelope . . . . 1·60 80
1429 100f. Duke of Edinburgh, King Hussein and Queen Alia . . . . 2·75 1·20

242 Mu'ta Military University, Karak City

1984. Jordanian Universities. Multicoloured.
1430 40f. Type **242** 70 25
1431 60f. Yarmouk University, Irbid City . . . . 1·00 50
1432 125f. Jordan University, Amman . . . . 1·70 1·10

243 Tombs of El-Hareth bin Omier el-Azdi and Derar bin el-Azwar

1984. Al Sahaba Tombs. Multicoloured.
1433 10f. Type **243** 25 10
1434 25f. Tombs of Sharhabil bin Hasna and Abu Obaidah Amer bin el-Jarrah . . . 60 15
1435 40f. Muath bin Jabal's tomb 85 25
1436 50f. Tombs of Zaid bin Haretha and Abdullah bin Rawaha 95 45
1437 60f. Tomb of Amer bin Abi Waqqas . . . . 1·10 70
1438 100f. Jafar bin Abi Taleb's tomb . . . . 1·90 1·10

244 Soldier descending Mountain and King Hussein

1985. Independence and Army Day. Mult.
1439 25f. Type **244** 50 15
1440 40f. Flags on map, King Abdullah and King Hussein 85 25
1441 60f. Flag, monument and arms . . . . 1·30 70
1442 100f. King Hussein, flag, King Abdullah and arms 2·20 1·60

245 Sir Rowland Hill (instigator of first stamps)

1985. Postal Celebrities. Multicoloured.
1443 40f. Type **245** 80 25
1444 60f. Heinrich von Stephan (founder of Universal Postal Union) . . . . . 1·10 70
1445 125f. Yacoub Sukker (first Jordanian stamp designer) 2·20 1·60

246 Emblem and Delegates round Table

1985. 1st Jordanians Abroad Conference. Mult.
1446 40f. Type **246** 80 25
1447 60f. Conference emblem and globe and hand over torch 1·10 70
1448 125f. Globe encircled by Jordanian flags . . . . . 2·40 1·60

247 I.Y.Y. Emblem

1985. International Youth Year. Multicoloured.
1449 10f. Type **247** 25 15
1450 25f. Arab couple on map, flag and emblem 60 25
1451 40f. Stylized figures flanking globe, flag and emblem 85 25
1452 60f. Part of cogwheel, laurel branch and ribbons in jug decorated with emblem 1·30 70
1453 125f. Stylized figures and emblem . . . . 2·40 1·60

248 El-Deir Temple, Petra

1985. 10th Anniv of World Tourist Organization. Multicoloured.
1454 10f. Type **248** 25 15
1455 25f. Temple of Artemis (ruins), Jerash 60 25
1456 40f. Amrah Palace 85 25
1457 50f. Hill town, Jordan valley 1·00 45
1458 60f. Sailing in Aqaba bay 1·30 85
1459 125f. Roman amphitheatre, Amman and city arms . . 2·20 1·90
MS1460 90 × 70 mm. 100f. Flower with emblem as vase and flag. Imperf . . . . 6·50 6·50

249 Mother and Baby and Hospital

1985. UNICEF Child Survival Campaign. Multicoloured.
1461 25f. Type **249** 60 15
1462 40f. Child being weighed . . 85 35
1463 60f. Childrens' heads as balloons . . . . 1·30 85
1464 125f. Mother feeding baby 2·20 1·90
MS1465 90 × 70 mm. 100f. Hands cradling children's heads. Imperf 11·00 11·00

250 Dancers

1985. 5th Anniv of Jerash Festival. Mult.
1466 10f. Opening ceremony, 1980 . . . . 25 15
1467 25f. Type **250** 60 25
1468 40f. Dancers (different) . . 85 35
1469 60f. Male choir at Roman theatre . . . . 1·30 85
1470 100f. King Hussein and his wife . . . . 2·20 1·70

251 Flag and Emblem forming "40"

1985. 40th Anniv of U.N.O.
1471 **251** 60f. multicoloured . . . 1·50 95
1472 125f. multicoloured . . . 2·20 1·70

252 Hussein comforting Boy

1985. 50th Birthday of King Hussein. Mult.
1473 10f. Type **252** 25 10
1474 25f. Hussein in Arab robes 60 25
1475 40f. Hussein piloting aircraft 85 35
1476 60f. Hussein in army uniform . . . . 1·30 85
1477 100f. Hussein in Arab headdress . . . . 2·20 1·70
MS1478 90 × 70 mm. 200f. Hussein in uniform, flags and Dome of the Rock, Jerusalem. Imperf 14·50 14·50

253 El Aqsa Mosque

1985. Compulsory Tax. Restoration of El Aqsa Mosque, Jerusalem.
1479 **253** 5f. multicoloured . . . . 1·00 1·00
1480 10f. multicoloured . . . 2·20 1·60

254 Policeman beside Car

1985. The Police. Multicoloured.
1481 40f. Type **254** 95 35
1482 60f. Policeman and crowd of children . . . . 1·30 50
1483 125f. Policeman taking oath 3·00 95

255 Satellite over Map of Arab Countries

1986. 1st Anniv of Launch of "Arabsat 1" Communications Satellite. Multicoloured.
1484 60f. Satellite 80 35
1485 100f. Type **255** . . . . . . 1·50 50

256 King presenting Colours

1986. 30th Anniv of Arabization of Jordanian Army. Multicoloured.
1486 40f. Type **256** 70 15
1487 60f. King Hussein shaking hands with soldier 95 35
1488 100f. King Hussein addressing Army . . . . 1·60 95
MS1489 90 × 70 mm. 100f. Text and Hussein addressing Army. Imperf . . . . 10·50 10·50

257 King Abdullah decorating Soldier

1986. 40th Anniv of Independence.
1490 **257** 160f. multicoloured . . . 2·50 1·50

258 King Hussein of Hejaz and Sons

1986. 70th Anniv of Arab Revolt. Multicoloured.
1491 40f. Type **258** 70 15
1492 60f. King Abdullah with armed men . . . . 1·20 45
1493 160f. King leading soldiers on horseback . . . . . 2·20 1·60
MS1494 90 × 70 mm. King Abdullah and Independence declaration. Imperf . . . . . 8·50 8·50

259 Emblem

1986. International Peace Year.
1495 **259** 160f. multicoloured . . . 2·20 1·50
1496 240f. black, orange & grn . . . . 3·00 2·10

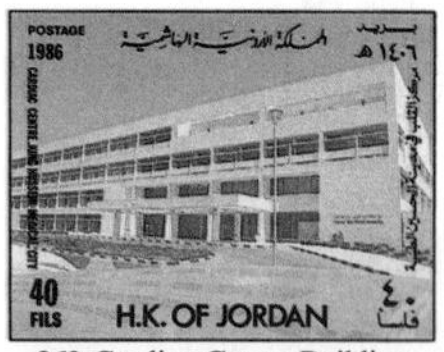
260 Cardiac Centre Building

1986. King Hussein Medical City. Multicoloured.
1497 40f. Type **260** 70 25
1498 60f. Patient undergoing operation . . . . 1·20 60
1499 100f. View of operating theatre during operation 1·70 1·00

261 Extract of King Hussein's Speech in Arabic

1986. 40th Anniv of U.N.O. Multicoloured.
1500 40f. Type **261** 70 15
1501 80f. Extract of speech in Arabic (different) . . . . 1·10 70
1502 100f. Extract of speech in English . . . . 1·60 95
MS1503 90 × 70 mm. 200f. Extracts of speech in Arabic and English and King Hussein making speech. Imperf . . . . 8·25 8·25

262 Head Post Office, Amman

1987. 35th Anniv of Arab Postal Union. Mult.
1504 80f. Type **262** 95 50
1505 160f. Ministry of Communications, Amman 1·70 1·30

263 Jaber ibn Hayyan al-Azdi

1987. Arab and Muslim Pharmacists. Mult.
1506 60f. Type **263** 80 35
1507 80f. Abu-al-Qasem al-Majreeti 95 50
1508 240f. Abu-Bakr al-Razi . . 2·50 2·20

264 Village

1987. S.O.S. Childrens' Village, Amman. Mult.
1509 80f. Type **264** . . . . . . 1·60 80
1510 240f. Child and mural . . . 2·75 2·20

265 Soldiers on Wall

1987. 40th Anniv of 4th Army Brigade. Multicoloured.
1511 60f. Type **265** . . . . . . 1·20 60
1512 80f. Mortar crew . . . . . . 1·70 80
MS1513 70 × 90 mm. 160f. Soldiers on parade . . . . 7·75 7·75

266 Black-headed Bunting

1987. Birds. Multicoloured.
1514 10f. Hoopoe 85 35
1515 40f. Palestine sunbird . . . 1·40 60
1516 50f. Type **266** . . . . . . 1·70 80
1517 60f. Spur-winged plover . . 2·10 85
1518 80f. Western greenfinch ("Greenfinch") . . . . . 2·75 1·50
1519 100f. Black-winged stilt . . 3·25 1·70

267 King Hussein

268 Horsemen Charging

1987.
1520 **267** 60f. multicoloured . . . 50 45
1521 80f. multicoloured . . . 80 60
1522 160f. multicoloured . . . 1·70 1·30
1523 240f. multicoloured . . . 2·40 1·70

1987. 800th Anniv of Battle of Hattin. Mult.
1524 60f. Type **268** . . . . . . 1·10 50
1525 80f. Horseman and Dome of the Rock . . . . 1·50 85
1526 100f. Saladin, horsemen and Dome of the Rock . . . 1·70 1·20
MS1527 90 × 70 mm. 100f. Saladin (29 × 44 mm). Perf or imperf 7·75 7·75

269 Arms

1987.
1528 **269** 80f. multicoloured . . . 95 70
1529 160f. multicoloured . . . 2·10 1·30

270 Amman Industrial Estate, Sahab

1987.
1530 **270** 80f. multicoloured . . . 95 25

271 University Crest

1987. 25th Anniv of Jordan University. Multicoloured.
1531 60f. Type **271** 80 25
1532 80f. Entrance to campus (47 × 32 mm) . . . . . . 1·00 45

272 Child's Head in Droplet

1987. UNICEF Child Survival Campaign. Multicoloured.
1533 60f. Type **272** 80 45
1534 80f. Hands reaching towards child and flag as "J" . . . 1·50 95
1535 160f. Baby on scales and children reading . . . . . 2·10 1·50

273 Parliament in Session, 1987

1987. 40th Anniv of Jordanian Parliament.
1536 – 60f. mauve and gold . . 85 60
1537 **273** 80f. multicoloured . . . 1·50 1·30
DESIGN: 60f. 1947 opening ceremony.

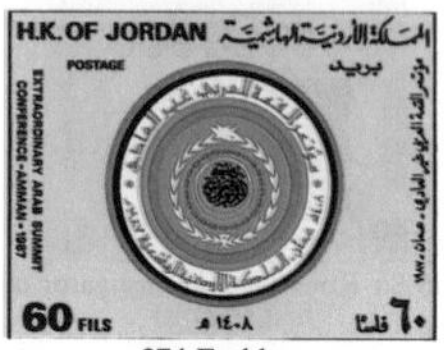
274 Emblem

1987. Extraordinary Arab Summit Conference, Amman.
1538 **274** 60f. multicoloured . . . 80 25
1539 80f. multicoloured . . . 1·00 45
1540 160f. multicoloured . . . 1·70 1·10
1541 240f. multicoloured . . . 2·50 1·70
MS1542 90 × 66 mm. 100f. Emblem, King Hussein and map. Imperf 7·25 7·25

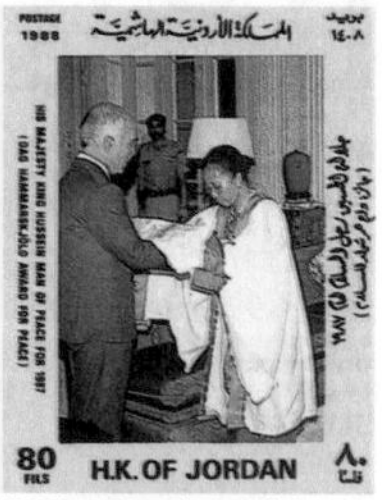
275 King Hussein receiving Cape

1988. Award of 1987 Dag Hammarskjold Peace Prize to King Hussein. Multicoloured.
1543 80f. Type **275** . . . . . . 1·00 45
1544 160f. King Hussein receiving Prize . . . . 1·70 1·10

276 Golden Sword

1988. Jordanian Victory in 1987 Arab Military Basketball Championship. Multicoloured.
1545 60f. Type **276** 80 25
1546 80f. King Hussein congratulating winners . . 1·00 60
1547 160f. Match scene . . . . . 2·20 1·70

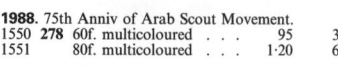

277 Anniversary Emblem and National Flag

278 Emblems and Globe

1988. 40th Anniv of W.H.O.
1548 **277** 60f. multicoloured . . . 95 35
1549 80f. multicoloured . . . 1·20 60

1988. 75th Anniv of Arab Scout Movement.
1550 **278** 60f. multicoloured . . . 95 35
1551 80f. multicoloured . . . 1·20 60

279 Crested Lark

1988. Birds. Multicoloured.
1552 10f. Type **279** . . . . . . 1·10 25
1553 20f. Stone-curlew . . . . . 1·10 25
1554 30f. Common redstart ("Redstart") . . . . . . 1·10 25
1555 40f. Blackbird . . . . . . 1·60 35
1556 50f. Feral rock pigeon ("Rock Dove") . . . . . 1·90 45
1557 160f. White-throated kingfisher ("Smyrna Kingfisher") . . . . . . 6·00 1·50
MS1558 70 × 90 mm. 310f. Birds as in Nos. 1552/7. Imperf . . . . 6·50 6·50

280 City cupped in Hands

282 Tennis

281 Um al-Rasas

1988. Restoration of Sana'a, Yemen Arab Republic.
1559 **280** 80f. multicoloured . . . 85 70
1560 160f. multicoloured . . . 1·90 1·40

1988. Historic Sites. Multicoloured.
1561 60f. Type **281** 70 50
1562 80f. Umm Qais 95 70
1563 160f. Iraq al-Amir . . . . . 1·90 1·40
MS1564 100 × 70 mm. Nos. 1561/3. Imperf . . . . 22·00 22·00

1988. Olympic Games, Seoul. Multicoloured.
1565 10f. Type **282** 35 25
1566 60f. Mascot 85 50
1567 80f. Running and swimming 1·10 70
1568 120f. Basketball . . . . . . 1·70 1·00
1569 160f. Football . . . . . . 2·40 1·40
MS1570 70 × 90 mm. 100f. Games emblem. Imperf . . . . 11·00 11·00

283 Flame and Figures

1988. 40th Anniv of Declaration of Human Rights.
1571 **283** 80f. multicoloured . . . 95 50
1572 160f. multicoloured . . . 1·50 85

284 El-Deir Temple, Petra

1988. 25th Anniv of Royal Jordanian Airline. Multicoloured.
1573 60f. Type **284** 85 60
1574 80f. Boeing 737 airliner and map of world . . . . . . 1·20 70

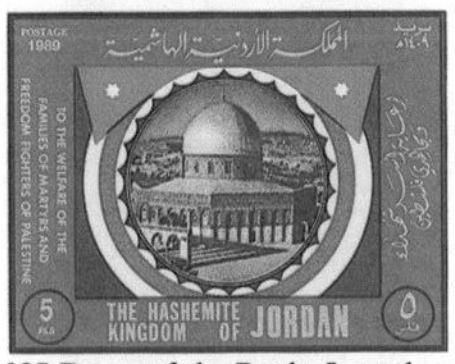

285 Dome of the Rock, Jerusalem

1989. Palestinian Welfare.
1575 **285** 5f. multicoloured 25 15
1576 10f. multicoloured 25 15

286 Treasury, Petra, Flags and King Hussein

1989. Formation of Arab Co-operation Council (economic grouping of four states). Multicoloured.
1577 10f. Type **286** 10 10
1578 30f. Sana'a, Yemen 35 15
1579 40f. Spiral Tower of Samarra, Iraq 45 25
1580 60f. Pyramids, Egypt . . . 70 35

287 Jordanian Parliament Building

1989. Centenary of Interparliamentary Union.
1581 **287** 40f. multicoloured . . . 25 15
1582 60f. multicoloured . . . 60 35

288 Modern Flats and Emblems

1989. Arab Housing Day and World Refugee Day. Multicoloured.
1583 5f. Type **288** 45 10
1584 40f. Hand supporting refugee family (horiz) . . 85 15
1585 60f. Modern blocks of flats (horiz) . . . . 1·50 25

289 King Abdullah, Mosque and King Hussein

1989. Inauguration of King Abdullah Ibn al-Hussein Mosque, Amman.
1586 **289** 40f. multicoloured . . . 45 15
1587 60f. multicoloured . . . 70 25
MS1588 90 × 70 mm. **289** 100f. multicoloured. Imperf . . . . 6·50 6·50

290 Horse's Head

1989. Arabian Horse Festival. Multicoloured.
1589 5f. Horse in paddock and emblem of Royal Stables (horiz) 45 10
1590 40f. Horse rearing and Treasury, Petra (horiz) . . 85 15
1591 60f. Type **290** . . . . . . 1·50 25
MS1592 90 × 70 mm. 100f. Mare and foal. Imperf . . . . 22·00 22·00

291 Trees

1989. 50th Anniv of Ministry of Agriculture. Multicoloured.
1593 5f. Type **291** 80 25
1594 40f. Tree and "50" 80 25
1595 60f. Orange trees and hives 1·00 35

292 Open Book, Globe and Flags

1989. Jordan Library Association.
1596 **292** 40f. multicoloured . . . 50 15
1597 60f. multicoloured . . . 70 25

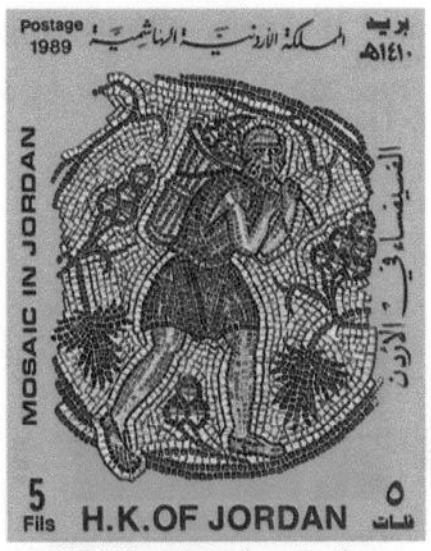

293 Man carrying Basket

1989. Mosaics. Multicoloured.
1598 5f. Type **293** 60 25
1599 10f. Philadelphia (modern Amman) 60 25
1600 40f. Deer . . . . 1·30 45
1601 60f. Man with stick . . . . 1·90 60
1602 80f. Jerusalem (horiz) . . . 2·50 85
MS1603 90 × 70 mm. 100f. As No. 1602. Imperf . . . . . . 14·50 14·50

294 Flags and Map

1990. 1st Anniv of Arab Co-operation Council.
1604 **294** 5f. multicoloured 25 25
1605 20f. multicoloured . . . 25 25
1606 60f. multicoloured . . . 70 45
1607 80f. multicoloured . . . 85 60

295 Wild Asses at Oasis

1990. Nature Conservation. Multicoloured.
1608 40f. Type **295** 25 25
1609 60f. Rock formation, Rum 45 25
1610 80f. Desert palm trees . . . 60 35

296 Horsemen and Building

1990. 70th Anniv of Arrival of Prince Abdullah in Ma'an.
1611 **296** 40f. multicoloured . . . 25 25
1612 60f. multicoloured . . . 35 25
MS1613 90x73 mm. 200f. multicoloured. Imperf . . . . 5·25 5·25
DESIGN: 200f. King Abdullah, Flags and horseman.

297 Emblem

1990. 40th Anniv of United Nations Development Programme.
1614 **297** 60f. multicoloured . . . 35 25
1615 80f. multicoloured . . . 45 25

298 King Hussein **299** Nubian Ibex

1990. Multicoloured, frame colour given.
1616 **298** 5f. yellow 25 25
1620 20f. green 25 25
1621 40f. red 25 25
1617 60f. blue 45 25
1618 80f. mauve 70 25
1622 240f. brown . . . . . 1·30 50
1623 320f. purple . . . . . 1·70 70
1624 1d. green . . . . 2·50 2·10

1991. Endangered Animals. Multicoloured.
1631 5f. Type **299** 15 15
1632 40f. Onager 45 15
1633 80f. Arabian gazelles . . . 85 35
1634 160f. Arabian oryx . . . . 1·70 80

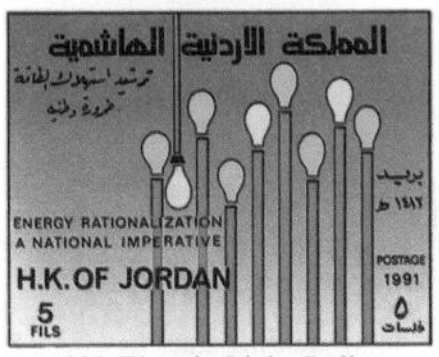

300 Electric Light Bulbs

1991. Energy Rationalization. Multicoloured.
1635 5f. Type **300** 25 25
1636 40f. Solar energy (vert) . . . 25 25
1637 80f. Angle-poise lamp by window (vert) 50 25

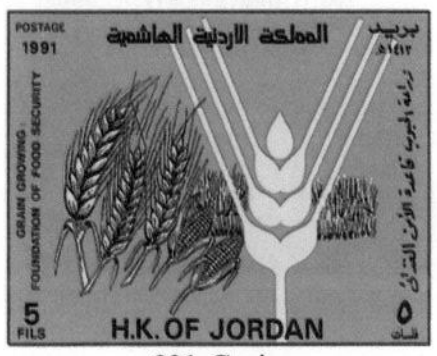

301 Grain

1991. Grain Production. Multicoloured.
1638 5f. Type **301** 25 25
1639 40f. Ear of wheat and leaves 25 25
1640 80f. Ear of wheat and field 50 25

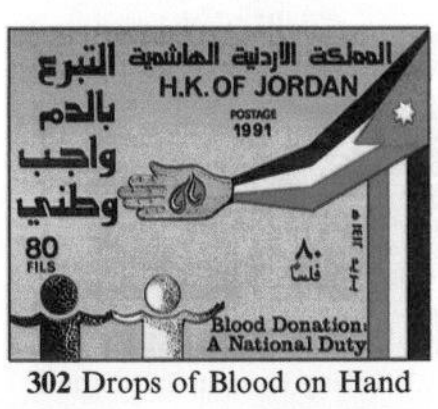

302 Drops of Blood on Hand

1991. National Blood Donation Campaign.
1641 **302** 80f. multicoloured . . . 80 45
1642 160f. multicoloured . . . 1·40 60

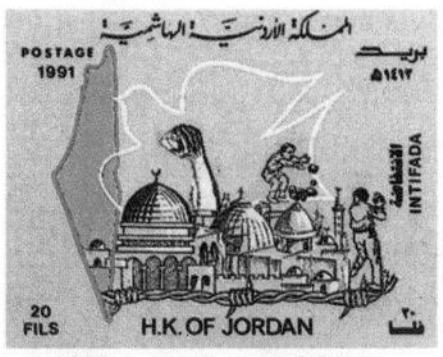

303 Jerusalem and Map

1991. Palestinian "Intifida" Movement.
1643 **303** 20f. multicoloured . . . 1·00 50

304 Emblem

1992. "Expo '92" World's Fair, Seville.
1644 **304** 80f. multicoloured . . . 45 25
1645 320f. multicoloured . . . 1·70 1·10

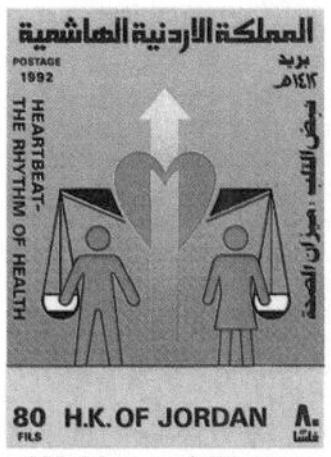

305 Man and Woman balancing Scales

1992. World Health Day. "Heartbeat—the Rhythm of Health".
1646 80f. Type **305** 60 25
1647 125f. Man and heart in balance and cardiograph (horiz) 85 15

306 Children

1992. S.O.S. Children's Village, Aqaba. Mult.
1648 80f. Type **306** 60 25
1649 125f. Village 85 45

307 Judo and Olympic Flame

1992. Olympic Games, Barcelona. Multicoloured.
1650 5f. Type **307** 25 10
1651 40f. Runners and track (vert) 25 25
1652 80f. Gymnast 45 25
1653 125f. Mascot (vert) 80 35
1654 160f. Table tennis 95 45
MS1655 70 × 90 mm. 100f. Motifs as Nos. 1650/4. Imperf . . . . . 13·00 13·00

308 King Hussein

1992. 40th Anniv of King Hussein's Accession. Multicoloured.
1656 40f. Type **308** 25 25
1657 80f. National colours, crown and King (horiz) 45 35

1658 125f. King and flags (horiz) 80 35
1659 160f. King, crown and anniversary emblem (horiz) 95 50
MS1660 90×70 mm. 200f. King Hussein and flame. Imperf 7·00 7·00

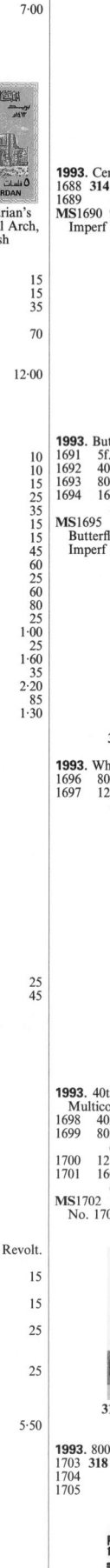

309 African Monarch

310 Hadrian's Triumphal Arch, Jerash

1992. Butterflies. Multicoloured.
1661 5f. Type **309** 15 15
1662 40f. Black-veined white 45 15
1663 80f. Swallowtail 85 35
1664 160f. "Pseudochazara telephassa" 1·70 70
MS1665 90×70 mm. 200f. Butterflies as in Nos. 1661/4. Imperf 12·00 12·00

1993. Variously dated "1992" to "1996".
1666 **310** 5f. brown, blue and black 10 10
1788 25f. brown, purple & blk 10 10
1718 40f. brown, green & blk 45 15
1798 50f. brown, yellow & blk 25 25
1799 75f. brown, cinn & blk 35 35
1667 80f. brown, green & blk 35 15
1668 100f. brown, red & black 45 15
1800 100f. brown, green & blk 45 45
1801 120f. brown, green & blk 60 60
1669 125f. brown, pink & blk 70 25
1721 125f. brown, blue & blk 60 60
1802 150f. brown, pink & blk 80 80
1670 160f. brown, yell & blk 70 25
1803 200f. brown, grey & blk 1·00 1·00
1671 240f. brown, pur & blk 95 25
1804 300f. brown, pink & blk 1·60 1·60
1672 320f. brown, chest & blk 1·30 35
1805 400f. brown, blue & blk 2·20 2·20
1793 500f. brown, ochre & blk 2·10 85
1674 1d. brown, yellow & blk 4·00 1·30

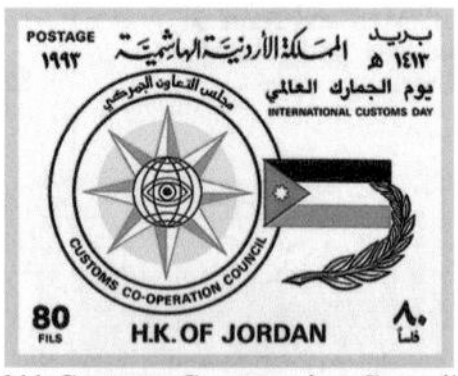

311 Customs Co-operation Council Emblem, Flag and Laurel

1993. International Customs Day.
1680 **311** 80f. multicoloured 60 25
1681 125f. multicoloured 85 45

312 King Hussein and Military Equipment

1993. Army Day and 77th Anniv of Arab Revolt. Multicoloured.
1682 5f. Type **312** 15 15
1683 40f. King Hussein, soldier, surgeons and tank 25 15
1684 80f. King Abdullah and Dome of the Rock 50 25
1685 125f. King Hussein of Hejaz, Dome of the Rock and horsemen 80 25
MS1686 90×70 mm. 100f. King Hussein, flags of Jordan and Palestine and army emblem. Imperf 5·50 5·50

313 Society Emblem and Natural Energy Resources

1993. 23rd Anniv of Royal Scientific Society.
1687 **313** 80f. multicoloured 50 35

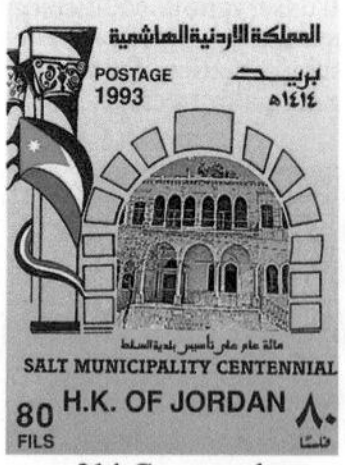

314 Courtyard

1993. Centenary of Salt Municipality.
1688 **314** 80f. multicoloured 60 25
1689 125f. multicoloured 85 45
MS1690 90×71 mm. Nos. 1688/9. Imperf (sold at 200f.) 6·00 6·00

315 Long-tailed Blue

1993. Butterflies. Multicoloured.
1691 5f. Type **315** 25 15
1692 40f. "Melanargria titea" 45 25
1693 80f. "Allancastria deyrollei" 70 35
1694 160f. "Gonepteryx cleopatra" 1·70 85
MS1695 91×72 mm. 100f. Butterflies as in Nos. 1691/4. Imperf 19·00 19·00

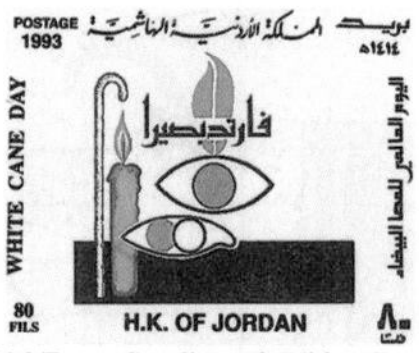

316 Eyes, Candle and White Cane

1993. White Cane Day. Multicoloured.
1696 80f. Type **316** 60 25
1697 125f. Globe, white cane and eye (vert) 85 45

317 King Hussein in Army Uniform

1993. 40th Anniv of King Hussein's Enthronement. Multicoloured.
1698 40f. Type **317** 25 25
1699 80f. King wearing Bedouin costume 50 35
1700 125f. King wearing suit 80 35
1701 160f. King with Queen Noor (horiz) 1·00 50
MS1702 90×71 mm. 100f. As No. 1701. Imperf 7·75 7·75

318 Saladin and Dome of the Rock, Jerusalem

1993. 800th Death Anniv of Saladin.
1703 **318** 40f. multicoloured 25 25
1704 80f. multicoloured 45 25
1705 125f. multicoloured 80 45

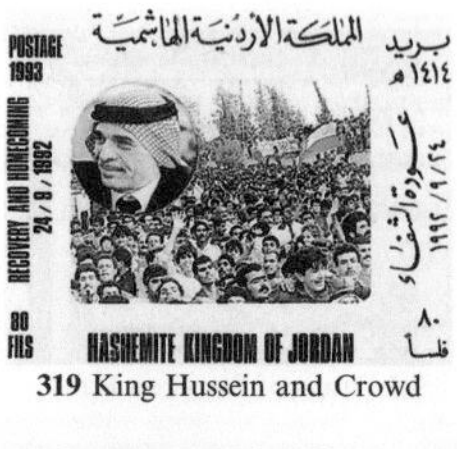

319 King Hussein and Crowd

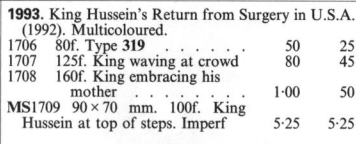

1993. King Hussein's Return from Surgery in U.S.A. (1992). Multicoloured.
1706 80f. Type **319** 50 25
1707 125f. King waving at crowd 80 45
1708 160f. King embracing his mother 1·00 50
MS1709 90×70 mm. 100f. King Hussein at top of steps. Imperf 5·25 5·25

320 Virus, Emblem and Silhouettes

1993. World AIDS Day.
1710 **320** 80f. multicoloured 50 35
1711 125f. multicoloured 80 50
MS1712 91×71 mm. Nos. 1710/11. Imperf (sold at 200f.) 6·00 6·00

321 Emblems and Flag

1993. 45th Anniv of United Nations Declaration of Human Rights.
1713 **321** 40f. multicoloured 25 25
1714 160f. multicoloured 1·00 50

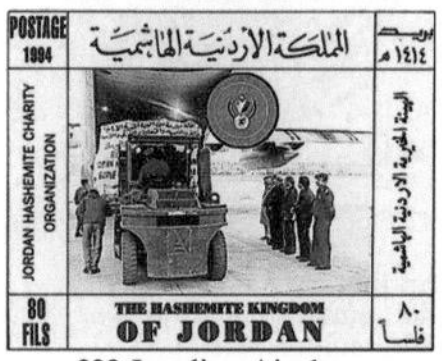

322 Loading Airplane

1994. Jordan Hashemite Charity Organization. Multicoloured.
1715 80f. Type **322** 50 35
1716 125f. Transport plane 80 50

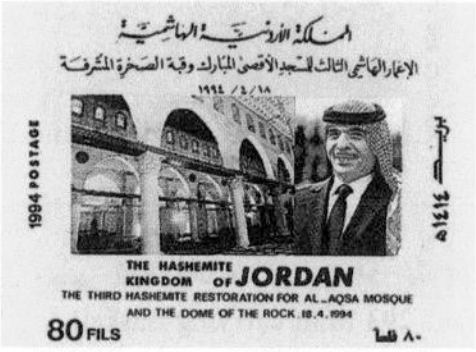

323 Mosque and King Hussein

1994. Refurbishment of El Aqsa Mosque and Dome of the Rock.
1726 80f. Type **323** 45 25
1727 125f. Dome of the Rock and King Hussein 60 35
1728 240f. Dome of the Rock and King Hussein (different) 1·30 60
MS1729 90×70 mm. 100f. King Hussein and interior and exterior view of dome. Imperf 7·75 7·75

324 Emblems on Doves

1994. 75th Anniv of International Red Cross and Red Crescent Societies. Multicoloured.
1730 80f. Child and emblems (horiz) 45 25
1731 160f. Type **324** 80 45
MS1732 70×90 mm. As Nos. 1721/2 but smaller (sold at 200f.) 10·50 10·50

325 Globe, Emblem and "75"

1994. 75th Anniv of I.L.O.
1733 **325** 80f. multicoloured 45 25
1734 125f. multicoloured 70 35

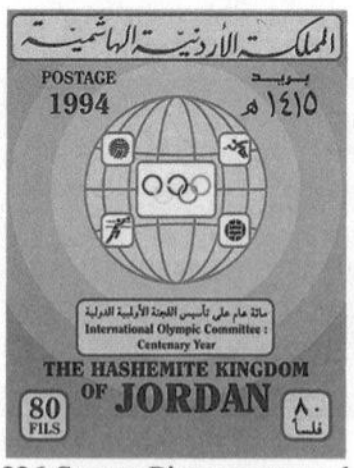

326 Sports Pictograms and Olympic Rings

1994. Centenary of International Olympic Committee. Multicoloured.
1735 80f. Type **326** 45 25
1736 125f. Sports pictograms, flame and "100" 80 45
1737 160f. Olympic rings, track and athlete (horiz) 95 45
1738 240f. Olympic rings and hand holding torch (horiz) 1·50 95
MS1739 90×70 mm. 100f. Olympic rings and Jordanian flag forming "J". Imperf 8·25 8·25

327 King Hussein greeting Soldiers

1994. Jordanian Participation in United Nations Peace-keeping Forces. Multicoloured.
1740 80f. Type **327** 45 25
1741 125f. King Hussein inspecting troops 70 45
1742 160f. U.N. checkpoint 80 45

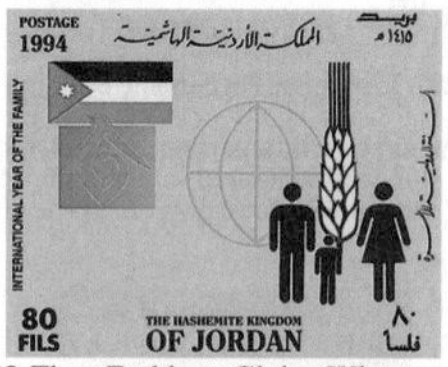

328 Flag, Emblem, Globe, Wheat and Family

1994. International Year of the Family.
1743 **328** 80f. multicoloured 45 25
1744 125f. multicoloured 80 45
1745 160f. multicoloured 95 45

329 Aircraft and Emblem

1994. 50th Anniv of I.C.A.O.
1746 **329** 80f. multicoloured 45 45
1747 125f. multicoloured 60 60
1748 160f. multicoloured 85 85

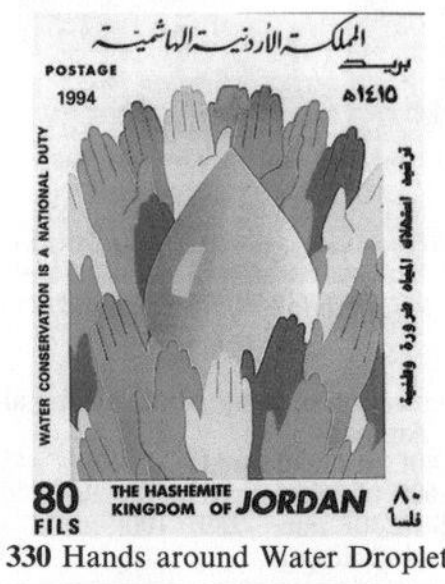

330 Hands around Water Droplet

1994. Water Conservation Campaign. Mult.
1749 80f. Type **330** 60 35
1750 125f. Glass beneath running tap, foodstuffs and industry 95 35
1751 160f. Water droplets and boy on lush hillside . . . 1·20 45

331 Crown Prince Hassan

1994. 10th Anniv of Crown Prince's Award.
1752 **331** 80f. multicoloured . . . 70 35
1753 125f. multicoloured . . . 85 35
1754 160f. multicoloured . . . 1·20 45

332 University Emblem

1995. Inauguration of Al al-Bayt University.
1755 **332** 80f. gold, blue and black 45 35
1756 125f. gold, green & black 80 35
MS1757 89×70 mm. Nos. 1734/4 (sold at 200f.) . . . . 3·50 3·50

333 U.N. Emblem and "50"

1995. 50th Anniv of U.N.O.
1758 **333** 80f. multicoloured . . . 60 35
1759 125f. multicoloured . . . 95 45

334 Labour Emblem and Crowd with Flag

1995. Labour Day. Multicoloured.
1760 80f. Type **334** 45 45
1761 125f. Emblem, world map and miner's head 60 60
1762 160f. Hands holding spanner and torch 85 85

335 Flags and Globe

1995. Jordan Week in Japan. Multicoloured.
1763 80f. Type **335** 50 35
1764 125f. Hemispheres and flags 85 35
1765 160f. Flags, brick wall and globe . . . . 1·00 50

336 Artefacts

1995. Petra, "The Rose City". Multicoloured.
1766 50f. Amphitheatre 50 35
1767 75f. Type **336** 70 35
1768 80f. Treasury seen through cleft in rocks (vert) . . . 80 35
1769 160f. Treasury (vert) . . . . 1·60 45
MS1770 90×70 mm. 200f. El-Deir Temple. Imperf . . . . 17·00 17·00

337 Emblem

1995. 50th Anniv of Arab League.
1771 **337** 80f. multicoloured . . . 45 45
1772 125f. multicoloured . . . 60 60
1773 160f. multicoloured . . . 85 85

338 Leaves and Emblem

1995. 50th Anniv of F.A.O. Multicoloured.
1774 80f. Type **338** 45 35
1775 125f. Ears of wheat and "50" incorporating F.A.O. emblem 80 35
1776 160f. United Nations emblem and "50" incorporating F.A.O. emblem . . . . 1·00 45

339 Knotted Ropes, Summit Emblem and National Flags

1995. Middle Eastern and North African Economic Summit, Amman.
1777 **339** 80f. multicoloured . . . 45 35
1778 125f. multicoloured . . . 80 35

340 King Hussein

1995. 60th Birthday of King Hussein. Mult.
1779 25f. Type **340** 35 35
1780 40f. Hussein within shield 35 35
1781 80f. Dove incorporating "60", El-Deir Temple (Petra) and Hussein . . . 45 35
1782 100f. Hussein in military uniform and anniversary emblem 60 35
1783 125f. King Hussein 70 45
1784 160f. Hussein, national flag and "60 60 60" . . . . . 1·00 45
MS1785 90×70 mm. 200f. Dome of the Rock and King Hussein within "60". Imperf . . . . 6·00 6·00

341 Hands and Hard of Hearing Emblem

1995. The Deaf. Multicoloured.
1786 80f. Type **341** 45 35
1787 125f. Emblems, sign language and hard of hearing emblem 80 35

342 Anniversary Emblem and Map of Jordan

1996. 50th Anniv of Independence. Mult.
1794 100f. Type **342** 60 35
1795 200f. King Hussein, map of Jordan and King Abdullah . . . . 1·10 60
1796 300f. King Hussein . . . . 1·60 95
MS1797 85×66 mm. 200f. King Hussein in military uniform. Imperf . . . . 5·25 5·25

343 Games Emblem, Olympic Rings and Pictograms

1996. Olympic Games, Atlanta. Multicoloured.
1806 50f. Type **343** 45 35
1807 100f. Games emblem and pictograms 80 35
1808 200f. Games emblem forming torch and figure 1·50 50
1809 300f. Games emblem, torch and national flag . . . . 2·10 80

344 Hand protecting Animals and Plants

1996. Protection of the Ozone Layer.
1810 **344** 100f. multicoloured . . . 1·20 45

345 Anniversary Emblem

1996. 50th Anniv of UNICEF Fund.
1811 **345** 100f. multicoloured . . . 50 35
1812 200f. multicoloured . . . 1·00 50

346 Playing Polo

1997. 50th Birthday of Crown Prince Hassan. Multicoloured.
1813 50f. Type **346** 35 35
1814 100f. Wearing western dress (vert) 50 35
1815 200f. In military uniform . . 1·00 50
MS1816 90×69 mm. 200f. Wearing graduation robes. Imperf . . . 6·00 6·00

347 Karak

1997. Centenary of Discovery of Madaba Mosaic Map. Multicoloured.
1817 100f. Type **347** 60 35
1818 200f. River Jordan (horiz) 1·30 45
1819 300f. Jerusalem . . . . . . 1·90 80
MS1820 90×70 mm. 100f. Remains of map. Imperf . . . . 10·50 10·50

348 Von Stephan

1997. Death Centenary of Heinrich von Stephan (founder of U.P.U.).
1821 **348** 100f. multicoloured . . . 80 35
1822 200f. multicoloured . . . 1·60 50

349 Sinai Rosefinch ("Rosefinch")

1997. Sinai Rosefinch ("The Jordanian Rosefinch").
1823 **349** 50f. multicoloured . . . 25 25
1824 100f. multicoloured . . . 60 60
1825 150f. multicoloured . . . 95 95
1826 200f. multicoloured . . . 1·30 1·30

350 Performers and Hadrian's Triumphal Arch

1997. 15th Anniv of Jerash Festival. Mult.
1827 50f. Type **350** 25 25
1828 100f. Orchestra, Festival emblem and Jerash ruins 60 60
1829 150f. Temple of Artemis and marching band 95 95
1830 200f. Women dancers and audience at performance 1·30 1·30
MS1831 90×70 mm. 200f. Torch-lighting ceremony. Imperf . . . 6·50 6·50

351 Current and Previous Parliament Buildings

1997. 50th Anniv of First National Parliament. Multicoloured.
1832 100f. Type **351** 50 50
1833 200f. King Hussein addressing, and view of, Chamber of Deputies . . 95 95

352 Meeting Emblem

1997. 53rd International Air Transport Assn Annual General Meeting, Amman.
1834 **352** 100f. multicoloured . . . 50 50
1835 200f. multicoloured . . . 95 95
1836 300f. multicoloured . . . 1·50 1·50

353 King Hussein and Queen Noor

1997. 62nd Birthday of King Hussein.

1837 **353** 100f. multicoloured . . . 50 50
1838 200f. multicoloured . . . 95 95
1839 300f. multicoloured . . . 1·50 1·50
MS1840 70 × 90 mm. 200f. As No. 1838 but 44 × 61 mm. . . 6·00 6·00

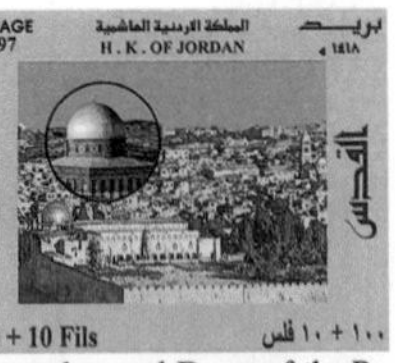

354 Jerusalem and Dome of the Rock

1997. Jerusalem.

1841 **354** 100f.+10f. multicoloured 50 50
1842 200f.+20f. multicoloured 1·10 1·10
1843 300f.+30f. multicoloured 1·60 1·60

355 Opening Ceremony

1997. Jordan, Arab Football Champion, 1997. Multicoloured.

1844 50f. Type **355** 25 25
1845 75f. Team saluting national anthem 35 35
1846 100f. Posing for team photograph and police officers patrolling crowd 50 50
MS1847 91 × 71 mm. 200f. King Hussein and Queen Noor among dignitaries and motorcade. Imperf 8·50 8·50

356 Women

1997. National Women's Forum. Mult.

1848 50f. Type **356** 25 25
1849 100f. National flag, women's profiles and emblems (horiz) 45 45
1850 150f. Forum meeting and emblem (horiz) 80 80

357 Air Pollution by Factories and Cars

1998. Earth Day. Children's Paintings. Mult.

1851 50f. Polluted air, land and water 25 25
1852 100f. Type **357** 45 45
1853 150f. "Earth" being strangled by pollution (vert) 80 80

358 King Abdullah and Camel in Desert

1998. 75th Anniv of Recognition of Transjordan as Autonomous State. Multicoloured.

1864 100f. Type **358** 50 50
1865 200f. King Hussein and camel in desert . . . . . 1·00 1·00
1866 300f. King Abdullah, King Hussein and May 1923 9p. stamp . . . . 1·60 1·60
MS1867 89 × 74 mm. 300f. As No. 1866 but 78 × 70 mm. Imperf 6·00 6·00

359 Thistle

1998. Flowers. Multicoloured.

1868 50f. Type **359** 25 25
1869 100f. Poppy 50 50
1870 150f. Carnation 80 80
MS1871 70 × 90 mm. 200f. Iris. Imperf . . . . 6·00 6·00

360 Animals and Trees

1998. Mosaics from Um ar-Rasas. Mult.

1872 100f. Type **360** 50 50
1873 200f. City buildings . . . . 1·00 1·00
1874 300f. Mosiac panel . . . . 1·60 1·60

361 Honey Bee and Honeycomb

1998. 2nd Arab Bee-keeping Conference. Mult.

1875 50f. Type **361** 35 25
1876 100f. Bee on flower (vert) 60 50
1877 150f. Bee, flower and honeycomb 95 80
MS1878 90 × 70 mm. 200f. Bees on flowers. Imperf . . . . 6·00 6·00

362 Dove with Stamp

1998. International Stamp Day. Multicoloured.

1879 50f. Type **362** 50 25
1880 100f. World map and U.P.U. emblem 85 50
1881 150f. Stamps encircling globe . . . . 1·40 80

363 King Hussein and Map of Jordan

1998. 63rd Birthday of King Hussein.

1882 **363** 100f. multicoloured . . . 50 50
1883 200f. multicoloured . . . 1·00 1·00
1884 300f. multicoloured . . . 1·60 1·60
MS1885 90 × 70 mm. 300f. King Hussein and map of Jordan (different). Imperf . . . . . . 6·00 6·00

364 King Hussein and Emblem

1998. 25th Anniv of Arab Police and Security Chiefs' Meeting. Multicoloured.

1886 100f. Type **364** 50 50
1887 200f. Flags of member countries of Arab League (vert) . . . . 1·00 1·00
1888 300f. Police beret and map of Jordan . . . . 1·60 1·60

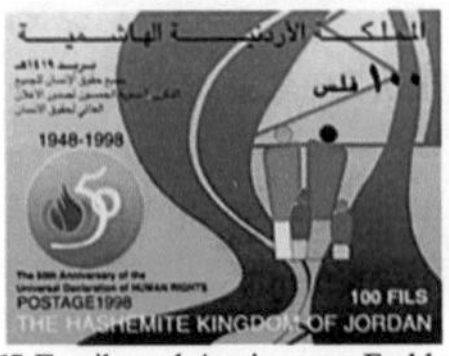

365 Family and Anniversary Emblem

1998. 50th Anniv of Universal Declaration of Human Rights. Multicoloured.

1889 100f. Type **365** 50 50
1890 200f. Silhouettes of people and United Nations emblem . . . . 1·00 1·00

366 Wahbi al Tal

1999. Birth Centenary and 50th Death Anniv of Mustafa Wahbi al Tal (poet).

1891 **366** 100f. multicoloured . . . 80 50

367 Mascot and Sports Pictograms

1999. 9th Arab Sports Tournament. Multicoloured.

1892 50f. Type **367** 45 45
1893 100f. Emblem, mascot and torch 60 60
1894 200f. Sportsmen, emblem and "9" (vert) . . . . . 1·40 1·40
1895 300f. Jordanian flag, mascot and emblem . . . . . . 1·90 1·90
MS1896 90 × 70 mm. 200f. Mascot and sports pictograms. Imperf 2·40 2·40

368 Railway Map, Station and Train

1999. Hijazi Railway Museum. Multicoloured.

1897 100f. Type **368** 70 70
1898 200f. Type **368** . . . . . . 1·40 1·40
1899 300f. Train and station building . . . . 2·10 2·10

369 *Pachyseris speciosa*

1999. Marine Life in the Gulf of Aqaba. Corals. Multicoloured.

1900 50f. Type **369** 25 25
1901 100f. *Acropora digitfera* . . 60 60
1902 200f. *Oxypora lacera* . . . 1·10 1·10
1903 300f. *Fungia echinata* . . . 1·60 1·60
MS1904 90 × 70 mm. 200f. Gorgonia. Imperf . . . . . . 5·50 5·50

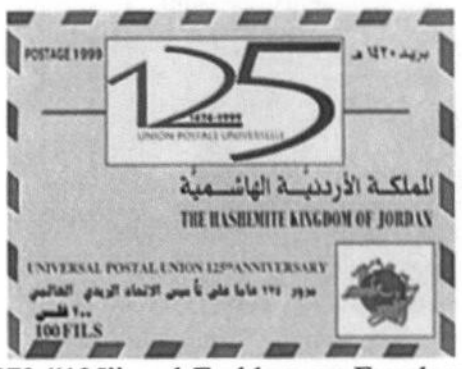

370 "125" and Emblem on Envelope

1999. 125th Anniv of Universal Postal Union. Multicoloured.

1905 100f. Type **370** 50 50
1906 200f. U.P.U. emblem on envelope, target and post emblem . . . . 1·10 1·10
MS1907 90 × 70 mm. 200f. As No. 1906. Imperf . . . . . . 1·10 1·10

371 Children helping Sick Globe

1999. Environmental Protection. Multicoloured.

1908 100f. Type **371** 45 45
1909 200f. Hands holding globe as apple 85 85

372 Aerial View of Temple

1999. Cradle of Civilizations. Multicoloured.

(a) Petra.

1910 100f. Type **372** 45 45
1911 200f. Front view of temple 85 85
1912 300f. Building in cliffs . . . 1·30 1·30

(b) Jerash.

1913 100f. Path between columns 45 45
1914 200f. Columns 85 85
1915 300f. Columns and ruined building . . . . 1·30 1·30

(c) Amman.

1916 100f. Auditorium 45 45
1917 200f. Columns 85 85
1918 300f. Statues . . . . 1·30 1·30

(d) Aqaba.

1919 100f. Camels, Wadi Rum . . 45 45
1920 200f. Building with wooden door 85 85
1921 300f. Fort . . . . 1·30 1·30

(e) Baptism Site.

1922 100f. Rushes at water's edge 45 45
1923 200f. Aerial view of site . . 85 85
1924 300f. Archaeological site . . 1·30 1·30

(f) Madaba.

1925 100f. Mosaic of man 45 45
1926 200f. Temple 85 85
1927 300f. Mosaic of town . . . 1·30 1·30

(g) Pella

1928 100f. Columns and steps . . 45 45
1929 200f. Columns and wall . . 85 85
1930 300f. Columns and sheep . . 1·30 1·30

(h) Ajloun

1931 100f. Castle 45 45
1932 200f. Castle from below . . 85 85
1933 300f. Hill top castle . . . . 1·10 1·10

(i) Um Quais

1934 100f. Arches and columns 45 45
1935 200f. Amphitheatre 85 85
1936 300f. Columns and rubble 1·10 1·10

(j) Desert Palaces

1937 100f. Mushatta 45 45
1938 200f. Kharaneh 85 85
1939 300f. Amra . . . . 1·10 1·10

373 Jordanian Stamps

1999. 20th Anniv of Jordan Philatelic Club. Multicoloured.
1940 100f. Type **373** 45 45
1941 200f. Jordanian stamps (different) 85 85

374 Assembly Room

1999. Museum of Political History. Multicoloured.
1942 100f. Type **374** 45 45
1943 200f. Courtyard 85 85
1944 300f. Entrance . . . . . . 1·30 1·30

375 Jordanian Flag and Emblems

1999. 50th Anniv of S.O.S. Children's Villages. Multicoloured.
1945 100f. Type **375** 45 45
1946 200f. Woman and children 85 85

376 King Abdullah II

1999. Coronation of King Abdullah II Bin Al-Hussein.
1947 **376** 100f. multicoloured . . . 45 45
1948 200f. multicoloured . . . 85 85
1949 300f. multicoloured . . . 1·30 1·30
MS1950 70 × 89 mm. 200f. No. 1948 but with gold border 85 85

377 King Abdullah II and Queen Rania

1999. Coronation of King Abdullah II Bin Al-Hussein and Queen Rania al-Abdullah.
1951 **377** 100f. multicoloured . . . 45 45
1952 200f. multicoloured . . . 85 85
1953 300f. multicoloured . . . 1·30 1·30
MS1954 70 × 89 mm. 200f. No. 1952 but with gold border 85 85

378 Crowned Portrait

2000. 38th Birth Anniv of King Abdullah II. Multicoloured.
1955 100f. Type **378** 45 45
1956 200f. King Abdullah II (horiz) 85 85
1957 300f. King Abdullah II and flag (horiz) . . . . 1·30 1·30

379 Red Cross Emblem and Jordanian Flag

2000. 50th Anniv of Geneva Red Cross Conventions. Multicoloured.
1959 **379** 100f. multicoloured . . . 45 45
1960 200f. multicoloured . . . 95 95
1961 300f. multicoloured . . . 1·40 1·40

380 Flag and "2000 A. D."

2000. New Millennium. Multicoloured.
1962 100f. Type **380** 45 45
1963 200f. Palms, sand and fish swimming 85 85
1964 300f. As No. 1957 but inscription in Arabic . . . 1·30 1·30

381 King Abdullah II, Roofs and Pope John Paul II

2000. 36th Anniv of Pope Paul VI's Visit to Jordan.
1965 **381** 100f. multicoloured . . . 45 45
1966 200f. multicoloured . . . 95 95
1967 300f. multicoloured . . . 1·40 1·40

382 Pope John Paul II, Trees and King Abdullah II

2000. Pope John Paul II's Visit to Jordan.
1968 100f. Type **382** 45 45
1969 200f. Pope John Paul II, river and King Abdullah II 95 95
1970 300f. Pope John Paul II, flags and King Abdullah II . . . . . . 1·40 1·40
MS1971 70 × 90 mm. 200f. Pope John Paul II. Imperf 95 95

383 Globe and Organization Emblem

2000. 50th Anniv of World Meteorological Organization. Multicoloured.
1972 100f. Type **383** 60 60
1973 200f. Globe and emblem (different) . . . . 1·10 1·10

384 Emblem, Flag and "90"

2000. 90th Anniv of Jordan Boy Scouts. Multicoloured.
1974 100f. Type **384** 70 70
1975 200f. Pyramids . . . . . . 1·40 1·40
1976 300f. "90", flag and pyramids . . . . 2·10 2·10
MS1977 90 × 70 mm. 200f. As No. 1974 but with design enlarged. Imperf . . . . 2·10 2·10

385 Clinic Building and Emblem

2000. Al-Amal Cancer Centre. Multicoloured.
1978 200f. Type **385** . . . . . . 1·10 1·10
1979 300f. Emblem and family . . 1·70 1·70

387 Scales enclosing Palace of Justice

2000. Palace of Justice, Amman. Multicoloured.
1980 100f. Type **387** 60 60
1981 200f. Building faade . . . . 1·10 1·10

388 Dove

2000. Endangered Species. Multicoloured.
1982 50f. Type **388** 25 25
1983 100f. Oryx 60 60
1984 150f. Caracal 95 95
1985 200f. Red fox . . . . 1·20 1·20
1986 300f. Iris . . . . 1·90 1·90
1987 400f. White broom . . . . 2·40 2·40

389 Iris

2000. World Conservation Union Conference, Amman.
1988 **389** 200f. multicoloured . . . 1·20 1·20
1989 300f. multicoloured . . . 1·90 1·90

390 Petra

2000. Tourism. Multicoloured.
1990 50f. Type **390** 25 25
1991 100f. Jerash 60 60
1992 150f. Mount Nebo 95 95
1993 200f. Dead Sea . . . . . . 1·20 1·20
1994 300f. Aqaba . . . . 1·90 1·90
1995 400f. Wadi Rum . . . . . 2·40 2·40

391 Column Capital

2000. Expo 2000, Hanover. Multicoloured.
1996 200f. Type **391** . . . . . . 1·20 1·20
1997 300f. Statuette . . . . . . 1·90 1·90
MS1998 90 × 70 mm. 200f. King Abdullah, Queen Rania Al-Abdullah and Expo 2000 buildings 2·20 2·20

392 King Hussein

2000. 1st Death Anniv of King Hussein. Multicoloured.
1999 50f. Type **392** 25 25
2000 150f. King Hussein enclosed in wreath (horiz) 95 95
2001 200f. Symbols of industry and King Hussein (horiz) 1·20 1·20
MS2002 90 × 70 mm. 200f. As No. 2000 but with design enlarged 1·20 1·20

393 Women and Child

2000. 50th Anniv of United Nations High Commissioner for Refugees (2001).
2003 200f. multicoloured . . . . 1·20 1·20
2004 300f. green, blue and black 1·90 1·90
DESIGN 300f. UNHCR emblem.

394 Conference Emblem and Jordanian Flag

2001. 13th Arab Summit Conference, Amman. Multicoloured.
2005 50f. Type **394** 25 25
2006 200f. Flags, emblem and map of Arab countries . . 1·00 1·00
2007 250f. King Abdullah II and emblem . . . . 1·30 1·30

395 Mohammed Al Dorra, his Father and Dome

2001. 1st Death Anniv of Mohammed Al Dorra. Multicoloured.
2008 200f. Type **395** . . . . . . 1·00 1·00
2009 300f. Mohammed Al Dorra and father . . . . 1·60 1·60

396 Dome of the Rock with Arms

2001. Al Asqa Intifada. Multicoloured.
2010 200f. Type **396** . . . . . . 1·00 1·00
2011 300f. Dome of the Rock and protesters . . . . 1·60 1·60

397 Wheelchair User

2001. Sports for Special Needs. Multicoloured.
2012 200f. Type **397** . . . . . . 1·00 1·00
2013 300f. Woman holding medal 1·60 1·60

398 School Children and No-Smoking Sign

2001. Campaign to stop Smoking amongst Young People. Multicoloured.
2014 200f. Type **398** . . . . . . 1·00 1·00
2015 300f. Stylized student holding no-smoking sign (vert) . . . . 1·60 1·60

399 Olive Branches and Map of Jordan

2001. Olive Cultivation. Multicoloured.
2016 200f. Type **399** . . . . . . 1·00 1·00
2017 300f. Girl holding olives (vert) . . . . 1·60 1·60

400 Family and World Map

2001. United Nations Year of Dialogue among Civilizations. Multicoloured.
2018 200f. Type **400** . . . . . . 1·00 1·00
2019 300f. Emblem, clasped hands and olive tree . . . 1·60 1·60

401 Sheik Hussein Bridge and Japanese and Jordanian Flags

2001. Japan—Jordan Co-operation. Multicoloured.
2020 200f. Type **401** . . . . . . 1·00 1·00
2021 300f. King Hussein bridge and clasped hands . . . . 1·60 1·60

402 Emblem, Star and National Colours

2002. Amman, Arab Cultural Capital, 2002. Multicoloured.
2022 100f. Type **402** 45 45
2023 200f. Flame and pen 85 85
2024 300f. Emblem and amphitheatre . . . . . . 1·30 1·30

403 Buildings

2002. Jordanian Artists. Multicoloured.
2025 100f. Type **403** 45 45
2026 150f. Abstract (Mahmoud Taha) (horiz) 65 65
2027 200f. Woman (Mohanna Durra) 85 85
2028 300f. Hilltop castle (Wijdan) (horiz) . . . . 1·30 1·30

404 Bird carrying Envelope

2002. 25th Anniv of Jordan—China Diplomatic Relations. Multicoloured.
2029 200f. Type **404** 85 85
2030 300f. King Abdullah II and Pres. Jiang Zemin . . . . 1·30 1·30

405 Goldfinch

2002. Birds. Multicoloured.
2031 100f. Type **405** 60 60
2032 200f. Rufous scrub robin (inscr "rufous bush robin") . . . . 1·10 1·10
2033 300f. Stork . . . . 1·70 1·70
MS2034 70 × 90 mm. 200f. Golden oriole, goshawk, bunting and hoopoe . . . . 7·25 7·25

406 Symbols of Industry

2002. "Jordan Vision 2002" (campaign for economic development). Multicoloured.
2035 200f. Type **406** 85 85
2036 300f. Hand and computer circuit board . . . . . . 1·30 1·30

407 Building Facade

2003. Archaeological Museum. Multicoloured.
2037 150f. Type **407** 65 25
2038 250f. Building from below 85 35

408 Sherif Hussein bin Ali

2003. Hashemite Dynasty. Sheet 230 × 90 mm containing T **408** and similar vert designs. Multicoloured.
MS2039 200f. × 5 Type **408**; King Abdullah; King Talal bin Abdullah; King Hussein bin Talal; King Abdullah II . . . . . . 2·10 2·00

409 *Cistanche tubulosa*

2003. Flora. Multicoloured.
2040 50f. Type **409** 30 30
2041 100f. *Ophioglossum polyphyllum* (vert) 60 60
2042 150f. *Narcissus tazetta* . . . 80 80
2043 200f. *Gynandriris sisyrinchium* (vert) . . . . 1·10 1·10

410 Italian Cypress (*Cupressus sempervirens*)

2003. Trees. Multicoloured.
2044 50f. Type **410** 60 60
2045 100f. *Pistacia atlantica* . . . 60 60
2046 200f. *Quercus aegilops* . . . 80 80

411 Short-toed Eagle (*Ciraetus gallicus*)

2003. Trees. Multicoloured.
2047 100f. Type **411** 60 60
2048 200f. Peregrine falcon (*Falco peregrinus*) . . . . 1·10 1·10
2049 300f. Northern sparrow hawk (*Accipter nisus*) . . 1·60 1·60
MS2050 70 × 90 mm 200f. *Ciraetus gallicus* (different). Imperf . . . 1·10 1·10

412 Company Emblem, Colours and Arch

2003. Jordan Post Company. Multicoloured.
2051 50f. Type **412** 30 30
2052 100f. Columns, stamp outline and emblem . . . 60 30

413 Ferrari F40 (1989)

2003. Royal Car Museum, Amman. Multicoloured.
2053 100f. Type **413** 60 60
2054 150f. Rolls Royce Phantom V (1968) 80 80
2055 300f. Mercedes Benz Cabriolet D (1961) . . . 1·60 1·60
MS2056 90 × 70 mm. 200f. Panther J72 convertible (1972), Mercedes Benz 300sc roadster (1956) and Cadillac 53 (1916). Imperf . . 1·10 1·10

OBLIGATORY TAX

T **36** Mosque in Hebron

T **43** Ruins at Palmyra, Syria

1947.
T264 T **36** 1m. blue 35 25
T265 2m. red 45 25
T266 3m. green 50 45
T267 5m. red 60 45
T268 – 10m. red 70 60
T269 – 15m. grey . . . . . . 1·00 70
T270 – 20m. brown . . . . . 1·50 85
T271 – 50m. violet . . . . . 2·50 1·70
T272 – 100m. red . . . . . . 7·25 5·25
T273 – 200m. blue . . . . . 22·00 13·00
T274 – 500m. green . . . . . 50·00 39·00
T275 – £P1 brown . . . . . . £100 85·00
DESIGNS: Nos. T268/71, Dome of the Rock; Nos. T272/75, Acre.

1950. Optd **Aid** in English and Arabic.
T290 T **28** 5m. orange . . . . . 12·00 12·00
T291 10m. violet . . . . . . 19·00 19·00
T292 15m. green . . . . . . 22·00 22·00

1950. Revenue stamps optd **Aid** in English and Arabic.
T296 T **43** 5m. orange . . . . . 19·00 14·50
T297 10m. violet . . . . . . 19·00 17·00

1951. Values in "FILS".
T302 T **36** 5f. red 60 60
T303 – 10f. red 60 60
T304 – 15f. black 70 70
T305 – 20f. brown 85 85
T306 – 100f. orange . . . . . 4·25 4·25
DESIGNS: Nos. T303/305, Dome of the Rock; No. T306, Acre.

1952. Nos. T264/75 optd **J.D.** (T344) or **FILS** (others).
T334 T **36** 1f. on 1m. blue 25 25
T335 2f. on 2m. red . . . . 75·00
T336 3f. on 3m. green . . . 35 25
T337 – 10f. on 10m. red . . . 45 25
T338 – 15f. on 15m. grey . . . 85 60
T339 – 20f. on 20m. brown . . 1·00 1·00
T340 – 50f. on 50m. violet . . 1·90 1·90
T341 – 100f. on 100m. orange 10·50 6·00
T342 – 200f. on 200m. blue . . 26·00 16·00
T343 – 500f. on 500m. green 60·00 43·00
T344 – 1d. on £P1 brown . . . £100 85·00

OFFICIAL STAMPS

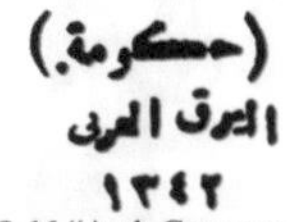

(O **16** "Arab Government of the East, 1342")

1924. Type **11** of Saudi Arabia optd with Type O **16**.
O117 ½p. red . . . . 23·00 £100

POSTAGE DUE STAMPS

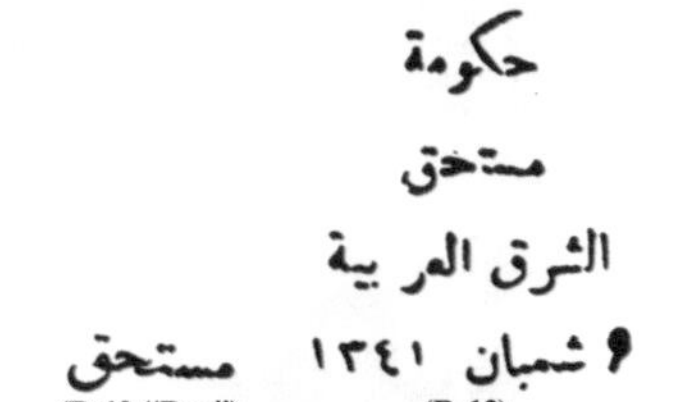

(D **12** "Due") (D **13**)

1923. Issue of 1923 (with opt T **10**) further optd.
(a) With Type D **12** (the 3p. also surch as T **12**).
D112 **11** ½p. on 3p. brown . . . . 19·00 22·00
D113 1p. blue . . . . 11·00 13·00
D114 1½p. lilac . . . . 14·00 15·00
D115 2p. orange . . . . 16·00 17·00

(b) With Type D **13** and surch as T **12**.
D116 **11** ½p. on 3p. brown . . . . 50·00 55·00

(D 14)

1923. Stamps of Saudi Arabia handstamped with Type D **14**.

D117	**11**	½p. red	1·50	3·75
D118		1p. blue	3·50	3·75
D119		1½p. violet	2·75	4·75
D120		2p. orange	4·25	5·50
D121		3p. brown	8·00	11·00
D122		5p. olive	8·50	17·00

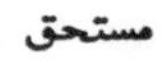

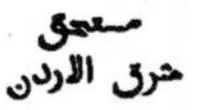 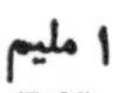

(D **20** "Due East of the Jordan") (D **21**)

1925. Stamps of Palestine (without Palestine opt) optd with Type D **20**.

D159	**3**	1m. brown	1·40	7·00
D160		2m. yellow	2·25	4·50
D161		4m. red	3·00	9·00
D162		8m. red	4·00	12·00
D163		13m. blue	5·00	12·00
D164		5p. purple	6·00	16·00

1926. Stamps of Palestine as last surch as Type D **21** ("DUE" and new value in Arabic).

D165	**3**	1m. on 1m. brown	6·00	7·00
D166		2m. on 1m. brown	4·75	7·00
D167		4m. on 3m. blue	5·00	8·00
D168		8m. on 3m. blue	5·00	8·00
D169		13m. on 13m. blue	8·00	9·00
D170		5p. on 13m. blue	9·00	13·00

The lower line of the surcharge differs for each value.

(D 25) D **26** D **50**

1928. Surch as Type D **25** or optd only.

D183	**22**	1m. on 3m. red	1·00	6·50
D184		2m. blue	1·50	6·50
D185		4m. on 15m. blue	1·50	7·50
D186		10m. red	2·75	7·50
D187	**23**	20m. on 100m. blue	4·00	17·00
D188		50m. purple	4·75	20·00

1929.

D244	D **26**	1m. brown	70	3·00
D245		2m. yellow	70	3·50
D246		4m. green	70	4·50
D247		10m. red	2·00	6·00
D193		20m. olive	8·00	13·00
D194		50m. blue	11·00	21·00

1952. Optd **FILS FILS** in English and Arabic.

D350	D **26**	1f. on 1m. brown	60	80
D351		2f. on 2m. yellow	60	80
D352		4f. on 4m. green	95	1·30
D353		10f. on 10m. red	2·50	3·00
D354		20f. on 20m. olive	7·25	7·25
D346		50f. on 50m. blue	5·25	5·25

1952. Inscr "THE HASHEMITE KINGDOM OF THE JORDAN".

D372	D **50**	1f. brown	50	70
D373		2f. yellow	50	70
D374		4f. green	50	70
D375		10f. red	1·00	1·20
D376		20f. brown	1·00	1·40
D377		50f. blue	3·00	3·25

1957. As Type D **50**, but inscr "THE HASHEMITE KINGDOM OF JORDAN".

D465		1f. brown	60	80
D466		2f. yellow	60	80
D467		4f. green	60	1·10
D468		10f. red	95	1·10
D469		20f. brown	1·60	2·20

JORDANIAN OCCUPATION OF PALESTINE Pt. 19

1948. Stamps of Jordan optd **PALESTINE** in English and Arabic.

P 1	**28**	1m. brown	45	45
P 2		2m. green	45	45
P 3		3m. green	45	45
P 4		3m. pink	25	25
P 5		4m. green	25	25
P 6		5m. orange	25	25
P 7		10m. violet	85	85
P 8		12m. red	85	50
P 9		15m. green	1·10	1·10
P10		20m. blue	1·50	85
P11	**29**	50m. purple	1·70	1·90
P12		90m. bistre	9·50	1·90
P13		100m. blue	10·50	5·50
P14		200m. violet	4·25	8·50
P15		500m. brown	36·00	16·00
P16		£P1 grey	75·00	40·00

1949. 75th Anniv of U.P.U. Stamps of Jordan optd **PALESTINE** in English and Arabic.

P30	**40**	1m. brown	45	45
P31		4m. green	45	45
P32		10m. red	70	70
P33		20m. blue	70	70
P34	–	50m. green (No. 289)	1·70	1·70

OBLIGATORY TAX

1950. Nos. T264/75 of Jordan optd **PALESTINE** in English and Arabic.

PT35	T **36**	1m. blue	15	45
PT36		2m. red	15	45
PT37		3m. green	45	50
PT38		5m. purple	50	45
PT39	–	10m. red	50	45
PT40	–	15m. black	1·70	50
PT41	–	20m. brown	2·75	95
PT42	–	50m. violet	4·00	1·90
PT43	–	100m. red	7·00	3·00
PT44	–	200m. blue	17·00	8·50
PT45	–	500m. green	50·00	26·00
PT46	–	£P1 brown	95·00	50·00

POSTAGE DUE STAMPS

1948. Postage Due stamps of Jordan optd **PALESTINE** in English and Arabic.

PD25	D **26**	1m. brown	2·20	3·00
PD26		2m. yellow	2·50	3·50
PD18		4m. green	2·50	3·50
PD28		10m. red	2·50	3·00
PD20		20m. olive	2·20	2·75
PD21		50m. blue	2·50	3·50

After a time the stamps of Jordan were used in the occupied areas.

JUBALAND Pt. 8

A district in E. Africa, formerly part of Kenya, ceded by Gt. Britain to Italy in 1925, and incorporated in Italian Somaliland.

100 centesimi = 1 lira.

1925. Stamps of Italy optd **OLTRE GIUBA**.

1	**30**	1c. brown	2·50	8·75
2	**31**	2c. brown	1·80	8·75
3	**37**	5c. green	1·50	4·50
4		10c. pink	1·50	4·50
5		15c. grey	1·50	6·25
6	**41**	20c. orange	1·50	6·25
39	**39**	20c. green	5·00	10·00
7		25c. blue	1·80	6·25
8		30c. brown	2·50	7·00
40		30c. grey	6·50	11·50
9		40c. brown	3·75	5·50
10		50c. mauve	3·75	5·50
11		60c. red	3·75	7·00
41	**44**	75c. red and carmine	30·00	35·00
12		1l. brown and green	7·00	8·75
42		1l.25 blue and ultramarine	42·00	44·00
13		2l. green and orange	47·00	24·00
43		2l.50 green and orange	55·00	80·00
14		5l. blue and pink	75·00	35·00
15		10l. green and pink	9·00	39·00

1925. Royal Jubilee stamps of Italy optd **OLTRE GIUBA**.

44B	**82**	60c. red	75	6·25
45B		1l. blue	75	10·75
46B		1l.25 blue	2·20	15·00

1926. St. Francis of Assisi stamps of Italy, as Nos. 191/6, optd **OLTRE GIUBA**.

47		20c. green	1·60	12·50
48		40c. violet	1·60	12·50
49		60c. red	1·60	18·00
50		1l.25 blue	1·60	27·00
51		5l.+2l.50 olive	4·50	39·00

8 Map of Jubaland

1926. 1st Anniv of Acquisition of Jubaland.

54	**8**	5c. orange	75	8·00
55		20c. green	75	8·00
56		25c. brown	75	8·00
57		40c. red	75	8·00
58		60c. purple	75	8·00
59		1l. blue	75	8·00
60		2l. grey	75	8·00

1926. As Colonial Propaganda T **6** of Cyrenaica, but inscr "OLTRE GIUBA".

61		5c.+5c. brown	65	4·25
62		10c.+5c. olive	65	4·25
63		20c.+5c. green	65	4·25
64		40c.+5c. red	65	4·25
65		60c.+5c. orange	65	4·25
66		1l.+5c. blue	65	7·00

EXPRESS LETTER STAMPS

1926. Express Letter stamps of Italy optd **OLTRE GUIBA**.

E52	E **35**	70c. red	18·00	25·00
E53	E **41**	2l.50 blue and pink	27·00	55·00

PARCEL POST STAMPS.

1925. Parcel Post stamps of Italy optd **OLTRE GIUBA**.

P16	P **53**	5c. brown	4·50	12·00
P17		10c. blue	2·75	12·00
P18		20c. black	2·75	12·00
P19		25c. red	2·75	12·00
P20		50c. orange	4·50	12·00
P21		1l. violet	3·75	28·00
P22		2l. green	7·00	28·00
P23		3l. yellow	20·00	38·00
P24		4l. grey	6·25	38·00
P25		10l. purple	39·00	55·00
P26		12l. brown	85·00	90·00
P27		15l. olive	75·00	90·00
P28		20l. purple	75·00	90·00

Unused prices are for complete stamps, used prices for half-stamps.

POSTAGE DUE STAMPS

1925. Postage Due stamps of Italy optd **OLTRE GIUBA**.

D29	D **12**	5c. purple and orange	8·00	7·00
D30		10c. purple and orange	8·00	7·00
D31		20c. purple and orange	8·00	11·00
D32		30c. purple and orange	8·00	11·00
D33		40c. purple and orange	8·00	12·50
D34		50c. purple and orange	10·00	16·00
D35		60c. brown and orange	10·00	18·00
D36		1l. purple and blue	14·00	25·00
D37		2l. purple and blue	65·00	90·00
D38		5l. purple and blue	80·00	90·00

KAMPUCHEA Pt. 21

Following the fall of the Khmer Rouge government, which had terminated the Khmer Republic, the People's Republic of Kampuchea was proclaimed on 10 January 1979.

Kampuchea was renamed Cambodia in 1989.

100 cents = 1 riel.

105 Soldiers with Flag and Independence Monument, Phnom Penh

106 Moscow Kremlin and Globe

1980. Multicoloured. Without gum.

402 0.1r. Type **105** . . . . . . 4·50 4·50
403 0.2r. Khmer people and flag 7·25 7·25
404 0.5r. Fisherman pulling in nets . . . . 11·00 11·00
405 1r. Armed forces and Kampuchean flag . . . . 18·00 18·00

1982. 60th Anniv of U.S.S.R. Multicoloured.

406 50c. Type **106** 35 20
407 1r. Industrial complex and map of U.S.S.R. 55 25

107 Arms of Kampuchea

1983. 4th Anniv of People's Republic of Kampuchea. Multicoloured.

408 50c. Type **107** 55 10
409 1r. Open book illustrating national flag and arms (horiz) 90 20
410 3r. Stylized figures and map 2·50 65
MS411 90 × 109 mm. 6r. Temple, Phnom Penh (28 × 35 mm) . . 4·75 90

108 Runner with Olympic Torch

109 Orange Tiger

1983. Olympic Games, Los Angeles (1984) (1st issue). Multicoloured.

412 20c. Type **108** 25 10
413 50c. Javelin throwing 35 10
414 80c. Pole vaulting 45 10
415 1r. Discus throwing 55 10
416 1r.50 Relay (horiz) 90 20
417 2r. Swimming (horiz) . . . . 1·30 20
418 3r. Basketball . . . . 2·00 20
MS419 92 × 64 mm. 6r. Football (31 × 39 mm) . . . . 4·25 90
See also Nos. 526/**MS**533.

1983. Butterflies. Multicoloured.

420 20c. Type **109** 20 10
421 50c. "Euploea althaea" . . . 25 10
422 80c. "Byasa polyeuctes" (horiz) 35 10
423 1r. "Stichophthalma howqua" (horiz) 55 10
424 1r.50 Leaf butterfly . . . . . 1·20 20
425 2r. Blue argus . . . . 1·30 20
426 3r. Lemon migrant . . . . . 2·00 20

110 Srah Srang

1983. Khmer Culture. Multicoloured.

427 20c. Type **110** 20 10
428 50c. Bakong 25 10
429 80c. Ta Som (vert) 35 10
430 1r. North gate, Angkor Thom (vert) 55 20
431 1r.50 Kennora (winged figures) (vert) . . . . . . 1·20 25
432 2r. Apsara (carved figures), Angkor (vert) . . . . . . 1·30 35
433 3r. Banteai Srei (goddess), Tevoda (vert) . . . . . . 2·00 55

111 Dancers with Castanets

1983. Folklore. Multicoloured.

434 50c. Type **111** 25 20
435 1r. Dancers with grass headdresses 90 25
436 3r. Dancers with scarves . . 2·00 65
MS437 94 × 63 mm. 6r. Warrior with blowpipe (31 × 39 mm) . . . . 4·00 90

112 Detail of Fresco

1983. 500th Birth Anniv of Raphael (artist).

438 **112** 20c. multicoloured 20 10
439 – 50c. multicoloured 25 10
440 – 80c. multicoloured 35 10
441 – 1r. multicoloured 80 20
442 – 1r.50 multicoloured . . . 1·30 25
443 – 2r. multicoloured . . . . 1·60 35
444 – 3r. multicoloured . . . . 2·20 55
MS445 97 × 75 mm. 6r. multicoloured (39 × 31 mm) . . 6·00 1·60

DESIGNS: Nos. 439/44, different details of frescoes by Raphael.

113 Montgolfier Balloon

1983. Bicentenary of Manned Flight. Mult.

446 20c. Type **113** 20 10
447 30c. "La Ville d'Orleans", 1870 . . . . 25 10
448 50c. Charles's hydrogen balloon 35 10
449 1r. Blanchard and Jeffries crossing Channel, 1785 . . 65 20
450 1r.50 Salomon Andree's balloon flight over Arctic 90 25
451 2r. Auguste Piccard's stratosphere balloon "F.N.R.S." . . . . 1·30 35
452 3r. Hot-air balloon race . . . 1·80 70
MS453 75 × 67 mm. 6r. Balloons over European town (vert) . . 5·75 1·10

114 Cobra

116 Sunflower

115 Rainbow Lory

1983. Reptiles. Multicoloured.

454 20c. Crested lizard (horiz) . . 20 10
455 30c. Type **114** 25 20
456 80c. Trionyx turtle (horiz) . . 45 20
457 1r. Chameleon 70 25
458 1r.50 Boa constrictor . . . . 1·30 45
459 2r. Crocodile (horiz) . . . . 1·60 65
460 3r. Turtle (horiz) . . . . . . 2·10 90

1983. Birds. Multicoloured.

461 20c. Type **115** 20 10
462 50c. Barn swallow 25 10
463 80c. Golden eagle (horiz) . . 45 10
464 1r. Griffon vulture (horiz) . . 90 10
465 1r.50 Javanese collared dove (horiz) . . . . 1·60 20
466 2r. Black-billed magpie . . . 2·00 20
467 3r. Great Indian hornbill . . 3·50 20

1983. Flowers. Multicoloured.

468 20c. Type **116** 20 10
469 50c. "Caprifoliaceae" 25 10
470 80c. "Bougainvillea" 35 10
471 1r. "Ranunculaceae" 65 20
472 1r.50 "Nyctagynaceae" . . . 1·30 20
473 2r. Cockscomb . . . . 1·60 25
474 3r. Roses . . . . 2·00 45

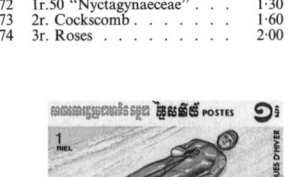

117 Luge

1983. Winter Olympic Games, Sarajevo (1984) (1st issue). Multicoloured.

475 1r. Type **117** 65 10
476 2r. Biathlon . . . . 1·40 20
477 4r. Ski-jumping . . . . . . 2·75 25
478 5r. Two-man bobsleigh . . . 3·25 35
479 7r. Ice hockey . . . . 4·75 45
MS480 81 × 68 mm. 6r. Skiing (35 × 28 mm) . . . . 5·25 90
See also Nos. 496/**MS**503.

118 Cyprinid

1983. Fishes. Multicoloured.

481 20c. Type **118** 20 10
482 50c. Loach 25 10
483 80c. Bubblebee catfish . . . 35 10
484 1r. Spiny eel 70 10
485 1r.50 Cyprinid (different) . . 1·30 20
486 2r. Cyprinid (different) . . . 1·80 20
487 3r. Aberrant fish . . . . . . 2·20 20

119 Factory and Gearwheel

1983. Festival of Rebirth. Multicoloured.

488 50c. Type **119** 25 20
489 1r. Tractor and cow (horiz) 90 20
490 3r. Bulk carrier, diesel locomotive, car and bridge 2·00 55
MS491 65 × 85 mm. 6r. Radio signal (31 × 39 mm) . . . . 5·25 90

120 Red Cross and Sailing Ship

1984. 5th Anniv of Liberation. Multicoloured.

492 50c. Type **120** 25 20
493 1r. Three soldiers, flags and temple 65 20
494 3r. Crowd surrounding temple . . . . 1·80 55
MS495 91 × 60 mm. 6r. Man carrying containers (31 × 39 mm) 5·25 1·20

121 Speed Skating

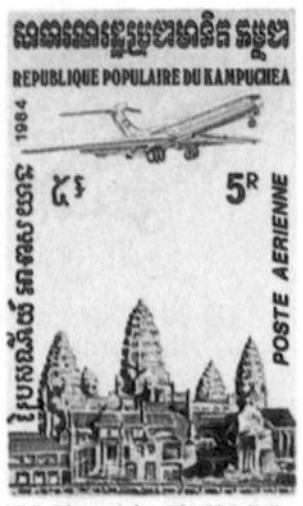

122 Ilyushin Il-62M Jet over Angkor Vat

1984. Winter Olympic Games, Sarajevo (2nd issue). Multicoloured.

496 20c. Type **121** 20 10
497 50c. Ice hockey 25 10
498 80c. Skiing 35 10
499 1r. Ski jumping 65 20
500 1r.50 Skiing (different) . . . 1·30 20
501 2r. Cross-country skiing . . . 1·60 25
502 3r. Ice skating (pairs) . . . . 2·00 45
MS503 120 × 80 mm. 6r. Ice skating (individual) (31 × 29 mm) . . . 5·25 1·10

1984. Air.

504 **122** 5r. multicoloured . . . . 4·00 20
505 10r. multicoloured . . . . 7·50 35
506 15r. multicoloured . . . . 11·00 45
507 25r. multicoloured . . . . 18·00 80

For design as Type **122** but inscribed "R.P. DU KAMPUCHEA", see Nos. 695/8.

123 Cattle Egret

124 Doves and Globe

1984. Birds. Multicoloured.

508 10c. Type **123** 20 10
509 40c. Black-headed shrike . . 65 10
510 80c. Slaty-headed parakeet 1·20 20
511 1r. Golden-fronted leafbird 1·60 20
512 1r.20 Red-winged crested cuckoo . . . . 1·80 25
513 2r. Grey wagtail . . . . . . 3·50 35
514 2r.50 Forest wagtail . . . . 3·75 45

1984. International Peace in South-East Asia Forum, Phnom Penh. Mult, background colour given.

515 **124** 50c. green 25 20
516 1r. blue 65 20
517 3r. violet . . . . 1·80 55

125 "Luna 2"

1984. Space Research. Multicoloured.

518 10c. "Luna 1" 20 10
519 40c. Type **125** 25 10
520 80c. "Luna 3" 35 10
521 1r. "Soyuz 6" and cosmonauts (vert) 65 10
522 1r.20 "Soyuz 7" and cosmonauts (vert) 90 20
523 2r. "Soyuz 8" and cosmonauts (vert) . . . . 1·30 20
524 2r.50 Book, rocket and S. P. Korolev (Russian spaceship designer) (vert) . . . . 1·80 20
MS525 81 × 80 mm. 6r. "Soyuz"-"Salyut" space complex and Earth (39 × 31 mm) . . . . 5·25 90

126 Throwing the Discus

1984. Olympic Games, Los Angeles (2nd issue). Multicoloured.

526	20c. Type **126**	20	10
527	50c. Long jumping	25	10
528	80c. Hurdling	35	10
529	1r. Relay	90	20
530	1r.50 Pole vaulting	1·20	20
531	2r. Throwing the javelin	1·40	25
532	3r. High jumping	2·00	45
MS533	79 × 59 mm. 76r. Sprinting	5·25	90

127 Hispano-Suiza "K6", 1933

1984. "Espana 84" International Stamp Exhibition, Madrid. Sheet 71 × 58 mm.

MS534	**127** 5r. multicoloured	5·25	1·80

128 Coyote

1984. Dog Family. Multicoloured.

535	10c. Type **128**	20	10
536	40c. Dingo	25	10
537	80c. Hunting dog	45	10
538	1r. Golden jackal	90	10
539	1r.20 Red fox	1·10	20
540	2r. Maned wolf (vert)	2·00	20
541	2r.50 Wolf	3·00	20

129 Class BB 1002 Diesel Locomotive, 1966, France

1984. Railway Locomotives. Multicoloured.

542	10c. Type **129**	20	10
543	40c. Class BB 1052 diesel locomotive, 1966, France	25	10
544	80c. Franco-Belgian-built steam locomotive, 1945, France	35	10
545	1r. Steam locomotive No. 231-505, 1929, France	80	10
546	1r.20 Class 803 diesel railcar, 1968, Germany	1·30	20
547	2r. Class BDE-405 diesel locomotive, 1957, France	1·60	20
548	2r.50 Class DS-01 diesel railcar, 1925, France	2·75	20

130 Magnolia

1984. Flowers. Multicoloured.

549	10c. Type **130**	20	10
550	40c. "Plumeria"		
551	80c. "Himenoballis" sp.	45	10
552	1r. "Peltophorum roxburghii"	1·10	20
553	1r.20 "Couroupita guianensis"	1·30	20
554	2r. "Lagerstroemia" sp.	2·20	20
555	2r.50 "Thevetia perubiana"	3·50	25

131 Mercedes Benz

1984. Cars. Multicoloured.

556	20c. Type **131**	20	10
557	50c. Bugatti	25	20
558	80c. Alfa Romeo	45	20
559	1r. Franklin	1·00	25
560	1r.50 Hispano-Suiza	1·40	35
561	2r. Rolls Royce	2·00	45
562	3r. Tatra	2·75	70
MS563	68 × 70 mm. 6r. Mercedes Benz (39 × 31 mm)	5·75	1·10

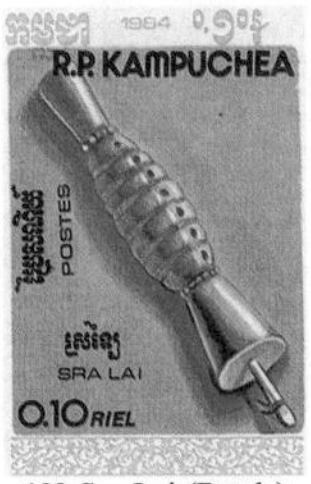

132 Sra Lai (Rattle)

133 Gazelle

1984. Musical Instruments. Multicoloured.

564	10c. Type **132**	20	10
565	40c. Skor drum (horiz)	25	10
566	80c. Skor drums (different)	35	10
567	1r. Thro khmer (stringed instrument) (horiz)	65	20
568	1r.20 Raneat ek (xylophone) (horiz)	1·30	35
569	2r. Raneat kong (bells) (horiz)	1·40	35
570	2r.50 Thro khe (stringed instrument) (horiz)	2·20	65

1984. Mammals. Multicoloured.

571	10c. Type **133**	20	10
572	40c. Roe deer	25	10
573	80c. Hare (horiz)	35	10
574	1r. Red deer	65	20
575	1r.20 Indian elephant	1·30	20
576	2r. Genet (horiz)	1·40	20
577	2r.50 Kouprey (horiz)	2·20	25

134 "Madonna and Child"

1984. 450th Death Anniv of Correggio (artist). Multicoloured.

578	20c. Type **134**	20	10
579	50c. Detail showing man striking monk	25	10
580	80c. "Madonna and Child" (different)	35	10
581	1r. "Madonna and Child" (different)	70	20
582	1r.50 "Mystical Marriage of St. Catherine"	1·30	20
583	2r. "Pieta"	1·50	20
584	3r. Detail showing man descending ladder	2·00	25
MS585	91 × 64 mm. 6r. "Coronation of the Virgin" (39 × 31 mm)	5·50	95

135 Bullock Cart

1985. National Festival (6th Anniv of People's Republic). Multicoloured.

586	50c. Type **135**	45	20
587	1r. Horse-drawn passenger cart	90	25
588	3r. Elephants	2·75	45
MS589	85 × 64 mm. 6r. Bullock-drawn passenger cart (31 × 39 mm)	5·75	90

136 Footballers

138 Glistening Ink Cap

137 Eska-Mofa Motor Cycle, 1939

1985. World Cup Football Championship, Mexico (1986) (1st issue). Designs showing footballers.

590	**136** 20c. multicoloured	20	10
591	– 50c. multicoloured	25	10
592	– 80c. multicoloured	35	10
593	– 1r. multicoloured (horiz)	65	20
594	– 1r.50 mult (horiz)	1·10	20
595	– 2r. multicoloured	1·30	20
596	– 3r. multicoloured	2·00	25
MS597	94 × 57 mm. 6r. multicoloured (39 × 31 mm)	5·25	90

See also Nos. 680/**MS**687.

1985. Centenary of Motor Cycle. Multicoloured.

598	20c. Type **137**	20	10
599	50c. Wanderer, 1939	25	10
600	80c. Premier, 1929	35	20
601	1r. Ardie, 1939	70	25
602	1r.50 Jawa, 1932	1·30	45
603	2r. Simson, 1983	1·50	70
604	3r. "CZ 125", 1984	2·00	90
MS605	100 × 85 mm. 6r. MBA, 1984 (39 × 31 mm)	5·75	90

1985. Fungi. Multicoloured.

606	20c. "Gymnophilus spectabilis" (horiz)	20	10
607	50c. Type **138**	35	10
608	80c. Panther cap	70	10
609	1r. Fairy cake mushroom	1·00	10
610	1r.50 Fly agaric	2·00	20
611	2r. Shaggy ink cap	2·75	20
612	3r. Caesar's mushroom	3·00	20

139 "Sputnik 1"

1985. Space Exploration. Multicoloured.

613	20c. Type **139**	20	10
614	50c. "Soyuz" rocket on transporter and Yuri Gagarin (first man in space)	25	20
615	80c. "Vostok 6" and Valentina Tereshkova (first woman in space)	35	20
616	1r. Space walker	65	25
617	1r.50 "Salyut"–"Soyuz" link	1·10	35
618	2r. "Lunokhod 1" (lunar vehicle)	1·30	45
619	3r. "Venera" (Venus probe)	2·00	70
MS620	94 × 59 mm. 6r. "Soyuz" preparing to dock with "Salyut" space station (39 × 31 mm)	5·25	1·40

140 Absara Dancer

140a Captured Nazi Standards, Red Square, Moscow

1985. Traditional Dances. Multicoloured.

621	50c. Absara group (horiz)	45	10
622	1r. Tepmonorom dance (horiz)	90	25
623	3r. Type **140**	1·80	70

1985. 40th Anniv of End of Second World War. Multicoloured.

623a	50c. Rejoicing soldiers in Berlin	35	10
623b	1r. Type **140a**	80	25
623c	3r. Tank battle	2·40	70

141 Tortoiseshell Cat

142 "Black Dragon" Lily

1985. Domestic Cats. Multicoloured.

624	20c. Type **141**	20	10
625	50c. Tortoiseshell (different)	25	20
626	80c. Tabby	45	20
627	1r. Long-haired Siamese	1·00	25
628	1t.50 Sealpoint Siamese	1·40	35
629	2r. Grey cat	2·00	45
630	3r. Black cat	2·75	70

1985. Flowers. Multicoloured.

631	20c. Type **142**	20	10
632	50c. "Iris delavayi"	25	10
633	80c. "Crocus aureus"	35	10
634	1r. "Cyclamen persicum"	70	20
635	1r.50 Fairy primrose	1·30	25
636	2r. Pansy "Ullswater"	1·80	35
637	3r. "Crocus purpureus grandiflorus"	2·10	55

143 "Per Italiani" (Antoine Watteau)

144 Lenin and Arms

1985. International Music Year. Multicoloured.

638	20c. Type **143**	20	10
639	50c. "St. Cecilia" (Carlos Saraceni)	25	10
640	80c. "Still Life with Violin" (Jean Baptiste Oudry) (horiz)	55	10
641	1r. "Three Musicians" (Fernand Leger)	65	20
642	1r.50 Orchestra	90	25
643	2r. "St. Cecilia" (Bartholomeo Schedoni)	1·30	35
644	3r. "Harlequin with Violin" (Christian Caillard)	1·80	55
MS645	55 × 89 mm. 6r. "The Fifer" (Edouard Manet) (31 × 39 mm)	6·50	1·40

1985. 115th Birth Anniv of Lenin. Multicoloured.

646	1r. Type **144**	1·10	35
647	3r. Lenin on balcony and map	2·10	70

145 Saffron-cowled Blackbird

1985. "Argentina '85" International Stamp Exhibition, Buenos Aires. Birds. Multicoloured.

648	20c. Type **145**	20	10
649	50c. Saffron finch (vert)	25	10
650	80c. Blue and yellow tanager (vert)	35	10
651	1r. Scarlet-headed blackbird	70	20
652	1r.50 Amazon kingfisher (vert)	1·30	25
653	2r. Toco toucan (vert)	1·80	35
654	3r. Rufous-bellied thrush	2·10	55

146 River Launch, Cambodia, 1942

1985. Water Craft. Multicoloured.

655	10c. Type **146**	20	10
656	40c. River launch, Cambodia, 1948	25	10
657	80c. Tug, Japan, 1913	35	10
658	1r. Dredger, Holland	65	20
659	1r.20 Tug, U.S.A.	90	25
660	2r. River freighter	1·30	35
661	2r.50 River tanker, Panama	1·80	55

147 "The Flood" (Michelangelo)

148 Son Ngoc Minh

1985. "Italia '85" International Stamp Exhibition, Rome. Paintings. Multicoloured.
662 20r. Type **147** 20 10
663 50r. "The Virgin of St. Marguerite" (Mazzola) 25 10
664 80r. "The Martyrdom of St. Peter" (Zampieri Domenichino) 35 10
665 1r. "Allegory of Spring" (detail) (Sandro Botticelli) 70 10
666 1r.50 "The Sacrifice of Abraham" (Caliari) . . . . 1·30 20
667 2r. "The Meeting of Joachim and Anne" (Giotto) . . . 1·80 20
668 3r. "Bacchus" (Michel Angelo Carravaggio) . . . 2·10 20
MS669 94 × 64 mm. 6r. Early steam locomotive, Berlin (31 × 39 mm) 6·50 1·40

1985. Festival of Rebirth.
670 **148** 50c. multicoloured 35 20
671 1r. multicoloured 55 25
672 3r. multicoloured . . . . 1·30 45

149 Tiger Barbs

1985. Fishes. Multicoloured.
673 20c. Type **149** 20 10
674 50c. Giant snakehead 25 10
675 80c. Veil-tailed goldfish . . . 35 10
676 1r. Pearl gourami 65 20
677 1r.50 Six-banded tiger barbs 1·10 25
678 2r. Siamese fighting fish . . . 1·30 35
679 3r. Siamese tigerfish . . . . 2·00 55

150 Footballers

152 "Mir" Space Station and Spacecraft

151 Cob

1986. World Cup Football Championship, Mexico (2nd issue).
680 **150** 20c. multicoloured 20 10
681 – 50c. multicoloured 25 10
682 – 80c. multicoloured 35 10
683 – 1r. multicoloured 65 20
684 – 1r.50 multicoloured . . . 90 25
685 – 2r. multicoloured . . . . 1·30 35
686 – 3r. multicoloured . . . . 1·80 55
MS687 95 × 92 mm. 6r. multicoloured (31 × 39 mm) . . . 5·25 90
DESIGNS: 50c. to 6r. Various footballing scenes.

1986. Horses. Multicoloured.
688 20c. Type **151** 20 10
689 50c. Arab 25 10
690 80c. Australian pony 35 10
691 1r. Appaloosa 70 20
692 1r.50 Quarter horse . . . . 1·30 20
693 2r. Vladimir heavy draught horse . . . . 1·50 20
694 3r. Andalusian . . . . 2·00 25

1986. 27th Russian Communist Party Congress. Multicoloured.
694a 50c. Type **152** 25 10
694b 1r. Lenin 80 35
694c 5r. Statue and launch of space rocket . . . . 3·00 65

1986. Air. As Nos. 504/7 but inscr "R.P. DU KAMPUCHEA".
695 **122** 5r. multicoloured . . . . 3·50 20
696 10r. multicoloured . . . . 7·25 35
697 15r. multicoloured . . . . 9·00 45
698 25r. multicoloured . . . . 16·00 80

153 Edaphosaurus (⅔-size illustration)

1986. Prehistoric Animals. Multicoloured.
699 20c. Type **153** 35 10
700 50c. Sauroctonus 45 10
701 80c. Mastodonsaurus 90 10
702 1r. Rhamphorhynchus (vert) 1·60 20
703 1r.50 "Brachiosaurus brancai" (vert) . . . . . . 2·50 25
704 2r. "Tarbosaurus bataar" (vert) . . . . 3·25 35
705 3r. Indricotherium (vert) . . 4·50 70

154 "Luna 16"

1986. 25th Anniv of First Man in Space. Multicoloured.
706 10c. Type **154** 20 10
707 40c. "Luna 3" 25 10
708 80c. "Vostok" 35 10
709 1r. Cosmonaut Leonov on space walk 65 20
710 1r.20 "Apollo" and "Soyuz" preparing to dock . . . . 1·10 20
711 2r. "Soyuz" docking with "Salyut" space station . . 1·30 20
712 2r.50 Yuri Gagarin (first man in space) and spacecraft . . 2·00 25

155 Baksei Chmkrong Temple, 920

1986. Khmer Culture. Multicoloured.
713 20c. Type **155** 20 10
714 50c. Buddha's head 25 10
715 80c. Prea Vihear monastery, Dangrek 35 10
716 1r. Fan with design of man and woman 45 20
717 1r.50 Fan with design of men fighting 65 25
718 2r. Fan with design of dancer 1·10 35
719 3r. Fan with design of dragon-drawn chariot . . . 1·50 70

156 Tricar, 1885

1986. Centenary (1985) of Motor Car. Mercedes Benz Models. Multicoloured.
720 20c. Type **156** 20 10
721 50c. Limousine, 1935 . . . . 25 10
722 80c. Open tourer, 1907 . . . 35 10
723 1r. Light touring car, 1920 65 20
724 1r.50 Cabriolet, 1932 . . . . 1·10 25
725 2r. "SKK" tourer, 1938 . . . 1·30 35
726 3r. "190", 1985 . . . . . . 2·00 70

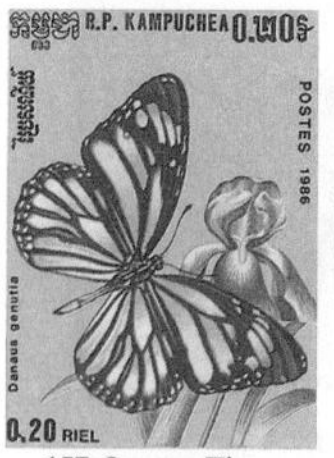

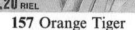

157 Orange Tiger

159 Solar System, Copernicus, Galileo and Tycho Brahe (astronomers)

158 English Kogge of Richard II's Reign

1986. Butterflies. Multicoloured.
727 20c. Type **157** 20 10
728 50c. Five-bar swallowtail . . 25 10
729 80c. Chequered swallowtail 35 10
730 1r. Chestnut tiger 70 20
731 1r.50 "Idea blanchardi" . . . 1·30 25
732 2r. Common mormon . . . 1·50 35
733 3r. "Dabasa payeni" . . . . 2·00 55

1986. Medieval Ships.
734 20c. Type **158** 20 10
735 50c. Kogge 25 10
736 80c. Knarr 35 10
737 1r. Galley 65 20
738 1r.50 Norman ship 90 25
739 2r. Mediterranean usciere . . 1·30 35
740 3r. French kogge . . . . . . 1·80 55

1986. Appearance of Halley's Comet. Multicoloured.
741 10c. Type **159** 20 10
742 20c. "Nativity" (Giotto) and comet from Bayeux Tapestry 20 10
743 50c. Comet, 1910, and Mt. Palomar observatory, U.S.A. 25 10
744 80c. Edmond Halley and "Planet A" space probe . . 45 20
745 1r.20 Diagram of comet's trajectory and "Giotto" space probe 70 25
746 1r.50 "Vega" space probe and camera 90 35
747 2r. Thermal pictures of comet 1·30 55
MS748 87 × 56 mm. 6r. "Vega" space probe (31 × 39 mm) . . . 4·25 1·10

160 Ruy Lopez

1986. "Stockholmia 86" International Stamp Exhibition. Chess. Multicoloured.
749 20c. Type **160** 20 10
750 50c. Francois-Andre Philidor 25 10
751 80c. Karl Anderssen and Houses of Parliament, London 35 10
752 1r. Wilhelm Steinitz and Charles Bridge, Prague . . 70 20
753 1r.50 Emanuel Lasker and medieval knight . . . . . 1·30 25
754 2r. Jose Raul Capablanca and Morro Castle, Cuba 1·80 35
755 3r. Aleksandr Alekhine . . . 2·10 70
MS756 62 × 72 mm. 6r. Chess pieces (39 × 31 mm) . . . . 6·50 1·40
No. 751 is wrongly inscribed "Andersen".

161 "Parodia maassii"

162 Bananas

1986. Cacti. Multicoloured.
757 20c. Type **161** 20 10
758 50c. "Rebutia marsoneri" . . 25 10
759 80c. "Melocactus evae" . . . 35 10
760 1r. "Gymnocalycium valnicekianum" 70 20
761 1r.50 "Discocactus silichromus" . . . . 1·30 25
762 2r. "Neochilenia simulans" 1·50 35
763 3r. "Weingartia chiquichuquensis" . . . . 2·00 55

1986. Fruit. Multicoloured.
764 10c. Type **162** 20 10
765 40c. Papaya 25 20
766 80c. Mangoes 35 20
767 1r. Breadfruit 45 20
768 1r.20 Lychees 65 35
769 2r. Pineapple . . . . 1·10 55
770 2r.50 Grapefruit (horiz) . . . 1·50 70

163 Concorde (⅔-size illustration)

1986. Aircraft. Multicoloured.
771 20c. Type **163** (wrongly inscr "Concord") 20 10
772 50c. Douglas DC-10 . . . . 25 10
773 80c. Boeing 747SP 35 10
774 1r. Ilyushin Il-62M 65 20
775 1r.50 Ilyushin Il-86 . . . . . 90 25
776 2r. Antonov An-24 (wrongly inscr "AN-124") . . . . . 1·30 35
777 3r. Airbus Industrie A300 . . 1·80 70

164 Elephant and Silver Containers on Tray

1986. Festival of Rebirth. Silverware. Mult.
778 50c. Type **164** 35 20
779 1r. Tureen 70 25
780 3r. Dish on stand . . . . . 2·10 45

165 Kouprey

1986. Endangered Animals. Cattle. Mult.
781 20c. Type **165** . . . . 1·10 20
782 20c. Gaur . . . . 1·60 25
783 80c. Bateng cow and calf . . 4·00 35
784 1r.50 Asiatic water buffalo 6·75 55

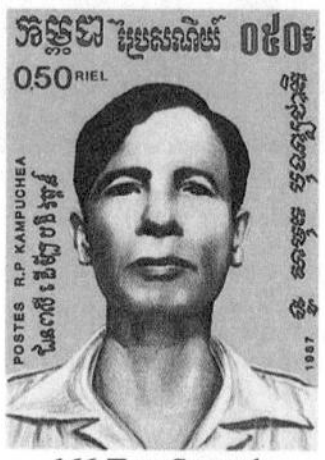

166 Tou Samuth (revolutionary)

1987. National Festival. 8th Anniv of People's Republic.
785 **166** 50c. multicoloured 25 20
786 1r. multicoloured 45 25
787 3r. multicoloured . . . . 1·10 45

167 Biathlon

1987. Winter Olympic Games, Calgary (1988) (1st issue). Multicoloured.
788 20c. Type **167** 20 10
789 50c. Figure skating 25 10
790 80c. Speed skating 35 10
791 1r. Ice hockey 65 20
792 1r.50 Two-man luge 90 25
793 2r. Two-man bobsleigh . . . 1·30 35
794 3r. Cross-country skiing . . . 1·80 70
MS795 91 × 65 mm. 6r. Skiing (39 × 31 mm) . . . . 4·25 1·10
See also Nos. 864/**MS**871.

168 Weightlifting

1987. Olympic Games, Seoul (1988) (1st issue). Designs showing ancient Greek and modern athletes. Multicoloured.

796	20c. Type **168**	20	10
797	50c. Archery (horiz)	25	10
798	80c. Fencing (horiz)	35	20
799	1r. Gymnastics	65	20
800	1r.50 Throwing the discus (horiz)	90	20
801	2r. Throwing the javelin	1·30	25
802	3r. Hurdling	1·80	35
MS803	93 × 63 mm. 6r. Wrestling (39 × 31 mm)	4·25	1·10

See also Nos. 875/**MS**882.

169 Papillon

1987. Dogs. Multicoloured.

804	20c. Type **169**	20	10
805	50c. Greyhound	25	10
806	80c. Great Dane	35	10
807	1r. Dobermann	70	20
808	1r.50 Samoyed	1·30	25
809	2r. Borzoi	1·80	35
810	3r. Rough collie	2·10	55

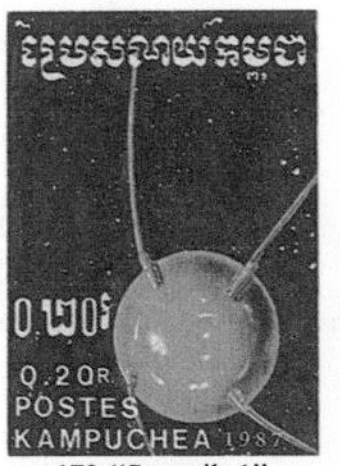
170 "Sputnik 1"

171 Flask

1987. Space Exploration. Multicoloured.

811	20c. Type **170**	20	10
812	50c. "Soyuz 10"	25	10
813	80c. "Proton"	35	10
814	1r. "Vostok 1"	65	20
815	1r.50 "Elektron 2"	90	25
816	2r. "Kosmos"	1·30	35
817	3r. "Luna 2"	1·80	70
MS818	71 × 48 mm. 6r. "Elektron 4" (39 × 31 mm)	4·25	1·10

1987. Metalwork. Multicoloured.

819	50c. Type **171**	25	20
820	1r. Repousse box (horiz)	70	25
821	1r.50 Teapot and cups on tray (horiz)	1·10	35
822	3r. Ornamental sword	2·00	55

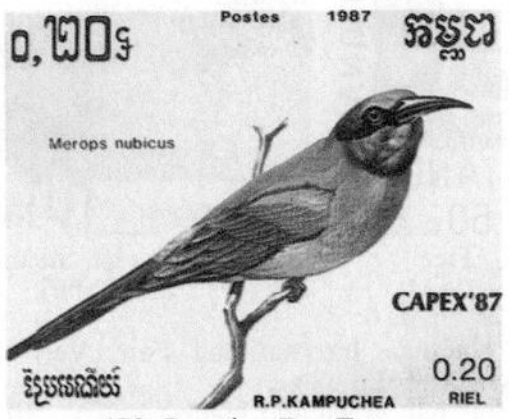
172 Carmine Bee Eater

1987. "Capex'87" International Stamp Exhibition, Toronto. Birds. Multicoloured.

823	20c. Type **172**	20	10
824	50c. Hoopoe (vert)	25	10
825	80c. South African crowned crane (vert)	35	10
826	1r. Barn owl (vert)	65	20
827	1r.50 Grey-headed kingfisher (vert)	1·10	25
828	2r. Red-whiskered bulbul	1·30	35
829	3r. Purple heron (vert)	2·00	55
MS830	70 × 94 mm. 6r. Asiatic paradise flycatcher (28 × 39 mm)	6·50	90

173 Horatio Phillip's "Multiplane" Model, 1893

1987. Experimental Aircraft Designs. Mult.

831	20c. Type **173**	20	10
832	50c. John Stringfellow's steam-powered model, 1848	25	10
833	80c. Thomas Moy's model "Aerial Steamer", 1875	35	10
834	1r. Leonardo da Vinci's "ornithopter", 1490	65	20
835	1r.50 Sir George Cayley's "convertiplane", 1843	1·10	20
836	2r. Sir Hiram Maxim's "Flying Test Rig", 1894	1·30	20
837	3r. William Henson's "Aerial Steam Carriage", 1842	2·00	25
MS838	98 × 83 mm. 6r. Leonardo da Vinci's drawing of "Flying Man" (31 × 39 mm)	4·25	90

No. 835 is wrongly dated "1840".

174 Giant Tortoise

1987. Reptiles. Multicoloured.

839	20c. Type **174**	20	10
840	50c. African spiny-tailed lizard	25	10
841	80c. Iguana	35	10
842	1r. Coast horned lizard	65	20
843	1r.50 Northern chuckwalla	90	25
844	2r. Glass lizard	1·30	35
845	3r. Common garter snake	1·80	55

175 Kamov Ka-15

1987. "Hafnia 87" International Stamp Exhibition, Copenhagen. Helicopters. Multicoloured.

846	20c. Type **175**	20	10
847	50c. Kamov Ka-18	25	10
848	80c. Westland Lynx	35	10
849	1r. Sud Aviation Gazelle	65	20
850	1r.50 Sud Aviation SA 330E Puma	90	20
851	2r. Boeing-Vertol CH-47 Chinook	1·30	20
852	3r. Boeing UTTAS	1·80	25
MS853	65 × 85 mm. 6r. Fairey rotodyne	4·25	1·10

176 Revolutionaries

178 Earth Station Dish Aerial

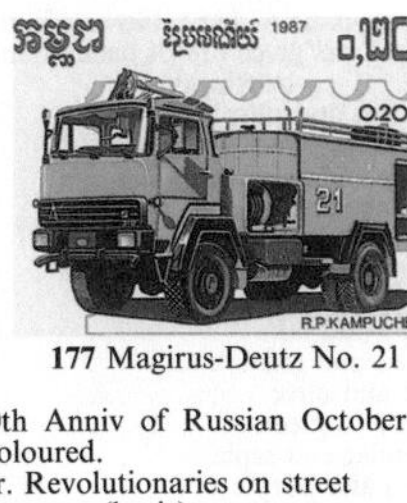
177 Magirus-Deutz No. 21

1987. 70th Anniv of Russian October Revolution. Multicoloured.

853a	2r. Revolutionaries on street corner (horiz)	1·10	20
853b	3r. Type **176**	1·30	45
853c	5r. Lenin receiving ticker-tape message (horiz)	3·00	70

1987. Fire Engines. Multicoloured.

854	20c. Type **177**	20	10
855	50c. "SIL-131" rescue vehicle	25	10
856	80c. "Cas-25" fire pump	35	10
857	1r. Sirmac Saab "424"	70	20
858	1r.50 Rosenbaum-Falcon	1·30	25
859	2r. Tatra "815-PRZ"	1·80	35
860	3r. Chubbfire "C-44-20"	2·10	55

1987. Telecommunications. Multicoloured.

861	50c. Type **178**	35	20
862	1r. Technological building with radio microwave aerial (27 × 44 mm)	70	25
863	3r. Intersputnik programme earth station (44 × 27 mm)	1·60	65

179 Speed Skating

1988. Winter Olympic Games, Calgary (2nd issue). Multicoloured.

864	20c. Type **179**	20	10
865	50c. Ice hockey	25	10
866	80c. Slalom	35	10
867	1r. Ski jumping	65	10
868	1r.50 Biathlon	90	20
869	2r. Ice dancing	1·30	20
870	3r. Cross-country skiing	1·80	20
MS871	66 × 89 mm. 6r. Four-man bobsleigh (31 × 39 mm)	4·25	90

180 Irrigation Canal Bed

1988. Irrigation Projects. Multicoloured.

872	50c. Type **180**	35	20
873	1r. Dam construction	70	25
874	3r. Dam and bridge	1·60	45

181 Beam Exercise

1988. Olympic Games, Seoul (2nd issue). Women's Gymnastics. Multicoloured.

875	20c. Type **181**	20	10
876	50c. Bar exercise (horiz)	25	10
877	80c. Ribbon exercise	35	10
878	1r. Hoop exercise	55	10
879	1r.50 Baton exercise	70	20
880	2r. Ball exercise (horiz)	1·20	20
881	3r. Floor exercise (horiz)	1·60	20
MS882	84 × 59 mm. 6r. Ball exercise (different) (28 × 36 mm)	4·25	90

182 Abyssinian

1988. "Juvalux 88" 9th Youth Philately Exhibition, Luxembourg. Cats. Multicoloured.

883	20c. White long-haired (horiz)	20	10
884	50c. Type **182**	25	10
885	80c. Ginger and white long-haired	35	10
886	1r. Tortoiseshell queen and kitten (horiz)	65	20
887	1r.50 Brown cat	1·10	25
888	2r. Black long-haired cat	1·30	35
889	3r. Grey cat	2·00	55
MS890	61 × 50 mm. 6r. Kittens (39 × 31 mm)	7·00	90

183 "Emerald Seas" (liner)

1988. "Essen 88" International Stamp Fair. Ships. Multicoloured.

891	20c. Type **183**	20	10
892	50c. Car ferry	25	10
893	80c. "Mutsu" (nuclear-powered freighter)	35	10
894	1r. "Kosmonavt Yury Gagarin" (research ship)	65	20
895	1r.50 Tanker	1·10	25
896	2r. Hydrofoil	1·30	35
897	3r. Hovercraft	2·00	55
MS898	95 × 70 mm. 6r. Hydrofoil (different) (39 × 31 mm)	4·75	90

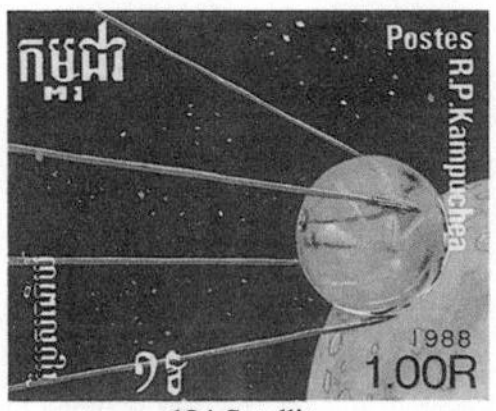
184 Satellite

1988. Space Exploration. Designs showing different satellites.

899	– 20c. multicoloured (vert)	20	10
900	– 50c. multicoloured (vert)	25	10
901	– 80c. multicoloured (vert)	35	10
902	**184** 1r. multicoloured	55	10
903	– 1r.50 multicoloured	80	20
904	– 2r. multicoloured	1·20	20
905	– 3r. multicoloured	1·60	20
MS906	103 × 63 mm. 6r. multicoloured (39 × 31 mm)	4·25	90

185 Swordtail

1988. "Finlandia 88" International Stamp Exhibition, Helsinki. Tropical Fish. Multicoloured.

907	20c. Type **185**	20	10
908	50c. Head-and-taillight tetra	25	10
909	80c. Paradise fish	35	20
910	1r. Black moor goldfish	65	20
911	1r.50 Cardinal tetra	1·10	20
912	2r. Sword-tailed characin	1·30	25
913	3r. Sail-finned molly	2·00	35
MS914	62 × 72 mm. 6r. Angel fish (31 × 39 mm)	5·75	90

186 Flowery Helicostyla

188 "Cattleya aclandiae"

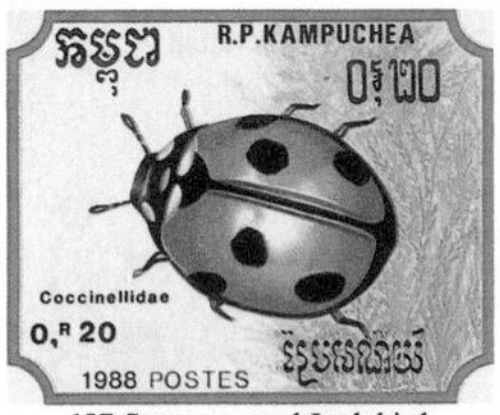
187 Seven-spotted Ladybird

1988. Sea Shells. Multicoloured.

915	20c. Type **186**	20	10
916	50c. Changing helicostyla	25	10
917	80c. Shining helicostyla	35	10
918	1r. Marinduque helicostyla	65	10
919	1r.50 Siren chlorena	1·10	20
920	2r. Miraculous helicostyla	1·30	20
921	3r. "Helicostyla limansauensis"	2·00	20

1988. Insects. Multicoloured.
922 20c. Type **187** 20 10
923 50c. "Zonabride geminata" (blister beetle) 25 10
924 80c. "Carabus auronitens" (ground beetle) 35 10
925 1r. Honey bee 65 10
926 1r.50 Praying mantis . . . . 1·10 20
927 2r. Dragonfly . . . . 1·30 20
928 3r. Soft-winged flower beetle 2·00 20

1988. Orchids. Multicoloured.
929 20c. Type **188** 20 10
930 50c. "Odontoglossum" "Royal Sovereign" 25 10
931 80c. "Cattleya labiata" . . . 35 10
932 1r. Bee orchid 65 10
933 1r.50 "Laelia anceps" 90 20
934 2r. "Laelia pumila" . . . . . 1·30 20
935 3r. "Stanhopea tigrina" (horiz) . . . . 1·80 20

189 Egyptian Banded Cobra

190 Walking Dance

1988. Reptiles. Multicoloured.
936 20c. Type **189** 20 10
937 50c. Common iguana 25 10
938 80c. Long-nosed vine snake (horiz) 35 10
939 1r. Common box turtle (horiz) 65 10
940 1r.50 Iguana (horiz) . . . . 1·10 20
941 2r. Viper (horiz) . . . . . . 1·30 20
942 3r. Common cobra . . . . . 2·00 20

1988. Festival of Rebirth. Khmer Culture. Multicoloured.
943 50c. Type **190** 35 20
944 1r. Peacock dance (horiz) . . 80 25
945 3r. Kantere dance (horiz) . . 2·00 65

191 Bridge

1989. Multicoloured.
946 50c. Type **191** 25 10
947 1r. More distant view of bridge 65 35
948 3r. Closer view of bridge . . 1·60 90

192 Cement Works

1989. National Festival. 10th Anniv of People's Republic of Kampuchea. Multicoloured.
949 3r. Bayon Earth Station (horiz) 25 10
950 12r. Electricity generating station 4 (horiz) 70 35
951 30r. Type **192** . . . . 2·00 90

193 Footballers

1989. World Cup Football Championship, Italy (1990).
952 **193** 2r. multicoloured 20 10
953 – 3r. multicoloured 25 10
954 – 5r. multicoloured 35 10
955 – 10r. multicoloured 80 10
956 – 15r. multicoloured . . . . 1·20 20
957 – 20r. multicoloured . . . . 1·60 20
958 – 35r. multicoloured . . . . 2·75 20
MS959 92 × 54 mm. 45r. multicoloured (goalkeeper) (31 × 39 mm) . . . . 4·25 90
DESIGNS: 3r. to 45r. Various footballing scenes. See also Nos. 1042/**MS**1049.

194 Tram

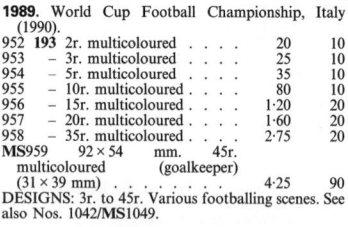

1989. Trams and Trains. Multicoloured.
960 2r. Type **194** 25 10
961 3r. ETR 401 Pendolino express train, 1976, Italy 35 10
962 5r. High speed train, Germany 45 10
963 10r. Theme park monorail train 80 10
964 15r. German Trans Europe Express (TEE) train . . . 1·20 20
965 20r. "Hikari" express train, Sanyo Shinkansenline, Japan . . . . 1·60 20
966 35r. TGV express train, France . . . . 3·00 20
MS967 85 × 55 mm. 45r. multicoloured (39 × 31 mm) . . 5·25 90

195 Fidel Castro

196 Scarlet Macaw

1989. 30th Anniv of Cuban Revolution.
968 **195** 12r. multicoloured . . . . 1·10 55

1989. Parrots. Multicoloured.
969 20c. Type **196** 20 10
970 80c. Sulphur-crested cockatoo 25 10
971 3r. Rose-ringed parakeet . . 35 10
972 6r. Blue and yellow macaw 70 10
973 10r. Brown-necked parrot . . 90 20
974 15r. Blue-fronted amazon . . 1·40 20
975 25r. White-capped parrot (horiz) . . . . 2·00 20
MS976 65 × 75 mm. 45r. Red-fronted parakeet (31 × 39 mm) 6·50 90

197 Skiing

1989. Winter Olympic Games, Albertville (1992). Multicoloured.
977 2r. Type **197** 20 10
978 3r. Biathlon 25 10
979 5r. Cross-country skiing . . . 35 10
980 10r. Ski jumping 80 10
981 15r. Speed skating . . . . . 1·10 20
982 20r. Ice hockey . . . . 1·30 20
983 35r. Two-man bobsleighing 2·75 20
MS984 75 × 89 mm. 45r. Figure skating (31 × 39 mm) . . . . 4·25 90
See also Nos.1069/**MS**1076 and 1152/**MS**1159.

198 "Nymphaea capensis" (pink)

1989. Water Lilies. Multicoloured.
985 20c. Type **198** 20 10
986 80c. "Nymphaea capensis" (mauve) 20 10
987 3r. "Nymphaea lotus dentata" 25 10
988 6r. "Dir. Geo. T. Moore" . . 45 10
989 10r. "Sunrise" 65 20
990 15r. "Escarboncle" . . . . . 1·30 20
991 25r. "Cladstoniana" . . . . 2·00 20
MS992 59 × 79 mm. 45r. "Paul Hariot" (31 × 39 mm) . . . . 4·25 90

199 Wrestling

1989. Olympic Games, Barcelona (1992). Multicoloured.
993 2r. Type **199** 20 10
994 3r. Gymnastics (vert) 25 10
995 5r. Putting the shot 35 10
996 10r. Running (vert) 70 10
997 15r. Fencing . . . . 1·10 20
998 20r. Canoeing (vert) . . . . 1·30 20
999 35r. Hurdling (vert) . . . . 2·75 20
MS1000 62 × 87 mm. 45r. Weightlifting (31 × 39 mm) . . 4·25 90
See also Nos. 1061/**MS**1068, 1163/**MS**1170, 1208/**MS**1213 and 1241/**MS**1246.

200 Downy Boletus

1989. Fungi. Multicoloured.
1001 20c. Type **200** 20 10
1002 80c. Red-staining inocybe 25 10
1003 3r. Honey fungus 35 10
1004 6r. Field mushroom 70 10
1005 10r. Brown roll-rim 90 20
1006 15r. Shaggy ink cap . . . . 1·40 20
1007 25r. Parasol mushroom . . 2·00 20

201 Shire Horse

1989. Horses. Multicoloured.
1008 2r. Type **201** 20 10
1009 3r. Brabant 25 10
1010 5r. Bolounais 35 10
1011 10r. Breton 80 10
1012 15r. Vladimir heavy draught horse . . . . 1·20 20
1013 20r. Italian heavy draught horse . . . . 1·60 20
1014 35r. Freiberger . . . . . . 2·75 20
MS1015 77 × 56 mm. 45r. Team of four white horses (39 × 31 mm) 5·25 90

KATANGA Pt. 14

The following stamps were issued by Mr. Tshombe's Government for independent Katanga. In 1963 Katanga was reunited with the Central Government of Congo.

1960. Various stamps of Belgian Congo optd **KATANGA** and bar or surch also. (a) Masks issue of 1948.
1 1f.50 on 1f.25 mauve and blue 80 20
2 3f.50 on 2f.50 green and brown 80 25
3 20f. purple and red . . . . . 2·75 85
4 50f. black and brown . . . . 6·50 3·00
5 100f. black and red . . . . . 48·00 21·00

(b) Flowers issue of 1952. Flowers in natural colours; colours given are of backgrounds and inscriptions.
6 10c. yellow and purple 20 20
7 15c. green and red 20 25
8 20c. grey and green 35 25
9 25c. orange and green 35 25
10 40c. salmon and green 35 25
11 50c. turquoise and red 45 35
12 60c. purple and green 45 35
13 75c. grey and lake 45 35
14 1f. lemon and red 55 45
15 2f. buff and olive 65 55
16 3f. pink and green 90 65
17 4f. lavender and sepia . . . 1·25 95
18 5f. green and purple . . . . 1·25 95
19 6f.50 lilac and red . . . . . 1·25 85
20 7f. brown and green . . . . . 1·75 1·25
21 8f. yellow and green . . . . 1·75 1·25
22 10f. olive and purple . . . . 28·00 17·00

(c) Wild animals issue of 1959.
23 10c. brown, sepia and blue . . 20 10
24 20c. blue and red . . . . . . 1·60 80
25 40c. brown and blue 20 10
26 50c. multicoloured 20 10
27 1f. black, green and brown . . 6·75 4·00
28 1f.50 black and yellow . . . . 11·00 7·50
29 2f. black, brown and red . . . 50 10
30 3f. black, purple and slate . . 4·25 3·00
31 5f. brown, green and sepia . . 75 30
32 6f.50 brown, yellow and blue 95 30
33 8f. bistre, violet and brown . . 1·40 35
34 10f. multicoloured . . . . . . 2·10 50

(d) Madonna.
35 **102** 50c. brown, ochre & chest 15 15
36 1f. brown, violet and blue 15 15
37 2f. brown, blue and slate 20 20

(e) African Technical Co-operation Commission. Inscr in French or Flemish.
38 **103** 3f. salmon and slate . . . 7·00 7·00
39 3f.50 on 3f. salmon & slate 2·10 2·10

1960. Independence. Independence issue of Congo optd **11 JUILLET DE L'ETAT DU KATANGA**.
40 **106** 20c. bistre 10 10
41 50c. red 10 10
42 1f. green 10 10
43 1f.50 brown 10 10
44 2f. mauve 10 10
45 3f.50 violet 15 10
46 5f. blue 15 10
47 6f.50 black 15 10
48 10f. orange 25 20
49 20f. blue 45 30

5

1961. Katanga Art.
50 **5** 10c. green 10 10
51 20c. violet 10 10
52 50c. blue 10 10
53 1f.50 green 10 10
54 2f. brown 10 10
55 – 3f.50 blue 10 10
56 – 5f. turquoise 10 10
57 – 6f. brown 10 10
58 – 6f.50 blue 10 10
59 – 8f. purple 15 10
60 – 10f. brown 15 10
61 – 20f. myrtle 25 20
62 – 50f. brown 50 40
63 – 100f. turquoise 85 70
DESIGNS: 3f.50 to 8f. "Preparing food"; 10f. to 100f. "Family circle".

6 Pres. Tshombe

1961. 1st Anniv of Independence. Portrait in brown.
64 **6** 6f.50+5f. red, green & gold 1·25 1·00
65 8f.+5f. red, green and gold 1·25 1·00
66 10f.+5f. red, green and gold 1·25 1·00

7 "Tree"

8 Early Aircraft, Steam Train and Safari

1961. Katanga International Fair. Vert symbolic designs as T **7**.
67 **7** 50c. red, green and black . . 10 10
68 – 1f. black and blue 10 10
69 – 2f.50 black and yellow . . . 15 15
70 **7** 3f.50 red, brown and black 15 15
71 – 5f. black and violet 25 25
72 – 6f.50 black and yellow . . . 30 30

1961. Air.
73 **8** 3f.50 multicoloured . . . . . 3·00 3·25
74 – 6f.50 multicoloured 65 65
75 **8** 8f. multicoloured . . . . . . 3·00 3·25
76 – 10f. multicoloured 65 65
DESIGNS: 6f.50, 10f. Tail of Boeing 707.

9 Gendarme in armoured Vehicle

1962. Katanga Gendarmerie.

77	9	6f. multicoloured	2·25	2·25
78		8f. multicoloured	35	35
79		10f. multicoloured	45	45

POSTAGE DUE STAMPS

1960. Postage Due stamps of Belgian Congo handstamped **KATANGA**. (a) On Nos. D270/4.

D50	D 86	10c. olive	80	80
D51		20c. blue	80	80
D52		50c. green	1·00	1·00
D53		1f. brown		
D54		2f. orange		

(b) On Nos. D330/6.

D55	D 99	10c. brown	3·25	3·25
D56		20c. purple	3·25	3·25
D57		50c. green	3·25	3·25
D58		1f. blue	1·00	1·00
D59		2f. red	2·00	2·00
D60		4f. violet	2·75	2·75
D61		6f. blue	3·25	3·25

KATHIRI STATE OF SEIYUN Pt. 1

The stamps of Aden were used in Kathiri State of Seiyun from 22 May 1937 until 1942.

1937. 16 annas = 1 rupee.
1951. 100 cents = 1 shilling.
1966. 1000 fils = 1 dinar.

1 Sultan of Seiyun

2 Seiyun

1942.

1	1	½a. green	20	70
2		¾a. brown	40	1·50
3		1a. blue	70	70
4	2	1½a. red	70	1·00
5	–	2a. brown	40	90
6	–	2½a. blue	1·25	1·00
7	–	3a. brown and red	1·75	2·50
8	–	8a. red	1·25	60
9	–	1r. green	3·75	2·25
10	–	2r. blue and purple	7·00	11·00
11	–	5r. brown and green	22·00	18·00

DESIGNS—VERT: 2a. Tarim; 2½a. Mosque at Seiyun; 1r. South Gate, Tarim; 5r. Mosque entrance, Tarim. HORIZ: 3a. Fortress at Tarim; 8a. Mosque at Seiyun; 2r. A Kathiri house.

1946. Victory. Optd **VICTORY ISSUE 8TH JUNE 1946.**

12	2	1½a. red	10	65
13	–	2½a. blue (No. 6)	10	10

1949. Royal Silver Wedding. As T **4b/c** of Pitcairn Islands.

14	1½a. red	30	2·50
15	5r. green	16·00	9·00

1949. 75th Anniv of U.P.U. As T **4d/g** of Pitcairn Islands surch with new values.

16	2½a. on 20c. blue	15	50
17	3a. on 30c. red	1·25	1·00
18	8a. on 50c. orange	25	1·00
19	1r. on 1s. blue	30	1·00

1951. 1942 stamps surch in cents or shillings.

20	1	5c. on 1a. blue	15	1·00
21	–	10c. on 2a. brown	30	65
22	–	15c. on 2½a. blue	15	1·25
23	–	20c. on 3a. brown and red	20	2·00
24	–	50c. on 8a. red	20	70
25	–	1s. on 1r. green	50	2·50
26	–	2s. on 2r. blue and purple	3·25	27·00
27	–	5s. on 5r. brown and green	20·00	38·00

1953. Coronation. As T **4h** of Pitcairn Islands.

28	15c. black and green	30	1·75

14 Sultan Hussein

29 "Telstar"

1954. As 1942 issue and new designs, but with portrait of Sultan Hussein as in T **14**.

29	14	5c. brown	10	10
30		10c. blue	15	10
31	2	15c. green	15	10
32	–	25c. red	15	10
33	–	35c. blue	15	10
34	–	50c. brown and red	15	10
39	–	70c. black	2·50	1·00
35	–	1s. orange	15	10
40	–	1s.25 green	2·50	7·50
41	–	1s.50 violet	2·50	7·50
36	–	2s. green	4·00	2·25
37	–	5s. blue and violet	7·50	6·50
38	–	10s. brown and violet	7·50	6·50

DESIGNS—VERT: 35c. Mosque at Seiyun; 70c. Qarn Adh Dhabi; 2s. South Gate, Tarim; 10s. Mosque entrance, Tarim. HORIZ: 50c. Fortress at Tarim; 1s. Mosque at Seiyun; 1s.25, Seiyun; 1s.50, Gheil Omer; 5s. Kathiri house.

1966. Nos. 29 etc surch **SOUTH ARABIA** in English and Arabic, with value and bar.

42	14	5f. on 5c.	15	10
43		5f. on 10c.	15	50
44	2	10f. on 15c.	15	50
45	–	15f. on 25c.	20	60
46	–	20f. on 35c.	15	30
47	–	25f. on 50c.	15	75
61	–	35f. on 70c.	2·00	80
49	–	50f. on 1s.	20	20
50	–	65f. on 1s.25	20	20
51	–	75f. on 1s.50	20	30
65	–	100f. on 2s.	3·25	2·50
53	–	250f. on 5s.	1·40	3·75
54	–	500f. on 10s.	1·75	3·75

Each value has two similar surcharges.

1966. Nos. 57, 59, 61/7 variously optd as given below, together with Olympic "rings".

68	10f. on 15c. (**LOS ANGELES 1932**)	35	35
69	20f. on 35c. (**BERLIN 1936**)	45	45
70	35f. on 70c. (**INTERNATIONAL COOPERATION**, etc)	45	45
71	50f. on 1s. (**LONDON 1948**)	50	55
72	65f. on 1s.25 (**HELSINKI 1952**)	50	1·00
73	75f. on 1s.50 (**MELBOURNE 1956**)	60	1·50
74	100f. on 2s. (**ROME 1960**)	70	1·75
75	250f. on 5s. (**TOKYO 1964**)	1·00	3·50
76	500f. on 10s. (**MEXICO CITY 1968**)	1·25	4·00

1966. World Cup Football Championship. Nos. 57, 59, 61/2, 65/7 optd **CHAMPIONS ENGLAND** (10f., 50f. and 250f.) or **FOOTBALL 1966** (others). Both with football symbol.

77	10f. on 15c.	70	30
78	20f. on 35c.	90	40
79	35f. on 70c.	1·25	40
80	50f. on 1s.	1·40	40
81	100f. on 2s.	3·75	2·00
82	250f. on 5s.	7·50	5·00
83	500f. on 10s.	9·50	8·00

1966. Centenary of I.T.U. (1965).

84	29	5f. green, black and violet	1·25	15
85	–	10f. purple, black and green	1·40	20
86	–	15f. blue, black and orange	1·75	20
87	29	25f. green, black and red	2·50	20
88	–	35f. purple, black and yellow	2·75	20
89	–	50f. blue, black and brown	3·25	25
90	29	65f. green, black and yellow	3·75	30

DESIGNS: 10, 35f. "Relay"; 15, 50f. "Ranger".

32 Churchill at Easel

1966. Sir Winston Churchill's Paintings. Mult.

91	5f. Type **32**	1·75	15
92	10f. "Antibes"	2·00	15
93	15f. "Flowers" (vert)	2·00	20
94	20f. "Tapestries"	2·00	35
95	25f. "Village, Lake Lugano"	2·00	35
96	35f. "Church, Lake Como" (vert)	2·00	40
97	50f. "Flowers at Chartwell" (vert)	2·25	65
98	65f. Type **32**	2·75	90

1967. "World Peace". Nos. 57, 59, 61/7 optd **WORLD PEACE** and names as given below.

99	10f. on 15c. (**PANDIT NEHRU**)	1·25	1·00
100	20f. on 35c. (**WINSTON CHURCHILL**)	4·50	2·25
101	35f. on 70c. (**DAG HAMMARSKJOLD**)	50	80
102	50f. on 1s. (**JOHN F. KENNEDY**)	60	90
103	65f. on 1s.25 (**LUDWIG ERHARD**)	70	1·10
104	75f. on 1s.50 (**LYNDON JOHNSON**)	80	1·25
105	100f. on 2s. (**ELEANOR ROOSEVELT**)	1·00	2·00
106	250f. on 5s. (**WINSTON CHURCHILL**)	13·00	10·00
107	500f. on 10s. (**JOHN F. KENNEDY**)	5·00	11·00

40 "Master Crewe as Henry VIII" (Sir Joshua Reynolds)

1967. Paintings. Multicoloured.

108	5f. Type **40**	30	25
109	10f. "The Dancer" (Degas)	35	30
110	15f. "The Fifer" (Manet)	40	35
111	20f. "Stag at Sharkey's" (boxing match, G. Bellows)	45	40
112	25f. "Don Manuel Osorio" (Goya)	50	45
113	35f. "St. Martin distributing his Cloak" (A. van Dyck)	70	65
114	50f. "The Blue Boy" (Gainsborough)	85	75
115	65f. "The White Horse" (Gauguin)	1·10	1·00
116	75f. "Mona Lisa" (Da Vinci) (45 × 62 mm)	1·40	1·25

1967. American Astronauts. Nos. 57, 59, 61/2 and 65/6 optd as below, all with space capsule.

117	10f. on 15c. (**ALAN SHEPARD JR.**)	55	1·25
118	20f. on 35c. (**VIRGIL GRISSOM**)	70	1·25
119	35f. on 70c. (**JOHN GLENN JR.**)	95	1·50
120	50f. on 1s. (**SCOTT CARPENTER**)	95	1·50
121	100f. on 2s. (**WALTER SCHIRRA JR.**)	2·25	3·75
122	250f. on 5s. (**GORDON COOPER JR.**)	3·50	7·00

50 Churchill Crown

1967. Churchill Commemoration.

123	50	75f. multicoloured	9·00	6·50

APPENDIX

The following stamps have either been issued in excess of postal needs or have not been made available to the public in reasonable quantities at face value.

1967.

Hunting. 20f.

Olympic Games, Grenoble. Postage 10, 25, 35, 50, 75f.; Air 100, 200f.

Scout Jamboree, Idaho. Air 150f.

Paintings—Renoir. Postage 10, 35, 50, 65, 75f.; Air 100, 200, 250f.

Paintings—Toulouse-Lautrec. Postage 10, 35, 50, 65, 75f.; Air 100, 200, 250f.

The National Liberation Front is said to have taken control of Kathiri State of Seiyun on 1 October 1967.

KAZAKHSTAN Pt. 10

Formerly a constituent republic of the Soviet Union, Kazakhstan declared its independence on 16 December 1991.

1992. 100 kopeks = 1 rouble.
1994. 100 tyin (ty.) = 1 tenge (t.).

1 "Golden Warrior"

(2)

1992. "Golden Warrior" (from 5th-century B.C. tomb).

1	1	50k. multicoloured	15	15

1992. Nos. 6079/80 of Russia optd as T **2**, in Cyrillic (2, 4) or English (3, 5) capitals.

2	12k. purple	2·75	2·25
3	12k. purple	2·75	2·25
4	13k. violet	2·75	2·25
5	13k. violet	2·75	2·25

(3)

4 Saiga

1992. Russian–French Space Flight. Nos. 6072/4 of Russia surch as T **3**.

6	30k. on 2k. brown	50	20
7	75k. on 3k. green	35	35
8	1r. on 1k. brown	45	45

1992.

9	4	75k. multicoloured	15	15

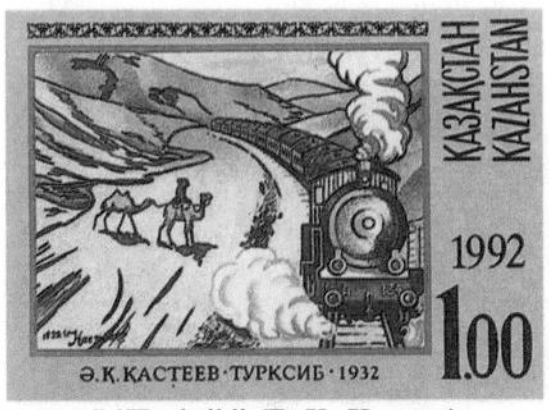

5 "Turksib" (E. K. Kasteev)

1992. Kazakh Art.

10	5	1r. multicoloured	25	25

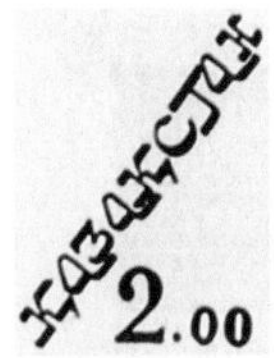

(6)

(7)

(8)

9 National Flag and Arms

1992. Various stamps of Russia surch as T **6** (11/12), **7** (13/14) or **8** (15/16).

11	1r.50 on 1k. brown (No. 5940)	15	10
12	2r. on 2k. brown (No. 6073)	40	20
13	3r. on 6k. blue (No. 4673)	25	20
14	5r. on 6k. blue (No. 4673)	25	20
15	10r. on 1k. brown (No. 5940)	40	30
16	24r.50 on 1k. brown (No. 5940)	40	30

1992. Republic Day.

17	9	5r. multicoloured	25	15

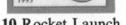

10 Rocket Launch

11 National Flag

1993.

18 10 1r. green 10 10
19 3r. red 10 10
20 10r. bistre 15 10
21 25r. violet 30 15
22 11 50r. yellow, blue and deep blue 60 30
See also Nos. 45 etc.

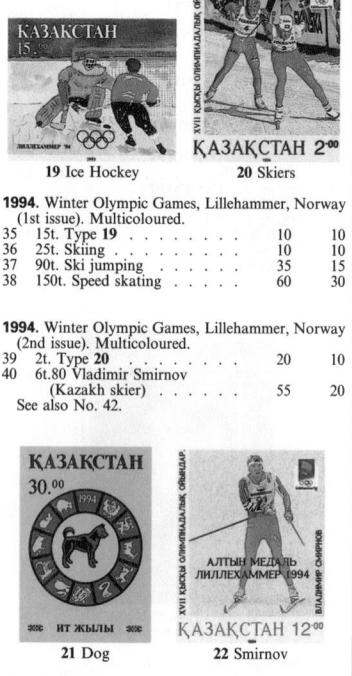

12 Rocket and Earth

1993. Space Mail.
23 12 100r. multicoloured 35 30

13 Cock

1993. New Year. Year of the Cock.
24 13 60r. black, red and yellow 35 30

14 Space Station

1993. Cosmonautics Day.
25 14 90r. multicoloured 35 30

15 Nazarbaev and Flag on Map

1993. President Nursultan Nazarbaev (1st series).
26 15 50r. multicoloured 35 25
See also No. 28.

16 Kalkaman-Uly

1993. 325th Birth Anniv of Bukar Zhyrau Kalkaman-Uly (poet).
27 16 15r. multicoloured 35 25

17 Arms, Flag on Map and Nazarbaev

1993. President Nursultan Nazarbaev (2nd series).
28 17 100r. multicoloured 35 25

18 Desert Dormouse

1993. Mammals. Multicoloured.
29 5r. Type 18 . . . . 10 10
30 10r. Porcupine 10 10
31 15r. Marbled polecat 20 10
32 20r. Asiatic wild ass 25 15
33 25r. Mouflon 30 15
34 30r. Cheetah 35 20

19 Ice Hockey

20 Skiers

1994. Winter Olympic Games, Lillehammer, Norway (1st issue). Multicoloured.
35 15t. Type 19 . . . . 10 10
36 25t. Skiing 10 10
37 90t. Ski jumping 35 15
38 150t. Speed skating 60 30

1994. Winter Olympic Games, Lillehammer, Norway (2nd issue). Multicoloured.
39 2t. Type 20 . . . . 20 10
40 6t.80 Vladimir Smirnov (Kazakh skier) 55 20
See also No. 42.

21 Dog

22 Smirnov

1994. New Year. Year of the Dog.
41 21 30t. black, blue and green 25 10

1994. Vladimir Smirnov, Winter Olympic Games Medals Winner. As No. 40 but face value changed and with additional inscription in Kazakh.
42 22 12t. multicoloured 75 35

23 Launch of "Soyuz TM16" at Baikonur

1994. Cosmonautics Day.
43 23 2t. multicoloured 25 10

24 Space Shuttle *Buran* on Baikonur Launch Pad and Toktar Aubakrirov

1994. 1st Space Flight of Kazakh Cosmonaut. Sheet 107 × 66 mm.
MS44 24 4 × 6t.80 multicoloured 1·10 1·10

1994.

45 10 15ty. blue 10 10
76 20ty. orange 10 10
77 25ty. yellow 10 10
78 50ty. grey 10 10
46 80ty. purple 15 10
79 1t. green 20 10
80 2t. blue 35 15
81 4t. mauve 60 25
82 6t. green 90 40
83 12t. mauve . . . . 1·90 90

25 Mt. Abay

1994. 5th "Asia Dauysy" International Music Festival, Almaty. Multicoloured.
47 10t. Type 25 . . . . 50 25
48 15t. Medeo Ice Stadium, Almaty 85 45

26 Horsfield's Tortoises

1994. Reptiles. Multicoloured.
49 1t. Type 26 . . . . 10 10
50 1t.20 Toad-headed agamas . . 10 10
51 2t. Halys vipers 10 10
52 3t. Turkestan plate-tailed geckos 15 10
53 5t. Steppe agamas 25 15
54 7t. Glass lizards 35 20
MS55 93 × 73 mm. 10t. Transcaspian desert monitor (*Varanus griseus*) 50 50

27 National Arms

1994. Republic Day.
56 27 2t. multicoloured 15 10

28 "Why does the Swallow have a Forked Tail?" (dir. Amen Khaidorov)

1994. Children's Fund. Kazakh Children's Films. Multicoloured.
57 1t.+30ty. Type 28 . . . . . 10 10
58 1t.+30ty. "The Calf and Hare seek a Better Life" (E. Abdrakhmanov) 10 10
59 1t.+30ty. Asses ("Lame Kulan" dir. Amen Khaidarov) 10 10

29 Entelodon

1994. Prehistoric Animals. Multicoloured.
60 1t. Type 29 . . . . 10 10
61 1t.20 Saurolophus 10 10
62 2t. Plesiosaurus 10 10
63 3t. "Sordes pilosus" 15 10
64 5t. Mosasaurus 25 15
65 7t. "Megaloceros giganteum" 35 20
MS66 92 × 72 mm. 10t. *Koelodonta antiquitatis* 50 50

1995. Nos. 45/6 surch.
67 24 1t. on 15ty. blue 10 10
68 2t. on 15ty. blue 15 10
69 3t. on 80ty. purple 25 10
70 4t. on 80ty. purple 35 15
71 6t. on 80ty. purple 45 20
72 8t. on 80ty. purple 50 25
73 12t. on 80ty. purple . . . . 1·10 50
74 20t. on 80ty. purple . . . . 2·10 85

31 Pig

32 Kunanbaev

1995. New Year. Year of the Pig.
75 31 10t. blue, black and light blue 50 50

1995. 150th Birth Anniv of Abai Kunanbaev (writer). Multicoloured.
86 4t. Type 32 . . . . 25 25
87 9t. Kunanbaev holding pen and book 50 50

33 Flight Path of "Soyuz" Spacecraft

1995. Cosmonautics Day. Multicoloured.
88 2t. Type 33 . . . . 80 40
89 10t. Yuri Malenchenko, Talgat Musabaev and Ulf Merbold (cosmonauts) . . . . 7·50 7·50

34 Manshuk Mametova and Battle Scene

1995. 50th Anniv of End of Second World War. Multicoloured.
90 1t. Type 34 . . . . 35 20
91 3t. Aliya Moldafulova and tank . . . . 1·00 75
92 5t. Wheat field, dove and eternal flame . . . . 3·75 3·25

35 "Spring" (S. Membeev)

1995. Paintings. Multicoloured.
93 4t. Type 35 . . . . 50 50
94 9t. "Mountains" (Zh. Shardenov) . . . . 1·00 1·00
95 15t. "Kulash Baiseitova in role of Kyz Zhibek" (G. Ismailova) (vert) . . . . 2·00 2·00
96 28t. "Kokpar" (K. Telzhanov) 4·00 4·00

1995. "Asia Dauysy" International Music Festival, Almaty. Nos. 47/8 optd **KAZAKSTAN '95 1995**.
97 10t. multicoloured . . . . . . 1·00 80
98 15t. multicoloured . . . . . . 1·50 1·25

37 Dauletkerei

1995. 175th Birth Anniv of Dauletkerei (composer and poet).
99 37 2t. multicoloured 35 25
100 28t. multicoloured . . . . 4·25 3·75

38 Gandhi, Temple and Spinning Wheel

1995. 125th Birth Anniv (1994) of Mahatma Gandhi.
101 38 9t. red and black . . . . . 1·00 80
102 22t. red and black . . . . 4·00 3·50

39 Anniversary Emblem

40 Cathedral of the Ascension

1995. 50th Anniv of U.N.O.
103 39 10t. gold and blue . . . . 1·00 80
104 36t. gold and blue . . . . 4·00 3·50

1995. Buildings in Almaty.
105 40 1t. green 15 15
106 – 2t. blue 20 10
107 – 3t. red 30 15
108 – 48t. brown . . . . 5·50 5·50
DESIGNS: 2t. Culture Palace; 3t. Opera and Ballet House; 48t. Theatre.
See also Nos. 124/5.

41 White-tailed Sea Eagle

1995. Birds of Prey. Multicoloured.

109	1t. Type **41**	10	10
110	3t. Osprey	20	10
111	5t. Lammergeier	35	15
112	6t. Himalayan griffon	40	20
113	30t. Saker falcon	2·10	1·00
114	50t. Golden eagle	3·50	1·75

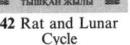

42 Rat and Lunar Cycle

43 Baikonur Launch Pad highlighted on Globe

1996. Chinese New Year. Year of the Rat.

115	**42**	25t. red, black and lilac	1·40	1·00

1996. Cosmonautics Day. Multicoloured.

116	6t. Type **43**	80	60
117	15t. Yuri Gagarin	1·90	1·50
118	20t. Proposed "Alpha" space station	3·00	2·50

44 Carancal (*Felis caracal*)

1996. "Save the Aral Sea". Sheet 128 × 108 mm containing T **44** and similar horiz designs. Multicoloured.
MS119 20t. Type **44**; 20t. Aral trout (*Salmo trutta aralensis*); 20t. Striped hyena (*Hyaena hyaena*); 20t. Kaufmann's shovelnose (*Pseudoscaphirhynchus kaufmanni*); 20t. Pike asp (*Aspiolucius esocinus*) . . . . . 3·00 2·00

45 Cycling

46 Zhabaev (after embroidery by G. Atknin)

1996. Olympic Games, Atlanta. Multicoloured.

120	4t. Type **45**	35	20
121	6t. Wrestling	55	25
122	30t. Boxing	2·75	1·40
MS123	92 × 69 mm. 50t. Hurdling (45 × 27 *mm*)	1·75	1·25

1996. As T **40** but smaller, size 24 × 19 mm.

124	1t. green	10	10
125	6t. green	20	10

DESIGNS: 1t. Circus; 6t. Academy of Sciences (50th anniv).

1996. 150th Birth Anniv of Zhambil Zhabaev (writer).

126	**46**	12t. multicoloured	70	50

47 Tomb, Dombauyl

1996. Ancient Buildings. Multicoloured.

127	1t. Type **47**	20	10
128	3t. Mausoleum, Aisha Biy	50	30
129	6t. Mausoleum, Syrly Tam	2·50	2·00
MS130	90 × 60 mm. 30t. Kozha Ahmet Yasavi Mausoleum, Turkestan	1·10	75

48 "Soyuz TM-13" docked with "Mir" Space Station

49 Map of Kazakhstan and Dove with Letter

1996. 5th Anniv of Toktar Aubakirov's (cosmonaut) Service on "Mir". Multicoloured.

131	46t. Type **48**	1·90	1·50
132	46t. Aubakirov	1·90	1·50

Nos. 131/2 were issued together, se-tenant, forming a composite design.

1996. World Post Day.

133	**49**	9t. blue	35	20
134	–	40t. orange	3·50	3·00

DESIGN: 40t. Dove with letter and Universal Postal Union emblem.

1996. Republic Day. No. 56 surch **KAZAKSTAN 1. 1996.**

135	**27**	21t. on 2t. multicoloured	1·00	75

51 "Saturnia schenki"

1996. Butterflies. Multicoloured.

136	4t. Type **51**	15	10
137	6t. "Parnassius patricius"	20	10
138	12t. "Parnasssius ariadne"	40	20
139	46t. "Colias draconis"	1·50	1·10

52 Borzois giving Chase

1996. Hunting Dogs.

140	**52**	5t. multicoloured	20	10
MS141	95 × 70 mm. **52**	100t. multicoloured	2·50	1·75

53 Bride before Yurte

54 Writing Materials and Books

1996. Traditional Costumes and Dwelling. Multicoloured.

142	10t. Type **53**	20	10
143	16t. Bridegroom before yurte	45	25
144	45t. Yurte interior	1·25	65

Nos. 142/4 were issued together, se-tenant, Nos. 142/3 forming a composite design.

1996. Bicentenary of National Archive.

145	**54**	4t. brown	15	10
146	–	68t. violet	2·50	2·10

DESIGN: 68t. Book and documents.

55 Scene from *Angel with Tyubetejka* by Shaken Aimanov

1996. Centenary (1995) of Motion Pictures. Sheet 135 × 148 mm containing T **55** and similar horiz designs. Multicoloured.
MS147 24t. Type **55**; 24t. *The Zhibek Girl* (S. Kozhykov); 24t. *His Time will Come* (M. Begalin); 24t. *My Name is Kozha* (A. Karsakbaev) 2·25 1·50

56 Head

1997. The Marbled Polecat. Multicoloured.

148	6t. Type **56**	15	10
149	10t. Adult with tail down	25	15
150	32t. Two polecats	80	45
151	46t. Adult with tail raised	1·10	70

57 Ox

58 Aries

1997. New Year. Year of the Ox.

152	**57**	40t. brown, black and green	1·00	70

1997. Star Signs. Each violet and purple.

153	1t. Type **58**	10	10
154	2t. Taurus	10	10
155	3t. Gemini	10	10
156	4t. Cancer	10	10
157	5t. Leo	10	10
158	6t. Virgo	10	10
159	7t. Libra	10	10
160	8t. Scorpio	10	10
161	9t. Sagittarius	10	10
162	10t. Capricorn	10	10
163	12t. Aquarius	25	20
164	20t. Pisces	40	30
MS165	109 × 164 mm. Nos. 153/64	1·50	1·50

59 Saturn and Automatic Transfer Vehicle

60 Emblem

1997. Cosmonautics Day. Multicoloured.

166	10t. Type **59**	25	20
167	10t. Space shuttle and "Mir" space station	25	20
168	10t. "Sputnik 1" and Earth	25	20

Nos. 166/8 were issued together, se-tenant, forming a composite design.

1997. World Book and Copyright Day.

169	**60**	15t. yellow and green	30	20
170		60t. yellow and green	1·10	85

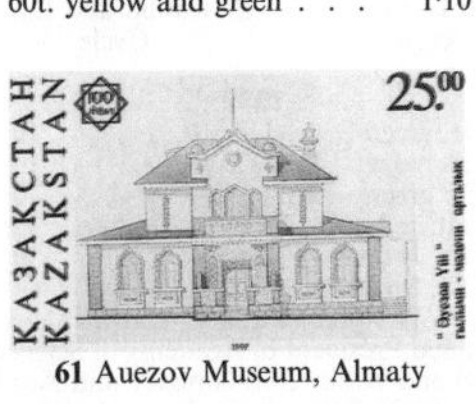

61 Auezov Museum, Almaty

1997. Birth Centenary of Mukhtar Auezov (philologist). Multicoloured.

171	25t. Type **61**	45	35
172	40t. Auezov at table (after Shcherkassky)	80	55

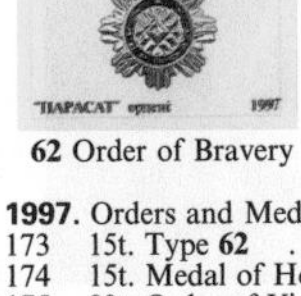

62 Order of Bravery

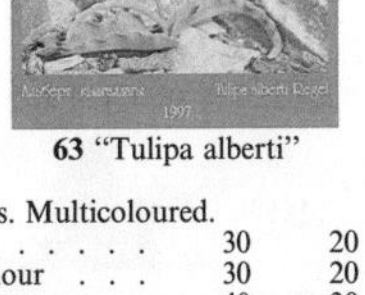

63 "Tulipa alberti"

1997. Orders and Medals. Multicoloured.

173	15t. Type **62**	30	20
174	15t. Medal of Honour	30	20
175	20t. Order of Victory	40	30
176	30t. National Order of Merit	55	40

1997. Tulips. Multicoloured.

177	15t. "Tulipa regelii"	30	20
178	35t. Type **63**	70	45
179	35t. "Tulipa greigii"	70	45

64 "Shepherd" (Sh. Sariev)

65 Moss Agate

1997. Paintings. Multicoloured.

180	25t. Type **64**	45	35
181	25t. "Fantastic Still Life" (S. Kalmykov)	45	35
182	25t. "Capturing Horse" (M. Kenbaev) (horiz)	45	35

1997. Minerals. Multicoloured.

183	15t. Type **65**	30	20
184	15t. Chalcedony	30	20
185	20t. Azurite	40	30
186	20t. Malachite	40	30
MS187	110 × 99 mm. Nos. 182/5	2·25	2·25

66 "Gylippus rickmersi"

67 Argali

1997. Arachnidae. Multicoloured.

188	30t. Type **66**	60	40
189	30t. "Latrodectus pallidus"	60	40
190	30t. "Oculicosa supermirabilis"	60	40
191	30t. "Anomalobuthus rickmersi"	60	40

1997. Karkaraly Nature Park. Sheet 114 × 148 mm containing T **67** and similar vert designs. Multicoloured.
MS192 30t. Type **67**; 30t. Common juniper; 30t. Cudgel stone . . . 1·90 1·50

68 Horse Race

1997. National Sports. Multicoloured.

193	20t. Type **68**	40	30
194	20t. Tearing goatskin ("Koknar")	40	30
195	20t. Wrestling	40	30
196	20t. Two-horse race	40	30

69 Ice Dancing

70 "Little Girl" (A. Ashkiyazara)

1998. Winter Sports. Multicoloured.

197	15t. Type **69**	30	20
198	30t. Biathlon	55	40

1998. Children's Paintings. Multicoloured.

199	15t. Type **70**	30	20
200	15t. "My House" (M. Tarakara) (horiz)	30	20

71 Tiger and Lunar Cycle

72 Kurmangazy

1998. New Year. Year of the Tiger.

201	**71**	30t. brown, black and yellow	55	40

1998. 175th Birth Anniv of Kurmangazy (composer).
202 **72** 30t. yellow, brown & black 55 40

73 Baitursynov

75 "Apollo 8" Spacecraft and Moon

74 Winged and Horned Beasts, Issyk Kurgan

1998. 125th Birth Anniv of Akhmet Baitursynov (writer).
203 **73** 30t. light brown, brown and black 55 40

1998. Archaeological Finds. Multicoloured.
204 15t. Type **74** 35 25
205 30t. Pendants, Aktasty (vert) 70 50
206 40t. Gold and jewel-studded open-work ornament depicting animals, Kargaly 95 65

1998. Cosmonautics Day. Multicoloured.
207 30t. Type **75** 55 40
208 30t. "Apollo 8", Earth and Moon 55 40
209 50t. "Vostok 6" orbiting Earth 90 60
Nos. 207/8 were issued together, se-tenant, forming a composite design.

76 Mosque

77 State Arms

1998. Astana. New Capital of Kazakhstan.
210 **76** 10t. brown 20 15
211 – 15t. blue (inscr "Akmola") 30 20
212 – 15t. blue (inscr "Astana") 1·00 90
213 – 20t. blue 40 30
214 – 25t. violet 30 20
MS215 99 × 73 mm. 100t. multicoloured . . . . 2·40 1·60
DESIGNS—VERT: 15t. Petroleum Ministry; 20t. Parliament. HORIZ: 25k. Presidents Palace. 43 × 25 mm.—100t. Presidents Palace.

1998.
216 **77** 1t. green 10 10
217 2t. blue 10 10
218 3t. red 10 10
219 4t. purple 10 10
220 5t. yellow 10 10
221 8t. orange 10 10
225 20t. orange 15 10
229 50t. blue 25 15

78 Climber fixing Tent

1998. Kazakhstan Expedition to Mt. Everest. Sheet 85 × 67 mm.
MS230 **78** 100t. multicoloured . . 2·40 1·60

79 Black Stork

1998. Birds. Multicoloured.
231 15t. Type **79** 30 20
232 30t. Greater flamingoes . . . 55 40
233 50t. Great white crane . . . 90 60

80 Lynx

82 Stamp and U.P.U. Emblem

81 Dove and Emblem

1998. Wild Cats. Multicoloured.
234 15t. Type **80** 30 20
235 30t. Sand dune cat 55 40
236 50t. Snow leopard 90 60

1998. Admission of Kazakhstan to Universal Postal Union. Sheet 104 × 84 mm.
MS237 **81** 50t. multicoloured . . 1·25 85

1998. World Post Day.
238 **82** 30t. bistre 35 25

83 Anniversary Emblem

84 Warrior with Sword

1998. 5th Anniv of the Tenge (currency unit).
239 **83** 40t. orange 50 30

1998. Kazakh Horsemen. Multicoloured.
240 20t. Type **84** 25 20
241 30t. Using bow and arrow . . 35 25
242 40t. With spear and shield . . 65 50

85 Rock Formation in Lake

1998. Environmental Protection. Buradai National Park. Sheet 110 × 98 mm containing T **85** and similar vert design. Multicoloured.
MS243 30t. Type **85**; 30t. View over lake . . . . 1·50 1·00

86 Family (census)

87 Rabbit and Lunar Cycle

1999.
244 **86** 1t. green 10 10
245 – 3t. red 10 10
246 – 9t. green 10 10
247 – 15t. red 25 15
248 – 20t. brown 30 20
249 – 30t. brown 40 25
DESIGNS—HORIZ: 15t. Kanyish Sambaev (geologist and President of Academy of Sciences, birth centenary) and book; 20t. Sambaev and Academy of Sciences. VERT: 3, 9, 30t. Dish aerial and "Intelsat" satellite.

1999. New Year. Year of the Rabbit.
250 **87** 40t. green, black and yellow 50 30

88 Steam Locomotive and Railway Route Map

89 Satellite

1999. Railway Locomotives. Multicoloured.
251 40t. Type **88** 50 30
252 50t. Electric locomotive . . . 60 55
253 60t. Diesel railcar 75 50
254 80t. Electric locomotive (different) . . . . 1·00 90

1999. Cosmonautics Day. Multicoloured.
255 50t. Type **89** 60 40
256 90t. Astronaut on Moon (30th anniv of first manned Moon landing) (horiz) . . 1·00 70

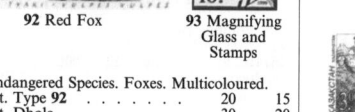

90 "Pseudoeremostachys severzowii"

91 Scene from *Turksib* (1929)

1999. Flowers. Multicoloured.
257 20t. Type **90** 25 20
258 30t. "Rhaphidophyton regelii" 35 25
259 90t. "Niedzwedzkia semiretschenskia" . . . . 1·00 70

1999. 70th Anniv of Kazak Cinema. Multicoloured.
260 15t. Type **91** 15 10
261 20t. M. Berkovich (director) and scenes from *Jambul's Youth* (1997) and *Wolf Cub among People* (1998) . . . 20 15
262 30t. Scenes from *The Devil Paths* (1935), *Our Dear Doctor* (1957) and *Amangeldy* (1938) 30 20
263 35t. Scenes from *Zama-ay* (1997), *Biography of a Young Accordionist* (1994) and *Who are you Rider?* (1989) 35 25
264 50t. Alfred Hitchcock (director) and scene from *The Birds* 50 35
265 60t. Sergei Eisenstein (director) 60 40

92 Red Fox

93 Magnifying Glass and Stamps

1999. Endangered Species. Foxes. Multicoloured.
266 20t. Type **92** 20 15
267 30t. Dhole 30 20
268 90t. Corsac fox 90 60

1999. 125th Anniv of Universal Postal Union.
269 **93** 10t. violet 10 10

94 Mushroom Cloud

1999. Environmental Protection Sheet 130 × 108, containing T **94** and similar horiz designs. Multicoloured.
MS270 15t. Type **94** (tenth Anniv of cessation of nuclear testing at Semipalatinsk); 45t. Emblem (International Day for Protection of the Ozone Layer); 60t. Butterflies and landscape . . . 1·30 1·30

95 Flower

96 T. Musabayev

1999. Endangered Flora (1st series).
271 **95** 4t. mauve 10 10
272 30t. green 30 20
See also Nos. 296/8, 310/11 and 357/63.

1999. Cosmonauts. Multicoloured.
273 40t. Type **96** 40 25
274 50t. T. Aubakirov (first Kazakhstan cosmonaut) (vert) 50 35

97 Ice Hockey Match

1999. Sports. Multicoloured.
275 20t. Type **97** 20 15
276 30t. Ice hockey team 30 20
277 40t. G. Kosanov (athlete) . . 40 25

99 Oil Rig

2000. Centenary of Oil Extraction in Kazakhstan.
279 **99** 7t. red 10 10

100 Yurt, Horse racing and Artifacts

101 Millennium Emblem

2000. Navruz Bayram Festival. Imperf.
280 **100** 20t. multicoloured 15 10

2000. New Millennium.
281 **101** 30t. blue, deep blue and orange 25 15

102 28th Guardsman-Panfilovs Memorial and Eternal Flame, Alma-Ata

103 "Stride into the Bright Future" (painting, Kostya Balakirev)

2000. 55th Anniv of End of Second World War.
282 **102** 3t. brown and red 10 10

2000. International Children's Day. New Millennium. Sheet 127 × 106 mm.
MS283 **103** 70t. multicoloured . . 60 60

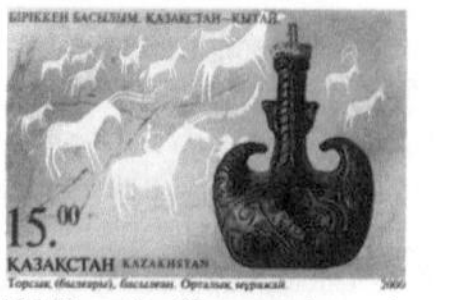
104 Koumiss (fermented mare's milk) Flask

2000. Joint issue with People's Republic of China. Pots. Multicoloured.
284 15t. Type **104** 10 10
285 50t. He-pot (Chinese wine vessel) 40 25

105 Mukanov

106 Dulati

2000. Birth Centenary of Sabit Mukanov (writer).
286 **105** 1t. green 10 10

2000. 500th Birth Anniv of Mukhammed Khaidar Dulti (historian) (1999).
287 **106** 8t. blue 10 10

107 Canoeing

108 "Echo" Telecom-munications Satellite

2000. Olympics Games, Sydney. Multicoloured.
288 35t. Type **107** 30 20
289 40t. Gymnastics 35 20
290 40t. Taekwondo 35 20
291 50t. Triathlon 40 25

2000.
292 **108** 5t. orange 10 10
293 15t. blue 10 10
294 20t. blue 15 10

109 Arystan Bab's Mausoleum

2000. 1500th Anniv of Turkestan (town). Sheet 160 × 140 mm containing T **109** and similar horiz designs. Multicoloured.
MS295 50t. Type **109**; 50t. Rabiy Sultan Begim's and Karashash Ana's mausolea; 70t. Kozhah Akhmet Yassauy's mausoleum 1·40 1·40
Stamps of a similar design were issued by Turkey.

110 Flower

111 Momysh-Uly and Gold Star of Hero of Soviet Union Medal

2000. Endangered Flora (2nd series).
296 **110** 1t. green 10 10
297 2t. blue 10 10
298 50t. blue 20 15

2000. 90th Birth Anniv of Baurdzhan Momyush-Uly (Soviet military leader).
299 **111** 4t. brown and black . . . 10 10

2001. Nos. 57/9 surch **2001 10.00.**
300 10t. on 1t. +30ty. multicoloured 10 10
301 10t. on 1t. +30ty. multicoloured 10 10
302 10t. on 1t. +30ty. multicoloured 10 10

113 Snail and Lunar Cycle

2001. New Year. Year of the Snail.
303 **113** 40t. black, blue and yellow 35 20

114 Rocket, Yuri Gagarin and Dogs

2001. Cosmonautics Day (2000). Multicoloured.
304 40t. Type **114** (40th anniv of space flight by Belka and Strelka (dogs)) 35 20
305 70t. Rocket launch (45th anniv of Baikonur cosmodrome) (vert) 60 30

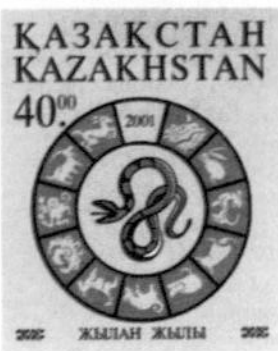
115 Snake and Lunar Cycle

2001. New Year. Year of the Snake.
306 **115** 40t. black, brown and green 35 20

116 Dove, Globe and Transport

2001. 10th Anniv of Ministry of Transportation and Communication. Sheet 100 × 70 mm.
MS307 **116** 100t. multicoloured 85 85

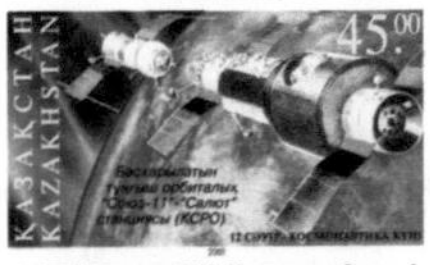
117 "Soyuz-II" Spacecraft and "Salyut" Space Station

118 *Aquilegia karatavica*

2001. Cosmonautics Day. Multicoloured.
308 45t. Type **117** 35 20
309 70t. Yuri Gagarin and earth (40th anniv of first manned space flight) 60 30

2001. Endangered Flora (3rd series).
310 **118** 3t. green 10 10
311 10t. green 10 10

119 Abulkhair-Khan (1693–1748)

120 Roborovski Hamster (*Phodopus roborovskii*)

2001. Khans (feudal rulers). Multicoloured.
312 50t. Type **119** 40 25
313 60t. Abylai-Khan (1711–1781) 50 30

2001. Fauna (1st series).
314 **120** 8t. orange 10 10
315 15t. blue 10 10
316 20t. blue 15 10
317 50t. brown 40 25
See also 351/4 and 386/92.

121 Northern Eagle Owl (*Bubo bubo*)

2001. Owls. Multicoloured.
318 30t. Type **121** 25 15
319 40t. Long-eared owl (*Asio otis*) 35 20
320 50t. Hawk owl (*Surnia ulula*) 40 25

122 Winged Lion and Fibre Optic Cable

123 Red Deer (*Cervus elaphus*)

2001. National Development Plan. Communications.
321 **122** 40t. multicoloured 35 20

2001. Fauna of Lake Markakol (national park). Sheet 110 × 98 mm containing T **123** and similar vert designs. Multicoloured.
MS322 Type **123**; 30t. Brown bear (*Ursus arctos*); 30t. Lenok (*Brachymystax lenok*) 70 70

124 Bobak Marmot (*Marmota bobak*)

2001. Flora and Fauna. Sheet 215 × 102 mm containing T **124** and similar horiz designs. Multicoloured.
MS323 Type **124**; 12t. Great bustard (*Otis tarda*); 25t. Relict gull (*Larus relictus*); 60t. African wildcat (*Felis silvestris libyca*); 90t. Water lily (*Nymphaea alba*); 100t. Dalmatian pelican (*Pelecanus crispus*) . . 3·00 3·00

125 Druzhba Station Facade

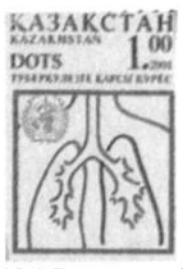
126 Lungs and United Nations Emblem

2001. Anniversaries. Sheet 105 × 74 mm containing T **125** and similar horiz designs. Multicoloured.
MS324 Type **125** (10th anniv of Kazakhstan–China railway); 20t. Steam locomotive (70th anniv of Turkestan–Siberia railway); 50t. Workmen (opening of Aksu–Delegen railway) 70 70

2001. Health.
325 **126** 1t. green, blue and black 10 10
326 – 5t. red, grey and black . . 10 10
DESIGNS: Type **126** (tuberculosis prevention campaign); 5t. Ribbon and book (AIDS prevention campaign).

127 River Charyn Cliffs

2001. International Year of Mountains. Multicoloured.
327 35t. Type **127** 30 15
328 60t. Mt. Khan Tegri 50 25

128 Alexej Leonov

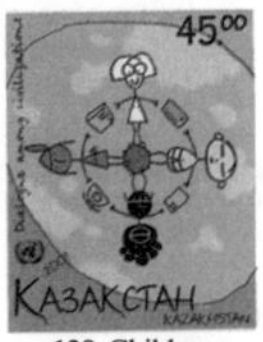
129 Children encircling Globe

2001. Space Anniversaries. Mlticoloured.
329 50t. Type **128** (35th anniv of 1st space walk) 40 20
330 70t. *Soyuz* and *Apollo* space craft (25th anniv of joint USSR–USA space flight) (horiz) 55 25

2001. United Nations Year of Dialogue among Civilizations.
331 **129** 45t. multicoloured 35 15

130 Wild Ass

2001. Endangered Species. Asiatic Wild Ass (*Equus heminus kulan*). Multicoloured.
332 9t. Type **130** 10 10
333 12t. Galloping 10 10
334 25t. Fighting 10 10
335 50t. Mare and foal 40 20

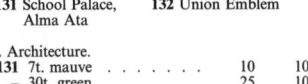

131 School Palace, Alma Ata

132 Union Emblem

2001. Architecture.
336 **131** 7t. mauve 10 10
337 – 30t. green 25 10
DESIGN: 30t. School Palace, Alma Ata (different).

2001. 10th Anniv of Union of Independent States.
338 **132** 40t. multicoloured 30 30

133 Pres. Nursultan Nazarbaev and Pope John Paul II

2001. Visit of Pope John Paul II to Kazakhstan. Multicoloured.
339 20t. Type **133** 15 10
340 50t. Pres. Nazarbaev and Pope John Paul II (different) 40 20

134 Independence Monument, Almaty

135 Celebration Emblem and Map

2001. 10th Anniv of Independence (1st issue). Sheet 110 × 96 mm containing T **134** and similar vert designs. Multicoloured.
MS341 Type **134**; 25t. Parliament House, Astana; 35t. Pres. Nursultan Nazarbaev 60 60
See also No. 342.

2001. 10th Anniv of Independence (2nd issue).
342 **135** 40t. yellow, blue and black 30 15

136 Man's Costume

138 Horse and Lunar Cycle

137 Women Ice Hockey Players

2001. Traditional Costumes. Multicoloured.
343 25t. Type **136** 20 10
344 35t. Woman's costume . . . 30 15
Nos. 343/4 were issued together, se-tenant, forming a composite design.

2002. Winter Olympic Games, Salt Lake City, USA. Multicoloured.
345 50t. Type **137** 40 20
346 150t. Freestyle ski jump . . . 1·20 1·20

2002. New Year. Year of the Horse.
347 **138** 50t. black, ochre and stone 40 20

139 Chestnut Horse

2002. Horses. Multicoloured.
348 9t. Type **139** 10 10
349 25t. Dark chestnut, two legs raised 20 10
350 60t. Grey 50 25

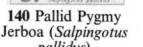

140 Pallid Pygmy Jerboa (*Salpingotus pallidus*)

142 *P-terygostemon spathulatus*

141 Denis Tito (passenger), Talgat Musabaev and Yury Baturin (crew of Soyuz TM-32)

2002. Fauna (2nd series).
351 **140** 5t. purple 10 10
352 15t. blue 10 10
353 40t. brown 30 15
354 50t. sepia 40 20

2002. Cosmonautics Day. Multicoloured.
355 30t. Type **141** 25 10
356 70t. Flags of USA, Kazakhstan and Russia . . 55 25

2002. Endangered Flora (4th series).
357 **142** 1t. green 10 10
358 2t. blue 10 10
359 3t. green 10 10
360 10t. violet 10 10
361 12t. mauve 10 10
362 25t. violet 20 10
363 35t. olive 30 15

143 Two Players

2002. World Cup Football Championships, Japan and South Korea. Multicoloured.
364 10t. Type **143** 10 10
365 10t. Player heading ball . . . 10 10

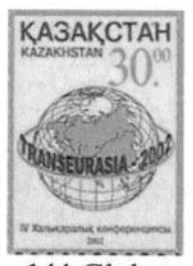
144 Globe

145 *Leontopodium fedtschenkoanum* (flower)

2002. TRANSEURASIA 2002 International Conference.
366 **144** 30t. blue, black and yellow 25 10

2002. Alatau National Park. Sheet 115 × 110 mm containing T **145** and similar vert designs. Multicoloured.
MS367 30t. × 3, Type **145**; Ermine (*Mustela erminea*); Aport Alexander apples 70 70

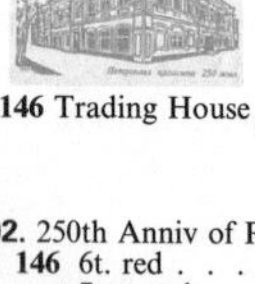
146 Trading House

147 "Kazakh Composition" (E. Sidorkin)

2002. 250th Anniv of Petropavlovsk.
368 **146** 6t. red 10 10
369 – 7t. purple 10 10
370 – 8t. orange (vert) 10 10
371 – 23t. blue (vert) 15 10
DESIGNS: 7t. No. 368; 8t. Karasai and Agyntai (heroes) monument; 23t. No. 371.

2002. Art.
372 **147** 8t. brown, bistre and black 10 10
373 – 9t. black and drab . . . 10 10
374 – 60t. sepia, bistre and black 50 25
DESIGNS: 9t. "Makhambet" (M. Kisametdinov); 60t. "Batyr" (E. Sidorkin).

148 Great Black-headed Gull (Pallas' Gull) (*Larus ichthyaetus Pallas*)

2002. Endangered Species. Birds. Multicoloured.
375 10t. Type **148** 10 10
376 15t. Demoiselle crane (*Anthropoides virgo*) . . . 10 10
Stamps of the same design were issued by Russia.

149 *Huso huso ponticus* (fish)

2002. Endangered Species. Marine Animals. Multicoloured.
377 20t. Type **149** 15 10
378 35t. Caspian seal (*Phoca caspica*) 30 15
Stamps of the same design were issued by Ukraine.

150 Mosque

2002. Bimillenary of Taraz. Sheet 115 × 80 mm.
MS379 **150** 70t. multicoloured . . 55 55

151 Altau Mountains

152 Gabiden Mustaphin

2002. International Year of Mountains. Sheet 90 × 70 mm.
MS380 **151** 50t. multicoloured . . 40 40

2002. Birth Centenary of Gabiden Mustaphin (writer).
381 **152** 10t. blue 10 10

153 Gani Muratbaev

154 Gabit Musrepov

2002. Birth Centenary of Gani Muratbaev (politician).
382 **153** 3t. brown 10 10

2002. Birth Centenary of Gabit Musrepov (writer).
383 **154** 20t. multicoloured 15 10

155 Ilyushin IL-86 over Almaty Airport

156 Desert Dormouse (*Selevinia betpakdalensis*)

2002. Aircraft. Multicoloured.
384 20t. Type **155** 15 10
385 40t. Tupelov TU-144 (25th Anniv of flight from Russia to Almaty) 35 15

2003. Fauna (3rd series).
386 **156** 4t. brown 10 10
387 5t. brown 10 10
388 6t. olive 10 10
389 7t. green 10 10
390 10t. blue 10 10
391 63t. red 50 25
392 150t. purple . . . . . . 1·20 60

157 Argali-Merino Ram

158 Sheep and Lunar Cycle

2003. Sheep. Multicoloured.
393 20t. Type **157** 15 10
394 40t. Ram (different) 30 15
395 50t. Argali ram 40 20

2003. New Year. ("Year of the Sheep").
396 **158** 50t. black, blue and light blue 40 20

2003. Fauna. Roborovski Hamster (*Phodopus roborovskii*) (2nd issue)).
397 **120** 35t. green 30 15

159 Sputnik "Pioner-10"

160 Memorial to Victims of Political Repression

2003. Cosmonautics Day. Multicoloured.
398 40t. Type **117** 30 15
399 70t. "Mir" space station (vert) 55 25

2003. 10th Anniv of Rehabilitation of Victims of Political Repression Law.
400 **160** 1t. magenta 10 10
401 8t. brown 10 10

161 IAAS Emblem

162 Couple wearing Kazakhstan Costumes

2003. 10th Anniv of the International Association of Academies of Sciences.
402 **161** 50t. multicoloured 40 20

2003. Traditional Costumes. Sheet 115 × 97 mm containing T **162** and similar vert designs(1st series). Multicoloured.
MS403 35t. × 3, Type **162**; Russian; Ukrainian 85 85
See also No. **MS**453.

163 Dombra

164 "Intelsat" Satellite

2003. Traditional Instruments. Multicoloured.
404 25t. Type **163** 20 10
405 50t. Kobyz 40 20

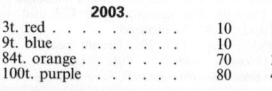

2003.
406 **164** 3t. red 10 10
407 9t. blue 10 10
408 84t. orange 70 35
409 100t. purple 80 40

165 Aldar Kose and Alasha Khan

2003. Fairy Tale Characters. Multicoloured.
410 30t. Type **165** 25 10
411 40t. Aldar Kose and Karynbaj 30 15

166 "Game of a Chess" (A. Richchi)

167 Aiteke Bi Baibekuly (1689–1766)

2003. Museum of Arts Exhibits. Multicoloured.
412 20t. Type **166** 10 10
413 35t. "Portrait of a Shepherd" (sculpture, H. Nauryzbaev) 30 15
414 45t. "Drinking Koumiss" (A. Galimbaeva) 35 15

2003. Judges. Multicoloured.
415 60t. Type **167** 30 15
416 60t. Kazibek Bi Keldibekuly (1667–1763) 30 15
417 60t. Tole Bi Alibekuly (1663–1756) 30 15

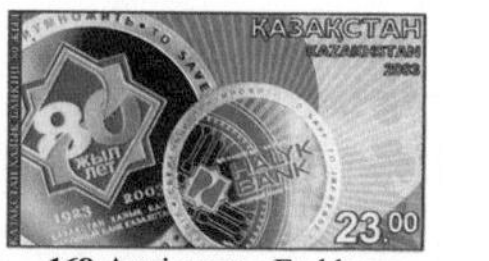
168 Anniversary Emblem

2003. 10th Anniv of Halyk Bank.
418 **168** 23t. multicoloured 20 10

169 Conference and UN Emblems

2003. International Ministerial Transport Co-operation Conference.
419 **169** 40t. multicoloured 30 15

170 Globe and UPU emblems

171 Central Mosque, Almaty

2003. World Post Day.
420 **170** 23t. violet and blue . . . 20 10

2003. Religious Buildings. Multicoloured.
421 50t. Type **171** 40 20
422 50t. Almaty Cathedral . . . 40 20

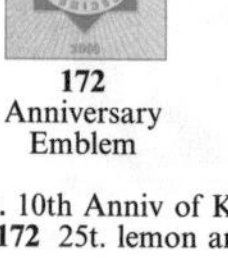
172 Anniversary Emblem

173 "Happiness" (S. Aitbaev) (1966)

2003. 10th Anniv of Kazakhstan Currency (tenge).
423 **172** 25t. lemon and blue . . . 20 10

2003. Paintings. Multicoloured.
424 100t. Type **173** 80 40
425 100t. "Morning Motherhood" (R. Ahmedov) (1962) . . . 80 40
Stamps of similar designs were issued by Uzbekistan.

174 *Populus diversifolia*

2003. Endangered Species. Asiatic Poplar.

426	**174**	100t. multicoloured	80	40

175 Cow

2003. Tamalgy—UNESCO World Heritage Site. Petroglyphs (carvings). Multicoloured.

427		25t. Type **175**	20	10
428		30t. Sun and bull (vert)	25	10

2004. No. 45 surch **200t.**

429		200t. on 80t. claret	1·60	80

177 Abylhan Kasteev

178 Monkey and Lunar Cycle

2004. Birth Centenary of Abylhan Kasteev (artist).

430	**177**	115t. multicoloured	95	40

2004. New Year. "Year of the Monkey".

431	**178**	35t. blue, ultramarine and ochre	30	15

179 Spacecraft "Mariner-10"

180 Kazakhstan Arms

2004. Cosmonautics Day. Multicoloured.

432		40t. Type **179**	30	15
433		50t. "Luna-3" space station (horiz)	40	20

2004.

434	**180**	1t. green	10	10
435		2t. blue	10	10
436		4t. purple	10	10
437		5t. yellow	10	10
438		10t. olive	10	10
439		16t. mauve	15	10
440		20t. mauve	15	10
441		35t. yellow	30	15
442		50t. emerald	40	20
443		72t. orange	60	30
444		100t. turquoise	80	40
445		200t. vermilion	1·60	80

181 National Flag

182 Electric Locomotive

2004.

451	**181**	25t. blue and lemon	20	10

2004. Centenary of Kazakhstan Railway. Sheet 101 × 71 mm.

MS452	**182**	150t. multicoloured	1·20	60

2004. Traditional Costumes (2nd series). Sheet 110 × 96 mm containing vert designs as T **162**. Multicoloured.

MS453		65t. × 2, Uzbekistan; German	1·00	1·00

183 Player and Emblem

2004. Centenary of FIFA (Federation Internationale de Football Association). Multicoloured.

454		100t. Type **183**	80	40
455		100t. Player facing right and emblem	80	40

184 Bayan Sulu (fairy tale)

185 Boxing

2004. Children's Drawings. Multicoloured.

456		45t. Type **184** (D. Ishanova)	30	15
457		45t. Mountains, yurts and sheep (A. Sadykov) (horiz)	30	15

2004. Olympic Games, Athens. Sheet 100 × 90 mm containing T **185** and similar horiz design. Multicoloured.

MS458		70t. Type **185**; 115t. Rifle shooting	1·50	1·50

186 Cinereous Vulture (*Aegypius monachus*) (inscr "Acgypius")

2004. Altyn Yemel National Park. Sheet 80 × 110 mm containing T **186** and similar horiz designs. Multicoloured.

MS459		50t. × 3 T **186**; Siberian ibex (*Capra sibirica*); Persian gazelle (*Gazella subgutturosa*)	1·20	1·20

187 Emblem

2004. 10th Anniv of Kazakhtelecom Company. Sheet 100 × 70 mm.

MS460	**187**	70t. multicoloured	55	25

188 Alkei Margulan

2004. Birth Centenary of Alkei Hakanovich Margulan (archaeologist).

461	**188**	115t. multicoloured	90	45

189 Flowers

2004. Greetings Stamp.

462	**189**	25t. multicoloured	20	10

2004. World Post Day.

463	**170**	3t. violet and blue	10	10
464		30t. lemon and blue	25	10

190 Bauble

2004. "Happy New Year".

465	**190**	65t. multicoloured	50	25

191 Adyrna

2004. Traditional Musical Instruments. Mult.

466		100t. Type **191**	80	40
467		100t. Gizhak	80	40

Stamps of the same design were issued by Tadjikistan.

192 Saken Seifullin

2004. 110th Birth Anniv of Saken Seifullin (writer). Multicoloured.

468	**192**	35t. multicoloured	30	15

193 Kazakh Woman's Headdress

194 Emblem

2004. Women's Headdress. Multicoloured.

469		72t. Type **193**	50	25
470		72t. Mongolian woman's headdress	50	25

Stamps of the same design were issued by Mongolia.

2005. Centenary of Research Institute of Veterinary Science.

471	**194**	7t. vermilion, blue and ultramarine	10	10

KEDAH Pt. 1

A state of the Federation of Malaya, incorporated in Malaysia in 1963.

100 cents = 1 dollar (Straits or Malayan).

1 Sheaf of Rice

2 Malay ploughing

1912.

1	**1**	1c. black and green	60	25
26		1c. brown	70	20
52		1c. black	1·00	10
27		2c. green	1·50	20
2		3c. black and red	4·50	30
19		3c. purple	65	1·00
53		3c. green	2·25	90
3		4c. red and grey	10·00	25
20		4c. red	4·00	30
54		4c. violet	1·00	10
4		5c. green and brown	2·25	3·00
55		5c. yellow	1·50	10
56		6c. red	1·75	65
5		8c. black and blue	3·75	3·50
57		8c. black	12·00	10
6	**2**	10c. blue and brown	2·25	90
58		12c. black and blue	4·50	3·50
31		20c. black and green	4·00	2·00
32		21c. mauve and purple	2·25	13·00
33		25c. blue and purple	2·25	9·00
34		30c. black and pink	3·00	11·00
59		35c. purple	8·50	29·00
9		40c. black and purple	3·50	14·00
36		50c. brown and blue	2·75	15·00
37w	–	$1 black and red on yellow	6·50	9·50
38	–	$2 green and brown	13·00	95·00
39	–	$3 black and blue on blue	70·00	95·00
40	–	$5 black and red	80·00	£150

DESIGN—As Type **2**: $1 to $5, Council Chamber.

1919. Surch in words.

24		50c. on $2 green and brown	70·00	75·00
25		$1 on $3 black and blue on blue	20·00	90·00

1922. Optd **MALAYA-BORNEO EXHIBITION.**

45	**1**	1c. brown	3·50	17·00
41		2c. green	3·50	25·00
46		3c. purple	3·00	42·00
47		4c. red	3·00	25·00
48	**2**	10c. blue and sepia	4·50	45·00
42		21c. purple	28·00	80·00
43		25c. blue and purple	28·00	80·00
44		50c. brown and blue	28·00	95·00

6 Sultan Abdul Hamid Halimshah

1937.

60	**6**	10c. blue and brown	4·50	1·25
61		12c. black and violet	40·00	7·50
62		25c. blue and purple	8·00	4·50
63		30c. green and red	8·00	10·00
64		40c. black and purple	4·00	16·00
65		50c. brown and blue	7·50	4·50
66		$1 black and green	4·00	10·00
67		$2 green and brown	£120	75·00
68		$5 black and red	32·00	£160

1948. Silver Wedding. As T **61/2** of Jamaica.

70		10c. violet	20	30
71		$5 red	27·00	32·00

1949. U.P.U. As T **63/66** of Pitcairn Islands.

72		10c. purple	25	75
73		15c. blue	1·75	1·50
74		25c. orange	65	1·50
75		50c. black	1·00	2·75

7 Sheaf of Rice

8 Sultan Badlishah

1950.

76	**7**	1c. black	50	30
77		2c. orange	50	15
78		3c. green	2·00	1·00
79		4c. brown	75	10
79ab		5c. purple	1·75	1·00
80		6c. grey	70	15
81		8c. red	1·75	2·75
81a		8c. green	1·00	1·75
82		10c. mauve	70	10
82a		12c. red	1·00	2·50
83		15c. blue	1·25	35
84		20c. black and green	1·50	2·50
84a		20c. blue	1·00	10
85	**8**	25c. purple and orange	1·50	30
85a		30c. red and purple	3·00	1·25
85b		35c. red and purple	1·00	1·50
86		40c. red and purple	2·75	6·00
87		50c. black and blue	2·25	35
88		$1 blue and purple	3·00	4·50
89		$2 green and red	20·00	23·00
90		$5 green and brown	42·00	45·00

1953. Coronation. As T **71** of Jamaica.

91		10c. black and purple	1·25	60

15 Fishing Craft

20 Sultan Abdul Halim Mu' Adzam Shah

1957. Inset portrait of Sultan Badlishah.

92	–	1c. black	10	60
93	–	2c. red	10	1·75
94	–	4c. sepia	10	1·00
95	–	5c. lake	10	75
96	–	8c. green	2·00	8·00
97	–	10c. sepia	65	40
98	**15**	20c. blue	2·75	2·50
99	–	50c. black and blue	2·50	3·50
100	–	$1 blue and purple	5·50	12·00
101	–	$2 green and red	25·00	32·00
102	–	$5 brown and green	40·00	35·00

DESIGNS—HORIZ: 1c. Copra; 2c. Pineapples; 4c. Ricefield; 5c. Masjid Alwi Mosque, Kangar; 8c. East Coast Railway "Golden Blowpipe" Express; $1 Govt Offices; $2 Bersilat (form of wrestling); $5 Weaving. VERT: 10c. Tiger; 50c. Aborigines with blowpipe.

1959. Installation of Sultan.

103	**20**	10c. yellow, brown and blue	10	10

21 Sultan Abdul Halim Shah

1959. As Nos. 92/102 but with inset portrait of Sultan Abdul Halim Shah as in T **21**.

104		1c. black	10	75
105		2c. red	10	2·00
106		4c. sepia	10	75
107		5c. lake	10	10
108		8c. green	3·50	3·50

109	10c. sepia	1·00	10
109a	10c. purple	5·00	40
110	20c. blue	1·00	1·00
111a	50c. black and blue	30	60
112	$1 blue and purple	1·75	2·25
113	$2 green and red	13·00	18·00
114	$5 brown and green	16·00	19·00

22 "Vanda hookeriana"

1965. Flowers. Multicoloured.

115	1c. Type **22**	10	1·25
116	2c. "Arundina graminifolia"	10	1·75
117	5c. "Paphiopedilum niveum"	10	10
118	6c. "Spathoglottis plicata"	15	60
119	10c. "Arachnis flos-aeris"	30	10
120	15c. "Rhyncostylis retusa"	1·50	10
121	20c. "Phalaenopsis violacea"	1·75	1·00

The higher values used in Kedah were Nos. 20/7 of Malaysia.

23 "Danaus melanippus"

1971. Butterflies. Multicoloured.

124	1c. "Delias ninus"	30	1·75
125	2c. Type **23**	50	1·75
126	5c. "Parthenos sylvia"	1·25	40
127	6c. "Papilio demoleus"	1·25	2·00
128	10c. "Hebomoia glaucippe"	1·25	10
129	15c. "Precis orithya"	1·25	10
130	20c. "Valeria valeria"	1·50	70

The higher values in use with this issue were Nos. 64/71 of Malaysia.

24 "Pterocarpus indicus"

1979. Flowers. Multicoloured.

135	1c. "Rafflesia hasseltii"	10	90
136	2c. Type **24**	10	90
137	5c. "Lagerstroemia speciosa"	10	60
138	10c. "Durio zibethinus"	15	10
139	15c. "Hibiscus rosa-sinensis"	15	10
140	20c. "Rhododendron scortechinii"	20	10
141	25c. "Etlingera elatior" (inscr "Phaeomeria speciosa")	40	20

25 Sultan Abdul Halim Shah

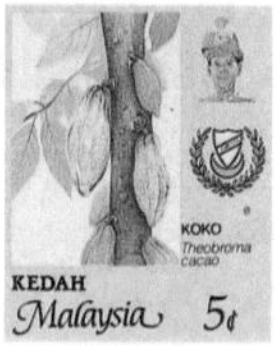

26 Cocoa

1983. Silver Jubilee of Sultan's Installation. Multicoloured.

142	20c. Type **25**	70	30
143	40c. Paddy fields (horiz)	1·75	1·75
144	60c. Paddy fields and Mount Jerai (horiz)	2·50	4·75

1986. Agricultural Products of Malaysia. Mult.

152	1c. Coffee	10	10
153	2c. Coconuts	10	10
154	5c. Type **26**	15	10
155	10c. Black pepper	15	10
156	15c. Rubber	25	10
157	20c. Oil palm	25	15
158	30c. Rice	30	15

KELANTAN Pt. 1

A state in the Federation of Malaya, incorporated in Malaysia in 1963.

100 cents = 1 dollar (Straits or Malayan).

1

3 Sultan Ismail

1911.

1a	1	1c. green	5·00	30
15		1c. black	1·00	50
16		2c. brown	7·00	3·75
16a		2c. green	4·00	40
2		3c. red	4·25	15
16b		3c. brown	4·50	1·00
17		4c. black and red	2·75	10
18		5c. green and red on yellow	1·50	10
19		6c. purple	3·25	1·50
19a		6c. red	4·00	5·50
5		8c. blue	5·50	1·00
20		10c. black and mauve	3·00	10
21		30c. purple and red	4·00	5·50
8		50c. black and orange	8·00	2·50
9		$1 green	48·00	40·00
9a		$1 green and brown	50·00	2·00
10		$2 green and red	1·50	4·00
11		$5 green and blue	4·00	7·50
12		$25 green and orange	42·00	85·00

1922. Optd **MALAYA BORNEO EXHIBITION**.

37	1	1c. green	3·50	48·00
30		4c. black and red	5·00	48·00
31		5c. green and red on yellow	6·00	48·00
38		10c. black and mauve	6·00	60·00
32		30c. purple and red	6·00	65·00
33		50c. black and orange	8·50	70·00
34		$1 green and brown	28·00	90·00
35		$2 green and red	70·00	£180
36		$5 green and blue	£170	£375

1928.

40	3	1c. olive and yellow	65	55
41		2c. green	4·50	20
42		4c. red	5·50	1·00
43		5c. brown	4·75	10
44		6c. black	11·00	9·00
45		8c. olive	4·75	10
46		10c. purple	22·00	2·75
47		12c. blue	4·00	6·00
48		25c. red and purple	5·50	3·50
49		30c. violet and red	40·00	20·00
50		40c. orange and green	8·50	26·00
51		50c. olive and orange	65·00	6·00
39		$1 blue	14·00	80·00
52		$1 violet and green	48·00	13·00
53		$2 brown and red	£225	£180
54		$5 red and lake	£400	£500

All except No. 39 are larger than T 3.

1948. Silver Wedding. As T **61/2** of Jamaica.

55	10c. violet	75	2·75
56	$5 red	27·00	48·00

1949. U.P.U. As T **63/6**of Jamaica.

57	10c. purple	25	30
58	15c. blue	2·00	1·00
59	25c. orange	40	3·00
40	50c. black	70	2·75

5 Sultan Ibrahim

6 Sultan Yahya Petra and Arms of Kelantan

1951.

61	5	1c. black	50	30
62		2c. orange	1·25	35
63		3c. green	4·50	2·00
64		4c. brown	75	15
65		5c. mauve	1·50	50
66		6c. grey	75	20
67		8c. red	2·00	3·50
68		8c. green	1·25	1·75
69		10c. purple	50	10
70		12c. red	2·75	2·25
71		15c. blue	4·25	60
72		20c. black and green	1·00	6·50
73		20c. blue	1·00	25
74		25c. purple and orange	1·50	55
75		30c. red and purple	1·25	2·00
76		35c. red and purple	1·25	1·50
77		40c. red and purple	9·00	13·00
78		50c. black and blue	3·75	40
79		$1 blue and purple	7·50	6·00
80		$2 green and red	27·00	29·00
81		$5 green and brown	48·00	42·00

1953. Coronation. As T **71** of Jamaica.

82	10c. black and purple	1·25	1·40

1957. As Nos. 92/102 of Kedah but inset portrait of Sultan Ibrahim.

83	1c. black	10	30
84	2c. red	75	1·50
85	4c. sepia	40	10
86	5c. lake	40	10
87	8c. green	1·00	3·00
88	10c. sepia	2·25	10
89	10c. purple	8·00	7·00
90	20c. blue	2·25	30
91	50c. black and blue	50	50
92	$1 blue and purple	6·00	1·50
93	$2 green and red	12·00	6·00
94	$5 brown and green	15·00	12·00

1961. Coronation of the Sultan.

95	6	10c. multicoloured	40	30

7 Sultan Yahya Petra

8 "Vanda hookeriana"

1961. As Nos. 83, etc, but with inset portrait of Sultan Yahya Petra as in T **7**.

96	1c. black	10	2·00
97	2c. red	10	2·00
98	4c. sepia	80	1·25
99	5c. lake	60	20
100	8c. green	8·00	10·00
101	10c. purple	1·75	25
102	20c. blue	4·75	1·50

1965. As Nos. 115/21 of Kedah but with inset portrait of Sultan Yahya Petra as in T **8**.

103	8	1c. multicoloured	10	1·00
104	–	2c. multicoloured	10	1·75
105	–	5c. multicoloured	15	30
106	–	6c. multicoloured	70	2·25
107	–	10c. multicoloured	30	25
108	–	15c. multicoloured	1·50	25
109	–	20c. multicoloured	1·50	1·50

The higher values used in Kelantan were Nos. 20/7 of Malaysia (National Issues).

9 "Parthenos sylvia"

1971. Butterflies. As Nos. 124/30 of Kedah but with portrait of Sultan Yahya Petra as in T **9**.

112	–	1c. multicoloured	30	2·25
113	–	2c. multicoloured	40	2·25
114	9	5c. multicoloured	1·50	60
115	–	6c. multicoloured	1·50	2·50
116	–	10c. multicoloured	1·50	30
117	–	15c. multicoloured	1·50	10
118	–	20c. multicoloured	2·00	1·50

The higher values in use with this series were Nos. 64/71 of Malaysia (National Issues).

10 "Lagerstroemia speciosa"

1979. Flowers. As Nos. 135/41 of Kedah but with portrait of Sultan Yahya Petra as in T **10**.

123	1c. "Rafflesia hasseltii"	10	1·00
124	2c. "Pterocarpus indicus"	10	1·00
125	5c. Type **10**	10	80
126	10c. "Durio zibethinus"	15	10
127	15c. "Hibiscus rosa-sinensis"	15	10
128	20c. "Rhododendron scortechinii"	20	10
129	25c. "Etlingera elatior" (inscr "Phaeomeria speciosa")	40	50

11 Sultan Tengku Ismail Petra

12 Black Pepper

1980. Coronation of Sultan Tengku Ismail Petra.

130	11	10c. multicoloured	40	75
131		15c. multicoloured	40	15
132		50c. multicoloured	90	2·75

1986. Agricultural Products of Malaysia. Mult.

140	1c. Coffee	10	30
141	2c. Coconuts	10	30
142	5c. Cocoa	50	10
143	10c. Type **12**	20	10
144	15c. Rubber	30	10
145	20c. Oil palm	20	15
146	30c. Rice	40	15

KENYA Pt. 1

Formerly part of Kenya, Uganda and Tanganyika (q.v.). Became independent in 1963 and a Republic in 1964.

100 cents = 1 shilling.

1 Cattle Ranching

4 Cockerel

3 National Assembly

1963. Independence.

1	1	5c. multicoloured	10	55
2	–	10c. brown	10	10
3	–	15c. mauve	1·00	10
4	–	20c. black and green	15	10
5	–	30c. black and yellow	15	10
6	–	40c. brown and blue	15	30
7	–	50c. red, black and green	15	10
8	–	65c. turquoise and yellow	55	65
9	3	1s. multicoloured	20	10
10	–	1s.30 brown, black & green	4·50	30
11	–	2s. multicoloured	1·25	40
12	–	5s. brown, blue and green	1·25	50
13	–	10s. brown and blue	8·50	3·00
14	–	20s. black and red	4·00	8·50

DESIGNS—As Type **1**: 10c. Wood-carving; 15c. Heavy industry; 20c. Timber industry; 30c. Jomo Kenyatta facing Mt. Kenya; 40c. Fishing industry; 50c. Kenya flag; 65c. Pyrethrum industry. As Type **3**: 1s.30, Tourism (Treetops hotel); 2s. Coffee industry; 5s. Tea industry; 10s. Mombasa Port; 20s. Royal College, Nairobi.

1964. Inauguration of Republic. Multicoloured.

15	15c. Type **4**	15	15
16	30c. Pres. Kenyatta	15	10
17	50c. African lion	15	10
18	1s.30 Hartlaub's turaco	2·50	50
19	2s.50 Nandi flame	30	3·75

5 Thomson's Gazelle

7 Greater Kudu

1966.

20	5	5c. orange, black and sepia	20	20
21	–	10c. black and green	10	10
22	–	15c. black and orange	10	10
23	–	20c. ochre, black and blue	10	15
24	–	30c. indigo, blue and black	20	10
25	–	40c. black and brown	60	30
26	–	50c. black and orange	60	10
27	–	65c. black and green	1·25	2·00
28	–	70c. black and purple	5·00	1·50
29	7	1s. brown, black and blue	30	10
30	–	1s.30 blue, green and black	4·00	20
31	–	1s.50 black, brown and green	3·00	2·25
32	–	2s.50 yellow, black & brown	3·25	1·25
33	–	5s. yellow, black and green	75	70
34	–	10s. ochre, black and brown	1·75	3·50
35	–	20s. multicoloured	5·50	13·00

DESIGNS—As Type **5**: 10c. Sable antelope; 15c. Aardvark ("Ant Bear"); 20c. Lesser bushbaby; 30c. Warthog; 40c. Common zebra; 50c. African buffalo; 65c. Black rhinoceros; 70c. Ostrich. As Type **7**: 1s.30, African elephant; 1s.50, Bat-eared fox; 2s.50, Cheetah; 5s. Savanna monkey ("Vervet Monkey"); 10s. Giant ground pangolin; 20s. Lion.

8 Perna Tellin

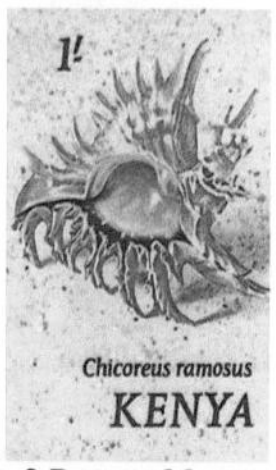

9 Ramose Murex

1971. Sea Shells. Multicoloured.

36	5c. Type **8**	10	30
37	10c. Episcopal mitre	15	10
38	15c. Purplish clanculus	15	20
39	20c. Humpback cowrie	15	20
40	30c. Variable abalone	20	10
41	40c. Flame top shell	20	10
42	50c. Common purple janthina	30	20
43	50c. Common purple janthina	11·00	3·00
44	60c. Bullmouth helmet	30	1·75

45	70c. Chambered or pearly nautilus	45	1·50
46	70c. Chambered or pearly nautilus	10·00	6·00
47a	1s. Type **9**	20	10
48	1s.50 Trumpet triton	1·00	10
49	2s.50 Trapezium horse conch	1·00	10
50a	5s. Great green turban	1·00	10
51	10s. Textile or cloth of gold cone	1·50	15
52a	20s. Scorpion conch	1·50	25

INSCRIPTIONS: No. 42, "Janthina globosa"; 43, "Janthina janthina"; 45, "Nautilus pompileus"; 46, "Nautilus pompilius".

Nos. 47/52 are larger, as Type **9**.

1975. Nos. 48/9 and 52a surch.

53	2s. on 1s.50 Trumpet triton	6·00	5·00
54	3s. on 2s.50 Trapezium horse conch	9·50	20·00
55	40s. on 20s. Scorpion conch	6·00	14·00

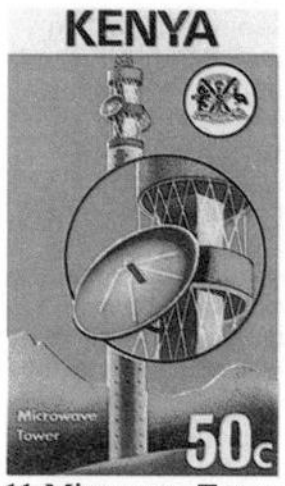

11 Microwave Tower

1976. Telecommunications Development. Mult.

56	50c. Type **11**	10	10
57	1s. Cordless switchboard (horiz)	10	10
58	2s. Telephones	20	30
59	3s. Message switching centre (horiz)	25	45
MS60	120 × 120 mm. Nos. 56/9. Imperf	1·10	2·50

12 Akii Bua, Ugandan Hurdler

1976. Olympic Games, Montreal. Multicoloured.

61	50c. Type **12**	10	10
62	1s. Filbert Bayi, Tanzanian runner	15	10
63	2s. Steve Muchoki, Kenyan boxer	45	35
64	3s. Olympic flame and East African flags	90	50
MS65	129 × 154 mm. Nos. 61/4	6·00	7·50

13 Diesel-hydraulic Train, Tanzania–Zambia Railway

1976. Railway Transport. Multicoloured.

66	50c. Type **13**	35	10
67	1s. Nile Bridge, Uganda	60	15
68	2s. Nakuru Station, Kenya	1·50	1·00
69	3s. Uganda Railway Class A steam locomotive, 1896	1·50	1·50
MS70	154 × 103 mm. Nos. 66/9	8·00	8·00

14 Nile Perch

1977. Game Fish of East Africa. Multicoloured.

71	50c. Type **14**	25	10
72	1s. Nile mouthbrooder ("Tilapia")	35	10
73	3s. Sailfish	75	60
74	5s. Black marlin	90	80
MS75	153 × 129 mm. Nos. 71/4	7·50	4·00

15 Maasai Manyatta (village), Kenya

1977. 2nd World Black and African Festival of Arts and Culture, Nigeria. Multicoloured.

76	50c. Type **15**	15	10
77	1s. "Heartbeat of Africa" (Ugandan dancers)	15	10
78	2s. Makonde sculpture, Tanzania	60	1·25
79	3s. "Early man and technology" (skinning hippopotamus)	75	2·00
MS80	132 × 109 mm. Nos. 76/9	4·00	5·50

16 Rally Car and Villagers

1977. 25th Anniv of Safari Rally. Multicoloured.

81	50c. Type **16**	15	10
82	1s. Pres. Kenyatta starting rally	15	10
83	2s. Car fording river	50	60
84	5s. Car and elephants	1·40	1·50
MS85	126 × 93 mm. Nos. 81/4	3·75	6·50

17 Canon Kivebulaya

1977. Centenary of Ugandan Church. Multicoloured.

86	50c. Type **17**	10	10
87	1s. Modern Namirembe Cathedral	10	10
88	2s. The first Cathedral	30	55
89	5s. Early congregation, Kigezi	50	1·25
MS90	126 × 94 mm. Nos. 86/9	1·40	2·50

18 Sagana Royal Lodge, Nyeri, 1952

1977. Silver Jubilee. Multicoloured.

91	2s. Type **18**	15	15
92	5s. Treetops Hotel (vert)	20	35
93	10s. Queen Elizabeth and Pres. Kenyatta	30	60
94	15s. Royal visit, 1972	45	1·00
MS95	Two sheets. (a) 140 × 60 mm. No. 94. (b) 152 × 127 mm. 50s. Queen and Prince Philip in Treetops Hotel Set of 2 sheets	2·00	1·40

19 Pancake Tortoise

1977. Endangered Species. Multicoloured.

96	50c. Type **19**	30	10
97	1s. Nile crocodile	40	10
98	2s. Hunter's hartebeest	1·60	40
99	3s. Red colobus monkey	1·75	50
100	5s. Dugong	2·00	75
MS101	127 × 101 mm. Nos. 97/100	7·00	8·50

20 Kenya-Ethiopia Border Point

1977. Nairobi–Addis Ababa Highway. Mult.

102	50c. Type **20**	15	10
103	1s. Archer's Post	15	10
104	2s. Thika Flyover	30	25
105	5s. Marsabit Game Lodge	50	75
MS106	144 × 91 mm. Nos. 102/5	2·25	3·50

21 Gypsum

22 Amethyst

1977. Minerals. Multicoloured.

107	10c. Type **21**	1·25	20
108	20c. Trona	2·00	20
109	30c. Kyanite	2·00	20
110	40c. Amazonite	1·40	10
111	50c. Galena	1·40	10
112	70c. Silicified wood	7·50	1·00
113	80c. Fluorite	7·50	60
114	1s. Type **22**	1·40	10
115	1s.50 Agate	1·50	30
116	2s. Tourmaline	1·50	20
117	3s. Aquamarine	1·75	55
118	5s. Rhodolite garnet	1·75	1·10
119	10s. Sapphire	1·75	1·50
120	20s. Ruby	4·50	2·50
121	40s. Green grossular garnet	18·00	20·00

23 Joe Kadenge (Kenya) and Forwards

1978. World Cup Football Championship, Argentina. Multicoloured.

122	50c. Type **23**	10	10
123	1s. Mohamed Chuma (Tanzania) and cup presentation	10	10
124	2s. Omari Kidevu (Zanzibar) and goalmouth scene	30	70
125	3s. Polly Ouma (Uganda) and three forwards	40	95
MS126	136 × 81 mm. Nos. 122/5	3·75	3·50

24 Boxing

1978. Commonwealth Games, Edmonton. Mult.

127	50c. Type **24**	15	10
128	1s. Welcoming the Olympic Games Team, 1968	15	10
129	3s. Javelin throwing	50	1·00
130	5s. Pres. Kenyatta admiring boxer's trophy	60	1·60

25 "Overloading is Dangerous"

1978. Road Safety. Multicoloured.

131	50c. Type **25**	50	10
132	1s. "Speed does not pay"	70	20
133	1s.50 "Ignoring Traffic Signs may cause death"	85	55
134	2s. "Slow down at School Crossing"	1·25	1·00
135	3s. "Never cross a continuous line"	1·40	2·50
136	5s. "Approach Railway Level Crossing with extreme caution"	2·00	3·50

26 Pres. Kenyatta at Mass Rally, 1963

1978. Kenyatta Day. Multicoloured.

137	50c. "Harambee Water Project"	15	10
138	1s. Handing over of Independence Instruments, 1963	15	10
139	2s. Type **26**	30	35
140	3s. "Harambee, 15 Great Years"	60	1·00
141	5s. "Struggle for Independence, 1952"	80	2·00

27 Freedom Fighters, Namibia

1978. International Anti-Apartheid Year.

142 **27**	50c. multicoloured	15	10
143 –	1s. black and blue	15	10
144 –	2s. multicoloured	30	30
145 –	3s. multicoloured	50	65
146 –	5s. multicoloured	55	1·00

DESIGNS: 1s. International seminar on apartheid; 2s. Steve Biko's tombstone; 3s. Nelson Mandela; 5s. Bishop Lamont.

28 Children Playing

1979. International Year of the Child. Multicoloured.

147	50c. Type **28**	15	10
148	2s. Boy fishing	40	60
149	3s. Children singing and dancing	55	1·10
150	5s. Children with camels	1·00	2·25

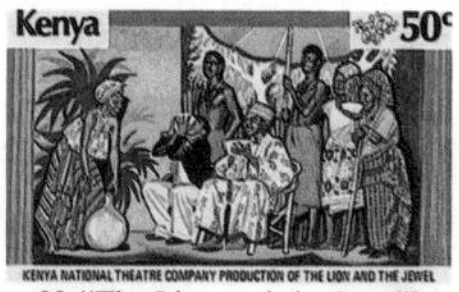

29 "The Lion and the Jewel"

1979. Kenya National Theatre. Multicoloured.

151	50c. Type **29**	15	10
152	1s. "Utisi"	15	10
153	2s. Theatre programmes	25	30
154	3s. Kenya National Theatre	35	45
155	5s. "Genesis"	50	75

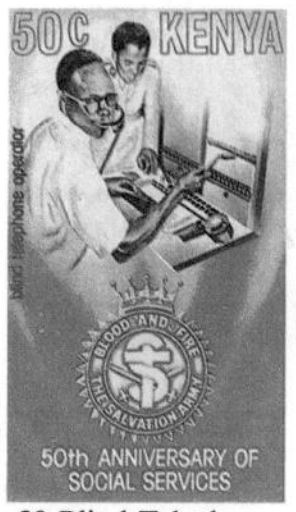

30 Blind Telephone Operator

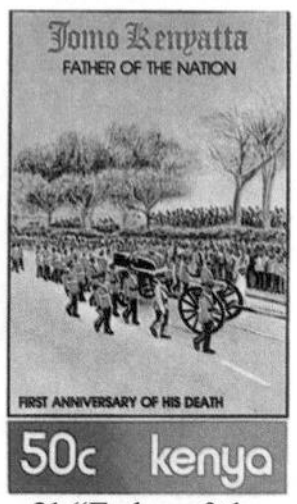

31 "Father of the Nation" (Kenyatta's funeral procession)

1979. 50th Anniv of Salvation Army Social Services.

156	50c. Type **30**	30	10
157	1s. Care for the aged	30	10
158	3s. Village polytechnic (horiz)	60	1·50
159	5s. Vocational training (horiz)	1·00	2·50

1979. 1st Death Anniv of President Kenyatta. Multicoloured.

160	50c. Type **31**	10	10
161	1s. "First President of Kenya" (Kenyatta receiving independence)	10	10
162	3s. "Kenyatta the politician" (speaking at rally)	30	50
163	5s. "A true son of Kenya" (Kenyatta as a boy carpenter)	40	95

32 British East Africa Company 1890 1a. Stamp

1979. Death Centenary of Sir Rowland Hill.

164 **32**	50c. multicoloured	15	10
165 –	1s. multicoloured	15	10
166 –	2s. black, red and brown	20	40
167 –	5s. multicoloured	35	1·00

DESIGNS: 1s. Kenya, Uganda and Tanganyika 1935 1s. stamp; 2s. Penny Black; 5s. 1964 2s.50 Inauguration of Republic commemorative.

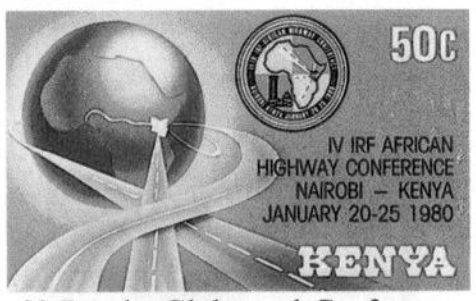

33 Roads, Globe and Conference Emblem

1980. International Road Federation. African Highway Conference, Nairobi. Multicoloured.

168	50c. Type **33**	15	10
169	1s. New weighbridge, Athi River	15	10
170	3s. New Nyali Bridge, Mombasa	40	85
171	5s. Highway to Jomo Kenyatta International Airport	50	2·00

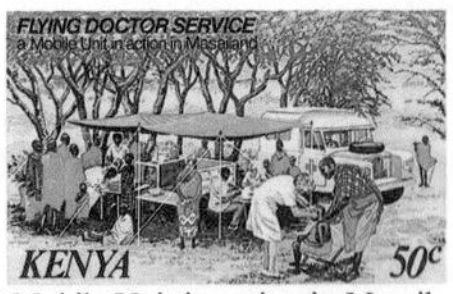

34 Mobile Unit in action in Masailand

1980. Flying Doctor Service. Multicoloured.

172	50c. Type **34**	10	10
173	1s. Donkey transport to Turkana airstrip (vert)	20	10
174	3s. Surgical team in action at outstation (vert)	65	1·00
175	5s. Emergency airlift from North Eastern Province	90	1·60
MS176	146 × 133 mm. Nos. 172/5	1·60	2·75

35 Statue of Sir Rowland Hill

37 Blue-spotted Stingray

36 Pope John Paul II

1980. "London 1980" International Stamp Exhibition.

177 **35**	25s. multicoloured	1·00	2·50
MS178	114 × 101 mm. No. 177	1·00	2·75

1980. Papal Visit. Multicoloured.

179	50c. Type **36**	40	10
180	1s. Pope, arms and cathedral (vert)	40	10
181	5s. Pope, flags and dove (vert)	75	85
182	10s. Pope, President Moi and map of Africa	1·25	1·75

1980. Marine Life. Multicoloured.

183	50c. Type **37**	30	10
184	2s. Allard's anemonefish	1·00	80
185	3s. Four-coloured nudibranch	1·25	1·75
186	5s. "Eretmochelys imbricata"	1·75	2·75

38 National Archives

1980. Historic Buildings. Multicoloured.

187	50c. Type **38**	10	10
188	1s. Provincial Commissioner's Office, Nairobi	15	10
189	1s.50 Nairobi House	20	20
190	2s. Norfolk Hotel	25	50
191	3s. McMillan Library	35	95
192	5s. Kipande House	55	1·60

39 "Disabled enjoys Affection"

1981. Int Year for Disabled Persons. Mult.

193	50c. Type **39**	15	10
194	1s. President Moi presenting flag to Disabled Olympic Games team captain	15	10
195	3s. Blind people climbing Mount Kenya, 1975	55	65
196	5s. Disabled artist at work	70	1·00

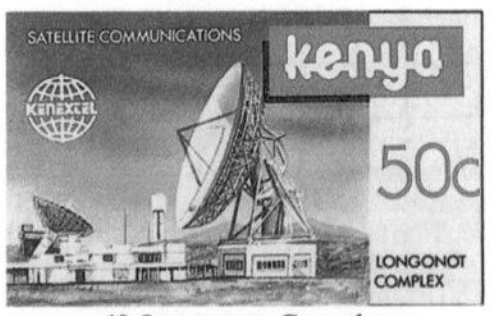

40 Longonot Complex

1981. Satellite Communications. Multicoloured.

197	50c. Type **40**	15	10
198	2s. "Intelsat V"	40	35
199	3s. "Longonot I"	45	55
200	5s. "Longonot II"	60	85

41 Kenyatta Conference Centre

1981. O.A.U. (Organization of African Unity) Summit Conference, Nairobi.

201 **41**	50c. multicoloured	15	10
202 –	1s. black, yellow and blue	15	10
203 –	3s. multicoloured	40	40
204 –	5s. multicoloured	70	65
205 –	10s. multicoloured	80	1·00
MS206	110 × 110 mm. No. 205	1·10	1·50

DESIGNS: 1s. "Panaftel" earth stations; 3s. Parliament Building; 5s. Jomo Kenyatta International Airport; 10s. O.A.U. flag.

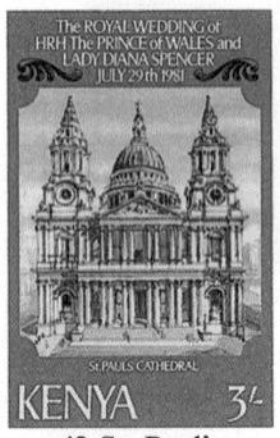

42 St. Paul's Cathedral

43 Giraffe

1981. Royal Wedding. Multicoloured.

207	50c. Prince Charles and President Daniel Arap Moi	10	10
208	3s. Type **42**	15	20
209	5s. Royal Yacht "Britannia"	25	30
210	10s. Prince Charles on safari in Kenya	40	55
MS211	85 × 102 mm. 25s. Prince Charles and Lady Diana Spencer	75	80

1981. Rare Animals. Multicoloured.

212	50c. Type **43**	15	10
213	2s. Bongo	25	25
214	5s. Roan antelope	40	1·00
215	10s. Agile mangabey	60	2·25

44 "Technical Development"

45 Kamba

1981. World Food Day. Multicoloured.

216	50c. Type **44**	10	10
217	1s. "Mwea rice projects"	15	10
218	2s. "Irrigation schemes"	30	55
219	5s. "Breeding livestock"	60	1·75

1981. Ceremonial Costumes (1st series). Mult.

220	50c. Type **45**	40	10
221	1s. Turkana	45	10
222	2s. Giriama	1·25	85
223	3s. Masai	1·60	2·25
224	5s. Luo	1·75	3·50

See also Nos. 329/33, 413/17 and 515/19.

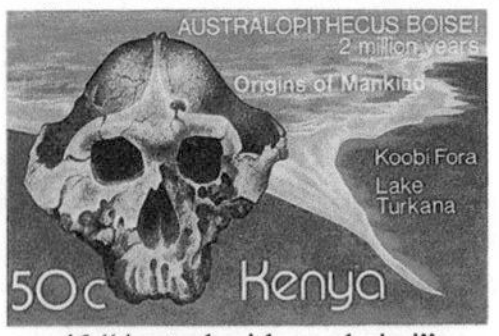

46 "Australopithecus boisei"

1982. "Origins of Mankind". Skulls. Multicoloured.

225	50c. Type **46**	1·75	30
226	2s. "Homo erectus"	3·25	1·50
227	3s. "Homo habilis"	3·25	3·75
228	5s. "Proconsul africanus"	3·75	5·00

47 Tree-planting

1982. 75th Anniv of Boy Scout Movement (Nos. 229, 231, 233 and 235) and 60th Anniv of Girl Guide Movement (Nos. 230, 232, 234 and 236). Multicoloured.

229	70c. Type **47**	50	80
230	70c. Paying homage	50	80
231	3s.50 "Be Prepared"	1·25	2·00
232	3s.50 "International Friendship"	1·25	2·00
233	5s. Helping disabled	1·50	2·50
234	5s. Community service	1·50	2·50
235	6s.50 Paxtu Cottage (Lord Baden-Powell's home)	1·50	2·75
236	6s.50 Lady Baden-Powell	1·50	2·75
MS237	112 × 112 mm. Nos. 229, 231, 233 and 235	3·75	3·00

48 Footballer displaying Shooting Skill

1982. World Cup Football Championship, Spain. Footballers silhouetted against Map of World. Multicoloured.

238	70c. Type **48**	1·50	65
239	3s.50 Heading	2·75	2·75
240	5s. Goalkeeping	3·75	4·25
241	10s. Dribbling	5·50	8·00
MS242	101 × 76 mm. 20s. Tackling	5·50	4·00

49 Cattle Judging

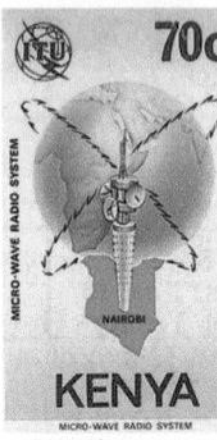

50 Micro-wave Radio System

1982. 80th Anniv of Agricultural Society of Kenya. Multicoloured.

243	70c. Type **49**	50	10
244	2s.50 Farm machinery	1·25	1·25
245	3s.50 Musical ride	1·50	2·50
246	6s.50 Agricultural Society emblem	2·00	4·25

1982. I.T.U. Plenipotentiary Conference, Nairobi. Multicoloured.

247	70c. Type **50**	50	10
248	3s.50 Sea-to-shore service link	1·75	1·75
249	5s. Rural telecommunications system	2·25	3·75
250	6s.50 I.T.U. emblem	2·50	4·50

1982. No. 113 surch **70c**.

251	70c. on 80c. Fluorite	1·00	1·25

52 Container Cranes

1983. 5th Anniv of Kenya Ports Authority. Mult.

252	70c. Type **52**	85	10
253	2s. Port by night	1·75	1·90
254	3s.50 Container cranes (different)	2·50	3·50
255	5s. Map of Mombasa Port	3·25	4·50
MS256	125 × 85 mm. Nos. 252/5	7·50	9·00

53 Shada Zambarau

54 Waridi Kikuba

1983. Flowers. Multicoloured.

257	10c. Type **53**	40	40
258	20c. Kilua Kingulima	55	40
259	30c. Mwalika Mwiya	55	40
260	40c. Ziyungi Buluu	55	40
261	50c. Kilua Habashia	55	30
262	70c. Chanuo Kato	60	20
262a	80c. As 40c.	4·50	4·75
262b	1s. Waridi Kikuba	4·50	80
263	1s. Type **54**	65	20
264	1s.50 Mshomoro Mtambazi	1·75	60
265	2s. Papatuo Boti	1·75	60
266	2s.50 Tumba Mboni	1·75	60
266a	3s. Mkuku Mrembo	14·00	9·00
267	3s.50 Mtongo Mbeja	1·50	1·50
267b	4s. Mnukia Muuma	4·75	7·00
268	5s. Nyungu Chepuo	1·25	1·50
268a	7s. Mlua Miba	6·50	10·00
269	10s. Muafunili	1·25	1·50
270	20s. Mbake Nyanza	1·25	2·50
271	40s. Njuga Pagwa	2·00	8·00

The 1s.50 to 40s. are in the same format as T **54**.

55 Coffee Plucking

56 Examining Parcels

1983. Commonwealth Day. Multicoloured.

272	70c. Type **55**	10	10
273	2s. President Daniel Arap Moi	15	20
274	5s. Satellite view of Earth (horiz)	35	45
275	10s. Masai dance (horiz)	65	1·00

1983. 30th Anniv of Customs Co-operation Council. Multicoloured.

276	70c. Type **56**	25	10
277	2s.50 Customs Headquarters, Mombasa	65	30
278	3s.50 Customs Council Headquarters, Brussels	75	40
279	10s. Customs patrol boat	2·40	2·50

57 Communications via Satellite

1983. World Communications Year. Multicoloured.

280	70c. Type **57**	60	10
281	2s.50 "Telephone and Postal Services"	1·50	1·75
282	3s.50 Communications by sea and air (horiz)	2·00	3·00
283	5s. Road and rail communications (horiz)	2·50	4·00

58 "Craftsman" (freighter) in Kilindini Harbour

1983. 25th Anniv of Intergovernmental Maritime Organization. Multicoloured.

284	70c. Type **58**	1·10	10
285	2s.50 Life-saving devices	2·25	1·75
286	3s.50 Mombasa container terminal	2·75	3·00
287	10s. Marine park	3·75	7·50

59 President Moi signing Visitors' Book

1983. 29th Commonwealth Parliamentary Conference. Multicoloured.
288 70c. Type **59** 25 10
289 2s.50 Parliament building, Nairobi (vert) . . . . . . 90 1·25
290 5s. State opening of Parliament (vert) . . . . . 1·60 3·00
MS291 122 × 141 mm. Nos. 288/90 2·50 6·00

60 Kenyan and British Flags

1983. Royal Visit. Multicoloured.
292 70c. Type **60** 50 10
293 3s.50 Sagana State Lodge . . 2·00 1·50
294 5s. Treetops Hotel . . . . . 2·25 2·75
295 10s. Queen Elizabeth II and President Moi . . . . . . 3·50 7·00
MS296 126 × 100 mm. 25s. Designs as Nos. 292/5, but without face values. Imperf . . . . 4·50 7·50

61 President Moi

1983. 20th Anniv of Independence. Mult.
297 70c. Type **61** 10 10
298 2s. President Moi planting tree 15 20
299 3s.50 Kenyan flag and emblem 25 35
300 5s. School milk scheme . . . 40 50
301 10s. People of Kenya . . . . 75 1·10
MS302 126 × 93 mm. 25s. Designs as Nos. 297 and 299/301, but without face values. Imperf . . . . . . 1·50 2·75

62 White-backed Night Heron

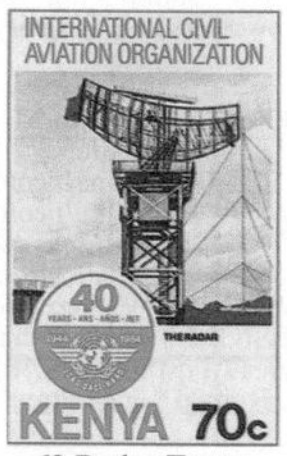

63 Radar Tower

1984. Rare Birds of Kenya. Multicoloured.
303 70c. Type **62** . . . . 1·75 30
304 2s.50 Quail plover . . . . . 3·00 2·50
305 3s.50 Taita olive thrush . . . 3·75 3·75
306 5s. Mufumbiri shrike . . . . 4·25 4·25
307 10s. White-winged apalis . . 5·50 7·00

1984. 40th Anniv of International Civil Aviation Organization. Multicoloured.
308 70c. Type **63** 20 10
309 2s.50 Kenya School of Aviation (horiz) 60 70
310 3s.50 Boeing 707 taking off from Moi airport (horiz) 90 1·40
311 5s. Air traffic control centre 1·25 2·00

64 Running

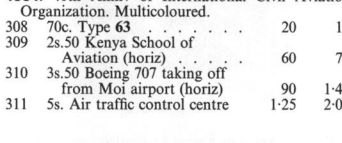

1984. Olympic Games, Los Angeles.
312 **64** 70c. black, green & dp green 30 10
313 – 2s.50 black, purple & violet 60 70
314 – 5s. black, blue & deep blue 1·50 2·50
315 – 10s. black, yellow & brown 3·50 6·00
MS316 130 × 121 mm. 25s. Designs as Nos. 312/15, but without face values. Imperf . . . . 3·25 3·25
DESIGNS: 2s.50, Hurdling; 5s. Boxing; 10s. Hockey.

65 Conference and Kenya Library Association Logos

1984. 50th Conference of the International Federation of Library Associations. Multicoloured.
317 70c. Type **65** 10 10
318 3s.50 Mobile library 50 60
319 5s. Adult library . . . . . . 65 1·25
320 10s. Children's library . . . 1·00 3·25

66 Doves and Cross

67 Export Year Logo

1984. 4th World Conference on Religion and Peace. As T **66**, each design showing a different central symbol. Multicoloured.
321 70c. Type **66** 30 10
322 2s.50 Arabic inscription . . . 1·25 1·50
323 3s.50 Peace emblem . . . . 1·60 2·50
324 6s.50 Star and Crescent . . . 2·00 4·00

1984. Kenya Export Year. Multicoloured.
325 70c. Type **67** 30 10
326 3s.50 Forklift truck with air cargo (horiz) . . . . . . 1·75 2·00
327 5s. Loading ship's cargo . . 2·50 3·00
328 10s. Kenyan products (horiz) 3·75 6·50

1984. Ceremonial Costumes (2nd series). As T **45**. Multicoloured.
329 70c. Luhya 80 15
330 2s. Kikuyu . . . . 2·00 1·75
331 3s.50 Pokomo . . . . 2·50 2·25
332 5s. Nandi . . . . 3·00 3·00
333 10s. Rendile . . . . 4·00 6·50

68 Staunton Knight and Nyayo National Stadium

1984. 60th Anniv of International Chess Federation. Multicoloured.
334 70c. Type **68** . . . . 2·25 40
335 2s.50 Staunton rook and Fort Jesus . . . . 3·25 1·75
336 3s.50 Staunton bishop and National Monument . . . 3·75 2·00
337 5s. Staunton queen and Parliament Building . . . 4·00 3·75
338 10s. Staunton king and Nyayo Fountain . . . . . 6·00 8·00

69 Cooking with Wood-burning Stove and Charcoal Fire

1985. Energy Conservation. Multicoloured.
339 70c. Type **69** 20 10
340 2s. Solar energy panel on roof 65 75
341 3s.50 Production of gas from cow dung . . . . 75 1·25
342 10s. Ploughing with oxen . . 2·25 6·00
MS343 110 × 85 mm. 20s. Designs as Nos. 339/42, but without face values . . . . 2·50 2·50

70 Crippled Girl Guide making Table-mat

1985. 75th Anniv of Girl Guide Movement. Multicoloured.
344 1s. Type **70** 75 15
345 3s. Girl Guides doing community service . . . . 1·75 1·50
346 5s. Lady Olave Baden-Powell (founder) . . . . 2·50 3·00
347 7s. Girl Guides gardening . . 4·00 6·50

71 Stylized Figures and Globe

1985. World Red Cross Day.
348 **71** 1s. black and red 80 15
349 – 4s. multicoloured . . . . . 3·00 3·00
350 – 5s. multicoloured . . . . . 3·25 3·50
351 – 7s. multicoloured . . . . . 4·50 6·50
DESIGNS: 4s. First Aid Team; 5s. Hearts containing crosses ("Blood Donation"); 7s. Cornucopia ("Famine Relief").

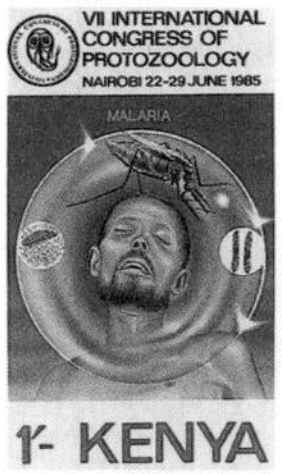

72 Man with Malaria

73 Repairing Water Pipes

1985. 7th International Congress of Protozoology, Nairobi. Multicoloured.
352 1s. Type **72** . . . . 2·00 25
353 3s. Child with Leishmaniasis 4·00 2·75
354 5s. Cow with Trypanosomiasis . . . . . 4·50 4·25
355 7s. Dog with Babesiosis . . . 7·50 8·50

1985. United Nations Women's Decade Conference. Multicoloured.
356 1s. Type **73** 20 10
357 3s. Traditional food preparation 60 70
358 5s. Basket-weaving . . . . . 75 1·25
359 7s. Dressmaking . . . . . . 1·00 3·00

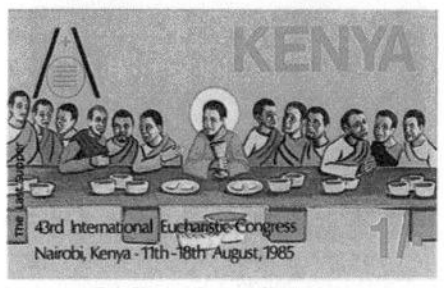

74 The Last Supper

1985. 43rd International Eucharistic Congress, Nairobi. Multicoloured.
360 1s. Type **74** 50 10
361 3s. Village family ("The Eucharist and the Christian Family") . . . . 2·25 2·00
362 5s. Congress altar, Uhuru Park . . . . 2·50 3·00
363 7s. St. Peter Claver's Church, Nairobi . . . . 3·00 5·00
MS364 117 × 80 mm. 25s. Pope John Paul II . . . . 8·00 7·00

75 Black Rhinoceros

1985. Endangered Animals. Multicoloured.
365 1s. Type **75** . . . . 2·75 40
366 3s. Cheetah . . . . 3·50 2·75
367 5s. De Brazza's monkey . . . 3·75 4·00
368 10s. Grevy's zebra . . . . . 7·50 9·00
MS369 129 × 122 mm. 25s. Endangered species (122 × 114 mm). Imperf . . . . 10·00 7·00

76 "Borassus aethiopum"

1986. Indigenous Trees. Multicoloured.
370 1s. Type **76** . . . . 1·00 15
371 3s. "Acacia xanthophloea" . . 3·25 2·50
372 5s. "Ficus natalensis" . . . . 4·25 4·25
373 7s. "Spathodea nilotica" . . . 5·50 8·50
MS374 117 × 96 mm. 25s. Landscape with trees (109 × 90 mm). Imperf 3·25 4·00

77 Dove and U.N. Logo (from poster)

78 Dribbling the Ball

1986. International Peace Year. Multicoloured.
375 1s. Type **77** 30 10
376 3s. U.N. General Assembly (horiz) . . . . 1·00 75
377 7s. Nuclear explosion . . . . 2·50 3·50
378 10s. Quotation from Wall of Isaiah, U.N. Building, New York (horiz) . . . . 6·00 6·50

1986. World Cup Football Championship, Mexico. Multicoloured.
379 1s. Type **78** . . . . 1·40 20
380 3s. Scoring from a penalty . . 3·00 1·25
381 5s. Tackling . . . . 3·75 2·25
382 7s. Cup winners . . . . . . 4·50 4·50
383 10s. Heading the ball . . . . 6·00 6·00
MS384 110 × 86 mm. 30s. Harambee Stars football team (102 × 78 mm). Imperf . . . . 4·25 3·75

79 Rural Post Office and Telephone

1986. "Expo '86" World Fair, Vancouver. Mult.
385 1s. Type **79** 50 15
386 3s. Container depot, Embakasi . . . . 2·75 1·75
387 5s. Piper Twin Commanche airplane landing at game park airstrip . . . . 5·50 3·00
388 7s. Container ship . . . . . 5·50 6·00
389 10s. Transporting produce to market . . . . 6·00 7·00

80 Telephone, Computer and Dish Aerial

1986. African Telecommunications. Multicoloured.
390 1s. Type **80** 35 10
391 3s. Telephones of 1876, 1936 and 1986 . . . . 1·00 85
392 5s. Dish aerial, satellite, telephones and map of Africa . . . . 1·25 1·25
393 7s. Kenyan manufacture of telecommunications equipment . . . . 1·75 2·25

81 Mashua

1986. Dhows of Kenya. Multicoloured.
394 1s. Type **81** . . . . 1·00 20
395 3s. Mtepe . . . . 2·50 1·50
396 5s. Dau La Mwao . . . . . 3·00 2·75
397 10s. Jahazi . . . . 5·50 6·00
MS398 118 × 80 mm. 25s. Lamu dhow and map of Indian Ocean 5·00 5·00

82 Nativity

83 Immunization

1986. Christmas. Multicoloured.
399 1s. Type **82** 40 10
400 3s. Shepherd and sheep . . . 1·25 55
401 5s. Angel and slogan "LOVE PEACE UNITY" (horiz) 1·90 1·40
402 7s. The Magi riding camels (horiz) . . . . 2·50 2·75

1987. 40th Anniv of UNICEF. Multicoloured.
403 1s. Type **83** 60 10
404 3s. Food and nutrition . . . 1·25 70
405 4s. Oral rehydration therapy 2·00 1·50
406 5s. Family planning . . . . 2·00 1·50
407 10s. Female literacy . . . . 2·75 4·00

84 Akamba Woodcarvers

1987. Tourism. Multicoloured.
408 1s. Type **84** 55 10
409 3s. Tourism on beach . . . . 3·25 1·75
410 5s. Tourist and guide at view point . . . . 4·00 4·00
411 7s. Pride of lions . . . . . . 6·00 7·00
MS412 118 × 81 mm. 30s. Geysers 11·00 11·00

1987. Ceremonial Costumes (3rd series). As T **45**. Multicoloured.
413 1s. Embu . . . . 1·00 10
414 3s. Kisii . . . . 2·75 70
415 5s. Samburu . . . . 3·25 1·75
416 7s. Taita . . . . 4·00 3·75
417 10s. Boran . . . . 4·25 4·25

85 Telecommunications by Satellite

1987. 10th Anniv of Kenya Posts and Telecommunications Corporation. Multicoloured.
418 1s. Type **85** 85 30
419 3s. Rural post office, Kajiado 1·90 1·90
420 4s. Awarding trophy, Welfare Sports . . . . 2·00 2·25
421 5s. Village and telephone box 2·25 2·50
422 7s. Speedpost labels and outline map of Kenya . . 3·25 4·00
MS423 110 × 80 mm. 25s. Corporation flag . . . . 2·50 2·75

86 Volleyball

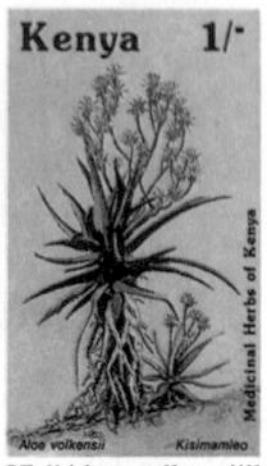

87 "Aloe volkensii"

1987. 4th All-Africa Games, Nairobi. Mult.
424 1s. Type **86** 20 10
425 3s. Cycling 85 45
426 4s. Boxing 35 75
427 5s. Swimming 40 85
428 7s. Steeplechasing . . . . . 60 1·60
MS429 117 × 80 mm. 30s. Kasarani Sports Complex (horiz) . . . . 2·50 2·75

1987. Medicinal Herbs. Multicoloured.
430 1s. Type **87** 75 10
431 3s. "Cassia didymobotrya" 1·75 1·00
432 5s. "Erythrina abyssinica" . . 2·50 2·25
433 7s. "Adenium obesum" . . . 3·00 3·75
434 10s. Herbalist's clinic . . . . 3·25 4·00

88 "Epamera sidus"

89 "Papilio rex"

1988. Butterflies. Multicoloured.
434a 10c. "Cyrestis camillus" . . 1·50 2·25
435 20c. Type **88** 35 70
436 40c. "Cynthia cardui" . . . 50 70
437 50c. "Colotis evippe" . . . 50 70
438 70c. "Precis westermanni" 50 70
439 80c. "Colias electo" 50 70
440 1s. "Eronia leda" 50 30
440a 1s.50 "Papilio dardanus" . . 5·50 30
441 2s. Type **89** 70 40
442 2s.50 "Colotis phisadia" . . . 75 90
443 3s. "Papilio desmondi" . . . 80 90
444 3s.50 "Papilio demodocus" 80 60
445 4s. "Papilio phorcas" 85 60
446 5s. "Charaxes druceanus" 90 70
447 7s. "Cymothoe teita" . . . 1·00 2·00
448 10s. "Charaxes zoolina" . . 1·00 1·75
449 20s. "Papilio dardanus" . . 1·25 3·25
450 40s. "Charaxes cithaeron" 2·00 6·00
The 10c. to 1s.50 are in the same format as T **88**.

90 Samburu Lodge and Crocodiles

1988. Kenyan Game Lodges. Multicoloured.
451 1s. Type **90** 70 10
452 3s. Naro Moru River Lodge and rock climbing . . . . 1·00 60
453 4s. Mara Serena Lodge and zebra with foal . . . . . . 1·25 1·40
454 5s. Voi Safari Lodge and buffalo . . . . 1·25 1·40
455 7s. Kilimanjaro Buffalo Lodge and giraffes . . . . 2·50 2·75
456 10s. Meru Mulika Lodge and rhinoceroses . . . . 2·75 3·25

91 Athletes and Stadium, Commonwealth Games, Brisbane, 1982

1988. "Expo '88" World Fair, Brisbane, and Bicent of Australian Settlement. Multicoloured.
457 1s. Type **91** 40 10
458 3s. Flying Doctor Service De Havilland Drover 3 and Piper Twin Commanche aircraft . . . . 2·75 1·25
459 4s. H.M.S. "Sirius" (frigate), 1788 . . . . 3·00 2·25
460 5s. Ostrich and emu . . . . 3·25 2·50
461 7s. Queen Elizabeth II, Pres. Arap Moi of Kenya and Prime Minister Hawke of Australia . . . . 3·00 3·75
MS462 117 × 80 mm. 30s. Entrance to Kenya Pavilion . . . . . . 1·90 2·00

92 W.H.O. Logo and Slogan

1988. 40th Anniv of W.H.O.
463 **92** 1s. blue, gold and deep blue 25 10
464 – 3s. multicoloured 85 70
465 – 5s. multicoloured . . . . . 1·25 1·25
466 – 7s. multicoloured . . . . . 1·75 2·25
DESIGNS: 3s. Mother with young son and nutritious food; 5s. Giving oral vaccine to baby; 7s. Village women drawing clean water from pump.

93 Handball

94 Calabashes

1988. Olympic Games, Seoul. Multicoloured.
467 1s. Type **93** 40 10
468 3s. Judo 65 55
469 5s. Weightlifting . . . . . . 85 1·00
470 7s. Javelin . . . . 1·00 1·50
471 10s. Relay racing . . . . . 1·40 2·25
MS472 110 × 78 mm. 30s. Tennis 2·25 2·50

1988. Kenyan Material Culture (1st issue). Mult.
473 1s. Type **94** 30 10
474 3s. Milk gourds 75 55
475 5s. Cooking pots (horiz) . . 85 85
476 7s. Winnowing trays (horiz) 1·25 1·60
477 10s. Reed baskets (horiz) . . 1·60 2·25
MS478 118 × 80 mm. 25s. Gourds, calabash and horn (horiz) . . . 1·50 1·60
See also Nos. 646/50.

95 Pres. Arap Moi taking Oath, 1978

1988. 10th Anniv of "Nyayo" Era. Mult.
479 1s. Type **95** 30 10
480 3s. Building soil conservation barrier . . . . 1·00 70
481 3s.50 Passengers boarding bus . . . . 3·00 1·40
482 4s. Metalwork shop . . . . 1·25 1·50
483 5s. Moi University, Eldoret 1·25 1·50
484 7s. Aerial view of hospital . . 3·00 3·50
485 10s. Pres. Arap Moi and Mrs. Thatcher at Kapsabet Telephone Exchange . . . 8·00 7·00

96 Kenya Flag

1988. 25th Anniv of Independence. Mult.
486 1s. Type **96** 75 10
487 3s. Coffee picking 80 50
488 5s. Proposed Kenya Posts and Telecommunications Headquarters building . . 1·00 1·10
489 7s. Kenya Airways Airbus Industrie A310-300 "Harambee Star" . . . . 5·50 3·00
490 10s. New diesel locomotive No. 9401 . . . . 7·50 5·00

97 Gedi Ruins, Malindi

1989. Historic Monuments. Multicoloured.
491 1s.20 Type **97** 50 10
492 3s.40 Vasco Da Gama Pillar, Malindi (vert) . . . . . . 1·25 1·25
493 4s.40 Ishiakani Monument, Kiunga . . . . 1·40 1·60
494 5s.50 Fort Jesus, Mombasa 1·60 1·90
495 7s.50 She Burnan Omwe, Lamu (vert) . . . . 2·50 3·50

98 125th Anniversary and Kenya Red Cross Logos

1989. 125th Anniv of International Red Cross. Multicoloured.
496 1s.20 Type **98** 50 10
497 3s.40 Red Cross workers with car crash victim . . . . . 1·25 90
498 4s.40 Disaster relief team distributing blankets . . . 1·40 1·40
499 5s.50 Henri Dunant (founder) 1·50 2·00
500 7s.70 Blood donor . . . . . 1·75 3·25

99 Female Giraffe and Calf

100 "Lentinus sajor-caju"

1989. Reticulated Giraffe. Multicoloured.
501 1s.20 Type **99** . . . . 1·75 30
502 3s.40 Giraffe drinking . . . 3·25 3·00
503 4s.40 Two giraffes . . . . . 3·75 4·00
504 5s.50 Giraffe feeding . . . . 4·50 5·50
MS505 80 × 110 mm. 30s. Designs as Nos. 501/4, but without face values . . . . 5·50 7·00
Designs from No. **MS**505 are without the Worldwide Fund for Nature logo.

1989. Mushrooms. Multicoloured.
506 1s.20 Type **100** . . . . . . 1·50 30
507 3s.40 "Agaricus bisporus" . . 2·50 2·00
508 4s.40 "Agaricus bisporus" (different) . . . . 2·75 2·50
509 5s.50 "Termitomyces schimperi" . . . . 3·50 3·50
510 7s.70 "Lentinus edodes" . . 4·25 5·50

101 Independence Monuments

1989. Birth Centenary of Jawaharlal Nehru (Indian statesman). Multicoloured.
511 1s.20 Type **101** . . . . . . 1·25 30
512 3s.40 Nehru with graduates and open book . . . . . 3·25 1·75
513 5s.50 Jawaharlal Nehru . . . 4·25 4·00
514 7s.70 Industrial complex and cogwheels . . . . 4·50 6·50

1989. Ceremonial Costumes (4th series). As T **45**. Multicoloured.
515 1s.20 Kipsigis . . . . 1·50 20
516 3s.40 Rabai . . . . 2·50 1·60
517 5s.50 Duruma . . . . 3·00 2·75
518 7s.70 Kuria . . . . 4·00 4·25
519 10s. Bajuni . . . . 4·25 6·00

102 EMS Speedpost Letters and Parcel

1990. 10th Anniv of Pan African Postal Union. Multicoloured.
520 1s.20 Type **102** 15 10
521 3s.40 Mail runner 35 35
522 5s.50 Mandera Post Office . . 55 70
523 7s.70 EMS Speedpost letters and globe (vert) . . . . . 80 1·60
524 10s. P.A.P.U. logo (vert) . . 90 1·60

103 "Stamp King" with Tweezers and Magnifying Glass

104 Moi Golden Cup

1990. "Stamp World London '90" International Stamp Exhibition.
525 **103** 1s.50 multicoloured . . . 35 10
526 – 4s.50 multicoloured . . . 1·25 1·25
527 – 6s.50 black, red and blue 1·40 1·60
528 – 9s. multicoloured . . . . 1·75 2·75
MS529 113 × 77 mm. Nos. 525/8 4·50 6·50
DESIGNS: 4s.50, Penny Black and Kenya Stamp Bureau postmark; 6s.50, Early British cancel-lations; 9s. Ronald Ngala Street Post Office, Nairobi.

1990. World Cup Football Championship, Italy. Trophies. Multicoloured.
530 1s.50 Type **104** 85 10
531 4s.50 East and Central Africa Challenge Cup . . . . . . 2·50 1·75
532 6s.50 East and Central Africa Club Championship Cup 3·50 3·50
533 9s. World Cup . . . . 3·75 6·00

105 K.A.N.U. Flag

1990. 30th Anniv of Kenya African National Union. Multicoloured.
534 1s.50 Type **105** 15 10
535 2s.50 Nyayo Monument . . . 15 15
536 4s.50 Party Headquarters . . 35 35
537 5s. Jomo Kenyatta (Party founder) 40 40
538 6s.50 President Arap Moi . . 50 85
539 9s. President Moi addressing rally . . . . 70 1·60
540 10s. Queue of voters . . . . 80 1·60

106 Desktop Computer

1990. 125th Anniv of I.T.U. Multicoloured.
541 1s.50 Type **106** 15 10
542 4s.50 Telephone switchboard assembly, Gilgil 35 50
543 6s.50 "125 YEARS" 45 1·00
544 9s. Urban and rural telecommunications 70 2·25

107 Queen Mother at British Museum, 1988

108 Queen Elizabeth at Hospital Garden Party, 1947

1990. 90th Birthday of Queen Elizabeth the Queen Mother.
545 **107** 10s. multicoloured 1·50 1·75
546 **108** 40s. black and green 3·25 5·00

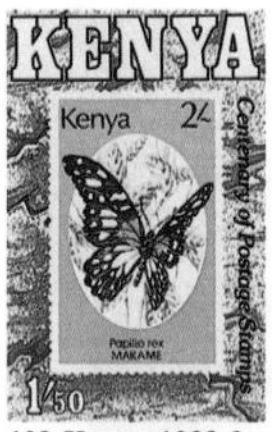
109 Kenya 1988 2s. Definitive

110 Adult Literacy Class

1990. Cent of Postage Stamps in Kenya. Mult.
547 1s.50 Type **109** 1·40 10
548 4s.50 East Africa and Uganda 1903 1a. 2·75 90
549 6s.50 British East Africa Co 1890 ½a. optd on G.B. 1d. 3·25 2·00
550 9s. Kenya and Uganda 1922 20c. 3·75 3·50
551 20s. Kenya, Uganda, Tanzania 1971 2s.50 railway commemorative 6·75 9·50

1990. International Literacy Year. Multicoloured.
552 1s.50 Type **110** 30 10
553 4s.50 Teaching by radio 1·00 1·10
554 6s.50 Technical training 1·25 1·75
555 9s. International Literacy Year logo 2·00 3·50

111 National Flag

1991. Olympic Games, Barcelona (1992) (1st issue). Multicoloured.
556 2s. Type **111** 1·10 10
557 6s. Basketball 2·75 1·40
558 7s. Hockey 2·75 2·25
559 8s.50 Table tennis 2·50 3·50
560 11s. Boxing 2·50 4·00
See also Nos. 580/4.

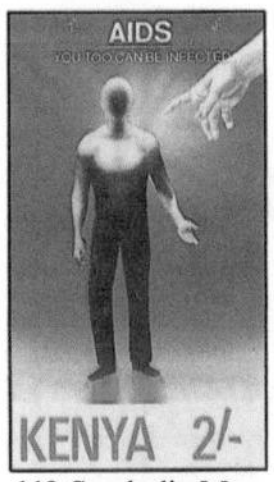
112 Symbolic Man and Pointing Finger

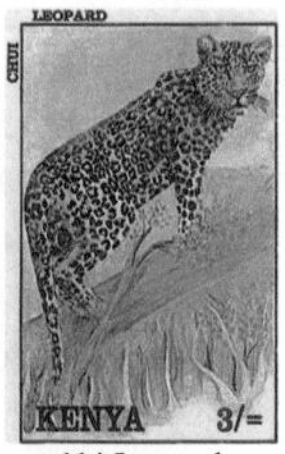
114 Leopard

113 Queen and Prince Philip with Pres. Moi

1992. AIDS Day. Multicoloured.
561 2s. Type **112** 1·00 15
562 6s. Victim and drugs 2·50 1·25
563 8s.50 Male and female symbols 3·00 3·50
564 11s. Symbolic figure and hypodermic syringe 4·50 5·00

1992. 40th Anniv of Queen Elizabeth II's Accession.
565 3s. Type **113** 50 10
566 8s. Marabou storks in tree 2·00 85
567 11s. Treetops Hotel 1·25 1·00
568 14s. Three portraits of Queen Elizabeth 1·25 1·25
569 40s. Queen Elizabeth II 2·50 4·50

1992. Kenya Wildlife. Multicoloured.
570 3s. Type **114** 1·75 30
571 8s. Lion 2·50 1·75
572 10s. Elephant 4·75 3·75
573 11s. Buffalo 2·50 3·75
574 14s. Black rhinoceros 6·50 7·00

115 International Harvester Safari Truck, 1926

1992. Vintage Cars. Multicoloured.
575 3s. Type **115** 1·75 20
576 8s. Fiat "509", 1924 3·00 1·75
577 10s. Hupmobile, 1923 3·25 2·75
578 11s. Chevrolet "Box Body", 1928 3·25 3·00
579 14s. Bentley/Parkward, 1934 3·75 4·25

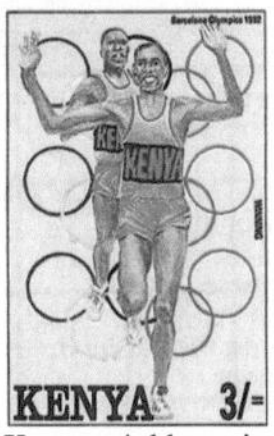
116 Kenyan Athlete winning Race

1992. Olympic Games, Barcelona (2nd issue). Mult.
580 3s. Type **116** 1·00 10
581 8s. Men's judo 2·00 1·25
582 10s. Kenyan women's volleyball players 2·50 2·25
583 11s. Kenyan men's 4 × 100 m relay runners 2·50 2·50
584 14s. Men's 10,000 m 2·75 4·00

117 Holy Child, Joseph and Animals

118 Asembo Bay Lighthouse, Lake Victoria

1992. Christmas. Multicoloured.
585 3s. Type **117** 30 10
586 8s. Mary with Holy Child 75 50
587 11s. Christmas tree 1·00 80
588 14s. Adoration of the Magi 1·25 2·00

1993. Lighthouses. Multicoloured.
589 3s. Type **118** 2·00 40
590 8s. Old Ras Serani lighthouse, Mombasa 3·00 1·50
591 11s. New Ras Serani lighthouse, Mombasa 3·25 2·75
592 14s. Gingira, Lake Victoria 4·00 4·50

119 Superb Starling

120 Yellow-billed Hornbill

1993. Birds. Multicoloured. (a) As T **119**.
593 50c. Type **119** 15 60
594 1s. Red and yellow barbet 25 50
594a 1s.50 Lady Ross's turaco 50 60
595 3s. Black-throated honeyguide ("Greater honeyguide") 50 10
595a 5s. African fish eagle 60 60
595b 6s. Vulturine guineafowl 3·50 75
596 7s. Malachite kingfisher 70 30
597 8s. Speckled pigeon 70 20
598 10s. Cinnamon-chested bee eater 70 20
599 11s. Scarlet-chested sunbird 70 25
600 14s. Bagalafecht weaver ("Reichenow's weaver") 75 30

(b) As T **120**.
601 50s. Type **120** 1·25 1·75
602 80s. Lesser flamingo 1·60 2·50
603 100s. Hadada ibis 1·90 2·75

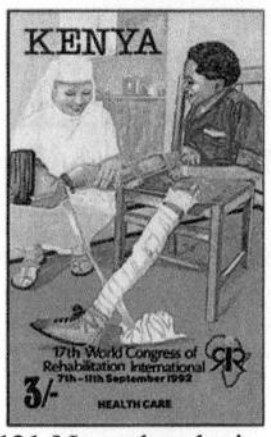
121 Nurse bandaging Boy's Legs

123 "Ansellia africana"

122 Maendeleo House, Nairobi

1993. 17th World Congress of Rehabilitation International.
611 **121** 3s. multicoloured 70 10
612 – 8s. multicoloured 1·10 70
613 – 10s. multicoloured 1·25 1·40
614 – 11s. multicoloured 1·25 1·60
615 – 14s. black, blue and orange 1·50 2·50
DESIGNS—HORIZ: 8s. Singing group on crutches; 10s. Vocational training; 11s. Wheelchair race. VERT: 14s. Congress emblem.

1994. 40th Anniv of Maendeleo Ya Wanawake Organization. Multicoloured.
616 3s.50 Type **122** 85 20
617 9s. Planting saplings 1·25 60
618 11s. Rural family planning clinic (vert) 1·50 1·25
619 12s.50 Women carrying water 1·75 2·25
620 15s.50 Improved wood-burning cooking stove (vert) 2·00 2·75

1994. Orchids. Multicoloured.
621 3s.50 Type **123** 1·75 30
622 9s. "Aerangis luteoalba var rhodosticta" 2·50 85
623 12s.50 "Polystachya bella" 2·75 2·25
624 15s.50 "Brachycorythis kalbreyeri" 3·00 3·00
625 20s. "Eulophia guineensis" 3·50 4·00

124 Emblem and K.I.C.C. Building, Nairobi

1994. 30th Anniv of African Development Bank. Multicoloured.
626 6s. Type **124** 75 25
627 25s. Isinya-Kajiado project 3·25 4·00

125 Kenyan Family

126 Paul Harris (founder of Rotary)

1994. International Year of the Family. Mult.
628 6s. Type **125** 75 10
629 14s.50 Nurse with mother and baby 2·75 1·40
630 20s. Schoolchildren and teacher (horiz) 3·00 3·25
631 25s. Emblem (horiz) 3·25 3·75

1994. 50th Anniv of Rotary Club of Mombasa. Multicoloured.
632 6s. Type **126** 30 10
633 14s.50 Anniversary logo 80 70
634 17s.50 Administering polio vaccine 1·10 1·75
635 20s. Women at stand pipe 1·10 1·90
636 25s. Rotary emblem 1·25 2·25

127 Donkey

128 Male Golfer in Bunker

1995. Kenya Society for Prevention of Cruelty to Animals. Multicoloured.
637 6s. Type **127** 30 10
638 14s.50 Cow 45 45
639 17s.50 Sheep 55 75
640 20s. Dog 1·50 2·00
641 25s. Cat 1·50 2·00

1995. Golf. Multicoloured.
642 6s. Type **128** 1·00 15
643 17s.50 Female golfer on fairway 2·25 1·75
644 20s. Male golfer teeing-off 2·25 2·75
645 25s. Head of golf club 2·50 3·00

129 Perfume Containers

1995. Kenyan Material Culture (2nd issue). Mult.
646 6s. Type **129** 30 10
647 14s.50 Basketry 75 75
648 17s.50 Preserving pots 85 1·25
649 20s. Gourds 1·10 1·75
650 25s. Wooden containers 1·25 2·00

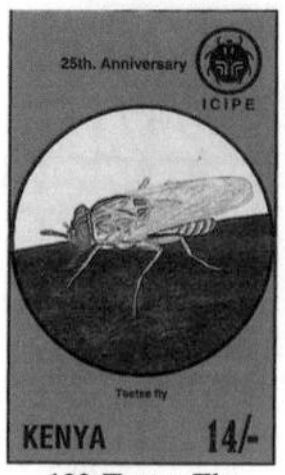
130 Tsetse Fly

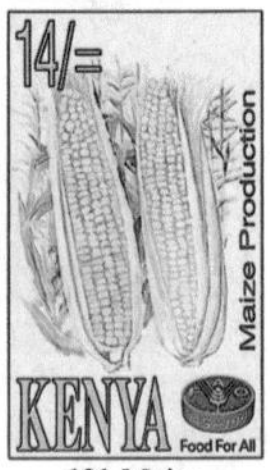
131 Maize

1995. 25th Anniv of I.C.I.P.E. Insect Pests. Multicoloured.
651 14s. Type **130** 50 30
652 26s. Tick 80 80
653 32s. Wild silkmoth 95 1·10
654 33s. Maize borer 1·00 1·75
655 40s. Locust 1·60 2·50

1995. 50th Anniv of F.A.O. Multicoloured.
656 14s. Type **131** 75 30
657 28s. Cattle 1·25 80
658 32s. Chickens 1·75 1·60
659 33s. Fisherman with catch 2·00 2·50
660 40s. Fruit 2·50 3·50

132 Kenyan and United Nations Flags over Headquarters, Nairobi

1995. 50th Anniv of United Nations.
661 **132** 23s. multicoloured 85 70
662 – 26s. multicoloured 95 95
663 – 32s. multicoloured 1·25 1·40
664 – 40s. blue, red and black 1·75 2·50
DESIGNS: 26s. Multi-racial group with emblem; 32s. United Nations helmet; 40s. 50th anniversary emblem.

133 Swimming

1996. Olympic Games, Atlanta (1st issue). Events and Gold Medal Winners. Multicoloured.
665 14s. Type **133** 1·00 1·10
666 20s. Archery 1·00 1·10
667 20s. Weightlifting 1·00 1·10
668 20s. Pole vault (vert) 1·00 1·10
669 20s. Equestrian (vert) 1·00 1·10
670 20s. Diving (vert) 1·00 1·10
671 20s. Sprinting (vert) 1·00 1·10
672 20s. Athlete carrying Olympic Torch (vert) 1·00 1·10
673 20s. Hurdling (vert) 1·00 1·10

674 20s. Kayak (vert) . . . . . 1·00 1·10
675 20s. Boxing (vert) . . . . . 1·00 1·10
676 20s. Gymnastics (vert) . . . 1·00 1·10
677 25s. Greg Louganis (U.S.A.) (diving, 1984 and 1988) (vert) . . . . 1·00 1·10
678 25s. Cassius Clay (U.S.A.) (boxing, 1960) (vert) . . . 1·00 1·10
679 25s. Nadia Comaneci (Rumania) (gymnastics, 1980) (vert) . . . . 1·00 1·10
680 25s. Daley Thompson (Great Britain) (decathlon, 1980 and 1984) (vert) . . . . . 1·00 1·10
681 25s. Kipchoge Keino (Kenya) (running, 1968) (vert) . . . 1·00 1·10
682 25s. Kornelia Enders (Germany) (swimming, 1976) (vert) . . . . 1·00 1·10
683 25s. Jackie Joyner-Kersee (U.S.A.) (long jump, 1988) (vert) . . . . 1·00 1·10
684 25s. Michael Jordan (U.S.A.) (basketball, 1984) (vert) . . 1·00 1·10
685 25s. Shun Fujimoto (Japan) (gymnastics, 1972) (vert) 1·00 1·10
686 32s. Javelin . . . . 1·00 1·10
687 40s. Fencing . . . . 1·10 1·25
688 50s. Discus . . . . 1·40 1·60
MS689 Two sheets, each 79 × 109 mm. (a) 100s. Athlete with medal (vert). (b) 100s. Athlete carrying Olympic Torch (different) (vert) Set of 2 sheets . . . . . 7·00 9·00

Nos. 665/7 with 686/8, 668/76 and 677/85 respectively were printed together, se-tenant, forming composite designs.

See also Nos. 702/6.

134 Lions

135 Water Buck

1996. Tourism. Multicoloured. (a) Designs as T **134**.
690 6s. Type **134** 30 10
691 14s. Mt. Kenya 35 30
692 20s. Sail boards 55 70
693 25s. Hippopotami . . . . . 1·25 1·40
694 40s. Couple in traditional dress . . . . 1·25 2·25
MS695 100 × 80 mm. 50s. Female giraffe and calf (vert) . . . . . 2·50 3·00

(b) Horiz designs as T **135**.
696 20s. Type **135** . . . . 1·25 1·50
697 20s. Pair of rhinoceroses . . 1·25 1·50
698 20s. Cheetah . . . . 1·25 1·50
699 20s. Group of oryx . . . . . 1·25 1·50
700 20s. Pair of giraffes . . . . . 1·25 1·50
701 20s. Monkey and bongo . . 1·25 1·50

136 Women's 10,000 Metres

137 Red Cross Emblem

1996. Olympic Games, Atlanta (2nd issue). Multicoloured.
702 6s. Type **136** 25 10
703 14s. Steeple-chasing 45 30
704 20s. Victorious athletes with flag 70 80
705 25s. Boxing . . . . 70 1·00
706 40s. Men's 1500 m . . . . . 1·25 2·00

1996. Kenya Red Cross Society.
707 **137** 6s. red and black 25 10
708 – 14s. multicoloured 45 35
709 – 20s. multicoloured 70 80
710 – 25s. multicoloured 80 95
711 – 40s. multicoloured . . . . 1·40 2·00

DESIGNS: 14s. Giving blood; 20s. Immunization; 25s. Refugee child with food; 40s. Cleaning the environment.

138 Impala

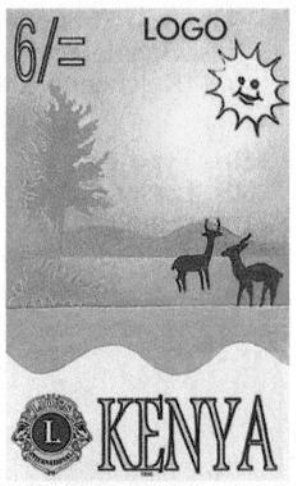

139 Kenya Lions Club Logo

1996. East African Wildlife Society. Multicoloured.
712 6s. Type **138** 20 10
713 20s. Colobus monkey 60 70
714 25s. African elephant . . . . 1·75 1·50
715 40s. Black rhinoceros . . . . 2·50 3·50

1996. Work of Lions Club International in Kenya. Multicoloured.
716 6s. Type **139** 15 10
717 14s. Eye operation 55 45
718 20s. Two disabled children in wheelchair . . . . 70 1·25
719 25s. Modern ambulance . . . 1·00 1·50

140 C.O.M.E.S.A. Logo

1997. Inauguration of Common Market for Eastern and Southern Africa. Multicoloured.
720 6s. Type **140** 15 15
721 20s. Kenyan flag and logo . . 85 1·10

141 "Haplochromis cinctus"

1997. Endangered Species. Lake Victoria Cichlid Fishes. Multicoloured.
722 25s. Type **141** . . . . 75 1·00
723 25s. "Haplochromis" "Orange Rock Hunter" . . 75 1·00
724 25s. "Haplochromis chilotes" 75 1·00
725 25s. "Haplochromis nigricans" . . . . 75 1·00

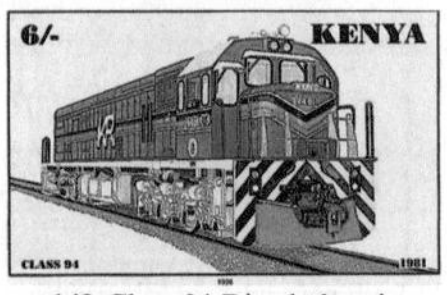

142 Class 94 Diesel-electric Locomotive No. 9401, 1981

1997. Kenya Railway Locomotives. Multicoloured.
726 6s. Type **142** 65 15
727 14s. Class 87 diesel-electric No. 8721, 1964 . . . . . 95 40
728 20s. Class 59 Garratt steam No. 5905, 1955 . . . . . 1·40 65
729 25s. Class 57 Garratt steam No. 5701, 1939 . . . . . 1·40 1·00
730 30s. Class 23 steam No. 2305, 1923 . . . . 1·50 1·60
731 40s. Class 10 steam No. 1001, 1914 . . . . 1·75 2·25

143 Orange

145 Girl Guides Anniversary Logo

144 Crocodile

1997. Fruits of East Africa. Multicoloured.
732 6s. Type **143** 55 15
733 14s. Pineapple . . . . 1·10 45
734 20s. Mango . . . . 1·75 1·60
735 25s. Pawpaw . . . . 2·00 2·25

1997. Local Tourist Attractions. Multicoloured.
736 10s. Type **144** . . . . 1·10 25
737 27s. Lake Bogoria hot springs 1·75 1·25
738 30s. Warthogs . . . . 1·75 1·60
739 33s. Windsurfing . . . . . . 1·75 1·90
740 42s. Traditional huts . . . . 1·90 3·00

1997. 75th Anniv of Kenyan Girl Guides Anniversary. Multicoloured.
741 10s. Type **145** 40 70
742 10s. Lord Baden-Powell . . . 40 70
743 27s. Girl guides hiking . . . 75 1·10
744 27s. Rangers in camp . . . . 75 1·10
745 33s. Girl guides planting seedlings . . . . 85 1·25
746 33s. Boy scouts giving first aid . . . . 85 1·25
747 42s. Boy scouts in camp . . . 90 1·25
748 42s. Brownies entertaining the elderly . . . . 90 1·25

146 Portuguese Ships arriving at Malindi

1998. 500th Anniv of Vasco da Gama's Arrival at Malindi. Multicoloured.
749 10s. Type **146** 45 25
750 24s. Portuguese ships 90 70
751 33s. Map of Africa . . . . . 1·10 1·50
752 42s. Vasco da Gama Pillar and harbour . . . . 1·25 1·90

147 Lion

1998. 18th Anniv of Pan African Postal Union. Wildlife. Multicoloured.
753 10s. Type **147** . . . . 1·00 25
754 24s. Buffalo . . . . 1·40 70
755 33s. Grant's gazelle . . . . . 1·60 2·00
756 42s. Cheetah . . . . 2·75 3·50
MS757 94 × 76 mm. 50s. Hirola gazelle . . . . 2·00 2·50

148 Pres. Arap Moi taking Oath, 1998

1998. Daniel Arap Moi's 5th Presidential Term.
758 **148** 14s. multicoloured . . . . 1·25 80

149 Leatherback Turtle

2000. Turtles. Multicoloured.
759 17s. Type **149** 90 35
760 20s. Green sea turtle . . . . 1·00 40
761 30s. Hawksbill turtle . . . . 1·40 1·00
762 47s. Olive Ridley turtle . . . 2·00 2·00
763 59s. Loggerhead turtle . . . 2·50 3·00

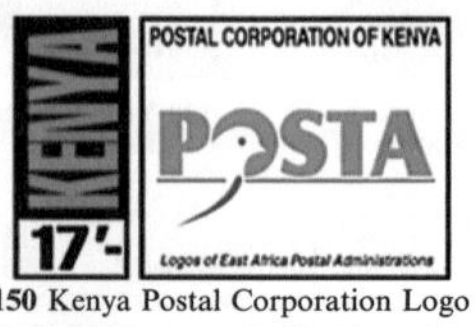

150 Kenya Postal Corporation Logo

2000. East Africa Postal Administrations' Co-operation. Multicoloured (except 17s.).
764 17s. Type **150** (red, blue and black) 65 35
765 35s. Uganda Post Ltd logo 1·25 1·00
766 50s. Tanzania Posts Corporation logo . . . . 1·75 2·25
MS767 100 × 80 mm. 70s. As 50s. 2·25 2·75

151 Cotton

152 Tea

2001. Crops. Multicoloured. (a) Vert designs as T **151**.
768 2s. Type **151** 10 10
769 4s. Bananas 10 10
770 5s. Avocado 10 10
771 6s. Cassava 10 10
772 8s. Arrowroot 10 15
773 10s. Pawpaw 15 20
774 19s. Orange 25 30
775 20s. Pyrethrum 30 35
776 30s. Groundnuts 40 45
777 35s. Coconut 50 55
778 40s. Sisal 55 60
779 50s. Cashew nuts 70 75

(b) Vert designs as T **152**.
780 60s. Type **152** 85 95
781 80s. Maize . . . . 1·10 1·20
782 100s. Coffee . . . . 1·40 1·50
783 200s. Finger millet . . . . . 2·75 3·00
784 400s. Sorghum . . . . 5·50 5·75
785 500s. Sugar cane . . . . . . 7·00 7·25

153 Source of the Nile, Jinja, Uganda

2002. Historical Sites of East Africa. Multicoloured.
786 19s. Type **153** 60 35
787 35s. Kamu Fort, Kenya (35 × 35 mm) . . . . . . 1·00 90
788 40s. Olduvai Gorge, Tanzania 2·00 1·75
789 50s. Thimlich Ohinga (ancient settlement), Kenya (35 × 35 mm) . . . . . . 2·00 2·25

154 Section of Mombasa Road

2003. 40th Anniv of Kenya—China Diplomatic Relations. Multicoloured.
790 21s. Type **154** 60 40
791 66s. Kasarani Stadium . . . 1·50 1·75

OFFICIAL STAMPS

Intended for use on official correspondence of the Kenya Government only, but there is no evidence that they were so used.

1964. Stamps of 1963 optd **OFFICIAL**.
O21 **46** 5c. multicoloured 10
O22 – 10c. brown 10
O23 – 15c. mauve . . . . 1·25
O24 – 20c. black and green . . . 20
O25 – 30c. black and yellow . . 30
O26 – 50c. red, black and green 2·75

POSTAGE DUE STAMPS

D 3

1967.
D13 **D 3** 5c. red . . . . 15 2·75
D41 10c. green . . . . 40 1·50
D42 20c. blue . . . . 40 1·50
D44 30c. brown 15 75
D45 40c. purple 15 75
D49 50c. green 10 10
D46 80c. red 20 90
D50 1s. orange 10 10
D51 2s. violet 10 10
D52 3s. blue 10 10
D53 5s. red 10 10

KENYA, UGANDA AND TANGANYIKA (TANZANIA) Pt. 1

From 1903 joint issues were made for British East Africa (later Kenya) and Uganda. In 1933 the postal administrations of Kenya, Uganda and Tanganyika were combined.

On independence of the constituent territories in the 1960s the postal administration became the East African Posts and Telecommunications Corporation. As well as separate issues for each state (q.v.), joint commemorative issues (which however were not valid in Zanzibar) were made until the dissolution of the Corporation in 1977.

1903. 16 annas = 100 cents = 1 rupee.
1922. 100 cents = 1 shilling.

1

2

1903.

17a	1	½a. green	8·00	3·25
2		1a. grey and red	1·75	1·00
19a		2a. purple	2·75	2·75
21		2½a. blue	7·50	17·00
22a		3a. purple and green	3·75	32·00
23		4a. green and black	7·50	18·00
24		5a. grey and brown	8·00	15·00
25		8a. grey and blue	7·00	8·50
9	2	1r. green	16·00	55·00
27		2r. purple	38·00	55·00
28		3r. green and black	55·00	£100
29		4r. grey and green	75·00	£140
30		5r. grey and red	85·00	£110
31		10r. grey and blue	£170	£200
15		20r. grey and stone	£550	£1100
16		50r. grey and brown	£1400	£2500

1907.

34	1	1c. brown	2·50	15
35		3c. green	13·00	70
36		6c. red	2·75	10
37		10c. lilac and olive	9·00	8·50
38		12c. purple	10·00	2·75
39		15c. blue	22·00	9·00
40		25c. green and black	8·50	7·00
41		50c. green and brown	12·00	12·00
42		75c. grey and blue	4·50	32·00

1912. As T **1/2** but portraits of King George V.

44		1c. black	30	1·75
45		3c. green	2·00	60
46		6c. red	70	60
47		10c. orange	2·00	50
48		12c. grey	2·75	50
49		15c. blue	2·75	80
50		25c. black and red on yellow	50	1·25
51		50c. black and lilac	1·50	1·25
52b		75c. black and green	6·00	7·50
53		1r. black and green	1·75	4·25
54		2r. red and black on blue	20·00	38·00
55		3r. violet and green	20·00	90·00
56		4r. red and green on yellow	45·00	£100
57		5r. blue and purple	48·00	£140
58		10r. red and green on green	£120	£190
59		20r. black and purple on red	£325	£325
60		20r. purple and blue on blue	£375	£425
61		50r. red and green	£600	£650
62		100r. purple and black on red	£4500	£2500
63		500r. green and red on green	£18000	

1919. No. 46 surch **4 cents**.

64		4c. on 6c. red	1·25	15

6

7

1922.

76	6	1c. brown	1·00	3·00
77		5c. violet	3·75	75
78		5c. green	2·00	50
79		10c. green	1·50	30
80		10c. black	4·00	20
81a		12c. black	4·50	26·00
82		15c. red	1·25	10
83		20c. orange	3·25	10
84		30c. blue	2·00	50
85		50c. grey	2·50	10
86		75c. olive	5·00	9·00
87	7	1s. green	4·25	2·50
88		2s. purple	8·00	9·50
89		2s.50 brown	18·00	75·00
90		3s. grey	17·00	6·50
91		4s. grey	22·00	85·00
92		5s. red	22·00	22·00
93		7s.50 orange	75·00	£160
94		10s. blue	48·00	48·00
95		£1 black and orange	£160	£250
96		£2 green and purple	£650	£1000
97		£3 purple and yellow	£900	
98		£4 black and mauve	£1700	
99		£5 black and blue	£1900	
100		£10 black and green	£8500	
101		£20 red and green	£17000	
102		£25 black and red	£21000	
103		£50 black and brown	£28000	
104		£75 purple and grey	£70000	
105		£100 red and black	£75000	

8 South African Crowned Cranes

9 Dhow on Lake Victoria

1935. King George V.

110	8	1c. black and brown	1·00	1·50
111	9	5c. black and green	1·75	40
112	–	10c. black and yellow	3·75	60
113	–	15c. black and red	2·25	10
114	8	20c. black and orange	3·50	20
115	–	30c. black and blue	2·50	1·00
116	9	50c. purple and black	1·75	10
117	–	65c. black and brown	3·00	2·00
118	–	1s. black and green	1·50	75
119	–	2s. red and purple	5·50	4·00
120	–	3s. blue and black	7·00	15·00
121	–	5s. black and red	17·00	27·00
122	8	10s. purple and blue	65·00	85·00
123	–	£1 black and red	£160	£190

DESIGNS—VERT: 10c., £1 Lion; 30c., 5s. Nile Railway Bridge, Ripon Falls. HORIZ: 15c., 2s. Kilimanjaro; 65c. Mt. Kenya; 1s., 3s. Lake Naivasha.

14a Windsor Castle

1935. Silver Jubilee.

124	14a	20c. blue and olive	75	10
125		30c. brown and blue	2·50	3·50
126		65c. green and blue	1·75	2·75
127		1s. grey and purple	2·00	2·50

14b King George VI and Queen Elizabeth

1937. Coronation.

128	14b	5c. green	20	10
129		20c. orange	40	30
130		30c. blue	60	1·75

15 Dhow on Lake Victoria

1938. As 1935 (except 10c.) but with portrait of King George VI as in T **15**.

131a	8	1c. black and brown	30	50
132	15	5c. black and green	4·25	50
133		5c. brown and orange	50	3·25
134	–	10c. brown and orange	2·25	10
135	–	10c. black and green	30	1·00
136	–	10c. brown and grey	1·25	55
137a	–	15c. black and red	5·50	3·75
138	–	15c. black and green	2·00	4·25
139b	8	20c. black and orange	6·50	10
140	15	25c. black and red	1·25	2·25
141b	–	30c. black and blue	2·75	10
142	–	30c. purple and brown	1·50	40
143	8	40c. black and blue	1·75	3·25
144e	15	50c. purple and black	6·00	55
145a	–	1s. black and brown	11·00	30
146b	–	2s. red and purple	21·00	30
147ac	–	3s. blue and black	26·00	3·50
148b	–	5s. black and red	26·00	1·25
149b	8	10s. purple and blue	42·00	3·75
150a	–	£1 black and red	23·00	16·00

DESIGN—HORIZ: 10c. Lake Naivasha.

1941. Stamps of South Africa surch **KENYA TANGANYIKA UGANDA** and value. Alternate stamps inscr in English or Afrikaans.

151	7	5c. on 1d. black and red	1·25	15
152	22a	10c. on 3d. blue	4·00	30
153	8	20c. on 6d. green and red	3·50	20
154	–	70c. on 1s. brown and blue (No. 120)	17·00	45

Prices for Nos. 151/4 are for unused pairs and used singles.

1946. Victory. As T **60** of Jamaica.

155		20c. orange	30	10
156		30c. blue	30	75

1948. Silver Wedding. As T **61/62** of Jamaica.

157		20c. orange	15	10
158		£1 red	38·00	55·00

1949. U.P.U. As T **63/3** of Jamaica.

159		20c. orange	15	10
160		30c. blue	1·75	1·75
161		50c. grey	45	20
162		1s. brown	50	40

1952. Visit of Queen Elizabeth II (as Princess) and Duke of Edinburgh. As Nos. 135 and 145ba but inscr "ROYAL VISIT 1952".

163		10c. black and green	10	1·50
164		1s. black and brown	30	2·25

1953. Coronation. As T **71** of Jamaica.

165		20c. black and orange	15	10

1954. Royal Visit. As No. 171 but inscr "ROYAL VISIT 1954".

166	18	30c. black and blue	40	15

18 Owen Falls Dam

21 Queen Elizabeth II

20 Royal Lodge, Sagana

1954.

167	18	5c. black and brown	75	50
168	–	10c. red	1·00	10
169a	–	15c. black and blue	55	1·25
170	–	20c. black and orange	1·25	10
171	18	30c. black and blue	80	10
172	–	40c. brown	1·25	75
173	–	50c. purple	2·00	10
174	–	65c. green and purple	2·75	1·50
175	–	1s. black and purple	1·75	10
176	–	1s.30 lilac and orange	10·00	10
177	–	2s. black and green	8·00	80
178	–	5s. black and orange	18·00	2·25
179	20	10s. black and blue	24·00	3·00
180	21	£1 red and black	16·00	13·00

DESIGNS—VERT (Size as Type **18**): 10, 50c. Giraffe; 20, 40c., 1s. Lion. HORIZ: 15c., 1s.30, 5s. Elephants; 65c., 2s. Mt. Kilimanjaro.

25 Map of E. Africa showing Lakes

1958. Centenary of Discovery of Lakes Tanganyika and Victoria by Burton and Speke.

181	25	40c. blue and green	30	40
182		1s.30 green and purple	30	1·40

26 Sisal

29 Queen Elizabeth II

28 Mt. Kenya and Giant Plants

1960.

183	26	5c. blue	10	15
184	–	10c. green	10	10
185	–	15c. purple	30	10
186	–	20c. mauve	20	10
187	–	25c. green	3·25	1·25
188	–	30c. red	15	10
189	–	40c. blue	15	20
190	–	50c. violet	15	10
191	–	65c. olive	30	1·50
192	28	1s. violet and purple	80	10
193	–	1s.30 brown and red	2·75	15
194	–	2s. indigo and blue	3·00	40
195	–	2s.50 olive and turquoise	5·00	2·75
196	–	5s. red and purple	3·75	60
197	–	10s. myrtle and green	8·00	6·50
198	29	20s. blue and lake	16·00	22·00

DESIGNS—As Type **26**: 10c. Cotton; 15c. Coffee; 20c. Blue wildebeest; 25c. Ostrich; 30c. Thomson's gazelle; 40c. Manta; 50c. Common zebra; 65c. Cheetah. As Type **28**: 1s.30, Murchison Falls and hippopotamus; 2s. Mt. Kilimanjaro and giraffe; 2s.50, Candelabra tree and black rhinoceros; 5s. Crater Lake and Mountains of the Moon; 10s. Ngorongoro Crater and African buffalo.

30 Land Tillage

1963. Freedom from Hunger.

199	30	15c. blue and olive	10	10
200	–	30c. brown and yellow	20	10
201	30	50c. blue and orange	30	10
202	–	1s.30 brown and blue	55	1·75

DESIGN: 30c., 1s.30, African with corncob.

31 Scholars and Open Book

1963. Founding of East African University.

203	31	30c. multicoloured	10	10
204		1s.30 multicoloured	20	20

32 Red Cross Emblem

1963. Centenary of Red Cross.

205	32	30c. red and blue	1·00	10
206		50c. red and brown	1·25	65

35 East African "Flags"

1964. Olympic Games, Tokyo.

207	–	30c. yellow and purple	10	10
208	–	50c. purple and yellow	15	10
209	35	1s.30 yellow, green and blue	40	10
210		2s.50 mauve, violet & blue	45	1·40

DESIGN—VERT: 30, 50c. Chrysanthemum emblem.

36 Rally Badge

1965. 13th East African Safari Rally.

211	36	30c. black, yellow & turq	10	10
212		50c. black, yellow & brown	10	10
213	–	1s.30 green, ochre and blue	25	10
214	–	2s.50 green, red and blue	40	1·50

DESIGN: 1s.30, 2s.50, Cars en route.

38 I.T.U. Emblem and Symbols

1965. Centenary of I.T.U. "I.T.U." and symbols in gold.

215	38	30c. brown and mauve	15	10
216		50c. brown and grey	15	10
217		1s.30 brown and blue	40	10
218		2s.50 brown and turquoise	75	2·25

39 I.C.Y. Emblem

1965. International Co-operation Year.

219	39	30c. green and gold	10	10
220		50c. black and gold	15	10
221		1s.30 blue and gold	30	10
222		2s.50 red and gold	75	2·50

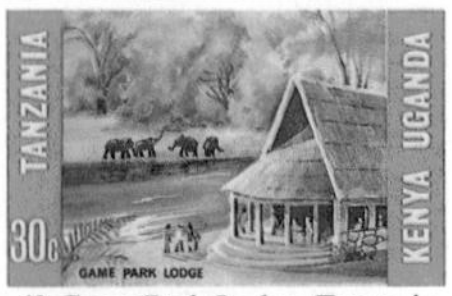

40 Game Park Lodge, Tanzania

1966. Tourism. Multicoloured.
223 30c. Type **40** 15 10
224 50c. Murchison Falls, Uganda 50 10
225 1s.30 Lesser flamingoes, Lake Nakuru, Kenya . . . . . 2·75 30
226 2s.50 Deep sea fishing, Tanzania . . . . 1·60 2·25

41 Games Emblem

1966. 8th British Empire and Commonwealth Games, Jamaica.
227 **41** 30c. multicoloured 10 10
228 50c. multicoloured 15 10
229 1s.30 multicoloured 20 10
230 2s.50 multicoloured . . . . 35 1·50

42 UNESCO Emblem

1966. 20th Anniv of UNESCO.
231 **42** 30c. black, green and red 30 10
232 50c. black, green and brown 35 10
233 1s.30 black, green and grey 1·00 15
234 2s.50 black, green & yellow 1·75 3·75

43 De Havilland Dragon Rapide

1967. 21st Anniv of East African Airways.
235 **43** 30c. violet, blue and green 30 10
236 – 50c. multicoloured 40 10
237 – 1s.30 multicoloured 85 30
238 – 2s.50 multicoloured . . . . 1·25 2·50
DESIGNS: 50c. Vickers Super VC-10; 1s.30, Hawker Siddeley Comet 4B; 2s.50, Fokker Friendship.

44 Pillar Tomb

1967. Archaeological Relics.
239 **44** 30c. ochre, black and purple 15 10
240 – 50c. red, black and brown 65 10
241 – 1s.30 black, yellow & green 85 15
242 – 2s.50 black, ochre and red 1·40 2·50
DESIGNS: 50c. Rock painting; 1s.30, Clay head; 2s.50, Proconsul skull.

48 Unified Symbols of Kenya, Tanzania and Uganda

1967. Foundation of East African Community.
243 **48** 5s. gold, black and grey . . 40 1·25

49 Mountaineering

1968. Mountains of East Africa. Multicoloured.
244 30c. Type **49** 15 10
245 50c. Mt. Kenya 30 10
246 1s.30 Mt. Kilimanjaro . . . 60 10
247 2s.50 Ruwenzori Mountains 90 2·25

50 Family and Rural Hospital

1968. World Health Organization.
248 **50** 30c. green, lilac and brown 10 10
249 – 50c. slate, lilac and black 15 10
250 – 1s.30 brown, lilac & lt brown 20 15
251 – 2s.50 grey, black and lilac 30 1·90
DESIGNS: 50c. Family and nurse; 1s.30, Family and microscope; 2s.50, Family and hypodermic syringe.

51 Olympic Stadium, Mexico City

1968. Olympic Games, Mexico.
252 **51** 30c. green and black . . . 10 10
253 – 50c. green and black . . . 15 10
254 – 1s.30 red, black and grey 25 15
255 – 2s.50 sepia and brown . . 35 1·50
DESIGNS—HORIZ: 50c. High-diving boards; 1s.30, Running tracks. VERT: 2s.50, Boxing ring.

52 "Umoja" (railway ferry)

1969. Water Transport.
256 **52** 30c. blue and grey 30 10
257 – 50c. multicoloured 35 10
258 – 1s.30 green and blue . . . 60 20
259 – 2s.50 orange and blue . . . 1·10 3·25
DESIGNS: 50c. S.S. "Harambee"; 1s.30, M.V. "Victoria"; 2s.50, "St. Michael".

53 I.L.O. Emblem and Agriculture

1969. 50th Anniv of Int Labour Organization.
260 **53** 30c. black, green and yellow 10 10
261 – 50c. multicoloured 10 10
262 – 1s.30 black, brown and orange 10 10
263 – 2s.50 black, blue & turq . . 20 90
DESIGNS—I.L.O. emblem and: 50c. Building-work; 1s.30, Factory-workers; 2s.50, Shipping.

54 Pope Paul VI and Ruwenzori Mountains

55 Euphorbia Tree shaped as Africa, and Emblem

1969. Visit of Pope Paul VI to Uganda.
264 **54** 30c. black, gold and blue 15 10
265 70c. black, gold and red . . 20 10
266 1s.50 black, gold and blue 25 20
267 2s.50 black, gold and violet 30 1·40

1969. 5th Anniv of African Development Bank.
268 **55** 30c. green and gold 10 10
269 70c. green, gold and violet 15 10
270 1s.50 green, gold and blue 30 10
271 2s.50 green, gold & brown 35 1·00

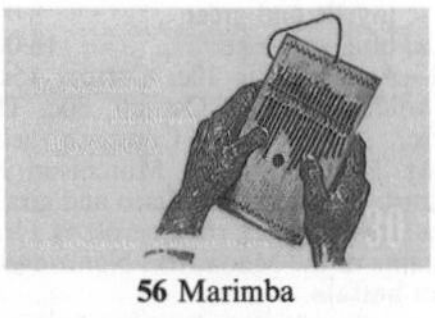

56 Marimba

1970. Musical Instruments.
272 **56** 30c. buff and brown . . . 15 10
273 – 70c. green, brown & yellow 25 10
274 – 1s.50 brown and yellow . . 50 10
275 – 2s.50 orange, yellow and brown . . . . 75 2·50
DESIGNS: 70c. Amadinda; 1s.50, Nzomari; 2s.50, Adeudeu.

57 Satellite Earth Station

1970. Inauguration of Satellite Earth Station.
276 **57** 30c. multicoloured 10 10
277 – 70c. multicoloured 15 10
278 – 1s.50 black, violet & orge 25 10
279 – 2s.50 multicoloured . . . . 55 2·25
DESIGNS: 70c. Transmitter—daytime; 1s.50, Transmitter—night; 2s. 50, Earth and satellite.

58 Athlete

1970. 9th Commonwealth Games.
280 **58** 30c. brown and black . . . 10 10
281 70c. green, brown and black 10 10
282 1s.50 lilac, brown and black 15 10
283 2s.50 blue, brown and black . . . . 20 1·25

59 "25" and U.N. Emblem

1970. 25th Anniv of United Nations.
284 **59** 30c. multicoloured 10 10
285 70c. multicoloured 10 10
286 1s.50 multicoloured 20 10
287 2s.50 multicoloured . . . . 45 2·00

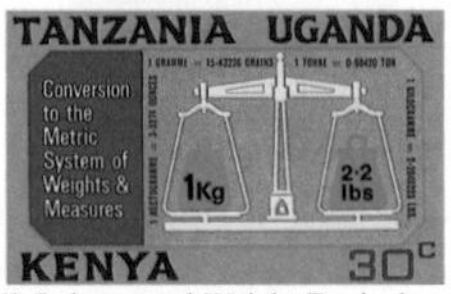

60 Balance and Weight Equivalents

1970. Conversion to Metric System. Multicoloured.
288 30c. Type **60** 10 10
289 70c. Fahrenheit and Centigrade thermometers 10 10
290 1s.50 Petrol pump and liquid capacities 15 10
291 2s.50 Surveyors and land measures . . . . 35 2·00

61 Class 11 Tank Locomotive

1971. Railway Transport. Multicoloured.
292 30c. Type **61** 30 10
293 70c. Class 90 diesel-electric locomotive 35 10
294 1s.50 Class 59 steam locomotive 50 20
295 2s.50 Class 30 steam locomotive . . . . 75 2·25
MS296 120 × 88 mm. Nos. 292/5 5·50 10·00

62 Syringe and Cow

1971. O.A.U. Rinderpest Campaign.
297 **62** 30c. black, brown and green 10 10
298 – 70c. black, blue and brown 10 10
299 **62** 1s.50 black, purple & brn 15 10
300 – 2s.50 black, red and brown 25 70
DESIGN: 70c., 2s.50, as Type **62** but with bull facing right.

63 Livingstone meets Stanley

1971. Centenary of Livingstone and Stanley meeting at Ujiji.
301 **63** 5s. multicoloured 30 75

64 Pres. Nyerere and Supporters

1971. 10th Anniv of Tanzanian Independence. Multicoloured.
302 30c. Type **64** 10 10
303 70c. Ujamaa village 15 10
304 1s.50 Dar-es-Salaam University 30 25
305 2s.50 Kilimanjaro International Airport . . . 1·00 3·25

65 Flags and Trade Fair Emblem

1972. All-Africa Trade Fair.
306 **65** 30c. multicoloured 10 10
307 70c. multicoloured 10 10
308 1s.50 multicoloured 10 10
309 2s.50 multicoloured 25 80

66 Child with Cup

1972. 25th Anniv of UNICEF. Multicoloured.
310 30c. Type **66** 10 10
311 70c. Children with ball . . . 10 10
312 1s.50 Child at blackboard . . 10 10
313 2s.50 Child and tractor . . . 25 80

67 Hurdling

1972. Olympic Games, Munich. Multicoloured.
314 40c. Type **67** 10 10
315 70c. Running 10 10
316 1s.50 Boxing 20 15
317 2s.50 Hockey . . . . 30 1·75
MS318 131 × 98 mm. Nos. 314/17 4·50 7·00

68 Ugandan Kobs

1972. 10th Anniv of Ugandan Independence. Multicoloured.
319 40c. Type **68** 20 10
320 70c. Conference Centre . . . 20 10
321 1s.50 Makerere University . . 45 30
322 2s.50 Coat of arms . . . . . 70 3·50
MS323 132 × 120 mm. Nos. 319/22 4·00 3·50

69 Community Flag

1972. 5th Anniv of East African Community.

324	69	5s. multicoloured	55	1·90

70 Run-of-the-wind Anemometer

1972. Centenary of IMO/WMO. Multicoloured.

325	40c. Type **70**	10	10
326	70c. Weather balloon (vert)	20	10
327	1s.50 Meteorological rocket	30	15
328	2s.50 Satellite receiving aerial	55	2·25

71 "Learning by Serving"

73 Police Dog-handler

72 Kenyatta Conference Centre

1973. 24th World Scouting Conference, Nairobi.

329	71	40c. multicoloured	15	10
330	–	70c. red, violet and black	20	10
331	–	1s.50 blue, violet and black	45	30
332	–	2s.50 multicoloured	1·00	2·25

DESIGNS: 70c. Baden-Powell's grave, Nyeri; 1s.50, World Scout emblem; 2s.50, Lord Baden-Powell.

1973. I.M.F./World Bank Conference.

333	72	40c. green, grey and black	10	10
334	–	70c. brown, grey and black	10	10
335	–	1s.50 multicoloured	25	35
336	–	2s.50 orange, grey & black	35	1·75
MS337		166×141 mm. Nos. 333/6. Imperf	1·40	3·75

DESIGNS: Nos. 334/6 show different arrangements of Bank emblems and the Conference Centre, the 1s.50 being vertical.

1973. 50th Anniv of Interpol.

338	73	40c. yellow, blue and black	55	15
339	–	70c. green, yellow and black	90	15
340	–	1s.50 violet, yellow & black	1·50	90
341	–	2s.50 green, orange & black	3·75	6·00
342	–	2s.50 green, orange & black	3·75	6·00

DESIGNS: 70c. East African policemen; 1s.50, Interpol emblem; 2s.50 (2), Interpol H.Q.

No. 341 is inscribed "St. Clans" and 342 "St. Cloud".

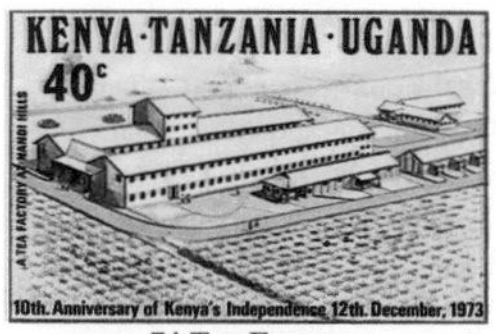

74 Tea Factory

1973. 10th Anniv of Kenya's Independence. Mult.

343	40c. Type **74**	10	10
344	70c. Kenyatta Hospital	15	10
345	1s.50 Nairobi Airport	50	20
346	2s.50 Kindaruma hydro-electric scheme	65	1·75

75 Party H.Q.

1973. 10th Anniv of Zanzibar's Revolution. Mult.

347	40c. Type **75**	10	10
348	70c. Housing scheme	15	10
349	1s.50 Colour T.V.	35	30
350	2s.50 Amaan Stadium	70	3·00

76 "Symbol of Union"

1974. 10th Anniv of Tanganyika–Zanzibar Union. Multicoloured.

351	40c. Type **76**	10	10
352	70c. Handclasp and map	15	10
353	1s.50 "Communications"	35	30
354	2s.50 Flags of Tanu, Tanzania and Afro-Shirazi Party	70	3·00

77 East African Family ("Stability of the Home")

1974. 17th Social Welfare Conference, Nairobi.

355	77	40c. yellow, brown & black	10	10
356	–	70c. multicoloured	10	10
357	–	1s.50 yellow, green & black	20	30
358	–	2s.50 red, violet and black	1·00	2·00

DESIGNS: 70c. Dawn and drummer (U.N. Second Development Plan); 1s.50, Agricultural scene (Rural Development Plan); 2s.50, Transport and telephone ("Communications").

78 New Postal H.Q., Kampala

1974. Centenary of U.P.U. Multicoloured.

359	40c. Type **78**	10	10
360	70c. Mail-train and post-van	20	10
361	1s.50 U.P.U. Building, Berne	15	20
362	2s.50 Loading mail into Vickers Super VC-10	55	1·50

79 Family-planning Clinic

1974. World Population Year.

363	79	40c. multicoloured	10	10
364	–	70c. mauve and red	10	10
365	–	1s.50 multicoloured	15	20
366	–	2s.50 blue, emerald and green	30	1·90

DESIGNS: 70c. "Tug of War"; 1s.50, "Population scales"; 2s.50, W.P.Y. emblem.

80 Seronera Wildlife Lodge, Tanzania

1975. East African Game Lodges. Multicoloured.

367	40c. Type **80**	15	10
368	70c. Mweya Safari Lodge, Uganda	20	10
369	1s.50 "Ark"—Aberdare Forest Lodge, Kenya	25	30
370	2s.50 Paraa Safari Lodge, Uganda	60	2·75

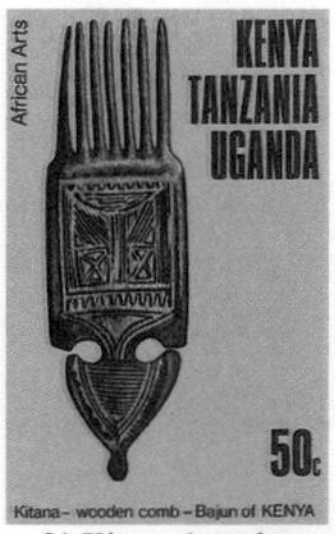

81 Kitana (wooden comb), Bajun of Kenya

83 Ahmed ("Presidential" Elephant)

82 International Airport, Entebbe

1975. African Arts. Multicoloured.

371	50c. Type **81**	10	10
372	1s. Earring, Chaga of Tanzania	15	10
373	2s. Okoco (armlet), Acholi of Uganda	35	70
374	3s. Kitete, Kamba gourd, Kenya	65	1·40

1975. O.A.U. Summit Conf, Kampala. Mult.

375	50c. Type **82**	30	10
376	1s. Map of Africa and flag (vert)	30	10
377	2s. Nile Hotel, Kampala	30	85
378	3s. Martyrs' Shrine, Namugongo (vert)	40	1·60

1975. Rare Animals. Multicoloured.

379	50c. Type **83**	50	10
380	1s. Albino buffalo	50	10
381	2s. Ahmed in grounds of National Museum	1·10	1·50
382	3s. Abbott's duiker	1·25	3·00

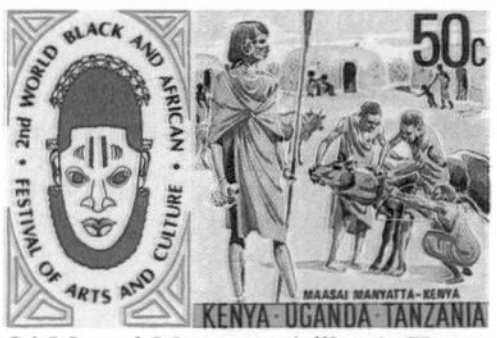

84 Maasai Manyatta (village), Kenya

1975. 2nd World Black and African Festival of Arts and Culture, Nigeria (1977). Multicoloured.

383	50c. Type **84**	15	10
384	1s. "Heartbeat of Africa" (Ugandan Dancers)	15	10
385	2s. Makonde sculpture, Tanzania	50	85
386	3s. "Early Man and Technology" (skinning animal)	75	1·40

85 Fokker Friendship at Nairobi Airport

1975. 30th Anniv of East African Airways. Multicoloured.

387	50c. Type **85**	1·00	40
388	1s. Douglas DC-9 at Kilimanjaro Airport	1·10	40
389	2s. Vickers Super VC-10 at Entebbe Airport	3·50	3·25
390	3s. East African Airways crest	3·75	3·75

Further commemorative sets were released during 1976–78 using common designs, but each inscribed for one republic only. See Kenya, Tanzania and Uganda.

Co-operation between the postal services of the three member countries virtually ceased after 30 June 1977. The postal services of Kenya, Tanzania and Uganda then operated independently.

OFFICIAL STAMPS

For use on official correspondence of the Tanganyika Government only.

1959. Stamps of 1954 optd **OFFICIAL**.

O 1	18	5c. black and brown	10	1·25
O 2	–	10c. red	15	1·25
O 3	–	15c. black and blue	30	1·25
O 4	–	20c. black and orange	20	20
O 5	18	30c. black and blue	15	85
O 6	–	50c. purple	20	20
O 7	–	1s. black and red	20	75
O 8	–	1s.30 orange and lilac	3·00	2·00
O 9	–	2s. black and green	1·25	1·00
O10	–	5s. black and orange	3·25	2·75
O11	20	10s. black and blue	2·00	3·25
O12	21	£1 red and black	6·50	15·00

1960. Stamps of 1960 optd **OFFICIAL**.

O13	26	5c. blue	10	1·25
O14	–	10c. green	10	1·25
O15	–	15c. purple	10	1·25
O16	–	20c. mauve	10	30
O17	–	30c. red	10	10
O18	–	50c. violet	30	85
O19	28	1s. violet and purple	30	10
O20	–	5s. red and purple	13·00	65

POSTAGE DUE STAMPS

D 1

D 2

1923.

D1	D 1	5c. violet	2·50	50
D2		10c. red	2·50	15
D3		20c. green	2·50	3·00
D4		30c. brown	17·00	14·00
D5		40c. blue	6·50	14·00
D6		1s. green	70·00	£130

1935.

D 7	D 2	5c. violet	2·75	1·75
D 8		10c. red	30	50
D 9		20c. green	40	50
D10		30c. brown	1·25	50
D11		40c. blue	1·50	3·00
D12		1s. grey	19·00	19·00

KHMER REPUBLIC Pt. 21

Cambodia was renamed Khmer Republic on 9 October 1970.

Following the fall of the Khmer Republic, the People's Republic of Kampuchea was proclaimed on 10 January 1979.

100 cents = 1 riel.

78 "Attack"

1971. Defence of Khmer Territory.

285	78	1r. multicoloured	15	10
286		3r. multicoloured	15	15
287		10r. multicoloured	50	25

79 "World Races" and U.N. Emblem

1971. Racial Equality Year.

288	79	3r. multicoloured	25	15
289		7r. multicoloured	40	25
290		8r. multicoloured	60	40

80 General Post Office, Phnom Penh

1971.

291	80	3r. multicoloured	15	10
292		9r. multicoloured	50	35
293		10r. multicoloured	60	40

81 Global Emblem

1971. World Telecommunications Day.

294	81	3r. multicoloured	25	15
295		4r. multicoloured	35	15
296	–	7r. multicoloured	40	25
297	–	8r. red, black and orange	50	25

DESIGN: 7, 8r. I.T.U. emblem.

82 Indian Coral Bean

1971. Wild Flowers. Multicoloured.

298	2r. Type **82**	40	15
299	3r. Orchid tree	50	40
300	6r. Flame-of-the-forest	1·00	40
301	10r. Malayan crape myrtle (vert)	1·20	65

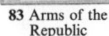

83 Arms of the Republic

84 Monument and Flag

1971. 1st Anniv of Republic.
302 **83** 3r. bistre and green 25 10
303 **84** 3r. multicoloured 25 10
304 4r. multicoloured 35 15
305 **83** 8r. bistre and orange . . . 40 15
306 10r. bistre and brown . . . 60 25
307 **84** 10r. multicoloured 50 35
MS308 Two sheets, each 130 × 100 mm. (a) Nos. 302 and 305/6 (sold for 25r.); (b) Nos. 303/4 and 307 (sold for 20r.) 4·75 4·00

85 UNICEF Emblem

86 Book Year Emblem

1971. 25th Anniv of UNICEF.
309 **85** 3r. purple 25 15
310 5r. blue 35 25
311 9r. red and violet 65 40

1972. International Book Year.
312 **86** 3r. green, purple and blue 25 15
313 8r. blue, green and purple 40 25
314 9r. bistre, blue and green 60 40
MS315 160 × 100 mm. Nos. 312/14 (sold at 25r.) . . . . 2·10 1·80

87 Lion of St. Mark's

1972. UNESCO "Save Venice" Campaign.
316 **87** 3r. brown, buff and purple 35 15
317 – 5r. brown, buff and green 60 25
318 – 10r. brown, blue and green 75 40
MS319 160 × 100 mm. Nos. 316/18 (sold at 23r.) . . . . 3·00 2·50
DESIGNS—HORIZ: 5r. St. Mark's Basilica. VERT: 10r. Bridge of Sighs.

88 U.N. Emblem

89 Dancing Apsaras (relief), Angkor

1972. 25th Anniv of Economic Commission for Asia and the Far East (C.E.A.E.O.).
320 **88** 3r. red 25 15
321 6r. blue 40 25
322 9r. red 60 40
MS323 141 × 101 mm. Nos. 320/3 (sold at 23r.) . . . . 1·90 1·70

1972.
324 **89** 1r. brown 25 15
325 3r. violet 25 15
326 7r. purple 40 25
327 8r. brown 40 25
328 9r. green 50 25
329 10r. blue 65 25
330 12r. purple 90 35
331 14r. blue . . . . 1·20 40

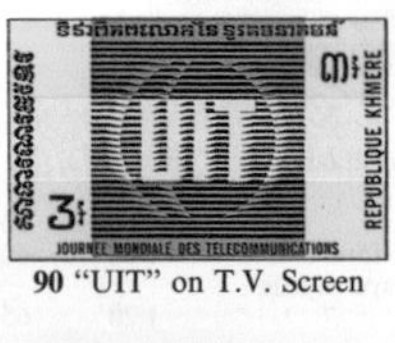

90 "UIT" on T.V. Screen

91 Conference Emblem

1972. World Telecommunications Day.
332 **90** 3r. black, blue and yellow 25 15
333 9r. black, blue and mauve 50 25
334 14r. black, blue and brown 75 40

1972. United Nations Environmental Conservation Conference, Stockholm.
335 **91** 3r. green, brown and violet 25 15
336 12r. violet and green . . . 40 25
337 15r. green and violet . . . 60 40
MS338 131 × 100 mm. Nos. 335/7 (sold at 35r.) . . . . 2·75 2·30

92 Javan Rhinoceros

94 Hoisting Flag

1972. Wild Animals.
339 **92** 3r. black, red and violet . . 40 15
340 – 4r. violet, bistre and purple 50 15
341 – 6r. brown, green and blue 90 35
342 – 7r. ochre, green and brown 1·30 35
343 – 8r. black, green and blue 1·50 40
344 – 10r. black, blue and green 2·00 60
DESIGNS: 4r. Mainland serow; 6r. Thamin; 7r. Banteng; 8r. Water buffalo; 10r. Gaur.

1972. Olympic Games, Munich. Nos. 164 of Cambodia and 302, 306 and 336/7 of Khmer Republic optd **XXe JEUX OLYMPIQUES MUNICH 1972**, Olympic rings and emblem.
345 **83** 3r. bistre and green 35 35
346 10r. bistre and brown . . . 1·20 65
347 – 12r. green and brown . . . 1·40 85
348 **91** 12r. violet and green . . . 1·40 85
349 15r. green and violet . . . 1·70 1·10

1972. 2nd Anniv of Republic.
350 **94** 3r. multicoloured 15 10
351 5r. multicoloured 25 15
352 9r. multicoloured 60 40

1972. Red Cross Aid for War Victims. No. 164 of Cambodia and 302, 306 and 336/7 of Khmer Republic surch **SECOURS AUX VICTIMES DE GUERRE**, red cross and value.
353 **83** 3r.+2r. bistre and green . . 25 25
354 10r.+6r. bistre and brown 65 65
355 – 12r.+7r. green and brown 75 65
356 **91** 12r.+7r. violet and green 75 75
357 15r.+8r. green and violet 1·30 1·30

96 Garuda

97 Crest and Temple

1973. Air.
358 **96** 3r. red 25 15
359 30r. blue . . . . 1·80 1·00
360 50r. lilac . . . . 3·25 1·80
361 100r. green . . . . 4·50 2·75

1973. New Constitution.
362 **97** 3r. multicoloured 15 10
363 12r. multicoloured 25 15
364 14r. multicoloured 40 35
MS365 130 × 100 mm. Nos. 362/4 (sold at 34r.) . . . . 1·60 1·40

98 Apsara

99 Interpol Emblem

1973. Angkor Sculptures.
366 **98** 3r. black 25 15
367 – 8r. blue 40 25
368 – 10r. brown 50 40
MS369 130 × 100 mm. Nos. 366/8 (sold at 25r.) . . . . 2·30 2·00
DESIGNS: 8r. Devata (12th century); 10f. Devata (10th century).

1973. 50th Anniv of International Criminal Police Organization (Interpol).
370 **99** 3r. green and turquoise . . 25 15
371 7r. green and red 35 25
372 10r. green and brown . . . 40 40
MS373 130 × 100 mm. Nos. 370/2 (sold at 30r.) . . . . 2·75 2·30

100 Marshal Lon Nol

1973. Honouring Marshal Lon Nol, 1st President of Republic.
374 **100** 3r. black, brown and green 15 15
375 8r. black, brown and green 25 25
376 14r. black, brown and agate 40 25
MS377 130 × 100 mm. Nos. 374/6 but background colours changed (sold at 50r.) . . . . 4·75 4·25

102 Copernicus and Space Rocket

1974. 500th Birth Anniv of Nicolas Copernicus (astronomer). Multicoloured.
382 1r. Type **102** (postage) . . . 20 20
383 5r. Copernicus and "Mariner II" 20 20
384 10r. Copernicus and "Apollo" 50 25
385 25r. Copernicus and "Telstar" . . . . 1·10 55
386 50r. Copernicus and space-walker . . . . 2·00 1·00
387 100r. Copernicus and spaceship landing on Moon 4·75 2·50
388 150r. Copernicus and Moon-landing craft leaving "Apollo" . . . . 7·00 4·00
389 200r. Copernicus and "Skylab III" (air) . . . . 8·50 4·00
390 250r. Copernicus and Concorde . . . . 14·00 7·50

1974. 4th Anniv of Republic. Various stamps optd **4E ANNIVERSAIRE DE LA REPUBLIQUE**.
391 **78** 10r. multicoloured 90 85
392 **77** 50r. on 3r. multicoloured 3·00 2·10
393 **94** 100r. on 5r. multicoloured 5·75 5·50
No. 392 is additionally optd **REPUBLIQUE KHMERE** in French and Cambodian.

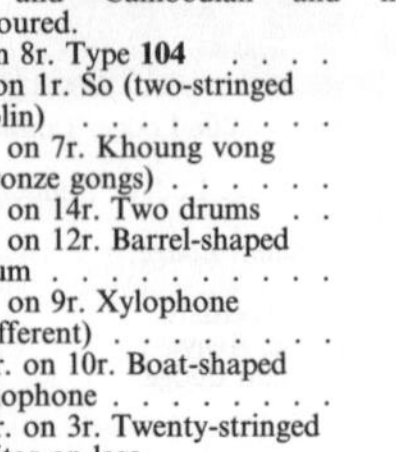

104 Xylophone

1975. Unissued stamps of Cambodia showing musical instruments, surch **REPUBLIQUE KHMERE** in French and Cambodian and new value. Multicoloured.
394 5r. on 8r. Type **104** . . . .
395 20r. on 1r. So (two-stringed violin) . . . .
396 160r. on 7r. Khoung vong (bronze gongs) . . . . . .
397 180r. on 14r. Two drums . .
398 235r. on 12r. Barrel-shaped drum . . . .
399 500r. on 9r. Xylophone (different) . . . .
400 1000r. on 10r. Boat-shaped xylophone . . . .
401 2000r. on 3r. Twenty-stringed guitar on legs . . . . . .
Set of 8 . . . . £250

POSTAGE DUE STAMPS

D 101 Frieze, Angkor Vat

1974.
D378 D **101** 2r. brown 25 25
D379 6r. green 35 35
D380 8r. red 50 50
D381 10r. blue 65 75

APPENDIX

The following stamps have either been issued in excess of postal needs or have not been available to the public in reasonable quantities at face value. Such stamps may later be given full listing if there is evidence of regular postal use.

1972.

Moon Landing of "Apollo 16". Embossed on gold foil. Air 900r. × 2.

Visit of Pres. Nixon to China. Embossed on gold foil. Air 900r. × 2.

Olympic Games, Munich. Embossed on gold foil. Air 900r. × 2.

1973.

Gold Medal Winners, Munich Olympics. Embossed on gold foil. Air 900r. × 2.

World Cup Football Championship, West Germany (1974). Embossed on gold foil. Air 900r. × 4.

1974.

Pres. Kennedy and "Apollo 11". Embossed on gold foil. Air 1100r. × 2.

500th Birth Anniv of Nicolas Copernicus (astronomer). Embossed on gold foil. Air 1200r.

Centenary of U.P.U. (1st issue). Postage 10, 60r.; Air 700; 1200r. embossed on gold foil.

1975.

Olympic Games, Montreal (1976). Postage 5, 10, 15, 25r.; Air 50, 100, 150, 200, 250r.; 1200r. embossed on gold foil.

World Cup Football Championship, West Germany (1974). Postage 1, 5, 10, 25r.; Air 50, 100, 150, 200, 250, 1200r. embossed on gold foil.

Centenary of U.P.U. (2nd issue). Postage 15, 20, 70, 160, 180, 235r.; Air 500, 1000, 2000, 2000r. embossed on gold foil.

KHOR FAKKAN Pt. 19

From 1965 various issues were produced for this dependency, some being overprinted on, or in the same designs as, issues for Sharjah.

APPENDIX

The following stamps have either been issued in excess of postal needs or have not been available to the public in reasonable quantities at face value. Such stamps may later be given full listing if there is evidence of regular postal use.

1965.

Views. Nos. 75/80 of Sharjah optd. Air 10, 20, 30, 40, 75, 100n.p.

Boy and Girl Scouts. Nos. 74 and 89 of Sharjah optd. 2, 2r.

Birds. Nos. 101/6 of Sharjah optd. Air 30, 40, 75, 150n.p., 2, 3r.

Olympic Games, Tokyo 1964. Nos. 95/7 of Sharjah optd. 40, 50n.p., 2r.

New York World's Fair. Nos. 81/3 of Sharjah optd. Air 20, 40n.p., 1r.

Pres. Kennedy Commem. Nos. 98/100 of Sharjah optd. Air 40, 60, 100n.p.

Centenary of I.T.U. Postage 1, 2, 3, 4, 5, 50n.p., 1r., 120n.p.

Pan-Arab Games, Cairo. 50p. × 5.

1966.

International Co-operation Year. 50n.p. × 8.

Churchill Commemoration. 2, 3, 4, 5r.

Roses. 20, 35, 60, 80n.p., 1r., 125n.p.

Fish. 1, 2, 3, 4, 5, 15, 20, 30, 40, 50, 75n.p., 1, 2, 3, 4, 5, 10r.

Int Stamp Exhibition, Washington D.C. (SIPEX). 80, 120n.p., 2r.

New Currency Surcharges in Rials and Piastres.

(a) 1965 I.T.U. Centenary issue. 10p. on 50n.p., 16p. on 120n.p., 1r. on 1r.

(b) Churchill issue. 1r. on 2r., 2r. on 3r., 3r. on 4r., 4r. on 5r.

(c) Roses issue. 1p. on 20n.p., 2p. on 35n.p., 4p. on 60n.p., 6p. on 80n.p., 10p. on 125n.p., 12p. on 1r.

New Currency Surcharges in Dirhams and Riyals.

(a) 1965 Pan-Arab Games issue. 20d. on 50p. × 5.

(b) Fish issue. 1d. on 1n.p., 2d. on 2n.p., 3d. on 3n.p., 4d. on 4n.p., 5d. on 5n.p., 15d. on 15n.p., 20d. on 20n.p., 30d. on 30n.p., 40d. on 40n.p., 50d. on 50n.p., 75d. on 75n.p., 1r. on 1r., 2r. on 2r., 3r. on 3r., 4r. on 4r., 5r. on 5r., 10r. on 10r.

3rd Death Anniv of Pres. J. Kennedy. Optd on Int Stamp Exhibition, Washington issue. 80d. on 80n.p., 120d. on 120n.p., 2r. on 2r.

World Football Cup Championship, England. ½r. × 7.

1967.

4th Death Anniv of Pres. J. Kennedy. Optd on 1966 Int Stamp Exhibition issue. 80d. on 80n.p., 120d. on 120n.p., 2r. on 2r.

1968.

Famous Paintings. Optd on Sharjah. Postage 1, 2, 3, 4, 5, 30, 40, 60, 75d.; Air 1, 2, 3, 4, 5r.

Winter Olympic Games, Grenoble. Optd on Sharjah. Postage 1, 2, 3, 4, 5d.; Air 1, 2, 3r.

Previous Olympic Games. Optd on Sharjah. Air 25, 50, 75d., 1r.50, 3, 4r.

Olympic Games, Mexico. Optd on Sharjah. 10, 20, 30d., 2, 2r.40, 5r.

1969.

12th World Jamboree. Optd on 1968 issue of Sharjah. Postage 1, 2, 3, 4, 5, 10d.; Air 30, 50, 60d., 1r.50.

Martyrs of Liberty. Optd on 1968 issue of Sharjah. Air 35d. × 4, 60d. × 4, 1r. × 4

Sportsmen and Women. Optd on 1968 issue of Sharjah. Postage 20, 30, 40, 60d., 1r.50, 2r.50; Air 35, 50d., 1, 2, 3r.25, 4, 4r.

A number of issues on gold or silver foil also exist, but it is understood that these were mainly for presentation purposes, although valid for postage.

In common with the other states of the United Arab Emirates the Khor Fakkan stamp contract was terminated on 1 August 1972, and any further new issues released after that date were unauthorised.

KIAUTSCHOU (KIAOCHOW) Pt. 7

A port in Shantung, China, leased by Germany from China in 1898. It was occupied by Japan in 1914, but reverted to China in 1922.

1900. 100 pfennige = 1 mark.
1905. 100 cents = 1 dollar (Chinese).

1900. No. 9 of German Post Offices in China surch **5 Pfg.**

3	5pf. on 10pf. red	55·00	60·00

1901. "Yacht" key-types inscr "KIAUTSCHOU".

11 N	3pf. brown	2·00	1·80
12	5pf. green	2·00	1·30
13	10pf. red	2·40	1·80
14	20pf. blue	7·50	8·75
15	25pf. black & red on yellow	13·50	18·00
16	30pf. black & orge on buff	13·50	18·00
17	40pf. black and red	18·00	22·00
18	50pf. black & purple on buff	18·00	27·00
19	80pf. black and red on pink	31·00	60·00
20 O	1m. red	60·00	£100
21	2m. blue	80·00	£120
22	3m. black	80·00	£225
23	5m. red and black	£225	£600

1905. Chinese currency. "Yacht" key-types inscr "KIAUTSCHOU".

34 N	1c. brown	45	1·60
35	2c. green	45	1·10
36	4c. red	90	1·30
37	10c. blue	1·10	3·50
38	20c. black and red	1·80	20·00
39	40c. black and red on pink	3·00	60·00
40 O	½d. red	5·00	60·00
41	1d. blue	5·75	65·00
42	1½d. black	7·50	£200
43	2½d. red and black	18·00	£550

KING EDWARD VII LAND Pt. 1

Stamp issued in connection with the Shackleton Antarctic Expedition in 1908. The expedition landed at Cape Royds in Victoria Land, instead of King Edward VII Land, the intended destination.

1908. Stamp of New Zealand optd **KING EDWARD VII LAND.**

A1 42	1d. red	£400	35·00

KIONGA Pt. 9

Part of German E. Africa, occupied by the Portuguese during the 1914/18 war, and now incorporated in Mozambique.

1916. "King Carlos" key-type of Lourenco Marques optd **REPUBLICA** and surch **KIONGA** and new value.

1 S	½c. on 100r. blue on blue	9·75	7·75
2	1c. on 100r. blue on blue	9·75	7·75
3	2½c. on 100r. blue on blue	9·75	7·75
4	5c. on 100r. blue on blue	9·75	7·75

KIRIBATI Pt. 1

This group of islands in the Pacific, formerly known as the Gilbert Islands, achieved independence on 12 July 1979 and was renamed Kiribati.

100 cents = 1 dollar.

15 National Flag

1979. Independence. Multicoloured.

84	10c. Type **15**	10	35
85	45c. Houses of Parliament and Maneaba ni Maungatabu (House of Assembly)	20	65

16 "Teraaka" (training ship)

1979. Multicoloured.

86	1c. Type **16**	10	90
122	3c. "Tautunu" (inter-island freighter)	15	30
123	5c. Hibiscus	10	15
124	7c. Catholic Cathedral, Tarawa	10	15
125	10c. Maneaba, Bikenibeu	10	15
91	12c. Betio Harbour	15	20
92	15c. Reef heron	35	25
93	20c. Flamboyant tree	20	25
129	25c. Moorish idol (fish)	30	30
95	30c. Frangipani	25	30
96	35c. G.I.P.C. Chapel, Tangintebu	25	30
97	50c. "Hypolimnas bolina" (butterfly)	75	55
133	$1 "Tabakea" (Tarawa Lagoon ferry)	50	75
134	$2 Evening scene	50	75
135	$5 National flag	1·00	2·00

17 Gilbert and Ellice Islands 1911 ½d. Stamp

18 Boy with Giant Clam Shell

1979. Death Cent of Sir Rowland Hill. Mult.

100	10c. Type **17**	10	10
101	20c. Gilbert & Ellice Islands 1956 2s.6d. definitive	15	20
102	25c. G.B. Edward VII 2s.6d.	15	20
103	45c. Gilbert and Ellice Islands 1924 10s.	25	35
MS104	113 × 110 mm. Nos. 100/3	70	1·00

1979. International Year of the Child. Mult.

105	10c. Type **18**	10	10
106	20c. Child climbing coconut palm (horiz)	10	10
107	45c. Girl reading	15	20
108	$1 Child in traditional costume	30	50

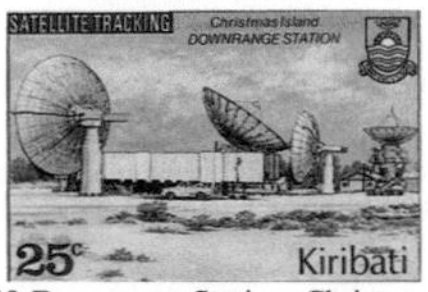

19 Downrange Station, Christmas Island

1980. Satellite Tracking. Multicoloured.

109	25c. Type **19**	10	10
110	45c. Map showing satellite trajectory	15	15
111	$1 Rocket launch, Tanegashima, Japan (vert)	30	35

20 T.S. "Teraaka"

1980. "London 1980" Int Stamp Exhibition. Mult.

112	12c. Type **20**	15	10
113	25c. Loading Air Tungaru Britten Norman Islander, Bonriki Airport	15	10
114	30c. Radio operator	15	10
115	$1 Bairiki Post Office	20	35
MS116	139 × 116 mm. Nos. 112/15	60	85

21 "Achaea janata"

1980. Moths. Multicoloured.

117	12c. Type **21**	10	10
118	25c. "Ethmia nigroapicella"	15	15
119	30c. "Utetheisa pulchelloides"	15	15
120	50c. "Anua coronata"	25	25

22 Captain Cook Hotel

1980. Development. Multicoloured.

136	10c. Type **22**	10	10
137	20c. Sports stadium	10	10
138	25c. International Airport, Bonriki	15	10
139	35c. National Library and Archives, Bairiki	15	10
140	$1 Otintai Hotel, Bikenibeu	20	40

23 "Acalypha godseffiana"

1981. Flowers. Multicoloured.

141	12c. Type **23**	10	10
142	30c. "Hibiscus schizopetalus"	15	15
143	35c. "Calotropis gigantea"	15	15
144	50c. "Euphorbia pulcherrima"	20	20

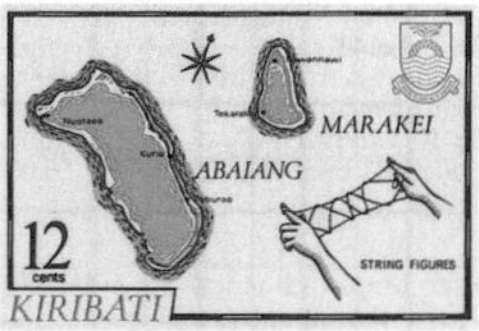

25 Maps of Abaiang and Marakei, and String Figures

1981. Islands (1st series). Multicoloured.

145	12c. Type **25**	15	10
146	30c. Maps of Little Makin and Butaritari, and village house	20	10
147	35c. Map of Maiana and coral road	25	15
148	$1 Map of Christmas Island, and Captain Cook's H.M.S. "Resolution"	70	75

See also Nos. 201/4, 215/18, 237/40, 256/60 and 270/3.

26 "Katherine"

27 Prince Charles and Lady Diana Spencer (½-size illustration)

1981. Royal Wedding. Royal Yachts. Multicoloured.

149	12c. Type **26**	10	15
150	12c. Type **27**	20	30
151	50c. "Osborne"	25	40
152	50c. Type **27**	50	75
153	$2 "Britannia"	35	80
154	$2 Type **27**	1·50	2·50
MS155	120 × 109 mm. $1.20 Type **27**	75	1·00

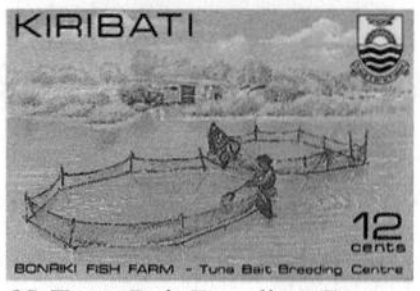

28 Tuna Bait Breeding Centre, Bonriki Fish Farm

1981. Tuna Fishing Industry. Multicoloured.

158	12c. Type **28**	15	10
159	30c. Tuna fishing	20	20
160	35c. Cold storage, Betio	20	25
161	50c. Government Tuna Fishing Vessel "Nei Manganibuka"	30	50
MS162	134 × 99 mm. Nos. 158/61	1·00	1·40

29 Pomarine Skua

1982. Birds. Multicoloured.

163	1c. Type **29**	15	15
164	2c. Mallard	15	15
165	4c. Collared petrel	20	20
166	5c. Blue-faced booby	20	20
167	7c. Friendly quail dove	20	20
168	8c. Common shoveler ("Shoveler")	20	20
169	12c. Polynesian reed warbler	20	20
170	15c. Pacific golden plover ("Pacific Plover")	25	25
171	20c. Reef heron	30	30
171a	25c. Common noddy ("Brown Noddy")	2·25	1·50
172	30c. Brown booby	30	30
173	35c. Audubon's shearwater	60	35
174	40c. White-throated storm petrel (vert)	35	40
175	50c. Bristle-thighed curlew (vert)	40	45
175a	55c. White tern ("Fairy Tern") (vert)	11·00	16·00
176	$1 Kuhl's lory ("Scarlet-breasted Lorikeet") (vert)	1·25	40
177	$2 Long-tailed koel ("Long-tailed Cuckoo") (vert)	1·25	55
178	$5 Great frigate bird (vert)	1·75	1·25

30 Riley Turbo Skyliner

1982. Air. Inaug of Tungaru Airline. Mult.

179	12c. Type **30**	15	10
180	30c. Britten Norman "short nose" Trislander	20	20
181	35c. Casa-212 Aviocar	20	25
182	50c. Boeing 727-200	30	35

No. 179 is inscr "De Havilland DH114 Heron" in error.

31 Mary of Teck, Princess of Wales, 1893

1982. 21st Birthday of Princess of Wales. Mult.

183	12c. Type **31**	10	10
184	50c. Coat of arms of Mary of Teck	20	35
185	$1 Diana, Princess of Wales	30	70

1982. Birth of Prince William of Wales. Nos. 183/5 optd **ROYAL BABY.**

186	12c. Type **31**	10	15
187	50c. Coat of arms of Mary of Teck	25	50
188	$1 Diana, Princess of Wales	40	70

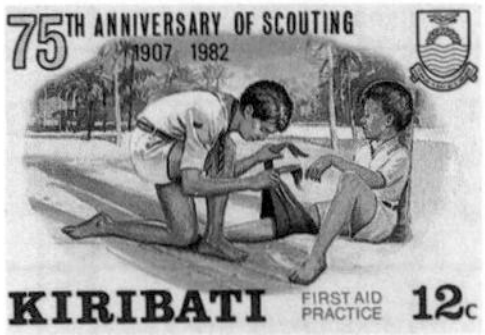

32 First Aid Practice

1982. 75th Anniv of Boy Scout Movement. Mult.
189 12c. Type **32** 20 15
190 25c. Boat repairs 20 30
191 30c. On parade 25 35
192 40c. Gilbert Islands 1977 8c. Scouting stamp and "75" 25 60

33 Queen and Duke of Edinburgh with Local Dancer

1982. Royal Visit. Multicoloured.
193 12c. Type **33** 15 15
194 25c. Queen, Duke of Edinburgh and outrigger canoe 20 20
195 35c. New Philatelic Bureau building 30 30
MS196 88 × 76 mm. 50c. Queen Elizabeth II 60 60

On No. **MS**196 the captions on the map for the islands of Teraina and Tabuaeran have been transposed.

34 "Obaia, The Feathered" (Kiribati legend)

1983. Commonwealth Day. Multicoloured.
197 12c. Type **34** 10 10
198 30c. Robert Louis Stevenson Hotel, Abemama 15 10
199 50c. Container ship off Betio 15 25
200 $1 Map of Kiribati 20 50

1983. Island Maps (2nd series). As T **25**. Mult.
201 12c. Beru, Nikunau and canoe 20 15
202 25c. Abemama, Aranuka, Kuria and fish 20 20
203 35c. Nonouti and reef fishing (vert) 25 35
204 50c. Tarawa and House of Assembly (vert) 30 50

35 Collecting Coconuts

1983. Copra Industry. Multicoloured.
205 12c. Type **35** 20 15
206 25c. Selecting coconuts for copra 35 25
207 30c. Removing husks 35 30
208 35c. Drying copra 35 35
209 50c. Loading copra at Betio 40 45

36 War Memorials

1983. 40th Anniv of Battle of Tarawa. Multicoloured.
210 12c. Type **36** 15 15
211 30c. Maps of Tarawa and Pacific Ocean 20 30
212 35c. Gun emplacement . . . 20 35
213 50c. Modern and war-time landscapes 25 55
214 $1 Aircraft carrier U.S.S. "Tarawa" 40 75

1983. Island Maps (3rd series). As T **25**. Mult.
215 12c. Teraina and Captain Fanning's ship "Betsey", 1798 . . . . 25 15
216 30c. Nikumaroro and hawksbill turtle 30 35
217 35c. Kanton and local postmark 35 40
218 50c. Banaba and flying fish 40 55

37 Tug "Riki"

1984. Kiribati Shipping Corporation. Mult.
219 12c. Type **37** 50 15
220 35c. Ferry "Nei Nimanoa" 90 35
221 50c. Ferry "Nei Tebaa" . . . 1·25 60
222 $1 Cargo ship "Nei Momi" 1·50 1·10
MS223 115 × 98 mm. Nos. 219/22 3·25 5·50

38 Water and Sewage Schemes

1984. "Ausipex" International Stamp Exhibition, Melbourne. Multicoloured.
224 12c. Type **38** 15 15
225 30c. "Nouamake" (game fishing boat) 20 30
226 35c. Overseas training schemes 20 40
227 50c. International communications link . . . 25 55

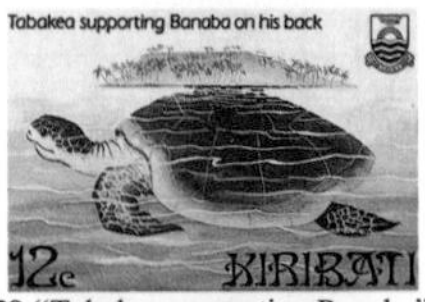

39 "Tabakea supporting Banaba"

1984. Kiribati Legends (1st series). Multicoloured.
228 12c. Type **39** 15 20
229 30c. "Nakaa, Judge of the Dead" 15 35
230 35c. "Naareau and Dragonfly" 15 45
231 50c. "Whistling Ghosts" . . 20 55

See also Nos. 245/8.

40 Sail-finned Tang

1985. Reef Fishes. Multicoloured.
232 12c. Type **40** 60 25
233 25c. Picasso triggerfish . . . 1·00 65
234 35c. Clown surgeonfish . . . 1·25 85
235 80c. Red squirrelfish . . . . 2·00 2·50
MS236 140 × 107 mm. Nos. 232/5 6·00 4·75

1985. Island Maps (4th series). As T **25**. Mult.
237 12c. Tabuaeran and great frigate bird ("Frigate Bird") . . . . 1·75 25
238 35c. Rawaki and germinating coconuts . . . . 2·25 40
239 50c. Arorae and xanthid crab 2·50 65
240 $1 Tamana and fish hook . . 3·00 1·50

41 Youths playing Football on Beach

1985. International Youth Year. Multicoloured.
241 15c. Type **41** 70 70
242 35c. Logos of I.Y.Y. and Kiribati Youth Year . . . 1·10 1·40
243 40c. Girl preparing food (vert) . . . . 1·25 1·60
244 55c. Map illustrating Kiribati's youth exchange links . . . . 1·40 2·25

1985. Kiribati Legends (2nd series). As T **39**. Mult.
245 15c. "Nang Kineia and the Tickling Ghosts" 50 35
246 35c. "Auriaria and Tituabine" 85 90
247 40c. "The first coming of Babai at Arorae" . . . . 1·00 1·40
248 55c. "Riiki and the Milky Way" . . . . 1·25 1·90

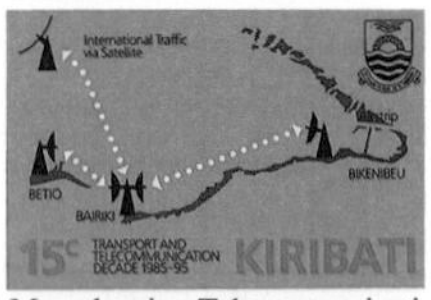

42 Map showing Telecommunications Satellite Link

1985. Transport and Telecommunications Decade (1st issue). Multicoloured.
249 15c. Type **42** . . . . 1·50 1·00
250 40c. M. V. "Moanaraoi" (Tarawa–Suva service) . . 2·75 3·00

See also Nos. 268/9, 293/4 and 314/15.

1986. 60th Birthday of Queen Elizabeth II. As T **246a** of Papua New Guinea. Multicoloured.
251 15c. Princess Elizabeth in Girl Guide uniform, Windsor Castle, 1938 . . . 15 15
252 35c. At Trooping the Colour, 1980 . . . . 20 30
253 40c. With Duke of Edinburgh in Kiribati, 1982 . . . . . 20 35
254 55c. At banquet, Austrian Embassy, London, 1966 . . 25 50
255 $1 At Crown Agents Head Office, London, 1983 . . . 45 1·25

1986. Island Maps (5th series). As T **25**. Mult.
256 15c. Manra and coconut crab 2·75 1·50
257 30c. Birnie and McKean Islands and cowrie shells 3·50 2·75
258 35c. Orona and red-footed booby . . . . 4·25 2·75
259 40c. Malden Island and whaling ship, 1844 . . . . 4·25 3·75
260 55c. Vostok, Flint and Caroline Islands and Bellingshausen's "Vostok", 1820 . . . . 4·25 4·25

43 "Lepidodactylus lugubris"

1986. Geckos. Multicoloured.
261 15c. Type **43** . . . . 1·50 70
262 35c. "Gehyra mutilata" . . . 1·75 1·50
263 40c. "Hemidactylus frenatus" 1·90 1·75
264 55c. "Gehyra oceanica" . . . 2·25 2·50

See also Nos. 274/7.

44 Maps of Australia and Kiribati

46 Henri Dunant (founder)

45 Freighter "Moamoa"

1986. America's Cup Yachting Championship. Multicoloured.
265 15c. Type **44** 20 65
266 55c. America's Cup and map of course . . . . 50 1·25
267 $1.50 "Australia II" (1983 winner) . . . . 1·00 1·50

1987. Transport and Telecommunications Decade (2nd issue). Multicoloured.
268 30c. Type **45** . . . . 2·75 2·50
269 55c. Telephone switchboard and automatic exchange . . 3·75 3·50

1987. Island Maps (6th series). As T **25**. Multicoloured.
270 15c. Starbuck and red-tailed tropic bird ("Red-tailed Tropicbird"!) 60 80
271 30c. Enderbury and white tern 70 85
272 55c. Tabiteuea and pandanus tree 70 90
273 $1 Onotoa and okai (house) 80 2·50

1987. Skinks. As T **43**. Multicoloured.
274 15c. "Emoia nigra" 30 45
275 35c. "Cryptoblepharus sp." 30 50
276 40c. "Emoia cyanura" 30 55
277 $1 "Lipinia noctua" . . . . . 45 1·50
MS278 130 × 114 mm. Nos. 274/7 1·10 3·25

1987. Royal Ruby Wedding. Nos. 251/5 optd **40TH WEDDING ANNIVERSARY**.
279 15c. Princess Elizabeth in Girl Guide uniform, Windsor Castle, 1938 . . . 15 25
280 35c. At Trooping the Colour, 1980 . . . . 20 30
281 40c. With Duke of Edinburgh in Kiribati, 1982 . . . . . 25 35
282 55c. At banquet, Austrian Embassy, London, 1966 . . 30 45
283 $1 At Crown Agents Head Office, London, 1983 . . . 50 1·25

1988. 125th Anniv of Int Red Cross. Mult.
284 15c. Type **46** 80 65
285 35c. Red Cross workers in Independence parade, 1979 1·25 1·50
286 40c. Red Cross workers with patient . . . . 1·25 1·60
287 55c. Gilbert & Ellice Islands 1970 British Red Cross Centenary 10c. stamp . . . 1·60 1·75

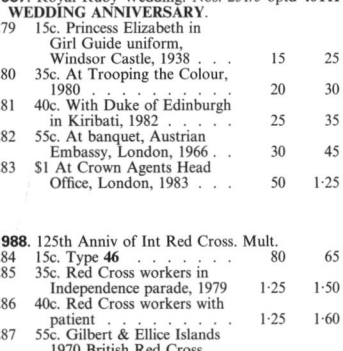

47 Causeway built by Australia

1988. Bicent of Australian Settlement and "Sydpex '88" National Stamp Exn, Sydney. Mult.
288 15c. Type **47** 25 20
289 35c. Capt. Cook and Pacific map 60 60
290 $1 Obverse of Australian $10 Bicentenary banknote . . . 1·25 1·75
291 $1 Reverse of $10 Bicentenary banknote . . . 1·25 1·75
MS292 95 × 76 mm. $2 "Logistic Ace" (container ship) (37 × 26 mm) . . . . 4·25 4·75

No. **MS**292 also commemorates the 150th anniversary of the first screw-driven steamship.

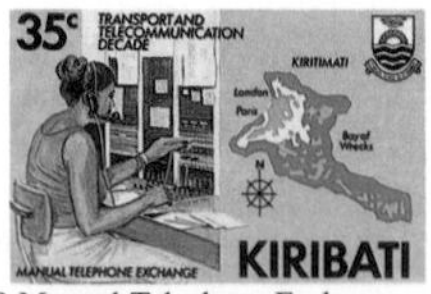

48 Manual Telephone Exchange and Map of Kiritimati

1988. Transport and Telecommunications Decade (3rd issue). Multicoloured.
293 35c. Type **48** 75 75
294 45c. Betio-Bairiki Causeway 1·00 1·00

49 "Hound" (brigantine), 1835

1989. Nautical History (1st series). Multicoloured.
295 15c. Type **49** 90 55
296 30c. "Phantom" (brig), 1854 1·50 1·10
297 40c. H.M.S. "Alacrity" (schooner), 1873 . . . . . 1·60 1·60
298 $1 "Charles W. Morgan" (whaling ship), 1851 . . . 3·00 3·75

See also Nos. 343/7 and 523/6.

50 Reef Heron ("Eastern Reef Heron")

51 House of Assembly

1989. Birds with Young. Multicoloured.
299 15c. Type **50** . . . . 1·25 1·50
300 15c. Reef heron ("Eastern Reef Heron") chicks in nest . . . . 1·25 1·50
301 $1 White-tailed tropic bird 2·50 3·25
302 $1 Young white-tailed tropic bird . . . . 2·50 3·25

Nos. 299/300 and 301/2 were each printed together, se-tenant, each pair forming a composite design.

1989. 10th Anniv of Independence. Mult.
303 15c. Type **51** 25 25
304 $1 Constitution . . . . . . 1·25 1·75

51a "Apollo 10" on Launch Gantry

1989. 20th Anniv of First Manned Landing on Moon. Multicoloured.

305 20c. Type **51a** 30 30
306 50c. Crew of "Apollo 10" (30 × 30 mm) 70 90
307 60c. "Apollo 10" emblem (30 × 30 mm) . . . . . . 80 1·00
308 75c. "Apollo 10" splashdown, Hawaii . . . . 95 1·25
MS309 82 × 100 mm. $2.50 "Apollo 11" command module in lunar orbit . . . . 6·50 7·50

51b Gilbert and Ellice Islands, 1949 75th Anniv of U.P.U. 3d. Stamp

51c Examining Fragment of Statue

1989. "Philexfrance 89" International Stamp Exhibition, Paris, and "World Stamp Expo '89", Washington (1st issue). Sheet 104 × 86 mm.

MS310 **51b** $2 multicoloured . . 3·50 5·00

1989. "Philexfrance 89" International Stamp Exhibition, Paris, and "World Stamp Expo '89", Washington (2nd issue). Designs showing Statue of Liberty. Multicoloured.

311 35c. Type **51c** . . . . 1·10 1·40
312 35c. Workman drilling Statue 1·10 1·40
313 35c. Surveyor with drawing 1·10 1·40

52 Telecommunications Centre

1989. Transport and Telecommunications Decade (4th issue). Multicoloured.

314 30c. Type **52** . . . . 1·50 1·25
315 75c. "Mataburo" (inter-island freighter) . . . . 3·50 4·00

1989. "Melbourne Stampshow '89". Nos. 301/2 optd with Exhibition emblem showing tram.

316 $1 White-tailed tropic bird 3·00 3·50
317 $1 Young white-tailed tropic bird . . . . 3·00 3·50

54 Virgin and Child (detail, "The Adoration of the Holy Child" (Denys Calvert))

1989. Christmas. Paintings. Multicoloured.

318 10c. Type **54** . . . . 1·00 55
319 15c. "The Adoration of the Holy Child" (Denys Calvert) . . . . 1·25 70
320 55c. "The Holy Family and St. Elizabeth" (Rubens) . . 3·00 1·25
321 $1 "Madonna with Child and Maria Magdalena" (School of Correggio) . . . . . . 4·50 7·00

55 Gilbert and Ellice Islands 1912 1d. and G.B. Twopence Blue Stamps

1990. 150th Anniv of the Penny Black and "Stamp World London 90" International Stamp Exhibition. Multicoloured.

322 15c. Type **55** . . . . 1·00 1·00
323 50c. Gilbert and Ellice Islands 1911 ½d. and G.B. Penny Black . . . . 2·50 2·75
324 60c. Kiribati 1982 1c. bird and G.B. 1870 ½d. . . . . 2·50 2·75
325 $1 Gilbert Islands 1976 1c. ship and G.B. 1841 1d. brown . . . . 2·75 3·50

56 Blue-barred Orange Parrotfish

1990. Fishes. Multicoloured.

326 1c. Type **56** 30 75
327 5c. Honeycomb grouper . . . 45 75
328 10c. Blue-finned trevally . . . 55 85
329 15c. Hump-backed snapper 70 50
330 20c. Variegated emperor . . 75 70
356 23c. Bennett's pufferfish . . . 1·25 1·50
331 25c. Rainbow runner 80 65
332 30c. Black-saddled coral grouper 90 65
333 35c. Great barracuda . . . . 1·00 75
334 40c. Convict tang . . . . . 1·00 80
335 50c. Violet squirrelfish . . . 1·25 90
336 60c. Stocky hawkfish . . . . 1·75 1·40
337 75c. Pennant coralfish . . . 1·90 1·60
338 $1 Common blue-striped snapper ("Yellow and blue sea perch") . . . . 2·25 1·90
339 $2 Sailfish . . . . 3·25 4·75
340 $5 White-tipped reef shark 6·50 9·50

1990. 90th Birthday of Queen Elizabeth the Queen Mother. As T **107** (75c.) or **108** ($2) of Kenya.

341 75c. multicoloured . . . . . 1·25 1·50
342 $2 black and green . . . . . 2·75 3·50

DESIGNS—21 × 36 mm: 75c. Queen Elizabeth the Queen Mother. 29 × 37 mm: $2 King George VI and Queen Elizabeth with air raid victim, London, 1940.

1990. Nautical History (2nd series). As T **49**. Multicoloured.

343 15c. "Herald" (whaling ship), 1851 . . . . 75 55
344 50c. "Belle" (barque), 1849 1·50 1·50
345 60c. "Supply" (schooner), 1851 . . . . 1·75 2·25
346 75c. "Triton" (whaling ship), 1848 . . . . 1·75 2·25
MS347 95 × 75 mm. $2 "Charlotte" (convict transport), 1789 . . . 7·50 8·50

57 Manta

1991. Endangered Species. Fishes. Multicoloured.

348 15c. Type **57** . . . . 1·10 55
349 20c. Manta (different) . . . . 1·25 90
350 30c. Whale shark . . . . . . 1·75 2·00
351 35c. Whale shark (different) 2·00 2·25

58 Queen Elizabeth II

1991. 65th Birthday of Queen Elizabeth II and 70th Birthday of Prince Philip. Multicoloured.

366 65c. Type **58** . . . . 1·25 1·50
367 70c. Prince Philip in R.A.F. uniform . . . . 1·25 1·50

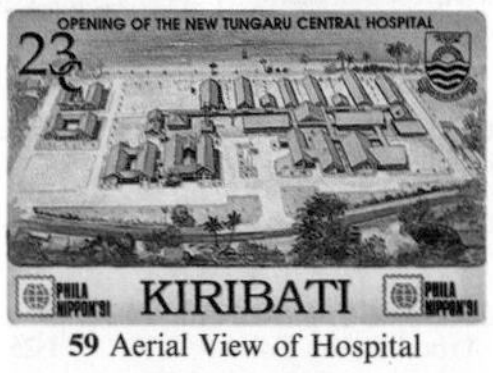

59 Aerial View of Hospital

1991. "Phila Nippon '91" International Stamp Exhibition, Tokyo, and Opening of Tungaru Central Hospital. Multicoloured.

368 23c. Type **59** 40 30
369 50c. Traditional dancers . . . 75 85
370 60c. Hospital entrance . . . 85 1·10
371 75c. Foundation stone and plaques . . . . 1·25 1·60
MS372 125 × 83 mm. $5 Casualty on trolley and ambulance . . . . 7·00 8·00

60 Mother and Child

1991. Christmas. Multicoloured.

373 23c. Type **60** 60 40
374 50c. The Holy Family in Pacific setting . . . . . . 1·10 90
375 60c. The Holy Family in traditional setting . . . . 1·25 1·50
376 75c. Adoration of the Shepherds . . . . 1·50 2·00

1992. 40th Anniv of Queen Elizabeth II's Accession. As T **214** of Lesotho. Multicoloured.

377 23c. Kiribati village 30 30
378 30c. Lagoon at sunset 40 45
379 50c. Tarawa waterfront . . . 60 70
380 60c. Three portraits of Queen Elizabeth 70 90
381 75c. Queen Elizabeth II . . . 90 1·10

1992. "EXPO '92" World's Fair, Seville. Nos. 356, 336/7 and 339 optd **EXPO'92 SEVILLA**.

382 23c. Bennett's pufferfish . . . 55 40
383 60c. Stocky hawkfish . . . . 1·25 1·50
384 75c. Pennant coralfish . . . 1·40 1·60
385 $2 Sailfish . . . . 3·00 4·00

62 Marine Training Centre Sign

1992. 25th Anniv of Marine Training Centre. Multicoloured.

386 23c. Type **62** 45 40
387 50c. Cadets on parade . . . 80 1·00
388 60c. Fire school . . . . . . 80 1·00
389 75c. Lifeboat training . . . . 1·10 1·40

63 Healthy Children

1992. United Nations World Health and Food and Agriculture Organizations. Multicoloured.

390 23c. Type **63** 55 50
391 50c. Fishing at night . . . . 1·00 1·00
392 60c. Fruit . . . . 1·25 1·50
393 75c. "Papuan Chief" (container ship) . . . . . 2·50 2·50

64 Phoenix Petrel

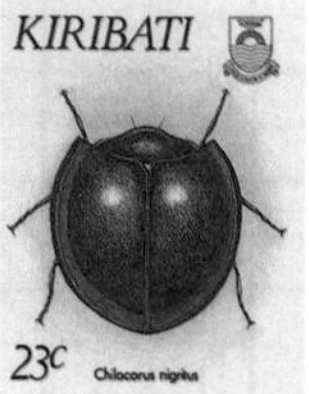

65 "Chilocorus nigritus"

1993. Birds. Multicoloured.

394 23c. Type **64** 40 70
395 23c. Cook's petrel 40 70
396 60c. Pintail ("Northern Pintail") . . . . 90 1·25
397 60c. European wigeon ("Eurasian Wigeon") . . . 90 1·25
398 75c. Spectacled tern . . . . 1·00 1·25
399 75c. Black-naped tern . . . . 1·00 1·25
400 $1 Australian stilt ("Stilt Wader") . . . . 1·25 1·40
401 $1 Wandering tattler . . . . 1·25 1·40

1993. Insects. Multicoloured.

402 23c. Type **65** . . . . 1·25 55
403 60c. "Rodolia pumila" (ladybird) . . . . 2·25 2·25
404 75c. "Rodolia cardinalis" (ladybird) . . . . 2·50 2·75
405 $1 "Cryptolaemus montrouzieri" . . . . . . 2·75 3·25

66 U.S. Air Reconnaissance Consolidated B-24 Liberator

1993. 50th Anniv of Battle of Tarawa. Multicoloured.

406 23c. Type **66** 75 75
407 23c. U.S.S. "Nautilus" (submarine) 75 75
408 23c. U.S.S. "Indianapolis" (cruiser) 75 75
409 23c. U.S.S. "Pursuit" (destroyer) 75 75
410 23c. Vought Sikorsky Kingfisher spotter seaplane 75 75
411 23c. U.S.S. "Ringgold" and "Dashiell" (destroyers) . . 75 75
412 23c. Sherman tank on seabed 75 75
413 23c. Grumman Hellcat fighter aircraft in lagoon 75 75
414 23c. Naval wreck on seabed 75 75
415 23c. First U.S. aircraft to land on Betio 75 75
416 75c. Landing craft leaving transports . . . . 1·25 1·25
417 75c. Marines landing on Betio . . . . 1·25 1·25
418 75c. Landing craft approaching beach . . . . 1·25 1·25
419 75c. Marines pinned down in surf . . . . 1·25 1·25
420 75c. U.S.S. "Maryland" (battleship) . . . . 1·25 1·25
421 75c. Aerial view of Betio Island . . . . 1·25 1·25
422 75c. U.S. Navy memorial . . 1·25 1·25
423 75c. Memorial to expatriates 1·25 1·25
424 75c. Japanese memorial . . . 1·25 1·25
425 75c. Plan of Betio Island . . 1·25 1·25

67 Shepherds and Angels

1993. Christmas. Pacific Nativity Scenes. Mult.

426 23c. Type **67** 40 30
427 40c. Three Kings 65 70
428 60c. Holy Family . . . . . . 85 1·25
429 75c. Virgin and Child . . . . 1·10 1·50
MS430 100 × 81 mm. $3 Virgin and Child (different) . . . . 3·75 5·50

68 Group of Dogs

1994. "Hong Kong '94" International Stamp Exhibition. Chinese New Year ("Year of the Dog"). Sheet 120 × 90 mm.

MS431 **68** $3 multicoloured . . . 4·00 5·50

69 Bryde's Whale and Calf

1994. Whales. Multicoloured.

432 23c. Type **69** . . . . 1·00 1·25
433 23c. Bryde's whale with two calves . . . . 1·00 1·25
434 40c. Blue whale and calf (face value at left) . . . . . . 1·25 1·40
435 40c. Blue whales and calf (face value at right) . . . . 1·25 1·40
436 60c. Humpback whale and calf (face value at left) . . 1·90 2·25
437 60c. Humpback whale and calf (face value at right) . . 1·90 2·25
438 75c. Killer whale and calf . . 1·90 2·25
439 75c. Killer whale and two calves . . . . 1·90 2·25

70 Family silhouetted on Beach

1994. 15th Anniv of Independence. Protecting the Environment. Multicoloured.
440 40c. Type **70** 60 60
441 60c. Fish and coral . . . . . . 1·00 1·25
442 75c. Great frigate birds in flight . . . . 1·25 1·50

71 "Diaphania indica" 72 "Nerium oleander"

1994. Butterflies and Moths. Multicoloured.
443 1c. Type **71** 10 15
444 5c. "Herpetogramma licarsisalis" 15 20
445 10c. "Parotis suralis" 25 20
446 12c. "Sufetula sunidesalis" . . 25 20
447 20c. "Aedia sericea" 35 25
448 23c. "Anomis vitiensis" . . . 35 25
449 30c. "Anticarsia irrorata" . . 45 30
450 35c. "Spodoptera litura" . . 55 40
451 40c. "Mocis frugalis" 65 50
452 45c. "Agrius convolvuli" . . 70 50
453 50c. "Cephonodes picus" . . 75 55
454 55c. "Gnathothlibus erotus" 80 60
455 60c. "Macroglossum hirundo" 80 60
456 75c. "Badamia exclamationis" 1·00 75
457 $1 "Precis villida" . . . . . 1·40 1·40
458 $2 "Danaus plexippus" . . . 2·25 2·50
459 $3 "Hypolimnas bolina" (male) . . . . 2·75 3·25
460 $5 "Hypolimnas bolina" (female) . . . . 3·75 4·50
See also No. **MS**527.

1994. Seasonal Flowers. Multicoloured.
461 23c. Type **72** 30 30
462 60c. "Catharanthus roseus" 80 1·25
463 75c. "Ipomea pes-caprae" . . 1·00 1·40
464 $1 "Calophyllum inophyllum" . . . . 1·40 2·00

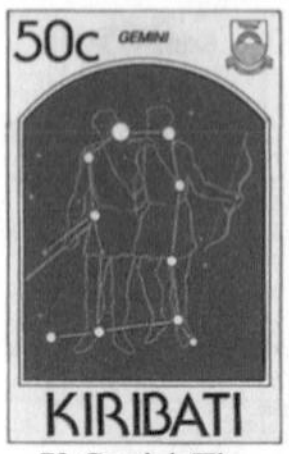

73 Gemini (The Twins) 74 Church and Traditional Meeting Hut

1995. Night Sky over Kiribati. Multicoloured.
465 50c. Type **73** 75 75
466 60c. Cancer (The Crab) . . . 85 1·00
467 75c. Cassiopeia (The Queen of Ethiopia) . . . . 1·00 1·40
468 $1 Southern Cross . . . . . 1·25 1·75

1995. Tourism. Multicoloured.
469 30c. Type **74** 85 95
470 30c. Fishermen and outrigger canoes 85 95
471 30c. Gun emplacement and map 85 95
472 30c. Children with marine creatures 85 95
473 30c. Sports 85 95
474 40c. Local girls in traditional costume 85 95
475 40c. Windsurfing 85 95
476 40c. Fishermen and wood carver 85 95
477 40c. Underwater sport . . . 85 95
478 40c. Women weaving 85 95

75 Grumman TBF Avenger

1995. 50th Anniv of End of Second World War. American Aircraft. Multicoloured.
489 23c. Type **75** 60 45
490 40c. Curtiss SOC.3-1 Seagull seaplane 80 70
491 50c. Consolidated B-24 Liberator bomber 90 90
492 60c. Grumman G-21 Goose amphibian . . . . 1·10 1·10
493 75c. Martin B-26 Marauder bomber . . . . 1·40 1·50
494 $1 Northrop P-61 Black Widow bomber . . . . . 1·60 1·75
MS495 75 × 85 mm. $2 Reverse of 1939–45 War Medal (vert) . . 2·50 3·00

76 Eclectus Parrots, Great Frigate Bird and Coconut Crabs

1995. Protecting the Environment. Multicoloured.
496 60c. Type **76** . . . . 85 1·10
497 60c. Red-tailed tropic birds, common dolphin and pantropical spotted dolphin 85 1·10
498 60c. Blue-striped snapper ("Yellow and blue sea perch"), blue-barred orange parrotfish and green turtle 85 1·10
499 60c. Red-breasted wrasse, pennant coralfish and violet squirrelfish . . . . 85 1·10

1995. "Jakarta '95" Stamp Exhibition, Indonesia. Nos. 496/9 optd **JAKARTA 95** within emblem.
500 60c. Type **76** . . . . 1·75 2·00
501 60c. Red-tailed tropic birds, common dolphin and pantropical spotted dolphin 1·75 2·00
502 60c. Blue-striped snapper, blue-barred orange parrotfish and green turtle 1·75 2·00
503 60c. Red-breasted wrasse, pennant coralfish and violet squirrelfish . . . . 1·75 2·00

78 Sow feeding Piglets

1995. "Singapore '95" International Stamp Exhibition and Beijing International Coin and Stamp Expo '95. Two sheets, each 113 × 85 mm, containing T **78**.
MS504 $2 multicoloured ("Singapore '95") . . . . . . 2·50 3·25
MS505 $2 multicoloured ("Beijing '95") . . . . 3·00 3·75
Nos. **MS**504/5 show the exhibition logos on the sheet margins.

79 "Teanoai" (police patrol boat)

1995. Police Maritime Unit. Multicoloured.
506 75c. Type **79** . . . . 1·40 1·75
507 75c. "Teanoai" at sea . . . . 1·40 1·75

80 Pantropical Spotted Dolphins

1996. Dolphins. Multicoloured.
508 23c. Type **80** . . . . 1·00 55
509 60c. Spinner dolphins . . . . 1·75 1·25
510 75c. Fraser's dolphins . . . . 1·90 1·75
511 $1 Rough-toothed dolphins 2·00 2·25

81 Tap and Top Left Segment of UNICEF Emblem

1996. 50th Anniv of UNICEF. Multicoloured.
512 30c. Type **81** 50 70
513 30c. Documents and top right segment 50 70
514 30c. Syringe and bottom left segment 50 70
515 30c. Open book and bottom right segment 50 70
Nos. 512/15 were printed together, se-tenant, with each block of 4 showing the complete emblem.

82 Chinese Dragon

1996. "CHINA '96" 9th Asian International Stamp Exhibition, Peking. Sheet 110 × 86 mm.
MS516 **82** 50c. multicoloured . . 1·00 1·50

83 L.M.S. No. 5609 "Gilbert and Ellice Islands" Locomotive

1996. "CAPEX '96" International Stamp Exhibition, Toronto. Sheet 111 × 80 mm.
MS517 **83** $2 multicoloured . . . 2·40 3·00

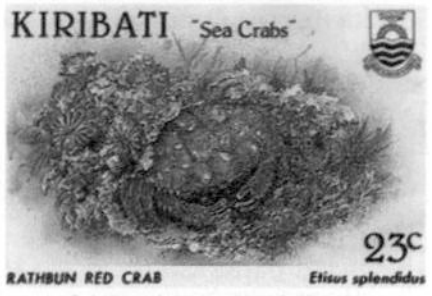

84 Rathbun Red Crab

1996. Sea Crabs. Multicoloured.
518 23c. Type **84** 50 40
519 60c. Red and white painted crab 90 80
520 75c. Red-spotted crab . . . . 1·10 1·10
521 $1 Red-spotted white crab . . 1·60 2·50

85 Kiribati Canoe

1996. "Taipei '96" International Stamp Exhibition, Taiwan. Sheet 110 × 86 mm.
MS522 **85** $1.50 multicoloured 3·00 3·50

1996. Nautical History (3rd series). As T **49**. Multicoloured.
523 23c. "Potomac" (whaling ship), 1843 . . . . . . 60 40
524 50c. "Southern Cross IV" (missionary ship), 1891 . . 90 90
525 60c. "John Williams III" (missionary sailing ship), 1890 . . . . 1·10 1·10
526 $1 H.M.S. "Dolphin" (frigate), 1765 . . . . . . 1·60 2·00

1997. "HONG KONG '97" International Stamp Exhibition. Sheet 130 × 90 mm, containing No. 457. Multicoloured.
MS527 $1 "Precis villida" . . . 1·10 1·60

1997. "Pacific '97" International Stamp Exhibition, San Francisco. Nos. 489/94 optd **PACIFIC 97 World Philatelic Exhibition San Francisco, California 29 May - 8 June**.
528 23c. Type **75** 40 35
529 40c. Curtiss SOC.3-1 Seagull seaplane 60 55
530 50c. Consolidated B-24 Liberator bomber 70 70
531 60c. Grumman G-21 Goose amphibian 80 90
532 75c. Martin B-26 Marauder bomber . . . . 90 1·10
533 $1 Northrop P-61 Black Widow bomber . . . . . 1·10 1·40
MS534 75 × 85 mm. $2 Reverse of 1939–45 War Medal (vert) . . 2·10 2·75

87 Queen Elizabeth II in 1996 88 Young Rock Dove

1997. Golden Wedding of Queen Elizabeth and Prince Philip. Multicoloured.
535 50c. Type **87** . . . . 1·25 1·50
536 50c. Prince Philip carriage-driving at Windsor Horse Show . . . . 1·25 1·50
537 60c. Queen in phaeton at Trooping the Colour . . . 1·25 1·50
538 60c. Prince Philip on Montserrat, 1993 . . . . . 1·25 1·50
539 75c. Queen Elizabeth and Prince Philip, 1989 . . . . 1·25 1·50
540 75c. Prince Edward on horseback . . . . 1·25 1·50
MS541 110 × 70 mm. $2 Queen Elizabeth and Prince Philip in Landau (horiz) . . . . 4·00 4·50
Nos. 535/6, 537/8 and 539/40 respectively were printed together, se-tenant, with the backgrounds forming composite designs.

1997. Birds. Multicoloured.
542 50c. Type **88** . . . . 1·00 1·25
543 50c. Adult rock dove . . . . 1·00 1·25
544 60c. Adult Pacific pigeon . . 1·00 1·25
545 60c. Young Pacific pigeon . . 1·00 1·25
546 75c. Adult Micronesian pigeon . . . . 1·00 1·25
547 75c. Young Micronesian pigeon . . . . 1·00 1·25

1997. "ASIA '97" Stamp Exhibition, Bangkok. Nos. 542/3 and 546/7 optd **ASIA '97 KIRIBATI 5 - 14 OCTOBER** and elephant.
548 50c. Type **88** . . . . 85 1·25
549 50c. Adult rock dove . . . . 85 1·25
550 75c. Adult Micronesian pigeon . . . . 1·00 1·40
551 75c. Young Micronesian pigeon . . . . 1·00 1·40

90 Spiny Lobster

1998. Endangered Species. Spiny Lobster. Multicoloured.
552 25c. Type **90** 40 60
553 25c. Facing right 40 60
554 25c. With coral in foreground 40 60
555 25c. On sponge 40 60
MS556 69 × 49 mm. $1.50 Spiny Lobster . . . . 1·90 2·50
No. **MS**556 does not show the W.W.F. panda emblem.

91 Diana, Princess of Wales, 1992

1998. Diana, Princess of Wales Commemoration.
557 **91** 25c. multicoloured 50 60
MS558 145 × 70 mm. 25c. Type **91**; 50c. Wearing black evening dress, 1981; 60c. With scarf over head, 1992; 75c. Wearing brown jacket, 1993 (sold at $2.10 + 50c. charity premium) . . . . 2·50 3·00

92 Children and Smiling Sun

1998. "Towards the Millennium" (1st issue). Sheet 102 × 69 mm.
MS559 **92** $1 multicoloured . . . 1·25 2·00
See also Nos. 580/4 and 594/8.

93 Indo-Pacific Humpbacked Dolphin

1998. Whales and Dolphins. Multicoloured.
560 25c. Type **93** 55 65
561 25c. Bottlenose dolphin . . . 55 65
562 60c. Short-snouted spinner dolphin . . . . 80 1·00
563 60c. Risso's dolphin . . . . 80 1·00
564 75c. Striped dolphin . . . . 1·00 1·10
565 75c. Sei whale . . . . 1·00 1·10
566 $1 Fin whale . . . . 1·25 1·40
567 $1 Minke whale . . . . . . 1·25 1·40

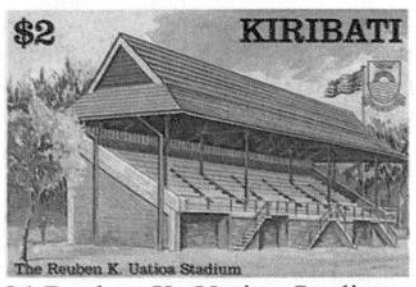

94 Reuben K. Uatioa Stadium, Kiribati

1998. "Italia '98" International Stamp Exhibition, Milan. Sheet 110 × 85 mm.

MS568	**94** $2 multicoloured	2·00	2·75

95 Pollutants and Harmful Emissions

1998. The Greenhouse Effect. Multicoloured.

569	25c. Type **95**	30	30
570	50c. Diagram of greenhouse effect	50	50
571	60c. Diagram of rising sea levels on Tarawa	60	65
572	75c. Diagram of rising sea levels on Kiritimati	70	85
MS573	103 × 69 mm. $1.50 Outrigger canoe	3·25	3·25

96 H.M.S. "Resolution" (Cook) at Christmas Island, 1777

1999. "Australia '99" World Stamp Exhibition, Melbourne. Sheet 136 × 56 mm.

MS574	**96** $2 multicoloured	2·25	2·75

97 Northern Shoveler (male)

1999. "iBRA '99" International Stamp Exhibition, Nuremberg. Ducks. Multicoloured.

575	25c. Type **97**	60	50
576	50c. Northern Shoveler (female) and ducklings	75	65
577	60c. Green-winged teal (male)	80	80
578	75c. Green-winged teal (female) and ducklings	90	1·00
MS579	100 × 70 mm. $3 Green-winged teal (male) and duckling	3·00	3·75

98 Map of Millennium Island

1999. "Towards the Millennium" (2nd issue). 20th Anniv of Independence. Multicoloured.

580	25c. Type **98**	80	80
581	60c. Map of Kiribati	1·25	1·25
582	75c. Map of Nikumaroro	1·25	1·25
583	$1 Amelia Earhart (aviator)	1·75	1·75
MS584	100 × 80 mm. Nos. 582/3	2·75	3·25

No. 581 shows Tarawa as "TAROWA" in error.

See also Nos. 594/8.

98a Buzz Aldrin (astronaut)

1999. 30th Anniv of First Manned Landing on Moon. Multicoloured.

585	25c. Type **98a**	35	35
586	60c. Service module docking with lunar module	65	75
587	75c. "Apollo 11" on Moon's surface	75	85
588	$1 Command module separating from service section	95	1·10
MS589	90 × 80 mm. $2 Kiribati as seen from Moon (circular, 40 mm diam)	1·90	2·50

99 Santa Claus in Sailing Canoe

1999. Christmas and 125th Anniv of Universal Postal Union. Multicoloured.

590	25c. Type **99**	35	25
591	60c. Santa and unloading freighter	65	65
592	75c. Santa in sleigh passing aircraft	80	85
593	$1 Santa using computer	1·00	1·40

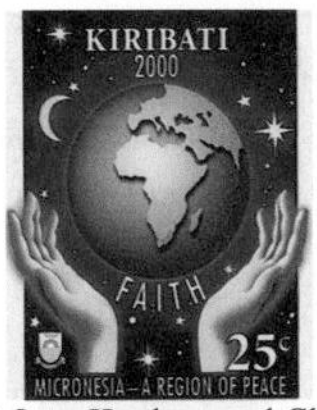

100 Open Hands around Globe ("FAITH")

2000. "Towards the Millennium" (3rd issue). "A Region of Peace". Multicoloured.

594	25c. Type **100**	30	35
595	40c. Solar eclipse ("HARMONY")	45	55
596	60c. Stars and Sun over Earth ("HOPE")	60	75
597	75c. Sun over Earth ("ENLIGHTENMENT")	75	90
598	$1 Dove over Earth ("PEACE")	90	1·10

101 Bert feeding Pigeons

2000. "Sesame Street" (children's T.V. programme). Multicoloured.

599	20c. Type **101**	20	30
600	20c. Little Bear flying kite	20	30
601	20c. Grover calling	20	30
602	20c. Elmo and Cookie Monster	20	30
603	20c. Telly leaning out of window	20	30
604	20c. Zoe painting house	20	30
605	20c. Ernie with bird	20	30
606	20c. Big Bird and Rosita reading	20	30
607	20c. Oscar the Grouch and Slimey in dustbin	20	30
MS608	139 × 86 mm. $1.50 Grover as postman	1·40	1·75

Nos. 599/607 were printed together, se-tenant, with the backgrounds forming a composite design.

102 Queen Elizabeth II in Kiribati, 1982

2000. "The Stamp Show 2000" International Stamp Exhibition, London. Sheet 80 × 70 mm.

MS609	**102** $5 multicoloured	4·25	5·00

2000. "EXPO 2000" World's Fair, Hanover. Nos. 444/5, 447, 457 and 459 optd **KIRIBATI AT EXPO 2000 1.06-31.10.2000.**

610	5c. *Herpetogramma licarsisalis*	15	25
611	10c. *Parotis suralis*	15	25
612	20c. *Aedia sericea*	25	30
613	$1 *Precis villida*	1·00	1·25
614	$3 *Hypolimnas bolina* (male)	2·75	3·25

104 Prince William as a Baby with Prince Charles

2000. 18th Birthday of Prince William. Each showing Prince William with Prince Charles. Multicoloured.

615	25c. Type **104**	40	35
616	60c. In Italy, 1985	75	75
617	75c. At Sandringham, Christmas, 1992	85	85
618	$1 At Balmoral, 1997	1·10	1·40

105 Wandering Whistling Duck

2001. Ducks. Multicoloured.

619	25c. Type **105**	45	45
620	25c. Green-winged teal	45	45
621	25c. Mallard	45	45
622	25c. Northern shoveler	45	45
623	25c. Pacific black duck	45	45
624	25c. Mountain duck ("Blue Duck")	45	45
MS625	85 × 75 mm. $1 Grey teal	2·00	2·25

106 Man with Tap (Tiare Hongkai)

2001. Water Conservation. Children's Drawings. Multicoloured.

626	25c. Type **106**	35	30
627	50c. Cooking pot on fire and house in rain (Gilbert Tluanga)	50	45
628	60c. Map in raindrop and cup (Mantokataake Tebaiuea) (vert)	55	50
629	75c. Hand holding drop (Tokaman Karanebo) (vert)	70	70
630	$2 Water management system (Taom Simon)	1·60	2·25

107 Betio Port

2001. "Philanippon '01" International Stamp Exhibition, Tokyo. Development Projects. Multicoloured.

631	75c. Type **107**	75	65
632	$2 New Parliament House complex	1·75	2·25

108 Norwegian Cruise Liner and Map of Route

2001. Tourism. Fanning Island. Multicoloured.

633	75c. Type **108**	75	60
634	$3 *Betsey* (full-rigged sealer) and map of Fanning Island	2·75	3·25

109 *Paracanthrus hepatus*

2002. Tropical Fish. Multicoloured.

635	5c. Type **109**	10	10
636	10c. *Centropyge flavissimus*	10	10
637	15c. *Anthias squamipinnis*	15	20
638	20c. *Centropyge loriculus*	15	20
639	25c. *Acanthurus lineatus*	20	25
640	30c. *Oxycirrhites typus*	25	30
641	40c. *Dascyllus trimaculatus*	35	40
642	50c. *Acanthurus achilles*	40	45
643	60c. *Pomacentrus caeruleus*	50	55
644	75c. *Acanthurus glaucopareius*	65	70
645	80c. *Thalassoma lunare*	65	70
646	90c. *Arothron meleagris*	75	80
647	$1 *Odonus niger*	85	90
648	$2 *Cephalopholis miniatus*	1·70	1·80
649	$5 *Pomacanthus imperator*	4·25	4·50
650	$10 *Balistoides conspicillum*	8·50	8·75

The 60c. is inscribed "coeruleus" in error.

110 Admiral Bellinghausen and *Vostok*, 1820

2002. Pacific Explorers. Multicoloured.

651	25c. Type **110**	40	35
652	40c. Captain Wilkes and the U.S.S. *Vincennes* (sail frigate), 1838–42	60	45
653	60c. Captain Fanning and *Betsey* (full-rigged sealer), 1798	70	65
654	75c. Captain Coffin and *Transit* (full-rigged ship), 1823	75	70
655	$1 Commodore Byron and H.M.S. *Dolphin* (frigate), 1765	90	1·00
656	$3 Captain Broughton and H.M.S. *Providence* (sloop), 1795	2·50	3·00
MS657	92 × 63 mm. $5 Captain Cook (vert)	5·00	5·50

111 Statue of Liberty with U.S. and Kiribati Flags

2002. In Remembrance. Victims of Terrorist Attacks on U.S.A. (11 September 2001).

658	**111** 25c. multicoloured	50	30
659	$2 multicoloured	2·00	2·50

112 Queen Elizabeth in 1953 **113** Woven "Parcel"

2002. Golden Jubilee. Featuring photographs by Dorothy Wilding. Multicoloured.

660	25c. Type **112**	60	60
MS661	135 × 110 mm. $2 Queen Elizabeth wearing Garter sash; $2 Queen Elizabeth in evening dress	4·50	5·00

2002. Christmas.

662	**113** 25c. multicoloured	35	25
663	– 60c. multicoloured	55	50
664	– 75c. multicoloured	70	60
665	– $1 multicoloured	80	80
666	– $2.50 multicoloured	2·25	2·50

DESIGNS: 60c. to $2.50 show different weave patterns.

114 *Cypraea mappa*

2003. Cowrie Shells of Kiribati. Multicoloured.

667	25c. Type **114**	20	25
668	50c. *Cypraea eglantine*	40	45
669	60c. *Cypraea mauritiana*	50	55
670	75c. *Cypraea cribraria*	65	70
671	$1 *Cypraea talpa*	85	90
672	$2.50 *Cypraea depressa*	2·10	2·20
MS673	130 × 95 mm. Nos. 667/72	4·75	5·00

115 Queen Elizabeth II and Duke of Edinburgh waving from Palace Balcony

2003. 50th Anniv of Coronation. Multicoloured.

674	25c. Type **114**	20	25
675	$3 Newly crowned Queen in Coronation ceremony	2·50	2·75
MS676	95 × 115 mm. $2 As Type **115**; $5 As $3	4·25	4·50

116 Sopwith Camel

2003. Centenary of Powered Flight. Multicoloured.

674	25c. Type **116**	20	25
675	50c. Northrop Alpha	40	45
676	60c. De Havilland D.H.106 Comet	50	55
677	75c. Boeing 727	65	70
678	$1 English Electric Canberra	85	90
679	$2.50 Lockheed Martin F22	2·10	2·25
MS680	115 × 65 mm. 40c. Mitsubishi A6M-5 Zero; 60c. Grumman F6F Hellcat	85	90

No. **MS**680 also commemorates the 60th anniversary of the Battle of Tarawa.

117 Teareba Teomeka, Tabwakea

118 Road Sign showing Car Accident

2003. Christmas. Churches of Christmas Island. Multicoloured.

681	25c. Type **117**	20	25
682	40c. Seventh-Day Adventist Church, London (Port Camp)	35	40
683	50c. St. Teresa Catholic Church, Tabakea Village	40	45
684	60c. Betaera Fou, London	50	55
685	75c. Children standing by church bells, London	75	80
686	$1.50 Emanuira Church, London	1·30	1·40
687	$2.50 Church of Christ (Ana Ekaretia Kristo) (58 × 22 mm)	2·10	2·20
MS688	144 × 82 mm. Nos. 681/7	5·50	6·00

2004. World Health Day. Road Safety. Multicoloured.

692	30c. Type **118**	25	30
693	40c. Road sign showing speeding car	35	40
694	50c. Road sign showing cigarette and alcohol	40	45
695	60c. Road sign showing children	50	55
MS696	165 × 58 mm. As Nos. 692/5	1·50	1·50

119 Pacific Golden Plover

2004. Bird Life International. Shore Birds. Multicoloured.

697	25c. Type **119**	20	25
698	40c. Whimbrel	35	40
699	50c. Wandering tattler (*Heteroscelus incanus*)	40	45
700	60c. Sanderling	50	55
701	75c. Bar-tailed godwit	60	65
702	$2.50 Ruddy turnstone	2·00	2·10
MS703	175 × 80 mm. $1 Head of Bristle-thighed curlew; $1 Front of Bristle-thighed curlew (vert); $1 Back of Bristle-thighed curlew (vert); $1 Two Bristle-thighed curlews; $1 Bristle-thighed curlews and tree	4·00	4·00

120 Athletes

2004. Olympic Games, Athens. Multicoloured.

704	25c. Type **120**	20	25
705	50c. Taekwondo	40	45
706	60c. Weight-lifting	50	55
707	75c. Sprinting	60	65
MS708	98 × 74 mm. $2.50 Athletes in training; $2.50 Athletes in front of Parliament House	4·00	4·00

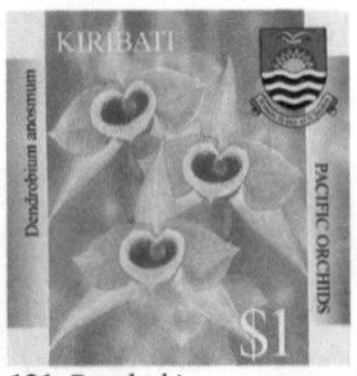

121 *Dendrobium anosmum*

2004. Orchids. Multicoloured.

709	$1 Type **121**	80	85
710	$1 *Dendrobium chrysotoxum*	80	85
711	$1 *Dendrobium laevifolium*	80	85
712	$1 *Dendrobium mohlianum*	80	85
713	$1 *Dendrobium pseudoglomeratum*	80	85
714	$1 *Dendrobium purpureum*	80	85
715	$1 *Grammatophyllum speciosum*	80	85
716	$1 *Dendrobium williamsianum*	80	85
717	$1 *Spathoglottis plicata*	80	85
718	$1 *Vanda hindsii*	80	85

Nos. 709/18 were printed together, se-tenant, with the backgrounds forming composite designs.

122 MV *Montelucia*

2004. Merchant Ships. Multicoloured.

719	50c. Type **122**	40	45
720	75c. MS *Pacific Princess*	60	65
721	$2.50 MS *Prinsendam*	2·00	2·10
722	$5 MS *Norwegian Wind*	4·00	4·25

OFFICIAL STAMPS

1981. Nos. 86/135 optd **O.K.G.S.**

O11	1c. Type **16**	10	50
O12	3c. M.V. "Tautunu" (inter-island freighter)	10	30
O13	5c. Hibiscus	10	20
O14	7c. Catholic Cathedral, Tarawa	10	20
O15	10c. Maneaba, Bikenibeu	10	20
O16	12c. Betio Harbour	30	30
O17	15c. Reef heron	1·75	30
O18	20c. Flamboyant tree	20	30
O19	25c. Moorish idol (fish)	30	30
O20	30c. Frangipani	30	35
O21	35c. G.I.P.C. Chapel, Tangintebu	35	40
O22	50c. "Hypolimnas bolina" (butterfly)	1·00	55
O23	$1 "Tabakea" (Tarawa Lagoon ferry)	65	50
O24	$2 Evening scene	70	70
O25	$5 National flag	1·25	1·75

1983. Nos. 169, 172/3, 175 and 177 optd **O.K.G.S.**

O36	12c. Polynesian reed warbler	40	30
O37	30c. Brown booby	70	50
O38	35c. Audubon's shearwater	80	60
O39	50c. Bristle-thighed curlew	1·00	80
O40	$2 Long-tailed koel	3·00	2·75

POSTAGE DUE STAMPS

D 1 Kiribati Coat of Arms

1981.

D1	**D 1**	1c. black and mauve	10	10
D2		2c. black and blue	10	10
D3		5c. black and green	10	10
D4		10c. black and brown	10	15
D5		20c. black and blue	15	25
D6		30c. black and brown	15	35
D7		40c. black and purple	20	45
D8		50c. black and green	20	50
D9		$1 black and red	30	75

KISHANGARH Pt. 1

A state of Rajasthan, India. Now uses Indian stamps.

12 pies = 1 anna; 16 annas = 1 rupee.

1

1899. Imperf or perf.

1	**1**	1a. green	22·00	55·00
3		1a. blue	£400	

2 (¼a.)

5 (2a.) Maharaja Sardul Singh

1899. Various arms designs. Perf or imperf.

21	**2**	¼a. green	£200	£400
22a		¼a. red	25	40
25		½a. green	13·00	16·00
8		½a. red	£2000	£1100
26a		½a. blue	85	50
7		½a. lilac	£130	£250
27		1a. grey	4·75	3·25
29		1a. mauve	75	1·00
12b		1a. pink	65·00	£180
15	**5**	2a. orange	4·50	4·50
31	**2**	4a. brown	2·00	5·50
32		1r. green	10·00	15·00
17		1r. lilac	20·00	32·00
33		1r. yellow	£750	
34		2r. red	35·00	50·00
35		5r. mauve	35·00	50·00

11 (½a.)

12 Maharaja Sardul Singh

1903. Imperf or perf.

39	**11**	½a. pink	11·00	3·00
40	**12**	2a. orange	3·00	6·00
41	**2**	8a. grey	5·00	7·50

13 Maharaja Madan Singh

14 Maharaja Madan Singh

1904.

42	**13**	¼a. red	45	75
43a		½a. brown	1·00	30
44a		1a. blue	1·75	2·00
45		2a. orange	15·00	7·00
46a		4a. brown	15·00	17·00
47		8a. violet	8·50	21·00
48		1r. green	25·00	38·00
49		2r. yellow	25·00	£150
50		5r. brown	23·00	£180

1912.

63	**14**	¼a. blue	20	45
64		½a. green	20	1·00
65		1a. red	1·00	2·50
54		2a. purple	2·50	5·00
67		4a. blue	6·00	8·00
68		8a. brown	7·00	40·00
69		1r. mauve	16·00	£120
70		2r. green	95·00	£350
71		5r. brown	40·00	£400

15

16 Maharaja Yagyanarayan Singh

1913.

59	**15**	¼a. blue	30	90
60		2a. purple	7·00	18·00

1928.

72	**16**	¼a. blue	80	2·00
73		½a. green	3·00	2·00
74	–	1a. red	75	1·50
75	–	2a. purple	3·00	8·50
76	**16**	4a. brown	1·50	1·75
77		8a. violet	3·75	27·00
78		1r. green	16·00	60·00
79		2r. yellow	28·00	£190
80		5r. red	38·00	£225

Nos. 74/5 are larger.

OFFICIAL STAMPS

1918. Optd **ON K S D**.

O 5	**2**	¼a. green	—	£120
O 6		¼a. pink	2·25	60
O 7		½a. blue	£160	40·00
O 9		1a. mauve	42·00	1·50
O10	**5**	2a. orange	—	£130
O11	**2**	4a. brown	55·00	16·00
O16		8a. grey	80·00	22·00
O12		1r. green	£160	£110
O13		2r. brown	—	£850
O14		5r. mauve	—	£1700

1918. Optd **ON K S D**.

O15	**12**	2a. orange	75·00	5·00

1918. Optd **ON K S D**.

O17	**13**	¼a. red	—	£275
O18		½a. brown	75	35
O19		1a. blue	8·50	4·00
O20		2a. orange	—	£900
O21		4a. brown	60·00	18·00
O22		8a. violet	£350	£200
O23		1r. green	£700	£650
O24		5r. brown		

1918. Optd **ON K S D**.

O28	**14**	¼a. blue	60	50
O29		½a. green	90	75
O30a		1a. red	1·00	1·00
O31		2a. purple	7·00	4·00
O32		4a. blue	23·00	15·00
O33		8a. brown	£120	42·00
O34		1r. mauve	£325	£325
O35		2r. green		
O36		5r. brown	£1600	

1918. Optd **ON K S D**.

O25	**15**	¼a. blue	6·00	
O27		2a. purple	£475	£500

For later issues see **RAJASTHAN.**

KOREA Pt. 18

A peninsula to the S. of Manchuria in E. Asia. Formerly an empire under Chinese suzerainty, it was annexed by Japan in 1910 and used Japanese stamps. After the defeat of Japan in 1945, Russian and United States Military administrations were set up in Korea to the north and south of the 38th Parallel respectively; in 1948 South Korea and North Korea became independent republics.

KOREAN EMPIRE

1884. 100 mon = 1 tempo.
1895. 5 poon = 1 cheun.
1900. 10 re (or rin) = 1 cheun; 100 cheun = 1 weun.

1 3 Korean Flag (4)

1894.

1	1	5m. pink	34·00	£4000
2	–	10m. blue	7·50	£2500

DESIGN: 10m. Central motif as in Type **1** but different frame and inscribed "CORGAN POST POST".

1895.

7	3	5p. green	14·00	12·00
8		10p. blue	18·00	10·00
9		25p. red	14·00	16·00
10a		50p. lilac	12·00	6·50

1897. Optd with T **4**.

12	3	5p. green	20·00	15·00
13		10p. blue	24·00	20·00
14		25p. red	30·00	24·00
16		50p. lilac	30·00	20·00

1899. Surch in Korean characters.

17	3	1(p.) on 5p. green (No. 7)	£1200	£750
20		1(p.) on 5p. green (No. 12)	£250	£200
18		1(p.) on 25p. red (No. 9)	£150	75·00
21		1(p.) on 25p. red (No. 14)	50·00	32·00

6 7 National Emblems 8

1900. T **6**, **7** (2ch.), **8** (2ch.) and similar designs.

22a		2r. grey	75	1·50
23		1ch. green	5·50	4·00
24		2ch. blue (T **7**)	35·00	38·00
25		2ch. blue (T **8**)	8·00	7·00
26		3ch. orange	7·50	7·50
27		4ch. red	10·00	9·00
28		5ch. pink	10·00	10·00
29		6ch. blue	12·00	11·00
30		10ch. purple	18·00	16·00
31a		15ch. purple	30·00	25·00
32		20ch. red	50·00	38·00
33		50ch. green and pink	£200	£140
34		1wn. multicoloured	£300	£200
35		2wn. green and purple	£500	£250

9 Imperial Crown 17 Falcon, Sceptre and Orb

1902. 40th Anniv of Emperor's Accession as King.

36	9	3ch. orange	32·00	25·00

(10) (11) (12) (16)

Types **10** to **12** are in two parts, the horizontal strokes (one, two or three) representing the value figures and the bottom part being the character for "cheun".

Some variation can be found in these woodblock overprints.

1902. (a) Surch as Types **10** to **12**.

37	3	1ch. on 25p. red (No. 9)	8·50	6·50
38		1ch. on 25p. red (No. 14)	45·00	45·00
39		2ch. on 25p. red (No. 9)	8·50	7·00
40		2ch. on 25p. red (No. 14)	42·00	40·00
42		2ch. on 50p. lilac (No 10a)	–	£350
43		3ch. on 25p. red (No. 9)	42·00	90·00
44		3ch. on 25p. red (No. 14)		
46		3ch. on 50p. lilac (No. 10a)	8·00	10·00
47		3ch. on 50p. lilac (No. 16)	12·00	12·00

(b) Surch as T **16** (Japanese "sen" character) and strokes.

49	3	3ch. on 50p. lilac	£650	£500

1903.

50	17	2r. grey	50	75
51		1ch. purple	4·50	4·50
52		2ch. green	4·50	4·50
53		3ch. orange	5·50	5·50
54		4ch. pink	6·50	6·00
55		5ch. brown	9·00	8·00
56		6ch. lilac	9·00	8·50
57		10ch. blue	12·00	10·00
58		15ch. red on yellow	22·00	22·00
59		20ch. purple on yellow	30·00	32·00
60		50ch. red on green	90·00	95·00
61		1wn. lilac on lilac	£150	£160
62		2wn. purple on orange	£250	£250

SOUTH KOREA

1946. 100 cheun = 1 weun.
1953. 100 weun = 1 hwan.
1962. 100 chon = 1 won.

A. UNITED STATES MILITARY GOVERNMENT

(31) 33 National Emblem

1946. Stamps of Japan surch as T **31**.

69		5ch. on 5s. purple (No. 396)	7·00	7·00
70		5ch. on 14s. red & brn (No. 324)	1·50	1·75
71		10ch. on 40s. purple (No. 407)	1·50	1·50
72		20ch. on 6s. blue (No. 397)	1·50	1·25
73		30ch. on 27s. red (No. 404)	1·50	1·25
74		5w. on 17s. violet (No. 402)	6·50	5·50

1946. Liberation from Japanese Rule.

75	–	3ch. orange	75	65
76	–	5ch. green	75	55
77	–	10ch. red	75	45
78	–	20ch. blue	75	45
79	33	50ch. purple	1·10	80
80		1w. brown	1·40	70

DESIGN : 3ch. to 20ch. Family and flag.

34 Dove of Peace and Map of Korea

1946. 1st Anniv of Liberation.

81	34	50ch. violet	5·00	2·75

35 U.S. and Korean Flags 36 Kyongju Observatory

39 Golden Crown of Silla 40 Admiral Li Sun Sin

1946. Resumption of Postal Service between Korea and U.S.A.

82	35	10w. red	6·00	4·00

1946.

83	36	50ch. blue	75	45
84	–	1w. brown	1·25	60
85	–	2w. blue	1·50	40
86	39	5w. mauve	14·00	6·00
87	40	10w. green	14·00	7·00

DESIGNS—As Type **36**: 1w. Hibiscus; 2w. Map of Korea.

41 Korean Alphabet 42 Li Jun, patriot

44 16th-century "Turtle" Ship 45 Letters Surrounding Globe

1946. 500th Anniv of Creation of Korean Alphabet.

88	41	50ch. blue	3·50	2·00

1947.

89	42	5w. green	8·50	3·00
90	–	10w. blue	8·50	3·00
91	–	20w. red	3·00	65
92	44	50w. brown	40·00	10·00

DESIGNS: 10w. Admiral Li Sun Sin; 20w. Independence Arch, Seoul.

1947. Resumption of Int Postal Service.

93	45	10w. blue	12·00	5·00

46 Douglas DC-4 Airliner

1947. Air. Inauguration of Air Mail Service.

94	46	50w. red	6·00	2·50
126		150w. blue	1·00	90
127		150w. green	8·50	4·00

47 Hand and Ballot Slip 48 Casting Votes

1948. South Korea Election.

95	47	2w. orange	10·00	7·00
96		5w. mauve	10·00	6·00
97		10w. violet	20·00	8·00
98	48	20w. red	30·00	16·00
99		50w. blue	28·00	17·00

49 Korean Flag and Laurel Wreath

1948. Olympic Games.

100	49	5w. green	65·00	35·00
101	–	10w. violet	25·00	14·00

DESIGN—VERT: 10w. Runner with torch.

50 Capitol and Ears of Rice

1948. Meeting of First National Assembly.

102	50	4w. brown	16·00	8·00

MINIATURE SHEETS. Many of the stamps from 1948 to 1956 exist in miniature sheets from limited printings which were presented to postal and government officials.

51 Korean Family

1948. Promulgation of Constitution.

103	51	4w. green	45·00	16·00
104	–	10w. brown	32·00	10·00

DESIGN—HORIZ: 10w. Flag of Korea.

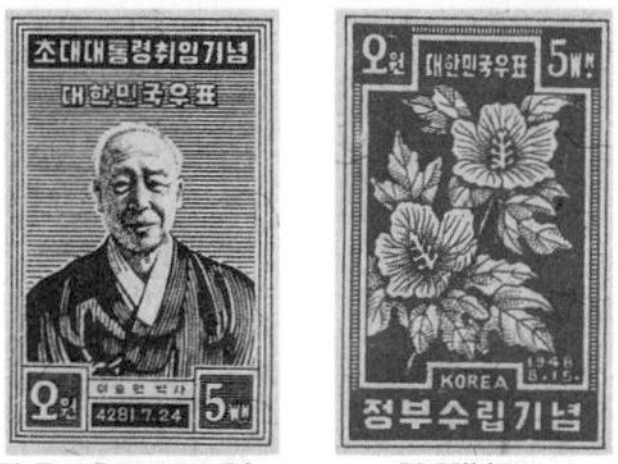

52 Dr. Syngman Rhee (First President) 53 Hibiscus

1948. Election of First President.

105	52	5w. blue	60·00	25·00

B. REPUBLIC OF KOREA

1948. Proclamation of Republic.

106	–	4w. blue	30·00	18·00
107	53	5w. mauve	26·00	16·00

DESIGN: 4w. Dove and olive branch.

54 Li Jun 55 Kyongju Observatory

1948.

108	54	4w. red	40	20
109	55	14w. blue	40	25

56 Doves and U.N. Emblem 57 Citizen and Date

1949. Arrival of U.N. Commission.

110	56	10w. blue	30·00	14·00

1949. National Census.

111	57	15w. violet	30·00	14·00

58 Children and Plant

1949. 20th Anniv of Children's Day.

112	58	15w. violet	15·00	7·00

59 Hibiscus 61 Dove and Globe

60 Map of Korea and Black-billed Magpies 62 Admiral Li Sun Sin

1949.

113	–	1w. red	3·00	1·50
114	–	2w. grey	1·50	60
115	–	5w. green	7·50	2·25
116	–	10w. green	2·75	1·40
117	59	15w. red	45	20
118	–	20w. brown	45	20
119	–	30w. green	50	20
120	–	50w. blue	45	20
121	60	65w. blue	2·10	1·40
122	–	100w. green	50	20
123	61	200w. green	60	35
124	–	400w. brown	60	40
125	62	500w. blue	60	45

DESIGNS—As Type **59**: 1w. Postman; 2w. Worker and factory; 5w. Harvesting rice; 10w. Manchurian cranes; 20w. Diamond Mountains; 30w. Ginseng plant; 50w. South Gate, Seoul; 100w. Tabo Pogoda, Kyongju. As Type **61**: 400w. Diamond Mountains.

63 Symbol and Phoenix

65 Korean Flag

64 Steam Train

1949. 1st Anniv of Independence.

128	**63**	15w. blue	18·00	7·50

1949. 50th Anniv of Korean Railways.

129	**64**	15w. blue	65·00	35·00

1949. 75th Anniv of U.P.U.

130	**65**	15w. multicoloured	12·00	8·00

66 Post-horse Warrant

67 Douglas DC-2 Airplane and Globe

1950. 50th Anniv of Membership of U.P.U.

131	**66**	15w. green	15·00	6·00
132		65w. brown	10·00	3·50

1950. Air. Opening of Internal Air Mail Service.

133	**67**	60w. blue	10·00	3·50

68 Demonstrators

69 Capitol, Seoul

1950. 31st Anniv of Abortive Proclamation of Independence.

134	**68**	15w. green	14·00	6·00
135		65w. violet	6·00	2·50

1950. 2nd South Korean Election.

136	**69**	30w. multicoloured	8·00	3·00

70 Dr. Syngman Rhee

71 Flag and Mountains

1950. Unification of Korea.

137	**70**	100w. blue	2·50	1·00
138	**71**	100w. green	3·50	1·00
139	–	200w. green	2·00	75

DESIGN—35 × 24 mm: 200w. Map of Korea and flags of U.N. and Korea.

73 Manchurian Crane

76 Post-horse Warrant

77 Fairy (8th cent painting)

1951. Perf or roul.

140	**73**	5w. brown	2·40	1·40
181	–	20w. violet	1·00	30
187	–	50w. green	2·00	30
183	**76**	100w. blue	1·25	25
193	**77**	1000w. green	2·25	40

DESIGNS—HORIZ: 20w. Astrological Tiger (ancient painting); 50w. Dove and Korean flag.

1951. Surch with new value.

145	**54**	100w. on 4w. red	2·75	75
146	**59**	200w. on 15w. red	4·50	2·00
147	**54**	300w. on 4w. red	1·50	1·00
156	–	300w. on 10w. green (116)	13·00	4·00
149	**55**	300w. on 14w. blue	2·25	75
150	**59**	300w. on 15w. red	1·75	75
151	–	300w. on 20w. brown (118)	2·50	85
152	–	300w. on 30w. green (119)	2·00	75
153	–	300w. on 50w. blue (120)	2·00	80
154	**60**	300w. on 65w. blue	5·75	3·50
155	–	300w. on 100w. green (122)	2·25	75

80 Statue of Liberty and Flags

1951. Participation in Korean War. Flags in national colours. A. As Type **80** in green. B. As Type **80** but showing U.N. Emblem and doves in blue.

158A	500w. Australia	6·00	6·00
159A	500w. Belgium	6·00	6·00
160A	500w. Britain	6·00	6·00
161A	500w. Canada	6·00	6·00
162A	500w. Colombia	6·00	6·00
163A	500w. Denmark	12·00	12·00
164A	500w. Ethiopia	6·00	6·00
165A	500w. France	6·00	6·00
166A	500w. Greece	6·00	6·00
167A	500w. India	10·00	10·00
168A	500w. Italy (with crown)	15·00	15·00
169A	500w. Italy (without crown)	7·00	7·00
170A	500w. Luxembourg	10·00	10·00
171A	500w. Netherlands	6·00	6·00
172A	500w. New Zealand	6·00	6·00
173A	500w. Norway	10·00	10·00
174A	500w. Philippines	6·00	6·00
175A	500w. Sweden	6·00	6·00
176A	500w. Thailand	6·00	6·00
177A	500w. Turkey	6·00	6·00
178A	500w. Union of South Africa	6·00	6·00
179A	500w. U.S.A.	5·00	5·00
158B	500w. Australia	6·00	6·00
159B	500w. Belgium	6·00	6·00
160B	500w. Britain	6·00	6·00
161B	500w. Canada	6·00	6·00
162B	500w. Colombia	6·00	6·00
163B	500w. Denmark	15·00	15·00
164B	500w. Ethiopia	6·00	6·00
165B	500w. France	6·00	6·00
166B	500w. Greece	6·00	6·00
167B	500w. India	10·00	10·00
168B	500w. Italy (with crown)	15·00	15·00
169B	500w. Italy (without crown)	7·00	7·00
170B	500w. Luxembourg	10·00	10·00
171B	500w. Netherlands	6·00	6·00
172B	500w. New Zealand	6·00	6·00
173B	500w. Norway	10·00	10·00
174B	500w. Philippines	6·00	6·00
175B	500w. Sweden	6·00	6·00
176B	500w. Thailand	6·00	6·00
177B	500w. Turkey	6·00	6·00
178B	500w. Union of South Africa	6·00	6·00
179B	500w. U.S.A.	5·00	5·00

1951. Air. No. **126** surch **500 WON**.

180	**46**	500w. on 150w. blue	2·50	75

82 Buddha of Sokkuram

83 Pulguksa Temple, Kyongju

84 Monument to King Muryol, Kyongju

85 Shrine of Admiral Li Sun Sin, Tongyong

1952. Inscr "KOREA".

184	**82**	200w. red	1·00	25
185	**83**	300w. green	80	25
191	**84**	500w. red	2·00	40
192		500w. blue	10·00	50·00
194	**85**	2000w. blue	1·50	40

See also Nos. 200/1 and 205.

86 President Syngman Rhee

1952. President's Election to 2nd Term of Office.

195	**86**	1000w. green	2·00	70

87 Douglas DC-3 over Freighter

1952. Air.

196	**87**	1200w. brown	1·10	40
197		1800w. blue	1·25	40
198		4200w. violet	1·50	50

For stamps in new currency, see Nos. 210/12.

88 Tree-planting

89 Monument to King Muryol, Kyongju

91 Pagoda Park, Seoul

92 Sika Deer

93 Sika Deer

1953. New currency. With character "hwan" after figure of value.

244	**88**	1h. blue	25	10
200	**84**	2h. blue	50	10
201		5h. green	60	10
202	**89**	5h. green	50	10
203	**88**	10h. green	1·00	10
204	–	10h. brown	2·50	10
205	**85**	20h. brown	3·25	10
206	**91**	30h. blue	1·00	10
242	**92**	100h. brown	7·50	30
243	**91**	200h. violet	3·50	25
208	**93**	500h. orange	28·00	1·60
209		1000h. brown	60·00	3·00

DESIGN: No. 204, "Metopta rectifasciata" (moth) and Korean flag.

For designs without character after figure of value, see 1955 issue (No. 273 etc).

1953. Air. Colours changed and new Currency.

210	**87**	12h. blue	1·25	35
211		18h. violet	1·50	40
212		42h. green	2·00	70

94 Field Hospital

1953. Red Cross Fund. Crosses in red.

213	**94**	10h.+5h. green	5·00	1·50
214	–	10h.+5h. blue	5·00	1·50

DESIGN—VERT: No. 214, Nurses supporting wounded soldier.

95 Y.M.C.A. Badge and Map

96 Douglas DC-6 over East Gate, Seoul

1953. 50th Anniv of Korean Young Men's Christian Association.

215	**95**	10h. red and black	2·00	70

1954. Air.

216	**96**	25h. brown	2·00	80
217		35h. purple	2·75	1·00
218		38h. green	2·75	1·10
219		58h. blue	2·50	1·25
258		70h. green	4·75	2·00
220		71h. blue	6·50	1·50
259		110h. brown	4·75	2·00
260		205h. mauve	7·00	2·00

98 Tokto Island

99 Erosion Control

1954.

221	–	2h. purple	1·00	15
222	–	5h. blue	80	15
223	**98**	10h. green	1·25	15

DESIGN: 2, 5h. Rocks off Tokto Island.

1954. 4th World Forestry Congress, Dehru Dun.

224	**99**	10h. light green and green	1·00	15
225		19h. light green and green	1·00	15

100 Presidents Syngman Rhee and Eisenhower

101 "Rebirth of Industry"

1954. Korea–United States Mutual Defence Treaty.

226	**100**	10h. blue	1·75	40
227		19h. brown	1·25	40
228		71h. green	2·50	85

1955. Reconstruction.

229	**101**	10h. brown	2·50	15
230		15h. violet	2·25	15
231		20h. blue	2·25	15
232		50h. mauve	3·00	25
269		50h. red	5·00	15

102 Rotary Emblem

103 Pres. Syngman Rhee

1955. 50th Anniv of Rotary International.

236	**102**	20h. violet	2·50	85
237		25h. green	1·25	45
238		71h. purple	1·50	50

1955. 80th Birthday of President.

239	**103**	20h. blue	3·25	1·00

104 Independence Arch, Seoul

1955. 10th Anniv of Liberation.

240	**104**	40h. green	2·00	70
241		100h. brown	2·00	1·00

105 Hibiscus

106 King Sejong

107 Kyongju Observatory

1955. Without character after figure of value.

273	**88**	2h. blue	25	10
309	**89**	4h. blue	60	10
310		5h. green	60	10
247	**105**	10h. mauve	1·00	10
277	–	10h. green	75	10
248	**106**	20h. purple	2·50	10
279	**105**	20h. mauve	60	15
280	–	30h. violet	75	15
281	**106**	40h. purple	85	15
249	**107**	50h. violet	2·75	10
315	–	55h. purple	2·00	10
250	**92**	100h. purple	12·00	10
284	**107**	100h. violet	2·75	15

285 **92** 200h. purple . . . . . . 3·25 15
286 **91** 400h. violet . . . . . . 32·00 35
251 **93** 500h. brown . . . . . . 28·00 40
288 1000h. brown . . . . . . 50·00 2·25
MS289 Set of 10 sheets (110 × 83 mm) each with one of Nos. 273/4, 277, 279/80, 283/6 £300
DESIGNS—HORIZ: No. 277, South Gate, Seoul; 280, Tiger. VERT: No. 315, Haegumgang (cliff face).

108 Runners and Torch

109 U.N. Emblem

1955. 36th National Athletic Meeting.
252 **108** 20h. purple . . . . 3·00 1·00
253 55h. green . . . . 3·00 1·00

1955. 10th Anniv of U.N.
254 **109** 20h. green . . . . 2·25 60
255 55h. blue . . . . 2·25 60

110 Admiral Li Sun Sin and 16th-century "Turtle" Ship

1955. 10th Anniv of Korean Navy.
256 **110** 20h. blue . . . . 3·00 1·50

111 Admiration Pagoda

112 Pres. Syngman Rhee

1956. 81st Birthday of President.
257 **111** 20h. green . . . . 3·00 1·00

1956. President's Election to Third Term of Office.
261 **112** 20h. brown . . . . 16·00 5·00
262 55h. blue . . . . 7·50 3·00

113 Torch and Olympic Rings

114 Central P.O., Seoul

1956. Olympic Games.
263 **113** 20h. brown . . . . 3·00 80
264 55h. green . . . . 3·00 80

1956. Stamp Day. Inscr "4289.12.4".
265 **114** 20h. turquoise . . . . . 3·00 55
266 – 50h. red . . . . 3·75 1·00
267 – 55h. green . . . . 1·50 55
DESIGNS—VERT: 50h. Stamp of 1884. HORIZ: 55h. Man leading post-pony.

MINIATURE SHEETS. Beginning in 1957 miniature sheets were put on sale at post offices. Miniature sheets of earlier issues were intended only for presentation purposes.

119 I.T.U. Emblem and Radio Mast

1957. 5th Anniv of Korea's Admission to I.T.U.
290 **119** 40h. blue . . . . 1·50 60
291 55h. green . . . . 1·50 60
MS292 110 × 3 mm. Nos. 290/1. Imperf. No gum. £500

120 Korean Scout and Badge

1957. 50th Anniv of Boy Scout Movement.
293 **120** 40h. purple . . . . 1·75 60
294 55h. purple . . . . 1·75 60
MS295 110 × 83 mm. Nos. 293/4. Imperf £1200

1957. Flood Relief Fund. As No. 281 but Korean inscr and premium added and colour changed.
299 **121** 40h.+10h. green . . . . . 2·50 50
MS300 110 × 84 mm. No. 299 . . £100

123 Mercury, Flags and Freighters

124 Star of Bethlehem and Pine Cone

1957. Korean–American Friendship Treaty.
301 **123** 40h. orange . . . . . . 1·25 60
302 205h. green . . . . 1·60 80
MS303 110 × 84 mm. Nos. 301/2. Imperf. No gum £600

1957. Christmas and New Year Issue.
304 **124** 15h. brown, green & orange . . . . 2·50 50
305 – 25h. green, red and yellow 2·50 30
306 – 30h. blue, green and yellow . . . . 4·25 1·25
MS307 Three sheets, each 90 × 60 mm. Nos. 304/6. Imperf £1400
DESIGNS: 25h. Christmas tree and tassels; 30h. Christmas tree and dog by window.

125 Winged Letter

126 Korean Children regarding future

1958. Postal Week.
321 **125** 40h. blue and red 80 25
MS322 90 × 60 mm. No. 321. Imperf £700

1958. 10th Anniv of Republic of Korea.
323 **126** 20h. grey 80 25
324 – 40h. red . . . . 1·25 25
MS325 110 × 84 mm. Nos. 323/4. Imperf £125 £125
DESIGN: 40h. Hibiscus flowers forming figure "10"

127 UNESCO Headquarters, Paris

128 Children flying Kites

1958. Inaug of UNESCO Building, Paris.
326 **127** 40h. orange and green . . 1·00 25
MS327 90 × 60 mm. No. 326. Imperf 75·00 60·00

1958. Christmas and New Year.
330 **128** 15h. green . . . . 1·00 30
331 – 25h. red, yellow and blue 1·00 30
332 – 30h. red, blue and yellow 2·00 50
MS333 Three sheets each 90 × 60 mm. Nos. 330/2. Imperf £100 £100
DESIGNS—VERT: 25h. Christmas tree, tassels and wicker basket (cooking sieve); 30h. Children in traditional festive costume.

129 Rejoicing Crowds in Pagoda Park, Flag and Torch

1959. 40th Anniv of Abortive Proclamation of Independence.
334 **129** 40h. purple and brown . . 1·00 25
MS335 90 × 60 mm. No. 334 . . 35·00 30·00

130 Marines going Ashore from Landing-craft

1959. 10th Anniv of Korean Marine Corps.
336 **130** 40h. bronze green . . . . 1·00 25
MS337 90 × 60 mm. No. 336. Imperf 7·50 6·00

1959. 3rd Postal Week. Sheet containing Nos. 311/4.
MS338 70 × 105 mm . . . . . . 6·00 4·00

131

1959. 10th Anniv of Korea's Admission to W.H.O.
339 **131** 40h. purple and pink . . 1·00 25
MS340 90 × 60 mm. No. 339. Imperf 8·00 6·00

132 Diesel Train

1959. 60th Anniv of Korean Railways.
341 **132** 40h. sepia and brown . . 1·75 75
MS342 90 × 60 mm. No. 341. Imperf 20·00 15·00

133 Runners in Relay Race

1959. 40th Korean National Games.
343 **133** 40h. brown and blue . . . 1·00 25
MS344 90 × 60 mm. No. 343. Imperf 10·00 8·00

134 Red Cross and Korea

1959. Red Cross. Inscr "1959 4292".
345 **134** 40h. red and green . . . 1·00 25
346 – 55h. red and mauve . . . 1·00 25
MS347 110 × 60 mm. Nos. 345/6. Imperf . . . . 22·00 16·00
DESIGN: 55h. Red Cross on globe.

135 Korean Postal Flags Old and New

136 Mice in Korean Costume and New Year Emblem

1959. 75th Anniv of Korean Postal Service.
348 **135** 40h. red and blue . . . . 1·00 25
MS349 90 × 60 mm. No. 348. Imperf 12·00 8·00

1959. Christmas and New Year.
350 **136** 15h. pink, blue and grey 1·00 15
351 – 25h. red, green and blue 80 15
352 – 30h. red, black and mauve 1·40 15
MS353 Three sheets each 90 × 60 mm. Nos. 350/2. Imperf 60·00 40·00
DESIGNS: 25h. Carol singers; 30h. Crane.

137 U.P.U. Monument

138 Honey Bee and Clover

1960. 60th Anniv of Admission of Korea to U.P.U.
354 **137** 40h. hocolate and blue . . 1·10 50
MS355 90 × 60 mm. No. 354. Imperf 12·00 6·00

1960. Children's Savings Campaign.
356 **138** 10h. yellow, brown and green 75 10
357 – 20h. brown, blue and pink 1·25 10
DESIGN: 20h. Snail and Korean money-bag.
For these stamps in new currency, see Nos. 452 etc.

139 "Uprooted Tree"

140 Pres. Eisenhower

1960. World Refugee Year.
358 **139** 40h. red, blue and green 80 10
MS359 90 × 60 mm. No. 358. Imperf 16·00 12·00

1960. Visit of President Eisenhower of United States.
360 **140** 40h. ultramarine, vermillion and green . . 3·00 80
MS361 90 × 60 mm. No. 360. Imperf 16·00 12·00

141 Schoolchildren

1960. 75th Anniv of Educational System.
362 **141** 40h. purple, chestnut & olive . . . . 1·00 25
MS363 90 × 60 mm. No. 362. Imperf 5·00 4·00

142 Assembly

143 "Liberation"

1960. Inauguration of House of Councillors.
364 **143** 40h. grey . . . . 1·00 25
MS365 90 × 60 mm. No. 364. Imperf 5·00 4·00

1960. 15th Anniv of Liberation.
366 **143** lake, blue and ochre . . . 1·00 25
MS367 90 × 60 mm. No. 366. Imperf 5·00 4·00

144 Weightlifting

145 Barn Swallow and Insulators

1960. Olympic Games.
368 **144** 20h. brown, flesh & turq 1·00 35
369 – 40h. brown, blue & turq 1·00 35
MS370 90 × 60 mm. Nos. 368/9. Imperf . . . . 16·00 10·00
DESIGN: 40h. South Gate, Seoul.

1960. 75th Anniv of Korean Telegraph Service.
371 **145** 40h. violet, grey and blue 1·10 60
MS372 90 × 60 mm. No. 371. Imperf 4·25 2·50

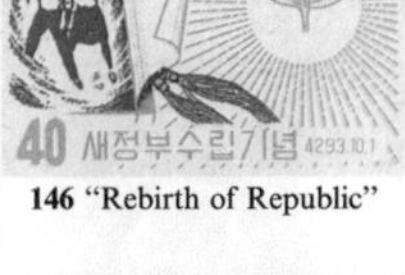
146 "Rebirth of Republic"

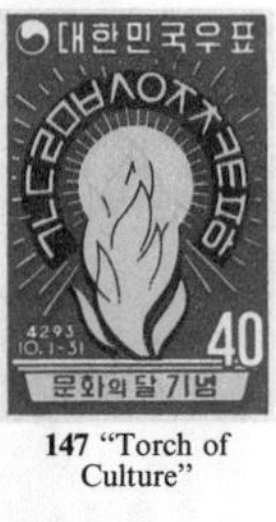
147 "Torch of Culture"

1960. Establishment of New Government.
373 **146** 40h. green, blue and orange . . . . 1·00 25
MS374 90 × 60 mm. No. 373. Imperf 4·00 3·00

1960. Postal Week and International Correspondence Week. Sheet containing Nos. 356/7. Imperf.
MS375 90 × 60 mm . . . . . . 3·00 2·00

1960. Cultural Month.
376 **147** 40h. yellow, lt blue & blue 1·00 25
MS377 90 × 60 mm. No. 376. Imperf 4·00 3·50

148 U.N. Flag

149 U.N. Emblem and Gravestones

1960. 15th Anniv of U.N.
378 **148** 40h. blue, green and mauve 1·00 25
MS379 90 × 60 mm. No. 378. Imperf 4·00 3·00

1960. Establishment of U.N. Memorial Cemetery.
380 **149** 40h. brown and orange 1·00 25
MS381 90 × 60 mm. No. 380. Imperf 4·00 3·50

150 "National Stocktaking"

151 Festival Stocking

1960. Census of Population and Resources.
382 **150** 40h. carmine, drab and blue 1·00 25
MS383 90 × 60 mm. No. 382. Imperf 4·00 3·00

1960. Christmas and New Year Issue.
384 – 15h. brown, yellow & grey 50 15
385 **151** 25h. red, green and blue 40 10
386 – 30h. red, yellow and blue 75 15
MS387 Three sheets, each 90 × 60 mm. Nos. 384/6. Imperf 18·00 14·00
DESIGNS: 15h. Ox's head; 30h. Girl bowing in New Year's greeting.

152 Wind-sock and Ancient Rain-gauge

1961. World Meteorological Day.
388 **152** 40h. ultramarine and blue 1·00 25
MS389 90 × 60 mm. No. 388. Imperf 3·00 2·50

153 Family, Sun and Globe

1961. World Health Day.
390 **153** 40h. brown and orange 1·00 25
MS391 90 × 60 mm. No. 390. Imperf 3·00 2·50

154 Students' Demonstration

1961. 1st Anniv of April Revolution (Overthrow of Pres. Syngman Rhee).
392 **154** 40h. green, red and blue 1·00 30
MS393 90 × 60 mm. No. 392. Imperf 6·00 4·25

155 Workers and Conference Emblem

157 Soldier's Grave

156 Girl Guide, Camp and Badge

1961. Int Community Development Conf, Seoul.
394 **155** 40h. green 80 25
MS395 90 × 60 mm. No. 394. Imperf 3·00 2·00

1961. 15th Anniv of Korean Girl Guide Movement.
396 **156** 40h. green 1·00 25
MS397 90 × 60 mm. No. 396. Imperf 7·00 5·50

1961. Memorial Day.
398 **157** 40h. black and drab 1·00 30
MS399 90 × 60 mm. No. 398. Imperf 3·50 3·00

158 Soldier with Torch

159 "Three Liberations"

1961. Revolution of 16 May (Seizure of Power by Gen. Pak Chung Hi).
400 **159** 40h. brown and yellow 1·00 30
MS401 90 × 60 mm. No. 400. Imperf 5·00 4·00

1961. Liberation Day.
402 **159** 40h. multicoloured 1·00 30
MS403 90 × 60 mm. No. 402. Imperf 3·50 2·75

160 Korean Forces, Flag and Destroyer

1961. Armed Forces Day.
404 **160** 40h. multicoloured 1·25 30
MS405 90 × 60 mm. No. 404. Imperf 3·25 2·25

161 "Korean Art" (Kyongbok Palace Art Gallery)

1961. 10th Korean Art Exhibition.
406 **161** 40h. chocolate and brown 1·00 25
MS407 90 × 60 mm. No. 406. Imperf 3·00 2·50

162 Birthday Candle

1961. 15th Anniv of UNESCO.
408 **162** 40h. blue and green 25 25
MS409 90 × 60 mm. No. 408. Imperf 2·00 2·50

163 Mobile X-Ray Unit

1961. Tuberculosis Vaccination Week.
410 **163** 40h. brown, black & lt brn 75 25
MS411 90 × 60 mm. No. 140. Imperf 3·00 2·50

164 Ginseng

165 King Sejong

166 White-bellied Black Woodpecker

167 Rice Harvester

168 Korean Drum

169 Douglas DC-8 Jetliner over Pagoda

1961.
412 **164** 20h. red 80 10
413 **165** 30h. purple 80 10
414 **166** 40h. blue and red 4·00 65
415 **167** 40h. green 1·10 10
416 **168** 100h. brown 1·75 10
See also 1962 issue (No. 537 etc), and for stamps inscribed "REPUBLIC OF KOREA", see Nos. 641 etc and 785/95.

1961. Air.
417 **169** 50h. violet and blue 10·00 3·50
418 – 100h. brown and blue 15·00 12·00
419 – 200h. brown and blue 20·00 6·00
420 – 400h. green and blue 20·00 6·50
DESIGNS—Plane over: 100h. West Gate, Suwon; 200h. Gateway and wall of Toksu Palace, Seoul; 400h. Pavilion, Kyongbok Palace, Seoul.
See also Nos. 454 etc.

170 I.T.U. Emblem as Satellite

1962. 10th Anniv of Admission to I.T.U.
421 **170** 40h. red and blue 1·25 40
MS422 90 × 59 mm. No. 421. Imperf 6·00 4·00

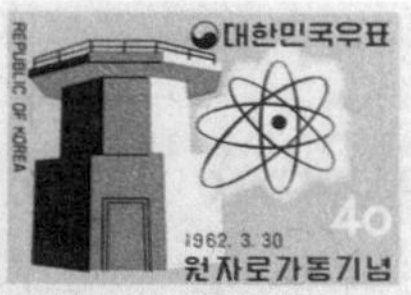
171 Triga Mark II Reactor

1962. 1st Korean Atomic Reactor.
423 **171** 40h. green, drab and blue 1·00 25

172 Mosquito and Emblem

1962. Malaria Eradication.
424 **172** 40h. red and green 50 25
MS425 90 × 60 mm. No. 424 3·00 2·50

173 Girl and Y.W.C.A. Emblem

1962. 40th Anniv of Korean Young Women's Christian Association.
426 **173** 40h. blue and orange 1·00 30

174 Emblem of Asian Film Producers' Federation

175 Soldiers crossing Han River Bridge

1962. 9th Asian Film Festival, Seoul.
427 **174** 40h. violet, red & turquoise 1·25 25

1962. 1st Anniv of 16th May Revolution.
428 – 30h. green and brown 1·50 50
429 **175** 40h. brown, green & turq 1·50 50
430 – 200h. yellow, red and blue 11·00 3·00
MS431 Three sheets, each 90 × 140 mm. Nos. 428/30. Imperf. Inscr in Korean 22·00 20·00
MS432 As last but sheets inscr in English 50·00 45·00
DESIGNS—HORIZ: 30h. "Industrial Progress" (men moving cogwheel up slope); 200h. "Egg" containing Korean badge and industrial skyline.

176 20-oared "Turtle" Ship

1962. 370th Anniv of Hansan Naval Victory over Japanese.
433 **176** 2w. blue and light blue 1·50 70
434 – 4w. black, violet & turq 2·75 1·00
DESIGN: 4w. 16-oared "turtle" ship.

177 Chindo Dog

178 "Hanabusaya asiatica"

179 Statue of Goddess Mikuk Besal

213 Longhorn Beetle

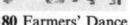

180 Farmers' Dance

181 12th-century Wine-jug

214 Factory, Fishes and Corn

182 Mison

183 13th-century Printing-block and Impression used for "Tripitaka Koreana"

191 Sika Deer

192 Bell of King Kyongdok

215 Boddhisatva, Sokkuram Shrine

216 Tile, Silla Dynasty

217 "Azure Dragon", Koguryo period

1962. New Currency.
537 **177** 20ch. brown 25 10
436 **178** 40ch. blue 30 10
785 – 40ch. green 40 10
539 **179** 50ch. brown 30 10
540 **213** 60ch. brown 40 10
541 **180** 1w. blue . . . . 1·00 10
542 **179** 1w.50 grey 30 10
543 **164** 2w. red . . . . 1·25 10
472 **165** 3w. purple . . . . 2·25 10
545 **167** 4w. green 30 10
442 **181** 5w. blue . . . . 4·25 10
547 **214** 7w. mauve . . . . 1·10 10
548 **168** 10w. brown . . . . 2·00 10
549 **182** 20w. mauve . . . . 3·00 10
550 **183** 40w. purple . . . . . . 4·50 10
551 **191** 50w. brown . . . . . . 6·00 15
552 **192** 100w. green . . . . . . 15·00 20
553 **215** 200w. deep green and green . . . . 5·00 10
554 **216** 300w. green and brown . . 10·00 10
555 **217** 500w. blue and light blue 7·00 10
DESIGN—18 × 72 mm: No. 785, motif as Type **178** but inscriptions differently arranged.
See also Nos. 607, 609 and 641/9.

184 Scout Badge and Korean Flag

185 Chub Mackerel, Trawler and Nets

1962. 40th Anniv of Korean Scout Movement.
446 **184** 4w. brown, red and blue 80 25
447 4w. green, red and blue 80 25
MS448 Two sheets, each 90 × 60 mm. (a) As No. 446; (b) As No. 447 . . . . 4·00 4·00

1962. 10th Indo-Pacific Fishery Council Meeting, Seoul.
449 **185** 4w. ultramarine and blue 1·40 30

186 I.C.A.O. Emblem

1962. 10th Anniv of Korea's Entry into I.C.A.O.
450 **186** 4w. blue and brown . . . 1·25 25
MS451 90 × 60 mm. No. 450. Imperf 5·50 3·25

1962. Children's Savings Campaign. As Nos. 356/7 but new currency.
452 1w. yellow, brown and green 3·25 10
453 2w. brown, blue and pink . . 8·25 65

1962. Air. New Currency.
454 **169** 5w. blue and violet . . . 12·50 2·40
512 – 10w. brown and green (As No. 418) . . . . 2·75 30
513 – 20w. brown and green (As No. 419) . . . . 3·50 35
563 **169** 39w. drab and blue . . . 4·75 35
514 – 40w. green and blue (As No. 420) . . . . 4·00 50
564 – 64w. green and blue (As No. 418) . . . . 2·10 25
565 – 78w. blue and green (As No. 419) . . . . 3·00 30
566 – 112w. green and blue (As No. 420) . . . . 3·00 30

187 Electric Power Plant

1962. Inauguration of 1st Korean Economic Five Year Plan.
458 **187** 4w. violet and orange . . 1·25 40
459 – 4w. ultramarine and blue 1·25 40
DESIGN: No. 459, Irrigation Dam.
See also Nos. 482/3, 528/9, 593/4 and 634/5.

188 Campaign Emblem

1963. Freedom from Hunger.
460 **188** 4w. green, buff and blue 75 25
MS461 90 × 60 mm. No. 460. Imperf 3·00 2·50

189 Globe and Letters

1963. 1st Anniv of Asian-Oceanic Postal Union.
462 **189** 4w. purple, green and blue 90 25
MS463 90 × 60 mm. No. 462. Imperf 3·00 2·25

190 Centenary Emblem and Map

1963. Centenary of Red Cross.
464 **190** 4w. red, grey and blue . . 90 25
465 4w. red, grey and orange 90 25
MS466 140 × 90 mm. Nos. 464/5. Imperf . . . . 6·00 5·00

1963. Flood Relief. As No. 545, but new colour and inscr with premium.
479 4w.+1w. blue . . . . 1·50 45

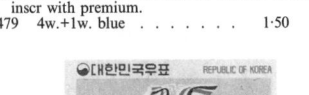

193 "15" and Hibiscus

1963. 15th Anniv of Republic.
480 **193** 4w. red, violet and blue 1·40 30

194 Nurse and Emblem

1963. 15th Anniv of Korean Army Nursing Corps.
481 **194** 4w. black, turquoise & grn . . . . 1·00 25

1963. Five Year Plan. Dated "1963". As T **187**.
482 4w. violet and blue 90 25
483 4w. chocolate and brown . . 4·25 85
DESIGNS: No. 482, Cement Factory, Mun'gyong, and bag of cement; 483, Miner and coal train, Samch'ok region.

195/6 Rock Temples of Abu Simbel

1963. Nubian Monuments Preservation.
484 **195** 3w. green and drab . . . 2·25 40
485 **196** 4w. green and drab . . . 2·25 40
MS486 90 × 60 mm. Nos. 484/5. Imperf . . . . 5·00 4·00
Nos. 484/5 were issued together, se-tenant, forming the composite design illustrated.

197 Rugby Football and Athlete

1963. 44th National Games.
487 **197** 4w. green, brown and blue . . . . 1·00 25

198 Nurse and Motor Clinic

1963. 10th Anniv of Korean Tuberculosis Prevention Society.
488 **198** 4w. blue and red . . . . 1·00 25

199 Eleanor Roosevelt

200 U.N. Headquarters

1963. 15th Anniv of Declaration of Human Rights.
489 **199** 3w. brown and blue . . . 80 25
490 – 4w. blue, green and buff 80 25
MS491 90 × 60 mm. Nos. 489/90. Imperf . . . . 3·25 2·75
DESIGN: 4w. Freedom torch and globe.

1963. 15th Anniv of U.N. Recognition of Korea.
492 **200** 4w. green, blue and black 1·00 25
MS493 90 × 60 mm. No. 492 . . 3·25 2·75

201 Pres. Pak Chong Hi and Capitol

1963. Inaug of President Pak Chong Hi.
494 **201** 4w. blue, turquoise & black . . . . 11·00 3·50

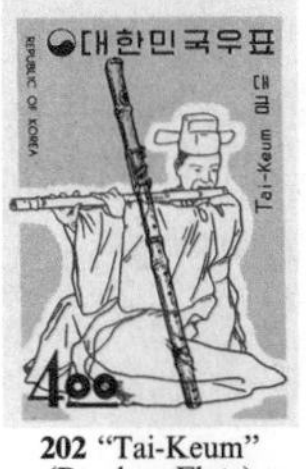

202 "Tai-Keum" (Bamboo Flute)

204 "UNESCO"

203 Symbols of Metric System

1963. Musical Instruments and Players. As T **202**.
495 4w. green, brown and drab 2·25 60
496 4w. black, blue and light blue 2·25 60
497 4w. green, mauve and pink 2·25 60
498 4w. brown, violet and grey 2·25 60
499 4w. blue, brown and pink . . 2·25 60
500 4w. turquoise, black and blue 2·25 60
501 4w. violet, bistre and yellow 2·25 60
502 4w. blue, brown and mauve 2·25 60
503 4w. black, blue and purple 2·25 60
504 4w. black, brown and pink 2·25 60
MUSICAL INSTRUMENTS (and players)—VERT: No. 495, Type **202**; 496, "Wul-keum" (banjo); 497, "Tang-piri" (flageolet); 498, "Na-bal" (trumpet); 499, "Hyang-pipa" (lute); 500, "Pyenkyeng" jade chimes; 501, "Taipyeng-so" (clarinet); 502, "Chang-ko" (double-ended drum). HORIZ: No. 503, "Wa-kong-hu" (harp); 504, "Kaya-ko" (zither).

1964. Introduction of Metric System in Korea.
505 **203** 4w. multicoloured 90 25

1964. 10th Anniv of Korean UNESCO Committee.
506 **204** 4w. ultramarine, red & blue 90 25

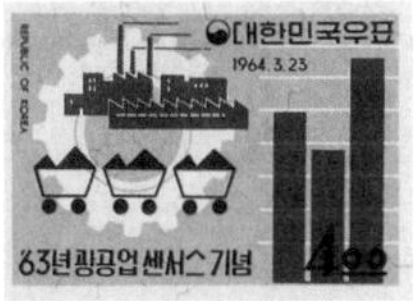

205 Symbols of Industry and Census

1964. National Industrial Census (1963).
507 **205** 4w. brown, black and grey . . . . 1·25 60

206 Y.M.C.A. Emblem and Profile of Young Man

1964. 50th Anniv of Korean Young Men's Christian Association.
508 **206** 4w. red, blue and green 75 25

207 Fair Emblem, Ginseng Root and Freighter

1964. New York World's Fair.
509 **207** 40w. brown, green & yellow . . . . 2·00 40
510 – 100w. ultramarine, brown and blue . . . . 9·00 1·50
MS511 90 × 60 mm. Nos. 509/10. Imperf . . . . 14·00 10·00
DESIGN: 100w. Korean pavilion at Fair.

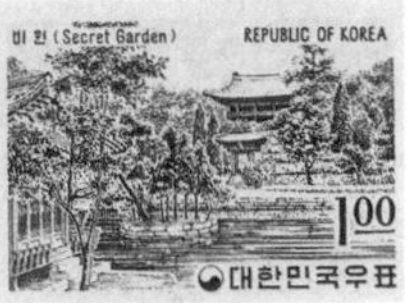

208 Secret Garden

1964. Background in light blue.
517 **208** 1w. green 60 20
518 – 2w. green . . . . 1·00 25
519 – 3w. green . . . . 1·00 25
520 – 4w. green . . . . 1·50 30
521 – 5w. violet . . . . 2·00 30
522 – 6w. blue . . . . 2·00 40
523 – 7w. brown . . . . 2·40 40
524 – 8w. brown . . . . 2·50 40
525 – 9w. violet . . . . 2·50 40
526 – 10w. green . . . . 2·75 45
MS527 Five sheets each 90 × 60 mm. 1w. and 10w.; 2w. and 9w.; 3w. and 8w.; 4w. and 7w.; 5w. and 6w. Imperf . . . . 20·00 16·00
DESIGNS: 2w. Whahong Gate; 3w. Uisang Pavilion; 4w. Mt. Songni; 5w. Paekma River; 6w. Anab Pond; 7w. Choksok Pavilion; 8w. Kwanghan Pavilion; 9w. Whaom Temple; 10w. Chonjeyon Falls.

1964. Five Year Plan. Dated "1964". As T **187**.
528 4w. black and blue . . . . . 1·50 30
529 4w. blue and yellow . . . . 1·00 30
DESIGNS: No. 528, Trawlers and fish; 529, Oil refinery and barrels.

209 Wheel and Globe

1964. Colombo Plan Day.
530 **209** 4w. lt brown, brown & grn 70 25
MS531 90 × 60 mm. No. 530. Imperf 3·00 2·50

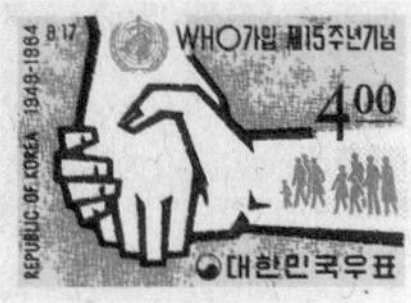
210 "Helping Hand"

1964. 15th Anniv of Korea's Admission to W.H.O.
532 **210** 4w. black, green and light green 50 25
MS533 90 × 60 mm. No. 532. Imperf 2·50 2·00

211 Running

1964. 45th National Games, Inchon.
534 **211** 4w. pink, green and purple . . . . 1·00 25

212 U.P.U. Monument, Berne, and Ribbons

1964. 90th Anniv of U.P.U.
535 **212** 4w. brown, blue and pink 75 25
MS536 90 × 60 mm. No. 535. Imperf 4·00 3·00

218 Federation Emblem

219 Olympic "V" Emblem

1964. 5th Meeting of Int Federation of Asian and Western Pacific Contractors' Assns.
556 **218** 4w. green, light green and brown 75 25

1964. Olympic Games, Tokyo.
557 **219** 4w. blue, turquoise & brn 1·50 60
558 – 4w. mauve, blue and green . . . . 1·50 60
559 – 4w. brown, ultram & blue 1·50 60
560 – 4w. red, brown and blue 1·50 60
561 – 4w. brown, purple and blue . . . . 1·50 60
MS562 Five sheets each 90 × 60 mm. As Nos. 557/61. Imperf . . . . 10·00 8·00
DESIGNS—HORIZ: No. 558, Running; 559, Rowing; 560, Horse-jumping; 561, Gymnastics.

220 Unissued 1884 100m. Stamp

221 Pine Cone

1964. 80th Anniv of Korean Postal Services.
567 **220** 3w. blue, violet and mauve . . . . 1·00 40
568 – 4w. black, violet and green . . . . 1·60 60
DESIGN: 4w. Hong Yong Sik, 1st Korean Postmaster-general.

1965. Korean Plants. Plants multicoloured, background colours given.
571 **221** 4w. green . . . . 1·25 40
572 – 4w. brown (Plum blossom) . . . . 1·25 40
573 – 4w. blue (Forsythia) . . . 1·25 40
574 – 4w. green (Azalea) . . . 1·25 40
575 – 4w. pink (Lilac) . . . . . 1·25 40
576 – 4w. grey (Wild rose) . . . 1·25 40
577 – 4w. green (Balsam) . . . 1·25 40
578 – 4w. grey (Hibiscus) . . . 1·25 40
579 – 4w. flesh (Crepe myrtle) 1·25 40
580 – 4w. blue (Ullung chrysanthemum) . . . 1·25 40
581 – 4w. buff (Paulownia, tree) 1·25 40
582 – 4w. blue (Bamboo) . . . 1·25 40
MS583 Twelve sheets each 90 × 60 mm. Nos. 571/82. Imperf 16·00 10·00

222 Folk Dancing

1965. Pacific Area Travel Assn Conf, Seoul.
584 **222** 4w. violet, brown & green 1·00 25
MS585 90 × 60 mm. No. 584. Imperf 2·40 2·00

223 Flag and Doves

1965. Military Aid for Vietnam.
586 **223** 4w. brown, blue and yellow 60 50
MS587 90 × 60 mm. No. 586. Imperf 2·40 2·00

224 "Food Production"

1965. Agricultural Seven Year Plan.
588 **224** 4w. brown, green and black 50 25

225 "Family Scales"

1965. Family Planning Month.
589 **225** 4w. green, drab & lt green 65 25
MS590 90 × 60 mm. No. 589. Imperf 1·60 1·40

226 I.T.U. Emblem and Symbols

1965. Centenary of I.T.U.
591 **226** 4w. black, red and blue 65 20
MS592 90 × 60 mm. No. 591. Imperf 2·00 1·60

1965. Five Year Plan. Dated "1965". As T **187**.
593 4w. blue and pink . . . . . 1·00 25
594 4w. sepia and brown 80 25
DESIGNS: No. 593, "Korea" (freighter) at quayside and crates; 594, Fertilizer plant and wheat.

227 Flags of Australia, Belgium, Great Britain, Canada and Colombia

1965. 15th Anniv of Outbreak of Korean War.
595 **227** 4w. multicoloured . . . . 1·00 40
596 – 4w. multicoloured . . . . 1·00 40
597 – 4w. multicoloured . . . . 1·00 40
598 – 4w. multicoloured . . . . 1·00 40
599 – 10w. multicoloured . . . 2·50 60
MS600 Five sheets each 90 × 60 mm. Nos. 595/9. Imperf . . . . . . 7·00 5·50
DESIGNS—U.N. Emblem and flags of: No. 596, Denmark, Ethiopia, France, Greece and India; 597, Italy, Luxembourg, Netherlands, New Zealand and Norway; 598, Philippines, Sweden, Thailand, Turkey and South Africa; 599, General MacArthur and flags of Korea, U.N. and U.S.A.

228 Flag and Sky-writing ("20")

229 Ants and Leaf

1965. 20th Anniv of Liberation.
601 **228** 4w. red, violet and blue 65 25
602 – 10w. red, blue and violet 1·10 40
DESIGN: 10w. South Gate and fireworks.

1965. Savings Campaign.
603 **229** 4w. brown, ochre and green 50 25

230 Hoisting Flag

231 Radio Aerial

1965. 15th Anniv of Recapture of Seoul.
604 **230** 3w. green, blue and orange . . . . 1·10 35

1965. 80th Anniv of Korean Telecommunications.
605 **231** 3w. green, black and blue 60 25
606 – 10w. black, blue and yellow . . . . 1·00 35
DESIGN: 10w. Telegraphist of 1885.

1965. Flood Relief. As No. 545 (1962 issue), but colour changed and inscr with premium.
607 4w.+2w. blue . . . . 1·00 30

232 Pole Vaulting

1965. National Athletic Meeting, Kwangju.
608 **232** 3w. multicoloured . . . . 1·00 40

1965. Aid for Children. As No. 545 (1962 issue), but colour changed and inscr with premium.
609 4w.+2w. purple . . . . . . 1·10 30

233 I.C.Y. Emblem

1965. International Co-operation Year and 20th Anniv of United Nations.
610 **233** 3w. red, green & dp green 50 25
611 – 10w. ultramarine, grn & bl . . . . 1·10 25
MS612 Two sheets each 90 × 60 mm. (a) No. 610; (b) No. 611 . . . 3·50 3·00
DESIGN—VERT: 10w. U.N. flag and headquarters, New York.

234 Child posting Letter

235 Children with Toboggan

1965. 10th Communications Day.
613 **234** 3w. multicoloured . . . . 1·00 25
614 – 10w. red, blue and green 1·60 30
DESIGN: 10w. Airmail envelope and telephone receiver.

1965. Christmas and New Year.
615 **235** 3w. blue, red and green 60 25
616 – 4w. blue, red and green 75 25
MS617 90 × 60 mm. Nos. 615/16. Imperf . . . . 2·50 2·25
DESIGN: 4w. Boy and girl in traditional costume.

236 Freedom House

1966. Opening of Freedom House, Panmunjom.
618 **236** 7w. black, emerald & grn 1·00 40
619 39w. black, lilac and green . . . . 4·25 60
MS620 90 × 60 mm. Nos. 618/19. Imperf . . . . 6·00 5·50

237 Mandarins

1966. Korean Birds. Multicoloured.
621 3w. Type **237** . . . . . . 2·40 1·25
622 5w. Manchurian crane . . . 2·50 1·25
623 7w. Common pheasant . . . 3·75 1·25
MS624 Three sheets each 90 × 60 mm. Nos. 621/3. Imperf 8·75 4·00

238 Pine Forest

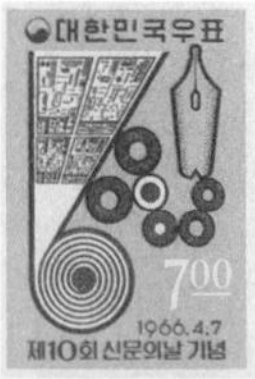
239 Printing Press and Pen

1966. Reafforestation Campaign.
625 **238** 7w. brown, green and light green 70 15

1966. 10th Newspaper Day.
626 **239** 7w. purple, yellow & green 60 15

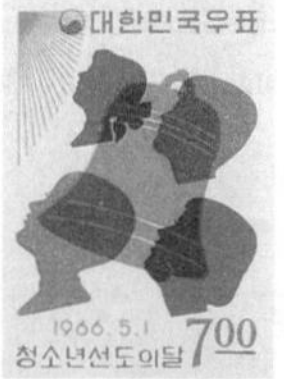
240 Curfew Bell and Young Koreans

241 W.H.O. Building

1966. Youth Guidance Month.
627 **240** 7w. orange, green and blue 60 15

1966. Inauguration of W.H.O. Headquarters, Geneva.
628 **241** 7w. black, blue and yellow . . . . 1·00 40
629 39w. red, grey and yellow 4·00 1·00
MS630 90 × 60 mm. No. 628. Imperf 3·00 2·50

242 Pres. Pak, Handclasp and Flags

1966. Pres. Pak Chung Hi's State Tour of South-East Asia.
631 **242** 7w. multicoloured . . . . 3·00 1·00

243 Girl Scout and Flag

1966. 20th Anniv of Korean Girl Scouts.
632 **243** 7w. black, green and yellow . . . . 1·00 20

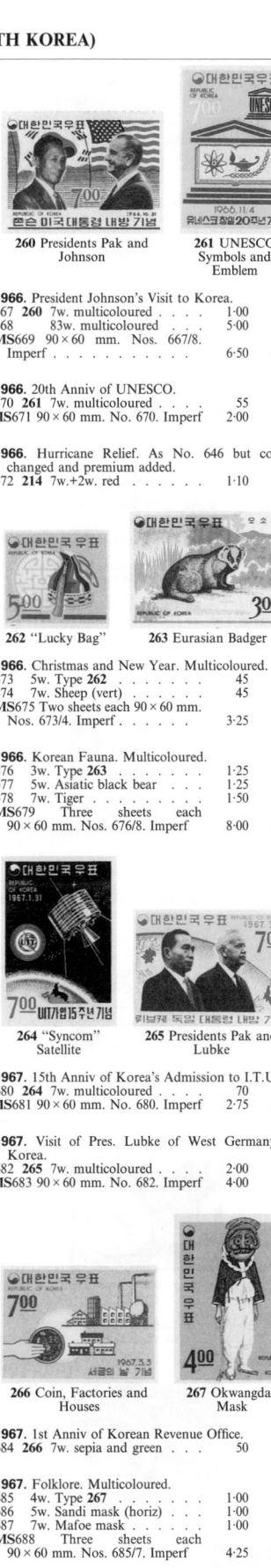

244 Student and Ehwa Women's University

1966. 80th Anniv of Korean Women's Education.
633 **244** 7w. multicoloured 65 20

1966. 5-Year Plan. Dated "1966". As T **187**.
634 7w. ultramarine and blue . . 1·75 60
635 7w. black and yellow . . . . 1·00 30
DESIGNS: No. 634, Map and transport; 635, Radar aerials and telephone.

245 Carrier Pigeons

1966. International Correspondence Week. Unissued sheet (90 × 60 mm) surch as shown in T **245** and optd **6**, **1966.6.13—19** with bars obliterating old inscr.
MS636 7(w.) on 40(h.) deep green, green and red . . . . 2·25 2·00

246 Wall-eyed Pollack

1966. Korean Fishes. Multicoloured.
637 3w. Type **246** . . . . 1·00 45
638 5w. Lenok . . . . 1·60 45
639 7w. Manchurian croaker . . 1·75 45
MS640 Three sheets each 90 × 60 mm. Nos. 637/9. Imperf 7·50 5·00

247 Incense-burner

249 Buddha, Kwanchok Temple

1966. As previous issues (some redrawn) and new designs, all inscr "REPUBLIC OF KOREA".
641 **213** 60ch. green 20 10
642 **180** 1w. green . . . . 1·10 10
643 **164** 2w. green 15 10
644 **165** 3w. brown 15 10
645 **181** 5w. blue . . . . 2·00 10
646 **214** 7w. blue . . . . 1·75 10
789 **168** 10w. blue (22 × 18 mm) 3·50 10
647 **247** 13w. blue . . . . 1·90 10
709 **182** 20w. green and light green 6·00 10
710 **183** 40w. green and olive . . . 7·00 10
793 40w. blue and pink (18 × 22 mm) . . . . . 6·50 10
711 **191** 50w. brown and bistre . . 5·75 10
648 – 60w. green . . . . 2·25 10
649 **249** 80w. green . . . . 2·25 10
DESIGN—As Type **247**: 60w. 12th-century porcelain vessel.

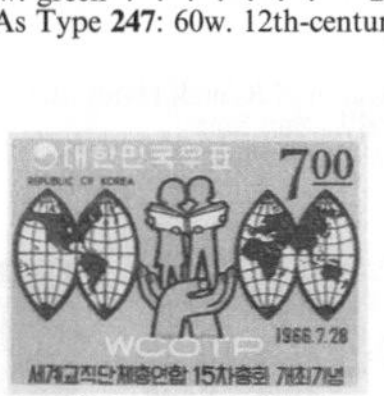
250 Children and Hemispheres

1966. 15th Assembly of World Conf of Teaching Profession (WCOTP), Seoul.
650 **250** 7w. violet, brown and blue 45 15
MS651 90 × 60 mm. No. 650. Imperf 1·50 1·40

251 Factory within Pouch

1966. Savings Campaign.
652 **251** 7w. multicoloured 45 15

252 People on Map of Korea

1966. National Census.
653 **252** 7w. multicoloured 45 15

253 "Lucida lateralis"

1966. Insects. Multicoloured.
654 3w. Type **253** 90 50
655 5w. "Hexacentrus japonicus" (grasshopper) 90 50
656 7w. "Sericinus montela" (butterfly) . . . . 1·00 50
MS657 Three sheets each 90 × 60 mm. (a) No. 654; (b) No. 655; (c) No. 656 . . . . . 3·25 2·00

254 C.I.S.M. Emblem and "Round Table" Meeting

1966. 21st General Assembly of International Military Sports Council (C.I.S.M.), Seoul.
658 **254** 7w. multicoloured 50 15
MS659 90 × 60 mm. No. 658. Imperf 1·60 1·40

255 Soldiers and Flags

1966. 1st Anniv of Korean Troops in Vietnam.
660 **255** 7w. multicoloured . . . . 3·00 90

256 Wrestling

1966. 47th Athletic Meeting, Seoul.
661 **256** 7w. multicoloured . . . . 2·00 45

257 Lions Emblem and Map

1966. 5th Orient and South-East Asian Lions Convention, Seoul.
662 **257** 7w. multicoloured 50 15
MS663 90 × 60 mm. No. 662. Imperf 2·00 1·50

258 University Emblem, "20" and Shields

1966. 20th Anniv of Seoul University.
664 **258** 7w. multicoloured 40 15

259 A.P.A.C.L. Emblem

1966. 12th Conference of Asian People's Anti-Communist League (A.P.A.C.L.), Seoul.
665 **259** 7w. multicoloured 50 25
MS666 90 × 60 mm. No. 665. Imperf 1·75 1·40

260 Presidents Pak and Johnson

261 UNESCO Symbols and Emblem

1966. President Johnson's Visit to Korea.
667 **260** 7w. multicoloured . . . . 1·00 25
668 83w. multicoloured . . . 5·00 70
MS669 90 × 60 mm. Nos. 667/8. Imperf . . . . 6·50 4·25

1966. 20th Anniv of UNESCO.
670 **261** 7w. multicoloured 55 20
MS671 90 × 60 mm. No. 670. Imperf 2·00 1·60

1966. Hurricane Relief. As No. 646 but colour changed and premium added.
672 **214** 7w.+2w. red . . . . . . 1·10 15

262 "Lucky Bag"

263 Eurasian Badger

1966. Christmas and New Year. Multicoloured.
673 5w. Type **262** 45 15
674 7w. Sheep (vert) 45 15
MS675 Two sheets each 90 × 60 mm. Nos. 673/4. Imperf . . . . . . 3·25 3·00

1966. Korean Fauna. Multicoloured.
676 3w. Type **263** . . . . 1·25 25
677 5w. Asiatic black bear . . . 1·25 25
678 7w. Tiger . . . . 1·50 25
MS679 Three sheets each 90 × 60 mm. Nos. 676/8. Imperf 8·00 6·00

264 "Syncom" Satellite

265 Presidents Pak and Lubke

1967. 15th Anniv of Korea's Admission to I.T.U.
680 **264** 7w. multicoloured 70 30
MS681 90 × 60 mm. No. 680. Imperf 2·75 2·25

1967. Visit of Pres. Lubke of West Germany to Korea.
682 **265** 7w. multicoloured . . . . 2·00 80
MS683 90 × 60 mm. No. 682. Imperf 4·00 3·75

266 Coin, Factories and Houses

267 Okwangdae Mask

1967. 1st Anniv of Korean Revenue Office.
684 **266** 7w. sepia and green . . . 50 25

1967. Folklore. Multicoloured.
685 4w. Type **267** . . . . 1·00 25
686 5w. Sandi mask (horiz) . . . 1·00 25
687 7w. Mafoe mask . . . . . . 1·00 25
MS688 Three sheets each 90 × 60 mm. Nos. 685/7. Imperf 4·25 3·50

268 J.C.I. Emblem and Pavilion

269 Map Emblem

1967. International Junior Chamber of Commerce Conference, Seoul.
689 **268** 7w. multicoloured 50 25
MS690 90 × 60 mm. No. 689. Imperf 2·00 1·75

1967. 5th Asian Pacific Dental Congress, Seoul.
691 **269** 7w. multicoloured 55 25
MS692 90 × 60 mm. No. 691. Imperf 2·00 1·60

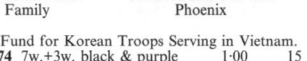

270 Korean Pavilion

271 Worker and Soldier

1967. World Fair, Montreal.
693 **270** 7w. black, red and yellow 1·00 35
694 83w. black, red and blue 6·50 70
MS695 90 × 60 mm. Nos. 693/4 6·00 5·00

1967. Veterans' Day.
696 **271** 7w. multicoloured 50 25

272 Railway Wheel and Rail

1967. 2nd Five Year Plan. Dated "1967".
697 **272** 7w. black, yellow & brown . . . . 2·40 1·10
698 – 7w. orange, brown & black . . . . 1·00 30
DESIGN: No. 698, Nut and bolt.
See also Nos. 773/4, 833/4, 895/6 and 981/2.

273 Sword Dance

1967. Folklore. Multicoloured.
699 4w. Type **273** 85 25
700 5w. Peace dance (vert) . . . 85 25
701 7w. Buddhist dance (vert) . . 1·10 25
MS702 Three sheets each 90 × 60 mm. Nos. 699/701. Imperf 4·00 3·00

274 Soldier and Family

275 President Pak and Phoenix

1967. Fund for Korean Troops Serving in Vietnam.
703 **274** 7w.+3w. black & purple 1·00 15

1967. Inaug of President Pak for 2nd Term.
704 **275** 7w. multicoloured . . . . 4·00 1·00
MS705 90 × 60 mm. No. 704. Imperf 12·00 10·00

276 Scout, Badge and Camp

1967. 3rd Korean Scout Jamboree. Multicoloured.
706 7w. Type **276** . . . . 1·00 30
707 20w. Scout badge, bridge and tent . . . . 2·50 50
MS708 Two sheets each 90 × 60 mm. Nos. 706/7. Imperf . . . . . . 5·00 4·00

280 Girls on Swing

1967. Folklore. Multicoloured.
712 4w. Type **280** . . . . 1·00 25
713 5w. Girls on seesaw (vert) . . 1·00 25
714 7w. Girls dancing (vert) . . . 1·40 25
MS715 Three sheet each 90 × 60 mm. Nos. 712/14. Imperf . . . . . 4·00 3·50

281 Freedom Centre **282** Boxing

1967. 1st World Anti-Communist League Conference, Taipei. Multicoloured.
716 5w. Type **281** 50 25
717 7w. Hand grasping chain (vert) 50 25
MS718 Two sheets each 90 × 60 mm. Nos. 716/17. Imperf . . . . . 3·75 3·00

1967. National Athletic Meeting, Seoul. Mult.
719 5w. Type **282** . . . . 1·10 25
720 7w. Basketball . . . . 1·10 25

283 Students' Memorial, Kwangjoo **284** Decade Emblem

1967. Students' Day.
721 **283** 7w. multicoloured 50 25

1967. International Hydrological Decade.
722 **284** 7w. multicoloured 50 25

285 Children spinning Top **286** Playing Shuttlecock

1967. Christmas and New Year.
723 **285** 5w. blue, red and pink . . 50 15
724 – 7w. brown, blue and bistre 50 15
MS725 Two sheets each 90 × 60 mm. Nos. 723/4. Imperf . . . . . . 3·50 2·50
DESIGN: 7w. Monkey and Signs of the Zodiac.

1967. Folklore. Multicoloured.
726 4w. Type **286** 90 25
727 5w. "Dalmaji" (horiz) . . . 90 25
728 7w. Archery . . . . 1·25 25
MS729 Three sheets each 90 × 60 mm. Nos. 726/8. Imperf 4·00 3·00

287 Microwave Transmitter

1967. Inaug of Microwave Telecommunications Service.
730 **287** 7w. black, green and blue 50 25
MS731 90 × 60 mm. No. 730. Imperf 2·50 2·00

288 Carving, King Songdok's Bell **289** 5th–6th century Earrings **290** Korean Flag

1968.
732 **288** 1w. brown and yellow . . 25 10
733 **289** 5w. yellow and green . . 1·25 10
734 **290** 7w. red and blue 70 10
787 7w. blue 45 10
788 7w. blue* 30 10
790 10w. blue* 60 10
*Nos. 788 and 790 have their face values shown as "7" or "10" only, omitting the noughts shown on Nos. 734 and 787.
For designs similar to Type **290** see Nos. 771, 780 and 827.

291 W.H.O. Emblem **292** E.A.T.A. Emblem and Korean Motif

1968. 20th Anniv of W.H.O.
735 **291** 7w. multicoloured 55 25
MS736 90 × 60 mm. No. 735. Imperf 2·75 2·00

1968. 2nd East Asia Travel Association Conference, Seoul.
737 **292** 7w. multicoloured 50 25
MS738 90 × 60 mm. No. 737. Imperf 2·75 2·00

293 C.A.C.C.I. Emblem, Korean Doorknocker and Factories

1968. 2nd Conference of Confederation of Asian Chambers of Commerce and Industry (C.A.C.C.I.), Seoul.
739 **293** 7w. multicoloured 50 25
MS740 90 × 60 mm. No. 739. Imperf 2·70 2·00

294 Pres. Pak and Emperor Haile Selassie

1968. Visit of Emperor of Ethiopia.
741 **294** 7w. multicoloured . . . . 2·00 75
MS742 90 × 60 mm. No. 741. Imperf 5·00 4·00

295 Post-bag

1968. Postman's Day. Multicoloured.
743 5w. Type **295** . . . . 1·25 50
744 7w. Postman 50 25

296 Atomic and Development Symbols

1968. Promotion of Science and Technology.
745 **296** 7w. blue, green and red 50 25

297 Kyung Hi University and Conference Emblem

1968. 2nd Conf of Int Assn of University Presidents.
746 **297** 7w. multicoloured 50 25
MS747 90 × 60 mm. No. 746. Imperf 4·00 3·00

298 "Liberation" **299** Reservist

1968. Liberation of Suppressed Peoples' Campaign.
748 **298** 7w. multicoloured 50 25

1968. Army Reservists' Fund.
749 **299** 7w.+3w. black & green 1·50 30

300 Stylized Peacock **301** Fair Entrance

1968. 20th Anniv of Republic.
750 **300** 7w. multicoloured 60 25

1968. 1st Korean Trade Fair, Seoul.
751 **301** 7w. multicoloured 50 25

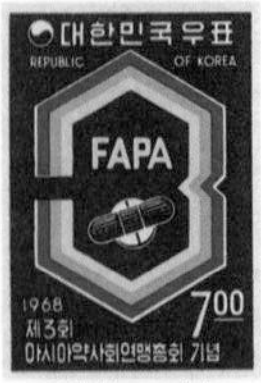

302 Assembly Emblem **303** Scout Badge

1968. 3rd General Assembly of Asian Pharmaceutical Association Federation.
752 **302** 7w. multicoloured 50 25

1968. 6th Far East Scout Conference, Seoul.
753 **303** 7w. multicoloured . . . . 1·25 25

304 Soldier and Battle Scene **305** Colombo Plan Emblem and Globe

1968. 20th Anniv of Korean Armed Forces.
754 **304** 7w. orange and green . . 2·00 40
755 – 7w. blue and light blue . . 2·00 40
756 – 7w. blue and orange . . . 2·00 40
757 – 7w. light blue and blue . . 2·00 40
758 – 7w. green and orange . . 2·00 40
DESIGNS: No. 755, Sailor and naval guns; 756, Servicemen and flags; 757, Airman and jet fighters; 758, Marine and landings.

1968. 19th Meeting of Colombo Plan Consultative Committee, Seoul.
759 **305** 7w. multicoloured 50 15

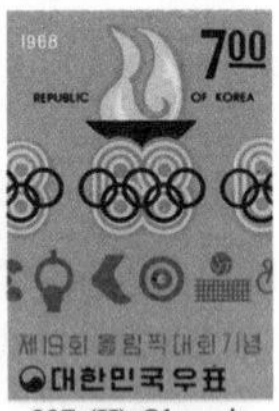

306 (I) Olympic Emblems **307** (II) Olympic Emblems

1968. Olympic Games, Mexico. Multicoloured.
760 7w. Type **306** . . . . 2·00 60
761 7w. Type **307** . . . . 2·00 60
762 7w. Cycling (I) . . . . 2·00 60
763 7w. Cycling (II) . . . . . . 2·00 60
764 7w. Boxing (I) . . . . 2·00 60
765 7w. Boxing (II) . . . . . . 2·00 60
766 7w. Wrestling (I) . . . . . . 2·00 60
767 7w. Wrestling (II) . . . . . 2·00 60
MS768 Four sheets each 90 × 60 mm. Imperf (a) Nos. 760/1; (b) Nos. 762/3; (c) Nos. 764/5; (d) Nos. 766/7 . . . . 20·00 12·00
The two types of each design may be identified by the position of the country name at the foot of the design—ranged right in types I, and left in types II. On three of the designs (excluding "Cycling") the figures of value are on left and right respectively. Types I and II of each design were issued together horizontally se-tenant within the sheets of 50 stamps.

308 Statue of Woman **309** Coin and Symbols

1968. 60th Anniv of Women's Secondary Education.
769 **308** 7w. multicoloured 50 20

1968. National Wealth Survey.
770 **309** 7w. multicoloured 50 20

1968. Disaster Relief Fund. As No. 734, but with additional inscr and premium added.
771 **290** 7w.+3w. red and blue . . 5·00 50
The face value on No. 771 is expressed as "7 00+3 00", see also Nos. 780 and 827.

310 Shin Eui Ju Memorial **311** Demonstrators

1968. Anniv of Student Uprising, Shin Eui Ju (1945).
772 **310** 7w. multicoloured 50 20

1968. 2nd Five Year Plan. As T **272**. Dated "1968". Multicoloured.
773 7w. Express motorway . . . 60 25
774 7w. "Clover-leaf" road junction 60 25

1968. Human Rights Year.
775 **311** 7w. multicoloured 50 20

312 Christmas Lanterns **314** Korean House and U.N. Emblems

1968. Christmas and New Year. Multicoloured.
776 5w. Type **312** 75 10
777 7w. Cockerel 75 10
MS778 Two sheets each 90 × 60 mm. Nos. 776/7. Imperf . . . . . . 6·00 4·00

1968. 20th Anniv of South Korea's Admission to U.N.
779 **314** 7w. multicoloured 50 20

1969. Military Helicopter Fund. As No. 734 but colours changed and inscr with premium added.
780 **290** 7w.+3w. red, blue & grn 1·25 40

315 Torch and Monument, Pagoda Park, Seoul **316** Hyun Choong Sa and "Turtle" Ships

1969. 50th Anniv of Samil (Independence) Movement.
781 **315** 7w. multicoloured 60 25

1969. Dedication of Rebuilt Hyun Choong Sa (Shrine of Admiral Li Sun Sin).
782 **316** 7w. multicoloured 80 25

317 President Pak and Yang di-Pertuan Agong **318** Stone Temple Lamp

1969. Visit of Yang di-Pertuan Agong (Malaysian Head-of-State).
783 **317** 7w. multicoloured . . . . 2·00 75
MS784 90 × 60 mm. No. 783. Imperf 7·50 4·25

1969.
786 **318** 5w. purple 50 10
791 – 20w. green . . . . 1·50 10
792 – 30w. green . . . . 2·25 10
794 – 40w. mauve and blue . . 1·75 10
795 – 100w. brown and purple 28·00 10
DESIGNS—As Type **318**. VERT: 20w. Wine jug; 40w. Porcelain Jar, Yi Dynasty; 100w. Seated Buddha (bronze). HORIZ: 30w. "Duck" vase.

323 "Red Cross" between Faces

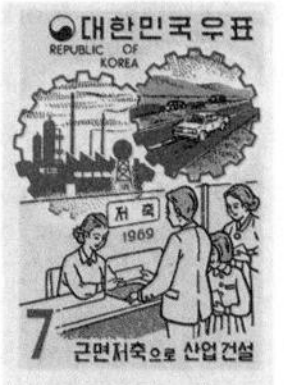

324 "Building the Nation's Economy"

1969. 50th Anniv of League of Red Cross Societies.
796 **323** 7w. multicoloured 85 20
MS797 90 × 60 mm. No. 796. Imperf 2·00 1·40

1969. "Second Economy Drive".
798 **324** 7w. multicoloured 40 15

325 Presidents Pak and Nguyen van Thieu

1969. Visit of President Nguyen van Thieu of South Vietnam.
799 **325** 7w. multicoloured . . . . 2·00 65
MS800 90 × 60 mm. No. 799. Imperf 7·50 3·25

326 Reafforestation and Flooded Fields

327 Ignition of Second-stage Rocket

1969. Flood and Drought Damage Prevention Campaign. Multicoloured.
801 7w. Type **326** 60 25
802 7w. Withered and flourishing plants 60 25

1969. First Man on the Moon.
803 **327** 10w. blue, black and red 1·50 50
804 – 10w. blue, black and red 1·50 50
805 – 20w. multicoloured . . . 1·50 50
806 – 20w. multicoloured . . . 1·50 50
807 – 40w. blue, red and black 1·50 50
MS808 160 × 110 mm. Nos. 803/7. Imperf . . . . 7·00 4·25
DESIGNS: No. 804, Separation of modules from rocket; 805, Diagram of lunar orbit; 806, Astronauts on Moon; 807, Splashdown of "Apollo 11".

328 Stepmother admonishing Kongji

332 Steam Locomotive of 1899

1969. Korean Fairy Tales (1st series). "Kongji and Patji". Multicoloured.
809 5w. Type **328** 65 25
810 7w. Kongji and sparrows . . 75 25
811 10w. Kongji and ox . . . . 1·10 40
812 20w. Kongji in sedan-chair 1·25 40
MS813 Four sheets each 90 × 60 mm. Imperf. (a) No.809; (b) No. 810; (c) No. 811; (d) No. 812 . . . . 6·00 4·00
See also Nos. 828/**MS**832, 839/**MS**843, 844/**MS**848 and 853/**MS**857.

1969. 70th Anniv of Korean Railways. Multicoloured.
814 7w. Type **332** . . . . 1·50 50
815 7w. Early steam and modern diesel locomotives . . . . 1·50 50

333 Northrop F-5A Freedom Jet Fighters

1969. 20th Anniv of Korean Air Force. Multicoloured.
816 10w. Type **333** . . . . . . 1·25 25
817 10w. McDonnell-Douglas F-4D Phantom II jet fighter . . . . 1·25 25

334 Game of Cha-jun

1969. 10th Korean Traditional Arts Contest, Taegu.
818 **334** 7w. multicoloured 60 15

335 Molecule and Institute Building

1969. Completion of Korean Institute of Science and Technology.
819 **335** 7w. multicoloured 60 15

336 Presidents Pak and Hamani

1969. Visit of President Hamani of Niger Republic.
820 **336** 7w. multicoloured . . . . 1·25 40
MS821 90 × 60 mm. No. 820. Imperf 4·00 3·00

337 Football

342 Students ringing "Education"

1969. 50th Anniv of National Athletic Meeting. Multicoloured.
822 10w. Type **337** . . . . 1·10 40
823 10w. Volleyball . . . . 1·10 40
824 10w. Korean wrestling (horiz) 1·10 40
825 10w. Fencing (horiz) . . . . 1·10 40
826 10w. Taekwondo (karate) (horiz) . . . . 1·10 40

1969. Searchlight Fund. As T **290** but with additional inscr and premium. Face value expressed as "7+3".
827 7w.+3w. red and blue 80 25

1969. Korean Fairy Tales (2nd series). "The Hare's Liver". As T **328**. Multicoloured.
828 5w. Princess and Doctors . . 65 30
829 7w. Hare arriving at Palace 70 30
830 10w. Preparing to remove the Hare's liver . . . . 1·10 40
831 20w. Escape of the Hare . . 1·25 40
MS832 Four sheets each 90 × 60 mm. Imperf. (a) No. 828; (b) No. 829; (c) No. 830; (d) No. 831 . . . . 6·00 4·00

1969. 2nd Five-year Plan. As T **272**. Dated "1969". Multicoloured.
833 7w. "Agriculture and Fisheries" 75 40
834 7w. Industrial emblems . . . 50 15

1969. 1st Anniv of National Education Charter.
835 **342** 7w. multicoloured 50 15

343 Toy Dogs

344 Woman with Letter and U.P.U. Monument, Berne

1969. Lunar New Year ("Year of the Dog"). Multicoloured.
836 5w. Type **343** 60 25
837 7w. Candle and lattice doorway 60 25

1970. 70th Anniv of Korea's Admission to U.P.U.
838 **344** 10w. multicoloured . . . 3·00 70

1970. Korean Fairy Tales (3rd series). "The Sun and the Moon". As T **328**. Multicoloured.
839 5w. Mother meets the tiger 65 25
840 7w. Tiger in disguise 70 25
841 10w. Children chased up a tree . . . . 1·10 40
842 20w. Children escape to Heaven . . . . 1·25 40
MS843 Four sheets each 90 × 60 mm. Imperf. (a) No. 839; (b) No. 840; (c) No. 841; (d) No. 842 . . . . 6·00 4·00

1970. Korean Fairy Tales (4th series). "The Woodcutter and the Fairy". As T **328**. Mult.
844 10w. Woodcutter hiding Fairy's dress . . . . 1·10 40
845 10w. Fairy as Woodcutter's Wife . . . . 1·10 40
846 10w. Fairy and children fly to Heaven . . . . 1·10 40
847 10w. Happy reunion . . . . 1·10 40
MS848 Four sheets each 90 × 60 mm. Imperf. (a) No. 844; (b) No. 845; (c) No. 846; (d) No. 847 . . . . 6·00 5·00

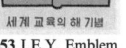

353 I.E.Y. Emblem on Open Book

354 Seated Buddha and Korean Pavilion

1970. International Education Year.
849 **353** 10w. multicoloured . . . 3·00 70

1970. "EXPO 70" World Fair, Osaka, Japan.
850 **354** 10w. multicoloured . . . 2·25 60

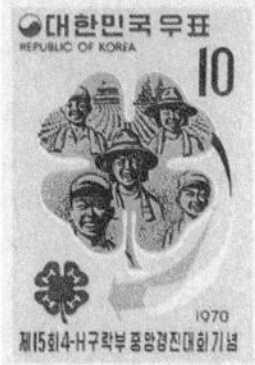

355 "4-11" Club Emblem

356 Bank Emblem and Cash

1970. 15th "4-11" Club (young farmers' organization) Central Contest, Suwon.
851 **355** 10w. multicoloured . . . 80 30

1970. 3rd General Meeting of Asian Development Bank, Seoul.
852 **356** 10w. multicoloured . . . 80 30

1970. Korean Fairy Tales (5th series). "Heungbu and Nolbu". As T **328**. Multicoloured.
853 10w. Heungbu tending swallow . . . . 1·00 25
854 10w. Heungbu finds treasure in pumpkin . . . . 1·00 25
855 10w. Nolbu with pumpkin . . 1·00 25
856 10w. Nolbu chased by devil 1·00 25
MS857 Four sheets each 90 × 60 mm. Imperf. (a) No. 853; (b) No. 854; (c) No. 855; (d) No. 856 . . . . 6·00 4·50

361 Royal Palanquin (Yi dynasty)

362 New Headquarters Building

1970. Early Korean Transport.
858 **361** 10w. multicoloured . . . 1·00 25
859 – 10w. multicoloured . . . 2·25 85
860 – 10w. multicoloured . . . 1·00 25
861 – 10w. black, stone and blue . . . . 1·25 25
DESIGNS—HORIZ: No. 859, Tramcar, 1899; 860, Emperor Sunjong's cadillac, 1903; 861, An Chang Nam's Nieuport 28 biplane, 1922.

1970. Opening of New U.P.U. Headquarters Building, Berne.
862 **362** 10w. multicoloured . . . 70 30

363 Dish Aerial and Hemispheres

1970. Inauguration of Satellite Communications Station, Kum San.
863 **363** 10w. multicoloured . . . 1·10 30

364 "PEN" and Quill Pen

366 Postal Code Symbol

365 Section of Motorway

1970. 37th International P.E.N. (literary organization) Congress, Seoul.
864 **364** 10w. multicoloured . . . 70 25

1970. Opening of Seoul–Pusan Motorway.
865 **365** 10w. multicoloured . . . 1·25 30

1970. Introduction of Postal Codes.
866 **366** 10w. multicoloured . . . 60 25

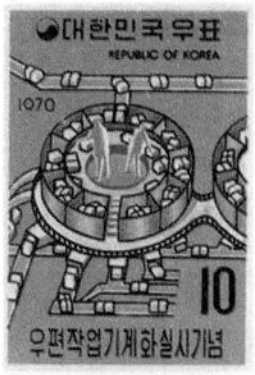

367 Parcel Sorting Area

368 Children's Hall and Boy

1970. Inauguration of Postal Mechanization.
867 **367** 10w. multicoloured . . . 60 25
MS868 130 × 90 mm. Nos. 866/7 × 2 15·00 19·00

1970. Opening of Children's Hall, Seoul.
869 **368** 10w. multicoloured . . . 60 30

369 "Mountain and River" (Yi In Moon)

1970. Korean Paintings of Yi Dynasty (1st series). Multicoloured.
870 10w. Type **369** . . . . . . 1·25 30
871 10w. "Jongyangsa Temple" (Chong Son) . . . . . . 1·25 30
872 10w. "Mountain and River by Moonlight" (Kim Doo Ryang) (vert) . . . . . . 1·25 30
MS873 Three sheets each 130 × 90 mm. Nos. 870/2 × 2 . . 6·00 4·25
See also Nos. 887/**MS**890, 897/**MS**900, 947/**MS**953, 956/**MS**953, 956/**MS**959 and 961/**MS**966.

370 P.T.T.I. Emblem

371 WAC and Corps Badge

1970. Councillors' Meeting, Asian Chapter of Postal, Telegraph and Telephone International (Post Office Trade Union Federation).
874 **370** 10w. multicoloured . . . 55 25

1970. 20th Anniv of Korean Women's Army Corps.
875 **371** 10w. multicoloured . . . 60 25

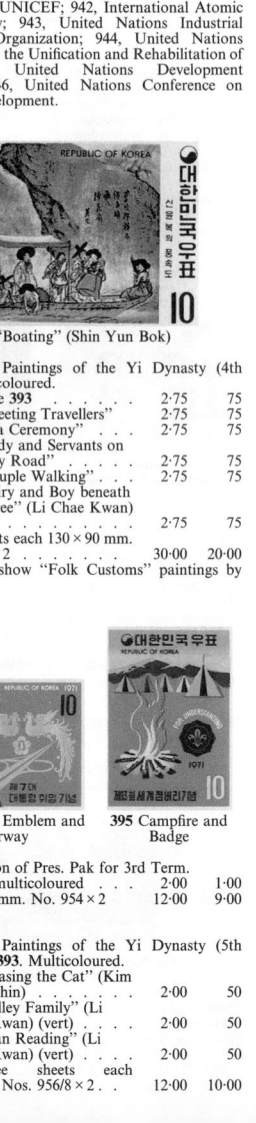

372 Pres. Pak and Flag

1970.
876 **372** 10w. multicoloured . . . 3·75 55
877 – 10w. black, green and blue . . . . 2·75 50
DESIGN—VERT: No. 877, Pres. Pak and industrial complex.

373 Presidents Pak and Sanchez Hernandez

1970. Visit of Pres. Sanchez Hernandez of El Salvador.
878 **373** 10w. multicoloured . . . 2·00 60
MS879 90 × 60 mm. No. 878. Imperf (inscr "SOLVADOL") . . . . 18·00 16·00

374 "People and Houses"

1970. National Census.
880 **374** 10w. multicoloured . . . 90 25

375 Diving

1970. 51st National Athletic Games, Seoul.
881 10w. Type **375** . . . . . . 1·40 50
882 10w. Hockey . . . . 1·40 50
883 10w. Baseball . . . . 1·40 50
MS884 Three sheets each 91 × 87 mm. Nos. 881/3 × 2. Imperf . . . . 9·00 8·00

376 Police Badge and Activities

377 Bell and Globe

1970. National Police Day.
885 **376** 10w. multicoloured . . . 1·00 30

1970. 25th Anniv of United Nations.
886 **377** 10w. multicoloured . . . 75 30

1970. Korean Paintings of the Yi Dynasty (2nd series). Vert designs at T **369**, showing animals. Multicoloured.
887 30w. "Fierce Tiger" (Shim Sa Yung) . . . . 2·50 75
888 30w. "Cats and Sparrows" (Pyun Sang Byuk) . . . . 2·50 75
889 30w. "Dog with Puppies" (Yi Am) . . . . 2·50 75
MS890 Three sheets each 130 × 90 mm. Nos. 887/9 × 2 . . 7·00 7·00

378 Kite and Reel

380 Fields ("Food Production")

379 Quotation and Emblems on Globe

1970. Lunar New Year ("Year of the Pig"). Multicoloured.
891 10w. Type **378** 65 20
892 10w. Toy pig 65 20
MS893 Two sheets each 90 × 60 mm. Nos. 891/2 × 3 . . . . 5·00 4·50

1970. 15th Communications Day.
894 **379** 10w. multicoloured . . . 65 30

1970. 2nd Five Year Plan. At T **272**. Dated "1970". Multicoloured.
895 10w. "Port Development" . . 50 20
896 10w. "House Construction" 50 20

1970. Korean Paintings of the Yi Dynasty (3rd series). Vert designs as T **369**. Multicoloured.
897 10w. "Chokpyokdo" (river cliff) (Kim Hong Do) . . . 1·75 30
898 10w. "Hen and Chicks" (Pyn Sang Byuk) . . . . 1·75 30
899 10w. "The Flute-player" (Shin Yun Bok) . . . . . 1·75 30
MS900 Three sheets each 90 × 60 mm. Nos. 897/9 × 2. Perf or imperf . . . . 14·00 10·00

1971. Economic Development (1st series). Mult.
901 10w. Type **380** 65 30
902 10w. Dam ("Electric Power") (horiz) 65 30
903 10w. Map on crate ("Exports") (horiz) 65 30
MS904 Three sheets each 90 × 60 mm. Nos. 901/3. Imperf 6·50 5·75
See also Nos. 905/7 and 910/12.

381 Coal-mining

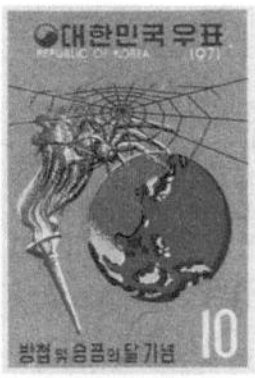

382 Globe, Torch and Spider

1971. Economic Development (2nd series). Mult.
905 10w. Type **381** . . . . . . 1·10 40
906 10w. Cement works (vert) . . 60 20
907 10w. Fertilizer plant 60 20
MS908 Three sheets each 90 × 60 mm. Nos. 905/7 × 2. Imperf . . . . 6·50 5·75

1971. Anti-espionage Month.
909 **382** 10w. multicoloured . . . 70 20

383 Motorway Junction

384 Reservist and Badge

1971. Economic Develepment (3rd series). Mult.
910 10w. Type **383** 60 20
911 10w. Scales ("Gross National Income") (horiz) 60 20
912 10w. Bee and coins ("Increased Savings") (horiz) 60 20
MS913 Three sheets each 90 × 60 mm. Nos. 910/12 × 2. Imperf . . . . 6·00 5·00

1971. 3rd Home Reserve Forces Day.
914 **384** 10w. multicoloured . . . 1·00 30

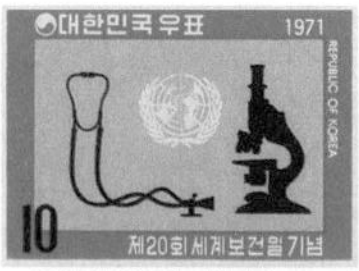

385 W.H.O. Emblem, Stethoscope and Microscope

386 Underground Train

1971. 20th World Health Day.
915 **385** 10w. multicoloured . . . 50 30

1971. Construction of Seoul Underground Railway System.
916 **386** 10w. multicoloured . . . 1·10 20

387 Footballer

388 Veteran and Association Flag

1971. 1st Asian Soccer Games, Seoul.
917 **387** 10w. multicoloured . . . 1·40 40

1971. 20th Korean Veterans' Day.
918 **388** 10w. multicoloured . . . 50 20

389 Girl Scouts

390 Torch and Economic Symbols

1971. 25th Anniv of Korean Girl Scouts Federation.
919 **389** 10w. multicoloured . . . 55 20

1971. 10th Anniv of May 16th Revolution.
920 **390** 10w. multicoloured . . . 50 20

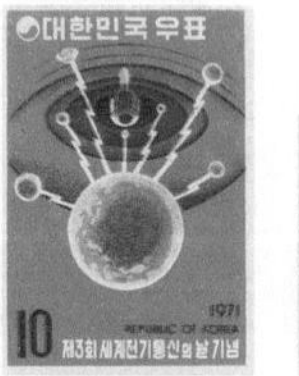

391 "Telecommunications"

392 F.A.O. Emblem

1971. 3rd World Telecommunications Day.
921 **391** 10w. multicoloured . . . 50 20

1971. "The Work of the United Nations Organization".
922 – 10w. mauve, black & green . . . . 1·50 50
923 **392** 10w. blue, black and mauve . . . . 1·50 50
924 – 10w. multicoloured . . . 1·50 50
925 – 10w. blue, black and mauve . . . . 1·50 50
926 – 10w. mauve, black & green . . . . 1·50 50
927 – 10w. blue, black and mauve . . . . 1·50 50
928 – 10w. mauve, black and blue . . . . 1·50 50
929 – 10w. black, green & mauve . . . . 1·50 50
930 – 10w. mauve, black and blue . . . . 1·50 50
931 – 10w. blue, black and mauve . . . . 1·50 50
932 – 10w. mauve, black and blue . . . . 1·50 50
933 – 10w. black, mauve & green . . . . 1·50 50
934 – 10w. mauve, blue and black . . . . 1·50 50
935 – 10w. black, mauve & green . . . . 1·50 50
936 – 10w. mauve, black and blue . . . . 1·50 50
937 – 10w. blue, black and mauve . . . . 1·50 50
938 – 10w. mauve, black and blue . . . . 1·50 50
939 – 10w. black, mauve & green . . . . 1·50 50
940 – 10w. mauve, black and blue . . . . 1·50 50
941 – 10w. blue, black and mauve . . . . 1·50 50
942 – 10w. mauve, black & green . . . . 1·50 50
943 – 10w. black, blue and mauve . . . . 1·50 50
944 – 10w. multicoloured . . . 1·50 50
945 – 10w. black, blue and mauve . . . . 1·50 50
946 – 10w. black, mauve & green . . . . 1·50 50
EMBLEMS: No. 992, I.L.O.; 924, General Assembly and New York Headquarters; 925, UNESCO; 926, W.H.O.; 927, World Bank; 928, International Development Association; 929, Security Council; 930, International Finance Corporation; 931, International Monetary Fund; 932, International Civil Aviation Organization; 933, Economic and Social Council; 934, South Korean flag; 935, Trusteeship Council; 936, U.P.U.; 937, I.T.U.; 938, World Meteorological Organization; 939, Int Court of Justice; 940, I.M.C.O.; 941, UNICEF; 942, International Atomic Energy Agency; 943, United Nations Industrial Development Organization; 944, United Nations Commission for the Unification and Rehabilitation of Korea; 945, United Nations Development Programme; 946, United Nations Conference on Trade and Development.

393 "Boating" (Shin Yun Bok)

1971. Korean Paintings of the Yi Dynasty (4th series). Multicoloured.
947 10w. Type **393** . . . . . . 2·75 75
948 10w. "Greeting Travellers" 2·75 75
949 10w. "Tea Ceremony" . . . 2·75 75
950 10w. "Lady and Servants on Country Road" . . . . . 2·75 75
951 10w. "Couple Walking" . . . 2·75 75
952 10w. "Fairy and Boy beneath Pine Tree" (Li Chae Kwan) (vert) . . . . 2·75 75
MS953 Six sheets each 130 × 90 mm. Nos. 947/52 × 2 . . . . 30·00 20·00
Nos. 947/51 show "Folk Customs" paintings by Shin Yun Bok.

394 Pres. Pak, Emblem and Motorway

395 Campfire and Badge

1971. Re-election of Pres. Pak for 3rd Term.
954 **394** 10w. multicoloured . . . 2·00 1·00
MS955 90 × 60 mm. No. 954 × 2 12·00 9·00

1971. Korean Paintings of the Yi Dynasty (5th series). As T **393**. Multicoloured.
956 10w. "Chasing the Cat" (Kim Deuk Shin) . . . . 2·00 50
957 10w. "Valley Family" (Li Chae Kwan) (vert) . . . . 2·00 50
958 10w. "Man Reading" (Li Chae Kwan) (vert) . . . . 2·00 50
MS959 Three sheets each 130 × 90 mm. Nos. 956/8 × 2 . . 12·00 10·00

1971. 13th World Scout Jamboree, Asagiri, Japan.
960 **395** 10w. multicoloured . . . 55 20

1971. Korean Paintings of the Yi Dynasty (6th series). As T **393** but vert. Multicoloured.
961 10w. "Classroom" . . . . . 2·50 85
962 10w. "Wrestling Match" . . 2·50 85
963 10w. "Dancer with Musicians" . . . . 2·50 85
964 10w. "Weavers" . . . . . . 2·50 85
965 10w. "Drawing Water at the Well" . . . . 2·50 85
MS966 Five sheets each 130 × 90 mm. Nos. 961/5 × 2 . . 30·00 22·00
Nos. 961/5 depict genre paintings by Kim Hong Do.

396 Cogwheel and Asian Map

1971. 3rd Asian Labour Minister's Conference, Seoul.
967 **396** 10w. multicoloured . . . 50 20
MS968 90 × 60 mm. No. 967 × 2 10·00 8·00

397 Judo

1971. 52nd National Athletic Meeting, Seoul. Multicoloured.
969 10w. Type **397** . . . . 1·25 40
970 10w. Archery . . . . 1·25 40
MS971 Two sheets each 91 × 87 mm. Nos. 969/70 × 3 . . . . 14·00 10·00

398 Korean Symbol on Palette

1971. 20th National Fine Art Exhibition.
972 **398** 10w. multicoloured . . . 50 20

399 Doctor and Globe **400** Emblems and "Vocational Skills"

1971. 7th Congress of Medical Associations from Asia and Oceania.
973 **399** 10w. multicoloured . . . 55 20

1971. 2nd National Vocational Skill Contest for High School Students.
974 **400** 10w. multicoloured . . . 50 20
MS975 90 × 60 mm. No. 974 × 2 8·00 5·00

401 Callipers and "K" Emblem

1971. 10th Anniv of Industrial Standardisation.
976 **401** 10w. multicoloured . . . 50 20

402 Fairy Tale Rats **403** Emblem and Hangul Alphabet

1971. Lunar New Year ("Year of the Rat"). Multicoloured.
977 10w. Type **402** . . . . 1·00 50
978 10w. Flying crane . . . . . 1·00 50
MS979 Two sheets each 90 × 60 mm. Nos. 977/8 × 3 . . . . 12·00 6·50

1971. 50th Anniv of Hangul Hakhoe (Korean Language Research Society).
980 **403** 10w. multicoloured . . . 50 20

1971. 2nd Five Year Plan. As T **272**. Dated "1971". Multicoloured.
981 10w. Atomic power plant . . 60 20
982 10w. Hydro-electric power project 65 20

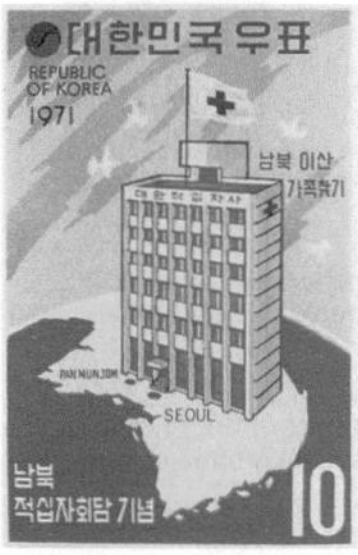

404 Korean Red Cross Building on Map **405** Globe and Open Book

1971. South–North Korean Red Cross Conference, Panmunjom.
983 **404** 10w. multicoloured . . . 1·00 30
MS984 125 × 90 mm. No. 983 × 2 5·00 4·00

1971. International Book Year.
985 **405** 10w. multicoloured . . . 60 20
MS986 90 × 60 mm. No. 985 × 2 5·00 4·00

406 "Intelsat 4" and Korean Earth Station **407** Speed Skating

1971. 20th Anniv of Korea's Membership of I.T.U.
987 **406** 10w. multicoloured . . . 50 20

1972. Winter Olympic Games, Sapporo, Japan. Multicoloured.
988 10w. Type **407** . . . . 1·00 30
989 10w. Figure-skating . . . . 1·00 30
MS990 90 × 60 mm. Nos. 988/9 6·50 4·50

408 Forestry Map **410** E.C.A.F.E. Emblem and Industrial Symbols

409 Scarab Beetles and Emblem

1972. "Trees for Unity" Campaign.
991 **408** 10w. multicoloured . . . 50 20

1972. 20th Anniv of Korean Junior Chamber of Commerce.
992 **409** 10w. multicoloured . . . 70 20

1972. 25th Anniv of U.N. Economic Commission for Asia and the Far East.
993 **410** 10w. multicoloured . . . 55 20

411 Flags of Member Countries **412** Reserve Forces' Flag

1972. 10th Anniv of Asian and Oceanic Postal Union.
994 **411** 10w. multicoloured . . . 50 20

1972. Home Reserve Forces Day.
995 **412** 10w. multicoloured . . . 1·00 30

413 Emblem and "Terias harina" **414** Rural Activities

1972. 50th Anniv of Korean Young Women's Christian Association.
996 **413** 10w. multicoloured . . . 1·75 50

1972. "New Community" (rural development) Movement.
997 **414** 10w. multicoloured . . . 50 20

415 "Anti-Espionage" and Korean Flag **416** Children with Balloons

1972. Anti-Espionage Month.
998 **415** 10w. multicoloured . . . 50 20

1972. 50th Children's Day.
999 **416** 10w. multicoloured . . . 50 20

417 Leaf Ornament from Gold Crown **418** Lake Paengnokdam, Mt. Halla Park

419 Kalkot, Koje Island, Hanryo Straits Park

1972. Treasures from King Munyong's Tomb. Multicoloured.
1000 10w. Type **417** 60 20
1001 10w. Gold earrings (horiz) 65 20

1972. National Parks (1st series).
1002 **418** 10w. multicoloured . . . 75 40
1003 **419** 10w. multicoloured . . . 75 40
See also Nos. 1018/19 and 1026/7.

420 Marguerite and Conference Emblem **421** Gwanghwa Gate and National Flags

1972. U.N. Environmental Conservation Conference, Stockholm.
1004 **420** 10w. multicoloured . . . 45 20
MS1005 90 × 60 mm. No. 1004 × 2 4·00 3·25

1972. 7th Asian and Pacific Council (ASPAC) Ministerial Meeting, Seoul.
1006 **421** 10w. multicoloured . . . 60 25

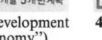

422 Pasture ("Development of Rural Economy") **423** "Love Pin"

1972. 3rd Five Year Plan. Dated "1972". Multicoloured.
1007 10w. Type **422** 60 25
1008 10w. Foundry ladle ("Heavy Industries") 60 25
1009 10w. Crate and Globe ("Increased Exports") . . 60 25

1972. Disaster Relief Fund.
1010 **423** 10w.+5w. red and blue 75 20

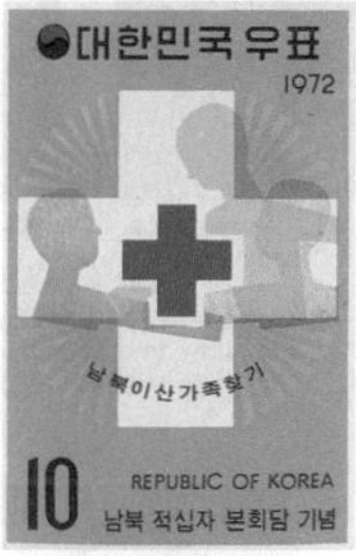

424 Judo **425** Family Reunion through Red Cross

1972. Olympic Games, Munich. Multicoloured.
1011 20w. Type **424** 75 20
1012 20w. Weightlifting 75 20
1013 20w. Wrestling 75 20
1014 20w. Boxing 75 20
MS1015 Two sheets each 90 × 60 mm. (a) Nos. 1011/12; (b) Nos. 1013/14 . . . . 7·00 6·00

1972. 1st Plenary Meeting of South–North Korean Red Cross Conference, Pyongyang.
1016 **425** 10w. multicoloured . . . 1·25 35
MS1017 125 × 90 mm. No. 1016 × 2 7·50 6·50

426 Bulkuk Temple, Kyongju Park **428** Conference Emblem within "5"

427 Statue and Bopju Temple, Mt. Sokri Park

1972. National Parks (2nd series).
1018 **426** 10w. multicoloured . . . 75 40
1019 **427** 10w. multicoloured . . . 75 40

1972. 5th Asian Judicial Conference, Seoul.
1020 **428** 10w. multicoloured . . . 55 20

429 Lions Badge between Korean Emblems

1972. 11th Orient and South-East Asian Lions Convention, Seoul.
1021 **429** 10w. multicoloured . . . 50 20

430 Scout taking Oath **431** Dolls and Ox's Head

1972. 50th Anniv of Korean Boy Scouts Movement.
1022 **430** 10w. multicoloured . . . 1·00 25

1972. Lunar New Year ("Year of the Ox"). Multicoloured.
1023 10w. Type **431** 60 20
1024 10w. Revellers in balloon . . 60 20
MS1025 Two sheets each 90 × 60 mm. Nos. 1023/4 × 2 . . 4·75 3·50

432 Temple, Mt. Naejang Park **433** Madeungryong Pass, Mt. Sorak Park

1972. National Parks (3rd series).
1026 **432** 10w. multicoloured . . . 75 40
1027 **433** 10w. multicoloured . . . 75 40

434 President Pak, Flag and "Development"

1972. Re-election of President Pak.
1028 **434** 10w. multicoloured . . . 2·00 65
MS1029 130 × 90 mm. Nos. 1028 × 2 12·00 10·00

435 National Central Museum, Kyongbok Palace **437** Korean Family

436 Temple, Mt. Sorak

1973. Korean Tourist Attractions (1st series).
1030 **435** 10w. multicoloured . . . 75 15
1031 **436** 10w. multicoloured . . . 75 15
See also Nos. 1042/3, 1048/9, 1057/8 and 1075/6.

1973. Korean Unification Campaign.
1032 **437** 10w. multicoloured . . . 50 15

438 "V" Sign and Flags **439** Construction Workers and Cogwheel

1973. Return of Korean Forces from South Vietnam.
1033 **438** 10w. multicoloured . . . 60 20

1973. 10th Workers' Day.
1034 **439** 10w. multicoloured . . . 50 15

440 W.M.O. Emblem and Satellite **442** Wonsam Costume (woman's ceremonial)

1973. Centenary of World Meteorological Organization.
1035 **440** 10w. multicoloured . . . 50 15
MS1036 90 × 60 mm. No. 1035 × 2 3·25 2·75

1973. Korean Court Costumes of the Yi Dynasty (1st series). Multicoloured. Background colours given.
1037 – 10w. orange . . . . . . 1·10 30
1038 **442** 10w. orange . . . . . . 1·10 30
MS1039 Two sheets each 125 × 90 mm. Nos. 1037/8 × 2 5·00 3·50
See also Nos. 1045/**MS**1047, 1053/**MS**1055, 1060/**MS**1062 and 1078/**MS**1080.
DESIGN: No. 1037, Kujangbok (king's ceremonial costume).

443 Nurse with Lamp **444** Reservists and Flag

1973. 50th Anniv of Korean Nurses' Association.
1040 **443** 10w. multicoloured . . . 65 15

1973. Home Reserve Forces Day.
1041 **444** 10w. multicoloured . . . 75 30

445 Palmi Island **446** Sain-am Rock, Mt. Dokjol

1973. Korean Tourist Attractions (2nd series).
1042 **445** 10w. multicoloured . . . 75 25
1043 **446** 10w. multicoloured . . . 75 25

447 Table Tennis Player

1973. Victory of South Korean Women's Team in World Table Tennis Championships, Sarajevo.
1044 **447** 10w. multicoloured . . . 1·25 30

1973. Korean Court Costumes of the Yi Dynasty (2nd series). As T **442**. Mult. Background colours given.
1045 10w. purple 80 15
1046 10w. green 80 15
MS1047 Two sheets each 125 × 90 mm. Nos. 1045/6 × 2 4·50 3·00
DESIGNS: No. 1045, Konryongpo (king's costume); 1046, Jokui (queen's ceremonial costume).

450 Admiral Li Sun Sin's Shrine, Asan **451** Limestone Cavern, Kusan-ni

1973. Korean Tourist Attractions (3rd series).
1048 **450** 10w. multicoloured . . . 80 25
1049 **451** 10w. multicoloured . . . 80 25

452 Children's Choir

1973. 20th Anniv of World Vision Int.
1050 **452** 10w. multicoloured . . . 75 25

453 Love Pin and "Disasters"

1973. Disaster Relief Fund.
1051 **453** 10w.+5w. mult 45 15

454 Steel Converter **457** Table Tennis Bat and Ball

1973. Inauguration of Pohang Steel Works.
1052 **454** 10w. multicoloured . . . 50 15

1973. Korean Court Costumes of the Yi Dynasty (3rd series). As T **442**. Mult. Background colours given.
1053 10w. blue . . . . 1·25 15
1054 10w. pink . . . . 1·25 15
MS1055 Two sheets each 125 × 90 mm. Nos. 1053/4 × 2 4·50 3·00
DESIGNS: No. 1053, Kangsapo (crown prince's) costume; 1054, Tangui (princess's) costume.

1973. Table Tennis Gymnasium Construction Fund.
1056 **457** 10w.+5w. mauve & grn 75 20

458 Namhae Suspension Bridge

459 Hongdo Island

1973. Korean Tourist Attractions (4th series).
1057 **458** 10w. multicoloured . . . 55 10
1058 **459** 10w. multicoloured . . . 55 10

460 Interpol and Korean Police Emblems

1973. 50th Anniv of International Criminal Police Organization (Interpol).
1059 **460** 10w. multicoloured . . . 65 10

1973. Korean Court Costumes of the Yi Dynasty (4th series). As T **442**. Mult. Background colours given.
1060 10w. yellow 75 10
1061 10w. blue 75 10
MS1062 Two sheets each 125 × 90 mm. Nos. 1060/1 × 2 3·25 2·50
DESIGNS: No. 1060, Kumkwanchobok (court official's) costume; 1061, Hwalot (queen's wedding) costume.

465 Manchurian Cranes **466** Sommal Lily **467** Motorway and Farm

1973.

1063	–	1w. brown	40	10
1063a	–	3w. black and blue . .	25	10
1064	–	5w. brown	10	10
1064a	–	6w. turquoise and green	30	10
1065	**465**	10w. ultramarine & blue	80	10
1066	**466**	10w. red, black & green	75	10
1067	**467**	10w. green and red . .	50	10
1068	–	30w. brown and yellow	65	10
1068a	–	50w. green and brown	50	10
1068b	–	60w. brown and yellow	50	10
1068c	–	80w. black and brown	75	10
1069	–	100w. yellow and brown	15·00	40
1069a	–	100w. red	1·00	15
1069b	–	200w. brown and pink	1·40	20
1069c	–	300w. red and lilac . .	2·00	25
1069d	–	500w. multicoloured . .	10·00	30
1069e	–	500w. purple and brown	4·00	25
1069f	–	1000w. green	5·00	60

DESIGNS—VERT: 1w. Mask of old man; 5w. Siberian chipmunk; 6w. Lily; 30w. Honey bee; 50w. Pot with lid; 60w. Jar; 100w. (No. 1069) Gold Crown, Silla dynasty; 100w. (No. 1069a) Admiral Yi Soon Shin; 300w. Pobjusa Temple; 500w. (No. 1069d) Gold Crown; 500w. (No. 1069e) Carved dragon (tile Backje Dynasty). LARGER 24 × 33 mm: 100w. Flying deities (relief from bronze bell, Sangweon Temple). HORIZ: 3w. Black-billed magpie; 80w. Ceramic horseman; 200w. Muryangsujeon Hall, Busok Temple.
For designs similar to Type **465** but with frame, see Type **703**.

470 Tennis

1973. 54th National Athletic Meeting, Pusan. Multicoloured.
1070 10w. Type **470** 65 15
1071 10w. Hurdling 65 15

471 Children with Stamp Albums

1973. Philatelic Week.
1072 **471** 10w. multicoloured . . . 40 10
MS1073 90 × 60 mm. No. 1072 × 2 4·00 3·75

472 Soyang River Dam

1973. Inauguration of Soyang River Dam.
1074 **472** 10w. multicoloured . . . 40 10

473 Mt. Mai, Chinan

474 Tangerine Grove, Cheju Island

1973. Korean Tourist Attractions (5th series).
1075 **473** 10w. multicoloured . . . 50 10
1076 **474** 10w. multicoloured . . . 50 10

475 Match, Cigarette and Flames **478** Tiger and Candles

1973. 10th Fire Prevention Day.
1077 **475** 10w. multicoloured . . . 40 10

1973. Korean Court Costumes of the Yi Dynasty (5th series). As T **442**. Mult. Background colours given.
1078 10w. orange 75 10
1079 10w. pink 75 10
MS1080 Two sheets each 125 × 90 mm. Nos. 1078/9 × 2 3·00 2·50
DESIGNS: No. 1078, Pyongsangbok (official's wife) costume; 1079, Kokunbok (military officer's) costume.

1973. Lunar New Year ("Year of the Tiger"). Multicoloured.
1081 10w. Type **478** 75 10
1082 10w. Decorated top 75 10
MS1083 Two sheets each 90 × 60 mm. Nos. 1081/2 × 2. . 6·00 5·00

479 Korean Girl and Flame Emblem

1973. 25th Anniv of Declaration of Human Rights.
1084 **479** 10w. multicoloured . . . 40 10

480 Boeing 747-200 Jetliner and Polar Zone

1973. Air.
1085 **480** 110w. blue and pink . . 3·00 30
1086 – 135w. red and green . . 3·00 30
1087 – 145w. red and blue . . . 3·00 30
1088 – 180w. yellow and lilac 3·00 30
DESIGNS—Boeing 747-200 jetliner and postal zones on map: 135w. South-east Asia; 145w. India, Australasia and North America; 180w. Europe, Africa and South America.

481 "Komunko" (zither)

1974. Traditional Musical Instruments (1st series). Multicoloured. Background colours given.
1089 **481** 10w. blue . . . . 1·00 10
1090 – 30w. orange . . . . . . 1·00 40
MS1091 Two sheets each 125 × 90 mm. (a) No. 1089 × 2; (b) No. 1090 × 2 . . . . 4·50 3·25
See also Nos. 1098/**MS**1100, 1108/**MS**1110, 1117/**MS**1119 and 1132/**MS**1134.
DESIGN: 30w. "Nagak" (trumpet triton).

483 Apricots

485 Reservist and Factory

1974. Fruits (1st series). Multicoloured.
1092 10w. Type **483** 30 10
1093 30w. Strawberries 60 15
MS1094 Two sheets each 90 × 60 mm. (a) No. 1092 × 2; (b) No. 1093 × 2 . . . . 3·25 3·00
See also Nos. 1104/**MS**1106, 1111**MS**1113, 1120/**MS**1122 and 1143/**MS**1145.

1974. Home Reserve Forces Day.
1095 **485** 10w. multicoloured . . . 30 10

486 W.P.Y. Emblem

489 Diesel Mail Train and Communications Emblem

1974. World Population Year.
1096 **486** 10w. multicoloured . . . 25 10
MS1097 90 × 60 mm. No. 1096 × 2 2·40 2·00

1974. Traditional Musical Instruments (2nd series). As T **481**. Multicoloured. Background colours given.
1098 10w. blue 75 10
1099 30w. green . . . . 1·50 15
MS1100 Two sheets each 125 × 90 mm. (a) No. 1098 × 2; (b) No. 1099 × 2 . . . . 5·50 2·25
DESIGNS: 10w. "Tchouk"; 30w. "Eu".

1974. Communications Day.
1101 **489** 10w. multicoloured . . . 75 15

490 C.A.F.E.A.-I.C.C. Emblem on Globe

491 Port Installations

1974. 22nd Session of International Chamber of Commerce's Commission on Asian and Far Eastern Affairs, Seoul.
1102 **490** 10w. multicoloured . . . 30 10

1974. Inaug of New Port Facilities, Inchon.
1103 **491** 10w. multicoloured . . . 40 10

1974. Fruits (2nd series). As T **483**. Mult.
1104 10w. Peaches 40 10
1105 30w. Grapes 60 15
MS1106 Two sheets each 90 × 60 mm. No. 1104/5 × 2 . . 2·25 1·40

494 UNESCO Emblem and Extended Fan

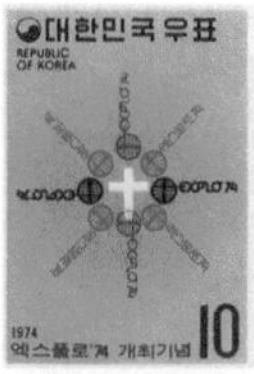
499 Cross and Emblems

1974. 20th Anniv of South Korean UNESCO Commission.
1107 **494** 10w. multicoloured . . . 30 10

1974. Traditional Musical Instruments (3rd series). As T **481**. Multicoloured. Background colours given.
1108 10w. orange 65 10
1109 30w. pink . . . . 1·25 15
MS1110 Two sheets each 125 × 90 mm. Nos. 1108/9 × 2 2·40 1·60
DESIGNS: 10w. "A-chaing" (stringed instrument); 30w. "Kyobang-ko" (drum).

1974. Fruits (3rd series). As T **483**. Multicoloured.
1111 10w. Pears 40 10
1112 30w. Apples 60 15
MS1113 Two sheets each 91 × 61 mm. Nos. 1111/12 × 2 2·40 1·60

1974. "Explo 74" 2nd International Training Congress on Evangelism. Multicoloured.
1114 10w. Type **499** 30 10
1115 10w. Emblem and Korean map on Globe 30 10

501 Underground Train

1974. Opening of Seoul Underground Railway.
1116 **501** 10w. multicoloured . . . 85 10

1974. Traditional Musical Instruments (4th series). As T **481**. Multicoloured. Background colours given.
1117 10w. blue 65 10
1118 30w. pink . . . . 1·10 15
MS1119 Two sheets each 125 × 90 mm. Nos. 1117/18 × 2 3·50 2·00
DESIGNS: 10w. "So ("Pan pipes"); 1118, Haikem (Two-stringed fiddle).

1974. Fruits (4th series). As T **483**. Multicoloured.
1120 10w. Cherries 40 10
1121 30w. Persimmons 60 10
MS1122 Two sheets each 91 × 61 mm. Nos. 1120/1 × 2 . . 2·00 1·10

506 Rifle Shooting

1974. 55th National Athletic Meeting, Seoul. Multicoloured.
1123 10w. Type **506** 30 10
1124 30w. Rowing 80 10

508 U.P.U. Emblem

509 Symbols of Member Countries

1974. Centenary of U.P.U.
1125 **508** 10w. multicoloured (postage) 30 10
1126 110w. multicoloured (air) 1·25 50
MS1127 Two sheets each 90 × 60 mm. Nos. 1125/6 × 2 . . 6·50 5·00

1974. 1st World Conference of People-to-People International.
1128 **509** 10w. multicoloured . . . 30 10

510 Korean Stamps of 1884

1974. Philatelic Week and 90th Anniv of First Korean Stamps.
1129 **510** 10w. multicoloured . . . 50 10
MS1130 91 × 61 mm. No. 1129 × 2 2·25 2·00

511 Taekwondo Contestants

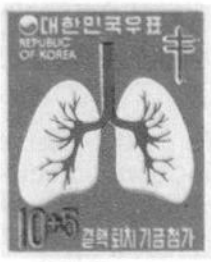
514 Lungs

1974. 1st Asian Taekwondo Championships, Seoul.
1131 **511** 10w. multicoloured . . . 50 10

1974. Traditional Musical Instruments (5th series). As T **481**. Multicoloured. Background colours given.
1132 10w. pink 50 10
1133 30w. ochre 75 15
MS1134 Two sheets each 125 × 90 mm. Nos. 1132/3 × 2 2·75 2·00
DESIGNS: 10w. Pak (clappers); 30w. Pyenchong (chimes).

1974. Tuberculosis Control Fund.
1135 **514** 10w.+5w. red & green 40 10

515 Presidents Pak and Ford

516 Yook Young Soo (wife of Pres. Pak)

1974. State Visit of President Ford of United States.
1136 **515** 10w. multicoloured . . . 55 20
MS1137 89 × 59 mm. No. 1136 × 2 5·00 4·50

1974. Yook Young Soo Memorial Issue.
1138 **516** 10w. green 50 15
1139 10w. orange 50 15
1140 10w. violet 50 15
1141 10w. blue 50 15
MS1142 91 × 125 mm. No. 1138/41 6·00 5·25

1974. Fruits (5th series). As T **483**. Multicoloured.
1143 10w. Tangerines 40 10
1144 30w. Chestnuts 50 15
MS1145 Two sheets each 91 × 61 mm. Nos. 1143/4 × 2. . 2·75 2·15

519 "Good Luck" Purse

521 U.P.U. Emblem and "75"

1974. Lunar New Year ("Year of the Rabbit"). Multicoloured.
1146 10w. Type **519** 40 10
1147 10w. Toy rabbits 40 10
MS1148 Two sheets each 91 × 61 mm. Nos. 1146/7 × 2 . . 3·25 2·25

1975. 75th Anniv of Korea's Membership of U.P.U. Multicoloured.
1149 10w. Type **521** 30 10
1150 10w. U.P.U. emblem and paper dart 30 10

523 Dove with "Good Luck" Card

1975. Inauguration of National Welfare Insurance System.
1151 **523** 10w. multicoloured . . . 20 10

524 Dr. Schweitzer, Map and Syringe

525 Salpuli Dancer

1975. Birth Centenary of Dr. Albert Schweitzer.
1152 **524** 10w. bistre 50 15
1153 10w. mauve 50 15
1154 10w. orange 50 15
1155 10w. green 50 15

1975. Korean Folk Dances (1st series). Multicoloured. Background colour given.
1156 **525** 10w. green 40 10
1157 – 10w. blue 40 10
MS1158 Two sheets each 90 × 60 mm. Nos. 1156/7 × 2 . . 2·00 1·40
DESIGN: No. 1157, Exorcism in dance.
See also Nos. 1168/**MS**1170, 1175/**MS**1177, 1193/**MS**1195 and 1028/**MS**1210.

527 Globe and Rotary Emblem

1975. 70th Anniv of Rotary International.
1159 **527** 10w. multicoloured . . . 25 10

528 Women and I.W.Y. Emblem

1975. International Women's Year.
1160 **528** 10w. multicoloured . . . 25 10

529 Violets

531 Saemaeul Township

1975. Flowers (1st series). Multicoloured.
1161 10w. Type **529** 40 10
1162 10w. Anemones 40 10
See also Nos. 1171/2, 1184/5, 1199/1200 and 1213/4.

1975. National Afforestation Campaign. Mult.
1163 10w. Type **531** 50 10
1164 10w. Lake and trees 50 10
1165 10w. "Green" forest 50 10
1166 10w. Felling timber 50 10
Nos. 1163/6 were issued together, se-tenant, forming a composite design.

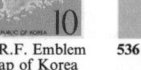

535 H.R.F. Emblem on Map of Korea

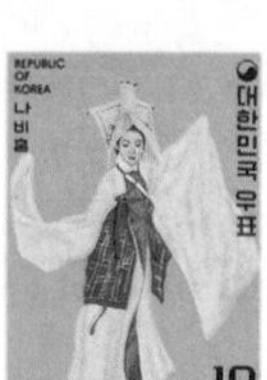
536 Butterfly Dance

1975. Homeland Reserve Forces Day.
1167 **535** 10w. multicoloured . . . 40 10

1975. Folk Dances (2nd series). Multicoloured. Background colour given.
1168 **536** 10w. green 45 10
1169 – 10w. yellow 45 10
MS1170 Two sheets each 90 × 60 mm. Nos. 1168/9 × 2 . . 1·75 1·40
DESIGN: No. 1169, Victory dance.

538 Rhododendron

540 Metric Symbols

1975. Flowers (2nd series). Multicoloured.
1171 10w. Type **538** 40 10
1172 10w. Clematis 40 10

1975. Centenary of Metric Convention.
1173 **540** 10w. multicoloured . . . 25 10

541 Soldier and Incense Pot

542 Mokjoong Dance

1975. 20th Memorial Day.
1174 **541** 10w. multicoloured . . . 25 10

1975. Folk Dances (3rd series). Multicoloured.
1175 **542** 10w. blue 45 10
1176 – 10w. pink 45 10
MS1177 Two sheets each 90 × 60 mm. Nos. 1175/6 × 2 . . 1·75 1·40
DESIGN: No. 1176, Malttungi dancer.

544 Flags of South Korea, U.N. and U.S.

1975. 25th Anniv of Korean War. Multicoloured.
1178 10w. Type **544** 45 10
1179 10w. Flags of Ethiopia, France, Greece, Canada and South Africa 45 10
1180 10w. Flags of Luxembourg, Australia, U.K., Colombia and Turkey 45 10
1181 10w. Flags of Netherlands, Belgium, Philippines, New Zealand and Thailand . . 45 10

548 Presidents Pak and Bongo

549 Iris

1975. State Visit of President Bongo of Gabon.
1182 **548** 10w. multicoloured . . . 40 10
MS1183 90 × 60 mm. No. 1182 × 2 2·00 1·60

1975. Flowers (3rd series). Multicoloured.
1184 10w. Type **549** 40 10
1185 10w. Thistle 40 10

551 Scout Scarf

552 Freedom Flame

1975. "Nordjamb 75" World Scout Jamboree, Norway. Multicoloured.
1186 10w. Type **551** 40 10
1187 10w. Scout oath 40 10
1188 10w. Scout camp 40 10
1189 10w. Axe and rope 40 10
1190 10w. Camp fire 40 10

1975. 30th Anniv of Liberation. Multicoloured.
1191 20w. Type **552** 45 10
1192 20w. Balloon emblems . . . 45 10

554 Drum Dance

556 Taekwondo Contestant

1975. Folk Dances (4th series). Multicoloured. Background colour given.
1193 **554** 20w. yellow 60 10
1194 – 20w. orange 60 10
MS1195 Two sheets each 90 × 60 mm. Nos. 1193/4 × 2 . . 2·25 1·60
DESIGN: No. 1194, Bara dance.

1975. 2nd World Taekwondo Championships, Seoul.
1196 **556** 20w. multicoloured . . . 30 10

557 Assembly Hall

1975. Completion of National Assembly Hall.
1197 **557** 20w. multicoloured . . . 30 10

558 Dumper Truck and Emblem

559 Broad-bell Flower

1975. Contractors' Association Convention, Seoul.
1198 **558** 20w. multicoloured . . . 40 10

1975. Flowers (4th series). Multicoloured.
1199 20w. Type **559** 45 10
1200 20w. Bush clover 45 10

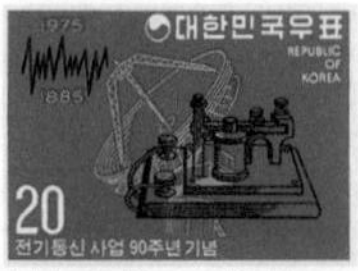

561 Morse Key and Dish Aerial

1975. 90th Anniv of Korean Telecommunications.
1201 **561** 20w. black, orange & pur 35 10

562 Yeongweol Caves

564 Flag and Missiles

1975. International Tourism Day. Multicoloured.
1202 20w. Type **562** 30 10
1203 20w. Mount Sorak 30 10

1975. Korean Armed Forces Day.
1204 **564** 20w. multicoloured . . . 30 10

565 "Gymnastics"

567 "Kangaroo" Collector

1975. 56th National Athletic Meeting. Multicoloured.
1205 20w. Type **565** 25 10
1206 20w. "Handball" 25 10

1975. Philatelic Week.
1207 **567** 20w. multicoloured . . . 30 10

568 Sogo Dance

570 U.N. Emblem and Handclasps

1975. Folk Dances (5th series). Multicoloured. Background colour given.
1208 **568** 20w. blue 45 10
1209 – 20w. yellow 55 10
MS1210 Two sheets each 90 × 60 mm. Nos. 1208/9 × 2 2·10 1·40
DESIGN: No. 1209, Bupo Nori dance.

1975. 30th Anniv of United Nations.
1211 **570** 20w. multicoloured . . . 25 10

571 Red Cross and Emblems

572 Camellia

1975. 70th Anniv of Korean Red Cross.
1212 **571** 20w. multicoloured . . . 35 10

1975. Flowers (5th series). Multicoloured.
1213 20w. Type **572** 50 10
1214 20w. Gentian 50 10

574 Union Emblem

575 Children Playing

1975. 10th Anniv of Asian Parliamentary Union.
1215 **574** 20w. multicoloured . . . 30 10

1975. Lunar New Year. Multicoloured.
1216 20w. Type **575** 30 10
1217 20w. Dragon ("Year of the Dragon") 30 10
MS1218 Two sheets each 90 × 60 mm. Nos. 1216/17 × 2 2·00 1·40

577 Electric Train

1975. Opening of Cross-country Electric Railway.
1219 **577** 20w. multicoloured . . . 50 10

578 "Dilipa fenestra"

1976. Butterflies (1st series). Multicoloured, background colour given.
1220 **578** 20w. red . . . . 1·00 10
1221 – 20w. blue . . . . 1·00 10
DESIGN: No. 1221, "Luehdorfia puziloi".
See also Nos. 1226/7, 1246/7, 1254/5 and 1264/5.

580 Institute Emblem and Science Emblems

581 Japanese White-naped Crane

1976. 10th Anniv of Korean Institute of Science and Technology.
1222 **580** 20w. multicoloured . . . 25 10

1976. Birds (1st series). Multicoloured.
1223 20w. Type **581** . . . . . . 1·00 30
1224 20w. Great bustard . . . . 1·00 30
See also Nos. 1243/4, 1251/2, 1257/8 and 1266/7.

583 Globe and Telephones

1976. Telephone Centenary.
1225 **583** 20w. multicoloured . . . 20 10

584 "Papilio xuthus"

1976. Butterflies (2nd series). Multicoloured, background colour given.
1226 **584** 20w. yellow . . . . . . 1·00 10
1227 – 20w. green . . . . . . 1·00 10
DESIGN: No. 1227, "Parnassius bremeri".

586 "National Development"

587 Eye and People

1976. Homeland Reserve Forces Day.
1228 **586** 20w. multicoloured . . . 30 10

1976. World Health Day. Prevention of Blindness.
1229 **587** 20w. multicoloured . . . 30 10

588 Pres. Pak and Flag

589 Ruins of Moenjodaro

1976. 6th Anniv of Saemaul Movement (community self-help programme). Multicoloured.
1230 20w. Type **588** 45 15
1231 20w. People ("Intellectual edification") 45 15
1232 20w. Village ("Welfare") . . 45 15
1233 20w. Produce and fields ("Production") 45 15
1234 20w. Produce and factory ("Increase of Income") . . 45 15

1976. Moenjodaro (Pakistan) Preservation Campaign.
1235 **589** 20w. multicoloured . . . 40 10

590 U.S. Flags of 1776 and 1976 **591** Camp Scene on Emblem

1976. Bicentenary of American Revolution. Each black, blue and red.

1236	100w. Type **590**	1·60	45
1237	100w. Statue of Liberty	1·60	45
1238	100w. Map of United States	1·60	45
1239	100w. Liberty Bell	1·60	45
1240	100w. American astronaut	1·60	45
MS1241	91 × 61 mm. No. 1236	2·75	2·25

1976. 30th Anniv of Korean Girl Scouts Federation.
1242 **591** 20w. multicoloured . . . 60 10

592 Blue-winged Pitta **594** Buddha and Temple

1976. Birds (2nd series). Multicoloured.

1243	20w. Type **592**	1·00	35
1244	20w. White-bellied black woodpecker	1·00	35

1976. UNESCO Campaign for Preservation of Borobudur Temple (in Indonesia).
1245 **594** 20w. multicoloured . . . 25 10

595 Eastern Pale Clouded Yellow

1976. Butterflies (3rd series). Multicoloured, background colour given.

1246 **595**	20w. olive	75	10
1247 –	20w. violet	75	10

DESIGN: No. 1247, Chinese windmill.

597 Protected Family **598** Volleyball

1976. National Life Insurance.
1248 **597** 20w. multicoloured . . . 30 10

1976. Olympic Games, Montreal. Multicoloured.

1249	20w. Type **598**	35	10
1250	20w. Boxing	35	10

600 Black Wood Pigeon **602** Children and Books

1976. Birds (3rd series). Multicoloured.

1251	20w. Type **600**	1·00	35
1252	20w. Oystercatcher	1·00	35

1976. Books for Children.
1253 **602** 20w. multicoloured . . . 25 10

603 "Hestina assimilis"

1976. Butterflies (4th series). Multicoloured, background colour given.

1254 **603**	20w. brown	75	10
1255 –	20w. drab	75	10

DESIGN: No. 1255, Blue triangle.

604a Corps Members and Flag **605** Black-faced Spoonbill

1976. 1st Anniv of Korean Civil Defence Corps.
1256 **604a** 20w. multicoloured . . 30 10

1976. Birds (4th series). Multicoloured.

1257	20w. Type **605**	1·00	35
1258	20w. Black stork	1·00	35

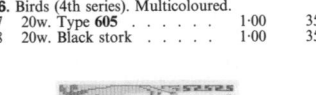

607 Chamsungdan, Mani Mountain

1976. International Tourism Day. Multicoloured.

1259	20w. Type **607**	40	10
1260	20w. Ilchumun Gate, Tongdosa	40	10

609 Cadet and Parade **610** "Musa basjoo" (flower arrangement, Cheong Jo the Great)

1976. 30th Anniv of Korean Military Academy.
1261 **609** 20w. multicoloured . . . 25 10

1976. Philatelic Week.

1262 **610**	20w. black, red and drab	25	10
MS1263	91 × 61 mm. No. 1262 × 2	1·40	1·40

611 Yellow-legged Tortoiseshell **613** Cinereous Vulture

1976. Butterflies (5th series). Multicoloured, background colour given.

1264 **611**	20w. light green	75	10
1265 –	20w. purple	75	10

DESIGN: No. 1265, "Fabriciana nerippe".

1976. Birds (5th series). Multicoloured.

1266	20w. Type **613**	3·75	1·25
1267	20w. Tundra swan	3·75	1·25

615 Snake (bas-relief, Kim Yu Shin's tomb) **619** Dish Aerial

617 "Training Technicians"

1976. Lunar New Year (Year of the Snake). Multicoloured.

1268	20w. Type **615**	50	10
1269	20w. Door knocker with Manchurian cranes	40	20
MS1270	Two sheets each 90 × 60 mm. Nos. 1268/9 × 2	1·60	1·40

1977. 4th Five Year Economic Development Plan. Multicoloured.

1271	20w. Type **617**	40	10
1272	20w. Tanker ("Heavy Industries")	50	10

1977. 25th Anniv of Korea's I.T.U. Membership.
1273 **619** 20w. multicoloured . . . 30 10

620 Korean Broadcasting Centre **621** Jar with Grape Design

1977. 50th Anniv of Broadcasting in Korea.
1274 **620** 20w. multicoloured . . . 35 10

1977. Korean Ceramics (1st series). Multicoloured, background colours given.

1275	20w. Type **621** (brown)	75	10
1276	20w. Celadon vase (grey)	75	10

See also Nos. 1285/6, 1287/8, 1290/1 and 1300/1.

623 "Two-children" Family **624** Reserve Soldier

1977. Family Planning.
1277 **623** 20w. green, turq & orge 30 10

1977. 9th Homeland Reserve Forces Day.
1278 **624** 20w. multicoloured . . . 35 10

625 Diagram of Brain **626** Medical Book and Equipment

1977. 10th Anniv of Science Day.
1279 **625** 20w. multicoloured . . . 25 10

1977. 35th International Military Medicine Meeting.
1280 **626** 20w. multicoloured . . . 45 10

627 Child with Flowers **628** Veterans' Flag and Emblem

1977. 20th Anniv of Children's Charter.
1281 **627** 20w. multicoloured . . . 25 10

1977. 25th Anniv of Korean Veterans' Day.
1282 **628** 20w. multicoloured . . . 40 10

629 Statue of Buddha, Sokkulam Grotto **630** Celadon Jar

1977. 2600th Birth Anniv of Buddha.

1283 **629**	20w. green and brown	40	10
MS1284	90 × 60 mm. No. 1283 × 2	1·75	1·50

1977. Korean Ceramics (2nd series). Multicoloured, background colours given.

1285	20w. Type **630** (pink)	45	10
1286	20w. Porcelain vase (blue) (vert)	45	10

632 "Buddha" Celadon Wine Jar

1977. Korean Ceramics (3rd series). Multicoloured, background colours given.

1287	20w. Type **632** (mauve)	45	10
1288	20w. Celadon vase (pale blue)	45	10

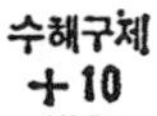

(634) **635** Celadon Vase, Black Koryo Ware

1977. Flood Relief. No. 791 surch with T **634**.
1289 20w.+10w. green . . . . . 1·25 40

1977. Korean Ceramics (4th series). Multicoloured, background colours given.

1290	20w. Type **635** (stone)	45	10
1291	20w. White porcelain bowl (green) (horiz)	45	10

637 Ulleung-do Island **639** Servicemen

1977. World Tourism Day. Multicoloured.

1292	20w. Type **637**	30	10
1293	20w. Haeundae Beach	30	10

1977. Armed Forces Day.
1294 **639** 20w. multicoloured . . . 20 10

640/1 "Mount Inwang Clearing-up after the Rain" (detail from drawing by Chung Seon)

1977. Philatelic Week.

1295 **640**	20w. multicoloured	40	10
1296 **641**	20w. multicoloured	40	10
MS1297	90 × 60 mm. Nos. 1285/6	1·50	1·25

Nos. 1295/6 were issued together, se-tenant, forming the composite design illustrated.

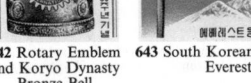

642 Rotary Emblem and Koryo Dynasty Bronze Bell **643** South Korean Flag over Everest

1977. 50th Anniv of Korean Rotary Club.
1298 **642** 20w. multicoloured . . . 50 10

1977. South Korean Conquest of Mount Everest.
1299 **643** 20w. multicoloured . . . 50 10

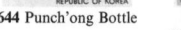

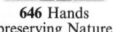

644 Punch'ong Bottle

646 Hands preserving Nature

1977. Korean Ceramics (5th series). Multicoloured, background colours given.
1300 20w. Type **644** (brown) . . 50 10
1301 20w. Celadon cylindrical bottle (pale brown) . . . 50 10

1977. Nature Conservation.
1302 **646** 20w. blue, green & brown 30 10

647 Children with Kites

649 Clay Pigeon Shooting

1977. Lunar New Year ("Year of the Horse"). Multicoloured.
1303 20w. Type **647** 30 10
1304 20w. Horse (bas-relief, Kim Yu Shin's tomb) 30 10
MS1305 Two sheets each 90 × 60 mm. (a) No. 1303 × 2; (b) No. 1304 × 2 . . . . 2·75 2·00

1977. 42nd World Shooting Championships, Seoul. Multicoloured.
1306 20w. Type **649** 35 10
1307 20w. Air pistol shooting . . . 35 10
1308 20w. Air rifle shooting . . . 35 10
MS1309 Three sheets each 90 × 60 mm. (a) No. 1306 × 2; (b) No. 1307 × 2; (c) No. 1308 × 2 7·50 5·00

652 Korean Airlines Boeing 747-200

1977. 25th Anniv of Korean Membership of I.C.A.O.
1310 **652** 20w. multicoloured . . . 45 10

653 "Exports"

1977. Korean Exports.
1311 **653** 20w. multicoloured . . . 35 10

654 Ships and World Map

1978. National Maritime Day.
1312 **654** 20w. multicoloured . . . 30 10

655 Three-storey Pagoda, Hwaom Temple

656 Seven-storey Pagoda, T'app'yong-ri

1978. Stone Pagodas (1st series).
1313 **655** 20w. multicoloured . . . 35 10
1314 **656** 20w. multicoloured . . . 35 10
See also Nos. 1319/20, 1322/5 and 1340/1.

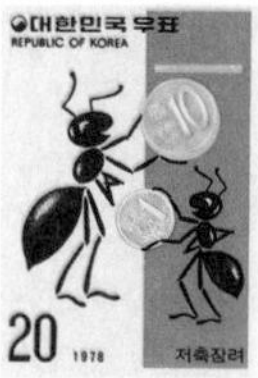
657 Ants with Coins

658 Seoul Sejong Cultural Centre, Hahoe Mask and Violin

1978. Savings Encouragement.
1315 **657** 20w. multicoloured . . . 30 10

1978. Opening of Seoul Sejong Cultural Centre.
1316 **658** 20w. multicoloured . . . 60 10

659 Standard Bearer

660 Pigeon and Young

1978. 10th Homeland Reserve Forces Day.
1317 **659** 20w. multicoloured . . . 25 10

1978. Family Planning.
1318 **660** 20w. black and green . . 35 10

661 Pagoda, Punhwang Temple

662 Pagoda, Miruk Temple

1978. Stone Pagodas (2nd series).
1319 **661** 20w. multicoloured . . . 35 10
1320 **662** 20w. multicoloured . . . 35 10

663 National Assembly

1978. 30th Anniv of National Assembly.
1321 **663** 20w. multicoloured . . . 25 10

664 Tabo Pagoda, Pulguk Temple

665 Three-storey Pagoda, Pulguk Temple

1978. Stone Pagodas (3rd series).
1322 **664** 20w. multicoloured . . . 35 10
1323 **665** 20w. multicoloured . . . 35 10

666 Ten-storey Pagoda, Kyongch'on Temple

667 Nine-storey Octagonal Pagoda, Wolchong Temple

1978. Stone Pagodas (4th series).
1324 **666** 20w. multicoloured . . . 45 10
1325 **667** 20w. multicoloured . . . 45 10

668 Emblem and Hands with Tools

669 Crater Lake, Mt. Baeguda and Bell of Joy

1978. 24th International Youth Skill Olympics, Pusan.
1326 **668** 20w. multicoloured . . . 25 10
MS1327 90 × 60 mm. No. 1326 × 1 50 1·25

1978. 30th Anniv of Republic of Korea.
1328 **669** 20w. multicoloured . . . 25 10

670 Army Nursing Officer

671 Sobaeksan Observatory and Telescope

1978. 30th Anniv of Army Nursing Corps.
1329 **670** 20w. multicoloured . . . 25 10

1978. Opening of Sobaeksan Observatory.
1330 **671** 20w. multicoloured . . . 40 10

672 Kyonghoeru Pavilion, Kyonbok Palace

673 Baeg-do Island

1978. World Tourism Day.
1331 **672** 20w. multicoloured . . . 30 10
1332 **673** 20w. multicoloured . . . 30 10

674 Customs Officers and Flag

1978. Centenary of Custom House.
1333 **674** 20w. multicoloured . . . 25 10

675 Armed Forces

676 Earthenware Figures, Silla Dynasty

1978. 30th Anniv of Korean Armed Forces.
1334 **675** 20w. multicoloured . . . 40 10

1978. Culture Month.
1335 **676** 20w. black and green . . 25 10

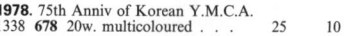

677 Painting of a Lady (Shin Yoon-bok)

678 Young Men and Y.M.C.A. Emblem

1978. Philatelic Week.
1336 **677** 20w. multicoloured . . . 35 10
MS1337 91 × 60 mm. No. 1336 × 2 1·75 1·00

1978. 75th Anniv of Korean Y.M.C.A.
1338 **678** 20w. multicoloured . . . 25 10

679 Hand smothering Fire

1978. Fire Prevention Campaign.
1339 **679** 20w. multicoloured . . . 25 10

680 Thirteen-storey Pagoda, Jeonghye Temple

681 Three-storey Pagoda, Jinjeon Temple

1978. Stone Pagodas (5th series).
1340 **680** 20w. multicoloured . . . 30 10
1341 **681** 20w. multicoloured . . . 30 10

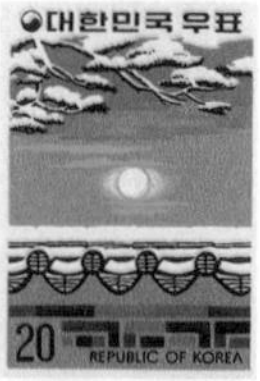
682 Snow Scene

684 People within Hibiscus

1978. Lunar New Year ("Year of the Sheep"). Multicoloured.
1342 20w. Type **682** 30 10
1343 20w. Sheep (bas-relief, Kim Yu Shin's tomb) 30 10
MS1344 Two sheets each 90 × 60 mm. Nos. 1342/3 × 2 . . 2·00 1·50

1978. 10th Anniv of National Education Charter.
1345 **684** 20w. multicoloured . . . 25 10

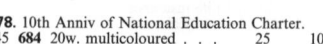

685 President Pak

1978. Re-election of President Pak.
1346 **685** 20w. multicoloured . . . 40 10
MS1347 90 × 60 mm. No. 1346 × 2 3·00 2·00

686 Golden Mandarinfish

687 Lace Bark Pine

1979. Nature Conservation.
1348 **686** 20w. multicoloured . . . 35 10
1349 **687** 20w. multicoloured . . . 35 10

688 Samil Monument

689 Worker and Bulldozer

1979. 60th Anniv of Samil Independence Movement.
1350 **688** 20w. multicoloured . . . 25 10

1979. Labour Day.
1351 **689** 20w. multicoloured . . . 25 10

690 Tabo Pagoda, Pulgak Temple

695 Hand holding Symbols of Security

1979. Korean Art. Multicoloured.
1352 20w. Type **690** 25 10
1353 20w. Gilt-bronze Maitreya 25 10
1354 20w. Gold crown of Silla . . 25 10
1355 20w. Celadon vase 25 10
1356 60w. "Tano Day Activities" (silk screen) (50 × 33 mm) 45 10
MS1357 90 × 126 mm. No. 1356 × 2 2·25 1·50

1979. Strengthening National Security.
1358 **695** 20w. multicoloured . . . 25 10

696 Pulguk Temple and P.A.T.A. Emblem

1979. 28th Pacific Area Travel Association Conference, Seoul.
1359 **696** 20w. multicoloured . . . 25 10

697 Presidents Pak and Senghor

1979. Visit of President Senghor of Senegal.
1360 **697** 20w. multicoloured . . . 25 10
MS1361 90 × 60 mm. No. 1360 × 2 1·00 90

698 Basketball

699 Children playing

1979. 8th World Women's Basketball Championships, Seoul.
1362 **698** 20w. multicoloured . . . 40 10

1979. International Year of the Child.
1363 **699** 20w. multicoloured . . . 30 10
MS1363a 90 × 60 mm. No. 1363 × 2 1·00 90

700 Children on Swing

1979. Family Planning.
1364 **700** 20w. multicoloured . . . 30 10

701 Mandarins

702 "Neofinettia falcata" (orchid)

1979. Nature Conservation.
1365 **701** 20w. multicoloured . . . 1·00 20
1366 **702** 20w. multicoloured . . . 40 10

703 Manchurian Cranes

1979.

1367	703	10w. black and green	65	15
1368	–	15w. deep green & green	15	10
1369	–	20w. bistre, black & blue	20	10
1370	–	30w. multicoloured . .	25	10
1371	–	40w. multicoloured . .	30	10
1372	–	50w. brown, red & orge	20	10
1373	–	60w. grey, purple & mve	30	10
1374	–	70w. multicoloured . .	50	10
1375	–	80w. yellow, black & red	60	10
1376	–	90w. buff, green and orange	75	10
1377	–	100w. purple and mauve	45	10
1377a	–	100w. black	45	10
1378	–	150w. black, bistre and blue	50	10
1379	–	200w. brown and green	1·10	10
1380	–	300w. blue	2·00	20
1381	–	400w. green, brown and deep green	2·25	20
1381a	–	400w. blue, ochre, brown and grey . . .	3·00	30
1382	–	450w. brown	1·60	40
1383	–	500w. dp green & green	2·00	40
1383a	–	550w. black	2·00	50
1384	–	600w. multicoloured . .	2·25	1·00
1385	–	700w. multicoloured . .	3·25	40
1386	–	800w. multicoloured . .	2·40	50
1387	–	1000w. lt brown & brn	3·25	40
1388	–	1000w. lt brown & brn	3·25	40
1389	–	5000w. multicoloured	18·00	4·00

DESIGNS—As T **703**: HORIZ: 15w. Mt. Sorak; 50w. Earthenware model of wagon; 90w. Paikryung Island; 1000w. Duck earthenware vessels (1387 facing right; 1388 facing left). VERT: 20w. Tolharubang (stone grandfather); 30w. National flag; 40w. "Hibiscus syriacus"; 60w. Porcelain jar, Yi Dynasty; 70w. Kyongju Observatory; 80w. Mounted warrior (pottery vessel); 100w. (1377) Ryu Kwan Soon; 100w. (1377a) Chung Yak Yong (writer); 150w. Porcelain jar, Chosun Dynasty; 200w. Ahn Joong Geun; 300w. Ahn Chang Ho; 400w. Koryo celadon incense burner; 450, 550w. Kim Ku (organizer of Korean Independence Party); 500w. Brick with mountain landscape; 600w. Hong Yung Sik (postal reformer); 700w. Duck (lid of incense burner). 29 × 41 mm: 800w. Dragon's head flagpole finial; 5000w. Tiger.
See also No. 1065.

725 People suffering from Traffic Pollution

1979. Environmental Protection.
1390 **725** 20w. brown and green 30 10

726 Common Goral

727 "Convallaria leiskei" Miquel

1979. Nature Conservation.
1391 **726** 20w. multicoloured . . . 40 10
1392 **727** 20w. multicoloured . . . 40 10

728 Presidents Pak and Carter

1979. Visit of President Carter of United States.
1393 **728** 20w. multicoloured . . . 20 10
MS1394 90 × 60 mm. No. 1393 × 2 1·10 95

729 Exhibition Building and Emblem

1979. Opening of Korea Exhibition Centre.
1395 **729** 20w. multicoloured . . . 20 10

730 Boeing 747-200 Jetliner and Globe

1979. 10th Anniv of Korean Air Lines.
1396 **730** 20w. multicoloured . . . 30 10

731 "The Courtesans' Sword Dance" (Shin Yun-bok)

1979. United States "5000 Years of Korean Art" Exhibition (1st issue).
1397 **731** 60w. multicoloured . . . 75 15
MS1398 89 × 125 mm. No. 1397 × 2 3·00 2·50
See also Nos. 1402/3, 1406/7, 1420/**MS**1422, 1426/7, 1433/4, 1441/2 and 1457/8.

732 Mount Mai, North Cholla Province

733 Dragon's Head Rock, Cheju Island

1979. World Tourism Day.
1399 **732** 20w. multicoloured . . . 25 10
1400 **733** 20w. multicoloured . . . 25 10

734 Heart, Donors and Blood Drop

1979. Blood Donors.
1401 **734** 20w. red and green . . . 50 10

735 White Porcelain Jar with Grape Design

736 Mounted Warrior (pottery vessel)

1979. "5000 Years of Korean Art" Exhibition (2nd issue).
1402 **735** 20w. multicoloured . . . 40 10
1403 **736** 20w. multicoloured . . . 40 10

737 "Moon Travel" (Park Chung Jae)

1979. Philatelic Week.
1404 **737** 20w. multicoloured . . . 20 10
MS1405 90 × 66 mm. No .1404 × 2 1·00 70

738 Hahoe Mask

739 Golden Amitabha with Halo

1979. "5000 Years of Korean Art" Exhibition (3rd issue).
1406 **738** 20w. multicoloured . . . 40 10
1407 **739** 20w. multicoloured . . . 40 10

740 Rain Frog

741 Asian Polypody

1979. Nature Conservation.
1408 **740** 20w. multicoloured . . . 45 10
1409 **741** 20w. multicoloured . . . 45 10

742 Monkey (bas-relief, Kim Yun Shin's tomb)

743 Children playing Yut

1979. Lunar New Year ("Year of the Monkey").
1410 **742** 20w. multicoloured . . . 20 10
1411 **743** 20w. multicoloured . . . 20 10
MS1412 Two sheets each 90 × 60 mm. (a) No. 1410 × 2; (b) No. 1411 × 2 . . . . 1·75 1·10

744 President Choi Kyu Hah

1979. Presidential Inauguration.
1413 **744** 20w. multicoloured . . . 30 10
MS1414 91 × 61 mm. No. 1413 × 2 1·40 1·10

745 Firefly

746 Meesun Tree

1980. Nature Conservation (5th series).
1415 **745** 30w. multicoloured . . . 45 10
1416 **746** 30w. multicoloured . . . 45 10

747 President Pak

748 Earthenware Kettle

749 "Landscape" (Kim Hong Do)

1980. President Pak Commemoration.
1417 **747** 30w. red 25 10
1418 30w. purple 25 10
MS1419 90 × 60 mm. Nos. 1417/18 1·50 1·25

1980. "5000 Years of Korean Art" Exhibition (4th issue).
1420 **748** 30w. multicoloured . . . 40 10
1421 **749** 60w. multicoloured . . . 55 10
MS1422 90 × 128 mm. No. 1421 × 2 2·00 1·50

750 "Lotus" 751 "Magpie and Tiger"

1980. Folk Paintings (1st series).
1423 **750** 30w. multicoloured . . . 50 20
1424 **751** 60w. multicoloured . . . 1·25 40
See also Nos. 1429/31, 1437/40 and 1453/6.

752 Merchant Ships

1980. Korean Merchant Navy.
1425 **752** 30w. multicoloured . . . 30 10

753 "Heavenly Horse" (tomb painting) 754 Banner Staff with Dragonhead Finial

1980. "5000 Years of Korean Art" Exhibition (5th series).
1426 **753** 30w. multicoloured . . . 40 10
1427 **754** 30w. multicoloured . . . 40 10

755 "Fruition"

1980. 10th Anniv of Saemaul Movement (community self-help programme).
1428 **755** 30w. multicoloured . . . 25 10

756 "Red Phoenix"

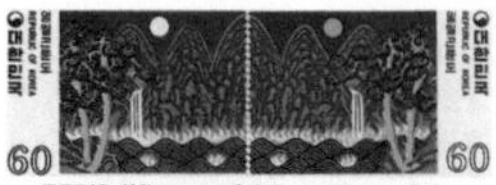
757/8 "Sun and Moon over Mt. Konryun" (½-size illustration)

1980. Folk Paintings (2nd series).
1429 **756** 30w. multicoloured . . . 30 10
1430 **757** 60w. multicoloured . . . 50 40
1431 **758** 60w. multicoloured . . . 50 40
MS1432 127 × 91 mm. Nos. 1430/1 2·00 1·60
Nos. 1430/1 were issued together, se-tenant, forming a composite design.

759 "Man on a Horse" (mural, Koguryo period) 760 "Tiger" (granite sculpture)

1980. "5000 Years of Korean Art" Exhibition (6th issue).
1433 **759** 30w. multicoloured . . . 40 10
1434 **760** 30w. multicoloured . . . 40 10

761 U.N. Flag and Rifle 762 "Venus de Milo" and Contestants

1980. 30th Anniv of Intervention of U.N. Forces in Korean War.
1435 **761** 30w. multicoloured . . . 30 10

1980. "Miss Universe" Beauty Contest, Seoul.
1436 **762** 30w. multicoloured . . . 30 10

763 "Rabbits pounding Grain in a Mortar" 764 "Dragon in Cloud"

1980. Folk Paintings (3rd series).
1437 **763** 30w. multicoloured . . . 40 10
1438 **764** 30w. multicoloured . . . 40 10

765 "Pine Tree" 766 "Flowers and Manchurian Cranes" (detail, folding screen)

1980. Folk Paintings (4th series).
1439 **765** 30w. multicoloured . . . 40 10
1440 **766** 30w. multicoloured . . . 75 20

767 Human faced Roof Tile 768 "White Tiger" (mural)

1980. "5000 Years of Korean Art" Exhibition (7th issue).
1441 **767** 30w. multicoloured . . . 30 10
1442 **768** 30w. multicoloured . . . 30 10

769 Football 770 President Chun Doo Hwan

1980. 10th President's Cup Football Tournament.
1443 **769** 30w. multicoloured . . . 30 10

1980. Presidential Inauguration.
1444 **770** 30w. multicoloured . . . 25 10
MS1445 90 × 60 mm. No. 1444 × 2 1·75 1·00

771 Woman Soldier and Emblem

1980. 30th Anniv of Women's Army Corps.
1446 **771** 30w. multicoloured . . . 25 10

772 River Baegma

773 Three Peaks of Dodam

1980. World Tourism Day.
1447 **772** 30w. pink and purple . . 30 10
1448 **773** 30w. yellow, green & blue 30 10

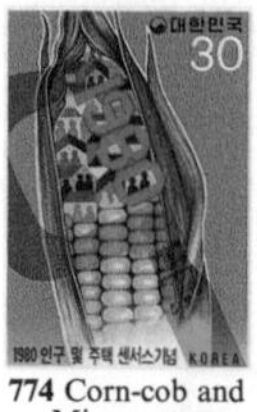

774 Corn-cob and Micrometer 775 Tree

1980. Population and Housing Census.
1449 **774** 30w. multicoloured . . . 30 10

1980. 75th Anniv of Korean Red Cross.
1450 **775** 30w. multicoloured . . . 35 10

776 "Angels delivering Mail" (Kim Ki Chul)

1980. Philatelic Week.
1451 **776** 30w. multicoloured . . . 25 10
MS1452 91 × 60 mm. No. 1451 × 2 1·00 75

777 "Ten Long-life Symbols" 781 Deva King (sculpture)

1980. Folk Paintings (5th series). Multicoloured.
1453 30w. Type **777** . . . . . . 1·40 25
1454 30w. "Herb of eternal youth" and deer 30 10
1455 30w. Pine and deer eating herb 30 10
1456 30w. Pine, water and rock 30 10
Nos. 1453/6 were issued together, se-tenant, forming a composite design.

1980. "5000 Years of Korean Art" Exhibition (8th series).
1457 **781** 30w. black 40 10
1458 30w. red 40 10

782 "Cable Enterprise" (cable ship) and Cross-section of Cable

1980. Inauguration of Korea–Japan Submarine Cable.
1459 **782** 30w. multicoloured . . . 35 10

783 Cock (bas-relief, Kim Yu Shin's tomb) 784 Cranes

1980. Lunar New Year ("Year of the Cock").
1460 **783** 30w. multicoloured . . . 30 10
1461 **784** 30w. multicoloured . . . 30 10
MS1462 Two sheets each 90 × 60 mm. (a) No. 1460 × 2; (b) No. 1461 × 2 . . . . 2·00 1·60

785 President Chun Doo Hwan and Factory within "Hibiscus syriacus"

1981. Presidential Inauguration.
1463 **785** 30w. multicoloured . . . 25 10
MS1464 90 × 60 mm. NO. 1463 × 2 90 70

786 "Korea Sun" (tanker) 787 "Asia Yukho" (freighter)

1981. Ships (1st series).
1465 **786** 30w. multicoloured . . . 55 15
1466 **787** 90w. multicoloured . . . 85 25
See also Nos. 1470/1, 1482/5 and 1501/2.

788 National Assembly Building

1981. Inaugural Session of 11th National Assembly.
1467 **788** 30w. brown and gold . . 30 10

789 Symbols of Disability and I.Y.D.P. Emblem 790 Disabled Person in Wheelchair at Foot of Steps

1981. International Year of Disabled Persons.
1468 **789** 30w. multicoloured . . . 30 10
1469 **790** 90w. multicoloured . . . 60 35

791 "Saturn" (bulk-carrier)

792 "Hanjin Seoul" (container ship)

1981. Ships (2nd series).
1470 **791** 30w. deep purple, purple and blue 55 15
1471 **792** 90w. grey, blue and red 85 25

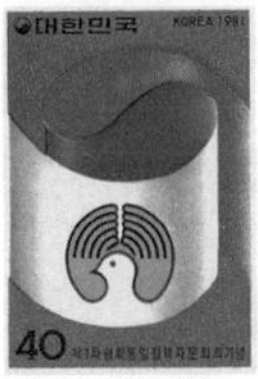
793 Council Emblem on Ribbon

1981. Advisory Council on Peaceful Unification Policy.
1472 **793** 40w. multicoloured . . . 30 10

794 "Clean Rivers and Air"

795 White Storks visiting Breeding Grounds

1981. World Environment Day.
1473 **794** 30w. multicoloured . . . 30 10
1474 **795** 90w. multicoloured . . . 65 20

796 Presidents Chun and Suharto of Indonesia

1981. Presidential Visit to A.S.E.A.N. Countries. Multicoloured.
1475 40w. Type **796** 50 10
1476 40w. Pres. Chun and Sultan of Malaysia 50 10
1477 40w. Handshake and flags of South Korea and Singapore 50 10
1478 40w. Pres. Chun and King of Thailand 50 10
1479 40w. Presidents Chun and Marcos of Philippines . . 50 10
1480 40w. Pres. Chun and flags of Korea, Singapore, Malaysia and Philippines (39 × 43 mm) 50 10
MS1481 Two sheets each 126 × 90 mm. (a) Nos. 1475/9; (b) No. 1480 × 2 . . . . 4·00 2·25

802 "Chung Ryong No. 3" (tug)

803 "Soo Gong No. 71" (trawler)

1981. Ships (3rd series).
1482 **802** 40w. multicoloured . . . 65 15
1483 **803** 100w. multicoloured . . 95 25

804 "Aldebaran" (log carrier)

805 "Hyundai No. 1" (car carrier)

1981. Ships (4th series).
1484 **804** 40w. multicoloured . . . 65 15
1485 **805** 100w. multicoloured . . 95 25

806 Korean with Flag and Dates on Graph

812 W.H.O. Emblem and Citizens

807 Glider

1981. 36th Anniv of Liberation.
1486 **806** 40w. multicoloured . . . 30 10

1981. 3rd Model Aeronautic Competition. Mult.
1487 10w. Type **807** 40 10
1488 20w. Elastic-powered airplane 40 10
1489 40w. Line-controlled airplane 40 15
1490 50w. Radio-controlled airplane 60 20
1491 80w. Radio-controlled helicopter 75 30

1981. 32nd Session of W.H.O. Regional Committee for the Western Pacific, Seoul.
1492 **812** 40w. multicoloured . . . 30 10

813 Seoul Communications Tower

814 Ulreung Island

1981. World Tourism Day.
1493 **813** 40w. multicoloured . . . 30 10
1494 **814** 40w. multicoloured . . . 30 10

815 Cycling

816 Swimming

1981. 62nd National Sports Meeting, Seoul.
1495 **815** 40w. multicoloured . . . 35 10
1496 **816** 40w. multicoloured . . . 35 10

817 Presidents Chun and Carazo Odio

818 Hand holding Plate with F.A.O. Emblem

1981. Visit of President Carazo Odio of Costa Rica.
1497 **817** 40w. multicoloured . . . 30 10

1981. World Food Day.
1498 **818** 40w. multicoloured . . . 30 10

819 Airliner and Clouds

820 South Gate of Seoul and Olympic Rings

1981. National Aviation Day.
1499 **819** 40w. orange, brown and silver 40 10

1981. Choice of Seoul as 1988 Olympic Host City.
1500 **820** 40w. multicoloured . . . 30 10

821 "Stolt Hawk" (chemical carrier)

822 Passenger Ferry

1981. Ships (5th series).
1501 **821** 40w. black 65 15
1502 **822** 100w. blue 95 25

823 "Hang-gliding" (Kim Kyung Jun)

1981. Philatelic Week.
1503 **823** 40w. multicoloured . . . 30 10
MS1504 90 × 60 mm. No. 1503 × 2 1·25 90

824 Camellia and Dog

825 Children flying Kite

1981. Lunar New Year ("Year of the Dog").
1505 **824** 40w. multicoloured . . . 30 10
1506 **825** 40w. multicoloured . . . 30 10
MS1507 Two sheets each 90 × 60 mm. (a) No. 1505 × 2; (b) No. 1506 × 2 . . . . 2·50 2·00

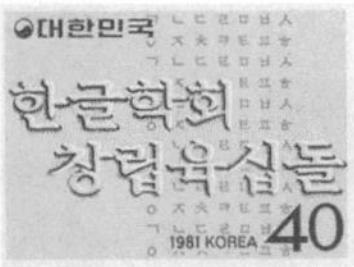
826 "Hangul Hakhoe"

1981. 60th Anniv of Hangul Hakhoe (Korean Language Society).
1508 **826** 40w. multicoloured . . . 35 10

827 Telephone and Dish Aerial

828 Scout Emblem and Logs forming "75"

1982. Inauguration of Korea Telecommunication Authority.
1509 **827** 60w. multicoloured . . . 40 10

1982. 75th Anniv of Boy Scout Movement.
1510 **828** 60w. multicoloured . . . 60 10

829 Young Woman

830 Dividers and World Map

1982. 60th Anniv of Korean Young Women's Christian Association.
1511 **829** 60w. multicoloured . . . 35 10

1982. Centenary of International Polar Year.
1512 **830** 60w. multicoloured . . . 50 10

831 Music and "Hibiscus syriacus"

1982. Children's Day.
1513 **831** 60w. multicoloured . . . 40 10

832 President Chun and Samuel Doe

1982. Visit of Samuel Doe (Liberian Head of State).
1514 **832** 60w. multicoloured . . . 35 10
MS1515 100 × 60 mm. No. 1514 × 2 1·00 80

833 Centenary Emblem

1982. Centenary of Korea–United States Friendship Treaty.
1516 **833** 60w. multicoloured . . . 30 10
1517 – 60w. multicoloured . . . 30 10
MS1518 90 × 60 mm. Nos. 1516/17 1·00 80
DESIGN: No. 1517, Statue of Liberty and Seoul South Gate.

835 Presidents Chun and Mobutu

1982. Visit of President Mobutu of Zaire.
1519 **835** 60w. multicoloured . . . 30 10
MS1520 100 × 60 mm. No. 1519 × 2. Imperf . . . . 1·00 80

836 "Territorial Expansion by Kwanggaeto the Great" (Lee Chong Sang)

837 "General Euljimunduck's Great Victory at Salsoo" (Park Kak Soon)

1982. Documentary Paintings (1st series).
1521 **836** 60w. multicoloured . . . 40 10
1522 **837** 60w. multicoloured . . . 40 10
See also Nos. 1523/4, 1537/8 and 1548/9.

838 "Shilla's Repulse of Invading Tang Army" (Oh Seung Woo)

839 "General Kang Kam Chan's Great Victory at Kyiju" (Lee Yong Hwan)

1982. Documentary Paintings (2nd series).
1523 **838** 60w. multicoloured . . . 40 10
1524 **839** 60w. multicoloured . . . 40 10

840 Convention Emblem and Globe

841 Presidents Chun and Moi of Kenya

1982. 55th International Y's Men's Club Convention, Seoul.
1525 **840** 60w. multicoloured . . . 20 10

1982. Presidential Visits to Africa and Canada. Multicoloured.
1526 60w. Type **841** 35 10
1527 60w. Presidents Chun and Shagari of Nigeria 35 10
1528 60w. Presidents Chun and Bongo of Gabon 35 10
1529 60w. Presidents Chun and Diouf of Senegal 35 10
1530 60w. Flags of South Korea and Canada 35 10
MS1531 Five sheets each 90 × 60 mm. (a) No. 1526 × 2; (b) No. 1527 × 2; (c) No. 1528 × 2; (d) No. 1529 × 2; (e) No. 1530 × 2 5·00 4·00

846 National Flag

1982. Centenary of National Flag.
1532 **846** 60w. multicoloured . . . 40 10
MS1533 90 × 60 mm. No. 1532 × 2 1·25 90

847 Emblem and Player

1982. 2nd Seoul Table Tennis Championships.
1534 **847** 60w. multicoloured . . . 40 10

848 Baseball Player

1982. 27th World Baseball Championship Series, Seoul.
1535 **848** 60w. brown 40 10

849 Exhibition Centre

1982. Seoul International Trade Fair.
1536 **849** 60w. multicoloured . . . 30 10

850 "Admiral Yi Sun Sin's Great Victory at Hansan" (Kim Hyung Ku)

851 "General Kim Chwa Jin's Chungsanri Battle" (Sohn Soo Kwang)

1982. Documentary Paintings (3rd series).
1537 **850** 60w. multicoloured . . . 60 15
1538 **851** 60w. multicoloured . . . 35 10

852 "Miners reading Consolatory Letters" (Um Soon Keun)

1982. Philatelic Week.
1539 **852** 60w. multicoloured . . . 45 10
MS1540 90 × 60 mm. No. 1539 × 2 70 60

853 Presidents Chung and Suharto

1982. Visit of President Suharto of Indonesia.
1541 **853** 60w. multicoloured . . . 30 10
MS1542 100 × 60 mm. No. 1541. Imperf × 2 . . . . 70 60

854 J.C.I. Emblem over World Map

855 "Intelsat 5" and "4-A" orbiting Globe

1982. 37th Junior Chamber International World Congress, Seoul.
1543 **854** 60w. multicoloured . . . 30 10

1982. Second U.N. Conference on the Exploration and Peaceful Uses of Outer Space, Vienna.
1544 **855** 60w. multicoloured . . . 30 10

856 Pig (bas-relief, Kim Yu Shin's tomb)

1982. Lunar New Year ("Year of the Pig").
1545 60w. Type **856** 35 10
1546 60w. Black-billed magpies and Korean moneybag . . 40 10
MS1547 Two sheets each 90 × 60 mm. (a) No. 1545 × 2; (b) No. 1546 × 2 . . . . 2·50 1·75

858 "General Kwon Yul's Great Victory at Haengju" (Oh Seung Woo)

859 "Kim Chong Suh's Exploitation of Yukin" (Kim Tae)

1982. Documentary Paintings (4th series).
1548 **858** 60w. multicoloured . . . 40 10
1549 **859** 60w. multicoloured . . . 40 10

860 Flags of South Korea and Turkey

861 Hand writing Letter

1982. Visit of President Evran of Turkey.
1550 **860** 60w. multicoloured . . . 35 10
MS1551 100 × 60 mm. No. 1550 × 2. Imperf 75 60

1982. Letter Writing Campaign.
1552 **861** 60w. multicoloured . . . 30 10

862 Emblem, Airliner, Container Ship and Cranes

1983. International Customs Day.
1553 **862** 60w. multicoloured . . . 50 15

863 Hyundai "Pony 2"

1983. Korean-made Vehicles (1st series). Multicoloured.
1554 60w. Type **863** 50 10
1555 60w. Keohwa Jeep 50 10
See also Nos. 1558/9, 1564/5, 1572/3 and 1576/7.

865 President Chun and Sultan of Malaysia

1983. Visit of King of Malaysia.
1556 **865** 60w. multicoloured . . . 30 10
MS1557 90 × 60 mm. No. 1556 × 2 70 55

866 Daewoo "Maepsy"

867 Kia "Bongo" Minibus

1983. Korean-made Vehicles (2nd series).
1558 **866** 60w. multicoloured . . . 50 10
1559 **867** 60w. multicoloured . . . 50 10

868 Former General Bureau of Postal Administration

869 Central Post Office, Seoul

1983. "Philakorea 84" International Stamp Exhibition, Seoul. Centenary of Korean Postal Service (1st series).
1560 **868** 60w. multicoloured . . . 30 10
1561 **869** 60w. multicoloured . . . 30 10
See also Nos. 1566/7, 1574/5 and 1603/6.

870 Old Village Schoolroom

1983. Teachers' Day.
1562 **870** 60w. multicoloured . . . 35 10
MS1563 90 × 60 mm. No. 1562 × 2 75 60

871 Asia Motor Co. Bus

872 Kia "Super Titan" Truck

1983. Korean-made Vehicles (3rd series).
1564 **871** 60w. multicoloured . . . 45 10
1565 **872** 60w. multicoloured . . . 45 10

873 Early Postman

1983. "Philakorea 84" International Stamp Exhibition, Seoul. Centenary of Korean Postal Service (2nd series).
1566 **873** 70w. multicoloured . . . 40 10
1567 – 70w. multicoloured . . . 40 10
DESIGN: No. 1567, Modern postman on motor-cycle.

875 "Communications in Outer Space" (Chun Ja Eun)

1983. World Communications Year.
1568 **875** 70w. multicoloured . . . 35 10
MS1569 90 × 60 mm. No. 1568 × 2 75 60

876 Whooper Swans at Sunrise

1983. Inaug of Communications Insurance.
1570 **876** 70w. multicoloured . . . 50 15

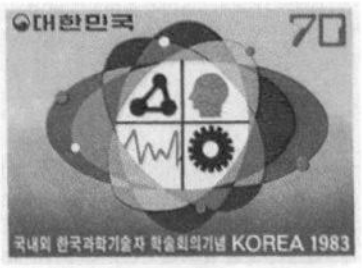
877 Emblems of Science and Engineering

1983. Korean Symposium on Science and Technology, Seoul.
1571 **877** 70w. multicoloured . . . 35 10

878 Daewoo Dump Truck

879 Hyundai Cargo Lorry

1983. Korean-made Vehicles (4th series).
1572 **878** 70w. multicoloured . . . 45 10
1573 **879** 70w. multicoloured . . . 45 10

880 Mail carried by Horse

1983. "Philakorea 84" International Stamp Exhibition, Seoul. Centenary of Korean Postal Service (3rd series). Multicoloured.
1574 70w. Type **880** 35 10
1575 70w. Mail truck and Douglas DC-8-60 Super Sixty jetliner 40 10

882 Dong-A Concrete Mixer Truck

883 Dong-A Tanker

1983. Korean-made Vehicles (5th series).
1576 **882** 70w. multicoloured . . . 50 10
1577 **883** 70w. multicoloured . . . 50 10

884 President Chun and King Hussein

1983. Visit of King Hussein of Jordan.
1578 **884** 70w. multicoloured . . . 35 10
MS1579 100 × 60 mm. No. 1578 × 2. Imperf 75 60

885 Woman with Fan

886 I.P.U. Emblem and Flags

1983. 53rd American Society of Travel Agents World Congress, Seoul.
1580 **885** 70w. multicoloured . . . 35 10

1983. 70th Inter-Parliamentary Union Conference, Seoul.
1581 **886** 70w. multicoloured . . . 35 10
MS1582 90 × 60 mm. No. 1581 × 2 80 60

887 Gymnastics

888 Football

1983. 64th National Sports Meeting, Inchon.
1583 **887** 70w. multicoloured . . . 40 10
1584 **888** 70w. multicoloured . . . 40 10

889 Presidents Chun and U San Yu of Burma

894 Rain Drops containing Symbols of Industry, Light and Food

1983. Presidential Visits. Multicoloured.
1585 70w. Type **889** 60 50
1586 70w. Presidents Chun and Giani Zail Singh of India 60 50
1587 70w. Presidents Chun and Jayewardene of Sri Lanka 60 50
1588 70w. Flags of South Korea and Australia 60 50
1589 70w. Flags of South Korea and New Zealand 60 50
MS1590 Five sheets each 90 × 60 mm. (a) No. 1585 × 2; (b) No. 1586 × 2; (c) No. 1587 × 2; (d) No. 1588 × 2; (e) No. 1589 × 2 8·75

1983. Development of Water Resources and 10th Anniv of Soyang-gang Dam.
1591 **894** 70w. multicoloured . . . 35 10

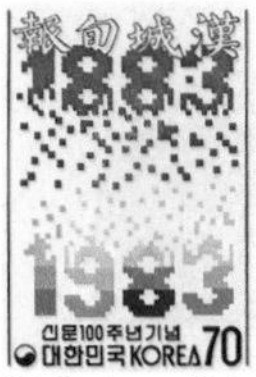
895 Centenary Dates

896 Tree with Lungs and Cross of Lorraine

1983. Centenary of 1st Korean Newspaper "Hansong Sunbo".
1592 **895** 70w. multicoloured . . . 35 10

1983. 30th Anniv of Korean National Tuberculosis Association.
1593 **896** 70w. multicoloured . . . 35 10

897 Presidents Chun and Reagan

898 Child collecting Stamps

1983. Visit of President Reagan of United States of America.
1594 **897** 70w. multicoloured . . . 35 10
MS1595 90 × 60 mm. No. 1594 × 2 75 55

1983. Philatelic Week.
1596 **898** 70w. multicoloured . . . 35 10
MS1597 90 × 60 mm. No. 1596 × 2 75 55

899 Rat (bas-relief, Kim Yu Shin's tomb)

1983. Lunar New Year ("Year of the Rat"). Multicoloured.
1598 70w. Type **899** 35 10
1599 70w. Manchurian cranes and pine 40 10
MS1600 Two sheets each 90 × 60 mm. (a) No. 1598 × 2; (b) No. 1599 × 2 . . . . 1·75 1·00

901 Bicentenary Emblem

902 5m. and 10m. Stamps, 1884

1984. Bicentenary of Catholic Church in Korea.
1601 **901** 70w. red, violet and silver 35 10
MS1602 90 × 60 mm. No. 1601 × 2 75 60

1984. "Philakorea 84" International Stamp Exhibition, Seoul. Centenary of Korean Postal Service (4th series). Multicoloured.
1603 70w. Type **902** 40 10
1604 70w. 5000w. stamp, 1983 . . 40 10

904 Old Postal Emblem and Post Box

1984. "Philakorea 84" International Stamp Exhibition, Seoul. Centenary of Korean Postal Service (5th series). Multicoloured.
1605 70w. Type **904** 40 10
1606 70w. Modern postal emblem and post box 40 10

906 President Chun and Sultan

1984. Visit of Sultan of Brunei.
1607 **906** 70w. multicoloured . . . 40 10
MS1608 100 × 60 mm. No. 1607 × 2 85 60

907 President Chun and Sheikh Khalifa

1984. Visit of Sheikh Khalifa of Qatar.
1609 **907** 70w. multicoloured . . . 35 10
MS1610 100 × 60 mm. No. 1609 × 2 80 60

908 Child posting Letter

1984. Centenary of Korean Postal Administration. Multicoloured.
1611 70w. Type **908** 35 10
1612 70w. Postman in city . . . 35 10
MS1613 Two sheets each 90 × 60 mm. (a) No. 1611 × 2; (b) No. 1612 × 2 . . . . 1·75 1·10

910 Pope John Paul II

911 Cogwheel, Worker's Tools and Flowers

1984. Visit of Pope John Paul II.
1614 **910** 70w. black 35 10
1615 70w. multicoloured . . . 35 10
MS1616 100 × 60 mm. Nos. 1614/15 1·10 70

1984. Labour Festival.
1617 **911** 70w. multicoloured . . . 30 10

912 Globe, Jetliner, Container Ship and Emblem

913 Map and Flags of S. Korea and Sri Lanka

1984. 63rd/64th Sessions of Customs Co-operation Council, Seoul.
1618 **912** 70w. multicoloured . . . 65 15

1984. Visit of President Jayewardene of Sri Lanka.
1619 **913** 70w. multicoloured . . . 35 10
MS1620 90 × 60 mm. No. 1619 × 2 75 45

914 Symbols and Punctuation Marks

915 Expressway

1984. 14th Asian Advertising Congress, Seoul.
1621 **914** 70w. multicoloured . . . 35 10

1984. Opening of 88 Olympic Expressway.
1622 **915** 70w. multicoloured . . . 35 10

916 Laurel, "Victory" and Olympic Rings

917 A.B.U. Emblem and Microphone

1984. 90th Anniv of International Olympic Committee.
1623 **916** 70w. multicoloured . . . 35 10

1984. 20th Anniv of Asia-Pacific Broadcasting Union.
1624 **917** 70w. multicoloured . . . 35 10

918 Flags of S. Korea and Senegal

1984. Visit of President Abdou Diouf of Senegal.
1625 **918** 70w. multicoloured . . . 35 10
MS1626 100 × 60 mm. No .1625 × 2. Imperf 75 60

919 Archery

921 Crucifixion

1984. Olympic Games, Los Angeles. Multicoloured.
1627 70w. Type **919** 40 10
1628 440w. Fencing . . . . . . 1·60 35

1984. Centenary of Korean Protestant Church. Multicoloured.
1629 70w. Type **921** 40 10
1630 70w. Cross, vine and dove 40 10
MS1631 80 × 100 mm. Nos. 1629/30 1·10 90

923 Man carrying Silk-covered Lantern

1984. Folk Customs (1st series). "Wedding" (Kim Kyo Man). Multicoloured.
1632 70w. Type **923** 40 10
1633 70w. Bridegroom on horse 40 10
1634 70w. Man playing clarinet 40 10
1635 70w. Bride in sedan chair (51 × 35 mm) 40 10
MS1636 90 × 61 mm. No. 1635 75 60
See also Nos. 1657/8, 1683/4, 1734/8, 1808/11, 1840/3, 1858/61 and 1915/18.

927 Pres. Chun and Mt. Fuji

1984. Pres. Chun's Visit to Japan.
1637 **927** 70w. multicoloured . . . 40 10
MS1638 100 × 60 mm. No. 1637 × 2. Imperf 90 75

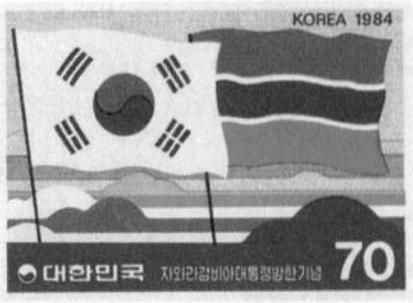
928 Flags of S. Korea and Gambia

1984. Visit of President Sir Dawada Kairaba Jawara of Gambia.
1639 **928** 70w. multicoloured . . . 40 10
MS1640 100 × 60 mm. No. 1639 × 2. Imperf 90 75

929 Symbols of International Trade

930 Namsan Tower and National Flags

1984. "Sitra '84" International Trade Fair, Seoul.
1641 **929** 70w. multicoloured . . . 40 10

1984. Visit of President El Hadj Omar Bongo of Gabon.
1642 **930** 70w. multicoloured . . . 40 10
MS1643 100 × 60 mm. No. 1642 × 2. Imperf 90 75

931 Badminton

932 Magnifying Glass and Exhibition Emblem

1984. 65th National Sports Meeting, Taegu. Multicoloured.
1644 70w. Type **931** 40 10
1645 70w. Wrestling 40 10

1984. "Philakorea 1984" International Stamp Exhibition, Seoul. Multicoloured.
1646 70w. Type **932** 40 10
1647 70w. South Gate, Seoul, and stamps (horiz) 40 10
MS1648 Two sheets each 124 × 90 mm. (a) Nos. 1646 × 2; (b) No. 1647 × 4 . . . . 3·00 2·75
MS1649 124 × 90 mm. 5000w. No. 1389 . . . . 15·00 12·00

934 Presidents Chun and Gayoom

1984. Visit of President Maumoon Abdul Gayoom of the Maldives.
1650 **934** 70w. multicoloured . . . 40 10
MS1651 100 × 60 mm. No. 1650 × 2. Imperf 90 75

935 "100" and Industrial Symbols

1984. Centenary of Korean Chamber of Commerce and Industry.
1652 **935** 70w. multicoloured . . . 40 10

936 Children playing Jaegi-chagi

937 Ox (bas-relief, Kim Yu Shin's tomb)

1984. Lunar New Year ("Year of the Ox").
1653 **936** 70w. multicoloured . . . 40 10
1654 **937** 70w. multicoloured . . . 40 10
MS1655 Two sheets each 90 × 60 mm. (a) No. 1653 × 2; (b) No. 1654 × 2 . . . . 1·75 1·00

938 I.Y.Y. Emblem

1985. International Youth Year.
1656 **938** 70w. multicoloured . . . 40 10

939 Pounding Rice for New Year Rice Cake

940 Welcoming Year's First Full Moon

1985. Folk Customs (2nd series).
1657 **939** 70w. multicoloured . . . 40 10
1658 **940** 70w. multicoloured . . . 40 10

941 Seoul Olympic Emblem

1985. Olympic Games, Seoul (1988) (1st issue). Multicoloured.
1659 70w.+30w. Type **941** . . . 45 20
1660 70w.+30w. Hodori (mascot) 45 20
MS1661 90 × 60 mm. Nos. 1659/60 1·00 75
See also Nos. 1673/4, 1678/8, 1694/5, 1703/10, 1747/50, 1752/5, 1784/7, 1814/17, 1826/7, 1835/6 and 1844/7.

943 "Still Life with Doll" (Lee Chong Woo)

944 "Rocky Mountain in Early Spring Morning" (Ahn Jung Shik)

1985. Modern Art (1st series).
1662 **943** 70w. multicoloured . . . 40 10
1663 **944** 70w. multicoloured . . . 40 10
See also Nos. 1680/1, 1757/60, 1791/4 and 1875/8.

945 Flags, Statue of Liberty and President Chun

946 Flags, Seoul South Gate and National Flower

1985. Presidential Visit to United States.
1664 **945** 70w. multicoloured . . . 40 10
MS1665 100 × 60 mm. No. 1664 × 2 90 70

1985. Visit of President Mohammed Zia-ul-Haq of Pakistan.
1666 **946** 70w. multicoloured . . . 40 10
MS1667 90 × 60 mm. No. 1666 × 2 90 70

947 Underwood Hall

1985. Centenary of Yonsei University.
1668 **947** 70w. black, buff and green 40 10

948 Flags and Map

1985. Visit of President Luis Alberto Monge of Costa Rica.
1669 **948** 70w. multicoloured . . . 40 10
MS1670 90 × 60 mm. No. 1669 × 2 90 70

949 Rasbora

950 Sailfish

1985. Fishes (1st series).
1671 **949** 70w. multicoloured . . . 75 15
1672 **950** 70w. multicoloured . . . 75 15
See also Nos. 1730/3, 1797/1800, 1881/4, 1903/6 and 1951/4.

951 Rowing

952 National Flags

1985. Olympic Games, Seoul (1988) (2nd issue). Multicoloured.
1673 70w.+30w. Type **951** . . . 45 30
1674 70w.+30w. Hurdling 45 30
MS1675 90 × 60 mm. Nos. 1673/4 1·00 75
For designs similar to Type **951** see Nos. 1687/**MS**1689 and 1694/**MS**1696.

1985. Visit of President Hussain Muhammed Ershad of Bangladesh.
1676 **952** 70w. multicoloured . . . 40 10
MS1677 90 × 60 mm. No. 1676 × 2. Imperf . . . . 1·00 75

953 National Flags

1985. Visit of President Joao Bernardo Vieira of Guinea-Bissau.
1678 **953** 70w. multicoloured . . . 40 10
MS1679 90 × 60 mm. No. 1678 × 2. Imperf . . . . 1·00 75

954 "Spring Day on the Farm" (Huh Paik Ryun)

955 "The Exorcist" (Kim Chung Hyun)

1985. Modern Art (2nd issue).
1680 **954** 70w. multicoloured . . . 40 10
1681 **955** 70w. multicoloured . . . 40 10

956 Heavenly Lake, Paekdu and National Flower

1985. 40th Anniv of Liberation.
1682 **956** 70w. multicoloured . . . 40 10

957 Wrestling

958 Janggi

1985. Folk Customs (3rd series).
1683 **957** 70w. multicoloured . . . 40 10
1684 **958** 70w. multicoloured . . . 40 10

959 "The Spring of My Home" (Lee Won Su and Hong Nan Pa)

960 "A Leaf Boat" (Park Hong Keun and Yun Yong Ha)

1985. Korean Music (1st series).
1685 **959** 70w. multicoloured . . . 45 10
1686 **960** 70w. multicoloured . . . 45 10
See also Nos. 1728/9, 1776/7, 1854/5, 1862/3, 1893/4, 1935/6, 1996/7 and 2064/5.

1985. Olympic Games, Seoul (1988) (3rd issue). As T **951**. Multicoloured.
1687 70w.+30w. Basketball . . . 45 20
1688 70w.+30w. Boxing 45 20
MS1689 90 × 60 mm. Nos. 1687/8 1·00 75

961 Satellite, "100" and Dish Aerial

962 Meetings Emblem

1985. Centenary of First Korean Telegraph Service.
1690 **961** 70w. multicoloured . . . 40 10

1985. World Bank and International Monetary Fund Meetings, Seoul.
1691 **962** 70w. multicoloured . . . 40 10

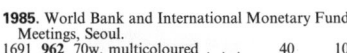

963 U.N. Emblem and Doves

1985. 40th Anniv of U.N.O.
1692 **963** 70w. multicoloured . . . 40 10

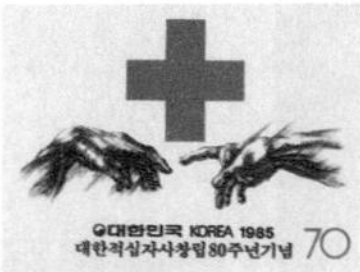

964 Red Cross and Hands (detail "Creation of Adam", Michelangelo)

1985. 80th Anniv of Korea Red Cross.
1693 **964** 70w. black, red and blue 45 10

1985. Olympic Games, Seoul (1988) (4th issue). As T **951**. Multicoloured.
1694 70w.+30w. Cycling 40 20
1695 70w.+30w. Canoeing . . . 40 20
MS1696 90 × 60 mm. Nos. 1694/5 1·00 75

965 Cancelled Stamp on Envelope

966 Tiger (bas-relief, Kim Yu Shin's tomb)

1985. Philatelic Week.
1697 **965** 70w. multicoloured . . . 40 10

1985. Lunar New Year ("Year of the Tiger").
1698 **966** 70w. multicoloured . . . 40 10

967 Mount Fuji and Boeing 747 Jetliner

1985. 20th Anniv of Korea–Japan Treaty on Basic Relations.
1699 **967** 70w. mult (postage) . . 45 10
1700 370w. multicoloured (air) 1·50 50

968 Doves and Globe

970 Pres. Chun, Big Ben and Korean and British Flags

1986. International Peace Year.
1701 **968** 70w. multicoloured . . . 35 10
1702 400w. multicoloured . . 1·75 40

1986. Olympic Games, Seoul (1988) (5th series). As T **951**. Multicoloured.
1703 70w.+30w. Show jumping (postage) 40 20
1704 70w.+30w. Fencing 40 20
1705 70w.+30w. Football 40 20
1706 70w.+30w. Gymnastics . . . 40 20
1707 370w.+100w. As No. 1703 (air) . . . . 1·60 70
1708 400w.+100w. As No. 1704 1·75 70
1709 440w.+100w. As No. 1705 1·90 70
1710 470w.+100w. As No. 1706 2·00 70

1986. Presidential Visit to Europe. Multicoloured.
1711 70w. Type **970** 40 10
1712 70w. Pres. Chun, Eiffel Tower and Korean and French flags 40 10
1713 70w. Pres. Chun, Belgian Parliament and Korean and Belgian flags 40 10
1714 70w. Pres. Chun, Cologne Cathedral and Korean and West German flags 40 10
MS1715 4 sheets each 100 × 60 mm. (a) No. 1711 × 2; (b) No. 1712 × 2; (c) No. 1713 × 2; (d) No. 1714 × 2 4·00 3·50

974/5 Kyongju and Kwanchon Observatories

1986. Science (1st series). Appearance of Halley's Comet.
1716 **974** 70w. multicoloured . . . 30 10
1717 **975** 70w. multicoloured . . . 30 10
See also Nos. 1781/2, 1833/4, 1864/5 and 1898/9.

976 General Assembly Emblem

977 Swallowtail and Flowers

1986. 5th Association of National Olympic Committees General Assembly, Seoul.
1718 **976** 70w. multicoloured . . . 45 10

1986. "Ameripex '86" International Stamp Exhibition, Chicago. Multicoloured.
1719 70w. Type **977** . . . . . . 2·00 75
1720 370w. "Papilio bianor" . . 2·00 75
1721 400w. Swallowtails . . . . 2·00 75
1722 440w. Swallowtail and frog 2·00 75
1723 450w. Swallowtail . . . . . 2·00 75
1724 470w. "Papilio bianor" . . 2·00 75
Nos. 1719/24 were printed together, se-tenant, forming a composite design.

983 Male and Female Symbols in Balance

1986. Centenary of Korean Women's Education.
1725 **983** 70w. multicoloured . . . 35 10

984 National Flags

1986. Visit of President Andre Kolingba of Central African Republic.
1726 **984** 70w. multicoloured . . . 35 10
MS1727 100 × 60 mm. No. 1726 × 2. Imperf 75 55

985 "Half Moon" (Yun Keuk Young)

986 "Let's Go and Pick the Moon" (Yun Seok Jung and Park Tae Hyun)

1986. Korean Music (2nd series).
1728 **985** 70w. multicoloured . . . 35 10
1729 **986** 70w. multicoloured . . . 35 10

987 Cyprinid Fish

988 Ayu

989 Black-spotted Sardine

990 Hammerheads

1986. Fishes (2nd series).
1730 **987** 70w. multicoloured . . . 85 20
1731 **988** 70w. multicoloured . . . 85 20
1732 **989** 70w. multicoloured . . . 85 20
1733 **990** 70w. multicoloured . . . 85 20

991 Flag Carrier and Gong Player

996 Child

1986. Folk Customs (4th series). Farm Music. Multicoloured.
1734 70w. Type **991** 30 10
1735 70w. Drummer and piper 30 10
1736 70w. Drummer and gong player 30 10
1737 70w. Men with ribbons . . 30 10
1738 70w. Man and woman with child 30 10
Nos. 1734/8 were printed together, se-tenant, forming a composite design.

1986. Family Planning.
1739 **996** 80w. multicoloured . . . 40 10

997 Bridge and "63" Building, Seoul

1986. Completion of Han River Development. Multicoloured.
1740 30w. Type **997** 85 25
1741 60w. Buildings and excursion boat 60 25
1742 80w. Rowing boat and Seoul Tower 40 10
Nos. 1740/2 were printed together, se-tenant, forming a composite design.

1000 Emblem

1986. 10th Asian Games, Seoul. (1st issue). Multicoloured.
1743 80w. Type **1000** 40 10
1744 80w. Firework display . . . 40 10
MS1745 Two sheets each 90 × 60 mm. (a) No. 1743 × 2; (b) No. 1744 × 2 . . . . 1·75 1·40
See also No. **MS**1751.

1002 "5", Delegates and Juan Antonio Samaranch (President of International Olympic Committee)

1986. 5th Anniv of Choice of Seoul as 1988 Olympic Games Host City.
1746 **1002** 80w. multicoloured . . 45 10

1986. Olympic Games, Seoul (1988) (6th issue). As T **951**. Multicoloured.
1747 80w.+50w. Weightlifting (postage) . . . . 1·25 60
1748 80w.+50w. Handball . . . . 1·25 60
1749 370w.+100w. As No. 1747 (air) . . . . 1·75 75
1750 400w.+100w. As No. 1748 1·90 75

1986. 10th Asian Games, Seoul (2nd issue). Sheet 130 × 90 mm.
MS1751 **1003**550w. multicoloured 1·75 1·25

1003 Main Stadium

1986. Olympic Games, Seoul (1988) (7th issue). As T **951**. Multicoloured.
1752 80w.+50w. Judo (postage) 1·10 60
1753 80w.+50w. Hockey . . . . 1·10 60
1754 440w.+100w. As No. 1752 (air) . . . . 1·75 70
1755 470w.+100w. As No. 1753 1·90 70

1004 Boy fishing for Stamp

1986. Philatelic Week.
1756 **1004** 80w. multicoloured . . 40 10

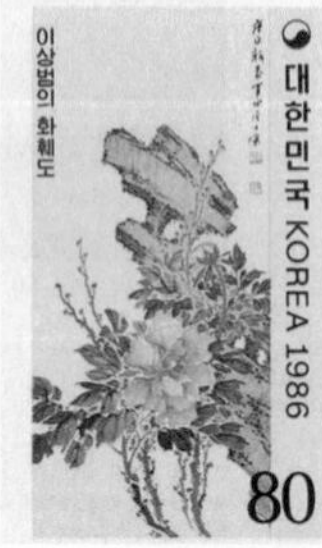

1005 "Chunhyang-do" (Kim Un Ho) **1006** "Flowers" (Lee Sang Bum)

1007 "Portrait of a Friend" (Ku Bon Wung)

1008 "Woman in a Ski Suit" (Son Ung Seng)

1986. Modern Art (3rd series).
1757 **1005** 80w. multicoloured . . 40 10
1758 **1006** 80w. multicoloured . . 40 10
1759 **1007** 80w. multicoloured . . 40 10
1760 **1008** 80w. multicoloured . . 40 10

1009 Rabbit **1010** Eastern Broad-billed Roller ("Roller")

1986. Lunar New Year ("Year of the Rabbit").
1761 **1009** 80w. multicoloured . . 35 10

1986. Birds. Multicoloured.
1762 80w. Type **1010** . . . . . 1·00 10
1763 80w. Japanese waxwing ("Waxwing") . . . . . . 1·00 10
1764 80w. Black-naped oriole ("Oriole") . . . . 1·00 10
1765 80w. Black-capped kingfisher ("Kingfisher") 1·00 10
1766 80w. Hoopoe . . . . 1·00 10

1011 Siberian Tiger **1012** Bleeding Heart ("Dicentra spectabilis")

1987. Endangered Animals. Multicoloured.
1767 80w. Type **1011** . . . . . 1·00 30
1768 80w. Leopard cat . . . . . 1·00 30
1769 80w. Red fox . . . . 1·00 30
1770 80w. Wild boar . . . . . . 1·00 30

1987. Flowers. Multicoloured.
1771 550w. Type **1012** . . . . . 1·50 25
1772 550w. Diamond bluebell ("Hanabusaya asiatica") 1·50 25
1773 550w. "Erythronium japonicum" . . . . 1·50 25
1774 550w. Pinks ("Dianthus chinensis") . . . . 1·50 25
1775 550w. "Chrysanthemum zawadskii" . . . . 1·50 25

1013 "Barley Field" (Park Wha Mok and Yun Yong Ha) **1014** "Magnolia" (Cho Young Shik and Kim Dong Jin)

1987. Korean Music (3rd series).
1776 **1013** 80w. multicoloured . . 40 10
1777 **1014** 80w. multicoloured . . 40 10

1015 National Flags and Korean National Flower

1987. Visit of President Ahmed Abdallah Abderemane of Comoros.
1778 **1015** 80w. multicoloured . . 35 10
MS1779 90 × 60 mm. No. 1778 × 2 75 50

1016 "100", Light Bulb and Hyang Woen Jeong

1987. Centenary of Electric Light in Korea.
1780 **1016** 80w. multicoloured . . 35 10

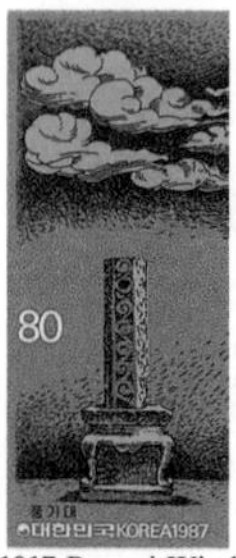

1017 Punggi Wind Observatory **1019** Globes, Crane and Ship

1987. Science (2nd series).
1781 **1017** 80w. dp brown & brown 40 10
1782 – 80w. brown & dp brown 40 10
DESIGN: No. 1782, Rain gauge.

1987. 15th International Association of Ports and Harbours General Session, Seoul.
1783 **1019** 80w. multicoloured . . 40 10

1987. Olympic Games, Seoul (1988) (8th issue). As T **951**. Multicoloured.
1784 80w.+50w. Wrestling . . . 80 25
1785 80w.+50w. Tennis 80 25
1786 80w.+50w. Diving 80 25
1787 80w.+50w. Show jumping 80 25
MS1788 Four sheets each 90 × 60 mm. (a) No. 1784 × 2; (b) No. 1785 × 2; (c) No. 1786 × 2; (d) No. 1787 × 2 . . . . 6·50 5·00

1020 Flags and Doves

1987. Visit of President U San Yu of Burma.
1789 **1020** 80w. multicoloured . . 40 10
MS1790 90 × 60 mm. No. 1789 × 2 85 50

1021 "Valley of Peach Blossoms" (Pyen Kwan Sik)

1022 "Rural Landscape" (Lee Yong Wu)

1023 "Man" (Lee Ma Dong)

1024 "Woman with Water Jar on Head" (sculpture, Yun Hyo Chung)

1987. Modern Art (4th series).
1791 **1021** 80w. multicoloured . . 35 10
1792 **1022** 80w. multicoloured . . 35 10
1793 **1023** 80w. multicoloured . . 35 10
1794 **1024** 80w. multicoloured . . 35 10

1025 Map and Digital Key Pad

1987. Completion of Automatic Telephone Network (1795) and Communications for Information Year (1796).
1795 80w. Type **1025** 35 10
1796 80w. Emblem 35 10

1027 Cyprinid Fishes

1028 Russell's Oarfish

1029 Cyprinid Fish

1030 Spine-tailed Mobula

1987. Fishes (3rd series).
1797 **1027** 80w. multicoloured . . 85 20
1798 **1028** 80w. multicoloured . . 85 20
1799 **1029** 80w. multicoloured . . 85 20
1800 **1030** 80w. multicoloured . . 85 20

1031 Statue of Indomitable Koreans (detail) and Flags

1033 Map and Pen within Profile

1987. Opening of Independence Hall. Mult.
1801 80w. Type **1031** 35 10
1802 80w. Monument of the Nation and aerial view of Hall 35 10
MS1803 Two sheets each 125 × 90 mm. (a) No. 1801 × 2; (b) No. 1802 × 2 . . . . 1·50 1·25

1987. 16th Pacific Science Congress, Seoul.
1804 **1033** 80w. multicoloured . . 35 10
MS1805 90 × 60 mm. No. 1804 × 2 80 50

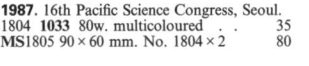

1034 Flags and Seoul South Gate

1987. Visit of President Virgilio Barco of Colombia.
1806 **1034** 80w. multicoloured . . 40 10
MS1807 90 × 60 mm. No. 1806 × 2 85 50

1035/1038 Festivities (½-size illustration)

1987. Folk Customs (5th series). Harvest Moon Day.
1808 **1035** 80w. multicoloured . . 35 10
1809 **1036** 80w. multicoloured . . 35 10
1810 **1037** 80w. multicoloured . . 35 10
1811 **1038** 80w. multicoloured . . 35 10
Nos. 1808/11 were issued together, se-tenant, forming a composite design.

1039 Telephone Dials forming Number

1040 Service Flags and Servicemen

1987. Installation of over 10,000,000 Telephone Lines.
1812 **1039** 80w. multicoloured . . 40 10

1987. Armed Forces Day.
1813 **1040** 80w. multicoloured . . 40 10

1987. Olympic Games, Seoul (1988) (9th issue). As T **951**. Multicoloured.
1814 80w.+50w. Table tennis . . 70 20
1815 80w.+50w. Shooting 70 20
1816 80w.+50w. Archery 70 20
1817 80w.+50w. Volleyball . . . 70 20
MS1818 4 sheets each 90 × 60 mm. (a) No. 1814 × 2; (b) No. 1815 × 2; (c) No. 1816 × 2; (d) No. 1817 × 2 . . . . 6·00 4·00

1041 Stamps around Child playing Trumpet

1042 Korean Scientist and Map

1987. Philatelic Week.
1819 **1041** 80w. multicoloured . . 35 10

1987. 1st Anniv of South Korea's Signing of Antarctic Treaty.
1820 **1042** 80w. multicoloured . . 80 30

1043 Dragon

1044 Scattered Sections of Apple

1987. Lunar New Year ("Year of the Dragon").
1821 **1043** 80w. multicoloured . . 35 10

1988. Compulsory Pension Programme.
1822 **1044** 80w. multicoloured . . 30 10

1045 Base and Gentoo Penguins

1046 Flag, Olympic Stadium and President Roh Tae Woo

1988. Completion of Antarctic Base.
1823 **1045** 80w. multicoloured . . 70 25

1988. Presidential Inauguration.
1824 **1046** 80w. multicoloured . . 30 10
MS1825 90 × 60 mm. No. 1824 × 2 1·50 1·25

1047 Dinghy Racing

1049 Crane

1988. Olympic Games, Seoul (1988) (10th issue). Multicoloured.
1826 80w.+20w. Type **1047** . . . 35 20
1827 80w.+20w. Taekwondo . . 35 20
MS1828 Two sheets each 90 × 60 mm. (a) No. 1826 × 2; (b) No. 1827 × 2 . . . . 1·50 1·25

1988. Japanese White-naped Crane. Mult.
1829 80w. Type **1049** . . . . . 1·25 60
1830 80w. Crane taking off . . . 1·25 60
1831 80w. Crane with wings spread . . . . 1·25 60
1832 80w. Two cranes in flight . . 1·25 60

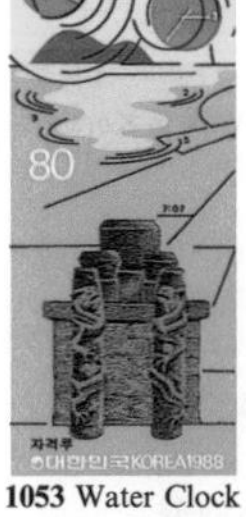

1053 Water Clock

1055 Torch Carrier

1988. Science (3rd series). Multicoloured.
1833 80w. Type **1053** 30 10
1834 80w. Sundial 30 10
Nos. 1833/4 were issued together, se-tenant, forming a composite design.

1988. Olympic Games, Seoul (1988) (11th issue). Multicoloured.
1835 80w.+20w. Type **1055** . . . 35 20
1836 80w.+20w. Stadium 35 20
MS1837 Two sheets each 90 × 60 mm. (a) No. 1835 × 2; (b) No. 1836 × 2 . . . . 1·50 1·25

1057 Globe and Red Cross as Candle

1058 Computer Terminal

1988. 125th Anniv of International Red Cross.
1838 **1057** 80w. multicoloured . . 30 10

1988. 1st Anniv of National Use of Telepress.
1839 **1058** 80w. multicoloured . . 30 10

1059 Woman sitting by Pool and Woman on Swing

1063 Olympic Flag and Pierre de Coubertin (founder of modern Games)

1988. Folk Customs (6th series). Tano Day. Multicoloured.
1840 80w. Type **1059** 65 35
1841 80w. Women dressing their hair 65 35
1842 80w. Woman on swing and boy smelling flowers . . . 65 35
1843 80w. Boys wrestling 65 35
Nos. 1840/3 were issued together, se-tenant, forming a composite design.

1988. Olympic Games, Seoul (1988) (12th issue). Multicoloured.
1844 80w. Type **1063** 30 10
1845 80w. Olympic monument . . 30 10
1846 80w. View of Seoul (vert) 30 10
1847 80w. Women in Korean costume (vert) 30 10
MS1848 Four sheets each 90 × 60 mm. (a) No. 1844 × 2; (b) No. 1845 × 2; (c) No. 1846 × 2; (d) No. 1847 × 2 . . . . 2·75 2·50

1067 Stamps forming Torch Flame

1068 Pouring Molten Metal from Crucible

1988. "Olymphilex '88" Olympic Stamps Exhibition, Seoul.
1849 **1067** 80w. multicoloured . . 30 10
MS1850 90 × 60 mm. No. 1849 × 2 65 40

1988. 22nd International Iron and Steel Institute Conference, Seoul.
1851 **1068** 80w. multicoloured . . 30 10

1069 Gomdoori (mascot)

1988. Paralympic Games, Seoul.
1852 80w. Type **1069** . . . . . 1·00 50
1853 80w. Archery 50 10

1071 "Homesick" (Lee Eun Sang and Kim Dong Jin)

1072 "The Pioneer" (Yoon Hae Young and Cho Doo Nam)

1988. Korean Music (4th series).
1854 **1071** 80w. multicoloured . . 35 10
1855 **1072** 80w. multicoloured . . 35 10

1073 Girls on See-saw

1075 Dancers

1074 Flags at Opening Ceremony

1988. Lunar New Year ("Year of the Snake").
1856 **1073** 80w. multicoloured . . 25 10

1988. Olympic Games, Seoul (13th issue). Sheet 130 × 90 mm.
MS1857 **1074** 550w. multicoloured 1·75 1·25

1989. Folk Customs (7th series). Mask Dance. Multicoloured.
1858 80w. Type **1075** 25 10
1859 80w. Dancer with fans . . . 25 10
1860 80w. Dancer holding branch 25 10
1861 80w. Dancer with "Lion" 25 10
Nos. 1858/61 were issued together, se-tenant, forming a composite design.

1079 "Arirang"

1080 "Doraji-taryong"

1989. Korean Music (5th series).
1862 **1079** 80w. multicoloured . . 25 10
1863 **1080** 80w. multicoloured . . 25 10

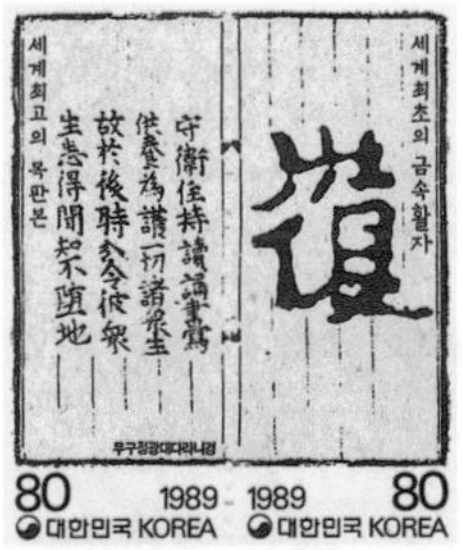

1081/2 Wooden and metal Type Printing

1989. Science (4th series).
1864 **1081** 80w. brown, bis & stone 25 10
1865 **1082** 80w. brown, bis & stone 25 10
Nos. 1864/5 were issued together, se-tenant, forming a composite design.

1083 Teeth, Globe, Pencil and Book

1084 Hand with Stick in Heart

1989. 14th Asian–Pacific Dental Congress.
1866 **1083** 80w. multicoloured . . 25 10

1989. Respect for the Elderly.
1867 **1084** 80w. multicoloured . . 25 10

1085 Emblem

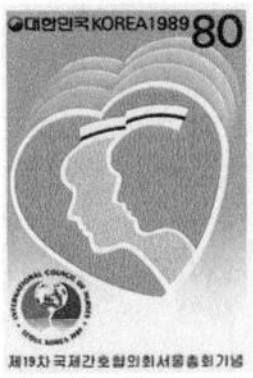

1086 Profiles within Heart

1989. Rotary Int Convention, Seoul.
1868 **1085** 80w. multicoloured . . 25 10

1989. 19th International Council of Nurses Congress, Seoul.
1869 **1086** 80w. multicoloured . . 25 10

1087 "Communication"

1088 "Longevity"

1989. National Information Technology Month.
1870 **1087** 80w. multicoloured . . 25 10

1989. World Environment Day.
1871 **1088** 80w. multicoloured . . 30 10

1089 Satellite, Globe and Dish Aerial

1090 "Liberty guiding the People" (detail, Eugene Delacroix)

1989. 10th Anniv of Asia–Pacific Telecommunity.
1872 **1089** 80w. multicoloured . . 25 10

1989. Bicentenary of French Revolution.
1873 **1090** 80w. multicoloured . . 25 10

1091 Apple and Flask

1989. 5th Asian and Oceanic Biochemists Federation Congress, Seoul.
1874 **1091** 80w. multicoloured . . 25 10

1092 "White Ox" (Lee Joong Sub)

1093 "Street Stall" (Park Lae Hyun)

1094 "Little Girl" (Lee Bong Sang)

1095 "Autumn Scene" (Oh Ji Ho)

1989. Modern Art (5th series).
1875 **1092** 80w. multicoloured . . 30 10
1876 **1093** 80w. multicoloured . . 30 10
1877 **1094** 80w. multicoloured . . 30 10
1878 **1095** 80w. multicoloured . . 30 10

1096 Hunting Scene

1097 Goddess of Law and Ancient Law Code

1989. Seoul Olympics Commemorative Festival and World Sports Festival for Ethnic Koreans.
1879 **1096** 80w. multicoloured . . 25 10

1989. 1st Anniv of Constitutional Court.
1880 **1097** 80w. multicoloured . . 25 10

1098 Banded Knifejaw

1099 Banded Loach

1100 Torrent Catfish

1101 Japanese Pinecone Fish

1989. Fishes (4th series).
1881 **1098** 80w. multicoloured . . 85 20
1882 **1099** 80w. multicoloured . . 85 20
1883 **1100** 80w. multicoloured . . 85 20
1884 **1101** 80w. multicoloured . . 85 20

1102 Emblem

1989. 44th International Eucharistic Congress, Seoul.
1885 **1102** 80w. multicoloured . . 25 10

1103 Control Tower and Boeing 747 Jetliner

1989. 29th International Civil Airports Association World Congress, Seoul.
1886 **1103** 80w. multicoloured . . 35 10

1104 Scissors cutting Burning Banner

1105 Lantern

1989. Fire Precautions Month.
1887 **1104** 80w. multicoloured . . 25 10

1989. Philatelic Week.
1888 **1105** 80w. multicoloured . . 25 10
MS1889 90 × 60 mm. No. 1888 × 2 70 50

1106 Cranes

1107 New Year Custom

1989. Lunar New Year ("Year of the Horse").
1890 **1106** 80w. multicoloured . . 25 10
1891 **1107** 80w. multicoloured . . 25 10
MS1892 Two sheets each 90 × 60 mm. (a) No. 1890 × 2; (b) No. 1891 × 2 . . . . 1·00 75

1108 "Pakyon Fall"

1109 "Chonan Samgori"

1990. Korean Music (6th series).
1893 **1108** 80w. multicoloured . . 25 10
1894 **1109** 80w. multicoloured . . 25 10

1110 Clouds, Umbrella and Satellite

1111 Child with Rose

1990. World Meteorological Day.
1895 **1110** 80w. multicoloured . . 40 10

1990. 40th Anniv of UNICEF Work in Korea.
1896 **1111** 80w. multicoloured . . 25 10

1112 Cable, Fish and Route Map

1990. Completion of Cheju Island–Kohung Optical Submarine Cable.
1897 **1112** 80w. multicoloured . . 40 10

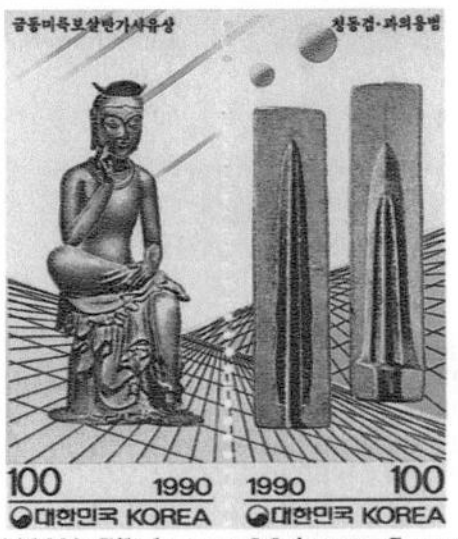

1113/4 Gilt-bronze Maitreya, Spear and Dagger Moulds

1990. Science (5th series). Metallurgy.
1898 **1113** 100w. multicoloured . . 30 15
1899 **1114** 100w. multicoloured . . 30 15
Nos. 1898/9 were issued together, se-tenant, forming the composite design illustrated.

1115 Housing and "20"

1990. 20th Anniv of Saemaul Movement (community self-help programme).
1900 **1115** 100w. multicoloured . . 30 15

1116 Youths

1117 Butterfly Net catching Pollution

1990. Youth Month.
1901 **1116** 100w. multicoloured . . 30 15

1990. World Environmental Day.
1902 **1117** 100w. multicoloured . . 30 15

1118 Belted Bearded Grunt

1119 Kusa Pufferfish

1120 Cherry Salmon

1121 Rosy Bitterling

1990. Fishes (5th series).
1903 **1118** 100w. multicoloured . . 75 20
1904 **1119** 100w. multicoloured . . 75 20
1905 **1120** 100w. multicoloured . . 75 20
1906 **1121** 100w. multicoloured . . 75 20

1122 Automatic Sorting Machines

1123 Bandaged Teddy Bear in Hospital Bed

1990. Opening of Seoul Mail Centre.
1907 **1122** 100w. multicoloured . . 30 15
MS1908 90 × 60 mm. No. 1907 × 2 70 60

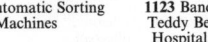

1990. Road Safety Campaign.
1909 **1123** 100w. multicoloured . . 75 30

1124 Campfire **1125** Lily

1990. 8th Korean Boy Scouts Jamboree, Kosong.
1910 **1124** 100w. multicoloured . . 30 15

1990. Wild Flowers (1st series). Multicoloured.
1911 370w. Type **1125** . . . . . 1·25 60
1912 400w. Asters . . . . 1·40 60
1913 440w. Pheasant's eye . . . 1·25 60
1914 470w. Scabious . . . . . . 1·90 60
See also Nos. 1956/9, 1992/5, 2082/5, 2133/6, 2162/5, 2191/4 and 2244/7.

1129 Washing Wool **1133** Church

1990. Folk Customs (8th series). Hand Weaving.
1915 **1129** 100w. red, yellow & blk 30 15
1916 – 100w. multicoloured . . 30 15
1917 – 100w. multicoloured . . 30 15
1918 – 100w. multicoloured . . 30 15
DESIGNS: No. 1916, Spinning; 1917, Dyeing spun yarn; 1918, Weaving.

1990. Centenary of Anglican Church in Korea.
1919 **1133** 100w. multicoloured . . 30 15

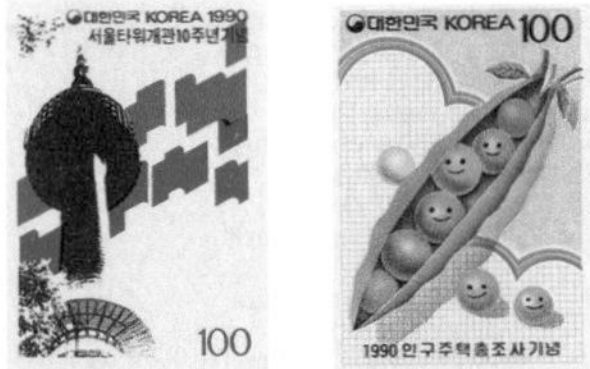

1134 Top of Tower **1135** Peas in Pod

1990. 10th Anniv of Seoul Communications Tower.
1920 **1134** 100w. black, blue & red 30 15

1990. Census.
1921 **1135** 100w. multicoloured . . 30 15

1136 "40" and U.N. Emblem **1137** Inlaid Case with Mirror

1990. 40th Anniv of U.N. Development Programme.
1922 **1136** 100w. multicoloured . . 30 15

1990. Philatelic Week.
1923 **1137** 100w. multicoloured . . 30 15
MS1924 90 × 60 mm. No. 1923 × 2 60 50

1138 Children feeding Ram **1140** Mascot

1990. Lunar New Year ("Year of the Sheep"). Multicoloured.
1925 100w. Type **1138** 30 15
1926 100w. Crane flying above mountains 30 15
MS1927 90 × 60 mm. Nos. 1925/6 60 50

1990. "Expo '93" World's Fair, Taejon (1st issue). Multicoloured.
1928 100w. Type **1140** 30 20
1929 440w. Yin and Yang (exhibition emblem) . . . 1·25 60
MS1930 Two sheets each 90 × 60 mm. (a) No. 1928 × 2; (b) No. 1929 × 2 . . . . 3·00 2·00
See also Nos.1932/**MS**1934, 20001/**MS**2002 and 2058/**MS**2062.

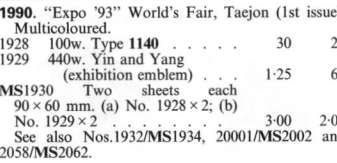

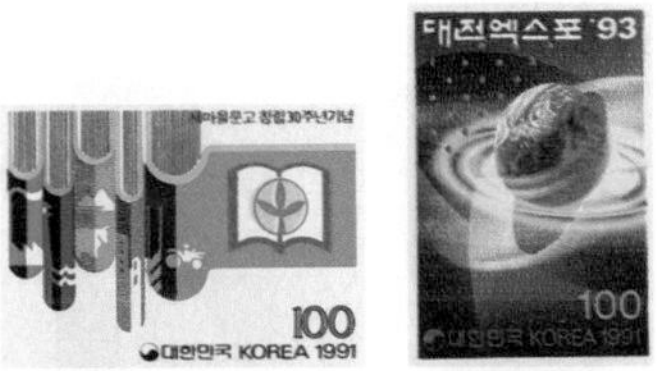

1142 Books and Emblem **1143** Earth

1991. 30th Anniv of Saemaul Minilibrary.
1931 **1142** 100w. multicoloured . . 30 15

1991. "Expo '93" World's Fair, Taejon (2nd issue). Multicoloured.
1932 100w. Type **1143** 30 15
1933 100w. Expo Tower 30 15
MS1934 Two sheets each 90 × 60 mm. (a) No. 1932 × 2; (b) No. 1933 × 2 . . . . 1·25 1·00

1145 "In a Flower Garden" (Uh Hyo Sun and Kwon Kil Sang) **1146** "Way to the Orchard" (Park Hwa Mok and Kim Kong Sun)

1991. Korean Music (7th series).
1935 **1145** 100w. multicoloured . . 30 15
1936 **1146** 100w. multicoloured . . 30 15

1147 Moth **1148** Beetle

1149 Butterfly **1150** Beetle

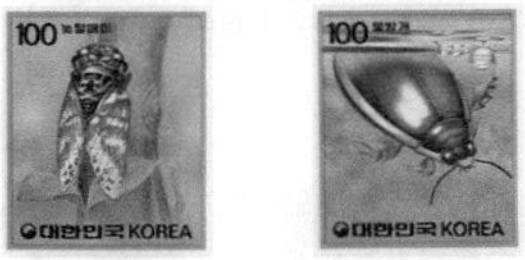

1151 Cicada **1152** Water Beetle

1153 Hornet **1154** Ladybirds

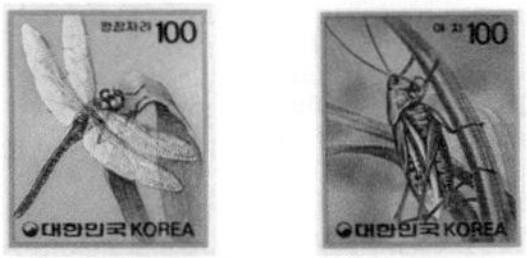

1155 Dragonfly **1156** Grasshopper

1991. Insects.
1937 **1147** 100w. multicoloured . . 40 15
1938 **1148** 100w. multicoloured . . 40 15
1939 **1149** 100w. multicoloured . . 40 15
1940 **1150** 100w. multicoloured . . 40 15
1941 **1151** 100w. multicoloured . . 40 15
1942 **1152** 100w. multicoloured . . 40 15
1943 **1153** 100w. multicoloured . . 40 15
1944 **1154** 100w. multicoloured . . 40 15
1945 **1155** 100w. multicoloured . . 40 15
1946 **1156** 100w. multicoloured . . 40 15

1157 Flautist and Centre **1158** Flag and Provisional Government Building

1991. 40th Anniv of Korean Traditional Performing Arts Centre.
1947 **1157** 100w. multicoloured . . 30 15

1991. 72nd Anniv of Establishment of Korean Provisional Government in Shanghai.
1948 **1158** 100w. multicoloured . . 30 15

1159 Urban Landscape and Emblem

1991. Employment for Disabled People.
1949 **1159** 100w. multicoloured . . 30 15

1160 Bouquet

1991. Teachers' Day.
1950 **1160** 100w. multicoloured . . 30 15

1161 Asian Minnow

1162 Majime Minnows

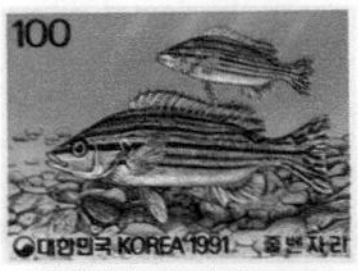

1163 Blotched Grunter

1164 Ijima's Left-eyed Flounder

1991. Fishes (6th series).
1951 **1161** 100w. multicoloured . . 65 25
1952 **1162** 100w. multicoloured . . 65 25
1953 **1163** 100w. multicoloured . . 65 25
1954 **1164** 100w. multicoloured . . 65 25

1165 Animals waiting to Board Bus **1166** "Aerides japonicum"

1991. "Waiting One's Turn" Campaign.
1955 **1165** 100w. multicoloured . . 30 15

1991. Wild Flowers (2nd series). Mult.
1956 100w. Type **1166** 35 15
1957 100w. "Heloniopsis orientalis" 35 15
1958 370w. "Aquilegia buergeriana" 90 40
1959 440w. "Gentiana zollingeri" 1·25 40

1167 Scout with Semaphore Flags **1168** "Y.M.C.A."

1991. 17th World Scout Jamboree.
1960 **1167** 100w. multicoloured . . 30 10
MS1961 90 × 60 mm. No. 1960 × 2 60 40

1991. Young Men's Christian Association World Assembly, Seoul.
1962 **1168** 100w. multicoloured . . 25 10

1169 Derelict Steam Locomotive and Family Members Reunited **1170** Globe, Rainbow, Dove and U.N. Emblem

1991. "North–South Reunification".
1963 **1169** 100w. multicoloured . . 90 20

1991. Admission of South Korea to United Nations Organization.
1964 **1170** 100w. multicoloured . . 25 10

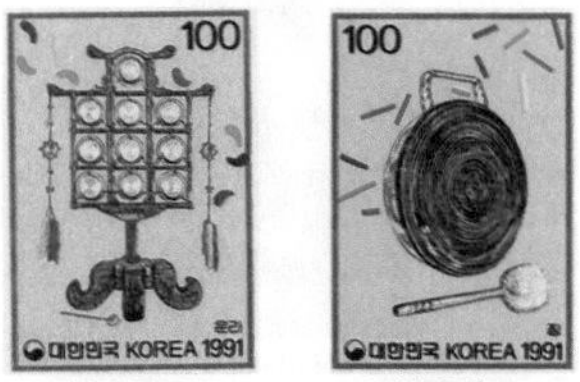

1171 Unra **1172** Jing

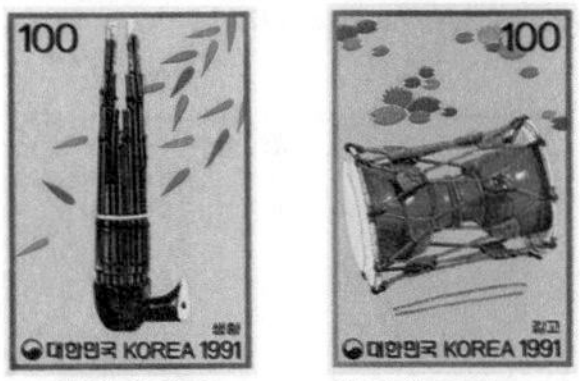

1173 Galgo **1174** Saeng-hwang

1991. Traditional Musical Instruments (1st series).
1965 **1171** 100w. multicoloured . . 40 20
1966 **1172** 100w. multicoloured . . 40 20
1967 **1173** 100w. multicoloured . . 40 20
1968 **1174** 100w. multicoloured . . 40 20
See also Nos. 1981/4.

1175 Film and Theatrical Masks **1176** Globe and Satellite

1991. Culture Month.
1969 **1175** 100w. multicoloured . . 25 10

1991. "Telecom 91" Int Telecommunications Exhibition, Geneva.
1970 **1176** 100w. multicoloured . . 25 10

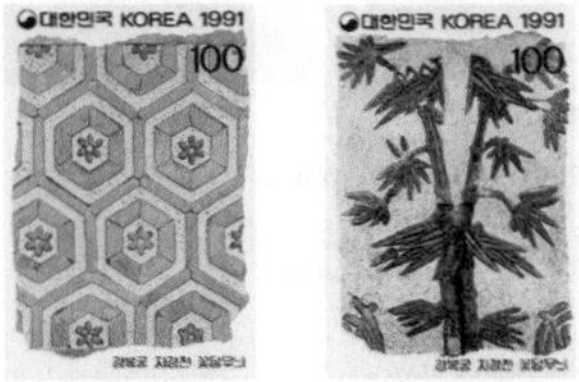

1177 Hexagonals **1178** Bamboo

1179 Geometric

1180 Tree

1991. Korean Beauty (1st series). Kottams (patterns on walls) from Jakyung Hall, Kyungbok Palace.
1971 **1177** 100w. multicoloured . . 55 25
1972 **1178** 100w. multicoloured . . 55 25
1973 **1179** 100w. multicoloured . . 55 25
1974 **1180** 100w. multicoloured . . 55 25
See also Nos. 2006/9, 2068/71, 2103/6, 2157/60, 2219/22, 2257/60, 2308/15, 2350/6 and 2437/40.

1181 Light Bulb turning off Switch

1182 "Longevity"

1991. Energy Saving Campaign.
1975 **1181** 100w. multicoloured . . 25 10

1991. Lunar New Year ("Year of the Monkey"). Multicoloured.
1976 100w. Type **1182** 40 10
1977 100w. Flying kites 55 10
MS1978 Two sheets each 90 × 60 mm. (a) No. 1976 × 2; (b) No. 1977 × 2 . . . . 1·25 1·75

1184 Stamps

1991. Philatelic Week.
1979 **1184** 100w. multicoloured . . 25 10
MS1980 90 × 60 mm. No. 1979 × 2 95 75

1185 Yonggo

1186 Chwago

1187 Kkwaenggwari

1188 T'ukchong

1992. Traditional Musical Instruments (2nd series).
1981 **1185** 100w. multicoloured . . 40 15
1982 **1186** 100w. multicoloured . . 40 15
1983 **1187** 100w. multicoloured . . 40 15
1984 **1188** 100w. multicoloured . . 40 15

1189 White Hibiscus

1191 Satellite

1992. "Hibiscus syriacus" (national flower). Multicoloured.
1985 100w. Type **1189** 45 25
1986 100w. Pink hibiscus 45 25

1992. Science Day.
1987 **1191** 100w. multicoloured . . 25 10

1192 Yoon Pong Gil

1193 Children and Heart

1992. 60th Death Anniv of Yoon Pong Gil (independence fighter).
1988 **1192** 100w. multicoloured . . 25 10

1992. Child Protection.
1989 **1193** 100w. multicoloured . . 30 10

1194 Japanese Warship attacking Korean Settlement

1195 Farmer

1992. 400th Anniv of Start of Im-Jin War.
1990 **1194** 100w. multicoloured . . 35 10

1992. 60th International Fertilizer Industry Association Conference, Seoul.
1991 **1195** 100w. multicoloured . . 25 10

1992. Wild Flowers (3rd series). As T **1166**. Multicoloured.
1992 100w. "Lychnis wilfordii" 30 10
1993 100w. "Lycoris radiata" . . 30 10
1994 370w. "Commelina communis" . . . . 1·00 45
1995 440w. "Calanthe striata" . . 1·00 45

1196 "Longing for Mt. Keumkang" (Han Sang Ok and Choi Young Shurp)

1197 "The Swing" (Kim Mal Bong and Geum Su Hyeon)

1992. Korean Music (8th series).
1996 **1196** 100w. multicoloured . . 30 10
1997 **1197** 100w. multicoloured . . 30 10

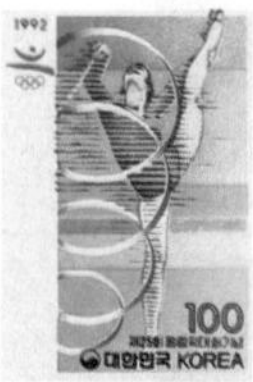
1198 Gymnastics

1199 Stylized View of Exhibition

1992. Olympic Games, Barcelona. Multicoloured.
1998 100w. Type **1198** 30 10
1999 100w. Pole vaulting 30 10

1992. "Expo '93" World's Fair, Taejon (3rd issue). Multicoloured.
2000 100w. Type **1199** 25 10
2001 100w. "Expo 93" 25 10
MS2002 Two sheets each 90 × 60 mm. (a) No. 2000 × 2; (b) No. 2001 × 2 . . . . 2·40 1·75

1201 Korea Exhibition Centre and South Gate, Seoul

1992. 21st Universal Postal Union Congress, Seoul (1st issue). Multicoloured.
2003 100w. Type **1201** 25 10
2004 100w. Tolharubang (stone grandfather), Cheju . . . 25 10
MS2005 Two sheets each 90 × 60 mm. (a) No. 2003 × 2; (b) No. 2004 × 2 . . . . 1·90 1·50
See also Nos. 2075/2077, 2088/**MS**2089 and 2112/**MS**2117.

1203 Woven Pattern

1204 Fruit and Flower Decorations

1205 Carved Decorations

1206 Coral, Butterfly and Pine Resin Decorations

1992. Korean Beauty (2nd series). Maedeups (tassels).
2006 **1203** 100w. multicoloured . . 40 15
2007 **1204** 100w. multicoloured . . 40 15
2008 **1205** 100w. multicoloured . . 40 15
2009 **1206** 100w. multicoloured . . 40 15

1207 Lee Pong Chang

1208 Hwang Young Jo (Barcelona, 1992)

1992. 60th Death Anniv of Lee Pong Chang (independence fighter).
2010 **1207** 100w. brown and orange 30 10

1992. Korean Winners of Olympic Marathon. Multicoloured.
2011 100w. Type **1208** 60 15
2012 100w. Shon Kee Chung (Berlin, 1936) 60 15
MS2013 90 × 60 mm. Nos. 2011/12 2·75 2·10

1209 Sails on Map of Americas

1210 Heads and Speech Balloon

1992. 500th Anniv of Discovery of America by Columbus.
2014 **1209** 100w. multicoloured . . 70 10

1992. Campaign for Purification of Language.
2015 **1210** 100w. multicoloured . . 70 10

1211 Flowers and Stamps

1212 Cockerels in Snow-covered Yard

1992. Philatelic Week.
2016 **1211** 100w. multicoloured . . 70 10
MS2017 60 × 90 mm. No. 2016 × 2 1·25 95

1992. Lunar New Year ("Year of the Cock"). Mult.
2018 100w. Type **1212** 60 10
2019 100w. Flying kites 60 10
MS2020 Two sheets each 90 × 60 mm. (a) No. 2018 × 2; (b) No. 2019 × 2 . . . . 1·60 1·25

1214 Emblem, Globe and Woman holding Bowl

1992. International Nutrition Conference, Rome.
2021 **1214** 100w. multicoloured . . 85 10

1215 View of Centre and Logo

1993. Inauguration of Seoul Arts Centre's Opera House.
2022 **1215** 110w. multicoloured . . 85 15

1216 Pres. Kim Young Sam, Flag and Mt. Paekdu Lake

1217 National Flag

1993. Inauguration of 14th President.
2023 **1216** 110w. multicoloured . . 85 15
MS2024 90 × 60 mm. No. 2023 × 2 4·00 3·00

1993. No. 2036a orange, black and pink, others multicoloured.
2025 10w. Type **1217** 10 10
2026 20w. White stork 40 10
2026a 20w. Black-crowned night heron 10 10
2027 30w. White magnolia . . . 10 10
2027a 30w. *Vitis amurensis* . . . 10 10
2028 40w. Korean white pine . . 10 10
2028a 40w. "Purpuricenus lituralus" (beetle) . . . 10 10
2028b 50w. Water cock 10 10
2029 60w. Squirrel 10 10
2030 70w. Chinese lanterns (plant) 10 10
2030a 80w. Japanese white eye on japonica branch . . . 10 10
2031 90w. Oriental scops owl . . 15 10
2031a 100w. Dishcloth gourd . . 35 10
2032 110w. "Hibiscus syriacus" (plant) 25 10
2033 120w. As 110w. 15 10
2034 130w. Narcissi 20 10
2034c 140w. As 130w. 15 10
2035 150w. Painted porcelain jar 25 10
2036 160w. Pine tree (horiz) . . 30 10
2036a 170w. Crayfish 20 10
2036c 170w. Far eastern curlew 20 10
2037 180w. Little tern (horiz) . . 50 15
2037a 190w. As 110w. 20 10
2038 200w. Turtle (horiz) . . . 30 10
2038a 200w. Snow crab (horiz) 30 10
2038b 210w. As 180w. 35 10
2038c 260w. As 180w. 25 10
2039 300w. Eurasian skylark (horiz) 45 15
2040 370w. Drum and drum dance (horiz) 65 15
2041 400w. Celadon cockerel water dropper (horiz) . . 65 15
2042 420w. As 370w. 65 15
2043 440w. Haho'i mask and Ssirum wrestlers (horiz) 80 15
2044 480w. As 440w. 75 15
2045 500w. Celadon pomegranate water dropper 80 15
2045a 600w. Hong Yong-sik (first Postmaster General) . . 90 15
2046 700w. Gilt-bronze Bongnae-san incense burner (23 × 34 mm) . . 1·10 25
2046a 700w. Cloud and crane jade ornament, Koryo Dynasty . . . . 1·10 25
2046b 710w. King Sejong and alphabet . . . . 1·25 25
2046c 800w. Cheju ponies . . . . 1·25 20
2047 900w. Gilt-bronze buddha triad (23 × 34 mm) . . . 1·60 30
2048 910w. As 710w. . . . . . 1·60 30
2049 930w. Celadon pitcher (blue background) (23 × 31 mm) . . . . . 1·50 25
2049a 930w. As No. 2049 (brown background) . . . . . . 1·60 25
2049b 1000w. Stone guardian animal (from tomb of King Muryong) (32 × 21 mm) . . . . . 1·60 35
2050 1050w. As 930w. . . . . . 1·60 40
2050a 1170w. Bronze incense burner . . . . 2·25 25
2050b 1190w. As 930w. . . . . . 2·75 30
2050c 2000w. Crown from tomb of Shinch'on-ni . . . . 3·00 35

1243 Student and Computer

1244 Emblem and Map

1993. Korean Student Inventions Exhibition.
2051 **1243** 110w. mauve and silver 85 10

1993. International Human Rights Conference, Vienna, Austria.
2052 **1244** 110w. multicoloured . . 85 10

1245 Hand scooping Globe from Water

1246 Matsu-take Mushroom ("Tricholoma matsutake")

1993. "Water is Life".
2053 **1245** 110w. multicoloured . . 85 10

1993. Fungi (1st series). Multicoloured.
2054 110w. Type **1246** 60 10
2055 110w. "Ganoderma lucidum" 60 10
2056 110w. "Lentinula edodes" 60 10
2057 110w. Oyster fungus ("Pleurotus ostreatus") . . 60 10
See also Nos. 2095/8, 2146/9, 2207/10, 2249/52 and 2293/6.

1247 Government Pavilion

1248 International Pavilion and Mascot

1249 Recycling Art Pavilion

1250 Telecom Pavilion

1993. "Expo '93" World's Fair, Taejon (4th issue).
2058 **1247** 110w. multicoloured . . 50 10
2059 **1248** 110w. multicoloured . . 50 10
2060 **1249** 110w. multicoloured . . 50 10
2061 **1250** 110w. multicoloured . . 50 10
MS2062 Four sheets each 90 × 60 mm. (a) No. 2058 × 2; (b) No. 2059 × 2; (c) No. 2060 × 2; (d) No. 2061 × 2 . . . . 2·25 2·00

1251 Emblems

1993. 19th Congress of International Society of Orthopaedic and Trauma Surgery.
2063 **1251** 110w. multicoloured . . 85 10

1252 "O Dol Ddo Gi" (Cheju Island folk song)

1253 "Ong He Ya" (barley threshing song)

1993. Korean Music (9th series).
2064 **1252** 110w. multicoloured . . 60 10
2065 **1253** 110w. multicoloured . . 60 10

1254 Janggu Drum Dance

1255 Emblem

1993. "Visit Korea" Year (1994) (1st issue).
2066 **1254** 110w. multicoloured . . 50 10
2067 **1255** 110w. multicoloured . . 50 10
See also Nos. 2086/7.

1256 "Twin Tigers" (military officials, 1st to 3rd rank)

1260 Campaign Emblem

1993. Korean Beauty (3rd series). Hyoongbae (embroidered insignia of the Chosun dynasty). Multicoloured.
2068 110w. Type **1256** 50 10
2069 110w. "Single Crane" (civil officials, 4th to 9th rank) 50 10
2070 110w. "Twin Cranes" (civil officials, 1st to 3rd rank) 50 10
2071 110w. "Dragon" (King) . . 50 10

1993. Anti-litter Campaign.
2072 **1260** 110w. multicoloured . . 50 10

1261 "Eggplant and Oriental Long-nosed Locust" (Shin Saim Dang)

1262 "Weaving"

1993. Philatelic Week.
2073 **1261** 110w. multicoloured . . 50 10
MS2074 90 × 60 mm. No. 2073 × 2 80 60

1993. 21st U.P.U. Congress, Seoul (2nd issue). Paintings by Kim Hong Do. Multicoloured.
2075 110w. Type **1262** 50 10
2076 110w. "Musicians and a Dancer" (vert) 50 10
MS2077 Two sheets each 90 × 60 mm. (a) No. 2075 × 2; (b) No. 2076 × 2 . . . . 1·60 1·25

1263 Ribbon and Globe as "30", Freighter and Ilyushin Il-86 Airliner

1993. 30th Trade Day.
2078 **1263** 110w. multicoloured . . 60 10

1264 Sapsaree and Kite

1993. Lunar New Year ("Year of the Dog"). Multicoloured.
2079 110w. Type **1264** 50 10
2080 110w. Puppy with New Year's Greetings bow . . 50 10
MS2081 Two sheets each 90 × 60 mm. (a) No. 2079 × 2; (b) No. 2080 × 2 . . . . 1·60 1·25

1993. Wild Flowers (4th series). As T **1166**.
2082 110w. "Weigela hortensis" 75 10
2083 110w. "Iris ruthenica" . . . 75 10
2084 110w. "Aceriphyllum rosii" 75 10
2085 110w. Marsh marigold ("Caltha palustris") . . . 75 10

1266 Flautist on Cloud

1267 T'alch'um Mask Dance

1994. "Visit Korea" Year (2nd issue).
2086 **1266** 110w. multicoloured . . 50 10
2087 **1267** 110w. multicoloured . . 50 10

1268 Map'ae, Horse, Envelope and Emblem

1269 Monument

1994. 21st U.P.U. Congress, Seoul (3rd issue).
2088 **1268** 300w. multicoloured . . 1·25 15
MS2089 90 × 60 mm. No. 2088 × 2 1·60 1·25
The map'ae was a token which gave authority to impress post horses.

1994. 75th Anniv of Samil (Independence) Movement.
2090 **1269** 110w. multicoloured . . 65 10

1270 Great Purple ("Sasakia charonda")

1994. Protection of Wildlife and Plants (1st series). Multicoloured.
2091 110w. Type **1270** (butterfly) 60 10
2092 110w. "Allomyrina dichotoma" (beetle) . . . 60 10
MS2093 Two sheets each 90 × 60 mm. (a) No. 2091 × 2; (b) No. 2092 × 2 . . . . 1·60 1·25
See also Nos. 2143/**MS**2145 and 2186/**MS**2188, 2241/**MS**2243, 2277/**MS**2279, 2326/**MS**2330, 2383/**MS**2387 and 2481/**MS**2485.
See also Nos. 2143/4, 2186/7, 2241/2, 2275/8, 2326/9, 2383/6 and 2481/4.

1271 Family of Mandarins

1994. International Year of the Family.
2094 **1271** 110w. multicoloured . . 65 10

1994. Fungi (2nd series). As T **1246**. Multicoloured.
2095 110w. Common morel ("Morchella esculenta") 50 10
2096 110w. "Gomphus floccosus" 50 10
2097 110w. "Cortinarius purpurascens" 50 10
2098 110w. "Oudemansiella platyphylla" 50 10
MS2099 2 sheets each 90 × 60 mm. (a) No. 2095 × 2; (b) No. 2096 × 2; (c) No. 2097 × 2; (d) No. 2098 × 2 3·25 2·50

1272 Museum

1994. Inauguration of War Memorial Museum, Yongsan (Seoul).
2100 **1272** 110w. multicoloured . . 65 10

1273 Text and Dove

1994. "Philakorea 1994" International Stamp Exhibition, Seoul (1st issue).
2101 **1273** 910w. multicoloured . . 2·00 40
MS2102 90 × 60 mm. No. 2101 2·40 2·00
See also Nos. 2107/**MS**2111.

See also Nos. 2107/9.

1274 Taeguk (Yin-Yang) Fan

1275 Crane Fan

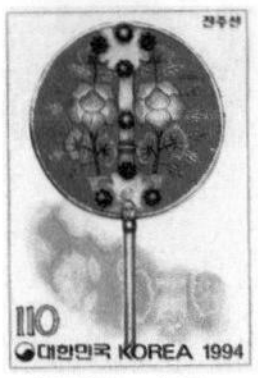

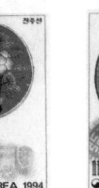

1276 Pearl Fan

1277 Wheel Fan

1994. Korean Beauty (4th series). Fans.
2103 **1274** 110w. multicoloured . . 50 10
2104 **1275** 110w. multicoloured . . 50 10
2105 **1276** 110w. multicoloured . . 50 10
2106 **1277** 110w. multicoloured . . 50 10

1278 "Wintry Days" (Kim Chong Hui)

1282 "Sword Dance" (Sin Yun Bok)

1994. "Philakorea 1994" International Stamp Exhibition, Seoul (2nd issue). (a). Multicoloured.
2107 130w. Type **1278** 50 10
2108 130w. "Grape" (Choe Sok Hwan) 50 10
2109 130w. "Riverside Scene" (Kim Duk Sin) 50 10
MS2110 Three sheets each 90 × 60 mm. (a) No. 2107 × 2; (b) No. 2108 × 2; (c) No. 2109 × 2 1·90 1·50
See also Nos. 2196/**MS**2198, 2234/**MS**22346, 2280/**MS**2282, 2322/**MS**2325; 2498/**MS**2501, 2594/**MS**2596 and 2697/**MS**2699.

(b).
MS2111 130w. Type **1281**; 300w. Manchurian cranes and sun; 370w. Manchurian cranes in treetops; 400w. Deer (vert); 440w. Turtle in stream (vert); 470w. Tree and stream (vert); 930w. Trees (vert) 5·00 3·75

1994. 21st U.P.U. Congress, Seoul (4th issue). Multicoloured.
2112 130w. Type **1282** 50 10
2113 130w. "Book Shelves" (detail of folk painting showing stamps) 50 10
2114 130w. Congress emblem . . 50 10
2115 130w. Hong Yung Sik (postal reformer) and Heinrich von Stephan (founder of U.P.U.) (horiz) 75 10
MS2116 Four sheets each 90 × 60 mm. (a) No. 2112 × 2; (b) No. 2113 × 2; (c) No. 2114 × 2; (d) No. 2115 × 2 . . . . 3·25 2·50
MS2117 125 × 86 mm. Nos. 2112/15 2·20 1·90

1283 Old Map

1284 Mail Van

1994. 600th Anniv of Adoption of Seoul as Capital of Korea (1st issue).
2118 **1283** 130w. multicoloured . . 60 10
See also No. 2139.

1994. Transport. Multicoloured.
2121 300w. Type **1284** 60 15
2122 330w. Airplane 80 15
2122a 340w. Airplane facing left 70 10
2122b 380w. As 340w. 60 10
2123 390w. Airplane (different) 1·10 15
2124 400w. As 330w. . . . . . 1·25 15
2126 540w. Streamlined diesel train . . . . 2·10 15
2127 560w. As 330w. . . . . . 2·25 15
2130 1190w. River cruiser . . . 3·75 25
2131 1300w. As 330w. . . . . . 4·00 40
2132 1340w. As 340w. . . . . . 4·25 35
2132a 1380w. As 340w. . . . . . 4·50 35

1994. Wild Flowers (5th series). As T **1166**. Multicoloured.
2133 130w. "Gentiana jamesii" 45 10
2134 130w. "Geranium eriostemon var. megalanthum" 45 10
2135 130w. "Leontopodium japonicum" 45 10
2136 130w. "Lycoris aurea" . . . 45 10

1285 "Water Melon and Field Mice" (detail of folding screen, Shin Saimdang)

1286 "600"

1994. Philatelic Week.
2137 **1285** 130w. multicoloured . . 65 10
MS2138 90 × 60 mm. No. 2137 × 2 65 50

1994. 600th Anniv of Seoul as Capital (2nd issue).
2139 **1286** 130w. multicoloured . . 65 10

1287 Pigs travelling in Snow

1994. Lunar New Year ("Year of the Pig"). Multicoloured.
2140 130w. Type **1287** 60 10
2141 130w. Family in forest . . . 60 10
MS2142 Two sheets each 90 × 60 mm. (a) No. 2140 × 2; (b) No. 2141 × 2 . . . . 1·25 95

1995. Protection of Wildlife and Plants (2nd series). Multicoloured.
2143 130w. Plancy's green pond frog ("Rana plancyi") . . 60 10
2144 130w. Common toad ("Bufo bufo") 60 10
MS2145 Two sheets each 125 × 86 mm. (a) No. 2143 × 2; (b) No. 2144 × 2 . . . . 1·25 95

1995. Fungi (3rd series). As T **1246**. Multicoloured.
2146 130w. Shaggy ink caps ("Coprinus comatus") . . 45 10
2147 130w. Chicken mushroom ("Laetiporus sulphureus") 45 10
2148 130w. "Lentinus lepideus" 45 10
2149 130w. Cracked green russula ("Russula virescens") . . 45 10
MS2150 Four sheets each 90 × 60 mm. (a) No. 2146 × 2; (b) No. 2147 × 2; (c) No. 2148 × 2; (d) No. 2149 × 2 . . . . 2·50 1·90

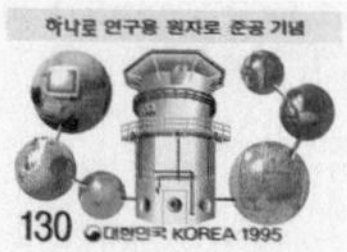
1290 Spheres around Reactor

1291 Scales of Justice

1995. Completion of Hanaro Research Reactor.
2151 **1290** 130w. multicoloured . . 65 10

1995. Centenary of Judicial System.
2152 **1291** 130w. multicoloured . . 65 10

1292 Tiger

1995. Centenary of Law Education.
2153 **1292** 130w. multicoloured . . 65 10

1293 Dooly the Little Dinosaur (Kim Soo Jeung)

1294 Kochuboo (Kim Yong Hwan)

1995. Cartoons (1st series). Multicoloured.
2154 **1293** 130w. multicoloured . . 70 10
2155 **1294** 440w. multicoloured . . 1·25 15
MS2156 Two sheets each 90 × 60 mm. (a) No. 2154; (b) No. 2155 . . . . 1·75 1·40
See also Nos. 2196/7, 2234/5, 2280/1, 2322/4 and 2498/500.

1295 Gate of Eternal Youth, Changdokkung Palace

1296 Fish Water Gate, Chuhamru Pavilion, Changdokkung Palace

1297 Pomosa Temple Gate, Pusan City

1298 Yangban Residence Gate, Hahoe Village

1995. Korean Beauty (5th series). Gates.
2157 **1295** 130w. multicoloured . . 50 10
2158 **1296** 130w. multicoloured . . 50 10
2159 **1297** 130w. multicoloured . . 50 10
2160 **1298** 130w. multicoloured . . 50 10

1299 Lion and Emblem

1995. 78th Convention of Lions Clubs International.
2161 **1299** 130w. multicoloured . . 65 10

1995. Wild Flowers (6th series). As T **1166**. Multicoloured.
2162 130w. "Halenia corniculata" 50 10
2163 130w. "Erythronium japonicum" 50 10
2164 130w. "Iris odaesanensis" 50 10
2165 130w. "Leontice microrrhyncha" 50 10

1300 National Flag

1301 Telescope

1995. 50th Anniv of Liberation. Multicoloured.
2166 130w. Type **1300** 60 10
2167 440w. Anniversary emblem (96 × 19 mm) . . . . . . 1·40 15
MS2168 Two sheets each 125 × 85 mm. (a) No. 2166 × 2; (b) No. 2167 . . . . 1·60 1·25

1995. Inauguration of Mt. Bohyun Optical Astronomy Observatory.
2169 **1301** 130w. multicoloured . . 65 10

1302 Turtle's Back Song

1303 Song from "Standards of Musical Science"

1995. Literature (1st series).
2170 **1302** 130w. multicoloured . . 60 10
2171 **1303** 130w. multicoloured . . 60 10
MS2172 Two sheets each 90 × 60 mm. (a) No. 2170 × 2; (b) No. 2171 × 2 . . . . 1·25 95
See also Nos. 2212/**MS**2214, 2269/**MS**2271, 2301/**MS**2303 and 2344/**MS**2348.

1304 "50 Th" incorporating Man with Wheat

1995. 50th Anniv of F.A.O.
2172 **1304** 150w. black and violet 70 10

1305 Open Bible

1306 Families in Houses

1995. Centenary of Korean Bible Society.
2174 **1305** 150w. multicoloured . . 70 10

1995. Population and Housing Census.
2175 **1306** 150w. multicoloured . . 70 10

1307 Dove of Flags

1995. 50th Anniv of United Nations Organization.
2176 **1307** 150w. multicoloured . . 70 10

1308 Rontgen

1309 "Water Pepper and Mantis" (detail of folding screen, Shin Saim Dang)

1995. Centenary of Discovery of X-Rays by Wilhelm Rontgen.
2177 **1308** 150w. multicoloured . . 70 10

1995. Philatelic Week.
2178 **1309** 150w. multicoloured . . 70 10
MS2179 90 × 60 mm. No. 2178 × 2 65 50

1310 Rat and Snowman

1312 Miroku Bosatsu, Koryu Temple, Kyoto

1995. Lunar New Year ("Year of the Rat"). Multicoloured.
2180 150w. Type **1310** 60 10
2181 150w. Cranes and pine trees (horiz) 60 10
MS2182 Two sheets each 90 × 60 mm. (a) No. 2180 × 2; (b) No. 2181 × 2 . . . . 1·10 85

1995. 30th Anniv of Resumption of Korea–Japan Diplomatic Relations.
2183 **1312** 420w. multicoloured . . 1·40 15

1313 Cable Route

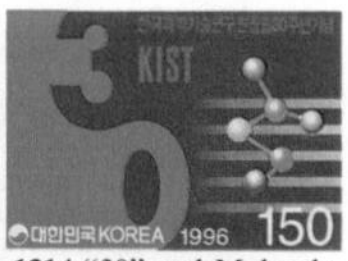
1314 "30" and Molecule

1996. Inauguration of Korea–China Submarine Cable.
2184 **1313** 420w. multicoloured . . 70 15

1996. 30th Anniv of Korea Institute of Science and Technology.
2185 **1314** 150w. multicoloured . . 70 10

1996. Protection of Wildlife and Plants (3rd series). As T **1270**. Multicoloured.
2186 150w. Black pond turtle ("Geoclemys reevesii") . . 60 10
2187 150w. Ground skink ("Scincella laterale") . . . 60 10
MS2188 Two sheets each 125 × 86 mm. (a) No. 2186 × 2; (b) No. 2187 × 2 . . . . 95 75

1315 Satellite and Launching Pad

1996. Launch of "Mugunghwa 2" Telecommunications Satellite.
2189 **1315** 150w. multicoloured . . 70 10

1316 So Chae P'il (founder) and Leader from First Issue

1996. Centenary of "Tongnip Shinmun" (first independent newspaper).
2190 **1316** 150w. multicoloured . . 70 10

1996. Wild Flowers (7th series). As T **1166**. Multicoloured.
2191 150w. "Cypripedium macranthum" 55 10
2192 150w. "Trilium tschonoskii" 55 10
2193 150w. "Viola variegata" . . 55 10
2194 150w. "Hypericum ascyron" 55 10

1317 Anniversary Emblem and Cadets

1996. 50th Anniv of Korean Military Academy.
2195 **1317** 150w. multicoloured . . 70 10

1318 Gobau (Kim Song Hwan)

1319 Battle between Kkach'i and Caesarius (Lee Hyun Se) (from film "Armageddon")

1996. Cartoons (2nd series).
2196 **1318** 150w. multicoloured . . 60 10
2197 **1319** 150w. multicoloured . . 60 10
MS2198 Two sheets each 90 × 60 mm. (a) No. 2196 × 2; (b) No. 2197 . . . . 50 40

1320 Anniversary Emblem

1321 Globe and Congress Emblem

1996. 50th Anniv of Korean Girl Scouts.
2199 **1320** 150w. multicoloured . . 70 10

1996. 35th World Congress of International Advertising Association, Seoul.
2200 **1321** 150w. multicoloured . . 70 10

1322 Syringes and Drugs

1996. International Anti-drug Day.
2201 **1322** 150w. multicoloured . . 70 10

1323 Skater

1324 Torch Bearer

1996. World University Students' Games, Muju and Chonju (1st issue). Multicoloured.
2202 150w. Type **1323** 90 10
2203 150w. Games emblem (vert) 90 10
See also Nos. 2228/9.

1996. Olympic Games, Atlanta. Multicoloured.
2204 150w. Type **1324** 65 10
2205 150w. Games emblem . . . 65 10

1325 Match Scene

1326 South Korean Team scoring Goal

1996. World Cup Football Championship (2002), South Korea and Japan. Two sheets each 134 × 78 mm. Multicoloured.
MS2206 Two sheets. (a) 400w. × 4, Type **1325**; (b) 400w. × 4, Type **1326** . . . . 5·00 3·75

1996. Fungi (4th series). As T **1246**. Multicoloured.
2207 150w. "Amanita inaurata" 70 10
2208 150w. "Paxillus atrotomentosus" 70 10
2209 150w. "Rhodophyllus crassipes" 70 10
2210 150w. "Sarcodon imbricatum" 70 10
MS2211 Four sheets each 90 × 60 mm. (a) No. 2207 × 2; (b) No. 2208 × 2; (c) No. 2209 × 2; (d) No. 2210 × 2 . . . . 2·00 1·50

1327 Requiem for a Deceased Sister

1328 Ode to Knight Kip'a

1996. Literature (2nd series).
2212 **1327** 150w. multicoloured . . 75 10
2213 **1328** 150w. multicoloured . . 75 10
MS2214 Two sheets, each 90 × 61 mm. (a) No. 2212 × 2; (b) No.2213 × 2 . . . . 3·00 2·50

1329 Alphabet

1330 Castle

1996. 550th Anniv of Han-Gul (Korean alphabet created by King Sejong).
2215 **1329** 150w. black and grey 70 10
MS2216 90 × 60 mm. No. 2215 × 2 1·40 1·00

1996. Bicentenary of Suwon Castle.
2217 **1330** 400w. multicoloured . . 1·90 15

1331 Front Gate, University Flag and Emblem

1996. 50th Anniv of Seoul National University.
2218 **1331** 150w. multicoloured . . 70 10

1332 Five-direction Pouch

1333 Chinese Phoenix Pouch (Queen's Court Pouch)

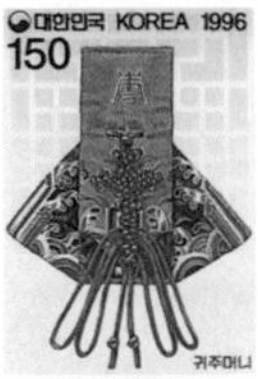

1334 Princess Pokon's Wedding Pouch

1335 Queen Yunbi's Pearl Pouch

1996. Korean Beauty (6th series). Pouches.
2219 **1332** 150w. multicoloured . . 70 10
2220 **1333** 150w. multicoloured . . 70 10
2221 **1334** 150w. multicoloured . . 70 10
2222 **1335** 150w. multicoloured . . 70 10

1336 "Poppy and Lizard" (detail of folding screen, Shin Saimdang)

1337 Children riding Ox

1996. Philatelic Week.
2223 **1336** 150w. multicoloured . . 70 10
MS2224 90 × 60 mm. No. 2223 × 2 1·40 1·00

1996. Lunar New Year ("Year of the Ox"). Multicoloured.
2225 150w. Type **1337** 95 10
2226 150w. Boy piper and resting ox 95 10
MS2227 Two sheets, each 90 × 60 mm. (a) No. 2225 × 2; (b) No. 2226 × 2 . . . . 4·00 2·75

1339 Figure Skating

1340 Coins forming "100"

1997. World University Students' Games, Muju and Chonju (2nd issue). Multicoloured.
2228 150w. Type **1339** 95 10
2229 150w. Skiing 95 10
MS2230 Two sheets, each 60 × 90 mm. (a) No. 2228 × 2; (b) No. 2229 × 2 . . . . 4·00 2·75

1997. Centenary of Foundation of Hansong Bank (first commercial bank in Korea).
2231 **1340** 150w. multicoloured . . 70 10

1341 "Auspicious Turtles"(painting)

1342 Globe, Pen and open Book (Jeon Chong Kwan)

1997. Interparliamentary Union Conference, Seoul.
2232 **1341** 150w. multicoloured . . 70 10

1997. World Book and Copyright Day.
2233 **1342** 150w. multicoloured . . 70 10

1343 A Long, Long Journey in Search of Mummy (Kim Chong Nae)

1344 Run, Run, Hannie (Lee Chin Ju)

1997. Cartoons (3rd series).
2234 **1343** 150w. multicoloured . . 70 10
2235 **1344** 150w. multicoloured . . 70 10
MS2236 Two sheets, each 90 × 60 mm. (a) No. 2234; (b) 2235 1·40 1·00

1345 Torch Bearer

1997. 2nd East Asian Games, Pusan.
2237 **1345** 150w. multicoloured . . 70 10

1346 Jules Rimet (founder)

1347 "Chukkuk" (Lee Chul Joo)

1997. World Cup Football Championship (2002), South Korea and Japan (1st issue).
2238 **1346** 150w. multicoloured . . 60 10
2239 **1347** 150w. multicoloured . . 60 10
MS2340 Two sheets, each 134 × 78 mm. (a) 2238 × 2; (b) 2242 × 2 . . . . 2·40 2·00
See also Nos. 2284/**MS**2288.

1997. Protection of Wildlife and Plants (4th series). As T **1270**. Multicoloured.
2241 150w. Chinese nine-spined sticklebacks ("Pungitius sinensis") 70 10
2242 150w. Spot-eared brook perch ("Coreoperca kawamebari") 70 10
MS2243 Two sheets, each 125 × 86 mm. (a) 2241 × 2; (b) No. 2242 × 2 . . . . 2·40 2·00

1997. Wild Flowers (8th series). As T **1166**. Multicoloured.
2244 150w. "Belamcanda chinensis" 75 10
2245 150w. "Belamcanda chinensis" 75 10
2246 150w. "Campanula takesimana" 75 10
2247 150w. "Magnolia sieboldii" 75 10

1348 Emblem and "97" forming Face

1349 Seoul South Gate and Emblem

1997. 2nd Art Biennale, Kwangju.
2248 **1348** 150w. multicoloured . . 70 10

1997. Fungi (5th series). As T **1246**. Multicoloured.
2249 150w. "Inocybe fastigiata" 75 10
2250 150w. "Panaeolus papilionaceus" 75 10
2251 150w. "Ramaria flava" . . 75 10
2252 150w. Fly agaric ("Amanita muscaria") 75 10
MS2253 Four sheets, each 90 × 60 mm. (a) No. 2249 × 2; (b) No. 2250 × 2; (c) No. 2251 × 2; (d) No. 2252 × 2 . . . . 6·00 5·50

1997. 85th World Dental Congress, Seoul.
2254 **1349** 170w. multicoloured . . 20 10

1350 Harbour and Score

1997. Centenary of Mokpo Port.
2255 **1350** 170w. multicoloured . . 70 10

1351 Main Building, Pyongyang

1997. Centenary of Founding of Soongsil Academy in Pyongyang (now situated in Seoul).
2256 **1351** 170w. multicoloured . . 70 10

1352 Concentric Squares

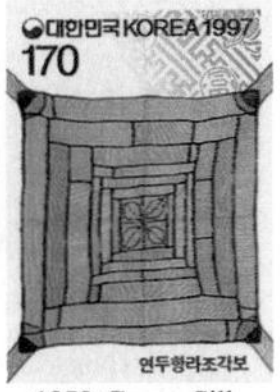

1353 Green Silk

1354 Pattern of Squares

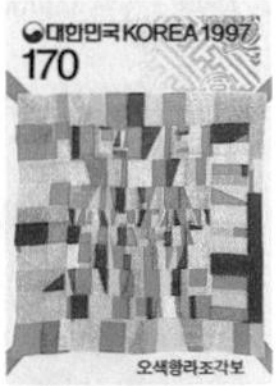

1355 Pattern of Squares and Triangles

1997. Korean Beauty (7th series). Patchwork Pojagi (wrapping cloths).
2257 **1352** 170w. multicoloured . . 65 10
2258 **1353** 170w. multicoloured . . 65 10
2259 **1354** 170w. multicoloured . . 65 10
2260 **1355** 170w. multicoloured . . 65 10

1356 "Hollyhock and Frog" (detail of folding screen, Shin Saimdang)

1357 Tiger's Head

1997. Philatelic Week.
2261 **1356** 170w. multicoloured . . 70 10
MS2262 90 × 60 mm. No. 2261 × 2 1·40 1·00

1997. Lunar New Year ("Year of the Tiger"). Multicoloured.
2263 170w. Type **1357** 70 10
2264 170w. "Magpie and Tiger" (folk painting) 70 10
MS2265 Two sheets, each 90 × 60 mm. (a) No. 2263 × 2; (b) No. 2264 × 2 . . . . 2·40 2·00

1359 Buddha, Sokkuram Shrine

1360 Pulguk Temple

1997. World Heritage Sites (1st series).
2266 **1359** 170w. multicoloured . . 20 10
2267 **1360** 380w. multicoloured . . 40 10
MS2268 144 × 88 mm. Nos. 2266/7 60 40
See also Nos. 2317/8, 2365/6, 2475//8 and 2533/4.

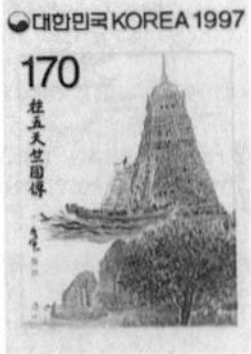

1361 "Poem to Sui General Yu Zhong Wen" (Ulchi Mundok)

1362 "Record of Travel to Five Indian Kingdoms" (Hye Ch'o)

1997. Literature (3rd series).
2269 **1361** 170w. multicoloured . . 70 10
2270 **1362** 170w. multicoloured . . 70 10
MS2271 Two sheets, each 90 × 60 mm. (a) No. 2269 × 2; (b) No. 2270 × 2 . . . . 2·40 2·00

1363 Neon Lights on Globe and Nuclear Power Plant

1998. Centenary of Introduction of Electricity to Korea.
2272 **1363** 170w. multicoloured . . 70 10

1364 Pres. Kim Dae Jung and Flag

1998. Inauguration of 15th President of South Korea.
2273 **1364** 170w. multicoloured . . 60 10
MS2274 120 × 110 mm. No. 2273 60 40

1998. Protection of Wildlife and Plants (5th series). Vert designs as T **1270**. Multicoloured.
2275 340w. Korean leopard ("Panthera pardus orientalis") . . . . 1·25 75
2276 340w. Asiatic black bears ("Selenarctos thibetanus") 1·25 75
2277 340w. European otters ("Lutra lutra") . . . . . 1·25 75
2278 340w. Siberian musk deers ("Moschus moschiferus") 1·25 75
MS2279 129 × 123 mm. Nos. 2275/8 5·00 4·50

1365 Aktong-i (Lee Hi Jae)

1366 Challenger (Park Ki Jong)

1998. Cartoons (4th series).
2280 **1365** 170w. multicoloured . . 40 10
2281 **1366** 340w. multicoloured . . 70 10
MS2282 Two sheets, each 90 × 60 mm. (a) No. 2280; (b) No. 2281 . . . . 1·10 80

1367 Assembly Building and Firework Display

1368 Player with Ball

1998. 50th Anniv of National Assembly.
2283 **1367** 170w. multicoloured . . 60 10

1998. World Cup Football Championship (2002), Korea and Japan (2nd issue). Multicoloured.
2284 170w. Type **1368** 50 10
2285 170w. Two players chasing ball 50 10
2286 170w. Players heading ball 50 10
2287 170w. Player kicking ball over head 50 10
MS2288 134 × 78 mm. No. 2284/7 2·00 1·40

1369 Writing on Stone Tablets

1998. Information Technology. Multicoloured.
2289 170w. Type **1369** 50 10
2290 170w. Pony Express 50 10
2291 170w. Man using telephone and post box 50 10
2292 170w. Old and modern forms of communication (68 × 22 mm) 50 10

1998. Fungi (6th series). As T **1246**. Multicoloured.
2293 170w. "Pseudocolus schellenbergiae" 50 10
2294 170w. "Cyptotrama asprata" 50 10
2295 170w. "Laccaria vinaceoavellanea" 50 10
2296 170w. "Phallus rugulosus" 50 10
MS2297 114 × 144 mm. Nos. 2293/6 2·00 1·40

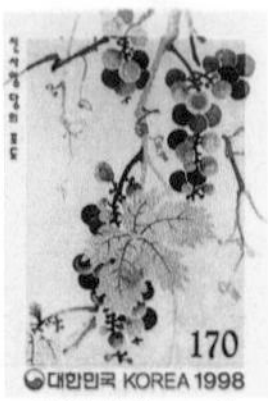

1373 Flag and Runners

1374 "Grapes" (Lady Shin Saimdang)

1998. 50th Anniv of Proclamation of Republic.
2298 **1373** 170w. multicoloured . . 60 10

1998. Philatelic Week.
2299 **1374** 170w. multicoloured . . 60 10
MS2300 90 × 60 mm. No. 2299 × 2 1·20 85

1375 Thinking of Mother

1376 Would You Leave Me Now?

1998. Literature (4th series). Sogyo Songs.
2301 **1375** 170w. multicoloured . . 60 10
2302 **1376** 170w. multicoloured . . 60 10
MS2303 Two sheets 90 × 20 mm. (a) No. 2301; (b) No. 2302 . . . . 1·20 85

1377 Film Strips and Masks

1998. 3rd Pusan International Film Festival.
2304 **1377** 170w. multicoloured . . 20 10

1378 Myungnyundang Hall

1998. 600th Anniv of Sungkyunkwan University.
2305 **1378** 170w. multicoloured . . 20 10

1379 National Constabulary, Badge and Lake Ch'onji

1380 Hot-air Balloon

1998. 50th Anniv of Korean Armed Forces.
2306 **1379** 170w. multicoloured . . 20 10

1998. World Stamp Day.
2307 **1380** 170w. multicoloured . . 20 10

1381 Peach

1382 Double Crane

1383 Carp

1384 Peach

1385 Toad

1386 Dragon and Cloud

1387 Monkey

1388 House

1998. Korean Beauty (8th series). Porcelain Water Droppers.
2308 **1381** 170w. multicoloured . . 20 10
2309 **1382** 170w. multicoloured . . 20 10
2310 **1383** 170w. multicoloured . . 20 10
2311 **1384** 170w. multicoloured . . 20 10
2312 **1385** 170w. multicoloured . . 20 10
2313 **1386** 170w. multicoloured . . 20 10
2314 **1387** 170w. multicoloured . . 20 10
2315 **1388** 170w. multicoloured . . 20 10

1389 Rabbits

1390 Tripitaka Koreana (scriptures engraved on wooden blocks)

1391 Changgyong P'anjon (woodblock repository)

1998. Lunar New Year ("Year of the Rabbit").
2316 **1389** 170w. multicoloured . . 20 10

1998. World Heritage Sites (2nd series). Haein Temple.
2317 **1390** 170w. multicoloured . . 20 10
2318 **1391** 380w. multicoloured . . 40 10
MS2319 144 × 88 mm. Nos. 2317/18 60 40

1392 Maize, Compass and Ship's Wheel

1999. Centenary of Kunsan Port.
2320 **1392** 170w. multicoloured . . 20 10

1393 Masan and Score of "I Want to Go" by Lee Eun Sang

1999. Centenary of Masan Port.
2321 **1393** 170w. multicoloured . . 20 10

1394 Rai-Fi (Kim San Ho)

1395 Tokgo T'ak (Lee Sang Mu)

1396 Im Kkuk Jung (Lee Du Ho)

1999. Cartoons (5th series).
2322 **1394** 170w. multicoloured . . 20 10
2323 **1395** 170w. multicoloured . . 20 10
2324 **1396** 170w. multicoloured . . 20 10
MS2325 Three sheets, each 88 × 58 mm. multicoloured. (a) 340w. Type **1394**; (b) 340w. No. 2323; (c) 340w. No. 2324 60 40

1999. Protection of Wildlife and Plants (6th series). Vert designs as T **1270**.
2326 170w. Peregrine falcon ("Falco peregrinus") . . . 20 10
2327 170w. Grey frog hawk ("Accipiter soloensis") . . 20 10
2328 340w. Steller's sea eagle ("Haliaeetus pelagicus") 35 10
2329 340w. Northern eagle owl ("Bubo bubo") 35 10
MS2330 136 × 133 mm. Nos. 2326/9 1·10 80

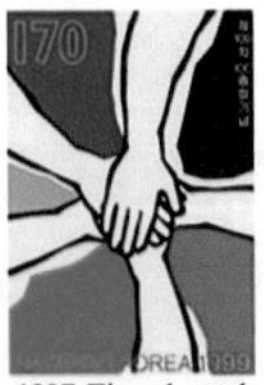

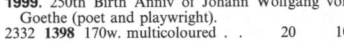

1397 Five clasped Hands

1398 Goethe (after Joseph Stieler)

1999. 109th International Olympic Committee Congress, Seoul.
2331 **1397** 170w. multicoloured . . 20 10

1999. 250th Birth Anniv of Johann Wolfgang von Goethe (poet and playwright).
2332 **1398** 170w. multicoloured . . 20 10

1399 "Kumgang Mountain" (Kyomjae Chong Son)

1999. Philatelic Week.

2334	**1399** 170w. multicoloured . .	20	10
MS2335	120 × 90 mm. **1399** 340w. multicoloured	20	15

1400 Mogul Tank Locomotive No. 101 (first locomotive in Korea)

1999. Centenary of Railway in Korea.

2336	**1400** 170w. multicoloured . .	20	10

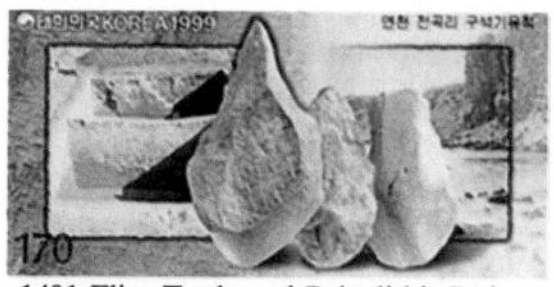
1401 Flint Tools and Paleolithic Ruins, Chungok-ri, Yonch'on

1999. New Millennium (1st series). Multicoloured.

2337	170w. Type **1401**	20	10
2338	170w. Comb-patterned pottery, burnt-out and reconstructed Neolithic dwellings, Amsa-dong, Seoul	20	10
2339	170w. Shell bracelets, bone spear heads and Neolithic shell mounds, Tongsam-dong, Pusan	20	10
2340	170w. Dolmen, Pukon-ri, Kanghwa-do Island . . .	20	10
2341	170w. Bronze and stone daggers and Bronze-age earthenware, Son-gguk-ri, Puyo	20	10
2342	170w. Rock carvings, Pan'gudae	20	10

See also Nos. 2357/62, 2374/8, 2388/92, 2397/2401, 2406/10, 2420/5, 2431/6, 2460/5, 2487/91 and 2511/15.

1402 Bird carrying Letter

1999. 125th Anniv of Universal Postal Union.

2343	**1402** 170w. multicoloured . .	20	10

1403 Little Odes on the Kwandong Area (Chong Ch'ol)

1404 Alas! How foolish I am! (Hwang Jin-i)

1405 Story of Hong Kil-dong (Ho Kyun)

1406 Story of Ch'unhyang

1999. Literature (5th series).

2344	**1403** 170w. multicoloured . .	20	10
2345	**1404** 170w. multicoloured . .	20	10
2346	**1405** 170w. multicoloured . .	20	10
2347	**1406** 170w. multicoloured . .	20	10
MS2348	Four sheets, each 90 × 60 mm. (a) No. 2344; (b) 90 × 60 mm. No. 2345; (c) 60 × 90 mm. No. 2346; (d) 60 × 90 mm. No. 2347	1·60	1·20

1407 Chrysanthemum, Bird and Duck

1408 Birds in Tree and Snake on Korean Character

1409 Pot Plant with Butterfly on Korean Character

1410 Fish on Korean Character

1411 Plant behind Tub of Fishes

1412 Crab on Korean Character

1413 Bird on Korean Character

1414 Chest and Plant behind Deer

1999. Korean Beauty (9th series).

2349	**1407** 340w. multicoloured . .	40	10
2350	**1408** 340w. multicoloured . .	40	10
2351	**1409** 340w. multicoloured . .	40	10
2352	**1410** 340w. multicoloured . .	40	10
2353	**1411** 340w. multicoloured . .	40	10
2354	**1412** 340w. multicoloured . .	40	10
2355	**1413** 340w. multicoloured . .	40	10
2356	**1414** 340w. multicoloured . .	40	10

1415 Ornament and Bird-shaped Vase

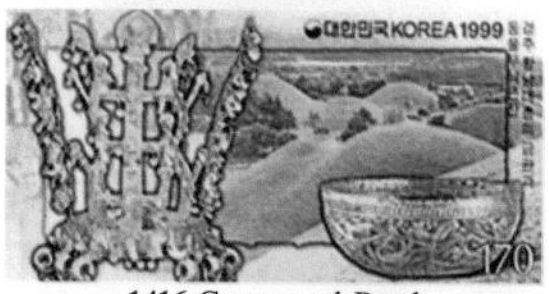
1416 Crown and Bowl

1417 Man on Horseback and Cave Paintings

1418 Gold Ornament and Jade Jewellery

1419 Stone Crafts

1420 Carved Stone Face

1999. New Millennium (2nd series).

2357	**1415** 170w. multicoloured . .	20	10
2358	**1416** 170w. multicoloured . .	20	10
2359	**1417** 170w. multicoloured . .	20	10
2360	**1418** 170w. multicoloured . .	20	10
2361	**1419** 170w. multicoloured . .	20	10
2362	**1420** 170w. multicoloured . .	20	10

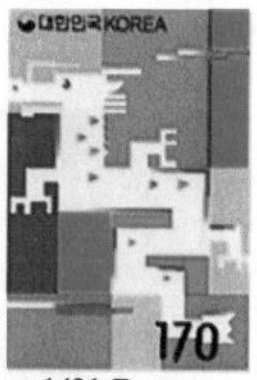
1421 Dragon

1999. Lunar New Year "Year of the Dragon".

2363	**1421** 170w. multicoloured . .	20	10
MS2364	90 × 61 mm. No. 2363 × 2	20	30

1422 Building

1423 Man and Musicians

1999. World Heritage Sites (3rd series).

2365	**1422** 170w. multicoloured . .	20	10
2366	**1423** 340w. multicoloured . .	40	10
MS2367	144 × 96 mm. Nos. 2365/6	60	40

1424 Player

1426 Sunset, Altar and Tablet

1425 Emblem

1999. World Cup Football Championship, Japan and Korea (2002). Multicoloured.

2368	170w. Type **1424**	20	10
2369	170w. Players tackling . . .	20	10
2370	170w. Player receiving ball	20	10
2371	170w. Goalkeeper catching ball	20	10
MS2372	134 × 78 mm. Nos. 2368/71	80	50

Nos. 2368/71 were issued together, se-tenant, forming a composite design.

2000. Centenary of South Korea's Membership of Universal Postal Union.

2373	**1425** 170w. multicoloured . .	20	10

2000. New Millennium (3rd series). Multicoloured.

2374	170w. Type **1426**	20	10
2375	170w. Cave painting of wrestlers	20	10
2376	170w. Inscribed bronze disc and warrior	20	10
2377	170w. Silhouettes of archers and inscribed standing stone	20	10
2378	170w. Junk and warrior . .	20	10

1427 Pashi Steam Locomotive

1428 Teho Steam Locomotive

1429 Mika Steam Locomotive

1430 Hyouki Steam Locomotive

2000. Railways (1st series).

2379	**1427** 170w. black, violet and mauve	20	10
2380	**1428** 170w. black, violet and mauve	20	10
2381	**1429** 170w. black, violet and grey	20	10
2382	**1430** 170w. black, violet and bistre	20	10

See also Nos. 2477/80, 2585/8 and 2682/5.

2000. Protection of Wildlife and Plants (7th series). As T **1270**. Multicoloured.

2383	170w. *Lilium cernum*	20	10
2384	170w. *Sedirea japonica* . . .	20	10
2385	170w. *Hibiscus hamabo* . . .	20	10
2386	170w. *Cypripedium japonicum*	20	10
MS2387	136 × 133 mm. Nos. 2383/6	80	50

Nos. 2383/**MS**2387 are impregnated with scent of flowers.

1431 State Civil Service Examination and Text

2000. New Millennium (4th series). Multicoloured.

2388	170w. Type **1431**	20	10
2389	170w. Man carving wood blocks	20	10
2390	170w. Pieces of metal type	20	10
2391	170w. An-Hyang (scholar) and Korean script	20	10
2392	170w. Mun Ik-jom (scholar), spinning wheel and cotton plant	20	10

1432 Children playing and House (Kim Chin Sook)

1433 Globe and Satellite

2000. World Water Day. Winning Design in Children's Painting Competition.

2393 **1432** 170w. multicoloured . . 20 10

2000. 50th Anniv of World Meteorological Organization.

2394 **1433** 170w. multicoloured . . 20 10

1434 Hand holding Rose

2000. "Share Love" (good neighbour campaign).

2395 **1434** 170w. multicoloured . . 20 10

No. 2395 is impregnated with the scent of roses.

1435 "2000"

2000. "CYBER KOREA 21".

2396 **1435** 170w. multicoloured . . 20 10

1436 King Sejong and Korean Script

2000. New Millennium (5th series). Multicoloured.

2397	170w. Type **1436**	20	10
2398	170w. Lady Shin Saimdang (caligrapher poet and painter) and detail of "Ch'ochung-do" (painting)	20	10
2399	170w. Yi Hwang and Yi I (founders of Confucian Academy)	20	10
2400	170w. Admiral Yi Sun-shin and model of "turle" ship	20	10
2401	170w. Sandae-nori (mask-dance drama)	20	10

1437 Park Soo Dong

1438 Bae Gum Taek

2000. Cartoons (6th series).

2402	**1437** 170w. multicoloured	20	10
2403	**1438** 170w. multicoloured	20	10
MS2404	Two sheets, each 90 × 60 mm. (a) No. 2402; (b) No. 2403	40	25

1439 Seedling on Map of Korean Peninsula

2000. Pyongyang, Korean Summit.

2405 **1439** 170w. multicoloured . . 20 10

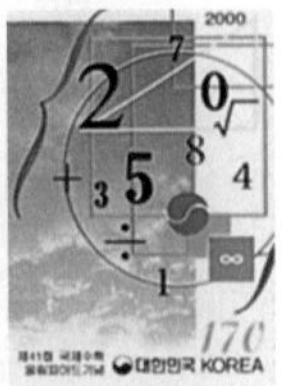

1440 Anatomical Diagram from *Tonui Pogam* (medical treatise by Huh Joan)

1441 Numbers and Mathematical Symbols

2000. Millennium (6th series). Multicoloured.

2406	170w. Type **1440**	20	10
2407	170w. "Dancer with Musicians" (illustration by Kim Hong Do)	20	10
2408	170w. "Plum Blossoms and Bird" (painting, Chong Yak Yong) and house in Kangjin where he served his exile	20	10
2409	170w. Map of Korea by Kim Chong Ho and wheel chart	20	10
2410	170w. Chon Bong Joan (revolutionary) and Tonghak Peasant Uprising monument	20	10

2000. International Mathematical Olympiad (high school mathematics competition).

2411 **1441** 170w. multicoloured . . 20 10

1442 *Yolha Diary* (Park Ji Won)

1443 *Fisherman's Calender*

1444 *The Nine-Cloud Dream*

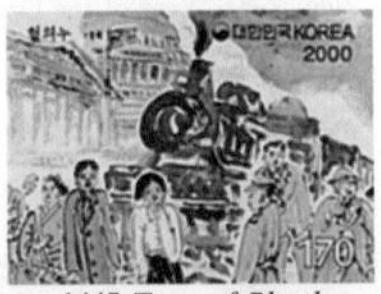

1445 *Tears of Blood*

1446 *From the Sea to a Child*

2000. Literature (6th series).

2412	**1442** 170w. multicoloured	20	10
2413	**1443** 170w. multicoloured	20	10
2414	**1444** 170w. multicoloured	20	10
2415	**1445** 170w. multicoloured	20	10
2416	**1446** 170w. multicoloured	20	10
MS2417	Five sheets. (a) 60 × 90 m. No. 2414; (b) 60 × 60 mm. No. 2413; (c) 90 × 60 mm. No. 2414; (d) 90 × 60 mm. No. 2415; (e) 90 × 60 mm. No. 2416	1·00	75

1447 Mountain

2000. Philately Week.

2418	**1447** 340w. multicoloured	40	10
MS2419	120 × 90 mm. No. 2418	40	25

1448 Porcelain

2000. Millennium (7th series). Multicoloured.

2420	170w. Type **1448**	20	10
2421	170w. "Bongjongsa" Temple (Paradise Pavilion)	20	10
2422	170w. Hahoe Tal masks	20	10
2423	170w. Royal Palace	20	10
2424	170w. Landscape painting	20	10
2425	170w. Water clock	20	10

1454 Taekwondo

2000. Olympic Games, Sydney.

2426 **1454** 170w. multicoloured . . 20 10

1455 Former Kyunngi High School Building, Hwadong

2000. Centenary of Public Secondary Schools.

2427 **1455** 170w. multicoloured . . 10 10

1456 "Returning to the Retirement House" (illustration from "Album of the Gathering of Old Statesmen")

2000. 3rd Asia-Europe Meeting, Seoul.

2428 **1456** 170w. multicoloured . . 10 10

1457 Emblem

2000. Icograde Millennium Congress, Seoul.

2429 **1457** 170w. black and yellow 10 10

1458 Mr. Gobau

2000. 50th Anniv of Mr. Gobau (cartoon character).

2430 **1458** 170w. multicoloured . . 10 10

1459 18th-Century Painting (Sin Yun Bok)

2000. Millennium (8th series). Multicoloured.

2431	170w. Type **1459**	10	10
2432	170w. Calligraphy by Kim Jeong Hui	10	10
2433	170w. Bongdon-Chiseong Hwaseong Fortress, Suwon	10	10
2434	170w. Myeongdong Cathedral	10	10
2435	170w. Wongaska theatre actors	10	10
2436	170w. The KITSat-satellite	10	10

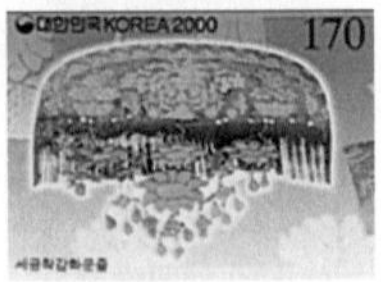

1460 Decorated Comb

2000. Korean Beauty (10th series). Multicoloured.

2437	170w. Type **1460**	10	10
2438	170w. Woman's ceremonial headdress	10	10
2439	170w. Butterfly-shaped hairpin	10	10
2440	170w. Hairpin with dragon decoration and jade hairpin with Chinese phoenix decoration	10	10

1461 Seoul World Cup Stadium

1462 Busan Sports Complex Main Stadium

1463 Daegu Sports Complex Stadium

1464 Incheon Munhak Stadium

1465 Gwangu World Cup Stadium

1466 Daejeon World Cup Stadium

1467 Ulsan Munsu Football Stadium

1468 Suwon World Cup Stadium

1469 Jeonju World Cup Stadium

1470 Jeju World Cup Stadium

2000. World Cup Football Championship (2002), South Korea and Japan.

2441 **1461** 170w. multicoloured . . 10 10
2442 **1462** 170w. multicoloured . . 10 10
2443 **1463** 170w. multicoloured . . 10 10
2444 **1464** 170w. multicoloured . . 10 10
2445 **1465** 170w. multicoloured . . 10 10
2446 **1466** 170w. multicoloured . . 10 10
2447 **1467** 170w. multicoloured . . 10 10
2448 **1468** 170w. multicoloured . . 10 10
2449 **1469** 170w. multicoloured . . 10 10
2450 **1470** 170w. multicoloured . . 10 10
MS2451 Five sheets each, 60 × 90 mm. (a) 170w. No. 2442; (b) 170w. Nos. 2443/4; (c) 170w. Nos. 2445/6; (d) 170w. Nos. 2447/8; (e) 170w. Nos. 2449/50 . . . . 1·00 75

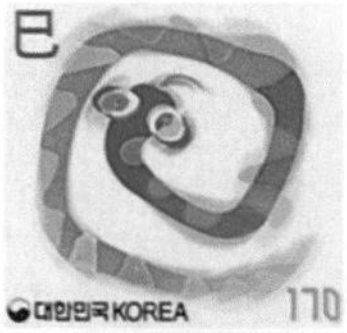

1471 Snake

2000. Lunar New Year "Year of the Snake". Ordinary or self-adhesive gum. (No. 2452).

2452 **1471** 170w. multicoloured . . 10 10
MS2453 170w. 107 × 69 mm. No. 2452 × 3 . . . . 30 20

1472 President Kim Dae Jung and Children

2000. Award of Nobel Peace Prize to President Kim Dae Jung.

2455 **1472** 170w. multicoloured . . 10 10
MS2456 118 × 70 mm. No. 2455 × 2 20 15

1473 Repository, Jeongjok Mountain and Taejo Sillok (script)

2000. World Heritage Sites (4th series). Multicoloured.

2457 340w. Type **1473** 35 10
2458 340w. King Sejong and script 35 10
MS2459 143 × 89 mm. Nos. 2457/8 70 55

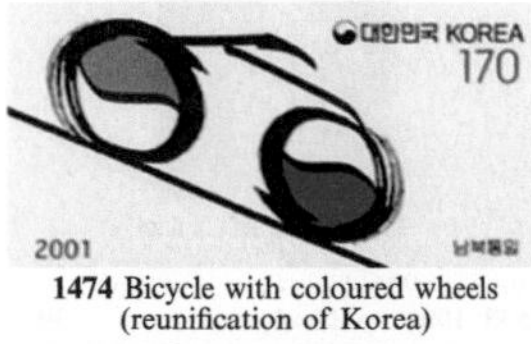

1474 Bicycle with coloured wheels (reunification of Korea)

2001. Millennium (9th series). Multicoloured.

2460 170w. Type **1474** 10 10
2461 170w. Rainbow (environmental protection) 10 10
2462 170w. Human D.N.A. and figure (eradication of incurable diseases) 10 10
2463 170w. Satellite and mobile telephone (communications technology) 10 10
2464 170w. Space (space travel) 10 10
2465 170w. Solar panels, solar-powered car and windmills (alternative energy sources) 10 10

1475 "Oksunn Peaks" (Kim Hong Do)

2001. Visit Korea Year 2001.

2466 **1475** 170w. multicoloured . . 10 10

1476 Plough

2001. Agricultural Implements. Multicoloured.

2467 170w. Type **1476** 10 10
2468 170w. Harrow 10 10
2469 170w. Sowing basket and namtae 10 10
2470 170w. Short-handled hoes 10 10
2471 170w. Manure barrel and fertilizer ash container . . 10 10
2472 170w. Water dipper 10 10
2473 170w. Winnower and thresher 10 10
2474 170w. Square straw drying mat and wicker tray . . . 10 10
2475 170w. Pestle, mortar and grinding stones 10 10
2476 170w. Rice basket and carrier 10 10

1486 2000 Series Diesel-electric Locomotive

1487 7000 Series Diesel-electric Locomotive

1488 Diesel Urban Commuter Train

1489 Diesel Saemaul Train

2001. Railways (2nd series).

2477 **1486** 170w. multicoloured . . 10 10
2478 **1487** 170w. multicoloured . . 10 10
2479 **1488** 170w. multicoloured . . 10 10
2480 **1489** 170w. multicoloured . . 10 10

2001. Protection of Wildlife and Plants (8th series). Vert designs as T **1270**. Multicoloured.

2481 170w. *Jeffersonia dubia* . . . 10 10
2482 170w. *Diapensia lapponica* 10 10
2483 170w. *Rhododendron aureum* 10 10
2484 170w. *Sedum orbiculatum* . . 10 10
MS2485 170w. 125 × 108 mm. Nos. 2481/4 . . . . 40 25

Nos. 2481/4 are impregnated with the scent of the Ume tree.

1490 Incheon Airport and Emblem

2001. Inauguration of Incheon Airport.

2486 **1490** 170w. multicoloured . . 10 10

1491 Kim Ku (leader of Independence Movement)

2001. Millennium (10th series). Multicoloured.

2487 170w. Type **1491** 10 10
2488 170w. Statue commemorating the March 1st Independence Movement 10 10
2489 170w. Interim Korean Government Headquarters, Shanghai and Members 10 10
2490 170w. Ahn Ik Tae (composer) and music score 10 10
2491 170w. Yun Dong Ju (poet) and *Seosi* (poem) 10 10

1492 Emblem

2001. International Olympic Fair, Seoul.

2492 **1492** 170w. multicoloured . . 10 10
MS2493 105 × 70 mm. No. 2492 × 2 15 15

1493 Bears hugging

2001. Greetings Stamps. Multicoloured.

2494 170w. Type **1493** 10 10
2495 170w. Flower 10 10
2496 170w. Trumpets (Congratulations) 10 10
2497 170w. Cake 10 10

1494 Iljimae (Ko Woo Young)

1495 Kkeobeongi (Kil Chang Duk)

2001. Cartoons (7th series).

2498 **1494** 170w. multicoloured . . 10 10
2499 **1495** 170w. multicoloured . . 10 10
MS2500 Two sheets, each 90 × 60 mm. (a) No. 2498. (b) No. 2499 Price for 2 sheets . . 15 15

1496 Players and Mountains (Switzerland, 1954)

2001. World Cup Football Championship, Japan and South Korea. Multicoloured.

2501 170w. Type **1496** 10 10
2502 170w. Players and Ancient settlement (Mexico, 1986) 10 10
2503 170w. Players and Coliseum (Italy, 1990) 10 10
2504 170w. Players and buildings (United States of America, 1994) 10 10
2505 170w. Players and Eiffel Tower (France, 1998) . . 10 10
MS2506 Five sheets, each 60 × 90 mm. (a) No. 2501 × 2. (b) No. 2502 × 2. (c) No. 2503 × 2. (d) No. 2504 × 2. (e) No. 2505 × 2 Set for 5 sheets 90 90

1497 Baechu Kimchi (Chinese Cabbage)

1498 Bossam Kimchi

1499 Dongchimi

1500 Klakdugi

2001. Korean Foods (1st series).

2507 **1497** 170w. multicoloured . . 10 10
2508 **1498** 170w. multicoloured . . 10 10
2509 **1499** 170w. multicoloured . . 10 10
2510 **1500** 170w. multicoloured . . 10 10

See also Nos. 2599/2602.

1501 Raising Flag (Liberation, 1945)

2001. Millennium (11th series). Multicoloured.

2511 170w. Type **1501** 10 10
2512 170w. Soldiers embracing (statue) (Korean War) . . 10 10
2513 170w. Seoul–Busan Expressway 10 10
2514 170w. Working in fields (Saemaul Undong movement) 10 10
2515 170w. Athletes forming emblem (Olympic Games, Seoul, 1988) 10 10

1502 Red Queen

1503 Pink Lady

2001. "Philakorea 2002" International Stamp Exhibition, Seoul. (1st issue). Roses.
2516 **1502** 170w. multicoloured . . 10 10
2517 **1503** 170w. multicoloured . . 10 10
MS2518 Two sheets, each 115 × 73 mm. (a) No. 2516 × 2. (b) No. 2517 × 2 Set for 2 sheets 35 35
See also Nos. 2604/**MS**2606 and 2639/**MS**2640.

1504 Roses in Heart

2001. Philately Week.
2519 **1504** 170w. multicoloured . . 30 10
MS2520 108 × 69 mm. No. 2519 × 2 60 60

1505 Goryeo Dynasty Porcelain Vase and Exhibition Emblem

2001. World Ceramics Expo, Icheon, Yeoju, and Gwangju.
2521 **1505** 170w. multicoloured . . 30 10

1506 Conference Emblem

2001. International Statistical Institute (ISI) Conference, Seoul.
2522 **1506** 170w. multicoloured . . 30 10

1507 Joseon Coin and Stamping Machine

2001. 50th Anniv of Korea Minting and Security Printing Corporation (KOMSEP).
2523 **1507** 170w. multicoloured . . 30 10

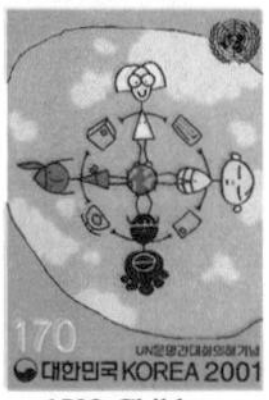

1508 Multicoloured Ball (Oullim Globe) **1509** Children encircling Globe

2001. International Council of Societies of Industrial Design (ICSID) Conference, Seoul.
2524 **1508** 170w. multicoloured . . 30 10

2001. United Nations Year of Dialogue among Civilizations.
2525 **1509** 170w. multicoloured . . 30 10

1510 Conference Emblem

2001. International Organization of Supreme Audit Institutions (INTOSAI) Conference, Seoul.
2526 **1510** 170w. ultramarine and vermilion 30 10

1511 *Dendrobium moniliforme* **1512** Snowflakes and Horse

2001. Orchids (1st series). Multicoloured.
2527 170w. Type **1511** 30 10
2528 170w. *Gymnadenia camtschatica* 30 10
2529 170w. *Habenaria radiate* . . 30 10
2530 170w. *Orchis cyclochila* . . . 20 10
Nos. 2527/30 are impregnated with the scent of orchid. See also Nos. 2670/3.

2001. New Year. Year of the Horse.
2531 **1512** 170w. multicoloured . . 30 10
MS2532 90 × 60 mm. No. 2531 × 2 60 60

1513 Seonjeongjeon Conference Hall, Changdeok Palace

2001. World Heritage Sites (5th series). Multicoloured.
2533 170w. Type **1513** 30 10
2534 340w. Injeongjeon coronation hall, Changdeok Palace (52 × 36 mm) 60 60
MS2535 144 × 96 mm. Nos. 2533/4

1514 *Limenitis populi*

2002. Fauna.
2536 60w. *Eophona migratoria* . . 10 10
2546 160w. Type **1514** 25 10
2547 210w. *Falco tinnunculus* . . 30 10
2548 280w. *Ficedula zanthopygia* 35 10

1515 Airplane, Locomotive and Lorry

2002. Transport.
2550 **1515** 280w. multicoloured 35 10
2551 310w. multicoloured 45 10
2551a 420w. multicoloured 50 10
2552 1380w. multicoloured 2·00 1·20
2553 1410w. multicoloured 2·10 1·20
2554 1580w. multicoloured 2·40 1·30
2555 1610w. multicoloured 2·40 1·30

1516 Kylin Roof Tile

2002. Roof Tiles. Multicoloured.
2565 1290w. Type **1516** . . . . . 2·00 1·20
2566 1310w. Ridge-end tile . . . 2·25 1·20
2567 1490w. As No. 2566 background colour altered 2·40 1·30
2568 1510w. As No. 2565 background colour altered 2·40 1·30

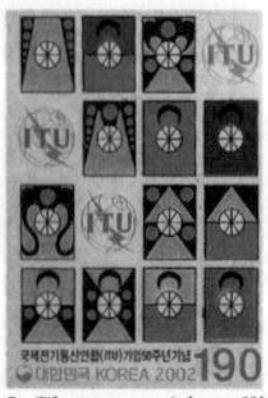

1518 Chungmu (signalling) Kites

2002. 50th Anniv of Membership of International Telecommunications Union.
2584 **1518** 190w. multicoloured . . 30 10

1519 EL8000 Electric Locomotive

1520 EL8100 Electric Locomotive

1521 Express Rail Car

1522 Express Electric Rail Car

2002. Railways (3rd series).
2585 **1519** 190w. multicoloured . . 30 10
2586 **1520** 190w. multicoloured . . 30 10
2587 **1521** 190w. multicoloured . . 30 10
2588 **1522** 190w. multicoloured . . 30 10

1523 Safflower (*Carthamus tinctorius*)

2002. Traditional Dye Plants. Multicoloured.
2589 190w. Type **1523** 30 10
2590 190w. *Lithospermum erythrorhizon* 30 10
2591 190w. Ash tree (*Fraxinus rhynchophylla*) 30 10
2592 190w. Indigo plant (*Persicaria tinctoria*) . . . 30 10

1524 Flowers

2002. International Flower Exhibition, Anmyeondo.
2593 **1524** 190w. multicoloured . . 30 10

1525 "Mengkkong-i-Seodang Village School" (Yoon Seung-woon)

1526 "Wogdoggle Dugdoggle" (Hwang Mi-na)

2002. Cartoons (8th series).
2594 **1525** 190w. multicoloured . . 30 10
2595 **1526** 190w. multicoloured . . 30 10
MS2596 Two sheets, each 90 × 60 mm. (a) No. 2594; (b) No. 2595. Set of 2 sheets . . . 60 60

1527 Campervan, Caravan and Tent

2002. 64th International Camping and Caravanning Rally.
2597 **1527** 190w. multicoloured . . 30 10

1528 Footballer (Europe)

2002. World Cup Football Championships, Japan and South Korea. Five sheets, each 60 × 90 mm containing T **1528** and similar circular designs. Multicoloured.
MS2598 (a) 190w. × 2, Type **1528** × 2; (b) 190w. × 2, Central & North America × 2; (c) 190w. × 2, Asia × 2; (d) 190w. × 2, South America × 2; (e) 190w. × 2, Africa × 2 . . . . 4·25 4·25

1529 Jeolpyeon

1530 Sirutteok

1531 Injeolmi

1532 Songpyeon

2002. Korean Foods (2nd series).
2599 **1529** 190w. multicoloured . . 30 10
2600 **1530** 190w. multicoloured . . 30 10
2601 **1531** 190w. multicoloured . . 30 10
2602 **1532** 190w. multicoloured . . 30 10

1533 Woman's Face

2002. Women's Week.
2603 **1533** 190w. multicoloured . . 30 10

1534 Child holding Flags

2002. Philakorea 2002 International Stamp Exhibition, Seoul (2nd issue). Multicoloured.

2604	190w. Type **1534**	30	10
2605	190w. Children and globe	30	10
MS2606	Two sheets, each 115 × 73 mm. (a) No. 2604 × 2; (b) No. 2605. Set of 2 sheets . . .	60	60

1535 Heung-injimun Fortress, Seoul

2002. Hometowns. Multicoloured.

2607	190w. Type **1535**	30	10
2608	190w. Two masked dancers, Seou	30	10
2609	190w. Basalt cliffs, Incheon	30	10
2610	190w. Dancers wearing white, Chamseongdan altar, Incheon	30	10
2611	190w. Freedom House, Paju, Gyeonggi	30	10
2612	190w. Yangjubyeol Sandaenori dancers one with raised arm, Gyeonggi	30	10
2613	190w. Ulsanbawi rock, Mt. Seoraksan, Gangwon . .	30	10
2614	190w. Two dancers one holding fan, Gangwon . .	30	10
2615	190w. Sail boat, Chungnam	30	10
2616	190w. Weaver, Chungnam	30	10
2617	190w. Tower, Expo Science Park, Daejeon	30	10
2618	190w. Scientist, Daedeok Science Town, Daejeon	30	10
2619	190w. Mt. Mai peaks, Jeonbuk	30	10
2620	190w. Iri folk band drummers, Jeonbuk . . .	30	10
2621	190w. Odong island, Jeonnam	30	10
2622	190w. Ganggang Sullae circle dance, Jeonnam . .	30	10
2623	190w. May 18th monument, Gwangju	30	10
2624	190w. Gossaum Nori tug of war, Gwangju	30	10
2625	190w. Beopju temple, Mt. Songni, Chungbuk . . .	30	10
2626	190w. Taekgyeon martial art, Chungbuk	30	10
2627	190w. Gwangbong Seokjoyeorae statue, Daegu	30	10
2628	190w. Dalseong forest, Daegu	30	10
2629	190w. Taejeondae cliffs, Busan	30	10
2630	190w. Three Dongnaeyaryu festival dancers, Busan . .	30	10
2631	190w. Dokdo islands, Gyeongbuk	30	10
2632	190w. Andongchajeon Nori log tying game, Gyeongbuk	30	10
2633	190w. Haegeumgang island, Gyeongnam	30	10
2634	190w. Goseong Ogwangdae clown dance, Gyeongnam	30	10
2635	190w. Cheonjeonnigakseok rock wall, Ulsan	30	10
2636	190w. Three Cheoyongmu masked dancers, Ulsan . .	30	10
2637	190w. Mt. Halla and Baeknokdam crater, Jeju	30	10
2638	190w. House, Jeju	30	10

1536 Exhibition Emblem and Talchum Masked Dancer

2002. Philakorea 2002 International Stamp Exhibition, Seoul (3rd issue).

2639	**1536** 190w. multicoloured . .	30	10
MS2640	90 × 60 mm. No.2639 × 2. Imperf	60	60

1537 Children and Dog

2002. Philately Week.

2641	**1537** 190w. multicoloured . .	30	10
MS2642	108 × 69 mm. Nos. 2641 × 2	60	60

1538 Guus Hiddink (coach)

2002. South Korea—Semi-Finalists, World Cup Football Championships, Japan and South Korea. Showing team members. Multicoloured.

2643	190w. Type **1538**	30	10
2644	190w. No.1 player	30	10
2645	190w. No.2	30	10
2646	190w. No.3	30	10
2647	190w. No.4	30	10
2648	190w. No.5	30	10
2649	190w. No.60	30	10
2650	190w. No.7	30	10
2651	190w. No.8	30	10
2652	190w. No.9	30	10
2653	190w. No.10	30	10
2654	190w. No.11	30	10
2655	190w. Goalkeeper	30	10
2656	190w. No.13	30	10
2657	190w. No.14	30	10
2658	190w. No.15	30	10
2659	190w. No.16	30	10
2660	190w. No.17	30	10
2661	190w. No.18	30	10
2662	190w. No.19	30	10
2663	190w. No.20	30	10
2664	190w. No.21	30	10
2665	190w. No.22	30	10
2666	190w. Goalkeeper (different)	30	10

1539 Stadium, Runner, Tower, Seagull and Diver

2002. 14th Asian Games, Busan.

2667	**1539** 190w. multicoloured . .	30	10
MS2668	120 × 70 mm. No. 2667 × 2	60	60

1540 Stylized Torch 1541 *Cymbidium kanran*

2002. 8th Far East and South Pacific Games for the Disabled (FESPIC), Busan.

2669	**1540** 190w. multicoloured . .	30	10

2002. Orchids (2nd series). Multicoloured.

2670	190w. Type **1541**	30	10
2671	190w. *Gastrodia elata* . . .	30	10
2672	190w. *Pogonia japonica* . .	30	10
2673	190w. *Cephalanthera falcate*	30	10

Each stamp impregnated with the scent of orchid.

1542 Taekwondo

2002. 10th Anniv of South Korea—China Diplomatic Relations. Martial Arts. Multicoloured.

2674	190w. Type **1542**	30	10
2675	190w. Wushu	30	10

1543 Sheep 1545 Dabo Pagoda, Bulguk Temple, Gyeongju

1544 Gongsimdon Observatory Tower

2002. New Year. "Year of the Sheep".

2676	**1543** 190w. multicoloured . .	30	10
MS2677	90 × 60 mm. No. 2676 × 2	60	60

2002. Hwaseong Fortress—UNESCO World Heritage Site. Sheet 145 × 232 mm containing T **1544** and similar horiz design. Multicoloured.

MS2678	190w. × 5 Type **1544**; 280w. Banghwasuryu Pavilion (52 × 36 mm)	1·90	1·90

2002. 10th Anniv of South Korea—Vietnam Diplomatic Relations. Multicoloured.

2679	190w. Type **1545**	30	10
2680	190w. One Pillar Pagoda, Hanoi	30	10

1546 American and Korean Flags Combined

2003. Centenary of Korean Emigration to United States of America.

2681	**1546** 190w. multicoloured . .	30	10

1547 Gondola Freight Car

1548 Box Car

1549 Tanker

1550 Hopper

2003. Railways (4th series).

2682	**1547** 190w. multicoloured . .	30	10
2683	**1548** 190w. multicoloured . .	30	10
2684	**1549** 190w. multicoloured . .	30	10
2685	**1550** 190w. multicoloured . .	30	10

1551 *Rubia akane* 1553 Flag

1552 Roh Moo Hyun

2003. Traditional Dye Plants (2nd series). Multicoloured.

2686	190w. Type **1551**	30	10
2687	190w. *Rhus javanica*	30	10
2688	190w. *Sophora japonica* . .	30	10
2689	190w. *Isatis tinctoria*	30	10

2003. Inauguration of President Roh Moo Hyun. Sheet 115 × 70 mm.

MS2690	**1552** 190w. multicoloured	30	30

2003.

2691	**1553** 10w. multicoloured . .	10	10

1554 Unhye (embroidered shoes) 1555 Tortoise-shaped Celadon Jug

2003. Traditional Culture (1st issue). Each chocolate, brown and indigo.

2692	190w. Type **1554**	30	10
2693	190w. Mokhwa (ankle boots)	30	10
2694	190w. Jipsin (straw shoes)	30	10
2695	190w. Namaksin (wooden clogs)	30	10

See also Nos. 2700/3, 2712/15 and 2720/3.

2003.

2696	**1555** 400w. multicoloured . .	60	35

1556 "Goblin's Cap" (Shin Moon Soo) 1557 "Sword of Fire" (Kim Hye Rin)

2003. Cartoons (9th series).

2697	**1556** 190w. multicoloured . .	30	10
2698	**1557** 190w. multicoloured . .	30	10
MS2699	Two sheets, each 90 × 60 mm. (a) No. 2697; (b) No. 2698 Set of 2 sheets . . .	60	60

2003. Traditional Culture (2nd issue). As T **1554**. Each black and brown.

2700	190w. Eoyeon (royal sedan chair)	30	10
2701	190w. Choheon (single-wheeled sedan chair) . . .	30	10
2702	190w. Saingyo (wedding sedan chair)	30	10
2703	190w. Namyeo (small open sedan chair)	30	10

Nos. 2700/3 were issued in horizontal se-tenant strips of four stamps within the sheet.

1558 Palmido Lighthouse

2003. Centenary of Lighthouse Building.

2704	**1558** 190w. multicoloured . .	30	10

1559 Yugwa

1560 Yeot Gangjeong

1561 Yakgwa

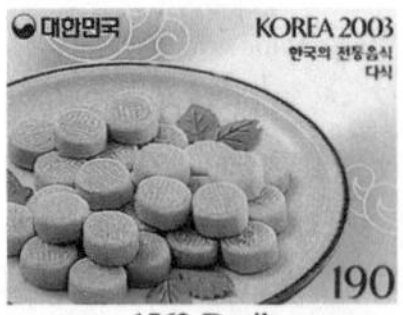
1562 Dasik

2003. Korean Foods (3rd series).
2705 **1559** 190w. multicoloured . . 30 10
2706 **1560** 190w. multicoloured . . 30 10
2707 **1561** 190w. multicoloured . . 30 10
2708 **1562** 190w. multicoloured . . 30 10

1563 *Malus asiatica*

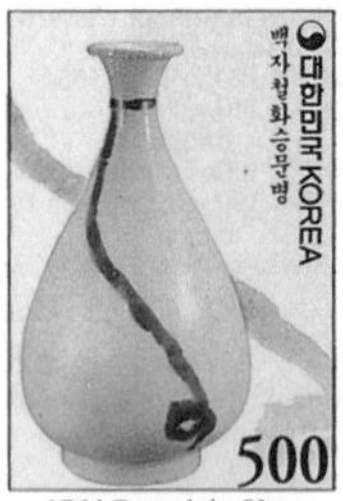
1564 Porcelain Vase

2003. Fruit and Flower. Multicoloured. Self-adhesive.
2709 190w. Type **1563** 30 10
2710 190w. *Aquilegia flabellate* (horiz) 30 10

2003.
2711 **1564** 500w. multicoloured . . 70 40

2003. Traditional Culture (3rd issue). As T **1554**. Each agate and chocolate.
2712 190w. Jojokdeung lantern 30 10
2713 190w. Deungjan (lamp-oil container) 30 10
2714 190w. Juchilmokje yukgakjedeung (hexagonal portable lantern) 30 10
2715 190w. Chot-dae (brass candlestick) 30 10

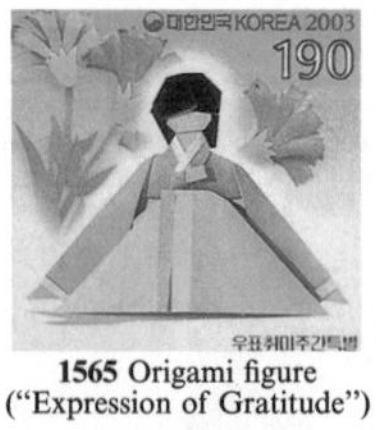
1565 Origami figure ("Expression of Gratitude")

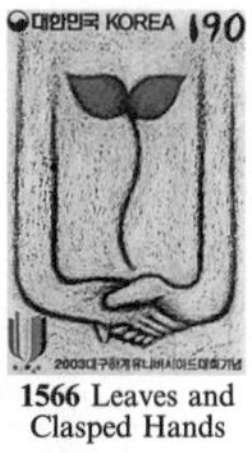
1566 Leaves and Clasped Hands

2003. Philately Week.
2716 **1565** 190w. multicoloured . . 30 10
MS2717 109 × 69 mm. Nos. 2716 × 2 Imperf 60 60

2003. Summer Universiade (games), Daegu.
2718 **1566** 190w. multicoloured . . 30 10
MS2719 91 × 60 mm. Nos. 2718 × 2 60 60

2003. Traditional Culture (4th issue). As T **1554**. Each indigo and claret.
2720 190w. Gujok-ban (table with decorated top) 30 10
2721 190w. Punghyeol-ban (tray table) 30 10
2722 190w. Ilju-ban (single stemmed table) 30 10
2723 190w. Haeju-ban (straight-sided table) 30 10

1567 Faces

1568 Stylised Teacher and Pupil

2003. Centenary of Korean YMCA (Young Men's Christian Association) Movement.
2724 **1567** 190w. multicoloured . . 30 10

2003. Centenary of Soong Eui Girl's School.
2725 **1568** 190w. multicoloured . . 30 10

1569 Hearts as TB Symbol

1570 *Cremastra appendiculata*

2003. 50th Anniv of National Tuberculosis Association.
2726 **1569** 190w. vermilion, ultramarine and grey 30 10

2003. Orchids (3rd series). Multicoloured.
2727 190w. Type **1570** 30 10
2728 190w. *Cymbidium lancifolium* 30 10
2729 190w. *Orchis graminifolia* . . 30 10
2730 190w. *Bulbophyllum drymoglossum* 30 10
Each stamp is impregnated with the scent of orchid.

1571 Monkey

1573 Cheomseongdae, Gyeongju

1572 Dolmen, Ganghwa

2003. New Year. "Year of the Monkey".
2731 **1571** 190w. multicoloured . . 30 10
MS2732 90 × 60 mm. No. 2731 × 2 60 60

2002. Ganghwa, Hwasoon and Gochang—UNESCO World Heritage Sites. Sheet 145 × 232 mm containing T **1572** and similar horiz design. Multicoloured.
MS2733 190w. × 5 Type **1572**; 280w. Dolmen (52 × 36 mm) . . . . 1·90 1·90

2003. 30th Anniv of South Korea—India Diplomatic Relations. Observatories. Multicoloured.
2734 190w. Type **1573** 30 10
2735 190w. Jantar Mantar, Jaipur 30 10

C. NORTH KOREAN OCCUPATION.

(**1** "Democratic People's Republic of Korea")

1950. Nos. 116 and 118/19 optd with Type **1**.
1 10w. green . . . . 45·00
2 20w. brown . . . . 12·50
3 30w. green . . . . 15·00

NORTH KOREA

100 cheun = 1 won.

GUM. All stamps of North Korea up to No. N1506 are without gum, except where otherwise stated.

A. RUSSIAN OCCUPATION

1 Hibiscus

2 Diamond Mountains

1946. Perf, roul or imperf.
N1 **1** 20ch. red . . . . 55·00 38·00
N2 **2** 50ch. green . . . . 17·00 15·00
N4b 50ch. red . . . . 10·00 10·00
N5b 50ch. violet . . . . 10·00 12·00

4 Gen. Kim Il Sung and Flag

5 Peasants

1946. 1st Anniv of Liberation from Japan.
N6 **4** 50ch. brown £190 £190

1947. Perf, roul or imperf.
N 7 **5** 1wn. green . . . . 5·00 4·00
N 8 1wn. violet . . . . 15·00 10·00
N 9 1wn. blue on buff . . . . 5·50 4·50
N10 1wn. blue . . . . 3·25 2·50

6

7

1948. 2nd Anniv of Labour Law.
N11 **6** 50ch. blue £225 £180

1948. 3rd Anniv of Liberation from Japan.
N12 **7** 50ch. red . . . . — £325

8

1948. Promulgation of Constitution.
N13 **8** 50ch. blue and red . . . . £160 40·00

B. KOREAN PEOPLE'S DEMOCRATIC REPUBLIC

9 North Korean Flag

10

1948. Establishment of People's Republic. Roul.
N16 **9** 25ch. violet . . . . 3·50 3·50
N17 50ch. blue . . . . 6·00 6·00

1949. Roul or perf.
N18 **10** 6wn. red and blue . . . . 2·00 2·00

11 Kim Il Sung University, Pyongyang

12 North Korean Flags

11a Kim Il Sung University, Pyongyang

1949. Roul.
N19 **11** 1wn. violet . . . . . . 45·00 20·00
N20 **11a** 1wn. blue . . . . 45·00 20·00

1949. 4th Anniv of Liberation from Japan. Roul or perf.
N22 **12** 1wn. red, green and blue 35·00 14·00

13 Order of the National Flag

14 Liberation Monument, Pyongyang

15 Soldier and Flags

16 Peasant and Worker

17 Tractor

18 Capitol, Seoul

1950. Perf, roul or imperf. Various sizes.
N24 **13** 1wn. green (A) . . . . . 4·00 1·00
N25 1wn. orange (A) . . . . . — 25·00
N26 1wn. orange (B) . . . . . 17·00 12·00
N27 1wn. green (C) . . . . . 4·00 1·25
N28 1wn. olive (D) . . . . . 7·00 4·50
SIZES: (A) 23½ × 37½ mm. (B) 20 × 32½ mm. (C) 22 × 35½ mm. (D) 22½ × 36½ mm.

1950. 5th Anniv of Liberation from Japan. Roul, perf or imperf. Various sizes.
N29 **14** 1wn. red, indigo and blue 1·25 90
N30 1wn. orange . . . . . . 7·00 5·00
N31 **15** 2wn. black, blue and red 1·25 90
N32 **16** 6wn. green (A) . . . . . 1·75 1·25
N36 6wn. red (B) . . . . . . 12·50 11·00
N33 **17** 10wn. brown (C) . . . . 2·50 2·00
N37 10wn. brown (D) . . . . 18·00 13·50
SIZES: (A) 20 × 30 mm. (B) 22 × 33 mm. (C) 20 × 28 mm. (D) 22 × 30 mm.

1950. Capture of Seoul by North Korean Forces. Roul.
N38 **18** 1wn. red, blue and green 40·00 32·00

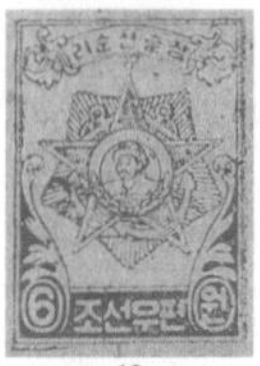
19

20 Kim Gi Ok and Aeroplane

1951. Order of Admiral Li Sun Sin. Imperf or perf.
N39 **19** 6wn. orange . . . . . . 6·50 5·00

1951. Air Force Hero Kim Gi Ok. Imperf.
N40 **20** 1wn. blue . . . . 8·00 3·00

21 Russian and North Korean Flags

22 Kim Ki U (hero)

23 N. Korean and Chinese Soldiers

1951. 6th Anniv of Liberation from Japan. Roul or perf.
N41 **21** 1wn. blue . . . . 3·50 2·50
N42 1wn. red . . . . 3·50 2·50
N43 **22** 1wn. blue . . . . 3·50 2·50
N44 1wn. red . . . . 3·75 2·50
N45 **23** 2wn. blue . . . . 6·50 5·00
N46 2wn. red . . . . 10·00 7·50
All values exist on buff and on white paper.

24 Order of Soldier's Honour — 25 — 26 Woman Partisan, Li Su Dok

1951. Imperf or perf.
N47 **24** 40wn. red . . . . 9·00 4·50

1951. Co-operation of Chinese People's Volunteers. Imperf or perf.
N49 **25** 10wn. blue . . . . 5·00 3·25

1952. Partisan Heroes. Imperf or perf.
N50 **26** 70wn. brown . . . . . . 4·00 1·00

27 — 28 Gen. P'eng Teh-huai — 29 Munition Worker

1952. Peace Propaganda. Imperf or perf.
N51 **27** 20wn. blue, green and red 6·00 2·00

1952. Honouring Commander of Chinese People's Volunteers. Imperf.
N52 **28** 10wn. purple . . . . . . 8·00 4·00

1952. Labour Day. Imperf or perf.
N53 **29** 10wn. red . . . . 17·00 17·00

30 — 31 — 32

1952. 6th Anniv of Labour Law. Imperf or perf.
N54a **30** 10wn. blue . . . . . . 11·00 11·00

1952. Anti-U.S. Imperialism Day. Imperf or perf.
N55 **31** 10wn. red . . . . 13·00 13·00

1952. North Korean and Chinese Friendship. Imperf or perf.
N56b **32** 20wn. deep blue . . . . 9·00 9·00

33 — 34

1952. 7th Anniv of Liberation from Japan. Imperf or perf.
N57 **33** 10wn. red . . . . 10·00 10·00
N58 **34** 10wn. red . . . . 12·00 12·00

35

1952. Int Youth Day. With gum. Imperf or perf.
N59 **35** 10wn. green . . . . . . 8·00 8·00

36 — 37

1953. 5th Anniv of People's Army. Imperf or perf.
N60 **36** 10wn. red . . . . 12·50 12·50
N61 **37** 40wn. purple . . . . . . 12·50 12·50

38 — 39

1953. Int Women's Day. With gum. Imperf or perf.
N62 **38** 10wn. red . . . . 10·00 8·00
N63 **39** 40wn. green . . . . . . 10·00 8·00

40 — 41

1953. Labour Day. Imperf or perf.
N64 **40** 10wn. green . . . . . . 7·50 7·50
N65 **41** 40wn. orange . . . . . . 7·50 7·50

42 — 43

1953. Anti-U.S. Imperialism Day. With gum. Imperf or perf.
N66 **42** 10wn. turquoise . . . . . 15·00 13·00
N67 **43** 40wn. red . . . . 15·00 13·00

44 — 45

1953. 4th World Youth Festival, Bucharest. With gum. Imperf or perf.
N68 **44** 10wn. blue and green . . 4·00 3·25
N69 **45** 20wn. green and pink . . 4·00 3·25

46 — 47

1953. Armistice and Victory Issue. With gum. Imperf or perf.
N70a **46** 10wn. brown and yellow 38·00 32·00

1953. 8th Anniv of Liberation from Japan. Imperf.
N71 **47** 10wn. red . . . . £120 90·00

48 — 49 Liberation Monument, Pyongyang

1953. 5th Anniv of People's Republic. Imperf or perf.
N72 **48** 10wn. blue and red . . . 11·00 11·00

1953. With gum. Imperf or perf.
N73 **49** 10wn. slate . . . . 3·75 3·50

(50) — (51)

1954. No. N18 optd "Fee Collected" in Korean characters, T **50**.
N74 **10** 6wn. red and blue £150 £150

1954. Nos. N18 and N39 surch with T **51**.
N75 **10** 5wn. on 6wn. red and blue 12·00 12·00
N76 **19** 5wn. on 6wn. orange . . . 55·00 45·00

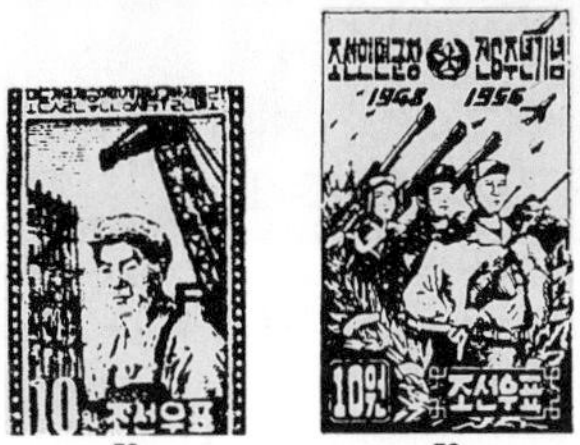

52 — 53

1954. Post-war Economic Reconstruction. With gum. Imperf or perf.
N77 **52** 10wn. blue . . . . 15·00 9·00

1954. 6th Anniv of People's Army. With gum. Imperf or perf.
N78 **53** 10wn. red . . . . 13·00 10·00

54 — 55

1954. Int Women's Day. With gum. Imperf or perf.
N79 **54** 10wn. red . . . . 5·50 5·50

1954. Labour Day. With gum. Imperf or perf.
N80 **55** 10wn. red . . . . 6·00 6·00

56 — 57 Taedong Gate, Pyongyang

1954. Anti-U.S. Imperialism Day. With gum. Imperf or perf.
N81 **56** 10wn. red . . . . 17·00 15·00

1954. Imperf or perf.
N82 **57** 5wn. lake . . . . 2·00 75
N83 5wn. brown . . . . 2·00 75

58 — 59 Soldier

1954. National Young Activists' Conference With gum. Imperf or perf.
N84 **58** 10wn. red, blue and slate 3·00 3·00

1954. 9th Anniv of Liberation from Japan. With gum. Imperf or perf.
N85 **59** 10wn. red . . . . 6·00 6·00

60 North Korean Flag — 61 Hwanghae Iron Works

62 Hwanghae Iron Works and Workers

1954. 6th Anniv of People's Republic. With gum. Imperf or perf.
N86 **60** 10wn. blue and red . . . 5·00 5·00

1954. Economic Reconstruction. Imperf or perf.
N87 **61** 10wn. blue . . . . 4·50 50
N88 **62** 10wn. brown . . . . . . 4·50 50

63 — 64

1955. 7th Anniv of People's Army. With gum. Imperf or perf.
N89 **63** 10wn. red . . . . 4·50 3·50

1955. Int Women's Day. With gum. Imperf or perf.
N90 **64** 10wn. deep blue . . . . . 5·00 3·50

65 — 66

1955. Labour Day. With gum. Imperf or perf.
N91 **65** 10wn. green . . . . . . 3·25 3·25
N92 **66** 10wn. red . . . . 3·25 3·25

67 Admiral Li Sun Sin — 68

1955. Imperf or perf.
N93 **67** 1wn. blue on green . . . 1·25 20
N94 2wn. red on buff . . . . 1·75 25
N95 2wn. red . . . . 3·00 50

1955. 9th Anniv of Labour Law. With gum. Imperf or perf.
N96 **68** 10wn. red . . . . 3·50 2·50

69 Liberation Monument and Flags

1955. 10th Anniv of Liberation from Japan. Imperf or perf.
N97 **69** 10wn. green . . . . . . 2·00 1·50
N98 10wn. red, blue and brown (29½ × 42½ mm) . . . . 1·25 1·00

70 — 71

1955. Soviet Union Friendship Month. Imperf or perf.
N 99 **70** 10wn. red . . . . 1·50 1·00
N100 10wn. red and blue . . . 2·25 1·50
N101 **71** 20wn. red and slate . . . 3·25 2·50
N102 20wn. red and blue . . . 1·50 1·25
SIZES: No. N99, 22 × 32½ mm; N100, 29½ × 43 mm; N101, 18½ × 32 mm; N102, 25 × 43 mm.

72 Son Rock — 73

1956. Haegumgang Maritime Park. Imperf or perf.
N103 **72** 10wn. blue on blue . . . 3·00 1·75

1956. 8th Anniv of People's Army. Imperf or perf.
N104 **73** 10wn. red on green . . . 5·50 5·50

74

1956. Labour Day. Imperf or perf.
N105 **74** 10wn. blue . . . . . . 4·50 2·75

75 Machinist — 76 Taedong Gate, Pyongyang

77 Woman Harvester — 78 Moranbong Theatre, Pyongyang

1956. Imperf or perf.
N106 **75** 1wn. brown . . . . . . 1·25 60
N107 **76** 2wn. blue 90 60
N108 **77** 10wn. red 90 60
N109 **78** 40wn. green . . . . . . 8·00 3·50

79 Miner — 80 Boy Bugler and Girl Drummer

1956. 10th Anniv of Labour Law. Imperf or perf.
N110 **79** 10wn. brown . . . . . . 2·50 1·00

1956. 10th Anniv of Children's Union. Imperf or perf.
N111 **80** 10wn. brown . . . . . . 4·00 2·75

81 Workers — 82 Industrial Plant

1956. 10th Anniv of Sex Equality Law. Imperf or perf.
N112 **81** 10wn. brown . . . . . . 2·00 1·40

1956. 10th Anniv of Nationalization of Industry. Imperf or perf.
N113 **82** 10wn. brown . . . . . . 45·00 16·00

83 Liberation Tower — 84 Kim Il Sung University

1956. 11th Anniv of Liberation from Japan. Imperf or perf.
N114 **83** 10wn. red . . . . 3·00 1·25

1956. 10th Anniv of Kim Il Sung University. Imperf or perf.
N115 **84** 10wn. brown . . . . . . 2·50 1·75

85 Boy and Girl — 86 Pak Ji Won

1956. 4th Democratic Youth League Congress. Imperf or perf.
N116 **85** 10wn. brown . . . . . . 2·50 1·50

1957. 220th Birth Anniv of Pak Ji Won "Yonam", (statesman). Imperf or perf.
N117 **86** 10wn. blue . . . . . . 1·50 90

87 Tabo Pagoda, Pulguksa — 88 Ulmil Pavilion, Pyongyang — 89 Furnaceman

1957. Imperf, perf or roul.
N118 **87** 5wn. blue . . . . 1·00 75
N119 **88** 40wn. green . . . . . . 2·00 1·25

1957. Production and Economy Campaign. With or without gum. Imperf or perf.
N121 **89** 10wn. blue . . . . . . 2·50 1·25

90 Furnaceman — 91 Voters and Polling Booth

1957. 2nd General Election. Imperf or perf.
N122 **90** 1wn. orange 75 30
N123 2wn. brown 75 30
N124 **91** 10wn. red . . . . 3·75 1·25

92 Ryongwangjong, Pyongyang — 93 Lenin and Flags

94 Kim Il Sung at Pochonbo — 95 Lenin — 96 Pouring Steel

1957. 1530th Anniv of Pyongyang. Imperf or perf.
N125 **92** 10wn. green . . . . . . 1·00 25

1957. 40th Anniv of Russian Revolution. Imperf or perf.
N126 **93** 10wn. green 75 40
N127 **94** 10wn. red 75 40
N128 **95** 10wn. blue 75 40
N129 **96** 10wn. orange . . . . . 2·00 40
No. N126 exists with gum.

97 Congress Emblem — 98 Liberation Monument, Spassky Tower and Flags

1957. 4th World Trade Unions Federation Congress. Leipzig. Imperf (with or without gum) or perf.
N130 **97** 10wn. blue and green . . 1·25 50

1957. Russian Friendship Month. Imperf or perf.
N131 **98** 10wn. green . . . . . . 1·75 50

99 Weighing a Baby — 100 Bandaging a Hand

1957. Red Cross. Imperf, perf or roul.
N132 **99** 1wn. red . . . . 6·00 1·00
N133 2wn. red . . . . 6·00 1·00
N134 **100** 10wn. red . . . . . . 15·00 2·75
No. N133 exists with or without gum.

101 Koryo Celadon Jug (12th century) — 102 Koryo Incense-burner (12th century)

1958. Korean Antiquities. Imperf (with or without gum) or perf.
N135 **101** 10wn. blue . . . . . . 4·50 75
N136 **102** 10wn. green . . . . . 4·50 75

103 Woljong Temple Pagoda — 104 Soldier

1958. With gum (5wn.), without gum (10wn.). Imperf or perf.
N137 **103** 5wn. green . . . . . . 1·00 50
N138 10wn. blue . . . . . . 1·50 75

1958. 10th Anniv of People's Army. No gum (No. N139) with or without gum (No. N140). Imperf or perf.
N139 **104** 10wn. blue . . . . . . 1·75 50
N140 – 10wn. red . . . . . . 4·50 65
DESIGN—HORIZ ($37\frac{1}{2}\times26$ mm): No. N140, Soldier, flag and Hwanghae Iron Works.

106 Lisunov Li-2 Airliner over Pyongyang

1958. Air. Imperf or perf.
N141 **106** 20wn. blue . . . . . . 5·50 1·00

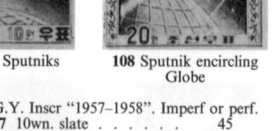

107 Sputniks — 108 Sputnik encircling Globe

1958. I.G.Y. Inscr "1957–1958". Imperf or perf.
N142 **107** 10wn. slate 45 10
N143 **108** 20wn. slate 45 10
N144 – 40wn. slate . . . . . . 1·75 30
N145 **107** 70wn. slate 50 20
DESIGN—HORIZ: 40wn. Sputnik over Pyongyang Observatory.
Nos. N142/4 exist with or without gum.

109 Furnaceman — 110 Hwanghae Iron Works

1958. Young Socialist Constructors' Congress, Pyongyang. Imperf or perf.
N146 **109** 10wn. blue . . . . . . 2·75 50

1958. Opening of Hwanghae Iron Works. Imperf or perf.
N147 **110** 10wn. blue . . . . . . 4·25 65

111 Commemorative Badge — 112 Federation Emblem

1958. Farewell to Chinese People's Volunteers (1st issue). Imperf or perf.
N148 **111** 10wn. purple and blue 1·50 40
See also No. N158.

1958. 4th International Women's Federation Democratic Congress. Imperf or perf.
N149 **112** 10wn. blue . . . . . . 1·00 35

113 Conference Emblem

1958. 1st World Young Workers' Trade Union Federation Conference, Prague. Imperf or perf.
N150 **113** 10wn. brown and green 1·75 35

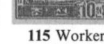

114 Flats, East Ward, Pyongyang — 115 Workers' Flats, Pyongyang

1958. Rehousing Progress. Imperf or perf.
N151 **114** 10wn. blue . . . . . . 2·00 50
N152 **115** 10wn. green . . . . . 2·00 50

117 Pyongyang Railway Station — 119 Textile Worker

1958. 10th Anniv of Korean People's Republic. Imperf or perf.
N153 – 10wn. green . . . . . 3·00 50
N154 **117** 10wn. green . . . . . 11·00 1·50
N155 – 10wn. brown and buff 1·50 50
N156 **119** 10wn. brown . . . . . 7·50 1·75
N157 – 10wn. brown . . . . . 6·50 1·00
DESIGNS—HORIZ: No. N153, Hungnam Fertiliser Plant; N157, Yongp'ung Dam, Pyongyang. VERT: No. N155, Arms of People's Republic.

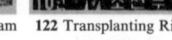

121 Volunteer and Steam Troop Train — 122 Transplanting Rice

1958. Farewell to Chinese People's Volunteers (2nd issue). Imperf or perf.
N158 **121** 10wn. sepia . . . . . . 24·00 8·00

1958. Imperf or perf.
N159 **122** 10wn. sepia 75 15

123 Winged Horse of Chollima — 124 N. Korean and Chinese Flags

1958. National Production Executives' Meeting, Pyongyang. With or without gum. Imperf or perf.
N160 **123** 10wn. red . . . . . . 1·60 30

1958. North Korean–Chinese Friendship Month. With or without gum. Imperf or perf.
N161 **124** 10wn. red, blue green 1·25 30

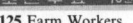

125 Farm Workers

126 Gen. Ulji Mun Dok

1959. National Co-operative Farming Congress, Pyongyang. With or without gum. Imperf or perf.
N162 **125** 10wn. blue 90 25

1959. With gum. Imperf or perf.
N163 **126** 10wn. red and yellow 2·00 50
See also Nos. N165/7 and N216/19.

127 Women with Banner

128 Rocket and Moon

1959. National Conference of Women Socialist Constructors, Pyongyang. With or without gum.
N164 **127** 10ch. brown and red . . 75 30

1959. Revalued currency. Portraits as T **126**. Imperf (with or without gum) or perf (with gum).
N165 – 2ch. blue on green . . . 60 10
N166 – 5ch. purple on buff . . 70 10
N167 **126** 10ch. red on cream . . 85 10
PORTRAITS: 2ch. General Kang Gam Chan; 5ch. General Chon Bong Jun.

1959. Launch of Soviet Moon Rocket. With or without gum. Imperf or perf.
N168 **128** 2ch. purple on buff . . 1·25 25
N169 10ch. blue on green . . 1·50 35

129 "Irrigation"

130 Inscribed Tree at Partisan H.Q., Chongbong

131 Kim Il Sung Statue

132 Mt. Paekdu

1959. Land Irrigation Project. Imperf or perf.
N170 **129** 10ch. multicoloured . . 3·75 65

1959. Partisan Successes against Japanese, 1937–39. With gum (No. N172) or no gum (others). Perf (N172) or imperf or perf (others).
N171 **130** 5ch. multicoloured . . . 2·75 45
N172 **131** 10ch. blue and turquoise 1·00 10
N173 **132** 10ch. violet . . . . . . 2·25 40

133 "Flying Horse" Tractor

1959. "Great Perspectives" (1st issue: Development of Industrial Mechanization). With or without gum. Perf, roul or imperf.
N174 **133** 1ch. red, olive and green 65 10
N175 – 2ch. multicoloured . . . 3·25 75
N176 – 2ch. red, pink and violet 60 10
N177 – 5ch. orange, brown and ochre 60 15
N178 – 10ch. blue, green & brn 70 15
N179 – 10ch. grn, lt grn & brn 1·50 25
DESIGNS: No. N175, Electric mine locomotive; N176, "Red Star 58" bulldozer; N177, "Flying Horse" excavator; N178, "SU-50" universal lathe; N179, "Victory 58" lorry.
See also Nos. N189a/200 and N275/79.

134 Armistice Building, Panmunjom

135 Protest Meeting

136 "Hoisting link between N. and S. Korea"

1959. Campaign for Withdrawal of U.S. Forces from S. Korea. With gum. Perf (20ch.) or imperf or perf (others).
N180 **134** 10ch. blue & ultramarine 55 20
N181 **135** 20ch. deep blue and blue 75 30
N182 **136** 70ch. brown, cream and purple . . . . 13·00 6·00

137 Emigration "Pickets"

1959. Campaign Against Emigration of South Koreans. With gum.
N183 **137** 20ch. brown and sepia 3·50 1·00

138 Korean Type of "1234"

139 Books breaking Chains

141 Korean Alphabet of 1443

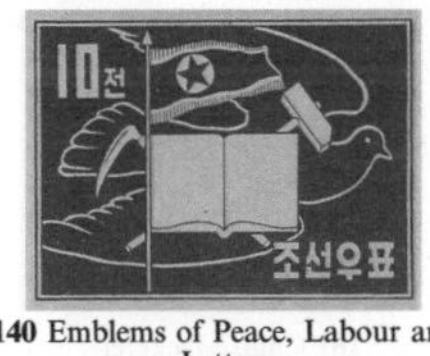
140 Emblems of Peace, Labour and Letters

1959. International Book Exibition, Leipzig. With gum (No. N184, N186) or no gum (others).
N184 **138** 5ch. sepia . . . . . . 15·00 5·00
N185 **139** 5ch. red and green . . . 4·50 1·50
N186 **140** 10ch. blue . . . . . . 4·50 1·50
N187 **141** 10ch. violet and blue . . 7·00 2·50
MSN187a 152 × 122 mm. Nos. N184/7 . . . . 65·00 35·00

142 Pig Farm

1959. Animal Husbandry. With gum (5ch.) or no gum (2ch.).
N188 – 2ch. brown, green & buff 75 15
N189 **142** 5ch. cream, blue & brn 1·00 20
DESIGN—HORIZ: 2ch. Cow-girl with Cattle.

143 Rotary Cement Kiln

1959. "Great Perspectives" (2nd issue: Production Targets). With gum (Nos. N190 and N192) or no gum (others). Perf (N197/8 and N200), perf or imperf (others).
N189a **143** 1ch. cinnamon, brn & bl 40 10
N190 – 2ch. multicoloured . . 60 10
N191 – 5ch. multicoloured . . 1·00 25
N192 – 10ch. multicoloured . . 1·25 35
N193 – 10ch. purple, yell & bl 60 10
N194 – 10ch. yellow, grn & red 90 10
N195 – 10ch. multicoloured . . 60 10
N196 – 10ch. blue, light blue and green 75 10
N197 – 10ch. multicoloured . . 60 10
N198 – 10ch. green, buff and brown 90 10
N199 – 10ch. brown and orange 60 10
N200 – 10ch. multicoloured . . 1·10 15
DESIGNS—VERT: No. N190, Electric power lines and dam; N191, Loading fertilizers into goods wagon. HORIZ: No. N192, Factory, electric power lines and dam; N163, Harvesting; N194, Sugar-beet, factory and pieces of sugar; N195, Steel furnace; N196, Trawlers; N197, Pig-iron workers; N198, Coal miners; N199, Girl picking apples; N200, Textile worker.

144 Sika Deer

145 Congress Emblem

1959. Game Preservation. No gum (5ch.), with gum (10ch.).
N201 – 5ch. multicoloured . . . 1·75 20
N202 – 5ch. yellow, brown & bl 1·75 10
N203 – 5ch. sepia, green & brn 1·75 10
N204 – 5ch. brown, black & blue . . . . 1·75 10
N205 **144** 10ch. multicoloured . . 1·75 25
N206 – 10ch. red, brown and green on cream . . . 12·00 1·75
DESIGNS—HORIZ: No. N201, Chinese water deer; N202, Siberian weasel; N203, Steppe polecat; N204, European otter; N206, Common pheasant.

1960. 3rd Korean Trade Unions Federation Congress. With gum.
N207 **145** 5ch. multicoloured . . . 45 20

146 "Chungnyon-ho" (freighter)

1959. Transport. With gum.
N208 – 5ch. purple . . . . . . 6·75 75
N209 **146** 10ch. green . . . . . . 2·50 60
DESIGN: 5ch. Electric train.

147 Soldier, Tractor and Plough

148 Knife Dance

1960. 12th Anniv of Korean People's Army. With gum.
N210 **147** 5ch. violet and blue . . 35·00 28·00

1960. Korean National Dances. Multicoloured.
N211 5ch. Type **148** . . . . . . 3·50 20
N212 5ch. Drum dance . . . . . 3·50 20
N213 10ch. Farmers' dance . . . 3·50 25

149 Women of Three Races

150 Kim Jong Ho (geographer)

1960. 50th Anniv of Int Women's Day. With gum.
N214 **149** 5ch. mauve and blue . . 90 15
N215 – 10ch. green and orange 90 25
DESIGN—VERT: 10ch. Woman operating lathe.

1960. Korean Celebrities. With gum.
N216 **150** 1ch. grey and green . . 75 10
N217 – 2ch. blue and yellow . . 90 10
N218 – 5ch. blue and yellow . . 3·00 20
N219 – 10ch. brown and ochre 85 10
PORTRAITS: 2ch. Kim Hong Do (painter); 5ch. Pak Yon (musician); 10ch. Chong Da San (scholar).

151 Grapes

152 Lenin

1960. Wild Fruits. Fruits in natural colours. With or without gum (N221/2), with gum (others).
N220 5ch. olive and turquoise . . 80 15
N221 5ch. drab and blue 80 15
N222 5ch. olive and blue 80 15
N223 10ch. olive and orange . . 1·25 20
N224 10ch. green and pink . . . 1·25 20
FRUITS: No. N220, T **151**; N221, Fruit of "Actinidia arguta planch"; N222, Pine-cone; N223, Hawthorn berries; N224, Horse-chestnut.

1960. 90th Birth Anniv of Lenin. With gum.
N225 **152** 10ch. purple 55 15

153 Koreans and American Soldier (caricature)

154 Arch of Triumph Square, Pyongyang

1960. Campaign Day for Withdrawal of U.S. Forces from South Korea. With gum.
N226 **153** 10ch. blue . . . . . . 3·25 40

1960. Views of Pyongyang.
N227 **154** 10ch. green 75 20
N228 – 20ch. slate . . . . . . 1·00 30
N229 – 40ch. green . . . . . . 2·25 50
N230 – 70ch. green . . . . . . 3·00 60
N231 – 1wn. blue . . . . . . 4·50 90
VIEWS OF PYONGYANG: 20ch. River Taedong promenade; 40ch. Youth Street; 70ch. People's Army Street; 1wn. Sungri Street.

155 Russian Flag on Moon (14.9.59)

156 "Mirror Rock"

1960. Russian Cosmic Rocket Flights. With gum (5ch.) or no gum (10ch.).
N232 – 5ch. turquoise . . . . . 2·00 1·10
N233 **155** 10ch. multicoloured . . 2·00 75
DESIGN: 5ch. "Lunik 3" approaching Moon (4.10.59).

1960. Diamond Mountains Scenery (1st issue). Multicoloured.
N234 5ch. Type **156** . . . . . . 1·00 10
N235 5ch. Devil-faced Rock . . . 1·00 10
N236 10ch. Dancing Dragon Bridge (horiz) . . . . . 3·00 25
N237 10ch. Nine Dragon Falls 3·50 25
N238 10ch. Mt. Diamond on the Sea (horiz) 90 10
See also Nos. N569/72, N599/601 and N1180/4.

157 Lily

158 Guerrillas in the Snow

1960. Flowers. Multicoloured. With gum (N242), with or without gum (others).
N239 5ch. Type **157** 90 15
N240 5ch. Rhododendron 90 15
N241 10ch. Hibiscus . . . . . . 1·75 20
N242 10ch. Blue campanula . . . 1·75 20
N243 10ch. Mauve campanula . . 1·75 20

1960. Revolutionary Leadership of Kim Il Sung.
N244 **158** 5ch. red 45 10
N245 – 10ch. blue 70 10
N246 – 10ch. red 70 10
N247 – 10ch. blue 70 10
N248 – 10ch. red 70 10
DESIGNS: No. N245, Kim Il Sung talks to guerrillas; N246, Kim Il Sung at Pochonbo; N247, Kim Il Sung on bank of Amnok River; N248, Kim Il Sung returns to Pyongyang.

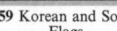

159 Korean and Soviet Flags

160 "North Korean–Soviet Friendship"

1960. 15th Anniv of Liberation from Japan.
N249 **159** 10ch. red, blue & brown 60 15

1960. North Korean–Soviet Friendship Month.
N250 **160** 10ch. lake on cream . . 35 15

161 Okryu Bridge, Pyongyang

1960. Pyongyang Buildings.
N251 **161** 10ch. blue . . . . . . 2·25 20
N252 – 10ch. violet . . . . . . 1·50 15
N253 – 10ch. green 75 10
DESIGNS: No. N252, Grand Theatre, Pyongyang; N253, Okryu Restaurant.

162 Tokro River Dam

1960. Inauguration of Tokro River Hydro-electric Power Station. With gum.
N254 **162** 5ch. blue 70 10

163

164 Quayside Welcome

1960. 15th Anniv of World Federation of Trade Unions.
N255 **163** 10ch. lt blue, ultram & bl 25 10

1960. Repatriation of Korean Nationals from Japan.
N256 **164** 10ch. purple . . . . . 2·50 35

165 Lenin and Workers

166 Football

1960. Korea–Soviet Friendship. With gum.
N257 **165** 10ch. brown and flesh 35 15

1960. Liberation Day Sports Meeting, Pyongyang. Multicoloured.
N258 5ch. Running (vert) 60 10
N259 5ch. Weightlifting (vert) . . 60 10
N260 5ch. Cycling (vert) . . . . 2·25 15
N261 5ch. Gymnastics (vert) . . 60 10
N262 5ch. Type **166** . . . . . . 1·10 15
N263 10ch. Swimming 60 10
N264 10ch. Moranbong Stadium, Pyongyang 60 10

167 Friendship Monument, Pyongyang

168 Federation Emblem

1960. 10th Anniv of Entry of Chinese Volunteers into Korean War. With gum.
N265 – 5ch. mauve 30 10
N266 **167** 10ch. blue 30 10
DESIGN—HORIZ: 5ch. Chinese and Korean soldiers celebrating.

1960. 15th Anniv of World Democratic Youth Federation.
N267 **168** 10ch. multicoloured . . 30 10

169 White-backed Woodpecker

170 Korean Wrestling

1960. Birds.
N268 **169** 2ch. multicoloured . . 9·00 15
N268a – 5ch. multicoloured . . 12·50 35
N269 – 5ch. brown, yellow & bl . . . . 17·00 70
N270 – 10ch. yellow, brn & grn . . . . 11·00 55
DESIGNS—HORIZ: 5ch. (N268a), Mandarins; 10ch. Black-naped oriole. VERT: 5ch. (N269), Oriental scops owl.

1960. Sports and Games. Multicoloured.
N271 5ch. Type **170** 60 10
N272 5ch. Riding on swing (vert) 60 10
N273 5ch. Archery . . . . 2·25 30
N274 10ch. Jumping on see-saw (vert) 60 10

171 Cogwheel and Textiles

172 Wild Ginseng (perennial herb)

1961. "Great Perspectives" (3rd issue: Targets of Seven-Year Plan, 1961–67. Inscr "1961"). Mult.
N275 5ch. Type **171** 60 10
N276 5ch. Cogwheel and Corn ("Mechanization of Rural Economy") . . . . . . 1·10 10
N277 10ch. Hammer, sickle and torch on flag (vert) . . . 30 10
N278 10ch. Cogwheels around power station 60 10
N279 10ch. Cogwheel and molten steel 45 10

1961. Multicoloured.
N280 5ch. Type **172** . . . . . . 1·50 10
N281 10ch. Cultivated ginseng . . 1·50 10

173 Aldehyde Shop

1961. Construction of Vinalon Factory. With gum.
N282 **173** 5ch. red and yellow . . 60 10
N283 – 10ch. green and yellow 1·10 10
N284 – 10ch. blue and yellow 1·10 10
N285 – 20ch. purple and yellow 1·25 15
DESIGNS: No. N283, Glacial acetic acid shop; N284, Polymerization and saponification shop; N285, Spinning shop.
See also Nos. N338/41.

174 Construction Work

175 Museum Building

1961. Construction of Children's Palace, Pyongyang. With gum.
N286 **174** 2ch. red on yellow . . . 35 15

1961. Completion of Museum of Revolution, Pyongyang. With gum.
N287 **175** 10ch. red 25 10

176 Cosmic Rocket

177 Wheat Harvester

1961. Launching of Soviet Venus Rocket.
N288 **176** 10ch. red, yellow & blue 60 15

1961. Agricultural Mechanization. With gum.
N289 – 5ch. violet 50 10
N290 – 5ch. green 50 10
N291 **177** 5ch. green 50 10
N292 – 10ch. blue 60 10
N293 – 10ch. purple 60 10
DESIGNS: No. N289, Tractor-plough; N290, Disc-harrow; N292, Maize-harvester; N293, Tractors.

178

179 Agriculture

1961. Opening of Training Institute.
N294 **178** 10ch. brown on buff . . 25 10

1961. 15th Anniv of Land Reform Law. With gum.
N295 **179** 10ch. green on yellow 45 15

180

182 Tractor-crane

181 Chub Mackerel

1961. 15th Anniv of National Programme. With gum.
N296 **180** 10ch. purple and yellow 20 10

1961. Marine Life.
N297 **181** 5ch. multicoloured . . . 1·25 10
N298 – 5ch. black and blue . . 2·00 25
N299 – 10ch. blue, black & lt bl 2·50 25
N300 – 10ch. multicoloured . . 1·25 10
N301 – 10ch. brown, yell & grn 1·25 10
DESIGNS: No. N298, Common dolphin; N299, Whale sp; N300, Yellow-finned tuna; N301, Pacific cod.

1961. With gum.
N302 **182** 1ch. brown 65 10
N303 – 2ch. brown 65 10
N304 – 5ch. green 90 10
N305 – 10ch. violet 90 20
DESIGNS—HORIZ: 2ch. Heavy-duty lorry; 5ch. Eight-metres turning lathe. VERT: 10ch. 3000-ton press.
See also Nos. N378/9c.

183 Tree-planting

184 "Peaceful Unification" Banner

1961. Re-afforestation Campaign. With gum.
N306 **183** 10ch. green . . . . . . 1·00 25

1961. Propaganda for Peaceful Reunification of Korea.
N307 **184** 10ch. multicoloured . . 6·50 1·50

185 Pioneers visiting Battlefield

1961. 15th Anniv of Children's Union. Mult.
N308 5ch. Pioneers bathing . . . 40 10
N309 10ch. Pioneer bugler . . . 1·25 20
N310 10ch. Type **185** 40 10

186 "Labour Law"

1961. 15th Anniv of Labour Law. With gum.
N311 **186** 10ch. blue on yellow . . 45 20

187 Apples

1961. Fruit. Multicoloured.
N312 5ch. Peaches 75 10
N313 5ch. Plums 75 10
N314 5ch. Type **187** 75 10
N315 10ch. Persimmons 75 10
N316 10ch. Pears 75 10

188 Yuri Gagarin and "Vostok 1"

1961. World's First Manned Space Flight.
N317 **188** 10ch. ultramarine & blue 35 10
N318 10ch. violet and blue . . 35 10

189 Power Station

1961. 15th Anniv of Nationalization of Industries Law. With gum.
N319 **189** 10ch. brown . . . . . 4·50 60

190 Women at Work

191 Children planting Tree

1961. 15th Anniv of Sex Equality Law. With gum.
N320 **190** 10ch. red 35 10

1961. Children. Multicoloured.
N321 5ch. Type **191** 60 10
N322 5ch. Reading book 30 10
N323 10ch. Playing with ball . . 30 10
N324 10ch. Building a house . . 30 10
N325 10ch. Waving flag 30 10

192 Poultry and Stock-breeding

193 Soldiers on March (statue)

1961. Improvement in Living Standards. Mult.
N326 5ch. Type **192** 60 10
N327 10ch. Fabrics and textile factory . . . . 1·10 10
N328 10ch. Trawler and fish (horiz) . . . . 1·50 20
N329 10ch. Grain-harvesting (horiz) 50 10

1961. 25th Anniv of Fatherland Restoration Association. With gum.
N330 – 10ch. violet 40 10
N331 – 10ch. violet 25 10
N332 **193** 10ch. blue and buff . . 25 10
DESIGNS—Marshal Kim Il Sung: No. N330, Seated under tree; N331, Working at desk.

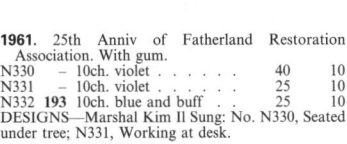

194 Party Emblem and Members

195 Miner

1961. 4th Korean Workers' Party Congress, Pyongyang. With gum.
N333 **194** 10ch. green 20 10
N334 – 10ch. purple 20 10
N335 – 10ch. red 20 10
DESIGNS—VERT: No. N334, "Chollima" statue, Pyongyang. HORIZ: No. N335, Marshal Kim Il Sung.

1961. Miners' Day. With gum.
N336 **195** 10ch. brown . . . . . 1·75 60

196 Pak in Ro

197 Aldehyde Shop

1961. 400th Birth Anniv of Pak in Ro (poet).
N337 **196** 10ch. indigo on blue . . 45 15

1961. Completion of Vinalon Factory. With gum.
N338 **197** 5ch. red and yellow . . 60 10
N339 – 10ch. brown and yellow 90 10
N340 – 10ch. blue and yellow 90 10
N341 – 20ch. purple and yellow 1·40 20
DESIGNS: No. N339, Glacial-acetic shop; N340, Polymerization and saponification shop; N341, Spinning shop.

198 Korean and Chinese Flags

199 Basketball

1961. North Korean Friendship Treaties with China and the U.S.S.R.
N342 – 10ch. multicoloured . . 40 10
N343 **198** 10ch. red, blue & yellow 40 10
DESIGN: No. N342, Korean and Soviet flags.

1961. Physical Culture Day. With gum.
N344 – 2ch. grey 75 10
N345 – 5ch. blue 90 10
N346 **199** 10ch. blue 90 10
N347 – 10ch. blue 90 10
N348 – 10ch. purple 90 10
N349 – 20ch. purple 75 10
DESIGNS: 2ch. Table tennis; 5ch. Flying model glider; 10ch. (N347) Rowing; 10ch. (N348) High jumping; 20ch. Sports emblem.

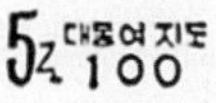
(**200**)

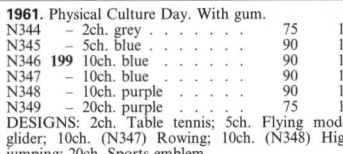

1961. Centenary of Publication of Map "Taidong Yu Jido" by Kim Jung Ho. No. N216 surch with T **200**.
N350 **150** 5ch. on 1ch. grey & grn 38·00 24·00

201 General Rock

202 "Agriculture and Industry"

1961. Mt. Chilbo Scenery. With gum.
N351 **201** 5ch. blue 75 10
N352 – 5ch. brown 75 10
N353 – 10ch. violet . . . . . . 1·40 20
N354 – 10ch. blue . . . . . . 1·40 20
N355 – 10ch. blue . . . . . . 1·40 20
DESIGNS—HORIZ: No. N352, Chonbul Peak; N354, Tiled House Rock; N355, Rainbow Rock. VERT: No. N353, Mansa Peak.

1961. With gum.
N356 **202** 10ch. green 35 10

203 Winged Horse and Congress Emblem

1961. 5th World Federation of Trade Unions Congress, Moscow. With gum.
N357 **203** 10ch. blue, purple & vio 25 10

204 Class "Red Banner" Electric Locomotive

1961. Railway Electrification. With gum.
N358 **204** 10ch. violet and yellow 4·00 1·60

205 Ice Hockey

1961. Winter Sports. With gum.
N359 – 10ch. brown and green 75 10
N360 – 10ch. brown and green 75 10
N361 **205** 10ch. brown and blue 75 10
N362 – 10ch. brown and blue 75 10
DESIGNS: No. N359, Figure skating; N360, Speed skating; N362, Skiing.

206 Grain Harvest

207 Tiger

1962. "Six Heights" of Production Targets (1st series). Inscr "1962". With gum.
N363 – 5ch. red, violet and grey 30 10
N364 – 5ch. brown and grey . . 1·75 30
N365 **206** 10ch. yellow, black & bl 30 10
N366 – 10ch. red, yellow & blue 90 10
N367 – 10ch. black and blue . . 1·10 15
N368 – 10ch. yellow, brown & bl 30 10
DESIGNS: No. N363, Ladle and molten steel; N364, Electric mine train; N366, Fabrics and mill; N367, Trawler and catch; N368, Construction of flats.
See also Nos. N440/5.

1962. Animals.
N369 **207** 2ch. multicoloured . . . 2·00 15
N370 – 2ch. brown and green 1·50 10
N371 – 5ch. yellow and green 1·50 10
N372 – 10ch. brown and green 1·75 15
ANIMALS—HORIZ: 2ch. (N370), Racoon-dog; 5ch. Chinese ferret-badger; 10ch. Asiatic black bear.

208 Kayagum Player

209 "Leuhdorfia puziloi"

1962. Musical Instruments and Players (1st series). Multicoloured.
N373 10ch. Type **208** . . . . . 1·75 20
N374 10ch. Man playing haegum (two-stringed bowed instrument) . . . . . . 1·75 20
N375 10ch. Woman playing wolgum (banjo) . . . . 1·75 20
N376 10ch. Man playing chotdae (flute) . . . . 1·75 20
N377 10ch. Woman playing wagonghu (harp) . . . . 1·75 20
See also Nos. N473/7.

1962. As T **182**. Inscr "1962". With gum (Nos. N379 and 379b), no gum (others).
N378 5ch. green 50 10
N379 10ch. blue 75 15
N379a 10ch. brown . . . . . . – 3·75
N379b 5wn. brown . . . . 9·50 3·00
N379c 10wn. purple . . . . . . 11·50 6·00
DESIGNS—VERT: 5ch. Hydraulic press; 10ch. (2), Three-ton hammer; 10wn. Tunnel drill. HORIZ: 5wn. Hobbing machine.
See also Nos. N415/22, N513/15 and N573.

1962. Butterflies. Multicoloured.
N380 5ch. Type **209** . . . . . . 2·50 15
N381 10ch. "Sericinus telamon" (purple background) . . 2·50 15
N382 10ch. Keeled apollo (lilac background) . . . . . . 2·50 15
N383 10ch. Peacock (green background) . . . . . . 2·50 15

210 G. S. Titov and "Vostok 2"

1962. 2nd Soviet Manned Space Flight.
N384 **210** 10ch. multicoloured . . 45 15

211 Marshal Kim Il Sung and (inset) addressing Workers

1962. Marshal Kim Il Sung's 50th Birthday. With gum.
N385 **211** 10ch. red 45 15
N386 – 10ch. green 45 15
N387 – 10ch. blue 45 10
DESIGN: No. 387, Kim Il Sung in fur hat and (inset) inspecting battle-front.

212 Kim Chaek

214 Black-faced Spoonbill

213 Mother with Children

1962. Korean Revolutionaries (1st series). With gum.
N388 **212** 10ch. sepia 35 10
N389 – 10ch. blue 35 10
N390 – 10ch. red 35 10
N391 – 10ch. purple 35 10
N392 – 10ch. green 35 10
N393 – 10ch. blue 35 10
N394 – 10ch. brown 35 10
PORTRAITS: No. N389, Kang Gon; N390, An Gil; N391, Ryu Gyong Su; N392/3, Kim Jong Suk; N394, Choe Chun Guk.
See also Nos. N478/82 and N733/5.

1962. National Mothers' Meeting, Pyongyang.
N395 **213** 10ch. multicoloured . . 30 10

1962. Birds. Inscr "1962". Multicoloured.
N396 5ch. Type **214** . . . . . . 1·75 20
N397 5ch. Brown hawk owl . . . 7·50 20
N398 10ch. Eastern broad-billed roller . . . . 4·25 50
N399 10ch. Black paradise flycatcher . . . . 4·25 50
N400 20ch. Tundra swan . . . . 6·50 90

215 Victory Flame

216 Japanese Croaker

1962. 25th Anniv of Battle of Pochonbo.
N401 **215** 10ch. multicoloured . . 55 10

1962. Fishes. Multicoloured.
N402 5ch. Type **216** . . . . . . 1·50 10
N403 5ch. Hairtail . . . . 1·50 10
N404 10ch. Dotted gizzard shad (head pointing to right) 1·75 20
N405 10ch. Japanese spotted seabass (blue background) . . . . . . 1·75 20
N406 10ch. Japanese croaker (green background) . . . 1·75 20

217 Waterdropper

218 Radial Drill

1962. Antiques. With gum.
N407 – 4ch. black and blue . . 1·00 10
N408 **217** 5ch. black and ochre . . 1·00 10
N409 A 10ch. black and green 1·25 10
N410 B 10ch. black and orange 1·25 10
N411 C 10ch. black and purple 1·25 10
N412 D 10ch. black and brown 1·25 10
N413 E 10ch. black and yellow 1·25 10
N414 – 40ch. black and grey . . 3·50 35
DESIGNS—VERT: 4ch. Brush pot; 40ch. Porcelain decanter. HORIZ: A, Inkstand; B, Brushstand; C, Turtle paperweight; D, Inkstone; E, Document case.

1962. Double frame-line. With gum.
N415 – 2ch. green 40 10
N415a – 2ch. brown . . . . . — 4·00
N416 – 4ch. blue . . . . . . 1·75 10
N417 **218** 5ch. blue 40 10
N418 – 5ch. purple 40 10
N419 – 10ch. purple 50 10
N420 – 40ch. blue . . . . . . 3·75 20
N421 – 90ch. blue . . . . . . 1·60 30
N422 – 1wn. brown . . . . . 4·75 50
DESIGNS—VERT: 2ch. Vertical milling machine; 5ch. (N418), Hydraulic hammer; 1wn. Spindle drill. HORIZ: 4ch. "Victory April 15" motor-car; 10ch. All-purpose excavator; 40ch. Trolley-bus; 90ch. Planing machine.
See also Nos. N513/15 and N573.

219 Chong Da San

220 Voter

1962. Birth Bicentenary of Chong Da San (philosopher).
N423 **219** 10ch. purple 35 10

1962. Election of Deputies to National Assembly. Multicoloured.
N424 10ch. Type **220** 80 10
N425 10ch. Family going to poll 80 10

221 Pyongyang

1962. 1535th Anniv of Pyongyang. With gum.
N426 **221** 10ch. black and blue . . 65 10

222 Globe and "Vostok 3" and "4"

223 Spiraea

1962. 1st "Team" Manned Space Flight.
N427 **222** 10ch. indigo, blue & red 60 20

1962. Korean Plants. Plants in natural colours; frame and inscr colours given.
N428 **223** 5ch. light green & green 1·25 10
N429 – 10ch. green and red . . 1·25 10
N430 – 10ch. blue and purple 1·25 10
N431 – 10ch. green and olive 1·25 10
PLANTS: No. N429, Ginseng; N430, Campanula; N431, "Rheumcoreanum makai (Polyonaceae)".

224 "Uibang Ryuchui"

225 Science Academy

1962. 485th Anniv of Publication of "Uibang Ryuchui" (medical encyclopaedia).
N432 **224** 10ch. multicoloured . . 3·50 30

1962. 10th Anniv of Korean Science Academy.
N433 **225** 10ch. blue and turquoise 1·00 10

226 Fisherwomen

227 European Mink

1962.
N434 **226** 10ch. blue . . . . . . 1·00 10

1962. Animals.
N435 **227** 4ch. brown and green 70 10
N436 – 5ch. blue, drab and green 70 10
N437 – 10ch. blue and yellow 90 10
N438 – 10ch. sepia and turquoise 90 10
N439 – 20ch. brown and blue 1·50 15
ANIMALS—HORIZ: No. N436, Chinese hare. VERT: No. N437, Eurasian red squirrel; N438, Common goral; N439, Siberian chipmunk.

228 Harvesting

1963. "Six Heights" of Production Targets (2nd issue). Inscr "1963". Multicoloured.
N440 5ch. Miner . . . . 1·00 20
N441 10ch. Type **228** 40 10
N442 10ch. Furnaceman 30 10
N443 10ch. Construction worker 30 10
N444 10ch. Textiles loom operator 65 10
N445 40ch. Fisherman and trawler . . . . 2·25 40

229 Soldier

230 Peony

1963. 15th Anniv of Korean People's Army. With gum.
N446 – 5ch. brown 50 10
N447 **229** 10ch. red 60 10
N448 – 10ch. blue 85 10
DESIGNS: 5ch. Airman; 10ch. Sailor.

1963. Korean Flowers. Multicoloured.
N449 5ch. Type **230** 60 10
N450 10ch. Rugosa rose 90 10
N451 10ch. Azalea 90 10
N452 20ch. Campion 90 10
N453 40ch. Orchid . . . . 2·50 35

231 "Sadang-ch'um" (Korean folk dance)

1963. International Music and Dancing Contest, Pyongyang. Multicoloured.
N454 10ch. Type **231** . . . . . 1·75 15
N455 10ch. Dancer with fan . . . 1·75 15

232 Revolutionaries

1963. 3rd Anniv of South Korean Rising of April, 1960.
N456 **232** 10ch. multicoloured . . 40 15

233 Karl Marx

234 Children in Chemistry Class

1963. 145th Birth Anniv of Karl Marx. With gum.
N457 **233** 10ch. blue 30 10

1963. Child Care and Amenities. Multicoloured.
N458 2ch. Type **234** 80 20
N459 5ch. Children running . . . 70 15
N460 10ch. Boy conducting choir 1·75 20
N461 10ch. Girl chasing butterfly 3·50 25

235 Armed Koreans and American Soldier (caricature)

1963. Campaign Month for Withdrawal of U.S. Forces from South Korea.
N462 **235** 10ch. multicoloured . . 45 10

236 "Cyrtoclytus capra"

237 Soldier with Flag

1963. Korean Beetles. Multicoloured designs. Colours of beetles given.
N463 5ch. Type **236** 75 10
N464 10ch. multicoloured . . . . 1·10 10
N465 10ch. red and blue . . . . 1·10 10
N466 10ch. indigo, blue and purple . . . . 1·10 10
BEETLES: No. N464, "Cicindela chinensis" (tiger beetle); N465, "Purpuricenus lituratus"; N466, "Agapanthia pilicornis".

1963. 10th Anniv of Victory in Korean War.
N467 **237** 10ch. multicoloured . . 50 10

238 North Korean Flag

239 Namdae Gate, Kaesong

1963. 15th Anniv of People's Republic. Mult.
N468 10ch. Type **238** 30 10
N469 10ch. North Korean Badge 30 10

1963. Ancient Korean Buildings (1st series). With gum.
N470 **239** 5ch. black 20 10
N471 – 10ch. blue 40 10
N472 – 10ch. brown 40 10
BUILDINGS: No. N471, Taedong Gate, Pyongyang; N472, Potong Gate, Pyongyang.
See also Nos. N537/8.

240 Ajaeng (bowed zither)

241 Nurse with Children

1963. Musical Instruments and Players (2nd series). Multicoloured. Nos. N473 and N476 with gum.
N473 3ch. Type **240** . . . . . . 1·25 15
N474 5ch. Pyongyon (jade chimes) . . . . 1·25 15
N475 10ch. Saenap (brass bowl) 1·50 15
N476 10ch. Rogo (drums in frame) . . . . 1·50 15
N477 10ch. Piri ("wooden pipe") 1·50 15

1963. Korean Revolutionaries (2nd issue). As T **212**. With gum.
N478 5ch. brown 40 10
N479 5ch. purple 40 10
N480 10ch. rose 50 10
N481 10ch. slate 50 10
N482 10ch. dull purple 50 10
PORTRAITS: No. N478, Kwon Yong Byok; N479, Ma Dong Hui; N480, Li Je Sun; N481, Pak Dal; N482, Kim Yong Bom.

1963. Child Welfare. Multicoloured.
N483 10ch. Type **241** 50 10
N484 10ch. Children in playground 50 10

242 Hwajang Hall

243 Furnaceman

1963. Mount Myohyang Resort. Multicoloured.
N485 5ch. Type **242** 35 10
N486 10c. Mountain stream and chalet 75 10
N487 10ch. Kwanum Pavilion and stone pagoda (horiz) 65 10
N488 10ch. Rope bridge across river (horiz) . . . . . . 1·75 15

1963. Seven Year Plan. With gum.
N489 **243** 5ch. red 20 10
N490 – 10ch. grey . . . . . . 1·50 20
N491 – 10ch. red . . . . 1·50 20
N492 – 10ch. lilac 85 10
DESIGNS—VERT: No. N490, Construction workers. HORIZ: No. N491, Power technicians; N492, Miners.

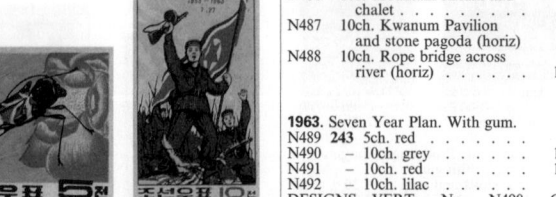

244 Children hoeing

1963. "Hung Bo" (fairytale). Multicoloured.
N493 5ch. Type **244** 30 10
N494 10ch. Tying up broken leg of swallow 90 10
N495 10ch. Barn swallow dropping gourd seed . . 90 15
N496 10ch. Sawing through giant gourd 50 10
N497 10ch. Treasure inside gourd 50 10

245 Marksman

1963. Marksmanship. Multicoloured.
N498 5ch. Type **245** 30 10
N499 10ch. Marksman with small-bore rifle 55 10
N500 10ch. Marksman with standard rifle 55 10

246 Sinuiju Chemical Fibre Factory

1964. Chemical Fibres Factories. With gum.
N501 **246** 10ch. slate 75 10
N502 – 10ch. purple 75 10
DESIGN: No. N502, Chongjin Chemical Fibre Factory.

247 Strikers

1964. 35th Anniv of Wonsan General Strike. With gum.
N503 **247** 10ch. brown 60 10

248 Korean Alphabet

1964. 520th Anniv of Korean Alphabet.
N504 **248** 10ch. green, buff & brn 60 20

249 Lenin

250 Whale-catcher

1964. 40th Death Anniv of Lenin. With gum.
N505 **249** 10ch. red 30 10

1964. Fishing Industry. Multicoloured.
N506 5ch. Type **250** 50 10
N507 5ch. Trawler No. 051 . . . 50 10
N508 10ch. Trawler No. 397 . . 1·00 20
N509 10ch. Trawler No. 738 . . 1·00 20

251 Insurgents

1964. 45th Anniv of Rising of 1st March. With gum.
N510 **251** 10ch. purple 30 10

252 Warring Peasants

1964. 70th Anniv of Kabo Peasants' War. With gum.
N511 **252** 10ch. purple 30 10

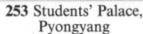

253 Students' Palace, Pyongyang

254 "Changbaek" Excavator

1964. With gum.
N512 **253** 10ch. green 30 10

1964. Single frame-line. Dated "1964" or "1965" (No. N573). With gum.
N513 – 5ch. violet 60 10
N514 **254** 10ch. green 90 10
N515 – 10ch. blue 90 10
N573 – 10ch. violet 75 20
DESIGNS—VERT: 5ch. 200 metre drill; 10ch. (N573) "Horning 500" machine. HORIZ: 10ch. (N515) 400 h.p. Diesel engine.

255 "On the March"

1964. 5th Korean Democratic Youth League Congress, Pyongyang.
N516 **255** 10ch. multicoloured . . 30 10

256 Electric Train

1964. Inauguration of Pyongyang–Sinuiju Electric Railway.
N517 **256** 10ch. multicoloured . . 2·50 20

257 Rejoicing in Chongsan-ri Village

1964. Popular Movement at Chongsan-ri. With gum.
N517a **257** 5ch. brown . . . . .

258 Drum Dance

259 "For the Sake of the Fatherland"

1964. Korean Dances.
N518 **258** 2ch. mauve, buff & black . . . . 1·50 15
N519 – 5ch. red, black & yellow 1·75 15
N520 – 10ch. multicoloured . . 2·00 15
DESIGNS: 5ch. "Ecstasy" (solo); 10ch. Tabor.

1964. Li Su Bok Commemorative. With gum.
N521 **259** 5ch. red 20 10

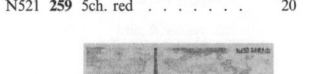

260 Nampo Smelting Works

1964. With gum.
N522 **260** 5ch. green . . . . . . 2·50 10
N523 – 10ch. slate . . . . . . 2·75 20
DESIGN: 10ch. Hwanghae iron works.

261 Torch, Chollima Statue and Cogwheel

1964. Asian Economic Seminar, Pyongyang. Multicoloured.
N524 5ch. Type **261** 25 10
N525 10ch. Flags, statue and cogwheel 30 10

262 Korean People and Statue of Kang Ho Yong (war hero)

1964. Struggle for Reunification of Korea.
N526 **262** 10ch. multicoloured . . 45 10

263 Hawk Fowl

1964. Domestic Poultry. Multicoloured.
N527 2ch. Type **263** 35 10
N528 4ch. White fowl 35 10
N529 5ch. Ryongyon fowl . . . 55 10
N530 5ch. Black fowl 55 10
N531 40ch. Helmet guineafowl . . 4·00 1·40

264 Skiing

1964. Winter Olympic Games, Innsbruck.
N532 **264** 5ch. red, blue and buff 50 10
N533 – 10ch. blue, green & buff 75 10
N534 – 10ch. blue, red and buff 75 10
DESIGNS: No. N533, Ice skating; N534, Skiing (slalom).

265 "Tobolsk" (passenger ship) and Flags

266 Tonggun Pavilion Uiju

1964. 5th Anniv of Agreement for Repatriation of Koreans in Japan.
N535 **265** 10ch. red, blue & lt blue 1·40 30
N536 – 30ch. multicoloured . . 1·10 15
DESIGN: 30ch. Return of repatriates.

1964. Ancient Korean Buildings (2nd series). With gum.
N537 **266** 5ch. purple 20 10
N538 – 10ch. green 30 10
DESIGN: 10ch. Inpang Pavilion, Kanggye City.

267 Cycling

268 Burning of the "General Sherman"

1964. Olympic Games, Tokyo.
N539 – 2ch. brown and blue . . 25 10
N540 **267** 5ch. brown and green 75 10
N541 – 10ch. orange and blue 35 10
N542 – 10ch. orange and green 35 10
N543 – 40ch. brown and blue 60 35
DESIGNS—HORIZ: 2ch. Rifle-shooting; 10ch. blue, Running. VERT: 10ch. green, Wrestling; 40ch. Volleyball.

1964. The "General Sherman" Incident, 1866. With gum.
N544 **268** 30ch. brown . . . . . 2·00 30

269 Organizing Guerrillas

1964. Guerrilla Operations in the 1930s against the Japanese. With gum.
N545 **269** 2ch. violet 25 10
N546 – 5ch. blue 35 10
N547 – 10ch. black 45 10
DESIGNS: 5ch. Kim Il Sung addressing guerillas; 10ch. Battle scene at Xiaowangqing.

270 Students attacking

271 Weightlifting

1964. Kwangju Students Rising, 1929. With gum.
N548 **270** 10ch. violet . . . . . . 1·60 15

1964. "GANEFO" Athletic Games, Djakarta, Indonesia (1963). Multicoloured.
N549 2ch. Type **271** 40 10
N550 5ch. Athlete breasting tape 40 10
N551 5ch. Boxing (horiz) 40 10
N552 10ch. Football (horiz) . . . 1·00 15
N553 10ch. Globe emblem (horiz) 40 15

272 Lynx

1964. Animals. With gum.
N554 2ch. sepia (Type **272**) . . . 75 10
N555 5ch. sepia (Leopard cat) . . 1·75 10
N556 10ch. brown (Leopard) . . 2·25 10
N557 10ch. sepia (Yellow-throated marten) . . . . 2·25 10

273 Vietnamese Attack

1964. Support for People of Vietnam.
N558 **273** 10ch. multicoloured . . 30 10

274 Prof. Kim Bong Han and Emblems

1964. Kyongrak Biological Systems.
N559 **274** 2ch. purple and olive . . 65 10
N560 – 5ch. green, orange & bl 90 10
N561 – 10ch. red, yellow & blue 1·25 10
DESIGNS—33 × 23½ mm: 5ch. "Bonghan" duct; 10ch. "Bonghan" corpuscle. Each include emblems as in Type **274**.

275 Farmers, Tractor and Lorry

1964. Agrarian Programme. Multicoloured.
N562 5ch. Type **275** 20 10
N563 10ch. Peasants with scroll and book 30 10
N564 10ch. Peasants, one writing in book 30 10

276 Chung Jin gets a Pistol

1964. The Struggle to capture Japanese Arms. With gum.
N565 **276** 4ch. brown 25 10

277 Girl with Korean Products

278 Three Fairies Rock

1964. Economic 7 Year Plan. Multicoloured. With gum (5ch.) or no gum (others).
N566 5ch. Type **277** 40 10
N567 10ch. Farm girl 40 10
N568 10ch. Couple on winged horse (23½ × 23½ mm) . . 25 10

1964. Diamond Mountains Scenery (2nd issue). Inscr "1964". Multicoloured. Without gum (2, 4ch.) or with gum (others).
N569 2ch. Type **278** 75 10
N570 4ch. Ryonju Falls . . . . 2·75 10
N571 10ch. The Ten Thousand Rocks, Manmulsang . . 75 10
N572 10ch. Chinju Falls . . . . 2·75 10

280 Soldiers Advancing, Fusong

1965. Guerrilla Operations against the Japanese, 1934–40. With gum.
N574 **280** 10ch. violet 50 10
N575 – 10ch. violet 50 10
N576 – 10ch. green 50 10
DESIGNS: No. N575, Soldiers descending hill, Hongqihe; N576, Soldiers attacking hill post, Luozigou.

281 Tuman River

1965. Korean Rivers. Multicoloured.
N577 2ch. Type **281** 60 10
N578 5ch. Taedong (vert) . . . . 1·75 15
N579 10ch. Amnok 75 10

282 Union Badge

1965. 1st Congress of Landworkers' Union, Pyongyang. With gum.
N580 **282** 10ch. multicoloured . . 30 10

283 Furnacemen and Workers

1965. 10 Major Tasks of 7 Year Plan. With gum.
N581 **283** 10ch. multicoloured . . 30 10

284 Miners' Strike, Sinhung Colliery

1965. 35th Anniv of Strikes and Peasants' Revolt. With gum.
N582 **284** 10ch. olive . . . . . . 1·25 15
N583 – 10ch. brown . . . . . 1·50 15
N584 – 40ch. purple . . . . . 1·00 15
DESIGNS: 10ch. Strikers at Pyongyang Rubber Factory; 40ch. Revolt of Tanchon peasants.

285 Embankment Construction

1965. Sunhwa River Works. With gum.
N585 **285** 10ch. multicoloured . . 30 10

286 Hand holding Torch

1965. 5th Anniv of South Korean Rising of April 19th. Multicoloured. With gum.
N586 10ch. Type **286** 20 10
N587 40ch. Student-hero, Kim Chio 45 20

287 Power Station under Construction

1965. Construction of Thermal Power Station, Pyongyang. With gum.
N588 **287** 5ch. brown and blue . . 25 10

288 African and Asian

1965. 10th Anniv of 1st Afro-Asian Conference, Bandung. With gum.
N589 **288** 10ch. multicoloured . . 30 10

289 Rejoicing of Koreans

1965. 10th Anniv of General Assn of Koreans in Japan. With gum.
N590 **289** 10ch. blue and red . . . 25 10
N591 – 40ch. indigo, blue & red 45 15
DESIGN: 40ch. Patriot and flag.

290 Workers in Battle **291** "Victory 64" 10-ton Lorry

1965. 2nd Afro-Asian Conf, Algiers. With gum.
N592 **290** 10ch. black, yellow red 75 10
N593 – 40ch. black, yellow red 1·25 25
DESIGN: 40ch. Korean and African soldiers.
The Algiers Conference did not take place.

1965. With gum.
N594 **291** 10ch. green . . . . . . 1·25 20

292 Kim Chang Gol

1965. War Heroes (1st series). With gum.
N595 **292** 10ch. green 30 10
N596 – 10ch. brown 30 10
N597 – 40ch. purple 75 20
PORTRAITS: No. N596, Cho Gun Sil and machine-gun; N597, An Hak Ryong and machine-gun.
See also Nos. N781/3 and N842/3.

293 Marx and Lenin

1965. Postal Ministers' Congress, Peking. With gum.
N598 **293** 10ch. black, yellow red 1·50 15

294 Lake Samil

1965. Diamond Mountains Scenery (3rd issue). Multicoloured. With gum.
N599 2ch. Type **294** 60 10
N600 5ch. Chipson Peak . . . . 1·00 10
N601 10ch. Kwanum Falls . . . 2·75 25

295 Amnok River, Kusimuldong

1965. Scenes of Japanese War. With gum.
N602 **295** 5ch. green and blue . . 35 10
N603 – 10ch. turquoise and blue 60 10
DESIGN: 10ch. Lake Samji.

296 Footballer and Games' Emblem **297** Workers and Map

1965. "GANEFO" Football Games, Pyongyang. Multicoloured. With gum.
N604 10ch. Type **296** . . . . . 1·25 10
N605 10ch. Games emblem and Moranbong Stadium . . 1·25 10

1965. 20th Anniv of Liberation from Japan. With gum.
N606 **297** 10ch. multicoloured . . 30 10

298 Engels **299** Pole Vaulting

1965. 145th Birth Anniv of Engels. With gum.
N607 **298** 10ch. brown 30 10

1965. Sports. Multicoloured. With gum.
N608 2ch. Type **299** 50 10
N609 4ch. Throwing the javelin 1·75 20
N610 10ch. Throwing the discus 50 10
N611 10ch. High jumping (horiz) 50 10
N612 10ch. Putting the shot (horiz) 50 10

301 Korean Fighters

1965. 20th Anniv of Korean Workers' Party. Each black, yellow and red. With gum.
N613 10ch. Type **301** 45 10
N614 10ch. Party emblem 45 10
N615 10ch. Lenin and Marx . . 45 10
N616 10ch. Workers marching . . 45 10
N617 10ch. Fighters 45 10
N618 40ch. Workers 45 10
MSN619 191 × 99 mm. Nos. N613/18 . . . . 9·50 4·25
Nos. N613/8 each have a red banner in the background and were issued together in blocks of 6 (3 × 2), forming a composite design, within the sheet.

302 Kim Chaek Iron Works **303** Grass Carp

1965. With gum.
N620 **302** 10ch. purple . . . . . 3·50 10
N621 – 10ch. brown . . . . . 3·50 10
DESIGN: No. 621, Chongjin Steel Works.

1965. Freshwater Fish. Multicoloured. With gum.
N622 2ch. Rainbow trout 70 10
N623 4ch. Dolly Varden charr . . 90 10
N624 10ch. Brown trout (surfacing water) . . . . 2·25 15
N625 10ch. Common carp diving (date at left) . . . . . . 2·25 15
N626 10ch. Type **303** . . . . . 2·25 15
N627 40ch. Crucian carp . . . . 3·25 55

304 Building House **305** Children in Workshop

1965. Kim Hong Do's Drawings. With gum.
N628 2ch. green (Type **304**) . . . 45 10
N629 4ch. purple (Weaving) . . . 90 10
N630 10ch. brown (Wrestling) . . 80 10
N631 10ch. blue (School class) . . 80 10
N632 10ch. red (Dancing) . . . . 1·25 10
N633 10ch. violet (Blacksmiths) 1·10 10

1965. Life at Pyongyang Children's and Students' Palace. Multicoloured. With gum.
N634 2ch. Type **305** 20 10
N635 4ch. Boxing 20 10
N636 10ch. Chemistry 75 10
N637 10ch. Playing violin and accordion 75 10

306 Whale-catcher

1965. Korean Fishing Boats. With gum.
N638 **306** 10ch. blue . . . . . . 1·40 25
N639 – 10ch. green . . . . . . 1·40 25
DESIGN: No. N639, Fishing fleet service vessel.

307 Great Tit **308** Silkworm Moth ("Bombyx mori") and Cocoon

1965. Korean Birds. Inscr "1965". Multicoloured. With gum.
N640 4ch. Black-capped kingfisher (vert) . . . . 2·40 50
N641 10ch. Type **307** . . . . . 3·50 1·25
N642 10ch. Pied wagtail (facing left) . . . . 3·50 1·25
N643 10ch. Azure-winged magpie (facing right) . . . . . 3·50 1·25
N644 40ch. Black-tailed hawfinch 8·00 4·50

1965. Korean Sericulture. With gum.
N645 **308** 2ch. green . . . . . . 5·00 20
N646 – 10ch. brown . . . . . 5·00 30
N647 – 10ch. purple . . . . . 5·00 30
MOTHS AND COCOONS: No. N646, Ailathus silk moth ("Samia cynthia"); N647, Chinese oak silk moth ("Antheraea pernyi").

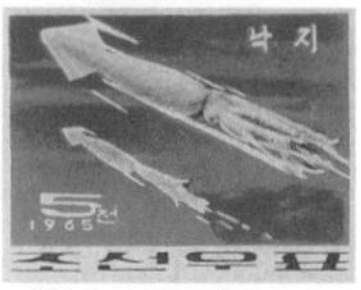

309 Hooded Crane **310** Japanese Common Squid

1965. Wading Birds. With gum.
N648 **309** 2ch. brown . . . . . . 4·25 15
N649 – 10ch. blue . . . . . . 4·50 45
N650 – 10ch. purple . . . . . 4·50 45
N651 – 40ch. green . . . . . . 8·75 90
BIRDS: No. N649, Japanese white-naped crane; N650, Manchurian crane; N651, Grey heron.

1965. Korean Molluscs. Multicoloured. With gum.
N652 5ch. Type **310** . . . . . . 1·25 10
N653 10ch. Giant Pacific octopus 1·75 10

311 Spotbill Duck

1965. Korean Ducks. Multicoloured. With gum.
N654 2ch. Type **311** . . . . . . 2·75 15
N655 4ch. Ruddy shelduck . . . 2·75 25
N656 10ch. Mallard . . . . . . 4·25 55
N657 40ch. Baikal teal . . . . . 6·25 1·25

312 Circus Theatre, Pyongyang **313** "Marvel of Peru" ("Mirabilis jalapa")

1965. Korean Circus. With gum except No. N661.
N658 **312** 2ch. blue, black & brown 75 10
N659 – 10ch. blue, red and black . . . . 1·50 10
N660 – 10ch. red, black & green 1·50 10
N661 – 10ch. orange, sepia & grn . . . . 1·50 10
N662 – 10ch. red, yellow & turq 1·50 10
DESIGNS—VERT: No. N659, Trapeze artistes; N660, Performer with hoops on seesaw; N661, Tightrope dancers; N662, Performer with revolving cap on stick.

1965. Korean Flowers. Multicoloured. With gum except No. N663.
N663 4ch. Type **313** . . . . . . 1·10 10
N664 10ch. Peony . . . . 1·50 10
N665 10ch. Moss rose . . . . . 1·50 10
N666 10ch. Magnolia . . . . . 1·50 10

314 "Finn" Class Dinghy

315 Cuban, Korean and African

1965. Yachts. Multicoloured. With gum.

N667	2ch. Type **314**	70	20
N668	10ch. "5.5m" class yacht	1·00	30
N669	10ch. "Dragon" class yacht	1·00	30
N670	40ch. "Star" class yacht	2·00	60

1966. African-Asian and Latin American Friendship Conference, Havana. With gum.

N671	**315** 10ch. multicoloured	30	10

316 Hosta

1966. Wild Flowers. Mult. With gum. (a) 1st series.

N672	2ch. Type **316**	50	10
N673	4ch. Dandelion	50	10
N674	10ch. Pink convolvulus	75	10
N675	10ch. Lily-of-the-valley	75	10
N676	40ch. Catalpa blossom	2·00	20

(b) 2nd series.

N677	2ch. Polyanthus	50	10
N678	4ch. Lychnis	50	10
N679	10ch. Adonis	75	10
N680	10ch. Orange lily	75	10
N681	90ch. Rhododendron	3·00	30

Nos. N672/6 exist imperf and without gum.

317 Farmer and Wife

1966. 20th Anniv of Land Reform Law. With gum.

N682	**317** 10ch. multicoloured	20	10

318 Troops advancing, Dashahe

319 Silla Bowl

1966. Paintings of Guerrilla Battles, 1937–39. With gum, except No. N684.

N683	**318** 10ch. red	30	10
N684	– 10ch. turquoise	30	10
N685	– 10ch. purple	30	10

DESIGNS AND BATTLES: No. N684, Troops firing from trees, Taehongdan; N685, Troops on hillside, Jiansanfeng.

1966. Art Treasures of Silla Dynasty. With gum.

N686	**319** 2ch. ochre	1·25	10
N687	– 5ch. black	1·25	10
N688	– 10ch. violet	1·25	10

DESIGNS: 5ch. Earthenware jug. 10ch. Censer.

320 Hands holding Torch, Rifle and Hammer

321 Torch and Patriots

1966. 80th Anniv of Labour Day. With gum.

N689	**320** 10ch. multicoloured	30	10

1966. 30th Anniv of Association for Restoration of Fatherland.

N690	**321** 10ch. red and yellow	30	10

322 Harvester

1966. Aid for Agriculture. Multicoloured.

N691	5ch. Type **322**	25	10
N692	10ch. Labourer	35	10

323 Young Pioneers

1966. 20th Anniv of Korean Children's Union. Without gum.

N693	**323** 10ch. multicoloured	50	10

324 Kangson Steel Works

1966. Korean Industries. With gum.

N694	**324** 10ch. grey	3·50	15
N695	– 10ch. red (Pongung Chemical Works)	3·50	15

325 Pacific Saury

1966. Korean Fishes. With gum, except Nos. N699/700.

N696	**325** 2ch. blue, green & purple	80	10
N697	– 5ch. purple, green & brn	1·00	10
N698	– 10ch. blue, buff & green	1·50	15
N699	– 10ch. purple and & green	1·50	15
N700	– 40ch. green, buff & blue	3·50	60

FISHES: 5ch. Pacific cod; 10ch. (N698), Chum salmon, (N699), Yellowfish; 40ch. Pink salmon.

326 Professor Kim Bong Han

1966. Kyungrak Biological System. With gum.

N701	**326** 2ch. blue, green & yellow	60	10
N702	– 4ch. multicoloured	60	10
N703	– 5ch. multicoloured	60	10
N704	– 10ch. multicoloured	60	10
N705	– 10ch. multicoloured	60	10
N706	– 10ch. multicoloured	60	10
N707	– 15ch. multicoloured	60	10
N708	– 40ch. multicoloured	60	10
MSN709	117×141 mm. Nos. N701/8	7·00	4·50

DESIGNS: No. N704, Kyongrak Institute; N708, Figure of Man; N702/3, 705/7, Diagram of system.

Nos. N701/8 were issued together, se-tenant, forming a composite design.

327 Leonov in Space ("Voskhod 2")

1966. Cosmonauts Day. Multicoloured.

N710	5ch. Type **327**	20	10
N711	10ch. "Luna 9"	55	10
N712	40ch. "Luna 10"	1·10	20

328 Footballers

1966. World Cup Football Championship. Mult.

N713	10ch. Type **328**	1·25	25
N714	10ch. Jules Rimet Cup, football and boots	1·25	25
N715	10ch. Goalkeeper saving goal (vert)	1·25	25

329 Defence of Seoul

1966. Korean War of 1950–53. With gum.

N716	**329** 10ch. green	35	10
N717	– 10ch. purple	35	10
N718	– 10ch. purple	35	10

DESIGNS: No. N717, Battle on Mt. Napal; N718, Battle for Height 1211.

330 Women in Industry

1966. 20th Anniv of Sex Equality Law.

N719	**330** 10ch. multicoloured	30	10

331 Industrial Workers

332 Water-jar Dance

1966. 20th Anniv of Industrial Nationalization.

N720	**331** 10ch. multicoloured	90	10

1966. Korean Dances. Multicoloured. 5, 40ch. with or without gum; others without.

N721	5ch. Type **332**	1·00	10
N722	10ch. Bell dance	1·75	15
N723	10ch. "Dancer in a Mural Painting"	1·75	15
N724	15ch. Sword dance	1·75	20
N725	40ch. Gold Cymbal dance	3·25	30

333 Korean attacking U.S. Soldier

334 Yakovlev Yak-12M Crop-spraying

1966. Korean Reunification Campaign. With gum.

N726	**333** 10ch. green	60	10
N727	– 10ch. purple	60	10
N728	– 10ch. lilac	3·75	45

DESIGNS: No. N727, Korean with young child; N728, Korean with shovel, industrial scene and electric train.

1966. Industrial Uses of Aircraft. With gum except 2 and 5ch.

N729	**334** 2ch. green and purple	50	10
N730	– 5ch. brown and green	6·00	20
N731	– 10ch. brown and blue	1·50	10
N732	– 40ch. brown and blue	1·50	10

DESIGNS: 5ch. Yakovlev Yak-18U (forest-fire observation); 10ch. Lisunov Li-2 (geological survey); 40ch. Lisunov Li-2 (detection of fish shoals).

1966. Korean Revolutionaries (3rd issue). As T **212**. With gum.

N733	10ch. violet (O Jung Hub)		
N734	10ch. green (Kim Gyong Sok)		
N735	10ch. blue (Li Dong Gol)		

335 Kim Il Sung University

1966. 20th Anniv of Kim Il Sung University. With gum.

N736	**335** 10ch. violet	50	10

336 Judo

1966. Ganefo Games, Phnom Penh.

N737	**336** 5ch. black, green & blue	60	10
N738	– 10ch. blk, grn & dp grn	60	10
N739	– 10ch. black and red	60	10

DESIGNS: No. N738, Basketball; N739, Table tennis.

337 Hoopoe

1966. Korean Birds. Multicoloured. Inscr "1966".

N740	2ch. Common rosefinch (horiz)	2·00	15
N741	5ch. Type **337**	2·40	20
N742	10ch. Black-breasted thrush (blue background) (horiz)	2·75	35
N743	10ch. Crested lark (green background) (horiz)	2·75	35
N744	40ch. White-bellied black woodpecker	6·00	90

338 Building Construction

1966. "Increased Production with Economy". Multicoloured. Without gum (40ch.) or with gum (others).

N745	5ch. Type **338**	25	10
N746	10ch. Furnaceman and graph	45	10
N747	10ch. Machine-tool production	45	10
N748	40ch. Miners and pit-head	1·40	15

339 Parachuting

1966. National Defence Sports. With gum.

N749	**339** 2ch. brown	75	10
N750	– 5ch. red	55	10
N751	– 10ch. blue	2·75	30
N752	– 40ch. green	1·60	20

DESIGNS: 5ch. Show jumping; 10ch. Motor cycle racing; 40ch. Radio receiving and transmitting competition.

340 "Samil Wolgan" (Association Magazine)

1966. 30th Anniv of "Samil Wolgan" Magazine.

N753	**340** 10ch. multicoloured	90	15

341 Red Deer

342 Blueberries

1966. Korean Deer. Multicoloured.

N754	2ch. Type **341**	30	10
N755	5ch. Sika deer	50	10
N756	10ch. Indian muntjac (erect)	90	10
N757	10ch. Reindeer (grazing)	90	10
N758	70ch. Fallow deer	2·25	25

1966. Wild Fruit. Multicoloured.

N759	2ch. Type **342**	50	10
N760	5ch. Wild pears	70	10
N761	10ch. Wild raspberries	90	10
N762	10ch. Schizandra	90	10

N763 10ch. Wild plums 90 10
N764 40ch. Jujube . . . . 2·25 15

343 Onpo Rest Home

1966. Korean Rest Homes. With gum.
N765 **343** 2ch. violet 25 10
N766 – 5ch. turquoise 35 10
N767 – 10ch. green 50 10
N768 – 40ch. black 80 20
REST HOMES: 5ch. Mt. Myohyang; 10ch. Songdowon; 40ch. Hongwon

344 Soldier

1967. 19th Anniv of Army Day. Without gum.
N769 **344** 10ch. green, yellow & red 25 10

345 Sow

1967. Domestic Animals. Multicoloured. Without gum. 40ch. also with gum.
N770 5ch. Type **345** 40 10
N771 10ch. Goat 50 10
N772 40ch. Ox . . . . 1·00 25

346 Battle Scene

1967. 30th Anniv of Battle of Pochonbo. With gum.
N773 **346** 10ch. orange, red & grn 50 10

347 Students

1967. Compulsory Technical Education for Nine Years.
N774 **347** 10ch. multicoloured . . 25 10

348 Table Tennis Player

1967. 29th Int Table Tennis Championships, Pyongyang. Designs showing players in action. 5ch. with or without gum.
N775 **348** 5ch. multicoloured . . . 40 10
N776 – 10ch. multicoloured . . 70 10
N777 – 40ch. multicoloured . . 1·10 15

349 Anti-aircraft Defences

1967. Paintings of Guerrilla War against the Japanese. With gum.
N778 **349** 10ch. blue 35 10
N779 – 10ch. purple . . . . . 3·00 25
N780 – 10ch. violet 35 10
PAINTINGS: No. N779, Blowing-up railway bridge; N780, People helping guerrillas in Wangyugou.

1967. War Heroes (2nd series). As T **292**. Designs showing portraits and combat scenes. With gum.
N781 10ch. slate 40 10
N782 10ch. violet 40 10
N783 10ch. blue 75 10
PORTRAITS: No. N781, Li Dae Hun and grenade-throwing; N782, Choe Jong Un and soldiers charging; N783, Kim Hwa Ryong and air dog-fighter aircraft.

350 Workers

1967. Labour Day.
N784 **350** 10ch. multicoloured . . 25 10

351 Card Game

1967. Korean Children. Multicoloured.
N785 5ch. Type **351** . . . . . . 1·00 10
N786 10ch. Children modelling tractor 60 10
N787 40ch. Children playing with ball . . . . 1·10 20

352 Victory Monument

1967. Unveiling of Battle of Ponchonbo Monument.
N788 **352** 10ch. multicoloured . . 30 10

353 Attacking Tank

354 "Polygonatum japonicum"

1967. Monuments to War of 1950–53. 2ch. with or without gum.
N789 **353** 2ch. green and turquoise 20 10
N790 – 5ch. sepia and green . . 85 10
N791 – 10ch. brown and buff 30 10
N792 – 40ch. brown and blue 60 15
MONUMENTS: 5ch. Soldier-musicians; 10ch. Soldier; 40ch. Soldier with children.

1967. Medicinal Plants. Mult; background colour of 10ch. values given to aid identification. Nos. 793/5 and 797 with or without gum.
N793 2ch. Type **354** . . . . . . 1·00 10
N794 5ch. "Hibiscus manihot" 1·00 10
N795 10ch. "Scutellaria baicalensis" (turquoise) 1·25 10
N796 10ch. "Pulsatilla koreana" (blue) . . . . 1·25 10
N797 10ch. "Rehmannian glutinosa" (yellow) . . . 1·25 10
N798 40ch. "Tanacetum boreale" 3·25 35

355 Servicemen

1967. People's Army. Multicoloured. 5ch. with or without gum.
N799 5ch. Type **355** 20 10
N800 10ch. Soldier and farmer 25 10
N801 10ch. Officer decorating soldier 25 10

356 Freighter "Chollima"

1967. With gum.
N802 **356** 10ch. green . . . . . . 1·10 10

357 "Reclamation of Tideland"

1967. "Heroic Struggle of the Chollima Riders". Paintings. Without gum (5ch.) or with gum (others).
N803 – 5ch. brown 40 10
N804 **357** 10ch. grey 55 10
N805 – 10ch. green 85 10
DESIGNS—VERT: 5ch. "Drilling Rock Precipice"; 10ch. (N805), "Felling Trees".

358 "Erimaculus isenbeckii"

1967. Crabs. Multicoloured.
N806 2ch. Type **358** 90 15
N807 5ch. "Neptunus trituberculatus" . . . . 1·10 15
N808 10ch. "Paralithodes camtschatica" . . . . . 1·60 15
N809 40ch. "Chionoecetes opilio" 2·50 40

359 Electric Train and Hand switching Points

1967. Propaganda for Reunification of Korea.
N810 **359** 10ch. multicoloured . . 2·25 40

360 Tongrim Waterfall

361 Chollima Flying Horse and Banners

1967. Korean Waterfalls. 2ch. with or without gum. Multicoloured.
N811 2ch. Type **360** . . . . . . 2·75 15
N812 10ch. Sanju waterfall, Mt. Myohyang . . . . 3·25 20
N813 40ch. Sambang waterfall, Mt. Chonak . . . . . . 5·00 45

1967. "The Revolutionary Surge Upwards". Various designs incorporating the Chollima Flying Horse.
N814 – 5ch. blue . . . . 1·40 20
N815 – 10ch. red 25 10
N816 – 10ch. green 25 10
N817 – 10ch. lilac 25 10
N817 **361** 10ch. red 20 10
DESIGNS—HORIZ: 5ch. Ship, electric train and lorry (Transport); N815, Bulldozers (Building construction); N816, Tractors (Rural development); N817, Heavy presses (Machine-building industry).

362 Lenin

1967. 50th Anniv of Russian October Revolution.
N819 **362** 10ch. brown, yell & red 25 10

363 Voters and Banner

1967. Korean Elections. Multicoloured.
N820 10ch. Type **363** 35 10
N821 10ch. Woman casting vote (vert) 35 10

364 Cinereous Black Vulture

1967. Birds of Prey. Multicoloured. With gum.
N822 2ch. Type **364** . . . . . . 3·00 45
N823 10ch. Booted eagle (horiz) 5·75 75
N824 40ch. White-bellied sea eagle . . . . 7·25 1·10

365 Chongjin

1967. North Korean Cities. With gum.
N825 **365** 5ch. green 70 10
N826 – 10ch. lilac 70 10
N827 – 10ch. violet 70 10
DESIGNS: No. N826, Humhung; N827, Sinuiju.

366 Soldier brandishing Red Book

1967. "Let us carry out the Decisions of the Workers' Party Conference!". Multicoloured.
N828 10ch. Type **366** 25 10
N829 10ch. Militiaman holding bayonet 25 10
N830 10ch. Foundryman and bayonet 25 10

367 Whaler firing Harpoon

1967. With gum.
N831 **367** 10ch. blue . . . . . . 2·00 25

368 Airman, Soldier and Sailor

1968. 20th Anniv of People's Army. Mult. With gum.

N832	10ch. Type **368**	30	10
N833	10ch. Soldier below attack in snow	30	10
N834	10ch. Soldier below massed ranks	30	10
N835	10ch. Soldier holding flag	30	10
N836	10ch. Soldier holding book	30	10
N837	10ch. Soldiers and armed workers with flag	30	10
N838	10ch. Furnaceman and soldier	30	10
N839	10ch. Soldier saluting . . .	30	10
N840	10ch. Charging soldiers . .	30	10
N841	10ch. Soldier, sailor and airman below flag . . .	30	10

1968. War Heroes (3rd series). As T **292**. With gum.

N842	10ch. violet	25	10
N843	10ch. purple	25	10

PORTRAITS: No. N842, Han Gye Ryol firing Bren gun; N843, Li Su Bok charging up hill.

369 Dredger "September 2"

370 Ten-storey Flats, East Pyongyang

371 Palace of Students and Children, Kaesong

1968. With gum.

N844	**369** 5ch. green	75	10
N845	**370** 10ch. blue	30	10
N846	**371** 10ch. blue	30	10

372 Marshal Kim Il Sung

1968. Marshal Kim Il Sung's 56th Birthday. With gum.

N847	**372** 40ch. multicoloured . .	65	40

373 Kim Il Sung with Mother

1968. Childhood of Kim Il Sung. Multicoloured.

N848	10ch. Type **373**	35	10
N849	10ch. Kim Il Sung with his father	35	10
N850	10ch. Setting out from home, aged 13	35	10
N851	10ch. Birthplace at Mangyongdae	35	10
N852	10ch. Mangyong Hill . . .	35	10

374 Matsu-take Mushroom

1968. Mushrooms. With gum.

N853	**374** 5ch. brown and green	4·25	50
N854	– 10ch. ochre, brn & grn	6·00	75
N855	– 10ch. brown and green	6·00	75

DESIGNS: No. N854, Black mushroom; N855, Cultivated mushroom.

375 Leaping Horseman

1968. 20th Anniv of Korean People's Democratic Republic. Multicoloured. With gum.

N856	10ch. Type **375**	1·25	10
N857	10ch. Four servicemen . .	1·25	10
N858	10ch. Soldier with bayonet	1·25	10
N859	10ch. Advancing with banners	1·25	10
N860	10ch. Statue	1·25	10
N861	10ch. Korean flag	1·25	10
N862	10ch. Soldier and peasant with flag	1·25	10
N863	10ch. Machine-gunner with flag	1·25	10

376 Domestic Products

377 Proclaiming the Ten Points

1968. Development of Light Industries. Multicoloured. With gum.

N864	2ch. Type **376**	25	10
N865	5ch. Textiles	1·00	10
N866	10ch. Tinned produce . . .	40	10

1968. Kim Il Sung's Ten Point Political Programme. Multicoloured.

N867	2ch. Type **377**	15	10
N868	5ch. Soldier and artisan (horiz)	20	10

378 Livestock

1968. Development of Agriculture. Mult. With gum.

N869	5ch. Type **378**	25	10
N870	10ch. Fruit-growing	25	10
N871	10ch. Wheat-harvesting . .	25	10

379 Yesso Scallop

1968. Shellfish. Multicoloured. With gum.

N872	5ch. Type **379**	1·10	10
N873	5ch. Meretrix chione (venus clam)	1·10	10
N874	10ch. "Modiolus hanleyi" (mussel)	1·75	20

380 Kim Il Sung at Head of Columns

1968. Battle of Pochonbo Monument. Detail of Monument. Multicoloured.

N875	10ch. Type **380**	25	10
N876	10ch. Head of right-hand column	25	10
N877	10ch. Tail of right-hand column	25	10
N878	10ch. Head of left-hand column	25	10
N879	10ch. Tail of left-hand column	25	10
N880	10ch. Centre of right-hand column	25	10
N881	10ch. Centre of left-hand column	25	10

SIZES—HORIZ: Nos. N876/8, 43 × 28 mm. 880/1, 56 × 28 mm.

The centrepiece of the Monument is flanked by two columns of soldiers, headed by Kim Il Sung.

381 Museum of the Revolution, Pochonbo

382 Grand Theatre, Pyongyang

1968.

N883	**381** 2ch. green	20	10
N884	**382** 10ch. brown	65	10

383 Irrigation

1969. Rural Development. Multicoloured.

N885	3ch. Type **383**	20	10
N886	5ch. Agricultural mechanization	20	10
N887	10ch. Electrification	40	10
N888	40ch. Applying fertilizers and spraying trees . . .	60	10

384 Grey Rabbits

1969. Rabbits. Mult. With or without gum.

N889	2ch. Type **384**	45	10
N890	10ch. Black rabbits	45	10
N891	10ch. Brown rabbits . . .	45	10
N892	10ch. White rabbits	45	10
N893	40ch. Doe and young . . .	1·40	15

385 "Age and Youth"

1969. Public Health Service.

N894	**385** 2ch. brown and blue . .	35	10
N895	– 10ch. blue and red . . .	75	10
N896	– 40ch. green and yellow	1·50	20

DESIGNS: 10ch. Nurse with syringe; 40ch. Auscultation by woman doctor.

386 Sowing Rice Seed

1969. Agricultural Mechanization.

N897	**386** 10ch. green	75	10
N898	– 10ch. orange	75	10
N899	– 10ch. black	75	10
N900	– 10ch. brown	75	10

DESIGNS: No. N898, Rice harvester; N899, Weed-spraying machine; N900, Threshing machine.

387 Ponghwa

1969. Revolutionary Historical Sites. Multicoloured.

N901	10ch. Type **387**	25	10
N902	10ch. Mangyongdae, birthplace of Kim Il Sung	25	10

388 Kim crosses into Manchuria, 1926, aged 13

1969. Kim Il Sung in Manchuria. Multicoloured. No. N907 with gum.

N903	10ch. Type **388**	40	10
N904	10ch. Leading strike of Yuwen Middle School boys, 1927	40	10
N905	10ch. Leading anti-Japanese demonstration in Kirin, 1928	40	10
N906	10ch. Presiding at meeting of Young Communist League, 1930	40	10
N907	10ch. Meeting of young revolutionaries	40	10

389 Birthplace at Chilgol

1969. Commemoration of Mrs. Kang Ban Sok, mother of Kim Il Sung. Multicoloured.

N908	10ch. Type **389**	30	10
N909	10ch. With members of Women's Association . .	30	10
N910	10ch. Resisting Japanese police	2·50	40

390 Pegaebong Bivouac

1969. Bivouac Sites in the Guerrilla War against the Japanese. Multicoloured.

N911	5ch. Type **390**	20	10
N912	10ch. Mupo site (horiz) . .	30	10
N913	10ch. Chongbong site . . .	30	10
N914	40ch. Konchang site (horiz)	1·00	20

391 Chollima Statue

392 Museum of the Revolution, Pyongyang

1969.

N915	**391** 10ch. blue	25	10
N916	**392** 10ch. green	25	10

393 Mangyong Chickens

395 Statue of Marshal Kim Il Sung

394 Marshal Kim Il Sung and Children

1969. Korean Poultry.
N917 **393** 10ch. blue 45 10
N918 – 10ch. violet . . . . . . 1·25 15
DESIGN: No. N918, Kwangpo ducks.

1969. Kim Il Sung's Educational System. Mult.
N919 2ch. Type **394** 25 10
N920 10ch. Worker with books 25 10
N921 40ch. Students with books 50 20

1969. Memorials on Pochonbo Battlefield. Inscr "1937.6.4". Multicoloured.
N922 5ch. Machine-gun post . . 25 10
N923 10ch. Type **395** 25 10
N924 10ch. "Aspen-tree" monument 25 10
N925 10ch. Glade Konjang Hill 25 10

396 Teaching at Myongsin School

1969. Commemoration of Kim Hyong Jik, father of Kim Il Sung. Multicoloured.
N926 10ch. Type **396** 30 10
N927 10ch. Secret meeting with Korean National Association members . . 30 10

397 Relay Runner

1969. 20th Anniv of Sports Day.
N928 **397** 10ch. multicoloured . . 35 10

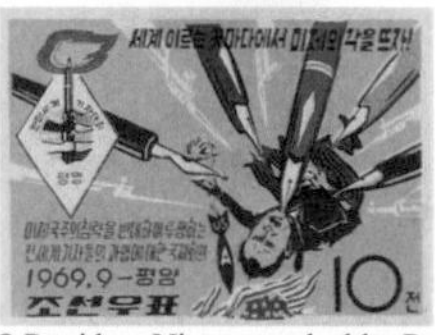

398 President Nixon attacked by Pens

1969. Anti-U.S. Imperialism Journalists' Conference, Pyongyang.
N929 **398** 10ch. multicoloured . . 35 10

399 Fighters and Battle

1969. Implementation of Ten-Point Programme of Kim Il Sung. Multicoloured.
N930 5ch. Type **399** (Reunification of Korea) 30 10
N931 10ch. Workers upholding slogan (vert) 30 10

400 Bayonet Attack over U.S. Flag

1969. Anti-American Campaign.
N932 **400** 10ch. multicoloured . . 35 10

401 Armed Workers

1969. Struggle for the Reunification of Korea. Multicoloured.
N933 10ch. Workers stabbing U.S. soldier (vert) . . . 20 10
N934 10ch. Kim Il Sung and crowd with flags (vert) 20 10
N935 50ch. Type **401** 50 20

402 Buri

1969. Korean Fishes. Multicoloured.
N936 5ch. Type **402** . . . . . . 1·00 10
N937 10ch. Eastern dace . . . . 1·75 10
N938 40ch. Flat-headed grey mullet . . . . 3·00 40

403 Freighter "Taesungsan"

1969.
N939 **403** 10ch. purple 75 10

405 Dahwangwai (1935)

407 Vietnamese Soldier and Furnaceman

406 Lake Chon

1970. Guerrilla Conference Places.
N940 **405** 2ch. blue and green . . 25 10
N941 – 5ch. brown and green 25 10
N942 – 10ch. lt green & green 25 10
DESIGNS: 5ch. Yaoyinggou (barn) (1935); 10ch. Xiaohaerbaling (tent) (1940).

1970. Mt. Paekdu, Home of Revolution (1st issue). Inscr "1970".
N943 **406** 10ch. black, brown & grn 60 10
N944 – 10ch. black, green & yell 60 10
N945 – 10ch. purple, blue & yell 60 10
N946 – 10ch. black, blue and pink 60 10
DESIGNS: No. N944, Piryu Peak; N945, Pyongsa (Soldier) Peak; N946, Changgun (General) Peak.
See also Nos. N979/81.

1970. Help for the Vietnamese People.
N947 **407** 10ch. green, brown & red 20 10

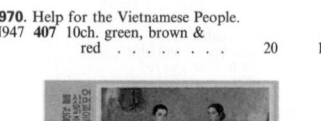

408 Receiving his Father's Revolvers from his Mother

1970. Revolutionary Career of Kim Il Sung. Multicoloured.
N948 10ch. Type **408** 65 20
N949 10ch. Receiving smuggled weapons from his mother 65 20
N950 10ch. Talking to farm workers 65 20
N951 10ch. At Kalun meeting, 1930 . . . . 65 20

409 Lenin

410 March of Koreans

1970. Birth Centenary of Lenin.
N952 **409** 10ch. brown & cinnamon 30 10
N953 – 10ch. brown and green 30 10
DESIGN: No. N953, Lenin making a speech.

1970. 15th Anniv of Association of Koreans in Japan.
N954 **410** 10ch. red 20 10
N955 10ch. purple 20 10

411 Uniformed Factory Worker

413 "Electricity Flows"

412 Students and Newspapers

1970. Workers' Militia.
N956 **411** 10ch. green, brn & mve 20 10
N957 – 10ch. green, brown & bl 20 10
DESIGN—HORIZ: No. N957, Militiaman saluting.

1970. Peasant Education. Multicoloured.
N958 2ch. Type **412** 35 10
N959 5ch. Peasant with book . . 20 10
N960 10ch. Students in class . . 20 10

1970. Commemoration of Army Electrical Engineers.
N961 **413** 10ch. brown 40 10

414 Soldier with Rifle

1970. Campaign Month for Withdrawal of U.S. Troops from South Korea.
N962 **414** 5ch. violet 15 10
N963 – 10ch. purple 30 10
DESIGN: 10ch. Soldier and partisan.

415 Rebel wielding Weapons

1970. Struggle in South Korea against U.S. Imperialism.
N964 **415** 10ch. violet 20 10

416 Labourer ("Fertilizers")

1970. Encouragement of Increased Productivity.
N965 **416** 10ch. green, pink & brn 40 10
N966 – 10ch. green, red & brn 70 10
N967 – 10ch. blue, green & brn 40 10
N968 – 10ch. bistre, brn & grn 40 10
N969 – 10ch. violet, green & brn 50 10
DESIGNS: No. N966, Furnaceman ("Steel"); N967, Operative ("Machines"); N968, Labourer ("Building Construction"); N969, Miner ("Mining").

417 Railway Guard

1970. "Speed the Transport System".
N970 **417** 10ch. blue, orange & grn . . . . 1·25 15

418 Agriculture

1970. Executive Decisions of the Workers' Party Congress. Designs embodying book.
N971 **418** 5ch. red 20 10
N972 – 10ch. green . . . . . . 1·10 15
N973 – 40ch. green . . . . . . 1·10 15
DESIGNS: 10ch. Industry; 40ch. The Armed Forces.

419 Chollima Statue and Workers' Party Banner

1970. 25th Anniv of Korean Workers' Party.
N974 **419** 10ch. red, brown & buff 20 10

420 Kim Il Sung and the People

1970. 5th Congress of Workers' Party. Miniature sheet (153 × 92 mm) comprising ten stamps as T **420** (10ch. values with symbols and inscr in panel at right).
MSN975 Multicoloured, comprising 40ch. T **420** and nine 10ch. stamps showing Family and new housing; Advance with Kim Il Sung's programme; People's army; Furnaceman and industry; Anti-U.S. Imperialism; Peasants and agriculture; Students with books; Schoolgirl with book; Collaboration with Freedom Fighters . . . . 13·50 5·50

421 Emblem of League

1971. 25th Anniv of League of Socialist Working Youth.
N976 **421** 10ch. red, brown & blue 20 10

422 Log Cabin, Nanhutou

1971. 35th Anniv of Nanhutou Guerrilla Conference.
N977 **422** 10ch. multicoloured . . 20 10

423 Tractor Driver

1971. 25th Anniv of Land Reform Law.
N978 **423** 2ch. red, green and black 20 10

1971. Mt. Paekdu, Home of Revolution (2nd issue). As T **406** but inscr "1971".
N979 2ch. black, olive and green 35 10
N980 5ch. pink, black and slate 2·25 15
N981 10ch. black, red and grey 60 10

DESIGNS—HORIZ: 2ch. General view; 10ch. Western peak. VERT: 5ch. Waterfall.

424 Popyong Museum

1971. Museum of the Revolution.

N982	**424**	10ch. brown and yellow	20	10
N983	–	10ch. blue and orange	20	10
N984	–	10ch. green and orange	20	10

DESIGNS: No. N983, Mangyongdae Museum; N984, Chunggang Museum.

425 Miner

1971. Six Year Plan for Coal Industry.

N985	**425**	10ch. multicoloured . .	40	10

426 Kim Il Sung

1971. Founding of Anti-Japanese Guerrilla Army. Multicoloured.

N986	10ch. Type **426**	35	10
N987	10ch. Kim Il Sung founding Anti-Japanese Guerrilla Army (horiz)	35	10
N988	10ch. Kim Il Sung addressing the people (horiz)	35	10
N989	10ch. Kim Il Sung and members of Children's Corps (horiz)	35	10

428 Hands holding Hammer and Rifle

1971. 85th Anniv of Labour Day.

N990	**428**	1wn. red, brown and buff	2·25	40

429 Soldiers and Map

430 Monument

1971. 35th Anniv of Association for Restoration of Fatherland.

N991	**429**	10ch. red, buff and black	35	10

1971. Battlefields in Musan Area, May 1939. Multicoloured.

N992	5ch. Type **430**	15	10
N993	10ch. Machine guns in perspex cases (horiz) . .	20	10
N994	40ch. Huts among birch trees (horiz)	55	15

431 Koreans Marching

432 Flame Emblem

1971. Solidarity of Koreans in Japan.

N995	**431**	10ch. brown	20	10

1971. 25th Anniv of Korean Childrens' Union.

N996	**432**	10ch. red, yellow and blue	20	10

433 Marchers and Banners

434 Foundryman

1971. 6th Congress of League of Socialist Working Youth.

N997	**433**	5ch. red, buff and black	10	10
N998	–	10ch. red, green & black	20	10

DESIGN: 10c. Marchers and banner under globe.

1971. 25th Anniv of Labour Law.

N999	**434**	5ch. black, purple & buff	20	10

435 Young Women

1971. 25th Anniv of Sex Equality Law.

N1000	**435**	5ch. multicoloured . .	20	10

436 Schoolchildren

1971. 15th Anniv of Compulsory Primary Education.

N1001	**436**	10ch. multicoloured . .	50	10

437 Choe Yong Do and Combat Scene

1971. Heroes of the Revolutionary Struggle in South Korea.

N1002	**437**	5ch. black and green	25	10
N1003	–	10ch. red and brown	25	10
N1004	–	10ch. black and red . .	25	10

DESIGNS: No. N1003, Revolutionary with book; N1004, Kim Jong Tae and scene of triumph.

438 Two Foundrymen

1971. 25th Anniv of Nationalization of Industry Law.

N1005	**438**	5ch. black, green & brn	1·50	10

439 Struggle in Korea

1971. The Anti-Imperialist and Anti-U.S. Imperialist Struggles.

N1006	**439**	10ch. red, black and brown	25	10
N1007	–	10ch. brown, black and blue	35	10
N1008	–	10ch. red, black and pink	50	10
N1009	–	10ch. black, olive and green	25	10
N1010	–	10ch. orange, black and red	50	10
N1011	–	40ch. green, black and pink	50	15

DESIGNS: No. N1007, Struggle in Vietnam; N1008, Soldier with rifle and airplane marked "EC"; N1009, Struggle in Africa; N1010, Cuban soldier and Central America; N1011, Bayoneting U.S. soldier.

440 Kim Il Sung University

1971. 25th Anniv of Kim Il Sung University.

N1012	**440**	10ch. grey, red & yellow	20	10

441 Iron-ore Ladle (Mining)

1971. Tasks of Six Year Plan. Multicoloured.

N1013	10ch. Type **441**	2·75	15
N1014	10ch. Workers and text . .	30	10
N1015	10ch. Electric train and track (Transport) . . .	2·75	15
N1016	10ch. Hand and wrench (Industry)	30	10
N1017	10ch. Mechanical scoop (Construction)	2·75	15
N1018	10ch. Manufactured goods (Trade)	30	10
N1019	10ch. Crate on hoists (Exports)	25	10
N1020	10ch. Lathe (Heavy Industries)	2·75	15
N1021	10ch. Freighter (Shipping)	60	10
N1022	10ch. Household equipment (Light Industries)	25	10
N1023	10ch. Corncob and wheat (Agriculture)	40	10

442 Technicians

1971. Cultural Revolution. Multicoloured.

N1024	2ch. Type **442**	20	10
N1025	5ch. Mechanic	25	10
N1026	10ch. Schoolchildren . . .	30	10
N1027	10ch. Chemist	50	10
N1028	10ch. Composer at piano	85	15

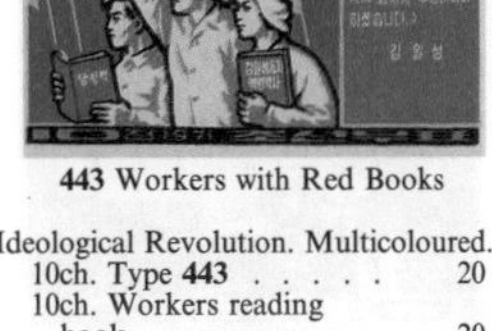
443 Workers with Red Books

1971. Ideological Revolution. Multicoloured.

N1029	10ch. Type **443**	20	10
N1030	10ch. Workers reading book	20	10
N1031	10ch. Workers' lecture . .	20	10
N1032	10ch. Worker and pneumatic drill	20	10

444 Korean Family

1971. Improvement in Living Standards.

N1033	**444**	10ch. multicoloured . .	15	10

445 Furnaceman

1971. Implementation of Decisions of Fifth Workers' Party Conference.

N1034	**445**	10ch. multicoloured . .	1·00	10

446

447 6000-ton Press

1971. Solidarity with South Korean Revolutionaries.

N1036	**446**	10ch. brown, bl & blk	30	10
N1037	–	10ch. brn, flesh & red	30	10
N1038	–	10ch. multicoloured . .	30	10
N1039	–	10ch. multicoloured . .	30	10

DESIGNS—VERT: No. N1037, U.S. soldier attacked by poster boards; N1038, Hands holding rifles aloft. HORIZ: No. N1039, Men advancing with rifles.

1971.

N1040	**447**	2ch. brown	70	10
N1041	–	5ch. blue	90	15
N1042	–	10ch. green	1·10	10
N1043	–	10ch. green	1·10	10

DESIGNS: No. N1041, Refrigerated freighter "Ponghwasan"; N1042, 300 h.p. bulldozer; N1043, "Sungrisan" lorry.

448 Title-page and Militants

1971. 35th Anniv of "Samil Wolgan" Magazine.

N1044	**448**	10ch. red, green & black	45	10

452 Poultry Chicks

1972. Poultry Breeding.

N1051	**452**	5ch. yellow, black and brown	25	10
N1052	–	10ch. orange, bistre and brown	35	10
N1053	–	40ch. blue, orange and deep blue	55	15

DESIGNS: 10ch. Chickens and battery egg house; 40ch. Eggs and fowls suspended from hooks.

453 Scene from "Village Shrine"

1972. Films of Guerrilla War.

N1054	**453**	10ch. grey and green	60	10
N1055	–	10ch. blue, pur & orge	60	10
N1056	–	10ch. purple, blue & yell	60	10

DESIGNS: No. N1055, Patriot with pistol ("A Sea of Blood"); N1056, Guerrilla using bayonet ("The Lot of a Self-Defence Corps Member").

454 Kim Il Sung acknowledging Greetings

1972. Kim Il Sung's 60th Birthday. Scenes in the life of Kim Il Sung, dated "1912–1972". Mult.

N1057	5ch. Type **454**	20	10
N1058	5ch. In campaign H.Q.	20	10
N1059	5ch. Military conference (horiz)	20	10
N1060	10ch. In wheatfield (horiz)	30	10
N1061	10ch. Directing construction (horiz)	2·00	40
N1062	10ch. Talking to foundry workers (horiz)	20	10
N1063	10ch. Aboard whaler (horiz)	55	10
N1064	10ch. Visiting a hospital (horiz)	75	10
N1065	10ch. Viewing orchard (horiz)	20	10
N1066	10ch. With survey party on Haeju–Hasong railway line (horiz)	2·00	40
N1067	10ch. Meeting female workers at silk factory (horiz)	1·00	15
N1068	10ch. Village conference (horiz)	20	10
N1069	10ch. Touring chicken factory (horiz)	35	10
N1070	40ch. Relaxing with children	45	20
N1071	1wn. Giant portrait and marchers	70	40
MSN1072	100 × 79 mm. 3wn. Kim Il Sung by Lake Chon (horiz). Imperf	3·75	1·50

455 Bugler sounding "Charge"

1972. 40th Anniv of Guerrilla Army.

N1073	**455** 10ch. multicoloured	45	10

456 Pavilion of Ryongpo

1972. Historic Sites of the 1950–53 War. Mult.

N1074	2ch. Type **456**	15	10
N1075	5ch. Houses at Onjong	15	10
N1076	10ch. Headquarters, Kosanjin	15	10
N1077	40ch. Victory Museum, Chonsung-dong	30	10

457 Volleyball

1972. Olympic Games, Munich. Multicoloured.

N1078	2ch. Type **457**	35	10
N1079	5ch. Boxing (horiz)	50	10
N1080	10ch. Judo	50	10
N1081	10ch. Wrestling (horiz)	50	10
N1082	40ch. Rifle-shooting	1·10	20

458 Chollima Street, Pyongyang

1971. Chollima Street, Pyongyang.

N1083	– 5ch. orange and black	1·60	15
N1084	**458** 10ch. yellow and black	60	15
N1085	– 10ch. green and black	60	15

DESIGNS: No. N1083, Bridge and skyscraper blocks; N1085, Another view looking up street.

459 Dredger

1972. Development of Natural Resources. Multicoloured.

N1086	5ch. Type **459**	35	10
N1087	10ch. Forestry	50	10
N1088	40ch. Reclaiming land from the sea	60	15

460 Ferrous Industry

1972. Tasks of the Six-Year Plan. The Metallurgical Industry. Inscr "1971–1976". Multicoloured.

N1089	10ch. Type **460**	1·40	10
N1090	10ch. Non-ferrous Industry	40	10

461 Iron Ore Industry

1972. Tasks of the Six-Year Plan. The Mining Industry. Inscr "1971–1976". Multicoloured.

N1091	10ch. Type **461**	40	10
N1092	10ch. Coal mining industry	1·50	15

462 Electronic and Automation Industry

1972. Tasks of the Six-Year Plan. The Engineering Industry. Inscr "1971–1976". Multicoloured.

N1093	10ch. Type **462**	60	10
N1094	10ch. Single-purpose machines	40	10
N1095	10ch. Machine tools	40	10

463 Clearing Virgin Soil

1972. Tasks of the Six-Year Plan. Rural Economy. Multicoloured.

N1096	10ch. Type **463**	45	10
N1097	10ch. Irrigation	45	10
N1098	10ch. Harvesting	45	10

464 Automation

1972. Tasks of the Six-Year Plan. Inscr "1971–1976". Multicoloured.

N1099	10ch. Type **464**	1·60	10
N1100	10ch. Agricultural mechanization	50	10
N1101	10ch. Lightening of household chores	50	10

465 Chemical Fibres and Materials

1972. Tasks of the Six-Year Plan. The Chemical Industry. Inscr "1971–1976". Multicoloured.

N1102	10ch. Type **465**	60	10
N1103	10ch. Fertilizers, insecticides and weed killers	60	10

466 Textiles

1972. Tasks of the Six-Year Plan. Consumer Goods. Inscr "1971–1976". Multicoloured.

N1104	10ch. Type **466**	65	10
N1105	10ch. Kitchen ware and overalls	45	10
N1106	10ch. Household goods	45	10

467 Fish, Fruit and Vegetables

1972. Tasks of the Six-Year Plan. The Food Industry. Multicoloured.

N1107	10ch. Type **467**	90	10
N1108	10ch. Tinned foods	65	10
N1109	10ch. Food packaging	65	10

468 Electrifying Railway Lines

1972. Tasks of the Six-Year Plan. Transport. Inscr "1971–1976". Multicoloured.

N1110	10ch. Type **468**	45	10
N1111	10ch. Laying new railway track	45	10
N1112	10ch. Freighters	55	10

469 Soldier with Shell

1972. North Korean Armed Forces. Multicoloured.

N1113	10ch. Type **469**	35	10
N1114	10ch. Marine	35	10
N1115	10ch. Air Force pilot	35	10

470 "Revolution of 19 April 1960"

1972. The Struggle for Reunification of Korea. Multicoloured.

N1116	10ch. Type **470**	15	10
N1117	10ch. Marchers with banner	15	10
N1118	10ch. Insurgents with red banner	15	10
N1119	10ch. Attacking U.S. and South Korean soldiers	15	10
N1120	10ch. Workers with posters	15	10
N1121	10ch. Workers acclaiming revolution	3·50	40
N1122	10ch. Workers and manifesto	15	10

471 Single-spindle Automatic Lathe

1972. Machine Tools.

N1123	**471** 5ch. green and purple	25	10
N1124	– 10ch. blue and green	35	10
N1125	– 40ch. green and brown	80	15

DESIGNS—HORIZ: 10ch. "Kusong-3" lathe; VERT: 40ch. 2,000 ton crank press.

472 Casting Vote

1972. National Elections. Multicoloured.

N1126	10ch. Type **472**	25	10
N1127	10ch. Election campaigner	25	10

475 Soldier

1973. 25th Anniv of Founding of Korean People's Army. Multicoloured.

N1130	5ch. Type **475**	20	10
N1131	10ch. Sailor	30	10
N1132	40ch. Airman	70	25

476 Wrestling Site

1973. Scenes of Kim Il Sung's Childhood, Mangyongdae. Multicoloured.

N1133	2ch. Type **476**	15	10
N1134	5ch. Warship rock	15	10
N1135	10ch. Swinging site (vert)	20	10
N1136	10ch. Sliding rock	20	10
N1137	40ch. Fishing site	60	15

477 Monument to Socialist Revolution and Construction, Mansu Hill

1973. Museum of the Korean Revolution.

N1138	**477** 10ch. multicoloured	25	10
N1139	– 10ch. multicoloured	25	10
N1140	– 40ch. multicoloured	50	15
N1141	– 3wn. green and yellow	2·50	60

DESIGNS—As Type **477**: 10ch. (N1139) Similar monument but men in military clothes; 40ch. Statue of Kim Il Sung. HORIZ—60 × 29 mm: 3wn. Museum building.

478 Karajibong Camp

1973. Secret Camps by Tuman-Gang in Guerrilla War, 1932. Multicoloured.

N1142 10ch. Type **478** 15 10
N1143 10ch. Soksaegol Camp . . 15 10

479

1973. Menace of Japanese Influence in South Korea.

N1144 **479** 10ch. multicoloured . . 20 10

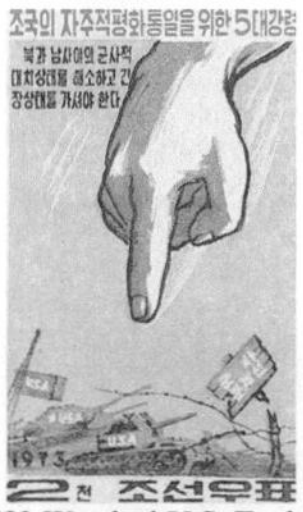

480 Wrecked U.S. Tanks

1973. Five-point Programme for Reunification of Korea. Multicoloured.

N1145 2ch. Type **480** 40 10
N1146 5ch. Electric train and crane lifting tractor . . 2·50 20
N1147 10ch. Leaflets falling on crowd 20 10
N1148 10ch. Hand holding leaflet and map of Korea . . . 40 10
N1149 40ch. Banner and globe 60 20

481 Lorries **482** Volleyball

1973. Lorries and Tractors. Multicoloured.

N1150 10ch. Type **481** 50 10
N1151 10ch. Tractors and earth-moving machine 50 10

1973. Socialist Countries' Junior Women's Volleyball Games, Pyongyang.

N1152 **482** 10ch. multicoloured . . 50 10

483 Battlefield

1973. 20th Anniv of Victory in Korean War.

N1153 **483** 10ch. green, pur & blk 20 10
N1154 – 10ch. brown, bl & blk 20 10

DESIGN: 10ch. Urban fighting.

484 "The Snow Falls"

1973. Mansudae Art Troupe. Dances. Multicoloured.

N1155 10ch. Type **484** 60 10
N1156 25ch. "A Bumper Harvest of Apples" . . . . . . 1·50 25
N1157 40ch. "Azalea of the Fatherland" . . . . . 1·75 30

485 Schoolchildren

1973. Ten Years Compulsory Secondary Education.

N1158 **485** 10ch. multicoloured . . 25 10

486 "Fervour in the Revolution"

1973. The Works of Kim Il Sung (1st series).

N1159 **486** 10ch. brown, red and yellow 15 10
N1160 – 10ch. brown, green and yellow 15 10
N1161 – 10ch. lake, brown and yellow 15 10

DESIGNS: No. N1160, Selected works; N1161, "Strengthen the Socialist System".

See also Nos. N1217/18.

487 Celebrating Republic

1973. 25th Anniv of People's Republic. Multicoloured.

N1162 5ch. Type **487** 10 10
N1163 10ch. Fighting in Korean War 10 10
N1164 40ch. Peace and reconstruction . . . . . 1·60 40

488 Pobwang Peak

1973. Mt. Myohyang. Multicoloured.

N1165 2ch. Type **488** 25 10
N1166 5ch. Inhodae Pavilion . . 35 10
N1167 10ch. Taeha Falls (vert) 1·75 30
N1168 40ch. Rongyon Falls (vert) 2·50 30

489 Party Memorial Building

1973. Party Memorial Building.

N1169 **489** 1wn. brn, grey & buff 1·25 30

490 Football and Handball

1973. National People's Sports Meeting. Mult.

N1170 2ch. Type **490** 60 10
N1171 5ch. High jumper and woman sprinter 40 10
N1172 10ch. Skaters and skiers 50 10
N1173 10ch. Wrestling and swinging 40 10
N1174 40ch. Parachutist and motor cyclists . . . . . 3·00 25

491 Weightlifting **492** Chongryu Cliff

1973. Junior Weightlifting Championships of Socialist Countries.

N1175 **491** 10ch. blue, brn & grn 50 10

1973. Scenery of Moran Hill, Pyongyang. Multicoloured.

N1176 2ch. Type **492** 70 15
N1177 5ch. Moran Waterfall . . 2·75 40
N1178 10ch. Pubyok Pavilion . . 75 10
N1179 40ch. Ulmil Pavilion . . . 90 15

493 Rainbow Bridge **494** Magnolia Flower

1973. Diamond Mountains Scenery (4th issue). Multicoloured.

N1180 2ch. Type **493** . . . . . 1·50 15
N1181 5ch. Suspension footbridge, Okryudong (horiz) . . . . 1·50 15
N1182 10ch. Chonnyo Peak . . . 75 10
N1183 10ch. Chilchung Rock and Sonji Peak (horiz) . . . 75 10
N1184 40ch. Sujong and Pari Peaks (horiz) 85 15

1973.

N1185 **494** 10ch. multicoloured . . 60 10

495 S. Korean Revolutionaries

1973. South Korean Revolution. Multicoloured.

N1186 10ch. Type **495** 30 10
N1187 10ch. Marching revolutionaries 30 10

496 Cock sees Butterflies

1973. Scenes from "Cock Chasing Butterflies". Fairy Tale. Multicoloured.

N1188 2ch. Type **496** . . . . . 1·50 10
N1189 5ch. Butterflies discuss how to repel cock . . . 1·50 10
N1190 10ch. Cock chasing butterflies with basket 2·00 15
N1191 10ch. Cock chasing butterfly up cliff . . . . 2·00 20
N1192 40ch. Cock chasing butterflies over cliff . . 2·25 25
N1193 90ch. Cock falls into sea and butterflies escape 2·75 30

497 Yonpung

1973. Historical Sites of War and Revolution (40ch.). Multicoloured.

N1196 2ch. Type **497** 10 10
N1197 5ch. Hyangha 10 10
N1198 10ch. Changgol 15 10
N1199 40ch. Paeksong 55 10

498 Science Library, Kim Il Sung University

1973. New Buildings in Pyongyang.

N1200 **498** 2ch. violet 50 10
N1201 – 5ch. green 15 10
N1202 – 10ch. brown 25 10
N1203 – 40ch. brown and buff 55 15
N1204 – 90ch. buff 95 30

DESIGNS—HORIZ: 10ch. Victory Museum; 40ch. People's Palace of Culture; 90ch. Indoor stadium. VERT: 5ch. Building No. 2, Kim Il Sung University.

499 Red Book

1973. Socialist Constitution of North Korea. Multicoloured.

N1205 10ch. Type **499** 15 10
N1206 10ch. Marchers with red book and banners . . . 15 10
N1207 10ch. Marchers with red book and emblem . . . 15 10

500 Oriental Great Reed Warbler

1973. Korean Songbirds. Multicoloured.

N1208 5ch. Type **500** . . . . . 2·40 40
N1209 10ch. Grey starling (facing right) . . . . 3·50 70
N1210 10ch. Daurian starling (facing left) . . . . . . 3·50 70

503 Chollima Statue

1974. The Works of Kim Il Sung (2nd series). Multicoloured.

N1217 10ch. Type **503** 65 10
N1218 10ch. Bayonets threatening U.S. soldier 15 10

504 Train in Station

1974. Opening of Pyongyang Metro. Multicoloured.

N1219 10ch. Type **504** 45 10
N1220 10ch. Escalators 45 10
N1221 10ch. Station hall 45 10

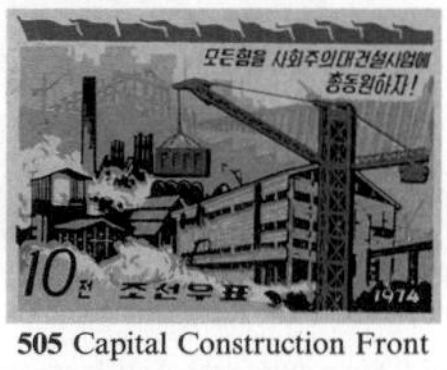

505 Capital Construction Front

1974. Five Fronts of Socialist Construction. Multicoloured.

N1222 10ch. Type **505** 15 10
N1223 10ch. Agricultural front 25 10
N1224 10ch. Transport front . . 1·25 15
N1225 10ch. Fisheries front . . . 90 15
N1226 10ch. Industrial front (vert) 25 10

506 Marchers with Banners

1974. 10th Anniv of Publication of "Theses on the Socialist Rural Question in Our Country". Multicoloured.

N1227	10ch. Type **506**	15	10
N1228	10ch. Book and rejoicing crowd	15	10
N1229	10ch. Tractor and banners	15	10

Nos. N1227/9 were issued together, se-tenant, forming a composite design.

507 Manure Spreader

1974. Farm Machinery.

N1230	**507**	2ch. green, black & red	60	10
N1231	–	5ch. red, black and blue	60	10
N1232	–	10ch. red, black and green	60	10

DESIGNS: 5ch. "Progress" tractor; 10ch. "Mount Taedoksan" tractor.

508 Archery (Grenoble)

1974. North Korean Victories at International Sports Meetings. Multicoloured.

N1233	2ch. Type **508**	1·00	15
N1234	5ch. Gymnastics (Varna)	25	10
N1235	10ch. Boxing (Bucharest)	40	10
N1236	20ch. Volleyball (Pyongyang)	25	10
N1237	30ch. Rifle shooting (Sofia)	60	10
N1238	40ch. Judo (Tbilisi)	80	15
N1239	60ch. Model aircraft flying (Vienna) (horiz)	1·25	20
N1240	1wn. 50 Table tennis (Peking) (horiz)	2·25	30

509 Book and Rejoicing Crowd

1974. The First Country with No Taxes.

N1241	**509**	10ch. multicoloured	20	10

510 Drawing up Programme in Woods

1974. Kim Il Sung during the Anti-Japanese Struggle. Multicoloured.

N1242	10ch. Type **510**	25	10
N1243	10ch. Giving directions to Pak Dal	25	10
N1244	10ch. Presiding over Nanhutou Conference	25	10
N1245	10ch. Supervising creation of strongpoint	25	10

511 Sun Hui loses her Sight

1974. Scenes from "The Flower Girl" (revolutionary opera). Multicoloured.

N1246	2ch. Type **511**	65	10
N1247	5ch. Death of Ggot Bun's mother	65	10
N1248	10ch. Ggot Bun throws boiling water at landlord	1·40	10
N1249	40ch. Ggot Bun joins revolutionaries	1·75	15
MSN1250	111 × 62 mm. 50ch. Ggot Bun amid flowers of revolution. Imperf	2·25	60

512 Leopard Cat

1974. 15th Anniv of Pyongyang Zoo. Multicoloured.

N1251	2ch. Type **512**	60	10
N1252	5ch. Lynx	60	10
N1253	10ch. Red fox	60	10
N1254	10ch. Wild boar	60	10
N1255	20ch. Dhole	60	15
N1256	40ch. Brown bear	75	25
N1257	60ch. Leopard	1·25	25
N1258	70ch. Tiger	1·75	30
N1259	90ch. Lion	2·00	35
MSN1260	140 × 100 mm. Diamond-shaped designs: 10ch. Wildcat; 30ch. Lynx; 50ch. Leopard; 60ch. Tiger. Imperf	4·25	90

513 "Rosa acucularis lindly"

1974. Roses. Multicoloured.

N1261	2ch. Type **513**	40	10
N1262	5ch. Yellow sweet briar	45	10
N1263	10ch. Pink aromatic rose	55	10
N1264	10ch. Aronia sweet briar (yellow centres)	55	10
N1265	40ch. Multi-petal sweet briar	1·40	10

514 Kim Il Sung greeted by Children (½-size illustration)

1974. 30th Anniv of Korean Children's Union. Sheet 126 × 95 mm.

MSN1266	**514**	1w.20 multicoloured	1·60	65

515 Weigela

1974. Flowering Plants of Mt. Paekdu. Mult.

N1267	2ch. Type **515**	50	10
N1268	5ch. Amaryllis	50	10
N1269	10ch. Red lily	50	10
N1270	20ch. Orange lily	65	10
N1271	40ch. Azalea	90	10
N1272	60ch. Yellow lily	1·50	10

516 Postwoman and Construction Site

1974. Centenary of U.P.U. and Admission of North Korea to Union. Multicoloured.

N1273	10ch. Type **516**	1·50	15
N1274	25ch. Chollima monument	25	10
N1275	40ch. Globe and Antonov An-12 transport planes	1·00	15

517 Common Pond Frog

1974. Amphibians. Multicoloured.

N1276	2ch. Type **517**	1·00	10
N1277	5ch. Oriental fire-bellied toad	1·25	10
N1278	10ch. Bullfrog	1·50	15
N1279	40ch. Common toad	2·00	25

518 "Women of Namgang Village"

1974. Korean Paintings. Multicoloured.

N1281	2ch. Type **518**	60	10
N1282	5ch. "An Old Man on the Rakdong River" (60 × 49 mm)	75	10
N1283	10ch. "Morning in the Nae-kumgang" (bridge)	1·50	10
N1284	20ch. "Mt. Kumgang" (60 × 49 mm)	1·25	15
MSN1285	116 × 115 mm. 1wn.50 "Evening Glow in Kangson". Imperf	3·25	90

519 "Elektron 1" and "Elektron 2", 1964

1974. Cosmonauts Day. Multicoloured.

N1286	10ch. Type **519**	15	10
N1287	20ch. "Proton 1", 1965	25	10
N1288	30ch. "Venera 3", 1966	40	10
N1289	40ch. "Venera 5" and "Venera 6", 1969	50	10
MSN1290	80 × 120 mm. 1wn. Dogs Belka and Strelka. Imperf	2·75	50

520 Satellite

1974. 4th Anniv of Launching of First Chinese Satellite. Sheet 80 × 120 mm. Imperf.

MSN1291	**520**	50ch. multicoloured	1·75	65

521 Antonov An-2 Biplane

1974. Civil Aviation. Multicoloured.

N1292	2ch. Type **521**	65	10
N1293	5ch. Lisunov Li-2	65	10
N1294	10ch. Ilyushin Il-14P	90	10
N1295	40ch. Antonov An-24	1·25	35
N1296	60ch. Ilyushin Il-18	2·00	50
MSN1297	96 × 68 mm. 90ch. Airliner. Imperf	3·75	85

522 "Rhododendron redowskianum"

1974. Plants of Mt. Paekdu. Multicoloured.

N1298	2ch. Type **522**	45	10
N1299	5ch. "Dryas octopetala"	45	10
N1300	10ch. "Potentilla fruticosa"	50	10
N1301	20ch. "Papaver somniferum"	65	10
N1302	40ch. "Phyllodoce caerulea"	90	20
N1303	60ch. "Oxytropis anertii"	1·50	40

523 "Sobaek River in the Morning"

1974. Modern Korean Paintings (1st series). Multicoloured.

N1304	10ch. Type **523**	60	10
N1305	20ch. "Combatants of Mt. Laohei" (60 × 40 mm)	65	10
N1306	30ch. "Spring in the Fields"	75	15
N1307	40ch. "Tideland Night"	5·25	60
N1308	60ch. "Daughter" (60 × 54 mm)	1·10	40

See also Nos. N1361/5, N1386/96 and N1485/9.

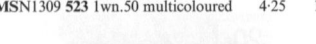

524 (½-size illustration)

1974. Bologna Exhibition for 50th Anniv of L'Unita (organ of the Italian communist party). Sheet 148 × 98 mm. Imperf.

MSN1309	**523**	1wn.50 multicoloured	4·25	1·50

525 Log Cabin, Unha Village

1974. Historic Sites of the Revolution. Multicoloured.

N1310	5ch. Munmyong	25	10
N1311	10ch. Type **525**	25	10

526 Sesame

1974. Oil-producing Plants. Multicoloured.

N1312	2ch. Type **526**	75	10
N1313	5ch. "Perilla frutescens"	80	10
N1314	10ch. Sunflower	90	10
N1315	40ch. Castor bean	1·25	40

527 Kim Il Sung as Guerrilla Leader

1974. Kim Il Sung. Multicoloured.

N1316	10ch. Type **527**	20	10
N1317	10ch. Commander of the People's Army (52 × 35 mm)	20	10
N1318	10ch. "The commander is also a son of the people" (52 × 35 mm)	20	10
N1319	10ch. Negotiating with the Chinese anti-Japanese unit (52 × 35 mm)	20	10

528

1974. Grand Monument on Mansu Hill. Mult.

N1320	10ch. Type **528**	15	10
N1321	10ch. As T **528** but men in civilian clothes	15	10
N1322	10ch. As T **528** but men facing left	15	10
N1323	10ch. As No. N1322 but men in civilian clothes	15	10

529 Factory Ship "Chilbosan"

1974. Deep-sea Fishing. Multicoloured.

N1324	2ch. Type **529**	70	25
N1325	5ch. Trawler support ship "Paekdusan"	70	25
N1326	10ch. Freighter "Moranbong"	70	25
N1327	20ch. Whale-catcher	70	25
N1328	30ch. Trawler	70	25
N1329	40ch. Stern trawler	70	25

539 Kim Il Sung crossing River Agrok

1975. 50th Anniv of Kim Il Sung's crossing of River Agrok.

N1349 **539**	10ch. multicoloured	25	10

540 Pak Yong Sun "World Table Tennis Queen"

1975. Pak Yong Sun, Winner of 33rd World Table Tennis Championships, Calcutta.

N1350 **540**	10ch. multicoloured	1·00	10
MSN1351	80 × 119 mm. 80ch. "Table Tennis Crown". Imperf	1·75	45

541 Common Zebra

1975. Pyongyang Zoo. Multicoloured.

N1352	10ch. Type **541**	30	10
N1353	10ch. African buffalo	30	10
N1354	20ch. Giant panda (horiz)	80	10
N1355	25ch. Bactrian camel	70	15
N1356	30ch. Indian elephant	1·25	20

542 "Blue Dragon"

1975. 7th-century Mural Paintings from Koguryo Tombs, Kangso.

N1357	10ch. Type **542**	75	10
N1358	15ch. "White Tiger"	1·00	10
N1359	25ch. "Red Phoenix" (vert)	1·25	10
N1360	40ch. "Snake-turtle"	1·75	25

543 "Spring in the Guerrilla Base" (1968)

1975. Modern Korean Paintings (2nd series). Anti-Japanese struggle. Multicoloured.

N1361	10ch. Type **543**	35	10
N1362	10ch. "Revolutionary Army landing at Unggi" (1969)	35	10
N1363	15ch. "Sewing Team Members" (1961)	55	10
N1364	20ch. "Girl Watering Horse" (1969)	1·00	15
N1365	30ch. "Kim Jong Suk giving Guidance to Children's Corps" (1970)	80	20

544 Cosmonaut

1975. Cosmonauts' Day. Multicoloured.

N1366	10ch. Type **544**	15	10
N1367	30ch. "Lunokhod" moon vehicle (horiz)	40	10
N1368	40ch. "Soyuz" spacecraft and "Salyut" space laboratory (horiz)	55	15

545 Victory Monument

1975. Commemoration of Battle of Pochonbo. Sheet 140 × 98 mm. Imperf.

MSN1369 **545**	1wn. multicoloured	1·75	55

546 The Beacon lit at Pochonbo, 1937

1975. Kim Il Sung during the Guerrilla War against the Japanese. Multicoloured.

N1370	10ch. Type **546**	25	10
N1371	10ch. "A Bowl of Parched-rice Powder", 1938	25	10
N1372	10ch. Guiding the Nanpaizi meeting, November, 1938	25	10
N1373	10ch. Welcoming helper	25	10
N1374	10ch. Lecturing the guerrillas	25	10
N1375	15ch. Advancing into the homeland, May 1939	35	10
N1376	25ch. By Lake Samji, May 1939	45	10
N1377	30ch. At Sinsadong, May 1939	55	10
N1378	40ch. Xiaohaerbaling meeting, 1940	65	15

547 Vase of Flowers and Kim Il Sung's Birthplace

1975. Kim Il Sung's 63rd Birthday. Multicoloured.

N1379	10ch. Type **547**	10	10
N1379a	40ch. Kim Il Sung's birthplace, Mangyongdae	35	10

548 South Korean Insurgent

1975. 15th Anniv of April 19th Rising.

N1380 **548**	10ch. multicoloured	15	10

549 "Kingfisher at a Lotus Pond"

1975. Paintings of Li Dynasty. Multicoloured.

N1381	5ch. Type **549**	1·50	10
N1382	10ch. "Crabs"	1·00	10
N1383	15ch. "Rose of Sharon"	1·75	20
N1384	25ch. "Lotus and Water Cock"	2·50	45
N1385	30ch. "Tree Peony and Red Junglefowl"	4·25	45

1975. Modern Korean Paintings (3rd series). Fatherland Liberation War. Dated designs as T **543**. Multicoloured.

N1386	5ch. "On the Advance Southward" (1966) (vert)	30	10
N1387	10ch. "The Assigned Post" (girl sentry) (1968) (vert)	40	10
N1388	15ch. "The Heroism of Li Su Bok" (1965)	40	10
N1389	25ch. "Retaliation" (woman machine-gunner) (1970)	65	20
N1390	30ch. "The awaited Troops" (1970)	80	20

1975. Modern Korean Paintings (4th series). Socialist Construction. As T **543**. Multicoloured.

N1391	10ch. "Pine Tree" (1966) (vert)	90	10
N1392	10ch. "The Blue Signal Lamp" (1960) (vert)	2·75	10
N1393	15ch. "A Night of Snowfall" (1963)	90	10
N1394	20ch. "Smelters" (1968)	1·00	15
N1395	25ch. "Tideland Reclamation" (1961)	1·00	15
N1396	30ch. "Mount Paekgum" (1966)	1·00	20

550 Flag and Building

552 "Feet first" entry (man)

551 Marathon Runners

1975. 20th Anniv of "Chongryon" Association of Koreans in Japan.

N1397 **550**	10ch. multicoloured	15	10
N1398	3wn. multicoloured	2·50	55

1975. Marathon Race of Socialist Countries. Sheet 105 × 74 mm. Imperf.

MSN1399 **551**	1wn. multicoloured	2·75	85

1975. Diving. Multicoloured.

N1400	10ch. Type **552**	25	10
N1401	25ch. Piked somersault (man)	50	10
N1402	40ch. "Head first" entry (woman)	1·00	15

553

1975. Campaign against U.S. Imperialism.
N1403 **553** 10ch. multicoloured . . 30 10

554 Silver Carp

1975. Fresh-water Fish. Multicoloured.
N1404 10ch. Type **554** 70 10
N1405 10ch. Elongate ilisha (swimming to right) . . 70 10
N1406 15ch. Banded minnow . . 1·00 15
N1407 25ch. Bare-headed bagrid 1·60 20
N1408 30ch. Amur catfish (swimming to right) . . 2·00 30
N1409 30ch. Chevron snakehead (swimming to left) . . . 2·00 30

555

1975. 10th Socialist Countries' Football Tournament, Pyongyang.
N1410 **555** 5ch. multicoloured . . 35 10
N1411 – 10ch. multicoloured . . 35 10
N1412 – 15ch. multicoloured . . 40 10
N1413 – 20ch. multicoloured . . 50 15
N1414 – 50ch. multicoloured . . 90 35
MSN1415 112 × 80 mm. 1wn. multicoloured. Imperf . . . . 3·00 95
DESIGNS: 10ch. to 1wn. Various footballers.

556 Blue and Yellow Macaw

557 Flats

1975. Birds. Multicoloured.
N1416 10ch. Type **556** . . . . . 1·50 20
N1417 15ch. Sulphur-crested cockatoo . . . . 1·75 25
N1418 20ch. Blyth's parakeet . . 2·25 40
N1419 25ch. Rainbow lory . . . 2·75 45
N1420 30ch. Budgerigar . . . . 3·25 60

1975. New Buildings in Pyongyang. Multicoloured.
N1421 90ch. Saesallim (formerly Sarguson) Street . . . . 1·50 40
N1422 1wn. Type **557** . . . . . 1·75 45
N1423 2wn. Potonggang Hotel 2·75 60

558 White Peach Blossom

559 Sejongbong

1975. Blossoms of Flowering Trees. Multicoloured.
N1424 10ch. Type **558** 40 10
N1425 15ch. Red peach blossom 40 10
N1426 20ch. Red plum blossom 60 15
N1427 25ch. Apricot blossom . . 75 15
N1428 30ch. Cherry blossom . . 1·00 20

1975. Landscapes in the Diamond Mountains. Multicoloured.
N1429 5ch. Type **559** 40 10
N1430 10ch. Chonsondae 65 10
N1431 15ch. Pisamun 85 10
N1432 25ch. Manmulsang . . . . 1·10 20
N1433 30ch. Chaehabong . . . . 1·25 20

560 Azalea

1975. Flowers of the Azalea Family. Multicoloured.
N1434 5ch. Type **560** 50 10
N1435 10ch. White azalea 50 10
N1436 15ch. Wild rhododendron 60 10
N1437 20ch. White rhododendron 60 15
N1438 25ch. Rhododendron . . . 80 15
N1439 30ch. Yellow rhododendron . . . . . 1·10 20

561 Gliders

1975. Training for National Defence. Mult.
N1440 5ch. Type **561** 60 10
N1441 5ch. Radio-controlled model airplane 60 10
N1442 10ch. "Free fall parachutist" (vert) . . . 75 10
N1443 10ch. Parachutist landing on target (vert) 75 10
N1444 20ch. Parachutist with bouquet of flowers (vert) 1·10 15
MSN1445 90 × 68 mm. 50ch. Three parachutists in circle. Imperf 1·50 45

562 Wild Apple

1975. Fruit Tree Blossom. Multicoloured.
N1446 10ch. Type **562** 40 10
N1447 15ch. Wild pear 40 10
N1448 20ch. Hawthorn 50 15
N1449 25ch. Chinese quince . . . 70 20
N1450 30ch. Flowering quince . . 80 20

563 Torch of Juche

1975. 30th Anniv of Korean Workers' Party. Multicoloured.
N1451 2ch. "Victory" and American graves 10 10
N1452 2ch. Sunrise over Mt. Paekdu-san 10 10
N1453 5ch. Type **563** 10 10
N1454 5ch. Chollima Statue and sunset over Pyongyang 10 10
N1455 10ch. Korean with Red Book 10 10
N1456 10ch. Chollima Statue . . 10 10
N1457 25ch. Crowds and burning building 35 10
N1458 70ch. Flowers and map of Korea 95 15
MSN1459 Two sheets (a) 85 × 120 mm. 90ch. Kim Il Sung delivering speech; (b) 120 × 85 mm. 1wn. Kim Il Sung leading crowd 2·75 1·25

564 Welcoming Crowd

1975. 30th Anniv of Kim Il Sung's Return to Pyongyang.
N1460 **564** 20ch. multicoloured . . 25 15

565 Workers holding "Juche" Torch

1975. 30th Anniv of "Rodong Simmun" (Journal of the Central Committee of the Worker's Party).
N1461 **565** 10ch. multicoloured . . 50 10
MSN1462 95 × 68 mm. **565** 1wn. multicoloured. Imperf . . . . 2·25 85

566 Hyonmu Gate

1975. Ancient Wall-Gates of Pyongyang. Mult.
N1463 10ch. Type **566** 10 10
N1464 10ch. Taedong Gate . . . 10 10
N1465 15ch. Potong Gate 20 10
N1466 20ch. Chongum Gate . . 35 15
N1467 30ch. Chilsong Gate (vert) 45 25

567

1975. Views of Mt. Chilbo.
N1468 **567** 10ch. multicoloured . . 40 10
N1469 – 10ch. multicoloured . . 40 10
N1470 – 15ch. multicoloured . . 65 10
N1471 – 20ch. multicoloured . . 75 15
N1472 – 30ch. multicoloured . . 85 20
DESIGNS: Nos. N1468/72, Various views.

568 Right-hand Section of Monument

1975. Historic Site of Revolution in Wangjaesan. Multicoloured.
N1473 10ch. Type **568** 10 10
N1474 15ch. Left-hand section of monument 20 10
N1475 25ch. Centre section of monument (38 × 60mm) 30 15
N1476 30ch. Centre section, close up (60 × 38mm) 40 20

569 Marchers with Flags

1976. 30th Anniv of Korean League of Socialist Working Youth. Multicoloured.
N1477 2ch. Flags and Emblem 15 10
N1478 70ch. Type **569** 90 40

570 Geese

1976. Ducks and Geese. Multicoloured.
N1479 10ch. Type **570** 40 10
N1480 20ch. "Perennial" duck . . 90 10
N1481 40ch. Kwangpo duck . . 1·60 20

571 "Oath"

1976. Korean Peoples Army (sculptural works). Multicoloured.
N1482 5ch. Type **571** 10 10
N1483 10ch. "Union of Officers with Men" (horiz) . . . 15 10
N1484 10ch. "This Flag to the Height" 15 10

572 "Rural Road at Evening"

1976. Modern Korean Paintings (5th series). Social Welfare. Multicoloured.
N1485 10ch. Type **572** 60 10
N1486 15ch. "Passing on Technique" (1970) . . . 70 10
N1487 25ch. "Mother (and Child)" (1965) 85 15
N1488 30ch. "Medical Examination at School" (1970) (horiz) . . . . . 1·50 15
N1489 40ch. "Lady Doctor of Village" (1970) (horiz) 1·75 20

573 Worker holding Text of Law

1976. 30th Anniv of Agrarian Reform Law.
N1490 **573** 10ch. multicoloured . . 20 10

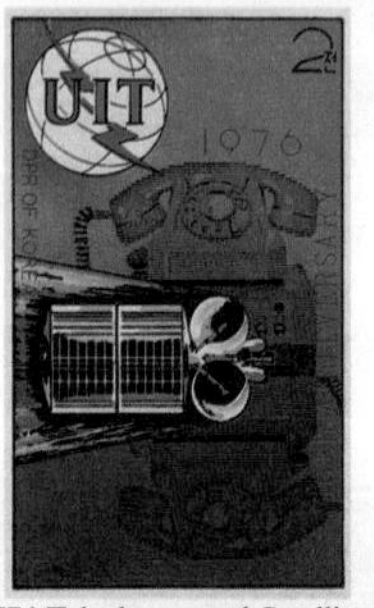
574 Telephones and Satellite

1976. Centenary of First Telephone Call. Multicoloured. With or without gum.
N1491 2ch. Type **574** 40 10
N1492 5ch. Satellite and antenna 40 10
N1493 10ch. Satellite and telecommunications systems 40 10
N1494 15ch. Telephone and linesman . . . . 1·10 10

N1495 25ch. Satellite and map of receiving stations . . . 1·50 15
N1496 40ch. Satellite and cable-laying barge . . . . . 1·75 20
MSN1497 94 × 70 mm. 50ch. Old telephone and satellite. Without gum . . . . 1·60 35

575 Cosmos

1976. Flowers. Multicoloured.
N1498 5ch. Type **575** 25 10
N1499 10ch. Dahlia 25 10
N1500 20ch. Zinnia 45 15
N1501 40ch. China aster 70 25

576 Fruit and Products

1976. Pukchong Meeting of Korean Workers' Party Presidium. Multicoloured.
N1502 5ch. Type **576** 75 10
N1503 10ch. Fruit and orchard scene 75 10

577 "Pulgungi" Electric Locomotive

1976. Railway Locomotives. Multicoloured.
N1504 5ch. Type **577** 40 10
N1505 10ch. "Chaju" underground train . . . 75 10
N1506 15ch. "Saebyol" diesel locomotive 95 15

GUM. All the following stamps were issued with gum, except where otherwise stated.

578 Satellite

1976. Space Flight. With or without gum.
N1507 **578** 2ch. multicoloured . . 15 10
N1508 – 5ch. multicoloured . . 15 10
N1509 – 10ch. multicoloured . . 20 10
N1510 – 15ch. multicoloured . . 30 10
N1511 – 25ch. multicoloured . . 45 15
N1512 – 40ch. multicoloured . . 70 20
MSN1513 77 × 98 mm. 50ch. Moon vehicle 85 35
DESIGNS: 5ch. to 50ch. Various satellite and space craft.

579 Kim Il Sung beside Car

1976. Kim Il Sung's 64th Birthday.
N1514 **579** 10ch. multicoloured . . 40 10
MSN1515 120 × 80 mm. 40ch. Kim Il Sung and rejoicing crowd . . 3·50 60

580 Bat and Ribbon

1976. 3rd Asian Table Tennis Championships. Multicoloured. Without gum.
N1516 5ch. Type **580** 40 10
N1517 10ch. Three women players with flowers . . 40 10
N1518 20ch. Player defending . . 65 10
N1519 25ch. Player making attacking shot . . . . . 1·00 15
MSN1520 74 × 99 mm. 50ch. Player making backhand shot. Imperf 1·60 60

581 Kim Il Sung announcing Establishment of Association

1976. 40th Anniv of Association for the Restoration of the Fatherland. Without gum.
N1521 **581** 10ch. multicoloured . . 10 10

582 Golden Pheasant

1976. Pheasants. Multicoloured. With or without gum.
N1522 2ch. Type **582** . . . . . 1·00 15
N1523 5ch. Lady Amherst's pheasant . . . . 1·10 15
N1524 10ch. Silver pheasant . . . 1·40 25
N1525 15ch. Reeves's pheasant 1·50 35
N1526 25ch. Temminck's tragopan . . . . 2·00 60
N1527 40ch. Common pheasant (albino) . . . . 2·40 1·00
MSN1528 77 × 58 mm. 50ch. Ring-necked pheasant . . . . 3·50 60

583 Monument and Map of River

585 Bronze Medal (Hockey, Pakistan)

584 Running

1976. Potong River Monument. Without gum.
N1529 **583** 10ch. brown and green 20 10

1976. Olympic Games, Montreal. Multicoloured.
N1530 2ch. Type **584** 30 10
N1531 5ch. Diving 30 10
N1532 10ch. Judo 30 10
N1533 15ch. Gymnastics 40 10
N1534 25ch. Gymnastics 80 15
N1535 40ch. Fencing . . . . . . 3·00 20
MSN1536 109 × 85 mm. 50ch. Runner with torch and Olympic Stadium . . . . 1·25 35

1976. Olympic Medal Winners (1st issue). Multicoloured.
N1537 2ch. Type **585** 75 10
N1538 5ch. Bronze medal (shooting, Rudolf Dollinger) 25 10
N1539 10ch. Silver medal (boxing, Li Byong Uk) 25 15
N1540 15ch. Silver medal (cycling, Daniel Morelon) . . . . 2·00 15
N1541 25ch. Gold medal (marathon, Waldemar Cierpinski) 90 20
N1542 40ch. Gold medal (boxing, Ku Yong Jo) . . . . . 1·10 25
MSN1543 109 × 84 mm. 50ch. Three medals . . . . 1·40 35

586 Boxing (Ku Yong Jo)

1976. Olympic Medal Winners (2nd issue). Multicoloured.
N1544 2ch. Type **586** 25 10
N1545 5ch. Gymnastics (Nadia Comaneci) 25 10
N1546 10ch. Pole vaulting (Tadeusz Slusarki) . . . 25 10
N1547 15ch. Hurdling (Guy Drut) 30 10
N1548 20ch. Cycling (Bernt Johansson) . . . . . . 2·50 15
N1549 40ch. Football (East Germany) . . . . . . 1·50 20
MSN1550 104 × 84 mm. 50ch. Ku Yong Jo (boxing champion) . . 1·60 35

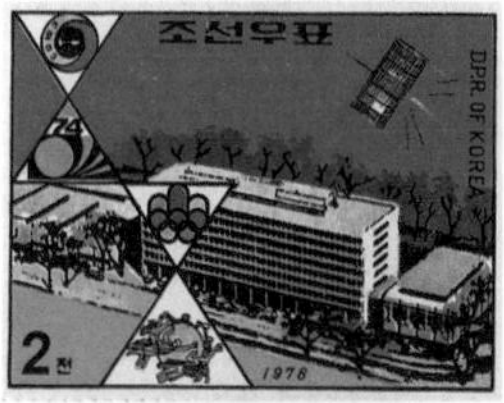

587 U.P.U. Headquarters, Berne

1976. International Festivities. Multicoloured.
N1551 2ch. Type **587** 40 10
N1552 5ch. Footballers (World Cup) 40 10
N1553 10ch. Olympic Stadium . . . 40 10
N1554 15ch. Olympic Village . . 40 10
N1555 25ch. Junk and satellite . . 70 20
N1556 40ch. Satellites 75 20
MSN1557 85 × 105 mm. 50ch. World map . . . . 1·25 35

588 Azure-winged Magpies

1976. Embroidery. Multicoloured. With or without gum.
N1558 2ch. Type **588** . . . . . 1·75 20
N1559 5ch. White magpie 90 15
N1560 10ch. Roe deer 30 10
N1561 15ch. Black-naped oriole and magnolias . . . . 2·10 20
N1562 25ch. Fairy with flute (horiz) 70 15
N1563 40ch. Tiger . . . . 1·60 40
MSN1564 94 × 105 mm. 50ch. Tiger (52 × 82 mm) . . . . 2·75 45

589 Roman "5" and Flame

1976. 5th Non-aligned States' Summit Conference, Colombo. Without gum.
N1565 **589** 10ch. multicoloured . . 10 10

590 Trophy and Certificate

1976. World Model Plane Championships (1975). Multicoloured. Without gum.
N1566 5ch. Type **590** 20 10
N1567 10ch. Trophy and medals 30 10
N1568 20ch. Model airplane and emblem 45 10
N1569 40ch. Model glider and medals 75 15

591 "Pulgungi" Diesel Shunting Locomotive

1976. Locomotives. Multicoloured.
N1570 2ch. Type **591** 40 10
N1571 5ch. "Saebyol" diesel locomotive 55 10
N1572 10ch. "Saebyol" diesel shunting locomotive . . 65 10
N1573 15ch. Electric locomotive 75 10
N1574 25ch. "Kumsong" diesel locomotive 95 15
N1575 40ch. "Pulgungi" electric locomotive . . . . . . 1·10 20
MSN1576 100 × 68 mm. 50ch. "Kumsong" type diesel locomotive. Imperf . . . . . . 5·00 2·50

592 House of Culture

1976. House of Culture. Without gum.
N1577 **592** 10ch. brown and black 15 10

593 Kim Il Sung visiting Tosongrang

1976. Revolutionary Activities of Kim Il Sung. Multicoloured.
N1578 2ch. Type **593** 20 10
N1579 5ch. Kim Il Sung visits pheasants 20 10
N1580 10ch. Kim Il Sung on hilltop 25 10
N1581 15ch. Kim Il Sung giving house to farmhand . . 30 10
N1582 25ch. Kim Il Sung near front line 70 10
N1583 40ch. Kim Il Sung walking in rain 70 15
MSN1584 105 × 85 mm. 50ch. Kim Il Sung with child at roadside 90 35

594 Kim Il Sung with Union Members

1976. 50th Anniv of Down-with-Imperialism Union. Without gum.

N1585	**594**	20ch. multicoloured . .	35	15

604 Searchlights and Kim Il Sung's Birthplace

605 Spring Costume

1977. New Year. Without gum.

N1589	**604**	10ch. multicoloured . .	10	10

1977. National Costumes of Li Dynasty. Mult.

N1590	10ch. Type **605** (postage)	45	10
N1591	15ch. Summer costume . .	60	10
N1592	20ch. Autumn costume . .	70	15
N1593	40ch. Winter costume (air)	1·10	20

606 Two Deva Kings (Koguryo Dynasty)

1977. Korean Cultural Relics. Multicoloured.

N1594	2ch. Type **606** (postage)	40	10
N1595	5ch. Gold-copper decoration, Koguryo Dynasty	40	10
N1596	10ch. Copper Buddha, Koryo Dynasty	60	10
N1597	15ch. Gold-copper Buddha, Paekje Dynasty	70	10
N1598	25ch. Gold crown, Koguryo Dynasty . . .	85	15
N1599	40ch. Gold-copper sun decoration, Koguryo Dynasty (horiz)	1·00	20
N1600	50ch. Gold crown, Silla Dynasty (air)	1·10	35

607 Worker with Five-point Programme

1977. Five-point Programme for Remaking Nature. Without gum.

N1601	**607**	10ch. multicoloured . .	20	10

608 Pine Branch and Map of Korea

1977. 60th Anniv of Korean National Association. Without gum.

N1602	**608**	10ch. multicoloured . .	35	10

609 Championship Emblem and Trophy

1977. 34th World Table Tennis Championships. Multicoloured. Without gum.

N1603	10ch. Type **609** (postage)	30	10
N1604	15ch. Pak Yong Sun . . .	40	10
N1605	20ch. Pak Yong Sun with trophy	70	15
N1606	40ch. Pak Yong Ok and Yang Ying (air)	1·10	20

610 Kim Il Sung founds Guerrilla Army at Mingyuegou

1977. Kim Il Sung's 65th Birthday. Multicoloured.

N1607	2ch. Type **610**	10	10
N1608	5ch. In command of army	10	10
N1609	10ch. Visiting steel workers in Kangson . .	25	10
N1610	15ch. Before battle	20	10
N1611	25ch. In schoolroom . . .	25	10
N1612	40ch. Viewing bumper harvest	35	10
MSN1613	85 × 94 mm. 50ch. "Kim Il Sung among the Artists" . .	65	30

611 "Chollima 72" Trolleybus

1977. Trolleybuses. Without gum.

N1614	**611**	5ch. blue, lilac and black	1·00	10
N1615	–	10ch. red, green & black	1·00	10

DESIGN: 10ch. "Chollima 74" trolleybus.

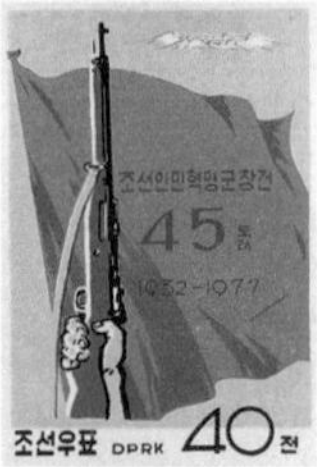

612 Red Flag and Hand holding Rifle

1977. 45th Anniv of Korean People's Revolutionary Army. Without gum.

N1616	**612**	40ch. red, yellow & blk	50	20

613 Proclamation and Watchtower

1977. 40th Anniv of Pochonbo Battle. Without gum.

N1617	**613**	10ch. multicoloured . .	10	10

614 Koryo White Ware Teapot

1977. Korean Porcelain. Multicoloured.

N1618	10ch. Type **614** (postage)	70	10
N1619	15ch. White vase, Li Dynasty	85	10
N1620	20ch. Celadon vase, Koryo Dynasty	1·00	10
N1621	40ch. Celadon vase with lotus decoration, Koryo Dynasty (air)	1·50	15

615 Postal Transport

1977. Postal Services. Multicoloured. Without gum.

N1623	2ch. Type **615**	1·00	15
N1624	10ch. Postwoman delivering letter	40	10
N1625	30ch. Mil Mi-8 helicopter	1·00	30
N1626	40ch. Ilyushin Il-18 airliner and world map	1·10	30

616 "Rapala arata"

1977. Butterflies and Dragonflies. Multicoloured.

N1627	2ch. Type **616** (postage)	60	10
N1628	5ch. "Colias aurora" . . .	80	10
N1629	10ch. Poplar admiral . . .	1·00	10
N1630	15ch. "Anax partherope" (dragonfly)	1·50	10
N1631	25ch. "Sympetrum pedemontanum" (dragonfly)	1·75	10
N1632	50ch. "Papilio maackii" (air)	2·25	20

617 Grey Cat

618

1977. Cats. Multicoloured.

N1634	2ch. Type **617**	1·25	10
N1635	10ch. Black and white cat	1·60	15
N1636	25ch. Ginger cat	2·75	20

1977. Dogs. Multicoloured.

N1638	5ch. Type **618** (postage)	1·00	10
N1639	15ch. Chow	1·25	10
N1640	50ch. Pungsang dog (air)	1·75	15

619 Kim Il Sung and President Tito

1977. Visit of President Tito.

N1642	**619**	10ch. multicoloured . .	10	10
N1643		15ch. multicoloured . .	15	10
N1644		20ch. multicoloured . .	20	10
N1645		40vh. multicoloured . .	25	10

620 Girl and Symbols of Education

1977. 5th Anniv of 11-year Compulsory Education. Without gum.

N1646	**620**	10ch. multicoloured . .	10	10

621 Chinese Mactra and Cobia

622 Students and "Theses"

1977. Shellfish and Fish. Multicoloured.

N1647	2ch. Type **621** (postage)	45	10
N1648	5ch. Bladder moon . . .	65	10
N1649	10ch. "Arca inflata" and pomfret	95	15
N1650	25ch. Thomas's rapa whelk and grouper . . .	1·40	40
N1651	50ch. Thomas's rapa whelk and globefish (air)	2·10	75

1977. Kim Il Sung's "Theses on Socialist Education". Multicoloured. Without gum.

N1653	10ch. Type **622**	20	10
N1654	20ch. Students, crowd and text	30	10

623 "Juche" Torch

624 Jubilant Crowd

1977. Seminar on the Juche Idea. Multicoloured. Without gum.

N1655	2ch. Type **623**	10	10
N1656	5ch. Crowd and red book	10	10
N1657	10ch. Chollima Statue and flags	10	10
N1658	15ch. Handclasp and red flag on world map . . .	10	10
N1659	25ch. Map of Korea and anti-U.S. slogans . . .	15	10
N1660	40ch. Crowd and Mt. Paekdu-san	20	10
MSN1661	117 × 78 mm. 50ch. Emblem of Juche seminar . . .	45	15

1977. Election of Deputies to Supreme People's Assembly. Without gum.

N1662	**624**	10ch. multicoloured . .	10	10

625 Footballers

1977. World Cup Football Championship, Argentina. Without gum.

N1663	**625**	10ch. multicoloured . .	90	15
N1664	–	15ch. multicoloured . .	1·25	20
N1665	–	40ch. multicoloured . .	2·00	25
MSN1666		132 × 82 mm. 50ch. Footballers	1·60	35

DESIGNS: 15ch. to 50ch. Different football scenes.

626 Kim Il Sung with Rejoicing Crowds

1977. Re-election of Kim Il Sung. Without gum.
N1667 **626** 10ch. multicoloured . . 20 10

627 Chollima Statue and Symbols of Communication

1977. 20th Anniv of Socialist Countries' Communication Organization. Without gum.
N1668 **627** 10ch. multicoloured . . 20 10

638 Chollima Statue and City Skyline

1978. New Year. Without gum.
N1687 **638** 10ch. multicoloured . . 20 10

639 Skater in 19th-century Costume

1978. Winter Olympic Games, Sapporo and Innsbruck. Multicoloured.
N1688 2ch. Type **639** (postage) 50 10
N1699 5ch. Skier 50 10
N1690 10ch. Woman skater . . . 50 10
N1691 15ch. Hunter on skis . . . 60 10
N1692 20ch. Woman (in 19th-century costume) on skis 60 10
N1693 25ch. Viking with longbow 2·75 15
N1694 40ch. Skier (air) . . . . 1·50 15
MSN1695 Two sheets. (a) 78 × 97 mm. 50ch. Innsbruck skyline; (b) 97 × 78 mm. 60ch. Skater . . . . 2·10 70

640 Post-rider and "Horse-ticket"

1978. Postal Progress. Multicoloured.
N1696 2ch. Type **640** (postage) 40 10
N1697 5ch. Postman on motor cycle . . . . 1·75 10
N1698 10ch. Electric train and post-van . . . . 1·75 15
N1699 15ch. Mail steamer and Mil Mi-8 helicopter . . 1·00 15
N1700 25ch. Tupolev Tu-154 jetliner and satellite . . 90 15
N1701 40ch. Dove and U.P.U. headquarters (air) . . . 60 15
MSN1702 Two sheets each 97 × 79 mm. (a) 50ch. Dove and UPU symbol; (b) 60ch. Dove and UPU headquarters . . . . . . 1·50 50

641 Self-portrait

1978. 400th Birth Anniv of Rubens.
N1703 **641** 2ch. multicoloured . . 25 10
N1704 5ch. multicoloured . . 25 10
N1705 40ch. multicoloured . . 1·50 20
MSN1706 96 × 79 mm. 50ch. multicoloured . . . . 1·50 35

642 "Chungsong" Tractor

1978. Farm Machines. Without gum.
N1707 **642** 10ch. red and black . . 45 10
N1708 – 10ch. brown and black 45 10
DESIGN: No. N1708, Sprayer.

643 Show Jumping

1978. Olympic Games, Moscow (1980) (1st issue). Equestrian Events. Multicoloured.
N1709 2ch. Type **643** 25 10
N1710 5ch. Jumping bar 35 10
N1711 10ch. Cross-country . . . 45 10
N1712 15ch. Dressage 50 10
N1713 25ch. Water splash . . . 75 15
N1714 40ch. Dressage (different) 1·25 15
MSN1715 75 × 111 mm. 50ch. Jumping triple bar . . . . . . 1·50 35
See also Nos. N1861/**MS**N1866, N1873/**MS**N1880 and N1887/**MS**N1893.

644 Soldier

1978. Korean People's Army Day. Multicoloured. Without gum.
N1716 5ch. Type **644** 10 10
N1717 10ch. Servicemen saluting 10 10

645 "Mangyongbong" (Freighter)

1978. Korean Ships. Multicoloured.
N1718 2ch. Type **645** (postage) 1·75 45
N1719 5ch. "Hyoksin" (freighter) 35 15
N1720 10ch. "Chongchongang" (gas carrier) 35 15
N1721 30ch. "Sonbong" (tanker) 60 20
N1722 50ch. "Taedonggang" (freighter) (air) . . . . 1·10 40

646 Uruguayan Footballer

1978. World Cup Football Championship Winners. Multicoloured.
N1724 5ch. Type **646** (postage) 50 10
N1725 10ch. Italian player . . . 50 10
N1726 15ch. West German player 50 10
N1727 25ch. Brazilian player . . 50 10
N1728 40ch. English player . . . 1·00 10
N1729 50ch. Hands holding World Cup (vert) (air) 1·50 15
MSN1730 110 × 74 mm. 50ch. Italian and North Korean players (air) . . . . 2·75 60

647 Footballers (1930 Winners, Uruguay)

1978. History of World Cup Football Championship. Multicoloured.
N1731 20ch. Type **647** (postage) 85 15
N1732 20ch. Italy, 1934 . . . . 85 15
N1733 20ch. France, 1938 . . . . 85 15
N1734 20ch. Brazil, 1950 . . . . 85 15
N1735 20ch. Switzerland, 1954 . . 85 15
N1736 20ch. Sweden, 1958 . . . 85 15
N1737 20ch. Chile, 1962 . . . . 85 15
N1738 20ch. England, 1966 . . . 85 15
N1739 20ch. Mexico, 1970 . . . 85 15
N1740 20ch. West Germany, 1974 85 15
N1741 20ch. Argentina, 1978 . . 85 15
N1742 50ch. Footballers and emblem (air) 85 15
MSN1743 73 × 98 mm. 50ch. World Cup and championship emblem 1·60 40

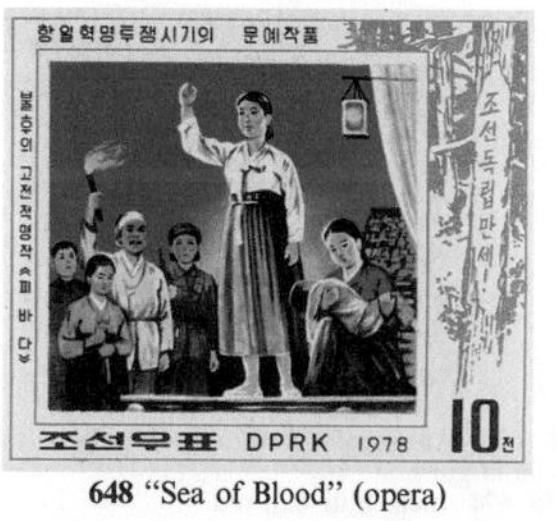

648 "Sea of Blood" (opera)

1978. Art from the Period of Anti-Japanese Struggle. Multicoloured.
N1744 10ch. Type **648** 40 10
N1745 15ch. Floral kerchief embroidered with map of Korea 50 10
N1746 20ch. "Tansimjul" (maypole dance) 75 15
MSN1747 100 × 69 mm. 40ch. Notation of "Song of Korea" 1·10 35

649 Red Flag and "7", Electricity and Coal

1978. Second 7 Year Plan. Multicoloured. Without gum.
N1748 5ch. Type **649** 25 10
N1749 10ch. Steel and non-ferrous metal 30 10
N1750 15ch. Engineering and chemical fertilizer . . . 35 10
N1751 30ch. Cement and fishing 70 10
N1752 50ch. Grain and tideland reclamation 75 10

650 Gymnastics (Alfred Flatow)

1978. Olympic Games History and Medal-winners. Multicoloured.
N1753 20ch. Type **650** 75 15
N1754 20ch. Runners (Michel Theato) 75 15
N1755 20ch. Runners (Wyndham Halswelle) 75 15
N1756 20ch. Rowing (William Kinnear) 75 15
N1757 20ch. Fencing (Paul Anspach) . . . . 1·50 25
N1758 20ch. Runners (Ugo Frigerio) 75 15
N1759 20ch. Runners (Ahmed El Quafi) 75 15
N1760 20ch. Cycling (Robert Charpentier) . . . . . 1·75 35
N1761 20ch. Gymnastics (Josep Stalder) 75 15
N1762 20ch. Boxing (Lazio Papp) 1·00 20
N1763 20ch. Runners (Ronald Delany) 75 15
N1764 20ch. High jump (Jolanda Balas) 75 15
N1765 20ch. High jump (Valery Brumel) 75 15
N1766 20ch. Gymnastics (Vera Caslavska) 75 15
N1767 20ch. Rifle shooting (Li Ho Jun) 75 15
MSN1768 105 × 95 mm. 50ch. Boxing (Ku Yong Jo) 95 35

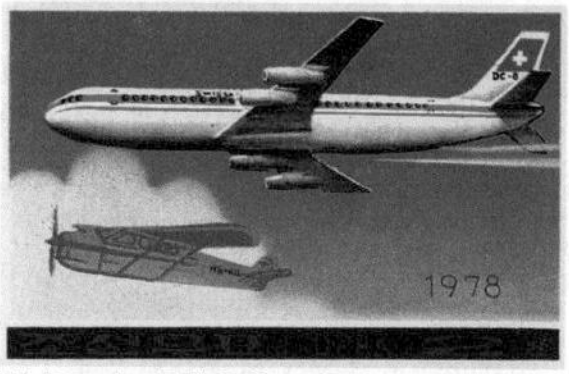

651 Douglas DC-8-63 and Comte Gentleman

1978. Airplanes. Multicoloured.
N1769 2ch. Type **651** 70 10
N1770 10ch. Ilyushin Il-62M and Avia BH-25 . . . . . 80 10
N1771 15ch. Douglas DC-8-63 and Savoia Marchetti S-71 . . . . 90 10
N1772 20ch. Tupolev Tu-144 and Kalinin K-5 . . . . . 1·10 10
N1773 25ch. Tupolev Tu-154 and Antonov An-2 biplane 1·10 10
N1774 30ch. Ilyushin Il-18 . . . 1·10 10
N1775 40ch. Concorde and Wibault 283 trimotor 2·25 40
MSN1776 102 × 75 mm. 50ch. Airbus Industries A300B2 jetliner and Focke Wulf A-17 Mowe 1·50 40

652 White-bellied Black Woodpecker and Map

1978. White-bellied Black Woodpecker Preservation. Multicoloured.
N1777 5ch. Type **652** . . . . . 1·50 15
N1778 10ch. Woodpecker and eggs . . . . 1·75 20
N1779 15ch. Woodpecker feeding young . . . . 2·25 30

N1780	25ch. Woodpecker feeding young (different)	2·75	60
N1781	50ch. Adult woodpecker on tree trunk	5·00	1·25

653 Demonstrators and Korean Map

1978. 30th Anniv of Democratic People's Republic of Korea. Multicoloured. Without gum.

N1783	10ch. Type **653**	10	10
N1784	10ch. Flag and soldiers	10	10
N1785	10ch. Flag and "Juche"	10	10
N1786	10ch. Red Flag	10	10
N1787	10ch. Chollima Statue and city skyline	10	10
N1788	10ch. "Juche" torch and men of three races	10	10

654 Cat and Pup

668 Red Flag and Pine Branch

655 Footballers

1978. Animal Paintings by Li Am. Multicoloured.

N1789	10ch. Type **654**	2·50	30
N1790	15ch. Cat up a tree	2·50	30
N1791	40ch. Wild geese	2·50	30

1978. Argentina's Victory in World Cup Football Championship. Without gum.

N1792	**655**	10ch. multicoloured	75	10
N1793	–	15ch. multicoloured	85	15
N1794	–	25ch. multicoloured	1·10	20
MSN1795		94×69 mm. 50ch. multicoloured	1·60	45

DESIGNS: 15ch. to 50ch. Different football scenes.

1979. New Year. Without gum.

N1812	**668**	10ch. multicoloured	15	10

669 Kim Il Sung with Children's Corps Members, Maanshan

1979. International Year of the Child (1st issue). Multicoloured. (a) Paintings of Kim Il Sung and children.

N1813	5ch. Type **669**	15	10
N1814	10ch. Kim Il Sung and Children's Corps members in classroom	25	10
N1815	15ch. New Year gathering	30	10
N1816	20ch. Kim Il Sung and children in snow	45	10
N1817	30ch. Kim Il Sung examines children's schoolbooks (vert)	50	10
	(b) Designs showing children		
N1818	10ch. Tug-of-war	15	10
N1819	15ch. Dance "Growing up Fast"	40	15
N1820	20ch. Children of many races and globe	40	10
N1821	25ch. Children singing	65	15
N1822	30ch. Children in toy spaceships	40	10
MSN1823	Two sheets (a) 90×72 mm. 50ch. Kim Il Sung visits a kindergarten (vert); (b) 124×85 mm. 50ch. As No. N1820	1·40	55

See also Nos. N1907/**MS**N1918.

670 Rose

1979. Roses. Multicoloured.

N1824	1wn. Red rose		
N1825	3wn. White rose		
N1826	5wn. Type **670**		
N1827	10wn. Deep pink rose		

See also Nos. N1837/42.

671 Warriors on Horseback

1979. "The Story of Two Generals". Multicoloured. Without gum.

N1828	5ch. Type **671**	20	10
N1829	10ch. Farm labourer blowing feather	30	10
N1830	10ch. Generals fighting on foot	30	10
N1831	10ch. Generals on horseback	30	10

672 Red Guard and Industrial Skyline

1979. 20th Anniv of Worker-Peasant Red Guards. Without gum.

N1832	**672**	10ch. multicoloured	15	10

673 Clement-Bayard Airship "Fleurus"

1979. Airships. Multicoloured. Without gum.

N1833	10ch. Type **673**	1·25	15
N1834	20ch. N.1 "Norge"	1·25	15
MSN1835	80×79 mm. 50ch. "Graf Zeppelin"	1·75	35

674 Crowd of Demonstrators

1979. 60th Anniv of 1st March Popular Uprising. Without gum.

N1836	**674**	10ch. blue and red	15	10

1979. Roses. As Nos. N1824/7. Multicoloured.

N1837	5ch. Type **670** (postage)	40	10
N1838	10ch. As No. N1827	45	10
N1839	15ch. As No. N1824	50	10
N1840	20ch. Yellow rose	60	10
N1841	30ch. As No. 1825	70	10
N1842	50ch. Deep pink rose (different) (air)	90	15

675 Table Tennis Trophy

1979. 35th World Table Tennis Championship, Pyongyang. Multicoloured. With or without gum.

N1843	5ch. Type **675**	20	10
N1844	10ch. Women's doubles	20	10
N1845	15ch. Women's singles	40	10
N1846	20ch. Men's doubles	60	10
N1847	30ch. Men's singles	80	10
MSN1848	84×108 mm. 50ch. Chollima Statue and championship emblem	85	30

676 Marchers with Red Flag

1979. Socialist Construction under Banner of Juche Idea. Multicoloured. Without gum.

N1849	5ch. Type **676**	10	10
N1850	10ch. Map of Korea	10	10
N1851	10ch. Juche torch	10	10

677 Badge

678 Emblem, Satellite orbiting Globe and Aerials

1979. Order of Honour of the Three Revolutions. Without gum.

N1852	**677**	10ch. blue	10	10

1979. World Telecommunications Day. Without gum.

N1853	**678**	10ch. multicoloured	25	10

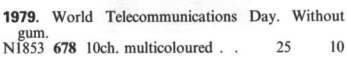

679 Advancing Soldiers and Monument

1979. 40th Anniv of Battle in Musan Area. Without gum.

N1854	**679**	10ch. mauve, light blue and blue	20	10

680 Exhibition Entrance

1979. Int Friendship Exhibition. Without gum.

N1855	**680**	10ch. multicoloured	10	10

681 "Peonies"

1979. 450th Death Anniv (1978) of Albrecht Durer (artist) (1st issue). Multicoloured.

N1856	15ch. Type **681**	75	20
N1857	20ch. "Columbines"	1·25	20
N1858	25ch. "A Great Tuft of Grass"	1·25	20
N1859	30ch. "Wing of a Bird"	2·10	55
MSN1860	92×67 mm. 50ch. As No. 1859	2·50	50

See also Nos. N2012/**MS**N2013.

682 Fencing

1979. Olympic Games, Moscow (2nd issue). Multicoloured. With gum (10, 40ch. only).

N1861	5ch. Type **682**	1·50	10
N1862	10ch. Gymnastics	40	10
N1863	20ch. Yachting	75	15
N1864	30ch. Athletics	60	15
N1865	40ch. Weightlifting	60	15
MSN1866	106×77 mm. 50ch. Equestrian event	85	30

683 Hunting

1979. Horse-riding (people of Koguryo Dynasty). Multicoloured.

N1867	5ch. Type **683**	65	10
N1868	10ch. Archery contest	65	10
N1869	15ch. Man beating drum on horseback	25	10
N1870	20ch. Man blowing horn	25	10
N1871	30ch. Man and horse, armoured with chainmail	25	10
N1872	50ch. Hawking (air)	2·00	15

684 Judo

685 Warrior's Costume

1979. Olympic Games, Moscow (3rd issue). Multicoloured. With gum (5, 15, 20, 30ch. only).

N1873	5ch. Type **684**	40	10
N1874	10ch. Volleyball	40	10
N1875	15ch. Cycling	1·50	25
N1876	20ch. Basketball	60	15
N1877	25ch. Canoeing	60	15
N1878	30ch. Boxing	90	25
N1879	40ch. Shooting	85	20
MSN1880	79×108 mm. 50ch. Gymnastics	85	30

1979. Warrior Costumes of Li Dynasty.

N1881	**685**	5ch. multicoloured	20	10
N1882	–	10ch. multicoloured	20	10
N1883	–	15ch. multicoloured	30	10
N1884	–	20ch. multicoloured	45	10
N1885	–	30ch. multicoloured	60	10
N1886	–	50ch. multicoloured (air)	90	15

DESIGNS: 10ch. to 50ch. Different costumes.

686 Wrestling

687 Monument

1979. Olympic Games, Moscow (4th issue). Multicoloured.
N1887 10ch. Type **686** 25 10
N1888 15ch. Handball 30 10
N1889 20ch. Archery . . . . . 1·60 25
N1890 25ch. Hockey . . . . . 1·60 45
N1891 30ch. Rowing 75 15
N1892 40ch. Football . . . . . 1·50 25
MSN1893 77 × 106 mm. 50ch. Equestrian events . . . . . . 2·50 1·00

1979. Chongbong Monument. Without gum.
N1894 **687** 10ch. multicoloured . . 20 10

688 Bottle-feeding Fawn

1979. Sika Deer. Multicoloured.
N1895 5ch. Type **688** (postage) 20 10
N1896 10ch. Doe and fawn . . . 20 10
N1897 15ch. Stag drinking from stream 20 15
N1898 20ch. Stag 25 15
N1899 30ch. Stag and doe . . . 35 25
N1900 50ch. Antlers and deer (air) 50 35

689 Moscovy Ducks

1979. Central Zoo, Pyongyang. Multicoloured.
N1901 5ch. Type **689** (postage) 40 10
N1902 10ch. Ostrich 85 10
N1903 15ch. Common turkey . . 1·10 10
N1904 20ch. Dalmatian pelican 1·25 10
N1905 30ch. Vulturine guineafowl 1·75 15
N1906 50ch. Mandarins (air) . . 2·75 20

690 Girl with Model Viking Ship

1979. International Year of the Child (2nd issue). Multicoloured.
N1907 20ch. Type **690** . . . . . 1·00 20
N1908 20ch. Boys with model steam railway locomotive . . . . . . 2·50 85
N1909 20ch. Boy with model biplane . . . . 1·25 20
N1910 20ch. Boy with model spaceman 80 20
N1911 30ch. Boy with model speedboat . . . . . . 1·50 30
N1912 30ch. Boy sitting astride toy electric train . . . . 2·50 85

N1913 30ch. Boy and model airplane . . . . 1·60 30
N1914 30ch. Boy and flying spaceman . . . . 1·00 30
MSN1915 Four sheets, each 77 × 104 mm. (a) 80ch. Boy and Concorde; (b) 80ch. Girl and satellite; (c) Boy and model liner; (d) 80ch. Children with model train . . . . 16·00 4·50

691 Footballers

1979. International Year of the Child (3rd issue). Multicoloured.
N1916 20ch. Type **691** . . . . . 1·25 20
N1917 30ch. Footballers (different) . . . . . . 1·75 30
MSN1918 104 × 78 mm. 80ch. Footballers (different) . . . . 3·00 75

692 Japanese Stonefish

1979. Marine Life. Multicoloured.
N1919 20ch. Type **692** . . . . . 1·25 10
N1920 30ch. Schlegel's redfish . . 1·40 20
N1921 50ch. Northern sealion . . 1·75 30

693 Cross-country Skiing (Sergei Saveliev)

1979. Winter Olympic Games, Lake Placid. Mult.
N1922 10ch. Figure skating (Irina Rodnina and Aleksandr Zaitsev) (horiz) 40 15
N1923 20ch. Ice hockey (Russian team) (horiz) 65 20
N1924 30ch. Women's 5 km relay (horiz) . . . . 1·10 25
N1925 40ch. Type **693** . . . . . 1·25 30
N1926 50ch. Women's speed skating (Tatiana Averina) . . . . 1·50 35
MSN1927 81 × 68 mm. 60ch. Ice dancing (Ludmila Pakhomova and Aleksandr Gorshkov) . . . . 2·75 75

694 The Honey Bee collecting Nectar

1979. The Honey Bee. Multicoloured.
N1928 20ch. Type **694** . . . . . 1·40 10
N1929 30ch. Bee and flowers . . 1·75 15
N1930 50ch. Bee hovering over flower . . . . 2·00 25

695 Kim Jong Suk's Birthplace, Heoryong

1979. Historic Revolutionary Sites.
N1931 **695** 10ch. multicoloured . . 15 10
N1932 – 10ch. brown, blue & blk 15 10
DESIGN: No. N1932, Sinpa Revolutionary Museum.

696 Mt. Paekdu

1980. New Year.
N1933 **696** 10ch. multicoloured . . 55 10

697 Student and Books

1980. Studying.
N1934 **697** 10ch. multicoloured . . 25 10

698 Conveyor Belt

1980. Unryul Mine Conveyor Belt.
N1935 **698** 10ch. multicoloured . . 55 10

699 Children of Three Races

1980. International Day of the Child. Multicoloured.
N1936 10ch. Type **699** 30 10
N1937 10ch. Girl dancing to accordion 50 10
N1938 10ch. Children in fairground airplane . . 40 10
N1939 10ch. Children as astronauts 30 10
N1940 10ch. Children on tricycles 1·25 30
N1941 10ch. Children with toy diesel train . . . . . . 1·75 45
N1942 10ch. "His loving care for the children, future of the fatherland" (59½ × 38 mm) 30 10
MSN1943 69 × 89 mm. 50ch. "Father Marshal visiting Kindergarten" (52 × 44 mm) . . 1·00 35

700 Monument

1980. Chongsan-ri Historic Site. Multicoloured.
N1944 5ch. Type **700** 10 10
N1945 10ch. Meeting place of the General Membership . . 15 10

701 Monument

1980. Monument marking Kim Jong Suk's Return.
N1946 **701** 10ch. multicoloured . . 15 10

702 Vasco Nunez de Balboa

1980. Conquerors of the Earth. Multicoloured.
N1947 10ch. Type **702** 50 10
N1948 20ch. Francisco de Orellana 75 20
N1949 30ch. Haroun Tazieff . . 1·00 35
N1950 40ch. Edmund Hillary and Sherpa Tenzing . . . . 1·50 45
MSN1951 75 × 105 mm. 70ch. Ibn Battuta . . . . 1·50 50

703 Museum

1980. Ryongpo Revolutionary Museum.
N1952 **703** 10ch. blue and black 20 10

704 Rowland Hill and Stamps

1980. Death Centenary (1979) of Sir Rowland Hill. Multicoloured.
N1953 30ch. Type **704** . . . . . 3·50 75
N1954 50ch. Rowland Hill and stamps (different) . . . 3·50 75

705 North Korean Red Cross Flag

1980. World Red Cross Day. Multicoloured.
N1955 10ch. Type **705** 70 20
N1956 10ch. Henri Dunant (founder) 70 20
N1957 10ch. Nurse and child . . 70 20
N1958 10ch. Polikarpov Po-2 biplane and ship . . . . 1·00 25
N1959 10ch. Mil Mi-4 helicopter 1·00 25
N1960 10ch. Children playing at nurses 70 20
N1961 10ch. Red Cross map over Korea and forms of transport . . . . 3·50 60
MSN1962 83 × 93 mm. 50ch. Nurse with syringe . . . . 2·00 90

706 Fernando Magellan

1980. Conquerors of the Sea. Multicoloured.
N1963 10ch. Type **706** . . . . . 1·75 25
N1964 20ch. Fridtjof Nansen . . 1·75 25

N1965 30ch. Auguste and Jacques Piccard . . . . 2·25 25
N1966 40ch. Jacques-Yves Cousteau . . . . 3·00 55
MSN1967 75 × 105 mm. 70ch. James Cook . . . . 4·75 75

707 Korean Stamps and Penny Black

1980. "London 1980" International Stamp Exhibition. Multicoloured.
N1968 10ch. Type **707** (postage) 2·00 40
N1969 20ch. Korean cover and British Guiana 1c. black and red . . . . 3·00 40
N1970 30ch. Early Korean stamp and modern cover . . . 2·00 40
N1971 50ch. Korean stamps . . . 2·50 35
N1972 40ch. Korean stamp and miniature sheet (air) . . 1·60 35
MSN1973 110 × 138 mm. 20ch. Type **707**; 30ch. As No. N1969; 50ch. As No. N1970 . . . . . 6·75 2·00

708 Wright Brothers

1980. Conquerors of Sky and Space. Multicoloured.
N1974 10ch. Type **708** 75 15
N1975 20ch. Louis Bleriot . . . 1·00 25
N1976 30ch. Anthony Fokker . . 1·50 40
N1977 40ch. Secondo Campini and Sir Frank Whittle 2·00 45
MSN1978 76 × 106 mm. 70ch. Count Ferdinand Zeppelin . . . . . 2·00 50

709 Space Station on Planet **710** Flag and Banners

1980. Conquerors of the Universe. Multicoloured.
N1979 10ch. Orbiting space station 20 10
N1980 20ch. Type **709** 25 20
N1981 30ch. Prehistoric animals and spaceships 90 35
N1982 40ch. Prehistoric animals and birds and spaceship 1·10 45
MSN1983 77 × 105 mm. 70ch. Planetary scene 90 30

1980. 25th Anniv of General Association of Korean Residents in Japan (Chongryon).
N1984 **710** 10ch. multicoloured . . 20 10

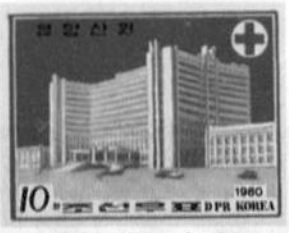
711 Hospital

1980. Pyongyang Maternity Hospital.
N1985 **711** 10ch. blue, purple & blk 45 15

712 Health Centre

1980. Changgangwon Health Centre, Pyongyang.
N1986 **712** 2ch. black and blue . . 25 10

713 Hand holding Rifle **714** Workers' Hostel, Samjiyon

1980. 50th Anniv of Revolutionary Army.
N1987 **713** 10ch. multicoloured . . 25 10

1980.
N1988 **714** 10ch. brown, blue & blk 30 10
N1989 – 10ch. black and green 50 20
N1990 – 10ch. black and red . . 50 20
N1991 – 10ch. black and yellow 50 20
N1992 – 10ch. multicoloured . . 30 10
N1993 – 10ch. multicoloured . . 30 10
N1994 – 10ch. multicoloured . . 1·00 35
N1995 – 10ch. green and black 75 25
N1996 – 10ch. grey, blue & black . . . . 3·50 60
N1997 – 10ch. multicoloured . . 6·00 85
DESIGNS: No. N1989, "Taedonggang" rice transplanter; N1990, "Chongsan-ri" rice harvester; N1991, Maize harvester; N1992, Revolutionary building, Songmun-ri; N1993, Revolutionary building, Samhwa; N1994, Sundial of 1438; N1995, 16th-century "turtle" ship; N1996, Pungsan dog; N1997, Japanese quail.

715 Party Emblem

1980. 6th Korean Workers' Party Congress. Multicoloured.
N1998 10ch. Type **715** 15 10
N1999 10ch. Students and Laurel leaf on globe 15 10
N2000 10ch. Group with accordion 45 15
N2001 10ch. Group with banner, microscope, book and trophy 25 10
N2002 10ch. Worker with book and flag 75 25
N2003 10ch. Worker with spanner and flag . . . 75 25
N2004 10ch. Marchers with torch and flags 15 10
N2005 10ch. Emblem, marchers and map 20 10
MSN2006 Two sheets each 94 × 77 mm. (a) 50ch. "The great Leader inspires and encourages Colliers on the Spot" (41 × 50 mm); (b) 50ch. "Leading the Van in the arduous March" (38 × 60 mm) . . . . 1·75 65

716 Dribbling Ball

1980. World Cup Football Championship, 1978–82. Multicoloured.
N2007 20ch. Type **716** . . . . . 2·50 60
N2008 30ch. Tackle . . . . . . 3·00 80
MSN2009 147 × 118 mm. 40ch. Tackling (different); 60ch. Moving in to tackle . . . . 5·00 1·50

717 Irina Rodnina and Aleksandr Zaitsev

1980. Winter Olympic Gold Winners. Multicoloured.
N2010 20ch. Type **717** . . . . 4·00 1·75
MSN2011 67 × 94 mm. 1wn. Natalia Linitshchnuk and Gennadi Karponosov . . . . 4·75 1·40

718 "Soldier with Horse" **719** Kepler, Astrolabe and Satellites

1980. 450th Death Anniv (1978) of Albrecht Durer (artist) (2nd issue). Multicoloured.
N2012 20ch. Type **718** . . . . . 5·00 1·50
MSN2013 81 × 106 mm. 1wn. "Horse and Rider" . . . . . 7·00 1·75

1980. 350th Death Anniv of Johannes Kepler (astronomer). Multicoloured.
N2014 20ch. Type **719** . . . . . 2·20 90
MSN2015 93 × 75 mm. 1wn. Kepler astrolabe and satellites (different) 4·50 1·50

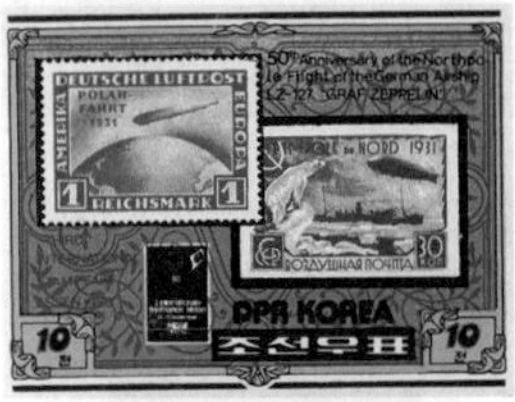

720 German 1m. and Russian 30k. Zeppelin Stamps

1980. 3rd International Stamp Fair, Essen. Mult.
N2016 10ch. Type **720** 85 25
N2017 20ch. German 2m. and Russian 35k. Zeppelin stamps . . . . 1·75 45
N2018 30ch. German 4m. and Russian 1r. Zeppelin stamps . . . . 2·50 65
MSN2019 137 × 82 mm. 50ch. Russian 2r. Polar Flight stamp and Korean 50ch. IYC stamp 5·75 2·25

721 Shooting (Aleksandr Melentev)

1980. Olympic Medal Winners. Multicoloured.
N2020 10ch. Type **721** 30 15
N2021 20ch. Cycling (Robert Dill-Bundi) . . . . . . 3·25 75
N2022 25ch. Gymnastics (Stoyan Deltchev) 50 25
N2023 30ch. Wrestling (Chang Se Hong and Li Ho Pyong) 50 25
N2024 35ch. Weightlifting (Ho Bong Chol) 50 25
N2025 40ch. Running (Marita Koch) 50 30
N2026 50ch. Modern Pentathlon (Anatoli Starostin) . . . 70 35
MSN2027 Two sheets. (a) 100 × 76 mm. 70ch. Boxing (Teofilo Stevenson); (b) 107 × 163 mm. 70ch. Ancient Greek rider on horse . . . . . 3·75 2·50

722 Tito

1980. President Tito of Yugoslavia Commemoration.
N2028 **722** 20ch. multicoloured . . 30 10

723 Convair CV 340 Airliner

1980. 25th Anniv of First Post-war Flight of Lufthansa. Multicoloured.
N2029 20ch. Type **723** . . . . . 4·75 1·75
MSN2030 90 × 75 mm. 1wn. Airbus A 300 . . . . 6·00 2·00

724 "The Rocket"

1980. 150th Anniv of Liverpool—Manchester Railway. Multicoloured.
N2301 20ch. Type **724** . . . . . 5·00 1·75
MSN2032 105 × 60 mm. 1wn. Locomotive drawing carriage and horsebox . . . . 6·00 2·00

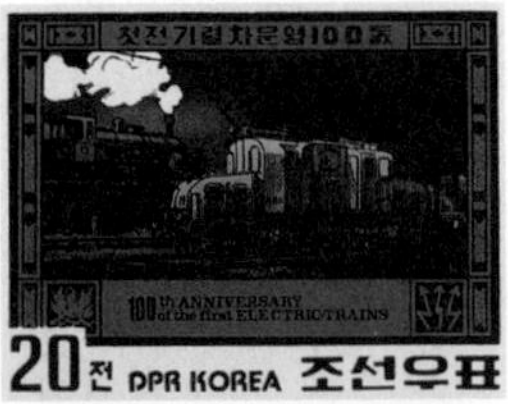

725 Steam and Electric Locomotives

1980. Centenary of First Electric Train. Multicoloured.
N2033 20ch. Type **725** . . . . . 5·00 1·75

726 Hammarskjold

1980. 75th Birth Anniv of Dag Hammarskjold (former Secretary General of United Nations). Multicoloured.
N2305 20ch. Type **726** MSN 2036 87 × 68 mm. 1wn. Hammarskjold (different) . . . . . . 3·75 1·50

727 Bobby Fischer and Boris Spassky

1980. World Chess Championship, Merano. Multicoloured.
N2037 20ch. Type **727** . . . . . 5·50 1·75
MSN2038 84 × 84 mm. 1wn. Viktor Korchnoi and Anatoly Karpov 7·00 1·75

728 Stolz

1980. Birth Centenary of Robert Stolz (composer). Multicoloured.
N2039 20ch. Type **728** . . . . . 2·50 75
MSN2040 94 × 76 mm. 1wn. Stolz examining stamp with magnifying glass . . . . 4·50 75

729 Chollima Statue **730** Russian Fairy Tale

1981. New Year. Without gum.
N2041 **729** 10ch. multicoloured . . 25 10

1981. International Year of the Child (1979) (4th issue). Fairy Tales. Multicoloured.
N2042 10ch. Type **730** . . . . . 1·10 30
N2043 10ch. Icelandic tale . . . 1·10 30
N2044 10ch. Swedish tale . . . . 1·10 30
N2045 10ch. Irish tale . . . . . 1·40 30
N2046 10ch. Italian tale . . . . 1·10 30
N2047 10ch. Japanese tale . . . 1·10 30
N2048 10ch. German tale . . . . 1·10 30
MSN2049 95 × 117 mm. 70ch. Korean tale . . . . 3·00 1·10

731 Changgwang Street

1981. Changgwang Street, Pyongyang.
N2050 **731** 10ch. multicoloured . . 35 10

732 Footballers

1981. World Cup Football Championship, Spain (1982) (1st issue). Multicoloured.
N2051 10ch. Type **732** . . . . . 2·25 45
N2052 20ch. Hitting ball past defender . . . . 2·25 45
N2053 30ch. Disputing possession of ball . . . . 2·25 45
MSN2054 95 × 103 mm. 70ch. Three players . . . . 3·75 1·25
See also Nos. N2055/**MS**N2060 and N2201/**MS**N2207.

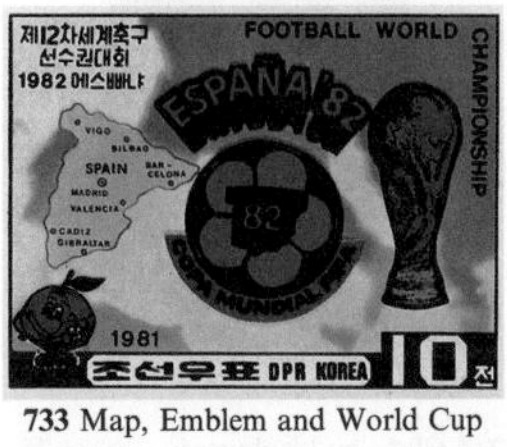

733 Map, Emblem and World Cup

1981. World Cup Football Championship, Spain (1982) (2nd issue). Multicoloured.
N2055 10ch. Type **733** . . . . . 1·50 30
N2056 15ch. Footballers . . . . 1·50 30
N2057 20ch. Heading ball . . . . 1·50 30
N2058 25ch. Footballers (different) . . . . . . 1·50 30
N2059 30ch. Footballers (different) . . . . . . 1·50 30
MSN2060 96 × 92 mm. 70ch. Footballers (different) . . . . 3·25 75

734 Workers with Book and Marchers with Banner

1981. Implementation of Decision of the 6th Koreans' Party Congress. Multicoloured.
N2061 2ch. Type **734** 10 10
N2062 10ch. Worker with book 10 10
N2063 10ch. Workers and industrial plant 25 10
N2064 10ch. Electricity and coal (horiz) . . . . 1·25 25
N2065 10ch. Steel and non-ferrous metals (horiz) 25 10
N2066 10ch. Cement and fertilizers (horiz) 25 10
N2067 30ch. Fishing and fabrics (horiz) 35 10
N2068 40ch. Grain and harbour (horiz) 25 10
N2069 70ch. Clasped hands . . . 20 10
N2070 1wn. Hand holding torch 30 15

735 Footballers

1981. Gold Cup Football Championship, Uruguay. Multicoloured.
N2071 20ch. Type **735** . . . . . 2·50 75
MSN2072 99 × 84 mm. 1wn. Goalkeeper diving for ball . . 3·00 1·10

736 Dornier Do-X Flying Boat

1981. "Naposta '81" International Stamp Exhibition, Stuttgart. Multicoloured.
N2073 10ch. Type **736** . . . . . 2·75 50
N2074 20ch. Airship LZ-120 "Bodensee" . . . . . . 2·75 50
N2075 30ch. "Gotz von Berlichingen" . . . . . 1·50 40
MSN2076 135 × 80 mm. 70ch. Mercedes-Benz "W 196" car 4·00 1·50

737 Telecommunications Equipment

1981. World Telecommunications Day.
N2077 **737** 10ch. multicoloured . . 1·75 20

738 "Iris pseudacorus"

1981. Flowers. Multicoloured.
N2078 10ch. Type **738** . . . . . 1·00 15
N2079 20ch. "Iris pallasii" . . . 1·25 20
N2080 30ch. "Gladiolus gandavensis" . . . . . 1·60 30

739 Austrian "WIPA 1981" and Rudolf Kirchschlager Stamps

1981. "WIPA 1981" International Stamp Exhibition, Vienna. Multicoloured.
N2081 20ch. Type **739** . . . . . 1·90 60
N2082 30ch. Austrian Maria Theresa and Franz Joseph stamps . . . . 2·50 80
MSN2083 133 × 87 mm. 50ch. Kim Il Sung and choir (38 × 60 mm) 3·00 1·00

740 Rings Exercise **741** Armed Workers

1981. Centenary of International Gymnastic Federation. Multicoloured.
N2084 10ch. Type **740** 50 20
N2085 15ch. Horse exercise . . . 60 20
N2086 20ch. Backwards somersault 80 20
N2087 25ch. Floor exercise . . . 90 25
N2088 30ch. Exercise with hoop 1·10 25
MSN2089 104 × 77 mm. 70ch. Exercise with wand (horiz) . . 1·75 75

1981. 50th Anniv of Mingyuehgou Meeting.
N2090 **741** 10ch. multicoloured . . 20 10

742 Farm Building, Sukchon

1981. 20th Anniv of Agricultural Guidance System and Taean Work System.
N2091 **742** 10ch. green, black and gold 20 10
N2092 – 10ch. blue, black and gold 20 10
DESIGN: No. N2092, Taean Revolutionary Museum.

743 Woman and Banner

1981. 55th Anniv of Formation of Women's Anti-Japanese Association.
N2093 **743** 5wn. multicoloured . . 2·75 75

743a Scene from Opera

1981. 10th Anniv of "Sea of Blood" (opera).
N2094 **743a** 10wn. multicoloured

744 Joan of Arc

1981. 550th Death Anniv of Joan of Arc. Multicoloured.
N2095 10ch. Type **744** . . . . . 2·00 50
N2096 10ch. Archangel Michael 2·25 50
N2097 70ch. Joan of Arc in armour . . . . 2·25 50
MSN2098 96 × 124 mm. No. N2097 4·00 1·50

745 Torch, Mountains and Flag

1981. 55th Anniv of Down with Imperialism Union.
N2099 **745** 1wn.50 multicoloured 40 20

746 "Young Girl by the Window"

1981. 375th Birth Anniv of Rembrandt (artist). Multicoloured.
N2100 10ch. Type **746** 70 25
N2101 20ch. "Rembrandt's Mother" . . . . 1·50 45
N2102 30ch. "Saskia van Uylenburgh" . . . . . 2·00 70
N2103 40ch. "Pallas Athene" . . 2·50 90
MSN2104 91 × 105 mm. 70ch. "Self-portrait" . . . . 4·00 1·90

747 Emblem and Banners over Pyongyang

1981. Symposium of Non-Aligned Countries on Food Self-Sufficiency, Pyongyang. Multicoloured.
N2105 10ch. Type **747** 20 10
N2106 50ch. Harvesting 50 10
N2107 90ch. Factories, tractors and marchers with banner 70 15

748 St. Paul's Cathedral

1981. Wedding of Prince of Wales (1st issue). Multicoloured.

N2108	10ch. Type **748**	1·40	35
N2109	20ch. Great Britain Prince of Wales Investiture stamp	1·40	35
N2110	30ch. Lady Diana Spencer	1·40	35
N2111	40ch. Prince Charles in military uniform	1·40	35
MSN2112	93 × 96 mm. 70ch. Engagement day portrait of couple	3·50	1·25

See also Nos. N2120/**MS**2124.

749 "Four Philosophers" (detail)

1981. Paintings by Rubens. Multicoloured.

N2113	10ch. Type **749**	40	20
N2114	15ch. "Portrait of Helena Fourment"	60	25
N2115	20ch. "Portrait of Isabella Brandt"	90	25
N2116	25ch. "Education of Maria de Medici"	1·10	30
N2117	30ch. "Helena Fourment and her Child"	1·40	35
N2118	40ch. "Helena Fourment in her Wedding Dress"	1·75	40
MSN2119	92 × 110 mm. 70ch. "Portrait of Nikolaas Rubens"	2·75	1·00

750 Royal Couple

1981. Wedding of Prince of Wales (2nd issue). Multicoloured.

N2120	10ch. Type **750**	1·75	45
N2121	20ch. Couple on balcony after wedding	1·75	45
N2122	30ch. Couple outside St. Paul's Cathedral	1·75	45
N2123	70ch. Full-length wedding portrait of couple	1·75	45
MSN2124	85 × 106 mm. 70ch. Royal couple and Queen Elizabeth on balcony	3·75	1·00

751 Rowland Hill and Stamps

1981. "Philatokyo '81" International Stamp Exhibition. Multicoloured.

N2125	10ch. Korean 2ch. Seminar on Juche Idea stamp (41 × 29 mm)	75	20
N2126	10ch. Korean and 70ch. stamps (41 × 29 mm)	2·00	75
N2127	10ch. Type **751**	2·00	75
N2128	20ch. Korean Fairy Tale stamps	1·75	40
N 2129	30ch. Japanese stamps	3·00	90
MSN2130	93 × 105 mm. 70ch. Medals, building and pigeon carrying letter	5·50	1·50

752 League Members and Flag

1981. Seventh League of Socialist Working Youth Congress, Pyongyang.

N2131	**752** 10ch. multicoloured	20	10
N2132	80ch. multicoloured	60	10

753 Government Palace, Sofia, Bulgarian Arms and Khan Asparuch

1981. 1300th Anniv of Bulgarian State.

N2133	**753** 10ch. multicoloured	25	10

754 Dimitrov

1981. Birth Centenary of Georgi Dimitrov (Bulgarian statesman).

N2134	**754** 10ch. multicoloured	25	10

755 Emblem, Boeing 747-200, City Hall and Mercedes "500"

1981. "Philatelia '81" International Stamp Fair, Frankfurt-am-Main.

N2135	**755** 20ch. multicoloured	2·50	35

756 Concorde, Airship "Graf Zeppelin" and Count Ferdinand von Zeppelin

1981. "Philexfrance 82" International Stamp Exhibition, Paris. Multicoloured. (a) As T **756**.

N2136	10ch. Type **756**	2·75	40
N2137	20ch. Concorde, Breguet Provence airliner and Santos-Dumont's biplane "14 bis"	3·25	75
N2138	30ch. "Mona Lisa" (Leonardo da Vinci) and stamps	1·75	30
MSN2139	99 × 105 mm. 60ch. French Rembrandt and Picasso stamps	5·50	1·50

(b) Size 32 × 53 mm.

N2140	10ch. Hotel des Invalides, Paris	1·00	45
N2141	20ch. President Mitterrand of France	1·00	45
N2142	30ch. International Friendship Exhibition building	1·00	45
N2143	70ch. Kim Il Sung	1·00	45

757 Rising Sun

758 Emblem and Flags

1982. New Year.

N2144	**757** 10ch. multicoloured	30	10

1982. "Prospering Korea". Multicoloured.

N2145	2ch. Type **758**	15	10
N2146	10ch. Industry	25	10
N2147	10ch. Agriculture	25	10
N2148	10ch. Mining	45	10
N2149	10ch. Arts	25	10
N2150	10ch. Al Islet lighthouse, Uam-ri	2·50	40
N2151	40ch. Buildings	50	15

759 "The Hair-do"

1982. Birth Centenary of Pablo Picasso (artist). Multicoloured.

N2152	10ch. Type **759**	75	20
N2153	10ch. "Paulo on a donkey"	1·75	35
N2154	20ch. "Woman leaning on Arm"	90	25
N2155	20ch. "Harlequin"	1·75	35
N2156	25ch. "Child with Pigeon"	1·90	50
N2157	25ch. "Reading a Letter"	1·75	35
N2158	35ch. "Portrait of Gertrude Stein"	1·50	30
N2159	35ch. "Harlequin" (different)	1·75	35
N2160	80ch. "Minotaur"	1·75	35
N2161	90ch. "Mother with Child"	1·75	35
MSN2162	Two sheets each 78 × 96 mm. (a) No. N2160; (b) No. 2161	6·00	2·00

760 Fireworks over Pyongyang

1982. Kim Il Sung's 70th Birthday. Multicoloured.

N2163	10ch. Kim Il Sung's birthplace, Mangyongdae	20	10
N2164	10ch. Type **760**	20	10
N2165	10ch. "The Day will dawn on downtrodden Korea" (horiz)	20	10
N2166	10ch. Signalling start of Pochonbo Battle (horiz)	20	10
N2167	10ch. Kim Il Sung starting Potong River project (horiz)	20	10
N2168	10ch. Embracing bereaved children (horiz)	20	10
N2169	10ch. Kim Il Sung as Supreme Commander (horiz)	20	10
N2170	10ch. "On the Road of Advance" (horiz)	20	10
N2171	10ch. Kim Il Sung kindling flame of Chollima Movement, Kansong Steel Plant (horiz)	75	25
N2172	10ch. Kim Il Sung talking to peasants (horiz)	20	10
N2173	10ch. Kim Il Sung fixing site of reservoir (horiz)	30	10
N2174	20ch. Kim Il Sung visiting Komdok Valley (horiz)	75	25
N2175	20ch. Kim Il Sung visiting Red Flag Company (horiz)	20	10
N2176	20ch. Kim Il Sung teaching Juche farming methods (horiz)	20	10
N2177	20ch. Kim Il Sung visiting iron works (horiz)	35	10
N2178	20ch. Kim Il Sung talking with smelters (horiz)	35	10
N2179	20ch. Kim Il Sung at chemical plant (horiz)	45	10
N2180	20ch. Kim Il Sung with fishermen (horiz)	40	10
MSN2181	Two sheets. (a) 93 × 82 mm. 60ch. Kim Il Sung as a boy (35 × 47 mm); (b) 60ch. "Long live Comrade Kim Il Sung" (35 × 46 mm)	3·00	1·25

761 Soldier saluting

1982. 50th Anniv of People's Army.

N2182	**761** 10ch. multicoloured	25	10

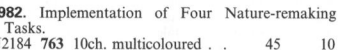

762 "The Bagpiper" (Durer)

763 Surveyors

1982. 4th Essen International Stamp Fair.

N2183	**762** 30ch. multicoloured	3·75	40

1982. Implementation of Four Nature-remaking Tasks.

N2184	**763** 10ch. multicoloured	45	10

764 Princess as Baby

765 Tower of the Juche Idea, Pyongyang

1982. 21st Birthday of Princess of Wales.

N2185	**764** 10ch. multicoloured	30	20
N2186	– 20ch. multicoloured	65	35
N2187	– 30ch. multicoloured	75	45
N2188	– 50ch. multicoloured	1·00	40
N2189	– 60ch. multicoloured	1·00	40
N2190	– 70ch. multicoloured	1·00	40
N2191	– 80ch. multicoloured	1·00	40
MSN2192	Two sheets each 88 × 100 mm. (a) 40ch. Princess with her brother; (b) No. N2191	6·25	2·00

DESIGNS: 20 to 80ch. Princess at various ages.

1982.

2193	**765** 2wn. multicoloured	1·25	30
2194	– 3wn. orange and black	1·75	40

DESIGN (26 × 38 mm): 3wn. Arch of Triumph.

766 Tiger

1982. Tigers.

N2195	**766** 20ch. multicoloured	1·25	35
N2196	– 30ch. multicoloured	1·90	35
N2197	– 30ch. mult (horiz)	2·75	45
N2198	– 40ch. mult (horiz)	2·75	45
N2199	– 80ch. mult (horiz)	2·75	45

MSN2200 105 × 54 mm. 80ch. multicoloured (horiz) . . . . . 3·50 90
DESIGNS: 30 to 80ch. Tigers.

767 Group 1 Countries

1982. World Cup Football Championship, Spain (3rd issue). Multicoloured.

N2201	10ch. Type **767**	45	20
N2202	20ch. Group 2 countries	1·00	25
N2203	30ch. Group 3 countries	1·40	30
N2204	40ch. Group 4 countries	1·75	40
N2205	50ch. Group 5 countries	2·00	50
N2206	60ch. Group 6 countries	2·25	50
MSN2207	133 × 92 mm. 1wn. World Cup, footballers and emblem	4·75	1·50

768 Rocket Launch

769 Charlotte von Stein

1982. The Universe. Multicoloured.

N2208	10ch. Type **768**	1·25	40
N2209	20ch. Spaceship over globe	1·25	40
N2210	80ch. Spaceship between globe and moon	1·50	40
MSN2211	71 × 103 mm. 80ch. Spaceship over crags	1·75	75

1982. 150th Death Anniv of Johann von Goethe (writer). Multicoloured.

N2212	10ch. Type **769**	50	25
N2213	10ch. Goethe's mother . .	1·50	45
N2214	20ch. Goethe's sister . . .	75	30
N2215	20ch. Angelika Kauffmann	1·50	45
N2216	25ch. Charlotte Buff . . .	90	35
N2217	25ch. Anna Amalia . . .	1·50	45
N2218	35ch. Lili Schonemann . .	1·25	40
N2219	35ch. Charlotte von Lengefeld	1·50	45
N2220	80ch. Goethe	1·60	45
MSN2221	126 × 84 mm. 80ch. Goethe (different)	3·50	1·50

770 Player holding aloft World Cup

1982. World Cup Football Championship Results. Multicoloured.

N2222	20ch. Type **770**	1·25	30
N2223	30ch. Group of players with World Cup	1·75	50
N2224	30ch. Type **770**	2·50	65
N2225	40ch. As No. N2203 . . .	2·50	65
N2226	80ch. King Juan Carlos of Spain and two players with World Cup	2·50	65
MSN2227	105 × 78 mm. No. N2226	4·00	1·90

771 Princess and Prince William of Wales

1982. 1st Wedding Anniv of Prince and Princess of Wales. Multicoloured.

N2228	30ch. Type **771**	2·75	90
MSN2229	135 × 102 mm. 80ch. Prince and Princess of Wales with Prince William	3·00	1·00

772 Royal Couple with Prince William

1982. Birth of Prince William of Wales. Mult.

N2230	10ch. Couple with Prince William (different) . . .	75	25
N2231	10ch. Princess of Wales holding bouquet	1·50	75
N2232	20ch. Couple with Prince William (different) . . .	90	30
N2233	20ch. Prince Charles carrying baby, and Princess of Wales . . .	1·50	75
N2234	30ch. Type **772**	1·00	40
N2235	30ch. Prince Charles carrying baby, and Princess of Wales (different)	1·50	75
N2236	40ch. Princess with baby	1·40	45
N2237	40ch. Prince and Princess of Wales (horiz)	2·40	95
N2238	50ch. Princess with baby (different)	1·75	50
N2239	50ch. Prince and Princess of Wales in evening dress (horiz)	2·40	95
N2240	80ch. Couple with Prince William (different) . . .	1·50	75
N2241	80ch. Prince Charles holding baby, and Princess of Wales (horiz)	2·40	95
MSN2242	Two sheets each 115 × 90 mm. (a) 80ch. Princess of Wales holding Prince William and royal family; (b) 80ch. Princess of Wales holding Prince William and godparents	13·00	5·75

773 Airship "Nulli Secundus II", 1908

1982. Bicentenary of Manned Flight (1st issue). Multicoloured.

N2243	10ch. Type **773**	1·25	40
N2244	10ch. Pauley and Durs Egg's dirigible balloon "The Dolphin", 1818	2·50	60
N2245	20ch. Tissandier Brothers' airship, 1883	1·50	50
N2246	20ch. Guyton de Morveau's balloon with oars, 1784	2·50	60
N2247	30ch. Parseval airship PL-VII, 1912	2·00	60
N2248	30ch. Sir George Cayley's airship design, 1837 . .	2·50	60
N2249	40ch. Count de Lennox's balloon "Eagle", 1834	2·25	60
N2250	40ch. Camille Vert's balloon "Poisson Volant", 1859	2·50	60
N2251	80ch. Dupuy de Lome's airship, 1872	2·50	60
MSN2252	71 × 100 mm. 80ch. Masse oar-powered balloon, 1784 (vert)	4·00	1·90

774 "Utopic Balloon Post" (Balthasar Antoine Dunker)

1982. Bicentenary of Manned Flight (2nd issue). Multicoloured.

N2253	10ch. Type **774**	1·50	40
N2254	10ch. Montgolfier balloon at Versailles, 1783 . . .	3·00	60
N2255	20ch. "... and they fly into heaven and have no wings ..."	2·00	50
N2256	20ch. Montgolfier Brothers' balloon, 1783	3·00	60
N2257	30ch. Pierre Testu-Brissy's balloon ascent on horseback, 1798	2·50	60
N2258	30ch. Charles's hydrogen balloon landing at Nesle, 1783	3·00	60
N2259	40ch. Gaston Tissandier's test flight of "Zenith", 1875	3·00	60
N2260	40ch. Blanchard and Jeffries' balloon flight over English Channel, 1785	3·00	60
N2261	80ch. Henri Giffard's balloon "Le Grand Ballon Captif" at World Fair, 1878	3·00	60
MSN2262	130 × 96 mm. 80ch. Night flight of balloon	4·00	1·90

775 Turtle with Scroll

1982. Tale of the Hare. Multicoloured.

N2263	10ch. Type **775**	1·00	15
N2264	20ch. Hare riding on turtle	1·50	20
N2265	30ch. Hare and turtle before Dragon King . .	1·75	30
N2266	40ch. Hare back on land	2·25	40

776 Flag, Red Book and City

777 Tower of Juche Idea

1982. 10th Anniv of Socialist Constitution.
N2267 **776** 10ch. multicoloured . . 25 10

1983. New Year.
N2268 **777** 10ch. multicoloured . . 15 10

778 Children reading "Saenal"

1983. 55th Anniv of "Saenal" Newspaper.
N2269 **778** 10ch. multicoloured . . 50 10

779 "Man in Oriental Costume"

1983. Paintings by Rembrandt. Multicoloured.

N2270	10ch. Type **779**	60	20
N2271	10ch. "Child with dead Peacocks" (detail) . . .	2·00	40
N2272	20ch. "The Noble Slav"	1·25	30
N2273	20ch. "Old Man in Fur Hat"	2·00	40
N2274	30ch. "Dr. Tulp's Anatomy Lesson" (detail)	3·25	50
N2275	30ch. "Portrait of a fashionable Couple" . .	2·00	40
N2276	40ch. "Two Scholars disputing"	1·50	35
N2277	40ch. "Woman with Child"	2·00	40
N2278	80ch. "Woman holding an Ostrich Feather Fan"	2·00	40
MSN2279	102 × 69 mm. 80ch. "Self-portrait"	3·00	1·60

780 Airships "Gross Basenach II" and "Graf Zeppelin" over Cologne

1983. "Luposta" International Air Mail Exhibition, Cologne. Multicoloured.

N2280	30ch. Type **780**	3·00	90
N2281	40ch. Parsevel airship PL-II over Cologne	3·00	90
MSN2282	86 × 95 mm. 80ch. "Virgin and Child" (Stephan Lochner) (vert)	2·50	1·00

781 Banner and Monument

1983. 50th Anniv of Wangjaesan Meeting.
N2283 **781** 10ch. multicoloured . . 20 10

782 Karl Marx

1983. Death Centenary of Karl Marx.
N2284 **782** 10ch. multicoloured . . 50 25

783 Scholar, Marchers and Map of Journey

1983. 60th Anniv of Thousand-ri Journey for Learning.
N2285 **783** 10ch. multicoloured . . 1·00 10

784 "Madonna of the Goldfinch"

1983. 500th Birth Anniv of Raphael. Multicoloured.

N2286	10ch. Type **784**	1·75	50
N2287	20ch. "The School of Athens" (detail)	1·50	40
N2288	30ch. "Madonna of the Grand Duke"	1·75	45
N2289	50ch. "Madonna of the Chair"	1·90	45
N2290	50ch. "Madonna of the Lamb"	1·50	50
N2291	80ch. "The Beautiful Gardener"	1·50	50
MSN2292	80 × 106 mm. 80ch. "Sistine Madonna"		

785 Department Store No. 1

1983. Pyongyang Buildings. Multicoloured.
N2293 2ch. Chongryu Restaurant 20 10
N2294 10ch. Part of Munsu Street 30 10
N2295 10ch. Ice Rink 40 10
N2296 40ch. Type **785** 60 15
N2297 70ch. Grand People's Study House 75 25

786 Emblem and Crowd **788** Satellite, Masts and Dish Aerial

787 Judo

1983. 5th Anniv of International Institute of Juche Idea.
N2298 **786** 10ch. multicoloured . . 15 10

1983. Olympic Games, Los Angeles (1st issue). Multicoloured.
N2299 20ch. Type **787** 65 40
N2300 20ch. Wrestling . . . . . 1·25 40
N2301 30ch. Judo (different) (value in gold) 65 40
N2302 30ch. Judo (different) (value in black) . . . . 1·25 40
N2303 40ch. Boxing 65 40
N2304 40ch. Li Ho Jun (1972 shooting gold medalist) 1·25 40
N2305 50ch. Weightlifting 65 40
N2306 50ch. Wrestling (different) 1·25 40
N2307 80ch. Boxing (different) 1·25 40
MSN2308 95 × 74 mm. 80ch. Judo (different) . . . . 2·25 1·00
See also Nos. N2359/**MS**N2365.

1983. World Communications Year (1st issue).
N2309 **788** 10ch. multicoloured . . 1·50 20
See also Nos. N2349/**MS**N2354.

789 Emblem, Giant Panda and Stamp

1983. "Tembal 83" International Thematic Stamp Exhibition, Basel. Multicoloured.
N2310 20ch. Type **789** . . . . . 1·75 35
N2311 30ch. Emblem, flag and Basel Town Post stamp 1·90 35

790 "Colourful Cow" (kogge), 1402

1983. Old Ships. Multicoloured.
N2312 20ch. Type **790** . . . . . 1·10 45
N2313 20ch. "Kwi-Sun" ("turtle" ship), 1592 . . . . . . 2·50 75
N2314 35ch. "Great Harry" (warship), 1555 . . . . 1·50 55
N2315 35ch. Admiral Li Sun Sin and "turtle" ship . . . 2·50 75
N2316 50ch. "Eagle of Lubeck" (galleon), 1567 . . . . 2·10 70
N2317 50ch. "Merkur" (full-rigged sailing ship), 1847 . . . . 2·50 75
N2318 80ch. "Herzogin Elisabeth" (cadet ship) 2·50 75
MSN2319 104 × 82 mm. 80ch. "Cristoforo Colombo" (cadet ship) . . . . 5·00 3·50

791 "Locomotion", 1825, Great Britain

1983. Railway Locomotives. Multicoloured.
N2320 20ch. Type **791** . . . . . 1·50 60
N2321 20ch. "Drache", 1848, Germany . . . . 4·75 1·00
N2322 35ch. "Adler", 1835, Germany . . . . 2·00 80
N2323 35ch. Korean steam locomotive . . . . . . 4·50 1·00
N2324 50ch. "Austria", 1837, Austria . . . . 3·25 80
N2325 50ch. Bristol and Exeter Railway steam locomotive, 1853 . . . 4·75 1·00
N2326 80ch. Caledonian Railway locomotive, 1859 . . . 4·75 1·00
MSN2327 106 × 64 mm. 80ch. "Ilmarinen", 1860 . . . . . . 6·00 1·90

792 Map, Hand and Weapons

1983. 10th Anniv of Publication of Five-point Policy for Korea's Reunification.
N2328 **792** 10ch. multicoloured . . 25 10

793 Emblem, Tower of Juche Idea and Fireworks

1983. World Conference on Journalists against Imperialism and for Friendship and Peace, Pyongyang. Multicoloured.
N2329 10ch. Type **793** 20 10
N2330 40ch. Emblem and rainbow and clasped hands 40 15
N2331 70ch. Emblem, map and hand with raised forefinger 50 20

794 Worker and Banners

1983. "Let's Create the Speed of the 80s".
N2332 **794** 10ch. multicoloured . . 25 10

795 Soldier and Rejoicing Crowd

1983. 30th Anniv of Victory in Liberation War.
N2333 **795** 10ch. multicoloured . . 25 10

796 "Gorch Fock" (cadet barque) and Korean 1978 2ch. Stamp

1983. "Bangkok 1983" International Stamp Exhibition. Multicoloured.
N2334 40ch. Type **796** . . . . . 3·00 1·25
MSN2335 195 × 71 mm. 80ch. Bangkok, Penny Black and Korean IYC stamp . . . . . 4·50 1·50

797 Skiing

1983. Winter Olympic Games, Sarajevo (1984). Multicoloured.
N2336 10ch. Type **797** 55 25
N2337 20ch. Figure skating (vert) 2·00 45
N2338 30ch. Skating (pair) . . . 1·60 55
N2339 50ch. Ski jumping . . . . 1·60 55
N2340 50ch. Ice hockey (vert) . . 2·00 45
N2341 80ch. Speed skating (vert) 2·00 45
MSN2342 74 × 87 mm. 80ch. Shooting (biathlon) (vert) . . . 3·00 1·10

798 Workers and Soldier with Books

1983. 35th Anniv of Korean People's Democratic Republic.
N2343 **798** 10ch. multicoloured . . 35 10

799 Archery **800** Girls holding Hands

1983. Folk Games. Multicoloured.
N2344 10ch. Type **799** . . . . . 2·50 40
N2345 10ch. Flying kites 65 20
N2346 40ch. See-sawing 65 20
N2347 40ch. Swinging 65 20

1983. Korean–Chinese Friendship.
N2348 **800** 10ch. multicoloured . . 50 10

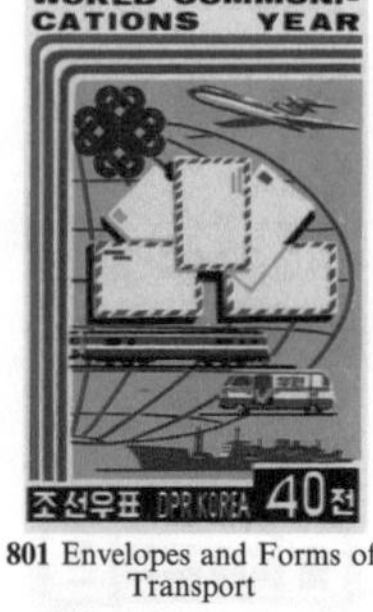

801 Envelopes and Forms of Transport

1983. World Communications Year (2nd issue). Multicoloured.
N2349 30ch. Mail van, motorcyclist and hand holding magazines . . . 4·75 90
N2350 30ch. Satellite, globe and dish aerial . . . . . . 1·25 40
N2351 40ch. Type **801** . . . . . 4·75 1·10
N2352 40ch. Television cameraman . . . . . . 1·25 40
N2353 80ch. Telephone and aerial 1·25 40
MSN2354 96 × 75 mm. 80ch. WCY emblem and satellite . . . . . 3·50 1·15

802 Portrait

1983. Paintings by Rubens. Multicoloured.
N2355 40ch. Type **802** . . . . . 1·40 60
N2356 40ch. Portrait (different) (horiz) . . . . 1·75 75
N2357 80ch. "The Sentencing of Midas" (horiz) . . . . 1·75 75
MSN2358 129 × 95 mm. 80ch. "The Bear Hunt" . . . . 2·50 90

803 Sprinting

1983. Olympic Games, Los Angeles (2nd issue). Multicoloured.
N2359 10ch. Type **803** 75 20
N2360 20ch. Show jumping . . . 1·75 45
N2361 30ch. Cycling . . . . . . 3·00 55
N2362 50ch. Handball . . . . . 2·00 60
N2363 50ch. Fencing . . . . . . 1·75 45
N2364 80ch. Gymnastics . . . . 1·75 45
MSN2365 109 × 75 mm. 80ch. Judo 3·50 1·50

804 "St. Catherine" **805** Kimilsungflower

804a Cat

1983. 450th Death Anniv (1984) of Antonio Correggio (artist). Multicoloured.
N2366 20ch. Type **804** . . . . . 1·75 60
N2367 20ch. "Morning" (detail) 2·50 75
N2368 35ch. "Madonna" . . . . 1·75 60
N2369 35ch. "Morning" (different) . . . . . . 2·50 75
N2370 50ch. "Madonna with St. John" . . . . 1·75 60
N2371 50ch. "St. Catherine" (different) . . . . . . 2·50 75
N2372 80ch. "Madonna and Child" . . . . 2·50 75
MSN2373 58 × 73 mm. 80ch. "Madonna and Child with Music-making Angels" . . . . 4·50 1·50

1983. Cats. Multicoloured, frame colour given.
N2373a **804a** 10ch. green . . . . 1·25 10
N2373b – 10ch. gold . . . . . 1·25 10
N2373c – 10ch. blue . . . . . 1·25 10
N2373d – 10ch. red . . . . . 1·25 10
N2373e – 10ch. silver . . . . 1·25 10
DESIGNS: Different cats' heads.

1983. New Year.
N2374 **805** 10ch. multicoloured . . 85 10

806 Worker and Workers' Party Flag

1984. "Under the Leadership of the Workers' Party". Multicoloured.
N2375 10ch. Type **806** 25 10
N2376 10ch. Ore-dressing plant No. 3, Komdok General Mining Enterprise, and Party Flag 40 10

807 Farm Worker, Rice and Maize

1984. 20th Anniv of Publication of "Theses of the Socialist Rural Question in Our Country".
N2377 **807** 10ch. multicoloured . . 25 10

808 Changdok School, Chilgol

1984. Kim Il Sung's 72nd Birthday.
N2378 **808** 5ch. green, black & blue 25 10
N2379 – 10ch. multicoloured . . 25 10
DESIGN: 10ch. Birthplace, Mangyongdae, and rejoicing crowd.

809 "Spanish Riding School" (Julius von Blaas)

1984. "Espana 84" International Stamp Exhibition, Madrid. Multicoloured.
N2380 10ch. Type **809** . . . . . 1·75 50
N2381 20ch. "Ferdinand of Austria" (Rubens) . . . 1·75 50
MSN2382 73 × 96 mm. 80ch. "Spanish Riding School" (Julius von Blaas) (different) . . . . . 4·50 1·50

810 "La Donna Velata" **812** Construction Site

811 Map and Second Stage Pumping Station

1984. 500th Birth Anniv (1983) of Raphael (artist). Multicoloured.
N2383 10ch. "Portrait of Agnolo Doni" . . . . 1·50 50
N2384 20ch. Type **810** . . . . . 1·50 50
N2385 30ch. "Portrait of Jeanne d'Aragon" . . . . . . 1·50 50
MSN2386 79 × 105 mm. 80ch. "St. Sebastian" . . . . 4·00 1·50

1984. 25th Anniv of Kiyang Irrigation System.
N2387 **811** 10ch. multicoloured . . 50 10

1984. Construction on Five District Fronts.
N2388 **812** 10ch. red, black & yell 50 10

813 Bobsleighing (East Germany)

1984. Winter Olympic Games Medal Winners. Multicoloured.
N2389 10ch. Ski jumping (Matti Nykaenen) . . . . . . 1·75 50
N2390 20ch. Speed skating (Karin Enke) . . . . 1·50 40
N2391 20ch. Slalom (Max Julen) 1·75 50
N2392 30ch. Type **813** . . . . . 1·50 40
N2393 30ch. Downhill skiing (Maria Walliser) . . . . 1·75 50
N2394 40ch. Cross-country skiing (Thomas Wassberg) . . 2·75 60
N2395 80ch. Cross-country skiing (Marja-Liisa Hamalainen) . . . . . 2·75 60
MSN2396 106 × 86 mm. 80ch. Biathlon (Peter Angerer) (vert) 3·50 1·50

814 Steam Locomotive, 1919

1984. Essen International Stamp Fair. Mult.
N2397 20ch. Streamlined steam locomotive, 1939 . . . 4·00 65
N2398 30ch. Type **814** . . . . . 4·00 65
MSN2399 94 × 86 mm. 80ch. Type "D" locomotive . . . . 6·75 1·50

815 "Mlle. Fiocre in the Ballet 'La Source' "

1984. 150th Birth Anniv of Edgar Degas (artist). Multicoloured.
N2400 10ch. Type **815** . . . . . 1·50 25
N2401 20ch. "The Dance Foyer at the Rue le Peletier Opera" . . . . 2·50 25
N2402 30ch. "Race Meeting" . . 3·75 40
MSN2403 108 × 89 mm. 80ch. "Dancers at the Barre" . . . . 3·50 1·50

816 Map of Pyongnam Irrigation System and Reservoir

1984. Irrigation Experts Meeting, Pyongyang.
N2404 **816** 2ch. multicoloured . . 40 10

817 Korean Stamp and Building **818** Crowd and Banners

1984. U.P.U. Congress Stamp Exn, Hamburg.
N2405 **817** 20ch. multicoloured . . 3·00 40
MSN2406 106 × 76 mm. 80ch. "Gorch Fock" (cadet barque) and Koren "turtle" stamp . . . . 4·50 3·50

1984. Proposal for Tripartite Talks.
N2407 **818** 10ch. multicoloured . . 40 10

819 Nobel experimenting

1984. 150th Birth Anniv (1983) of Alfred Bernhard Nobel (inventor). Multicoloured.
N2408 20ch. Type **819** . . . . . 3·00 45
N2409 30ch. Portrait of Nobel . . 3·00 45
MSN2410 109 × 99 mm. 80ch. Portrait of Nobel (different) . . 5·25 1·10

820 Drinks, Tinned Food, Clothes and Flats

1984. Improvements of Living Standards.
N2411 **820** 10ch. multicoloured . . 55 10

821 Sunhwa School, Mangyongdae

1984. School of Kim Hyong Jik (Kim Il Sung's Father).
N2412 **821** 10ch. multicoloured . . 40 10

822 Armed Crowd with Banners

1984. 65th Anniv of Kuandian Conference.
N2413 **822** 10ch. multicoloured . . 40 10

823 "Thunia bracteata"

1984. Flowers. Multicoloured.
N2414 10ch. "Cattleya loddigesii" 1·00 10
N2415 20ch. Type **823** . . . . . 1·25 25
N2416 30ch. "Phalaenopsis amabilis" . . . . 1·75 40
MSN2417 67 × 94 mm. Kimilsung flower . . . . 4·00 1·50

824 Swordfish and Trawler

1984. Fishing Industry. Multicoloured.
N2418 5ch. Type **824** . . . . . 1·25 15
N2419 10ch. Blue marlin and trawler . . . . 1·75 25
N2420 40ch. Sailfish and game fishing launch . . . . . 4·50 1·25

825 Revolutionary Museum, Chilgol

1984.
N2421 **825** 10ch. multicoloured . . 40 10

826 Kim Hyok, Cha Gwang Su and Youth **828** Clock Face

827 Inauguration of a French Railway Line, 1860

1984. "Let's All become the Kim Hyoks and Cha Gwang Sus of the '80s".
N2422 **826** 10ch. multicoloured . . 60 10

1984. Centenary (1983) of "Orient Express". Multicoloured.
N2423 10ch. Type **827** . . . . . 1·40 25
N2424 20ch. Opening of a British railway line, "1821" . . 2·50 50
N2425 30ch. Inauguration of Paris–Rouen line, 1843 3·00 90
MSN2426 11 × 81 mm. Interiors of Wagons-lits Car, 1905 . . . . 6·00 2·25

1984. Centenary of Greenwich Meridian. Multicoloured.
N2427 10ch. Type **828** . . . . . 2·50 1·00
MSN2428 112 × 81 mm. 80ch. Cholliuma statue, buildings and clock . . . . 4·50 1·50

829 Grand Theatre, Hamburg **830** Turning on Machinery

1984.
N2429 **829** 10ch. blue 40 10

1984. Automation of Industry.
N2430 **830** 40ch. multicoloured . . 60 30

831 "Dragon Angler"

1984. Paintings. Multicoloured.
N2431 10ch. Type **831** . . . . . 1·00 10
N2432 20ch. "Ox Driver" (Kim Du Ryang) (47 × 35 mm) . . . . . 1·25 25
N2433 30ch. "Bamboo" (Kim Jin U) (47 × 35 mm) . . . . 1·75 40

832 Tsiolkovsky

1984. K. E. Tsiolkovsky (space scientist). Mult.
N2435 20ch. Type **832** 90 25
N2436 30ch. "Sputnik" orbiting Earth . . . . 1·25 40
MSN2437 100 × 70 mm. 80ch. Rocket launch . . . . 3·25 1·00

833 "Pongdaesan"

1984. Container Ships. Multicoloured.
N2438 10ch. Type **833** 95 10
N2439 20ch. "Ryongnamsan" . . 1·10 35
N2440 30ch. "Rungrado" . . . . 1·50 55
MSN2441 97 × 107 mm. 80ch. "Kumgangsan" . . . . 4·75 50

834 Caracal

1984. Animals. Multicoloured.
N2442 10ch. Spotted hyenas . . . 60 10
N2443 20ch. Type **834** 90 25
N2444 30ch. Black-backed jackals 1·25 40
N2445 40ch. Foxes . . . . 1·60 60
MSN2446 80 × 104 mm. 80ch. Lanner falcon (vert) . . . . . 6·00 1·50

835 Marie Curie

836 Chestnut-eared Aracari ("Toucan")

1984. 50th Anniv of Marie Curie (physicist). Multicoloured.
N2447 10ch. Type **835** . . . . . 2·00 25
MS2448 78 × 103 mm. 80ch. Portrait of Marie Curie . . . . 4·00 1·50

1984. Birds. Multicoloured.
N2449 10ch. Hoopoe . . . . . . 1·40 20
N2450 20ch. South African crowned cranes ("Crowned Crane") . . 1·75 50
N2451 30ch. Saddle-bill stork ("Stork") . . . . 2·50 70
N2452 40ch. Type **836** . . . . . 3·50 90
MS2453 104 × 74 mm 80ch. Black kite . . . . 6·50 1·75

837 Cosmonaut

1984. Space Exploration. Multicoloured.
N2454 10ch. Type **837** 50 10
N2455 20ch. Cosmonaut on space-walk 75 25
N2456 30ch. Cosmonaut (different) . . . . 1·00 40
MSN2457 77 × 90 mm. 80ch. Moon vehicle . . . . 2·75 90

838 "Arktika"

1984. Russian Ice-breakers. Multicoloured.
N2458 20ch. Type **838** . . . . . 1·25 35
N2459 30ch. "Ermak" . . . . . . 1·75 50
MSN2460 97 × 67 mm. 80c. "Lenin" 4·75 1·50

839 Mendeleev

1984. 150th Birth Anniv of Dmitiri Mendeleev (chemist). Multicoloured.
N2461 10ch. Type **839** 95 10
MSN2462 95 × 65 mm. 80ch. Seated statue of Mendeleev . . . . . 4·00 1·50

840 Kim Il Sung in U.S.S.R.

1984. Kim Il Sung's Visits to Eastern Europe. Multicoloured.
N2463 10ch. Type **840** 60 10
N2464 10ch. In Poland 60 10
N2465 10ch. In German Democratic Republic . . 60 10
N2466 10ch. In Czechoslovakia 60 10
N2467 10ch. In Hungary 60 10
N2468 10ch. In Bulgaria 60 10
N2469 10ch. In Rumania 60 10

841 Freesia

1985. New Year.
N2471 **841** 10ch. multicoloured . . 75 10

842 Journey Route, Steam Locomotive and Memorials

1985. 60th Anniv of 1000 ri Journey by Kim Il Sung. Multicoloured.
N2472 5ch. Type **842** . . . . . 1·25 10
N2473 10ch. Boy trumpeter and schoolchildren following route 50 10
Nos. N2472/3 were issued together, se-tenant, forming a composite design.

843 Cugnot's Steam Car, 1769

844 Camp, Mt. Paekdu

1985. History of the Motor Car (1st series). Multicoloured.
N2474 10ch. Type **843** . . . . . 1·40 10
N2475 15ch. Goldsworthy Gurney steam omnibus, 1825 . . . . 1·40 15
N2476 20ch. Gottlieb Daimler diesel car, 1885 . . . . 1·40 25
N2477 25ch. Benz three-wheeled diesel car, 1886 . . . . 1·60 35
N2478 30ch. Peugeot diesel car, 1891 . . . . 2·00 40
MSN2479 92 × 75 mm. 80c. black and gold (Wind car) . . . . . 4·00 1·50
See also Nos. N2562/**MS**N2567.

1985. Korean Revolution Headquarters.
N2480 **844** 10ch. multicoloured . . 40 20

845 Taechodo Lighthouse

846 Hedgehog challenges Tiger

1985. Lighthouses. Multicoloured.
N2481 10ch. Type **845** . . . . . 1·75 10
N2482 20ch. Sodo . . . . 1·90 30
N2483 30ch. Pido . . . . 2·25 45
N2484 40ch. Suundo . . . . . . 2·75 70

1985. "The Hedgehog defeats the Tiger" (fable). Multicoloured.
N2485 10ch. Type **846** 60 10
N2486 20ch. Tiger goes to stamp on rolled-up hedgehog 90 25
N2487 30ch. Hedgehog clings to tiger's nose . . . . . . 1·25 40
N2488 35ch. Tiger flees . . . . . 1·40 50
N2489 40ch. Tiger crawls before hedgehog . . . . 1·60 60

847 "Pleurotus cornucopiae"

848 West Germany v. Hungary, 1954

1985. Fungi. Multicoloured.
N2490 10ch. Type **847** . . . . . 1·10 10
N2491 20ch. Oyster fungus . . . 1·40 25
N2492 30ch. "Catathelasma ventricosum" . . . . . 1·90 40

1985. World Cup Football Championship Finals.
N2493 **848** 10ch. black, buff & brn 60 10
N2494 – 10ch. multicoloured . . 60 10
N2495 – 20ch. black, buff & brn 90 25
N2496 – 20ch. multicoloured . . 90 25
N2497 – 30ch. black, buff & brn 1·25 40
N2498 – 30ch. multicoloured . . 1·25 40
N2499 – 40ch. black, buff & brn 1·60 60
N2500 – 40ch. multicoloured . . 1·60 60
MSN2501 Two sheets, (a) 105 × 75 mm. 80ch. black, cinnamon and gold; (b) 94 × 95 mm. 80ch.multicoloured 8·00 3·00
DESIGNS—VERT: No. N2493, Type **848**; N2496, West Germany v. Netherlands, 1974; N2499, England v. West Germany,**MS**N2501 (b), Azieca Stadium, Mexico (venue of 1966 final). HORIZ: N2494, Brazil v. Italy, 1970; N2495, Brazil v. Sweden, 1958. N2497, Brazil v. Czechoslovakia, 1963; N2498 Argentina v Netherlands, 1968. **MS**N2500, Italy v West Germany, 1982; **MS**N2501 (a) North Korea's quarter-final place, 1966.

849 Date and Kim Il Sung's Birthplace

850 Horn Player

1985. 73rd Birthday of Kim Il Sung.
N2502 **849** 10ch. multicoloured . . 40 10

1985. 4th-century Musical Instruments. Mult.
N2503 10ch. Type **850** . . . . . 1·40 10
N2504 20ch. So (pipes) player . . 1·40 25

851 Chongryon Hall, Tokyo

852 Common Marmoset

1985. 30th Anniv of Chongryon (General Association of Korean Residents in Japan).
N2505 **851** 10ch. brown 40 10

1985. Mammals. Multicoloured.
N2506 5ch. Type **852** 85 10
N2507 10ch. Ring-tailed lemur . . 85 10

853 National Emblem

1985. Sheet 51 × 70 mm.
MSN2508 **853** 80ch. multicoloured 1·50 50

854 Buenos Aires and Argentina 1982 Stamp

855 Dancer and Gymnast

1985. "Argentina '85" International Stamp Exhibition, Buenos Aires. Multicoloured.
N2509 10ch. Type **854** 75 10
N2510 20ch. Iguacu Falls and Argentina 1984 and North Korea 1978 stamps (horiz) . . . . . 2·50 25
MSN2511 73 × 100 mm. 80ch. Gaucho . . . . 4·00 1·50

1985. 12th World Youth and Students' Festival, Moscow. Multicoloured.
N2512 10ch. Type **855** 60 10
N2513 20ch. Spassky Tower, Moscow, and Festival emblem 90 25
N2514 40ch. Youths of different races . . . . 1·60 60

856 Peace Pavilion, Youth Park

857 Liberation Celebrations

1985. Pyongyang Buildings.
N2515 **856** 2ch. black and green 20 10
N2516 – 40ch. brown & lt brn 45 20
DESIGN: 40ch. Multi-storey flats, Chollima Street.

1985. 40th Anniv of Liberation.
N2517 – 5ch. red, black and blue 20 10
N2518 – 10ch. multicoloured . . 40 10
N2519 – 10ch. brown, blk & grn 40 10
N2520 – 10ch. multicoloured . . 40 10
N2521 **857** 10ch. yellow, blk & red 40 10
N2522 – 10ch. red, orange & blk 40 10
N2523 – 40ch. multicoloured . . 60 20
MSN2524 68 × 50 mm. 90ch. multicoloured . . . . 2·00 75
DESIGNS—HORIZ: No. N2517, Soldiers with rifles and flag; N2518, Crowd with banners and Flame of Juche; N2519, Korean and Soviet soldiers raising arms; N2520, Japanese soldiers laying down weapons; N2523, Students bearing banners. VERT: No. N2522, Liberation Tower, Moran Hill, Pyongyang; **MS**2524, Monument.

858 Halley and Comet

1985. Appearance of Halley's Comet. Multicoloured.
N2525 10ch. Type **858** 90 10
N2526 20ch. Diagram of comet's flight and space probe 1·25 25
MS2527 144 × 128 mm. 80ch. ultramarine and gold (Comet's trajectory) . . . . 4·00 1·50

859 "Camellia japonica"

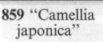

861 Party Founding Museum

860 "Hunting"

1985. Flowers. Multicoloured.
N2528 10ch. "Hippeastrum hybridum" 90 10
N2529 20ch. Type **859** . . . . . 1·25 25
N2530 30ch. "Cyclamen persicum" . . . . . . 1·75 40

1985. Koguryo Culture.
N2531 10ch. "Hero" (vert) . . . 60 10
N2532 15ch. "Heroine" (vert) . . 75 15
N2533 20ch. "Flying Fairy" 90 25
N2534 25ch. Type **860** . . . . 1·10 35
MSN2535 90 × 80 mm. 80ch. "Pine Tree" (28 × 48 mm) . . . . . 3·00 1·00

1985. 40th Anniv of Korean Workers' Party. Multicoloured.
N2536 5ch. Type **861** 20 10
N2537 10ch. Soldier with gun and workers 40 10
N2538 10ch. Soldiers and flag . . 40 10
N2539 40ch. Statue of worker, peasant and intellectual holding aloft party emblem 60 20
MSN2540 60 × 75 mm. 90ch. People with flowers . . . . 1·75 60

862 Arch of Triumph, Pyongyang

863 Colosseum, Rome, and N. Korea 1975 10ch. Stamp

1985. 40th Anniv of Kim Il Sung's Return.
N2541 **862** 10ch. brown and green 40 10

1985. "Italia '85" International Stamp Exhibition, Rome. Multicoloured.
N2542 10ch. Type **863** 60 10
N2543 20ch. "The Holy Family" (Raphael) (vert) 90 25
N2544 30ch. Head of "David" (statue, Michelangelo) (vert) . . . . 1·25 40
MSN2545 67 × 47 mm. 80ch. Pantheon, Rome . . . . . 4·00 1·50

864 Mercedes Benz Type "300"

1985. South-West German Stamp Fair, Sindelfingen. Multicoloured.
N2546 10ch. Type **864** . . . . . 1·00 10
N2547 15ch. Mercedes Benz Type "770" . . . . . . 1·40 15
N2548 20ch. Mercedes Benz "W 150" . . . . 1·75 25
N2549 30ch. Mercedes Type "600" . . . . . . 2·00 40
MSN2550 84 × 57 mm. 80ch. Mercedes Benz "W31" . . . . 4·25 90

865 Tackle

1985. World Cup Football Championship, Mexico (1st issue). Multicoloured.
N2551 20ch. Type **865** . . . . . 1·10 25
N2552 30ch. Three players . . . 1·40 40
MSN2553 106 × 76 mm. 80ch. Goalkeeper and Mexican monuments . . . . 4·00 1·50
See also Nos. N2558/**MS**N2560 and 2577/**MS**N2583.

866 Dancers

1985. International Youth Year. Multicoloured.
N2554 10ch. Type **866** 60 10
N2555 20ch. Sports activities . . 90 25
N2556 30ch. Technology . . . . 1·25 40
MSN2557 75 × 60 mm. 80ch. Young people . . . . 3·00 90

867 Players

1985. World Cup Football Championship, Mexico (2nd issue). Multicoloured.
N2558 20ch. Type **867** . . . . . 1·25 25
N2559 30ch. Goalkeeper and players . . . . 1·60 40
MSN2560 102 × 80 mm. 80ch. Goalkeeper and bullfighter . . 4·00 1·50

868 Juche Torch

869 Amedee Bollee and Limousine, 1901

1986. New Year.
N2561 **868** 10ch. multicoloured . . 40 10

1986. History of the Motor Car (2nd series). Multicoloured.
N2562 10ch. Type **869** 75 10
N2563 20ch. Stewart Rolls, Henry Royce and "Silver Ghost", 1906 . . . . . 1·25 25
N2564 25ch. Giovanni Agnelli and Fiat car, 1912 . . . 1·40 35
N2565 30ch. Ettore Bugatti and "Royal" coupe, 1928 . . 1·60 40
N2566 40ch. Louis Renault and fiacre, 1906 . . . . . . 2·25 60
MSN2567 75 × 80 mm. 80ch. Gottiebo Daimler, Karl Benz and Mercedes "S", 1927 . . . . . 4·50 95

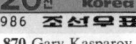

870 Gary Kasparov

872 Tongdu Rock, Songgan

871 Cemetery Gate

1986. World Chess Championship, Moscow.
N2568 **870** 20ch. multicoloured . . 2·25 25
MSN2569 60 × 82 mm. 80ch. Anatoly Karpov and Kasparov 4·25 1·50

1986. Revolutionary Martyrs' Cemetery, Pyongyang. Multicoloured.
N2570 5ch. Type **871** 20 10
N2571 10ch. Bronze sculpture (detail) 55 10

1986. 37th Anniv of Pres. Kim Il Sung's Visit to Songgan Revolutionary Site.
N2572 **872** 10ch. multicoloured . . 40 10

873 Buddhist Scriptures Museum

1986. Mt. Myohyang Buildings.
N2573 **873** 10ch. brown and green 40 10
N2574 – 20ch. violet and red . . 50 10
DESIGN: 20ch. Taeung Hall.

874 Tomato Anemonefish

1986. Fishes. Multicoloured.
N2575 10ch. Pennant coralfish . . 1·50 20
N2576 20ch. Type **874** . . . . . 2·25 45

875 Footballers and Flags of Italy, Bulgaria and Argentina

1986. World Cup Football Championship, Mexico (3rd issue). Designs showing footballers and flags of participating countries. Multicoloured.
N2577 10ch. Type **875** 60 10
N2578 20ch. Mexico, Belgium, Paraguay and Iraq . . . 90 25
N2579 25ch. France, Canada, U.S.S.R. and Hungary 1·10 35
N2580 30ch. Brazil, Spain, Algeria and Northern Ireland . . . . 1·25 40
N2581 35ch. West Germany, Uruguay, Scotland and Denmark . . . . 1·40 50
N2582 40ch. Poland, Portugal, Morocco and England 1·60 60
MSN2583 100 × 70 80ch. Ball, boots, footballers and trophy . . . . 4·00 1·50

876 Singer, Pianist and Emblem

1986. 4th Spring Friendship Art Festival, Pyongyang.
N2584 **876** 1wn. multicoloured . . 1·25 55

877 Daimler "Motorwagen", 1886

878 Mangyong Hill

1986. 60th Anniv of Mercedes-Benz (car manufacturers). Multicoloured.
N2585 10ch. Type **877** 75 10
N2586 10ch. Benz "velo", 1894 75 10
N2587 20ch. Mercedes car, 1901 1·00 25
N2588 20ch. Benz limousine, 1909 1·00 25
N2589 30ch. Mercedes "tourenwagen", 1914 . . 1·40 40
N2590 30ch. Mercedes-Benz "170" 6-cylinder, 1931 1·40 40
N2591 40ch. Mercedes-Benz "380", 1933 . . . . . 1·75 60
N2592 40ch. Mercedes-Benz "540 K", 1936 . . . . 1·75 60
MSN2593 75 × 60 mm. 80ch. Mercedes-Simplex "phaeton", 1904 . . . . 4·00 1·50

1986. 74th Birthday of Kim Il Sung.
N2594 **878** 10ch. multicoloured . . 30 10

879 Crowd

1968. 50th Anniv of Association for the Restoration of the Fatherland.
N2595 **879** 10ch. multicoloured . . 30 10

880 Dove carrying Letter

1986. International Peace Year. Multicoloured.
N2596 10ch. Type **880** 50 10
N2597 20ch. U.N. Headquarters, New York 80 25
N2598 30ch. Dove, globe and broken missiles . . . . 1·10 40
MSN2599 72 × 90 mm. 80ch. Sculpture . . . . 3·00 95

881 "Mona Lisa" (Leonardo da Vinci)

1986.
N2600 **881** 20ch. multicoloured . . 90 25

882 Pink Iris

883 Kim Un Suk

1986. Irises. Multicoloured.
N2601 20ch. Type **882** . . . . . 1·25 25
N2602 30ch. Violet iris . . . . . 1·75 40
MSN2603 84 × 64 80ch. Magenta iris . . . . 4·00 1·50

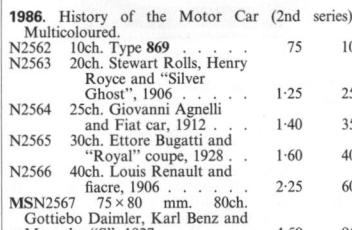

1986. Tennis Players. Multicoloured.
N2604 10ch. Type **883** (postage) 2·00 35
N2605 20ch. Ivan Lendl . . . . 2·00 35
N2606 30ch. Steffi Graf . . . . 2·00 35
N2607 50ch. Boris Becker (air) 2·00 35

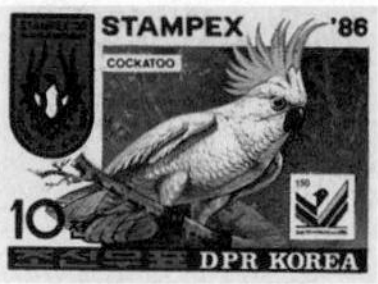
884 Sulphur-crested Cockatoo ("Cockatoo")

1986. "Stampex '86" Stamp Exhibition. Adelaide, Australia. Multicoloured.
N2608 10ch. Type **884** . . . . . 1·60 20
MSN2609 75 × 60 mm. 80ch. Kangaroo . . . . 4·00 1·50

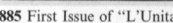

885 First Issue of "L'Unita"

886 "Express II" (icebreaker) and Sweden 1872 20 ore Stamp

1986. National "L'Unita" (Italian Communist Party newspaper) Festival, Milan. Multicoloured.
N2610 10ch. Type **885** 60 10
N2611 20ch. Milan Cathedral . . 90 25
N2612 30ch. "Pieta" (Michelangelo) (vert) . . 1·25 40
MSN2613 85 × 65 mm. 80ch. Enrico Berlingoer (former General Secretary of Italian Communist Part) (vert) . . . . 1·90 65

1986. "Stockholmia 86" International Stamp Exhibition, Stockholm.
N2614 10ch. multicoloured . . . 2·00 10
MSN2615 86 × 60 mm. 80ch. UPU emblem, mail coach and Swedish stamps (horiz) . . . . 4·00 1·25

887 Reprint of First Stamp

1986. 40th Anniv of First North Korean Stamps (1st issue). Multicoloured.
N2616 10ch. Type **887** (postage) 75 10
N2617 15ch. Imperforate reprint of first stamp 50 35
N2618 50ch. 1946 50ch. violet stamp (air) . . . . . . 2·00 75
See also Nos. N2619/21.

888 Postal Emblems and 1962 and 1985 Stamps

1986. 40th Anniv of First North Korean Stamps (2nd issue). Multicoloured.
N2619 10ch. Type **888** (postage) 2·00 25
N2620 15ch. General Post Office and 1976 and 1978 stamps . . . . 2·00 35
N2621 50ch. Kim Il Sung, first stamp and reprint (vert) (air) . . . . 1·60 45

1986. World Cup Football Championship Results. Nos. N2577/82 optd **1st: ARG 2nd: FRG 3rd: FRA 4th: BEL.**
N2622 10ch. multicoloured . . . 80 10
N2623 20ch. multicoloured . . . 1·10 25
N2624 25ch. multicoloured . . . 1·40 35
N2625 30ch. multicoloured . . . 1·50 40
N2626 35ch. multicoloured . . . 1·60 50
N2627 40ch. multicoloured . . . 1·90 60
MSN2628 100 × 70 mm. 80ch. multicoloured . . . . 4·50 1·00

890 Flag and Man with raised Fist

892 Schoolchildren

891 Gift Animals House

1986. 60th Anniv of Down-with-Imperialism Union.
N2629 **890** 10ch. multicoloured . . 30 10

1986. 1st Anniv of Gift Animals House, Central Zoo, Pyongyang.
N2630 **891** 2wn. multicoloured . . 3·00 1·10

1986. 40th Anniv of UNESCO. Multicoloured.
N2631 10ch. Type **892** 60 10
N2632 50ch. Anniversary emblem, Grand People's Study House and telecommunications (horiz) . . . . 1·50 75

893 Communications Satellite

1986. 15th Anniv of Intersputnik.
N2633 **893** 5wn. multicoloured . . 7·00 3·00

894 Oil tanker leaving Lock

1986. West Sea Barrage.
N2634 **894** 10ch. multicoloured . . 50 10
N2635 – 40ch. grn, blk & gold 1·25 20
N2636 – 1wn. 20 multicoloured 2·75 60
DESIGNS: 20ch. Aerial view of dam; 1wn.20, Aerial view of lock.

895 Common Morel

1986. Minerals and Fungi. Multicoloured.
N2637 10ch. Lengenbachite (postage) . . . . 2·00 25
N2638 10ch. Common funnel cap 2·00 25
N2639 15ch. Rhodochrosite . . . 2·00 25
N2640 15ch. Type **895** . . . . . 2·00 25
N2641 50ch. Annabergite (air) . . 2·00 25
N2642 50ch. Blue russula . . . . 2·00 25

896 Machu Picchu, Peru, and N. Korea Taedong Gate Stamp

1986. North Korean Three-dimensional Photographs and Stamp Exhibition, Lima, Peru. Multicoloured.
N2643 10ch. Type **896** . . . . .
MSN2644 110 × 75 mm. 80ch. Korean and Peruvian children 4·00 1·50

897 Pine Tree

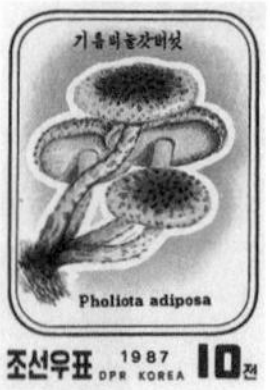
898 "Pholiota adiposa"

1987. New Year. Multicoloured.
N2645 10ch. Type **897** 75 15
N2646 40ch. Hare 90 25

1987. Fungi. Multicoloured.
N2647 10ch. Type **898** . . . . . 1·50 20
N2648 20ch. Chanterelle . . . . 1·75 20
N2649 30ch. "Boletus impolitus" 2·00 30
MS2650 50 × 70 mm. 80ch. "Gomphidius rutilus" . . . . 3·75 1·00

899 Kim Ok Song (composer)

901 East Pyongyang Grand Theatre

900 King Jong Il (½-size illustration)

1987. Musicians' Death Anniversaries. Mult.
N2651 10ch. Maurice Ravel (composer, 50th anniv) 1·50 20
N2652 10ch. Type **899** (22nd anniv) . . . . 1·50 20
N2653 20ch. Giovanni Lully (composer, 300th anniv) 1·50 20
N2654 30ch. Franz Liszt (composer, centenary (1986)) . . . . 1·50 20
N2655 40ch. Violins (250th anniv of Antonio Stradivari (violin maker)) . . . . 1·50 20
N2656 40ch. Christoph Gluck (composer, bicent) . . . 1·50 20

1997. Kim Jong Il's Birthday. Sheet 85 × 105 mm.
MSN2657 **900** 80ch. multicoloured 1·10 40

1987. Buildings.
N2658 **901** 5ch. green 35 10
N2659 – 10ch. brown 45 10
N2660 – 3wn. blue . . . . . . 3·00 90
DESIGNS—VERT: 10ch. Pyongyang Koryo Hotel. HORIZ: 3wn. Rungnado Stadium.

902 "Gorch Fock" (German cadet barque)

1987. Sailing Ships. Multicoloured.
N2661 20ch. Type **902** (postage) 70 20
N2662 30ch. "Tovarishch" (Russian cadet barque) (vert) . . . . 1·00 30
N2663 50ch. "Belle Poule" (cadet schooner) (vert) (air) . . 1·50 50
N2664 50ch. "Sagres II" (Portuguese cadet barque) (vert) . . . . . 1·50 50
N2665 1wn. Koryo period merchantman . . . . . 3·00 1·00
N2666 1wn. "Dar Mlodziezy" (Polish cadet full-rigged ship) (vert) . . . . . . 3·00 1·00

903 Road Signs

1987. Road Safety.
N2667 **903** 10ch. blue, red and black (postage) . . . 1·00 10
N2668 – 10ch. red and black . . 1·00 10
N2669 – 20ch. blue, red & black 1·25 20
N2670 – 50ch. red and black (air) . . . . 1·50 50
DESIGNS: Nos. N2668/70, Different road signs.

904 Fire Engine

1987. Fire Engines.
N2671 **904** 10ch. mult (postage) 1·75 25
N2672 – 20ch. multicoloured . . 1·90 25
N2673 – 30ch. multicoloured . . 2·50 30
N2674 – 50ch. multicoloured (air) . . . . 3·25 50
DESIGNS: N2672/4, 20ch. to 50ch. Different machines.

905 "Apatura ilia" and Spiraea

1987. Butterflies and Flowers. Multicoloured.
N2675 10ch. Type **905** 70 10
N2676 10ch. "Ypthima argus" and fuchsia 70 10
N2677 20ch. "Neptis philyra" and aquilegia . . . . . 1·00 20
N2678 20ch. "Papilio protenor" and chrysanthemum . . 1·00 20
N2679 40ch. "Parantica sita" and celosia . . . . 1·60 40
N2680 40ch. "Vanessa indica" and hibiscus . . . . . 1·60 40

906 Association Monument, Pyongyang

907 Doves, Emblem and Tree

1987. 70th Anniv of Korean National Association (independence movement).
N2681 **906** 10ch. red, silver & black 25 10

1987. 5th Spring Friendship Art Festival, Pyongyang.
N2682 **907** 10ch. multicoloured . . 25 10

908 Mangyong Hill

909 Bay

1987. 75th Birthday of Kim Il Sung. Mult.
N2683 10ch. Type **908** 25 10
N2684 10ch. Kim Il Sung's birthplace, Mangyongdae (horiz) 25 10

N2685 10ch. "A Bumper Crop of Pumpkins" (62 × 41 mm) 25 10
N2686 10ch. "Profound Affection for the Working Class" 25 10

1987. Horses. Multicoloured.

N2687	10ch. Type **909**	40	10
N2688	10ch. Bay (different) . . .	40	10
N2689	40ch. Grey rearing	1·25	40
N2690	40ch. Grey on beach . . .	1·25	40

910 "Sputnik 1" (first artificial satellite)

1987. Transport. Multicoloured.

N2691	10ch. "Juche" high speed train (horiz)	40	10
N2692	10ch. Electric locomotive "Mangyongdae" (horiz)	40	10
N2693	10ch. Type **910** (30th anniv of flight)	40	10
N2694	20ch. Laika (30th anniv of first animal in space) . .	70	20
N2695	20ch. Tupolev Tu-144 supersonic airliner (horiz)	70	20
N2696	20ch. Concorde (11th anniv of first commercial flight) (horiz)	70	20
N2697	30ch. Count Ferdinand von Zeppelin (70th death anniv) and airship LZ-4 (horiz)	1·00	30
N2698	80ch. Zeppelin and diagrams and drawings of airships (horiz) . . .	3·00	1·00

911 Musk Ox

1987. "Capex '87" International Stamp Exhibition, Toronto. Multicoloured.

N2699	10ch. Type **911**	65	10
N2700	40ch. Jacques Cartier, his ship "Grande Hermine" and "Terry Fox" (ice-breaker) (horiz)	1·75	40
N2701	60ch. Ice hockey (Winter Olympics, Calgary, 1988) (horiz)	1·75	60

912 Trapeze Artistes

1987. International Circus Festival, Monaco. Multicoloured.

N2702	10ch. Type **912**	40	10
N2703	10ch. "Brave Sailors" (North Korean acrobatic act) (vert) . .	40	10
N2704	20ch. Clown and elephant (vert)	70	20
N2705	20ch. North Korean artiste receiving "Golden Clown" award	70	20
N2706	40ch. Performing horses and cat act	2·10	40
N2707	50ch. Prince Rainier and his children applauding	1·50	50

913 Attack on Watch Tower

1987. 50th Anniv of Battle of Pochonbo.
N2708 **913** 10ch. brown, black and ochre 25 10

914 Sports

1987. Angol Sports Village.

N2709	**914** 5ch. brown and gold	15	10
N2710	– 10ch. blue and gold . .	25	10
N2711	– 40ch. brown and gold	75	25
N2712	– 70ch. blue and gold . .	1·25	40
N2713	– 1wn. red and gold . .	1·90	60
N2714	– 1wn.20 violet	2·25	70

DESIGNS: Exteriors of—10ch. Indoor swimming pool; 40ch. Weightlifting gymnasium; 70ch. Table tennis gymnasium; 1wn. Football stadium; 1wn.20, Handball gymnasium.

915 Mandarins

1987. Mandarins. Multicoloured.

N2715	20ch. Type **915**	1·50	40
N2716	20ch. Mandarins on shore	1·50	40
N2717	20ch. Mandarins on branch	1·50	40
N2718	40ch. Mandarins in water	2·25	60

916 Exhibition Site and 1987 3wn. Stamp

1987. "Olymphilex '87" Olympic Stamps Exhibition, Rome. Multicoloured.
N2719 10ch. Type **916** 90 10
MS2720 95 × 80 mm. 80ch. Exhibition emblem and 5ch. and 1wn. Angol Sports Village stamps 3·00 1·00

917 Underground Station and Guard

1987. Railway Uniforms. Multicoloured.

N2721	10ch. Type **917**	40	10
N2722	10ch. Underground train and station supervisor	40	10
N2723	20ch. Guard and electric train	60	15
N2724	30ch. Guard with flag and electric train	85	20
N2725	40ch. "Orient Express" guard and steam locomotive	1·10	25
N2726	40ch. German ticket controller and diesel train	1·10	25

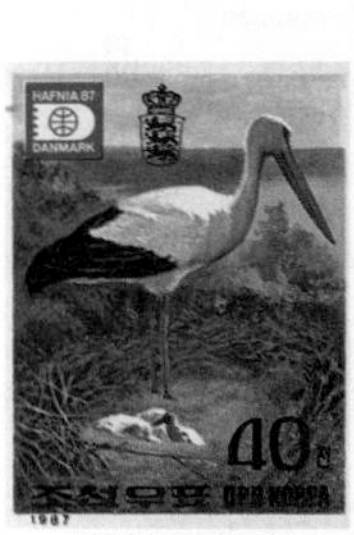

918 White Stork

920 Victory Column

919 Ice Skating

1987. "Hafnia 87" International Stamp Exhibition, Copenhagen. Multicoloured.

N2727	40ch. Type **918**	2·40	50
N2728	60ch. "Danmark" (cadet full-rigged ship) and "Little Mermaid", Copenhagen	1·75	40

1987. Winter Olympic Games, Calgary (1988). Multicoloured.

N2729	40ch. Type **919**	1·00	30
N2730	40ch. Ski jumping	1·00	30
N2731	40ch. Skiing (value on left) (horiz)	1·00	30
N2732	40ch. Skiing (value on right) (horiz)	1·00	30
MSN2733	73 × 100 mm. 80ch. Skiing	3·00	1·00

1987. 750th Anniv of Berlin and "Philatelia '87" International Stamp Exhibition, Cologne. Mult.

N2734	10ch. Type **920**	40	10
N2735	20ch. Reichstag (horiz) . .	70	20
N2736	30ch. Pfaueninsel Castle	1·00	30
N2737	40ch. Charlottenburg Castle (horiz)	1·25	40
MSN2738	77 × 94 mm. 80ch. Olympic stadium (horiz) . . .	3·00	1·00

921 Garros and Bleriot XI

1987. Birth Centenary of Roland Garros (aviator) and Tennis as an Olympic Sport. Multicoloured.

N2739	20ch. Type **921**	1·50	20
N2740	20ch. Ivan Lendl (tennis player)	2·25	20
N2741	40ch. Steffi Graf (tennis player)	3·00	40
MSN2742	80 × 102 mm. 80ch. Steffi Graf (different)	4·00	1·00

922 Kim Jong Suk ($\frac{1}{2}$-size illustration)

1878. 70th Birth Anniv of Kim Jong Suk (revoloutionary). Sheet 80 × 100 mm.
MSN2743 **922** 80ch. multicoloured 1·10 50

923 Pyongyang Buildings

1988. New Year. Multicoloured.

N2744	10ch. Type **923**	20	10
N2745	40ch. Dragon	75	25

924 Banner and Newspaper

925 Birthplace, Mt. Paekdu

1988. 60th Anniv of "Saenal" Newspaper.
N2746 **924** 10ch. multicoloured . . 45 10

1988. King Jongs Il's Birthday. Multicoloured.

N2747	109 × 85 mm. 10ch. Type **925**	20	10
MSN2748	109 × 85 mm. Kim Jong Il (41 × 63 mm.)	1·10	50

926 Henry Dunant (founder)

1988. 125th Anniv of International Red Cross. Multicoloured.

N2749	10ch. Type **926**	75	10
N2750	20ch. North Korean Red Cross emblem and map	1·00	15
N2751	20ch. International Committee headquarters, Geneva	1·10	15
N2752	40ch. Pyongyang Maternity Hospital, doctor and baby	1·25	25
MSN2753	70 × 100 mm. 80ch. Red Cross and Red Crescent flags and anniversary emblem	2·00	50

927 "Santa Maria"

1988. 500th Anniv (1992) of Discovery of America by Christopher Columbus. Multicoloured.

N2754	10ch. Type **927**	1·25	10
N2755	20ch. "Pinta"	1·25	20
N2756	30ch. "Nina"	1·25	30
MSN2757	80 × 102 mm. 80ch. "Columbus on the deck of his Flagship (detail, Karl von Piloty)	2·75	50

Nos. N2754/6 were issued together, se-tenant, forming a composite design of Columbus's ships leaving Palos.

928 Montgolfier Balloon and Modern Hot-air Balloons

929 Dancers

1988. "Juvalux '88" International Youth Stamp Exhibition, Luxembourg. Multicoloured.

N2758	40ch. Type **928**	90	25
N2759	60ch. Steam locomotive and railway map of Luxembourg, 1900 . . .	1·60	35

1988. 6th Spring Friendship Art Festival, Pyongyang. Multicoloured.
N2760 10ch. Singer (poster) . . . 20 10
N2761 1wn.20 Type **929** . . . . 1·90 75

930 Inaugural Congress Emblem

931 Birthplace, Mangyongdae

1988. 10th Anniv of International Institute of the Juche Idea.
N2762 **930** 10ch. multicoloured . . 20 10

1988. 76th Birthday of Kim Il Sung. Multicoloured.
N2763 10c. Type **931** 20 10
MSN2764 135 × 95 mm. 80ch. Kim Il Sung and schoolchildren (40 × 62 mm.) . . . . 1·10 50

932 "Urho" (ice-breaker)

1988. "Finlandia 88" International Stamp Exhibition, Helsinki. Multicoloured.
N2765 40ch. Type **932** . . . . . 1·40 25
N2766 60ch. Matti Nykaenen (Olympic Games ski-jumping medallist) . . . 1·10 35

933 Postcard for 1934 Championship

934 Emblem

1988. World Cup Football Championship, Italy (1st issue). Multicoloured.
N2767 10ch. Football match . . 50 10
N2768 20ch. Type **933** 85 15
N2769 30ch. Player tackling (horiz) . . . . 1·25 20
MSN2770 100 × 75 mm. 80ch. Winning Italian team, 1982 (horiz) 2·00 50
See also Nos. N2924/7.

1988. 13th World Youth and Students' Festival, Pyongyang (1st issue). Multicoloured.
N2771 5ch. Type **934** 10 10
N2772 10ch. Dancer 40 10
N2773 10ch. Gymnast and gymnasium, Angol Sports Village 20 10
N2774 10ch. Map of Korea, globe and doves 30 10
N2775 10ch. Finger pointing at shattered nuclear rockets 75 10
N2776 1wn.20 Three differently coloured hands and dove . . . . 2·10 75
See also Nos. N2860/3 and N2879/80.

935 Fairy

936 Mallards

1988. "Eight Fairies of Mt. Kumgang" (tale). Multicoloured.
N2777 10ch. Type **935** 20 10
N2778 15ch. Fairy at pool and fairies on rainbow . . . 30 10
N2779 20ch. Fairy and woodman husband 40 15
N2780 25ch. Couple with baby 70 20
N2781 30ch. Couple with son and daughter 55 20
N2782 35ch. Family on rainbow 1·00 35

1988. "Praga '88" International Stamp Exhibition, Prague. Multicoloured.
N2783 20ch. Type **936** . . . . . 1·90 25
N2784 40ch. Vladimir Remek (Czechoslovak cosmonaut) 75 25

937 Red Crossbill

1988. Birds. Multicoloured.
N2785 10ch. Type **937** 70 20
N2786 15ch. Common stonechat 1·00 30
N2787 20ch. Eurasian nuthatch 1·40 35
N2788 25ch. Great spotted woodpecker . . . . . . 1·60 45
N2789 30ch. River kingfisher . . 2·00 50
N2790 35ch. Bohemian waxwing 2·10 65

938 Fair Emblem

1988. 40th International Stamp Fair, Riccione. Multicoloured.
N2791 20ch. Type **938** 40 15
MSN2792 101 × 75 mm. 80ch. Drum dancer (vert) . . . . 1·50 50

939 Emu

1988. Bicentenary of Australian Settlement. Mult.
N2793 10ch. Type **939** 60 15
N2794 15ch. Satin bowerbirds . . 85 20
N2795 25ch. Laughing kookaburra (vert) . . . . 1·40 35
MSN2796 101 × 73 mm. 80ch. HMS "Resolution" (Cook's ship) . . 2·20 70

940 Floating Crane "5-28"

1988. Ships. Multicoloured.
N2797 10ch. Type **940** 40 15
N2798 20ch. Freighter "Hwanggumsan" . . . 60 20
N2799 30ch. Freighter "Changjasan Chongnyon-ho" 75 25
N2800 40ch. Liner "Samjiyon" 1·00 30

941 "Hansa"

1988. 150th Birth Anniv of Count Ferdinand von Zeppelin (airship pioneer). Multicoloured.
N2801 10ch. Type **941** 40 10
N2802 20ch. "Schwaben" 75 15
N2803 30ch. "Viktoria Luise" . . 90 20
N2804 40ch. LZ-3 . . . . 1·25 25
MSN2805 102 × 80 mm. 1wn. Portrait of Zeppelin (vert) . . 1·90 65

942 Kim Il Sung and Jambyn Batmunkh

1988. Kim Il Sung's Visit to Mongolia.
N2806 **942** 10ch. multicoloured . . 20 10

943 Hero and Labour Hero of the D.P.R.K. Medals

1988. National Heroes Congress.
N2807 **943** 10ch. multicoloured . . 20 10

944 Tower of Juche Idea

1988. 40th Anniv of Democratic Republic. Multicoloured.
N2808 5ch. Type **944** 10 10
N2809 10ch. Smelter and industrial buildings . . 20 10
N2810 10ch. Soldier and Mt. Paekdu 20 10
N2811 10ch. Map of Korea and globe 20 10
N2812 10ch. Hand holding banner, globe and doves 20 10
MSN2813 118 × 105 mm. 1wn.20 Kim Il Sung designing national flag and emblem (41 × 63 mm) 2·25 35

945 "Sunflowers" (Vincent van Gogh)

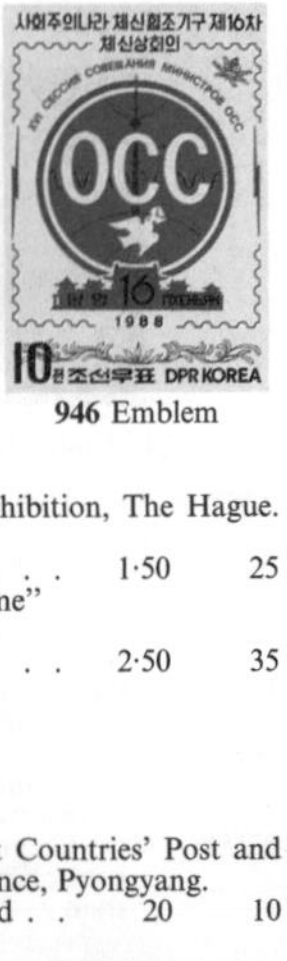

946 Emblem

1988. "Filacept 88" Stamp Exhibition, The Hague. Multicoloured.
N2814 40ch. Type **945** . . . . . 1·50 25
N2815 60ch. "The Chess Game" (Lucas van Leyden) (horiz) . . . . 2·50 35

1988. 16th Session of Socialist Countries' Post and Telecommunications Conference, Pyongyang.
N2816 **946** 10ch. multicoloured . . 20 10

947 Chaju "82" 10-ton Truck

948 "Owl"

1988. Tipper Trucks. Multicoloured.
N2817 20ch. Type **947** 40 15
N2818 40ch. Kumsusan-ho 40-ton truck 75 25

1988. Paintings by O Un Byol. Multicoloured.
N2819 10ch. Type **948** . . . . . 2·25 25
N2820 15ch. "Dawn" (red junglefowl) . . . . . . 1·00 25
N2821 20ch. "Beautiful Rose received by Kim Il Sung" 60 15
N2822 25ch. "Sun and Bamboo" 75 15
N2823 30ch. "Autumn" (fruit tree) . . . . 1·10 35

949 "Chunggi" Steam Locomotive No. 35

1988. Railway Locomotives. Multicoloured.
N2824 10ch. Type **949** 70 10
N2825 20ch. "Chunggi" steam locomotive No. 22 . . . 95 15
N2826 30ch. "Chongiha" electric locomotive No. 3 . . . 1·10 20
N2827 40ch. "Chunggi" steam locomotive No. 307 . . 1·40 25

950 Pirmen Zurbriggen (downhill skiing)

1988. Winter Olympic Games, Calgary, Medal Winners. Multicoloured.
N2828 10ch. Type **950** 20 10
N2829 20ch. Yvonne van Gennip (speed skating) 40 15
N2830 30ch. Marjo Matikainen (cross-country skiing) 55 20
N2831 40ch. U.S.S.R. (ice hockey) (horiz) 75 25
MSN2832 Two sheets, each 105 × 95 mm. (a) 80ch. Katarina Witt (figure skating); (b) 80ch. As sheet (a) but with names of winners printed in margin . . . 3·00 1·00

951 Yuri Gagarin

1988. 1st Man and Woman in Space. Mult.
N2833 20ch. Type **951** 40 15
N2834 40ch. Valentina Tereshkova 75 25

952 Nehru 953 Chollima Statue

1988. Birth Centenary of Jawaharlal Nehru (Indian statesman) and "India 89" International Stamp Exhibition, New Delhi.

N2835	**952** 20ch. purple, black and gold	60	15
MSN2836	90 × 74 mm. 60ch. multicoloured (Dancer)	1·10	35

1989. New Year. Multicoloured.

N2837	10ch. Type **953**	20	10
N2838	20ch. "The Dragon Angler" (17th-century painting)	60	15
N2839	40ch. "Tortoise and Serpent" (Kangso tomb painting) (horiz)	90	25

954 Archery

1989. National Defence Training. Multicoloured.

N2840	10ch. Type **954**	90	10
N2841	15ch. Rifle shooting . . .	30	10
N2842	20ch. Pistol shooting . . .	40	15
N2843	25ch. Parachuting	50	15
N2844	30ch. Launching model glider	55	20

955 Dobermann Pinscher 957 Agriculture

1989. Animals presented to Kim Il Sung. Mult.

N2845	10ch. Type **955**	50	10
N2846	20ch. Labrador	70	15
N2847	25ch. German shepherd	1·00	15
N2848	30ch. Rough collies (horiz)	1·00	20
N2849	35ch. Serval (horiz) . . .	1·25	20
MSN2850	95 × 75 mm. 80ch. "Felis libica" (horiz)	2·25	50

1989. 25th Anniv of Publication of "Theses on the Socialist Rural Question in our Country" by Kim Il Sung.

N2852	**957** 10ch. multicoloured . .	40	10

958 The Gypsy and Grapes 959 Korean Girl

1989. Fungi and Fruits. Multicoloured.

N2853	10ch. Type **958**	50	10
N2854	20ch. Caesar's mushroom and magnolia vine . . .	80	15
N2855	25ch. "Lactarius hygrophoides" and "Eleagnus crispa" . . .	1·10	15
N2856	30ch. "Agaricus placomyces" and Chinese gooseberries . .	1·25	20
N2857	35ch. Horse mushroom and "Lycium chinense"	1·50	20
N2858	40ch. Elegant boletus and "Juglans cordiformis"	1·75	25
MSN2859	100 × 78 mm. 1wn. "Gomphidius roseus" and Diospyros lotus" (48 × 30 mm)	3·50	65

1989. 13th World Youth and Students' Festival, Pyongyang (2nd issue). Multicoloured.

N2860	10ch. Type **959**	20	10
N2861	20ch. Children of different races	40	15
N2862	30ch. Fairy and rainbow	55	20
N2863	40ch. Young peoples and Tower of Juche Idea . .	45	25

960 "Parnassius eversmanni"

1969. Insects. Multicoloured.

N2864	10ch. Type **960**	50	15
N2865	15ch. "Colias heos" . . .	60	15
N2866	20ch. "Dilipa fenestra" . .	70	15
N2867	25ch. "Buthus martensis"	80	15
N2868	30ch. "Trichogramma ostriniae"	95	15
N2869	40ch. "Damaster constricticollis"	1·00	15
MSN2870	82 × 65 mm. 80ch. "Parnassius nomion"	2·25	50

961 Dancers (poster) 962 Birthplace, Mangyongdae

1989. Spring Friendship Art Festival, Pyongyang.

N2871	**961** 10ch. multicoloured . .	45	10

1989. 77th Birthday of Kim Il Sung.

N2872	**962** 10ch. multicoloured . .	20	10

963 Battle Plan and Monument to the Victory

1989. 50th Anniv of Battle of the Musan Area.

N2873	**963** 10ch. blue, flesh and red	60	10

964 Modern Dance

1989. Chamo System of Dance Notation. Multicoloured.

N2874	10ch. Type **964**	55	10
N2875	20ch. Ballet	70	15
N2876	25ch. Modern dance (different)	85	15
N2877	30ch. Traditional dance	1·00	20
MSN2878	85 × 105 mm. 80ch. Dancers	2·25	50

965 Hands supporting Torch 966 Victorious Badger

1989. 13th World Youth and Students' Festival, Pyongyang (3rd issue).

N2879	**965** 5ch. blue	10	10
N2880	– 10ch. brown	20	10

DESIGN: 10ch. Youth making speech.

1989. "Badger measures the Height" (cartoon film). Multicoloured.

N2881	10ch. Cat, bear and badger race to flag pole	80	10
N2882	40ch. Cat and bear climb pole while badger measures shadow . . .	1·25	25
N2883	50ch. Type **966**	1·50	30

967 Kyongju Observatory and Star Chart 969 Pele (footballer) and 1978 25ch. Stamp

1989. Astronomy.

N2884	20ch. multicoloured . . .	1·00	15
MSN2885	102 × 85 mm. 80ch. Planet Saturn (horiz)	2·40	50

968 "Liberty guiding the People" (Eugene Delacroiz)

1989. "Philexfrance 89" International Stamp Exhibition, Paris. Sheet 107 × 88 mm.

MSN2886	**968** 70ch. multicoloured	1·25	45

1989. "Brasiliana 89" International Stamp Exhibition, Rio de Janeiro.

N2887	**969** 40ch. multicoloured . .	1·25	25

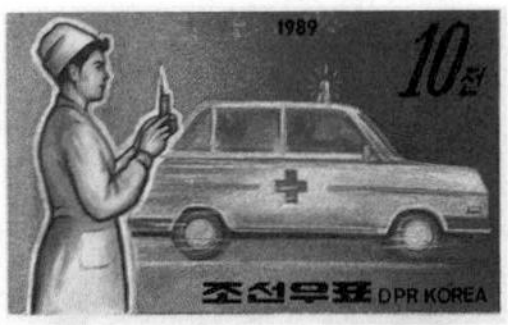

970 Nurse and Ambulance

1989. Emergency Services. Multicoloured.

N2888	10ch. Type **970**	20	10
N2889	20ch. Surgeon and ambulance	30	15
N2890	30ch. Fireman and fire engine	2·25	20
N2891	40ch. Fireman and engine (different)	2·25	25

971 Kaffir Lily 972 Air Mail Letter and Postal Transport

1989. Plants presented to Kim Il Sung. Mult.

N2892	10ch. Type **971**	40	10
N2893	15ch. Tulips	50	10
N2894	20ch. Flamingo lily . . .	75	15
N2895	25ch. "Rhododendron obtusum"	90	15
N2896	30ch. Daffodils	1·00	20
MSN2897	84 × 104 mm. 80ch. "Gerbera hybrida"	2·10	50

1989. 150th Anniv of the Penny Black and "Stamp World London 90" International Stamp Exhibition (1st issue). Multicoloured.

N2898	5ch. Type **972**	40	10
N2899	10ch. Post box and letters	55	10
N2900	20ch. Stamps, tweezers and magnifying glass . .	60	15
N2901	30ch. First North Korean stamps	75	20
N2902	40ch. Universal Postal Union emblem and headquarters, Berne . .	1·00	25
N2903	50ch. Sir Rowland Hill and Penny Black . . .	1·25	30

See also No. N2956/**MS**N2957

973 "Bistorta incana"

1989. Alpine Flowers. Multicoloured.

N2904	10ch. "Iris setosa"	50	10
N2905	15ch. "Aquilegia japonica"	60	10
N2906	20ch. Type **973**	75	15
N2907	25ch. "Rodiola elongata"	90	15
N2908	30ch. "Sanguisorba sitchensis"	95	20
MSN2909	62 × 49 mm. 80ch. "Trollius japonicus"	2·00	50

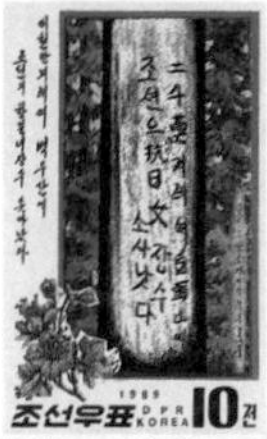

974 Tree, Mt. Paekdu 975 Skipping

1989. Slogan-bearing Trees (1st series). Mult.

N2910	10ch. Type **974**	20	10
N2911	3wn. Tree, Oun-dong, Pyongyang	5·50	1·75
N2912	5wn. Tree, Mt. Kanbaek	9·50	3·25

See also No. N2931.

1989. Children's Games. Multicoloured.

N2913	10ch. Type **975**	20	10
N2914	20ch. Windmill	1·25	15
N2915	30ch. Kite	55	20
N2916	40ch. Whip and top . . .	75	25

976 Marches

1989. International March for Peace and Reunification of Korea. Sheet 100 × 77 mm.

MSN2917	**976** 80ch. multicoloured	1·50	50

977 Diesel Train and Sinpa Youth Station

1989. Railway Locomotives. Multicoloured.

N2918	10ch. Type **977**	40	10
N2919	20ch. "Pulgungi" electric locomotive	60	15
N2920	25ch. Diesel goods train	70	15
N2921	30ch. Diesel train	85	20
N2922	40ch. Steam locomotive	1·00	25
N2923	50ch. Steam locomotive (different)	1·10	30

978 Players and Map of Italy

1989. World Cup Football Championship, Italy (2nd issue). Multicoloured.

N2924	10ch. Type **978**	1·00	10
N2925	20ch. Free kick	50	15
N2926	30ch. Goal mouth scrimmage	75	20
N2927	40ch. Goalkeeper diving for ball	95	25

979 Magellan (navigator) and his Ship "Vitoria"

1989. "Descobrex '89" International Stamp Exhibition, Portugal.
N2928 **979** 30ch. multicoloured . . 1·25 20

980 Mangyong Hill and Pine Branches **981** Ryukwoli

1990. New Year. Multicoloured.
N2929 10ch. Type **980** 20 10
N2930 20ch. Koguryo mounted archers 90 15

1990. Slogan-bearing Trees (2nd series). As T **974**. Multicoloured.
N2931 5ch. Tree, Mt. Paekdu . . 25 10

1990. Dogs. Multicoloured.
N2932 20ch. Type **981** . . . . . 1·25 20
N2933 30ch. Palryuki . . . . . 1·25 20
N2934 40ch. Komdungi . . . . 1·25 20
N2935 50ch. Oulruki . . . . . . 1·25 20

982 Birthplace, Mt. Paekdu **983** Stone Instruments and Primitive Man

1990. Birthday of Kim Jong Il.
N2936 **982** 10ch. brown 20 10

1990. Evolution of Man. Multicoloured.
N2937 10ch. Type **983** 45 10
N2938 40ch. Palaeolithic and Neolithic man 90 25

984 Rungna Bridge, Pyongyang

1990. Bridges. Multicoloured.
N2939 10ch. Type **984** 45 10
N2940 20ch. Potong bridge, Pyongyang 60 15
N2941 30ch. Sinuiji-Ryucho Island Bridge 85 20
N2942 40ch. Chungsongui Bridge, Pyongyang . . . . . . 1·10 25

985 Infantryman **987** Dancers

986 "Atergatis subdentatus"

1990. Warriors' Costumes. Multicoloured.
N2943 20ch. Type **985** 40 15
N2944 30ch. Archer 55 20
N2945 50ch. Military commander in armour 95 30
N2946 70ch. Officer's costume, 10th–14th centuries . . 1·25 40

Nos. N2943/5 depict costumes from the 3rd century B.C. to the 7th century A.D.

1990. Crabs. Multicoloured.
N2947 20ch. Type **986** 60 15
N2948 30ch. "Platylambrus validus" 75 20
N2949 50ch. "Uca arcuata" . . . 1·10 30

1990. Spring Friendship Art Festival, Pyongyang.
N2950 **987** 10ch. multicoloured . . 30 10

988 Monument at Road Folk, Mangyongdae **989** "Gymnocalycium sp."

1990. 78th Birthday of Kim Il Sung.
N2951 **988** 10ch. green and gold 20 10
MSN2952 85 × 105 mm. 80ch. multicoloured (Kim Il Sung) (38 × 60 mm) . . . . 1·10 50

1990. Cacti. Multicoloured.
N2953 10ch. Type **989** 50 10
N2954 30ch. "Pyllocactus hybridus" 90 20
N2955 50ch. "Epiphyllum truncatum" . . . . . . 1·50 30

990 Exhibition Emblem **991** Congo Peafowl

1990. "Stamp World London 90" International Stamp Exhibition (2nd issue).
N2956 **990** 20ch. red and black . . 40 15
MSN2957 49 × 66 mm. 70ch. grey, black and gold . . . . 1·25 40
DESIGN: 70ch. Sir Rowland Hill.

1990. Peafowl. Multicoloured.
N2958 10ch. Type **991** 75 25
N2959 20ch. Common peafowl 2·00 60
MSN2960 96 × 82 mm. 70ch. Common peafowl displaying tail 1·75 55

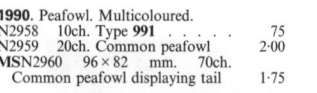

992 Dolphin and Submarine

1990. Bio-engineering. Multicoloured.
N2961 10ch. Type **992** . . . . . 1·10 25
N2962 20ch. Bat and dish aerial 1·10 25
N2963 30ch. Owl and Tupolev Tu-154 jetliner . . . . 1·25 35
N2964 40ch. Squid, "Soyuz" rocket and Concorde supersonic jetliner . . . 1·10 25

993 "Self-portrait" (Rembrandt) **994** K. H. Rummenigge (footballer)

1990. "Belgica 90" International Stamp Exhibition, Brussels. Multicoloured.
N2965 10ch. Type **993** 30 10
N2966 20ch. "Self-portrait" (Raphael) 60 15
N2967 30ch. "Self-portrait" (Rubens) 75 20

1990. "Dusseldorf '90" International Youth Stamp Exhibition. Multicoloured.
N2968 20ch. Steffi Graf (tennis player) 85 15
N2969 30ch. Exhibition emblem 55 20
N2970 70ch. Type **994** . . . . . 1·25 40

995 Workers' Stadium, Peking, and Games Mascot

1990. 11th Asian Games, Peking (Nos. N2971/2) and 3rd Asian Winter Games, Samjiyon (N2973). Multicoloured.
N2971 10ch. Type **995** 30 10
N2972 30ch. Chollima Statue and sportsmen 75 20
N2973 40ch. Sportsmen and Games emblem . . . . 1·00 25

996 Ball

1990. West Germany, Winners of World Cup Football Championship. Multicoloured.
N2974 15ch. Emblem of F.I.F.A. (International Federation of Football Associations) 40 10
N2975 20ch. Jules Rimet 50 15
N2976 25ch. Type **996** 60 15
N2977 30ch. Olympic Stadium, Rome (venue of final) 65 20
N2978 35ch. Goalkeeper 75 20
N2979 40ch. Emblem of West German Football Association 90 25
MSN2980 106 × 92 mm. 80ch. German Football Association emblem and trophy (horiz) . . 1·40 45

997 Kakapo and Map of New Zealand

1990. "New Zealand 1990" International Stamp Exhibition, Auckland.
N2981 **997** 30ch. multicoloured . . 1·60 50

998 "Summer at Chipson Peak"

1990. "Europa 90" International Stamp Fair, Riccione. Sheet 90 × 70 mm.
MSN2982 **998** 80cn. multicoloured 1·50 50

999 Head of Procession

1990. Koguryo Wedding Procession. Mult.
N2983 10ch. Type **999** . . . . . 1·00 20
N2984 30ch. Bridegroom . . . . 1·00 20
N2985 50ch. Bride in carriage . . 1·00 20
N2986 1wn. Drummer on horse 1·00 20
Nos. N2983/6 were issued together, se-tenant, forming a composite design.

1000 Marchers descending Mt. Paekdu

1990. Rally for Peace and Reunification of Korea. Multicoloured.
N2987 10ch. Type **1000** 20 10
MSN2988 106 × 70 mm. 1wn. Crowd watching dancers . . . . . . 1·25 50

1001 Praying Mantis

1990. Insects. Multicoloured.
N2989 20ch. Type **1001** 40 15
N2990 30ch. Ladybird 55 20
N2991 40ch. "Pheropsophus jessoensis" 75 25
N2992 70ch. "Phyllium siccifolium" . . . . . . 1·25 40

1002 Footballers

1990. North–South Reunification Football Match, Pyongyang. Multicoloured.
N2993 10ch. Type **1002** 75 10
N2994 20ch. Footballers (different) 75 15
MSN2995 105 × 80 mm. 1wn. Teams parading . . . . 1·90 65

1003 Concert Emblem **1004** Ox

1990. National Reunification Concert.
N2996 **1003** 10ch. multicoloured 20 10

1990. Farm Animals.
N2997 **1004** 10ch. brown and green 20 10
N2998 – 20ch. lilac and yellow 40 15
N2999 – 30ch. grey and red . . 55 20
N3000 – 40ch. green and yellow 75 25
N3001 – 50ch. brown and blue 95 30
DESIGNS: 20ch. Pig; 30ch. Goat; 40ch. Sheep; 50ch. Horse.

1005 Chinese and North Korean Soldiers

1990. 40th Anniv of Participation of Chinese Volunteers in Korean War. Multicoloured.
N3002 10ch. Type **1005** 20 10
N3003 20ch. Populace welcoming volunteers (horiz) . . . 40 15

N3004 30ch. Rejoicing soldiers and battle scene (horiz) . . 50 20
N3005 40ch. Post-war reconstruction (horiz) . . 60 25
MSN3006 95×75 mm. 80ch. Friendship Tower, Moran Hill, Pyongyang . . . . 1·10 65

1006 Anniversary Emblem

1990. 40th Anniv of United Nations Development Programme.
N3007 **1006** 1wn. blue, silver & blk . . . . 1·90 65

1007 Mikado Sturgeon
1008 Sheep

1990. Fishes.
N3008 **1007** 10ch. brown and green 25 10
N3009 – 20ch. green and blue . . 55 15
N3010 – 30ch. blue and purple . . 75 25
N3011 – 40ch. brown and blue . . 1·00 30
N3012 – 50ch. violet and green . . 1·25 35
DESIGNS: 20ch. Large-headed sea bream; 30ch. Agoo flyingfish; 40ch. Fat greenling; 50ch. Tobij-ei eagle ray.

1990. New Year.
N3013 **1008** 40ch. multicoloured . . 75 25

1009 Moorhen
1010 Giant Panda

1990. Birds.
N3014 **1009** 10ch. blue, green & blk 55 15
N3015 – 20ch. brown, bistre and black 90 30
N3016 – 30ch. green, grey and black . . . . . . 1·10 50
N3017 – 40ch. brown, orange and black . . . . 1·75 60
N3018 – 50ch. ochre, brown and black . . . . 2·25 70
DESIGNS: 20ch. Jay; 30ch. Three-toed woodpecker; 40ch. Whimbrel; 50ch. Water rail.

1991. "Phila Nippon '91" International Stamp Exhibition, Tokyo. Multicoloured.
N3019 10ch. Type **1010** 30 10
N3020 20ch. Two giant pandas feeding 50 15
N3021 30ch. Giant panda clambering onto branch . . 70 20
N3022 40ch. Giant panda on rock 90 25
N3023 50ch. Two giant pandas . . 1·10 30
N3024 60ch. Giant panda in tree fork . . . . 1·25 35
MSN3025 115×85 mm. Giant panda . . . . 1·90 65

1011 Changsan

1991. Revolutionary Sites.
N3026 5ch. Type **1011** 10 10
N3027 10ch. Oun 20 10

1012 Black-faced Spoonbills
1014 Hedgehog Fungus

1013 "Clossiana angarensis"

1991. Endangered Birds. Multicoloured.
N3028 10ch. Type **1012** 30 10
N3029 20ch. Grey herons 60 15
N3030 30ch. Great egrets 85 25
N3031 40ch. Manchurian cranes . . 1·10 30
N3032 50ch. Japanese white-naped cranes . . . . . 1·75 35
N3033 70ch. White storks . . . . 2·25 50

1991. Alpine Butterflies. Multicoloured.
N3034 10ch. Type **1013** 25 10
N3035 20ch. "Erebia embla" . . 40 15
N3036 30ch. Camberwell beauty . . 60 20
N3037 40ch. Comma 75 30
N3038 50ch. Eastern pale clouded yellow 90 35
N3039 60ch. "Theela betulae" . . 1·10 45

1991. Fungi. Multicoloured.
N3040 10ch. Type **1014** 25 10
N3041 20ch. "Phylloporus rhodoxanthus" 45 15
N3042 30ch. "Calvatia craniiformis" 60 20
N3043 40ch. Cauliflower clavaria . . 80 30
N3044 50ch. "Russula integra" . . 1·00 35

1015 Kumchon

1991. Revolutionary Sites. Multicoloured.
N3045 10ch. Type **1015** 15 10
N3046 40ch. Samdung 60 30

1016 Dr. Kye Ung Sang (researcher)
1017 Emblem and Venue

1991. Silkworm Research. Multicoloured.
N3047 10ch. Type **1016** 15 10
N3048 20ch. Chinese oak silk moth 30 15
N3049 30ch. "Attacus ricini" . . 45 20
N3050 40ch. "Antheraea yamamai" 60 30
N3051 50ch. Silkworm moth . . 75 35
N3052 60ch. "Aetias artemis" . . 90 45

1991. 9th Spring Friendship Art Festival, Pyongyang.
N3053 **1017** 10ch. multicoloured 10 10

1018 Emperor Penguins
1020 Map and Kim Jong Ho

1019 People's Palace of Culture (venue)

1991. Antarctic Exploration. Multicoloured.
N3054 10ch. Type **1018** 35 20
N3055 20ch. Research station . . 40 15
N3056 30ch. Elephant seals . . . 75 20
N3057 40ch. Research ship . . . 90 40
N3058 50ch. Southern black-backed gulls . . . . . 1·60 40
MSN3059 75×105 mm. 80ch. National flag and map of Antarctica . . . . 1·25 50

1991. 85th Interparliamentary Union Conference, Pyongyang.
N3060 **1019** 10ch. dp green, grn & sil 15 10
N3061 – 1wn.50 multicoloured 2·25 1·10
DESIGN: 1wn.50, Conference emblem and azalea.

1991. 130th Anniv of Publication of Kim Jong Ho's Map "Taidong Yu Jido".
N3062 **1020** 90ch. black, brn & sil 1·40 70

1021 Cynognathus

1991. Dinosaurs. Multicoloured.
N3063 10ch. Type **1021** 25 10
N3064 20ch. Brontosaurus . . . 40 15
N3065 30ch. Stegosaurus and allosaurus 55 20
N3066 40ch. Pterosauria 70 30
N3067 50ch. Ichthyosaurus . . . 85 35

1022 Sprinting

1991. Olympic Games, Barcelona (1992) (1st issue). Multicoloured.
N3068 10ch. Type **1022** 15 10
N3069 10ch. Hurdling 15 10
N3070 20ch. Long jumping 30 15
N3071 20ch. Throwing the discus 30 15
N3072 30ch. Putting the shot . . 45 20
N3073 30ch. Pole vaulting . . . 45 20
N3074 40ch. High jumping . . . 60 30
N3075 40ch. Throwing the javelin 60 30
MSN3076 Two sheets, each 105×85 mm. (a) 80ch. Breasting the tape; (b) 80ch. Running . . 2·40 1·10
See also Nos. N3142/MS3148.

1023 Cats and Eurasian Tree Sparrows

1991. Cats. Multicoloured.
N3077 10ch. Type **1023** 50 35
N3078 20ch. Cat and rat 40 15
N3079 30ch. Cat and butterfly . . 55 20
N3080 40ch. Cats with ball . . . 75 30
N3081 50ch. Cat and frog . . . 90 35

1024 "Wisteria Flowers and Pups" (detail)

1991. "Riccione '91" Stamp Fair and Exhibition, Italy. Sheet 116×80 mm. International.
MSN3082 **1024** 80ch. multicoloured 1·25 60

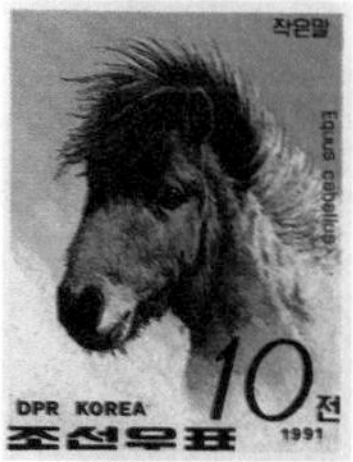

1025 Wild Horse

1991. Horses. Multicoloured.
N3083 10ch. Type **1025** 25 10
N3084 20ch. Hybrid of wild ass and wild horse 40 15
N3085 30ch. Przewalski's horse 60 20
N3086 40ch. Wild ass 75 30
N3087 50ch. Wild horse (different) 90 35

1026 Pennant Coralfish

1991. Fishes. Multicoloured.
N3088 10ch. Type **1026** (postage) 40 10
N3089 20ch. Clown triggerfish . . 75 25
N3090 30ch. Tomato anemonefish 1·00 30
N3091 40ch. Palette surgeonfish 1·40 45
N3092 50ch. Freshwater angelfish (air) . . . . 1·60 55
MSN3093 88×60 mm. 80ch. Tetras ("Hyhessobrycon innesi") (51×31 mm) . . . . 1·10 55

1027 Rhododendrons

1991. Flowers. Multicoloured.
N3094 10ch. Begonia 25 10
N3095 20ch. Gerbera 40 15
N3096 30ch. Type **1027** 55 20
N3097 40ch. Phalaenopsis 70 30
N3098 50ch. "Impatiens sultanii" 85 35
N3099 60ch. Streptocarpus . . . 1·00 45
Nos. N3097/9 commemorate "CANADA '92" international youth stamp exhibition, Montreal.

1028 Panmunjom

1991.
N3100 **1028** 10ch. multicoloured 15 10

1029 Magnolia
1030 Players

1991. National Flower.

N3101	**1029** 10ch. multicoloured	40	10

1991. Women's World Football Championship, China. Multicoloured.

N3102	10ch. Type **1030**	25	10
N3103	20ch. Dribbling the ball	40	15
N3104	30ch. Heading the ball	55	20
N3105	40ch. Overhead kick	70	30
N3106	50ch. Tackling	85	35
N3107	60ch. Goalkeeper	1·10	45

1031 Squirrel Monkeys

1992. Monkeys. Multicoloured.

N3108	10ch. Type **1031**	25	10
N3109	20ch. Pygmy marmosets	40	15
N3110	30ch. Red-handed tamarins	60	20
MSN3111	65 × 91 mm. 80ch. Monkey leaping (33 × 51 mm)	1·25	60

1032 Eagle Owl

1992. Birds of Prey. Multicoloured.

N3112	10ch. Type **1032**	25	20
N3113	20ch. Common buzzard	55	30
N3114	30ch. African fish eagle	2·00	60
N3115	40ch. Steller's sea eagle	1·25	65
N3116	50ch. Golden eagle	1·40	75
MSN3117	78 × 59 mm. 80ch. Common kestrel (41 × 31 mm)	1·25	60

1033 Birthplace, Mt. Paekdu

1992. Birthday of Kim Jong Il. Mt. Paekdu. Multicoloured.

N3118	10ch. Type **1033**	15	10
N3119	20ch. Mountain summit	30	15
N3120	30ch. Lake Chon (crater lake)	45	20
N3121	40ch. Lake Sarryi	60	30
MSN3122	162 × 87 mm. 80ch. "Snowstorm on Mt. Paekdu" (41 × 63 mm)	1·25	60

1034 Service Bus

1992. Transport.

N3123	**1034** 10ch. multicoloured	25	10
N3124	– 20ch. multicoloured	40	15
N3125	– 30ch. multicoloured	60	20
N3126	– 40ch. multicoloured	75	30
N3127	– 50ch. multicoloured	90	35
N3128	– 60ch. multicoloured	1·10	45

DESIGNS: 20ch. to 60ch. Different buses and electric trams.

1035 Dancers and Emblem

1992. Spring Friendship Art Festival, Pyongyang.

N3129	**1035** 10ch. multicoloured	30	10

1036 Birthplace, Mangyongdae

1992. 80th Birthday of Kim Il Sung. Revolutionary Sites. Multicoloured.

N3130	10ch. Type **1036** (postage)	15	10
N3131	10ch. Party emblem and Turubong monument	15	10
N3132	10ch. Map and Ssuksom	15	10
N3133	10ch. Statue of soldier and Tongchang	15	10
N3134	40ch. Cogwheels and Taean	60	30
N3135	40ch. Chollima Statue and Kangson	60	30
N3136	1wn.20 Monument and West Sea Barrage (air)	1·75	85
MSN3137	160 × 160 mm. 80ch. "April spring Friendship Art Festival" (41 × 63 mm)	1·25	60

1037 Kang Ban Sok

1992. Birth Centenary of Kang Ban Sok (mother of Kim Il Sung). Sheet 80 × 103 mm.

MSN3138	**1037** 80ch. multicoloured	1·25	60

1038 Soldiers on Parade

1992. 60th Anniv of People's Army. Multicoloured.

N3139	10ch. Type **1038**	15	10
N3140	10ch. Couple greeting soldier	15	10
N3141	10ch. Army, air force and navy personnel	15	10

1039 Hurdling

1992. Olympic Games, Barcelona (2nd issue). Multicoloured.

N3142	10ch. Type **1039**	25	10
N3143	20ch. High jumping	40	15
N3144	30ch. Putting the shot	60	20
N3145	40ch. Sprinting	75	30
N3146	50ch. Long jumping	90	35
N3147	60ch. Throwing the javelin	1·10	45
MSN3148	105 × 85 mm. 80ch. Running	1·10	55

1040 Planting Crops

1992. Evolution of Man. Designs showing life in the New Stone Age (10, 20ch.) and the Bronze Age (others). Multicoloured.

N3149	10ch. Type **1040** (postage)	15	10
N3150	20ch. Family around cooking pot	30	15
N3151	30ch. Ploughing fields	45	20
N3152	40ch. Performing domestic chores	60	30
N3153	50ch. Building a dolmen (air)	75	35

1041 White-bellied Black Woodpecker **1042** Map and Hands holding Text

1992. Birds. Multicoloured.

N3154	10ch. Type **1041**	20	15
N3155	20ch. Common pheasant	40	25
N3156	30ch. White stork	60	35
N3157	40ch. Blue-winged pitta	85	55
N3158	50ch. Pallas's sandgrouse	1·10	60
N3159	60ch. Black grouse	1·25	80
MSN3160	98 × 63 mm. 80ch. Daurian starling	1·25	60

1992. 20th Anniv of Publication of North–South Korea Joint Agreement.

N3161	**1042** 1wn.50 multicoloured	90	30
MSN3162	112 × 76 mm. No. 3161 × 2	4·00	2·00

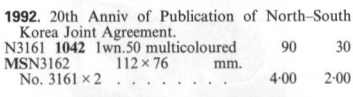

1043 "Bougainvillea spectabilis" **1044** Venus, Earth, Mars and Satellite

1992. Flowers. Multicoloured.

N3163	10ch. Type **1043**	25	10
N3164	20ch. "Ixora chinensis"	40	15
N3165	30ch. "Dendrobium taysuwie"	60	20
N3166	40ch. "Columnea gloriosa"	75	30
N3167	50ch. "Crinum"	90	35
N3168	60ch. "Ranunculus asiaticus"	1·10	45

1992. The Solar System. Multicoloured.

N3169	50ch. Type **1044**	90	35
N3170	50ch. Jupiter	90	35
N3171	50ch. Saturn	90	35
N3172	50ch. Uranus	90	35
N3173	50ch. Neptune and Pluto	90	35
MSN3174	90 × 71 mm. 80ch. Planet Earth	1·10	55

Nos. N3169/73 were issued together, se-tenant, forming a composite design.

1045 "470" Dinghy **1046** Moreno Mannini (defender)

1992. "Riccione '92" Stamp Fair. Multicoloured.

N3175	10ch. Type **1045**	15	10
N3176	20ch. Sailboard	30	15
N3177	30ch. Sailing dinghy	45	20
N3178	40ch. "Finn" dinghy	60	30
N3179	50ch. "420" dinghy	75	35
N3180	60ch. Fair emblem	90	45

1992. Sampdoria, Italian Football Champion, 1991. Multicoloured.

N3181	20ch. Type **1046**	30	15
N3182	30ch. Gianluca Vialli (forward)	45	30
N3183	40ch. Pietro Vierchowod (defender)	60	30
N3184	50ch. Fausto Pari (defender)	75	35
N3185	60ch. Roberto Mancini (forward)	90	45
N3186	1wn. Paolo Mantovani (club president)	1·50	75
MSN3187	92 × 66 mm. 1wn. Vialli and Riccardo Garrone (president of club sponsor) (51 × 33 mm)	1·50	75

1047 Black-belts warming up

1992. 8th World Taekwondo Championship, Pyongyang. Multicoloured.

N3188	10ch. Type **1047** (postage)	15	10
N3189	30ch. "Roundhouse" kick	45	30
N3190	50ch. High kick	75	35
N3191	70ch. Flying kick	1·00	50
N3192	90ch. Black-belt breaking tiles with fist	1·40	70
MSN3193	93 × 75 mm. 1wn.20 Flight scene (33 × 51 mm) (air)	1·75	85

1048 Common Toad ("Bufo bufo")

1992. Frogs and Toads. Multicoloured.

N3194	40ch. Type **1048** (postage)	75	30
N3195	40ch. Moor frog ("Rana arvalis")	75	30
N3196	40ch. "Rana chosenica"	75	30
N3197	70ch. Common pond frog ("Rana nigromaculata")	1·25	50
N3198	70ch. Japanese tree toad ("Hyla japonica")	1·25	50
N3199	70ch. "Rana coreana" (air)	1·25	50

1049 "Rhododendron mucronulatum"

1992. World Environment Day. Multicoloured.

N3200	10ch. Type **1049** (postage)	15	10
N3201	30ch. Barn swallow	55	35
N3202	40ch. "Stewartia koreana" (flower)	60	30
N3203	50ch. "Dictyoptera aurora" (beetle)	75	35
N3204	70ch. "Metasequoia glyptostroboides" (tree)	1·00	50
N3205	90ch. Chinese salamander	1·40	70
N3206	1wn. 20 "Ginkgo biloba" (tree) (air)	1·75	85
N3207	1wn. 40 Alpine bullhead	3·00	1·25

1050 Fin Whale ("Balaenoptera physalus")

1992. Whales and Dolphins. Multicoloured.

N3208	50ch. Type **1050** (postage)	1·00	35
N3209	50ch. Common dolphin ("Delphinus delphis")	1·00	35
N3210	50ch. Killer Whale ("Orcinus orca")	1·00	35
N3211	50ch. Hump-backed whale ("Megaptera nodosa")	1·00	35
N3212	50ch. Bottle-nosed whale ("Berardius bairdii")	1·00	35
N3213	50ch. Sperm whale ("Physeter catadon") (air)	1·00	35

1051 Mother and Chicks

1992. New Year. Roosters in various costumes. Multicoloured.

N3214	10ch. Type **1051**	15	10
N3215	20ch. Lady	30	15
N3216	30ch. Warrior	45	20
N3217	40ch. Courtier	60	30
N3218	50ch. Queen	75	35
N3219	60ch. King	90	45
MSN3220	112 × 80 mm. 1wn.20 Sultan	1·75	85

1052 Choe Chol Su (boxing)

1992. Gold Medal Winners at Barcelona Olympics. Multicoloured.
N3221 10ch. Type **1052** 15 10
N3222 20ch. Pae Kil Su (gymnastics) 30 15
N3223 50ch. Ri Hak Son (freestyle wrestling) . . 75 35
N3224 60ch. Kim Il (freestyle wrestling) 90 45
MSN3225 28 × 120 mm. Nos. N3221/4; 30ch. Flags of Spain and North Korea, flame, gold medal and archer; 40ch. Church of the Holy Family (Barcelona), games mascot and emblem . . . . . 2·75 1·25

1053 Golden Mushroom

1055 League Members and Flag

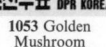

1054 "Keumkangsania asiatica"

1993. Fungi. Multicoloured.
N3227 10ch. Type **1053** 15 10
N3228 20ch. Shaggy caps 30 15
N3229 30ch. "Ganoderma lucidum" 45 20
N3230 40ch. Brown mushroom 60 30
N3231 50ch. "Volvaria bombycina" 75 35
N3232 60ch. "Sarcodon aspratus" 90 45
MSN3233 59 × 60 mm. 1wn. Scarlet caterpillar fungus . . . . . . 1·50 75

1993. Plants. Multicoloured.
N3234 10ch. Type **1054** 25 10
N3235 20ch. "Echinosophora koreensis" 80 15
N3236 30ch. "Abies koreana" . . 55 20
N3237 40ch. "Benzoin angustifolium" 75 30
N3238 50ch. "Abeliophyllum distichum" 85 35
N3239 60ch. "Abelia mosanensis" 1·00 45
MSN3240 73 × 93 mm. 1wn. "Pentactina rupicola" (27 × 38 mm) . . . . 1·50 75

1993. 8th League of Socialist Working Youth Congress. Multicoloured.
N3241 10ch. Type **1055** 15 10
N3242 40ch. Flame, League emblem and text 60 30

1056 Phophyong Revolutionary Site Tower and March Corps Emblem

1057 Tower of Juche Idea and Grand Monument, Mt. Wangjae

1993. 70th Anniv of 1000-ri Journey for Learning.
N3243 **1056** 10ch. multicoloured 15 10

1993. 60th Anniv of Wangjaesan Meeting.
N3244 **1057** 5ch. multicoloured . . 10 10

1058 "Kimjomgil" (begonia)

1993. 51st Birthday if Kim Jong Li. Multicoloured.
N3245 10ch. Type **1058** 40 10
MSN3246 170 × 95 mm. 1wn. Kim Il Sung writing paean to Kim Jong Il on his 59th birthday (50 × 41 mm) 1·50 75

1059 Pilot Fish

1993. Fishes. Multicoloured.
N3247 10ch. Type **1059** 25 10
N3248 20ch. Japanese stingray . . 55 20
N3249 30ch. Opah 80 30
N3250 40ch. Coelacanth . . . . 1·10 45
N3251 50ch. Moara grouper . . 1·25 50
MSN3252 96 × 70 mm. 1wn.20 Mako shark . . . . 1·75 85

1060/1064 "Spring on the Hill" (½-size illustration)

1993. 18th-century Korean Painting.
N3253 **1060** 40ch. multicoloured 60 30
N3254 **1061** 40ch. multicoloured 60 30
N3255 **1062** 40ch. multicoloured 60 30
N3256 **1063** 40ch. multicoloured 60 30
N3257 **1064** 40ch. multicoloured 60 30
Nos. N3253/7 were issued together, se-tenant, forming the composite design illustrated.

1065 Violinist, Dancers and Emblem

1993. Spring Friendship Art Festival, Pyongyang.
N3258 **1065** 10ch. multicoloured 15 10

1066 Books

1993. 81st Birthday of Kim Li Sung and Publication of his Reminiscences "With the Country". Multicoloured.
N3259 10ch. Type **1066** 15 10
MSN3260 140 × 105 mm. 1wn. Kim Il Sung writing (62 × 412 mm) 1·50 75

1067 Kwangbok Street

1993. Pyongyang. Multicoloured.
N3261 10ch. Type **1067** 15 10
N3262 20ch. Chollima Street . . 30 15
N3263 30ch. Munsu Street . . . 45 20
N3264 40ch. Moranbong Street 60 30
N3265 50ch. Thongil Street . . . 75 35
MSN3266 115 × 74 mm. 1wn. Changgwang street . . . . . . 1·50 75

1068 "Trichogramma dendrolimi" (fly)

1993. Insects. Multicoloured.
N3267 10ch. Type **1068** 15 10
N3268 20ch. "Brachymeria obscurata" (fly) 30 15
N3269 30ch. "Metrioptera brachyptera" (cricket) 45 20
N3270 50ch. European field cricket 75 35
N3271 70ch. "Geocoris pallidipennis" (beetle) 1·00 50
N3272 90ch. "Cyphonony x dorsalis" (wasp) fighting spider . . . . 1·40 70

1069 Ri In Mo

1071 Grey-headed Woodpecker

1070 Footballers

1993. Return from Imprisonment of Ri in Mo (war correspondent). Multicoloured.
N3273 10ch. Type **1069** 15 10
MSN3274 110 × 80 mm. 1wn.20 Ri in Mo and flowers (47 × 35 mm) 1·75 85

1993. World Cup Football Championship, U.S.A.
N3275 **1070** 10ch. multicoloured 25 10
N3276 – 20ch. multicoloured 40 15
N3277 – 30ch. multicoloured 60 20
N3278 – 50ch. multicoloured 90 35
N3279 – 70ch. multicoloured 1·25 50
N3280 – 90ch. multicoloured 1·75 70
DESIGNS: 20ch. to 90ch. Various footballing scenes.

1993. Birds. Multicoloured.
N3281 10ch. Type **1071** 20 15
N3282 20ch. King bird of paradise 40 20
N3283 30ch. Lesser bird of paradise 45 35
N3284 40ch. Paradise whydah . . 80 55
N3285 50ch. Magnificent bird of paradise . . . . 1·00 60
N3286 60ch. Greater bird of paradise . . . . 1·25 80
Nos. N3283/4 also commemorate "Indopex '93" international stamp exhibition, Surabaya.

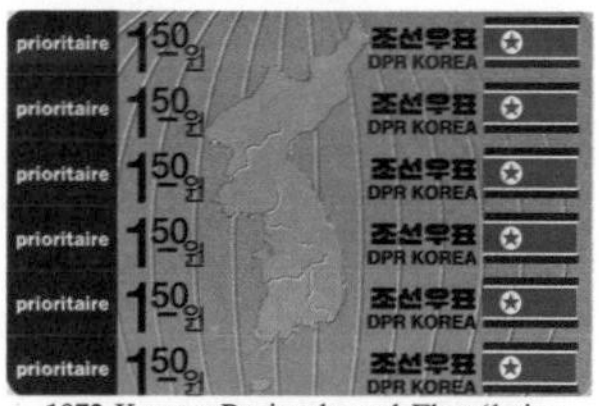
1072 Korean Peninsula and Flag (½-size illustration)

1993. Self-adhesive. Roul.
N3287 **1072** 1wn.50 multicoloured 2·00 30
No. N3287 is for any one of the six stamps which together make up the design illustrated. They are peeled from a card backing.

1073 Kim Myong Nam (weightlifting, 1990)

1993. World Champions. Multicoloured.
N3293 10ch. Type **1073** 15 10
N3294 20ch. Kim Kwang Suk (gymnastics, 1991) . . . 30 15
N3295 30ch. Pak Yong Sun (table tennis, 1975, 1977) . . . 45 20
N3296 50ch. Kim Yong Ok (radio direction-finding, 1990) 75 35
N3297 70ch. Han Yun Ok (taekwondo, 1987, 1988, 1990) . . . . 1·00 50
N3298 90ch. Kim Yong Sik (free-style wrestling, 1986, 1989) . . . . 1·40 70

1074 Cabbage and Chilli Peppers

1075 State Arms

1993. Fruits and Vegetables. Multicoloured.
N3299 10ch. Type **1074** 15 10
N3300 20ch. Squirrels and horse chestnuts 30 15
N3301 30ch. Grapes and peach 45 20
N3302 40ch. Birds and persimmon 60 30
N3303 50ch. Tomatoes, aubergine and cherries 75 35
N3304 60ch. Radish, onion and garlic 90 45

1993.
N3305 **1075** 10ch. red 15 10

1076 Soldiers and Civilians

1993. 40th Anniv of Victory in Liberation War. Multicoloured.
N3306 10ch. Type **1076** 15 10
N3307 10ch. Officer and soldier 15 10
N3308 10ch. Guided missiles on low-loaders on parade 15 10
N3309 10ch. Anti-aircraft missiles on lorries on parade . . 15 10
N3310 10ch. Self-propelled missile launchers (tracked vehicles) on parade . . 15 10
N3311 10ch. Machine gun emplacement (30 × 48 mm) 15 10
N3312 10ch. Soldier holding flag (bronze statue) (30 × 48 mm) 15 10
N3314 10ch. Kim Il Sung at strategic policy meeting 15 10
N3315 10ch. Kim Il Sung directing battle for Height 1211 . . . . . 15 10
N3316 10ch. Kim Il Sung at munitions factory . . . 15 10
N3317 10ch. Kim Il Sung with tank commanders . . . 15 10
N3318 10ch. Kim Il Sung with triumphant soldiers . . 15 10
N3319 20ch. Kim Il Sung with artillery unit 30 15
N3320 20ch. Kim Il Sung encouraging machine gun crew 30 15
N3321 20ch. Kim Il Sung studying map of Second Front 30 15
N3322 20ch. Kim Il Sung with airmen 30 15
N3323 20ch. Musicians ("Alive is art of Korea") 30 15
N3313 40ch. Soldiers and flags ("Let us become Kim Jims and Ri Su Boks of the 90s") (30 × 48 mm) 60 30
MSN3324 Four sheets, (a) 150 × 90 mm; 80ch. Kim Il Sung beside tank (39 × 50 mm); (b) 131 × 75 mm. 80ch. Kim Il Sung and victory celebrations (33 × 51 mm); (c) 1wn. Kim Il sung making speech (47 × 35 mm); (d) 190 × 93 mm. 1wn. king Il Sung taking salute (38 × 49 mm) . . 4·75 2·25

1077 Choe Yong Do

1078 "Robinia sp."

1993. National Reunification Prize Winners. Multicoloured.
N3325 10ch. Type **1077** 15 10
N3326 20ch. Kim Ku 30 15
N3327 30ch. Hong Myong Hui 45 20
N3328 40ch. Ryo Un Hyong . . 60 30
N3329 50ch. Kim Jong Thae . . 75 35
N3330 60ch. Kim Chaek 90 45

1993. "Taipei '93" International Stamp Exhibition, Taipeh. Multicoloured.
N3331 20ch. Type **1078** 40 15
N3332 30ch. "Hippeastrum" . . . 60 20
MSN3333 75 × 105 mm. 1wn. Deer (33 × 51 mm) . . . . 1·50 70

1079 Newton

1080 King Tongmyong shooting Bow

1993. 350th Birth Anniv (1992) of Sir Isaac Newton (mathematician and scientist). Multicoloured.
N3334 10ch. Type **1079** 25 10
N3335 20ch. Apple tree and formula of law of gravitation 40 15
N3336 30ch. Satellite, reflecting telescope, dish aerial, globe and rocket . . . 60 20
N3337 50ch. Formula of binomial theorem 90 35
N3338 70ch. Newton's works and statue . . . . 1·10 50

1993. Restoration of King Tongmyong of Koguryo's Tomb. Multicoloured.
N3339 10ch. Type **1080** 15 10
N3340 20ch. King Tongmyong saluting crowd 30 15
N3341 30ch. Restoration monument 45 20
N3342 40ch. Temple of the Tomb of King Tongmyong (horiz) 60 30
N3343 50ch. Tomb (horiz) . . . 75 35
MSN3344 95 × 105 mm. 80ch. Kim Il Sung visiting tomb (41 × 63 mm) 1·10 85

1081 First North Korea and Thailand Stamps

1993. "Bangkok 1993" International stamp Exhibition, Thailand. Sheet 76 × 81 mm.
MSN3345 **1081** 1wn. 20 multicoloured . . . . 1·75 85

1082 "Cyrtopodium andresoni"

1084 Mao Tse-tung at Yanan, 1944

1993. Orchids. Multicoloured.
N3346 10ch. Type **1082** 25 10
N3347 20ch. "Cattleya" 40 15
N3348 30ch. "Cattleya intermedia" "Oculata" 60 20
N3349 40ch. Potinaria "Maysedo godensia" 75 30
N3350 50ch. Kim Il Sung flower 1·00 35

모택동탄생100돐
毛泽东诞生100周年
1893-1993

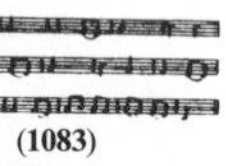
(1083)

1993. Birth Centenary of Mao Tse-tung (1st issue). No. **MS**N3006 optd with T **1083**.
MSN3351 95 × 75 mm. 80ch. multicoloured . . . . 1·25 60
See also Nos. N3352/**MS**N3357.

1993. Birth Centenary of Mao Tse-tung. Multicoloured.
N3352 10ch. Type **1084** 15 10
N3353 20ch. Seated portrait (Peking, 1960) 30 15
N3354 30ch. Casting a vote, 1953 45 20
N3355 40ch. With pupils at Shaoshan Secondary School, 1959 . . . . . 60 30
MSN3356 110 × 70 mm. 1wn. Mao Tse-tung and Pres. Kim Il Sung of North Korea (47 × 35 mm) . . 1·50 75
MSN3357 169 × 130 mm. Nos. N3352/MSN3356 25ch. Mao Tse-tung proclaiming foundation of Chinese People's Republic, 1949 (47 × 35 mm); 25ch. Mao Tse-tung with son Mao An-ying (47 × 35 mm) . . . . 3·25 1·60

1085 Phungsan

1086 Purple Hyosong Flower

1994. New Year. Dogs. Multicoloured.
N3358 10ch. Type **1085** 15 10
N3359 20ch. Yorkshire terriers 30 15
N3360 30ch. Gordon setter . . . 45 20
N3361 40ch. Pomeranian 60 30
N3362 50ch. Spaniel with pups 75 35
MSN3363 80 × 66 mm. 1wn. Pointer 1·50 75

1994. 52nd Birthday of Kim Jong Il. Multicoloured.
N3364 10ch. Type **1086** 25 10
N3365 40ch. Yellow hyosong flower 80 30
MSN3366 156 × 82 mm. 1wn. Kim Il Sung and Kim Jong surrounded by flowers (44 × 53 mm) . . . 1·50 75

1087 Red and Black Dragon-eyed

1994. Goldfishes. Multicoloured.
N3367 10ch. Type **1087** 20 10
N3368 30ch. Red and white bubble-eyed 70 30
N3369 50ch. Red and white veil-tailed wenyu . . . . . 1·10 50
N3370 70ch. Red and white fringe-tailed . . . . . . 1·60 75

1088 Crowd with Banners

1089 Wheat, Banner and Woman writing

1994. 20th Anniv of Publication of "Programme for Modelling the Whole Society on the Juche Idea" by Kim Jong Il. Multicoloured.
N3371 20ch. Type **1088** 30 15
MSN3372 145 × 95 mm. 1wn.20 Kim Jong Il making speech (41 × 63 mm) . . . . 1·75 85

1994. 30th Anniv of Publication of "Theses on the Socialist Rural Question in Our Country" by Kim Il Sung. Multicoloured.
N3373 10ch. Type **1089** 15 10
N3374 10ch. Electricity generating systems and pylon . . . 15 10
N3375 10ch. Lush fields, grain and tractor 15 10
N3376 40ch. Modern housing, books, food crops and laboratory technician . . 60 30
N3377 40ch. Revellers 60 30
MS3378 Two sheets, each 134 × 111 mm. (a) 1wn. KimIl Sung in field (38 × 59 mm); (b) 1wn. Peasants with Kim Il Jong (41 × 63 mm) . . . . 2·75 1·40

1090 "Mangyongbong-92" (ferry)

1091 National Flag

1994. Ships. Multicoloured.
N3379 20ch. Type **1090** 30 15
N3380 30ch. "Osandok" (freighter) 45 20
N3381 40ch. "Ryongaksan" (stern trawler) 60 30
N3382 50ch. Stern trawler 75 35
MSN3383 131 × 112 mm. Nos. 3379/82; 80ch. × 2 "Maekjon-1" (passenger ship) 4·00 2·00

1994.
N3384 **1091** 10ch. red and blue . . 15 10

1092 Birthplace and Magnolia (national flower)

1093 "Chrysosplenium sphaerospermum"

1994. 82nd Birthday of Kim Il Sung. Multicoloured.
N3385 10ch. Type **1092** 15 10
N3386 40ch. Birthplace, Manyongdae, and Kim Il Sung flower 60 30
MSN3387 162 × 103 mm. 40ch. × 5 Composite design of Lake Chon (crater lake of Mt. Paekdu) and score of "Song of General Kim Il Sung" . . . . 2·75 1·40

1994. Alpine Plants on Mt. Paekdu. Multicoloured.
N3388 10ch. Type **1093** 25 10
N3389 20ch. "Campanula cephalotes" 40 15
N3390 40ch. "Trollius macropetalus" 75 30
N3391 40ch. "Gentiana algida" 75 30
N3392 50ch. "Sedum kamtschaticum" 90 35
MSN3393 78 × 64 mm. 1wn. "Dianthus repens" . . . . . . 1·50 75

1094 National Olympic Committee Emblem

1095 Red Cross Launch ("Relief on the Sea")

1994. Centenary of International Olympic Committee. Multicoloured.
N3394 10ch. Type **1094** 15 10
N3395 20ch. Pierre de Coubertin (founder) 30 15
N3396 30ch. Olympic flag and flame 45 20
N3397 50ch. Emblem of Centennial Olympic Congress, Paris 75 35
MSN3398 Two sheets, each 75 × 105 mm. (a) 1wn. Torch carrier; (b) 1wn. Juan Antonio Samaranch (!OC President) and entrance headquarters . . . . 2·25 1·25

1994. 75th Anniv of International Red Cross and Red Crescent Federation. Multicoloured.
N3399 10ch. Electric tram, pedestrians on footbridge and traffic lights ("Prevention of Traffic Accident") . . . 45 10
N3400 20ch. Type **1095** 30 15
N3401 30ch. Planting tree ("Protection of Environment") 45 20
N3402 40ch. Dam ("Prevention of Drought Damage") 60 30

1994. No. N3287 surch **160** in circle.
N3403 **1072** 1wn.60 on 1wn.50 multicoloured . . . 2·10 1·00

1097 Northern Fur Seal

1994. Marine Mammals. Multicoloured.
N3404 10ch. Type **1097** 25 10
N3405 40ch. Southern elephant seal 75 30
N3406 60ch. Southern sealion . . 1·10 45
MSN3407 Two sheets, (a) 80 × 130 mm. 20ch. Californian sealion; 30ch. Ringed seal; 50ch. Walrus. (b) 80 × 88nn. 1wn. Harp seal . . . . 2·75 1·40

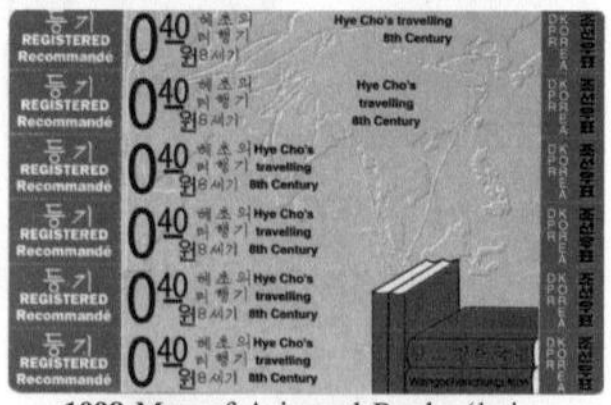
1098 Map of Asia and Books (½-size illustration)

1994. 8th-century Travels of Hye Cho. Self-adhesive. Roul.
N3408 **1098** 40ch. multicoloured 55 25
No. N3408 is for any one of the six stamps which together make up the design illustrated. They are peeled from a card backing.

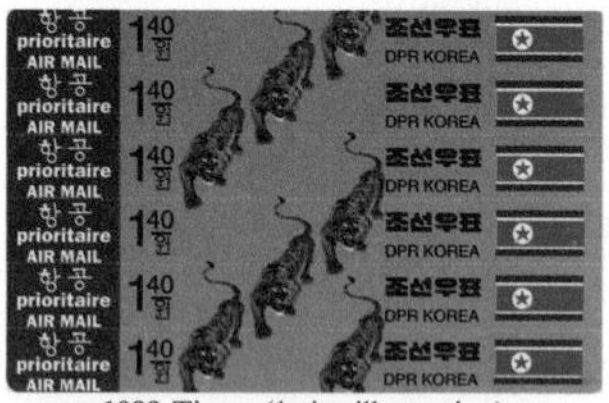
1099 Tigers (½-size illustration)

1994. Self-adhesive. Roul.
N3409 **1099** 1wn.40 multicoloured 1·90 95
No. N3409 is for any one of the six stamps which together make up the design illustrated. They are peeled from a card backing.

1100 Kim Jong Il on Mt. Paekdu

1994. 30th Anniv of Kim Jong Il's Leadership of Korean Workers' Party. Two Sheets containing multicoloured designs as T **1100** showing various scenes featuring Kim Jong Il.
MSN3410 Two sheets. (a) 148 × 182 mm. 40ch. Type **1100**; 40ch With engineers surveying bay; 40ch. Visiting the set of "Star of Korea" (film); 40ch. Visiting Chongryu Restaurant; 40ch. Reviewing tank corps; 40k. Shaking hands with international figures. (b) 145 × 95 mm. 1wn. At desk (41 × 63 mm) . . . . . . 4·00 2·00

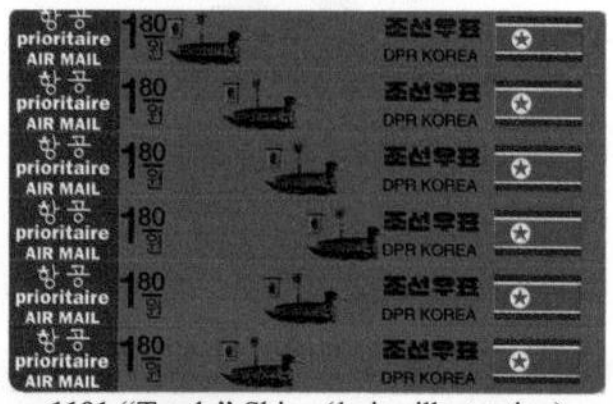
1101 "Turtle" Ships (½-size illustration)

1994. Self-adhesive. Roul.
N3411 **1101** 1wn.80 multicoloured 2·40 1·10
No. N3411 is for any one of the six stamps which together make up the design illustrated. They are peeled from a card backing.

1102 Striped Bonnet

1994. Molluscs. Multicoloured.
N3412 30ch. Type **1102** 60 20
N3413 40ch. Equilateral venus . . 1·00 30
MSN3414 103 × 75 mm. 1wn.20 Bladder moon . . . . 1·75 85
MSN3415 Two sheets, each 127 × 73 mm. (a) Nos. N3413/**MS**N3414; 10ch. "Cardium muticum" (cockle). (b) Nos. N3412 and **MS**N3412 and **MS**N3414; 20ch. "Buccinum bayani (whelk) . . . . 4·50 2·25

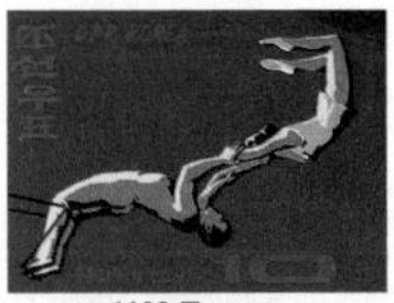
1103 Trapeze

1994. Circus Acrobatics. Multicoloured.
N3416 10ch. Type **1103** 15 10
N3417 20ch. Reino (Swedish acrobat) performing rope dance 30 15
N3418 30ch. Seesaw performer 45 20
N3419 40ch. Unicycle juggler . . 60 30

1104 Korean Script and "100"

1994. Birth Centenary of Kim Hyong Jik (father of Kim Il Sung). Multicoloured.
N3420 10c. Type **1104** 10 10
MSN3421 61 × 85 mm. 1wn. Kim Hyong Jik (30 × 48 mm) . . . 1·50 75

1105 Jon Pong Jun and Battle Scene

1994. Centenary of Kabo Peasant War.
N3422 **1105** 10ch. multicoloured 15 10

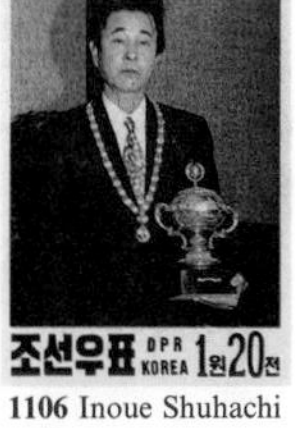

1106 Inoue Shuhachi

1994. Award of First International Kim Il Sung Prize to Inoue Shuhachi (Director Genaral to Juche Idea International Institute). Sheet 103 × 78 mm.
MSN3423 **1106** 1wn.20 multicoloured . . . . 1·75 85
See also Nos. N3458/**MS**N3464.

1107 Workers and Banner

1109 "Acorus calamus"

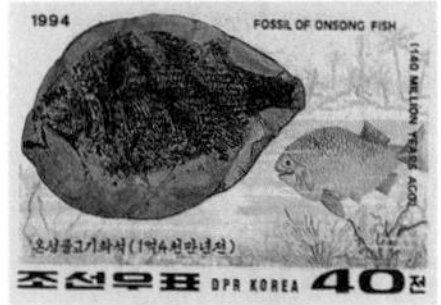

1108 Onsong Fish

1994. Revolutionary Economic Strategy.
N3424 **1107** 10ch. multicoloured 15 10

1994. Fossils. Multicoloured.
N3425 40ch. Type **1108** 90 30
N3426 40ch. Metasequoia 75 30
N3427 40ch. Mammoth teeth . . 75 30
N3428 80ch. Archaeopteryx . . . 1·60 2·50

1994. Medicinal Plants. Multicoloured.
N3429 20ch. Type **1109** 30 15
N3430 30ch. "Arctium lappa" . . 45 20
MSN3431 Two sheet. (a) 133 × 86 mm. 80ch. "Lilium lancifolium"; 80ch. "Codonopsis lanceolata". (b) 56 × 83 mm. 1wn. Ginseng (vert) . . . . 3·50 1·25

1110 Ribbon Exercise

1111 Chou En-lai at Tianjun, 1919

1994. Callisthenics. Multicoloured.
N3432 10ch. Type **1110** 15 10
N3433 20ch. Ball exercise 30 15
N3434 30ch. Hoop exercise . . . 45 20
N3435 40ch. Ribbon exercise (different) 60 30
N3436 50ch. Club exercise . . . 75 35

1994. 96th Birth Anniv of Chou En-lai (Chinese statesman). Multicoloured.
N3437 10ch. Type **1111** 15 10
N3438 20ch. Arrival in Northern Shanxi from Long March 30 15
N3439 30ch. At Conference of Asian and African Countries, Bandung, Indonesia, 1955 . . . . 45 20
N3440 40ch. Surrounded by children in Wulumuqi, Xinjiang Province . . . 60 30
MSN3441 106 × 70 mm. 80ch. green, silver and black (Kim Il Sung proposing to Chou En-li during Korean visit, 1970) (46½ × 35 mm) 1·10 55
MSN3442 Two sheets, each 144 × 110 mm. (a) Nos. N3440/**MS**N3441; 20ch. Leading Nanchang Uprising, 1927 (46½ × 35 mm). (b) N3438/9 and **MS**3441; 20ch. At airport on return from foreign visit (46½ × 35 mm) . . . . 4·00 2·00

1113 Kim Il Sung as Youth, 1927

1994. Kim Il Sung Commemoration (1st issue). (a) As T **1113**. Each red, gold and black.
N3444 40ch. Type **1113** 60 30
N3445 40ch. Kim Il Sung and Kim Jong Suk 60 30
N3446 40ch. Kim Il Sung as young man 60 30

(b) Horiz designs as T **1115**. Each purple, gold and black.
N3447 40ch. Kim Il Sung making speech, Pyongyang, 1945 . . . . 60 30
N3448 40ch. Kim Il Sung sitting at desk 60 30
N3449 40ch. Kim Il Sung at microphone 60 30

(c) Miniature sheet.
MSN3450 78 × 106 mm. 1wn. Kim Il Sung smiling (35 × 46 mm) . . 1·50 75
See also Nos. N3459/63.

1114 Player No. 4

1994. World Cup Football Championship, U.S.A. Multicoloured.
N3451 10ch. Type **1114** 15 10
N3452 20ch. Player No. 5 . . . . 30 15
N3453 30ch. Player No. 6 . . . . 45 20
N3454 40ch. Player No. 7 . . . . 60 30
N3455 1wn. Player No. 8 . . . . 1·50 75
N3456 1wn.50 Player No. 9 . . . 2·25 1·10
MSN3457 Two sheets. (a) 79 × 112 mm. 2wn.50 Stadium, players and trophy (41 × 48 mm); (b) 200 × 223 mm. 1wn. × 6, each depicting player, trophy and different view . . . . 11·00 5·00

1115 Kim Il Sung making Radio Broadcast, 1950

1994. Kim Il Sung Commemoration (2nd issue). (a) Each green, gold and black.
N3458 40ch. Type **1115** 60 30
N3459 40ch. Kim Il Sung with four soldiers, 1951 . . . 60 30
N3460 40ch. Kim Il Sung and crowd of soldiers, 1953 60 30

(b) Multicoloured (N3463) or lilac, gold and black (others).
N3461 40ch. Kim Il Sung with workers at Chongjin Steel Plant, 1959 . . . 60 30
N3462 40ch. Kim Il Sung on Onchon Plain 60 30
N3463 40ch. Kim Il Sung at desk using telephone 60 30

(c) Miniature sheet.
MSN3464 78 × 106 mm. 1wn. Kim Il Sung and Kim Jong Il (35 × 47 mm) . . . . 1·50 75

1116 National Flags and Flowers

1117 Ri Myon Sang and Score of "Snow Falls"

1994. Korean—Chinese Friendship. Multicoloured.
N3465 10ch. Type **1116** 60 30
MSN3466 79 × 100 mm. 1wm.20 black, grey and gold (Mao Tse-tung and Kim Il Sung) (53 × 44 mm) . . . . 1·75 85

1994. Composers. Multicoloured.
N3467 50ch. Type **1117** . . . . 1·00 35
N3468 50ch. Pak Han Kyu and score of "Nobody Knows" . . . . 1·00 35
N3469 50ch. Ludwig van Beethoven and score of piano sonata No. 14 . . 1·00 35
N3470 50ch. Wolfgang Amadeus Mozart and score of symphony No. 39 . . . 1·00 35

1118 National Emblem

1994.
N3471 **1118** 1wn. green . . . . . 1·50 75
N3472 3wn. brown . . . . . 4·00 2·00

1119 P. Wiberg (Alpine combined skiing)

1994. Winter Olympic Games, Lillehammer, Gold Medal Winners. Multicoloured.
N3473 10ch. Type **1119** 15 10
N3474 20ch. D. Compagnoni (slalom) 30 15
N3475 30ch. O. Baiul (figure skating) 45 20
N3476 40ch. D. Jansen (speed skating) 60 30
N3477 1wn. L. Yegorova (cross-country sking) . . . . 1·50 75
N3478 1wn.50 B. Blair (speed skating) . . . . 2·25 1·10
MSN3479 Seven sheets, each 102 × 75 mm (a/f) or 131 × 895 mm (g). (a) 1wn. Norwegian skiing team and B. Daehile (Alpine combine); (b) 1wn. Gordeyeva and Grinkov (pairs figure skating); (c) 1wn. G. Hackl (luge); (e) 1wn. J. Weissflog (ski jumping); (f) 1wn. Kono, Ogiwara and Abe (cross-country skiing); (g.) 2wn.50 T. Moe (downhill) (50 × 35 mm) 11·00 5·50

1120 Pig Couple

1121 Pison Waterfalls, Mt. Myohyang

1995. New Year. Year of the Pig. Multicoloured.
N3480 20ch. Type **1120** 45 15
N3481 40ch. Pigs carrying bucket and spade 80 30
MSN3482 40ch. Two sheets, each 72 × 70 mm. (a) 1wn. Adult pig greeting young pigs; (b) 1wn. Pig couple carrying pumpkin . . . 2·75 1·40
See also No. **MS**3533.

1995. 20th Anniv of World Tourism Organization. Multicoloured.
N3483 30ch. Tower of Juche Idea, Pyongyang . . . 45 20
N3484 30ch. Type **1121** 45 20
N3485 30ch. Myogilsang (cliff-face carving of Buddha), Mt. Kumgang 45 20

1122 Mangyongdae, Badaogou and Badge

1123 Monument bearing 50th Birthday Ode, Mt. Paekdu

1995. 70th Anniv of 1000-ri (250 mile) Journey by Kim Il Sung to Restore Fatherland.
N3486 **1122** 40ch. multicoloured 60 30

1995. 53rd Birthday of Kim Jung Il. Multicoloured.
N3487 10ch. Type**1123** 15 10
MSN3488 Tree sheets. (a) 75 × 90 mm. 20ch. Kim Il Sung and Kim Jong Il (horiz); 80ch, Kim Jong Il on balcony overlooking West Sea Barrage (horiz); (b) 90 × 75 mm. 40ch. Kim Jong Il in public park; 50ch. Kim Jong before memorial in Taesongsan Revolutionary Martyrs' Cemetery; (c) 96 × 75 mm. 1wn. Kim Jong Il on visit to Tyongsong Machine Complex, 1984 (31 × 50 mm) 3·75 1·75

1124 Reconstruction Monument

1125 Jamaedo Lighthouse

1995. Completion of Reconstruction of King Tangun's Tomb. Multicoloured.
N3489 10ch. Type **1124** 15 10
N3490 30ch. Bronze dagger on plinth 45 20
N3491 50ch. Monument inscribed with exploits of King Tangun 75 15
N3492 70ch. Gateway (horiz) . . 1·00 50
MSN3493 103 × 60 mm. 1wn.40 King Tangun . . . . 2·10 1·00

1995. Lighthouses. Multicoloured.
N3494 20ch. Type **1125** 30 15
N3495 1wn. Phido Lighthouse, West Sea Barrage . . . 1·75 85

1126 Cracked Green Russula

1127 Couple planting Tree

1995. Fungi. Multicoloured.
N3496 20ch. Type **1126** 50 15
N3497 30ch. "Russula atropurpurea" 75 20
MS3498 68 × 90 mm. 1wm. Kim Il Sung and children (29 × 41 mm) 1·50 75

1995. Tree Planting Day.
N3499 **1127** 10ch. multicoloured 30 10

1128 Birthplace, Mangyongdae

1995. 20th Anniv of Kim Il Sung's Visit to China.
N3500 1129 10ch. multicoloured 15 10
N3501 40ch. multicoloured . . . 60 30
MSN3501 84 × 80 mm. 50ch. purple, gold and black 75 35
DESIGNS: As T **1129** but vert—20ch. Deng Xiaoping of China sitting in armchair. 60 × 38 mm—50ch. Kim Il Sung and Deng Xiaoping.

1129 Deng Xiaoping waving

1995. 20th Anniv of Kim Il Sung's Visit to China. Multicoloured.
N3503 10ch. Type **1129** 15 10
N3504 20ch. Deng Xiaoping of China sitting in armchair (vert) 30 15

1130 Venue

1995. 40th Anniv of Asian–African Conference, Bandung.
N3506 **1130** 10ch. black, buff and red 15 10
N3507 – 50ch. brown, gold and black 75 35
MSN3508 88 × 85 mm. 1wn. brown and black . . . . 1·50 75
DESIGN: 50ch. Kim Il Sung receiving honorary Doctorate at Indonesia University.

1131 Emblem

1132 Amethyst

1995. International Sports and Cultural Festival for Peace, Pyongyang. Multicoloured.
N3509 20ch. Type **1131** 30 15
N3510 40ch. Dancer 60 30
N3511 40ch. Inoki Kanji (leader of Sports Peace Party of Japan) 60 30
MSN3512 87 × 70 mm. 1wn. Rikidozan (wrestler) . . . . . 1·50 75

1995. Minerals.
N3513 **1132** 20ch. multicoloured 50 15

1133 Eurasian Tree Sparrow

1134 Ostrea

1995. White Animals. Multicoloured.
N3514 40ch. Type **1133** 60 30
N3515 40ch. "Stichopus japonicus" (sea slug) . . 60 30

1995. Fossils. Multicoloured.
N3516 50ch. Type **1134** . . . . 1·00 35
N3517 1wn. Cladophlebis (fern) 1·50 75

1135 Chess

1136 National Flag and Korean Hall, Tokyo

1995. Traditional Games. Multicoloured.
N3518 30ch. Type **1135** 50 20
N3519 60ch. Taekwondo . . . . 1·00 45
N3520 70ch. Yut . . . . 1·25 50

1995. 40th Anniv of Association of Koreans in Japan.
N3521 **1136** 1wn. multicoloured 1·50 75

1137 Weightlifting

1138 "Russula citrina"

1995. Olympic Games, Atlanta (1996). Multicoloured.
N3522 50ch. Type **1137** 90 35
N3523 50ch. Boxing 90 35
MSN3524 62 × 78 mm. 1wn. Clay-pigeon shooting . . . . 1·50 75
DESIGNS: 50ch. Kim Il Sung receiving honorary Doctorate at Indonesia University. 1wn. Kim Il Sung and Kim Jong Il at conference tenth anniversary ceremony, Djakarta.

1995. Fungi. Multicoloured.
N3525 40ch. Type **1138** 75 30
N3526 60ch. Black trumpets . . . 1·00 45
N3527 80ch. Shaggy caps . . . . 1·40 60

1139 Kim Il Sung greeting Pres. Mugabe of Zimbabwe

1995. 1st Death Anniv of Kim Il Sung. Four sheets containing designs as T **1139** inscriptions in black, frames in gold, centre colour listed.
MSN3528 Four sheets (a) 109 × 85 mm. 10ch. blue; 70ch. sepia. (b) 130 × 66 mm. 20ch. blue; 50ch. chocolate. (c) 129 × 66 mm. 30ch. blue; 40ch. purple. (d) 80 × 107 mm. 1wn. plum . . . 4·25 2·10
DESIGNS—VERT: 70ch. With King Norodom Sihanouk of Cambodia. HORIZ: Kim Il Sung being awarded title of Honorary Doctor of Algeria University, 1975; 30ch. With Pres. Ho Chi Minh of Vietnam; 40ch. Greeting Che Cuevara; 50ch. With Pres. Fidel Castro of Cuba; 1wm. Giving speech.

1140 Mt. Paekdu and Revolutionaries

1141 Markswoman

1995. 50th Anniv of Liberation. Multicoloured.
N3529 10ch. Type **1140** 15 10
N3530 30ch. Map of Korea and family 45 20
N3531 60ch. Medal 90 45
MS3532 Two sheets, each 120 × 110 mm. (a) 2 × 20ch. Revolutionary and crowd with banners; (b) No. N3530 × 2; 2 × 40ch. Revolutionaries . . . 3·25 1·00

1995.
MSN3533 Nos. N3480/1, each × 2 1·60 80

1995. 1st Military World Games, Rome.
N3534 **1141** 40ch. multicoloured 60 30

1142 Kim Il Sung With Prime Minister Chou En-Lai of China, 1970

1995. Korean—Chinese Friendship, Three sheets containing designs as T **1142** inscriptions in black, frames in gold, centre colour listed below.
MSN3535 Three sheets. (a) 50ch. purple (Type **1142**); 50ch. green (With Deng Ying-chao of China, 1979). (b) 85 × 100 mm. 80ch. green (Greeting Mao Tse-tung of China, 1958) (vert). (c) 85 × 100 mm. 80ch. purple (In Hamburg with Prime Minister Chou En-lai of China) (vert) 3·50 1·75

1143 Emblem and Banner

1144 Arch of Triumph, Pyongyang

1995. 50th Anniv of Korean Workers' Party. Multicoloured.
N3536 10ch. Type **1143** 15 10
N3537 20ch. Statue of worker, peasant and intellectual 30 15
N3538 30ch. Party monument . . 45 20
MS3539 108 × 75 mm. 1wn. Kim Il Sung (founder) (38 × 50 mm) 1·50 75

1995. 50th Anniv of Kim Il Sung's Return to Homeland.
N3540 **1144** 10ch. multicoloured 15 10

1145 Tuna

1147 Guinea Pig

1146 Kim Hyong Gwon

1995. Designs as T **1145**. Each brown and black.
(a) Fishes.
N3541 40ch. Type **1145** 70 30
N3542 50ch. Pennant coralfish (with two bands) . . . 90 35
N3543 50ch. Needlefish 90 35
N3544 60ch. Seascorpion . . . . 1·00 45
N3545 5wn. Emperor angelfish 6·50 3·25
(b) Buildings on Kwangbok Street, Pyongyang.
N3546 60ch. Circus 90 45
N3547 70ch. Flats . . . . 1·00 50
N3548 80ch. Ryanggang Hotel . . 1·25 60
N3549 90ch. Tower apartment block (vert) . . . . . . 1·40 70
N3550 1wn. Sosan Hotel (vert) 1·50 75
(c) Machines.
N3551 10ch. Kamsusan tipper truck 15 10
N3552 20ch. Bulldozer 30 15
N3553 30ch. Excavator 45 20
N3554 40ch. Earth mover (vert) 60 30
N3555 10wn. "Chollima 80" tractor (vert) . . . . 13·00 6·50
(d) Animals.
N3556 30ch. Giraffe (vert) . . . 45 20
N3557 40ch. Ostrich (vert) . . . 60 30
N3558 60ch. Bluebuck (vert) . . 90 45
N3559 70ch. Bactrian camel . . 1·00 50
N3560 3wn. Indian rhinoceros . . 4·25 2·00
(e) Sculptures of Children.
N3561 30ch. Boy holding bird (vert) 45 20
N3562 40ch. Boy with goose (vert) 60 30
N3563 60ch. Girl with geese (vert) 90 45
N3564 70ch. Boy and girl with football (vert) . . . . 1·00 50
N3565 2wn. Boy and girl arguing over football (vert) . . . 3·00 1·50

1995. 90th Birth Anniv of Hyong Gwon (uncle of Kim Il Sung). Sheet 90 × 70 mm.
MSN3566 **1146** 1wn. black and gold 1·50 75

1996. Rodents. Multicoloured.
N3567 20ch. Type **1147** 50 15
N3568 20ch. Squirrel 50 15
N3569 30ch. White mouse . . . 70 20

1148 Emblem, Badge and Flag

1149 Restoration Mounument

1996. 50th Anniv of League of Socialist Working Youth.
N3570 **1148** 10ch. multicoloured 15 10

1996. Reconstruction of Tomb of King Wanggon. Multicoloured.
N3571 30ch. Type **1149** 60 20
N3572 40ch. Entrance gate . . . 75 30
N3573 50ch. Tomb 90 35

1150 Teng Li-Chuang (singer)

1996. Sheet 130 × 86 mm.
MSN3574 **1150** 49ch. multicoloured 60 30

1151 Kim Song Sung

1996. 3rd Asian Games, Harbin, China. Speed Skaters. Sheet 130 × 81 containing T **1151** and similar vert design. Multicoloured.
MSN3575 30ch. Type **1551**; 30ch. Ye Qiaobo 90 45

1152 Jong Il Peak and Kim Jong Il Flower

1153 Pairs Skating

1996. 54th Birthday of Kim Jong Il. Multicoloured.
N3576 10ch. Type **1152** 40 10
MSN3577 96 × 78 mm. 80ch. Kim Jong Il and servicemen in snow (35 × 78 mm) . . . . 1·25 60

1996. 5th Paektusan Prize Figure Skating Championships. Multicoloured.
N3578 10ch. Type **1153** 25 10
N3579 20ch. Pairs skating (different) 40 15
N3580 30ch. Pairs skating (different) 60 20
N3581 50ch. Women's individual skating 90 35
MSN3582 100 × 116 mm. No. 3575/82. . . . . 1·75 85

1154 Left-hand detail

1996. "Folk Tail" (screen painting) by Ryu Suk. Sheet 206 × 84 mm containing T **1154** and similar vert designs. Multicoloured.
MSN3583 8 × 20ch. Composite design of the painting . . . . 2·10 2·00

1155 Farm Worker

1156 1946 20ch. Stamp and Tower of Juche Idea

1996. 50th Anniv of Agrarian Reform Law.
N3584 **1155** 10ch. multicoloured 15 10

1996. 50th Anniv of First North Korean Stamps.
N3585 **1156** 1wn. multicoloured 1·40 70

1157 Yangzhou, China

1996. Centenary of founding of Chinese Imperial Post. Two sheets each 108 × 90 mm containing Type **1157** or similar horiz designs. Multicoloured.
MSN3586 Two sheets (a) 50ch. Type **1157**; (b) 50ch. Taihu Lake, Jiangsu . . . . 1·40 70

1158 Birthplace, Mangyongdae

1996. 83rd Birthday of Kim Il Sung. Multicoloured.
N3587 10ch. Type **1158** 15 10
MSN3588 105 × 115 mm. 1wn. "Eternal Image" (portrait of Kim Il Sung) (41 × 62 mm) . . . . 1·40 70

1159 Gateway

1996. "China '96" Asian International Stamp Exhibition, Peking. Landmarks in Zhejiang. Multicoloured.
N3589 10ch. Type **1159** 25 10
N3590 10ch. Haiyin Pool 25 10
MSN3591 105 × 80 mm. Pantuo Stone (60 × 38 mm) 80 40

1160 Hopscotch

1161 Association Pamphlets

1996. Children's Games. Multicoloured.
N3592 20ch. Type **1160** 40 15
N3593 40ch. Shuttlecock 75 30
N3594 50ch. Sledging 90 35

1996. 60th Anniv of Association for Restoration of the Fatherland.
N3595 **1161** 10ch. multicoloured 15 10

1162 Ri Po lk

1996. 120th Birth Anniv of Ri Po lk (grandmother of Kim Il Sung). Sheet 80 × 90 mm.
MSN3595 **1162** 1wn. grey, black and gold . . . . 1·40 70

1163 Arctic Fox

1164 Boy Saluting

1996. Polar Animals. Multicoloured.
N3597 50ch. Type **1163** 75 35
N3598 50ch. Polar bear 75 35
N3599 50ch. Emperor penguins 75 35
N3600 50ch. Leopard seals . . . 75 35

1996. 50th Anniv of Korean Children's Union. Multicoloured.
N3601 10ch. Type **1164** 15 10
MSN3602 83 × 98 mm. 1wn. "There's Nothing to envy in the World" (painting of Kim Il Sung with Union members) (33 × 51 mm) . . . . 1·40 70

1165 Steam Locomotive

1166 Kim Chol Ju

1996. Railway Locomotives. Multicoloured.
N3603 50ch. Type **1165** 75 35
N3604 50ch. Electric locomotive (green livery) 75 35
N3605 50ch. Steam locomotive (facing right) 75 35
N3606 50ch. Diesel locomotive (red and yellow livery) 75 35

1996. 80th Birth Anniv of Kim Chol Ju (brother of Kim Il Sung). Sheet 58 × 77 mm.
MSN3607 **1166** 1wn.50 brown, gold black . . . . 2·10 50

1167 Open Book and Characters

1168 Worker using Microphone

1996. 760th Anniv of Publication of "Complete Collection of Buddhist Scriptures printed from 80,000 Wooden Blocks".
N3608 **1167** 40ch. multicoloured 60 30

1996. 50th Anniv of Labour Law.
N3609 **1168** 50ch. multicoloured 75 35

1169 Eastern Broad-billed Roller

1996. Birds. (1st series). 110 × 92 mm containing T **1169** and similar horiz designs. Multicoloured.
MSN3610 **10ch.** Type **1169**; 40ch. Yellow-rumped flycatcher; 50ch. European cuckoo . . . . . . 1·50 75

1170 Ye Qiaboo

1996. 3rd Asian Winter Games, Harbin, China (2nd issue). As No. **MSN3575** but with right hand-stamp changed.
MSN3611 30ch. Type **1151**; 30ch. Type **1170** 90 40

1171 Kumsusan Memorial Palace

1996. 2nd Death Anniv of Kim Il Sung. Multicoloured.
N3612 10ch. Type **1171** 15 10
MSN3613 Three sheets. (a) 116 × 71 mm. 1wn. Statue of Kim Il Sung, Kumsusan Memorial Palace (29 × 41 mm). (b) 80 × 106 mm. 1wn. Bars of "The Leader will always be with Us" (44 × 53 mm). (c) 115 × 105 mm. 1wn. Crowd visiting statue of Kim Il Sung, Manus Hill (34 × 51 mm) Set of 3 sheets . . . . 1·70 40

1172 Kim Il Sung meeting Jiang Zemin of China, 1991

1173 Football and Ancient Greek Athletes

1996. 35th Anniv of Korean–Chinese Treaty for Friendship, Co-operation and Mutual Assistance.
N3614 **1172** 10ch. brown, gold and black 15 10
N3615 – 10ch. green, gold and black 15 10
MSN3616 70 × 80 mm. 80ch. ultramarine, gold and black . . 45 10
DESIGNS—VERT: 10ch. Kim Il Sung meeting Pres. Mao Zedong of China, 1954. HORIZ: 80ch. Kim Il Sung meeting Deng Xiaoping of China, 1982.

1996. Centenary of Modern Olympic Games and Olympic Games, Atlanta. Multicoloured.
N3617 50ch. Type **1173** 85 35
N3618 50ch. Tennis, Olympic Anthem and 1896 5l. Greek stamp 85 35
N3619 50ch. Throwing the hammer and advertisement poster for first modern olympics 85 35
N3620 50ch. Baseball and Olympic stadium, Atlanta 85 35

1174 Couple

1175 State Arms and Symbols of Industry and Communications

1996. Birds (2nd series). Sheet 110 × 92 mm containing horiz design as T **1169**. Multicoloured.
N3621 **1174** 50ch. multicoloured 70 35
MSN3622 10ch. crested shelduck; 40ch. Demoiselle crane; 50c. Mute Swan 55 30

1996. 50th Anniv of Nationalization of Industries.
N3623 **1175** 50ch. bistre and brown 65 30

1176 Boy with Ball

1996. 50th Anniv of UNICEF. Multicoloured.
N3624 10ch. Type **1176** 25 10
N3625 20ch. Boy with building blocks 35 15
N3626 50ch. Boy eating melon . . 75 30
N3627 60ch. Girl playing accordion 90 40

1177 Pae Kil Su (men's pommel) (N. Korea)

1996. 1st Asian Gymnastics Championships, Changsha, China. Sheet 167 × 127 mm containing T **1177** and similar vert designs. Multicoloured.
MSN3628 15ch. Type **1177**; 15ch. Li Jing (China); 15ch. Chen Cui Ting on rings (China); 15ch. Kim Kwang Suk (asymmetrical bars) (N. Korea) 25 10

1178 University Buildings, Pyongyang

1996. 50th Anniv of Kim Il Sung University.

N3629	**1178** 10ch. multicoloured	15	10

1179 Tiger

1180 Red Flag and Tower of Juche Idea

1996. World Conservation Union Congress, Montreal, Canada. Multicoloured.

N3630	50ch. Type **1179**	75	30
N3631	50ch. Royal spoonbill	75	30
MSN3632	80 × 66 mm. 80ch. Dove-hand protecting sapling growing from globe (horiz)	45	10

1996. 70th Anniv of Down-with-Imperialism Union.

N3633	**1180** 10ch. multicoloured	30	10

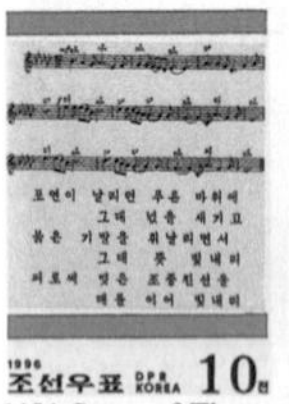

1181 Score of Theme Song from "Red Mountain Ridge" (film)

1182 Archeozoic Era

1996. 44th Death Anniv of Huang Ji Guang (Chinese volunteer in Korean War).

MSN3634	142 × 80 mm. 10ch. multicoloured (Type **1181**); 30ch. brown, silver and black (Huang Ji Guang); 30ch. multicoloured Huang Ji Guang) blocking gun muzzle with body)	40	10

1996. History of the Earth. Sheet 160 × 70 mm containing T **1182** and similar vert designs. Multicoloured.

MSN3635	50ch. Type **1182**; 50ch. Proterozoic era; 50ch. Palaeozoic era; 50ch. Mesozoic era; 50ch. Cainozoic era	1·40	35

1183 Japanese Eel

1996. Freshwater Fishes. Multicoloured.

N3636	20ch. Type **1183**	70	15
N3637	20ch. Menada grey mullet ("Liza haematocheila")	70	15
MSN3638	74 × 53 mm. 80ch. Silver carp	45	10

1184 Soldiers and Supreme Commander's Flag

1996. 5th Anniv of Appointment of Kim Jong Il as Supreme Commander of the People's Army.

N3639	**1184** 20ch. multicoloured	50	15

1185 "Ox Driver" (Kim Tu Ryang)

1997. New Year. Year of the Ox. Multicoloured.

N3640	70ch. Type **1185**	2·25	45
N3641	70ch. Bronze ritual plate of two bulls and a tiger	2·25	45
N3642	70ch. Boy with bull (ceramic)	2·25	45
N3643	70ch. Boy flautist sitting on bull (sculpture)	2·25	45
MSN3644	83 × 82 mm. 80ch. "People's support of the Front" (drawing, Jong Jong Yo) (60 × 38 mm)	45	10

1186 Left-hand Detail

1187 Kitten with Dogs in Basket

1997. "Flowers and Butterflies" by Nam Kye U. Multicoloured.

N3645	50ch. Type **1186**	1·25	30
N3646	50ch. Centre detail	1·25	30
N3647	50ch. Right-hand detail	1·25	30

Nos. N3645/7 were issued together, se-tenant, forming a composite design of the painting.

1997. Paintings of Cats and Dogs. Multicoloured.

N3648	50ch. Type **1187**	1·25	30
N3649	50ch. Pup in vine-wreathed basket, kitten and pumpkin	1·50	30
MSN3650	Two sheets, each 96 × 114 mm. (a) 50ch. × 2, Kitten in basket of vegetables, pup, fruit and flowers; 50ch. Kitten in basket of flowers, pup and ball of wool; No. N3648. (b) 50c. × 2, Kittens, pup and vegetables (as in sheet a); No. 3649 Set of 2 sheets	1·70	35

1188 Bank of China

1997. Return of Hong Kong to China. Sheet 145 × 100 mm containing T **1188** and similar vert designs. Multicoloured.

MSN3651	20ch. Type **1188**; 20ch. Building with spire; 20ch. High-rise buildings	35	10

1189 Birthplace, Mt. Paekdu

1997. 55th Birthday of Kim Jong Il. Multicoloured.

N3652	10ch. Type **1189**	40	10
MSN3653	Two sheets, each 64 × 86 mm. (a) 1wn. Kim Jong Il inspecting farm equipment (47 × 53 mm); (b) 1wn. Kim Jong Il receiving flowers from soldier (47 × 35 mm) Set of 2 sheets	1·10	25

1190 Pair

1997. 6th Paektusan Prize International Figure Skating Championships, Pyongyang. Multicoloured.

N3654	50ch. Type **1190**	1·50	30
N3655	50ch. Pair (mauve)	1·50	30
N3656	50ch. Pair (green)	1·50	30

1191 Kye Sun Hui

1997. North Korean Gold Medal in Women's judo at Olympic Games, Atlanta.

MSN3657	**1191** 80ch. multicoloured	75	35

1192 Choe Un A

1997. Choe Un A (competitor in World go championships at seven years). Sheet 90 × 110 mm.

MSN3658	**1192** 80ch. multicoloured	45	10

1193 "Prunus ansu"

1194 Foundation Monument

1997. Apricots. Multicoloured.

N3659	50ch. Type **1193**	1·40	30
N3660	50ch. "Prunus mandshurica"	1·40	30
N3661	50ch. Hoeryong white apricot ("Prunus armeniaca")	1·40	30
N3662	50ch. Puksan apricot ("Prunus sibirica")	1·40	30

1997. 80th Anniv of Foundation of Korean National Association.

N3663	**1194** 10ch. brown and green	50	10

1195 Sapling

1196 Birthplace, Mangyongdae

1997. 50th Anniv of Reforestation Day. Multicoloured.

N3664	10ch. Type **1195**	50	10
MS3665	90 × 100 mm. 1wn. Kim Il Sung planting sapling on Munsa Hill	55	

1997. 85th Birth Anniv of Kim Il Sung. Multicoloured.

N3666	10ch. Type **1196**	50	10
N3667	20ch. Sliding Rock (horiz)	1·00	10
N3668	40ch. Warship Rock (horiz)	1·25	25
MSN3669	Two sheets. (a) 110 × 90 mm. 1wn. Kim Il Sung in crowd (50 × 41 mm). (b) 100 × 120 mm. 1wn. Kim Il Sung on flowered hill-top (33 × 51 mm) Set of 2 sheets	1·10	25

1197 Cap Badge and Modern Weapons

1997. 65th Anniv of People's Army. Multicoloured.

N3670	10ch. Type **1197**	10	10
MSN3671	75 × 90 mm. 1wn. Soldier applauding Kin Il Sung and Kim Jong Il (35 × 49 mm)	55	30

1198 Map of Korea

1199 Tower of Juche Idea, People and Flag

1997. 25th Anniv of Publication of North—South Korea joint Agreement.

N3672	10ch. Type **1198**	10	10
MSN3673	105 × 70 mm. 1wn. Kim Il Sung's Autograph Monument, Phammunjom (60 × 38 mm)	55	30

1997. Posters reflecting Joint New Year Newspaper Editorials. Multicoloured.

N3674	10ch. Type **1199**	10	10
N3675	10ch. Man with flag	10	10
N3676	10ch. Soldier, miner, farmer, intellectual and bugler	10	10

1200 Exhibition Centre

1997. International Friendship Exhibition, Myohyang Mountains. Four sheetd containing designs as T **1200**. Multicoloured.

MSN3677	Four sheets, each 105 × 120 mm. (a) 70ch. Type **1200**. (b) 70ch. Statue of Kim Il Sung in entrance hall; (c) 70ch. "Native Home in Mangyongdae (ivory sculpture from China) (horiz); (d) 70ch. Stuffed crocodile holding cups on salver and wooden ash tray (from Nicaragua) Set of 4 sheets	80	20

1201 Memorial Post and Blazing Fortress

1997. 60th Anniv of Battle of Pochonbo.

N3678	**1201** 40ch. multicoloured	35	15

1202 Kim Il Sung transplanting Rice

1997. 50th Anniv of Kim Il Sung's Visit to Mirin Plain Paddy-fields. Two sheets, each 75 × 105 mm, containing designs as T **1202**.
MSN3679 Two sheets. (a) 1wn. black and gold (Type **1202**); (b) 1wn. multicoloured (Kim Il Sung inspecting rice-transplanting machine) Set of 2 sheets . . . 1·10 30

1203 Signing Nanjing Treaty, 1842

1997. Return og Hong Kong to China. Two sheets containing multicoloured designs as T **1203**.
MSN3680 Two sheets. (a) 124 × 117 mm. 20ch. Type **1203**; 20ch. Signing China—Britain Joint Statement, Peking, 1984; 20ch. Deng Xiaoping and Margaret Thatcher; 20ch. Jiang Zemin and Tong Jiahua (Mayor of Hong Kong), 1996. (b) 124 × 95 mm. 97 mm. Deng Xiaoping (circular, diameter 42 mm) (pair sold at 1wn.80) Set of 2 sheets . . . . 1·00 25

1204 "Redlichia chinensis"

1997. Fossils. Multicoloured.
N3681 50ch. Type **1204** 45 20
N3682 1wn. "Ptychoparia coreanica" 90 45

1205 Kim Il Sung at Kim Chaek Ironworks, June 1985

1207 Spring

1206 Blindman's Buff

1997. 3rd Death Anniv of Kim Il Sung. Multicoloured.
N3683 50ch. Kim Il Sung at microphones (party conference, October 1985) 45 20
N3684 50ch. Type **1205** 45 20
N3685 50ch. Kim Il Sung and farmers holding wheat (Songsin Co-operative Farm, Sadong District, 1993) 45 20
N3686 50ch. Performing artists applauding Kim Il Sung, 1986 . . . . . . 45 20
N3687 50ch. Kim Il Sung at Jonchon Factory, Jagang Province, 1991 45 20
N3688 50ch. Kim Il Sung receiving flowers at People's Army Conference, 1989 . . . 45 20

1997. Children's Games. Multicoloured.
N3689 30ch. Type **1206** 30 15
N3690 60ch. Five stones 55 25
N3691 70ch. Arm wrestling . . . 65 30

1997. Women's National Costumes. Multicoloured.
N3692 10ch. Type **1207** 10 10
N3693 40ch. Summer 35 15
N3694 50ch. Autumn 45 20
N3695 60ch. Winter 55 25

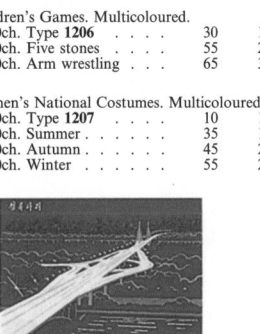

1208 Aerial View

1997. Chongryu Bridge, Pyongyang. Multicoloured.
N3696 50ch. Type **1208** 45 20
N3697 50ch. Chongryu Bridge and birds 45 20

1209 Sun, Magnolias and Balloons

1997. 85th Anniv of Juche Era and Sun Day. Multicoloured.
N3698 10ch. Type **1209** 15 10
MSN3699 85 × 115 mm. 1wn. Kim Il Sung (circular, diameter 45 mm) 55 30

1210 Korean Text and Kim Il Sung University

1997. 20th Anniv of Publication of Theses on Socialist Education.
N3700 **1210** 10ch. multicoloured 10 10

1211 Tupolev Tu-134

1997. 20th Anniv of Korean Membership of International Civil Aviation Oraganization. Three sheets, each 165 × 58 mm. containing designs as T **1211**. Multicoloured.
MSN3701 Tree sheets. (a) 2 × 20ch. Type **1211**; (b) 2 × 30ch. Tupolev Tu-154; (c) 2 × 50ch. Illyushin IL-62 . . . . 2·10 55

1212 Chonbul Peak

1997. 10th Anniv of Korean Membership of World Tourism Organization. Mt Chilbo. Multicoloured.
N3702 50ch. Type **1212** 45 20
N3703 50ch. Sea-Chilbo (coast) 45 20
N3704 50ch. Rojok Peak 45 20

1213 Podok Hermitage

1997. Kumgang Mountains. Multicoloured.
N3705 50ch. Type **1213** 45 20
N3706 50ch. Kumgang Gate . . 45 20

1214 School, Pupil and Mt. Paekdu

1997. 50th Anniv of Mangyongdae Revolutionary School.
N3707 **1214** 40ch. multicoloured 35 15

1215 Lion

1997. Animals presented as Gifts to Kim Il Sung. Multicoloured.
N3708 20ch. Type **1215** (Ethiopia, 1987) 15 10
N3709 30ch. Jaguar (Japan, 1992) 30 15
N3710 50ch. Barbary sheep (Czechoslovakia, 1992) 45 20
N3711 80ch. Scarlet macaw (Austria, 1979) 70 35

1216 Bust

1997. 27th Anniv of Participation in Korean War of the Chinese People's Volunteers. Qu Shao Yun. Sheet 145 × 80 mm containing T **126** and similar vert designs. Multicoloured.
MSN3712 10ch. Statue; 30ch. Type **1216**; 30ch. Qu Shao Yun on fire 40 10

1217 Ten-pin Bowling

1997. Sports. Multicoloured.
N3713 50ch. Type **1217** 45 20
N3714 50ch. Golf 45 20
N3715 50ch. Fencing 45 20

1218 Snails

1997. Snails. Multicoloured.
N3716 50ch. Type **1218** 45 20
N3717 50ch. Two snails on leaf 45 20
N3718 50ch. Snail laying eggs . . 45 20

1219 Shanghai

1997. International Stamp and Coin Exhibition, Shanghai. Sheet 145 × 199 mm containing T **1219** and similar vert design.
MSN3719 30ch. Type **1219**; 50ch. Shanghai (different) 75 35

1220 "Juche 87" and Temple

1997. New Year. Year of the Tiger. Multicoloured.
N3720 10ch. Type **1220** 10 10
N3721 50ch. Tiger in rocket (24 × 34 mm) 45 20
N3722 50ch. Tiger steering ship (24 × 34 mm) 45 20
MSN3723 112 × 75 mm. 80ch. Tiger driving train (24 × 34 mm) . . 45 15

1221 Birthplace, Hoeryong

1997. 80th Birth Anniv of Kim Jong Sok (revolutionary). Multicoloured.
N3724 10ch. Type **1221** 15 10
MSN3725 85 × 115 mm. 1wn. Kim Jong Suk (41 × 50 mm) 55 30

1222 Skiing

1223 Birthdate and Celebration Ribbon

1998. Winter Olympic Ganes, Nagano, Japan. Multicoloured.
N3726 20ch. Type **1222** 15 10
N3727 40ch. Speed skating . . . 35 15

1998. 50th birth Anniv of Kim Jong Il. Multicoloured.
N3728 10ch. Type **1223** 15 10
MSN3729 3wn. Log cabin (birthplace, Mt. Paekdu) . . . 1·70 40

1224 Korean Tigers

1998. Wildlife Paintings. Multicoloured.
N3730 50ch. Type **1224** 45 20
N3731 50ch. Manchurian cranes 45 20
MSN3732 102 × 157 mm. 50ch. Nos. N3730/1; 50ch. Bears; 50ch. Racoon dogs 80 20

1225 Route Map, Birthplace at Mangyongdae and Trail Followers

1998. 75th Anniv of 1000-ri (250 mile) Journey by Kim Il Sung.
N3733 **1225** 10ch. multicoloured 10 10

1226 Soldiers and Balloons

1998. 5th Anniv of Appointment of Kim Jong Il as Chairman of National Defence Commission.
N3734 **1226** 10ch. multicoloured 10 10

1227 Flags and Birthplace, Mangyongdae

1229 United Front Tower and Moranbong Theatre

1228 Kim Il Sung as Child

1998. 86th Birth Anniv of Kim Il Sung. Multicoloured.
N3735 **1227** 10ch. multicoloured . . . 15 10
MSN3736 Eight sheets, each 84 × 155 mm. (a) 80ch. Type **1228**; (b) 80ch. As student (wearing cap with rectangular badge); (c) 80ch. Commander of revolutionary army (wearing cap with star badge); (d) 80ch. In jacket and tie (three-quarter face) 80ch. In army uniform; (f) 80ch. In Mao jacket; (g) 80ch. In jacket and tie (full-face); (h) 80ch. Wearing glasses Set of 8 sheets 2·75 70

1998. 50th Anniv of North–South Conference, Pyongyang.
N3737 **1229** 10ch. brown, blue and black 10 10

1230 Players and Championship Emblem

1231 Cabbages

1998. World Cup Football Championship, France. Multicoloured.
N3738 30ch. Type **1230** 30 15
N3739 50ch. Player winning ball and emblem 45 20
MSN3740 62 × 87 mm. 80ch. Tackling and emblem 45 10

1998. Vegetables. Multicoloured.
N3741 10ch. Type **1231** 10 10
N3742 40ch. Radishes 35 15
N3743 50ch. Spring onions . . . 45 20
N3744 60ch. Cucumbers 55 25
N3745 70ch. Pumpkins 65 30
N3746 80ch. Carrots 70 35
N3747 90ch. Garlic 80 40
N3748 1wn. Peppers 90 45

1232 "Countryside in May" (Jong Jong Yo)

1998. Paintings. Multicoloured.
N3749 60ch. Type **1232** 55 25
N3750 1wn.40 "Dance" (Kim Yong Jun) . . . . 1·25 65
MSN3751 80 × 80 mm. 3wn. "Heart to Heart talk with a Peasant" (Yu Yong Gwan) (59 × 58 mm.) 1·70 40

1233 Model of Automatic Space Station (from U.S.S.R.)

1998. International Friendship Exhibition, Myohyang Mountains (2nd series). Multicoloured.
N3752 1wn. Type **1233** 90 45
N3753 1wn. Ceramic flower vase (from Egypt) 90 45
N3754 1wn. "Crane" (statuette, from Billy Graham (evangelist)) 90 45
MSN3755 86 × 100 mm. 1wn. claret and black (Kim Il Sung) (35 × 56 mm) 55

1234 Research Ship, Buoy and Dolphins in Globe and Hydro-meteorological Headquarters

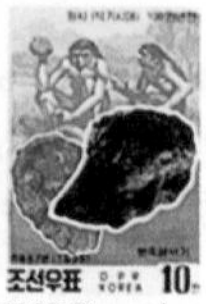

1235 Stone Age Implement

1998. International Year of the Ocean. Multicoloured.
N3756 10ch. Type **1234** 10 10
N3757 80ch. Sailing dinghies and mother with child . . . 70 35
MSN3758 128 × 105 mm. 5wn. Vasco da Gama (vert) . . . . 2·75 70

1998. Korean Central History Museum, Pyongyang. Multicoloured.
N3759 10ch. Type **1235** 10 10
N3760 2wn.50 Fossil skull of monkey . . . . 2·25 1·10
MSN3761 80 × 75 mm. 4wn. claret, grey and black (Kim Il Sung visiting museum) (60 × 38 mm) 2·25 55

1236 Commander of Hedgehog Unit and Squirrel

1998. "Squirrels and Hedgehogs" (cartoon film). Multicoloured.
N3762 20ch. Type **1236** 15 10
N3763 30ch. Commander of hedgehog unit receiving invitation to banquet . . 30 15
N3764 60ch. Weasel ordering mouse to poison bear 55 25
N3765 1wn.20 Squirrel with poisoned bear . . . . . 1·10 55
N3766 2wn. Weasel and mice invade Flower Village 1·75 90
N3767 2wn.50 Hedgehog scout rescues squirrel . . . . 2·25 1·10

1237 Ri Sung Gi and Molecular Model

1998. 2nd Death Anniv of Ri Sung Gi (inventor of vinalon material). Multicoloured.
N3768 40ch. Type **1237** 20 10
MSN3769 80 × 65 mm. 80ch. Ri Sung Gi working in laboratory 55 15

1238 Tiger Cub

1239 "Victory" (Liberation War Monument, Pyongyang) and Medal

1998. Young Mammals. Multicoloured.
N3770 10ch. Type **1238** 10 10
N3771 50ch. Donkey foal 45 20
N3772 1wn.60 Elephant . . . . 1·50 75
N3773 2wn. Two lion cubs . . . 1·75 90

1998. 45th Anniv of Victory in Liberation War.
N3774 **1239** 45ch. brown and pink 25 10
MSN3775 Two sheets, each 62 × 87 mm. multicoloured. (a) 45ch. "Gaz-67" jeep and route map of Kim Il Sung's wartime inspections (30 × 48 mm). (b) 2wn. "Kim Il Sung inspecting Frontline" (painting) (48 × 30 mm) Set of 2 sheets . . 1·40 35

1240 "White Herons in Forest"

1241 Pouch

1998. Embroidery. Multicoloured.
N3776 10ch. Type **1240** 10 10
N3777 40ch. "Carp" 35 20
N3778 1wn.20 "Hollyhock" . . . 1·10 55
N3779 1wn.50 "Cockscomb" . . 1·40 70
MSN3780 80 × 65 mm. 4wn. "Pine and Cranes" . . . . 2·25 55

1998. Traditional Costume Adornments. Multicoloured.
N3781 10ch. Type **1241** 10 10
N3782 50ch. Tassels 45 25
N3783 1wn.50 Hairpin . . . . . 1·40 70
N3784 1wn.90 Silver knife . . . 1·75 90

1242 Rocket and State Flag

1243 Kim Jong Il Flower

1998. Launch of first Korean Artificial satellite "Kwangmyongsong 1".
N3785 40ch. Type **1242** 20 10
MSN3786 81 × 115 mm. 1wn.50 Rocket and satellite orbit (41 × 63 mm) 80 20

1998. Re-election of Kim Jung Il as Chairman of National dfefence Commission. Multicoloured.
N3787 10ch. Type **1243** 10 10
MSN3788 69 × 94 mm. 1wn. Kim Jonh Il (circular, diameter 42 mm) . . . . 1·50 75

1244 Tower of Juche Idea, State Arms and Flag

1998. 50th Anniv of Democratic Republic (1st issue). Multicoloured.
N3789 10ch. Type **1244** 10 10
N3790 1wn. Painting "The Founding of the Democratic People's Republic of Korea, Our Glorious Fatherland" (Kim Il Sung waving from balcony) (48 × 30 mm) 90 45
N3791 1wn. Painting "Square of Victory" (Kim Il Sung and crowd with banners) (48 × 30 mm) 90 45
N3792 1wn. Poster "The Sacred Marks of the Great Leader Kim Il Sung will shine on this Land of Socialism" (Kim Il Sung with produce against panoramic background of Korea) (48 × 30 mm) 90 45

1245 "Let Us Push Ahead with the Forced March for Final Victory"

1247 Cycling

1998.
N3793 **1245** 10ch. multicoloured 10 10

1246 State Flag and Arms forming "50"

1998. 50th Anniv of Democratic Republic (2nd issue). Two sheets containing T **1246**or similar multicoloured design.
MSN3794 Two sheets. (a) 108 × 84 mm. 40ch. Type **1246**; (b) 108 × 125 mm. 1wn. Celebration Parade (31 × 38 mm) Set of 2 sheets 75 15

1998. Olympic Games, Sydney, Australia (2000). Multicoloured.
N3795 20ch. Type **1247** 15 10
N3796 50ch. Football 45 25
N3797 80ch. Show jumping . . . 70 35
N3798 1wn.50 Throwing the javelin . . . . 1·40 70
MSN3799 57 × 80 mm. 2wn.50 Basketball . . . . 1·40 35

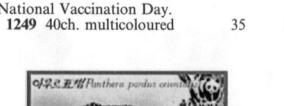

1248 "Cyclamen persicum"

1249 Oral Vaccination

1998. Plants presented as Gifts to Kim Jong Il. Multicoloured.
N3800 20ch. Type **1248** (France, 1994) 15 10
N3801 2wn. "Dianthus chinensis" var. "laciniatus" (Japan, 1994) . . . . 1·75 90

1998. National Vaccination Day.
N3802 **1249** 40ch. multicoloured 35 20

1250 Leopard

1998. The Leopard. Multicoloured.
N3803 1wn. Type **1250** 90 45
N3804 1wn. Leopard in snow . . 90 45
N3805 1wn. Leopard looking to left 90 45
N3806 1wn. Leopard's face . . . 90 45

1251 Canal

1998. Land and Environment Conservation Day. Multicoloured.
N3807 10ch. Type **1251** 10 10
N3808 40ch. Motorway, tower blocks and lorry 35 20
MSN3809 85 × 71 mm. 1wn. Kim Il Sung shovelling earth to signal start of Pothong River improvement 55 15

1252 Emblem and Milan Cathedral

1998. "Italia98" International Stamp Exhibition, Milan, Italy. Sheet 108 × 90 mm.
MSN3810 **1252** 2wn. multicoloured . . . 1·10 30

1253 Peng Dehuai and Kim Il Sung

1998. Birth Centenary of Peng Dehuai (commander of Chinese People's Volunteers in Korea Liberation War). Sheet 131 × 112 mm containing T **1253** and similar multicoloured designs.
MSN3811 20ch. Type **1253**; 20ch. Mao Tse-tung (Chinese communist leader), Chou Enlai (Chinese statesman) and Peng Dehuai; 30ch. Peng Dehuai in marshal's uniform (27 × 38 mm); 30ch. "On the Front" (painting), He Kong De) (27 × 38 mm) . . 55 15

1254 Liu Shaoqi

1255 Victory in Yonsong Monument, Yonan Fortress and Banners

1998. Birth Centenary of Liu Shaoqi (Chairman of Chinese People's Republic, 1959–68). Multicoloured.
N3812 10ch. Type **1254** 10 10
N3813 20ch. Liu Shaoqi and Mao Tse-tung 15 10
N3814 30ch. Liu Shaoqi and his daughter, Xiao Xiao . . 30 15
N3815 40ch. Liu Shaoqi and his wife, Wang Guangmei 35 15
MSN3816 100 × 70 mm. 1wn. Liu Shaoqi and Kim Il Sung (46½ × 35 mm.) 55 15

1998. 400th Anniv of Victory in Korean–Japanese War. Multicoloured.
N3817 10ch. Type **1255** 10 10
N3818 30ch. Naval Victory in Myongryang Monument, General Ri Sun Sin and "turtle" ship 30 15
N3819 1wn.60 Monument to Hyujong in Kwangwon province, Hyujong (Buddhist priest), sword and helmet 90 45
MSN3820 12 × 68 mm. 10wn. "Sea Battle off Hansan Islet in 1592" (painting) . . . . 5·50 1·40

1256 Dish Aerial, Artificial Satellite, Globe and Relay Tower

1257 Goat

1998. 15th Anniv of North Korean Membership of Intersputnik.
N3821 **1256** 1wn. dp grn & grn . . 90 45

1998.
N3822 **1257** 10ch. black and green 10 10
N3823 1wn. black and red 90 45

1258 "A Floral Carriage of Happiness" (sculpture) and Palace

1259 Emblem

1998. Mangyongdae School-children' palace. Multicoloured.
N3824 40ch. Type **1258** 20 10
MSN3825 85 × 4? mm. 1wn. Quotation of Kim Il Sung "Children are the treasure of our country. Korea of the future is theirs" 55 10

1998. 50th Anniv of Universal Declaration of Human Rights.
N3826 **1259** 20ch. multicoloured 15 10

1260 Reeves's Turtle

1261 Thajong Rock

1998. Reptiles and Amphibians. Multicoloured.
N3827 10ch. Type **1260** 10 10
N3828 40ch. Skink 35 15
N3829 60ch. Loggerhead turtle 55 25
N3830 1wn.20 Leatherback turtle 1·10 55
Nos. N3827/30 were issued together, se-tenant, forming a composite design.

1998. Mt. Chilbo. Multicoloured.
N3831 30ch. Type **1261** 30 15
N3832 50ch. Peasant Rock . . . 45 20
N3833 1wn.70 Couple Rock . . . 1·50 75

1262 Ri Mong Ryong marrying Song Chun Hyang

1263 Chollima Statue

1998. Tale of Chun Hyang. Multicoloured.
N3834 40ch. Type **1262** 35 15
N3835 1wn.60 Pyon Hak Do watching Chun Hyang 1·50 75
N3836 2wn.50 Ri Mong Ryong and Chun Hyang . . . 2·40 1·10
MS3837 110 × 95 mm. Nos. N3834/6; 2wn. Chun Hyang in wedding veil . . . . 1·10 30

1998. Pyongyang Monuments.
N3838 **1263** 10ch. red 10 10
N3839 A 10ch. red 10 10
N3840 B 10ch. red 10 10
N3841 A 20ch. orange 15 10
N3842 **1263** 30ch. orange 30 15
N3843 A 40ch. yellow 35 15
N3844 B 40ch. yellow 35 15
N3845 **1263** 70ch. green 65 30
N3846 B 70ch. green 65 30
N3847 1wn.20 green . . . . 1·00 50
N3848 **1263** 1wn.50 green . . . . 1·40 70
N3849 A 2wn. blue . . . . . 1·75 85
N3850 B 3wn. blue . . . . . 2·75 1·40
N3851 **1263** 5wn. blue . . . . . 4·50 2·25
N3852 A 10wn. violet . . . . 9·00 4·50
DESIGNS: A, Arch of Triumph; B, Tower of Juche Idea.

1264 Rabbit meeting Lion

1265 Automatic Rifle and Star

1999. New Year. Year of the Rabbit. Multicoloured.
N3853 10ch. Type **1264** 10 10
N3854 1wn. Rabbit with mirror and lion . . . . 1·40 70
N3855 1wn.50 Lion in trap . . . 2·00 1·00
N3856 2wn.50 Rabbit . . . . . 3·50 1·75
MSN3857 160 × 70 mm. 10ch. Type **1264**; 1wn. No. N3854; 1wn.50 No. N3855; 2wn.50 No. N3856 . . . . 2·75 70

1999. 40th Anniv of Worker-Peasant Red Guards.
N3858 **1265** 10ch. multicoloured 10 10

1266 Log Cabin (birthplace, Mt. Paekdu)

1267 Cranes, Rice Sheaf and "35"

1999. 57th Birth Anniv of Kim Jong Il.
N3859 **1266** 40ch. multicoloured 30 15

1999. 35th Anniv of Publication of *Theses on the Socialist Rural Question in Our Country* by Kim Il Sung.
N3860 **1267** 10ch. multicoloured 10 10

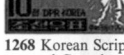

1268 Korean Script and Crowd

1270 Birthplace, Mangyondae

1269 16th-century "Turtle" Ship

1999. 80th Anniv of 1 March Uprising.
N3861 **1268** 10ch. black and brown 10 10

1999. "Australia '99" International Stamp Exhibition, Melbourne.
N3862 **1269** 2wn. multicoloured 1·40 70
MSN3863 100 × 75 mm. **1269** 2wn. multicoloured . . . . 1·10 30

1999. 87th Birth Anniv of Kim Il Sung.
N3864 **1270** 10ch. brown, flesh and grey 10 10
MSN3865 68 × 95 mm. 2wn. multicoloured (Kim Il Sung 94 × 62 mm) . . . . 1·10 30

1271 Player

1999. 45th Table Tennis Championship, Belgrade, Yugoslavia.
N3866 **1271** 1wn.50 multicoloured 1·10 55

1272 Korean Sports Stamps and Emblem

1999. "iBRA'99" International Stamp Exhibition, Nuremberg, Germany.
N3867 **1272** 1wn. multicoloured 80 40

1273*Benzoin obtus*

1274 Chimpanzee and Rhinoceros

1999. 40th Anniv of Central Botanical Garden, Mt. Taesong, Pyongyang. Multicoloured.
N3868 10ch. Type **1273** 10 10
N3869 30ch. *Styrax obassia* . . . 20 10
N3870 70ch. *Petunia hybrida* . . 45 20
N3871 90ch. *Impatiens hybrida* 60 30
MSN3872 65 × 75 mm. 2wn. Kimilsung-flower and Kimjongil (begonia) . . . . 1·10 30

1999. 40th Anniv of Central Zoo, Mt. Taesong, Pyongyang. Multicoloured.
N3873 50ch. Type **1274** 35 15
N3874 60ch. Manchurian crane and deer 45 20
N3875 70ch. Common zebra and kangaroo 50 25
MSN3876 95 × 75 mm. 2wn. Tiger 1·10 30

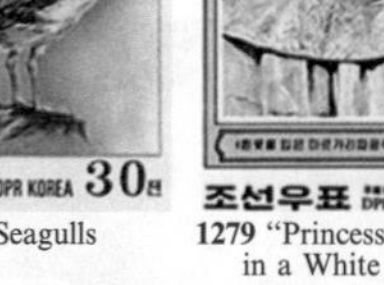

1275 Light Industry Hall

1999. Three Revolutions Museum, Ryonmotdong, Pyongyang. Multicoloured.
N3877 60ch. Type **1275** 45 20
N3878 80ch. Heavy Industry Hall 60 30

1276 Methods of Communication, Satellite and Globe

1999. 20th Anniv of Asia–Pacific Telecommunications Union.
N3879 **1276** 1wn. multicoloured 75 35

1277 Monument

1999. 60th Anniv of Victory in Battle of Musan.
N3880 **1277** 10ch. multicoloured 10 10

1278 Seagulls

1279 "Princess Margarita in a White Dress"

1999. 190th Birth Anniv of Charles Darwin (naturalist). Multicoloured.
N3881 30ch. Type **1278** 15 10
N3882 50ch. Bats 35 15
N3883 1wn. Dolphins 75 35
N3884 1wn.20 Man on horseback 1·00 50
N3885 1wn.50 Dancer . . . . . 1·10 55
MSN3886 76 × 67 mm. 2wn. Charles Darwin (26 × 39 mm) . . . . . 1·10 30

1999. 400th Birth Anniv of Diego Velazquez (artist). Multicoloured.
N3887 50ch. Type **1279** 35 15
N3888 50ch. "Men drawing Water from a Well" . . 35 15
N3889 3wn.50 "Self-portrait" . . 3·75 2·00
MSN3890 68 × 118 mm. No. N3889 25 15

1280 Rimyongsu Power Station

1999. Hydro-electric Power Stations. Multicoloured.
N3891 50ch. Type **1280** 35 15
N3892 1wn. Jangjasan Power Station 75 35

1281 Players tackling

1999. 3rd Women's World Football Championship, U.S.A. Multicoloured.

N3893 1wn. Type **1281** 75 35
N3894 1wn.50 Player No. 3 and player wearing blue and white strip tackling . . 1·10 55
N3895 1wn.50 Player and goalkeeper . . . . . . 1·10 55
N3896 2wn. Player No. 7 and player wearing blue strip 1·50 75

1282 The Earth, Space Rocket and Mars

1999. Exploration of Planet Mars. Sheet 110 × 75 mm. containing T **1282** and similar vert designs. Multicoloured.

MSN3897 2wn. Type **1282**; 2wn. Satellite orbiting Mars; 2wn. Probe landing on Mars . . . . 3·25 80

1283 Man with Candlesticks

1999. *The Nation and Destiny* (Korean film). Scenes from the film. Multicoloured.

N3898 1wn. Type **1283** 80 40
N3899 1wn. Woman holding gun and man in white suit 80 40
N3900 1wn. Man behind bars . . 80 40
N3901 1wn. Man with protective goggles on head 80 40

1284 Samil Lagoon

1999. Mt. Kumgang. Multicoloured.

N3902 20ch. Type **1284** 15 10
N3903 40ch. Samson Rocks (vert) 30 15
N3904 60ch. Rock, Kumgang Sea 45 20
N3905 80ch. Kuryong Waterfall (vert) 60 30
N3906 1wn. Kwimyon Rock (vert) . . . . 1·10 55

1285 Emblem, Girl and Dove

1999. 125th Anniv of Universal Postal Union. Sheet 87 × 67 mm.

MSN3907 **1285** 2wn. multicoloured 1·10 30

1286 France 1870 20c. Stamp and North Korea 20ch. 1946 Stamp

1999. "Philexfrance99" International Stamp Exhibition, Paris. Sheet 102 × 77 mm.

MSN3908 **1286** 2wn.50 multicoloured . . . . 1·40 35

1287 Mercedes Motor Car

1999. 5th Death Anniv of Kim Il Sung. Multicoloured.

N3909 1wn. Type **1287** 70 35
N3910 1wn. Railway carriage . . 70 35

1288 Chinese Characters and Mangyong Hill

1999. 105th Birth Anniv of Kim Hyong Jik (revolutionary).

N3911 **1288** 10ch. multicoloured 10 10

1289 Patterned Vessel

1999. Ceramics. Multicoloured.

N3912 70ch. Type **1289** 50 25
N3913 80ch. Wit and Beauty jar 60 50
N3914 1wn. Patterned vase . . . 80 40
N3915 1wn.50 Celadon kettle . . 1·10 55
N3916 2wn.50 White china vase 1·75 85

1290 Silver Carp

1999. Fish Breeding. Multicoloured.

N3917 50ch. Type **1290** 35 15
N3918 1wn. Common carp . . . 80 40
N3919 1wn.50 Spotted silver carp 1·10 55

1291 Map and Crowd

1999. Year of National Independence and Solidarity.

N3920 **1291** 40ch. multicoloured 35 15

1292 Samjiyon with Maps of Japan and Korea

1999. 40th Anniv of Repatriation of Korean Nationals in Japan.

N3921 **1292** 1wn.50 multicoloured 1·10 55

1293 Symbols of Prosperity

1999.

N3922 **1293** 40ch. multicoloured 55 25

1294 100 m Race

1295 *Acalypha hispida*

1999. World Athletics Championships, Seville, Spain. Multicoloured.

N3923 30ch. Type **1294** 40 20
N3924 40ch. Hurdles 55 25
N3925 80ch. Discus . . . . . . 1·10 55

1999. Plants presented to Kim Il Sung. Multicoloured.

N3926 40ch. Type **1295** 55 25
N3927 40ch. *Allamanda neriifolia* 55 25
N3928 40ch. *Begonia x hiemalis* 55 25
N3929 40ch. *Fatsia japonica* . . 55 25
N3930 40ch. *Streptocarpus hybrida* 55 25
N3931 40ch. *Streptocarpus rexii* 55 25

Nos. N3926/31 were issued together, se-tenant, forming a composite design.

1296 "Play a Flute to call the Phoenix"

1999. "CHINA 1999" International Stamp Exhibition and 22nd UPU Congress, Beijing. T **1296** and similar vert designs. Multicoloured.

MSN3932 40ch. Type **1296**; 40ch. "Relics kept in Bamboo Field"; 40ch. "Six Friends in a Pine Forest"; 40ch. "Lady's Morning Dressing" . . . . 1·80 45

1297 *Grifola frondosa*

1999. Mushrooms. Multicoloured.

N3933 40ch. Type **1297** 55 25
N3934 60ch. *Lactarius volemus* 80 40
N3935 1wn. *Coriolus versicolor* 1·40 70

1298 *Aporocactus flagelliformis*

1299 Rat

1999. Cacti. Multicoloured.

N3936 40ch. Type **1298** 55 25
N3937 50ch. *Astrophytum ornatum* 70 35
N3938 60ch. *Gymnocalycium michano vichii* 80 40

1999. Animals of Eastern Zodiac. Two sheets, each 110 × 160 mm containing T **1299** and similar circular multicoloured designs.

MSN3942 Two sheets (a) 10ch. Type **1299**; 10ch. Ox; 10ch. Tiger; 10ch Rabbit; 10ch. Dragon; 10ch. Snake. (b) 10ch. Horse; 10ch. Sheep; 10ch. Monkey; 10ch. Cockerel; 10ch. Dog; Sow and piglets (each sold at 1wn.) . . 55 15

1300 Shrimp

1999. Crustacea. Multicoloured.

N3943 50ch. Type **1300** 70 35
N3944 70ch. Shrimp 95 45
N3945 80ch. Lobster . . . . . . 1·10 55

1301 Jong Song Ok (marathon runner)

1999. Victory of Jong Song Ok at World Athletic Championship, Seville.

N3946 40ch. Type **1301** 20 10
MSN3947 90 × 70 mm. 2wn. Jong Song Ok (vert) . . . . 1·10 30

1302 Mt. Kumgang, North Korea

1999. 50th Anniv of North Korean–China Diplomatic Relations. Multicoloured.

N3948 40ch. Type **1302** 30 15
N3949 60ch. Mt. Lushan, China 40 20
MSN3950 142 × 93 mm. Nos. N3948/9 . . . . 55 15

1303 Deng Xiaoping

1999. Return of Macao to China. Four sheets containing T **1303** and similar multicoloured designs.

MSN3591 Four sheets. (a) 155 × 100m. 20ch. Type **1303** (green frame); 20ch. Jiang Zemin (President of People's Republic of China) and He Houba (mayor of Macao Special Administrative Region) (green frame); 80ch. Mao Tse-tung (green frame); (b) 155 × 100 mm. As No. **MSN3951a** but gold frames; (c) 90 × 122 mm. 1wn. Jiang Zemin (green frame) (circular design); (d) As **MSN3951c** but with gold frame 2·00 50

1304 Steel Worker holding Torch

1305 Yellow Dragon

2000. New Year. 40th Anniv of 19 April Rising.

N3952 **1304** 10ch. multicoloured 10 10

2000. Koguryo Era Tomb Murals, Jian. Multicoloured.

N3953 70ch. Type **1305** 40 10
MSN3954 90 × 60 mm. 1wn.60 Blue dragon (51 × 33 mm) 90 25

1306 Weeding

2000. "Rural Life" (anon). Showing details from the painting. Multicoloured.
N3955 40ch. Type **1306** 30 10
N3956 40ch. Hemp cloth weaving 30 10
N3957 40ch. Threshing 30 10
N3958 40ch. Riverside market . . 30 10

1307 Views across Lake Chou

2000. Mt. Paektu. Multicoloured.
N3959 20ch. Type **1307** 15 10
N3960 20ch. Eagle-shaped rock formation 15 10
N3961 20ch. Owl-shaped rock formation 15 10

1308 Chuibari Mask Dance

1309 Cat

2000. Pongsan Mask Dance. Depicting masks and characters from component dances. Multicoloured.
N3962 50ch. Type **1308** 35 15
N3963 80ch. Ryangban Mask Dance 55 25
N3964 1wn. Malttugi Mask Dance 70 35

2000. Cats. Multicoloured.
N3965 50ch. Type **1309** 35 15
N3966 50ch. Three kittens . . . 35 15
N3967 50ch. Mother and kittens 35 15

1310 Singapura Cat

1312 Styracosaurus

1311 Log Cabin (birthplace, Mt. Paekdu)

2000. Fauna. Multicoloured.
N3968 2wn. Type **1310** . . . . . 1·10 25
N3969 2wn. Blue Abyssinian cat 1·10 25
N3970 2wn. Oriental cat . . . . 1·10 25
N3971 2wn. Scottish fold tabby cat . . . . 1·10 25
N3972 2wn. Shiba inu . . . . . 1·10 25
N3973 2wn. Yorkshire terrier . . 1·10 25
N3974 2wn. Japanese chin . . . 1·10 25
N3975 2wn. Afghan hound . . . 1·10 25
N3976 2wn. Przewalski's horse 1·10 25
N3977 2wn. Grey cob . . . . . 1·10 25
N3978 2wn. White horse rearing 1·10 25
N3979 2wn. Donkeys . . . . . . 1·10 25
N3980 2wn. Panda in tree . . . . 1·10 25
N3981 2wn. Panda eating . . . . 1·10 25
N3982 2wn. Panda scratching against tree . . . . . . 1·10 25
N3983 2wn. Mother and cub . . 1·10 25
N3984 2wn. Two polar bears (*Ursus maritimus*) . . . 1·10 25
N3985 2wn. Mother and cub . . 1·10 25
N3986 2wn. Standing bear . . . 1·10 25
N3987 2wn. Bear lying down . . 1·10 25
N3988 2wn. Mexican lance-headed rattlesnake (*Crotalus polystictus*) . . 1·10 25
N3989 2wn. Scarlet king snake (*Lampropeltis triangulum elapsoides*) . . . . . . 1·10 25
N3990 2wn. Green tree python (*Chondropython viridis*) 1·10 25
N3991 2wn. Blood python (*Python curtus*) . . . . 1·10 25
N3992 2wn. Corythosaurus . . . 1·10 25
N3993 2wn. Psittacosaurus . . . 1·10 25
N3994 2wn. Megalosaurus . . . 1·10 25
N3995 2wn. Muttaburrasaurus . . 1·10 25
N3996 2wn. Burmeister's porpoise (*Phocoena spinipinnis*) 1·10 25
N3997 2wn. Finless porpoise (*Neophocaena phocaenoides*) . . . . . 1·10 25
N3998 2wn. Bottle-nosed dolphin (*Tursiops truncatus*) . . 1·10 25
N3999 2wn. Curvier's beaked whale (*Ziphius cavirostris*) . . . . . . 1·10 25
N4000 2wn. Port Jackson shark (*Heterodontus portusjacksoni*) . . . . 1·10 25
N4001 2wn. Great hammerhead shark (*Sphyrna mokarran*) (inscr "mokkarran") . . . . . 1·10 25
N4002 2wn. Zebra shark (*Stegostoma fasciatum*) 1·10 25
N4003 2wn. Ornate wobbegong (*Orectolobus ornatus*) . . 1·10 25
N4004 2wn. Ruddy shelduck (*Tadorna ferruginea*) . . 1·10 25
N4005 2wn. European widgeon (*Anas penelope*) . . . . 1·10 25
N4006 2wn. Mandarin drake (*Aix galericulata*) . . . . . 1·10 25
N4007 2wn. Hottentot teal (*Anas hottentota*) . . . . . 1·10 25
N4008 2wn. Little owl (*Athene noctua*) . . . . 1·10 25
N4009 2wn. Ural owl (*Strix uralensis*) . . . . 1·10 25
N4010 2wn. Great horned owl (*Bubo virginianus*) . . . 1·10 25
N4011 2wn. Snowy owl (*Nyctea scandiaca*) . . . . . . 1·10 25
N4012 2wn. Slaty-headed parakeet (*Psittacula himalayana*) . . . . . . 1·10 25
N4013 2wn. Male eclectus parrot (*Eclectus roratus*) . . . 1·10 25
N4014 2wn. Major Mitchell's cockatoo (*Cacatua leadbeateri*) . . . . . . 1·10 25
N4015 2wn. Female eclectus parrot (*Eclectus roratus*) 1·10 25
N4016 2wn. Indian leaf butterfly (*Kallima paralekta*) . . 1·10 25
N4017 2wn. Spanish festoon (*Zerynthia rumina*) . . . 1·10 25
N4018 2wn. Male and female emerald swallowtails (*Papilio palinurus*) . . . 1·10 25
N4019 2wn. *Bhutanitis lidderdalii* 1·10 25
N4020 2wn. Bumble bee . . . . 1·10 25
N4021 2wn. Bumble bee on flower . . . . 1·10 25
N4022 2wn. Honey bee (*Apis mellifera*) . . . . 1·10 25
N4023 2wn. Honey bee attacking spider . . . . 1·10 25
N4024 2wn. *Micrommata virescens* (spider) . . . 1·10 25
N4025 2wn. *Araneus quadratus* (spider) . . . . 1·10 25
N4026 2wn. *Dolomedes fimbriatus* (spider) . . . . 1·10 25
N4027 2wn. *Aculepeira ceropegia* (spider) . . . . 1·10 25

Nos. N3980/3 are wrongly inscr "Aculepeira ceropegia".

2000. 58th Birth Anniv of Kim Jong II.
N4028 **1311** 40ch. multicoloured 20 10

2000. Dinosaurs. Sheet 120 × 80 mm, containing T **1312** and similar multicoloured designs.
MSN4029 1wn. Type **1312**; 1wn. Saltasaurus (29 × 41 mm); 1wn. Tyrannosaurus . . . . 1·75 40

1313 Peacock (*Inachis io*)

2000. Butterflies. Multicoloured.
N4030 40ch. Type **1313** 20 10
N4031 60ch. Swallowtail (*Papilio machaon*) 35 10
N4032 80ch. Mimic (*Hypolimnas misippus*) 45 10
N4034 1wn.20 *Papilio bianor Cramer* 70 15

1314 Patas Monkey (*Erythrocebus patas*)

1315 Red Flag, Top of Chollima Statue and Emblem

2000. Primates. Multicoloured.
N4035 50ch. Type **1314** 30 10
N4036 50ch. Western tarsier (*Tarsius spectrm*) . . . 30 10
MSN4037 Sheet 75 × 65 mm. 2wn. Mona monkey (*Cercopithecus mona*) . . . . 1·10 25

2000. 55th Anniv of Korean Worker's Party (1st issue).
N4038 **1315** 10ch. multicoloured 10 10
See also Nos. N4083/**MS**N4084.

1316 Demonstrators

2000. 40th Anniv of 19 April Uprising, South Korea.
N4039 **1316** 40ch. multicoloured 20 10

1317 Kim Il Sun Flower

2000. 88th Birth Anniv of Kim II Sung.
N4040 **1317** 40ch. multicoloured 20 10

1318 Mun Ik Hwan

1319 Symbols of Technology, Globe, Flag and Chollima Statue

2000. 6th Death Anniv of Mun Ik Hwan (National Reunification Prize winner).
N4041 **1318** 50ch. multicoloured 30 10

2000. New Millennium. 55th Anniv of Korean Worker's Party. Multicoloured.
N4042 40ch. Type **1319** 20 10
N4043 1wn.20 Dove with envelope, globe and satellites 70 15

1320 *Cattleya intermedia*

2000. Orchids. Multicoloured.
N4044 20ch. Type **1320** 10 10
N4045 50ch. *Dendrobium moschatum* 30 10
N4046 70ch. *Brassolaeliocattleya* 40 10
MSN4047 85 × 60 mm. 2wn. *Laeliocattleya* . . . . 1·10 25

1321 Okryu Bridge (River Taedong)

2000. Bridges.
N4048 20ch. Type **1321** 10 10
N4049 30ch. Ansan Bridge (River Pothong) 15 10
N4050 1wn. Rungna Bridge (River Taedong) 60 15

1322 Okryugum and Jaengggang Dancers

1323 Half Moon (Yun Kuk Yong)

2000. Air. "WIPA 2000" International Stamp Exhibition, Vienna. Traditional Instruments and Folk Dances. Sheet 150 × 84 mm, containing T **1322** and similar vert designs. Multicoloured.
MSN4051 1wn. Type **1322**; 1wn.50 Oungum and Full Moon Viewing; 1wn.50 Janggo (drum) and Trio 1·75 40
The 1wn. stamp does not carry an airmail inscription.

2000. Children's Songs. Multicoloured.
N4052 40ch. Type **1323** 20 10
N4053 60ch. Kangnam Nostalgia (Kim Sok Song and An Ki Yong) 35 10
MSN4054 95 × 80 mm. 2wn. Spring in Home Village (Ri Won Su and Hong Ran Pha) . . . . 1·10 25

1324 Pearly Nautilus (*Nautilus pompilius*)

1325 Drake and Duck

2000. Cephalopods. Multicoloured.
N4055 40ch. Type **1324** 20 10
N4056 60ch. Common octopus (*Octopus vulgaris*) . . . 35 10
N4057 1w.50 Squid (*Ommastrephes sloanei pacificus*) 85 20
MSN4058 60 × 70 mm. 1wn.50 No. N4057 . . . . 85 20

2000. Mandarin Ducks. Multicoloured.
N4059 50ch. Type **1325** 30 10
N4060 50ch. Drake with duck and couple on bridge 30 10
MSN4061 92 × 75 mm. 1wn. Duck, drake and ducklings 60 15

1326 Table Tennis

2000. "World Expo 2000" International Stamp Exhibition, Anaheim, California. Sport. Multicoloured.
N4062 80ch. Type **1326** 45 10
N4063 1wn. Basketball 60 15
N4064 1wn.20 Baseball 70 15

1327 Sungri-61 NA

2000. Trucks. Multicoloured.
N4065 40ch. Type **1327** 20 10
N4066 70ch. Tipper truck 40 10
N4067 1wn.50 Konsol 25 ton dump truck 85 20

1328 Ri Tae Hun (artillery company commander) and 76 mm Field Gun

2000. Weaponry. Multicoloured.
N4068 60ch. Type **1328** 35 10
N4069 80ch. Ko Hyon Bin (tank commander) and T-34 tank 45 10
N4070 1wn. Squadron leader Paek Ki Rak and Yakovlev Yak-9P pursuit plane 60 15

1329 Fluorite

2000. Minerals. Multicoloured.
N4071 30ch. Type **1329** 15 10
N4072 60ch. Graphite 35 10
N4073 1w.60 Magnesite 90 20
MSN4074 74 × 74 mm. 1w.60 No. N4073 . . . . 90 20

2000. "Indonesia 2000" International Stamp Exhibition, Jakarta. Nos. N4059/**MS**N4061 optd **WORLD PHILATELIC EXHIBITION JAKARTA 15-21 AUGUST 2000** and emblem, No. **MS**N4061 optd in the margin.
N4075 50ch. multicoloured . . . 30 10
N4076 50ch. multicoloured . . . 30 10
MSN4077 1wn. multicoloured . . 60 15

1331 Swimming

2000. Olympic Games, Sydney. Triathlon. Sheet 78 × 110 mm, containing T **1331** and similar horiz designs. Multicoloured.
MSN4078 80ch. Type **1331**; 1w.20 Cycling; 2w. Running . . . . 2·00 50

1332 Sanju Falls

2000. Myohyang Mountain. Multicoloured.
N4079 40ch. Type **1332** 20 10
N4080 40ch. Inho rock 20 10
N4081 1w.20 Sangwon valley . . 70 15

2000. "Espana 2000" International Stamp Exhibition, Madrid. No. **MS**N4029 optd **Exposioion Mundial de Filatolia 2000. 0.6 - 14.** in the margin.
MSN4082 120 × 80 mm. 1w. Type **1312**; 1w. Saltasaurus; 1w. Tyrannosaurus . . . . 1·10 25

1334 Anniversary Emblem and Party Museum

2000. 55th Anniv of Korean Worker's Party (2nd issue). Multicoloured.
N4083 40ch. Type **1334** 20 10
MSN4084 120 × 85 mm. 50ch. Kim Il Sung (35 × 56 mm); 50ch. Kim Jong Il (35 × 56 mm); 50ch. Kim Jong Suk (35 × 56 mm) 80 20

1335 Flag, Bulldozer and Fields

2000. Land Re-organization.
N4085 **1335** 10ch. multicoloured 10 10

1336 Potatoes, Pigs, Fields and Scientist

2000. Taehongdan (potato production centre). Multicoloured.
N4086 40ch. Type **1336** 20 10
MSN4087 110 × 92 mm. 2w. Kim Il Sung with farmers in potato field (42 × 34 mm) . . . . 1·10 25

1337 Kim Jong Il and Pres. Jiang Zemin

2000. Visit of Kim Jong Il to People's Republic of China. Sheet 110 × 80 mm.
MSN4088 **1337** 1w.20 multicoloured 70 15

1338 Kim Jong Il and Pres. Kim Dae Jung

2000. North Korea–South Korea Summit Meeting, Pyongyang. Sheet 85 × 110 mm.
MSN4089 **1338** 2w. multicoloured 1·10 25

1339 Kim Jong Il and Pres. Putin

2000. Visit of Pres. Vladimir Putin of Russian Federation. Sheet 94 × 108 mm.
MSN4090 **1339** 1w.50 multicoloured 85 20

1340 Soldiers crossing River Amnok

2000. 50th Anniv of Chinese People's Volunteers Participation in Korean War (1st issue). Sheet 139 × 164 mm, containing T **1340** and similar horiz designs. Multicoloured.
MSN4091 10ch. Type **1340**; 10ch. Battle; 50ch. Chinese and Korean soldiers; 50ch. Mao Tse-tung and Chinese leaders; 80ch. Soldiers and gun emplacement . . . . . . 1·10 25

1341 Chinese and Korean Soldiers

1342 *Aquilegia oxysepala*

2000. 50th Anniv of Chinese People's Volunteers Participation in Korean War (2nd issue).
N4092 **1341** 30ch. multicoloured 15 10

2000. Alpine Flowers. Multicoloured.
N4093 30ch. Type **1342** 15 10
N4094 50ch. Brilliant campion (*Lychnis fulgens*) 25 10
N4095 70ch. Self-heal (*Prunela vulgaris*) 40 10

1343 Women presenting Prisoners with Flowers (½-size illustration)

2000. Repatriation of Long-term Prisoners of War. Sheets containing horiz designs as T **1343**. Multicoloured.
MSN4096 Two sheets. (a) 139 × 87 mm. 80ch. Type **1343**. (b) 165 × 120 mm. 1w.20 Prisoners and crowd. Price for 2 sheets 1·10 25

1344 Flag, Factories and Trees

2001. New Year (1st issue).
N4097 **1344** 10ch. multicoloured 10 10

1345 White Snake meeting Xu Xian

2001. New Year (2nd issue). Tale of the White Snake. Multicoloured.
N4098 10ch. Type **1345** 10 10
N4099 40ch. Stealing the Immortal Grass 20 10
N4100 50ch. White and Green snakes and Xu Xian . . 25 10
N4101 80ch. Flooding of Jinshan Hill 45 10
MSN4102 105 × 80 mm. 1wn.20 White snake and Green snake (32 × 52 mm) 70 15

1346 E. Lasker and J-R. Capablanca

2001. World Chess Champions. 165th Birth Anniv of Wilhelm Steinitz (19th-century champion) (**MS**N4109). Multicoloured.
N4103 10ch. Type **1346** 10 10
N4104 20ch. A. Alekhine and M. Euwe 10 10
N4105 30ch. M. Botvinnik and V. Smylov 15 10
N4106 40ch. T. Petrosian and M. Tal 20 10
N4107 50ch. B. Spassky and R. Fisher 25 10
N4108 1wn. A. Karpov and G. Kasparov 50 10
MSN4109 105 × 80 mm. 2wn.50 Wilhelm Steinitz (32 × 52 mm) 1·40 30

1347 White Suit and Black Hat

2001. Ri-Dynasty Men's Costumes. Multicoloured.
N4110 10ch. Type **1347** 10 10
N4111 40ch. White suit with blue waistcoat 20 10
N4112 50ch. White trousers, brown jacket and pagoda-shaped hat . . . 25 10
N4113 70ch. Knee-length pale blue coat, black hat and stick 40 10
MSN4114 110 × 80 mm. 1wn.50 Blue knee-length coat with ornamental cummerbund and black boots 85 20

1348 Small Appliance (fire)

2001. Fire Engines. Designs showing engines and fire hazards. Multicoloured.
N4115 20ch. Type **1348** 10 10
N4116 30ch. Large engine with hydraulic ladder (oil can) 15 10
N4117 40ch. Small engine with two-door cab and closed back (match) 20 10
N4118 60ch. Small engine with ladder, spotlight and external hose reel (gas canister) 30 10
N4119 2wn. Older-style engine (cigarette) 80 20
MSN4120 95 × 90 mm. 2wn. As No. N4119 (32 × 52 mm) . . . . . 1·10 25

1349 Black-naped Oriole (*Oriolus chinensis*)

2001. "HONG KONG 2001" International Stamp Exhibition. Sheet 72 × 80 mm.
MSN4121 **1349** 1wn.40 mult . . 80 20

1350 Jjong Il Peak and Flower

2001. 59th Birth Anniv of Kim Jong Il.
N4122 **1350** 10ch. multicoloured 10 10

1351 Flag and Symbols of Industry and Agriculture

2001. New Millennium. Rodong Sinmun, Josoninmingun and Chongnyonjonwi Newspapers Joint Editorial.
N4123 **1351** 10ch. multicoloured 10 10

1352 Log Cabin (revolutionary headquarters, Mt. Paekdu)

2001.

N4124 **1352** 40ch. multicoloured 20 10

1353 Family Home, Mangyongdae

2001. 89th Birth Anniv of Kim Il Sung. Multicoloured.

N4125 10ch. Type **1353** 10 10
MSN4126 170 × 103 mm. 80ch. × 8, Eight different portraits of Kim Il Sung (vert) . . . . 3·25 3·25

1354 Kim Jong Il

2001. Army as Priority. Sheet 140 × 75 mm.

MSN4127 **1354** 1w. multicoloured 60 15

1355 Pyongyang—Kaesong Motorway

2001. Roads. Multicoloured.

N4128 40ch. Type **1355** 20 10
N4129 70ch. Pyongyang—Hyanngsan expressway 40 10
N4130 1w. 20 Pyongyang—Nampo motorway . . . 70 15
N4131 1w. 50 Pyongyang—Wonsan expressway . . 85 20

1356 Ryongwang Pavilion, Pyongyang

2001. Cultural Heritage. Pavilions. Multicoloured.

N4132 40ch. Type **1356** 20 10
N4133 80ch. Inphung, Kanggye 60 15
N4134 1w. 50 Paeksang, Anju . . 85 20
N4135 2w. Thonggun, Uiju . . . 1·10 25

1357 Man with raised Arm

2001.

N4136 **1357** 10ch. Multicoloured 10 10

1358 Blue-throat (*Luscinia svecica*)

2001. Birds. Multicoloured.

N4137 10ch. Type **1358** 10 10
N4138 40ch. Grey lag goose (*Anser anser*) 20 10
N4139 80ch. Short-tailed albatross (*Diomedea albatrus*) 60 15
N4140 1w. Little ring plover (*Charadrius dubius*) . . 65 15
N4141 1w. 20 Common guillemot (*Uria aalge*) 70 15
N4142 1w. 50 House martin (*Delichon urbica*) . . . 85 20

1359 Mao Zedong (⅔-size illustration)

2001. 80th Anniv of Chinese Communist Party. Three sheets, each 152 × 67 mm containing T **1359** and similar horiz designs. Multicoloured.

MSN4143 (a) 80ch. Type **1359**; (b) 80ch. Deng Xiaping; (c) 80ch. Jiang Zemin . . . . 1·20 1·20

1360 Woljong Temple, Mt. Kuwol

2001. Kumol Mountain. Multicoloured.

N4144 10ch. Type **1360** 10 10
N4145 40ch. Revolutionary building 20 10
N4146 70ch. Potnamu Pavilion 40 10
N4147 1w. 30 Tak Peak 70 15
N4148 1w. 50 Ryongyon Falls . . 85 20

1361 *Rheum coreanum*

2001. Endangered Species. Plants. Multicoloured.

N4149 10ch. Type **1361** 10 10
N4150 40ch. *Forsythia densiflora* 20 10
N4151 1w. *Rhododendron yedoense* 65 15
N4152 2w. *Iris setosa* . . . . . . 1·10 25

1362 *Eria pannea*

2001. Orchids. Multicoloured.

N4153 10ch. Type **1362** 10 10
N4154 40ch. *Cymbidium* 20 10
N4155 90ch. *Sophrolaeliocattleya* 65 15
N4156 1w. 60 *Cattleya trianae* . . 90 25
N4157 2w. *Cypripedium macranthum* . . . . . . 1·10 25
MSN4158 142 × 96 mm. No. N4157 1·10 1·10

1363 Pibaldo Lighthouse

2001. Lighthouses. Multicoloured.

N4159 40ch. Type **1363** 20 10
N4160 70ch. Soho, Hamhung . . 40 10
N4161 90ch. Komalsan, Chongjin 65 15
N4162 1w. 50 Alsom, Rason . . 85 20
MSN4163 81 × 95 mm. No. N4162 85 85

1364 Kim Po Hyon

2001. 130th Birth Anniv of Kim Po Hyon. Sheet 80 × 90 mm.

MSN4164 **1364** 1w. black and bronze 65 15

1365 Black Stork (*Ciconia nigra*)

2001. Endangered Species. Fauna. Multicoloured.

N4165 40ch. Type **1365** 20 10
N4166 40ch. Cinereous vulture (*Aegypius monchus*) . . 20 10
N4167 70ch. Chinese water deer (*Hydropotes inermis*) . . 40 10
N4168 90ch. Goral (*Nemorhaedus goral*) 65 15
N4169 1w. 30 Northern eagle owl (*Bubo bubo*) 75 20
MSN4170 106 × 81 mm. No. N4169 75 75

1366 Deng Ya Ping receiving Gold Medal for Table Tennis from Juan Antonio Samaranch (Olympic president)

2001. Olympic Games 2008, Beijing. Sheet 152 × 115 mm containing T **1366** and similar circular designs. Multicoloured.

MSN4171 56ch. × 5, Type **1366**; Jiang Zemin (pres. People's Republic of China); Wang Jun Xia (athletics); Li Ning (gymnast); Fu Ming Xia (diver) . . . . . . 1·20 1·20

1367 Cycle Football

2001. Cycling. Sheet 90 × 145 mm containing T **1367** and similar vert designs. Multicoloured.

MSN4172 10ch. Type **1367**; 40ch. Road racing; 1w. Cyclo-cross; 2w. Indoor racing . . . . 2·00 2·00

1368 Yuri Gagarin

2001. Space Exploration. Multicoloured.

N4173 10ch. Type **1368** (cosmonaut) 10 10
N4174 40ch. Apollo 11 space ship 20 10
N4175 1w. 50 Kwangmyongsong satellite 85 20
N4176 2w. Edmund Halley (astronomer). Halley's comet and Giotto satellite . . . . 1·10 25
MSN4177 140 × 197 mm. Nos. N4173/6 . . . . 2·25 2·25

1369 Presidents Vladimir Putin and Kim Jong Il

2001. Visit of Kim Jong Il to Russia. Sheet 92 × 105 mm.

MSN4178 **1369** 1w.50 multicoloured 2·00 2·00

1370 Presidents Kim Jong Il and Jiang Zemin

2001. Meeting between Pres. Kim Jong Il and Jiang Zemin (pres. People's Republic of China). Sheet 72 × 104 mm.

MSN4179 **1370** 1w.50 multicoloured 2·00 2·00

1371 Kim Jong Suk protecting Kim Il Sung during Battle

2001. 84th Birth Anniv of Kim Jong Suk (revolutionary fighter). Sheet 168 × 100 mm.

MSN4180 **1371** 1w.60 multicoloured 2·30 2·30

1372 Kim Jong Il inspecting Troops

2001. 10th Anniv of Kim Jong Il's election as Supreme Commander of Korean People's Army. Sheet 90 × 110 mm.

MSN4181 **1372** 1w. multicoloured 1·40 1·40

1373 Chollima Statue

2002.
N4182 **1373** 10ch. multicoloured 20 10

1374 Grey Horse

2002. New Year ("Year of the Horse"). "Ten Horses" (paintings by Wang Zhi Cheng) (Nos. N4183/6). Multicoloured.
N4183 10ch. Type **1374** 10 10
N4184 40ch. Bay 20 10
N4185 60ch. Skewbald 25 10
N4186 1w.30 Piebald 75 20
MSN4187 (a) 106 × 80 mm. 1w.60. "Jiu Fang Gao" (painting by Xu Bei Hong) (36 × 57 mm); (b) 168 × 104 mm. Nos. N4183/6 and **MS**4187a . . . . 3·10 3·10

1375 Flower Basket
1377 Banner, Torch and Soldiers

1376 Zeppelin LZ1

2002. 60th Birth Anniv of Kim Jong Il. Multicoloured.
N4188 10ch. Type **1375** 10 10
MSN4189 (a) 124 × 94 mm. 1w.20 × 3, Kim Il Sung (father) (32 × 52 mm); Kim Jong Il as child (32 × 52 mm); Kim Jong Suk (mother) (32 × 52 mm). (b) 105 × 85 mm. 1w.50 Kim Jong Il with soldiers (45 × 34 mm). (c) 77 × 117 mm. 2w. Kim Jong Il as young man (42 × 64 mm) . . . 3·50 3·50

2002. Centenary of First Zeppelin Airship Flight. Multicoloured.
N4190 40ch. Type **1376** 20 10
N4191 80ch. LZ 60 15
N4192 1w. 20 Zeppelin NT . . . 70 15
MSN4193 (a) 110 × 80 mm. 2w.40 Zeppelin NT (different). (b) 132 × 110 mm. Nos. N4190/**MS**N4193a . . . . 3·25 3·25

2002. *Rodong Sinmun*, *Josoninmingun* and *Chongnyonjonwi* Newspapers Joint Editorial.
N4194 **1377** 10ch. multicoloured 10 10

1378 *Collybia confluens*

2002. Fungi.
N4195 10ch. Type **1378** 10 10
N4196 40ch. *Sparassis laminose* 25 10
N4197 80ch. Grisette (*Amanita vaginata*) (inscr "Amanjta") 60 15
N4198 1w. 20 *Russla integra* . . . 70 15
N4199 1w. 50 Scaly pholita (*Pholita squarrosa*) . . . 85 20

1379 Family Home, Mangyongdae
1381 Emblem, Doves, Dancers and Music

1380 Kang Pan Sok

2002. 90th Birth Anniv of Kim Il Sung. Multicoloured.
N4200 10ch. Type **1379** 10 10
MSN4201 (a) 105 × 85 mm. 1w.50 Kim Il Sung as young man (45 × 54 mm). (b) 105 × 85 mm. 1w.50 With Kim Jong Suk (wife) (45 × 54 mm). (c) 105 × 85 mm. 1w.50 With Kim Chaeck (revolutionary) (45 × 54 mm). (d) 76 × 117 mm. 2w. Wearing black jacket (42 × 64 mm) . . . . . 5·50 5·50

2002. 110th Birth Anniv of Kang Pan Sok (mother of Kim Il Sung). Sheet 70 × 100 mm.
MSN4202 **1380** 1w. multicoloured 40 10

2002. 20th April Spring Friendship Art Festival.
N4203 **1381** 10ch. multicoloured 10 10

1382 Electric Locomotive

2002. 20th-century Locomotives. Multicoloured.
N4204 10ch. Type **1382** 10 10
N4205 40ch. Electric locomotive (different) 20 10
N4206 1w. 50 Steam locomotive 85 20
N4207 2w. Steam locomotive (different) . . . . . . 1·10 25
MSN4208 65 × 55 mm. 2w. Diesel locomotive . . . . 1·10 1·10

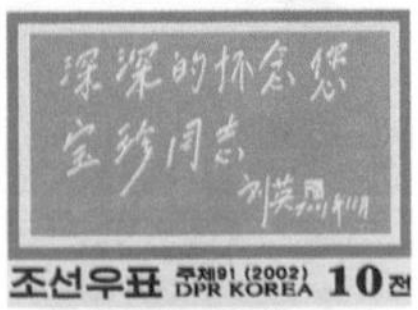

1383 Inscription

2002. Birth Centenary of He Baozhen (first wife of Liu Shaoqi (Chinese politician)). Sheet 150 × 110 mm containing T **1383** and similar multicoloured designs.
MSN4209 10ch. Type **1383**; 20ch. Arch; 30ch. Building; 40ch. Family (33 × 45 mm); 1w. He Baozhen and Liu Shaoqi (33 × 45 mm) 95 95

1384 *Cristaria plicata*

2002. Shellfish. Multicoloured.
N4210 10ch. Type **1384** 10 10
N4211 40ch. *Lanceolaria cospidata* 20 10
N4212 1w. *Schistodesmus lampreyanus* 60 15
N4213 1w. 50 *Lamprotula coreana* 85 20

1385 Soldiers

2002. 70th Anniv of Korean People's Army. Multicoloured.
N4214 10ch. Type **1385** 10 10
MSN4215 60 × 85 mm. 1w.60 Kim Il Sung and Kim Jong Il (39 × 51 mm). Perf or imperf 90 20

1386 Actors

2002. Arirang Festival. Multicoloured.
N4216 10ch. Type **1386** 10 10
N4217 20ch. Animation and cartoon characters . . . 10 10
N4218 30ch. Dancer holding fan 15 10
N4219 40ch. Dancers 20 10
MSN4220 120 × 93 mm. 1w. Woman holding tambourine (54 × 45 mm) 60 15

1387 Ri Rang and Song Bu

2002. Arirang Legend. Sheet 176 × 88 mm containing T **1387** and similar vert designs. Multicoloured.
MSN4221 10ch. Type **1387**; 40ch. As young adults; 50ch. Ri Rang killing landlord; 1w.50 Song Bu 1·30 1·30

1388 Symbols of Modern Industry

2002. Science and Technology.
N4222 **1388** 10ch. multicoloured 10 10

1389 Squid-shaped Stalactite

2002. Ryongmun Cavern. Sheet 160 × 105 mm containing T **1389** and similar vert designs. Multicoloured.
MSN4223 10ch. Type **1389**; 20ch. Chandelier-shaped stalactite; 30ch. Hill-shaped stalagmite; 40ch. Stalagmite with rough surface 60 15

1390 Monument

2002. 30th Anniv of Charter of Three Principles for Re-unification.
N4224 **1390** 10ch. multicoloured 10 10

1391 *Stauropus fagi*

2002. Butterflies. Multicoloured.
N4225 10ch. Type **1391** 10 10
N4226 40ch. *Agrias claudina* . . . 20 10
N4227 1w. 50 *Catocala nupta* . . 85 20
N4228 2w. Blue morpho (*Morpho rhetenor*) . . . . 1·10 25

조선우표 DPR KOREA 주체91(2002) 80전
(1392)

2002. 16th Chinese Communist Party Conference, Beijing. Nos. **MS**N4143a/c optd in the margin with T **1392**.
MSN4229 (a) 80ch. Type **1359**. (b) 80ch. Deng Xiaping. (c) 80ch. Jiang Zemin . . . . 1·20 1·20

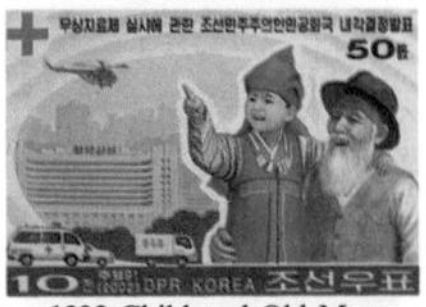

1393 Child and Old Man

2002. 50th Anniv of Free Medical Care.
N4230 **1393** 50ch. multicoloured 25 10

1394 Kim Jong Suk as Child
1395 Workers, Soldiers and Symbols of Industry

2002. 85th Birth Anniv of Kim Jong Suk (wife of Kim Il Sung). Sheet containing T **1394** and similar vert designs. Multicoloured.
MSN4231 10ch. Type **1394**; 40ch. As young woman; 1w. Wearing uniform; 1w.50 In middle age 1·70 1·70

2002. 30th Anniv of Constitution.
N4232 **1395** 10ch. multicoloured 10 10

1396 Returnees
1397 Hong Chang Su

2002. Red Cross and Red Crescent (humanitarian organizations) Day. Multicoloured.
N4233 3w. Type **1396** 10 10
N4234 12w. Red Cross workers 10 10
N4235 80w. Family (AIDS awareness) 10 10
N4336 150w. Humanitarian aid to flood victims 20 10
MSN4237 (a) 150 × 115 mm. Nos. N4233/4 and N4326, each × 2. (b) 85 × 113 mm. No. N4325 . . . 90 90

2002. Hong Chang Su—2000 World Super-Flyweight Champion. Sheet 110 × 75 mm.
N4238 **1397** 75w. multicoloured 10 10

1398 Kim Jong Il and President Vladimir Putin

2002. Kim Jong Il's Visit to Russia. Two sheets containing T **1398** and similar multicoloured design.
MSN4239 (a) 85 × 70 mm. 70w. Type **1398**; (b) 120 × 100 mm. 120w. President Putin and Kim Jong Il shaking hands (vert) . . 20 20

1399 Seal-point Shorthair Cat

2002. Cats and Dogs. Multicoloured.
N4240 3w. Type **1399** 10 10
N4241 12w. Pungsan dog 10 10
N4242 100w. White shorthair cat 15 10
N4243 150w. Black and white shorthair cat 20 10
MSN4244 57 × 70 mm. 150w. Cavalier King Charles spaniel 20 20

1400 Iron Pyrite

2002. Minerals. Multicoloured.
N4245 3w. Type **1400** 10 10
N4246 12w. Magnetite 10 10
N4247 130w. Calcite 15 10
N4248 150w. Galena 15 10

1401 Prime Minister Koizumi Junichiro and Kim Jong Il signing Declaration

2002. Japan—Korea Bilateral Declaration. Two sheets containing T **1401** and similar horiz design. Multicoloured.
MSN4249 (a) 90 × 80 mm. 120w. Type **1401**; (b) 75 × 65 mm. 150w. Prime Minister Junichiro and Kim Jong Il shaking hands 35 10

1402 Family Home, Mangyongdae

2002. National Symbols.
N4250 **1402** 1w. brown 10 10
N4251 – 3w. green (vert) . . . 10 10
N4252 – 5w. agate 10 10
N4253 – 10w. crimson (vert) 10 10
N4254 – 12w. claret (17 × 26 mm) 10 10
N4255 – 20w. scarlet and ultramarine (17 × 26 mm) . . . 10 10
N4256 – 30w. red (vert) . . . 10 10
N4257 – 40w. blue (vert) . . . 10 10
N4258 – 50w. brown (17 × 26 mm) . . . 10 10
N4259 – 70w. sepia (17 × 26 mm) . . . 10 10
N4260 – 100w. brown (17 × 26 mm) . . . 15 10
N4261 – 200w. crimson (17 × 26 mm) . . . 25 10

DESIGNS: Type **1402**; 3w. Mount Paeku; 5w. Hoeryong; 10w. Kimilsungia; 12w. Torch (Tower of Juche Idea); 20w. Flag; 30w. Kimjongilia; 40w. Magnolia blossom; 50w. National emblem; 70w. Chollima statue; 100w. Victorious Fatherland monument; 200w. Workers Party monument.

1403 Workers and Soldiers

2003. New Year.
N4262 **1403** 3w. multicoloured . . 10 10

1404 Bald Eagle steals Young Antelope

2003. Antelope defeats Bald Eagle (fairy tale). Multicoloured.
N4263 3w. Type **1404** 10 10
N4264 50w. Antelopes unite to defeat eagle 10 10
N4265 70w. Eagle eating fish poisoned by antelopes 10 10
N4266 100w. Mother antelope and rescued baby . . . 15 10
MSN4267 110 × 80 mm. 150w. Antelopes carrying fruit (54 × 45 mm) 20 20

1405 Greeting Full Moon (January 15th festival)

2003. Folk Festivals. Multicoloured.
N4268 3w. Type **1405** 10 10
N4269 12w. Dance greeting full moon (January 15th) . . 10 10
N4270 40w. Swinging (Surinal festival) 10 10
N4271 70w. Woman and child (Hangawi festival) . . . 10 10
N4272 140w. Peasant dance (Hangawi) 15 10
MSN4273 110 × 90 mm. 112w. Wrestling (Surinal) 15 15

1406 Soldier

1407 Weapons

2003. *Rodong Sinmun*, *Josoninmingun* and *Chongnyonjonwi* Newspapers Joint Editorial.
N4274 **1406** 12w. multicoloured 10 10

2003. Withdrawal from NPT.
N4275 **1407** 30w. multicoloured 10 10

1408 Ode Monument

2003. 61st Birth Anniv of Kim Jong Il. Multicoloured.
N4276 3w. Type **1408** 10 10
MSN4277 90 × 60 mm. 75w. Mt. Paektu (64 × 42 mm) 10 10

1409 *Paekmagang* (cargo ship)

2003. Ships. Multicoloured.
N4278 15w. Type **1409** 10 10
N4279 50w. *Konsol* (dredger) . . 10 10
N4280 70w. *Undok No. 2* (passenger ship) 10 10
N4281 112w. *Piryugang* (cargo ship) 15 10
MSN4282 78 × 52 mm. 150w. *Pyongyang No. 1* (pleasure cruiser) 20 20

1410 Zis

2003. Kim Il Sung's Presidential Cars. Multicoloured.
N4283 3w. Type **1410** 10 10
N4284 14w. Gaz 10 10
N4285 70w. Pobeda 10 10
N4286 90w. Merceds Benz . . . 10 10
MSN4287 100 × 80 mm. 150w. "Delaying His Urgent Journey" (painting by Kim Sam Gon) (64 × 42 mm) 20 20

1411 Book Cover

1412 Trumpeter and Symbols of Journey

2003. 30th Anniv of Publication of "On the Art of the Cinema" by Kim Jong Il. Sheet 95 × 75 mm.
MSN4288 **1411** 120w. multicoloured 15 15

2003. 80th Anniv of Kim Il Sung's 250 Mile Journey for Learning.
N4289 **1412** 15w. multicoloured 10 10

1413 Soldier and Workers

1414 Flags and Emblem

2003. Korean People's Army.
N4290 **1413** 3w. multicoloured . . 10 10

2003. 10th Anniv of Election of Kim Jong Il as Chairman of National Defence Commission. Multicoloured.
N4291 3w. Type **1414** 10 10
MSN4292 175 × 75 mm. 12w. Kim Jong Il with computers (51 × 49 mm); 70w. With soldiers (51 × 49 mm); 112w. With raised hand (51 × 49 mm) 25 25

1415 Birthplace, Mangyongdae and Kimilsungia

2003. 91st Birth Anniv of Kim Il Sung.
N4293 **1415** 3w. multicoloured . . 10 10

1416 Order of Suhbaatar (Mongolia)

2003. Kim Il Sung's Medals and Orders. Multicoloured.
N4294 12w. Type **1416** 10 10
N4295 35w. Order of Grand Cross (Madagascar) . . 10 10
N4296 70w. Order of Lenin (USSR) 10 10
N4297 140w. Order of Playa Giron (Cuba) 15 15
MSN4298 108 × 91 mm. 120w. Fidel Castro (president of Cuba) and Kim Il Sung (horiz) 15 15

1417 *Pantala flavescens*

2003. Insects. Multicoloured.
N4299 15w. Type **1417** 10 10
N4300 70w. *Tibicen japonicus* . . 10 10
N4301 220w. *Xylotrupes dichotomus* 25 10
N4302 300w. *Lycaena dispar* . . 35 10
MSN4303 150 × 85 mm. Nos. N4299/302 . . . . 80 80

1418 Glutinous Rice Cakes

2003. Traditional Food. Multicoloured.
N4304 3w. Type **1418** 10 10
N4305 30w. Tongkimchi 10 10
N4306 70w. Sinsollo 10 10
MSN4307 100 × 83 mm. 120w. Pyongyang raengmyon 15 15

1419 Victory Monument, Taechongdan Hill

2003. Sheet 98 × 71 mm.
MSN4308 **1419** 90w. multicoloured 10 10

1420 Manse Pavilion

2003. Ryangchon Temple, Kowon, South Hamgyong Province. Multicoloured.
N4309 3w. Type **1420** 10 10
N4310 12w. Three statues 10 10

N4311	40w. Buddha and two saints (painting)	10	10
N4312	50w. Buddha and four saints (painting)	10	10
MSN4313	100 × 80 mm. 120w. Taeung Hall	15	15

APPENDIX

The following stamps have either been issued in excess of postal needs or have not been available to the public in reasonable quantities at face value. Such stamps may later be given full listing if there is evidence of regular postal use.

1976.

Olympic Games, Montreal. Three-dimensional stamps showing Olympic events. 5, 10, 15, 20, 25, 40ch.

1977.

Olympic Games, Montreal. Three-dimensional stamps showing medals. 5, 10, 15, 20, 25, 40ch.

Olympic Games, Montreal. 1976 Olympic Games issue optd with winners' names. 5, 10, 15, 20, 25, 40ch.

1979.

XIII Winter Olympic Games, 1980. Nos. N1688/94 optd. 2, 5, 10, 15, 20, 25, 40ch.

1981.

Nobel Prizes for Medicine. Nos. N1955/61 optd. 7 × 10ch.

World Cup Football Championship, Spain (1982). Nos. N1731/41 optd. 12 × 20ch.

World Cup Football Championship, Spain (1982). Three-dimensional stamps. Air 20, 30ch.

1982.

21st Birthday of Princess of Wales. Nos. N2108/11 and N2120/3 optd. 10, 20, 30, 40ch.; 10, 20, 30, 70ch.

Birth of Prince William of Wales. Nos. N2185/91 optd. 10, 20, 30, 50, 60, 70, 80ch.

World Cup Football Championship, Spain, Results. Nos. N2201/6 optd. 10, 20, 30, 40, 50, 60ch.

Birth of Prince William of Wales. Three-dimensional stamps. 3 × 30ch.

1983.

XXIII Olympic Games, Los Angeles, 1984. Nos. N2084/8 optd. 10, 15, 20, 25, 30ch.

1984.

European Royal History. 81 × 10ch.

KOUANG TCHEOU (KWANGCHOW) Pt. 17

An area and port of S. China, leased by France from China in April 1898. It was returned to China in February 1943.

1906. 100 centimes = 1 franc.
1919. 100 cents = 1 piastre.

Unless otherwise stated the following are optd or surch on stamps of Indo-China.

1906. Surch **Kouang Tcheou-Wan** and value in Chinese.

1	**8**	1c. green	4·25	4·25
2		2c. red on yellow	4·00	4·00
3		4c. mauve on blue	4·00	4·25
4		5c. green	4·50	5·00
5		10c. red	4·50	4·50
6		15c. brown on blue	10·50	10·50
7		20c. red on green	5·00	4·75
8		25c. blue	4·50	4·75
9		30c. brown on cream	5·75	6·25
10		35c. black on yellow	8·25	8·25
11		40c. black on grey	5·75	5·50
12		50c. brown on cream	25·00	25·00
13	D	75c. brown on orange	32·00	32·00
14	**8**	1f. green	32·00	35·00
15		2f. brown on yellow	32·00	35·00
16	D	5f. mauve on lilac	£160	£160
17	**8**	10f. red on green	£180	£200

1908. Native types surch **KOUANG-TCHEOU** and value in Chinese.

18	**10**	1c. black and brown	85	65
19		2c. black and brown	45	1·60
20		4c. black and blue	1·25	1·75
21		5c. black and green	1·75	1·25
22		10c. black and red	1·75	1·90
23		15c. black and violet	3·00	3·50
24	**11**	20c. black and violet	3·75	5·00
25		25c. black and blue	6·00	6·25
26		30c. black and brown	8·25	11·00
27		35c. black and green	14·00	15·00
28		40c. black and brown	12·50	15·00
29		50c. black and red	16·00	16·00
30	**12**	75c. black and orange	16·00	16·00
31	–	1f. black and red	19·00	19·00
32	–	2f. black and green	35·00	38·00
33	–	5f. black and blue	65·00	70·00
34	–	10f. black and violet	65·00	£110

1919. Nos. 18/34 surch in figures and words.

35	**10**	⅖ on 1c. black and brown	60	2·50
36		⅘c. on 2c. black and brown	35	2·75
37		1⅗c. on 4c. black and blue	1·10	2·25
38		2c. on 5c. black and green	3·00	3·25
39		4c. on 10c. black and red	4·00	2·50
40		6c. on 15c. black and violet	2·75	3·00
41	**11**	8c. on 20c. black and violet	5·00	4·75
42		10c. on 25c. black and blue	13·50	12·50
43		12c. on 30c. black & brown	3·75	3·75
44		14c. on 35c. black and green	4·00	3·50
45		16c. on 40c. black & brown	3·25	3·25
46		20c. on 50c. black and red	3·50	3·25
47	**12**	30c. on 75c. black & orange	7·75	8·75
48	–	40c. on 1f. black and red	11·00	9·50
49	–	80c. on 2f. black and green	11·50	10·00
50	–	2p. on 5f. black and blue	£130	£120
51	–	4p. on 10f. black and violet	21·00	25·00

1923. Native types optd **KOUANG-TCHEOU** only. (Value in cents and piastres).

52	**10**	⅒c. red and grey	15	2·75
53		⅕c. black and blue	15	3·00
54		⅖c. black and brown	15	2·50
55		⅘c. black and red	15	3·00
56		1c. black and brown	30	2·75
57		2c. black and green	55	3·25
58		3c. black and violet	45	3·25
59		4c. black and orange	55	3·00
60		5c. black and red	1·25	2·50
61	**11**	6c. black and red	55	3·50
62		7c. black and green	40	3·00
63		8c. black on lilac	1·75	3·25
64		9c. black and yellow on green	2·50	3·25
65		10c. black and blue	1·75	3·25
66		11c. black and violet	2·75	3·25
67		12c. black and brown	3·00	3·25
68		15c. black and orange	3·50	4·00
69		20c. black and blue on buff	3·00	3·75
70		40c. black and red	4·25	4·75
71		1p. black and green on green	9·25	13·00
72		2p. black and purple on pink	15·00	20·00

1927. Pictorial types optd **KOUANG-TCHEOU**.

73	**22**	⅒c. green	15	2·75
74		⅕c. yellow	20	2·50
75		⅖c. blue	25	3·00
76		⅘c. brown	20	2·25
77		1c. orange	85	3·00
78		2c. green	35	3·00
79		3c. blue	95	3·25
80		4c. pink	55	3·00
81		5c. violet	80	3·25
82	**23**	6c. red	55	2·25
83		7c. brown	1·10	3·25
84		8c. green	1·60	3·00
85		9c. purple	1·50	3·00
86		10c. blue	1·90	3·00
87		11c. orange	3·00	3·50
88		12c. grey	1·75	3·00
89	**24**	15c. brown and red	3·50	4·00
90		20c. grey and violet	3·75	4·00
91	–	25c. mauve and brown	3·50	4·00
92	–	30c. olive and blue	3·50	3·50
93	–	40c. blue and red	3·25	3·25
94	–	50c. grey and green	3·50	3·50
95	–	1p. black, yellow and blue	4·75	6·25
96	–	2p. blue, orange and red	6·25	7·00

1937. International Exhibition, Paris. As No. **MS**246*a* of Indo-China (Diane de Poitiers) but colour changed and optd "KOUANG-TCHEOU" in black.

MS97 30c. green . . . .

1937. 1931 issue optd **KOUANG-TCHEOU.**

98	**33**	⅒c. blue	15	2·75
99		⅕c. lake	15	3·00
100		⅖c. red	15	3·00
101		½c. brown	15	2·75
102		⅘c. violet	30	2·75
103	**33**	1c. brown	15	2·75
104		2c. green	15	2·50
126	–	3c. brown	50	30
105	–	3c. green	75	3·00
106	–	4c. blue	2·50	3·25
127	–	4c. green	50	30
128	–	4c. yellow	1·75	1·00
107	–	5c. purple	2·50	3·00
129	–	5c. green	50	35
108	–	6c. red	20	3·00
130	–	7c. black	50	45
131	–	8c. lake	50	45
132	–	9c. black on yellow	50	45
109	–	10c. blue	2·50	3·00
133	–	10c. blue on pink	75	55
110	–	15c. blue	70	3·00
134	–	18c. blue	30	30
111	–	20c. red	20	3·00
112	–	21c. green	20	3·00
135	–	22c. green	50	35
113	–	25c. purple	2·00	1·60
136	–	25c. blue	70	45
114	–	30c. brown	3·50	4·75
115	**36**	50c. brown	1·40	3·00
116		60c. purple	35	3·25
137		70c. blue	40	3·25
117		1p. green	2·00	3·25
118		2p. red	2·75	3·75

1939. New York World's Fair. As T **28** of Mauritania.

119	13c. red	75	3·25
120	23c. deep blue and blue	1·40	3·25

1939. 150th Anniv of French Revolution. As T **29** of Mauritania.

121	6c.+2c. green	6·00	9·25
122	7c.+3c. brown	6·00	9·25
123	9c.+4c. orange	7·25	9·25
124	13c.+10c. red	5·50	9·25
125	23c.+20c. blue	6·75	9·25

KUWAIT Pt. 1, Pt. 19

An independent Arab Shaikhdom on the N.W. coast of the Persian Gulf with Indian and later British postal administration. On 1 February 1959 the Kuwait Government assumed responsibility for running its own postal service. In special treaty relations with Great Britain until 19 June 1961 when Kuwait became completely independent.

1923. 12 pies = 1 anna; 16 annas = 1 rupee.
1957. 100 naye paise = 1 rupee.
1961. 1000 fils = 1 dinar.

Stamps of India optd **KUWAIT**.

1923. King George V.

16	**56**	½a. green	3·25	1·40
16b	**79**	½a. green	4·50	1·40
2	**57**	1a. brown	2·75	3·25
17b	**81**	1a. brown	5·50	1·25
3	**58**	1½a. brown (No. 163)	2·25	4·50
4	**59**	2a. lilac	3·75	4·00
19c		2a. orange	4·50	2·50
18	**70**	2a. lilac	3·25	1·25
19		2a. orange	20·00	85·00
5	**61**	2a.6p. blue	2·75	8·00
6	**62**	3a. orange	4·25	20·00
20		3a. blue	2·75	1·75
21		3a. red	5·50	4·25
22	**71**	4a. green	25·00	80·00
22a	**63**	4a. green	6·50	14·00
9	**64**	6a. bistre	8·50	13·00
23	**65**	8a. mauve	19·00	13·00
11	**66**	12a. red	14·00	42·00
12	**67**	1r. brown and green	21·00	35·00
26		2r. red and orange	10·00	65·00
27		5r. blue and violet	85·00	£225
28		10r. green and red	£180	£400
29		15r. blue and olive	£550	£800

1933. Air.

31	**72**	2a. green	14·00	27·00
32		3a. blue	3·00	2·50
33		4a. olive	90·00	£170
34		6a. bistre	3·75	4·50

1939. King George VI.

36	**91**	½a. brown	7·00	1·75
38		1a. red	7·00	1·50
39	**92**	2a. orange	7·00	2·75
41	–	3a. green	7·00	2·00
43	–	4a. brown	38·00	19·00
44	–	6a. turquoise	25·00	9·00
45	–	8a. violet	28·00	32·00
46	–	12a. lake	20·00	60·00
47	**93**	1r. slate and brown	14·00	3·50
48		2r. purple and brown	4·00	16·00
49		5r. green and blue	14·00	19·00
50		10r. purple and red	60·00	75·00
51		15r. brown and green	£170	£225

1942. King George VI stamps of 1940.

52	**100a**	3p. slate	2·25	4·00
53		½a. purple	1·75	3·25
54		9p. green	3·75	9·50
55		1a. red	1·50	2·25
56	**101**	1½a. violet	4·25	8·50
57		2a. red	4·25	3·75
58		3a. violet	5·50	6·00
59		3½a. blue	4·25	8·50
60	**102**	4a. brown	5·50	3·00
60a		6a. turquoise	14·00	9·50
61		8a. violet	7·00	4·50
62		12a. lake	8·00	4·50
63	–	14a. purple (No. 277)	15·00	18·00

From 1948 onwards, for stamps with similar surcharges, but without name of country, see British Postal Agencies in Eastern Arabia.

Stamps of Great Britain surch **KUWAIT** and new values in Indian currency.

1948. King George VI.

64	**128**	½a. on ½d. green	1·50	1·75
84		½a. on ½d. orange	2·50	1·50
65		1a. on 1d. red	1·50	1·75
85		1a. on 1d. blue	2·00	1·60
66		1½a. on 1½d. brown	2·00	1·75
86		1½a. on 1½d. green	2·00	2·25
67		2a. on 2d. orange	1·75	1·75
87		2a. on 2d. brown	2·00	1·50
68		2½a. on 2½d. blue	2·00	1·00
88		2½a. on 2½d. red	2·00	2·75
69		3a. on 3d. violet	1·50	80
89	**129**	4a. on 4d. blue	2·00	1·50
70		6a. on 6d. purple	1·50	75
71	**130**	1r. on 1s. brown	3·50	2·00
72	**131**	2r. on 2s.6d. green	3·75	4·50
73		5r. on 5s. red	5·50	4·50
73a	–	10r. on 10s. blue (No. 478a)	38·00	6·00

1948. Silver Wedding.

74	**137**	2½a. on 2½d. blue	2·00	2·25
75	**138**	15r. on £1 blue	32·00	32·00

1948. Olympic Games.

76	**139**	2½a. on 2½d. blue	1·00	2·50
77	**140**	3a. on 3d. violet	1·00	2·50
78	–	6a. on 5d. purple	1·25	2·50
79	–	1r. on 1s. brown	1·25	2·50

1949. U.P.U.

80	**143**	2½a. on 2½d. blue	1·00	2·50
81	**144**	3a. on 3d. violet	1·00	3·25
82	–	6a. on 6d. purple	1·00	3·25
83	–	1r. on 1s. brown	1·00	1·25

1951. Pictorial high values.

90	**147**	2r. on 2s.6d. green	15·00	4·75
91	–	5r. on 5s. red (No. 510)	23·00	5·00
92	–	10r. on 10s. blue (No. 511)	30·00	8·00

1952. Queen Elizabeth II.

93	**154**	½a. on ½d. orange	20	1·50
94		1a. on 1d. blue	20	10
95		1½a. on 1½d. green	15	1·25
96		2a. on 2d. brown	35	10
97	**155**	2½a. on 2½d. red	15	1·25
98		3a. on 3d. lilac	40	10
99		4a. on 4d. blue	1·25	1·00
100	**157**	6a. on 6d. purple	1·50	10
101	**160**	12a. on 1s.3d. green	5·00	2·50
102		1r. on 1s.6d. blue	4·50	10

1953. Coronation.

103	**161**	2½a. on 2½d. red	3·50	3·25
104	–	4a. on 4d. blue	3·50	3·25
105	**163**	12a. on 1s.3d. green	5·00	5·50
106	–	1r. on 1s.6d. blue	4·00	1·25

1955. Pictorials.

107	**166**	2r. on 2s.6d. brown	8·00	2·25
108	–	5r. on 5s. red	8·50	6·50
109	–	10r. on 10s. blue	8·50	4·75

1957. Queen Elizabeth II.

120	**157**	1n.p. on 5d. brown	10	70
121	**154**	3n.p. on ½d. orange	60	3·50
122		6n.p. on 1d. blue	60	1·25
123		9n.p. on 1½d. green	60	2·50
124		12n.p. on 2d. brown	60	3·50
125	**155**	15n.p. on 2½d. red	60	3·50
126		20n.p. on 3d. lilac	60	30
127		25n.p. on 4d. blue	2·25	3·25
128	**157**	40n.p. on 6d. purple	1·00	30
129	**158**	50n.p. on 9d. olive	5·50	4·00
130	**160**	75n.p. on 1s.3d. green	5·50	4·50

20 Shaikh Abdullah

21 Dhow

1958.

131	**20**	5n.p. green	55	10
132a		10n.p. red	30	10
133		15n.p. brown	25	15
134		20n.p. violet	25	15
135		25n.p. orange	40	25
136		40n.p. purple	2·10	65
137	**21**	40n.p. blue	50	15
138	–	50n.p. red	40	15
139	–	75n.p. green	50	30
140	–	1r. purple	55	40
141	–	2r. blue and brown	2·75	70
142	–	5r. green	4·50	2·00
143	–	10r. lilac	14·50	4·75

DESIGNS—HORIZ: As Type **21**: 50n.p. Oil pipelines; 75n.p. Shuwaikh Power Station. 36 × 20 mm: 1r. Oil rig; 2r. Single-masted dhow; 5r. Kuwait Mosque; 10r. Main Square, Kuwait Town.

22 Shaikh Abdullah and Flag

1960. 10th Anniv of Shaikh's Accession.

144	**22**	40n.p. red and green	50	15
145		60n.p. red and blue	70	25

1961. As 1958 issue but currency changed and new designs.

146	**20**	1f. green	10	10
147		2f. red	10	10
148		4f. brown	10	10
149		5f. violet	10	10
150		8f. red	10	10
151		15f. purple	15	10
152	–	20f. green (as No. 142)	25	15
153	–	25f. blue	40	25
154	–	30f. blue and brown (as No. 141)	50	25
155	–	35f. black and red	55	25
156	**21**	40f. blue (32 × 22 mm)	65	25
157	–	45f. brown	65	25
158	–	75f. brown & grn (as No. 141)	1·00	55
159	–	90f. brown and blue	95	50
160	–	100f. red	1·20	25
161	**21**	250f. green (32 × 22 mm)	8·00	1·20
162	–	1d. orange	14·50	4·00
163	–	3d. red (as No. 142)	32·00	24·00

NEW DESIGNS—37 × 20 mm: 25, 100f. Vickers Viscount 700 airliner over South Pier, Mina al Ahmadi; 35, 90f. Shuwaikh Secondary School; 45f., 1d. Wara Hill.

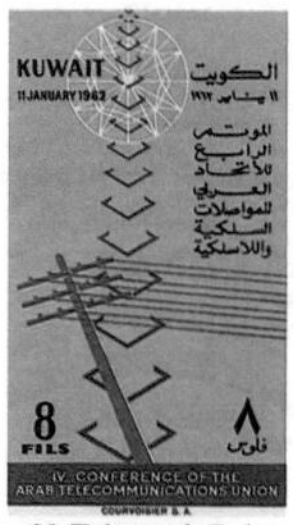
23 Telegraph Pole

1962. 4th Arab Telecommunications Union Conference.

164	**23**	8f. blue and black	30	10
165		20f. red and black	70	40

1962. Arab League Week. As T **76** of Libya.

166	20f. purple	25	15
167	45f. brown	55	50

25 Mubarakiya School, Shaikh Abdullah and Shaikh Mubarak

1962. Golden Jubilee of Mubarakiya School.

168	**25**	8f. multicoloured	30	10
169		20f. multicoloured	65	30

26 National Flag and Crest

27 Campaign Emblem

1962. National Day.

170	**26**	8f. multicoloured	15	15
171		20f. multicoloured	40	25
172		45f. multicoloured	90	30
173		90f. multicoloured	1·40	90

1962. Malaria Eradication.

174	**27**	4f. green and turquoise	15	10
175		25f. grey and green	65	55

28 "Industry and Progress"

1962. Bicentenary of Sabah Dynasty.

176	**28**	8f. multicoloured	15	10
177		20f. multicoloured	50	25
178		45f. multicoloured	95	50
179		75f. multicoloured	1·60	80

29 Mother and Child

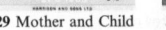

31 "Education from Oil"

30 Campaign Emblem, Palm and Domestic Animals

1963. Mothers' Day. Centres black and green; value black; country name red.

180	**29**	8f. yellow	15	10
181		20f. blue	40	30
182		45f. olive	80	50
183		75f. grey	1·50	55

1963. Freedom from Hunger. Design in brown and green. Background colours given.

184	**30**	4f. blue	25	15
185		8f. yellow	50	30
186		20f. lilac	90	55
187		45f. pink	1·60	1·40

1963. Education Day.

188	**31**	4f. brown, blue and yellow	15	10
189		20f. green, blue and yellow	55	25
190		45f. purple, blue and yellow	1·00	50

32 Shaikh Abdullah and Flags

1963. 2nd Anniv of National Day. Flags in green, black and red; values in black.

191	**32**	4f. blue	65	50
192		5f. ochre	95	80
193		20f. violet	4·75	3·50
194		50f. brown	9·75	6·00

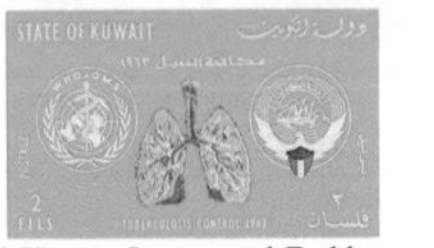

33 Human Lungs, and Emblems of W.H.O. and Kuwait

1963. W.H.O. "Tuberculosis Control" Campaign. Emblem yellow; arms black, green and red.

195	**33**	2f. black and stone	15	10
196		4f. black and green	15	10
197		8f. black and blue	40	15
198		20f. black and red	1·40	55

34 Municipal Hall and Scroll

1963. New Constitution. Centres dull purple; Amir red.

199	**34**	4f. red	15	10
200		8f. green	25	10
201		20f. purple	50	25
202		45f. brown	80	50
203		75f. violet	1·40	95
204		90f. blue	1·80	1·20

35 Football

36 Scales of Justice and Globe

1963. Arab Schools Games. Multicoloured.

205	1f. Type **35**	15	10
206	4f. Basketball	15	10
207	5f. Swimming (horiz)	15	10
208	8f. Running	25	10
209	15f. Throwing the javelin (horiz)	55	25
210	20f. Pole vaulting (horiz)	80	25
211	35f. Gymnastics (horiz)	1·60	55
212	45f. Gymnastics	2·40	1·20

1963. 15th Anniv of Declaration of Human Rights.

213	**36**	8f. black, green and violet	15	10
214		20f. black, yellow and grey	70	40
215		25f. black, brown and blue	1·10	65

37 Shaikh Abdullah

38 Rameses II in War Chariot

1964. Multicoloured, frame colours given.

216	**37**	1f. grey	15	10
217		2f. blue	15	10
218		4f. brown	15	10
219		5f. brown	15	10
220		8f. brown	25	10
221		10f. green	30	10
222		15f. green	40	10
223		20f. blue	40	10
224		25f. green	50	25
225		30f. green	55	25
226		40f. violet	90	30
227		45f. violet	95	40
228		50f. yellow	1·00	40
229		70f. purple	1·20	50
230		75f. red	1·60	55
231		90f. blue	2·40	55
232		100f. lilac	2·75	50
233		250f. brown (25 × 30 mm)	6·75	2·00
234		1d. purple (25 × 30 mm)	24·00	8·00

1964. Nubian Monuments Preservation.

235	**38**	8f. purple, blue and buff	30	10
236		20f. violet, blue & light blue	70	40
237		30f. violet, blue & turquoise	95	50

39 Mother and Child

1964. Mother's Day.

238	**39**	8f. blue, green and grey	15	10
239		20f. blue, green and red	50	15
240		30f. blue, green and bistre	65	30
241		45f. indigo, green and blue	80	50

40 Nurse giving B.C.G. Vaccine to Patient, and Bones of Chest

41 Dhow and Microscope

1964. World Health Day.

242	**40**	8f. green and brown	50	10
243		20f. red and green	1·10	40

1964. Education Day.

244	**41**	8f. multicoloured	15	10
245		15f. multicoloured	25	15
246		20f. multicoloured	40	25
247		30f. multicoloured	55	50

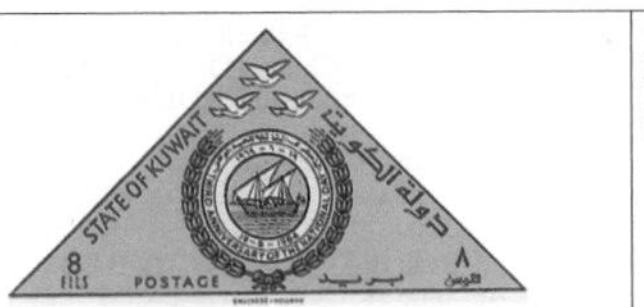

42 Dhow and Doves

1964. 3rd Anniv of National Day. Badge in blue, brown, black, red and green.

248	**42**	8f. black and brown	25	15
249		20f. black and green	40	25
250		30f. black and grey	65	40
251		45f. black and blue	90	55

43 A.P.U. Emblem

44 Hawker Siddeley Comet 4C and Douglas DC-3 Airliners

1964. 10th Anniv of Arab Postal Union's Permanent Office, Cairo.

252	**43**	8f. brown and blue	40	10
253		20f. blue and yellow	55	25
254		45f. brown and green	1·00	65

1964. Air. 10th Anniv of Kuwait Airways. Sky in blue; aircraft blue, red and black.

255	**44**	20f. black and bistre	55	25
256		25f. black and brown	70	25
257		30f. black and green	80	40
258		45f. black and brown	1·10	55

45 Conference Emblem

46 Dhow, Doves and Oil-drilling Rig

1965. 1st Arab Journalists' Conference, Kuwait.

259	**45**	8f. multicoloured	30	10
260		20f. multicoloured	55	25

1965. 4th Anniv of National Day.

261	**46**	10f. multicoloured	25	10
262		15f. multicoloured	55	15
263		20f. multicoloured	80	30

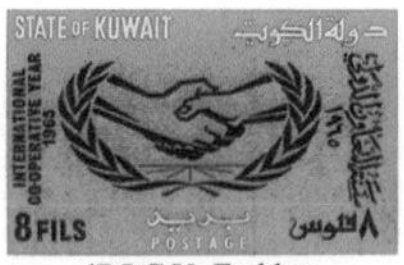

47 I.C.Y. Emblem

48 Mother and Children

1965. International Co-operation Year.

264	**47**	8f. black and red	30	15
265		20f. black and blue	55	25
266		30f. black and green	1·10	40

The stamps are inscribed "CO-OPERATIVE".

1965. Mothers' Day.

267	**48**	8f. multicoloured	30	10
268		15f. multicoloured	50	30
269		20f. multicoloured	80	50

49 Weather Kite

1965. World Meteorological Day.

270	**49**	4f. blue and yellow	40	10
271		5f. blue and orange	40	15
272		20f. blue and green	1·60	80

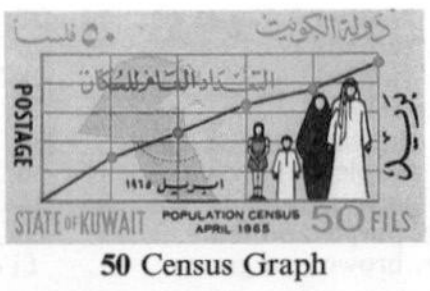

50 Census Graph

1965. Population Census.

273	**50**	8f. black, brown and blue	25	10
274		20f. black, pink and green	65	25
275		50f. black, green and red	1·50	65

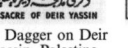

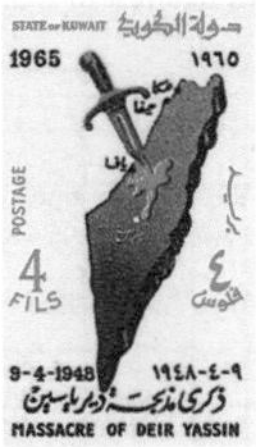

50a Dagger on Deir Yassin, Palestine

51 Atomic Symbol and Tower of Shuwaikh Secondary School

1965. Deir Yassin Massacre.

276	**50a**	4f. red and blue	30	25
277		45f. red and green	2·10	95

1965. Education Day.

278	**51**	4f. multicoloured	25	10
279		20f. multicoloured	55	30
280		45f. multicoloured	1·20	80

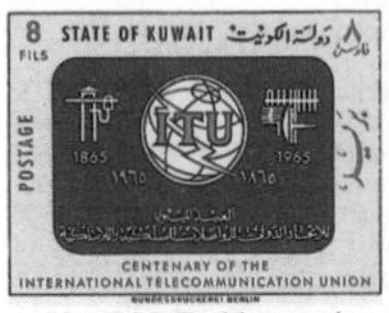

52 I.T.U. Emblem and Symbols

53 Saker Falcon

52a Lamp and Burning Library

1965. I.T.U. Centenary.

281	**52**	8f. red and blue	25	15
282		20f. red and green	95	25
283		45f. blue and red	2·40	95

1965. Reconstitution of Burnt Algiers Library.

284	**52a**	8f. green, red and black	50	15
285		15f. red, green and black	1·30	30

1965. Centre in brown.

286	**53**	8f. purple	2·00	25
287		15f. green	1·60	25
288		20f. blue	2·75	40
289		25f. red	3·00	55
290		30f. green	3·50	65
291		45f. blue	6·75	95
292		50f. purple	8·00	1·00
293		90f. red	13·00	2·10

54 Open Book

55 Shaikh Sabah

1966. Education Day.

294	**54**	8f. multicoloured	25	10
295		20f. multicoloured	70	30
296		30f. multicoloured	1·00	50

1966.

297	**55**	4f. multicoloured	10	10
298		5f. multicoloured	15	10
299		20f. multicoloured	40	10
300		30f. multicoloured	55	15
301		40f. multicoloured	70	25
302		45f. multicoloured	90	30
303		70f. multicoloured	2·00	80
304		90f. multicoloured	2·40	1·20

56 Pomfrets and Ears of Wheat

1966. Freedom from Hunger.

305	**56**	20f. multicoloured	2·00	55
306		45f. multicoloured	3·00	1·00

57 Eagle and Scales of Justice

1966. 5th Anniv of National Day.
307 57 20f. multicoloured . . . . 1·20 25
308 25f. multicoloured . . . . 1·20 40
309 45f. multicoloured . . . . 2·50 95

58 Cogwheel and Map of Arab States

1966. Arab Countries Industrial Development Conference, Kuwait.
310 58 20f. green black and blue 65 25
311 50f. green, black and brown . . . . 1·10 55

59 Mother and Children

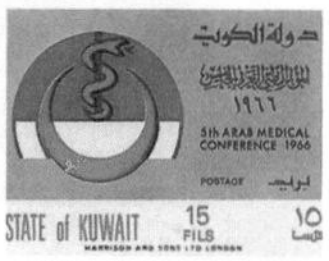
60 Red Crescent and Emblem of Medicine

1966. Mothers' Day.
312 59 20f. multicoloured 55 25
313 45f. multicoloured . . . . 1·20 55

1966. 5th Arab Medical Conference, Kuwait.
314 60 15f. red and blue 40 65
315 30f. red, blue and pink . . 90 65

61 "Man and his Cities"

62 W.H.O. Building

1966. World Health Day.
316 61 8f. multicoloured 55 15
317 10f. multicoloured 80 15

1966. Inaug of W.H.O. Headquarters, Geneva.
318 62 5f. green, blue and red . . 55 15
319 10f. green, blue & turquoise . . . . 1·00 15

62a Traffic Signals

63 Symbol of Blood Donation

1966. Traffic Day.
320 62a 10f. red, emerald and green 55 15
321 20f. emerald, red and green 80 30

1966. Blood Bank Day.
322 63 4f. multicoloured 50 15
323 8f. multicoloured . . . . . 1·10 40

64 Shaikh Ahmad and "British Fusilier" (tanker)

1966. 20th Anniv of 1st Crude Oil Shipment.
324 64 20f. multicoloured 80 40
325 45f. multicoloured . . . . 1·80 80

65 Ministry Building

1966. Inauguration of Ministry of Guidance and Information Building.
326 65 4f. red and brown 15 10
327 5f. brown and green . . . 15 10
328 8f. green and violet 30 10
329 20f. orange and blue . . . 70 25

66 Dhow, Lobster, Fish and Crab

67 U.N. Flag

1966. F.A.O. Near East Countries Fisheries Conference, Kuwait.
330 66 4f. multicoloured 55 15
331 20f. multicoloured . . . . 1·60 70

1966. U.N. Day.
332 67 20f. multicoloured 95 25
333 45f. multicoloured . . . . 2·00 95

68 UNESCO Emblem

1966. 20th Anniv of UNESCO.
334 68 20f. multicoloured 80 15
335 45f. multicoloured . . . . 2·00 80

69 Ruler and University Shield

1966. Opening of Kuwait University.
336 69 8f. multicoloured 30 10
337 10f. multicoloured 30 10
338 20f. multicoloured 80 25
339 45f. multicoloured . . . . 1·60 95

70 Ruler and Heir-Apparent

1966. Appointment of Heir-Apparent.
340 70 8f. multicoloured 30 10
341 20f. multicoloured 70 25
342 45f. multicoloured . . . . 1·60 90

71 Scout Badge

72 Symbols of Learning

1966. 30th Anniv of Kuwait Scouts.
343 71 4f. brown and green . . . 1·10 30
344 20f. green and brown . . . 3·00 1·10

1967. Education Day.
345 72 10f. multicoloured 30 10
346 45f. multicoloured 80 30

73 Fertiliser Plant

1967. Inauguration of Chemical Fertiliser Plant.
347 73 8f. multicoloured 40 10
348 20f. multicoloured . . . . 1·00 30

74 Ruler, Dove and Olive-branch

76 Arab Family

75 Map and Municipality Building

1967. 6th Anniv of National Day.
349 74 8f. multicoloured 30 10
350 20f. multicoloured 80 30

1967. 1st Arab Cities Organization Conf, Kuwait.
351 75 20f. multicoloured . . . . 1·20 40
352 30f. multicoloured . . . . 2·00 1·00

1967. Family's Day.
353 76 20f. multicoloured . . . . 1·20 40
354 45f. multicoloured . . . . 2·00 1·00

77 Arab League Emblem

78 Sabah Hospital

1967. Arab Cause Week.
355 77 8f. blue and grey 30 10
356 10f. green and yellow . . . 65 15

1967. World Health Day.
357 78 8f. multicoloured 65 10
358 20f. multicoloured . . . . 1·80 40

79 Nubian Statues

1967. Arab Week for Nubian Monuments Preservation.
359 79 15f. green, brown and yellow 70 15
360 20f. green, purple and blue 1·30 40

80 Traffic Policeman

1967. Traffic Day.
361 80 8f. multicoloured 80 25
362 20f. multicoloured . . . . 2·00 55

81 I.T.Y. Emblem

1967. International Tourist Year.
363 81 20f. black, blue & turquoise 80 15
364 45f. black, blue and mauve 1·60 80

82 "Reaching for Knowledge"

83 Map of Palestine

1967. "Eliminate Illiteracy" Campaign.
365 82 8f. multicoloured . . . . . 1·00 10
366 20f. multicoloured . . . . 1·80 50

1967. U.N. Day.
367 83 20f. red and blue 55 15
368 45f. red and orange . . . 1·20 55

84 Factory and Cogwheels

1967. 3rd Arab Labour Ministers' Conference.
369 84 20f. yellow and red 80 15
370 45f. yellow and grey . . . 1·80 1·00

85 Open Book and Kuwaiti Flag

86 Oil Rig and Map

1968. Education Day.
371 85 20f. multicoloured 50 10
372 45f. multicoloured . . . . 1·50 90

1968. 30th Anniv of Oil Discovery in Greater Burgan Field.
373 86 10f. multicoloured 80 15
374 20f. multicoloured . . . . 1·60 80

87 Ruler and Sun's Rays

88 Book, Eagle and Sun

1968. 7th Anniv of National Day.
375 87 8f. multicoloured 30 10
376 10f. multicoloured 30 15
377 15f. multicoloured 40 15
378 20f. multicoloured 55 15

1968. Teachers' Day.
379 88 8f. multicoloured 30 10
380 20f. multicoloured 70 15
381 45f. multicoloured . . . . 1·40 80

89 Family Picnicking

1968. Family Day.
382 89 8f. multicoloured 25 10
383 10f. multicoloured 30 10
384 15f. multicoloured 40 10
385 20f. multicoloured 55 15

90 Ruler, W.H.O. and State Emblems

1968. World Health Day and 20th Anniv of W.H.O.

386	**90**	20f. multicoloured	80	40
387		45f. multicoloured	1·60	95

91 Dagger on Deir Yassin, and Scroll

1968. 20th Anniv of Deir Yassin Massacre.

388	**91**	20f. red and blue	95	40
389		45f. red and violet	3·00	80

92 Pedestrians on Road Crossing

93 Torch and Map

1968. Traffic Day.

390	**92**	10f. multicoloured	80	25
391		15f. multicoloured	1·20	40
392		20f. multicoloured	2·40	55

1968. Palestine Day.

393	**93**	10f. multicoloured	1·00	30
394		20f. multicoloured	1·60	40
395		45f. multicoloured	3·50	1·40

94 Palestine Refugees

1968. Human Rights Year.

396	**94**	20f. multicoloured	25	15
397		30f. multicoloured	40	30
398		45f. multicoloured	80	40
399		90f. multicoloured	1·60	1·40

95 National Museum

96 Man reading Book

1968.

400	**95**	1f. green and brown	10	10
401		2f. green and purple	10	10
402		5f. red and black	15	10
403		8f. green and brown	25	10
404		10f. purple and blue	30	10
405		20f. blue and brown	50	15
406		25f. orange and blue	55	15
407		30f. green and blue	80	25
408		45f. deep purple and purple	1·30	50
409		50f. red and green	1·60	80

1968. International Literacy Day.

410	**96**	15f. multicoloured	30	10
411		20f. multicoloured	80	25

97 Refugee Children and U.N. Headquarters

1968. United Nations Day.

412	**97**	20f. multicoloured	30	10
413		30f. multicoloured	50	30
414		45f. multicoloured	80	40

98 Chamber of Commerce Building

1968. Inauguration of Kuwait Chamber of Commerce and Industry Building.

415	**98**	10f. purple and orange	30	10
416		15f. blue and mauve	30	15
417		20f. green and brown	50	30

99 Conference Emblem

1968. 14th Arab Chambers of Commerce, Industry and Agriculture Conference.

418	**99**	10f. multicoloured	30	10
419		15f. multicoloured	30	10
420		20f. multicoloured	50	30
421		30f. multicoloured	65	40

100 Refinery Plant

101 Holy Koran, Scales and People

1968. Inauguration of Shuaiba Refinery.

422	**100**	10f. multicoloured	40	10
423		20f. multicoloured	70	15
424		30f. multicoloured	90	40
425		45f. multicoloured	1·60	80

1968. 1,400th Anniv of the Holy Koran.

426	**101**	8f. multicoloured	40	10
427		20f. multicoloured	80	15
428		30f. multicoloured	1·20	40
429		45f. multicoloured	1·60	70

102 Boeing 707 Airliner

1969. Inauguration of Boeing 707 Aircraft by Kuwait Airways.

430	**102**	10f. multicoloured	40	15
431		20f. multicoloured	80	30
432		25f. multicoloured	1·20	55
433		45f. multicoloured	2·10	70

103 Globe and Symbols of Engineering and Science

1969. Education Day.

434	**103**	15f. multicoloured	50	15
435		20f. multicoloured	65	50

104 Hilton Hotel

105 Family and Teachers' Society Emblem

1969. Inauguration of Kuwait Hilton Hotel.

436	**104**	10f. multicoloured	30	15
437		20f. multicoloured	70	25

1969. Education Week.

438	**105**	10f. multicoloured	30	15
439		20f. multicoloured	70	25

106 Flags and Laurel

107 Emblem, Teacher and Class

1969. 8th Anniv of National Day.

440	**106**	15f. multicoloured	30	15
441		20f. multicoloured	50	25
442		30f. multicoloured	65	40

1969. Teachers' Day.

443	**107**	10f. multicoloured	30	15
444		20f. multicoloured	55	40

108 Kuwaiti Family

1969. Family Day.

445	**108**	10f. multicoloured	40	15
446		20f. multicoloured	80	25

109 Ibn Sina, Nurse with Patient and W.H.O. Emblem

110 Motor-cycle Police

1969. World Health Day.

447	**109**	15f. multicoloured	80	15
448		20f. multicoloured	95	25

1969. Traffic Day.

449	**110**	10f. multicoloured	1·20	15
450		20f. multicoloured	2·40	40

111 I.L.O. Emblem

1969. 50th Anniv of I.L.O.

451	**111**	10f. gold, black and red	30	15
452		20f. gold, black and green	65	25

112 Tanker "Al Sabahiah"

1969. 4th Anniv of Kuwait Shipping Company.

453	**112**	20f. multicoloured	95	40
454		45f. multicoloured	2·30	1·10

113 Woman writing Letter

1969. International Literacy Day.

455	**113**	10f. multicoloured	30	10
456		20f. multicoloured	65	30

114 Amir Shaikh Sabah

115 "Appeal to World Conscience"

1969. Portraits mult; background colours given.

457	**114**	8f. blue	30	10
458		10f. pink	30	10
459		15f. grey	40	15
460		20f. yellow	40	15
461		25f. lilac	55	25
462		30f. orange	80	30
463		45f. grey	1·10	40
464		50f. green	1·30	50
465		70f. blue	1·40	55
466		75f. blue	2·00	65
467		90f. brown	2·00	80
468		250f. purple	6·50	2·10
469		500f. green	12·00	7·75
470		1d. purple	21·00	13·00

1969. United Nations Day.

471	**115**	10f. blue, black and green	40	10
472		20f. blue, black and stone	90	15
473		45f. blue, black and red	1·90	70

116 Earth Station

1969. Inauguration of Kuwait Satellite Communications Station. Multicoloured.

474		20 Type **116**	1·30	15
475		45f. Dish aerial on Globe (vert)	2·10	80

117 Refugee Family

118 Globe, Symbols and I.E.Y. Emblem

1969. Palestinian Refugee Week.

476	**117**	20f. multicoloured	1·60	40
477		45f. multicoloured	3·50	1·50

1970. International Education Year.

478	**118**	20f. multicoloured	50	15
479		45f. multicoloured	1·10	70

119 Shoue

1970. Kuwait Sailing Dhows. Multicoloured.

480		8f. Type **119**	50	15
481		10f. Sambuk	55	25
482		15f. Baggala	90	30
483		20f. Battela	1·10	50
484		25f. Bum	1·40	55
485		45f. Baggala	2·40	1·00
486		50f. Dhow-building	2·75	1·20

120 Kuwaiti Flag

1970. 9th Anniv of National Day.

487	**120**	15f. multicoloured	70	25
488		20f. multicoloured	90	25

121 Young Commando and Dome of the Rock, Jerusalem

1970. Support for Palestinian Commandos. Multicoloured.

489		10f. Type **121**	1·10	65
490		20f. Commando in battle-dress	2·10	1·30
491		45f. Woman commando	4·75	3·00

122 Parents with "Children"

1970. Family Day.

492	**122**	20f. multicoloured	40	15
493		30f. multicoloured	70	25

123 Arab League Flag, Emblem and Map

1970. 25th Anniv of Arab League.

494	**123**	20f. brown, green and blue	55	15
495		45f. violet, green and orange	80	40

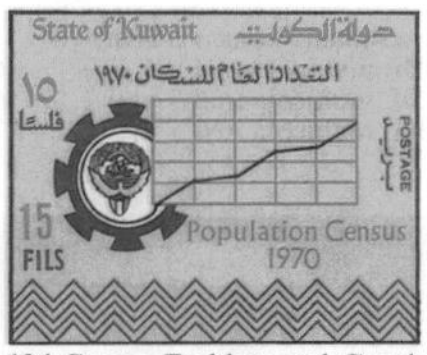

124 Census Emblem and Graph

1970. Population Census.

496	**124**	15f. multicoloured	30	10
497		20f. multicoloured	50	55
498		30f. multicoloured	65	40

125 Cancer the Crab in "Pincers"
126 Traffic Lights and Road Signs

1970. World Health Day.

499	**125**	20f. multicoloured	80	40
500		30f. multicoloured	1·30	55

1970. Traffic Day.

501	**126**	20f. multicoloured	1·20	50
502		30f. multicoloured	1·60	80

127 Red Crescent

1970. International Red Cross and Crescent Day.

503	**127**	10f. multicoloured	50	10
504		15f. multicoloured	70	30
505		30f. multicoloured	2·00	55

128 New Headquarters Building

1970. Opening of New U.P.U. Headquarters Building, Berne.

506	**128**	20f. multicoloured	70	25
507		30f. multicoloured	1·00	55

129 Amir Shaikh Sabah
130 U.N. Symbols

1970.

508	**129**	20f. multicoloured	70	15
509		45f. multicoloured	1·90	80
MS510		127 × 101 mm. Nos. 508/9. Imperf	4·50	4·50

1970. 25th Anniv of United Nations.

511	**130**	20f. multicoloured	40	15
512		45f. multicoloured	80	40

131 "Medora" (tanker) at Sea Island Jetty

1970. Oil Shipment Facilities, Kuwait.

513	**131**	20f. multicoloured	1·20	25
514		45f. multicoloured	2·00	80

132 Kuwaiti and U.N. Emblems and Hand writing

1970. International Literacy Day.

515	**132**	10f. multicoloured	80	15
516		15f. multicoloured	95	40

133 Guards and Badge

1970. First Graduation of National Guards.

517	**133**	10f. multicoloured	55	15
518		20f. multicoloured	1·20	40

134 Symbols and Flag
136 Map of Palestine on Globe

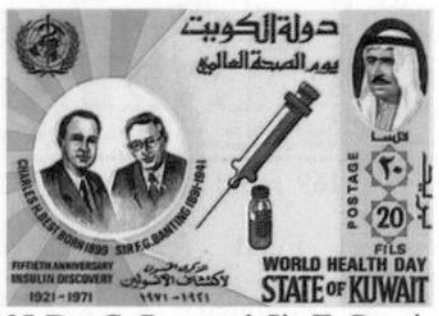

135 Dr. C. Best and Sir F. Banting (discoverers of insulin) and Syringe

1971. 10th Anniv of National Day.

519	**134**	20f. multicoloured	80	30
520		30f. multicoloured	1·20	40

1971. World Health Day, and 50th Anniv of Discovery of Insulin.

521	**135**	20f. multicoloured	1·20	30
522		45f. multicoloured	2·40	55

1971. Palestine Week.

523	**136**	20f. multicoloured	1·20	15
524		45f. multicoloured	2·40	80

137 I.T.U. Emblem

1971. World Telecommunications Day.

525	**137**	20f. black, brown and silver	80	25
526		45f. black, brown and gold	1·80	55

138 "Three Races"

1971. Racial Equality Year.

527	**138**	15f. multicoloured	50	15
528		30f. multicoloured	90	50

139 A.P.U. Emblem

1971. 25th Anniv of Founding of Arab Postal Union at Sofar Conference.

529	**139**	20f. multicoloured	70	25
530		45f. multicoloured	1·40	55

140 Book, Pupils, Globes and Pen

1971. International Literacy Day.

531	**140**	25f. multicoloured	65	15
532		60f. multicoloured	1·60	80

141 Footballers

1971. Regional Sports Tournament, Kuwait. Multicoloured.

533		20f. Type **141**	1·10	40
534		30f. Footballer blocking attack	1·60	70

142 Emblems of UNICEF and Kuwait

1971. 25th Anniv of UNICEF.

535	**142**	25f. multicoloured	40	25
536		60f. multicoloured	1·00	55

143 Book Year Emblem

1972. International Book Year.

537	**143**	20f. black and brown	55	30
538		45f. black and green	1·30	70

144 Crest and Laurel

1972. 11th Anniv of National Day.

539	**144**	20f. multicoloured	80	10
540		45f. multicoloured	1·60	70

145 Telecommunications Centre

1972. Inauguration of Telecommunications Centre, Kuwait.

541	**145**	20f. multicoloured	1·20	25
542		45f. multicoloured	3·25	95

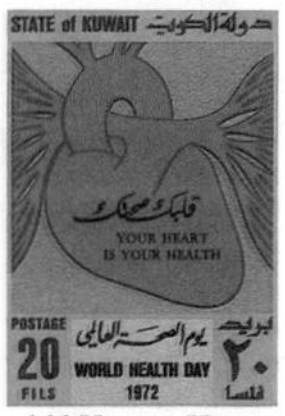

146 Human Heart
147 Nurse and Child

1972. World Health Day and World Heart Month.

543	**146**	20f. multicoloured	1·20	40
544		45f. multicoloured	3·25	95

1972. International Red Cross and Crescent Day.

545	**147**	8f. multicoloured	55	25
546		40f. multicoloured	3·00	95

148 Football

1972. Olympic Games, Munich. Multicoloured.

547		2f. Type **148**	10	10
548		4f. Running	15	10
549		5f. Swimming	15	10
550		8f. Gymnastics	30	10
551		10f. Throwing the discus	30	10
552		15f. Show jumping	55	15
553		20f. Basketball	70	15
554		25f. Volleyball	90	40

149 Produce and Fishing Boat
151 Ancient Capitals

150 Bank Emblem

1972. 11th F.A.O. Near East Regional Conference, Kuwait.

555	149 5f. multicoloured	30	30
556	10f. multicoloured	1·10	80
557	20f. multicoloured	2·30	1·60

1972. 20th Anniv of National Bank of Kuwait.

558	150 10f. multicoloured	30	10
559	35f. multicoloured	1·30	65

1972. Archaeological Excavations on Failaka Island. Multicoloured.

560	2f. Type **151**	15	15
561	5f. View of excavations	30	10
562	10f. "Leaf" capital	50	15
563	15f. Excavated building	1·00	25

152 Floral Emblem

153 Interpol Emblem

1973. 12th Anniv of National Day.

564	152 10f. multicoloured	30	10
565	20f. multicoloured	65	25
566	30f. multicoloured	1·00	50

1973. 50th Anniv of International Criminal Police Organization (Interpol).

567	153 10f. multicoloured	65	15
568	15f. multicoloured	1·20	30
569	20f. multicoloured	1·40	70

154 C.I.S.M. Badge and Flags

155 Airways Building

1973. 25th Anniv of International Military Sports Council (C.I.S.M.).

570	154 30f. multicoloured	80	40
571	40f. multicoloured	1·20	55

1973. Opening of Kuwait Airways H.Q. Building.

572	155 10f. multicoloured	40	10
573	15f. multicoloured	55	15
574	20f. multicoloured	70	30

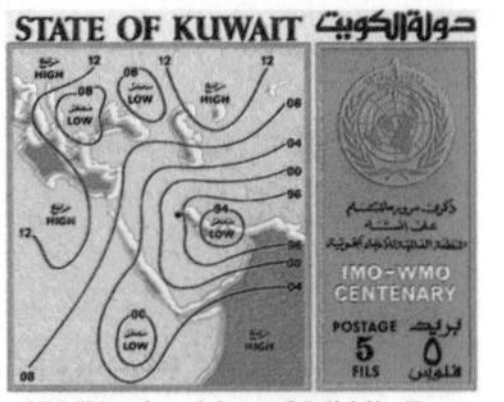
156 Weather Map of Middle East

1973. Centenary of World Meteorological Organization.

575	156 5f. multicoloured	40	15
576	10f. multicoloured	65	25
577	15f. multicoloured	95	50

157 Shaikhs Ahmed and Sabah

1973. 50th Anniv of 1st Kuwait Stamp Issue (overprints on India of 1923).

578	157 10f. multicoloured	50	10
579	20f. multicoloured	90	15
580	70f. multicoloured	2·75	1·10

158 Mourning Dove

1973. Birds and Hunting Equipment. Multicoloured. (a) Size 32 × 32 mm.

581	5f. Type **158**	55	15
582	5f. Hoopoe ("Upupa epops")	55	15
583	5f. Feral rock pigeon ("Columba livia")	55	15
584	5f. Stone-curlew ("Burhinus oedicnemus")	55	15
585	8f. Great grey shrike ("Lanius excubitor")	90	15
586	8f. Red-backed shrike ("Lanius collurio")	90	15
587	8f. Black-headed shrike ("Lanius schach")	90	15
588	8f. Golden oriole ("Orielus chinensis")	90	15
589	10f. Willow warbler ("Phylloscopus trochilus")	90	15
590	10f. Great reed warbler ("Acrocephalus arundinaceus")	90	15
591	10f. Blackcap ("Sylvia atricapilla")	90	15
592	10f. Barn swallow ("Hirundo rustica")	90	15
593	15f. Rock thrush ("Monticola solitarius")	1·30	30
594	15f. Common redstart ("Phoenicurus phoenicurus")	1·30	30
595	15f. Northern wheatear ("Oenanthe oenanthe")	1·30	30
596	15f. Bluethroat ("Luscinia svecica")	1·30	30
597	20f. Houbara bustard ("Chlamydotis undulata")	1·80	40
598	20f. Pin-tailed sandgrouse ("Pterocles alchata")	1·80	40
599	20f. Greater wood rail ("Aramides ypecaha")	1·80	40
600	20f. Spotted crake ("Porzana porzana")	1·80	40

(b) Size 38 × 38 mm.

601	25f. American kestrel ("Falco sparverius")	2·40	50
602	25f. Great black-backed gull ("Larus marinus")	2·40	50
603	25f. Purple heron ("Ardea purpurea")	2·40	50
604	25f. Wryneck ("Jynx torquilla")	2·40	50
605	30f. European bee eater ("Merops apiaster")	2·50	55
606	30f. Saker falcon ("Accipiter")	2·50	55
607	30f. Grey wagtail ("Motacilla cinerea")	2·50	55
608	30f. Pied wagtail ("Motacilla alba")	2·50	55
609	45f. Bird traps	3·75	1·20
610	45f. Driving great grey shrikes into net	3·75	1·20
611	45f. Stalking Feral rock pigeon with hand net	3·75	1·20
612	45f. Great grey shrike and disguised lure	3·75	1·20

159 Flame Emblem

160 Congress Emblem

1973. 25th Anniv of Declaration of Human Rights.

613	159 10f. multicoloured	40	30
614	40f. multicoloured	1·20	40
615	75f. multicoloured	2·00	1·10

1974. 4th Congress of Arab Veterinary Union, Kuwait.

616	160 30f. multicoloured	70	30
617	40f. multicoloured	1·00	70

161 Flag and Wheat Ear Symbol

163 Tournament Emblem

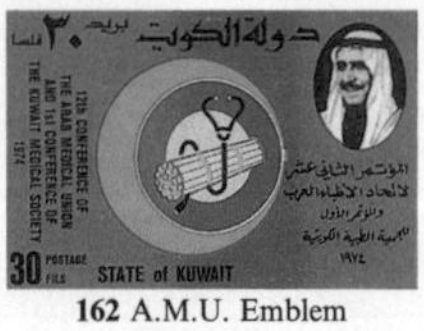
162 A.M.U. Emblem

1974. 13th Anniv of National Day.

618	161 20f. multicoloured	40	15
619	30f. multicoloured	65	25
620	70f. multicoloured	1·40	1·20

1974. 12th Conference of Arab Medical Union and 1st Conference of Kuwait Medical Society.

621	162 30f. multicoloured	1·40	40
622	40f. multicoloured	2·30	80

1974. 3rd Arabian Gulf Trophy Football Tournament, Kuwait.

623	163 25f. multicoloured	1·10	30
624	45f. multicoloured	1·90	80

164 Institute Buildings

1974. Inauguration of Kuwait Institute for Scientific Research.

625	164 15f. multicoloured	1·10	30
626	20f. multicoloured	1·50	50

165 Emblems of Kuwait, Arab Postal Union and U.P.U.

1974. Centenary of U.P.U.

627	165 20f. multicoloured	30	15
628	30f. multicoloured	30	30
629	60f. multicoloured	55	55

166 Symbolic Telephone Dial

167 Council Emblem and Flags of Member States

1974. World Telecommunications Day.

630	166 10f. multicoloured	30	15
631	30f. multicoloured	90	40
632	40f. multicoloured	1·30	50

1974. 17th Anniv of Signing Arab Economic Unity Agreement.

633	167 20f. green, black and red	70	30
634	30f. red, black and green	80	50

168 "Population Growth"

1974. World Population Year.

635	168 30f. multicoloured	80	15
636	70f. multicoloured	2·00	1·10

169 Fund Building

1974. Kuwait Fund for Arab Economic Development.

637	169 10f. multicoloured	55	15
638	20f. multicoloured	90	30

170 Shuaiba Emblem

1974. 10th Anniv of Shuaiba Industrial Area.

639	170 10f. multicoloured	50	15
640	20f. multicoloured	1·10	30
641	30f. multicoloured	1·60	70

171 Arms of Kuwait and "14"

1975. 14th Anniv of National Day.

642	171 20f. multicoloured	50	10
643	70f. multicoloured	1·30	90
644	75f. multicoloured	1·90	1·10

172 Census Symbols

1975. Population Census.

645	172 8f. multicoloured	10	10
646	20f. multicoloured	30	15
647	30f. multicoloured	50	30
648	70f. multicoloured	1·40	80
649	100f. multicoloured	2·30	95

173 I.W.Y. and Kuwait Women's Union Emblems

1975. International Women's Year.

650	173 15f. multicoloured	65	15
651	20f. multicoloured	65	25
652	30f. multicoloured	1·20	50

174 Classroom within Open Book

1975. International Literacy Day.

653	174 20f. multicoloured	55	15
654	30f. multicoloured	1·00	50

175 I.S.O. Emblem

176 U.N. Flag, Rifle and Olive-branch

1975. World Standards Day.

655	175 10f. multicoloured	30	15
656	20f. multicoloured	65	30

1975. 30th Anniv of U.N.O.

657	176 20f. multicoloured	55	15
658	45f. multicoloured	1·30	55

177 Shaikh Sabah

1975.

659	177 8f. multicoloured	25	10
660	20f. multicoloured	65	15
661	30f. multicoloured	1·00	30
662	50f. multicoloured	1·60	50
663	90f. multicoloured	3·00	90
664	100f. multicoloured	3·25	95

178 Kuwait "Skyline"

1976. 15th Anniv of National Day.

665	178	10f. multicoloured	55	15
666		20f. multicoloured	1·00	25

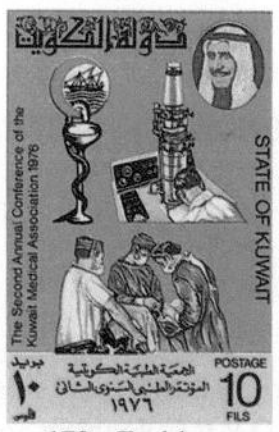

178a Emblem, Microscope and Operation

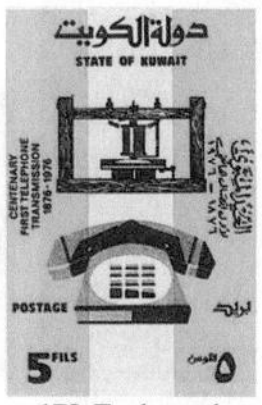

179 Early and Modern Telephones

1976. 2nd Annual Conference of Kuwait Medical Association.

667	178a	5f. multicoloured	50	15
668		10f. multicoloured . . .	95	30
669		30f. multicoloured . . .	2·50	1·10

1976. Telephone Centenary.

670	179	5f. black and orange . . .	30	15
671		15f. black and blue . . .	70	25

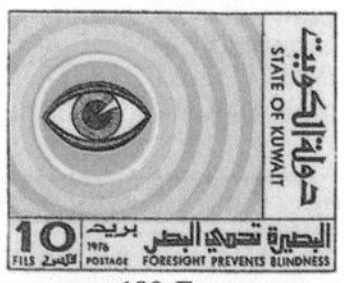

180 Eye

1976. World Health Day.

672	180	10f. multicoloured	50	15
673		20f. multicoloured	80	25
674		30f. multicoloured	1·50	65

181 Red Crescent Emblem

1976. 10th Anniv of Kuwait Red Crescent Society.

675	181	20f. multicoloured	50	15
676		30f. multicoloured	80	40
677		45f. multicoloured	1·50	65
678		75f. multicoloured	2·40	1·60

182 Suburb of Manama

183 Basketball

1976. U.N. Human Settlements Conference.

679	182	10f. multicoloured	40	15
680		20f. multicoloured	90	25

1976. Olympic Games, Montreal. Multicoloured.

681	4f. Type **183**	10	10
682	8f. Running	15	10
683	10f. Judo	25	10
684	15f. Handball	30	15
685	20f. Figure-skating	40	25
686	30f. Volleyball	55	40
687	45f. Football	90	55
688	70f. Swimming	1·40	80

184 Ethnic Heads and Map of Sri Lanka

1976. Non-Aligned Countries' Congress, Colombo.

689	184	20f. multicoloured	50	15
690		30f. multicoloured	65	40
691		45f. multicoloured	95	55

185 Torch, UNESCO. Emblem and Kuwaiti Arms

1976. 30th Anniv of UNESCO.

692	185	20f. multicoloured	50	15
693		45f. multicoloured	1·10	40

186 Pot-throwing

187 Diseased Knee

1977. Popular Games. Multicoloured.

694	5f. Type **186**	25	10
695	5f. Kite-flying	25	10
696	5f. Balancing sticks	25	10
697	5f. Spinning tops	25	10
698	10f. Blind-man's-buff (horiz)	50	25
699	10f. Rowing (horiz)	50	25
700	10f. Rolling hoops (horiz) . .	50	25
701	10f. Rope game (horiz) . . .	50	25
702	15f. Skipping	70	40
703	15f. Marbles	70	40
704	15f. Carting	70	40
705	15f. Teetotum (tops)	70	40
706	20f. Halma (horiz)	95	50
707	20f. Model boating (horiz) . .	95	50
708	20f. Pot and candle (horiz)	95	50
709	20f. Hide-and-seek (horiz) . .	95	50
710	30f. Knucklebones	1·50	70
711	30f. Hiding the stone	1·50	70
712	30f. Hopscotch	1·50	70
713	30f. Catch-as-catch-can . . .	1·50	70
714	40f. Bowls (horiz)	1·90	95
715	40f. Hockey (horiz)	1·90	95
716	40f. Guessing which hand (horiz)	1·90	95
717	40f. Jacks (horiz)	1·90	95
718	60f. Hiding the cake (horiz)	3·00	1·50
719	60f. Chess (horiz)	3·00	1·50
720	60f. Story-telling (horiz) . . .	3·00	1·50
721	60f. Treasure hunt (horiz) . .	3·00	1·50
722	70f. Hobby horses (horiz) . .	3·50	1·60
723	70f. Hide-and-seek (horiz) . .	3·50	1·60
724	70f. Catch shadow (horiz) . .	3·50	1·60
725	70f. Throwing game (horiz)	3·50	1·60

1977. World Rheumatism Year.

726	187	20f. multicoloured	50	15
727		30f. multicoloured	65	25
728		45f. multicoloured	1·00	40
729		75f. multicoloured	1·20	1·20

188 Shaikh Sabah

1977. 16th National Day.

730	188	10f. multicoloured	15	10
731		15f. multicoloured	30	15
732		30f. multicoloured	70	25
733		80f. multicoloured	1·60	65

189 Kuwait Tower

190 A.P.U. Emblem and Flags

1977. Inauguration of Kuwait Tower.

734	189	30f. multicoloured	65	15
735		80f. multicoloured	1·80	80

1977. 25th Anniv of Arab Postal Union.

736	190	5f. multicoloured	15	10
737		15f. multicoloured	25	15
738		30f. multicoloured	55	25
739		80f. multicoloured	1·60	80

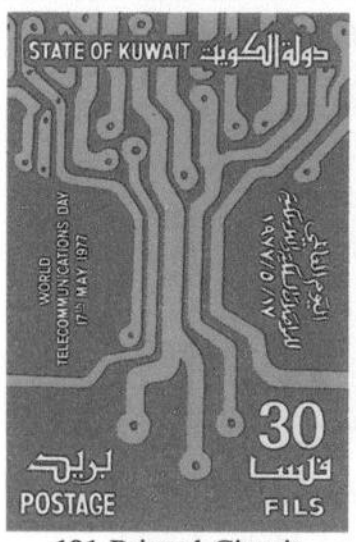

191 Printed Circuit

192 Shaikh Sabah

1977. World Telecommunications Day.

740	191	30f. orange and brown . .	90	15
741		80f. orange and green . .	2·30	1·10

1977.

742	192	15f. brown, black and blue	1·00	25
743		25f. brown, black & yellow	1·60	30
744		30f. brown, black and red	1·80	40
745		80f. brown, black and lilac	4·00	1·20
746		100f. brown, black & orge	5·25	1·40
747		150f. brown, black & blue	8·00	2·00
748		200f. brown, black & green	10·50	3·25

192a Aerogramme stamp

193 Championship Emblem

1977. Aerogramme stamp. Imperf.

748a	192a	55f. red and blue . . .		

No. 748a was applied before sale to aerogrammes to uprate the imprinted 25f. stamp. It was not available separately.

1977. 4th Asian Youth Basketball Championships.

749	193	30f. multicoloured	80	15
750		80f. multicoloured	1·60	80

194 "Popular Dancing" (O. Al-Nakeeb)

1977. Children's Paintings. Multicoloured.

751	15f. Type **194**	25	10
752	15f. "Al Deirah" (A. M. al-Onizi)	25	10
753	30f. "Fishing" (M. al-Jasem)	55	15
754	30f. "Dugg al-Harees" (B. al-Sa'adooni) (vert)	55	15
755	80f. "Fraisa Dancing" (M. al-Mojaibel) (vert)	1·60	80
756	80f. "Kuwaiti Girl" (K. Ghazi) (vert)	1·60	80

195 Dome of the Rock and Palestinian Freedom Fighters

1978. Palestinian Freedom Fighters.

757	195	30f. multicoloured	1·60	80
758		80f. multicoloured	4·00	1·60

196 Dentist treating Patient

1978. 10th Arab Dental Union Congress.

759	196	30f. multicoloured	80	15
760		80f. multicoloured	1·80	1·00

197 Carrying Water from Dhows

1978. Water Resources. Multicoloured.

761	5f. Type **197**	15	10
762	5f. Camel	15	10
763	5f. Water carrier	15	10
764	5f. Pushing water in cart . .	15	10
765	10f. Irrigation with donkey	30	10
766	10f. Water troughs in desert	30	10
767	10f. Pool by a town	30	10
768	10f. Watering crops	30	10
769	15f. Bedouin watering sheep	50	15
770	15f. Bedouin women by pool	50	15
771	15f. Camels watered by pipeline	50	15
772	15f. Water skins in Bedouin tent	50	15
773	20f. Oasis with wells	65	25
774	20f. Washing and drinking at home	65	25
775	20f. Water urn	65	25
776	20f. Filling vessels from taps	65	25
777	25f. Desalination plant . . .	80	25
778	25f. Water tanker	80	25
779	25f. Filling water tankers . .	80	25
780	25f. Modern water tanks . .	80	25
781	30f. Catching water during storm (vert)	95	30
782	30f. Water tank (vert)	95	30
783	30f. Sheet to catch rain (vert)	95	30
784	30f. Trees by water tanks (vert)	95	30
785	80f. Carrying water on donkey (vert)	2·50	90
786	80f. Woman carrying water-can (vert)	2·50	90
787	80f. Woman with water-skins (vert)	2·50	90
788	80f. Tanker delivering water to house (vert)	2·50	90
789	100f. Tanker delivering to courtyard tank (vert) . . .	3·25	1·00
790	100f. Household cistern (vert)	3·25	1·00
791	100f. Filling cistern (vert) . .	3·25	1·00
792	100f. Drawing water from well (vert)	3·25	1·00

198 Symbols of Development

1978. 17th National Day.

793	198	30f. multicoloured	40	15
794		80f. multicoloured	1·20	55

199 Face of Smallpox Victim

1978. Global Eradication of Smallpox.

795	199	30f. multicoloured	50	15
796		80f. multicoloured	1·30	70

200 Microwave Antenna

201 Shaikh Jabir

1978. 10th World Telecommunications Day.

797	200	30f. multicoloured	40	15
798		80f. multicoloured	1·20	65

1978. Portrait in brown; background colour given.

799	201	15f. green	40	25
800		30f. orange	90	40
801		80f. purple	2·00	95
802		100f. green	2·10	1·10
803		130f. brown	3·50	1·60
804		180f. violet	5·25	2·10
805		1d. red (24 × 29 mm) . . .	16·00	9·75
806		4d. blue (24 × 29 mm) . .	55·00	24·00

202 Mount Arafat, Pilgrims and Kaaba

1978. Pilgrimage to Mecca.
807 **202** 30f. multicoloured 65 15
808 80f. multicoloured . . . . 1·80 80

203 U.N. and Anti-Apartheid Emblems

1978. International Anti-Apartheid Year.
809 **203** 30f. multicoloured 50 25
810 80f. multicoloured . . . . 1·10 80
811 180f. multicoloured . . . 2·40 1·60

204 Refugees

1978. 30th Anniv of Declaration of Human Rights.
812 **204** 30f. multicoloured 55 25
813 80f. multicoloured . . . . 1·50 55
814 100f. multicoloured . . . 1·90 1·20

205 Information Centre

1978. Kuwait Information Centre.
815 **205** 5f. multicoloured 10 10
816 15f. multicoloured 25 15
817 30f. multicoloured 55 25
818 80f. multicoloured . . . . 1·50 70

206 Kindergarten

207 Kuwaiti Flag and Doves

1979. International Year of the Child.
819 **206** 30f. multicoloured 55 15
820 80f. multicoloured . . . . 1·50 80

1979. 18th National Day.
821 **207** 30f. multicoloured 40 30
822 80f. multicoloured . . . . 1·00 80

208 Crops and Greenhouse

1979. 4th Arab Agriculture Ministers' Congress.
823 **208** 30f. multicoloured 40 15
824 80f. multicoloured . . . . 1·20 80

209 World Map, Koran and Symbols of Arab Achievements

1979. The Arabs.
825 **209** 30f. multicoloured 50 15
826 80f. multicoloured . . . . 1·30 80

210 Children flying Kites

1979. Children's Paintings. Multicoloured.
827 30f. Type **210** 80 40
828 30f. Girl and doves 80 40
829 30f. Crowd and balloons . . 80 40
830 80f. Boys smiling (horiz) . . 1·90 95
831 80f. Children in landscape (horiz) . . . . 1·90 95
832 80f. Tug-of-war (horiz) . . . 1·90 95

211 Wave Pattern and Television Screen

212 International Military Sports Council Emblem

1979. World Telecommunications Day.
833 **211** 30f. multicoloured 40 15
834 80f. multicoloured . . . . 1·20 70

1979. 29th International Military Football Championship.
835 **212** 30f. multicoloured 50 25
836 80f. multicoloured . . . . 1·40 95

213 Child and Industrial Landscape

1979. World Environment Day.
837 **213** 30f. multicoloured 90 40
838 80f. multicoloured . . . . 2·40 1·20

214 Children supporting Globe

215 Children with Television

1979. 50th Anniv of Int Bureau of Education.
839 **214** 30f. multicoloured 40 15
840 80f. multicoloured . . . . 1·20 70
841 130f. multicoloured . . . 1·60 1·10

1979. 25th Anniv of Kuwaiti Kindergartens. Children's Drawings. Multicoloured.
842 30f. Type **215** 50 15
843 80f. Children with flags . . . 1·30 70

216 The Kaaba, Mecca

1979. Pilgrimage to Mecca.
844 **216** 30f. multicoloured 65 15
845 80f. multicoloured . . . . 1·80 70

217 Figure, with Dove and Torch, clothed in Palestinian Flag

1979. Int Day of Solidarity with Palestinians.
846 **217** 30f. multicoloured . . . . 1·60 55
847 80f. multicoloured . . . . 4·00 1·50

218 Boeing 747 and Douglas DC-3 Airliners

1979. 25th Anniv of Kuwait Airways.
848 **218** 30f. multicoloured 80 40
849 80f. multicoloured . . . . 2·00 1·20

219 "Pinctada" Shell bearing Map of Kuwait

1980. 19th National Day.
850 **219** 30f. multicoloured 50 15
851 80f. multicoloured . . . . 1·30 70

220 Graph with Human Figures

1980. Population Census.
852 **220** 30f. black, silver and blue 55 25
853 80f. black, gold and orange . . . . 1·40 70

221 Campaign Emblem

1980. World Health Day. Anti-smoking Campaign.
854 **221** 30f. multicoloured 80 15
855 80f. multicoloured . . . . 1·80 90

222 Municipality Building

1980. 50th Anniv of Kuwait Municipality.
856 **222** 15f. multicoloured 30 10
857 30f. multicoloured 55 25
858 80f. multicoloured . . . . 1·50 90

223 "The Future"

1980. Children's Imagination of Future Kuwait. Multicoloured.
859 30f. Type **223** 65 30
860 80f. Motorways . . . . 1·80 90

224 Hand blotting out Factory

1980. World Environment Day.
861 **224** 30f. multicoloured 65 30
862 80f. multicoloured . . . . 1·60 65

225 Volleyball

226 O.P.E.C. Emblem and Globe

1980. Olympic Games, Moscow. Multicoloured.
863 15f. Type **225** 30 15
864 15f. Tennis 30 15
865 30f. Swimming 40 25
866 30f. Weightlifting 40 25
867 30f. Basketball 40 25
868 30f. Judo 40 25
869 80f. Gymnastics . . . . . 1·00 80
870 80f. Badminton . . . . . . 1·00 80
871 80f. Fencing . . . . 1·00 80
872 80f. Football . . . . 1·00 80

1980. 20th Anniv of Organization of Petroleum Exporting Countries.
873 **226** 30f. multicoloured 70 25
874 80f. multicoloured . . . . 1·50 90

227 Mosque and Kaaba, Mecca

1980. 1400th Anniv of Hegira.
875 **227** 15f. multicoloured 30 15
876 30f. multicoloured 70 30
877 80f. multicoloured . . . . 1·80 95

228 Dome of the Rock

1980. International Day of Solidarity with Palestinian People.
878 **228** 30f. multicoloured . . . . 1·60 65
879 80f. multicoloured . . . . 4·00 1·80

229 Ibn Sina (Avicenna)

1980. Birth Millenary of Ibn Sina (philosopher and physician).
880 **229** 30f. multicoloured 55 15
881 80f. multicoloured . . . . 1·60 90

230 Islamic Symbols

231 Person in Wheelchair playing Snooker

1981. 1st Islamic Medicine Conference, Kuwait.
882 **230** 30f. multicoloured 65 15
883 80f. multicoloured . . . . 1·50 1·10

1981. International Year of Disabled Persons. Multicoloured.

884 30f. Type **231** 65 25
885 80f. Girl in wheelchair . . . 1·80 95

232 Symbols of Development and Progress

1981. 20th National Day.

886 **232** 30f. multicoloured 65 25
887 80f. multicoloured . . . . 1·60 95

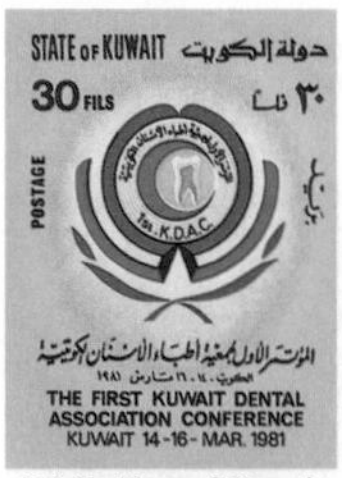

233 Emblem of Kuwait Dental Association

234 "Lamp"

1981. 1st Kuwait Dental Association Conference.

888 **233** 30f. multicoloured . . . . 1·50 55
889 80f. multicoloured . . . . 3·75 1·50

1981. World Red Cross and Red Crescent Day.

890 **234** 30f. multicoloured 70 45
891 80f. multicoloured . . . . 2·00 1·20

235 Emblems of I.T.U. and W.H.O. and Ribbons forming Caduceus

236 Tanker polluting Sea and Car polluting Atmosphere

1981. World Telecommunications Day.

892 **235** 30f. multicoloured 95 15
893 80f. multicoloured . . . . 2·30 1·30

1981. World Environment Day.

894 **236** 30f. multicoloured . . . . 1·00 30
895 80f. multicoloured . . . . 2·50 1·30

237 Sief Palace

1981.

896 **237** 5f. multicoloured 10 10
897 10f. multicoloured 10 10
898 15f. multicoloured 15 10
899 25f. multicoloured 25 10
900 30f. multicoloured 30 10
901 40f. multicoloured 40 15
902 60f. multicoloured 55 25
903 80f. multicoloured 80 25
904 100f. multicoloured . . . 95 30
905 115f. multicoloured . . . 1·10 40
906 130f. multicoloured . . . 1·30 50
907 150f. multicoloured . . . 1·50 55
908 180f. multicoloured . . . 1·80 65
909 250f. multicoloured . . . 2·40 90
910 500f. multicoloured . . . 4·75 1·80
911 1d. multicoloured . . . . 9·75 3·50
912 2d. multicoloured . . . . 19·00 6·75
913 3d. multicoloured . . . . 29·00 10·50
914 4d. multicoloured . . . . 39·00 13·50

Nos. 911/14 are larger, 33 × 28 mm and have a different border.

238 Pilgrims

1981. Pilgrimage to Mecca.

915 **238** 30f. multicoloured 95 30
916 80f. multicoloured . . . . 2·40 95

239 Palm Trees, Sheep, Camel, Goat and F.A.O. Emblem

1981. World Food Day.

917 **239** 30f. multicoloured 95 30
918 80f. multicoloured . . . . 2·40 95

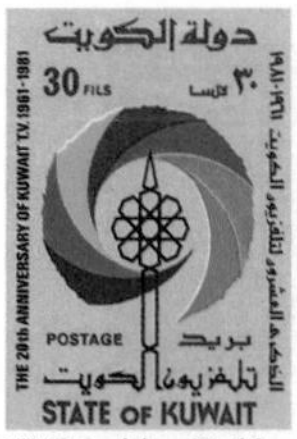

240 Television Emblem

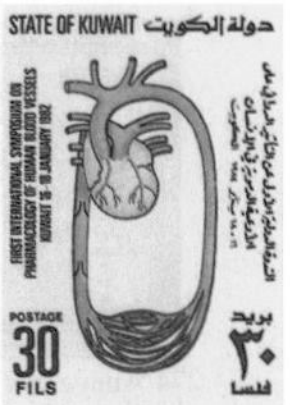

241 Blood Circulation Diagram

1981. 20th Anniv of Kuwait Television.

919 **240** 30f. multicoloured 95 30
920 80f. multicoloured . . . . 2·40 95

1982. 1st International Symposium on Pharmacology of Human Blood Vessels.

921 **241** 30f. multicoloured . . . . 1·10 90
922 80f. multicoloured . . . . 2·50 1·30

242 Symbols of Development, Progress and Peace

1982. 21st National Day.

923 **242** 30f. multicoloured 65 30
924 80f. multicoloured . . . . 1·60 90

243 Emblem of Kuwait Boy Scouts Association on Globe

1982. 75th Anniv of Boy Scout Movement.

925 **243** 30f. multicoloured 90 50
926 80f. multicoloured . . . . 2·40 1·10

244 Emblem of Arab Pharmacists Union

1982. Arab Pharmacists Day.

927 **244** 30f. multicoloured . . . . 1·20 30
928 80f. multicoloured . . . . 2·75 1·10

245 Red Crescent, Arab and W.H.O. Emblem

246 A.P.U. Emblem

1982. World Health Day.

929 **245** 30f. multicoloured . . . . 1·10 70
930 80f. multicoloured . . . . 3·50 2·00

1982. 30th Anniv of Arab Postal Union.

931 **246** 30f. black, orange and green . . . . 1·20 30
932 80f. black, green and orange . . . . 2·75 1·10

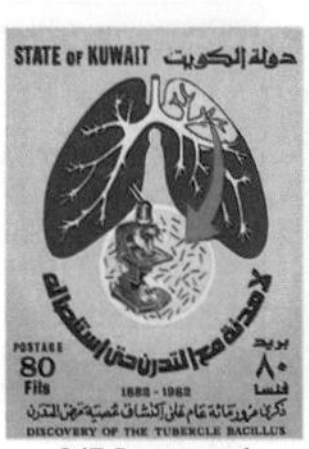

247 Lungs and Microscope

249 Museum Exhibits

248 Crest and Emblems of Kuwait Football Association and Olympic Committee

1982. Centenary of Discovery of Tubercle Bacillus.

933 **247** 30f. multicoloured . . . . 1·60 65
934 80f. multicoloured . . . . 4·75 1·80

1982. World Cup Football Championship, Spain.

935 **248** 30f. multicoloured . . . . 1·00 30
936 80f. multicoloured . . . . 2·50 1·10

1982. 10th Anniv of Science and Natural History Museum.

937 **249** 30f. multicoloured . . . . 2·40 40
938 80f. multicoloured . . . . 4·75 1·80

250 "Al-Wattyah" (container ship)

1982. 6th Anniv of United Arab Shipping Company. Multicoloured.

939 30f. Type **250** 90 30
940 80f. "Al-Salimiah" (freighter) 2·40 95

251 Palm Trees

253 Desert Flower

252 Pilgrims

1982. Arab Palm Tree Day.

941 **251** 30f. multicoloured 65 30
942 80f. multicoloured . . . . 1·50 95

1982. Pilgrimage to Mecca.

943 **252** 15f. multicoloured 50 10
944 30f. multicoloured 95 30
945 80f. multicoloured . . . . 2·50 95

1983. Desert Plants. As T **253**. Multicoloured; background colours given. (a) Vert designs.

946 10f. green 10 10
947 10f. violet 10 10
948 10f. salmon 10 10
949 10f. pink (blue flowers) . . . 10 10
950 10f. bistre 10 10
951 10f. green 10 10
952 10f. light orange 10 10
953 10f. red (poppy) 10 10
954 10f. brown 10 10
955 10f. blue 10 10
956 15f. green 15 15
957 15f. purple 15 15
958 15f. blue 15 15
959 15f. blue (iris) 15 15
960 15f. olive 15 15
961 15f. red 15 15
962 15f. brown 15 15
963 15f. blue (bellflowers) 15 15
964 15f. mauve 15 15
965 15f. pink 15 15
966 30f. brown 40 30
967 30f. mauve 40 30
968 30f. blue 40 30
969 30f. green 40 30
970 30f. pink 40 30
971 30f. blue 40 30
972 30f. green 40 30
973 30f. mauve 40 30
974 30f. bistre 40 30
975 30f. yellow 40 30

(b) Horiz designs.

976 40f. red (fungi) 55 40
977 40f. green (fungi) 55 40
978 40f. violet 55 40
979 40f. blue 55 40
980 40f. grey 55 40
981 40f. green 55 40
982 40f. mauve 55 40
983 40f. brown 55 40
984 40f. blue 55 40
985 40f. green (daisies) 55 40
986 80f. violet . . . . 1·20 65
987 80f. green . . . . 1·20 65
988 80f. yellow (yellow flowers) 1·20 65
989 80f. brown (green leaves) . . 1·20 65
990 80f. blue . . . . 1·20 65
991 80f. yellow . . . . 1·20 65
992 80f. green . . . . 1·20 65
993 80f. violet (red berries) . . . 1·20 65
994 80f. brown (yellow flowers) 1·20 65
995 80f. yellow (red and blue flowers) . . . . 1·20 65

DESIGNS: Various plants.

254 Peace Dove on Map of Kuwait

1983. 22nd National Day.

996 **254** 30f. multicoloured 65 25
997 80f. multicoloured . . . . 1·80 95

255 I.M.O. Emblem

1983. 25th Anniv of International Maritime Organization.

998 **255** 30f. multicoloured 40 25
999 80f. multicoloured . . . . 1·20 65

256 Virus and Map of Africa

1983. 3rd International Conference on Impact of Viral Diseases on Development of Middle East and African Countries.

1000 **256** 15f. multicoloured . . . 30 15
1001 30f. multicoloured . . . 65 30
1002 80f. multicoloured . . . 1·60 1·10

257 Stylized Figures exercising

1983. World Health Day.

1003 **257** 15f. multicoloured . . . 50 25
1004 30f. multicoloured . . . 95 50
1005 80f. multicoloured . . . 2·40 1·50

258 U.P.U., W.C.Y. and I.T.U. Emblems

1983. World Communications Year.

1006	258	15f. multicoloured	40	25
1007		30f. multicoloured	80	50
1008		80f. multicoloured	2·00	1·50

259 Map of Kuwait and Dhow

1983. World Environment Day.

1009	259	15f. multicoloured	50	25
1010		30f. multicoloured	95	50
1011		80f. multicoloured	2·50	1·50

260 Walls of Jerusalem

1983. World Heritage Convention.

1012	260	15f. multicoloured	40	15
1013		30f. multicoloured	70	30
1014		80f. multicoloured	1·90	1·10

261 Pilgrims in Mozdalipha

1983. Pilgrimage to Mecca.

1015	261	15f. multicoloured	40	15
1016		30f. multicoloured	80	30
1017		80f. multicoloured	2·30	1·10

262 Arab within Dove

1983. International Day of Solidarity with Palestinian People.

1018	262	15f. multicoloured	50	25
1019		30f. multicoloured	95	50
1020		80f. multicoloured	2·50	1·30

263 Kuwait Medical Association and Congress Emblems

1984. 21st Pan-Arab Medical Congress.

1021	263	15f. multicoloured	50	25
1022		30f. multicoloured	90	50
1023		80f. multicoloured	2·30	1·40

264 State Arms within Key

1984. Inauguration of New Health Establishments.

1024	264	15f. multicoloured	40	15
1025		30f. multicoloured	70	30
1026		80f. multicoloured	1·90	1·10

265 Dove and Globe

266 Symbols of Medicine within Head

1984. 23rd National Day.

1027	265	15f. multicoloured	40	15
1028		30f. multicoloured	90	30
1029		80f. multicoloured	2·30	1·10

1984. 2nd International Medical Science Conference.

1030	266	15f. multicoloured	50	25
1031		30f. multicoloured	95	50
1032		80f. multicoloured	2·50	1·30

267 Douglas DC-3 Airliner

1984. 30th Anniv of Kuwait Airways Corporation.

1033	267	30f. blue, dp blue & yell	90	65
1034		80f. blue, dp blue & mve	2·40	1·30

268 Magazine Covers

269 Family and Emblems

1984. 25th Anniv of "Al-Arabi" (magazine).

1035	268	15f. multicoloured	40	15
1036		30f. multicoloured	80	30
1037		80f. multicoloured	2·10	1·10

1984. World Health Day.

1038	269	15f. multicoloured	40	15
1039		30f. multicoloured	80	30
1040		80f. multicoloured	2·30	1·10

270 Sudanese Orphan and Village

1984. Hanan Kuwaiti Village, Sudan.

1041	270	15f. multicoloured	40	15
1042		30f. multicoloured	90	30
1043		80f. multicoloured	2·30	1·10

271 I.C.A.O., Kuwait Airport and Kuwait Airways Emblems

1984. 40th Anniv of I.C.A.O.

1044	271	15f. multicoloured	50	25
1045		30f. multicoloured	90	50
1046		80f. multicoloured	2·40	1·40

272 Map of Arab Countries and Youths

1984. Arab Youth Day.

1047	272	30f. multicoloured	95	50
1048		80f. multicoloured	2·40	1·30

273 Swimming

1984. Olympic Games, Los Angeles. Multicoloured.

1049	30f. Type 273	40	40
1050	30f. Hurdling	40	40
1051	80f. Judo	1·20	1·20
1052	80f. Equestrian	1·20	1·20

274 Anniversary Emblem, Camera, Airplane, Al-Aujairy Observatory and Wind Tower

1984. 10th Anniv of Science Club.

1053	274	15f. multicoloured	50	25
1054		30f. multicoloured	95	50
1055		80f. multicoloured	2·50	1·40

275 Stoning the Devil

1984. Pilgrimage to Mecca.

1056	275	30f. multicoloured	95	55
1057		80f. multicoloured	2·30	1·50

276 Anniversary Emblem

1984. 20th Anniv of International Telecommunications Satellite Consortium (Intelsat).

1058	276	30f. multicoloured	95	55
1059		80f. multicoloured	2·30	1·50

277 Council Emblem

278 Hands breaking Star

1984. 5th Supreme Council Session of Gulf Co-operation Council.

1060	277	30f. multicoloured	95	65
1061		80f. multicoloured	2·30	1·60

1984. International Day of Solidarity with Palestinian People.

1062	278	30f. multicoloured	95	55
1063		80f. multicoloured	2·30	1·50

279 Company Emblem as Satellite

280 I.Y.Y. Emblem

1984. 50th Anniv of Kuwait Oil Company.

1064	279	30f. multicoloured	95	55
1065		80f. multicoloured	2·30	1·50

1985. International Youth Year.

1066	280	30f. multicoloured	55	25
1067		80f. multicoloured	1·50	90

281 "24", Hand holding Flame and Dove

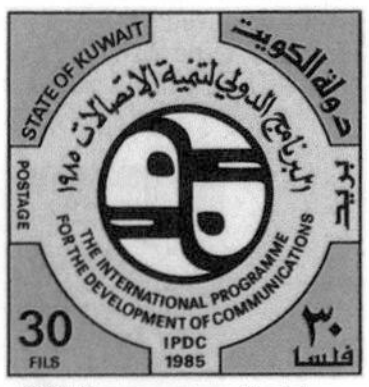

282 Programme Emblem

1985. 24th National Day.

1068	281	30f. multicoloured	80	30
1069		80f. multicoloured	2·30	90

1985. International Programme for Communications Development.

1070	282	30f. multicoloured	80	30
1071		80f. multicoloured	2·00	1·10

283 Emblem

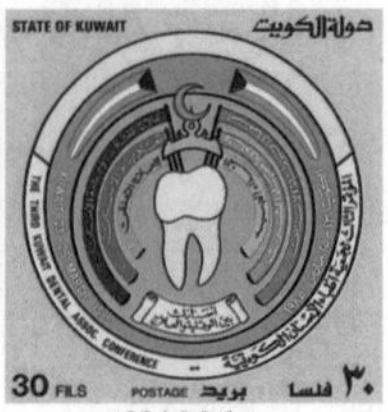

284 Molar

1985. 1st Arab Gulf Social Work Week.

1072	283	30f. multicoloured	80	30
1073		80f. multicoloured	2·00	1·10

1985. 3rd Kuwait Dental Association Conference.

1074	284	30f. multicoloured	80	55
1075		80f. multicoloured	1·80	1·50

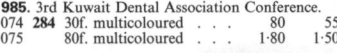

285 Emblem

286 Globe and Figures

1985. Population Census.

1076	285	30f. multicoloured	90	30
1077		80f. multicoloured	2·40	1·10

1985. World Health Day.

1078	286	30f. multicoloured	95	40
1079		80f. multicoloured	1·90	1·20

287 Arabic Script

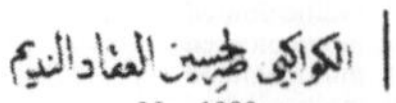

No. 1080

No. 1081

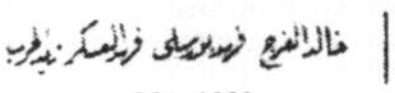

No. 1082

No. 1083

No. 1084

No. 1085

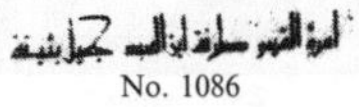

No. 1086

No. 1087

1985. 50th Anniv of Central Library. Designs showing titles of books and names of authors in Arabic script (first line of text illustrated above).
1080 30f. gold . . . . 1·00 55
1081 30f. gold . . . . 1·00 55
1082 30f. gold . . . . 1·00 55
1083 30f. gold . . . . 1·00 55
1084 80f. black and gold . . . . 2·50 1·00
1085 80f. black and gold . . . . 2·50 1·00
1086 80f. black and gold . . . . 2·50 1·00
1087 80f. black and gold . . . . 2·50 1·00

288 Seascape

1985. World Environment Day.
1088 **288** 30f. multicoloured . . . 1·10 55
1089 80f. multicoloured . . . 3·00 1·50

289 Anniversary Emblem

1985. 25th Anniv of Organization of Petroleum Exporting Countries.
1090 **289** 30f. ultramarine, bl & mve 90 40
1091 80f. ultramarine, bl & brn . . . . 2·40 1·20

290 Emblem and Heads

1985. Introduction of Civilian Identity Cards.
1092 **290** 30f. multicoloured . . . 90 30
1093 80f. multicoloured . . . 2·40 1·10

291 Flag on Globe within Symbolic Design

1985. International Day of Solidarity with Palestinian People.
1094 **291** 15f. multicoloured . . . 55 30
1095 30f. multicoloured . . . 1·20 65
1096 80f. multicoloured . . . 3·25 1·80

292 Birds

1986. 25th National Day.
1097 **292** 15f. multicoloured . . . 50 25
1098 30f. multicoloured . . . 95 50
1099 80f. multicoloured . . . 2·50 1·40

293 Emblem

294 W.H.O. Emblem as Flower

1986. 20th Anniv of Kuwait Red Crescent.
1100 **293** 20f. multicoloured . . . 80 25
1101 25f. multicoloured . . . 95 40
1102 70f. multicoloured . . . 2·75 1·40

1986. World Health Day.
1103 **294** 20f. multicoloured . . . 80 50
1104 25f. multicoloured . . . 1·00 55
1105 70f. multicoloured . . . 3·00 1·80

295 I.P.Y. Emblem

1986. International Peace Year.
1106 **295** 20f. green, blue and black 80 25
1107 25f. blue, yellow and black 95 40
1108 70f. blue, mauve and black . . . . 2·75 1·40

296 "Al Mirqab"

1986. 10th Anniv of United Arab Shipping Company. Container Ships. Multicoloured.
1109 20f. Type **296** 80 40
1110 70f. "Al Mubarakiah" . . . 3·25 1·40

297 Bank Emblem on Map

1986. 25th Anniv of Gulf Bank.
1111 **297** 20f. multicoloured . . . 80 40
1112 25f. multicoloured . . . 95 50
1113 70f. multicoloured . . . 2·75 1·30

298 Zig-zags and Diamonds

1986. Sadu Art. Multicoloured.
1114 20f. Type **298** 55 25
1115 70f. Triangles and symbols 1·90 95
1116 200f. Stripes and triangles 5·75 2·75

299 Dove on Manacled Hand pointing to Map

1986. International Day of Solidarity with Palestinian People.
1117 **299** 20f. multicoloured . . . 1·10 40
1118 25f. multicoloured . . . 1·50 55
1119 70f. multicoloured . . . 3·75 1·50

300 Conference Emblem

1987. 5th Islamic Summit Conference.
1120 **300** 25f. multicoloured . . . 70 25
1121 50f. multicoloured . . . 1·50 55
1122 150f. multicoloured . . . 4·50 1·60

301 Map in National Colours and Symbols of Development

1987. 26th National Day.
1123 **301** 50f. multicoloured . . . 1·20 40
1124 150f. multicoloured . . . 3·50 1·40

302 Health Science Centre

1987. 3rd Kuwait International Medical Sciences Conference: Infectious Diseases in Developing Countries.
1125 **302** 25f. multicoloured . . . 55 25
1126 150f. multicoloured . . . 3·50 1·40

303 Campaign Emblem

1987. World Health Day. Child Immunization Campaign.
1127 **303** 25f. multicoloured . . . 65 25
1128 50f. multicoloured . . . 1·30 50
1129 150f. multicoloured . . . 3·75 1·40

304 Jerusalem

1987. "Jerusalem is an Arab City".
1130 **304** 25f. multicoloured . . . 65 25
1131 50f. multicoloured . . . 1·30 55
1132 150f. multicoloured . . . 3·75 1·80

305 Pilgrims in Miqat Wadi Mihrim

1987. Pilgrimage to Mecca.
1133 **305** 25f. multicoloured . . . 65 25
1134 50f. multicoloured . . . 1·30 55
1135 150f. multicoloured . . . 3·75 1·80

306 Emblem

308 Project Monument and Site Plan

307 Buoy and Container Ship

1987. Arab Telecommunications Day.
1136 **306** 25f. multicoloured . . . 55 25
1137 50f. multicoloured . . . 1·00 55
1138 150f. multicoloured . . . 3·25 1·80

1987. World Maritime Day.
1139 **307** 25f. multicoloured . . . 70 25
1140 50f. multicoloured . . . 1·50 50
1141 150f. multicoloured . . . 4·50 1·40

1987. Al-Qurain Housing Project.
1142 **308** 25f. multicoloured . . . 55 15
1143 50f. multicoloured . . . 1·10 40
1144 150f. multicoloured . . . 3·50 1·00

309 Unloading Container Ship

1987. 10th Anniv of Ports Public Authority.
1145 **309** 25f. multicoloured . . . 70 25
1146 50f. multicoloured . . . 1·50 55
1147 150f. multicoloured . . . 4·50 1·80

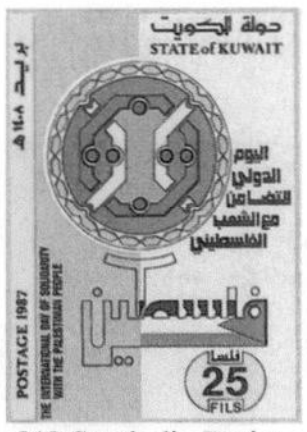
310 Symbolic Design

311 Emblem

1987. International Day of Solidarity with Palestinian People.
1148 **310** 25f. multicoloured . . . 55 25
1149 50f. multicoloured . . . 1·00 50
1150 150f. multicoloured . . . 3·25 1·40

1988. 25th Anniv of Women's Cultural and Social Society.
1151 **311** 25f. multicoloured . . . 50 15
1152 50f. multicoloured . . . 90 40
1153 150f. multicoloured . . . 2·75 1·00

312 Emblem

313 Hands holding W.H.O. Emblem

1988. 27th National Day.
1154 **312** 25f. multicoloured . . . 50 15
1155 50f. multicoloured . . . 90 40
1156 150f. multicoloured . . . 2·75 1·00

1988. World Health Day. 40th Anniv of W.H.O.
1157 **313** 25f. multicoloured . . . 55 25
1158 50f. multicoloured . . . 1·10 50
1159 150f. multicoloured . . . 3·50 1·40

314 Regional Maritime Protection Organization Symbol

315 Society Emblem

1988. 10th Anniv of Kuwait Regional Convention for Protection of Marine Environment.
1160 **314** 35f. ultram, blue & brn 80 25
1161 50f. ultram, blue & grn 1·20 55
1162 150f. ultram, blue & pur 3·50 1·80

1988. 25th Anniv of Kuwait Teachers' Society.
1163 **315** 25f. multicoloured . . . 55 15
1164 50f. multicoloured . . . 1·00 40
1165 150f. multicoloured . . . 3·25 1·20

316 Pilgrims at al-Sail al-Kabir Miqat

1988. Pilgrimage to Mecca.
1166 **316** 25f. multicoloured . . . 65 15
1167 50f. multicoloured . . . 1·30 40
1168 150f. multicoloured . . . 3·75 1·20

317 Gang of Youths lying in wait for Soldiers

318 Ring of Dwellings around Key

1988. Palestinian "Intifida" Movement.
1169 **317** 50f. multicoloured . . . 2·00 40
1170 150f. multicoloured . . . 5·25 1·20

1988. Arab Housing Day.
1171 **318** 50f. multicoloured . . . 95 40
1172 100f. multicoloured . . . 2·00 80
1173 150f. multicoloured . . . 3·00 1·20

319 Map of Palestine highlighted on Globe

320 Volunteers embracing Globe

1988. International Day of Solidarity with Palestinian People.
1174 **319** 50f. multicoloured . . . 95 40
1175 100f. multicoloured . . . 2·00 80
1176 150f. multicoloured . . . 3·00 1·20

1988. International Volunteer Day.
1177 **320** 50f. multicoloured . . . 95 40
1178 100f. multicoloured . . . 1·90 80
1179 150f. multicoloured . . . 2·75 1·20

321 Conference, Kuwait Society of Engineers and Arab Engineers Union Emblems

1989. 18th Arab Engineering Conference.
1180 **321** 50f. multicoloured . . . 90 40
1181 100f. multicoloured . . . 1·80 80
1182 150f. multicoloured . . . 2·50 1·20

322 Flags as Figures supporting Map

323 Conference Emblem

1989. 28th National Day.
1183 **322** 50f. multicoloured . . . 90 40
1184 100f. multicoloured . . . 1·80 80
1185 150f. multicoloured . . . 2·50 1·20

1989. 5th Kuwait Dental Association Conference.
1186 **323** 50f. multicoloured . . . 80 40
1187 150f. multicoloured . . . 2·40 80
1188 250f. multicoloured . . . 4·00 2·00

324 Emblems

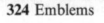

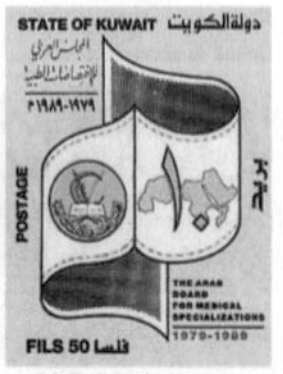
325 Anniversary Emblem

1989. World Health Day.
1189 **324** 50f. multicoloured . . . 65 30
1190 150f. multicoloured . . . 2·00 95
1191 250f. multicoloured . . . 3·50 1·60

1989. 10th Anniv of Arab Board for Medical Specializations.
1192 **325** 50f. multicoloured . . . 65 30
1193 150f. multicoloured . . . 2·00 95
1194 250f. multicoloured . . . 3·50 1·60

326 Torch, Pen and Flag

1989. 25th Anniv of Kuwait Journalists' Association.
1195 **326** 50f. multicoloured . . . 70 40
1196 200f. multicoloured . . . 3·00 1·60
1197 250f. multicoloured . . . 3·50 2·00

327 Attan'eem Miqat, Mecca

1989. Pilgrimage to Mecca.
1198 **327** 50f. multicoloured . . . 80 40
1199 150f. multicoloured . . . 2·40 1·20
1200 200f. multicoloured . . . 3·25 1·60

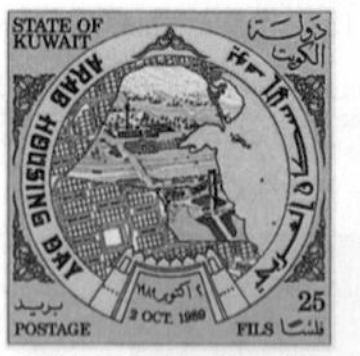
328 Al-Qurain Housing Project

329 Tree

1989. Arab Housing Day.
1201 **328** 25f. multicoloured . . . 65 15
1202 50f. multicoloured . . . 1·40 40
1203 150f. multicoloured . . . 4·00 1·20

1989. Greenery Week.
1204 **329** 25f. multicoloured . . . 65 15
1205 50f. multicoloured . . . 1·40 40
1206 150f. multicoloured . . . 4·00 1·20

330 Dhow

331 Emblem and Map

1989. Coil Stamps.
1207 **330** 50f. gold and green . . . 1·50 1·50
1208 100f. gold and blue . . . 3·00 3·00
1209 200f. gold and red . . . 6·00 6·00

1989. 5th Anniv of Gulf Investment Corporation.
1210 **331** 25f. multicoloured . . . 65 15
1211 50f. multicoloured . . . 1·40 40
1212 150f. multicoloured . . . 4·00 1·20

332 Emblem

333 Zakat House

1989. 1st Anniv of "Declaration of Palestine State".
1213 **332** 50f. multicoloured . . . 80 40
1214 150f. multicoloured . . . 2·40 1·20
1215 200f. multicoloured . . . 3·25 1·60

1989. Orphanage Sponsorship Project.
1216 **333** 25f. multicoloured . . . 50 25
1217 50f. multicoloured . . . 90 55
1218 150f. multicoloured . . . 2·75 1·60

334 Shaikh Sabah al-Salem as-Sabah (former Chief) and Officers

335 Globe and Dove

1989. 50th Anniv (1988) of Kuwait Police.
1219 **334** 25f. multicoloured . . . 50 25
1220 50f. multicoloured . . . 90 55
1221 150f. multicoloured . . . 2·75 1·60

1990. 29th National Day.
1222 **335** 25f. multicoloured . . . 50 25
1223 50f. multicoloured . . . 90 55
1224 150f. multicoloured . . . 2·75 1·60

336 Earth, Clouds and Weather Balloon

1990. World Meteorological Day.
1225 **336** 50f. multicoloured . . . 90 50
1226 100f. multicoloured . . . 1·80 95
1227 150f. multicoloured . . . 2·50 1·50

337 Map bordered by National Flag

338 Lanner Falcon

1990. World Health Day.
1228 **337** 50f. multicoloured . . . 90 50
1229 100f. multicoloured . . . 1·80 95
1230 150f. multicoloured . . . 2·50 1·50

1990.
1231 **338** 50f. gold and blue . . . 6·50 6·50
1232 100f. gold and red . . . 6·50 6·50
1233 150f. gold and green . . . 6·50 6·50

339 Soldiers carrying Kuwait Flag

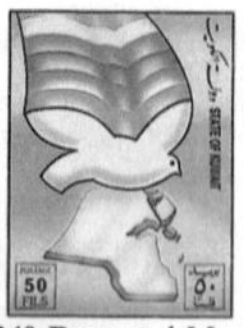
340 Dove and Map

1991. Liberation (1st issue).
1234 **339** 25f. multicoloured . . . 50 30
1235 50f. multicoloured . . . 1·00 65
1236 150f. multicoloured . . . 3·00 1·90
See also Nos. 1243/**MS**1285.

1991. Peace.
1237 **340** 50f. multicoloured . . . 1·00 55
1238 100f. multicoloured . . . 2·10 1·30
1239 150f. multicoloured . . . 3·00 1·80

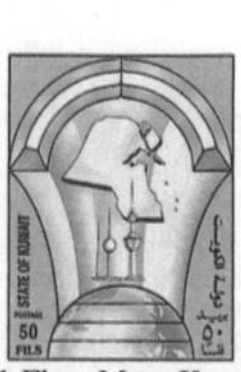
341 Flag, Map, Kuwait Towers and Globe

1991. Reconstruction.
1240 **341** 50f. multicoloured . . . 95 65
1241 150f. multicoloured . . . 3·00 1·80
1242 200f. multicoloured . . . 3·75 2·40

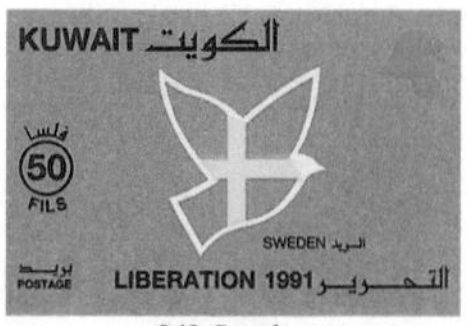
342 Sweden

1991. Liberation (2nd issue). Each showing a dove coloured with the flag of one of the assisting nations. Multicoloured.
1243 50f. Type **342** 95 80
1244 50f. Soviet Union 95 80
1245 50f. United States of America 95 80
1246 50f. Kuwait 95 80
1247 50f. Saudi Arabia 95 80
1248 50f. United Nations 95 80
1249 50f. Singapore 95 80
1250 50f. France 95 80
1251 50f. Italy 95 80
1252 50f. Egypt 95 80
1253 50f. Morocco 95 80
1254 50f. United Kingdom . . . 95 80
1255 50f. Philippines 95 80
1256 50f. United Arab Emirates 95 80
1257 50f. Syria 95 80
1258 50f. Poland 95 80
1259 50f. Australia 95 80
1260 50f. Japan 95 80
1261 50f. Hungary 95 80
1262 50f. Netherlands 95 80
1263 50f. Denmark 95 80
1264 50f. New Zealand 95 80
1265 50f. Czechoslovakia 95 80
1266 50f. Bahrain 95 80
1267 50f. Honduras 95 80
1268 50f. Turkey 95 80
1269 50f. Greece 95 80
1270 50f. Oman 95 80
1271 50f. Qatar 95 80
1272 50f. Belgium 95 80
1273 50f. Sierra Leone 95 80
1274 50f. Argentina 95 80
1275 50f. Norway 95 80
1276 50f. Canada 95 80
1277 50f. Germany 95 80
1278 50f. South Korea 95 80
1279 50f. Bangladesh 95 80
1280 50f. Bulgaria 95 80
1281 50f. Senegal 95 80
1282 50f. Spain 95 80
1283 50f. Niger 95 80
1284 50f. Pakistan 95 80
MS1285 87 × 134 mm. 1d. Flag and dove. Imperf . . . . 16·00 16·00

343 "Human Terror"

344 Emblem

1991. 1st Anniv of Iraqi Invasion. Multicoloured.
1286 50f. Type **343** . . . . . . 1·00 65
1287 100f. "Invasion of Kuwait" 2·00 1·20
1288 150f. "Environmental Terrorism" (horiz) . . . . 3·00 1·80
MS1289 90 × 65 mm. 250f. "Desert Storm" (liberation campaign). Imperf . . . . 5·75 5·75

1991. 30th Anniv (1990) of Organization of Petroleum Exporting Countries.
1290 **344** 25f. multicoloured . . . 50 30
1291 50f. multicoloured . . . 1·00 65
1292 150f. multicoloured . . . 3·00 1·90

345 National Flag, Arabic Script and Broken Chains

1991. Campaign to Free Kuwaiti Prisoners of War. Each black and yellow.
1293 50f. Type **345** 95 40
1294 150f. Prison bars, "Don't Forget Our P.O.W.'s" and broken chains . . . . . 2·75 1·40
MS1295 121 × 101 mm. No. 1293 × 2; No. 1294 × 2 . . 8·00 7·25

346 Names of Member Countries forming Tree

1991. 12th Gulf Co-operation Council Summit Conference, Kuwait. Multicoloured.
1296 25f. Type **346** 40 30
1297 150f. National flags as leaves of plant . . . . . 2·50 1·60
MS1298 Two sheets, each 100 × 120 mm. (a) No. 1296 × 2, No. 1297 × 2; (b) No. 1297 × 2; 2 × 25f. Simialr to No. 1296 but with tree multicoloured . . . . 13·00 12·00

347 I.L.Y. Emblem

1992. International Literacy Year (1990).
1299 **347** 50f. blue and brown . . 90 55
1300 100f. blue and yellow . . 1·80 1·10
1301 150f. blue and mauve . . 2·50 1·60

348 Doves and National Flag

1992. 31st National Day (1302) and 1st Anniv of Liberation (1303).
1302 **348** 50f. black, green and red 50 30
1303 – 150f. multicoloured . . . 1·60 1·00
MS1304 120 × 99 mm. No. 1302 × 2; No. 1303 × 2 . . . . 4·50 4·00
DESIGN: 150f. Assisting nations' flags.

349 Dromedaries

1992.
1305 **349** 25f. multicoloured . . . 30 30
1306 50f. multicoloured . . . 65 65
1307 150f. multicoloured . . . 1·90 1·90
1308 200f. multicoloured . . . 2·40 2·40
1309 350f. multicoloured . . . 4·50 4·50

350 Paddle, La Giralda Tower and Kuwaiti Pavilion

1992. "Expo '92" World's Fair, Seville. Multicoloured.
1310 50f. Type **350** 50 50
1311 50f. Dhows 50 50
1312 50f. Dhow 50 50
1313 50f. Kuwaiti Pavilion and dhow 50 50
1314 150f. Kuwaiti Pavilion on Spanish flag . . . . . . 1·40 1·40
1315 150f. Paddle and La Giralda Tower on hoist of Kuwaiti flag . . . . . . 1·40 1·40
1316 150f. Paddle, La Giralda Tower and dhow on Spanish flag . . . . . . 1·40 1·40
1317 150f. Kuwaiti Pavilion and dhow on fly of Kuwaiti flag . . . . 1·40 1·40
MS1318 120 × 169 mm. Nos. 1310/17 . . . . 7·75 7·75

351 Snake around Top of Palm Tree

1992. 2nd U.N. Conference on Environment and Development, Rio de Janeiro, Brazil. Mult.
1319 150f. Type **351** . . . . . . 1·60 1·00
1320 150f. Snakes, Kuwait colours on map and palm tree . . . . 1·60 1·00
1321 150f. Skull, snake around tree trunk and dead fish 1·60 1·00
1322 150f. Snake around camel's neck and bird . . . . . 1·60 1·00
MS1323 121 × 101 mm. Nos. 1319/22 . . . . 7·75 7·25
Nos. 1319/22 were issued together, se-tenant, forming a composite design of the painting "Environmental Terrorism".

352 Palace of Justice

1992.
1324 **352** 25f. multicoloured . . . 25 15
1325 50f. multicoloured . . . 55 30
1326 100f. multicoloured . . . 1·00 65
1327 150f. multicoloured . . . 1·60 95
1328 250f. multicoloured . . . 2·50 1·60

353 Running and Handball

1992. Olympic Games, Barcelona. Multicoloured.
1329 50f. Swimming and football 80 50
1330 100f. Type **353** . . . . . . 1·60 95
1331 150f. Judo and show jumping . . . . 2·40 1·50
Each value also portrays the Olympic flag and Prince Fahed al-Ahmad al-Sabah, President of several sports organizations, who was killed in the Iraqi invasion.

354 Tanks, Demonstrators with Placards and Executed Civilians

1992. 2nd Anniv of Iraqi Invasion. Children's Drawings. Multicoloured.
1332 50f. Type **354** 50 50
1333 50f. Soldiers rounding up civilians 50 50
1334 50f. Military vehicles and Kuwait Towers 50 50
1335 50f. Battle scene 50 50
1336 150f. Tanks, bleeding eye and soldiers . . . . . . 1·40 1·40
1337 150f. Battle scene around fortifications . . . . . . 1·40 1·40
1338 150f. Liberation . . . . . . 1·40 1·40
1339 150f. Soldiers and military vehicles . . . . 1·40 1·40
MS1340 121 × 171 mm. Nos. 1332/9 7·25 6·75

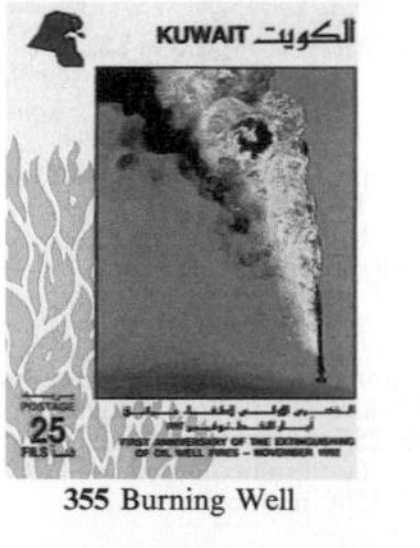
355 Burning Well

1992. 1st Anniv of Extinguishing of Oil Well Fires. Multicoloured.
1341 25f. Type **355** 25 25
1342 50f. Spraying dampener on fire 50 50
1343 150f. Close-up of spraying 1·40 1·40
1344 250f. Extinguished well (horiz) . . . . 2·40 2·40

356 Kuwait Towers

357 Laying Bricks to form "32"

1993.
1345 **356** 25f. multicoloured . . . 25 25
1346 100f. multicoloured . . . 90 90
1347 150f. multicoloured . . . 1·40 1·40

1993. 32nd National Day.
1348 **357** 25f. multicoloured . . . 25 25
1349 50f. multicoloured . . . 50 50
1350 150f. multicoloured . . . 1·40 1·40

358 Symbols of Oppression and Freedom

359 Hands Signing

1993. 2nd Anniv of Liberation.
1351 **358** 25f. multicoloured . . . 25 25
1352 50f. multicoloured . . . 50 50
1353 150f. multicoloured . . . 1·40 1·40

1993. Deaf Child Week.
1354 **359** 25f. multicoloured . . . 25 25
1355 50f. multicoloured . . . 50 50
1356 150f. multicoloured . . . 1·40 1·40
1357 350f. multicoloured . . . 3·25 3·25

360 Chained Prisoner

361 Hand scratching Map

1993. Campaign to Free Kuwaiti Prisoners of War. Multicoloured.
1358 50f. Type **360** 50 50
1359 150f. Chained hand, hoopoe and barred window (horiz) . . . . 1·40 1·40
1360 200f. Screaming face on wall of empty cell . . . . . . 1·80 1·80

1993. 3rd Anniv of Iraqi Invasion.
1361 **361** 50f. multicoloured . . . 40 40
1362 150f. multicoloured . . . 1·40 1·40

362 Emblem

1993. 40th Anniv of Kuwait Air Force.
1363 **362** 50f. multicoloured . . . 40 40
1364 150f. multicoloured . . . 1·40 1·40

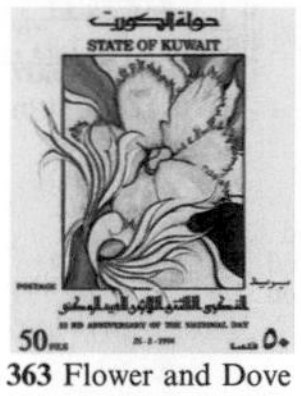
363 Flower and Dove

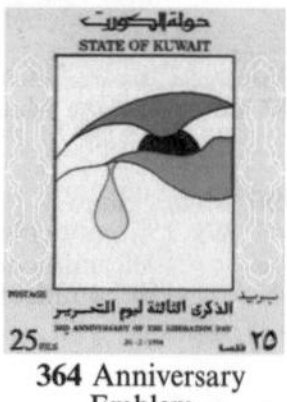
364 Anniversary Emblem

1994. 33rd National Day.
1365 **363** 25f. multicoloured . . . 25 25
1366 50f. multicoloured . . . 50 50
1367 150f. multicoloured . . . 1·40 1·40

1994. 3rd Anniv of Liberation.
1368 **364** 25f. multicoloured . . . 25 25
1369 50f. multicoloured . . . 50 50
1370 150f. multicoloured . . . 1·40 1·40

365 Anniversary Emblem

366 Stylized Emblems

1994. 25th Anniv of Central Bank of Kuwait.
1371 **365** 25f. multicoloured . . . 25 25
1372 50f. multicoloured . . . 50 50
1373 150f. multicoloured . . . 1·50 1·50

1994. Int Year of the Family. Mult.
1374 50f. Type **366** 50 50
1375 150f. Three I.Y.F. emblems 1·50 1·50
1376 200f. Globe, emblem and spheres (horiz) . . . . . 2·00 2·00

367 Emblem on Sky

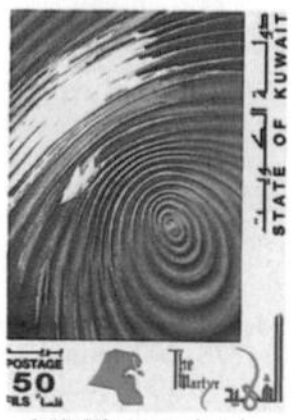
368 Fingerprint in Water

1994. 20th Anniv of Industrial Bank of Kuwait.
1377 **367** 50f. multicoloured . . . 50 50
1378 100f. gold, blue and black 95 95
1379 150f. multicoloured . . . 1·50 1·50

1994. Martyrs' Day. Multicoloured.
1380 50f. Type **368** 50 50
1381 100f. Fingerprint in sand . . 95 95
1382 150f. Fingerprint in national colours . . . . 1·50 1·50
1383 250f. Fingerprint in clouds over Kuwait Towers . . . 2·40 2·40
MS1384 91 × 111 mm. Nos. 1380/3 5·25 5·25

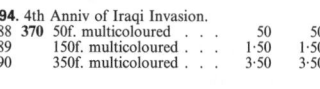

369 Anniversary Emblem

370 Free and Imprisoned Doves

1994. 75th Anniv of I.L.O.
1385 **369** 50f. multicoloured . . . 50 50
1386 150f. multicoloured . . . 1·50 1·50
1387 350f. gold, blue and black . . . . 3·50 3·50

1994. 4th Anniv of Iraqi Invasion.
1388 **370** 50f. multicoloured . . . 50 50
1389 150f. multicoloured . . . 1·50 1·50
1390 350f. multicoloured . . . 3·50 3·50

371 Emblem

372 Anniversary Emblem

1994. Kuwait Ports Authority.
1391 **371** 50f. multicoloured . . . 50 50
1392 150f. multicoloured . . . 1·50 1·50
1393 350f. multicoloured . . . 3·50 3·50

1994. 20th Anniv of Kuwait Science Club.
1394 **372** 50f. multicoloured . . . 50 50
1395 100f. multicoloured . . . 95 95
1396 150f. multicoloured . . . 1·50 1·50

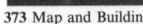

373 Map and Building

374 I.C.A.O. and Kuwait International Airport Emblems

1994. Inauguration of Arab Towns Organization Permanent Headquarters. Multicoloured.
1397 50f. Type **373** 50 50
1398 100f. Close-up of arched facade 95 95
1399 150f. Door . . . . 1·50 1·50

1994. 50th Anniv of I.C.A.O. Mult.
1400 100f. Type **374** . . . . . . 1·00 1·00
1401 150f. Emblems and control tower . . . . 1·50 1·50
1402 350f. Airplane and "50 years" . . . . 3·50 3·50

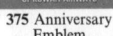

375 Anniversary Emblem

376 Family

1994. 40th Anniv of Kuwait Airways.
1403 **375** 50f. multicoloured . . . 50 50
1404 100f. multicoloured . . . 95 95
1405 150f. multicoloured . . . 1·50 1·50

1995. Population Census.
1406 **376** 50f. multicoloured . . . 50 50
1407 100f. multicoloured . . . 95 95
1408 150f. multicoloured . . . 1·50 1·50

377 Children waving Flags

378 Falcon dragging Kuwaiti Flag from Snake's Grip

1995. 34th National Day.
1409 **377** 25f. multicoloured . . . 25 25
1410 50f. multicoloured . . . 50 50
1411 150f. multicoloured . . . 1·50 1·50

1995. 4th Anniv of Liberation.
1412 **378** 25f. multicoloured . . . 25 25
1413 50f. multicoloured . . . 50 50
1414 150f. multicoloured . . . 1·50 1·50

379 Conference Venue

1995. International Medical Conference. Mult.
1415 50f. Type **379** 50 50
1416 100f. Lecture 95 95
1417 150f. Emblem on map of Kuwait in national colours . . . . 1·50 1·50

380 Anniversary Emblem and Flags

381 Emblem

1995. 50th Anniv of Arab League. Multicoloured.
1418 50f. Type **380** 50 50
1419 100f. Kuwaiti and League flags and League emblem (horiz) 95 95
1420 150f. Handshake and League emblem . . . . . 1·50 1·50

1995. World Health Day. "A World without Polio".
1421 **381** 50f. multicoloured . . . 50 50
1422 150f. multicoloured . . . 1·50 1·50
1423 200f. multicoloured . . . 2·00 2·00

382 "100"

383 Olive Branch falling from Wounded Dove's Beak

1995. Centenary of Volleyball.
1424 **382** 50f. multicoloured . . . 50 50
1425 100f. multicoloured . . . 1·00 1·00
1426 150f. multicoloured . . . 1·50 1·50

1995. 5th Anniv of Iraqi Invasion.
1427 **383** 50f. multicoloured . . . 50 50
1428 100f. multicoloured . . . 1·00 1·00
1429 150f. multicoloured . . . 1·50 1·50

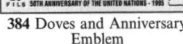

384 Doves and Anniversary Emblem

385 Farmer with Animals

1995. 50th Anniv of U.N.O.
1430 **384** 25f. multicoloured . . . 25 25
1431 50f. multicoloured . . . 50 50
1432 150f. multicoloured . . . 1·50 1·50

1995. 50th Anniv of F.A.O. Multicoloured.
1433 50f. Type **385** 50 50
1434 100f. Fish market . . . . . 1·00 1·00
1435 150f. Agriculture . . . . . 1·50 1·50
MS1436 120 × 70 mm. Nos. 1433/5 3·00 3·00

386 Emblems within Ruler

387 "Onobrychis ptolemaica"

1995. World Standards Day. Multicoloured.
1437 50f. Type **386** 50 50
1438 100f. Emblems and aspects of industry (48 × 27 mm) 1·00 1·00
1439 150f. As No. 1438 . . . . . 1·50 1·50

1995. Flowers. Multicoloured.
1440 5f. Type **387** 10 10
1441 15f. "Convolvulus oxyphyllus" 25 25
1442 25f. Corn poppy 50 50
1443 50f. "Moltkiopsis ciliata" . . 80 80
1444 150f. "Senecio desfontainei" 2·40 2·40

388 Coins forming Map of Kuwait

389 Boy Scout in Watchtower

1996. Money Show.
1445 **388** 25f. multicoloured . . . 25 25
1446 100f. multicoloured . . . 95 95
1447 150f. multicoloured . . . 1·40 1·40

1996. 60th Anniv of Scout Movement in Kuwait. Multicoloured.
1448 50f. Type **389** 65 65
1449 100f. Scout drawing water from well . . . . 1·40 1·40
1450 150f. Scouts planting sapling 2·00 2·00

390 Hands supporting Ear of Wheat

391 Saker Falcon trailing National Colours, Falcon and City

1996.
1451 **390** 50f. multicoloured . . . 50 50
1452 100f. multicoloured . . . 95 95
1453 150f. multicoloured . . . 1·50 1·50

1996. 35th National Day.
1454 **391** 25f. multicoloured . . . 25 25
1455 50f. multicoloured . . . 50 50
1456 150f. multicoloured . . . 1·40 1·40

392 Horses

393 View through Gateway

1996. 5th Anniv of Liberation.
1457 **392** 25f. multicoloured . . . 25 25
1458 50f. multicoloured . . . 50 50
1459 150f. multicoloured . . . 1·40 1·40

1996. Arab City Day.
1460 **393** 50f. multicoloured . . . 50 50
1461 100f. multicoloured . . . 95 95
1462 150f. multicoloured . . . 1·50 1·50

394 Emblem

395 Figures holding Open Book within Bird

1996. 7th Kuwait Dental Association Conference.
1463 **394** 25f. multicoloured . . . 25 25
1464 50f. multicoloured . . . 50 50
1465 150f. multicoloured . . . 1·40 1·40

1996. 50th Anniv of UNESCO.
1466 **395** 25f. multicoloured . . . 25 25
1467 100f. multicoloured . . . 95 95
1468 150f. multicoloured . . . 1·40 1·40

396 Flags, Anniversary Emblem and Tanker

397 Shaikh Mubarak al-Sabah

1996. 50th Anniv of First Oil Shipment from Kuwait.
1469 **396** 25f. multicoloured . . . 25 25
1470 100f. multicoloured . . . 95 95
1471 150f. multicoloured . . . 1·40 1·40

1996. Centenary of Accession as Emir of Shaikh Mubarak al-Sabah. Multicoloured.
1472 25f. Type **397** 25 25
1473 50f. Shaikh Mubarak al-Sabah and ribbons . . . 50 50
1474 150f. Type **397** . . . . . . 1·40 1·40

398 Rifle Shooting

399 Festival Emblem

1996. Olympic Games, Atlanta. Multicoloured.
1475 25f. Type **398** 25 25
1476 50f. Running 50 50
1477 100f. Weightlifting 95 95
1478 150f. Fencing . . . . 1·50 1·50

1996. National Council for Culture, Art and Letters. First Children's Cultural Festival.
1479 **399** 25f. multicoloured . . . 25 25
1480 100f. multicoloured . . . 95 95
1481 150f. multicoloured . . . 1·40 1·40

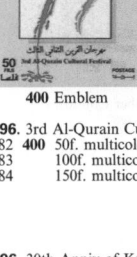

400 Emblem

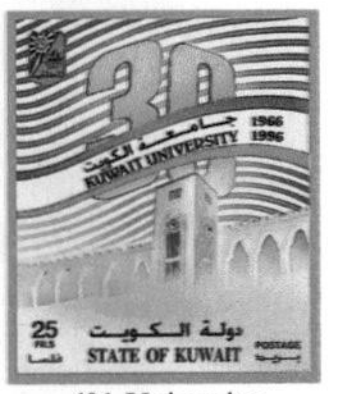

401 University

1996. 3rd Al-Qurain Cultural Festival.
1482 **400** 50f. multicoloured . . . 50 50
1483 100f. multicoloured . . . 95 95
1484 150f. multicoloured . . . 1·50 1·50

1996. 30th Anniv of Kuwait University.
1485 **401** 25f. multicoloured . . . 25 25
1486 100f. multicoloured . . . 95 95
1487 150f. multicoloured . . . 1·40 1·40

402 Liberation Tower

403 Sehel's Grey Mullet

1996.
1488 **402** 5f. multicoloured 10 10
1489 10f. multicoloured . . . 15 15
1490 15f. multicoloured . . . 25 25
1491 25f. multicoloured . . . 30 30
1492 50f. multicoloured . . . 70 70
1493 100f. multicoloured . . . 1·40 1·40
1494 150f. multicoloured . . . 2·10 2·10
1495 200f. multicoloured . . . 2·75 2·75
1496 250f. multicoloured . . . 3·50 3·50
1497 350f. multicoloured . . . 4·75 4·75

1997. Marine Life. Multicoloured. (a) Fishes.
1498 25f. Type **403** 25 25
1499 50f. Yellow-finned seabream 50 50
1500 100f. Greasy grouper . . . 95 95
1501 150f. Silver-backed seabream 1·50 1·50
1502 200f. Silver grunt . . . . . 1·90 1·90
1503 350f. Silver pomfret . . . . . 3·50 3·50

(b) Shrimps.
1504 25f. Tail and body segments of shrimps 25 25
1505 25f. Head and body segments of shrimps . . . 25 25
1506 25f. Underside of fish and body and legs of shrimp 25 25
1507 25f. Head of shrimp, fish and body and legs of shrimp 25 25
1508 50f. Tail and body segments of two shrimps 50 50
1509 50f. Legs and body segments of shrimp 50 50
1510 50f. Body segments of shrimp and fish 50 50
1511 50f. Head of shrimp, seaweed and body and legs of shrimp 95 95
1512 100f. Tail and body segments of two shrimps 95 95
1513 100f. Head, legs and body segments of shrimps . . . 95 95
1514 100f. Body of shrimp . . . 95 95
1515 100f. Part of head, legs, tail and body of three shrimps 95 95
1516 150f. Body segments of two shrimps and upper half of fish . . . . 1·50 1·50
1517 150f. Front part of bodies of two shrimps and tail of fish . . . . 1·50 1·50
1518 150f. Heads of two shrimps, complete shrimp and fish 1·50 1·50
1519 150f. Body segments of two shrimps and front part of shrimps head . . . . . 1·50 1·50

Nos. 1504/19 were issued together, se-tenant, forming a composite design of shrimps in a marine environment.

404 Flag, Cupped Hands and Sunflower

1997. 36th National Day.
1520 **404** 25f. multicoloured . . . 25 25
1521 50f. multicoloured . . . 50 50
1522 150f. multicoloured . . . 1·40 1·40

405 Flag, rejoicing Crowd and Shaikh Jabir

1997. 6th Anniv of Liberation.
1523 **405** 25f. multicoloured . . . 25 25
1524 50f. multicoloured . . . 50 50
1525 150f. multicoloured . . . 1·40 1·40

406 Emblem **407** Emblem

1997. 10th Anniv of Montreal Protocol (on reduction of use of chlorofluorocarbons).
1526 **406** 25f. multicoloured . . . 25 25
1527 50f. multicoloured . . . 50 50
1528 150f. multicoloured . . . 1·50 1·50

1997. Kuwait Industries Exhibition.
1529 **407** 25f. multicoloured . . . 25 25
1530 50f. multicoloured . . . 50 50
1531 150f. multicoloured . . . 1·50 1·50

408 Signs of Zodiac and Whale

1997. 25th Anniv of Educational Science Museum.
1532 25f. Type **408** 25 25
1533 50f. Space shuttle orbiting Earth, whale, astronaut and dinosaur (horiz) . . . 50 50
1534 150f. Symbols of past, present and future around whale . . . . 1·50 1·50
MS1535 100 × 75 mm. 150f. Coelacanth (horiz) . . . . . . 9·75 9·75

409 National Council for Culture, Arts and Letters Emblem

1997. 22nd Kuwait Arabic Book Exhbition.
1536 **409** 25f. multicoloured . . . 25 25
1537 50f. multicoloured . . . 50 50
1538 150f. multicoloured . . . 1·50 1·50

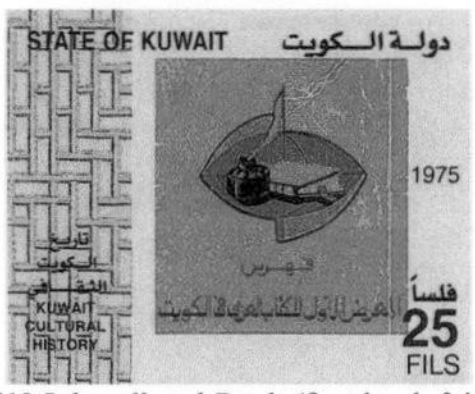

410 Ink-well and Book (first book fair, 1975)

1997. Kuwait Cultural History.
1539 25f. Type **410** 25 25
1540 25f. Front page of "Kuwait Magazine" (1928) 25 25
1541 25f. Front page "A'lam al-Fikr" (periodical) (1970) 25 25
1542 25f. Pyramids and dhow ("Al'Bitha" magazine, 1946) 25 25
1543 25f. Rising sun over open book and quill ("Al'am al Ma'rifa" (periodical), 1978) 25 25
1544 25f. Book with dhow on front cover ("Dalil Almohtar Fi Alaam Al-Bihar", 1923) 25 25
1545 25f. Arabic script and "brick" design ("Al-Arabi" magazine, 1958) 25 25
1546 25f. Open book (inauguration of first public library, 1923) . . . 25 25
1547 25f. Two covers showing Arabic script in boxes and cosmic explosion ("Al Thaqafa Al-Alamiya" (periodical), 1981) 25 25
1548 25f. Actors and curtain ("The World Theatre" (periodical), 1969) 25 25
1549 50f. Entrance to Qibliya Girls' School (1937) . . . 40 30
1550 50f. Scissors cutting ribbon (first Fine Arts Exhibition, 1959) 40 30
1551 50f. Mubarakiya School (1912) 40 30
1552 50f. Family entering Kuwait National Museum (1958) 40 30
1553 50f. Shuwaikh Secondary School (1953) 40 30
1554 50f. Door and three windows (Al-Marsam Al-Hor, 1959) 40 30
1555 50f. Decorated screen (Alma'had Aldini, 1947) 40 30
1556 50f. Courtyard of Folklore Centre (1956) 40 30
1557 50f. Three columns of Arabic script (Al Ma'arif printing press, 1947) . . . 40 30
1558 50f. Class photograph (Literary Club, 1924) . . 40 30
1559 150f. Heads and curtains (Folk Theatre Group, 1956) . . . . 1·60 1·00
1560 150f. Musical instruments and notes (Academy of Music, 1972) . . . . . . 1·60 1·00
1561 150f. Film frames, audience and camera (opening of Al-Sharqiya cinema, 1955) 1·60 1·00
1562 150f. Curtains around couple at oasis (Theatrical Academy, 1967) . . . . . 1·60 1·00
1563 150f. Marine views in film frame ("Bas Ya Bahar" (first Kuwaiti feature film), 1970) . . . . 1·60 1·00

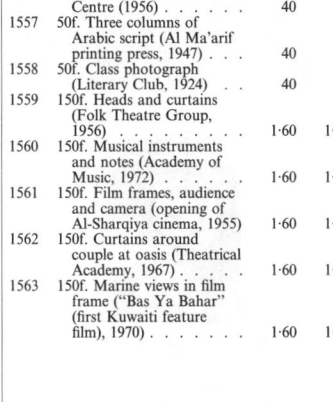

411 Doves flying over Members' Flags

1997. 18th Gulf Co-operation Council Summit, Kuwait. Multicoloured.
1564 25f. Type **411** 30 30
1565 50f. Members' flags forming doves wheeling over map (horiz) 65 65
1566 150f. Doves perched atop wall of members' flags . . 1·90 1·90

412 State Flag

1998. 37th National Day.
1567 **412** 25f. multicoloured . . . 30 30
1568 50f. multicoloured . . . 65 65
1569 150f. multicoloured . . . 1·90 1·90

413 Flag, Map and Dove

1998. 7th Anniv of Liberation.
1570 **413** 25f. multicoloured . . . 30 30
1571 50f. multicoloured . . . 65 65
1572 150f. multicoloured . . . 1·90 1·90

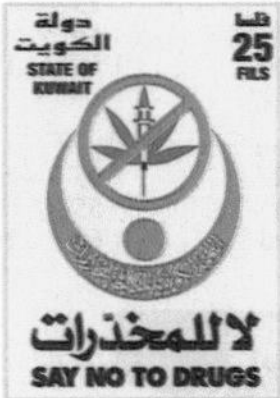

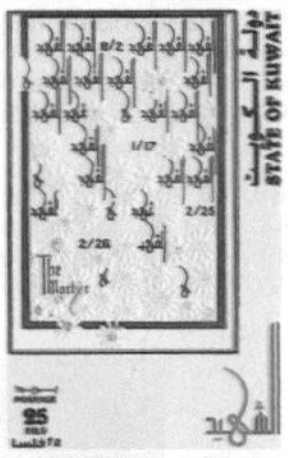

414 Emblem **415** Text on Open Page with Flowers

1998. Anti-drugs Campaign.
1573 **414** 25f. multicoloured . . . 30 30
1574 50f. multicoloured . . . 65 65
1575 150f. multicoloured . . . 1·90 1·90

1998. Martyrs' Day. Multicoloured.
1576 25f. Type **415** 30 30
1577 50f. Tree 65 65
1578 150f. Calligraphy . . . . . 1·90 1·90
MS1579 60 × 54 mm. 500f. Shaikh Jabir; 500f. People of Kuwait 13·00 13·00

416 Woman selling Cooked Vegetables **417** Child's Face

1998. Life in Pre-Oil Kuwait (1st series). Mult.
1580 25f. Type **416** 30 20
1581 50f. Ship-building 65 50
1582 100f. Sailor strapping his box . . . . 1·30 1·00
1583 150f. Pearl divers wading out to boat . . . . 2·00 1·80
1584 250f. Delivering fresh water 3·50 2·30
1585 350f. Pigeon trainer . . . . 4·50 3·25
See also Nos. 1599/604.

1998. 12th Anniv of Chernobyl Nuclear Disaster.
1586 **417** 25f. multicoloured . . . 30 30
1587 50f. multicoloured . . . 65 65
1588 150f. multicoloured . . . 1·90 1·90

418 World Map and Emblem

1998. International Year of the Ocean. Multicoloured.
1589 25f. Type **418** 30 30
1590 50f. Motifs as in Type **418** but differently arranged in rectangle (27 × 37 mm) . . 65 65
1591 150f. Type **418** . . . . . . 1·90 1·90

419 Emblem

1998. 25th Anniv of Union of Consumer Co-operative Societies. Multicoloured.
1592 **419** 25f. multicoloured . . . 25 25
1593 50f. multicoloured . . . 55 55
1594 150f. multicoloured . . . 1·80 1·80

420 Men on Crutches

1998. Anti-landmine Campaign. Details from painting by Jafar Islah. Multicoloured.
1595 25f. Type **420** 25 25
1596 50f. Man on crutch 55 55
1597 150f. Man on crutches and woman helping child . . 1·80 1·80
MS1598 96 × 89 mm. 500f. Motifs of Nos. 1596/7 . . . . 5·75 5·75

1998. Life in Pre-Oil Kuwait (2nd series). As T **416**. Multicoloured.
1599 25f. Hairdresser 30 25
1600 50f. Hand-grinding 55 40
1601 100f. Tailor . . . . 1·10 60
1602 150f. Artist . . . . 1·60 1·00
1603 250f. Potter . . . . 2·75 1·30
1604 350f. Hand-spinning . . . . 4·00 1·90

421 New Postal Emblem

1998.
1605 **421** 25f. multicoloured . . . 25 20
1606 50f. multicoloured . . . 55 30
1607 100f. multicoloured . . . 1·00 60
1608 150f. multicoloured . . . 1·60 1·00
1609 250f. multicoloured . . . 2·50 1·80

422 Child's Painting

1998. Children's Cultural House.
1610 **422** 25f. multicoloured . . . 25 25
1611 50f. multicoloured . . . 55 55
1612 150f. multicoloured . . . 1·60 1·60

423 Collage **424** Falcon

1998. 50th Anniv of Universal Declaration of Human Rights.
1613 **423** 25f. multicoloured . . . 25 25
1614 50f. multicoloured . . . 55 55
1615 150f. multicoloured . . . 1·60 1·60

1998.
1616 25f. Type **424** 50 50
1617 50f. Young camels 95 95
1618 150f. Dhow . . . . 2·50 2·50

425 Emblem

1998. 25th Anniv of Public Authority for Applied Education and Training.
1619 **425** 25f. multicoloured . . . 25 25
1620 50f. multicoloured . . . 50 50
1621 150f. multicoloured . . . 1·40 1·40

426 Entrance and Palm Trees

1999. Seif Palace. Different views of the Palace. Mult.
1622 25f. Type **426** 15 15
1623 50f. Palace buildings 40 30
1624 100f. Tower 80 50
1625 150f. Type **426** . . . . . 1·30 70
1626 250f. As No. 1623 . . . . . 2·10 1·20
1627 350f. As No. 1624 . . . . . 3·00 1·90

427 "38"

1999. 38th National Day.
1628 **427** 50f. multicoloured . . . 40 40
1629 150f. multicoloured . . . 1·20 1·20

428 Building, Dove and "8"

1999. 8th Anniv of Liberation.
1630 **428** 50f. multicoloured . . . 40 40
1631 150f. multicoloured . . . 1·20 1·20

429 Liver and Kuwait Flag

1999. 20th Anniv of Organ Transplantation in Kuwait. Multicoloured.
1632 50f. Type **429** 40 40
1633 150f. Heart and Kuwait flag 1·20 1·20

430 Emblem and Kuwait Flag

432 "2000" and Emblem

431 Emblem

1999. 40th Anniv of *Al-Arabi* (magazine).
1634 **430** 50f. multicoloured . . . 40 40
1635 150f. multicoloured . . . 1·20 1·20

2000. International Civil Aviation Day.
1636 **431** 50f. multicoloured . . . 50 50
1637 150f. multicoloured . . . 1·50 1·50
1638 250f. multicoloured . . . 2·40 2·40

2000. Kuwait International Airport.
1639 **432** 50f. multicoloured . . . 50 50
1640 150f. multicoloured . . . 1·50 1·50
1641 250f. multicoloured . . . 2·40 2·40

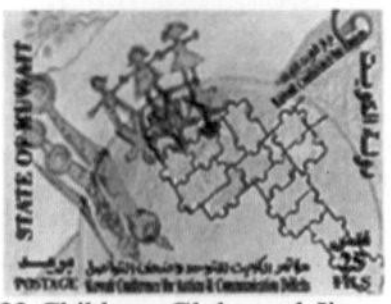

433 Children, Globe and Jigsaw Pieces

2000. International Conference on Autism and Communication Deficiencies, Kuwait. Children's paintings. Multicoloured.
1642 25f. Type **433** 25 25
1643 50f. Globe and children . . 55 55
1644 150f. Children holding hands . . . . 1·60 1·60

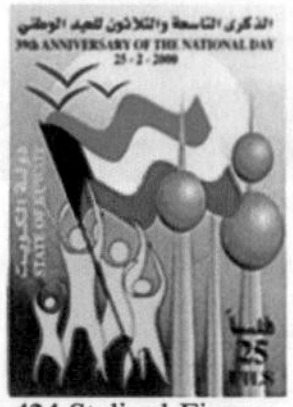

434 Stylized Figures and Flag

435 State Flag

2000. 39th National Day.
1645 **434** 25f. multicoloured . . . 25 25
1646 50f. multicoloured . . . 55 55
1647 150f. multicoloured . . . 1·60 1·60

2000. 9th Anniv of Liberation.
1648 **435** 25f. multicoloured . . . 25 25
1649 50f. multicoloured . . . 55 55
1650 150f. multicoloured . . . 1·60 1·60

436 Emblem

2000. 25th Anniv (1999) of Kuwait Science Club.
1651 **436** 50f. multicoloured . . . 50 50
1652 150f. multicoloured . . . 1·50 1·50
1653 350f. multicoloured . . . 3·50 3·50

437 Emblem

2000. International Investment Forum, Kuwait.
1654 **437** 25f. multicoloured . . . 25 25
1655 50f. multicoloured . . . 55 55
1656 150f. multicoloured . . . 1·60 1·60

438 View over City

439 Emblem and Hand holding Scroll

2000. Kuwait City.
1657 **438** 50f. multicoloured . . . 40 40
1658 150f. multicoloured . . . 1·10 1·10
1659 350f. multicoloured . . . 2·50 2·50

2000. 3rd Private Education Week.
1660 **439** 50f. multicoloured . . . 40 40
1661 150f. multicoloured . . . 1·10 1·10
1662 350f. multicoloured . . . 2·50 2·50

440 Emblem and Stamps Encircling Globe

2000. 125th Anniv of Universal Postal Union.
1663 **440** 50f. multicoloured . . . 40 40
1664 150f. multicoloured . . . 1·10 1·10
1665 350f. multicoloured . . . 2·50 2·50
MS1666 100 × 75 mm. 1d. Stamps encircling globes . . . . 7·25 7·25

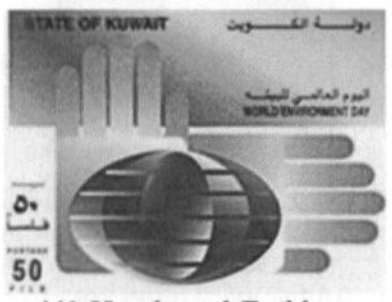

441 Hands and Emblem

2000. World Environment Day.
1667 **441** 50f. multicoloured . . . 40 40
1668 150f. multicoloured . . . 1·10 1·10
1669 350f. multicoloured . . . 2·50 2·50

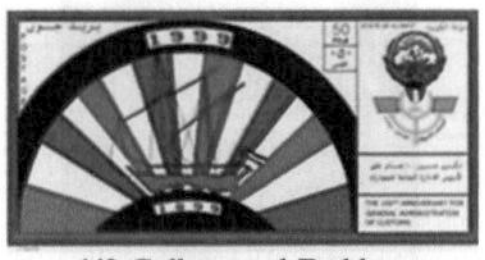

442 Galleon and Emblem

2000. Cent of General Customs' Administration.
1670 **442** 50f. multicoloured . . . 40 40
1671 150f. multicoloured . . . 1·10 1·10
1672 350f. multicoloured . . . 2·50 2·50
MS1673 100 × 5 mm. **442** 1d. multicoloured . . . . 7·25 7·25

443 Emblem

2000. 10th Anniv of Committee for Missing and Prisoners of War Affairs. Multicoloured.
1674 25f. Type **443** 15 15
1675 50f. Emblem and chains . . 40 40
1676 150f. Emblem forming "10" 1·00 1·00

444 Kick-boxing and Emblem

2000. Olympic Games, Sydney. Multicoloured.
1677 25f. Type **444** 15 15
1678 50f. Shooting 40 20
1679 150f. Swimming . . . . . . 1·10 60
1680 200f. Weight-lifting . . . . 1·50 85
1681 250f. Running . . . . . . 1·90 1·00
1682 350f. Football . . . . . . 2·50 1·60

A 1d. imperforate miniature sheet, the design consisting of the emblem and pictograms as depicted on the stamps, exists in a cover inscribed "With the Compliments of Ministry of Communications - Post Sector".

445 Emblem and Outline of Tooth

2000. 25th Anniv of Kuwait Dental Association.
1683 **445** 50f. multicoloured . . . 40 40
1684 150f. multicoloured . . . 1·10 1·10
1685 350f. multicoloured . . . 2·50 2·50

446 Emblem

2000. 6th Gulf Cooperation Council (G.C.C.) Joint Stamp Exhibition, Kuwait.
1686 **446** 25f. multicoloured . . . 25 25
1687 50f. multicoloured . . . 55 55
1688 150f. multicoloured . . . 1·60 1·60
MS1689 146 × 111 mm. 1d. Emblems of current and previous exhibitions. Imperf . . . . . . 6·50 6·50

447 Building and "15" in Laurel Wreath

2000. 15th Anniv of Gulf Investment Corporation and Inauguration of New Headquarters Building. Multicoloured.
1690 25f. Type **447** 25 25
1691 50f. Building in centre with "15" at left 55 55
1692 150f. Building at right with "15" in centre . . . . . 1·60 1·60

448 Letters and Book

2000. National Council for Culture, Arts and Letters.
1693 **448** 25f. multicoloured . . . 25 25
1694 50f. multicoloured . . . 55 55
1695 150f. multicoloured . . . 1·60 1·60
MS1695a **448** 500f. multicoloured (85 × 95 mm) . . . . 4·75 4·75

449 Map and Emblems

2001. Arab Cultural Capital.
1696 **449** 25f. multicoloured . . . 25 25
1697 50f. multicoloured . . . 55 55
1698 150f. multicoloured . . . 1·60 1·60

450 Emblem

451 Anniversary Emblem

2001. "Long Live February".
1699 **450** 25f. multicoloured . . . 25 25
1700 50f. multicoloured . . . 55 55
1701 150f. multicoloured . . . 1·60 1·60

2001. 40th Anniv of National Day.
1702 **451** 25f. multicoloured . . . 25 25
1703 50f. multicoloured . . . 55 55
1704 150f. multicoloured . . . 1·60 1·60

452 Doves

453 Buildings

2001. 10th Anniv of Liberation Day.
1705 **452** 25f. multicoloured . . . 25 25
1706 50f. multicoloured . . . 55 55
1707 150f. multicoloured . . . 1·60 1·60

2001. 40th Anniv of Kuwait Fund For Arab Economic Development.
1708 **453** 25f. multicoloured . . . 25 25
1709 50f. multicoloured . . . 55 55

454 Anniversary Emblem

2001. 50th Anniv of United Nations Commissioner for Refugees. Multicoloured.
1710 25f. Type **454** 25 25
1711 50f. Anniversary emblem (vertical blue band) . . . 55 55
1712 150f. Anniversary emblem (different) . . . . 1·60 1·60

455 Pierced Flag

2001. Prisoners.
1713 **455** 25f. multicoloured . . . 25 25
1714 50f. multicoloured . . . 55 55
1715 150f. multicoloured . . . 1·60 1·60

456 Anniversary Emblem

2001. 50th Anniv of Radio Kuwait.

1716	**456**	25f. multicoloured . . .	25	25
1717		50f. multicoloured (vert)	55	55
1718		150f. multicoloured (vert)	1·60	1·60

457 Mosque and Colours

2001. Al Aqsa Uprising. Multicoloured.

1719	25f. Type **457**	25	25
1720	50f. Mosque dome and uprising	55	55
1721	150f. Mosque dome and uprising (different) . . .	1·60	1·60

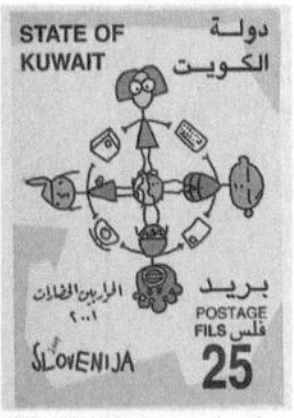

458 Children encircling Globe

459 Script

2001. United Nations Year of Dialogue among Civilizations.

1722	**458**	25f. multicoloured . . .	25	25
1723		50f. multicoloured . . .	55	55
1724		150f. multicoloured . . .	1·60	1·60

2001. Heritage Management Foundation. Multicoloured.

1725	25f. Type **459**	25	25
1726	50f. Sheikh Abdulla	55	55
1727	150f. Sheikh Jabir	1·60	1·60

460 Stylised Tree with Nine Leaves

461 Face covered by Hands

2001. 25th Anniv of Tourism Enterprise. Multicoloured.

1728	25f. Type **460**	25	20
1729	50f. Twig with six long leaves	55	40
1730	100f. Many-branched tree with falling leaves	1·20	60
1731	150f. Tree with two branches	1·60	90
MS1732	60 × 80 mm. 250f. As Nos. 1728/31. Imperf	2·75	2·75

2001. Human Rights. Multicoloured.

1733	25f. Type **461**	25	25
1734	50f. Faces and barbed wire (horiz)	55	55
1735	150f. Chains, globe and child's face (horiz)	1·60	1·60

462 Metal Artefact

2001. 10th Anniv of Scientific Diving Team. Multicoloured.

1736	25f. Type **462**	25	25
1737	50f. Divers	55	55
1738	150f. Turtle (vert)	1·60	1·60

463 Original Building Facade

2002. 50th Anniv of National Bank. Multicoloured.

1739	50f. Type **463**	25	25
1740	100f. Modern building . . .	55	55
1741	150f. Anniversary emblem and camels	1·60	1·60

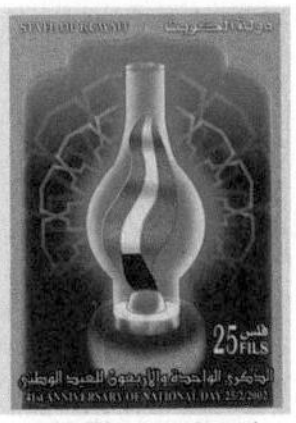

464 Flag enclosed Lamp

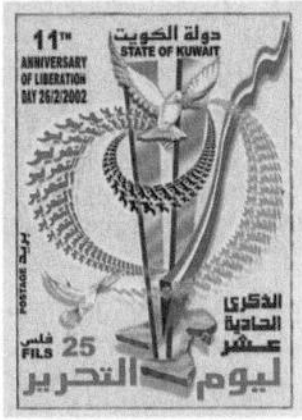

465 Monument, Doves, Flag and Map

2002. 1st Anniv of National Day. Multicoloured.

1742	**464**	25f. multicoloured . . .	25	25
1743		50f. multicoloured . . .	55	55
1744		150f. multicoloured . . .	1·60	1·60

2002. 11th Anniv of Liberation Day. Multicoloured.

1745	**465**	25f. multicoloured . . .	25	25
1746		50f. multicoloured . . .	55	55
1747		150f. multicoloured . . .	1·60	1·60

466 Camel Caravan

467 Emblem and Gas Tower

2002. Arab Nomads. Multicoloured.

1748	**466**	25f. multicoloured . . .	25	25
1749		50f. multicoloured . . .	55	55
1750		150f. multicoloured . . .	1·60	1·60

2002. Rehabilitation of Al-Qurain Landfill Site. Multicoloured.

1751	**467**	25f. multicoloured . . .	25	25
1752		50f. multicoloured . . .	55	55
1753		150f. multicoloured . . .	1·60	1·60

468 Northern Lapwing

469 Adult and Child's Hands

2002. Kuwait Scientific Centre. Multicoloured.

1754	25f. Type **468**	80	80
1755	25f. Spur-winged plover . .	80	80
1756	25f. Otter	80	80
1757	25f. Crocodile	80	80
1758	25f. Fennec fox	80	80
1759	25f. Caracal	80	80
1760	25f. Protoreaster	80	80
1761	25f. Sepia	80	80
1762	25f. Nurse shark	80	80
1763	25f. Lionfish	80	80
1764	25f. Kestrel	80	80
1765	25f. Fruit bat	80	80
1766	50f. Centre building (45 × 27 mm)	1·60	1·60
MS1767	80 × 60 mm. 250f. Dock and building. Imperf	6·00	6·00

2002. 10th Anniv of Social Development Office. Multicoloured.

1768	**469**	25f. multicoloured . . .	25	25
1769		50f. multicoloured . . .	55	55

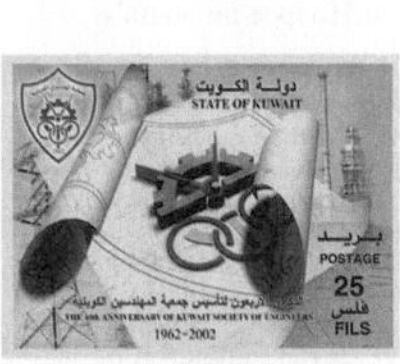

470 Engineering Symbols

2002. 40th Anniv of Society of Engineers. Multicoloured.

1770	**470**	25f. multicoloured . . .	25	25
1771		50f. multicoloured . . .	55	55
1772		150f. multicoloured . . .	1·60	1·60

471 Anniversary Emblems

2002. 25th Anniv of Science Foundation. Multicoloured.

1773	25f. Type **471**	25	25
1774	50f. Building	55	55
1775	150f. Map of Kuwait (vert)	1·60	1·60

472 Organization Emblem

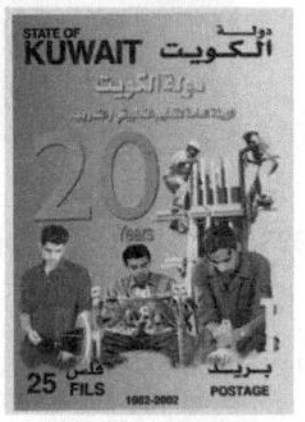

473 Engineering Workers

2002. International Year of Volunteers. KNPVC (welfare organization).

1776	**472**	25f. multicoloured . . .	25	25
1777		50f. multicoloured . . .	55	55
1778		150f. multicoloured . . .	1·60	1·60

2002. 20th Anniv of Professional Education Programme. Multicoloured.

1779	25f. Type **473**	25	25
1780	50f. Theatre nurse	55	55
1781	100f. Man checking dials . .	1·00	1·00
1782	150f. Flag and "20"	1·60	1·60
1783	250f. Emblem	2·50	2·50

474 Traditional Boat

475 Greek Ruins, Failaka Island

2003.

1784	**474**	100f. multicoloured . . .	1·20	1·20

2003. 42nd Anniv of National Day. Multicoloured.

1785	**475**	25f. multicoloured . . .	30	30
1786		50f. multicoloured . . .	65	65
1787		150f. multicoloured . . .	1·90	1·90

476 Bureau Emblem and Boat

2003. The Martyrs' Bureau. Multicoloured.

1788	25f. Type **476**	30	30
1789	50f. National flag on Qarow Island	65	65
1790	150f. Fingerprint on stone	1·90	1·90
1791	350f. "746" and map . . .	3·00	3·00

477 Leafless Tree and Dunes

2003. International Day to Combat Desertification. Multicoloured.

1792	25f. Type **477**	30	30
1793	50f. Log in valley	65	65
1794	150f. Oasis	1·90	1·90

478 Statuette

2003. Kuwait Design. Multicoloured.

1795	25f. Type **478**	30	30
1796	100f. Statuette (different) . .	1·20	1·20
1797	150f. Group of statuettes . .	1·90	1·90

479 "43" and Star

2003. 43rd Anniv of Commercial Bank. Multicoloured.

1798	25f. Type **479**	30	30
1799	50f. "43" and original building	65	65
1800	150f. "43" and modern building	1·90	1·90

480 Stylised Family

2004. 10th Anniv of Awqaf Public Foundation. Multicoloured.

1801	50f. Type **480**	65	65
1802	100f. Hand	1·20	1·20
1803	150f. Scholar and minaret	1·90	1·90

481 Palm Tree as Flag

2004. 43rd Anniv of National Day. Multicoloured.

1804	25f. Type **481**		
1805	50f. Pearl shell as flag and "43" as pearl		
1806	150f. Flags flying above gateway		
1807	350f. Boat and towers . . .		

OFFICIAL STAMPS

1923. Stamps of India (King George V) optd **KUWAIT SERVICE.**

O 1	**56**	½a. green	2·25	26·00
O 2	**57**	1a. brown	3·00	15·00
O 3	**58**	1½a. brown (No. 163) . .	3·50	38·00
O 4	**59**	2a. lilac	5·50	27·00
O17	**70**	2a. lilac	55·00	£170
O 5	**61**	2a.6p. blue	4·50	65·00
O 6	**62**	3a. orange	3·50	65·00
O19		3a. blue	4·50	£700
O 8	**63**	4a. green	3·50	6·00
O20	**71**	4a. green	4·25	2·00
O 9	**65**	8a. mauve	6·00	90·00
O22	**66**	12a. red	26·00	£170
O10	**67**	1r. brown and green . . .	18·00	£150
O11		2r. red and orange . . .	18·00	£200
O12		5r. blue and violet	75·00	£400
O13		10r. green and red	£120	£350
O14		15r. blue	£180	£475

POSTAGE DUE STAMPS

D 34

D 51

1963.

D199	**D 34**	1f. brown and black	10	25
D200		2f. lilac and black . .	25	30
D201		5f. blue and black . .	30	25
D202		8f. green and black . .	65	40
D203		10f. yellow and black	80	80
D204		25f. red and black . .	1·90	2·40

The above stamps were not sold to the public unused until 1 July 1964.

1965.

D276	**D 51**	4f. pink and yellow . .	15	25
D277		15f. red and blue . . .	55	40
D278		40f. blue and green . .	1·20	90
D279		50f. green and mauve	1·60	1·30
D280		100f. blue and yellow	3·00	2·40

KYRGYZSTAN Pt. 10

Formerly Kirghizia, a constituent republic of the Soviet Union, Kyrgyzstan became independent in 1991. Its capital Frunze reverted to its previous name of Bishkek.

1992. 100 kopeks = 1 rouble.
1993. 100 tyin = 1 som.

1 Sary-C'helek Nature Reserve

2 Golden Eagle

1992.

1 1 15k. multicoloured 15 15

1992.

2 2 50k. multicoloured 25 20

3 "Cattle at Issyk-Kule" (G. A. Aitiev)

1992.

3 3 1r. multicoloured 25 15

4 Carpet and Samovar

1992.

4 4 1r.50 multicoloured 25 15

5 Cave Paintings

1993. National Monuments. Multicoloured.
5 10k. Type **5** 10 10
6 50k. 11th-century tower, Burana (vert) 10 10
7 1r.+25k. Mausoleum of Manas, Talas (vert) 10 10
8 2r.+50k. Mausoleum, Uzgen 15 10
9 3r. Yurt 20 15
10 5r.+50k. Statue of Manas, Bishkek 35 25
11 9r. Cultural complex, Bishkek 55 35
MS12 61 × 91 mm. 10r. Cockle jewellery . . . . 1·25 1·00
The premium on Nos. 7/8 and 10 were used for the financing of a Manas museum.

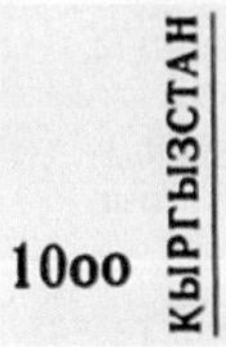
(6)

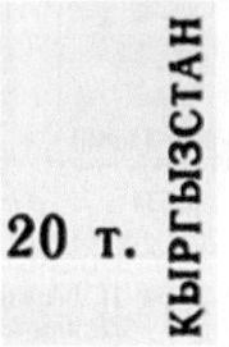
(7)

1993. Nos. 5940, 6073 and 4671 of Russia surch as T **6**.
13 10k. on 1k. brown 15 10
14 20k. on 2k. brown 40 20
15 30k. on 3k. red 60 40

1993. Nos. 4672/3 of Russia surch as T **7**.
16 20t. on 4k. red 20 10
17 30t. on 6k. blue 40 30

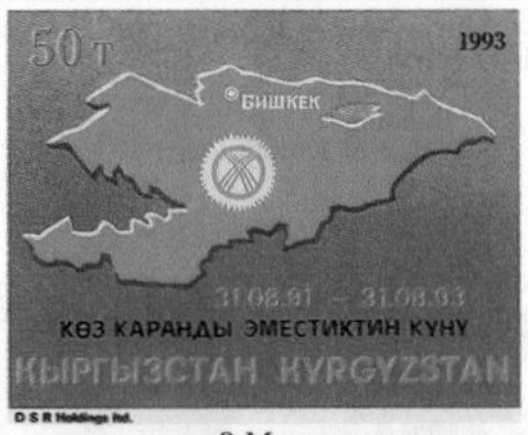
8 Map

1993. 2nd Anniv of Independence (18) and 1st Anniv of Admission to United Nations (19). Multicoloured.
18 50t. Type **8** 35 25
19 60t. U.N. emblem, national flag and Government Palace, Bishkek (vert) 45 30
See also No. **MS**35.

9 Komuz

1993. Music.
20 9 30t. multicoloured 25 15

10 Dog

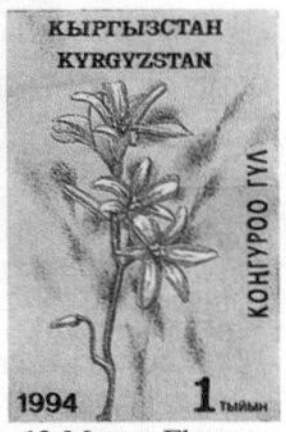
12 Mauve Flowers

11 Adult and Cub

1994. New Year. Year of the Dog.
22 10 60t. multicoloured 20 15
MS21 84 × 67 mm. 140t. Similar design to Type **9** but with motifs reversed (51 × 39 mm) . . . . 4·00 3·00

1994. The Snow Leopard. Multicoloured.
23 10t. Type **11** 15 10
24 20t. Lying curled-up 35 20
25 30t. Sitting 45 30
26 40t. Head 60 40

1994. Flowers. Multicoloured.
27 1t. Type **12** 10 10
28 3t. Daisies (horiz) 10 10
29 10t. Tulip 10 10
30 16t. Narcissi 10 10
31 20t. Deep pink flower 15 10
32 30t. White flower 20 15
33 40t. Yellow flower 30 25
MS34 70 × 90 mm. 50t. *Trollius altaicum* 35 35

1994. 3rd Anniv of Independence and Second Anniv of Admission to United Nations. Sheet containing stamps as Nos. 18/19 but with face values changed. Multicoloured.
MS35 110 × 80 mm. 120t. Type **8**; 130t. As No. 19 . . . . 1·75 1·75

13 Fluorite

15 Woman with Rug

14 Turkestan Catfish

1994. Minerals. Multicoloured.
36 80t. Type **13** 20 15
37 90t. Calcite 20 15
38 100t. Getchellite 20 15
39 110t. Barite 25 20
40 120t. Auripigment 25 20
41 140t. Antimonite 30 20
MS42 135 × 95 mm. 200t. Cinnabar 75 75

1994. Fishes. Multicoloured.
43 110t. Type **14** 30 20
44 120t. Schmidt's dace 40 30
45 130t. Scaleless osman 50 40
46 140t. Spotted stone loach . . . 60 45
MS47 82 × 57 mm. 200t. Common carp (*Cyprinus carpio*) 75 75

1995. Traditional Costumes. Multicoloured.
48 50t. Type **15** 10 10
49 50t. Musician 10 10
50 100t. Falconer 25 15
51 100t. Woman with long plaits 25 15

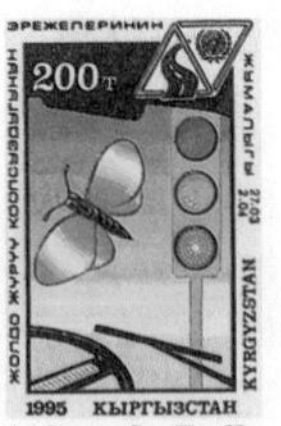
16 Butterfly, Traffic Lights and Emblem

17 Brown Bear

1995. Road Safety Week.
52 16 200t. multicoloured 30 20

1995. Animals. Multicoloured.
53 110t. Type **17** 10 10
54 120t. Snow leopard (horiz) . . 15 10
55 130t. Golden eagle 30 15
56 140t. Menzbier's marmot (horiz) 25 15
57 150t. Short-toed eagle (horiz) 35 15
58 160t. Golden eagle (different) 40 20
59 190t. Red fox (horiz) 35 20
MS60 90 × 70 mm. 130t. Golden eagle (*different*); 170t. Argali 60 60

18 Memorial Flame, Bishkek

1995. 50th Anniv of End of Second World War. Sheet 90 × 70 mm.
MS61 18 150t. multicoloured . . 40 40

19 Aitschurek (wife of Manas)

20 Osprey

1995. Millenary of "Manas" (epic poem). Each blue and gold.
62 10t.+5t. Type **19** 10 10
63 20t.+10t. Hoopoe on youth's wrist 10 10
64 30t.+10t. Birth of Semetey, son of Manas 10 10
65 30t.+10t. Woman carrying spear and leading horse . . 10 10
66 40t.+15t. Warrior astride dead dragon 15 10
67 50t.+15t. Jakyp, father of Manas 20 15
68 50t.+15t. Manas on horseback 20 15
69 50t.+15t. Seytek, grandson of Manas 20 15
MS70 Two sheets. (a) 166 × 107 mm. 2s. + 50t. Saryakbai (Manas singer) cradling injured warrier (37 × 51 mm). (b) 148 × 131 mm. 2s.+50t. Sagymbai (Manas singer) (37 × 51 mm) 90 90

1995. Birds. Multicoloured.
71 10t. Type **20** 10 10
72 50t. Tawny eagle 10 10
73 100t. Lammergeier 20 15
74 140t. Saker falcon 25 15
75 150t. Short-toed eagle 25 15
76 200t. Lammergeier 35 25
77 300t. Golden eagle 50 30
MS78 90 × 70 mm. 600t. White-tailed sea eagle (*Haliaeetus albicilla*) (29 × 40 mm) . . . . 1·00 1·00

21 Envelopes on Map and U.P.U. Emblem

22 State Arms

1995. Postage Stamp Week.
79 21 200t. multicoloured 30 20

1995.
80 22 20t. violet 10 10
81 50t. blue 10 10
82 100t. brown 15 10
83 500t. green 65 50

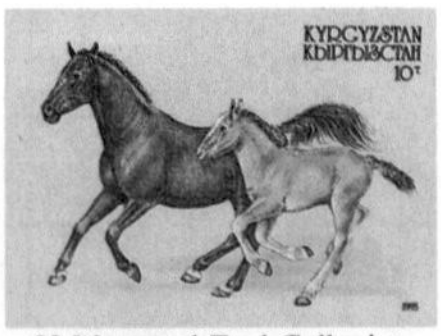
23 Mare and Foal Galloping

1995. Horses. Multicoloured.
89 10t. Type **23** 10 10
90 50t. Palamino mare and foal (vert) 10 10
91 100t. Brown mare and foal (vert) 20 15
92 140t. Chestnut mare and foal (vert) 25 15
93 150t. Chestnut mare and foal 25 15
94 200t. Grey mare and foal . . . 35 25
95 300t. Pair of foals 50 30
MS96 91 × 71 mm. 600t. brown and cream (Mongolian wild horses) (*Equus caballus*) (vert) 90 90

24 Headquarters, New York

1995. 50th Anniv of United Nations Organization. Sheet 71 × 91 mm containing T **24** and similar horiz design. Multicoloured.
MS97 100t. Type **24**; 100t. Rainbow and mountains 35 35

25 River Nile, Egypt

1995. Natural Wonders of the World. Multicoloured.
98 10t. Type **25** 10 10
99 50t. Mt. Kilimanjaro, Tanzania 10 10
100 100t. Sahara Desert, Algeria 15 10
101 140t. Amazon River, Brazil (vert) 20 15
102 150t. Grand Canyon, U.S.A. (vert) 20 15
103 200t. Victoria Falls, Zimbabwe (vert) 25 20
104 350t. Mt. Everest, Nepal . . 50 35
105 400t. Niagara Falls, Canada 55 40
MS106 Two sheets, each 90 × 70 mm. (a) Gull over Issyk-Kule lake, Kyrgyzstan; (b) Eagle over Issyk-Kule lake . . . . . 1·90 1·90
No. 98 is wrongly inscribed "Egipt".

26 Steppe Ribbon Snake

1996. Reptiles. Multicoloured.
107 20t. Type **26** 10 10
108 50t. Fat-tailed panther gecko 10 10
109 50t. Tessellated water snake 10 10
110 100t. Central Asian viper . . 15 10
111 150t. Arguta 25 20
112 200t. Dione snake 35 25
113 250t. "Asyblepharus sp." (wrongly inscr "Asymblepharus") 40 30
MS114 91 × 71 mm. 500t. Sand lizard (*Lacerta agilis*) 75 75

27 Kaufmann's Shovelnose (*Pseudoscphirhyncus kafmanni*)

1996. "Save the Aral Sea". Sheet 128 × 108 mm containing T **27** and similar horiz designs. Multicoloured.
MS115 100t. Caracal (*Felis caracal*); 100t. Aral trout (*Salmo trutta aralensis*); 100t. Striped hyena (*Hyaena hyaena*); 100t. Type **27**; 100t. Pike asp (*Aspiolucius esocinus*) . . . . 1·10 1·10

28 Show Jumping and Traditional Horse Race

1996. Olympic Games, Atlanta, U.S.A. Multicoloured.

116	100t.+20t. Type **28**	25	15
117	140t.+30t. Boxing and traditional wrestling match	35	25
118	150t.+30t. Archer and mounted archer shooting at eagle	50	40
119	300t.+50t. Judo competitor, ballooning, yachting and water-skiing	85	65

29 Golden Eagle

1997. Animals.

120	600t. Type **29**	85	60
121	600t. Markhor ("Capra falconeri")	85	60
122	600t. Argali ("Ovis ammon")	85	60
123	600t. Himalayan griffon ("Gyps himalayensis") . .	85	60
124	600t. Asiatic wild ass ("Equus hemionus")	85	60
125	600t. Wolf ("Canis lupus")	85	60
126	600t. Brown bear ("Ursus arctos") (wrongly inscr "arctor")	85	60
127	600t. Saiga ("Saiga tatarica")	85	60

30 Tiger

1998. New Year. Year of the Tiger.

128	**30**	600t. multicoloured	65	45

31 "Parnassius actius"

1998. Butterflies. Multicoloured.

129	600t. Type **31** (wrongly inscr "Parnasius")	65	45
130	600t. "Colias christophi" . .	65	45
131	600t. Swallowtail ("Papilio machaon")	65	45
132	600t. "Colias thisoa"	65	45
133	600t. "Parnassius delphius"	65	45
134	600t. "Parnassius tianschanicus"	65	45

32 Roe Deer

1998. Animals. Multicoloured.

135	600t. Type **32**	60	45
136	600t. Osprey ("Pandion haliaetus")	60	45
137	600t. Hoopoe ("Upupa epops")	60	45
138	600t. White stork ("Ciconia ciconia")	60	45
139	1000t. Golden oriole ("Oriolus oriolus")	60	45
140	1000t. Snow leopard	60	45
141	1000t. River kingfisher ("Alcedo althis")	60	45
142	1000t. Common kestrel ("Falco tinnunculus") . . .	60	45

33 Andrei Dimitriyevich Sakharov (physicist)

1998. 50th Anniv of Universal Declaration of Human Rights. Multicoloured.

143	10s. Type **33**	80	45
144	10s. Crowd cheering	80	45
145	10s. Martin Luther King (civil rights leader)	80	45
146	10s. Mahatma Ghandi (Indian leader)	80	45
147	10s. Eleanor Roosevelt (humanitarian)	80	45

34 Tyrannosaurus

1998. Prehistoric Animals. Multicoloured.

148	10s. Type **34**	80	45
149	10s. Saurolophus	80	45
150	10s. Gallimimus (horiz) . . .	80	45
151	10s. Euoplocephalus (horiz)	80	45
152	10s. Protoceratops (horiz) . .	80	45
153	10s. Velociraptor (horiz) . .	80	45

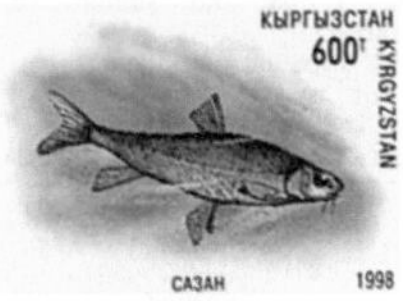

35 Fish

1998. Fauna. Multicoloured.

154	600t. Type **35**	50	30
155	600t. Fish (with orange tail and fins)	50	30
156	1000t. Bar-headed goose . .	80	45
157	1000t. Chukar partridge . . .	80	45
158	1000t. Goosander by water	80	45
159	1000t. Common shelduck swimming	80	45
160	1000t. Rodent	80	45
161	1000t. Himalayan snowcock standing on one leg	80	45

36 Map of Kyrgyzstan

1998. 5th Anniv of Constitution.

162	**36**	1000t. multicoloured . . .	80	45

37 Fox

1999. "iBRA" International Stamp Exhibition, Nuremberg, Germany. The Corsac Fox (*Vulpes corsac*). Multicoloured.

163	10s. Type **37**	85	50
164	10s. Fox sleeping	85	50
165	30s. Two foxes standing . . .	2·50	1·50
166	50s. Mother and cubs	4·25	2·50

38 Fox

1999. The Corsac Fox (*Vulpes corsac*). Multicoloured.

167	10s. Type **38**	85	50
168	10s. Fox sleeping	85	50
169	30s. Two foxes standing . . .	2·50	1·50
170	50s. Mother and cubs	4·25	2·50

39 "The Fisherman and the Golden Fish" (poem)

40 State Arms

1999. Birth Bicentenary of Alexander Sergeevich Pushkin. Multicoloured.

171	36t. "Ruslan and Lyudmila" (poem)	10	10
172	6s. Type **39**	50	30
173	10s. "Tsar Saltan" (poem) . .	85	50
174	10s. "The Golden Cockerel" (fairy tale)	85	50
MS175	74 × 99 mm. 20s. Pushkin	1·70	1·70

1999.

176	**40**	20t. blue	10	10

41 Giant Panda (*Ailuropoda melanoleuca*)

1999. "China '99" International Stamp Exhibition, Beijing, China. Sheet 90 × 90 mm containing T **41** and similar horiz design. Multicoloured.
MS180 10s. Type **41**; 15s. Brown wood owl (*Strix leptogrammica*) 2·20 2·20

42 State Flag and Emblem

1999. World Kick Boxing Championships, Bishkek. Multicoloured.

181	3s. Type **42**	20	15
182	3s. Emblem on blue background with Cyrillic championship title in red	20	15
183	3s. "WORLD" in green across globe and emblem	20	15
MS184	121 × 62 mm. 6s. "WORLD" in blue across globe and emblem (different); 6s. "KICKBOXING" and emblem on yellow rectangle	1·00	1·00

43 Envelopes and Emblem

1999. 125th Anniv of Universal Postal Union. Multicoloured.

185	3s. Type **43**	25	15
186	6s. Airplane, envelopes, horseman and emblem . .	50	30

44 Anniversary Emblem

2000. 3000th Anniv of Osh. Sheet 139 × 109 mm containing Multicoloured.
MS187 6s.+25t. Type **44**; 6s.+25t. Ravat Abdullakhan Mosque; 6s.+25t. Tahti Suleiman Mosque; 6s.+25t. Asaf ibn Burhia tower 2·20 2·20

45 Taigan

2000. Asian Dogs. Multicoloured.

188	3s. Type **45**	25	15
189	6s. Tasy	50	30
190	6s. Afghan hound	50	30
191	10s. Saluki	85	50
192	15s. Mid-Asian shepherd . .	1·25	75
193	15s. Akbash	1·25	75
194	20s. Chow Chow	1·70	1·00
195	25s. Akita-inu	2·00	1·30

46 Minjilkiev

2000. 60th Birth Anniv of Bulat Minzhilkiev (opera singer).

196	**46**	5s. multicoloured	40	25

No. 196 is wrongly inscribed "1940–1998" instead of "1940–1997".

47 Private Cholponbai Tuleberdiev and Medal

2000. 55th Anniv of End of Second World War. Showing recipients of Gold Star of Hero of Soviet Union Medal. Multicoloured.

197	6s. Type **47**	50	30
198	6s. Major-General Ivan Vasilievich Panfilov (vert)	50	30
199	6s. Private Duishenkul Shopokov	50	30

2000. No. 27 surch **36t.**

200	36t. on 1t. multicoloured . .	10	10

49 Wrestling

2000. Olympic Games, Sydney. Multicoloured.

201	1s. Type **49**	20	20
202	3s. Hurdling (vert)	30	30
203	6s. Boxing	60	60
204	10s. Weightlifting (vert) . . .	75	75

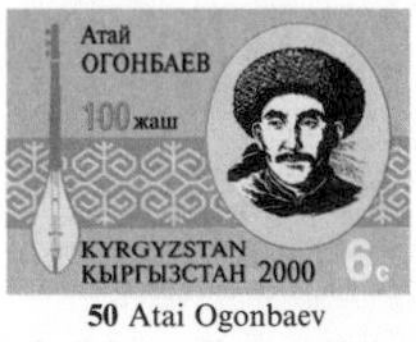

50 Atai Ogonbaev

2000. Birth Centenary of Atai Ogonbaev (musician).

205	**50**	6s. multicoloured	60	60

51 Dark Green Fritillary (*Argynnis aglaja*)

2000. Butterflies. Multicoloured.

206 3s. Type **51** 30 30
207 3s. Swallowtail (*Papilo machaon*) 30 30
208 3s. Peacock (*Inachis io*) . . . 30 30
209 3s. Apollo (*Parnassius Apollo*) 30 30
210 3s. Small tortoiseshell (*Aglais urticae*) 30 30
211 3s. *Colias thisoa* 30 30

52 Khan-Tegri

2000. International Year of Mountains (1st series). Multicoloured.

212 10s. Type **52** 75 75
213 10s. Lenin Peak 75 75
214 10s. Victory Peak 75 75

See also Nos. 228/**MS**231.

53 Dank Medal (bravery)

2001. Orders and Medals. Multicoloured.

215 36t. Type **53** 10 10
216 48t. Baatyrene (women's medal) 10 10
217 1s. Manas 3rd class order . . 10 10
218 2s. Manas 2nd class order . . 20 20
219 3s. Manas 1st class order . . 30 30
220 6s. Danaker order (bravery) 60 60
221 10s. Ak Shumkar (Hero of Kyrgyz Republic) 75 75

54 Crying Child and Military Aircraft

2001. 50th Anniv of United Nations High Commissioner for Refugees.

222 **54** 10s. multicoloured 75 75

55 Snake

2001. New Year. Year of the Snake.

223 **55** 6s. multicoloured 60 60

56 Children encircling Globe

2001. United Nations Year of Dialogue among Civilizations.

224 **56** 10s. multicoloured 75 75

57 Communication House

2001. Bishkek.

225 **57** 48t. green 10 10
226 – 1s. green 10 10
227 – 3s. brown 30 30

DESIGNS: 1s. Government House; 3s. National Opera House.

58 Yaks in Pasture

2001. International Year of Mountains (2nd series). Multicoloured.

228 10s. Type **58** 75 75
229 10s. Horses crossing river . . 75 75
230 10s. Forested slopes 75 75
MS231 10 × 83 mm. Designs as Nos. 228/30 . . . . 2·25 2·25

59 Yacht on Lake Issyk-Kul

2001. International Year of Eco-tourism. Multicoloured.

232 10s. Type **59** 75 75
233 10s. Lake Sary-Chelek . . . 75 75
234 10s. Suusamyr Valley 75 75
MS235 119 × 89 mm. 10s. Mosque, Naryn (vert) 75 75

60 Ak-Shumkar (legendary bird) and Khan-Tengri Mountain

2001. 10th Anniv of Independence. Multicoloured.

236 1s.50 Type **60** 10 10
237 7s. Pres. Askar Akaev and national flag 60 60
MS238 126 × 90 mm. 11s.50 Government House, Bishkek 85 85

61 Kurmanbek (statue), Djalal-Abad

2001. 500th Birth Anniv of Kurmanbek Khan (military leader).

239 **61** 1s.50 multicoloured 10 10

2001. 40th Anniv of Worldwide Fund for Nature. Nos. 163/6 overprinted **40th Anniversary 1961–2001** or surcharged.

240 25s. on 10s. Fox . . . . . .
241 25s. on 10s. Fox sleeping . . 85 85
242 30s. Two foxes standing . . . 1·75 1·75
243 50s. Mother and cubs . . . . 1·75 1·75

Nos. 240/1 with both change of face value and celebratory inscription, and Nos. 242/3 with only celebratory inscription.

63 Kurmandjan Datka

2001. 190th Birth Anniv of Kurmandjan Dakta (aka Alai Queen, female tribal leader).

244 **63** 10s.+70t. black 75 75

64 RCC and Kyrgyzstan Post **65** Union Emblem Office Emblems

2001. 10th Anniv of Regional Communications Community.

245 **64** 7s. multicoloured 60 60

2001. 10th Anniv of Union of Independent States.

246 **65** 6s. blue and yellow 60 60

66 Skating

2002. Olympic Games, Salt Lake City, USA. Multicoloured.

247 50t. Type **66** 10 10
248 1s.50 Biathlon 20 20
249 7s. Hockey 80 80
250 10s. Ski jumping 90 90
MS251 88 × 89 mm. 50s. Alpine skiing . . . . 1·50 1·50

67 Horse

2002. Chinese New Year ("Year of the Horse").

252 **67** 1s. multicoloured 15 15

68 Two Players **69** Kyrgyzstan and Pakistan Flags and Dove

2002. World Cup Football Championships, Japan and South Korea. Sheet 136 × 118 mm containing T **68** and similar vert designs. Multicoloured.

MS253 1s.50 Type **68**; 3s. Players tackling for ball; 7s.20 Player dribbling ball; 12s. Player defending; 24s. Players jumping for ball; 60s. Player chasing another . . . . 14·00 14·00

2002. 10th Anniv of Kyrgyzstan—Pakistan Diplomatic Relations.

254 **69** 12s. multicoloured 75 75

2002. No. **MS**253 surch **Final BRAZIL 2 : 0 GREMANY Third Place TURKEY : KOREA** in either gold or silver.

MS255 (a) As No. **MS**253 (gold ovpt) (b) As No. **MS**253 (silver ovpt) . . . . 14·00 14·00

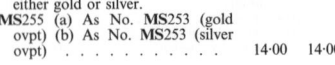

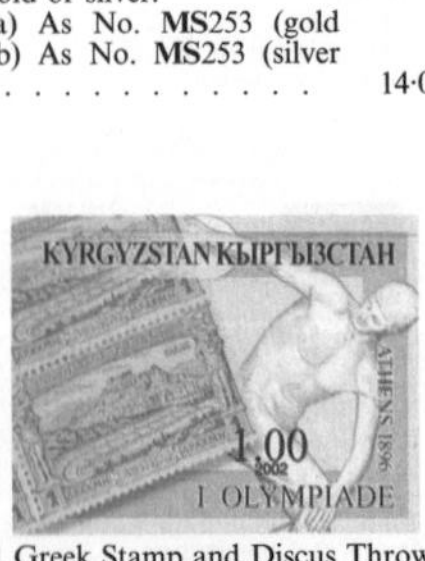

71 Greek Stamp and Discus Thrower (Athens, 1896)

2002. History of Summer Olympic Games. Four sheets, each 140 × 110 mm containing T **71** and similar horiz designs. Multicoloured.

MS256 (a) 1s. Type **71**; 2s. Boxer and French stamp (Paris 1900); 3s. Diver and American stamp (St. Louis 1904); 5s. Weightlifting and English stamp (London 1908); 7s. Rower and Swedish stamp (Stockholm 1912). 7s. Athlete and Belgian stamp (Antwerp 1920). (b) 1s. Gymnast and French stamp (Paris 1924); 2s. Diver and Dutch stamp (Amsterdam 1928); 3s. Table tennis and American stamp (Los Angeles 1932); 5s. Runner and German stamp (Berlin 1936); 7s. Fencing and English stamp (London 1948); 7s. Gymnast and Finnish stamp (Helsinki 1952). (c) 1s.50 Volleyball and Australian stamp (Melbourne 1956); 3s. Tennis and Italian stamp (Rome 1960); 5s. Swimmer and Japan stamp (Tokyo 1964); 5s. Wrestlers and Mexican stamp (Mexico 1968); 7s.20 Kayaker and German stamp (Munich 1972); 12s. Yacht and Canadian stamp (Montreal 1976). (d) 1s. Gymnast and USSR stamp (Moscow 1980); 3s. Synchronised swimmer and USA stamp (Los Angeles 1984); 5s. Cyclist and Korean stamp (Seoul 1988); 5s. High jumper and Spanish stamp (Barcelona 1992); 7s.20 Wind surfer and USA stamp (Atlanta 1996); 12s. Gymnast and Australian stamp (Sydney 2000) 10·00 10·00

72 Zhalal-Abad **76** Olmoskhan Atabekova

2002. Regional Cities.

257 **72** 20t. purple 10 10
258 – 50t. purple 10 10
259 – 60t. purple 10 10
260 – 1s. blue 15 15
261 – 1s.50 blue 20 20
262 – 2s. slate 25 25
263 – 3s. slate 35 35
264 – 7s. slate 80 80
265 – 10s. blue 90 90

DESIGNS: 20t. Zhalal-Abad; 50t. Talas; 60t. Osh; 1s. Zhalal-Abad; 1s.50 Talas; 2s. Osh; 3s. Zhalal-Abad; 7s. Talas; 10s. Osh.

2002. No. 27 surch **2000 1.50**.

266 1s.50 on 1t. multicoloured . . 20 20

2002. No. 28 surch **3.60**.

267 3s.60 on 3t. multicoloured . . 35 35

2002. No. 29 surch **7.00 2002**.

268 7s. on 10t. multicoloured . . 80 80

2003. 80th (2002) Birth Anniversary of Olmoskhan Atabekova (war heroine).

269 **76** 7s.20 multicoloured 80 80

77 Atomic Symbol and Association Emblem

2003. 10th Anniversary of the International Association of Academies of Sciences. Multicoloured.

270 1s.50 Type **77** 20 20
271 7s.20 Emblem 80 80

78 Figurines

2003. 2200th Anniv of Nationhood (1st issue). Saki Tribal Gold and Bronze Artefacts. Two sheets containing T **78** and similar horiz designs. Multicoloured. Imperf (**MS**272a) or imperf (**MS**272).

MS272 (a) 119 × 140 mm. 1s.50 Type **78**; 3s. Shield; 3s.60 Lion; 5s. Horned head; 7s. Bird; 10s. Two goat heads with joined horns; 20s.Coin; 42s. Animal headed staff.(b) 125 × 89 mm. 42s. Mask	5·00	5·00

See also No. **MS**277.

79 Airplane and Post Office Building, Bishkek

2003. 125th Anniv of Bishkek Post Office. Multicoloured.

273		1s. Type **79**	15	15
274		3s. Wagon, jeep and building	35	35
275		7s. Building, dove and wagon	80	80
MS276		119 × 88 mm. 50s. Dove and building (different). Imperf	1·50	1·50

80 Barsbek

2003. 2200th Anniv of Nationhood (2nd issue). Rulers. Sheet 99 × 160 mm containing T **80** and similar horiz designs. Multicoloured.

MS277 1s.50 Type **80** (7th-century leader); 3s. Alp Sol; 3s.60 Mukhammed; 5s. Manap; 7s.20 Zharban; 10s. Kubatbek; 18s. Azhy; 20s. Ormon; 25s. Alymbek; 30s. Shabdan	9·00	9·00

81 Rabat

2003. Tourism. Issyk Kul Resorts. Sheet 167 × 148 mm containing T **81** and similar horiz designs showing resorts. Multicoloured.

MS278 1s. Type **81**; 1s.50 Raduga; 2s. Teltoru; 3s. Kyrgyzskoe Vzmorije; 3s.60 Tamga; 5s. Solnyshko; 7s. Vityaz; 8s. AkBermet; 12s. Royal Beach; 20s. Inscr "Luchezarnoe poberejie"	4·00	4·00

82 Rat

2003. Chinese Lunar Calendar. Sheet 210 × 171 mm containing T **82** and similar horiz designs showing Chinese lunar animals. Multicoloured.

MS279 1.50 "Year of the Rat"; 3s. "Year of the Ox"; 5s. "Year of the Tiger"; 7s. "Year of the Rabbit"; 12s. "Year of the Dragon"; 12s. "Year of the Snake"; 15s. "Year of the Horse"; 15s. "Year of the Sheep"; 20s. "Year of the Monkey"; 20s. "Year of the Cock"; 25s. "Year of the Dog"; 25s. "Year of the Pig"	9·00	9·00

83 Flag

2003. National Symbols.

280	**83**	3s. vermilion, yellow and black	30	30
281	–	3s. black	30	30
282	–	5s. multicoloured	40	50
MS283		(a) 136 × 81 mm. Nos. 280/2 (b) 103 × 74 mm. 12s. multicoloured (52 × 37 mm)	1·60	1·60

DESIGNS: Type **83**; 3s. Anthem; 5s. National arms; 12s. "Notes" (written by Syma Tsjan (Chinese historian).

84 Sheep

2003. New Year. "Year of the Sheep".

284	**84**	1s.50 multicoloured	20	20

LA AGUERA Pt. 9

An administrative district of Spanish Sahara, whose stamps it later used.

1920. Rio de Oro stamps optd **LA AGUERA**.

1	**15**	1c. green	1·90	1·90
2		2c. brown	1·90	1·90
3		5c. green	1·90	1·90
4		10c. red	1·90	1·90
5		15c. yellow	1·90	1·90
6		20c. violet	1·90	1·90
7		25c. blue	1·90	1·90
8		30c. brown	1·90	1·90
9		40c. pink	1·90	1·90
10		50c. blue	6·25	6·25
11		1p. red	11·50	11·50
12		4p. purple	36·00	36·00
13		10p. orange	70·00	70·00

2

1923.

14	**2**	1c. blue	85	85
15		2c. green	85	85
16		5c. green	85	85
17		10c. red	85	85
18		15c. brown	85	85
19		20c. yellow	85	85
20		25c. blue	85	85
21		30c. brown	85	85
22		40c. red	1·10	1·10
23		50c. purple	3·50	3·50
24		1p. mauve	7·25	7·25
25		4p. violet	19·00	19·00
26		10p. orange	30·00	30·00

LABUAN Pt. 1

An Island off the N. coast of Borneo, ceded to Great Britain in 1846, and a Crown Colony from 1902. Incorporated with Straits Settlements in 1906, it used Straits stamps till it became part of N. Borneo in 1946.

100 cents = 1 dollar.

1

18

1879.

17	**1**	2c. green	19·00	27·00
39		2c. red	5·00	3·50
6		6c. orange	£110	£120
40		6c. green	8·00	4·50
7		8c. red	£110	£110
41		8c. violet	5·00	8·00
43		10c. brown	12·00	8·00
9		12c. red	£275	£325
45		12c. blue	6·50	6·50
10		16c. blue	80·00	80·00
46		16c. grey	6·50	9·50
47		40c. orange	20·00	32·00

1880. (a) Surch **8**.

11x	**1**	8 on 12c. red	£1200	£750

(b) Surch **6 6** or **8 8**.

12	**1**	6 on 16c. blue	£2250	£900
13		8 on 12c. red	£1600	£1000

1881. Surch **EIGHT CENTS**.

14	**1**	8c. on 12c. red	£325	£375

1881. Surch **Eight Cents**.

15	**1**	8c. on 12c. red	£120	£130

1883. Manuscript surch **one Dollar A.S.H.**

22	**1**	$1 on 16c. blue	£3500	

1885. Surch **2 CENTS** horiz.

23	**1**	2c. on 8c. red	£225	£400
24		2c. on 16c. blue	£950	£850

1885. Surch **2 Cents** horiz.

25	**1**	2c. on 16c. blue	£110	£160

1885. Surch with large **2 Cents** diag.

26	**1**	2c. on 8c. red	65·00	£110

1891. Surch **6 Cents**.

35	**1**	6c. on 8c. violet	9·50	8·50
37		6c. on 16c. blue	£2000	£1800
38		6c. on 40c. orange	£9000	£4500

1892. Surch as **Two CENTS** or **Six CENTS**.

49	**1**	2c. on 40c. orange	£170	90·00
50		6c. on 16c. grey	£375	£150

Most issues from 1894 exist cancelled-to-order with black bars. Our prices are for stamps postally used, cancelled-to-order examples being worth considerably less.

1894. Types of North Borneo (different colours) optd **LABUAN**.

62	**24**	1c. black and mauve	1·50	8·50
63	**25**	2c. black and blue	2·50	8·00
64a	**26**	3c. black and yellow	8·50	9·00
65a	**27**	5c. black and green	38·00	14·00
67	**28**	6c. black and red	2·50	15·00
69	**29**	8c. black and pink	7·00	23·00
70	**30**	12c. black and orange	23·00	48·00
71	**31**	18c. black and brown	22·00	55·00
74a	**32**	24c. blue and mauve	13·00	45·00
80	**10**	25c. green	25·00	29·00
81	–	50c. purple (as No. 82)	25·00	29·00
82	–	$1 blue (as No. 83)	60·00	55·00

1895. No. 83 of North Borneo surch **LABUAN** and value in cents.

75		4c. on $1 red	1·25	2·00
76		10c. on $1 red	4·25	1·40
77		20c. on $1 red	28·00	10·00
78		30c. on $1 red	32·00	40·00
79		40c. on $1 red	28·00	30·00

1896. Jubilee of Cession of Labuan to Gt. Britain. Nos. 62/8 optd **1846 JUBILEE 1896**.

83	**24**	1c. black and mauve	18·00	22·00
84d	**25**	2c. black and blue	38·00	16·00
85	**26**	3c. black and yellow	35·00	22·00
86	**27**	5c. black and green	55·00	16·00
87	**28**	6c. black and red	27·00	21·00
88b	**29**	8c. black and pink	40·00	12·00

1897. Stamps of North Borneo, Nos. 92 to 106 (different colours), optd **LABUAN**. Opt at top of stamp.

89		1c. black and purple	4·00	4·75
90		2c. black and blue	15·00	4·25
91b		3c. black and yellow	8·50	6·50
92a		5c. black and green	50·00	55·00
93b		6c. black and red	6·50	21·00
94a		8c. black and pink	18·00	12·00
95a		12c. black and orange	32·00	50·00

Overprint at foot of stamp.

98a	–	12c. black and orange (as No. 106)	42·00	50·00

Opt at foot. Inscr "POSTAL REVENUE".

96b	–	18c. black and bistre (as No. 108)	12·00	45·00

Opt at foot. Inscr "POSTAGE AND REVENUE".

99a	–	18c. black and bistre (as No. 110)	80·00	60·00

Opt at top. Inscr "POSTAGE AND REVENUE".

101b	–	18c. black and bistre (as No. 110)	38·00	55·00

Opt at top. "POSTAGE AND REVENUE" omitted.

97a	–	24c. blue and lilac (as No. 109)	12·00	50·00

Opt at top. Inscr "POSTAGE AND REVENUE".

100	–	24c. blue and mauve (No. 111)	29·00	55·00

1899. Stamps of Labuan surch 4 **CENTS**.

102	4c. on 5c. black & grn (92a)	35·00	26·00
103	4c. on 6c. black & red (93b)	23·00	19·00
104a	4c. on 8c. black and pink (94a)	30·00	32·00
105	4c. on 12c. black and orange (98a)	38·00	35·00
106	4c. on 18c. black and olive (101b)	26·00	18·00
107a	4c. on 24c. blue and mauve (100)	20·00	25·00
108	4c. on 25c. green (80)	6·00	7·50
109	4c. on 50c. purple (81)	6·50	7·50
110	4c. on $1 blue (82)	6·50	7·50

1900. Stamps of North Borneo, as Nos. 95 to 107, optd **LABUAN**.

111		2c. black and green	3·75	2·50
112		4c. black and brown	8·50	42·00
113a		4c. black and red	5·00	9·50
114		5c. black and blue	20·00	18·00
115		10c. brown and grey	50·00	80·00
116		16c. green and brown	50·00	£110

1902.

117	**18**	1c. black and purple	4·50	7·00
118		2c. black and green	4·00	5·00
119		3c. black and brown	3·25	12·00
120		4c. black and red	3·25	3·50
121		8c. black and orange	10·00	9·00
122		10c. brown and blue	3·25	12·00
123		12c. black and yellow	7·00	14·00
124		16c. green and brown	4·75	18·00
125		18c. black and brown	3·25	22·00
126		25c. green and blue	7·50	18·00
127		50c. purple and lilac	10·00	42·00
128		$1 red and orange	8·50	50·00

1904. Surch **4 cents**.

129	–	4c. on 5c. black and green (92a)	40·00	40·00
130	–	4c. on 6c. black and red (93b)	12·00	38·00
131	–	4c. on 8c. black and pink (94a)	25·00	42·00
132	–	4c. on 12c. black and orange (98a)	19·00	42·00
133	–	4c. on 18c. black and olive (101b)	23·00	45·00
134a	–	4c. on 24c. blue and mauve (100)	27·00	38·00
135	**10**	4c. on 25c. green (80)	8·50	24·00
136		4c. on 50c. purple (81)	8·50	24·00
137		4c. on $1 blue (82)	8·50	24·00

POSTAGE DUE STAMPS

1901. Optd **POSTAGE DUE**.

D1	2c. black and green (111)	16·00	24·00
D2	3c. black and yellow (91)	20·00	85·00
D3b	4c. black and red (113)	35·00	85·00
D4	5c. black and blue (114)	50·00	£100
D5	6c. black and red (93b)	30·00	95·00
D6	8c. black and pink (94a)	60·00	90·00
D7b	12c. black and orange (98a)	85·00	£110
D8	18c. black and olive (101b)	23·00	£100
D9c	24c. blue and mauve (100)	48·00	85·00

LAGOS Pt. 1

A British colony on the southern coast of Nigeria. United with Southern Nigeria in 1906 to form the Colony and Protectorate of Southern Nigeria.

12 pence = 1 shilling;
20 shillings = 1 pound.

1

3

1874.

21	**1**	½d. green	2·00	80
17		1d. mauve	19·00	10·00
22		1d. red	2·00	80
11		2d. blue	45·00	13·00
23		2d. grey	60·00	5·50
19		3d. brown	15·00	5·00
5		4d. red	85·00	40·00
24		4d. lilac	£100	8·50
25		6d. green	8·00	42·00
26		1s. orange	7·00	20·00
27		2s.6d. black	£300	£275
28		5s. blue	£550	£450
29		10s. brown	£1500	£1000

1887.

30	**1**	2d. mauve and blue	3·50	2·00
31		2½d. blue	3·75	1·75
32		3d. mauve and brown	2·50	3·25
33		4d. mauve and black	2·25	1·75
34		5d. mauve and green	2·00	11·00
35		6d. mauve	4·75	3·00
35a		6d. mauve and red	5·00	12·00
36		7½d. mauve and red	2·25	30·00
37		10d. mauve and yellow	3·25	13·00
38		1s. green and black	5·50	24·00
39		2s.6d. green and red	23·00	80·00
40		5s. green and blue	40·00	£150
41		10s. green and brown	80·00	£200

1893. Surch **HALF PENNY** and bars.

42	**1**	½d. on 4d. mauve and black	4·25	2·50

1904.

44	**3**	½d. green	1·50	5·50
45		1d. purple and black on red	1·00	15
56		2d. purple and blue	2·25	2·00
47		2½d. purple and blue on blue	1·00	1·50
48		3d. purple and brown	2·25	1·75
59a		6d. purple and mauve	4·25	1·50
60a		1s. green and black	23·00	2·25
61		2s.6d. green and red	16·00	55·00
62		5s. green and blue	22·00	95·00
63		10s. green and brown	60·00	£200

LAOS Pt. 21

Previously part of French Indo-China, the Kingdom of Laos was proclaimed in 1947. In 1949 it became an Associated State within the French Union and in 1953 it became fully independent within the Union.

Laos left the French Union in 1956. In 1976 it became a Republic.

1951. 100 cents = 1 piastre.
1955. 100 cents = 1 kip.

1 River Mekong

2 King Sisavang Vong

1951.
1 **1** 10c. green and turquoise . . 35 35
2 20c. red and purple 35 35
3 30c. blue and indigo . . . . 1·50 1·10
4 – 50c. brown and deep brown 35 35
5 – 60c. orange and red 35 35
6 – 70c. turquoise and blue . . . 35 35
7 – 1p. violet and deep violet . . 75 75
8 **2** 1p.50 purple and brown . . . 1·10 1·10
9 – 2p. green and turquoise . . . 15·00 5·50
10 – 3p. red and purple . . . . . 1·10 90
11 – 5p. blue and indigo . . . . 1·50 1·10
12 – 10p. purple and brown . . . 2·20 1·50
DESIGNS—As Type **1**: 50c. to 70c. Luang Prabang; 1p. and 2p. to 10p. Vientiane.

3 Laotian Woman

4 Laotian Woman Weaving

1952.
13 **3** 30c. violet and blue (postage) 75 35
14 80c. turquoise and green . . 75 35
15 1p.10 red and crimson . . . 75 75
16 1p.90 blue and indigo . . . . 1·10 1·10
17 3p. deep brown and brown 1·10 1·10
18 – 3p.30 violet and deep violet (air) . . . . 1·10 75
19 **4** 10p. green and blue . . . . 1·80 1·10
20 20p. red and crimson . . . . 3·75 2·50
21 30p. brown and black . . . . 5·50 5·50
DESIGN—As Type **4**: 3p.30, Vat Pra Keo shrine.

1952. Anniv of First Issue of Laos Stamps. Souvenir booklet containing 26 sheets inscr "ROYAUME DU LASO" in French and Laotian. Nos. 1/2, 13/17, 19/21 and D22/7.
MS21b 26 sheets each 130 × 90 mm £325

5 King Sisavang Vong and U.P.U. Monument

1952. 1st Anniv of Admission to U.P.U.
22 **5** 80c. violet, bl & ind (postage) 1·10 1·10
23 1p. brown, red and lake . . . 1·10 1·10
24 1p.20 blue and violet . . . . 1·10 1·10
25 1p.50 brown, emerald & grn 1·10 1·10
26 1p.90 turquoise and sepia . . 1·10 1·10
27 25p. indigo and blue (air) . . 4·50 4·50
28 50p. sepia, purple and brown 4·50 4·50

6 Girl carrying her Brother **7** Court of Love

1953. Red Cross Fund. Cross in red.
29 **6** 1p.50+1p. purple and blue . . 2·50 2·50
30 3p.+1p.50 red and green . . 2·50 2·50
31 3p.90+2p.50 purple & brn . . 3·00 3·00

1953.
32 **7** 4p.50 turquoise and blue . . 95 75
33 6p. brown and slate 95 75

8 Buddha

1953. Air. Statues of Buddha.
34 – 4p. green 95 75
35 – 6p.50 green . . . . 1·30 95
36 – 9p. green . . . . 1·90 1·30
37 **8** 11p.50 orange, brown and red . . . . 3·00 2·50
38 – 40p. purple . . . . 7·00 2·50
39 – 100p. green . . . . 13·50 9·50
DESIGNS—HORIZ: 4p. Reclining. VERT: 6p.50, Seated; 9p. Standing (full-face); 40p. Standing (facing right); 100p. Buddha and temple dancer.

9 Vientiane

1954. Golden Jubilee of King Sisavang Vong.
40 **9** 2p. violet and blue (postage) 48·00 31·00
41 3p. red and brown . . . . . 48·00 34·00
42 50p. turquoise and blue (air) £150 £150

10 Ravana

1955. Air. "Ramayana" (dramatic poem).
43 **10** 2k. blue, emerald and green 95 75
44 – 4k. red and brown . . . . 1·30 1·10
45 – 5k. green, brown and red . . 2·50 1·50
46 – 10k. black, orange and brown . . . . 4·50 3·00
47 – 20k. olive, green and violet 5·50 3·75
48 – 30k. black, brown and blue 7·50 5·25
DESIGNS—HORIZ: 4k. Hanuman, the white monkey; 5k. Ninh Laphath, the black monkey. VERT: 10k. Sita and Rama; 20k. Luci and Ravana's friend; 30k. Rama.

11 Buddha and Worshippers

1956. 2500th Anniv of Buddhist Era.
49 **11** 2k. brown (postage) . . . . 3·00 2·50
50 3k. black . . . . 3·75 2·50
51 5k. sepia . . . . 5·50 3·00
52 20k. carmine and red (air) 34·00 27·00
53 30k. green and bistre . . . 35·00 32·00
Nos. 49/53 were wrongly inscribed as commemorating the birth anniversary of Buddha.

12 U.N. Emblem **13** U.N. Emblem

1956. 1st Anniv of Admission to U.N.
54 **12** 1k. black (postage) 75 60
55 2k. blue 95 90
56 4k. red . . . . 1·30 95
57 6k. violet . . . . 1·60 1·30
58 **13** 15k. blue (air) . . . . . . 6·25 6·25
59 30k. red . . . . 8·75 8·75

14 Flute Player

1957. Native Musicians.
60 **14** 2k. multicoloured (postage) 1·80 1·30
61 – 4k. multicoloured . . . . . 1·80 1·30
62 – 8k. blue, brown and orange 3·25 1·50
63 – 12k. multicoloured (air) . . 2·50 2·50
64 – 14k. multicoloured . . . . 3·00 3·00
65 – 20k. multicoloured . . . . 3·75 3·75
DESIGNS—VERT: 4k. Piper; 14k. Violinist; 20k. Drummer. HORIZ: 8k. Xylophonist; 12k. Bells player.

15 Harvesting Rice

1957. Rice Cultivation.
66 **15** 3k. multicoloured . . . . . 1·10 60
67 – 5k. brown, red and green . . 1·10 75
68 – 16k. violet, olive and blue 2·20 1·30
69 – 26k. chocolate, brown & grn 3·00 2·20
DESIGNS—VERT: 5k. Drying rice; 16k. Winnowing rice. HORIZ: 26k. Polishing rice.

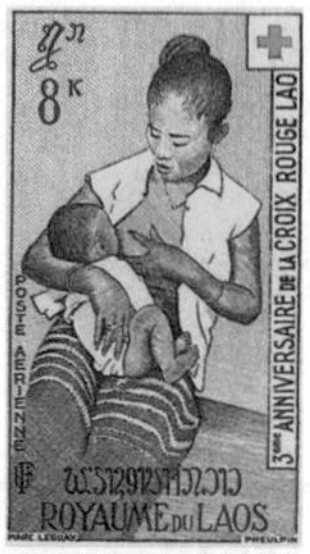

16 "The Offertory" **18** Mother and Child

17 Carrier Elephants

1957. Air. Buddhism.
70 **16** 10k. multicoloured 90 90
71 – 15k. brown, yellow & choc 1·30 1·30
72 – 18k. yellow and green . . . 1·60 1·60
73 – 24k. red, black and yellow 3·75 3·75
DESIGNS—As T **16**: HORIZ: 15k. "Meditation" (children on river craft). 48 × 36½ mm: 24k. "The Great Renunciation" (dancers with horse). VERT: 18k. "Serenity" (head of Buddhist).

1958. Laotian Elephants. Multicoloured.
74 10c. Type **17** 50 35
75 20c. Elephant's head with head-dress 50 35
76 30c. Elephant with howdah (vert) 50 35
77 2k. Elephant hauling log . . . 1·00 35
78 5k. Elephant walking with calf (vert) . . . . 2·40 1·10
79 10k. Caparisoned elephant (vert) . . . . 3·00 1·10
80 13k. Elephant bearing throne (vert) . . . . 4·00 2·20

1958. Air. 3rd Anniv of Laotian Red Cross. Cross in red.
81 **18** 8k. black and grey . . . . 1·10 1·10
82 12k. olive and brown . . . 1·10 1·10
83 15k. turquoise and green . . 1·30 1·30
84 20k. violet and bistre . . . 1·50 1·50

19

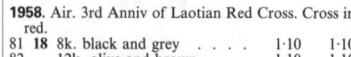

1958. Inauguration of UNESCO Headquarters Building, Paris.
85 **19** 50c. blue, orange and red 35 20
86 – 60c. violet, brown and green 35 20
87 – 70c. blue, brown and red . . 35 20
88 – 1k. red, blue and bistre . . 75 45
DESIGNS—VERT: 60c. Woman, children and part of exterior of UNESCO building; 70c. Woman and children hailing UNESCO building superimposed on globe. HORIZ: 1k. General view of UNESCO building and Eiffel Tower.

20 King Sisavang Vong

1959.
89 **20** 4k. lake 50 50
90 6k.50 red 50 50
91 9k. mauve 50 50
92 13k. green 75 75

21 Stage Performance **22** Portal of Vat Phou Temple, Pakse

1959. Education and Fine Arts.
93 **21** 1k. multicoloured 35 20
94 – 2k. lake, violet and black . . 35 20
95 – 3k. black, green and purple 75 20
96 – 5k. green, yellow and violet 75 45
DESIGNS—VERT: 2k. Student and "Lamp of Learning"; 5k. Stage performers and Buddhist temple. HORIZ: 3k. Teacher and children with "Key to Education".

1959. Laotian Monuments. Multicoloured.
97 50c. Type **22** 20 15
98 1k.50 That Ing Hang, Savannakhet (horiz) . . . 35 20
99 2k.50 Vat Phou Temple, Pakse (horiz) 45 35
100 7k. That Luang, Vientiane . . 75 45
101 11k. As 7k., but different view (horiz) 80 65
102 12k.50 Phou-Si Temple, Luang Prabang . . . . . 1·10 80

1960. World Refugee Year. Nos. 89 and 79 surch **ANNEE MONDIALE DU REFUGIE 1959–1960** and premium.
103 4k.+1k. red . . . . 3·75 3·75
104 10k.+1k. multicoloured . . . 5·50 5·50

24 Plain of Jars, Xieng Khouang **25** Funeral Urn

1960. Air. Tourism.
105 **24** 9k.50 red, bistre and blue 75 75
106 – 12k. brown, violet and green 95 95
107 – 15k. red, green and brown 1·20 1·20
108 – 19k. brown, orange and green . . . . 1·40 1·40
DESIGNS—HORIZ: 12k. Phapheng Falls, Champassak; 15k. Pair of bullocks with cart. VERT: 19k. Buddhist monk and village.

1961. Funeral of King Sisavang Vong.
109 **25** 4k. bistre, black and red 1·10 1·10
110 – 6k.50 brown and black . . 1·10 1·10
111 – 9k. brown and black . . . 1·10 1·10
112 – 25k. black . . . . 3·00 3·00
DESIGNS: 6k.50, Urn under canopy; 9k. Catafalque on dragon carriage; 25k. King Sisavang Vong.

26 Temples and Statues ("Pou Gneu Nha Gneu")

27 King Savang Vatthana

1962. Air. Festival of Makha Bousa.

113	**26**	11k. brown, red and green	75	75
114	–	14k. blue and orange . . .	90	90
115	–	20k. green, yellow and mauve	1·30	1·30
116	–	25k. red, blue and green	1·60	1·60

DESIGNS—As T **26**: 14k. Bird ("Garuda"); 20k. Flying deities ("Hanuman"). 36 × 48 mm: 25k. Warriors ("Nang Teng One").

1962.

117	**27**	1k. brown, red and blue . .	20	20
118		2k. brown, red and mauve	45	20
119		5k. brown, red and blue . .	45	35
120		10k. brown, red and bistre	80	45

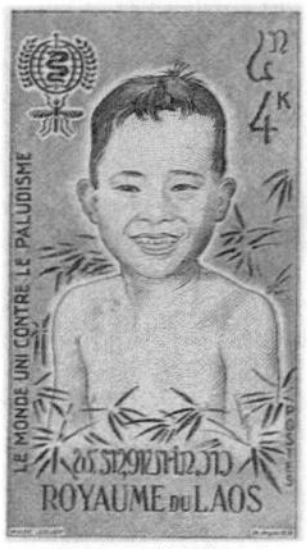

28 Laotian Boy

29 Royal Courier

1962. Malaria Eradication.

121	**28**	4k. olive, black and green	35	15
122	–	9k. brown, black & turq	45	35
123	–	10k. red, yellow and green	80	45
MS123a		130 × 100 mm. Nos. 121/2. Imperf	£225	

DESIGN: 9k. Laotian girl; 10k. Campaign emblem

1962. Philatelic Exhibition, Vientiane, and Stamp Day.

124	–	50c. multicoloured	50	50
125	–	70c. multicoloured	50	50
126	–	1k. black, green and red	1·10	1·10
127	**29**	1k.50 multicoloured . . .	90	90
MS127a		Two sheets (each 129 × 100 mm) containing Nos. 124/5 and 126/7	75·00	
MS127b		As above but imperf . .	75·00	

DESIGNS—HORIZ: 50c. Modern mail transport; 70c. Dancer and globe. VERT: 1k. Royal courtier on elephant.

30 Fisherman

1963. Freedom from Hunger.

128	**30**	1k. bistre, violet and green	35	20
129	–	4k. blue, brown and green	50	35
130	–	5k. blue, bistre and green	50	45
131	–	9k. blue, green and brown	90	50
MS131a		220 × 100 mm. Nos. 128/31. Imperf	3·75	3·75

DESIGNS—VERT: 4k. Threshing rice; 9k. Harvesting rice. HORIZ: 5k. Ploughing paddy field.

31 Queen of Laos

1963. Red Cross Centenary.

132	**31**	4k. red, blue and brown . .	50	50
133		6k. multicoloured	60	60
134		10k. red, blue and brown	95	95
MS134a		140 × 100 mm. Nos. 132/4	4·50	4·50

32 Laotian supporting U.N. Emblem

1963. 15th Anniv of Declaration of Human Rights.

135	**32**	4k. purple, blue and red . .	1·30	90

33 Temple, Map and Rameses II

1964. Nubian Monuments Preservation.

136	**33**	4k. multicoloured	35	35
137		6k. multicoloured	50	50
138		10k. multicoloured	75	75
MS138a		185 × 100 mm. Nos. 136/8 (sold at 25k.)	2·75	2·75

34 Offertory Vase and Horn

1964. "Constitutional Monarchy". Multicoloured.

139	10k. Type **34**	45	20
140	15k. Seated Buddha of Vat Pra Keo	50	30
141	20k. Laotians walking across map	60	45
142	40k. Royal Palace, Luang Prabang	1·10	60
MS142a	140 × 140 mm. Nos. 139/42	3·75	3·75

35 Phra Vet and Wife

36 Meo Warrior

1964. Folklore. Phra Vet Legend. Multicoloured.

143	10k. Type **35**	45	45
144	32k. "Benediction"	65	65
145	45k. Phame and wife	95	95
146	55k. Arrest of Phame	1·30	1·30
MS146a	140 × 80 mm. Nos. 143/6. Imperf	6·25	6·25

1964. "People of Laos".

147	–	25k. black, brown and green (postage)	75	75
148	**36**	5k. multicoloured (air) . .	30	15
149	–	10k. pink, grey and purple	45	20
150	–	50k. brown, drab and lilac	1·60	90
MS150a		150 × 115 mm. Nos. 147/50	4·50	5·50

DESIGNS: 10k. Kha hunter; 25k. Girls of three races; 50k. Thai woman.

37 Red Lacewing

1965. Butterflies and Moths.

151	**37**	10k. chestnut, brown and green (postage)	95	50
152	–	25k. blue, black and yellow	1·90	75
153	–	40k. yellow, brown & green	4·00	1·50
154	–	20k. red and yellow (air)	2·20	1·10

BUTTERFLIES—As Type **37**: 25k. Yellow pansy. 48 × 27 mm: 20k. Atlas moth; 40k. "Dysphania militaris" (moth).

38 Wattay Airport ("French Aid")

1965. Foreign Aid.

155	**38**	25k. mauve, brown & turq	35	20
156	–	45k. brown and green . . .	50	45
157	–	55k. brown and blue . . .	75	60
158	–	75k. multicoloured	1·10	80

DESIGNS—VERT: 45k. Mother bathing child (water resources: "Japanese Aid"); 75k. School and plants (education and cultivation: "American Aid"). HORIZ: 55k. Studio of radio station ("British Aid").

39 Hophabang

1965.

159	**39**	10k. multicoloured	30	20

40 Teleprinter Operator, Globe and Map

1965. I.T.U. Centenary.

160	**40**	5k. brown, violet and purple	35	20
161	–	30k. brown, blue and green	50	45
162	–	50k. multicoloured	95	80
MS162a		150 × 100 mm. Nos. 160/2	2·75	2·75

DESIGNS: 30k. Globe, map, telephonist and radio operator; 50k. Globe, radio receiver and mast.

1965. Nos. 89/90 surch.

163	**20**	1k. on 4k. lake	15	10
164		5k. on 6k.50 brown . . .	20	15

42 Mother and Baby

43 Leopard Cat

1965. 6th Anniv of U.N. "Protection of Mother and Child".

MS165a	130 × 100 mm. No. 165	3·75	3·75

1965. Air. Laotian Fauna.

166	**43**	25k. yellow, brown & green	45	35
167	–	55k. brown, sepia and blue	75	65
168	–	75k. brown and green . . .	90	80
169	–	100k. brown, black & yell	1·60	1·10
170	–	200k. black and red . . .	3·75	2·50

DESIGNS: 55k. Phayre's flying squirrel; 75k. Javan mongoose; 100k. Chinese porcupine; 200k. Binturong.

44 U.N. Emblem on Map

45 Bulls in Combat

1965. 20th Anniv of U.N.

171	**44**	5k. blue, grey and green . .	20	20
172		25k. blue, grey and mauve	45	35
173		40k. blue, grey and turquoise	65	65

1965. Laotian Pastimes.

174	**45**	10k. brown, black and orange	35	20
175	–	20k. blue, red and green	35	30
176	–	25k. red, blue and green	50	35
177	–	50k. multicoloured	75	60

DESIGNS: 20k. Tikhy (form of hockey); 25k. Pirogue race; 50k. Rocket festival.

46 Slaty-headed Parakeet

1966. Birds.

178	**46**	5k. green, brown and red	50	45
179	–	15k. brown, black & turq	75	50
180	–	20k. sepia, ochre and blue	1·30	90
181	–	45k. blue, sepia and violet	3·00	2·20

BIRDS: 15k. White-crested laughing thrush; 20k. Osprey; 45k. Indian roller (or "blue jay").

47 W.H.O. Building

1966. Inaug of W.H.O. Headquarters, Geneva.

182	**47**	10k. blue and turquoise . .	35	20
183		25k. green and red	35	30
184		50k. black and blue . . .	75	60
MS185		150 × 100 mm. Nos. 182/4 (sold at 150k.)	16·00	16·00

48 Ordination of Priests

1966. Laotian Ceremonies. Multicoloured.

186	10k. Type **48**	35	20
187	25k. Sand-hills ceremony . .	45	35
188	30k. "Wax pagoda" procession (vert)	65	45
189	40k. "Sou-Khouan" ceremony (vert)	80	50

49 UNESCO Emblem

1966. 20th Anniv of UNESCO.

190	**49**	20k. orange and black . .	20	20
191		30k. blue and black . . .	45	35
192		40k. green and black . . .	50	45
193		60k. red and black	75	65
MS194		140 × 140 mm. Nos. 190/3 (sold at 250k.)	2·75	2·75

50 Letter, Carrier Pigeon and Emblem

1966. International Correspondence Week.

195	**50**	5k. blue, brown and red . .	20	15
196		20k. purple, black and green	45	30
197		40k. brown, red and blue	50	35
198		45k. black, green and purple	75	60
MS199		130 × 100 mm. Nos. 195/8 (sold at 240k.)	3·00	3·00

51 Flooded Village

52 Carving, Siprapouthbat Pagoda

1967. Mekong Delta Flood Relief. Multicoloured.
200 20k.+5k. Type **51** 50 50
201 40k.+10k. Flooded market-place 80 80
202 60k.+15k. Flooded airport . . 1·30 1·30
MS203 150 × 100 mm. Nos. 200/2 (sold at 250k.) . . . . 4·50 4·50

1967. Buddhist Art.
204 **52** 5k. green and brown . . . 20 20
205 – 20k. blue and sepia 45 20
206 – 50k. purple and sepia . . . 95 60
207 – 70k. grey and brown . . . 1·30 90
DESIGNS (carvings in temple pagodas, Luang Prabang): 30k. Visoun; 50k. Xiengthong; 70k. Visoun (different).

53 General Post Office

1967. Opening of New G.P.O. Building, Vientiane.
208 **53** 25k. brown, green & purple 30 15
209 50k. blue, green and slate 45 35
210 70k. red, green and brown 75 60

54 Giant Snakehead **55** "Cassia fistula"

1967. Fishes.
211 **54** 20k. black, bistre and blue 50 35
212 – 35k. slate, bistre and blue 60 45
213 – 45k. sepia, ochre and green 1·10 65
214 – 60k. black, bistre and green 1·50 75
DESIGNS: 35k. Giant catfish; 45k. Tire-track spiny eel; 60k. Bronze knifefish.

1967. Flowers.
215 **55** 30k. yellow, green and mauve 50 35
216 – 55k. red, green and orange 75 45
217 – 75k. red, green and blue 1·10 80
218 – 80k. yellow, mauve and green . . . . 1·50 90
DESIGNS: 55k. "Cucuma singulario"; 75k. "Poinciana regia"; 80k. "Plumeria acutifolia".

56 Harvesting

1967. 10th Anniv of Laotian Red Cross.
219 **56** 20k.+5k. multicoloured . . 35 35
220 50k.+10k. multicoloured 75 75
221 60k.+15k. multicoloured 1·20 1·20
MS222 185 × 99 mm. Nos. 219/21 (sold at 250k.+30k.) . . . . . 2·50 2·50

57 Banded Krait

1967. Reptiles.
223 **57** 5k. blue, yellow and green 35 35
224 – 40k. brown, bistre and green 75 60
225 – 100k. chocolate, brown and green . . . . 2·75 1·60
226 – 200k. black, brown and green . . . . 5·25 3·00
DESIGNS: 40k. Marsh crocodile; 100k. Pit viper; 200k. Water monitor.

58 Human Rights Emblem

1968. Human Rights Year. Emblem in red and green.
227 **58** 20k. green 35 20
228 30k. brown 35 20
229 50k. blue 75 50
MS230 190 × 100 mm. Nos. 227/9 (sold at 250k.) . . . . 2·75 2·75

59 Military Parade

1968. Army Day. Multicoloured.
231 15k. Type **59** (postage) . . . 35 20
232 20k. Soldiers and tank in battle 35 30
233 60k. Soldiers and Laotian flag 65 50
234 200k. Parade of colours before National Assembly building (air) . . . . . . 1·30 90
235 300k. As No. 234 . . . . . 2·10 1·30
MS236 80 × 110 mm. Nos. 231/5 (sold at 600k.) . . . . 5·25 5·25

60 W.H.O. Emblem

1968. 20th Anniv of W.H.O.
237 **60** 15k. brown, red and purple 20 20
238 30k. brown, green and blue 35 30
239 70k. brown, purple and red 60 35
240 110k. light brown, purple and brown 95 75
241 250k. brown, blue and green . . . . 2·20 1·60
MS242 130 × 115 mm. Nos. 237/41 (sold at 500k.) . . . . 5·25 5·25

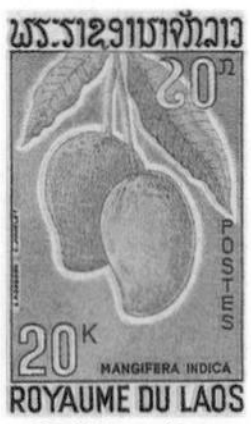

61 "Chrysochroa mnizechi" **62** "Mangifera indica"

1968. Beetles.
243 **61** 30k. blue, yellow and green (postage) 60 35
244 – 50k. black, orange & purple 95 45
245 – 90k. blue, orange and ochre . . . . 1·60 80
246 – 120k. black and orange (air) . . . . 1·30 50
247 – 160k. multicoloured . . . 1·90 80
INSECTS—VERT: 50k. "Aristobia approximator"; 90k. "Eutaenia corbetti". HORIZ: 120k. "Dorysthenes walkeri"; 160k. "Megaloxantha bicolor".

1968. Laotian Fruits.
248 **62** 20k. green, blue and black 35 20
249 – 50k. green, red and blue 50 30
250 – 180k. green, brown & orge 1·80 1·10
251 – 250k. green, brown & yell 2·50 1·60
DESIGNS—VERT: 50k. "Tamarindus indica". HORIZ: 180k. "Artocarpus intregrifolia"; 250k. "Citrullus vulgaris".

63 Hurdling

1968. Olympic Games, Mexico.
252 **63** 15k. green, blue & brown 20 20
253 – 80k. brown, turquoise & blue 60 45
254 – 100k. blue, brown and green 75 50
255 – 110k. brown, red and blue 80 60
DESIGNS: 80k. Tennis; 100k. Football; 110k. High jumping.

64 Oriental Door, Wat Ongtu (detail)

1969. Wat Ongtu Temple.
256 **64** 150k. gold, black and red 1·80 1·10
257 – 200k. gold, black and red 2·40 1·60
DESIGN: 200k. Central door, Wat Ongtu.

65 "Pharak praying to the Gods"

1969. Laotian "Ballet Royal". Designs showing dance characters. Multicoloured.
258 10k. Type **65** (postage) . . . 35 20
259 15k. "Soukhib ordered to attack" 50 35
260 20k. "Thotsakan reviewing troops" 60 50
261 30k. "Nang Sida awaiting punishment" 95 60
262 40k. "Pharam inspecting his troops" . . . . 1·30 75
263 60k. "Hanuman about to rescue Nang Sida" . . . . 1·90 1·30
264 110k. "Soudagnou battling with Thotsakan" (air) . . . 2·75 2·20
265 300k. "Pharam dancing with Thotsakkan" . . . . . . 6·25 4·00
MS266 Two sheets, each 106 × 106 mm. (a) Nos. 258/60, 265 (sold at 650k.); (b) Nos. 261/4 (sold at 480k.). Imperf . . . . 8·75 8·75

66 Handicrafts Workshop, Vientiane

1969. 10th Anniv of I.L.O.
267 **66** 30k. violet & purple (postage) 35 35
268 60k. brown and green . . . 75 65
269 – 300k. black & brown (air) 4·00 2·75
DESIGN: 300k. Elephants moving logs.

67 Chinese Pangolin

1969. "Wild Animals" (1st series). Multicoloured.
270 15k. Type **67** (postage) . . . 35 15
271 30k. Type **67** 75 35
272 70k. Sun bear (air) 95 60
273 120k. Common gibbon (vert) 1·80 1·10
274 150k. Tiger . . . . 2·40 1·30
See also Nos. 300/3 and 331/5.

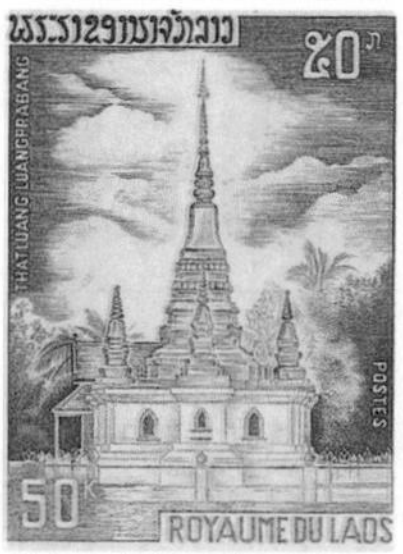

68 Royal Mausoleum, Luang Prabang

1969. 10th Death Anniv of King Sisavang Vong.
275 **68** 50k. ochre, blue and green 75 50
276 – 70k. ochre and lake . . . 75 50
DESIGN: 70k. King Sisavang Vong (medallion).

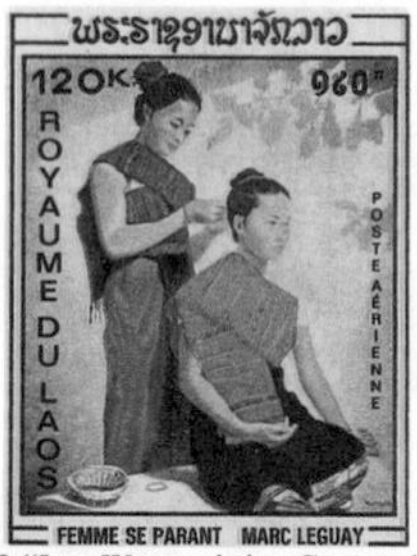

69 "Lao Woman being Groomed" (Leguay)

1969. Air. Paintings by Marc Leguay (1st series). Multicoloured.
277 10k. Type **69** . . . . 1·50 75
278 150k. "Village Market" (horiz) . . . . 2·20 1·10
See also Nos. 285, 307/9 and 357/61.

70 Carved Capital, Wat Xiengthong

1970. Laotian Pagodas. Multicoloured.
279 70k. Type **70** (postage) . . . 1·10 75
280 100k. Library, Wat Sisaket (air) 90 35
281 120k. Wat Xiengthong (horiz) 1·30 75

71 "Noon" Drum

1970. Laotian Drums.
282 **71** 30k. mult (postage) 75 60
283 – 55k. black, green and brown . . . . 1·10 90
284 – 125k. brown, yellow and flesh (air) . . . . . . 2·20 1·50
DESIGNS—HORIZ: 55k. Bronze drum. VERT: 125k. Wooden drum.

1970. Air. Paintings by Marc Leguay (2nd series). As T **69**. Multicoloured.
285 150k. "Banks of the Mekong" (horiz) . . . . . 1·80 1·30

72 Franklin D. Roosevelt

1970. Air. 25th Death Anniv of Franklin D. Roosevelt (American statesman).
286 **72** 120k. slate and green . . . 1·80 1·10

73 "Lenin explaining Electrification Plan" (L. Shmatko)

1970. Birth Centenary of Lenin.
287 **73** 30k. multicoloured . . . . 1·30 45
288 70k. multicoloured 80 60

1970. "Support for War Victims". Nos. 258/65 ("Ballet Royal") surch **Soutien aux Victimes de la Guerre** and premium.
289 10k.+5k. mult (postage) . . . 45 45
290 15k.+5k. multicoloured . . . 45 45
291 20k.+5k. multicoloured . . . 45 45
292 30k.+5k. multicoloured . . . 45 45
293 40k.+5k. multicoloured . . . 90 90
294 60k.+5k. multicoloured . . . 1·00 1·00
295 110k.+5k. mult (air) . . . . 2·20 2·20
296 300k.+5k. multicoloured . . 3·25 3·25

75 Weaving Silk

1970. "EXPO 70" World Fair, Osaka, Japan. Laotian Silk Industry.
297 **75** 30k. bl, brn & red (postage) 45 30
298 – 70k. multicoloured 90 60
299 – 125k. multicoloured (air) 1·30 90
DESIGNS: 70k. Silk-spinning; 125k. Winding skeins.

76 Wild Boar

77 Buddha, U.N. Emblem and New York H.Q.

1970. Wild Animals (2nd series).
300 **76** 20k. brown & grn (postage) 45 20
301 – 60k. brown and olive . . . 90 45
302 – 210k. brown, red and yellow (air) . . . . . . 2·20 1·60
303 – 500k. green, brown & orge 4·50 3·00
ANIMALS: 210k. Leopard; 500k. Gaur.

1970. 25th Anniv of U.N.O.
304 **77** 30k. brown, mauve and blue (postage) 60 35
305 70k. brown, blue and green 90 50
306 – 125k. multicoloured (air) 1·90 1·10
DESIGN—26 × 36 mm: 125k. Nang Thorani ("Goddess of the Earth") and New York Headquarters.

1970. Air. Paintings by Marc Leguay (3rd series). As T **69**. Multicoloured.
307 100k. "Village Track" . . . 1·10 50
308 120k. "Paddy-field in the Rainy Season" (horiz) . . 1·50 60
309 150k. "Village Elder" . . . . 1·60 80

78 "Nakhanet"

1971. Laotian Mythology (1st series). Frescoes from Triumphal Arch, Vientiane. Multicoloured.
310 **78** 70k. orange, brown and red (postage) 60 45
311 – 85k. green, yellow and blue 75 50
312 – 125k. multicoloured (air) 1·50 80
DESIGNS: As T **78**: 85k. "Rahu". 49 × 36 mm: 125k. "Underwater duel between Nang Matsa and Hanuman".
See also Nos. 352/4 and 385/7.

79 Silversmiths

1971. Laotian Traditional Crafts. Multicoloured.
313 30k. Type **79** 20 20
314 50k. Potters 35 20
315 70k. Pirogue-builder (49 × 36 mm) 65 35

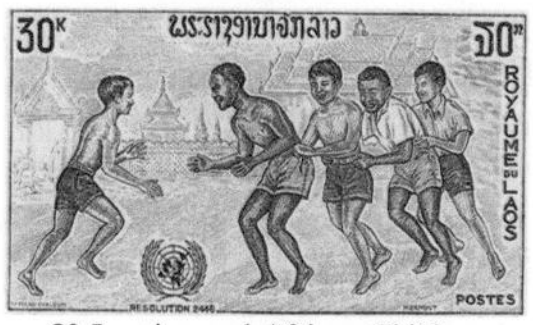

80 Laotian and African Children

1971. Racial Equality Year.
316 **80** 30k. blue, red and green 30 20
317 – 60k. violet, red and yellow 50 30
DESIGN: 60k. Laotian dancers and musicians.

81 Buddhist Monk at That Luang

1971. 50th Anniv of Vientiane Rotary Club.
318 **81** 30k. violet, brown and blue 35 20
319 – 70k. grey, red and blue . . 1·10 50
DESIGN—VERT: 70k. Laotian girl on "Dragon" staircase.

82 "Dendrobium agregatum"

83 Dancers from France and Laos

1971. Laotian Orchids. Multicoloured.
320 30k. Type **82** (postage) . . . 75 35
321 40k. "Rynchostylis giganterum" 75 50
322 50k. "Ascocentrum miniatur" (horiz) . . . . 1·10 45
323 60k. "Paphiopedilum exul" 1·30 75
324 70k. "Trichoglottis fasciata" (horiz) . . . . 1·50 80
325 80k. Cattleya (horiz) . . . . 1·60 80
326 125k. Brazilian cattleya (horiz) (air) . . . . . . 3·25 1·10
327 150k. "Vanda teres" (horiz) 3·75 1·30
Nos. 321, 323 and 325 are smaller, 22 × 36 or 36 × 22 mm. Nos. 326/7 are larger, 48 × 27 mm.

1971. Air. "Twin Cities" of St. Astier (France) and Keng-Kok (Laos).
328 **83** 30k. brown and light brown 20 15
329 70k. purple and plum . . . 35 15
330 100k. green and deep green 50 20

84 Common Palm Civet

1971. Wild Animals (3rd series).
331 **84** 25k. black, violet and blue (postage) 50 30
332 40k. black, green and olive 75 45
333 – 50k. orange and green . . 1·10 60
334 – 85k. brown, green & emerald . . . . 1·80 95
335 – 300k. brown and green (air) . . . . 4·00 2·40
DESIGNS: 50k. Lesser Malay chevrotain; 85k. Sambar; 300k. Javan rhinoceros.

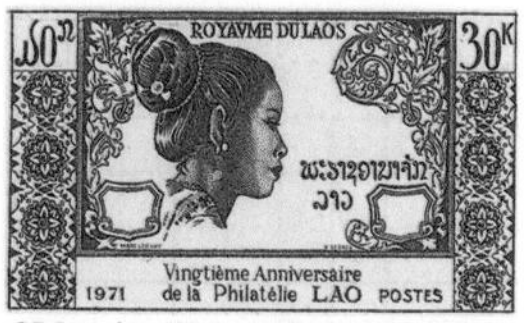

85 Laotian Woman (design from 1952 issue)

1971. 20th Anniv of Laotian Stamps.
336 **85** 30k. chocolate, brown and violet (postage) 20 15
337 – 40k. multicoloured 45 20
338 – 50k. black, flesh and blue 60 35
339 – 125k. violet, brn & grn (air) . . . . 1·40 90
MS340 180 × 110 mm. **85** 30k. chocolate, brown and violet; 60k. red and brown; 85k. deep green, green and blue . . . . . . 3·00 3·00
DESIGNS: 36 × 48 mm—40k. Violinist (1957 issue); 50k. Rama (1965 issue); 125k. "The Offertory" 1957 issue).

86 "Sunset on the Mekong"

1971. Air. Paintings by Chamnane Prisayane. Mult.
341 125k. Type **86** . . . . 1·20 90
342 150k. "Quiet Morning at Ban Tane Pieo" . . . . 1·60 1·10

87 Children reading Book

1972. International Book Year.
343 **87** 30k. green (postage) . . . 20 15
344 – 70k. brown 50 35
345 – 125k. violet (air) . . . . . 1·10 80
DESIGNS—22 × 27 mm: 70k. Laotian illustrating manuscript. 48 × 27 mm: 125k. Father showing manuscripts to children.

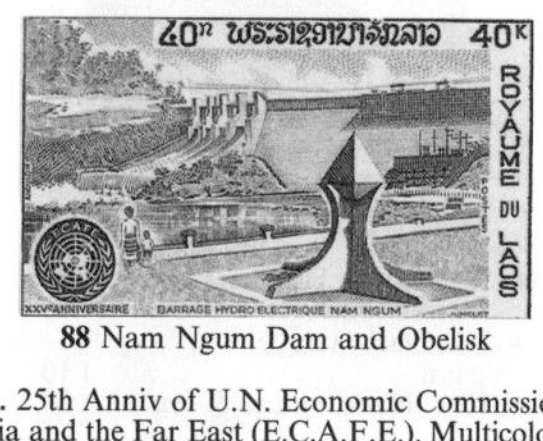

88 Nam Ngum Dam and Obelisk

1972. 25th Anniv of U.N. Economic Commission for Asia and the Far East (E.C.A.F.E.). Multicoloured.
346 40k. Type **88** (postage) . . . 30 20
347 80k. Type **88** 60 35
348 145k. Lake and spill-way, Nam Ngum Dam (air) . . 1·10 75

89 "The Water-carrier"

1972. 25th Anniv of UNICEF Drawings by Lao Schoolchildren. Multicoloured.
349 50k. Type **89** (postage) . . . 60 35
350 80k. "Teaching Bamboo-weaving" 75 45
351 120k. "Riding a Water-buffalo" (air) . . . . . . 1·10 80

90 "Nakharath"

1972. Air. Laotian Mythology (2nd series).
352 **90** 100k. turquoise 75 60
353 – 120k. lilac 95 75
354 – 150k. brown . . . . 1·30 90
DESIGNS: 120k. "Nang Kinnali"; 150k. "Norasing".

91 Festival Offerings

1972. Air. That Luang Religious Festival.
355 **91** 110k. brown 75 50
356 – 125k. purple . . . . 1·10 75
DESIGN: 125k. Festival procession.

1972. Air. Paintings by Marc Leguay (4th series). As T **69**. Multicoloured.
357 50k. "In the Paddy Field" (detail) 45 35
358 50k. "In the Paddy Field" (different detail) 45 35
359 70k. "Village in the Rainy Season" (detail) 65 45
360 70k. "Village in the Rainy Season" (different detail) 65 45
361 120k. "Laotian Mother" . . 1·50 90
Nos. 357/8 and 359/60 when placed together form the complete painting in each case.

92 Attopeu Religious Costume

93 "Lion" Guardian, That Luang

1973. Regional Costumes.
362 **92** 40k. yellow, mauve & brown (postage) 45 20
363 – 90k. black, red and brown 95 45
364 – 120k. brown, sepia and mauve (air) 90 60
365 – 150k. ochre, red and brown 1·10 80
DESIGNS: 90k. Phongsaly festival costume; 120k. Luang Prabang wedding costume; 150k. Vientiane evening dress.

1973. 55th Anniv of Lions International.
366 **93** 40k. red, pur & bl (postage) 45 20
367 80k. red, yellow and blue 75 45
368 – 150k. multicoloured (air) 1·20 90
DESIGN—48 × 27 mm: 150k. Lions emblems and statue of King Saysetthathirath, Vientiane.

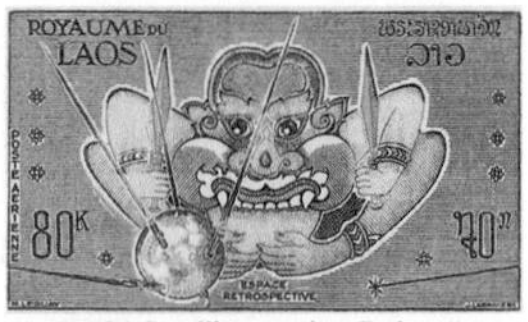

94 Satellite passing Rahu

1973. Traditional and Modern Aspects of Space. Multicoloured.
369 80k. Type **94** 50 35
370 150k. Landing module and Laotian festival rocket . . 95 50

95 Dr. Gerhard Hansen and Map of Laos

1973. Centenary of Identification of Leprosy Bacillus by Hansen.
371 **95** 40k. purple, dp pur & orge 50 35
372 80k. purple, brown & yell 95 45

96 "Benediction" **97** "Nang Mekhala". (Goddess of the Sea)

1973. 25th Anniv of Laotian Boy Scouts Association.
373 **96** 70k. yellow & brn (postage) 65 35
374 – 110k. violet and orange (air) 65 35
375 – 150k. blue, drab and brown 90 50
DESIGNS—48 × 27 mm: 110k. Campfire entertainment; 150k. Scouts helping flood victims, Vientiane, 1966.

1973. Air. Centenary of World Meteorological Organization.
376 **97** 90k. lilac, red and brown 65 35
377 – 150k. brown, red & lt brn 1·20 50
DESIGN—HORIZ: 150k. "Chariot of the Sun".

99 Interpol H.Q., Paris

1973. 50th Anniv of Int Criminal Police Organization (Interpol).
382 **99** 40k. blue (postage) 30 20
383 80k. brown and light brown 45 30
384 – 150k. violet, red and green (air) 90 50
DESIGN—48 × 27 mm: 150k. Woman in opium poppy field.

100 "Phra Sratsvady"

1974. Air. Laotian Mythology (3rd series).
385 **100** 100k. red, brown and lilac 75 45
386 – 110k. brown, lilac and red 95 50
387 – 150k. violet, brown and light brown . . . . . 1·50 80
DESIGNS: 110k. "Phra Indra"; 150k. "Phra Phrom".

101 Boy and Postbox **102** "Eranthemum nervosum"

1974. Centenary of U.P.U.
388 **101** 70k. brown, green and blue (postage) 50 35
389 80k. brown, blue and green 60 50
390 – 200k. brown and red (air) 2·20 1·50
DESIGN—48 × 36 mm: 200k. Laotian girls with letters, and U.P.U. Monument, Berne (Type **105**).

1974. Laotian Flora.
391 **102** 30k. violet & grn (postage) 50 35
392 – 50k. multicoloured . . . 75 45
393 – 80k. red, green and brown 1·10 75
394 – 500k. green & brown (air) 4·00 2·50
DESIGNS—As T **102**: HORIZ: 50k. Water lily; 80k. Red silk-cotton. 36 × 36 mm: 500k. Pitcher plant.

103 Mekong Ferry carrying Bus

1974. Laotian Transport.
395 **103** 25k. brown & orge (postage) 35 20
396 – 90k. brown and bistre . . 1·80 90
397 – 250k. brown & green (air) 1·90 1·10
DESIGNS—VERT: 90k. Bicycle rickshaw. HORIZ: 250k. Mekong house boat.

104 Marconi, and Laotians with Transistor Radio

1974. Birth Centenary of Guglielmo Marconi (radio pioneer).
398 **104** 60k. grey, green and brown (postage) 35 20
399 90k. grey, brown and green . . . . 1·80 90
400 – 200k. blue and brown (air) . . . . 1·90 1·10
DESIGN: 200k. Communications methods.

105 U.P.U. Monument and Laotian Girls

1974. Air Centenary of U.P.U.
401 **105** 500k. lilac and red . . . 4·50 2·75
MS402 135 × 105 mm. No. 401 4·50 4·50
For 200k. as T **105** see No. 390.

106 "Diastocera wallichi"

1974. Beetles.
403 **106** 50k. brown, black and green (postage) 75 45
404 – 90k. black, turquoise & grn . . . . 1·10 60
405 – 100k. black, orange & brn 1·50 90
406 – 110k. violet, red & grn (air) . . . . 1·30 50
DESIGNS: 90k. "Macrochenus isabellunus"; 100k. "Purpuricenus malaccensis"; 110k. "Sternocera multipunctata".

107 Pagoda and Sapphire

1974. "Mineral Riches".
407 **107** 100k. brown, green & blue 75 50
408 – 110k. brown, blue & yellow 90 50
DESIGN: 110k. Gold-panning and necklace.

108 King Savang Vatthana, Prince Souvanna Phouma and Prince Souvanouvong

1975. 1st Anniv (1974) of Laotian Peace Treaty.
409 **108** 80k. brown, ochre & green 75 35
410 300k. brown, ochre & pur 1·30 1·10
411 420k. brown, ochre and turquoise . . . . 1·50 1·10

109 Fortune-teller's Chart

1975. Chinese New Year ("Year of the Rabbit").
413 **109** 40k. brown and green . . 50 20
414 – 200k. black, brown and green . . . . 1·30 50
415 – 350k. brown, green and blue . . . . 2·40 1·30
DESIGNS—HORIZ: 200k. Fortune-teller. VERT: 350k. Woman riding hare.

110 U.N. Emblem and Frieze **112**

111 King Savang Vatthana, Prince Souvanna Phouma and Prince Souvanouvong

1975. International Women's Year.
416 **110** 100k. blue and turquoise 35 30
417 – 200k. orange and green 75 35
MS418 130 × 100 mm. Nos. 416/17 4·75 4·75
DESIGN: 200k. IWY emblem.

1975. 1st Laotian Peace Treaty (2nd issue). Sheet 90 × 70 mm.
MS419 **111** 2000k. gold, red and green . . . . 8·75 8·75

1975. "Pravet Sandone" Religious Festival.
420 **112** 80k. multicoloured . . . 50 30
421 – 110k. multicoloured . . . 50 35
422 – 120k. multicoloured . . . 65 45
423 – 130k. multicoloured . . . 1·10 60
DESIGNS: 110k. to 130k. Various legends.

113 Buddha and Stupas

1975. UNESCO Campaign for Preservation of Borobudur Temple (in Indonesia).
424 **113** 100k. green, blue & brown 65 35
425 – 200k. ochre, green & brown . . . . 1·30 80
MS426 130 × 100 mm. Nos. 424/5 1·50 1·50
DESIGN: 200k. Temple sculptures.

114 Laotian Arms **115** Thathiang, Vien-Tran

1976. Multicoloured, background colour given.
427 **114** 1k. blue 15 15
428 2k. mauve 15 15
429 5k. green 20 15
430 10k. violet 45 35
431 200k. orange . . . . . . 3·00 2·20
MS432 165 × 70 mm. Nos. 427/31 11·00 11·00

1976. Pagodas. Multicoloured.
433 1k. Type **115** 15 15
434 2k. Phonsi, Luang Prabang 20 15
435 30k. Type **115** 75 50
436 80k. As 2k. . . . . 1·50 1·10
437 100k. As 2k. . . . . 2·20 1·50
438 300k. Type **115** . . . . . . 3·75 2·75
MS439 Two sheets, each 113 × 75 mm. (a) Nos. 433, 435 and 438; (b) Nos. 434 and 436/7 8·00 8·00

116 Silversmith

1977. Laotian Crafts. Multicoloured.
440 1k. Type **116** 10 10
441 2k. Weaver 15 10
442 20k. Potter 75 20
443 50k. Basket-weaver (vert) . . 1·30 45
MS444 Four sheets, 90 × 81 mm (d) or 81 × 90 mm (others). (a) No. 440 × 2; (b) No. 441 × 2; (c) No. 442 × 2; (d) No. 443 × 2 . . 11·00 11·00

117 Gubarev, Grechko and "Salyut" Space Station

1977. 60th Anniv of Russian Revolution. Mult.
445 5k. Type **117** 10 10
446 20k. Lenin 20 15
447 50k. As 20k. 50 30
448 60k. Type **117** 60 45
449 100k. Government Palace, Vientiane, and Kremlin, Moscow (horiz) . . . . . 1·00 75
450 250k. As 100k. . . . . . . 2·40 1·90
MS451 Two sheets, each 141 × 81 mm. (a) Nos. 445, 447 and 450; (b) Nos. 446 and 448/9 8·75 8·75

118 Laotian Arms **119** Soldiers with Flag

1978.

452 **118** 5k. yellow and black . . . 15 15
453 10k. sepia and black . . . 15 15
454 50k. purple and black . . 50 15
455 100k. green and black . . 95 50
456 250k. violet and black . . 1·90 1·10

1978. Army Day. Multicoloured.

457 20k. Type **119** 15 15
458 40k. Soldiers attacking village (horiz) 20 15
459 300k. Anti-aircraft guns . . . 1·80 1·10

120 Marchers with Banner

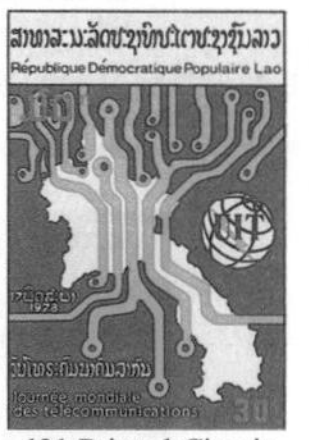

121 Printed Circuit and Map of Laos

1978. National Day. Multicoloured.

460 20k. Type **120** 35 15
461 50k. Women with flag . . . 35 15
462 400k. Dancer . . . . 2·20 1·50
MS463 Two sheets, each 160 × 105 mm, each containing Nos. 460/2, arranged from left (a) 20, 50, 400k.; (b) 400, 50, 20k. Imperf . . . . 8·75 8·75

1979. World Telecommunications Day.

464 **121** 30k. orange, brown & sil 15 10
465 – 250k. multicoloured . . . 1·50 80

DESIGN: 250k. Printed circuit, map of Laos and transmitter tower.

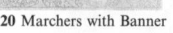

122 Woman posting Letter

1979. 15th Anniv of Asian-Oceanic Postal Union. Multicoloured.

466 5k. Type **122** 10 10
467 10k. Post Office counter . . . 10 10
468 80k. As 10k. 80 35
469 100k. Type **122** 95 50

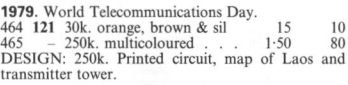

123 Children playing Ball

1979. International Year of the Child (1st issue). Multicoloured. Without gum.

470 20k. Type **123** 20 15
471 50k. Children at school (horiz) 45 15
472 200k. Mother feeding child 2·20 80
473 500k. Nurse immunising child 6·25 1·80
MS474 215 × 110 mm. Nos. 470/3. Imperf . . . . 15·00 15·00

See also Nos. 479/**MS**482.

124 Elephant, Buffalo and Pirogues

1979. Transport. Multicoloured.

475 5k. Type **124** 15 15
476 10k. Buffalo carts 15 15
477 70k. As No. 476 . . . . . . 75 20
478 500k. Type **124** . . . . . . 2·75 1·50

125 Dancing Child

1979. International Year of the Child (2nd issue). Multicoloured. Without gum.

479 100k. Children playing musical instruments (horiz) 50 35
480 200k. Child releasing dove . . 95 75
481 600k. Type **125** . . . . . . 3·25 1·80
MS482 189 × 109 mm. Nos. 479/81. Imperf . . . . 12·50 12·50

126 Forest and Paddy Field

1980. 5th Anniv of Republic (1st issue) and 25th Anniv of People's Front. Mult. Without gum.

483 30c. Type **126** 15 15
484 50c. Classroom and doctor examining baby (horiz) . . 35 15
485 1k. Three women 50 35
486 2k. Dam and electricity pylons (horiz) . . . . . . 1·30 1·10
MS487 170 × 99 mm. Nos. 483/6. Imperf . . . . 8·75 7·50

127 Lenin Reading

1980. 110th Birth Anniv of Lenin. Multicoloured.

488 1k. Type **127** 20 15
489 2k. Lenin writing 45 20
490 3k. Lenin and Red Flag (vert) 60 35
491 4k. Lenin making speech (vert) . . . . 1·10 50
MS492 136 × 95 mm. Nos. 488/91. Imperf . . . . 4·50 4·50

128 Workers in Field

1980. 5th Anniv of Republic (2nd issue). Multicoloured. Without gum.

493 50c. Type **128** 15 10
494 1k.60 Loading logs on lorry and elephant hauling logs 35 15
495 4k.60 Veterinary workers tending animals 75 30
496 5k.40 Workers in paddy field 1·10 45
MS497 207 × 165 mm. Nos. 193/6. Imperf . . . . 8·75 7·50

129 Emblems of Industry, Technology, Transport, Sport and Art

1981. 26th P.C.U.S. (Communist Party) Congress. Multicoloured.

498 60c. Type **129** 15 10
499 4k.60 Communist star breaking manacles and globe . . . . 1·50 45
500 5k. Laurel branch and broken bomb . . . . 2·10 50
MS501 140 × 106 mm. Nos. 498/500 (sold at 15k.) . . . . 6·25 4·00

130 Giant Pandas

1981. "Philatokyo 81" International Stamp Exhibition, Tokyo. Sheet 90 × 60 mm.

MS502 **130** 10k. multicoloured 5·50 2·20

131 Player heading Ball

132 Disabled Person on Telephone

1981. World Cup Football Championship, Spain (1982) (1st issue). Multicoloured.

503 1k. Type **131** 15 10
504 2k. Receiving ball 35 15
505 3k. Passing ball 50 15
506 4k. Goalkeeper diving for ball (horiz) 80 15
507 5k. Dribbling . . . . 1·10 35
508 6k. Kicking ball . . . . . . 1·60 45

See also Nos. 545/50.

1981. International Year of Disabled Persons. Multicoloured.

509 3k. Type **132** . . . . 1·10 35
510 5k. Disabled teacher . . . . 1·30 75
511 12k. Person in wheelchair mending net . . . . 3·25 1·10

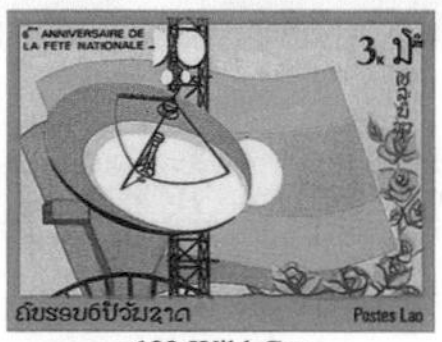

133 Wild Cat

1981. Wild Cats. Multicoloured.

512 10c. Type **133** 15 15
513 20c. Fishing cat 15 15
514 30c. Caracal 15 15
515 40c. Clouded leopard 15 15
516 50c. Flat-headed cat 15 15
517 9k. Jungle cat . . . . 3·25 65

134 Dish Aerial and Flag

1981. 6th National Day Festival. Multicoloured.

518 3k. Type **134** 45 30
519 4k. Soldier and flag 65 35
520 5k. Girls presenting flowers to soldier, flag and map of Laos 95 45

135 Indian Elephant

1982. Indian Elephant. Multicoloured.

521 1k. Type **135** 20 15
522 2k. Elephant carrying log . . 50 15
523 3k. Elephant with passengers 65 20
524 4k. Elephant in trap 90 30
525 5k. Elephant and young . . . 1·20 35
526 5k.50 Herd of elephants . . . 1·50 50

136 Laotian Wrestling

1982. Wrestling.

527 **136** 50c. multicoloured 15 15
528 – 1k.20 multicoloured . . . 15 15
529 – 2k. multicoloured 35 15
530 – 2k.50 multicoloured . . . 60 20
531 – 4k. multicoloured 95 35
532 – 5k. multicoloured . . . . 1·50 50

DESIGNS: 1k.20 to 5k. Various wrestling scenes.

137 "Nymphaea zanzibariensis"

1982. Water Lilies. Multicoloured.

533 30c. Type **137** 15 15
534 40c. "Nelumbo nucifera" "Gaertn Rose" 15 15
535 60c. "Nymphaea rosea" . . . 15 15
536 3k. "Nymphaea nouchali" . . 65 35
537 4k. "Nymphaea" White . . . 95 35
538 7k. "Nelumbo nucifera" "Gaertn White" . . . . . 1·90 45

138 Barn Swallow

1982. Birds. Multicoloured.

539 50c. Type **138** 15 15
540 1k. Hoopoe 15 15
541 2k. River kingfisher 50 15
542 3k. Black-naped blue monarch 75 20
543 4k. Grey wagtail (horiz) . . . 1·00 20
544 10k. Long-tailed tailor bird (horiz) . . . . 2·50 75

139 Football

1982. World Cup Football Championship, Spain (2nd issue).

545 **139** 1k. multicoloured 20 15
546 – 2k. multicoloured 35 15
547 – 3k. multicoloured 50 15
548 – 4k. multicoloured 75 20

549 **139** 5k. multicoloured 95 30
550 – 6k. multicoloured . . . . 1·30 45
MS551 81 × 63 mm. 15k. multicoloured (footballer and flag) (36 × 28 mm) . . . . 3·50 1·30
DESIGNS: 2, 3, 4, 6, 15k. Various football scenes.

140 "Herona marathus"

1982. Butterflies. Multicoloured.
552 1k. Type **140** 20 15
553 2k. "Neptis paraka" 45 15
554 3k. "Euripus halitherses" . . 65 20
555 4k. "Lebadea martha" . . . 95 20
556 5k. "Iton semamora" (42 × 26 mm) . . . . . . 1·50 35
557 6k. Common palm fly (59 × 41 mm) . . . . . . 1·80 45

141 Buddhist Temple, Vientiane

1982. "Philexfrance 82" International Stamp Exhibition, Paris. Sheet 86 × 64 mm.
MS558 **141** 10k. multicoloured 2·75 1·30

142 River Raft

1982. River Craft. Multicoloured.
559 50c. Type **142** 15 15
560 60c. River sampan 15 15
561 1k. River house boat 20 15
562 2k. River passenger steamer 50 15
563 3k. River ferry 65 20
564 8k. Self-propelled barge . . . 1·60 50

143 Vat Chanh

1982. Pagodas. Multicoloured.
565 50c. Type **143** 15 15
566 60c. Vat Inpeng 15 15
567 1k. Vat Dong Mieng 20 15
568 2k. Ho Tay 50 15
569 3k. Vat Ho Pha Keo 65 20
570 8k. Vat Sisaket . . . . . . 1·60 50

1982. Various stamps optd **1982**.
571 **114** 1k. multicoloured . . . .
572 **116** 1k. multicoloured . . . .
573 – 2k. multicoloured (441)
574 **117** 5k. multicoloured . . . .
575 **118** 5k. yellow and black . . .
576 **122** 5k. multicoloured . . . .
577 **124** 5k. multicoloured . . . .
578 – 10k. multicoloured (467)
579 – 10k. multicoloured (476)
580 – 20k. multicoloured (446)
581 **119** 20k. multicoloured . . .
582 **121** 30k. orange, brown & sil
583 – 40k. multicoloured (458)
584 – 50k. multicoloured (443)
585 – 70k. multicoloured (477)
586 – 80k. multicoloured (468)
587 **122** 100k. multicoloured . . .
588 **114** 200k. multicoloured . . .
589 **121** 250k. multicoloured . . .

145 Poodle

1982. Dogs. Multicoloured.
591 50c. Type **145** 15 15
592 60c. Samoyed 15 15
593 1k. Boston terrier 20 15
594 2k. Cairn terrier 65 15
595 3k. Chihuahua 90 35
596 8k. Bulldog . . . . 2·40 60

146 Woman watering Crops

1982. World Food Day. Multicoloured.
597 7k. Type **146** . . . . 1·30 45
598 8k. Woman transplanting rice 1·50 50

147 Fiat, 1925

1982. Cars. Multicoloured.
599 50c. Type **147** 15 15
600 60c. Peugeot, 1925 . . . . . 15 15
601 1k. Berliet, 1925 . . . . . . 30 15
602 2k. Ballot, 1925 . . . . . . 60 15
603 3k. Renault, 1926 . . . . . 90 35
604 8k. Ford, 1925 . . . . 1·80 60

148 President Souphanouvong

1982. 7th Anniv of Republic. Multicoloured.
605 50c. Type **148** 15 15
606 1k. Tractors (horiz) 20 15
607 2k. Cow (horiz) 30 15
608 3k. Lorry passing dish aerial (horiz) 50 20
609 4k. Nurse examining child . . 75 35
610 5k. Classroom (horiz) . . . . 1·00 35
611 6k. Dancer . . . . 1·50 45

149 Dimitrov, Flag and Arms of Bulgaria

1982. Birth Centenary of Georgi Dimitrov (Bulgarian statesman).
612 **149** 10k. multicoloured . . . 1·60 90

150 Kremlin and Arms of U.S.S.R.

151 Hurdling

1982. 60th Anniv of U.S.S.R. Multicoloured.
613 3k. Type **150** 50 35
614 4k. Doves and maps of U.S.S.R. and Laos 95 50
MS615 96 × 92 mm. Nos. 613/14 3·25 1·30

1983. Olympic Games, Los Angeles (1984) (1st issue). Multicoloured.
616 50c. Type **151** 15 15
617 1k. Javelin 20 15
618 2k. Basketball 30 15
619 3k. Diving 50 15
620 4k. Gymnastics 75 35
621 10k. Weightlifting . . . . . 2·20 75
MS622 91 × 62 mm. 15k. Football (31 × 39 mm) . . . . 3·25 1·30
See also Nos. 708/**MS**715.

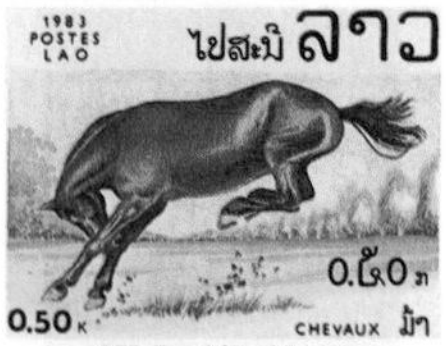
152 Bucking Horse

1983. Horses. Multicoloured.
623 50c. Type **152** 15 15
624 1k. Rearing black horse . . . 20 15
625 2k. Trotting brown horse . . 35 15
626 3k. Dappled grey horse . . . 65 20
627 4k. Wild horse crossing snow 80 30
628 10k. Horse in paddock . . . 2·50 75

153 "St. Catherine of Alexandria"

1983. 500th Birth Anniv of Raphael (artist). Multicoloured.
629 50c. Type **153** 15 15
630 1k. "Adoration of the Kings" 20 15
631 2k. "Madonna of the Grand Duke" 35 15
632 3k. "St. George and the Dragon" 65 20
633 4k. "The Vision of Ezekiel" 80 30
634 10k. "Adoration of the Kings" (different) . . . . 2·50 75
MS635 74 × 123 mm. 10k. "Coronation of the Virgin" (39 × 31 mm) . . . . 3·00 90

154 A. Gubarev (Soviet) and V. Remek (Czechoslovak)

1983. Cosmonauts. Multicoloured.
636 50c. Type **154** 15 15
637 50c. P. Klimuk (Soviet) and Miroslaw Hermaszewski (Polish) 15 15
638 1k. V. Bykovsky (Soviet) and Sigmund Jahn (East German) 20 15
639 1k. Nikolai Rukavishnikov (Soviet) and Georgi Ivanov (Bulgarian) 20 15
640 2k. V. Kubasov (Soviet) and Bertalan Farkas (Hungarian) 35 15
641 3k. V. Dzhanibekov (Soviet) and Gurragchaa (Mongolian) 60 20
642 4k. L. Popov (Soviet) and D. Prunariu (Rumanian) 75 20
643 6k. Soviet cosmonaut and Arnaldo Tamayo (Cuban) 1·10 35
644 10k. Soviet and French cosmonauts . . . . . . 2·20 75
MS645 92 × 90 mm. 10k. V. Gorbatko (Soviet) and Pham Tuan (Vietnamese) (28 × 35 mm) 2·50 90

155 Jacques Charles's Hydrogen Balloon, 1783

1983. Bicentenary of Manned Flight. Mult.
646 50c. Type **155** 15 15
647 1k. Blanchard and Jeffries' balloon, 1785 . . . . . . 20 15
648 2k. Vincenzo Lunardi's balloon (London–Ware flight), 1784 . . . . . . 35 15
649 3k. Modern hot-air balloon over city 75 20
650 4k. Massed balloon ascent, 1890 . . . . 90 35
651 10k. Auguste Piccard's stratosphere balloon "F.N.R.S.", 1931 . . . . 2·50 75
MS652 100 × 83 mm. 10k. Balloon "Double Eagle II" (312 × 39 mm) 2·50 95

156 German Maybach Car

1983. "Tembal 83" Stamp Exhibition, Basle. Sheet 95 × 63 mm.
MS653 **156** 10k. multicoloured 3·00 95

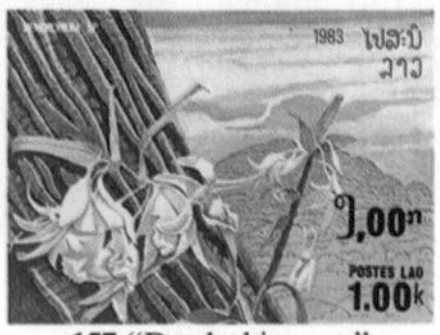
157 "Dendrobium sp."

1983. Flowers. Multicoloured.
654 1k. Type **157** 20 15
655 2k. "Aerides odoratum" . . 35 15
656 3k. "Dendrobium aggregatum" 60 20
657 4k. "Dendrobium" 75 20
658 5k. "Moschatum" . . . . . 1·00 30
659 6k. "Dendrobium sp." (different) . . . . 1·50 45

158 Downhill Skiing

1983. Winter Olympic Games, Sarajevo (1984) (1st issue). Multicoloured.
660 50c. Type **158** 15 15
661 1k. Slalom 20 15
662 2k. Ice hockey 35 15
663 3k. Speed skating 65 20
664 4k. Ski jumping 80 30
665 10k. Luge . . . . 2·20 75
MS666 91 × 57 mm. 15k. Bobsleigh (39 × 31 mm) . . . . 3·25 1·10
See also Nos. 696/**MS**703.

159 Boatman on Tachin River

1983. "Bangkok 1983" International Stamp Exhibition. Sheet 93 × 72 mm.
MS667 **159** 10k. multicoloured 2·50 90

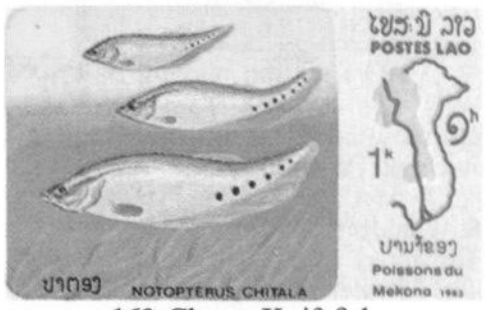
160 Clown Knifefish

1983. Fishes of Mekong River. Multicoloured.
668 1k. Type **160** 20 15
669 2k. Common carp 35 15
670 3k. Lesser Mekong catfish . . 65 20
671 4k. Giant barb 75 20
672 5k. Black shark . . . . . . 1·20 30
673 6k. Nile mouthbrooder . . . 1·60 45

161 Magellan and "Vitoria"

1983. Explorers and their Ships. Multicoloured.
674 1k. Type **161** 20 15
675 2k. Jacques Cartier and "Grande Hermine" 35 15
676 3k. Columbus and "Santa Maria" 75 20
677 4k. Pedro Alvares Cabral and "El Ray" 90 20
678 5k. Cook and H.M.S. "Resolution" . . . . . . 1·10 30
679 6k. Charcot and "Pourquoi-pas?" . . . . 1·60 45
No. 679 is wrongly inscribed "Cabot".

162 Tabby Cat

1983. Domestic Cats. Multicoloured.
680 1k. Type **162** 20 15
681 2k. Long-haired Persian . . . 75 15
682 3k. Siamese 65 20
683 4k. Burmese 80 20
684 5k. Persian . . . . 1·20 30
685 6k. Tortoiseshell . . . . . . 1·60 45

1983. Nos. 430 and 466 optd **1983**.
685a **122** 5k. multicoloured . . .
685b **114** 10k. multicoloured . . .

163 Marx, Book, Sun and Signature

1983. Death Centenary of Karl Marx. Mult.
686 1k. Marx, dove, globe and flags 30 15
687 4k. Type **163** . . . . 1·00 15
688 6k. Marx and flags . . . . . 1·80 50

164 Elephant dragging Log

1983. 8th Anniv of Republic. Multicoloured.
689 1k. Type **164** 30 15
690 4k. Cattle and pig (horiz) . . 1·00 15
691 6k. Crops . . . . 1·80 50

165 Carrier Pigeon and Telex Machine

1983. World Communications Year. Multicoloured.
692 50c. Type **165** 15 15
693 1k. Early telephone, handset and receiver 20 15
694 4k. Television tube and aerial 90 30
695 6k. Satellite and dish aerial 1·50 50

166 Ice Skating **167** Tiger

1984. Winter Olympic Games, Sarajevo (2nd issue). Multicoloured.
696 50c. Type **166** 15 15
697 1k. Speed skating 20 15
698 2k. Biathlon 35 15
699 3k. Luge (horiz) 90 30
700 4k. Downhill skiing (horiz) . . 95 30
701 5k. Ski jumping . . . . . . 1·30 45
702 6k. Slalom . . . . 1·60 50
MS703 89 × 55 mm. 10k. Ice hockey (31 × 39 mm) . . . . 2·50 90

1984. Endangered Animals. The Tiger. Mult.
704 25c. Type **167** 35 15
705 25c. Tigers (horiz) 35 15
706 3k. Tiger and cubs (horiz) . . 4·00 50
707 4k. Tiger cubs . . . . 6·25 1·00

168 Diving

1984. Olympic Games, Los Angeles (2nd issue). Multicoloured.
708 50c. Type **168** 15 15
709 1k. Volleyball 30 15
710 2k. Running 60 15
711 4k. Basketball . . . . 1·20 15
712 5k. Judo . . . . 1·30 30
713 6k. Football . . . . 1·80 35
714 7k. Gymnastics . . . . 2·10 45
MS715 98 × 81 mm. 10k. Wrestling (31 × 39 mm) . . . . 2·50 90

169 Tuned Drums

1984. Musical Instruments. Multicoloured.
716 1k. Type **169** 20 15
717 2k. Xylophone 45 15
718 3k. Pair of drums 80 20
719 4k. Hand drum . . . . . . 1·00 30
720 5k. Barrel drum . . . . . . 1·30 30
721 6k. Pipes and string instrument . . . . 2·10 45

170 National Flag **171** Chess Game

1984. National Day. Multicoloured.
722 60c. Type **170** 20 15
723 1k. National arms 45 15
724 2k. As No. 723 . . . . . . 60 20

1984. 60th Anniv of World Chess Federation. Multicoloured.
725 50c. Type **171** 15 15
726 1k. Renaissance game from "The Three Ages of Man" (miniature attr. to Estienne Porchier) 20 15
727 2k. Woman teaching girls . . 50 15
728 2k. Margrave Otto IV of Brandenburg playing chess with his wife 50 15
729 3k. Four men at chessboard 90 30
730 4k. Two women playing . . . 1·30 30
731 8k. Two men playing . . . . 2·75 45
MS732 87 × 70 mm. 10k. Human chess game (31 × 39 mm) . . . 2·50 90
Nos. 725, 727 and 729/31 show illustrations from King Alfonso X's "Book of Chess, Dice and Tablings".

172 "Cardinal Nino de Guevara" (El Greco) **173** "Adonis aestivalis"

1984. "Espana 84" International Stamp Exhibition, Madrid. Multicoloured.
733 50c. Type **172** 15 15
734 1k. "Gaspar de Guzman, Duke of Olivares, on Horseback" (Velazquez) . . 30 15
735 2k. "The Annunciation" (Murillo) 45 15
736 2k. "Portrait of a Lady" (Zurbaran) 45 15
737 3k. "The Family of Charles IV" (Goya) 65 30
738 4k. "Two Harlequins" (Picasso) 95 30
739 8k. "Abstract" (Miro) . . . 1·90 45
MS740 63 × 80 mm. 10k. "Burial of the Count of Orgaz" (El Gerco) 2·50 90

1984. Woodland Flowers. Multicoloured.
741 50c. Type **173** 15 15
742 1k. "Alpinia speciosa" . . . 20 15
743 2k. "Cassia lechenaultiana" 45 15
744 2k. "Aeschynanthus speciosus" 45 15
745 3k. "Datura meteloides" . . 75 30
746 4k. "Quamoclit pennata" . . 95 30
747 8k. "Commelina benghalensis" . . . . . . 1·90 45

174 Nazzaro

1984. 19th Universal Postal Union Congress Philatelic Salon, Hamburg. Cars. Multicoloured.
748 50c. Type **174** 15 15
749 1k. Daimler 20 15
750 2k. Delage 45 15
751 2k. Fiat "S 57/14B" 45 15
752 3k. Bugatti 90 30
753 4k. Itala . . . . 1·30 30
754 8k. Blitzen Benz . . . . . 2·40 45
MS755 79 × 52 mm. 10k. Winton "Bullet" . . . . 2·50 95

175 "Madonna and Child"

1984. 450th Death Anniv of Correggio (artist). Multicoloured.
756 50c. Type **175** 15 15
757 1k. Detail showing horsemen resting 30 15
758 2k. "Madonna and Child" (different) 50 15
759 2k. "Mystical Marriage of St. Catherine" 50 15
760 3k. "Four Saints" 75 30
761 4k. "Noli me Tangere" . . . 1·10 30
762 8k. "Christ bids Farewell to the Virgin Mary" . . . . 2·20 45
MS763 80 × 107 mm. 10k. "Madonna and Child" (different) (31 × 39 mm) . . . . 3·25 95

176 "Luna 1"

1984. Space Exploration. Multicoloured.
764 50c. Type **176** 15 15
765 1k. "Luna 2" 20 15
766 2k. "Luna 3" 45 15
767 2k. Kepler and "Sputnik 2" 45 15
768 3k. Newton and Lunokhod 2 95 20
769 4k. Jules Verne and "Luna 13" . . . . 1·30 35
770 8k. Copernicus and space station . . . . 2·40 60

177 Malaclemys Terrapin

1984. Reptiles. Multicoloured.
771 50c. Type **177** 15 15
772 1k. Banded krait 20 15
773 2k. Indian python (vert) . . . 45 15
774 2k. Reticulated python . . . 45 15
775 3k. Tokay gecko 95 20
776 4k. "Natrix subminiata" (snake) . . . . 1·30 35
777 8k. Dappled ground gecko 2·50 60

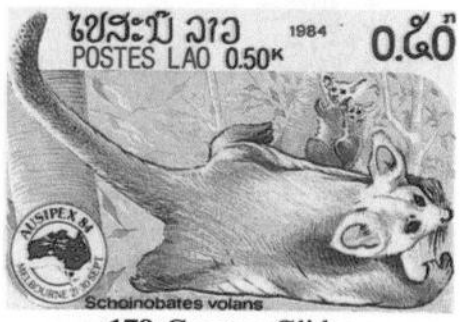

178 Greater Glider

1984. "Ausipex 84" International Stamp Exhibition, Melbourne. Marsupials. Mult.
778 50c. Type **178** 15 15
779 1k. Platypus 30 15
780 2k. Southern hairy-nosed wombat ("Lasiorhinus latifrons") 45 15
781 2k. Tasmanian devil ("Sarcophilus harrisii") . . 45 15
782 3k. Thylacine 95 20
783 4k. Tiger cat . . . . 1·20 35
784 8k. Wallaby . . . . 2·10 60
MS785 95 × 58 mm. 10k. Red kangaroo (31 × 39 mm) . . . . 2·50 90

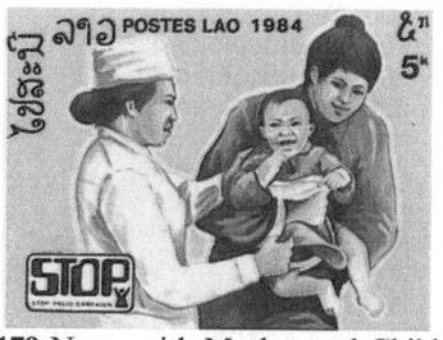

179 Nurse with Mother and Child

1984. Anti-poliomyelitis Campaign. Multicoloured.
786 5k. Type **179** . . . . 1·10 50
787 6k. Doctor inoculating child 1·30 50

180 Dragon Stair-rail

1984. Laotian Art. Multicoloured.
788 50c. Type **180** 15 15
789 1k. Capital of column . . . 20 15
790 2k. Decorative panel depicting god 35 15
791 2k. Decorative panel depicting leaves 35 15
792 3k. Stylized leaves (horiz) . . 75 20
793 4k. Triangular flower decoration (horiz) . . . . 1·30 35
794 8k. Circular lotus flower decoration . . . . 2·40 60

181 River House Boats

1984. 9th Anniv of Republic. Multicoloured.
795 1k. Type **181** 45 15
796 2k. Passengers boarding Fokker Friendship airliner 65 20
797 4k. Building a bridge . . . . 1·30 60
798 10k. Building a road . . . . 2·75 1·20

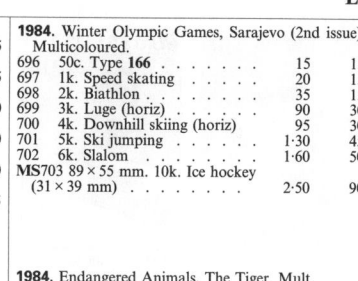

182 Players with Ball

1985. World Cup Football Championship, Mexico (1986) (1st issue). Multicoloured.

799	50c. Type **182**	15	15
800	1k. Heading the ball	20	15
801	2k. Defending the ball	60	15
802	3k. Running with ball	90	15
803	4k. Taking possession of ball	1·30	30
804	5k. Heading the ball (different)	1·60	35
805	6k. Saving a goal	1·90	60
MS806	56 × 72 mm. 10k. Flag, player and ball (31 × 39 mm)	2·75	90

See also Nos. 868/**MS**875.

183 Motor Cycle

1985. Centenary of Motor Cycle. Multicoloured.

807	50c. Type **183**	15	15
808	1k. Gnome Rhone, 1920	20	15
809	2k. F.N. "M67C", 1928	50	15
810	3k. Indian "Chief", 1930	75	15
811	4k. Rudge Multi, 1914	1·10	30
812	5k. Honda "Benly J", 1953	1·30	35
813	6k. CZ, 1938	1·60	60

1985. Various stamps optd **1985**.

813a	–	40k. multicoloured (458)
813b	–	50k. multicoloured (443)
813c	–	50k. multicoloured (447)
813d	–	70k. multicoloured (477)
813e	–	80k. multicoloured (468)
813f	–	100k. multicoloured (449)
813g	**122**	100k. multicoloured
813h	**114**	200k. multicoloured
813i	–	250k. multicoloured (450)
813j	**118**	250k. violet and black
813k	**121**	250k. multicoloured
813m	–	300k. multicoloured (459)

184 Fly Agaric

1985. Fungi. Multicoloured.

814	50c. Type **184**	15	15
815	1k. Cep	20	15
816	2k. Shaggy ink cap ("Coprinus comatus")	50	15
817	2k. The blusher ("Amanita rubescens")	50	15
818	3k. Downy boletus	1·00	30
819	4k. Parasol mushroom	1·60	35
820	8k. Brown roll-rim	2·75	65

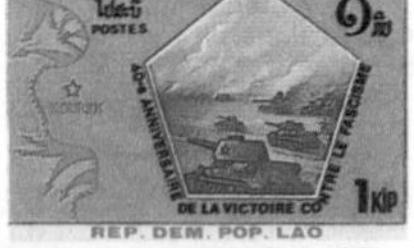

184a Battle Plan, Kursk, and Tanks

1985. 40th Anniv of End of Second World War. Multicoloured.

820a	1k. Type **184a**	35	15
820b	2k. Monument and military parade, Red Square, Moscow	65	15
820c	4k. Street battle and battle plan, Stalingrad	1·30	35
820d	5k. Battle plan and Reichstag, Berlin	1·60	45
820e	6k. Soviet Memorial, Berlin-Treptow, and military parade at Brandenburg Gate	1·90	50

185 Lenin reading "Pravda"

1985. 115th Birth Anniv of Lenin. Multicoloured.

821	1k. Type **185**	35	15
822	2k. Lenin (vert)	60	15
823	10k. Lenin addressing meeting (vert)	2·50	75

186 "Cattleya percivaliana"

1985. "Argentina '85" International Stamp Exhibition, Buenos Aires. Orchids. Multicoloured.

824	50c. Type **186**	15	15
825	1k. "Odontoglossum luteo-purpureum"	20	15
826	2k. "Cattleya lueddemanniana"	45	15
827	2k. "Maxillaria sanderiana"	45	15
828	3k. "Miltonia vexillaria"	75	20
829	4k. "Oncidium varicosum"	1·00	30
830	8k. "Cattleya dowiana"	2·20	60
MS831	82 × 63 mm. 10k. "Catasetum fimbriatum" (31 × 39 mm)	3·00	95

187 Rhesus Macaque

188 "Saturn" Rocket on Launch Pad

1985. Mammals. Multicoloured.

832	2k. Type **187**	30	15
833	3k. Kouprey	60	15
834	4k. Porcupine (horiz)	90	30
835	5k. Asiatic black bear (horiz)	1·10	30
836	10k. Chinese pangolin	2·40	60

1985. 10th Anniv of "Apollo"–"Soyuz" Space Link. Multicoloured.

837	50c. Type **188**	15	15
838	1k. Soviet rocket on launch pad	30	15
839	2k. "Apollo" approaching "Soyuz 19" (horiz)	45	15
840	2k. "Soyuz 19" approaching "Apollo" (horiz)	45	15
841	3k. "Apollo" and crew T. Stafford, V. Brand and D. Stayton (horiz)	75	20
842	4k. "Soyuz 19" and crew A. Leonov and V. Kubasov (horiz)	1·00	30
843	8k. "Apollo" and "Soyuz 19" docked (horiz)	2·10	60

189 Fiat Biplane

1985. "Italia '85" International Stamp Exhibition, Rome. Multicoloured. (a) Aircraft. As T **189**.

844	50c. Type **189**	15	15
845	1k. Cant Z.501 Gabbiano flying boat	20	15
846	2k. Marina Fiat MF.5 flying boat	45	15
847	3k. Macchi Castoldi MC-100 flying boat	65	20
848	4k. Anzani biplane	90	30
849	5k. Ambrosini biplane	95	30
850	6k. Piaggio P-148	1·30	45
MS851	86 × 54 mm. 10k. Marina Fiat MF.4 flying boat (39 × 31 mm)	2·50	1·00

(b) Columbus and his Ships. Size 40 × 29 mm.

852	1k. "Pinta"	20	15
853	2k. "Nina"	45	15
854	3k. "Santa Maria"	65	20
855	4k. Christopher Columbus	90	30
856	5k. Map of Columbus's first voyage	1·10	35

190 U.N. and National Flags on Globe

191 Woman feeding Child

1985. 40th Anniv of U.N.O. Multicoloured.

857	2k. Type **190**	65	20
858	3k. U.N. emblem and Laotian arms on globe	95	30
859	10k. Map on globe	2·75	95

1985. Lao Health Services. Multicoloured.

860	1k. Type **191**	20	15
861	3k. Red Cross nurse injecting child (horiz)	80	15
862	4k. Red Cross nurse tending patient (horiz)	1·00	30
863	10k. Mother breast-feeding baby	2·20	75

192 Soldier, Workers and Symbols of Industry and Agriculture

1985. 10th Anniv of Republic. Multicoloured.

864	3k. Type **192**	65	20
865	10k. Soldier, workers and symbols of transport and communications	2·50	90

193 Soldier with Flag and Workers

1985. 30th Anniv of Lao People's Revolutionary Party. Multicoloured.

866	2k. Type **193**	90	15
867	8k. Soldier with flag and workers (different)	2·75	60

194 Footballers

1986. World Cup Football Championship, Mexico (2nd issue).

868	**194**	50c. multicoloured	15	15
869	–	1k. multicoloured	20	15
870	–	2k. multicoloured	45	15
871	–	3k. multicoloured	65	20
872	–	4k. multicoloured	75	20
873	–	5k. multicoloured	95	30
874	–	6k. multicoloured	1·30	35
MS875		92 × 92 mm. 10k. multicoloured (39 × 31 mm)	3·75	90

DESIGNS: 1k. to 10k. Various football scenes.

194a Cosmonaut, "Mir" Space Complex and Earth

1986. 17th Soviet Communist Party Congress. Multicoloured.

875a	4k. Type **194a**	1·00	30
875b	20k. Lenin and Red Flag	4·00	95

195 "Pelargonium grandiflorum"

196 "Aporia hippia"

1986. Flowers. Multicoloured.

876	50c. Type **195**	15	15
877	1k. Columbine	20	15
878	2k. "Fuchsia globosa"	45	15
879	3k. "Crocus aureus"	65	20
880	4k. Hollyhock	75	20
881	5k. "Gladiolus purpureo"	95	30
882	6k. "Hyacinthus orientalis"	1·30	35

1986. Butterflies. Multicoloured.

883	50c. Type **196**	15	15
884	1k. "Euthalia irrubescens"	20	15
885	2k. "Japonica lutea"	45	15
886	3k. "Pratapa ctesia"	65	20
887	4k. Leaf butterfly	75	20
888	5k. Yellow orange-tip	95	30
889	6k. Chestnut tiger	1·30	35

197 Rocket launch at Baikanur Space Centre

1986. 25th Anniv of First Man in Space. Mult.

890	50c. Type **197**	15	15
891	1k. "Molniya" communications satellite	30	15
892	2k. "Salyut" space station (horiz)	45	15
893	3k. Yuri Gagarin, "Sputnik 1" and rocket debris (horiz)	80	15
894	4k. "Luna 3" and Moon	1·10	20
895	5k. Vladimir Komarov on first space walk	1·60	35
896	6k. "Luna 16" lifting off from Moon	1·80	45
MS897	88 × 66 mm. 10k. "Soyuz" preparing to dock with "Salyut" (39 × 31 mm)	2·50	90

198 Giraffe

1986. Animals. Multicoloured.

898	50c. Type **198**	15	15
899	1k. Lion	20	15
900	2k. African elephant	45	15
901	3k. Red kangaroo	65	20
902	4k. Koala	90	20
903	5k. Greater flamingo	1·00	30
904	6k. Giant panda	1·80	50
MS905	80 × 60 mm. 10k. American bison (31 × 39 mm)	2·50	1·00

199 Boeing 747-100

1986. Air. Aircraft. Multicoloured.

906	20k. Type **199**	3·75	30
907	50k. Ilyushin Il-86	8·75	80

200 Great Argus Pheasant (½-size illustration)

1986. Pheasants. Multicoloured.

908	50c. Type **200**	15	15
909	1k. Silver pheasant	20	15
910	2k. Common pheasant	45	15
911	3k. Lady Amherst's pheasant	65	20
912	4k. Reeves's pheasant	75	20
913	5k. Golden pheasant	95	30
914	6k. Copper pheasant	1·30	35

201 Scarlet King Snake

1986. Snakes. Multicoloured.

915	50c. Corn snake	15	15
916	1k. Type **201**	20	15
917	1k. Richard's blind snake (vert)	45	15
918	2k. Western ring-necked snake	65	20
919	4k. Mangrove snake	75	20
920	5k. Indian python	95	30
921	6k. Common cobra (vert)	1·30	35

202 Bayeux Tapestry (detail) and Comet Head

1986. Appearance of Halley's Comet. Multicoloured.

922	50c. Comet over Athens (65 × 21 mm)	15	15
923	1k. Type **202**	20	15
924	2k. Edmond Halley (astronomer) and comet tail (20 × 21 mm)	45	15
925	3k. "Vega" space probe and comet head	65	20
926	4k. Galileo and comet tail (20 × 21 mm)	75	20
927	5k. Comet head (20 × 21 mm)	95	30
928	6k. "Giotto" space probe and comet tail	1·30	35
MS929	100 × 45 mm. 10k. Surface of Earth and comet head (39 × 31 mm)	2·50	90

Nos. 923/4, 925/6 and 927/8 resepctively were issued together, se-tenant, each pair forming a composite design.

203 Keeshond

204 "Mammillaria matudae"

1986. "Stockholmia 86" International Stamp Exhibition. Dogs. Multicoloured.

930	50c. Type **203**	15	15
931	1k. Elkhound (horiz)	20	15
932	2k. Bernese (horiz)	50	15
933	3k. Pointing griffon (horiz)	80	20
934	4k. Collie (horiz)	80	20
935	5k. Irish water spaniel (horiz)	1·00	30
936	6k. Briard (horiz)	1·60	50
MS937	78 × 60 mm. 10k. Brittany spaniels chasing grey partridge (39 × 31 mm)	2·50	1·00

1986. Cacti. Multicoloured.

938	50c. Type **204**	15	15
939	1k. "Mammillaria theresae"	20	15
940	2k. "Ariocarpus trigonus"	45	15
941	3k. "Notocactus crassigibbus"	65	20
942	4k. "Astrophytum asterias" hybrid	75	20
943	5k. "Melocactus manzanus"	95	30
944	6k. "Astrophytum ornatum" hybrid	1·30	35

205 Arms and Dove on Globe

206 Vat Phu Champasak

1986. International Peace Year.

945	**205** 3k. multicoloured	80	20
946	– 5k. black, blue and red	1·30	35
947	– 10k. multicoloured	2·50	90

DESIGNS: 5k. Dove on smashed bomb; 10k. People supporting I.P.Y. emblem.

1987. 40th Anniv of UNESCO. Multicoloured.

948	3k. Type **206**	65	20
949	4k. Dish aerial and map of Laos on globe	90	30
950	9k. People reading books (horiz)	1·80	60

207 Speed Skating

1987. Winter Olympic Games, Calgary (1988) (1st issue). Multicoloured.

951	50c. Type **207**	15	15
952	1k. Biathlon	20	15
953	2k. Figure skating (pairs)	45	15
954	3k. Luge (horiz)	65	20
955	4k. Four-man bobsleigh (horiz)	75	20
956	5k. Ice hockey (horiz)	95	30
957	6k. Ski jumping (horiz)	1·30	35
MS958	78 × 58 mm. 10k. Skiing (31 × 39 mm)	2·50	1·00

See also Nos. 1046/**MS**1052.

208 Gymnast and Urn

1987. Olympic Games, Seoul (1988) (1st issue). Sports and Greek Pottery. Multicoloured.

959	50c. Type **208**	15	15
960	1k. Throwing the discus and vase (horiz)	20	15
961	2k. Running and urn	45	15
962	3k. Show jumping and bowl (horiz)	65	20
963	4k. Throwing the javelin and plate	75	20
964	5k. High jumping and bowl with handles (horiz)	95	30
965	6k. Wrestling and urn	1·30	35
MS966	82 × 55 mm. 10k. Runner leaving blocks (39 × 31 mm)	2·20	90

See also Nos. 1053/**MS**1060.

209 Great Dane

1987. Dogs. Multicoloured.

967	50c. Type **209**	15	15
968	1k. Black labrador	20	15
969	2k. St. Bernard	45	15
970	3k. Tervuren shepherd dog	75	20
971	4k. German shepherd	80	20
972	5k. Beagle	1·30	30
973	6k. Golden retriever	1·50	50

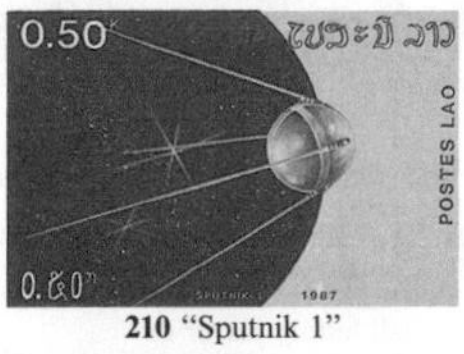

210 "Sputnik 1"

1987. 30th Anniv of Launch of First Artificial Satellite. Multicoloured.

974	50c. Type **210**	15	15
975	1k. "Sputnik 2"	20	15
976	2k. "Cosmos 97"	45	15
977	3k. "Cosmos"	65	20
978	4k. "Mars"	75	20
979	5k. "Luna 1"	95	30
980	9k. "Luna 3" (vert)	1·50	45

211 "MONTREAL" Handstamp on Letter to Quebec and Schooner

1987. "Capex 87" International Stamp Exhibition, Toronto. Ships and Covers. Multicoloured.

981	50c. Type **211**	15	15
982	1k. "PAID MONTREAL" on letter and schooner	20	15
983	2k. Letter from Montreal to London and "William D. Lawrence" (full-rigged ship)	45	15
984	3k. 1840 letter to Williamsburgh and "Neptune" (steamer)	65	20
985	4k. 1844 letter to London and "Athabasca" (screw-steamer)	75	20
986	5k. 1848 letter and "Chicora" (paddle-steamer)	95	30
987	6k. 1861 letter and "Passport" (river paddle-steamer)	1·30	35
MS988	80 × 60 mm. 10k. 1949 4c. Canadian stamp (39 × 31 mm)	2·20	90

212 Horse

1987. Horses. Multicoloured.

989	50c. Type **212**	15	15
990	1k. Chestnut (vert)	20	15
991	2k. Black horse with sheepskin noseband (vert)	45	15
992	3k. Dark chestnut (vert)	65	20
993	4k. Black horse (vert)	75	20
994	5k. Chestnut with plaited mane (vert)	95	30
995	6k. Grey (vert)	1·30	35

213 Volvo "480"

1987. Motor Cars. Multicoloured.

996	50c. Type **213**	15	15
997	1k. Alfa Romeo "33"	20	15
998	2k. Ford "Fiesta"	45	15
999	3k. Ford "Fiesta" (different)	75	20
1000	4k. Ford "Granada"	80	20
1001	5k. Citroen "AX"	1·30	30
1002	6k. Renault "21"	1·50	50
MS1003	65 × 52 mm. 10k. Skoda "Estelle" (39 × 31 mm)	2·75	95

214 "Vanda teres"

1987. Orchids. Multicoloured.

1004	3k. Type **214**	15	15
1005	7k. "Laeliocattleya" sp.	15	15
1006	10k. "Paphiopedilum" hybrid	20	15
1007	39k. "Sobralia" sp.	80	20
1008	44k. "Paphiopedilum" hybrid (different)	90	30
1009	47k. "Paphiopedilum" hybrid (different)	1·00	35
1010	50k. "Cattleya trianaei"	1·20	35
MS1011	52 × 75 mm. 95k. "Vanda tricolour" (31 × 39 mm)	2·50	90

215 Elephants

1987. "Hafnia 87" International Stamp Exhibition, Copenhagen. Elephants. Multicoloured.

1012	50c. Type **215**	15	15
1013	1k. Three elephants	20	15
1014	2k. Elephant feeding	45	15
1015	3k. Elephant grazing on grass	65	20
1016	4k. Adult with calf	75	20
1017	5k. Elephant walking	95	30
1018	6k. Elephant (vert)	1·30	35
MS1019	64 × 44 mm. 10k. Adults and calf (39 × 31 mm)	2·20	90

216 Building Bamboo House

1987. International Year of Shelter for the Homeless. Multicoloured.

1020	1k. Type **216**	15	15
1021	27k. Building wooden house	60	20
1022	46k. House on stilts	1·20	30
1023	70k. Street of houses on stilts	1·80	60

217 Clown Loach

1987. Fishes. Multicoloured.

1024	3k. Type **217**	15	15
1025	7k. Harlequin filefish	15	15
1026	10k. Silver-spotted squirrelfish	20	15
1027	39k. Mandarin fish	80	20
1028	44k. Coral hind	90	30
1029	47k. Zebra lionfish	1·00	35
1030	50k. Semicircle angelfish	1·20	35

218 Watering Seedlings

1987. World Food Day. Multicoloured.

1031	1k. Type **218**	15	15
1032	3k. Harvesting maize (vert)	15	15
1033	5k. Harvesting rice	15	15
1034	63k. Children with fish (vert)	1·30	45
1035	142k. Tending pigs and poultry	3·00	90

219 Wounded Soldiers on Battlefield

1987. 70th Anniv of Russian Revolution. Multicoloured.

1036	1k. Type **219**	20	15
1037	2k. Mother and baby	45	20
1038	4k. Storming the Winter Palace	80	20
1039	8k. Lenin amongst soldiers and sailors	1·60	45
1040	10k. Lenin labouring in Red Square	2·20	60

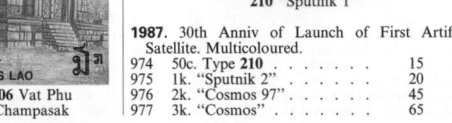

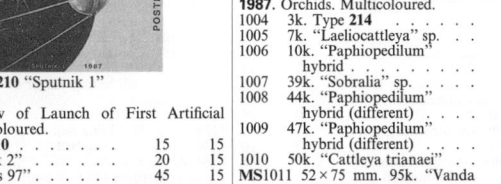

220 Hoeing

1987. Rice Culture in Mountain Regions. Mult.
1041 64k. Type **220** . . . . . . 1·40 30
1042 100k. Working in paddy fields . . . . 2·40 75

221 Laotheung Costume

1987. Ethnic Costumes. Multicoloured.
1043 7k. Type **221** 15 15
1044 38k. Laoloum costume . . . 80 20
1045 144k. Laosoun costume . . 3·00 1·00

222 Two-man Bobsleigh

1988. Winter Olympic Games, Calgary (2nd issue). Multicoloured.
1046 1k. Type **222** 15 15
1047 4k. Biathlon (shooting) . . . 15 15
1048 20k. Cross-country skiing 45 15
1049 42k. Ice hockey 90 30
1050 63k. Speed skating . . . . 1·30 45
1051 70k. Slalom . . . . 1·50 50
MS1052 74 × 45 mm. 95k. Skiing (39 × 31 mm) . . . . 2·20 90

223 Throwing the Javelin

1988. Olympic Games, Seoul (2nd issue). Mult.
1053 2k. Type **223** 15 15
1054 5k. Triple jumping 15 15
1055 10k. Men's gymnastics . . . 20 15
1056 12k. Pirogue racing 35 15
1057 38k. Women's gymnastics 1·00 20
1058 46k. Fencing . . . . 1·30 30
1059 100k. Wrestling . . . . . . 2·75 65
MS1060 100 × 67 mm. 95k. Men's gymnastics (36 × 38 mm) . . . 2·20 90

224 Tyrannosaurus

1988. "Juvalux 88" Youth Philately Exhibition, Luxembourg. Prehistoric Animals. Multicoloured.
1061 3k. Type **224** (wrongly inscr "Trachodon") 15 15
1062 7k. "Ceratosaurus nasicornis" (vert) 20 15
1063 39k. "Iguanodon bernissartensis" (vert) . . 1·10 20
1064 44k. Scolosaurus (vert) . . . 1·10 35
1065 47k. "Phororhacus" sp. (vert) . . . . 1·10 35
1066 50k. Anatosaurus (wrongly inscr "Tyrannosaurus") 1·50 35
MS1067 73 × 94 mm. 95k. Pteranodon (39 × 31 mm) . . . 2·40 90

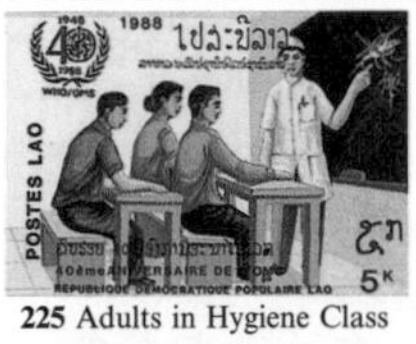

225 Adults in Hygiene Class

1988. 40th Anniv of W.H.O. Multicoloured.
1068 5k. Type **225** 15 15
1069 27k. Fumigating houses . . 50 15
1070 164k. Woman pumping fresh water (vert) . . . . 3·50 1·20

226 "Sans Pareil", 1829

227 Red Frangipani

1988. "Essen 88" International Stamp Fair. Early Railway Locomotives. Multicoloured.
1071 6k. Type **226** 15 15
1072 15k. "Rocket", 1829 . . . . 35 15
1073 20k. "Royal George", 1827 (horiz) 45 15
1074 25k. Trevithick's locomotive, 1803 (horiz) 60 20
1075 30k. "Novelty", 1829 (horiz) 90 20
1076 100k. "Tom Thumb", 1829 (horiz) . . . . 2·40 75
MS1077 82 × 70 mm. 95k. Stephenson's "Locomotion", 1825 (34 × 28 mm) . . . . 2·75 95

1988. "Finlandia 88" International Stamp Exhibition, Helsinki. Flowers. Multicoloured.
1078 8k. Type **227** 15 15
1079 9k. Hollyhock 20 15
1080 15k. Flame-of-the forest . . 30 15
1081 33k. Golden shower 65 20
1082 64k. "Dahlia coccinea" (red) 1·30 45
1083 69k. "Dahlia coccinea" (yellow) . . . . 1·50 50
MS1084 76 × 58 mm. 95k. Hollyhock, frangipani and flame-of-the-forest (31 × 39 mm) . . . 2·75 1·00

228 Sash Pattern

1988. Decorative Stencil Patterns.
1085 **228** 1k. multicoloured . . . 15 15
1086 – 2k. yellow, red and black 15 15
1087 – 3k. multicoloured . . . 20 15
1088 – 25k. multicoloured . . . 65 20
1089 – 163k. multicoloured . . . 3·25 1·40
DESIGNS (stencils for)—VERT: 2k. Pagoda doors; 3k. Pagoda walls. HORIZ: 25k. Pagoda pillars; 163k. Skirts.

229 Dove and Figures

230 Stork-billed Kingfisher

1988. 125th Anniv of Red Cross Movement. Multicoloured.
1090 4k. Type **229** 15 15
1091 52k. Red Cross workers with handicapped people 1·20 50
1092 144k. Red Cross worker vaccinating baby (horiz) 4·00 1·60

1988. Birds. Multicoloured.
1093 6k. Type **230** 15 15
1094 10k. Japanese quail 20 15
1095 13k. Blossom-headed parakeet 30 15
1096 44k. Orange-breasted green pigeon 65 20
1097 63k. Black-crested bulbul . . 1·30 45
1098 64k. Mountain imperial pigeon . . . . 1·50 50

231 Red Cross Workers loading Supplies into Pirogue

1988. Completion of 1st Five Year Plan. Multicoloured.
1099 20k. Type **231** 50 20
1100 40k. Library 90 35
1101 50k. Irrigating fields . . . . 1·30 50
1102 100k. Improvement in communications . . . . . 2·20 1·00

232 Ruy Lopez Segura

1988. Chess Masters. Multicoloured.
1103 1k. Type **232** 15 15
1104 2k. Karl Anderssen 15 15
1105 3k. Paul Morphy (wrongly inscr "Murphy") 15 15
1106 6k. Wilhelm Steinitz 20 15
1107 7k. Emanuel Lasker 30 15
1108 12k. Jose Raul Capablanca 45 20
1109 172k. Aleksandr Alekhine 4·00 1·00

233 Tortoiseshell and White

1989. "India 89" International Stamp Exhibition, New Delhi. Cats. Multicoloured.
1110 5k. Type **233** 15 15
1111 6k. Brown tabby 15 15
1112 10k. Black and white . . . 35 15
1113 20k. Red tabby 60 15
1114 50k. Black . . . . 1·20 35
1115 172k. Silver tabby and white 4·00 90
MS1116 70 × 94 mm. 95k. Brown tabby and white (31 × 39 mm) 2·75 1·10

234 Gunboat, Tank, Soldiers and Flags

1989. 40th Anniv of People's Army. Multicoloured.
1117 1k. Type **234** 15 15
1118 2k. Soldier teaching mathematics (vert) 15 15
1119 3k. Army medics vaccinating civilians 15 15
1120 250k. Peasant, revolutionary, worker and soldiers . . . . 6·75 95

235 Footballers

1989. World Cup Football Championship, Italy (1990) (1st issue). Multicoloured.
1121 10k. Type **235** 20 15
1122 15k. Footballer looking to pass ball 30 15
1123 20k. Ball hitting player on chest 45 15
1124 25k. Tackle 60 20
1125 45k. Dribbling ball 90 30
1126 105k. Kicking ball . . . . . 2·40 75
MS1127 52 × 65 mm. 95k. Players and goalkeeper (38 × 29 mm) 2·20 1·10
See also Nos. 1168/**MS**1174.

236 Couple planting Sapling

1989. Preserve Forests Campaign. Multicoloured.
1128 4k. Type **236** 15 15
1129 10k. Burning and fallen trees 20 15
1130 12k. Man felling tree (vert) 20 20
1131 200k. Trees on map (vert) 4·50 90

237 Camilo Cienfuegos, Fidel Castro and Flag

238 Skaters

1989. 30th Anniv of Cuban Revolution. Multicoloured.
1132 45k. Type **237** . . . . . . 1·10 35
1133 50d. Cuban and Laotian flags . . . . 1·10 35

1989. Winter Olympic Games, Albertville (1992) (1st issue). Figure Skating. Multicoloured.
1134 9k. Type **238** 20 15
1135 10k. Pair (horiz) 30 15
1136 15k. Ice dancing 45 15
1137 24k. Female skater 50 20
1138 29k. Pair 65 20
1139 114k. Male skater . . . . . 2·75 90
MS1140 49 × 78 mm. 95k. Pair (different) (31 × 39 mm) . . . . 2·20 1·10
See also. Nos. 1195/**MS**1202, 1237/**MS**1242 and 1276/**MS**1281.

239 High Jumping

241 Sapodillas

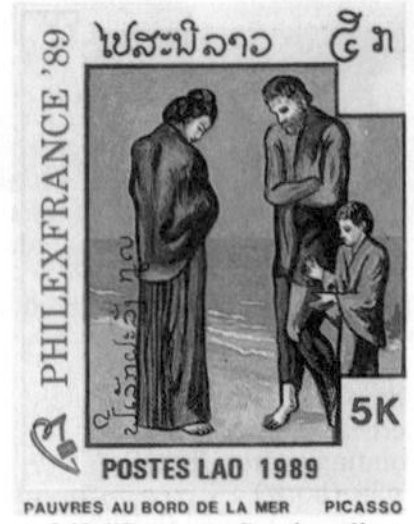

240 "Poor on Seashore"

1989. Olympic Games, Barcelona (1992) (1st issue). Multicoloured.
1141 5k. Type **239** 15 15
1142 15k. Gymnastics 30 15
1143 20k. Cycling (horiz) 45 20
1144 25k. Boxing (horiz) 50 30
1145 70k. Archery . . . . 1·30 50
1146 120k. Swimming . . . . . 2·75 60
MS1147 65 × 91 mm. 95k. Baseball (31 × 39 mm) . . . . 2·20 1·10
See also Nos. 1179/**MS**1185, 1231/**MS**1236 and 1282/**MS**1287.

1989. "Philexfrance '89" International Stamp Exhibition, Paris. Paintings by Picasso. Mult.
1148 5k. Type **240** 15 15
1149 7k. "Motherhood" 20 15
1150 8k. "Portrait of Jaime S. le Bock" 20 15
1151 9k. "Harlequins" 45 20
1152 105k. "Boy with Dog" . . . 2·75 60
1153 114k. "Girl on Ball" . . . . 2·75 75
MS1154 65 × 75 mm. 95k. "Woman in Hat" (31 × 39 mm) . . . . 2·75 1·10

1989. Fruits. Multicoloured.
1155 5k. Type **241** 15 15
1156 20k. Sugar-apples 50 20
1157 20k. Guavas 50 20
1158 30k. Durians 75 30
1159 50k. Pomegranates . . . . . 1·30 45
1160 172k. "Moridica charautia" 4·50 90

242 Sikhotabong Temple, Khammouane

243 Nehru and Woman

1989. Temples. Multicoloured.
1161 5k. Type **242** 15 15
1162 15k. Dam Temple, Vientiane 30 20
1163 61k. Ing Hang Temple, Savannakhet . . . . . . 1·20 50
1164 161k. Ho Vay Phra Luang Temple, Vientiane . . . . 3·75 1·00

1989. Birth Centenary of Jawaharlal Nehru (Indian statesman). Multicoloured.
1165 1k. Type **243** 15 15
1166 60k. Nehru and group of children (horiz) . . . . . 1·30 45
1167 200k. Boy garlanding Nehru 4·50 1·00

244 Footballer

1990. World Cup Football Championship, Italy (2nd issue).
1168 **244** 10k. multicoloured . . . 20 15
1169 – 15k. multicoloured . . . 30 15
1170 – 20k. multicoloured . . . 45 15
1171 – 25k. multicoloured . . . 50 20
1172 – 45k. multicoloured . . . 95 30
1173 – 105k. multicoloured . . 2·40 75
MS1174 90 × 67 mm. 95k. multicoloured (31 × 39 mm) . . 2·20 1·10
DESIGNS: 15 to 95k. Different football scenes.

245 Teacher and Adult Class

1990. International Literacy Year. Multicoloured.
1175 10k. Type **245** 20 15
1176 50k. Woman teaching child (vert) . . . . 1·20 65
1177 60k. Monk teaching adults 1·30 45
1178 150k. Group reading and writing under tree . . . . 3·25 1·00

246 Basketball

1990. Olympic Games, Barcelona (1992) (2nd issue). Multicoloured.
1179 10k. Type **246** 20 15
1180 30k. Hurdling 60 15
1181 45k. High jumping 95 20
1182 50k. Cycling . . . . 1·20 30
1183 60k. Throwing the javelin 1·30 45
1184 90k. Tennis . . . . 2·20 75
MS1185 86 × 102 mm. 95k. Gymnastics (31 × 39 mm) . . . 2·20 1·10

247 Great Britain 1840 Penny Black and Mail Coach

1990. "Stamp World London 90" International Stamp Exhibition. Multicoloured.
1186 15k. Type **247** 30 15
1187 20k. U.S 1847 5c. stamp and early steam locomotive 45 20
1188 40k. France 1849 20c. stamp and mail balloons, Paris, 1870 . . . . 90 20
1189 50k. Sardinia 1851 5c. stamp and post rider . . . . . 1·00 30
1190 60k. Indo-China 1892 1c. stamp and elephant . . . 1·30 45
1191 100k. Spain 1850 6c. stamp and Spanish galleon . . . 1·90 65
MS1192 54 × 54 mm. 95k. Laos 1976 1k. stamp and Douglas DC-8 airliner (36 × 28 mm) . . . . . 2·20 1·10

248 Ho Chi Minh addressing Crowd

1990. Birth Centenary of Ho Chi Minh. Mult.
1193 40k. Type **248** . . . . . . 1·00 45
1194 60k. Ho Chi Minh and Laotian President . . . . 1·60 60
1195 160k. Ho Chi Minh and Vietnamese flag (vert) . . 4·50 1·60

249 Speed Skating

1990. Winter Olympic Games, Albertville (1992) (2nd issue). Multicoloured.
1196 10k. Type **249** 20 15
1197 25k. Cross-country skiing (vert) 50 15
1198 30k. Downhill skiing . . . 60 20
1199 35k. Tobogganing 90 20
1200 80k. Figure skating (pairs) (vert) . . . . 1·60 50
1201 90k. Biathlon . . . . . . 2·10 60
MS1202 97 × 83 mm. 95k. Ice hockey (31 × 39 mm) . . . . . 2·20 1·10

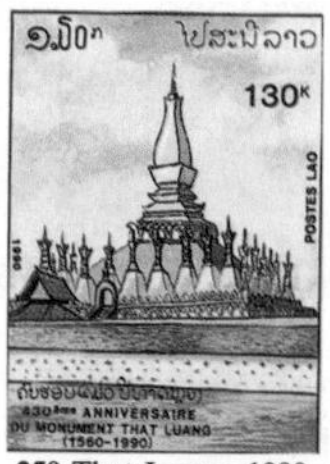

250 That Luang, 1990

1990. 430th Anniv of That Luang. Multicoloured.
1203 60k. That Luang, 1867 (horiz) . . . . 1·60 45
1204 70k. That Luang, 1930 (horiz) . . . . 2·20 60
1205 130k. Type **250** . . . . . 3·75 1·00

251 Parson Bird

1990. "New Zealand 1990" International Stamp Exhibition, Auckland. Multicoloured.
1206 10k. Type **251** 20 15
1207 15k. Eurasian sky lark . . . 30 15
1208 20k. Oystercatcher 45 20
1209 50k. Variable cormorant . . 1·30 30
1210 60k. Great Reef heron . . . 1·50 45
1211 100k. Brown kiwi . . . . . 2·75 75
MS1212 56 × 82 mm. 95k. Rough-faced cormorant (30 × 37 mm) 2·75 1·10

252 Brown-antlered Deer

1990. Mammals. Multicoloured.
1213 10k. Type **252** 20 15
1214 20k. Gaur 45 15
1215 40k. Wild water buffalo . . 95 20
1216 45k. Kouprey . . . . 1·10 30
1217 120k. Javan rhinoceros . . . 2·75 90

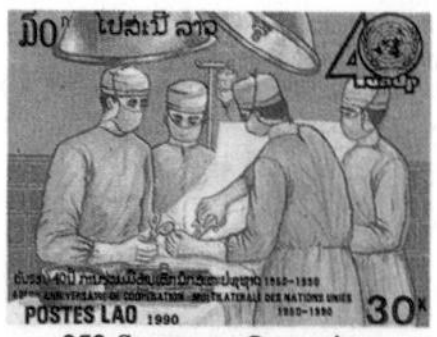

253 Surgeons Operating

1990. 40th Anniv of United Nations Development Programme. Multicoloured.
1218 30k. Type **253** 90 30
1219 45k. Fishermen inspecting catch . . . . 1·50 30
1220 80k. Air-traffic controller (vert) . . . . 2·20 90
1221 90k. Electricity plant workers . . . . 2·50 1·20

254 Rice Ceremony

1990. New Year. Multicoloured.
1222 5k. Type **254** 20 15
1223 10k. Elephant in carnival parade 30 15
1224 50k. Making offerings at temple . . . . 1·10 30
1225 150k. Family ceremony . . 3·25 1·10

255 Memorial, Wreath and Eternal Flame

1990. 15th National Day Festival. Multicoloured.
1226 15k. Type **255** 45 20
1227 20k. Celebration parade . . 65 45
1228 80k. Hospital visit . . . . . 2·20 90
1229 120k. Girls parading with banner . . . . 3·25 1·20

256 West German World Cup Football Champion

1991. West Germany, World Cup Football Champion. Sheet 86 × 58 mm.
MS1230 **256** 95k. multicoloured 2·20 1·10

257 Two-man Kayak

1991. Olympic Games, Barcelona (1992) (3rd issue). Multicoloured.
1231 22k. Type **257** 15 15
1232 32k. Canoeing 15 15
1233 285k. Diving (vert) 90 20
1234 330k. Racing dinghies (vert) 1·10 30
1235 1000k. Swimming . . . . . 2·75 90
MS1236 83 × 55 mm. 700k. Two-man canoeing (39 × 31 mm) . . 2·75 1·10

258 Bobsleighing

1991. Winter Olympic Games, Albertville (1992) (3rd issue). Multicoloured.
1237 32k. Type **258** 15 15
1238 135k. Cross-country skiing (horiz) 45 15
1239 250k. Ski jumping (horiz) 75 20
1240 275k. Biathlon (horiz) . . . 90 30
1241 900k. Speed skating (horiz) 2·75 90
MS1242 80 × 63 mm. 700k. Skiing (31 × 39 mm) . . . . 2·75 1·10

259 Pha Pheng Falls, Champassak

1991. Tourism. Multicoloured.
1243 155k. Type **259** 50 20
1244 220k. Pha Tang mountains, Vangvieng 75 30
1245 235k. Tat Set waterfall, Saravane (vert) 90 50
1246 1000k. Plain of Jars, Xieng Khouang (vert) . . . . . 3·50 1·10

260 Match Scene

1991. World Cup Football Championship, U.S.A. (1994) (1st issue). Multicoloured.
1247 32k. Type **260** 15 15
1248 330k. Goalkeeper catching ball 95 20
1249 340k. Player controlling ball (vert) . . . . 1·20 20
1250 400k. Player dribbling ball 1·50 30
1251 500k. Tackle . . . . 1·80 75
MS1252 75 × 57 mm. 700k. Player shooting at goal (31 × 39 mm) 2·75 1·10
See also Nos. 1292/**MS**1297, 1370/**MS**1375 and 1386/**MS**1391.

261 Planting Saplings

1991. National Tree Planting Day. Multicoloured.
1253 350k. Type **261** 75 30
1254 700k. Planting saplings (different) . . . . 2·20 75
1255 800k. Removing saplings from store . . . . 2·50 1·10

262 "Mallard", 1938, Great Britain

1991. "Espamer '91" Spain–Latin America Stamp Exhibition, Buenos Aires. Railway Locomotives. Multicoloured.
1256 25k. Type **262** 15 15
1257 32k. Class 4500 steam locomotive, France (inscr "Pacific 231") 20 15
1258 285k. Streamlined steam locomotive, U.S.A. . . . 95 30
1259 650k. Canadian Pacific Class T1b steam locomotive, 1938 . . . . 1·90 65
1260 750k. East African Railways Class 59 steam locomotive, 1955 . . . . 2·75 95
MS1261 80 × 64 mm. 700k. Class VT601 diesel-hydraulic intercity express (39 × 31 mm) . . . . . 2·75 1·10

263 Spindle Festival

1991. Traditional Music. Multicoloured.

1262	20k. Type **263**	15	15
1263	220k. Mong player (vert)	65	20
1264	275k. Siphandone singer (vert)	75	30
1265	545k. Khap ngum singer	1·80	65
1266	690k. Phouthaydam dance	2·20	90

264 Great Purple

1991. "Phila Nippon '91" International Stamp Exhibition, Tokyo. Butterflies. Multicoloured.

1267	55k. Type **264**	20	15
1268	90k. "Luehdorfia puziloi" (wrongly inscr "Luendorfia")	30	15
1269	255k. "Papilio bianor"	90	20
1270	285k. Swallowtail	1·00	30
1271	900k. Mikado swallowtail	3·00	90
MS1272	60 × 77 mm. 700k. Common map butterfly (39 × 31 mm)	2·75	1·10

265 Emblem and Pattern **266** Bobsleighing

1991. International Decade for Cultural Development (1988–97). Multicoloured.

1273	285k. Type **265**	75	30
1274	330k. Emblem and drum	90	30
1275	1000k. Emblem and pipes	2·75	1·10

1992. Winter Olympic Games, Albertville (4th issue). Multicoloured.

1276	200k. Type **266**	50	15
1277	220k. Slalom skiing	65	20
1278	250k. Downhill skiing (horiz)	75	20
1279	500k. One-man luge	1·60	30
1280	600k. Figure skating	1·80	75
MS1281	77 × 61 mm. 700k. Speed skating (31 × 39 mm)	2·75	90

267 Running **269** Argentinian and Italian Players and Flags

268 Pest Control

1992. Olympic Games, Barcelona (4th issue). Multicoloured.

1282	32k. Type **267**	15	15
1283	245k. Baseball	65	20
1284	275k. Tennis	90	20
1285	285k. Basketball	90	30
1286	900k. Boxing (horiz)	3·00	75
MS1287	71 × 59 mm. 700k. Diving (39 × 31 mm)	2·75	90

1992. World Health Day. Multicoloured.

1288	200k. Type **268**	60	20
1289	255k. Anti-smoking campaign	65	30
1290	330k. Donating blood	95	60
1291	1000k. Vaccinating child (vert)	3·00	1·20

1992. World Cup Football Championship, U.S.A. (1994) (2nd issue). Multicoloured.

1292	260k. Type **269**	60	15
1293	305k. German and English players and flags	80	20
1294	310k. United States flag, ball and trophy	90	30
1295	350k. Italian and English players and flags	1·30	45
1296	800k. German and Argentinian players and flags	2·75	90
MS1297	60 × 88 mm. 700k. Goalkeeper catching ball (31 × 39 mm)	3·00	90

270 Common Cobra

1992. Snakes. Multicoloured.

1298	280k. Type **270**	80	20
1299	295k. Common cobra	80	20
1300	420k. Wagler's pit viper	1·30	45
1301	700k. King cobra (vert)	2·75	90

271 Doorway and Ruins

1992. Restoration of Wat Phou. Multicoloured.

1302	185k. Type **271**	60	35
1303	220k. Doorway (different)	65	35
1304	1200k. Doorway with collapsed porch (horiz)	4·00	1·60

272 "Pinta" and Juan Martinez's Map

1992. "Genova '92" International Thematic Stamp Exhibition. Multicoloured.

1305	100k. Type **272**	20	15
1306	300k. Piri Reis's letter and caravelle (vert)	90	20
1307	350k. Magellan's ship and Paolo del Pozo Toscanelli's world map	1·20	20
1308	400k. Gabriel de Vallesca's map and Vasco da Gama's flagship "Sao Gabriel"	1·30	45
1309	455k. Juan Martinez's map and Portuguese four-masted caravel	1·60	65
MS1310	94 × 63 mm. 700k. "Santa Maria" (39 × 31 mm)	3·00	90

273 Woman in Traditional Costume **274** Boy Drumming

1992. Traditional Costumes of Laotian Mountain Villages.

1311 **273**	25k. multicoloured	15	15
1312 –	55k. multicoloured	20	15
1313 –	400k. multicoloured	1·30	45
1314 –	1200k. multicoloured	4·00	1·20

DESIGNS: 55 to 1200k. Different costumes.

1992. International Children's Day. Children at Play. Multicoloured.

1315	220k. Type **274**	60	20
1316	285k. Girls skipping (horiz)	80	20
1317	330k. Boys racing on stilts	1·20	30
1318	400k. Girls playing "escape" game (horiz)	1·50	60

275 Praying before Buddha **276** Crested Gibbon

1992. National Customs. Multicoloured.

1319	100k. Type **275**	30	15
1320	140k. Wedding (horiz)	45	20
1321	160k. Religious procession (horiz)	75	20
1322	1500k. Monks receiving alms (horiz)	4·75	2·20

1992. Climbing Mammals. Multicoloured.

1323	10k. Type **276**	20	15
1324	100k. Variegated langur	30	20
1325	250k. Pileated gibbon	80	30
1326	430k. Francois's monkey	1·50	45
1327	800k. Lesser slow loris	3·00	80

277 New York

1993. 130th Anniv of Underground Railway Systems. Multicoloured.

1328	15k. Type **277**	15	15
1329	50k. West Berlin	20	15
1330	100k. Paris	30	20
1331	200k. London	80	30
1332	900k. Moscow	3·00	1·20
MS1333	85 × 55 mm. 700k. Royal Mail underground system, London (31 × 39 mm)	3·00	90

278 Malayan Bullfrog

1993. Amphibians. Multicoloured.

1334	55k. Type **278**	20	15
1335	90k. Muller's clawed frog	30	15
1336	100k. Glass frog (vert)	45	20
1337	185k. Giant toad	65	30
1338	1200k. Common tree frog (vert)	4·00	1·20

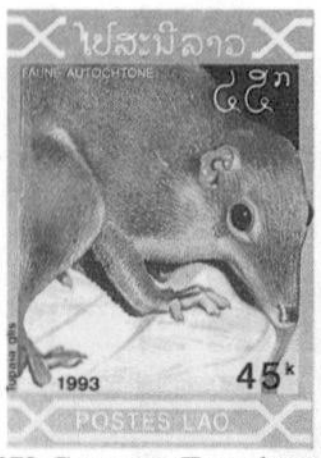

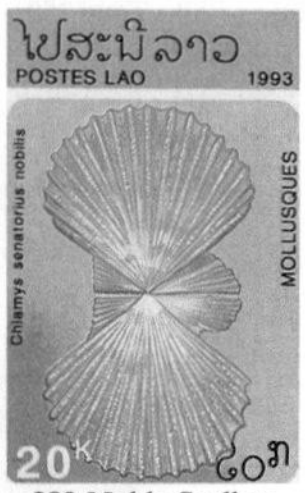

279 Common Tree-shrew **280** Noble Scallop

1993. Mammals. Multicoloured.

1339	45k. Type **279**	20	15
1340	60k. Philippine flying lemur	20	15
1341	120k. Loris	45	20
1342	500k. Eastern tarsier	1·60	65
1343	600k. Giant gibbon	1·90	1·20

1993. Molluscs. Multicoloured.

1344	20k. Type **280**	15	15
1345	30k. Precious wentletrap	15	15
1346	70k. Spider conch	30	20
1347	500k. Aulicus cone	1·60	65
1348	1000k. Milleped spider conch	3·00	1·20

281 Drugs and Skull smoking

1993. Anti-drugs Campaign. Multicoloured.

1349	200k. Type **281**	65	30
1350	430k. Burning seized drugs	1·40	60
1351	900k. Instructing on dangers of drugs	3·00	1·20

282 House **283** Greater Spotted Eagle

1993. Traditional Houses. Multicoloured.

1352	32k. Type **282**	15	15
1353	200k. Thatched house with gable end (horiz)	75	20
1354	650k. Thatched house (horiz)	1·90	60
1355	750k. House with tiled roof (horiz)	2·40	1·20

1993. Birds of Prey. Multicoloured.

1356	10k. Type **283**	15	15
1357	100k. Spotted little owl	45	20
1358	330k. Pied harrier (horiz)	1·60	45
1359	1000k. Short-toed eagle	4·00	1·30

284 Fighting Forest Fire

1993. Environmental Protection. Multicoloured.

1360	32k. Type **284**	15	15
1361	40k. Wildlife on banks of River Mekong	15	15
1362	260k. Paddy fields	90	30
1363	1100k. Oxen in river	4·00	1·20

285 "Narathura atosia"

1993. "Bangkok 1993" International Stamp Exhibition. Butterflies. Multicoloured.

1364	35k. Type **285**	15	15
1365	80k. "Parides philoxenus"	20	15
1366	150k. "Euploea harrisi"	45	20
1367	220k. Yellow orange-tip	65	30
1368	500k. Female common palm fly	1·90	80
MS1369	85 × 69 mm. 700k. "Stichophtlalma Louisa" (39 × 31 mm)	3·00	90

286 Footballer

1993. World Cup Football Championship, U.S.A. (3rd issue). Multicoloured.

1370	10k. Type **286**	15	15
1371	20k. Brazil player	15	15
1372	285k. Uruguay player	80	20
1373	400k. Germany player	1·40	45
1374	800k. Forward challenging goalkeeper	2·75	1·20
MS1375	99 × 72 mm. 700k. Ball on pitch (31 × 39 mm)	3·00	90

287 Hesperornis

1994. Prehistoric Birds. Multicoloured.
1376 10k. Type **287** 15 15
1377 20k. Mauritius dodo 15 15
1378 150k. Archaeopteryx 60 20
1379 600k. Phororhachos . . . . 1·80 45
1380 700k. Giant moa . . . . . 2·50 90
MS1381 80 × 65 mm. 700k. *Teratornis mirabilis* (Teratornis) (39 × 31 mm) . . . . 3·00 90

288 Olympic Flag and Flame

289 Bridge and National Flags

1994. Centenary of International Olympic Committee. Multicoloured.
1382 100k. Type **288** 30 15
1383 250k. Ancient Greek athletes (horiz) 80 20
1384 1000k. Pierre de Coubertin (founder) and modern athlete . . . . 3·50 1·40

1994. Opening of Friendship Bridge between Laos and Thailand.
1385 **289** 500k. multicoloured . . 1·90 1·20

290 World Map and Players

1994. World Cup Football Championship, U.S.A. (4th issue).
1386 **290** 40k. multicoloured . . . 15 15
1387 – 50k. multicoloured . . . 20 15
1388 – 60k. multicoloured . . . 20 15
1389 – 320k. multicoloured . . . 1·20 45
1390 – 900k. multicoloured . . 3·50 1·20
MS1391 82 × 59 mm. 700k. multicoloured (31 × 39 mm) . . 2·50 90
DESIGNS: 50 to 900k. Different players on world map.

291 Pagoda

1994. Pagodas.
1392 **291** 30k. multicoloured . . . 15 15
1393 – 150k. multicoloured . . 45 20
1394 – 380k. multicoloured . . 1·20 30
1395 – 1100k. multicoloured . . 3·50 1·20
DESIGNS: 150 to 1100k. Different gabled roofs.

292 Bear eating

1994. The Malay Bear. Multicoloured.
1396 50k. Type **292** 35 15
1397 90k. Bear's head 80 20
1398 200k. Adult and cub . . . . 1·80 30
1399 220k. Bear . . . . 1·90 45

293 Grass Snake

1994. Amphibians and Reptiles. Multicoloured.
1400 70k. Type **293** 20 15
1401 80k. Tessellated snake . . . 20 15
1402 90k. Fire salamander . . . 30 15
1403 600k. Alpine newt . . . . . 1·90 60
1404 800k. Green lizard (vert) . . 2·50 1·20
MS1405 79 × 50 mm. 700k. Great crested newt (39 × 31 mm) . . 2·50 90

294 Phra Xayavoraman 7

295 Family supporting Healthy Globe

1994. Buddhas. Multicoloured.
1406 15k. Type **294** 15 15
1407 280k. Phra Thong Souk . . 90 30
1408 390k. Phra Manolom . . . 1·30 45
1409 800k. Phra Ongtu . . . . . 2·50 1·20

1994. International Year of the Family. Multicoloured.
1410 200k. Type **295** 65 30
1411 500k. Mother taking child to school (horiz) . . . . 1·60 80
1412 700k. Mother and children 2·40 1·20
MS1413 50 × 70 mm. 700k. Family and flag . . . . 2·50 90

296 Kong Hang

1994. Traditional Laotian Drums. Multicoloured.
1414 370k. Type **296** . . . . . 1·30 35
1415 440k. Kong Leng (portable drum) . . . . 1·50 45
1416 450k. Kong Toum (drum on stand) . . . . 1·50 45
1417 600k. Kong Phene (hanging drum) . . . . 2·10 65

297 Elephant in Procession

1994. Ceremonial Elephants. Multicoloured.
1418 140k. Type **297** 45 20
1419 400k. Elephant in pavilion 1·30 80
1420 890k. Elephant in street procession (vert) . . . . 2·75 1·30

298 Theropodes

1994. Prehistoric Animals. Multicoloured.
1421 50k. Type **298** 20 15
1422 380k. Iguanodontides . . . 1·80 60
1423 420k. Sauropodes . . . . . 2·10 65

299 Playing Musical Instruments

1995. 20th Anniv of World Tourism Organization. Multicoloured.
1424 60k. Type **299** 20 15
1425 250k. Women dancing . . . 80 20
1426 400k. Giving alms to monks 1·30 45
1427 650k. Waterfall (vert) . . . 1·80 80
MS1428 40 × 83 mm. 700k. Close-up view of waterfall in No. 1427 (31 × 39 mm) . . . . 2·40 80

300 Trachodon

302 Children and Emblem

301 Indian Jungle Mynah

1995. Prehistoric Animals. Multicoloured.
1429 50k. Type **300** 15 15
1430 70k. Protoceratops 15 15
1431 300k. Brontosaurus 80 30
1432 400k. Stegosaurus . . . . . 1·10 45
1433 600k. Tyrannosaurus . . . 1·80 65

1995. Birds. Multicoloured.
1434 50k. Type **301** 15 15
1435 150k. Jerdon's starling . . . 45 15
1436 300k. Common mynah . . . 90 35
1437 700k. Southern grackle . . . 1·90 80

1995. 25th Anniv of Francophonie. Multicoloured.
1438 50k. Type **302** 15 15
1439 380k. Golden roof decorations . . . . 1·20 60
1440 420k. Map . . . . 1·30 65

303 Pole Vaulting

304 Chalice

1995. Olympic Games, Atlanta, U.S.A. (1st issue). Multicoloured.
1441 60k. Type **303** 15 15
1442 80k. Throwing the javelin 20 15
1443 200k. Throwing the hammer 60 20
1444 350k. Long jumping . . . . 1·00 35
1445 700k. High jumping . . . . 2·10 80
MS1446 90 × 60 mm. 700k. Baseball (39 × 31 mm) . . . . 2·40 80
See also Nos. 1484/**MS**1489.

1995. Antique Vessels. Multicoloured.
1447 70k. Type **304** 15 15
1448 200k. Resin and silver bowl (horiz) 50 20
1449 450k. Geometrically decorated bowl (horiz) . . 1·30 50
1450 600k. Religious chalice (horiz) . . . . 1·80 65

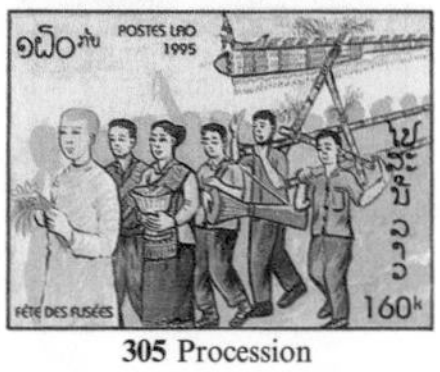
305 Procession

1995. Rocket Festival. Multicoloured.
1451 80k. Launching rocket (vert) 20 15
1452 160k. Type **305** 45 15
1453 500k. Musicians in procession . . . . 1·40 50
1454 700k. Crowds and rockets 2·10 80

306 Red Tabby Longhair

1995. Cats. Multicoloured.
1455 40k. Type **306** 15 15
1456 50k. Siamese sealpoint . . . 20 15
1457 250k. Red tabby longhair (different) 80 20
1458 400k. Tortoiseshell shorthair 1·30 30
1459 650k. Head of tortoiseshell shorthair (vert) . . . . . 1·60 65
MS1460 49 × 70 mm. 700k. Tortoiseshell shorthair (different) (39 × 31 mm) . . . . 2·40 80

307 "Nepenthes villosa"

1995. Insectivorous Plants. Multicoloured.
1461 90k. Type **307** 20 15
1462 100k. "Dionaea muscipula" 30 15
1463 350k. "Sarracenia flava" . . 1·00 30
1464 450k. "Sarracenia purpurea" 1·30 30
1465 500k. "Nepenthes ampullaria" . . . . . . 1·50 60
MS1466 59 × 77 mm. 1000k. *Nepenthes gracillis* (31 × 39 mm) 3·00 90

308 Stag Beetle

1995. Insects. Multicoloured.
1467 40k. Type **308** 15 15
1468 50k. May beetle 20 15
1469 500k. Blue carpenter beetle 1·40 45
1470 800k. Great green grasshopper . . . . . . 2·40 80

309 Cattle grazing

1995. 50th Anniv of F.A.O. Multicoloured.
1471 80k. Type **309** 20 15
1472 300k. Working paddy-field 90 45
1473 1000k. Agriculture . . . . 3·00 1·20

310 At Meeting

1995. 50th Anniv of U.N.O. Peoples of Different Races. Multicoloured.
1474 290k. Type **310** 80 35
1475 310k. Playing draughts . . . 90 45
1476 440k. Children playing . . . 1·40 65

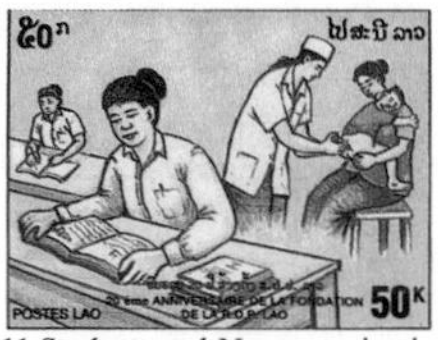
311 Students and Nurse vaccinating Child

1995. 20th Anniv of Republic. Multicoloured.
1477 50k. Type **311** 15 15
1478 280k. Agricultural land . . 80 45
1479 600k. Bridge . . . . 1·80 90

312 Mong

1996. Traditional New Year Customs. Multicoloured.

1480	50k. Type **312**	15	15
1481	280k. Phouthai	90	30
1482	380k. Ten Xe	1·20	45
1483	420k. Lao Loum	1·30	45

313 Cycling

1996. Olympic Games, Atlanta, U.S.A. (2nd issue). Multicoloured.

1484	30k. Type **313**	15	15
1485	150k. Football	30	15
1486	200k. Basketball (vert)	45	20
1487	300k. Running (vert)	65	30
1488	500k. Shooting	1·20	60
MS1489	80 × 60 mm. 1000k. High jumping (38 × 30 mm)	2·20	2·20

314 Sun Bear

1996. Animals. Multicoloured.

1490	40k. Type **314**	15	15
1491	60k. Grey pelican	15	15
1492	200k. Leopard	45	20
1493	250k. Swallowtail	60	30
1494	700k. Indian python	1·50	80

315 Weaving

1996. International Women's Year. Multicoloured.

1495	20k. Type **315**	15	15
1496	290k. Physical training instructress	65	30
1497	1000k. Woman feeding child (vert)	2·20	1·10

316 Rat

317 Players

1996. New Year. Year of the Rat.

1498	**316** 50k. multicoloured	15	15
1499	– 340k. multicoloured	1·20	60
1500	– 350k. multicoloured	1·30	60
1501	– 370k. multicoloured	1·30	65

DESIGNS: 340k. to 370k. Different rats.

1996. World Cup Football Championship, France (1998) (1st issue).

1502	**317** 20k. multicoloured	15	15
1503	– 50k. multicoloured	15	15
1504	– 300k. multicoloured	65	30
1505	– 400k. multicoloured	90	45
1506	– 500k. multicoloured	1·10	50
MS1507	63 × 92 mm. 1000k. multicoloured (30 × 37 mm)	2·20	2·20

DESIGNS: 50k. to 1000k. Different football scenes.

See also Nos. 1589/**MS**1595.

318 Village Women grinding Rice

1996. Children's Drawings. Multicoloured.

1508	180k. Type **318**	65	30
1509	230k. Women picking fruit	80	35
1510	310k. Village women preparing food	1·10	50
1511	370k. Women tending vegetable crops	1·30	65

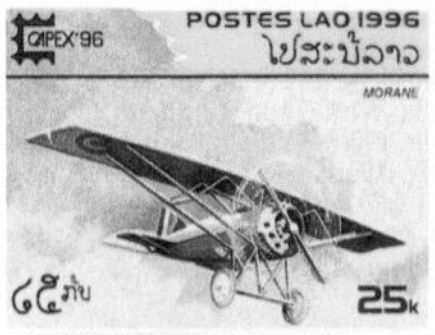

319 Morane Monoplane

1996. "Capex'96" International Stamp Exhibition, Toronto, Canada. Aircraft. Multicoloured.

1512	25k. Type **319**	15	15
1513	60k. Sopwith Camel biplane	15	15
1514	150k. De Havilland D.H.4 biplane	30	15
1515	250k. Albatros biplane	50	30
1516	800k. Caudron biplane	1·80	90

320 Front View

1996. Ox-carts. Multicoloured.

1517	50k. Type **320**	15	10
1518	100k. Side view	20	15
1519	440k. Oxen pulling cart	1·00	50

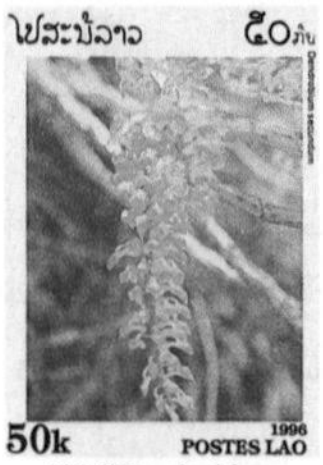

321 "Dendrobium secundum"

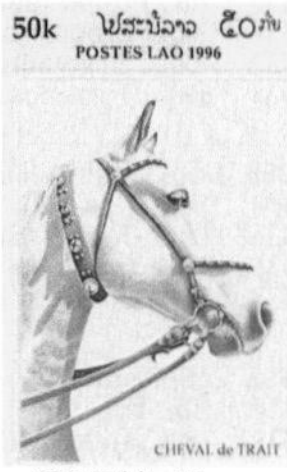

322 White Horse

1996. Orchids (1st series). Multicoloured.

1520	50k. Type **321**	15	15
1521	200k. "Ascocentrum miniatum"	45	20
1522	500k. "Aerides multiflorum"	1·10	60
1523	520k. "Dendrobium aggregatum"	1·30	60

See also Nos. 1563/**MS**1569, 1626/9, 1685/**MS**1689 and 1836/46.

1996. Saddle Horses. Multicoloured.

1524	50k. Type **322**	15	15
1525	80k. Horse with red and black bridle	15	15
1526	200k. Bay horse with white bridle and reins	45	20
1527	400k. Horse with red and yellow cords braided into mane	90	45
1528	600k. Chestnut horse with white blaze	1·30	65
MS1529	89 × 69 mm. 1000k. Horse with ornate yellow and red bridle (28 × 36 mm)	2·20	2·20

323 Pupils displaying Slates to Teacher

1996. 50th Anniv of UNICEF. Multicoloured.

1530	200k. Type **323**	65	30
1531	500k. Mother breastfeeding (vert)	1·80	80
1532	600k. Woman drawing water at public well	2·10	1·10

324 Leatherback Turtle

1996. 25th Anniv of Greenpeace (environmental organization). Turtles. Multicoloured.

1533	150k. Type **324**	50	20
1534	250k. Leatherback turtle at water's edge	90	45
1535	400k. Hawksbill turtle	1·50	75
1536	450k. "Chelonia agassizi"	1·60	80

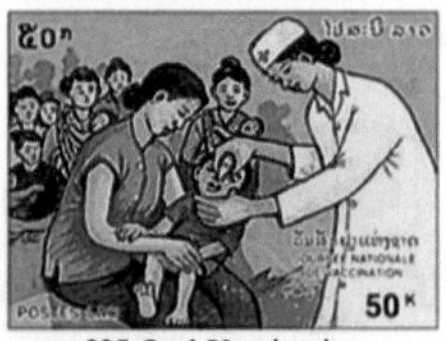

325 Oral Vaccination

1997. National Vaccination Day. Multicoloured.

1537	50k. Type **325**	15	15
1538	340k. Nurse injecting child's leg	1·20	60
1539	370k. Nurse pushing child in wheelchair	1·30	65

326 George Stephenson and "Pioneer", 1836

1997. Steam Railway Locomotives. Multicoloured.

1540	100k. "Kinnaird", 1846 (44 × 27 mm)	20	15
1541	200k. Type **326**	45	20
1542	300k. Robert Stephenson and long-boiler express locomotive, 1848	65	30
1543	400k. Stephenson locomotive "Adler", 1835, Germany	90	45
1544	500k. "Lord of the Isles", 1851–84	1·20	60
1545	600k. "The Columbine", 1845	1·40	65
MS1546	69 × 93 mm. 2000k. South Carolina Railroad locomotive *Best Friend of Charleston*, 1830 (39 × 31 mm)	4·50	4·50

The 200 and 300k. are wrongly inscr "Stepheson".

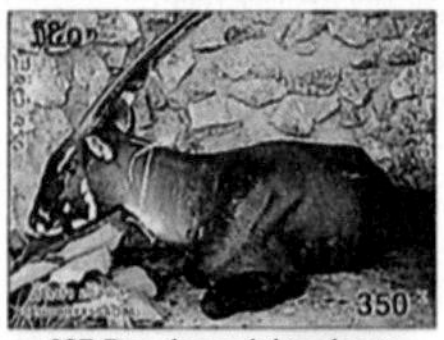

327 Pseudoryx lying down

1997. Pseudoryx (Saola). Multicoloured.

1547	350k. Type **327**	1·30	1·30
1548	380k. Grazing (vert)	1·40	1·40
1549	420k. Scratching with hind leg	1·50	1·50

328 Masked Lovebirds ("Agapornis personata")

330 Steaming Rice

329 Signs of the Chinese Zodiac

1997. Lovebirds. Multicoloured.

1550	50k. Type **328**	15	15
1551	150k. Grey-headed lovebird ("Agapornis cana")	30	15
1552	200k. Nyasa lovebirds ("Agapornis lilianae")	45	20
1553	400k. Fischer's lovebirds ("Agapornis fischeri")	90	45
1554	500k. Black-cheeked lovebirds ("Agapornis nigregenis")	1·10	60
1555	800k. Peach-faced lovebird ("Agapornis roseicollis")	1·90	90
MS1556	91 × 74 mm. 2000k. Black-winged lovebirds (31 × 38 mm)	4·50	4·50

1997. New Year. Year of the Ox. Multicoloured.

1557	50k. Type **329**	15	15
1558	300k. Woman riding ox (vert)	1·20	1·20
1559	440k. Ox on float in procession	1·60	1·60

1997. Food Preparation. Multicoloured.

1560	50k. Type **330**	15	15
1561	340k. Water containers (horiz)	75	35
1562	370k. Table laid with meal (horiz)	80	35

331 "Vanda roeblingiana"

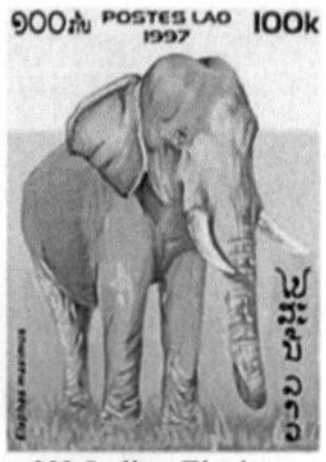

332 Indian Elephant ("Elephas maximus")

1997. Orchids (2nd series). Multicoloured.

1563	50k. Type **331**	15	15
1564	100k. "Dendrobium findleyanum"	20	15
1565	150k. "Dendrobium crepidatum"	30	15
1566	250k. "Sarcanthus birmanicus"	50	30
1567	400k. "Cymbidium lowianum"	90	45
1568	1000k. "Dendrobium gratiosissimum"	2·40	1·10
MS1569	95 × 70 mm. 2000k. *Paphiopedilum chamberlainanum* (31 × 37 mm)	4·50	4·50

See also Nos. 1626/9, 1685/**MS**1689 and 1836/46.

1997. Elephants. Multicoloured.

1570	100k. Type **332**	20	15
1571	250k. Indian elephant carrying log (horiz)	50	30
1572	300k. Indian elephant with young (horiz)	65	30
1573	350k. African elephant ("Loxodonta africana") (horiz)	80	35
1574	450k. African elephant in water (horiz)	1·00	50
1575	550k. African elephant with ears flapping	1·30	60
MS1576	117 × 74 mm. 2000k. Forequarter of African elephant (31 × 39 mm)	4·50	4·50

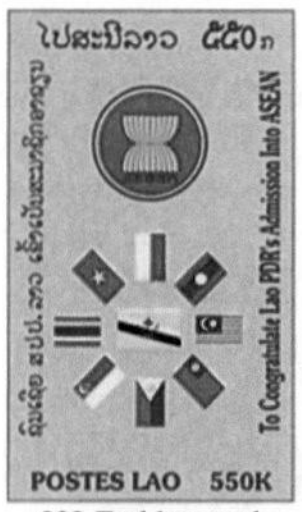

333 Emblem and Brunei Flag

336 Players

335 Headquarters, Djakarta, Indonesia

1997. Admission of Laos into Association of South East Asian Nations. Members' flags, centre flag given.

1577	550k. Type **333**	80	80
1578	550k. Indonesia (red and white bands)	80	80
1579	550k. Laos (red, blue with white circle, red bands)	80	80
1580	550k. Malaysia (crescent and star on blue quarter, red and white stripes)	80	80
1581	550k. Myanmar (flower and stars on blue quarter, red)	80	80
1582	550k. Philippines (sun and stars on white triangle, blue and red bands)	80	80
1583	550k. Singapore (crescent and five stars on red band, white band)	80	80
1584	550k. Thailand (red, white, blue, red bands)	80	80
1585	550k. Vietnam (yellow star on red)	80	80
MS1586	Nine sheets, each 138 × 110 mm. (a) No. 1577; (b) No. 1578; (c) No. 1582; (d) No. 1580; (e) No. 1581; (f) No. 1582; (g) No. 1583; (h) No. 1584; (i) No. 1585	7·25	7·25

1997. 30th Anniv of Association of South East Asian Nations. Multicoloured.

1587	150k. Type **335**	60	60
1588	600k. Map of Laos and state flag	2·50	2·50

1997. World Cup Football Championship, France (1998) (2nd issue).

1589	**336**	100k. multicoloured	20	15
1590	–	200k. multicoloured	45	20
1591	–	250k. multicoloured	50	30
1592	–	300k. multicoloured	65	30
1593	–	350k. multicoloured	80	35
1594	–	700k. multicoloured	1·50	75
MS1595		111 × 84 mm. 2000k. multicoloured	4·50	4·50

DESIGNS: 200k. to 2000k. Various football scenes.

337 Phoenician Nef

1997. Sailing Ships. Multicoloured.

1596	50k. Type **337**	15	15
1597	100k. 13th-century nef	20	15
1598	150k. 15th-century nef	30	15
1599	200k. 16th-century Portuguese caravel	45	20
1600	400k. 17th-century Dutch ship	90	45
1601	900k. H.M.S. "Victory" (Nelson's flagship)	2·10	1·00
MS1602	80 × 60 mm. 2000k. "Great Harry" (sail warship), 1514	4·50	4·50

338 Headdress

1997. Headdresses and Masks. Multicoloured.

1603	50k. Type **338**	15	15
1604	100k. Headdress with flower at left	20	15
1605	150k. Mask with curved tusks (horiz)	30	15
1606	200k. Mask tipped with headdress decorated with two faces	50	20
1607	350k. Mask with green face	75	35

339 Two Pirogues

1997. Pirogue Race. Multicoloured.

1608	50k. Type **339**	15	15
1609	100k. Crowd cheering competitors from land	20	15
1610	300k. Side view of two competing pirogues	65	30
1611	500k. People cheering on spectator boat	1·10	50

340 Sunken Net

1998. Traditional Fishing Methods. Multicoloured.

1612	50k. Type **340**	15	15
1613	100k. Fisherman throwing net (horiz)	30	30
1614	450k. Funnel net	1·40	1·40
1615	650k. Lobster pots (horiz)	1·90	1·90

341 Man riding Tiger

1998. New Year. Year of the Tiger.

1616	**341**	150k. multicoloured	60	60
1617		350k. multicoloured	1·40	1·40
1618		400k. multicoloured	1·80	1·80

342 Wat Sisaket Shrine

344 Buddha, Luang Phabang Temple

343 Boat and Pole

1998. Temples. Multicoloured.

1619	10000k. Type **342**	7·50	7·50
1620	25000k. Wat Phou temple, Pakse (horiz)	15·00	15·00
1621	45000k. That Luang (royal mausoleum) (horiz)	22·00	22·00

1998. Water Transport. Multicoloured.

1622	1100k. Type **343**	1·10	1·10
1623	1200k. Covered canoe	1·20	1·20
1624	2500k. Motorized canoe	2·50	2·50

1998.

1625	**344**	3000k. multicoloured	2·10	2·10

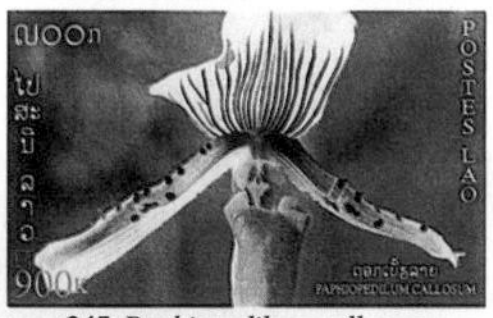

345 *Paphiopedilum callosum*

1998. Orchids (3rd series). Multicoloured.

1626	900k. Type **345**	1·40	1·40
1627	950k. *Paphiopedilum concolor*	1·50	1·50
1628	1000k. *Dendrobium thyrsiflorum* (vert)	1·60	1·60
1629	1050k. *Dendrobium lindleyi* (vert)	1·60	1·60

See also Nos. 1685/**MS**1689 and 1836/46.

346 Children in Classroom

1998. 50th Anniv of Universal Declaration of Human Rights. Multicoloured.

1630	300k. Type **346**	35	35
1631	1700k. Woman posting vote into ballot box	2·20	2·20

347 Gaeng

1998. Wind Instruments. Multicoloured.

1632	900k. Type **347**	1·30	1·30
1633	1200k. Khuoy (flute)	1·80	1·80
1634	1500k. Khaen (bamboo pipes of various lengths)	2·20	2·20

348 Military Personnel and Flag

1999. 50th Anniv of People's Army. Multicoloured.

1635	1300k. Type **348**	1·10	1·10
1636	1500k. Soldier with upraised arm and jungle fighters (vert)	1·30	1·30

349 Inscribed Monument (world heritage)

1999. UNESCO World Heritage Site. Luang Prabang. Multicoloured.

1637	400k. Type **349**	35	35
1638	1150k. House with veranda and dovecote (horiz)	95	95
1639	1250k. Wat Xiengthong (horiz)	1·00	1·00

350 Yao Children celebrating New Year, Muong Sing

1999. Tourism Year (1st issue). Multicoloured.

1640	200k. Type **350**	15	15
1641	500k. Phadeang, Vangvieng district	35	35
1642	1050k. Wat That Makmo, Luang Prabang	80	80
1643	1300k. Patuxay (victory monument), Vientiane (vert)	1·00	1·00

See also No. **MS**1653 and 1714/17.

351 Rabbit and Chinese Zodiac Animals

353 Collared Owlet (*Glaucidium brodiei*)

352 Iron Plough

1999. New Year. Year of the Rabbit. Multicoloured.

1644	1500k. Type **351**	75	75
1645	1600k. White rabbit (horiz)	1·60	1·60

1999. Traditional Farming Implements. Multicoloured.

1646	1500k. Type **352**	1·10	1·10
1647	2000k. Harrow	1·50	1·50
1648	3200k. Wooden plough	2·40	2·40

1999. Owls and Bat. Multicoloured.

1649	900k. Type **353**	75	75
1650	1600k. Collared scops owl (*Otus lempiji*)	1·50	1·50
1651	2100k. Barn owl (*Tyto alba*)	2·20	2·20
1652	2800k. Black capped fruit bat (*Chironax melanocephalus*)	3·00	3·00

354 Patuxay (victory monument), Vientiane

1999. Tourism (2nd issue). Sheet 135 × 100 mm containing T **354** and similar horiz designs.

MS1653	2500k. Type **354**; 4000k. Ho Phra Keo, Vientiane; 5500k. Wat Xieng Thong, Luang Prabang; 8000k. Pha That Luang, Vientiane	10·50	10·50

355 Envelope and Globe

1999. 125th Anniv of Universal Postal Union. Multicoloured.

1654	2600k. Type **355**	1·80	1·80
1655	3400k. Postman delivering letter	2·50	2·50

356 Carved Tree Stump

1999. International Horticultural Exposition, Kunming, China. Exposition buildings. Multicoloured.

1656	300k. Type **356**	20	20
1657	900k. China Hall	45	45
1658	2300k. Science and Technology Hall	1·20	1·20
1659	2500k. Traditional Laotian house	1·40	1·40

357 Javan Rhino (*Rhinoceros sondaicus*)

1999. Animals. Multicoloured.

1660	700k. Type **357**	50	50
1661	900k. Water buffalo (*Bubalus bubalis*) (vert)	65	65
1662	1700k. Spotted linsang (*Prionodon pardicolor*)	1·30	1·30
1663	1800k. Sambar deer (*Cervus unicolor*)	1·30	1·30
1664	1900k. Lion (*Panthera leo*) (vert)	1·40	1·40

358 Airport and Hospital

2000. Millennium (1st issue). Multicoloured.

1665	2000k. Type **358**	75	75
1666	2000k. Temple	75	75
1667	2000k. Building with portico	75	75
1668	2000k. River and traditional buildings	75	75
MS1669	124 × 181 mm. Nos. 1665/8	3·00	3·00

Nos. 1665/8 were issued together, se-tenant, forming a composite design.

See also Nos. 1718/19.

359 Kor Loma

360 *Dendrobium draconis*

2000. Women's Regional Costumes (1st series). Multicoloured.

1670	100k. Type **359**	10	10
1671	200k. Kor Pchor	10	10
1672	500k. Nhuan Krom	15	15
1673	900k. Taidam	30	30
1674	2300k. Yao	65	65
1675	2500k. Meuy	75	75
1676	2600k. Sila	80	80
1677	2700k. Hmong	80	80
1678	2800k. Yao (different)	80	80
1679	3100k. Kor Nukkuy	90	90
1680	3200k. Kor Pouxang	95	95
1681	3300k. Yao Lanten	1·00	1·00
1682	3400k. Khir	1·10	1·10
1683	3500k. Kor	1·00	1·00
1684	3900k. Hmong (different)	1·20	1·20

See also Nos.1777/87.

2000. Orchids (4th series). Bangkok 2000 International Stamp Exhibition (**MS**1689) Multicoloured.

1685	500k. Type **360**	15	15
1686	900k. *Paphiopedilum hirsutissimum*	30	30
1687	3000k. *Dendrobium sulcatum*	95	95
1688	3400k. *Rhynchostylis gigantean*	1·10	1·10
MS1689	111 × 145 mm. Nos. 1686/90	3·00	3·00

See also Nos. 1836/46

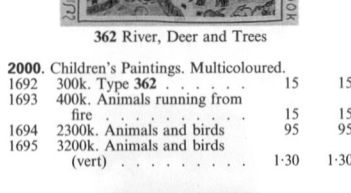

361 Dragon and Chinese Zodiac

2000. Year of the Dragon. Multicoloured.

1690	1800k. Type **361**	50	50
1691	2300k. Dragon swimming	75	75

362 River, Deer and Trees

2000. Children's Paintings. Multicoloured.

1692	300k. Type **362**	15	15
1693	400k. Animals running from fire	15	15
1694	2300k. Animals and birds	95	95
1695	3200k. Animals and birds (vert)	1·30	1·30

363 Peacock

2000. The Peacock. Multicoloured.

1696	700k. Type **363**	20	20
1697	1000k. With tail displayed	35	35
1698	1800k. Peahen (horiz)	60	60
1699	3500k. Pair (horiz)	1·20	1·20
MS1700	146 × 110 mm. 10000k. Front showing tail displayed	3·50	3·50

364 Bridge

2000. Pakse Bridge over Mekong River. Multicoloured.

1701	900k. Type **364**	30	30
1702	2700k. Overview of bridge	95	95
1703	3200k. Bridge from right	1·10	1·10
MS1704	180 × 122 mm. 4000k. No. 1701; 7500k. No. 1702; 8500k. No. 1703r	6·75	6·75

365 Cycling

2000. Olympic Games, Sydney. Multicoloured.

1705	500k. Type **365**	15	15
1706	900k. Boxing	30	30
1707	2600k. Kick boxing	90	90
1708	3600k. Canoeing	1·30	1·30
MS1709	124 × 180 mm. Nos. 1705/8	3·25	3·25

366 Lao Theung

367 Phousy Stupa, Luang Prabang

2000. Regional Wedding Costumes. Multicoloured.

1710	800k. Type **366**	30	30
1711	2300k. Lao Lum	75	75
1712	3400k. Lao Sung	1·20	1·20

2000. Tourism (3rd issue). Multicoloured.

1713	300k. Type **367**	15	15
1714	600k. Tham Chang cave	20	20
1715	2800k. Inhang Stupa	1·20	1·20
1716	3300k. Buddha, Phiawal temple, Xiengkhuang	1·40	1·40

368 Building Facade

2000. 25th Anniv of Republic of Laos.

1717	**368** 4000k. multicoloured	1·30	1·30

369 Satellites and Child writing

371 Yao mane Huaphanh

370 Roadway

2001. Millennium (2nd issue). Multicoloured.

1718	3200k. Type **369**	1·00	1·00
1719	4000k. Electricity pylons and dam	1·30	1·30

2001. Route 13 Highway Improvement Project. Sheet 120 × 190 mm containing T **370** and similar horiz designs. Multicoloured.

MS1720	4000k. Type **370**; 4000k. Bridge and mountains; 4000k. Bridge (different)	4·00	4·00

2001. Men's Regional Costumes. Multicoloured.

1721	100k. Type **371**	10	10
1722	200k. Gnaheun Champasak	10	10
1723	500k. Katou Sarvane	15	15
1724	2300k. Hmong Dam Oudomxay	80	80
1725	2500k. Harlak Xekong	90	90
1726	2600k. Kui Luangnamtha	90	90
1727	2700k. Krieng Xekong	95	95
1728	3100k. Khmu Nhuan Luangnamtha	1·10	1·10
1729	3200k. Ta Oy Saravane	1·10	1·10
1730	3300k. TaiTheng Bolihamxay	1·20	1·20
1731	3400k. Hmong Khao Huaphanh	1·20	1·20
1732	3500k. Gnor Khammouane	1·30	1·30
1733	3600k. Phouthai Na Gnom ZVK	1·30	1·30
1734	4000k. Yao Ventiane	1·40	1·40
1735	5000k. Hmong LPQ	1·80	1·80

372 Cocks

2001. Fighting Cocks. Multicoloured.

1736	500k. Type **372**	20	20
1737	900k. Pair with wings outstretched	35	35
1738	3200k. Pair, one in flight	1·30	1·30
1739	3500k. Pair resting	1·40	1·40
MS1740	140 × 111 mm. 10000k. Cock crowing (36 × 51 mm)	4·00	4·00

373 Pou Nyer and Nya Nyer

2001. Luang Prabang New Year Celebrations. Multicoloured.

1741	300k. Type **373**	10	10
1742	600k. Hae Nang Sangkhan	20	20
1743	1000k. Sand Stupa (horiz)	35	35
1744	2300k. Hae Prabang	80	80
1745	4000k. Takbat	1·50	1·50

374 Snake

2001. Year of the Snake. Multicoloured.

1746	900k. Type **374**	30	30
1747	3500k. Snake and Chinese zodiac symbols	1·20	1·20

375 That Luang, Ventiane and Forbidden City, Beijing ($\frac{1}{2}$-size illustration)

2001. 40th Anniv of Laos–China Diplomatic Relations.

1748	**375** 1000k. multicoloured	35	35

376 Nurse, Mother and Children

2001. Polio Eradication Campaign. Sheet 135 × 101 mm containing T **376** and similar horiz design.

MS1749	900k. Type **376**; 2500k. Family and map	1·10	1·10

377 Mekong River

2001. Mekong River at Twilight. Multicoloured.

1750	900k. Type **377**	30	30
1751	2700k. River with boats in foreground	90	90
1752	3400k. River (different)	1·10	1·10

378 Poppy Field

2001. Anti-Drug Campaign. Multicoloured.

1753	100k. Type **378**	35	35
1754	4000k. Burning seized drugs	1·10	1·10

379 Intermediate Egret (*Egretta intermedia*)

2001. Birds. Philanippon '01 International Stamp Exhibition. Multicoloured.

1755	700k. Type **379**	20	20
1756	800k. Bulbucus ibis (33 × 49 mm)	20	20
1757	3100k. Grey heron (*Ardea cinera*) (33 × 49 mm)	95	95
1758	3400k. Great egret (*Egretta alba*)	1·00	1·00
MS1759	200 × 146 mm. Nos. 1755/8	3·00	3·00

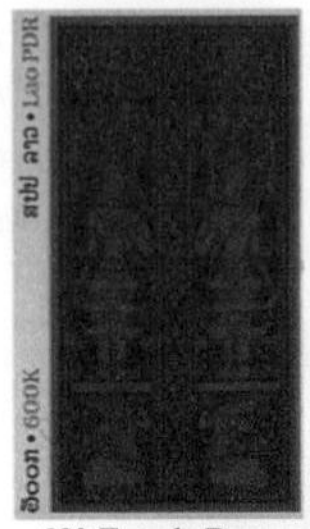

380 Temple Door

382 Women using Pestles and Mortar

381 White Frangipani

2001. Buddhist Temple Doors.

1760	**380** 600k. multicoloured	20	20
1761	– 2300k. multicoloured	80	80
1762	– 2500k. multicoloured	90	90
1763	– 2600k. multicoloured	90	90

DESIGNS: 2300k. to 2600k. Different temple doors.

2001. The Frangipani. Multicoloured.

1764	1000k. Type **381**	35	35
1765	2500k. Pink frangipani (vert)	90	90
1766	3500k. Red frangipani	1·20	1·20
MS1767	145 × 111 mm. Nos. 1764/6	2·40	2·40

2001. Traditional Mortars. Multicoloured.

1768	900k. Type **382**	30	30
1769	2600k. Wheel driven pestle and mortar (horiz)	80	80
1770	3500k. Fulcrum and lever pestle and mortar	1·10	1·10

383 Himavanta

2001. Vessantara (Buddhist story illustrating charity). Multicoloured.

1771	200k. Type **383**	10	10
1772	900k. Vanapavesa	35	35
1773	3200k. Kumarakanda	1·30	1·30
1774	3600k. Sakkapabba	1·50	1·50
MS1775	120 × 151 mm. Nos. 1772/4	3·25	3·25

384 People and Emblem

2001. International Year of Volunteers.

1776	**384** 1000k. multicoloured	35	35

2002. Women's Regional Costumes (2nd series). As T **359**. Multicoloured.

1777	200k. Meuy	10	10
1778	300k. Leu	10	10
1779	500k. Tai Kouane	15	15
1780	700k. Tai Dam	25	25
1781	1000k. Tai Man	30	30
1782	1500k. Lanten	45	45
1783	2500k. Hmong	80	80
1784	3000k. Phouxang	95	95
1785	3500k. Taitheng	1·10	1·10
1786	4000k. Tai O	1·20	1·20
1787	5000k. Tai Dam (different)	1·50	1·50

385 Phou Phamane

2002. International Year of Mountains. Multicoloured.

1788	1500k. Type **385**	55	55
1789	1500k. Pha Tang	55	55

386 Horse

2002. Chinese New Year ("Year of the Horse"). Multicoloured.

1790	1500k. Type **386**	55	55
1791	3500k. Galloping horse	1·10	1·10

387 Two Men carrying Parcels on Pole

2002. 50th Anniv of Laos Admission to Universal Postal Union.

1792	**387** 3000k. black	85	85

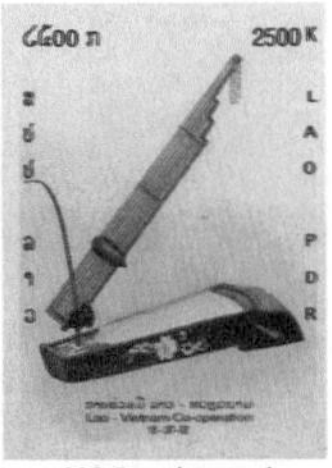

388 Laotian and Vietnamese Musical Instruments

389 *Sagra femorata*

2002. 40th Anniv of Laos—Vietnam Diplomatic Relations. 25th Anniv of Friendship Treaty.

1793	**388** 2500k. multicoloured	70	70
1794	– 3500k. black and orange (horiz)	1·00	1·00

DESIGNS: 2500k. Type **388**; 3500k. Prince Souvanna Vong and Ho Chi Minh (Vietnamese leader).

2002. Beetles. PhilaKorea 2002. Multicoloured.

1795	1000k. Type **389**	25	25
1796	1000k. *Cerambycidae*	25	25
1797	1000k. *Chrysoxhroa mniszechii*	25	25
1798	1000k. *Anoplophora*	25	25
1799	1000k. *Chrysochroa saundersi*	25	25
1800	1000k. *Mouhotia batesi*	25	25
1801	1000k. *Megaloxantha assamensis*	25	25
1802	1000k. *Eupatorus gracillicornis*	25	25
MS1803	150 × 210 mm. 1000k. × 8, *Sagra femorata* (different); *Cerambycidae* (different); *Chrysoxhroa mniszechii* (different); *Anoplophora* (different); *Chrysochroa saundersi* (different); *Mouhotia batesi* (different); *Megaloxantha assamensis* (different); *Eupatorus gracillicornis* (different)	2·00	2·00

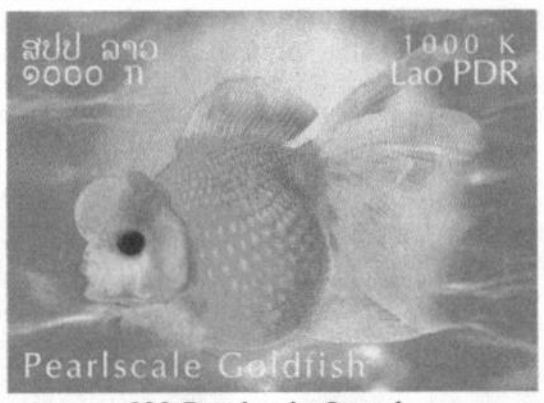

390 Pearlscale Oranda

2002. Goldfish. Multicoloured.

1804	1000k. Type **390**	35	35
1805	1000k. Moor	35	35
1806	1000k. Bubble eye	35	35
1807	1000k. Red-capped oranda	35	35
1808	1000k. Lionhead	35	35
1809	1000k. Pom pom	35	35
1810	1000k. Ranchu	35	35
1811	1000k. Fantail	35	35
1812	1000k. Celestial	35	35
1813	1000k. Ryukin	35	35
1814	1000k. Brown oranda	35	35
1815	1000k. Veiltail (inscr "Veitail")	35	35

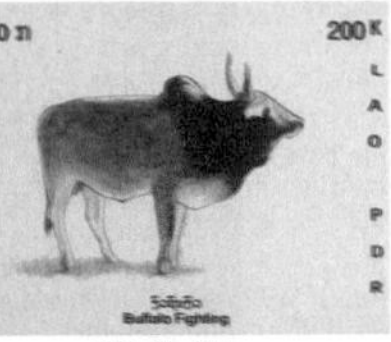

391 Buffalo

2002. Buffalo Fighting. Multicoloured.

1816	200k. Type **391**	15	15
1817	300k. Two buffalos with raised heads	15	15
1818	3000k. Two with locked horns	85	85
1819	4000k. Two chasing one another	1·10	1·10

392 Roadway

2002. Route 9 Highway Improvement Project. Sheet 190 × 116 mm containing T **392** and similar horiz designs. Multicoloured.

MS1820	1500k. × 3, Type **392**; Road junction; Open road	1·40	1·40

393 Arched Doorway

2003. World Heritage Site. Wat Phou Temple, Champasak. Multicoloured.

1821	1500k. Type **393**	30	30
1822	3000k. Wat Phou (horiz)	70	70
1823	4000k. Internal doorway and Buddha	1·20	1·20
MS1824	145 × 150 mm. 10000k. Carving showing three-headed elephant (96 × 30 mm)	2·60	2·60

394 Great Mormon (*Papillio memnon*)

2003. Butterflies. Multicoloured.

1825	1000k. Type **394**	30	30
1826	1000k. *Pachliopta aristolochiae*	30	30
1827	1000k. Inscr "Dalias pasithoe"	30	30
1828	1000k. *Castalius rosimon*	30	30
1829	1000k. *Polyura Schreiber*	30	30
1830	1000k. Blue triangle (*Graphium sarpedon*)	30	30
1831	1000k. *Spindasis lohita*	30	30
1832	1000k. *Hasora schoenherr*	30	30
MS1833	156 × 129 mm. 1000k. *Danaus genutia*	2·60	2·60

No. **MS**1833 was cut round in the shape of a butterfly.

395 Two Goats

2003. New Year ("Year of the Goat"). Multicoloured.

1834	2500k. Type **395**	70	70
1835	5000k. Goat wearing bell and saddle cloth	1·40	1·40

396 *Phalaenopsis paifang*

2003. Orchids (5th series). Multicoloured.

1836	200k. Type **396**	10	10
1837	300k. *Coelogyne lentiginosa*	15	15
1838	500k. *Phalaenopsis sumatrana*	25	25
1839	1000k. *Phalaenopsis bellina*	30	30
1840	1500k. *Paphiopedilum appletonianum*	30	30
1841	2000k. *Vanda bensonii*	50	50
1842	2500k. *Dendrobium harveyanum*	60	60
1843	3000k. *Paphiopedilum glaucophyllum*	75	75
1844	3500k. *Paphiopedilum gratrixianum*	90	90
1845	4000k. *Vanda roeblingiana*	1·00	1·00
1846	5000k. *Phalaenopsis Lady Sakara*	1·30	1·30

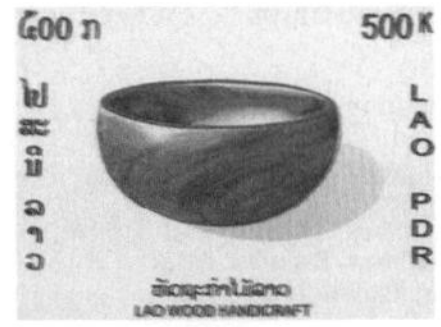

397 Bowl

2003. Wooden Crafts. Multicoloured.

1847	500k. Type **397**	15	10
1848	1500k. Drinks set	40	40
1849	2500k. Flower-shaped bowl	65	65
1850	3500k. Vase (vert)	95	95

398 Children using Coconut Feet Lifters

2003. Traditional Sports and Games. Multicoloured.

1851	1000k. Type **398**	30	30
1852	3000k. Spinning tops	80	80
1853	4000k. Tee knee (hockey)	1·00	1·00

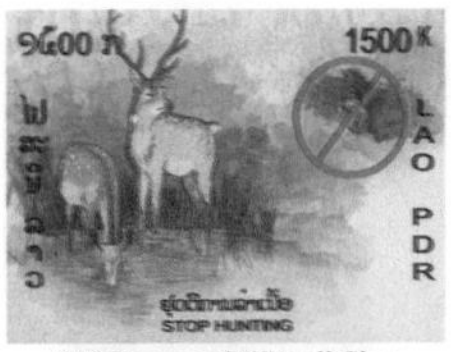

399 Deer and "Stop" Sign

2003. "Stop Hunting" Campaign. Multicoloured.

1854	1500k. Type **399**	40	40
1855	2000k. Rifle and bow	50	50
1856	4500k. Prey animals	1·20	1·20

400 Mango

2003. Fruit. Multicoloured.

1857	500k. Type **400**	15	15
1858	1500k. Water melon	40	40
1859	2500k. Custard apple	65	65
1860	4000k. Pineapple	1·00	1·00

401 Monk writing on Palm Leaf

402 Buddha (Pha Sene Souk)

2003. Palm Leaf Manuscripts. Multicoloured.

1861	500k. Type **401**	15	15
1862	1500k. Manuscript book	30	30
1863	2500k. Manuscript casket	55	55
1864	3000k. Ho Tai temple archive	65	65

2003. Luang Prabang Statues. Statues of Buddha. Multicoloured.

1865	500k. Type **402**	15	15
1866	1500k. Pha Gnai	30	30
1867	3000k. Pha Ong Luang	55	55
1868	3500k. Pha Ong Sene	65	65
MS1869	110 × 144 mm. 1000k. Pha Attharatsa (30 × 96 mm)	2·50	2·50

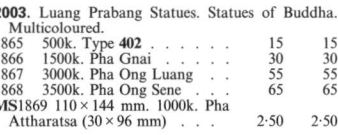

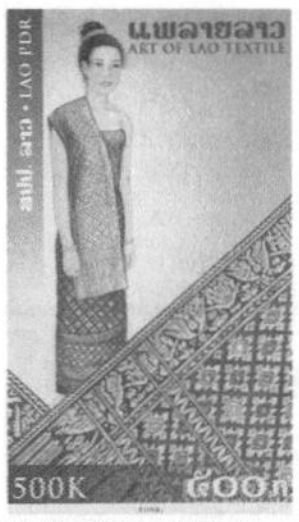

403 Traditional Cloth and Woman wearing Sin Mai (skirt) and Bieng Phae (scarf)

2003. Laotian Textiles. Showing cloth and woman. Multicoloured.

1870	500k. Type **403**	15	15
1871	1000k. Woman at right and brown patterned cloth	25	25
1872	3000k. Woman at left and green patterned cloth	65	65
1873	4000k. Woman at right and block patterned cloth	80	80

404 Haw Pha Keaw (Installed Emerald Buddha), Vientiane

2004.

1874	**404** 5500k. multicoloured	1·20	1·20

406 Two Dolphins

2004. Endangered Species. Irrawaddy Dolphins. Multicoloured.

1883	1500k. Type **406**	30	30
1884	2500k. Leaping	55	55
1885	3500k. With heads raised	65	65

407 Two Monkeys

2004. New Year "Year of the Monkey". Multicoloured.

1886	500k. Type **407**	15	15
1887	4500k. Monkey king	1·10	1·10

POSTAGE DUE STAMPS

D 5 Vat Sisaket Shrine — D 6 Sampans — D 98 Serpent

1952.

D22	D 5	10c. brown	15	15
D23		20c. violet	15	15
D24		50c. red	15	15
D25		1p. green	20	20
D26		2p. blue	20	20
D27		5p. purple	75	75
D28	D 6	10p. blue	1·10	1·10

1973.

D378	D 98	10k. black, brn & yell	15	15
D379		15k. black, yell & grn	15	15
D380		20k. black, green & bl	15	15
D381		50k. black, blue & red	35	35

APPENDIX

The following stamps have either been issued in excess of postal needs or have not been available to the public in reasonable quantities at face value. Such stamps may later be given full listing if there is evidence of regular postal use.

1975.

Centenary of U.P.U. Postage 10, 15, 30, 40k.; Air 1000, 1500k. On gold foil 2500, 3000k.

"Apollo–Soyuz" Space Link. Postage 125, 150, 200, 300k.; Air 450, 700k.

Bicentenary of American Revolution. Postage 10, 15, 40, 50, 100, 125, 150, 200k.; Air 1000, 1500k.

LAS BELA Pt. 1

A state of Baluchistan. Now part of Pakistan.

12 pies = 1 anna; 16 annas = 1 rupee.

1

1897.

1	1	½a. black on white	24·00	16·00
11		½a. black on blue	13·00	7·50
3		½a. black on grey	14·00	8·00
12		½a. black on green	13·00	7·50
8	–	1a. black on orange	19·00	21·00

The 1a. has the English inscription in a circle with the native inscription across the centre.

LATAKIA Pt. 19

The former state of the Alaouites which changed its name to Latakia in 1930.

Latakia was merged with Syria in 1936.

100 centimes = 1 piastre.

1931. As 1930 stamps of Syria (T **26/7**) optd **LATTAQUIE** in French and Arabic.

65	0p.10 mauve	2·00	2·50
66	0p.20 blue	25	2·50
67	0p.20 red	1·80	4·00
68	0p.25 green	1·30	4·00
69	0p.25 violet	2·75	4·75
70	0p.50 violet	2·25	4·50
71	0p.75 red	3·25	4·75
72	1p. green	1·80	2·25
73	1p.50 brown	4·50	6·25
74	1p.50 green	6·25	6·50
75	2p. violet	3·25	2·50
76	3p. green	7·25	7·00
77	4p. orange	4·00	2·25
78	4p.50 red	6·00	8·00
79	6p. green	6·50	8·00
80	7p.50 blue	6·00	6·25
81	10p. brown	7·25	10·00
82	15p. green	13·50	16·00
83	25p. purple	23·00	32·00
84	50p. brown	27·00	30·00
85	100p. red	65·00	80·00

1931. Air. As 1931 air stamps of Syria optd **LATTAQUIE** in French and Arabic.

86	0p.50 yellow	1·60	2·50
87	0p.50 brown	2·50	3·75
88	1p. brown	2·25	2·50
89	2p. blue	4·25	4·50
90	3p. green	3·50	4·75
91	5p. purple	7·25	11·00
92	10p. blue	9·50	9·00
93	15p. red	10·50	14·50
94	25p. orange	26·00	38·00
95	50p. black	32·00	42·00
96	100p. mauve	34·00	34·00

POSTAGE DUE STAMPS

1931. Nos. D197/8 of Syria optd **LATTAQUIE** in French and Arabic.

D86	8p. black on blue	26·00	38·00
D87	15p. black on pink	15·00	20·00

LATVIA Pt. 10

A country on the Baltic Sea. Previously part of the Russian Empire, Latvia was independent from 1918 to 1940 when it became part of the U.S.S.R.

Following the dissolution of the U.S.S.R. in 1991, Latvia once again became an independent republic.

1918. 100 kapeikas = 1 rublis.
1923. 100 santimu = 1 lats.
1991. 100 kopeks = 1 (Russian) rouble.
1992. 100 kopeks = 1 Latvian rouble.
1993. 100 santimu = 1 lats.

1 — 4 — 5 Rising Sun

1918. Printed on back of German war maps. Imperf or perf.

15	1	3k. lilac	10	10
16		5k. red	10	10
17		10k. blue	10	10
18		15k. green	10	10
41		20k. orange	10	10
20		25k. grey	50	35
21		35k. brown	20	20
42		40k. purple	30	10
22		50k. violet	20	20
44		75k. green	25	15
29		3r. red and blue	1·25	75
30		5r. red and brown	1·25	60

1919. Liberation of Riga. Imperf.

24	4	5k. red	20	20
25		15k. green	20	20
26		35k. brown	35	45

For stamps of Types **1** and **4** optd with a cross, with or without Russian letters "Z A", see under North-West Russia Nos. 21/42.

1919. Imperf or perf.

27	5	10k. blue	50	35

6 — 7

1919. 1st Anniv of Independence. (a) Size 33 × 45 mm.

32	6	10k. red and brown	35	35

(b) Size 28 × 38 mm.

33	6	10k. red and brown	20	20
34		35k. green and blue	20	20
35		1r. red and green	75	75

1919. Liberation of Courland.

36	7	10k. red and brown	10	10
37		25k. green and blue	20	20
38		35k. blue and black	30	30
39		1r. brown and green	55	55

8

1920. Red Cross stamps. (a) On backs of blue Bolshevist notes. Perf.

46	8	20-30k. red and brown	50	1·50
47		40-55k. red and blue	50	1·50
48		50-70k. red and green	50	1·75
49		1r.-1r.30 red and grey	75	2·00

(b) On backs of green Western Army notes. Perf.

50	8	20-30k. red and brown	40	90
51		40-55k. red and blue	40	90
52		50-70k. red and green	60	90
53		1r.-1r.30 red and grey	75	1·75

(c) On backs of red, green and brown Bolshevist notes. Imperf.

54	8	20-30k. red and brown	1·00	2·75
55		40-55k. red and blue	1·00	2·75
56		50-70k. red and green	1·00	2·75
57		1r.-1r.30 red and grey	2·00	4·00

CHARITY PREMIUMS. In the above and later issues where two values are expressed, the lower value represents the franking value and the higher the price charged, the difference being the charity premium.

9 — 10

1920. Liberation of Latgale.

58	9	50k. pink and green	20	30
59		1r. brown and green	30	40

1920. 1st Constituent Assembly.

60	10	50k. red	50	20
61		1r. blue	50	15
62		3r. green and brown	90	70
63		5r. purple and grey	1·00	80

1920. Surch in white figures on black oval.

64	6	10r. on 1r. red and green	2·00	1·10
65		20r. on 1r. red and green	3·50	2·50
66		30r. on 1r. red and green	4·50	4·00

1920. Surch **2 DIWI RUBLI.** Perf.

67	1	2r. on 10k. blue	2·00	1·25
68	4	2r. on 35k. brown	50	30

1920. (a) Surch **WEENS** or **DIVI**, value and **RUBLI.**

69	7	1 (WEENS) r. on 35k. blue and black	30	30
70		2 (DIVI) r. on 10k. red and brown	45	40
71		2 (DIVI) r. on 25k. green and blue	70	30

(b) Surch **DIWI RUBLI 2.**

72	6	2r. on 35k. green and blue	90	70

(c) Surch **DIVI 2 RUB. 2.**

73	10	2r. on 50k. red	25	40

(d) Surch **Desmit rubli.**

74	6	10r. on 10r. on 1r. red and green (No. 64)	1·00	65

1921. Red Cross. Nos. 51/3 surch **RUB 2 RUB.**

75	8	2r. on 20-30k. red and brown	2·50	4·50
76		2r. on 40-55k. red and blue	2·50	4·50
77		2r. on 50-70k. red and green	2·50	4·50
78		2r. on 1r.-1r.30k. red and grey	2·50	4·50

1921. Surch in figures and words over thick bar of crossed lines.

79	9	10r. on 50k. pink and green	90	70
80		20r. on 50k. pink and green	4·25	3·25
81		30r. on 50k. pink and green	4·00	3·00
82		50r. on 50k. pink and green	7·00	6·50
83		100r. on 50k. pink and green	18·00	15·00

19 Bleriot XI

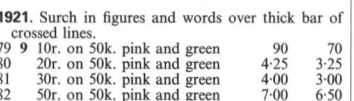

1921. Air. Value in "RUBLU". Imperf or perf.

84	19	10r. green	5·00	3·00
85		20r. blue	5·00	1·50

See also Nos. 155/7.

21 Latvian Coat of Arms — 22 Great Seal of Latvia

1921. Value in "Kopeks" or "Roubles".

86	21	50k. violet	25	10
87b		1r. yellow	25	25
88		2r. green	20	10
89		3r. green	30	25
90		5r. red	80	10
91		6r. red	1·25	75
92		9r. orange	90	25
93		10r. blue	1·10	10
94		15r. blue	4·50	1·00
95c		20r. lilac	11·00	1·50
96	22	50r. brown	20·00	5·00
97		100r. blue	24·00	4·25

1923. Value in "Santimi" or "Lats".

127	21	1s. mauve	15	10
129		2s. yellow	15	10
130		3s. red	15	10
100		4s. green	45	10
132		5s. green	30	10
133		6s. green and yellow	10	10
134		7s. green	30	15
103		10s. red	85	10
136d		10s. green and yellow	7·00	10
104		12s. mauve	25	20
105c		15s. purple and orange	2·75	10
107		20s. blue	1·50	10
139		20s. pink	3·00	20
108		25s. blue	20	10
109		30s. pink	4·00	10
140		30s. blue	1·25	10
141		35s. blue	1·50	10
110		40s. purple	1·50	15
143		50s. grey	3·00	15
144	22	1l. brown and bistre	6·00	15
116		2l. blue and light blue	14·00	90
117		5l. green and light green	48·00	3·75
118		10l. red and light red	6·00	15·00

1923. Charity. War Invalids. Surch **KARA INVALIDIEM S.10S.** and cross.

112	21	1s.+10s. mauve	50	1·00
113		2s.+10s. yellow	50	1·00
114		4s.+10s. green	50	1·00

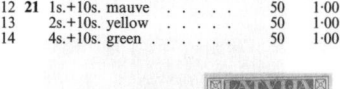

24 Town Hall — 28 Pres. J. Cakste

1925. 300th Anniv of City of Libau.

119	–	6-12s. blue and red	1·75	4·50
120	24	15-25s. brown and blue	90	3·50
121	–	25-35s. green and violet	1·75	3·50
122	–	30-40s. lake and blue	4·00	14·00
123	–	50-60s. violet and green	5·00	16·00

DESIGNS—HORIZ: 6-12s. Harbour and lighthouse; 25-35s. Spa health pavilion. VERT: 30-40s. St. Anna's Church; 50-60s. Arms of Libau.

1927. Surch.

124	1	15s. on 40k. purple	50	40
125		15s. on 50k. violet	1·10	1·25
126	10	1l. on 3r. green and brown	7·50	12·00

1928. Death of President Cakste and Memorial Fund.

150	28	2-12s. orange	2·50	4·00
151		6-16s. green	2·50	4·00
152		15-25s. lake	2·50	4·00
153		25-35s. blue	2·50	4·00
154		30-40s. red	2·50	4·00

1928. Air. Value in "SANTIMU" or "SANTIMI".

193	19	10s. green	1·50	75
156		15s. red	2·00	1·00
157		25s. blue	3·50	1·75

29 Ruins at Rezekne — 30 Venta

1928. 10th Anniv of Independence. Views.

158	29	6s. purple and green	50	15
159	–	15s. green and brown	40	15
160	–	20s. green and red	90	50
161	–	30s. brown and blue	1·10	20
162	–	50s. pink and grey	2·50	2·50
163	–	1l. sepia and brown	3·00	1·75

DESIGNS: 15s. Jelgava (Mitau); 20s. Cesis (Wenden); 30s. Liepaja (Libau); 50s. Riga; 1l. National Theatre, Riga.

1928. Liberty Memorial Fund. Imperf or perf.

164	30	6-16s. green	2·25	2·25
165	–	10-20s. red	2·25	2·25
166	–	15-25s. brown	2·25	2·25
167	–	30-40s. blue	2·25	2·25
168	–	50-60s. black	2·25	2·25
169	–	1l.-1l.10s. purple	3·50	3·50

DESIGNS: 10-20s. "Latvia" (Woman); 15-25s. Mitau; 30-40s. National Theatre, Riga; 50-60s. Wenden; 1l.-1l.10s. Trenches, Riga Bridge.

32 Z. A. Meierovics — 33 J. Rainis

1929. 3rd Death Anniv of Meierovics (Foreign Minister). Imperf or perf.

170	32	2-4s. yellow	3·00	3·00
171		6-12s. green	3·00	3·00
172		15-25s. purple	3·00	3·00
173		25-35s. blue	3·00	3·00
174		30-40s. blue	3·00	3·00

1930. Memorial Fund for J. Rainis (writer and politician). Imperf or perf.

175	33	1-2s. purple	75	1·75
176		2-4s. orange	75	1·75
177		4-8s. green	75	1·75
178		6-12s. brown and green	75	1·75
179		10-20s. red	15·00	32·00
180		15-30s. green and brown	15·00	32·00

34 Klemm KI-20 over Durbe Castle

1930. Air. J. Rainis Memorial Fund. Imperf or perf.

181	**34**	10-20s. green and red	10·00	11·50
182		15-30s. red and green	10·00	11·50

35

36

1930. Anti-T.B. Fund.

183	–	1-2s. red and purple	50	50
184	–	2-4s. red and orange	50	50
185	**35**	4-8s. red and green	65	80
186	–	5-10s. brown and green	75	1·10
187	–	6-12s. yellow and green	75	1·10
188	–	10-20s. black and red	1·00	1·60
189	–	15-30s. green and brown	1·50	1·50
190	–	20-40s. blue and red	1·50	1·75
191	–	25-50s. lilac, blue and red	2·00	2·50
192	**36**	30-60s. lilac, green and blue	2·75	3·00

DESIGNS—VERT: As Type **35**: 1-2s., 2-4s. The Crusaders' Cross; 5-10s. G. Zemgalis; 6-12s. Tower; 10-20s. J. Cakste; 15-30s. Floral design; 20-40s. A. Kviesis. HORIZ: As Type **36**: 25-50s. Sanatorium.

1931. Nos. 183/92 surch.

196	9 on 6-12s. yellow and green	65	1·00
197	16 on 1-2s. red and purple	10·00	20·00
198	17s. on 2-4s. red and orange	1·25	2·25
199	19 on 4-8s. red and green	3·00	7·00
200	20 on 5-10s. brown and green	2·00	8·00
201	23 on 15-30s. green and brown	75	1·00
202	25 on 10-20s. black and red	2·00	3·75
203	35 on 20-40s. blue and red	3·75	4·50
204	45 on 25-50s. lilac, blue and red	12·00	16·00
205	55 on 30-60s. lilac, green & bl	13·00	17·00

1931. Air. Charity. Nos. 155/7 surch **LATVIJAS AIZSARGI** and value. Imperf or perf.

206	**19**	50 on 10s. green	13·00	18·00
207		1l. on 15s. red	13·00	18·00
208		1l.50 on 2s. blue	13·00	18·00

38 Foreign Invasion

1932. Militia Maintenance Fund. Imperf or perf.

209	–	1-11s. blue and purple	1·90	2·10
210	**38**	2-17s. orange and olive	1·90	2·10
211	–	3-23s. red and brown	1·90	2·10
212	–	4-34s. green	1·90	2·10
213	–	5-45s. green	1·90	2·10

DESIGNS: 1-11s. The Holy Oak and Kriva telling stories; 3-23s. Lacplesis, the deliverer; 4-34s. The Black Knight (enemy) slaughtered; 5-45s. Laimdota, the spirit of Latvia, freed.

39 Infantry Manoeuvres

1932. Militia Maintenance Fund. Imperf or perf.

214	–	6-25s. purple and brown	4·00	4·50
215	**39**	7-35s. blue and green	4·00	4·50
216	–	10-45s. sepia and green	4·00	4·50
217	–	12-55s. green and red	4·00	4·50
218	–	15-75s. violet and red	4·00	4·50

DESIGNS—HORIZ: 6-25s. Troops on march. VERT: 10-45s. First aid to soldier; 12-55s. Army kitchen; 15-75s. Gen. J. Balodis.

41

1932. Air. Charity. Imperf or perf.

219	**41**	10-20s. black and green	12·00	18·00
220		15-30s. red and grey	12·00	18·00
221		25-50s. blue and grey	12·00	18·00

1932. Riga Exn of Lettish Products. Optd **Latvijas razojumu izstade Riga. 1932.g.10.-18.IX.**

222	**21**	3s. red	50	40
223		10s. green on yellow	1·50	80
224		20s. pink	1·50	70
225		35s. blue	2·40	1·60

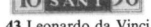

43 Leonardo da Vinci

44 "Mourning Mother" Memorial, Riga

1932. Air. Charity. Pioneers of Aviation. Imperf or perf.

226	–	5-25s. green and brown	10·00	15·00
227	**43**	10-50s. green and brown	10·00	15·00
228	–	15-75s. green and red	13·50	17·00
229	–	20-100s. mauve and green	13·50	17·00
230	–	25-125s. blue and brown	13·50	17·00

DESIGNS—VERT: 5s. Icarus; 15s. Jacques Charles's hydrogen balloon, 1783 (inscr "Charliers"). HORIZ: 20s. Wright Type A biplane; 25s. Bleriot XI monoplane.

1933. Air. Wounded Latvian Airmen Fund. Imperf or perf.

231	–	2-52s. brown and black	6·00	14·00
232	**44**	3-53s. red and black	6·00	14·00
233	–	10-60s. green and black	6·00	14·00
234	–	20-70s. red and black	6·00	14·00

DESIGNS: 2s. Fall of Icarus; 10s., 20s. Proposed tombs for airmen.

1933. Air. Charity. Riga–Bathurst Flight. Nos. 155/7 optd **LATVIJA-AFRIKA 1933** or surch also.

235	10s. green	15·00	50·00
236	15s. red	15·00	50·00
237	25s. blue	18·00	50·00
238	50s. on 15s. red	£120	£325
239	100s. on 25s. blue	£120	£325

In the event the aircraft crashed at Neustettin, Germany, and the mail was forwarded by ordinary post.

46 Biplane under Fire at Riga

1933. Air. Charity. Wounded Latvian Airmen Fund. Imperf or perf.

240	–	3-53s. blue and orange	20·00	24·00
241	**46**	7-57s. brown and blue	20·00	24·00
242	–	35-135s. black and blue	20·00	24·00

DESIGNS: 3s. Monoplane taking off; 35s. Map and aircraft.

47 Glanville Brothers' Gee Bee Super Sportster

1933. Air. Charity. Wounded Latvian Airmen Fund. Imperf or perf.

243	**47**	8-68s. grey and brown	30·00	50·00
244	–	12-112s. green and purple	30·00	50·00
245	–	30-130s. grey and blue	30·00	50·00
246	–	40-190s. blue and purple	30·00	50·00

DESIGNS: 12s. Supermarine S6B seaplane; 30s. Airship "Graf Zeppelin" over Riga; 40s. Dornier Do-X flying boat.

48 President's Palace

50 A. Kronvalds

51

1934. 15th Anniv of New Constitution.

247	**48**	3s. red	10	15
248	–	5s. green	15	10
249	–	10s. green	1·75	10
250	–	20s. red	1·75	10
251	–	35s. blue	10	15
252	**48**	40s. brown	20	15

DESIGNS: 5, 10s. Arms and shield; 20s. Allegory of Latvia; 35s. Government Building.

1936. Lettish Intellectuals.

253	**50**	3s. red	1·10	4·00
254	–	10s. green	1·10	4·00
255	–	20s. mauve	1·10	5·00
256	–	35s. blue	1·10	5·00

PORTRAITS: 10s. A. Pumpurs; 20s. J. Maters; 35s. Auseklis.

1936. White Cross Fund. Designs incorporating Cross and Stars device as in T **51**.

257	**51**	3s. red	1·50	4·00
258	–	10s. green	1·50	4·00
259	–	20s. mauve	1·50	5·00
260	–	35s. blue	1·50	5·00

DESIGNS: 10s. Oak leaves; 20s. Doctors and patient; 35s. Woman holding shield.

53 Independence Monument, Rauna (Ronneburg)

54 President Ulmanis

1937. Monuments.

261	**53**	3s. red	35	1·40
262	–	5s. green	35	60
263	–	10s. green	35	35
264	–	20s. red	85	1·00
265	–	30s. blue	90	1·25
266	–	35s. blue	1·40	1·50
267	–	40s. brown	2·25	2·50

DESIGNS—VERT: 10s. Independence Monument, Jelgava (Mitau); 20s. War Memorial, Valka (Walk); 30s. Independence Monument, Iecava (Eckau); 35s. Independence Monument, Riga; 40s. Col. Kalpak's Grave, Visagalas Cemetery. HORIZ: 5s. Cemetery Gate, Riga.

1937. President Ulmanis's 60th Birthday.

268	**54**	3s. red and orange	15	10
269		5s. light green and green	15	15
270		10s. deep green and green	25	35
271		20s. purple and red	55	35
272		25s. grey and blue	85	70
273		30s. deep blue and blue	85	60
274		35s. indigo and blue	75	50
275		40s. light brown and brown	85	75
276		50s. green and black	90	80

55 Palace of Justice

1938. National Building Fund. Sheet 140 × 100 mm comprising 35 (s.) blue (T **55**) and 40 (s.) brown (Power Station, Kegums).

MS277 Sold at 2l. . . . 11·00 3·00

56 Gaizinkalns, Livonia

57 General J. Balodis

1938. 20th Anniv of Independence.

278	**56**	3s. red	10	10
279	–	5s. green	10	10
280	**57**	10s. green	30	10
281	–	20s. mauve	20	10
282	–	30s. blue	60	20
283	–	35s. slate	90	10
284	–	40s. mauve	80	15

DESIGNS: As Type **56**: 5s. Latgale landscape; 30s. City of Riga; 35s. Rumba waterfall, Courland; 40s. Zemgale landscape. As Type **57**: 20s. President Ulmanis.

58 Elementary School, Riga

1939. 5th Anniv of Authoritarian Government.

285	**58**	3s. brown	30	60
286	–	5s. green	30	60
287	–	10s. green	95	20
288	–	20s. red	95	65
289	–	30s. blue	1·40	1·00
290	–	35s. blue	1·40	1·50
291	–	40s. purple	1·75	1·00
292	–	50s. black	2·00	1·25

DESIGNS: 5s. Jelgava Castle; 10s. Riga Castle; 20s. Independence Monument; 30s. Eagle and National Flag; 35s. Town Hall, Daugavpils; 40s. War Museum and Powder-magazine, Riga; 50s. Pres. Ulmanis.

1939. 5th Year of Office of Pres. Ulmanis. Sheet as **MS**277 optd "1934 1939 14/V".

MS293 Sold at 2l. . . . 14·00 40·00

59 Reaping

60 Arms of Courland, Livonia and Latgale

61 Arms of Latvian Soviet Socialist Republic

1939. Harvest Festival. Dated "8 X 1939".

294	**59**	10s. green	40	40
295	–	20s. red (Apples)	70	30

1940.

296	**60**	1s. violet	25	50
297		2s. yellow	30	50
298		3s. red	10	15
299		5s. brown	10	10
300		7s. green	10	60
301		10s. green	75	15
302		20s. red	75	10
303		30s. brown	90	40
304		35s. blue	10	85
305		50s. green	1·00	50
306		1l. olive	2·00	60

1940. Incorporation of Latvia in U.S.S.R.

307	**61**	1s. violet	15	20
308		2s. yellow	15	15
309		3s. red	10	10
310		5s. olive	10	10
311		7s. green	10	45
312		10s. green	30	10
313		20s. red	65	10
314		30s. blue	80	30
315		35s. blue	10	55
316		40s. brown	60	20
317		50s. grey	90	25
318		1l. brown	2·00	35
319		5l. green	11·00	5·50

64 Latvian Arms

65 Latvian Arms

1991.

320	**64**	5k. silver, brown & lt brn	35	20
321		10k. silver, brown & drab	15	10
322		15k. silver, sepia & brown	15	10
323		20k. silver, blue & lt blue	60	20
324		40k. silver, green and light green	1·25	40
325		50k. silver, brown and lilac	1·40	45
326	**65**	100k. multicoloured	2·75	80
327		200k. multicoloured	5·00	1·40

1991. Nos. 6073 and 6077a of Russia surch **LATVIJA** and new value.

332	100k. on 7k. blue	10	10
333	300k. on 2k. brown	35	25
334	500k. on 2k. brown	60	40
335	1000k. on 2k. brown	1·25	70

67 Main Statue, Liberty Monument, Riga

68 Olympic Committee Symbol

1991.

336	**67**	10k. multicoloured	10	10
337		15k. multicoloured	10	10
338		20k. multicoloured	15	10
339		30k. multicoloured	25	15
340		50k. multicoloured	40	20
341		100k. multicoloured	80	45

1992. Recognition of Latvian Olympic Committee.

342	**68**	50k.+25k. red, silver and drab	40	20
343	–	50k.+25k. red, silver and grey	40	20
344	**68**	100k.+50k. red, gold and bistre	80	45

DESIGN: No. 343, as T **68** but symbols smaller and inscribed "BERLIN 18.09.91." at left.

69 Vaidelotis

72 Children in Fancy Dress around Christmas Tree

1992. Statues from the base of the Liberty Monument, Riga.
345 – 10k. black and brown . . . 10 10
346 **69** 20k. brown and grey . . . 15 10
347 – 30k. deep lilac and lilac . . 25 15
348 **69** 30k. deep brown and brown 25 15
349 – 40k. blue and grey 35 20
350 **69** 50k. green and grey . . . 40 25
351 – 50k. black and grey . . . 40 25
352 – 100k. purple and mauve . . 85 45
353 – 200k. deep blue and blue 1·60 80
DESIGNS: Nos. 345, 347, 353, Kurzeme (warrior with shield); 349, 351/2, Lachplesis (two figures).

1992. Nos. 4672, 6073 and 6077a of Russia surch **LATVIJA** and new value.
354a 1r. on 7k. blue 10 10
355 3r. on 2k. brown 10 10
356 5r. on 2k. brown 20 10
357 10r. on 2k. brown 40 20
358 25r. on 4k. red 95 45

1992. Birds of the Baltic. As Nos. 506/9 of Lithuania.
359 5r. black and red 50 45
360 5r. brown, black and red . . 50 45
361 5r. sepia, brown and red . . 50 45
362 5r. brown, black and red . . 50 45
DESIGNS: Nos 359, Osprey ("Pandion haliaetus"); 360, Black-tailed godwit ("Limosa limosa"); 361, Goosander ("Mergus merganser"); 362, Common shelducks ("Tadorna tadorna").

1992. Christmas. Multicoloured.
363 2r. Type **72** 20 10
364 3r. Angel choir 30 15
365 10r. Type **72** 50 20
366 15r. Adoration of the Kings 65 30

1993. Nos. 4855, 5296 and 5295 of Russia surch **LATVIJA** and new value.
367 50r. on 6k. multicoloured . . 75 35
368 100r. on 6k. multicoloured 1·50 75
369 300r. on 6k. multicoloured 3·25 1·60

74 Kuldiga Couple

75 Emblem

1993. Traditional Costumes. Multicoloured.
370 5s. Type **74** 15 10
371 10s. Alsunga 30 20
372 20s. Lielvarde 55 35
373 50s. Rucava . . . . 1·40 1·00
374 100s. Zemgale . . . . 3·00 2·00
375 500s. Ziemellatgale . . . . 13·50 9·00
MS376 103 × 88 mm. Nos. 370/5 18·00 8·00
See also Nos. 428/**MS**429, 442/**MS**443, 467/**MS**468 and 491/**MS**492.

1993. National Song Festival.
377 **75** 3s. black, gold and brown 15 10
378 5s. black, gold and lilac . . 30 15
379 – 15s. multicoloured . . . . 1·00 50
DESIGN: 15s. Abstract.

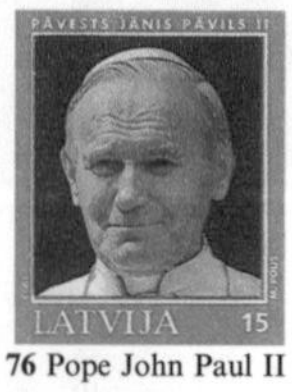

76 Pope John Paul II

77 Flags

1993. Papal Visit.
380 **76** 15s. multicoloured 50 35

1993. 75th Anniv of First Republic.
381 **77** 5s. multicoloured 15 10
382 15s. multicoloured 45 35

78 Valters

79 Biathlon

1994. 100th Birthday of Evalds Valters (actor).
383 **78** 15s. brown, light brown and gold 50 35

1994. Winter Olympic Games, Lillehammer, Norway. Multicoloured.
384 5s. Type **79** 15 10
385 10s. Two-man bobsleigh . . 25 15
386 15s. One-man luge 50 35
387 100s. Figure skating . . . . 2·75 1·50
MS388 55 × 80 mm. 200s. As No. 385 . . . . 4·75 4·75

80 Reed Hut

1994. 70th Anniv of Latvian Ethnological Open-air Museum, Bergi.
389 **80** 5s. multicoloured 25 10

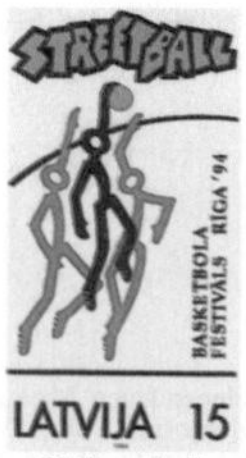

81 Streetball

82 Kurzeme

1994. Basketball Festival, Riga.
390 **81** 15s. black, grey and orange 50 35

1994. Arms (1st series). (a) Size 18 × 21 mm.
391 **82** 1s. red, black and silver 10 10
392 – 2s. multicoloured 10 10
393 – 3s. silver, black and blue 10 10
394 – 5s. silver, black and red 10 10
395 – 8s. silver, black and blue 20 10
396 – 10s. silver, black and blue 25 10
396a – 10s. multicoloured 20 10
397 – 13s. black, gold and silver 30 15
397a – 16s. multicoloured 35 15
398 – 20s. silver, black and grey 50 25
398a – 20s. multicoloured 45 20
399 – 24s. green, black and silver 55 25
399a – 28s. multicoloured 60 30
400 – 30s. multicoloured 65 30
401 – 36s. silver, black and red 75 35
402 – 50s. multicoloured . . . . 1·10 55

(b) Size 29 × 23½ mm.
403 – 100s. multicoloured . . . . 2·10 1·00
404 – 200s. multicoloured . . . . 4·25 1·10
DESIGNS: 2s. Auce; 3s. Zemgale; 5s. Vidzeme; 8s. Livani; 10s. (396) Latgale; 10s. (396a) Valmiera; 13s. Preila; 16s. Ainazi; 20s. (398) Grobina; 20s. (398a) Rezekne; 24s. Tukums; 28s. Madona; 30, 100s. Riga; 36s. Priekule; 50, 200s. State arms.
See also Nos. 501/6.

83 Emblem

84 Coins in Scales

1994. 75th Anniv of Latvia University.
405 **83** 5s. gold, blue and green . . 10 10

1994. Europa. Multicoloured.
406 10s. Type **84** 25 20
407 50s. Money chest and notes in scales . . . . 1·25 60

85 Eating Cherries

86 Angel

1994. The Fat Dormouse. Multicoloured.
408 5s. Type **85** 15 10
409 10s. Eating strawberries . . . 30 15
410 10s. On leafy branch 30 15
411 15s. On branch of apple tree 60 30

1994. Christmas. Multicoloured.
412 3s. Type **86** 10 10
413 8s. Angels playing violin and flute 30 15
414 13s. Angels singing 50 25
415 100s. Wreath of candles . . . 2·75 1·40

87 Gnome with Candle

88 Emblem

1994. 80th Birthday of Margarita Staraste (children's writer and illustrator). Multicoloured.
416 5s. Type **87** 15 10
417 10s. Bear 30 15
418 10s. Child on sledge 30 15

1994. Road Safety Year.
419 **88** 10s. multicoloured 35 10

89 Emblem

90 Bauska Castle (Latvia)

1995. 50th Anniv of U.N.O.
420 **89** 15s. blue, red and silver . . 50 25

1995. Via Baltica Motorway Project. Multicoloured.
421 8s. Type **90** 30 15
MS422 100 × 110 mm. 18s. Beach Hotel, Parnu (Estonia); 18s. Type **90**; 18s. Kaunas (Lithuania) 1·60 1·60

91 White-backed Woodpecker

92 Vaivods

1995. European Nature Conservation Year. Birds. Multicoloured.
423 8s. Type **91** 30 15
424 20s. Corncrake 75 40
425 24s. White-winged black tern 95 50

1995. Birth Centenary of Cardinal Julijans Vaivods.
426 **92** 8s. multicoloured 20 10

93 Sun and Open Book

1995. 60th Anniv of Karlis Ulmaris Schools Appeal.
427 **93** 8s. multicoloured 20 10

1995. Traditional Costumes. As T **74**. Multicoloured.
428 8s. Nica 30 15
MS429 100s. As No. 428 . . . . 2·25 2·25

94 National Opera House

95 Lacplesis, the Bear Slayer

1995. 800th Anniv of Riga (1st issue). Multicoloured.
430 8s. Type **94** 25 10
431 16s. National Theatre 45 20
432 24s. Art School (44 × 26 mm) 70 35
433 36s. Art Museum (44 × 26 mm) 95 45
See also Nos. 456/9, 479/82, 493/6, 522/5, 540/3 and 560/3.

1995. European Peace and Freedom. Multicoloured.
434 16s. Type **95** 50 25
435 50s. Spidola . . . . 1·60 80

96 Christmas Tree at Night

97 Stradins

1995. Christmas. Multicoloured.
436 6s. Type **96** 20 10
437 6s. Elf flying with candle . . 20 10
438 15s. Cottage at night 40 20
439 24s. Elf with dog and cat . . 75 35

1996. Birth Centenary of Pauls Stradins (surgeon).
440 **97** 8s. multicoloured 20 10

98 Zenta Maurina (writer)

99 Children with Toys

1996. Europa. Famous Women.
441 **98** 36s. multicoloured . . . . 1·10 50

1996. Traditional Costumes. As T **74**. Multicoloured.
442 8s. Barta 25 15
MS443 100 × 70 mm. 100s. As No. 422 . . . . 2·75 2·75

100 Cycling

101 Swallowtail

1996. Sheet 96 × 97 mm.
MS444 **99** 48s. multicoloured . . 1·50 1·50

1996. Olympic Games, Atlanta. Multicoloured.
445 8s. Type **100** 20 10
446 16s. Basketball 40 20
447 24s. Walking 65 30
448 36s. Canoeing (horiz) . . . . 1·00 50
MS449 85 × 60 mm. 100s. Throwing the javelin (horiz) . . . . . . 2·75 2·75

1996. Butterflies. Multicoloured.
450 8s. Type **101** 25 10
451 24s. Clifden's nonpareil . . . 75 40
452 80s. Large tiger moth . . . . 2·00 1·00

102 1912 Russo-Balt Fire Engine

103 Apartment Block (E. Laube)

1996. Latvian Car Production. Multicoloured.
453 8s. Type **102** 25 10
454 24s. 1899 Leutner-Russia carriage 70 35
455 36s. 1939 Ford-Vairogs motor car . . . . 1·00 50

1996. 800th Anniv of Riga (2nd issue). Multicoloured.
456 8s. Type **103** 25 10
457 16s. Stained glass window (F. Sefels) (30 × 26 mm) . . 45 20
458 24s. Turreted buildings (E. Laube) (38 × 26 mm) 75 35
459 30s. Couple welcoming charioteer (mural, J. Rozentals) (38 × 26 mm) 1·00 50

104 Elves and Presents

1996. Christmas. Multicoloured.
460 6s. Type **104** 15 10
461 14s. Children with dog and Father Christmas on skis 35 20
462 20s. Child at tree and Father Christmas in armchair . . 50 25

105 European Nightjar

106 Symbols of Independence

1997. 75th Anniv of Birdlife International (conservation organization). Multicoloured.
463 10s. Type **105** 30 15
464 20s. Greater spotted eagle . . 75 35
465 30s. Aquatic warbler . . . . 1·10 55

1997. 6th Anniv of Independence.
466 **106** 10s. multicoloured 30 15

1997. Traditional Costumes. As T **74**. Multicoloured.
467 10s. Rietumvidzeme 20 10
MS468 100 × 70 mm. 100s. As No. 467 . . . . 1·75 1·75

107 Turaidas Roze

108 "Wappen der Herzogin von Kurland" (galleon)

1997. Europa. Tales and Legends.
469 **107** 32s. multicoloured 90 45

1997. Baltic Sailing Ships. Multicoloured.
470 10s. Type **108** 30 15
MS471 110 × 70 mm. 20s. As No. 470 but with different frame; 20s. Kurshes ship (Lithuania); 20s. Maasilinn ship (Estonia) . . . 2·75 2·75

109 Hermes and Neptune

1997. Centenary of Ventspils International Commercial Port.
472 **109** 20s. blue, silver and yellow 60 30

110 Stamp Collecting

1997. Children's Leisure Pursuits. Multicoloured.
473 10s. Type **110** 25 10
474 12s. Motor cycle trials (vert) 40 20
475 20s. Ice hockey and skiing (vert) 60 30
476 30s. Tennis, football and basketball . . . . 1·00 50

111 Moricsala

1997. Nature Reserves. Multicoloured.
477 10s. Type **111** 25 10
478 30s. Slitere 75 35

112 Woman, Wooden Building and Jewellery (12th century)

1997. 800th Anniv of Riga (3rd issue). 12th–16th Centuries. Multicoloured.
479 10s. Type **112** 25 10
480 20s. 13th-century Cathedral cloister, statue (K. Bernevics) and seal of Bishop Albert, rosary beads and writing implement 55 25
481 30s. Livonian Order's castle, statue of V. von Plettenberg (Order Master) and weapons 80 40
482 32s. "Three Brothers" terrace, statue of St. John and seal (27 × 27 mm) 90 45

113 Man and Bear

1997. Christmas. Mummers. Multicoloured.
483 8s. Type **113** 20 10
484 18s. Witches 50 25
485 28s. Horse 70 35

114 Flames

115 Sculpture of Character

1998. Winter Olympic Games, Nagano, Japan.
486 **114** 20s. multicoloured 55 25

1998. Spridisi Memorial (to Anna Brigadere (writer)) Museum, Tervete.
487 **115** 10s. multicoloured 25 10

116 Song Festival

1998. Europa. National Festivals.
488 **116** 30s. multicoloured 65 30

117 Grini

1998. Nature Reserves. Multicoloured.
489 10s. Type **117** 20 10
490 30s. Teici 65 30

1998. Traditional Costumes. As T **74**. Multicoloured.
491 10s. Krustpils 20 10
MS492 100 × 69 mm. 100s. As No. 491 but man with Midsummer Festival headdress . . . . . . 2·10 2·10

118 Dannenstern House, Wooden Sculpture and Polish and Swedish Coins

1998. 800th Anniv of Riga (4th issue). 16th–20th Centuries. Multicoloured.
493 10s. Type **118** 20 10
494 20s. Library, medallion and monument to G. Herder (poet and philosopher) . . 45 20
495 30s. Arsenal, Victory column, octant and compass . . . 65 30
496 40s. Entrance gate to Warrior's Cemetery, "Mother Latvia" (statue) and 5l. coin 85 40

1998. Arms (2nd series). As T **82**.
497 5s. multicoloured 10 10
497a 5s. multicoloured 10 10
497b 5s. multicoloured 10 10
499 10s. multicoloured 20 10
499a 10s. multicoloured 20 10
499b 10s. black, red and silver . . 20 10
500 15s. multicoloured 30 15
501 15s. black, blue and silver 30 15
502 15s. multicoloured 30 15
503 15s. multicoloured 30 15
504 15s. black, silver and red . . 30 15
504a 15s. multicoloured 30 15
504b 15s. silver and black 30 15
504c 20s. multicoloured 35 15
504d 15s. multicoloured 30 15
504e 15s. multicoloured 30 15
504f 15s. multicoloured 30 15
505 30s. multicoloured 65 30
505a 20s. blue, silver and black 35 15
506 40s. multicoloured 75 35
509 40s. multicoloured 80 40
DESIGNS: No. 497, Smiltene; 497a, Ludza; 497b, Valka; 499, Valmiera; 499a, Dobeje; 499b, Balvi; 500, Bauska; 501, Ogre; 502, Daugavpils; 503, Jurmala; 504, Kuldiga; 504a, Sigulda; 504b, Gulbene; 504c, Ventspils; 504d, Cesis; 504e, Talsi; 504f, Aluksne; 505, Liepaja; 505a, Saldus; 506, Jelgava; 509, Jekabpils.

119 1918 5k. Stamp

120 Dome Church, Riga

1998. 70th Anniv of First Latvian Stamp.
510 **119** 30s. red, cream and grey 65 30

1998. Churches.
511 **120** 10s. multicoloured 20 10

121 Janis Cakste (1922–27)

122 State Flag

1998. Presidents.
512 **121** 10s. multicoloured 20 10

1998. 80th Anniv of Declaration of Independence. Multicoloured.
513 10s. Type **122** 20 10
514 30s. State arms and flags . . 65 30

123 Elves building Snowman

1998. Christmas. Multicoloured.
515 10s. Type **123** 20 10
516 20s. Elves decorating tree . . 40 20
517 30s. Elves sledging 65 30

124 Krustkalnu Nature Reserve

125 Playing Cards and Edgars (from novel "Purva Bridejs")

1999. Europa. Parks and Gardens.
518 30s. Type **124** 65 30
519 60s. Gauja National Nature Park . . . . 1·25 60

1999. Latvian Literature. Rudolfs Blaumanis.
520 **125** 110s. multicoloured . . . 2·25 1·10

126 Council Emblem

1999. 50th Anniv of Council of Europe.
521 **126** 30s. multicoloured 65 30

127 "Widwud" (schooner)

1999. 800th Anniv of Riga (5th issue). Transport. Multicoloured.
522 10s. Electric tramcar No. 258 (30 × 26½ mm) 20 10
523 30s. Type **127** 65 30
524 40s. Biplane 75 35
525 70s. Steam locomotive No. Tk-236 . . . . 1·50 75

128 Aglona Basilica

129 Family and State Flag

1999. Churches.
526 **128** 15s. multicoloured 30 15

1999. 10th Anniv of Baltic Chain (human chain uniting capitals of Latvia, Lithuania and Estonia).
527 **129** 15s. multicoloured 30 15
MS528 110 × 72 mm. 30s. Type **129**; 30s. Family and Lithuanian flag; 30s. Family and Estonian flag 1·90 1·90

130 Rundale Palace

1999. Palaces.
529 **130** 20s. multicoloured 40 20

131 "Perse"

1999. 90th Death Anniv of Julijs Feders (painter).
530 **131** 15s. multicoloured 30 15

132 Gustavs Zemgals (1927–30)

133 Harbour, Letters and Emblem

1999. Presidents.
531 **132** 15s. multicoloured 35 15

1999. 125th Anniv of Universal Postal Union.
532 **133** 40s. multicoloured 90 45

134 Father Christmas and Candle

135 "Artist's Model" (J. Rosentals)

1999. Christmas. Multicoloured.
533 12s. Type **134** 25 10
534 15s. Children watching television 35 15
535 40s. Father Christmas placing toys under tree 90 45

2000.
536 **135** 40s. multicoloured 90 45

136 Scene from *The Wagon Driver* (poem) **137** "Building Europe"

2000. 50th Death Anniv of Aleksandrs Caks (poet).
537 **136** 40s. multicoloured 90 45

2000. Europa.
538 **137** 60s. multicoloured . . . . 1·40 70

138 Ice Hockey Players

2000. Ice Hockey.
539 **138** 70s. multicoloured . . . . 1·50 75

140 Central Market

2000. 800th Anniv of Riga (6th issue). Tourist Sights. Multicoloured.
540 20s. Type **140** 45 20
541 40s. Dome Church organ (25 × 30 mm) 90 45
542 40s. Zoo (44 × 26 mm) . . . 90 45
543 70s. The Powder Tower (25 × 30 mm) . . . . . . 1·50 75

141 Jelgava Palace

2000. Palaces.
544 **141** 40s. multicoloured 45 20

142 Globe and Olympic Rings

2000. Olympic Games, Sydney.
545 **142** 40s. multicoloured 45 20
546 70s. multicoloured . . . . 1·60 80

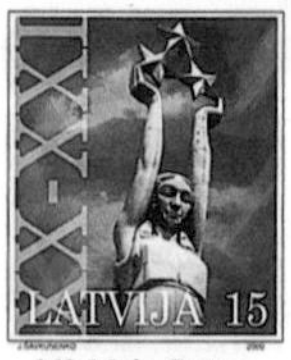

143 Main Statue, Liberty Monument, Riga (Karlis Zale) **144** Alberts Kviesis (1930–36)

2000. New Millennium. Multicoloured.
547 15s. Type **143** 30 15
548 50s. Brotherhood of Blackheads meeting house, Riga . . . . 1·10 55

2000. Presidents.
549 **144** 15s. multicoloured 30 15

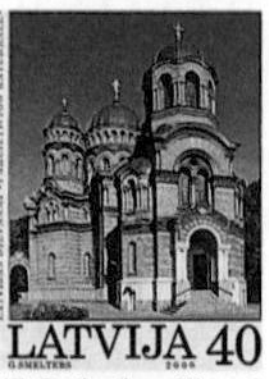

145 Orthodox Church, Riga **146** Nurses tending to Elderly Lady

2000. Churches.
550 **145** 40s. multicoloured 45 20

2000. Latvian Red Cross.
551 **146** 15s. multicoloured 30 15

147 Elf and Sleigh **148** People around Bonfire

2000. Christmas. Multicoloured.
552 12s. Type **147** 25 10
553 15s. Cherubs 30 15
554 15s. Mary and baby Jesus . . 30 15

2001. Sovereignty.
555 **148** 40s. multicoloured 45 20

149 "When Silava's Forest Wakes" (V. Purvitis)

2001.
556 **149** 40s. multicoloured 45 20

150 Karlis Ulmanis (1936–40) **152** Ventas Rumba (waterfall), Kuldiga

151 ML Series Steam Locomotive

2001. Presidents.
557 **150** 15s. multicoloured 30 15

2001. Narrow-gauge Railway.
558 **151** 40s. multicoloured 45 20

2001. Europa. Water Resources.
559 **152** 60s. multicoloured . . . . 1·40 70

153 Modern View of Riga

2001. 800th Anniv of Riga (7th issue). Multicoloured.
560 15s. Type **153** 30 15
561 15s. Modern View of Riga with three spires 30 15
562 60s. 16th-century view of Riga . . . . 1·40 70
563 70s. 17th-century view of Riga . . . . 1·50 75
Nos. 560/1 were issued together, se-tenant, forming a composite design.

154 Cat with Pipe ("Pussy's Water Mill" (fairytale))

2001. Literature. Karlis Skalbe (writer) Commemoration.
564 **154** 40s. multicoloured 45 20

155 Tals

2001. 10th Death Anniv of Mikhail Nekhemevich Tal (World Chess Champion, 1960–1961). Sheet 98 × 68 mm.
MS565 **155** 100s. multicoloured 2·25 2·25

156 Beach, Vidzeme, Latvia

2001. Baltic Sea Coast. Multicoloured.
566 15s. Type **156** 30 15
MS567 125 × 60 mm. 30s. As Type **156**; 30s. Sand dunes, Palanga, Lithuania; 30s. Rocky coastline, Lahemaa, Estonia . . 2·00 2·00
Stamps in similar designs were issued by Estonia and Lithuania.

157 Cesvaines Palace

2001. Palaces.
568 **157** 40s. multicoloured 45 20

158 Synagogue, Riga **160** White Rabbits

159 Krisjanis Valdemars (½-size illustration)

2001.
569 **158** 70s. multicoloured . . . . 1·50 75

2001. Ship Building, Trade and Discovery. Multicoloured.
570 15s. Type **159** (founder of Naval College and ship builder) 30 15
571 70s. Hercogs Jekabs, Duke of Courland (ship builder) . . 1·50 75

2001. Christmas. Multicoloured.
572 12s. Type **160** 25 10
573 15s. Dog and rabbit 30 15
574 15s. Sheep 30 15

161 Cross-country Skiers

2002. Winter Olympic Games, Salt Lake City.
575 **161** 40s. multicoloured 80 40

162 Downhill Skier **163** "Refugees" (Jekabs Kazaks)

2002. Winter Paralympic Games, Salt Lake City.
576 **162** 15s. multicoloured 30 15

2002. Art.
577 **163** 40s. multicoloured 80 40

164 Clowns

2002. Europa. Circus.
578 **164** 60s. multicoloured . . . . 1·20 60

165 Lady's Slipper Orchid **166** Soldier and Flag (*Cypripedium calceolus*)

2002. Plants. Multicoloured.
579 15s. Type **165** 50 15
580 40s. Water chestnut (*Trapa natans*) 80 40

2002. Armed Forces.
581 **166** 40s. multicoloured 80 40

167 Jancis standing in Brook ("The White Book") **169** Atlantic Cod (*Gadus morhua*)

168 Kristians Johan Dals

2002. Literature. 40th Death Anniv of Janis Jaunsudrabins (writer).
582 **167** 40s. multicoloured 80 40

2002. Kristians Johan Dals (sailor and founder of maritime school) Commemoration.
584 **168** 70s. multicoloured . . . . 1·40 70

2002. Fish. Multicoloured.
585 15s. Type **169** 30 15
586 40s. Wels (*Silurus glanis*) . . 80 40

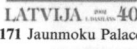

170 Bridge over River Venta

2002. Sheet 100 × 70 mm.
MS587 **170** 100s. multicoloured 2·00 1·00

171 Jaunmoku Palace **172** Grebenschikov Old Believers Praying House, Riga

2002. Palaces.
588 **171** 40s. multicoloured 80 40

2002. Churches.
589 **172** 70s. multicoloured . . . . 1·40 70

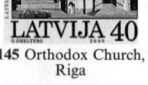

173 Mittens and Couple wearing Traditional Winter Clothes

2002. Mittens (1st series).
590 **173** 15s. multicoloured 30 15
See also Nos. 606 and 628.

174 Christmas Tree and Elf Musician
175 Man enters Room (Niklavs Srtunke)

2002. Christmas. Multicoloured.
591 12s. Type **174** 25 10
592 15s. Elf musicians on present 30 15
593 15s. Angel 30 15

2003. Art.
594 **175** 40s. multicoloured 80 40

176 Fly Orphide (*Ophrys insectifera*)
177 Scene from "Straumei" (poem)

2003. Plants. Multicoloured.
595 15s. Type **176** 30 15
596 40s. Yew (*Taxus baccata*) . . 80 40

2003. Literature. 40th Death Anniv of Edvarts Virza (writer).
597 **177** 40s. multicoloured 80 40

178 "Riga's Towers" (Valda Batraks)
179 Kolka Lighthouse

2003. Europa. Poster Art.
598 **178** 60s. multicoloured . . . . 1·20 60

2003.
599 **179** 60s. multicoloured . . . . 1·20 60

180 Baptist Church, Riga

2003. Churches.
600 **180** 70s. multicoloured . . . . 1·40 70

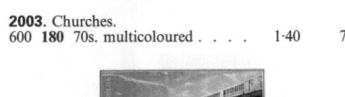

181 Bridge over River Gauja, Sigulda.

2003. Sheet 100 × 70 mm.
MS601 **181** 100s. multicoloured 2·00 1·00

182 *Thymallus thymallus*

2003. Fish. Multicoloured.
602 15s. Type **182** 30 15
603 30s. *Salmo salar* 60 30

183 Pied Wagtail (*Motacilla alba*)

2003.
604 **183** 15s. multicoloured 30 15

184 Birinu Palace

2003. Palaces.
605 **184** 40s. multicoloured 80 40

185 Mittens and Couple, Liv

2003. Mittens (2nd series).
606 **185** 15s. multicoloured 30 15
See also No. 628.

186 Motorcycle and Sidecar

2003. Motor Sports.
607 **186** 70s. multicoloured . . . . 1·40 70

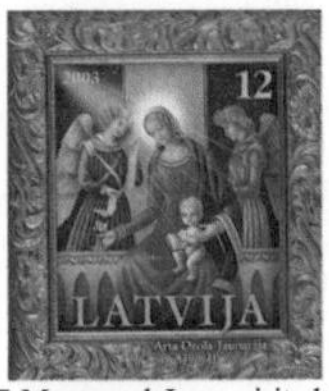

187 Mary and Jesus visited by Angels

2003. Christmas. Multicoloured.
608 12s. Type **187** 25 10
609 15s. Holy Family 30 15
610 15s. Annunciation of Mary 30 15

188 "Still Life with Triangular Ruler" (Romans Suta)

2004. Art.
611 **188** 40s. multicoloured 80 40

189 Scene from "Times of Land Surveyors"

2004. Literature. Reinis and Matiss Kaudzites (writers) Commemoration.
612 **189** 40s. multicoloured 80 40

190 Gentian (*Gentiana cruciata*)

2004. Plants. Multicoloured.
613 15s. Type **190** 30 15
614 30s. *Onobrychis arenaria* . . 60 30

191 Crowd of Fans

2004. International Ice Hockey Federation Championship, Riga (2006).
615 **191** 30s. multicoloured 60 30

192 Stars

2004. Enlargement of European Union. Multicoloured.
616 30s. Type **192** 60 30
617 30s. Flags of new members 60 30

193 Family in Rowing Boat

2004. Europa. Holidays.
618 **193** 60s. multicoloured . . . . 1·20 60

194 Footballers

2004. Euro 2004 Football Championship, Portugal.
619 **194** 30s. multicoloured 60 30

195 *Oncrhynchus mykiss*

2004. Fish. Multicoloured.
620 15s. Type **195** 30 15
621 30s. *Psetta maxima* 60 30

196 Statues of Liberty, New York and Riga

2004. 10th Anniv of Visit of Bill Clinton (president of USA, 1993–2001).
622 **196** 40s. multicoloured 80 40

197 Bridge over River Daugava, Riga.

2004. Sheet 100 × 70 mm.
MS623 **197** 100s. multicoloured 2·00 2·00

198 Wrestlers

2004. Olympic Games, Athens.
624 **198** 30s. multicoloured 60 30

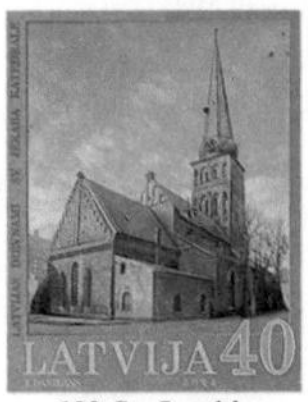

199 St. Jacob's Cathedral, Riga
200 Mikelbaka Lighthouse

2004. Churches.
625 **199** 40s. multicoloured 80 40

2004.
626 **200** 60s. multicoloured . . . . 1·20 60

201 Jaunpils Palace
203 Heart, Rabbit, Bluebird and Children

202 Mittens and Couple, Piebalga

2004. Palaces.
627 **201** 40s. multicoloured 80 40

2004. Mittens (3rd series).
628 **202** 15s. multicoloured 30 15

2004. Christmas.
629 12s. Type **203** 25 10
630 15s. Snowman 30 15
631 15s. Angel 30 15

204 Revolution Monument, Riga

2005. Centenary of Russian Revolution.
632 **204** 12s. multicoloured 25 10

205 Gentian (*Pulsatilla patens*)

2005. Plants. Multicoloured.
633 15s. Type **205** 30 15
634 30s. *Allium ursinum* 60 30

206 St. Jacob's Cathedral, Riga

2005. Churches.
635 **206** 40s. multicoloured 80 40

LEBANON Pt. 19

A territory north of the Holy Land, formerly part of the Turkish Empire, Greater Lebanon was given a separate status under French Mandate in 1920. Until September 1923, the French occupation stamps of Syria were used and these were followed by the joint issue of 1923, Nos. 97 etc., of Syria. Independence was proclaimed in 1941, but the country was not evacuated by French troops until 1946.

100 centimes = 1 piastre;
100 piastres = 1 Lebanese pound.

1924. Stamps of France surch **GRAND LIBAN** and value. (a) Definitive stamps.
1 **11** 10c. on 2c. purple 80 1·70
2 **18** 25c. on 5c. orange 1·30 90
3 50c. on 10c. green 1·70 85
4 **15** 75c. on 15c. green 2·30 4·25
5 **18** 1p. on 20c. brown 2·75 95
6 1,25p. on 25c. blue 3·75 2·50
7 1,50p. on 30c. orange 3·25 5·00
8 1,50p. on 30c. red 3·00 5·00
9 **15** 2,50p. on 50c. blue 2·30 85
10 **13** 2p. on 40c. red and blue 1·60 95
11 3p. on 60c. violet and blue 7·25 10·00
12 5p. on 1f. red and yellow 8·75 8·25
13 10p. on 2f. orange and green 17·00 13·50
14 25p. on 5f. blue and buff 29·00 44·00

(b) Pasteur issue.
15 **30** 50c. on 10c. green 1·40 3·25
16 1,50p. on 30c. red 2·75 6·00
17 2,50p. on 50c. blue 1·10 3·75

(c) Olympic Games issue.
18 **31** 50c. on 10c. green and light green 28·00 65·00
19 – 1,25p. on 25c. deep red and red 11·50 65·00
20 – 1,50p. on 30c. red and black 17·00 50·00
21 – 2,50p. on 50c. blue 11·50 55·00

1924. Air. Stamps of France surch **Poste par Avion GRAND LIBAN** and value.
22 **13** 2p. on 40c. red and blue 10·50 23·00
23 3p. on 60c. violet and blue 11·00 23·00
24 5p. on 1f. red and yellow 10·00 11·00
25 10p. on 2f. orange and green 11·00 21·00

1924. Stamps of France surch **Grand Liban** (T **13**) or **Gd Liban** (others) and value in French and Arabic. (a) Definitive stamps.
26 **11** 0p.10 on 2c. purple 20 95
27 **18** 0p.25 on 5c. orange 1·10 1·00
28 0p.50 on 10c. green 2·75 3·00
29 **15** 0p.75 on 15c. green 75 3·25
30 **18** 1p. on 20c. brown 90 20
31 1p.25 on 25c. blue 2·75 3·50
32 1p.50 on 30c. red 1·90 2·30
33 1p.50 on 30c. orange 60·00 60·00
34 2p. on 35c. violet 2·30 5·25
35 **13** 2p. on 40c. red and blue 3·00 35
36 2p. on 45c. green and blue 21·00 24·00
37 3p. on 60c. violet and blue 2·75 1·80
38 **15** 3p. on 60c. violet 3·25 6·00
39 4p. on 85c. red 75 3·00
40 **13** 5p. on 1f. red and yellow 2·50 2·50
41 10p. on 2f. orange and green 7·25 16·00
42 25p. on 5f. blue and buff 11·00 21·00

(b) Pasteur issue.
43 **30** 0p.50 on 10c. green 60 15
44 0p.75 on 15c. green 3·00 5·25
45 1p.50 on 30c. red 2·75 55
46 2p. on 45c. red 4·00 6·25
47 2p.50 on 50c. blue 75 25
48 4p. on 75c. blue 2·00 2·75

(c) Olympic Games issue.
49 **31** 0p.50 on 10c. green and light green 16·00 50·00
50 – 1p.25 on 25c. deep red and red 22·00 55·00
51 – 1p.50 on 30c. red and black 16·00 50·00
52 – 2p.50 on 50c. ultramarine and blue 26·00 42·00

(d) Ronsard issue.
53 **35** 4p. on 75c. blue on bluish 65 6·50

1924. Air. Stamps of France surch **Gd Liban Avion** and value in French and Arabic.
54 **13** 2p. on 40c. red and blue 6·25 21·00
55 3p. on 60c. violet and blue 5·75 21·00
56 5p. on 1f. red and yellow 5·00 21·00
57 10p. on 2f. orange and green 7·25 23·00

5 Cedar of Lebanon

7 Tripoli

6 Beirut

1925. Views.
58 **5** 0p.10c. violet 10 1·30
59 **6** 0p.25c. black 70 1·20
60 – 0p.50c. green (Tripoli) 1·30 1·20
61 – 0p.75c. red (Beit ed-Din) 1·60 3·50
62 – 1p. purple (Baalbek ruins) 2·00 30
63 – 1p.25 green (Mouktara) 2·75 3·00
64 – 1p.50 pink (Tyre) 1·30 40
65 – 2p. brown (Zahle) 2·00 10
66 – 2p.50 blue (Baalbek) 1·20 30
67 – 3p. brown (Deir el-Kamar) 95 65
68 – 5p. violet (Sidon) 6·25 6·75
69 **7** 10p. purple 7·00 5·75
70 – 25p. blue (Beirut) 10·00 27·00

1925. Air. Nos. 65 and 67/9 optd **AVION** in French and Arabic.
71 – 2p. brown 4·00 8·25
72 – 3p. brown 4·25 7·50
73 – 5p. violet 4·50 7·75
74 **7** 10p. purple 4·00 5·50

1926. Air. Nos. 65 and 67/9 optd with Bleriot XI airplane.
75 – 2p. brown 4·00 9·00
76 – 3p. brown 3·00 9·25
77 – 5p. violet 4·00 9·50
78 **7** 10p. purple 2·75 9·00

1926. War Refugee Charity. Various stamps surch **Secours aux Refugies Afft** and premium in French and Arabic. (a) Postage. Stamps of 1925.
79 **6** 0p.25+0p.25 black 2·00 5·75
80 – 0p.50+0p.25 green 2·75 9·00
81 – 0p.75+0p.25 red 1·50 8·00
82 – 1p.+0p.50 purple 2·30 8·00
83 – 1p.25+0p.50 green 2·00 10·00
84 – 1p.50+0p.50 pink 4·00 8·50
85 – 2p.+0p.75 brown 4·50 7·75
86 – 2p.50+0p.75 blue 2·50 12·00
87 – 3p.+1p. brown 3·00 11·00
88 – 5p.+1p. violet 6·25 13·00
89 **7** 10p.+2p. purple 6·50 17·00
90 – 25p.+5p. blue 7·00 21·00

(b) Air. Nos. 75/78 surch.
91 – 2p.+1p. brown 4·25 14·50
92 – 3p.+2p. brown 4·00 13·00
93 – 5p.+3p. violet 3·50 13·00
94 **7** 10p.+5p. purple 4·00 19·00

1926. Stamps of 1925 surch in English and Arabic.
95 – 3p.50 on 0p.75 red 2·75 3·25
96 **6** 4p. on 0p.25 black 3·50 3·75
98 – 4p.50 on 0p.75 red 3·50 3·25
99 – 6p. on 2p.50 blue 3·50 3·50
100 – 7p.50 on 2p.50 blue 3·25 85
101 – 12p. on 1p.25 green 2·50 3·75
102 – 15p. on 25p. blue 4·50 1·50
103 – 20p. on 1p.25 green 8·25 11·00

1927. Stamps of 1925 and provisional stamps of Lebanon optd **Republique Libanaise**.
104 **5** 0p.10 violet 45 1·60
105 – 0p.50 green 1·00 55
106 – 1p. purple 35 10
107 – 1p.50 pink 1·60 1·60
108 – 2p. brown 3·25 1·90
109 – 3p. brown 1·30 45
110 **6** 4p. on 0p.25 black (No. 96) 1·50 30
111 – 4p.50 on 0p.75 red (No. 98) 1·00 25
112 – 5p. violet 3·25 3·75
113 – 7p.50 on 2p.50 bl (No. 100) 1·80 55
114 **7** 10p. purple 4·25 4·00
115 – 15p. on 25p. blue (No. 102) 10·00 5·50
117 – 25p. blue 10·00 28·00

1927. Air. Nos. 75/78 optd **Republique Libanaise**.
118 – 2p. brown 5·00 9·00
119 – 3p. brown 3·25 7·75
120 – 5p. violet 5·00 8·75
121 **7** 10p. purple 3·75 8·75

الجمهورية اللبنانية
(10)

1928. Nos. 104/117 optd with T **10** or surch also.
145 **5** 05 on 0p.10 violet 10 1·00
124 0p.10 violet 45 25
125 – 0p.50 green 2·50 1·90
146 – 0p.50 on 0p.75 red 35 30
126 – 1p. purple 1·30 30
127 – 1p.50 pink 3·00 3·00
128 – 2p. brown 4·75 6·75
147 – 2p. on 1p.25 green 1·20 25
129 – 3p. brown 2·75 65
148 **6** 4p. on 0p.25 black 3·00 10
131 – 4p.50 on 0p.75 red 2·50 2·30
132a – 5p. violet 2·75 5·75
149 – 7p.50 on 2p.50 blue 2·00 15
134 **7** 10p. purple 9·00 9·50
123 – 15p. on 25p. blue 11·50 23·00
136 – 25p. blue 10·50 13·50

1928. Air. Optd or surch with airplane, **Republique Libanaise** and line of Arabic as T **10**.
151 – 0p.50 green 80 4·25
152 – 0p.50 on 0p.75 red (No. 146) 1·30 2·30
153 – 1p. purple 2·00 3·25
141 – 2p. brown 3·75 6·75
154 – 2p. on 1p.25 grn (No. 147) 2·30 2·50
142 – 3p. brown 2·50 4·25
143 – 5p. violet 4·25 5·25
144 **7** 10p. purple 4·25 3·25
155 – 15p. on 25p. blue (No. 123) £170 £190
156 – 25p. blue £110 £110

14 Silkworm Larva, Cocoon and Moth

1930. Silk Congress.
157 **14** 4p. sepia 12·00 25·00
158 4½p. red 12·50 24·00
159 7½p. blue 10·00 22·00
160 10p. violet 15·00 22·00
161 15p. green 17·00 21·00
162 25p. purple 11·50 21·00

15 Cedars of Lebanon

16a Baalbek

1930. Views.
163b – 0p.10 orange (Beirut) 1·50 35
164 **15** 0p.20 brown 1·00 1·40
165a – 0p.25 blue (Baalbek) 1·20 25
166 – 0p.50 brown (Bickfaya) 95 55
166b – 0p.75 brown (Baalbek) 3·75 2·50
167 – 1p. green (Saida) 5·00 40
167a – 1p. purple (Saida) 7·00 55
168 – 1p.50 purple (Beit ed-Din) 4·00 1·20
168a – 1p.50 green (Beit ed-Din) 9·75 40
169 – 2p. blue (Tripoli) 6·00 75
170 – 3p. sepia (Baalbek) 7·00 75
171 – 4p. brown (Nahr-el-Kalb) 7·00 45
172 – 4p.50 red (Beaufort) 6·00 65
173 – 5p. green (Beit ed-Din) 3·00 50
251 – 5p. blue (Nahr el-Kalb) 2·75 50
174 – 6p. purple (Tyre) 8·00 75
175 **16a** 7p.50 blue 6·00 50
176 – 10p. green (Hasbaya) 9·00 85
177 – 15p. purple (Afka Falls) 10·00 75
178 – 25p. green (Beirut) 10·00 95
179 – 50p. green (Deir el-Kamar) 46·00 13·00
180 – 100p. black (Baalbek) 40·00 20·00

17 Jebeil (Byblos)

1930. Air. Potez 29-4 biplane and views as T **17**.
181 0p.50 purple (Rachaya) 1·50 1·70
182 1p. green (Broumana) 60 85
183 2p. orange (Baalbek) 65 1·30
184 3p. red (Hasroun) 2·00 1·70
185 5p. green (Byblos) 1·70 1·50
186 10p. red (Kadisha) 2·30 1·40
187 15p. brown (Beirut) 1·90 1·10
188 25p. violet (Tripoli) 2·50 2·00
189 50p. lake (Kabelais) 6·25 5·00
190 100p. brown (Zahle) 7·50 9·00

18 Skiing

1936. Air. Tourist Propaganda.
191 **18** 0p.50 green 3·00 2·50
192 – 1p. orange 3·75 3·75
193 **18** 2p. violet 2·00 2·75
194 – 3p. green 2·75 2·75
195 **18** 5p. red 5·00 4·50
196 – 10p. brown 5·25 5·50
197 – 15p. red 38·00 30·00
198 **18** 25p. green £100 £120
DESIGN: 1, 3, 10, 15p. Jounieh Bay.

20 Cedar of Lebanon

21 President Edde

22 Lebanese Landscape

1937.
199 **20** 0p.10 red 10 10
200 0p.20 blue 20 4·00
201 0p.25 lilac 30 3·25
202 0p.50 mauve 10 10
203 0p.75 brown 25 1·40
207 **21** 3p. violet 3·75 1·40
208 4p. brown 1·60 10
209 4p.50 red 2·30 10
211 **22** 10p. red 3·25 15
212 12½p. blue 1·20 10
213 15p. green 3·25 15
214 20p. brown 3·50 10
215 25p. red 4·75 45
216 50p. violet 9·75 2·00
217 100p. sepia 10·50 3·75

23 Exhibition Pavilion, Paris

1937. Air. Paris International Exhibition.
218 **23** 0p.50 black 1·50 1·80
219 1p. green 70 3·00
220 2p. brown 1·50 3·00
221 3p. green 1·10 2·50
222 5p. green 1·30 3·00
223 10p. red 10·00 14·00
224 15p. purple 6·50 12·00
225 25p. brown 14·00 25·00

25 Ruins of Baalbek

1937. Air.
226 – 0p.50 blue 10 30
227 – 1p. red 1·40 1·60
228 – 2p. sepia 2·00 1·50
229 – 3p. red 4·50 3·50
230 – 5p. green 2·30 85
231 **25** 10p. violet 1·30 10
232 – 15p. blue 1·50 2·30
233 – 25p. violet 5·50 2·75
234 – 50p. green 11·50 1·40
235 – 100p. brown 5·00 5·50
DESIGN: 0p.50 to 5p. Beit ed-Din.

1938. Nos. 207/8 surch in English and Arabic figures.
236 **21** 2p. on 3p. violet 1·20 15
237 2½p. on 4p. brown 1·70 15

27 Medical College, Beirut

32 Emir Bechir Chehab

28 Maurice Nogues and Liore et Olivier LeO H.24-3 Flying Boat over Beirut

1938. Air. Medical Congress.
238 **27** 2p. green 2·75 4·50
239 3p. orange 3·75 4·50
240 5p. violet 4·00 7·00
241 10p. red 10·00 17·00

1938. Air. 10th Anniv of 1st Air Service between France and Lebanon.
242 **28** 10p. purple . . . . 5·00 9·00
MS242a 161 × 120 mm. No. 242 in block of four . . . . 55·00 60·00

1938. Surch.
243 **16a** 6p. on 7p.50 blue . . . . 2·75 80
244 – 7p.50 on 50p. grn (No. 179) . . . . . . 3·00 2·30
245 – 7p.50 on 100p. blk (No. 180) . . . . . . 2·30 2·75
246 **22** 12p.50 on 7p.50 blue . . 4·50 1·30
247 12½p. on 7p.50 blue . . . 2·00 20

1939. As T **16a**, but with differing figures and Arabic inscriptions in side panels, and imprint at foot "IMP. CATHOLIQUE-BEYROUTH-LIBAN" instead of "HELIO VAUGIRARD".
248 1p. green 85 65
249 1p.50 purple . . . . 1·30 40
250 7p.50 red . . . . 2·00 30
DESIGN: 1p. to 7p.50, Beit ed-Din.

1942. 1st Anniv of Proclamation of Independence.
252 **32** 0p.50 green (postage) . . . 2·10 2·10
253 1p.50 purple . . . . 2·10 2·10
254 6p. red . . . . 2·10 2·10
255 15p. blue . . . . 2·10 2·10
256 – 10p. purple (air) . . . . . 3·50 3·50
257 – 50p. green . . . . 4·25 4·25
DESIGN: 10, 50p. Airplane over mountains.

1943. Surch in English and Arabic and with old values cancelled with ornaments.
258 **21** 2p. on 4p. brown . . . . 4·25 3·75
261 – 2p. on 5p. blue (No. 251) 70 40
262 – 3p. on 5p. blue (No. 251) 70 40
259 – 6p. on 7p.50 red (No. 250) 95 70
263 **22** 6p. on 12½p. blue 95 70
264 7½p. on 12½p. blue . . . . 1·40 1·50
260 10p. on 12½p. blue . . . . 1·40 60

37 Parliament House

38 Bechamoun

1944. 2nd Anniv of Proclamation of Independence.
265 **37** 25p. red (postage) . . . . 8·50 8·50
266 – 50p. blue . . . . 8·50 8·50
267 **37** 150p. blue . . . . 8·50 8·50
268 – 200p. purple . . . . 8·50 8·50
DESIGN: 50p., 200p. Government House.

269 **38** 25p. green (air) . . . . . 3·50 2·20
270 50p. orange . . . . 3·50 2·20
271 – 100p. brown . . . . 3·50 3·00
272 – 200p. violet . . . . 4·25 3·00
273 – 300p. green . . . . 14·50 14·50
274 – 500p. brown . . . . 39·00 27·00
DESIGNS: 100p., 200p. Rachaya Citadel; 300p., 500p. Beirut.

38a Beirut Isolation Hospital

(**39**)

1944. 6th Medical Congress. Optd with T **39**.
275 **38a** 10p. red (postage) . . . . 4·75 4·75
276 20p. blue . . . . 4·75 4·75
277 – 20p. orange (air) . . . . 2·20 2·20
278 – 50p. blue . . . . 3·00 3·00
279 – 100p. purple . . . . 3·75 3·75
DESIGN: Nos. 277/9, Bhannes Sanatorium.

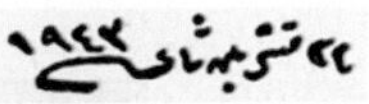
(**40** Trans "Nov. 23, 1943")

1944. 1st Anniv of President's Return to Office. Nos. 265/74 optd with T **40**.
280 **37** 25p. red (postage) . . . . 10·00 10·00
281 – 50p. blue . . . . 10·00 10·00
282 **37** 150p. blue . . . . 10·00 10·00
283 – 200p. purple . . . . 10·00 10·00
284 **38** 25p. green (air) . . . . . 4·25 4·25
285 – 50p. orange . . . . 8·50 8·50
286 – 100p. brown . . . . 9·25 9·25
287 – 200p. violet . . . . 17·00 17·00
288 – 300p. green . . . . 22·00 22·00
289 – 500p. brown . . . . 42·00 42·00

41 Crusader Castle, Byblos

42 Falls of R. Litani

1945.
397 **41** 7p.50 red (postage) . . . . 2·50 15
398 10p. purple . . . . 3·75 25
399 12p.50 blue . . . . 9·25 25
290 15p. brown . . . . 2·50 2·10
291 20p. green . . . . 2·50 2·10
292 – 25p. blue . . . . 2·50 2·10
400 **41** 25p. violet . . . . 17·00 60
293 – 50p. red . . . . 5·00 2·50
401 **41** 50p. green . . . . 39·00 4·25
294 **42** 25p. brown (air) . . . . . 1·90 1·30
295 50p. purple . . . . 2·50 1·90
296 – 200p. violet . . . . 8·50 3·00
297 – 300p. black . . . . 19·00 6·25
DESIGNS—HORIZ: Nos. 292/3, Crusader Castle, Tripoli; 296/7, Cedar of Lebanon and skier.

43 V(ictory) and National Flag

44 V(ictory) and Lebanese Soldiers at Bir-Hakeim

1946. Victory. "V" in design. (a) Postage.
298 **43** 7p.50 brown, red and pink 70 10
299 10p. purple, pink and red 1·00 10
300 12p.50 purple, blue and red 1·50 10
301 15p. green, emerald and red . . . . 2·50 15
302 20p. myrtle, green and red 2·20 15
303 25p. blue, light blue and red . . . . 3·50 35
304 50p. blue, violet and red 5·50 1·90
305 100p. black, blue and red 9·25 3·50

(b) Air.
306 **44** 15p. blue, yellow and red 60 15
307 20p. red and blue 70 40
308 25p. blue, yellow and red 70 40
309 50p. black, violet and red 1·50 40
310 100p. violet and red . . . 3·75 1·30
311 150p. brown and red . . . 4·75 2·10
MS311a 142 × 230 mm. Nos. 298/311. Colours changed. Text in brown (with gum) or blue (without gum) . . . . 85·00 85·00

1946. As T **43** but without "V" sign.
312 7p.50 lake, red and mauve . . 1·00 15
313 10p. violet, mauve and red 1·50 15
314 12p.50 brown, green and red 2·10 15
315 15p. brown, pink and red . . 3·00 25
316 20p. blue, orange and red . . 2·50 25
317 25p. myrtle, green and red . . 4·75 35
318 50p. blue, light blue and red 8·50 1·50
319 100p. black, blue and red . . 13·50 3·50

45 Grey Herons

1946.
320 **45** 12p.50 red (postage) . . . 19·00 1·40
321 10p. orange (air) . . . . . 6·75 1·00
322 25p. blue . . . . 8·50 50
323 50p. green . . . . 19·00 1·40
324 100p. purple . . . . 34·00 6·25

46 Cedar of Lebanon

47

1946.
325 **46** 0p.50 brown 40 15
326 1p. purple 85 15
327 2p.50 violet . . . . 3·00 15
328 5p. red . . . . 3·00 15
329 6p. grey . . . . 3·00 15

1946. Air. Arab Postal Congress.
330 **47** 25p. blue . . . . 1·00 60
331 50p. green . . . . 1·40 95
332 75p. red . . . . 2·30 1·50
333 150p. violet . . . . 5·50 2·75

48 Cedar of Lebanon

49 President, Bridge and Tablet

1947.
333a **48** 0p.50 brown . . . . . . 1·20 10
333b 2p.50 green . . . . . . 1·70 10
333c 5p. red . . . . 3·00 25

1947. Air. Evacuation of Foreign Troops from Lebanon.
334 **49** 25p. blue . . . . 1·00 40
335 50p. red . . . . 1·40 85
336 75p. black . . . . 3·00 1·30
337 150p. green . . . . 5·00 2·50

50 Crusader Castle, Tripoli

51 Jounieh Bay

1947.
338 **50** 12p.50 red (postage) . . . 7·75 35
339 25p. blue . . . . 9·25 40
340 50p. green . . . . 30·00 85
341 100p. violet . . . . 38·00 6·75
342 **51** 5p. green (air) 35 10
343 10p. mauve 40 10
344 15p. red 70 10
403 15p. green . . . . 8·50 1·30
345 20p. orange . . . . 1·30 15
345a 20p. red . . . . 1·40 25
346 25p. blue . . . . 1·70 15
347 50p. red . . . . 3·50 35
348 100p. purple . . . . 7·75 60
349 – 150p. purple . . . . 15·00 1·30
350 – 200p. slate . . . . 22·00 6·00
351 – 300p. black . . . . 36·00 13·50
DESIGN: 150p. to 300p. Grand Serail Palace.

54 Phoenician Galley

1947. Air. 12th Congress of U.P.U., Paris.
352 – 10p. blue 95 40
353 – 15p. red . . . . 1·40 60
354 – 25p. blue . . . . 1·90 1·00
355 **54** 50p. green . . . . 4·25 1·20
356 – 75p. violet . . . . 5·50 1·70
357 – 100p. brown . . . . 7·75 3·75
DESIGN—VERT: 10p. to 25p. Posthorn.

55 Faraya Bridge and Statue

1947. Air. Red Cross Fund. Cross in red.
358 **55** 12p.50+25p. green . . . . 7·75 6·00
359 25p.+50p. blue . . . . . 8·50 6·75
360 – 50p.+100p. brown . . . . 11·00 8·50
361 – 75p.+150p. violet . . . . 22·00 17·00
362 – 100p.+200p. grey . . . . 42·00 30·00
DESIGN: 50p. to 100p. Djounie Bay and statue.

56 Cedar of Lebanon

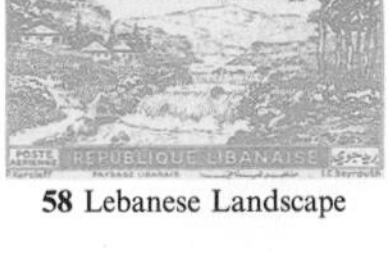
58 Lebanese Landscape

1948.
363 **56** 0p.50 blue (postage) . . . 15 10
364 1p. brown 40 10
395 1p. orange . . . . 1·00 10
365 2p.50 mauve 70 10
366 3p. green . . . . 1·70 10
367 5p. red . . . . 2·20 10
368 – 7p.50 red . . . . 6·00 25
369 – 10p. purple . . . . 3·75 25
370 – 12p.50 blue . . . . 9·25 25
371 – 25p. blue . . . . 13·50 75
372 – 50p. green . . . . 32·00 6·00
373 **58** 5p. red (air) 35 10
374 10p. mauve . . . . 1·00 10
375 15p. brown . . . . 3·00 15
376 20p. slate . . . . 4·75 15
377 25p. blue . . . . 8·50 1·20
378 50p. black . . . . 14·50 1·70
DESIGN—As T **58**: Nos. 368/72, Zebaide Aqueduct.

59 Europa on Bull

61 Apollo on Sun Chariot

1948. 3rd Meeting of UNESCO, Beirut.
379 **59** 10p. orange and red (postage) . . . . 2·20 1·50
380 12p.50 mauve and violet 3·00 2·20
381 25p. green and light green 3·50 2·20
382 – 30p. buff and brown . . . 4·75 2·75
383 – 40p. green and turquoise 6·75 2·75
DESIGN—VERT: 30, 40p. Avicenna (philosopher and scientist).

384 **61** 7p.50 blue & lt blue (air) 1·90 1·50
385 15p. black and grey . . . 2·20 1·50
386 20p. brown and pink . . . 3·75 2·20
387 – 35p. red . . . . 6·25 3·00
388 – 75p. green . . . . 12·50 6·75
MS388a 142 × 205 mm. Nos. 379/88. Imperf. No gum £250 £250
DESIGN—HORIZ: 35, 75p. Symbolic figure.

63 Camel

64 Sikorsky S-51 Helicopter

1949. 75th Anniv of U.P.U.
389 **63** 5p. violet (postage) . . . . 1·20 85
390 7p.50 red . . . . 1·70 1·50
391 12p.50 blue . . . . 2·75 1·90
392 **64** 25p. blue (air) . . . . . . 6·00 3·00
393 50p. green . . . . 9·25 4·75
MS393a 135 × 190 mm. Nos. 389/93. Imperf (sold at 150p.) . . . . 70·00 70·00

65 Cedar of Lebanon

66 Nahr el-Kalb Bridge

1950.
407 **65** 0p.50 red 25 15
408 1p. red 75 15
409 2p.50 violet . . . . 1·20 15
410 5p. purple . . . . 2·20 15
411 **66** 7p.50 red . . . . 2·75 15
412 10p. lilac . . . . 3·50 15
413 12p.50 blue . . . . 5·50 25
414 25p. blue . . . . 10·00 1·10
415 50p. green . . . . 30·00 6·00

67 Congressional Flags

1950. Lebanese Emigrants' Congress. Inscr "MOIS DES EMIGRES–ETE 1950".
416 **67** 7p.50 green (postage) . . . 75 25
417 12p. mauve 75 25
418 – 5p. blue (air) . . . . . . 2·20 60
419 – 15p. violet . . . . 3·00 85
420 – 25p. brown . . . . 1·50 85
421 – 35p. green . . . . 3·00 1·50
MS421a 134 × 184 mm. Nos. 416/21. Imperf. No gum . . . . . 70·00 70·00
DESIGNS: 5, 15p. House martins; 25, 35p. Pres. Bishara al-Khoury and building.

70 Crusader Castle, Sidon

1950. Air.
422 **70** 10p. brown 60 10
423 15p. green 95 10
424 20p. red . . . . 3·00 40

425 25p. blue . . . . 5·00 1·00
426 50p. grey . . . . 8·50 2·50

1950. Surch with figures and bars.
427 **56** 1p. on 3p. green 60 25
428 **46** 2p.50 on 6p. grey 85 25

73 Cedar of Lebanon

74 Nahr el-Kalb Bridge

75 Crusader Castle, Sidon

1951.
429 **73** 0p.50 red (postage) 25 10
430 1p. brown 60 10
431 2p.50 grey . . . . 3·00 10
432 5p. purple . . . . 3·50 10
433 **74** 7p.50 red . . . . 3·50 35
434 10p. purple . . . . 4·75 25
435 12p.50 turquoise . . . . . 8·50 40
436 25p. blue . . . . 13·50 1·50
437 50p. green . . . . 31·00 8·00

438 **75** 10p. turquoise (air) 95 15
439 15p. brown . . . . 2·10 15
440 20p. red . . . . 2·10 25
441 25p. blue . . . . 2·20 25
442 35p. mauve . . . . 6·00 3·00
443 50p. blue . . . . 11·00 2·20

Type **74** is similar to Type **66** but left value tablets differ.

For design as Type **74** but inscr "LIBAN", see Nos. 561/3.

76 Cedar of Lebanon

77 Baalbek

1952.
444 **76** 0p.50 green (postage) . . . 70 10
445 1p. brown 70 10
446 2p.50 blue . . . . 1·10 25
447 5p. red . . . . 1·90 25
448 **77** 7p.50 red . . . . 2·50 50
449 10p. violet . . . . 5·50 60
450 12p.50 blue . . . . 5·50 60
451 25p. blue . . . . 6·75 1·50
452 – 50p. green . . . . 20·00 2·75
453 – 100p. brown . . . . 42·00 8·50

454 – 5p. red (air) 35 10
455 – 10p. grey 50 15
456 – 15p. mauve 95 15
457 – 20p. orange . . . . 1·50 35
458 – 25p. blue . . . . 1·50 40
459 – 35p. blue . . . . 2·50 50
460 – 50p. green . . . . 8·50 60
461 – 100p. blue . . . . 60·00 2·50
462 – 200p. green . . . . 34·00 4·75
463 – 300p. sepia . . . . . . 47·00 10·00

DESIGNS—As Type **77**: Nos. 452/3, Beaufort Castle; 454/9, Beirut Airport; 460/3, Amphitheatre, Byblos.

78 Cedar of Lebanon

79 General Post Office

80 Douglas DC-4

1953.
559 **78** 0p.50 blue (postage) . . . 25 15
465 1p. red 85 10
466 2p.50 violet . . . . 1·10 25
560 2p.50 purple 70 15
467 5p. green . . . . 1·10 25
468 **79** 7p.50 red . . . . 3·00 40
469 10p. green . . . . 3·50 60
470 12p.50 turquoise . . . . . 5·00 70
471 25p. blue . . . . 7·75 1·40
472 50p. brown . . . . 13·50 3·00

473 **80** 5p. green (air) 35 10
474 10p. red 70 10
475 15p. red 95 10
476 20p. turquoise . . . . . . 1·50 10
477 25p. blue . . . . 3·75 15
478 35p. brown . . . . 5·50 25
479 50p. blue . . . . 7·75 50
480 100p. sepia . . . . 14·50 5·00

For 20p. green as Type **79** see No. 636.

81 Cedar of Lebanon

82 Beit ed-Din Palace

83 Baalbek

1954.
481 **81** 0p.50 blue (postage) . . . 25 10
482 1p. orange 40 10
483 2p.50 violet 70 15
484 5p. green . . . . 1·40 25
485 **82** 7p.50 red . . . . 2·20 50
486 10p. green . . . . 3·50 50
487 12p.50 blue . . . . 5·50 70
488 25p. deep blue . . . . . . 7·75 2·75
489 50p. turquoise . . . . . . 13·50 4·25
490 100p. sepia . . . . 21·00 4·75

491 **83** 5p. green (air) 40 10
492 10p. lilac 85 10
493 15p. red 95 10
494 20p. brown . . . . 1·40 10
495 25p. blue . . . . 1·50 25
496 35p. sepia . . . . 2·10 25
497 – 50p. green . . . . 6·75 40
498 – 100p. red . . . . 11·00 70
499 – 200p. sepia . . . . 22·00 2·20
500 – 300p. blue . . . . 38·00 4·75

DESIGN—As T **83**: 50p. to 300p. Litani Irrigation Canal.

For other values as Nos. 497/500, see Nos. 564/7.

84 Khalde Airport, Beirut

1954. Air. Opening of Beirut International Airport.
501 **84** 10p. red and pink 60 15
502 25p. blue and ultramarine 1·50 40
503 35p. brown and sepia . . . 2·10 75
504 65p. green and turquoise 5·00 3·00

84a

1955. Arab Postal Union.
505 **84a** 12p.50 green (postage) . . 60 40
506 25p. violet 85 40
507 2p.50 brown (air) 40 35

85 Rotary Emblem

86 Cedar of Lebanon

87 Jeita Grotto

88 Skiers

1955. Air. 50th Anniv of Rotary International.
508 **85** 35p. green . . . . 1·10 85
509 65p. blue . . . . 1·90 1·30

1955.
510 **86** 0p.50 blue (postage) . . . 25 15
511 1p. red 25 15
512 2p.50 violet 50 15
552 2p.50 blue . . . . 7·25 15
513 5p. green 85 15
514 **87** 7p.50 orange . . . . . . 1·10 15
515 10p. green . . . . 1·90 15
516 12p.50 blue . . . . 1·90 15
517 25p. blue . . . . 4·75 35
518 50p. green . . . . 6·75 85

519 **88** 5p. turquoise (air) 60 40
520 15p. red . . . . 1·00 25
521 20p. violet . . . . 1·70 25
522 25p. blue . . . . 3·50 35
523 35p. brown . . . . 5·00 60
524 50p. brown . . . . 9·25 85
525 65p. blue . . . . 17·00 2·75

The face value on No. 510 reads "0.50 PIASTRE"; on No. 512 the "2" and "50" are different sizes and the 1 and 5p. have no dash under "P".

For other colours and new values as Type **88** see Nos. 568/70 and for redrawn Type **86** see Nos. 582/5, 686 and 695/7.

89 Visitor from Abroad

90 Cedar of Lebanon

91 Globe and Columns

92 Oranges

1955. Air. Tourist Propaganda.
526 **89** 2p.50 slate and purple . . 15 10
527 12p.50 blue & ultramarine 40 25
528 25p. blue and indigo . . . 95 40
529 35p. blue and green . . . 1·30 60
MS529a 159 × 110 mm. Nos. 526/9. Imperf . . . . 17·00 17·00

1955.
530 **90** 0.50p. blue (postage) . . . 10 10
531 1p. orange 15 10
532 2p.50 violet 35 10
533 5p. green 60 10
534 **91** 7p.50 red and orange . . . 85 10
535 10p. green and brown . . . 95 10
536 12p.50 blue and green . . 1·00 10
537 25p. blue and mauve . . . 2·10 20
538 50p. green and blue . . . 3·00 40
539 100p. brown and orange 4·75 1·00

540 **92** 5p. yellow and green (air) 40 15
541 10p. orange and green . . 85 15
542 15p. orange and green . . 1·00 15
543 20p. orange and brown . . 1·30 15
544 – 25p. violet and blue . . . 1·90 15
545 – 35p. purple and green . . 3·00 25
546 – 50p. yellow and black . . 3·50 25
547 – 65p. yellow and green . . 6·25 35
548 – 100p. orange and green . . 8·50 95
549 – 200p. red and green . . . 17·00 4·75

DESIGNS—VERT: 25p. to 50p. Grapes. HORIZ: 4p. to 200p. Quinces.

93 U.N. Emblem

1956. Air. 10th Anniv of U.N.
550 **93** 35p. blue . . . . 4·75 3·75
551 65p. green . . . . 6·25 4·75
MS551a 90 × 70 mm. Nos. 550/1. Imperf . . . . 85·00 85·00

94 Masks, Columns and Gargoyle

1956. Air. Baalbek International Drama Festival. Inscr "FESTIVAL INTERNATIONAL DE BAALBECK".
553 **94** 2p.50 sepia 40 15
554 10p. green 60 25
555 – 12p.50 blue 70 40
556 – 25p. violet . . . . 1·00 50
557 – 35p. purple . . . . 2·20 85
558 – 65p. slate . . . . 3·50 1·90

DESIGNS—HORIZ: 12p.50, 25p. Temple ruins at Baalbek. VERT: 35p., 65p. Double bass, masks and columns.

1957. As earlier designs but redrawn. (a) Postage. As T **74** but inscr "LIBAN".
561 7p.50 red . . . . 1·40 15
562 10p. brown . . . . 1·90 15
563 12p.50 blue . . . . 2·20 15

(b) Air. Arabic inscription changed. New values and colours.
564 – 10p. violet 35 10
565 – 15p. orange 40 10
566 – 20p. green 50 15
567 – 25p. blue 85 15
568 **88** 35p. green . . . . 2·50 25
569 65p. purple . . . . 4·75 70
570 100p. brown . . . . 7·25 1·40

DESIGN: 10p. to 25p. As Nos. 497/500.

95 Pres. Chamoun and King Faisal II of Iraq

1957. Air. Arab Leaders' Conference, Beirut.
571 **95** 15p. orange 75 40
572 – 15p. blue 75 40
573 – 15p. maroon 75 40
574 – 15p. purple 75 40
575 – 15p. green 75 40
576 – 25p. turquoise 85 40
577 – 100p. brown . . . . 5·00 2·75
MS577a 106 × 151 mm. Nos. 571/6. Imperf . . . . 70·00 70·00

DESIGNS—As T **95**: 15p. values show Pres. Chamoun and: King Hussein of Jordan (No. 572), Abdallah Khalil of Sudan (No. 573), Pres. Shukri Bey al-Quwatli of Syria (No. 574) and King Saud of Saudi Arabia (No. 575); 25p. Map and Pres. Chamoun. 44 × 44 mm (Diamond shape): 100p. The six Arab Leaders.

97 Runners

98 Miners

1957. 2nd Pan-Arabian Games, Beirut.
578 **97** 2p.50 sepia (postage) . . . 75 40
579 – 12p.50 blue . . . . 1·10 60

580 – 35p. purple (air) . . . . . 3·00 1·20
581 – 50p. green . . . . 3·75 1·70
MS581a 132 × 185 mm. Nos. 576/81. Imperf. No gum £100 £100

DESIGNS—VERT: 12p.50, Footballers. HORIZ: 35p. Fencers; 50p. Stadium.

1957.
582 **86** 0p.50 blue ($16\frac{1}{2} \times 20\frac{1}{2}$ mm) (postage) 15 15
582a 0p.50 violet ($17 \times 21\frac{1}{2}$ mm) 25 15
583 1p. brown ($16\frac{1}{2} \times 20\frac{1}{2}$ mm) 25 15
583a 1p. purple ($17 \times 21\frac{1}{2}$ mm) 25 15
584 2p.50 violet ($16\frac{1}{2} \times 20\frac{1}{2}$ mm) 40 15
584a 2p.50 blue ($17 \times 21\frac{1}{2}$ mm) 40 15
585 5p. green ($16\frac{1}{2} \times 20\frac{1}{2}$ mm) 60 15
586 **98** $7\frac{1}{2}$p. pink 95 15
587 10p. brown . . . . 1·20 15
588 $12\frac{1}{2}$p. blue . . . . 1·70 15
589 – 25p. blue . . . . 1·70 15
590 – 50p. green . . . . 3·00 35
591 – 100p. brown . . . . 5·00 1·00

592 – 5p. green (air) 25 10
593 – 10p. orange 25 10
594 – 15p. brown 25 10
595 – 20p. purple 40 15
596 – 25p. blue 60 15
597 – 35p. purple 95 35
598 – 50p. green . . . . 1·70 50
599 – 65p. brown . . . . 3·00 50
600 – 100p. grey . . . . 3·75 1·40

DESIGNS: POSTAGE—As Type **86**: 50c. inscr "0 P.50", 2p.50, Figures in uniform size; 1p., 5p. Short dash under "P". As Type **98**: VERT: 25p. to 100p. Potter. AIR—As Type **98**: HORIZ: 5p. to 25p. Cedar of Lebanon with signs of the Zodiac, bird and ship; 35 to 100p. Chamoun Electric Power Station.

99 Cedar of Lebanon

100 Soldier and Flag

101 Douglas DC-6B at Khalde Airport

1959.
601 **99** 0p.50 blue (postage) . . . 15 15
602 1p. orange 25 15
603 2p.50 violet 40 15
604 5p. green 60 15
605 **100** 12p.50 blue . . . . . . 1·20 15
606 25p. blue . . . . 1·40 15
607 50p. brown . . . . . . 2·20 25
608 100p. sepia . . . . . . 4·25 50
609 **101** 5p. green (air) 70 10
610 10p. purple 70 10
611 15p. violet 95 10
612 20p. red . . . . 1·30 15
613 25p. violet . . . . . . 1·70 25
614 – 35p. myrtle . . . . . . 1·40 25
615 – 50p. turquoise . . . . . 1·70 25
616 – 65p. sepia . . . . . . 3·50 50
617 – 100p. blue . . . . . . 3·75 85
DESIGN—HORIZ: Nos. 614/17, Factory, cogwheel and telegraph pylons.

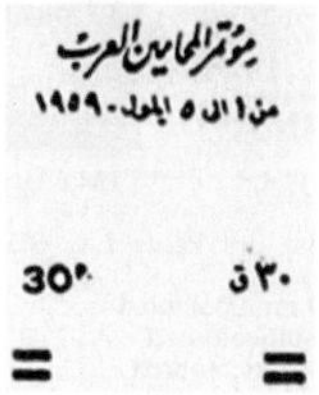
(102)

1959. Lawyers' Conference. Nos. 538 and 546 surch as T **102**.
618 30p. on 50p. myrtle and blue (postage) 85 60
619 40p. on 50p. yellow & blk (air) . . . . 1·40 85

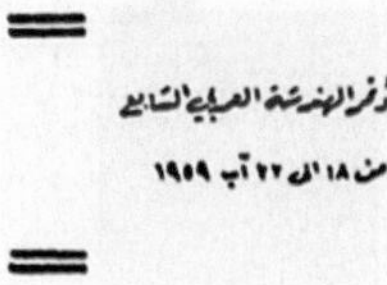
(103)

1959. Air. Engineers' Conference. Nos. 614 and 616 surch as T **103**.
620 30p. on 35p. myrtle . . . . . 1·40 70
621 40p. on 65p. sepia . . . . . 1·40 75

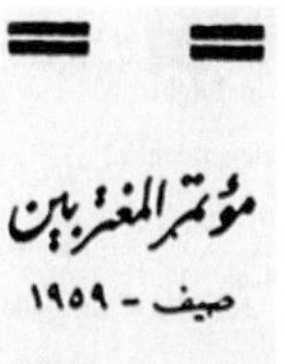
(104)

105 Discus Thrower

1959. Emigrants' Conference. No. 590 surch as T **104**.
622 30p. on 50p. green 85 25
623 40p. on 50p. green . . . . . 1·30 50

1959. Air. 3rd Mediterranean Games, Beirut.
624 **105** 15p. green 60 25
625 – 30p. brown 85 40
626 – 40p. blue . . . . 2·00 75
MS626a 106 × 130 mm. Nos. 624/6. Imperf (sold at 100p.) £170 £170
MS626b As last but with sheet values in margins . . . . 65·00 65·00
DESIGNS—VERT: 30p. Weightlifting. HORIZ: 40p. Games emblem.

106 Soldiers with Standard

108 Planting Tree

1959. Air. 16th Anniv of Independence.
627 **106** 40p. red and black . . . 1·10 55
628 60p. red and green . . . 1·40 70

1959. Surch.
629 **100** 7p.50 on 12p.50 blue . . 40 10
630 10p. on 12p.50 blue . . . 50 10
631 15p. on 25p. blue 60 15
632 – 40p. on 50p. green (No. 590) . . . . . . 1·40 40
633 **88** 40p. on 65p. purple (No. 569) (air) . . . . 3·00 50

1960. Air. 25th Anniv of Friends of the Tree Society.
634 **108** 20p. purple and green . . 85 60
635 40p. sepia and green . . . 1·40 85

1960. Air. As T **79** but colours of name and value tablets reversed.
636 20p. green 85 50

109 Pres. Chehab

111 "Uprooted Tree"

110 Arab League Centre

1960. Air.
637 **109** 5p. green 10 10
638 10p. blue 10 10
639 15p. brown 15 10
640 20p. sepia 15 10
641 30p. olive 35 15
642 40p. red 35 20
643 50p. blue 70 25
644 70p. purple . . . . . . 1·30 35
645 100p. green . . . . . . 2·50 70

1960. Inaug of Arab League Centre, Cairo.
646 **110** 15p. turquoise 60 40

1960. Air. World Refugee Year. (a) Size $20\frac{1}{2} \times 36\frac{1}{2}$ mm.
647 **111** 25p. brown 85 60
648 40p. green . . . . 1·40 85
MS648a 90 × 110 mm. Nos. 647/8. Imperf (sold at 150p.) . . . . 42·00 42·00

(b) Size $19\frac{3}{4} \times 35\frac{1}{4}$ mm.
648b **111** 25p. brown . . . . . . 1·20 1·20
648c 40p. green . . . . . . 1·40 1·40

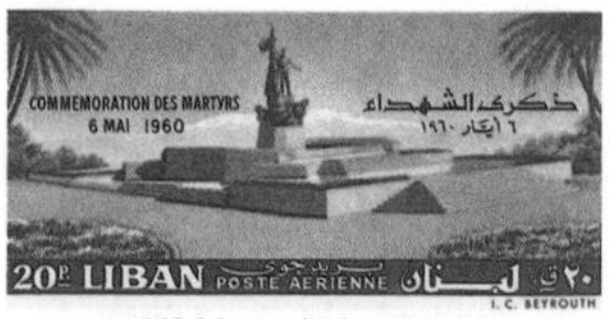
112 Martyrs' Monument

1960. Air. Martyrs' Commemoration.
649 **112** 20p. purple and green . . 60 35
650 40p. blue and green . . . 85 60
651 – 70p. olive and black . . . 2·00 85
DESIGN—VERT: 70p. Detail of statues on monument.

113 Pres. Chehab and King Mohammed V

114 Pres. Chehab

1960. Air. Visit of King Mohammed V of Morocco.
652 **113** 30p. chocolate and brown 95 40
653 70p. brown and black . . 1·90 70

1960.
654 **114** 50c. green 15 15
655 2p.50 olive 15 15
656 5p. green 15 15
657 7p.50 red 35 15
658 15p. blue 60 25
659 50p. purple . . . . . . 1·40 35
660 100p. brown . . . . . . 3·00 60

115 Child

116 Dove, Map and Flags

1960. Air. Mother and Child Days.
661 **115** 20p. red and yellow . . . 40 15
662 20p.+10p. red and yellow 60 25
663 – 60p. blue and light blue 1·40 1·00
664 – 60p.+15p. blue & lt bl . . 2·20 1·10
DESIGN: Nos. 663/4, Mother and child.

1960. Air. World Lebanese Union Meeting, Beirut. Multicoloured.
665 20p. Type **116** 25 25
666 40p. Cedar of Lebanon and homing pigeons 85 40
667 70p. Globes and Cedar of Lebanon (horiz) . . . . . 1·00 60
MS667a 110 × 139 mm. Nos. 665/7. Imperf (sold at 150p.) . . . . 13·50 13·50

(117)

1960. Arabian Oil Congress, Beirut. Optd with T **117**.
668 **86** 5p. green (No. 585) . . . 35 10
669 **110** 15p. turquoise 75 40

1960. Air. World Refugee Year. Nos. 648b/c surch in English and Arabic.
669a **111** 20p.+10p. on 40p. grn 8·50 8·50
669b 30p.+15p. on 25p. brn 12·00 12·00

119 Boxing

1961. Olympic Games.
670 **119** 2p.50+2p.50 brown and blue (postage) 15 15
671 – 5p.+5p. brown & orge . . 35 25
672 – 7p.50+7p.50 brn & vio . . 50 40
673 – 15p.+15p. brown & red (air) . . . . 2·75 2·50
674 – 25p.+25p. brown & grn 2·75 2·50
675 – 35p.+35p. brown & bl . . 3·00 2·50
MS675a 137 × 118 mm. Nos. 673/5. Imperf (sold at 150p.) . . . . 31·00 31·00
DESIGNS: 5p. Wrestling; 7p.50, Putting the shot; 15p. Fencing; 25p. Cycling; 35p. Swimming.

120 Pres. Chehab

121 Pres. Chehab and Map of Lebanon

122 U.N. Emblem and Map

1961.
676 **120** 2p.50 ultramarine and blue (postage) 15 10
677 7p.50 violet and mauve 15 10
678 10p. brown and yellow . . 40 10
679 **121** 5p. green & lt green (air) 15 10
680 10p. brown and ochre . . 40 10
681 70p. violet and mauve . . 2·10 50
682 – 200p. blue and bistre . . 4·75 2·10
DESIGN—HORIZ: 200p. Casino, Maameltein.

1961. Air. 15th Anniv of U.N.O.
683 **122** 20p. purple and blue . . 50 25
684 – 30p. green and brown . . 85 40
685 – 50p. blue and ultramarine 1·40 70
MS685a 100 × 132 mm. Nos. 683/5. Imperf (sold at 125p.) . . . . 8·50 8·50

DESIGNS—VERT: 30p. U.N. emblem and Baalbek ruins. HORIZ: 50p. View of U.N. Headquarters and Manhattan.

123 Cedar of Lebanon

124 Bay of Maameltein

1961. Redrawn version of T **86** (different arrangement at foot). Shaded background.
686 **123** 2p.50 myrtle 50 10
See also Nos. 695/7.

1961. Air.
687 **124** 15p. lake 40 15
688 30p. blue 70 35
689 40p. sepia . . . . 1·00 50

125 Weaving

1961. Air. Labour Day.
690 – 30p. red . . . . 1·40 70
691 **125** 70p. blue . . . . 2·75 1·40
DESIGN: 30p. Pottery.

126 Water-skiers

1961. Air. Tourist Month.
692 – 15p. violet and blue . . . 70 35
693 **126** 40p. blue and flesh . . . 1·40 50
694 – 70p. olive and flesh . . . 2·10 1·10
DESIGNS—VERT: 15p. Firework display. HORIZ: 70p. Tourists in punt.

1961. As T **123** but plain background.
695 2p.50 yellow 40 15
696 5p. lake 40 15
697 10p. black 60 15

127 G.P.O., Beirut

1961.
698 **127** 2p.50 mauve (postage) . . 40 15
699 5p. green 60 15
700 15p. blue 70 25
701 – 35p. green (air) 60 35
702 – 50p. brown . . . . 1·00 40
703 – 100p. black . . . . 1·40 70
DESIGN: 35p. to 100p. Motor highway, Dora.

128 Cedars of Lebanon

129 Tyre Waterfront

1961.
704 **128** 0p.50 green (postage) . . 15 15
705 1p. brown 15 15
706 2p.50 blue 15 15
707 5p. red 35 15
708 7p.50 violet 50 15
709 – 10p. purple . . . . 1·10 15
710 – 15p. blue . . . . 1·50 35
711 – 50p. green . . . . 1·70 1·00
712 – 100p. black . . . . 4·25 1·50
713 **129** 5p. red (air) 25 15
714 10p. violet 35 15
715 15p. blue 60 15
716 20p. orange 60 15
717 30p. green 70 20
718 – 40p. purple . . . . 1·00 35
719 – 50p. blue . . . . 1·30 50
720 – 70p. green . . . . 1·70 85
721 – 100p. sepia . . . . 3·00 1·40
DESIGNS—HORIZ: Nos. 709/12, Zahle. VERT: Nos. 718/21, Afka Falls.
See also Nos. 729/34.

130 UNESCO Building, Beirut

1961. Air. 15th Anniv of UNESCO. Mult.
722 20p. Type **130** 50 20
723 30p. UNESCO emblem and cedar (vert) 70 40
724 50p. UNESCO Building, Paris . . . . 1·40 65

131 Tomb of Unknown Soldier

132 Scout Bugler

1961. Independence and Evacuation of Foreign Troops Commemoration. Multicoloured.
725 10p. Type **131** (postage) . . . 40 10
726 15p. Soldier and flag 50 15
727 25p. Cedar emblem (horiz) (air) 40 40
728 50p. Emirs Bashir and Fakhreddine (horiz) . . . 60 50

1962. As Nos. 704/21 but with larger figures of value.
729 **128** 50c. green (postage) . . . 25 15
730 1p. brown 35 15
731 2p.50 blue 40 15
732 – 15p. blue . . . . 3·00 25
733 **129** 5p. red (air) 15 10
734 – 40p. purple . . . . 6·75 85

1962. Lebanese Scout Movement Commemorative.
735 ½p. black, yell & grn (postage) 10 10
736 1p. multicoloured 10 10
737 2½p. green, black and red . . 15 10
738 6p. multicoloured 40 10
739 10p. yellow, black and blue 70 10
740 15p. multicoloured (air) . . . 85 15
741 20p. yellow, black and violet 95 25
742 25p. multicoloured . . . . . 1·40 85
DESIGNS—VERT: ½p. Type **132**; 6p. Lord Baden-Powell; 20p. Saluting hand. HORIZ: 1p. Scout with flag, cedar and badge; 2½p. Stretcher party, badge and laurel; 10p. Scouts at campfire; 15p. Cedar and Guide badge; 25p. Cedar and Scout badge.

133 Arab League Centre, Cairo, and Emblem

134 Blacksmith

1962. Air. Arab League Week.
743 **133** 20p. ultramarine and blue 40 25
744 30p. lake and pink . . . 50 40
745 50p. green and turquoise 95 70
See also Nos. 792/5.

1962. Air. Labour Day.
746 **134** 5p. green and blue . . . 15 10
747 10p. blue and pink . . . 25 10
748 – 25p. violet and pink . . . 60 25
749 – 35p. mauve and blue . . 85 40
DESIGN—HORIZ: 25, 35p. Tractor.

1962. European Shooting Championships. Nos. 670/5 optd **CHAMPIONNAT D'EUROPE DE TIR 2 JUIN 1962** in French and Arabic.
750 **119** 2p.50+2p.50 (postage) . . 25 25
751 – 5p.+5p. 60 60
752 – 7p.50+7p.50 . . . . . . 70 70
753 – 15p.+15p. (air) . . . . . 1·00 1·00
754 – 25p.+25p. . . . . 2·30 2·30
755 – 35p.+35p. . . . . 2·75 2·75

136 Hand grasping Emblem

137 Rock Temples of Abu Simbel

1962. Air. Malaria Eradication.
756 **136** 30p. brown & light brown 85 50
757 – 70p. violet and lilac . . . 1·40 95
DESIGN: 70p. Campaign emblem.

1962. Nubian Monuments.
758 **137** 5p. bl & ultram (postage) 50 15
759 15p. lake and brown . . . 70 25
760 – 30p. yellow and green (air) . . . . 1·70 60
761 – 50p. olive and grey . . . 3·25 1·30
DESIGNS: 30, 50p. Bas-relief.

138 Playing-card Symbols

139 Schoolboy

1962. Air. European Bridge Championships.
762 **138** 25p. multicoloured . . . 3·50 2·10
763 40p. multicoloured . . . 3·50 2·10

1962. Schoolchildren's Day.
764 **139** 30p. mult (postage) . . . 60 25
765 – 45p. multicoloured (air) 85 50
DESIGN: 45p. Teacher.

140

141 Cherries

1962. Air. 19th Anniv of Independence.
766 **140** 25p. green, red & turq . . 95 50
767 25p. violet, red & turq . . 95 50
768 25p. blue, red & turquoise 95 50

1962. Fruits. Multicoloured.
769 0p.50 Type **141** (postage) . . 25 10
770 1p. Figs 40 10
771 2p.50 Type **141** 50 10
772 5p. Figs 60 10
773 7p.50 Type **141** 25 10
774 10p. Grapes 40 15
775 17p.50 Grapes 85 15
776 30p. Grapes . . . . 1·50 25
777 50p. Oranges . . . . . . 2·75 60
778 100p. Pomegranates . . . . 5·50 1·50
779 5p. Apricots (air) 15 10
780 10p. Plums 35 15
781 20p. Apples 60 15
782 30p. Plums 85 35
783 40p. Apples 95 35
784 50p. Pears . . . . 1·10 40
785 70p. Medlars . . . . . . 1·70 50
786 100p. Lemons . . . . . . 3·00 1·00

142 Reaping

143 Nurse tending Baby

1963. Air. Freedom from Hunger.
787 **142** 2p.50 yellow and blue . . 10 10
788 5p. yellow and green . . . 10 10
789 7p.50 yellow and purple 25 15
790 – 15p. green and red . . . 60 15
791 – 20p. green and red . . . 85 40
DESIGN—HORIZ: 15, 20p. Three ears of wheat within hand.

1963. Air. Arab League Week. As T **133** but inscr "1963".
792 5p. violet and blue 10 10
793 10p. green and blue 25 25
794 15p. brown and blue 40 35
795 20p. grey and blue 70 60

1963. Air. Red Cross Centenary.
796 – 5p. green and red 10 10
797 – 20p. blue and red 35 15
798 **143** 35p. red and black . . . 60 35
799 40p. violet and red . . . 1·00 50
DESIGN—HORIZ: 5, 20p. Blood transfusion.

144 Allegory of Music

145 Flag and rising Sun

1963. Air. Baalbek Festival.
800 **144** 35p. orange and blue . . 1·00 50

1963. Air. 20th Anniv of Independence. Flag and sun in red and yellow.
801 **145** 5p. turquoise 10 15
802 10p. green 35 40
803 25p. blue 60 60
804 40p. drab . . . . 1·00 95

146 Cycling

147 Hyacinth

1964. 4th Mediterranean Games, Naples (1963).
805 **146** 2p.50 brown and purple (postage) 15 10
806 – 5p. orange and blue . . . 25 10
807 – 10p. brown and violet . . 40 15
808 – 15p. orange and green (air) 40 25
809 – 17p.50 brown and blue . . 50 35
810 – 30p. brown and turquoise 85 50
MS810a 152 × 112 mm. Nos. 808/10. Imperf (sold at 100p.) . . . . 12·50 12·50
DESIGNS—VERT: 5p. Basketball; 10p. Running; 15p. Tennis. HORIZ: 17p.50, Swimming; 30p. Skiing.

1964. Flowers. Multicoloured.
811 0p.50 Type **147** (postage) . . 10 10
812 1p. Type **147** 10 10
813 2p.50 Type **147** 10 10
814 5p. Cyclamen 15 10
815 7p.50 Cyclamen 15 10
816 10p. Poinsettia (vert) . . . 35 15
817 17p.50 Anemone (vert) . . . 70 20
818 30p. Iris (vert) . . . . . . 1·40 50
819 50p. Poppy (vert) . . . . . 3·50 85
820 5p. Lily (vert) (air) 35 25
821 10p. Ranunculus (vert) . . . 60 25
822 20p. Anemone (vert) 75 25
823 40p. Tuberose (vert) . . . . 1·40 50
824 45p. Rhododendron (vert) . . 1·40 50
825 50p. Jasmine (vert) . . . . . 1·70 50
826 70p. Yellow broom (vert) . . 2·50 85
Nos. 816/26 are size 26½ × 37 mm.

148 Cedar of Lebanon

149 Cedar of Lebanon

1964.
827 **148** 0p.50 green 40 15
828 **149** 0p.50 green 25 15
829 2p.50 blue 25 15
830 5p. mauve 35 15
831 7p.50 orange 70 15
832 17p.50 purple . . . . . . 1·30 15

150 Child on Rocking-horse

152 "Flame of Freedom"

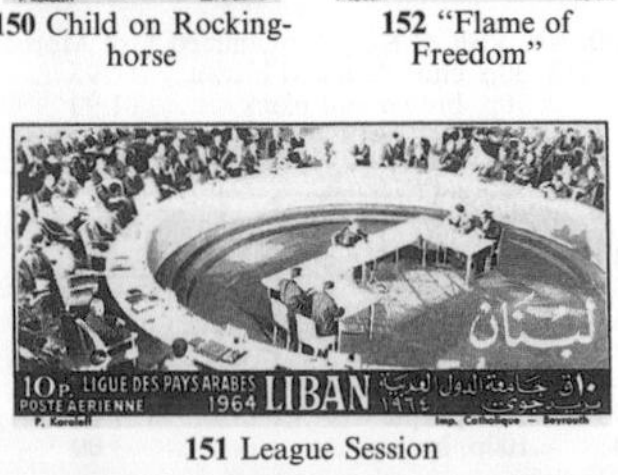
151 League Session

1964. Air. Children's Day.
833 – 5p. red, orange and green 15 10
834 – 10p. red, orange and brown 25 15
835 **150** 20p. orange, blue and ultramarine 50 40
836 40p. yellow, blue and purple . . . . 1·00 70
DESIGN—HORIZ: 5, 10p. Girls skipping.

1964. Air. Arab League Meeting.
837 **151** 5p. buff, brown and black 40 25
838 10p. black 50 25
839 15p. turquoise 75 35
840 20p. mauve, brn & sepia 1·20 50

1964. Air. 15th Anniv of Declaration of Human Rights.
841 **152** 20p. red, pink and brown 25 15
842 – 40p. orange, blue and light blue 50 25
DESIGN: 40p. Flame on pedestal bearing U.N. emblem.

153 Sick Child

154 Clasped Wrists

1964. Air. "Bal des Petits Lits Blancs" (Ball for children's charity).
843 **153** 2p.50 multicoloured . . . 10 10
844 5p. multicoloured 15 10
845 15p. multicoloured . . . 20 15
846 – 17p.50 multicoloured . . 50 50
847 – 20p. multicoloured . . . 60 50
848 – 40p. multicoloured . . . 1·00 35
DESIGN—55 × 25½ mm: 17p.50 to 40p. Children in front of palace (venue of ball).

1964. Air. World Lebanese Union Congress, Beirut.
849 **154** 20p. black, yellow & green 60 25
850 40p. black, yellow & pur 1·10 60

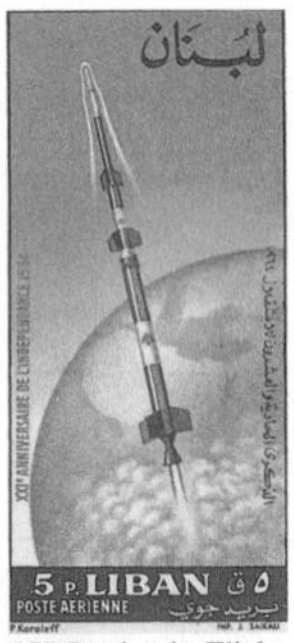
155 Rocket in Flight

1964. Air. 21st Anniv of Independence.
851 **155** 5p. multicoloured 25 15
852 10p. multicoloured . . . 25 15
853 – 40p. blue and black . . . 95 60
854 – 70p. purple and black . . 1·70 1·30
DESIGNS—HORIZ: 40p. to 70p. "Struggle for Independence" (battle scene).

156 Temple Columns

1965. Baalbek Festival.
855 **156** 2p.50 black and orange (postage) 15 15
856 – 7p.50 black and blue . . 40 25
857 – 10p. multicoloured (air) 15 10
858 – 15p. multicoloured . . . 35 10
859 – 25p. multicoloured . . . 60 40
860 – 40p. multicoloured . . . 1·20 50
DESIGNS—28 × 55 mm: 10, 15p. Man in costume; 25, 40p. Woman in costume.

157 Swimming

1965. Olympic Games, Tokyo.
861 **157** 2p.50 black, blue and mauve (postage) . . . 15 10
862 – 7p.50 purple, green & brn 85 60
863 – 10p. grey, brown & green 1·10 70
864 – 15p. black and green (air) 25 10

865 – 25p. green and purple 60 25
866 – 40p. brown and blue 95 40
MS866a 140 × 100 mm. Nos. 864/6. Imperf (sold at 100p.) 14·50 14·50
DESIGNS—HORIZ: 7p.50, Fencing; 15p. Horse-jumping; 40p. Gymnastics. VERT: 10p. Basketball; 25p. Rifle-shooting.

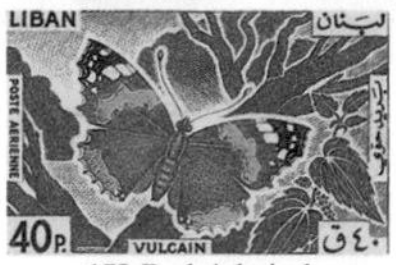

158 Red Admiral

1965. (a) Postage. Birds.
867 – 5p. multicoloured 40 10
868 – 10p. multicoloured 60 10
869 – 15p. chocolate, orange & brn 1·10 10
870 – 17p.50 purple, red and blue 1·60 15
871 – 20p. black, yellow and green 1·90 15
872 – 32p.50 yellow, brown & grn 4·75 75

(b) Air. Butterflies.
873 – 30p. yellow, brown and red 85 15
874 – 35p. blue, red and bistre 1·30 25
875 **158** 40p. brown, red and green 1·60 25
876 – 45p. brown, yellow & blue 2·00 40
877 – 70p. multicoloured 3·00 60
878 – 85p. black, orange & green 3·50 75
879 – 100p. blue and plum 5·00 85
880 – 200p. brown, blue & pur 9·25 1·00
881 – 300p. sepia, yellow & green 13·50 3·00
882 – 500p. brown, blue and light blue 25·00 6·00
DESIGNS—As T **158**. BIRDS: 5p. Northern bullfinch; 10p. Eurasian goldfinch; 15p. Hoopoe; 17p.50, Red-legged partridge; 20p. Golden oriole; 32p.50, European bee eater. BUTTERFLIES: 30p. Large tiger moth; 35p. Small postman; 45p. Common grayling; 70p. Swallowtail; 85p. Orange-tip; 100p. Blue morpho; 200p. "Erasmia sanguiflua"; 300p. "Papilio crassus". 35½ × 25 mm: 500p. Amelia's charakes.

159 Pope Paul and Pres. Helou

1965. Air. Pope Paul's Visit to Lebanon.
883 **159** 45p. violet and gold 4·25 1·90
MS883a 100 × 81 mm. No. 883. Imperf (sold at 100p.) 38·00 38·00

160 Sheep

1965.
884 – 50c. multicoloured 60 15
885 – 1p. grey, black and mauve 75 15
886 **160** 2p.50 yellow, sepia & grn 85 15
DESIGNS: 50c. Cow and calf; 1p. Rabbit.

161 "Cedars of Friendship"

162 "Silk Manufacture"

1965. Air.
887 **161** 40p. multicoloured 1·40 25

1965. Air. World Silk Congress, Beirut. Mult.
888 2p.50 Type **162** 20 15
889 5p. Type **162** 20 15
890 7p.50 Type **162** 25 15
891 15p. Weaver and loom 25 15
892 30p. As 15p. 75 25
893 40p. As 15p. 1·10 40
894 50p. As 15p. 1·40 60

163 Parliament Building

1965. Air. Centenary of Lebanese Parliament.
895 **163** 35p. brown, ochre and red 50 25
896 40p. brown, ochre & green 70 40

164 U.N. Emblem and Headquarters

165 Playing-card "King"

1965. Air. 20th Anniv of U.N.O.
897 **164** 2p.50 blue 10 10
898 10p. red 15 10
899 17p.50 violet 20 15
900 30p. green 40 25
901 40p. brown 50 50
MS901a 101 × 80 mm. No. 901 in violet. Imperf (sold at 50p.) 14·50 14·50

1965. Air. World Bridge Championships, Beirut.
902 **165** 2p.50 multicoloured 15 10
903 15p. multicoloured 60 15
904 17p.50 multicoloured 95 20
905 40p. multicoloured 1·90 85
MS905a 105 × 85 mm. Nos. 903 and 905. Imperf or perf (sold at 75p.) 19·00 19·00

166 Dagger on Deir Yassin, Palestine

167 I.T.U. Emblem and Symbols

1965. Air. Deir Yassin Massacre.
906 **166** 50p. multicoloured 3·50 95

1966. Air. Centenary (1965) of I.T.U.
907 **167** 2p.50 multicoloured 10 10
908 15p. multicoloured 35 10
909 17p.50 multicoloured 50 15
910 25p. multicoloured 1·10 25
911 40p. multicoloured 1·50 40

168 Stage Performance

1966. Air. Baalbek Festival. Multicoloured.
912 2p.50 Type **168** 15 15
913 5p. Type **168** 15 15
914 7p.50 Ballet performance (vert) 15 15
915 15p. Ballet performance (vert) 35 15
916 30p. Concert 75 35
917 40p. Concert 1·10 40

169 Tabarja

1966. Tourism. Multicoloured.
918 50c. Hippodrome, Beirut (postage) 15 10
919 1p. Pigeon Grotto, Beirut 15 10
920 2p.50 Type **169** 15 10
921 5p. Ruins, Beit-Mery 15 10
922 7p.50 Ruins, Anjar 15 10
923 10p. Djezzine Falls (air) 15 10
924 15p. Sidon Castle 20 10
925 20p. Amphitheatre, Byblos 30 10
926 30p. Sun Temple, Baalbek 40 15
927 50p. Palace, Beit ed-Din 1·10 15
928 60p. Nahr-el Kalb 1·30 20
929 70p. Tripoli 1·90 40

170 W.H.O. Building

1966. Air. Inauguration of W.H.O. Headquarters, Geneva.
930 **170** 7p.50 green 25 15
931 17p.50 red 40 30
932 25p. blue 75 40

171 Skiing

1966. Air. International Cedars Festival.
933 **171** 2p.50 brown, red & green 15 15
934 – 5p. multicoloured 15 15
935 – 17p.50 multicoloured 35 25
936 – 25p. red, brown and green 1·00 40
DESIGNS: 5p. Tobogganing; 17p.50, Cedar in snow; 25p. Ski-lift.

172 Inscribed Sarcophagus

1966. Air. Phoenician Invention of the Alphabet.
937 **172** 10p. brown, black & green 10 10
938 – 15p. brown, ochre & mve 35 15
939 – 20p. sepia, blue and ochre 40 25
940 – 30p. brown, orange & yell 85 40
DESIGNS: 15p. Phoenician sailing ship; 20p. Mediterranean route map showing spread of Phoenician alphabet; 30p. Kadmus with alphabet tablet.

173 Child in Bath

174 Decade Emblem

1966. Air. Int Children's Day. Multicoloured.
941 2p. Type **173** 10 10
942 5p. Boy and doll in rowing boat 10 10
943 7p.50 Girl skiing 25 10
944 15p. Girl giving food to bird 60 15
945 20p. Boy doing homework 85 40
MS946 100 × 69½ mm. 50p. Children of various races (horiz). Imperf 6·00 6·00

1966. Air. International Hydrological Decade.
947 **174** 5p. ultramarine, bl & orge 10 10
948 10p. red, blue and orange 15 10
949 – 15p. sepia, green & orange 25 15
950 – 20p. blue, green & orange 60 25
DESIGN: 15p., 20p. Similar "wave" pattern.

175 Rev. Daniel Bliss (founder)

176 I.T.Y. Emblem

177 Beit ed-Din Palace

1966. Air. Centenary of American University, Beirut.
951 **175** 20p. brown, yellow & grn 40 20
952 – 30p. green, brown and blue 50 30
MS953 125 × 85 mm. 50p. brown, orange and green. Imperf 2·10 2·10
DESIGNS—VERT: 30p. University Chapel. Horiz (59 × 37 mm)—50p. Rev. Daniel Bliss, University and emblem.

1967. International Tourist Year (1st issue).
(a) Postage.
954 **176** 50c. multicoloured 10 10
955 1p. multicoloured 10 10
956 2p.50 multicoloured 10 10
957 5p. multicoloured 10 10
958 7p.50 multicoloured 15 10

(b) Air. Multicoloured.
959 10p. Tabarja 15 10
960 15p. Pigeon Rock, Beirut 25 10
961 17p.50 Type **177** 35 10
962 20p. Sidon 35 10
963 25p. Tripoli 35 15
964 30p. Byblos 40 15
965 35p. Ruins, Tyre 60 15
966 40p. Temple, Baalbek 95 15
See also Nos. 977/MS980a.

178 Signing Pact, and Flags

1967. Air. 22nd Anniv of Arab League Pact.
967 **178** 5p. multicoloured 10 10
968 10p. multicoloured 15 10
969 15p. multicoloured 25 25
970 20p. multicoloured 60 35

179 Veterans War Memorial Building, San Francisco

1967. Air. San Francisco Pact of 1945. Mult.
971 2p.50 Type **179** 60 20
972 5p. Type **179** 60 20
973 7p.50 Type **179** 60 20
974 10p. Scroll and flags of U.N. and Lebanon 20 20
975 20p. As 10p. 35 20
976 30p. As 10p. 70 20

180 Temple Ruins, Baalbek

1967. Air. International Tourist Year (2nd issue). Multicoloured.
977 5p. Type **180** 10 10
978 10p. Ruins, Anjar 15 10
979 15p. Ancient bridge, Nahr-Ibrahim 25 15
980 20p. Grotto, Jeita 40 15
MS980a 112 × 90 mm. 50p. Beirut (plus flag and map of Lebanon). Imperf 21·00 21·00

181

1967. Air. India Day.
981 **181** 2p.50 red 15 15
982 5p. purple 15 15
983 7p.50 brown 15 15
984 10p. blue 15 15
985 15p. green 40 15

182

1967. Air. 22nd Anniv of Lebanon's Admission to U.N.O.
986 **182** 2p.50 red 10 10
987 5p. blue 10 10

988	7p.50 green	10	10
989	– 10p. red	10	15
990	– 20p. blue	25	15
991	– 30p. green	40	15
MS991a	109 × 85 mm. 100p. red (T **182**). Imperf	6·00	6·00

DESIGN: 10, 20, 30p. U.N. Emblem.

183 Goat and Kid

1967. Animals and Fishes. Multicoloured.

992	50c. Type **183** (postage)	15	10
993	1p. Cattle	15	10
994	2p.50 Sheep	15	10
995	5p. Dromedaries	15	10
996	10p. Donkey	40	10
997	15p. Horses	85	15
998	20p. Basking shark (air)	85	10
999	30p. Garfish	85	15
1000	40p. Pollack	1·30	15
1001	50p. Cuckoo wrasse	1·40	20
1002	70p. Striped red mullet	3·75	25
1003	100p. Rainbow trout	4·75	25

184 Ski Jumping

1968. Air. International Ski Congress, Beirut.

1004 **184**	2p.50 multicoloured	15	10
1005	– 5p. multicoloured	20	10
1006	– 7p.50 multicoloured	25	10
1007	– 10p. multicoloured	25	15
1008	– 25p. multicoloured	85	25
MS1008a	121 × 91 mm. 50p. multicoloured. Imperf	6·75	6·75

DESIGNS: 5p. to 10p. Skiing (all different); 25p. Congress emblem of Cedar and skis.

185 Princess Khaskiah

1968. Air. Emir Fakhreddine II Commem. Mult.

1009	2p.50 Type **185**	10	15
1010	5p. Emir Fakhreddine II	10	15
1011	10p. Sidon Citadel (horiz)	15	15
1012	15p. Chekif Citadel (horiz)	25	15
1013	17p.50 Beirut Citadel (horiz)	40	15
MS1013a	120 × 86 mm. 50p. Battle of Anjar. Imperf	11·00	11·00

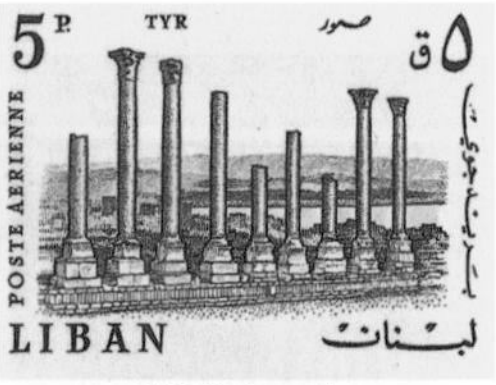

186 Colonnade

1968. Air. Tyre Antiquities.

1014	– 2p.50 brn, cream & pink	10	10
1015 **186**	5p. brown, blue & yellow	15	10
1016	– 7p.50 brown, buff & grn	25	15
1017	– 10p. brown, blue & orange	40	25
MS1018	120 × 80 mm. 10p. brown and blue. Perf or imperf (sold at 50p.)	21·00	21·00

DESIGNS—VERT: 2p.50, Roman bust; 10p. Bas-relief. HORIZ: 7p.50, Arch.

187 Justinian and Mediterranean Map

1968. Air. 1st Anniv of Faculty of Law, Beirut.

1019	5p. Justinian (vert)	10	10
1020	10p. Justinian (vert)	10	10
1021	15p. Type **187**	15	10
1022	20p. Type **187**	25	15

188 Arab League Emblem

1968. Air. Arab Appeal Week.

1023 **188**	5p. multicoloured	10	10
1024	10p. multicoloured	15	10
1025	15p. multicoloured	25	10
1026	20p. multicoloured	40	15

189 Cedar on Globe

1968. Air. 3rd World Lebanese Union Congress, Beirut.

1027 **189**	2p.50 multicoloured	10	10
1028	5p. multicoloured	15	10
1029	7p.50 multicoloured	20	10
1030	10p. multicoloured	25	25

190 Jupiter's Temple Ruins, Baalbek

1968. Air. Baalbek Festival. Multicoloured.

1031	5p. Type **190**	10	10
1032	10p. Bacchus's Temple	15	15
1033	15p. Corniche, Jupiter's Temple	25	15
1034	20p. Portal, Bacchus's Temple	40	25
1035	25p. Columns, Bacchus's Temple	60	40

191 Long Jumping and Atlantes

1968. Air. Olympic Games, Mexico.

1036 **191**	5p. black, yellow and blue	10	10
1037	– 10p. black, blue & purple	15	15
1038	– 15p. multicoloured	25	15
1039	– 20p. multicoloured	40	25
1040	– 25p. brown	60	35

DESIGNS (each incorporating Aztec relic): 10p. High jumping; 15p. Fencing; 20p. Weightlifting; 25p. "Sailing boat" with oars.

192 Lebanese driving Tractor ("Work protection")

193 Minshiya Stairs

1968. Air. Human Rights Year. Multicoloured.

1041	10p. Type **192**	10	10
1042	15p. Citizens ("Social Security")	15	15
1043	25p. Young men of three races ("Unity")	35	30

1968. Air. Centenary of 1st Municipal Council (Deir el-Kamar). Multicoloured.

1044	10p. Type **193**	10	10
1045	15p. Serai kiosk	15	15
1046	25p. Ancient highway	35	30

194 Nurse and Child

1969. Air. UNICEF. Multicoloured.

1047 **194**	5p. black, brown and blue	10	10
1048	– 10p. black, green & yell	10	10
1049	– 15p. black, red and purple	15	10
1050	– 20p. black, blue & yellow	25	15
1051	– 25p. black, ochre & mve	35	15

DESIGNS: 10p. Produce; 15p. Mother and child; 20p. Child with book; 25p. Children with flowers.

195 Ancient Coin

1969. Air. 20th Anniv of International Museums Council (I.C.O.M.). Exhibits in National Museum, Beirut. Multicoloured.

1052	2p.50 Type **195**	10	10
1053	5p. Gold dagger, Byblos	15	10
1054	7p.50 Detail of Ahiram's Sarcophagus	25	10
1055	30p. Jewelled pectoral	50	25
1056	40p. Khalde "bird" vase	75	70

196 Water-skiing

1969. Air. Water Sports. Multicoloured.

1057	2p.50 Type **196**	10	10
1058	5p. Water-skiing (group)	15	10
1059	7p.50 Paraskiing (vert)	20	10
1060	30p. Racing dinghies (vert)	60	35
1061	40p. Racing dinghies	75	70

197 Frontier Guard

1969. Air. 25th Anniv of Independence. The Lebanese Army.

1062	2p. Type **197**	10	10
1063	5p. Unknown Soldier's Tomb	10	10
1064	7p.50 Army Foresters	15	10
1065	15p. Road-making	25	15
1066	30p. Military ambulance and Sud Aviation Alouette III helicopter	60	35
1067	40p. Skiing patrol	85	40

198 Concentric Red Crosses

1971. Air. 25th Anniv of Lebanese Red Cross.

1068 **198**	15p. red and black	40	15
1069	– 85p. red and black	1·60	1·00

DESIGN: 85p. Red Cross in shape of cedar of Lebanon.

199 Foil and Flags of Arab States

1971. Air. 10th International Fencing Championships. Multicoloured.

1070	10p. Type **199**	10	10
1071	15p. Foil and flags of foreign nations	15	15
1072	35p. Contest with foils	60	40
1073	40p. Epee contest	70	50
1074	50p. Contest with sabres	1·00	60

200 "Farmers at Work" (12th-century Arab painting)

1971. Air. 50th Anniv (1969) of I.L.O.

1075 **200**	10p. multicoloured	15	10
1076	40p. multicoloured	75	40

201 U.P.U. Monument and New H.Q. Building, Berne

1971. Air. New U.P.U. Headquarters Building, Berne.

1077 **201**	15p. red, black and yellow	15	10
1078	35p. yellow, black and orange	75	40

202 "Ravens setting fire to Owls" (14th-century painting)

1971. Air. Children's Day. Multicoloured.

1079	15p. Type **202**	40	15
1080	85p. "The Lion and the Jackal" (13th-century painting) (39 × 29 mm)	1·90	85

203 Arab League Flag and Map

1971. Air. 25th Anniv of Arab League.

1081 **203**	30p. multicoloured	40	20
1082	70p. multicoloured	95	65

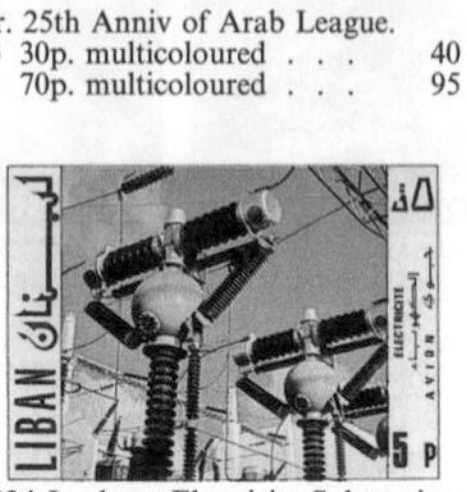

204 Jamhour Electricity Sub-station

1971. Air. Multicoloured.

1083	5p. Type **204**	15	10
1084	10p. Maameltein Bridge	15	10
1085	15p. Hoteliers' School	15	10
1086	20p. Litani Dam	15	10
1087	25p. Interior of T.V. set	25	10
1088	35p. Bziza Temple	50	15
1089	40p. Jounieh Harbour	60	15
1090	45p. Radar scanner, Beirut Airport	75	25
1091	50p. Hibiscus	1·00	25
1092	70p. School of Sciences Building	1·50	25
1093	85p. Oranges	1·70	40
1094	100p. Satellite Communications Station, Arbanieh	2·40	85

205 Insignia of Imam al Ouzai (theologian)

1971. Air. Lebanese Celebrities.

1095	**205**	25p. brown, gold & green	35	20
1096	–	25p. brown, gold & yell	35	20
1097	–	25p. brown, gold & yell	35	20
1098	–	25p. brown, gold & green	35	20

PORTRAITS: No. 1096, Bechara el Khoury (poet and writer); 1097, Hassan Kamel el Sabbah (scientist); 1098, Gibran Khalil Gibran (writer).

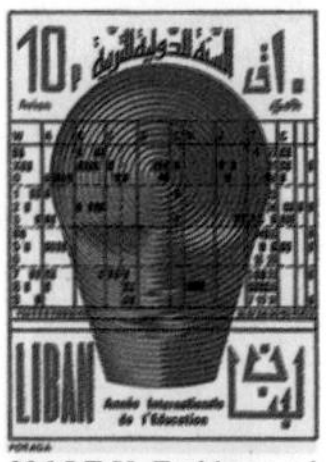
206 I.E.Y. Emblem and Computer Card

1971. Air. International Education Year.

1099	**206**	10p. black, blue and violet	10	10
1100		40p. black, yellow and red	60	35

207 Dahr-el-Basheq Sanatorium

208 "Solar Wheel" Emblem

1971. Air. Tuberculosis Relief Campaign.

1101	**207**	50p. multicoloured	95	40
1102	–	100p. multicoloured	1·40	70

DESIGN: 100p. Different view of Sanatorium.

1971. Air. 16th Baalbek Festival.

1103	**208**	15p. orange and blue	15	15
1104	–	85p. black, blue & orange	95	60

DESIGN: 85p. Corinthian capital.

209 Field-gun

1971. Air. Army Day. Multicoloured.

1105	15p. Type **209**	35	15
1106	25p. Dassault Mirage IIICJ jet fighters	60	25
1107	40p. Army Command H.Q.	95	40
1108	70p. "Tarablous" (naval patrol boat)	1·90	85

210 Interior Decoration

212 U.N. Emblem

211 Lenin

1971. Air. 2nd Anniv of Burning of Al-Aqsa Mosque, Jerusalem.

1109	**210**	15p. brown and deep brown	50	15
1110		35p. brown and deep brown	1·10	50

1971. Air. Birth Centenary of Lenin. Mult.

1111	30p. Type **211**	50	25
1112	70p. Lenin in profile	1·10	70

1971. Air. 25th Anniv of United Nations.

1113	**212**	15p. multicoloured	15	10
1114		85p. multicoloured	1·10	60

213 "Europa" Mosaic, Byblos

1971. Air. World Lebanese Union.

1115	**213**	10p. multicoloured	15	10
1116		40p. multicoloured	1·10	35

1972. Various stamps surch.

1117	5p. on 7p.50 (No. 922) (postage)	15	15
1118	5p. on 7p.50 (No. 958)	15	15
1119	25p. on 32p.50 (No. 872)	1·00	15
1120	5p. on 7p.50 (No. 1016) (air)	25	15
1121	100p. on 300p. (No. 881)	4·25	2·10
1122	100p. on 500p. (No. 882)	4·25	2·10
1123	200p. on 300p. (No. 881)	7·25	4·25

217 Morning Glory

218 Ornate Arches

1973. Air. Multicoloured.

1124	2p.50 Type **217**	10	10
1125	5p. Roses	15	10
1126	15p. Tulips	25	10
1127	25p. Lilies	40	10
1128	40p. Carnations	60	15
1129	50p. Iris	95	10
1130	70p. Apples	1·40	15
1131	75p. Grapes	1·40	15
1132	100p. Peaches	2·20	70
1133	200p. Pears	3·75	50
1134	300p. Cherries	5·00	1·10
1135	500p. Oranges	7·25	1·90

1973. Air. Lebanese Domestic Architecture.

1136	–	35p. multicoloured	60	15
1137	**218**	50p. multicoloured	85	35
1138	–	85p. multicoloured	1·40	50
1139	–	100p. multicoloured	1·50	70

DESIGNS: Nos. 1136 and 1138/39, Various Lebanese dwellings.

219 Girl with Lute

1973. Air. Ancient Costumes. Multicoloured.

1140	5p. Woman with rose	15	15
1141	10p. Shepherd	25	15
1142	20p. Horseman	25	20
1143	25p. Type **219**	40	20

220 Swimming

1973. Air. 5th Pan-Arab Schools' Games, Beirut. Multicoloured.

1144	5p. Type **220**	15	10
1145	10p. Running	15	10
1146	15p. Gymnastics	25	10
1147	20p. Volleyball	40	15
1148	25p. Basketball	40	15
1149	50p. Table-tennis	95	35
1150	75p. Handball	1·40	40
1151	100p. Football	2·20	1·30
MS1152	121 × 71 mm. No. 1151. Imperf	3·50	3·50

221 Brasilia

1973. Air. 150th Anniv of Brazil's Independence. Multicoloured.

1153	5p. Type **221**	15	15
1154	20p. Salvador (Bahia) in 1823	25	15
1155	25p. Map and Phoenician galley	40	15
1156	50p. Emperor Pedro I and Emir Fakhreddine II	1·00	40

222 Marquetry

223 Cedar of Lebanon

1973. Air. Lebanese Handicrafts. Multicoloured.

1157	10p. Type **222**	15	10
1158	20p. Weaving	25	10
1159	35p. Glass-blowing	50	15
1160	40p. Pottery	65	25
1161	50p. Metal-working	75	35
1162	70p. Cutlery-making	1·20	40
1163	85p. Lace-making	1·60	60
1164	100p. Handicrafts Museum	1·70	1·10

1974.

1165	**223**	50c. green, brown & orge	20	10

224 Camp Site and Emblems

1974. Air. 11th Arab Scout Jamboree, Smar-Jubeil, Lebanon. Multicoloured.

1166	2p.50 Type **224**	15	15
1167	5p. Scout badge and map	15	15
1168	7p.50 Map of Arab countries	35	15
1169	10p. Lord Baden-Powell and Baalbek	35	15
1170	15p. Guide and camp	35	15
1171	20p. Lebanese Guide and Scout badge	50	15
1172	25p. Scouts around campfire	75	15
1173	30p. Globe and Scout badge	85	35
1174	35p. Flags of participating countries	1·20	35
1175	50p. Scout chopping wood for old man	1·70	60

225 Mail Train

1974. Centenary of U.P.U. Multicoloured.

1176	5p.50 Type **225**	85	50
1177	20p. Container ship	60	15
1178	25p. Congress building, Lausanne, and U.P.U. H.Q., Berne	60	15
1179	50p. Mail plane	1·00	60

226 Congress Building, Sofar

227 "Mountain Road" (O. Onsi)

1974. Air. 25th Anniv of Arab Postal Union. Multicoloured.

1180	5p. Type **226**	15	15
1181	20p. View of Sofar	35	15
1182	25p. A.P.U. H.Q., Cairo	40	15
1183	50p. Ministry of Posts, Beirut	1·90	1·00

1974. Air. Lebanese Paintings. Multicoloured.

1184	50p. Type **227**	1·10	60
1185	50p. "Clouds" (M. Farroukh)	1·10	60
1186	50p. "Woman" (G. K. Gebran)	1·10	60
1187	50p. "Embrace" (C. Gemayel)	1·10	60
1188	50p. "Self-portrait" (H. Serour)	1·10	60
1189	50p. "Portrait" (D. Corm)	1·10	60

228 Hunter killing Lion

1974. Air. Hermel Excavations. Multicoloured.

1190	5p. Type **228**	15	10
1191	10p. Astarte	25	10
1192	25p. Dogs hunting boar	1·30	40
1193	35p. Greco-Roman tomb	2·75	1·40

229 Book Year Emblem

1974. Air. International Book Year (1972).

1194	**229**	5p. multicoloured	10	10
1195		10p. multicoloured	25	10
1196		25p. multicoloured	1·30	40
1197		35p. multicoloured	1·90	1·40

230 Magnifying Glass

231 Georgina Rizk in Lebanese Costume

1974. Air. Stamp Day. Multicoloured.

1198	5p. Type **230**	15	15
1199	10p. Linked posthorns	15	15
1200	15p. Stamp-printing	35	15
1201	20p. "Stamp" in mount	60	35

1974. Air. Miss Universe 1971 (Georgina Rizk). Multicoloured.

1202	5p. Type **231**	10	10
1203	20p. Head-and-shoulders portrait	60	25
1204	25p. Type **231**	75	35
1205	50p. As 20p.	1·60	1·10
MS1206	156 × 112 mm. Nos. 1202/5. Imperf	6·00	6·00

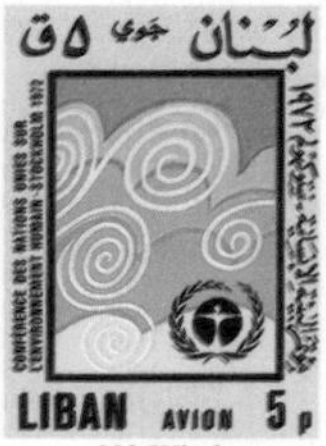
232 Winds

234 Discus-throwing

233 UNICEF Emblem and Sikorsky S-55 Helicopter

1974. Air. U.N. Conference on Human Environment, Stockholm, 1972. Multicoloured.

1207	5p. Type **232**	10	10
1208	25p. Mountains and plain	60	10
1209	30p. Trees and flowers	60	25
1210	40p. Sea	75	60
MS1211	153 × 113 mm. Nos. 1207/1210. Imperf	5·50	5·50

1974. Air. 25th Anniv of UNICEF. Multicoloured.
1212 20p. Type **233** 70 15
1213 25p. Emblem and child welfare clinic 35 15
1214 35p. Emblem and kindergarten class 70 25
1215 70p. Emblem and schoolgirls in laboratory . . . . . . 1·30 35
MS1216 158 × 112 mm. Nos. 1212/1215. Imperf . . . 4·25 4·25

1974. Air. Olympic Games, Munich (1972). Mult.
1217 5p. Type **234** 15 15
1218 10p. Putting the shot . . . 15 15
1219 15p. Weight-lifting 15 15
1220 35p. Running 70 35
1221 50p. Wrestling 85 35
1222 85p. Javelin-throwing . . . 1·70 50
MS1223 175 × 130 mm. Nos. 1217/22. Imperf . . . . . 6·00 6·00

235 Symbols of Archaeology

1975. Air. Beirut—"University City". Mult.
1224 20p. Type **235** 35 10
1225 25p. Science and medicine 35 15
1226 35p. Justice and commerce 70 50
1227 70p. Industry and commerce 1·40 70

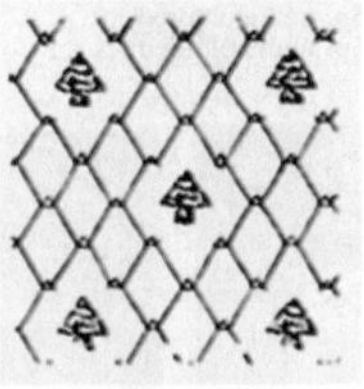
(236)

1978. Air. Various stamps optd with different patterns as T **236**. (a) Tourist Views. Nos. 1090, 1092/3.
1228 45p. Radar scanner, Beirut Airport . . . . 1·00 35
1229 70p. School of Sciences Building . . . . 2·10 40
1230 85p. Oranges . . . . 2·30 70

(b) Flowers and Fruits. Nos. 1124/35.
1231 2p.50 Type **217** 25 20
1232 5p. Roses 25 20
1233 15p. Tulips 50 20
1234 25p. Lilies . . . . 1·00 20
1235 40p. Carnations . . . . . . 1·00 35
1236 50p. Iris . . . . 1·40 35
1237 70p. Apples . . . . 2·10 40
1238 75p. Grapes . . . . 2·50 40
1239 100p. Peaches . . . . . . 2·75 85
1240 200p. Pears . . . . 6·00 2·50
1241 300p. Cherries . . . . . . 8·50 4·25
1242 500p. Oranges . . . . . . 12·50 6·75

(c) Lebanese Domestic Architecture. Nos. 1136/9.
1243 – 35p. multicoloured . . . 1·20 20
1244 **218** 50p. multicoloured . . . 1·20 35
1245 – 85p. multicoloured . . . 2·30 70
1246 – 100p. multicoloured . . 2·75 85

(d) Ancient Costumes. Nos. 1140/3.
1247 5p. Woman with rose . . . 25 20
1248 10p. Shepherd 35 20
1249 20p. Horseman 60 20
1250 25p. Type **219** . . . . . . 1·10 20

(e) Lebanese Handicrafts. Nos. 1157/8, 1160/4.
1251 10p. Type **222** 20 20
1252 20p. Weaving 60 20
1253 40p. Pottery . . . . 1·00 35
1254 50p. Metal-working . . . . 1·70 35
1255 70p. Cutlery-making . . . . 2·10 40
1256 85p. Lace-making . . . . . 2·30 70
1257 100p. Handicraft Museum 2·75 85

237 Mikhail Naimy (poet) and View of al-Chakroub Baskinta

1978. Air. Mikhail Naimy Festival Week. Mult.
1258 25p. Mikhail Naimy and Sannine mountains . . . 35 10
1259 50p. Type **237** 70 35
1260 75p. Mikhail Naimy (vert) 1·10 60

238 Heart and Arrow

239 Army Badge

1978. Air. World Health Day. "Down with Blood Pressure".
1261 **238** 50p. blue, red and black 1·00 50

1980. Army Day. Multicoloured.
1262 25p. Type **239** (postage) . . 50 25
1263 50p. Statue of Emir Fakhr el Dine on horseback (air) 85 35
1264 75p. Soldiers with flag (horiz) . . . . 1·30 35

240 13th-century European King

1980. Air. 50th Anniv (1974) of International Chess Federation. Multicoloured.
1265 50p. Rook, knight and Jubilee emblem (horiz) . . 1·30 85
1266 75p. Type **240** . . . . . . 2·10 1·70
1267 100p. Rook and Lebanon Chess Federation emblem 3·50 2·50
1268 150p. 18th-century French rook, king and knight . . 4·75 3·50
1269 200p. Painted faience rook, queen and bishop . . . . 6·00 4·25

241 Congress, U.P.U. and Lebanon Post Emblems

1981. Air. 18th U.P.U. Congress, Rio de Janeiro (1979).
1270 **241** 25p. blue, brown and black . . . . 1·30 60
1271 50p. pink, brown & black . . . . 2·10 1·10
1272 75p. green, brown and black . . . . 3·50 1·70

242 Children on Raft

1981. Air. International Year of the Child (1979).
1273 **242** 100p. multicoloured . . 4·25 2·50

243 President Sarkis

1981. 5th Anniv of Election of President Sarkis.
1274 **243** 125p. multicoloured . . 1·30 70
1275 300p. multicoloured . . 3·75 1·50
1276 500p. multicoloured . . 6·25 2·10

244 Society Emblem and Children

1981. Air. Centenary (1978) of Al-Makassed Islamic Welfare Society. Multicoloured.
1277 50p. Type **244** 70 15
1278 75p. Institute building . . . 1·00 25
1279 100p. Al-Makassed (founder) . . . . 1·30 40

245 Stork carrying Food

1982. World Food Day (1981). Multicoloured.
1280 50p. Type **245** 75 25
1281 75p. Ear of wheat and globe 1·20 35
1282 100p. Fruit, fish and grain 1·50 60

246 W.C.Y. Emblem

247 Phoenician Galley flying Scout Flag

1983. World Communications Year.
1283 **246** 300p. multicoloured . . 3·75 1·90

1983. 75th Anniv of Boy Scout Movement. Multicoloured.
1284 200p. Type **247** . . . . . 2·50 1·30
1285 300p. Scouts lowering flag and signalling by semaphore . . . . 3·50 1·70
1286 500p. Camp . . . . 6·25 2·50

248 "The Soul is Back"

1983. Birth Centenary of Gibran (poet and painter). Multicoloured.
1287 200p. Type **248** . . . . . 2·50 1·30
1288 300p. "The Family" . . . . 3·50 1·70
1289 500p. "Gibran" . . . . . . 6·25 2·50
1290 1000p. "The Prophet" . . . 12·00 6·25
MS1291 130 × 151 mm. Nos. 1287/90. Imperf (sold at L£25) . . . . 36·00 36·00

249 Cedar of Lebanon

250 Iris

1984.
1292 **249** 5p. multicoloured . . . 50 10

1984. Flowers. Multicoloured.
1293 10p. Type **250** 35 15
1294 25p. Periwinkle 60 35
1295 50p. Barberry . . . . 1·30 50

251 Dove with Laurel over Buildings

1984. Lebanese Army. Multicoloured.
1296 75p. Type **251** . . . . . . 1·30 50
1297 150p. Cedar and soldier holding rifle . . . . . . 2·50 1·20
1298 300p. Broken chain, hand holding laurel wreath and cedar . . . . 6·25 2·50

252 Temple Ruins, Fakra

1984. Multicoloured.
1299 100p. Type **252** . . . . . 1·30 50
1300 200p. Temple ruins, Bziza 2·50 1·20
1301 500p. Roman arches and relief, Tyre . . . . 6·25 1·70

253 President taking Oath

1988. Installation of President Amin Gemayel.
1302 **253** L£25 multicoloured . . . 85 60

254 Map of South America and Cedar of Lebanon

1988. 1st World Festival of Lebanese Youth in Uruguay.
1303 **254** L£5 multicoloured . . . 35 15

255 Satellite, Flags and Earth

256 Children

1988. "Arabsat" Telecommunications Satellite.
1304 **255** L£10 multicoloured . . . 50 35

1988. UNICEF Child Survival Campaign.
1305 **256** L£15 multicoloured . . . 85 50

257 Arabic "75" and Scout Emblems

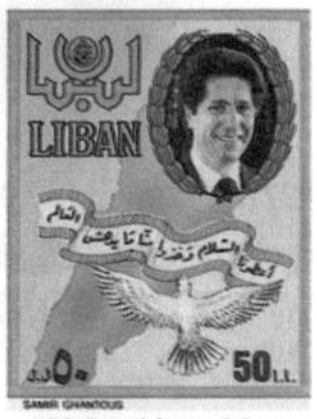
258 President, Map and Dove

1988. 75th Anniv (1987) of Arab Scouts Movement.
1306 **257** L£20 multicoloured . . . 1·00 60

1988. International Peace Year (1986).
1307 **258** L£50 multicoloured . . . 1·70 85

259 Red Cross and Figures

260 Cedar of Lebanon

1988. Red Cross.
1308 **259** L£10+L£1 red, silver and black 50 35
1309 – L£20+L£2 multicoloured 85 60
1310 – L£30+L£3 silver, green and red . . . . 1·40 85
DESIGNS: L£20, Helmeted heads; L£30, Globe, flame, and dove holding map of Lebanon.

1989.
1311 **260** L£50 green and mauve . . . 35 15
1312 L£70 green and brown . . . 50 25
1313 L£100 green and yellow . . . 85 40
1314 L£200 green and blue . . 1·70 85
1315 L£500 deep green & green . . . . 4·75 2·10

261 Dining in the Open at Zahle, 1883

1993. 50th Anniv of Independence. Multicoloured.
1316 L£200 Type **261** 85 70
1317 L£300 Castle ruins, Saida (vert) . . . . 1·70 1·20
1318 L£500 Presidential Palace, Baabda . . . . 2·50 1·70
1319 L£1000 Sword ceremony (vert) . . . . 4·25 2·50
1320 L£3000 Model for the rebuilding of central Beirut . . . . 8·50 5·00
1321 L£5000 President Elias Hrawi and state flag (vert) 17·00 10·00
MS1322 130 × 149 mm. L£10000 As Nos. 1319/24 but smaller and without face values. Imperf . . 25·00 25·00

262 Protection of Plants

263 Martyrs' Monument, Beirut

1994. Environmental Protection. Multicoloured.
1323 L£100 Type **262** 40 25
1324 L£200 Protection against forest fires 60 40
1325 L£500 Reforesting with cedars . . . . 1·50 1·00
1326 L£1000 Creation of urban green zones . . . . 3·00 2·10
1327 L£2000 Trees . . . . 5·00 3·50
1328 L£5000 Green tree in town 15·00 10·00

1995. Martyrs' Day.
1329 **263** L£1500 multicoloured . . 5·00 5·00

264 Arabic Script under Magnifying Glass and Headquarters

1996. Anniversaries and Events. Multicoloured.
1330 L£100 Type **264** (inauguration of Postal Museum, Arab League Headquarters, Cairo) . . 40 40
1331 L£500 Anniversary emblem (50th anniv of UNICEF) (horiz) . . . . 2·10 2·10
1332 L£500 Ears of wheat and anniversary emblem (50th anniv (1995) of F.A.O.) 2·10 2·10
1333 L£1000 U.N. Building (New York) and anniversary emblem (50th anniv (1995) of U.N.O.) . . . . 4·25 4·25
1334 L£1000 Emblem (International Year of the Family (1994)) (horiz) . . 4·25 4·25
1335 L£2000 Anniversary emblem (75th anniv (1994) of I.L.O.) (horiz) . . . . . 8·50 8·50
1336 L£2000 Emblem (50th anniv of Arab League) . . . . 8·50 8·50
1337 L£3000 Emblem (75th anniv (1994) of Lebanese Law Society) . . . . 12·50 12·50
1338 L£3000 Rene Moawad (former President, 70th birth anniv (1995)) . . . 12·50 12·50

265 Commemorative Medallion

1997. 1st Anniv of Shelling of Cana Refugee Camp.
1339 **265** L£1100 multicoloured . . 6·75 6·75

266 Pope John Paul II and President Hrawi

1998. Papal Visit.
1340 **266** L£10000 multicoloured 65·00 65·00

1999. Various stamps optd with a Fleuon values unchanged. Original numbers given.
1341 L£100 multicoloured (No. 1330) . . . . 2·00 2·00
1342 L£200 multicoloured (No. 1316) . . . . 4·25 4·25
1343 L£500 multicoloured (No. 1318) . . . . 10·50 10·50
1344 L£500 multicoloured (No. 1319) . . . . 10·50 10·50
1346 L£500 multicoloured (No. 1331) . . . . 10·50 10·50
1347 L£500 multicoloured (No. 1332) . . . . 10·50 10·50
1348 L£1000 multicoloured (No. 1326) . . . . 21·00 21·00
1349 L£1000 multicoloured (No. 1333) . . . . 21·00 21·00
1350 L£1100 multicoloured (No. 1339) . . . . 25·00 25·00
1351 L£1500 multicoloured (No. 1329) . . . . 32·00 32·00
1352 L£2000 multicoloured (No. 1335) . . . . 32·00 32·00
1353 L£3000 multicoloured (No. 1337) . . . . 65·00 65·00
1354 L£5000 multicoloured (No. 1328) £110 £110
1355 L£10000 multicoloured (No. 1340) £225 £225

268 Cedar of Lebanon

1999.
1356 **268** L£100 red 25 25
1359 L£300 turquoise . . . . 1·10 1·10
1357 L£500 grey 70 70
1358 L£1000 blue . . . . . . 2·10 2·10
1360 L£1100 brown . . . . . 2·40 2·40
1361 L£1500 violet . . . . . 17·00 17·00

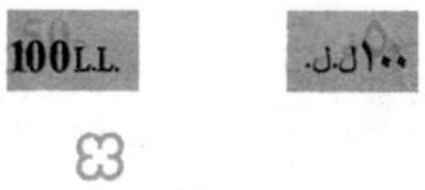
(269)

(270)

1999. Nos. 1295/6 surch as T **269**. No. 1092 surch as T **270**.
1368 L£100 on L£50 multicoloured 50 50
1369 L£300 on L£75 multicoloured . . . . . . 1·20 1·20
1370 L£1100 on L£70 multicoloured . . . . . . 4·25 4·25

271 Emir Chehab's Palace, Hasbaya

272 Flag and Soldiers

1999. Buildings. Multicoloured.
1371 L£100 Type **271** 40 40
1372 L£300 UN Economic and Social Commission for Western Asia, Beirut . . . 85 85
1373 L£500 Emir Fakhreddine's Palace, Deir-el-Kamar (horiz) . . . . 1·70 1·70
1374 L£1100 Grand Serail, Beirut (horiz) . . . . 3·75 3·75

1999. Nos. 1335 and 1338 optd with a Fleuron, values unchanged.
1375 L£2000 multicoloured . . . 8·50 8·50
1376 L£3000 multicoloured . . . 12·50 12·50

2001. Return of South Lebanon (1st series).
1377 **272** L£1100 multicoloured . . 2·40 2·40
See also No. **MS**1991.

273 Ibrahim Abd el Al

2001. 93rd Birth Anniv of Ibrahim Abd el Al (engineer).
1378 **273** L£1000 multicoloured . . 2·30 2·30

274 Hand and Bars

2001. Prisoners.
1379 **274** L£500 multicoloured . . 1·10 1·10

275 Emblem

2001. SOS Children's Villages.
1380 **275** L£300 multicoloured . . 70 70

276 Hand holding "50"

2001. 50th Anniversaries.
1381 **276** L£500 olive (Geneva Convention) . . . . . 1·10 1·10
1382 – L£1100 lilac (Geneva Convention) . . . . . 2·10 2·10
1383 – L£1500 multicoloured (Red Cross and Red Crescent) . . . . . 3·25 3·25
DESIGNS: L£500 Type **276**; L£1100 Fist around bars and "50"; L£1500 Hand holding stylized people.

277 Ahas Abu Chabke

2001. 97th Birth Anniv of Ahas Abu Chabke (writer).
1384 **277** L£1500 multicoloured . . 3·00 3·00

278 Father Monnot and Emblem

2001. 125th Anniv of Saint Joseph University, Beirut.
1385 **278** L£5000 multicoloured . . 10·00 10·00

279 Abdallah Zakher

2001. 319th Birth Anniv of Abdallah Zakher (first Arab printer).
1386 **279** L£1000 multicoloured . . 2·10 2·10

280 UN Emblem

2001. 25th. Anniv of UN Economic and Social Commission for Western Asia.
1387 **280** L£10000 ultramarine, blue and mauve . . . 21·00 21·00

281 Arabic Script

2002. Day of the Arab Woman.
1388 **281** L£1000 multicoloured . . 2·10 2·10

282 Emblem

2002. Arab Summit Conference, Beirut. Multicoloured.
1389 L£2000 Type **282** . . . . . 4·25 4·25
1390 L£3000 Cedar tree and Pres. Emile Lahoud . . . . . 6·25 6·25

283 Pres. Emile Lahoud

2002. Return of Southern Lebanon (2nd series). Sheet 160 × 108 mm containing T **283** and similar vert designs. Multicoloured.
MS1391 L£1100 × 4 Type **283**; Pres. Lahoud with raised arm; Pres. Lahoud and map; Sword ceremony . . . . 10·00 10·00

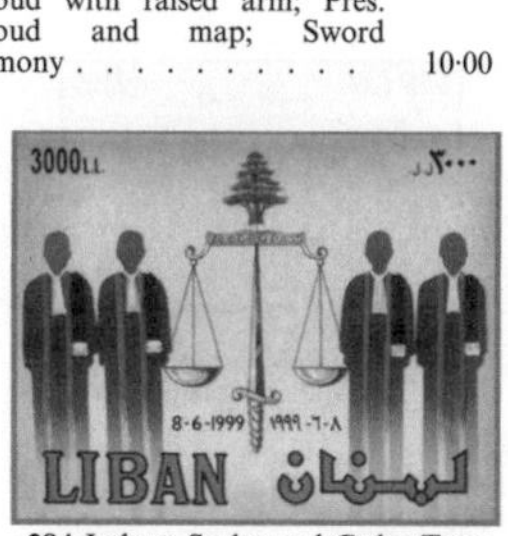
284 Judges, Scales and Cedar Tree

2002. Martyrs. Sheet 120 × 90 mm.

MS1392	**284**	L£3000 multicoloured	6·25	6·25

285 UPU Emblem and Cedar Tree

2002. 125th Anniv of Universal Postal Union.

1393	**285**	L£2000 multicoloured . .	3·50	3·50

286 Men seated at Table, Zouk Mikael

2002. Souks. Multicoloured.

1394	L£100 Type **286**	15	15
1395	L£300 Vendor with wheeled stall, Saida Souk	50	50
1396	L£500 Byblos (UNESCO world heritage site) . . .	85	85
1397	L£1000 Carpet mender, Tripoli	1·70	1·70

287 Emblem and National Colours

2002. 9th Francophile States Summit, Beirut. Multicoloured.

1398	L£1500 Type **287**	2·50	2·50
1399	L£1500 Pres. Lahoud . . .	2·50	2·50

288 Emblem

2002. Beirut, Arab Culture Capital, 2002.

1400	**288**	L£2000 multicoloured . .	3·50	3·50

289 Roman Temple, Bziza

2002. Ruins. Multicoloured.

1401	L£1100 Type **289**	1·70	1·70
1402	L£1500 Arqa	2·50	2·50
1403	L£2000 Niha	3·50	3·50
1404	L£3000 Castle, Mousailaha	6·25	6·25

290 Lebanese Amber

2002. Fossils. Multicoloured.

1405	L£5000 Type **290**	10·00	10·00
1406	L£10000 *Nematonotus longispinus*	20·00	20·00

291 Tree, Signatures, Lebanese and French Leaders

2003. 60th Anniv of Independence. Multicoloured.

1407	L£1250 Type **291**	90	90
1408	L£1250 Tree, signatures and parade	90	90
1409	L£1750 Tree, signatures and dignitaries	1·30	1·30
1410	L£1750 Tree and signatures	1·30	1·30
MS1411	160 × 110 mm. L£6000 Nos. 1407/10. Imperf	4·25	4·25

292 Postal Building before Restoration, Riad El Solh–Beirut

2004. Restoration of Posts and Telecommunications Buildings. Multicoloured.

1412	L£100 Type **292**	10	10
1413	L£300 Restored building . .	20	20

293 Snow Scene, Faqra

2004. Tourism.

1414	**293**	L£500 multicoloured . .	35	35

294 Musical Score and Emblem

2004. Al Bustan Music Festival, Riad El Solh–Beirut.

1415	**294**	L£1000 multicoloured . .	70	70

295 Kamouaa

2004. Tourism. Ski Resorts. Multicoloured.

1416	L£100 Type **295**	10	10
1417	L£100 Aayoun Siman . . .	10	10
1418	L£250 Laklouk (vert) . . .	20	20
1419	L£300 Zaarour	20	20
1420	L£300 Kanat Bakish	20	20
1421	L£1000 Cedres	70	70

296 Anniversary Emblem and Hospital (½-size illustration)

2004. 125th Anniv of St. Georges Hospital, Beirut.

1422	**296**	L£3000 multicoloured . .	2·20	2·20

297 Baalbeck International Festival

2004. Festivals. Multicoloured.

1423	L£500 Type **297**	35	35
1424	L£1250 Tyre (vert)	90	90
1425	L£1400 Beiteddine (vert) . .	1·00	1·00
1426	L£1750 Byblos (vert) . . .	1·30	1·30

POSTAGE DUE STAMPS

1924. Postage Due stamps of France surch **GRAND LIBAN** and value in "CENTIEMES" or "PIASTRES".

D26	D **11**	50c. on 10c. brown . .	1·90	3·00
D27		1p. on 20c. green . . .	3·50	10·50
D28		2p. on 30c. red	2·50	8·00
D29		3p. on 50c. purple . . .	2·30	7·50
D30		5p. on 1f. purple on yellow	1·40	5·25

1924. Postage Due stamps of France surch **Gd Liban** and value in French and Arabic.

D58	D **11**	0p.50 on 10c. brown . .	95	5·50
D59		1p. on 20c. green . . .	1·60	5·00
D60		2p. on 30c. red	1·30	4·00
D61		3p. on 50c. purple . . .	1·30	5·50
D62		5p. on 1f. purple on yell	70	6·00

D **7** Nahr el-Kalb

1925.

D75	D **7**	0p.50 brown on yellow	1·10	3·00
D76	–	1p. red on pink	90	4·25
D77	–	2p. black on blue . . .	2·00	3·25
D78	–	3p. brown on orange . .	2·30	7·00
D79	–	5p. black on green . . .	1·70	6·50

DESIGNS—HORIZ: 1p. Pine Forest, Beirut; 2p. Pigeon Grotto, Beirut; 3p. Beaufort Castle; 5p. Baalbeck.

1927. Optd **Republique Libanaise**.

D122	D **7**	0p.50 brown on yellow	40	3·25
D123	–	1p. red on pink	60	4·25
D124	–	2p. black on blue . . .	1·90	5·50
D125	–	3p. brown on orange	2·00	4·00
D126	–	5p. black on green . .	3·25	9·75

1928. Nos. D122/6 optd with T **10**.

D145	D **7**	0p.50 brown on yellow	2·00	4·25
D146	–	1p. red on pink	1·90	5·00
D147	–	2p. black on blue . . .	1·80	5·00
D148	–	3p. brown on orange	2·30	8·50
D149	–	5p. black on green . .	2·75	12·50

D **18**

D **19** Bas-relief from Sarcophagus of King Ahiram at Byblos

D **32**

1931.

D191	D **18**	0p.50 black on pink	80	1·60
D192	–	1p. black on blue . .	1·60	1·00
D193	–	2p. black on yellow . .	2·30	1·80
D194	–	3p. black on green . .	3·25	2·30
D195	D **32**	5p. black on orange	8·75	10·00
D196	D **19**	8p. black on pink . .	5·50	6·75
D252	D **32**	10p. green	9·75	11·00
D197	–	15p. black	3·75	5·00

DESIGNS: 1p. Bas-relief of Phoenician galley; 2p. Arabesque; 3p. Garland; 15p. Statuettes.

D **43** National Museum

1945.

D298	D **43**	2p. black on lemon . .	3·00	2·40
D299		5p. blue on pink . . .	3·50	2·75
D300		25p. blue on green . .	5·00	4·00
D301		50p. purple on blue . .	6·00	4·75

D **53**

1947.

D352	D **53**	5p. black on green . .	4·75	1·20
D353		25p. black on yellow	47·00	3·00
D354		50p. black on blue . .	25·00	7·50

D **59** Monument at Hermel

1948.

D379	D **59**	2p. black on yellow . .	3·00	75
D380		3p. black on pink . .	6·75	2·75
D381		10p. black on blue . .	17·00	5·00

D **67**

1950.

D416	D **67**	1p. red	85	15
D417		5p. blue	4·25	70
D418		10p. green	6·00	1·40

D **78**

1952.

D464	D **78**	1p. mauve	25	10
D465		2p. violet	40	20
D466		3p. green	50	20
D467		5p. blue	75	25
D468		10p. brown	1·40	50
D469		25p. black	11·00	1·20

D **81** D **93**

1953.

D481	D **81**	1p. red	15	10
D482		2p. green	15	15
D483		3p. orange	15	15
D484		5p. purple	25	20
D485		10p. brown	75	25
D486		15p. blue	1·40	60

1955.

D550	D **93**	1p. brown	15	15
D551		2p. green	15	15
D552		3p. turquoise	15	15
D553		5p. purple	15	15
D554		10p. green	50	20
D555		15p. blue	50	20
D556		25p. purple	1·30	70

D **178** D **184** Emir Fakhreddine II

1967.

D967	D **178**	1p. green	10	10
D968		5p. mauve	15	15
D969		15p. blue	35	40

1968.

D1004	D **184**	1p. slate and grey	10	10
D1005		2p. turquoise & green	10	10
D1006		3p. orange & yellow	10	15
D1007		5p. purple and red	10	15
D1008		10p. olive and yellow	15	15
D1009		15p. blue and violet	35	35
D1010		25p. blue & lt blue	60	55

POSTAL TAX STAMPS

These were issued between 1945 and 1962 for compulsory use on inland mail (and sometimes on mail to Arab countries) to provide funds for various purposes.

T 41

(T 42)

1945. Lebanese Army. Fiscal stamp as Type T 41 surch with Type T **42**.

T289	T **41**	5p. on 30c. brown	£500	2·40

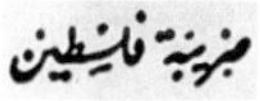
(T 50)

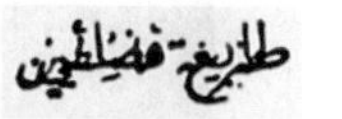
(T 51)

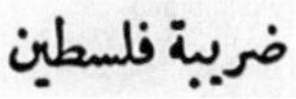

(T 52)

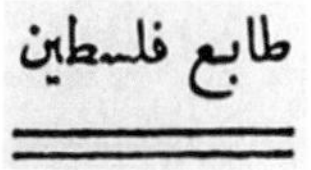

(T 56 "Palestine stamp")

1947. Aid to War in Palestine. Surch as Type T **42**.

(a) With top line Type T **50**.

T338	T **41**	5p. on 25c. green	21·00	1·70
T339		5p. on 30c. brown	27·00	3·50
T340		5p. on 60c. blue	42·00	2·40
T341		5p. on 3p. pink	21·00	3·00
T342		5p. on 15p. blue	21·00	1·20

(b) With top line Type T **51**.

T343	T **41**	5p. on 10p. red	85·00	4·00

(c) With top line Type T **52**.

T344	T **41**	5p. on 3p. pink	21·00	1·70

(d) As No. T344 but with figure "5" at left instead of "0" and without inscr between figures.

T345	T **41**	5p. on 3p. pink	£375	22·00

1948. Palestine Aid. No. T289 optd with Type T **56**.

T363	T **41**	5p. on 30c. brown	21·00	2·20

T **95** Family and Ruined House

1956. Earthquake Victims.

T559	T **95**	2p.50 brown	3·00	20

T **99** Rebuilding

T **100** Rebuilding

1957. Earthquake Victims.

T601	T **99**	2p.50 brown	3·00	20
T602		2p.50 green	1·40	20
T603	T **100**	2p.50 brown	2·10	10

T **132** Rebuilding

T **133** Rebuilding

1961. Earthquake Victims.

T729	T **132**	2p.50 brown	1·70	10
T730	T **133**	2p.50 blue	1·40	10

LEEWARD ISLANDS Pt.1

A group of islands in the Br. W. Indies, including Antigua, Barbuda, British Virgin Islands, Dominica (till end of 1939), Montserrat, Nevis and St. Christopher (St. Kitts). Stamps of Leeward Islands were used concurrent with the issues for the respective islands until they were withdrawn on the 1 July 1956.

1890. 12 pence = 1 shilling;
20 shillings = 1 pound.
1951. 100 cents = 1 West Indian dollar.

1

(3)

1890.

1	**1**	½d. mauve and green	3·50	1·25
2		1d. mauve and red	4·00	20
3		2½d. mauve and blue	5·00	20
4		4d. mauve and orange	4·75	8·50
5		6d. mauve and brown	11·00	13·00
6		7d. mauve and grey	5·00	12·00
7		1s. green and red	20·00	50·00
8		5s. green and blue	£120	£250

1897. Diamond Jubilee. Optd with T **3**.

9	**1**	½d. mauve and green	4·25	14·00
10		1d. mauve and red	4·75	14·00
11		2½d. mauve and blue	5·00	14·00
12		4d. mauve and orange	38·00	70·00
13		6d. mauve and brown	50·00	90·00
14		7d. mauve and grey	50·00	90·00
15		1s. green and red	£120	£190
16		5s. green and blue	£450	£750

1902. Surch **One Penny**.

17	**1**	1d. on 4d. mauve and orange	3·50	5·50
18		1d. on 6d. mauve and brown	4·50	11·00
19		1d. on 7d. mauve and grey	4·00	7·50

1902. As T **1**, but portrait of King Edward VII.

29		½d. purple and green	3·50	2·00
21		1d. purple and red	7·00	20
22		2d. purple and brown	2·75	4·25
23		2½d. purple and blue	5·50	2·25
24		3d. purple and black	4·75	7·50
25		6d. purple and brown	2·50	8·00
26		1s. green and red	3·50	19·00
27		2s.6d. green and black	27·00	70·00
28		5s. green and blue	48·00	75·00

1907. As last, but colours changed.

36		¼d. brown	2·75	1·75
37		½d. green	3·50	1·25
38		1d. red	10·00	80
39		2d. grey	3·50	7·50
40		2½d. blue	7·00	4·25
41		3d. purple and yellow	3·50	7·50
42		6d. purple	8·50	7·00
43		1s. black on green	5·50	21·00
44		2s.6d. black and red on blue	40·00	48·00
45		5s. green and red on yellow	42·00	65·00

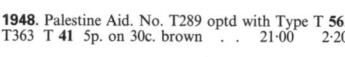

10 King George V

14 King George VI

1912.

46	**10**	¼d. brown	1·75	1·00
59		½d. green	1·00	75
60		1d. red	2·25	55
61		1d. violet	2·25	1·00
63		1½d. red	3·25	2·00
64		1½d. brown	1·25	10
65		2d. grey	2·00	80
67		2½d. blue	3·50	1·25
66		2½d. yellow	6·50	50·00
69		3d. purple on yellow	1·50	6·50
68		3d. blue	4·75	26·00
70		4d. black and red on yellow	3·00	21·00
71		5d. purple and green	2·50	4·25
53		6d. purple	3·00	8·00
54		1s. black on green	3·00	8·00
74a		2s. purple and blue on blue	7·50	48·00
75		2s.6d. black and red on blue	6·50	23·00
76		3s. green and violet	12·00	25·00
77		4s. black and red	12·00	42·00
57b		5s. green and red on yellow	28·00	70·00

Larger type, as T **15** of Malta.

79	**13**	10s. green and red on green	55·00	85·00
80		£1 purple and black on red	£225	£250

1935. Silver Jubilee. As T **14a** of Kenya, Uganda and Tanganyika.

88	1d. blue and red	1·60	1·50
89	1½d. blue and grey	2·25	70
90	2½d. brown and blue	2·25	3·50
91	1s. grey and purple	10·00	19·00

1937. Coronation. As T **14b** of Kenya, Uganda and Tanganyika.

92	1d. red	30	20
93	1½d. brown	70	70
94	2½d. blue	80	1·25

1938.

95a	**14**	¼d. brown	30	1·75
96		½d. green	70	70
97		½d. grey	1·00	1·50
99		1d. red	2·25	1·75
100		1d. green	55	15
101		1½d. brown	1·00	50
102		1½d. orange and black	85	40
103		2d. grey	3·00	1·25
104		2d. red	1·40	1·25
105a		2½d. blue	80	1·25
106		2½d. black and purple	55	15
107a		3d. orange	50	85
108		3d. blue	65	15
109a		6d. purple	6·50	2·25
110b		1s. black on green	4·25	1·00
111a		2s. purple and blue on blue	10·00	2·00
112b		5s. green and red on yellow	32·00	15·00
113c	–	10s. green and red on green	£120	75·00
114b	–	£1 purple and black on red	35·00	24·00

The 10s. and £1 are as Type **15** of Bermuda but with portrait of King George VI.

1946. Victory. As T **60** of Jamaica.

115	1½d. brown	15	50
116	3d. orange	15	50

1949. Silver Wedding. As T **61/2** of Jamaica.

117	2½d. blue	10	10
118	5s. green	4·25	3·25

1949. U.P.U. As T **63/66** of Jamaica.

119	2½d. black	15	1·75
120	3d. blue	2·00	1·75
121	6d. mauve	15	1·75
122	1s. turquoise	15	1·75

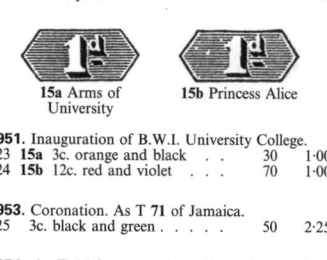

15a Arms of University

15b Princess Alice

1951. Inauguration of B.W.I. University College.

123	**15a**	3c. orange and black	30	1·00
124	**15b**	12c. red and violet	70	1·00

1953. Coronation. As T **71** of Jamaica.

125	3c. black and green	50	2·25

1954. As T **14** but portrait of Queen Elizabeth II facing left.

126	½c. brown	10	60
127	1c. grey	1·25	1·25
128	2c. green	1·75	10
129	3c. yellow and black	2·50	1·00
130	4c. red	1·75	10
131	5c. black and purple	2·25	1·00
132	6c. yellow	2·25	60
133	8c. blue	2·50	10
134	12c. purple	2·00	10
135	24c. black and green	2·00	20
136	48c. purple and blue	6·50	2·75
137	60c. brown and green	6·00	2·25
138	$1.20 green and red	5·00	3·25

Larger type as T **15** of Malta, but portrait of Queen Elizabeth II facing left.

139	$2.40 green and red	7·00	5·50
140	$4.80 purple and black	7·00	7·00

LESOTHO Pt. 1

Formerly Basutoland, attained independence on 4 October 1966 and changed its name to Lesotho.

1966. 100 cents = 1 rand.
1979. 100 lisente = 1 (ma)loti.

33 Moshoeshoe I and Moshoeshoe II

1966. Independence.

106	**33**	2½c. brown, black and red	10	10
107		5c. brown, black and blue	10	10
108		10c. brown, black and green	15	10
109		20c. brown, black and purple	20	15

1966. Nos. 69 etc. of Basutoland optd **LESOTHO**.

110A	**8**	½c. black and sepia	10	10
111A	–	1c. black and green	10	10
112A	–	2c. blue and orange	60	10
113B	**26**	2½c. sage and red	50	10
114A	–	3½c. indigo and blue	30	10
115A	–	5c. brown and green	10	10
116A	–	10c. bronze and purple	10	10
117B	–	12½c. brown and turquoise	30	20
118A	–	25c. blue and red	20	20
119B	–	50c. black and red	70	50
120B	**9**	1r. black and purple	65	75

35 "Education, Culture and Science"

36 Maize

1966. 20th Anniv of UNESCO.

121	**35**	2½c. yellow and green	10	10
122		5c. green and olive	15	10
123		12½c. blue and red	35	15
124		25c. orange and blue	60	75

1967.

125	**36**	½c. green and violet	10	10
126	–	1c. sepia and red	10	10
149	–	2c. yellow and green	10	10
128	–	2½c. black and ochre	10	10
151	–	3c. chocolate, green & brn	15	15
152	–	3½c. blue and yellow	15	10
130	–	5c. bistre and blue	20	10
131	–	10c. brown and grey	10	10
132	–	12½c. black and orange	20	10
133	–	25c. black and blue	55	20
134	–	50c. black, blue & turquoise	4·50	1·25
135	–	1r. multicoloured	65	75
136	–	2r. black, gold and purple	1·00	1·75

DESIGNS—HORIZ: 1c. Cattle; 2c. Aloes; 2½c. Basotho hat; 3c. Sorghum; 3½c. Merino sheep ("Wool"); 5c. Basotho pony; 10c. Wheat; 12½c. Angora goat ("Mohair"); 25c. Maletsunyane Falls; 50c. Diamonds; 1r. Arms of Lesotho. VERT: 2r. Moshoeshoe II.

See also Nos. 191/203.

46 Students and University

1967. 1st Conferment of University Degrees.

137	**46**	1c. sepia, blue and orange	10	10
138		2½c. sepia, ultramarine & bl	10	10
139		12½c. sepia, blue and red	10	10
140		25c. sepia, blue and violet	15	15

47 Statue of Moshoeshoe I

1967. 1st Anniv of Independence.

141	**47**	2½c. black and green	10	10
142	–	12½c. multicoloured	25	15
143	–	25c. black, green and ochre	35	25

DESIGNS: 12½c. National flag; 25c. Crocodile (national emblem).

50 Lord Baden-Powell and Scout Saluting

1967. 60th Anniv of Scout Movement.

144	**50**	15c. multicoloured	20	10

51 W.H.O. Emblem and World Map

1968. 20th Anniv of World Health Organization.

145	**51**	2½c. blue, gold and red	15	10
146	–	25c. multicoloured	45	60

DESIGN: 25c. Nurse and child.

55 Running Hunters

1968. Rock Paintings.

160	**55**	3c. brown, turquoise & grn	25	10
161	–	3½c. yellow, olive and sepia	30	10
162	–	5c. red, ochre and brown	35	10
163	–	10c. yellow, red and purple	45	10
164	–	15c. buff, yellow and brown	75	30
165	–	20c. green, yellow & brown	90	55
166	–	25c. yellow, brown & black	1·00	75

DESIGNS—HORIZ: 3½c. Baboons; 10c. Archers; 20c. Eland; 25c. Hunting scene. VERT: 5c. Javelin thrower; 15c. Blue cranes.

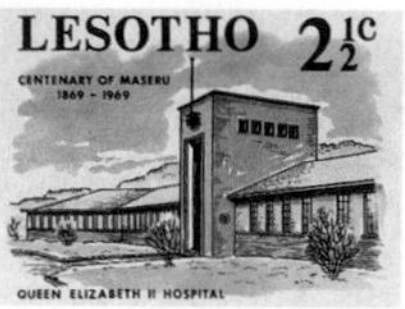

62 Queen Elizabeth II Hospital

1969. Centenary of Maseru (capital). Mult.

167	2½c. Type **62**	10	10
168	10c. Lesotho Radio Station	10	10

169	12½c. Leabua Jonathan Airport	35	10
170	25c. Royal Palace	25	15

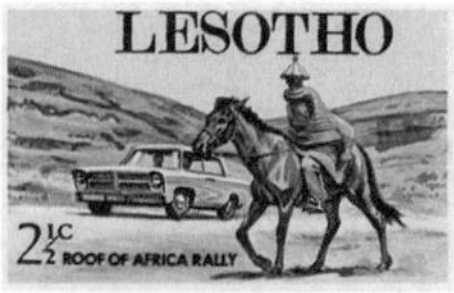

66 Rally Car passing Basuto Tribesman

1969. "Roof of Africa" Car Rally.

171	**66**	2½c. yellow, mauve & plum	15	10
172	–	12½c. blue, yellow and grey	20	10
173	–	15c. blue, black and mauve	20	10
174	–	20c. black, red and yellow	20	10

DESIGNS: 12½c. Rally car on mountain road; 15c. Chequered flags and "Roof of Africa" Plateau; 20c. Map of rally route and Independence Trophy.

71 Gryponyx and Footprints

1970. Prehistoric Footprints (1st series).

175	–	3c. brown and sepia	90	70
176	**71**	5c. purple, pink and sepia	1·10	30
177	–	10c. yellow, black and sepia	1·40	35
178	–	15c. yellow, black and sepia	2·00	2·25
179	–	25c. blue and black	2·75	2·25

DESIGNS: 3c. Dinosaur footprints at Moyeni; 10c. Plateosauravus and footprints; 15c. Tritylodon and footprints; 25c. Massospondylus and footprints.

No. 175 is larger, 60 × 23 mm.

See also Nos. 596/8.

75 Moshoeshoe I as a Young Man

1970. Death Centenary of Chief Moshoeshoe I.

180	**75**	2½c. green and mauve	10	10
181	–	25c. blue and brown	20	20

DESIGN: 25c. Moshoeshoe I as an old man.

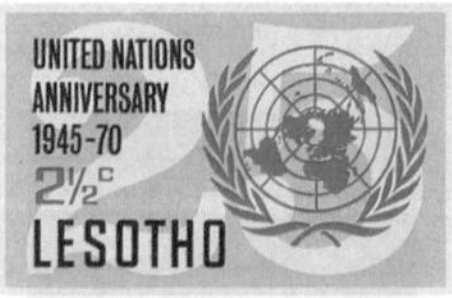

77 U.N. Emblem and "25"

1970. 25th Anniv of United Nations.

182	**77**	2½c. pink, blue and purple	10	10
183	–	10c. multicoloured	10	10
184	–	12½c. red, blue and drab	10	25
185	–	25c. multicoloured	15	65

DESIGNS: 10c. U.N. Building; 12½c. "People of the World"; 25c. Symbolic dove.

78 Gift Shop, Maseru

1970. Tourism. Multicoloured.

186	2½c. Type **78**	10	10
187	5c. Trout fishing	20	10
188	10c. Pony trekking	25	10
189	12½c. Skiing, Maluti Mountains	50	10
190	20c. Holiday Inn, Maseru	40	50

79 Maize **80** Lammergeier

1971. As Nos. 147/58 but in new format omitting portrait, as in T **79**. New designs for 4c., 2r.

191	**79**	½c. green and violet	10	10
192	–	1c. brown and red	10	10
193	–	2c. yellow and green	10	10
194	–	2½c. black, green & yellow	10	10
195	–	3c. brown, green & yellow	10	10
196	–	3½c. blue and yellow	10	10
196a	–	4c. multicoloured	20	10
197	–	5c. brown and blue	15	10
198	–	10c. brown and grey	15	10
199	–	12½c. brown and orange	25	30
200	–	25c. slate and blue	60	40
201	–	50c. black, blue and green	6·00	4·50
202	–	1r. multicoloured	1·25	1·75
401	–	2r. brown and blue	70	2·25

DESIGNS—HORIZ: 4c. National flag. VERT: 2r. Statue of Moshoeshoe I.

1971. Birds. Multicoloured.

204	2½c. Type **80**	2·50	20
205	5c. Bald ibis	3·50	2·50
206	10c. Orange-breasted rockjumper	3·50	2·00
207	12½c. Blue bustard ("Blue korhaan")	3·75	3·50
208	15c. Painted-snipe	4·25	4·50
209	20c. Golden-breasted bunting	4·25	4·50
210	25c. Ground woodpecker	4·75	4·50

81 Lionel Collett Dam

1971. Soil Conservation. Multicoloured.

211	4c. Type **81**	10	10
212	10c. Contour ridges	10	10
213	15c. Earth dams	25	10
214	25c. Beaver dams	35	35

82 Diamond Mining

1971. Development. Multicoloured.

215	4c. Type **82**	75	40
216	10c. Pottery	30	10
217	15c. Weaving	45	60
218	20c. Construction	55	1·50

83 Mail Cart

1972. Centenary of Post Office.

219	**83**	5c. brown and pink	15	20
220	–	10c. multicoloured	15	10
221	–	15c. blue, black and brown	20	15
222	–	20c. multicoloured	30	90

DESIGNS—HORIZ: 10c. Postal bus; 20c. Maseru Post Office. VERT: 15c. 4d. Cape of Good Hope stamp of 1876.

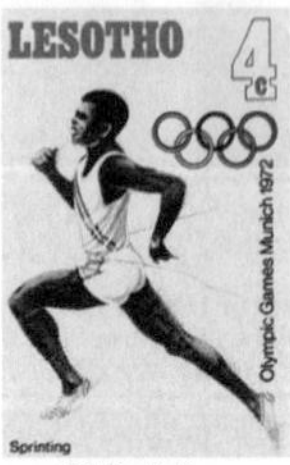

84 Sprinting

1972. Olympic Games, Munich. Multicoloured.

223	4c. Type **84**	15	10
224	10c. Shot putting	20	10
225	15c. Hurdling	30	10
226	25c. Long-jumping	35	55

85 "Adoration of the Shepherds" (Matthias Stomer)

1972. Christmas.

227	**85**	4c. multicoloured	10	10
228		10c. multicoloured	10	10
229		25c. multicoloured	15	20

86 W.H.O. Emblem

1973. 25th Anniv of W.H.O.

230	**86**	20c. yellow and blue	30	30

1973. O.A.U. 10th Anniv. Nos. 194 and 196a/8 optd **O.A.U. 10th Anniversary Freedom in Unity**.

231	2½c. black, green and brown	10	10
232	4c. multicoloured	10	10
233	5c. brown and blue	10	10
234	10c. brown and blue	15	15

88 Basotho Hat and W.F.P. Emblem

1973. 10th Anniv of World Food Programme. Multicoloured.

235	4c. Type **88**	10	10
236	15c. School feeding	20	15
237	20c. Infant feeding	20	20
238	25c. "Food for work"	25	25

89 "Aeropetes tulbaghia"

1973. Butterflies. Multicoloured.

239	4c. Type **89**	75	10
240	5c. "Papilio demodocus"	85	50
241	10c. "Cynthia cardui"	1·25	50
242	15c. "Precis hierta"	2·25	1·75
243	20c. "Precis oenone"	2·25	1·75
244	25c. "Danaus chrysippus"	2·50	2·75
245	30c. "Colotis evenina"	2·50	3·75

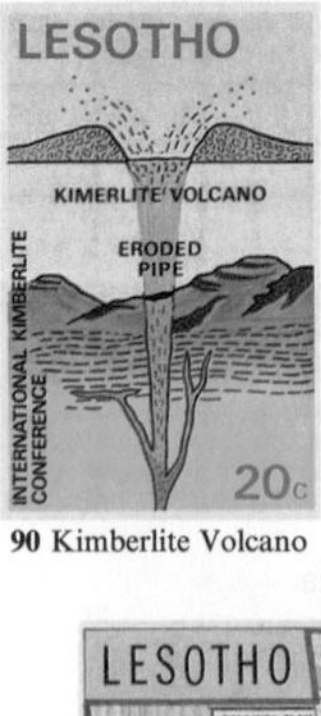

90 Kimberlite Volcano **92** Open Book and Wreath

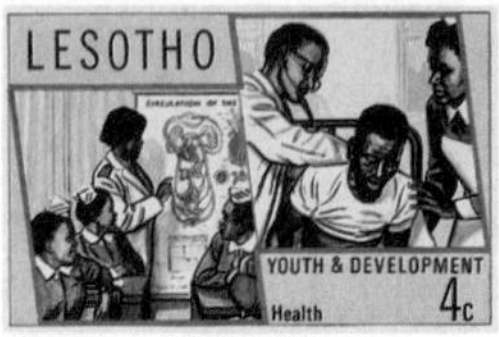

91 "Health"

1973. International Kimberlite Conference. Mult.

246	10c. Map of diamond mines (horiz)	2·00	50
247	15c. Kimberlite-diamond rock (horiz)	2·25	2·25
248	20c. Type **90**	2·25	2·50
249	30c. Diamond prospecting	3·75	7·00

1974. Youth and Development. Multicoloured.

250	4c. Type **91**	10	10
251	10c. "Education"	15	10
252	20c. "Agriculture"	20	10
253	25c. "Industry"	30	20
254	30c. "Service"	30	25

1974. 10th Anniv of U.B.L.S. Multicoloured.

255	10c. Type **92**	15	10
256	15c. Flags, mortar-board and scroll	20	20
257	20c. Map of Africa	25	25
258	25c. King Moshoeshoe II capping a graduate	25	65

93 Senqunyane River Bridge, Marakabei

1974. Rivers and Bridges. Multicoloured.

259	4c. Type **93**	10	10
260	5c. Tsoelike River and bridge	10	10
261	10c. Makhaleng River Bridge	20	10
262	15c. Seaka Bridge, Orange/Senqu River	35	35
263	20c. Masianokeng Bridge, Phuthiatsana River	40	40
264	25c. Mahobong Bridge, Hlotse River	45	45

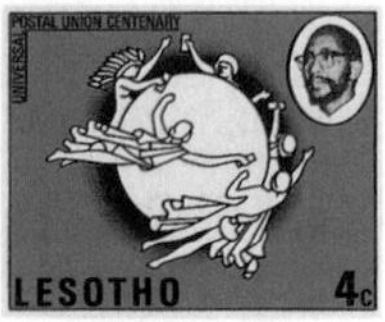

94 U.P.U. Emblem

1974. Centenary of U.P.U.

265	**94**	4c. green and black	10	10
266	–	10c. orange, yellow & black	15	10
267	–	15c. multicoloured	20	60
268	–	20c. multicoloured	45	85

DESIGNS: 10c. Map of airmail routes; 15c. Post Office H.Q., Maseru; 20c. Horseman taking rural mail.

95 Siege of Thaba-Bosiu

1974. 150th Anniv of Siege of Thaba-Bosiu. Multicoloured.

269	4c. Type **95**	10	10
270	5c. The wreath-laying	10	10
271	10c. Moshoeshoe I (vert)	25	10
272	20c. Makoanyane, the warrior (vert)	90	55

96 Mamokhorong

1974. Basotho Musical Instruments. Multicoloured.

273	4c. Type **96**	10	10
274	10c. Lesiba	10	10
275	15c. Setolotolo	15	20
276	20c. Meropa	15	20
MS277	108 × 92 mm. Nos. 273/6	1·00	2·00

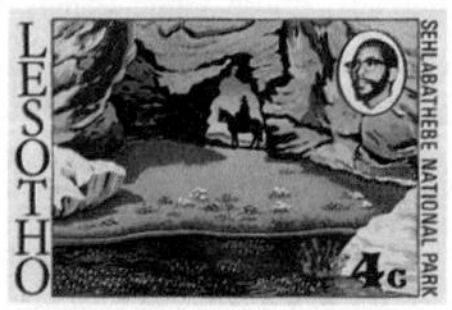

97 Horseman in Rock Archway

1975. Sehlabathebe National Park. Mult.

278	4c. Type **97**	30	10
279	5c. Mountain view through arch	30	10
280	15c. Antelope by stream	50	45
281	20c. Mountains and lake	50	50
282	25c. Tourists by frozen waterfall	65	75

98 Morena Moshoeshoe I   99 Mokhibo Dance

1975. Leaders of Lesotho.
283 **98** 3c. black and blue 10 10
284 – 4c. black and mauve . . . 10 10
285 – 5c. black and pink 10 10
286 – 6c. black and brown . . . 10 10
287 – 10c. black and red 10 10
288 – 15c. black and red 20 20
289 – 20c. black and green . . . 25 30
290 – 25c. black and blue 25 40
DESIGNS: 4c. King Moshoeshoe II; 5c. Morena Letsie I; 6c. Morena Lerotholi; 10c. Morena Letsie II; 15c. Morena Griffith; 20c. Morena Seeiso Griffith Lerotholi; 25c. Mofumahali Mantsebo Seeiso, O.B.E.
The 25c. also commemorates International Women's Year.

1975. Traditional Dances. Multicoloured.
291 4c. Type **99** 15 10
292 10c. Ndlamo 20 10
293 15c. Baleseli 35 75
294 20c. Mohobelo . . . . 40 1·25
MS295 111 × 100 mm. Nos. 291/4 3·75 3·50

100 Enrolment

1976. 25th Anniv of Lesotho Red Cross. Mult.
296 4c. Type **100** 50 10
297 10c. Medical aid 70 10
298 15c. Rural service . . . . . 1·00 1·25
299 25c. Relief supplies . . . . . 1·40 2·50

101 Tapestry

1976. Multicoloured.
300 2c. Type **101** 10 35
301 3c. Mosotho horseman . . . 20 30
302 4c. Map of Lesotho . . . . 1·50 10
303 5c. Lesotho Brown diamond 75 1·00
304 10c. Lesotho Bank 30 10
305 15c. Lesotho and O.A.U. flags . . . . 2·00 1·00
306 25c. Sehlabathebe National Park 60 35
307 40c. Pottery . . . . 60 1·00
308 50c. Prehistoric rock art . . . 2·75 2·00
309 1r. King Moshoeshoe II (vert) . . . . 60 1·75

102 Football   **103** "Rising Sun"

1976. Olympic Games, Montreal. Mult.
310 4c. Type **102** 15 10
311 10c. Weightlifting 15 10
312 15c. Boxing 35 35
313 25c. Throwing the discus . . 50 80

1976. 10th Anniv of Independence. Multicoloured.
314 4c. Type **103** 10 10
315 10c. Open gates 10 10
316 15c. Broken chains 40 20
317 25c. Britten Norman Islander aircraft over hotel 50 35

104 Telephones, 1876 and 1976

1976. Centenary of Telephone. Multicoloured.
318 4c. Type **104** 10 10
319 10c. Early handset and telephone-user, 1976 . . . 15 10
320 15c. Wall telephone and telephone exchange 25 20
321 25c. Stick telephone and Alexander Graham Bell . . 45 50

105 "Aloe striatula"   **106** Large-toothed Rock Hyrax

1977. Aloes and Succulents. Multicoloured.
322 3c. Type **105** 25 10
323 4c. "Aloe aristata" 25 10
324 5c. "Kniphofia caulescens" 25 10
325 10c. "Euphorbia pulvinata" 35 10
326 15c. "Aloe saponaria" . . . 1·00 30
327 20c. "Caralluma lutea" . . . 1·00 50
328 25c. "Aloe polyphylla" . . . 1·25 70
See also Nos. 347/54.

1977. Animals. Multicoloured.
329 4c. Type **106** . . . . 3·50 30
330 5c. Cape porcupine . . . . . 3·50 75
331 10c. Zorilla (polecat) . . . . 3·50 30
332 15c. Klipspringer . . . . . . 11·00 2·50
333 25c. Chacma baboon . . . . 12·00 3·75

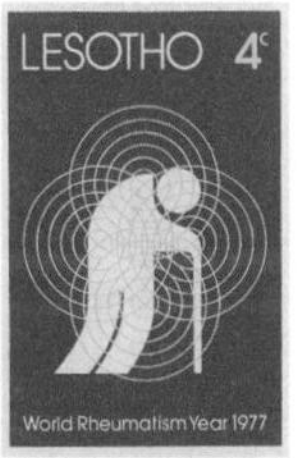

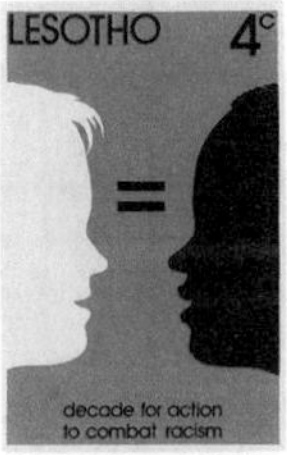

107 "Rheumatic Man"   **110** Black and White Heads

108 Small-mouthed Yellowfish

1977. World Rheumatism Year.
334 **107** 4c. yellow and red 10 10
335 – 10c. blue and deep blue 15 10
336 – 15c. yellow and blue . . . 30 10
337 – 25c. red and black 40 45
DESIGNS—Each show the "Rheumatic Man" as Type **107**: 10c. Surrounded by "pain"; 15c. Surrounded by "chain"; 25c. Supporting globe.

1977. Fish. Multicoloured.
338 4c. Type **108** 30 10
339 10c. Mudfish 45 10
340 15c. Rainbow trout . . . . . 1·00 35
341 25c. Barnard's mudfish . . . 1·10 60

1977. No. 198 surch **3**.
342 3c. on 10c. brown and blue 1·00 1·00

1977. Decade for Action to Combat Racism.
343 **110** 4c. black and mauve . . . 10 10
344 – 10c. black and blue . . . 10 10
345 – 15c. black and orange . . 15 15
346 – 25c. black and green . . . 25 25
DESIGNS: 10c. Jigsaw pieces; 15c. Cogwheels; 25c. Handshake.

1978. Flowers. As T **105**. Multicoloured.
347 2c. "Papaver aculeatum" . . 10 50
348 3c. "Diascia integerrima" . . 10 50
349 4c. "Helichrysum trilineatum" 10 10
350 5c. "Zaluzianskya maritima" 10 10
351 10c. "Gladiolus natalensis" 15 10
352 15c. "Chironia krebsii" . . . 20 40
353 25c. "Wahlenbergia undulata" . . . . 35 1·00
354 40c. "Brunsvigia radulosa" 65 2·00

111 Edward Jenner vaccinating Child   **112** Tsoloane Falls

1978. Global Eradication of Smallpox. Mult.
355 5c. Type **111** 25 35
356 25c. Head of child and W.H.O. emblem 75 90

1978. Waterfalls. Multicoloured.
357 4c. Type **112** 15 10
358 10c. Qiloane Falls 25 10
359 15c. Tsoelikana Falls 35 60
360 25c. Maletsunyane Falls . . . 55 1·75

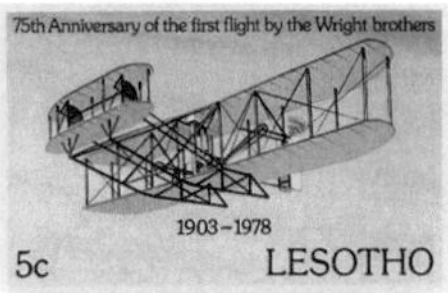

113 Wright Flyer III, 1903

1978. 75th Anniv of First Powered Flight. Mult.
361 5c. Type **113** 15 30
362 25c. Wilbur and Orville Wright 40 60

114 "Orthetrum farinosum"   **115** Oudehout Branch in Flower

1978. Insects. Multicoloured.
363 4c. Type **114** 10 10
364 10c. "Phymateus viridipes" 20 10
365 15c. "Belonogaster lateritis" 30 50
366 25c. "Sphodromantis gastrica" 50 90

1979. Trees. Multicoloured.
367 4c. Type **115** 15 10
368 10c. Wild olive 20 10
369 15c. Blinkblaar 35 80
370 25c. Cape holly . . . . . . 70 1·50

116 Mampharoane

1979. Reptiles. Multicoloured.
371A 4s. Type **116** 10 10
372A 10s. Qoaane 20 10
373A 15s. Leupa 30 70
374A 25s. Masumu . . . . . . 60 1·40

117 Basutoland 1933 1d. Stamp   **118** Detail of painting "Children's Games" by Brueghel

1979. Death Centenary of Sir Rowland Hill.
375 **117** 4s. multicoloured 10 10
376 – 15s. multicoloured 30 20
377 – 25s. black, orange & bistre 40 30
MS378 118 × 95 mm. 50s. multicoloured 60 80
DESIGNS: 15s. Basutoland 1962 ½c. new currency definitive; 25s. Penny Black; 50s. 1972 15c. Post Office Centenary commemorative.

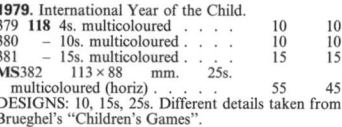

1979. International Year of the Child.
379 **118** 4s. multicoloured 10 10
380 – 10s. multicoloured 10 10
381 – 15s. multicoloured 15 15
MS382 113 × 88 mm. 25s. multicoloured (horiz) 55 45
DESIGNS: 10, 15s, 25s. Different details taken from Brueghel's "Children's Games".

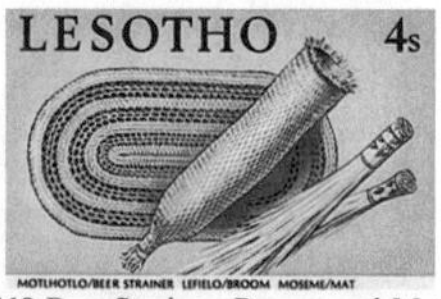

119 Beer Strainer, Broom and Mat

1980. Grasswork. Multicoloured.
383 4s. Type **119** 10 10
384 10s. Winnowing basket . . . 10 10
385 15s. Basotho hat 20 25
386 25s. Grain storage 35 40

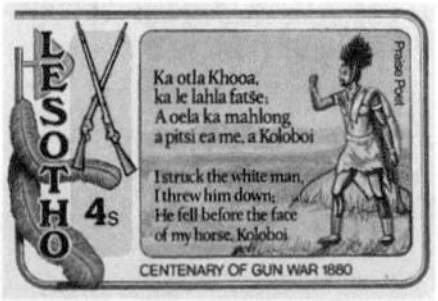

120 Praise Poet

1980. Centenary of Gun War. Multicoloured.
387 4s. Type **120** 15 10
388 5s. Lerotholi, Commander of Basotho Army 15 10
389 10s. Ambush at Qalabane . . 20 10
390 15s. Snider and Martini-Henry rifles 60 45
391 25s. Map showing main areas of action 70 55

121 Olympic Flame, Flags and Kremlin

1980. Olympic Games, Moscow. Multicoloured.
392 25s. Type **121** 25 25
393 25s. Doves, flame and flags 25 25
394 25s. Football 25 25
395 25s. Running 25 25
396 25s. Opening ceremony . . . 25 25
MS397 110 × 85 mm. 1m.40 Ancient and modern athletes carrying Olympic torch . . . . 1·10 1·25

1980. Nos. 203 and 300/9 surch **s** or new value.
402A 2s. on 2c. Type **101** . . . 10 10
403A 3s. on 3c. Mosotho horseman 20 10
410A 5s. on 5c. Lesotho Brown diamond . . . . 1·50 10
404B 6s. on 4c. Map of Lesotho 70 10
411B 10s. on 10c. Lesotho Bank 10 10
412A 25s. on 25c. Sehlabathebe National Park 25 30
406A 40s. on 40c. Pottery 45 50
414A 50s. on 50c. Prehistoric rock art . . . . 2·00 55
415B 75s. on 15c. Lesotho and O.A.U. flags . . . . . 1·50 75
409A 1m. on 1r. King Moshoeshoe II . . . . . 80 1·00
417A 2m. on 2r. Statue of King Moshoeshoe I . . . . . 80 1·40

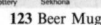

123 Beer Mug   **124** Queen Elizabeth the Queen Mother with Prince Charles

1980. Pottery. Multicoloured.
418 4s. Type **123** 10 10
419 10s. Beer brewing pot 10 10
420 15s. Water pot 15 15
421 25s. Pot shapes 25 30
MS422 150 × 110 mm. 40s. × 4 Wedgwood plaques of Prince Philip; Queen Elizabeth II; Prince Charles; Princess Anne (each 22 × 35 mm). 50 90
No. **MS**422 was issued to commemorate the 250th birth anniversary of Josiah Wedgwood.

1980. 80th Birthday of The Queen Mother. Mult.

423	5s. Type **124**	25	25
424	10s. The Queen Mother	25	25
425	1m. 1947 Basutoland Royal Visit 2d. stamp (54×43 mm)	90	90

125 Lesotho Evangelical Church, Morija

1980. Christmas. Multicoloured.

426	4s. Type **125**	10	10
427	15s. St. Agnes' Anglican Church, Teyateyaneng	10	10
428	25s. Cathedral of Our Lady of Victories, Maseru	15	10
429	75s. University Chapel, Roma	45	50
MS430	110×85 mm. 1m.50 Nativity scene (43×29 mm)	50	80

126 "Voyager" Satellite and Jupiter

1981. Space Exploration. Multicoloured.

431	25c. Type **126**	30	25
432	25c. "Voyager" and Saturn	30	25
433	25c. "Voyager" passing Saturn	30	25
434	25c. "Space Shuttle" releasing satellite	30	25
435	25c. "Space Shuttle" launching into space	30	25
MS436	111×85 mm. 1m.40 Saturn	1·40	1·00

127 Greater Kestrel

128 Wedding Bouquet from Lesotho

1981. Birds. Multicoloured.

437	1s. Type **127**	15	40
438	2s. Speckled pigeon ("Rock Pigeon") (horiz)	15	40
439	3s. South African crowned crane ("Crowned Crane")	20	40
440	5s. Bokmakierie shirike ("Bokmakierie")	20	40
504	6s. Cape robin chat ("Cape Robin")	30	10
505	7s. Yellow canary	30	10
506	10s. Red-billed pintail ("Red-billed Teal") (horiz)	30	10
507	25s. Malachite kingfisher	80	30
508	40s. Yellow-tufted malachite sunbird ("Malachite Sunbird") (horiz)	1·00	45
509	60s. Cape longclaw ("Orange-throated Longclaw") (horiz)	1·25	90
510	75s. Hoopoe ("African Hoppoe") (horiz)	1·50	90
448	1m. Red bishop (horiz)	75	75
449	2m. Egyptian goose (horiz)	1·00	1·50
450	5m. Lilac-breasted roller (horiz)	1·25	4·00

1981. Royal Wedding (1st issue). Multicoloured.

451	25s. Type **128**	10	10
452	50s. Prince Charles riding	20	25
453	75s. Prince Charles and Lady Diana Spencer	30	50

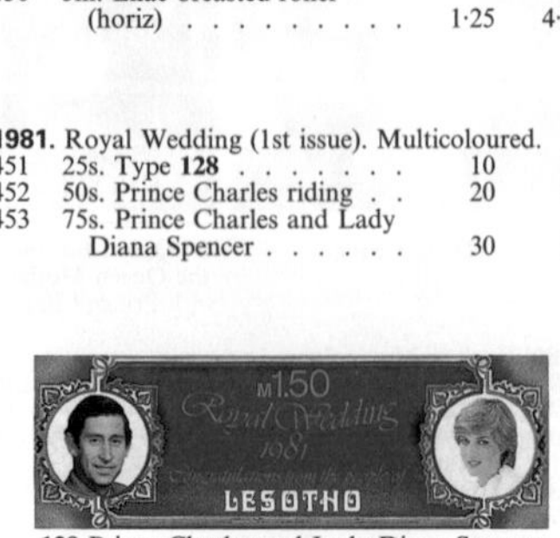

129 Prince Charles and Lady Diana Spencer (½-size illustration)

1981. Royal Wedding (2nd issue). Sheet 115×90 mm.

MS454	**129** 1m.50, multicoloured	1·00	1·25

130 "Santa planning his Annual Visit"

1981. Christmas. Paintings by Norman Rockwell. Multicoloured.

455	6s. Type **130**	15	10
456	10s. "Santa reading his Mail"	25	10
457	15s. "The Little Spooners"	30	20
458	20s. "Raleigh Rockwell Travels"	30	25
459	25s. "Ride 'em Cowboy"	30	30
460	60s. "The Discovery"	50	1·00
MS461	111×85 mm. 1m.25 "Mystic Nativity" (48×31 mm)	1·10	1·10

131 Duke of Edinburgh, Award Scheme Emblem and Flags

1981. 25th Anniv of Duke of Edinburgh Award Scheme. Multicoloured.

462	6s. Type **131**	10	10
463	7s. Tree planting	10	10
464	25s. Gardening	25	20
465	40s. Mountain climbing	40	40
466	75s. Award Scheme emblem	70	75
MS467	111×85 mm. 1m.40 Duke of Edinburgh (45×30 mm)	1·25	1·25

132 Wild Cat

1981. Wildlife. Multicoloured.

468	6s. Type **132**	1·25	30
469	20s. Chacma baboon (44×31 mm)	2·00	70
470	25s. Cape eland	2·50	75
471	40s. Porcupine	3·25	1·75
472	50s. Oribi (44×31 mm)	3·25	1·75
MS473	111×85 mm. 1m.50 Black-backed Jackal (47×31 mm)	2·75	1·90

133 Scout Bugler

1982. 75th Anniv of Boy Scout Movement. Multicoloured.

474	6s. Type **133**	30	25
475	30s. Scouts hiking	35	50
476	40s. Scout sketching	40	60
477	50s. Scout with flag	40	65
478	75s. Scouts saluting	45	80
MS479	117×92 mm. 1m.50 Lord Baden-Powell	1·00	2·00

134 Jules Rimet Trophy with Footballers and Flags of 1930 Finalists (Argentina and Uruguay)

1982. World Cup Football Championship, Spain. Each showing Trophy with Players and Flags from Past Finals. Multicoloured.

480	15s. Type **134**	25	25
481	15s. Czechoslovakia and Italy, 1934	25	25
482	15s. Hungary and Italy, 1938	25	25
483	15s. Brazil and Uruguay, 1950	25	25
484	15s. Hungary and W. Germany, 1954	25	25
485	15s. Sweden and Brazil, 1958	25	25
486	15s. Czechoslovakia and Brazil, 1962	25	25
487	15s. W. Germany and England, 1966	25	25
488	15s. Italy and Brazil, 1970	25	25
489	15s. Holland and W. Germany, 1974	25	25
490	15s. Holland and Argentina, 1978	25	25
491	15s. Map of World on footballs	25	25
MS492	118×93 mm. 1m.25 Bernabeu Stadium, Madrid (47×35 mm)	1·10	1·25

Nos. 480/8 show the Jules Rimet Trophy and Nos. 489/91 the World Cup Trophy.

135 Portrait of George Washington

1982. 250th Birth Anniv of George Washington. Multicoloured.

493	6s. Type **135**	10	10
494	7s. Washington with step-children and dog	10	10
495	10s. Washington with Indian chief	15	10
496	25s. Washington with troops	30	30
497	40s. Washington arriving in New York	40	40
498	1m. Washington on parade	1·00	1·10
MS499	117×92 mm. 1m.25 Washington crossing the Delaware	1·00	1·00

136 Lady Diana Spencer in Tetbury, May 1981

137 Mosotho reading Sesotho Bible

1982. 21st Birthday of Princess of Wales. Mult.

514a	30s. Lesotho coat of arms	40	40
515	50s. Type **136**	60	60
516	75s. Wedding picture at Buckingham Palace	80	1·00
517	1m. Formal portrait	1·25	1·40

1982. Centenary of Sesotho Bible. Multicoloured.

518	6s. Type **137**	15	20
519	15s. Sesotho bible and Virgin Mary holding infant Jesus	20	25
520	1m. Sesotho bible and Cathedral (62×42 mm)	50	75

138 Birthday Greetings

1982. Birth of Prince William of Wales. Mult.

521	6s. Type **138**	2·25	2·75
522	60s. Princess Diana and Prince William	1·00	1·00

139 "A Partridge in a Pear Tree"

1982. Christmas. "The Twelve Days of Christmas". Walt Disney cartoon characters. Multicoloured.

523	2s. Type **139**	10	10
524	2s. "Two turtle doves"	10	10
525	3s. "Three French hens"	10	10
526	3s. "Four calling birds"	10	10
527	4s. "Five golden rings"	10	10
528	4s. "Six geese a-laying"	10	10
529	75s. "Seven swans a-swimming"	1·40	1·75
530	75s. "Eight maids a-milking"	1·40	1·75
MS531	126×101 mm. 1m.50, "Nine ladies dancing, ten lords a-leaping, eleven pipers piping, twelve drummers drumming"	2·40	2·75

140 "Lepista caffrorum"

1983. Fungi. Multicoloured.

532	10s. Type **140**	15	10
533	30s. "Broomeia congregata"	30	40
534	50s. "Afroboletus luteolus"	60	90
535	75s. "Lentinus tuber-regium"	90	1·40

141 Ba-Leseli Dance

1983. Commonwealth Day. Multicoloured.

536	5s. Type **141**	10	10
537	30s. Tapestry weaving	20	30
538	60s. Queen Elizabeth II (vert)	35	65
539	75s. King Moshoeshoe II (vert)	40	80

142 "Dancers in a Trance" (rock painting from Ntloana Tsoana)

1983. Rock Paintings. Multicoloured.

540	6s. Type **142**	20	10
541	25s. "Baboons", Sehonghong	55	35
542	60s. "Hunters attacking Mountain Reedbuck", Makhetha	60	1·10
543	75s. "Eland", Lehaha la Likhomo	65	1·60
MS544	166×84 mm. Nos. 540/3 and 10s. "Cattle herding", Sehonghong (52×52 mm)	1·25	3·50

143 Montgolfier Balloon, 1783

1983. Bicentenary of Manned Flight. Mult.

545	7s. Type **143**	15	10
546	30s. Wright brothers and Flyer I	30	40
547	60s. First airmail flight	50	1·25
548	1m. Concorde	2·25	2·50
MS549	180×92 mm. Nos. 545/8 and 6s. Dornier Do-28D Skyservant of Lesotho Airways (60×60 mm)	2·75	2·75

144 Rev. Eugene Casalis

1983. 150th Anniv of Arrival of the French Missionaries. Multicoloured.

550	6s. Type **144**	10	10
551	25s. The founding of Morija	10	10
552	40s. Baptism of Libe	10	15
553	75s. Map of Lesotho	20	25

145 Mickey Mouse and Pluto greeted by Friends

1983. Christmas. Walt Disney Characters in scenes from "Old Christmas" (Washington Irving's sketchbook). Multicoloured.

554	1s. Type **145**	10	10
555	2s. Donald Duck and Pluto	10	10
556	3s. Donald Duck with Huey, Dewey and Louie	10	10
557	4s. Goofy, Donald Duck and Mickey Mouse	10	10
558	5s. Goofy holding turkey, Donald Duck and Mickey Mouse	10	10
559	6s. Goofy and Mickey Mouse	10	10
560	75s. Donald and Daisy Duck	2·00	2·40
561	1m. Goofy and Clarabell	2·50	2·75
MS562	132 × 113 mm. 1m.75 Scrooge McDuck, Pluto and Donald Duck	3·25	4·50

146 "Danaus chrysippus"

1984. Butterflies. Multicoloured.

563	1s. Type **146**	30	40
564	2s. "Aeropetes tulbaghia"	30	40
565	3s. "Colotis evenina"	35	40
566	4s. "Precis oenone"	35	40
567	5s. "Precis hierta"	35	40
568	6s. "Catopsilia florella"	35	10
569	7s. "Phalanta phalantha"	35	10
570	10s. "Acraea stenobea"	40	10
571	15s. "Cynthia cardui"	75	10
572	20s. "Colotis subfasciatus"	75	10
573	30s. "Charaxes jasius"	75	30
574	50s. "Terias brigitta"	75	40
575	60s. "Pontia helice"	75	50
576	75s. "Colotis regina"	75	50
577	1m. "Hypolimnas misippus"	75	1·50
578	5m. "Papilio demodocus"	1·50	7·50

147 "Thou shalt not have Strange Gods before Me"

1984. Easter. The Ten Commandments. Mult.

579	20s. Type **147**	30	30
580	20s. "Thou shalt not take the name of the Lord thy God in vain"	30	30
581	20s. "Remember thou keep holy the Lord's Day"	30	30
582	20s. "Honour thy father and mother"	30	30
583	20s. "Thou shalt not kill"	30	30
584	20s. "Thou shalt not commit adultery"	30	30
585	20s. "Thou shalt not steal"	30	30
586	20s. "Thou shalt not bear false witness against thy neighbour"	30	30
587	20s. "Thou shalt not covet thy neighbour's wife"	30	30
588	20s. "Thou shalt not covet thy neighbour's goods"	30	30
MS589	102 × 73 mm. 1m.50 Moses with Tablets (45 × 28 mm)	1·00	2·25

148 Torch Bearer

1984. Olympic Games, Los Angeles. Multicoloured.

590	10s. Type **148**	10	10
591	30s. Horse-riding	10	10
592	50s. Swimming	15	20
593	75s. Basketball	20	25
594	1m. Running	25	30
MS595	101 × 72mm. 1m.50 Olympic Flame and flags	1·25	2·50

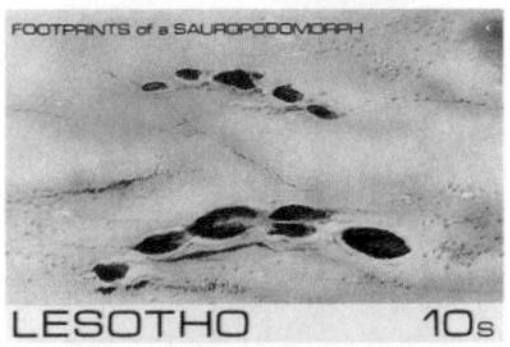

149 Sauropodomorph Footprints

1984. Prehistoric Footprints (2nd series). Mult.

596	10s. Type **149**	50	30
597	30s. Lesothosaurus footprints	60	1·25
598	50s. Footprint of carnivorous dinosaur	70	2·00

150 Wells Fargo Coach, 1852

1984. "Ausipex" Int Stamp Exhibition, Melbourne. Bicent of First Mail Coach Run. Mult.

599	6s. Type **150**	10	10
600	7s. Basotho mail cart, circa 1900	10	10
601	10s. Bath mail coach, 1784	10	10
602	30s. Cobb coach, 1853	15	15
603	50s. Exhibition logo and Royal Exhibition Buildings, Melbourne (82 × 25 mm)	50	80
MS604	147 × 98 mm. 1m.75 G.B. Penny Black, Basutoland 1934 "OFFICIAL" optd 6d. and Western Australia 1854 4d. with frame inverted (82 × 25 mm)	2·25	3·75

151 "The Orient Express" (1900)

1984. Railways of the World. Multicoloured.

605	6s. Type **151**	30	15
606	15s. Class 05 streamlined steam locomotive No. 001, Germany (1935)	30	30
607	30s. Caledonian Railway steam locomotive "Cardean" (1906)	35	60
608	60s. Atchison, Topeka & Santa Fe "Super Chief" express (1940)	40	1·75
609	1m. L.N.E.R. "Flying Scotsman" (1934)	40	2·00
MS610	108 × 82mm. 2m. South African Railways "The Blue Train" (1972)	1·00	2·50

152 Eland Calf

1984. Baby Animals. Multicoloured.

611	15s. Type **152**	35	20
612	20s. Young chacma baboons	35	25
613	30s. Oribi calf	35	40
614	75s. Young Natal red hares	50	1·60
615	1m. Black-backed jackal pups (46 × 27 mm)	50	2·00

153 Crown of Lesotho

154 Christ condemned to Death

1985. Silver Jubilee of King Moshoeshoe II. Mult.

616	6s. Type **153**	10	10
617	30s. King Moshoeshoe in 1960	20	30
618	75s. King Moshoeshoe in traditional dress, 1985	50	75
619	1m. King Moshoeshoe in uniform, 1985	70	1·10

1985. Easter. The Stations of the Cross. Mult.

620	20s. Type **154**	25	35
621	20s. Christ carrying the Cross	25	35
622	20s. Falling for the first time	25	35
623	20s. Christ meets Mary	25	35
624	20s. Simon of Cyrene helping to carry the Cross	25	35
625	20s. Veronica wiping the face of Christ	25	35
626	20s. Christ falling a second time	25	35
627	20s. Consoling the women of Jerusalem	25	35
628	20s. Falling for the third time	25	35
629	20s. Christ being stripped	25	35
630	20s. Christ nailed to the Cross	25	35
631	20s. Dying on the Cross	25	35
632	20s. Christ taken down from the Cross	25	35
633	20s. Christ being laid in the sepulchre	25	35
MS634	138 × 98 mm. 2m. "The Crucifixion" (Mathias Grunewald)	1·50	3·50

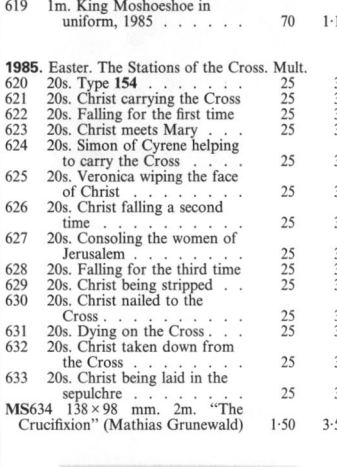

155 Duchess of York with Princess Elizabeth, 1931

1985. Life and Times of Queen Elizabeth the Queen Mother. Multicoloured.

635	10s. Type **155**	35	10
636	30s. The Queen Mother in 1975	70	50
637	60s. Queen Mother with Queen Elizabeth and Princess Margaret, 1980	80	90
638	2m. Four generations of Royal Family at Prince Harry's christening, 1984	1·25	2·50
MS639	139 × 98 mm. 2m. Queen Elizabeth with the Princess of Wales and her children at Prince Harry's christening (37 × 50 mm)	2·25	2·75

156 B.M.W. "732i"

1985. Century of Motoring. Multicoloured.

640	6s. Type **156**	25	15
641	10s. Ford "Crown Victoria"	35	15
642	30s. Mercedes-Benz "500SE"	75	50
643	90s. Cadillac "Eldorado Biarritz"	1·50	2·50
644	2m. Rolls-Royce "Silver Spirit"	2·00	4·00
MS645	139 × 98 mm. 2m. Rolls-Royce "Silver Ghost Tourer", 1907 (37 × 50 mm)	4·00	6·00

157 American Cliff Swallow

158 Two Youths Rock-climbing

1985. Birth Bicentenary of John J. Audubon (ornithologist). Designs showing original paintings. Multicoloured.

646	5s. Type **157**	40	30
647	6s. Great crested grebe (horiz)	40	30
648	10s. Vesper sparrow ("Vester Sparrow") (horiz)	55	30
649	30s. Common greenshank ("Greenshank") (horiz)	1·25	75
650	60s. Stilt sandpiper (horiz)	1·75	2·75
651	2m. Glossy ibis (horiz)	2·50	6·00

1985. International Youth Year and 75th Anniv of Girl Guide Movement. Multicoloured.

652	10s. Type **158**	20	10
653	30s. Young technician in hospital laboratory	50	40
654	75s. Three guides on parade	1·00	1·25
655	2m. Guide saluting	1·75	3·00
MS656	138 × 98 mm. 2m. "Olave, Lady Baden-Powell" (Grace Wheatley) (37 × 50 mm)	2·40	2·75

159 U.N. (New York) 1951 1c. Definitive and U.N. Flag

160 Cosmos

1985. 40th Anniversary of U.N.O.

657 **159**	10s. multicoloured	25	10
658 –	30s. multicoloured	60	35
659 –	50s. multicoloured	95	85
660 –	2m. black and green	5·00	6·50

DESIGNS—VERT: 30s. Ha Sofonia Earth Satellite Station; 2m. Maimonides (physician, philosopher and scholar). HORIZ: 50s. Lesotho Airways Fokker F.27 Friendship at Maseru Airport.

1985. Wild Flowers. Multicoloured.

661	6s. Type **160**	40	15
662	10s. Small agapanthus	55	15
663	30s. Pink witchweed	1·10	70
664	60s. Small iris	1·50	2·00
665	90s. Wild geranium or cranesbill	1·75	3·00
666	1m. Large spotted orchid	3·00	5·00

160a Mrs Jumbo and Baby Dumbo

1985. 150th Birth Anniv of Mark Twain. Walt Disney cartoon characters illustrating various Mark Twain quotations. Multicoloured.

667	6s. Type **160a**	40	15
668	50s. Uncle Scrooge and Goofy reading newspaper	1·25	1·00
669	90s. Winnie the Pooh, Tigger, Piglet and Owl	1·75	2·00
670	1m.50 Goofy at ship's wheel	2·75	3·00
MS671	127 × 102 mm. 1m.25 Mickey Mouse as astronaut	4·75	3·75

160b Donald Duck as the Tailor

1985. Birth Bicentenaries of Grimm Brothers (folklorists). Walt Disney cartoon characters in scenes from "The Wishing Table". Mult.

672	10s. Type **160b**	50	20
673	60s. The second son (Dewey) with magic donkey and gold coins	1·50	1·50
674	75s. The eldest son (Huey) with wishing table laden with food	1·75	1·75
675	1m. The innkeeper stealing the third son's (Louie) magic cudgel	2·00	2·75
MS676	127 × 102 mm. 1m.50 The tailor and eldest son with wishing table	4·75	5·50

161 Male Lammergeier on Watch

162 Two Players chasing Ball

1986. Flora and Fauna of Lesotho. Multicoloured.

677	7s. Type **161**	1·75	65
678	9s. Prickly pear	70	20
679	12s. Stapelia	70	20
680	15s. Pair of lammergeiers	2·50	60
681	35s. Pig's ears	1·10	60

682 50s. Male lammergeier in flight . . . . 3·75 2·75
683 1m. Adult and juvenile lammergeiers . . . . . . 3·75 4·75
684 2m. Columnar cereus . . . . 3·75 6·50
MS685 125 × 106 mm. 2m. Verreaux's eagle ("Black Eagle") 8·50 12·00

1986. World Cup Football Championship, Mexico. Multicoloured.
686 35s. Type **162** . . . . 1·25 50
687 50s. Goalkeeper saving goal 1·75 1·25
688 1m. Three players chasing ball . . . . 3·00 2·75
689 2m. Two players competing for ball . . . . 5·00 5·00
MS690 104 × 74 mm. 3m. Player heading ball . . . . 9·00 8·50

162a Galileo and 200 inch Hale Telescope at Mount Palomar Observatory, California

1986. Appearance of Halley's Comet. Multicoloured.
691 9s. Type **162a** 50 15
692 15s. Halley's Comet and "Pioneer Venus 2" spacecraft 75 20
693 70s. Halley's Comet of 684 A.D. (from "Nuremberg Chronicle", 1493) . . . . 1·60 1·40
694 3m. Comet and landing of William the Conqueror, 1066 . . . . 4·00 5·50
MS695 101 × 70 mm. 4m. Halley's Comet over Lesotho . . . . . 6·50 7·00

163 International Year of the Child Gold Coin

1986. 1st Anniv of New Currency (1980). Mult.
696 30s. Type **163** . . . . 4·00 6·50
697 30s. Five maloti banknote . . 4·00 6·50
698 30s. Fifty lisente coin . . . . 4·00 6·50
699 30s. Ten maloti banknote . . 4·00 6·50
700 30s. One sente coin . . . . . 4·00 6·50
These stamps were prepared in 1980, but were not issued at that time.

163a Princess Elizabeth in Pantomime

1986. 60th Birthday of Queen Elizabeth II.
701 **163a** 90s. black and yellow . . 50 60
702 – 1m. multicoloured . . . 55 65
703 – 2m. multicoloured . . . 90 1·40
MS704 119 × 85 mm. 4m. black and grey-brown . . . . 1·75 3·25
DESIGNS: 1m. Queen at Windsor Horse Show, 1971; 2m. At Royal Festival Hall, 1971; 4m. Princess Elizabeth in 1934.

163b Statue of Liberty and Bela Bartok (composer)

1986. Centenary of Statue of Liberty. Immigrants to the U.S.A. Multicoloured.
705 15s. Type **163b** 85 30
706 35s. Felix Adler (philosopher) 85 30
707 1m. Victor Herbert (composer) . . . . 3·00 2·00
708 3m. David Niven (actor) . . 4·25 4·25
MS709 103 × 74 mm. 3m. Statue of Liberty (vert) . . . . 3·50 5·00

163c Mickey Mouse and Goofy as Japanese Mail Runners

1986. "Ameripex" International Stamp Exhibition, Chicago. Walt Disney cartoon characters delivering mail. Multicoloured.
710 15s. Type **163c** 80 20
711 35s. Mickey Mouse and Pluto with mail sledge . . . . . 1·10 30
712 1m. Goofy as postman riding Harley-Davidson motorcycle . . . . 2·25 2·75
713 2m. Donald Duck operating railway mailbag apparatus 2·50 4·00
MS714 127 × 101 mm. 4m. Goofy driving mail to aircraft . . . . 6·50 7·00

1986. Various stamps surch. (a) On Nos. 437 etc (Birds)
729 9s. on 5s. Bokmakierie shrike 75 20
715 9s. on 10s. Red-billed pintail (horiz) . . . . 3·50 1·25
716 15s. on 1s. Type **127** . . . . 7·00 3·00
717 15s. on 2s. Speckled pigeon (horiz) . . . . 4·00 4·50
718 15s. on 5s. Bokmakierie shrike . . . . 2·25 35
719 15s. on 60s. Cape longclaw (horiz) 20 10
730 16s. on 25s. Malachite kingfisher . . . . 2·75 1·00
731 35s. on 25s. Malachite kingfisher . . . . 1·50 60
721 35s. on 75s. Hoopoe . . . . 16·00 15·00

(b) On Nos. 563 etc (Butterflies).
722 9s. on 30s. "Charaxes jasius" 15 10
723 9s. on 60s. "Pontia helice" 3·25 4·00
724 15s. on 1s. Type **146** . . . . 2·00 2·25
725 15s. on 2s. "Aeropetes tulbaghia" 20 20
726 15s. on 3s. "Colotis evenina" 20 20
727 15s. on 5s. "Precis hierta" . . 20 20
732 20s. on 4s. "Precis oenone" 10 10
728 35s. on 75s. "Colotis regina" 35 35
733 40s. on 7s. "Phalanta phalantha" 15 20

(c) No. 722 further surch.
734 3s. on 9s. on 30s. "Charaxes jasius" . . . . 1·00 1·00
735 7s. on 9s. on 30s. "Charaxes jasius" . . . . 1·25 1·00

170a Prince Andrew and Miss Sarah Ferguson

1986. Royal Wedding. Multicoloured.
736 50s. Type **170a** 40 40
737 1m. Prince Andrew 70 80
738 3m. Prince Andrew piloting helicopter . . . . 2·75 2·25
MS739 88 × 88 mm. 4m. Prince Andrew and Miss Sarah Ferguson (different) . . . . 3·50 4·50

171 Basotho Pony and Rider

1986. 20th Anniv of Independence. Multicoloured.
740 9s. Type **171** 40 10
741 15s. Basotho woman spinning mohair 40 15
742 35s. Crossing river by rowing boat 50 30
743 3m. Thaba Tseka Post Office 1·00 3·00
MS744 109 × 78 mm. 4m. King Moshoeshoe I . . . . 4·75 8·00

171a Chip'n' Dale pulling Christmas Cracker

1986. Christmas. Walt Disney cartoon characters. Multicoloured.
745 15s. Type **171a** 80 20
746 35s. Mickey and Minnie Mouse . . . . 1·10 30
747 1m. Pluto pulling Christmas taffy . . . . 1·90 2·75
748 2m. Aunt Matilda baking . . 2·25 4·00
MS749 126 × 102 mm. 5m. Huey and Dewey with gingerbread house 5·50 7·00

172 Rally Car

173 Lawn Tennis

1987. Roof of Africa Motor Rally. Multicoloured.
750 9s. Type **172** 30 10
751 15s. Motorcyclist 35 15
752 35s. Motorcyclist (different) 55 35
753 4m. Rally car (different) . . . 3·00 5·00

1987. Olympic Games, Seoul (1988) (1st issue). Multicoloured.
754 9s. Type **173** 70 10
755 15s. Judo 70 15
756 20s. Athletics 75 20
757 35s. Boxing 85 30
758 1m. Diving . . . . 1·10 1·75
759 3m. Ten-pin bowling . . . . 2·75 5·50
MS760 Two sheets, each 75 × 105 mm. (a) 2m. Lawn tennis (different). (b) 4m. Football. Set of 2 sheets . . . . 6·00 5·00
See also Nos. 838/41.

174 Isaac Newton and Reflecting Telescope

1987. Great Scientific Discoveries. Multicoloured.
761 5s. Type **174** 30 10
762 9s. Alexander Graham Bell and first telephone 30 15
763 75s. Robert Goddard and liquid fuel rocket 80 75
764 4m. Chuck Yeager and Bell XS-1 rocket plane . . . . 2·75 4·50
MS765 98 × 68 mm. 4m. "Mariner 10" spacecraft . . . . 2·75 3·00

175 Grey Rhebuck

1987. Flora and Fauna. Multicoloured.
766 5s. Type **175** 40 15
767 9s. Cape clawless otter . . . 40 15
768 15s. Cape grey mongoose . . 55 20
769 20s. Free State daisy (vert) 60 20
770 35s. River bells (vert) 75 30
771 1m. Turkey flower (vert) . . 1·75 2·50
772 2m. Sweet briar (vert) . . . . 2·25 3·75
773 3m. Mountain reedbuck . . . 2·75 5·00
MS774 Two sheets, each 114 × 98 mm. (a) 2m. Pig-Lily (vert). (b) 4m. Cape Wildebeest. Set of 2 sheets . . . . 5·50 9·00

176 Scouts hiking

178 "Madonna and Child" (detail)

177 Spotted Trunkfish and Columbus's Fleet

1987. World Scout Jamboree, Australia. Mult.
775 9s. Type **176** 60 20
776 15s. Scouts playing football 65 20
777 35s. Kangaroos 80 50
778 75s. Scout saluting . . . . . 1·75 1·25
779 4m. Australian scout windsurfing . . . . 3·75 6·50
MS780 96 × 66 mm. 4m. Outline map and flag of Australia . . . 3·25 4·00

1987. 500th Anniv (1992) of Discovery of America by Columbus. Multicoloured.
781 9s. Type **177** 65 20
782 15s. Green turtle and ships 80 20
783 35s. Columbus watching common dolphins from ship . . . . 1·00 40
784 5m. White-tailed tropic bird and fleet at sea . . . . . 6·00 7·50
MS785 105 × 76 mm. 4m. "Santa Maria" and Cuban Amazon in flight . . . . 5·00 4·00
No. 782 is inscribed "Carribbean" in error.

1987. Christmas. Paintings by Raphael. Mult.
786 9s. Type **178** 30 10
787 15s. "Marriage of the Virgin" 45 15
788 35s. "Coronation of the Virgin" (detail) 90 40
789 90s. "Madonna of the Chair" 2·00 3·50
MS790 75 × 100 mm. 3m. "Madonna and Child enthroned with Five Saints" (detail) . . . . 3·00 3·00

179 Lesser Pied Kingfisher

1988. Birds. Multicoloured.
791 2s. Type **179** 20 30
792 3s. Three-banded plover . . . 20 30
793 5s. Spur-winged goose . . . 20 30
794 10s. Clapper lark 20 20
795 12s. Red-eyed bulbul 30 10
796 16s. Cape weaver 30 10
797 20s. Paradise sparrow ("Red-headed Finch") 30 10
798 30s. Mountain wheater ("Mountain Chat") 35 20
799 40s. Common stonechat ("Stone Chate") 40 20
800 55s. Pied barbet 50 25
801 60s. Red-shouldered glossy starling 55 50
802 75s. Cape sparrow 60 60
803 1m. Cattle egret 60 80
804 3m. Giant kingfisher . . . . 90 2·50
805 10m. Helmeted guineafowl 1·90 7·00

1988. Royal Ruby Wedding. Nos. 701/3 optd **40TH WEDDING ANNIVERSARY H.M. QUEEN ELIZABETH II H.R.H. THE DUKE OF EDINBURGH**.
806 90s. black and yellow 80 65
807 1m. multicoloured 90 80
808 2m. multicoloured . . . . . 1·60 1·40
MS809 119 × 85 mm. 4m. black and grey-brown . . . . 3·00 2·75

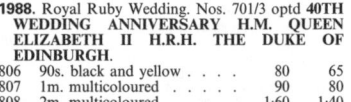

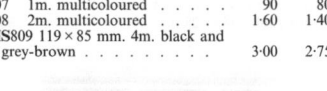

181 Mickey Mouse and Goofy outside Presidential Palace, Helsinki

1988. "Finlandia '88" International Stamp Exhibition, Helsinki. Designs showing Walt Disney cartoon characters in Finland. Mult.

810 1s. Type **181** 10 10
811 2s. Goofy and Mickey Mouse in sauna 10 10
812 3s. Goofy and Mickey Mouse fishing in lake 10 10
813 4s. Mickey and Minnie Mouse and Finlandia Hall, Helsinki 10 10
814 5s. Mickey Mouse photographing Goofy at Sibelius Monument, Helsinki 10 10
815 10s. Mickey Mouse and Goofy pony trekking . . . 10 10
816 3m. Goofy, Mickey and Minnie Mouse at Helsinki Olympic Stadium . . . . . 4·00 3·00
817 5m. Mickey Mouse and Goofy meeting Santa at Arctic Circle . . . . 5·00 4·00
MS818 Two sheets, each 127 × 102 mm. (a) 4m. Mickey Mouse and nephew as Lapps. (b) 4m. Daisy Duck, Goofy, Mickey and Minnie Mouse by fountain, Helsinki. Set of 2 sheets . . . 5·50 7·00

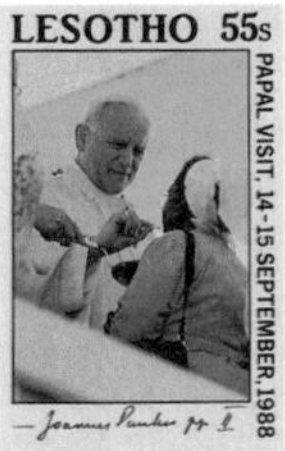

182 Pope John Paul II giving Communion

183 Large-toothed Rock Hyrax

1988. Visit of Pope John Paul II. Mult.

819 55s. Type **182** 40 25
820 2m. Pope leading procession 1·25 1·50
821 3m. Pope at airport . . . . 1·75 2·00
822 4m. Pope John Paul II . . . 2·25 2·75
MS823 98 × 79 mm. 5m. Archbishop Morapeli (horiz) . . . . 5·00 4·50

1988. Small Mammals of Lesotho. Mult.

824 16s. Type **183** 55 15
825 40s. Ratel and black-throated honey guide (bird) . . . . 1·75 55
826 75s. Small-spotted genet . . . 1·50 85
827 3m. Yellow mongoose . . . 3·25 5·50
MS828 110 × 78 mm. 4m. Meerkat 3·25 4·00

184 "Birth of Venus" (detail) (Botticelli)

1988. Famous Paintings. Multicoloured.

829 15s. Type **184** 30 15
830 25s. "View of Toledo" (El Greco) 35 20
831 40s. "Maids of Honour" (detail) (Velasquez) 45 25
832 50s. "The Fifer" (Manet) . . 55 30
833 55s. "Starry Night" (detail) (Van Gogh) 55 30
834 75s. "Prima Ballerina" (Degas) 70 70
835 2m. "Bridge over Water Lilies" (Monet) . . . . . 1·75 2·25
836 3m. "Guernica" (detail) (Picasso) . . . . 1·75 2·75
MS837 Two sheets, each 110 × 95 mm. (a) 4m. "The Presentation of the Virgin in the Temple" (Titian). (b) 4m. "The Miracle of the Newborn Infant" (Titian). Set of 2 sheets . . . . 4·00 4·50

185 Wrestling

1988. Olympic Games, Seoul (2nd series). Mult.

838 12s. Type **185** 10 10
839 16s. Show jumping (vert) . . 10 10
840 55s. Shooting 20 30
841 3m.50 As 16s. (vert) . . . . 1·40 2·00
MS842 108 × 77 mm. 4m. Olympic flame (vert) . . . . 2·75 3·50

186 Yannick Noah and Eiffel Tower, Paris

1988. 75th Anniv of Int Tennis Federation. Mult.

843 12s. Type **186** 60 25
844 20s. Rod Laver and Sydney Harbour Bridge and Opera House . . . . 1·00 30
845 30s. Ivan Lendl and Prague 65 25
846 65s. Jimmy Connors and Tokyo (vert) 80 40
847 1m. Arthur Ashe and Barcelona (vert) . . . . . 1·25 60
848 1m.55 Althea Gibson and New York (vert) . . . . 1·25 90
849 2m. Chris Evert and Vienna (vert) . . . . 1·50 1·25
850 2m.40 Boris Becker and Houses of Parliament, London (vert) . . . . . . 1·75 1·75
851 3m. Martina Navratilova and Golden Gate Bridge, San Francisco . . . . 2·00 2·00
MS852 98 × 72 mm. 4m. Steffi Graf and Berlin . . . . 3·00 3·75
No. 844 is inscribed "SIDNEY" in error.

186a "The Averoldi Polyptych" (detail)

1988. Christmas. 500th Birth Anniv of Titian (artist). Multicoloured.

853 12s. Type **186a** 20 10
854 20s. "Christ and the Adulteress" (detail) 20 10
855 35s. "Christ and the Adulteress" (different detail) 30 20
856 45s. "Angel of the Annunciation" 40 30
857 65s. "Saint Dominic" 55 50
858 1m. "The Vendramin Family" (detail) 75 80
859 2m. "Mary Magdalen" . . . 1·25 1·75
860 3m. "The Tribute Money" . . 1·75 2·50
MS861 (a) 94 × 110 mm. 5m. "Mater Dolorosa". (b) 110 × 94 mm. 5m. "Christ and the Woman taken in Adultery" (horiz). Set of 2 sheets 6·00 8·00

187 Pilatus PC-6 Turbo Porter

1989. 125th Anniv of International Red Cross. Aircraft. Multicoloured.

862 12s. Type **187** 50 10
863 20s. Unloading medical supplies from Cessna Caravan I 60 20
864 55s. De Havilland D.H.C.6 Twin Otter 200/300 . . . . 90 50
865 3m. Douglas DC-3 . . . . . 2·75 3·50
MS866 109 × 80 mm. 4m. Red Cross logo and Douglas DC-3 (vert) 6·50 3·75

187a "Dawn Mist at Mishima"

1989. Japanese Art. Paintings by Hiroshige. Mult.

867 12s. Type **187a** 30 10
868 16s. "Night Snow at Kambara" 35 10
869 20s. "Wayside Inn at Mariko Station" 35 10
870 35s. "Shower at Shono" . . 55 10
871 55s. "Snowfall on the Kisokaido near Oi" . . . 65 40
872 1m. "Autumn Moon at Seba" 85 85
873 3m.20 "Evening Moon at Ryogoku Bridge" . . . . 2·25 3·00
874 5m. "Cherry Blossoms at Arashiyama" . . . . . . 2·75 3·75
MS875 Two sheets, each 102 × 76 mm. (a) 4m. "Listening to the Singing Insects at Dokanyama". (b) 4m. "Moonlight, Nagakubo". Set of 2 sheets . . . . 6·00 7·00

188 Mickey Mouse as General

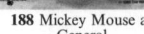

189 "Paxillus involutus"

1989. "Philexfrance 89" International Stamp Exhibition, Paris. Designs showing Walt Disney cartoon characters in French military uniforms of the Revolutionary period. Multicoloured.

876 1s. Type **188** 10 10
877 2s. Ludwig von Drake as infantryman 10 10
878 3s. Goofy as grenadier . . . 10 10
879 4s. Horace Horsecollar as cavalryman 10 10
880 5s. Pete as hussar 10 10
881 10s. Donald Duck as marine 10 10
882 3m. Gyro Gearloose as National Guard . . . . . 3·25 3·25
883 5m. Scrooge McDuck as admiral . . . . 4·00 4·25
MS884 Two sheets, each 127 × 102 mm. (a) 4m. Mickey and Minnie Mouse as King Louis XVI and Marie Antoinette with Goofy as a National Guard (horiz). (b) 4m. Mickey Mouse as drummer. Set of 2 sheets . . . . 7·50 9·00
No. 879 is inscribed "CALVARYMAN" in error.

1989. Fungi. Multicoloured.

900 12s. Type **189** 20 10
901 16s. "Ganoderma applanatum" 20 15
902 55s. "Suillus granulatus" . . 45 35
903 5m. "Stereum hirsutum" . . 3·25 4·50
MS904 96 × 69 mm. 4m. "Scleroderma cepa" ("flavidum") 5·00 5·50

190 Sesotho Huts

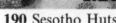

192 Launch of "Apollo 11"

191 Marsh Sandpiper

1989. Maloti Mountains. Multicoloured.

905 1m. Type **190** . . . . 70 1·00
906 1m. American aloe and mountains . . . . 70 1·00
907 1m. River valley with waterfall . . . . 70 1·00
908 1m. Sesotho tribesman on ledge . . . . 70 1·00
MS909 86 × 117 mm. 4m. Spiral Aloe . . . . 3·00 4·00
Nos. 905/8 were printed together, se-tenant, forming a composite design.

1989. Migrant Birds. Multicoloured.

910 12s. Type **191** 80 30
911 65s. Little stint . . . . 1·50 70
912 1m. Ringed plover . . . . . 2·00 1·50
913 4m. Curlew sandpiper . . . 3·50 5·50
MS914 97 × 69 mm. 5m. Ruff (vert) 8·50 9·00

1989. 20th Anniv of First Manned Landing on Moon. Multicoloured.

915 12s. Type **192** 25 10
916 16s. Lunar module "Eagle" landing on Moon (horiz) 25 15
917 40s. Neil Armstrong leaving "Eagle" 45 25
918 55s. Edwin Aldrin on Moon (horiz) 50 30
919 1m. Aldrin performing scientific experiment (horiz) 85 85
920 2m. "Eagle" leaving Moon (horiz) . . . . 1·50 1·75
921 3m. Command module "Columbia" in Moon orbit (horiz) . . . . 2·00 2·25
922 4m. Command module on parachutes . . . . 2·50 2·75
MS923 81 × 111 mm. 5m. Astronaut on Moon . . . . 5·00 6·00

193 English Penny Post Paid Mark, 1680

1989. "World Stamp Expo '89" International Stamp Exhibition, Washington (1st issue). Stamps and Postmarks.

924 **193** 75s. red, black and stone 70 75
925 – 75s. black, grey and red 70 75
926 – 75s. violet, black & brown 70 75
927 – 75s. brown, black & lt brn 70 75
928 – 75s. black and yellow . . 70 75
929 – 75s. multicoloured 70 75
930 – 75s. black and lilac . . . 70 75
931 – 75s. black, red and brown 70 75
932 – 75s. red, black and yellow 70 75

DESIGNS: No. 925, German postal seal and feather, 1807; 926, British Post Office in Crete 1898 20pa. stamp; 927, Bermuda 1848 Perot 1d. provisional; 928, U.S.A. Pony Express cancellation, 1860; 929, Finland 1856 5k. stamp; 930, Fiji 1870 "Fiji Times" 1d. stamp, 1870; 931, Sweden newspaper wrapper handstamp, 1823; 932, Bhor 1879 ½a. stamp.

193a Cathedral Church of St. Peter and St. Paul, Washington

1989. "World Stamp Expo '89" International Stamp Exhibition, Washington (2nd issue). Sheet 78 × 61 mm.

MS933 **193a** 4m. multicoloured 2·50 3·00

193b "The Immaculate Conception"

1989. Christmas. Paintings by Velazquez. Mult.

934 12s. Type **193b** 10 10
935 20s. "St. Anthony Abbot and St. Paul the Hermit" . . . 15 10
936 35s. "St. Thomas the Apostle" 25 25
937 55s. "Christ in the House of Martha and Mary" 35 35
938 1m. "St. John writing The Apocalypse on Patmos" . . 60 75
939 3m. "The Virgin presenting the Chasuble to St. Ildephonsus" . . . . . 1·60 2·25
940 4m. "The Adoration of the Magi" . . . . 2·00 2·75
MS941 71 × 96 mm. 5m. "The Coronation of the Virgin" . . 6·50 7·50

194 Scene from 1966 World Cup Final, England

1989. World Cup Football Championship, Italy. Scenes from past finals. Multicoloured.

942 12s. Type **194** 50 10
943 16s. 1970 final, Mexico . . . 50 15
944 55s. 1974 final, West Germany . . . . 1·00 40
945 5m. 1982 final, Spain . . . . 3·75 5·50
MS946 106 × 85 mm. 4m. Player's legs and symbolic football . . 6·00 7·00

1990. No. 889 and 798/9 surch **16 s**.

948	16s. on 12s. Red-eyed bulbul	1·50	20
948e	16s. on 30s. Common wheater	60	15
948f	16s. on 40s. Common stonechat	60	15

197 "Byblia anvatara"

198a Lady Elizabeth Bowes-Lyon and Brother in Fancy Dress

198 "Satyrium princeps"

1990. Butterflies. Multicoloured.

949	12s. Type **197**	70	15
950	16s. "Cynthia cardui"	80	15
951	55s. "Precis oenone"	1·25	40
952	65s. "Pseudacraea boisduvali"	1·25	65
953	1m. "Precis orithya"	2·00	1·25
954	2m. "Precis sophia"	3·00	2·50
955	3m. "Danaus chrysippus"	4·00	4·25
956	4m. "Druryia antimachus"	5·00	6·50
MS957	105 × 70 mm. 5m. "Papilio demodocus"	7·50	9·00

1990. "EXPO 90" International Garden and Greenery Exhibition, Osaka. Local Orchids. Multicoloured.

958	12s. Type **198**	55	15
959	16s. "Huttonaea pulchra"	60	15
960	55s. "Herschelia graminifolia"	1·25	30
961	1m. "Ansellia gigantea"	1·75	75
962	1m.55 "Polystachya pubescens"	2·00	1·75
963	2m.40 "Penthea filicornis"	2·00	2·25
964	3m. "Disperis capensis"	2·25	3·25
965	4m. "Disa uniflora"	3·00	4·00
MS966	95 × 68 mm. 5m. "Stenoglottis longifolia"	7·50	9·00

1990. 90th Birthday of Queen Elizabeth the Queen Mother.

967	**198a** 1m.50 black and mauve	1·25	1·25
968	– 1m.50 black and mauve	1·25	1·25
969	– 1m.50 black and mauve	1·25	1·25
MS970	90 × 75 mm. 5m. brown, black and mauve	4·00	4·00

DESIGNS: No. 968, Lady Elizabeth Bowes-Lyon in evening dress; 969, Lady Elizabeth Bowes-Lyon wearing hat; **MS**970, Lady Elizabeth Bowes-Lyon as a child.

199 King Moshoeshoe II and Prince Mohato wearing Seana-Marena Blankets

200 Filling Truck at No. 1 Quarry

1990. Traditional Blankets. Multicoloured.

971	12s. Type **199**	10	10
972	16s. Prince Mohato wearing Seana-Marena blanket	10	10
973	1m. Pope John Paul II wearing Seana-Marena blanket	1·75	1·10
974	3m. Basotho horsemen wearing Matlama blankets	2·00	3·00
MS975	85 × 104 mm. 5m. Pope John Paul II wearing hat and Seana-Marena blanket (horiz)	4·50	4·75

1990. Lesotho Highlands Water Project. Mult.

976	16s. Type **200**	75	10
977	20s. Tanker lorry on Pitseng–Malibamatso road	80	10
978	55s. Piers for Malibamatso Bridge	90	30
979	2m. Excavating Mphosong section of Pitseng–Malibamatso road	3·00	3·75
MS980	104 × 85 mm. 5m. Sinking blasting borcholes on Pitseng–Malibamatso road	6·50	7·50

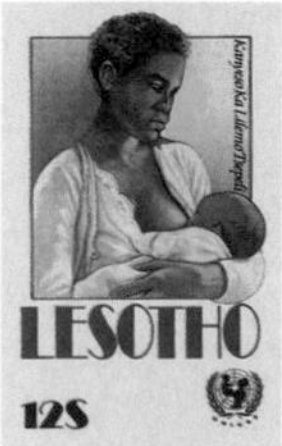

201 Mother breastfeeding Baby

202 Men's Triple Jump

1990. UNICEF Child Survival Campaign. Multicoloured.

981	12s. Type **201**	60	10
982	55s. Baby receiving oral rehydration therapy	1·10	45
983	1m. Weight monitoring	1·75	2·75

1990. Olympic Games, Barcelona (1992). Mult.

984	16s. Type **202**	65	10
985	55s. Men's 200 m race	85	25
986	1m. Men's 5000 m race	1·40	1·25
987	4m. Show jumping	4·00	6·00
MS988	100 × 70 mm. 5m. Olympic flame (horiz)	6·50	7·50

203 "Virgin and Child" (detail, Rubens)

1990. Christmas. Paintings by Rubens. Mult.

989	12s. Type **203**	20	10
990	16s. "Adoration of the Magi" (detail)	20	10
991	55s. "Head of One of the Three Kings"	45	25
992	80s. "Adoration of the Magi" (different detail)	60	60
993	1m. "Virgin and Child" (different detail)	70	70
994	2m. "Adoration of the Magi" (different detail)	1·25	1·75
995	3m. "Virgin and Child" (different detail)	2·00	2·50
996	4m. "Adoration of the Magi" (different detail)	2·25	3·25
MS997	71 × 100 mm. 5m. "Assumption of the Virgin" (detail)	4·00	5·50

204 Mickey Mouse at Nagasaki Peace Park

1991. "Phila Nippon '91" International Stamp Exhibition, Tokyo. Walt Disney cartoon characters in Japan. Multicoloured.

998	20s. Type **204**	70	15
999	30s. Mickey Mouse on Kamakura Beach	75	20
1000	40s. Mickey and Donald Duck with Bunraku puppet	85	25
1001	50s. Mickey and Donald eating soba	95	35
1002	75s. Mickey and Minnie Mouse at tea house	1·25	70
1003	1m. Mickey running after "Hikari" express train	1·25	1·00
1004	3m. Mickey Mouse with deer at Todaiji Temple, Nara	3·00	3·50
1005	4m. Mickey and Minnie outside Imperial Palace	3·00	4·00
MS1006	Two sheets, each 127 × 112 mm. (a) 5m. Mickey Mouse skiing. (b) 5m. Mickey and Minnie having a picnic. Set of 2 sheets	7·00	8·00

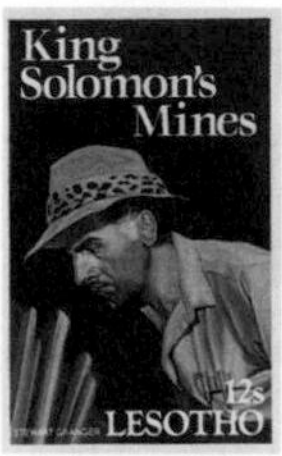

205 Stewart Granger ("King Solomon's Mines")

207 Victim of Drug Abuse

206 "Satyrus aello"

1991. Famous Films with African Themes. Mult.

1007	12s. Type **205**	35	20
1008	16s. Johnny Weissmuller ("Tarzan the Ape Man")	35	20
1009	30s. Clark Gable and Grace Kelly ("Mogambo")	50	35
1010	55s. Sigourney Weaver and gorilla ("Gorillas in the Mist")	75	55
1011	70s. Humphrey Bogart and Katharine Hepburn ("The African Queen")	90	80
1012	1m. John Wayne and capture of rhinoceros ("Hatari!")	1·25	1·00
1013	2m. Meryl Streep and De Havilland Gipsy Moth light aircraft ("Out of Africa")	2·00	2·25
1014	4m. Arsenio Hall and Eddie Murphy ("Coming to America")	2·75	3·50
MS1015	108 × 77 mm. 5m. Elsa the Lioness ("Born Free")	3·75	4·50

1991. Butterflies. Multicoloured.

1016B	2s. Type **206**	10	30
1017B	3s. "Erebia medusa"	10	30
1018A	5s. "Melanargia galathea"	10	30
1019B	10s. "Erebia aethiops"	15	30
1020A	20s. "Coenonympha pamphilus"	20	10
1021B	25s. "Pyrameis atalanta"	20	10
1022B	30s. "Charaxes jasius"	25	10
1023B	40s. "Colias palaeno"	25	10
1024B	50s. "Colias cliopatra"	30	10
1025B	60s. "Colias philodice"	30	10
1026B	70s. "Rhumni gonepterix"	30	10
1027B	1m. "Colias caesonia"	50	25
1028B	2m. "Pyrameis cardui"	90	75
1029cA	3m. "Danaus chrysippus"	1·40	1·75
1030B	10m. "Apatura iris"	4·00	4·50

1991. "Say No To Drugs" Campaign.

1031	**207** 16s. multicoloured	1·50	60

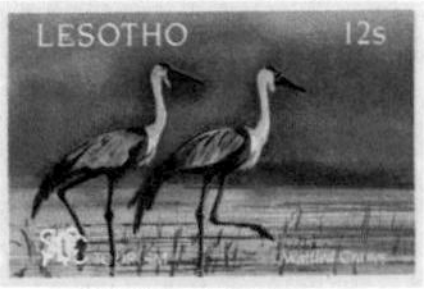

208 Wattled Cranes

1991. Southern Africa Development Co-ordination Conference Tourism Promotion. Multicoloured.

1032	12s. Type **208**	1·25	1·00
1033	16s. Butterfly on flowers	1·25	1·00
1034	25s. Zebra and tourist bus at Mukorob (rock formation), Namibia	1·50	60
MS1035	75 × 117 mm. 3m. Basotho women in ceremonial dress	3·75	4·50

209 De Gaulle in 1939

211 "St. Anne with Mary and the Child Jesus"

210 Prince and Princess of Wales

1991. Birth Centenary of Charles de Gaulle (French statesman).

1036	**209** 20s. black and brown	80	15
1037	– 40s. black and purple	1·00	25
1038	– 50s. black and green	1·00	40
1039	– 60s. black and blue	1·00	70
1040	– 4m. black and red	3·50	5·50

DESIGNS: 40s. General De Gaulle as Free French leader; 50s. De Gaulle as provisional President of France, 1944–46; 60s. Charles de Gaulle in 1958; 4m. Pres. De Gaulle.

1991. 10th Wedding Anniv of Prince and Princess of Wales. Multicoloured.

1041	50s. Type **210**	1·50	25
1042	70s. Prince Charles at polo and Princess Diana holding Prince Harry	1·50	45
1043	1m. Prince Charles with Prince Harry and Princess Diana in evening dress	1·60	70
1044	3m. Prince William and Prince Harry in school uniform	2·25	3·00
MS1045	68 × 91 mm. 4m. Portraits of Prince with Princess and sons	5·50	4·25

1991. Christmas. Drawings by Albrecht Durer.

1046	**211** 20s. black and mauve	60	10
1047	– 30s. black and blue	75	20
1048	– 50s. black and green	90	25
1049	– 60s. black and red	95	30
1050	– 70s. black and yellow	1·00	60
1051	– 1m. black and orange	1·25	1·10
1052	– 2m. black and purple	2·50	2·75
1053	– 4m. black and blue	3·50	6·00
MS1054	Two sheets, each 102 × 127 mm. (a) 5m. black and red. (b) 5m. black and blue. Set of 2 sheets	6·00	7·50

DESIGNS: 30s. "Mary on Grass Bench"; 50s. "Mary with Crown of Stars"; 60s. "Mary with Child beside Tree"; 70s. "Mary with Child beside Wall"; 1m. "Mary in Halo on Crescent Moon"; 2m. "Mary breastfeeding Child"; 4m. "Mary with Infant in Swaddling Clothes".

212 Mickey Mouse and Pluto pinning the Tail on the Donkey

1991. Children's Games. Walt Disney cartoon characters. Multicoloured.

1055	20s. Type **212**	65	15
1056	30s. Mickey playing mancala	70	20
1057	40s. Mickey rolling hoop	80	20
1058	50s. Minnie Mouse hula-hooping	90	25
1059	70s. Mickey and Pluto throwing a frisbee	1·25	75
1060	1m. Donald Duck with a diabolo	1·60	1·40
1061	2m. Donald's nephews playing marbles	2·50	3·00
1062	3m. Donald with Rubik's cube	3·00	4·00
MS1063	Two sheets, each 127 × 112 mm. (a) 5m. Donald's and Mickey's nephews playing tug-of-war. (b) 5m. Mickey and Donald mock fighting. Set of 2 sheets	8·00	9·00

213 Lanner Falcon

1992. Birds. Multicoloured.

1064	30s. Type **213**	65	60
1065	30s. Bateleur	65	60
1066	30s. Paradise sparrow (inscr "Red-headed Finch")	65	60
1067	30s. Lesser striped swallow	65	60
1068	30s. Alpine swift	65	60
1069	30s. Didric cuckoo ("Diederik Cuckoo")	65	60

1070 30s. Yellow-tufted malachite sunbird ("Malachite Sunbird") 65 60
1071 30s. Burchell's gonolek ("Crimson-breasted Shrike") 65 60
1072 30s. Pin-tailed whydah . . . 65 60
1073 30s. Lilac-breasted roller . . 65 60
1074 30s. Black bustard ("Korhaan") 65 60
1075 30s. Black-collared barbet 65 60
1076 30s. Secretary bird 65 60
1077 30s. Red-billed quelea . . . 65 60
1078 30s. Red bishop 65 60
1079 30s. Ring-necked dove . . . 65 60
1080 30s. Yellow canary 65 60
1081 30s. Cape longclaw ("Orange-throated Longclaw") 65 60
1082 30s. Cordon-bleu (inscr "Blue Waxbill") 65 60
1083 30s. Golden bishop 65 60
Nos. 1064/83 were printed together, se-tenant, forming a composite design.

214 Queen Elizabeth and Cooking at a Mountain Homestead

1992. 40th Anniv of Queen Elizabeth II's Accession. Multicoloured.
1084 20s. Type **214** 35 15
1085 30s. View from mountains 35 20
1086 1m. Cacti and mountain . . 1·00 65
1087 4m. Thaba-Bosiu . . . . . 3·00 3·50
MS1088 75 × 97 mm. 5m. Mountains at sunset . . . . 4·25 4·50

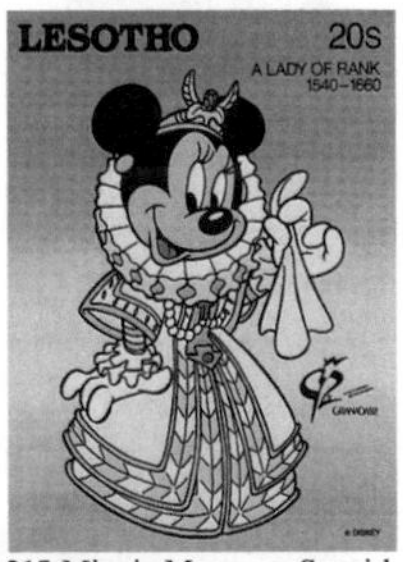

215 Minnie Mouse as Spanish Lady, 1540–1660

1992. International Stamp Exhibitions. Walt Disney cartoon characters. Multicoloured. (a) "Granada '92", Spain. Traditional Spanish Costumes.
1089 20s. Type **215** 80 20
1090 50s. Mickey Mouse as Don Juan at Lepanto, 1571 . . 95 40
1091 70s. Donald in Galician costume, 1880 . . . . . 1·25 70
1092 2m. Daisy Duck in Aragonese costume, 1880 2·50 3·25
MS1093 127 × 112 mm. 5m. Goofy the bullfighter . . . . 4·50 5·00

(b) "World Columbian Stamp Expo '92". Red Indian Life.
1094 30s. Donald Duck making arrowheads 70 30
1095 40s. Goofy playing lacrosse 75 40
1096 1m. Mickey Mouse and Donald Duck planting corn . . . . 1·25 1·10
1097 3m. Minnie Mouse doing bead work . . . . 2·75 3·25
MS1098 127 × 112 mm. 5m. Mickey paddling canoe . . . . 4·50 5·00

216 Stegosaurus

1992. Prehistoric Animals. Multicoloured.
1099 20s. Type **216** 90 30
1100 30s. Ceratosaurus . . . . . 1·00 35
1101 40s. Procompsognathus . . 1·25 45
1102 50s. Lesothosaurus . . . . 1·50 55
1103 70s. Plateosaurus . . . . . 1·50 70
1104 1m. Gasosaurus . . . . . . 1·75 1·25
1105 2m. Massospondylus . . . 2·25 2·75
1106 3m. Archaeopteryx . . . . 2·50 3·50
MS1107 Two sheets, each 105 × 77 mm. (a) 5m. As 50s. (b) 5m. As 3m. Set of 2 sheets . . 11·00 9·50

217 Men's Discus **218** "Virgin and Child" (Sassetta)

1992. Olympic Games, Albertville and Barcelona. Multicoloured.
1108 20s. Type **217** 20 15
1109 30s. Men's long jump . . . 25 15
1110 40s. Women's 4 × 100 m relay 30 25
1111 70s. Women's 100 m 50 50
1112 1m. Men's parallel bars . . 70 70
1113 2m. Men's double luge (horiz) . . . . 1·40 1·75
1114 3m. Women's 30k cross-country skiing (horiz) . . 1·75 2·50
1115 4m. Men's biathlon . . . . 2·00 2·75
MS1116 Two sheets, each 100 × 70 mm. (a) 5m. Women's figure skating. (b) 5m. Ice hockey (horiz). Set of 2 sheets . . . . 6·75 7·50

1992. Christmas. Religious Paintings. Mult.
1117 20s. Type **218** 45 15
1118 30s. "Coronation of the Virgin" (Master of Bonastre) 55 20
1119 40s. "Virgin and Child" (Master of SS. Cosmas and Damian) 65 25
1120 70s. "The Virgin of Great Panagia" (detail) (12th-century Russian school) . . . . 1·00 55
1121 1m. "Madonna and Child" (Vincenzo Foppa) . . . . 1·60 1·10
1122 2m. "Madonna and Child" (School of Lippo Memmi) 2·25 2·50
1123 3m. "Virgin and Child" (Barnaba da Modena) . . 2·75 3·25
1124 4m. "Virgin and Child with Saints" (triptych) (Simone dei Crocifissi) . . . . . . 3·00 3·50
MS1125 Two sheets, each 76 × 102 mm. (a) 5m. "Virgin and Child with Saints" (different detail) (Simone dei Crocifissi). (b) 5m. "Virgin and Child enthroned and surrounded by Angels" (Cimabue). Set of 2 sheets . . 8·00 10·00

219 World Trade Centre, New York

1992. Postage Stamp Mega Event, New York. Sheet 100 × 70 mm.
MS1126 **219** 5m. multicoloured 5·50 6·50

220 Baby Harp Seal (Earth Summit '92, Rio)

1993. Anniversaries and Events. Multicoloured.
1127 20s. Type **220** 85 40
1128 30s. Giant panda (Earth Summit '92, Rio) . . . . 1·10 40
1129 40s. Airship "Graf Zeppelin" over globe (75th death anniv of Count Ferdinand von Zeppelin) . . . . 1·10 40
1130 70s. Woman grinding maize (International Conference on Nutrition, Rome) . . . 60 45
1131 4m. Lt. Robinson's Royal Aircraft Factory B.E.2C shooting down Schutte Lanz SL-11 airship (75th death anniv of Count Ferdinand von Zeppelin) 3·50 4·25
1132 5m. Valentina Tereshkova and "Vostok 6" (30th anniv of first woman in space) . . . . 3·50 4·25
MS1133 Two sheets, each 100 × 70 mm. (a) 5m. Dr. Ronald McNair ("Challenger" astronaut) (International Space Year). (b) 5m. South African crowned crane (Earth Summit '92, Rio). Set of 2 sheets . . . . 9·00 9·00

221 "Orpheus and Eurydice" (detail)

1993. Bicentenary of the Louvre, Paris. Paintings by Poussin. Multicoloured.
1134 70s. Type **221** 80 80
1135 70s. "Rape of the Sabine Women" (left detail) . . . 80 80
1136 70s. "Rape of the Sabine Women" (right detail) . . 80 80
1137 70s. "The Death of Sapphira" (left detail) . . 80 80
1138 70s. "The Death of Sapphira" (right detail) 80 80
1139 70s. "Echo and Narcissus" (left detail) 80 80
1140 70s. "Echo and Narcissus" (right detail) 80 80
1141 70s. "Self-portrait" 80 80
MS1142 70 × 100 mm. 5m. "The Money Lender and his Wife" (57 × 89 mm) (Metsys) . . . . 4·75 5·00

222 Aloe

1993. Flowers. Multicoloured.
1143 20s. Type **222** 40 10
1144 30s. Calla lily 45 15
1145 40s. Bird of paradise plant 45 15
1146 70s. Amaryllis 75 40
1147 1m. Agapanthus 90 60
1148 2m. Crinum . . . . 2·75 2·25
1149 4m. Watsonia . . . . 2·50 3·25
1150 5m. Gazania . . . . 2·50 3·50
MS1151 Two sheets, each 98 × 67 mm. (a) 7m. Plumbago. (b) 7m. Desert Rose. Set of 2 sheets 7·50 8·50

223 "Precis westermanni"

1993. Butterflies. Multicoloured.
1152 20s. Type **223** 40 15
1153 40s. "Precis sophia" 50 20
1154 70s. "Precis terea" 65 45
1155 1m. "Byblia acheloia" . . . 75 75
1156 2m. "Papilio antimachus" 1·25 1·50
1157 5m. "Pseudacraea boisduvali" . . . . 1·75 3·00
MS1158 Two sheets, each 96 × 62 mm. (a) 7m. "Precis oenone". (b) 7m. "Precis octavia". Set of 2 sheets . . . . 7·00 7·00
No. 1157 is inscribed "Pesudacraea boisduvali" in error.

224 Queen Elizabeth II at Coronation (photograph by Cecil Beaton)

1993. 40th Anniv of Coronation.
1159 **224** 20s. multicoloured . . . 80 85
1160 – 40s. multicoloured . . . 1·00 1·10
1161 – 1m. black and green . . 1·40 1·50
1162 – 5m. multicoloured . . . 3·25 3·50
MS1163 70 × 100 mm. 7m. multicoloured ($42\frac{1}{2} \times 28\frac{1}{2}$ mm) 6·00 6·50
DESIGNS—VERT: 40s. St. Edward's Crown and Sceptre; 1m. Queen Elizabeth the Queen Mother; 5m. Queen Elizabeth II and family. HORIZ: 7m. "Conversation Piece at Royal Lodge, Windsor" (detail) (Sir James Gunn).

225 East African Railways Vulcan Steam Locomotive, 1929

1993. African Railways. Multicoloured.
1164 20s. Type **225** 75 25
1165 30s. Beyer-Garratt Class 15A steam locomotive, Zimbabwe Railways, 1952 85 30
1166 40s. Class 25 steam locomotive, South African Railways, 1953 . . . . . 90 30
1167 70s. Class A 58 steam locomotive, East African Railways . . . . 1·25 60
1168 1m. Class 9E electric locomotives, South African Railways . . . . 1·40 85
1169 2m. Class 87 diesel-electric locomotive, East African Railways, 1971 . . . . . 1·75 1·60
1170 3m. Class 92 diesel locomotive, East African Railways, 1971 . . . . . 2·00 2·25
1171 5m. Class 26 steam locomotive No. 3450, South African Railways, 1982 . . . . 2·50 3·50
MS1172 Two sheets, each 104 × 82 mm. (a) 7m. Class 6E electric locomotive, South African Railways, 1969. (b) 7m. Class 231-132BT steam locomotive, Algerian Railways, 1937. Set of 2 sheets . . . . 10·00 10·00

226 Court-house

1993. Traditional Houses. Multicoloured.
1173 20s. Type **226** 50 10
1174 30s. House with reed fence 55 15
1175 70s. Unmarried girls' house 1·00 40
1176 4m. Hut made from branches . . . . 3·50 5·00
MS1177 81 × 69 mm. 4m. Decorated houses . . . . 3·00 4·00

227 Black and White Shorthair

1993. Domestic Cats. Multicoloured.
1178 20s. Type **227** 60 25
1179 30s. Shorthair tabby lying down 60 25
1180 70s. Head of shorthair tabby 80 40
1181 5m. Black and white shorthair with shorthair tabby . . . . 2·75 4·00
MS1182 113 × 89mm. 5m. Shorthair Tabby with rat (vert) . . . . . 3·75 4·00

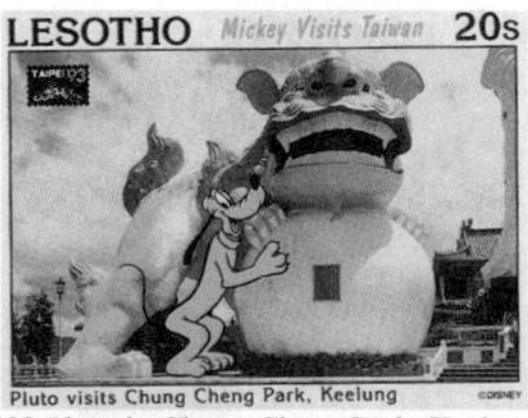

228 Pluto in Chung Cheng Park, Keelung

1993. "Taipei '93" Asian International Stamp Exhibition, Taiwan. Walt Disney cartoon characters in Taiwan. Multicoloured.

1183 20s. Type **228** 65 10
1184 30s. Donald Duck at Chiao-Tienkung Temple Festival 75 15
1185 40s. Goofy with lantern figures 85 20
1186 70s. Minnie Mouse shopping at temple festival 1·25 40
1187 1m. Daisy Duck at Queen's Head Rock, Yehliu (vert) 1·50 70
1188 1m.20 Mickey and Minnie at National Concert Hall (vert) 1·60 1·60
1189 2m. Donald at Chiang Kai-shek Memorial Hall (vert) 1·75 2·00
1190 2m.50 Donald and Daisy at the Grand Hotel, Taipei 2·00 2·75
MS1191 Two sheets, each 128 × 102 mm. (a) 5m. Goofy over National Palace Museum, Taipei. (b) 6m. Mickey and Minnie at Presidential Palace Museum, Taipei (vert). Set of 2 sheets 8·50 8·50

229 Tseliso "Frisco" Khomari (Lesotho)

230 King Letsie III signing Oath of Office

1994. World Cup Football Championship, U.S.A. Multicoloured.

1192 20s. Type **229** 50 10
1193 30s. Thato "American Spoon" Mohale (Lesotho) 55 15
1194 40s. Jozic Davor (Yugoslavia) and Freddy Rincorn (Colombia) 65 20
1195 50s. Lefika "Mzee" Lekhotla (Lesotho) 70 25
1196 70s. Litsiso "House-on-fire" Khali (Lesotho) 85 55
1197 1m. Roger Milla (Cameroun) 1·00 85
1198 1m.20 David Platt (England) 1·50 2·00
1199 2m. Karl Heinz Rummenigge (Germany) and Soren Lerby (Denmark) 1·75 2·50
MS1200 Two sheets, each 100 × 70 mm. (a) 6m. Klaus Lindenberger (Czechoslovakia). (b) 6m. Franco Baresi (Italy) and Ivan Hasek (Czechoslovakia) (horiz). Set of 2 sheets 8·50 8·50

1994. 1st Anniv of Restoration of Democracy. Multicoloured.

1201 20s. Type **230** 20 15
1202 30s. Parliament building (horiz) 25 15
1203 50s. Swearing-in of Dr. Ntsu Mokhehle as Prime Minister (horiz) 40 20
1204 70s. Maj-Gen P. Ramaema handing Instruments of Government to Dr. Ntsu Mokhehle (horiz) 70 40

231 Aquatic River Frog

1994. "Philakorea '94" International Stamp Exhibition, Seoul. Frogs and Toads. Mult.

1205 35s. Type **231** 25 10
1206 50s. Bubbling kassina 35 15
1207 1m. Guttural toad 60 60
1208 1m.50 Common river frog 80 1·25
MS1209 Two sheets, each 102 × 72 mm. (a) 5m. Jade frog (sculpture). (b) 5m. Black Spotted frog and oriental white-eye (bird) (vert). Set of 2 sheets 8·50 8·50

232 De Havilland D.H.C.6 Twin Otter and Emblem

1994. 50th Anniv of I.C.A.O. Multicoloured.

1210 35s. Type **232** 40 15
1211 50s. Fokker F.27 Friendship on runway 55 20
1212 1m. Fokker F.27 Friendship over Moshoeshoe I International Airport 90 70
1213 1m.50 Cessna light aircraft over mountains 1·25 1·50

1995. No. 1022 surch **20s**.

1214a 20s. on 30s. "Charaxes jasius" 1·00 65

234 "Tagetes minuta"

235 Pius XII College, 1962

1995. Medicinal Plants. Multicoloured.

1215 35s. Type **234** 20 10
1216 50s. "Plantago lanceolata" 25 15
1217 1m. "Amaranthus spinosus" 45 45
1218 1m.50 "Taraxacum officinale" 80 1·10
MS1219 120 × 91 mm. 5m. "Dativa stramonium" 2·00 2·25

1995. 50th Anniv of University Studies in Lesotho. Multicoloured.

1220 35s. Type **235** 15 10
1221 50s. Campus, University of Basutoland, Bechuanaland and Swaziland, 1966 20 15
1222 70s. Campus, University of Botswana, Lesotho and Swaziland, 1970 30 15
1223 1m. Administration Block, University of Botswana, Lesotho and Swaziland, 1975 45 40
1224 1m.50 Administration Block, National University of Lesotho, 1988 65 85
1225 2m. Procession of Vice-Chancellors, National University of Lesotho, 1995 80 1·40

236 Qiloane Pinnacle, Thaba-Bosiu

237 "Peace"

1995. 20th Anniv of World Tourism Organization. Multicoloured.

1226 35s. Type **236** 25 10
1227 50s. Ha Mohalenyane rock formation 30 15
1228 1m. Botsoela Falls (vert) 55 45
1229 1m.50 Backpackers in Makhaleng River Gorge 80 1·25
MS1230 143 × 88 mm. 4m. Red Hot Pokers (38 × 57 mm) 2·00 2·25

No. **MS**1230 is inscribed "RED HOT PORKERS" in error.

1995. 50th Anniv of United Nations. Multicoloured.

1231 35s. Type **237** 30 10
1232 50s. "Justice" (scales) 40 20
1233 1m.50 "Reconciliation" (clasped hands) (horiz) 1·00 1·40

238 "Sutter's Gold Rose"

240 Adding Iodized Salt to Cooking Pot

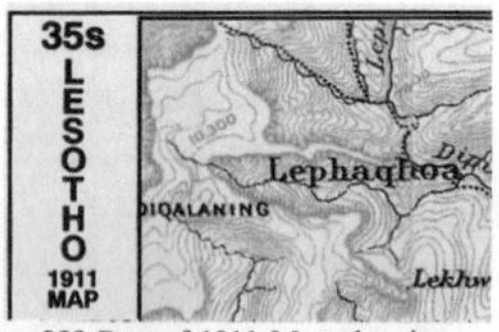

239 Part of 1911 Map showing Lephaqhoa

1995. Christmas. Roses. Multicoloured.

1234 5s. Type **238** 10 30
1235 50s. "Michele Meilland" 35 10
1236 1m. "J. Otto Thilow" 60 40
1237 2m. "Papa Meilland" 95 1·40

1996. Completion of New Standard Map of Lesotho (1994). Map Sections of Malibamatso Valley. Multicoloured. (a) 1911 Map.

1238 35s. Type **239** 30 30
1239 35s. Boritsa Tsuene 30 30
1240 35s. Molapo 30 30
1241 35s. Nkeu 30 30
1242 35s. Three rivers flowing east 30 30
1243 35s. Tibedi and Rafanyane 30 30
1244 35s. Two rivers flowing east 30 30
1245 35s. Madibatmatso River 30 30
1246 35s. Bokung River 30 30
1247 35s. Semena River 30 30

(b) 1978 Map.

1248 35s. Mountains and river valley 30 30
1249 35s. Pelaneng and Lepaqoa 30 30
1250 35s. Mamohau 30 30
1251 35s. Ha Lejone 30 30
1252 35s. Ha Thoora 30 30
1253 35s. Ha Mikia 30 30
1254 35s. Ha Kosetabole 30 30
1255 35s. Ha Seshote 30 30
1256 35s. Ha Rapooane 30 30
1257 35s. Bokong Ha Kennan 30 30

(c) 1994 Map.

1258 35s. Mafika-Lisiu Pass 30 30
1259 35s. Ha Lesaoana 30 30
1260 35s. Ha Masaballa 30 30
1261 35s. Ha Nkisi 30 30
1262 35s. Ha Rafanyane 30 30
1263 35s. Laitsoka Pass 30 30
1264 35s. "Katse Reservoir" 30 30
1265 35s. Seshote 30 30
1266 35s. Sephareng 30 30
1267 35s. Katse Dam 30 30

Nos. 1238/47, 1248/57 and 1258/67 respectively were printed together, se-tenant, forming composite designs.

1996. 50th Anniv of UNICEF. Multicoloured.

1268 35s. Type **240** 25 10
1269 50s. Herdboys with livestock (horiz) 35 20
1270 70s. Children in class (horiz) 45 20
1271 1m.50 Boys performing traditional dance (horiz) 90 1·25

241 U.S.A. Basketball Team, 1936

1996. Olympic Games, Atlanta. Previous Gold Medal Winners. Multicoloured.

1272 1m. Type **241** 50 20
1273 1m.50 Brandenburg Gate and stadium, Berlin, 1936 50 30
1274 1m.50 Glen Morris (U.S.A.) (decathlon, 1936) (vert) 50 50
1275 1m.50 Saidi Aouita (Morocco) (5000 m running, 1984) (vert) 50 50
1276 1m.50 Arnie Robinson (U.S.A.) (long jump, 1976) (vert) 50 50
1277 1m.50 Hans Woellke (Germany) (shot put, 1936) (vert) 50 50
1278 1m.50 Renate Stecher (Germany) (100 m running, 1972) (vert) 50 50
1279 1m.50 Evelyn Ashford (U.S.A.) (100 m running, 1984) (vert) 50 50
1280 1m.50 Willie Davenport (U.S.A.) (110 m hurdles, 1968) (vert) 50 50
1281 1m.50 Bob Beamon (U.S.A.) (long jump, 1968) (vert) 50 50
1282 1m.50 Heidi Rosendhal (Germany) (long jump, 1972) (vert) 50 50
1283 2m. Jesse Owens (U.S.A.) (track and field, 1936) (vert) 65 70
1284 3m. Speed boat racing 85 1·00
MS1285 Two sheets, each 110 × 80 mm. (a) 8m. Michael Gross (Germany) (swimming, 1984) (vert). (b) 8m. Kornelia Ender (Germany) (swimming, 1976) (vert). Set of 2 sheets 6·50 7·00

No. 1273 is inscribed "BRANDEBOURG GATE" in error. No. 1274 incorrectly identifies Glen Morris as the gold medal winner in the 1936 long jump.

Nos. 1274/82 were printed together, se-tenant, with the backgrounds forming a composite design.

242 Class WP Steam Locomotive (India)

1996. Trains of the World. Multicoloured.

1286 1m.50 Type **242** 75 75
1287 1m.50 Canadian Pacific steam locomotive No. 2471 (Canada) 75 75
1288 1m.50 The "Caledonian" (Great Britain) 75 75
1289 1m.50 Steam locomotive "William Mason" (U.S.A.) 75 75
1290 1m.50 "Trans-Siberian Express" (Russia) 75 75
1291 1m.50 Steam train (Switzerland) 75 75
1292 1m.50 ETR 450 high speed train (Italy) 75 75
1293 1m.50 TGV express train (France) 75 75
1294 1m.50 XPT high speed train (Australia) 75 75
1295 1m.50 "Blue Train" (South Africa) 75 75
1296 1m.50 Intercity 225 express train (Great Britain) 75 75
1297 1m.50 "Hikari" express train (Japan) 75 75
MS1298 Two sheets, each 98 × 68 mm. (a) 8m. Class 52 steam locomotive (Germany) (57 × 43 mm). (b) 8m. ICE high speed train (Germany) (57 × 43 mm). Set of 2 sheets 7·50 8·00

243 Mothers' Union Member, Methodist Church

1996. Christmas. Mothers' Unions. Multicoloured.

1299 35s. Type **243** 25 10
1300 50s. Roman Catholic Church 30 10
1301 1m. Lesotho Evangelical Church 55 35
1302 1m.50 Anglican Church 80 1·25

No. 1302 is inscribed "Anglian" in error.

244 Hand Clasp (Co-operation for Development)

245 Land Reclamation

1997. 10th Anniv of Lesotho Highland Water Project (1996). Multicoloured.

1303 35s. Type **244** 25 10
1304 50s. Lammergeier and rock painting (Nature and Heritage) 50 20
1305 1m. Malibamatso Bridge (Engineering) 60 40
1306 1m.50 Katse Valley in 1986 and 1996 (75 × 28 mm) 90 1·25

No. 1305 is inscribed "Developement" in error.

1997. Environment Protection. Multicoloured.

1307 35s. Type **245** 25 10
1308 50s. Throwing rubbish into bin 30 15
1309 1m. Hands holding globe and tree 55 30
1310 1m.20 Recycling symbol and rubbish 65 65
1311 1m.50 Collecting rain water 75 85

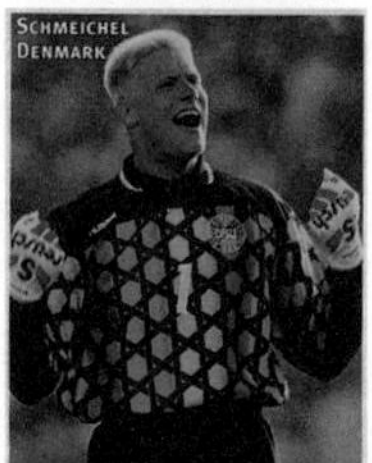

246 Schmeichel, Denmark

1997. World Cup Football Championship, France (1998). Multicoloured.

1312 1m. Type **246** 40 20
1313 1m.50 Bergkamp, Netherlands 55 55
1314 1m.50 Argentine players celebrating 55 55
1315 1m.50 Argentine and Dutch players competing for ball 55 55
1316 1m.50 Players heading ball 55 55
1317 1m.50 Goalkeeper deflecting ball 55 55
1318 1m.50 Goal-mouth melee 55 55
1319 1m.50 Argentine player kicking ball 55 55
1320 2m. Southgate, England 70 70
1321 2m.50 Asprilla, Colombia 80 85
1322 3m. Gascoigne, England 90 95
1323 4m. Giggs, Wales 1·10 1·25
MS1324 Two sheets, each 127 × 102 mm. (a) 8m. Littbarski, West Germany (horiz). (b) 8m. Shearer, England. Set of 2 sheets 6·50 7·00

247 "Spialia spio"

1997. Butterflies. Multicoloured.

1325 1m.50 Type **247** 60 60
1326 1m.50 "Leptotes pirithous" 60 60
1327 1m.50 "Acratea satis" 60 60
1328 1m.50 "Belenois aurota aurota" 60 60
1329 1m.50 "Spindasis natalensis" 60 60
1330 1m.50 "Torynesis orangica" 60 60
1331 1m.50 "Lepidochysops variabilis" 60 60
1332 1m.50 "Pinacopteryx eriphia" 60 60
1333 1m.50 "Anthene butleri livida" 60 60
MS1334 Two sheets, each 106 × 76 mm. (a) 8m. "Bematistes aganice". (b) 8m. "Papilio demodocus". Set of 2 sheets 6·50 6·50

Nos. 1325/33 were printed together, se-tenant, with the backgrounds forming a composite design.

No. 1326 is inscribed "Cyclyrius pirithous", No. 1332 "Pinacopteryx eriphea" and No. **MS**1334(b) "Papalio demodocus", all in error.

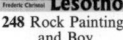

248 Rock Paintings and Boy **249** Diana, Princess of Wales

1998. 40th Anniv of Morija Museum and Archives. Multicoloured.

1335 35s. Type **248** 10 10
1336 45s. Hippopotamus and lower jaw bone (horiz) 10 10
1337 50s. Woman and cowhide skirt 10 10
1338 1m. Drum and "thomo" (musical bow) 15 20
1339 1m.50 Warrior with "khau" (gorget awarded for valour) 25 30
1340 2m. Herders with ox (horiz) 35 40

1998. Diana, Princess of Wales Commemoration. Multicoloured.

1341 3m. Type **249** 1·10 1·25
1342 3m. Wearing grey jacket 1·10 1·25
1343 3m. Wearing white polo-necked jumper 1·10 1·25
1344 3m. Wearing pearl necklace 1·10 1·25
1345 3m. Wearing white evening dress 1·10 1·25
1346 3m. Wearing pale blue jacket 1·10 1·25
MS1347 70 × 100 mm. 9m. Accepting bouquet 6·50 6·50

250 Atitlan Grebe

1998. Fauna of the World. Multicoloured. (a) Vert designs as T **250**.

1348 1m. Type **250** 15 20
1349 1m. Cabot's tragopan 15 20
1350 1m. Spider monkey 15 20
1351 1m. Dibatag 15 20
1352 1m. Right whale 15 20
1353 1m. Imperial amazon ("Imperial Parrot") 15 20
1354 1m. Cheetah 15 20
1355 1m. Brown-eared pheasant 15 20
1356 1m. Leatherback turtle 15 20
1357 1m. Imperial woodpecker 15 20
1358 1m. Andean condor 15 20
1359 1m. Barbary deer 15 20
1360 1m. Grey gentle lemur 15 20
1361 1m. Cuban amazon ("Cuban Parrot") 15 20
1362 1m. Numbat 15 20
1363 1m. Short-tailed albatross 15 20
1364 1m. Green turtle 15 20
1365 1m. White rhinoceros 15 20
1366 1m. Diademed sifaka 15 20
1367 1m. Galapagos penguin 15 20

(b) Horiz designs, each 48 × 31 mm.

1368 1m.50 Impala 25 30
1369 1m.50 Black bear 25 30
1370 1m.50 American buffalo 25 30
1371 1m.50 African elephant 25 30
1372 1m.50 Kangaroo 25 30
1373 1m.50 Lion 25 30
1374 1m.50 Giant panda 25 30
1375 1m.50 Tiger 25 30
1376 1m.50 Zebra 25 30
MS1377 Four sheets, each 98 × 68 mm. (a) 8m. White-bellied sunbird. (b) 8m. Golden-shouldered parrot. (c) 8m. Snail darter. (d) 8m. Monkey (47 × 31 mm). Set of 4 sheets 5·25 5·50

251 Cape Vulture

1998. Endangered Species. Cape Vulture. Mult.

1378 1m. Type **251** 15 20
1379 1m. Looking towards ground 15 20
1380 1m. Looking over shoulder 15 20
1381 1m. Facing right 15 20

252 Siamese

1998. Cats of the World. Multicoloured.

1382 70s. Type **252** 10 10
1383 1m. Chartreux 15 20
1384 2m. Korat 35 40
1385 2m. Japanese bobtail 35 40
1386 2m. British white 35 40
1387 2m. Bengal 35 40
1388 2m. Abyssinian 35 40
1389 2m. Snowshoe 35 40
1390 2m. Scottish fold 35 40
1391 2m. Maine coon 35 40
1392 2m. Balinese 35 40
1393 2m. Persian 35 40
1394 2m. Javanese 35 40
1395 2m. Turkish angora 35 40
1396 2m. Tiffany 35 40
1397 3m. Egyptian mau 50 55
1398 4m. Bombay 65 70
1399 5m. Burmese 85 90
MS1400 Two sheets, each 98 × 69 mm. (a) 8m. Tonkinese. (b) 8m. Singapura. Set of 2 sheets 2·75 3·00

Nos. 1385/90 and 1391/6 respectively were printed together, se-tenant, with the backgrounds forming composite designs.

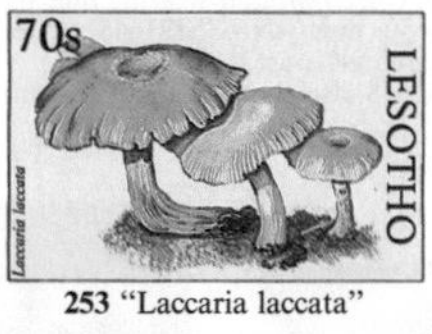

253 "Laccaria laccata"

1998. Fungi of the World. Multicoloured.

1401 70s. Type **253** 10 15
1402 1m. "Mutinus caninus" 15 20
1403 1m. "Hygrophorus psittacinus" 15 20
1404 1m. "Cortinarius obtusus" 15 20
1405 1m. "Volvariella bombycina" 15 20
1406 1m. "Cortinarius caerylescens" 15 20
1407 1m. "Laccaria amethystina" 15 20
1408 1m. "Tricholoma aurantium" 15 20
1409 1m. "Amanita excelsa (spissa)" 15 20
1410 1m. "Clavaria helvola" 15 20
1411 1m. Unidentified species (inscr "Cortinarius caerylescens") 15 20
1412 1m. "Russula queletii" 15 20
1413 1m. "Amanita phalloides" 15 20
1414 1m. "Lactarius deliciosus" 15 20
1415 1m.50 "Tricholoma lascivum" 25 30
1416 2m. "Clitocybe geotropa" 35 40
1417 3m. "Amanita excelsa" 50 55
1418 4m. Red-capped bolete 65 70
MS1419 Two sheets, each 98 × 68 mm. (a) 8m. "Amanita pantherina". (b) 8m. "Boletus satanas". Set of 2 sheets 2·75 3·00

Nos. 1406, 1407, 1414, 1416 and **MS**1419b are inscribed "Continarius caerylescens", "Laccaria amethystea", "Lactarius delicious", "Clitocybe geotrapa" and "Boletys satanus", all in error.

254 "Simba"

1998. World Cinema. Multicoloured. (a) Films about Africa.

1420 2m. Type **254** 35 40
1421 2m. "Call to Freedom" 35 40
1422 2m. "Cry the Beloved Country" 35 40
1423 2m. "King Solomon's Mines" 35 40
1424 2m. "Flame and the Fire" 35 40
1425 2m. "Cry Freedom" 35 40
1426 2m. "Bopha!" 35 40
1427 2m. "Zulu" 35 40

(b) Japanese Film Stars.

1428 2m. Takamine Hideko 35 40
1429 2m. James Shigeta 35 40
1430 2m. Miyoshi Umeki 35 40
1431 2m. May Ishimara 35 40
1432 2m. Sessue Hayakawa 35 40
1433 2m. Miiko Taka 35 40
1434 2m. Mori Masayuki 35 40
1435 2m. Hara Setsuko 35 40
1436 2m. Kyo Machiko 35 40
MS1437 Two sheets. (a) 68 × 98 mm. 10m. Lion cubs from "Born Free" (horiz). (b) 70 × 100 mm. 10m. Toshiro Mifune. Set of 2 sheets 3·25 3·50

Nos. 1420/7 and 1428/36 respectively were printed together, se-tenant, with the backgrounds forming composite designs.

No. 1423 is inscribed "KING SOLOMAN'S MINES" in error.

255 Ceresiosaurus

1998. Prehistoric Animals. Multicoloured.

1438 2m. Type **255** 35 40
1439 2m. Rhomaleosaurus 35 40
1440 2m. Anomalocaris 35 40
1441 2m. Mixosaurus 35 40
1442 2m. Stethacanthus 35 40
1443 2m. Dunklosteus 35 40
1444 2m. Tommotia 35 40
1445 2m. Sanctacaris 35 40
1446 2m. Ammonites 35 40
1447 2m. Rhamphorhynchus 35 40
1448 2m. Brachiosaurus 35 40
1449 2m. Mamenchisaurus hochuanensis 35 40
1450 2m. Ceratosaurus nasicornis 35 40
1451 2m. Archaeopteryx 35 40
1452 2m. Leaellynasaura amicagraphica 35 40
1453 2m. Chasmosaurus belli 35 40
1454 2m. Deinonychus and Pachyrhinosaurus 35 40
1455 2m. Deinonychus 35 40
1456 2m. Nyctosaurus 35 40
1457 2m. Volcanoes 35 40
1458 2m. Eudimorphodon 35 40
1459 2m. Apatosaurus 35 40
1460 2m. Peteinosaurus 35 40
1461 2m. Tropeognathus 35 40
1462 2m. Pteranodon ingens 35 40
1463 2m. Ornithodesmus 35 40
1464 2m. Wuerhosaurus 35 40
MS1465 Three sheets, each 100 × 70 mm. (a) 10m. Coelophysis (vert). (b) 10m. Tyrannosaurus (vert). (c) 10m. Woolly Rhinoceros. Set of 3 sheets 5·00 5·25

Nos. 1438/46, 1447/55 and 1456/64 respectively were printed together, se-tenant, with the backgrounds forming composite designs.

256 Treefish

1998. Year of the Ocean. Fishes. Multicoloured.

1466 1m. Type **256** 15 20
1467 1m. Tigerbarb 15 20
1468 1m. Bandtail puffer 15 20
1469 1m. Cod 15 20
1470 1m.50 Clown loach 25 30
1471 1m.50 Christy's lyretail 25 30
1472 1m.50 Filefish 25 30
1473 1m.50 Sicklefin killie 25 30
1474 2m. Brook trout 35 40
1475 2m. Emerald betta 35 40
1476 2m. Pacific electric ray 35 40
1477 2m. Bighead searobin 35 40
1478 2m. Weakfish 35 40
1479 2m. Red drum 35 40
1480 2m. Blue marlin 35 40
1481 2m. Yellowfin tuna 35 40
1482 2m. Barracuda 35 40
1483 2m. Striped bass 35 40
1484 2m. White shark 35 40
1485 2m. Permit 35 40
1486 2m. Purple firefish 35 40
1487 2m. Harlequin sweetlips 35 40
1488 2m. Clown wrasse 35 40
1489 2m. Bicolour angelfish 35 40
1490 2m. False cleanerfish 35 40
1491 2m. Mandarinfish 35 40
1492 2m. Regal tang 35 40
1493 2m. Clownfish 35 40
1494 2m. Bluegill 35 40
1495 2m. Grayling 35 40
1496 2m. Walleye 35 40
1497 2m. Brown trout 35 40
1498 2m. Atlantic salmon 35 40
1499 2m. Northern pike 35 40
1500 2m. Large-mouth bass 35 40
1501 2m. Rainbow trout 35 40
1502 2m. Platy variatus 35 40
1503 2m. Archerfish 35 40
1504 2m. Clown knifefish 35 40
1505 2m. Angelicus 35 40
1506 2m. Black arowana 35 40
1507 2m. Spotted scat 35 40
1508 2m. Kribensis 35 40
1509 2m. Golden pheasant 35 40
1510 3m. Harlequin tuskfish 50 55
1511 4m. Half-moon angelfish 65 70
1512 5m. Spotted trunkfish 85 90
1513 6m. Wolf eel 1·00 1·10
1514 7m. Cherubfish 1·20 1·30
MS1515 Four sheets, each 98 × 73 mm. (a) 12m. Common Carp. (b) 12m. Sockeye Salmon. (c) 12m. Winter Flounder. (d) 12m. Horn Shark. Set of 4 sheets 8·00 8·25

Nos. 1470/3 show the face value as "M1.5".

257 Crowning of King Letsie III

1998. 1st Anniv of Coronation of King Letsie III. Multicoloured.

1516 1m. Type **257** 15 20
1517 1m. King saluting Basotho nation 15 20
1518 1m. King Letsie in profile 15 20

258 "Pelargonium sidoides"

1998. Flowers. Multicoloured.

1519 10s. Type **258** 10 10
1520 15s. "Aponogeton ranunculiflorus" 10 10
1521 20s. "Sebaea leiostyla" 10 10
1522 40s. "Sebaea grandis" 10 10
1523 50s. "Satyrium neglectum" 10 10
1524 60s. "Massonia jasminiflora" 10 10
1525 70s. "Ajuga ophrydis" 10 15
1526 80s. "Nemesia fruticans" 10 15
1527 1m. "Aloe broomii" 15 20
1528 2m. "Wahlenbergia androsacea" 35 40
1529 2m.50 "Phygelius capensis" 40 45
1530 3m. "Dianthus basuticus" 50 55
1531 4m.50 "Rhodohypoxis baurii" 75 80
1532 5m. "Turbina oblongata" 85 90
1533 6m. "Hibiscus microcarpus" 1·00 1·10
1534 10m. "Lobelia erinus" ("Moraea stricta") 1·70 1·80

259 Japanese Akita

1999. Dogs. Multicoloured.

1535 70s. Type **259** 10 15
1536 1m. Canaan dog 15 20

1537 2m. Husky ("ESKIMO DOG") 35 40
1538 2m. Cirneco dell'Etna . . . 35 40
1539 2m. Afghan hound 35 40
1540 2m. Finnish spitz 35 40
1541 2m. Dalmatian 35 40
1542 2m. Basset hound 35 40
1543 2m. Shar-pei 35 40
1544 2m. Boxer 35 40
1545 2m. Catalan sheepdog . . . 35 40
1546 2m. English toy spaniel . . 35 40
1547 2m. Greyhound 35 40
1548 2m. Keeshond 35 40
1549 2m. Bearded collie 35 40
1550 4m.50 Norwegian elkhound 75 80
MS1551 Two sheets, each 98 × 69 mm. (a) 8m. Rough Collie. (b) 8m. Borzoi. Set of 2 sheets 2·75 3·00

Nos. 1538/43 and 1544/9 were printed together, se-tenant, with the backgrounds forming composite designs.

260 Belted Kingfisher

1999. Birds. Multicoloured.
1552 70s. Type **260** 10 15
1553 1m.50 Palm cockatoo (vert) 25 30
1554 2m. Red-tailed hawk 35 40
1555 2m. Evening grosbeak . . . 35 40
1556 2m. Blue-winged pitta ("Lesser Blue-winged Pitta") 35 40
1557 2m. Lichtenstein's oriole ("Atlamira Oriole") . . . 35 40
1558 2m. Rose-breasted grosbeak 35 40
1559 2m. Yellow warbler 35 40
1560 2m. Akiapolaau 35 40
1561 2m. American goldfinch . . 35 40
1562 2m. Common flicker ("Northern Flicker") . . 35 40
1563 2m. Western tanager 35 40
1564 2m. Blue jay (vert) 35 40
1565 2m. Common cardinal ("Northern Cardinal") (vert) 35 40
1566 2m. Yellow-headed blackbird (vert) 35 40
1567 2m. Red crossbill (vert) . . 35 40
1568 2m. Cedar waxwing (vert) 35 40
1569 2m. Vermilion flycatcher (vert) 35 40
1570 2m. Pileated woodpecker (vert) 35 40
1571 2m. Western meadowlark (vert) 35 40
1572 2m. Belted kingfisher ("Kingfisher") (vert) . . . 35 40
1573 3m. Tufted puffin 50 55
1574 4m. Reddish egret 65 70
1575 5m. Hoatzin (vert) 85 90
MS1576 Two sheets. (a) 76 × 106 mm. 8m. Great egret. (b) 106 × 76 mm. 8m. Chestnut-flanked white-eye "Zosterops erythropleura". Set of 2 sheets 2·75 3·00

No. 1553 shows the face value as "M1.5".

Nos. 1555/63 and 1564/72 were printed together, se-tenant, with the backgrounds forming composite designs.

261 "Cattleya dowiana"

1999. Orchids of the World. Multicoloured.
1577 1m.50 Type **261** 25 30
1578 2m. "Cochleanthes discolor" 35 40
1579 2m. "Cischweinfia dasyandra" 35 40
1580 2m. "Ceratostylis retisquama" 35 40
1581 2m. "Comparettia speciosa" 35 40
1582 2m. "Cryptostylis subulata" 35 40
1583 2m. "Cycnoches ventricosum" 35 40
1584 2m. "Dactylorhiza maculata" 35 40
1585 2m. "Cypripedium calceolus" 35 40
1586 2m. "Cymbidium finlaysonianum" 35 40
1587 2m. "Apasia epidendroides" 35 40
1588 2m. "Barkaria lindleyana" 35 40
1589 2m. "Bifrenaria tetragona" 35 40
1590 2m. "Bulbophyllum graveolens" 35 40
1591 2m. "Brassavola flagellaris" 35 40
1592 2m. "Bollea lawrenceana" 35 40
1593 2m. "Caladenia carnea" . . 35 40
1594 2m. "Catasetum macrocarpum" 35 40
1595 2m. "Cattleya aurantiaca" 35 40
1596 2m. "Dendrobium bellatulum" 35 40
1597 2m. "Dendrobium trigonopus" 35 40
1598 2m. "Dimerandra emarginata" 35 40
1599 2m. "Dressleria eburnea" . . 35 40
1600 2m. "Dracula tubeana" . . . 35 40
1601 2m. "Disa kirstenbosch" . . 35 40
1602 2m. "Encyclia alata" . . . 35 40
1603 2m. "Epidendrum pseudepidendrum" . . . 35 40
1604 2m. "Eriopsis biloba" . . . 35 40
1605 3m. "Diurus behrii" 50 55
1606 4m. "Ancistrochilus rothchildianus" 65 70
1607 5m. "Aerangis curnowiana" 85 90
1608 7m. "Arachnis flos-aeris" . . 1·20 1·30
1609 8m. "Aspasia principissa" 1·30 1·40
MS1610 Four sheets, each 110 × 82 mm. (a) 10m. "Paphiopedilum tonsum". (b) 10m. "Ansellia africana". (c) 10m. "Laelia rubescens". (d) 10m. "Ophrys apifera". Set of 4 sheets 6·75 7·00

No. 1583 was inscribed "Cycnoches ventricsum" in error.

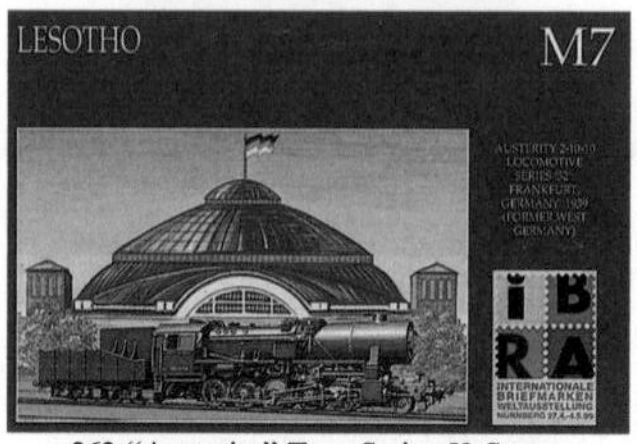

262 "Austerity" Type Series 52 Steam Locomotive, Frankfurt, 1939

1999. "iBRA '99" International Stamp Exhibition, Nuremburg. Railway Locomotives. Multicoloured.
1611 7m. Type **262** . . . . . . 1·20 1·30
1612 8m. "Adler" and Brandenburg Gate, Berlin, 1835 . . . . 1·30 1·40

263 "View of Sumida River in Snow"

1999. 150th Death Anniv of Katsushika Hokusai (Japanese artist). Multicoloured.
1613 3m. Type **263** 50 55
1614 3m. "Two Carp" 50 55
1615 3m. "The Blind" (woman with eyes closed) 50 55
1616 3m. "The Blind" (woman with one eye open) . . . 50 55
1617 3m. "Fishing by Torchlight" 50 55
1618 3m. "Whaling off the Goto Islands" 50 55
1619 3m. "Makamaro watching the Moon from a Hill" 50 55
1620 3m. "Peonies and Butterfly" 50 55
1621 3m. "The Blind" (old man with open eyes) 50 55
1622 3m. "The Blind" (old man with one eye open) . . . 50 55
1623 3m. "People crossing an Arched Bridge" (four people on bridge) 50 55
1624 3m. "People crossing an Arched Bridge" (two people on bridge) 50 55
MS1625 Two sheets, each 102 × 72 mm. (a) 10m. "Bell-flower and Dragonfly" (vert). (b) 10m. "Moon above Yodo River and Osaka Castle" (vert). Set of 2 sheets . . . . 3·25 3·50

264 African Boy

1999. 10th Anniv of United Nations Rights of the Child Convention. Multicoloured.
1626 2m. Type **264** 35 40
1627 2m. Asian girl 35 40
1628 2m. European boy 35 40

Nos. 1626/8 were printed together, se-tenant, the backgrounds forming a composite design.

265 Mephistopheles appearing as Dog in Faust's Study

1999. 250th Birth Anniv of Johann von Goethe (German writer).
1629 **265** 6m. multicoloured . . . 1·00 1·10
1630 – 6m. blue, lilac and black . . 1·00 1·10
1631 – 6m. multicoloured . . . 1·00 1·10
MS1632 76 × 106 mm. 12m. red, violet and black . . . . 2·00 2·10

DESIGNS—HORIZ: No. 1630, Goethe and Schiller; 1631, Mephistopheles disguised as a dog scorching the Earth. VERT: No. **MS**1632, Mephistopheles.

No. 1629, in addition to the normal country name, shows "GUYANA" twice in violet across the centre of the design.

266 "Water Lily at Night" (Pan Tianshou)

267 Queen Elizabeth, 1938

1999. "China '99" International Stamp Exhibition, Beijing. Paintings of Pan Tianshou (Chinese artist). Multicoloured.
1633 1m.50 Type **266** 25 30
1634 1m.50 "Hen and Chicks" . . 25 30
1635 1m.50 "Plum Blossom and Orchid" 25 30
1636 1m.50 "Plum Blossom and Banana Tree" 25 30
1637 1m.50 "Crane and Pine" . . 25 30
1638 1m.50 "Swallows" 25 30
1639 1m.50 "Eagle on the Pine" (bird looking up) 25 30
1640 1m.50 "Palm Tree" 25 30
1641 1m.50 "Eagle on the Pine" (bird looking down) . . . 25 30
1642 1m.50 "Orchids" 25 30
MS1643 138 × 105 mm. 6m. "Sponge Gourd" (51 × 39 mm); 6m. "Dragonfly" (51 × 39 mm) . . 2·00 2·10

1999. "Queen Elizabeth the Queen Mother's Century".
1644 **267** 5m. black and gold . . . 85 90
1645 – 5m. multicoloured . . . 85 90
1646 – 5m. black and gold . . . 85 90
1647 – 5m. multicoloured . . . 85 90
MS1648 153 × 152 mm. 15m. multicoloured . . . . 2·50 2·75

DESIGNS: No. 1645, King George VI and Queen Elizabeth, 1948; 1646, Queen Mother wearing tiara, 1963; 1647, Queen Mother wearing blue hat, Canada, 1989. 37 × 50 mm.—No. **MS**1648, Queen Mother outside Clarence House.

No. **MS**1648 also shows the Royal Arms embossed in gold.

268 Chinese Soldier firing Rocket, 1150

270 King Letsie III and Miss Karabo Anne Motsoeneng

269 U.S.S. "New Jersey" (battleship)

1999. New Millennium. People and Events of Twelfth Century (1150–99). Multicoloured.
1649 1m.50 Type **268** 25 30
1650 1m.50 Burmese temple guardian, 1150 . . . . . 25 30
1651 1m.50 Troubadour serenading Lady, 1150 . . 25 30
1652 1m.50 Abbot Suger (advisor to French Kings), 1150 25 30
1653 1m.50 Pope Adrian IV, 1154 25 30
1654 1m.50 Henry II of England, 1154 . . . . 25 30
1655 1m.50 Bust of Frederick Barbarossa, King of Germany, and Holy Roman Emperor, 1155 . . 25 30
1656 1m.50 Shogun Yoritomo of Japan, 1156 . . . . . . 25 30
1657 1m.50 Count and Countess of Vaudemont (Crusader monument), 1165 . . . . 25 30
1658 1m.50 Ibn Rushd (Arab translator), 1169 . . . . 25 30
1659 1m.50 Archbishop Thomas a Becket, 1170 . . . . . 25 30
1660 1m.50 Leaning Tower of Pisa, 1174 . . . . 25 30
1661 1m.50 Pivot windmill, 1180 25 30
1662 1m.50 Saladin (Saracen general), 1187 . . . . . 25 30
1663 1m.50 King Richard the Lionheart of England, 1189 . . . . 25 30
1664 1m.50 Moai (statues), Easter Island, 1150 (59 × 39 mm) 25 30
1665 1m.50 Crusader, 1189 . . . 25 30

1999. Maritime Developments 1700–2000. Mult.
1666 4m. Type **269** 65 70
1667 4m. "Aquila" (Italian aircraft carrier) 65 70
1668 4m. "De Zeven Provincien" (Dutch cruiser) 65 70
1669 4m. H.M.S. "Formidable" (aircraft carrier) 65 70
1670 4m. "Vittorio Veneto" (Italian cruiser) 65 70
1671 4m. H.M.S. "Hampshire" (destroyer) 65 70
1672 4m. "France" (French liner) 65 70
1673 4m. "Queen Elizabeth 2" (liner) 65 70
1674 4m. "United States" (American liner) 65 70
1675 4m. "Queen Elizabeth" (liner) 65 70
1676 4m. "Michelangelo" (Italian liner) 65 70
1677 4m. "Mauretania" (British liner) 65 70
1678 4m. "Shearwater" (British hydrofoil ferry) 65 70
1679 4m. British Class M submarine 65 70
1680 4m. SRN 130 hovercraft . . 65 70
1681 4m. Italian Second World War submarine 65 70
1682 4m. SRN 3 hovercraft . . . 65 70
1683 4m. "Soucoupe Plongeante" (oceanographic submersible) 65 70
1684 4m. "James Watt" (early steamship) 65 70
1685 4m. "Savannah" (steam/sail ship), 1819 . . . . 65 70
1686 4m. "Amistad" (slave schooner) 65 70
1687 4m. American Navy brig . . 65 70
1688 4m. "Great Britain" (liner) 65 70
1689 4m. "Sirius" (paddle steamer) 65 70
MS1690 Four sheets, each 106 × 76 mm. (a) 15m. U.S.S. "Enterprise" (aircraft carrier) (vert). (b) 15m. "Titanic" (liner). (c) 15m. German U-boat. (d) 15m. "E. W. Morrison" (Great Lakes schooner) (vert). Set of 4 sheets 10·00 10·50

Nos. 1686 and 1687 both have their names wrongly inscribed as "ARMISTAD" and "BRICK" on the sheet margin.

2000. Wedding of King Letsie III. Multicoloured.
1691 1m. Type **270** 15 20
1692 1m. Miss Karabo Anne Motsoeneng 15 20
1693 1m. King Letsie III 15 20
1694 1m. King Letsie III and Miss Karabo Motsoeneng in traditional dress . . . 15 20

271 "Apollo 18" and "Soyuz 19" docked in Orbit

2000. 25th Anniv of "Apollo–Soyuz" Joint Project. Multicoloured.
1695 8m. Type **271** . . . . . . 1·30 1·40
1696 8m. "Apollo 18" and docking module . . . . . 1·30 1·40
1697 8m. "Soyuz 19" . . . . . . 1·30 1·40
MS1698 106 × 76mm. 15m. Docking module and "Soyuz 19" . . . 2·50 2·75

272 Gena Rowlands (actress), 1978

274 Johann Sebastian Bach

273 George Stephenson

2000. 50th Anniv of Berlin Film Festival. Showing actors, directors and film scenes with awards. Multicoloured.

1699	6m. Type **272**	1·00	1·10
1700	6m. Vlastimil Brodsky (actor), 1975	1·00	1·10
1701	6m. Carlos Saura (director), 1966	1·00	1·10
1702	6m. Scene from *La Collectionneuse*, 1967	1·00	1·10
1703	6m. Scene from *Le Depart*, 1967	1·00	1·10
1704	6m. Scene from *Le Diable Probablement*, 1977	1·00	1·10
MS1705	97 × 103 mm. 15m. Scene from *Stammheim*, 1986	2·50	2·75

No. 1704 is inscribed "LE DIIABLE PROBABLEMENT" in error.

2000. 175th Anniv of Stockton and Darlington Line (first public railway). Multicoloured.

1706	8m. Type **273**	1·30	1·40
1707	8m. Stephenson's Patent locomotive	1·30	1·40
1708	8m. Robert Stephenson's Britannia Tubular Bridge, Menai Straits	1·30	1·40

2000. 250th Death Anniv of Johann Sebastian Bach (German composer). Sheet 105 × 101 mm.

MS1709	**274** 15m. multicoloured	2·50	2·75

275 Albert Einstein

2000. Election of Albert Einstein (mathematical physicist) as *Time Magazine* "Man of the Century". Sheet 117 × 91 mm.

MS1710	**275** 15m. multicoloured	2·50	2·75

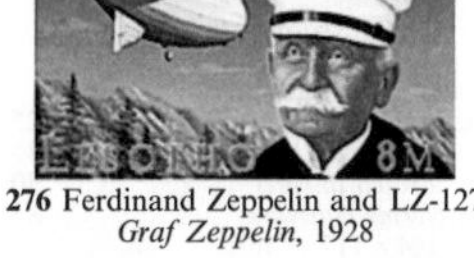

276 Ferdinand Zeppelin and LZ-127 *Graf Zeppelin*, 1928

2000. Centenary of First Zeppelin Flight. Mult.

1711	8m. Type **276**	1·30	1·40
1712	8m. LZ-130 *Graf Zeppelin II*, 1938	1·30	1·40
1713	8m. LZ-10 *Schwaben*, 1911	1·30	1·40
MS1714	83 × 119 mm. 15m. LZ-130 *Graf Zeppelin II*, 1938 (50 × 37 mm)	2·50	2·75

277 Nedo Nadi (Italian fencer), 1920

2000. Olympic Games, Sydney. Multicoloured.

1715	6m. Type **277**	1·00	1·10
1716	6m. Swimming (butterfly stroke)	1·00	1·10
1717	6m. Aztec Stadium, Mexico City, 1968	1·00	1·10
1718	6m. Ancient Greek boxing	1·00	1·10

278 Prince William in Evening Dress

279 Spotted-leaved Arum

2000. 18th Birthday of Prince William. Multicoloured.

1719	4m. Type **278**	65	70
1720	4m. Wearing coat and scarf	65	70
1721	4m. Wearing striped shirt and tie	65	70
1722	4m. Getting out of car	65	70
MS1723	100 × 80 mm. 15m. Prince William (37 × 50 mm)	2·50	2·75

2000. African Flowers. Multicoloured.

1724	3m. Type **279**	50	55
1725	3m. Christmas bells	50	55
1726	3m. Lady Monson	50	55
1727	3m. Wild pomegranate	50	55
1728	3m. Blushing bride	50	55
1729	3m. Bot River protea	50	55
1730	3m. Drooping agapanthus	50	55
1731	3m. Yellow marsh Afrikander	50	55
1732	3m. Weak-stemmed painted lady	50	55
1733	3m. Impala lily	50	55
1734	3m. Beatrice Watsonia	50	55
1735	3m. Pink arum	50	55
1736	3m. Starry gardenia	50	55
1737	3m. Pink hibiscus	50	55
1738	3m. Dwarf poker	50	55
1739	3m. Coast kaffirboom	50	55
1740	3m. Rose cockade	50	55
1741	3m. Pride of Table Mountain	50	55
1742	4m. Moore's crinum	65	70
1743	5m. Flame lily	85	90
1744	6m. Cape clivia	1·00	1·10
1745	8m. True sugarbush	1·30	1·40
MS1746	Two sheets, each 107 × 77 mm. (a) 15m. Red Hairy Erika (horiz). (b) 15m. Green Arum. Set of 2 sheets	5·00	5·25

Nos. 1724/9, 1730/5 and 1736/41 were each printed together, se-tenant, with the backgrounds forming composite designs.

No. 1733 is inscribed "LIly", No. 1736 "Gardenia thunbengii" and No. 1741 "Disa unoflora", all in error.

280 Black Rhinoceros

2000. "The Stamp Show 2000", International Stamp Exhibition, London. Endangered Wildlife. Multicoloured.

1747	4m. Type **280**	65	70
1748	4m. Leopard	65	70
1749	4m. Roseate tern	65	70
1750	4m. Mountain gorilla	65	70
1751	4m. Mountain zebra	65	70
1752	4m. Zanzibar red colobus monkey	65	70
1753	4m. Cholo alethe	65	70
1754	4m. Temminck's pangolin	65	70
1755	4m. Cheetah	65	70
1756	4m. African elephant	65	70
1757	4m. Chimpanzee	65	70
1758	4m. Northern white rhinoceros	65	70
1759	5m. Blue wildebeest	85	90
1760	5m. Tree hyrax	85	90
1761	5m. Red lechwe	85	90
1762	5m. Eland	85	90
MS1763	Two sheets, each 65 × 118 mm. (a) 15m. Dugong (vert). (b) 15m. West African Manatee (vert). Set of 2 sheets	5·00	5·25

Nos. 1747/52, 1753/8 and 1759/62 were each printed together, se-tenant, with the backgrounds forming composite designs.

281 Cadillac Eldorado Seville (1960)

2000. Classic Cars. Multicoloured.

1764	3m. Type **281**	50	55
1765	3m. Citroen DS (1955–75)	50	55
1766	3m. Ford Zephyr Zodiac MK II (1961)	50	55
1767	3m. MG TF (1945–55)	50	55
1768	3m. Porsche 356 (1949–65)	50	55
1769	3m. Ford Thunderbird (1955)	50	55
1770	3m. Cisitalia 202 Coupe (1948–52)	50	55
1771	3m. Dodge Viper (1990s)	50	55
1772	3m. TVR Vixen SI (1968–69)	50	55
1773	3m. Lotus 7 (1957–70)	50	55
1774	3m. Ferrari 275 GTB/4 (1964–68)	50	55
1775	3m. Pegasus - Touring Spider (1951–58)	50	55
1776	4m. Fiat Type O (1913)	65	70
1777	4m. Stutz Bearcat (1914)	65	70
1778	4m. French Leyat (1924)	65	70
1779	4m. Benz gasoline-driven Motorwagon (1886)	65	70
1780	4m. Isotta Fraschini Type 8A (1925)	65	70
1781	4m. Markus Motor Carriage (1887)	65	70
1782	4m. Morris Minor (1951)	65	70
1783	4m. Hispano-Suiza Type 68 (1935)	65	70
1784	4m. MG TC (1949)	65	70
1785	4m. Morgan 4/4 (1955)	65	70
1786	4m. Jaguar XK120 (1950)	65	70
1787	4m. Triumph 1800/2000 Roadster (1946–49)	65	70
MS1788	Four sheets. (a) 110 × 85 mm. 15m. AC ACE (1953–63). (b) 110 × 85 mm. 15m. Morris Minor 1000 (1948–71). (c) 85 × 110 mm. 15m. Ferrari F 40 (vert). (d) 110 × 85 mm. 15m. Bersey Electric Cab (1896). Set of 4 sheets	10·00	10·50

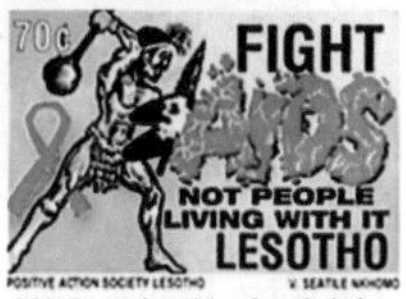

282 Basotho Warrior fighting "AIDS"

2001. Fight Against Aids. Multicoloured.

1789	70c. Type **282**	10	15
1790	1m. "Speed Kills So Does Aids"	15	20
1791	1m.50 "People with Aids need friends not rejection"	25	30
1792	2m.10 "Even when you're off duty protect the nation"	35	40

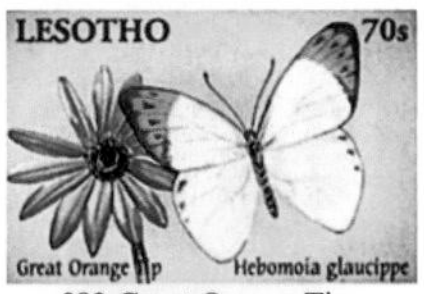

283 Great Orange Tip

2001. Butterflies. Multicoloured.

1793	70s. Type **283**	10	15
1794	1m. Red-banded pereute	15	20
1795	1m.50 Sword grass brown	25	30
1796	2m. Striped blue crow	35	40
1797	2m. Orange-banded sulphur	35	40
1798	2m. Large wood nymph	35	40
1799	2m. The postman	35	40
1800	2m. Palmfly	35	40
1801	2m. Gulf fritillary	35	40
1802	2m. Cairns birdwing	35	40
1803	2m. Common morpho	35	40
1804	2m. Common dotted border	35	40
1805	2m. African migrant	35	40
1806	2m. Large oak blue	35	40
1807	2m. The wanderer	35	40
1808	2m. Tiger swallowtail	35	40
1809	2m. Union jack	35	40
1810	2m. Saturn	35	40
1811	2m. Broad-bordered grass yellow	35	40
1812	2m. Hewitson's uraneis	35	40
1813	3m. Bertoni's antwren bird	50	55
1814	3m. Clorinde	50	55
1815	3m. Iolas blue	50	55
1816	3m. Mocker swallowtail	50	55
1817	3m. Common Indian crow	50	55
1818	3m. Grecian shoemaker	50	55
1819	3m. Small flambeau	50	55
1820	3m. Orchid swallowtail	50	55
1821	3m. Alfalfa butterfly	50	55
1822	4m. Doris butterfly	65	70
MS1823	Two sheets, each 70 × 100 mm. (a) 15m. Forest Queen. (b) 15m. Crimson Tip. Set of 2 sheets	5·00	5·25

Nos. 1797/1804, 1805/12 and 1813/20 were each printed together, se-tenant, with the backgrounds forming composite designs.

284 Roman General and Soldiers from "Battle of Lepanto and Map of the World" (anon)

2001. "Philanippon 01" International Stamp Exhibition, Tokyo. Paintings from Momoyama Era. Multicoloured.

1824	1m.50 Type **284**	25	30
1825	2m. Pikemen and musketeers from "Battle of Lepanto and Map of the World"	35	40
1826	3m. Manchurian crane from "Birds and Flowers of the Four Seasons" (Kano Eitoku)	50	55
1827	4m. Travellers in the mountains from "Birds and Flowers of the Four Seasons"	65	70
1828	5m. "Portrait of a Lady" (24½ × 81½ mm)	85	90
1829	5m. "Honda Tadakatsu" (24½ × 81½ mm)	85	90
1830	5m. "Wife of Goto Tokujo" (24½ × 81½ mm)	85	90
1831	5m. "Emperor Go-Yozei" (Kano Takanobu) (24½ × 81½ mm)	85	90
1832	5m. "Tenzuiin Hideyoshi's Mother, Hoshuku Sochin" (24½ × 81½ mm)	85	90
1833	6m. "Hosokawa Yusai" (Ishin Suden) (24½ × 81½ mm)	1·00	1·10
1834	6m. "Sen No Rikyu" (attr Hasegawa Tohaku) (24½ × 81½ mm)	1·00	1·10
1835	6m. "Oichi No Kata" (24½ × 81½ mm)	1·00	1·10
1836	6m. "Inaba Ittetsu" (attr Hasegawa Tohaku) (24½ × 81½ mm)	1·00	1·10
1837	6m. "Oda Nobunaga" (Kokei Sochin) (24½ × 81½ mm)	1·00	1·10
1838	7m. "Viewing the Maples at Mount Takao"	1·20	1·30
1839	8m. "The Four Accomplishments" (Kaiho Yusho)	1·30	1·40
MS1840	Two sheets. (a) 98 × 131 mm. 15m. "Tokugawa Ieyasu". (b) 114 × 134 mm. 15m. "Toyotomi Hideyoshi". Set of 2 sheets	5·00	5·25

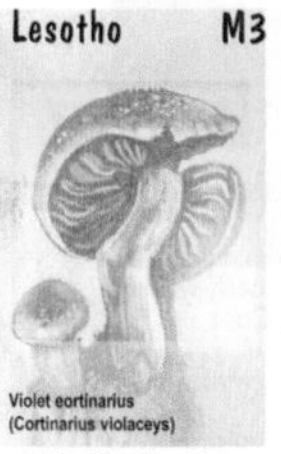

285 *Cortinarius violaceus*

287 Black Kite

286 "Woman with Baby in Sunset" (Leila Hall)

2001. "Belgica 2001" International Stamp Exhibition, Brussels. African Fungi. Multicoloured.

1841	3m. Type **285**	50	55
1842	3m. *Pleurocybella porrigens*	50	55
1843	3m. *Collybia velutibes*	50	55
1844	3m. *Lentinellus cochleatus*	50	55
1845	3m. *Anthurua aseroiformis*	50	55
1846	3m. Caesar's mushroom	50	55
1847	4m. *Cortinarius traganus*	65	70
1848	4m. *Peziza sarcosphaera*	65	70
1849	4m. *Russula emetica*	65	70
1850	4m. *Stropharia ambigua*	65	70
1851	4m. *Phlogiotis helvelloides*	65	70
1852	4m. *Clitocybe odora*	65	70
1853	5m. Golden false pholiota	85	90
1854	5m. *Coprinus micaceus*	85	90
1855	5m. *Hygrophorus camarophyllus*	85	90
1856	5m. *Panaeolus campanulatus*	85	90
MS1857	Two sheets, each 75 × 55 mm. (a) 15m. *Boletus parasiticus* (horiz). (b) 15m. *Hygrophorus hygrocybe conicus* (horiz). Set of 2 sheets	5·00	5·25

No. 1841 is inscribed "violaceys", 1842 "Pleyrocybella", 1844 "Cochleathus", 1852 "Clitoeybe" and 1856 "Panaelus companulatus" all in error.

2001. Winners of United Nations Children's Art Competition. Multicoloured.

1858	70s. Type **286**	10	15
1859	1m. "Herdboy with Lamb" (Chambeli Ramathe)	15	20
1860	1m.50 "Girl with A.I.D.S. Ribbon" (Chambeli Ramathe) (vert)	25	30
1861	2m.10 "Satellite Dish and Map seen through Keyhole" (Mika Sejake) (vert)	35	40

2001. Birds of Prey. Multicoloured.

1862 70s. Type **287** 10 15
1863 1m. Martial eagle 15 20
1864 1m.50 Bateleur 25 30
1865 2m.10 African goshawk 35 40
1866 2m.50 Lammergeier ("Bearded Vulture") 40 45
1867 3m. Jackal buzzard 50 55

No. 1865 is inscribed "GASHAWK" in error.

288 Grass Owl

2001. Wildlife of Southern Africa. Multicoloured.

1868 1m. Type **288** 15 20
1869 2m.10 Klipspringer 35 40
1870 3m. Saddle-backed jackal 50 55
1871 4m. Aardvark 65 70
1872 4m. Common kestrel ("Rock Kestrel") 65 70
1873 4m. Black-footed cat 65 70
1874 4m. Springhare 65 70
1875 4m. Aardwolf 65 70
1876 4m. Rock hyrax 65 70
1877 4m. Damara zebra 65 70
1878 4m. Bontebok 65 70
1879 4m. Eland 65 70
1880 4m. Lion 65 70
1881 4m. Saddle-backed jackal 65 70
1882 4m. Black kite ("Yellow-billed Kite") 65 70
1883 5m. Black wildebeest 85 90
MS1884 Two sheets, each 90 × 64 mm. (a) 15m. Black-shouldered kite. (b) 15m. Caracal (vert). Set of 2 sheets 5·00 5·25

Nos. 1871/6 and 1877/82 were each printed together, se-tenant, with the backgrounds forming composite designs.

289 Queen Elizabeth wearing Purple Coat

2002. Golden Jubilee. Multicoloured.

1885 8m. Type **289** 1·30 1·40
1886 8m. Queen Elizabeth with Duke of Edinburgh on launch 1·30 1·40
1887 8m. Queen Elizabeth with mayor 1·30 1·40
1888 8m. Duke of Edinburgh wearing sunglasses 1·30 1·40
MS1889 76 × 108 mm. 20m. Queen Elizabeth inspecting R.A.F. guard of honour 3·25 3·50

290 Homer Wood (Rotary pioneer)

2002. 25th Anniv of Rotary International in Lesotho. Multicoloured.

1890 8m. Type **290** 1·30 1·40
1891 10m. Paul Harris (founder of Rotary International) 1·70 1·80
MS1892 Two sheets. (a) 60 × 75 mm. 25m. Coloured globe and Rotary logo. (b) 75 × 60 mm. 25m. Golden Gate Bridge, San Francisco, and Rotary logo (horiz) 8·25 8·50

No. 1890 is inscribed "HORNER" in error.

291 Machache

2002. International Year of Mountains. Showing Lesotho mountains (except No. **MS**1897). Multicoloured.

1893 8m. Type **291** 1·30 1·40
1894 8m. Thabana-li-Mele 1·30 1·40
1895 8m. Qiloane 1·30 1·40
1896 8m. Thaba-Bosiu 1·30 1·40
MS1897 64 × 83 mm. 25m. The Matterhorn, Switzerland (vert) 4·25 4·50

No. **MS**1897 is inscribed "Mount Rainer" in error.

292 Boys with Calf, Lithabaneng

2002. S.O.S. Children's Villages (Kinderdorf International).

1898 **292** 10m. multicoloured 1·70 1·80

293 Spiral Aloe

2002. U.N. Year of Eco Tourism. Multicoloured.

1899 6m. Type **293** 1·00 1·10
1900 6m. Athrixia gerradii (flower) 1·00 1·10
1901 6m. Horseman and packhorse 1·00 1·10
1902 6m. Lion 1·00 1·10
1903 6m. Frog 1·00 1·10
1904 6m. Thatched building 1·00 1·10
MS1905 77 × 83 mm. 20m. European bee eater (vert) 3·25 3·50

294 U.S. Flag as Statue of Liberty with Lesotho Flag

2002. "United We Stand". Support for Victims of 11 September 2001 Terrorist Attacks.

1906 **294** 7m. multicoloured 1·20 1·30

295 Sheet Bend Knot

2002. 20th World Scout Jamboree, Thailand. Multicoloured.

1907 9m. Type **295** 1·50 1·60
1908 9m. Pup and forester tents 1·50 1·60
1909 9m. Scouts in canoe 1·50 1·60
1910 9m. Life-saving 1·50 1·60
MS1911 75 × 59 mm. 25m. Scouts asleep in tent 4·25 4·50

296 Angel's Fishing Rod (*Dierama pulcherrimum*)

2002. Flowers, Orchids and Insects. Multicoloured.

MS1912 100 × 180 mm. 6m. Type **296**; 6m. Marigold (*Calendula officinalis*); 6m. Dianthus "Joan's Blood"; 6m. Mule pink (*Dianthus plumarius*); 6m. Tiger lily (*Lilium lancifolium*); 6m. Clematis viticella "Comtesse de Bouchaud" 6·00 6·25
MS1913 180 × 100 mm. 6m. Leaf grasshopper (*Brochopeplu exalatus*); 6m. Golden-ringed dragonfly (*Cordulegaster boltoni*); 6m. Weevil-hunting wasp (*Cerceris arenaria*); 6m. European grasshopper (*Oedipoda miniata*); 6m. Thread-waisted Wasp (Ammophilia alberti); 6m. Mantid (*Mantis acontista*) (all horiz) 6·00 6·25
MS1914 95 × 103 mm. 6m. *Phragmipedium besseae*; 6m.*Cypripedium calceolus*; 6m. Cattleya "Louise Georgiana"; 6m.*Brassocattleya binosa*; 6m. *Laelia gouldiana*; 6m. *Paphiopedilum maudiae* "Alba" 6·00 6·25
MS1915 Three sheets. (a) 63 × 75 mm. 20m. Bleeding heart(*Dicentra spectabilis*. (b) 75 × 63 mm. 20m. Orb web spider (*Argiope bruennichi*). (c) 75 × 63 mm. 20m. *Brassavola tuberculata* Set of 3 10·00 10·50

297 Bleriot's Canard at Bagatelle, 1906

2004. Centenary of Powered Flight. Multicoloured.

MS1916 177 × 97 mm. 6m. Type **297**; 6m. Bleriot's Double-winged Libellule, 1907; 6m. Bleriot's No. VIII in Toury–Artenay cross-country flight, 1908; 6m. Bleriot's X12 Test Flight, 1909 3·00 3·25
MS1917 66 × 97 mm. 15m. Louis Bleriot's No. XI 2·50 2·75

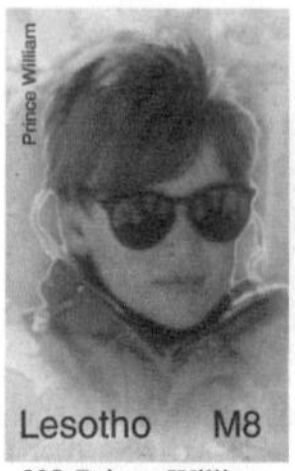

298 Prince William

299 Queen Elizabeth II

2004. 21st Birthday of Prince William. Multicoloured.

MS1918 77 × 148 mm. 8m. Type **298**; 8m. Wearing grey suit and tie; 8m. Wearing yellow polo shirt 4·00 4·25
MS1919 98 × 68 mm. 15m. Young Prince William 2·50 2·75

2004. 50th Anniv (2003) of Coronation. Multicoloured.

MS1920 148 × 85 mm. 8m. Type **299**; 8m. Wearing ivory suit and hat; 8m. Wearing royal uniform 4·00 4·25
MS1921 68 × 97 mm. 15m. Queen Elizabeth II 2·50 2·75

300 *Bematistes aganice*

2004. Butterflies. Multicoloured.

1922 1m.50 *Acraea rabbaiae* 25 30
1923 2m.10 *Alaena margaritacea* 35 40
1924 4m Type **300** 65 70
1925 6m. *Acraea quirina* 1·00 1·10
MS1926 117 × 116 mm. 6m. *Bematistes excise* (male); 6m. *Bematistes excise* (female); 6m. *Bematistes epiprotea*; 6m. *Bematistes poggei* 4·00 4·25
MS1927 67 × 98 mm. 15m. *Acraea satis* 2·50 2·75

301 Secretary Bird

2004. Birds. Multicoloured.

1928 1m.50 Type **301** 25 30
1929 2m.10 South African crowned crane ("Gray-crowned Crane") 35 40
1930 3m. Pied avocet 50 55
1931 5m. Common kestrel 85 90
MS1932 108 × 136 mm. 6m. European roller; 6m. European cuckoo ("Common Cuckoo"); 6m. Great spotted cuckoo; 6m. Pel's fishing owl 4·00 4·25
MS1933 68 × 97 mm. 15m. Kori bustard 2·50 2·75

302 Bald Ibis

2004. Endangered Species. Bald Ibis. Multicoloured.

1934 3m. Type **302** 50 55
1935 3m. Bald Ibis at rest 50 55
1936 3m. Bald Ibis on nest 50 55
1937 3m. Bald Ibis in flight (facing right) 50 55
MS1938 207 × 132 mm. Designs as Nos. 1934/6 and 1937 (Bald Ibis facing left), each × 2 4·00 4·25

303 Cape Porcupine

2004. Animals. Multicoloured.

1939 1m. Type **303** 15 20
1940 1m.50 Brown rat 25 30
1941 2m.10 Springhare (vert) 35 40
1942 5m. South African galago (vert) 85 90
MS1943 117 × 136 mm. 5m. Striped grass mouse; 5m. Greater galago; 5m. Ground pangolin; 5m. Banded mongoose 2·50 2·75

304 *Sparaxis grandiflora*

2004. Flowers. Multicoloured.

1945 1m.50 Type **304** 25 30
1946 2m.10 *Agapanthus africanus* 35 40
1947 3m. *Protea linearis* 50 55
1948 5m *Nerine cultivars* 85 90
MS1949 104 × 117 mm. 5m. *Kniphofia uvaria*; 5m. *Amaryllis belladonna*; 5m. *Gazania splendens*; 5m. *Erica coronata* 3·25 3·50
MS1950 68 × 98 mm. 15m. *Saintpaulia cultivars* 2·50 2·75

305 Qiloane Falls

2004. International Year of Freshwater. T **305** and similar horiz designs. Multicoloured.

MS1951 85 × 167 mm. 8m. Type **305**; 8m. Halfway down Qiloane Falls; 8m. Base of Qiloane Falls 4·00 4·25
MS1952 118 × 84 mm. 15m. Orange River 2·50 2·75

306 Mokhoro (Round House and Cooking Hut)

2005. Basotho Houses. Multicoloured.

1953	70s. Type **306**	10	10
1954	1m. Heisi (Rectangular house) Type **306**	15	20
1955	1m.50 Typical homestead	25	30
1956	2m.10 Mathule (Round house with porch)	35	40

No. 1953 is inscribed "70L" and No. 1956 "Mohlongoa-fat'se", both in error.

POSTAGE DUE STAMPS

1966. Nos. D9/10 of Basutoland optd **LESOTHO**.

D11	D **2**	1c. red	30	75
D12		5c. violet	30	90

D 1

D 2

1967.

D13	D **1**	1c. blue	15	3·00
D14		2c. red	15	3·50
D15		5c. green	20	3·50

1986.

D19	D **2**	2s. green	20	1·25
D20		5s. blue	20	1·25
D21		35s. violet	60	1·50

APPENDIX

The following stamps have either been issued in excess of postal needs, or have not been available to the public in reasonable quantities at face value.

1981.

15th Anniv of Independence. Classic Stamps of the World. 10m. × 40, each embossed on gold foil.

LIBERIA Pt. 13

A republic on the W. coast of Africa, founded as a home for freed slaves.

100 cents = 1 dollar.

1

2

1860.

7	**1**	6c. red	23·00	32·00
8		12c. blue	20·00	32·00
9		24c. green	23·00	32·00

1880.

13	**1**	1c. blue	3·25	4·75
14		2c. red	2·25	3·25
15		6c. mauve	4·25	5·50
16		12c. yellow	4·25	6·00
17		24c. red	5·00	6·75

1881.

18	**2**	3c. black	4·25	4·00

3

4

5 "Alligator" (first settlers' ship)

1882.

47	**3**	8c. blue	3·25	3·25
20		16c. red	4·25	3·25

1886.

49	**3**	1c. red	95	95
50		2c. green	95	1·00
23		3c. mauve	1·00	1·00
52		4c. brown	1·10	1·00
27		6c. grey	1·50	1·50
54	**4**	8c. grey	2·75	2·75
55		16c. yellow	4·25	4·25
29	**5**	32c. blue	17·00	17·00

7 Liberian Star

8 African Elephant

9 Oil Palm

10 Pres. H. R. W. Johnson

11 Vai Woman

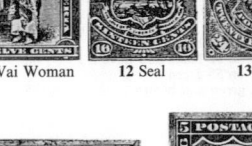

12 Seal

13 Star

15 Hippopotamus

17 President Johnson

1892.

75	**7**	1c. red	30	30
76		2c. blue	30	30
77	**8**	4c. black and green	2·10	1·60
78	**9**	6c. green	85	75
79	**10**	8c. black and brown	60	75
80	**11**	12c. red	60	85
81	**12**	16c. lilac	2·10	1·60
82	**13**	24c. green on yellow	1·50	1·25
83	**12**	32c. blue	3·00	2·50
84	**15**	$1 black and blue	10·00	5·75
85	**13**	$2 brown on buff	4·25	3·75
86	**17**	$5 black and red	5·50	5·50

1893. Surch **5 5 Five Cents**.

103	**9**	5c. on 6c. green	1·50	1·50

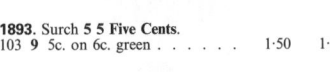

24

1894. Imperf or roul.

117	**24**	5c. black and red	6·25	6·25

35

36

1897.

144	**9**	1c. purple	70	35
145		1c. green	85	50
146	**15**	2c. black and bistre	1·50	1·10
147		2c. black and red	1·60	1·40
148	**8**	5c. black and lake	1·60	1·10
149		5c. black and blue	3·00	2·00
150	**10**	10c. blue and yellow	60	50
151	**11**	15c. black	60	65
152	**12**	20c. red	1·90	1·25
153	**13**	25c. green	1·25	85
154	**12**	30c. blue	4·25	3·00
155	**35**	50c. black and brown	2·10	2·75

1897.

156	**36**	3c. red and green	25	40

1901. Official stamps of 1892–98 optd **ORDINARY**.

175	**9**	1c. purple (No. O157)	50·00	35·00
176		1c. green (O158)	28·00	32·00
177	**7**	2c. blue (O120)	75·00	80·00
178	**15**	2c. black and brown (O159)	£100	45·00
179		2c. black and red (O160)	28·00	32·00
180	**24**	5c. green and lilac (O130)	£225	£225
181	**8**	5c. black and red (O161)	£150	£150
182		5c. black and blue (O162)	22·00	28·00
183	**10**	8c. black and brown (O122)	75·00	
184		10c. blue and yellow (O163)	28·00	32·00
169	**11**	12c. red (O92)	£100	£100
185		15c. black (O164)	28·00	32·00
170	**12**	16c. lilac (O93)		
186		16c. lilac (O124)	£325	£325
187		20c. red (O165)	32·00	38·00
171	**13**	24c. green and yellow (O94)	£300	£300
188		24c. green on yellow (O125)	32·00	38·00
189		25c. green (O166)	32·00	38·00
190	**12**	30c. blue (O167)	28·00	32·00
191	**13**	32c. blue (O126)	£150	£150
192	**35**	50c. black & brown (O168)	38·00	42·00
172	**15**	$1 black and blue (O96)	£1300	£1300
193		$1 black and blue (O127)	£225	£250
194	**13**	$2 brown on buff (O128)	£1300	£1300
174	**17**	$5 black and red (O98)	£3000	£3000
196		$5 black and red (O129)	£1400	£1400

1902. Surch **75c.** and bar.

206	**15**	75c. on $1 black and blue	8·25	7·75

40 Liberty

1903.

209	**40**	3c. black	25	15

1903. Surch in words.

216	**12**	10c. on 16c. lilac	2·50	4·50
217	**13**	15c. on 24c. green on yell	3·00	5·00
218	**12**	20c. on 32c. blue	4·25	5·25

1904. Surch.

219	**9**	1c. on 5c. on 6c. green (No. 103)	60	80
220	**8**	2c. on 4c. black and green (No. O89)	2·50	3·25
221	**12**	2c. on 30c. blue (No. 154)	6·25	9·25

50 African Elephant

51 Head of Mercury

52 Mandingo Tribesmen

53 Pres. Barclay and Executive Mansion

1906.

224	**50**	1c. black and green	1·00	50
225	**51**	2c. black and red	15	15
226	–	5c. black and blue	2·00	75
227	–	10c. black and red	3·00	90
228	–	15c. green and violet	7·00	2·75
229	–	20c. black and orange	7·25	2·50
230	–	25c. grey and blue	75	20
231	–	30c. violet	70	15
232	–	50c. black and green	75	20
233	–	75c. black and brown	7·00	2·10
234	–	$1 black and pink	1·90	25
235	**52**	$2 black and green	3·00	35
236	**53**	$5 grey and red	5·75	50

DESIGNS—As Type **50**: 5c. Chimpanzee; 15c. Agama lizard; 75c. Pygmy hippopotamus. As Type **51**: 10c. Great blue turaco; 20c. Great egret; 25c. Head of Liberty on coin; 30c. Figures "30"; 50c. Liberian flag. As Type **53**: $1 Head of Liberty.

55 Coffee Plantation

56 Gunboat "Lark"

57 Commerce

1909†. The 10c. is perf or roul.

250	**55**	1c. black and green	25	15
251	–	2c. black and red	25	15
252	**56**	5c. black and blue	1·75	35
254	**57**	10c. black and purple	25	20
255	–	15c. black and blue	1·25	35
256	–	20c. green and red	2·50	50
257	–	25c. black and brown	1·75	35
258	–	30c. brown	1·75	35
259	–	50c. black and green	2·75	60
260	–	75c. black and brown	2·25	45

DESIGNS—As Type **55**: 2c. Pres. Barclay; 15c. Vai woman spinning cotton; 20c. Pepper plant; 25c. Village hut; 30c. Pres. Barclay (in picture frame). As Type **56**: 50c. Canoeing; 75c. Village (design shaped like a book).

1909. No. 227 surch **Inland 3 Cents**.

261	3c. on 10c. black and red	4·75	5·25

1910†. Surcharged **3 CENTS INLAND POSTAGE**. Perf or rouletted.

274	**57**	3c. on 10c. black and purple	35	25

1913. Various types surch with new value and bars or ornaments.

322	–	1c. on 2c. black and red (No. 251)	2·25	3·00
290	**57**	+ 2c. on 3c. on 10c. black and purple	60	2·00
323	**56**	2c. on 5c. black and blue	2·25	3·00
292	–	2c. on 15c. black and blue (No. 255)	1·25	1·25
279	–	2c. on 25c. grey & blue (A) (No. 230)	7·50	3·75
281	–	2c. on 25c. black and brown (A) (No. 257)	7·50	3·75
295	–	2c. on 25c. black and brown (B) (No. 257)	6·25	6·25
296	–	5c. on 20c. green and red (No. 256)	85	4·50
280	–	5c. on 30c. violet (C) (No. 231)	7·50	3·75
282	–	5c. on 30c. brown (C) (No. 258)	7·50	3·75
297	–	5c. on 30c. brown (D) (No. 258)	3·75	3·75
278	**36**	8c. on 3c. red and green	60	30
283	–	10c. on 50c. black and green (E) (No. 259)	9·25	5·75
299	–	10c. on 50c. black and green (F) (No. 259)	6·75	6·75
303	–	20c. on 75c. black and brown (No. 260)	3·25	6·25
304	**53**	25c. on $1 black and pink	32·00	32·00
305	–	50c. on $2 black and green (No. 235)	9·25	9·25
308	–	$1 on $5 grey and red (No. 236)	42·00	42·00

Descriptions of surcharges. (A) **1914 2 CENTS**. (B) **2** over ornaments. (C) **1914 5 CENTS**. (D) **5** over ornaments. (E) **1914 10 CENTS**. (F) **10** and ornaments.

64 House on Providence Is

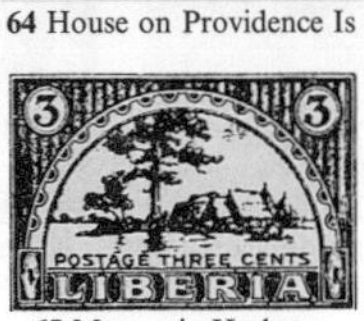

65 Monrovia Harbour, Providence Is

1915.

288	**64**	2c. red	20	10
289	**65**	3c. violet	20	10

1916. Liberian Frontier Force. Surch **LFF 1 C**.

332	**9**	1c. on 1c. green	£120	£120
333	**50**	1c. on 1c. black and green	£375	£375
334	**55**	1c. on 1c. black and green	2·75	4·25
335	–	1c. on 2c. black and red (No. 251)	2·75	4·25

1916. Surch **1916** over new value.

339	**1**	3c. on 6c. mauve	32·00	32·00
340		5c. on 12c. yellow	4·00	4·00
341		10c. on 24c. red	3·25	3·75

1917. Surch **1917** and value in words.

342	**13**	4c. on 25c. green	8·25	9·25
343	**52**	5c. on 30c. violet (No. 231)	60·00	65·00

1918. Surch **3 CENTS**.

345	**57**	3c. on 10c. black & purple	2·40	3·75

91 Bongo

93

92 African Palm Civet

94 Traveller's Tree

1918.

349	**91**	1c. black and green	65	25
350	**92**	2c. black and red	65	25
351	–	5c. black and blue	15	10
352	**93**	10c. green	20	10
353	–	15c. green and black	2·50	20
354	–	20c. black and red	50	15
355	**94**	25c. green	3·25	25
356	–	30c. black and mauve	11·00	95
357	–	50c. black and blue	13·00	1·10
358	–	75c. black and olive	1·00	25
359	–	$1 blue and brown	4·25	25
360	–	$2 black and violet	6·00	30
361	–	$5 brown	6·00	40

DESIGNS—As Type **91**: 5c. Coat of Arms; 15c. Oil palm; 20c. Statue of Mercury; 75c. Heads of Mandingos; $5 "Liberia" seated. As Type **92**: 50c. West African mudskipper; $1 Coast view; $2 Liberia College. As Type **93**: 30c. Palm-nut Vulture.

1918. Geneva Red Cross Fund. Surch **TWO CENTS** and red cross.

375	**91**	1c.+2c. black and green	75	75
376	**92**	2c.+2c. black and red	75	75
377	–	5c.+2c. black and blue	25	1·00
378	**93**	10c.+2c. green	50	1·00
379	–	15c.+2c. green and black	2·40	1·75
380	–	20c.+2c. black and red	1·50	3·00
381	**94**	25c.+2c. green	3·25	3·25
382	–	30c.+2c. black and mauve	10·50	5·75
383	–	50c.+2c. black and blue	7·00	5·75
384	–	75c.+2c. black and olive	2·10	5·25
385	–	$1+2c. blue and brown	4·25	7·00
386	–	$2+2c. black and violet	5·75	11·50
387	–	$5+2c. brown	14·00	23·00

1920. Surch **1920** and value and two bars.

393	**91**	3c. on 1c. black & green	1·50	2·75
394	**92**	4c. on 2c. black and red	1·50	3·00
395	R **42**	5c. on 10c. black & blue	3·75	4·25
396		5c. on 10c. black and red	3·75	4·25
397		5c. on 10c. black & grn	3·75	4·25
398		5c. on 10c. black & vio	3·75	4·25
399		5c. on 10c. black and red	3·75	4·25

100 Cape Mesurado

101 Pres. D. E. Howard

1921.

402	**100**	1c. green	20	10
403	**101**	5c. black and blue	25	10
404	–	10c. blue and red	80	10
405	–	15c. green and purple	3·00	50
406	–	20c. green and red	1·50	25
407	–	25c. black and yellow	2·75	50
408	–	30c. purple and green	1·00	15
409	–	50c. blue and yellow	1·00	25
410	–	75c. sepia and red	1·00	40
411	–	$1 black and red	17·00	1·00
412	–	$2 violet and yellow	24·00	1·40
413	–	$5 red and purple	22·00	1·50

DESIGNS—VERT: 10c. Arms. HORIZ: 15c. Crocodile; 20c. Pepper plant; 25c. Leopard; 30c. Village; 50c. "Kru" boatman; 75c. St. Paul's River; $1 Bongo (antelope); $2 Great Indian hornbill; $5 African elephant.

1921. Optd **1921**.

414	**100**	1c. green	9·25	50
415	**64**	2c. red	9·25	50
416	**65**	3c. violet	12·50	50
417	**101**	5c. black and blue	2·75	50
418	–	10c. blue and red	20·00	50
419	–	15c. green and purple	11·50	1·00
420	–	20c. green and red	5·25	60
421	–	25c. black and yellow	11·50	1·00
422	–	30c. purple and green	3·00	50
423	–	50c. blue and yellow	3·00	70
424	–	75c. sepia and red	3·75	50
425	–	$1 black and red	30·00	1·50
426	–	$2 violet and yellow	28·00	1·60
427	–	$5 red and purple	32·00	5·25

107 Arrival of First Settlers in "Alligator"

1923. Centennial issue.

466	**107**	1c. black and blue	14·00	70
467		2c. brown and red	17·00	70
468		5c. blue and olive	17·00	70
469		10c. mauve and green	4·75	70
470		$1 brown and red	7·00	70

108 J. J. Roberts Memorial

109 House of Representatives, Monrovia

110 Rubber Plantation

1923.

471	**108**	1c. green	3·75	10
472	**109**	2c. brown and red	3·75	10
473	–	3c. black and lilac	25	10
474	–	5c. black and blue	42·00	15
475	–	10c. brown and grey	25	10
476	–	15c. blue and bistre	18·00	50
477	–	20c. mauve and green	2·00	50
478	–	25c. brown and red	65·00	50
479	–	30c. mauve and brown	50	20
480	–	50c. orange and purple	1·00	40
481	–	75c. blue and grey	1·50	65
482	**110**	$1 violet and red	3·75	1·00
483	–	$2 blue and orange	4·00	65
484	–	$5 brown and green	10·00	65

DESIGNS—As Type **108**: 3c. Star; 5, 10c. Pres. King; 50c. Pineapple. As Type **109**: 15c. Hippopotamus; 20c. Kob (antelope); 25c. African buffalo; 30c. Natives making palm oil; 75c. Carrying elephant tusk. As Type **110**: $2 Stockton lagoon; $5 Styles of huts.

1926. Surch **Two Cents** and thick bar or wavy lines or ornamental scroll.

504	**91**	2c. on 1c. black and green	3·00	3·25

116 Palm Trees

117 Map of Africa

118 President King

1928.

511	**116**	1c. green	40	15
512		2c. violet	20	20
513		3c. brown	35	20
514	**117**	5c. blue	55	35
515	**118**	10c. grey	70	35
516	**117**	15c. purple	3·75	1·40
517		$1 brown	42·00	15·00

1936. Nos. O518 and 512/13 surch **AIR MAIL SIX CENTS.**

525	**116**	6c. on 1c. green	£170	90·00
526		6c. on 2c. violet	£170	90·00
527		6c. on 3c. brown	£170	90·00

122 Ford "Tin Goose"

1936. Air. 1st Air Mail Service of 28th February.

530	**122**	1c. black and green	25	10
531		2c. black and red	25	10
532		3c. black and violet	40	10
533		4c. black and orange	40	15
534		5c. black and blue	45	15
535		6c. black and green	45	20

1936. Nos. 350/61 surch **1936** and new values in figures.

536		1c. on 2c. black and red	30	50
537		3c. on 5c. black and blue	30	45
538		4c. on 10c. green	25	40
539		6c. on 15c. green and black	30	55
540		8c. on 20c. black and red	20	60
541		12c. on 30c. black and mauve	1·25	1·40
542		14c. on 50c. black and blue	1·50	1·75
543		16c. on 75c. black and olive	50	60
544		18c. on $1 blue and brown	60	80
545		22c. on $2 black and violet	60	95
546		24c. on $5 brown	75	1·25

1936. Nos. O363/74 optd with star and **1936** or surch also in figures and words.

547		1c. on 2c. black and red	30	50
548		3c. on 5c. black and blue	25	50
549		4c. on 10c. green	20	45
550		6c. on 15c. green and brown	25	60
551		8c. on 20c. black and lilac	30	60
552		12c. on 30c. black and violet	95	1·25
553		14c. on 50c. black and brown	1·00	1·50
554		16c. on 75c. black and brown	45	60
555		18c. on $1 blue and olive	50	65
556		22c. on $2 black and olive	60	90
557		24c. on $5 green	75	95
558		25c. green and brown	75	1·25

126 Hippopotamus

1937.

559	–	1c. black and green	1·25	60
560	–	2c. black and red	1·00	30
561	–	3c. black and purple	1·00	35
562	**126**	4c. black and orange	1·50	60
563	–	5c. black and blue	1·75	85
564	–	6c. black and green	45	20

DESIGNS: 1c. Black and white casqued hornbill; 2c. Bushbuck; 3c. African buffalo; 5c. Western reef heron; 6c. Pres. Barclay.

127 Tawny Eagle in Flight

128 Three-engine Flying Boat

129 Little Egrets

1938. Air.

565	**127**	1c. green	25	20
566	**128**	2c. red	15	10
567	–	3c. olive	35	20
568	**129**	4c. orange	50	10
569	–	5c. green	65	20
570	**128**	10c. violet	25	10
571	–	20c. mauve	30	15
572	–	30c. grey	1·25	20
573	**127**	50c. brown	1·75	20
574	–	$1 blue	1·40	25

DESIGNS—VERT: 20c., $1 Sikorsky S-43 amphibian. HORIZ: 3, 30c. Lesser black-backed gull in flight.

130 Immigrant Ships nearing Liberian Coast

1940. Centenary of Founding of Liberian Commonwealth.

575	**130**	3c. blue	50	15
576	–	5c. brown	20	10
577	–	10c. green	25	15

DESIGNS: 5c. Seal of Liberia and Flags of original Settlements; 10c. Thos. Buchanan's house and portrait.

1941. Centenary of First Postage Stamps. Nos. 575/7 optd **POSTAGE STAMP CENTENNIAL 1840–1940** and portrait of Rowland Hill.

578	**130**	3c. blue (postage)	1·75	1·75
579	–	5c. brown	1·75	1·75
580	–	10c. green	1·75	1·75
581	**130**	3c. blue (air)	1·40	1·40
582	–	5c. brown	1·40	1·40
583	–	10c. green	1·40	1·40

Nos. 581/3 are additionally optd with airplane and **AIR MAIL**.

1941. Red Cross Fund. Nos. 575/7 surch **RED CROSS** plus Red Cross and **TWO CENTS**.

584	**130**	+ 2c. on 3c. bl (postage)	1·40	1·40
585	–	+ 2c. on 5c. brown	1·40	1·40
586	–	+ 2c. on 10c. green	1·40	1·40
587	**130**	+ 2c. on 3c. blue (air)	1·40	1·40
588	–	+ 2c. on 5c. brown	1·40	1·40
589	–	+ 2c. on 10c. green	1·40	1·40

Nos. 587/9 are additionally optd with airplane and **AIR MAIL**.

1941. Air. 1st Flight to U.S.A. Nos. 565/74 surch **First Flight LIBERIA - U.S. 1941 50c** and bar.

594	**127**	50c. on 1c.	£2500	£225
595	**128**	50c. on 2c.	£150	75·00
596	–	50c. on 3c.	£180	90·00
597	**129**	50c. on 4c.	60·00	38·00
598		50c. on 5c.	60·00	38·00
599	**128**	50c. on 10c.	45·00	38·00
600	–	50c. on 20c.	£1500	£150
601	–	50c. on 30c.	60·00	24·00
602	**127**	50c. brown	60·00	24·00
603	–	$1 blue	45·00	30·00

The first flight was cancelled and covers were sent by ordinary mail. The flight took place in 1942 and the stamps were reissued but with the date obliterated.

1942. As Nos. 594/601 but with date "1941" obliterated by two bars.

604	**127**	50c. on 1c. green	7·00	7·00
605	**128**	50c. on 2c. red	6·00	6·75
606	–	50c. on 3c. green	5·50	4·75
607	**129**	50c. on 4c. orange	4·00	6·25
608		50c. on 5c. green	2·40	2·40
609	**128**	50c. on 10c. violet	5·25	6·25
610	–	50c. on 20c. mauve	5·25	6·25
611	–	5c. on 30c. grey	4·00	4·00
612	**127**	50c. brown	4·00	4·00
613	–	$1 blue	6·25	7·50

138 Miami–Monrovia Air Route

1942. Air.

614	**138**	10c. red	20	10
615	–	12c. blue	30	10
616	–	24c. green	35	10
617	**138**	30c. green	35	10
618		35c. lilac	40	15
619		50c. purple	50	15
620		70c. olive	55	30
621		$1.40 red	75	50

DESIGN: 12, 24c. Boeing 247 airliner over Liberian Agricultural and Industrial Fair.

139 Bushbuck

1942.

622	–	1c. brown and violet	80	20
623	–	2c. brown and blue	80	20
624	–	3c. brown and green	1·25	45
625	**139**	4c. red and black	2·00	70
626	–	5c. brown and olive	1·75	70
627	–	10c. black and red	3·75	1·10

DESIGNS—HORIZ: 1c. Royal antelope; 2c. Water chevrotain; 3c. Jentink's duiker; 5c. Banded duiker. VERT: 10c. Diana monkey.

1944. Stamps of 1928 and 1937 surch.

628	**116**	1c. on 2c. violet	7·50	7·50
634	**126**	1c. on 4c. black & orange	48·00	40·00
629	**118**	1c. on 10c. grey	10·00	6·25
635	–	2c. on 3c. black and purple (No. 561)	50·00	40·00
630	**117**	2c. on 5c. blue	3·25	3·25

632 116 3c. on 2c. violet . . . . . 27·00 30·00
636 – 4c. on 5c. black and blue (No. 563) . . . . . . 18·00 18·00
633 118 4c. on 10c. grey . . . . . 3·25 3·25
637 – 5c. on 1c. black and green (No. 559) . . . . . . 85·00 45·00
638 – 6c. on 2c. black and red (No. 560) . . . . . . 12·50 12·50
639 – 10c. on 6c. black and green (No. 564) . . . . 14·00 12·50

1944. Air stamps of 1936 and 1938 surch.
643 128 10c. on 2c. red . . . . . 27·00 30·00
644 129 10c. on 5c. green . . . . 9·50 9·50
640 122 30c. on 1c. black & green 80·00 50·00
645 30c. on 3c. olive (No. 567) £120 55·00
646 129 30c. on 4c. orange . . . . 9·50 9·50
641 122 50c. on 3c. black & violet 20·00 23·00
642 70c. on 2c. black and red 50·00 50·00
647 – $1 on 3c. olive (No. 567) 25·00 25·00
648 127 $1 on 50c. brown . . . . 35·00 25·00

150 Pres. Roosevelt reviewing Troops

1945. Pres. Roosevelt Memorial.
650 150 3c. black & pur (postage) 15 15
651 5c. black and blue 30 25
652 70c. black and brown (air) 1·00 1·00

151 Opening Monrovia Harbour Project

1946. Opening of Monrovia Harbour Project by Pres. Tubman.
653 151 5c. blue (postage) 25 15
654 24c. green (air) . . . . . 1·90 2·10

1947. As T 151, but without inscr at top.
655 5c. violet (postage) 15 15
656 25c. red (air) . . . . 1·00 1·10

152 1st Postage Stamps of United States and Liberia

1947. U.S. Postage Stamps Centenary and 87th Anniv of Liberian Postal Issues.
657 152 5c. red (postage) 30 15
658 12c. green (air) 40 15
659 22c. violet 50 20
660 50c. blue 60 25

153 Matilda Newport Firing Canon

1947. 125th Anniv of Defence of Monrovia.
662 153 1c. black & green (postage) 15 10
663 3c. black and violet . . . 20 10
664 5c. black and blue . . . 20 15
665 10c. black and yellow . . 1·50 45
666 25c. black and red (air) 1·40 35

154 Liberty

156 Douglas DC-3

1947. Centenary of National Independence.
667 – 1c. green (postage) . . . 20 10
668 154 2c. purple 20 10
669 – 3c. purple 30 15
670 – 5c. blue 40 15
671 – 12c. orange (air) 60 20
672 – 25c. red 75 35
673 – 50c. brown 90 70
DESIGNS—VERT: 1c. Liberian star; 3c. Arms of Liberia; 4c. Map of Liberia; 12c. J. J. Roberts Monument; 25c. Liberian Flag; 50c. (26½ × 33 mm) Centenary Monument.

1948. Air. 1st Liberian International Airways Flight (Monrovia–Dakar).
674 156 25c. red . . . . 1·50 1·00
675 50c. blue . . . . 2·40 1·50

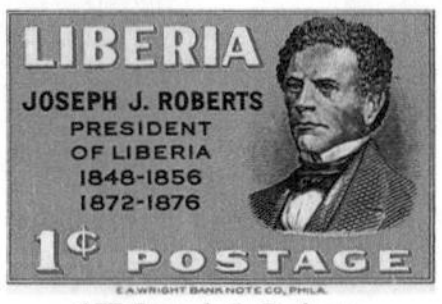

157 Joseph J. Roberts

1949. Liberian Presidents. Portrait and name in black. (a) Postage.
676 – 1c. green (Roberts) . . . 1·60 3·25
677 157 1c. green 15 10
678 – 1c. pink (Roberts) 25 15
679 – 2c. pink (Benson) 35 35
680 – 2c. yellow (Benson) . . . 35 15
681 – 3c. mauve (Warner) . . . 35 35
682 – 4c. olive (Payne) 35 55
683 – 5c. blue (Mansion) . . . 45 55
684 – 6c. orange (Roye) 55 95
685 – 7c. green (Gardner and Russell) . . . . 70 1·25
686 – 8c. red (Johnson) . . . . 70 1·40
687 – 9c. purple (Cheeseman) 1·10 1·10
688 – 10c. yellow (Coleman) . . 75 35
689 – 10c. grey (Coleman) . . . 40 20
690 – 15c. orange (Gibson) . . 85 40
691 – 15c. blue (Gibson) 25 15
692 – 20c. grey (A. Barclay) . . 1·25 70
693 – 20c. red (A. Barclay) . . 50 45
694 – 25c. red (Howard) . . . . 1·60 1·10
695 – 25c. blue (Howard) . . . 50 45
696 – 50c. turquoise (King) . . 3·25 95
697 – 50c. purple (King) 70 60
698 – $1 mauve (E. Barclay) . . 5·75 70
699 – $1 brown (E. Barclay) . . 4·00 55

(b) Air.
700 – 25c. blue (Tubman) . . . . 1·00 55
701 – 25c. green (Tubman) 75 35
Nos. 676 and 678 have a different portrait of Roberts wearing a moustache.

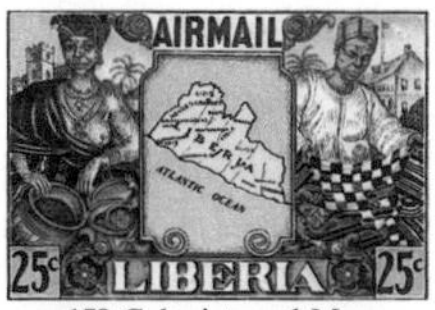

158 Colonists and Map

1949. Multicoloured.
702 1c. Settlers approaching village (postage) 50 75
703 2c. Rubber tapping and planting 50 75
704 3c. Landing of first colonists in 1822 . . . . 1·00 1·50
705 5c. Jehudi Ashmun and Matilda Newport defending stockade 50 75
706 25c. Type 158 (air) . . . . . 1·25 1·50
707 50c. Africans and coat of arms . . . . 2·75 3·25

159 Hand holding Book

1950. National Literacy Campaign.
708 159 5c. blue (postage) 20 15
709 – 25c. red (air) 70 70
DESIGN—VERT: 25c. Open book and rising sun.

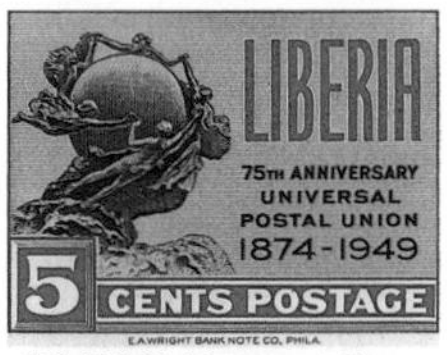

160 U.P.U. Monument, Berne

1950. 75th Anniv of U.P.U.
711 160 5c. black and green (post) 20 15
712 – 10c. black and mauve . . 30 30
713 – 25c. purple & orange (air) 3·25 3·25
DESIGNS—HORIZ: 10c. Standehaus, Berne. VERT: 25c. U.P.U. Monument, Berne.

161 Carey, Ashmun and Careysburg

162 U.N. Headquarters

163 Flags and U.N. Emblem

1952. Designs all show portrait of Ashmun.
715 – 1c. green (postage) . . . 10 10
716 161 2c. blue and red 10 10
717 – 3c. green and purple . . . 10 10
718 – 4c. green and brown . . . 15 10
719 – 5c. red and blue 20 15
720 – 10c. blue and red 25 20
721 – 25c. black and purple (air) 35 35
722 – 50c. red and blue . . . . 1·00 45
DESIGNS—VERT: 1c. Seal of Liberia; 3c. Harper and Harper City; 5c. Buchanan and Upper Buchanan. HORIZ: 4c. Marshall and Marshall City; 10c. Roberts and Robertsport; 25c. Monroe and Monrovia; 50c. Tubman and map.

1952. U.N. Commemoration.
724 162 1c. blue (postage) 10 10
725 – 4c. blue and pink 15 10
726 – 10c. brown and yellow . . 25 20
727 163 25c. red and blue (air) . . 55 45
DESIGNS—HORIZ: 4c. Liberian and U.N. flags and scroll; 10c. Liberian and U.N. emblems.

164 Modern Road-building

1953. Air. Transport.
729 164 12c. brown 15 15
730 – 25c. purple 75 30
731 – 35c. violet . . . . 1·60 30
732 – 50c. orange 65 25
733 – 70c. green . . . . 1·25 40
734 – $1 blue . . . . 1·40 55
DESIGNS: 25c. "African Glen" (freighter) in Monrovia Harbour; 35c. Diesel locomotive; 50c. Free Port of Monrovia; 70c. Roberts Field Airport; $1 Tubman Bridge.

165 Garden Bulbul ("Pepper Bird")

166 Blue-throated Roller ("Roller")

1953. Imperf or perf.
735 165 1c. red and blue . . . . 1·00 20
736 166 3c. blue and salmon . . . 1·00 25
737 – 4c. brown and yellow . . 1·50 30
738 – 5c. turquoise and mauve 1·75 35
739 – 10c. mauve and green . . 1·75 35
740 – 12c. orange and brown . . 2·75 50
BIRDS: As Type 165: 4c. Yellow-casqued hornbill ("Hornbill"); 5c. Giant kingfisher ("Kingfisher"). As Type 166: 10c. African jacana ("Jacana"); 12c. Broad-tailed paradise whydah ("Weaver").

167 Hospital

1954. Liberian Govt. Hospital Fund.
741 – 5c.+5c. black and purple (postage) 20 15
742 – 10c.+5c. black and red (air) 15 20
743 167 20c.+5c. black & green . . 25 25
744 – 25c.+5c. black, red and blue 30 20
DESIGNS—As Type 167: 5c. Medical research workers; 10c. Nurses. 46 × 35 mm: 25c. Doctor examining patient.

168 Children of the World

1954. Air. UNICEF.
745 168 $5 ultramarine, red and blue . . . . 27·00 23·00

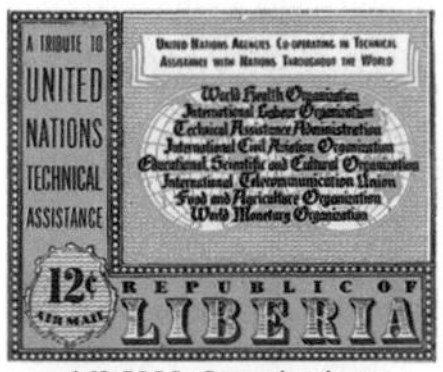

169 U.N. Organizations

1954. Air. U.N. Technical Assistance.
746 169 12c. black and blue . . . 25 15
747 – 15c. brown and yellow . . 25 15
748 – 20c. black and green . . . 30 20
749 – 25c. blue and red 35 25
DESIGNS: 15c. Printers; 20c. Mechanic; 25c. Teacher and students.

1954. Air. Visit of President Tubman to U.S.A. As Nos. 729/34 but colours changed and inscr "COMMEMORATING PRESIDENTIAL VISIT U.S.A.—1954".
750 12c. orange 20 20
751 25c. blue 80 25
752 35c. red . . . . 4·00 1·50
753 50c. mauve 80 30
754 70c. brown . . . . 1·10 50
755 $1 green . . . . 1·60 3·25

170 Football

171 "Callichilia stenosepala"

1955. Sports.
756 – 3c. red and green (postage) 15 10
757 170 5c. black and orange . . 15 10
758 – 25c. violet and yellow . . 25 20
759 – 10c. blue and mauve (air) 20 15
760 – 12c. brown and blue . . . 15 15
761 – 25c. red and green 20 20
DESIGNS—VERT: 3c. Tennis; 25c. Boxing (No. 758). HORIZ: 10c. Baseball; 12c. Swimming; 25c. Running (No. 761).

1955. Flowers.
763 171 6c. yellow, salmon and green (postage) 15 10
764 – 7c. red, yellow and green 15 10
765 – 8c. buff, blue and green 20 10
766 – 9c. green and orange . . 25 15
767 – 20c. yellow, green and violet (air) 15 15
768 – 25c. yellow, green and red 20 20
FLOWERS—VERT: 7c. "Gomphia subcordata"; 8c. "Listrostachys chudata"; 9c. "Mussaenda isertiana". HORIZ: 20s. "Costus"; 25c. "Barteria nigritiana".

172 U.N. General Assembly
173 Tapping Rubber and Rotary Emblem

1955. Air. 10th Anniv of U.N.
769 – 10c. blue and red 20 10
770 **172** 15c. black and violet . . . 25 15
771 – 25c. brown and green . . 35 15
772 – 50c. green and red . . . . 1·00 20
DESIGNS—VERT: 10c. U.N. emblem; 25c. Liberian Secretary of State signing U.N. Charter. HORIZ: 50c. Page from U.N. Charter.

1955. 50th Anniv of Rotary International.
773 **173** 5c. green & yell (postage) 25 15
774 – 10c. blue and red (air) . . 15 50
775 – 15c. brown, yellow and red 20 65
DESIGNS: 10c. Rotary International H.Q., Evanston; 15c. View of Monrovia.

174 Coliseum, New York

1956. 5th Int Philatelic Exhibition, New York.
777 – 3c. brown and green (postage) 15 10
778 **174** 4c. brown and green . . . 10 25
779 – 6c. purple and black . . . 20 10
780 **174** 10c. blue and red (air) . . 25 15
781 – 12c. violet and orange . . 20 15
782 – 15c. purple and turquoise 25 20
DESIGNS—VERT: 3c., 15c. Statue of Liberty. HORIZ: 6c., 12c. The Globe.

175 Chariot Race

1956. Olympic Games.
784 – 4c. brown & olive (postage) 10 10
785 – 6c. black and green . . . 15 10
786 – 8c. brown and blue . . . 20 10
787 **175** 10c. black and red 25 10
788 – 12c. purple and green (air) 20 15
789 – 20c. multicoloured 30 20
DESIGNS—HORIZ: 4c. Olympic rings, eastern grey kangaroo and emu; 8c. Goddess of Victory; 12c., 20c. Olympic torch superimposed on map of Austrialia. VERT: 6c. Discus thrower.

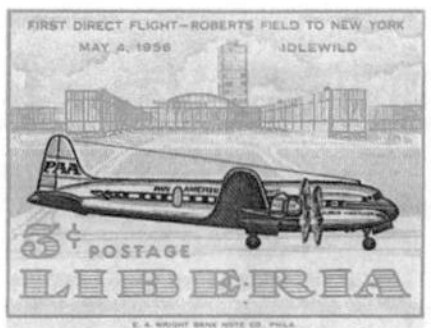

176 Douglas DC-6B "John Alden" at Idlewild Airport

1957. 1st Anniv of Inauguration of Liberia–U.S. Direct Air Service.
791 **176** 3c. blue & orange (postage) 15 15
792 – 5c. black and mauve . . . 20 20
793 **176** 12c. blue and green (air) 30 25
794 – 15c. black and brown . . 30 25
795 **176** 25c. blue and red 45 25
796 – 50c. black and blue . . . 85 30
DESIGN: 5, 15, 50c. President Tubman and "John Alden" at Roberts Field, Liberia.

177 Children's Playground

1957. Inauguration of Antoinette Tubman Child Welfare Foundation. Inscr as in T **177**.
797 **177** 4c. green and red (postage) 10 10
798 – 5c. brown and turquoise 15 10
799 – 6c. violet and bistre . . . 15 10
800 – 10c. blue and red 20 15
801 – 15c. brown and blue (air) 20 15
802 – 35c. purple and grey . . . 35 25
DESIGNS: 5c. Teacher with pupil; 6c. National anthem with choristers; 10c. Children viewing welfare home; 15c. Nurse inoculating youth; 35c. Kamara triplets.

178 German Flag and Brandenburg Gate

1958. Pres. Tubman's European Tour. Flags in national colours.
804 **178** 5c. blue (postage) 15 10
805 – 5c. brown 15 10
806 – 5c. red 15 10
807 – 10c. black (air) 25 15
808 – 15c. green 25 20
809 – 15c. blue 25 20
810 – 15c. violet 25 20
DESIGNS: Flags of: Netherlands and windmill (No. 805); Sweden and Royal Palace, Stockholm (No. 806); Italy and Colosseum (No. 807); France and Arc de Triomphe (No. 808); Switzerland and Alpine chalet (No. 809); Vatican City and St. Peter's Basilica (No. 810).

179 Map of the World
180 Africans and Map

1958. 10th Anniv of Declaration of Human Rights.
811 **179** 3c. blue and black 25 15
812 – 5c. brown and blue . . . 20 20
813 – 10c. orange and black . . 30 75
814 – 12c. black and red 40 35
DESIGNS: 5c. U.N. Emblem and H.Q. building; 10c. U.N. Emblem; 12c. U.N. Emblem and initials of U.N. agencies.

1959. Africa Freedom Day.
816 **180** 20c. orge & brn (postage) 30 30
817 – 25c. brown and blue (air) 35 20
DESIGN: 25c. Two Africans looking at Pres. Tubman's declaration of Africa Freedom Day.

181
182 Abraham Lincoln

1959. Inaug of UNESCO Building, Paris.
818 **181** 25c. purple & grn (postage) 35 40
819 – 25c. red and blue (air) . . 35 30
DESIGN—HORIZ: No. 819 UNESCO Headquarters, Paris.

1959. 150th Birth Anniv of Abraham Lincoln.
821 **182** 10c. black & blue (postage) 25 30
822 15c. black and orange . . 30 30
823 25c. black and green (air) 55 50

183 Presidents Toure, Tubman and Nkrumah at Conference Table
184 "Care of Refugees"

1960. "Big Three" Conf, Saniquellie, Liberia.
825 **183** 25c. black & red (postage) 35 25
826 – 25c. black, bl & buff (air) 35 25
DESIGN: No. 826, Medallion portraits of Presidents Toure (Guinea), Tubman (Liberia) and Nkrumah (Ghana).

1960. World Refugee Year.
827 **184** 25c. green & blk (postage) 35 30
828 25c. blue and black (air) 55 40

185
186 Weightlifting

1960. 10th Anniv of African Technical Co-operation Commission (C.C.T.A.).
830 **185** 25c. green & blk (postage) 35 50
831 – 25c. brown and blue (air) 45 35
DESIGN: No. 831, Map of Africa with symbols showing fields of assistance.

1960. Olympic Games, Rome.
832 **186** 5c. brown & grn (postage) 20 15
833 – 10c. brown and purple . . 40 75
834 – 15c. brown and orange . . 35 30
835 – 25c. brown and blue (air) 70 80
DESIGNS—HORIZ: 10c. Rowing; 25c. Javelin-throwing. VERT: 15c. Walking.

187 Stamps of 1860 and Map
188 "Guardians of Peace"

1960. Liberian Stamp Centenary. Stamps, etc., in green, red and blue. Colours of map and inscriptions given.
837 **187** 5c. black (postage) . . . 25 15
838 20c. brown 40 40
839 25c. blue (air) 50 40

1961. Membership of U.N. Security Council.
841 **188** 25c. blue and red (postage) 45 35
842 – 25c. blue and red (air) . . 45 25
DESIGN—HORIZ: No. 842, Dove of Peace, Globe and U.N. Emblem.

189 Anatomy Class, University of Liberia
190 President Roberts

1961. 15th Anniv of UNESCO.
845 **189** 25c. brown & grn (postage) 35 35
846 – 25c. brown and violet (air) 35 25
DESIGN: No. 846, Science class, University of Liberia.

1961. 150th Birth Anniv of Joseph J. Roberts (first President of Liberia).
848 **190** 5c. sepia & orge (postage) 20 15
849 – 10c. sepia and blue . . . 35 15
850 – 25c. sepia and green (air) 45 35
DESIGNS—HORIZ: 10c. Pres. Roberts and old and new presidential mansions; 25c. Pres. Roberts and Providence Is.

191 Scout and Sports

1961. Liberian Boy Scout Movement.
852 **191** 5c. sepia & violet (postage) 25 20
853 – 10c. ochre and blue . . . 30 20
854 – 25c. sepia and green (air) 40 30
DESIGNS—HORIZ: 10c. Scout badge and scouts in camp. VERT: 25c. Scout and badge.

192 Hammarskjold and U.N. Emblem
193 Campaign Emblem

1962. Dag Hammarskjold Commem.
856 **192** 20c. black & blue (postage) 30 20
857 25c. black and purple (air) 35 25

1962. Malaria Eradication.
859 **193** 25c. green & red (postage) 35 25
860 – 25c. orange and violet (air) 35 25
DESIGN—HORIZ: No. 860, Campaign emblem and slogan.

194 Pres. Tubman and New York Skyline

1962. Air. President's Visit to U.S.A.
862 **194** 12c. multicoloured 25 15
863 25c. multicoloured 35 30
864 50c. multicoloured 70 55

195 U.N. Emblem

1962. U.N. Day.
865 **195** 20c. bistre & grn (postage) 35 30
866 – 25c. blue & deep blue (air) 45 30
DESIGN: 25c. U.N. emblem and flags.

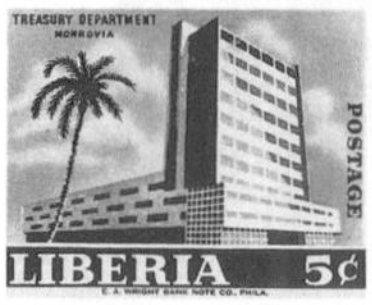

196 Treasury Building
197 F.A.O. Emblem, Bowl and Spoon

1962. Liberian Government Buildings.
868 – 1c. orange & blue (postage) 10 15
869 **196** 5c. violet and blue 15 10
870 – 10c. brown and buff . . . 20 15
871 – 15c. blue and salmon . . 25 20
872 – 80c. yellow and brown . . 1·60 1·00
873 – 12c. red and green (air) 25 15
874 – 50c. blue and orange . . 1·00 90
875 – 70c. blue and mauve . . . 1·40 1·00
876 **196** $1 black and orange . . . 2·00 1·10
BUILDINGS: 1, 80c. Executive; 10, 50c. Information; 12, 15, 70c. Capitol.

1963. Freedom from Hunger.
877 **197** 5c. purple & turq (postage) 15 10
878 – 25c. yellow and green (air) 35 20
DESIGN: 25c. F.A.O. emblem and Globe.

198 Rocket

1963. Space Exploration.
880 **198** 10c. yellow & bl (postage) 20 15
881 – 15c. brown and blue . . . 35 40
882 – 25c. green and orange (air) 45 30
DESIGNS—HORIZ: 15c. Space capsule. VERT: 25c. "Telstar" TV satellite.

199 Red Cross

200 "Unity" Scroll

1963. Red Cross Centenary.
884 **199** 5c. green and red (postage) 15 15
885 – 10c. grey and red 20 20
886 – 25c. violet and red (air) 35 30
887 – 50c. blue and red . . . . 1·00 85
DESIGNS—VERT: 10c. Emblem and torch. HORIZ: 25c. Red Cross and Globe; 50c. Emblem and Globe.

1963. Conference of African Heads of State, Addis Ababa.
888 **200** 20c. brn & grn (postage) 40 35
889 – 25c. red and green (air) 45 30
DESIGN: 25c. Map of Africa (inscr "AFRICAN SUMMIT CONFERENCE").

201 Ski-jumping

202 President Kennedy

1963. Winter Olympic Games, Innsbruck. (1964).
890 **201** 5c. blue and red (postage) 20 20
891 – 10c. red and blue (air) . . 25 25
892 – 25c. orange and green . . 35 35
DESIGNS—VERT: 10c. Olympic flame. HORIZ: 25c. Olympic rings. All have mountain scenery as backgrounds.

1964. President Kennedy Memorial Issue.
894 **202** 20c. black & blue (postage) 35 20
895 – 25c. black and purple (air) 45 25
DESIGN—VERT: 25c. Pres. Kennedy, full face portrait.

203 "Relay I" Satellite

204 Mt. Fuji

1964. Space Communications.
897 – 10c. orange and green . . 20 15
898 **203** 15c. blue and mauve . . . 25 20
899 – 25c. yellow, black and blue 45 25
SATELLITES—HORIZ: 10c. "Syncom"; 25c. "Mariner II".

1964. Olympic Games, Tokyo.
901 **204** 10c. green and yellow . . 15 10
902 – 15c. purple and red . . . 20 15
903 – 25c. red and buff 45 20
DESIGNS: 15c. Japanese arch and Olympic Flame; 25c. Cherry blossom and stadium.

205 Scout Bugle

206 "The Great Emancipator" (statue)

1965. Liberian Boy Scouts.
905 – 5c. brown and blue (postage) 25 15
906 **205** 10c. ochre and green . . . 40 25
907 – 25c. blue and red (air) . . 50 35
DESIGNS—VERT: 5c. Scout badge and saluting hand; 25c. Liberian flag within scout badge.

1965. Death Centenary of Abraham Lincoln.
909 **206** 5c. brown and sepia . . . 20 25
910 – 20c. green and light brown 35 30
911 – 25c. blue and purple . . . 40 40
DESIGNS—HORIZ: 20c. Bust of Lincoln, and Pres. Kennedy. VERT: 25c. Lincoln statue, Chicago (after St. Gaudens).

207 I.C.Y. Emblem

1965. International Co-operation Year.
913 **207** 12c. brown and orange . . 70 25
914 25c. brown and blue . . . 40 25
915 50c. brown and green . . 80 70

208 I.T.U. Emblem and Symbols

1965. Centenary of I.T.U.
917 **208** 25c. brn & grn (postage) 40 50
918 35c. mauve and black . . 60 50
919 50c. blue and red (air) . . 80 45

209 Pres. Tubman and Flag

210 Sir Winston Churchill

1965. Pres. Tubman's 70th Birthday. Multicoloured.
921 25c. Type **209** (postage) . . . 35 30
922 25c. President and Liberian arms (air) 35 25

1966. Churchill Commemoration.
924 **210** 15c. black & orge (postage) 30 30
925 – 20c. black and green . . . 35 25
926 – 25c. black and blue (air) 40 30
DESIGNS—HORIZ: 20c. Churchill in uniform of Trinity House Elder Brother; 25c. Churchill and Houses of Parliament.

211 Pres. Roberts

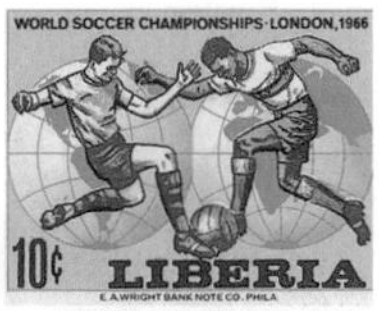

212 Footballers and Hemispheres

1966. Liberian Presidents.
928 **211** 1c. black & pink (postage) 10 10
929 – 2c. black and yellow . . . 10 10
930 – 3c. black and violet . . . 10 10
931 – 4c. black and yellow . . . 75 50
932 – 5c. black and orange . . 10 10
933 – 10c. black and green . . . 15 10
934 – 25c. black and blue . . . 35 20
935 – 50c. black and mauve . . 70 65
936 – 80c. black and red . . . . 1·25 95
937 – $1 black and brown . . . 1·40 15
938 – $2 black and purple . . . 3·25 2·75
939 – 25c. black and green (air) 35 25
PRESIDENTS: 2c. Benson; 3c. Warner; 4c. Payne; 5c. Roye; 10c. Coleman; 25c. (postage) Howard; 25c. (air) Tubman; 50c. King; 80c. Johnson; $1 Barclay; $2 Cheesman.

1966. World Cup Football Championships.
940 **212** 10c. brown and turquoise 15 15
941 – 25c. brown and mauve . . 35 30
942 – 35c. brown and orange . . 50 45
DESIGNS—VERT: 25c. Presentation cup, football and boots; 35c. Footballer.

213 Pres. Kennedy taking Oath

1966. 3rd Death Anniv of Pres. Kennedy.
944 **213** 15c. black & red (postage) 25 15
945 – 20c. purple and blue . . . 35 20
946 – 25c. blue, black and ochre (air) 45 30
947 – 35c. blue and pink . . . 85 45
DESIGNS: 20c. Kennedy stamps of 1964; 25c. U.N. General Assembly and Pres. Kennedy; 35c. Pres. Kennedy and rocket on launching pad.

214 Children on See-saw

1966. 20th Anniv of UNICEF.
949 **214** 5c. blue and red 20 20
950 – 80c. brown and green . . 1·50 1·50
DESIGN: 80c. Child playing "Doctors".

215 Giraffe

216 Scout Emblem and Various Sports

1966. Wild Animals. Multicoloured.
951 2c. Type **215** 10 10
952 3c. Lion 20 15
953 5c. Crocodile (horiz) 15 10
954 10c. Chimpanzees 40 20
955 15c. Leopard (horiz) 50 25
956 20c. Black rhinoceros (horiz) 60 40
957 25c. African elephant 70 50

1967. World Scout Jamboree, Idaho.
958 – 10c. purple and green . . 20 15
959 **216** 25c. red and blue 35 50
960 – 40c. brown and green . . 85 60
DESIGNS—VERT: 10c. Jamboree emblem. HORIZ: 40c. Scout by campfire, and Moon landing.

217 Pre-Hispanic Sculpture

218 W.H.O. Building, Brazzaville

1967. Publicity for Olympic Games, Mexico (1968).
962 **217** 10c. violet and orange . . 75 85
963 – 25c. orange, black and blue 35 40
964 – 40c. red and green 60 65
DESIGNS—VERT: 25c. Aztec calendar. HORIZ: 40c. Mexican sombrero, guitar and ceramics.

1967. Inauguration of W.H.O.'s Regional Office, Brazzaville.
966 **218** 5c. yellow and blue . . . 20 20
967 – 80c. green and yellow . . 1·25 1·25
DESIGN—VERT: 80c. As Type **218** but in vertical format.

219 Boy with Rattle

220 Ice-hockey

1967. Musicians and Instruments. Multicoloured.
968 2c. Type **219** 15 15
969 3c. Tomtom and soko violin (horiz) 20 20
970 5c. Mang harp (horiz) . . . 25 25
971 10c. Alimilim 30 30
972 15c. Xylophone drums . . . 35 35
973 25c. Tomtoms 50 40
974 35c. Oral harp 75 60

1967. Publicity for Winter Olympic Games, Grenoble (1968).
975 **220** 10c. blue and green . . . 15 20
976 – 25c. violet and blue . . . 35 30
977 – 40c. brown and orange . . 85 50
DESIGNS: 25c. Ski-jumping; 40c. Tobogganing.

221 Pres. Tubman

222 Human Rights Emblem

1967. Re-election of Pres. Tubman for 6th Term.
979 **221** 25c. brown and blue . . . 35 25

1968. Human Rights Year.
981 **222** 3c. blue and red 10 10
982 80c. green and brown . . 1·60 1·60

223 Dr. King and Hearse

224 Throwing the Javelin and Statue of Diana

1968. Martin Luther King Commemoration.
984 **223** 15c. brown and blue . . . 25 20
985 – 25c. brown and blue . . . 40 30
986 – 35c. black and olive . . . 60 65
DESIGNS—VERT: 25c. Dr. Martin Luther King. HORIZ: Dr. King and Lincoln Monument.

1968. Olympic Games, Mexico.
988 **224** 15c. violet and brown . . 25 15
989 – 25c. blue and red . . . 35 15
990 – 35c. brown and green . . 50 30
DESIGNS: 25c. Throwing the discus and Quetzalcoatl sculpture; 35c. High-diving and Xochilcalco bas-relief.

225 President Tubman

1968. 25th Anniv of Pres. Tubman's Administration.
992 **225** 25c. black, brown & silver 1·10 50

226 I.L.O. Symbol

1969. 50th Anniv of I.L.O.
994 **226** 25c. blue & gold (postage) 35 35
995 – 80c. green and gold (air) 1·50 1·40
DESIGN: 80c. As Type **226** but vert.

227 "Prince Balthasar Carlos" (Velasquez)

228 Bank Emblem on "Tree"

1969. Paintings (1st series). Multicoloured.
996 3c. Type **227** 10 10
997 5c. "Red Roofs" (Pissarro) (horiz) 20 10
998 10c. "David and Goliath" (Caravaggio) (horiz) . . . 30 15
999 12c. "Still Life" (Chardin) (horiz) 30 15

1000 15c. "The Last Supper" (Leonardo da Vinci) (horiz) . . . 35 15
1001 20c. "Regatta at Argenteuil" (Monet) (horiz) . . . 50 20
1002 25c. "Judgement of Solomon" (Giorgione) . . 45 25
1003 35c. "The Sistine Madonna" (Raphael) . . . 85 30

See also Nos. 1010/1017.

1969. 5th Anniv of African Development Bank.
1004 **228** 25c. brown and blue . . 45 40
1005 80c. red and green . . . 1·50 1·10

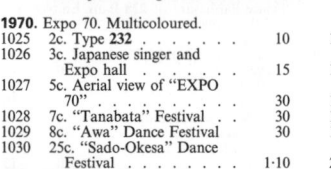

229 Memorial Plaque

1969. 1st Man on the Moon.
1006 **229** 15c. blue and ochre . . . 25 15
1007 – 25c. blue and orange . . 70 20
1008 – 35c. red and slate . . . 1·00 25
DESIGNS—VERT: 25c. Moon landing and Liberian; 35c. "Kennedy" stamp of 1966; 35c. Module lifting off from Moon.

1969. Paintings (2nd series). As T **227**. Multicoloured.
1010 3c. "The Gleaners" (Millet) (horiz) . . . 15 10
1011 5c. "View of Toledo" (El Greco) . . . 20 15
1012 10c. "Heads of Negroes" (Rubens) (horiz) . . . 30 15
1013 12c. "The Last Supper" (El Greco) (horiz) . . . 30 20
1014 15c. "Peasants Dancing" (Brueghel) (horiz) . . . 35 20
1015 20c. "Hunters in the Snow" (Brueghel) (horiz) . . . 40 25
1016 25c. "Descent from the Cross" (detail, Weyden) 45 30
1017 35c. "The Conception" (Murillo) . . . 60 40

230 Peace Dove and Emblems

1970. 25th Anniv of United Nations.
1018 **230** 5c. green & sil (postage) 15 25
1019 – $1 blue and silver (air) 1·25 1·00
DESIGN: $1, U.N. emblem and olive branch.

231 World Cup "Football" Emblem

1970. World Cup Football Championship, Mexico.
1020 **231** 5c. brown and blue . . . 20 15
1021 – 10c. brown and green . . 25 20
1022 – 25c. gold and purple . . 45 30
1023 – 35c. red and blue . . . 60 45
DESIGN—VERT: 10c. Tialoc, Mexican Rain God; 25c. Jules Rimet Cup. HORIZ: 35c. Football in sombrero.

232 Japanese Singer and Festival Plaza

1970. Expo 70. Multicoloured.
1025 2c. Type **232** . . . 10 10
1026 3c. Japanese singer and Expo hall . . . 15 10
1027 5c. Aerial view of "EXPO 70" . . . 30 10
1028 7c. "Tanabata" Festival . . 30 10
1029 8c. "Awa" Dance Festival 30 15
1030 25c. "Sado-Okesa" Dance Festival . . . 1·10 25

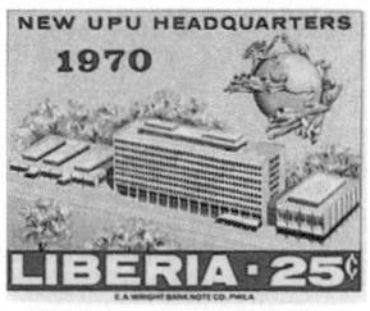

233 New H.Q. Building

1970. Inauguration of New U.P.U. Headquarters Building, Berne.
1032 **233** 25c. brown and blue . . 35 35
1033 – 80c. brown and chestnut 1·50 1·50
DESIGN—VERT: 80c. Similar to Type **233** but with larger U.P.U. monument.

234 "The First Consul" (Vien)

1970. Birth Bicentenary of Napoleon Bonaparte. Multicoloured.
1034 3c. Type **234** . . . 20 10
1035 5c. "Napoleon visiting school" (unknown artist) 30 15
1036 10c. "Napoleon Bonaparte" (detail, Isabey) . . . 35 15
1037 12c. "The French Campaign" (Meissonier) 40 20
1038 20c. "The Abdication" (Bouchot) . . . 80 30
1039 25c. "Meeting of Napoleon and Pope Pius VII" (Demarne) . . . 1·50 35
Design of 10c. is incorrectly attributed to Gerard on the stamp.

235 Pres. Tubman

1970. Pres. Tubman's 75th Birthday.
1041 **235** 25c. multicoloured . . . 75 25

236 "Adoration of the Magi" (Van der Weyden)

1970. Christmas. "The Adoration of the Magi" by artists as below. Multicoloured.
1043 3c. Type **236** . . . 10 10
1044 5c. H. Memling . . . 15 10
1045 10c. S. Lochner . . . 25 15
1046 12c. A. Altdorfer (vert) . . 30 15
1047 20c. H. van der Goes . . . 35 15
1048 25c. H. Bosch (vert) . . . 40 30

237 Bapende Mask

239 Pres. Tubman and Women at Ballot Box

238 Astronauts on Moon

1971. African Ceremonial Masks. Masks from different tribes. Multicoloured.
1050 2c. Type **237** . . . 10 10
1051 3c. Dogon . . . 15 10
1052 5c. Baoule . . . 15 15
1053 6c. Dedougou . . . 20 15
1054 9c. Dan . . . 25 15
1055 15c. Bamileke . . . 30 20
1056 20c. Bapende (different) . . 40 30
1057 25c. Bamileke costume . . 60 30

1971. "Apollo 14" Moon Mission. Multicoloured.
1058 3c. Type **238** . . . 15 10
1059 5c. Astronaut and Moon vehicle . . . 15 10
1060 10c. Erecting U.S. flag on Moon . . . 20 10
1061 12c. Splashdown . . . 40 15
1062 20c. Astronauts leaving capsule . . . 45 15
1063 25c. "Apollo 14" crew . . 60 20

1971. 25th Anniv of Liberian Women's Suffrage.
1065 **239** 3c. blue and brown . . . 15 30
1066 – 80c. brown and green . . 1·50 1·50
DESIGN—HORIZ: 80c. Pres. Tubman, women and map.

240 Hall of Honour, Munich

1971. Olympic Games, Munich (1972) (1st issue). Views of Munich. Multicoloured.
1067 3c. Type **240** . . . 15 10
1068 5c. View of central Munich 15 10
1069 10c. National Museum . . 20 10
1070 12c. Max Joseph's Square 25 10
1071 20c. Propylaen, King's Square . . . 40 15
1072 25c. Liesel-Karistadt Fountain . . . 60 20

241 American Scout

242 Pres. William Tubman

1971. World Scout Jamboree, Asagiri, Japan. Scouts in national uniforms. Multicoloured.
1074 3c. Type **241** . . . 15 10
1075 5c. West Germany . . . 15 10
1076 10c. Australia . . . 20 15
1077 12c. Great Britain . . . 25 15
1078 20c. Japan . . . 40 20
1079 25c. Liberia . . . 60 30

1971. Pres. Tubman Memorial Issue.
1081 **242** 3c. brown, blue and black . . . 10 10
1082 25c. brown, purple & blk 35 35

243 Common Zebra and Foal

1971. 25th Anniv of UNICEF. Animals with young. Multicoloured.
1083 5c. Type **243** . . . 20 10
1084 7c. Koalas . . . 30 15
1085 8c. Guanaco . . . 35 15
1086 10c. Red fox and cubs . . . 45 15
1087 20c. Savanna monkeys . . . 65 25
1088 25c. Brown bears . . . 90 35

244 Cross-country Skiing and Sika Deer

1971. Winter Olympic Games, Sapporo, Japan. Sports and Hokkaido Animals. Multicoloured.
1090 2c. Type **244** . . . 10 10
1091 3c. Tobogganing and black woodpecker . . . 70 20
1092 5c. Ski-jumping and brown bear . . . 15 10
1093 10c. Bobsleighing and common guillemots . . . 1·00 20
1094 15c. Figure-skating and northern pika . . . 30 20
1095 25c. Slalom skiing and Manchurian cranes . . . 2·00 50

245 A.P.U. Emblem, Dove and Letter

1971. 10th Anniv of African Postal Union.
1097 **245** 25c. orange and blue . . 35 50
1098 80c. brown and grey . . 1·10 1·00

246 "Elizabeth" (emigrant ship) at Providence Island

1972. 150th Anniv of Liberia.
1099 **246** 3c. green and blue . . . 70 50
1100 – 20c. blue and orange . . 35 20
1101 **246** 25c. purple and orange 2·00 55
1102 – 35c. purple and green . . 1·10 75
DESIGNS—VERT: 20, 35c. Arms and Founding Fathers Monument, Monrovia.

247 Pres. Tolbert and Map

1972. Inaug of Pres. Wm. R. Tolbert Jnr.
1104 **247** 25c. brown and green . . 35 25
1105 – 80c. brown and blue . . 1·60 80
DESIGN—VERT: 80c. Pres. Tolbert standing by desk.

248 Football

1972. Olympic Games, Munich (2nd issue). Multicoloured.
1106 3c. Type **248** . . . 10 10
1107 5c. Swimming . . . 15 10
1108 10c. Show-jumping . . . 25 10
1109 12c. Cycling . . . 30 15
1110 20c. Long-jumping . . . 45 20
1111 25c. Running . . . 60 25

249 Globe and Emblem

251 Emperor Haile Selassie

250 Astronaut and Moon Rover

1972. 50th Anniv of Int Y's Men's Clubs.
1113 **249** 15c. violet and gold . . 40 15
1114 – 90c. green and blue . . . 1·75 1·75
DESIGN: 90c. Club emblem on World Map.

1972. Moon Mission of "Apollo 16". Mult.
1115 3c. Type **250** 10 10
1116 5c. Reflection on visor . . . 10 10
1117 10c. Astronauts with cameras 15 10
1118 12c. Setting up equipment 50 15
1119 20c. "Apollo 16" emblem 65 20
1120 25c. Astronauts in Moon Rover 90 50

1972. Emperor Haile Selassie of Ethiopia's 80th Birthday.
1122 **251** 20c. green and yellow . . 40 30
1123 25c. purple and yellow 45 40
1124 35c. brown and yellow 85 85

252 H.M.S. "Ajax" (ship of the line), 1809

1972. Famous Ships of the British Royal Navy. Multicoloured.
1125 3c. Type **252** 35 25
1126 5c. HMS "Hogue" (screw ship of the line), 1848 . . 65 25
1127 7c. HMS "Ariadne" (frigate), 1816 . . . . . 85 30
1128 15c. HMS "Royal Adelaide" (ship of the line), 1828 . . 1·00 55
1129 20c. HMS "Rinaldo" (screw sloop), 1860 . . . . . . 1·40 70
1130 25c. HMS "Nymphe" (screw sloop), 1888 . . . . . . 1·90 1·00

253 Pres. Tolbert taking Oath

1972. 1st Year of President Tolbert Presidency.
1132 **253** 15c. multicoloured . . . 65 55
1133 25c. multicoloured . . . 95 95

254 Klaus Dibiasi and Italian Flag

1973. Olympic Games, Munich. Gold-medal Winners. Multicoloured.
1135 5c. Type **254** 10 10
1136 8c. Borzov and Soviet flag 15 10
1137 10c. Yanagida and Japanese flag 15 10
1138 12c. Spitz and U.S. flag . . 20 15
1139 15c. Keino and Kenyan flag 25 15
1140 25c. Meade and Union Jack 35 25

255 Astronaut on Moon

1973. Moon Flight of "Apollo 17". Multicoloured.
1142 2c. Type **255** 10 10
1143 3c. Testing lunar rover at Cape Kennedy 10 10
1144 10c. Collecting Moon rocks 15 10
1145 15c. Lunar rover on Moon 20 15
1146 20c. "Apollo 17" crew at Cape Kennedy 30 20
1147 25c. Astronauts on Moon 35 25

256 Steam Locomotive, Great Britain

1973. Historical Railways. Steam locomotives of 1895–1905 Multicoloured.
1149 2c. Type **256** 25 10
1150 3c. Netherlands 35 10
1151 10c. France 65 15
1152 15c. No. 1800, U.S.A. . . . 95 20
1153 20c. Class 150 No. 1, Japan 2·00 25
1154 25c. Germany . . . . . . 3·00 30

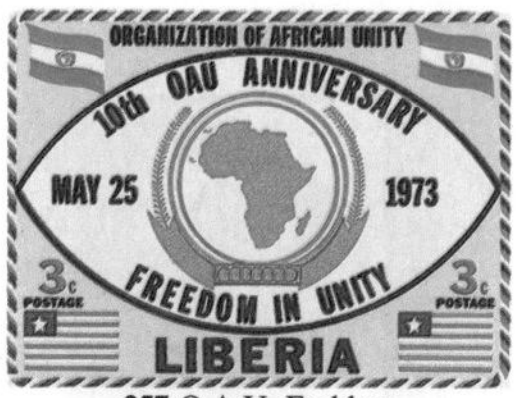
257 O.A.U. Emblem

1973. 10th Anniv of Organization of African Unity.
1156 **257** 3c. multicoloured 10 10
1157 5c. multicoloured 10 10
1158 10c. multicoloured . . . 15 10
1159 15c. multicoloured . . . 20 15
1160 25c. multicoloured . . . 35 25
1161 50c. multicoloured . . . 1·00 1·00

258 Edward Jenner and Roses

1973. 25th Anniv of W.H.O. Multicoloured.
1162 1c. Type **258** 15 10
1163 4c. Sigmund Freud and violets 15 10
1164 10c. Jonas Salk and chrysanthemums 25 10
1165 15c. Louis Pasteur and scabious 40 15
1166 20c. Emil von Behring and mallow 45 20
1167 25c. Sir Alexander Fleming and rhododendrons . . . 85 25

259 Stanley Steamer, 1910

1973. Vintage Cars. Multicoloured.
1169 2c. Type **259** 10 10
1170 3c. Cadillac Model A, 1903 10 10
1171 10c. Clement-Bayard, 1904 15 10
1172 15c. Rolls-Royce Silver Ghost tourer, 1907 . . . 25 15
1173 20c. Maxwell gentleman's speedster, 1905 . . . . 35 20
1174 25c. Chadwick, 1907 . . . . 50 25

260 Copernicus, Armillary Sphere and Satellite Communications System

1973. 500th Birth Anniv of Copernicus. Mult.
1176 1c. Type **260** 10 10
1177 4c. Eudoxus solar system . . 10 10
1178 10c. Aristotle, Ptolemy and Copernicus 15 10
1179 15c. "Saturn" and "Apollo" spacecraft 25 15
1180 20c. Astronomical observatory satellite . . . 35 20
1181 25c. Satellite tracking-station 50 25

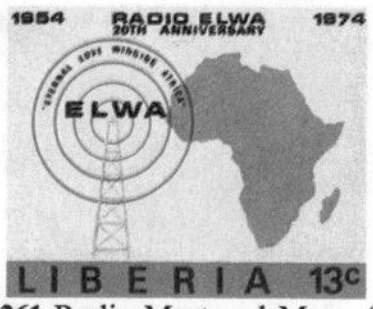
261 Radio Mast and Map of Africa

1974. 20th Anniv of "Eternal Love Winning Africa". Radio Station. Multicoloured.
1183 13c. Type **261** 25 25
1184 15c. Radio mast and map of Liberia 35 25
1185 17c. Type **261** 35 50
1186 25c. As 15c. 50 40

262 "Thomas Coutts" (full-rigged sailing ship) and "Aureol" (liner)

1974. Cent of U.P.U. Multicoloured.
1187 2c. Type **262** 20 10
1188 3c. Boeing 707 airliner and "Brasil" (liner), satellite and Monrovia Post Office 30 10
1189 10c. U.S. and Soviet Telecommunications satellites 15 10
1190 15c. Postal runner and Boeing 707 airliner . . . 25 20
1191 20c. British Advanced Passenger Train (APT) and Liberian mail-van . . 1·50 25
1192 25c. American Pony Express rider 50 35

263 Fox Terrier

1974. Dogs. Multicoloured.
1194 5c. Type **263** 15 10
1195 10c. Boxer 20 10
1196 16c. Chihuahua 30 15
1197 19c. Beagle 35 20
1198 25c. Golden retriever . . . 40 25
1199 50c. Collie . . . . 1·10 50

264 West Germany v. Chile Match

1974. World Cup Football Championship, West Germany. Scenes from semi-final matches. Multicoloured.
1201 1c. Type **264** 10 10
1202 2c. Australia v. East Germany 10 10
1203 5c. Brazil v. Yugoslavia . . 15 10
1204 10c. Zaire v. Scotland . . . 20 10
1205 12c. Netherlands v. Uruguay 25 15
1206 15c. Sweden v. Bulgaria . . 30 15
1207 20c. Italy v. Haiti 40 20
1208 25c. Poland v. Argentina . . 60 25

265 "Chrysiridia madagascariensis"

1974. Tropical Butterflies. Multicoloured.
1210 1c. Type **265** 10 10
1211 2c. "Catagramma sorana" 10 10
1212 5c. "Erasmia pulchella" . . 20 10
1213 17c. "Morpho cypris" . . . 50 25
1214 25c. "Agrias amydon" . . . 70 35
1215 40c. "Vanessa cardui" . . . 1·40 45

266 Pres. Tolbert and Gold Medallion

1974. "Family of Man" Award to President Tolbert. Multicoloured.
1217 3c. Type **266** 10 25
1218 $1 Pres. Tolbert, medallion and flag . . . . 1·40 1·40

267 Churchill with Troops

1975. Birth Centenary of Sir Winston Churchill. Multicoloured.
1219 3c. Type **267** 10 10
1220 10c. Churchill and aerial combat 30 10
1221 15c. Churchill aboard "Liberty" ship in Channel 55 15
1222 17c. Churchill reviewing troops in desert 30 15
1223 20c. Churchill crossing Rhine 40 20
1224 25c. Churchill with Roosevelt 50 25

268 Marie Curie

1975. International Women's Year. Multicoloured.
1226 2c. Type **268** 10 10
1227 3c. Mahalia Jackson 10 10
1228 5c. Joan of Arc 10 10
1229 10c. Eleanor Roosevelt . . . 15 10
1230 25c. Matilda Newport . . . 50 25
1231 50c. Valentina Tereshkova 70 55

269 Old State House, Boston, and U.S. 2c. "Liberty Bell" Stamp of 1926

1975. Bicentenary of American Independence.
1233 5c. Type **269** 15 10
1234 10c. George Washington and 1928 "Valley Forge" stamp 30 10
1235 15c. Philadelphia and 1937 "Constitution" stamp . . 45 15
1236 20c. Benjamin Franklin and 1938 "Ratification" stamp 50 15
1237 25c. Paul Revere's Ride and 1925 "Lexington-Concord" stamp 70 20
1238 50c. "Santa Maria" and 1893 "Columbus' Landing" stamp . . . . 2·25 55

270 Dr. Schweitzer, Yellow Baboon and Lambarene Hospital

1975. Birth Centenary of Dr Albert Schweitzer. Multicoloured.
1240 1c. Type **270** 10 10
1241 3c. Schweitzer, African elephant and canoe . . . 15 10
1242 5c. Schweitzer, African buffalo and canoe 25 20
1243 6c. Schweitzer, kob and dancer 30 10
1244 25c. Schweitzer, lioness and village woman 75 25
1245 50c. Schweitzer, common zebras and clinic scene . . 1·40 65

271 "Apollo" Spacecraft

1975. "Apollo–Soyuz" Space Link. Multicoloured.

1247	5c. Type **271**	10	10
1248	10c. "Soyuz" spacecraft	15	10
1249	15c. American–Russian handclasp	20	15
1250	20c. Flags and maps of America and Russia	25	15
1251	25c. Leonov and Kubasov	35	20
1252	50c. Slayton, Brand and Stafford	95	50

272 Presidents Tolbert and Stevens, and Signing Ceremony

1975. Liberia–Sierra Leone Mano River Union Agreement.

1254	**272**	2c. multicoloured	10	10
1255		3c. multicoloured	10	10
1256		5c. multicoloured	10	10
1257		10c. multicoloured	15	10
1258		25c. multicoloured	35	25
1259		50c. multicoloured	70	70

273 Figure Skating

1976. Winter Olympic Games, Innsbruck. Multicoloured.

1260	1c. Type **273**	10	10
1261	4c. Ski jumping	20	20
1262	10c. Skiing (slalom)	30	20
1263	25c. Ice hockey	60	30
1264	35c. Speed skating	90	40
1265	50c. Two-man bobsledding	1·25	65

274 Pres. Tolbert taking Oath

1976. Inauguration of President William R. Tolbert, Jr. Multicoloured.

1267	3c. Type **274**	10	10
1268	25c. Pres. Tolbert in Presidential Chair (vert)	35	25
1269	$1 Liberian crest, flag and commemorative gold coin	1·90	1·40

275 Weightlifting

1976. Olympic Games, Montreal. Multicoloured.

1270	2c. Type **275**	10	10
1271	3c. Pole-vaulting	10	10
1272	10c. Hammer and shot-put	30	15
1273	25c. "Tempest" dinghies	65	35
1274	35c. Gymnastics	90	60
1275	50c. Hurdling	1·25	65

276 Bell's Telephone and Receiver

1976. Telephone Centenary. Multicoloured.

1277	1c. Type **276**	10	10
1278	4c. Mail-coach	10	10
1279	5c. "Intelsat 4" satellite	15	10
1280	25c. Cable-ship "Dominia", 1926	1·25	30
1281	40c. British Advanced Passenger Train (APT)	1·60	50
1282	50c. Wright Flyer I, airship "Graf Zeppelin" and Concorde	1·75	60

277 Gold Nugget Pendant

1976. Liberian Products (1st series). Multicoloured.

1284	1c. Mano River Bridge	10	10
1285	3c. Type **277**	10	10
1286	5c. "V" ring	10	10
1286a	7c. As No. 1286	15	25
1287	10c. Rubber tree and tyre	15	10
1287a	15c. Combine harvester	20	10
1287b	17c. As No. 1289	45	10
1287c	20c. Hydro-electric plant	60	45
1288	25c. Mesurado shrimp	75	25
1288a	27c. Dress and woman tie-dying cloth	80	60
1289	55c. Great barracuda	1·40	35
1289a	$1 Train carrying iron ore	4·50	60

For designs as T **277** but in a smaller size, see Nos. 1505/8.

278 Black Rhinoceros

1976. Animals. Multicoloured.

1290	2c. Type **278**	10	10
1291	3c. Bongo	10	10
1292	5c. Chimpanzee (vert)	15	10
1293	15c. Pygmy hippopotamus	40	15
1294	25c. Leopard	80	40
1295	$1 Gorilla	3·00	90

279 Statue of Liberty and Unification Monument on Maps of U.S.A. and Liberia

1976. Bicentenary of American Revolution. Multicoloured.

1297	25c. Type **279**	35	25
1298	$1 Presidents Washington and Ford (U.S.A.), Roberts and Tolbert (Liberia)	1·75	65

280 Baluba Masks

1977. Second World Black and African Festival of Arts and Culture, Lagos (Nigeria). Tribal Masks. Multicoloured.

1300	5c. Type **280**	10	10
1301	10c. Bateke	15	10
1302	15c. Basshilele	20	15
1303	20c. Igungun	30	15
1304	25c. Maisi	60	20
1305	50c. Kifwebe	1·10	45

281 Latham's Francolin

1977. Liberian Wild Birds. Multicoloured.

1307	5c. Type **281**	50	10
1308	10c. Narina's trogon ("Narina Trogon")	80	15
1309	15c. Rufous-crowned roller	80	20
1310	20c. Brown-cheeked hornbill	85	25
1311	25c. Garden bulbul ("Pepper Bird")	1·00	35
1312	50c. African fish eagle ("Fish Eagle")	1·10	85

282 Alwin Schockemohle (individual jumping)

1977. Olympic Games, Montreal. Equestrian Gold-medal Winners. Multicoloured.

1314	5c. Edmund Coffin (military dressage) (postage)	15	10
1315	15c. Type **282**	40	20
1316	20c. Christine Stuckelberger (dressage)	50	30
1317	25c. "Nations Prize" (French team)	70	35
1318	55c. Military dressage (U.S.A. team) (air)	1·25	70

283 Queen Elizabeth II

1977. Silver Jubilee of Queen Elizabeth II. Multicoloured.

1320	15c. Type **283**	35	15
1321	25c. Queen Elizabeth and Prince Philip with President and Mrs. Tubman of Liberia	55	25
1322	80c. Queen Elizabeth, Prince Philip and Royal Arms	2·40	70

284 "Blessing the Children"

1977. Christmas. Multicoloured.

1324	20c. Type **284**	50	25
1325	25c. "The Good Shepherd"	70	35
1326	$1 "Jesus and the Woman of Samaria at the Well"	2·00	1·00

285 Dornier Do-X Flying Boat

1978. "Progress in Aviation". Multicoloured.

1327	2c. Type **285**	10	10
1328	3c. Space shuttle "Enterprise" on Boeing 747	10	10
1329	5c. Edward Rickenbacker and Douglas DC-3	10	10
1330	25c. Charles Lindbergh and "Spirit of St. Louis"	45	20
1331	35c. Louis Bleriot and Bleriot XI monoplane	65	35
1332	50c. Wright Brothers and Flyer I	90	55

286 Santos-Dumont's Airship "Ballon No. 9 La Badaleuse", 1903

1978. 75th Anniv of First Zeppelin Flight. Multicoloured.

1334	2c. Type **286**	10	10
1335	3c. Thomas Baldwin's airship "U.S. Military No. 1", 1908	10	10
1336	5c. Tissandier brothers' airship, 1883	10	10
1337	25c. Parseval airship PL-VII, 1912	40	20
1338	40c. Airship "Nulli Secundus II", 1908	75	35
1339	50c. Beardmore airship R-34, 1919	85	55

287 Tackling

1978. World Cup Football Championship, Argentina.

1341	**287**	2c. multicoloured	10	10
1342	–	3c. multicoloured (horiz)	10	10
1343	–	10c. multicoloured (horiz)	15	10
1344	–	25c. multicoloured (horiz)	60	20
1345	–	35c. multicoloured	80	25
1346	–	50c. multicoloured (horiz)	1·25	50

DESIGNS: Nos. 1342/6, Different match scenes.

288 Coronation Chair

1978. 25th Anniv of Coronation. Multicoloured.

1348	5c. Type **288**	10	25
1349	25c. Imperial State Crown	35	25
1350	$1 Buckingham Palace (horiz)	1·75	1·00

289 Mohammed Ali Jinnah and Flags

1978. Birth Centenary of Mohammed Ali Jinnah (first Governor-General of Pakistan).

1352	**289**	30c. multicoloured	1·50	1·50

290 Carter and Tolbert Families

1978. Visit of President Carter of U.S.A. Mult.

1353	5c. Type **290**	10	10
1354	25c. Presidents Carter and Tolbert with Mrs. Carter at microphones	50	45
1355	$1 Presidents Carter and Tolbert in open car	2·00	2·00

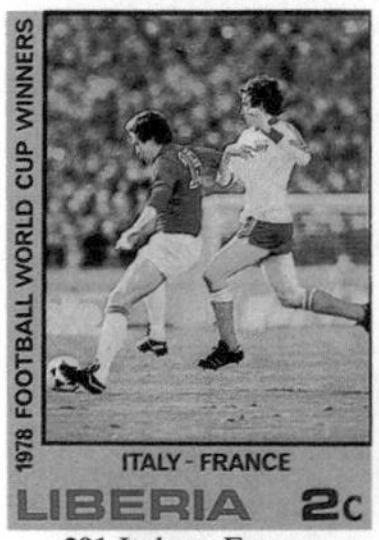

291 Italy v. France **292** Timber Truck

1978. Argentina's Victory in World Cup Football Championship. Multicoloured.

1356	1c. Brazil v. Spain (horiz)	10	10
1357	2c. Type **291**	10	10
1358	10c. Poland v. West Germany (horiz)	15	10
1359	27c. Peru v. Scotland	65	25
1360	35c. Austria v. West Germany	80	55
1361	50c. Argentinian players with Cup	1·25	80

1978. 8th World Forestry Congress, Djakarta. Multicoloured.

1363	5c. Chopping up log (horiz)	10	10
1364	10c. Type **292**	15	10
1365	25c. Felling trees (horiz)	60	20
1366	50c. Loggers (horiz)	1·10	70

293 Presidents Gardner and Tolbert with Monrovia Post Office

1979. Centenary of U.P.U. Membership. Mult.

1367	5c. Type **293**	10	10
1368	35c. Presidents Gardner and Tolbert with U.P.U. emblem	90	90

294 "25" and Radio Waves

1979. 25th Anniv of Radio ELWA. Multicoloured.

1369	35c. Type **294**	75	75
1370	$1 Radio tower	2·10	2·10

295 I.Y.C., Decade of the African Child and S.O.S. Villages Emblems

1979. International Year of the Child. Multicoloured.

1371	5c. Type **295**	10	10
1372	25c. As Type **295** but with UNICEF instead of S.O.S. Villages emblem	25	20
1373	35c. Type **295**	50	25
1374	$1 As No. 1372	1·40	1·40

296 Clasped Arms and Torches

1979. Organization for African Unity Summit Conference, Monrovia. Multicoloured.

1375	5c. Type **296**	10	10
1376	27c. Masks	40	25
1377	35c. African animals	50	50
1378	50c. Thatched huts and garden bulbuls	1·50	65

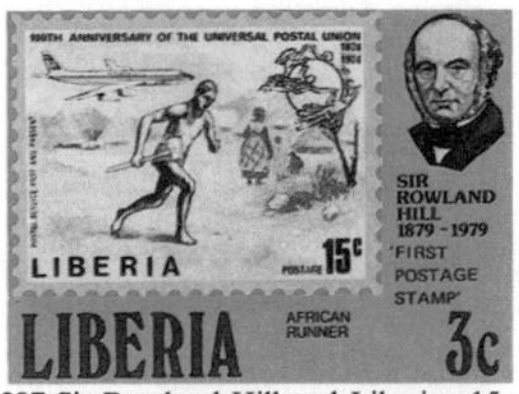

297 Sir Rowland Hill and Liberian 15c. Stamp, 1974

1979. Death Centenary of Sir Rowland Hill. Multicoloured.

1379	3c. Type **297**	10	10
1380	10c. Pony Express rider	15	10
1381	15c. British mail coach	20	35
1382	25c. "John Penn" (paddle-steamer)	75	55
1383	27c. Class "Coronation" streamlined steam locomotive No. 6235, Great Britain	1·10	25
1384	50c. Concorde	1·50	90

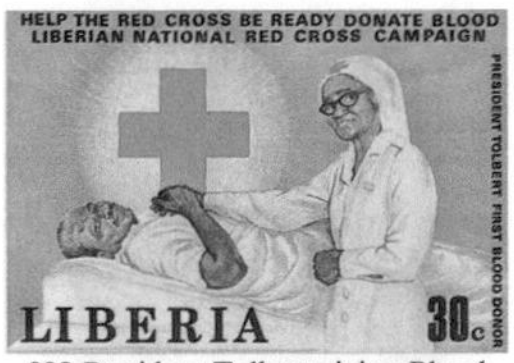

298 President Tolbert giving Blood

1979. National Red Cross Blood Donation Campaign. Multicoloured.

1386	30c. Type **298**	45	25
1387	50c. President Tolbert and Red Cross	1·00	1·00

299 "World Peace" (tanker)

1979. 2nd World Maritime Day and 30th Anniv of Liberia Maritime Programme. Multicoloured.

1388	5c. Type **299**	30	15
1389	$1 "World Peace" (different)	2·25	2·00

300 "A Good Turn"

1979. Scout Paintings by Norman Rockwell. Multicoloured.

1390	5c. Scout giving first aid to pup ("A Good Scout")	20	15
1391	5c. Type **300**	20	15
1392	5c. "Good Friends"	20	15
1393	5c. "Spirit of America"	20	15
1394	5c. "Scout Memories"	20	15
1395	5c. "The Adventure Trail"	20	15
1396	5c. "On My Honour"	20	15
1397	5c. "A Good Scout"	20	15
1398	5c. "The Right Way"	20	15
1399	5c. "The Scoutmaster"	20	15
1400	10c. "A Scout is Loyal"	40	25
1401	10c. "An Army of Friendship"	35	20
1402	10c. "Carry on"	35	20
1403	10c. "A Good Scout"	35	20
1404	10c. "The Campfire Story"	35	20
1405	10c. "High Adventure"	35	20
1406	10c. "Mighty Proud"	35	20
1407	10c. "Tomorrow's Leader"	35	20
1408	10c. "Ever Onward"	35	20
1409	10c. "Homecoming"	35	20
1410	15c. "Scouts of Many Trails"	40	25
1411	15c. "America builds for Tomorrow"	40	25
1412	15c. "The Scouting Trail"	40	25
1413	15c. "A Scout is Reverent"	40	25
1414	15c. "A Scout is Helpful"	40	25
1415	15c. "Pointing the Way"	40	25
1416	15c. "A Good Sign All Over the World"	40	25
1417	15c. "To Keep Myself Physically Strong"	40	25
1418	15c. "A Great Moment"	40	25
1419	15c. "Growth of a Leader"	40	25
1420	25c. "A Scout is Loyal"	60	35
1421	25c. "A Scout is Friendly"	60	35
1422	25c. "We Too, Have a Job to Do"	60	35
1423	25c. "I Will do my Best"	60	35
1424	25c. "A Guiding Hand"	60	35
1425	25c. "Breakthrough for Freedom"	1·25	40
1426	25c. "Scouting is Outing"	60	35
1427	25c. "Beyond the Easel"	60	35
1428	25c. "Come and Get It"	60	35
1429	25c. "America's Manpower begins with Boypower"	60	35
1430	35c. "All Together"	80	45
1431	35c. "Men of Tomorrow"	80	45
1432	35c. "Friend in Need"	80	45
1433	35c. "Our Heritage"	80	45
1434	35c. "Forward America"	80	45
1435	35c. "Can't Wait"	80	45
1436	35c. "From Concord to Tranquility"	80	45
1437	35c. "We Thank Thee"	80	45
1438	35c. "So Much Concern"	80	45
1439	35c. "Spirit of '76"	80	45

301 Mrs. Tolbert and Children

1979. S.O.S. Children's Village, Monrovia. Multicoloured.

1440	25c. Mrs. Tolbert and children (different) (horiz)	35	50
1441	40c. Type **301**	90	90

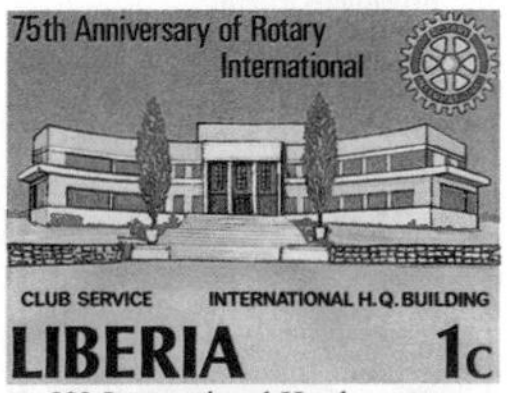

302 International Headquarters, Evanston, Illinois

1979. 75th Anniv of Rotary International. Multicoloured.

1442	1c. Type **302**	10	10
1443	5c. Vocational services	10	10
1444	17c. Wheelchair patient and nurse (community service) (vert)	20	35
1445	27c. Flags (international service)	40	50
1446	35c. Different races holding hands around globe (health, hunger and humanity)	50	50
1447	50c. President Tolbert and map of Africa (17th anniv of Monrovia Rotary Club) (vert)	1·00	1·00

303 Ski Jumping

1980. Winter Olympic Games, Lake Placid. Multicoloured.

1449	1c. Type **303**	10	10
1450	5c. Pairs figure skating	10	10
1451	17c. Bobsleigh	20	35
1452	27c. Cross-country skiing	75	75
1453	35c. Speed skating	75	75
1454	50c. Ice hockey	1·00	1·00

304 Presidents Tolbert of Liberia and Stevens of Sierra Leone and View of Mano River

1980. 5th Anniv of Mano River Union and 1st Anniv (1979) of Postal Union.

1456	**304** 8c. multicoloured	15	10
1457	27c. multicoloured	45	50
1458	35c. multicoloured	80	75
1459	80c. multicoloured	1·75	1·75

305 Redemption Horn

1981. People's Redemption Council (1st series). Multicoloured.

1460	1c. Type **305**	10	10
1461	10c. M/Sgt. Doe and allegory of redemption (horiz)	10	10
1462	14c. Map, soldier and citizens (horiz)	15	15
1463	$2 M/Sgt. Samuel Doe (chairman of Council)	3·75	3·75

See also Nos. 1475/8.

306 Players and Flags of Argentine, Uruguay, Italy and Czechoslovakia

1981. World Cup Football Championship, Spain (1982). Multicoloured.

1464	3c. Type **306**	10	10
1465	5c. Players and flags of Hungary, Italy, Germany, Brazil and Sweden	10	10
1466	20c. Players and flags of Italy, Germany, Brazil and Sweden	20	20
1467	27c. Players and flags of Czechoslovakia, Brazil, Great Britain and Germany	25	25
1468	40c. Players and flags of Italy, Brazil, Germany and Netherlands	60	60
1469	55c. Players and flags of Netherlands and Uruguay	1·10	1·10

307 M/Sgt. Doe and Crowd

1981. 1st Anniv of People's Redemption Council. Multicoloured.

1471	22c. Type **307**	20	20
1472	27c. M/Sgt. Doe and national flag	25	25
1473	30c. Hands clasping arms, sunrise and map	45	45
1474	$1 M/Sgt. Doe, "Justice" and soldiers	1·75	1·75

1981. People's Redemption Council (2nd series).

1475	6c. Type **305**	10	10
1476	23c. As No. 1461	20	20
1477	31c. As No. 1462	45	45
1478	41c. As No. 1463	60	60

308 John Adams

1981. Presidents of the United States (1st series). Multicoloured.

1479 4c. Type **308** 10 10
1480 5c. William Henry Harrison 10 10
1481 10c. Martin Van Buren . . 15 15
1482 17c. James Monroe 20 20
1483 20c. John Quincy Adams . . 25 25
1484 22c. James Madison 25 25
1485 27c. Thomas Jefferson . . . 35 30
1486 30c. Andrew Jackson . . . 55 50
1487 40c. John Tyler 80 70
1488 80c. George Washington . . 1·50 1·50

See also Nos. 1494/1503, 1519/27 and 1533/42.

309 Prince Charles and Lady Diana Spencer

1981. British Royal Wedding. Multicoloured.

1490 31c. Type **309** 30 30
1491 41c. Intertwined initials . . 40 40
1492 62c. St. Paul's Cathedral . . 1·10 1·10

1981. Presidents of the United States (2nd series). As T **308**. Multicoloured.

1494 6c. Rutherford B. Hayes . . 10 10
1495 12c. Ulysses S. Grant . . . 15 15
1496 14c. Millard Fillmore . . . 20 15
1497 15c. Zachary Taylor 20 15
1498 20c. Abraham Lincoln . . . 25 20
1499 27c. Andrew Johnson . . . 30 25
1500 31c. James Buchanan . . . 50 45
1501 41c. James A. Garfield . . . 70 60
1502 50c. James K. Polk 80 70
1503 55c. Franklin Pierce . . . . 1·00 85

1981. Liberian Products (2nd series). As T **277**, but smaller, 33 × 20 mm. Multicoloured.

1504a 1c. Mano River Bridge . . 10 10
1505 3c. Type **277** 10 10
1506 6c. Rubber tree and tyre 10 10
1506a 15c. Combine harvester . . 20 15
1507 25c. Mesurado shrimp . . 35 35
1508 31c. Hydro-electric plant 70 70
1509 41c. Dress and woman tie-dying cloth 60 55
1509a 80c. Great barracuda . . . 2·50 1·50
1510 $1 Diesel train carrying iron ore . . . . 5·75 1·60

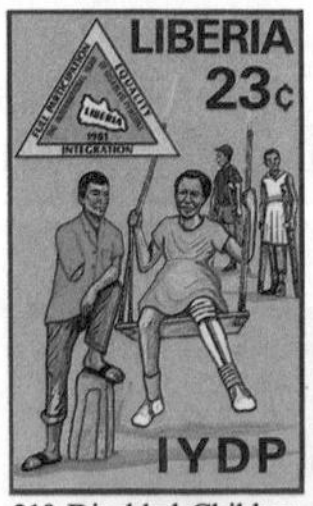

310 Disabled Children

312 Lady Diana Spencer

311 Examination Room

1982. International Year of Disabled People (1981). Multicoloured.

1515 23c. Type **310** 35 35
1516 62c. Child leading blind woman . . . . 1·25 95

1982. 30th Anniv of West African Examination Council.

1517 **311** 6c. multicoloured 10 10
1518 31c. multicoloured . . . 45 45

1982. Presidents of the United States (3rd series). As T **308**. Multicoloured.

1519 4c. William Taft 10 25
1520 5c. Calvin Coolidge 10 10
1521 6c. Benjamin Harrison . . . 15 15
1522 10c. Warren Harding . . . 20 25
1523 22c. Grover Cleveland . . . 45 45
1524 27c. Chester Arthur 50 70
1525 31c. Woodrow Wilson . . . 60 60
1526 41c. William McKinley . . 70 80
1527 80c. Theodore Roosevelt . . 1·50 1·60

1982. Princess of Wales. 21st Birthday. Mult.

1529 31c. Type **312** 70 70
1530 41c. Lady Diana Spencer (different) 85 85
1531 62c. Lady Diana accepting flower . . . . 1·25 1·25

1982. Presidents of the United States (4th series). As T **308**. Multicoloured.

1533 4c. Jimmy Carter 10 10
1534 6c. Gerald Ford 15 15
1535 14c. Harry Truman 25 25
1536 17c. Franklin D. Roosevelt 30 30
1537 23c. Lyndon B. Johnson . . 40 40
1538 27c. Richard Nixon 45 50
1539 31c. John F. Kennedy . . . 50 60
1540 35c. Ronald Reagan 60 80
1541 50c. Herbert Hoover 80 90
1542 55c. Dwight D. Eisenhower 1·00 1·00

1982. Birth of Prince William of Wales. Nos. 1529/31 optd **ROYAL BABY 21-6-82 PRINCE WILLIAM.**

1544 31c. Type **312** 45 45
1545 41c. Lady Diana Spencer (different) 60 60
1546 62c. Lady Diana accepting flower 95 95

314 Lt. Col. Fallah nGaida Varney

1983. 3rd Anniv of National Redemption Day. Multicoloured.

1548 3c. Type **314** 10 10
1549 6c. Commander-in-Chief Samuel Doe 10 10
1550 10c. Major-General Jlatoh Nicholas Podier 15 15
1551 15c. Brigadier-General Jeffery Sei Gbatu 20 15
1552 31c. Brigadier-General Thomas Gunkama Quiwonkpa 50 45
1553 41c. Colonel Abraham Doward Kollie 60 80

315 National Archives Centre

1983. Opening of National Archives Centre. Multicoloured.

1555 6c. Type **315** 10 10
1556 31c. National Archives Centre 50 45

316 "Circumcision of Christ"

1983. Christmas. 500th Birth Anniv of Raphael. Multicoloured.

1557 6c. Type **316** 10 10
1558 15c. "Adoration of the Magi" (detail) 20 15
1559 25c. "The Annunciation" (detail) 40 35
1560 31c. "Madonna of the Baldachino" 50 45
1561 41c. "Holy Family" (detail) 60 55
1562 62c. "Madonna and Child with Five Saints" (detail) 90 85

317 Graduates of M.U.R. Training Programmes

1984. 10th Anniv (1983) of Mano River Union. Multicoloured.

1564 6c. Type **317** 10 10
1565 25c. Map of Africa 40 35
1566 31c. Presidents and map of member states 50 45
1567 41c. President of Guinea signing Accession Agreement 70 85

318 Redemption Day Hospital, New Kru Town

1984. 4th Anniv of National Redemption Day. Multicoloured.

1569 3c. Type **318** 10 10
1570 10c. Ganta–Harpa Highway project 15 15
1571 20c. Opening of Constitution Assembly . . 35 30
1572 31c. Commander-in-Chief Doe launching Ganta–Harper Highway project 50 45
1573 41c. Presentation of Draft Constitution 70 85

319 "Adoration of the Magi"

1984. Rubens Paintings (1st series). Multicoloured.

1574 6c. Type **319** 10 10
1575 15c. "Coronation of Catherine" 25 20
1576 25c. "Adoration of the Magi" 70 70
1577 31c. "Madonna and Child with Halo" 85 85
1578 41c. "Adoration of the Shepherds" . . . . 1·10 1·10
1579 62c. "Madonna and Child with Saints" . . . . . . 1·75 1·75

See also Nos. 1612/17.

320 Jesse Owens

1984. Olympic Games, Los Angeles. Multicoloured.

1581 3c. Type **320** 10 10
1582 4c. Rafer Johnson 10 10
1583 25c. Miruts Yifter 65 65
1584 41c. Kipchoge Keino . . . . 1·10 1·10
1585 62c. Muhammad Ali . . . . 1·75 1·75

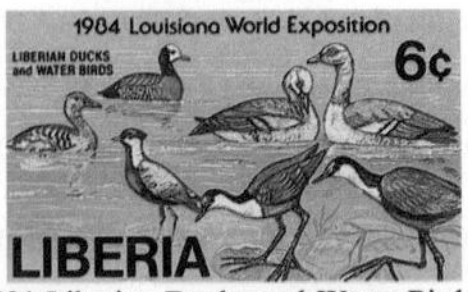

321 Liberian Ducks and Water Birds

1984. Louisiana World Exposition. Multicoloured.

1587 6c. Type **321** 20 20
1588 31c. Bulk carrier loading ore at Buchanan Harbour . . 1·60 75
1589 41c. Peters' mormyrid, electric catfish, Nile perch, krib and jewel cichlid . . 1·50 1·10
1590 62c. Diesel train carrying iron ore . . . . 1·75 90

322 Mother and Calf

1984. Pygmy Hippopotami. Multicoloured.

1591 6c. Type **322** 20 10
1592 10c. Pair of hippopotami . . 80 80
1593 20c. Close-up of hippopotamus . . . . . 1·40 1·40
1594 31c. Hippopotamus and map . . . . 2·10 2·10

323 Mrs. Doe and Children

1984. Indigent Children's Home, Bensonville. Multicoloured.

1595 6c. Type **323** 10 10
1596 31c. Mrs. Doe and children (different) 50 50

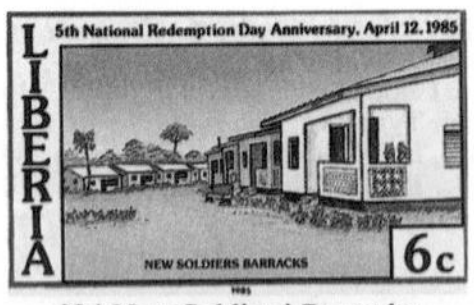

324 New Soldiers' Barracks

1985. 5th Anniv of National Redemption Day. Multicoloured.

1597 6c. Type **324** 10 10
1598 31c. Pan-African Plaza . . . 50 50

325 Bohemian Waxwing

1985. Birth Bicentenary of John J. Audubon (ornithologist). Multicoloured.

1599 1c. Type **325** 15 10
1600 3c. Bay-breasted warbler . . 30 10
1601 6c. White-winged crossbill 35 15
1602 31c. Grey phalarope ("Red Phalarope") . . . . . . 2·00 1·00
1603 41c. Eastern bluebird . . . 2·50 1·50
1604 62c. Common cardinal ("Northern Cardinal") . . 3·50 2·40

326 Germany v. Morocco, 1970

1985. World Cup Football Championship, Mexico (1986). Multicoloured.

1605 6c. Type **326** 10 10
1606 15c. Zaire v. Brazil, 1974 . . 20 15
1607 25c. Tunisia v. Germany, 1978 . . . . 60 60
1608 31c. Cameroun v. Peru, 1982 (vert) 75 75
1609 41c. Algeria v. Germany, 1982 . . . . 95 95
1610 62c. Senegal team . . . . . . 1·40 1·40

327 "Mirror of Venus" (detail)

328 Women transplanting Rice

1985. Rubens Paintings (2nd series). Mult.

1612	6c. Type **327**	10	10
1613	15c. "Adam and Eve in Paradise" (detail)	20	15
1614	25c. "Andromeda" (detail)	60	60
1615	31c. "The Three Graces" (detail)	75	75
1616	41c. "Venus and Adonis" (detail)	95	95
1617	62c. "The Daughters of Leucippus" (detail)	1·40	1·40

1985. World Food Day.

1619 **328**	25c. multicoloured	1·25	85
1620	31c. multicoloured	1·50	1·10

329 Queen Mother in Garter Robes

330 Alamo, San Antonio, Texas

1985. 85th Birthday of Queen Elizabeth the Queen Mother. Multicoloured.

1621	31c. Type **329**	35	30
1622	41c. At the races	80	75
1623	62c. Waving to the crowds	1·10	1·10

1986. "Ameripex '86" International Stamp Exhibition, Chicago. Multicoloured.

1625	25c. Type **330**	60	60
1626	31c. Liberty Bell, Philadelphia	75	75
1627	80c. Magnifying glass, emblem and Liberian stamps	3·00	2·25

331 Unveiling Ceremony, 1886 (after E. Moran)

333 Royal Theatre. Gendarmenmarkt

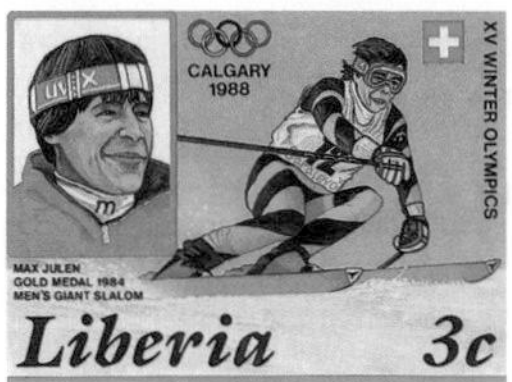

332 Max Julen (Men's Giant Slalom)

1986. Centenary of Statue of Liberty. Multicoloured.

1628	20c. Type **331**	30	50
1629	31c. Frederic-Auguste Bartholdi (sculptor) and statue	75	75
1630	$1 Head of statue	2·40	2·40

1987. Winter Olympic Games, Calgary (1988). 1984 Games Gold Medallists. Multicoloured.

1631	3c. Type **332**	10	10
1632	6c. Debbi Armstrong (women's giant slalom)	10	10
1633	31c. Peter Angerer (biathlon)	35	55
1634	60c. Bill Johnson (men's downhill)	1·10	1·10
1635	80c. East German team (four-man bobsleigh)	1·40	1·40

1987. Liberian–German Friendship. 750th Anniv of Berlin. Multicoloured.

1637	6c. Type **333**	10	10
1638	31c. Kaiser Friedrich Museum, River Spree	35	55
1639	60c. Charlottenburg Palace	1·10	1·10
1640	80c. Kaiser Wilhelm Memorial Church	1·40	1·40

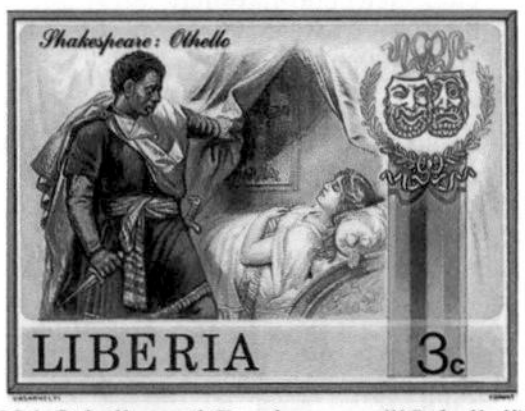

334 Othello and Desdemona ("Othello")

1987. William Shakespeare. Multicoloured.

1642	3c. Type **334**	10	10
1643	6c. Romeo and Juliet ("Romeo and Juliet")	10	10
1644	10c. Falstaff ("The Merry Wives of Windsor")	15	10
1645	15c. Falstaff, Doll Tearsheet and Prince Hal ("Henry IV", Part 2)	20	15
1646	31c. Hamlet holding Yorick's skull ("Hamlet")	60	50
1647	60c. Macbeth and the three witches ("Macbeth")	1·25	1·25
1648	80c. Lear and companions in the storm ("King Lear")	1·75	1·75
1649	$2 William Shakespeare and Globe Theatre, Southwark	4·00	4·00

335 Emblem

1987. Amateur Radio Week. 25th Anniv of Liberia Radio Amateur Association. Multicoloured.

1650	10c. Type **335**	15	10
1651	10c. Amateur radio enthusiasts	15	10
1652	35c. Certificate awarded to participants in anniversary "On the Air" activity	80	70
1653	35c. Globe, flags and banner	80	70

336 Illuminated Torch Flame

1987. Centenary of Statue of Liberty. Multicoloured.

1654	6c. Type **336**	10	10
1655	6c. Scaffolding around statue's head	10	10
1656	6c. Men working on head	10	10
1657	6c. Men working on crown	10	10
1658	6c. Statue's toes	10	10
1659	15c. Statue behind "Sir Winston Churchill" (cadet schooner)	45	20
1660	15c. "Bay Queen" (harbour ferry)	45	20
1661	15c. Posters on buildings and crowd	20	15
1662	15c. Tug and schooner in bay	45	20
1663	15c. Decorated statues around building	20	15
1664	31c. Fireworks display around statue	60	50
1665	31c. Statue floodlit	60	50
1666	31c. Statue's head	60	50
1667	31c. Fireworks display around statue (different)	60	50
1668	31c. Statue (half-length)	60	50
1669	60c. Wall poster on building (vert)	1·10	1·00
1670	60c. Yachts and cabin cruisers on river (vert)	1·50	1·00
1671	60c. Measuring statue's nose (vert)	1·10	1·00
1672	60c. Plastering nose (vert)	1·10	1·00
1673	60c. Finishing off repaired nose (vert)	1·10	1·00

337 Dr. Doe (President), Dr. Moniba (Vice-President), Flags and Hands

1988. 2nd Anniv of Second Republic.

1674 **337**	10c. multicoloured	15	10
1675	35c. multicoloured	65	55

338 Breast-feeding

1988. UNICEF Child Survival and Development Campaign. Multicoloured.

1676	3c. Type **338**	10	10
1677	6c. Oral rehydration therapy (vert)	10	10
1678	31c. Immunization	60	50
1679	$1 Growth monitoring (vert)	2·00	2·00

339 Chief Justice Emmanuel N. Gbalazeh swearing-in Dr. Samuel Kanyon Doe

1988. Inauguration of Second Republic.

1680 **339**	6c. multicoloured	10	10

340 Footballer and Stadium

1988. 2nd Anniv of Opening of Samuel Kanyon Doe Sports Complex.

1681 **340**	31c. multicoloured	60	50

341 Child and Volunteer reading

1988. 25th Anniv of U.S. Peace Corps in Liberia.

1682 **341**	10c. multicoloured	10	10
1683	35c. multicoloured	70	60

342 Pres. Doe, Farm Workers and Produce

1988. Green Revolution.

1684 **342**	10c. multicoloured	25	10
1685	35c. multicoloured	85	35

344 Emblem

345 Type GP10 Diesel Locomotive, Nimba

1988. 25th Anniv of Organization of African Unity.

1687 **344**	10c. multicoloured	10	10
1688	35c. multicoloured	70	60
1689	$1 multicoloured	2·00	2·00

1988. Locomotives. Multicoloured.

1690	10c. Type **345**	25	15
1691	35c. Triple-headed diesel iron ore train	85	50

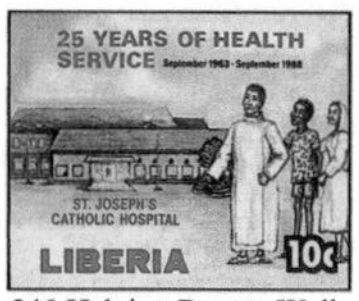

346 Helping Boy to Walk

347 Baseball

1988. 25th Anniv of St. Joseph's Catholic Hospital. Multicoloured.

1693	10c. Type **346**	10	10
1694	10c. Medical staff and hospital	10	10
1695	35c. Monk, child, candle and hospital	65	65
1696	$1 Map behind doctor with nurse holding baby	1·90	1·90

1988. Olympic Games, Seoul. Multicoloured.

1697	10c. Type **347**	10	10
1698	35c. Hurdling	65	65
1699	45c. Fencing	80	80
1700	80c. Synchronized swimming	1·40	1·40
1701	$1 Yachting	1·75	1·75

348 Monkey Bridge

349 Tending Crops

1988.

1703	10c. Type **348**	10	10
1704	35c. Sasa players (horiz)	40	60
1705	45c. Snake dancers	70	75

1988. 10th Anniv of International Fund for Agricultural Development. Multicoloured.

1706	10c. Type **349**	10	10
1707	35c. Farmers tending livestock and spraying crops	70	60

350 Destruction of Royal Exchange, 1838

1988. 300th Anniv of Lloyd's of London. Multicoloured.

1708	10c. Type **350**	10	10
1709	35c. Britten Norman Islander airplane (horiz)	60	60
1710	45c. "Chevron Antwerp" (tanker) (horiz)	70	75
1711	$1 "Lakonia" (liner) ablaze, 1963	2·00	2·00

351 Honouring Head of Operational Smile Team

1989. 3rd Anniv of Second Republic.

1712 **351**	10c. black and blue	10	10
1713	35c. black and red	80	85
1714 –	50c. black and mauve	1·25	1·25

DESIGN: 50c. Pres. Samuel Doe at John F. Kennedy Memorial Hospital.

1989. Presidents of United States (5th series). As T **308**. Multicoloured.

1715	$1 George Bush	2·50	2·50

352 "Harmony"

353 Union Glass Factory, Gardersville, Monrovia

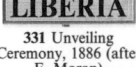

1989. Liberia–Japan Friendship. 50th Anniv of Rissho Kosei-Kai (lay Buddhist association). Multicoloured.
1716 10c. Type **352** 10 10
1717 10c. Nikkyo Niwano (founder and president of association) 10 10
1718 10c. Rissho Kosei-Kai headquarters, Tokyo . . . 10 10
1719 50c. Eternal Buddha, Great Sacred Hall . . . . . . 1·40 1·40

1989. 15th Anniv of Mano River Union. Mult.
1721 10c. Type **353** 15 10
1722 35c. Presidents of Guinea, Sierra Leone and Liberia 70 60
1723 45c. Monrovia–Freetown highway 85 80
1724 50c. Flags, map and mail van 85 85
1725 $1 Presidents at 1988 Summit . . . . 2·00 1·90

354 Symbols of International Co-operation

357 Helicopter Carrier U.S.S. "Okinawa"

1989. World Telecommunications Day.
1726 **354** 50c. multicoloured . . . 85 85

1989. 20th Anniv of First Manned Landing on Moon. Multicoloured.
1728 10c. Type **357** 60 15
1729 35c. Edwin Aldrin, Neil Armstrong and Michael Collins (crew) (28 × 28 mm) 70 60
1730 45c. "Apollo 11" flight emblem (28 × 28 mm) . . 1·00 1·00
1731 $1 Aldrin descending to Moon's surface . . . . . 2·00 2·00

358 Renovation of Statue of Liberty

360 Nehru and Flag

1989. "Philexfrance '89" International Stamp Exhibition, Paris, and "World Stamp Expo '89" International Stamp Exhibition, Washington D.C. Multicoloured.
1733 25c. Type **358** 55 45
1734 25c. French contingent at statue centenary celebrations 55 45
1735 25c. Statue, officials and commemorative plaque 55 45

1989. Birth Centenary of Jawaharlal Nehru (Indian statesman). Multicoloured.
1737 45c. Type **360** 85 70
1738 50c. Nehru 95 80

361 Close View of Station

1990. New Standard A Earth Satellite Station. Multicoloured.
1739 10c. Type **361** 15 10
1740 35c. Distant view of station 85 85

362 Emblem

1990. 25th Anniv of United States Educational and Cultural Foundation in Liberia. Multicoloured.
1741 10c. Type **362** 15 10
1742 45c. Similar to Type **362** but differently arranged . . . 85 70

363 Flags, Arms, Map and Union Emblem

364 Bomi County

1990. 10th Anniv of Pan-African Postal Union.
1743 **363** 35c. multicoloured . . . 70 55

1990. County Flags. Multicoloured.
1744 10c. Type **364** 10 10
1745 10c. Bong 10 10
1746 10c. Grand Bassa 10 10
1747 10c. Grand Cape Mount . . 10 10
1748 10c. Grand Gedeh 10 10
1749 10c. Grand Kru 10 10
1750 10c. Lofa 10 10
1751 10c. Margibi 10 10
1752 10c. Maryland 10 10
1753 10c. Montserrado 10 10
1754 10c. Nimba 10 10
1755 10c. Rivercress 10 10
1756 10c. Sinoe 10 10
1757 35c. Type **364** 65 55
1758 35c. Bong 65 55
1759 35c. Grand Bassa 65 55
1760 35c. Grand Cape Mount . . 65 55
1761 35c. Grand Gedeh 65 55
1762 35c. Grand Kru 65 55
1763 35c. Lofa 65 55
1764 35c. Margibi 65 55
1765 35c. Maryland 65 55
1766 35c. Montserrado 65 55
1767 35c. Nimba 65 55
1768 35c. Rivercress 65 55
1769 35c. Sinoe 65 55
1770 45c. Type **364** 85 70
1771 45c. Bong 85 70
1772 45c. Grand Bassa 85 70
1773 45c. Grand Cape Mount . . 85 70
1774 45c. Grand Gedeh 85 70
1775 45c. Grand Kru 85 70
1776 45c. Lofa 85 70
1777 45c. Margibi 85 70
1778 45c. Maryland 85 70
1779 45c. Montserrado 85 70
1780 45c. Nimba 85 70
1781 45c. Rivercress 85 70
1782 45c. Sinoe 85 70
1783 50c. Type **364** . . . . . . 1·10 1·10
1784 50c. Bong . . . . 1·10 1·10
1785 50c. Grand Bassa . . . . . 1·10 1·10
1786 50c. Grand Cape Mount . . 1·10 1·10
1787 50c. Grand Gedeh . . . . . 1·10 1·10
1788 50c. Grand Kru . . . . . . 1·10 1·10
1789 50c. Lofa . . . . 1·10 1·10
1790 50c. Margibi . . . . 1·10 1·10
1791 50c. Maryland . . . . . . 1·10 1·10
1792 50c. Montserrado . . . . . 1·10 1·10
1793 50c. Nimba . . . . 1·10 1·10
1794 50c. Rivercress . . . . . . 1·10 1·10
1795 50c. Sinoe . . . . 1·10 1·10
1796 $1 Type **364** . . . . . . 2·00 2·00
1797 $1 Bong . . . . 2·00 2·00
1798 $1 Grand Bassa . . . . . . 2·00 2·00
1799 $1 Grand Cape Mount . . . 2·00 2·00
1800 $1 Grand Gedeh . . . . . . 2·00 2·00
1801 $1 Grand Kru . . . . 2·00 2·00
1802 $1 Lofa . . . . 2·00 2·00
1803 $1 Margibi . . . . 2·00 2·00
1804 $1 Maryland . . . . 2·00 2·00
1805 $1 Montserrado . . . . . . 2·00 2·00
1806 $1 Nimba . . . . 2·00 2·00
1807 $1 Rivercress . . . . 2·00 2·00
1808 $1 Sinoe . . . . 2·00 2·00

365 Lady Elizabeth Bowes-Lyon as Girl

368 Boxing

367 Clasped Hands and Map

1991. 90th Birthday (1990) of Queen Elizabeth the Queen Mother. Multicoloured.
1809 10c. Type **365** 15 10
1810 $2 As Duchess of York (29 × 36½ mm) . . . . . 4·00 4·00

1991. National Unity. Multicoloured.
1812 35c. Type **367** 65 50
1813 45c. National flag and map of Africa (ECOMOG (West African States Economic Community peace-keeping forces)) . . 85 65
1814 50c. Brewer, Konneh and Michael Francis (co-chairmen) and national flag (All-Liberia Conference) 95 75

1992. Olympic Games, Barcelona. Multicoloured.
1815 45c. Type **368** 85 65
1816 50c. Football 95 75
1817 $1 Weightlifting . . . . . . 1·90 1·75
1818 $2 Water polo . . . . . . 3·75 3·50

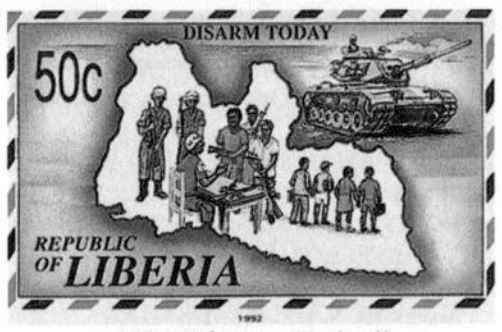

369 "Disarm Today"

1993. Peace and Redevelopment. Multicoloured.
1820 50c. Type **369** 95 70
1821 $1 "Join your Parents and build Liberia" . . . . . 1·90 1·40
1822 $2 "Peace must prevail in Liberia" . . . . 3·75 2·75

OFFICIAL STAMPS

1892. Stamps of 1892 optd **OFFICIAL**.
O 87 **7** 1c. red 30 40
O 88 2c. blue 30 50
O 89 **8** 4c. black and green . . . 50 50
O104 **9** 5c. on 6c. green (No. 89) 80 80
O 90 6c. green 60 50
O 91 **10** 8c. black and brown . . 45 45
O 92 **11** 12c. red . . . . 1·10 1·10
O 93 **12** 16c. lilac . . . . 1·10 1·10
O 94 **13** 24c. green on yellow . . 1·10 1·10
O 95 **12** 32c. blue . . . . 1·10 1·10
O 96 **15** $1 black and blue . . . 22·00 8·75
O 97 **13** $2 brown on buff . . . 9·00 6·25
O 98 **17** $5 black and red . . . . 13·50 5·75

1894. Stamps of 1892 optd **O S**.
O119 **7** 1c. red 30 20
O120 2c. blue 60 25
O121 **8** 4c. black and green . . . 95 35
O122 **10** 8c. black and brown . . 80 35
O123 **11** 12c. red . . . . 1·10 40
O124 **12** 16c. lilac . . . . 1·10 40
O125 **13** 24c. green on yellow . . 1·10 45
O126 **12** 32c. blue . . . . 1·60 55
O127 $1 black and blue . . . 13·50 13·50
O128 $2 brown on buff . . . 13·50 13·50
O129 $5 black and red . . . . 80·00 55·00

1894. Stamp of 1894 in different colours optd **O S**. Imperf or roul.
O130 **24** 5c. green and lilac . . . 1·75 2·00

1898. Stamps of 1897 optd **O S**.
O157 **9** 1c. purple 35 35
O158 1c. green 35 35
O159 **15** 2c. black and bistre . . . 1·00 30
O160 2c. black and red . . . . 1·50 70
O161 **8** 5c. black and lake . . . 1·50 70
O162 5c. black and blue . . . 1·90 70
O163 **10** 10c. blue and yellow . . 85 80
O164 **11** 15c. black 85 80
O165 **12** 20c. red . . . . 1·40 95
O166 **13** 25c. green 85 80
O167 **12** 30c. blue . . . . 2·40 1·40
O168 **35** 50c. black and brown . . 2·10 1·40

1903†. Stamp of 1903, but different colour, optd **O S**.
O210 **40** 3c. green 20 15

1904. Nos. O104 and 167 surch **ONE O.S.** and bars or **OS 2** and bars.
O222 **9** 1c. on 5c. on 6c. green 1·10 1·10
O223 **12** 2c. on 30c. blue . . . . 7·75 7·50

1906†. Stamps of 1906, but different colours, optd **OS**.
O237 **50** 1c. black and green . . . 50 50
O238 **51** 2c. black and red 15 15
O239 – 5c. black and blue . . . 55 35
O240 – 10c. black and violet . . 2·50 60
O241 – 15c. black and brown . . 2·00 40
O242 – 20c. black and green . . 2·50 50
O243 – 25c. grey and purple . . 30 15
O244 – 30c. brown 50 15
O245 – 50c. green and brown . . 50 20
O246 – 75c. black and blue . . 1·10 75
O247 – $1 black and green . . . 55 25
O248 **52** $2 black and purple . . . 1·50 25
O249 **53** $5 black and orange . . . 3·75 30

1909†. Stamps of 1909, but different colours, optd **OS**. 10c. perf or roul.
O262 **55** 1c. black and green . . . 15 10
O263 – 2c. brown and red . . . 15 10
O264 **56** 5c. black and blue . . . 1·00 15
O266 **57** 10c. blue and black . . . 50 25
O267 – 15c. black and purple . . 50 25
O268 – 20c. green and bistre . . 75 45
O269 – 25c. green and blue . . 70 50
O270 – 30c. blue 60 40
O271 – 50c. green and brown . . 2·25 40
O272 – 75c. black and violet . . 1·10 40

1910. No. O266 surch **3 CENTS INLAND POSTAGE**. Perf or roul.
O276 **57** 3c. on 10c. blue and black 55 45

1914. Official stamps surch: (A) **1914 2 CENTS**. (B) **+2c**. (C) **5**. (D) **CENTS 20 OFFICIAL**.
O291 **57** +2c. on 3c. on 10c. blue and black (B) (No. O275) . . . . 60 1·60
O284 – 2c. on 25c. grey and purple (A) (No. O243) 15·00 6·25
O285 – 5c. on 30c. blue (C) (No. O270) . . . . 5·25 3·00
O286 – 20c. on 75c. black and violet (D) (No. O272) 7·00 3·00

1914. No. 233 surch **CENTS 20 OFFICIAL**.
O287 20c. on 75c. black and brown . . . . 5·25 3·00

1915. Official stamps of 1906 and 1909 surch in different ways.
O325 – 1c. on 2c. brown and red (No. O263) . . . . . 2·25 2·50
O326 **56** 2c. on 5c. black and blue (No. O264) . . . . . 2·50 3·00
O310 – 2c. on 15c. black and purple (No. O267) . . 65 45
O311 – 2c. on 25c. green and blue (No. O269) . . . 3·75 3·75
O312 – 5c. on 20c. green and bistre (No. O268) . . . 65 50
O313 – 5c. on 30c. green and brown (No. O270) . . 5·75 5·75
O314 – 10c. on 50c. green and brown (No. O271) . . 6·50 7·50
O316 – 20c. on 75c. black and violet (No. O272) . . . 2·00 2·00
O317 – 25c. on $1 black and green (No. O247) . . . 13·50 13·50
O318 **52** 50c. on $2 black and purple (No. O248) . . 15·00 15·00
O320 **53** $1 on $5 black and orange (No. O249) . . 15·00 15·00

1915. No. O168 surch **10 10** and ornaments and bars.
O321 **35** 10c. on 50c. black & brn 9·75 9·75

1915. Military Field Post. Official stamps surch **L E F 1 c.**
O336 **50** 1c. on 1c. black and green (No. O237) . . . £325 £325
O337 **55** 1c. on 1c. black and green (No. O262) . . . 3·00 3·50
O338 – 1c. on 2c. brown and red (No. O263) . . . . . 2·40 2·50

1917. No. O244 surch **FIVE CENTS 1917** and bars.
O344 5c. on 30c. brown . . . . 15·00 15·00

1918. No. O266 surch **3 CENTS**.
O348 **57** 3c. on 10c. blue and black . . . . 1·40 1·50

1918†. Stamps of 1918, but in different colours, optd **O S**.
O362 **91** 1c. brown and green . . 50 15
O363 **92** 2c. black and red 50 15
O364 – 5c. black and blue . . . 75 10
O365 **93** 10c. blue 35 10
O366 – 15c. green and brown . . 1·75 40
O367 – 20c. black and lilac . . . 55 10
O368 **94** 25c. green and brown . . 3·25 45
O369 – 30c. black and violet . . 4·75 15
O370 – 50c. black and brown . . 5·00 50
O371 – 75c. black and brown . . 2·00 15
O372 – $1 blue and olive . . . 3·75 30
O373 – $2 black and olive . . . 6·25 20
O374 – $5 green . . . . 8·25 20

1920. Nos. O362/3 surch **1920** and value and two bars.
O400 **91** 3c. on 1c. brown & green 95 50
O401 **92** 4c. on 2c. black and red 60 50

1921†. Stamps of 1915 and 1921, in different colours, optd **O S** or **OFFICIAL**.
O428 **100** 1c. green 70 10
O429 **64** 2c. red . . . . 4·50 10
O430 **65** 3c. brown 70 10
O431 **101** 5c. brown and blue . . . 70 10
O432 – 10c. black and purple . . 35 15
O433 – 15c. green and black . . 2·75 50
O434 – 20c. blue and brown . . 1·10 25
O435 – 25c. green and orange . . 3·75 50
O436 – 30c. red and brown . . 75 15
O437 – 50c. green and black . . 75 25
O438 – 75c. purple and blue . . 1·90 25
O439 – $1 black and blue . . . 12·50 55
O440 – $2 green and orange . . 16·00 1·00
O441 – $5 blue and green . . . 17·00 1·75

1921†. Nos. O400/41 optd **1921**.
O442 **100** 1c. green . . . . 4·00 20
O443 **64** 2c. red . . . . 4·00 20
O444 **65** 3c. brown . . . . 4·00 25
O445 **101** 5c. brown and blue . . . 2·40 25
O446 – 10c. black and purple . . 4·00 25
O447 – 15c. green and black . . 4·25 15
O448 – 20c. blue and brown . . 4·25 35
O449 – 25c. green and orange . . 5·00 20
O450 – 30c. red and brown . . 4·00 30
O451 – 50c. green and black . . 4·75 15
O452 – 75c. purple and blue . . 2·75 15
O453 – $1 black and blue . . . 8·75 1·10
O454 – $2 green and orange . . 15·00 1·75
O455 – $5 blue and green . . . 16·00 3·00

1923†. Stamps of 1923, but different colours, optd **O S.**

O485	**108**	1c. black and green	5·25	10
O486	**109**	2c. brown and red	5·25	10
O487	–	3c. black and blue	5·25	10
O488	–	5c. green and orange	5·25	10
O489	–	10c. purple and olive	5·25	10
O490	–	15c. blue and green	75	40
O491	–	20c. blue and lilac	75	40
O492	–	25c. brown	16·00	40
O493	–	30c. brown and blue	70	20
O494	–	50c. brown and bistre	70	30
O495	–	75c. green and grey	70	25
O496	**110**	$1 green and red	1·50	40
O497	–	$2 red and purple	2·00	50
O498	–	$5 brown and blue	3·75	50

1926. No. O362 surch **Two Cents** and either thick bar, wavy lines, ornamental scroll or two bars.

O506	**91**	2c. on 1c. brown & green	90	80

1928. Stamps of 1928 optd **OFFICIAL SERVICE.**

O518	**116**	1c. green	70	35
O519		2c. violet	1·40	50
O520		3c. brown	1·40	15
O521	**117**	5c. blue	80	15
O522	**118**	10c. grey	2·40	1·00
O523	**117**	15c. lilac	1·40	60
O524		$1 brown	40·00	16·00

1944. No. O522 surch.

O649	**118**	4c. on 10c. grey	8·00	8·00

POSTAGE DUE STAMPS

1892. Stamps of 1886 surch **POSTAGE DUE** and value in frame.

D 99	**4**	3c. on 3c. mauve	1·25	1·25
D100		6c. on 6c. grey	6·25	6·25

D 23

1894.

D110	D **23**	2c. black and orange on yellow	95	55
D111		4c. black & red on rose	95	55
D112		6c. black & brn on buff	95	75
D113		8c. black & blue on bl	1·00	75
D114		10c. black and green on mauve	1·25	95
D115		20c. black and violet on grey	1·25	95
D116		40c. black and brown on green	2·50	1·75

REGISTRATION STAMPS

R 22

1893.

R105	R **22**	(10c.) black (Buchanan)	£275	£350
R106		(10c.) blk ("Grenville")	£1000	£1250
R107		(10c.) black (Harper)	£1000	£1250
R108		(10c.) black (Monrovia)	40·00	£175
R109		(10c.) blk (Robertsport)	£500	£575

1894. Surch **10 CENTS 10** twice.

R140	R **22**	10c. blue on pink (Buchanan)	3·75	3·75
R141		10c. green on buff (Harper)	3·75	3·75
R142		10c. red on yellow (Monrovia)	3·75	3·75
R143		10c. red on blue (Robertsport)	3·75	3·75

R 42 Pres. Gibson

1904†.

R211	R **42**	10c. black and blue (Buchanan)	1·50	25
R212		10c. black and red ("Grenville")	1·50	25
R213		10c. black and green (Harper)	1·50	25
R214		10c. black and violet (Monrovia)	1·50	25
R215		10c. black and purple (Robertsport)	1·50	25

R **96** Patrol Boat "Quail"

1919. Roul or perf.

R388	R **96**	10c. blue and black (Buchanan)	90	5·75
R389		10c. black and brown ("Grenville")	90	7·50
R390		10c. black and green (Harper)	90	5·25
R391		10c. blue and violet (Monrovia)	90	5·75
R392		10c. black and red (Robertsport)	90	7·50

R **106** Gabon Viper

1921†.

R456	R **106**	10c. black and red (Buchanan)	23·00	2·50
R457		10c. black and red (Greenville)	14·00	2·50
R458		10c. black and blue (Harper)	18·00	2·50
R459		10c. black and orange (Monrovia)	14·00	2·50
R460		10c. black and green (Robertsport)	14·00	2·50

1921†. Optd **1921.**

R461	R **106**	10c. black and lake	20·00	4·25
R462		10c. black and red	20·00	4·25
R463		10c. black and blue	20·00	4·25
R464		10c. black and orange	20·00	4·25
R465		10c. black and green	20·00	4·25

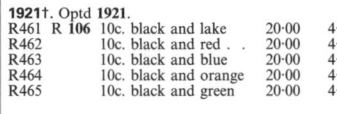

R **111** Sailing Skiff (Buchanan)

1923†. Various sea views.

R499	R **111**	10c. red and black	8·50	55
R500	–	10c. green and black	8·50	55
R501	–	10c. orange and black	8·50	55
R502	–	10c. blue and black	8·50	55
R503	–	10c. violet and black	8·50	55

DESIGNS: No. R500, Lighter (Greenville); R501, Full-rigged sailing ship (Harper); R502, "George Washington" (liner) (Monrovia); R503, Canoe (Robertsport).

1941. No. 576 surch **REGISTERED 10 CENTS 10.**

R592	10c. on 5c. brown (postage)	1·40	1·40
R593	10c. on 5c. brown (air)	1·40	1·40

No. R593 is additionally optd with airplane and **AIR MAIL.**

SPECIAL DELIVERY STAMPS

1941. No. 576 surch with postman and **SPECIAL DELIVERY 10 CENTS 10.**

S590	10c. on 5c. brown (postage)	1·40	1·40
S591	10c. on 5c. brown (air)	1·40	1·40

No. S591 is additionally optd with airplane and **AIR MAIL.**

LIBYA Pt. 8; Pt. 13

A former Italian colony in N. Africa, comprising the governorates of Cyrenaica and Tripolitania. From the end of 1951 an independent kingdom including the Fezzan also. Following a revolution in 1969 the country became the Libyan Arab Republic.

1912. 100 centesimi = 1 lira.
1952. 1000 milliemes = 1 Libyan pound.
1972. 1000 dirhams = 1 dinar.

A. ITALIAN COLONY

1912. Stamps of Italy optd **LIBYA** (No. 5) or **Libia** (others).

1	**30**	1c. brown	85	85
2	**31**	2c. brown	85	50
3	**37**	5c. green	85	35
4		10c. red	85	35
5	**41**	15c. grey	£100	1·70
6	**37**	15c. grey	3·50	3·50
7	**33**	20c. orange	2·40	35
8	**41**	20c. orange	2·75	3·50
9	**39**	25c. blue	2·75	35
10		40c. brown	5·25	1·00
11	**33**	45c. green	22·00	17·00
12	**39**	50c. violet	17·00	1·40
13		60c. red	12·00	13·50
14	**34**	1l. brown and green	50·00	1·70
15		5l. blue and red	£275	£200
16		10l. green and pink	24·00	80·00

1915. Red Cross stamps of Italy optd **LIBIA.**

17	**53**	10c.+5c. red	2·10	8·50
18	**54**	15c.+5c. grey	11·00	19·00
19		20c. on 15c.+5c. grey	11·00	19·00
20		20c.+5c. orange	3·50	19·00

1916. No. 100 of Italy optd **LIBIA.**

21	**41**	20c. on 15c. grey	27·00	5·25

4 Roman Legionary

5 Goddess of Plenty

6 Roman Galley leaving Tripoli

7 Victory

1921.

22A	**4**	1c. brown and black	35	2·50
23A		2c. brown and black	35	2·50
24A		5c. green and black	50	45
50		7½c. brown and black	35	4·00
51	**5**	10c. pink and black	35	25
52		15c. orange and brown	4·25	1·00
27A		25c. blue and deep blue	50	15
54	**6**	30c. brown and black	25	50
55		50c. green and black	25	50
30A		55c. violet and black	3·50	7·50
57	**7**	75c. red and purple	1·90	10
58		1l. brown	6·00	35
59	**6**	1l.25 blue and indigo	25	10
32A	**7**	5l. blue and black	21·00	13·50
33A		10l. green and blue	£150	75·00

1922. Victory stamps of Italy optd **LIBIA.**

34	**62**	5c. green	1·20	5·25
35		10c. red	1·20	5·25
36		15c. grey	1·20	6·75
37		25c. blue	1·20	6·75

1922. Nos. 9 and 12 of Libya surch.

38	**39**	40c. on 50c. mauve	2·20	1·70
39		80c. on 25c. blue	2·20	5·25

9 "Libyan Sibyl" by Michelangelo

10 Bedouin Woman

1924.

41	**9**	20c. green	70	10
42		40c. brown	1·70	50
43		60c. blue	70	10
44		1l.75 orange	25	10
45		2l. red	2·10	85
46		2l.55 violet	4·00	5·75

1928. Air. Air stamps of Italy optd **Libia.**

63	**88**	50c. pink	6·75	8·50
64		80c. brown and purple	21·00	33·00

1928. Types of Italy optd **LIBIA** (No. 67) or Libia (others).

65	**92**	7½c. brown	5·25	26·00
66	**34**	1l.25 blue	38·00	13·50
67	**91**	1l.75 brown	43·00	1·70

1936. 10th Tripoli Trade Fair.

68	**10**	50c. violet	1·20	2·40
69		1l.25 blue	1·40	6·25

1936. Air. Nos. 96 and 99 of Cyrenaica optd **LIBIA.**

70	–	50c. violet	1·70	35
71	**17**	1l. black	3·50	17·00

1937. Air. Stamps of Tripolitania optd **LIBIA.**

72	**18**	50c. red	10	10
73		60c. red	60	
74		75c. blue	60	17·00
75		80c. purple	60	31·00
76	**19**	1l. blue	1·50	85
77		1l.20 brown	60	38·00
78		1l.50 orange	60	
79		5l. green	60	

11 Triumphal Arch

12 Roman Theatre, Sabrata

1937. Inauguration of Coastal Highway.

80	**11**	50c. red (postage)	2·20	3·50
81		1l.25 blue	2·20	7·75
82	**12**	50c. purple (air)	2·20	4·25
83		1l. black	2·20	4·25

1937. 11th Tripoli Trade Fair. Optd **XI FIERA DI TRIPOLI.**

84	**11**	50c. red (postage)	10·50	24·00
85		1l.25 blue	10·50	24·00
86	**12**	50c. purple (air)	10·50	24·00
87		1l. black	10·50	24·00

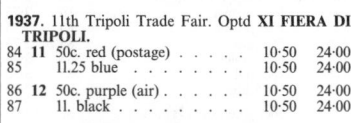

14 Benghazi Waterfront

1938. 12th Tripoli Trade Fair.

88	**14**	5c. brown (postage)	10	1·00
89	–	10c. brown	10	70
90	**14**	25c. green	45	1·20
91	–	50c. violet	50	50
92	**14**	75c. red	85	1·70
93	–	1l.25 blue	95	3·50

DESIGN: 10c., 50c., 1l.25, Fair Buildings.

94	50c. brown (air)	1·00	1·90
95	1l. blue	1·00	4·00

DESIGN—VERT: View of Tripoli.

16 Statue of Augustus

17 Eagle and Serpent

1938. Birth Bimillenary of Augustus the Great.

96	**16**	5c. green (postage)	10	1·00
97	–	10c. red	10	1·00
98	**16**	25c. green	50	60
99	–	50c. mauve	50	45
100	**16**	75c. red	1·50	3·25
101	–	1l.25 blue	1·50	2·20
102	**17**	50c. brown (air)	35	1·40
103		1l. mauve	50	3·00

DESIGN: 10, 50c., 1l.25, Statue of Goddess of Plenty.

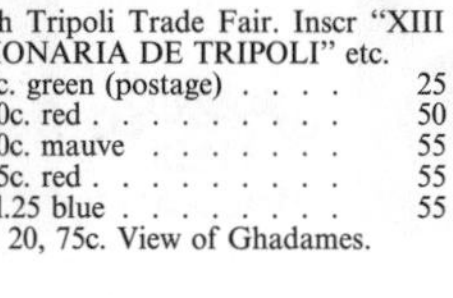

18 Agricultural Landscape

1939. 13th Tripoli Trade Fair. Inscr "XIII FIERA CAMPIONARIA DE TRIPOLI" etc.

104	**18**	5c. green (postage)	25	85
105	–	20c. red	50	85
106	**18**	50c. mauve	55	85
107	–	75c. red	55	1·70
108	**18**	1l.25 blue	55	2·50

DESIGN: 20, 75c. View of Ghadames.

109	–	25c. green (air)	25	1·30
110	–	50c. green	35	1·30
111	–	1l. mauve	45	1·70

DESIGNS—Fiat G18V airplane over: 25c., 1l. Arab and camel in desert; 50c. Fair entrance.

19 Buildings

1940. Naples Exhibition.

112	19	5c. brown (postage)	1·50	1·00
113	–	10c. orange	1·00	70
114	–	25c. green	60	1·00
115	19	50c. violet	60	70
116	–	75c. red	70	2·20
117	–	1l.25 blue	85	3·75
118	–	2l.+75c. red	85	13·00

DESIGNS—HORIZ: 10, 75c., 2l. Oxen and plough. VERT: 25c., 1l.25, Mosque.

119	–	50c. black (air)	50	85
120	–	1l. brown	50	1·70
121	–	2l.+75c. blue	85	5·25
122	–	5l.+2l.50 brown	85	7·75

DESIGNS—HORIZ: 50c., 2l. Savoia Marchetti S.M.75 airplane over city; 1, 5l. Savoia Marchetti S-73 airplane over oasis.

19a Hitler and Mussolini

1941. Rome–Berlin Axis Commemoration.

123	19a	5c. orange (postage)	10	2·75
124		10c. brown	10	2·75
125		20c. purple	85	2·75
126		25c. green	85	2·75
127		50c. violet	85	2·75
128		75c. red	85	8·50
129		1l.25 blue	85	8·50
130		50c. green (air)	85	12·00

B. INDEPENDENT

ليبيا
LIBYA
(20)

-- ليبيا -- ليبيا
٤ ليرة ع.
4 MAL.
LIBYA
(21)

-- ليبيا --
٨ فـرنك
8 FRANCS
LIBYA
(22)

1951. Stamps of Cyrenaica optd. (a) For use in Cyrenaica, optd as T **20**.

131	24	1m. brown	15	15
132		2m. red	20	20
133		3m. yellow	25	25
134		4m. green	28·00	19·00
135		5m. brown	35	35
136		8m. orange	40	40
137		10m. violet	60	60
138		12m. red	1·10	1·10
139		20m. blue	1·50	1·50
140	25	50m. blue and brown	8·75	8·75
141		100m. red and black	14·50	14·50
142		200m. violet and blue	45·00	40·00
143		500m. yellow and green	£150	£130

(b) For use in Tripolitania. Surch as T **21** in Military Authority lire.

151	24	1mal. on 2m. red	25	25
152		2mal. on 4m. green	25	25
153		4mal. on 8m. orange	25	25
154		5mal. on 10m. violet	35	35
155		6mal. on 12m. red	35	35
156		10mal. on 20m. blue	65	65
157	25	24 mal. on 50m. blue and brown	3·00	3·00
158		48mal. on 100m. red	11·00	11·00
159		96mal. on 200m. violet and blue	27·00	27·00
160		240mal. on 500m. yellow and green	70·00	70·00

(c) For use in Fezzan. Surch as T **22**.

166	24	2f. on 2m. red	20	20
167		4f. on 4m. green	30	30
168		8f. on 8m. orange	35	40
169		10f. on 10m. violet	50	50
170		12f. on 12m. red	75	75
171		20f. on 20m. blue	2·00	2·00
172	25	48f. on 50m. blue & brown	38·00	35·00
173		96f. on 100m. red and black	40·00	35·00
174		192f. on 200m. violet and blue	£110	80·00
175		480f. on 500m. yellow and green	£190	£190

23 King Idris

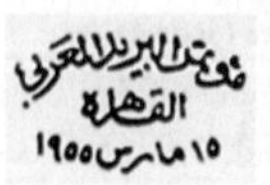

(28)

30

1952.

176	23	2m. brown	10	10
177		4m. grey	10	10
178		5m. green	12·50	35
179		8m. red	40	25
180		10m. violet	12·50	15
181		12m. red	75	15
182		20m. blue	13·50	45
183		25m. brown	13·50	45
184	–	50m. blue and brown	1·75	65
185	–	100m. red and black	3·75	1·90
186	–	200m. violet and blue	6·00	3·50
187	–	500m. orange and green	25·00	17·00

Nos. 184/7 are larger.

1955. Arab Postal Union. As T **84a** of Lebanon but inscr "LIBYE" at top.

200		5m. brown	1·25	60
201		10m. green	1·90	90
202		30m. violet	4·25	2·00

1955. 2nd Arab Postal Congress, Cairo. Nos. 200/2 optd with T **28**.

203		5m. brown	40	30
204		10m. green	95	50
205		30m. violet	2·25	1·25

1955. No. 177 surch.

206	23	5m. on 4m. grey	1·25	45

1955.

207	30	1m. black on yellow	10	10
208		2m. bistre	1·40	50
209		2m. brown	10	10
210		3m. blue	10	10
211		4m. black	1·50	50
212		4m. lake	20	15
213		5m. green	40	20
214		10m. lilac	65	25
215		18m. red	15	10
216		20m. orange	25	15
217		30m. blue	50	20
218		35m. brown	65	25
219		40m. lake	1·10	40
220		50m. olive	85	25
221	–	100m. purple and slate	1·75	50
222	–	200m. lake and blue	9·25	1·40
223	–	500m. orange and green	15·00	7·25
224	–	£L1 green, brown and sepia on yellow	21·00	11·50

Nos. 221/4 are larger, 27 × 32 mm.
See also Nos. 242/57.

33 Immam's Tomb at Djaghboub

1956. Death Centenary of Imam Essayed Mohamed Aly el Senussi.

225	33	5m. green	20	20
226		10m. lilac	35	20
227		15m. red	95	75
228		30m. blue	1·60	1·25

34 Map of Libya

35

1956. 1st Anniv of Admission to U.N.

229	34	15m. buff and blue	30	15
230		35m. buff, purple and blue	1·00	30

1957. Arab Postal Congress, Tripoli.

231	35	15m. blue	1·75	90
232		500m. brown	12·50	6·50

36

39

37 F.A.O. Emblem and Date Palms

1958. 10th Anniv of Declaration of Human Rights.

233	36	10m. violet	20	15
234		15m. green	25	20
235		30m. blue	95	50

1959. 1st Int Dates Conf, Tripoli.

236	37	10m. black and violet	20	15
237		15m. black and green	50	20
238		45m. black and blue	1·00	50

1960. Inauguration of Arab League Centre, Cairo. As T **110** of Lebanon, but with Arms of Libya and inscr "LIBYA".

239		10m. black and green	50	20

1960. World Refugee Year.

240	39	10m. black and violet	25	15
241		45m. black and blue	1·25	75

1960. As Nos. 207 etc. On coloured paper.

242	30	1m. black on grey	10	10
243		2m. brown on buff	10	10
244		3m. indigo on blue	10	10
245		4m. lake on red	10	10
246		5m. green on green	10	10
247		10m. lilac on violet	10	10
248		15m. sepia on buff	10	10
249		20m. orange on orange	20	10
250		30m. red on pink	20	15
251		40m. lake on red	30	20
252		45m. blue on blue	35	20
253		50m. olive on bistre	35	20
254	–	100m. purple & slate on blue	1·25	35
255	–	200m. lake and blue on blue	3·25	1·40
256	–	500m. orange and green on green	23·00	5·50
257	–	£L1 green, brown and sepia	23·00	11·00

40 Palm Tree and Radio Mast

41 Military Watchtower (medallion)

1960. 3rd Arab Telecommunications Conf, Tripoli.

258	40	10m. violet	15	10
259		15m. turquoise	20	10
260		45m. lake	1·40	65

1961. Army Day.

261	41	5m. brown and green	20	10
262		15m. brown and blue	60	15

42 Zelten Field and Marsa Brega Port

1961. Inaug of First Libyan Petrol Pipeline.

263	42	15m. green and buff	25	10
264		50m. brown and lavender	75	40
265		100m. blue and light blue	2·25	90

43 Broken Chain and Agricultural Scenes

1961. 10th Anniv of Independence.

266	43	15m. sepia, turquoise and green	15	10
267	–	50m. sepia, brown and buff	45	25
268	–	100m. sepia, blue & salmon	2·10	80

DESIGNS—(embodying broken chain): 50m. Modern highway and buildings; 100m. Industrial machinery.

44 Tuareg Camel Riders

1962. International Fair, Tripoli.

269	44	10m. chestnut and brown	60	10
270	–	15m. green and purple	75	25
271	–	50m. blue and green	2·00	1·60

DESIGNS: 15m. Well; 50m. Oil derrick.

45 Campaign Emblem

46 Ahmed Rafik

1962. Malaria Eradication.

273	45	15m. multicoloured	25	20
274		50m. multicoloured	1·10	90

1962. 1st Death Anniv of Ahmed Rafik el Mehdawi (poet).

276	46	15m. green	15	10
277		20m. brown	55	20

47 Scout Badge and Handclasp

48 City within Oildrop

1962. 3rd Boy Scouts' Meeting, Tripoli.

278	47	5m. sepia, red and yellow	10	10
279	–	10m. sepia, yellow and blue	20	10
280	–	15m. sepia, yellow and grey	25	20

DESIGNS: 10m. Scouts and badge; 15m. Badge and camp.

1962. Inauguration of Essider Terminal, Sidrah Oil Pipeline.

282	48	15m. purple and green	45	15
283		50m. olive and brown	1·10	45

49 Red Crescent encircling Globe

1963. International Red Cross Centenary.

284	49	10m. multicoloured	20	15
285		15m. multicoloured	25	20
286		20m. multicoloured	90	60

50 Rainbow over Map of Tripoli

1963. International Trade Fair, Tripoli.

287	50	15m. multicoloured	25	20
288		30m. multicoloured	70	20
289		50m. multicoloured	1·40	60

51 Palm and Well

1963. Freedom from Hunger.

290	51	10m. green, brown and blue	20	10
291	–	15m. ochre, purple & green	25	20
292	–	45m. sepia, blue and salmon	1·10	75

DESIGNS: 15m. Camel and sheep; 45m. Farmer sowing and tractor.

52 "Emancipation"

1963. 15th Anniv of Declaration of Human Rights.

293	52	5m. brown and blue	10	10
294		15m. purple and blue	20	10
295		50m. green and blue	45	30

54 Map and Fair Entrance

55 Child playing in Sun

1964. International Fair, Tripoli.

300	54	10m. green, brown and red	75	15
301		15m. green, brown & purple	1·00	50
302		30m. green, brown and blue	1·40	75

1964. Children's Day. Sun gold.

303	55	5m. violet, red and pink	10	10
304	–	15m. brown, bistre and buff	20	15
305	55	45m. violet, blue & lt blue	1·25	65

DESIGN: 15m. Child in bird's nest.

56 Lungs and Stethoscope

1964. Anti-tuberculosis Campaign.

307	56	20m. violet	90	25

57 Crown and Map

58 Libyan Woman, Silk Moth and Cocoon

1964. 1st Anniv of Libyan Union.

308	57	5m. orange and green	15	10
309		50m. yellow and blue	1·00	50

1964. Emancipation of Libyan Women.

310	58	10m. blue and green	15	10
311		20m. blue and yellow	55	35
312		35m. blue and pink	85	80

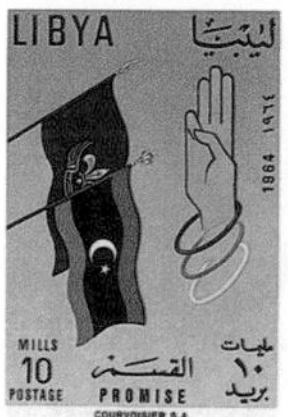

59 Flags and Scout Salute

60 Bayonet

1964. Libyan Scouts. Multicoloured.

314		10m. Type 59	65	20
315		20m. Scout badge and saluting hands	1·25	60

1964. Foundation of the Senussi Army.

317	60	10m. brown and green	15	10
318		20m. black and orange	65	40

61 Ahmed Bahloul (poet)

62 Football

1964. Ahmed Bahloul El-Sharef Commem.

319	61	15m. purple	20	10
320		20m. blue	65	20

1964. Olympic Games, Tokyo. Rings in Gold.

321		5m. black and blue (Type 62)	25	20
322		10m. black & purple (Cycling)	25	20
323		20m. black and red (Boxing)	50	20
324		30m. black and buff (Runner)	65	50
325		35m. black and olive (High-diving)	65	50
326		50m. black & green (Hurdling)	65	50

Nos. 321/6 were arranged together se-tenant in the sheets, each block of six being superimposed with the Olympic "rings" symbol.

63 A.P.U. Emblem

64 I.C.Y. Emblem

1964. 10th Anniv of Arab Postal Union.

328	63	10m. blue and yellow	10	10
329		15m. brown and lilac	20	10
330		30m. brown and green	95	65

1965. International Co-operation Year.

331	64	5m. gold and blue (postage)	25	10
332		15m. gold and red	90	25
333		50m. gold and violet (air)	1·50	35

65 European Bee Eater

1965. Birds. Multicoloured.

335		5m. Long-legged buzzard (vert)	1·10	30
336		10m. Type 65	1·50	30
337		15m. Black-bellied sandgrouse	2·25	30
338		20m. Houbara bustard	2·75	55
339		30m. Spotted sandgrouse	3·50	90
340		40m. Barbary partridge (vert)	4·25	1·25

66 Fair Emblem

1965. International Trade Fair, Tripoli.

341	66	50m. multicoloured	75	50

67 Compass, Rocket and Balloons

1965. World Meteorological Day.

342	67	10m. multicoloured	10	10
343		15m. multicoloured	20	15
344		50m. multicoloured	1·00	70

68 I.T.U. Emblem and Symbols

1965. Centenary of I.T.U.

345	68	10m. brown	10	10
346		20m. purple	15	10
347		50m. mauve	90	65

69 Lamp and Burning Library

70 Rose

1965. Reconstitution of Burnt Algiers Library.

348	69	15m. multicoloured	20	10
349		50m. multicoloured	90	25

1965. Flowers. Multicoloured.

351		1m. Type 70	10	10
352		2m. Iris	10	10
353		3m. Cactus flower	10	10
354		4m. Sunflower	50	10

71 Sud Aviation Super Caravelle over Globe

72 Forum, Cyrene

1965. Inaug of Kingdom of Libya Airlines.

355	71	5m. multicoloured	10	10
356		10m. multicoloured	20	10
357		15m. multicoloured	70	10

1965.

358	72	50m. olive and blue	70	25
359	–	100m. brown and blue	1·25	45
360	–	200m. blue and purple	3·00	95
361	–	500m. green and red	6·50	2·75
362	–	£L1 brown and green	14·00	6·50

DESIGNS–VERT: 100m. Trajan's Arch, Leptis Magna; 200m. Apollo's Temple, Cyrene. HORIZ: 500m. Antonine Temple, Sabratha; £L1 Theatre, Sabratha.

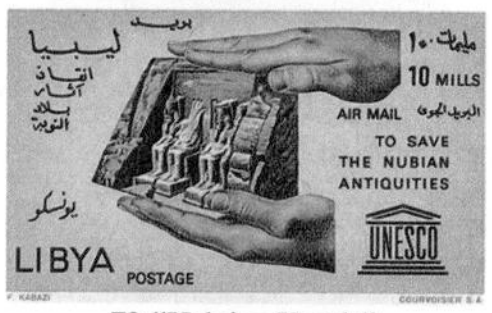

73 "Helping Hands"

1966. Air. Nubian Monuments Preservation.

363	73	10m. brown and bistre	20	10
364		15m. brown and green	25	10
365		40m. brown and chestnut	1·10	50

74 Germa Mausoleum

1966.

367	74	70m. violet and brown	1·40	75

See also No. E368.

75 Globe and Satellites

1966. International Trade Fair, Tripoli.

369	75	15m. black, gold and green	20	10
370		45m. black, gold and blue	70	20
371		55m. black, gold and purple	95	60

76 League Centre, Cairo, and Emblem

77 W.H.O. Building

1966. Arab League Week.

372	76	20m. red, green and black	10	10
373		55m. blue, red and black	65	50

1966. Air. Inaug of W.H.O. Headquarters, Geneva.

374	77	20m. black, yellow and blue	20	10
375		50m. black, green and red	65	25
376		65m. black, salmon and lake	95	70

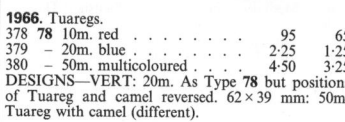

78 Tuareg with Camel

80 Leaping Deer

1966. Tuaregs.

378	78	10m. red	95	65
379	–	20m. blue	2·25	1·25
380	–	50m. multicoloured	4·50	3·25

DESIGNS—VERT: 20m. As Type 78 but positions of Tuareg and camel reversed. 62 × 39 mm: 50m. Tuareg with camel (different).

1966. 1st Arab Girl Scouts Camp (5m.) and 7th Arab Boy Scouts Camp (25 and 65m.). Multicoloured.

382		5m. Type 80	10	10
383		25m. Boy scouts Camp emblem (vert)	20	10
384		65m. As 25m.	1·00	50

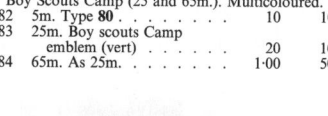

81 Airline Emblem

1966. Air. 1st Anniv of Kingdom of Libya Airlines.

385	81	25m. multicoloured	20	15
386		60m. multicoloured	1·00	75
387		85m. multicoloured	1·40	1·00

82 UNESCO Emblem

83 Castle of Columns, Tolemaide

1967. 20th Anniv of UNESCO.

388	82	15m. multicoloured	20	10
389		25m. multicoloured	90	20

1967. Tourism.

390	83	25m. black, brown & violet	20	10
391	–	55m. brown, violet & black	90	50

DESIGN—HORIZ: 55m. Sebba Fort.

84 "British Confidence" (tanker) at Oil Terminal

1967. Inaug of Marsa al Hariga Oil Terminal.

392	84	60m. multicoloured	1·75	65

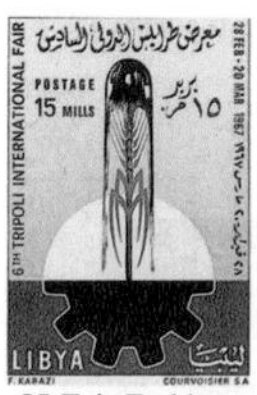

85 Fair Emblem

86 I.T.Y. Emblem

1967. International Fair, Tripoli.

393	85	15m. multicoloured	50	10
394		55m. multicoloured	75	50

1967. International Tourist Year.

395	86	5m. black and blue	10	10
396		10m. blue and black	10	10
397		45m. black, blue and pink	60	15

87 Running

88 Open Book and Arab League Emblem

1967. Mediterranean Games, Tunisia. Designs showing action "close-ups".
398 **87** 5m. black, orange and blue 10 10
399 – 10m. black, brown and blue 10 10
400 – 15m. black, violet and blue 10 10
401 – 45m. black, red and blue 30 25
402 – 75m. black, green and blue 75 30
DESIGNS: 10m. Throwing the javelin; 15m. Cycling; 45m. Football; 75m. Boxing.

1967. Literacy Campaign.
403 **88** 5m. orange and violet 10 10
404 10m. green and violet 10 10
405 15m. purple and violet 15 10
406 25m. blue and violet 20 15

89 Human Rights Emblem

90 Cameleers, Fokker Friendship, Oil Rig and Map

1968. Human Rights Year.
407 **89** 15m. red and green 15 10
408 60m. blue and orange 65 25

1968. International Fair, Tripoli.
409 **90** 55m. multicoloured 95 30

91 Arab League Emblem

1968. Arab League Week.
410 **91** 10m. red and blue 10 10
411 45m. green and orange 65 50

92 Children "Wrestling" (statue)

93 W.H.O. Emblem and Reaching Hands

1968. Children's Day. Multicoloured.
412 25m. Type **92** 45 15
413 55m. Libyan mother and children 80 55

1968. 20th Anniv of W.H.O.
414 **93** 25m. blue and purple 25 15
415 55m. brown and blue 40 25

94 Oil Pipeline Map

1968. Inauguration of Zueitina Oil Terminal.
416 **94** 10m. multicoloured 20 10
417 60m. multicoloured 1·10 65

95 "Teaching the People"

1968. "Eliminate Illiteracy".
418 **95** 5m. mauve 10 10
419 10m. orange 10 10
420 15m. blue 10 10
421 20m. green 20 20

96 Conference Emblem

1968. 4th Session of Arab Labour Ministries Conference, Tripoli.
422 **96** 10m. multicoloured 10 10
423 15m. multicoloured 20 10

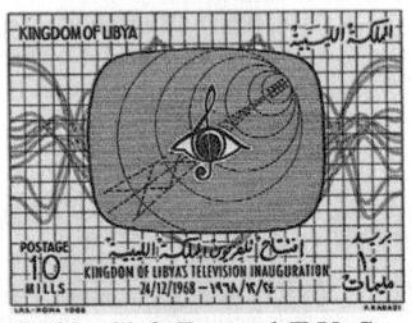
97 Treble Clef, Eye and T.V. Screen

1968. Inauguration of Libyan Television Service.
424 **97** 10m. multicoloured 10 10
425 30m. multicoloured 65 20

98 Bridge, Callipers and Road Sign

1968. Opening of Wadi El Kuf Bridge.
426 **98** 25m. multicoloured 15 15
427 60m. multicoloured 70 25

99 Melons

100 Fair Emblem

1969. Fruits. Multicoloured.
428 5m. Type **99** 10 10
429 10m. Dates 10 10
430 15m. Lemons 10 10
431 20m. Oranges 15 10
432 25m. Peaches 50 15
433 35m. Pears 90 50

1969. 8th International Trade Fair, Tripoli.
434 **100** 25m. multicoloured 15 10
435 35m. multicoloured 25 15
436 40m. multicoloured 60 20

101 Hoisting Weather Balloon

1969. World Meteorological Day.
437 **101** 60m. multicoloured 1·10 65

102 Family on Staircase within Cogwheel

103 I.L.O. Emblem

1969. 10th Anniv of Libyan Social Insurance.
438 **102** 15m. multicoloured 15 10
439 55m. multicoloured 30 25

1969. 50th Anniv of I.L.O.
440 **103** 10m. green, black & turq 10 10
441 60m. green, black and red 70 50

104 Emblem and Desert Scene

1969. African Tourist Year.
442 **104** 15m. multicoloured 15 10
443 30m. multicoloured 65 50

105 Members of the Armed Forces and Olive Branch

106 Dish Aerial and Flags

1969. Revolution of 1st September.
444 **105** 5m. multicoloured 25 10
445 10m. multicoloured 35 20
446 15m. multicoloured 55 25
447 25m. multicoloured 85 40
448 45m. multicoloured 1·00 60
449 60m. multicoloured 2·10 1·00
On Nos. 444/9 the value is in white and the designer's name appears at the foot of design.

1970. 5th Anniv of Arab Satellite Communications Co-operation Agreement.
450 **106** 15m. multicoloured 50 15
451 20m. multicoloured 75 20
452 25m. multicoloured 1·00 25
453 40m. multicoloured 1·50 75

107 Arab League Flag, Arms and Map

1970. Silver Jubilee of Arab League.
454 **107** 10m. sepia, green and blue 10 10
455 15m. brown, green & orge 15 15
456 20m. purple, green & olive 50 25

1970. Revolution of 1 September. Designs as T **105**, but without imprint "M. A. Siala" at foot, and figures of value differently inscr.
457 **87** 5m. multicoloured 25 10
458 10m. multicoloured 35 20
459 15m. multicoloured 55 25
460 25m. multicoloured 85 40
461 45m. multicoloured 1·00 60
462 60m. multicoloured 2·10 1·00

108 New Headquarters Building

109 Arms and Soldiers

1970. New U.P.U. Headquarters Building, Berne.
463 **108** 10m. multicoloured 15 10
464 25m. multicoloured 20 20
465 60m. multicoloured 95 60

1970. Nos. 358 and 360/2 with "KINGDOM OF LIBYA" inscriptions obliterated.
465a **72** 50m. olive and blue
466 – 200m. blue and purple
467 – 500m. green and pink
468 – £L1 brown and green
These stamps were sold only for use on parcel post items. Other values may exist so overprinted, but were unauthorized.
See also Nos. 518/23.

1970. Evacuation of Foreign Military Bases in Libya.
469 **109** 15m. black and red 15 15
470 25m. yellow, blue and red 45 20
471 45m. yellow, red and green 1·25 30

110 Soldiers and Libyan Flag

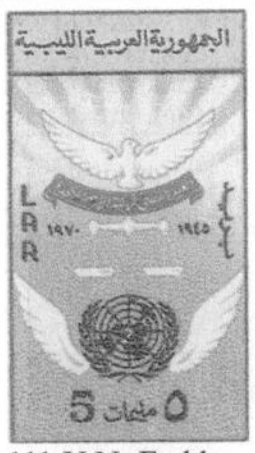
111 U.N. Emblem, Dove and Scales

1970. 1st Anniv of Libyan Arab Republic.
472 **110** 20m. multicoloured 55 15
473 25m. multicoloured 70 15
474 30m. multicoloured 1·25 75

1970. 25th Anniv of United Nations.
475 **111** 5m. brown, red and green 25 10
476 10m. green, red & emerald 65 15
477 60m. green, red and blue 1·75 75

112 Map and Flags

113 Dove, U.N. Emblem and Globe

1970. Signing of Tripoli Charter of Co-operation.
478 **112** 15m. green, black and red 5·00 1·50

1971. 10th Anniv of U.N. De-colonisation Declaration.
479 **113** 15m. multicoloured 50 15
480 20m. multicoloured 75 20
481 60m. multicoloured 1·90 75

114 Education Year Emblem

115 Palestinian Guerrilla

1971. International Education Year.
482 **114** 5m. brown, red and black 15 10
483 10m. green, red and black 50 10
484 20m. blue, red and black 1·10 15

1971. "Al-Fatah" Movement for the Liberation of Palestine.
485 **115** 5m. multicoloured 15 10
486 10m. multicoloured 50 15
487 100m. multicoloured 1·75 1·00

116 Fair Emblem

117 O.P.E.C. Emblem

1971. 9th International Trade Fair, Tripoli.
488 **116** 15m. multicoloured 15 10
489 30m. multicoloured 65 20

1971. Organization of Petroleum Exporting Countries (O.P.E.C.).
490 **117** 10m. brown and yellow 15 10
491 70m. violet and pink 1·25 65

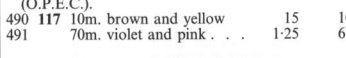

118 Global Symbol

1971. World Telecommunications Day (Nos. 494/5) and Pan-African Telecommunications Network.
492 – 5m. multicoloured 10 10
493 – 15m. multicoloured 10 10
494 **118** 25m. multicoloured 20 15
495 35m. multicoloured 50 25
DESIGN: 5m., 15m. Telecommunications map of Africa.

119 Soldier, Torch and Flag

120 Ramadan Suehli

1971. 1st Anniv of Evacuation of Foreign Troops.
496 **119** 5m. multicoloured 10 10
497 10m. multicoloured . . . 15 10
498 15m. multicoloured . . . 20 15

1971. Ramadan Suehli (patriot). Commem.
499 **120** 15m. multicoloured . . . 15 10
500 55m. multicoloured . . . 75 35
For similar portraits see Nos. 503/4, 507/8, 526/7 and 553/4.

121 Palm and Dates

122 Pres. Gamal Nasser

1971. 2nd Anniv of 1 September Revolution.
501 **121** 5m. multicoloured 20 10
502 15m. multicoloured . . . 1·00 15

1971. 40th Death Anniv of Omar el Mukhtar (patriot). As T **120**.
503 5m. multicoloured 10 10
504 100m. multicoloured . . . . 1·75 90

1971. 1st Death Anniv of Pres. Nasser of Egypt.
505 **122** 5m. black, green & purple 10 10
506 15m. black, purple & green 95 10

1971. 21st Death Anniv of Ibrahim Usta Omar (poet). As T **120**.
507 25m. multicoloured 25 15
508 30m. multicoloured 80 20

123 Racial Equality Year Emblem

124 A.P.U. Emblem

1971. Racial Equality Year.
509 **123** 25m. multicoloured . . . 25 15
510 35m. multicoloured . . . 70 15

1971. 25th Anniv of Founding of Arab Postal Union at Sofar Conference.
511 **124** 5m. multicoloured 10 10
512 10m. multicoloured . . . 20 10
513 15m. multicoloured . . . 15 10

125 Arab Postal Union Emblem and Envelopes

126 Book Year Emblem

1971. 10th Anniv of African Postal Union. Mult.
514 10m. Type **125** 10 10
515 15m. Type **125** 15 10
516 25m. A.P.U. Emblem and dove with letter 25 15
517 55m. As 25m. 95 35

1971. Nos. 423/33 with "KINGDOM OF LIBYA" inscriptions obliterated.
518 5m. Type **99** . . . .
519 10m. Dates . . . .
520 15m. Lemons . . . .
521 20m. Oranges . . . .
522 25m. Peaches . . . .
523 35m. Pears . . . .

1972. International Book Year.
524 **126** 15m. multicoloured . . . 15 10
525 20m. multicoloured . . . 25 20

1972. Ahmed Gnaba (poet) Commem. As T **120**.
526 20m. multicoloured 25 10
527 35m. multicoloured 65 20

127 Libyan Arms

128 Tombs, Ghirza

1972. Values in Milliemes.
528 **127** 5m. multicoloured 10 10
529 10m. multicoloured . . . 10 10
530 25m. multicoloured . . . 15 10
531 30m. multicoloured . . . 20 10
532 35m. multicoloured . . . 25 10
533 40m. multicoloured . . . 50 15
534 45m. multicoloured . . . 60 15
535 55m. multicoloured . . . 85 20
536 60m. multicoloured . . . 1·00 35
537 90m. multicoloured . . . 1·60 90
For values in dirhams and dinars see Nos. 555/62.

1972. Libyan Antiquities. Multicoloured.
538 5m. Type **128** 10 10
539 10m. Cufic inscription, Ajdabiya 10 10
540 15m. Marcus Aurelius' Arch, Tripoli (horiz) 15 10
541 25m. Exchanging Weapons (cave painting, Wadi Zigza) 65 15
542 55m. Garamantian chariot (wall drawing, Wadi Zigza) 1·40 65
543 70m. "Libya crowning Cyrene" (Roman relief, Cyrene) . . . . 2·50 90

129 Fair Emblem

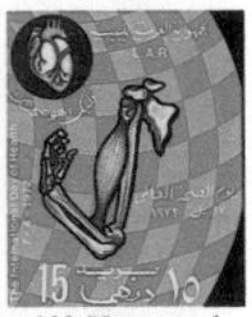

130 Heart and Skeletal Arm

1972. 10th International Trade Fair, Tripoli.
544 **129** 25m. multicoloured . . . 20 15
545 35m. multicoloured . . . 25 20
546 50m. multicoloured . . . 95 25
547 70m. multicoloured . . . 1·40 35

1972. World Health Day.
548 **130** 15m. multicoloured . . . 1·10 25
549 25m. multicoloured . . . 2·25 75

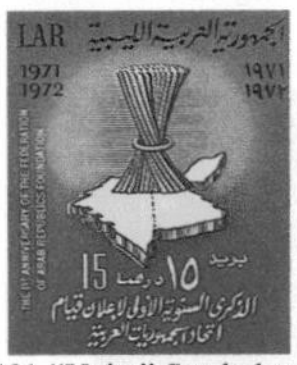

131 "Unity" Symbol on Map

132

1972. 1st Anniv of Libyan–Egyptian Federation Agreement.
550 **131** 15m. yellow, blue and black 10 10
551 20m. yellow, green & emer 20 10
552 25m. yellow, red and black 80 20

1972. Birth Centenary (1970) of Suleiman el Baruni (writer). As T **120**.
553 10m. multicoloured 95 15
554 70m. multicoloured . . . . . 1·25 75

1972. New Currency (Dirhams and Dinars). As T **127**. (a) Size 19 × 24 mm.
555 **127** 15dh. multicoloured . . . 10 10
556 65dh. multicoloured . . . 75 50
557 70dh. multicoloured . . . 90 65
558 80dh. multicoloured . . . 1·25 65

(b) Size 27 × 32 mm.
559 **127** 100dh. multicoloured . . 1·75 2·00
560 200dh. multicoloured . . 3·25 1·60
561 500dh. multicoloured . . 7·50 5·00
562 1D. multicoloured . . . . 13·50 10·00

1972.
563 **132** 5m. multicoloured . . . . 1·90 50
564 20m. multicoloured . . . . 7·50 1·40
565 50m. multicoloured . . . 18·00 3·75
Nos. 563/5 were also issued with the Arabic face values expressed in the new currency.
See also Nos. 657/9.

133 Environmental Emblem

134 Olympic Emblems

1972. U.N. Environmental Conservation Conference, Stockholm.
566 **133** 15dh. multicoloured . . . 50 10
567 55dh. multicoloured . . . 1·10 35

1972. Olympic Games, Munich.
568 **134** 25dh. multicoloured . . . 1·50 35
569 35dh. multicoloured . . . 2·25 90

135 Symbolic Tree and "Fruit"

136 Dome of the Rock

1972. 3rd Anniv of 1 September Revolution.
570 **135** 15dh. multicoloured . . . 15 10
571 25dh. multicoloured . . . 70 15

1973. Dome of the Rock, Jerusalem.
572 **136** 10dh. multicoloured . . . 10 10
573 25dh. multicoloured . . . 50 15

137 Nicolas Copernicus

138 Libyan Eagle and Fair

1973. 500th Birth Anniv of Copernicus. Mult.
574 15dh. Type **137** 15 10
575 25dh. "Copernicus in his Observatory" (horiz) . . . 50 15

1973. 11th International Trade Fair, Tripoli.
576 **138** 5dh. multicoloured . . . 15 10
577 10dh. multicoloured . . . 50 10
578 15dh. multicoloured . . . 90 15

139 Blind Persons and Occupations

140 Map and Laurel

1973. Role of the Blind in Society.
579 **139** 20dh. multicoloured . . . 5·50 1·25
580 25dh. multicoloured . . . 10·00 2·50

1973. 10th Anniv of Organization of African Unity.
584 **140** 15dh. multicoloured . . . 20 10
585 25dh. multicoloured . . . 65 45

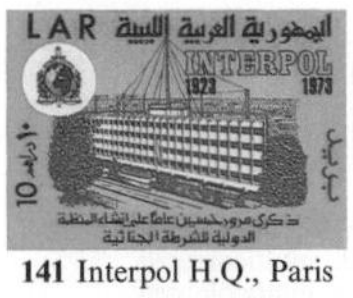

141 Interpol H.Q., Paris

1973. 50th Anniv of International Criminal Police Organization (Interpol).
586 **141** 10dh. multicoloured . . . 10 10
587 15dh. multicoloured . . . 15 10
588 25dh. multicoloured . . . 60 20

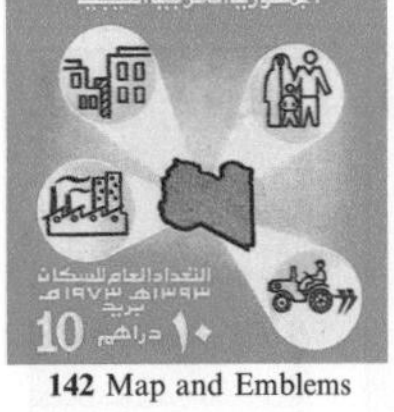

142 Map and Emblems

143 W.M.O. Emblem

1973. Census.
589 **142** 10dh. blue, black and red 3·00 65
590 25dh. green, black and blue . . . . 4·25 1·25
591 35dh. orange, black and grn . . . . 8·00 2·50

1973. W.M.O. Centenary.
592 **143** 5dh. blue, black and red 10 10
593 10dh. blue, black and green 15 10

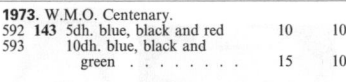

144 Footballers

1973. 2nd Palestine Cup Football Championship.
594 **144** 5dh. brown and green . . 45 20
595 25dh. brown and red . . 80 15

145 Revolutionary Torch

146 "Writing Ability"

1973. 4th Anniv of 1 September Revolution.
596 **145** 15dh. multicoloured . . . 20 10
597 25dh. multicoloured . . . 85 10

1973. Literacy Campaign.
598 **146** 25dh. multicoloured . . . 50 15

147 Doorway of Old City Hall

148 Militiamen and Flag

1973. Cent of Tripoli Municipality. Mult.
599 10dh. Type **147** 20 10
600 25dh. Khondok fountain . . 50 10
601 35dh. Clock tower 75 40

1973. Libyan Militia.
602 **148** 15dh. multicoloured . . . 15 10
603 25dh. multicoloured . . . 55 10

149 Arabic Quotation from Speech of 15 April 1973

1973. Declaration of Cultural Revolution by Col. Gaddafi. Multicoloured.
604 25dh. Type **149** 20 10
605 70dh. As Type **149** but text in English 60 30

150 Ploughing with Camel

151 Human Rights Emblem

1973. 10th Anniv of World Food Programme.
606 **150** 10dh. multicoloured . . . 10 10
607 25dh. multicoloured . . . 20 10
608 35dh. multicoloured . . . 55 15

1973. 25th Anniv of Declaration of Human Rights.
609 **151** 25dh. red, purple and blue 20 10
610 70dh. red, green and blue 1·10 30

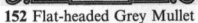

152 Flat-headed Grey Mullet

154 Emblem formed with National Flags

153 Lookout Post and Scout Salute

1973. Fishes. Multicoloured.

611		5dh. Type **152**	15	10
612		10dh. Zebra seabream . . .	70	10
613		15dh. Grouper	1·00	15
614		20dh. Painted comber	1·50	20
615		25dh. Yellow-finned tunny . .	2·75	30

1974. 20th Anniv of Scouting in Libya.

616	**153**	5dh. multicoloured . . .	95	10
617		20dh. multicoloured . . .	2·50	50
618		25dh. multicoloured . . .	4·00	1·25

1974. 12th International Trade Fair, Tripoli.

619	**154**	10dh. multicoloured . . .	50	10
620		25dh. multicoloured . . .	75	15
621		35dh. multicoloured . . .	1·25	35

155 Family within Protective Hands

156 Minaret within Star

1974. World Health Day.

622	**155**	5dh. multicoloured . . .	15	10
623		25dh. multicoloured . . .	50	20

1974. Inauguration of Benghazi University.

624	**156**	10dh. multicoloured . . .	20	10
625		25dh. multicoloured . . .	75	15
626		35dh. multicoloured . . .	1·10	25

157 U.P.U. Emblem within Star

158 Traffic Lights and Signs

1974. Centenary of U.P.U.

627	**157**	25dh. multicoloured . . .	5·50	75
628		70dh. multicoloured . . .	10·00	1·50

1974. Motoring and Touring Club of Libya.

629	**158**	5dh. multicoloured . . .	10	10
630		10dh. multicoloured . . .	15	10
631		25dh. multicoloured . . .	15	10

159 Tank, Refinery and Pipeline

160 W.P.Y. Emblem and People

1974. 5th Anniv of 1 September Revolution.

632	**159**	5dh. multicoloured . . .	10	10
633		20dh. multicoloured . . .	15	10
634		25dh. multicoloured . . .	15	10
635		35dh. multicoloured . . .	20	15

1974. World Population Year.

637	**160**	25dh. multicoloured . . .	20	10
638		35dh. multicoloured . . .	50	20

161

162 Congress Emblem

1975. 13th International Trade Fair, Tripoli. Libyan Costumes.

639	**161**	5dh. multicoloured . . .	10	10
640	–	10dh. multicoloured . . .	10	10
641	–	15dh. multicoloured . . .	10	10
642	–	20dh. multicoloured . . .	20	10
643	–	25dh. multicoloured . . .	75	10
644	–	50dh. multicoloured . . .	1·10	20

DESIGNS: 10dh. to 50dh. Various costumes.

1975. Arab Workers' Congress.

645	**162**	10dh. multicoloured . . .	10	10
646		25dh. multicoloured . . .	15	15
647		35dh. multicoloured . . .	50	15

163 Teacher at Blackboard

1975. Teachers' Day.

648	**163**	10dh. multicoloured . . .	10	10
649		25dh. multicoloured . . .	20	10

164 Human Figures, Text and Globe

1975. World Health Day.

650	**164**	20dh. multicoloured . . .	15	10
651		25dh. multicoloured . . .	20	10

165 Readers and Bookshelves

166 Festival Emblem

1975. Arab Book Exhibition.

652	**165**	10dh. multicoloured . . .	10	10
653		20dh. multicoloured . . .	20	10
654		25dh. multicoloured . . .	50	15

1975. 2nd Arab Youth Festival.

655	**166**	20dh. multicoloured . . .	15	10
656		25dh. multicoloured . . .	20	15

1975. As Nos. 563/5 but without "L.A.R.".

657	**132**	5dh. black, orange & blue	35	10
658		20dh. black, yellow & blue	75	10
659		50dh. black, green and blue	1·40	15

167 Games Emblem

168 Dove of Peace

1975. 7th Mediterranean Games, Algiers.

660	**167**	10dh. multicoloured . . .	10	10
661		25dh. multicoloured . . .	45	10
662		50dh. multicoloured . . .	85	20

1975. 6th Anniv of 1 September Revolution. Multicoloured.

663		25dh. Type **168**	20	10
664		70dh. Peace dove with different background . . .	95	25

169 Khalil Basha Mosque

170 Arms and Crowds

1975. Mosques. Multicoloured.

666		5dh. Type **169**	10	10
667		10dh. Sidi Abdulla El Shaab	10	10
668		15dh. Sidi Ali El Fergani . .	10	10
669		20dh. Al Kharruba (vert) . .	15	10
670		25dh. Katiktha (vert)	20	10
671		30dh. Murad Agha (vert) . .	45	15
672		35dh. Maulai Mohamed (vert)	55	15

1976. National People's Congress.

673	**170**	35dh. multicoloured . . .	20	10
674		40dh. multicoloured . . .	25	10

171 Dialogue Emblem

172 Woman blowing Bugle

1976. Islamic–Christian Dialogue Seminar.

675	**171**	40dh. multicoloured . . .	50	15
676		115dh. multicoloured . .	1·40	60

1976. International Trade Fair, Tripoli. Mult.

677		10dh. Type **172**	10	10
678		20dh. Lancer	15	10
679		30dh. Drummer	65	10
680		40dh. Bagpiper	75	20
681		100dh. Woman with jug on head	1·90	35

173 Early and Modern Telephones

1976. Telephone Centenary. Multicoloured.

682		40dh. Type **173**	1·60	15
683		70dh. Alexander Graham Bell	2·75	50

174 Mother and Child

175 Hands supporting Eye

1976. International Children's Day.

685	**174**	85dh. multicoloured . . .	75	30
686		110dh. multicoloured . .	1·10	40

1976. World Health Day.

687	**175**	30dh. multicoloured . . .	20	10
688		35dh. multicoloured . . .	20	10
689		40dh. multicoloured . . .	50	15

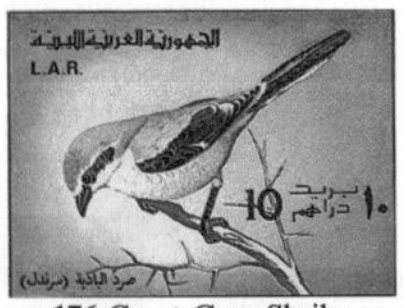

176 Great Grey Shrike

1976. Libyan Birds. Multicoloured.

690		5dh. Little bittern	75	25
691		10dh. Type **176**	1·40	40
692		15dh. Fulvous babbler . . .	2·00	50
693		20dh. European bee eater (vert)	2·75	70
694		25dh. Hoopoe	3·00	95

177 Barabekh Plant

178 Cycling

1976. Natural History Museum. Multicoloured.

695		10dh. Type **177**	10	10
696		15dh. Fin whale (horiz) . . .	15	10
697		30dh. Lizard (horiz)	20	10
698		40dh. Elephant's skull (horiz)	70	15
699		70dh. Bonnelli's eagle	4·50	55
700		115dh. Barbary sheep	2·00	40

1976. Olympic Games, Montreal. Multicoloured.

701		15dh. Type **178**	10	10
702		25dh. Boxing	20	10
703		70dh. Football	95	20

179 Global "Tree"

180 Agricultural and Industrial Symbols

1976. Non-Aligned Countries' Colombo Conference.

705	**179**	115dh. multicoloured . .	95	35

1976. 7th Anniv of Revolution.

706	**180**	30dh. multicoloured . . .	15	10
707		40dh. multicoloured . . .	45	15
708		100dh. multicoloured . .	90	55

181 Various Sports

182 Chessboard and Pieces

1976. 5th Arab Games, Damascus.

710	**181**	15dh. multicoloured . . .	10	10
711		30dh. multicoloured . . .	15	10
712		100dh. multicoloured . .	1·00	55

1976. Arab Chess Olympiad, Tripoli.

714	**182**	15dh. multicoloured . . .	95	15
715		30dh. multicoloured . . .	1·60	60
716		100dh. multicoloured . .	5·00	95

183 Ratima

186 Kaaba, Mecca

184 Emblem and Text

1976. Libyan Flora. Multicoloured.

717		15dh. Type **183**	15	10
718		20dh. "Sword of Crow" . . .	15	10
719		35dh. "Lasef"	50	10
720		40dh. "Yadid"	80	15
721		70dh. Esparto grass	1·90	25

1976. International Archives Council.

722	**184**	15dh. multicoloured . . .	10	10
723		35dh. multicoloured . . .	15	10
724		70dh. multicoloured . . .	55	20

1976. Pilgrimage to Mecca.
729 **186** 15dh. multicoloured . . . 10 10
730 30dh. multicoloured . . . 15 10
731 70dh. multicoloured . . . 30 20
732 100dh. multicoloured . . 75 30

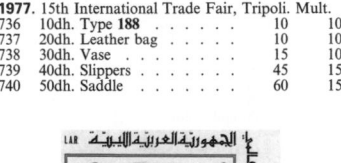

187

188 Basket

1977. Coil Stamps.
733 **187** 5dh. multicoloured . . . 10 10
734 20dh. multicoloured . . . 10 10
735 50dh. multicoloured . . . 55 40

1977. 15th International Trade Fair, Tripoli. Mult.
736 10dh. Type **188** 10 10
737 20dh. Leather bag 10 10
738 30dh. Vase 15 10
739 40dh. Slippers 45 15
740 50dh. Saddle 60 15

189 Girl with Flowers

1977. Children's Day. Multicoloured.
742 10dh. Type **189** 10 10
743 30dh. Clothes shop 15 10
744 40dh. Orchard 20 15

190 Fighters and Machine-gun

191 Protected Child

1977. 9th Anniv of Battle of Al-Karamah.
745 **190** 15dh. multicoloured . . . 10 10
746 25dh. multicoloured . . . 15 10
747 70dh. multicoloured . . . 80 25

1977. World Health Day.
748 **191** 15dh. multicoloured . . . 10 10
749 30dh. multicoloured . . . 15 10

192 A.P.U. Emblem

1977. 25th Anniv of Arab Postal Union.
750 **192** 15dh. multicoloured . . . 10 10
751 20dh. multicoloured . . . 15 10
752 40dh. multicoloured . . . 20 15

193 Maps of Libya and Africa

194 Heart on Map of Libya

1977. Organization of African Unity Conference, Tripoli.
753 **193** 40dh. multicoloured . . . 1·00 20
754 70dh. multicoloured . . . 1·50 30

1977. Red Crescent Commemoration.
755 **194** 5dh. multicoloured . . . 10 10
756 10dh. multicoloured . . . 15 10
757 30dh. multicoloured . . . 65 15

195 Messenger and Jet Fighter

1977. Communications Progress. Multicoloured.
758 20dh. Type **195** 15 10
759 25dh. Arab rider and Concorde 30 15
760 60dh. Satellite and aerial . . 55 20
761 115dh. Television relay via satellite . . . . 1·10 65
762 150dh. Camel rider and Boeing 727 airliner loading 1·75 90
763 200dh. "Apollo–Soyuz" link 2·25 1·10

196 Mosque

197 Archbishop Capucci

1977. Libyan Mosques.
765 **196** 40dh. multicoloured . . . 20 15
766 – 50dh. multicoloured (vert) 50 15
767 – 70dh. multicoloured . . . 70 20
768 – 90dh. multicoloured . . . 85 30
769 – 100dh. multicoloured (vert) . . . . 1·00 35
770 – 115dh. multicoloured . . 1·25 75
DESIGNS: 50dh. to 115dh. Various mosques.

1977. 3rd Anniv of Archbishop Capucci's Imprisonment.
771 **197** 30dh. multicoloured . . . 15 10
772 40dh. multicoloured . . . 20 15
773 115dh. multicoloured . . 1·25 60

198 Clasped Hands and Emblems

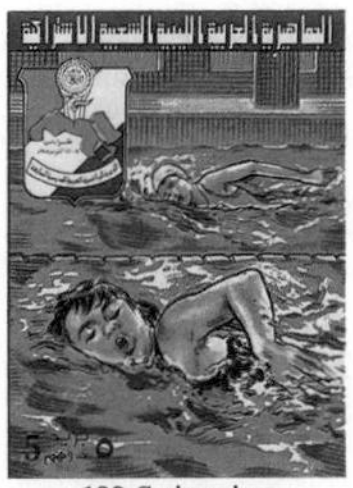
199 Swimming

1977. 8th Anniv of Revolution.
774 **198** 15dh. multicoloured . . . 10 10
775 30dh. multicoloured . . . 15 10
776 85dh. multicoloured . . . 80 25

1977. Arab School Sports. Multicoloured.
778 5dh. Type **199** 10 10
779 10dh. Handball (horiz) . . . 10 10
780 15dh. Football 15 10
781 25dh. Table tennis (horiz) . . 50 20
782 40dh. Basketball . . . . . . 1·10 65

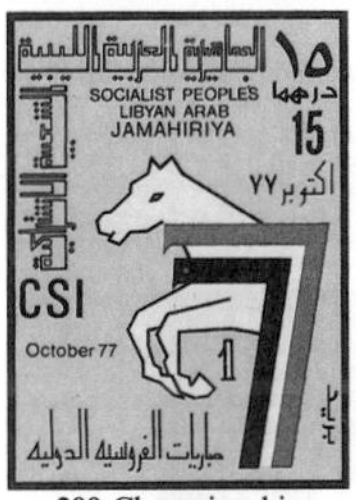
200 Championship Emblem

201 Dome of the Rock

1977. 1st International Turf Championships, Tripoli. Multicoloured.
783 5dh. Horse jumping fence (facing left) 10 10
784 10dh. Arab horseman 10 10
785 15dh. Type **200** 15 10
786 45dh. Horse jumping fence (facing right) 55 15
787 115dh. Arab horseman racing 1·40 80

1977. Palestine Welfare.
789 **201** 5dh. multicoloured . . . 10 10
790 10dh. multicoloured . . . 10 10

202 Fort, and Hands writing Arabic Script in Book

203 Emblem

1977. "The Green Book". Multicoloured.
791 35dh. Type **202** 15 10
792 40dh. Type **202** (text in English) 20 15
793 115dh. Dove with "Green Book" and map . . . . . 1·25 70

1977. World Standards Day.
794 **203** 5dh. multicoloured . . . 10 10
795 15dh. multicoloured . . . 10 10
796 30dh. multicoloured . . . 15 10

204 Giraffe

1978. Rock Drawings from Wadi Mathendous. Multicoloured.
797 10dh. Crocodiles (horiz) . . . 10 10
798 15dh. Elephant hunt (horiz) 10 10
799 20dh. Type **204** 15 10
800 30dh. Antelope (horiz) . . . 45 15
801 40dh. Elephant (horiz) . . . 65 20

205 Silver Pendant

206 Compass and Lightning Flash

1978. 16th Tripoli International Fair.
802 **205** 5dh. silver, black and red 10 10
803 – 10dh. silver, black & violet 10 10
804 – 20dh. silver, black & green 10 10
805 – 25dh. silver, black and blue 15 10
806 – 115dh. silver, black & blue . . . . 1·10 70
DESIGNS: 10dh. Silver ornamental plate; 20dh. Necklace with three pendants; 25dh. Crescent-shaped silver brooch; 115dh. Silver armband.

1978. Arab Cultural Education Organization.
807 **206** 30dh. multicoloured . . . 20 15
808 115dh. multicoloured . . 1·40 65

207 Dancing a Round

1978. Children's Day. Children's Paintings. Multicoloured.
809 40dh. Type **207** 20 15
810 40dh. Children with placards 20 15
811 40dh. Shopping street 20 15
812 40dh. Playground 20 15
813 40dh. Wedding ceremony . . 20 15

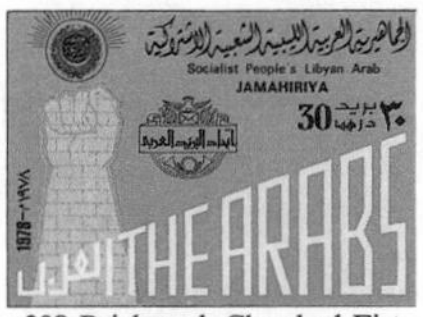
208 Brickwork Clenched Fist

1978. The Arabs.
814 **208** 30dh. multicoloured . . . 20 15
815 115dh. multicoloured . . 1·10 35

209 Blood Pressure Meter

211 Games Emblem

210 Microwave Antenna

1978. World Hypertension Month.
816 **209** 30dh. multicoloured . . . 15 15
817 115dh. multicoloured . . 1·25 35

1978. World Telecommunications Day.
818 **210** 30dh. multicoloured . . . 15 15
819 115dh. multicoloured . . 1·00 35

1978. 3rd African Games, Algiers.
820 **211** 15dh. copper, violet & blk 10 10
821 30dh. silver, lilac and black 15 10
822 115dh. gold, purple & blk 1·10 35

212 Aerial View of Airport

1978. Inauguration of Tripoli International Airport. Multicoloured.
823 40dh. Type **212** 30 10
824 115dh. Terminal building . . 1·25 65

213 Ankara

1978. Turkish–Libyan Friendship.
825 **213** 30dh. multicoloured . . . 15 10
826 35dh. multicoloured . . . 15 10
827 115dh. multicoloured . . 1·10 35

214 "Armed Forces"

215 Crater

1978. 9th Anniv of 1 September Revolution. Multicoloured.
828 30dh. Type **214** 60 15
829 35dh. Tower, Green Book and symbols of progress 15 10
830 115dh. "Industry" 95 70

1978. 2nd Symposium on Geology of Libya. Multicoloured.
832 30dh. Type **215** 15 10
833 40dh. Oasis 20 15
834 115dh. Crater (different) . . 1·10 60

216 "Green Book" and Different Races

1978. International Anti-Apartheid Year.
835 **216** 30dh. multicoloured . . . 15 10
836 40dh. multicoloured . . . 20 15
837 115dh. multicoloured . . 85 35

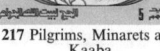

217 Pilgrims, Minarets and Kaaba

218 Clasped Hands and Globe

1978. Pilgrimage to Mecca.

838	**217**	5dh. multicoloured	10	10
839		10dh. multicoloured	10	10
840		15dh. multicoloured	10	10
841		20dh. multicoloured	15	10

1978. U.N. Conference for Technical Co-operation between Developing Countries.

842	**218**	30dh. multicoloured	15	10
843		40dh. multicoloured	20	15
844		115dh. multicoloured	85	35

219 Workers, Rifles, Torch and Flag

220 Human Figure and Scales

1978. Arab Countries Summit Conference. Multicoloured.

845	30dh. Type **219**	15	10
846	40dh. Map of Middle East, eagle and crowd (horiz)	20	15
847	115dh. As	40	
848	145dh. Type **219**	1·00	45

1978. 30th Anniv of Declaration of Human Rights.

849	**220**	15dh. multicoloured	10	10
850		30dh. multicoloured	20	15
851		115dh. multicoloured	50	35

221 Horse Racing and Fort

222 Lilienthal's Biplane Glider

1978. Libyan Study Centre.

852	**221**	20dh. multicoloured	15	10
853		40dh. multicoloured	20	15
854		115dh. multicoloured	95	60

1978. 75th Anniv of First Powered Flight. Mult.

855	20dh. Type **222**	10	10
856	25dh. Lindbergh's "Spirit of St. Louis"	10	10
857	30dh. Admiral Richard Byrd's Trimotor "Floyd Bennett"	80	25
858	50dh. Bleriot 5190 Santos Dumont flying boat and airship "Graf Zeppelin"	95	35
859	115dh. Wright brothers and Wright Type A	1·10	75

223 Libyans, Torch and Laurel Wreath

224 Mounted Dorcas Gazelle Head

1979.

861	**223**	5dh. multicoloured	10	10
862		10dh. multicoloured	10	10
863		15dh. multicoloured	10	10
864		30dh. multicoloured	20	10
865		50dh. multicoloured	20	10
866		60dh. multicoloured	25	15
867		70dh. multicoloured	30	15
868		100dh. multicoloured	75	25
869		115dh. multicoloured	85	30
870		200dh. multicoloured	1·10	45
871		250dh. multicoloured	1·90	65
871		500dh. multicoloured	3·50	65
872		1000dh. multicoloured	6·75	3·50
872a		1500dh. multicoloured	12·50	4·25
872b		2500dh. multicoloured	23·00	7·50

Nos. 861/9 measure 18 × 23 mm and Nos. 870/2b 26 × 32 mm.

1979. Coil Stamps.

873	**224**	5dh. multicoloured	15	10
874		20dh. multicoloured	25	10
875		50dh. multicoloured	80	25

225 Tortoise

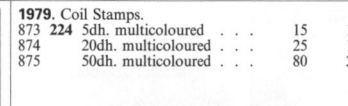

1979. Libyan Animals. Multicoloured.

876	5dh. Type **225**	10	10
877	10dh. Addax (vert)	10	10
878	15dh. Algerian hedgehog	20	10
879	20dh. North African crested porcupine	20	10
880	30dh. Dromedaries	30	15
881	35dh. Wild cat (vert)	40	15
882	45dh. Dorcas gazelle (vert)	95	25
883	115dh. Cheetah	1·90	75

226 Carpet

1979. 17th Tripoli International Trade Fair.

884	**226**	10dh. multicoloured	10	10
885	–	15dh. multicoloured	10	10
886	–	30dh. multicoloured	15	10
887	–	45dh. multicoloured	15	10
888	–	115dh. multicoloured	85	35

DESIGNS: 15dh. to 115dh. Different carpets

227 Aircraft and People

1979. International Year of the Child. Children's Paintings (1st series). Multicoloured.

889	20dh. Type **227**	10	10
890	20dh. Shepherd with flock	10	10
891	20dh. Open air cafe	10	10
892	20dh. Boat in storm	10	10
893	20dh. Policeman on traffic duty	10	10

See also Nos. 975/9.

228 World Map, Koran and Symbols of Arab Achievements

229 Radar Tower and Map

1979. The Arabs.

894	**228**	45dh. multicoloured	20	15
895		70dh. multicoloured	55	20

1979. World Meteorological Day.

896	**229**	15dh. multicoloured	10	10
897		30dh. multicoloured	15	10
898		50dh. multicoloured	20	15

230 Medical Care

1979. World Health Day.

899	**230**	40dh. multicoloured	20	15

231 "Carpobrotus acinaciformis"

1979. Libyan Flowers. Multicoloured.

900	10dh. Type **231**	10	10
901	15dh. "Caralluma europaea"	10	10
902	20dh. "Arum cirenaicum"	10	10
903	35dh. "Lavatera arborea"	50	15
904	40dh. "Capparis spinosa"	50	15
905	50dh. "Ranunculus asiaticus"	60	15

232 Farmer and Sheep

1979. 10th Anniv of Revolution. Mult.

906	15dh. Type **232**	10	10
907	15dh. Crowd with Green Book	10	10
908	15dh. Oil field	10	10
909	15dh. Refinery	10	10
910	30dh. Dish aerial	15	10
911	30dh. Hospital	15	10
912	30dh. Doctor examining patient	15	10
913	30dh. Surgeon	15	10
914	40dh. Street, Tripoli	20	15
915	40dh. Steel mill	20	15
916	40dh. Tanks	20	15
917	40dh. Tuareg horsemen	20	15
918	70dh. Revolutionaries and Green Book	70	20
919	70dh. Crowd within map of Libya	70	20
920	70dh. Mullah	70	20
921	70dh. Student	70	20

233 Volleyball

234 Emblem

1979. "Universiada '79" World University Games, Mexico City. Multicoloured.

923	45dh. Type **233**	20	15
924	115dh. Football	1·10	30

1979. 3rd World Telecommunications Exhibition, Geneva.

925	**234**	45dh. multicoloured	20	15
926		115dh. multicoloured	1·25	30

235 Seminar Emblem and Crowd

1979. International Seminar on the "Green Book". Multicoloured.

927	10dh. Type **235**	10	10
928	35dh. Seminar in progress (horiz) (70 × 43 mm)	45	15
929	100dh. Colonel Gaddafi with "Green Book"	1·00	30

236 Horsemen in Town

1979. Evacuation of Foreign Forces. Multicoloured.

931	30dh. Type **236**	15	10
932	40dh. Tuareg horsemen	20	15

237 Football Match

1979. Mediterranean Games, Split.

934	**237**	15dh. multicoloured	10	10
935		30dh. multicoloured	50	10
936		70dh. multicoloured	1·25	20

238 Cyclist and Emblem

1979. Junior Cycling Championships, Tripoli. Multicoloured.

937	15dh. Type **238**	10	10
938	30dh. Cyclists and emblem	15	10

239 Horse-jumping

1979. Pre-Olympics. Multicoloured.

939	45dh. Type **239**	20	15
940	60dh. Javelin	55	15
941	115dh. Hurdles	1·10	55
942	160dh. Football	1·40	65

Nos. 939/42 exist from sheets on which an overall Moscow Olympics emblem in silver was superimposed on the stamps.

240 Figure clothed in Palestinian Flag

1979. Solidarity with Palestinian People.

944	**240**	30dh. multicoloured	15	10
945		115dh. multicoloured	1·10	30

241 Ploughing

1980. World Olive Oil Year.

946	**241**	15dh. multicoloured	10	10
947		30dh. multicoloured	15	10
948		45dh. multicoloured	20	15

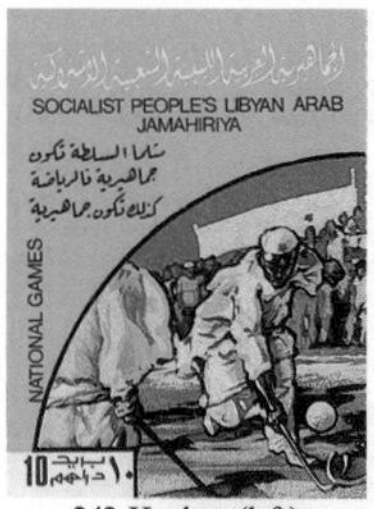

242 Hockey (left) 243 Pipes

1980. National Sports. Multicoloured.

949	10dh. Type **242**	10	10
950	10dh. Hockey (right)	10	10
951	10dh. Leap-frog (left)	10	10
952	10dh. Leap-frog (right) . . .	10	10
953	15dh. Long jump (left) . . .	10	10
954	15dh. Long jump (right) . . .	10	10
955	15dh. Ball catching (left) . .	10	10
956	15dh. Ball catching (right) . .	10	10
957	20dh. Wrestling (left)	10	10
958	20dh. Wrestling (right) . . .	10	10
959	20dh. Stone throwing (left)	10	10
960	20dh. Stone throwing (right)	10	10
961	30dh. Tug-of-war (left) . . .	15	10
962	30dh. Tug-of-war (right) . .	15	10
963	30dh. Jumping (left)	15	10
964	30dh. Jumping (right)	15	10
965	45dh. Horsemen (left)	45	15
966	45dh. Horsemen (right) . . .	45	15
967	45dh. Horsemen with whips (left)	45	15
968	45dh. Horsemen with whips (right)	45	15

Nos. 949/68 were issued together, divided into se-tenant blocks of four within the sheet, each horizontal pair forming a composite design.

1980. 18th Tripoli International Fair. Multicoloured.

969	5dh. Drum (horiz)	10	10
970	10dh. Drum (different) (horiz)	10	10
971	15dh. Type **243**	10	10
972	20dh. Bagpipes (horiz) . . .	10	10
973	25dh. Stringed instrument and bow (horiz)	15	10

1980. International Year of the Child (1979) (2nd issue). As T **227**. Multicoloured.

975	20dh. "Horse Riding" . . .	10	10
976	20dh. "Beach scene"	10	10
977	20dh. "Fish"	10	10
978	20dh. "Birthday party" . . .	10	10
979	20dh. "Sheep Festival" . . .	10	10

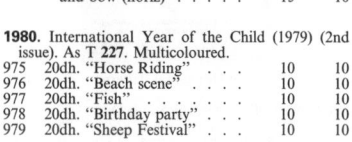

244 Mosque and Kaaba

1980. 400th Anniv of Hejira.

980 **244**	50dh. multicoloured . . .	25	15
981	115dh. multicoloured . .	1·10	55

245 Surgical Operation and Hospital

1980. World Health Day.

982 **245**	20dh. multicoloured . . .	10	10
983	50dh. multicoloured . . .	50	15

246 Battle of Shoghab "Shahat", 1913

1980. Battles (1st series). Multicoloured.

984	20dh. Gardabia, 1915	20	15
986	20dh. Type **246**	10	10
988	20dh. Fundugh al-Shibani "Garian"	10	10
990	20dh. Yefren	10	10
992	20dh. Ghira "Brak"	20	15
994	20dh. El Hani (Shiat)	35	15
996	20dh. Sebah	20	15
998	20dh. Sirt	10	10
985	35dh. Gardabia	10	10
987	35dh. Shoghab "Shahat" . .	20	15
989	35dh. Fundagh al-Shibani "Garian"	20	15
991	35dh. Yefren	20	15
993	35dh. Ghira "Brak"	20	15
995	35dh. El Hani (Shiat) . . .	60	25
997	35dh. Sebah	20	15
999	35dh. Sirt	10	10

The two values commemorating each battle were issued in se-tenant pairs, each pair forming a composite design.

See also Nos. 1027/50, 1140/63 and 1257/80.

247 Flame 248 Ghadames

1980. Sheikh Zarruq Festival.

1000 **247**	40dh. multicoloured . .	20	15
1001	115dh. multicoloured . .	1·00	65

1980. Arabian Towns Organization. Mult.

1003	15dh. Type **248**	10	10
1004	30dh. Derna	15	10
1005	50dh. Ahmad Pasha Mosque, Tripoli	50	15

249 Guides on Hike

1980. 14th Pan-Arab Scout Jamboree. Multicoloured.

1006	15dh. Type **249**	10	10
1007	30dh. Guides cooking . . .	15	10
1008	50dh. Cub Scouts cooking	25	15
1009	115dh. Scouts map-reading	1·10	60

250 Oil Refinery

1980. 11th Anniv of Revolution. Multicoloured.

1011	5dh. Type **250**	10	10
1012	10dh. Recreation and youth	10	10
1013	15dh. Agriculture	10	10
1014	25dh. Boeing 727-200 airplane and liner	60	15
1015	40dh. Education	20	15
1016	115dh. Housing	95	30

251 Camels, Map of Libya and Conference Emblem

1980. World Tourism Conference, Manila. Mult.

1018	45dh. Type **251**	20	15
1019	115dh. Emblem, map and camel riders	95	30

252 Figures supporting O.P.E.C. Emblem

1980. 20th Anniv of Organization of Petroleum Exporting Countries. Multicoloured.

1020	45dh. O.P.E.C. emblem and globe	20	15
1021	115dh. Type **252**	95	30

253 Death of Omar el Mukhtar

1980. 49th Death Anniv of Omar el Mukhtar (patriot).

1022 **253**	20dh. multicoloured . .	10	10
1023	35dh. multicoloured . .	20	15

253a Map of Libya and Science Symbols

1980. Birth Millenary of Avicenna (philosopher) and School Scientific Exhibition. Multicoloured.

1025	45dh. Type **253a**	20	15
1026	115d. Avicenna and Exhibition Emblem . . .	1·10	30

1981. Battles (2nd series). As T **246**. Mult.

1027	20dh. Zuara	10	10
1029	20dh. Tawargha	10	10
1031	20dh. Dernah	10	10
1033	20dh. Bir Tagreft	10	10
1035	20dh. Funduk El Jamel "Misurata"	10	10
1037	20dh. Sidi El Khemri "Gusbat"	10	10
1039	20dh. El Khoms	10	10
1041	20dh. Roghdalin "Menshia"	10	10
1043	20dh. Ain Zara "Tripoli"	10	10
1045	20dh. Rughbat el Naga "Benina"	10	10
1047	20dh. Tobruk	10	10
1049	20dh. Ikshadia "Werfella"	10	10
1028	35dh. Zuara	15	15
1030	35dh. Tawargha	15	15
1032	35dh. Dernah	15	15
1034	35dh. Bir Tagreft	15	15
1036	35dh. Funduk El Jamel "Misurata"	15	15
1038	35dh. Sidi El Khemri "Gusbat"	15	15
1040	35dh. El Khoms	15	15
1042	35dh. Roghdalin "Menshia"	15	15
1044	35dh. Ain Zara "Tripoli"	15	15
1046	35dh. Rughbat el Naga "Benina"	15	15
1048	35dh. Tobruk	15	15
1050	35dh. Ikshadia "Werfella"	15	15

The two values commemorating each battle were issued in se-tenant pairs, each pair forming a composite design.

254 Tent, Trees and Sun

1981. Children's Day. Children's Paintings. Multicoloured.

1051	20dh. Type **254**	10	10
1052	20dh. Women	10	10
1053	20dh. Picnic	10	10
1054	20dh. Aeroplane and playing children	10	10
1055	20dh. Mosque and man with camel	10	10

255 Central Bank 257 Crowd and "Green Book" Stamp of 1977

256 Pots

1981. 25th Anniv of Central Bank of Libya.

1056 **255**	45dh. multicoloured . .	15	15
1057	115dh. multicoloured . .	95	35

1981. Tripoli International Fair. Multicoloured.

1059	5dh. Type **256**	10	10
1060	10dh. Silver coffee pot (vert)	10	10
1061	15dh. Long-necked vase (vert)	10	10
1062	45dh. Round-bellied vase . .	45	15
1063	115dh. Jug	1·10	35

1981. People's Authority Declaration.

1064 **257**	50dh. multicoloured . .	15	15
1065	115dh. multicoloured . .	95	35

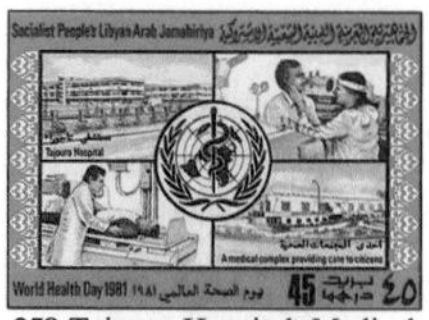

258 Tajoura Hospital, Medical Complex, Patients receiving Treatment and W.H.O. Emblem

1981. World Health Day.

1066 **258**	45dh. multicoloured . .	15	15
1067	115dh. multicoloured . .	95	35

259 Eye and Man on Crutches

1981. International Year of Disabled People.

1068 **259**	20dh. green, blue & black	10	10
1069 –	45dh. green, black & blue	15	15
1070 –	115dh. blue and green	1·00	35

DESIGNS: 45dh. Globe and I.Y.D.P. emblem; 115dh. Hands holding shield with I.Y.D.P. emblem, eye and man on crutch.

260 Horse

1981. Libyan Mosaics. Multicoloured.

1071	10dh. Type **260**	10	10
1072	20dh. Ship	10	10
1073	30dh. Birds, fish and flowers	10	10
1074	40dh. Leopard	40	15
1075	50dh. Man playing musical instrument	50	15
1076	115dh. Fishes	1·10	35

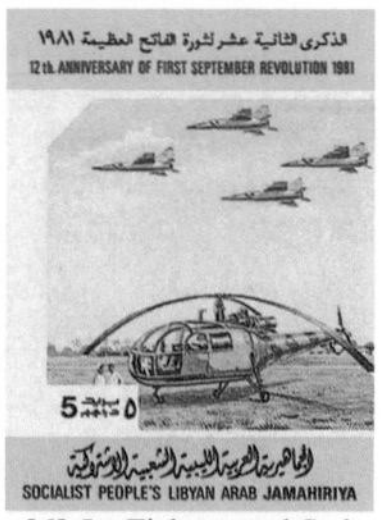

261 Racial Discrimination Emblem 262 Jet Fighters and Sud Aviation Alouette III Helicopter (left-hand stamp)

1981. Int Year Against Racial Discrimination.

1077 **261**	45dh. multicoloured . .	25	25
1078	50dh. multicoloured . .	55	30

1981. 12th Anniv of Revolution.

1079 262 5dh. blue and light blue 15 10
1080 – 5dh. blue and light blue 15 10
1081 – 5dh. blue and light blue 10 10
1082 – 5dh. blue and light blue 10 10
1083 – 10dh. black and blue . . 10 10
1084 – 10dh. black and blue . . 10 10
1085 – 10dh. black and blue . . 10 10
1086 – 10dh. black and blue . . 10 10
1087 – 15dh. brown & lt brown 10 10
1088 – 15dh. brown & lt brown 10 10
1089 – 15dh. brown & lt brown 10 10
1090 – 15dh. brown & lt brown 10 10
1091 – 20dh. blue and green . . 15 15
1092 – 20dh. blue and green . . 15 15
1093 – 20dh. blue and green . . 15 15
1094 – 20dh. blue and green . . 15 15
1095 – 25dh. brown and yellow 15 15
1096 – 25dh. brown and yellow 15 15
1097 – 25dh. brown and yellow 15 15
1098 – 25dh. brown and yellow 15 15

DESIGNS—VERT: No. 1080, Jet fighter (right-hand stamp); 1081/2, Parachutists; 1083/4, Tank parade; 1085/6, Marching frogmen; 1087/8, Anti-aircraft rocket trucks; 1089/90, Missile trucks. HORIZ: 1091/2, Marching sailors; 1093/4, Jeeps and anti-aircraft rocket trucks; 1095/6, Armoured vehicles and landrovers; 1097/8, Tank parade.

Each pair forms a horizontal composite design, the first number being the left-hand stamp in each instance.

263 Wheat and Plough

1981. World Food Day.

1100 263 45dh. multicoloured . . 25 25
1101 200dh. multicoloured . . 1·75 95

264 "Pseudotergumia fidia"

1981. Butterflies. Multicoloured.

1102 5dh. Type 264 . . . . . . 15 10
1103 5dh. "Chazara prieuri" (sun in background) 15 10
1104 5dh. "Polygonia c-album" (trees in background) . . 15 10
1105 5dh. "Colias crocea" (mosque in background) 15 10
1106 10dh. "Anthocharis bellia" (face value bottom right) 15 10
1107 10dh. "Pandoriana pandora" (face value bottom left) 15 10
1108 10dh. "Melanargia ines" (face value top right) . . 15 10
1109 10dh. "Charaxes jasius" (face value top left) . . . 15 10
1110 15dh. "Nymphales antiopa" (face value bottom right) 30 30
1111 15dh. "Eurodryas desfontainii" (face value bottom left) 30 30
1112 15dh. "Iphiclides podalirius" (face value top right) . . 30 30
1113 15dh. "Glaucopsyche melanops" (face value top left) 30 30
1114 25dh. "Spialia sertorius" (face value bottom right) 50 45
1115 25dh. "Pieris brassicae" (face value bottom left) 50 45
1116 25dh. "Lysandra albicans" (face value top right) . . 50 45
1117 25dh. "Celastrina argiolus" (face value top left) . . . 50 45

The four designs of each value were issued together in small sheets of four, showing composite background designs.

265 Grapes

266 I.Y.D.P. Emblem and Globe

1981. Fruit. Multicoloured.

1119 5dh. Type 265 . . . . . . 10 10
1120 10dh. Dates 10 10
1121 15dh. Lemons 10 10
1122 20dh. Oranges 15 15
1123 35dh. Barbary figs 20 20
1124 55dh. Pomegranate 65 30

1981. International Year of Disabled Persons.

1125 266 45dh. multicoloured . . 25 25
1126 115dh. multicoloured . . 90 55

267 Animals (looking right)

1982. Libyan Mosaics. Multicoloured.

1127 45dh. Type 267 . . . . . 50 25
1128 45dh. Orpheus 50 25
1129 45dh. Animals (looking left) 50 25
1130 45dh. Fishes 50 25
1131 45dh. Fishermen 50 25
1132 45dh. Fishes and ducks . . 50 25
1133 45dh. Farm 50 25
1134 45dh. Birds and fruit . . . 50 25
1135 45dh. Milking 50 25

268 Koran Texts leading to Ka'aba

269 Grinding Flour

1982. 3rd Koran Reading Contest. Multicoloured.

1136 10dh. Type 268 . . . . . 10 10
1137 35dh. Koran and formation of the World 20 20
1138 115dh. Reading the Koran 95 55

1982. Battles (3rd series). As T 246. Multicoloured.

1140 20dh. Hun "Gioffra" . . . 15 15
1142 20dh. Gedabia 15 15
1144 20dh. El Asaba "Gianduba" 15 15
1146 20dh. El Habela 15 15
1148 20dh. Suk El Ahad "Tarhuna" 15 15
1150 20dh. El Tangi 15 15
1152 20dh. Sokna 15 15
1154 20dh. Wadi Smalus "Jabel El Akdar" 15 15
1156 20dh. Sidi Abuagela "Agelat" 15 15
1158 20dh. Sidi Surur "Zeliten" 15 15
1160 20dh. Kuefia 15 15
1162 20dh. Abunjeim 15 15
1141 35dh. Hun "Gioffra" . . . 20 20
1143 35dh. Gedabia 20 20
1145 35dh. El Asaba "Gianduba" 20 20
1147 35dh. El Habela 20 20
1149 35dh. Suk El Ahad "Tarhuna" 20 20
1151 35dh. El Tangi 20 20
1153 35dh. Sokna 20 20
1155 35dh. Wadi Smalus "Jabel El Akdar" 20 20
1157 35dh. Sidi Abuagela "Agelat" 20 20
1159 35dh. Sidi Surur "Zeliten" 20 20
1161 35dh. Kuefia 20 20
1163 35dh. Abunjeim 20 20

The two values commemorating each battle were issued in se-tenant pairs, each pair forming a composite design.

1982. Tripoli International Fair. Multicoloured.

1164 5dh. Type 269 . . . . . 10 10
1165 10dh. Ploughing 10 10
1166 25dh. Stacking hay 15 15
1167 35dh. Weaving 20 20
1168 45dh. Cooking 50 25
1169 100dh. Harvesting 95 50

270 "ALFATAH" forming Farm Vehicle

1982. People's Authority Declaration. Multicoloured.

1170 100dh. Type 270 . . . . . 75 50
1171 200dh. Colonel Gaddafi, old man, "Green Book" and guns . . . . 1·75 95
1172 300dh. Rejoicing crowd . . 2·50 1·40

271 Scout flying Model Airship

272 Map of Africa and A.F.C. Emblem

1982. 75th Anniv of Boy Scout Movement. Mult.

1173 100dh. Type 271 . . . . . 75 50
1174 200dh. Scouts helping injured dog . . . . 1·75 95
1175 300dh. Scout reading to old man . . . . 1·75 1·40
1176 400dh. Scout with model rocket . . . . 3·75 2·25

1982. African Football Cup Competition.

1178 272 100dh. multicoloured . . 95 50
1179 200dh. multicoloured . . 1·90 95

273 Footballer

1982. World Cup Football Championship, Spain. Multicoloured.

1180 45dh. Type 273 . . . . . 25 25
1181 100dh. Footballer (different) 75 50
1182 200dh. As No. 1173 . . . . 1·60 95
1183 300dh. Footballer and goalkeeper . . . . 2·25 1·40

274 Palestinian Children

1982. Palestinian Children's Day. Multicoloured.

1185 20dh. Type 274 . . . . . 15 15
1186 20dh. Girl with dish 15 15
1187 20dh. Child with turban . . 15 15
1188 20dh. Young child 15 15
1189 20dh. Young boy 15 15

275 Lanner Falcon

277 Map of Libya and A.P.U. Emblem

276 Nurses' Class, Operating Theatre and Doctor examining Child

1982. Birds. Multicoloured.

1190 15dh. Type 275 . . . . . 35 25
1191 15dh. Eurasian swift 35 25
1192 15dh. Peregrine falcon . . . 35 25
1193 15dh. Greater flamingo . . 35 25
1194 25dh. Whitethroat 60 35
1195 25dh. Turtle dove 60 35
1196 25dh. Black-bellied sandgrouse 60 35
1197 25dh. Egyptian vulture . . . 60 35
1198 45dh. Golden oriole . . . . 1·00 60
1199 45dh. European bee eater 1·00 60
1200 45dh. River kingfisher . . . 1·00 60
1201 45dh. European roller . . . 1·00 60
1202 95dh. Barbary partridge . . 2·00 1·25
1203 95dh. Barn owl . . . . . . 2·00 1·25
1204 95dh. Cream-coloured courser . . . . 2·00 1·25
1205 95dh. Hoopoe . . . . . . 2·00 1·25

The four designs of each value were printed together in se-tenant blocks of four, forming a composite design.

1982. Teaching Hospitals.

1207 276 95dh. multicoloured . . 85 50
1208 100dh. multicoloured . . 85 50
1209 205dh. multicoloured . . 2·00 1·10

1982. 30th Anniv of Arab Postal Union.

1210 277 100dh. multicoloured . . 95 50
1211 200dh. multicoloured . . 1·90 95

278 19th-century Chinese King and Diagram of Fischer v Spassky, 1972

1982. World Chess Championship, Moscow. Mult.

1212 100dh. Type 278 . . . . . 1·25 50
1213 100dh. African king and diagram of Karpov v Korchnoi, 1978 . . . . . 1·25 50
1214 100dh. Modern bishop and diagram of Smyslov v Karpov, 1971 . . . . . . 1·25 50
1215 100dh. 19th-century European rook and diagram of Tal v Vadasz, 1977 . . . . 1·25 50

Nos. 1212/15 were printed together, se-tenant, forming a composite design.

279 Hexagonal Pattern

1982. World Telecommunications Day.

1217 279 100dh. multicoloured . . 75 50
1218 200dh. multicoloured . . 1·50 95

280 Map of Libya and "Green Book"

1982. 51st Anniv of International Philatelic Federation (F.I.P.).

1219 280 200dh. multicoloured . . 1·75 95

281 Family and Flag

283 Palm Tree and Red Crescent

282 Pres. Gaddafi and Jet Aircraft

1982. Organization of African Unity Summit. Multicoloured.

1221 50dh. Type 281 . . . . . 30 30
1222 100dh. Map, dove and symbols of industry and agriculture 75 50
1223 200dh. Pres. Gaddafi and crowd with "Green Book" (65 × 36 mm.) . . . . . . 1·90 95

1982. 13th Anniv of Revolution. Multicoloured.

1225	15dh. Type **282**	15	10
1226	20dh. Gaddafi, soldiers and rockets	15	10
1227	30dh. Gaddafi, sailors and naval vessels	50	25
1228	45dh. Gaddafi, soldiers and tanks	25	25
1229	70dh. Gaddafi, and armed forces	60	35
1230	100dh. Gaddafi and women soldiers	90	50

1982. 25th Anniv of Libyan Red Crescent. Multicoloured.

1232	100dh. Type **283**	95	50
1233	200dh. "25" within crescents	1·90	95

284 Globe, Dove and Rifle

286 Philadelphus

285 Gaddafi, Crowd, "Green Book" and Emblems

1982. Solidarity with Palestinian People.

1234	**284**	100dh. black, mauve and green	95	40
1235		200dh. black, blue and green	1·90	80

1982. Al Fateh University Symposium on the "Green Book". Multicoloured.

1236	100dh. Type **285**	95	45
1237	200dh. Gaddafi, "Green Book", map and emblems	1·90	95

1983. Flowers. Multicoloured.

1238	25dh. Type **286**	15	10
1239	25dh. Hypericum	15	10
1240	25dh. Antirrhinum	15	10
1241	25dh. Lily	15	10
1242	25dh. Capparis	15	10
1243	25dh. Tropaeolum	15	10
1244	25dh. Roses	15	10
1245	25dh. Chrysanthemum	15	10
1246	25dh. "Nigella damascena"	15	10
1247	25dh. "Guilladia lanceolata"	15	10
1248	25dh. Dahlia	15	10
1249	25dh. "Dianthus caryophyllus"	15	10
1250	25dh. "Notobasis syriaca"	15	10
1251	25dh. "Nerium oleander"	15	10
1252	25dh. "Iris histroides"	15	10
1253	25dh. "Scolymus hispanicus"	15	10

287 Customs Council Building, Brussels, and Warrior on Horseback

288 Camel

1983. 30th Anniv of Customs Co-operation Council. Multicoloured.

1254	25dh. Type **287**	15	10
1255	50dh. Customs building	25	20
1256	100dh. Customs building and warrior with sword	50	45

1983. Battles (4th series). As T **246**. (a) Battle of Ghaser Ahmed.

1257	50dh. multicoloured	25	20
1258	50dh. multicoloured	25	20

(b) Battle of Sidi Abuarghub.

1259	50dh. multicoloured	25	20
1260	50dh. multicoloured	25	20

(c) Battle of Ghar Yunes.

1261	50dh. multicoloured	25	20
1262	50dh. multicoloured	25	20

(d) Battle of Bir Otman.

1263	50dh. multicoloured	25	20
1264	50dh. multicoloured	25	20

(e) Battle of Sidi Sajeh.

1265	50dh. multicoloured	25	20
1266	50dh. multicoloured	25	20

(f) Battle of Ras el-Hamam.

1267	50dh. multicoloured	25	20
1268	50dh. multicoloured	25	20

(g) Battle of Zawiet Ishghefa.

1269	50dh. multicoloured	25	20
1270	50dh. multicoloured	25	20

(h) Battle of Wadi Essania.

1271	50dh. multicoloured	25	20
1272	50dh. multicoloured	25	20

(i) Battle of El-Meshiashta.

1273	50dh. multicoloured	25	20
1274	50dh. multicoloured	25	20

(j) Battle of Gharara.

1275	50dh. multicoloured	25	20
1276	50dh. multicoloured	25	20

(k) Battle of Abughelan.

1277	50dh. multicoloured	20	20
1278	50dh. multicoloured	20	20

(l) Battle of Mahruka.

1279	50dh. multicoloured	20	20
1280	50dh. multicoloured	20	20

The two values for each battle were printed together in se-tenant pairs, forming composite designs.

1983. Farm Animals. Multicoloured.

1281	25dh. Type **288**	15	10
1282	25dh. Cow	15	10
1283	25dh. Horse	15	10
1284	25dh. Bull	15	10
1285	25dh. Goat	15	10
1286	25dh. Sheep dog	15	10
1287	25dh. Ewe	15	10
1288	25dh. Ram	15	10
1289	25dh. Greylag goose	35	25
1290	25dh. Helmeted guineafowl	35	25
1291	25dh. Rabbit	15	10
1292	25dh. Wood pigeon	35	25
1293	25dh. Common turkey	35	25
1294	25dh. Cockerel	15	10
1295	25dh. Hen	15	10
1296	25dh. Goose	15	10

289 Musician with Twin-horned Pipe

1983. Tripoli International Fair. Multicoloured.

1297	40dh. Type **289**	20	15
1298	45dh. Bagpipes (horiz)	25	20
1299	50dh. Horn	25	20
1300	55dh. Flute (horiz)	30	25
1301	75dh. Pipe	65	35
1302	100dh. Man and woman at well	90	45

290 Phoenician Galley

1983. 25th Anniv of International Maritime Organization. Multicoloured.

1303	100dh. Type **290**	1·25	55
1304	100dh. Ancient Greek galley	1·25	55
1305	100dh. Ancient Egyptian ship	1·25	55
1306	100dh. Roman sailing ship	1·25	55
1307	100dh. Viking longship	1·25	55
1308	100dh. Libyan xebec	1·25	55

291 Motorist

1983. Children's Day. Multicoloured.

1309	20dh. Type **291**	10	10
1310	20dh. Tractor and trailer	10	10
1311	20dh. Child with dove and globe	10	10
1312	20dh. Scout camp	10	10
1313	20dh. Dinosaur	10	10

292 Pres. Gaddafi with Children

1983. World Health Day. Multicoloured.

1314	25dh. Type **292**	15	10
1315	50dh. Gaddafi and old man in wheelchair	25	20
1316	100dh. Gaddafi visiting sick girl (horiz)	80	45

293 Gaddafi, Map and "Green Book"

294 Economic Emblems on Map of Africa

1983. 1st World "Green Book" Symposium. Mult.

1317	50dh. Type **293**	25	20
1318	70dh. Syposium in session and emblem (56 × 37 mm)	60	30
1319	80dh. Gaddafi, "Green Book", emblem and "Jamahiriya"	65	35

1983. 25th Anniv of African Economic Committee.

1321	**294**	50dh. multicoloured	25	20
1322		100dh. multicoloured	90	45
1323		250dh. multicoloured	1·90	1·10

296 Cuckoo Wrasse ("Labrus bimaculatus")

1983. Fishes. Multicoloured.

1325	25dh. Type **296**	30	15
1326	25dh. Streaked gurnard ("Trigoporus lastoviza")	30	15
1327	25dh. Peacock wrasse ("Thalassoma pavo")	30	15
1328	25dh. Mediterranean cardinal-fish ("Apogon imberbis")	30	15
1329	25dh. Atlantic mackerel ("Scomber scombrus")	30	15
1330	25dh. Black seabream ("Spondyliosoma cantharus")	30	15
1331	25dh. Greater weaver ("Trachinus draco")	30	15
1332	25dh. Peacock blenny ("Blennius pavo")	30	15
1333	25dh. Lesser red scorpionfish ("Scorpaena notata")	30	15
1334	25dh. Painted comber ("Serranus scriba")	30	15
1335	25dh. Angler ("Lophius piscatorius")	30	15
1336	25dh. Stargazer ("Uranoscopus scaber")	30	15
1337	25dh. Frigate mackerel ("Auxis thazard")	30	15
1338	25dh. John dory ("Zeus faber")	30	15
1339	25dh. Flying gurnard ("Dactylopterus volitans")	30	15
1340	25dh. Corb ("Umbrina cirrosa")	30	15

297 "Still-life" (Gauguin)

1983. Paintings. Multicoloured.

1341	50dh. Type **297**	25	20
1342	50dh. Abstract	25	20
1343	50dh. "The Conquest of Tunis by Charles V" (Rubens)	25	20
1344	50dh. "Arab Band in Horse-drawn Carriage"	25	20
1345	50dh. "Apotheosis of Gaddafi" (vert)	25	20
1346	50dh. Horses (detail of Raphael's "The Triumph of David over the Assyrians") (vert)	25	20
1347	50dh. "Workers" (vert)	25	20
1348	50dh. "Sunflowers" (Van Gogh) (vert)	25	20

298 Basketball

1983. Olympic Games, Los Angeles. Mult.

1349	10dh. Type **298**	10	10
1350	15dh. High jumping	10	10
1351	25dh. Running	15	10
1352	50dh. Gymnastics	25	20
1353	100dh. Windsurfing	80	45
1354	200dh. Shot-putting	1·50	95

299 I.T.U. Building, Antenna and W.C.Y. Emblem

1983. World Communications Year.

1356	**299**	10dh. multicoloured	10	10
1357		50dh. multicoloured	25	20
1358		100dh. multicoloured	75	45

300 "The House is to be served by its Residents"

1983. Extracts from the Green Book. Mult.

1359	10dh. Type **300**	10	10
1360	15dh. "Power, wealth and arms are in the hands of the people"	10	10
1361	20dh. "Masters in their own castles" (vert)	10	10
1362	35dh. "No democracy without popular congresses"	20	15
1363	100dh. "The authority of the people" (vert)	50	45
1364	140dh. "The Green Book is the guide of humanity for final release"	1·10	70

301 Handball

1983. 2nd African Youth Festival. Multicoloured.

1366	100dh. Type **301**	85	45
1367	100dh. Basketball	85	45
1368	100dh. High jumping	85	45
1369	100dh. Running	85	45
1370	100dh. Football	85	45

302 Marching Soldiers

1983. 14th Anniv of September Revolution. Mult.

1371	65dh. Type **302**	35	30
1372	75dh. Weapons and communications training	40	35
1373	90dh. Women with machine-guns and bazookas	70	40

1374 100dh. Machine-gun training 75 45
1375 150dh. Bazooka training . . 1·10 70
1376 250dh. Rifle training . . . . 2·00 1·10

303 Saluting Scouts

1983. Scout Jamborees. Multicoloured.
1378 50dh. Type **303** 25 20
1379 100dh. Scouts around camp fire 90 45
EVENTS. 50dh. Second Islamic Scout Jamboree; 100dh. 15th Pan Arab Scout Jamboree.

304 Traffic Cadets

305 Saadun

1983. Traffic Day. Multicoloured.
1381 30dh. Type **304** 40 15
1382 70dh. Traffic policeman . . 70 30
1383 200dh. Police motorcyclists 1·90 1·25

1983. 90th Birth Anniv of Saadun (patriot soldier).
1384 **305** 100dh. multicoloured . . 90 45

306 Walter Wellman's airship "America", 1910

1983. Bicentenary of Manned Flight. Mult.
1385 100dh. Type **306** . . . . . 1·00 55
1386 100dh. Airship "Nulli Secundus", 1907 . . . . 1·00 55
1387 100dh. Jean-Baptiste Meusnier's balloon design, 1784 . . . . 1·00 55
1388 100dh. Blanchard and Jeffries' Channel crossing, 1785 (vert) . . . . 1·00 55
1389 100dh. Pilatre de Rozier's hydrogen/hot-air balloon flight, 1784 (vert) . . . . 1·00 55
1390 100dh. First Montgolfier balloon, 1783 (vert) . . . 1·00 55

307 Globe and Dove

1983. Solidarity with Palestinian People.
1393 **307** 200dh. green, blue & blk 1·60 95

308 Gladiators fighting

1983. Mosaics. Multicoloured.
1394 50dh. Type **308** 50 20
1395 50dh. Gladiators fighting (different) 50 20
1396 50dh. Gladiators and slave 50 20
1397 50dh. Two musicians . . . 50 20
1398 50dh. Three musicians . . . 50 20
1399 50dh. Two gladiators . . . 50 20
1400 50dh. Two Romans and bound victim 50 20

1401 50dh. Leopard and man hunting deer 50 20
1402 50dh. Deer and man with boar 50 20

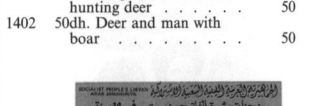

309 Traditional Architecture

1983. Achievements of the Revolution. Mult.
1403 10dh. Type **309** 10 10
1404 15dh. Camels drinking and mechanization of farming 10 10
1405 20dh. Computer operator and industrial scene . . . 10 10
1406 35dh. Modern architecture 15 10
1407 100dh. Surgeons and nurses treating patients and hospital 90 40
1408 140dh. Airport and airplane 1·25 75

310 Flooding a River Bed

311 Mahmud Burkis

1983. Colonel Gaddafi—River Builder. Multicoloured.
1410 50dh. Type **310** 20 15
1411 50dh. Irrigation pipe and agricultural produce . . . 20 15
1412 100dh. Colonel Gaddafi, irrigation pipe and farmland (62 × 44 mm) . . 1·00 40
1413 100dh. Colonel Gaddafi and map (68 × 32 mm) . . . . 1·00 40
1414 150dh. Colonel Gaddafi explaining irrigation project (35 × 32 mm) . . . 1·40 65
Nos. 1410/12 were printed together in se-tenant strips of three forming a composite design.

1984. Personalities. Multicoloured.
1416 100dh. Type **311** . . . . . 1·00 40
1417 100dh. Ahmed el-Bakbak . . 1·00 40
1418 100dh. Mohamed el-Misurati . . . . 1·00 40
1419 100dh. Mahmud Ben Musa 1·00 40
1420 100dh. Abdulhamid el-Sherif 1·00 40
1421 100dh. Mehdi el-Sherif . . 1·00 40
1422 100dh. Mahmud Mustafa Dreza . . . . 1·00 40
1423 100dh. Hosni Fauzi el-Amir 1·00 40
1424 100dh. Ali Haidar el-Saati 1·00 40
1425 200dh. Ahmed el-Feghi Hasan . . . . 1·50 80
1426 200dh. Bashir el-Jawab . . 1·50 80
1427 200dh. Ali el-Gariani . . . 1·50 80
1428 200dh. Muktar Shakshuki 1·50 80
1429 200dh. Abdurrahman el-Busayri . . . . 1·50 80
1430 200dh. Ibbrahim Bakir . . . 1·50 80
1431 200dh. Mahmud el-Janzuri 1·50 80

312 Windsurfing

313 Col. Gaddafi with Schoolchildren

1984. Water Sports. Multicoloured.
1432 25dh. Type **312** 30 10
1433 25dh. Dinghy sailing (orange and red sails) . . 30 10
1434 25dh. Dinghy sailing (mauve sails) 30 10
1435 25dh. Hang-gliding on water skis 20 10
1436 25dh. Water-skiing 20 10
1437 25dh. Angling from boat . . 30 10
1438 25dh. Men in speed boat . . 30 10
1439 25dh. Water-skiing (different) 20 10
1440 25dh. Fishing 30 10
1441 25dh. Canoeing 20 10
1442 25dh. Surfing 20 10
1443 25dh. Water-skiing (different) 20 10
1444 25dh. Scuba diving 30 10
1445 25dh. Diving 30 10

1446 25dh. Swimming in snorkel and flippers 30 10
1447 25dh. Scuba diving for fish 30 10

1984. African Children's Day. Multicoloured.
1448 50dh. Type **313** 50 15
1449 50dh. Colonel Gaddafi and children in national dress 50 15
1450 100dh. Colonel Gaddafi on map and children at various activities (62 × 43 mm) . . . . . . 1·90 60

314 Women in National, Casual and Military Dress

1984. Libyan Women's Emancipation. Multicoloured.
1451 55dh. Type **314** 50 20
1452 70dh. Women in traditional, casual and military dress (vert) 75 25
1453 100dh. Colonel Gaddafi and women in military dress 95 40

315 Theatre, Sabratha

1984. Roman Ruins of Cyrenaica. Multicoloured.
1454 50dh. Type **315** 20 15
1455 60dh. Temple, Cyrene . . . 50 20
1456 70dh. Monument, Sabratha (vert) 60 25
1457 100dh. Amphitheatre, Leptis Magna 90 40
1458 150dh. Temple, Cyrene (different) . . . . 1·40 65
1459 200dh. Basilica, Leptis Magna . . . . 1·90 80

316 Silver Dirham, 115h.

318 Muktar Shiaker Murabet

317 Men at Tea Ceremony

1984. Arabic Islamic Coins (1st series).
1460 **316** 200dh. silver, yellow and black . . . . 1·90 85
1461 – 200dh. silver, mauve and black . . . . 1·90 85
1462 – 200dh. silver, green and black . . . . 1·90 85
1463 – 200dh. silver, orange and black . . . . 1·90 85
1464 – 200dh. silver, blue and black . . . . 1·90 85
DESIGNS: No. 1461, Silver dirham, 93h; 1462, Silver dirham, 121h; 1463, Silver dirham, 49h; 1464, Silver dirham, 135h.
See also Nos. 1643/5.

1984. International Trade Fair, Tripoli. Mult.
1465 25dh. Type **317** 15 10
1466 35dh. Woman making tea 15 15
1467 45dh. Men taking tea . . . 20 15
1468 55dh. Family taking tea . . . 50 20
1469 75dh. Veiled women pouring tea 70 30
1470 100dh. Robed men taking tea . . . . 1·00 40

1984. Musicians. Multicoloured.
1471 100dh. Type **318** . . . . . 1·25 65
1472 100dh. El-Aref el-Jamal . . 1·25 65
1473 100dh. Ali Shiaalia . . . . 1·25 65
1474 100dh. Bashir Fehmi . . . . 1·25 65

319 Playing among Trees

1984. Children's Day. Designs showing children's paintings. Multicoloured.
1475 20dh. Type **319** 10 10
1476 20dh. A rainy day 10 10
1477 20dh. Weapons of war . . . 10 10
1478 20dh. Playing on the swing 10 10
1479 20dh. Playing in the park 10 10

320 Crest and "39"

1984. 39th Anniv of Arab League.
1480 **320** 30dh. multicoloured . . 15 15
1481 40dh. multicoloured . . 20 15
1482 50dh. multicoloured . . 55 20

321 Red Four-seater Car

1984. Motor Cars and Steam Locomotives. Mult.
1483 100dh. Type **321** . . . . 1·25 65
1484 100dh. Red three-seater car 1·25 65
1485 100dh. Yellow two-seater car with three lamps . . . 1·25 65
1486 100dh. Covered red four-seater car . . . . 1·25 65
1487 100dh. Yellow two-seater car with two lamps . . . 1·25 65
1488 100dh. Cream car with spare wheel at side . . . . . 1·25 65
1489 100dh. Green car with spare wheel at side . . . . . . 1·25 65
1490 100dh. Cream four-seater car with spare wheel at back . . . . 1·25 65
1491 100dh. Locomotive pulling wagon and coach . . . . 1·40 45
1492 100dh. Purple and blue locomotive . . . . 1·40 45
1493 100dh. Cream locomotive 1·40 45
1494 100dh. Lilac and brown locomotive . . . . 1·40 45
1495 100dh. Lilac and black locomotive with red wheels . . . . 1·40 45
1496 100dh. Cream and red locomotive . . . . 1·40 45
1497 100dh. Purple and black locomotive with red wheels . . . . 1·40 45
1498 100dh. Green and orange locomotive . . . . 1·40 45

322 Stylized People and Campaign Emblem

1984. World Health Day. Anti-Polio Campaign. Multicoloured.
1499 20dh. Type **322** 10 10
1500 30dh. Stylized people and 1981 20dh. stamp 15 15
1501 40dh. Stylized people and Arabic emblem 50 15

323 Man making Slippers

1984. Handicrafts. Multicoloured.

1502	150dh. Type **323**	1·60	65
1503	150dh. Man making decorative harness	1·60	65
1504	150dh. Women forming cotton into skeins	1·60	65
1505	150dh. Woman spinning by hand	1·60	65
1506	150dh. Man weaving	1·60	65
1507	150dh. Women weaving	1·60	65

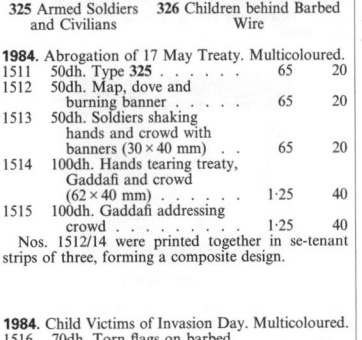

324 Telephones, Dial and Mail

1984. Postal and Telecommunications Union Congress. Multicoloured.

1508	50dh. Type **324**	50	20
1509	50dh. Woman working at computer console, dial and man working on computer	50	20
1510	100dh. Satellite, map, laurel branches and telephone handset	1·00	40

325 Armed Soldiers and Civilians 326 Children behind Barbed Wire

1984. Abrogation of 17 May Treaty. Multicoloured.

1511	50dh. Type **325**	65	20
1512	50dh. Map, dove and burning banner	65	20
1513	50dh. Soldiers shaking hands and crowd with banners (30 × 40 mm)	65	20
1514	100dh. Hands tearing treaty, Gaddafi and crowd (62 × 40 mm)	1·25	40
1515	100dh. Gaddafi addressing crowd	1·25	40

Nos. 1512/14 were printed together in se-tenant strips of three, forming a composite design.

1984. Child Victims of Invasion Day. Multicoloured.

1516	70dh. Torn flags on barbed wire	70	25
1517	100dh. Type **326**	1·00	40

327 "The Party System Aborts Democracy" 328 Man in Brown Robes

1984. Quotations from "The Green Book". Multicoloured.

1518	100dh. Type **327**	95	40
1519	100dh. Colonel Gaddafi	95	40
1520	100dh. "Partners not wage-workers"	95	40
1521	100dh. "No representation in lieu of the people. Representation is falsification"	95	40
1522	100dh. The Green Book	95	40
1523	100dh. "Committees everywhere"	95	40
1524	100dh. "Forming parties splits societies"	95	40
1525	100dh. Skyscraper and earthmover	95	40
1526	100dh. "No democracy without popular congresses"	95	40

1984. Costumes. Multicoloured.

1527	100dh. Type **328**	1·25	65
1528	100dh. Woman in green dress and red shawl	1·25	65
1529	100dh. Man in ornate costume and turban	1·25	65
1530	100dh. Man in short trousers and plain shirt	1·25	65
1531	100dh. Woman in shift and trousers with white shawl	1·25	65
1532	100dh. Man in long white robe and red shawl	1·25	65

329 Footballer tackling

1984. World Cup Football Championship. Mult.

1533	70dh. Type **329**	70	25
1534	70dh. Footballers in magenta and green shirts	70	25
1535	70dh. Footballers in orange and lemon shirts	70	25
1536	70dh. Goalkeeper failing to save ball	70	25
1537	70dh. Footballers in yellow and brown shirts	70	25
1538	70dh. Top of Trophy and footballer in green striped shirt	70	25
1539	70dh. Top of Trophy and footballers in blue and pink shirts	70	25
1540	70dh. Footballers in black and white striped and green and red striped shirts	70	25
1541	70dh. Footballers in green and red striped shirts	70	25
1542	70dh. Foot of trophy and footballers in orange striped and blue shirts	70	25
1543	70dh. Foot of trophy and goalkeeper	70	25
1544	70dh. Goalkeeper saving headed ball	70	25
1545	70dh. Referee and footballers	70	25
1546	70dh. Footballers in white with red striped sleeves and orange shirts	70	25
1547	70dh. Footballers in white and green striped and orange shirts	70	25
1548	70dh. Footballer in pink shirt	70	25

Nos. 1533/48 were printed in sheetlets of 16 stamps, the backgrounds to the stamps forming an overall design of a stadium.

330 Football 331 Palm Trees

1984. Olympic Games, Los Angeles. Mult.

1549	100dh. Type **330**	1·25	65
1550	100dh. Swimming	1·25	65
1551	100dh. Throwing the discus	1·25	65
1552	100dh. Windsurfing	1·25	65
1553	100dh. Basketball	1·25	65
1554	100dh. Running	1·25	65

1984. 9th World Forestry Congress. Mult.

1556	100dh. Four types of forest	1·10	40
1557	200dh. Type **331**	2·10	1·10

332 Modern Building

1984. 15th Anniv of Revolution. Multicoloured.

1558	25dh. Type **332**	15	10
1559	25dh. Front of building	15	10
1560	25dh. Building by pool	15	10
1561	25dh. Col. Gaddafi (three-quarter portrait)	15	10
1562	25dh. High-rise block	15	10
1563	25dh. Crane and mosque	15	10
1564	25dh. Motorway interchange	15	10
1565	25dh. House and garden	15	10
1566	25dh. Shepherd and flock	15	10
1567	25dh. Combine harvester	15	10
1568	25dh. Tractors	15	10
1569	25dh. Scientific equipment	15	10
1570	25dh. Col. Gaddafi (full face)	15	10
1571	25dh. Water pipeline	15	10
1572	25dh. Lighthouse	15	10
1573	25dh. Liner at quay	45	10

333 Armed Man

334 Soldier flogging Civilian

1984. Evacuation of Foreign Forces. Mult.

(a) As T **333**.

1574	50dh. Type **333**	50	20
1575	50dh. Armed man (different)	50	20
1576	100dh. Men on horseback charging (62 × 40 mm)	1·00	40

(b) As T **334**.

1577	100dh. Type **334**	1·00	40
1578	100dh. Girl on horse charging soldiers	1·00	40
1579	100dh. Mounted soldiers and wounded being tended by women	1·00	40

335 Woman riding Skewbald Showjumper

1984. Equestrian Events. Multicoloured.

1580	25dh. Type **335**	15	10
1581	25dh. Man riding black showjumper (stands in background)	15	10
1582	25dh. Jockey riding chestnut horse (stands in background)	15	10
1583	25dh. Man on chestnut horse jumping in cross-country event	15	10
1584	25dh. Man riding bay horse in showjumping competition	15	10
1585	25dh. Woman on black horse in dressage competition	15	10
1586	25dh. Man on black horse in dressage competition	15	10
1587	25dh. Woman riding chestnut horse in cross-country event	15	10
1588	25dh. Jockey riding bay horse	15	10
1589	25dh. Woman on bay horse in dressage competition	15	10
1590	25dh. Man on grey horse in dressage competition	15	10
1591	25dh. Jockey riding grey steeplechaser	15	10
1592	25dh. Woman riding grey showjumper	15	10
1593	25dh. Woman riding through water in cross-country competition	15	10
1594	25dh. Woman on chestnut horse in cross-country competition	15	10
1595	25dh. Man riding dun showjumper	15	10

Nos. 1580/95 were printed together in sheetlets of 16 stamps, the backgrounds of the stamps forming an overall design of an equestrian ring.

336 Man cleaning Corn 337 Map and Pharmaceutical Equipment

1984. Traditional Agriculture. Multicoloured.

1596	100dh. Type **336**	1·25	65
1597	100dh. Man using oxen to draw water from well	1·25	65
1598	100dh. Man making straw goods	1·25	65
1599	100dh. Shepherd with sheep	1·25	65
1600	100dh. Man treating animal skin	1·25	65
1601	100dh. Man climbing coconut tree	1·25	65

1984. 9th Conference of Arab Pharmacists Union.

1602 **337**	100dh. multicoloured	1·25	40
1603	200dh. multicoloured	2·50	1·10

338 Crowd with Banner showing Map of North Africa

1984. Arab–African Unity. Multicoloured.

1604	100dh. Type **338**	1·25	65
1605	100dh. Crowd and men holding flags	1·25	65

339 1982 and 1983 Solidarity Stamps and Map of Palestine

1984. Solidarity with Palestinian People.

1606 **339**	100dh. multicoloured	1·25	40
1607	150dh. multicoloured	1·90	1·00

340 Boeing 747SP, 1975

1984. 40th Anniv of International Civil Aviation Organization. Multicoloured.

1608	70dh. Type **340**	95	30
1609	70dh. Concorde, 1969	95	30
1610	70dh. Lockheed TriStar 500, 1978	95	30
1611	70dh. Airbus Industrie A310, 1982	95	30
1612	70dh. Tupolev Tu-134A, 1962	95	30
1613	70dh. Shorts 360, 1981	95	30
1614	70dh. Boeing 727-100, 1963	95	30
1615	70dh. Sud Aviation Caravelle 10R, 1965	95	30
1616	70dh. Fokker Friendship, 1955	95	30
1617	70dh. Lockheed Constellation, 1946	95	30
1618	70dh. Martin M-130 flying boat, 1955	95	30
1619	70dh. Douglas DC-3, 1936	95	50
1620	70dh. Junkers Ju-52/3m, 1932	95	30
1621	70dh. Lindbergh's "Spirit of St. Louis", 1927	95	30
1622	70dh. De Havilland Moth, 1925	95	30
1623	70dh. Wright Flyer I, 1903	95	30

Nos. 1608/23 were printed together in sheetlets of 16 stamps, the backgrounds of the stamps forming an overall design of a runway.

341 Coin 342 Mother and Son

1984. 20th Anniv of African Development Bank. Multicoloured.

1624	50dh. Type **341**	55	20
1625	70dh. Map of Africa and "20"	1·00	25
1626	100dh. "20" and symbols of industry and agriculture	1·25	65

1985. UNICEF Child Survival Campaign. Multicoloured.

1627 70dh. Type **342** . . . . . 1·00 50
1628 70dh. Couple and children 1·00 50
1629 70dh. Col. Gaddafi and children . . . . 1·00 50
1630 70dh. Boys in uniform . . . 1·00 50

343 Mohamed Hamdi

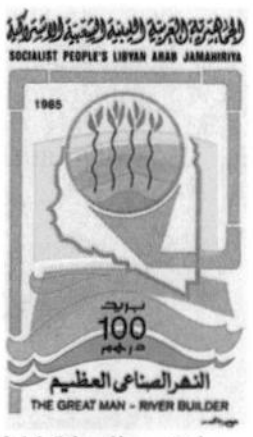

344 Pipeline, River, Plants and Map

1985. Musicians and Instruments. Multicoloured.

1631 100dh. Kamel el-Ghadi . . 1·25 65
1632 100dh. Fiddle rebab . . . . 1·25 65
1633 100dh. Ahmed el-Khogia . . 1·25 65
1634 100dh. Violin . . . . 1·25 65
1635 100dh. Mustafa el-Fallah . . 1·25 65
1636 100dh. Zither . . . . 1·25 65
1637 100dh. Type **343** . . . . . 1·25 65
1638 100dh. Mask . . . . 1·25 65

1985. Col. Gaddafi—River Builder. Multicoloured.

1639 100dh. Type **344** . . . . . 1·25 65
1640 100dh. Water droplet, river and flowers . . . . 1·25 65
1641 100dh. Dead tree with branch thriving in water droplet . . . . 1·25 65

345 Gold Dinar, 105h.

1985. Arabic Islamic Coins (2nd series). Mult.

1643 200dh. Type **345** . . . . . 2·50 1·25
1644 200dh. Gold dinar, 91h. . . 2·50 1·25
1645 200dh. Gold dinar, 77h. . . 2·50 1·25

346 Fish

347 Gaddafi in Robes and Hat

1985. Fossils. Multicoloured.

1647 150dh. Type **346** . . . . . 3·00 90
1648 150dh. Frog . . . . 1·90 55
1649 150dh. Mammal . . . . . 1·90 55

1985. People's Authority Declaration. Mult.

1650 100dh. Type **347** . . . . . 1·25 65
1651 100dh. Gaddafi in black robe holding book . . . 1·25 65
1652 100dh. Gaddafi in dress uniform without cap . . . 1·25 65
1653 100dh. Gaddafi in black dress uniform with cap . . 1·25 65
1654 100dh. Gaddafi in white dress uniform . . . . . 1·25 65

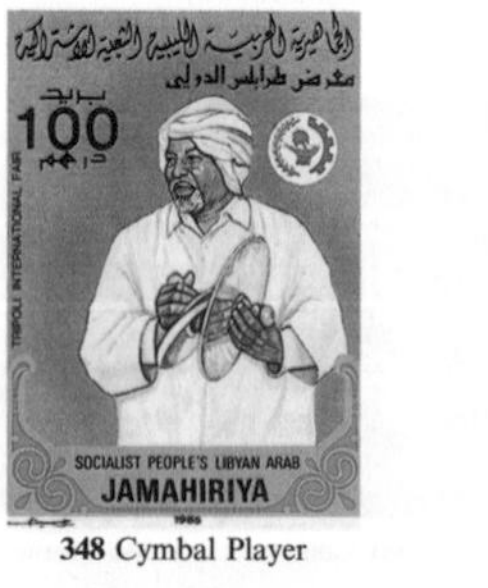

348 Cymbal Player

1985. International Trade Fair, Tripoli. Mult.

1655 100dh. Type **348** . . . . . 1·25 65
1656 100dh. Piper and drummer 1·25 65
1657 100dh. Drummer and bagpipes player . . . . . 1·25 65
1658 100dh. Drummer . . . . . . 1·25 65
1659 100dh. Tambour player . . 1·25 65

349 Goalkeeper catching Ball

350 Emblem, Radio Transmitter and Satellite

1985. Children's Day. Multicoloured.

1660 20dh. Type **349** 10 10
1661 20dh. Child on touchline with ball 10 10
1662 20dh. Letters of alphabet as players 10 10
1663 20dh. Goalkeeper saving ball 10 10
1664 20dh. Player heading ball 10 10

1985. International Communications Development Programme.

1665 **350** 30dh. multicoloured . . 15 10
1666 70dh. multicoloured . . 75 25
1667 100dh. multicoloured . . 1·10 65

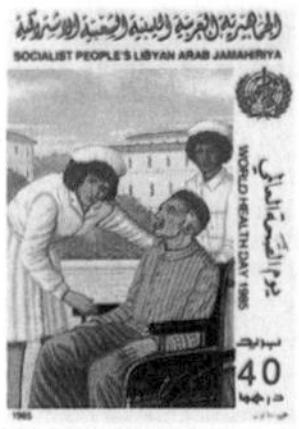

351 Nurses and Man in Wheelchair

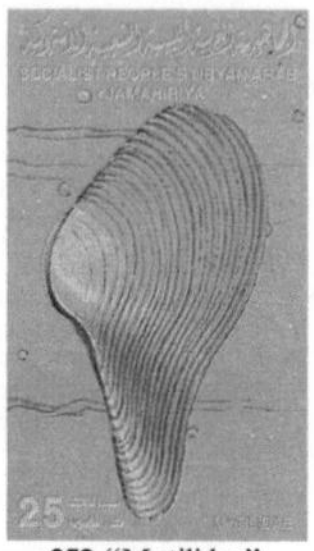

352 "Mytilidae"

1985. World Health Day. Multicoloured.

1668 40dh. Type **351** 50 10
1669 60dh. Nurses and doctors 75 15
1670 100dh. Nurse and child . . 1·25 65

1985. Sea Shells. Multicoloured.

1671 25dh. Type **352** 40 15
1672 25dh. Purple dye murex ("Muricidae") 40 15
1673 25dh. Tuberculate cockle ("Cardiidae") 40 15
1674 25dh. "Corallophilidae" . . 40 15
1675 25dh. Trunculus murex ("Muricidae") 40 15
1676 25dh. "Muricacea" 40 15
1677 25dh. "Turridae" 40 15
1678 25dh. Nodose paper nautilus ("Argonautidae") 40 15
1679 25dh. Giant tun ("Tonnidae") 40 15
1680 25dh. Common pelican's-foot ("Aporrhaidae") . . 40 15
1681 25dh. "Trochidae" 40 15
1682 25dh. "Cancellariidae" . . . 40 15
1683 25dh. "Epitoniidae" 40 15
1684 25dh. "Turbinidae" 40 15
1685 25dh. Zoned mitre ("Mitridae") 40 15
1686 25dh. Cat's-paw scallop ("Pectinidae") 40 15

Nos. 1671/86 were printed se-tenant, the backgrounds forming an overall design of the sea bed.

353 Books and Emblem

354 Girls Skipping

1985. International Book Fair, Tripoli.

1687 **353** 100dh. multicoloured . . 1·25 60
1688 200dh. multicoloured . . 2·25 1·25

1985. International Youth Year. Multicoloured.

1689 20dh. Type **354** 10 10
1690 20dh. Boys playing with stones 10 10
1691 20dh. Girls playing hopscotch 10 10
1692 20dh. Boys playing with sticks 10 10
1693 20dh. Boys playing with spinning top 10 10

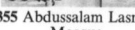

355 Abdussalam Lasmar Mosque

356 Jamila Zemerli

1985. Minarets. Multicoloured.

1695 50dh. Type **355** 50 15
1696 50dh. Zaoviat Kadria Mosque 50 15
1697 50dh. Zaoviat Amura Mosque 50 15
1698 50dh. Gurgi Mosque . . . 50 15
1699 50dh. Mizran Mosque . . . 50 15
1700 50dh. Salem Mosque . . . 50 15
1701 50dh. Ghat Mosque 50 15
1702 50dh. Ahmed Karamanli Mosque 50 15
1703 50dh. Atya Mosque 50 15
1704 50dh. El Kettani Mosque 50 15
1705 50dh. Benghazi Mosque . . 50 15
1706 50dh. Derna Mosque . . . 50 15
1707 50dh. El Derug Mosque . . 50 15
1708 50dh. Ben Moussa Mosque 50 15
1709 50dh. Ghadames Mosque 50 15
1710 50dh. Abdulwahab Mosque 50 15

1985. Teachers' Day. Multicoloured.

1711 100dh. Type **356** . . . . . 1·25 65
1712 100dh. Hamida El-Anezi . . 1·25 65

357 "Philadelphia" exploding

358 Gaddafi and Followers

1985. Battle of the "Philadelphia". Multicoloured.

1713 50dh. Type **357** 60 20
1714 50dh. Men with swords . . 60 20
1715 100dh. Men fighting and ship's rigging (59 × 45 mm) . . . . . . 1·25 45

Nos. 1713/15 were printed together, se-tenant, forming a composite design.

1986. Colonel Gaddafi's Islamic Pilgrimage. Multicoloured.

1716 200dh. Gaddafi writing . . 2·50 1·25
1717 200dh. Gaddafi praying . . 2·50 1·25
1718 200dh. Gaddafi, crowds and Kaaba . . . . 2·50 1·25
1719 200dh. Gaddafi and mirror 2·50 1·25
1720 200dh. Type **358** . . . . . 2·50 1·25

359 "Leucopaxillus lepistoides"

1985. Mushrooms. Multicoloured.

1722 50dh. Type **359** . . . . . 1·10 25
1723 50dh. "Amanita caesarea" 1·10 25
1724 50dh. "Coriolus hirsutus" 1·10 25
1725 50dh. "Cortinarius subfulgens" . . . . 1·10 25
1726 50dh. "Dermocybe pratensis" . . . . 1·10 25
1727 50dh. "Macrolepiota excoriata" . . . . 1·10 25
1728 50dh. "Amanita curtipes" 1·10 25
1729 50dh. "Trametes ljubarskyi" 1·10 25
1730 50dh. "Pholiota aurivella" 1·10 25
1731 50dh. "Boletus edulis" . . . 1·10 25
1732 50dh. "Geastrum sessile" . . 1·10 25
1733 50dh. "Russula sanguinea" 1·10 25
1734 50dh. "Cortinarius herculeus" . . . . 1·10 25
1735 50dh. "Pholiota lenta" . . . 1·10 25
1736 50dh. "Amanita rubescens" 1·10 25
1737 50dh. "Seleroderma polyrhizum" . . . . . . 1·10 25

Nos. 1722/37 were printed together, se-tenant, the backgrounds of the stamps forming an overall design of map of Mediterranean.

360 Woman in Purple Striped Dress

361 "In Need Freedom is Latent"

1985. Traditional Women's Costumes. Multicoloured.

1738 100dh. Type **360** . . . . . 1·25 65
1739 100dh. Woman in robes covering her face . . . . 1·25 65
1740 100dh. Woman in colourful robes with heavy jewellery 1·25 65
1741 100dh. Woman in long blue striped dress . . . . . 1·25 65
1742 100dh. Woman in red dress and trousers . . . . . . 1·25 65

1985. Quotations from "The Green Book".

1743 **361** 100dh. lt green, grn & blk 45 35
1744 – 100dh. multicoloured . . 45 35
1745 – 100dh. lt green, grn & blk 45 35
1746 – 100dh. lt green, grn & blk 45 35
1747 – 100dh. multicoloured . . 45 35
1748 – 100dh. lt green, grn & blk 45 35
1749 – 100dh. lt green, grn & blk 45 35
1750 – 100dh. multicoloured . . 45 35
1751 – 100dh. lt green, grn & blk 45 35

DESIGNS: No. 1744, Gaddafi in uniform reading; 1745, "To make a party you split society"; 1746, "Public sport is for all the masses"; 1747, "Green Books" and doves; 1748, "Wage-workers are a type of slave, however improved their wages may be"; 1749, "People are only harmonious with their own arts and heritages"; 1750, Gaddafi addressing crowd; 1751, "Democracy means popular rule not popular expression".

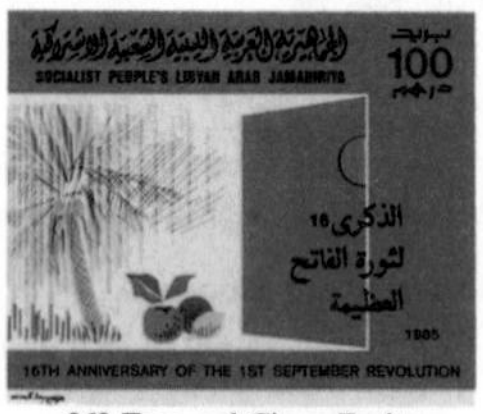

362 Tree and Citrus Fruits

1985. 16th Anniv of Revolution. Multicoloured.

1752 100dh. Type **362** . . . . . 1·25 65
1753 100dh. Oil pipeline and tanks . . . . 1·25 65
1754 100dh. Capital and olive branch . . . . 1·25 65
1755 100dh. Mosque and modern buildings . . . . 1·25 65
1756 100dh. Flag and mountains 1·25 65
1757 100dh. Telecommunications 1·25 65

363 Zauiet Amoura, Janzour

364 Players in Red No. 5 and Green Shirts

1985. Mosque Gateways. Multicoloured.

1759 100dh. Type **363** . . . . . 1·25 65
1760 100dh. Shiaieb El-Ain, Tripoli . . . . 1·25 65
1761 100dh. Zauiet Abdussalam El-Asmar, Zliten . . . . 1·25 65
1762 100dh. Karamanli, Tripoli 1·25 65
1763 100dh. Gurgi, Tripoli . . . 1·25 65

1985. Basketball. Multicoloured.

1764 25dh. Type **364** 15 10
1765 25dh. Players in green number 7 and red shirts 15 10
1766 25dh. Players in green number 8 and red shirts 15 10
1767 25dh. Players in red number 6 and green shirts 15 10
1768 25dh. Players in red number 4 and green number 7 shirts 15 10
1769 25dh. Players in green numbers 6 and 5 and red number 9 shirts 15 10
1770 25dh. Basket and one player in red and two in green shirts 15 10

1771 25dh. Players in red number 8 and green number 7 shirts 15 10
1772 25dh. Two players in green shirts and two in red shirts, one number 4 . . . 15 10
1773 25dh. Players in red numbers 4 and 7 and green shirts 15 10
1774 25dh. Players in red numbers 4 and 9 and green numbers 7 and 4 shirts 15 10
1775 25dh. Players in red number 6 and green shirts 15 10
1776 25dh. Players in red number 9 and green number 8 shirts 15 10
1777 25dh. Players in red number 8 and green number 5 shirts 15 10
1778 25dh. Players in red number 4 and green shirts 15 10
1779 25dh. Players in red number 5 and green number 10 shirts 15 10

Nos. 1764/79 were printed together se-tenant, the backgrounds of the stamps forming an overall design of basketball court and basket.

365 People in Light Ray

1985. Evacuation of Foreign Forces. Multicoloured.

1780 100dh. Man on crutches in web and light shining on tree . . . . 1·25 65
1781 100dh. Hands pulling web away from man . . . . . 1·25 65
1782 100dh. Type **365** . . . . . 1·25 65

366 Stockbook, Magnifying Glass and Stamps

367 Players

1985. Stamp Day. "Italia '85" International Stamp Exhibition, Rome. Multicoloured.

1783 50dh. Man and desk on flying stamp above globe 65 15
1784 50dh. Type **366** 65 15
1785 50dh. Stamps escaping from wallet 65 15

1986. World Cup Football Championship, Mexico (1st issue). Multicoloured.

1786 100dh. Type **367** . . . . . 1·25 65
1787 100dh. Players in red and white number 10 and yellow shirts . . . . . . 1·25 65
1788 100dh. Goalkeeper and player defending goal against attack . . . . . 1·25 65
1789 100dh. Goalkeeper diving to make save . . . . . . 1·25 65
1790 100dh. Goalkeeper jumping to make save . . . . . . 1·25 65
1791 100dh. Player in red and white shirt tackling player in lime shirt . . . . . . 1·25 65

See also Nos. 1824/9.

368 Hands releasing Dove

1985. Solidarity with Palestinian People.

1793 **368** 100dh. multicoloured . . 95 35
1794 150dh. multicoloured . . 1·60 75

370 Headquarters and Dish Aerial

371 Paper and Quill in Hand

1986. 1st Anniv of General Posts and Telecommunications Corporation.

1807 **370** 100dh. multicoloured . . 1·00 30
1808 150dh. multicoloured . . 1·50 75

1986. Peoples' Authority Declaration. Multicoloured.

1809 50dh. Type **371** 65 40
1810 50dh. Paper and globe in hand 65 40
1811 100dh. "Green Books" and dove (53 × 37 mm) . . . 1·25 65

372 Flute

1986. International Trade Fair, Tripoli. Mult.

1812 100dh. Type **372** . . . . . 1·25 65
1813 100dh. Drums . . . . 1·25 65
1814 100dh. Double pipes . . . . 1·25 65
1815 100dh. Tambourines . . . . 1·25 65
1816 100dh. Drum hung from shoulder . . . . 1·25 65

373 Boy Scout with Fish on Hook

1986. Children's Day. Multicoloured.

1817 50dh. Type **373** . . . . . 1·10 25
1818 50dh. Boy on camel 65 15
1819 50dh. Boy catching butterflies 65 15
1820 50dh. Boy playing drum . . 65 15
1821 50dh. Boy and giant goalkeeper on football pitch 65 15

374 Emblem, Man and Skull in Blood Droplet

1986. World Health Day. Multicoloured, background colours given.

1822 **374** 250dh. silver . . . . . . 2·50 1·25
1823 250dh. gold . . . . . . 2·50 1·25

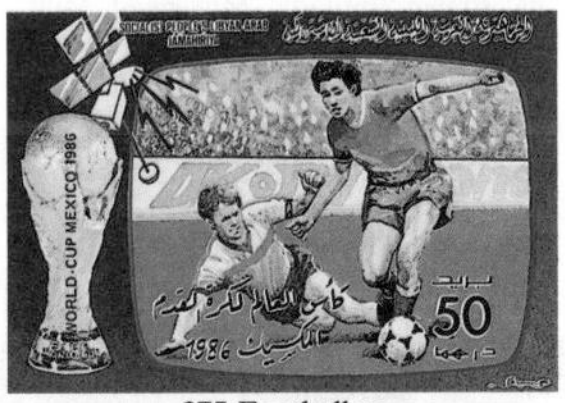

375 Footballers

1986. World Cup Football Championship, Mexico (2nd issue). Multicoloured.

1824 50dh. Type **375** 65 15
1825 50dh. Player jumping over player on ground 65 15
1826 50dh. Referee and players 65 15
1827 50dh. Goalkeeper trying to save ball 65 15
1828 50dh. Player about to tackle 65 15
1829 50dh. Player jumping over ball 65 15

376 Peas

377 Health Programmes

1986. Vegetables. Multicoloured.

1831 50dh. Type **376** 45 15
1832 50dh. Marrow 45 15
1833 50dh. Beans 45 15
1834 50dh. Aubergine 45 15
1835 50dh. Corn on the cob . . . 45 15
1836 50dh. Tomato 45 15
1837 50dh. Red pepper 45 15
1838 50dh. Zucchini 45 15
1839 50dh. Garlic 45 15
1840 50dh. Cabbage 45 15
1841 50dh. Cauliflower 45 15
1842 50dh. Celery 45 15
1843 50dh. Onions 45 15
1844 50dh. Carrots 45 15
1845 50dh. Potato 45 15
1846 50dh. Radishes 45 15

Nos. 1831/46 were printed together in sheetlets of 16 stamps, the backgrounds of the stamps forming an overall design of a garden.

1986. Jamahiriya Thought. Multicoloured.

1847 50dh. Type **377** 50 15
1848 50dh. Education programmes 50 15
1849 100dh. "Green Book", agricultural scenes and produce (agriculture programmes) (62 × 41 mm) . . . . . . 1·75 45

378 Gaddafi studying Plan

1986. Colonel Gaddafi, "Great man-made River Builder". Multicoloured.

1850 100dh. Type **378** 95 30
1851 100dh. Gaddafi showing planned route on map . . 95 30
1852 100dh. Gaddafi and old well 95 30
1853 100dh. Gaddafi in desert . . 95 30
1854 100dh. Gaddafi and pipe . . 95 30
1855 100dh. Gaddafi at pumping station 95 30
1856 100dh. Gaddafi and storage tank 95 30
1857 100dh. Workers' hut 95 30
1858 100dh. Water in cupped hands and irrigation equipment 95 30
1859 100dh. Gaddafi turning wheel at opening ceremony 95 30
1860 100dh. Laying pipes 95 30
1861 100dh. Pipe sections on lorries 95 30
1862 100dh. Gaddafi in robes holding "Green Book" . . 95 30
1863 100dh. Boy giving Gaddafi bowl of fruit 95 30
1864 100dh. Boy drinking from tap 95 30
1865 100dh. Gaddafi praying . . 95 30

379 Gaddafi with Children

1986. Colonel Gaddafi, "Man of Peace". Mult.

1866 100dh. Type **379** . . . . . 1·10 30
1867 100dh. Reading book in tent 1·10 30
1868 100dh. With his mother . . 1·10 30
1869 100dh. Praying in tent with his sons . . . . 1·10 30
1870 100dh. Talking to hospital patient . . . . 1·10 30
1871 100dh. Driving tractor . . . 1·10 30

380 General Dynamics F-111 Exploding above Man with injured Child

381 Gaddafi, Ruined buildings and Stretcher-bearers

1986. Battle of the U.S.S. "Philadelphia" and American Attack on Libya. Multicoloured. (a) As T **380**.

1872 50dh. Type **380** 40 25
1873 50dh. American aircraft carrier and escaping family 60 25
1874 100dh. "Philadelphia" exploding (59 × 38 mm) 1·25 50

(b) As T **381**.

1875 70dh. Type **381** 80 20
1876 70dh. Burning wreckage of car and man and boy in rubble 80 20
1877 70dh. Woman and child by burning ruin 80 20
1878 70dh. Men running from bomb strike 80 20
1879 70dh. Covered body and rescue workers searching ruins 80 20
1880 70dh. Libyans and General Dynamics F-111 airplane tail and wing 80 25
1881 70dh. Libyans waving fists 80 20
1882 70dh. Rescue workers lifting child from rubble 80 20
1883 70dh. Weeping women and soldier carrying baby . . 80 20
1884 70dh. Libyans and glare of explosion 80 20
1885 70dh. Libyans and General Dynamics F-111 airplane wing and nose 80 25
1886 70dh. Man carrying girl . . 80 20
1887 70dh. Coffins held aloft by crowd 80 20
1888 70dh. Crowd carrying pictures of Gaddafi . . . 80 20
1889 70dh. Wounded being tended 80 20
1890 70dh. Hands tending wounded baby 80 20

(c) Size 89 × 32 mm.

1891 100dh. General Dynamics F-111 bombers, Gaddafi and anti-aircraft rockets 1·25 35

Nos. 1872/4 were printed together in se-tenant strips of three within the sheet, each strip forming a composite design.

382 "The House must be served by its own Tenant"

1986. Quotations from the "Green Book".

1892 **382** 100dh. lt green, grn & blk . . . . 1·00 30
1893 – 100dh. multicoloured . . 1·00 30
1894 – 100dh. lt green, grn & blk . . . . 1·00 30
1895 – 100dh. lt green, grn & blk . . . . 1·00 30
1896 – 100dh. multicoloured . . 1·00 30
1897 – 100dh. lt green, grn & blk . . . . 1·00 30
1898 – 100dh. lt green, grn & blk . . . . 1·00 30
1899 – 100dh. multicoloured . . 1·00 30
1900 – 100dh. lt green, grn & blk . . . . 1·00 30

DESIGNS: No. 1893, Gaddafi; 1894, "The Child is raised by his mother"; 1895, "Democracy is the Supervision of the People by the People"; 1896, "Green Books"; 1897, "Representation is a Falsification of Democracy"; 1898, "The Recognition of Profit is an Acknowledgement of Exploitation"; 1899, Vase of roses, iris, lilies and jasmine; 1900, "Knowledge is a Natural Right of every Human Being which Nobody has the Right to deprive him of under any Pretext".

383 Map, Chrysanthemum and Health Services

1986. 17th Anniv of Revolution. Multicoloured.
1901 200dh. Type **383** . . . . . 2·50 95
1902 200dh. Map, sunflower and agriculture programme . . 2·50 95
1903 200dh. "Sunflowers" (Van Gogh) . . . . 2·50 95
1904 200dh. Map, rose and defence programme . . . 2·50 95
1905 200dh. Map, campanula and oil exploration programme . . . . 2·50 95

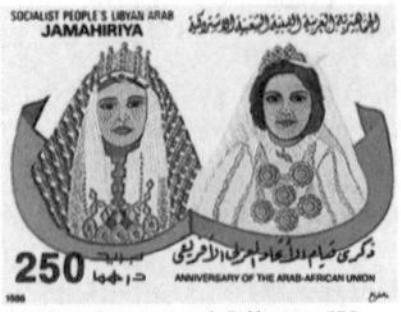

384 Moroccan and Libyan Women

1986. Arab–African Union. Multicoloured.
1906 250dh. Type **384** . . . . . 2·50 80
1907 250dh. Libyan and Moroccan horsemen . . . 2·50 80

385 Libyan Horseman

1986. Evacuation of Foreign Forces. Multicoloured.
1908 50dh. Type **385** 50 15
1909 100dh. Libyan horsemen trampling Italian soldiers 1·10 30
1910 150dh. Italian soldiers charging . . . . 1·50 50

386 Globe and Rose

1986. International Peace Year. Multicoloured, background colours given.
1911 **386** 200dh. green . . . . . 1·90 70
1912 200dh. blue . . . . . . 1·90 70

387 Brick "Fists" and Maps within Laurel Wreath

1986. Solidarity with Palestinian People. Multicoloured, background colours given.
1913 **387** 250dh. blue . . . . . . 2·50 80
1914 250dh. red . . . . . . 2·50 80

388 Drummer

1986. Folk Music. Multicoloured.
1915 70dh. Type **388** 95 20
1916 70dh. Masked stick dancer 95 20
1917 70dh. Woman dancer with pot headdress 95 20
1918 70dh. Bagpipe player . . . 95 20
1919 70dh. Tambour player . . . 95 20

389 Gazelles

1987. Endangered Animals. Sand Gazelle. Multicoloured.
1920 100dh. Type **389** . . . . . 1·25 30
1921 100dh. Mother and calf . . 1·25 30
1922 100dh. Gazelle drinking . . 1·25 30
1923 100dh. Gazelle lying down 1·25 30

390 Oil Derricks and Crowd **391** Sheep and Shepherd

1987. People's Authority Declaration. Multicoloured.
1924 500dh. Type **390** . . . . . 4·00 1·75
1925 500dh. Buildings and crowd 4·00 1·75
1926 1000dh. Gaddafi addressing crowd and globe (40 × 38 mm) . . . . . . 8·00 3·25

1987. 18th Anniv of Revolution. Multicoloured.
1927 150dh. Type **391** . . . . . 1·50 50
1928 150dh. Col. Gaddafi in robes . . . . 1·50 50
1929 150dh. Mosque . . . . 1·50 50
1930 150dh. Water flowing from irrigation pipe . . . . . 1·50 50
1931 150dh. Combine harvester 1·50 50
1932 150dh. Col. Gaddafi in army uniform with microphone 1·50 50
1933 150dh. Harvesting crop . . 1·50 50
1934 150dh. Irrigation . . . . . 1·50 50
1935 150dh. Soldier with rifle . 1·50 50
1936 150dh. Buildings behind Libyan with rifle . . . . 1·50 50
1937 150dh. Fountain . . . . . 1·50 50
1938 150dh. Buildings and beach 1·50 50
1939 150dh. Fort and girls . . . 1·50 50
1940 150dh. Children and hand on rifle butt . . . . . . 1·50 50
1941 150dh. Theatre . . . . . . 1·50 50
1942 150dh. Couple . . . . . . 1·50 50

392 Omar Abed Anabi al Mansusri

1988. Personalities. Multicoloured.
1943 100dh. Type **392** 75 30
1944 200dh. Ahmed Ali al Emrayd . . . . 1·50 70
1945 300dh. Khalifa Said Ben Asker . . . . 2·50 1·00
1946 400dh. Mohamed Ben Farhat Azawi . . . . . . 3·00 1·10
1947 500dh. Mohamed Souf al Lafi al Marmori . . . . 3·75 1·50

393 Gaddafi and Crowd with Raised Fists around Earthmover Bucket

1988. Freedom Festival Day.
1948 **393** 100dh. multicoloured . . 95 30
1949 150dh. multicoloured . . 1·60 75
1950 250dh. multicoloured . . 2·50 1·25

394 Woman and Children running

1988. 2nd Anniv of American Attack on Libya. Multicoloured.
1951 150dh. Type **394** . . . . . 1·40 50
1952 150dh. Gaddafi playing chess with boy . . . . . 1·40 50
1953 150dh. Gaddafi and children 1·40 50
1954 150dh. Gaddafi in robes . . 1·40 50
1955 150dh. Gaddafi and boys praying . . . . 1·40 50
1956 150dh. Gaddafi and injured girl . . . . 1·40 50
1957 150dh. Gaddafi in robes with children (horiz) . . . 1·40 50
1958 150dh. Gaddafi making speech (horiz) . . . . . 1·40 50
1959 150dh. Gaddafi and family (horiz) . . . . 1·40 50

395 Roses

1988. 19th Anniv of Revolution.
1961 **395** 100dh. multicoloured . . 75 30
1962 250dh. multicoloured . . 2·00 80
1963 300dh. multicoloured . . 2·25 1·00
1964 500dh. multicoloured . . 4·25 1·50

396 Relay **397** Dates

1988. Olympic Games, Seoul. Multicoloured.
1965 150dh. Type **396** . . . . . 1·25 50
1966 150dh. Cycling . . . . . . 1·25 50
1967 150dh. Football . . . . . . 1·25 50
1968 150dh. Tennis . . . . . . 1·25 50
1969 150dh. Running . . . . . . 1·25 50
1970 150dh. Showjumping . . . 1·25 50

1988. The Palm Tree. Multicoloured.
1972 500dh. Type **397** . . . . . 4·25 1·50
1973 1000dh. Tree . . . . 8·00 3·75

398 Petrol Bomb, Sling and Map **399** Globe, Declaration and Dove

1988. Palestinian "Intifada" Movement. Mult.
1974 100dh. Type **398** 95 30
1975 200dh. Boy holding stones (45 × 38 mm) . . . . . 1·60 70
1976 300dh. Map and flag . . . 2·50 1·00

1989. People's Authority Declaration.
1977 **399** 260dh. multicoloured . . 1·10 65
1978 500dh. multicoloured . . 2·00 1·25

400 Crowd and Green Books (½-size illustration)

1989. 20th Anniv of Revolution. Multicoloured.
1979 150dh. Type **400** . . . . . 1·25 40
1980 150dh. Soldiers, Colonel Gaddafi and water pipeline . . . . 1·25 40
1981 150dh. Military hardware, Gaddafi in uniform, education, communications and medicine . . . . 1·25 40
1982 150dh. Armed horsemen . . 1·25 40
1983 150dh. U.S.S. "Philadelphia" exploding 1·25 55

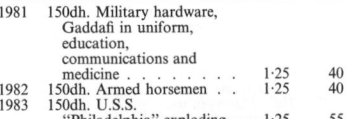

401 Execution Victims, Soldiers and Colonel Gaddafi

1989. 78th Anniv of Deportation of Libyans to Italy. Multicoloured.
1985 100dh. Type **401** 40 25
1986 100dh. Colonel Gaddafi and Libyans 40 25
1987 100dh. Soliders, deportees and Gaddafi 40 25
1988 100dh. Deportees on jetty and in boats 55 25
1989 100dh. Gaddafi and corpses 40 25

402 Demoliton of Wall **403** Emblem of Committee for supporting "Intifida"

1989. "Demolition of Borders".
1991 **402** 150dh. multicoloured . . 1·60 1·60
1992 200dh. multicoloured . . 2·10 2·10

1989. Palestinian "Intifada" Movement. Mult.
1993 100dh. Type **403** . . . . . 1·10 1·10
1994 300dh. Crowd of youths . . 3·00 3·00
1995 500dh. Emblem (1st anniv of declaration of state of Palestine) . . . . 4·75 4·75

404 Circulation Diagram and Annafis

1989. Ibn Annafis (physician) Commemoration.
1996 **404** 100dh. multicoloured . . 1·25 1·25
1997 150dh. multicoloured . . 1·90 1·90

405 Green Books and Fort **406** Libyan People and Soldier

1990. People's Authority Declaration.
1998 **405** 300dh. multicoloured . . 2·75 2·75
1999 500dh. multicoloured . . 5·00 5·00

1990. 20th Anniv of American Forces Evacuation.
2000 **406** 100dh. multicoloured . . 1·00 1·00
2001 400dh. multicoloured . . 4·00 4·00

407 Eagle **408** Anniversary Emblem

1990. 21st Anniv of Revolution.
2002 **407** 100dh. multicoloured . . 1·00 1·00
2003 400dh. multicoloured . . 4·00 4·00
2004 1000dh. multicoloured 10·50 10·50

1990. 30th Anniv of Organization of Petroleum Exporting Countries.

2006	**408**	100dh. multicoloured . .	1·00	1·00
2007		400dh. multicoloured . .	4·00	4·00

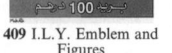

409 I.L.Y. Emblem and Figures

410 Player, Globe and Ball

1990. International Literacy Year.

2008	**409**	100dh. multicoloured . .	1·10	1·10
2009		300dh. multicoloured . .	3·00	3·00

1990. World Cup Football Championship, Italy.

2010	**410**	100dh. multicoloured . .	1·00	1·00
2011		400dh. multicoloured . .	4·00	4·00
2012		500dh. multicoloured . .	5·00	5·00

411 Hand holding Ears of Wheat

412 Members' Flags

1990. World Food Day. Multicoloured.

2014	500dh. Type **411**	5·00	5·00
2015	2000dh. Ploughing	20·00	20·00

1991. 2nd Anniv of Union of Arab Maghreb.

2016	**412**	100dh. multicoloured . .	1·10	1·10
2017		300dh. multicoloured . .	3·00	3·00

413 Flame, Scroll and Koran

1991. People's Authority Declaration.

2018	**413**	300dh. multicoloured . .	2·75	2·75
2019		400dh. multicoloured . .	3·75	3·75

414 Girl and International Year of the Child Emblem

415 World Health Organization Emblem

1991. Children's Day. Multicoloured.

2020	100dh. Type **414**	95	95
2021	400dh. Boy and Day of the African Child emblem . .	3·75	3·75

1991. World Health Day. Multicoloured.

2022	100dh. Type **415**	95	95
2023	200dh. As Type **415** but with emblem additionally inscr "WHO OMS" . . .	1·90	1·90

416 Wadi el Hayat

1991. Scenes from Libya. Multicoloured.

2024	100dh. Type **416**	95	95
2025	250dh. Mourzuk (horiz) . .	2·50	2·50
2026	500dh. Ghadames (horiz) . .	5·00	5·00

417 Digging Riverbed and laying Pipes

1991. Great Man-made River. Multicoloured.

2027	50dh. Type **417**	25	15
2028	50dh. Col. Gaddafi, agricultural projects and livestock (59 × 37 mm) . .	25	15
2029	50dh. Produce	25	15

Nos. 2027/9 were printed together, se-tenant, forming a composite design.

418 "22", Roses and Broken Chain

1991. 22nd Anniv of Revolution. Multicoloured.

2030	300dh. Type **418**	2·75	2·75
2031	400dh. "22" within wheat/ cogwheel wreath and broken chain	3·75	3·75

419 Emblem and Globe

1991. "Telecom 91" International Telecommunications Exhibition, Geneva. Multicoloured.

2033	100dh. Type **419**	95	95
2034	500dh. Buildings and dish aerial (horiz)	4·50	4·50

420 Monument and Soldier

1991. 80th Anniv of Deportation of Libyans to Italy. Multicoloured.

2035	100dh. Type **420**	95	95
2036	400dh. Naval transport, Libyans and soldiers . . .	3·75	3·75

421 Map

1991. Arab Unity.

2038	**421**	50dh. multicoloured . .	20	10
2039		100dh. multicoloured . .	40	20

422 Lorry

424 State Arms

423 Gaddafi and Camels

1991. Paris–Dakar Trans-Sahara Rally. Mult.

2040	50dh. Type **422**	20	10
2041	50dh. Blue lorry	20	10
2042	50dh. African Product lorry	20	10
2043	50dh. Tomel lorry	20	10
2044	50dh. All-terrain vehicle No. 173	20	10
2045	50dh. Mitsusuki all-terrain vehicle	20	10
2046	50dh. Michedop all-terrain vehicle	20	10
2047	50dh. All-terrain vehicle No. 401	20	10
2048	50dh. Motor cycle No. 100	20	10
2049	50dh. Rider pushing red motor cycle	20	10
2050	50dh. Rider pushing white motor cycle	20	10
2051	50dh. Motor cycle No. 98	20	10
2052	50dh. Motor cycle No. 101	20	10
2053	50dh. Motor cycle No. 80	20	10
2054	50dh. Motor cycle No. 12	20	10
2055	50dh. Motor cycle No. 45	20	10

1992. "Gaddafi, Man of Peace 1992". Multicoloured, colour of frame given.

2056	**423**	100dh. green	40	20
2057		100dh. grey	40	20
2058		100dh. red	40	20
2059		100dh. ochre	40	20

1992.

2061	**424**	100dh. green, brn & yell	40	20
2062		150dh. green, brn & grey	60	30
2063		200dh. green, brown & bl	85	45
2064		250dh. green, brn & orge	1·10	55
2065		300dh. green, brn & vio	1·25	65
2066		400dh. green, brn & mve	1·75	90
2067		450dh. emerald, brn & grn	1·90	95

425 1991 100dh. Stamp, Tweezers, Magnifying Glass and Stamps

1992. 3rd Anniv of Union of Arab Maghreb.

2068	**425**	75dh. multicoloured . .	30	15
2069		80dh. multicoloured . .	35	20

426 Horse-drawn Carriage

1992. International Trade Fair, Tripoli. Mult.

2070	50dh. Type **426**	20	10
2071	100dh. Horse-drawn cart . .	40	20

427 Emblem

1992. People's Authority Declaration.

2072	**427**	100dh. multicoloured . .	40	20
2073		150dh. multicoloured . .	60	30

428 Emblem and Camel Rider

1992. African Tourism Year.

2074	**428**	50dh. multicoloured . .	20	10
2075		100dh. multicoloured . .	40	20

429 Big-eyed Tuna

1992. Fishes. Multicoloured.

2076	100dh. Type **429**	75	30
2077	100dh. Mackerel scad . . .	75	30
2078	100dh. Little tuna (seven spines on back)	75	30
2079	100dh. Seabream (continuous dorsal fin) . .	75	30
2080	100dh. Spanish mackerel (four spines on back) . .	75	30
2081	100dh. Striped red mullet (with whiskers)	75	30

430 Horsewoman with Rifle

1992. Horse Riders. Multicoloured.

2082	100dh. Type **430**	40	20
2083	100dh. Man on rearing white horse	40	20
2084	100dh. Man on brown horse with ornate bridle	40	20
2085	100dh. Roman soldier on brown horse	40	20
2086	100dh. Man in blue coat on brown horse	40	20
2087	100dh. Arab on white horse	40	20

431 Long Jumping

1992. Olympic Games, Barcelona. Multicoloured.

2089	50dh. Type **431**	20	10
2090	50dh. Throwing the discus	20	10
2091	50dh. Tennis	20	10

432 Palm Trees

1992. Achievements of the Revolution. Mult.

2093	100dh. Type **432**	40	20
2094	150dh. Ingots and foundry	60	30
2095	250dh. Container ship . . .	1·10	55
2096	300dh. Airplane	1·25	65
2097	400dh. Assembly hall . . .	1·75	90
2098	500dh. Water pipes and Gaddafi	2·10	1·10

433 Gaddafi

434 Laurel Wreath, Torch and "23"

1992. Multicoloured, background colours given.

2099	**433**	500dh. green	2·50	1·10
2100		1000dh. pink	5·00	2·50
2101		2000dh. blue	10·00	5·00
2102		5000dh. violet	25·00	12·50
2103		6000dh. orange	32·00	16·00

1992. 23rd Anniv of Revolution. Multicoloured.

2104	50dh. Type **434**	20	10
2105	100dh. Laurel wreath, flag, sun and "23"	40	20

435 Antelope drinking

436 Horse and Broken Chain

1992. Oases. Multicoloured.

2107	100dh. Type **435**	40	20
2108	200dh. Sun setting behind camel train (vert)	85	45
2109	300dh. Camel rider	1·25	65

1992. Evacuation of Foreign Forces. Multicoloured.

2110	75dh. Type **436**	30	15
2111	80dh. Flag and broken chain	35	20

437 Monument and Dates

1992. 81st Anniv of Deportation of Libyans to Italy.

2112 **437**	100dh. multicoloured	40	20
2113	250dh. multicoloured	1·10	55

438 Dome of the Rock and Palestinian

1992. Palestinian "Intifada" Movement. Mult.

2114	100dh. Type **438**	40	20
2115	300dh. Map, Dome of the Rock, flag and fist (vert)	1·25	65

439 Red and White Striped Costume

440 Mohamed Ali Imsek

1992. Women's Costumes. Multicoloured.

2116	50dh. Type **439**	20	10
2117	50dh. Large red hat with silver decorations, white tunic and red wrap	20	10
2118	50dh. Brown and orange striped costume with small gold necklace and horseshoe brooch	20	10
2119	50dh. Purple and white costume	20	10
2120	50dh. Orange striped costume	20	10

1993. Physicians.

2121 **440**	40dh. black, yellow and silver	15	10
2122 –	60dh. black, green and gold	20	15

DESIGN: 60dh. Aref Adhani Arif.

441 Globe, Crops and Spoon-feeding Man

1993. International Nutrition Conference, Rome.

2123 **441**	70dh. multicoloured	35	25
2124	80dh. multicoloured	40	30

442 Gaddafi, Eagle and Oil Refinery

1993. People's Authority Declaration.

2125 **442**	60dh. multicoloured	20	15
2126	65dh. multicoloured	25	15
2127	75dh. multicoloured	25	15

443 Crowd with Tambours

445 Girl

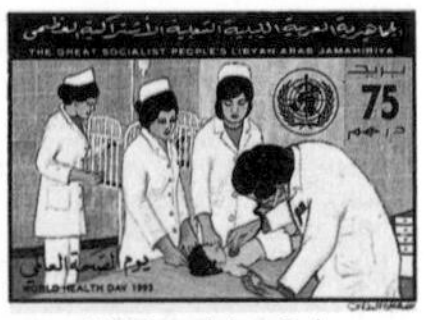

444 Examining Baby

1993. International Trade Fair, Tripoli. Mult.

2128	60dh. Type **443**	20	15
2129	60dh. Crowd with camel	20	15
2130	60dh. Dance of veiled men (horiz)	20	15
2131	60dh. Women preparing food (horiz)	20	15

1993. World Health Day. Multicoloured.

2133	75dh. Type **444**	25	15
2134	85dh. Medical staff attending patient	30	20

1993. Children's Day. Multicoloured.

2135	75dh. Type **445**	25	15
2136	75dh. Girl wearing blue and white veil and gold cuff	25	15
2137	75dh. Girl with white fluted collar and silver veil	25	15
2138	75dh. Girl with hands clasped	25	15
2139	75dh. Girl wearing blue scallop-edged veil	25	15

446 Phoenician Ship

1993. Ships. Multicoloured.

2140	50dh. Type **446**	20	15
2141	50dh. Arab galley	20	15
2142	50dh. Pharaonic ship	20	15
2143	50dh. Roman bireme	20	15
2144	50dh. Carvel	20	15
2145	50dh. Yacht (globe showing Italy)	20	15
2146	50dh. Yacht (globe showing Greece)	20	15
2147	50dh. Galeasse	20	15
2148	50dh. Nau	20	15
2149	50dh. Yacht (globe showing left half of Libya)	20	15
2150	50dh. Yacht (globe showing right half of Libya)	20	15
2151	50dh. "Santa Maria"	20	15
2152	50dh. "France" (liner)	20	15
2153	50dh. Schooner	20	15
2154	50dh. Sail/steam warship	20	15
2155	50dh. Modern liner	20	15

Nos. 2140/55 were issued together, se-tenant, the centre four stamps forming a composite design.

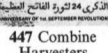

447 Combine Harvesters

448 Woman tending Youth

1993. 24th Anniv of Revolution. Multicoloured.

2156	50dh. Type **447**	20	15
2157	50dh. Col. Gaddafi	20	15
2158	50dh. Cattle behind men filling sack with grain	20	15
2159	50dh. Chickens behind shepherd with flock	20	15
2160	50dh. Oil rig	20	15
2161	50dh. Eagle and camel	20	15
2162	50dh. Industrial plant	20	15
2163	50dh. Water pipeline	20	15
2164	50dh. Man harvesting dates	20	15
2165	50dh. Man in field and boxes of produce	20	15
2166	50dh. Pile of produce	20	15
2167	50dh. Man picking courgettes	20	15
2168	50dh. Children reading	20	15
2169	50dh. Typist and laboratory worker	20	15
2170	50dh. Hand-picking crop and ploughing with tractor	20	15
2171	50dh. Tractor towing circular harrow	20	15

Nos. 2156/71 were issued together, se-tenant, forming several composite designs.

1993. 82nd Anniv of Deportation of Libyans to Italy. Multicoloured.

2172	50dh. Type **448**	20	15
2173	50dh. Soldiers and Libyan family	20	15
2174	50dh. Col. Gaddafi (in turban)	20	15
2175	50dh. Libyans in food queue	20	15
2176	50dh. Man being flogged	20	15
2177	50dh. Horseman charging between soldiers and Libyans	20	15
2178	50dh. Soldier with manacled Libyan before court	20	15
2179	50dh. Libyans gazing at hanged man	20	15
2180	50dh. Crowd of Libyans and two soldiers	20	15
2181	50dh. Soldiers guarding procession of Libyans	20	15
2182	50dh. Soldiers and manacled Libyans on quayside	20	15
2183	50dh. Deportees in boat	20	15
2184	50dh. Col. Gaddafi (bare-headed)	20	15
2185	50dh. Two Libyan families and branch of palm tree	20	15
2186	50dh. Soldiers in disarray (ruins in background)	20	15
2187	50dh. Libyan horsemen	20	15

Nos. 2172/87 were issued together, se-tenant, forming several composite designs.

449 Brooch

451 Player and Trophy

450 Gaddafi, Soldiers and Jet Fighters

1994. Silver Jewellery. Multicoloured.

2188	55dh. Type **449**	20	15
2189	55dh. Armlet	20	15
2190	55dh. Pendant	20	15
2191	55dh. Pendants hanging from oblong	20	15
2192	55dh. Necklace	20	15
2193	55dh. Slippers	20	15

1994. 25th Anniv of Revolution. Multicoloured.

2194	100dh. Type **450**	35	25
2195	100dh. Libyan tribesmen and Gaddafi in uniform (59 × 38 mm)	35	25
2196	100dh. Peaceful pursuits and elderly couple	35	25

Nos. 2194/6 were issued together, se-tenant, forming a composite design.

1994. World Cup Football Championship, U.S.A. Multicoloured.

2198	100dh. Type **451**		
2199	100dh. Kicking ball with inside of foot	35	25
2200	100dh. Kicking ball in air	35	25
2201	100dh. Goalkeeper	35	25
2202	100dh. Running with ball	35	25
2203	100dh. Player taking ball on chest	35	25

452 Gaddafi

1994. 83rd Anniv of Deportation of Libyans to Italy. Multicoloured.

2205	95dh. Type **452**	35	25
2206	95dh. Light plane over rifleman	35	25
2207	95dh. Couple running from biplane	35	25
2208	95dh. Biplane flying over men and boy	35	25
2209	95dh. Man trapped beneath fallen horse	35	25
2210	95dh. Soldiers and Libyans fighting (camel's head and neck in foreground)	35	25
2211	95dh. Soldiers surrounding fallen Libyan	35	25
2212	95dh. Man carrying boy	35	25
2213	95dh. Soldier with whip raised	35	25
2214	95dh. Robed man shouting	35	25
2215	95dh. Tank and battle scene	35	25
2216	95dh. Women fleeing mounted soliers	35	25
2217	95dh. Man being flogged and woman cradling head of fallen Libyan	35	25
2218	95dh. Soldiers and Libyans fighting (camels in background)	35	25
2219	95dh. Women and soldiers on quayside	35	25
2220	95dh. Deportees in two boats	35	25

Nos. 2205/20 were issued together, se-tenant, forming several composite designs.

453 Darghut

454 Armed Forces

1994. Mosques. Multicoloured.

2221	70dh. Type **453**	25	15
2222	70dh. Benghazi	25	15
2223	70dh. Kabao	25	15
2224	70dh. Gouzgu	25	15
2225	70dh. Siala	25	15
2226	70dh. El Kettani	25	15

1994. People's Authority Declaration. Multicoloured.

2227	80dh. Type **454**	30	20
2228	80dh. Truck, hand holding Green Book and ears of wheat	30	20
2229	80dh. Pipes on trailers, water pipeline and family	30	20
2230	80dh. Crowd with Green Books	30	20
2231	80dh. Col. Gaddafi	30	20
2232	80dh. Youths and produce	30	20

Nos. 2227/32 were issued together, se-tenant, forming a composite design.

455 Sun over Cemetery, National Flag, Dove and Footprints

457 Declaration and Flowers

456 Men with Weapons and Troops in Background

1994. Evacuation of Foreign Forces.

2233	**455** 65dh. multicoloured	25	15
2234	95dh. multicoloured	35	20

1994. Gaddafi Prize for Human Rights. Multicoloured.

2235	95dh. Type **456**	35	20
2236	95dh. Men with weapons	35	20
2237	95dh. President Nelson Mandela of South Africa	35	20
2238	95dh. President Gaddafi	35	20
2239	95dh. Amerindian meditating	35	20
2240	95dh. Warriors on horseback	35	20
2241	95dh. Amerindian chief	35	20
2242	95dh. Amerindian	35	20
2243	95dh. Riflemen and aircraft	35	20
2244	95dh. Bomber, women, fire and left page of book	35	20
2245	95dh. Right page of book and surgeon operating	35	20
2246	95dh. Surgeons operating	35	20
2247	95dh. Masked revolutionaries with flag	35	20
2248	95dh. Revolutionaries raising arms with flag	35	20
2249	95dh. Young boys with stones	35	20
2250	95dh. Revolutionaries, fire and troops	35	20

Nos. 2235/50 were issued together, se-tenant, forming a composite design.

1995. People's Authority Declaration. Multicoloured, colour of background given.

2251	**457** 100dh. yellow	35	20
2252	100dh. blue	35	20
2253	100dh. green	35	20

458 Emblem, Members' Flags and Map showing Member Countries

1995. 50th Anniv of Arab League. Multicoloured, frame colour given.

2254	**458** 200f. blue	70	45
2255	200f. green	70	45

459 Messaud Zentuti

1995. 60th Anniv of National Football Team. Designs showing players. Multicoloured.

2257	100dh. Type **459**	35	20
2258	100dh. Salem Shermit	35	20
2259	100dh. Ottoman Marfua	35	20
2260	100dh. Ghaleb Siala	35	20
2261	100dh. Team, 1935	35	20
2262	100dh. Senussi Mresila	35	20

Nos. 2257/62 were issued together, se-tenant, forming a composite design.

460 Dromedary

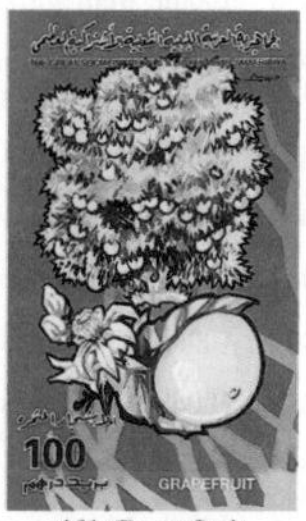

461 Grapefruit

1995. Libyan Zoo. Multicoloured.

2263	100dh. Type **460**	35	20
2264	100dh. Secretary bird	35	20
2265	100dh. African wild dog	35	20
2266	100dh. Oryx	35	20
2267	100dh. Baboon	35	20
2268	100dh. Golden jackal	35	20
2269	100dh. Crowned eagle	35	20
2270	100dh. Desert eagle owl ("Eagle Owl")	35	20
2271	100dh. Desert hedgehog	35	20
2272	100dh. Sand gerbil	35	20
2273	100dh. Addax	35	20
2274	100dh. Fennec fox	35	20
2275	100dh. Lanner falcon	35	20
2276	100dh. Desert wheatear	35	20
2277	100dh. Pin-tailed sandgrouse	35	20
2278	100dh. Jerboa	35	20

Nos. 2263/78 were issued together, se-tenant, the backgrounds forming a composite design.

1995. Fruit. Multicoloured.

2279	100dh. Type **461**	35	20
2280	100dh. Wild cherry	35	20
2281	100dh. Mulberry	35	20
2282	100dh. Strawberry	35	20
2283	100dh. Plum	35	20
2284	100dh. Pear	35	20
2285	100dh. Apricot	35	20
2286	100dh. Almond	35	20
2287	100dh. Prickly pear	35	20
2288	100dh. Lemon	35	20
2289	100dh. Peach	35	20
2290	100dh. Dates	35	20
2291	100dh. Olive	35	20
2292	100dh. Orange	35	20
2293	100dh. Fig	35	20
2294	100dh. Grape	35	20

Nos. 2279/94 were issued together, se-tenant, the backgrounds forming a composite design.

462 Students

1995. 26th Anniv of Revolution. Multicoloured.

2295	100dh. Type **462**	35	20
2296	100dh. Mosque, teacher and students	35	20
2297	100dh. President Gaddafi	35	20
2298	100dh. Laboratory workers	35	20
2299	100dh. Hospital patient, doctor examining child, and nurse	35	20
2300	100dh. Surgeons operating	35	20
2301	100dh. Cobblers and keyboard operator	35	20
2302	100dh. Sound engineers and musician	35	20
2303	100dh. Crane and apartment block	35	20
2304	100dh. Silos	35	20
2305	100dh. Oil rig platform	35	20
2306	100dh. Airplane and ships	35	20
2307	100dh. Animals grazing and farmer	35	20
2308	100dh. Pipeline	35	20
2309	100dh. Camels at trough and crops	35	20
2310	100dh. Crops and farm vehicle	35	20

Nos. 2295/2310 were issued together, se-tenant, forming a composite design.

463 Scout Badge and Wildlife

1995. Scouting. Multicoloured.

2311	250dh. Type **463**	85	55
2312	250dh. Badge, butterflies and scouts with animals (59 × 39 mm)	85	55
2313	250dh. Badge and scouts	85	55

Nos. 2311/13 were issued together, se-tenant, forming a composite design.

464 Warships and Rocket

1995. 9th Anniv of American Attack on Libya. Multicoloured.

2314	100dh. Type **464**	35	20
2315	100dh. Bombers, helicopters, warships and Libyans (59 × 49 mm)	35	20
2316	100dh. Bomber and woman holding baby	35	20

Nos. 2314/16 were issued together, se-tenant, forming a composite design.

465 Gaddafi on Horseback

466 Dromedary and Woman with Water Jars

1995. International Trade Fair, Tripoli. Multicoloured.

2317	100dh. Type **465**	35	20
2318	100dh. Horseman	35	20
2319	100dh. Horseman (horse galloping to right)	35	20
2320	100dh. Horsemen with whips (horiz)	35	20
2321	100dh. Horseman holding rifle (horiz)	35	20
2322	100dh. Horsewoman brandishing rifle in air (horiz)	35	20

1995. City of Ghadames. Multicoloured.

2324	100dh. Type **466**	35	20
2325	100dh. Making cheeses	35	20
2326	100dh. Woman holding jar	35	20
2327	100dh. Feeding chickens	35	20
2328	100dh. Spinning wool	35	20
2329	100dh. Woman in traditional costume	35	20
2330	100dh. Drying grain	35	20
2331	100dh. Milking goat	35	20
2332	100dh. Making shoes	35	20
2333	100dh. Weaving	35	20
2334	100dh. Engraving brass tabletops	35	20
2335	100dh. Harvesting dates	35	20
2336	100dh. Reading scriptures	35	20
2337	100dh. Potter	35	20
2338	100dh. Washing clothes in well	35	20
2339	100dh. Picking fruit	35	20

467 Family with Torch and National Flag

1995. Evacuation of Foreign Forces.

2340	**467** 50dh. multicoloured	20	10
2341	100dh. multicoloured	35	20
2342	200dh. multicoloured	70	45

468 Honeycomb and Bees on Flowers

1995. Arab Beekeepers' Association. Multicoloured, colour of border given.

2343	**468** 100dh. mauve	35	20
2344	100dh. lilac	35	20
2345	100dh. green	35	20

469 Stubbing out Cigarette and holding Rose

470 Dr. Mohamed Feituri

1995. World Health Day. Multicoloured, colour of central band given.

2346	**469** 100dh. yellow	35	20
2347	100dh. orange	35	20

1995.

2348	**470** 200dh. multicoloured	70	45

471 Gaddafi and Horsemen

1995. 84th Anniv of Deportation of Libyans to Italy. Multicoloured.

2349	100dh. Type **471**	35	20
2350	100dh. Horsemen	35	20
2351	100dh. Battle scene	35	20
2352	100dh. Bomber over battle scene	35	20
2353	100dh. Libyans with rifles	35	20
2354	100dh. Soldiers fighting with Libyans	35	20
2355	100dh. Soldiers with weapons and man on ground	35	20
2356	100dh. Soldiers with rifles and building in background	35	20
2357	100dh. Libyans	35	20
2358	100dh. Soldiers charging men on ground	35	20
2359	100dh. Soldiers shooting at horseman	35	20
2360	100dh. Soldiers pushing Libyan to ground	35	20
2361	100dh. Horsemen charging	35	20
2362	100dh. Horses falling to ground	35	20
2363	100dh. Children	35	20
2364	100dh. Deportees in boats	35	20

Nos. 2349/64 were issued together, se-tenant, forming a composite design.

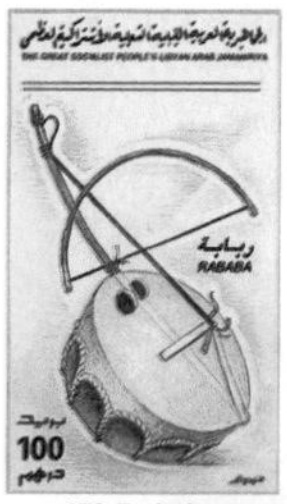

472 Rababa

473 Blue Door

1995. Musical Instruments. Multicoloured.

2365	100dh. Type **472**	35	20
2366	100dh. Nouba	35	20
2367	100dh. Clarinet	35	20
2368	100dh. Drums	35	20
2369	100dh. Magruna	35	20
2370	100dh. Zukra	35	20
2371	100dh. Zil	35	20
2372	100dh. Kaman	35	20
2373	100dh. Guitar	35	20
2374	100dh. Trumpet	35	20
2375	100dh. Tapla	35	20
2376	100dh. Gonga	35	20
2377	100dh. Saxophone	35	20
2378	100dh. Piano	35	20
2379	100dh. Ganoon	35	20
2380	100dh. Ood	35	20

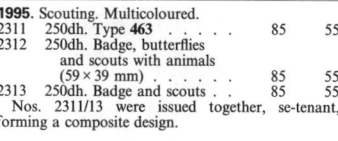

1995. Doors from Mizda. Multicoloured.

2381 100dh. Type **473** 35 20
2382 100dh. Door with arch detail 35 20
2383 100dh. Door made of logs 35 20
2384 100dh. Arched door 35 20
2385 100dh. Wide door with bolts 35 20

474 Sports within Olympic Rings

1995. Centenary of International Olympic Committee. Multicoloured, colour of face value given.

2386 **474** 100dh. black 35 20
2387 100dh. red 35 20

475 Baryonyx

1995. Prehistoric Animals. Multicoloured.

2388 100dh. Type **475** 35 20
2389 100dh. Oviraptor 35 20
2390 100dh. Stenonychosaurus 35 20
2391 100dh. Tenontosaurus 35 20
2392 100dh. Yangchuanosaurus 35 20
2393 100dh. Stegotetrabelodon (facing right) 35 20
2394 100dh. Stegotetrabelodon (facing left) 35 20
2395 100dh. Psittacosaurus 35 20
2396 100dh. Heterodontosaurus 35 20
2397 100dh. "Loxodonta atlantica" 35 20
2398 100dh. "Mammuthus africanavus" 35 20
2399 100dh. Erlikosaurus 35 20
2400 100dh. Cynognathus 35 20
2401 100dh. Plateosaurus 35 20
2402 100dh. Staurikosaurus 35 20
2403 100dh. Lystrosaurus 35 20

Nos. 2388/2403 were issued together, se-tenant, the backgrounds forming a composite design.

476 Child and Dinosaur walking with Stick

1995. Children's Day. Multicoloured.

2405 100dh. Type **476** 35 20
2406 100dh. Child on mammoth's back 35 20
2407 100dh. Child on way to school and tortoise under mushroom 35 20
2408 100dh. Dinosaur playing football 35 20
2409 100dh. Child pointing rifle at pteranodon 35 20

477 Helicopter, Soldier and Stone-thrower

1995. Palestinian "Intifada" Movement. Mult.

2410 100dh. Type **477** 35 20
2411 100dh. Dome of the Rock and Palestinian with flag 35 20
2412 100dh. Women with flag 35 20

Nos. 2410/12 were issued together, se-tenant, forming a composite design.

478 Airplane, Control Tower and Tailfin

1995. 50th Anniv of I.C.A.O. Multicoloured, colour of face value given.

2413 **478** 100dh. blue 35 20
2414 100dh. black 35 20

479 Headquarters, New York

480 "Iris germanica"

1995. 50th Anniv of U.N.O. Multicoloured, colour of background given.

2415 **479** 100dh. pink 35 20
2416 100dh. lilac 35 20

1995. Flowers. Multicoloured.

2417 200dh. Type **480** 35 20
2418 200dh. "Canna edulis" 35 20
2419 200dh. "Nerium oleander" 35 20
2420 200dh. Corn poppy ("Papaver rhoeas") 35 20
2421 200dh. Bird of Paradise flower ("Strelitzia reginae") 35 20
2422 200dh. "Amygdalus communis" 35 20

481 Open Hand

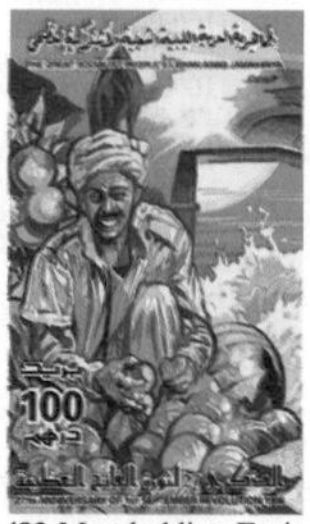

483 Man holding Fruit

482 Football

1996. People's Authority Declaration. Multicoloured.

2423 **481** 100dh. multicoloured 35 20
2424 150dh. multicoloured 50 30
2425 200dh. multicoloured 65 40

1996. Olympic Games, Atlanta, U.S.A. Multicoloured.

2426 100dh. Type **482** 35 20
2427 100dh. Long jumping 35 20
2428 100dh. Tennis 35 20
2429 100dh. Cycling 35 20
2430 100dh. Boxing 35 20
2431 100dh. Equestrian show jumping 35 20

Nos. 2426/31 were issued together, se-tenant, the background forming a composite design of the Games emblem.

1996. 27th Anniv of Revolution. Multicoloured.

2433 100dh. Type **483** 35 20
2434 100dh. Water flowing along chute and out of pipe 35 20
2435 100dh. Tractor, water and women with flowers 35 20
2436 100dh. Man working on pipe by water 35 20
2437 100dh. Man sewing 35 20
2438 100dh. Woman textile worker 35 20
2439 100dh. President Gaddafi in white shirt and red cape 35 20
2440 100dh. Women laboratory workers 35 20
2441 100dh. Anatomy instruction and man using microscope 35 20
2442 100dh. Child holding hand to face 35 20
2443 100dh. Woman praying before open Koran 35 20
2444 100dh. Man weaving 35 20
2445 100dh. Two aircraft 35 20
2446 100dh. Man on camel, liner and dish aerial 35 20
2447 100dh. Stern of liner and television camera 35 20
2448 100dh. Woman using microphone and woman being filmed 35 20

Nos. 2433/48 were issued together, se-tenant, forming a composite design.

484 Bomb Exploding

1996. 10th Anniv of American Attack on Libya. Multicoloured.

2449 100dh. Type **484** 35 20
2450 100dh. Man with raised arms 35 20
2451 100dh. Woman carrying child 35 20
2452 100dh. Injured man on ground and fighter plane 35 20
2453 100dh. Fireman hosing down burning car 35 20
2454 100dh. Exploding plane 35 20
2455 100dh. Head of President Gaddafi 35 20
2456 100dh. Airplane bombing tented camp 35 20
2457 100dh. Rescuers helping two women 35 20
2458 100dh. Man with bandaged head and hand 35 20
2459 100dh. Woman with hankerchief to mouth 35 20
2460 100dh. Stretcher bearers 35 20
2461 100dh. Explosion and man being carried away 35 20
2462 100dh. Explosion and man with injured hand 35 20
2463 100dh. Rescuers helping injured mother with baby 35 20
2464 100dh. Burning car and helpers tending injured boy 35 20

Nos. 2449/64 were issued together, se-tenant, forming a composite design.

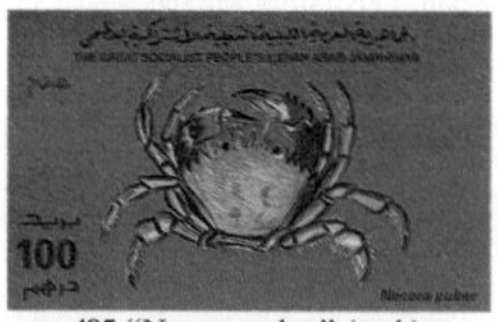

485 "Necora puber" (crab)

1996. Crustaceans. Multicoloured.

2465 100dh. Type **485** 35 20
2466 100dh. "Lissa chiragra" (crab) 35 20
2467 100dh. Rock lobster ("Palinurus elephas") 35 20
2468 100dh. "Scyllarus arctus" 35 20
2469 100dh. Green crab ("Carcinus maenas") 35 20
2470 100dh. Helmet crab ("Calappa granulata") 35 20
2471 100dh. "Parapenaeus longirostris" (prawn) 35 20
2472 100dh. Norway lobster ("Nephrops norvegicus") 35 20
2473 100dh. "Eriphia verrucosa" (crab) 35 20
2474 100dh. Edible crab ("Cancer pagurus") 35 20
2475 100dh. "Penaeus kerathurus" (prawn) 35 20
2476 100dh. Mantis shrimp ("Squilla mantis") 35 20
2477 100dh. Spider crab ("Maja squinado") 35 20
2478 100dh. "Pilumnus hirtellus" (crab) 35 20
2479 100dh. "Pagurus alatus" (crab) 35 20
2480 100dh. "Macropodia tenuirostris" 35 20

Nos. 2465/80 were issued together, se-tenant, the backgrounds forming a composite design.

486 Mats

487 Woman kneeling over Boy

1996. Maghreb Handicrafts Day. Basketwork. Multicoloured.

2481 100dh. Type **486** 35 20
2482 100dh. Lidded storage vessel 35 20
2483 100dh. Bowl 35 20
2484 100dh. Mug and teapot 35 20
2485 100dh. Box with open lid 35 20
2486 100dh. Bird's-eye view of dish 35 20
2487 100dh. Pot with wide base and mouth and narrower neck 35 20
2488 100dh. Lidded pot with carrying handle 35 20
2489 100dh. Bulbous bottle-shaped carrier 35 20
2490 100dh. Large dish 35 20
2491 100dh. Oval dish with well in centre 35 20
2492 100dh. Straight-sided bottle-shaped carrier 35 20
2493 100dh. Vessel with double carrying handles and open lid 35 20
2494 100dh. Dish on stand 35 20
2495 100dh. Pot with wide base and narrow mouth 35 20
2496 100dh. Bag with lid 35 20

1996. 85th Anniv of Deportation of Libyans to Italy. Multicoloured.

2497 100dh. Type **487** 35 20
2498 100dh. Horseman leading prisoner 35 20
2499 100dh. President Gaddafi wearing turban 35 20
2500 100dh. Old man holding stick in camp 35 20
2501 100dh. Man being flogged 35 20
2502 100dh. Horseman, soldiers and crowd wearing fezzes 35 20
2503 100dh. Prisoner, advocate and man in tricolour sash 35 20
2504 100dh. Family and soldier 35 20
2505 100dh. Soldiers guarding prisoners (boy at front) 35 20
2506 100dh. Soldiers escorting woman on camel and man on donkey 35 20
2507 100dh. Prisoners being escorted through street 35 20
2508 100dh. Prisoners in boat 35 20
2509 100dh. President Gaddafi in white embroided shirt with open hand 35 20
2510 100dh. Group of prisoners including man with raised arm 35 20
2511 100dh. Horsemen charging and soldiers 35 20
2512 100dh. Horseman with rifle 35 20

Nos. 2497/2512 were issued together, se-tenant, forming several composite designs.

488 Bay

1996. Horses. Multicoloured.

2513 100dh. Type **488** 35 20
2514 100dh. Light brown horse under tree (branches at right of stamp) 35 20
2515 100dh. Light brown horse by lake under tree (branch at left) 35 20
2516 100dh. Dark brown horse (edge of lake at left) 35 20
2517 100dh. Black horse with hoof raised 35 20
2518 100dh. Chestnut horse 35 20
2519 100dh. Grey horse running 35 20
2520 100dh. Piebald 35 20
2521 100dh. Head of grey and tail of black horses 35 20
2522 100dh. Head of black and tail of chestnut horses 35 20
2523 100dh. Head and rump of chestnut horses 35 20
2524 100dh. Head of chestnut horse with white mane 35 20
2525 100dh. Head of black horse and parts of three other horses 35 20

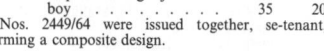

2526	100dh. Head of chestnut horse with blond mane and parts of three other horses	35	20
2527	100dh. Head of dark brown horse and parts of three other horses	35	20
2528	100dh. Head of dark brown and part of chestnut horses	35	20

Nos. 2513/28 were issued together, se-tenant, forming a composite design.

489 Camel

490 Photographer, Newspapers and Computer

1996. Camels. Multicoloured.

2529	200dh. Type **489**	65	40
2530	200dh. Head of camel	65	40
2531	200dh. Dark brown dromedary	65	40
2532	200dh. Long-haired Bactrian camel	65	40
2533	200dh. Light brown Bactrian camel	65	40
2534	200dh. Brown Bactrian camel with white stripe and tail	65	40

Nos. 2529/34 were issued together, se-tenant, forming a composite design.

1996. The Press and Information. Multicoloured.

2535	100dh. Type **490**	35	20
2536	200dh. Television, control desk, musicians, computer and dish aerial	65	40

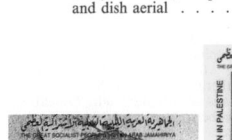

491 "Mene rhombea"

492 Palestinian Flag and Hands holding up Stones

1996. Fossils. Multicoloured.

2537	200dh. Type **491**	65	40
2538	200dh. "Mesodon macrocephalus"	65	40
2539	200dh. "Eyron arctiformis"	65	40
2540	200dh. Stegosaurus	65	40
2541	200dh. Pteranodon	65	40
2542	200dh. Allosaurus	65	40

1996. Palestinian "Intifada" Movement.

2543 **492**	100dh. multicoloured	35	20
2544	150dh. multicoloured	50	30
2545	200dh. multicoloured	65	40

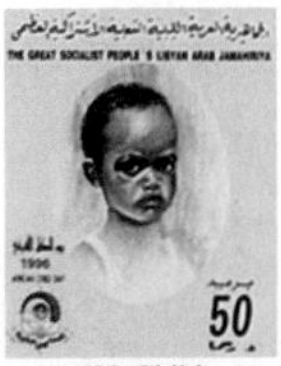
493 Child

494 Cat

1996. African Child Day. Multicoloured.

2546	50dh. Type **493**	10	10
2547	150dh. Type **493**	40	25
2548	200dh. Mother and child	50	35

1996. Children's Day. Cats. Multicoloured.

2549	100dh. Type **494**	25	15
2550	100dh. Tabby (back view with head turned)	25	15
2551	100dh. Colourpoint (black and white)	25	15
2552	100dh. Tabby adult and kitten	25	15
2553	100dh. Tortoiseshell white (sitting)	25	15

495 Family and Tower Block

1996. World Family Day. Multicoloured.

2554	150dh. Type **495**	40	25
2555	150dh. Family and car parked by palm trees	40	25
2556	200dh. Family, symbolic globe and flowers (45 × 26 mm)	50	35

Nos. 2554/6 were issued together, se-tenant, forming a composite design.

496 Mohamed Kamel el-Hammali

1996. Libyan Teachers. Multicoloured.

2557	100dh. Type **496**	25	15
2558	100dh. Mustafa Abdalla ben-Amer	25	15
2559	100dh. Mohamed Messaud Fesheka	25	15
2560	100dh. Kairi Mustafa Serraj	25	15
2561	100dh. Muftah el-Majri	25	15
2562	100dh. Mohamed Hadi Arafa	25	15

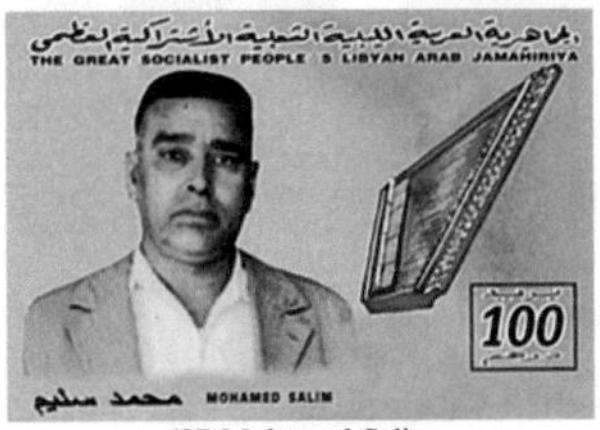
497 Mohamed Salim

1996. Libyan Singers. Multicoloured.

2563	100dh. Type **497**	25	15
2564	100dh. Mohamed M. Sayed Bumedyen	25	15
2565	100dh. Otman Najim	25	15
2566	100dh. Mahmud Sherif	25	15
2567	100dh. Mohamed Ferjani Marghani	25	15
2568	100dh. Mohamed Kabazi	25	15

498 Snake

1996. Reptiles. Multicoloured.

2569	100dh. Type **498**	25	15
2570	100dh. Diamond-back snake beside river	25	15
2571	100dh. Turtle on water (segmented shell and large flippers)	25	15
2572	100dh. Snake wrapped around tree branch	25	15
2573	100dh. Brown lizard on tree trunk	25	15
2574	100dh. Coiled snake with head raised and mouth open	25	15
2575	100dh. Snake with head raised beside water	25	15
2576	100dh. Turtle on water (flat shell, pointed snout and small flippers)	25	15
2577	100dh. Green lizard on tree trunk	25	15
2578	100dh. Snake with wavy pattern on ground	25	15
2579	100dh. Snake with horns	25	15
2580	100dh. Chameleon	25	15
2581	100dh. Tortoise on ground (facing right)	25	15
2582	100dh. Snake on rock with head raised	25	15
2583	100dh. Tortoise on ground (facing left)	25	15
2584	100dh. Grey lizard on rock	25	15

Nos. 2569/84 were issued together, se-tenant, forming a composite design.

499 Mirror and Clothes Brush

1996. International Trade Fair, Tripoli. Each silver, pink and black.

2585	100dh. Type **499**	25	15
2586	100dh. Decanter on tray	25	15
2587	100dh. Two round-bottomed flasks	25	15
2588	100dh. Two long-necked flasks	25	15
2589	100dh. Covered bowl	25	15
2590	100dh. Backs of hairbrush and mirror	25	15

500 Gaddafi and Symbolic Scenes

501 Scouts and Stamp Album

1997. People's Authority Declaration.

2591 **500**	100dh. multicoloured	25	15
2592	200dh. multicoloured	25	15
2593	300dh. multicoloured	25	15

1997. Postal Savings Bank. Multicoloured.

2594	50dh. Type **501**	10	10
2595	50dh. Two Girl Guides and albums	10	10
2596	100dh. Bank books and butterflies	25	15

Nos. 2594/6 were issued together, se-tenant, forming a composite design.

502 Scientist with Test Tubes

503 Death enveloping Man's Head

1997. World Health Day. Multicoloured.

2597	50dh. Type **502**	10	10
2598	50dh. Scientist at microscope	10	10
2599	100dh. Doctor and nurse examining baby	25	15

Nos. 2597/9 were issued together, se-tenant, forming a composite design.

1997. Anti-drugs Campaign.

2600 **503**	100dh. multicoloured	25	15
2601	150dh. multicoloured	40	25
2602	200dh. multicoloured	50	35

504 Library

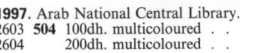

1997. Arab National Central Library.

2603 **504**	100dh. multicoloured	25	15
2604	200dh. multicoloured	50	35

505 Dancer and Local Crafts

1997. Arab Tourism Year.

2606 **505**	100dh. multicoloured	25	15
2607	200dh. multicoloured	50	25
2608	250dh. multicoloured	65	45

CONCESSIONAL LETTER POST

1929. No. CL227 of Italy optd **LIBIA**.

CL68 CL **93**	10c. blue	22·00	17·00

1941. No. CL267 of Italy optd **LIBIA**.

CL123 CL **109**	10c. brown	8·50	8·50

EXPRESS LETTER STAMPS

A. ITALIAN ISSUES

1915. Express Letter stamps of Italy optd **Libia**.

E17 E **35**	25c. pink	19·00	8·50
E18 E **41**	30c. blue and pink	5·25	22·00

E **8**

1921.

E34 E **8**	30c. red and blue	1·70	5·25
E35	50c. brown and red	2·50	6·75
E42	60c. brown and red	5·25	10·50
E43	2l. red and blue	8·50	21·00

Nos. E34 and E43 are inscribed "EXPRES".

1922. Nos. E17/18 surch.

E40 E **35**	60c. on 25c. pink	9·50	11·00
E41 E **41**	1l.60 on 30c. blue and pink	11·00	23·00

1926. Nos. E42/3 surch.

E62 E **8**	70 on 60c. brown and red	5·25	10·50
E64	1l.25 on 60c. brown and red	4·25	1·50
E63	2.50 on 2l. red and blue	8·50	21·00

B. INDEPENDENT ISSUES

1966. Design similar to T **74** inscr "EXPRES".

E368	90m. red and green	2·30	1·30

DESIGN—HORIZ: 90m. Saracen Castle, Zuela.

OFFICIAL STAMPS

1952. Optd **Official** in English and Arabic.

O192 **23**	2m. brown	40	35
O193	4m. grey	65	50
O194	5m. green	4·50	1·60
O195	8m. red	2·50	75
O196	10m. violet	3·75	1·25
O197	12m. red	6·75	2·50
O198	20m. blue	13·50	5·25
O199	25m. brown	17·00	6·75

PARCEL POST STAMPS

Unused prices are for complete pairs, used prices for a half.

1915. Parcel Post stamps of Italy optd **LIBIA** on each half of the stamp.

P17 P **53**	5c. brown	85	3·50
P18	10c. blue	85	3·50
P19	20c. black	1·00	3·50
P20	25c. red	1·00	3·50
P21	50c. orange	1·90	3·50
P22	1l. violet	1·90	5·25
P23	2l. green	2·75	5·25
P24	3l. yellow	3·50	5·25
P25	4l. grey	3·50	5·25
P26	10l. purple	43·00	39·00
P27	12l. brown	85·00	£110
P28	15l. green	85·00	£140
P29	20l. purple	£110	£150

1927. Parcel Post stamps of Italy optd **LIBIA** on each half of the stamp.

P62 P **92**	5c. brown	£9000	
P63	10c. blue	2·10	3·50
P64	25c. red	2·10	3·50
P65	30c. blue	35	1·70
P66	50c. orange	48·00	£100
P67	60c. red	35	1·70
P68	1l. violet	19·00	50·00
P69	2l. green	22·00	50·00
P70	3l. bistre	1·00	4·25
P71	4l. black	1·00	7·75
P72	10l. mauve	£180	£200
P73	20l. purple	£180	£250

POSTAGE DUE STAMPS
A. ITALIAN ISSUES

1915. Postage Due stamps of Italy optd **Libia**.

D17	D **12**	5c. mauve and orange	1·40	4·25
D18		10c. mauve and orange	1·50	2·50
D19		20c. mauve and orange	2·10	3·50
D20		30c. mauve and orange	2·50	4·25
D21		40c. mauve and orange	3·75	6·00
D22		50c. mauve and orange	2·50	3·50
D23		60c. mauve and orange	4·00	7·75
D24		60c. brown and orange	60·00	85·00
D25		1l. mauve and blue	2·50	7·75
D26		2l. mauve and blue	38·00	50·00
D27		5l. mauve and blue	50·00	75·00

1934. Postage Due stamps of Italy optd **LIBIA**.

D68	D **141**	5c. brown	10	2·10
D69		10c. blue	10	2·10
D70		20c. red	1·00	1·20
D71		25c. green	1·00	1·20
D72		30c. red	1·00	4·25
D73		40c. brown	1·00	3·00
D74		50c. violet	1·20	35
D75		60c. blue	1·50	10·50
D76	D **142**	1l. orange	1·40	35
D77		2l. green	38·00	10·50
D78		5l. violet	60·00	21·00
D79		10l. blue	10·50	31·00
D80		20l. red	10·50	41·00

B. INDEPENDENT ISSUES

1951. Postage Due stamps of Cyrenaica optd. (a) For use in Cyrenaica. Optd as T **20**.

D144	D **26**	2m. brown	5·00	5·00
D145		4m. green	5·00	5·00
D146		8m. red	6·75	6·25
D147		10m. orange	7·50	6·25
D148		20m. yellow	11·00	10·00
D149		40m. blue	30·00	20·00
D150		100m. black	40·00	23·00

(b) For use in Tripolitania. Surch as T **21**.

D161	D **26**	1mal. on 2m. brown	5·50	5·00
D162		2mal. on 4m. green	7·50	5·50
D163		4mal. on 8m. red	12·50	10·00
D164		10mal. on 20m. yellow	27·00	20·00
D165		20mal. on 40m. blue	45·00	35·00

D **25**

D **53** Government Building, Tripoli 1952.

1951.

D188	D **25**	2m. brown	65	25
D189		5m. green	95	50
D190		10m. red	2·25	95
D191		50m. blue	7·50	2·25

1964.

D296	D **53**	2m. brown	10	10
D297		6m. green	20	10
D298		10m. red	70	45
D299		50m. blue	1·25	85

D **185** Men in Boat

1976. Ancient Mosaics. Multicoloured.

D725	5dh. Type D **185**	10	10
D726	10dh. Head of Medusa	10	10
D727	20dh. Peacock	10	10
D728	50dh. Fish	80	25

LIECHTENSTEIN Pt. 8

A small independent principality lying between Austria and Switzerland.

1912. 100 heller = 1 krone.
1921. 100 rappen = 1 franc (Swiss).

1 Prince John II

1912.

4	**1**	5h. green	8·75	6·00
2		10h. red	40·00	6·00
3		25h. blue	40·00	20·00

2

3

1917.

7	**2**	3h. violet	75	55
8		5h. green	75	55
9	**3**	10h. purple	95	85
10		15h. brown	95	75
11		20h. green	95	85
12		25h. blue	95	75

1918. 60th Anniv of Prince John's Accession. As T **3** but dated "1858–1918" in upper corners.

13	**3**	20h. green	60	1·00

1920. Optd with a scroll pattern.

14	**2**	5h. green	1·60	4·50
15	**3**	10h. purple	1·60	4·50
16		25h. blue	1·60	4·50

1920. Surch.

17	**2**	40h. on 3h. violet	1·60	4·50
18	**3**	1k. on 15h. brown	1·60	4·50
19		2½k. on 20h. green	1·60	4·50

7

8 Castle of Vaduz

1920. Imperf.

20	**7**	5h. bistre	15	2·40
21		10h. orange	15	2·40
22		15h. blue	15	2·40
23		20h. brown	15	2·40
24		25h. green	15	2·40
25		30h. grey	15	2·40
26		40h. red	15	2·40
27	**8**	1k. blue	15	2·40

9 Prince John I

10 Arms

1920. Perf.

28	**7**	5h. bistre	10	35
29		10h. orange	10	35
30		15h. blue	10	35
31		20h. brown	10	35
32	–	25h. green	10	35
33	**7**	30h. grey	10	35
34	–	40h. purple	10	35
35	–	50h. green	10	35
36	–	60h. brown	10	35
37	–	80h. pink	10	35
38	**8**	1k. lilac	20	55
39	–	2k. blue	25	60
40	**9**	5k. black	40	70
41	–	7½k. grey	55	90
42	**10**	10k. brown	60	1·00

DESIGNS—As Type **8**: 25h. St. Mamertus Chapel; 40h. Gutenberg Castle; 50h. Courtyard, Vaduz Castle; 60h. Red House, Vaduz; 80h. Church Tower, Schaan; 2k. Bendern. As Type **9**: 7½k. Prince John II.

11 Madonna

14 Arms

15 St. Mamertus Chapel

16 Vaduz

1920. Prince John's 80th Birthday. Imperf or perf.

43	**11**	50h. green	50	1·80
44		80h. red	50	1·80
45		2k. blue	50	1·80

1921. Surch **2 Rp.** and bars.

47	**7**	2r. on 10h. orange (No. 21)	40	13·50

1921.

47a	**14**	2r. yellow	65	6·00
48		2½r. brown	55	6·00
49		3r. orange	65	5·00
50		5r. green	6·50	85
51		7½r. blue	7·25	20·00
65		10r. green	14·00	3·00
53		13r. brown	5·00	43·00
54		15r. violet	10·50	11·50
55	**15**	20r. black and violet	30·00	85
56	–	25r. black and red	1·90	3·00
57	–	30r. black and green	38·00	5·75
66	–	30r. black and blue	9·75	90
58	–	35r. black and brown	2·75	6·25
59	–	40r. black and blue	4·75	2·50
60	–	50r. black and green	5·75	3·25
61	–	80r. black and grey	16·00	38·00
62	**16**	1f. black and red	31·00	23·00

DESIGNS—As Type **15**: 25r. Vaduz Castle; 30r. Bendern; 35r. Prince John II; 40r. Church Tower at Schaan; 50r. Gutenberg Castle; 80r. Red House, Vaduz.

1924. Surch.

63	**14**	5 on 7½r. blue	75	1·10
64		10 on 13r. brown	55	1·60

19 Vine-dresser

21 Government Bldg. and Church, Vaduz

1924.

67	**19**	2½r. mauve and green	85	3·50
68		5r. blue and brown	1·20	55
69		7½r. brown and green	90	4·00
70	–	10r. green	8·50	50
71	**19**	15r. green and purple	4·75	17·00
72	–	20r. red	20·00	60
73	**21**	1½f. blue	60·00	50·00

DESIGN—As Type **19**: 10, 20r. Castle of Vaduz.

22 Prince John II

23

1925. 85th Birthday of Prince John.

74	**22**	10+5r. green	21·00	9·25
75		20+5r. red	15·00	9·25
76		30+5r. blue	4·75	2·00

1927. 87th Birthday of Prince. Arms multicoloured.

77	**23**	10+5r. green	5·75	13·50
78		20+5r. purple	5·75	13·50
79		30+5r. blue	5·50	12·50

24 Salvage Work by Austrian soldiers

1928. Flood Relief.

80	–	5r.+5r. brown and purple	13·50	18·00
81	–	10r.+10r. brown and green	13·00	16·00
82	**24**	20r.+10r. brown and red	13·00	16·00
83	–	30r.+10r. brown and blue	8·75	16·00

DESIGNS: 5r. Railway bridge between Buchs and Schaan; 10r. Village of Ruggell; 30r. Salvage work by Swiss soldiers.

26 Prince John II, 1858–1928

1928. 70th Anniv of Accession of Prince John II.

84	–	10r. green and brown	2·10	2·30
85	–	20r. green and red	4·75	5·75
86	–	30r. green and blue	11·00	13·00
87	–	60r. green and mauve	35·00	65·00
88	**26**	1f.20 blue	36·00	65·00
89		1f.50 brown	65·00	£160
90		2f. red	65·00	£160
91		5f. green	65·00	£200

DESIGN—VERT: 10r. to 60r. Prince John II.

28 Prince Francis I

31 Girl Vintager

32 Prince Francis I and Princess Elsa

34 Monoplane over Vaduz Castle and Rhine Valley

1929. Accession of Prince Francis I.

92	–	10r. green	50	1·60
93	**28**	20r. red	75	2·10
94	–	30r. blue	1·10	12·00
95	–	70r. brown	10·50	60·00

PORTRAITS: 10r. Prince Francis I as a boy; 30r. Princess Elsa; 70r. Prince Francis and Princess Elsa.

1930.

96	**31**	3r. red	45	65
97	–	5r. green	1·00	75
98	–	10r. lilac	1·00	50
99	–	20r. red	21·00	80
100	–	25r. green	5·00	18·00
101	–	30r. blue	5·00	1·10
102	–	35r. green	6·25	10·50
103	–	40r. brown	6·25	3·50
104	–	50r. black	60·00	9·50
105	–	60r. green	60·00	18·00
106	–	90r. purple	60·00	£100
107	–	1f.20 brown	80·00	£160
108	–	1f.50 blue	34·00	42·00
109	**32**	2f. brown and green	48·00	75·00

DESIGNS—VERT: 5r. Mt. Three Sisters–Edelweiss; 10r. Alpine cattle-alpine roses; 20r. Courtyard of Vaduz Castle; 25r. Mt. Naafkopf; 30r. Valley of Samina; 35r. Rofenberg Chapel; 40r. St. Mamertus' Chapel; 50r. Kurhaus at Malbun; 60r. Gutenberg Castle; 90r. Schellenberg Monastery; 1f.20, Vaduz Castle; 1f.50, Pfaelzer club hut.

1930. Air.

110	–	15r. brown	4·50	6·00
111	–	20r. green	11·50	12·00
112	–	25r. brown	5·75	19·00
113	–	35r. blue	9·00	13·00
114	**34**	45r. green	25·00	44·00
115		1f. purple	40·00	30·00

DESIGNS—VERT: 15, 20r. Biplane over snowy mountain peak. HORIZ: 25, 35r. Biplane over Vaduz Castle.

35 Airship "Graf Zeppelin" over Alps

1931. Air.

116	**35**	1f. green	28·00	24·00
117	–	2f. blue	80·00	£225

DESIGN: 2f. Airship "Graf Zeppelin" (different).

37 Princess Elsa

38 Mt. Naafkopf

39 Prince Francis I

1932. Youth Charities.

118	–	10r.+5r. green	14·50	22·00
119	**37**	20r.+5r. red	15·00	23·00
120	–	30r.+10r. blue	17·00	27·00

DESIGNS—22 × 29 mm: 10r. Arms of Liechtenstein. As Type **37**: 30r. Prince Francis.

1933.

121	**38**	25r. orange	£190	60·00
122	–	90r. green	6·50	48·00
123	–	1f.20 brown	48·00	£180

DESIGNS: 90r. Gutenberg Castle; 1f.20, Vaduz Castle.

1933. Prince Francis's 80th Birthday.

124	**39**	10r. violet	13·00	33·00
125		20r. red	13·00	33·00
126		30r. blue	13·00	33·00

40

41 "Three Sisters"

42 Vaduz Castle

44 Prince Francis I

45 Arms of Liechtenstein

46 Golden Eagle

1933.

127	**40**	3r. red	20	45
128	**41**	5r. green	2·50	45
129	–	10r. violet	65	35
130	–	15r. orange	25	85
131	–	20r. red	60	45
132	–	25r. brown	15·00	40·00
133	–	30r. blue	3·25	85
134	–	35r. green	85	3·50
135	–	40r. brown	95	2·40
136	**42**	50r. brown	17·00	11·00
137	–	60r. purple	1·70	4·00
138	–	90r. green	5·25	13·50
139	–	1f.20 blue	1·90	12·50
140	–	1f.50 brown	2·30	16·00
141	–	2f. brown	42·00	£130
142	**44**	3f. blue	55·00	£130
143	**45**	5f. purple	£300	£650

DESIGNS—As Type **41**: 10r. Schaan Church; 15r. Bendern am Rhein; 20r. Town Hall, Vaduz; 25r. Saminatal. As Type **44**: 2f. Princess Elsa. As Type **42**: 30r. Saminatal (different); 35r. Schellenberg ruins; 40r. Government Building, Vaduz; 60r. Vaduz Castle (different); 90r. Gutenberg Castle; 1f.20, Pfalzer Hut, Bettlerjoch; 1f.50, Valuna.

See also Nos. **MS**144, **MS**153, 174, 225/6 and 258.

1934. Vaduz First Liechtenstein Philatelic Exhibition. Sheet 105 × 125 mm.

MS144 **45**	5f. chocolate	£1100	£1700

1934. Air.

145	**46**	10r. violet	5·25	13·50
146	–	15r. orange	13·00	30·00
147	–	20r. red	14·00	30·00
148	–	30r. blue	14·00	30·00
149	–	50r. green	20·00	25·00

DESIGNS: 10r. to 20r. Golden eagles in flight; 30r. Ospreys in nest; 50r. Golden eagle on rock.

1935. Air. No. 115 surch **60 Rp.**

150	**34**	60r. on 1f. purple	21·00	32·00

49 "Hindenburg" and Schaan Church

1936. Air.

151	**49**	1f. red	26·00	55·00
152	–	2f. violet	22·00	55·00

DESIGN: 2f. "Graf Zeppelin" over Schaan Airport.

1936. 2nd Liechtenstein Philatelic Exhibition and Opening of Postal Museum, Vaduz. Sheet 165 × 119 mm containing two each of Nos. 131 and 133.

MS153	Sold at 2fr.	35·00	35·00

51 Masescha am Triesenberg

52 Schellenberg Castle

1937.

154	–	3r. brown	20	13·50
155	**51**	5r. green and buff	15	20
156	–	10r. violet and buff	15	15
157	–	15r. black and buff	40	50
158	–	20r. red and buff	25	30
159	–	25r. brown and buff	60	2·20
160	–	30r. blue and buff	1·40	55
161	**52**	40r. green and buff	1·40	1·20
162	–	50c. brown and buff	95	1·80
163	–	60r. purple and buff	1·40	1·70
164	–	90r. violet and buff	7·50	8·75
165	–	1f. purple and buff	1·30	8·25
166	–	1f.20 brown and buff	6·00	11·50
167	–	1f.50 grey and buff	3·00	12·00

DESIGNS—As Type **51**: 3r. Schalun ruins; 10r. Knight and Vaduz Castle; 15r. Upper Saminatal; 20r. Church and Bridge at Bendern; 25r. Steg Chapel and girl. As Type **52**: 30r. Farmer and orchard, Triesenberg; 50r. Knight and Gutenberg Castle; 60r. Baron von Brandis and Vaduz Castle; 90r. "Three Sisters" mountain; 1f. Boundary-stone on Luziensteig; 1f.20, Minstrel and Gutenberg Castle; 1f.50, Lawena (Schwarzhorn).

53 Roadmakers at Triesenberg

1937. Workers' Issue.

168	–	10r. mauve	80	45
169	**53**	20r. red	1·10	75
170	–	30r. blue	1·50	1·60
171	–	50r. brown	95	2·10

DESIGNS: 10r. Bridge at Malbun; 30r. Binnen Canal Junction; 50r. Francis Bridge, near Planken.

1938. 3rd Liechtenstein Philatelic Exhibition, Vaduz. Sheet 100 × 135 mm containing stamps as No. 175 in different colour in a block of four.

MS173 **54**	50r. blue	35·00	21·00

1938. Death of Prince Francis I.

174	**44**	3f. black on yellow	6·25	49·00

54 Josef Rheinberger

55 Black-headed Gulls

1939. Birth Centenary of Rheinberger (composer).

175	**54**	50r. grey	55	2·75

1939. Air.

176	–	10r. violet (Barn swallows)	25	50
177	**55**	15r. orange	40	1·40
178	–	20r. red (Herring gull)	80	45
179	–	30r. blue (Common buzzard)	80	1·10
180	–	50r. green (Northern goshawk)	2·75	1·70
181	–	1f. red (Lammergeier)	2·20	11·00
182	–	2f. violet Lammergeier	1·90	11·50

56 Offering Homage to First Prince

1939. Homage to Francis Joseph II.

183	**56**	20r. red	75	1·20
184		30r. blue	75	1·20
185		50r. green	75	1·30

57 Francis Joseph II

1939.

186	–	2f. green on cream	5·00	25·00
187	–	3f. violet on cream	4·50	25·00
188	**57**	5f. brown on cream	10·50	21·00

DESIGNS: 2f. Cantonal Arms; 3f. Arms of Principality.

58 Prince John when a Child

1940. Birth Centenary of Prince John II.

189	**58**	20r. red	50	1·40
190	–	30r. blue	70	2·20
191	–	50r. green	1·10	5·75
192	–	1f. violet	6·50	43·00
193	–	1f.50 black	5·25	42·00
194	–	3f. brown	3·50	12·00

DESIGNS—As Type **58**: Portraits of Prince John in early manhood (30r.), in middle age (50r.) and in later life (1f.), and Memorial tablet (1f.50). As Type **44**: 3f. Framed portrait of Prince John II.

60 Wine Press

1941. Agricultural Propaganda.

195	–	10r. brown	45	40
196	**60**	20r. purple	65	75
197	–	30r. blue	75	1·40
198	–	50r. green	2·30	10·50
199	–	90r. violet	2·30	11·50

DESIGNS: 10r. Harvesting maize; 30r. Sharpen-ing scythe; 50r. Milkmaid and cow; 90r. Girl wearing traditional headdress.

61 Madonna and Child

62 Prince Hans Adam

1941.

200	**61**	10f. purple on stone	33·00	70·00

1941. Princes (1st issue).

201	**62**	20r. red	35	1·20
202	–	30r. blue (Wenzel)	65	1·90
203	–	1f. grey (Anton Florian)	1·90	11·00
204	–	1f.50 green (Joseph)	1·90	11·50

See also Nos. 210/13 and 217/20.

63 St. Lucius preaching

1942. 600th Anniv of Separation from Estate of Montfort.

205	**63**	20r. red on pink	75	65
206	–	30r. blue on pink	70	1·40
207	–	50r. green on pink	1·60	5·00
208	–	1f. brown on pink	2·00	9·75
209	–	2f. violet on pink	2·30	9·75

DESIGNS: 30r. Count of Montfort replanning Vaduz; 50r. Counts of Montfort-Werdenberg and Sargans signing treaty; 1f. Battle of Gutenberg; 2f. Homage to Prince of Liechtenstein.

64 Prince John Charles

65 Princess Georgina

1942. Princes (2nd issue).

210	**64**	20r. pink	25	75
211	–	30r. blue (Francis Joseph I)	45	1·40
212	–	1f. purple (Alois I)	1·40	9·50
213	–	1f.50 brown (John I)	1·40	9·50

1943. Marriage of Prince Francis Joseph II and Countess Georgina von Wildczek.

214	–	10r. purple	50	70
215	**65**	20r. red	50	1·10
216	–	30r. blue	50	1·10

PORTRAITS—VERT: 10r. Prince Francis Joseph II. HORIZ (44 × 25 mm): 30r. Prince and Princess.

66 Alois II

67 Marsh Land

1943. Princes (3rd issue).

217	**66**	20r. brown	50	50
218	–	30r. blue	80	95
219	–	1f. brown	1·30	5·50
220	–	1f.50 green	1·30	5·50

PORTRAITS: 30r. John II; 1f. Francis I; 1f.50, Francis Joseph II.

1943. Completion of Irrigation Canal.

221	**67**	10r. violet	20	35
222	–	30r. blue	35	1·70
223	–	50r. green	65	6·25
224	–	2f. brown	1·60	9·75

DESIGNS: 30r. Draining the canal; 50r. Ploughing reclaimed land; 2f. Harvesting crops.

1943. Castles. As T **41**.

225	10r. grey (Vaduz)	40	55
226	20r. brown (Gutenberg)	35	70

69 Planken

70 Prince Francis Joseph II

1944. Various designs. Buff backgrounds.

227	**69**	3r. brown	20	20
228	–	5r. green (Bendern)	20	15
228a	–	5r. brown (Bendern)	10·00	45
229	–	10r. grey (Triesen)	12·00	45
230	–	15r. grey (Ruggell)	40	55
231	–	20r. red (Vaduz)	40	35
232	–	25r. brown (Triesenberg)	45	55
233	–	30r. blue (Schaan)	50	40
234	–	40r. brown (Balzers)	65	1·10
235	–	50r. blue (Mauren)	1·50	1·70
236	–	60r. green (Schellenberg)	4·25	3·25
237	–	90r. green (Eschen)	4·25	3·50
238	–	1f. purple (Vaduz Castle)	3·00	3·75
239	–	1f.20 brown (Valunatal)	3·25	4·00
240	–	1f.50 blue (Lawena)	3·25	3·75

1944.

241	**70**	2f. brown and buff	4·00	10·00
242	–	3f. green and buff	3·50	8·00

DESIGN: 3f. Princess Georgina.

See also Nos. 302/3.

72

73

1945. Birth of Crown Prince Johann Adam Pius (known as Prince Hans Adam).

243	**72**	20r. red, yellow and gold	65	40
244		30r. blue, yellow and gold	80	1·00
245		100r. grey, yellow and gold	2·10	4·00

1945.

246	**73**	5f. blue on buff	16·00	18·00
247		5f. brown on buff	17·00	27·00

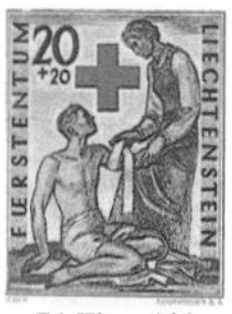
74 First Aid

75 St. Lucius

1945. Red Cross. Cross in red.

248	–	10r.+10r. purple and buff	1·40	1·40
249	**74**	20r.+20r. purple and buff	1·40	2·00
250	–	1f.+1f.40 blue and buff	6·25	18·00

DESIGNS: 10r. Mother and children; 1f. Nurse and invalid.

1946.

251	**75**	10f. grey on buff	24·00	22·00

1946. 4th Liechtenstein Philatelic Exhibition, Vaduz and 25th Anniv of Postal Agreement with Switzerland. Sheet 84 × 60 mm.

MS251a	10r. (× 2) Old Postal Coach (*horiz*), violet, brown and buff (sold at 3f.)	28·00	38·00

76 Red Deer Stag

79 Wilbur Wright

1946. Wild Life.

252	**76**	20r. red	1·20	1·30
255	–	20r. red (Chamois)	2·00	2·10
283	–	20r. red (Roebuck)	7·75	2·30
253	–	30r. blue (Arctic hare)	1·60	2·10
256	–	30r. blue (Alpine marmot)	3·00	2·75
284	–	30r. green (Black grouse)	13·50	7·75
285	–	80r. brown (Eurasian badger)	27·00	30·00
254	–	1f.50 green (Western capercaillie)	5·75	8·50
257	–	1f.50 brown (Golden eagle)	6·75	12·00

1947. Death of Princess Elsa. As No. 141.

258	–	2f. black on yellow	2·20	9·25

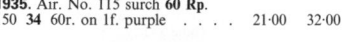

1948. Air. Pioneers of Flight.
259 – 10r. green 65 20
260 – 15r. violet 65 1·00
261 – 20r. brown 80 25
262 – 25r. red 1·10 1·25
263 – 40r. blue 1·30 1·60
264 – 50r. blue 1·70 1·60
265 – 1f. purple 3·50 2·40
266 – 2f. purple 4·00 3·75
267 **79** 5f. green 5·25 4·75
268 – 10f. black 28·00 14·00
PORTRAITS: 10r. Leoardo da Vinci; 15r. Joseph Montgolfier; 20r. Jakob Degen; 25r. Wilhelm Kress; 40r. Etienne Robertson; 50r. William Henson; 1f. Otto Lilienthal; 2f. Salomon Andree; 10f. Icarus

80 "Ginevra de Benci" (Da Vinci)

1949. Paintings.
269 **80** 10r. green 45 25
270 – 20r. red 95 50
271 – 30r. brown 2·50 1·20
272 – 40r. blue 5·25 60
273 – 50r. violet 4·50 5·25
274 – 60r. grey 9·25 4·75
275 – 80r. brown 2·30 3·25
276 – 90r. green 9·25 4·00
277 – 120r. mauve 2·30 4·00
DESIGNS: 20r. "Portrait of a Young Girl" (Rubens); 30r. Self-portrait of Rembrandt in plumed hat; 40r. "Stephan Gardiner, Bishop of Winchester" (Quentin Massys); 50r. "Madonna and Child" (Hans Memling); 60r. "Franz Meister in 1456" (Jehan Fouquet); 80r. "Lute Player" (Orazio Gentileschi); 90r. "Portrait of a Man" (Bernhardin Strigel); 120r. "Portrait of a Man (Duke of Urbino)" (Raphael).

1949. No. 227 surch **5 Rp.** and bars.
278 **69** 5r. on 3r. brown and buff 50 35

82 Posthorn and Map of World

1949. 75th Anniv of U.P.U.
279 **82** 40r. blue 2·75 3·25

1949. 5th Liechtenstein Philatelic Exhibition, Vaduz. Sheet 122 × 70 mm containing paintings as 1949 issue in new colours.
MS279a 10r. green (as 10r.); 20r. mauve (as 80r.); 40r. blue (as 120r.). Sold at 3f. 90·00 £110

83 Rossauer Castle

86 Boy cutting Loaf

1949. 250th Anniv of Acquisition of Domain of Schellenberg.
280 **83** 20r. purple 1·50 1·40
281 – 40r. blue 5·25 6·00
282 – 1f.50 red 8·00 7·50
DESIGN—HORIZ: 40r. Bendern Church. VERT: 1f.50, Prince Johann Adam I.

1950. Surch **100 100**.
286 **82** 100r. on 40r. blue 19·00 31·00

1951. Agricultural scenes.
287 **86** 5r. mauve 25 10
288 – 10r. green 50 10
289 – 15r. brown 4·25 4·75
290 – 20r. brown 95 20
291 – 25r. purple 4·25 4·75
292 – 30r. green 2·50 50
293 – 40r. blue 7·50 4·25
294 – 50r. purple 6·50 3·00
295 – 60r. brown 6·25 3·00
296 – 80r. brown 6·25 6·75
297 – 90r. green 13·00 4·50
298 – 1f. blue 42·00 5·50
DESIGNS: 10r. Man whetting scythe; 15r. Mowing; 20r. Girl and sweet corn; 25r. Haywain; 30r. Gathering grapes; 40r. Man with scythe; 50r. Herdsman with cows; 60r. Ploughing; 80r. Girl carrying basket of fruit; 90r. Woman gleaning; 1f. Tractor hauling corn.

87 "Lock on the Canal" (Aelbert Cuyp)

88 "Willem von Heythuysen, Burgomaster of Haarlem" (Frans Hals)

1951. Paintings.
299 **87** 10r.+10r. green 7·50 5·25
300 **88** 20r.+10r. brown 8·00 10·50
301 – 40r.+10r. blue 6·75 7·00
DESIGN—As Type **87**: 40r. "Landscape" (Jacob van Ruysdael).

90 Vaduz Castle

96 Lord Baden-Powell

1951.
302 **70** 2f. blue 12·50 22·00
303 – 3f. brown £110 75·00
304 **90** 5f. green £130 £110
DESIGN: 3f. Princess Georgina.

1952. No. 281 surch **1.20**.
308 1f.20 on 40r. blue 17·00 37·00

1952. Paintings from Prince's Collection. (a) As T **80** but size 25 × 30 mm.
309 10r. green 1·00 65
305 20r. purple 25·00 2·20
307 40r. blue 9·00 3·75
312 40r. blue 24·00 34·00
PAINTINGS: No. 309, "Portrait of a Young Man" (A. G.); 305, "Portrait" (Giovanni Salvoldo); 307, "St. John" (Andrea del Sarto); 312, "Leonhard, Count of Hag" (Hans von Kulmbach).

(b) As T **88** (22½ × 24 mm).
310 20r. brown 11·00 1·70
306 30r. green 17·00 5·75
311 30r. brown 22·00 5·25
PAINTINGS: No. 310, "St. Nicholas" (Bartholomaus Zeitblom); 306, "Madonna and Child" (Sandro Botticelli); 311, "St. Christopher" (Lucas Cranach the elder).

1953. 14th International Scout Conference.
313 **96** 10r. green 1·40 90
314 20r. brown 9·50 1·50
315 25r. red 9·00 15·00
316 40r. blue 8·75 3·25

97 Alemannic Ornamental Disc, (c. A.D. 600)

98 Prehistoric Walled Settlement, Borscht

1953. Opening of National Museum, Vaduz.
317 **97** 10r. brown 7·00 8·25
318 **98** 20r. green 7·00 8·00
319 – 1f.20 blue 36·00 24·00
DESIGN—VERT: 1f.20, Rossen jug (3000 B.C.).

99 Footballers

100 Madonna and Child

1954. Football.
320 **99** 10r. brown and red 1·60 75
321 – 20r. deep green and green 5·75 2·00
322 – 25r. deep brown and brown 13·00 21·00
323 – 40r. violet and grey 11·50 7·25
DESIGNS: 20r. Footballer kicking ball; 25r. Goalkeeper; 40r. Two footballers.
For stamps in similar designs see Nos. 332/5, 340/3, 351/4 and 363/6.

1954. Nos. 299/301 surch in figures.
324 **87** 35r. on 10r.+10r. green 3·00 1·60
325 **88** 60r. on 20r.+10r. brown 11·00 8·25
326 – 65r. on 40r.+10r. blue 6·50 5·75

1954. Termination of Marian Year.
327 **100** 20r. brown 2·50 2·75
328 40r. black 13·00 14·00
329 1f. brown 14·00 13·50

101 Princess Georgina

102 Crown Prince John Adam Pius

1955.
330 – 2f. brown 55·00 31·00
331 **101** 3f. green 55·00 31·00
PORTRAIT: 2f. Prince Francis Joseph II.

1955. Mountain Sports. As T **99**.
332 10r. purple and blue 1·70 75
333 20r. green and bistre 4·00 75
334 25r. brown and blue 13·00 12·50
335 40r. green and red 11·50 3·50
DESIGNS: 10r. Slalom racer; 20r. Mountaineer hammering in piton; 25r. Skier; 40r. Mountaineer resting on summit.

1955. 10th Anniv of Liechtenstein Red Cross. Cross in red.
336 **102** 10r. violet 1·30 40
337 – 20r. green 3·00 1·20
338 – 40r. brown 5·00 5·25
339 – 60r. red 5·00 3·50
PORTRAITS: 20r. Prince Philip; 40r. Prince Nicholas; 60r. Princess Nora.
See also No. 350.

1956. Athletics. As T **99**.
340 10r. green and brown 90 50
341 20r. purple and green 2·50 75
342 40r. brown and blue 3·75 4·25
343 1f. brown and red 7·50 8·75
DESIGNS: 10r. Throwing the javelin; 20r. Hurdling; 40r. Pole vaulting; 1f. Running.

103

104 Prince Francis Joseph II

1956. 150th Anniv of Sovereignty of Liechtenstein.
344 **103** 10r. purple and gold 2·00 60
345 1f.20 blue and gold 8·50 3·25

1956. 50th Birthday of Prince Francis Joseph II.
346 **104** 10r. green 1·30 35
347 15r. blue 2·10 2·10
348 25r. purple 2·10 2·10
349 60r. brown 6·00 2·10

1956. 6th Philatelic Exhibition, Vaduz. As T **102** but inscr "6. BRIEFMARKEN-AUSSTELLUNG".
350 20r. green 2·30 40

1956. Gymnastics. As T **99**.
351 10r. green and pink 2·00 70
352 15r. purple and green 4·25 4·75
353 25r. green and drab 5·00 6·25
354 1f.50 brown and yellow 13·00 11·00
DESIGNS: 10r. Somersaulting; 15r. Vaulting; 25r. Exercising with rings; 1f.50, Somersaulting on parallel bars.

105 Norway Spruce

106 Lord Baden-Powell

1957. Liechtenstein Trees and Bushes.
355 **105** 10r. purple 2·75 1·40
356 – 20r. red 3·00 50
357 – 1f. green 5·00 5·00
DESIGNS: 20r. Wild rose bush; 1f. Silver birch.
See also Nos. 369/71, 375/7 and 401/3.

1957. 50th Anniv of Boy Scout Movement and Birth Centenary of Lord Baden-Powell (founder).
358 – 10r. blue 1·00 1·00
359 **106** 20r. brown 1·00 1·00
DESIGN: 10r. Torchlight procession.

107 St. Mamertus Chapel

108 Relief Map of Liechtenstein

1957. Christmas.
360 **107** 10r. brown 70 20
361 – 40r. blue 2·20 5·00
362 – 1f.50 purple 7·75 8·00
DESIGNS—(from St. Mamertus Chapel): 40r. Altar shrine; 1f.50, "Pieta" (sculpture).
See also Nos. 372/4 and 392/4.

1958. Sports. As T **99**.
363 15r. violet and blue 90 1·00
364 30r. green and purple 3·00 5·25
365 40r. green and orange 5·00 5·50
366 90r. brown and green 2·75 3·50
DESIGNS: 15r. Swimmer; 30r. Fencers; 40r. Tennis player; 90r. Racing cyclists.

1958. Brussels International Exhibition.
367 **108** 25r. violet, stone and red 50 50
368 40r. purple, blue and red 65 55

1958. Liechtenstein Trees and Bushes. As T **105**.
369 20r. brown (Sycamore) 2·30 50
370 50r. green (Holly) 9·00 3·75
371 90r. violet (Yew) 2·30 2·50

1958. Christmas. As T **107**.
372 20r. green 2·20 1·90
373 35r. violet 2·20 2·50
374 80r. brown 2·50 2·10
DESIGNS: 20r. "St. Maurice and St. Agatha"; 35r. "St. Peter"; 80r. St. Peter's Chapel, Mals-Balzers.

1959. Liechtenstein Trees and Bushes. As T **105**.
375 20r. lilac (Red-berried larch) 3·75 1·90
376 50r. red (Red-berried elder) 3·50 2·10
377 90r. green (Linden) 3·00 2·50

109

111 Harvester

110 Flags of Vaduz Castle and Rhine Valley

1959. Pope Pius XII Mourning.
378 **109** 30r. purple and gold 60 60

1959. Views.
379 – 5r. brown 10 10
380 **110** 10r. purple 10 10
381 – 20r. mauve 25 10
382 – 30r. red 35 25
383 – 40r. green 70 40
384 – 50r. blue 50 40
385 – 60r. blue 65 50
386 **111** 75r. brown 95 1·10
387 – 80r. green 85 65
388 – 90r. purple 1·00 95
389 – 1f. brown 1·00 80
390 – 1f.20 red 1·30 1·20
390a – 1f.30 green 1·30 1·40
391 – 1f.50 blue 1·50 1·50
DESIGNS—HORIZ: 5r. Bendern Church; 20r. Rhine Dam; 30r. Gutenberg Castle; 40r. View from Schellenberg; 50r. Vaduz Castle; 60r. Naafkopf-Falknis Mountains (view from the Bettlerjoch); 1f.20, Harvesting apples; 1f.30, Farmer and wife; 1f.50, Saying grace at table. VERT: 80r. Alpine haymaker; 90r. Girl in vineyard; 1f. Mother in kitchen.

1959. Christmas. As T **107**.
392 5r. green 50 20
393 60r. brown 5·00 3·75
394 1f. purple 3·00 2·00
DESIGNS: 5r. Bendern Church belfry; 60r. Relief on bell of St. Theodul's Church; 1f. Sculpture on tower of St. Lucius's Church.

112 Bell 47J Ranger Helicopter

1960. Air. 30th Anniv of 1st Liechtenstein Air Stamps.
395 **112** 30r. red . . . . 1·80 1·90
396 – 40r. blue . . . . 4·00 1·90
397 – 50r. purple . . . . 6·00 3·75
398 – 75r. green . . . . 2·00 2·00
DESIGNS: 40r. Boeing 707 jetliner; 50r. Convair Coronado jetliner; 75r. Douglas DC-8 jetliner.

1960. World Refugee Year. Nos. 367/8 surch **WELTFLUCHTLINGSJAHR 1960**, uprooted tree and new value.
399 **108** 30+10r. on 40r. purple, blue and red 80 80
400 50+10r. on 25r. violet, stone and red . . . . . 1·20 1·20

1960. Liechtenstein Trees and Bushes. As T **105**.
401 20r. brown (Beech) . . . . . 5·50 5·25
402 30r. purple (Juniper) . . . . 6·25 8·00
403 50r. turquoise (Mountain pines) . . . . 18·00 10·00

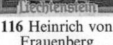

114 Europa "Honeycomb"

115 Princess Gina

1960. Europa.
404 **114** 50r. multicoloured . . . . 65·00 44·00

1960.
404a – 1f.70 violet . . . . . . 1·40 1·00
405 **115** 2f. blue . . . . 1·90 1·60
406 – 3f. brown . . . . 2·40 1·60
PORTRAITS: 1f.70, Crown Prince Hans Adam; 3f. Prince Francis Joseph II.

116 Heinrich von Frauenberg

117 "Power Transmission"

1961. Minnesingers (1st issue). Multicoloured. Reproduction from the Manessian Manuscript of Songs.
407 15r. Type **116** 30 30
408 25r. Ulrich von Liechtenstein 50 45
409 35r. Ulrich von Gutenberg 70 60
410 1f. Konrad von Altstatten . . 1·10 1·00
411 1f.50 Walther von der Vogelweide . . . . 4·75 7·25
See also Nos. 415/18 and 428/31.

1961. Europa.
412 **117** 50r. multicoloured 30 30

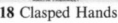

117a Prince John II

1962. 50th Anniv of First Liechtenstein Postage Stamps. Sheet 133 × 118 mm. T **117a** and similar horiz design.
MS412a 5r. green; 10r. red; 25r. blue. Sold at 2f.60 . . . . 8·25 4·50
DESIGNS: 0r. Prince Francis I; 25r. Prince Francis Joseph I.

118 Clasped Hands

119 Campaign Emblem

1962. Europa.
413 **118** 50r. red and blue 40 40

1962. Malaria Eradication.
414 **119** 50r. blue 35 35

1962. Minnesingers (2nd issue). As T **116**. Mult.
415 20r. King Konradin 25 25
416 30r. Kraft von Toggenburg 65 70
417 40r. Heinrich von Veldig . . 65 70
418 2f. Tannhauser . . . . . . 1·90 2·00

120 Pieta

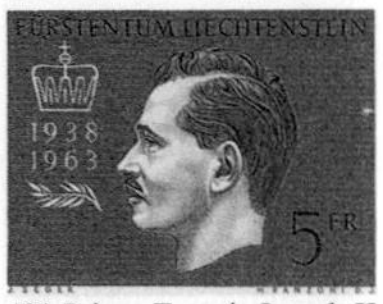

121 Prince Francis Joseph II

1962. Christmas.
419 **120** 30r. mauve 40 45
420 – 50r. red 55 55
421 – 1f.20 blue . . . . 1·20 1·20
DESIGNS: 50r. Fresco with angel; 1f.20, View of Mauren.
See also Nos. 438/40.

1963. 25th Anniv of Reign of Prince Francis Joseph II.
422 **121** 5f. green . . . . 3·50 2·50

122 Milk and Bread

1963. Freedom from Hunger.
423 **122** 50r. brown, purple and red 35 40

123 "Angel of Annunciation"

124 "Europa"

1963. Red Cross Cent. Cross in red; background grey.
424 **123** 20r. yellow and green . . 25 25
425 – 80r. violet and mauve . . 40 55
426 – 1f. blue and ultramarine 95 75
DESIGNS: 80r. "The Epiphany"; 1f. "Family".

1963. Europa.
427 **124** 50r. multicoloured 60 50

1963. Minnesingers (3rd issue). As T **116**. Mult.
428 25r. Heinrich von Sax . . . 20 20
429 30r. Kristan von Hamle . . . 35 35
430 75r. Werner von Teufen . . . 60 60
431 1f.70 Hartmann von Aue . . 1·40 1·40

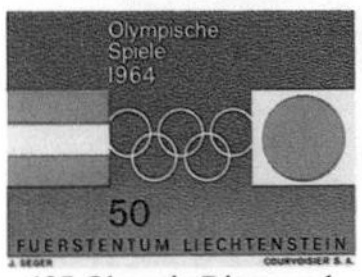

125 Olympic Rings and Flags

126 Arms of Counts of Werdenberg, Vaduz

1964. Olympic Games, Tokyo.
432 **125** 50r. red, black and blue 35 40

1964. Arms (1st issue). Multicoloured.
433 20f. Type **126** 20 20
434 30f. Barons of Brandis . . . 25 25
435 80r. Counts of Sulz 70 70
436 1f.50 Counts of Hohenems 90 95
See also Nos. 443/6.

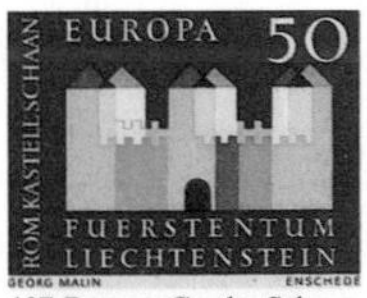

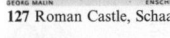

127 Roman Castle, Schaan

128 P. Kaiser

1964. Europa.
437 **127** 50f. multicoloured 65 45

1964. Christmas. As T **120**.
438 10r. purple 10 10
439 40r. blue 20 20
440 1f.30 purple 85 85
DESIGNS: 10r. Masescha Chapel; 40r. "Mary Magdalene" (altar painting); 1f.30, "St. Sebastian, Madonna and Child, and St. Rochus" (altar painting).

1964. Death Centenary of Peter Kaiser (historian).
441 **128** 1f. green on cream . . . 55 45

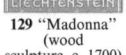

129 "Madonna" (wood sculpture, c. 1700)

130 Europa "Links" (ancient belt-buckle)

1965.
442 **129** 10f. red . . . . 7·25 3·00

1965. Arms (2nd issue). As T **126**. Multicoloured.
443 20r. Von Schellenberg . . . 20 20
444 30r. Von Gutenberg 30 20
445 80r. Von Frauenberg 80 70
446 1f. Von Ramschwag 80 70

1965. Europa.
447 **130** 50r. brown, grey and blue 45 35

131 "Jesus in the Temple"

1965. Birth Centenary of Ferdinand Nigg (painter).
448 – 10r. deep green and green 15 15
449 – 30r. brown and orange . . 20 20
450 **131** 1f.20 green and blue . . . 85 85
DESIGNS—VERT: 10r. "The Annunciation"; 30r. "The Magi".

132 Princess Gina and Prince Franz (after painting by Pedro Leitao)

133 Telecommunications Symbols

1965. Special Issue.
451 **132** 75r. multicoloured 45 45
See also No. 457.

1965. Centenary of I.T.U.
452 **133** 25r. multicoloured 20 25

134 Tree ("Wholesome Earth")

1966. Nature Protection.
453 **134** 10r. green and yellow . . 10 10
454 – 20r. blue and light blue 10 10
455 – 30r. blue and green . . 10 10
456 – 1f.50 red and yellow . . 55 55
DESIGNS: 20r. Bird ("Pure Air"); 30r. Fish ("Clean Water"); 1f.50, Sun ("Protection of Nature").

1966. Prince Franz Joseph II's 60th Birthday. As T **132**, but with portrait of Prince Franz and inscr "1906–1966".
457 1f. multicoloured 45 45

135 Arms of Herren von Richenstein

136 Europa "Ship"

1966. Arms of Triesen Families. Multicoloured.
458 20r. Type **135** 10 10
459 30r. Jinker Vaistli 15 15
460 60r. Edle von Trisun 40 40
461 1f.20 Die von Schiel 55 55

1966. Europa.
462 **136** 50r. multicoloured 35 35

137 Vaduz Parish Church

138 Cogwheels

1966. Restoration of Vaduz Parish Church.
463 **137** 5r. green and red 10 10
464 – 20r. purple and bistre . . 10 10
465 – 30r. blue and red 10 15
466 – 1f.70 brown and green . . 65 70
DESIGNS: 20r. St. Florin; 30r. Madonna; 1f.70, God the Father.

1967. Europa.
467 **138** 50r. multicoloured 35 35

139 "The Man from Malanser"

140 Crown Prince Hans Adam

1967. Liechtenstein Sagas (1st series). Multicoloured.
468 20r. Type **139** 10 15
469 30r. "The Treasure of Gutenberg" 25 25
470 1f.20 "The Giant of Guflina" 70 60
See also Nos. 492/4 and 516/18.

1967. Royal Wedding. Sheet 86 × 95 mm comprising T **140** and similar vert design.
MS471 1f.50 indigo and blue (T **140**); 1f.50 brown and light brown (Princess Marie) . . . . 2·50 2·20

141 "Alpha and Omega"

1967. Christian Symbols. Multicoloured.
472 20r. Type **141** 10 10
473 30r. "Tropaion" (Cross as victory symbol) 10 10
474 70r. Christ's monogram . . . 75 55

142 Father J. B. Buchel (educator, historian and poet)

143 "E.F.T.A."

1967. Buchel Commemoration.
475 **142** 1f. red and green 60 50

1967. European Free Trade Association.
476 **143** 50r. multicoloured 35 30

144 "Peter and Paul", Mauren

145 Campaign Emblem

1967. "Patrons of the Church". Multicoloured.
477 5r. "St. Joseph", Planken . . 10 10
478 10r. "St. Lawrence", Schaan 10 10
479 20r. Type **144** 20 10
480 30r. "St. Nicholas", Balzers 25 15
480a 40r. "St. Sebastian", Nendeln 50 25
481 50r. "St. George", Schellenberg 60 30
482 60r. "St. Martin", Eschen 60 35
483 70r. "St. Fridolin", Ruggell 60 45
484 80r. "St. Gallus", Triesen 75 55

485 1f. "St. Theodolus", Triesenberg 85 55
486 1f.20 "St. Anna", Vaduz Castle . . . . 1·20 80
487 1f.50 "St. Marie", Bendern-Camprin . . . . 1·70 1·10
488 2f. "St. Lucius", (patron saint of Liechtenstein) . . 1·90 1·30

1967. "Technical Assistance".
489 **145** 50r.+20r. multicoloured 50 35

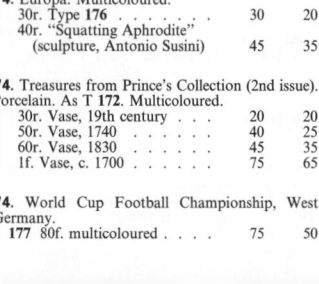

146 Europa "Key"

1968. Europa.
490 **146** 50r. multicoloured 35 35

147 Arms of Liechtenstein and Wilczek **148** Sir Rowland Hill

1968. Silver Wedding Anniv of Prince Francis Joseph II and Princess Gina.
491 **147** 75r. multicoloured 50 55

1968. Liechtenstein Sagas (2nd series). As T **139**. Multicoloured.
492 30r. "The Treasure of St. Mamerten" 10 10
493 50r. "The Hobgoblin in the Bergerwald" 25 25
494 80r. "The Three Sisters" . . 70 60

1968. "Pioneers of Philately" (1st series).
495 **148** 20r. green 10 10
496 – 30r. brown 10 10
497 – 1f. black 85 70
PORTRAITS: 30r. Philippe de Ferrary; 1f. Maurice Burrus.
See also Nos. 504/5 and 554/6.

150 Arms of Liechtenstein **151** Colonnade

1969.
498 **150** 3f.50 brown . . . . . . 2·50 1·20

1969. Europa.
499 **151** 50r. multicoloured 60 40

152 "Biology"

1969. 250th Anniv of Liechtenstein. Multicoloured.
500 10r. Type **152** 10 10
501 30r. "Physics" 10 15
502 50r. "Astronomy" 35 30
503 80r. "Art" 60 60

1969. "Pioneers of Philately" (2nd series). As T **148**.
504 80r. brown 50 50
505 1f.20 blue . . . . 1·10 85
PORTRAITS: 80r. Carl Lindenberg; 1f.20, Theodore Champion.

153 Arms of St. Luzi Monastery **154** Symbolic "T"

1969. Arms of Church Patrons. Multicoloured.
506 20r. St. Johann's Abbey . . . 20 25
507 30r. Type **153** 30 25
508 30r. Ladies' Priory, Schanis 25 20
509 30r. Knights Hospitallers, Feldkirch 35 25
510 50r. Pfafers Abbey 30 40
511 50r. Weingarten Abbey . . . 40 45
512 75r. St. Gallen Abbey 55 65
513 1f.20 Ottobeuren Abbey . . . 1·40 1·00
514 1f.50 Chur Episcopate . . . 1·30 1·20

1969. Centenary of Liechtenstein Telegraph System.
515 **154** 30r. multicoloured 25 25

1969. Liechtenstein Sagas (3rd series). As T **139**. Multicoloured.
516 20r. "The Cheated Devil" . . 10 10
517 50r. "The Fiery Red Goat" 40 35
518 60r. "The Grafenberg Treasure" 60 50

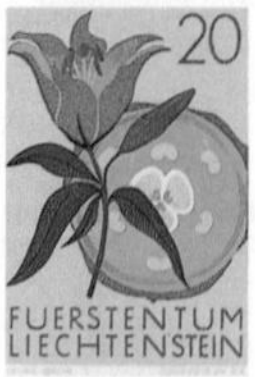

155 Orange Lily **156** "Flaming Sun"

1970. Nature Conservation Year. Multicoloured.
519 20r. Type **155** 20 10
520 30r. Wild orchid 25 20
521 50r. Ranunculus 40 35
522 1f.20 Bog bean 85 85
See also Nos. 532/5 and 548/51.

1970. Europa.
523 **156** 50r. yellow, blue and green 45 35

157 Prince Wenzel **158** Prince Francis Joseph II

1970. 25th Anniv of Liechtenstein Red Cross.
524 **157** 1f. multicoloured 85 70

1970. 800th Anniv of Wolfram von Eschenbach. Sheet 73 × 96 mm containing vert designs similar to T **116** from the "Codex Manaesse". Multicoloured.
MS525 30r. Wolfram von Eschenbach; 50r. Reinmar the Fiddler; 80r. Hartmann von Starkenberg; 1f.20 Friedrich von Hausen. Sold for 3f. . . . . . 2·50 2·50

1970.
526 – 1f.70 green . . . . . . 2·00 1·50
526a – 2f.50 blue . . . . . . 2·10 1·70
527 **158** 3f. black . . . . 2·50 1·80
DESIGNS: 1f.70, Prince Hans Adam; 2f.50, Princess Gina.

159 "Mother and Child" (R. Schadler) **160** Bronze Boar (La Tene period)

1970. Christmas.
528 **159** 30r. multicoloured 30 20

1971. National Museum Inauguration.
529 **160** 25r. black, blue & ultram 20 20
530 – 30r. green and brown . . 25 20
531 – 75r. multicoloured 55 50
DESIGNS: 30r. Ornamental peacock (Roman, 2nd-century); 75r. Engraved bowl (13th-century).

1971. Liechtenstein Flowers (2nd series). As T **155**. Multicoloured.
532 10r. Cyclamen 20 10
533 20r. Moonwort 20 20
534 50r. Superb pink 40 35
535 1f.50 Alpine columbine . . . 1·30 1·00

161 Europa Chain

1971. Europa.
536 **161** 50r. yellow, blue & black 40 40

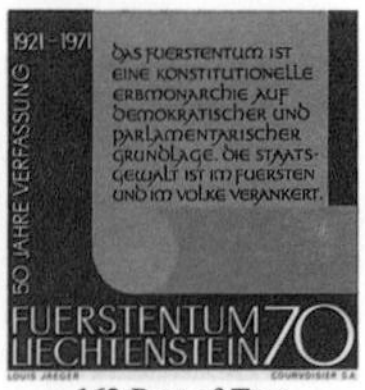

162 Part of Text **163** Cross-country Skiing

1971. 50th Anniv of 1921 Constitution. Mult.
537 70r. Type **162** 65 55
538 80r. Princely crown 70 60

1971. Winter Olympic Games, Sapporo, Japan (1972). Multicoloured.
539 15r. Type **163** 20 10
540 40r. Ice hockey 35 30
541 65r. Downhill skiing 60 35
542 1f.50 Figure skating . . . . 1·60 1·10

164 "Madonna and Child" (sculpture, Andrea della Robbia) **165** Gymnastics

1971. Christmas.
543 **164** 30r. multicoloured 30 20

1972. Olympic Games, Munich. Multicoloured.
544 10r. Type **165** 10 10
545 20r. High jumping 15 10
546 40r. Running 30 25
547 60r. Throwing the discus . . 45 35

1972. Liechtenstein Flowers (3rd series). As T **155**. Multicoloured.
548 20r. Sulphur anemone . . . 15 10
549 30r. Turk's-cap lily 25 15
550 60r. Alpine centaury 50 40
551 1f.20 Reed-mace 95 75

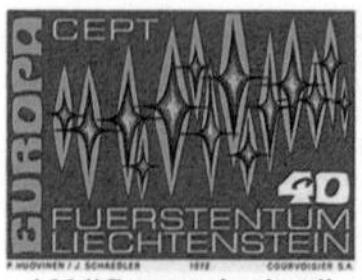

166 "Communications" **168** "Faun"

167 Bendern

1972. Europa.
552 **166** 40r. multicoloured 30 30

1972. "Liba '72" Stamp Exhibition, Vaduz. Sheet 101 × 65 mm containing T **167** and similar horiz design.
MS553 1f. violet; 2f. red . . . . 2·50 2·50
DESIGN: 2f. Vaduz castle.

1972. "Pioneers of Philately" (3rd series). As T **148**.
554 30r. green 25 25
555 40r. purple 30 30
556 1f.30 blue . . . . 1·10 85
PORTRAITS: 30r. Emilio Diena; 40r. Andre de Cock; 1f.30, Theodore E. Steinway.

1972. "Natural Art". Motifs fashioned from roots and branches. Multicoloured.
557 20r. Type **168** 10 10
558 30r. "Dancer" 20 20
559 1f.10 "Owl" 85 80

169 "Madonna with Angels" (F. Nigg) **170** Lawena Springs

1972. Christmas.
560 **169** 30r. multicoloured 30 20

1972. Landscapes.
561 – 5r. purple and yellow . . 15 10
562 **170** 10r. green and light green 10 10
563 – 15r. brown and green . . 10 10
564 – 25r. purple and blue . . . 30 20
565 – 30r. purple and brown . . 35 30
566 – 40r. purple and brown . . 45 30
567 – 50r. blue and lilac 40 35
568 – 60r. green and yellow . . 60 50
569 – 70r. blue and cobalt . . . 70 60
570 – 80r. green and light green 80 60
571 – 1f. brown and green . . . 1·00 75
572 – 1f.30 blue and green . . . 1·10 1·00
573 – 1f.50 brown and blue . . 1·40 1·20
574 – 1f.80 brown & lt brown 1·70 1·50
575 – 2f. brown and blue . . . 2·20 1·50
DESIGNS: 5r. Silum; 15r. Ruggeller Reed; 25r. Steg Kirchlispitz; 30r. Feld Schellenberg; 40r. Rennhof Mauren; 50r. Tidrufe; 60r. Eschner Riet; 70r. Mittagspitz; 80r. Schaan Forest; 1f. St. Peter's Chapel, Mals; 1f.30, Frommenhaus; 1f.50, Ochsenkopf; 1f.80, Hehlawangspitz; 2f. Saminaschlucht.

171 Europa "Posthorn"

1973. Europa.
576 **171** 30r. multicoloured 35 20
577 40r. multicoloured 40 30

172 Chambered Nautilus Goblet **173** Arms of Liechtenstein

1973. Treasures from Prince's Collection (1st issue). Drinking Vessels. Multicoloured.
578 30r. Type **172** 25 20
579 70r. Ivory tankard 60 45
580 1f.10 Silver cup 85 70
See also Nos. 589/92.

1973.
581 **173** 5f. multicoloured . . . . 4·75 3·00

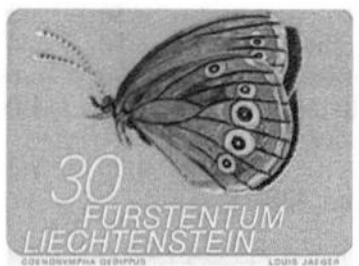

174 False Ringlet **175** "Madonna" (Bartolomeo di Tommaso da Foligno)

1973. Small Fauna of Liechtenstein (1st series). Multicoloured.
582 30r. Type **174** 20 20
583 40r. Curlew 90 35
584 60r. Edible frog 35 40
585 80r. Grass snake 70 55
See also Nos. 596/9.

1973. Christmas.
586 **175** 30r. multicoloured 30 25

176 "Shouting Horseman" (sculpture, Andrea Riccio) **177** Footballers

1974. Europa. Multicoloured.
587 30r. Type **176** 30 20
588 40r. "Squatting Aphrodite" (sculpture, Antonio Susini) 45 35

1974. Treasures from Prince's Collection (2nd issue). Porcelain. As T **172**. Multicoloured.
589 30r. Vase, 19th century . . . 20 20
590 50r. Vase, 1740 . . . . . . 40 25
591 60r. Vase, 1830 . . . . . . 45 35
592 1f. Vase, c. 1700 . . . . . . 75 65

1974. World Cup Football Championship, West Germany.
593 **177** 80f. multicoloured 75 50

178 Posthorn and U.P.U. Emblem

179 Bishop Marxer

1974. Centenary of Universal Postal Union.
594 **178** 40r. black, green and gold . . . 35 25
595 60r. black, red and gold . . . 45 35

1974. Small Fauna of Liechtenstein (2nd series). As T **174**. Multicoloured.
596 15r. Mountain newt 10 10
597 25r. Adder 10 10
598 70r. Cynthia's fritillary (butterfly) 80 55
599 1f.10 Three-toed woodpecker 1·20 80

1974. Death Centenary of Bishop Franz Marxer.
600 **179** 1f. multicoloured 75 50

180 Prince Francis Joseph II and Princess Gina

1974.
601 **180** 10f. brown and gold . . . 9·25 6·25

181 "St. Florian"

182 Prince Constantin

1974. Christmas. Glass Paintings. Multicoloured.
602 30r. Type **181** 25 15
603 50r. "St. Wendelin" 50 30
604 60r. "St. Mary, Anna and Joachim" 65 35
605 70r. "Jesus in Manger" . . . 85 55

1975. Liechtenstein Princes.
606 **182** 70r. green and gold . . . 55 50
607 – 80r. purple and gold . . . 70 70
608 – 1f.20 blue and gold . . . 1·00 90
PORTRAITS: 80r. Prince Maximilian; 1f.20, Prince Alois.

183 "Cold Sun" (M. Frommelt)

184 Imperial Cross

1975. Europa. Paintings. Multicoloured.
609 30r. Type **183** 25 20
610 60r. "Village" (L. Jager) . . 70 55

1975. Imperial Insignia (1st series). Multicoloured.
611 30r. Type **184** 30 20
612 60r. Imperial sword 45 35
613 1f. Imperial orb 90 65
614 1f.30 Imperial robe (50 × 32 mm) . . . . . . 6·25 4·75
615 2f. Imperial crown . . . . . 2·75 1·90
See also Nos. 670/3.

185 "Red Cross Activities"

186 St. Mamerten, Triesen

1975. 30th Anniv of Liechtenstein Red Cross.
616 **185** 60r. multicoloured 75 45

1975. European Architectural Heritage Year. Multicoloured.
617 40r. Type **186** 30 25
618 50r. Red House, Vaduz . . . 35 30
619 70r. Prebendary buildings, Eschen 60 55
620 1f. Gutenberg Castle, Balzers 90 80

187 Speed Skating

188 "Daniel in the Lions' Den"

1975. Winter Olympic Games, Innsbruck (1976). Multicoloured.
621 20r. Type **187** 20 10
622 25r. Ice hockey 25 20
623 70r. Downhill skiing 65 55
624 1f.20 Slalom . . . . 1·10 90

1975. Christmas and Holy Year. Capitals in Chur Cathedral.
625 **188** 30r. violet and gold . . . 25 20
626 – 60r. green and gold . . . 50 35
627 – 90r. red and gold 70 85
DESIGNS: 60r. "Madonna"; 90r. "St. Peter".

189 Mouflon

190 Crayfish

1976. Europa. Ceramics by Prince Hans von Liechtenstein. Multicoloured.
628 40r. Type **189** 50 30
629 80r. "Ring-necked Pheasant and Brood" 75 70

1976. World Wildlife Fund. Multicoloured.
630 25r. Type **190** 30 30
631 40r. Turtle 60 30
632 70r. European otter 85 70
633 80r. Northern lapwing . . . 1·70 90

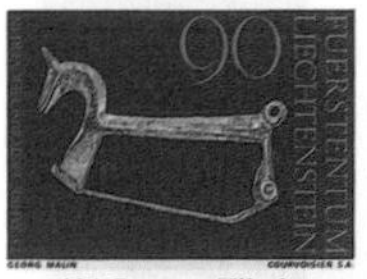

191 Roman Fibula

193 Judo

192 Obverse of 50f. Coin depicting portrait of Prince

1976. 75th Anniv of National Historical Society.
634 **191** 90r. multicoloured 85 60

1976. 70th Birthday of Prince Francis Joseph II. Sheet 102 × 65 mm containing T **192** and similar horiz design. Multicoloured.
MS635 1f. Type **192**; 1f. Reverse of 50f. coin depicting Arms of Liechtenstein . . . . 1·70 2·00

1976. Olympic Games, Montreal. Multicoloured.
636 35r. Type **193** 30 25
637 50r. Volleyball 35 40
638 80r. Relay 60 50
639 1f.10 Long jumping 85 75

194 "Singing Angels"

195 "Pisces"

1976. 400th Birth Anniv (1977) of Peter Paul Rubens (painter). Multicoloured.
640 50r. Type **194** 60 65
641 70r. "Sons of the Artist" . . 90 85
642 1f. "Daughters of Cecrops" (49 × 39 mm) . . . . . . 3·50 3·50

1976. Signs of the Zodiac (1st series). Multicoloured.
643 20r. Type **195** 20 20
644 40r. "Aries" 30 25
645 80r. "Taurus" 60 55
646 90r. "Gemini" 85 70
See also Nos. 666/9 and 710/13.

196 "Child Jesus of Prague"

197 Sarcophagus Statue, Chur Cathedral

1976. Christmas. Monastic Wax Sculptures. Mult.
647 20r. Type **196** 20 10
648 50r. "The Flight into Egypt" (vert) 60 35
649 80r. "Holy Trinity" (vert) . . 90 55
650 1f.50 "Holy Family" . . . . 1·40 1·00

1976. Bishop Ortlieb von Brandis of Chur Commemoration.
651 **197** 1f.10 brown and gold . . 1·00 70

199 Map of Liechtenstein, 1721 (J. Heber)

200 Coin of Emperor Constantine II

1977. Europa. Multicoloured.
664 40r. Type **199** 25 25
665 80r. "View of Vaduz, 1815" (F. Bachmann) 60 60

1977. Signs of the Zodiac (2nd series). As T **195**. Multicoloured.
666 40r. "Cancer" 30 25
667 70r. "Leo" 60 55
668 80r. "Virgo" 75 70
669 1f.10 "Libra" 85 90

1977. Imperial Insignia (2nd series). As T **184**. Multicoloured.
670 40r. Holy Lance and Reliquary with Particle of the Cross 30 25
671 50r. "St. Matthew" (Imperial Book of Gospels) 35 50
672 80r. St. Stephen's Purse . . . 50 50
673 90r. Tabard of Imperial Herald 70 75

1977. Coins (1st series). Multicoloured.
674 35r. Type **200** 30 30
675 70r. Lindau Brakteat 55 55
676 80r. Coin of Ortlieb von Brandis 65 55
See also Nos. 707/9.

201 Frauenthal Castle, Styria

202 Children in Costume

1977. Castles.
677 **201** 20r. green and gold . . . 25 20
678 – 50r. red and gold . . . 50 40
679 – 80r. lilac and gold 75 60
680 – 90r. blue and gold 80 70
DESIGNS: 50r. Gross-Ullersdorf, Moravia; 80r. Liechtenstein Castle, near Modling, Austria; 90r. Palais Liechtenstein, Alserbachstrasse, Vienna.

1977. National Costumes. Multicoloured.
681 40r. Type **202** 30 25
682 70r. Two girls in traditional costume 45 45
683 1f. Woman in festive costume 65 65

203 Princess Tatjana

1977. Princess Tatjana.
684 **203** 1f.10 lt brn, brn & gold 95 95

204 "Angel"

205 Palais Liechtenstein, Bankgasse, Vienna

1977. Christmas. Sculptures by Erasmus Kern. Multicoloured.
685 20r. Type **204** 15 15
686 50r. "St. Rochus" 40 35
687 80r. "Madonna" 65 60
688 1f.50 "God the Father" . . . 1·00 1·00

1978. Europa.
689 **205** 40r. blue and gold 35 30
690 – 80r. red and gold 80 60
DESIGN: 80r. Feldsberg Castle.

206 Farmhouse, Triesen

207 Vaduz Castle

1978. Buildings. Multicoloured.
691 10r. Type **206** 10 10
692 20r. Upper village of Triesen 15 15
693 35r. Barns at Balzers 30 30
694 40r. Monastery building, Bendern 30 25
695 50r. Rectory tower, Balzers-Mals 40 40
696 70r. Rectory, Mauren 55 55
697 80r. Farmhouse, Schellenberg 65 65
698 90r. Rectory, Balzers 75 85
699 1f. Rheinberger House, Vaduz 80 80
700 1f.10 Vaduz Mitteldorf . . . 85 90
701 1f.50 Town Hall, Triesenberg 1·20 1·20
702 2f. National Museum and Administrator's residence, Vaduz . . . . 1·70 1·60

1978. 40th Anniv of Prince Francis Joseph II's Accession. Royal Residence. Multicoloured.
703 40r. Type **207** 35 35
704 50r. Courtyard 35 35
705 70r. Hall 65 55
706 80r. High Altar, Castle Chapel 70 60

208 Coin of Prince Charles

209 "Portrait of a Piebald" (J. G. von Hamilton and A. Faistenberger)

1978. Coins (2nd series). Multicoloured.
707 40r. Type **208** 30 30
708 50r. Coin of Prince John Adam 40 35
709 80r. Coin of Prince Joseph Wenzel 65 60

1978. Signs of the Zodiac (3rd series). As T **195**. Multicoloured.
710 40r. "Scorpio" 30 25
711 50r. "Sagittarius" 40 35
712 80r. "Capricorn" 65 55
713 1f.50 "Aquarius" . . . . . 1·10 1·00

1978. Paintings. Multicoloured.
714 70r. Type **209** 60 60
715 80r. "Portrait of a Blackish-brown Stallion" (J. G. von Hamilton) 80 80
716 1f.10 "Golden Carriage of Prince Joseph Wenzel" (Martin von Meytens) ($48\frac{1}{2} \times 38$ mm) . . . . . . 1·00 1·00

210 "Adoration of the Shepherds"

211 Comte AC-8 Mail Plane "St. Gallen" over Schaan

1978. Christmas. Church Windows, Triesenberg. Multicoloured.
717 20r. Type **210** 15 15
718 50r. "Enthroned Madonna with St. Joseph" 40 40
719 80r. "Adoration of the Magi" 70 75

1979. Europa. Multicoloured.
720 40r. Type **211** 55 50
721 80r. Airship "Graf Zeppelin" over Vaduz Castle 95 75

212 Child Drinking

213 Ordered Wave-field

1979. International Year of the Child. Multicoloured.
722 80r. Type **212** 50 60
723 90r. Child eating 55 70
724 1f.10 Child reading . . . . . 1·00 85

1979. 50th Anniv of International Radio Consultative Committee (CCIR).
725 **213** 50r. blue and black . . . 40 35

214 Abstract Composition

215 Sun rising over Continents

1979. Liechtenstein's Entry into Council of Europe.
726 **214** 80r. multicoloured 70 60

1979. Development Aid.
727 **215** 1f. multicoloured 85 75

216 Arms of Carl Ludwig von Sulz

1979. Heraldic Windows in the Liechtenstein National Museum. Multicoloured.
728 40r. Type **216** 35 30
729 70r. Arms of Barbara von Sulz 70 60
730 1f.10 Arms of Ulrich von Ramschwag and Barbara von Hallwil 90 80

217 Sts. Lucius and Florian (fresco, Waltensberg-Vuorz Church)

1979. Patron Saints.
731 **217** 20f. multicoloured . . . . 16·00 11·00

218 Base of Ski Slope, Valuna

1979. Winter Olympic Games, Lake Placid (1980). Multicoloured.
732 40r. Type **218** 30 25
733 70r. Malbun and Ochsenkopf 65 60
734 1f.50 Ski-lift, Sareis . . . . . 1·20 1·00

219 "The Annunciation"

1979. Christmas. Embroideries by Ferdinand Nigg. Multicoloured.
735 20r. Type **219** 20 40
736 50r. "Christmas" 40 35
737 80r. "Blessed are the Peacemakers" 60 75

220 Maria Leopoldine von Esterhazy (bust by Canova)

221 Arms of Andreas Buchel, 1690

1980. Europa.
738 **220** 40r. green, turq & gold 50 50
739 – 80r. brown, red and gold 80 75
DESIGN: 80r. Maria Theresia von Liechtenstein (after Martin von Meytens).

1980. Arms of Bailiffs (1st series). Multicoloured.
740 40r. Type **221** 30 25
741 70r. Georg Marxer, 1745 . . 60 55
742 80r. Luzius Frick, 1503 . . . 70 85
743 1f.10 Adam Oehri, 1634 . . . 85 75
See also Nos. 763/6, and 788/91.

222 3r. Stamp of 1930

223 Milking Pail

1980. 50th Anniv of Postal Museum.
744 **222** 80r. red, green and grey 70 65

1980. Alpine Dairy Farming Implements. Mult.
745 20r. Type **223** 20 10
746 50r. Wooden heart dairy herd descent marker 40 35
747 80r. Butter churn 65 60

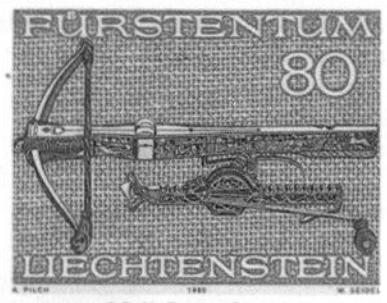

224 Crossbow

1980. Hunting Weapons.
748 **224** 80r. brown and lilac . . . 65 60
749 – 90r. black and green . . . 75 65
750 – 1f.10 black and stone . . 90 80
DESIGNS: 90r. Spear and knife; 1f.10, Rifle and powder-horn.

225 Triesenberg Costumes

1980. Costumes. Multicoloured.
751 40r. Type **225** 30 30
752 70r. Dancers, Schellenberg . . 65 60
753 80r. Brass band, Mauren . . 75 70

226 Beech Trees, Matrula (spring)

227 Angel bringing Shepherds Good Tidings

1980. The Forest in the Four Seasons. Multicoloured.
754 40r. Type **226** 30 30
755 50r. Firs in the Valorsch (summer) 40 35
756 80r. Beech tree, Schaan (autumn) 65 55
757 1f.50 Edge of forest at Oberplanken (winter) . . . 1·10 1·20

1980. Christmas. Multicoloured.
758 20r. Type **227** 20 45
759 50r. Crib 40 35
760 80r. Epiphany 60 60

228 National Day Procession

229 Prince Alois and Princess Elisabeth with Francis Joseph

1981. Europa. Multicoloured.
761 40r. Fireworks at Vaduz Castle 35 25
762 80r. Type **228** 80 70

1981. Arms of Bailiffs (2nd series). As T **221**. Multicoloured.
763 40r. Anton Meier, 1748 . . . 25 25
764 70r. Kaspar Kindle, 1534 . . 55 45
765 80r. Hans Adam Negele, 1600 . . . . 65 55
766 1f.10 Peter Matt, 1693 . . . 80 75

1981. 75th Birthday of Prince Francis Joseph II. Sheet 120 × 87 mm containing T **229** and similar vert designs. Multicoloured.
MS767 70r. Type **229**; 80r. Princes Alois and Francis Joseph; 150r. Prince Francis Joseph II . . . 3·00 3·00

230 Scout Emblems

1981. 50th Anniv of Liechtenstein Boy Scout and Girl Guide Movements.
768 **230** 20r. multicoloured 45 35

231 Symbols of Disability

232 St. Theodul (sculpture)

1981. International Year of Disabled Persons.
769 **231** 40r. multicoloured 35 35

1981. 1600th Birth Anniv of St. Theodul.
770 **232** 80r. multicoloured 65 60

233 "Xanthoria parietina"

1981. Mosses and Lichens. Multicoloured.
771 40r. Type **233** 25 25
772 50r. "Parmelia physodes" . . 50 40
773 70r. "Sphagnum palustre" . . 65 60
774 80r. "Amblystegium serpens" 75 70

234 Gutenberg Castle

1981. Gutenberg Castle. Multicoloured.
775 20r. Type **234** 20 20
776 40r. Courtyard 25 30
777 50r. Parlour 45 35
778 1f.10 Great Hall . . . . . . 1·00 90

235 Cardinal Karl Borromaus von Mailand

236 St. Nicholas blessing Children

1981. Famous Visitors to Liechtenstein (1st series). Multicoloured.
779 40r. Type **235** 30 30
780 70r. Johann Wolfgang von Goethe (writer) 70 75
781 89r. Alexander Dumas the younger (writer) 75 65
782 1f. Hermann Hesse (writer) 85 75
See also Nos. 804/7 and 832/5.

1981. Christmas. Multicoloured.
783 20r. Type **236** 20 20
784 50r. Adoration of the Kings 40 40
785 80r. Holy Family 75 65

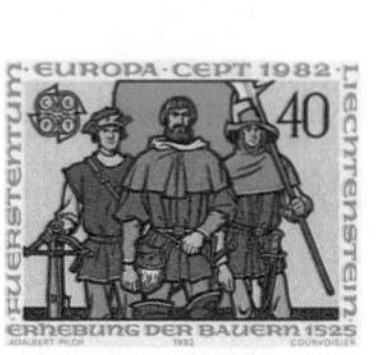

237 Peasant Revolt, 1525

1982. Europa. Multicoloured.
786 40r. Type **237** 35 35
787 80r. King Wenceslaus with Counts (Imperial direct rule, 1396) 75 70

1982. Arms of Bailiffs (3rd series). As T **221**. Multicoloured.
788 40r. Johann Kaiser, 1664 . . 35 25
789 70r. Joseph Anton Kaufmann, 1748 . . . . . 65 50
790 80r. Christoph Walser, 1690 75 60
791 1f.10 Stephan Banzer, 1658 1·00 95

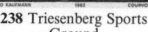

238 Triesenberg Sports Ground — **239** Crown Prince Hans Adam

1982. World Cup Football Championship, Spain. Multicoloured.

792	15r. Type **238**	15	60
793	25r. Eschen/Mauren playing fields	25	25
794	1f.80 Rheinau playing fields, Balzers	1·50	1·40

1982. "Liba 82" Stamp Exhibition. Multicoloured.

795	1f. Type **239**	85	85
796	1f. Princess Marie Aglae	85	85

240 Tractor (agriculture)

1982. Rural Industries. Multicoloured.

797	30r. Type **240**	25	20
798	50r. Cutting flowers (horticulture)	45	35
799	70r. Workers with logs (forestry)	60	55
800	150r. Worker and milk (dairy farming)	1·30	1·20

241 "Neu Schellenberg"

1982. 150th Birth Anniv of Mortiz Menzinger (artist). Multicoloured.

801	40r. Type **241**	30	30
802	50r. "Vaduz"	60	45
803	100r. "Bendern"	95	90

242 Angelika Kauffmann (artist, self-portrait) — **243** Angel playing Lute

1982. Famous Visitors to Liechtenstein (2nd series). Multicoloured.

804	40r. Emperor Maximilian I (after Benhard Strigel)	25	25
805	70f. Georg Jenatsch (liberator of Grisons)	55	50
806	80r. Type **242**	65	55
807	1f. St. Fidelis of Sigmaringen	85	80

1982. Christmas. Details from High Altar by Jakob Russ, Chur Cathedral. Multicoloured.

808	20r. Type **243**	15	15
809	50r. Madonna and child	45	35
810	80r. Angel playing organ	70	65

244 Notker Balbulus of St. Gall — **245** Shrove Thursday

1983. Europa. Multicoloured.

811	40r. Type **244**	30	25
812	80r. Hildegard of Bingen	80	55

1983. Shrovetide and Lent Customs. Mult.

813	40r. Type **245**	30	25
814	70r. Shrovetide carnival	70	50
815	1f.80 Lent Sunday bonfire	1·70	1·40

246 River Bank — **247** "Schaan"

1983. Anniversaries and Events. Multicoloured.

816	20r. Type **246**	35	20
817	40r. Montgolfier Brothers' balloon	50	35
818	50r. Airmail envelope	55	45
819	80r. Plant and hands holding spade	75	65

EVENTS: 20r. Council of Europe river and coasts protection campaign; 40r. Bicentenary of manned flight; 50r. World Communications Year; 80r. Overseas aid.

1983. Landscape Paintings by Anton Ender. Mult.

820	40r. Type **247**	35	25
821	50r. "Gutenberg Castle"	60	45
822	200r. "Steg Reservoir"	2·50	1·90

248 Princess Gina — **249** Pope John Paul II

1983. Multicoloured.

823	2f.50 Type **248**	2·75	2·50
824	3f. Prince Francis Joseph II	3·25	3·00

1983. Holy Year.

825	**249**	80r. multicoloured	1·20	80

250 Snowflakes and Stripes — **251** Seeking Shelter

1983. Winter Olympic Games, Sarajevo. Mult.

826	40r. Type **250**	30	25
827	80r. Snowflake	85	75
828	1f.80 Snowflake and rays	1·70	1·70

1983. Christmas. Multicoloured.

829	20r. Type **251**	15	20
830	50r. Infant Jesus	55	35
831	80r. Three Kings	80	70

252 Aleksandr Vassilievich Suvorov (Russian general) — **253** Bridge

1984. Famous Visitors to Liechtenstein (3rd series). Multicoloured.

832	40r. Type **252**	40	30
833	70r. Karl Rudolf von Buol-Schauenstein, Bishop of Chur	70	60
834	80r. Carl Zuckmayer (dramatist)	80	65
835	1f. Curt Goetz (actor)	95	90

1984. Europa. 25th Anniv of E.P.T. Conf.

836	**253**	50r. blue and deep blue	55	40
837		80r. pink and brown	80	80

254 The Warning Messenger — **255** Pole Vaulting

1984. Liechtenstein Legends. The Destruction of Trisona. Each brown, grey and blue.

838	35r. Type **254**	25	25
839	50r. The buried town	55	40
840	80r. The spared family	80	70

1984. Olympic Games, Los Angeles. Mult.

841	70r. Type **255**	65	65
842	80r. Throwing the discus	80	80
843	1f. Putting the shot	1·00	1·00

256 Currency (trade and banking)

1984. Occupations. Multicoloured.

844	5r. Type **256**	10	10
845	10r. Plumber adjusting pipe (building trade)	10	10
846	20r. Operating machinery (industry—production)	25	25
847	35r. Draughtswoman (building trade—planning)	35	35
848	45r. Office worker and world map (industry—sales)	50	50
849	50r. Cook (tourism)	50	25
850	60r. Carpenter (building trade—interior decoration)	60	50
851	70r. Doctor injecting patient (medical services)	70	70
852	80r. Scientist (industrial research)	80	75
853	100r. Bricklayer (building trade)	1·00	85
854	120r. Flow chart (industry—administration)	1·20	1·40
855	150r. Handstamping covers (post and communications)	1·90	1·40

257 Princess Marie — **258** Annunciation

1984. Multicoloured.

856	1f.70 Type **257**	1·40	1·40
857	2f. Crown Prince Hans Adam	1·40	1·70

1984. Christmas. Multicoloured.

858	35r. Type **258**	40	30
859	50r. Holy Family	35	40
860	80r. The Three Kings	65	70

259 Apollo and the Muses playing Music (detail from 18th-century harpsichord lid)

1985. Europa. Music Year. Multicoloured.

861	50r. Type **259**	60	50
862	80r. Apollo and the Muses playing music (different)	85	75

260 St. Elisabeth Convent, Schaan

1985. Monasteries. Multicoloured.

863	50r. Type **260**	60	45
864	1f. Schellenberg Convent	1·10	1·00
865	1f.70 Gutenberg Mission, Balzers	1·50	1·50

261 Princess Gina and handing out of Rations

1985. 40th Anniv of Liechtenstein Red Cross. Multicoloured.

866	20r. Type **261**	30	25
867	50r. Princess Gina and Red Cross ambulance	55	60
868	120r. Princess Gina with refugee children	95	1·20

262 Justice — **263** Papal Arms

1985. Cardinal Virtues. Multicoloured.

869	35r. Type **262**	35	30
870	50r. Temperance	55	50
871	70r. Prudence	70	65
872	1f. Fortitude	75	85

1985. Papal Visit. Sheet 100 × 67 mm containing T **263** and similar vert designs. Multicoloured.

MS873	50r. Type **263**; 80r. St. Maria zum Trost Chapel; 170r. Our Lady of Liechtenstein (statue) (29 × 43 mm)	3·25	3·25

264 "Portrait of a Canon" (Quentin Massys)

1985. Paintings in Metropolitan Museum, New York. Multicoloured.

874	50r. Type **264**	70	60
875	1f. "Clara Serena Rubens" (Rubens)	1·10	1·10
876	1f.20 "Duke of Urbino" (Raphael)	70	1·20

265 Halberd used by Charles I's Bodyguard

1985. Guards' Weapons and Armour. Mult.

877	35r. Type **265**	45	35
878	50r. Morion used by Charles I's bodyguard	55	50
879	80r. Halberd used by Carl Eusebius's bodyguard	75	70

266 Frankincense — **267** Puppets performing Tragedy

1985. Christmas. Multicoloured.

880	35r. Type **266**	40	30
881	50r. Gold	65	60
882	80r. Myrrh	65	75

1985. Theatre. Multicoloured.

883	50r. Type **267**	65	65
884	80r. Puppets performing comedy	85	80
885	1f.50 Opera	1·30	1·20

268 Courtyard — **269** Barn Swallows

1986. Vaduz Castle. Multicoloured.

886	20r. Type **268**	25	20
887	25r. Keep	40	35
888	50r. Castle	60	55
889	90r. Inner gate	90	75
890	1f.10 Castle from gardens	1·20	1·00
891	1f.40 Courtyard (different)	1·50	1·30

1986. Europa. Birds. Multicoloured.

892		50r. Type **269**	60	55
893		90r. European robin	95	85

270 "Offerings"

271 Palm Sunday

1986. Lenten Fast.

894	**270**	1f.40 multicoloured	1·40	1·40

1986. Religious Festivals. Multicoloured.

895		35r. Type **271**	45	30
896		50r. Wedding	55	35
897		70r. Rogation Day procession	80	55

272 Karl Freiherr Haus von Hausen

273 Francis Joseph II

1986. 125th Anniv of Liechtenstein Land Bank.

898	**272**	50r. brown, ochre and buff	55	55

1986. 80th Birthday of Prince Francis Joseph II.

899	**273**	3f.50 multicoloured	3·25	3·00

274 Roebuck in Ruggeller Riet

275 Cabbage and Beetroot

1986. Hunting. Multicoloured.

900		35r. Type **274**	45	45
901		50r. Chamois at Rappenstein	70	70
902		1f.70 Stag in Lawena	1·50	1·50

1986. Field Crops. Multicoloured.

903		50r. Type **275**	50	50
904		80r. Red cabbages	85	85
905		90r. Potatoes, onions and garlic	95	95

276 Archangel Michael

277 Silver Fir

1986. Christmas. Multicoloured.

906		35r. Type **276**	30	30
907		50r. Archangel Gabriel	65	65
908		90r. Archangel Raphael	90	90

1986. Tree Bark. Multicoloured.

909		35r. Type **277**	30	30
910		90r. Norway spruce	95	95
911		1f.40 Pedunculate oak	1·50	1·50

278 Gamprin Primary School

280 Niklaus von Flue

1987. Europa. Multicoloured.

912		50r. Type **278**	60	55
913		90r. Schellenberg parish church	95	90

1987. 500th Death Anniv of Niklaus von Flue (martyr).

914	**280**	1f.10 multicoloured	1·20	1·20

281 Bullhead

282 Prince Alois (frame as in first stamps)

1987. Fishes (1st series). Multicoloured.

915		50r. Type **281**	55	55
916		90r. Brown trout	85	85
917		1f.10 European grayling	1·40	1·40

See also Nos. 959/61.

1987. 75th Anniv of First Liechtenstein Stamps.

918	**282**	2f. multicoloured	2·20	2·20

283 Staircase

284 Arms

1987. Liechtenstein City Palace, Vienna. Multicoloured.

919		35r. Type **283**	35	35
920		50r. Minoritenplatz doorway	75	70
921		90r. Staircase (different)	1·00	1·00

1987. 275th Anniv of Transfer of County of Vaduz to House of Liechtenstein.

922	**284**	1f.40 multicoloured	1·50	1·50

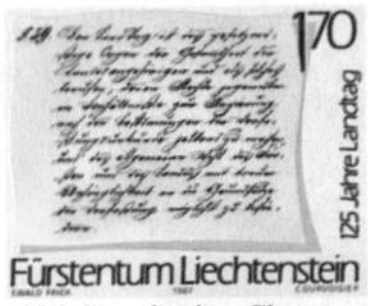

285 Constitution Charter, 1862

286 St. Matthew

1987. 125th Anniv of Liechtenstein Parliament.

923	**285**	1f.70 multicoloured	1·80	1·80

1987. Christmas. Illuminations from Golden Book of Pfafers Abbey. Multicoloured.

924		35r. Type **286**	40	35
925		50r. St. Mark	60	60
926		60r. St. Luke	65	65
927		90r. St. John	1·20	1·20

287 "The Toil of the Cross-country Skier"

288 Dish Aerial

1987. Winter Olympic Games, Calgary (1988). Multicoloured.

928		25r. Type **287**	35	35
929		90r. "The Courageous Pioneers of Skiing"	1·00	1·00
930		1f.10 "As our Grandfathers used to ride on a Bobsled"	1·40	1·40

1988. Europa. Transport and Communications. Mult.

931		50r. Type **288**	40	40
932		90r. Maglev monorail	1·10	1·00

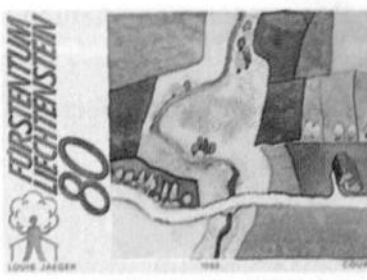

289 Agriculture

1988. European Campaign for Rural Areas. Multicoloured.

933		80r. Type **289**	80	80
934		90r. Village centre	1·20	1·20
935		1f.70 Road	1·90	1·90

290 Headphones on Books (Radio Broadcasts)

291 Crown Prince Hans Adam

1988. Costa Rica–Liechtenstein Cultural Co-operation.

936	**290**	50r. multicoloured	60	60
937	–	1f.40 red, brown and green	1·50	1·50

DESIGN: 1f.40, Man with pen and radio (Adult education).

1988. 50th Anniv of Accesion of Prince Francis Joseph II. Sheet 100 × 68 mm containing T **291** and similar vert designs. Multicoloured.

MS938		50r. Type **291**; 50r. Prince Alois; 2f. Prince Francis Joseph II	4·50	4·25

292 St. Barbara's Shrine, Balzers

1988. Wayside Shrines. Multicoloured.

939		25r. Type **292**	35	35
940		35r. Shrine containing statues of Christ, St. Peter and St. Paul at Oberdorf, Vaduz	40	40
941		50r. St. Anthony of Egypt's shrine, Fallagass, Ruggel	50	50

293 Cycling

294 Joseph and Mary

1988. Olympic Games, Seoul. Multicoloured.

942		50r. Type **293**	45	45
943		80r. Gymnastics	80	85
944		90r. Running	1·00	1·10
945		1f.40 Equestrian event	1·80	1·90

1988. Christmas. Multicoloured.

946		35r. Type **294**	35	30
947		50r. Baby Jesus	65	70
948		90r. Wise Men presenting gifts to Jesus	1·10	1·10

295 Letter beside Footstool (detail)

296 "Cat and Mouse"

1988. "The Letter" (portrait of Marie-Theresa, Princesse de Lamballe by Anton Hickel). Multicoloured.

949		50r. Type **295**	65	75
950		90r. Desk and writing materials (detail)	1·00	1·10
951		2f. "The Letter" (complete painting)	2·10	2·40

1989. Europa. Children's Games. Multicoloured.

952		50r. Type **296**	65	65
953		90r. "Hide and Seek"	1·20	1·20

298 Rheinberger and Score

299 Little Ringed Plover

1989. 150th Birth Anniv of Josef Gabriel Rheinberger (composer).

954	**298**	2f.90 black, blue & purple	3·50	3·75

1989. Endangered Animals. Multicoloured.

955		25r. Type **299**	65	30
956		35r. Green tree frog	45	45
957		50r. "Libelloides coccajus" (lace-wing)	65	60
958		90r. Polecat	1·30	1·20

300 Northern Pike

1989. Fishes (2nd series). Multicoloured.

959		50r. Type **300**	50	55
960		1f.10 Brown trout	1·20	1·30
961		1f.40 Stone loach	1·70	1·90

301 Return of Cattle from Alpine Pastures

302 Falknis

1989. Autumn Customs. Multicoloured.

962		35r. Type **301**	40	45
963		50r. Peeling corn cobs	70	75
964		80r. Cattle market	80	80

1989. Mountains. Watercolours by Josef Schadler.

965	–	5r. multicoloured	10	10
966	–	10r. multicoloured	10	10
967	–	35r. multicoloured	30	35
968	–	40r. multicoloured	40	50
969	–	45r. multicoloured	45	55
970	**302**	50r. multicoloured	45	55
971	–	60r. multicoloured	55	60
972	–	70r. multicoloured	65	75
973	–	75r. multicoloured	70	80
974	–	80r. violet, brown & black	75	85
975	–	1f. multicoloured	90	1·10
976	–	1f.20 multicoloured	1·10	1·20
977	–	1f.50 multicoloured	1·50	1·40
978	–	1f.60 multicoloured	1·90	1·70
979	–	2f. multicoloured	1·60	1·75

DESIGNS: 5r. Augstenberg; 10r. Hahenespiel; 35r. Nospitz; 40r. Ochsenkopf; 45r. Three Sisters; 60r. Kuhgrat; 70r. Galinakopf; 75r. Plassteikopf; 80pf. Naafkopf; 1f. Schonberg; 1f.20, Bleikaturm; 1f.50, Garselliturm; 1f.60, Schwarzhorn; 2f. Scheienkopf.

303 "Melchior and Balthasar"

304 Mace Quartz

1989. Christmas. Details of triptych by Hugo van der Goes. Multicoloured.

981		35r. Type **303**	55	45
982		50r. "Kaspar and Holy Family" (27 × 34 mm)	55	65
983		90r. "St. Stephen"	90	90

1989. Minerals. Multicoloured.

984		50r. Type **304**	60	60
985		1f.10 Globe pyrite	1·50	1·50
986		1f.50 Calcite	1·90	1·90

305 Nendeln Forwarding Agency, 1864

306 Penny Black

1990. Europa. Post Office Buildings. Mult.
987 50r. Type **305** 65 65
988 90r. Vaduz post office, 1976 1·00 1·00

1990. 150th Anniv of the Penny Black.
989 **306** 1f.50 multicoloured . . . 1·90 1·80

307 Footballers

308 Tureen, Oranges and Grapes

1990. World Cup Football Championship, Italy.
990 **307** 2f. multicoloured . . . . 2·30 2·20

1990. 9th Death Anniv of Benjamin Steck (painter). Multicoloured.
991 50r. Type **308** 75 75
992 80r. Apples and pewter bowl 1·00 1·00
993 1f.50 Basket, apples, cherries and pewter jug . . . . . . 1·50 1·50

309 Princess Gina

310 Common Pheasant

1990. Prince Francis Joseph II and Princess Gina Commemoration. Multicoloured.
994 2f. Type **309** . . . . 2·10 2·10
995 3f. Prince Francis Joseph II 3·25 3·25

1990. Game Birds. Multicoloured.
996 25r. Type **310** 35 35
997 50r. Black grouse 65 65
998 2f. Mallard . . . . 2·40 2·40

311 Annunciation

312 St. Nicholas

1990. Christmas. Paintings. Multicoloured.
999 35r. Type **311** 45 45
1000 50r. Nativity 55 60
1001 90r. Adoration of the Magi 1·00 1·00

1990. Winter Customs. Multicoloured.
1002 35r. Type **312** 45 45
1003 50r. Awakening on New Year's Eve 55 55
1004 1f.50 Giving New Year greetings . . . . 1·60 1·60

313 Mounted Courier

314 "Olympus 1" Satellite

1990. 500th Anniv of Regular European Postal Services.
1005 **313** 90r. multicoloured . . . 1·00 1·00

1991. Europa. Europe in Space. Multicoloured.
1006 50r. Type **314** 60 60
1007 90r. "Meteosat" satellite . . 1·00 1·00

315 St. Ignatius de Loyola (founder of Society of Jesus)

316 U.N. Emblem and Dove

1991. Anniversaries. Multicoloured.
1008 80r. Type **315** (500th birth anniv) 95 90
1009 90r. Wolfgang Amadeus Mozart (composer, death bicentenary) . . . . . . 1·00 1·00

1991. Admission to U.N. Membership (1990).
1010 **316** 2f.50 multicoloured . . . 2·75 2·75

317 Non-Commissioned Officer and Private

318 "Near Maloja" (Giovanni Giacometti)

1991. 125th Anniv of Last Mobilization of Liechtenstein's Military Contingent (to the Tyrol). Multicoloured.
1011 50r. Type **317** 55 60
1012 70r. Tunic, chest and portrait 75 70
1013 1f. Officer and private . . . 1·20 1·20

1991. 700th Anniv of Swiss Confederation. Paintings by Swiss artists. Multicoloured.
1014 50r. Type **318** 55 55
1015 80r. "Rhine Valley" (Ferdinand Gehr) 90 85
1016 90r. "Bergell" (Augusto Giacometti) 95 95
1017 1f.10 "Hoher Kasten" (Hedwig Scherrer) . . . . 1·20 1·20

319 Stampless and Modern Covers

320 Princess Marie

1991. "Liba 92" National Stamp Exhibition, Vaduz.
1018 **319** 90r. multicoloured . . . 1·00 1·00

1991. Multicoloured.
1019 3f. Type **320** . . . . 3·25 3·25
1020 3f.40 Prince Hans Adam II 3·50 3·50

321 Virgin of the Annunciation (exterior of left wing)

322 Cross-country Skiers and Testing for Drug Abuse

1991. Christmas. Details of the altar from St. Mamertus Chapel, Triesen. Multicoloured.
1021 50r. Type **321** 55 55
1022 80r. Madonna and Child (wood-carving attr. Jorg Syrlin, inner shrine) . . . 85 85
1023 90r. Angel Gabriel (exterior of right wing) 95 90

1991. Winter Olympic Games, Albertville. Mult.
1024 70r. Type **322** 80 80
1025 80r. Ice hockey player tackling opponent and helping him after fall . . 85 85
1026 1f.60 Downhill skier and fallen skier caught in safety net . . . . 1·90 1·80

323 Relay Race, Drugs and Shattered Medal

324 Aztecs

1992. Olympic Games, Barcelona. Multicoloured.
1027 50r. Type **323** 50 55
1028 70r. Cycling road race . . . 95 90
1029 2f.50 Judo . . . . 2·75 2·75

1992. Europa. 500th Anniv of Discovery of America by Columbus. Multicoloured.
1030 80r. Type **324** 80 80
1031 90r. Statue of Liberty and New York skyline 95 90

325 Clown in Envelope ("Good Luck")

327 "Blechnum spicant"

326 Arms of Liechtenstein—Kinsky Alliance

1992. Greetings Stamps. Multicoloured.
1032 50r. Type **325** 50 50
1033 50r. Wedding rings in envelope and harlequin violinist 50 50
1034 50r. Postman blowing horn (31 × 21 mm) 50 50
1035 50r. Flying postman carrying letter sealed with heart (31 × 21 mm) . . . 50 50

1992. "Liba '92" National Stamp Exhibition. Silver Wedding Anniv of Prince Hans Adam and Princess Marie. Sheet 100 × 67 mm containing T **326** and similar vert design. Multicoloured.
MS1036 2f. Type **326**; 2f.50 Royal couple (photo by Anthony Buckley) . . . . 5·50 5·25

1992. Ferns. Multicoloured.
1037 40r. Type **327** 40 40
1038 50r. Maidenhair spleenwort 55 50
1039 70r. Hart's-tongue 75 70
1040 2f.50 "Asplenium ruta-muraria" . . . . 2·40 2·50

328 Reading Edict

329 Chapel of St. Mamertus, Triesen

1992. 650th Anniv of County of Vaduz.
1041 **328** 1f.60 multicoloured . . . 1·70 1·70

1992. Christmas. Multicoloured.
1042 50r. Type **329** 55 50
1043 90r. Crib, St. Gallus's Church, Triesen 95 95
1044 1f.60 St. Mary's Chapel, Triesen . . . . 1·70 1·70

330 Crown Prince Alois

331 "Nafkopf and Huts, Steg"

1992.
1045 **330** 2f.50 multicoloured . . . 2·50 2·40

1993. 1400th Birth Anniv of Hans Gantner (painter). Multicoloured.
1046 50r. Type **331** 40 40
1047 60r. "Hunting Lodge, Sass" 70 70
1048 1f.80 "Red House, Vaduz" 2·20 2·20

332 "910805" (Bruno Kaufmann)

333 "Tale of the Ferryman" (painting)

1993. Europa. Contemporary Art. Multicoloured.
1049 80r. Type **332** . . . . . . 1·00 1·00
1050 1f. "The Little Blue" (Evi Kliemand) . . . . 1·20 1·20

1993. Tibetan Collection in the National Museum. Multicoloured.
1051 60r. Type **333** 75 70
1052 80r. Religious dance mask 75 90
1053 1f. "Tale of the Fish" (painting) . . . . 1·10 1·40

334 "Tree of Life"

335 "The Black Hatter"

1993. Missionary Work.
1054 **334** 1f.80 multicoloured . . . 2·20 2·00

1993. Homage to Liechtenstein.
1055 **335** 2f.80 multicoloured . . . 3·75 3·75

336 Crown Prince Alois and Duchess Sophie of Bavaria

1993. Royal Wedding. Sheet 100 × 67 mm.
MS1056 **336** 4f. multicoloured . . 5·00 5·00

337 Origanum

338 Eurasian Badger

1993. Flowers. Illustrations from "Hortus Botanicus Liechtensteinsis". Multicoloured.
1057 50r. Type **337** 75 65
1058 60r. Meadow sage 85 70
1059 1f. "Seseli annuum" . . . . 1·40 1·10
1060 2f.50 Large self-heal . . . . 2·20 2·75

1993. Animals. Multicoloured.
1061 60r. Type **338** 70 75
1062 80r. Beech marten . . . . . 1·00 1·00
1063 1f. Red fox . . . . 1·30 1·30

339 "Now that the Quiet Days are Coming ..." (Rainer Maria Rilke)

340 Ski Jump

1993. Christmas. Multicoloured.
1064 60r. Type **339** 70 70
1065 80r. "Can You See the Light ..." (Th. Friedrich) 1·00 1·00
1066 1f. "Christmas, Christmas ..." (R. A. Schroder) . . . 1·10 1·10

1993. Winter Olympic Games, Lillehammer, Norway (1994). Multicoloured.
1067 60r. Type **340** 90 90
1068 80r. Slalom . . . . 1·10 1·10
1069 2f.40 Bobsleighing . . . . . 2·50 2·50

341 Seal and Title Page

342 Andean Condor

1994. Anniversaries. Multicoloured.
1070 60r. Type **341** (275th anniv of Principality) 75 75
1071 1f.80 State, Prince's and Olympic flags (centenary of International Olympic Committee) . . . . . . 2·10 2·10

1994. Europa. Discoveries of Alexander von Humboldt. Multicoloured.
1072 80r. Type **342** 95 95
1073 1f. "Rhexia cardinalis" (plant) . . . . 1·20 1·20

343 Football Pitch and Hopi Indians playing Kickball

344 Elephant with Letter

1994. World Cup Football Championship, U.S.A.
1074 **343** 2f.80 multicoloured . . . 3·25 3·25

1994. Greetings Stamps. Multicoloured.
1075 60r. Type **344** 75 75
1076 60r. Cherub with flower and hearts 75 75
1077 60r. Pig with four-leaf clover 75 75
1078 60r. Dog holding bunch of tulips 75 75

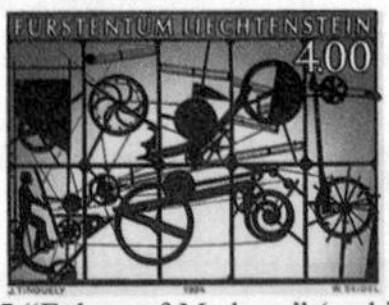

345 "Eulogy of Madness" (mobile, Jean Tinguely)

1994. Homage to Liechtenstein.
1079 **345** 4f. black, pink and violet 5·00 5·00

346 Spring

1994. Seasons of the Vine. Multicoloured.
1080 60r. Type **346** 75 75
1081 60r. Vine leaves (Summer) 75 75
1082 60r. Trunk in snowy landscape (Winter) . . . 75 75
1083 60r. Grapes (Autumn) . . . 75 75
Nos. 1080/3 were issued together, se-tenant, forming a composite design.

347 Strontium

1994. Minerals. Multicoloured.
1084 60r. Type **347** 85 90
1085 80r. Quartz . . . . 1·10 1·10
1086 3f.50 Iron dolomite . . . . 4·00 3·75

348 "The True Light"

349 Earth

1994. Christmas. Multicoloured.
1087 60r. Type **348** 70 70
1088 80r. "Peace on Earth" . . . 95 95
1089 1f. "Behold, the House of God" . . . . 1·20 1·20

1994. The Four Elements. Multicoloured.
1090 60r. Type **349** 75 75
1091 80r. Water 95 95
1092 1f. Fire . . . . 1·20 1·20
1093 2f.50 Air . . . . 2·75 2·75

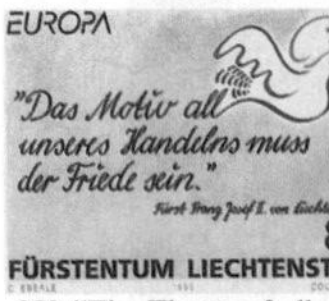

350 "The Theme of all our Affairs must be Peace"

351 U.N. Flag and Bouquet of Flowers

1995. Europa. Peace and Freedom. Quotations of Franz Josef II. Multicoloured.
1094 80r. Type **350** 95 95
1095 1f. "Through Unity comes Strength and the Bearing of Sorrows" . . . . . . 1·30 1·30

1995. Anniversaries and Event. Multicoloured.
1096 60r. Princess Marie with children (50th anniv of Liechtenstein Red Cross) (horiz) 75 75
1097 1f.80 Type **351** (50th anniv of U.N.O.) . . . . 2·20 2·20
1098 3f.50 Alps (European Nature Conservation Year) . . . . 4·25 4·25

352 "Falknis Mountains"

353 "One Heart and One Soul"

1995. Birth Centenary of Anton Frommelt (painter). Multicoloured.
1099 60r. Type **352** 75 75
1100 80r. "Three Oaks" . . . . 1·00 1·00
1101 4f.10 "The Rhine" . . . . 4·75 4·75

1995. Greetings Stamps. Multicoloured.
1102 60r. Type **353** 75 75
1103 60r. Bandage round sunflower ("Get Well") 75 75
1104 60r. Baby arriving over rainbow ("Hurrah! Here I am") 75 75
1105 60r. Delivering letter by hot-air balloon ("Write again") 75 75

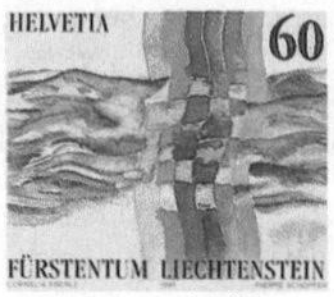

354 Coloured Ribbons woven through River

355 Arnica

1995. Liechtenstein–Switzerland Co-operation.
1106 **354** 60r. multicoloured . . . 75 75

No. 1106 was valid for use in both Liechtenstein and Switzerland (see No. 1308 of Switzerland).

1995. Medicinal Plants. Multicoloured.
1107 60r. Type **355** 70 75
1108 80r. Giant nettle 95 75
1109 1f.80 Common valerian . . 2·20 2·20
1110 3f.50 Fig-wort . . . . . . 3·50 3·75

356 Angel (detail of painting)

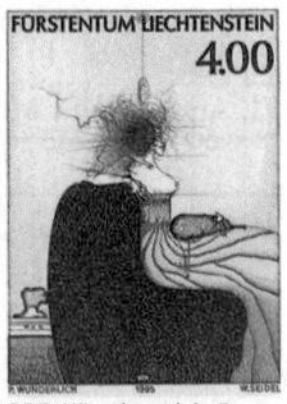

357 "Lady with Lap-dog" (Paul Wunderlich)

1995. Christmas. Painting by Lorenzo Monaco. Multicoloured.
1111 60r. Type **356** 70 70
1112 80r. "Virgin Mary with Infant and Two Angels" 95 95
1113 1f. Angel facing left (detail of painting) . . . . . . 1·20 1·20

1995. Homage to Liechtenstein.
1114 **357** 4f. multicoloured . . . . 4·75 4·75

358 Eschen

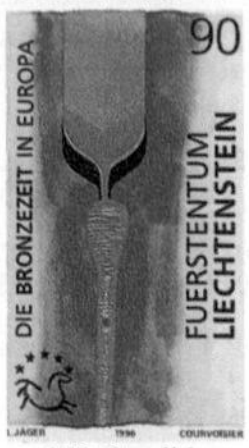

359 Crucible

1996. Scenes. Multicoloured.
1115 10r. Type **358** 10 10
1116 20r. Planken 25 25
1117 50r. Ruggell 55 55
1117a 60r. Balzers 60 60
1117b 70r. Schellenberg 75 75
1118 80r. Ruggell 85 85
1120 1f. Nendeln . . . . 1·10 1·10
1120a 1f.10 Eschen . . . . . . 1·20 1·20
1122 1f.20 Triesen . . . . . . 1·30 1·30
1123 1f.30 Triesen . . . . . . 1·40 1·40
1124 1f.40 Mauren . . . . . . 1·50 1·50
1125 1f.70 Schaanwald . . . . 1·80 1·80
1125a 1f.80 Malbun . . . . . . 1·90 1·90
1125b 1f.90 Schaan . . . . . . 2·10 2·10
1126 2f. Gamprin . . . . 2·10 2·10
1126a 2f.20 Balzers . . . . . . 2·30 2·30
1127 4f. Triesenberg . . . . . 4·25 4·25
1127a 4f.50 Bendern . . . . . 4·75 4·75
1128 5f. Vaduz Castle . . . . . 5·25 5·25

1996. Bronze Age in Europe.
1130 **359** 90r. multicoloured . . . 1·10 1·10

360 Kinsky and Diary Extract, 7 March 1917

1996. Europa. Famous Women. Nora, Countess Kinsky (mother of Princess Gina of Liechtenstein).
1131 **360** 90r. grey, purple and blue . . . . 1·00 1·00
1132 – 1f.10 grey, blue and purple . . . . . . 1·20 1·20
DESIGN: 1f.10, Kinsky and diary extract for 28 February 1917.

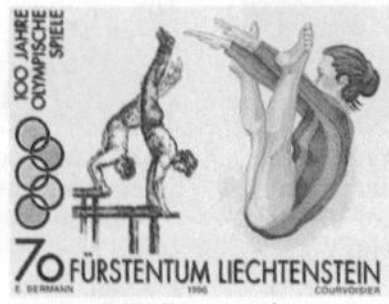

361 Gymnastics

1996. Centenary of Modern Olympic Games. Multicoloured.
1133 70r. Type **361** 75 75
1134 90r. Hurdling 95 95
1135 1f.10 Cycling . . . . 1·30 1·30

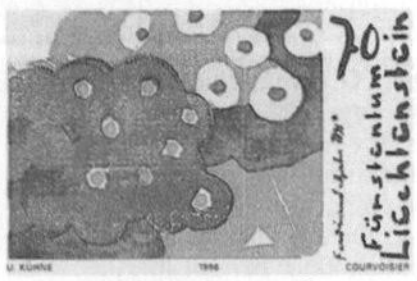

362 "Primroses"

1996. Birth Centenary of Ferdinand Gehr (painter). Multicoloured.
1136 70r. Type **362** 80 80
1137 90r. "Daisies" . . . . . . 1·00 1·00
1138 1f.10 "Poppy" . . . . . . 1·20 1·20
1139 1f.80 "Buttercups" (33 × 23 mm) . . . . . . 2·00 2·00

363 State Arms

1996.
1140 **363** 10f. multicoloured . . . 10·50 10·50

364 Veldkirch, 1550

1996. Millenary of Austria.
1141 **364** 90r. multicoloured . . . 1·10 1·10

365 "Poltava"

366 St. Matthew

1996. 43rd Death Anniv of Eugen Zotow (painter). Multicoloured.
1142 70r. Type **365** 75 75
1143 1f.10 "Three Bathers in a Berlin Park" 75 75
1144 1f.40 "Vaduz" . . . . . . 1·00 1·00

1996. Christmas. Illustrations from Illuminated Manuscript "Liber Viventium Fabariensis". Multicoloured.
1145 70r. Type **366** 80 75
1146 90r. Emblems of St. Mark 1·00 95
1147 1f.10 Emblems of St. Luke 1·20 1·20
1148 1f.80 Emblems of St. John 2·00 2·00

367 Schubert

368 The Wild Gnomes

1997. Birth Bicent of Franz Schubert (composer).
1149 **367** 70r. multicoloured . . . 85 85

1997. Europa. Tales and Legends. Multicoloured.
1150 90r. Type **368** 90 90
1151 1f.10 Man, pumpkin and rabbit (The Foal of Planken) . . . . 1·20 1·20

369 "Madonna and Child with St. Lucius and St. Florinus" (Gabriel Dreher)

1997. National Patron Saints.
1152 **369** 20f. multicoloured . . . 17·00 17·00

370 "Phaeolepiota aurea"

1997. Fungi (1st series). Multicoloured.
1153 70r. Type **370** 70 70
1154 90r. "Helvella silvicola" . . 90 90
1155 1f.10 Orange peel fungus . . 1·20 1·20
See also Nos. 1238/40.

371 Steam Train, Schaanwald Halt

372 "Girl with Flower" (Enrico Baj)

1997. 125th Anniv of Liechtenstein Railways. Mult.
1156 70r. Type **371** 75 75
1157 90r. Diesel-electric train, Nendeln station 95 95
1158 1f.80 Electric train, Schaan-Vaduz station . . . . . . 1·90 1·90

1997. Homage to Liechtenstein.
1159 **372** 70r. multicoloured . . . 75 75

373 Basket of Roses

374 Cross-country skiing

1997. Christmas. Glass Tree Decorations. Multicoloured.
1160 70r. Type **373** 70 70
1161 90r. Bell 90 90
1162 1f.10 Bauble . . . . 1·10 1·10

1997. Winter Olympic Games, Nagano, Japan (1998). Skiing. Multicoloured.
1163 70r. Type **374** 70 70
1164 90r. Slalom 95 95
1165 1f.80 Downhill . . . . . . 1·90 1·90

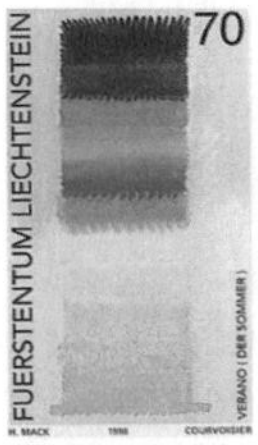

375 "Verano" (The Summer)"

1998. Homage to Liechtenstein. Paintings by Heinz Mack. Multicoloured.
1166 70r. Type **375** 70 70
1167 70r. "Homage to Liechtenstein" 70 70
1168 70r. "Between Day and Dream" 70 70
1169 70r. "Salute Cirico!" 70 70

376 Prince's Festival Procession, Vaduz

1998. Europa. National Festivals. Multicoloured.
1170 90r. Type **376** 95 95
1171 1f.10 Music Societies Festival, Gutenberg Castle, Balzers . . . . . 1·20 1·20

377 National Flags on Bridge

1998. 75th Anniv of Liechtenstein–Switzerland Customs Treaty.
1172 **377** 1f.70 multicoloured . . . 1·80 1·80

378 Goalkeeper

1998. World Cup Football Championship, France.
1173 **378** 1f.80 multicoloured . . . 1·90 1·90

379 Clown with Queen of Hearts

380 Wooden Milk Vat

1998. Greeting Stamps. Clowns. Multicoloured.
1174 70r. Type **379** 70 70
1175 70r. Clown holding four-leaf clovers 70 70
1176 70r. Clown raising hat . . . 70 70
1177 70r. Clown holding heart . . 70 70

1998. Traditional Crafts (1st series). Multicoloured.
1178 90r. Type **380** 90 90
1179 2f.20 Clog . . . . 2·20 2·20
1180 3f.50 Wheel . . . . 3·50 3·50
See also Nos. 1257/9.

381 Expelling Johann Langer from Liechtenstein

1998. 150th Anniv of 1848 Revolutions in Europe.
1181 **381** 1f.80 multicoloured . . . 1·90 1·90

382 Virgin Mary

1998. Christmas. Multicoloured.
1182 70r. Type **382** 75 75
1183 90r. "The Nativity" (35 × 26 mm) 90 90
1184 1f.10 Joseph . . . . 1·20 1·20
Nos. 1182 and 1184 show details of the complete relief depicted on No. 1183.

383 Zum Lowen Guest House

384 Automatic and Manual Switchboards

1998. Preservation of Historical Environment. Hinterschellenberg. Multicoloured.
1185 90r. Type **383** 90 95
1186 1f.70 St. George's Chapel (vert) . . . . 1·90 1·90
1187 1f.80 Houses . . . . 1·90 1·90

1998. Centenary of Telephone in Liechtenstein.
1188 **384** 2f.80 multicoloured . . . 3·00 3·00

385 Eschen

1999. 300th Anniv of Purchase of Unterland by Prince Johann Adam. Sheet 107 × 68 mm containing T **385** and similar horiz design. Multicoloured.
MS1189 90r. × 5 plus label, Composite design of the Unterland showing the villages of Eschen, Gamprin, Mauren, Ruggell and Schellenberg . . . 4·50 4·50

386 Smooth Snake and Schwabbrunnen-Aescher Nature Park

387 Council Anniversary Emblem and Silhouettes

1999. Europa. Parks and Gardens. Multicoloured.
1190 90r. Type **386** . . . . . . 1·00 1·00
1191 1f.10 Corn crake and Ruggell marsh . . . . . 1·10 1·10

1999. Anniversaries and Event. Multicoloured.
1192 70r. Type **387** (50th anniv of Council of Europe and European Convention on Human Rights) 75 75
1193 70r. Bird with envelope in beak (125th anniv of U.P.U.) 75 75
1194 70r. Heart in hand (75th anniv of Caritas Liechtenstein (welfare organization)) 75 75

388 Judo

1999. 8th European Small States Games, Liechtenstein. Multicoloured.
1195 70r. Type **388** 70 70
1196 70r. Swimming 70 70
1197 70r. Throwing the javelin . . 70 70
1198 90r. Cycling 95 95
1199 90r. Shooting 95 95
1200 90r. Tennis 95 95
1201 90r. Squash 95 95
1202 90r. Table tennis 95 95
1203 90r. Volleyball 95 95

389 "Herrengasse"

1999. Paintings by Eugen Verling. Multicoloured.
1204 70r. Type **389** 85 85
1205 2f. "Old Vaduz with Castle" 1·20 1·20
1206 4f. "House in Furst-Franz-Josef Street, Vaduz" . . . 5·00 5·00

390 Scene from "Faust", Act I

1999. 250th Birth Anniv of Johann Wolfgang Goethe (poet and playwright). Multicoloured.
1207 1f.40 Type **390** . . . . . . 1·50 1·50
1208 1f.70 Faust and the Devil sealing wager . . . . . . 1·80 1·80

391 "The Annunciation"

392 Identification Mark on Door, Ubersaxen

1999. Christmas. Paintings by Joseph Walser from Chapel of Our Lady of Comfort, Dux. Mult.
1209 70r. Type **391** 75 75
1210 90r. "Nativity" 95 95
1211 1f.10 "Adoration" . . . . . 1·20 1·20

1999. Walser Identification Marks. Multicoloured.
1212 70r. Type **392** 75 75
1213 90r. Mark on mural 95 95
1214 1f.80 Mark on axe . . . . . 1·90 1·90

393 Gutenberg

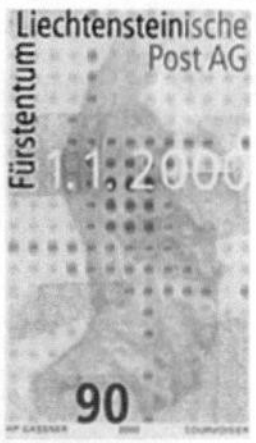

395 Emblem

394 "The Adoration of the Shepheards" (Matthia Stomer)

1999. 600th Birth Anniv of Johannes Gutenberg (inventor of printing press).
1215 **393** 3f.60 multicoloured . . . 2·75 2·75

2000. 2000 Years of Christianity. Sheet 108 × 68 mm containing T **394** and similar square design. Multicoloured.
MS1216 70r. Type **394**; 1f.10 "Three Kings" (Ferdinand Gehr) . . . 1·75 1·75

2000. Provision of Postal Services by Liechtenstein Post in Partnership with Swiss Post.
1217 **395** 90r. multicoloured . . . 95 95

396 "Mars and Rhea Silvia" (Peter Paul Rubens)

2000. Paintings. Multicoloured.
1218 70r. Type **396** 75 75
1219 1f.80 "Cupid with Soap-Bubble" (Rembrandt) . . 1·90 1·90

397 "Fragrance of Humus"

398 "Building Europe"

2000. "EXPO 2000" World's Fair, Hanover, Germany. Paintings by Friedensreich Hundertwasser. Multicoloured.
1220 70r. Type **397** 75 75
1221 90r. "Do Not Wait Houses-Move" . . . . 1·00 1·00
1222 1f.10 "The Car: a Drive Towards Nature and Creation" . . . . 1·20 1·20

2000. Europa.
1223 **398** 1f.10 multicoloured . . . 1·10 1·10

399 "Dove of Peace" (Antonio Martini)

2000. "Peace 2000". Paintings by members of Association of Mouth and Foot Painting Artists. Mult.
1224 1f.40 Type **399** . . . . . . 1·50 1·50
1225 1f.70 "World Peace" (Alberto Alvarez) . . . . 1·80 1·80
1226 2f.20 "Rainbow" (Eiichi Minami) . . . . 2·30 2·30

400 Koalas on Rings (Gymnastics)

2000. Olympic Games, Sydney. Multicoloured.
1227 80r. Type **400** 80 80
1228 1f. Joey leaping over crossbar (High jump) . . 95 95
1229 1f.30 Emus approaching finish line (Athletics) . . . 1·40 1·40
1230 1f.80 Duckbill platypuses in swimming race . . . . . 1·90 1·90

401 "The Dreaming Bee" (Joan Miro)

2000. Inauguration of Art Museum. Multicoloured.
1231 80r. Type **401** 85 85
1232 1f.20 "Cube" (Sol LeWitt) 1·30 1·30
1233 2f. "Bouquet of Flowers" (Raelant Savery) (31 × 46 mm) . . . . . . 2·00 2·00

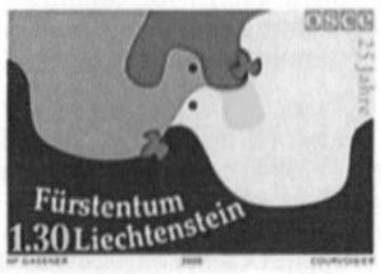

402 "Peace Doves"

2000. 25th Anniv of Organization for Security and Co-operation in Europe.
1234 **402** 1f.30 multicoloured . . . 1·40 1·40

403 Root Crib

2000. Christmas. Cribs. Multicoloured.
1235 80r. Type **403** 80 80
1236 1f.30 Oriental crib . . . . . 1·40 1·40
1237 1f.80 Crib with cloth figures 1·90 1·90

2000. Fungi (2nd series). As T **370**. Multicoloured.
1238 90r. Mycena adonis 90 90
1239 1f.10 Chalciporus amarellus 1·20 1·20
1240 2f. Pink waxcap . . . . . . 2·10 2·10

404 Postman delivering Parcel

2001. Greetings Stamps. Multicoloured.
1241 70r. Type **404** 75 75
1242 70r. Postman delivering flowers 75 75

Nos. 1241/2 are for the stamps with the parcel (1241) and flowers (1242) intact. The parcel and flowers can be scratched away to reveal a greetings message.

405 Silver Easter Egg **406** Mountain Spring

2001. Decorated Easter Eggs. Multicoloured.
1243 1f.20 Type **405** . . . . . . 1·30 1·30
1244 1f.80 Cloissonne egg . . . . 2·00 2·00
1245 2f. Porcelain egg . . . . . 2·00 2·00

2001. Europa. Water Resources.
1246 **406** 1f.30 multicoloured . . . 1·40 1·40

407 Emblem

2001. Liechtenstein Presidency of Council of Europe.
1247 **407** 1f.80 multicoloured . . . 1·90 1·90

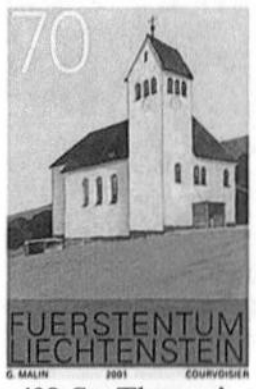

408 Carolingian Cruciform Fibula **409** St. Theresa's Chapel, Schaanwald

2001. Centenary of Historical Association. Multicoloured.
1248 70r. Type **408** 75 75
1249 70r. "Mars of Gutenberg" (statue) 75 75

2001. Preservation of Historical Environment (2nd series). Multicoloured.
1250 70r. Type **409** 75 75
1251 90r. St. Johann's Torkel (wine press), Mauren . . 1·00 1·00
1252 1f.10 Pirsch Transformer Station, Schaanwald . . . 1·10 1·10

See also Nos. 1274/5, 1292/3 and 1358/9.

410 Mary and kneeling Votant (Chapel of Our Lady, Dux, Schann)

2001. Votive Paintings. Multicoloured.
1253 70r. Type **410** 70 70
1254 1f.20 Mary and Jesus, St. George among other Saints, and text of vow (St. George's Chapel, Schellenberg) . . . . . . 1·20 1·20
1255 1f.30 Mary, St. Joseph of Arimathea, St. Christopher, Johann Christoph Walser (votant) and text of vow (Chapel of Our Lady, Dux, Schann) . . . . 1·50 1·50

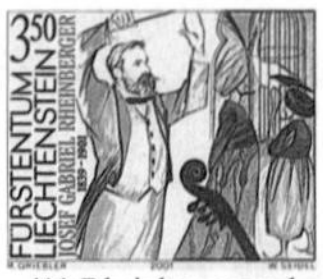

411 Rheinberger and Scene from *Zauberwort* (song cycle) **412** "Annunciation"

2001. Death Centenary of Josef Gabriel Rheinberger (composer).
1256 **411** 3f.50 multicoloured . . . 3·75 3·75

2001. Traditional Crafts (2nd series). As T **380**. Multicoloured.
1257 70r. Agricultural implements and horseshoe 75 75
1258 90r. Rake . . . . 1·00 1·00
1259 1f.20 Harness . . . . 1·30 1·30

2001. Christmas. Medallions from The Joyful, Sorrowful and Glorious Rosary Cycle. Multicoloured.
1260 70r. Type **412** 70 70
1261 90r. Nativity 90 90
1262 1f.30 Presentation of Jesus at the Temple . . . . . . 1·50 1·50

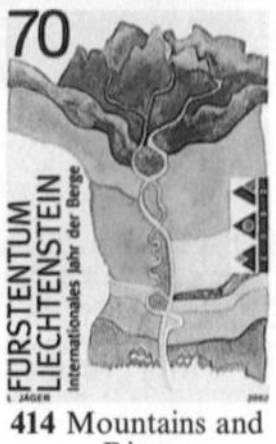

413 Square **414** Mountains and River

2001. Paintings by Gottfried Honeggar. Mult.
1263 1f.80 Type **413** . . . . . . 2·00 2·00
1264 2f.20 Circle . . . . 2·20 2·20

2002. International Year of Mountains and 50th Anniv of the International Commission of Alpine Protection. Multicoloured.
1265 70r. Type **414** 65 65
1266 1f.20 Stylized mountains . . 1·10 1·10

415 "Schellenberg"

2002. 30th Death Anniv of Friedrich Kaufmann (artist). Multicoloured.
1267 70r. Type **415** 65 65
1268 1f.30 "Schaan" . . . . . . 1·20 1·20
1269 1f.80 "Steg" . . . . 3·50 3·50

416 Space Shuttle and Bee

2002. Liechtenstein's participation in N.A.S.A. Space Technology and Research Students Project.
1270 **416** 90r. multicoloured . . . 85 85

The project submitted by the Liechtenstein Gymnasium concerned the study of the effects of space on carpenter bees.

417 Man on Tightrope

2002. Europa. Circus. Multicoloured.
1271 90r. Type **417** 85 85
1272 1f.30 Juggler . . . . 1·20 1·20

418 Emblem

2002. "Liba '02" National Stamp Exhibition, Vaduz (1st issue).
1273 **418** 1f.20 multicoloured . . . 1·10 1·10

See also Nos. 1282/3 and 1318/20.

419 Houses, Popers

2002. Preservation of Historical Environment (2nd series). Multicoloured.
1274 70r. Type **419** 65 65
1275 1f.20 House, Weiherring . . 1·10 1·10

420 Footballers

2002. World Cup Football Championship, Japan and South Korea.
1276 **420** 1f.80 multicoloured . . . 1·70 1·70

421 Princess Marie

2002. The Royal Couple. Multicoloured.
1277 3f. Type **421** . . . . 2·75 2·75
1278 3f.50 Prince Hans-Adam II 3·25 3·25

422 Ghost Orchid (*Epipogium aphyllum*) **423** Stamps and Emblem

2002. Orchids. Multicoloured.
1279 70r. Type **422** 65 65
1280 1f.20 Fly orchid (*Ophrys insectifera*) . . . . 1·10 1·10
1281 1f.30 Black vanilla orchid (*Nigritella nigra*) . . . . 1·20 1·20

2002. "Liba 02" National Stamp Exhibition, Vaduz (2nd issue). 90th Anniv of First Liechtenstein Stamps. Multicoloured.
1282 90r. Type **423** 85 85
1283 1f.30 Stamps showing royal family . . . . 1·20 1·20

424 Princess Sophie

2002. Prince Alois and Princess Sophie. Multicoloured.
1284 2f. Type **424** . . . . 1·90 1·90
1285 2f.50 Prince Alois . . . . . 2·30 2·30

425 Mary and Joseph

2002. Christmas. Batik. Multicoloured.
1286 70r. Type **425** 65 65
1287 1f.20 Nativity . . . . . . 1·10 1·10
1288 1f.80 Flight into Egypt . . . 1·70 1·70

426 The Eagle, Vaduz

2002. Inn Signs. Multicoloured.
1289 1f.20 Type **426** . . . . . . 1·10 1·10
1290 1f.80 The Angel, Balzers . . 1·70 1·70
1291 3f. The Eagle, Bendern . . . 2·75 2·75

427 St. Fridolin Parish Church **429** Pruning Vines

428 Postal Emblem

2003. Preservation of Historical Environment (3rd series). Multicoloured.
1292 70r. Type **427** 60 60
1293 2f.50 House, Spidach (horiz) 2·10 2·10

2003. Europa. Poster Art.
1294 **428** 1f.20 multicoloured . . . 1·10 1·10

2003. Viticulture (1st issue). Multicoloured.
1295 1f.30 Type **429** 1·10 1·10
1296 1f.80 Tying up vines 1·60 1·60
1297 2f.20 Hoeing 2·00 2·00
See also Nos. 1301/3, 1304/6 and 1312/14.

430 Bridge

2003. 50th Anniv of Liechtenstein Association for the Disabled.
1298 **430** 70r. multicoloured 60 60

431 Renovated Buildings and Ammonite

2003. Renovation of National Museum. Multicoloured.
1299 1f.20 Type **431** 1·10 1·10
1300 1f.30 Verweserhaus building and bailiff's shield 1·10 1·10

2003. Viticulture (2nd issue). As T **429**. Multicoloured.
1301 1f.20 Looping the tendrils 1·10 1·10
1302 1f.80 Removing leaves from around grapes 1·60 1·60
1303 3f.50 Reducing top growth 3·00 3·50

2003. Viticulture (3rd issue). As T **429**. Multicoloured.
1304 70r. Thinning out 60 60
1305 90r. Harvesting 80 80
1306 1f.10 Pressing the grapes 1·00 1·00

432 St. George

433 Parents and Young on Nest

2003. Saints (1st series). Multicoloured.
1307 1f.20 Type **432** 1·10 1·10
1308 1f.20 St. Blaise 1·10 1·10
1309 1f.30 St. Vitus 1·10 1·10
1310 1f.30 St. Erasmus 1·10 1·10
See also Nos. 1323/8.

2003. Conservation of White Storks in Rhine Valley.
1311 **433** 2f.20 multicoloured 2·00 2·00

2003. Viticulture (4th issue). As T **429**. Multicoloured.
1312 70r. Tasting 60 60
1313 90r. Harvesting ice-wine grapes 80 80
1314 1f.20 Bottling 1·10 1·10

434 Archangel Gabriel appearing to Mary

2003. Christmas. Multicoloured.
1315 70r. Type **434** 60 60
1316 90r. Nativity 80 80
1317 1f.30 Three Kings 1·10 1·10

435 Cow (Laura Beck)

2003. "Liba 02" National Stamp Exhibition, Vaduz (3rd issue). Children's Drawing Competition Winners. Multicoloured.
1318 70r. Type **435** 60 60
1319 1f.80 Bee (Laura Lingg) 1·60 1·60
1320 1f.80 Apple tree (Patrick Marxer) (vert) 1·60 1·60

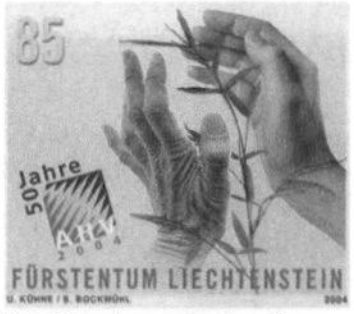

436 Hands enclosing Leaves

2004. 50th Anniv of AHV (retirement insurance).
1321 **436** 85r. multicoloured 75 75

437 Hot Air Balloon

2004. Europa. Holidays.
1322 **437** 1f.30 multicoloured 1·10 1·10

2004. Saints (2nd series). As T **432**. Multicoloured.
1323 1f. St. Achatius 90 90
1324 1f. St. Margaret 90 90
1325 1f.20 St. Christopher 1·10 1·10
1326 1f.20 St. Pantaleon 1·10 1·10
1327 2f.50 St. Cyriacus 2·00 2·00
1328 2f.50 St. Aegidius 2·00 2·00

438 Bendern

2004. Tourism. Aerial views of Liechtenstein. Multicoloured.
1329 15r. Type **438** 15 15
1330 85r. Gross-Teg 75 75
1331 1f. Tuass 90 90
1332 6f. Gutenberg 5·50 5·50

439 Olympic Torch

440 Bee Orchid (*Ophrys apifera*)

2004. Olympic Games, Athens 2004.
1350 **439** 85r. multicoloured 75 75

2004. Orchids. Multicoloured.
1351 85r. Type **440** 75 75
1352 1f. *Orchis ustulata* 90 90
1353 1f.20 *Epipactis purpurata* 1·00 1·00

441 Mathematical Symbols

2004. Science. Multicoloured.
1354 85r. Type **441** 75 75
1355 1f. Atomic diagram (physics) 90 90
1356 1f.30 Molecular structure (chemistry) 1·10 1·10
1357 1f.80 Star map and Saturn (astronomy) 1·60 1·60

442 Two-storied House on Unterdorfstrasse (street)

2004. Preservation of Historical Environment (4th series). Multicoloured.
1358 2f.20 Type **442** 2·00 2·00
1359 2f.50 Unterdorfstrasse (street) 2·20 2·20

443 The Annunciation

2004. Christmas. Multicoloured.
1360 85r. Type **443** 75 75
1361 1f. Nativity 90 90
1362 1f.80 Adoration of the Magi 1·60 1·60

444 Ammonite

445 Map of Europe as Manuscript (emblem of Rinascimento Virtuale)

2004. Fossils. Multicoloured.
1363 1f.20 Type **444** 1·00 1·00
1364 1f.30 Sea urchin 1·10 1·10
1365 2f.20 Shark's tooth 2·00 2·00

2004. Rinascimento Virtuale (Europe-wide co-operation in digital palimpsest (old manuscripts) research).
1366 **445** 2f.50 multicoloured 2·20 2·20

2005. Saints (2nd issue). As T **432**. Multicoloured.
1367 85r. St. Eustachius 75 75
1368 85r. St. Dionysius 75 75
1369 1f.80 St. Barbara 1·60 1·60
1370 1f.80 St. Katharina 1·60 1·60

446 Female Customer, Waiters and Chef

447 "Venus in Front of the Mirror" (Peter Paul Rubens)

2005. Europa. Gastronomy.
1371 **446** 1f.30 multicoloured 1·10 1·10

2005. Liechtenstein Museum, Garden Palace, Vienna.
1372 **447** 2f.20 multicoloured 2·25 2·25
A stamp of the same design was issued by Austria.

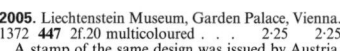

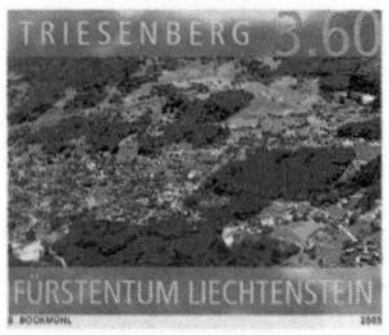

448 Triesenberg

2005. Tourism.
1373 **448** 3f.60 multicoloured 3·50 3·50

OFFICIAL STAMPS

1932. Stamps of 1930 optd **REGIERUNGS DIENSTSACHE** under crown.
O118 5r. green 8·00 6·25
O119 10r. lilac 40·00 6·25
O120 20r. red 40·00 6·25
O121 30r. blue 8·75 8·00
O122 35r. green 6·25 16·00
O123 50r. black 36·00 10·00
O124 60r. green 7·50 21·00
O125 1f.20 brown 90·00 £225

1933. Nos. 121 and 123 optd **REGIERUNGS DIENSTSACHE** in circle round crown.
O126 **38** 25r. orange 25·00 25·00
O127 – 1f.20 brown 55·00 £170

1934. Nos. 128 etc. optd **REGIERUNGS DIENSTSACHE** in circle round crown.
O150 **41** 5r. green 1·00 1·20
O151 – 10r. violet 2·50 95
O152 – 15r. orange 30 1·50
O153 – 20r. red 35 95
O155 – 25r. brown 1·90 9·25
O156 – 30r. blue 2·50 5·00
O157 **42** 50r. brown 1·00 1·90
O158 – 90r. green 5·50 25·00
O159 – 1f.50 brown 32·00 £110

1937. Stamps of 1937 optd **REGIERUNGS DIENSTSACHE** in circle round crown.
O174 **51** 5r. green and buff 20 20
O175 – 10r. violet and buff 35 60
O176 – 20r. red and buff 95 1·10
O177 – 25r. brown and buff 55 1·40
O178 – 30r. blue and buff 1·10 1·40
O179 – 50r. brown and buff 60 1·10
O180 – 1f. purple and buff 75 5·50
O181 – 1f.50 grey and buff 2·20 8·00

1947. Stamps of 1944 optd **DIENSTMARKE** and crown.
O255 5r. green 1·10 75
O256 10r. violet 1·10 95
O257 20r. red 1·60 1·00
O258 30r. blue 1·70 1·40
O259 50r. grey 1·70 2·75
O260 1f. red 7·50 9·25
O261 1f.50 blue 7·50 9·25

O **86**

O **198** Government Building, Vaduz

1950. Buff paper.
O287 O **86** 5r. purple and grey 10 10
O288 10r. green and mauve 10 10
O289 20r. brown and blue 25 25
O290 30r. purple and red 35 35
O291 40r. blue and brown 50 50
O292 55r. green and red 85 1·00
O293 60r. grey and mauve 1·40 1·10
O294 80r. orange and grey 95 95
O295 90r. brown and blue 1·00 1·00
O296 1f.20 turquoise and orange 1·40 1·40

1968. White paper.
O495 O **86** 5r. brown and orange 10 10
O496 10r. violet and red 10 10
O497 20r. red and green 25 25
O498 30r. green and red 35 35
O499 50r. blue and red 60 60
O500 60r. orange and blue 60 60
O501 70r. purple and green 75 75
O502 80r. green and red 75 75
O503 95r. green and red 1·20 1·20
O504 1f. purple & turquoise 1·00 1·00
O505 1f.20 brown & turq 1·20 1·20
O506 2f. brown and orange 2·50 2·50

1976.
O652 O **198** 10r. brown and violet 10 10
O653 20r. red and blue 10 25
O654 35r. blue and red 20 60
O655 40r. violet and green 30 30
O656 50r. green and mauve 35 30
O657 70r. purple and green 45 50
O658 80r. green and purple 50 60
O659 90r. violet and blue 55 60
O660 1f. grey and purple 60 50
O661 1f.10 brown and blue 75 1·20
O662 1f.50 green and red 95 75
O663 2f. orange and blue 1·20 60
O664 5f. purple and orange 8·75 7·50

POSTAGE DUE STAMPS

D **11**

D **25**

D **58**

1920.
D43 D **11** 5h. red 20 35
D44 10h. red 20 35
D45 15h. red 20 35
D46 20h. red 20 35
D47 25h. red 20 35
D48 30h. red 20 35
D49 40h. red 20 35
D50 50h. red 20 35
D51 80h. red 20 35
D52 1k. blue 20 35
D53 2k. blue 20 35
D54 5k. blue 20 35

1928.
D84 D **25** 5r. red and violet 60 1·90
D85 10r. red and violet 1·20 1·70
D86 15r. red and violet 2·50 10·00
D87 20r. red and violet 2·10 1·90

D88		25r. red and violet	2·10	7·50
D89		30r. red and violet	5·00	9·25
D90		40r. red and violet	6·75	10·50
D91		50r. red and violet	6·75	15·00

1940.

D189	D **58**	5r. red and blue	1·20	2·50
D190		10r. red and blue	50	1·00
D191		15r. red and blue	60	5·00
D192		20r. red and blue	75	1·20
D193		25r. red and blue	1·40	2·75
D194		30r. red and blue	2·75	5·00
D195		40r. red and blue	2·75	4·25
D196		50r. red and blue	3·00	5·00

LITHUANIA Pt. 10

A country on the Baltic Sea, under Russian rule until occupied by the Germans in the first World War (see German Eastern Command). It was an independent republic from 1918 to 1940, when it was incorporated into the U.S.S.R.

Lithuania declared its independence in 1990, and the U.S.S.R. formally recognized the republic in 1991.

1918. 100 skatiku = 1 auksinas.
1922. 100 centu = 1 litas.
1990. 100 kopeks = 1 rouble.
1992. Talons.
1993. 100 centu = 1 litas.

1

2

1918.

3	1	10s. black on buff	40·00	22·00
4		15s. black on buff	35·00	22·00
5		20s. black on buff	4·50	3·25
6		30s. black on buff	4·50	3·25
7		40s. black on buff	12·00	6·00
8		50s. black on buff	4·50	3·25

1919.

9	2	10s. black on buff	5·50	1·90
10		15s. black on buff	5·50	1·90
11		20s. black on buff	5·50	1·90
12		30s. black on buff	5·50	1·90

3

4

1919.

13	3	10s. black on buff	1·60	1·00
14		15s. black on buff	1·60	1·00
15		20s. black on buff	1·60	1·00
16		30s. black on buff	1·60	1·00
17		40s. black on buff	1·60	1·00
18		50s. black on buff	1·60	1·00
19		60s. black on buff	1·60	1·40

1919.

20	4	10s. black on buff	2·00	1·00
21		15s. black on buff	2·00	1·00
22		20s. black on buff	2·00	1·00
23		30s. black on buff	2·00	1·00
24		40s. black on buff	2·00	1·50
25		50s. black on buff	2·00	1·50
26		60s. black on buff	2·00	2·00

5 Arms

6

7

1919. "auksinas" in lower case letters on 1 to 5a.

40	5	10s. pink	15	15
50		10s. orange	15	10
51		15s. violet	15	10
52		20s. blue	15	10
43		30s. orange	15	15
53		30s. bistre	15	10
54		40s. brown	15	10
55	6	50s. green	15	10
56		60s. red and violet	15	10
57		75s. red and yellow	15	10
37	7	1a. red and grey	35	20
38		3a. red and brown	35	20
39		5a. red and green	40	30

1921. As T 7, but "AUKSINAS" or "AUKSINAI" in capital letters.

58	7	1a. red and grey	15	10
59		3a. red and brown	25	15
60		5a. red and green	40	25

11 Lithuania receiving Independence

12 Lithuania arises

1920. 2nd Anniv of Independence.

65	11	10s. lake	1·50	2·00
66		15s. lilac	1·50	2·00
67		20s. blue	1·50	2·00
68	12	30s. brown	1·50	2·00
69	–	40s. green and brown	1·50	2·00
70	12	50s. red	1·50	2·00
71		60s. lilac	1·50	2·00
72	–	80s. red and violet	1·50	2·00
73	–	1a. red and green	1·50	2·00
74	–	3a. red and brown	1·60	2·00
75	–	5a. red and green	1·60	2·00

DESIGNS—VERT: 40s., 80s., 1a. Lithuania with chains broken; 3, 5a. (25×25 mm) Arms.

16 Arms

17 Vytautas

1920. National Assembly.

76	16	10s. red	40	30
77		15s. violet	50	40
78	17	20s. green	50	40
79	16	30s. brown	60	50
80	–	40s. violet and green	60	50
81	17	50s. brown and orange	60	50
82		60s. red and orange	60	50
83	–	80s. red, grey and black	60	60
84	–	1a. yellow and black	60	60
85	–	3a. green and black	75	70
86	–	5a. violet and black	2·00	1·75

DESIGNS—As Type 17: 40s., 80s. Gediminas. As Type 16: 1a. to 5a. Sacred Oak and Altar.

20 Sower

21 Kestutis

22 Reaper

23

28 Allegory of Flight

24 Flying Posthorn

25 Junkers F-13 over River Niemen

1921.

87	20	10s. red	30	1·75
88		15s. mauve	15	1·00
89		20s. blue	10	10
90	22	30s. brown	50	4·25
91	21	40s. red	15	10
92	22	50s. olive	10	10
93		60s. mauve and green	40	5·00
94	21	80s. red and orange	20	15
95		1a. green and brown	15	10
96		2a. red and blue	15	10
97	23	3a. blue and brown	50	2·00
124	20	4a. blue and yellow	30	75
98	23	5a. red and grey	60	3·25
125	20	8a black and green	35	1·00
99	23	10a. mauve and red	75	35
100		25a. green and brown	1·40	1·25
101		100a. grey and red	6·00	6·00

1921. Air. Inauguration of Kaunas–Konigsberg Air Service.

102	24	20s. blue	65	55
103		40s. orange	65	55
104		60s. green	75	65
105		80s. red	75	65
106	25	1a. green and red	2·00	1·25
107	–	2a. brown and blue	2·00	1·50
108	–	5a. grey and yellow	2·75	2·75

DESIGNS—As Type 25: 2a. Three Junkers F-13 monoplanes; 5a. Junkers F-13 over Gediminas Castle.

1921. Air. Inauguration of Air Mail Service.

109	28	20s. lilac and orange	90	1·50
110		40s. red and blue	90	1·50
111		60s. olive and blue	1·00	1·60
112		80s. green and yellow	1·00	1·60
113		1a. blue and green	90	1·60
114		2a. red and grey	1·50	1·75
115		5a. green and purple	1·50	1·75

1922. Surch **4 AUKSINAI** with or without frame.

116	6	4a. on 75s. red and yellow	40	40

30 Junkers F-13

1922. Air.

118	30	1a. red and brown	1·40	2·00
119		3a. green and violet	1·40	2·00
120		5a. yellow and blue	1·90	2·75

31 Junkers F-13 over Gediminas Castle

33 Pte. Luksis

1922. Air.

121	31	2a. red and blue	1·25	1·00
122		4a. red and brown	1·25	1·00
123		10a. blue and black	2·00	1·50

1922. "De jure" Recognition of Lithuania by League of Nations. Inscr "LIETUVA DE JURE".

126	33	20s. red and black	50	50
127	–	40s. violet and green	40	40
128	–	50s. blue and purple	40	40
129	–	60s. orange and violet	40	40
130	–	1a. blue and red	40	40
131	–	2a. brown and blue	50	50
132	–	3a. blue and brown	50	50
133	–	4a. purple and green	50	50
134	–	5a. red and brown	50	50
135	–	6a. blue	60	50
136	–	8a. yellow and blue	60	50
137	–	10a. green and violet	90	75

DESIGNS—VERT: 40s. Lt. Juozapavicius; 50s. Dr. Basanavicius; 60s. Mrs. Petkevicaite; 1a. Prof. Voldemaras; 2a. Dovidaitis; 3a. Dr. Slezevicius; 4a. Dr. Galvanauskas; 5a. Dr. Grinius; 6a. Dr. Stulginskis; 8a. Pres. Smetona. HORIZ: (39×27 mm): 10a. Stauguitis, Pres. Smetona and Silingas.

1922. Surch.

138	5	1c. on 10s. orange (postage)	50	5·00
139		1c. on 15s. violet	50	5·00
143		1c. on 20s. blue	50	4·00
144		1c. on 30s. orange	40·00	£100
145		1c. on 30s. bistre	20	40
146		1c. on 40s. brown	50	4·00
148	22	1c. on 50s. olive	10	15
149	6	2c. on 50s. green	75	4·00
150		2c. on 60s. red and violet	10	10
151		2c. on 75s. red and yellow	50	5·00
152	20	3c. on 10s. red	1·10	6·00
153		3c. on 15s. mauve	15	15
154		3c. on 20s. blue	20	3·00
155	22	3c. on 30s. brown	90	8·50
156	21	3c. on 40s. red	15	15
157	7	3c. on 1a. (No. 37)	75·00	£120
158		3c. on 1a. (No. 58)	25	1·25
159		3c. on 3a. (No. 38)	60·00	£100
160		3c. on 3a. (No. 59)	10	65
161		3c. on 5a. (No. 39)	32·00	55·00
162		3c. on 5a. (No. 60)	20	80
163	22	5c. on 50s. olive	10	10
164		5c. on 60s. mauve & green	2·75	16·00
165	21	5c. on 80s. red and orange	20	40
166	6	5c. on 4a. on 75s. red and yellow	50	11·00
168	21	10c. on 1a. green & brown	25	10
169		10c. on 2a. red and blue	10	10
170	20	15c. on 4a. blue and yellow	20	10
171	23	25c. on 3a. blue and green	5·00	24·00
172		25c. on 5a. red and grey	3·00	8·50
173		25c. on 10a. mauve and red	75	1·60
174	20	30c. on 8a. black and green	25	25
175	23	50c. on 25a. green & brown	1·10	3·00
176		1l. on 100 a grey and red	2·00	3·25
177	24	10c. on 20s. blue (air)	1·00	3·50
178		10c. on 40s. orange	1·25	5·00
179		10c. on 60s. green	1·00	5·00
180		10c. on 80s. red	1·25	5·00
181	25	20c. on 1a. green and red	4·75	12·50
182	–	20c. on 2a. (No. 107)	8·00	18·00
183	31	25c. on 2a. red and blue	1·00	85
184		30c. on 4a. red and brown	1·00	80
185	–	50c. on 5a. (No. 108)	1·40	1·25
186	31	50c. on 10a. blue and black	65	1·25
187	30	1l. on 5a. yellow and blue	12·50	27·00

38 Wayside Cross

39 Ruins of Kaunas Castle

40 Seminary Church

1923.

201	38	2c. brown	60	30
202		3c. bistre	85	25
203		5c. green	85	10
204		10c. violet	1·50	10
189		15c. red	1·00	10
190		20c. green	1·00	15
191		25c. blue	1·00	10
206		36c. brown	7·50	65
192	39	50c. green	1·00	10
193		60c. red	1·10	15
194	40	1l. orange and green	5·50	10
195		3l. red and grey	5·50	55
196		5l. brown and blue	7·00	90

43 Arms of Memel

44 Ruins of Trakai

1923. Union of Memel with Lithuania.

210	43	1c. red and green	80	1·25
211	–	2c. mauve	80	1·25
212	–	3c. yellow	80	1·25
213	43	5c. buff and blue	80	1·25
214	–	10c. red	1·50	1·50
215	–	15c. green	1·50	1·50
216	44	25c. violet	2·00	1·75
217	–	30c. red	2·00	2·50
218	–	60c. green	4·50	4·75
219	–	1l. green	3·00	3·00
220	–	2l. red	5·00	6·00
221	44	3l. blue	5·50	7·00
222	–	5l. blue	13·50	14·50

DESIGNS—As Type 43: 3c., 2l. Chapel of Biruta; 10c., 15c. War Memorial Kaunas; As Type 44: 2, 30c. Arms of Lithuania; 60c., 5l. Memel Lighthouse; 1l. Memel Harbour.

45 Biplane

46 Biplane

1924. Air.

223	45	20c. yellow	1·40	70
224		40c. green	1·40	70
225		60c. red	1·50	75
226	46	1l. brown	3·25	65

1924. Charity. War Orphans Fund. Surch **KARO NASLAICIAMS** and premium.

227	38	2c.+2c. bistre (postage)	1·00	1·50
228		3c.+3c. bistre	1·00	1·50
229		5c.+5c. green	1·00	1·50
231		10c.+10c. violet	1·00	2·50
232		15c.+15c. red	1·00	2·50
233		20c.+20c. olive	2·00	3·00
235		25c.+25c. blue	4·00	7·00
236		36c.+34c. brown	6·00	9·00
237	39	50c.+50c. green	6·00	9·00
238		60c.+60c. red	7·50	12·00
239	40	1l.+1l. orange and green	7·50	12·00
240		3l.+2l. red and grey	12·00	16·00
241		5l.+3l. brown and blue	18·00	25·00
242	45	20c.+20c. yellow (air)	8·00	10·00
243		40c.+40c. green	8·00	10·00
244		60c.+60c. red	8·00	10·00
245	46	1l.+1l. brown	12·00	14·00

49 Barn Swallow carrying Letter

56

57

1926. Air.

246	49	20c. red	1·25	55
247		40c. orange and mauve	1·25	55
248		60c. black and blue	2·75	65

1926. Charity. War Invalids. Nos. 227/39 surch with new values and small ornaments.

249	38	1c.+1c. on 2c.+2c.	1·00	1·25
250		2c.+2c. on 3c.+3c.	1·00	1·25
251		2c.+2c. on 5c.+5c.	1·00	1·25
253		5c.+5c. on 10c.+10c.	1·75	2·00
254		5c.+5c. on 15c.+15c.	1·75	2·00
255		10c.+10c. on 20c.+20c.	1·75	2·00
257		10c.+10c. on 25c.+25c.	4·00	5·00
258		14c.+14c. on 36c.+34c.	6·00	7·00
259	39	20c.+20c. on 50c.+50c.	4·00	5·00
260		25c.+25c. on 60c.+60c.	6·00	9·00
261	40	30c.+30c. on 1l.+1l.	10·00	15·00

1926. Charity. War Orphans. Nos. 227/39 surch **V.P.** and new values in circular ornament.

262	38	1c.+1c. on 2c.+2c.	1·00	1·25
263		2c.+2c. on 3c.+3c.	1·00	1·25
264		2c.+2c. on 5c.+5c.	1·00	1·25
266		5c.+5c. on 10c.+10c.	2·00	2·50
267		10c.+10c. on 15c.+15c.	2·00	2·50
268		15c.+15c. on 20c.+20c.	2·50	2·50
270		15c.+15c. on 25c.+25c.	5·00	5·00
271		19c.+19c. on 36c.+34c.	5·00	6·00
272	39	25c.+25c. on 50c.+50c.	6·00	7·50
273		30c.+30c. on 60c.+60c.	9·00	12·00
274	40	50c.+50c. on 1l.+1l.	12·00	18·00

1927.

275	56	2c. orange	75	10
276		3c. brown	75	10
277		5c. green	1·00	10
278		10c. violet	2·00	10
279		15c. red	1·75	10
280		25c. blue	1·75	10
283		30c. blue	12·00	1·00

1927. Dr. Basanavicius Mourning Issue.

285	57	15c. red	90	1·00
286		25c. blue	90	1·00
287		50c. green	1·10	1·00
288		60c. violet	2·00	2·75

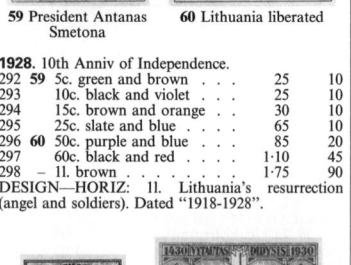

58 "Vytis" of the Lithuanian Arms

1927.

289	58	1l. green and grey	1·25	50
290		3l. violet and green	3·25	50
291		5l. brown and grey	5·00	1·25

59 President Antanas Smetona

60 Lithuania liberated

1928. 10th Anniv of Independence.

292	59	5c. green and brown	25	10
293		10c. black and violet	25	10
294		15c. brown and orange	30	10
295		25c. slate and blue	65	10
296	60	50c. purple and blue	85	20
297		60c. black and red	1·10	45
298	–	1l. brown	1·75	90

DESIGN—HORIZ: 1l. Lithuania's resurrection (angel and soldiers). Dated "1918-1928".

62

63

64 J. Tubelis

66 Railway Station, Kaunas

1930. 500th Death Anniv of Grand Duke Vytautas.

299	62	2c. brown (postage)	25	10
300		3c. violet and brown	25	10
301		5c. red and green	25	10
302		10c. green and violet	25	10
303		15c. violet and red	25	10
304		30c. purple and blue	25	10
305		36c. olive and purple	35	15
306		50c. blue and green	35	20
307		60c. red and blue	60	10
308	63	1l. purple, grey and green	1·50	40
309		3l. violet, pink and mauve	3·25	1·25
310		5l. red, grey and brown	4·00	1·75
311		10l. black and blue	13·00	18·00
312		25l. green and brown	35·00	48·00
313	64	5c. brown, yellow and black (air)	35	35
314		10c. black, drab and blue	40	40
315		15c. blue, grey and purple	40	40
316	–	20c. red, orange and brown	1·00	55
317	–	40c. violet, light blue & blue	1·40	80
318	–	60c. black, lilac and green	1·60	1·40
319	–	1l. black, lilac and red	3·00	1·50

DESIGNS—HORIZ: 20c., 40c. Vytautas and Kaunas; 60c., 1l. Vytautas and Smetona.

1932. Orphans' Fund. Imperf or perf.

320	66	5c. blue and brown	1·00	1·00
321		10c. purple and brown	1·00	1·00
322	–	15c. brown and green	30	30
323	–	25c. blue and green	45	50
324	–	50c. grey and olive	70	1·25
325	–	60c. grey and mauve	1·00	4·25
326	–	1l. blue and grey	2·50	3·25
327	–	3l. purple and green	4·50	5·00

DESIGNS—As Type **66**: 15, 25c. "The Two Pines" (painting); 50c. G.P.O. VERT: 60c., 1, 3l. Vilnius Cathedral.

68 Map of Lithuania, Memel and Vilna

1932. Air. Orphans' Fund. Imperf or perf.

328	68	5c. red and green	25	25
329		10c. purple and brown	25	25
330	–	15c. blue and buff	40	40
331	–	20c. black and brown	2·40	2·00
332	–	40c. purple and yellow	2·00	2·50
333	–	60c. blue and buff	3·00	5·50
334	–	1l. purple and green	3·50	5·50
335	–	2l. blue and green	3·75	5·50

DESIGNS: 15, 20c. Airplane over R. Niemen; 40, 60c. Town Hall, Kaunas; 1, 2l. Vytautas Church, Kaunas.

69 Vytautas escapes from Prison

71 Coronation of Mindaugas

1932. 15th Anniv of Independence. Imperf or perf.

336	69	5c. purple and red (postage)	50	50
337		10c. brown and grey	50	50
338	–	15c. green and red	50	50
339	–	25c. brown and purple	75	1·25
340	–	50c. brown and green	1·00	1·25
341	–	60c. red and green	2·50	5·00
342	–	1l. black and blue	3·25	3·25
343	–	3l. green and purple	3·50	5·50
344	–	5c. lilac and green (air)	15	20
345	–	10c. red and green	15	25
346	71	15c. brown and violet	20	30
347	–	20c. black and red	45	45
348	–	40c. black and purple	65	1·25
349	–	60c. black and orange	1·90	6·00
350	–	1l. green and violet	3·00	3·50
351	–	2l. brown and blue	3·25	6·00

DESIGNS—POSTAGE. As Type **69**: 15, 25c. Vytautas and Jagello preaching the gospel; 50, 60c. Battle of Grunewald; 1, 3l. Proclamation of Independence. AIR. As Type **71**: 5, 10c. Battle of Saules; 40c. Gediminas in Council; 60c. Founding of Vilnius; 1l. Russians surrendering to Gediminas; 2l. Algirdas before Moscow.

72 A. Visteliauskas

1933. 50th Anniv of Publication of "Ausra".

352	72	5c. red and green	20	25
353		10c. red and blue	20	25
354	–	15c. red and orange	20	25
355	–	25c. brown and blue	55	75
356	–	50c. blue and green	65	1·00
357	–	60c. deep brown & lt brown	2·00	5·00
358	–	1l. purple and red	2·50	3·75
359	–	3l. purple and blue	3·50	6·00

PORTRAITS: 15, 25c. P. Vileisis; 50, 60c. J. Sliupas; 1, 3l. J. Basanavicius.

73 Trakai Castle

1933. Air. 550th Death Anniv of Grand Duke Kestutis.

360	73	5c. blue and green	20	35
361		10c. brown and violet	20	35
362	–	15c. violet and blue	20	35
363	–	20c. purple and brown	55	80
364	–	40c. purple and blue	90	1·60
365	–	60c. blue and red	2·25	7·00
366	–	1l. blue and green	3·00	4·50
367	–	2l. green and violet	3·75	9·00

DESIGNS: 15, 20c. Kestutis encounters Birute; 40, 60c. Birute; 1, 2l. Kestutis and Algirdas.

74 Mother and Child

75 J. Tumas Vaizgantas

1933. Child Welfare. (a) Postage.

373	74	5c. brown and green	15	20
374		10c. blue and red	15	20
375	–	15c. purple and green	20	25
376	–	25c. black and orange	40	75
377	–	50c. red and green	55	1·00
378	–	60c. orange and black	1·90	4·50
379	–	1l. blue and brown	2·50	3·50
380	–	3l. green and purple	3·50	6·00

DESIGNS—VERT: 15, 25c. Boy reading a book; 50, 60c. Boy with building bricks; 1, 3l. Mother and child weaving.

(b) Air. Various medallion portraits in triangular frames.

381	–	5c. blue and red	15	15
382	–	10c. green and violet	15	15
383	75	15c. brown and green	15	15
384		20c. blue and red	25	35
385	–	40c. green and lake	85	1·25
386	–	60c. brown and blue	1·75	3·25
387	–	1l. blue and yellow	1·90	2·75
388	–	2l. lake and green	3·25	4·00

DESIGNS: 5, 10c. Maironis; 40, 60c. Vincas Kudirka; 1, 2l. Zemaite.

76 Captains S. Darius and S. Girenas

78 "Flight" mourning over Wreckage

81 President A. Smetona

1934. Air. Death of Darius and Girenas (trans-Atlantic airmen).

389	76	20c. red and black	10	10
390	–	40c. blue and red	10	10
391	76	60c. violet and black	10	10
392	78	1l. black and red	35	15
393	–	3l. orange and green	1·00	2·00
394	–	5l. blue and brown	4·00	4·25

DESIGNS—HORIZ: 40c. Bellanca monoplane "Lituanica" over Atlantic. VERT: 3l. "Lituanica" and globe; 5l. "Lituanica" and Vytis.

1934. President's 60th Birthday.

395	81	15c. red	3·00	10
396		30c. green	5·00	15
397		60c. blue	10·00	30

82

83

84 Gleaner

85

1934.

398	82	2c. red and orange	25	10
399		5c. green	30	10
400	83	10c. brown	75	10
401	84	25c. brown and green	2·00	10
402	83	35c. red	2·00	10
403	84	50c. blue	3·50	10
404	85	1l. purple and red	18·00	10
405		3l. green	20	10
406	–	5l. purple and blue	20	20
407	–	10l. brown and yellow	1·25	1·25

DESIGNS—HORIZ: as Type **85**: 5l., 10l. Knight.

For design as Type **82** but smaller, see Nos. 411/12.

1935. Air. Honouring Atlantic Flyer Vaitkus. No. 390 optd **F. VAITKUS nugalejo Atlanta 21-22-IX-1935.**

407a		40c. blue and red	£190	£300

87 Vaitkus and Air Route

88 President Smetona

1936. Air. Felix Vaitkus's New York–Ireland Flight.

408	87	15c. purple	1·40	45
409		30c. green	1·60	1·10
410		60c. blue	2·50	1·10

1936. As T **82** but smaller (18 × 23 mm).

411	82	2c. orange	10	10
412		5c. green	10	10

1936.

413	88	15c. red	4·00	10
414		30c. green	9·00	10
415		60c. blue	7·50	10

89

90 Archer

1937.

416	89	10c. green	1·10	10
417		25c. mauve	10	10
418		35c. red	60	10
419		50c. brown	30	10
419a		1l. blue	15	30

1938. 1st National Olympiad Fund.

420	90	5c.+5c. green	7·00	9·00
421	–	15c.+5c. red	9·00	10·00
422	–	30c.+10c. blue	12·00	14·00
423	–	60c.+15c. brown	18·00	20·00

DESIGNS: 15c. Throwing the javelin; 30c. Diving; 60c. Relay runner breasting tape.

1938. Scouts' and Guides' National Camp Fund. Nos. 420/3 optd **TAUTINE SKAUCIU** (or **SKAUTU) STOVYKLA** and badge.

424	90	5c.+5c. green	7·00	8·50
425	–	15c.+5c. red	9·00	9·50
426	–	30c.+10c. blue	12·00	14·00
427	–	60c.+15c. brown	17·00	19·00

92 President Smetona

93 Scoring a Goal

1939. 20th Anniv of Independence.

428	–	15c. red	30	10
429	92	30c. green	30	10
430	–	35c. mauve	55	25
431	92	60c. blue	60	25
MS431a		148 × 105 mm. Nos. 430/1	7·00	30·00
MS431b		Do. but imperf	35·00	80·00

DESIGN: 15, 35c. Dr. Basanvicius proclaiming Lithuanian independence.

1939. 3rd European Basketball Championship and Physical Culture Fund.

432	–	15c.+10c. brown	7·50	7·50
433	93	30c.+15c. green	7·50	7·50
434	–	60c.+40c. violet	15·00	17·00

DESIGNS—VERT: 15c. Scoring a goal. HORIZ: (40½ × 36 mm); 60c. International flags and ball.

1939. Recovery of Vilnius. Nos. 428/31 optd **VILNIUS 1939-X-10** and trident.

435	–	15c. red	75	30
436	92	30c. green	75	40
437	–	35c. mauve	1·00	55
438	92	60c. blue	1·40	85

95 Vytis

96 Vilnius

1940. "Liberty" Issue.
439 **95** 5c. brown 10 10
440 – 10c. green 40 30
441 – 15c. orange 10 10
442 – 25c. brown 10 30
443 – 30c. green 15 10
444 – 35c. orange 20 45
DESIGNS: 10c. Angel; 15c. Woman releasing a dove; 25c. Mother and children; 30c. "Liberty Bell"; 35c. Mythical animal.

1940. Recovery of Vilnius.
445 **96** 15c. brown 30 15
446 – 30c. green 55 25
447 – 60c. blue . . . . 1·10 90
MS447a 140×106 mm. Nos. 445/7 with gold frames . . . . . . 7·50 16·00
DESIGNS—VERT: 30c. Portrait of Gediminas. HORIZ: 60c. Ruins of Trakai Castle.

1940. Incorporation of Lithuania in U.S.S.R. Optd **LTSR 1940 VII 21.**
448 **82** 2c. red and orange 15 40
449 **95** 5c. brown 15 40
450 – 10c. green (No. 440) . . . 3·25 5·00
451 – 15c. orange (No. 441) . . . 15 50
452 – 25c. brown (No. 442) . . . 20 75
453 – 30c. green (No. 443) . . . 25 80
454 – 35c. orange (No. 444) . . . 25 1·50
455 **89** 50c. brown . . . . 25 1·40

From 1940 to 1990 Lithuania used stamps of Russia.

99 Angel and Map

1990. No gum. Imperf.
456 **99** 5k. green 10 10
457 10k. lilac 10 10
458 20k. blue 20 10
459 50k. red 75 40

1990. No gum. Imperf (simulated perfs).
460 **99** 5k. green and brown . . . 10 10
461 10k. purple and brown . . 10 10
462 20k. blue and brown . . . 30 20
463 50k. red and brown . . . 90 45

100 Vytis

101 Hill of Crosses, Siauliai

1991.
464 **100** 10k. black, gold and brown 10 10
465 15k. black, gold and green 10 10
466 20k. black, gold and blue 10 10
467 30k. black, gold and red 15 10
468 40k. black and gold . . . 10 10
469 50k. black, gold and violet 10 10
470 **101** 50k. brown, chestnut & blk 10 10
471 **100** 100k. black, gold & green 10 10
472 – 200k. brown, chest & blk 80 40
473 **100** 500k. black, gold and blue 40 20
DESIGN: As T **101**—200k. Lithuanian Liberty Bell.
See also Nos. 482 and 488/9.

102 Liberty Statue, Kaunas

103 Angel with Trumpet

1991. National Day.
480 **102** 20k. mauve, silver & black 15 10

1991. 1st Anniv of Declaration of Independence from U.S.S.R.
481 **103** 20k. deep green and green 15 10

1991. No gum. Imperf (simulated perfs).
482 **100** 15k. green and black . . 10 10

104 Wayside Crosses

1991.
483 **104** 40k. green and silver . . . 15 10
484 – 70k. brown, buff and gold 30 15
485 – 100k. brown, yellow & sil 45 20
DESIGNS: 70k. "Madonna" (icon from Pointed Gate Chapel, Vilnius); 100k. Towers of St. Anne's Church, Vilnius.

105 Candle

1991. 50th Anniv of Resistance to Soviet and German Occupations.
486 **105** 20k. yellow, black & bistre 10 10
487 – 50k. rose, black and red 25 10
488 – 70k. multicoloured . . . 35 15
DESIGNS: 50k. Shield pierced by swords; 70k. Sword and wreath.

1991. No gum. Imperf.
489 **100** 25k. black and brown . . 10 10
490 30k. black and purple . . 15 10

106 World Map and Games Emblem

107 National Flag in Ice-axe and Mt. Everest

1991. 4th International Lithuanians' Games.
491 **106** 20k. green, black & yellow 20 10
492 – 50k.+25k. green, black and yellow 55 25
DESIGN: 50k. Symbolic female athlete.

1991. Lithuanian Expedition to Mt. Everest.
493 **107** 20k. multicoloured . . . 20 10
494 70k. multicoloured . . . 55 25

108 Trakai Castle

109 Black Storks

1991. 650th Death Anniv of Grand Duke Gediminas. Each brown, ochre and green.
495 30k. Type **108** 15 10
496 50k. Gediminas 25 15
497 70k. Vilnius in 14th century 40 20

1991. Birds in the Red Book. Multicoloured.
498 30k.+15k. Type **109** . . . . 1·10 75
499 50k. Common cranes . . . . 1·40 90

110 U.N. and National Emblems and National Flag

111 National Team Emblem and Colours

1992. Admission to U.N.O.
500 **110** 100k. multicoloured . . . 15 10

1992. Winter Olympic Games, Albertville, and Summer Games, Barcelona. Multicoloured.
501 50k.+25k. Type **111** 15 10
502 130k. Winter Games emblem 30 15
503 280k. Summer Games emblem 55 25

112 Slipper Orchid

113 Goosander ("Mergus merganser")

1992. Plants in the Red Book. Multicoloured.
504 200k. Type **112** 30 15
505 300k. Sea holly 50 25

1992. Birds of the Baltic. No value expressed.
506 **113** B (15t.) black and green 70 45
507 – B (15t.) brown, blk & grn 70 45
508 – B (15t.) sepia, brown & grn 70 45
509 – B (15t.) brown, blk & grn 70 45
DESIGNS: No. 506, Osprey ("Pandion haliaetus"); 507, Black-tailed godwit ("Limosa limosa"); 509, Common shelduck ("Tadorna tadorna").

114 Kedainiai

115 Couple

1992. Arms. Multicoloured.
510 2t. Type **114** 10 10
511 3t. Vilnius 10 10
512 10t. State arms 30 15
See also Nos. 531/3, 569/71, 594/5, 628/30, 663/5, 682/4, 712/14, 742/4, 769/71 and 781/3.

1992. Costumes of Suvalkija.
513 **115** 2t. multicoloured 15 10
514 – 5t. multicoloured 30 15
515 – 7t. multicoloured 45 20
DESIGNS: 5, 7t. Different costumes.

116 Zapyskis Church

1993. Churches.
516 **116** 3t. black and stone . . . 10 10
517 – 10t. black and blue . . . 25 10
518 – 15t. black and grey . . . 40 20
DESIGNS: 10t. Church of St. Peter and St. Paul, Vilnius; 15t. Church of the Resurrection, Kaunas.

1993. Nos. 467, 490 and 468 surch.
519 **100** 1t. on 30k. blk, gold & red 10 10
520 1t. on 30k. black & purple 10 10
521 3t. on 40k. black and gold 15 10

118 Jonas Basanavicius (statesman)

1993. National Day. No value expressed.
522 **118** A (3t.) red, cinn & brn . . 10 10
523 – B (15t.) grn, stone & brn 55 25
DESIGN: No. 523, Jonas Vileisis (politician).

119 Vytautas

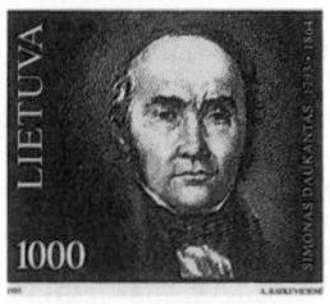
120 Simonas Daukantas (historian)

1993. 600th Anniv (1987) of Accession of Grand Duke Vytautas.
524 – 5t. gold, red and black . . 10 10
525 **119** 10t. green, black and red 25 10
526 – 15t. black, yellow and red 40 20
MS527 80×120 mm. 50t. olive, black and red . . . . 1·10 70
DESIGNS: 5t. Seal; 15t. "Battle of Grunwald" (Jan Matejka) 50t. Type **119**.

1993. Birth Anniversaries. Each brown and yellow.
528 10t. Type **120** (bicent) 15 10
529 20t. Vydunas (125th anniv) 35 20
530 45t. Vincas Mykolaitis-Putinas (philosopher, centenary) 80 40

1993. Town Arms. As T **114**. Multicoloured.
531 5c. Skuodas 10 10
532 30c. Telsiai 20 10
533 50c. Klaipeda 35 15

121 "Watchtower" (M. K. Ciurlionis)

122 State Arms

1993. World Unity Day (5c.) and Transatlantic Flight (80c.). Multicoloured.
534 5c. Type **121** 10 10
535 80c. Steponas Dariaus and Stasys Gireno 50 25

1993. No value expressed.
536 **122** A, green, brown and red 10 10
537 B, red, green and bistre 35 20

123 Pope John Paul II and View of Siluva

124 Couple

1993. Papal Visit. Multicoloured.
538 60c. Type **123** 35 20
539 60c. Pope and Hill of Crosses 35 20
540 80c. Pope and Kaunas . . . 50 25
541 80c. Pope and Ausra Gates, Vilnius 50 25

1993. Costumes of Dzukai.
542 **124** 60c. multicoloured 25 10
543 – 80c. multicoloured 40 20
544 – 1l. multicoloured 55 25
DESIGNS: 80c. to 1l. Different costumes.

125 Klaipeda Post Office

1993. 75th Anniv of First Lithuanian Postage Stamps.
545 **125** 60c. multicoloured 35 15
546 – 60c. multicoloured 30 15
547 – 80c. multicoloured 50 25
548 – 1l. black, brown and green 60 30
DESIGNS: No. 546, Kaunas post office; 547, Ministry for Post and Information, Vilnius; 548, First Lithuanian stamp.

126 "The Ladle Carver" (A. Gudaitis)

127 European Pond Turtle

1993. Europa. Contemporary Art.
549 **126** 80c. multicoloured 45 25

1993. Pond Life. Multicoloured.
550 80c. Type **127** 40 20
551 1l. Running toad 45 25

128 Games Emblem and Team Colours

130 Kristijonas Donelaitis

129 Antanas Smetona (President 1919–22 and 1926–40)

1994. Winter Olympic Games, Lillehammer, Norway.
552 **128** 1l.10 multicoloured . . . 45 20

1994. National Day.
553 **129** 1l. red and black 30 15
554 – 1l. brown and black . . . 30 15
DESIGN: No. 554, Aleksandras Stulginskis (President 1922–26).

1994. Writers. Each cream, brown and orange.
555 60c. Type **130** 25 10
556 80c. Vincas Kudirka 35 15
557 1l. Jonas Maciulis Maironis 45 20

131 State Arms

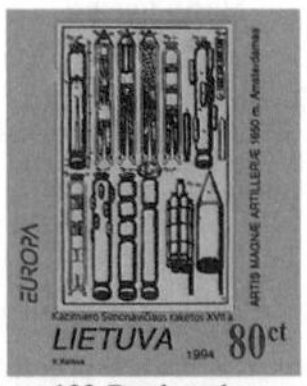

132 Rockets by Kazimieras Simonavicius (illus from "Artis Magnae Artilleriae")

1994.
558 **131** 5c. brown 10 10
559 10c. lilac 10 10
560 20c. green 10 10
612 40c. purple 15 10
613 50c. blue 20 10

1994. Europa. Inventions and Discoveries.
561 **132** 80c. multicoloured 45 20

1994. 100th Postage Stamp. Sheet 80 × 62 mm.
MS562 **99** 10l. green and red (sold at 12l.) . . . . 4·75 4·75

133 Couple

134 Music Note, Globe and Flag

1994. 19th-century Costumes of Zemaiciai (Lowlands).
563 **133** 5c. multicoloured 10 10
564 – 80c. multicoloured 35 15
565 – 1l. multicoloured 45 20
DESIGNS: 80c., 1l., Different costumes from Zemaiciai.

1994. Lithuanians of the World Song Festival.
566 **134** 10c. multicoloured 10 10

135 State Arms

136 Common Bat

1994.
567 **135** 2l. multicoloured 80 40
568 3l. multicoloured . . . . 1·25 60
See also **MS**580.

1994. Town Arms. As T **114** but size 25 × 32 mm. Multicoloured.
569 10c. Punia 10 10
570 60c. Alytus 25 10
571 80c. Perloja 35 15

1994. Mammals. Multicoloured.
572 20c. Type **136** 15 10
573 20c. Fat dormouse 15 10

137 Kaunas Town Hall

1994. Town Halls.
574 **137** 10c. black and mauve . . 10 10
575 – 60c. black and blue . . . 25 10
576 – 80c. black and green . . . 35 15
DESIGNS: 60c. Kedainiai; 80c. Vilnius.

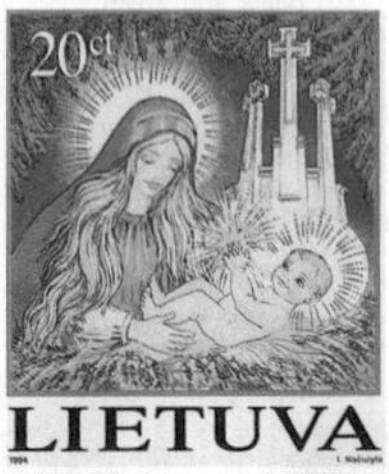

138 Madonna and Child

1994. Christmas.
577 **138** 20c. multicoloured 15 10

139 Steponas Kairys

1995. National Day. Signatories to 1918 Declaration of Independence.
578 **139** 20c. lilac, grey and black 10 10
579 – 20c. blue, grey and black 10 10
DESIGN: No. 579, Pranas Dovydaitis (Head of Government, March–April 1919).

1995. 5th Anniv of Independence. Sheet 75 × 105 mm.
MS580 **135** 4 × 1l. multicoloured 1·90 1·90

140 Kaunas (Lithuania)

141 "Lithuanian School, 1864–1904" (P. Rimsa)

1995. Via Baltica Motorway Project. Multicoloured.
581 20c. Type **140** 10 10
MS582 100 × 110 mm. 1l. Beach Hotel, Parnu (Estonia); 1l. Bauska Castle (Latvia); 1l. Type **140** 1·50 1·50

1995. Europa. Peace and Freedom.
583 **141** 1l. multicoloured 40 20

142 Couple

143 Motiejus Valancius (120th death)

1995. Costumes of the Highlands.
584 – 20c. multicoloured 10 10
585 – 70c. multicoloured 25 15
586 **142** 1l. multicoloured 40 20
DESIGNS: 70c. to 1l. Different 19th-century costumes.

1995. Anniversaries.
587 **143** 30c. cream, pur & yell . . 10 10
588 – 40c. cream, grn & orge . . 20 10
589 – 70c. cream, dp bl & pink 30 15
DESIGNS: 40c. Zemaite (150th birth); 70c. Kipras Petrauskas (110th birth).

144 Pieta

145 Torch-bearer

1995. Day of Mourning and Hope.
590 **144** 20c. multicoloured 10 10

1995. 5th World Lithuanians Games.
591 **145** 30c. multicoloured 15 10

146 "Baptria tibiale"

147 "Valerija Mesalina"

1995. Butterflies and Moths in "The Red Book". Multicoloured.
592 30c. Type **146** 20 10
593 30c. Cream-spot tiger moth ("Arctia villica") 20 10

1995. Town Arms. As T **114**. Multicoloured.
594 40c. Virbalis 20 10
595 1l. Kudirkos Naumiestis (horiz) 40 20

1995. 250th Birth Anniv of Pranciskus Smuglevicius (painter).
596 **147** 40c. multicoloured 20 10

148 Trakai Island Castle

1995. Castles.
597 – 40c. multicoloured 15 10
598 **148** 70c. blue, dp blue & black 30 15
599 – 1l. multicoloured 35 20
DESIGNS: 40c. Vilnius Upper Castle; 1l. Birzai Castle.

149 Star over Winter Scene

150 Bison

1995. Christmas. Multicoloured.
600 40c. Type **149** 20 10
601 1l. Churchgoers with lanterns 40 20

1996. The European Bison. Multicoloured.
602 30c. Type **150** 10 10
603 40c. Pair of bison 15 10
604 70c. Adult and calf 25 10
605 1l. Parents and calf 30 15

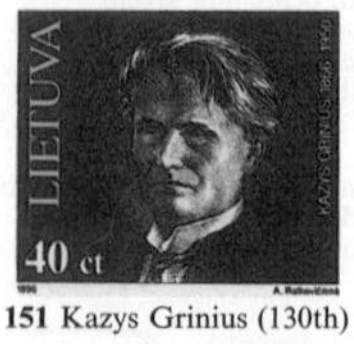

151 Kazys Grinius (130th)

1996. Birth Anniversaries.
606 **151** 40c. cream, brown & blue 15 10
607 – 1l. cream, bistre & yellow 40 20
608 – 1l. cream, blue and red 40 20
DESIGNS: No. 607, Antanas Zmuidzinavicius (120th); 608, Balys Sruoga (centenary).

152 Vladas Mironas

1996. National Day. Signatories to 1918 Declaration of Independence.
609 **152** 40c. cream, grey and black 15 10
610 – 40c. bistre, brown and black 15 10
DESIGN: No. 610, Jurgis Saulys.

153 Barbora Radvilaite

154 Couple

1996. Europa. Famous Women.
611 **153** 1l. multicoloured 30 15

1996. Costumes of Klaipeda. 19th-century costumes. Multicoloured.
618 40c. Type **154** 15 10
619 1l. Woman in red skirt and man in frock-coat 45 20
620 1l. Woman in black skirt and man in blue waistcoat . . 45 20

155 Angel

156 "The Discus Thrower"

1996. Day of Mourning and Hope.
621 **155** 40c. blue, red and black 20 10
622 – 40c. green, red and black 20 10
DESIGN: No. 622, Head of crucifix.

1996. Olympic Games, Atlanta. Multicoloured.
623 1l. Type **156** 35 15
624 1l. Basketball 35 15

157 "Sacrifice"

158 Players

1996. 85th Death Anniv of Mikolajus Ciurlionis (artist). Multicoloured.
625 40c. Type **157** 15 10
626 40c. "Cemetery" 15 10
MS627 80 × 102 mm. 3l. "Sonata of the Andante" (25 × 36 mm); 3l. "Sonata of the Stars—Allegro" (25 × 36 mm) . . . .

1996. Town Arms. As T **114** but size 25 × 32 mm.
628 50c. multicoloured 20 10
629 90c. red, black and yellow . . 40 20
630 1l.20 multicoloured 50 25
DESIGN: 50c. Seduva; 90c. Panevezys; 1l.20, Zarasai.

1996. Lithuanian Basketball Team, Bronze Medallist, Olympic Games, Atlanta. Sheet 50 × 72 mm.
MS631 **158** 4l.20 multicoloured 1·40 1·40

159 Angels heralding

1996. Christmas. Multicoloured.
632 50c. Type **159** 20 10
633 1l.20 Elf riding on "Pegasus" 40 20

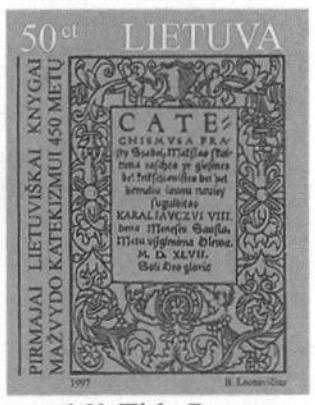

160 Ieva Simonaityte (writer, birth centenary)
161 Title Page

1997. Anniversaries.
634 **160** 50c. stone, brown and green 15 10
635 – 90c. stone, grey and yellow 35 20
636 – 1l.20 stone, grn & orge . . 40 20
MS638 94 × 56 mm. **161** 4l.80 brown and grey (26 × 36 mm) . . . . 1·90 1·25
DESIGNS: 90c. Jonas Sliupas (physician, 53rd death); 1l.20, Vladas Jurgutis (financier, 31st death).

1997. 450th Anniv of Publication of "Catechism of Mazvydas" (first Lithuanian book).
637 **161** 50c. brown and grey . . . 20 10

162 Mykolas Birziska

1997. National Day. Signatories to 1918 Declaration of Independence.
639 **162** 50c. green, lt grn & blk 20 10
640 – 50c. purple, stone and black 20 10
DESIGN: No. 640, Kazimieras Saulys.

163 Flag on Mountain Peak

1997. Completion of Ascent of World's Highest Mountains by Vladas Vitauskas. Sheet 80 × 60 mm.
MS641 **163** 4l.80 multicoloured 1·90 1·25

164 "Little Witch" (Jovita Jankeviciute)
165 Lecture

1997. Europa. Tales and Legends. Multicoloured.
642 1l.20 Type **164** 45 20
643 1l.20 "Rainbow" (Ieva Staseviciute) (horiz) 45 20

1997. 600th Anniv of First Lithuanian School.
644 **165** 50c. multicoloured 20 10

166 Kurshes Ship

1997. Baltic Sailing Ships. Multicoloured.
645 50c. Type **166** 20 10
MS646 110 × 70 mm. 1l.20 Kushes ship (as in T **166** but with frame etc); 1l.20 Maasilinn ship (Estonia); 1l.20 *Wappen der Herzogin von Kurland* (galleon) (Estonia) . . . . 1·50 1·50

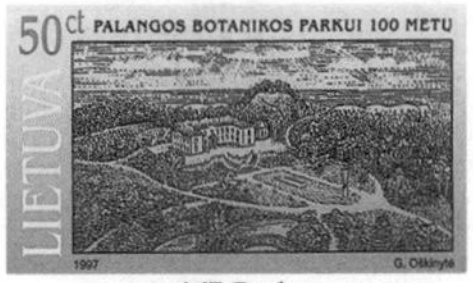

167 Park

1997. Centenary of Palanga Botanical Park.
647 **167** 50c. yellow, black and brown 20 10

168 Ship of Flags
169 Elk's-horn Staff, 3000 B.C.

1997. 2nd Baltic Sea Games, Lithuania.
648 **168** 90c. multicoloured 35 15

1997. Museum Exhibits. Multicoloured.
649 90c. Type **169** 35 15
650 1l.20 Silver coins of Grand Duke Kazimierz IV, 15th century A.D. 45 20

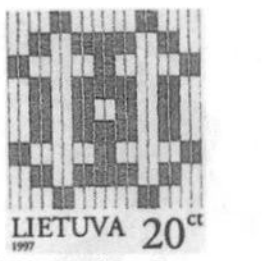

170 Vytis's Cross
171 Black Morel

1997.
651 **170** 5c. yellow & light yellow 10 10
652 10c. yellow and cream . . 10 10
653 20c. green and brown . . 10 10
654 35c. purple and lilac . . 10 10
655 50c. brown and cinnamon 15 10
656 70c. yellow and cream . . 20 10

1997. Fungi in the Red Book. Multicoloured.
660 1l.20 Type **171** 50 25
661 1l.20 Bronze boletus 50 25

172 Letter and Seal
173 Cherub holding Lantern above Town

1997. 674th Anniv of Letters of Invitation for Migrants sent by Grand Duke Gediminas to European Cities.
662 **172** 50c. multicoloured 20 10

1997. Town Arms. As T **114** but size 25 × 33 mm.
663 50c. Neringa 15 10
664 90c. Vilkaviskis 30 15
665 1l.20 Pasvalys 40 20

1997. Christmas. Multicoloured.
666 50c. Type **173** 15 10
667 1l.20 Snow-covered trees . . 40 20

174 Figure Skaters

1998. Winter Olympic Games, Nagano, Japan.
668 **174** 1l.20 ultramarine and blue 35 15

175 Alfonsas Petrulis (priest)

1998. National Day. Signatories to 1918 Declaration of Independence.
669 **175** 50c. green, grey and black 15 10
670 – 90c. brown, lt brn & blk 30 15
DESIGN: No. 670, Jokubas Sernas (lawyer and politician).

176 Text of Declaration and State Emblem
177 Lyrics and Kudirka's Memorial

1998. 80th Anniv of Declaration of Independence. Sheet 123 × 50 mm.
MS671 **176** 6l.60 multicoloured 2·00 2·00

1998. Centenary of *Tautiskai giesmei* (national anthem) by Vincas Kudirka (lyricist). Sheet 90 × 64 mm.
MS672 **177** 5l.20 multicoloured 1·60 1·60

178 Gustaitis and ANBO-41 (reconnaissance plane)

1998. Birth Centenary of Antanas Gustaitis (pilot and aircraft constructor). Multicoloured.
673 2l. Type **178** 60 30
674 3l. ANBO-VIII (light bomber) and diagrams . . 90 45

179 National Song Festival
180 Tadas Ivanauskas (zoologist, 27th death anniv)

1998. Europa. National Festivals.
675 **179** 1l.20 multicoloured . . . 35 15

1998. Anniversaries.
676 **180** 50c. green, lt yell & yell 15 10
677 – 90c. red, yellow & orge 30 15
678 – 90c. green, yellow & orge 30 15
DESIGNS—45 × 25 mm: No. 677, Stasys Lozoraitis (diplomat, birth centenary) and Stasys Lozoraitis (diplomat, 10th death anniv); No. 678, Jurgis Baltrusaitis (writer and diplomat, 125th birth anniv) and Jurgis Baltrusaitis (art historian, 4th death anniv).

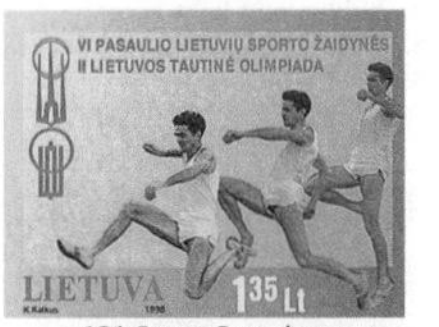

181 Long Jumping

1998. 6th World Lithuanian Games and Second National Games.
679 **181** 1l.35 multicoloured . . . 40 20

182 Atlantic Salmon

1998. Fishes in the Red Book. Multicoloured.
680 1l.40 Type **182** 45 20
681 1l.40 Whitefish ("Coregonus lavaretus") 45 20

1998. Town Arms. As T **114** but size 25 × 33 mm. Multicoloured.
682 70c. Kernave 20 10
683 70c. Trakai 20 10
684 1l.35 Kaunas 40 20

183 Vilnius–Cracow Postal Service, 1562

1998. Postal History. Multicoloured.
685 70c. Type **183** 20 10
MS686 55 × 86 mm. 13l. Hologram of posthorn and map of Europe, Africa and Asia (80th anniv of first Lithuanian stamps) (39 × 29 mm) 4·00 4·00

184 "All Night Long" (Antanas Zmuidzinavicius)

1998. Paintings. Multicoloured.
687 70c. Type **184** 20 10
688 1l.35 "Vilnius: Bernardines' Garden" (Juozapas Marsevskis) 40 20

185 Girl holding Church

1998. Christmas. Multicoloured.
689 70c. Type **185** 20 10
690 1l.35 Couple going into tree house 40 20

186 Mickiewicz (statue, G. Jokuonis)
187 Angwels holding Title Page

1998. Birth Bicentenary of Adam Mickiewicz (poet).
691 **186** 70c. multicoloured 20 10

1999. 400th Anniv of Publication of Translation into Lithuanian by Mikalojus Dauksa of *Postilla Catholicka* by Jacob Wujek. Sheet 60 × 67 mm.
MS692 **187** 5l.90 brown and silver 1·90 1·90

188 Petras Klimas (historian and diplomat)

1999. National Day. Signatories to 1918 Declaration of Independence.
693 **188** 70c. red and black 20 10
694 – 70c. blue and black . . . 20 10
DESIGN: No. 694, Donatas Malinauskas (diplomat).

189 Augustinas Gricius (dramatist)
190 Emblem and State Flag

1999. Birth Centenaries.
695 **189** 70c. black, cream & orge 20 10
696 – 70c. brown, cream & pink 20 10
697 – 1l.35 green, cream and orange 40 20

DESIGNS: No. 696, Juozas Matulis (chemist); 697, Pranas Skardzius (philologian).

1999. 50th Anniv of North Atlantic Treaty Organization.
698 **190** 70c. multicoloured 20 10

191 Aukstaitija National Park

1999. Europa. Parks and Gardens. Multicoloured.
699 1l.35 Type **191** 40 20
700 1l.35 Curonian Spit National Park 40 20

192 Council Flag **193** Boarded Clay Windmill, Melniai

1999. 50th Anniv of Council of Europe.
701 **192** 70c. multicoloured 20 10

1999. Windmills. Multicoloured.
702 70c. Type **193** 20 10
703 70c. Red-brick windmill, Pumpenai 20 10

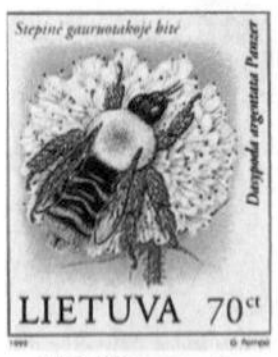

194 "Dasypoda argentata" **195** Sculpture of U.P.U. Emblem, Berne

1999. Bumble Bees. Multicoloured.
704 70c. Type **194** 20 10
705 2l. "Bombus pomorum" . . 60 30

1999. 125th Anniv of Universal Postal Union.
706 **195** 70c. multicoloured 20 10

196 1918 and 1990 Stamps and Society Emblems

1999. 75th Anniv of Lithuanian Philatelic Society.
707 **196** 1l. multicoloured 30 15

197 Cast and Producers

1999. Centenary of First Public Performance of Lithuanian Drama (*America in the Bath* by Keturakis). Sheet 99 × 59 mm containing T **197** and similar vert design. Multicoloured.
MS708 4l. Type **197**; 4l. Playbill 2·50 2·50

198 Family and State Flag **199** Emblem

1999. 10th Anniv of the Baltic Chain (human chain uniting the capitals of Lithuania, Estonia and Latvia). Multicoloured.
709 1l. Type **198** 30 15
MS710 110 × 72 mm. 2l. Type **198**; 2l. Family and Estonian flag; 2l. Family and Latvian flag . . . 1·75 85

1999. 50th Anniv of Establishment of Lithuanian Freedom Fight Movement.
711 **199** 70c. multicoloured 20 10

1999. Town Arms. Designs as T **114** but size 25 × 33 mm. Multicoloured.
712 70c. Marijampole 20 10
713 1l. Siauliai 30 15
714 1l.40 Rokiskis 40 20

200 Sword of General S. Zukauskas, 1927 **201** "Horse and Bear" (fable)

1999. Exhibits in Vytautas Magnus War Museum. Multicoloured.
715 70c. Type **200** 20 10
716 3l. 17th-century Hussar's armour 90 45

1999. Birth Bicentenary of Simonas Stanevicius (writer).
717 **201** 70c. multicoloured 20 10

202 "Winter Symphony" **203** Top of Monument

1999. Christmas. Multicoloured.
718 70c. Type **202** 20 10
719 1l.35 Cathedral, candles and bell 40 20

2000. Ironwork.
720 **203** 10c. blue and brown . . . 10 10
721 – 20c. blue and stone . . . 10 10
722 – 1l. blue and pink 30 15
723 – 1l.30 blue and green . . . 40 20
724 – 1l.70 blue and light blue 50 25
DESIGNS: 20c. to 1l.70, Different examples of ornamental ironwork.

204 Jonas Vailokaitis

2000. National Day. Signatories to 1918 Declaration of Independence.
725 **204** 1l.30 orange, stone & blk 40 25
726 – 1l.70 brown, stone & blk 50 25
DESIGN: 1l.70, Jonas Smilgevicius.

205 Declaration

2000. 10th Anniv of Restoration of Independence. Sheet 86 × 71 mm.
MS727 **205** 7l.40 multicoloured 2·25 2·25

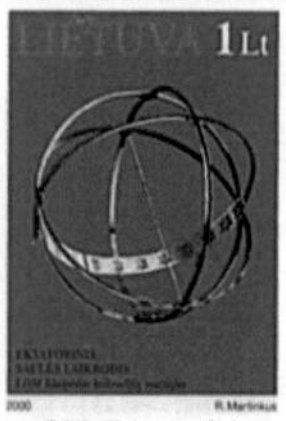

206 Vincas Pietaris (writer, 150th anniv) **207** Equatorial Sundial

2000. Birth Anniversaries.
728 **206** 1l. green, black and purple 30 15
729 – 1l.30 blue, black & brown 40 20
730 – 1l.70 brown, black & bl 50 25
DESIGNS: 1l.30, Kanutas Ruseckas (painter, bicentenary); 1l.70, Povilas Visinskis (literary critic, 125th anniv).
See also Nos. 753/5.

2000. Exhibits in Klaipeda Clock Museum. Mult.
731 1l. Type **207** 35 15
732 2l. Renaissance-style clock case 70 35

208 "Building Europe" **209** Osprey

2000. Europa.
733 **208** 1l.70 multicoloured . . . 60 30

2000. Birds of Prey. Multicoloured.
734 1l. Type **209** 35 15
735 2l. Black kite 70 35

210 Grey Seal

2000. Lithuanian Marine Museum, Kopgalis. Mult.
736 1l. Type **210** 35 15
737 1l. Magellanic penguin (*Spheniscus magellanicus*) 35 15

211 Cycling

2000. Olympic Games, Sydney. Multicoloured.
738 1l. Type **211** 35 15
739 3l. Swimming . . . . 1·00 50

212 "Fairy Tail Castle" (Ciurlionis)

2000. 125th Birth Anniv of Mikalojus Konstantinas Ciurlionis (artist and composer). Sheet 59 × 56 mm.
MS740 **212** 4l. multicoloured . . 1·25 1·25

213 Tree and Emblem

2000. 10th Anniv of Lithuanian Postal Service.
741 **213** 1l. multicoloured 35 15

2000. Town Arms. As T **114** but size 25 × 33 mm. Multicoloured.
742 1l. Raseiniai 35 15
743 1l. Taurage 35 15
744 1l.30 Utena 45 20

214 Snow-covered Village **215** The Nativity

2000. Christmas. Multicoloured.
745 1l. Type **214** 35 15
746 1l.70 Snow-covered church 60 30

2000. Holy Year (2000). Sheet 69 × 87 mm containing T **215** and similar vert designs. Multicoloured.
MS747 2l. Type **215**; 2l. Jesus with James and John; 2l. Crucifixion; 2l. Jesus entering Heaven . . . 2·50 2·50

216 Neolithic Amber Artefact

2000. New Millennium.
748 **216** 1l. multicoloured 35 15

217 Medals

2000. Lithuanian Victories in Olympic Games, Sydney. Sheet 65 × 102 mm.
MS749 **217** 4l. multicoloured . . 1·25 1·25

218 Vilnius Television Tower and Flag **220** Lake Galve

219 Saliamonas Banaitis

2001. 10th Anniv of Soviet Action in Vilnius.
750 **218** 1l. multicoloured 35 15

2001. National Day. Signatories to 1918 Declaration of Independence.
751 **219** 1l. brown, grey and black 35 15
752 – 2l. lilac, grey and black 70 35
DESIGN: 2l. Justinas Staugaitis.

2001. Anniversaries. As T **206**.
753 1l. blue, red and black . . . 35 15
754 1l. green, red and black . . . 35 15
755 1l.70 brown, violet and black 60 30
DESIGNS: No. 753, Juozas MikEnas (artist, birth centenary); 754, Pranas Vaicaitis (poet, death centenary); 755, Petras Vileisis (civil engineer, 150th birth anniv).

2001. Europa. Water Resources. Multicoloured.
756 1l.70 Type **220** 60 30
757 1l.70 River Nemunas 60 30

221 Floating Bogbean (*Nymphoides peltata*)

2001. Plants in the Red Book. Multicoloured.
758 2l. Type **221** 70 35
759 3l. Crossleaf heather (*Erica tetralix*) . . . . 1·10 55

222 Paplauja Bridge, Vilnius

2001. Bridges. Multicoloured.
760 1l. Type **222** 35 15
761 1l.30 Pakruojis, Kruoja . . . 50 25

223 National Flag

2001. Millenary of Lithunania. Sheet 125×100 mm containing T **223** and similar horiz designs. Multicoloured.
MS762 2l. Type **223**; 2l. State emblem; 2l. Map of Lithuania; 2l. Map of Europe . . . . 1·90 1·90

224 Sand Dunes, Palanga, Lithuania

2001. Baltic Sea Coast. Multicoloured.
763 1l. Type **224** 35 15
MS764 125×60 mm. 2l. As Type **224** but with Palanga at left; 2l. Rocky coastline, Lahemaa, Estonia; 2l. Beach, Vidzeme, Latvia . . . . 1·90 1·90

225 19th-century Cottage, Kirdeikiai, Utena District

2001. 35th Anniv of Open Air Museum, Rumsiskes. Multicoloured.
765 1l. Type **225** 35 15
766 2l. Farmer's house, Darlenai, Kretinga district 70 35

226 "Sadness" (sculpture)

2001. 120th Birth Anniv of Juozas Zikaras (artist).
767 **226** 3l. multicoloured . . . . 1·10 55

227 Charter and King Stephan I Batory of Poland

2001. 418th Anniv of Introduction of Postal Rates based on Weight.
768 **227** 1l. multicoloured 35 15

2001. Town Arms. As T **114** but size 25×33 mm. Multicoloured.
769 1l. Lazdijai 35 15
770 1l.30 Birzai 50 25
771 1l.70 Veliuona 60 30

228 Birds on Straw and Pine Pyramid ("Winter troubles")

2001. Christmas and New Year. Multicoloured.
772 1l. Type **228** 40 20
773 1l.70 Birds and crib ("Jesus' cradle") 70 35

229 Basanavicius **230** Skier

2001. 150th Birth Anniv of Jonas Basanavicius (politician and signatory to 1918 Declaration of Independence). Sheet 82×60 mm.
MS774 **229** 5l. multicoloured . . 2·10 2·10

2002. Winter Olympic Games, Salt Lake City, U.S.A.
775 **230** 1l.30 multicoloured . . . 70 35

231 Kazys Bizauskas

2002. National Day. Signatories to 1918 Declaration of Independence.
776 **231** 1l. sepia, brown and black 40 20
777 – 1l. violet, brown and black 40 20
DESIGN: No. 777 Stanislovas Narutavicius (politician).

232 Antanas Salys

2002. Birth Anniversaries. Multicoloured.
778 1l. Type **232** (linguist, centenary) 40 20
779 1l.30 Satrijos Ragana (writer, 125th anniv) 55 25
780 1l.70 Oskaras Milasius (poet, 125th anniv) 70 35

2002. Town Arms. As T **114** but size 25×33 mm. Multicoloured.
781 1l. Birstonas 40 20
782 1l. Anyksciai 40 20
783 1l.70 Prienai 70 35

233 Book, Archives and Seal

2002. 150th Anniv of State Archives.
784 **233** 1l. multicoloured 40 20

234 Stoat (*Mustela erminea*)

2002. Endangered Species. Multicoloured.
785 1l. Type **234** 40 20
786 3l. Lynx (*Lynx (Felis) lynx*) 1·10 55

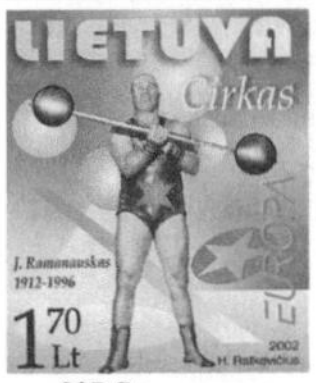

235 Strongman

2002. Europa. Circus.
787 **235** 1l.70 multicoloured . . . 65 30

236 Ford 350 Fire Engine

2002. Bicentenary of Vilnius Fire and Rescue Service.
788 **236** 1l. multicoloured 40 20

237 Diesel Locomotive TU 2

2002. Narrow-gauge Railway. Multicoloured.
789 1l.30 Type **237** 50 25
790 2l. Steam locomotive PT 4 75 35

238 Flint Tool

2002. Millenary of Lithuania (2009). Sheet 126×100 mm containing T **238** and similar horiz designs. Multicoloured.
MS791 2l. Type **238**; 2l. Publius Cornelius Tacitus (chronicler); 2l. Viking ship; 2l. Annals of Quedlinburg (manuscript containing first reference to Lithuania) . . . . 3·00 1·50

239 Rooftops **240** Script and Exhibits

2002. 750th Anniv of Klaipeda. Sheet 88×59 mm.
MS792 **239** 5l. multicoloured . . 2·00 1·00

2002. Maironis Literature Museum, Kaunas. Multicoloured.
793 1l. Type **240** 40 20
794 3l. Museum buildings . . . . 1·10 55

241 King Zigmantas Vaza (founder of postal system)

2002. Postal History.
795 **241** 1l. multicoloured 40 20

242 Star and Clock-face **243** Mother and Child (Danielius Peciulis)

2002. Christmas and New Year. Multicoloured.
796 1l. Type **242** 40 20
797 1l.70 Christmas tree 65 30

2002. European Children's Day.
798 **243** 1l. multicoloured 40 20

244 Laurynas Stuoka-Gucevicius (architect)

2003. Personalities. Multicoloured.
799 1l. Type **244** 40 20
800 1l. Juozas Eretas (writer) . . 40 20

245 Gargzdai **246** Pervalka Lighthouse

2003. Town Arms. Multicoloured.
801 1l. Type **245** 40 20
802 1l. Kretinga 40 20
803 1l. Palanga 40 20
804 1l. Papile 40 20
805 1l. Rietavas 40 20
See also Nos. 827/9.

2003. Lighthouses. Multicoloured.
806 1l. Type **246** 40 20
807 3l. Uostadvaris . . . . . . 1·10 55

247 Face and Pencils

2003. Europa. Poster Art.
808 **247** 1l.70 multicoloured . . . 65 30

248 Royal Palace, Vilnius

2003. Royal Palace Restoration.
809 **248** 1l. multicoloured 40 20

249 Observatory Building **250** *Cerambyx cerdo*

2003. 250th Anniv of Astronomical Observatory, Vilnius University.
810 **249** 1l. multicoloured 40 20

2002. Endangered Species. Beetles. Multicoloured.
811 3l. Type **250** . . . . 1·10 55
812 3l. Stag beetle (*Lucanus cervus*) . . . . 1·10 55

251 Fortifications, 1183

2003. Lithuania Millenary. Sheet 125×100 mm containing T **251** and similar horiz designs. Multicoloured.
MS813 2l. Type **251**; 2l. The Battle of Shiauliai, 1236; 2l. The Coronation of King Mindaugas, 1253; 2l. Vilnius, 1323 . . . . 3·00 1·50

252 King Mindaugas

2003. 750th Anniv of Coronation of King Mindaugas. Sheet 87 × 58 mm.
MS814 **252** 5l. multicoloured . . 2·00 2·00

253 Hot Air Balloons

2003. 13th European Hot Air Balloon Championships, Vilnius.
815 **253** 1l.30 multicoloured . . . 50 25

254 Cardinal Sladkevicius

255 City Arms

2003. 3rd Death Anniv of Cardinal Vincentas Sladkevicius.
816 **254** 1l. multicoloured 40 20

2003. 500th Anniv of Panevezys City.
817 **255** 1l. multicoloured 40 20

256 Post Office, Map and Postal Seal

2003. Postal History.
818 **256** 1l. multicoloured 40 20

257 Christmas Tree, Church and Houses

258 Trophy and Basketball

2003. Christmas. Multicoloured.
819 1l. Type **257** 40 20
820 1l.70 Street lamps through houses 40 20

2003. Lithuania, European Men's Basketball Champions, 2003. Sheet 62 × 75 mm.
MS821 **258** 5l. multicoloured . . 2·00 2·00

259 Plastic Glider BK-7

2003. Aviation Museum, Kaunas.
822 1l. Type **259** 40 20
823 1l. Training glider BRO-12 40 20

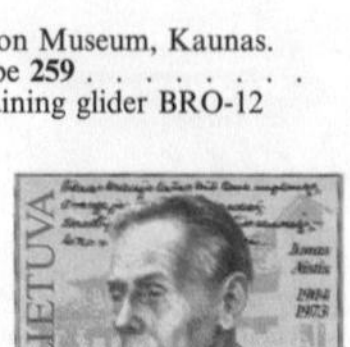
260 Jonas Aistis

2004. Anniversaries. Multicoloured.
824 1l. Type **260** (writer) (birth centenary) 40 20
825 1l. Kazimieras Buga (philologist) (80th death anniv) 40 20
826 1l. Adolfas Jucys (scientist) (birth centenary) 40 20

2004. Town Arms. As T **245**. Multicoloured.
827 1l. Mazeikiai 40 20
828 1l.30 Radviliskis 40 20
829 1l.40 Ukmerge Palanga . . . 40 20

261 King Steponas Batoras, Petras Skarga

262 Parasol on Beach and University Building

2004. 425th Anniv of Vilnius University.
830 **261** 1l. multicoloured 40 20

2004. Europa. Holidays. Multicoloured.
831 1l.70 Type **262** 65 30
832 1l.70 Yacht at sea 65 30

263 Frontispieces

2004. Centenary of the Re-establishment of printing using Latin Characters.
833 **263** 1l.30 multicoloured . . . 50 25

264 Lithuania Flag, Map of Europe, Stars and Shield

2004. Lithuania's Accession to the European Union. Multicoloured.
834 1l.70 Type **264** 65 30
835 1l.70 Flags of new members 65 30

265 Football

2004. Centenary of FIFA (Federation Internationale de Football Association).
836 **265** 3l. multicoloured . . . . 1·10 55

266 Chiune Sugihara

267 Burning of Pilenai, 1336

2004. Chiune Sugihara (Japanese Consul 1939–40) Commemoration.
837 **266** 1l. multicoloured 40 20

2004. Lithuania Millenary. Sheet 125 × 100 mm containing T **267** and similar vert designs.
MS838 2l. × 4, Type **267**; Algirdas (leader of Siniye Vody battle), 1362; Jagaila establishing Lithuania as Catholic country; Battle of Zalgiris (detail) (painting by Janas Mateika) . . . . . . 3·00 3·00

268 Iguana

2004. Tadas Ivanauskas Zoology Museum. Multicoloured.
839 1l. Type **268** 40 20
840 1l. Aquila chryaetos 40 20

269 Show Jumping

2004. Olympic Games, Athens. Multicoloured.
841 2l. Type **269** 80 40
842 3l. Canoeing . . . . 1·20 60

270 Northern Eagle Owl (*Bubo bubo*)

271 Aleksotas Funicular Railway

2004. Endangered Species. Owls. Multicoloured.
843 1l.30 Type **270** 55 25
844 3l. Short-eared owl (*Asio flammeus*) . . . . 1·20 60

2004. Funicular Railways. Multicoloured.
845 1l. Type **271** 40 20
846 1l.30 Zaliakalnis 55 25

272 Snow-covered Tree

2004. Christmas. Multicoloured.
847 1l. Type **272** 40 20
848 1l.70 Bullfinch 65 30

273 Kazys Boruta

274 Pink and Yellow Flowers

2005. Anniversaries. Multicoloured.
849 1l. Type **273** (writer) (birth centenary) 40 20
850 1l. Petras Kalpokas (artist) (60th death anniv) 40 20
851 1l. Jonas Puzinas (archaeologist) (birth centenary) 40 20

2005. Greetings Stamps. Multicoloured. Self-adhesive.
852 1l. Type **274** 40 20
853 1l. Orange flowers 40 20

275 Horses pulling Sulkies

2005. Centenary of Horse Races, Sartai Lake, Dusetos.
854 **275** 1l. multicoloured 40 20

2005. Town Arms. As T **245**. Multicoloured.
855 1l. Druskininkai 40 20
856 1l. Vabalninkas 40 20

276 White Cheese ("Baltas varskes suris")

2005. Europa. Gastronomy. Multicoloured.
857 1l.70 Type **276** 40 20
858 1l.70 Black bread ("Juoda duona") 40 20

LOMBARDY AND VENETIA Pt. 2

Formerly known as Austrian Italy. Although these provinces used a different currency the following issues were valid throughout Austria. Lombardy was annexed by Sardinia in 1859 and Venetia by Italy in 1866.

1850. 100 centesimi = 1 lira.
1858. 100 soldi = 1 florin.
100 kreuzer = 1 gulden.

1 Arms of Austria

1850. Imperf.
1c **1** 5c. orange . . . . £1000 75·00
2c 10c. black . . . . £1900 70·00
7 15c. red . . . . £475 2·75
4a 30c. brown . . . . £1700 5·50
5e 45c. blue . . . . £4500 13·50

1859. As T **4** and **5** of Austria (Emperor Francis Joseph I) but value in soldi. Perf.
16 **5** 2s. yellow . . . . £350 70·00
17 **4** 3s. black £1600 £190
18 3s. green . . . . £225 50·00
19 **5** 5s. red . . . . £150 3·00
20 10s. brown . . . . £250 38·00
21 15s. blue . . . . £1100 13·50

3 Emperor Francis Joseph I

4 Arms of Austria

1861.
25 **3** 5s. red . . . . £1000 1·70
26 10s. brown . . . . £1600 17·00

1863.
27 **4** 2s. yellow . . . . 65·00 £120
33 3s. green . . . . 6·25 12·50
34 5s. red . . . . 2·10 1·00
35 10s. blue . . . . 12·50 3·75
36 15s. brown . . . . 45·00 37·00

JOURNAL STAMPS

J 5

1858. Imperf.
J22 **J 5** 1k. black £1100 £3000
J23 2k. red . . . . £170 60·00
J24 4k. red £2750

LOURENCO MARQUES Pt. 9

A Portuguese colony in E. Africa, now part of Mozambique, whose stamps it uses.

1895. 1000 reis = 1 milreis.
1913. 100 centavos = 1 escudo.

1895. "Figures" key-type inscr "LOURENCO MARQUES".
1 **R** 5r. yellow 30 30
2 10r. mauve 30 30
3 15r. brown 75 55
4 20r. lilac 75 55
10 25r. green 60 30
12 50r. blue . . . . 1·50 1·20
18 75r. pink . . . . 1·40 90
14 80r. green . . . . 4·00 2·50
7 100r. brown on yellow . . . 1·70 90
16 150r. red on pink . . . . . 3·25 2·50
8 200r. blue on blue . . . . . 3·00 1·90
9 300r. blue on brown . . . . 3·00 1·90

1895. 700th Death Anniv of St. Anthony. Optd **L. MARQUES CENTENARIO DE S. ANTONIO MDCCCXCV** on (a) "Embossed" key-type inscr "PROVINCIA DE MOCAMBIQUE".

19	Q	5r. black	14·00	11·50
20		10r. green	15·00	11·50
21		20r. red	17·00	13·00
22		25r. purple	21·00	13·00
23		40r. brown	21·00	13·00
27a		50r. blue	14·00	13·00
25		100r. brown	70·00	65·00
26		200r. violet	28·00	23·00
27		300r. orange	45·00	39·00

(b) "Figures" key-type inscr "MOCAMBIQUE"

28	R	5r. orange	14·00	8·00
29		10r. mauve	21·00	13·00
30		50r. blue	35·00	26·00
35		75r. pink	42·00	32·00
32		80r. green	55·00	45·00
33		100r. brown on yellow	£100	95·00
35a		150r. red on pink	35·00	26·00

1897. No. 9 surch **50 reis.**

36	R	50r. on 300r. blue on brown	£170	£160

1898. "King Carlos" key-type inscr "LOURENCO MARQUES". Name and value in black.

37	S	2½r. grey	25	25
38		5r. orange	25	25
39		10r. green	25	25
40		15r. brown	1·00	75
83		15r. green	65	45
41		20r. lilac	60	35
42		25r. green	60	35
84		25r. red	45	25
43		50r. blue	1·00	75
85		50r. brown	85	65
86		65r. blue	3·25	2·75
44		75r. pink	2·00	1·20
87		75r. purple	1·30	90
45		80r. mauve	1·60	1·10
46		100r. blue on blue	1·30	75
88		115r. brown on pink	3·75	3·50
89		130r. brown on yellow	3·75	3·50
47		150r. brown on yellow	2·00	1·20
48		200r. purple on pink	3·00	1·50
49		300r. blue on pink	2·10	1·50
90		400r. blue on yellow	4·25	3·75
50		500r. black on blue	4·25	2·10
51		700r. mauve on yellow	23·00	9·75

1899. Green and brown fiscal stamps of Mozambique, as T **9** of Macao, bisected and each half surch **Correio de Lourenco Marques** and value. Imperf.

55	–	5r. on half of 10r.	2·75	1·90
56	–	25r. on half of 10r.	2·75	1·90
57	–	50r. on half of 30r.	2·75	1·90
58	–	50r. on half of 800r.	7·00	5·25

1899. No. 44 surch **50 Reis**.

59	S	50r. on 75r. pink	4·50	2·75

1902. "Figures" and "Newspaper" key-types surch.

60	V	65r. on 2½r. brown	2·10	1·70
62	R	65r. on 5r. yellow	2·10	1·60
63		65r. on 15r. brown	2·10	1·60
64		65r. on 20r. lilac	2·10	1·60
66		115r. on 10r. mauve	2·10	1·60
67		115r. on 200r. blue on blue	2·10	1·60
68		115r. on 300r. blue on brn	2·10	1·60
70		130r. on 25r. green	1·90	1·70
72		130r. on 80r. green	2·10	1·70
73		130r. on 150r. red on pink	2·10	1·70
74		400r. on 50r. blue	7·00	3·00
76		400r. on 75r. pink	5·50	3·00
78		400r. on 100r. brown on yellow	3·75	2·75

1902. "King Carlos" key-type inscr "LOURENCO MARQUES" optd **PROVISORIO**.

79	S	15r. brown	1·30	90
80		25r. green	1·30	65
81		50r. blue	1·70	95
82		75r. pink	2·40	1·50

1905. No. 86 surch **50 REIS**.

91	S	50r. on 65r. blue	2·50	2·10

1911. "King Carlos" key-type inscr "LOURENCO MARQUES" optd **REPUBLICA**.

92	S	2½r. grey	25	20
93		5r. orange	25	20
94		10r. green	45	35
95		15r. green	45	35
96		20r. lilac	45	35
97		25r. red	85	50
98		50r. brown	75	50
99		75r. purple	1·20	50
100		100r. blue on blue	75	50
178		115r. brown on pink	1·20	1·00
102		130r. brown on yellow	85	50
103		200r. purple on pink	85	50
104		400r. blue on yellow	1·30	1·10
105		500r. black on blue	1·40	1·10
106		700r. mauve on yellow	1·70	1·10

1913. Surch **REPUBLICA LOURENCO MARQUES** and value on "Vasco da Gama" issues of (a) Portuguese Colonies.

107		¼c. on 2½r. green	1·30	1·00
108		½c. on 5r. red	1·30	1·00
109		1c. on 10r. purple	1·30	1·00
110		2½c. on 25r. green	1·30	1·00
111		5c. on 50r. blue	1·30	1·00
112		7½c. on 75r. brown	3·25	2·40
113		10c. on 100r. brown	1·70	1·00
114		15c. on 150r. brown	1·70	1·00

(b) Macao.

115		¼c. on ½a. green	95	75
116		½c. on 1a. red	95	75
117		1c. on 2a. purple	95	75
118		2½c. on 4a. green	95	75
119		5c. on 8a. blue	95	75
120		7½c. on 12a. brown	1·70	1·30
121		10c. on 16a. brown	1·30	65
122		15c. on 24a. brown	1·30	1·00

(c) Timor.

123		¼c. on ½a. green	95	75
124		½c. on 1a. red	95	75
125		1c. on 2a. purple	95	75
126		2½c. on 4a. green	95	75
127		5c. on 8a. blue	95	75
128		7½c. on 12a. brown	1·70	1·30
129		10c. on 16a. brown	1·30	65
130		15c. on 24a. brown	1·30	1·00

1914. "Ceres" key-type inscr "LOURENCO MARQUES".

147	U	¼c. green	25	20
148		½c. black	25	20
149		1c. green	25	20
150		1½c. brown	25	25
151		2c. red	25	25
152		2½c. violet	25	25
153		5c. blue	60	55
154		7½c. brown	60	55
155		8c. grey	60	55
140		10c. red	1·10	65
157		15c. purple	1·00	75
142		20c. green	1·30	95
143		30c. brown on green	1·10	90
144		40c. brown on pink	4·25	3·25
145		50c. orange on orange	1·90	1·50
146		1e. green on blue	1·90	1·50

1914. Provisionals of 1902 overprinted **REPUBLICA**.

166	R	115r. on 10r. mauve	65	55
167		115r. on 200r. blue on blue	75	55
168		115r. on 300r. blue on brn	75	55
161		130r. on 25r. green	1·10	1·00
164		130r. on 80r. green	1·70	1·30
169		130r. on 150r. red on pink	75	55
184		400r. on 50r. blue	1·30	90
185		400r. on 75r. pink	1·90	1·50

1915. Nos. 93 and 148 perf diagonally and each half surch ½.

170	S	½ on half of 5r. orange	2·30	1·80
171	U	½ on half of ¼c. black	2·30	1·80

Prices for Nos. 170/1 are for whole stamps.

1915. Surch **Dois centavos.**

172	S	2c. on 15r. (No. 83)	1·00	75
173		2c. on 15c. (No. 95)	1·00	75

1918. Red Cross Fund. "Ceres" key-type inscr "LOURENCO MARQUES", optd **9-3-18** and Red Cross or surch with value in figures and bars also.

188	U	¼c. green	2·10	1·90
189		½c. black	2·10	1·90
190		1c. green	2·10	1·90
191		2½c. violet	2·10	1·90
192a		5c. blue	2·10	1·90
193		10c. red	2·40	2·30
194		20c. on 1½c. brown	2·40	2·30
195		30c. brown on green	2·75	2·50
196		40c. on 2c. red	2·75	2·50
197		50c. on 7½c. brown	2·75	2·50
198		70c. on 8c. grey	2·75	2·50
199		1e. on 15c. purple	2·50	2·50

1920. No. 166 surch **Um quarto de centavo.**

200	R	¼c. on 115r. on	75	55

1920. No. 152 surch in figures or words.

201	U	1c. on 2½c. violet	60	35
202		1½c. on 2½c. violet	60	35
203		4c. on 2½c. violet	20	15

For other surcharges on "Ceres" key-type of Lourenco Marques, see Mozambique Nos. 309/10 and Nos. D44 and 46.

NEWSPAPER STAMPS

1893. "Newspaper" key-type inscr "LOURENCO MARQUES".

N1	V	2½r. brown	35	30

1895. 700th Death Anniv of St. Anthony. "Newspaper" key-type inscr "MOCAMBIQUE" optd **L. MARQUES CENTENARIO DE S. ANTONIO MDCCCXCV.**

N36	V	2½r. brown	5·25	3·50

LUBECK Pt. 7

Formerly one of the free cities of the Hanseatic League. In 1868 joined the North German Confederation.

16 schilling = 1 mark.

1

3

1859. Imperf.

9	1	½s. lilac	15·00	£1700
10		1s. orange	28·00	£1700
3		2s. brown	21·00	£225
4		2½s. red	43·00	£800
6		4s. green	21·00	£600

1863. Rouletted.

11	3	½s. green	43·00	65·00
13		1s. orange	£130	£170
14		2s. red	26·00	55·00
16		2½s. blue	£110	£400
17		4s. bistre	47·00	£110

4

5

1864. Imperf.

19	4	1¼s. brown	26·00	£110

1865. Roul.

21	5	1½s. mauve	26·00	85·00

LUXEMBOURG Pt. 4

An independent Grand Duchy lying between Belgium and the Saar District. Under German Occupation from 1940 to 1944.

1852. 12½ centimes = 1 silver groschen.
100 centimes = 1 franc.
1940. 100 pfennig = 1 reichsmark.
1944. 100 centimes = 1 franc (Belgian).
2002. 100 cents = 1 euro.

1 Grand Duke William III

3

4

1852. Imperf.

2	1	10c. black	£1900	32·00
3a		1s. red	£1200	£100

1859. Imperf or roul.

23	3	1c. brown	30·00	7·25
21		1c. orange	25·00	5·75
17		2c. black	14·00	10·50
8		4c. yellow	£160	£150
20		4c. green	30·00	21·00
10	4	10c. blue	£160	13·50
24		10c. purple	£100	1·60
25		10c. lilac	£110	2·50
28		12½c. red	£140	4·50
30		20c. brown	£120	10·50
12		25c. brown	£325	£225
32		25c. blue	£1000	9·00
13		30c. purple	£220	£190
14		37½c. green	£275	£140
35		37½c. bistre	£650	£225
39		40c. orange	42·00	75·00

1872. Surch **UN FRANC**. Roul.

37	4	1f. on 37½c. bistre	£900	55·00

1874. Perf.

57a	3	1c. brown	6·50	6·00
58a		2c. black	6·00	1·25
42		4c. green	1·00	9·00
43		5c. yellow	£150	12·00
60a	4	10c. lilac	£150	75
61		12½c. red	£160	£160
62a		20c. brown	14·00	13·50
63a		25c. blue	£225	3·75
64		30c. red	2·75	15·00
55		40c. orange	85	5·00

1879. Surch **Un Franc.** Perf.

56	4	1f. on 37½c. bistre	6·25	42·00

7 Agriculture and Trade

8 Grand Duke Adolf

9

1882.

81a	7	1c. grey	20	50
82c		2c. brown	10	25
83c		4c. bistre	30	1·50
84c		5c. green	55	25
85a		10c. red	4·50	75
86a		12½c. blue	1·00	21·00
87c		20c. orange	2·00	1·75
88a		25c. blue	£130	1·50
89a		30c. green	13·00	11·00
90c		50c. brown	1·00	6·25
91a		1f. lilac	60	23·00
92a		5f. orange	28·00	£150

1891.

125a	8	10c. red	15	25
126b		12½c. green	45	50
128		20c. orange	11·00	65
129c		25c. blue	85	40
130b		30c. green	1·00	85
131b		37½c. green	2·40	2·75
132b		50c. brown	6·00	3·25
133a		1f. purple	11·00	11·50
134		2½f. black	1·50	19·00
135		5f. lake	32·00	60·00

1895.

152	9	1c. grey	1·40	30
153		2c. brown	15	15
154		4c. bistre	20	70
155		5c. green	1·40	15
156		10c. red	6·50	15

10

11 Grand Duke William IV

13 Grand Duchess Adelaide

1906.

157	10	1c. grey	10	15
158		2c. brown	10	15
159		4c. bistre	15	20
160		5c. green	25	15
231		5c. mauve	10	15
161		6c. lilac	20	30
161a		7½c. orange	15	2·10
162	11	10c. red	1·50	10
163		12½ slate	1·50	30
164		15c. brown	1·50	50
165		20c. orange	3·00	45
166		25c. blue	45·00	30
166a		30c. olive	70	50
167		37½c. green	75	55
168		50c. brown	4·25	70
169		87½c. blue	1·75	6·25
170		1f. purple	4·75	1·25
171		2½f. red	50·00	60·00
172		5f. purple	7·00	42·00

1912. Surch **62½ cts.**

173	11	62½c. on 87½c. blue	1·25	1·75
173a		62½c. on 2½f. red	1·40	3·00
173b		62½c. on 5f. purple	55	1·90

1914.

174	13	10c. purple	10	10
175		12½c. green	10	10
176		15c. brown	10	10
176a		17½c. brown	10	30
177		25c. blue	10	10
178		30c. brown	10	40
179		35c. blue	10	30
180		37½c. brown	10	30
181		40c. red	15	30
182		50c. grey	25	40
183		62½c. green	35	1·90
183a		87½c. orange	35	1·90
184		1f. brown	2·00	60
185		2½f. red	45	1·90
186		5f. violet	7·00	32·00

1916. Surch in figures and bars.

187	10	2½ on 5c. green	10	10
188		3 on 2c. brown	10	10
212		5 on 1c. grey	10	15
213		5 on 4c. bistre	10	20
214		5 on 7½c. orange	10	15
215		6 on 2c. brown	25	25
189	13	7½ on 10c. red	10	10
190		17½ on 30c. brown	10	35
191		20 on 17½c. brown	10	20
216		25 on 37½c. sepia	10	20
217		75 on 62½c. green	10	20
218		80 on 87½c. orange	10	20
192		87½ on 1f. brown	55	6·25

17 Grand Duchess Charlotte

18 Vianden Castle

1921. Perf.
194 **17** 2c. brown 10 15
195 3c. green 10 15
196 6c. purple 10 15
197 10c. green 10 15
193a 15c. red* 10 15
198 15c. green 10 15
234 15c. orange 10 30
199 20c. orange 15 30
235 20c. green 10 30
200 25c. green 15 15
201 30c. red 15 15
202 40c. orange 15 15
203 50c. blue 15 35
236 50c. red 10 25
204 75c. red 15 1·25
237 75c. blue 10 25
205 80c. black 15 65
206a **18** 1f. red 20 35
238 1f. blue 25 40
207 – 2f. blue 40 55
239 – 2f. brown 2·40 1·40
208 – 5f. violet 12·00 6·00
DESIGNS—As Type **18**: 2f. Factories at Esch; 5f. Railway viaduct over River Alzette.
*No. 193a was originally issued on the occasion of the birth of Crown Prince Jean.
See also Nos. 219/20.

21 Monastery at Clervaux

1921. War Monument Fund.
209 **21** 10c.+5c. green 30 2·40
210 – 15c.+10c. orange 30 4·25
211 – 25c.+10c. green 30 2·40
DESIGNS—HORIZ: 15c. Pfaffenthal; 25c. as Type **26**.

1922. Philatelic Exhibition. Imperf.
219 **17** 25c. green 1·75 4·50
220 30c. red 1·75 4·50

26 Luxembourg

28 Echternach

1923. Birth of Princess Elisabeth. Sheet 78 × 59 mm to 79 × 61 mm.
MS221 **26** 10f. green £1000 £1700

1923.
222a **26** 10f. black 4·00 8·75

1923. Unveiling of War Memorial by Prince Leopold of Belgium. Nos. 209/11 surch **27 mai 1923** and additional values.
223 **21** 10+5+25c. green 1·40 14·00
224 – 15+10+25c. orange 1·40 19·00
225 – 25+10+25c. green 1·40 14·00

1923.
226a **28** 3f. blue 75 55

1924. Charity. Death of Grand Duchess Marie Adelaide. Surch **CARITAS** and new value.
227 **13** 12½c.+7½c. green 15 1·75
228 35c.+10c. blue 15 1·75
229 2½f.+1f. red 75 19·00
230 5f.+2f. violet 60 13·50

1925. Surch 5.
240 **17** 5 on 10c. green 10 15

31

32 Grand Duchess Charlotte

1925. Anti-T.B. Fund.
241 **31** 5c.+5c. violet 25 50
242 30c.+5c. orange 25 2·25
243 50c.+5c. brown 25 4·25
244 1f.+10c. blue 65 10·50

1926.
245 **32** 5c. mauve 10 15
246 10c. olive 10 20
246a 15c. black 10 20
247 20c. orange 25 25
248 25c. green 25 30
248a 25c. brown 20 25
248b 30c. green 20 25
248c 30c. violet 20 20
248d 35c. violet 1·75 20
248e 35c. green 10 15
249 40c. brown 10 20
250 50c. brown 10 20
250a 60c. green 1·75 20
251 65c. brown 20 1·40
251a 70c. violet 10 10
252 75c. red 15 45
252a 75c. brown 10 20
253 80c. brown 20 1·10
253a 90c. red 50 10
254 1f. black 55 30
254a 1f. red 35 30
255 1¼f. blue 10 35
255a 1¼f. yellow 6·00 95
255b 1¼f. green 35 25
255c 1¼f. red 9·00 1·60
255d 1½f. blue 1·10 1·25
255e 1¾f. blue 75 30

33 Prince Jean

34 Grand Duchess and Prince Felix

1926. Child Welfare.
256 **33** 5c.+5c. black and mauve 15 35
257 40c.+10c. black & green 15 75
258 50c.+15c. black & yellow 15 75
259 75c.+20c. black and red 30 8·00
260 1f.50+30c. black & bl 3·00 8·50

1927. International Philatelic Exhibition.
261 **34** 25c. purple 1·25 11·00
262 50c. green 1·75 15·00
263 75c. red 1·25 11·00
264 1f. black 1·25 11·00
265 1½f. blue 1·25 11·00

35 Princess Elisabeth

37 Clervaux

1927. Child Welfare.
266 **35** 10c.+5c. black and blue 15 40
267 50c.+10 black and brown 15 75
268 75c.+20c. black & orange 15 1·10
269 1f.+30c. black and red 30 8·00
270 1½f.+50c. black and blue 30 8·00

1927. Stamps of 1921 and 1926 surch.
270a **32** 10 on 30c. green 35 30
271 **17** 15 on 20c. green 10 20
272 **32** 15 on 25c. green 15 50
273 **17** 35 on 40c. orange 15 15
274 **32** 60 on 65c. brown 15 35
275 **17** 60 on 75c. blue 15 25
276 **32** 60 on 75c. red 15 35
277 **17** 60 on 80c. black 15 35
278 **32** 60 on 80c. brown 15 45
278a 70 on 75c. brown 4·50 30
278b 75 on 90c. red 1·40 55
278c 1¾ on 1½f. blue 3·25 1·25

1928. Perf.
279a **37** 2f. black 85 60
See also No. 339.

38 Princess Marie Adelaide

39 Princess Marie Gabrielle

1928. Child Welfare.
280 **38** 10c.+5c. purple & green 20 85
281 60c.+10c. olive & brown 30 2·25
282 75c.+15c. green and red 50 5·00
283 1f.+25c. brown & green 1·25 16·00
284 1½f.+50c. blue & yellow 1·25 16·00

1928. Child Welfare.
285 **39** 10c.+10c. green & brown 20 55
286 35c.+15c. brown & green 85 4·75
287 75c.+30c. black and red 85 6·50
288 1¼f.+50c. green and red 2·00 17·00
289 1¾f.+75c. black and blue 2·50 22·00

40 Prince Charles

41 Arms of Luxembourg

1930. Child Welfare.
290 **40** 10c.+5c. brown & green 20 90
291 75c.+10c. green & brown 1·40 4·75
292 1f.+25c. violet and red 3·00 17·00
293 1¼f.+75c. black & yellow 4·25 24·00
294 1¾f.+1f.50 brown & blue 5·00 24·00

1930.
295 **41** 5c. red 35 35
296 10c. green 45 20

42 Biplane over River Alzette

43 Luxembourg, Lower Town

1931. Air.
296a **42** 50c. green 60 1·10
297 75c. brown 60 1·25
298 1f. red 60 1·40
299 1¼f. purple 60 1·40
300 1¾f. blue 60 1·40
300a 3f. black 90 5·00

1931.
301 **43** 20f. green 3·25 19·00

44 Princess Alix

45 Countess Ermesinde

46 Emperor Henry VII

1931. Child Welfare.
302 **44** 10c.+5c. grey and brown 20 85
303 75c.+10c. green and red 3·50 11·00
304 1f.+25c. grey and green 6·00 23·00
305 1¼f.+75c. green and violet 6·00 23·00
306 1¾f.+1f.50 grey and blue 10·50 45·00

1932. Child Welfare.
307 **45** 10c.+5c. brown 35 90
308 75c.+10c. violet 2·10 13·50
309 1f.+25c. red 9·25 38·00
310 1¼f.+75c. lake 9·25 38·00
311 1¾f.+1f.50 blue 9·25 38·00

1933. Child Welfare.
312 **46** 10c.+5c. brown 35 80
313 75c.+10c. purple 4·25 13·00
314 1f.+25c. red 12·00 32·00
315 1¼f.+75c. brown 14·50 40·00
316 1¾f.+1f.50 blue 14·50 60·00

47 Gateway of the Three Towers

48 Arms of John the Blind

1934.
317 **47** 5f. green 1·00 7·25

1934. Child Welfare.
318 **48** 10c.+5c. violet 10 85
319 35c.+10c. green 2·75 9·25
320 75c.+15c. red 2·75 9·25
321 1f.+25c. red 14·50 40·00
322 1¼f.+75c. orange 16·00 50·00
323 1¾f.+1½f. blue 15·00 50·00

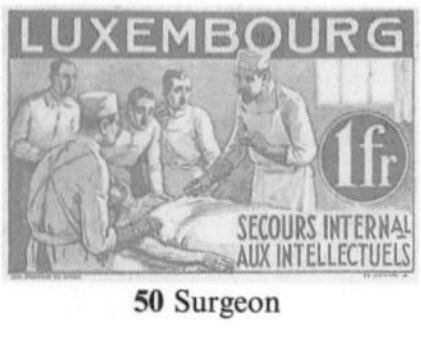
50 Surgeon

1935. International Relief Fund for Intellectuals.
324 – 5c. violet 20 1·00
325 – 10c. red 40 1·00
326 – 15c. olive 35 1·75
327 – 20c. orange 55 3·00
328 – 35c. green 80 4·00
329 – 50c. black 95 5·50
330 – 70c. green 2·00 6·00
331 **50** 1f. red 2·00 6·00
332 – 1f.25 turquoise 8·00 50·00
333 – 1f.75 blue 10·00 50·00
334 – 2f. brown 30·00 £110
335 – 3f. brown 42·00 £150
336 – 5f. blue 70·00 £275
337 – 10f. purple £180 £475
338 **50** 20f. green £200 £575
DESIGNS—HORIZ: 5c., 10f. Schoolteacher; 15c., 3f. Journalist; 20c., 1f.75, Engineer; 35c., 1f.25, Chemist. VERT: 10c., 2f. "The Arts"; 50c., 5f. Barrister; 70c. University.
This set was sold at the P.O. at double face value.

1935. Esch Philatelic Exhibition. Imperf.
339 **37** 2f.(+50c.) black 6·00 16·00

52 Vianden

1935.
340 **52** 10f. green 1·40 9·00

53 Charles I

54 Town Hall

1935. Child Welfare.
341 **53** 10c.+5c. violet 10 40
342 35c.+10c. green 35 60
343 70c.+20c. brown 85 1·50
344 1f.+25c. red 12·50 38·00
345 1f.25+75c. brown 12·50 38·00
346 1f.75+1f.50 blue 12·50 48·00

1936. 11th Int Philatelic Federation Congress.
347 **54** 10c. brown 35 40
348 35c. green 45 75
349 70c. orange 55 1·10
350 1f. red 1·60 6·50
351 1f.25 violet 2·75 8·50
352 1f.75 blue 1·60 7·25

55 Wenceslas I

56 Wenceslas II

1936. Child Welfare.
353 **55** 10c.+5c. brown 10 25
354 35c.+10c. green 15 45
355 70c.+20c. slate 35 60
356 1f.+25c. red 2·10 10·00
357 1f.25+75c. violet 4·00 23·00
358 1f.75+1f.50 blue 4·00 14·50

1937. Dudelange Philatelic Exhibition. Sheet 125 × 85 mm. As No. 207 (pair) in new colour.
MS359 2f. (+3f.) brown 1·40 9·50

1937. Child Welfare.
360 **56** 10c.+5c. black and red 10 20
361 35c.+10c. green & purple 25 35
362 70c.+20c. red and blue 25 35
363 1f.+25c. red and green 1·25 11·00
364 1f.25+75c. purple & brn 1·60 11·50
365 1f.75+1f.50 blue & blk 1·75 13·00

57 St. Willibrord

61 Sigismond of Luxembourg

1938. Echternach Abbey Restoration Fund (1st issue). 1200th Death Anniv of St. Willibrord.
366 **57** 35c.+10c. green 35 45
367 – 70c.+10c. black 85 55
368 – 1f.25+25c. red 1·40 2·25
369 – 1f.75+50c. blue 2·40 2·40
370 – 3f.+2f. red 6·25 7·50
371 – 5f.+5f. violet 7·00 7·25
DESIGNS—As Type **57**: 70c. Town Hall, Echternach; 1f.25, Pavilion, Echternach Municipal Park. 31 × 51 mm: 1f.75, St. Willibrord (from miniature). 42 × 38 mm: 3f. Echternach Basilica; 5f. Whitsuntide dancing procession.
See also Nos. 492/7 and 569/70.

1938. Child Welfare.
372 **61** 10c.+5c. black & mauve 10 35
373 35c.+10c. black & green 25 40
374 70c.+20c. black & brown 35 40
375 1f.+25c. black and red 2·00 11·50

376 1f.25+75c. black & grey . . 2·00 11·50
377 1f.75+1f.50 black & bl . . 2·75 17·00

62 Arms of Luxembourg

63 William I

1939. Centenary of Independence.
378 **62** 35c. green 15 20
379 **63** 50c. orange 20 20
380 – 70c. green 10 20
381 – 75c. olive 45 75
382 – 1f. red . . . . 1·00 1·50
383 – 1f.25 violet 15 30
384 – 1f.75 blue 15 30
385 – 3f. brown 30 45
386 – 5f. black . . . . 30 3·00
387 – 10f. red . . . . 85 7·00
PORTRAITS—As Type **63**: 70c. William II; 75c. William III; 1f. Prince Henry; 1f.25 Grand Duke Adolphe; 1f.75 William IV; 3f. Marie-Anne, wife of William IV; 5f. Grand Duchess Marie Adelaide; 10f. Grand Duchess Charlotte.

1939. Surch in figures.
388 **32** 30c. on 60c. green . . . . 15 1·60

65 Allegory of Medicinal Spring

66 Prince Jean

1939. Mondorf-les-Bains Propaganda.
389 **65** 2f. red . . . . 40 2·50

1939. 20th Anniv of Reign and of Royal Wedding.
390 **66** 10c.+5c. brn on cream . . 10 40
391 – 35c.+10c. green on cream 25 1·25
392 – 70c.+20c. black on cream 95 1·60
393 **66** 1f.+25c. red on cream . . 4·00 35·00
394 – 1f.25+75c. violet on cream 5·00 48·00
395 – 1f.75+1f.50 blue on cream 6·00 65·00
PORTRAITS: 35c., 1f.25, Prince Felix; 70c., 1f.75, Grand Duchess Charlotte.

1939. Twentieth Year of Reign of Grand Duchess Charlotte. Sheet 144 × 163 mm with designs as T **66** but without "CARITAS".
MS395a 2f. red (T **66**); 3f. green (Prince Felix); 5f. blue (Grand Duchess Charlotte) . . . . . 35·00 75·00

1940. Anti-T.B. Fund. Surch with Cross of Lorraine and premium.
396 **65** 2f.+50c. grey . . . . . . 1·25 13·00

1940–44. GERMAN OCCUPATION.

1940. T **94** of Germany optd **Luxemburg**.
397 **94** 3pf. brown 10 35
398 4pf. blue 10 40
399 5pf. green 10 40
400 6pf. green 10 35
401 8pf. red 10 35
402 10pf. brown 10 40
403 12pf. red 10 30
404 15pf. purple 20 65
405 20pf. blue . . . . 20 1·10
406 25pf. blue . . . . 45 1·25
407 30pf. green . . . . . . 45 1·00
408 40pf. mauve . . . . . . 45 1·25
409 50pf. black and green . . . 45 1·60
410 60pf. black and purple . . 1·75 3·25
411 80pf. black and blue . . 2·40 12·00
412 100pf. black and yellow . . 90 4·25

1940. Types of Luxembourg surch.
413 **32** 3 Rpf. on 15c. black . . . 10 50
414 4 Rpf. on 20c. orange . . 10 50
415 5 Rpf. on 35c. green . . 10 50
416 6 Rpf. on 10c. green . . . 10 50
417 8 Rpf. on 25c. brown . . . 10 50
418 10 Rpf. on 40c. brown . . 10 50
419 12 Rpf. on 60c. green . . . 10 50
420 15 Rpf. on 1f. red . . . 10 3·50
421 20 Rpf. on 50c. brown . . 10 85
422 25 Rpf. on 5c. mauve . . . 30 2·75
423 30 Rpf. on 70c. violet . . . 10 85
424 40 Rpf. on 75c. brown . . 10 1·10
425 50 Rpf. on 1¼f. green . . . 10 85
426 **65** 60 Rpf. on 2f. red . . . 1·25 18·00
427 **47** 80 Rpf. on 5f. green . . . 20 3·25
428 **52** 100 Rpf. on 10f. green . . 20 3·25

1941. Nos. 739/47 of Germany optd **Luxemburg**.
429 3pf.+2pf. brown 20 75
430 4pf.+3pf. blue 20 75
431 5pf.+3pf. green 20 75
432 6pf.+4pf. green 20 75
433 8pf.+4pf. orange 20 75
434 12pf.+6pf. red 20 75
435 15pf.+10pf. purple . . . . 1·40 5·50
436 25pf.+15pf. blue . . . . . 1·40 6·00
437 40pf.+35pf. purple . . . . . 1·40 6·00

1944. INDEPENDENCE REGAINED.

70 Grand Duchess Charlotte

71 "Britannia"

1944.
438 **70** 5c. brown 10 15
439 10c. slate 10 15
440 20c. orange 30 15
441 25c. brown 10 15
442 30c. red 40 35
443 35c. green 15 30
444 40c. blue 40 35
445 50c. violet 15 15
445a 60c. orange . . . . . . 2·25 15
446 70c. red 15 20
447 70c. green . . . . . . 75 1·10
448 75c. brown 40 20
449 1f. olive 10 15
450 1¼f. orange 20 55
451 1½f. orange 40 20
452 1¾f. blue 10 45
453 2f. red . . . . 3·50 30
454 2½f. mauve . . . . . . 8·00 5·50
455 3f. green 75 60
456 3½f. blue 90 75
457 5f. green 10 40
458 10f. red . . . . 15 1·10
459 20f. blue . . . . 50 19·00

1945. Liberation.
460 – 60c.+1f.40 green 20 25
461 – 1f.20+1f.80 red 20 25
462 **71** 2f.50+3f.50 blue 20 25
463 – 4f.20+4f.80 violet 20 25
DESIGNS: 60c. Ship symbol of Paris between Cross of Lorraine and Arms of Luxembourg; 1f.20, Man killing snake between Arms of Russia and Luxembourg; 4f.20, Eagle between Arms of U.S.A. and Luxembourg.

72 Statue of the Madonna in Procession

74 Lion of Luxembourg

73 Altar and Shrine of the Madonna

1945. Our Lady of Luxembourg.
464 **72** 60c.+40c. green . . . . . 30 1·00
465 – 1f.20+80c. red . . . . . 30 1·00
466 – 2f.50+2f.50 blue . . . . . 40 5·50
467 – 5f.50+6f.50 violet . . . . 1·25 65·00
468 **73** 20f.+20f. brown . . . . . 1·25 65·00
MS468a 83 × 96 mm. 50f+50f. grey (as 1f.20) . . . . 2·00 38·00
DESIGNS: As Type **72**: 1f.20, The Madonna; 2f.50, The Madonna and Luxembourg; 5f.50, Portal of Notre Dame Cathedral.

1945.
469 **74** 20c. black 20 20
470 30c. green 20 20
470a 60c. violet 20 25
471 75c. brown 20 20
472 1f.20 red 20 20
473 1f.50 violet 20 15
474 2f.50 blue 30 30

75 Members of the Maquis

76

1945. National War Victims Fund.
475 **75** 20c.+30c. green and buff 20 1·00
476 – 1f.50+1f. red and buff . . 20 1·00
477 – 3f.50+3f.50 blue & buff . . 40 9·25
478 – 5f.+10f. brown and buff . . 35 9·25
MS478a 100 × 110 mm. Designs and colours as Nos. 475/8 but values changed; 2f.50+2f.50, 3f.50+6f.50, 5f.+15f., 20f.+20f. . . . . . 20·00 £275
DESIGNS: 1f.50, Mother and children; 3f.50, Political prisoner; 5f. Executed civilian.

1946. Air.
479 – 1f. green and blue 35 20
480 **76** 2f. brown and yellow . . . 20 35
481 – 3f. brown and yellow . . . 35 20
482 – 4f. violet and grey 50 30
483 **76** 5f. purple and yellow . . . 45 30
484 – 6f. purple and blue 50 35
485 – 10f. brown and yellow . . 1·75 50
486 **76** 20f. blue and grey . . . . 2·10 1·25
487 – 50f. green and light green 4·00 1·50
DESIGNS: 1, 4, 10f. Airplane wheel; 3, 6, 50f. Airplane engine and castle.

76a Old Rolling Mill, Dudelange

1946. National Stamp Exhibition, Dudelange. Sheet 100 × 80 mm.
MS487a **76a** 50f. (+5f.) blue on buff 14·00 35·00

77 John the Blind, King of Bohemia

78 Exterior Ruins of St. Willibrord Basilica

79 St. Willibrord

1946. 600th Death Anniv of John the Blind.
488 **77** 60c.+40c. green and grey 30 1·60
489 1f.50+50c. red and buff . . 35 2·10
490 3f.50+3f.50 blue & grey . . 1·75 23·00
491 5f.+10f. brown and grey 1·00 19·00

1947. Echternach Abbey Restoration (2nd issue). Inscr "ECHTERNACH".
492 **78** 20c.+10c. black 35 30
493 – 60c.+10c. green 55 60
494 – 75c.+25c. red 85 75
495 – 1f.50c.+50c. brown . . . . 1·00 70
496 – 3f.50c.+ 2f.50 blue . . . . 5·00 4·50
497 **79** 25f.+25f. purple . . . . 27·00 21·00
DESIGNS—As Type **78**: 60c. Statue of Abbot Bertels; 75c. Echternach Abbey emblem; 1f.50, Ruined interior of Basilica; 3f.50, St. Irmine and Pepin II carrying model of Abbey.

80 U.S. Military Cemetery, Hamm

82 Michel Lentz (national poet)

1947. Honouring Gen. George S. Patton.
498 **80** 1f.50 red and buff 40 20
499 – 3f.50 blue and buff . . . . 2·25 2·25
500 **80** 5f. green and grey . . . . 2·25 2·25
501 – 10f. purple and grey . . . 9·25 35·00
PORTRAIT: 3f.50, 10f. Gen. G. S. Patton.

1947. National Welfare Fund.
502 **82** 60c.+40c. brown & buff . . 65 75
503 1f.50+50c. pur & buff . . 75 75
504 3f.50+3f.50 blue & grey . . 6·00 17·00
505 10f.+5f. green and grey . . 6·50 17·00

83 L'Oesling

85 "Dicks" (Edmund de la Fontaine)

1948. Tourist Propaganda.
505a – 2f.50 brown and chocolate . . . . . . 1·75 35
505b – 3f. violet . . . . 5·00 95
505c – 4f. blue . . . . 3·75 95
506 **83** 7f. brown . . . . 15·00 65
507 – 10f. green . . . . 1·90 20
508 – 15f. red . . . . 1·90 35
509 – 20f. blue . . . . 1·90 35
DESIGNS—HORIZ: 2f.50, Television transmitter, Dudelange; 3f. Radio Luxembourg; 4f. Victor Hugo's house, Vianden; 10f. River Moselle; 15f. Mining district. VERT: 20f. Luxembourg.

1948. National Welfare Fund.
510 **85** 60c.+40c. brown & bistre 45 75
511 1f.50+50c. red and pink . . 70 85
512 3f.50+3f.50 blue & grey . . 9·25 18·00
513 10f.+5f. green and grey . . 11·50 18·00

86 Grand Duchess Charlotte

87 Date-stamp and Map

1948.
513a **86** 5c. orange 10 20
513b 10c. blue 10 25
514 15c. olive 10 20
514a 20c. purple 20 20
515 25c. grey 10 20
515a 30c. olive 20 20
515b 40c. red 40 40
515c 50c. orange 40 20
516 60c. bistre 30 25
517 80c. green 30 20
518 1f. red 85 20
518a 1f.20 black 85 30
518b 1f.25 brown 85 35
519 1f.50 turquoise 85 15
520 1f.60 grey . . . . 1·25 1·25
521 2f. purple 85 15
521a 2f.50 red . . . . 1·40 30
521b 3f. blue . . . . 10·00 40
521c 3f.50 red . . . . 3·25 45
522 4f. blue . . . . 3·25 45
522a 5f. violet . . . . 8·00 40
523 6f. purple . . . . 6·00 55
524 8f. green . . . . 4·50 1·00

1949. 30th Year of Reign of Grand Duchess Charlotte. Sheet 110 × 75 mm.
MS524a **86** 8f.+3f. blue; 12f.+5f. green; 15f.+7f. brown . . . . . 75·00 35·00

1949. 75th Anniv of U.P.U.
525 **87** 80c. green, lt green & black 60 55
526 2f.50 red, pink and black 2·75 1·60
527 4f. ultramarine, blue & black . . . . 5·00 5·25
528 8f. brown, buff and black 16·00 26·00

88 Michel Rodange

89 Young Girl

1949. National Welfare Fund.
529 **88** 60c.+40c. green and grey 55 45
530 2f.+1f. purple and claret 5·50 4·50
531 4f.+2f. blue and grey . . . 9·00 9·00
532 10f.+5f. brown and buff . . 9·00 17·00

1950. War Orphans Relief Fund.
533 – 60c.+15c. turquoise . . . . 1·75 75
534 **89** 1f.+20c. red . . . . 4·50 1·10
535 – 2f.+30c. brown . . . . . . 2·10 1·10
536 **89** 4f.+75c. blue . . . . . . 12·00 14·00
537 – 8f.+3f. black . . . . . . 32·00 38·00
538 **89** 10f.+5f. purple . . . . . 32·00 38·00
DESIGN: 60c., 2f., 8f. Mother and boy.

90 J. A. Zinnen (composer)

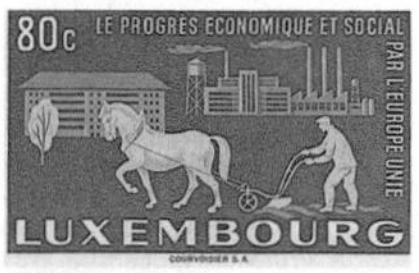

91 Ploughman and Factories

1950. National Welfare Week.

539	**90**	60c.+10c. violet and grey	55	25
540		2f.+15c. red and buff . . .	70	35
541		4f.+15c. blue and grey . .	5·50	6·00
542		8f.+5f. brown and buff . .	19·00	23·00

1951. To Promote United Europe.

543	**91**	80c. green and light green	10·05	8·25
544	–	1f. violet and light violet	4·50	50
545	–	2f. brown and grey	21·00	50
546	**91**	2f.50 red and orange . . .	21·00	17·00
547	–	3f. brown and yellow . . .	35·00	26·00
548	–	4f. blue and light blue . .	50·00	35·00

DESIGNS: 1, 3f. Map, people and "Rights of Man" Charter; 2, 4f. Scales balancing "United Europe" and "Peace".

92 L. Menager (composer)

1951. National Welfare Fund.

549	**92**	60c.+10c. black and grey	40	35
550		2f.+15c. green and grey . .	40	35
551		4f.+15c. blue and grey . .	4·50	3·00
552		8f.+5f. purple and grey . .	24·00	27·00

92a T 1 and 86

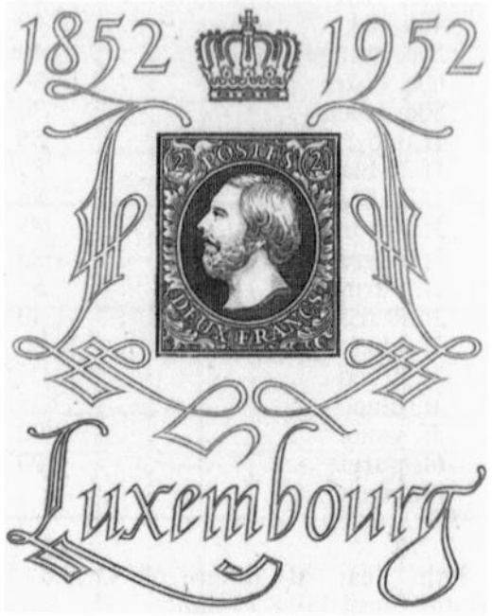

92b T 1

1952. National Philatelic Exhibition ("CENTILUX") and Stamp Centenary.

552a	**92a**	80c. black, pur & grn (air)	50	55
552b		2f.50 black, purple & red	1·25	1·40
552c		4f. black, purple and blue	3·25	3·25
552d		8f. black, purple and red	40·00	50·00
552e		10f. black, purple & brn	35·00	42·00
552f	**92b**	2f. blk & grn (postage)	26·00	35·00
552g		4f. red and green	26·00	35·00

93 Hurdling

1952. 15th Olympic Games, Helsinki.

553	**93**	1f. black and green	55	40
554	–	2f. blk & lt brn (Football)	2·25	40
555	–	2f.50 blk & pink (Boxing)	3·50	1·25
556	–	3f. blk & drab (Water polo)	4·50	1·40
557	–	4f. black and blue (Cycling)	21·00	6·75
558	–	8f. black and lilac (Fencing)	13·50	4·00

94 J. B. Fresez (painter)

95 Prince Jean and Princess Josephine Charlotte

1952. National Welfare Fund.

559	**94**	60c.+15c. green and blue	40	40
560		2f.+25c. brown & orange	40	40
561		4f.+25c. violet and grey . .	3·50	3·50
562		8f.+4f.75 purple & lt pur	25·00	32·00

1953. Royal Wedding.

563	**95**	80c. violet and deep mauve	45	35
564		1f.20 deep brown & brown	45	35
565		2f. deep green and green	1·40	35
566		3f. deep purple and purple	1·40	55
567		4f. deep blue and blue . .	6·00	1·00
568		9f. brown and red	6·00	1·00

96 Echternach Basilica

97 Pierre D'Aspelt

1953. Echternach Abbey Restoration (3rd issue).

569	**96**	2f. red	3·50	35
570	–	2f.50 olive	5·00	5·25

DESIGN: 2f.50, Interior of Basilica.

1953. 7th Birth Centenary of Pierre D'Aspelt.

571	**97**	4f. black	8·25	4·50

98 "Candlemas Singing"

99 Foils, Mask and Gauntlet

1953. National Welfare Fund.

572	**98**	25c.+15c. carmine and red	40	40
573	–	80c.+20c. blue and brown	40	40
574	–	1f.20+30c. green & turq . .	95	75
575	**98**	2f.+25c. brown and red . .	50	40
576	–	4f.+50c. blue & turquoise	6·75	6·50
577	–	7f.+3f.35 lilac and violet	19·00	18·00

DESIGNS: 80c., 4f. "The Rattles"; 1f.20, 7f. "The Easter-eggs".

1954. World Fencing Championships.

578	**99**	2f. deep brown and brown on cream	4·25	60

100 Fair Emblem

101 Earthenware Whistle

1954. Luxembourg International Fair.

579	**100**	4f. multicoloured	10·00	4·00

1954. National Welfare Fund.

580	**101**	25c.+5c. red and orange	50	45
581	–	80c.+20c. grey & black . .	50	45
582	–	1f.20+30c. green and cream	1·75	1·40
583	**101**	2f.+25c. brown and buff	70	55
584	–	4f.+50c. dp blue & blue	6·50	6·25
585	–	7f.+3f.45 violet & mve . .	26·00	22·00

DESIGNS: 80c., 4f. Sheep and drum; 1f.20, 7f. Merry-go-round horses.

102 Tulips

103

1955. Mondorf-les-Bains Flower Show.

586	**102**	80c. red, green and brown	25	25
587	–	2f. yellow, green and red	35	25
588	–	3f. purple, green & emer	2·75	4·50
589	–	4f. orange, green and blue	4·50	4·50

FLOWERS: 2f. Daffodils; 3f. Hyacinths; 4f. Parrot tulips.

1955. 1st National Crafts Exhibition.

590	**103**	2f. black and grey	1·50	35

104 "Charter"

105 "Christmas Day"

1955. 10th Anniv of U.N.

591	**104**	80c. blue and black . . .	65	55
592	–	2f. brown and red	5·00	30
593	–	4f. red and blue	3·75	3·00
594	–	9f. green and brown . . .	1·60	85

SYMBOLIC DESIGNS: 2f. "Security"; 4f. "Justice"; 9f. "Assistance".

1955. National Welfare Fund.

595	–	25c.+5c. red and pink . .	35	30
596	**105**	80c.+20c. black and grey	35	30
597	–	1f.20+30c. deep green and green	60	80
598	–	2f.+25c. deep brown and brown	70	30
599	**105**	4f.+50c. blue & lt blue . .	6·50	9·50
600	–	7f.+3f.45 purple & mve	13·00	13·50

ALLEGORICAL DESIGNS: 25c., 2f. "St. Nicholas's Day"; 1f.20, 7f. "Twelfth Night".

1956. Mondorf-les-Bains Flower Show. As T **102** but inscription at top in one line. Multicoloured.

601	2f. Anemones	75	25
602	3f. Crocuses	3·00	1·60

1956. Roses. As T **102** but inscr at top "LUXEMBOURG-VILLE DES ROSES". Multicoloured.

603	2f.50 Yellow roses	5·00	4·00
604	4f. Red roses	2·50	2·25

108 Steel Plant and Girder

109 Blast Furnaces and Map

1956. 50th Anniv of Esch-sur-Alzette.

605	**108**	2f. red, black & turquoise	2·75	45

1956. European Coal and Steel Community. Inscr as in T **109**.

606	**109**	2f. red	26·00	50
607	–	3f. blue	26·00	20·00
608	–	4f. green	5·00	4·25

DESIGNS—VERT: 3f. Girder supporting City of Luxembourg. HORIZ: 4f. Chain and miner's lamp.

110

111 Luxembourg Central Station

1956. Europa.

609	**110**	2f. black and brown . . .	£250	35
610		3f. red and orange	42·00	35·00
611		4f. deep blue and blue . .	2·50	2·50

1956. Electrification of Luxembourg Railways.

612	**111**	2f. sepia and black . . .	2·00	45

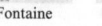

112 I. de la Fontaine

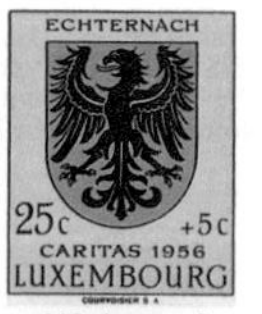

113 Arms of Echternach

1956. Council of State Centenary. Inscr as in T **112**.

613	**112**	2f. sepia	1·40	35
614	–	7f. purple	2·75	75

DESIGN: 7f. Grand Duchess Charlotte.

1956. National Welfare Fund. Inscr "CARITAS 1956". Arms. Multicoloured.

615	25c.+5c. Type **113**	30	35
616	80c.+20c. Esch-sur-Alzette . .	30	35
617	1f.20+30c. Grevenmacher . .	45	70
618	2f.+25c. Type **113**	35	35
619	4f.+50c. Esch-sur-Alzette . .	3·50	4·00
620	7f.+3f.45 Grevenmacher . . .	7·50	11·50

114 Lord Baden-Powell and Scout Emblems

115 Prince Henri

1957. Birth Centenary of Lord Baden-Powell, and 50th Anniv of Scouting Movement.

621	**114**	2f. brown and green . . .	1·00	25
622	–	2f.50 red and violet . . .	2·50	2·40

DESIGN: 2f.50, as Type **114** but showing Girl Guide emblems.

1957. "Prince Jean and Princess Josephine-Charlotte Foundation" Child Welfare Clinic.

623	**115**	2f. deep brown and brown	1·00	25
624	–	3f. deep green and green	3·50	3·00
625	–	4f. deep blue and blue . .	2·50	2·50

DESIGNS—HORIZ: 3f. Children's Clinic Project. VERT: 4f. Princess Marie-Astrid.

116 "Peace"

117 Fair Entrance and Flags

1957. Europa.

626	**116**	2f. brown	2·40	25
627		3f. red	38·00	15·00
628		4f. purple	32·00	15·00

1957. National Welfare Fund. Arms as T **113** inscr "CARITAS 1957". Multicoloured.

629	25c.+5c. Luxembourg	35	40
630	80c.+20c. Mersch	35	40
631	1f.20+30c. Vianden	45	60
632	2f.+25c. Luxembourg	30	35
633	4f.+50c. Mersch	3·50	4·50
634	7f.+3f.45 Vianden	5·50	7·00

1958. 10th Anniv of Luxembourg Int Fair.

635	**117**	2f. multicoloured	30	25

118 Luxembourg Pavilion

119 St. Willibrord holding Child (after Puseel)

1958. Brussels Exhibition.

636	**118**	2f.50 blue and red	30	25

1958. 1300th Birth Anniv of St. Willibrord.

637	–	1f. red	30	30
638	**119**	2f.50 sepia	35	20
639	–	5f. blue	90	85

DESIGNS: 1f. St. Willibrord and St. Irmina holding inscribed plaque; 5f. St. Willibrord and suppliant. (Miracle of the wine-cask).

119a Europa

120 Open-air Theatre at Wiltz

1958. Europa.

640	**119a**	2f.50 blue and red . . .	15	15
641		3f.50 brown and green . .	2·50	25
642		5f. red and blue	65	65

1958. Wiltz Open-air Theatre Commemoration.

643	**120**	2f.50 sepia and grey . . .	55	15

121 Vineyard

122 Grand Duchess Charlotte

1958. Bimillenary of Moselle Wine Industry.
644 **121** 2f.50 brown and green . . 55 15

1958. National Welfare Fund. Arms as T **113** inscr "CARITAS 1958". Multicoloured.
645 30c.+10c. Capellen 35 30
646 1f.+25c. Diekirch 35 30
647 1f.50+25c. Redange 55 45
648 2f.50+50c. Capellen 35 30
649 5f.+50c. Diekirch . . . . . . 3·25 4·00
650 8f.50+4f.60 Redange . . . . 5·00 6·75

1959. 40th Anniv of Accession of Grand Duchess Charlotte.
651 **122** 1f.50 deep green & green 70 35
652 2f.50 brown & lt brown 70 35
653 5f. lt blue and ultramarine 1·40 1·10

123 N.A.T.O. Emblem

123a Europa

1959. 10th Anniv of N.A.T.O.
654 **123** 2f.50 blue and olive . . . 20 15
655 8f.50 blue and brown . . 55 40

1959. Mondorf-les-Bains Flower Show. As T **102** but inscr "1959".
656 1f. violet, yellow and turquoise 30 30
657 2f.50 red, green and blue . . 40 25
658 3f. blue, green and purple . . 65 60
FLOWERS: 1f. Iris; 2f.50, Peony; 3f. Hortensia.

1959. Europa.
659 **123a** 2f.50 green 45 20
660 5f. blue 75 85

124 Steam Locomotive and First Bars of Hymn "De Feierwon"

1959. Railways Centenary.
661 **124** 2f.50 blue and red . . . . 1·90 40

1959. National Welfare Fund. Arms as T **113** inscr "CARITAS 1959". Multicoloured.
662 30c.+10c. Clervaux 35 30
663 1f.+25c. Remich 35 30
664 1f.50+25c. Wiltz 60 45
665 2f.50+50c. Clervaux 35 30
666 5f.+50c. Remich . . . . . . 1·50 1·90
667 8f.50+4f.60 Wiltz . . . . . . 6·50 9·50

125 Refugees seeking Shelter

126 Steel Worker

1960. World Refugee Year.
668 **125** 2f.50 blue and salmon . . 20 15
669 – 5f. blue and violet 35 40
DESIGN—HORIZ: 5f. "The Flight into Egypt" (Biblical scene).

1960. 10th Anniv of Schuman Plan.
670 **126** 2f.50 lake 30 25

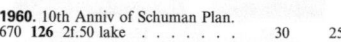

127 European School, Luxembourg

128 Grand Duchess Charlotte

1960. European School Commemoration.
671 **127** 5f. black and blue 95 95

1960.
672 **128** 10c. red 10 25
673 20c. red 10 25
673a 25c. orange 20 25
674 30c. drab 10 15
675 50c. green 50 15
676 1f. violet 50 15
677 1f.50 mauve 50 15
678 2f. turquoise 55 25
679 2f.50 purple 85 25
680 3f. dull purple . . . . . 2·40 15
680a 3f.50 turquoise . . . . . 2·50 1·75
681 5f. brown . . . . 1·25 25
681a 6f. turquoise . . . . . . 2·40 25

129 Heraldic Lion, and Tools

1960. 2nd National Crafts Exhibition.
682 **129** 2f.50 multicoloured . . . 1·40 35

129a Conference Emblem

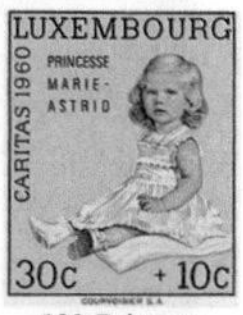

130 Princess Marie-Astrid

1960. Europa.
683 **129a** 2f.50 green and black . . 40 15
684 5f. black and red 65 35

1960. National Welfare Fund. Inscr "CARITAS 1960". Centres and inscr in sepia.
685 **130** 30c.+10c. blue 20 25
686 – 1f.+25c. pink 20 25
687 – 1f.50+25c. turquoise . . . 50 60
688 **130** 2f.50+50c. yellow 40 35
689 – 5f.+50c. lilac . . . . . 85 2·40
690 – 8f.50+4f.60 sage . . . . 3·25 12·00
DESIGNS: Princess Marie-Astrid standing (1, 5f.), sitting with book on lap (1f.50, 8f.50).

131 Great Spotted Woodpecker

132 Patton Monument, Ettelbruck

1961. Animal Protection Campaign. Inscr "PROTECTION DES ANIMAUX".
691 **131** 1f. multicoloured 20 25
692 – 1f.50 buff, blue and black 25 25
693 – 3f. brown, buff and violet 40 40
694 – 8f.50 multicoloured . . . 60 70
DESIGNS—VERT: 8f.50, Dachshund. HORIZ: 1f.50, Cat; 3f. Horse.

1961. Tourist Publicity.
695 **132** 2f.50 blue and black . . . 50 25
696 – 2f.50 green 50 25
DESIGN—VERT: No. 696, Clervaux.

133 Doves

134 Prince Henri

1961. Europa.
697 **133** 2f.50 red 15 15
698 5f. blue 25 25

1961. National Welfare Fund. Inscr "CARITAS 1961". Centres and inscr in sepia.
699 **134** 30c.+10c. mauve 35 35
700 – 1f.+25c. lavender 35 35
701 – 1f.50+25c. salmon 45 50
702 **134** 2f.50+50c. green 45 35
703 – 5f.+50c. yellow . . . . 2·40 2·40
704 – 8f.50+4f.60 grey . . . . 4·00 6·50
DESIGNS: Prince Henri when young boy (1, 5f.); youth in formal dress (1f.50, 8f.50).

135 Cyclist carrying Cycle

136 Europa "Tree"

1962. World Cross-country Cycling Championships, Esch-sur-Alzette.
705 **135** 2f.50 multicoloured . . . 30 25
706 – 5f. multicoloured (Emblem) 30 40

1962. Europa.
707 **136** 2f.50 multicoloured . . . 25 15
708 5f. brown, green & purple 35 30

137 St. Laurent's Church, Diekirch

138 Prince Jean and Princess Margaretha as Babies

1962.
709 **137** 2f.50 black and brown . . 45 25

1962. National Welfare Fund. inscr "CARITAS 1962". Centres and inscr in sepia.
710 **138** 30c.+10c. buff 30 25
711 – 1f.+25c. blue 30 25
712 – 1f.50+25c. olive 35 40
713 – 2f.50+50c. pink 35 25
714 – 5f.+50c. green . . . . . 1·40 2·40
715 – 8f.50+4f.60 violet . . . 3·25 4·50
PORTRAITS—VERT: 1f., 2f.50, Prince Jean and: 2f.50, 5f. Princess Margaretha, at various stages of childhood. HORIZ: 8f.50, The Royal Children.

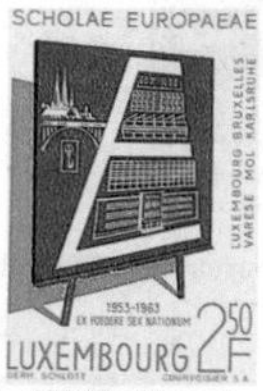

139 Blackboard

140 Benedictine Abbey, Munster

1963. 10th Anniv of European Schools.
716 **139** 2f.50 green, red and grey 20 15

1963. Millenary of City of Luxembourg and International Philatelic Exhibition. (a) Horiz views.
717 – 1f. blue 20 25
718 **140** 1f.50 red 20 25
719 – 2f.50 green 20 25
720 – 3f. brown 20 25
721 – 5f. violet 45 60
722 – 11f. blue . . . . 1·40 1·75
VIEWS: 1f. Bock Rock; 2f.50, Rham Towers; 3f. Grand Ducal Palace; 5f. Castle Bridge; 11f. Millenary Buildings.

(b) Vert multicoloured designs.
723 1f. "Three Towers" Gate 20 25
724 1f.50 Great Seal 20 30
725 2f.50 "The Black Virgin" (statue), St. John's Church 20 30
726 3f. Citadel 35 30
727 5f. Town Hall 20 45

141 Colpach Castle

1963. Red Cross Centenary.
728 **141** 2f.50 red and slate 30 25

142 "Human Rights"

1963. 10th Anniv of European "Human Rights" Convention.
729 **142** 2f.50 blue on gold 20 25

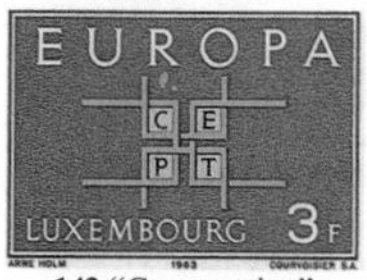

143 "Co-operation"

144 Brown trout snapping Bait

1963. Europa.
730 **143** 3f. green, orange & turq 20 15
731 6f. orange, red and brown 35 35

1963. World Fishing Championships, Wormeldange.
732 **144** 3f. slate 25 15

145 Telephone Dial

146 St. Roch (patron saint of bakers)

1963. Inauguration of Automatic Telephone System.
733 **145** 3f. green, black and blue 25 15

1963. National Welfare Fund. Patron Saints of Crafts and Guilds. Inscr "CARITAS 1963". Multicoloured.
734 50c.+10c. Type **146** 20 25
735 1f.+25c. St. Anne (tailors) . . 20 25
736 2f.+25c. St. Eloi (smiths) . . 20 35
737 3f.+50c. St. Michel (haberdashers) 20 25
738 6f.+50c. St. Barthelemy (butchers) . . . . 1·00 1·90
739 10f.+5f.90 St. Thibaut (seven crafts) . . . . 1·75 3·25

147 Power House

148 Barge entering Canal

1964. Inauguration of Vianden Reservoir.
740 **147** 2f. blue, brown and red 20 15
741 – 3f. blue, turq & red . . . 20 15
742 – 6f. brown, blue and green 30 30
DESIGNS—HORIZ: 3f. Upper reservoir. VERT: 6f. Lohmuhle Dam.

1964. Inauguration of Moselle Canal.
743 **148** 3f. indigo and blue . . . 30 15

149 Europa "Flower"

150 Students thronging "New Athenaeum"

1964. Europa.
744 **149** 3f. blue, brown and cream 20 15
745 6f. sepia, green and yellow 30 25

1964. Opening of "New Athenaeum" (education centre).
746 **150** 3f. black and green . . . 20 25

150a King Baudouin, Queen Juliana and Grand Duchess Charlotte

1964. 20th Anniv of "BENELUX".
747 **150a** 3f. brown, yellow & blue 20 25

151 Grand Duke Jean and Princess Josephine-Charlotte

152 Three Towers

1964. Accession of Grand Duke Jean.
748 **151** 3f. deep blue and light blue 30 15
749 6f. sepia and light brown 35 30

1964. National Welfare Fund. Inscr "CARITAS 1964". Multicoloured.
750 50c.+10c. Type **152** 20 25
751 1f.+25c. Grand Duke Adolphe Bridge 20 25
752 2f.+25c. Lower Town 20 25
753 3f.+50c. Type **152** 20 25
754 6f.+50c. Grand Duke Adolphe Bridge . . . . . 85 1·75
755 10f.+5f.90 Lower Town . . . 1·40 2·50

153 Rotary Emblem and Cogwheels

154 Grand Duke Jean

1965. 60th Anniv of Rotary International.
756 **153** 3f. multicoloured 20 15

1965.
757 **154** 25c. brown 20 10
758 50c. red 20 10
759 1f. blue 20 10
760 1f.50 purple 10 10
761a 2f. red 35 10
762 2f.50 orange 35 30
763a 3f. green 45 10
763b 3f.50 brown 45 45
764a 4f. purple 50 10
764ba 5f. green 45 10
765a 6f. lilac 55 10
765b 7f. orange 50 20
765c 8f. blue 70 25
766 9f. green 70 25
766a 10f. black 50 10
767 12f. red . . . . . . 1·00 25
767a 14f. blue 70 40
767b 16f. green . . . . . 1·00 30
767c 18f. green 35 45
767d 20f. blue 85 25
767e 22f. brown . . . . . 1·25 85

155 I.T.U. Emblem and Symbols

1965. Centenary of I.T.U.
768 **155** 3f. blue, lake and violet 30 25

156 Europa "Sprig"

157 "The Roman Lady of the Titelberg"

1965. Europa.
769 **156** 3f. turquoise, red and black 20 25
770 6f. brown, blue and green 30 30

1965. National Welfare Fund. Fairy Tales. Inscr "CARITAS 1965". Multicoloured.
771 50c.+10c. Type **157** 15 25
772 1f.+25c. "Schappchen, the Huntsman" 15 25
773 2f.+25c. "The Witch of Koerich" 20 25
774 3f.+50c. "The Goblins of Schoendels" 20 25
775 6f.+50c. "Tollchen, Watchman of Hesperange" 35 1·10
776 10f.+5f.90 "The Old Spinster of Heispelt" . . . . 1·10 3·00

158 "Flag" and Torch

159 W.H.O. Building

1966. 50th Anniv of Luxembourg Workers' Union.
777 **158** 3f. red and grey 20 15

1966. Inaug of W.H.O. Headquarters, Geneva.
778 **159** 3f. green 20 15

160 Golden Key

161 Europa "Ship"

1966. Tercentenary of Solemn Promise to Our Lady of Luxembourg.
779 **160** 1f.50 green 10 15
780 – 2f. red 10 15
781 – 3f. blue 15 15
782 – 6f. brown 30 30
DESIGNS: 2f. Interior of Luxembourg Cathedral (after painting by J. Martin); 3f. Our Lady of Luxembourg (after engraving by R. Collin); 6f. Gallery pillar, Luxembourg Cathedral (after sculpture by D. Muller).

1966. Europa.
783 **161** 3f. blue and grey 20 25
784 6f. green and brown . . . 35 30

162 Class 1800 Diesel-electric Locomotive

1966. Luxembourg Railwaymen's Philatelic Exhibition. Multicoloured.
785 1f.50 Type **162** 50 25
786 3f. Class 3600 electric locomotive 50 30

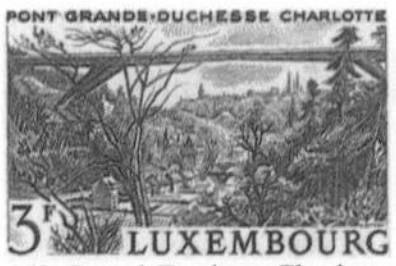

163 Grand Duchess Charlotte Bridge

164 Kirchberg Building and Railway Viaduct

1966. Tourism.
787 **163** 3f. lake 20 15
See also Nos. 807/8, 828 and 844/5.

1966. "Luxembourg-European Centre".
788 **164** 1f.50 green 20 25
789 – 13f. blue (Robert Schuman monument) 50 35

165 "Mary, Veiled Matron of Wormeldange"

166 City of Luxembourg, 1850 (after engraving by N. Liez)

1966. National Welfare Fund. Luxembourg Fairy Tales. Multicoloured.
790 50c.+10c. Type **165** 15 25
791 1f.50+25c. "Jekel Warden of the Wark" 15 25
792 2f.+25c. "The Black Gentleman of Vianden" . . 15 30
793 3f.+50c. "The Gracious Fairy of Rosport" 20 25
794 6f.+1f. "The Friendly Shepherd of Donkolz" . . 45 85
795 13f.+6f.90 "The Little Sisters of Trois-Vierges" . . . . . 60 2·50

1967. Centenary of Treaty of London.
796 **166** 3f. brown, blue and green 20 25
797 – 6f. red, brown and blue 30 30
DESIGN—VERT: 6f. Plan of Luxembourg fortress c. 1850 (after T. de Cederstolpe).

167 Cogwheels

168 Lion on Globe

1967. Europa.
798 **167** 3f. purple, grey and buff 35 25
799 6f. sepia, purple and blue 40 35

1967. 50th Anniv of Lions International.
800 **168** 3f. yellow, purple & black 20 25

169 European Institutions Building, Luxembourg

170 Hikers and Hostel

1967. N.A.T.O. Council Meeting, Luxembourg.
801 **169** 3f. turquoise and green 20 25
802 6f. red and pink 35 40

1967. Luxembourg Youth Hostels.
803 **170** 1f.50 multicoloured . . . 15 25

171 Shaving-dish (after Degrotte)

172 "Gardener"

1967. "200 Years of Luxembourg Pottery".
804 **171** 1f.50 multicoloured . . . 20 25
805 – 3f. multicoloured 20 25
DESIGN—VERT: 3f. Vase, c. 1820.

1967. "Family Gardens" Congress, Luxembourg.
806 **172** 1f.50 orange and green . . 15 25

1967. Tourism. As T **163**.
807 3f. indigo and blue 30 25
808 3f. purple, green and blue . . 45 25
DESIGNS—HORIZ: No. 807, Moselle River and quayside, Mertert. VERT: No. 808, Moselle, Church and vines, Wormeldange.

173 Prince Guillaume

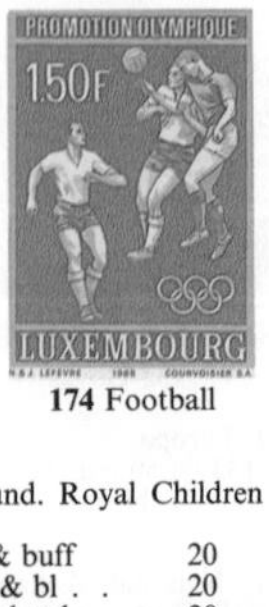

174 Football

1967. National Welfare Fund. Royal Children and Residence.
809 **173** 50c.+10c. brown & buff 20 25
810 – 1f.50+25c. brown & bl . . 20 25
811 – 2f.+25c. brown and red 20 25
812 – 3f.+50c. brown & yell . . 65 25
813 – 6f.+1f. brown & lav . . . 45 1·00
814 – 13f.+6f.90 brn, grn & bl 60 3·25
DESIGNS: 1f.50, Princess Margaretha; 2f. Prince Jean; 3f. Prince Henri; 6f. Princess Marie-Astrid; 13f. Berg Castle.

1968. Olympic Games, Mexico.
815 – 50c. light blue and blue 20 15
816 **174** 1f.50 green and emerald 20 15
817 – 2f. yellow and green . . . 25 15
818 – 3f. light orange and orange 20 15
819 – 6f. green and blue 25 25
820 – 13f. red and crimson . . . 45 35
DESIGNS: 50c. Diving; 2f. Cycling; 3f. Running; 6f. Walking; 13f. Fencing.

175 Europa "Key"

1968. Europa.
821 **175** 3f. brown, black and green 35 15
822 6f. green, black and orange 40 35

176 Thermal Bath Pavilion, Mondorf-les-Bains

1968. Mondorf-les-Bains Thermal Baths.
823 **176** 3f. multicoloured 25 15

177 Fair Emblem

1968. 20th Anniv of Luxembourg Int Fair.
824 **177** 3f. multicoloured 25 25

178 Village Project

179 "Blood Transfusion"

1968. Luxembourg SOS Children's Village.
825 **178** 3f. purple and green . . . 30 15
826 – 6f. black, blue and purple 35 30
DESIGN—VERT: 6f. Orphan with foster-mother.

1968. Blood Donors of Luxembourg Red Cross.
827 **179** 3f. red and blue 40 25

180 Fokker Friendship over Luxembourg

181 Cap Institute

1968. Tourism.
828 **180** 50f. dp blue, brown & blue . . . . 2·50 25

1968. National Welfare Fund. Luxembourg Handicapped Children.
829 **181** 50c.+10c. brown and blue 20 25
830 – 1f.50+25c. brn & grn . . 20 25
831 – 2f.+25c. brown & yell . . 30 35
832 – 3f.+50c. brown and blue 30 25
833 – 6f.+1f. brown and buff . . 50 90
834 – 13f.+6f.90 brown and pink . . . . 1·25 3·00
DESIGNS: 1f.50, Deaf and dumb child; 2f. Blind child; 3f. Nurse supporting handicapped child; 6f. and 13f. Mentally handicapped children (different).

182

183 Colonnade

1969. "Juventus 1969" Junior International Philatelic Exhibition. Sheet 111 × 70 mm containing T **182** and similar vert designs. Multicoloured.
MS835 3f. Type **182**; 6f. "Sport"; 13f. Sun, open book and ball 2·50 3·25

1969. Europa.
836 **183** 3f. multicoloured 35 15
837 6f. multicoloured 40 35

184 "The Wooden Horse" (Kutter)

1969. 75th Birth Anniv of Joseph Kutter (painter). Multicoloured.
838 3f. Type **184** 50 25
839 6f. "Luxembourg" (Kutter) 50 40

185 ILO Emblem

186 National Colours

1969. 50th Anniv of Int Labour Organization.
840 **185** 3f. gold, violet and green 30 15

1969. 25th Anniv of "BENELUX" Customs Union.
841 **186** 3f. multicoloured 30 15

187 N.A.T.O. Emblem

188 Ear of Wheat and Agrocentre, Mersch

1969. 20th Anniv of N.A.T.O.
842 **187** 3f. orange and brown . . 35 15

1969. "Modern Agriculture".
843 **188** 3f. grey and green 20 15

189 Echternach

190 Vianden Castle

1969. Tourism.
844 **189** 3f. indigo and blue . . . 30 25
845 – 3f. blue and green 30 25
DESIGN: No. 845, Wiltz.

1969. National Welfare Fund. Castles (1st series). Multicoloured.
846 50c.+10c. Type **190** 15 25
847 1f.50+25c. Lucilinburhuc . . 15 25
848 2f.+25c. Bourglinster . . . 20 25
849 3f.+50c. Hollenfels 20 25
850 6f.+1f. Ansembourg . . . . 50 1·40
851 13f.+6f.90 Beaufort . . . . . 85 3·25
See also Nos. 862/7.

191 Pasque Flower

192 Firecrest

1970. Nature Conservation Year. Multicoloured.
852 3f. Type **191** 20 25
853 6f. West European hedgehogs 35 40

1970. 50 Years of Bird Protection.
854 **192** 1f.50 green, black & orge 20 20

193 "Flaming Sun"

1970. Europa.
855 **193** 3f. multicoloured 35 15
856 6f. multicoloured 40 40

194 Road Safety Assoc. Emblem and Traffic

1970. Road Safety.
857 **194** 3f. black, red and lake . . 20 15

195 "Empress Kunegonde and Emperor Henry II" (stained-glass windows, Luxembourg Cathedral)

1970. Centenary of Luxembourg Diocese.
858 **195** 3f. multicoloured 20 25

196 Population Pictograph

1970. Population Census.
859 **196** 3f. red, blue and green . . 20 15

197 Facade of Town Hall, Luxembourg

1970. 50th Anniv of Union of Four Suburbs with Luxembourg City.
860 **197** 3f. brown, ochre and blue 20 15

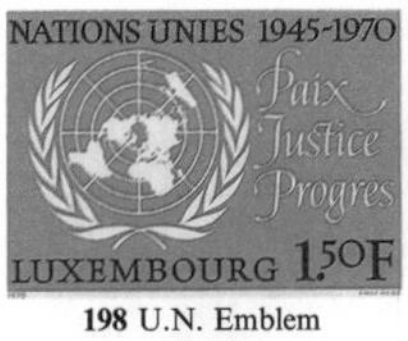

198 U.N. Emblem

199 Monks in the Scriptorium

1970. 25th Anniv of United Nations.
861 **198** 1f.50 violet and blue . . . 10 15

1970. National Welfare Fund. Castles (2nd series). Designs as T **190**.
862 50c.+10c. Clervaux 15 25
863 1f.50+25c. Septfontaines . . 15 25
864 2f.+25c. Bourscheid 20 25
865 3f.+50c. Esch-sur-Sure . . . 20 25
866 6f.+1f. Larochette . . . . . 50 1·40
867 13f.+6f.90 Brandenbourg . . 80 3·25

1971. Medieval Miniatures produced at Echternach. Multicoloured.
868 1f.50 Type **199** 20 25
869 3f. Vine-growers going to work 20 15
870 6f. Vine-growers at work and returning home 20 25
871 13f. Workers with spades and hoe 50 55

200 Europa Chain

1971.
872 **200** 3f. black, brown and red 35 15
873 6f. black, brown and green 50 55

201 Olympic Rings and Arms of Luxembourg

202 "50" and Emblem

1971. Int Olympic Committee Meeting, Luxembourg.
874 **201** 3f. red, gold and blue . . 20 25

1971. 50th Anniv of Luxembourg's Christian Workers' Union (L.C.G.B.).
875 **202** 3f. purple, orange & yell 20 15

203 Artificial Lake, Upper Sure Valley

204 Child with Coin

1971. Man-made Landscapes.
876 **203** 3f. blue, grey and brown 35 15
877 – 3f. brown, green and blue 35 25
878 – 15f. black, blue and brown 65 15
DESIGNS: No. 877, Water-processing plant, Esch-sur-Sure; No. 878, ARBED (United Steelworks) Headquarters Building, Luxembourg.

1971. Schoolchildren's Saving Campaign.
879 **204** 3f. multicoloured 25 25

205 "Bethlehem Children"

206 Coins of Belgium and Luxembourg

1971. National Welfare Fund. "The Nativity"–wood-carvings in Beaufort Church. Multicoloured.
880 1f.+25c. Type **205** 30 25
881 1f.50+25c. "Shepherds" . . . 30 25
882 3f.+50c. "Virgin, Child Jesus and St. Joseph" 30 25
883 8f.+1f. "Herdsmen" . . . . 85 2·40
884 18f.+6f.50 "One of the Magi" 1·60 5·25

1972. 50th Anniv of Belgium–Luxembourg Economic Union.
885 **206** 1f.50 silver, black & green 20 25

207 Bronze Mask (1st cent)

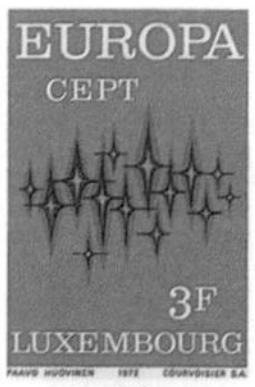

208 "Communications"

1972. Gallo-Roman Exhibits from Luxembourg State Museum. Multicoloured.
886 1f. Samian bowl (2nd century) (horiz) 20 15
887 3f. Type **207** 35 15
888 8f. Limestone head (2nd/3rd century) 65 75
889 15f. Glass "head" flagon (4th century) 60 65

1972. Europa.
890 **208** 3f. multicoloured 35 15
891 8f. multicoloured 85 85

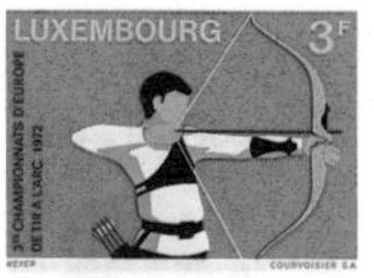

209 Archer

210 R. Schuman (after bronze by R. Zilli)

1972. 3rd European Archery Championships, Luxembourg.
892 **209** 3f. multicoloured 35 15

1972. 20th Anniv of Establishment of European Coal and Steel Community in Luxembourg.
893 **210** 3f. green and grey 45 15

211 National Monument

212 "Renert"

1972. Monuments and Buildings.
894 **211** 3f. brown, green and violet 35 25
895 – 3f. brown, green and blue 55 25
DESIGN: No. 895, European Communities' Court of Justice.

1972. Cent of Publication of Michel Rodange's "Renert" (satirical poem).
896 **212** 3f. multicoloured 30 25

213 "Angel"

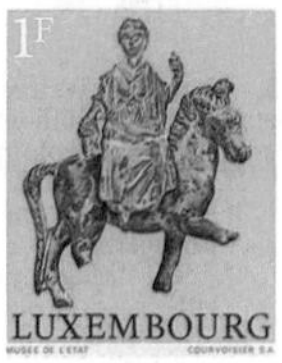

214 "Epona on Horseback"

1972. National Welfare Fund. Stained Glass Windows in Luxembourg Cathedral. Multicoloured.
897 1f.+25c. Type **213** 20 25
898 1f.50+25c. "St. Joseph" . . . 20 25
899 3f.+50c. "Holy Virgin with Child Jesus" 20 25
900 8f.+1f. "People of Bethlehem" . . . . 85 2·40
901 18f.+6f.50 "Angel" (facing left) . . . . 2·50 6·00

1973. Archaeological Relics. Multicoloured.
902 1f. Type **214** 20 15
903 4f. "Panther attacking swan" (horiz) 30 25
904 8f. Celtic gold coin 85 85
905 15f. Bronze boar (horiz) . . . 70 60

215 Europa "Posthorn"

216 Bee on Honeycomb

1973. Europa.
906 **215** 4f. orange, blue and violet 35 25
907 8f. green, yellow & purple 1·00 90

1973. Bee-keeping.
908 **216** 4f. multicoloured 45 15

217 Nurse and Child

218 Capital, Vianden Castle

1973. Day Nurseries in Luxembourg.
909 **217** 4f. multicoloured 35 15

1973. Romanesque Architecture in Luxembourg.
910 **218** 4f. purple and green . . . 30 15
911 – 8f. blue and brown . . . 70 75
DESIGN: 8f. Detail of altar, St. Irmina's Chapel, Rosport.

219 Labour Emblem

220 J. de Busleyden

1973. 50th Anniv of Luxembourg Board of Labour.
912 **219** 3f. multicoloured 25 15

1973. 500th Anniv of Great Council of Malines.
913 **220** 4f. purple and brown . . 30 15

221 Monument, Wiltz

222 Joachim and St. Anne

1973. National Strike Monument.
914 **221** 4f. green, brown and grey 35 15

1973. National Welfare Fund. "The Nativity". Details from 16th-century reredos, Hachiville Hermitage. Multicoloured.
915 1f.+25c. Type **222** 20 25
916 3f.+25c. "Mary meets Elizabeth" 20 25
917 4f.+50c. "Magus presenting gift" 25 25
918 8f.+1f. "Shepherds at the manger" . . . . 85 2·25
919 15f.+7f. "St. Joseph with Candle" . . . . 2·50 6·75

223 Princess Marie-Astrid, Association President

224 Flame Emblem

1974. Luxembourg Red Cross Youth Association.
920 **223** 4f. multicoloured . . . . 1·40 30

1974. 50th Anniv of Luxembourg Mutual Insurance Federation.
921 **224** 4f. multicoloured 45 30

225 Seal of Henry VII, King of the Romans

226 "Hind" (A. Tremont)

1974. Seals in Luxembourg State Archives.
922 **225** 1f. brown, yellow & purple 20 15
923 – 3f. brown, yellow & green 30 30
924 – 4f. dk brown, yellow & brn 35 25
925 – 19f. brown, yellow & blue 85 75
DESIGNS: 3f. Equestrian seal of John the Blind, King of Bohemia; 4f. Municipal seal of Diekirch; 19f. Seal of Marienthal Convent.

1974. Europa. Sculptures. Multicoloured.
926 4f. Type **226** 80 25
927 8f. "Abstract" (L. Wercollier) 1·90 1·50

227 Churchill Memorial, Luxembourg

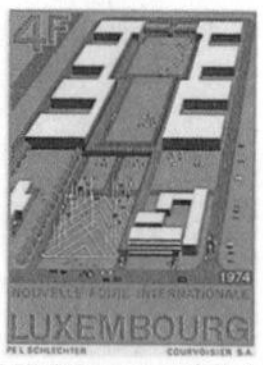

228 Diagram of Fair

1974. Birth Centenary of Sir Winston Churchill.
928 **227** 4f. multicoloured 35 15

1974. New International Fair, Luxembourg-Kirchberg.
929 **228** 4f. multicoloured 35 15

229 "Theis the Blind" (artist unknown)

230 "Crowning of St. Cecily and St. Valerien" (Hollenfels Church)

1974. 150th Death Anniv of "Theis the Blind" (Mathias Schou, folk singer).
930 **229** 3f. multicoloured 35 40

1974. Gothic Architecture.
931 **230** 4f. brown, green and violet 30 15
932 – 4f. black, brown and blue 30 15
DESIGN: No. 932, Interior of Septfontaines Church.

231 U.P.U. Emblem on "100"

1974. Centenary of Universal Postal Union.
933 **231** 4f. multicoloured 25 25
934 8f. multicoloured 35 75

232 "Benelux"

1974. 30th Anniv of Benelux (Customs Union).
935 **232** 4f. turquoise, green & blue 85 25

233 Differdange

1974. Tourism.
936 **233** 4f. purple 85 15

234 "Annunciation"

235 "Crucifixion"

1974. National Welfare Fund. Illustrations from "Codex Aureus Epternacensis". Multicoloured.
937 1f.+25c. Type **234** 20 25
938 3f.+25c. "Visitation" 20 25
939 4f.+50c. "Nativity" 25 25
940 8f.+1f. "Adoration of the Magi" . . . . 1·00 2·40
941 15f.+7f. "Presentation at the Temple" . . . . 1·90 5·25

1974. 50th Anniv of Christmas Charity Stamps. Detail of cover from "Codex Aureus Epternacensis". Sheet 80 × 90 mm.
MS942 **235** 20f.+10f. multicoloured 3·50 8·25

236 The Fish Market, Luxembourg

1975. European Architectural Heritage Year.
943 **236** 1f. green 35 25
944 – 3f. brown 85 35
945 – 4f. lilac . . . . 1·00 25
946 – 19f. red . . . . 1·00 90
DESIGNS—HORIZ: 3f. Bourglinster Castle; 4f. Market Square, Echternach. VERT: 19f. St. Michael's Square, Mersch.

237 "Joseph Kutter" (self-portrait)

238 Dr. Albert Schweitzer

1975. Luxembourg Culture, and Europa. Paintings. Multicoloured.
947 1f. Type **237** 30 25
948 4f. "Remich Bridge" (N. Klopp) (horiz) . . . . 1·00 30
949 8f. "Still Life" (J. Kutter) (horiz) . . . . 2·00 1·75
950 20f. "The Dam" (D. Lang) 1·25 50

1975. Birth Centenary of Dr. Albert Schweitzer (medical missionary).
951 **238** 4f. blue 55 25

239 Robert Schuman, G. Martino and P.-H. Spaak

240 Civil Defence Emblem

1975. 25th Anniv of Robert Schuman Declaration for European Unity.
952 **239** 4f. black, gold and green 55 25

1975. 15th Anniv of Civil Defence Reorganization.
953 **240** 4f. multicoloured 50 25

241 Ice Skating

242 Fly Orchid

1975. Sports. Multicoloured.
954 **241** 3f. purple, blue and green 35 30
955 – 4f. brown, green & dp brn 50 15
956 – 15f. blue, brown and green . . . . 1·00 70
DESIGNS—HORIZ: 4f. Water-skiing. VERT: 15f. Rock-climbing.

1975. National Welfare Fund. Protected Plants (1st series). Multicoloured.
957 1f.+25c. Type **242** 20 25
958 3f.+25c. Pyramid orchid . . . 40 30
959 4f.+50c. Marsh helleborine 50 15
960 8f.+1f. Pasque flower . . . . 1·10 1·75
961 15f.+7f. Bee orchid . . . . . 2·50 5·00
See also Nos. 976/80 and 997/1001.

243 Grand Duchess Charlotte (80th)

244 7th-century Disc-shaped Brooch

1976. Royal Birthdays. Multicoloured.
962 6f. Type **243** . . . . 1·25 35
963 6f. Prince Henri (21st) . . . 1·25 35

1976. Luxembourg Culture. Ancient Treasures from Merovingian Tombs. Multicoloured.
964 2f. Type **244** 20 15
965 5f. 5th-6th century glass beaker (horiz) 30 30
966 6f. Ancient pot (horiz) 30 25
967 12f. 7th century gold coin . . 90 90

245 Soup Tureen

1976. Europa. 19th-century Pottery. Multicoloured.
968 6f. Type **245** 65 25
969 12f. Bowl . . . . 1·50 1·40

246 Independence Hall, Philadelphia

247 Symbol representing "Strength and Impetus"

1976. Bicentenary of American Revolution.
970 **246** 6f. multicoloured 35 30

1976. Olympic Games, Montreal.
971 **247** 6f. gold, magenta and mauve 35 30

248 Association Emblem and "Sound Vibrations"

249 "Virgin and Child"

1976. 30th Anniv of "Jeunesses Musicales" (Youth Music Association).
972 **248** 6f. multicoloured 35 30

1976. Renaissance Art. Multicoloured.
973 6f. Type **249** 35 25
974 12f. Bernard de Velbruck, Lord of Beaufort (funeral monument) 85 85

250 Alexander Graham Bell

1976. Telephone Centenary.
975 **250** 6f. green 35 25

1976. National Welfare Fund. Protected Plants (2nd series). As T **242**. Multicoloured.
976 2f.+25c. Gentian 20 25
977 5f.+25c. Wild daffodil . . . 20 25
978 6f.+50c. Red helleborine (orchid) 30 25
979 12f.+1f. Late spider orchid 85 2·00
980 20f.+8f. Twin leaved squill 2·50 5·00

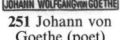

251 Johann von Goethe (poet)

252 Fish Market, Luxembourg

1977. Luxembourg Culture. Famous Visitors to Luxembourg.
981 **251** 2f. purple 20 15
982 – 5f. violet 30 30
983 – 6f. black 50 25
984 – 12f. violet 65 70
DESIGNS: 5f. Joseph Mallard William Turner (painter); 6f. Victor Hugo (writer); 12f. Franz Liszt (musician).

1977. Europa. Multicoloured.
985 6f. Type **252** 45 30
986 12f. Grand Duke Adolphe railway bridge and European Investment Bank 1·40 1·25

253 Esch-sur-Sure

254 Marguerite de Busbach (founder)

1977. Tourism.
987 **253** 5f. blue 45 25
988 – 6f. brown 35 25
DESIGNS 6f. Ehnen.

1977. Anniversaries. Multicoloured.
989 6f. Type **254** 40 25
990 6f. Louis Braille (after Filippi) 40 25
ANNIVERSARIES: No. 989, 350th anniv of foundation of Notre Dame Congregation; No. 990, 125th death anniv.

255 10c. and 1sgr. Stamps of 1852

1977. 125th Anniv of Luxembourg Stamps. Sheet 90 × 60 mm.
MS991 **255** 40f. black, chestnut and grey . . . . 4·00 5·25

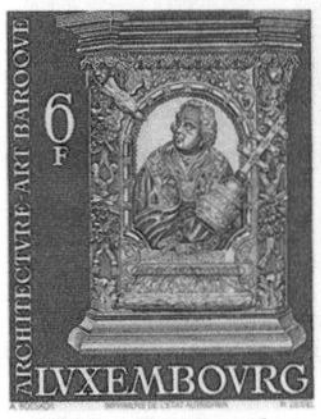

256 St. Gregory the Great

257 Head of Medusa

1977. Baroque Art. Sculpture from Feulen Parish Church pulpit attributed to J.-G. Scholtus.
992 **256** 6f. purple 40 25
993 – 12f. grey 70 80
DESIGN: 12f. St. Augustine.

1977. Roman Mosaic at Diekirch.
994 **257** 6f. multicoloured 70 25

258 Scene from "Orpheus and Eurydice" (Gluck)

1977. 25th Wiltz International Festival.
995 **258** 6f. multicoloured 65 25

259 Map of E.E.C. and "Europa" (R. Zilli)

1977. 20th Anniv of Rome Treaties.
996 **259** 6f. multicoloured 55 25

1977. National Welfare Fund. Protected Plants (3rd series). As T **242**. Multicoloured.
997 2f.+25c. Lily of the valley 20 25
998 5f.+25c. Columbine 30 30
999 6f.+50c. Mezereon 50 30
1000 12f.+1f. Early spider orchid 1·40 2·40
1001 20f.+8f. Spotted orchid . . 2·40 5·00

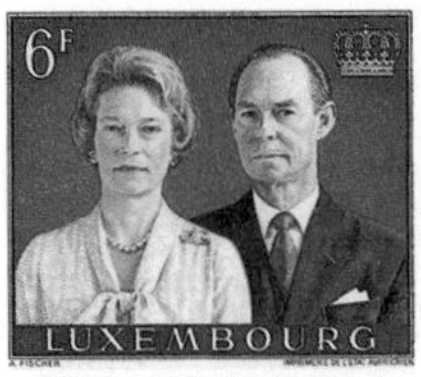

260 Grand Duke Jean and Duchess Josephine-Charlotte

261 Fountain and Youth

1978. Royal Silver Wedding. Sheet 116 × 67 mm.
MS1002 **260** 6f., 12f. multicoloured 1·25 1·50

1978. "Juphilux 78" Junior International Philatelic Exhibition. Sheet 103 × 72 mm containing T **261** and similar vert designs. Multicoloured.
MS1003 5f. Type **261**; 6f. Streamer; 20f. Dancing youths . . . . . 3·00 4·50
MS1003 was on sale at 60f., including entrance fee of 29f., at the Exhibition, by postal application and at post offices.

262 Charles IV

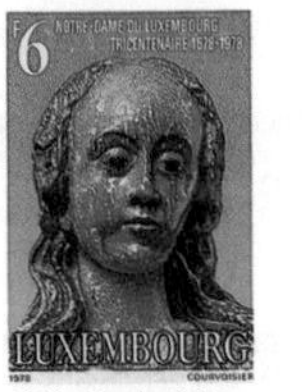

263 Head of Our Lady of Luxembourg

1978. Europa.
1004 **262** 6f. lilac 35 25
1005 – 12f. red . . . . 1·00 1·10
DESIGN: 12f. Pierre d'Aspelt (funeral monument, Mainz Cathedral).

1978. Anniversaries. Multicoloured.
1006 6f. Type **263** (300th anniv of election as patron saint) 35 30
1007 6f. Trumpeters (135th anniv of Grand Ducal Military Band) 35 30

264 Emile Mayrisch (after T. van Rysselberghe)

265 Child with Ear of Millet

1978. 50th Death Anniv of Emile Mayrisch (iron and steel magnate).
1008 **264** 6f. multicoloured 85 25

1978. "Solidarity 1978". Multicoloured.
1009 2f. Type **265** (Terre des Hommes) 20 15
1010 5f. Flower and lungs (70th anniv of Luxembourg Anti-tuberculosis League) 20 25
1011 6f. Open cell (Amnesty International and 30th anniv of Declaration of Human Rights) 30 25

266 Perfect Ashlar

267 "St. Matthew"

1978. 175th Anniv of Luxembourg Grand Lodge.
1012 **266** 6f. blue 35 30

1978. National Welfare Fund. Glass Paintings (1st series). Multicoloured.
1013 2f.+25c. Type **267** 15 25
1014 5f.+25c. "St. Mark" 30 30
1015 6f.+50c. "Nativity" 40 30
1016 12f.+1f. "St. Luke" . . . . 1·40 65
1017 20f.+8f. "St. John" . . . . 1·75 4·50
See also Nos. 1035/9 and 1055/8.

268 Denarius of Gaius Julius Caesar

269 Mondorf-les-Bains

1979. Luxembourg Culture. Roman Coins in the State Museum. Multicoloured.
1018 5f. Type **268** 30 25
1019 6f. Sestertius of Faustina I 50 25
1020 9f. Follis of Helena 70 45
1021 26f. Solidus of Valens . . . 1·40 1·25
See also Nos. 1040/3 and 1060/3.

1979. Tourism.
1022 **269** 5f. green, brown and blue 50 15
1023 – 6f. red 85 15
DESIGN: 6f. Luxembourg Central Station.

270 Stage Coach

271 Antoine Meyer (poet)

1979. Europa. Multicoloured.
1024 6f. Type **270** . . . . 2·40 25
1025 12f. Old wall telephone (vert) . . . . 2·40 1·50

1979. Anniversaries.
1026 – 2f. purple 45 25
1027 **271** 5f. red 35 25
1028 – 6f. turquoise 35 25
1029 – 9f. grey-black 35 35
DESIGNS—36 × 36 mm: 2f. Michel Pintz on trial (after L. Piedboeuf) and monument to rebels (180th anniv of peasant uprising against French). 22 × 36 mm: 5f. Type **271** (150th anniv of first publication in Luxembourg dialect); 6f. S. G. Thomas (cent of purchase of Thomas patent for steel production); 9f. "Abundance crowning Work and Saving" (ceiling painting by August Vinet) (50th anniv of Stock Exchange).

272 "European Assembly"

273 Blindfolded Cherub with Chalice

1979. First Direct Elections to European Assembly.
1030 **272** 6f. multicoloured . . . . 1·10 60

1979. Rococo Art. Details from altar of St. Michael's Church by Barthelemy Namur. Multicoloured.
1031 6f. Type **273** 35 30
1032 12f. Cherub with anchor . . 50 75

274 Child with Traffic Symbol Balloons jumping over Traffic

1979. International Year of the Child.
1033 **274** 2f. blue, brown and red 20 15

275 Radio Waves, "RTL" and Dates

1979. 50th Anniv of Broadcasting in Luxembourg.
1034 **275** 6f. blue and red 45 25

1979. National Welfare Fund. Glass Paintings (2nd series). As T **267**. Multicoloured.
1035 2f.+25c. "Spring" 15 20
1036 5f.+25c. "Summer" 30 30
1037 6f.+50c. "Charity" 40 30
1038 12f.+1f. "Autumn" 70 15
1039 20f.+8f. "Winter" . . . . . 1·25 4·50

1980. Luxembourg Culture. Medieval Coins in the State Museum. As T **268**. Multicoloured.
1040 2f. Grosso of Emperor Henry VII 15 15
1041 5f. Grosso of John the Blind of Bohemia 20 25
1042 6f. "Mouton d'or" of Wenceslas I and Jeanne, Duke and Duchess of Brabant 65 25
1043 20f. Grosso of Wenceslas II, Duke of Luxembourg . . 1·60 75

276 State Archives Building

277 Jean Monnet (statesman)

1980. Tourism.
1044 **276** 6f. purple, ultram & bl 50 15
1045 – 6f. red and brown . . . 60 15
DESIGN—VERT: No. 1045, Ettelbruck Town Hall.

1980. Europa.
1046 **277** 6f. black 50 25
1047 – 12f. olive . . . . 1·00 90
DESIGN: 12f. St. Benedict of Nursia (founder of Benedictine Order) (statue in Echternach Abbey).

278 Sports Equipment

279 Gloved Hand protecting Worker from Machinery

1980. "Sports for All".
1048 **278** 6f. black, orange & green 1·40 30

1980. 9th World Congress on the Prevention of Accidents at Work and Occupational Diseases, Amsterdam.
1049 – 2f. multicoloured 20 15
1050 **279** 6f. brown, grey and red 40 25
DESIGN—VERT: 2f. Worker pouring molten iron.

280 "Mercury" (Jean Mich)

281 Postcoded Letter

1980. Art Nouveau Sculpture. Statues beside entrance to State Savings Bank.
1051 **280** 8f. lilac 45 30
1052 – 12f. blue 65 60
DESIGN: 12f. "Ceres" (Jean Mich).

1980. Postcode Publicity.
1053 **281** 4f. brown, ochre and red 50 15

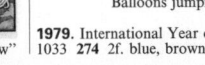

282 Policemen and Patrol Car

1980. 50th Anniv of National Police Force.
1054 **282** 8f. multicoloured 55 25

1980. National Welfare Fund. Glass Paintings (3rd series). As T **267**. Multicoloured.
1055 4f.+50c. "St. Martin" . . . 30 25
1056 6f.+50c. "St. Nicholas" . . 30 25
1057 8f.+1f. "Virgin and child" 40 1·00
1058 30f.+10f. "St. George" . . . 2·25 4·50

283 Grand Duke Jean

1981. Grand Duke Jean's 60th Birthday. Sheet 115 × 73 mm containing T **283** and similar vert design.
MS1059 8f. Type **283**; 12f. Grand Duke Jean's coat of arms; 30f. Type **283** . . . . 1·75 2·10

1981. Luxembourg Culture. Coins in the State Museum. As T **268**.
1060 4f. Patagon of Philip IV of Spain, 1635 . . . . . . 20 25
1061 6f. 12 sols coin of Maria Theresa, 1775 . . . . . . 30 30
1062 8f. 12 sols coin of Emperor Joseph II, 1789 . . . . . 30 30
1063 30f. Siege crown of Emperor Francis II, 1795 . . . . . 1·00 1·00

284 European Parliament Building, Luxembourg

285 Cock-shaped Whistle sold at Easter Monday Market

1981. Tourism.
1064 **284** 8f. brown and blue . . . 35 25
1065 – 8f. red and blue 35 25
DESIGN: No. 1065, National Library.

1981. Europa. Multicoloured.
1066 8f. Procession of beribboned sheep and town band to local fair 45 25
1067 12f. Type **285** 70 65

286 Staunton Knight on Chessboard

287 Prince Henri and Princess Maria Teresa

1981. Anniversaries.
1068 **286** 4f. multicoloured 30 25
1069 – 8f. ochre, brown & silver 40 30
1070 – 8f. multicoloured 40 30
DESIGNS—VERT: 4f. Type **286** (50th anniv of Luxembourg Chess Federation); 8f. (1070), Pass-book and State Savings Bank (125th anniv of State Savings Bank). HORIZ: 8f. (1069), First Luxembourg banknote (125th anniv of International Bank of Luxembourg's issuing rights).

1981. Royal Wedding.
1071 **287** 8f. multicoloured 55 50

288 Gliders over Useldange

289 Flame

1981. Aviation. Multicoloured.
1072 8f. Type **288** 45 30
1073 16f. Cessna 172F Skyhawk and 182H Skylane sports planes 70 65
1074 35f. Boeing 747-200F 182H over Luxembourg-Findel airport terminal . . . . . 1·40 90

1981. Energy Conservation.
1075 **289** 8f. multicoloured 50 20

290 Arms of Petange

291 "Apple Trees in Blossom" (Frantz Seimetz)

1981. National Welfare Fund. Arms of Local Authorities (1st series). Multicoloured.
1076 4f.+50c. Type **290** 20 25
1077 6f.+50c. Larochette 25 25
1078 8f.+1f. "Adoration of the Magi" (School of Rubens) 40 35
1079 16f.+2f. Stadtbredimus . . . 70 1·75
1080 35f.+12f. Weiswampach . . 2·50 4·50
See also Nos. 1097/1101 and 1119/23.

1982. Luxembourg Culture. Landscapes through the Four Seasons. Multicoloured.
1081 4f. Type **291** 30 30
1082 6f. "Landscape" (Pierre Blanc) 40 40
1083 8f. "The Larger Hallerbach" (Guido Oppenheim) . . . 45 30
1084 16f. "Winter Evening" (Eugene Mousset) 85 80

292 Cross of Hinzert and Statue "Political Prisoner" (Lucien Wercollier)

293 Treaty of London, 1867, and Luxembourg Fortress

1982. National Monument of the Resistance and Deportation, Notre-Dame Cemetery.
1085 **292** 8f. multicoloured 40 20

1982. Europa. Multicoloured.
1086 8f. Type **293** 50 30
1087 16f. Treaty of Paris, 1951, and European Coal and Steel Community Building, Luxembourg . . 85 80

294 St. Theresa of Avila (wood statue, Carmel Monastery)

295 State Museum

1982. Anniversaries. Multicoloured.
1088 4f. Type **294** (400th death anniv) 20 15
1089 8f. Raoul Follereau (social worker for lepers, 5th death anniv) 35 25

1982. Tourism.
1090 **295** 8f. brown, blue and black 40 20
1091 – 8f. buff, black and blue 40 20
DESIGN: No. 1091, Luxembourg Synagogue.

296 Bourscheid Castle

297 Key in Lock

1982. Classified Monuments (1st series).
1092 **296** 6f. blue 30 20
1093 – 8f. red 45 20
DESIGN—HORIZ: 8f. Vianden Castle.
See also Nos. 1142/3 and 1165/6.

1982. Anniversaries. Multicoloured.
1094 4f. Type **297** (50th anniv of International Youth Hostel Federation) . . . 45 30
1095 8f. Scouts holding hands around globe (75th anniv of Scouting Movement) (vert) 70 30

298 Monument to Civilian and Military Deportation

1982. Civilian and Military Deportation Monument, Hollerich Station.
1096 **298** 8f. multicoloured 40 30

1982. National Welfare Fund. Arms of Local Authorities (2nd series) and Stained Glass Window (8f.). As T **290**. Multicoloured.
1097 4f.+50c. Bettembourg . . . 25 25
1098 6f.+50c. Frisange 30 25
1099 8f.+1f. "Adoration of the Shepherds" (Gustav Zanter, Hoscheid parish church) 45 80
1100 16f.+2f. Mamer . . . . . . 85 1·75
1101 35f.+12f. Heinerscheid . . . 2·40 4·75

299 Modern Fire Engine

300 "Mercury" (Auguste Tremont)

1983. Centenary of National Federation of Fire Brigades. Multicoloured.
1102 8f. Type **299** 45 30
1103 16f. Hand fire-pump (18th century) 70 75

1983. Anniversaries and Events.
1104 **300** 4f. multicoloured 30 30
1105 – 6f. multicoloured 30 30
1106 – 8f. brown, black and blue 40 30
1107 – 8f. deep blue and blue 40 30
DESIGNS: No. 1104, Type **300** (25th Congress of International Association of Foreign Exchange Dealers); 1105, N.A.T.O. emblem surrounded by flags of member countries (25th anniv of N.A.T.O.); 1106, Echternach Cross of Justice (30th Congress of International Union of Barristers); 1107, Globe and customs emblem (30th anniv of Customs Co-operation Council).

301 Robbers attacking Traveller

1983. Europa. Miniatures from "Codex Aureus Escorialensis", illustrating Parable of the Good Samaritan. Multicoloured.
1108 8f. Type **301** . . . . 1·25 40
1109 16f. Good Samaritan helping traveller . . . . . 2·75 1·25

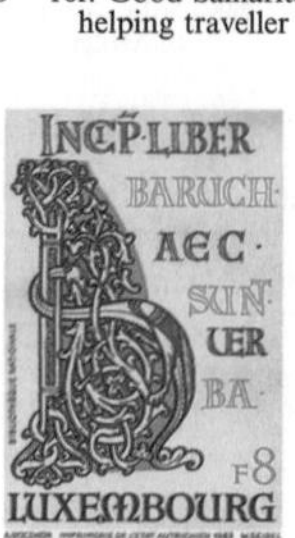

302 Initial "H" from "Book of Baruch"

303 Despatch Rider and Postcode

1983. Luxembourg Culture. Echternach Abbey Giant Bible. Multicoloured.
1110 8f. Type **302** 45 35
1111 35f. Initial "B" from letter of St. Jerome to Pope Damasius I . . . . 1·40 1·10

1983. World Communications Year. Mult.
1112 8f. Type **303** 85 20
1113 8f. Europan Communications Satellite (horiz) . . . . 1·75 30

304 St. Lawrence's Church, Diekirch

305 Basketball

1983. Tourism.
1114 **304** 7f. orange, brown and blue 35 20
1115 – 10f. orange, brown & bl 55 20
DESIGN—HORIZ: 10f. Dudelange Town Hall.

1983. Anniversaries and Events. Multicoloured.
1116 7f. Type **305** (50th anniv of Luxembourg basketball Federation) 45 35
1117 10f. Sheepdog (European Working Dog Championships) 65 35
1118 10f. City of Luxembourg ("The Green Heart of Europe") . . . . 1·10 35

1983. National Welfare Fund. Arms of Local Authorities (3rd series) and Painting. As T **290**. Multicoloured.
1119 4f.+1f. Winseler 30 30
1120 7f.+1f. Beckerich 40 35
1121 10f.+1f. "Adoration of the Shepherds" (Lucas Bosch) 45 50
1122 16f.+2f. Feulen . . . . . . 85 1·75
1123 40f.+13f. Mertert . . . . . 2·40 4·25

306 Lion and First Luxembourg Stamp

307 Pedestrian Precinct

1984. Anniversaries. Each black, red and blue.
1124 10f. Type **306** 70 35
1125 10f. Lion and ministry buildings 70 35
1126 10f. Lion and postman's bag 70 35
1127 10f. Lion and diesel locomotive 70 35
ANNIVERSARIES: No. 1124, 50th anniv of Federation of Luxembourg Philatelic Societies; 1125, 75th anniv of Civil Service Trade Union Movement; 1126, 75th anniv of Luxembourg Postmen's Trade Union; 1127, 125th anniv of Luxembourg Railways.

1984. Environmental Protection. Multicoloured.
1128 7f. Type **307** 45 35
1129 10f. City of Luxembourg sewage treatment plant . . 45 35

308 Hands supporting European Parliament Emblem

309 Bridge

1984. 2nd Direct Elections to European Parliament.
1130 **308** 10f. multicoloured . . . 70 40

1984. Europa. 25th Anniv of European Post and Telecommunications Conference.
1131 **309** 10f. green, dp green & blk . . . . 1·60 35
1132 16f. orange, brown & blk 3·25 1·40

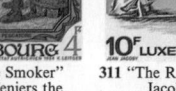

310 "The Smoker" (David Teniers the Younger)

311 "The Race" (Jean Jacoby)

1984. Paintings. Multicoloured.
1133 4f. Type **310** 50 30
1134 7f. "Young Turk caressing his Horse" (Eugene Delacroix) (horiz) 65 35

1135 10f. "Ephiphany" (Jan Steen) (horiz) 85 35
1136 50f. "The Lacemaker" (Pieter van Slingelandt) 3·50 2·50

1984. Olympic Games, Los Angeles.
1137 **311** 10f. orange, black & blue 65 30

312 "Pecten sp."

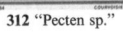

313 "American Soldier" (statue by Michel Heitz at Clervaux)

1984. Luxembourg Culture. Fossils in the Natural History Museum. Multicoloured.
1138 4f. Type **312** 45 20
1139 7f. Devil's toe-nail 50 35
1140 10f. "Coeloceras raquinianum" (ammonite) 85 35
1141 16f. Dapedium (fish) . . . . 1·00 85

1984. Classified Monuments (2nd series). As T **296**.
1142 7f. turquoise 35 35
1143 10f. brown 45 30
DESIGNS: 7f. Hollenfels Castle; 10f. Larochette Castle.

1984. 40th Anniv of Liberation.
1144 **313** 10f. black, red and blue 1·40 30

314 Infant astounded by Surroundings

315 Jean Bertels (abbot of Echternach Abbey)

1984. National Welfare Fund. The Child. Mult.
1145 4f.+1f. Type **314** 35 35
1146 7f.+1f. Child dreaming . . . 50 50
1147 10f.+1f. "Nativity (crib, Steinsel church) 85 55
1148 16f.+2f. Child sulking . . . 2·40 2·50
1149 40f.+13f. Girl admiring flower . . . . 6·00 6·75

1985. Luxembourg Culture. Portrait Medals in State Museum (1st series). Multicoloured.
1150 4f. Type **315** (steatite medal, 1595) 25 30
1151 7f. Emperor Charles V (bronze medal, 1537) . . 35 35
1152 10f. King Philip II of Spain (silver medal, 1555) . . . 45 35
1153 30f. Maurice of Orange-Nassau (silver medal, 1615) . . . . 1·40 1·00
See also Nos. 1173/6.

316 Fencing

317 Papal Arms

1985. Anniversaries. Multicoloured.
1154 10f. Type **316** (50th anniv of Luxembourg Fencing Federation) 60 30
1155 10f. Benz "Velo" (centenary of automobile) 60 30
1156 10f. Telephone within concentric circles (centenary of Luxembourg telephone service) 60 30

1985. Visit of Pope John Paul II.
1157 **317** 10f. multicoloured . . . 45 30

318 Treble Clef within Map of National Anthem

319 Maquisards Badge and "Wounded Soldiers" (sculpture, Rene Weyland)

1965. Europa. Music Year. Multicoloured.
1158 10f. Type **318** (Grand Duke Adolphe Union of choral, instrumental and folklore societies) . . . . 1·50 35
1159 16f. Neck of violin, music school and score of Beethoven's Violin Concerto opus 61 . . . . 3·00 1·60

1985. 40th Anniv of V.E. (Victory in Europe) Day. Sheet 120 × 72 mm containing T **319** and similar vert designs.
MS1160 10f. multicoloured (Type **319**); 10f. brown, black and blue (War medal); 10f. multicoloured (Union of Resistance Movements badge); 10f. black, red and blue (dove and barbed wire hands) (liberation of prison camps) . . . . 2·40 2·75

320 Little Owl

1985. Endangered Animals. Multicoloured.
1161 4f. Type **320** 85 35
1162 7f. European wildcat (horiz) 1·75 50
1163 10f. Red admiral (horiz) . . 2·50 40
1164 50f. European tree frog . . 3·50 2·40

1985. Classified Monuments (3rd series). As T **296**.
1165 7f. red 35 30
1166 10f. green 35 30
DESIGNS—HORIZ: 7f. Echternach orangery. VERT: 10f. Mohr de Waldt house.

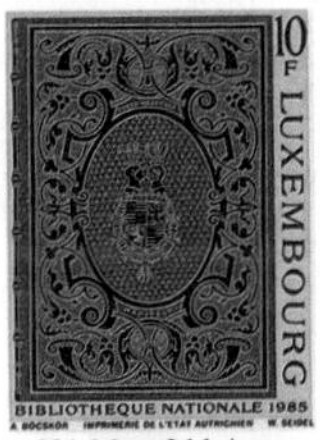

321 Mansfeld Arms (book binding)

322 Application

1985. Luxembourg Culture.
1167 **321** 10f. multicoloured . . . 50 35

1985. National Welfare Fund. Multicoloured.
1168 4f.+1f. Type **322** 40 30
1169 7f.+1f. Friendship 55 45
1170 10f.+1f. "Adoration of the Magi" (16th century alabaster sculpture) . . . 85 45
1171 16f.+2f. Child identifying with his favourite characters . . . . 2·50 2·50
1172 40f.+13f. Shame . . . . . 6·25 8·25

1986. Luxembourg Culture. Portrait Medals in State Museum (2nd series). As T **315**.
1173 10f. multicoloured 45 35
1174 12f. multicoloured 50 30
1175 18f. black, grey and blue . . 70 60
1176 20f. multicoloured . . . . . 1·00 75
DESIGNS: 10f. Count of Monterey (silver medal, 1675); 12f. Louis XIV of France (silver medal, 1684); 18f. Pierre de Weyms (president of Provincial Council) (pewter medal, 1700); 20f. Duke of Marlborough (silver medal, 1706).

323 Bee on Flower

324 Forest and City

1986. Anniversaries. Multicoloured.
1177 12f. Type **323** (centenary of Federation of Luxembourg Beekeeper's Associations) 70 30
1178 12f. Table tennis player (50th anniv of Luxembourg Table Tennis Federation) 70 30
1179 11f. Mosaic of woman with water jar (centenary of Mondorf State Spa) . . . 70 30

1986. Europa. Multicoloured.
1180 12f. Type **324** . . . . . . 1·00 35
1181 20f. Mankind, industry and countryside . . . . 1·60 1·10

325 Fort Thungen

326 Schuman

1986. Luxembourg Town Fortifications. Mult.
1182 15f. Type **325** . . . . . . 1·25 50
1183 18f. Invalids' Gate (vert) . . 1·25 50
1184 50f. Malakoff Tower (vert) 2·00 65

1986. Birth Centenary of Robert Schuman (politician).
1185 **326** 2f. black and red 15 15
1186 10f. black and blue . . . 40 35

327 Road through Red Triangle on Map

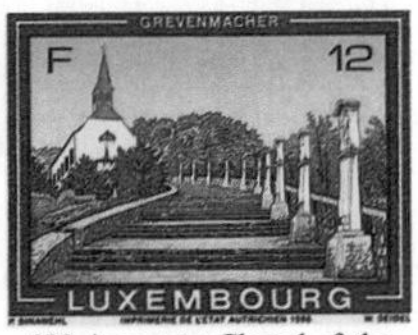

328 Ascent to Chapel of the Cross, Grevenmacher

1986. European Road Safety Year.
1187 **327** 10f. multicoloured . . . 50 30

1986. Tourism.
1188 **328** 12f. multicoloured . . . 65 30
1189 – 12f. brown, stone and red 65 30
DESIGN: No. 1189, Relief from Town Hall facade, Esch-sur-Alzette.

329 Presentation of Letter of Freedom to Echternach (after P. H. Witkamp)

330 Annunciation

1986. 800th Birth Anniv of Countess Ermesinde of Luxembourg.
1190 **329** 12f. brown and stone . . 55 35
1191 – 30f. buff, black and grey 1·60 1·00
DESIGN: 30f. Seal, 1238.

1986. National Welfare Fund. Illustrations from 15th-century "Book of Hours". Multicoloured.
1192 6f.+1f. Type **330** 85 35
1193 10f.+1f. Angel appearing to shepherds 45 35
1194 12f.+2f. Nativity 85 45
1195 18f.+2f. Adoration of the Magi . . . . 2·50 3·00
1196 20f.+8f. Flight into Egypt 4·25 5·50

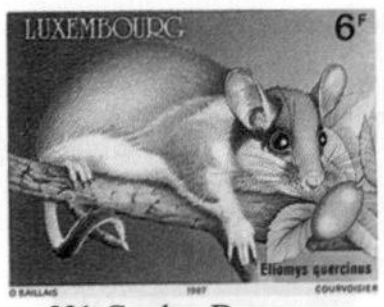

331 Garden Dormouse

332 Network Emblem

1987. Endangered Animals. Multicoloured.
1197 6f. Type **331** 65 65
1198 10f. Banded agrion (vert) . . 1·00 40
1199 12f. White-throated dipper (vert) . . . . 1·50 40
1200 25f. Salamander . . . . . . 2·40 1·25

1987. 50th Anniversaries. Multicoloured.
1201 12f. Type **332** (Amateur Short Wave Network) . . 45 40
1202 12f. Anniversary Emblem (International Fair) . . . 45 30

333 "St. Bernard of Siena and St. John the Baptist"

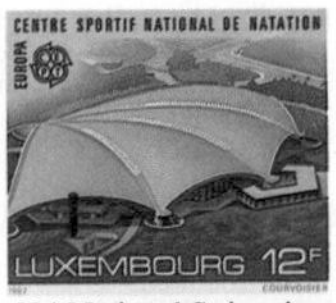

334 National Swimming Centre (Roger Taillibert)

1987. Paintings by Giovanni Ambrogio Bevilacqua in State Museum. Multicoloured.
1203 10f. Type **333** 45 40
1204 18f. "St. Jerome and St. Francis of Assisi" . . 70 80

1987. Europa. Architecture. Multicoloured.
1205 12f. Type **334** . . . . . . 1·00 40
1206 20f. European Communities' Court of Justice . . . . . 2·40 1·25

335 "Consecration" (stained glass window by Gustav Zanter)

336 Charles Metz (first President) (after Jean-Baptiste Fresez)

1987. Millenary of St. Michael's Church. Multicoloured.
1207 12f. Type **335** 45 30
1208 20f. Baroque organ-chest . . 85 80

1987. Chamber of Deputies.
1209 **336** 6f. brown 30 30
1210 – 12f. blue 55 50
DESIGN: 12f. Chamber of Deputies building.

337 Hennesbau, Niederfeulen

338 Annunciation

1987. Rural Architecture. Each ochre, brown and blue.
1211 10f. Type **337** 50 35
1212 12f. 18th-century dwelling house converted to health centre, Mersch 50 20
1213 100f. 18th-century house converted to Post Office, Bertrange . . . . 3·25 1·10

1987. National Welfare Fund. Illustrations from 15th-century Paris "Book of Hours". Multicoloured.
1214 6f.+1f. Type **338** 60 55
1215 10f.+1f. Visitation . . . . . 95 1·00
1216 12f.+2f. Adoration of the Magi . . . . 1·25 1·00
1217 18f.+2f. Presentation in the Temple . . . . 2·40 2·40
1218 20f.+8f. Flight into Egypt 5·00 5·00

339 Lilies and Water-lily

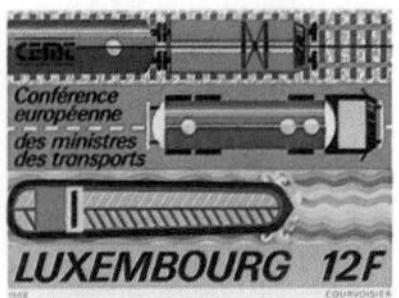

340 Rail, Road and Water Transport

1988. Luxembourg Culture. Flower Illustrations by Pierre-Joseph Redoute. Multicoloured.
1219 6f. Type **339** 60 35
1220 10f. Primulas and double narcissus 60 40
1221 12f. Tulips and chrysanthemums . . . . 1·00 45
1222 50f. Irises and gorterias . . 3·25 2·10

1988. European Conference of Ministers of Transport, Luxembourg (1223) and 25th Anniv of Eurocontrol (air safety organization) (1224). Multicoloured.
1223 12f. Type **340** 55 30
1224 20f. Boeing 747 airplane . . 1·00 85

341 Princess Maria Teresa

342 Wiltz Town Hall and Cross of Justice

1988. "Juvalux 88" Ninth Youth Philately Exhibition, Luxembourg. Sheet 11×72 mm containing T **341** and similar vert designs. Multicoloured.
MS1225 12f. Type **341**; 18f. Princes Guillaume, Felix and Louis; 50f. Crown Prince Henri . . . . . 5·00 5·75

1988. Tourism. Multicoloured.
1226 10f. Type **342** 60 40
1227 12f. Differdange Castle (vert) 60 40
See also Nos. 1254/5 and 1275/6.

343 Athletes

1988. 50th Anniv of League of Luxembourg Student Sports Associations.
1228 **343** 12f. multicoloured . . . 70 45

344 Automated Mail Sorting

1988. Europa. Transport and Communications. Multicoloured.
1229 12f. Type **344** . . . . . . 2·40 35
1230 20f. Electronic communications . . . . . 2·50 1·75

345 Jean Monnet (statesman, birth centenary) **346** Emblem and Flame

1988. European Anniversaries.
1231 **345** 12f. pink, brn & lt brn 50 35
1232 – 12f. brown and green . . 85 35
DESIGN: No. 1232, European Investment Bank headquarters, Kirchberg (30th anniv).

1988. Olympic Games, Seoul.
1233 **346** 12f. multicoloured . . . 50 35

347 Septfontaines Castle **348** Annunciation to Shepherds

1988. Doorways.
1234 **347** 12f. black and brown . . 60 30
1235 – 25f. black and green . . 1·25 90
1236 – 50f. black and brown . . 2·25 1·40
DESIGNS: 25f. National Library; 50f. Holy Trinity Church.

1988. National Welfare Fund. Illustrations from 16th-century "Book of Hours". Multicoloured.
1237 9f.+1f. Type **348** 45 45
1238 12f.+2f. Adoration of the Magi 50 50
1239 18f.+2f. Madonna and Child 2·40 2·40
1240 20f.+8f. Pentecost . . . . . 1·50 2·50

349 C. M. Spoo (promoter of Luxembourgish) **350** Grand Ducal Family Vault Bronze (Auguste Tremont)

1989. Anniversaries.
1241 **349** 12f. black, red and brown 50 45
1242 – 18f. multicoloured . . . 85 60·00
1243 – 20f. red, black and grey 1·25 1·00
DESIGNS: 12f. Type **349** (75th death anniv); 18f. Stylized inking pad (125th anniv of Book Workers' Federation); 20f. Henri Dunant (founder of International Red Cross) (75th anniv of Luxembourg Red Cross).

1989. 150th Anniv of Independence.
1244 **350** 12f. multicoloured . . . 65 30

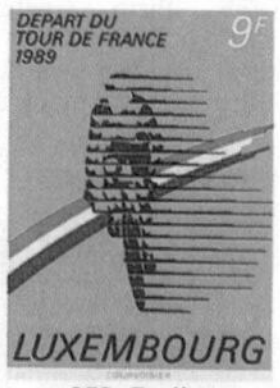

351 "Astra" Satellite and Map on T.V. Screens **352** Cyclist

1989. Launch of 16-channel T.V. Satellite.
1245 **351** 12f. multicoloured . . . 60 40

1989. Start in Luxembourg of Tour de France Cycling Race.
1246 **352** 9f. multicoloured 65 40

353 Assembly and Flag **354** Emblem

1989. 40th Anniv of Council of Europe.
1247 **353** 12f. multicoloured . . . 65 30

1989. Centenary of Interparliamentary Union.
1248 **354** 12f. yellow, blue & indigo 70 30

355 Hands **356** "Three Children in a Park" (anon)

1989. 3rd Direct Elections to European Parliament.
1249 **355** 12f. multicoloured . . . 65 30

1989. Europa. Children's Games and Toys. Multicoloured.
1250 12f. Type **356** 65 35
1251 20f. "Child with Drum" (anon) . . . . 1·40 1·00

357 Grand Duke Jean **358** Charles IV

1989. 25th Anniv of Accession of Grand Duke Jean.
1252 **357** 3f. black and orange . . 1·00 75
1253 9f. black and green . . . 1·00 95

1989. Tourism. As T **342**. Multicoloured.
1254 12f. Clervaux Castle 50 30
1255 18f. 1st-century bronze wild boar, Titelberg 85 70

1989. Luxembourg History. Stained Glass Windows by Joseph Oterberger, Luxembourg Cathedral. Multicoloured.
1256 12f. Type **358** 60 40
1257 20f. John the Blind 85 90
1258 25f. Wenceslas II . . . . . 1·00 1·10

359 St. Lambert and St. Blase, Fennange **360** Funfair (650th anniv of Schueberfouer)

1989. National Welfare Fund. Restored Chapels (1st series). Multicoloured.
1259 9f.+1f. Type **359** 50 50
1260 12f.+2f. St. Quirinus, Luxembourg (horiz) . . . 60 65
1261 18f.+3f. St. Anthony the Hermit, Reisdorf (horiz) 2·00 2·00
1262 25f.+8f. The Hermitage, Hachiville . . . . 3·00 3·00
See also Nos. 1280/3 and 1304/7.

1990. Anniversaries.
1263 **360** 9f. multicoloured 65 35
1264 – 12f. brown, pink & black 50 35
1265 – 18f. multicoloured . . . 80 75
DESIGNS: 12f. Batty Weber (writer, 50th death anniv); 18f. Dish aerial (125th anniv of International Telecommunications Union).

361 Troops at Fortress

1990. Luxembourg Culture. Etchings of the Fortress by Christoph Wilhelm Selig. Multicoloured.
1266 9f. Type **361** 45 40
1267 12f. Soldiers by weir 50 40
1268 20f. Distant view of fortress 1·25 90
1269 25f. Walls . . . . 1·60 1·10

362 Paul Eyschen (75th anniv) **363** "Psallus pseudoplatini" (male and female) on Maple

1990. Statesmen's Death Anniversaries.
1270 **362** 9f. brown and blue . . . 45 40
1271 – 12f. blue and brown . . 55 35
DESIGN: 12f. Emmanuel Servais (centenary).

1990. Centenary of Luxembourg Naturalists' Society.
1272 **363** 12f. multicoloured . . . 60 35

364 General Post Office, Luxembourg City **365** Hammelsmarsch Fountain (Will Lofy)

1990. Europa. Post Office Buildings.
1273 **364** 12f. black and brown . . 1·50 35
1274 – 20f. black and blue . . . 2·10 1·25
DESIGN—VERT: 20f. Esch-sur-Alzette Post Office.

1990. Tourism. As T **342**. Multicoloured.
1275 12f. Mondercange administrative offices . . 60 30
1276 12f. Schifflange town hall and church 60 30

1990. Fountains. Multicoloured.
1277 12f. Type **365** 50 35
1278 25f. Doves Fountain . . . . 1·00 90
1279 50f. Maus Ketty Fountain, Mondorf-les-Bains (Will Lofy) . . . . 2·00 2·40

366 Congregation of the Blessed Virgin Mary, Vianden **367** Grand Duke Adolf

1990. National Welfare Fund. Restored Chapels (2nd series). Multicoloured.
1280 9f.+1f. Type **366** 60 60
1281 12f.+2f. Notre Dame, Echternach (horiz) 85 70
1282 18f.+3f. Consoler of the Afflicted, Grentzingen (horiz) . . . . 1·75 1·75
1283 25f.+8f. St. Pirmin, Kaundorf . . . . 3·00 2·75

1990. Centenary of Nassau-Weilbourg Dynasty. Sheet 115×160 mm containing T **367** and similar vert designs. Multicoloured.
MS1284 12f. Type **367**; 12f. Grand Duchess Marie Adelaide; 18f. Grand Ducal arms; 18f. Grand Duchess Charlotte; 20f. Grand Duke William IV; 20f. Grand Duke Jean . . . . 6·00 6·75

368 "Geastrum varians" **370** Dicks (after Jean Goedert)

369 "View from the Trier Road"

1991. Fungi. Illustrations by Pierre-Joseph Redoute. Multicoloured.
1285 14f. Type **368** 65 40
1286 14f. "Agaricus (Gymnopus) thiebautii" 65 50
1287 18f. "Agaricus (Lepiota) lepidocephalus" 85 95
1288 25f. "Morchella favosa" . . 1·40 1·25

1991. Luxembourg Culture. 50th Death Anniv of Sosthene Weis (painter). Multicoloured.
1289 14f. Type **369** 60 40
1290 18f. "Vauban Street and the Viaduct" 70 75
1291 25f. "St. Ulric Street" (vert) 1·25 1·10

1991. Death Centenary of Edmond de la Fontaine (pen-name Dicks) (poet).
1292 **370** 14f. multicoloured . . . 70 45

371 Claw grasping Piece of Metal (after Emile Kirscht) **372** National Miners' Monument, Kayl

1991. 75th Anniv of Trade Union Movement in Luxembourg.
1293 **371** 14f. multicoloured . . . 70 45

1991. Tourism. Multicoloured.
1294 14f. Type **372** 70 40
1295 14f. Magistrates' Court, Redange-sur-Attert (horiz) 70 40

373 Earth and Orbit of "Astra 1A" and "1B" Satellites **374** Telephone

1991. Europa. Europe in Space. Multicoloured.
1296 14f. Type **373** . . . . . . 1·10 45
1297 18f. Betzdorf Earth Station 1·75 1·00

1991. Posts and Telecommunications.
1298 **374** 4f. brown . . . . 2·00 1·40
1299 – 14f. blue 55 55
DESIGN: 14f. Postbox.

375 1936 International Philatelic Federation Congress Stamp

376 Girl's Head

1991. 50th Stamp Day.
1300 **375** 14f. multicoloured . . . 70 40
The stamp illustrated on No. 1300 incorrectly shows a face value of 10f.

1991. Mascarons (stone faces on buildings) (1st series).
1301 **376** 14f. black, buff & brown 60 40
1302 – 25f. black, buff and pink 1·10 90
1303 – 50f. black, buff and blue 1·90 1·75
DESIGNS: 25f. Woman's head; 50f. Man's head.
See also Nos. 1320/22.

377 Chapel of St. Donatus, Arsdorf

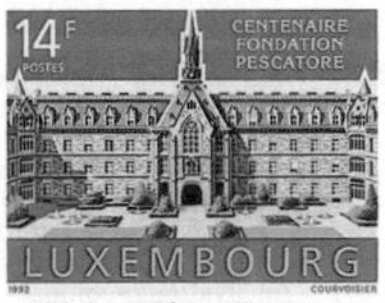

378 Jean-Pierre Pescatore Foundation

1991. National Welfare Fund. Restored Chapels (3rd series). Multicoloured.
1304 14f.+2f. Type **377** 85 70
1305 14f.+2f. Chapel of Our Lady of Sorrows, Brandenbourg (horiz) 85 90
1306 18f.+3f. Chapel of Our Lady, Luxembourg (horiz) 1·75 1·25
1307 22f.+7f. Chapel of the Hermitage, Wolwelange 2·50 2·75

1992. Buildings. Multicoloured.
1308 14f. Type **378** 70 50
1309 14f. Higher Technology Institute, Kirchberg . . . 70 50
1310 14f. New Fairs and Congress Centre, Kirchberg 70 50

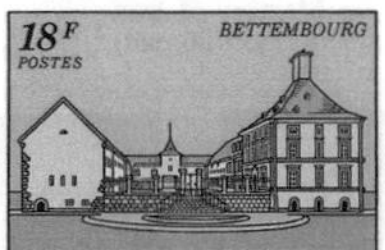

379 Inner Courtyard, Bettembourg Castle

1992. Tourism. Multicoloured.
1311 18f. Type **379** 70 65
1312 25f. Walferdange railway station . . . . 1·00 95

380 Athlete (detail of mural, Armand Strainchamps)

1992. Olympic Games, Barcelona.
1313 **380** 14f. multicoloured . . . 1·25 35

381 Luxembourg Pavilion

382 Lions Emblem

1992. "Expo '92" World's Fair, Seville.
1314 **381** 14f. multicoloured . . . 65 40

1992. 75th Anniv of Lions International.
1315 **382** 14f. multicoloured . . . 60 40

383 Memorial Tablet (Lucien Wercollier)

384 Nicholas Gonner (editor)

1992. 50th anniv of General Strike.
1316 **383** 18f. brown, grey and red 70 70

1992. Europa. 500th anniv of Discovery of America by Columbus. Luxembourg Emigrants to America.
1317 **384** 14f. brown, black & green 85 45
1318 – 22f. blue, black & orange 1·40 1·25
DESIGN: 22f. Nicolas Becker (writer).

385 Star and European Community Emblem

386 Posthorn and Letters

1992. Single European Market.
1319 **385** 14f. multicoloured . . . 65 40

1992. Mascarons (2nd series). As T **376**.
1320 14f. black, buff and green 55 40
1321 22f. black, buff and blue . . 1·10 1·00
1322 50f. black, buff and purple 1·75 1·60
DESIGNS: 14f. Ram's head; 22f. Lion's head; 50f. Goat's head.

1992. 150th Anniv of Post and Telecommunications Office. Designs showing stained glass windows by Auguste Tremont. Mult.
1323 14f. Type **386** 50 45
1324 22f. Post rider . . . . . . 1·40 1·25
1325 50f. Telecommunications . . 1·60 1·60

387 Hazel Grouse

388 Grand Duke Jean

1992. National Welfare Fund. Birds (1st series). Multicoloured.
1326 14f.+2f. Type **387** 85 95
1327 14f.+2f. Golden oriole (vert) 85 95
1328 18f.+3f. Black stork . . . . 2·40 2·10
1329 22f.+7f. Red kite (vert) . . . 3·00 3·00
See also Nos. 1364/7 and 1383/6.

1993.
1330 **388** 1f. black and yellow . . 10 10
1331 2f. black and green . . . 10 10
1332 5f. black and yellow . . 20 20
1333 7f. black and brown . . 30 20
1334 8f. black and green . . . 30 25
1335 9f. black and mauve . . 35 35
1336 10f. black and blue . . . 45 30
1337 14f. black and purple . . 1·40 30
1338 15f. black and green . . 50 45
1339 16f. black and orange . . 50 45
1340 18f. black and yellow . . 70 40
1341 20f. black and red . . . 70 55
1342 22f. black and green . . 90 55
1343 25f. black and blue . . . 85 70
1344 100f. black and brown 3·00 2·00

389 Old Ironworks Cultural Centre, Steinfort

1993. Tourism. Multicoloured.
1350 14f. Type **389** 65 35
1351 14f. "Children with Grapes" Fountain, Schwebsingen 65 35

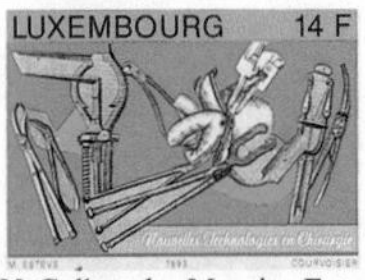

390 Collage by Maurice Esteve

1993. New Surgical Techniques.
1352 **390** 14f. multicoloured . . . 60 40

391 Hotel de Bourgogne (Prime Minister's offices)

1993. Historic Houses. Multicoloured.
1353 14f. Type **391** 55 40
1354 20f. Simons House (now Ministry of Agriculture) 85 70
1355 50f. Cassal House . . . . . 2·40 1·75

392 "Rezlop" (Fernand Roda)

1993. Europa. Contemporary Art. Multicoloured.
1356 14f. Type **392** 70 45
1357 22f. "So Close" (Sonja Roef) . . . . 1·40 1·00

393 Monument (detail, D. Donzelli), Tetange Cemetery

394 Emblem

1993. 75th Death Anniv of Jean Schortgen (first worker elected to parliament).
1358 **393** 14f. multicoloured . . . 60 40

1993. Centenary of Artistic Circle of Luxembourg.
1359 **394** 14f. mauve and violet . . 60 40

395 European Community Ecological Label

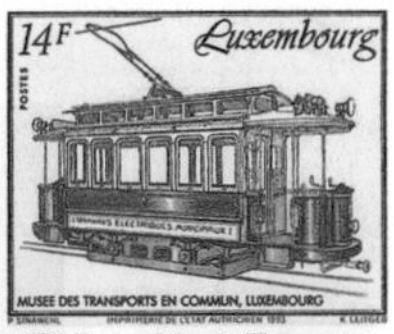

396 Tram No. 1 (Transport Museum, Luxembourg)

1993. Protection of Environment.
1360 **395** 14f. blue, green & emerald 60 40

1993. Museum Exhibits (1st series). Multicoloured.
1361 14f. Type **396** 70 40
1362 22f. Iron ore tipper wagon (National Mining Museum, Rumelange) . . 1·00 1·00
1363 60f. Horse-drawn carriage (Arts and Ancient Crafts Museum, Wiltz) . . . . . 2·40 4·75
See also Nos. 1404/6 and 1483/4.

1993. National Welfare Fund. Birds (2nd series). As T **387**. Multicoloured.
1364 14f.+2f. Common snipe ("Becassine") 70 70
1365 14f.+2f. River kingfisher ("Martin-Pecheur") (vert) 70 70
1366 18f.+3f. Little ringed plover ("Petit Gravelot") . . . . 1·40 1·40
1367 22f.+7f. Sand martin ("Hirondelle de Rivage") (vert) . . . . 2·50 2·50

397 "Snow-covered Landscape" (Joseph Kutter)

1994. Artists' Birth Centenaries. Multicoloured.
1368 14f. Type **397** 60 40
1369 14f. "The Moselle" (Nico Klopp) 60 40

398 Members' Flags

399 17th-century Herald's Tabard

1994. 4th Direct Elections to European Parliament.
1370 **398** 14f. multicoloured . . . 60 40

1994. Congresses. Multicoloured.
1371 14f. Type **399** (21st International Genealogy and Heraldry Congress) 60 40
1372 18f. International Police Association emblem on map (14th World Congress) 70 40

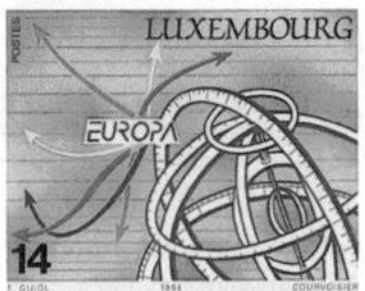

400 Arrows and Terrestrial Globe

1994. Europa. Discoveries. Multicoloured.
1373 14f. Type **400** 85 45
1374 22f. Chart, compass rose and sails . . . . 1·40 1·25

401 "Family" (Laura Lammar)

1994. International Year of the Family.
1375 **401** 25f. multicoloured . . . 1·00 95

402 Crowds cheering American Soldiers

1994. 50th Anniv of Liberation.
1376 **402** 14f. multicoloured . . . 60 50

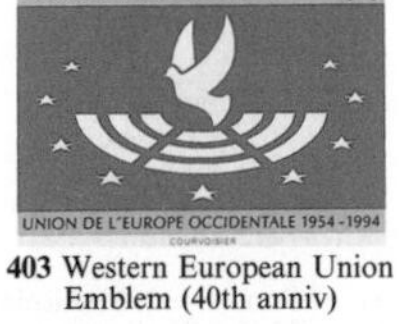

403 Western European Union Emblem (40th anniv)

1994. Anniversaries and Campaign.
1377 **403** 14f. blue, lilac and ultramarine 70 50
1378 – 14f. multicoloured . . . 70 45
1379 – 14f. multicoloured . . . 2·40 70
DESIGNS—No. 1378, Emblem (25th anniv in Luxembourg of European Communities' Office for Official Publications); 1379, 10th-century B.C. ceramic bowl from cremation tomb, Bigelbach (European Bronze Age Campaign).

404 Munster Abbey (General Finance Inspectorate)

1994. Former Refuges now housing Government Offices. Multicoloured.
1380 15f. Type **404** 70 65
1381 25f. Holy Spirit Convent (Ministry of Finance) . . 85 1·00
1382 60f. St. Maximine Abbey of Trier (Ministry of Foreign Affairs) . . . . 2·00 2·75

1994. National Welfare Fund. Birds (3rd series). As T **387**. Multicoloured.
1383 14f.+2f. Common stonechat ("Traquet Patre") (vert) 70 85
1384 14f.+2f. Grey partridge ("Perdix Grise") 70 85
1385 18f.+3f. Yellow wagtail ("Bergeronnette Printaniere") . . . . . . 1·40 1·40
1386 22f.+7f. Great grey shrike ("Pie-Grieche Grise") (vert) . . . . 2·50 2·50

405 "King of the Antipodes"

406/409 Panoramic View of City (½-size illustration)

1995. Luxembourg, European City of Culture.
1387 **405** 16f. multicoloured . . . 1·00 65
1388 – 16f. multicoloured . . . 1·00 65
1389 – 16f. multicoloured . . . 1·00 65
1390 **406** 16f. multicoloured . . . 70 60
1391 **407** 16f. multicoloured . . . 70 60
1392 **408** 16f. multicoloured . . . 70 60
1393 **409** 16f. multicoloured . . . 70 60
1394 – 16f. multicoloured . . . 70 60
DESIGNS—As T **405**: No. 1388, "House with Arcades and Yellow Tower"; 1389, "Small Path" (maze). 35 × 26 mm: No. 1394, Emblem.
Nos. 1390/3 were issued together, se-tenant, forming the composite design illustrated.

410 Landscape and Slogan

411 Colour Spectrum and Barbed Wire

1995. European Nature Conservation Year.
1395 **410** 16f. multicoloured . . . 70 40

1995. Europa. Peace and Freedom. 50th Anniv of Liberation of Concentration Camps. Mult.
1396 16f. Type **411** 70 65
1397 25f. Wire barbs breaking through symbolic sky and earth . . . . 1·10 1·10

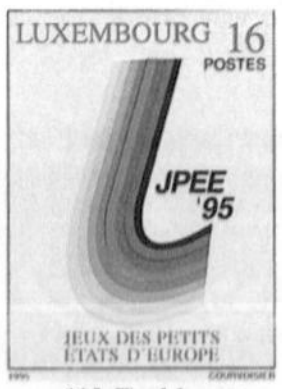

412 Emblem

1995. Anniversaries and Event. Multicoloured.
1398 16f. Type **412** (6th Small European States Games, Luxembourg) 60 60
1399 32f. Diagram of section through Earth (27th anniv of underground Geodynamics Laboratory, Walferdange) (33 × 34 mm) . . . . . . 1·25 1·25
1400 80f. Anniversary emblem (50th anniv of U.N.O.) 2·75 2·75

413 Boeing 757

1995. 40th Anniv of Luxembourg–Iceland Air Link.
1401 **413** 16f. multicoloured . . . 60 60

414 Erpeldange Castle

415 Stained Glass Window from Alzingen Church

1995. Tourism. Multicoloured.
1402 16f. Type **414** 60 65
1403 16f. Schengen Castle 60 65

1995. Museum Exhibits (2nd series). Vert designs as T **396**. Multicoloured.
1404 16f. Churn (Country Art Museum, Vianden) . . . 70 70
1405 32f. Wine-press (Wine Museum, Ehnen) . . . . 1·25 1·50
1406 80f. Sculpture of potter (Leon Nosbusch) (Pottery Museum, Nospelt) . . . . 3·25 3·00

1995. Christmas.
1407 **415** 16f.+2f. multicoloured 1·00 1·25

416 Broad-leaved Linden ("Tilia platyphyllos")

417 Mayrisch (after Theo van Rysselberghe)

1995. National Welfare Fund. Trees (1st series). Multicoloured.
1408 16f.+2f. Type **416** 70 95
1409 16f.+2f. Horse chestnut ("Aesculus hippocastanum") (horiz) 70 95
1410 20f.+3f. Pedunculate oak (horiz) . . . . 1·25 1·40
1411 32f.+7f. Silver birch . . . . 2·25 2·40
See also Nos. 1432/5 and 1458/61.

1996. 68th Death Anniv of Emile Mayrisch (engineer).
1412 **417** A (16f.) multicoloured 70 65

418 Mounument, Place Clairefontaine (Jean Cardot)

420 "Marie Munchen"

419 Electric Railcar

1996. Birth Centenary of Grand Duchess Charlotte.
1413 **418** 16f. multicoloured . . . 85 60

1996. 50th Anniv of Luxembourg National Railway Company. Multicoloured.
1414 16f. Type **419** 70 70
1415 16f. Linked cars 70 70
1416 16f. Train (right-hand detail) 70 70

Nos. 1414/16 were issued together, se-tenant, forming a composite design of a Series 2000 electric railcar set.

1996. 96th Death Anniv of Mihaly Munkacsy (painter). Multicoloured.
1417 16f. Type **420** 70 80
1418 16f. Munkacsy (after Edouard Charlemont) (horiz) 70 80

421 Workers and Emblem

422 Marie de Bourgogne

1996. Anniversaries.
1419 **421** 16f. green, orge & blk 60 65
1420 – 20f. multicoloured . . . 70 90
1421 – 25f. multicoloured . . . 1·00 1·25
1422 – 32f. multicoloured . . . 1·25 1·40
DESIGNS—HORIZ: 16f. Type **421** (75th anniv of Luxembourg Confederation of Christian Trade Unions); 32f. Film negative (centenary of motion pictures). VERT: 20f. Transmitter and radio waves (centenary of Guglielmo Marconi's patented wireless telegraph); 25f. Olympic flame and rings (centenary of modern Olympic Games).

1996. Europa. Famous Women. Duchesses of Luxembourg. Multicoloured.
1423 16f. Type **422** 60 65
1424 25f. Maria-Theresa of Austria . . . . 1·00 1·25

423 Handstamp

1996. Bicentenary (1995) of Registration and Property Administration.
1425 **423** 16f. multicoloured . . . 60 65

424 Children of different Cultures (Michele Dockendorf)

1996. "Let us Live Together". Multicoloured.
1426 16f. Type **424** 65 65
1427 16f. "L'Abbraccio" (statue, Marie-Josee Kerschen) (vert) 65 65

425 Eurasian Badger

1996. Mammals. Multicoloured.
1428 16f. Type **425** 65 65
1429 20f. Polecat 65 70
1430 80f. European otter . . . . 3·00 3·25

426 "The Birth of Christ" (icon, Eva Mathes)

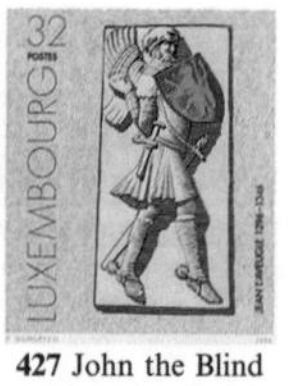

427 John the Blind

1996. Christmas.
1431 **426** 16f.+2f. multicoloured 1·40 1·40

1996. National Welfare Fund. Trees (2nd series). As T **416**. Multicoloured.
1432 16f.+2f. Willow ("Salix sp.") (horiz) 65 85
1433 16f.+2f. Ash ("Fraxinus excelsior") 65 85
1434 20f.+3f. Mountain ash (horiz) . . . . 1·25 1·60
1435 32f.+7f. Common beech . . 2·40 2·75

1996. 700th Birth Anniv of John the Blind (King of Bohemia and Count of Luxembourg).
1436 **427** 32f. multicoloured . . . 1·25 1·40

428 Koerich Church

1997. Tourism. Multicoloured.
1437 16f. Type **428** 70 50
1438 16f. Servais House, Mersch (horiz) 70 50

429 Birthplace of Robert Schuman (politician), Luxembourg-Clausen

1997. Anniversaries. Multicoloured.
1439 16f. Type **429** (40th anniv of Treaties of Rome establishing European Economic Community and European Atomic Energy Community) . . . 70 50
1440 20f. National colours forming wing of Mercury (75th anniv of Belgium–Luxembourg Economic Union) 85 75

430 "Grand Duchess Charlotte"

1997. 11th World Federation of Rose Societies Congress, Belgium, Mondorf (Luxembourg) and the Netherlands. Roses. Multicoloured.
1441 16f. Type **430** 70 70
1442 20f. "The Beautiful Sultana" (33 × 26 mm) 70 80
1443 80f. "In Memory of Jean Soupert" (33 × 26 mm) . . 2·75 2·50

431 Badge, Luxembourg Fortress, Shako and Sword

432 The Beautiful Melusina

1997. Anniversaries.
1444 **431** 16f. multicoloured . . . 60 60
1445 – 16f. black, blue and red 60 60
1446 – 16f. brown, green and pink 60 60
DESIGNS—As T **431**: No. 1444, Type **431** (bicentenary of Grand Ducal Gendarmerie Corps); 1445, Cock and rabbit (75th anniv of Luxembourg Union of Small Domestic Animals Farming Societies). 33 × 33 mm: No. 1446, Bather and attendant, early 1900s (150th anniv of Mondorf spa).

1997. Europa. Tales and Legends. Multicoloured.
1447 16f. Type **432** 70 65
1448 25f. The Hunter of Hollenfels . . . . 1·00 1·25

433 Face on Globe

1997. "Juvalux 98" Youth Stamp Exhibition (1st issue). Multicoloured.

1449	16f. Type **433**	70	65
1450	80f. Postmen (painting, Michel Engels)	2·75	2·75

See also Nos. 1475/8.

434 Emblem

1997. Sar–Lor–Lux (Saarland–Lorraine–Luxembourg) European Region.

1451	**434** 16f. multicoloured	70	65

Stamps in similar designs were issued by France and Germany.

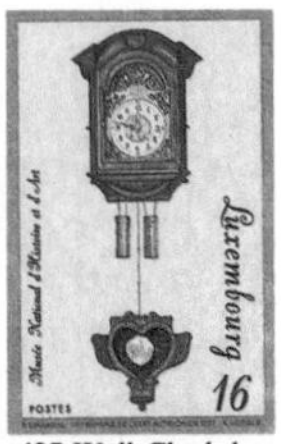

435 Wall Clock by Dominique Nauens, 1816

436 "Kalborn Mill"(Jean-Pierre Gleis)

1997. Clocks. Multicoloured.

1452	16f. Type **435**	70	65
1453	32f. Astronomical clock by J. Lebrun, 1850 (26 × 44 mm)	1·10	1·40
1454	80f. Wall clock by Mathias Hebeler, 1815	2·75	2·50

1997. Water Mills. Multicoloured.

1455	16f. Type **436**	70	65
1456	50f. Interior of Ramelli mill, 1588 (from book "The Water Wheel" by Wilhelm Wolfel) (vert)	1·75	2·10

437 Holy Family

438 Count Henri V

1997. Christmas.

1457	**437** 16f.+2f. multicoloured	1·25	1·25

1997. National Welfare Fund. Trees (3rd series). As T **416**. Multicoloured.

1458	16f.+2f. Wych elm ("Ulmus glabra")	70	85
1459	16f.+2f. Norway maple ("Acer platanoides")	70	85
1460	20f.+3f. Wild cherry	1·00	1·00
1461	32f.+7f. Walnut (horiz)	1·75	1·75

1997. 750th Anniv of Accession of Henri V, Count of Luxembourg.

1462	**438** 32f. multicoloured	1·25	1·00

439 Rodange Church

440 Cog and "50"

1998. Tourism. Multicoloured.

1463	16f. Type **439**	70	65
1464	16f. Back of local authority building, Hesperange (horiz)	70	65

1998. Anniversaries.

1465	**440** 16f. multicoloured	70	65
1466	– 16f. multicoloured	70	65
1467	– 20f. multicoloured	70	90
1468	– 50f. black, red and stone	1·75	2·10

DESIGNS: No. 1465, Type **440** (50th anniv of Independent Luxembourg Trade Union); 1466, Festival poster (Rene Wismer) (50th anniv of Broom Festival, Wiltz); 1467, Memorial (death centenary of Jean Antoine Zinnen (composer of national anthem)); 1468, Typewriter keys and page from first issue of "Luxemburger Wort" (150th anniv of abolition of censorship).

441 Brown Trout

1998. Freshwater Fishes. Multicoloured.

1469	16f. Type **441**	70	65
1470	25f. Bullhead	1·00	1·25
1471	50f. Riffle minnow	2·00	2·10

442 Henri VII and Flags outside Fair Venue, Kirchberg

1998. 700th Anniv of Granting to Count Henri VII of Right to Hold a Fair. Value indicated by letter.

1472	**442** A (16f.) multicoloured	70	70

443 Fireworks over Adolphe Bridge (National Day)

444 Town Postman, 1880

1998. Europa. National Festivals. Multicoloured.

1473	16f. Type **443**	85	70
1474	25f. Stained-glass window and flame (National Remembrance Day)	1·00	1·25

1998. "Juvalux '98" Youth Stamp Exhibition (2nd issue). Multicoloured.

1475	16f. Type **444**	70	65
1476	25f. Letter, 1590 (horiz)	80	1·25
1477	50f. Rural postman, 1880	1·75	2·10
MS1478	125 × 76 mm 16f., 80f. Railway viaduct and city (composite design)	4·50	5·00

445 Masonic Symbols (Paul Moutschen)

1998. 150th Anniv of St. John of Hope Freemason Lodge.

1479	**445** 16f. multicoloured	60	65

446 Echternach

1998. 1300th Anniv of Echternach Abbey. Multicoloured.

1480	16f. Type **446**	60	65
1481	48f. Buildings in Echternach	2·40	2·10
1482	60f. Echternach Abbey	2·00	2·25

447 Spanish Morion (late 16th century)

1998. Museum Exhibits (3rd series). City of Luxembourg History Museum. Multicoloured.

1483	16f. Type **447**	70	65
1484	80f. Wayside Cross from Hollerich (1718)	2·75	3·00

448 "Nativity" (altarpiece by Georges Saget, St. Mauritius Abbey, Clervaux)

1998. Christmas.

1485	**448** 16f.+2f. multicoloured	1·40	1·10

449 "Bech"

1998. National Welfare Fund (1st series). Villages. 16th-century drawings by Jean Bertels. Multicoloured.

1486	16f.+2f. Type **449**	70	85
1487	16f.+2f. "Ermes Turf" (now Ermsdorf)	70	85
1488	20f.+3f. "Itsich" (now Itzig)	1·00	1·25
1489	32f.+7f. "Stein Hem" (now Steinheim)	1·75	1·90

See also Nos. 1510/13 and 1550/3.

450 Globe and Jigsaw

1998. 40th Anniv of North Atlantic Maintenance and Supply Agency.

1490	**450** 36f. multicoloured	1·40	1·50

451 Council Building and Emblem

1999. 50th Anniv of Council of Europe.

1491	**451** 16f. multicoloured	70	70

452 Euro Coin and Map

1999. Introduction of the Euro (European currency). Value expressed by letter.

1492	**452** A (16f.) multicoloured	1·00	65

453 Tawny Owl

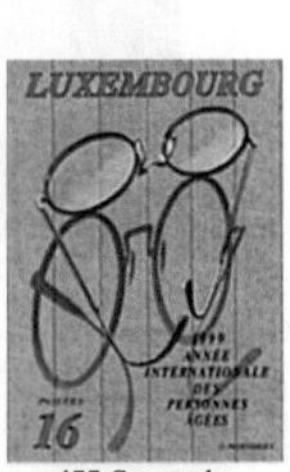

455 Spectacles

454 Globe and Emblem

1999. Owls. Multicoloured.

1493	A (16f.) Type **453**	70	65
1494	32f. Eagle owl (horiz)	1·25	1·25
1495	60f. Barn owl (horiz)	2·50	3·00

1999. 50th Anniv of N.A.T.O.

1496	**454** 80f. multicoloured	3·00	3·50

1999. International Year of the Elderly.

1497	**455** 16f. multicoloured	70	65

456 Emblem and Envelopes

1999. 125th Anniv of Universal Postal Union.

1498	**456** 16f. multicoloured	70	65

457 Haute-Sure National Park

1999. Europa. Parks and Gardens. Multicoloured.

1499	16f. Type **457**	70	70
1500	25f. Ardennes-Eifel National Park	1·00	1·25

458 Emblem

1999. Anniversaries. Multicoloured.

1501	16f. Type **458** (75th anniv of National Federation of Mutual Societes)	70	65
1502	32f. Camera and roll of film (50th anniv of Luxembourg Federation of Amateur Photographers)	1·40	1·40
1503	80f. Gymnasts (centenary of Luxembourg Gymnastics Federation)	3·50	3·50

459 Prince Guillaume

461 A. Mayrisch de Saint-Hubert

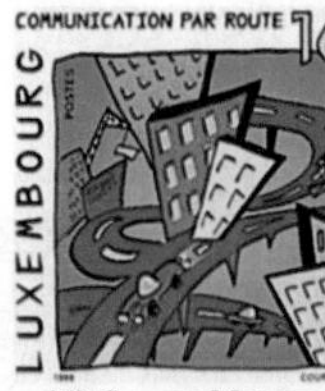

460 Cars on Motorway

1999. 18th Birthday of Prince Guillaume.

1504	**459** 16f. multicoloured	70	70

1999. Communications of the Future. Mult.

1505	16f. Type **460**	60	70
1506	20f. Earth and satellite	70	85
1507	80f. Planets and spacecraft	3·00	3·00

1999. 125th Birth Anniv of Aline Mayrisch de Saint-Hubert (President of Luxembourg Red Cross).

1508	**461** 20f. multicoloured	70	80

462 Decorated Church Tower

1999. Christmas.

1509	**462** 16f.+2f. multicoloured	1·00	90

1999. National Welfare Fund. Villages (2nd series). As T **449**, showing 6th-century drawings by Jean Bertels. Multicoloured.
1510 16f.+2f. “Oswiler” (now Osweiler) 70 80
1511 16f.+2f. “Bettem Burch” (now Bettembourg) . . . 70 80
1512 20f.+3f. “Cruchte auf der Alset” (now Cruchten) . . 80 1·00
1513 32f.+7f. “Berchem” . . . . 2·00 2·10

463 “Gateway” (sketch by Goethe)

1999. 250th Birth Anniv of Johann Wolfgang von Goethe (poet and playwright).
1514 **463** 20f. chestnut, cream & brn 70 80

464 “2000”

2000. New Millennium. Value expressed by letter. Multicoloured. Self-adhesive.
1515 A (16f.) Type **464** (blue streaks emanating from bottom right) 70 65
1516 A (16f.) Blue streaks emanating from bottom left 70 65
1517 A (16f.) Blue streaks emanating from top right 70 65
1518 A (16f.) Blue streaks emanating from top left 70 65

465 Charles V

2000. 500th Birth Anniv of Emperor Charles V. Value expressed by letter.
1519 **465** A (16f.) multicoloured 70 60

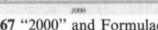

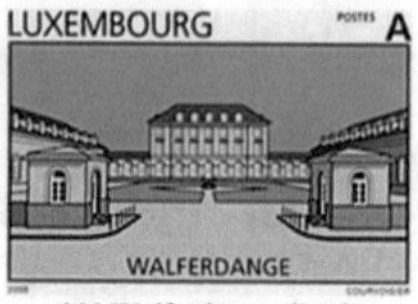
466 Walferdange Castle

2000. Tourism. Value expressed by letter. Multicoloured.
1520 A (16f.) Type **466** 70 60
1521 A (16f.) Local government offices, Wasserbillig (vert) 70 60

467 “2000” and Formulae

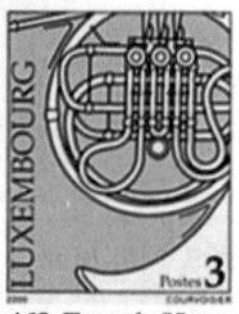
468 French Horn

2000. World Mathematics Year.
1522 **467** 80f. multicoloured . . . 2·75 3·00

2000. Musical Instruments.
1523 **468** 3f. black and violet . . . 20 10
1524 – 9f. black and green . . . 40 35
1525 – 12f. black and yellow . . . 45 40
1526 – 21f. black and pink . . . 75 75
1527 – 24f. black and blue . . . 80 55
1528 – 30f. black and pink . . . 85 65
DESIGNS: 9f. Electric guitar; 12f. Saxophone; 21f. Violin; 24f. Accordion; 30f. Grand piano.

469 Production and Storage Facilities, 1930s (Harry Rabinger)

2000. Centenary (1999) of Esch-sur-Alzette Gas Works.
1535 **469** 18f. multicoloured . . . 70 75

470 Mallard

471 “Building Europe”

2000. Ducks. Multicoloured.
1536 18f. Type **470** 70 75
1537 24f. Common pochard (vert) 80 80
1538 30f. Tufted duck (vert) . . . 1·00 85

2000. Europa.
1539 **471** 21f. multicoloured . . . 85 70

472 Jean Monnet and Robert Schuman

2000. 50th Anniv of Schuman Plan (proposal for European Coal and Steel Community).
1540 **472** 21f. black, blue & yellow 85 70

473 Blast Furnace

2000. 20th Anniv of Blast Furnace “B”, Esch-Belval.
1541 **473** A (18f.) multicoloured 55 35

474 Castle Walls and Tower (Wenzel Walk)

2000. Circular City Walks. Multicoloured.
1542 18f. Type **474** 55 35
1543 42f. Bridge and tower (Vauban walk) . . . . . 1·25 75

475 Will Kesseler

2000. Modern Art (1st series). Showing paintings by artist named. Multicoloured.
1544 21f. Type **475** 55 35
1545 24f. Joseph Probst (vert) . . 85 85
1546 36f. Mett Hoffmann 65 40
See also Nos. 1612/14.

476 Prince Henri in Uniform and Princess Maria

2000. Swearing in of Prince Henri as Head of State of Grand Duchy of Luxembourg. Multicoloured.
1547 18f. Type **476** 70 45
MS1548 125 × 90 mm. 100f. Prince Henri in civilian clothes and Princess Maria . . . . 4·50 5·00

477 Child before Christmas Tree

2000. Christmas.
1549 **477** 18f.+2f. multicoloured 85 85

2000. National Welfare Fund. Villages (3rd series). As T **449** showing 16th-century drawings by Jean Bertels. Multicoloured.
1550 18f.+2f. “Lorentzwiller” (now dorentzweiler) . . . 70 70
1551 21f.+3f. “Coosturf” (now Consdorf) 95 95
1552 24f.+3f. “Elfingen” (now Elvange) 95 95
1553 36f.+7f. “Sprenckigen” (now Sprinkange) . . . . . . 1·75 1·75

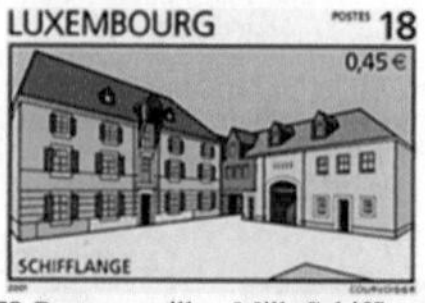
478 Bestgensmillen Mill, Schifflange

2001. Tourism. Multicoloured.
1554 18f. Type **478** 70 50
1555 18f. Vineyard, Wormeldange (vert) 70 50

479 Nik Welter

2001. Writers’ Death Anniversaries. Multicoloured.
1556 18f. Type **479** (50th anniv) 70 50
1557 24f. Andre Gide (50th anniv) . . . . 1·00 65
1558 30f. Michel Rodange (125th anniv) . . . . 1·40 1·00

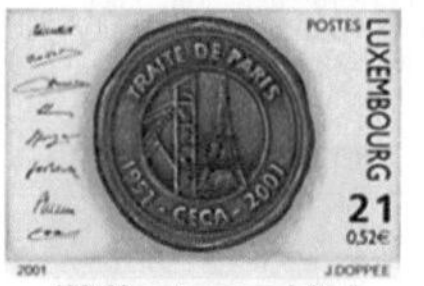
480 Signatures and Seal

2001. 50th Anniv of Treaty of Paris.
1559 **480** 21f. multicoloured . . . 85 65

481 Citroen 2CV Mini-Van

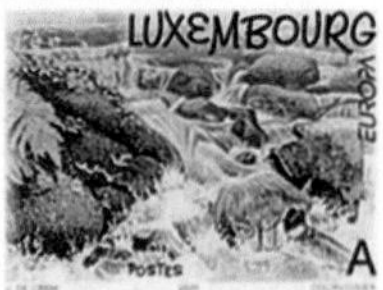
482 Stream, Mullerthal

2001. Postal Vehicles. Mult. Self-adhesive.
1560 3f. Type **481** 20 15
1561 18f. Volkswagen Beetle . . . 65 50

2001. Europa. Water Resources. Multicoloured. Value expressed by letter (No. 1562) or with face value (No. 1563).
1562 A (18f.) Type **482** 70 70
1563 21f. Pond and Kaltreis water tower (vert) . . . . 1·00 70

483 “Mother and Child” (Ger Maas)

484 Helicopter and Rescuer

2001. Humanitarian Projects. Multicoloured.
1564 18f. Type **483** (humanitarian aid) 65 50
1565 24f. International Organization for Migration emblem 85 65

2001. Rescue Services. Multicoloured.
1566 18f. Type **484** 65 50
1567 30f. Divers and rubber dinghy . . . . 1·00 85
1568 45f. Fire engine and fireman wearing protective clothing . . . . 1·75 1·40

DENOMINATION. From No. 1569 Luxembourg stamps are denominated in euros only.

485 Five Cent Coin

486 Grand Duke Henri

2001. Euro Currency. Coins. Multicoloured.
1569 5c. Type **485** 20 20
1570 10c. Ten cent coin 20 20
1571 20c. Twenty cent coin . . . 35 35
1572 50c. Fifty cent coin 65 65
1573 €1 One euro coin . . . . 1·40 1·40
1574 €2 Two euro coin . . . . 2·75 2·75

2001. Grand Duke Henri.
1575 1c. indigo, blue and ultramarine 10 10
1576 3c. olive, green and ultramarine 10 10
1580 **486** 7c. dp blue, blue & red 10 10
1583 22c. sepia, brown & red 35 30
1584 25c. lilac and ultramarine 35 30
1585 30c. dp green, grn & red 40 35
1588 45c. dp violet, vio & red 60 40
1589 50c. black and ultramarine 60 45
1590 52c. brown, buff and red 65 40
1591 59c. deep blue, blue and red 75 45
1592 60c. black, green and blue 75 45
1593 74c. brown, stone and red 95 55
1594 80c. agate, green and blue 95 55
1595 89c. mauve, brown and red . . . . 1·10 80

487 Emblem

2001. European Year of Languages. Value expressed by letter.
1596 **487** A (45c.) multicoloured 60 50

488 Sun, Wind-powered Generators and Houses (renewable energy)

2001. Environment and Medicine of the Future. Multicoloured.
1597 45c. Type **488** 65 55
1598 59c. Tyre, tins, bottle and carton (recycling) . . . 85 65
1599 74c. Microscope and test-tubes (biological research) 1·00 1·00

489 St. Nicholas

2001. Christmas.
1600 **489** 45c.+5c. multicoloured 60 45

490 Squirrel

2001. National Welfare Fund. Animals (1st issue). Multicoloured.
1601 45c.+5c. Type **490** 60 45
1602 52c.+8c. Wild boar 75 55
1603 59c.+11c. Hare (vert) . . . 90 65
1604 89c.+21c. Wood pigeon (vert) . . . . 1·40 1·40
See also Nos. 1632/5 and 1660/3.

491 Emblem

2001. Kiwanis International (community organization).
1605 **491** 52c. dp blue, bl & gold 65 40

New Currency. 100 cents = 1 euro.

492 Snowboarding

493 Mortiz Ney

2002. Sports. Self-adhesive. Multicoloured.
1606 7c. Type **492** 10 10
1607 7c. Skateboarding 10 10
1608 7c. Inline skating 10 10
1609 45c. BMX biking 55 35
1610 45c. Beach volleyball . . . 55 35
1611 45c. Street basketball . . . 55 35

2002. Modern Art (2nd series). Showing works by artist named. Multicoloured.
1612 22c. Type **493** 30 20
1613 45c. Dany Prum (horiz) . . 55 35
1614 59c. Christiane Schmit . . . 75 45

494 Map of Europe and "1977"

2002. Anniversaries. Multicoloured.
1615 45c. Type **494** (25th anniv of European Court of Auditors) 55 35
1616 52c. Scales of Justice and map of Europe (50th anniv of European Communities Court of Justice) 65 40

495 Tightrope Walker

2002. Europa. The Circus. Multicoloured.
1617 45c. Type **495** 55 35
1618 52c. Clown juggling 65 40

496 Emblem

2002. 2002 Tour de France (starting in Luxembourg). Multicoloured.
1619 45c. Type **496** 55 35
1620 52c. Francois Faber (winner of 1909 Tour de France) (vert) 65 40
1621 €2.45 "The Champion" (Joseph Kutter) (vert) . . 3·00 1·90

497 Orchestra on Stage (50th Anniv of Festival of Wiltz)

2002. Cultural Anniversaries. Value expressed by letter (No. 1622) or face value (No. 1623). Multicoloured.
1622 A (45c.) Type **497** 55 35
1623 €1.12 Victor Hugo and signature (birth bicentenary) . . . . . . 1·40 85

498 Grand Duke William III of Netherlands

2002. 150th Anniv of First Luxembourg Stamp (1st issue). Sheet 121 × 164 mm, containing T **498** and similar horiz designs. Multicoloured.
MS1624 45c. Type **498**; 45c. Grand Duke Adolphe; 45c. Grand Duchess Charlotte; 45c. Grand Duke Henri . . . . 2·25 2·25
See also Nos. 1630/1.

499 Water Droplet on Spruce

2002. Natural History Museum. Multicoloured. Value expressed by letter. Self-adhesive.
1625 A (45c.) Type **499** 55 35
1626 A (45c.) Mocker swallowtail 55 35
1627 A (45c.) Houseleek 55 35
1628 A (45c.) Blackthorn berries 55 35

500 Emblem

501 Postmen in Flying Vehicles (Clare Nothumb)

2002. 750th Anniv of Grevenmacher City Charter.
1629 **500** 74c. multicoloured . . . 90 55

2002. 150th Anniv of First Luxembourg Stamp (2nd issue). Winning Entries in Stamp Design Competition. (a) With face value.
1630 22c. Type **501** 30 15

(b) Value expressed by letter.
1631 A (45c.) Symbols of communications and flying saucer orbiting planet (Christine Hengen) (horiz) 55 35

502 Fox

503 Place d'Armes

2002. Christmas.
1636 **503** 45c.+5c. multicoloured 60 45

2002. National Welfare Fund. Animals (2nd series). Multicoloured.
1632 45c.+5c. Type **502** 60 45
1633 52c.+8c. Hedgehog (vert) . . 75 60
1634 59c.+11c. Pheasant 90 65
1635 89c.+21c. Deer (vert) . . . 1·40 1·40

No. 1636 was issued in se-tenant sheetlets of 12 stamps, the margins of which were impregnated with the scent of cinnamon.

504 Grand Duke Jean and Grand Duchess Josephine-Charlotte

2003. Golden Wedding Anniversary of Grand Duke Jean and Grand Duchess Josephine-Charlotte.
1637 **504** 45c. multicoloured . . . 65 40

505 Catherine Schleimer-Kill

2003. 30th Death Anniversaries. Multicoloured.
1638 45c. Type **505** (political pioneer) 65 40
1639 45c. Lou Koster (composer) 65 40

506 Citeaux Abbey, Differdange

2003. Tourism. Multicoloured.
1640 50c. Type **506** 70 40
1641 €1 Mamer Castle . . . . . 1·40 85
1642 €2.50 St. Joseph Church, Esch-sur-Alzette (vert) . . 3·50 2·10

507 Pamphlets and Compact Discs

2003. 50th Anniv of Official Journal of European Communities (daily publication of official reports).
1643 **507** 52c. multicoloured . . . 75 45

508 Head and Symbols

2003. 400th Anniv of the Athenee (secondary school), Luxembourg.
1644 **508** 45c. multicoloured . . . 60 35

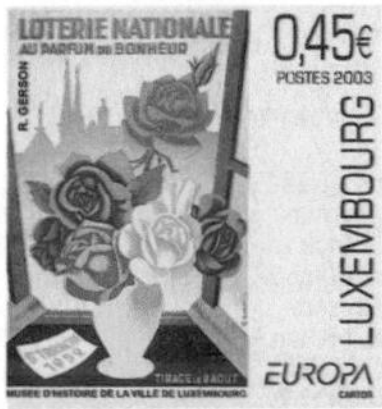

509 1952 National Lottery Poster (Roger Gerson)

2003. Europa. Poster Art. Multicoloured.
1645 45c. Type **509** 60 35
1646 52c. Tiger (1924 Commercial Fair poster) (Auguste Tremont) 70 40

510 Adolphe Bridge

2003. Bridges and Viaducts. Multicoloured.
1647 45c. Type **510** (centenary) 60 35
1648 59c. Stierchen bridge (14th-century) (38 × 28 mm) 80 60
1649 89c. Victor Bodson bridge (Hesperange viaduct) (38 × 28 mm) . . . . . . 1·20 90

511 Woman Hoeing

2003. 75th Anniv of Gaart an Heem (gardening association). Multicoloured.
1650 25c. Type **511** 35 20
1651 A (45c.) Woman holding rake 60 35
1652 €2 Children . . . . 2·75 2·00

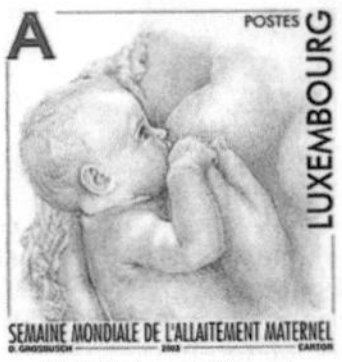

512 Baby at Breast

513 Light Bulb

2003. Breastfeeding Campaign.
1653 **512** A (45c.) brown, chestnut and black 60 35

2003. 75th Anniv of Electricity.
1654 **513** A (45c.) multicoloured 60 35

514 Engineering Steel Sheet Piles

2003. Made in Luxembourg. Multicoloured.
1655 60c. Type **514** 80 60
1656 70c. Medical valve 90 55
1657 80c. Technician and polyester film . . . . . . 1·10 65

515 Church and Cloud containing Buildings

2003. Christmas. Multicoloured.
1658 50c.+5c. Type **515** 85 85
1659 50c.+5c. Child, church and Christmas tree 85 85

516 Roe-deer

2003. Fauna (3rd series). Multicoloured.
1660 50c.+5c. Type **516** 85 85
1661 60c.+10c. Raccoon (horiz) 90 90
1662 70c.+10c. Weasel . . . . . 1·10 1·10
1663 €1 +25c. Goshawk (horiz) 1·60 1·60

517 *Cantharellus tubaeformis*

2004. Fungi. Multicoloured. Self-adhesive.
1664 10c. Type **517** 15 10
1665 10c. *Ramaria flava* 15 10
1666 10c. *Stropharia cynea* . . . 15 10
1667 50c. *Helvella lacunosa* . . . 65 40

1668		50c. *Anthurus archeri*	65	40
1669		50c. *Clitopilus prunulus*	65	40

518 Annual Street Market, Luxembourg-Ville

2004. Anniversaries. Multicoloured.

1670		50c. Type **518** (75th anniv)	65	40
1671		50c. Haberdashery (centenary of Esch-sur-Alzette Commercial Union)	65	40

519 Edward Steichen

2004. Birth Anniversaries. Multicoloured.

1672	**519**	50c. lilac, brown and black	65	40
1673	–	70c. blue, buff and black	95	60

DESIGNS: 50c. Type **519** (photographer) (125th); 70c. Hugo Gernsback (science fiction writer) (120th and centenary of his emigration to USA).

520 Stylized Figures

2004. European Elections.

1674	**520**	50c. multicoloured	65	40

521 Hikers on Bridge, Mullerthal

2004. Europa. Holidays. Multicoloured.

1675		50c. Type **521**	65	40
1676		60c. Camp site, Bourscheid-Beach	80	60

522 Runners carrying Olympic Flame (A. Bilska)

2004. Sport. Winning Entries in Children's Drawing Competition. Multicoloured.

1677		50c. Type **522** (Olympic Games, Athens, 2004)	60	40
1678		60c. Basketball (L. Eyschen) (European Year of Education through Sport)	80	60

523 Building and Anniversary Emblem

2004. 50th Anniv of European School, Luxembourg.

1679	**523**	70c. multicoloured	95	55

524 Breads and Beer

2004. Made in Luxembourg. Food. Multicoloured.

1680		35c. Type **524**	45	25
1681		60c. Meat products	80	50
1682		70c. Dairy products	95	55

525 Bull and Bear

2004. 75th Anniv of Luxembourg Stock Exchange.

1683	**525**	50c. multicoloured	65	40

526 Museum Building (Marc Angel)

2004. National Museum of History and Art. Multicoloured.

1684		50c. Type **526**	65	50
1685		€1.10 "Young Woman with a Fan" (Luigi Rubio)	1·50	90
1686		€3 "Charity" (Lucas Cranach)	4·00	2·50

527 Carol Singers

2004. Christmas.

1687	**527**	50c.+5c. multicoloured	75	75

528 Skiing

2004. Sport. Multicoloured.

1688		50c.+5c. Type **528**	75	75
1689		60c.+10c. Running (vert)	95	95
1690		70c.+10c. Swimming	1·10	1·10
1691		€1+25c. Football (vert)	1·70	1·70

529 Tank, Soldiers and Liberation Monument, Schumannseck (Carlo Losch)

2004. Liberation of Luxembourg (1944–45).

1692	**529**	70c. multicoloured	95	55

OFFICIAL STAMPS

1875. Stamps of 1859–72 optd **OFFICIEL**. Roul.

O79	**3**	1c. brown	26·00	35·00
O80		2c. black	26·00	35·00
O81	**4**	10c. lilac	£1900	£1900
O82		12½c. red	£425	£450
O83		20c. brown	35·00	55·00
O84		25c. blue	£225	£150
O85		30c. purple	29·00	70·00
O88b		40c. orange	£250	£250
O87		1f. on 37½c. bistre (No. 37)	£100	23·00

1875. Stamps of 1874–79 optd **OFFICIEL**. Perf.

O 89	**3**	1c. brown	8·00	32·00
O 90		2c. black	10·00	32·00
O 91		4c. green	85·00	£130
O 92		5c. yellow	48·00	70·00
O 93a	**4**	10c. lilac	75·00	80·00
O111		12½c. red	60·00	£100
O 99a		25c. blue	3·00	2·50
O 96		1f. on 37½c. bistre (No. 56)	29·00	40·00

1881. Stamp of 1859 optd **S. P.** Roul.

O116	**3**	40c. orange	32·00	60·00

1881. Stamps of 1874–79 optd **S. P.** Perf.

O121	**3**	1c. brown	23·00	50·00
O122		2c. black	23·00	50·00
O118		4c. green	£140	£170
O123		5c. yellow	70·00	85·00
O124	**4**	10c. lilac	95·00	£140
O125		12½c. red	£110	£140
O126		20c. brown	60·00	£100
O127		25c. blue	60·00	£100
O128		30c. red	70·00	£100
O120		1f. on 37½c. bistre (No. 56)	30·00	42·00

1882. Stamps of 1882 optd **S. P.**

O141	**7**	1c. grey	30	40
O142		2c. brown	30	40
O143		4c. olive	35	50
O144		5c. green	35	55
O145		10c. red	16·00	15·00
O146		12½c. blue	2·50	4·00
O147		20c. orange	2·50	4·00
O148		25c. blue	17·00	23·00
O149		30c. olive	5·25	8·50
O150		50c. brown	1·00	2·25
O151		1f. lilac	1·00	2·75
O152		5f. orange	16·00	30·00

1891. Stamps of 1891 optd **S. P.**

O188	**8**	10c. red	30	45
O189		12½c. green	6·00	6·00
O190		20c. orange	9·50	7·00
O191a		25c. blue	30	40
O192		30c. green	6·50	6·75
O193a		37½c. green	6·00	7·50
O194		50c. brown	5·00	8·25
O195a		1f. purple	5·00	10·00
O196		2½f. black	38·00	60·00
O197		5f. lake	29·00	55·00

1898. Stamps of 1895 optd **S. P.**

O213	**9**	1c. grey	1·90	1·75
O214		2c. brown	1·40	1·50
O215		4c. bistre	1·40	1·50
O216		5c. green	3·25	4·00
O217		10c. red	40·00	32·00

1908. Stamps of 1906 optd **Officiel**.

O218	**10**	1c. grey	10	30
O219		2c. brown	10	30
O220		4c. bistre	10	30
O221		5c. green	10	30
O271		5c. mauve	10	30
O222		6c. lilac	10	30
O223		7½c. yellow	25	30
O224		10c. red	30	45
O225		12½c. slate	30	50
O226		15c. brown	40	65
O227		20c. orange	40	65
O228		25c. blue	40	60
O229		30c. olive	4·50	4·50
O230		37½c. green	70	75
O231		50c. brown	1·10	1·40
O232		87½c. blue	1·75	3·25
O233		1f. purple	2·50	3·50
O234		2½f. red	70·00	65·00
O235		5f. purple	65·00	40·00

1915. Stamps of 1914 optd **Officiel**.

O236	**13**	10c. purple	20	60
O237		12½c. green	20	60
O238		15c. brown	20	60
O239		17½c. brown	20	60
O240		25c. blue	20	60
O241		30c. brown	1·40	3·75
O242		35c. blue	25	25
O243		37½c. brown	25	1·00
O244		40c. red	35	95
O245		50c. grey	35	85
O246		62½c. green	35	1·25
O247		87½c. orange	35	1·40
O248		1f. brown	35	1·25
O249		2½f. red	40	2·50
O250		5f. violet	40	3·25

1922. Stamps of 1921 optd **Officiel**.

O251	**17**	2c. brown	15	20
O252		3c. green	15	15
O253		6c. purple	15	30
O272		10c. green	10	30
O273		15c. green	10	30
O274		15c. orange	10	30
O256		20c. orange	25	40
O275		20c. green	10	30
O257		25c. green	25	40
O258		30c. red	25	40
O259		40c. orange	25	40
O260		50c. blue	30	55
O276		50c. red	15	35
O261		75c. red	30	55
O277		75c. blue	20	45
O266		80c. black	25	50
O263	**18**	1f. red	50	1·50
O278		1f. blue	40	1·25
O267	–	2f. blue	40	1·75
O279	–	2f. brown	1·50	4·75
O269	–	5f. violet	5·00	8·50

1922. Stamps of 1923 optd **Officiel**.

O268b	**28**	3f. blue	40	1·40
O270	**26**	10f. black	9·50	25·00

1926. Stamps of 1926 optd **Officiel**.

O280	**32**	5c. mauve	10	20
O281		10c. green	10	20
O298		15c. black	30	95
O282		20c. orange	10	20
O283		25c. green	10	20
O300		25c. brown	35	70
O301		30c. green	30	1·25
O302		30c. violet	40	1·00
O303		35c. violet	40	35
O304		35c. green	40	95
O286		40c. brown	15	25
O287		50c. brown	15	25
O307		60c. green	40	75
O288		65c. brown	15	40
O308		70c. violet	1·90	6·00
O289		75c. red	15	40
O309		75c. brown	40	75
O291		80c. brown	25	45
O292		90c. red	35	65
O293		1f. black	30	50
O312		1f. red	45	1·50
O294		1¼f. blue	15	15
O313		1¼f. yellow	1·40	4·00
O314		1¼f. green	2·50	4·75
O315		1½f. blue	40	1·25
O316		1¾f. blue	45	1·25

1928. Stamp of 1928 optd **Officiel**.

O317	**37**	2f. black	55	1·40

1931. Stamp of 1931 optd **Officiel**.

O318	**43**	20f. green	2·40	6·50

1934. Stamp of 1934 optd **Officiel**.

O319	**47**	5f. green	1·75	5·00

1935. No. 340 optd **Officiel**.

O341	**52**	10f. green	1·60	6·75

POSTAGE DUE STAMPS

D 12 Arms of Luxembourg

D 77

1907.

D173	**D 12**	5c. black and green	10	20
D174		10c. black and green	85	20
D175		12½c. black and green	30	85
D176		20c. black and green	55	60
D177		25c. black and green	17·00	1·10
D178		50c. black and green	45	3·00
D179		1f. black and green	30	3·25

1920. Surch.

D193	**D 12**	15 on 12½c. blk & grn	2·00	5·25
D194		30 on 25c. black & grn	2·50	7·50

1922.

D221	**D 12**	5c. red and green	10	30
D222		10c. red and green	10	30
D223		20c. red and green	25	30
D224		25c. red and green	30	45
D225		30c. red and green	30	50
D226		35c. red and green	40	65
D227		50c. red and green	40	65
D228		60c. red and green	40	60
D229		70c. red and green	4·50	4·50
D230		75c. red and green	70	75
D231		1f. red and green	1·10	1·40
D232		2f. red and green	1·75	3·25
D233		3f. red and green	2·50	3·50

1946.

D488	**D 77**	5c. green	35	65
D489		10c. green	35	45
D490		20c. green	35	45
D491		30c. green	35	45
D492		50c. green	35	35
D493		70c. green	45	70
D494		75c. green	1·40	30
D495		1f. red	35	30
D496		1f.50 red	35	30
D497		2f. red	45	30
D498		3f. red	70	30
D499		5f. red	1·00	35
D500		10f. red	1·75	3·50
D501		20f. red	3·50	20·00

MACAO Pt. 9; Pt. 17

A former Portuguese territory in China at the mouth of the Canton River.

1884. 1000 reis = 1 milreis.
1894. 78 avos = 1 rupee.
1913. 100 avos = 1 pataca.

1884. "Crown" key-type inscr "MACAU".
10 P 5r. black . . . . 7·75 5·75
2 10r. orange . . . . 11·50 10·50
21 10r. green . . . . 11·00 9·00
12 20r. bistre . . . . 19·00 14·50
27 20r. red . . . . 19·00 17·00
13 25r. red . . . . 11·50 5·50
22 25r. lilac . . . . 11·00 9·25
14 40r. blue . . . . 35·00 32·00
23 40r. buff . . . . 21·00 14·50
15 50r. green . . . . 42·00 34·00
24 50r. blue . . . . 11·50 11·50
31 80r. grey . . . . 37·00 29·00
16 100r. lilac . . . . 19·00 17·00
17 200r. orange . . . . 21·00 17·00
9 300r. brown . . . . 22·00 18·00

1885. "Crown" key type of Macao surch **80 reis** in circle. No gum.
19 P 80r. on 100r. lilac . . . . . 50·00 32·00

1885. "Crown" key type of Macao surch in Reis. With gum (43, 44, 45), no gum (others).
32 P 5r. on 25r. pink . . . . . . 12·50 8·25
43 5r. on 80r. grey . . . . . . 8·25 7·00
46 5r. on 100r. lilac . . . . . . 45·00 37·00
33 10r. on 25r. pink . . . . . . 21·00 13·50
38 10r. on 50r. green . . . . . 70·00 70·00
44 10r. on 80r. grey . . . . . . 24·00 26·00
47 10r. on 200r. orange . . . . 44·00 37·00
35 20r. on 50r. green . . . . . 16·00 10·00
45 20r. on 80r. grey . . . . . . 30·00 21·00
40 40r. on 50r. green . . . . . 60·00 45·00

1885. "Crown" key-type of Macao surch with figure of value only and bar. No gum.
41 P 5 on 25r. red . . . . 30·00 18·00
42a 10 on 50r. green . . . . . . 22·00 16·00

9

1887. Fiscal stamps as **T 9** surch **CORREIO** and new value. No gum.
50 5r. on 10r. green and brown 90·00 80·00
51 5r. on 20r. green and brown 90·00 80·00
52 5r. on 60r. green and brown 90·00 80·00
53 10r. on 10r. green and brown £110 90·00
54 10r. on 60r. green and brown £110 90·00
55 40r. on 20r. green and brown £180 £130

1888. "Embossed" key-type inscr "PROVINCIA DE MACAU".
56 Q 5r. black . . . . 8·50 4·00
57 10r. green . . . . 8·50 6·75
58 20r. red . . . . 14·50 6·75
59 25r. mauve . . . . 14·50 6·75
60 40r. brown . . . . 14·50 6·75
61 50r. blue . . . . 14·50 6·75
62 80r. grey . . . . 17·00 11·50
63 100r. brown . . . . 19·00 12·50
71 200r. lilac . . . . 30·00 17·00
72 300r. orange . . . . 29·00 17·00

1892. No. 71 surch **30 30**.
73 Q 30 on 200r. lilac . . . . . . 30·00 23·00

1894. "Embossed" key-type of Macao surch **PROVISORIO**, value and Chinese characters. No gum.
75b Q 1a. on 5r. black . . . . . 7·25 3·75
76 3a. on 20r. red . . . . . . 10·00 4·25
77 4a. on 25r. violet . . . . . 12·00 7·00
89 5a. on 30 on 200r. lilac (No. 73) . . . . 60·00 55·00
78 6a. on 40r. brown . . . . 10·00 7·00
79 8a. on 50r. blue . . . . . 27·00 11·50
80 13a. on 80r. grey . . . . . 13·00 10·00
81 16a. on 100r. brown . . . . 18·00 8·25
82 31a. on 200r. lilac . . . . 55·00 32·00
83 47a. on 300r. orange . . . 60·00 17·00

1894. "Figures" key-type inscr "MACAU".
91 R 5r. yellow . . . . 5·00 2·50
92 10r. mauve . . . . 5·00 2·50
93 15r. brown . . . . 6·00 4·00
94 20r. lilac . . . . 10·00 4·00
95 25r. green . . . . 15·00 9·25
96 50r. blue . . . . 22·00 9·25
97 75r. pink . . . . 40·00 28·00
98 80r. green . . . . 27·00 18·00
99 100r. brown on buff . . . . 28·00 14·50
100 150r. red on pink . . . . . 32·00 14·50
101 200r. blue on blue . . . . 45·00 19·00
102 300r. blue on brown . . . 55·00 19·00

1898. As Vasco da Gama types of Portugal but inscr "MACAU".
104 ½a. green . . . . 3·25 2·50
105 1a. red . . . . 3·25 2·50
106 2a. purple . . . . 3·25 2·50
107 4a. green . . . . 4·00 2·50
108 8a. blue . . . . 7·00 3·75
109 12a. brown . . . . 8·00 4·25
110 16a. brown . . . . 8·00 3·75
111 24a. brown . . . . 11·00 7·25

1898. "King Carlos" key-type inscr "MACAU". Name and value in black.
112 S ½a. grey . . . . 1·40 75
113 1a. yellow . . . . 1·40 75
114 2a. green . . . . 1·60 55
115 2½a. brown . . . . 2·50 1·40
116 3a. lilac . . . . 2·50 1·40
174 3a. grey . . . . 3·25 1·60
117 4a. green . . . . 4·25 2·50
175 4a. red . . . . 3·00 1·60
176 5a. brown . . . . 4·00 2·50
177 6a. brown . . . . 4·25 3·00
119 8a. blue . . . . 4·75 2·50
178 8a. brown . . . . 5·00 2·50
120 10a. blue . . . . 5·00 3·25
121 12a. pink . . . . 7·00 5·75
179 12a. purple . . . . 17·00 11·00
122 13a. mauve . . . . 8·50 6·00
180 13a. lilac . . . . 8·75 5·50
123 15a. green . . . . 17·00 11·50
124 16a. blue on blue . . . . . 8·00 5·75
181 18a. brown on pink . . . . 16·00 13·00
125 20a. brown on cream . . . 9·50 8·25
126 24a. brown on yellow . . . 12·50 6·75
127 31a. purple . . . . 15·00 6·75
182 31a. purple on pink . . . . 15·00 13·50
128 47a. blue on pink . . . . . 24·00 11·00
183 47a. blue on yellow . . . . 25·00 22·00
129 78a. black on blue . . . . 29·00 14·00

1900. "King Carlos" key-type of Macao surch **PROVISORIO** and new value.
132 S 5 on 13a. mauve . . . . . 4·50 3·75
133 10 on 16a. blue on blue . . . 6·00 4·00
134 15 on 24a. brown on yellow 14·00 4·00
135 20 on 31a. purple . . . . . 18·00 4·00

1902. Various types of Macao surch.
138 Q 6a. on 5r. black . . . . . 3·75 2·50
142 R 6a. on 5r. yellow . . . . . 3·50 2·50
136 P 6a. on 10r. yellow . . . . 12·00 7·00
137 6a. on 10r. green . . . . . 8·00 5·50
139 Q 6a. on 10r. green . . . . . 3·75 2·50
143 R 6a. on 10r. mauve . . . . 8·00 5·00
144 6a. on 15r. brown . . . . . 8·00 9·25
145 6a. on 25r. green . . . . . 4·75 3·25
140 Q 6a. on 40r. brown . . . . . 3·75 2·50
146 R 6a. on 80r. green . . . . . 3·50 2·50
148 6a. on 100r. brown on buff 11·00 3·50
149 6a. on 200r. blue on blue 3·50 2·50
151 V 18a. on 2½r. brown . . . . 4·75 4·00
153 Q 18a. on 20r. red . . . . . 12·00 4·25
162 R 18a. on 20r. lilac . . . . . 12·00 4·75
154 Q 18a. on 25r. mauve . . . . 60·00 28·00
163 R 18a. on 50r. blue . . . . . 12·00 4·75
165 18a. on 75r. pink . . . . . 12·00 4·75
155 Q 18a. on 80r. grey . . . . . 80·00 44·00
156 18a. on 100r. brown . . . . 9·25 8·25
166 R 18a. on 150r. red on pink 8·75 4·75
158 Q 18a. on 200r. lilac . . . . 70·00 45·00
160 18a. on 300r. orange . . . 15·00 7·00
167 R 18a. on 300r. blue on brn 12·00 6·00

1902. "King Carlos" type of Macao optd **PROVISORIO**.
168 S 2a. green . . . . 8·25 4·75
169 4a. green . . . . 8·25 4·75
170 8a. blue . . . . 8·25 4·75
171 10a. blue . . . . 8·75 5·50
172 12a. pink . . . . 14·50 8·25

1905. No. 179 surch **10 AVOS** and bar.
184 S 10a. on 12a. purple . . . . 15·00 9·75

1910. "Due" key-type of Macao, but with words "PORTEADO" and "RECEBER" cancelled.
185 W ½a. green . . . . 7·50 5·25
186 1a. green . . . . 7·50 5·25
187 2a. grey . . . . 7·50 5·25

1911. "King Carlos" key-type of Macao optd **REPUBLICA**.
188 S ½a. grey 70 60
189 1a. orange 70 60
190 2a. green 70 60
191 3a. grey 70 60
192 4a. red . . . . 2·50 2·30
193 5a. brown . . . . 2·50 1·90
194 6a. brown . . . . 2·50 1·90
195 8a. brown . . . . 2·50 1·90
196 10a. blue . . . . 2·50 1·90
197 13a. lilac . . . . 3·75 2·00
198 16a. blue on blue . . . . . 3·75 2·00
199 18a. brown on pink . . . . 8·50 5·75
200 20a. brown on cream . . . 8·50 5·75
201 31a. purple on pink . . . . 8·50 5·75
202 47a. blue on yellow . . . . 12·00 9·00
203 78a. black on blue . . . . 20·00 13·00

30

32

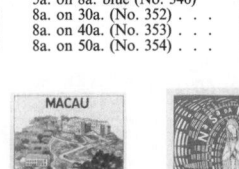

1911. Fiscal stamp surch **POSTAL 1 AVO** and bar.
204 30 1a. on 5r. brown, yellow and black . . . . 7·50 3·75

1911. Stamps bisected and surch.
205 S 2a. on half of 4a. red (No. 175) . . . . 20·00 10·00
206 5a. on half of 10a. blue (No. 120) £160 £160
207 5a. on half of 10a. blue (No. 171) . . . . 65·00 60·00

1911.
210 32 1a. black £325 £325
211 2a. black £350 £350

1913. Provisionals of 1902 surch in addition with new value and bars over old value and optd **REPUBLICA**.
212 R 2a. on 18a. on 20r. lilac (No. 162) . . . . 6·00 2·50
213 2a. on 18a. on 50r. blue (No. 163) . . . . 6·00 2·50
215 2a. on 18a. on 75r. pink (No. 165) . . . . 7·00 2·50
216 2a. on 18a. on 150r. red on pink (No. 166) . . . . 7·00 2·50

1913. Provisionals of 1902 and 1905 optd **REPUBLICA**.
218 Q 6a. on 5r. (No. 138) . . . . 4·25 3·75
284 R 6a. on 5r. (No. 142) . . . . 2·50 2·10
217 P 6a. on 10r. (No. 137) . . . 13·00 8·75
285 Q 6a. on 10r. (No. 139) . . . 9·25 8·75
286 R 6a. on 10r. (No. 143) . . . 4·75 4·75
287 6a. on 15r. (No. 144) . . . 4·25 3·25
288 6a. on 25r. (No. 145) . . . 4·50 4·00
220 Q 6a. on 40r. (No. 140) . . . 4·50 3·25
289 R 6a. on 80r. (No. 146) . . . 4·50 3·25
291 6a. on 100r. (No. 148) . . . 11·00 8·25
292 6a. on 200r. (No. 149) . . . 3·00 1·70
281 S 8a. (No. 170) . . . . . . 2·10 1·80
282 10a. (No. 171) . . . . . . 2·10 1·80
283 10a. on 12a. (No. 184) . . . 2·10 1·80
293 V 18a. on 2½r. (No. 151) . . . 1·90 1·70
229 Q 18a. on 20r. (No. 153) . . . 7·25 5·25
295 R 18a. on 20r. (No. 162) . . . 4·25 3·25
296 18a. on 50r. (No. 163) . . . 4·75 3·75
298 18a. on 75r. (No. 165) . . . 4·75 3·75
230 Q 18a. on 100r. (No. 156) . . 35·00 27·00
299 R 18a. on 150r. (No. 166) . . 4·75 3·75
233 Q 18a. on 300r. (No. 160) . . 13·50 10·50
300 R 18a. on 300r. (No. 167) . . 9·75 5·50

1913. Stamps of 1911 issue surch.
252 S ½a. on 5a. brown . . . . . 3·75 2·50
255 1a. on 13a. lilac . . . . . 4·75 3·75
253 4a. on 8a. brown . . . . . 4·75 3·75

1913. Vasco da Gama stamps of Macao optd **REPUBLICA**, and the 12a. surch **10 A.**
256 ½a. green . . . . 2·50 1·50
257 1a. red . . . . 4·25 1·60
258 2a. purple . . . . 4·25 1·60
259 4a. green . . . . 3·75 1·60
260 8a. blue . . . . 4·25 2·00
261 10a. on 12a. brown . . . . 12·00 4·00
262 16a. brown . . . . 6·00 2·50
263 24a. brown . . . . 8·00 3·25

1913. "Ceres" key-type inscr "MACAU".
264 U ½a. green . . . . 1·40 70
310 1a. black . . . . 1·40 70
311 1½a. green . . . . 1·10 60
280 2a. green . . . . 1·40 70
313 3a. orange . . . . 3·25 2·30
267 4a. red . . . . 2·50 1·50
315 4a. yellow . . . . 2·75 2·50
268 5a. brown . . . . 3·00 2·00
269 6a. violet . . . . 3·00 2·00
270 8a. brown . . . . 3·00 2·00
271 10a. blue . . . . 3·00 2·00
272 12a. brown . . . . 3·00 2·00
320 14a. mauve . . . . 8·25 8·50
321 16a. grey . . . . 5·50 4·25
274 20a. red . . . . 7·75 5·25
322 24a. green . . . . 8·25 7·00
323 32a. brown . . . . 11·50 9·75
275 40a. purple . . . . 8·00 5·25
324 56a. pink . . . . 18·00 15·00
276 58a. brown on green . . . 14·50 11·00
325 72a. brown . . . . 32·00 11·50
277 76a. brown on pink . . . . 15·00 12·50
278 1p. orange on orange . . . 19·00 15·00
326 1p. orange . . . . 40·00 23·00
279 3p. green on blue . . . . . 65·00 47·00
327 3p. turquoise . . . . £100 80·00
328 5p. red £160 £120

1919. Surch.
301 U ½a. on 5a. brown (No. 268) 32·00 25·00
330 1a. on 24a. grn (No. 322) 2·75 2·30
302 R 2 on 6a. on 25r. green (No. 288) . . . . £150 80·00
303 2 on 6a. on 80r. green (No. 289) . . . . 46·00 36·00
304 S 2a. on 6a. (No. 177) . . . 28·00 25·00
331 U 2a. on 32a. (No. 323) . . . 2·75 2·30
332 4a. on 12a. (No. 272) . . . 2·75 2·30
329 5a. on 6a. violet (No. 269) 3·75 3·50
334 7a. on 8a. brn (No. 270) . . 16·00 10·00
335 12a. on 14a. (No. 320) . . . 3·75 3·25
336 15a. on 16a. (No. 321) . . . 3·75 3·75
337 20a. on 56a. pink (No. 324) 32·00 23·00

50 "Portugal" and Galeasse

1934.
338 50 ½a. brown 35 35
339 1a. brown 35 35
340 2a. green 60 55
341 3a. mauve 60 55
342 4a. black 70 65
343 5a. grey 70 65
344 6a. brown 70 65
345 7a. red 95 85
346 8a. blue 95 85
347 10a. red . . . . 1·50 90
348 12a. blue . . . . 1·50 90
349 14a. green . . . . 1·50 90
350 15a. purple . . . . 1·50 90
351 20a. orange . . . . 1·50 90
352 30a. green . . . . 4·00 2·75
353 40a. violet . . . . 4·00 2·50
354 50a. brown . . . . 7·50 4·75
355 1p. blue . . . . 18·00 10·00
356 2p. brown . . . . 25·00 15·00
357 3p. green . . . . 40·00 22·00
358 5p. mauve . . . . 85·00 29·00

1936. Air. Stamps of 1934 optd **Aviao** and with Greek characters or surch also.
359 40 2a. green . . . . 3·00 1·80
360 3a. mauve . . . . 3·00 1·80
361 5a. on 6a. brown . . . . . 3·00 1·80
362 7a. red . . . . 3·00 1·80
363 8a. blue . . . . 5·75 4·25
364 15a. purple . . . . 17·00 9·50

54 Vasco da Gama

56 Airplane over Globe

1938. Name and value in black.
365 54 1a. green (postage) 60 50
366 2a. brown 60 50
367 3a. violet 60 50
368 4a. green 60 50
369 – 5a. red 60 50
370 – 6a. grey . . . . 1·50 95
371 – 8a. purple . . . . 1·50 95
372 – 10a. mauve . . . . 2·00 1·10
373 – 12a. red . . . . 2·00 1·10
374 – 15a. orange . . . . 2·00 1·10
375 – 20a. blue . . . . 3·25 1·70
376 – 40a. black . . . . 6·00 2·40
377 – 50a. brown . . . . 6·00 2·40
378 – 1p. red . . . . 18·00 7·25
379 – 2p. green . . . . 32·00 11·00
380 – 3p. blue . . . . 50·00 18·00
381 – 5p. brown . . . . 85·00 22·00

382 56 1a. red (air) 45 40
383 2a. violet 55 40
384 3a. orange 55 40
385 5a. blue . . . . 1·30 75
386 10a. red . . . . 2·20 1·20
387 20a. green . . . . 3·50 2·00
388 50a. brown . . . . 6·00 2·75
389 70a. red . . . . 11·50 5·00
390 1p. mauve . . . . 22·00 7·25

DESIGNS: Nos. 369/71, Mousinho de Albuquerque; 372/4, Henry the Navigator; 375/7, Dam; 378/81, Afonso de Albuquerque.

1940. Surch.
391 50 1a. on 6a. brown (No. 344) 5·25 4·25
394 2a. on 6a. brown (No. 344) 2·30 2·20
395 3a. on 6a. brown (No. 344) 2·30 2·10
401 – 3a. on 6a. grey (No. 370) 50·00 41·00
396 50 5a. on 7a. red (No. 345) 2·30 2·20
397 5a. on 8a. blue (No. 346) 2·30 2·20
398 8a. on 30a. (No. 352) . . . 5·00 3·00
399 8a. on 40a. (No. 353) . . . 5·00 3·00
400 8a. on 50a. (No. 354) . . . 5·50 4·75

61 Mountain Fort

62 Our Lady of Fatima

1948.
410 – 1a. brown and orange . . 1·40 25
427 – 1a. violet and pink . . . . 2·10 85
411 61 2a. purple 85 25
428 2a. brown and yellow . . . 2·10 85
412 – 3a. purple . . . . 2·50 70
429 – 3a. orange . . . . 3·25 85
413 – 8a. red . . . . 3·00 1·00
430 – 8a. grey . . . . 2·00 85
414 – 10a. purple . . . . 3·50 85
431 – 10a. brown and orange . . 4·75 1·10
415 – 20a. blue . . . . 6·00 1·60
416 – 30a. grey . . . . 6·50 1·20
432 – 30a. blue . . . . 10·00 2·50
417 – 50a. brown and buff . . . 8·00 1·80
433 – 50a. olive and green . . . 22·00 2·50
418 – 1p. green . . . . 80·00 11·50
419 – 1p. blue . . . . 85·00
434 – 1p. brown . . . . 43·00 7·75
420 – 2p. red . . . . 55·00 14·50
421 – 3p. green . . . . 80·00 40·00
422 – 5p. violet . . . . 90·00 17·00

DESIGNS—HORIZ: 1a. Macao house; 3a. Port of Macao; 8a. Praia Grande Bay; 10a. Leal Senado Sq; 20a. Sao Jerome Hill; 30a. Street scene, Macao; 50a. Relief of goddess of Ma (allegory); 5p. Forest road. VERT: 1p. Cerco Gateway; 2p. Barra Pagoda, Ma-Cok-Miu; 3p. Post Office.

1948. Honouring the Statue of Our Lady of Fatima.
423 62 8a. red . . . . 15·00 4·25

64 Globe and Letter

65 Bells and Dove

1949. 75th Anniv of U.P.U.
424 **64** 32a. purple . . . . 80·00 19·00

1950. Holy Year.
425 **65** 32a. black . . . . 10·00 3·75
426 – 50a. red . . . . 13·00 5·00
DESIGN: 50a. Angel holding candelabra.

66 Arms and Dragon

1950.
435 **66** 1a. yellow on cream . . . 1·40 90
436 2a. green on green . . . . 1·40 90
437 10a. purple on green . . . 1·40 90
438 10a. mauve on green . . . 1·40 90

67 F. Mendes Pinto

68 Junk

1951.
439 **67** 1a. indigo and blue 40 20
440 – 2a. brown and green . . . 70 20
441 – 3a. green and light green 1·40 25
442 – 6a. violet and blue . . . . 2·75 30
443 – 10a. brown and orange . . 4·00 95
444 **67** 20a. purple and light purple . . . . 12·00 2·30
445 – 30a. brown and green . . . 16·00 2·40
446 – 50a. red and orange . . . 32·00 10·50
DESIGNS: 2, 10a. St. Francis Xavier; 3, 50a. J. Alvaras; 6, 30a. L. de Camoens.

1951.
447 – 1p. ultramarine and blue 26·00 2·50
448 – 3p. black and blue . . . . 85·00 6·75
449 **68** 5p. brown and orange . . £100 22·00
DESIGNS—HORIZ: 1p. Sampan. VERT: 3p. Junk.

69 Our Lady of Fatima

71 St. Raphael Hospital

1951. Termination of Holy Year.
450 **69** 60a. mauve and pink . . . 20·00 6·00

1952. 1st Tropical Medicine Congress, Lisbon.
451 **71** 6a. lilac and black . . . . 5·75 3·50

72 St. Francis Xavier Statue

73 The Virgin

1952. 400th Death Anniv of St. Francis Xavier.
452 **72** 3a. black on cream . . . . 1·20 50
453 – 16a. brown on buff . . . . 4·00 1·50
454 – 40a. black on blue . . . . 8·25 3·25
DESIGNS: 16a. Miraculous Arm of St. Francis; 40a. Tomb of St. Francis.

1953. Missionary Art Exhibition.
455 **73** 8a. brown and drab . . . 1·90 45
456 10a. blue and brown . . . 5·00 1·80
457 50a. green and drab . . . 14·00 3·00

74 Honeysuckle

75 Portuguese Stamp of 1853 and Arms of Portuguese Overseas Provinces

1953. Indigenous Flowers.
458 **74** 1a. yellow, green and red 40 40
459 – 3a. purple, green and yellow 40 40
460 – 5a. red, green and brown 70 75
461 – 10a. multicoloured 70 80
462 – 16a. yellow, green & brown 70 80
463 – 30a. pink, brown and green 2·30 2·75
464 – 39a. multicoloured . . . . 2·40 2·75
465 – 1p. yellow, green and purple . . . . 5·50 3·00
466 – 3p. red, brown and grey 14·00 5·25
467 – 5p. yellow, green and red 25·00 7·75
FLOWERS: 3a. Myosotis; 5a. Dragon claw; 10a. Nunflower; 16a. Narcissus; 30a. Peach blossom; 39a. Lotus blossom; 1p. Chrysanthemum; 3p. Plum blossom; 5p. Tangerine blossom.

1954. Portuguese Stamp Centenary.
468 **75** 10a. multicoloured . . . . 8·00 2·00

76 Father M. de Nobrega and View of Sao Paulo

77 Map of Macao

1954. 4th Centenary of Sao Paulo.
469 **76** 39a. multicoloured . . . . 6·00 5·50

1956. Map multicoloured. Values in red, inscr in brown. Colours given are of the backgrounds.
470 **77** 1a. drab 45 30
471 3a. slate 45 30
472 5a. brown 45 30
473 10a. buff . . . . 1·90 75
474 30a. blue . . . . 2·40 75
475 40a. green . . . . 3·25 1·50
476 90a. grey . . . . 8·50 2·75
477 1p.50 pink . . . . 14·00 3·00

78 Exhibition Emblem and Atomic Emblems

79 "Cinnamomum camphora"

1958. Brussels International Exhibition.
478 **78** 70a. multicoloured . . . . 5·00 1·90

1958. 6th International Congress of Tropical Medicine.
479 **79** 20a. multicoloured . . . . 5·25 3·50

80 Globe girdled by Signs of the Zodiac

81 Boeing 707 over Ermida da Penha

1960. 500th Death Anniv of Prince Henry the Navigator.
480 **80** 2p. multicoloured . . . . 9·50 2·75

1960. Air. Multicoloured.
481 50a. Praia Grande Bay . . . 2·25 55
482 76a. Type **81** . . . . 4·00 55
483 3p. Macao . . . . 4·50 1·50
484 5p. Mong Ha . . . . 16·00 1·40
485 10p. Shore of Praia Grande Bay . . . . 23·00 2·20

82 Hockey

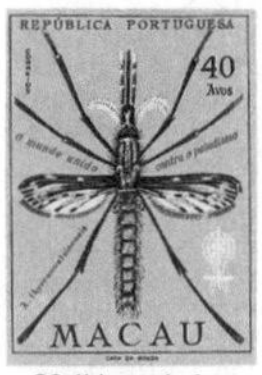

83 "Anopheles hycranus sinensis"

1962. Sports. Multicoloured.
486 10a. Type **82** 30 25
487 16a. Wrestling . . . . 2·75 1·80
488 20a. Table tennis . . . . . . 2·00 1·60
489 50a. Motor cycle racing . . . 3·50 2·30
490 1p.20 Relay racing . . . . . 9·00 4·00
491 2p.50 Badminton . . . . . . 20·00 7·25

1962. Malaria Eradication.
492 **83** 40a. multicoloured . . . . 5·50 2·75

84 Bank Building

85 I.T.U. Emblem and St. Gabriel

1964. Centenary of National Overseas Bank.
493 **84** 20a. multicoloured . . . . 8·50 3·00

1965. Centenary of I.T.U.
494 **85** 10a. multicoloured . . . . 4·25 1·00

86 Infante Dom Henrique Academy and Visconde de Sao Januario Hospital

87 Drummer, 1548

1966. 40th Anniv of Portuguese National Revolution.
495 **86** 10a. multicoloured . . . . 6·00 1·80

1966. Portuguese Military Uniforms. Mult.
496 10a. Type **87** . . . . 1·00 35
497 15a. Soldier, 1548 . . . . . 2·00 35
498 20a. Arquebusier, 1649 . . . 2·00 35
499 40a. Infantry officer, 1783 . . 3·50 1·00
500 50a. Infantryman, 1783 . . . 3·75 1·40
501 60a. Infantryman, 1902 . . . 5·00 1·40
502 1p. Infantryman, 1903 . . . 7·50 2·00
503 3p. Infantryman, 1904 . . . 17·00 8·00

88 O. E. Carmo and Patrol Boat "Vega"

89 Arms of Pope Paul VI, and "Golden Rose"

1967. Centenary of Military Naval Assn. Mult.
504 10a. Type **88** . . . . 1·30 85
505 20a. Silva Junior and sail frigate "Don Fernando" 5·50 2·20

1967. 50th Anniv of Fatima Apparitions.
506 **89** 50a. multicoloured . . . . 5·00 1·50

90 Cabral Monument, Lisbon

91 Adm. Gago Coutinho with Sextant

1968. 500th Birth Anniv of Pedro Cabral (explorer). Multicoloured.
507 20a. Type **90** . . . . 3·50 1·00
508 70a. Cabral's statue, Belmonte . . . . 5·00 2·20

1969. Birth Centenary of Admiral Gago Coutinho.
509 **91** 20a. multicoloured . . . . 3·25 1·40

92 Church and Convent of Our Lady of the Reliquary, Vidigueira

93 L. A. Rebello da Silva

1969. 500th Birth Anniv of Vasco da Gama (explorer).
510 **92** 1p. multicoloured . . . . 8·00 1·20

1969. Centenary of Overseas Administrative Reforms.
511 **93** 90a. multicoloured . . . . 3·25 2·20

94 Bishop D. Belchoir Carneiro

95 Facade of Mother Church, Golega

1969. 400th Anniv of Misericordia Monastery, Macao.
512 **94** 50a. multicoloured . . . . 3·25 95

1969. 500th Birth Anniv of King Manoel I.
513 **95** 30a. multicoloured . . . . 5·50 95

96 Marshal Carmona

97 Dragon Mask

1970. Birth Centenary of Marshal Carmona.
514 **96** 5a. multicoloured . . . . 2·00 95

1971. Chinese Carnival Masks. Multicoloured.
515 5a. Type **97** . . . . 1·10 40
516 10a. Lion mask . . . . . . 2·00 40

98 Portuguese Traders at the Chinese Imperial Court

1972. 400th Anniv of Camoens' "The Lusiads" (epic poem).
517 **98** 20a. multicoloured . . . . 8·00 4·50

99 Hockey

1972. Olympic Games, Munich.
518 **99** 50a. multicoloured . . . . 2·50 95

100 Fairey IIID Seaplane "Santa Cruz" arriving at Rio de Janeiro

1972. 50th Anniv of First Flight from Lisbon to Rio de Janeiro.
519 **100** 5p. multicoloured . . . . 14·00 7·00

101 Lyre Emblem and Theatre Facade

102 W.M.O. Emblem

1972. Centenary of Pedro V Theatre, Macao.

520	**101**	2p. multicoloured	9·00	2·40

1973. Centenary of W.M.O.

521	**102**	20a. multicoloured . . .	2·75	1·70

103 Visconde de Sao Januario

104 Chinnery (self-portrait)

1974. Centenary of Visconde de Sao Januario Hospital. Multicoloured.

522		15a. Type **103**	95	35
523		60a. Hospital buildings of 1874 and 1974	3·50	95

1974. Birth Bicent of George Chinnery (painter).

524	**104**	30a. multicoloured . . .	3·00	1·20

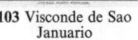

105 Macao–Taipa Bridge

1975. Inauguration of Macao–Taipa Bridge. Multicoloured.

525		20a. Type **105**	1·40	45
526		2p.20 View of Bridge from below	8·00	2·00

106 Man waving Banner

1975. 1st Anniv of Portuguese Revolution.

527	**106**	10a. multicoloured . . .	2·30	2·75
528		1p. multicoloured	10·00	6·25

107 Pou Chai Pagoda

1976. Pagodas. Multicoloured.

529		10p. Type **107**	12·50	5·75
530		20p. Tin Hau Pagoda	21·00	8·25

108 Symbolic Figure

1977. Legislative Assembly.

531	**108**	5a. blue, dp blue & black	7·00	2·50
532		2p. brown and black . . .	37·00	10·00
533		5p. yellow, green and black	26·00	9·75

1979. Nos. 462, 464, 469, 482, 523 and 526 surch.

536	–	10a. on 16a. yellow, green and brown	8·25	4·75
537	–	30a. on 39a. multicoloured	9·50	4·75
538	76	30a. on 39a. multicoloured	37·00	25·00
539	–	30a. on 60a. multicoloured	6·75	5·25
540	81	70a. on 76a. multicoloured	34·00	8·75
541	–	2p. on 2p.20 multicoloured	8·25	7·25

111 Camoes and Macao Harbour

113 Buddha and Macao Cathedral

1981. 400th Death Anniv (1980) of Camoes (Portuguese poet).

542	**111**	10a. multicoloured . . .	35	35
543		30a. multicoloured . . .	55	35
544		1p. multicoloured	1·60	1·40
545		3p. multicoloured	3·75	2·10

1981. Transcultural Psychiatry Symposium.

547	**113**	15a. multicoloured . . .	65	30
548		40a. multicoloured . . .	65	40
549		50a. multicoloured . . .	1·10	65
550		60a. multicoloured . . .	1·10	65
551		1p. multicoloured	1·90	90
552		2p.20 multicoloured . . .	4·50	1·80

115 Health Services Buildings

1982. Buildings.

554	–	10a. grey, blue and yellow	15	15
555	–	20a. black, green & lt grn	15	15
556	**115**	30a. green, grey and stone	20	20
557	–	40a. yellow, lt green & grn	25	20
558	–	60a. orange, chocolate and brown	45	15
559	–	80a. pink, green & brown	45	15
560	–	90a. purple, blue and red	75	30
561	–	1p. multicoloured	60	55
562	–	1p.50 yellow, brn & grey	1·10	45
563	–	2p. purple, ultramarine and blue	1·60	95
564	–	2p.50 ultramarine, pink and blue	1·90	1·20
565	–	3p. yellow, green and olive	1·90	95
566	–	7p.50 lilac, blue and red	5·50	2·00
567	–	10p. grey, lilac and mauve	6·50	3·25
568	–	15p. yellow, brown and red	9·50	4·25

DESIGNS: 10a. Social Welfare Institute; 20a. Holy House of Mercy; 40a. Guia lighthouse; 60a. St. Lawrence's Church; 80a. St. Joseph's Seminary; 90a. Pedro V Theatre; 1p. Cerco city gate; 1p.50, St. Domenico's Church; 2p. Luis de Camoes Museum; 2p.50, Ruins of St. Paul's Church; 3p. Palace of St. Sancha (Governor's residence); 7p.50, Senate House; 10p. Schools Welfare Service building; 15p. Barracks of the Moors (headquarters of Port Captaincy and Maritime Police).

116 Heng Ho (Moon goddess)

1982. Autumn Festival. Multicoloured.

569		40a. Type **116**	25	15
570		1p. Decorated gourds	95	40
571		2p. Paper lantern	1·30	1·10
572		5p. Warrior riding lion . . .	3·25	2·30

117 Aerial View of Macao, Taipa and Coloane Islands

118 "Switchboard Operators" (Lou Sok Man)

1982. Macao's Geographical Situation. Mult.

573		50a. Type **117**	55	35
574		3p. Map of South China . .	1·80	1·90

1983. World Communications Year. Children's Drawings. Multicoloured.

575		60a. Type **118**	35	25
576		3p. Postman and pillar box (Lai Sok Pek)	2·00	1·60
577		6p. Globe with methods of communication (Loi Chak Keong)	4·00	2·75

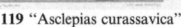

119 "Asclepias curassavica"

120 Galleon and Map of Macao (left)

1983. Medicinal Plants. Multicoloured.

578		20a. Type **119**	55	50
579		40a. "Acanthus ilicifolius" . .	95	50
580		60a. "Melastoma sanguineum"	1·20	1·00
581		70a. Indian lotus ("Nelumbo nucifera")	1·80	1·20
582		1p.50 "Bombax malabaricum"	3·50	2·10
583		2p.50 "Hibiscus mutabilis"	6·50	4·00
MS584		143 × 90 mm. Nos. 578/83 (sold at 6p.50)	38·00	22·00

1983. 16th Century Portuguese Discoveries. Multicoloured.

585		4p. Type **120**	2·75	1·70
586		4p. Galleon, astrolabe and map of Macao (right) . . .	2·75	1·70

Nos. 585/6 were printed together, se-tenant, forming a composite design.

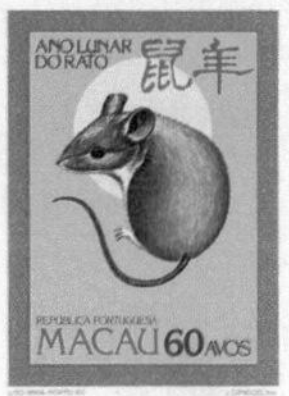

121 Rat

122 Detail of First Macao Stamp, 1884

1984. New Year. "Year of the Rat".

587	**121**	60a. multicoloured . . .	4·75	4·25

1984. Centenary of Macao Stamps.

588	**122**	40a. black and red . . .	45	25
589		3p. black and red	2·00	1·30
590		5p. black and brown . . .	3·50	2·10
MS591		116 × 139 mm. Nos. 588/90	13·50	11·00

123 Jay

1984. "Ausipex 84" International Stamp Exhibition, Melbourne. Birds. Multicoloured.

592		30a. White-throated and river kingfishers	60	25
593		40a. Type **123**	75	30
594		50a. Japanese white-eye . . .	1·00	35
595		70a. Hoopoe	1·30	55
596		2p.50 Pekin robin	4·00	1·80
597		6p. Mallard	9·00	2·75

124 Hok Lou T'eng

1984. "Philakorea 84" International Stamp Exhibition, Seoul. Fishing Boats. Multicoloured.

598		20a. Type **124**	15	15
599		60a. Tai Tong	40	30
600		2p. Tai Mei Chai	1·50	1·00
601		5p. Ch'at Pong T'o	3·50	2·75

125 Ox and Moon

126 Open Hand with Stylized Doves

1985. New Year. Year of the Ox.

602	**125**	1p. multicoloured	3·75	3·75

1985. International Youth Year. Multicoloured.

603		2p.50 Type **126**	1·40	95
604		3p. Open hands and plants	2·10	1·30

127 Pres. Eanes

1985. Visit of President Ramalho Eanes of Portugal.

605	**127**	1p.50 multicoloured . . .	1·30	60

128 Riverside Scene

129 "Euploea midamus"

1985. 25th Anniv of Luis de Camoes Museum. Paintings by Cheng Chi Yun. Multicoloured.

606		2p.50 Type **128**	3·50	1·00
607		2p.50 Man on seat and boy filling jar from river . . .	3·50	1·00
608		2p.50 Playing harp in summerhouse	3·50	1·00
609		2p.50 Three men by river . .	3·50	1·00

1985. World Tourism Day. Butterflies. Mult.

610		30a. Type **129**	35	15
611		50a. Great orange-tip	35	20
612		70a. "Lethe confusa"	55	25
613		2p. Purple sapphire	1·30	90
614		4p. "Euthalia phemius seitzi"	2·50	1·40
615		7p.50 Common birdwing . .	4·75	2·40
MS616		95 × 120 mm. Nos. 610/15	22·00	14·00

130 Tou (sailing barge)

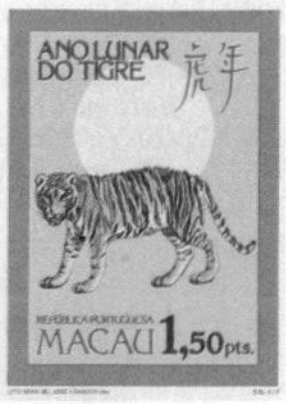

131 Tiger and Moon

1985. "Italia '85" International Stamp Exhibition, Rome. Cargo Boats. Multicoloured.

617		50a. Type **130**	35	20
618		70a. "Veng Seng Lei" (motor junk)	45	30
619		1p. "Tong Heng Long No. 2" (motor junk) . . .	60	45
620		6p. "Fong Vong San" (container ship)	3·50	1·70

1986. New Year. Year of the Tiger.

621	**131**	1p.50 multicoloured . . .	1·80	1·00

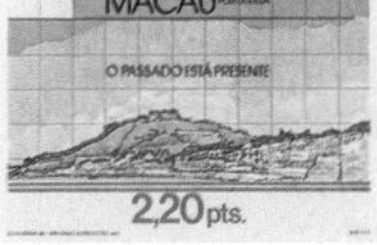

132 View of Macao

133 Suo-na

1986. Macao, "the Past is still Present".

622	**132**	2p.20 multicoloured . . .	1·40	90

1986. "Ameripex '86" International Stamp Exn, Chicago. Musical Instruments. Multicoloured.

623		20a. Type **133**	15	15
624		50a. Sheng (pipes)	35	25
625		60a. Er-hu (bowed instrument)	35	25
626		70a. Ruan (string instrument)	50	45
627		5p. Cheng (harp)	5·50	2·20
628		8p. Pi-pa (lute)	9·00	5·00
MS629		119 × 111 mm. Nos. 623/8	28·00	20·00

134 "Flying Albatros" (hydrofoil)

1986. "Stockholmia 86" International Stamp Exhibition. Passenger Ferries. Multicoloured.

630		10a. Type **134**	15	25
631		40a. "Tejo" (hovercraft) . . .	25	35
632		3p. "Tercera" (jetfoil)	1·70	1·50
633		7p.50 "Cheung Kong" (high speed ferry)	4·50	3·50

135 Taipa Fortress **136** Sun Yat-sen

1986. 10th Anniv of Security Forces. Fortresses. Multicoloured.
634 2p. Type **135** . . . . 1·70 1·10
635 2p. St. Paul on the Mount . . 1·70 1·10
636 2p. St. Francis . . . . 1·70 1·10
637 2p. Guia . . . . 1·70 1·10
Nos. 634/7 were printed together, se-tenant, forming a composite design.

1986. 120th Birth Anniv of Dr. Sun Yat-sen. Multicoloured.
638 70a. Type **136** . . . . 3·50 3·00
MS639 95 × 70 mm. 1p.30 Dr. Sun Yat-sen (*different*) . . . . . . 15·00 10·00

137 Hare and Moon **138** Wa To (physician)

1987. New Year. Year of the Hare.
640 **137** 1p.50 multicoloured . . . 2·75 85

1987. Shek Wan Ceramics. Multicoloured.
641 2p.20 Type **138** . . . . . . 1·80 85
642 2p.20 Choi San, God of Fortune . . . . 1·80 85
643 2p.20 Yi, Sun God . . . . . . 1·80 85
644 2p.20 Cung Kuei, Keeper of Demons . . . . 1·80 85

139 Boats

1987. Dragon Boat Festival. Multicoloured.
645 50a. Type **139** 55 30
646 5p. Dragon boat prow . . . 3·25 2·00

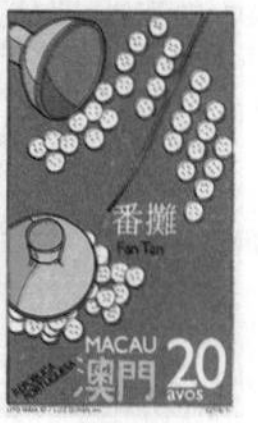

140 Circular Fan **141** Fantan

1987. Fans. Multicoloured.
647 30a. Type **140** 50 30
648 70a. Folding fan with tree design . . . . 1·00 40
649 1p. Square-shaped fan with peacock design . . . . . 3·00 1·00
650 6p. Heart-shaped fan with painting of woman and tree . . . . 7·50 2·40
MS651 113 × 139 mm. Nos. 647/50 48·00 38·00

1987. Casino Games. Multicoloured.
652 20a. Type **141** 35 20
653 40a. Cussec 55 25
654 4p. Baccarat . . . . 2·50 1·30
655 7p. Roulette . . . . 7·00 3·00

142 Goods Hand-cart **143** Dragon and Moon

1987. Traditional Vehicles. Multicoloured.
656 10a. Type **142** 30 20
657 70a. Open sedan chair . . . 1·00 45
658 90a. Rickshaw . . . . 1·40 60
659 10p. Cycle rickshaw . . . . 7·00 4·00
MS660 90 × 65 mm. 7p.50 Covered sedan chair . . . . 12·50 10·50

1988. New Year. Year of the Dragon.
661 **143** 2p.50 multicoloured . . . 2·30 1·50

144 West European Hedgehog

1988. Protected Mammals. Multicoloured.
662 3p. Type **144** . . . . 2·30 1·00
663 3p. Eurasian badger . . . . 2·30 1·00
664 3p. European otter . . . . . 2·30 1·00
665 3p. Chinese pangolin . . . . 2·30 1·00

145 Breastfeeding

1988. 40th Anniv of W.H.O. Multicoloured.
666 60a. Type **145** 45 20
667 80a. Vaccinating child . . . 80 30
668 2p.40 Donating blood . . . 1·60 1·10

146 Bicycles

1988. Transport. Multicoloured.
669 20a. Type **146** 20 20
670 50a. Lambretta and Vespa . . 45 45
671 3p.30 Open-sided motor car 1·60 1·20
672 5p. Renault delivery truck, 1912 . . . . 2·75 2·75
MS673 68 × 57 mm. 7p.50 Rover (1907) . . . . 12·50 10·50

147 Hurdling **148** Intelpost (electronic mail)

1988. Olympic Games, Seoul. Multicoloured.
674 40a. Type **147** 45 45
675 60a. Basketball 60 50
676 1p. Football . . . . 1·50 60
677 8p. Table tennis . . . . . . 4·75 2·50
MS678 112 × 140 mm. Nos. 673/6; 5p. Taekwondo . . . . 9·25 9·25

1988. New Postal Services. Multicoloured.
679 13p.40 Type **148** . . . . . 6·25 5·75
680 40p. Express Mail Service (EMS) . . . . 20·00 8·50

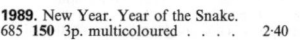

149 B.M.W. Saloon Car **150** Snake and Moon

1988. 35th Macao Grand Prix. Multicoloured.
681 80a. Type **149** 45 35
682 2p.80 Motor cycle . . . . . 1·10 1·10
683 7p. Formula 3 car . . . . . 3·75 2·10
MS684 115 × 139 mm. Nos. 681/3 17·00 15·00

1989. New Year. Year of the Snake.
685 **150** 3p. multicoloured . . . . 2·40 2·10

151 Water Carrier **152** White Building

1989. Traditional Occupations (1st series). Multicoloured.
686 50a. Type **151** 30 30
687 1p. Tan-kya (boat) woman 80 45
688 4p. Tin-tin man (pedlar) . . 1·80 1·40
689 5p. Tao-fu-fa (soya bean cheese) vendor . . . . . . 2·30 2·00
See also Nos. 714/17 and 743/6.

1989. Paintings by George Vitalievich Smirnoff in Luis Camoes Museum. Multicoloured.
690 2p. Type **152** . . . . 1·40 95
691 2p. Building with railings . . 1·40 95
692 2p. Street scene . . . . . . 1·40 95
693 2p. White thatched cottage 1·40 95

153 Common Cobra **154** Talu

1989. "Philexfrance 89" International Stamp Exhibition, Paris. Snakes of Macao. Mult.
694 2p.50 Type **153** . . . . . . 1·60 1·00
695 2p.50 Banded krait ("Bungarus fasciatus") . . 1·60 1·00
696 2p.50 Bamboo pit viper ("Trimeresurus albolabris") 1·60 1·00
697 2p.50 Rat snake ("Elaphe radiata") . . . . 1·60 1·00

1989. Traditional Games. Multicoloured.
698 10a. Type **154** 15 15
699 60a. Triol (marbles) 35 30
700 3p.30 Chiquia (shuttlecock) 1·90 1·00
701 5p. Chinese chequers . . . . 2·50 1·80

155 Piaggio P-136L Flying Boat **156** Malacca

1989. Aircraft. Multicoloured.
702 50a. Type **155** 25 15
703 70a. Martin M-130 flying boat 55 25
704 2p.80 Fairey 111D seaplane 1·40 90
705 4p. Hawker Osprey seaplane 2·20 1·70
MS706 105 × 82 mm. 7p.50 De Havilland D.H.80A Puss Moth 9·75 8·25

1989. "World Stamp Expo '89" International Stamp Exhibition, Washington D.C. Portuguese Presence in Far East. Multicoloured.
707 40a. Type **156** 30 15
708 70a. Thailand 55 25
709 90a. India 55 30
710 2p.50 Japan . . . . 1·50 85
711 7p.50 China . . . . 3·25 1·80
MS712 14? × 130 mm. Nos. 707/11; 3p. Macao . . . . 8·50 8·00

157 Horse and Moon **159** Long-finned Grouper ("Epinephelus megachir")

158 Penny Black and Sir Rowland Hill (postal reformer)

1990. New Year. Year of the Horse.
713 **157** 4p. multicoloured . . . . 1·60 1·20

1990. Traditional Occupations (2nd series). As T **151**. Multicoloured.
714 30a. Long-chau singer . . . 25 15
715 70a. Cobbler 60 25
716 1p.50 Travelling penman . . 90 60
717 7p.50 Fisherman with wide nets . . . . 3·25 1·80

1990. 150th Anniv of the Penny Black. Sheet 91 × 130 mm.
MS718 **158** 10p. multicoloured 7·75 6·00

1990. Fishes. Multicoloured.
719 2p.40 Type **159** . . . . . . 1·00 60
720 2p.40 Malabar snapper ("Lutianus malabaricus") 1·00 60
721 2p.40 Spotted snakehead ("Ophiocepalus maculatus") . . . . 1·00 60
722 2p.40 Paradise fish ("Macropodus opercularis") . . . . . . 1·00 60

160 Porcelain

1990. "New Zealand 1990" International Stamp Exhibition, Auckland. Industrial Diversification. Multicoloured.
723 3p. Type **160** . . . . 1·20 85
724 3p. Furniture . . . . 1·20 85
725 3p. Toys . . . . 1·20 85
726 3p. Artificial flowers . . . . 1·20 85
MS727 131 × 95 mm. Nos. 723/6 10·00 9·00

161 Cycling **162** Rose by Lazaro Luis

1990. 11th Asian Games, Peking. Multicoloured.
728 80a. Type **161** 45 30
729 1p. Swimming 55 45
730 3p. Judo . . . . 1·20 90
731 4p.20 Shooting . . . . 2·20 1·70
MS732 95 × 140 mm. Nos. 728/31; 6p. Athlete with bamboo pole 5·00 4·25

1990. Compass Roses. Designs showing roses from ancient charts by cartographer named. Mult.
733 50a. Type **162** 30 20
734 1p. Diogo Homem 55 25
735 3p.50 Diogo Homem (different) . . . . 1·30 75
736 6p.50 Fernao Vaz Dourado 3·00 1·70
MS737 107 × 100 mm. 5p. Luiz Teixeira (29 × 39 mm) . . . . 23·00 19·00

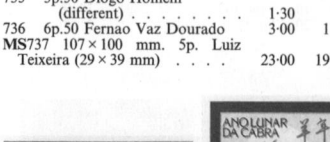

163 Cricket Fight **164** Goat and Moon

1990. Betting on Animals. Multicoloured.
738 20a. Type **163** 15 15
739 80a. Melodious laughing thrush fight 35 20
740 1p. Greyhound racing . . . 60 30
741 10p. Horse racing . . . . . 3·75 2·50

1991. New Year. Year of the Goat.
742 **164** 4p.50 multicoloured . . . 1·70 1·40

1991. Traditional Occupations (3rd series). As T **151**. Multicoloured.

743	80a. Knife-grinder	30	15
744	1p.70 Flour-puppets vendor	70	30
745	3p.50 Street barber	1·20	65
746	4p.20 Fortune-teller	1·70	1·00

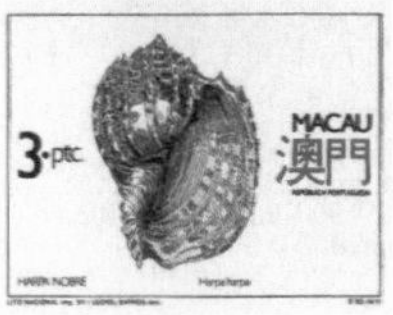

165 True Harp ("Harpa harpa")

1991. Sea Shells. Multicoloured.

747	3p. Type **165**	1·20	70
748	3p. Oil-lamp tun ("Tonna zonata")	1·20	70
749	3p. Bramble murex ("Murex pecten")	1·20	70
750	3p. Rose-branch murex ("Chicoreus rosarius")	1·20	70

The Latin names on Nos. 749/50 are incorrect.

166 Character and Backcloth

1991. Chinese Opera. Multicoloured.

751	**166**	60a. multicoloured	20	10
752	–	80a. multicoloured	35	15
753	–	1p. multicoloured	50	25
754	–	10p. multicoloured	3·75	2·00

DESIGNS: Nos. 752/4, Different backcloths and costumes.

167 "Delonix regia" and Lou Lim Ioc Garden

1991. Flowers and Gardens (1st series). Mult.

755	1p.70 Type **167**	55	25
756	3p. "Ipomoea cairica" and Sao Francisco Garden	1·00	55
757	3p.50 "Jasminum mesyi" and Sun Yat Sen Park	1·10	70
758	4p.20 "Bauhinia variegata" and Seac Pai Van Park	1·40	75
MS759	95 × 137 mm. Nos. 755/8	8·00	6·00

See also Nos. 815/**MS**19.

168 Portuguese Traders unloading Boats

169 Firework Display

1991. Cultural Exchange. Nambam Paintings attr. Kano Domi. Multicoloured.

760	4p.20 Type **168**	1·40	70
761	4p.20 Portuguese traders displaying goods to buyers	1·40	70
MS762	107 × 74 mm. Nos. 760/1	5·25	4·50

1991. Christmas. Multicoloured.

763	1p.70 Type **169**	45	25
764	3p. Father Christmas	95	45
765	3p.50 Man dancing	1·10	60
766	4p.20 January 1st celebrations	1·50	80

170 Concertina Door

1992. Doors and Windows. Multicoloured.

767	1p.70 Type **170**	55	20
768	3p. Window with four shutters	95	45
769	3p.50 Window with two shutters	1·10	65
770	4p.20 Louvred door	1·40	95

171 Monkey and Moon

172 T'it Kuai Lei

1992. New Year. Year of the Monkey.

771	**171**	4p.50 multicoloured	1·60	1·30

1992. Gods of Chinese Mythology (1st series). Multicoloured.

772	3p.50 (1) Type **172**	1·60	95
773	3p.50 (2) Chong Lei Kun	1·60	95
774	3p.50 (3) Cheong Kuo Lou on donkey	1·60	95
775	3p.50 (4) Loi Tong Pan	1·60	95

See also Nos. 796/9.

173 Lion Dance

1992. "World Columbian Stamp Expo '92", Chicago. Chinese Dances. Multicoloured.

776	1p. Type **173**	30	15
777	2p.70 Lion dance (different)	85	40
778	6p. Dragon dance	1·90	95

174 High Jumping

1992. Olympic Games, Barcelona. Multicoloured.

779	80a. Type **174**	20	15
780	4p.20 Badminton	1·20	55
781	4p.70 Roller hockey	1·50	1·00
782	5p. Yachting	2·75	1·00
MS783	137 × 95 mm. Nos. 779/82	17·00	14·00

175 Na Cha Temple

1992. Temples (1st series). Multicoloured.

784	1p. Type **175**	30	15
785	1p.50 Kun Iam	45	20
786	1p.70 Hong Kon	65	35
787	6p.50 A Ma	2·10	1·10

See also Nos. 792/5 and 894/8.

176 Tung Sin Tong Services

1992. Centenary of Tung Sin Tong (medical and educational charity).

788	**176**	1p. multicoloured	35	15

177 Rooster and Dragon

1992. Portuguese–Chinese Friendship.

789	**177**	10p. multicoloured	3·00	1·50
MS790	109 × 74 mm. **177**	10p. multicoloured	6·75	5·50

178 Red Junglefowl

179 Children carrying Banners

1992. New Year. Year of the Cock.

791	**178**	5p. multicoloured	1·80	1·10

See also No. **MS**917.

1993. Temples (2nd series). As T **175**. Mult.

792	50a. T'am Kong	15	10
793	2p. T'in Hau	70	30
794	3p.50 Lin Fong	1·20	60
795	8p. Pau Kong	2·40	1·20

1993. Gods of Chinese Mythology (2nd series). As T **172**. Multicoloured.

796	3p.50 (1) Lam Ch'oi Wo flying on crane	1·50	95
797	3p.50 (2) Ho Sin Ku (goddess) on peach blossom	1·50	95
798	3p.50 (3) Hon Seong Chi crossing sea on basket of flowers	1·50	95
799	3p.50 (4) Ch'ou Kuok K'ao crossing river on plank	1·50	95

1993. Chinese Wedding. Multicoloured.

800	3p. Type **179**	95	50
801	3p. Bride	95	50
802	3p. Bridegroom	95	50
803	3p. Wedding guests	95	50
MS804	124 × 106 mm. 8p. Bride and groom (50 × 40 mm)	11·50	7·75

Nos. 800/3 were issued together, se-tenant, forming a composite design.

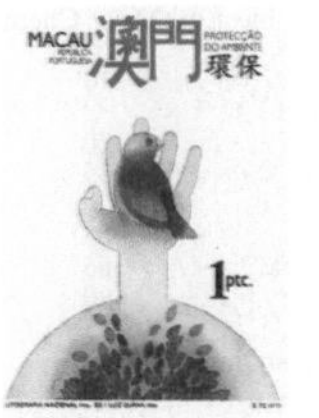

180 Bird perched on Hand

181 Eurasian Scops Owl

1993. Environmental Protection.

805	**180**	1p. multicoloured	55	20

1993. Birds of Prey. Multicoloured.

806	3p. Type **181**	95	60
807	3p. Barn owl ("Tyto alba")	95	60
808	3p. Peregrine falcon ("Falco peregrinus")	95	60
809	3p. Golden eagle ("Aquila obrysaetos")	95	60
MS810	107 × 128 mm. Nos. 806/9	11·50	9·50

182 Town Hall

1993. Union of Portuguese-speaking Capital Cities.

811	**182**	1p.50 green, blue and red	40	20

183 Portuguese Missionaries

1993. 450th Anniv of First Portuguese Visit to Japan. Multicoloured.

812	50a. Japanese man with musket	15	10
813	3p. Type **183**	90	45
814	3p.50 Traders carrying goods	1·00	55

184 "Spathodea campanulata" and Luis de Camoes Garden

1993. Flowers and Gardens (2nd series). Multicoloured.

815	1p. Type **184**	30	15
816	2p. "Tithonia diversifolia" and Montanha Russa Garden	60	25
817	3p. "Rhodomyrtus tomentosa" and Cais Garden	90	40
818	8p. "Passiflora foetida" and Flora Garden	2·20	1·20
MS819	90 × 120 mm. Nos. 815/18	4·75	3·50

185 Caravel

1993. 16th-century Sailing Ships. Multicoloured.

820	1p. Type **185**	30	15
821	2p. Caravel (different)	60	25
822	3p.50 Nau	95	60
823	4p.50 Galleon	1·20	60
MS824	160 × 105 mm. Nos. 820/3	3·75	3·00

186 Saloon Car

1993. 40th Anniv of Macao Grand Prix. Multicoloured.

825	1p.50 Type **186**	40	15
826	2p. Motor cycle	60	25
827	4p.50 Racing car	1·30	70

187 Chow-chow and Moon

1994. New Year. Year of the Dog.

828	**187**	5p. multicoloured	1·40	70

See also No. **MS**917.

188 Map and Prince Henry (½-size illustration)

1994. 600th Birth Anniv of Prince Henry the Navigator.

829	**188**	3p. multicoloured	85	40

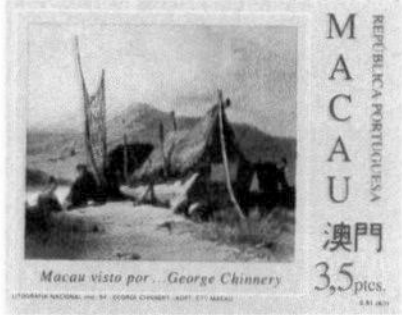

189 Lakeside Hut

1994. Birth Bicentenary of George Chinnery (artist). Multicoloured.

830	3p.50 Type **189**	1·00	50
831	3p.50 Fisherman on sea wall	1·00	50
832	3p.50 Harbour	1·00	50
833	3p.50 Sao Tiago Fortress	1·00	50
MS834	138 × 87 mm. Nos. 830/3	4·75	4·75

190 Lai Sis Exchange

1994. Spring Festival of Lunar New Year. Multicoloured.
835 1p. Type **190** 30 15
836 2p. Flower and tangerine tree decorations 55 25
837 3p.50 Preparing family meal 1·00 50
838 4p.50 Paper decorations bearing good wishes . . . 1·40 70

191 "Longevity" **192** Footballer

1994. Legends and Myths (1st series). Chinese Gods. Multicoloured.
839 3p. Type **191** 85 40
840 3p. "Prosperity" 85 40
841 3p. "Happiness" 85 40
MS842 138 × 90 mm. Nos. 839/41 3·00 2·50
See also Nos. 884/**MS**888, 930/**MS**933 and 994/**MS**998.

1994. World Cup Football Championship, U.S.A. Multicoloured.
843 2p. Type **192** 60 25
844 3p. Tackling 85 40
845 3p.50 Heading ball . . . . . 1·00 55
846 4p.50 Goalkeeper saving goal 1·30 75
MS847 138 × 90 mm. Nos. 843/6 3·50 3·25

193 Rice Shop **194** Astrolabe

1994. Traditional Chinese Shops. Multicoloured.
848 1p. Type **193** 25 10
849 1p.50 Medicinal tea shop . . 35 15
850 2p. Salt-fish shop 55 20
851 3p.50 Pharmacy . . . . . . 1·00 60

1994. Nautical Instruments. Multicoloured.
852 3p. Type **194** 75 35
853 3p.50 Quadrant 95 50
854 4p.50 Sextant . . . . 1·20 65

195 Fencing

1994. 12th Asian Games, Hiroshima, Japan. Multicoloured.
855 1p. Type **195** 25 10
856 2p. Gymnastics 50 20
857 3p. Water-polo 75 35
858 3p.50 Pole vaulting . . . . . 1·00 60

196 Nobre de Carvalho Bridge

1994. Bridges. Multicoloured.
859 1p. Type **196** 30 15
860 8p. Friendship Bridge . . . . 2·10 1·10

197 Carp **199** Pig and Moon

198 Angel's Head (stained glass window, Macao Cathedral)

1994. Good Luck Signs. Multicoloured.
861 3p. Type **197** 75 35
862 3p.50 Peaches 95 50
863 4p.50 Water lily . . . . . . 1·20 65

1994. Religious Art. Multicoloured.
864 50a. Type **198** 10 10
865 1p. Holy Ghost (stained glass window, Macao Cathedral) 25 10
866 1p.50 Silver sacrarium . . . 40 15
867 2p. Silver salver 55 25
868 3p. "Escape into Egypt" (ivory statuette) 75 50
869 3p.50 Gold and silver cup . . 1·00 70

1995. New Year. Year of the Pig.
870 **199** 5p.50 multicoloured . . . 1·60 80

200 "Lou Lim Iok Garden"

1995. Paintings of Macao by Lio Man Cheong. Multicoloured.
871 50a. Type **200** 10 10
872 1p. "Guia Fortress and Lighthouse" 20 10
873 1p.50 "Barra Temple" . . . 35 15
874 2p. "Avenida da Praia, Taipa" 55 25
875 2p.50 "Kun Iam Temple" . . 65 30
876 3p. "St. Paul's Seminary" . . 80 40
877 3p.50 "Penha Hill" 95 55
878 4p. "Gates of Understanding Monument" . . . . 1·20 80

201 Magnifying Glass over Goods

1995. World Consumer Day.
879 **201** 1p. multicoloured 25 15

202 Pangolin **203** Kun Sai Iam

1995. Protection of Chinese ("Asian") Pangolin. Multicoloured.
880 1p.50 In fork of tree 35 30
881 1p.50 Hanging from tree by tail 35 30
882 1p.50 On leafy branch . . . 35 30
883 1p.50 Type **202** 35 30

1995. Legends and Myths (2nd series). Kun Sai Iam (Buddhist god). Multicoloured.
884 3p. Type **203** 80 40
885 3p. Holding baby 80 40
886 3p. Sitting behind water lily 80 40
887 3p. With water lily and dragonfish 80 40
MS888 138 × 90 mm. 8p. Kun Sai Iam (*different*) . . . . 3·25 2·10

204/7 Senado Square (¼-size illustration)

1995. Senado Square.
889 **204** 2p. multicoloured 50 25
890 **205** 2p. multicoloured 50 25
891 **206** 2p. multicoloured 50 25
892 **207** 2p. multicoloured 50 25
MS893 138 × 90 mm. 8p. multicoloured (Leal Senado building and Post Office Clock tower) (*horiz*) . . . . 2·10 2·00
Nos. 889/92 were issued together, se-tenant, forming the composite design illustrated.

1995. Temples (3rd series). As T **175**. Multicoloured.
894 50a. Kuan Tai 10 10
895 1p. Pak Tai 25 10
896 1p.50 Lin K'ai 35 15
897 3p. Se Kam Tong 75 40
898 3p.50 Fok Tak 95 55

208 Pekin Robin ("Leiothrix lutea")

1995. "Singapore'95" International Stamp Exhibition. Birds. Multicoloured.
899 2p.50 Type **208** 65 35
900 2p.50 Japanese white-eye ("Zosterops japonica") . . 65 35
901 2p.50 Island canary ("Serinus canarius canarius") 65 35
902 2p.50 Melodious laughing thrush ("Gurrulax canonus") 65 35
MS903 137 × 90 mm. 10p. Magpie robin (*Copyschus saularis*) . . . 2·75 2·50

209 Pipa

1995. International Music Festival. Musical Instruments. Multicoloured.
904 1p. Type **209** 25 10
905 1p. Erhu (string instrument) 25 10
906 1p. Gong (hand-held drum) 25 10
907 1p. Sheng (string instrument) 25 10
908 1p. Xiao (flute) 25 10
909 1p. Tambor (drum) 25 10
MS910 137 × 90 mm. 8p. Two players with instruments (40 × 29 mm) . . . . 2·10 2·00

210 Anniversary Emblem, World Map and U.N. Headquarters, New York

1995. 50th Anniv of United Nations Organization.
911 **210** 4p.50 multicoloured . . . 1·10 60

211 Terminal Building

1995. Inauguration of Macao International Airport. Multicoloured.
912 1p. Type **211** 25 10
913 1p.50 Terminal (different) . . 35 20
914 2p. Loading airplane and cargo building 55 25
915 3p. Control tower 80 45
MS916 137 × 90 mm. 8p. Airplane taking off . . . . 2·10 1·00

1995. Lunar Cycle. Sheet 180 × 216 mm containing previous New Year designs.
MS917 12 × 1p.50. As Nos. 791, 828, 870, 587, 771, 602, 742, 621, 713, 685, 661 and 640 . . . . . . 4·75 3·75

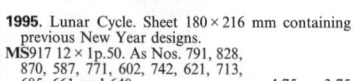

212 Rat

1996. New Year. Year of the Rat.
918 **212** 5p. multicoloured . . . . 1·30 65
MS919 137 × 90 mm. **212** 10p. multicoloured . . . . 2·75 2·50

213 Cage

1996. Traditional Chinese Cages.
920 **213** 1p. multicoloured 20 10
921 – 1p.50 multicoloured . . . 35 15
922 – 3p. multicoloured 75 40
923 – 4p.50 multicoloured . . . 1·20 60
MS924 137 × 90 mm. 10p. multicoloured . . . . 2·75 2·50
DESIGNS: 1p.50 to 10p., Different cages.

214 Street **215** Tou Tei (God of Earth)

1996. Paintings of Macao by Herculano Estorninho. Multicoloured.
925 50a. Fishing boats (horiz) . . 10 10
926 1p.50 Town square 35 15
927 3p. Type **214** 75 35
928 5p. Townscape (horiz) . . . 1·30 70
MS929 137 × 90 mm. 10p. Colonnaded entrance . . . . . 2·75 2·50

1996. Legends and Myths (3rd series). Multicoloured.
930 3p.50 Type **215** 90 50
931 3p.50 Choi San (God of Fortune) 90 50
932 3p.50 Chou Kuan (God of the Kitchen) 90 50
MS933 137 × 89 mm. Nos. 930/2 2·75 2·30

216 Customers

1996. Traditional Chinese Tea Houses. Mult.
934 2p. Type **216** 50 25
935 2p. Waiter with tray of steamed stuffed bread . . . 50 25
936 2p. Newspaper vendor . . . 50 25
937 2p. Waiter pouring tea at table 50 25
MS938 138 × 90 mm. 8p. Jar and food snacks . . . . 2·10 3·75
Nos. 934/7 were issued together, se-tenant, forming a composite design.

217 Get Well Soon

1996. Greetings stamps. Multicoloured.
939 50a. Type **217** 10 10
940 1p.50 Congratulations on new baby 35 15
941 3p. Happy birthday 75 35
942 4p. Wedding congratulations 1·10 55

218 Swimming

1996. Olympic Games, Atlanta, U.S.A. Mult.

943	2p. Type **218**	45	20
944	3p. Football	75	35
945	3p.50 Gymnastics	95	40
946	4p.50 Sailboarding	1·20	70
MS947	137 × 90 mm. 10p. Boxing	2·75	2·50

219 Crane (civil, 1st rank)

1996. Civil and Military Insignia of the Mandarins (1st series). Multicoloured.

948	2p.50 Type **219**	60	30
949	2p.50 Lion (military, 2nd rank)	60	30
950	2p.50 Golden pheasant (civil, 2nd rank)	60	30
951	2p.50 Leopard (military, 3rd rank)	60	30

See also Nos. 1061/4.

220 Trawler with Multiple Nets

1996. Nautical Sciences: Fishing Nets. Mult.

952	3p. Type **220**	75	35
953	3p. Modern trawler with net from stern	75	35
954	3p. Two sailing junks with common net	75	35
955	3p. Junk with two square nets at sides	75	35

Nos. 952/5 were issued together, se-tenant, forming a composite design.

221 National Flag and Statue (½-size illustration)

1996. 20th Anniv of Legislative Assembly.

956	**221** 2p.80 multicoloured	70	35
MS957	138 × 90 mm. **221** 8p. multicoloured	2·00	2·00

222 Dragonfly

1996. Paper Kites. Multicoloured.

958	3p.50 Type **222**	85	50
959	3p.50 Butterfly	85	50
960	3p.50 Owl	85	50
961	3p.50 Swallow	85	50
MS962	138 × 90 mm. 8p.Chinese dragon (50 × 37 mm)	2·00	2·00

223 Doll

1996. Traditional Chinese Toys. Multicoloured.

963	50a. Type **223**	10	10
964	1p. Fish	25	10
965	3p. Painted doll	75	35
966	4p.50 Dragon	1·10	60

224 Ox

1997. New Year. Year of the Ox.

967	**224** 5p.50 multicoloured	1·30	75
MS968	137 × 89 mm. **224** 10p. multicoloured	2·50	2·50

225 Colourful and Gold Twos

1997. Lucky Numbers. Multicoloured.

969	2p. Type **225**	45	20
970	2p.80 Eights	75	35
971	3p. Threes	75	35
972	3p.90 Nines	1·00	55
MS973	137 × 90 mm. 9p. Numbers around doorway of café	2·30	2·20

No. **MS**973 also commemorates "Hong Kong '97" International Stamp Exhibition.

226 "Sail Boats" **227** Elderly Woman

1997. Paintings of Macao by Kwok Se. Multicoloured.

974	2p. Type **226**	45	20
975	3p. "Fortress on the Hill"	70	35
976	3p.50 "Asilum"	85	55
977	4p.50 "Portas do Cerco"	1·20	65
MS978	138 × 90 mm. 8p. "Rua de Sao Paulo" (detail) (horiz)	2·00	2·00

1997. Tan-Ka (boat) People. Multicoloured.

979	1p. Type **227**	20	50
980	1p.50 Elderly woman holding tiller	35	50
981	2p.50 Woman with child on back	65	50
982	5p.50 Man mending fishing nets	1·40	50

228 Entrance to Temple **229** Dragon Dancers

1997. A-Ma Temple. Multicoloured.

983	3p.50 Type **228**	75	50
984	3p.50 Wall and terraces of Temple	75	50
985	3p.50 View of incense smoke through gateway	75	50
986	3p.50 Incense smoke emanating from pagoda	75	50
MS987	138 × 90 mm. Ship (representative of land reclamation in front of temple)	2·00	2·00

1997. Drunken Dragon Festival. Multicoloured.

988	2p. Type **229**	45	20
989	3p. Dragon dancer	75	35
990	5p. Dancer holding "tail" of dragon	1·30	65
MS991	138 × 90 mm. Dancer with dragon's head (horiz)	2·30	2·20

230 Frois with Japanese Man

1997. 400th Death Anniv of Father Luis Frois (author of "The History of Japan"). Multicoloured.

992	2p.50 Type **230**	60	35
993	2p.50 Father Frois and church (vert)	60	35

231 Wat Lot

1997. Legends and Myths (4th series). Door Gods. Multicoloured.

994	2p.50 Type **231**	60	35
995	2p.50 San Su	60	35
996	2p.50 Chon Keng	60	35
997	2p.50 Wat Chi Kong	60	35
MS998	138 × 90 mm. 10p. Chon Keng and Wat Chi Kong on doors (39 × 39 mm)	2·50	2·50

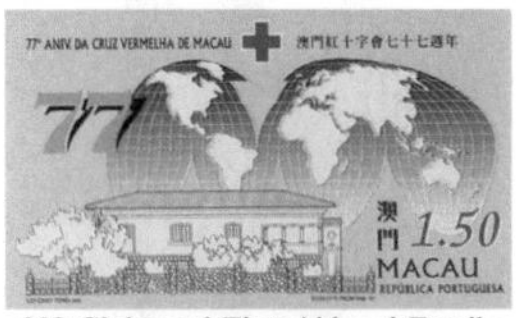

232 Globe and First Aid and Family Health School

1997. 77th Anniv of Macao Red Cross.

999	**232** 1p.50 multicoloured	35	25

233 Balconies

1997. Balconies.

1000	**233** 50a. multicoloured	10	10
1001	– 1p. multicoloured	20	10
1002	– 1p.50 multicoloured	35	15
1003	– 2p. multicoloured	45	20
1004	– 2p.50 multicoloured	60	30
1005	– 3p. multicoloured	80	40
MS1006	137 × 90 mm. 8p. multicoloured (29 × 39 mm)	2·00	1·90

DESIGNS: 1p. to 8p. Various balcony styles.

234 Plant Leaf Fan

1997. Fans. Multicoloured.

1007	50a. Type **234**	10	10
1008	1p. Paper fan	20	10
1009	3p.50 Silk fan	80	40
1010	4p. Feather fan	1·00	55
MS1011	138 × 90 mm. 9p. Woman holding sandalwood fan	2·20	2·20

235 Wood **236** Kung Fu

1997. Feng Shui. The Five Elements. Mult.

1012	50a. Type **235**	10	10
1013	1p. Fire	20	10
1014	1p.50 Earth	35	15
1015	2p. Metal	35	20
1016	2p.50 Water	70	40
MS1017	138 × 90 mm. 10p. Centre of geomancer's chart	2·50	2·40

1997. Martial Arts. Multicoloured.

1018	1p.50 Type **236**	35	15
1019	3p.50 Judo	80	40
1020	4p. Karate	1·00	50

237 Tiger

1998. New Year. Year of the Tiger.

1021	**237** 5p.50 multicoloured	1·30	65
MS1022	138 × 90 mm. **237** 10p. multicoloured	2·50	2·40

238 Soup Stall

1998. Street Traders. Multicoloured.

1023	1p. Type **238**	20	10
1024	1p.50 Snack stall	35	15
1025	2p. Clothes stall	45	20
1026	2p.50 Balloon stall	60	30
1027	3p. Flower stall	70	35
1028	3p.50 Fruit stall	90	50
MS1029	138 × 90 mm. 6p. Fruit stall (different)	1·50	1·40

239 Beco da Se

1998. Gateways. Multicoloured.

1030	50a. Type **239**	10	10
1031	1p. Patio da Ilusao	20	10
1032	3p.50 Travessa das galinhas	80	40
1033	4p. Beco das Felicidades	1·00	55
MS1034	138 × 90 mm. 9p. St. Joseph's Seminary	2·30	2·20

240 Woman and Child

1998. Legends and Myths (5th series). Gods of Ma Chou. Multicoloured.

1035	4p. Type **240**	95	50
1036	4p. Woman and man's face in smoke	95	50
1037	4p. Woman with children playing instruments	95	50
1038	4p. Goddess and sailing barges	95	50
MS1039	138 × 90 mm. 10p. Head of goddess	2·50	2·40

241 "Sao Gabriel" (flagship)

1998. 500th Anniv of Vasco da Gama's Voyage to India via Cape of Good Hope. Multicoloured.

(a) Wrongly dated "1598 1998".

1040	1p. Type **241**	20	10
1041	1p.50 Vasco da Gama	35	15
1042	2p. "Sao Gabriel" and map of India	50	30
MS1043	138 × 90 mm. 8p. Compass rose	2·20	2·20

(b) Correctly dated "1498 1998".

1044	1p. Type **241**	20	10
1045	1p.50 As No. 1041	35	15
1046	2p. As No. 1042	50	30
MS1047	138 × 90 mm. 8p. As No. **MS**1043	2·00	1·90

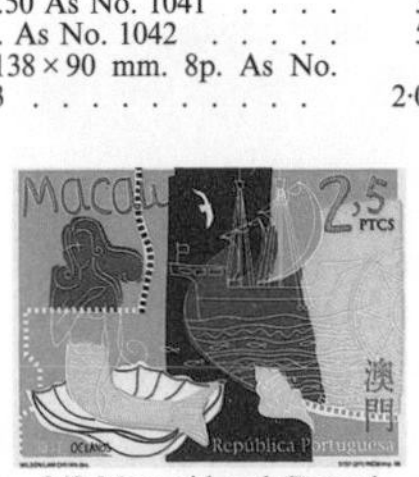

242 Mermaid and Caravel

1998. International Year of the Ocean. Mult.
1048 2p.50 Type **242** 60 30
1049 3p. Whale and oil-rig . . . 70 35
MS1050 138 × 90 mm. Caravel and whale . . . . 2·00 1·90

243 Players

1998. World Cup Football Championship, France. Multicoloured.
1051 3p. Type **243** 70 35
1052 3p.50 Players competing for ball 80 40
1053 4p. Player kicking ball clear while being tackled . . . 95 50
1054 4p.50 Player beating another to ball . . . . 1·10 65
MS1055 138 × 90 mm. 9p. Players and ball . . . . 2·20 2·20

244 Lio Seak Chong Mask

1998. Chinese Opera Masks. Multicoloured.
1056 1p.50 Type **244** 35 15
1057 2p. Wat Chi Kong 45 20
1058 3p. Kam Chin Pao 70 35
1059 5p. Lei Kwai . . . . 1·20 65
MS1060 138 × 90 mm. Opera mask 2·00 1·90

1998. Civil and Military Insignia of the Mandarins (2nd series). As T **219**. Multicoloured.
1061 50a. Lion (military, 2nd rank) 10 10
1062 1p. Bear (military, 5th rank) 20 10
1063 1p.50 Golden pheasant (civil, 2nd rank) 35 15
1064 2p. Silver pheasant (civil, 5th rank) 55 30
MS1065 138 × 90 mm. 9p. Crane (civil, 1st rank) . . . . 2·20 2·20

245 Smiling Buddha

1998. Kun Iam Temple. Multicoloured.
1066 3p.50 Type **245** 80 40
1067 3p.50 Pavilion and temple gardens 80 40
1068 3p.50 Temple gateway . . . 80 40
1069 3p.50 Pagoda, stream and gardens 80 40
MS1070 138 × 90 mm. 10p. Temple 2·40 2·30
Nos. 1066/9 were issued together, se-tenant, forming a composite design.

246 Carriage in Street

1998. Paintings of Macao by Didier Rafael Bayle. Multicoloured.
1071 2p. Type **246** 45 20
1072 3p. Street (horiz) 65 35
1073 3p.50 Building (horiz) . . . 80 40
1074 4p.50 Kiosk in square . . . 1·10 60
MS1075 138 × 90 mm. 8p. Balcony (horiz) . . . . 1·90 1·90

247 Dragon

1998. Tiles by Eduardo Nery (from panel at Departure Lounge of Macao Airport). Multicoloured.
1076 1p. Type **247** 20 10
1077 1p.50 Galleon 35 15
1078 2p.50 Junk 60 30
1079 5p.50 Phoenix . . . . . . 1·30 65
MS1080 138 × 90 mm. 10p. Guia Lighthouse . . . . 2·40 2·30

248 Rabbit

1999. New Year. Year of the Rabbit.
1081 **248** 5p.50 multicoloured . . 1·30 65
MS1082 138 × 90 mm. **248** 10p. multicoloured . . . . 1·30 65

249 Jia Bao Yu

1999. Literature. Characters from "A Dream of Red Mansions" by Cao Xue Qin. Multicoloured.
1083 2p. Type **249** 45 25
1084 2p. Lin Dai Yu holding pole and cherry blossom . . . 45 25
1085 2p. Bao Chai holding fan 45 25
1086 2p. Wang Xi Feng sitting in chair 45 25
1087 2p. You San Jie holding sword 45 25
1088 2p. Qing Wen sewing "peacock" cloak 45 25
MS1089 138 × 90 mm. 8p. Jia Bao Yu and Lin Dai Yu . . . . . 1·90 1·90

250 Sailing Ships

1999. "Australia'99" International Stamp Exhibition, Melbourne. Oceans and Maritime Heritage. Multicoloured.
1090 1p.50 Type **250** 35 15
1091 2p.50 Marine life 60 30
MS1092 138 × 90 mm. 6p. Head of whale (vert) . . . . 1·40 1·40

251 De Havilland D.H.9 Biplane

1999. 75th Anniv of Sarmento de Beires and Brito Pais's Portugal–Macao Flight. Multicoloured.
1093 3p. Breguet 16 Bn2 Patria 70 35
1094 3p. Type **251** 70 35
MS1095 137 × 104 mm. Nos. 1093/4 1·40 1·40

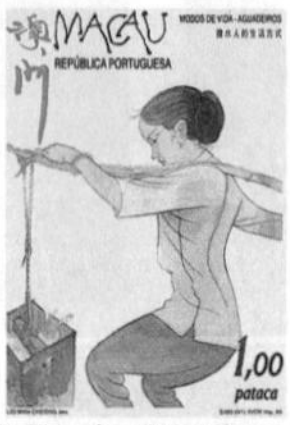

252 Carrying Containers on Yoke

1999. The Water Carrier. Multicoloured.
1096 1p. Type **252** 20 10
1097 1p.50 Filling containers from pump 35 15
1098 2p. Lowering bucket down well 45 20
1099 2p.50 Filling containers from tap 60 35
MS1100 138 × 90 mm. 7p. Woman with containers on yoke climbing steps . . . . 1·70 1·60

253 "Sea-Me-We-3" Undersea Fibre Optic Cable

1999. Telecommunications Services. Multicoloured.
1101 50a. Type **253** 10 10
1102 1p. Dish aerial at Satellite Earth Station 25 10
1103 3p.50 Analogue mobile phone 80 40
1104 4p. Televisions 90 45
1105 4p.50 Internet and e-mail . . 1·10 60
MS1106 138 × 90 mm. 8p. Emblem and computer mouse (horiz) 1·90 1·90

254 Macao Cultural Centre

1999. Modern Buildings. Multicoloured.
1107 1p. Type **254** 25 10
1108 1p.50 Museum of Macao . . 35 15
1109 2p. Macao Maritime Museum 45 25
1110 2p.50 Ferry Terminal . . . 55 30
1111 3p. Macao University . . . 75 35
1112 3p.50 Public Administration building (vert) 80 45
1113 4p.50 Macao World Trade Centre (vert) . . . . . . 1·00 55
1114 5p. Coloane kart-racing track (vert) . . . . 1·20 60
1115 8p. Bank of China (vert) . . 1·80 95
1116 12p. National Overseas Bank (vert) . . . . 2·75 1·40

255 Health Department

1999. Classified Buildings in Tap Seac District. Multicoloured.
1117 1p.50 Type **255** 35 20
1118 1p.50 Central Library (face value in salmon) 35 20
1119 1p.50 Centre of Modern Art of the Orient Foundation (face value in yellow) . . 35 20
1120 1p.50 Portuguese Institute of the Orient (face value in light blue) 35 20
MS1121 138 × 90 mm. 10p. I.P.O.R. building . . . . 2·40 2·30
Nos. 1117/20 were issued together, se-tenant, forming a composite design.

256 Teapot and Plate of Food

258 Chinese and Portuguese Ships, Christ's Cross and Yin Yang

257 "Portuguese Sailor and Chinese Woman" (Lagoa Henriques), Company of Jesus Square

1999. Dim Sum. Multicoloured.
1122 2p.50 Type **256** 55 30
1123 2p.50 Plates of food, chopsticks and left half of bowls 55 30
1124 2p.50 Plates of food, glass, cups and right half of bowls 55 30
1125 2p.50 Plates of food and large teapot 55 30
MS1126 138 × 90 mm. 9p. Plates of food . . . . 2·40 2·30
Nos. 1122/5 were issued together, se-tenant, forming a composite design.

1999. Contemporary Sculptures (1st series). Multicoloured.
1127 1p. Type **257** 25 10
1128 1p.50 "The Gate of Understanding" (Charters de Almeida), Praia Grande Bay (vert) 35 20
1129 2p.50 "Statue of the Goddess Kun Iam" (Cristina Leiria), Macao Cultural Centre (vert) . . 55 20
1130 3p.50 " Taipa Viewing Point" (Dorita Castel-Branco), Nobre de Carvalho Bridge, Taipa 80 35
MS1131 138 × 90 mm. 10p. "The Pearl" (Jose Rodrigues), Amizade rounderbout . . . . 2·40 2·30
See also Nos. 1186/**MS**1190.

1999. Portuguese–Chinese Cultural Mix. Mult.
1132 1p. Type **258** 20 10
1133 1p.50 Ah Mah Temple and Portuguese and Macanese architecture 35 20
1134 2p. Bridge, steps and Chinese architecture . . . 45 20
1135 3p. Macanese architecture and Portuguese terrace . . 65 35
MS1136 138 × 90 mm. Enlargement of right-hand part of design in No. 1135 . . . . 2·40 2·30
Nos. 1132/5 were issued together, se-tenant, forming a composite design.

259 Globe

1999. Macao Retrospective. Multicoloured.
1137 1p. Type **259** 25 10
1138 1p.50 Roof terrace 35 20
1139 2p. Portuguese and Chinese people 55 30
1140 3p.50 Modern Macao . . . 80 45
MS1141 138 × 90 mm. 9p. City coat of arms . . . . 2·20 2·10

260 Gateway

1999. Establishment of Macao as Special Administrative Region of People's Republic of China. Multicoloured.
1142 1p. Type **260** 20 10
1143 1p.50 Bridge and boat race 25 20
1144 2p. Wall of ruined church 35 25
1145 2p.50 Lighthouse and racing cars 40 30
1146 3p. Building facade 55 45
1147 3p.50 Stadium and orchestra 60 50
MS1148 138 × 90 mm. 8p. Pink flower . . . . 2·10 2·10

261 Sight-seeing Tower

2000. A New Era. Sheet 138 × 90 mm.
MS1149 **261** 8p. multicoloured . . 2·10 2·10

262 Dragon

2000. New Year. Year of the Dragon.
1150 **262** 5p.50 multicoloured . . 95 75
MS1151 138 × 90 mm. **262** 10p. multicoloured . . . . 2·50 2·50

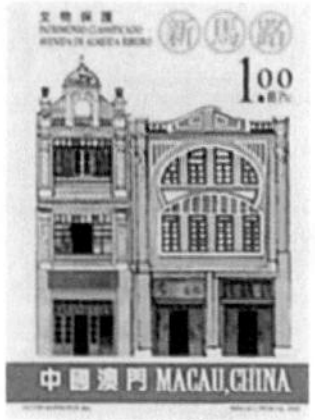

263 Buildings

2000. Classified Buildings in Almeida Ribeiro Avenue, Macao City. Multicoloured.
1152 1p. Type **263** 20 15
1153 1p.50 Yellow and pink buildings 25 20
1154 2p. Yellow building 35 25
1155 3p. Purple, green and pink buildings 55 45
MS1156 138 × 90 mm. 9p. Beige building . . . . 2·10 2·10

SERIAL NUMBERS. In sets containing several stamps of the same denomination, the serial number is quoted in brackets to assist identification. This is the last figure in the bottom right corner of the stamp.

264 Zhong (Leong Pai Wan)

2000. Arts in Macao. Chinese Calligraphy. Showing Chinese characters by named calligraphy masters. Each black and red.
1157 3p. (1) Type **264** 55 45
1158 3p. (2) Guo (Lin Ka Sang) 55 45
1159 3p. (3) Shu (Lok Hong) . . 55 45
1160 3p. (4) Fa (Sou Su Fai) . . 55 45
MS1161 138 × 90 mm. 8p. Zhong, guo, shu and fa . . . . 2·10 2·10

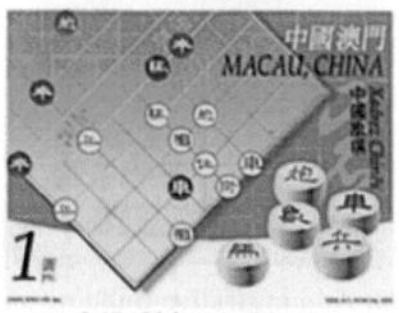

265 Chinese Chess

2000. Board Games. Multicoloured.
1162 1p. Type **265** 20 15
1163 1p.50 Chess 25 20
1164 2p. Go 35 25
1165 2p.50 Flying chess 40 30
MS1166 138 × 90 mm. 9p. Chinese checkers . . . . 2·20 2·20

266 Group of Friends

2000. Tea. Multicoloured.
1167 2p. Type **266** 35 25
1168 3p. Family drinking tea . . 55 45
1169 3p.50 Women drinking tea 60 50
1170 4p.50 Men drinking tea 80 65
MS1171 138 × 90 mm. 8p. Woman making tes . . . . 2·20 2·20

267 Tricycle Driver and Foreign Tourists

2000. Tricycle Drivers. Multicoloured.
1172 2p. (1) Type **267** 35 25
1173 2p. (2) With couple in carriage 35 25
1174 2p. (3) With empty carriage 35 25
1175 2p. (4) With feet resting on saddle 35 25
1176 2p. (5) Sitting in carriage . . 35 25
1177 2p. (6) Mending tyre 35 25
MS1178 138 × 90 mm. 8p. Standing beside tricycle (vert) . . . . . 2·20 2·20

268 Monkey King standing on Tiger Skin

2000. Classical Literature. *Journey to the West* (Ming dynasty novel). Multicoloured.
1179 1p. Type **268** 20 15
1180 1p.50 Monkey King tasting the heavenly peaches . . 25 20
1181 2p. Monkey King, Prince Na Zha and flaming wheels 35 25
1182 2p.50 Erlang Deity with spear 40 30
1183 3p. Heavenly Father Lao Jun 55 45
1184 3p.50 Monkey King in Buddha's hand 60 55
MS1185 138 × 90 mm. 9p. Monkey King holding baton (horiz) . . 2·30 2·30

269 "Wing of Good Winds" (Augusto Cid), Pac On Roundabout, Taipa

2000. Contemporary Sculptures (2nd series). Multicoloured.
1186 1p. Type **269** 15 10
1187 2p. "The Embrace" (Irene Vilar), Luis de Camoes Garden (vert) 35 25
1188 3p. Monument (Soares Branco), Guia's Tunnel, Outer Harbour (vert) . . 55 40
1189 4p. "The Arch of the Orient" (Zulmiro de Carvalho), Avienda Rodrigo Rodrigues Viaduct 70 55
MS1190 90 × 138 mm. 10p. "Goddess A-Ma" (Leong Man Lin). Coloane Iland . . . . . 2·75 2·75

270 Decorated Pot

2000. Ceramics. Multicoloured.
1191 2p.50 (1) Type **270** 45 35
1192 2p.50 (2) Vase, dish and teapot 45 35
1193 2p.50 (3) Blue vase 45 35
1194 2p.50 (4) Cabbage-shaped pot and leaf-shaped dish 45 35
1195 2p.50 (5) Plate and fishes . . 45 35
1196 2p.50 (6) Blue and white vase 45 35
MS1197 138 × 90 mm. 8p. Decorated plate (round-design) . . . . 2·20 2·20
Nos. 1191/6 were issued together, se-tenant, with the backgrounds forming a composite design.

271 Phoenix crouching, Shang Dynasty

2000. Jade Ornaments. Multicoloured.
1198 1p.50 Type **271** 25 20
1199 2p. Archer's white jade ring, Warring States period . . 35 25
1200 2p.50 Dragon and phoenix, Six Dynasties 45 35
1201 3p. Pendant with dragon decoration, Western Han Dynasty 55 40
MS1202 138 × 90 mm. 9p. Medallion (detail) (vert) . . . . 2·30 2·30

272 Dancers with National and Special Administrative Flags

2000. 1st Anniv of Macau as Special Administrative Region of People's Republic of China. Multicoloured.
1203 2p. Type **272** 35 25
1204 3p. Chinese dragons and lotus flower 55 40
MS1205 138 × 90 mm. 18p. Flags, statesmen and lotus flower (59 × 39 mm) . . . . 4·75 4·75
Nos. 1203/4 were issued together, se-tenant, forming a composite design.

273 Snake

2001. New Year. Year of the Snake.
1206 **273** 5p.50 multicoloured . . 95 75
MS1207 138 × 90 mm. **272** 10p. multicoloured . . . . 2·50 2·50

274 Man holding Bottle ("Nursing Vengeance despite Hardships")

2001. Ancient Proverbs. Multicoloured.
1208 2p. (1) Type **274** 35 25
1209 2p. (2) Man waiting for a rabbit ("Trusting to Chance and Windfalls") 35 25
1210 2p. (3) Fox and tiger ("Bullying Others by Flaunting One's Powerful Connections") 35 25
1211 2p. (4) Mother with child ("Selecting a Proper Surrounding to Bring up Children") 35 25
MS1212 138 × 90 mm. 8p. Man stealing bell ("Burying Ones' Head in the Sand) . . . . 2·20 2·20

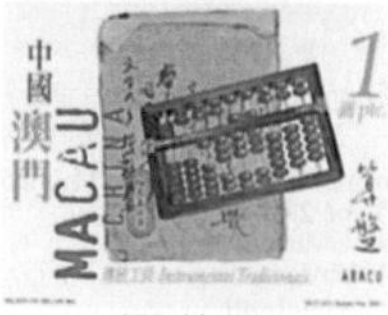

275 Abacus

2001. Traditional Tools. Multicoloured.
1213 1p. Type **275** 15 10
1214 2p. Plane 35 25
1215 3p. Iron 55 40
1216 4p. Scales 70 55
MS1217 138 × 90 mm. 8p. Text, scales and iron . . . . 2·20 2·20

276 Buddha

2001. Religions. Multicoloured.
1218 1p. Type **276** 15 10
1219 1p.50 Worshippers 25 20
1220 2p. Man carrying Cross and religious procession . . . 35 25
1221 2p.50 Procession 45 35
MS1222 138 × 90 mm. 8p. Religious Symbols (circular design)(59 × 59 mm) . . . . . 2·30 2·30
Nos. 1218/19 and 1220/1 respectively were issued together, se-tenant, forming a composite design.

277 Fireman and Platform Car

2001. Fire Brigade. Multicoloured.
1223 1p.50 Type **277** 25 20
1224 2p.50 Fireman wearing chemical protection suit using portable flammable gases detector and Pumping Tank vehicle . . 45 35
1225 3p. Foam car and fireman wearing asbestos suit using foam hose 55 40
1226 4p. Fire officers in dress uniforms and ambulance 70 55
MS1227 138 × 90 mm. 8p. Fireman (59 × 39 mm) . . . . 2·30 2·30

278 Electronic Keys

2001. E-Commerce. Multicoloured.
1228 1p.50 Type **278** 25 20
1229 2p. Hands passing letter (e-mail) 35 25
1230 2p.50 Mobile phone 45 35
1231 3p. Palm hand-held computer 55 40
MS1232 138 × 90 6p. Laptop computers (59 × 39 mm) . . . 1·60 1·60

279 Emblem

2001. Choice of Beijing as 2008 Olympic Games Host City.
1233 **279** 1p. multicoloured . . . 15 10

280 Praying

2001. Classical Literature. *Romance of the Three Kingdoms* (novel by Luo Guanzhong). Multicoloured.
1234 3p. (1) Type **280** 55 40
1235 3p. (2) Soldier and man fighting 55 40
1236 3p. (3) Men talking 55 40
1237 3p. (4) Man dreaming . . . 55 40
MS1238 138 × 90 mm. 7p. Head of Soldier (horiz) . . . . 1·90 1·90

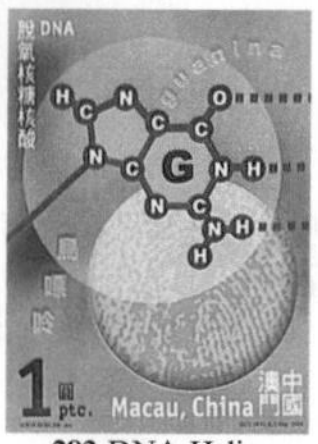

281 Baby, Doctor and Schoolchildren

283 DNA Helix containing Guanine Base

282 Municipal Market

2001. National Census. Multicoloured.
1239 1p. Type **281** 15 10
1240 1p.50 Street scene 25 20
1241 2p.50 Suspension bridge and crowd 45 35
MS1242 137 × 90 mm. 6p. Subjects as Nos. 1239/41 (86 × 37 mm) 1·60 1·60

2001. Macau Markets. Multicoloured.
1243 1p.50 Type **282** 25 20
1244 2p.50 Building and road-side stall 45 35
1245 3p.50 Covered market . . . 60 45
1246 4p.50 Multi-storey building 80 60
MS1247 138 × 90 mm. 7p. Bus station building (59 × 38 mm) 1·90 1·90

2001. Science and Technology. Composition and Structure of DNA. Showing chemical bases of DNA. Multicoloured.
1248 1p. Type **283** 15 10
1249 2p. Helix containing cytosine base 35 25
1250 3p. Helix containing adenine base 55 40
1251 4p. Helix containing thymine base 70 55
MS1252 137 × 90 mm. 8p. Helix containing adenine base (different) (44 × 29 mm) . . . . 2·20 2·20

284 Commander Ho Yin's Garden

2001. Parks and Gardens. Multicoloured.
1253 1p.50 Type **284** 25 20
1254 2p.50 Mong Há Hill municipal park 45 35
1255 3p. City of Flowers Garden 55 40
1256 4p.50 Great Taipa Natural Park 80 60
MS1257 138 × 90 mm. 8p. Garden of Art . . . . 2·20 2·20

285 Trigrams and Dragons

2001. Pa Kua (martial art) (1st series). Multicoloured.
1258 2p. (1) Type **285** 35 25
1259 2p. (4) Trigrams, couple and deer 35 25
1260 2p. (7) Trigrams, fields and buffaloes 35 25
1261 2p. (3) Trigrams and volcano 35 25
1262 2p. (6) Trigrams and three men crawling 35 25
1263 2p. (2) Trigrams, man and donkey 35 25
1264 2p. (5) Trigrams, horse and carriage 35 25
1265 2p. (8) Trigrams, men with gifts and potentate . . . 35 25
MS1266 15 × 90 mm. 8p. Yu Fu (Pa Kua master) (59 × 27 mm) . . 2·20 2·20
See also Nos. 1323/**MS**1331.

286 Horse's Head

2002. New Year. Year of the Horse. Multicoloured.
1267 5p.50 Type **286** . . . . . . 1·00 60
MS1268 138 × 91 mm. 10p. As No. 1267 but design enlarged 2·75 2·75

287 Lao Lao visiting Fidalgo's House

289 Facade and bas-relief of St. Paul

288 Cantao San Kong Opera Performers

2002. Classical Literature. Dream of Red Mansions. Multicoloured.
1269 2p. Type **287** 35 20
1270 2p. Jin Chuan suffering injustice 35 20
1271 2p. Proof of Dada's love for Zi Juan 35 20
1272 2p. Xiang Yun adorned with peony flowers 35 20
1273 2p. Liu Lang combing her hair 35 20
1274 2p. Miao Yu offering tea . . 35 20
MS1275 139 × 90 mm. 8p. Woman reading (The wonderful dream of love) . . . . 2·30 2·30

2002. Festivals. Tou-Tei (God of Earth) Festival. Multicoloured.
1276 1p.50 Type **288** 25 15
1277 2p.50 Respected elders dinner 45 25
1278 3p.50 Burning of cult objects 60 35
1279 4p.50 Cooking suckling pig 80 50
MS1280 139 × 90 mm. 8p. Bearded man with sword (vert) . . . . 2·30 2·30

2002. 400th Anniv St. Paul's Church, Macao. Multicoloured.
1281 1p. Type **289** 20 10
1282 3p.50 Corner of faade and ornament 60 35
MS1283 139 × 90 mm. 8p. Statue in alcove (30 × 40 mm) . . . . . 2·30 2·30

290 Goalkeeper diving for Ball

2002. World Cup Football Championships, Japan and South Korea. Multicoloured.
1284 1p. Type **290** 20 10
1285 1p.50 Players tackling for ball 25 15

291 Underwater Animals and Oil Refinery

2002. Environmental Protection. Multicoloured.
1286 1p. Type **291** (marine conservation) 20 10
1287 1p.50 Boy planting tree (reforestation) 25 15
1288 2p. Emblem and bins (recycling) 35 20
1289 2p.50 Spoonbills (wetland conservation) 40 25
1290 3p. Energy plant and waste truck (energy regeneration) 50 30
1291 3p.50 Boy sweeping leaves (clean urban environment) 60 35
1292 4p. Girl blowing bubbles (air purification) 70 35
1293 4p.50 Nurse and elderly patient (health and hygiene) 80 50
1294 8p. Owl (improving city living) . . . . 1·40 85

292 Zheng Guanying at Home

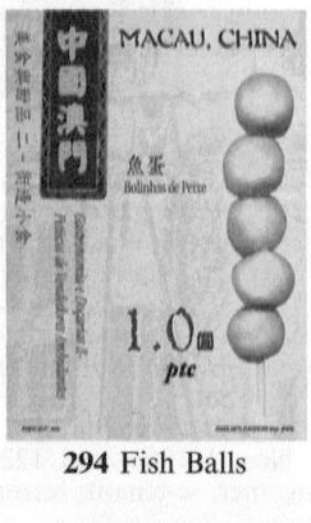

294 Fish Balls

293 Macau Tower and Skyline

2002. 160th Birth Anniv of Zheng Guanying (industrialist, reformer and philanthropist). Multicoloured.
1295 1p. Type **292** 20 10
1296 2p. As young man and docks 35 20
1297 3p. As young man and alms giving 55 35
1298 3p.50 As older man and writing 60 35
MS1299 138 × 90 mm. 6p. Seated at table (40 × 60 mm) . . . . . . 1·60 1·60

2001. Honesty and Transparency. Multicoloured.
1300 1p. Type **293** 20 10
1301 3p.50 Macau skyline from Monte Fort 55 35

2002. Street Vendor's Food. Multicoloured.
1302 1p. Type **294** 20 10
1303 1p.50 Dried beef 25 15
1304 2p. Tongue roll 35 20
1305 2p.50 Sat Kei Ma 45 30
MS1306 138 × 91 mm. 7p. Cookie (50 × 50 mm) . . . . 1·90 1·90

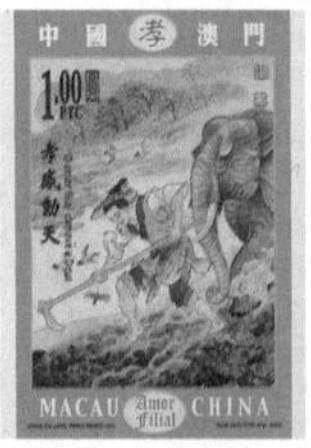

295 Shun ploughing

296 Electroweak Unification with the help of Elephant Diagram

2002. The Twenty-four Paragons of Filial Devotion (book by Guo Jujing). Multicoloured.
1307 1p. Type **295** 20 10
1308 1p.50 Huang Xiang cooling his father's bed with fan 25 15
1309 2p. Meng Zong crying over bamboo shoots for mother 35 20
1310 2p.50 Wang Xiang melting ice to get fish for stepmother 45 30
1311 4p.50 Min Ziqian pleading for cruel stepmother . . . 80 50
1312 4p.50 Jiang Shi, wife and bubbling spring 80 50
1313 4p.50 Bin Chen surrendering to be with mother 80 50
1314 4p.50 Wang Gang pleading for father's body 80 50
MS1315 95 × 139 mm. 7p. Tanzi bringing deer milk to his parents 1·90 1·90

2002. Science and Technology. Particle Physics. Multicoloured.
1316 1p.50 Type **296** 25 15
1317 1p.50 Scales (spontaneous symmetry breaking) . . . 25 15
1318 1p.50 Higgs boson diagram 25 15
1319 1p.50 Three families Z decay curve diagram 25 15
1320 1p.50 Quark groups (quantum cromodynamics) 25 15
1321 1p.50 Graph showing interactions and predicted interactions 25 15
MS1322 138 × 90 mm. 8p. DELPHI detector . . . . 2·20 2·20

2002. Pa Kua (martial art) (2nd series). As T **285**. Multicoloured.
1323 2p. (1) Trigrams, stream and tiger 35 20
1324 2p. (4) Trigrams, man and woman 35 20
1325 2p. (7) Trigrams, couple feeding elderly person . . 35 20
1326 2p. (3) Trigrams, birds, men and path 35 20
1327 2p. (6) Trigrams and man sat in tree 35 20
1328 2p. (2) Trigrams and two men bowing 35 20
1329 2p. (5) Trigrams, yin/yang symbols and storks . . . 35 20
1330 2p. (8) Trigrams and potentate 35 20
MS1331 135 × 90mm. 8p. Woman with jug (59 × 27 mm) . . . . 2·20 2·20

297 Goat's Head

2003. Year of the Goat. Multicoloured.
1332 5p.50 Type **297** 75 75
MS1333 138 × 90 mm. Goat's head (detail) 75 75

298 Classmates

2003. Folk Tales. Liang Shanbo and Zhu Yingtai. Multicoloured.
1334 3p.50 (1) Type **298** 45 30
1335 3p.50 (2) Saying goodbye . . 45 30
1336 3p.50 (3) On terrace 45 30
1337 3p.50 (4) Yingtai's parents arranging marriage . . . 45 30
MS1338 138 × 90 mm. 9p.Turning into butterflies (40 × 60 mm) . . 1·20 1·20

299 Song Jiang

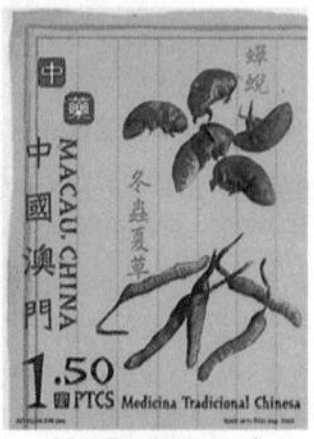

301 Fungus and Chrysalis

300 Administrative Building and Doves

2003. Classical Literature. Outlaws of the Marsh. Multicoloured.
1339 2p. (1) Type **299** 25 15
1340 2p. (2) Lin Chong 25 15
1341 2p. (3) Wu Song 25 15
1342 2p. (4) Lu Zhishen 25 15
1343 2p. (5) Wu Yong 25 15
1344 2p. (6) Hua Rong 25 15
MS1345 138 × 90 mm. 8p. Two outlaws . . . . 1·10 1·10

2003. 10th Anniv of Proclamation of Basic Law of Macao. Multicoloured.
1346 1p. Type **300** 15 10
1347 4p.50 Flags, children, book and doves 60 35

2003. Traditional Chinese Medicine. Multicoloured.
1348 1p.50 Type **301** 20 10
1349 2p. Flowers and fruit . . . 25 15
1350 3p. Gingko leaves and dried stems 40 30
1351 3p.50 Liquorice root and angelica 50 30
MS1352 139 × 90 mm. 8p. Seated man holding tea cup (horiz) . . 1·10 1·10

302 Two-storied Building

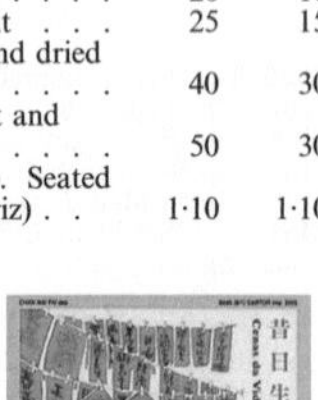

303 Scribe

2003. Cultural Heritage. Architecture of Taipa and Coloane Islands. Multicoloured.
1353 1p. Type **302** 15 10
1354 1p.50 Single-storied building 20 10
1355 2p. Two buildings and dog 25 15
1356 3p.50 Dog, tree, buildings and fish 50 30
MS1357 139 × 90 mm. 9p. Building with bell tower (horiz) . . . . 1·20 1·20
Nos. 1353/6 were issued together, se-tenant, forming a composite design.

2003. Traditional Scenes from Everyday Life. Multicoloured.
1358 1p.50 Type **303** 20 10
1359 1p.50 Puppeteer 20 10
1360 1p.50 Street vendor and children 20 10
1361 1p.50 Washer woman 20 10
1362 1p.50 Lantern seller 20 10
1363 1p.50 Man carrying tray on head 20 10
1364 1p.50 Photographer 20 10
1365 1p.50 Man wearing cockerel costume 20 10
MS1366 138 × 90 mm. 8p. Barber 1·10 1·10

2003. Pa Kua (martial art) (3rd series). As T **285**. Multicoloured.
1367 2p. (1) Trigrams, people and castle 25 15
1368 2p. (4) Trigrams and women with raised arms 25 15
1369 2p. (7) Trigrams and horsemen 25 15
1370 2p. (3) Trigrams and ox 25 15
1371 2p. (6) Trigrams and water wheels 25 15
1372 2p. (2) Trigrams, masked figures and leopard 25 15
1373 2p. (5) Trigrams and seated men and women 25 15
1374 2p. (8) Trigrams, bird and sunset 25 15
MS1375 135 × 90 mm. 8p. Woman and child (59 × 27 mm) 1·10 1·10
Nos. 1367/74 were issued together, se-tenant, each showing two trigrams and a descriptive painting.

304 Astronaut

2003. 1st Chinese Manned Space Flight. Multicoloured.
1376 1p. Type **304** 15 10
1377 1p.50 Ship and satellite 20 10

305 Triumph TR2

2003. 50th Anniv of Macao Grand Prix. Two sheets containing T **305** and similar multicoloured designs.
MS1378 (a) 225 × 156 mm. 1p. Type **305**; 1p.50 Early Brabham race car; 2p. Formula 3 race car; 3p. Grand Prix motorcyclist; 3p.50 Saloon car; 4p.50 Dallara race car. (b) 138 × 91 mm.12p. Anniversary emblem (38 × 38 mm) (circular) 3·75 3·75

306 Hua Tuo (detail, ceramic sculpture) (Pan Yushu)

2003. Macao Museum of Art. Multicoloured.
1379 1p. Type **306** 15 10
1380 1p.50 "View of Praia Grande and Penha Hill at Sunset" (George Smirnoff) 20 10
1381 2p. "Ruins of S. Paulo" (George Chinnery) 25 15
1382 2p.50 "Music in the Garden" (Su Liupeng) 35 20
MS1383 138 × 90 mm. 7p. "Macao, The Praia Grande" (58 × 55 mm) 95 95

307 Monkey's Head

2004. Year of the Monkey. Multicoloured.
1384 5p.50 Type **307** 75 75
MS1385 138 × 90 mm. 10p. Monkey's head (detail) 1·40 1·40

2004. Pa Kua (martial art) (4th series). As T **285**. Multicoloured.
1386 2p. (1) Trigrams, men and sack 25 15
1387 2p. (4) Trigrams and storm over hill 25 15
1388 2p. (7) Trigrams and men eating 25 15
1389 2p. (3) Trigrams and imprisoned animal 25 15
1390 2p. (6) Trigrams, waterfall and family on horseback 25 15
1391 2p. (2) Trigrams and climbers 25 15
1392 2p. (5) Trigrams and junks (boats) 25 15
1393 2p. (8) Trigrams counting 25 15
MS1394 135 × 90 mm. 8p. Stone carver (59 × 27 mm) 1·10 1·10
Nos. 1386/93 were issued together, se-tenant, each showing two trigrams and a descriptive painting.

309 Li Sao and Chariot Steeds

310 Guan Di

2004. Classical Literature. Li Sao (poem by Qu Yuan). Showing scenes from poem. Multicoloured.
1395 1p.50 Type **309** 20 10
1396 1p.50 Cultivating orchids 20 10
1397 1p.50 With sister 20 10
1398 1p.50 With phoenix 20 10
1399 1p.50 With cart drawn by dragons 20 10
1400 1p.50 In garden 20 15
MS1401 138 × 90 mm. 8p. With arm outstretched (vert) 1·10 1·10

2004. Myths and Legends. Guan Di (war god). Multicoloured.
1402 1p.50 Type **310** 20 10
1403 1p.50 Wearing armour 20 10
1404 1p.50 On horseback 20 10
1405 1p.50 Wearing robes 20 10
MS1406 138 × 90 mm. 8p. Facing left 1·10 1·10

311 Running

2004. Olympic Games, Athens. Multicoloured.
1407 1p. Type **311** 15 10
1408 1p.50 Long jump 20 10
1409 2p. Discus 25 15
1410 3p.50 Javelin 50 30

312 "Lotus Flower in Full Bloom" (statue) and Deng Xiaoping wearing Uniform

2004. Birth Centenary of Deng Xiaoping (leader of China, 1978–89). Multicoloured.
1411 1p. Type **312** 15 10
1412 1p.50 Deng Xiaoping and St. Paul's Church 20 10
MS1413 138 × 90 mm. 8p. As young man and lotus flower (40 × 40 mm) (circular) 1·10 1·10

313 Fireworks over Waterfront (⅔-size illustration)

2004. International Firework Display Competition. Multicoloured.
1414 1p. Type **313** 15 10
1415 1p.50 Large burst and Macao Tower 20 10
1416 2p. Two large bursts and Macao Bridge 25 15
1417 4p.50 Large burst over Monte Hill 60 35
MS1418 138 × 90 mm. 9p. Trophy (vert) 1·20 1·20

314 People's Republic of China Flag

2004. 55th Anniv of People's Republic of China. Multicoloured.
1419 1p. Type **314** 15 10
1420 1p.50 Macao flag 20 10
1421 2p. People's Republic emblem 25 15
1422 3p. Macao emblem 40 25
MS1423 138 × 90 mm. 7p. Imperial Palace, Beijing (59 × 39 mm) 95 95

315 Graph showing Expanding Universe

2004. Science and Technology. Cosmology. Multicoloured.
1424 1p. Type **315** 15 10
1425 1p.50 Graph showing cosmic radiation 20 10
1426 2p. Galaxies (fluctuating galaxies) 25 15
1427 3p.50 Tetrahedron divided into dark matter, dark energy and the known universe 50 30
MS1428 138 × 90 mm. 8p. Mathematical shapes (Big Bang theory) 1·10 1·10

316 Soldier and Flag

2004. People's Republic of China Garrison, Macao. Multicoloured.
1429 1p. Type **316** 15 10
1430 1p. Tank soldier saluting 15 10
1431 1p.50 St. Paul's Church and convoy 20 10
1432 1p.50 Nursing corps 20 10
1433 3p.50 Soldier at attention 50 30
1434 3p.50 Soldier charging 50 30
MS1435 138 × 90 mm. 8p. Soldiers carrying Flag (39 × 60 mm) 1·10 1·10

317 Lotus Blossom

2004. 5th Anniv of Macao Special Administrative Region. Multicoloured.
1436 1p.50 Type **317** 20 10
1437 2p. Blossoms and Cultural Centre 25 15
1438 2p.50 Blossoms and Monte Hill buildings 35 20
1439 3p. Blossoms, Macao Tower and Lisboa Hotel 40 25
MS1440 138 × 90 mm. 10p. Lotus blossom (different) 1·40 1·40
Nos. 1436/9 were issued together, se-tenant, forming a composite design.

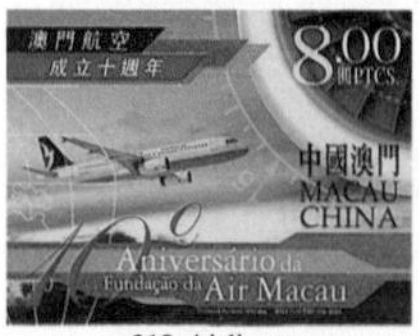
318 Airliner

2004. 10th Anniv of Air Macao. Sheet 138 × 90 mm.
MS1441 **318** 8p. multicoloured 1·10 1·10

319 Rooster

2005. New Year. "Year of the Rooster".
1442 **319** 5p. multicoloured
MS1443 138 × 90 mm. **319** $10 multicoloured 1·40 1·40

CHARITY TAX STAMPS

The notes under this heading in Portugal also apply here.

43

C 48 Our Lady of Charity (altarpiece, Macao Cathedral)

1919. Fiscal stamp optd **TAXA DE GUERRA**.
C305 **43** 2a. green 5·00 3·50
C306 11a. green 7·25 6·75
The above was for use in Timor as well as Macao.

1925. As Marquis de Pombal issue of Portugal but inscr "MACAU".
C329 C **73** 2a. red 1·50 1·40
C330 – 2a. red 1·80 1·70
C331 C **75** 2a. red 1·90 1·70

1930. No gum.
C332 C **48** 5a. brown and buff 32·00 26·00

1945. As Type C **48** but values in Arabic and Chinese numerals left and right, at bottom of design. No gum.
C486 1a. olive and green 1·00 50
C487 2a. purple and grey 1·00 50
C415 5a. brown and yellow 23·00 21·00
C416 5a. blue and light blue 29·00 26·00
C417 10a. green and light green 21·00 16·00
C488 10a. blue and green 1·00 50
C418 15a. orange and light orange 20·00 15·00
C419 20a. red and orange 30·00 25·00
C489 20a. brown and yellow 2·10 80
C420 50a. lilac and buff 30·00 25·00
C472 50a. red and pink 20·00 7·00

1981. No. C487 and similar higher (fiscal) values surch **20 avos** and Chinese characters.
C546 20a. on 2a. purple on grey 3·00 1·50
C534 20a. on 1p. green & lt green 3·50 2·50
C535 20a. on 3p. black and pink 3·00 1·00
C536 20a. on 5p. brown & yellow

1981. No. C418 surch **10 avos** and Chinese characters.
C553 10a. on 15a. orange and light orange 3·00 1·50

NEWSPAPER STAMPS

1892. "Embossed" key-type of Macao surch **JORNAES** and value. No gum.
N73 Q 2½r. on 10r. green 11·00 3·75
N74 2½r. on 40r. brown 11·00 3·75
N75 2½r. on 80r. grey 11·00 3·75

1893. "Newspaper" key-type inscr "Macau".
N80 V 2½r. brown 3·50 2·30

1894. "Newspaper" key-type of Macao surch ½ **avo PROVISORIO** and Chinese characters.
N82 V ½a. on 2½r. brown 6·00 2·50

POSTAGE DUE STAMPS

1904. "Due" key-type inscr "MACAU". No gum (12a. to 1p.), with or without gum (others).
D184 W ½a. green 1·00 90
D185 1a. green 1·00 90
D186 2a. grey 1·00 90
D187 4a. brown 1·10 90
D188 5a. orange 1·90 1·40
D189 8a. brown 2·20 1·40
D190 12a. brown 2·75 2·10
D191 20a. blue 6·75 4·50
D192 40a. red 7·50 6·00
D193 50a. orange 15·00 12·00
D194 1p. lilac 32·00 23·00

1911. "Due" key-types of Macao optd **REPUBLICA**.

D204	W	½a. green	90	90
D205		1a. green	90	90
D206		2a. grey	90	90
D207		4a. brown	90	90
D208		5a. orange	90	90
D209		8a. brown	90	90
D287		12a. brown	3·25	2·10
D211		20a. blue	3·75	2·00
D212		40a. red	8·00	3·25
D290		50a. orange	13·00	5·75
D291		1p. lilac	14·50	12·00

1925. Marquis de Pombal issue, as Nos. C329/31 optd **MULTA**.

D329	C 73	4a. red	1·50	1·50
D330	–	4a. red	1·50	1·50
D331	C 75	4a. red	1·50	1·50

1947. As Type D **1** of Portuguese Colonies, but inscr "MACAU".

D410	D 1	1a. black and purple	3·75	1·90
D411		2a. black and violet	3·75	1·90
D412		4a. black and blue	3·75	1·90
D413		5a. black and brown	3·75	1·90
D414		8a. black and purple	3·75	1·90
D415		12a. black and brown	3·75	1·90
D416		20a. black and green	7·00	4·25
D417		40a. black and red	12·00	6·50
D418		50a. black and yellow	16·00	8·50
D419		1p. black and blue	18·00	11·00

1949. Postage stamps of 1934 surch **PORTEADO** and new value.

D424	50	1a. on 4a. black	2·50	1·40
D425		2a. on 6a. brown	2·50	1·40
D426		4a. on 8a. blue	2·50	1·40
D427		5a. on 10a. red	2·50	1·40
D428		8a. on 12a. blue	3·75	2·30
D429		12a. on 30a. green	6·00	2·75
D430		20a. on 40a. violet	7·00	3·25

1951. Optd **PORTEADO** or surch also.

D439	66	1a. yellow on cream	1·20	1·20
D440		2a. green on green	1·20	1·20
D441		7a. on 10a. mauve on green	1·20	1·20

D 70

1952. Numerals in red. Name in black.

D451	D 70	1a. blue and green	70	55
D452		3a. brown and salmon	80	65
D453		5a. slate and blue	80	65
D454		10a. red and blue	1·40	1·10
D455		30a. blue and brown	2·40	1·80
D456		1p. brown and grey	4·25	3·25

MACEDONIA Pt. 3

Part of Austro-Hungarian Empire until 1918 when it became part of Yugoslavia. Separate stamps were issued during German Occupation in the Second World War.

In 1991 Macedonia became an independent republic.

A. GERMAN OCCUPATION

100 stotinki = 1 lev.

Македония
8. IX. 1944
1 лв.

(G 1)

1944. Stamps of Bulgaria, 1940–44. (a) Surch as Type G **1**.

G1	1l. on 10st. orange	3·50	14·00
G2	3l. on 15st. blue	3·50	14·00

(b) Surch similar to Type G **1** but larger.

G3	6l. on 10st. blue	4·00	18·00
G4	9l. on 15st. green	4·00	18·00
G5	9l. on 15st. green	5·00	24·00
G6	15l. on 4l. black	12·00	50·00
G7	20l. on 7l. blue	12·00	50·00
G8	30l. on 14l. brown	20·00	50·00

B. INDEPENDENT REPUBLIC

1991. 100 paras = 1 dinar.
1992. 100 deni (de.) = 1 denar (d.).

1 Trumpeters

2 Emblems and Inscriptions

1991. Obligatory Tax. Independence.

1	1	2d.50 black and orange	35	35

1992. Obligatory Tax. Anti-cancer Week. (a) T **2** showing Red Cross symbol at bottom left.

2	2	5d. mauve, black and blue	55	55
3	–	5d. multicoloured	55	55
4	–	5d. multicoloured	55	55
5	–	5d. multicoloured	55	55

DESIGNS: No. 3, Flowers, columns and scanner; 4, Scanner and couch; 5, Computer cabinet.

(b) As T **2** but with right-hand inscr reading down instead of up and without Red Cross symbol.

6	5d. mauve, black & blue (as No. 2)	25	25
7	5d. multicoloured (as No. 3)	25	25
8	5d. multicoloured (as No. 4)	25	25
9	5d. multicoloured (as No. 5)	25	25

3 Red Cross Aircraft dropping Supplies

1992. Obligatory Tax. Red Cross Week. Multicoloured.

10	10d. Red Cross slogans (dated "08–15 MAJ 1992")	15	15
11	10d. Type **3**	15	15
12	10d. Treating road accident victim	15	15
13	10d. Evacuating casualties from ruined building	15	15

The three pictorial designs are taken from children's paintings.

4 "Skopje Earthquake"

6 Nurse with Baby

5 "Wood-carvers Petar and Makarie" (icon), St. Joven Bigorsk Monastery, Debar

1992. Obligatory Tax. Solidarity Week.

14	4	20d. black and mauve	15	15
15	–	20d. multicoloured	15	15
16	–	20d. multicoloured	15	15
17	–	20d. multicoloured	15	15

DESIGNS: No. 15, Red Cross nurse with child; 16, Mothers carrying toddlers at airport; 17, Family at airport.

1992. 1st Anniv of Independence.

18	5	30d. multicoloured	35	35

For 40d. in same design see No. 33.

1992. Obligatory Tax. Anti-tuberculosis Week. Multicoloured.

19	20d. Anti-tuberculosis slogans (dated "14–21.IX.1992")	10	10
20	20d. Type **6**	10	10
21	20d. Nurse giving oxygen	10	10
22	20d. Baby in cot	10	10

7 "The Nativity" (fresco, Slepce Monastery)

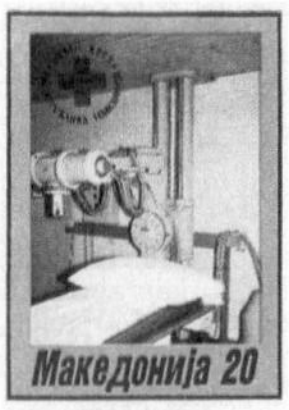

9 Radiography Equipment

8 Mixed Bouquet

1992. Christmas. Multicoloured.

23	100d. Type **7**	50	50
24	500d. "Madonna and Child" (fresco), Zrze Monastery	1·75	1·75

1993. Obligatory Tax. Red Cross Fund. Multicoloured.

25	20d. Red Cross slogans	10	10
26	20d. Marguerites	10	10
27	20d. Carnations	10	10
28	20d. Type **8**	10	10

1993. Obligatory Tax. Anti-cancer Week. Multicoloured.

29	20d. Anti-cancer slogans (dated "1–8 MART 1993")	10	10
30	20d. Type **9**	10	10
31	20d. Overhead treatment unit	10	10
32	20d. Scanner	10	10

1993. As No. 18 but changed value.

33	5	40d. multicoloured	40	40

10 Macedonian Flag

1993.

34	10	10d. multicoloured	10	10
35		40d. multicoloured	45	45
36		50d. multicoloured	55	55

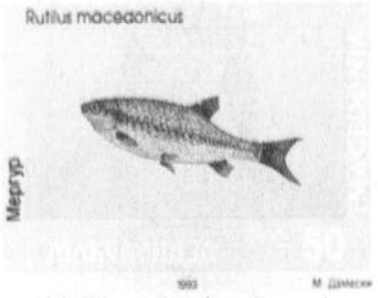

11 Macedonian Roach

1993. Fishes from Lake Ohrid. Multicoloured.

37	50d. Type **11**	15	15
38	100d. Lake Ohrid salmon	20	20
39	1000d. Type **11**	2·00	2·00
40	2000d. As No. 38	3·00	3·00

12 Crucifix, St. George's Monastery

1993. Easter.

41	12	300d. multicoloured	70	70

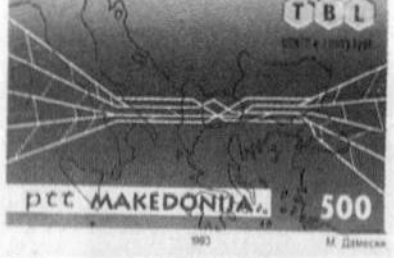

13 Diagram of Telecommunications Cable and Map

1993. Opening of Trans-Balkan Telecommunications Line.

42	13	500d. multicoloured	70	70

14 Red Cross Worker with Baby

1993. Obligatory Tax. Red Cross Week. Multicoloured.

43	50d. Red Cross inscriptions (dated "08–15 MAJ 1993")	10	10
44	50d. Type **14**	10	10
45	50d. Physiotherapist and child in wheelchair	10	10
46	50d. Stretcher party	10	10

See also No. 73.

15 Unloading UNICEF Supplies from Lorry

1993. Obligatory Tax. Solidarity Week.

47	–	50de. black, mauve and silver	10	10
48	15	50de. multicoloured	10	10
49	–	50de. multicoloured	10	10
50	–	50de. multicoloured	10	10

DESIGNS: No. 47, "Skopje Earthquake"; 49, Labelling parcels in warehouse; 50, Consignment of parcels on fork-lift truck.

See also No. 72.

16 U.N. Emblem and Rainbow

1993. Admission to United Nations Organization.

51	16	10d. multicoloured	1·00	1·00

17 "Insurrection" (detail), (B. Lazeski)

19 Tapestry

18 Children in Meadow

1993. 90th Anniv of Macedonian Insurrection.

52	17	10d. multicoloured	1·00	1·00
MS53		116×73 mm. 30d. multicoloured	2·75	2·75

1993. Obligatory Tax. Anti-tuberculosis Week. Multicoloured.

54	50de. Anti-tuberculosis slogans (dated "14–21.09.1993")	10	10
55	50de. Type **18**	10	10
56	50de. Bee on flower	10	10
57	50de. Goat behind boulder	10	10

See also No. 71.

1993. Centenary of Founding of Inner Macedonia Revolutionary Organization.

58		4d. Type **19**	30	30
MS59		90×75 mm. 40d. Two motifs as Type **19**	2·75	2·75

20 "The Nativity" (fresco from St. George's Monastery, Rajcica)

1993. Christmas. Multicoloured.
60 2d. Type **20** 25 25
61 20d. "The Three Kings" (fresco from Slepce Monastery) . . . . 1·00 1·00

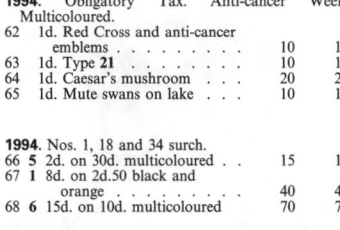

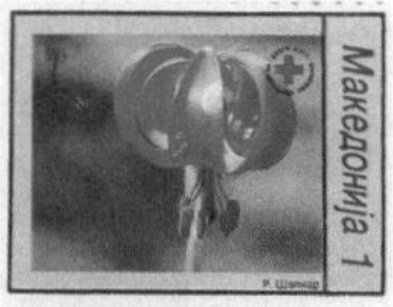

21 Lily

1994. Obligatory Tax. Anti-cancer Week. Multicoloured.
62 1d. Red Cross and anti-cancer emblems 10 10
63 1d. Type **21** 10 10
64 1d. Caesar's mushroom . . . 20 20
65 1d. Mute swans on lake . . . 10 10

1994. Nos. 1, 18 and 34 surch.
66 **5** 2d. on 30d. multicoloured . . 15 15
67 **1** 8d. on 2d.50 black and orange 40 40
68 **6** 15d. on 10d. multicoloured 70 70

23 Decorated Eggs **24** Kosta Racin (writer)

1994. Easter.
69 **23** 2d. multicoloured 25 25

1994. Obligatory Tax. Red Cross Week. As previous designs but values, and date (70), changed. Multicoloured.
70 1d. Red Cross inscriptions (dated "8–15 MAJ 1994") 10 10
71 1d. Type **18** 10 10
72 1d. As No. 50 . . . . 10 10
73 1d. Type **14** 10 10

1994. Revolutionaries. Portraits by Dimitar Kondovski. Multicoloured.
74 8d. Type **24** 45 45
75 15d. Grigor Prlicev (writer) . . 1·00 1·00
76 20d. Nikola Vaptsarov (Bulgarian poet) . . . . . . 1·75 1·75
77 50d. Goce Delcev (founder of Internal Macedonian–Odrin Revolutionary–Organization) . . . . 2·40 2·40

25 "Skopje Earthquake" **26** Tree and Family

1994. Obligatory Tax. Solidarity Week.
78 **25** 1d. black, red and silver . . 10 10

1994. Census.
79 **26** 2d. multicoloured 25 25

27 St. Prohor Pcinski Monastery (venue) **28** Swimmer

1994. 50th Anniv of Macedonian National Liberation Council. Multicoloured.
805d. Type **27** 30 30
MS81 108 × 73 mm. 50d. Aerial view of Monastery . . . . 2·75 2·75

1994. Swimming Marathon, Ohrid.
82 **28** 8d. multicoloured 45 45

29 Turkish Cancellation and 1992 30d. Stamp on Cover

1994. 150th Anniv (1993) of Postal Service in Macedonia.
83 **29** 2d. multicoloured 20 20

30 Mastheads

1994. 50th Anniversaries of "Nova Makedonija", "Mlad Borec" and "Makedonka" (newspapers).
84 **30** 2d. multicoloured 25 25

31 Open Book

1994. 50th Anniv of St. Clement of Ohrid Library. Multicoloured.
85 2d. Type **31** 15 15
86 10d. Page of manuscript (vert) 50 50

32 Globe **33** Wireless and Gramophone Record

1994. Obligatory Tax. Anti-AIDS Week.
87 – 2d. red and black 10 10
88 **32** 2d. black, red and blue . . 10 10
89 – 2d. black, yellow and red . . 10 10
90 – 2d. black and red 10 10
DESIGNS: No. 87, Inscriptions in Cyrillic (dated "01-08.12.1994"); 89, Exclamation mark in warning triangle; 90, Safe sex campaign emblem.

1994. 50th Anniv of Macedonian Radio.
91 **33** 2d. multicoloured 20 20

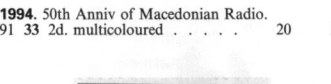

34 Macedonian Pine

1994. Flora and Fauna. Multicoloured.
92 5d. Type **34** 35 35
93 10d. Lynx 80 80

1995. Nos. 35 and 33 surch.
94 **10** 2d. on 40d. multicoloured 35 35
96 **5** 5d. on 40d. multicoloured 35 35

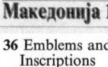

36 Emblems and Inscriptions **38** Voluntary Workers

37 Fresco

1995. Obligatory Tax. Anti-cancer Week. Multicoloured.
97 1d. Type **36** 10 10
98 1d. White lilies 10 10
99 1d. Red lilies 10 10
100 1d. Red roses 10 10

1995. Easter.
101 **37** 4d. multicoloured 30 30

1995. Obligatory Tax. Red Cross. Multicoloured.
102 1d. Cross and inscriptions in Cyrillic (dated "8–15 MAJ 1995") 10 10
103 1d. Type **38** 10 10
104 1d. Volunteers in T-shirts . . 10 10
105 1d. Globe, red cross and red crescent 10 10

39 Troops on Battlefield

1995. 50th Anniv of End of Second World War.
106 **39** 2d. multicoloured 25 25

40 Anniversary Emblem

1995. 50th Anniv of Macedonian Red Cross.
107 **40** 2d. multicoloured 20 20

41 Rontgen and X-Ray Lamp

1995. Centenary of Discovery of X-Rays by Wilhelm Rontgen.
108 **41** 2d. multicoloured 20 20

42 "Skopje Earthquake"

1995. Obligatory Tax. Solidarity Week.
109 **42** 1d. black, red and gold . . 10 10

43 Cernodrinski (dramatist)

1995. 50th Anniv of Vojdan Cernodrinski Theatre Festival.
110 **43** 10d. multicoloured 50 50

44 Kraljevic (fresco, Markov Monastery, Skopje)

1995. 600th Death Anniv of Marko Kraljevic (Serbian Prince).
111 **44** 20d. multicoloured . . . . 1·00 1·00

45 Puleski

1995. Death Centenary of Gorgi Puleski (linguist and revolutionary).
112 **45** 2d. multicoloured 20 20

46 Manuscript, Bridge and Emblem

1995. Writers' Festival, Struga.
113 **46** 2d. multicoloured 25 25

47 Robert Koch (discoverer of tubercule bacillus) **48** Child holding Parents' Hands

1995. Obligatory Tax. Anti-tuberculosis Week.
114 **47** 1d. brown, black and red 10 10

1995. Obligatory Tax. Childrens' Week. Self-adhesive. Imperf.
115 **48** 2d. blue 10 10

49 Maleshevija **50** Interior of Mosque

1995. Buildings. Multicoloured.
116 2d. Type **49** 15 15
117 20d. Krakornica . . . . . . 1·10 1·10

1995. Tetovo Mosque.
118 **50** 15d. multicoloured 90 90

51 Lumiere Brothers (inventors of cine-camera)

1995. Centenary of Motion Pictures. Multicoloured.
119 10d. Type **51** 55 55
120 10d. Milton and Janaki Manaki (Macedonian cinematographers) 55 55
Nos. 119/20 were issued together, se-tenant, forming a composite design.

52 Globe in Nest within Frame

1995. 50th Anniv of U.N.O. Multicoloured.
121 20d. Type **52** 80 80
122 50d. Sun within frame . . . 2·50 2·50

53 Male and Female Symbols

1995. Obligatory Tax. Anti-AIDS Week.
123 **53** 1d. multicoloured 10 10

54 Madonna and Child

1995. Christmas.
124 **54** 15d. multicoloured 75 75

55 Dalmatian Pelican

1995. Birds. Multicoloured.
125 15d. Type **55** 75 75
126 40d. Lammergeier . . . . . 2·00 2·00

56 Letters of Alphabet and Jigsaw Pieces

1995. 50th Anniv of Alphabet Reform.
127 **56** 5d. multicoloured 35 35

57 St. Clement of Ohrid (detail of fresco)

1995. 700th Anniv of Fresco, St. Bogorodica's Church, Ohrid.
128 **57** 8d. multicoloured 45 45
MS129 85 × 67 mm. **57** 50d. multicoloured. Imperf . . . . 20·00 20·00

58 Postal Headquarters, Skopje

1995. 2nd Anniv of Membership of U.P.U.
130 **58** 10d. multicoloured 60 60

59 Zip joining Flags

1995. Entry to Council of Europe and Organization for Security and Co-operation in Europe.
131 **59** 20d. multicoloured . . . . 1·10 1·10

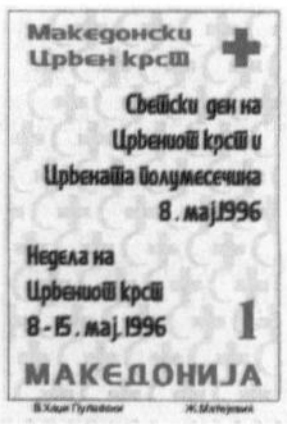

60 Hand holding out Apple **61** Inscriptions

1996. Obligatory Tax. Anti-cancer Week.
132 **60** 1d. multicoloured 10 10

1996. Obligatory Tax. Red Cross Week. Each red, black and yellow.
133 1d. Type **61** 10 10
134 1d. Red Cross principles in Macedonian 10 10
135 1d. Red Cross principles in English 10 10
136 1d. Red Cross principles in French 10 10
137 1d. Red Cross principles in Spanish 10 10

62 Canoeing

1996. Olympic Games, Atlanta. Designs showing statue of discus thrower and sport. Multicoloured.
138 2d. Type **62** 10 10
139 8d. Basketball (vert) 40 40
140 15d. Swimming 75 75
141 20d. Wrestling 95 95
142 40d. Boxing (vert) . . . . . 1·75 1·75
143 50d. Running (vert) . . . . 2·25 2·25

63 "Skopje Earthquake"

1996. Obligatory Tax. Solidarity Week.
144 **63** 1d. gold, red and black . . 10 10

64 Scarecrow Drug Addict **65** Boy

1996. United Nations Anti-drugs Decade.
145 **64** 20d. multicoloured 75 75

1996. Children's Week. Children's Drawings. Multicoloured.
146 2d. Type **65** 10 10
147 8d. Girl 35 35

66 Fragment from Tomb and Tsar Samuel (after Dimitar Kondovski)

1996. Millenary of Crowning of Tsar Samuel (ruler of Bulgaria and Macedonia).
148 **66** 40d. multicoloured . . . . 1·50 1·50

67 Petrov

1996. 75th Death Anniv of Gorce Petrov (revolutionary).
149 **67** 20d. multicoloured 75 75

68 Ohrid Seal, 1903, and State Flag

1996. 5th Anniv of Independence.
150 **68** 10d. multicoloured 40 40

69 Lungs on Globe **70** Vera Ciriviri-Trena (freedom fighter)

1996. Obligatory Tax. Anti-tuberculosis Week.
151 **69** 1d. red, blue and black . . 10 10

1996. Europa. Famous Women. Multicoloured.
152 20d. Type **70** 65 65
153 40d. Mother Teresa (Nobel Peace Prize winner and founder of Missionaries of Charity) . . . . 1·25 1·25

71 Hand holding Syringe

1996. Obligatory Tax. Anti-AIDS Week.
154 **71** 1d. black, red and yellow 10 10

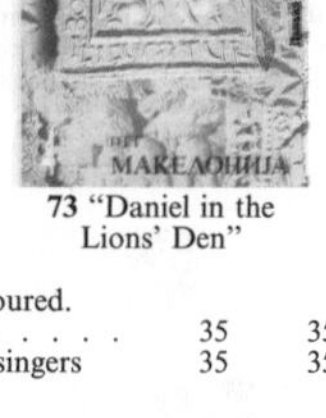

72 Candle, Nuts and Fruit **73** "Daniel in the Lions' Den"

1996. Christmas. Multicoloured.
155 10d. Type **72** 35 35
156 10d. Tree and carol singers 35 35

1996. Early Christian Terracotta Reliefs. (a) Green backgrounds.
157 4d. Type **73** 15 15
158 8d. St. Christopher and St. George 25 25
159 20d. Joshua and Caleb . . . 60 60
160 50d. Unicorn . . . . 1·40 1·40

(b) Blue backgrounds.
161 4d. Type **73** 15 15
162 8d. As No. 158 . . . . . . 25 25
163 20d. As No. 159 . . . . . . 60 60
164 50d. As No. 160 . . . . . . 1·40 1·40

74 Nistrovo **76** UNICEF Coach

75 "Pseudochazara cingovskii"

1996. Traditional Houses. Multicoloured.
165 2d. Type **74** 10 10
166 8d. Brodec 30 30
167 10d. Niviste 35 35

1996. Butterflies. Multicoloured.
168 4d. Type **75** 15 15
169 40d. Danube clouded yellow 1·25 1·25

1996. 50th Anniversaries. Multicoloured.
170 20d. Type **76** (UNICEF) . . 65 65
171 40d. Church in Mtskheta, Georgia (UNESCO) . . . 1·40 1·40

77 Skier

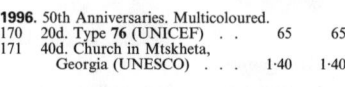

1997. 50 Years of Ski Championships at Sar Planina.
172 **77** 20d. multicoloured 70 70

78 Bell

1997. 150th Birth Anniv of Alexander Graham Bell (telephone pioneer).
173 **78** 40d. multicoloured . . . . 1·40 1·40

79 Family and Healthy Foodstuffs **81** Red Cross on Globe

80 Hound

1997. Obligatory Tax. Anti-cancer Week.
174 **79** 1d. multicoloured 10 10

1997. Roman Mosaics from Heraklia. Mult.
175 2d. Type **80** 10 10
176 8d. Steer 25 25
177 20d. Lion 70 70
178 40d. Leopard with prey . . . 1·25 1·25
MS179 85 × 60 mm. 50d. Deer and plant tub. Imperf . . . . . . 2·75 2·75

1997. Obligatory Tax. Red Cross Week.
180 **81** 1d. mult 10 10

82 Gold Plate

1997. 1100th Anniv of Cyrillic Alphabet. Mult.
181 10d. Type **82** 30 30
182 10d. Sts. Cyril and Methodius 30 30

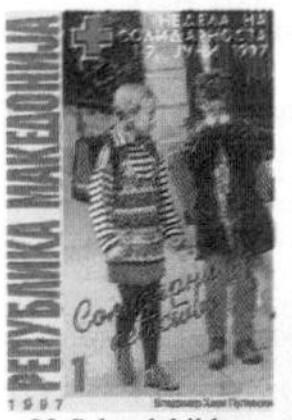

83 Schoolchildren 84 Mountain Flowers

1997. Obligatory Tax. Solidarity Week.
183 **83** 1d. multicoloured 10 10

1997. 5th Anniv of Ecological Association.
184 **84** 15d. multicoloured 55 55

85 Itar Pejo 86 St. Naum and St. Naum's Church, Ohrid

1997. Europa. Tales and Legends. Multicoloured.
185 20d. Type **85** 70 70
186 40d. Stork-men . . . . . . 1·25 1·25

1997. 1100th Birth Anniv of St. Naum.
187 **86** 15d. multicoloured 55 55

87 Diseased Lungs 88 Stibnite

1997. Obligatory Tax. Anti-tuberculosis Week.
188 **87** 1d. multicoloured 10 10

1997. Minerals. Multicoloured.
189 27d. Type **88** 95 95
190 40d. Lorandite . . . . 1·40 1·40

89 Dove and Sun above Child in Open Hand

1997. International Children's Day.
191 **89** 27d. multicoloured 95 95

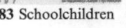

90 Chanterelle

1997. Fungi. Multicoloured.
192 2d. Type **90** 10 10
193 15d. Bronze boletus 50 50
194 27d. Caesar's mushroom . . 95 95
195 50d. "Morchella conica" . . 1·75 1·75

91 Group of Children 92 Gandhi

1998. Obligatory Tax. Anti-AIDS Week.
196 **91** 1d. multicoloured 10 10

1998. 50th Death Anniv of Mahatma Gandhi (Indian independence campaigner).
197 **92** 30d. multicoloured . . . . 1·00 1·00

93 Formula of Pythagoras's Theory

1998. 2500th Death Anniv of Pythagoras (philosopher and mathematician).
198 **93** 16d. multicoloured 55 55

94 Alpine Skiing

1998. Winter Olympic Games, Nagano, Japan. Multicoloured.
199 4d. Type **94** 15 15
200 30d. Cross-country skiing . . 1·00 1·00

95 Novo Selo

1998. Traditional Houses. Multicoloured.
201 1d. Bogomila 10 10
201a 2d. Type **95** 10 10
201b Jachintse 10 10
202 4d. Jablanica 15 15
202a 4d. Svekani 10 10
202b 5d. Teovo 10 10
202c 6d. Zdunje 15 10
202d 6d. Mitrasinci 15 15
202e 9d. Ratevo 20 20
203 16d. Kiselica 35 35
204 20d. Konopnica 70 70
205 30d. Ambar . . . . 1·00 1·00
206 50d. Galicnik . . . . 1·75 1·75

96 "Exodus" (Kole Manev)

1998. 50th Anniv of Exodus of Children during Greek Civil War.
215 **96** 30d. multicoloured . . . . 1·00 1·00

97 "Proportions of Man" (Leonardo da Vinci)

1998. Obligatory Tax. Anti-cancer Week.
216 **97** 1d. multicoloured 10 10

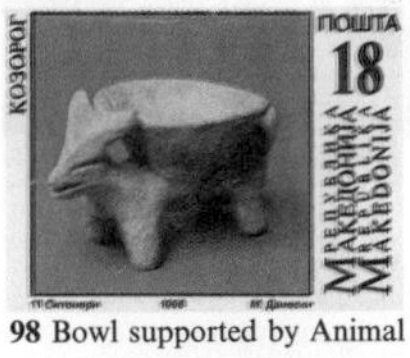

98 Bowl supported by Animal

1998. Archaeological Finds from Nedit. Mult.
217 4d. Carafes 15 15
218 18d. Type **98** 60 60
219 30d. Sacred female figurine 1·00 1·00
220 60d. Stemmed cup . . . . . 2·10 2·10

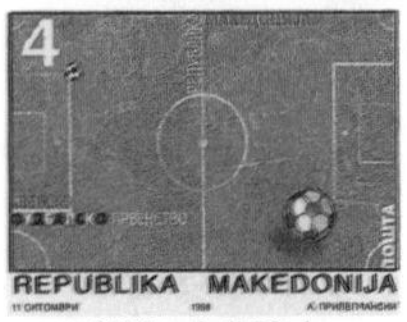

99 Football Pitch

1998. World Cup Football Championship, France. Multicoloured.
221 4d. Type **99** 15 15
222 30d. Globe and football pitch 1·00 1·00

100 Folk Dance

1998. Europa. National Festivals. Multicoloured.
223 30d. Type **100** . . . . . . 1·00 1·00
224 40d. Carnival . . . . 1·40 1·40

101 Profiles

1998. Obligatory Tax. Red Cross Week.
225 **101** 2d. multicoloured 10 10

102 Carnival Procession 103 Hands and Red Cross

1998. 18th Congress of Carnival Towns, Strumica.
226 **102** 30d. multicoloured . . . 1·00 1·00

1998. Obligatory Tax. Solidarity Week.
227 **103** 2d. multicoloured 10 10

104 Flower 105 Cupovski

1998. Environmental Protection. Multicoloured.
228 4d. Type **104** 15 15
229 30d. Polluting chimney uprooting tree . . . . . . 1·00 1·00

1998. 120th Birth Anniv of Dimitrija Cupovski.
230 **105** 16d. multicoloured . . . 55 55

106 Steam Locomotive and Station 107 Doctor and Patient

1997. 150th Anniv of Railways in Macedonia. Multicoloured.
231 30d. Type **106** . . . . . . 1·00 1·00
232 60d. Steam locomotive, 1873 (horiz) . . . . 2·10 2·10

1998. Obligatory Tax. Anti-tuberculosis Week.
233 **107** 2d. multicoloured 10 10

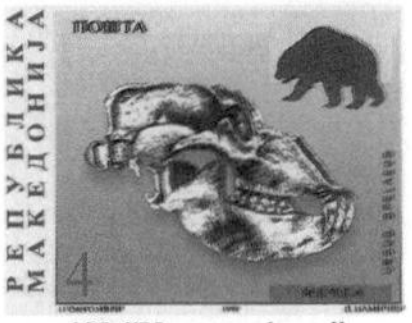

108 "Ursus spelaeus"

1998. Fossilized Skulls. Multicoloured.
234 4d. Type **108** 10 10
235 8d. "Mesopithecus pentelici" 15 15
236 18d. "Tragoceros" 40 40
237 30d. "Aceratherium incsivum" 65 65

109 Atanos Badev (composer) and Score

1998. Centenary of "Zlatoustova Liturgy".
238 **109** 25d. multicoloured . . . 50 50

110 Child with Kite

1998. Children's Day.
239 **110** 30d. multicoloured . . . 65 65

111 "Cerambyx cerdo" (longhorn beetle)

1998. Insects. Multicoloured.
240 4d. Type **111** 10 10
241 8d. Alpine longhorn beetle 15 15
242 20d. European rhinoceros beetle 40 40
243 40d. Stag beetle 85 85

112 Reindeer and Snowflakes

1998. Christmas and New Year. Multicoloured.
244 4d. Type **112** 10 10
245 30d. Bread and oak leaves . . 65 65

113 Ribbon and Gender Symbols

1998. Obligatory Tax. Anti-AIDS Week.
246 **113** 2d. multicoloured 10 10

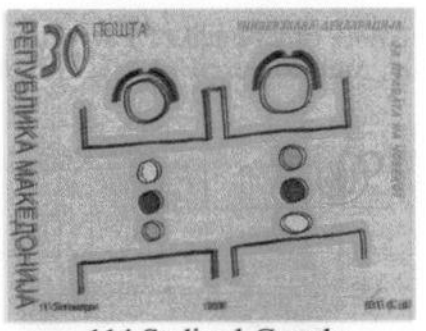

114 Stylized Couple

1998. 50th Anniv of Universal Declaration of Human Rights.
247 **114** 30d. multicoloured . . . 65 65

115 Sharplaninec

1999. Dogs.
248 **115** 15d. multicoloured . . . 30 30

116 Girl's Face

117 "The Annunciation" (Demir Hisar, Slepce Monastery)

1999. Obligatory Tax. Anti-cancer Week.
249 **116** 2d. multicoloured 10 10

1999. Icons. Multicoloured.
250 4d. Type **117** 10 10
251 8d. "Saints" (St. Nicholas's Church, Ohrid) 15 15
252 18d. "Madonna and Child" (Demir Hisar, Slepce Monastery) 40 40
253 30d. "Christ the Redeemer" (Zrze Monastery, Prilep) 65 65
MS254 53 × 74 mm. 50d. "Christ and Archangels" (Archangel Michael Church, Lesnovo Monastery, Probiotip) . . . . 2·75 2·75

118 Pandilov and "Hay Harvest"

1999. Birth Centenary of Dimitar Pandilov (painter).
255 **118** 4d. multicoloured 10 10

119 Telegraph Apparatus

1999. Centenary of the Telegraph in Macedonia.
256 **119** 4d. multicoloured 10 10

120 University and Sts. Cyril and Methodius

1999. 50th Anniv of Sts. Cyril and Methodius University.
257 **120** 8d. multicoloured 15 15

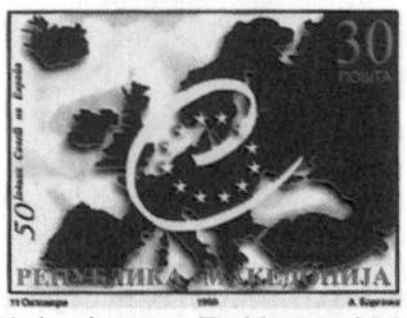

121 Anniversary Emblem and Map of Europe

1999. 50th Anniv of Council of Europe.
258 **121** 30d. multicoloured . . . 65 65

122 Pelister National Park

1999. Europa. Parks and Gardens. Multicoloured.
259 30d. Type **122** 65 65
260 40d. Mavrovo National Park 85 85

123 Figures linking Raised Arms

1999. Obligatory Tax. Red Cross Week.
261 **123** 2d. multicoloured 10 10

124 People running round Globe

125 Tree

1999. Obligatory Tax. Solidarity Week.
262 **124** 2d. multicoloured 10 10

1999. Environmental Protection.
263 **125** 30d. multicoloured . . . 65 65

126 Tsar Petur Delyan

1999. Medieval Rulers of Macedonia. Mult.
264 4d. Type **126** 10 10
265 8d. Prince Gjorgji Vojteh . . 15 15
266 18d. Prince Dobromir Hrs . . 40 40
267 30d. Prince Strez 65 65
Nos. 264/7 were issued together, se-tenant, forming a composite design.

127 Kuzman Shaikarev (author)

1999. 125th Anniv of First Macedonian Language Primer.
268 **127** 4d. multicoloured 10 10

128 Faces in Outline of Lungs

129 "Crocus scardicus"

1999. Obligatory Tax. Anti-tuberculosis Week.
269 **128** 2d. multicoloured 10 10

1999. Flowers. Multicoloured.
270 4d. Type **129** 10 10
271 8d. "Astragalus mayeri" . . 15 15
272 18d. "Campanula formanekiana" 40 40
273 30d. "Viola kosaninii" . . . 65 65

130 Child

1999. Children's Week.
274 **130** 30d. multicoloured . . . 60 60

131 Emblem

1999. 125th Anniv of Universal Postal Union. Mult.
275 5d. Type **131** 10 10
276 30d. Emblem (different) . . . 60 60

132 Men on Horseback

133 Misirkov

1999. 1400th Anniv of Slavs in Macedonia.
277 **132** 5d. multicoloured 10 10

1999. 125th Birth Anniv (2000) of Krste Petkov Misirkov (writer).
278 **133** 5d. multicoloured 10 10

134 Pine Needles

1999. Christmas. Multicoloured.
279 5d. Type **134** 10 10
280 30d. Traditional pastry (vert) 60 60

135 Stylized Figures supporting Globe

1999. Obligatory Tax. Anti-AIDS Week.
281 **135** 2d.50 multicoloured . . . 10 10

136 Altar Cross (19th-century), St. Nikita Monastery

2000. Bimillenary of Christianity. Multicoloured.
282 5d. Type **136** 10 10
283 10d. "Akathist of the Holy Mother of God" (14th-century fresco), Marko's Monastery (horiz) 20 20
284 15d. "St. Clement" (14th-century icon), Ohrid 30 30
285 30d. "Paul the Apostle" (14th-century fresco), St. Andrew's Monastery . . 60 60
MS286 70 × 50 mm. 50d. Cathedral Church of St. Sophia (11th-century), Ohrid (29 × 31 mm) . . . . 2·75 2·75

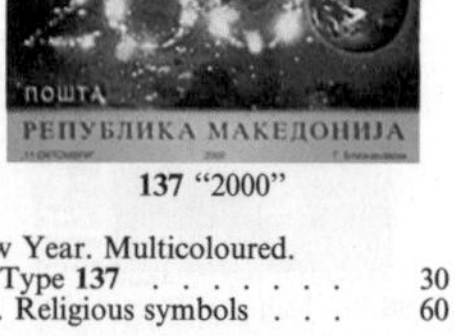

137 "2000"

2000. New Year. Multicoloured.
287 5d. Type **137** 30 30
288 30d. Religious symbols . . . 60 60

138 Globe Unravelling and Medical Symbols

139 Jewelled Brooch with Icon, Ohrid

2000. Obligatory Tax. Anti-cancer Week.
289 **138** 2d.50 multicoloured . . . 10 10

2000. Jewellery. Multicoloured.
290 5d. Type **139** 10 10
291 10d. Bracelet, Bitola 20 20
292 20d. Earrings, Ohrid 40 40
293 30d. Butterfly brooch, Bitola 60 60

140 Magnifying Glass and Perforation Gauge

2000. 50th Anniv of Philately in Macedonia.
294 **140** 5d. multicoloured 10 10

141 Globe and Emblem

2000. 50th Anniv of World Meteorological Organization.
295 **141** 30d. multicoloured . . . 60 60

142 Men with Easter Eggs

144 "Building Europe"

143 Stylized Figures

2000. Easter.
296 **142** 5d. multicoloured 10 10

2000. Obligatory Tax. Red Cross Week.
297 **143** 2d.50 multicoloured . . . 10 10

2000. Europa.
298 **144** 30d. multicoloured . . . 60 60

145 Running

2000. Olympic Games, Sydney. Multicoloured.
299 5d. Type **145** 10 10
300 30d. Wrestling 60 60

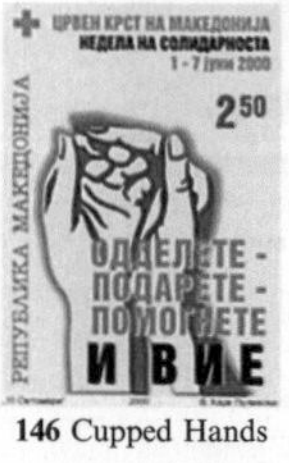

146 Cupped Hands

147 Flower and Globe

2000. Obligatory Tax. Solidarity Week.
301 **146** 2d.50 multicoloured . . . 10 10

2000. International Environmental Protection Day.
302 **147** 5d. multicoloured 10 10

148 Teodosija Sinaitski (printing pioneer)

150 Faces and Hands

149 Mother Teresa

2000. Printing. Multicoloured.
303 6d. Type **148** 10 10
304 30d. Johannes Gutenberg (inventor of printing press) 60 60

2000. 3rd Death Anniv of Mother Teresa (Order of Missionaries of Charity).
305 **149** 6d. multicoloured 10 10

2000. Obligatory Tax. Red Cross Week.
306 **150** 3d. multicoloured 10 10

151 Little Egret

2000. Birds. Multicoloured.
307 6d. Type **151** 10 10
308 10d. Grey heron 20 20
309 20d. Purple heron 40 40
310 30d. Glossy ibis 60 60

152 Children and Tree

2000. Children's Week.
311 **152** 6d. multicoloured 15 15

153 Dimov

154 Emblem

2000. 125th Birth Anniv of Dimo Hadzi Dimov (revolutionary).
312 **153** 6d. multicoloured 15 15

2000. 50th Anniv of Faculty of Economics, St. Cyril and St. Methodius University, Skopje.
313 **154** 6d. multicoloured 15 15

155 Church and Frontispiece

2000. 250th Birth Anniv of Joakim Krcovski (writer).
314 **155** 6d. multicoloured 15 15

156 Nativity

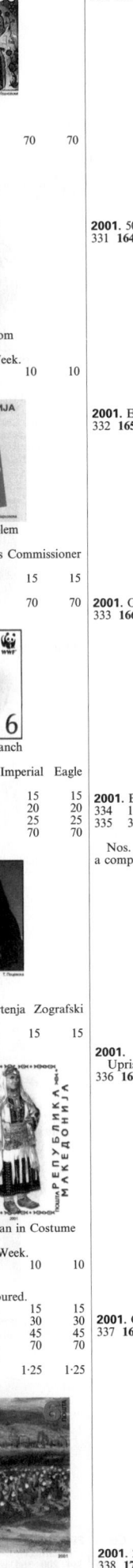

2000. Christmas.
315 **156** 30d. multicoloured . . . 70 70

157 Hand holding Condom

2000. Obligatory Tax. Anti-AIDS. Week.
316 **157** 3d. multicoloured 10 10

158 Handprints and Emblem

2001. 50th Anniv of United Nations Commissioner for Human Rights. Multicoloured.
317 6d. Type **158** 15 15
318 30d. Hands forming Globe (vert) 70 70

159 Imperial Eagle on Branch

2001. Endangered Species. The Imperial Eagle (*Aquila heliaca*). Multicoloured.
319 6d. Type **159** 15 15
320 8d. With chick 20 20
321 10d. Flying 25 25
322 30d. Head 70 70

160 Zografski

2001. 125th Death Anniv of Partenja Zografski (historian).
323 **160** 6d. multicoloured 15 15

161 Emblem

162 Woman in Costume

2001. Obligatory Tax. Anti-Cancer Week.
324 **161** 3d. multicoloured 10 10

2001. Regional Costumes. Multicoloured.
325 6d. Type **162** 15 15
326 12d. Couple in costume . . . 30 30
327 18d. Woman in costume . . . 45 45
328 30d. Couple in costume . . . 70 70
MS329 76 × 64 mm. 50d. Women working (30 × 30 mm). Imperf 1·25 1·25

163 Landscape

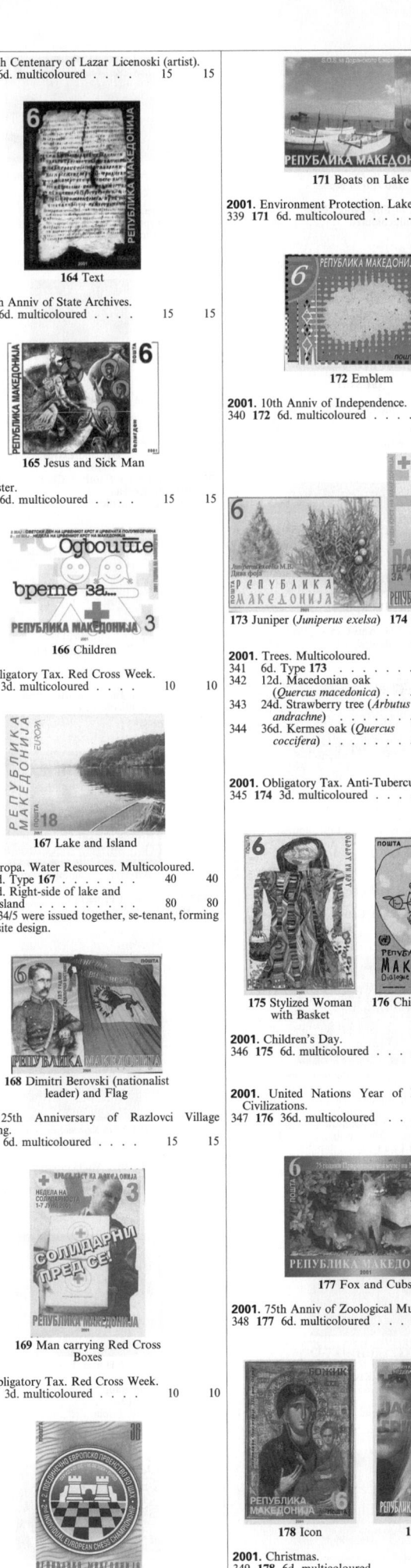

2001. Birth Centenary of Lazar Licenoski (artist).
330 **163** 6d. multicoloured 15 15

164 Text

2001. 50th Anniv of State Archives.
331 **164** 6d. multicoloured 15 15

165 Jesus and Sick Man

2001. Easter.
332 **165** 6d. multicoloured 15 15

166 Children

2001. Obligatory Tax. Red Cross Week.
333 **166** 3d. multicoloured 10 10

167 Lake and Island

2001. Europa. Water Resources. Multicoloured.
334 18d. Type **167** 40 40
335 36d. Right-side of lake and island 80 80

Nos. 334/5 were issued together, se-tenant, forming a composite design.

168 Dimitri Berovski (nationalist leader) and Flag

2001. 125th Anniversary of Razlovci Village Uprising.
336 **168** 6d. multicoloured 15 15

169 Man carrying Red Cross Boxes

2001. Obligatory Tax. Red Cross Week.
337 **169** 3d. multicoloured 10 10

170 Championship Emblem

2001. 2nd Individual Chess Championship, Ohrid.
338 **170** 36d. multicoloured . . . 80 80

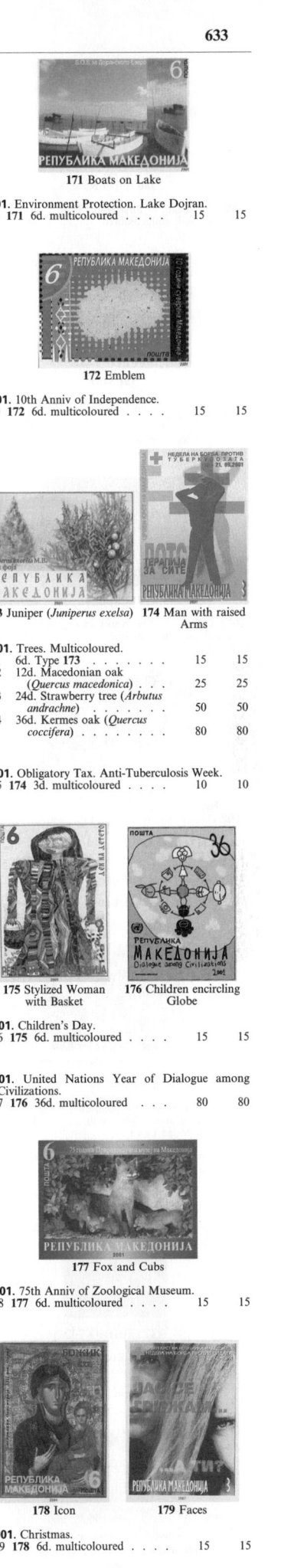

171 Boats on Lake

2001. Environment Protection. Lake Dojran.
339 **171** 6d. multicoloured 15 15

172 Emblem

2001. 10th Anniv of Independence.
340 **172** 6d. multicoloured 15 15

173 Juniper (*Juniperus exelsa*)

174 Man with raised Arms

2001. Trees. Multicoloured.
341 6d. Type **173** 15 15
342 12d. Macedonian oak (*Quercus macedonica*) . . . 25 25
343 24d. Strawberry tree (*Arbutus andrachne*) 50 50
344 36d. Kermes oak (*Quercus coccifera*) 80 80

2001. Obligatory Tax. Anti-Tuberculosis Week.
345 **174** 3d. multicoloured 10 10

175 Stylized Woman with Basket

176 Children encircling Globe

2001. Children's Day.
346 **175** 6d. multicoloured 15 15

2001. United Nations Year of Dialogue among Civilizations.
347 **176** 36d. multicoloured . . . 80 80

177 Fox and Cubs

2001. 75th Anniv of Zoological Museum.
348 **177** 6d. multicoloured 15 15

178 Icon

179 Faces

2001. Christmas.
349 **178** 6d. multicoloured 15 15

2001. Obligatory Tax. Anti-AIDS Week.
350 **179** 3d. multicoloured 10 10

180 Alfred Nobel

2001. Centenary of First Nobel Prize.
351 **180** 36d. multicoloured . . . 80 80

181 Skier

2002. Winter Olympic Games, Salt Lake City, USA. Multicoloured.
352 6d. Type **181** 15 15
353 36d. Skier (different) 80 80

182 Sunrise

2002. Obligarory Tax. Anti-Cancer Week.
354 **182** 3d. multicoloured 10 10

183 Likej (coin)

2002. Ancient Coins. Coins. Multicoloured.
355 6d. Type **183** 15 15
356 12d. Alexander III tetradrachm 25 25
357 24d. Lichnidos 50 50
358 36d. Philip II gold coin (stater) 80 80
MS359 85 × 62 mm. 50d. Coin 1·10 1·10

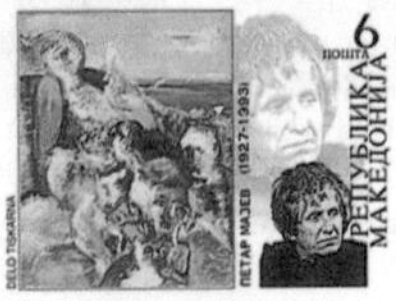
184 Painting and Petar Mazev

2002. Artists Birth Anniversaries. Multicoloured.
360 6d. Type **184** (75th anniv) . . 15 15
361 6d. Triptych, 1978 (Dimitar Kondovski, 75th anniv) . . 15 15
362 36d. Mona Lisa (La Gioconda) and Leonardo da Vinci (550th anniv) . . 80 80

185 "The Risen Christ"

2002. Easter.
363 **185** 6d. multicoloured 15 15

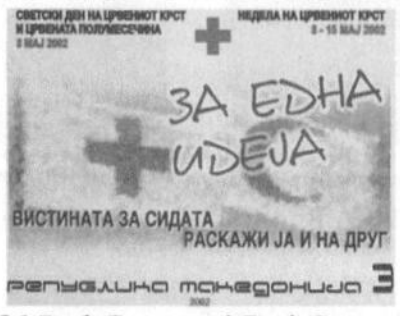
186 Red Cross and Red Crescent Flags

2002. Obligatory Tax. Red Cross Week.
364 **186** 3d. multicoloured 10 10

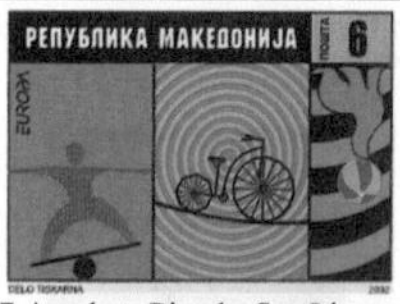
187 Acrobat, Bicycle, Sea Lion and Ball

2002. Europa. Circus. Multicoloured.
365 6d. Type **187** 15 15
366 36d. Circles, bicycle and ball 80 80

188 Championship Emblem, Ball and Player

2002. World Cup Football Championships, Japan and South Korea.
367 **188** 6d. multicoloured 15 15

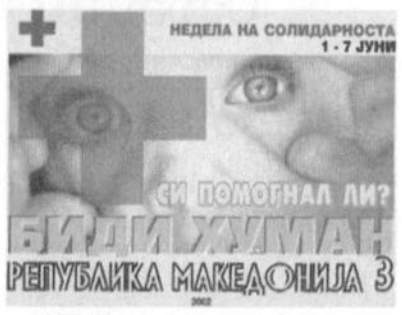
189 Red Cross and Face

2002. Obligatory Tax. Solidarity Week.
368 **189** 3d. multicoloured 10 10

190 Tree containing Shapes

2002. Environment Protection.
369 **190** 6d. multicoloured 15 15

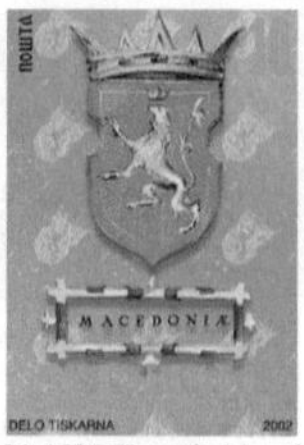
191 1595 Korenic Neonic Coat of Arms

2002. National Arms. Multicoloured.
370 10d. Type **191** 20 20
371 36d. 1620 Coat of Arms . . 80 80

192 House, Krusevo

2002. City Architecture. Multicoloured.
372 36d. Type **192** 80 80
373 50d. House, Bitola . . . . . 1·10 1·10

193 Metodija Andonov-Cento

2002. Birth Centenary of Metodija Andonov-Cento (first Macedonian president).
374 **193** 6d. multicoloured 15 15

194 Nikola Karev

2002. 125th Birth Anniv of Nikola Karev (revolutionary leader).
375 **194** 18d. multicoloured . . . 40 40

195 Grey Partridge (*Perdix perdix*)

2002. Fauna. Multicoloured.
376 6d. Type **195** 15 15
377 12d. Wild Pig (*Sus scrofa*) . . 25 25
378 24d. Chamois (*Rupicapra rupicapra*) 50 50
379 36d. Rock Partridge (*Alectoris graeca*) 80 80

196 Face

2002. Obligatory Tax. Anti-Tuberculosis Week.
380 **196** 3d. multicoloured 10 10

197 House and People (child's drawing)

2002. Children's Day.
381 **197** 6d. multicoloured 15 15

198 Mary and Jesus (14th-century icon)

2002. Christmas.
382 **198** 9d. multicoloured 20 20

199 Clock, Numbers and Face

2002. Obligatory Tax. Anti-AIDS Week.
383 **199** 3d. multicoloured 10 10

200 Andreja Damjanov and Building Facade

2003. 125th Death Anniv of Andreja Damjanov (architect).
384 **200** 36d. multicoloured . . . 1·10 1·10

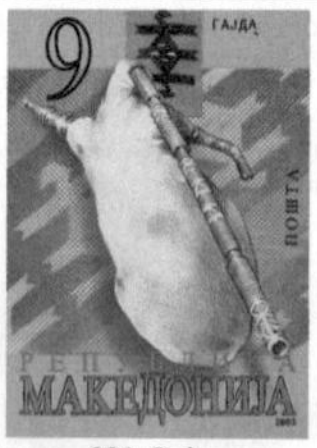
201 Gajga

2003. Traditional Musical Instruments. Multicoloured.
385 9d. Type **201** 30 30
386 10d. Tambura 30 30
387 20d. Kemene 60 60
388 50d. Tapan . . . . 1·50 1·50

202 Scouts and Campsite

2003. 50th Anniv of Scouting in Macedonia.
389 **202** 9d. multicoloured 30 30

203 Face surrounded by Petals

2003. Obligatory Tax. Anti-Cancer Week.
390 **203** 4d. multicoloured 20 20

204 Krste Petkov Misirkov (founder)

2003. 50th Anniv of Krste Petkov Misirkov Macedonian Language Institute.
391 **204** 9d. multicoloured 30 30

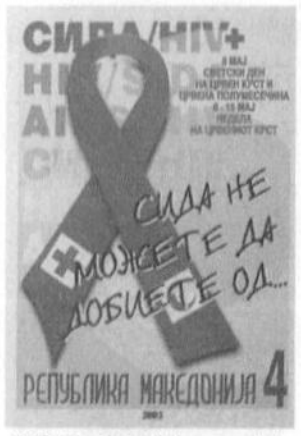
205 Red Ribbon with Red Cross and Red Crescent Emblems

206 International Graphic Art Triennial, Bitola (1994)

2003. Obligatory Tax. Red Cross Week.
392 **205** 3d. multicoloured 20 20

2003. Europa. Poster Art. Multicoloured.
393 36d. Type **206** . . . . 1·10 1·10
394 36d. "Ohrider Sommer" (1966) . . . . 1·10 1·10

207 Outstretched Hand

209 Handball Player

208 Brown Bear (*Ursus arctos*)

2003. Obligatory Tax. Solidarity Week. Litho.
395 **207** 4d. multicoloured 20 20

2003.
396 **208** 9d. multicoloured 20 20

2003. City Architecture. As T **192**. Multicoloured.
397 10d. House, Skopje 10 10
398 20d. House, Resen 30 30

2003. National Arms. As T **191**. Multicoloured.
399 9d. 17th-century arms 30 30
400 36d. 1694 Coat of Arms . . 1·10 1·10

2003. World Youth Handball Championships.
401 **209** 36d. multicoloured . . . 1·10 1·10

210 Seal and Revolutionaries

2003. Centenary of Ilinden Uprising. Multicoloured.
402 9d. Type **210** 30 30
403 36d. Leaders and Mechen Kamen monument . . . . 1·10 1·10
MS404 60 × 75 mm. 50d. Revolutionaries (different) . . 1·50 1·50

211 "Self Portrait" (Nikola Martinovski)

2003. Artists' Anniversaries. Multicoloured.
405 9d. Type **211** (birth centenary) 30 30
406 36d. "Moulin de Galette" (Vincent van Gogh) (150th birth anniv) (horiz) . . . . 1·50 1·50

212 Stylized Figure

2003. Obligatory Tax. Anti-Tuberculosis Week.
407 **212** 4d. multicoloured 20 20

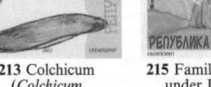

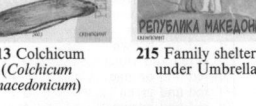

213 Colchicum (*Colchicum macedonicum*)

215 Family sheltering under Umbrella

214 Said Najdeni

2003. Flowers. Multicoloured.
408 9d. Type **213** 30 30
409 20d. Viola (*Viola allchariensis*) 60 60
410 36d. *Tulipa mariannae* . . . 1·20 1·20
411 50d. *Thymus oehmianus* . . . 1·50 1·50

2003. Death Centenaries. Multicoloured.
412 9d. Type **214** (Albanian writer and reformer) . . . 30 30
413 9d. Jeronim de Rada (Italian-Albanian writer) 30 30

2003. Children's Day.
414 **215** 9d. multicoloured 30 30

216 Seal and Armed Revolutionaries

2003. 125th Anniv of Kresna Uprising.
415 **216** 9d. multicoloured 30 30

217 Dimitir Vlahov

2003. 50th Death Anniv of Dimitir Vlahov (politician).
416 **217** 9d. multicoloured 30 30

218 Mary and Jesus (fresco)

2003. Christmas.
417 **218** 9d. multicoloured 30 30

219 Ribbon

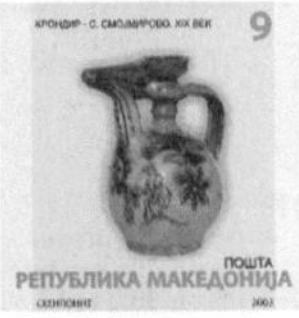

220 19th-century Jug, Smojmirovo

2003. Obligatory Tax. Anti-AIDS Week.
418 **219** 4d. vermilion 25 25

2003. Cultural Artifacts. Multicoloured.
419 3d. Amphora 15 15
420 5d. Tassel, Vrutok 30 30
422 9d. Type **220** 30 30
423 10d. Kettle, Ohrid 30 30
425 12d. Albastron (alabaster incense pot) 40 40
430 20d. Chest decoration, Galicnik 60 60

221 Wilbur and Orville Wright and *Wright Flyer*

2003. Centenary of Powered Flight.
440 **221** 50d. multicoloured . . . 1·50 1·50

222 Street Scene (Tomo Vladimirski)

2004. Artists' Birth Centenaries. Multicoloured.
441 9d. Type **222** 30 30
442 9d. Ohrid Street (Vangel Kodzoman) 30 30

223 Breast Examination

224 Knives and Armour

2004. Obligatory Tax. Anti-Cancer Week.
443 **223** 4d. multicoloured 25 25

2004. Cultural Heritage. Weapons. Multicoloured.
444 10d. Type **224** 30 30
445 20d. 19th-century sword . . . 60 60
446 36d. 18th-century pistol . . . 90 90
447 50d. 18th-century rifle . . . 1·50 1·50

225 Carpet

226 Kostandin Kristoforidhi (writer)

2004. Traditional Carpets. Multicoloured.
448 36d. Type **225** 95 95
449 50d. Carpet (different) . . . 1·50 1·50

2004. Centenary of Publication of First Albanian Dictionary in Macedonia.
450 **226** 36d. multicoloured . . . 95 95

227 House, Kratovo

2004. City Architecture.
451 **227** 20d. multicoloured . . . 60 60

228 Parasol and Woman Reading

229 Profiles

2004. Europa. Holidays. Multicoloured.
452 50d. Type **228** . . . . 1·40 1·40
453 50d. Yacht and island . . . 1·40 1·40
Nos. 452/3 were issued together, se-tenant, forming a composite design of a beach scene.

2004. Obligatory Tax. Red Cross Week.
454 **229** 4d. multicoloured 25 25

230 Stars

2004. Application to join European Union.
455 **230** 36d. multicoloured . . . 90 90

231 Hands enclosing Globe

232 Pelican and Lake

2004. Obligatory Tax. Solidarity Week.
456 **231** 6d. multicoloured 30 30

2004. Prespa National Park.
457 **232** 36d. multicoloured . . . 90 90

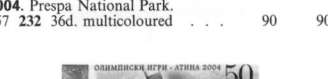

233 Flags as Interlocking Rings

2004. Olympic Games, Athens. Multicoloured.
458 50d. Type **233** . . . . 1·20 1·20
459 50d. Rings (different) . . . . 1·20 1·20
Nos. 458/9 were issued together, se-tenant, forming a composite design of Olympic rings.

234 Sami Frasheri

2004. Death Centenary of Sami Frasheri (Albanian writer).
460 **234** 12d. multicoloured . . . 30 30

235 Emblem, Feet and Ball

2004. Centenary of FIFA (Federation Internationale de Football Association).
461 **235** 100d. multicoloured . . . 2·20 2·20

236 Marko Cepenkov

2004. Anniversaries. Multicoloured.
462 12d. Type **236** (writer) (175th birth) 30 30
463 12d. Vasil Glavinov (politician) (75th death) (vert) 30 30

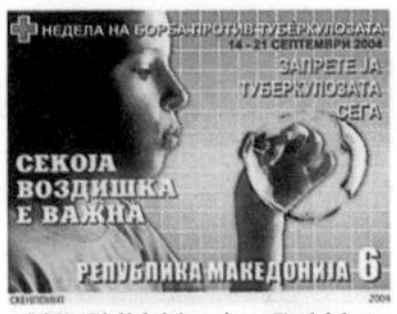

237 Child blowing Bubbles

2004. Obligatory Tax. Anti-Tuberculosis Week.
464 **237** 4d. multicoloured 10 10

238 Bohemian Waxwing (*Bombycilla garrulous*)

2004. Birds. Multicoloured.

465		12d. Type **238**	30	30
466		24d. Woodchat shrike (*Lanius senato*)	55	55
467		36d. Rock thrush (*Monticola saxatilis*)	90	90
468		48d. Northern bullfinch (*Pyrrhula pyrrhula*)	1·20	1·20
MS469		86×61 mm. 60d. Wall creeper (*Tichodroma muraria*). Imperf	2·00	2·00

239 Children

2004. Children's Day.

470	**239**	12d. multicoloured	30	30

240 Binary Code

2004. World Summit on Information Technology Society (WSIS).

471	**240**	36d. multicoloured	90	90

241 Manuscript

2004. Millenary of Publication of Asseman Gospel (Glagolitic (early Slavonic language) liturgical gospel).

472	**241**	12d. multicoloured	30	30

242 Marco Polo

2004. 750th Birth Anniv of Marco Polo (traveller).

473	**242**	36d. multicoloured	90	90

243 Star, Ribbons, Snowflakes and Holly

2004. Christmas.

474	**243**	12d. multicoloured	30	30

244 Hands

2004. Obligatory Tax. AIDS Week.

475	**244**	6d. multicoloured	30	30

MADAGASCAR Pt. 6

A large island in the Indian Ocean off the east coast of Africa. French Post Offices operated there from 1885.

In 1896 the island was declared a French colony, absorbing Diego-Suarez and Ste. Marie de Madagascar in 1898 and Nossi-Be in 1901.

Madagascar became autonomous as the Malagasy Republic in 1958; it reverted to the name of Madagascar in 1992.

100 centimes = 1 franc.

A. FRENCH POST OFFICES

1889. Stamps of French Colonies "Commerce" type surch with value in figures.

1	J	05 on 10c. black on lilac	£525	£150
2		05 on 25c. black on red	£525	£140
4		05 on 40c. red on yellow	£130	80·00
5		5 on 10c. black on lilac	£170	90·00
6		5 on 25c. black on red	£170	£100
7		15 on 25c. black on red	£120	75·00
3		25 on 40c. red on yellow	£475	£130

5

1891. No gum. Imperf.

9	**5**	5c. black on green	£120	11·50
10		10c. black on blue	90·00	25·00
11		15c. blue on blue	95·00	18·00
12		25c. brown on buff	21·00	14·50
13		1f. black on yellow	£900	£225
14		5f. black and lilac on lilac	£1800	£900

1895. Stamps of France optd **POSTE FRANCAISE Madagascar**.

15	**10**	5c. green	6·00	6·50
16		10c. black on lilac	45·00	32·00
17		15c. blue	50·00	12·00
18		25c. black on red	60·00	8·25
19		40c. red on yellow	70·00	10·00
20		50c. red	£110	12·50
21		75c. brown on orange	£100	50·00
22		1f. olive	£120	42·00
23		5f. mauve on lilac	£150	80·00

1896. Stamps of France surch with value in figures in oval.

29	**10**	5c. on 1c. black on blue	£4250	£1600
30		15c. on 2c. brown on yellow	£1700	£800
31		25c. on 3c. grey	£2250	£800
32		25c. on 4c. red on grey	£4750	£1500
33		25c. on 40c. red on yellow	£1000	£600

B. FRENCH COLONY OF MADAGASCAR AND DEPENDENCIES

1896. "Tablet" key-type inscr "MADAGASCAR ET DEPENDANCES".

1	D	1c. black and red on blue	85	25
2		2c. brown and blue on buff	45	1·40
2a		2c. brown & blk on buff	6·75	7·00
3		4c. brown and blue on grey	95	1·25
17		5c. green and red	3·00	15
6		10c. black and blue on lilac	11·00	1·25
18		10c. red and blue	2·75	15
7		15c. blue and red	9·00	1·00
19		15c. grey and red	4·00	65
8		20c. red and blue on green	6·25	1·90
9		25c. black and red on pink	10·50	25
20		25c. blue and red	23·00	35·00
10		30c. brown & bl on drab	8·50	2·25
21		35c. black and red on yellow	42·00	4·00
11		40c. red and blue on yellow	8·25	1·25
12		50c. red and blue on pink	15·00	1·40
22		50c. brown and red on blue	27·00	27·00
13		75c. violet & red on orge	2·75	3·25
14		1f. green and red	17·00	2·50
15		1f. green and blue	27·00	16·00
16		5f. mauve and blue on lilac	42·00	30·00

1902. "Tablet" key-type stamps as above surch.

27	D	0,01 on 2c. brown and blue on buff	5·25	3·75
27a		0,01 on 2c. brown and black on buff	3·75	9·00
29		0,05 on 30c. brown and blue on drab	3·75	5·25
23		05 on 50c. red and blue on pink	2·25	2·25
31		0,10 on 50c. red and blue on pink	3·25	5·00
24		10 on 5f. mauve and blue on lilac	18·00	13·50
32		0,15 on 75c. violet and red on orange	1·50	1·50
33		0,15 on 1f. green and red	3·50	3·75
25		15 on 1f. green and red	3·50	1·25

1902. Nos. 59 and 61 of Diego-Suarez surch.

34	D	0,05 on 30c. brown and blue on drab	£110	£100
36		0,10 on 50c. red and blue on pink	£3750	£3750

4 Zebu and Lemur

5 Transport in Madagascar

1903.

38	**4**	1c. purple	50	25
39		2c. brown	50	35
40		4c. brown	40	1·00
41		5c. green	6·75	35
42		10c. red	8·75	35
43		15c. red	9·00	30
44		20c. orange	2·75	1·50
45		25c. blue	30·00	1·40
46		30c. red	30·00	13·00
47		40c. lilac	38·00	4·00
48		50c. brown	60·00	28·00
49		75c. yellow	48·00	25·00
50		1f. green	50·00	35·00
51		2f. blue	55·00	32·00
52		5f. black	55·00	80·00

1908.

53a	**5**	1c. green and violet	10	20
54		2c. green and red	10	20
55		4c. brown and green	10	1·25
56		5c. olive and green	1·25	20
90		5c. red and black	30	15
57		10c. brown and pink	1·60	20
91		10c. olive and green	30	30
92		10c. purple and brown	45	30
58		15c. red and lilac	35	20
93		15c. green and olive	45	2·75
94		15c. red and blue	65	3·75
59		20c. brown and orange	1·00	80
60		25c. black and blue	5·00	95
95		25c. black and violet	25	25
61		30c. black and brown	4·50	4·25
96		30c. brown and red	45	1·25
97		30c. purple and green	35	20
98		30c. light green and green	2·25	3·00
62		35c. black and red	1·75	1·50
63		40c. black and brown	90	70
64		45c. black and green	1·50	2·75
99		45c. red and scarlet	60	2·75
100		45c. purple and lilac	2·75	3·50
65		50c. black and violet	1·00	1·10
101		50c. black and blue	65	30
102		50c. yellow and black	20	40
103		60c. violet on pink	45	1·90
104		65c. blue and black	2·00	3·25
66		75c. black and red	90	40
105		85c. red and green	1·25	3·50
67		1f. green and brown	30	40
106		1f. blue	35	1·40
107		1f. green and mauve	6·75	9·25
108		1f.10 green and brown	1·60	3·25
68		2f. green and blue	2·75	1·40
69		5f. brown and violet	16·00	8·25

1912. "Tablet" key-type surch.

70	D	05 on 15c. grey and red	25	75
71		05 on 20c. red and blue on green	80	1·75
72		05 on 30c. brown and blue on drab	50	3·00
73		10 on 75c. violet and red on orange	2·50	14·50
81		0.60 on 75c. violet and red on orange	9·75	11·00
82		1f. on 5f. mauve and blue on lilac	1·25	3·00

1912. Surch.

74	**4**	05 on 2c. brown	25	2·75
75		05 on 20c. orange	55	1·40
76		05 on 30c. red	45	3·00
77		10 on 40c. lilac	1·10	3·25
78		10 on 50c. brown	1·50	4·25
79		10 on 75c. brown	3·50	11·50
83		1f. on 5f. black	90·00	90·00

1915. Surch **5c** and red cross.

80	**5**	10c.+5c. brown and pink	50	1·60

1921. Surch **1 cent.**

84	**5**	1c. on 15c. red and lilac	20	1·60

1921. Type **5** (some colours changed) surch.

109	**5**	25c. on 15c. red and lilac	60	3·00
85		0,25 on 35c. black and red	6·50	7·00
86		0,25 on 40c. black and brown	4·50	5·75
87		0,25 on 45c. black and green	3·50	4·75
111		25c. on 2f. green and blue	40	1·90
112		25c. on 5f. brown and violet	40	3·00
88		0,30 on 40c. black and brown	85	2·25
113		50c. on 1f. green and brown	1·25	25
89		0,60 on 75c. black and red	2·75	3·25
114		60 on 75c. violet on pink	80	50
115		65c. on 75c. black and red	2·25	3·00
116		85c. on 45c. black and green	1·50	3·25
117		90c. on 75c. pink and red	80	2·25
118		1f.25 on 1f. blue	1·00	2·50
119		1f.50 on 1f. lt blue & blue	1·75	20
120		3f. on 5f. violet and green	2·25	2·75
121		10f. on 5f. mauve and red	8·00	7·50
122		20f. on 5f. blue and mauve	12·00	9·25

14 Sakalava Chief

15 Zebus

17 Betsileo Woman

18 General Gallieni

1930.

123	**18**	1c. blue	15	2·75
124	**15**	1c. green and blue	15	15
125	**14**	2c. brown and red	10	10
177	**18**	3c. blue	15	1·50
126a	**14**	4c. mauve and brown	25	25
127	**15**	5c. red and green	15	15
128	–	10c. green and red	10	10
129	**17**	15c. red	10	10
130	**15**	20c. blue and brown	10	15
131	–	25c. brown and lilac	20	10
132	**17**	30c. green	35	20
133	**14**	40c. red and green	55	30
134	**17**	45c. lilac	1·90	2·00
178	**18**	45c. green	1·25	1·75
179		50c. brown	25	10
180		60c. mauve	15	1·75
136	**15**	65c. mauve and brown	2·75	2·25
181	**18**	70c. red	1·50	2·50
137	**17**	75c. brown	2·25	20
138	**15**	90c. red	2·75	1·10
182	**18**	90c. brown	40	15
139	–	1f. blue and brown	3·25	2·50
140	–	1f. red and scarlet	1·25	1·25
140a	–	1f.25 brown and blue	2·75	1·50
183	**18**	1f.40 orange	2·75	2·75
141	**14**	1f.50 ultramarine and blue	10·00	65
142		1f.50 red and brown	80	95
278		1f.50 brown and red	10	1·25
184	**18**	1f.60 violet	2·25	2·75
143	**14**	1f.75 red and brown	5·50	55
185	**18**	2f. red	40	20
186a		3f. green	60	1·50
146	**14**	5f. brown and mauve	8·75	2·75
147	**18**	10f. orange	1·90	1·40
148	**14**	20f. blue and brown	6·50	4·50

DESIGN—VERT: 10c., 25c., 1f., 1f.25, Hova girl.

1931. "Colonial Exhibition" key-types inscr "MADAGASCAR".

149	E	40c. black and green	2·50	3·00
150	F	50c. black and mauve	3·25	3·00
151	G	90c. black and red	2·75	3·00
152	H	1f.50 black and blue	3·75	3·00

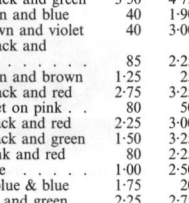

19 Bloch 120 over Madagascar

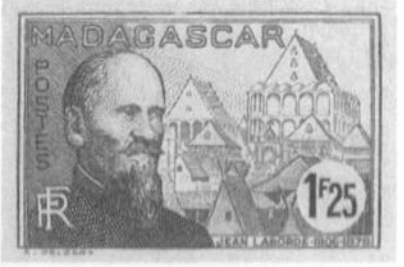

20 J. Laborde and Tananarivo Palace

1935. Air.

153	**19**	50c. red and green	1·75	1·90
154		90c. red and green	30	2·75
155		1f.25 red and lake	1·50	2·25
156		1f.50 red and blue	1·50	2·25
157		1f.60 red and blue	55	2·25
158		1f.75 red and orange	9·00	5·75
159		2f. red and blue	1·60	2·00
160		3f. red and orange	70	2·25
161		3f.65 red and black	1·40	1·00
162		3f.90 red and green	40	2·50
163		4f. red and carmine	29·00	3·25
164		4f.50 red and black	16·00	60
165		5f.50 red and green	1·10	2·75
166		6f. red and mauve	85	2·50
167		6f.90 red and purple	60	2·50
168		8f. red and mauve	2·75	3·25
169		8f.50 red and green	3·00	3·25
170		9f. red and green	1·25	2·75
171		12f. red and brown	40	2·25
172		12f.50 red and violet	3·25	3·25
173		15f. red and orange	40	2·25
174		16f. red and green	3·00	4·00
175		20f. red and brown	4·00	3·75
176		50f. red and blue	5·50	7·00

1937. International Exhibition, Paris. As T **16** of Mauritania.

187		20c. violet	80	3·25
188		30c. green	1·75	3·25
189		40c. red	40	1·50
190		50c. brown and agate	35	75
191		90c. red	35	1·90
192		1f.50 blue	50	2·00

1938. 60th Death Anniv of Jean Laborde (explorer).

193	20	35c. green	75	40
194		55c. violet	55	65
195		65c. red	1·00	50
196		80c. purple	1·00	50
197		1f. red	65	50
198		1f.25 red	2·00	2·75
199		1f.75 blue	45	90
200		2f.15 brown	2·00	3·25
201		2f.25 blue	1·75	3·25
202		2f.50 brown	30	30
203		10f. green	40	80

1938. Int Anti-cancer Fund. As T **22** of Mauritania.

204		1f.75+50c. blue	4·50	13·50

1939. New York World's Fair. As T **28** of Mauritania.

205		1f.25 red	2·25	1·75
206		2f.25 blue	2·50	2·50

1939. 150th Anniv of French Revolution. As T **29** of Mauritania.

207		45c.+25c. green and black (postage)	5·75	13·50
208		70c.+30c. brown and black	7·25	13·50
209		90c.+35c. orange and black	5·25	13·50
210		1f.25+1f. red and black	5·75	13·50
211		2f.25+2f. blue and black	5·75	13·50
212		4f.50+4f. black and orange (air)	9·50	22·00

1942. Surch **50** and bars.

213	15	50 on 65c. mauve & brown	3·25	50

1942. Free French Administration. Optd **FRANCE LIBRE** or surch also.

214	14	2c. brown and red (postage)	2·75	3·25
215	18	3c. blue	£120	£120
216	15	0,05 on 1c. green and blue	1·75	1·40
217	20	0,10 on 55c. violet	50	3·50
218	17	15c. red	15·00	14·50
219	20	0,30 on 65c. red	40	3·00
220	15	0f.50 on 0,05 on 1c. green and blue	2·25	3·25
221		50 on 65c. mauve & brown	1·25	10
222	18	50 on 90c. brown	2·00	10
223	15	65c. mauve and brown	3·25	3·25
224	18	70c. red	2·25	3·00
225	20	80c. purple	4·00	3·50
226	–	1,00 on 1f.25 brown and blue (No. 140a)	3·75	3·75
227	20	1,00 on 1f.25 red	9·75	8·50
228	18	1f.40 orange	2·75	2·75
229	5	1f.50 on 1f. blue	3·25	3·25
230	14	1f.50 ultramarine and blue	2·50	3·25
231		1f.50 red and brown	3·50	3·25
232	18	1,50 on 1f.60 violet	2·50	2·75
233	14	1,50 on 1f.75 red & brown	2·75	1·60
234	20	1,50 on 1f.75 blue	2·25	2·50
235	18	1f.60 violet	2·75	2·75
236	20	2,00 on 2f.15 brown	1·75	85
237		2f.25 blue	2·75	3·00
238	–	2f.25 blue (No. 206)	2·75	2·75
239	20	2f.50 brown	5·00	4·75
240	5	10f. on 5f. mauve and red	13·50	11·00
241	20	10f. green	5·25	5·00
242	5	20f. on 5f. blue and mauve	17·00	16·00
243	14	20f. blue and brown	£700	£800
244	19	1,00 on 1f.25 red and lake (air)	7·00	7·00
245		1f.50 red and blue	8·25	9·25
246		1f.75 red and orange	90·00	£100
247		3,00 on 3f.65 red and black	2·75	15
248		8f. red and purple	3·25	3·25
249		8,00 on 8f.50 red and green	2·75	70
250		12f. red and brown	4·25	4·00
251		12f.50 red and violet	3·25	3·25
252		16f. red and green	7·25	7·25
253		50f. red and blue	6·00	6·00

24 Traveller's Tree

29 Gen. Gallieni

25a Legionaries by Lake Chad

1943. Free French Issue.

254	24	5c. brown	10	2·75
255		10c. mauve	10	10
256		25c. green	10	2·00
257		30c. orange	10	10
258		40c. blue	55	20
259		80c. purple	60	20
260		1f. blue	50	15
261		1f.50 red	60	15
262		2f. yellow	75	15
263		2f.50 blue	60	10
264		4f. blue and red	1·25	40
265		5f. green and black	60	10
266		10f. red and blue	85	15
267		20f. violet and brown	1·25	20

1943. Free French Administration. Air. As T **19a** of Oceanic Settlements, but inscr "MADAGASCAR".

268		1f. orange	30	1·50
269		1f.50 red	30	1·25
270		5f. purple	25	35
271		10f. black	1·00	1·60
272		25f. blue	90	2·50
273		50f. green	90	80
274		100f. red	1·10	35

1944. Mutual Aid and Red Cross Funds. As T **19b** of Oceanic Settlements.

275		5f.+20f. green	75	3·00

1944. Surch **1f.50**.

276	24	1f.50 on 5c. brown	20	60
277		1f.50 on 10c. mauve	70	3·00

1945. Eboue. As T **20a** of Oceanic Settlements.

279		2f. black	15	25
280		25f. green	70	3·50

1946. Air. Victory. As T **20b** of Oceanic Settlements.

281		8f. red	20	20

1945. Surch with new value.

282	24	50c. on 5c. brown	30	40
283		60c. on 5c. brown	40	2·50
284		70c. on 5c. brown	40	2·50
285		1f.20 on 5c. brown	25	2·25
286		2f.40 on 25c. green	45	60
287		3f. on 25c. green	45	30
288		4f.50 on 25c. green	1·50	2·00
289		15f. on 2f.50 blue	50	85

1946. Air. From Chad to the Rhine.

290	25a	5f. blue	55	3·00
291	–	10f. red	80	2·50
292	–	15f. green	1·00	3·25
293	–	20f. brown	90	3·00
294	–	25f. violet	85	3·25
295	–	50f. red	60	3·00

DESIGNS: 10f. Battle of Koufra; 15f. Tank Battle, Mareth; 20f. Normandy Landings; 25f. Liberation of Paris; 50f. Liberation of Strasbourg.

1946.

296	–	10c. green (postage)	10	60
297	–	30c. orange	10	20
298	–	40c. olive	10	40
299	–	50c. purple	10	10
300	–	60c. blue	10	1·60
301	–	80c. green	10	1·60
302	–	1f. sepia	10	10
303	–	1f.20 green	20	1·40
304	29	1f.50 red	10	10
305	–	2f. black	10	10
306	–	3f. purple	25	10
307	–	3f.60 red	90	2·25
308	–	4f. blue	35	10
309	–	5f. orange	40	15
310	–	6f. blue	15	10
311	–	10f. lake	45	20
312	–	15f. brown	50	10
313	–	20f. blue	30	20
314	–	25f. brown	55	25
315	–	50f. blue and red (air)	1·10	1·25
316	–	100f. brown and red	85	45
317	–	200f. brown and green	2·25	2·50

DESIGNS—As T **29**. VERT: 10 to 50c. Native with spear; 6, 10f. Gen. Duchesne; 15, 20, 25f. Lt.-Col. Joffre. HORIZ: 60, 80c. Zebus; 1f., 1f.20, Sakalava man and woman; 3f.60, 4, 5f. Betsimisaraka mother and child. 49 × 28 mm: 50f. Aerial view of Port of Tamatave. 28 × 51 mm: 100f. Allegory of flight. 51 × 28 mm: Douglas DC-2 airplane and map of Madagascar.

36 Gen. Gallieni and View

1946. 50th Anniv of French Protectorate.

318	36	10f.+5f. purple	20	3·00

1948. Air. Discovery of Adelie Land, Antarctic. No. 316 optd **TERRE ADELIE DUMONT D'URVILLE 1840.**

319		100f. brown and red	26·00	55·00

1949. Air. 75th Anniv of U.P.U. As T **38** of New Caledonia.

320		25f. multicoloured	1·40	1·75

1950. Colonial Welfare Fund. As T **39** of New Caledonia.

321		10f.+2f. purple and green	3·50	9·25

38 Cacti and Succulents

39 Long-tailed Ground Roller

40 Woman and Forest Road

1952.

322	38	7f.50 green & blue (postage)	35	20
323	39	8f. lake	90	40
324		15f. blue and green	2·40	40
325	–	50f. green and blue (air)	2·50	30
326	–	100f. black, brown and blue	6·00	1·40
327	–	200f. brown and green	20·00	8·00
328	40	500f. brown, sepia & green	30·00	7·50

DESIGNS—As Type **40**: 50f. Palm trees; 100f. Antsirabe Viaduct; 200f. Ring-tailed lemurs.

1952. Military Medal Centenary As T **40** of New Caledonia.

329		15f. turquoise, yellow & green	1·10	1·50

1954. Air. 10th Anniv of Liberation. As T **42** of New Caledonia.

330		15f. purple and violet	2·25	1·25

41 Marshal Lyautey

1954. Birth Centenary of Marshal Lyautey.

331	41	10f. indigo, blue & ultram	45	10
332		40f. lake, grey and black	55	10

42 Gallieni School

43 Cassava

1956. Economic and Social Development Fund.

333	–	3f. brown and grey	25	10
334	42	5f. brown and chestnut	25	10
335	–	10f. blue and grey	30	10
336	–	15f. green and turquoise	40	10

DESIGNS: 3f. Tamatave and tractor; 10f. Dredging canal; 15f. Irrigation.

1956. Coffee. As T **44** of New Caledonia.

337		20f. sepia and brown	20	10

1957. Plants.

338	43	2f. green, brown and blue	25	10
339	–	4f. red, brown and green	15	10
340	–	12f. green, brown and violet	70	10

DESIGNS: 4f. Cloves; 12f. Vanilla.

Issues of 1958–92. For issues between these dates, see under MALAGASY REPUBLIC.

362 Children with Mascot

363 Environmental Projects

1992. School Sports Festival (1990).

910	362	140f. multicoloured	35	10

1992. Air. World Environment Day.

911	363	140f. multicoloured	10	10

364 Post Box and Globe

365 Basenji

1992. Air. World Post Day.

912	364	500f. multicoloured	75	25

1992. Domestic Animals. Multicoloured.

913		140f. Type **365**	10	10
914		500f. Anglo-Arab horse	90	25
915		640f. Tortoiseshell cat and kitten	1·10	30
916		1025f. Siamese and colourpoint (cats)	1·60	50
917		1140f. Holstein horse	2·25	60
918		5000f. German shepherd dogs	6·50	75

366 Foodstuffs

1992. International Nutrition Conference, Rome.

920	366	500f. multicoloured	1·10	25

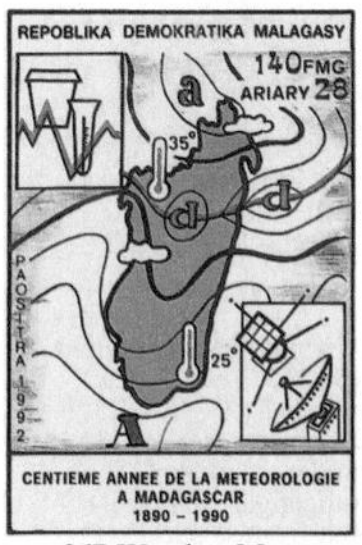

367 Weather Map

1992. Centenary of Meteorological Service.

921	367	140f. multicoloured	35	10

368 "Eusemia bisma"

1992. Butterflies and Moths. Multicoloured.

922		15f. Type **368**	10	10
923		35f. Tailed comet moth (vert)	10	10
924		65f. "Alcides aurora"	10	10
925		140f. "Agarista agricola"	35	10
926		600f. "Trogonoptera croesus"	1·40	30
927		850f. "Trogonodtera priamus"	1·75	45
928		1300f. "Pereute leucodrosime"	2·25	70

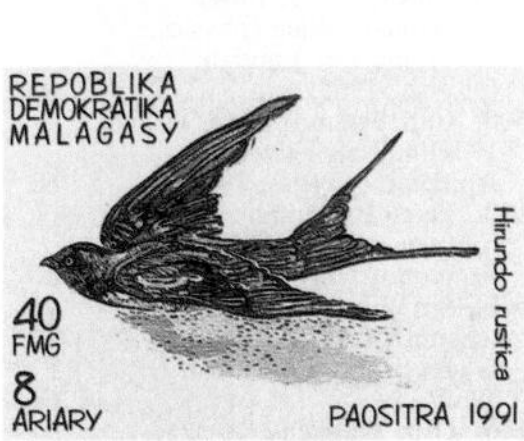

369 Barn Swallow

1992. Birds. Multicoloured.

930		40f. Type **369**	10	10
931		55f. Pied harrier (vert)	10	10
932		60f. European cuckoo (vert)	10	10
933		140f. Sacred ibis	10	10
934		210f. Purple swamphen	45	10
935		500f. Common roller	1·10	25
936		2000f. Golden oriole	4·00	1·10

370 Gymnastics

1992. Olympic Games, Barcelona. Multicoloured.

938	65f. Type **370**	10	10
939	70f. High jumping	10	10
940	120f. Archery	10	10
941	140f. Cycling	35	10
942	675f. Weightlifting	1·10	30
943	720f. Boxing	1·40	35
944	1200f. Two-man kayak	1·75	60

371 Pusher-tug, Pangalanes Canal

1993.

946 **371** 140f. multicoloured . . . 35 10

372 BMW

373 Hyacinth Macaw

1993. Motor Cars. Multicoloured.

947	20f. Type **372**	10	10
948	40f. Toyota "Carina"	10	10
949	60f. Cadillac	10	10
950	65f. Volvo	10	10
951	140f. Mercedes-Benz	10	10
952	640f. Ford "Sierra"	1·00	30
953	3000f. Honda "Concerto"	4·50	90

1993. Parrot Family. Multicoloured.

955	50f. Type **373**	10	10
956	60f. Cockatiel	10	10
957	140f. Budgerigar	10	10
958	500f. Jandaya conure	60	25
959	675f. Budgerigar (different)	1·10	35
960	800f. Red-fronted parakeet	1·40	45
961	1750f. Kea	2·75	65

375 Albert Einstein (physics, 1921) and Niels Bohr (physics, 1922)

1993. Nobel Prize Winners. Multicoloured.

964	500f. Type **375**	60	25
965	500f. Wolfgang Pauli (physics, 1945) and Max Born (physics, 1954)	60	25
966	500f. Joseph Thomson (physics, 1906) and Johannes Stark (physics, 1919)	60	25
967	500f. Otto Hahn (physics, 1944) and Hideki Yukawa (physics, 1949)	60	25
968	500f. Owen Richardson (physics, 1928) and William Shockley (physics, 1956)	60	25
969	500f. Albert Michelson (physics, 1907) and Charles Townes (physics, 1964)	60	25
970	500f. Wilhelm Wien (physics, 1911) and Lev Landau (physics, 1962)	60	25
971	500f. Carl Braun (physics, 1909) and Sir Edward Appleton (physics, 1947)	60	25
972	500f. Percy Bridgman (physics, 1946) and Nikolai Semyonov (physics, 1956)	60	25
973	500f. Sir William Ramsay (chemistry, 1904) and Glenn Seaborg (chemistry, 1951)	60	25
974	500f. Otto Wallach (chemistry, 1910) and Hermann Staudinger (chemistry, 1953)	60	25
975	500f. Richard Synge (chemistry, 1952) and Axel Theorell (chemistry, 1955)	60	25
976	500f. Thomas Morgan (medicine, 1933) and Hermann Muller (medicine, 1946)	60	25
977	500f. Allvar Gullstrand (medicine, 1911) and Willem Einthoven (medicine, 1924)	60	25
978	500f. Sir Charles Sherrington (medicine, 1932) and Otto Loewi (medicine, 1936)	60	25
979	500f. Jules Bordet (medicine, 1936) and Sir Alexander Fleming (medicine, 1945)	60	25

376 1956 Bugatti

1993. Racing Cars and Railway Locomotives. Multicoloured.

980	20f. Type **376**	10	10
981	20f. 1968 Ferrari	10	10
982	20f. 1948 Class C62 steam locomotive, 1948, Japan	10	10
983	20f. Electric train, 1975, Russia	10	10
984	140f. 1962 Lotus Mk 25	10	10
985	140f. 1970 Matra	10	10
986	140f. Diesel locomotive, 1954, Norway	10	10
987	140f. Class 26 steam locomotive, 1982, South Africa	10	10
988	1250f. 1963 Porsche	90	65
989	1250f. 1980 Ligier JS 11	90	65
990	1250f. Metroliner electric train, 1967, U.S.A.	90	65
991	1250f. Diesel train, 1982, Canada	90	65
992	3000f. 1967 Honda	2·10	1·50
993	3000f. 1992 Benetton B 192	2·10	1·50
994	3000f. Union Pacific Railroad diesel-electric locomotive, 1969, U.S.A.	2·10	2·10
995	3000f. TGV Atlantique express train, 1990, France	2·10	2·10

377 Pharaonic Ship

1993. Ships. Multicoloured.

996	5f. Type **377**	10	10
997	5f. Mediterranean carrack	10	10
998	5f. "Great Western" (sail paddle-steamer), 1837	10	10
999	5f. "Mississippi" (paddle-steamer), 1850	10	10
1000	15f. Phoenician bireme	10	10
1001	15f. Viking ship	10	10
1002	15f. "Clermont" (first commercial paddle-steamer), 1806	10	10
1003	15f. "Pourquoi Pas?" (Charcot's ship), 1936	10	10
1004	140f. "Santa Maria" (Columbus's ship), 1492	10	10
1005	140f. H.M.S. "Victory" (ship of the line), 1765	10	10
1006	140f. Motor yacht	10	10
1007	140f. "Bremen" (liner), 1950	10	10
1008	10000f. "Sovereign of the Seas" (galleon), 1637	9·25	80
1009	10000f. "Cutty Sark" (clipper)	9·25	80
1010	10000f. "Savannah" (nuclear-powered freighter)	9·25	80
1011	10000f. "Condor" (hydrofoil)	9·25	80

No. 999 is wrongly inscribed "Mississipi".

378 Johannes Gutenberg and Printing Press

1993. Inventors. Multicoloured.

1012	500f. Type **378**	60	25
1013	500f. Sir Isaac Newton and telescope	60	25
1014	500f. John Dalton and atomic theory	60	25
1015	500f. Louis Jacques Daguerre and camera	60	25
1016	500f. Michael Faraday and electric motor	60	25
1017	500f. Wright brothers and "Flyer"	60	25
1018	500f. Alexander Bell and telephone	60	25
1019	500f. Thomas Edison and telegraph	60	25
1020	500f. Karl Benz and motor vehicle	60	25
1021	500f. Sir Charles Parsons and "Turbina"	60	25
1022	500f. Rudolf Diesel and diesel locomotive	60	35
1023	500f. Guglielmo Marconi and early radio	60	25
1024	500f. Lumiere brothers and cine-camera	60	35
1025	500f. Herman Oberth and space rocket	60	25
1026	500f. John Mauchly, J. Prosper Eckert and computer	60	25
1027	500f. Arthur Shawlow, compact disc and laser	60	25

379 Leonardo da Vinci and "Virgin of the Rocks"

1993. Painters. Multicoloured.

1028	50f. Type **379**	10	10
1029	50f. Titian and "Sacred and Profane Love"	10	10
1030	50f. Rembrandt and "Jeremiah crying"	10	10
1031	50f. J. M. W. Turner and "Ulysses"	10	10
1032	640f. Michelangelo and the Doni Tondo	70	30
1033	640f. Peter Paul Rubens and "Self-portrait"	70	30
1034	640f. Francisco Goya and "Don Manuel Osorio de Zuniga"	70	30
1035	640f. Eugene Delacroix and "Christ on Lake Gennesaret"	70	30
1036	1000f. Claude Monet and "Poppyfield"	95	50
1037	1000f. Paul Gauguin and "Two Tahitians"	95	50
1038	1000f. Henri Marie de Toulouse-Lautrec and "Woman with a Black Boa"	95	50
1039	1000f. Salvador Dali and "St. James of Compostela"	95	50
1040	2500f. Pierre Auguste Renoir and "Child carrying Flowers"	2·75	90
1041	2500f. Vincent Van Gogh and "Dr. Paul Gachet"	2·75	90
1042	2500f. Pablo Picasso and "Crying Woman"	2·75	90
1043	2500f. Andy Warhol and "Portrait of Elvis"	2·75	90

380 Sunset Moth ("Chrysiridia madagascariensis")

1993. Butterflies, Moths and Birds. Multicoloured.

1044	45f. Type **380**	10	10
1045	45f. African monarch ("Hypolimnas misippus")	10	10
1046	45f. Southern crested Madagascar coucal ("Coua verreauxi")	10	10
1047	45f. African marsh owl ("Asio helvola")	10	10
1048	60f. "Charaxes antamboulou"	10	10
1049	60f. "Papilio antenor"	10	10
1050	60f. Crested Madagascar coucal ("Coua cristata")	10	10
1051	60f. Helmet bird ("Euryceros prevostii")	10	10
1052	140f. "Hypolimnas dexithea"	10	10
1053	140f. "Charaxes andronodorus"	10	10
1054	140f. Giant Madagascar coucal ("Couca gigas")	10	10
1055	140f. Madagascar red fody ("Foudia madagascarensis")	10	10
1056	3000f. "Euxanthe madagascarensis"	3·25	45
1057	3000f. "Papilio grosesmithi"	3·25	45
1058	3000f. Sicklebill ("Falculea palliata")	3·25	45
1059	3000f. Madagascar serpent eagle ("Eutriorchis astur")	3·25	45

Nos. 1044/59 were issued together, se-tenant, the butterfly and bird designs respectively forming composite designs.

381 Henri Dunant and Volunteers unloading Red Cross Lorry

1993. Anniversaries and Events. Multicoloured.

1060	500f. Type **381** (award of first Nobel Peace Prize, 1901)	35	25
1061	640f. Charles de Gaulle and battlefield (50th anniv of Battle of Bir-Hakeim (1992))	45	30
1062	1025f. Crowd at Brandenburg Gate (bicentenary (1991) and fourth anniv of breach of Berlin Wall)	1·10	55
1063	1500f. Doctors giving health instruction to women (Rotary International and Lions International)	1·60	55
1064	3000f. Konrad Adenauer (German chancellor 1949–63, 24th death anniv (1991))	3·25	60
1065	3500f. "LZ-4" (airship), 1908, and Count Ferdinand von Zeppelin (75th death anniv (1992))	4·00	60

382 Guides and Anniversary Emblem

383 Player, Trophy and Ficklin Home, Macon

1993. Air. 50th Anniv of Madagascan Girl Guides.

1067 **382** 140f. multicoloured . . . 10 10

1993. World Cup Football Championship, United States (1992). Multicoloured.

1068	140f. Type **383**	10	10
1069	640f. Player, trophy and Herndon Home, Atlanta	65	35
1070	1025f. Player, trophy and Cultural Centre, Augusta	1·40	55
1071	5000f. Player, trophy and Old Governor's Mansion, Milledgeville	6·00	1·00

1993. Various stamps optd with emblem and inscription. (a) Germany, World Cup Football Champion, 1990. Nos. 778/81 optd **VAINQUEUR: ALLEMAGNE.**

1073	**328**	350f. multicoloured	25	15
1074	–	1000f. multicoloured	90	50
1075	–	1500f. multicoloured	1·50	80
1076	–	2500f. multicoloured	2·75	1·00

(b) Gold Medallists at Winter Olympic Games, Albertville (1992). Nos. 812/15 optd with Olympic rings, **"MEDAILLE D'OR"** and further inscr as below.

1077	350f. **BOB A QUATRE (AUT) INGO APPELT HARALD WINKLER GERHARD HAIDACHER THOMAS SCROLL**	25	15
1078	1000f. **1000 M. - OLAF ZINKE (GER)**	90	50
1079	1500f. **50 KM LIBRE BJOERN DAEHLIE (NOR)**	1·50	80
1080	2500f. **SUPER G MESSIEURS KJETIL-ANDRE AAMODT (NOR)**	2·75	1·25

(c) Anniversaries. Nos. 1060, 675 and 707 optd as listed below.

1082	500f. Red Cross and **130e ANNIVERSAIRE DE LA CREATION DE LA CROIX-ROUGE 1863–1993**	2·25	1·10
1083	550f. Lions emblem and **75eme ANNIVERSAIRE LIONS**	2·25	1·10
1084	1500f. Guitar and **THE ELVIS'S GUITAR 15TH ANNIVERSARY OF HIS DEATH 1977–1992**	1·75	80
1085	1500f. Guitar and **GUITARE ELVIS 15eme ANNIVERSAIRE DE SA MORT 1977–1992**	1·75	80

(d) 50th Death Anniv of Robert Baden-Powell (founder of Boy Scouts). Optd **50eme ANNIVERSAIRE DE LA MORT DE BADEN POWEL** and emblem. (i) On Nos. 870/5 with scout badge in wreath.

1086 **354** 140f. multicoloured . . . 10 10
1087 – 500f. multicoloured . . . 35 25
1088 – 640f. multicoloured . . . 45 30
1089 – 1025f. multicoloured . . 1·10 30
1090 – 1140f. multicoloured . . 1·10 35
1091 – 3500f. multicoloured . . 3·25 1·10

(ii) On No. 676 with profile of Baden-Powell.

1093 1500f. multicoloured . . . . 1·75 80

(e) Bicentenary of French Republic. Nos. 761/5 optd **Republique Francaise** and emblem within oval and **BICENTENAIRE DE L'AN I DE LA REPUBLIQUE FRANCAISE**.

1094 250f. multicoloured 20 15
1095 350f. multicoloured 25 15
1096 1000f. multicoloured . . . . 1·10 50
1097 1500f. multicoloured . . . . 1·75 50
1098 2500f. multicoloured . . . . 2·75 90

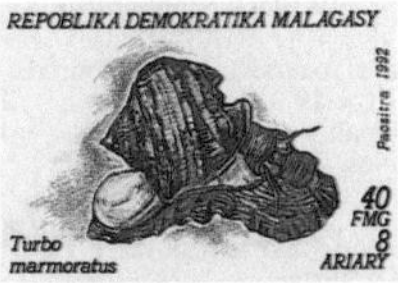

385 Great Green Turban

1993. Molluscs. Multicoloured.

1100 40f. Type **385** 10 10
1101 60f. Episcopal mitre 10 10
1102 65f. Common paper nautilis . 10 10
1103 140f. Textile cone 10 10
1104 500f. European sea hare . . 90 25
1105 675f. "Harpa amouretta" . . 1·10 35
1106 2500f. Tiger cowrie . . . . 3·50 70

386 Tiger Shark

1993. Sharks. Multicoloured.

1108 10f. Type **386** 10 10
1109 45f. Japanese sawshark . . 10 10
1110 140f. Whale shark 15 10
1111 270f. Smooth hammerhead 30 20
1112 600f. Oceanic white-tipped shark 65 35
1113 1200f. Zebra shark . . . . 1·25 80
1114 1500f. Goblin shark . . . . 1·90 1·10

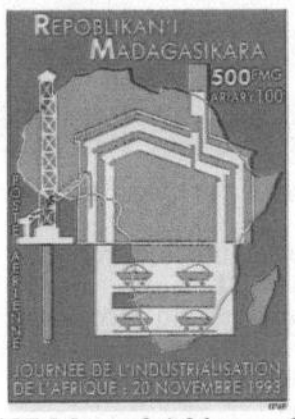
387 Map of Africa and Industry

1993. Air. African Industrialization Day.

1116 **387** 500f. red, yellow and blue 80 50

388 "Superviem Odoriko" Express Train

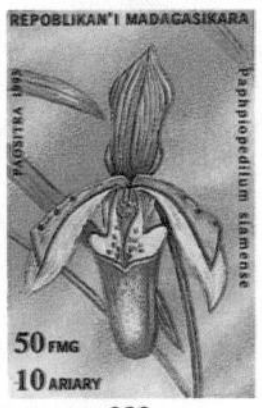

389 "Paphiopedilum siamense"

1993. Locomotives. Multicoloured.

1117 5f. Type **388** 10 10
1118 15f. Morrison Knudsen diesel locomotive No. 801 10 10
1119 140f. ER-200 diesel train, Russia 10 10
1120 265f. General Motors GP60 diesel-electric locomotive No. EKD-5, U.S.A. . . . 20 15
1121 300f. New Jersey Transit diesel locomotive, U.S.A. 20 15
1122 575f. ICE high speed train, Germany 40 30
1123 2500f. X2000 high speed train, Sweden . . . . . . 1·75 1·25

1993. Orchids. Multicoloured.

1125 50f. Type **389** (wrongly inscr "Paphpiopedilum") . . . 10 10
1126 65f. "Cypripedium calceolus" 10 10
1127 70f. "Ophrys oestrifera" . . 10 10
1128 140f. "Cephalanthera rubra" 10 10
1129 300f. "Cypripedium macranthon" 20 15
1130 640f. "Calanthe vestita" . . 80 30
1131 2500f. "Cypripedium guttatum" . . . . 3·25 90

390 "Necrophorus tomentosus"

392 Fork and Spoon, Sakalava

391 Lufthansa Airliner, Germany

1994. Beetles. Multicoloured.

1133 20f. Type **390** 10 10
1134 60f. "Dynastes tityus" . . . 10 10
1135 140f. "Megaloxanta bicolor" 10 10
1136 605f. Searcher 40 10
1137 720f. "Chrysochroa mirabilis" 50 15
1138 1000f. "Crioceris asparaqi" 70 25
1139 1500f. Rose chafer . . . . 1·10 35

1994. Aircraft. Multicoloured.

1141 10f. Type **391** 10 10
1142 10f. British Aerospace/ Aerospatiale Concorde supersonic jetliner of Air France 10 10
1143 10f. Air Canada airliner . . 10 10
1144 10f. ANA airliner, Japan . . 10 10
1145 60f. Boeing 747 jetliner of British Airways 10 10
1146 60f. Dornier Do-X flying boat, Germany 10 10
1147 60f. Shinmeiwa flying boat, Japan 10 10
1148 60f. Royal Jordanian airliner 10 10
1149 640f. Alitalia airliner 45 15
1150 640f. French-European Development Project Hydro 2000 flying boat 45 15
1151 640f. Boeing 314 flying boat 45 15
1152 640f. Air Madagascar airliner 45 15
1153 5000f. Emirates Airlines airliner, United Arab Emirates . . . . 3·50 1·10
1154 5000f. Scandinavian Airways airliner . . . . 3·50 1·10
1155 5000f. KLM airliner, Netherlands . . . . . . 3·50 1·10
1156 5000f. Air Caledonie airliner, New Caledonia 3·50 1·10

Nos. 1141/56 were issued together, se-tenant, Nos. 1146/7 and 1150/1 forming a composite design.

1994. Traditional Crafts. Multicoloured.

1157 30f. Silver jewellery, Mahafaly 10 10
1158 60f. Type **392** 10 10
1159 140f. Silver jewellery, Antandroy 10 10
1160 430f. Silver jewellery on table, Sakalava 30 10
1161 580f. Frames of decorated paper, Ambalavao 40 10
1162 1250f. Silver jewellery, Sakalava 90 30
1163 1500f. Marquetry table, Ambositra . . . . 1·10 35

393 "Chicoreus torrefactus" (shell)

1994. Marine Life. Multicoloured.

1165 15f. Type **393** 10 10
1166 15f. "Fasciolaria filamentosa" (shell) . . . 10 10
1167 15f. Regal angelfish ("Pigopytes diacanthus") 10 10
1168 15f. Coelacanth ("Latimeria chalumnae") 10 10
1169 30f. "Stellaria solaris" (shell) 10 10
1170 30f. Ventral harp ("Harpa ventricosa") 10 10
1171 30f. Blue-tailed boxfish ("Ostracion cyanurus") 10 10
1172 30f. Clown wrasse ("Coris gaimardi") 10 10
1173 1250f. Lobster ("Panulirus sp.") 90 30
1174 1250f. "Stenopus hispidus" (crustacean) 90 30
1175 1250f. Undulate triggerfish ("Balistapus undulatus") 90 30
1176 1250f. Forceps butterflyfish ("Forcipiger longirostris") 90 30
1177 1500f. Hermit crab ("Pagure") . . . . 1·10 35
1178 1500f. Hermit crab ("Bernard l'Hermite") . . 1·10 35
1179 1500f. Diadem squirrelfish ("Adioryx diadema") . . 1·10 35
1180 1500f. Lunulate lionfish ("Pterois lunulata") . . . 1·10 35

Nos. 1165/80 were issued together, se-tenant, the backgrounds forming a composite design.

394 Arms

395 Troops landing on Beach

1994. Air. Junior Economic Chamber Zone A (Africa, Middle East and Indian Ocean) Conference, Antananarivo. Multicoloured.

1181 140f. Type **394** 10 10
1182 500f. Arms as in Type **394** but with inscriptions differently arranged (vert) 70 20

1994. 50th Anniv of Allied Landings at Normandy. Multicoloured.

1183 1500f. Type **395** . . . . . 1·10 35
1184 3000f. German troops defending ridge and allied troops (as T **397**) . . . . 2·25 75
1185 3000f. Airplanes over battle scene, trooper with U.S. flag and German officer (as T **397**) . . . . 2·25 75

Nos. 1183/5 were issued together, se-tenant, forming a composite design.

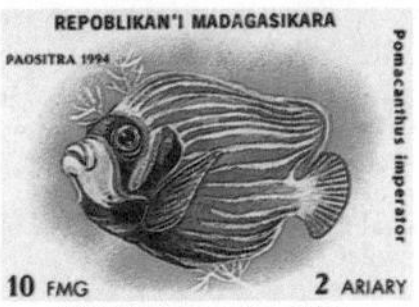

396 Emperor Angelfish

1994. Aquarium Fishes. Multicoloured.

1186 10f. Type **396** 10 10
1187 30f. Siamese fighting fish . . 10 10
1188 45f. Pearl gourami 10 10
1189 95f. Cuckoo-wrasse 10 10
1190 140f. Blotched upsidedown catfish ("Synodontis nigreventris") 10 10
1191 140f. Jack Dempsey ("Cichlasoma biocellatum") 10 10
1192 3500f. Mummichog . . . . 2·50 80

397 Notre Dame Cathedral, Armed Resistance Fighters and Rejoicing Crowd

1994. 50th Anniv of Liberation of Paris by Allied Forces. Multicoloured.

1194 1500f. Crowd and Arc de Triomphe (as T **395**) . . . 55 15
1195 3000f. Type **397** . . . . . . 1·10 35
1196 3000f. Eiffel Tower and tank convoy . . . . 1·10 35

Nos. 1194/6 were issued together, se-tenant, forming a composite design.

398 Emblem and "75"

1994. 75th Anniv of I.L.O.

1197 **398** 140f. multicoloured . . . 10 10

399 Biathlon

1994. Winter Olympic Games, Lillehammer, Norway. Multicoloured. (a) Without overprints.

1198 140f. Type **399** 10 10
1199 1250f. Ice hockey 45 15
1200 2000f. Figure skating . . . 75 25
1201 2500f. Skiing (downhill) . . 95 30

(b) Gold Medal Winners. Nos. 1198/1201 optd.

1203 140f. Optd **M. BEDARD CANADA** 10 10
1204 1250f. Optd **MEDAILLE D'OR SUEDE** 45 15
1205 2000f. Optd **O. BAYUL UKRAINE** 75 25
1206 2500f. Optd **M. WASMEIER ALLEMAGNE** 95 30

401 Majestic performing Dressage Exercise and Windsor Hotel, 1892

1994. Olympic Games, Atlanta, U.S.A. Mult.

1208 640f. Type **401** 25 10
1209 1000f. Covington Courthouse, 1884, and putting the shot 35 10
1210 1500f. Table tennis and Carolton Community Activities Centre 55 15
1211 3000f. Newman Commercial Court Square, 1800, and footballer . . . . 1·10 35

402 Spider on Map of Madagascar

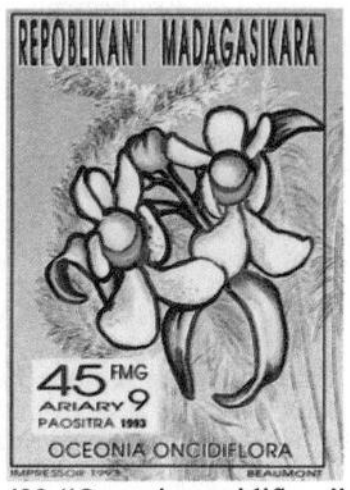

403 "Oceonia oncidiflora"

1994. "Archaea workmani" (spider).

1213 **402** 500f. multicoloured . . . 20 15

1994. Flowers, Fruit, Fungi and Vegetables. Multicoloured.

1214 45f. Type **403** 10 10
1215 45f. Breadfruit ("Artocarpus altilis") 10 10
1216 45f. "Russula annulata" . . 10 10
1217 45f. Sweet potato 10 10
1218 60f. "Cymbidella rhodochica" 10 10
1219 60f. "Eugenia malaceensis" 10 10
1220 60f. "Lactarius claricolor" 10 10
1221 60f. Yam 10 10
1222 140f. Vanilla orchid ("Vanilla planifolia") . . 10 10
1223 140f. "Jambosa domestica" 10 10
1224 140f. "Russula tuberculosa" 10 10
1225 140f. Avocado 10 10
1226 3000f. "Phaius humblotii" 1·10 35
1227 3000f. Papaya . . . . . . 1·10 35
1228 3000f. "Russula fistulosa" 1·10 35
1229 3000f. Manioc . . . . . . 1·10 35

Nos. 1214/29 were issued together, se-tenant, the backgrounds forming a composite design.

PARCEL POST STAMPS

1919. Receipt stamp of France surch **MADAGASCAR ET DEPENDANCES 0fr.10 COLIS POSTAUX**.

P81 0f.10 on 10c. grey . . . . . 5·50 4·75

1919. Fiscal stamp of Madagascar surch **COLIS POSTAUX 0f.10**.

P82 0f.10 on 1f. pink . . . . . . 70·00 42·00

1919. Fiscal stamps surch **Madagascar et Dependances** (in capitals on No. P83) **COLIS POSTAUX 0f.10.**

P83	0f.10 pink	12·00	6·75
P84	0f.10 red and green	3·50	3·75
P85	0f.10 black and green	3·50	3·25

POSTAGE DUE STAMPS

1896. Postage Due stamps of Fr. Colonies optd **Madagascar et DEPENDANCES.**

D17 U	5c. blue	5·50	9·00
D18	10c. brown	5·50	7·00
D19	20c. yellow	4·75	8·00
D20	30c. red	8·50	7·75
D21	40c. mauve	60·00	48·00
D22	50c. violet	5·00	5·00
D23	1f. green	90·00	60·00

D 6 Governor's Palace, Tananarive

D 37

1908.

D70 D 6	2c. red	10	10
D71	4c. violet	10	15
D72	5c. green	10	80
D73	10c. red	10	10
D74	20c. olive	10	1·90
D75	40c. brown on cream	15	2·50
D76	50c. brown on blue	15	1·75
D77	60c. red	35	2·75
D78	1f. blue	30	1·50

1924. Surch in figures.

D123 D 6	60c. on 1f. red	55	3·75
D124	2f. on 1f. purple	30	3·00
D125	3f. on 1f. blue	35	3·00

1942. Free French Administration. Optd **FRANCE LIBRE** or surch also.

D254 D 6	10c. red	1·40	3·25
D255	20c. green	35	3·25
D256	0,30 on 5c. green	2·75	3·25
D257	40c. brown on cream	2·25	3·25
D258	50c. brown and blue	2·00	3·25
D259	60c. red	2·25	3·25
D260	1f. blue	30	3·00
D261	1f. on 2c. purple	7·00	8·50
D262	2f. on 4c. violet	3·75	4·25
D263	2f. on 1f. mauve	2·00	3·25
D264	3f. on 1f. blue	2·50	3·00

1947.

D319 D 37	10c. mauve	10	2·25
D320	30c. brown	10	2·75
D321	50c. green	10	2·75
D322	1f. brown	10	2·00
D323	2f. red	90	1·60
D324	3f. brown	95	1·75
D325	4f. blue	90	2·50
D326	5f. red	1·40	2·75
D327	10f. green	1·10	45
D328	20f. blue	1·25	3·50

APPENDIX

The following stamps have either been issued in excess of postal needs or have not been available to the public in reasonable quantities at face value.

1992.

Olympic Games, Barcelona. 500f. (on gold foil).

1993.

Bicentenary of French Republic. 1989 "Philexfrance 89" issue optd. 5000f.

1994.

Elvis Presley (entertainer). 10000f. (on gold foil).

World Cup Football Championship, U.S.A. 10000f. (on gold foil).

Winter Olympic Games, Lillehammer, Norway. 10000f. (on gold foil).

Olympic Games, Atlanta, U.S.A. 5000f. (on gold foil).

MADEIRA — Pt. 9

A Portuguese island in the Atlantic Ocean off the N.W. coast of Africa. From 1868 to 1929 and from 1980 separate issues were made.

1868. 1000 reis = 1 milreis.
1912. 100 centavos = 1 escudo.
2002. 100 cents = 1 euro.

Nos. 1/78b are stamps of Portugal optd **MADEIRA**.

1868. With curved value label. Imperf.

1 **14**	20r. bistre	£140	£110
2	50r. green	£140	£110
3	80r. orange	£150	£110
4	100r. lilac	£200	£110

1868. With curved value label. Perf.

10 **14**	5r. black	40·00	30·00
13	10r. yellow	65·00	55·00
14	20r. bistre	£110	80·00
15	25r. red	40·00	9·00
16	50r. green	£130	£120
17	80r. orange	£130	£120
19	100r. mauve	£130	£120
20	120r. blue	80·00	65·00
21	240r. mauve	£400	£375

1871. With straight value label.

30 **15**	5r. black	6·50	4·50
47	10r. yellow	25·00	14·00
72a	10r. green	80·00	60·00
48	15r. brown	15·00	8·50
49	20r. bistre	23·00	16·00
34	25r. pink	8·50	5·00
51	50r. green	50·00	23·00
71	50r. blue	£130	70·00
36	80r. orange	90·00	60·00
53	100r. mauve	90·00	55·00
38	120r. blue	£130	90·00
55	150r. blue	£180	£150
74	150r. yellow	£300	£275
39	240r. lilac	£750	£550
67	300r. lilac	80·00	75·00

1880. Stamps of 1880.

79 **16**	5r. black	28·00	22·00
78	25r. grey	30·00	11·50
78b	25r. brown	30·00	11·50
77 **17**	25r. grey	30·00	22·00

1898. Vasco da Gama. As Nos. 378/85 of Portugal.

134	2½r. green	2·50	1·30
135	5r. red	2·50	1·30
136	10r. purple	3·25	1·50
137	25r. green	3·00	1·40
138	50r. blue	9·25	3·50
139	75r. brown	11·50	7·75
140	100r. brown	12·00	8·00
141	150r. brown	18·00	13·00

For Nos. 134/41 with **REPUBLICA** overprint, see Nos. 455/62 of Portugal.

6 Ceres

7 20r. Stamp, 1868

1929. Funchal Museum Fund. Value in black.

148 **6**	3c. violet	60	55
149	4c. yellow	60	55
150	5c. blue	60	55
151	6c. brown	85	75
152	10c. red	85	75
153	15c. green	85	75
154	16c. brown	85	75
155	25c. purple	90	85
156	32c. green	90	85
157	40c. brown	90	85
158	50c. grey	90	85
159	64c. blue	90	85
160	80c. brown	90	85
161	96c. red	3·75	3·50
162	1e. black	75	75
163	1e.20 pink	75	75
164	1e.60 blue	75	75
165	2e.40 yellow	1·10	1·10
166	3e.36 green	1·60	1·50
167	4e.50 red	1·60	1·50
168	7e. blue	3·50	3·75

1980. 112th Anniv of First Overprinted Madeira Stamps.

169 **7**	6e.50 black, bistre and green	20	10
170 –	19e.50 black, purple and red	90	60
MS171	140 × 115 mm. Nos. 169/70 (sold at 30e.)	4·00	4·00

DESIGN: 19e.50, 100r. stamp, 1868.

8 Ox Sledge

1980. World Tourism Conference, Manila, Philippines. Multicoloured.

172	50c. Type **8**	10	10
173	1e. Wine and grapes	10	10
174	5e. Map of Madeira	50	10
175	6e.50 Basketwork	50	15
176	8e. Orchid	90	35
177	30e. Fishing boat	1·70	60

9 O Bailinho (folk dance)

1981. Europa.

178 **9**	22e. multicoloured	1·40	70
MS179	141 × 115 mm. No. 178 × 2	4·25	4·25

10 Portuguese Caravel approaching Madeira

11 "Dactylorhiza foliosa"

1981. 560th Anniv (1980) of Discovery of Madeira. Multicoloured.

180	8e.50 Type **10**	50	10
181	33e.50 Prince Henry the Navigator and map of Atlantic Ocean	1·80	60

1981. Regional Flowers. Multicoloured.

182	7e. Type **11**	35	15
183	8e.50 "Geranium maderense"	40	15
184	9e. "Goodyera macrophylla"	50	10
185	10e. "Armeria maderensis"	50	10
186	12e.50 "Matthiola maderensis"	20	10
187	20e. "Isoplexis sceptrum"	70	40
188	27e. "Viola paradoxa"	1·20	55
189	30e. "Erica maderensis"	85	30
190	33e.50 "Scilla maderensis"	1·20	75
191	37e.50 "Cirsium latifolium"	90	60
192	50e. "Echium candicans"	1·60	80
193	100e. "Clethra arborea"	2·30	90

12 First Sugar Mill

13 Dancer holding Dolls on Staff

1982. Europa.

199 **12**	33e.50 multicoloured	1·90	75
MS200	139 × 115 mm. No. 199 × 3	10·50	10·50

1982. O Brinco Dancing Dolls. Multicoloured.

201	27e. Type **13**	1·20	65
202	33e.50 Dancers	1·80	90

14 Los Levadas Irrigation Channels

1983. Europa.

203 **14**	37e.50 multicoloured	1·50	60
MS204	114 × 140 mm. No. 203 × 3	13·00	13·00

15 Flag of Madeira

16 Rally Car

1983. Flag.

205 **15**	12e.50 multicoloured	75	10

1984. Europa. As T **398** of Portugal but additionally inscr "MADEIRA".

206	51e. multicoloured	2·00	1·10
MS207	113 × 140 mm. No. 206 × 3	10·00	10·00

1984. 25th Anniv of Madeira Rally. Multicoloured.

208	16e. Type **16**	50	10
209	51e. Rally car (different)	1·80	65

17 Basket Sledge

18 Braguinha Player

1984. Transport (1st series). Multicoloured.

210	16e. Type **17**	30	10
211	35e. Hammock	95	55
212	40e. Borracheiros (wine carriers)	1·40	55
213	51e. Carreira local sailing boat	1·70	75

See also Nos. 218/21.

1985. Europa.

214 **18**	60e. multicoloured	2·10	90
MS215	140 × 115 mm. No. 214 × 3	12·00	12·00

19 Black Scabbardfish

1985. Fishes (1st series). Multicoloured.

216	40e. Type **19**	1·30	50
217	60e. Opah	1·80	75

See also Nos. 222/3 and 250/3.

1985. Transport (2nd series). As T **17**. Mult.

218	20e. Ox sledge	35	10
219	40e. Mountain railway	1·00	45
220	46e. Fishing boat and basket used by pesquitos (itinerant fish sellers)	1·40	90
221	60e. Coastal ferry	1·60	75

1986. Fishes (2nd series). As T **19**. Multicoloured.

222	20e. Big-eyed tuna	60	10
223	75e. Alfonsino	3·00	80

20 Cory's Shearwater and Tanker

1986. Europa.

224 **20**	68e.50 multicoloured	2·40	1·00
MS225	140 × 114 mm. No. 224 × 3	12·50	12·50

21 Sao Lourenco Fort, Funchal

1986. Fortresses. Multicoloured.

226	22e.50 Type **21**	55	15
227	52e.50 Sao Joao do Pico Fort, Funchal	1·70	75
228	68e.50 Sao Tiago Fort, Funchal	2·50	1·00
229	100e. Nossa Senhora do Amparo Fort, Machico	3·50	85

22 Firecrest

24 Funchal Cathedral

23 Social Services Centre, Funchal (Raul Chorao Ramalho)

1987. Birds (1st series). Multicoloured.

230	25e. Type **22**	55	10
231	57e. Trocaz pigeon	1·80	90
232	74e.50 Barn owl	2·50	1·20
233	125e. Soft-plumaged petrel	3·25	1·40

See also Nos. 240/3.

1987. Europa. Architecture.

234 **23**	74e.50 multicoloured	2·20	1·00
MS235	140 × 113 mm. No. 234 × 4	12·50	12·50

1987. Historic Buildings. Multicoloured.

236	51e. Type **24**	1·60	75
237	74e.50 Old Town Hall, Santa Cruz	1·90	75

25 "Maria Cristina" (mail boat)

1988. Europa. Transport and Communications.
238 **25** 80e. multicoloured . . . . 2·30 85
MS239 139 × 112 mm. As No. 238 × 4 but with cream background 12·50 12·50

1988. Birds (2nd series). As T **22** but horiz. Multicoloured.
240 27e. European robin 50 10
241 60e. Streaked rock sparrow 1·60 85
242 80e. Chaffinch . . . . 2·20 90
243 100e. Northern sparrowhawk 2·50 90

26 Columbus and Funchal House **27** Child flying Kite

1988. Christopher Columbus's Houses in Madeira. Multicoloured.
244 55e. Type **26** . . . . 1·70 65
245 80e. Columbus and Porto Santo house (horiz) . . . . 1·90 75

1989. Europa. Children's Games and Toys. Multicoloured.
246 80e. Type **27** . . . . 2·10 90
MS247 139 × 112 mm. 80e. × 2, Type **27**; 80e. × 2, Child flying kite (*different*) . . . . 12·50 12·50

28 Church of St. John the Evangelist **29** Spiny Hatchetfish

1989. "Brasiliana 89" Stamp Exhibition, Rio de Janeiro. Madeiran Churches. Multicoloured.
248 29e. Type **28** 50 15
249 87e. St. Clara's Church and Convent . . . . 2·10 1·00

1989. Fishes (3rd series). Multicoloured.
250 29e. Type **29** 50 10
251 60e. Dog wrasse . . . . . . 1·40 75
252 87e. Rainbow wrasse . . . . 2·10 95
253 100e. Madeiran scorpionfish 2·20 1·30

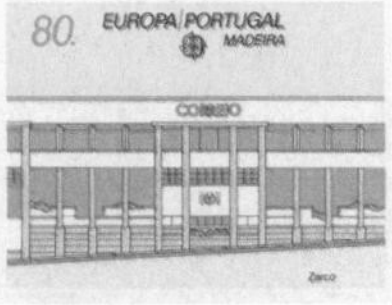

30 Zarco Post Office **31** Bananas

1990. Europa. Post Office Buildings. Multicoloured.
254 80e. Type **30** . . . . 1·50 75
MS255 139 × 111 mm. 80e. × 2, Type **30**; 80e. × 2, Porto da Cruz Post Office . . . . 11·00 11·00

1990. Sub-tropical Fruits. Multicoloured.
256 5e. Type **31** 15 10
257 10e. Thorn apple 15 10
258 32e. Avocado 50 20
259 35e. Mangoes 50 20
260 38e. Tomatoes 50 20
261 60e. Sugar apple . . . . . . 1·40 60
262 65e. Surinam cherries . . . . 1·10 55
263 70e. Brazilian guavas . . . . 1·40 65
264 85e. Delicious fruits . . . . 1·40 75
265 100e. Passion fruit . . . . . 2·10 95
266 110e. Papayas . . . . 1·80 70
267 125e. Guava . . . . 1·80 75

32 Tunny Boat

1990. Boats. Multicoloured.
270 32e. Type **32** 50 10
271 60e. Desert Islands boat . . . 1·10 50
272 70e. Maneiro . . . . 1·30 75
273 95e. Chavelha . . . . 2·00 1·00

33 Trocaz Pigeon

1991. The Trocaz Pigeon. Multicoloured.
274 35e. Type **33** 75 20
275 35e. Two pigeons 75 20
276 35e. Pigeon on nest 75 20
277 35e. Pigeon alighting on twig 75 20
Nos. 264/7 were issued together, se-tenant, forming a composite design.

34 European Remote Sensing ("ERS1") Satellite

1991. Europa. Europe in Space. Multicoloured.
278 80e. Type **34** . . . . 1·50 85
MS279 140 × 112 mm. 80e. × 2, Type **34**; 80e. × 2, "Spot" satellite 11·50 11·50

35 Columbus and Funchal House

1992. Europa. 500th Anniv of Discovery of America by Columbus.
280 **35** 85e. multicoloured . . . . 1·20 60

36 "Gaviao" (ferry)

1992. Inter-island Ships. Multicoloured.
281 38e. Type **36** 50 15
282 65e. "Independencia" (catamaran ferry) 95 50
283 85e. "Madeirense" (car ferry) 1·20 60
284 120e. "Funchalense" (freighter) . . . . 1·60 70

37 "Shadow thrown by Christa Maar" (Lourdes Castro) **39** Window of St. Francis's Convent, Funchal

38 Seals Swimming

1993. Europa. Contemporary Art. Multicoloured.
285 50e. Type **37** . . . . 1·40 60
MS286 140 × 112 mm. 90e. × 2, Type **37**; 90e. × 2, "Shadow thrown by Dahlia" . . . . . 7·50 7·50

1993. Mediterranean Monk Seal. Multicoloured.
287 42e. Type **38** 60 30
288 42e. Seal basking 60 30
289 42e. Two seals on rocks . . . 60 30
290 42e. Mother suckling young 60 30
Nos. 287/90 were issued together, se-tenant, forming a composite design.

1993. Regional Architecture. Multicoloured.
291 42e. Type **39** 50 20
292 130e. Window of Mercy, Old Hospital, Funchal . . . . 1·90 85

40 Native of Cape of Good Hope and Explorer with Model Caravel

1992. Europa. Discoveries. Multicoloured.
293 90e. Type **40** 85 60
MS294 140 × 112 mm. 100e. × 2, Type **40**; 100e. × 2, Palm tree and explorer with model caravel . . 6·25 6·25

41 Embroidery

1994. Traditional Crafts (1st series). Multicoloured.
295 45e. Type **41** 45 20
296 75e. Tapestry 90 45
297 100e. Boots . . . . 1·10 60
298 140e. Wicker chair back . . . 1·70 80
See also Nos. 301/4.

42 Funchal **43** Bread Dough Figures

1994. District Arms. Multicoloured.
299 45e. Type **42** 45 20
300 140e. Porto Santo . . . . . 1·50 75

1995. Traditional Crafts (2nd series). Mult.
301 45e. Type **43** 50 20
302 80e. Inlaid wooden box . . . 85 35
303 95e. Bamboo cage 95 55
304 135e. Woollen bonnet . . . . 1·30 65

44 Guiomar Vilhena (entrepreneur)

1996. Europa. Famous Women. Multicoloured.
305 98e. Type **44** 95 50
MS306 140 × 112 mm. No. 305 × 3 3·00 3·00

45 "Adoration of the Magi"

1996. Religious Paintings by Flemish Artists. Multicoloured.
307 47e. Type **45** 45 20
308 78e. "St. Mary Magdalene" 80 45
309 98e. "The Annunciation" (horiz) 95 50
310 140e. "Saints Peter, Paul and Andrew" (horiz) . . . . . 1·20 70

46 "Eumichtis albostigmata" (moth)

1997. Butterflies and Moths. Multicoloured.
311 49e. Type **46** 45 20
312 80e. Menophra maderae (moth) 75 30
313 100e. Painted lady 90 50
314 140e. Large white . . . . . 1·30 70

47 Robert Achim and Anne of Arfet (Legend of Machico)

1997. Europa. Tales and Legends. Multicoloured.
315 100e. Type **47** . . . . 1·00 50
MS316 140 × 106 mm. No. 315 × 3 3·00 3·00

48 New Year's Eve Fireworks Display, Funchal

1998. Europa. National Festival. Multicoloured.
317 100e. Type **48** 90 45
MS318 140 × 109 mm. No. 317 × 3 2·75 2·75

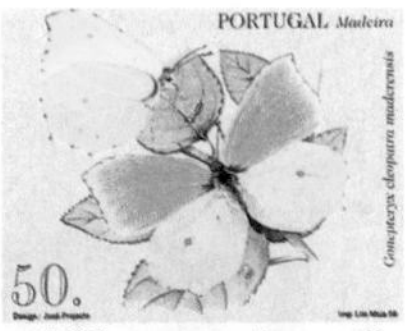

49 "Gonepteryx cleopatra"

1998. Butterflies and Moths. Multicoloured.
319 50e. Type **49** 45 20
320 85e. "Xanthorhoe rupicola" 70 35
321 100e. "Noctua teixeirai" . . 90 45
322 140e. "Xenochlorodes nubigena" . . . . 1·20 65

50 Madeira Island Nature Park

1999. Europa. Parks and Gardens. Multicoloured.
323 100e. Type **50** 85 45
MS324 153 × 108 mm. No. 323 × 3 2·50 2·50

51 Medieval Floor Tile

1999. Tiles from Frederico de Freitas Collection, Funchal. Multicoloured.
325 51e. Type **51** 45 20
326 80e. English art-nouveau tile (19th–20th century) 70 35
327 95e. Persian tile (14th century) 85 45
328 100e. Spanish Moor tile (13th century) 90 45
329 140e. Dutch Delft tile (18th century) . . . . 1·20 60
330 210e. Syrian tile (13th–14th century) . . . . 1·70 90

52 "Building Europe"

2000. Europa. Multicoloured.

332	100e. Type **52**	85	45
MS333	154 × 108 mm. Nos. 332 × 3	2·50	2·50

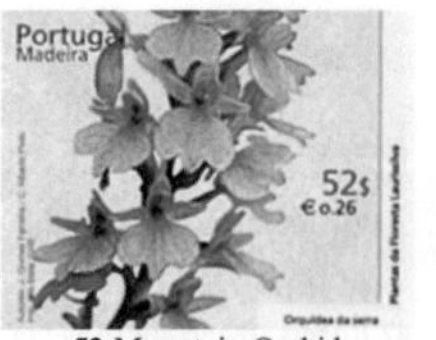

53 Mountain Orchid

2000. Plants of Laurissilva Forest. Multicoloured.

334	52e. Type **53**	40	20
335	85e. White orchid	70	35
336	100e. Leafy plant	80	40
337	100e. Laurel	80	40
338	140e. Barbusano	90	60
339	350e. Visco	2·75	1·40

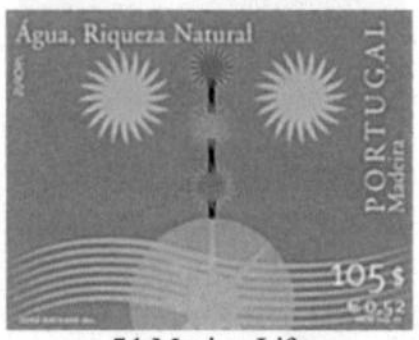

54 Marine Life

2001. Europa. Water Resources. Multicoloured.

341	105e. Type **54**	85	45
MS342	140 × 110 mm. No. 341 × 3	2·50	2·50

55 Musicians

2001. Traditions of Madeira. Multicoloured.

343	53e. Type **55**	40	20
344	85e. Couple carrying produce	65	35
345	105e. Couple selling goods	80	40
MS346	140 × 112 mm. 350e. Man carrying birds	2·75	2·75

56 Clown

2002. Europa. Circus.

347 **56**	54c. multicoloured	85	40
MS348	140 × 110 mm. No. 347 × 3	2·50	2·50

57 Turtle Doves (*Streptopelia turtur*)

2002. Birds. Multicoloured.

349	28c. Type **57**	40	20
350	28c. Perching dove	40	20
351	28c. Dove with raised wings	40	20
352	28c. Dove with chicks	40	20

58 1992 Theatre Festival Poster (José Brandao)

2003. Europa. Poster Art.

353 **58**	55c. multicoloured	75	35
MS354	140 × 113 mm. No. 353 × 2	1·60	1·60

59 Bird of Paradise Flower, Figure and Yachts

2004. Europa. Holidays.

355 **59**	56c. multicoloured	55	25
MS356	141 × 112 mm. No. 355 × 2	1·60	1·60

60 Selvagens White-faced Storm-Petrel (*Pelagodroma marina hypoleuca*)

2004. Selvagens Islands. Multicoloured.

357	30c. Type **60**	40	20
358	45c. *Monathes lowei* (plant) and beetle	60	30
359	72c. *Tarentola bischoffi*	1·00	50
MS360	140 × 112 mm. Nos. 357/9	2·10	2·10

No. **MS**360 has the stamps arranged so as to make a composite design with a description of the islands below.

CHARITY TAX STAMPS

The note under this heading in Portugal also applies here.

1925. As Marquis de Pombal stamps of Portugal but inscr "MADEIRA".

C142 C **73**	15c. grey	1·70	1·40
C143 –	15c. grey	1·70	1·40
C144 C **75**	15c. grey	1·70	1·40

NEWSPAPER STAMP

1876. Newspaper stamp of Portugal optd **MADEIRA**.

N69 N **17**	2½r. green	9·25	4·75

POSTAGE DUE STAMPS

1925. Marquis de Pombal stamps as Nos. C1/3 optd **MULTA**.

D145 C **73**	30c. grey	1·40	1·30
D146 –	30c. grey	1·40	1·30
D147 C **75**	30c. grey	1·40	1·30

MAFEKING Pt. 1

A town in the Cape of Good Hope. Special stamps issued by British garrison during Boer War.

12 pence = 1 shilling;
20 shillings = 1 pound.

1900. Surch **MAFEKING, BESIEGED.** and value.

(a) On Cape of Good Hope stamps.

1 **6**	1d. on ½d. green	£200	65·00
2 **17**	1d. on ½d. green	£250	75·00
3	3d. on 1d. red	£225	50·00
4 **6**	6d. on 3d. mauve	£26000	£250
5	1s. on 4d. olive	£6000	£325

(b) On stamps of Bechuanaland Protectorate (opts on Great Britain).

6 **71**	1d. on ½d. red (No. 59)	£200	60·00
7 **57**	3d. on 1d. lilac (No. 61)	£850	90·00
13 **73**	6d. on 2d. green and red (No. 62)	£1100	75·00
9 **75**	6d. on 3d. purple on yellow (No. 63)	£5000	£275
14 **79**	1s. on 6d. purple on red (No. 65)	£4500	90·00

(c) On stamps of British Bechuanaland (opts on Great Britain).

10 **3**	6d. on 3d. lilac and black (No. 12)	£350	65·00
11 **76**	1s. on 4d. green and brown (No. 35)	£1300	80·00
15 **79**	1s. on 6d. purple on red (No. 36)	£15000	£700
16 **82**	2s. on 1s. green (No. 37)	£8500	£375

3 Cadet Sgt.-Major Goodyear

4 General Baden-Powell

1900.

17 **3**	1d. blue on blue	£800	£275
20 **4**	3d. blue on blue	£1200	£350

MAHRA SULTANATE OF QISHN AND SOCOTRA Pt. 1

The National Liberation Front took control on 1 October 1967, and full independence was granted by Great Britain on 30 November 1967. Subsequently part of Southern Yemen.

1000 fils = 1 dinar.

1 Mahra Flag

1967.

1 **1**	5f. multicoloured	1·75	40
2	10f. multicoloured	1·75	40
3	15f. multicoloured	1·75	40
4	20f. multicoloured	1·75	40
5	25f. multicoloured	1·75	40
6	35f. multicoloured	1·75	40
7	50f. multicoloured	1·75	40
8	65f. multicoloured	1·75	40
9	100f. multicoloured	1·75	40
10	250f. multicoloured	1·75	45
11	500f. multicoloured	1·75	60

APPENDIX

The following stamps have either been issued in excess of postal needs or have not been available to the public in reasonable quantities at face value.

1967.

Scout Jamboree, Idaho. 15, 75, 100, 150f.

President Kennedy Commemoration. Postage 10, 15, 25, 50, 75, 100, 150f.; Air 250, 500f.

Olympic Games, Mexico (1968). Postage 10, 25, 50f.; Air 250, 500f.

For later issues see **SOUTHERN YEMEN** and **YEMEN PEOPLE'S DEMOCRATIC REPUBLIC** in Volume 4.

MALACCA Pt. 1

A British Settlement on the Malay Peninsula which became a state of the Federation of Malaya, incorporated in Malaysia in 1963.

100 cents = 1 dollar (Malayan).

1948. Silver Wedding. As T **4b/c** of Pitcairn Islands.

1	10c. violet	30	1·75
2	$5 brown	29·00	38·00

1949. As T **58** of Straits Settlements.

3	1c. black	30	70
4	2c. orange	80	45
5	3c. green	30	1·75
6	4c. brown	30	10
6a	5c. purple	60	1·50
7	6c. grey	75	85
8	8c. red	75	6·00
8a	8c. green	2·00	4·75
9	10c. mauve	30	10
9a	12c. red	2·00	6·00
10	15c. blue	2·50	60
11	20c. black and green	50	7·00
11a	20c. blue	4·00	2·50
12	25c. purple and orange	50	70
12a	35c. red and purple	1·75	3·00
13	40c. red and purple	1·25	11·00
14	50c. black and blue	1·00	1·25
15	$1 blue and purple	8·50	21·00
16	$2 green and red	21·00	21·00
17	$5 green and brown	45·00	35·00

1949. U.P.U. As T **63/66** of Jamaica.

18	10c. purple	30	50
19	15c. blue	2·00	1·75
20	25c. orange	85	4·75
21	50c. black	60	4·75

1953. Coronation. As T **71** of Jamaica.

22	10c. black and purple	1·00	1·50

1 Queen Elizabeth II

1954.

23 **1**	1c. black	10	60
24	2c. orange	30	1·25
25	4c. brown	40	10
26	5c. mauve	30	2·50
27	6c. grey	10	40
28	8c. green	40	2·75
29	10c. purple	1·00	10
30	12c. red	30	3·00
31	20c. blue	20	1·25
32	25c. purple and orange	20	1·50
33	30c. red and purple	20	30
34	35c. red and purple	20	1·50
35	50c. black and blue	75	2·50
36	$1 blue and purple	7·00	8·00
37	$2 green and red	22·00	35·00
38	$5 green and brown	23·00	42·00

1957. As Nos. 92/102 of Kedah but inset portrait of Queen Elizabeth II.

39	1c. black	10	40
40	2c. red	10	40
41	4c. sepia	40	10
42	5c. lake	30	10
43	8c. green	1·25	2·50
44	10c. sepia	30	10
45	20c. blue	40	50
46	50c. black and blue	30	1·00
47	$1 blue and purple	2·75	3·00
48	$2 green and red	12·00	21·00
49	$5 brown and green	14·00	38·00

2 Copra

1960. As Nos. 39/49 but with inset picture of Melaka tree and Pelandok (mouse-deer) as in T **2**.

50	1c. black	10	30
51	2c. red	10	65
52	4c. sepia	10	10
53	5c. lake	10	10
54	8c. green	3·00	3·00
55	10c. purple	30	10
56	20c. blue	1·00	80
57	50c. black and blue	70	80
58	$1 blue and purple	2·50	2·50
59	$2 green and red	7·00	9·50
60	$5 brown and green	9·50	14·00

3 "Vanda hookeriana"

1965. As Nos. 115/21 of Kedah but with Arms of Malacca inset and inscr "MELAKA" as in T **3**.

61 **3**	1c. multicoloured	10	1·50
62 –	2c. multicoloured	10	1·50
63 –	5c. multicoloured	10	40
64 –	6c. multicoloured	30	80
65 –	10c. multicoloured	20	10
66 –	15c. multicoloured	1·75	40
67 –	20c. multicoloured	2·25	1·00

The higher values used in Malacca were Nos. 20/7 of Malaysia.

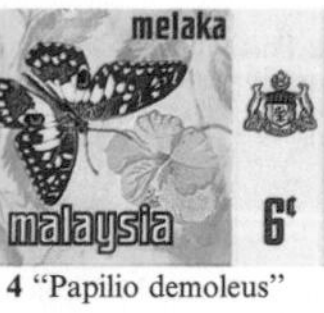

4 "Papilio demoleus"

1971. Butterflies. As Nos. 124/30 of Kedah but with Arms of Malacca as in T **4**. Inscr "melaka".

70 –	1c. multicoloured	60	2·25
71 –	2c. multicoloured	1·00	2·25
72 –	5c. multicoloured	1·50	1·00
73 **4**	6c. multicoloured	1·50	3·00
74 –	10c. multicoloured	1·50	60
75 –	15c. multicoloured	2·25	20
76 –	20c. multicoloured	2·25	2·50

The higher values in use with this issue were Nos. 64/71 of Malaysia.

5 "Durio zibethinus"

6 Rubber

1979. Flowers. As Nos. 135/41 of Kedah but with Arms of Malacca and inscr "melaka" as in T **5**.

82	1c. "Rafflesia hasseltii"	10	1·25
83	2c. "Pterocarpus indicus"	10	1·25
84	5c. "Lagerstroemia speciosa"	15	1·00
85	10c. Type **5**	20	35
86	15c. "Hibiscus rosa-sinesis"	20	10
87	20c. "Rhododendron scortechinii"	25	10
88	25c. "Etlingera elatior" (inscr "Phaeomeria speciosa")	45	80

1986. As Nos. 152/8 of Kedah but with Arms of Malacca and inscr "MELAKA" as in T **6**.

96	1c. Coffee	10	10
97	2c. Coconuts	10	10
98	5c. Cocoa	10	10
99	10c. Black pepper	10	10
100	15c. Type **6**	10	10
101	20c. Oil palm	10	10
102	30c. Rice	10	15

MALAGASY REPUBLIC Pt. 6; Pt. 13

The former areas covered by Madagascar and Dependencies were renamed the Malagasy Republic within the French Community on 14 October 1958. It became independent on 26 June 1960. In 1992 it reverted to the name of Madagascar.

1958. 100 centimes = 1 franc.
1976. 5 francs = 1 ariary.

1958. 10th Anniv of Declaration of Human Rights. As T **48** of New Caledonia.

1	10f. brown and blue	65	45

1959. Tropical Flora. As T **47** of New Caledonia.

2	6f. green, brown and yellow	25	25
3	25f. multicoloured	75	35

DESIGNS—HORIZ: 6f. "Datura"; 25f. Poinsettia.

2a Malagasy Flag and Assembly Hall

1959. Proclamation of Malagasy Republic and "French Community" Commemorative (60f.).

4 **2a**	20f. red, green and purple	35	25
5 –	25f. red, green and grey	45	25
6 –	60f. multicoloured	1·10	55

DESIGNS—VERT: 25f. Malagasy flag on map of Madagascar; 60f. Natives holding French and Malagasy flags.

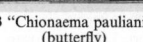

3 "Chionaema pauliani" (butterfly)

3a Reafforestation

1960.

7 –	30c. multicoloured (postage)	15	10
8 –	40c. brown, chocolate & green	15	10
9 –	50c. turquoise and purple	15	10
10 **3**	1f. red, purple and black	20	10
11 –	3f. black, red and olive	20	10
12 –	5f. green, brown and red	20	20
13 –	6f. yellow and green	20	20
14 –	8f. black, green and red	20	20
15 –	10f. green, brown & turquoise	40	20
16 –	15f. green and brown	50	20
17 –	30f. multicoloured (air)	70	40
18 –	40f. brown and turquoise	1·25	30
19 –	50f. multicoloured	2·50	50
20 –	100f. multicoloured	4·00	85
21 –	200f. yellow and violet	5·50	1·50
22 –	500f. brown, blue and green	9·50	2·25

BUTTERFLIES—As Type **2**: 30c. Purple-tip; 40c. "Acraea hova"; 50c. Clouded mother-of-pearl; 3f. "Hypolimnas dexithea". 48 × 27 mm: 50f. "Charaxes antamboulou"; 100f. Sunset moth. 27 × 48 mm: 200f. Tailed comet moth.
OTHER DESIGNS—As Type **2**: HORIZ: 5f. Sisal; 8f. Pepper; 15f. Cotton. VERT: 6f. Ylang ylang (flower); 10f. Rice. 48½ × 27 mm: 30f. Sugar cane trucks; 40f. Tobacco plantation; 500f. Mandrare Bridge.

1960. Trees Festival.

23 **3a**	20f. brown, green and ochre	55	35

4

5 Pres. Philibert Tsiranana

1960. 10th Anniv of African Technical Co-operation Commission.

24 **4**	25f. lake and green	55	35

1960.

25 **5**	20f. brown and green	35	35

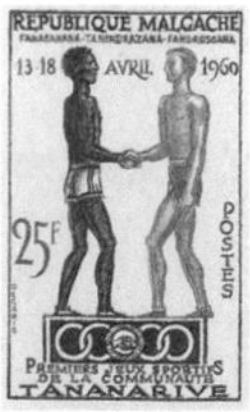

6 Young Athletes

7 Pres. Tsiranana

1960. 1st Youth Games, Tananarive.

26 **6**	25f. brown, chestnut and blue	65	35

1960.

27 **7**	20f. black, red and green	25	10

1960. Independence. Surch **+10 F FETES DE L'INDEPENDANCE**.

28 **7**	20f.+10f. black, red & grn	55	35

9 Ruffed Lemur

1961. Lemurs.

29 –	2f. purple & turq (postage)	15	15
30 **9**	4f. black, brown and myrtle	20	15
31 –	12f. brown and green	50	30
32 –	65f. brown, sepia and myrtle (air)	2·25	65
33 –	85f. black, sepia and green	2·25	1·00
34 –	250f. purple, black & turq	6·50	2·75

LEMURS—VERT: As Type **9**: 2f. Grey gentle lemur; 12f. Mongoose-lemur. 48 × 27 mm: 65f. Diadem sifaka; 85f. Indris; 250f. Verreaux's sifaka.

10 Diesel Train

1962.

35 **10**	20f. myrtle	1·50	45
36 –	25f. blue	35	15

DESIGN: 25f. President Tsirianana Bridge.

11 U.N. and Malagasy Flags, and Govt. Building, Tananarive

1962. Admission into U.N.O.

37 **11**	25f. multicoloured	35	20
38	85f. multicoloured	1·40	55

1962. Malaria Eradication. As T **43** of Mauritania.

39	25f.+5f. green	80	80

12 Ranomafana

1962. Tourist Publicity.

40 **12**	10f. purple, myrtle and blue (postage)	20	15
41 –	30f. purple, blue and myrtle	40	15
42 –	50f. blue, myrtle and purple	60	25
43 –	60f. myrtle, purple and blue	80	35
44 –	100f. brown, myrtle and blue (air)	1·75	95

DESIGNS—As Type **12**: 30f. Tritriva Lake; 50f. Foulpointe; 60f. Fort Dauphin. 27 × 47½ mm: 100f. Boeing 707 airliner over Nossi-Be.

13 G.P.O., Tamatave

1962. Stamp Day.

45 **13**	25f.+5f. brn, myrtle & bl	35	40

14 Malagasy and UNESCO. Emblems

1962. UNESCO. Conference on Higher Education in Africa, Tananarive.

46 **14**	20f. black, green and red	35	25

1962. 1st Anniv of Union of African and Malagasy States. As T **45** of Mauritania.

47	30f. green	45	35

15 Hydro-electric Station

1962. Malagasy Industrialization.

48 **15**	5f. multicoloured	10	10
49 –	8f. multicoloured	15	10
50 –	10f. multicoloured	20	10
51 –	15f. brown, black and blue	35	15
52 –	20f. multicoloured	35	20

DESIGNS—HORIZ: 8f. Atomic plant; 15f. "Esso Gasikara" (tanker); 20f. Hertzian aerials at Tananarive-Fianarantsoa. VERT: 10f. Oilwell.

16 Globe and Factory

1963. International Fair, Tamatave.

53 **16**	25f. orange and black	30	20

1963. Freedom from Hunger. As T **51** of Mauritania.

54	25f.+5f. lake, brown and red	60	60

17 Douglas DC-8 Airliner

1963. Air. Malagasy Commercial Aviation.

55 **17**	500f. blue, red and green	8·50	3·25

18 Central Post Office, Tananarive

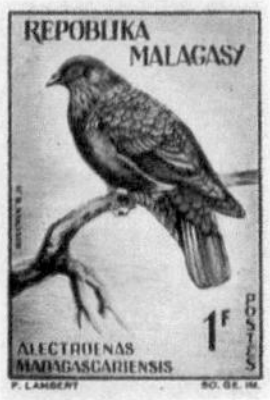

19 Madagascar Blue Pigeon

1963. Stamp Day.

56 **18**	20f.+5f. brown & turq	55	35

1963. Malagasy Birds and Orchids (8f. to 12f.). Multicoloured. (a) Postage as T **19**.

57	1f. Type **19**	70	35
58	2f. Blue Madagascar coucal	70	35
59	3f. Madagascar red fody	70	35
60	6f. Madagascar pygmy kingfisher	70	35
61	8f. "Gastrorchis humblotii"	20	15
62	10f. "Eulophiella roempleriana"	65	25
63	12f. "Angraecum sesquipedale"	65	25
	(b) Air. Horiz: 49½ × 28 mm.		
64	40f. Helmet bird	2·75	60
65	100f. Pitta-like ground roller	6·50	1·25
66	200f. Crested wood ibis	8·75	2·75

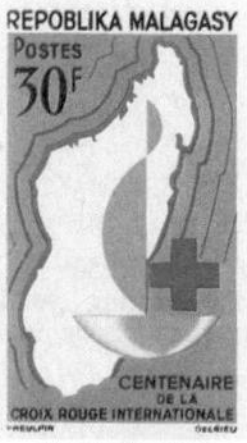

20 Centenary Emblem and Map

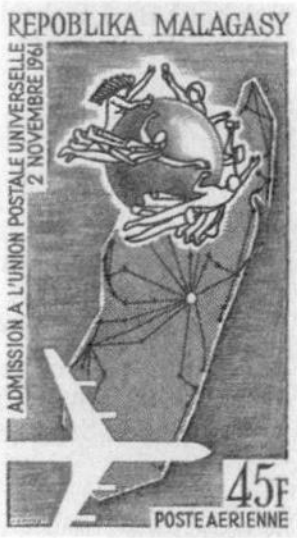

21 U.P.U. Monument, Berne, and Map of Malagasy

1963. Red Cross Centenary.

67 **20**	30f. multicoloured	80	60

1963. Air. African and Malagasy Posts and Telecommunications Union. As T **56** of Mauritania.

68	85f. multicoloured	1·40	90

1963. Air. 2nd Anniv of Malagasy's Admission to U.P.U.

69 **21**	45f. blue, red and turquoise	50	25
70	85f. blue, red and violet	90	50

22 Arms of Fianarantsoa

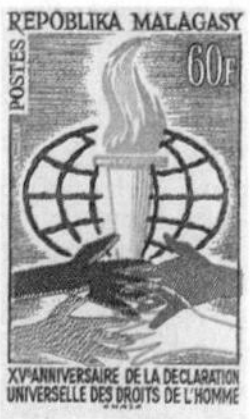

23 Flame, Globe and Hands

1963. Town Arms (1st series). Multicoloured.

71	1f.50 Antsirabe	10	10
72	5f. Antalaha	15	10
73	10f. Tulear	20	10
74	15f. Majunga	30	15
75	20f. Type **22**	40	15
75a	20f. Manajary	25	10
76	25f. Tananarive	45	15
76a	30f. Nossi Be	35	15
77	50f. Diego-Suarez	85	50
77a	90f. Antsohihy	1·40	55

See also Nos. 174/7 and 208/9.

1963. 15th Anniv of Declaration of Human Rights.

78 **23**	60f. ochre, bronze and mauve	55	45

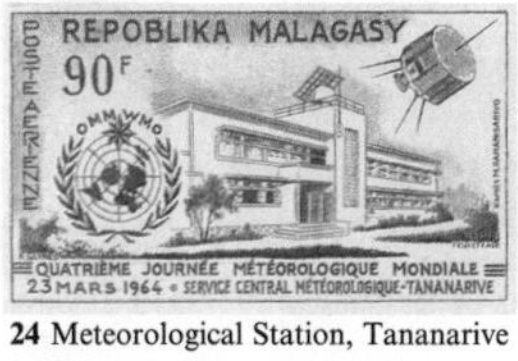

24 Meteorological Station, Tananarive

1964. Air. World Meteorological Day.

79 **24**	90f. brown, blue and grey	1·50	1·25

25 Postal Cheques and Savings Bank Building, Tananarive
26 Scouts beside Campfire

1964. Stamp Day.
80 **25** 25f.+5f. brown, bl & grn . . 50 60

1964. 40th Anniv of Malagasy Scout Movement.
81 **26** 20f. multicoloured 55 25

27 Symbolic Bird and Globe within "Egg"
28 Statuette of Woman

1964. "Europafrique".
82 **27** 45f. brown and green . . . 45 35

1964. Malagasy Art.
83 **28** 6f. brown, blue and indigo (postage) 25 15
84 – 30f. brown, bistre & green 45 20
85 – 100f. brown, red & vio (air) 1·50 95
DESIGNS: 30f. Statuette of squatting vendor. 27 × 48½ mm: 100f. Statuary of peasant family, ox and calf.

1964. French, African and Malagasy Co-operation. As T **68** of Mauritania.
86 25f. brown, chestnut and black 40 25

29 Tree on Globe
30 Cithern

1964. University of Malagasy Republic.
87 **29** 65f. black, red and green . . 50 25

1965. Malagasy Musical Instruments.
88 – 3f. brown, blue and mauve (postage) 20 10
89 **30** 6f. sepia, purple and green 25 10
90 – 8f. brown, black and green 35 10
91 – 25f. multicoloured 90 50
92 – 200f. brown, orange and green (air) . . . . 4·00 2·25
DESIGNS—As Type **30**: 3f. Kabosa (lute); 8f. Hazolahy (sacred drum). LARGER—VERT: 35½ × 48 mm: 25f. "Valiha Player" (after E. Ralambo). 27 × 48 mm: 200f. Bara violin.

31 Foulpointe Post Office

1965. Stamp Day.
93 **31** 20f. brown, green and orange 20 15

32 I.T.U. Emblem
33 J.-J. Rabearivelo (poet)

1965. I.T.U. Centenary.
94 **32** 50f. green, blue and red . . 1·00 45

1965. Rabearivelo Commemorative.
95 **33** 40f. brown and orange . . . 40 25

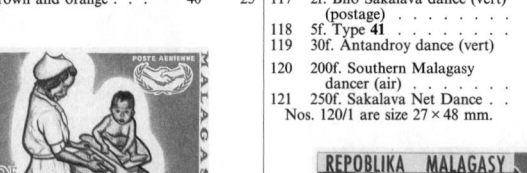

34 Nurse weighing Baby

1965. Air. International Co-operation Year.
96 **34** 50f. black, bistre and blue 60 35
97 – 100f. purple, brown and blue . . . . 1·25 60
DESIGN: 100f. Boy and girl.

35 Pres. Tsiranana
36 Bearer

1965. Pres. Tsiranana's 55th Birthday.
98 **35** 20f. multicoloured 25 15
99 25f. multicoloured 30 20

1965. Postal Transport.
102 – 3f. violet, blue and brown 30 15
103 – 4f. blue, brown and green 25 15
104 **36** 10f. multicoloured 25 15
105 – 12f. multicoloured 30 20
106 – 20f. multicoloured 90 20
107 – 25f. multicoloured 80 20
108 – 30f. red, brown and blue 2·25 1·60
109 – 65f. brown, blue and violet 1·50 50
DESIGNS—HORIZ: 3f. Early car; 4f. Filanzane (litter); 12f. Pirogue; 20f. Horse-drawn mail-cart; 25f. Bullock cart; 30f. Early railway postal carriage; 65f. Hydrofoil, "Porthos", Betsiboka.

37 Diseased Hands

1966. World Leprosy Day.
110 **37** 20f. purple, red and green 35 20

38 Planting Trees

1966. Reafforestation Campaign.
111 **38** 20f. violet, brown & turq 35 20

39 "Cicindelidae chaetodera andriana"

1966. Malagasy Insects. Multicoloured.
112 1f. Type **39** 10 10
113 6f. "Mantodea tisma freiji" 20 10
114 12f. "Cerambycini mastododera nodicollis" . . 45 20
115 45f. "Trachelophoru giraffa" 85 30

40 Madagascar 1c. Stamp of 1903
41 Betsileo Dance

1966. Stamp Day.
116 **40** 25f. bistre and red 35 25

1966. Folk Dances. Multicoloured.
117 2f. Bilo Sakalava dance (vert) (postage) 15 10
118 5f. Type **41** 25 15
119 30f. Antandroy dance (vert) 55 20
120 200f. Southern Malagasy dancer (air) . . . . 3·50 1·50
121 250f. Sakalava Net Dance . . 4·00 2·25
Nos. 120/1 are size 27 × 48 mm.

43 "Tree" of Emblems

1966. O.C.A.M. Conference, Tananarive.
122 **43** 25f. multicoloured 30 15
The above was issued with "Janvier 1966" obliterated by bars, and optd **JUIN 1966**.

44 Singing Anthem
45 UNESCO. Emblem

1966. National Anthem.
123 **44** 20f. brown, mauve & green 25 10

1966. 20th Anniv of UNESCO..
124 **45** 30f. blue, bistre and red . . 35 20

46 Lions Emblem
47 Harvesting Rice

1967. 50th Anniv of Lions Int.
125 **46** 30f. multicoloured 40 20

1967. International Rice Year.
126 **47** 20f. multicoloured 30 15

48 Adventist Temple, Tanambao-Tamatave

1967. Religious Buildings (1st series).
127 **48** 3f. ochre, blue and green 10 10
128 – 5f. lilac, purple and green 10 10
129 – 10f. purple, blue and green 25 10
BUILDINGS—VERT: 5f. Catholic Cathedral, Tananarive. HORIZ: 10f. Mosque, Tamatave.
See also Nos. 148/50.

49 Raharisoa at Piano

1967. 4th Death Anniv of Norbert Raharisoa (composer).
130 **49** 40f. multicoloured 55 20

50 Jean Raoult's Bleriot XI, 1911

1967. "History of Malagasy Aviation".
131 **50** 5f. brown, blue and green (postage) 35 15
132 – 45f. black, blue and brown 90 35
133 – 500f. black, blue and ochre (air) . . . . 8·75 3·75
DESIGNS: 45f. Bernard Bougault and flying boat, 1926. 48 × 27 mm: 500f. Jean Dagnaux and Breguet 19A2 biplane, 1927.

51 Ministry of Communications, Tananarive
52 Church, Torch and Map

1967. Stamp Day.
134 **51** 20f. green, blue and orange 25 15

1967. Air. 5th Anniv of U.A.M.P.T. As T **101** of Mauritania.
135 100f. mauve, bistre and red 1·25 60

1967. Centenary of Malagasy Lutheran Church.
136 **52** 20f. multicoloured 30 15

53 Map and Decade Emblem
54 Woman's Face and Scales of Justice

1967. Int Hydrological Decade.
137 **53** 90f. brown, red and blue 85 45

1967. Women's Rights Commission.
138 **54** 50f. blue, ochre and green 50 25

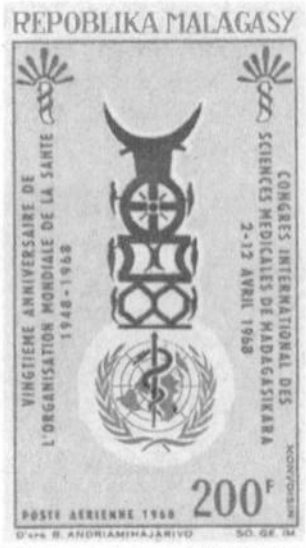

55 Human Rights Emblem
56 Congress and W.H.O. Emblems

1968. Human Rights Year.
139 **55** 50f. red, green and black 40 25

1968. Air. 20th Anniv of W.H.O. and Int Medical Sciences Congress, Tananarive.
140 **56** 200f. red, blue and ochre 2·40 1·25

57 International Airport, Tananarive-Ivato

1968. Air. Stamp Day.
141 **57** 500f. blue, green and brown . . . . 6·75 3·25

1968. Nos. 33 and 38 surch.
142 **11** 20f. on 85f. (postage) . . . 40 30
143 – 20f. on 85f. (No. 33) (air) 50 30

59 "Industry and Construction"
61 Isotry Protestant Church, Fitiavana, Tananarive

60 Church and Open Bible

1968. Five-year Plan (1st issue).

144	**59**	10f. plum, red and green	15	10
145	–	20f. black, red and green	20	15
146	–	40f. blue, brown & ultram	2·10	60

DESIGNS—VERT: 20f. "Agriculture". HORIZ: 40f. "Transport".
See also Nos. 156/7.

1968. 150th Anniv of Christianity in Madagascar.
147 **60** 20f. multicoloured 25 10

1968. Religious Buildings (2nd series).

148	**61**	4f. brown, green and red	10	10
149	–	12f. brown, blue and violet	20	10
150	–	50f. indigo, blue and green	45	25

DESIGNS: 12f. Catholic Cathedral, Fianarantsoa; 50f. Aga Khan Mosque, Tananarive.

62 President Tsiranana and Wife

63 Cornucopia, Coins and Map

1968. 10th Anniv of Republic.

151	**62**	20f. brown, red and yellow	20	10
152		30f. brown, red and blue	25	15

1968. 50th Anniv of Malagasy Savings Bank.
154 **63** 20f. multicoloured 25 10

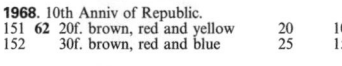

64 "Dance of the Whirlwind"

1968. Air.
155 **64** 100f. multicoloured . . . . 1·50 65

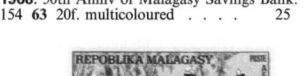

65 Malagasy Family

1968. Five-year Plan (2nd issue).

156	**65**	15f. red, yellow and blue	15	10
157	–	45f. multicoloured	40	25

DESIGN—VERT: 45f. Allegory of "Achievement".

1968. Air. "Philexafrique" Stamp Exn, Abidjan (1969) (1st issue). As T **113a** of Mauritania.
158 100f. multicoloured . . . . . 2·75 80
DESIGN: 100f. "Young Woman sealing a Letter" (J. B. Santerre).

1969. Air. "Philexafrique" Stamp Exn, Abidjan, Ivory Coast (2nd issue). As T **114a** of Mauritania.
159 50f. red, green and drab . . . 1·60 90
DESIGN: 50f. Malagasy Arms, map and Madagascar stamp of 1946.

68 "Queen Adelaide receiving Malagasy Mission, London" (1836–37)

1969.
160 **68** 250f. multicoloured . . . . 4·50 3·25

69 Hand with Spanner, Cogwheels and I.L.O. Emblem

1969. 50th Anniv of I.L.O.
161 **69** 20f. multicoloured 25 15

70 Post and Telecommunications Building, Tananarive

1969. Stamp Day.
162 **70** 30f. multicoloured 35 20

71 Map, Steering Wheel and Vehicles

72 President Tsiranana making Speech

1969. 20th Anniv of Malagasy Motor Club.
163 **71** 65f. multicoloured 60 35

1969. 10th Anniv of President Tsiranana's Assumption of Office.
164 **72** 20f. multicoloured 20 10

73 Bananas

74 Start of Race and Olympic Flame

1969. Fruits.

165	**73**	5f. green, brown and blue	15	10
166	–	15f. red, myrtle and green	30	10

DESIGN: 15f. Lychees.

1969. Olympic Games, Mexico (1968).
167 **74** 15f. brown, red and green 25 20

75 "Malagasy Seashore, East Coast" (A. Razafinjohany)

1969. Air. Paintings by Malagasy Artists. Multicoloured.

168	100f. Type **75**	1·25	80
169	150f. "Sunset on the High Plateaux" (H. Ratovo) . .	2·50	1·40

76 Imerino House, High Plateaux

77 Ambalavao Arms

1969. Malagasy Traditional Dwellings (1st series).

170	–	20f. red, blue and green . .	20	10
171	–	20f. brown, red and blue	20	10
172	**76**	40f. red, blue and indigo	40	20
173	–	60f. purple, green and blue	60	25

HOUSES—HORIZ: 20f. (No. 170), Tsimihety hut, East Coast; 60f. Betsimisaraka dwellings, East Coast. VERT: 20f. (No. 171), Betsileo house, High Plateaux.
See also Nos. 205/6.

1970. Town Arms (2nd series). Multicoloured.

174	10f. Type **77**	20	10
175	25f. Morondava	35	15
176	25f. Ambatondrazaka	35	15
177	80f. Tamatave	90	35

See also Nos. 208/9.

78 Agate

80 U.N. Emblem and Symbols

1970. Semi-precious Stones. Multicoloured.

178	5f. Type **78**	1·60	55
179	20f. Ammonite	3·25	1·10

1970. New U.P.U. Headquarters Building, Berne. As T **81** of New Caledonia.
180 20f. blue, brown and mauve 30 20

1970. 25th Anniv of United Nations.
181 **80** 50f. black, blue and orange 65 25

81 Astronaut and Module on Moon

1970. Air. 1st Anniv of "Apollo 11" Moon-landing.
182 **81** 75f. green, slate and blue 1·10 40

82 Malagasy Fruits

1970.
183 **82** 20f. multicoloured 30 15

83 Delessert's Lyria

1970. Sea Shells (1st series). Multicoloured.

184	5f. Type **83**	50	15
185	10f. Bramble murex	65	25
186	20f. Thorny oyster	1·40	50

84 Aye-aye

1970. International Nature Conservation Conference, Tananarive.
187 **84** 20f. multicoloured 40 30

85 Boeing 737 in Flight

1970. Air.
188 **85** 200f. red, green and blue 2·40 1·25

86 Pres. Tsiranana

87 Calcite

1970. Pres. Tsiranana's 60th Birthday.
189 **86** 30f. brown and green . . . 30 15

1971. Minerals. Multicoloured.

190	12f. Type **87**	1·60	45
191	15f. Quartz	2·25	65

88 Soap Works, Tananarive

1971. Malagasy Industries.

192	**88**	5f. multicoloured	15	10
193	–	15f. black, brown and blue	25	10
194	–	50f. multicoloured	55	15

DESIGNS: 15f. Chrome works, Comina-Andriamena; 50f. Textile complex, Sotema-Majunga.

89 Globe and Emblems

1971. Council Meeting of Common Market Countries with African and Malagasy Associated States, Tananarive.
195 **89** 5f. multicoloured 15 15

90 Rural Mobile Post Office

1971. Stamp Day.
196 **90** 25f. multicoloured 35 15

91 Gen. De Gaulle

1971. Death (1970) of Gen. Charles de Gaulle.
197 **91** 30f. black, red and blue . . 70 35

92 Palm Beach Hotel, Nossi-Be

93 Forestry Emblem

1971. Malagasy Hotels.

198	**92**	25f. multicoloured	30	20
199	–	65f. brown, blue and green	60	30

DESIGN: 65f. Hilton Hotel, Tananarive.

1971. Forest Preservation Campaign.
200 **93** 3f. multicoloured 15 10

94 Jean Ralaimongo

1971. Air. Malagasy Celebrities.
201 **94** 25f. brown, red and orange 30 15
202 – 65f. brown, myrtle & green 40 25
203 – 100f. brown, ultram & bl 90 40
CELEBRITIES: 65f. Albert Sylla; 100f. Joseph Ravoahangy Andrianavalona.

1971. Air. 10th Anniv of African and Malagasy Posts and Telecommunications Union. As T **139a** of Mauritania.
204 100f. U.A.M.P.T. H.Q., Brazzaville, and painting "Mpisikidy" (G. Rakotovao) . . . . . 1·00 60

96 Vezo Dwellings, South-east Coast

1971. Malagasy Traditional Dwellings (2nd series). Multicoloured.
205 5f. Type **96** 15 10
206 10f. Antandroy hut, South coast 20 10

97 "Children and Cattle in Meadow" (G. Rasoaharijaona)

1971. 25th Anniv of UNICEF.
207 **97** 50f. multicoloured 65 30

1972. Town Arms (3rd series). As T **77**. Mult.
208 1f. Maintirano Arms 10 10
209 25f. Fenerive-Est 35 20

99 Cable-laying train

1972. Co-axial Cable Link, Tananarive–Tamatave.
210 **99** 45f. brown, green and red 2·75 1·25

100 Telecommunications Station

1972. Inauguration of Philibert Tsiranana Satellite Communications Station.
211 **100** 85f. multicoloured 75 45

101 Pres. Tsiranana and Voters

102 "Moped" Postman

1972. Presidential Elections.
212 **101** 25f. multicoloured 40 35

1972. Stamp Day.
213 **102** 10f. multicoloured 40 20

1972. De Gaulle Memorial. No. 197 surch **MEMORIAL +20F.**
214 **91** 30f.+20f. black, red & bl 60 60

104 Exhibition Emblem and Stamps

1972. 2nd National Stamp Exn, Antanarive.
215 **104** 25f. multicoloured 35 30
216 40f. multicoloured 60 35
217 100f. multicoloured . . . 1·25 75

105 Road and Monument

1972. Opening of Andapa–Sambava Highway.
219 **105** 50f. multicoloured 35 25

106 Petroleum Refinery, Tamatave

1972. Malagasy Economic Development.
220 **106** 2f. blue, green and yellow 20 10
221 – 100f. multicoloured . . . 3·00 30
DESIGN: 100f. 3600 CV diesel locomotive.

107 R. Rakotobe

1972. Air. 1st Death Anniv of Rene Rakotobe (poet).
222 **107** 40f. brown, purple & orge 40 20

108 College Buildings

1972. 150th Anniv of Razafindrahety College, Tananarive.
223 **108** 10f. purple, brown & blue 15 10

109 Volleyball

1972. African Volleyball Championships.
224 **109** 12f. black, orange & brn 40 15

110 Runners breasting Tape

1972. Air. Olympic Games, Munich. Multicoloured.
225 100f. Type **110** . . . . . . 1·40 60
226 200f. Judo . . . . 2·25 90

111 Hospital Complex

1972. Inauguration of Ravoahangy Andrianavalona Hospital.
227 **111** 6f. multicoloured 20 15

112 Mohair Goat

1972. Air. Malagasy Wool Production.
228 **112** 250f. multicoloured . . . 3·75 2·25

113 Ploughing with Oxen

1972. Agricultural Expansion.
229 **113** 25f. multicoloured 25 15

114 "Virgin and Child" (15th-cent Florentine School)

1972. Air. Christmas. Religious Paintings. Mult.
230 85f. Type **114** 85 55
231 150f. "Adoration of the Magi" (A. Mantegna) (horiz) . . . . 2·00 85

115 Betsimisarka Women

1972. Traditional Costumes. Multicoloured.
232 10f. Type **115** 20 10
233 15f. Merina mother and child 30 20

116 Astronauts on Moon

1973. Air. Moon Flight of "Apollo 17".
234 **116** 300f. purple, brown & grey . . . . 3·25 1·75

117 "Natural Produce"

1973. 10th Anniv of Malagasy Freedom from Hunger Campaign Committee.
235 **117** 25f. multicoloured 30 15

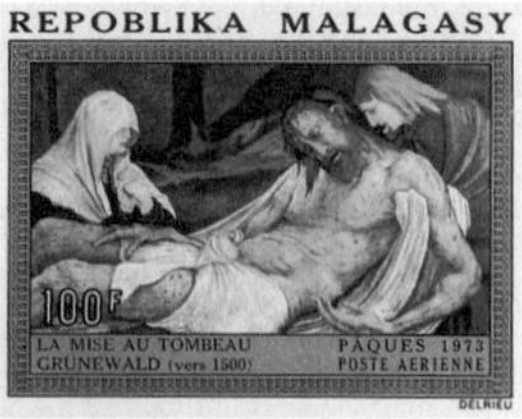

118 "The Entombment" (Grunewald)

1973. Air. Easter. Multicoloured.
236 100f. Type **118** . . . . . . 1·00 55
237 200f. "The Resurrection" (Grunewald) (vert) . . . . 2·25 1·10

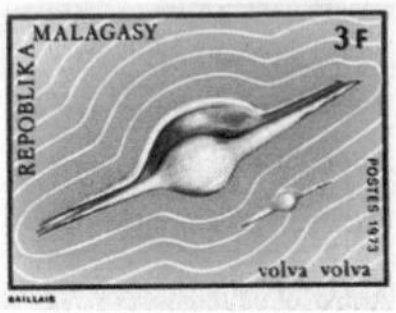

119 Shuttlecock Volva

1973. Sea Shells (2nd series). Multicoloured.
238 3f. Type **119** 15 10
239 10f. Arthritic spider conch . . 25 20
240 15f. Common harp 50 30
241 25f. Type **119** 70 45
242 40f. As 15f. . . . . 1·10 50
243 50f. As 10f. . . . . 2·25 60

120 Postal Courier, Tsimandoa

121 "Africa" within Scaffolding

1973. Stamp Day.
244 **120** 50f. blue, green and brown 45 20

1973. 10th Anniv of Organization of African Unity.
245 **121** 25f. multicoloured 30 15

122 "Cameleon campani"

1973. Malagasy Chameleons. Multicoloured.
246 1f. Type **122** 10 10
247 5f. "Cameleon nasutus" (male) 10 10
248 10f. "Cameleon nasutus" (female) 15 10
249 40f. As 5f. 55 25
250 60f. Type **122** 85 35
251 85f. As 10f. . . . . 1·25 65

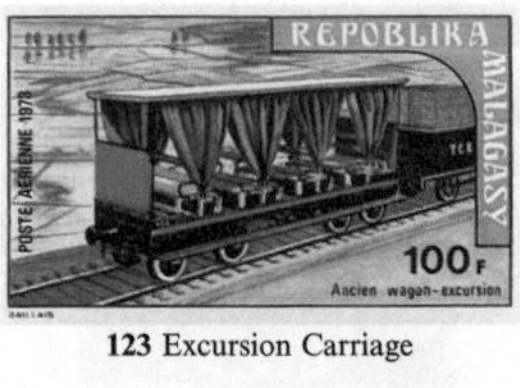

123 Excursion Carriage

1973. Air. Early Malagasy Railways. Multicoloured.
252 100f. Type **123** . . . . . . 1·75 85
253 150f. Mallet steam locomotive No. 24, 1907 . . . . . . 2·50 1·40

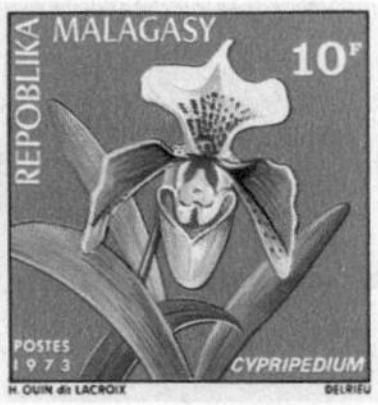

124 "Cypripedium"

1973. Orchids. Multicoloured.
254 10f. Type **124** 30 15
255 25f. "Nepenthes pervillei" . . 50 20
256 40f. As 25f. . . . . 1·00 35
257 100f. Type **124** . . . . . . 2·25 85

1973. Pan African Drought Relief. No. 235 surch **SECHERESSE SOLIDARITE AFRICAINE** and value.
258 **117** 100f. on 25f. multicoloured . . . . . 1·10 60

126 Dish Aerial and Meteorological Station **129** Pres. Kennedy

128 Greater Dwarf Lemur

1973. Air. W.M.O. Centenary.
259 **126** 100f. orange, blue & black 1·25 65

1973. 12th Anniv of African and Malagasy Posts and Telecommunications. As T **155a** of Mauritania.
260 100f. red, violet and green . . 90 45

1973. Malagasy Lemurs.
261 **128** 5f. brown, green and purple (postage) 55 15
262 – 25f. brown, sepia & green 1·10 65
263 – 150f. brn, grn & sepia (air) . . . . 2·75 1·25
264 **128** 200f. brown, turq & blue 4·00 1·75
DESIGN—VERT: 25f., 150f. Weasel-lemur.

1973. Air. 10th Death Anniv of Pres. John Kennedy.
265 **129** 300f. multicoloured . . . 3·25 1·75

130 Footballers

1973. Air. World Cup Football Championship. West Germany.
266 **130** 500f. mauve, brown and light brown . . . . . 5·50 2·50

CURRENCY. Issues from No. 267 to No. 389 have face values shown as "Fmg". This abbreviation denotes the Malagasy Franc which was introduced in 1966.

131 Copernicus, Satellite and Diagram

1974. Air. 500th Birth Anniv of Copernicus.
267 **131** 250f. blue, brown & green 3·25 1·50

1974. No. 76a surch.
268 25f. on 30f. multicoloured . . 25 15

133 Agricultural Training **135** Family and House

134 Male Player, and Hummingbird on Hibiscus

1974. 25th World Scouting Conference, Nairobi, Kenya.
269 **133** 4f. grey, blue and green (postage) 10 10
270 – 15f. purple, green and blue 20 15
271 – 100f. ochre, red & blue (air) 80 45
272 – 300f. brown, blue & black 3·50 1·75
DESIGNS—VERT: 15f. Building construction. HORIZ: 100f. First Aid training; 300f. Fishing.

1974. Air. Asia, Africa and Latin America Table-Tennis Championships, Peking.
273 **134** 50f. red, blue and brown 80 30
274 – 100f. red, blue and violet 1·60 70
DESIGN: 100f. Female player and stylized bird.

1974. World Population Year.
275 **135** 25f. red, orange and blue 25 10

136 Micheline Railcar

1974. Air. Malagasy Railway Locomotives.
276 **136** 50f. green, red and brown 75 25
277 – 85f. red, blue and green 1·25 30
278 – 200f. blue, lt blue & brown . . . . 3·25 80
DESIGNS: 85f. Track-inspection trolley; 200f. Garratt steam locomotive, 1926.

137 U.P.U. Emblem and Letters

1974. Air. Centenary of U.P.U.
279 **137** 250f. red, blue and violet 3·00 1·40

138 Rainibetsimisaraka

1974. Rainibetsimisaraka Commemoration.
280 **138** 25f. multicoloured 35 20

1974. Air. West Germany's Victory in World Cup Football Championship. No. 266 optd **R.F.A. 2 HOLLANDE 1**.
281 **130** 500f. mauve, brown and light brown . . . . . 5·00 2·75

140 "Apollo" and "Soyuz" spacecraft

1974. Air. Soviet–U.S. Space Co-operation.
282 **140** 150f. orange, green & blue 1·10 60
283 – 250f. green, blue & brown 2·00 1·00
DESIGN: No. 283, As Type **140** but different view.

141 Marble Slabs

1974. Marble Industry. Multicoloured.
284 4f. Type **141** 55 15
285 25f. Quarrying . . . . 1·40 25

1974. Air. Universal Postal Union Centenary (2nd issue). No. 279 optd **100 ANS DE COLLABORATION INTERNATIONALE**.
286 **137** 250f. red, blue and violet 1·75 1·00

143 Faces and Maps

1974. Europafrique.
287 **143** 150f. brown, red & orange 1·40 70

144 "Food in Hand"

1974. "Freedom from Hunger".
288 **144** 80f. blue, brown and grey 65 35

145 "Coton" **146** Malagasy People

1974. Malagasy Dogs. Multicoloured.
289 50f. Type **145** . . . . 1·40 45
290 100f. Hunting dog . . . . . 2·25 1·10

1974. Founding of "Fokonolona" Commune.
291 **146** 5f. multicoloured 15 10
292 10f. multicoloured 15 10
293 20f. multicoloured 20 10
294 60f. multicoloured 60 30

147 "Discovering Talent"

1974. National Development Council.
295 **147** 25f. multicoloured 20 10
296 35f. multicoloured 30 15

148 "Adoration of the Magi" (David)

1974. Air. Christmas. Multicoloured.
297 200f. Type **148** . . . . . . 2·25 95
298 300f. "Virgin of the Cherries and Child" (Metzys) . . . 3·25 1·25

149 Malagasy Girl and Rose

1975. International Women's Year.
299 **149** 100f. brown, orange & grn 85 40

150 Colonel Richard Ratsimandrava (Head of Government)

1975.
300 **150** 15f. brown, black & yellow 15 10
301 25f. brown, black and blue 20 15
302 100f. brown, black & green 80 35

151 Sofia Bridge

1975.
303 **151** 45f. multicoloured 50 20

152 U.N. Emblem and Part of Globe

1975. Air. 30th Anniv of U.N. Charter.
304 **152** 300f. multicoloured . . . 2·75 1·25

153 De Grasse (after Mauzaisse) and "Randolph"

1975. Bicentenary of American Revolution (1st issue). Multicoloured.
305 40f. Type **153** (postage) . . . 85 25
306 50f. Lafayette, "Lexington" and H.M.S. "Edward" . . 95 30
307 100f. D'Estaing and "Languedoc" (air) . . . . 1·75 50
308 200f. Paul Jones, "Bonhomme Richard" and H.M.S. "Serapis" . . . . 2·50 1·10
309 300f. Benjamin Franklin, "Millern" and "Montgomery" . . . . . 3·50 1·60

154 "Euphorbia viguieri"

1975. Malagasy Flora. Multicoloured.
311 15f. Type **154** (postage) . . . 25 15
312 25f. "Hibiscus rosesinensis" 40 20
313 30f. "Plumeria rubra acutitolia" 55 20
314 40f. "Pachypodium rosulatum" . . . . 1·00 30
315 85f. "Turraea sericea" (air) 1·75 1·00

1975. Air. "Apollo"–"Soyuz" Space Link. Nos. 282/3 optd **JONCTION 17 JUILLET 1975.**
316 **140** 150f. orange, green & blue 1·00 60
317 – 250f. green, blue & brown 2·25 1·00

156 Temple Frieze

1975. Air. "Save Borobudur Temple" (in Indonesia) Campaign.
318 **156** 50f. red, orange and blue 1·00 50

157 "Racial Unity"

1975. Namibia Day.
319 **157** 50f. multicoloured 45 20

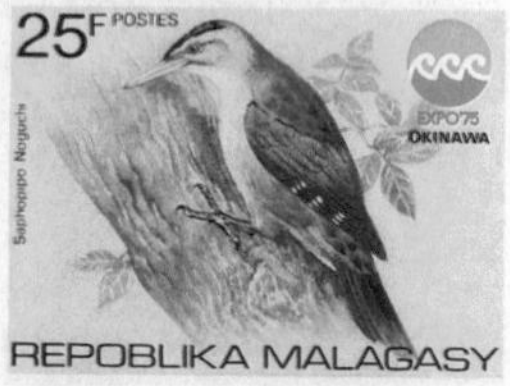

158 Pryer's Woodpecker

1975. International Exposition, Okinawa. Fauna. Multicoloured.
320 25f. Type **158** (postage) . . . 50 25
321 40f. Ryukyu rabbit 50 20
322 50f. Toad 70 30
323 75f. Tortoise . . . . 1·40 40
324 125f. Sika deer (air) . . . . 1·50 55

159 Lily Waterfall

1975. Lily Waterfall. Multicoloured.
326 25f. Type **159** 40 15
327 40f. Lily Waterfall (distant view) 60 15

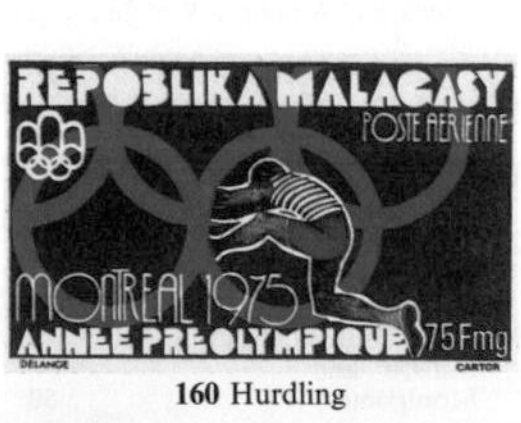

160 Hurdling

1975. Air. "Pre-Olympic Year". Olympic Games, Montreal (1976). Multicoloured.
328 75f. Type **160** 60 35
329 200f. Weightlifting (vert) . . 2·00 75

161 Bobsleigh "Fours"

1975. Winter Olympic Games, Innsbruck. Multicoloured.
330 75f. Type **161** (postage) . . . 50 25
331 100f. Ski-jumping 80 35
332 140f. Speed-skating . . . . . 1·25 50
333 200f. Cross-country skiing (air) . . . . 2·00 75
334 245f. Downhill skiing . . . . 2·25 90

162 Pirogue

1975. Malagasy Sailing-vessels. Multicoloured.
336 8f. Type **162** 55 15
337 45f. Malagasy schooner . . . 1·10 25

163 Canoeing

1976. Olympic Games, Montreal. Multicoloured.
338 40f. Type **163** (postage) . . . 25 15
339 50f. Sprinting and hurdling 35 20
340 100f. Putting the shot, and long-jumping (air) 90 35
341 200f. Gymnastics-horse and parallel bars . . . . 1·75 75
342 300f. Trampoline-jumping and high-diving . . . . . 2·40 1·00

164 "Apollo 14" Lunar Module and Flight Badge

1976. Air. 5th Anniv of "Apollo 14" Mission.
344 **164** 150f. blue, red and green 1·25 65

1976. Air. 5th Anniv of "Apollo 14" Mission. No. 344 optd **5e Anniversaire de la mission APOLLO XIV.**
345 **164** 150f. blue, red and green 1·25 75

166 "Graf Zeppelin" over Fujiyama

1976. 75th Anniv of Zeppelin. Multicoloured.
346 40f. Type **166** (postage) . . . 35 15
347 50f. "Graf Zeppelin" over Rio de Janeiro 40 15
348 75f. "Graf Zeppelin" over New York 80 25
349 100f. "Graf Zeppelin" over Sphinx and pyramids . . . 95 35
350 200f. "Graf Zeppelin" over Berlin (air) . . . . 2·25 75
351 300f. "Graf Zeppelin" over London . . . . 4·00 1·00

167 "Prevention of Blindness"

1976. World Health Day.
353 **167** 100f. multicoloured . . . 1·25 55

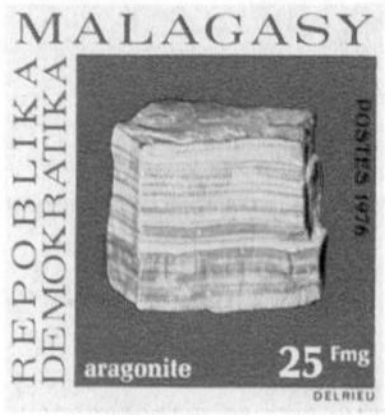

168 Aragonite

1976. Minerals and Fossils. Multicoloured.
354 25f. Type **168** 50 15
355 50f. Fossilized wood . . . . 1·10 55
356 150f. Celestyte . . . . 3·25 1·60

169 Alexander Graham Bell and Early Telephone

1976. Telephone Centenary. Multicoloured.
357 25f. Type **169** 15 10
358 50f. Cable maintenance, 1911 30 15
359 100f. Telephone operator and switchboard, 1895 . . . . 60 25
360 200f. "Emile Baudot" cable ship . . . . 2·25 90
361 300f. Man with radio-telephone . . . . 2·25 80

170 Children reading Book

1976. Children's Books Promotion. Multicoloured.
363 10f. Type **170** 15 10
364 25f. Children reading book (vert) 35 15

1976. Medal winners, Winter Olympic Games, Innsbruck. Nos. 330/4 optd **VAINQUEUR** and medal winner.
365 75f. Type **161** (postage) . . . 50 25
366 100f. Ski-jumping 80 40
367 140f. Skating . . . . 1·25 50
368 200f. Cross-country skiing (air) . . . . 1·40 75
369 245f. Downhill skiing . . . . 1·90 1·00
OPTS: 75f. **ALLEMAGNE FEDERALE**; 100f. **KARL SCHNABL, AUTRICHE**; 140f. **SHEILA YOUNG, ETATS-UNIS**; 200f. **IVAR FORMO, NORVEGE**; 245f. **ROSI MITTERMAIER, ALLEMAGNE DE L'OUEST.**

The subject depicted on No. 367 is speed-skating, an event in which the gold medal was won by J. E. Storholt, Norway.

1976. Bicentenary of American Revolution (2nd issue). Nos. 305/9 optd **4 JUILLET 1776–1976** in frame.
371 **153** 40f. multicoloured (postage) 35 25
372 – 50f. multicoloured 40 30
373 – 100f. multicoloured (air) 75 50
374 – 200f. multicoloured . . . 1·50 85
375 – 300f. multicoloured . . . 2·25 1·25

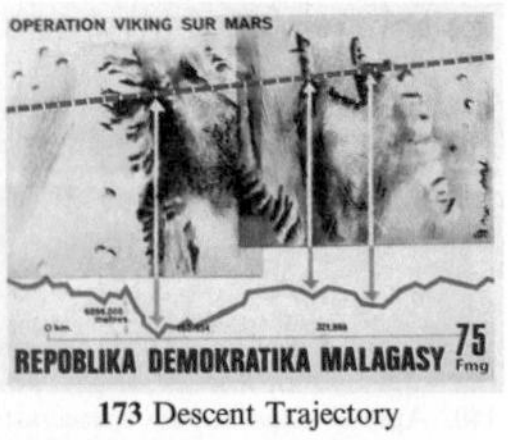

173 Descent Trajectory

1976. "Viking" Landing on Mars. Multicoloured.
377 75f. Type **173** 40 20
378 100f. "Viking" landing module separation 60 25
379 200f. "Viking" on Martian surface . . . . 1·25 55
380 300f. "Viking" orbiting Mars 2·00 80

174 Rainandriamampandry

175 Doves over Globe

1976. 30th Anniv of Treaties signed by Rainandriamampandry (Foreign Minister).
382 **174** 25f. multicoloured 30 20

1976. Indian Ocean—"Zone of Peace". Multicoloured.
383 60f. Type **175** 35 20
384 160f. Doves flying across Indian Ocean (horiz) . . . 1·10 55

1976. Olympic Games Medal Winners. Nos. 338/42 optd with names of two winners on each stamp.
385 **163** 40f. multicoloured (postage) 25 15
386 – 50f. multicoloured 35 25
387 – 100f. multicoloured (air) 70 40
388 – 200f. multicoloured . . . 1·40 65
389 – 300f. multicoloured . . . 2·00 1·00
OVERPRINTS: 40f. **V. DIBA, A. ROGOV**; 50f. **H. CRAWFORD, J. SCHALLER**; 100f. **U. BEYER, A. ROBINSON**; 200f. **N. COMANECI, N. ANDRIANOV**; 300f. **K. DIBIASI, E. VAYTSEKHOVSKAIA.**

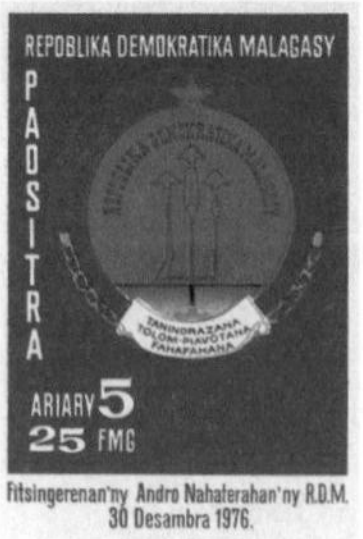

177 Malagasy Arms

1976. 1st Anniv of Malagasy Democratic Republic.
391 **177** 25f. multicoloured 20 10

178 Rabezavana (Independence Movement Leader)

1977. National Heroes. Multicoloured.
392 25f. Type **178** 20 10
393 25f. Lt. Albert Randriamaromanana . . . 20 10
394 25f. Ny Avana Ramanantoanina (politician) 20 10
395 100f. Fasam-Pirenena National Mausoleum, Tananarive (horiz) 75 40

179 Family

1977. World Health Day.
396 **179** 5f. multicoloured 15 10

180 Medical School, Antananarivo

1977. 80th Anniv of Medical School, Antananarivo.
397 **180** 250f. multicoloured . . . 2·00 95

181 Rural Post Van

1977. Rural Mail.
398 **181** 35f. multicoloured 30 15

182 Morse Key and Man with Headphones

1977. 90th Anniv of Antananarivo–Tamatave Telegraph.
399 **182** 15f. multicoloured 15 10

183 Academy Emblem

1977. 75th Anniv of Malagasy Academy.
400 **183** 10f. multicoloured 15 10

184 Lenin and Russian Flag

1977. 60th Anniv of Russian Revolution.
401 **184** 25f. multicoloured . . . . 1·10 10

185 Raoul Follereau

1978. 25th Anniv of World Leprosy Day.
402 **185** 5f. multicoloured 90 10

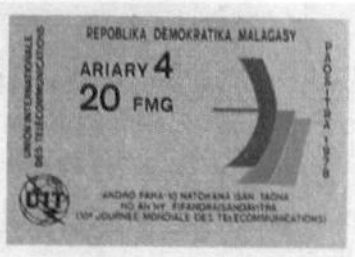

186 Microwave Antenna

187 "Co-operation"

1978. World Telecommunications Day.
403 **186** 20f. multicoloured 15 10

1978. Anti-Apartheid Year.
404 **187** 60f. red, black and yellow 40 25

188 Children with Instruments of Revolution

189 Tractor, Factory and Labourers

1978. "Youth—Pillar of the Revolution".
405 **188** 25f. multicoloured 75 45

1978. Socialist Co-operatives.
406 **189** 25f. multicoloured 15 10

190 Women at Work

191 Children with Books, Instruments and Fruit

1979. "Women, Pillar of the Revolution".
407 **190** 40f. multicoloured 25 15

1979. International Year of the Child.
408 **191** 10f. multicoloured 20 10

192 Ring-tailed Lemur

193 J. V. S. Razakandraina

1979. Animals. Multicoloured.
409 25f. Type **192** (postage) . . . 25 15
410 125f. Black lemur . . . . . 1·40 30
411 1000f. Malagasy civet . . . . 8·50 2·25
412 20f. Tortoise (air) 20 20
413 95f. Black lemur (different) 1·00 40

1979. J. V. S. Razakandraina (poet) Commem.
414 **193** 25f. multicoloured 15 10

194 "Centella asiatica"

1979. Medicinal Plant.
415 **194** 25f. multicoloured 15 10

195 Map of Malagasy and Ste. Marie Telecommunications Station

1979. Telecommunications.
416 **195** 25f. multicoloured 20 10

196 Post Office, Antsirabe

1979. Stamp Day.
417 **196** 500f. multicoloured . . . 3·25 1·10

197 Palestinians with Flag

1979. Air. Palestinian Solidarity.
418 **197** 60f. multicoloured 50 20

198 Concorde and Map of Africa

1979. 20th Anniv of ASECNA (African Air Safety Organization).
419 **198** 50f. multicoloured 60 20

199 Lenin addressing Meeting

1980. 110th Birth Anniv of Lenin.
420 **199** 25f. multicoloured 45 10

200 Taxi-bus

201 Map illuminated by Sun

1980. 5th Anniv of Socialist Revolution.
421 **200** 30f. multicoloured 20 10

1980. 20th Anniv of Independence.
422 **201** 75f. multicoloured 50 30

202 Military Parade

1980. 20th Anniv of Army.
423 **202** 50f. multicoloured 35 15

203 Joseph Raseta

1980. Dr. Joseph Raseta Commemoration.
424 **203** 30f. multicoloured 20 10

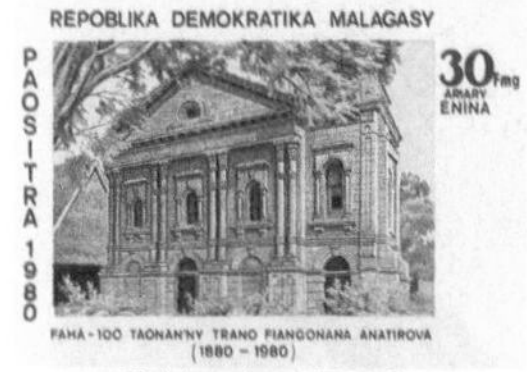

204 Anatirova Temple

1980. Anatirova Temple Centenary.
425 **204** 30f. multicoloured 20 10

205 Boxing

1980. Olympic Games, Moscow. Multicoloured.
426 30f. Hurdling 45 10
427 75f. Type **205** 90 25
428 250f. Judo . . . . 1·75 75
429 500f. Swimming . . . . . . 3·25 1·50

206 Emblem, Map and Sun

1980. 5th Anniv of Malagasy Democratic Republic.
430 **206** 30f. multicoloured 20 10

207 Skier

1981. Winter Olympic Games, Lake Placid (1980).
431 **207** 175f. multicoloured . . . 1·10 55

208 "Angraecum leonis"

209 Handicapped Student

1981. Flowers. Multicoloured.
432 5f. Type **208** 10 10
433 80f. "Angraecum famosum" 60 25
434 170f. "Angraecum sesquipedale" . . . . . . 1·25 55

1981. International Year of Disabled People. Mult.
435 25f. Type **209** 20 10
436 80f. Disabled carpenter . . . 55 25

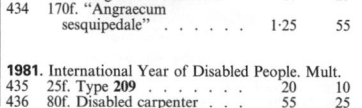

210 Ribbons forming Caduceus, I.T.U. and W.H.O. Emblems

1981. World Telecommunications Day.

437	**210**	15f. blue, black and yellow	15	10
438		45f. multicoloured	35	15

211 Valentina Tereshkova (first woman in space)

1981. Space Achievements. Multicoloured.

439		30f. Type **211**	15	10
440		80f. Astronaut on Moon	55	25
441		90f. Yuri Gagarin (first man in space)	65	30

212 Raphael-Louis Rafiringa

1981. Raphael-Louis Rafiringa Commemoration.

442	**212**	30f. multicoloured	20	10

213 Child writing Alphabet

1981. World Literacy Day.

443	**213**	30f. multicoloured	20	10

214 Ploughing and Sowing

1981. World Food Day.

444	**214**	200f. multicoloured	1·25	60

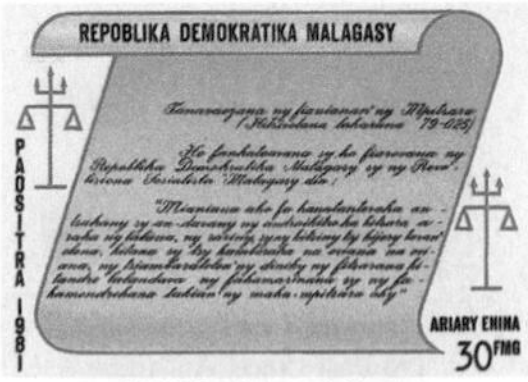

215 Magistrates' Oath

1981. Renewal of Magistrates' Oath.

445	**215**	30f. mauve and black	20	10

216 "Dove"

1981. Birth Centenary of Pablo Picasso.

446	**216**	80f. multicoloured	60	25

217 U.P.U. Emblem and Malagasy Stamps

1981. 20th Anniv of Admission to U.P.U.

447	**217**	5f. multicoloured	10	10
448		30f. multicoloured	20	10

218 Stamps forming Map of Malagasy

1981. Stamp Day.

449	**218**	90f. multicoloured	65	30

219 Hook-billed Vanga

1982. Birds. Multicoloured.

450		25f. Type **219**	95	10
451		30f. Courol	95	10
452		200f. Madagascar fish eagle (vert)	7·25	85

220 Vaccination

221 Jeannette Mpihira

1982. Centenary of Discovery of Tubercule Bacillus.

453	**220**	30f. multicoloured	30	15

1982. Jeannette Mpihira Commemoration.

454	**221**	30f. multicoloured	20	10

222 Woman's Head formed from Map of Africa

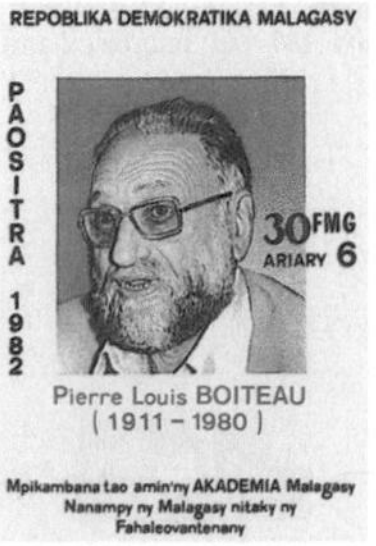

223 Pierre Louis Boiteau

1982. Air. 20th Anniv of Pan-African Women's Organization.

455	**222**	80f. multicoloured	60	30

1982. Pierre Louis Boiteau Commemoration.

456	**223**	30f. multicoloured	20	15

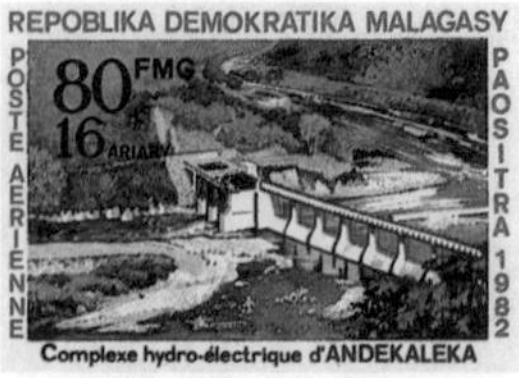

224 Andekaleka Dam

1982. Air. Andekaleka Hydro-electric Complex.

457	**224**	80f. multicoloured	60	30

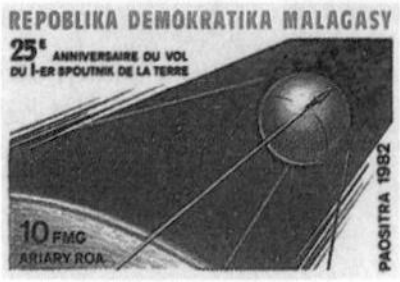

225 "Sputnik I"

1982. 25th Anniv of First Artificial Satellite. Multicoloured.

458		10f. Type **225**	10	10
459		80f. Yuri Gagarin	60	30
460		100f. "Soyuz"–"Salyut" space station	75	35

226 Heading Ball

1982. World Cup Football Championship, Spain. Multicoloured.

461		30f. Type **226**	20	10
462		40f. Running with ball	30	15
463		80f. Tackle	60	30

227 Ploughing, Sowing and F.A.O. Emblem

1982. World Food Day.

465	**227**	80f. multicoloured	50	30

228 Bar Scene

1982. 150th Anniv of Edouard Manet (artist). Multicoloured.

466		5f. Type **228**	45	15
467		30f. Woman in white	65	10
468		170f. Man with pipe	2·75	65

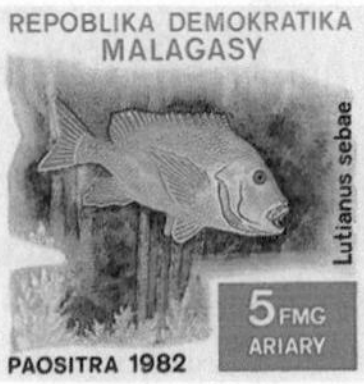

229 Emperor Snapper

1982. Fishes. Multicoloured.

470		5f. Type **229**	20	20
471		20f. Sailfish	30	20
472		30f. Lionfish	40	20
473		50f. Yellow-finned tuna	65	20
474		200f. Black-tipped grouper	3·00	85

230 Fort Mahavelona

1982. Landscapes. Multicoloured.

476		10f. Type **230** (postage)	10	10
477		30f. Ramena coast	20	10
478		400f. Jacarandas in flower (air)	2·75	1·50

231 Flags of Russia and Malagasy, Clasped Hands and Tractors

1982. 60th Anniv of U.S.S.R. Multicoloured.

479		10f. Type **231**	10	10
480		15f. Flags, clasped hands and radio antenna	10	10
481		30f. Map of Russia, Kremlin and Lenin	15	10
482		150f. Flags, clasped hands, statue and arms of Malagasy	1·00	45

232 Television, Drums, Envelope and Telephone

1983. World Communications Year. Multicoloured.

483		30f. Type **232**	15	10
484		80f. Stylized figures holding cogwheel	2·75	60

233 Axe breaking Chain on Map of Africa

234 Henri Douzon

1983. 20th Anniv of Organization of African Unity.

485	**233**	30f. multicoloured	20	10

1983. Henri Douzon (lawyer) Commemoration.

486	**234**	30f. multicoloured	20	10

237 Ruffed Lemur

1984. Lemurs. Multicoloured.
489 30f. Type **237** 35 20
490 30f. Verreaux's sifaka 35 20
491 30f. Lesser mouse-lemur (horiz) 35 20
492 30f. Aye-aye (horiz) 35 20
493 200f. Indri (horiz) . . . . . 2·75 1·10

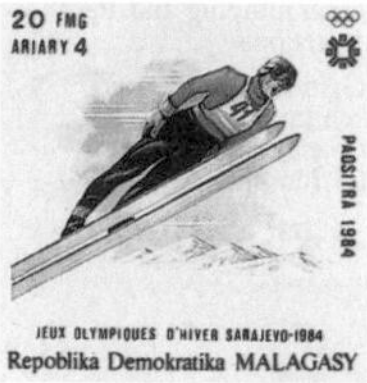

238 Ski Jumping

1984. Winter Olympic Games, Sarajevo. Mult.
495 20f. Type **238** 15 10
496 30f. Ice hockey 20 10
497 30f. Downhill skiing 20 10
498 30f. Speed skating 20 10
499 200f. Ice dancing . . . . . . 1·40 70

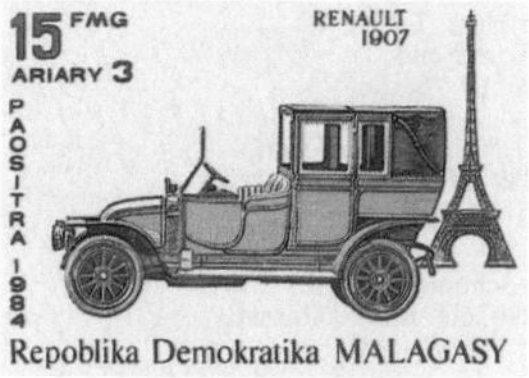

239 Renault, 1907

1984. Early Motor Cars. Multicoloured.
501 15f. Type **239** 20 10
502 30f. Benz, 1896 . . . . . . 30 15
503 30f. Baker, 1901 . . . . . . 30 15
504 30f. Blake, 1901 . . . . . . 30 15
505 200f. F.I.A.L., 1908 . . . . 2·00 75

240 Pastor Ravelojaona

241 "Noli me Tangere"

1984. Pastor Ravelojaona (encylopaedist) Commemoration.
507 **240** 30f. multicoloured 20 15

1984. 450th Death Anniv of Correggio. Paintings by Artist.
508 **241** 5f. multicoloured 10 10
509 – 20f. multicoloured 15 10
510 – 30f. multicoloured 25 15
511 – 80f. multicoloured 45 25
512 – 200f. multicoloured . . . 1·40 65

242 Paris Landmarks and Emblem

243 Football

1984. 60th Anniv of International Chess Federation. Multicoloured.
514 5f. Type **242** 15 15
515 20f. Wilhelm Steinitz and stylized king 20 15
516 30f. Vera Menchik and stylized queen 35 15
517 30f. Anatoly Karpov and trophy 35 15
518 215f. Nona Gaprindashvili and trophy . . . . 2·75 90

1984. Olympic Games, Los Angeles.
520 **243** 100f. multicoloured . . . 45 30

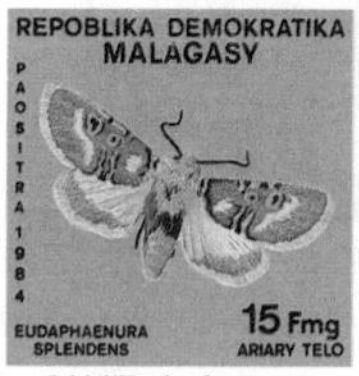

244 "Eudaphaenura splendens"

245 Ralaimongo

1984. Butterflies. Multicoloured.
521 15f. Type **244** 20 15
522 50f. "Acraea hova" 60 20
523 50f. "Othreis boesae" 60 20
524 50f. "Pharmocophagus antenor" 60 20
525 200f. "Epicausis smithii" . . 2·25 1·00

1984. Birth Centenary of Jean Ralaimongo (politician).
527 **245** 50f. multicoloured 30 15

246 Children in Brief-case

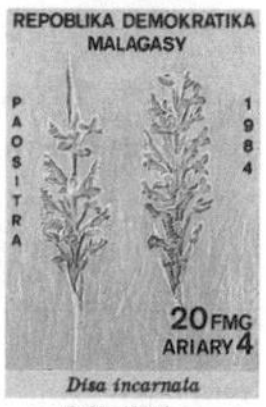

247 "Disa incarnata"

1984. 25th Anniv of Children's Rights Legislation.
528 **246** 50f. multicoloured 40 15

1984. Orchids. Multicoloured.
529 20f. Type **247** (postage) . . . 20 10
530 235f. "Eulophiella roempleriana" . . . . . . 2·25 85
531 50f. "Eulophiella roempleriana" (horiz) (air) 60 25
532 50f. "Grammangis ellisii" (horiz) 60 25
533 50f. "Grammangis spectabilis" 60 25

248 U.N. Emblem and Cotton Plant

1984. 20th Anniv of United Nations Conference on Commerce and Development.
535 **248** 100f. multicoloured . . . 60 30

249 "Sun Princess" (Sadio Diouf)

1984. 40th Anniv of International Civil Aviation Organization.
536 **249** 100f. multicoloured . . . 65 30

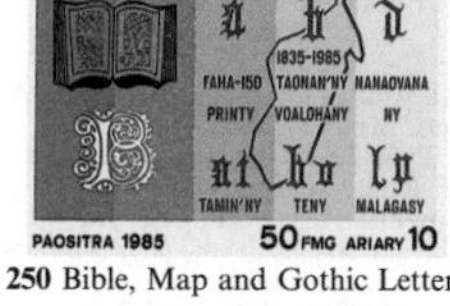

250 Bible, Map and Gothic Letters

1985. 150th Anniv of First Bible in Malagasy Language.
537 **250** 50f. brown, pink and black 30 15

251 Farming Scenes, Census-taker and Farmer

252 Lap-dog

1985. Agricultural Census.
538 **251** 50f. grey, black and mauve 30 15

1985. Cats and Dogs. Multicoloured.
539 20f. Type **252** 20 15
540 20f. Siamese cat 20 15
541 50f. Abyssinian cat (vert) . . 60 20
542 100f. Cocker spaniel (vert) . . 1·25 35
543 235f. Poodle . . . . 2·50 90

253 Russian Soldiers in Berlin

1985. 40th Anniv of Victory in Second World War.
545 20f. Type **253** 15 10
546 50f. Arms of French squadron and fighter planes 40 15
547 100f. Victory parade, Red Square, Moscow 75 30
548 100f. French troops entering Paris (vert) . . . . 1·25 30

254 Parade in Stadium

1985. 10th Anniv of Malagasy Democratic Republic.
549 **254** 50f. multicoloured 40 15

255 Medal and Independence Obelisk

256 Peace Dove and Stylized People

1985. 25th Anniv of Independence.
550 **255** 50f. multicoloured 40 15

1985. 12th World Youth and Students' Festival, Moscow.
551 **256** 50f. multicoloured 40 15

257 I.Y.Y. Emblem and Map of Madagascar

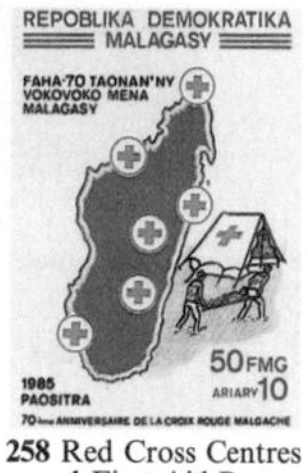

258 Red Cross Centres and First Aid Post

1985. International Youth Year.
552 **257** 100f. multicoloured . . . 60 25

1985. 70th Anniv of Malagasy Red Cross.
553 **258** 50f. multicoloured 60 25

259 "View of Sea at Saintes-Maries" (Vincent van Gogh)

1985. Impressionist Paintings. Multicoloured.
554 20f. Type **259** 45 10
555 20f. "Rouen Cathedral in the Evening" (Claude Monet) (vert) 45 10
556 45f. "Young Girls in Black" (Pierre-Auguste Renoir) (vert) 80 20
557 50f. "Red Vineyard at Arles" (van Gogh) 80 20
558 100f. "Boulevard des Capucines, Paris" (Monet) 1·40 40

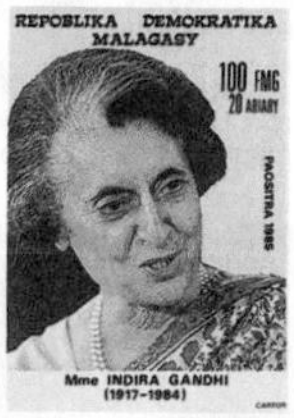

260 Indira Gandhi

1985. Indira Gandhi (Indian Prime Minister) Commemoration.
560 **260** 100f. multicoloured . . . 80 30

261 Figures and Dove on Globe and Flag

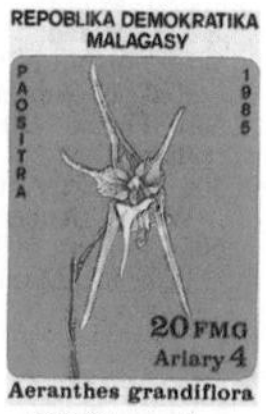

262 "Aeranthes grandiflora"

1985. 40th Anniv of U.N.O.
561 **261** 100f. multicoloured . . . 65 25

1985. Orchids. Multicoloured.
562 20f. Type **262** 20 10
563 45f. "Angraecum magdalenae" and "Nephele oenopion" (insect) (horiz) 35 15
564 50f. "Aerangis stylosa" . . . 35 15
565 100f. "Angraecum eburneum longicalcar" and "Hippotion batschi" (insect) 80 35
566 100f. "Angraecum sesquipedale" and "Xanthopan morganipredicta" (insect) 80 35

263 Russian and Czechoslovakian Cosmonauts

1985. Russian "Interkosmos" Space Programme. Multicoloured.
568 20f. Type **263** 15 10
569 20f. Russian and American flags and "Apollo"–"Soyuz" link 15 10
570 50f. Russian and Indian cosmonauts 30 15
571 100f. Russian and Cuban cosmonauts 50 25
572 200f. Russian and French cosmonauts . . . . 1·25 60

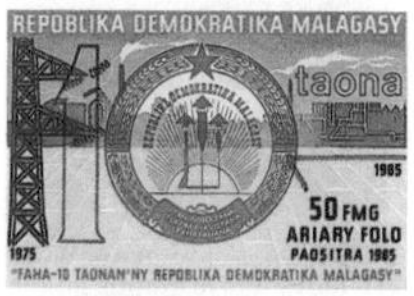

264 Emblem in "10"

1985. 10th Anniv of Malagasy Democratic Republic.
574 **264** 50f. multicoloured 30 15

265 Headquarters

1986. 10th Anniv of ARO (State insurance system).
575 **265** 50f. yellow and brown . . 30 15

266 "David and Uriah" (Rembrandt)

268 Sombrero, Football and Player

267 Comet

1986. Foreign Paintings in Hermitage Museum, Leningrad. Multicoloured.

576	20f. Type **266**	20	10
577	50f. "Portrait of Old Man in Red" (Rembrandt)	50	30
578	50f. "Danae" (Rembrandt) (horiz)	50	30
579	50f. "Marriage of Earth and Water" (Rubens)	50	30
580	50f. "Portrait of Infanta Isabella's Maid" (Rubens)	50	30

1986. Air. Appearance of Halley's Comet.
582 **267** 150f. multicoloured . . . 1·00 50

1986. Russian Paintings in the Tretyakov Gallery, Moscow. As T **266**. Multicoloured.

583	20f. "Fruit and Flowers" (I. Khroutsky) (horiz)	15	10
584	50f. "The Rooks have Returned" (A. Savrasov)	60	25
585	50f. "Unknown Woman" (I. Kramskoi) (horiz)	30	20
586	50f. "Aleksandr Pushkin" (O. Kiprenski)	30	20
587	100f. "March, 1895" (I. Levitan) (horiz)	90	40

1986. World Cup Football Championship, Mexico.
589 **268** 150f. multicoloured . . . 1·10 30

269 Child Care

270 Jungle Cat

1986. UNICEF Child Survival Campaign.
590 **269** 60f. multicoloured 40 15

1986. Wild Cats. Multicoloured.

591	10f. Type **270**	20	10
592	10f. Wild cat	20	10
593	60f. Caracal	45	20
594	60f. Leopard cat	45	20
595	60f. Serval	45	20

271 Dove above Hands holding Globe

1986. International Peace Year. Multicoloured.

597	60f. Type **271**	40	15
598	150f. Doves above emblem and map	1·00	45

272 U.P.U. Emblem on Dove

273 U.P.U. Emblem on Globe

1986. World Post Day.

599	**272**	60f. multicoloured (postage)	40	15
600		150f. blue, black and red (air)	1·10	50

1986. Air. 25th Anniv of Admission to U.P.U.
601 **273** 150f. multicoloured . . . 1·10 50

274 Giant Madagascar Coucal

1986. Birds. Multicoloured.

602	60f. Type **274**	1·10	30
603	60f. Crested Madagascar coucal	1·10	30
604	60f. Rufous vangas (vert)	1·10	30
605	60f. Red-tailed vangas (vert)	1·10	30
606	60f. Sicklebill	1·10	30

275 Tortoise

1987. Endangered Animals. Multicoloured.

608	60f. Type **275**	65	25
609	60f. Crocodile	65	25
610	60f. Crested wood ibis (vert)	65	25
611	60f. Vasa parrot	65	25

276 Crowd in "40"

1987. 40th Anniv of Anti-colonial Uprising.

613	**276**	60f. brown, red and yellow	35	15
614	–	60f. multicoloured	35	15

DESIGN: No. 614, Hands in broken manacles, map, rifleman and spearman.

277 Emblems, Map and Pictogram

1987. 1st Indian Ocean Towns Games.

615	**277**	60f. multicoloured	35	15
616		150f. multicoloured	1·10	35

278 "Sarimanok"

1987. The "Sarimanok" (replica of early dhow). Multicoloured.

617	60f. Type **278**	50	20
618	150f. "Sarimanok" (different)	1·25	40

279 Coffee Plant

280 Rifle Shooting and Satellite

1987. 25th Anniv of African and Malagasy Coffee Producers Organization. Multicoloured.

619	60f. Type **279**	35	15
620	150f. Map showing member countries	1·10	35

1987. Winter Olympic Games, Calgary (1988). Multicoloured.

621	60f. Type **280**	25	10
622	150f. Slalom	60	20
623	250f. Luge	1·25	40
624	350f. Speed skating	1·40	50
625	400f. Ice hockey	1·60	60
626	450f. Ice skating (pairs)	2·00	70

281 "Giotto" Space Probe

1987. Appearance of Halley's Comet (1986). Space Probes. Multicoloured.

628	60f. Type **281**	25	10
629	150f. "Vega 1"	60	20
630	250f. "Vega 2"	1·25	40
631	350f. "Planet A 1"	1·40	50
632	400f. "Planet B 1"	1·60	60
633	450f. "I.C.E."	2·00	70

282 Piper Aztec

283 Rabearivelo

1987. Air. 25th Anniv of Air Madagascar. Mult.

635	60f. Type **282**	40	20
636	60f. De Havilland Twin Otter	40	20
637	150f. Boeing 747-200	1·00	40

1987. 50th Death Anniv of Jean-Joseph Rabearivelo (poet).
638 **283** 60f. multicoloured 30 15

284 Communications Equipment Robot and Print-out Paper

285 Emblem

1987. National Telecommunications Research Laboratory.
639 **284** 60f. green, black and red 30 15

1987. 150th Anniv of Execution of Rafaravavy Rasalama (Christian martyr).
640 **285** 60f. black, deep blue and blue 30 15

286 Hand using Key and Telegraphist

1987. Cent of Antananarivo–Tamatave Telegraph.
641 **286** 60f. multicoloured 30 15

287 Bartholomeu Dias and Departure from Palos, 1492

1987. 500th Anniv (1992) of Discovery of America by Columbus. Multicoloured.

642	60f. Type **287**	30	20
643	150f. Route around Samana Cay and Henry the Navigator	60	25
644	250f. Columbus and crew disembarking, 1492, and A. de Marchena	75	30
645	350f. Building Fort Navidad and Paolo del Pozzo Toscanelli	1·10	40
646	400f. Columbus in Barcelona, 1493, and Queen Isabella of Spain	1·60	65
647	450f. Columbus and "Nina"	1·75	70

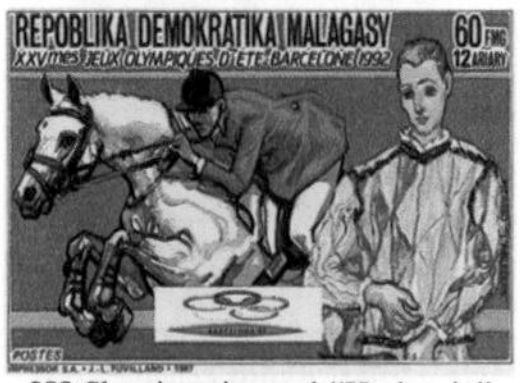

288 Showjumping and "Harlequin" (Picasso)

1987. Olympic Games, Barcelona (1992). Multicoloured.

649	60f. Type **288** (postage)	15	10
650	150f. Weightlifting and Barcelona Cathedral	40	20
651	250f. Hurdling and Canaletas Fountain	70	30
652	350f. High jumping and Parc d'Attractions	1·00	40
653	400f. Gymnast on bar and church (air)	1·40	50
654	450f. Gymnast with ribbon and Triumphal Arch	1·75	50

289 Anniversary Emblem, T.V. Tower and Interhotel "Berlin"

290 Musician and Dancers

1987. 750th Anniv of Berlin.
656 **289** 150f. multicoloured . . . 25 15

1987. Schools Festival.
657 **290** 60f. multicoloured 15 10

291 Madagascar Pasteur Institute and Pasteur

1987. Centenary of Pasteur Institute, Paris.
658 **291** 250f. multicoloured . . . 60 25

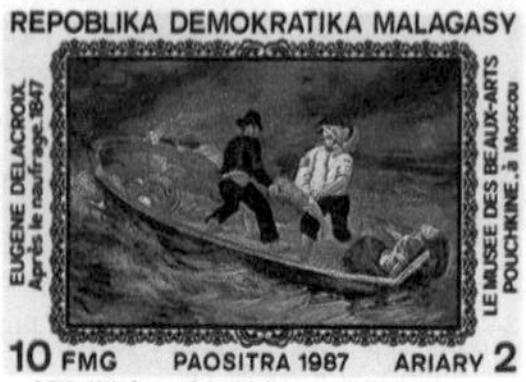

292 "After the Shipwreck" (Eugene Delacroix)

1987. Paintings in Pushkin Museum of Fine Arts, Moscow. Multicoloured.

659	10f. Type **292**	15	10
660	60f. "Jupiter and Callisto" (Francois Boucher) (vert)	15	10
661	60f. "Still Life with Swan" (Frans Snyders)	15	10
662	60f. "Chalet in the Mountains" (Gustave Courbet)	15	10
663	150f. "At the Market" (Joachim Bueckelaer)	40	15

293 Emblem

294 Family and House on Globe

1987. 10th Anniv of Pan-African Telecommunications Union.
665 **293** 250f. multicoloured . . . 40 20

1988. International Year of Shelter for the Homeless (1987). Multicoloured.
666 80f. Type **294** 15 10
667 250f. Hands forming house protecting family from rain 35 20

295 Lenin addressing Crowd

1988. 70th Anniv of Russian Revolution. Mult.
668 60f. Type **295** 15 10
669 60f. Revolutionaries 15 10
670 150f. Lenin in crowd 25 15

296 Broad-nosed Gentle Lemur

1988. Endangered Species. Multicoloured.
671 60f. Type **296** 15 10
672 150f. Diadem sifaka 20 15
673 250f. Indri 35 15
674 350f. Ruffed lemur 60 25
675 550f. Purple herons (horiz) 1·60 50
676 1500f. Nossi-be chameleon (horiz) . . . . 2·40 1·25

297 Ice Skating

1988. Winter Olympic Games, Calgary. Mult.
678 20f. Type **297** 10 10
679 60f. Speed-skating 10 10
680 60f. Slalom 10 10
681 100f. Cross-country skiing . . 20 10
682 250f. Ice hockey 45 20

298 Dove, Axe breaking Chain and Map

1988. 25th Anniv of Organization of African Unity.
684 **298** 80f. multicoloured 15 10

299 Institute Building

1988. 20th Anniv of National Posts and Telecommunications Institute.
685 **299** 80f. multicoloured 15 10

300 College

1988. Centenary of St. Michael's College.
686 **300** 250f. multicoloured . . . 30 20

301 Pierre and Marie Curie in Laboratory **302** Emblem

1988. 90th Anniv of Discovery of Radium.
687 **301** 150f. brown and mauve 40 15

1988. 10th Anniv of Alma-Ata Declaration (on health and social care).
688 **302** 60f. multicoloured 15 10

303 Emblem **304** Ring-tailed Lemurs on Island

1988. 40th Anniv of W.H.O.
689 **303** 150f. brown, blue and black 20 15

1988. 50th Anniv of Tsimbazaza Botanical and Zoological Park. Multicoloured.
690 20f. Type **304** 15 10
691 80f. Ring-tailed lemur with young (25 × 37 mm) 20 10
692 250f. Palm tree and ring-tailed lemur within "Zoo" (47 × 32 mm) 40 20

305 Hoopoe and Blue Madagascar Coucal **306** Cattle grazing

1988. Scouts, Birds and Butterflies. Multicoloured.
694 80f. Type **305** 10 10
695 250f. "Chrysiridia croesus" (butterfly) 40 20
696 270f. Nelicourvi weaver and red forest fody 50 10
697 350f. "Papilio dardanus" (butterflies) 60 40
698 550f. Crested Madagascar coucal . . . . 1·00 25
699 1500f. "Argema mittrei" (butterfly) . . . . 2·50 2·00

1988. 10th Anniv of International Fund for Agricultural Development.
701 **306** 250f. multicoloured . . . 30 20

307 Karl Bach and Clavier **308** Books

1988. Musicians' Anniversaries. Multicoloured.
702 80f. Type **307** (death bicentenary) 15 10
703 250f. Franz Schubert and piano (160th death) 40 15
704 270f. Georges Bizet and scene from "Carmen" (150th birth) 40 20
705 350f. Claude Debussy and scene from "Pelleas et Melisande" (70th death) . . 50 25
706 550f. George Gershwin at piano writing score of "Rhapsody in Blue" (90th birth) 75 45
707 1500f. Elvis Presley (10th death (1987)) . . . . . . 2·75 1·25

1988. "Ecole en Fete" Schools Festival.
709 **308** 80f. multicoloured 15 10

309 "Black Sea Fleet at Feodosiya" (Ivan Aivazovski) **310** "Tragocephala crassicornis"

1988. Paintings of Sailing Ships. Multicoloured.
710 20f. Type **309** 40 15
711 80f. "Lesnoie" (N. Semenov) 40 15
712 80f. "Seascape with Sailing Ships" (Simon de Vlieger) 40 15
713 100f. "Orel" (N. Golitsine) (horiz) 45 15
714 250f. "Naval Battle Exercises" (Adam Silo) . . 90 25

1988. Endangered Beetles. Multicoloured.
716 20f. Type **310** 15 10
717 80f. "Polybothris symptuosa-gema" 55 25
718 250f. "Euchroea auripigmenta" . . . . . . 1·25 60
719 350f. "Stellognata maculata" 1·60 80

311 Stretcher Bearers and Anniversary Emblem **312** Symbols of Human Rights

1988. 125th Anniv of International Red Cross. Multicoloured.
720 80f. Type **311** 15 10
721 250f. Red Cross services, emblem and Henri Dunant (founder) 35 20

1988. 40th Anniv of Declaration of Human Rights. Multicoloured.
722 80f. Type **312** 15 10
723 250f. Hands with broken manacles holding "40" . . 35 15

313 Mercedes-Benz "Blitzen-Benz", 1909

1989. Cars and Trains. Multicoloured.
724 80f. Type **313** 15 10
725 250f. Micheline diesel railcar "Tsikirity", 1952, Tananarive–Moramanga line . . . . 1·50 15
726 270f. Bugatti coupe binder, "41" 40 20
727 350f. Class 1020 electric locomotive, Germany . . . 1·90 25
728 1500f. Souleze 701 diesel train, Malagasy . . . . . 4·75 1·25
729 2500f. Opel racing car, 1913 3·50 2·00

314 Tyrannosaurus

1989. Prehistoric Animals. Multicoloured.
731 20f. Type **314** 15 10
732 80f. Stegosaurus 20 10
733 250f. Arsinoitherium 40 15
734 450f. Triceratops 80 30

315 "Tahitian Girls"

1989. Woman in Art. Multicoloured.
736 20f. Type **315** 10 10
737 80f. "Portrait of a Girl" (Jean-Baptiste Greuze) . . 15 10
738 80f. "Portrait of a Young Woman" (Titian) 15 10
739 100f. "Woman in Black" (Auguste Renoir) 20 10
740 250f. "The Lace-maker" (Vasily Tropinine) 35 15

316 "Sobennikoffia robusta" **317** Nehru

1989. Orchids. Multicoloured.
742 5f. Type **316** 15 10
743 10f. "Grammangis fallax" (horiz) 15 10
744 80f. "Angraecum sororium" 20 10
745 80f. "Cymbidiella humblotii" 20 10
746 250f. "Oenia oncidiiflora" . . 60 20

1989. Birth Centenary of Jawaharlal Nehru (Indian statesman).
748 **317** 250f. multicoloured . . . 45 15

318 Mahamasina Sports Complex, Lake Anosy and Ampefiloha Quarter

1989. Antananarivo. Multicoloured.
749 5f. Type **318** 10 10
750 20f. Andravoahangy and Anjanahary Quarters . . . 10 10
751 80f. Zoma market and Faravohitra Quarter . . . 15 10
752 80f. Andohan' Analekely Quarter and 29 March Column 15 10
753 250f. Avenue de l'Independance and Jean Ralaimongo Column . . . 35 15
754 550f. Lake Anosy, Queen's Palace and Andohalo School 70 35

319 Rose Quartz

1989. Ornamental Minerals. Multicoloured.
755 80f. Type **319** 20 10
756 250f. Fossilized wood 60 20

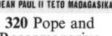

320 Pope and Rasoamanarivo **321** Map and Runner with Torch

1989. Visit of Pope John Paul II and Beatification of Victoire Rasoamanarivo. Multicoloured.
757 80f. Type **320** 20 10
758 250f. Map and Pope 55 20

1989. Town Games.
759 **321** 80f.+20f. multicoloured 15 15

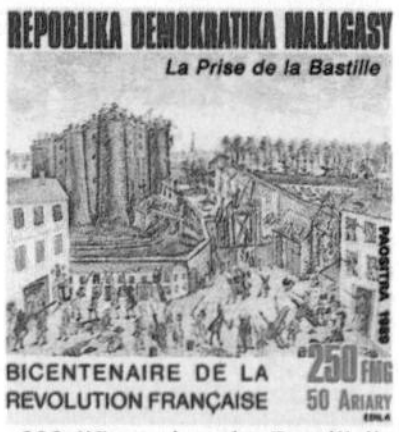

322 "Storming the Bastille"

1989. Bicentenary of French Revolution (1st issue).
760 **322** 250f. multicoloured . . . 35 15
See also Nos. 773/5.

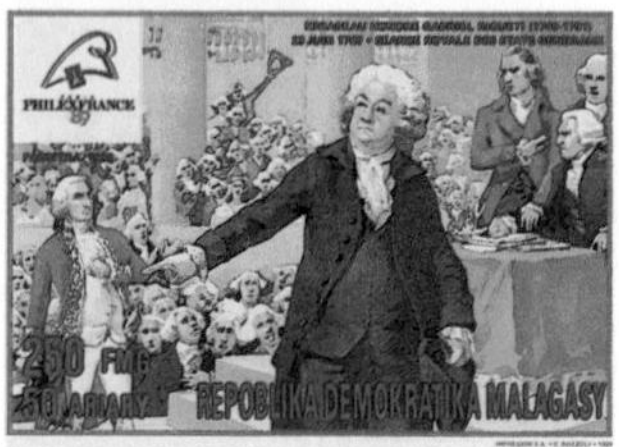

323 Mirabeau and Gabriel Riqueti at Meeting of States General

1989. "Philexfrance 89" International Stamp Exhibition, Paris. Multicoloured.
761 250f. Type **323** 30 15
762 350f. Camille Desmoulins' call to arms 45 20
763 1000f. Lafayette and crowd demanding bread . . . . . 1·25 60
764 1500f. Trial of King Louis XVI . . . . 2·00 80
765 2500f. Assassination of Marat 3·25 1·25

324 "Mars 1"

1989. Space Probes. Multicoloured.
767 20f. Type **324** 10 10
768 80f. "Mars 3" 15 10
769 80f. "Zond 2" 15 10
770 250f. "Mariner 9" 35 15
771 270f. "Viking 2" 40 20

325 "Liberty guiding the People" (Eugene Delacroix)

1989. Bicentenary of French Revolution (2nd issue). Multicoloured.
773 5f. Type **325** (postage) . . . 10 10
774 80f. "La Marseillaise" (Francois Rude) 15 10
775 250f. "Oath of the Tennis Court" (Jacques Louis David) (air) 35 15

326 Rene Cassin (founder) **327** Mother and Young on Bamboo

1989. 25th Anniv of International Human Rights Institute for French Speaking Countries.
776 **326** 250f. multicoloured . . . 30 15

1989. Golden Gentle Lemur.
777 **327** 250f. multicoloured . . . 40 20

328 Footballer and Cavour Monument, Turin **330** Long Jumping

329 Pennant Coralfish

1989. World Cup Football Championship, Italy. Multicoloured.
778 350f. Type **328** 50 20
779 1000f. Footballer and Christopher Columbus monument, Genoa . . . . 1·40 50
780 1500f. Florentine footballer, 1530, and "David" (sculpture, Michelangelo) 2·00 75
781 2500f. Footballer and "Rape of Proserpina" (sculpture, Bernini), Rome . . . . . 3·25 1·40

1990. Fishes. Multicoloured.
783 5f. Type **329** 10 10
784 20f. Snub-nosed parasitic eel (vert) 20 10
785 80f. Manta ray (vert) 35 15
786 250f. Black-tipped grouper 90 30
787 320f. Smooth hammerhead 1·25 45

1990. Olympic Games, Barcelona (1992). Mult.
789 80f. Type **330** 10 10
790 250f. Pole vaulting 35 15
791 550f. Hurdling 65 25
792 1500f. Cycling . . . . 2·00 60
793 2000f. Baseball . . . . 2·50 80
794 2500f. Tennis . . . . 3·25 1·25

331 "Queen of the Isalo" (rock)

1990. Natural Features. Multicoloured.
796 70f. Type **331** 15 10
797 150f. Lonjy Island (as T **332**) 25 15

332 Pipe

1990. Sakalava Craft. Multicoloured.
798 70f. Type **332** 15 10
799 150f. Combs (as T **331**) . . . 25 15

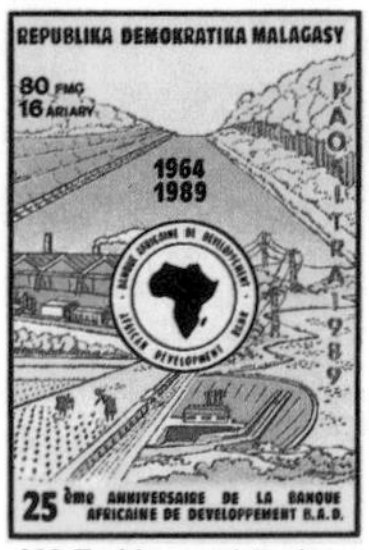

333 Emblem and Projects

1990. 25th Anniv of African Development Bank.
800 **333** 80f. multicoloured 15 10

334 "Voyager II" and Neptune

1990. 20th Anniv of First Manned Landing on Moon. Multicoloured.
801 80f. Type **334** 15 10
802 250f. Hughes Hercules flying boat, Boeing 747 airliner and flying boat "of the future" 40 15
803 550f. "Noah" satellite tracking elephants 70 25
804 1500f. Venus and "Magellan" space probe . . . . 1·25 55
805 2000f. Halley's Comet and Concorde . . . . 2·25 90
806 2500f. "Apollo 11" landing capsule and crew . . . . . 3·25 1·00

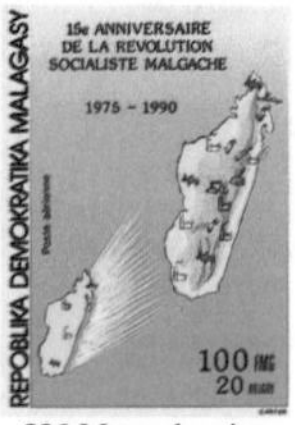

335 Liner on Globe **336** Maps showing Development between 1975 and 1990

1990. 30th Anniv of International Maritime Organization.
808 **335** 250f. ultramarine, bl & blk 55 15

1990. Air. 15th Anniv of Malagasy Socialist Revolution.
809 **336** 100f. multicoloured . . . 15 10
810 – 350f. black and grey . . . 45 25
DESIGN: 350f. Presidential Palaces, 1975 and 1990.

337 Oral Vaccination **338** Four-man Bobsleigh

1990. Anti-Polio Campaign.
811 **337** 150f. multicoloured . . . 30 15

1990. Winter Olympic Games, Albertville (1992) (1st issue). Multicoloured.
812 350f. Type **338** 40 20
813 1000f. Speed skating . . . . . 1·25 40
814 1500f. Cross-country skiing 2·00 65
815 2500f. Super G . . . . 3·00 1·10
See also Nos. 862/8.

339 Society Emblem **340** Mascot

1990. Air. 25th Anniv of Malagasy Bible Society.
817 **339** 25f. multicoloured 10 10
818 – 100f. blue, black and green 15 10
DESIGN—VERT: 100f. Society emblem.

1990. 3rd Indian Ocean Island Games, Malagasy (1st issue).
819 **340** 100f.+20f. on 80f.+20f. multicoloured 15 15
820 350f.+20f. on 250f.+20f. multicoloured 75 40
The games were originally to be held in 1989 and the stamps were printed for release then. The issued stamps are handstamped with the correct date and new value.
See also Nos. 822/3.

341 Symbols of Agriculture and Industry **342** Torch

1990. 30th Anniv of Independence.
821 **341** 100f. multicoloured . . . 15 10

1990. 3rd Indian Ocean Island Games, Malagasy (2nd issue).
822 **342** 100f. multicoloured . . . 15 10
823 350f. multicoloured . . . 45 20

343 Envelopes forming Map and Mail Transportation

1990. Air. World Post Day.
824 **343** 350f. multicoloured . . . 2·00 55

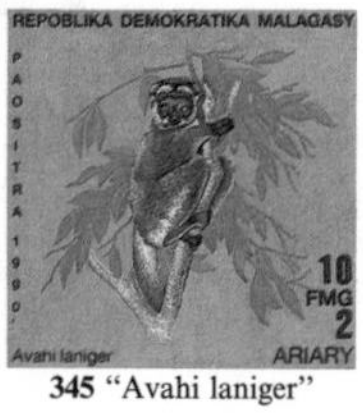

344 Ho Chi Minh **345** "Avahi laniger"

1990. Birth Centenary of Ho Chi Minh (President of North Vietnam, 1945–69).
825 **344** 350f. multicoloured . . . 40 20

1990. Lemurs. Multicoloured.
826 10f. Type **345** 10 10
827 20f. "Lemur fulvus albifrons" 10 10
828 20f. "Lemur fulvus sanfordi" 10 10
829 100f. "Lemur fulvus collaris" 25 15
830 100f. "Lepulemur ruficaudatus" 25 15

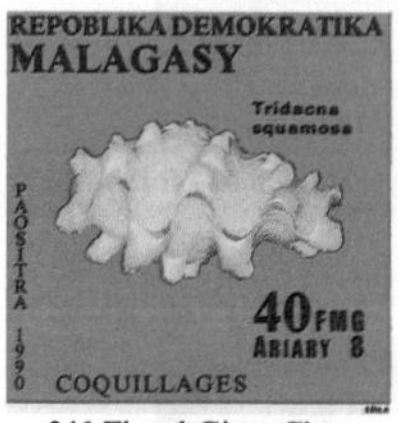

346 Fluted Giant Clam **347** Letters in Book

1990. Shells. Multicoloured.
832 40f. Type **346** 25 15
833 50f. Dimidiate and subulate augers 35 15

1990. International Literacy Year. Multicoloured.
834 20f. Type **347** 10 10
835 100f. Open book and hand holding pen (horiz) 20 15

348 Cep

349 De Gaulle, Leclerc and Parod under Arc de Triomphe, 1944

1991. Fungi. Multicoloured.

836	25f. Type **348**	10	10
837	100f. Butter mushroom	35	10
838	350f. Fly agaric	55	20
839	450f. Scarlet-stemmed boletus	75	25
840	680f. Flaky-stemmed witches' mushroom	1·10	40
841	800f. Brown birch bolete	1·25	45
842	900f. Orange birch bolete	1·40	55

1991. Multicoloured.

844	100f. Type **349**	10	10
845	350f. "Galileo" space probe near Jupiter	55	10
846	800f. Crew of "Apollo 11" on Moon	1·10	25
847	900f. De Gaulle and Free French emblem, 1942	1·40	30
848	1250f. Concorde aircraft and German ICE high speed train	3·25	80
849	2500f. Gen. Charles de Gaulle (French statesman)	3·25	95

350 Industrial and Agricultural Symbols and Arms

351 Baobab Tree

1991. 15th Anniv (1990) of Republic.

851	**350** 100f. multicoloured	10	10

1991. Trees. Multicoloured.

852	140f. Type **351**	55	10
853	500f. "Dideria madagascariensis"	1·10	45

352 Whippet

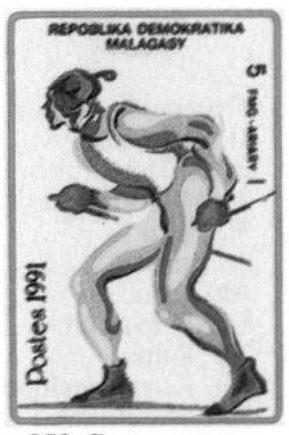

353 Cross-country Skiing

1991. Dogs. Multicoloured.

854	30f. Type **352**	35	10
855	50f. Japanese spaniel	45	10
856	140f. Toy terrier	90	10
857	350f. Chow-chow	65	10
858	500f. Chihuahua	90	15
859	800f. Afghan hound	1·10	25
860	1140f. Papillon	1·75	65

1991. Winter Olympic Games, Albertville (2nd issue). Multicoloured.

862	5f. Type **353**	10	10
863	15f. Biathlon	10	10
864	60f. Ice hockey	35	10
865	140f. Skiing	45	10
866	640f. Ice skating	45	30
867	1000f. Ski jumping	1·90	50
868	1140f. Speed skating	2·75	60

354 "Helictopleurus splendidicollis"

1992. Scouts, Insects and Fungi. Multicoloured.

870	140f. Type **354**	10	10
871	500f. "Russula radicans" (mushroom)	90	25
872	640f. "Cocles contemplator" (insect)	1·10	30
873	1025f. "Russula singeri" (mushroom)	1·60	50
874	1140f. "Euchroea oberthurii" (beetle)	1·75	60
875	3500f. "Lactariopsis pandani" (mushroom)	5·50	2·00

355 Former and Present Buildings

1992. 90th Anniv (1991) of Paul Minault College.

877	**355** 140f. multicoloured	45	10

356 Repairing Space Telescope

1992. Space. Multicoloured.

878	140f. Type **356**	10	10
879	500f. "Soho" sun probe	65	25
880	640f. "Topex-Poseidon" oceanic survey satellite	90	30
881	1025f. "Hipparcos" planetary survey satellite	1·25	50
882	1140f. "Voyager 2" Neptune probe	1·40	60
883	5000f. "ETS-VI" Japanese test communications satellite	6·75	1·25

357 Ryuichi Sakamoto

1992. Entertainers. Multicoloured.

885	100f. Type **357**	10	10
886	350f. John Lennon	55	15
887	800f. Bruce Lee	1·40	40
888	900f. Sammy Davis jun	1·60	45
889	1250f. John Wayne	1·60	60
890	2500f. James Dean	3·25	1·25

358 Lychees

1992. Fruits. Multicoloured.

892	10f. Type **358**	10	10
893	50f. Oranges	10	10
894	60f. Apples	10	10
895	140f. Peaches	35	10
896	555f. Bananas (vert)	1·10	30
897	800f. Avocados (vert)	1·40	40
898	1400f. Mangoes (vert)	2·40	75

359 9th-century Galley

360 Couple in Heart

1992. Sailing Ships. Multicoloured.

900	15f. Type **359**	10	10
901	65f. Full-rigged sailing ship, 1878	10	10
902	140f. "Golden Hind" (Drake's flagship)	45	10
903	500f. 18th-century dhow	1·00	25
904	640f. "Ostrust" (galleon), 1721 (vert)	1·10	30
905	800f. Dutch caravel, 1599 (vert)	1·40	40
906	1025f. "Santa Maria" (Columbus's flagship), 1492	1·75	50

1992. Anti-AIDS Campaign.

908	**360** 140f. black and mauve	35	10

361 Tending Trees

1992. Reforestation.

909	**361** 140f. dp green, black & grn	10	10

POSTAGE DUE STAMPS

D **13** Independence Obelisk

1962.

D45	D **13** 1f. green	10	10
D46	2f. brown	10	10
D47	3f. violet	10	10
D48	4f. slate	10	10
D49	5f. red	10	10
D50	10f. green	15	15
D51	20f. purple	20	20
D52	40f. blue	50	45
D53	50f. red	75	70
D54	100f. black	1·40	1·25

APPENDIX

The following stamps have either been issued in excess of postal needs or have not been available to the public in reasonable quantities at face value.

1987.

Winter Olympic Games, Calgary (1988). 1500f. (on gold foil).

1989.

Scout and Butterfly. 5000f. (on gold foil).

"Philexfrance 89" Int Stamp Exhibition, Paris. 5000f. (on gold foil).

World Cup Football Championship, Italy. 5000f. (on gold foil).

1990.

Winter Olympic Games, Albertville (1992). 5000f. (on gold foil).

1991.

Birth Centenary of De Gaulle. 5000f. (on gold foil).

1992.

Olympic Games, Barcelona. 500f. (on gold foil).

1993.

Bicentenary of French Republic. 1989 "Philexfrance 89" issue optd. 5000f.

1994.

Elvis Presley (entertainer). 10000f. (on gold foil).

World Cup Football Championship, U.S.A. 10000f. (on gold foil).

Winter Olympic Games, Lillehammer, Norway. 10000f. (on gold foil).

Olympic Games, Atlanta, U.S.A. 5000f. (on gold foil).

For further issues see under **MADAGASCAR**.

MALAWI Pt. 1

Formerly Nyasaland, became an independent Republic within the Commonwealth on 6 July 1966.

1964. 12 pence = 1 shilling;
20 shillings = 1 pound.
1970. 100 tambalas = 1 kwacha.

44 Dr. H. Banda (Prime Minister) and Independence Monument

1964. Independence.

211	**44** 3d. olive and sepia	10	10
212	– 6d. multicoloured	10	10
213	– 1s.3d. multicoloured	35	10
214	– 2s.6d. multicoloured	45	1·25

DESIGNS—each with Dr. Hastings Banda: 6d. Rising sun; 1s.3d. National flag; 2s.6d. Coat of arms.

48 Tung Tree

1964. As Nos. 199/210 of Nyasaland but inscr "MALAWI" as in T **48**. The 9d., 1s.6d. and £2 are new values and designs.

252	$\frac{1}{2}$d. violet	10	10
216	1d. black and green	10	10
217	2d. brown	10	10
218	3d. brown, green and bistre	15	10
219	4d. blue and yellow	85	15
220	6d. purple, green and blue	75	10
221	9d. brown, green and yellow	30	15
258	1s. brown, blue and yellow	25	10
223	1s.3d. green and brown	50	60
259	1s.6d. brown and green	30	10
224	2s.6d. brown and blue	1·10	1·00
225	5s. multicoloured (I)	65	3·00
225a	5s. multicoloured (II)	7·50	90
226	10s. green, salmon and black	1·50	2·00
227	£1 brown and yellow	7·00	5·50
262	£2 multicoloured	25·00	24·00

DESIGNS (New): 1s.6d. Burley tobacco; £2 "Cyrestis camillus" (butterfly).

Two types of 5s. I, inscr "LAKE NYASA". II, inscr "LAKE MALAWI".

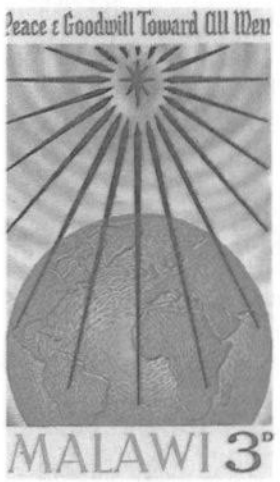

49 Christmas Star and Globe

1964. Christmas.

228	**49** 3d. green and gold	10	10
229	6d. mauve and gold	10	10
230	1s.3d. violet and gold	10	10
231	2s.6d. blue and gold	20	50
MS231a	83 × 126 mm. Nos. 228/31. Imperf	1·00	1·75

50 Coins

1964. Malawi's First Coinage. Coins in black and silver.

232	**50** 3d. green	10	10
233	9d. mauve	20	10
234	1s.6d. purple	25	10
235	3s. blue	35	85
MS235a	126 × 104 mm. Nos. 232/5. Imperf	1·40	1·10

1965. Nos. 223/4 surch.

236	1s.6d. on 1s.3d. green & brown	10	10
237	3s. on 2s.6d. brown and blue	20	20

52 Chilembwe leading Rebels

1965. 50th Anniv of 1915 Rising.

238	**52** 3d. violet and green	10	10
239	9d. olive and orange	10	10
240	1s.6d. brown and blue	15	10
241	3s. turquoise and blue	20	25
MS241a	127 × 83 mm. Nos. 238/41	5·00	6·00

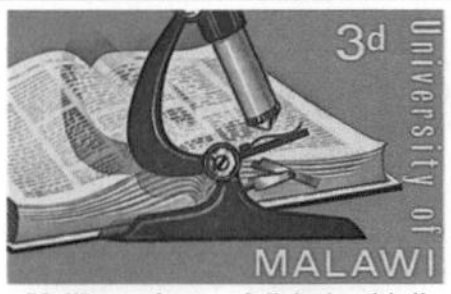

53 "Learning and Scholarship"

1965. Opening of Malawi University.

242	53	3d. black and green . . .	10	10
243		9d. black and mauve . . .	10	10
244		1s.6d. black and violet . .	10	10
245		3s. black and blue	15	40
MS246		127 × 84 mm. Nos. 242/5	2·50	2·50

54 "Papilio ophidicephalus"

1966. Malawi Butterflies. Multicoloured.

247		4d. Type **54**	80	10
248		9d. "Papilio desmondi" (magdae)	1·25	10
249		1s.6d. "Epamera handmani"	1·75	30
250		3s. "Amauris crawshayi" . .	2·75	6·00
MS251		130 × 100 mm. Nos. 247/50	17·00	11·00

58 British Central Africa 6d. Stamp of 1891

59 President Banda

1966. 75th Anniv of Postal Services.

263	58	4d. blue and green	10	10
264		9d. blue and red	15	10
265		1s.6d. blue and lilac . . .	20	10
266		3s. grey and blue	30	70
MS267		83 × 127 mm. Nos. 263/6	5·00	3·25

1966. Republic Day.

268	59	4d. brown, silver and green	10	10
269		9d. brown, silver and mauve	10	10
270		1s.6d. brown, silver & violet	15	10
271		3s. brown, silver and blue	25	15
MS272		83 × 127 mm. Nos. 268/71	2·00	3·00

60 Bethlehem

1966. Christmas.

273	60	4d. green and gold	10	10
274		9d. purple and gold . . .	10	10
275		1s.6d. red and gold	15	10
276		3s. blue and gold	40	80

61 "Ilala I"

1967. Lake Malawi Steamers.

277	61	4d. black, yellow and green	40	10
278	–	9d. black, yellow and mauve	45	10
279	–	1s.6d. black, red and violet	65	20
280	–	3s. black, red and blue . .	1·25	1·75

DESIGNS: 9d. "Dove"; 1s.9d. "Chauncy Maples I" (wrongly inscr "Chauncey"); 3s. "Gwendolen".

62 Golden Mbuna (female)

1967. Lake Malawi Cichlids. Multicoloured.

281		4d. Type **62**	40	10
282		9d. Scraped-mouthed mbuna	55	10
283		1s.6d. Zebra mbuna	70	20
284		3s. Orange mbuna	1·75	1·75

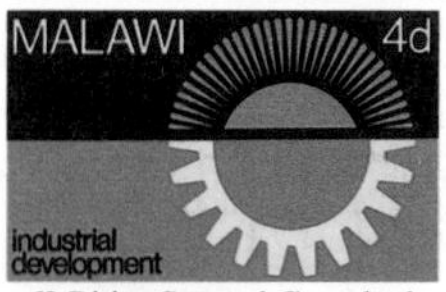

63 Rising Sun and Gearwheel

1967. Industrial Development.

285	63	4d. black and green . . .	10	10
286		9d. black and red	10	10
287		1s.6d. black and violet . .	10	10
288		3s. black and blue	15	30
MS289		134 × 108 mm. Nos. 285/8	75	1·40

64 Mary and Joseph beside Crib

1967. Christmas.

290	64	4d. blue and green	10	10
291		9d. blue and red	10	10
292		1s.6d. blue and yellow . .	10	10
293		3s. deep blue and blue . .	15	30
MS294		114 × 100 mm. Nos. 290/3	1·00	3·00

65 "Calotropis procera"

1968. Wild Flowers. Multicoloured.

295		4d. Type **65**	15	10
296		9d. "Borreria dibrachiata" . .	15	10
297		1s.6d. "Hibiscus rhodanthus"	15	10
298		3s. "Bidens pinnatipartita"	20	95
MS299		135 × 91 mm. Nos. 295/8	1·25	3·00

66 Bagnall Steam Locomotive No. 1 "Thistle"

1968. Malawi Locomotives.

300	66	4d. green, blue and red . .	25	10
301	–	9d. red, blue and green . .	30	15
302	–	1s.6d. multicoloured . . .	40	30
303	–	3s. multicoloured	70	3·00
MS304		120 × 88 mm. Nos. 300/3	2·00	6·00

DESIGNS: 9d. Class G steam locomotive No. 49; 1s.6d. Class "Zambesi" diesel locomotive No. 202; 3s. Diesel railcar No. DR1.

67 "The Nativity" (Piero della Francesca)

1968. Christmas. Multicoloured.

305		4d. Type **67**	10	10
306		9d. "The Adoration of the Shepherds" (Murillo) . . .	10	10
307		1s.6d. "The Adoration of the Shepherds" (Reni)	10	10
308		3s. "Nativity, with God the Father and Holy Ghost" (Pittoni)	15	15
MS309		115 × 101 mm. Nos. 305/8	35	1·60

69 Nyassa Lovebird

70 Carmine Bee Eater

1968. Birds (1st series). Multicoloured.

310		1d. Scarlet-chested sunbird (horiz)	15	10
311		2d. Violet starling (horiz) . .	20	10
312		3d. White-browed robin chat (horiz)	30	10
313		4d. Red-billed fire finch (horiz)	50	40
314		6d. Type **69**	1·25	15
315		9d. Yellow-rumped bishop . .	1·25	60
316		1s. Type **70**	1·00	15
317		1s.6d. Grey-headed bush shrike	5·00	8·00
318		2s. Paradise whydah	5·00	8·00
319		3s. African paradise flycatcher (vert)	6·00	4·25
320		5s. Bateleur (vert)	7·00	4·25
321		10s. Saddle-bill stork (vert)	5·50	7·50
322		£1 Purple heron (vert) . . .	10·00	18·00
323		£2 Green turaco ("Livingstone's Loerie") . .	42·00	48·00

SIZES: 1d. to 9d. as Type **69**; 1s.6d. to £2 as Type **70**.

See also Nos. 473/85.

71 I.L.O. Emblem

1969. 50th Anniv of Int Labour Organization.

324	71	4d. gold and green	10	10
325		9d. gold and brown . . .	10	10
326		1s.6d. gold and brown . .	10	10
327		3s. gold and blue	15	15
MS328		127 × 89 mm. Nos. 324/7	1·00	4·75

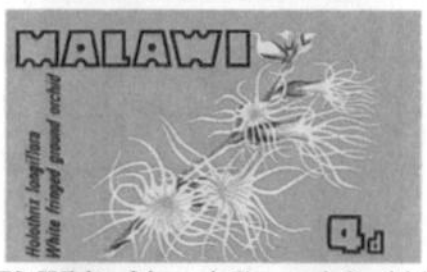

72 White-fringed Ground Orchid

1969. Orchids of Malawi. Multicoloured.

329		4d. Type **72**	15	10
330		9d. Red ground orchid . . .	20	10
331		1s.6d. Leopard tree orchid . .	30	20
332		3s. Blue ground orchid . . .	60	2·00
MS333		118 × 86 mm. Nos. 329/32	1·10	3·75

73 African Development Bank Emblem

74 Dove over Bethlehem

1969. 5th Anniv of African Development Bank.

334	73	4d. yellow, brown and ochre	10	10
335		9d. yellow, ochre and green	10	10
336		1s.6d. yellow, ochre & brn	10	10
337		3s. yellow, ochre and blue	15	15
MS338		102 × 137 mm. Nos. 334/7	50	90

1969. Christmas.

339	74	2d. black and yellow . . .	10	10
340		4d. black and turquoise . .	10	10
341		9d. black and red	10	10
342		1s.6d. black and violet . .	10	10
343		3s. black and blue	15	15
MS344		130 × 71 mm. Nos. 339/43	1·00	1·75

75 "Zonocerus elegans" (grasshopper)

77 Runner

1970. Insects of Malawi. Multicoloured.

345		4d. Type **75**	15	10
346		9d. "Mylabris dicincta" (beetle)	15	10
347		1s.6d. "Henosepilachna elaterii" (ladybird)	20	10
348		3s. "Sphodromantis speculabunda" (mantid) . .	35	65
MS349		86 × 137 mm. Nos. 345/8	1·25	2·25

1970. Rand Easter Show. No. 317 optd **Rand Easter Show 1970**.

350		1s.6d. multicoloured	50	2·25

1970. 9th Commonwealth Games, Edinburgh.

351	77	4d. blue and green	10	10
352		9d. blue and red	10	10
353		1s.6d. blue and yellow . .	10	10
354		3s. deep blue and blue . .	15	15
MS355		146 × 96 mm. Nos. 351/4	55	90

1970. Decimal Currency. Nos. 316 and 318 surch.

356		10t. on 1s. multicoloured . .	2·25	25
357		20t. on 2s. multicoloured . .	2·75	3·50

79 "Aegocera trimeni"

1970. Moths. Multicoloured.

358		4d. Type **79**	20	10
359		9d. "Faidherbia bauhiniae"	30	10
360		1s.6d. "Parasa karschi" . . .	50	20
361		3s. "Teracotona euprepia" . .	1·25	3·50
MS362		112 × 92 mm. Nos. 358/61	4·25	6·00

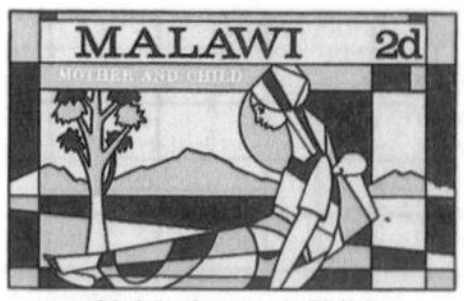

80 Mother and Child

1970. Christmas.

363	80	2d. black and yellow . . .	10	10
364		4d. black and green . . .	10	10
365		9d. black and red	10	10
366		1s.6d. black and purple . .	10	10
367		3s. black and blue	15	15
MS368		166 × 100 mm. Nos. 363/7	1·00	2·25

1971. No. 319 surch **30t Special United Kingdom Delivery Service.**

369		30t. on 3s. multicoloured . .	50	2·00

No. 369 was issued for use on letters carried by an emergency airmail service from Malawi to Great Britain during the British postal strike. The fee of 30t. was to cover the charge for delivery by a private service, and ordinary stamps to pay the normal airmail postage had to be affixed as well. These stamps were in use from 8 February to 8 March.

82 Decimal Coinage and Cockerel

83 Greater Kudu

1971. Decimal Coinage.

370	82	3t. multicoloured	15	10
371		8t. multicoloured	20	10
372		15t. multicoloured	25	20
373		30t. multicoloured	35	1·50
MS374		140 × 101 mm. Nos. 370/3	1·00	1·75

1971. Decimal Currency. Antelopes. Mult.

375		1t. Type **83**	10	10
376		2t. Nyala	15	10
377		3t. Mountain reedbuck . . .	20	50
378		5t. Puku	40	1·25
379		8t. Impala	45	1·00
380		10t. Eland	60	10
381		15t. Klipspringer	1·00	20
382		20t. Suni	1·50	90
383		30t. Roan antelope	9·50	1·00
384		50t. Waterbuck	1·00	65
385		1k. Bushbuck	1·50	85
386		2k. Red forest duiker . . .	2·75	1·50
387		4k. Common duiker	20·00	19·00

Nos. 380/7 are larger, size 25 × 42 mm.

No. 387 is incorrectly inscr "Gray Duiker".

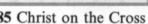

85 Christ on the Cross

87 "Holarrhena febrifuga"

1971. Easter. Multicoloured.

388	85	3t. black and green	10	25
389	–	3t. black and green	10	25
390	85	8t. black and red	10	25
391	–	8t. black and red	10	25
392	85	15t. black and violet . . .	15	30
393	–	15t. black and violet . . .	15	30
394	85	30t. black and blue	20	45
395	–	30t. black and blue	20	45
MS396		Two sheets, each 95 × 145 mm. (a) Nos. 388, 390, 392 and 394. (b) Nos. 389, 391, 393 and 395 Set of 2 sheets . .	1·50	3·50

DESIGN: Nos. 389, 391, 393, 395, The Resurrection. Both designs from "The Small Passion" (Durer).

1971. Flowering Shrubs and Trees. Mult.
397 3t. Type **87** 10 10
398 8t. "Brachystegia spiciformis" 10 10
399 15t. "Securidaca longepedunculata" 15 10
400 30t. "Pterocarpus rotundifolius" . . . . . . 30 1·00
MS401 102 × 135 mm. Nos. 397/400 1·00 2·00

88 Drum Major

89 "Madonna and Child" (William Dyce)

1971. 50th Anniv of Malawi Police Force.
402 **88** 30t. multicoloured . . . . 65 1·25

1971. Christmas. Multicoloured.
403 3t. Type **89** 10 10
404 8t. "The Holy Family" (M. Schongauer) 15 10
405 15t. "The Holy Family with St. John" (Raphael) . . . 20 20
406 30t. "The Holy Family" (Bronzino) . . . . 50 1·40
MS407 101 × 139 mm. Nos. 403/6 1·10 2·50

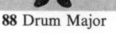

90 Vickers Viscount 700

1972. Air. Malawi Aircraft. Multicoloured.
408 3t. Type **90** 30 10
409 8t. Hawker Siddeley H.S.748 50 10
410 15t. Britten Norman Islander 75 30
411 30t. B.A.C. One Eleven . . . 1·25 2·25
MS412 143 × 94 mm. Nos. 408/11 8·00 5·50

91 Figures (Chencherere Hill)

1972. Rock Paintings.
413 **91** 3t. green and black 25 10
414 – 8t. red, grey and black . . 30 10
415 – 15t. multicoloured 35 30
416 – 30t. multicoloured . . . . 45 1·00
MS417 121 × 97 mm. Nos. 413/16 2·75 2·75
DESIGNS: 8t. Lizard and cat (Chencherere Hill); 15t. Schematics (Diwa Hill); 30t. Sun through rain (Mikolongwe Hill).

92 Boxing

1972. Olympic Games, Munich.
418 **92** 3t. multicoloured 10 10
419 8t. multicoloured 15 10
420 15t. multicoloured 20 10
421 30t. multicoloured 35 45
MS422 110 × 92 mm. Nos. 418/21 1·25 1·75

93 Arms of Malawi

1972. Commonwealth Parliamentary Conf.
423 **93** 15t. multicoloured 30 35

94 "Adoration of the Kings" (Orcagna)

1972. Christmas. Multicoloured.
424 3t. Type **94** 10 10
425 8t. "Madonna and Child Enthroned" (Florentine School) 10 10
426 15t. "Virgin and Child" (Crivelli) 20 10
427 30t. "Virgin and Child with St. Anne" (Flemish School) 45 70
MS428 95 × 121 mm. Nos. 424/7 1·10 2·00

95 "Charaxes bohemani"

1973. Butterflies. Multicoloured.
429 3t. Type **95** 50 10
430 8t. "Uranothauma crawshayi" 75 10
431 15t. "Charaxes acuminatus" 1·00 30
432 30t. "Amauris ansorgei" (inscr in error "EUPHAEDRA ZADDACHI") . . . . . 4·00 8·50
433 30t. "Amauris ansorgei" (inscr corrected) . . . . . 3·75 8·50
MS434 145 × 95 mm. Nos. 429/32 7·00 11·50

96 Livingstone and Map

1973. Death Cent of David Livingstone (1st issue).
435 **96** 3t. multicoloured 10 10
436 8t. multicoloured 15 10
437 15t. multicoloured 20 10
438 30t. multicoloured 35 60
MS439 144 × 95 mm. Nos. 435/8 1·00 1·50
See also No. 450/**MS**451.

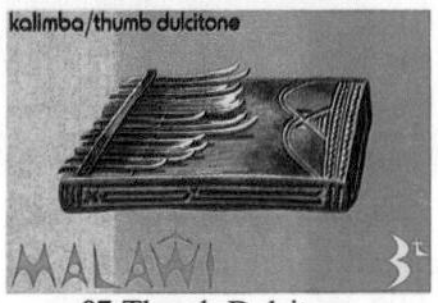

97 Thumb Dulcitone

1973. Musical Instruments. Multicoloured.
440 3t. Type **97** 10 10
441 8t. Hand zither (vert) . . . 15 10
442 15t. Hand drum (vert) . . . 25 10
443 30t. One-stringed fiddle . . . 45 60
MS444 120 × 103 mm. Nos. 440/3 2·75 2·00

98 The Magi

1973. Christmas.
445 **98** 3t. blue, lilac & ultramarine 10 10
446 8t. red, lilac and brown . . 10 10
447 15t. mauve, blue & dp mve 15 10
448 30t. yellow, lilac and brown 30 70
MS449 165 × 114 mm. Nos. 445/8 75 1·40

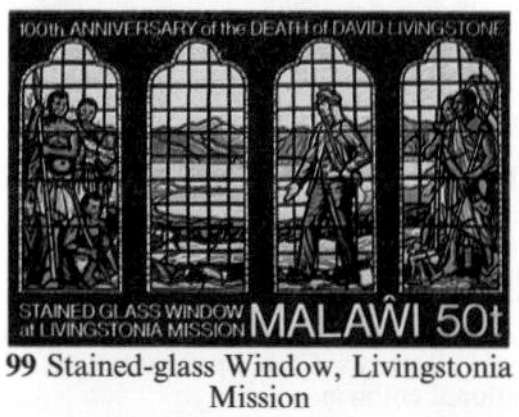

99 Stained-glass Window, Livingstonia Mission

1973. Death Cent of David Livingstone (2nd issue).
450 **99** 50t. multicoloured . . . . 45 1·00
MS451 71 × 77 mm. No. 450 . . 80 1·60

100 Large-mouthed Black Bass

1974. 35th Anniv of Malawi Angling Society. Multicoloured.
452 3t. Type **100** 20 10
453 8t. Rainbow trout 25 10
454 15t. Silver alestes ("Lake salmon") 40 20
455 30t. Tigerfish . . . . 70 1·75
MS456 169 × 93 mm. Nos. 452/5 2·50 2·50

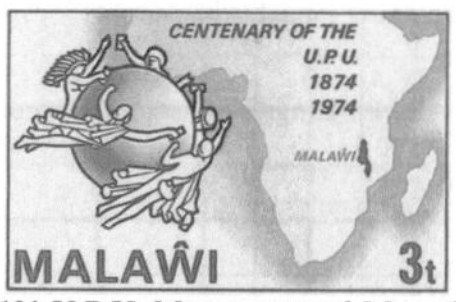

101 U.P.U. Monument and Map of Africa

1974. Centenary of U.P.U.
457 **101** 3t. green and brown . . . 10 10
458 8t. red and brown 10 10
459 15t. violet and brown . . 15 10
460 30t. blue and brown . . . 30 1·10
MS461 115 × 146 mm. Nos. 457/60 65 1·75

102 Capital Hill, Lilongwe

1974. 10th Anniv of Independence.
462 **102** 3t. multicoloured 10 10
463 8t. multicoloured 10 10
464 15t. multicoloured 10 10
465 30t. multicoloured 25 35
MS466 120 × 86 mm. Nos. 462/5 45 1·00

103 "Madonna of the Meadow" (Bellini)

1974. Christmas. Multicoloured.
467 3t. Type **103** 10 10
468 8t. "The Holy Family with Sts. John and Elizabeth" (Jordaens) 10 10
469 15t. "The Nativity" (Pieter de Grebber) 15 10
470 30t. "Adoration of the Shepherds" (Lorenzo di Credi) 30 50
MS471 163 × 107 mm. Nos. 467/70 60 1·25

104 Arms of Malawi

105 African Snipe

106 Spur-winged Goose ("Spurwing Goose")

1975.
472 **104** 1t. blue 20 40
472a 5t. red . . . . 65 2·00

1975. Birds (2nd series). Multicoloured. (a) As T **105**.
473 1t. Type **105** . . . . 1·50 2·00
474 2t. Double-banded sandgrouse (horiz) . . . . 1·50 2·00
475 3t. Indian blue quail ("Blue Quail") (horiz) . . . . . . 1·50 1·50
476 5t. Red-necked spurfowl ("Red-necked Francolin") 3·50 1·25
477 8t. Harlequin quail (horiz) . . 4·75 1·00

(b) As T **106**.
502 10t. Type **106** . . . . 2·00 1·50
503 15t. Denham's bustard ("Stanley Bustard") . . . 2·00 2·00
480 20t. Comb duck ("Knob-billed Duck") . . . . . . 1·00 2·25
481 30t. Helmeted guineafowl ("Crowned Guinea Fowl") 1·25 70
482 50t. African pygmy goose ("Pigmy Goose") (horiz) 2·00 1·60
483 1k. Garganey . . . . 3·00 8·50
504 2k. White-faced whistling duck ("White Face Tree Duck") . . . . 5·00 11·00
485 4k. African green pigeon ("Green Pigeon") . . . . 13·00 16·00

107 M.V. "Mpasa"

1975. Ships of Lake Malawi. Multicoloured.
486 3t. Type **107** 30 10
487 8t. M.V. "Ilala II" 40 10
488 15t. M.V. "Chauncy Maples II" 75 30
489 30t. M.V. "Nkwazi" . . . . 1·00 3·00
MS490 105 × 142 mm. Nos. 486/9 2·25 4·25

108 "Habenaria splendens"

109 Thick-tailed Bushbaby

1975. Malawi Orchids. Multicoloured.
491 3t. Type **108** 40 10
492 10t. "Eulophia cucullata" . . 50 10
493 20t. "Disa welwitschii" . . . 80 25
494 40t. "Angraecum conchiferum" . . . . . . 1·10 1·50
MS495 127 × 111 mm. Nos. 491/4 7·00 8·00

1976. Malawi Animals. Multicoloured.
496 3t. Type **109** 10 10
497 10t. Leopard 35 10
498 20t. Roan antelope 55 35
499 40t. Common zebra . . . . 1·00 2·75
MS500 88 × 130 mm. Nos. 496/9 2·50 3·50

1975. 10th Africa, Caribbean and Pacific Ministerial Conference. No. 482 optd **10th ACP Ministerial Conference 1975.**
514 50t. African pygmy goose . . 1·00 2·25

111 "A Castle with the Adoration of the Magi"

1975. Christmas. Religious Medallions. Mult.
515 3t. Type **111** 10 10
516 10t. "The Nativity" 15 10
517 20t. "Adoration of the Magi" (different) 20 10
518 40t. "Angel appearing to Shepherds" . . . . 50 2·25
MS519 98 × 168 mm. Nos. 515/18 1·50 3·25

112 Alexander Graham Bell

113 President Banda

1976. Centenary of Telephone.
520 **112** 3t. green and black . . . 10 10
521 10t. purple and black . . 10 10

522 20t. violet and black . . . 20 10
523 40t. blue and black . . . 50 1·40
MS524 137 × 114 mm. Nos. 520/3 1·10 1·75

1976. 10th Anniv of Republic. Multicoloured.
525 **113** 3t. green 10 10
526 10t. purple 10 10
527 20t. blue 20 10
528 40t. blue . . . . 50 1·40
MS529 102 × 112 mm. Nos. 524/8 1·00 2·50

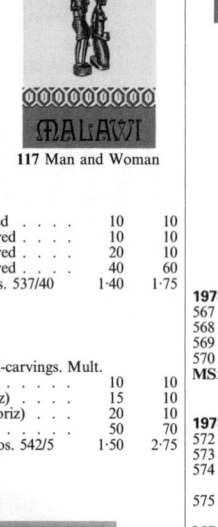

114 Bagnall Diesel Shunter No. 100

1976. Malawi Locomotives. Multicoloured.
530 3t. Type **114** 40 15
531 10t. Class "Shire" diesel locomotive No. 503 . . . 70 15
532 20t. Nippon Sharyo diesel-hydraulic locomotive No. 301 . . . . 1·40 45
533 40t. Hunslet diesel-hydraulic locomotive No. 110 . . . 2·10 6·50
MS534 130 × 118 mm. Nos. 530/3 4·25 7·00

1976. Centenary of Blantyre Mission. Nos. 479 and 481 optd **Blantyre Mission Centenary 1876–1976.**
535 15t. Denham's bustard . . . 1·50 1·50
536 30t. Helmeted guineafowl . . 1·75 3·50

116 Child on Bed of Straw

117 Man and Woman

1976. Christmas.
537 **116** 3t. multicoloured 10 10
538 10t. multicoloured 10 10
539 20t. multicoloured 20 10
540 40t. multicoloured 40 60
MS541 135 × 95 mm. Nos. 537/40 1·40 1·75

1977. Handicrafts. Wood-carvings. Mult.
542 4t. Type **117** 10 10
543 10t. Elephant (horiz) 15 10
544 20t. Rhinoceros (horiz) . . . 20 10
545 40t. Antelope 50 70
MS546 153 × 112 mm. Nos. 542/5 1·50 2·75

118 Chileka Airport

1977. Transport. Multicoloured.
547 4t. Type **118** 40 10
548 10t. Blantyre–Lilongwe Road 40 10
549 20t. M.V. "Ilala II" . . . . 1·00 35
550 40t. Blantyre–Nacala rail line 1·50 4·75
MS551 127 × 83 mm. Nos. 547/50 3·00 4·50

119 Blue-grey Mbuna

1977. Fish of Lake Malawi. Multicoloured.
552B 4t. Type **119** 30 10
553B 10t. Livingston mbuna . . 50 20
554A 20t. Zebra mbuna . . . . 1·40 30
555B 40t. Malawi scale-eater . . 1·50 1·25
MS556A 147 × 99 mm. Nos. 552A/5B . . . . 3·00 4·50

120 "Madonna and Child with St. Catherine and the Blessed Stefano Maconi" (Borgognone)

121 "Entry of Christ into Jerusalem" (Giotto)

1977. Christmas.
557 **120** 4t. multicoloured 10 10
558 – 10t. multicoloured 10 10
559 – 20t. multicoloured 20 10
560 – 40t. multicoloured . . . . 50 1·00
MS561 150 × 116 mm. Nos. 557/60 2·50 3·00
DESIGNS: 10t. "Madonna and Child with the Eternal Father and Angels" (Borgognone); 20t. Bottigella altarpiece (detail, Foppa); 40t. "Madonna of the Fountain" (van Eyck).

1978. Easter. Paintings by Giotto. Multicoloured.
562 4t. Type **121** 10 10
563 10t. "The Crucifixion" . . . 15 10
564 20t. "Descent from the Cross" 30 10
565 40t. "Jesus appears before Mary" 50 55
MS566 150 × 99 mm. Nos. 562/5 1·90 2·40

122 Nyala

124 "Vanilla polylepis"

123 Malamulo Seventh Day Adventist Church

1978. Wildlife. Multicoloured.
567 4t. Type **122** . . . . 2·50 10
568 10t. Lion (horiz) . . . . . 7·00 40
569 20t. Common zebra (horiz) . 10·00 1·00
570 40t. Mountain reedbuck . . . 11·00 7·50
MS571 173 × 113 mm. Nos. 567/70 30·00 11·00

1978. Christmas. Multicoloured.
572 4t. Type **123** 10 10
573 10t. Likoma Cathedral . . . 10 10
574 20t. St. Michael's and All Angels', Blantyre 20 10
575 40t. Zomba Catholic Cathedral . . . . 40 1·50
MS576 190 × 105 mm. Nos. 572/5 70 1·50

1979. Orchids. Multicoloured.
577 1t. Type **124** 50 30
578 2t. "Cirrhopetalum umbellatum" 50 30
579 5t. "Calanthe natalensis" . . 50 10
580 7t. "Ansellia gigantea" . . . 50 50
581 8t. "Tridactyle bicaudata" . . 50 30
582 10t. "Acampe pachyglossa" . . 50 10
583 15t. "Eulophia quartiniana" . 50 15
584 20t. "Cyrtorchis arcuata" . . 50 50
585 30t. "Eulophia tricristata" . . 1·25 30
586 50t. "Disa hamatopetala" . . 85 50
587 75t. "Cynorchis glandulosa" . 2·00 6·50
588 1k. "Aerangis kotschyana" . 1·60 1·75
589 1k.50 "Polystachya dendrobiiflora" . . . . . 1·75 6·00
590 2k. "Disa ornithantha" . . . 1·25 2·00
591 4k. "Cyrtorchis praetermissa" 1·50 4·50

125 Tsamba

1979. National Tree Planting Day. Mult.
592 5t. Type **125** 20 10
593 10t. Mulanje cedar 25 10
594 20t. Mlombwa 40 20
595 40t. Mbawa . . . . 70 2·50
MS596 118 × 153 mm. Nos. 592/5 1·40 3·00

126 Train crossing Viaduct

1979. Opening of Salima–Lilongwe Railway Line. Multicoloured.
597 5t. Type **126** 25 15
598 10t. Diesel railcar at station 40 15
599 20t. Diesel train rounding bend 60 30
600 40t. Diesel train passing through cutting . . . . . 85 2·00
MS601 153 × 103 mm. Nos. 597/600 4·00 4·50

127 Young Child

1979. International Year of the Child. Designs showing young children. Multicoloured; background colours given.
602 **127** 5t. green 10 10
603 – 10t. red 10 10
604 – 20t. mauve 25 10
605 – 40t. blue . . . . 45 1·40

128 1964 3d. Independence Commemorative Stamp

1979. Death Centenary of Sir Rowland Hill. Designs showing 1964 Independence Commemorative Stamps. Multicoloured.
606 **127** 5t. Type **128** 10 10
607 10t. 6d. value 10 10
608 20t. 1s.3d. value 20 10
609 40t. 2s.6d. value 35 60
MS610 163 × 108 mm. Nos. 606/9 75 1·40

129 River Landscape

1979. Christmas. Multicoloured.
611 5t. Type **129** 10 10
612 10t. Sunset 10 10
613 20t. Forest and hill 25 15
614 40t. Plain and mountains . . 50 2·50

130 Limbe Rotary Club Emblem

132 Agate Nodule

131 Mangochi District Post Office

1980. 75th Anniv of Rotary International.
615 **130** 5t. multicoloured 10 10
616 – 10t. multicoloured 10 10
617 – 20t. blue, gold and red . . 30 15
618 – 40t. gold and blue . . . . 75 2·25
MS619 105 × 144 mm. Nos. 615/18 1·10 2·25
DESIGNS: 10t. Blantyre Rotary Club pennant; 20t. Lilongwe Rotary Club pennant; 40t. Rotary International emblem.

1980. "London 1980" International Stamp Exhibition.
620 **131** 5t. black and green . . . 10 10
621 – 10t. black and red 10 10
622 – 20t. black and violet . . . 15 10
623 – 1k. black and blue . . . 65 1·10
MS624 114 × 89 mm. Nos. 620/3 1·25 2·25
DESIGNS: 10t. New Blantyre Sorting Office; 20t. Mail transfer hut, Walala; 1k. First Nyasaland Post Office, Chiromo.

1980. Gemstones. Multicoloured.
625 5t. Type **132** 60 10
626 10t. Sunstone 80 10
627 20t. Smoky quartz . . . . . 1·40 30
628 1k. Kyanite crystal . . . . . 3·50 6·00

133 Elephants

1980. Christmas. Children's Paintings. Mult.
629 5t. Type **133** 40 10
630 10t. Flowers 30 10
631 20t. Class "Shire" diesel train 75 20
632 1k. Malachite kingfisher . . . 1·60 2·00

134 Suni

1981. Wildlife. Multicoloured.
633 7t. Type **134** 15 10
634 10t. Blue duiker 20 10
635 20t. African buffalo 30 15
636 1k. Lichtenstein's hartebeest 1·25 1·60

135 "Kanjedza II" Standard "A" Earth Station

1981. International Communications. Mult.
637 7t. Type **135** 10 10
638 10t. Blantyre International Gateway Exchange 15 10
639 20t. "Kanjedza I" standard "B" earth station 25 15
640 1k. "Satellite communications" . . . . 1·50 1·90
MS641 101 × 151 mm. Nos. 637/40 1·75 3·00

136 Maize

1981. World Food Day. Agricultural Produce. Multicoloured.
642 7t. Type **136** 15 10
643 10t. Rice 20 10
644 20t. Finger-millet 30 20
645 1k. Wheat . . . . 1·00 1·40

137 "The Adoration of the Shepherds" (Murillo)

138 Impala Herd

1981. Christmas. Paintings. Multicoloured.
646 7t. Type **137** 20 10
647 10t. "The Holy Family" (Lippi) (horiz) 25 10
648 20t. "The Adoration of the Shepherds" (Louis le Nain) (horiz) 45 15
649 1k. "The Virgin and Child, St. John the Baptist and an Angel" (Paolo Morando) 1·10 1·75

1982. National Parks. Wildlife. Multicoloured.
650 7t. Type **138** 20 10
651 10t. Lions 35 10

652 20t. Greater kudu 50 20
653 1k. Greater flamingoes . . . 1·75 5·50

139 Kamuzu Academy

1982. Kamuzu Academy.
654 **139** 7t. multicoloured 15 10
655 – 20t. multicoloured 20 10
656 – 30t. multicoloured 30 45
657 – 1k. multicoloured . . . . 1·00 3·75
DESIGNS: 20t. to 1k. Various views of the Academy.

140 Attacker challenging Goalkeeper

1982. World Cup Football Championship, Spain. Multicoloured.
658 7t. Type **140** 75 25
659 20t. FIFA World Cup trophy 1·60 1·25
660 30t. Football stadium . . . . 1·90 3·25
MS661 80 × 59 mm. 1k. Football 1·75 1·60

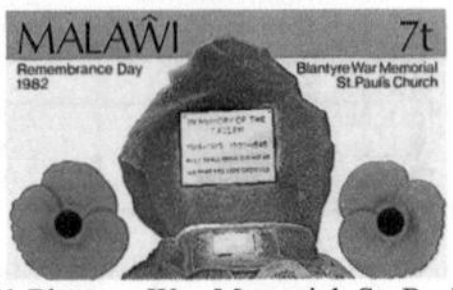

141 Blantyre War Memorial, St. Paul's Church

1982. Remembrance Day. Multicoloured.
662 7t. Type **141** 10 10
663 20t. Zomba war memorial . . 15 10
664 30t. Chichiri war memorial 20 30
665 1k. Lilongwe war memorial 65 4·25

142 Kwacha International Conference Centre

1983. Commonwealth Day. Multicoloured.
666 7t. Type **142** 10 10
667 20t. Tea-picking, Mulanje . . 20 10
668 30t. World map showing position of Malawi 25 30
669 1k. Pres. Dr. H. Kamuzu Banda . . . . 60 1·50

143 "Christ and St. Peter" 144 Pair by Lake

1983. 500th Birth Anniv of Raphael. Details from the cartoon for "The Miraculous Draught of Fishes" Tapestry. Multicoloured.
670 7t. Type **143** 35 10
671 20t. "Hauling in the Catch" 75 80
672 30t. "Fishing Village" (horiz) 90 2·50
MS673 110 × 90 mm. 1k. "Apostle" 1·60 1·60

1983. African Fish Eagle. Multicoloured.
674 30t. Type **144** . . . . 1·60 1·90
675 30t. Making gull-like call . . 1·60 1·90
676 30t. Diving on prey . . . . . 1·60 1·90
677 30t. Carrying fish . . . . . 1·60 1·90
678 30t. Feeding on catch . . . . 1·60 1·90

145 Kamuzu International Airport

1983. Bicentenary of Manned Flight. Mult.
679 7t. Type **145** 10 10
680 20t. Kamuzu International Airport (different) 25 15
681 30t. B.A.C. One Eleven . . . 40 45
682 1k. Short Empire "C" Class flying boat at Cape Maclear . . . . 1·10 2·50
MS683 100 × 121 mm. Nos. 679/82 2·00 4·00

146 "Clerodendrum myricoides" 147 Golden Mbuna

1983. Christmas. Flowers. Multicoloured.
684 7t. Type **146** 40 10
685 20t. "Gloriosa superba" . . . 90 15
686 30t. "Gladiolus laxiflorus" . . 1·00 60
687 1k. "Aframomum angustifolium" . . . . . . 2·25 7·00

1984. Fishes. Multicoloured.
688 1t. Type **147** . . . . 30 1·00
689 2t. Malawi eyebiter . . . . . 30 1·00
690 5t. Blue mbuna . . . . . . 30 1·00
691 7t. Lombardo's mbuna . . . 30 30
692 8t. Golden zebra mbuna . . 30 30
693 10t. Fairy cichlid 30 10
694 15t. Crabro mbuna 30 10
695 20t. Marbled zebra mbuna 30 10
696 30t. Sky-blue mbuna 50 20
697 40t. Venustus cichlid 60 30
698 50t. Thumbi emperor cichlid 2·25 3·25
699 75t. Purple mbuna . . . . . 2·75 5·50
700 1k. Zebra mbuna . . . . . 3·00 5·00
701 2k. Fairy cichlid (different) 4·00 7·00
702 4k. Mbenje emperor cichlid 5·00 11·00
Nos. 688 and 691/7 exist with different imprint dates at foot.

148 Smith's Red Hare

1984. Small Mammals. Multicoloured.
703 7t. Type **148** 20 10
704 20t. Gambian sun squirrel . . 35 50
705 30t. South African hedgehog 35 1·10
706 1k. Large-spotted genet . . . 50 5·50

149 Running 150 "Euphaedra neophron"

1984. Olympic Games, Los Angeles. Mult.
707 7t. Type **149** 15 10
708 20t. Boxing 35 20
709 30t. Cycling 75 70
710 1k. Long jumping . . . . . 1·00 3·75
MS711 90 × 128 mm. Nos. 707/10 2·40 5·00

1984. Butterflies.
712 **150** 7t. multicoloured 95 30
713 – 20t. yellow, brown and red . . . . 2·25 45
714 – 30t. multicoloured . . . . 2·50 1·10
715 – 1k. multicoloured . . . . 4·25 9·00
DESIGNS: 20t. "Papilio dardanus"; 30t. "Antanartia schaeneia"; 1k. "Spindasis nyassae".

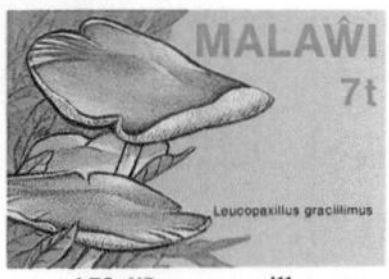

151 "Virgin and Child" (Duccio) 152 "Leucopaxillus gracillimus"

1984. Christmas. Religious Paintings. Mult.
716 7t. Type **151** 55 10
717 20t. "Madonna and Child" (Raphael) . . . . 1·40 20
718 30t. "Virgin and Child" (ascr to Lippi) . . . . 1·90 70
719 1k. "The Wilton Diptych" . . 3·50 8·00

1985. Fungi. Multicoloured.
720 7t. Type **152** . . . . 1·25 30
721 20t. "Limacella guttata" . . 2·50 45
722 30t. "Termitomyces eurrhizus" . . . . 3·00 1·25
723 1k. "Xerulina asprata" . . . 5·50 9·50

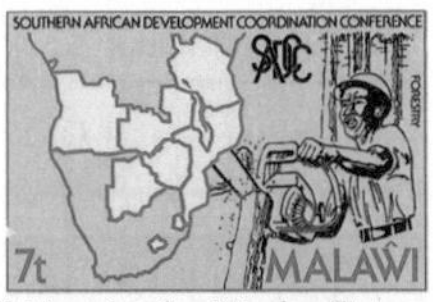

153 Map showing Member States and Lumberjack (Forestry)

1985. 5th Anniv of Southern African Development Co-ordination Conference. Designs showing map and aspects of development.
724 **153** 7t. black, green and light green 75 10
725 – 15t. black, red and pink 1·25 20
726 – 20t. black, violet and mauve . . . . 4·00 1·75
727 – 1k. black, blue and light blue . . . . 4·50 10·00
DESIGNS: 15t. Radio mast (Communications); 20t. Diesel locomotive (Transport); 1k. Trawler and net (Fishing).

154 M.V. "Ufulu"

1985. Ships of Lake Malawi (2nd series). Mult.
728 7t. Type **154** 90 10
729 15t. M.V. "Chauncy Maples II" . . . . 1·75 20
730 20t. M.V. "Mtendere" . . . 2·25 65
731 1k. M.V. "Ilala II" . . . . . 4·50 6·00
MS732 120 × 84 mm. Nos. 728/31 8·00 8·00

155 Stierling's Woodpecker 156 "The Virgin of Humility" (Jaime Serra)

1985. Birth Bicentenary of John J. Audubon (ornithologist). Multicoloured.
733 7t. Type **155** . . . . 1·25 30
734 15t. Lesser seedcracker . . . 2·25 30
735 20t. East coast akelat ("Gunning's Akalat") . . . 2·25 65
736 1k. Boehm's bee eater . . . 4·25 7·00
MS737 130 × 90 mm. Nos. 733/6 10·00 10·00

1985. Christmas. Nativity Paintings. Mult.
738 7t. Type **156** 30 10
739 15t. "The Adoration of the Magi" (Stefano da Zevio) 75 15
740 20t. "Madonna and Child" (Gerard van Honthorst) . . 85 25
741 1k. "Virgin of Zbraslav" (Master of Vissy Brod) . . 2·25 5·50

157 Halley's Comet and Path of "Giotto" Spacecraft

1986. Appearance of Halley's Comet. Mult.
742 8t. Type **157** 60 10
743 15t. Halley's Comet above Earth 65 15
744 20t. Comet and dish aerial, Malawi . . . . 1·00 30
745 1k. "Giotto" spacecraft . . . 2·00 6·00

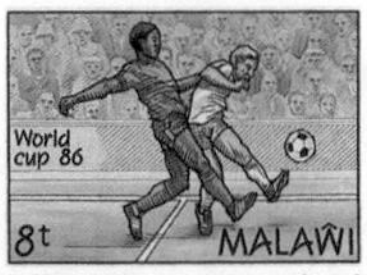

158 Two Players competing for Ball

1986. World Cup Football Championship, Mexico. Multicoloured.
746 8t. Type **158** 70 10
747 15t. Goalkeeper saving goal 95 20
748 20t. Two players competing for ball (different) . . . . 1·10 35
749 1k. Player kicking ball . . . 4·00 5·50
MS750 108 × 77 mm. Nos. 746/9 10·00 11·00

159 President Banda 160 "Virgin and Child" (Botticelli)

1986. 20th Anniv of Republic. Multicoloured.
751 8t. Type **159** . . . . 1·50 2·75
752 15t. National flag 80 15
753 20t. Malawi coat of arms . . 85 25
754 1k. Kamuzu International Airport and emblem of national airline . . . . . 3·50 6·00

1986. Christmas. Multicoloured.
755 8t. Type **160** 45 10
756 15t. "Adoration of the Shepherds" (Guido Reni) 80 15
757 20t. "Madonna of the Veil" (Carlo Dolci) . . . . . . 1·25 35
758 1k. "Adoration of the Magi" (Jean Bourdichon) . . . . 3·75 9·00

161 Wattled Crane

1987. Wattled Crane. Multicoloured.
759 8t. Type **161** . . . . 1·50 40
760 15t. Two cranes . . . . . . 2·25 50
761 20t. Cranes at nest . . . . . 2·25 80
762 75t. Crane in lake . . . . . 4·50 12·00

162 Bagnall Steam Locomotive No. 2 "Shamrock"

1987. Steam Locomotives. Multicoloured.
767 10t. Type **162** . . . . 2·00 40
768 25t. Class D steam locomotive No. 8, 1914 . . 2·75 50
769 30t. Bagnall steam locomotive No. 1 "Thistle" . . . . . 3·00 85
770 1k. Kitson steam locomotive No. 6, 1903 . . . . 6·00 12·00

163 Hippopotamus grazing 164 "Stathmostelma spectabile"

1987. Hippopotamus. Multicoloured.
771 10t. Type **163** . . . . 1·50 40
772 25t. Hippopotami in water 2·25 50
773 30t. Female and calf in water 2·25 75
774 1k. Hippopotami and cattle egret . . . . 6·00 12·00
MS775 78 × 101 mm. Nos. 771/4 11·00 12·00

1987. Christmas. Wild Flowers. Multicoloured.
776 10t. Type **164** 65 10
777 25t. "Pentanisia schweinfurthii" . . . . . 1·50 25
778 30t. "Chironia krebsii" . . . 1·75 55
779 1k. "Ochna macrocalyx" . . 3·00 9·00

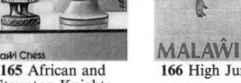

165 African and Staunton Knights

166 High Jumping

1988. Chess. Local and Staunton chess pieces. Multicoloured.

780	15t. Type **165**	1·25	30
781	35t. Bishops	1·75	70
782	50t. Rooks	2·00	1·50
783	2k. Queens	6·00	12·00

1988. Olympic Games, Seoul. Multicoloured.

784	15t. Type **166**	30	10
785	35t. Javelin throwing	50	20
786	50t. Tennis	75	50
787	2k. Shot-putting	1·60	3·00
MS788	91 × 121 mm. Nos. 784/7	3·50	3·50

167 Evergreen Forest Warbler ("Eastern Forest Scrub Warbler")

167a Rebuilt Royal Exchange, 1844

1988. Birds. Multicoloured.

789	1t. Type **167**	20	80
790	2t. Yellow-throated woodland warbler ("Yellow-throated Warbler")	30	80
791	5t. Moustached green tinkerbird	50	80
792	7t. Waller's red-winged starling ("Waller's Chestnut-wing Starling")	50	80
793	8t. Oriole-finch	50	80
794	10t. White starred robin ("Starred Robin")	2·75	80
795	15t. Bar-tailed trogon	50	10
796	20t. Green-backed twin-spot ("Green Twinspot")	50	10
797	30t. African grey cuckoo shrike ("Grey Cuckoo Shrike")	50	10
798	40t. Black-fronted bush shrike	60	10
799	50t. White-tailed crested flycatcher	3·25	1·25
800	75t. Green barbet	70	1·00
801	1k. Lemon dove ("Cinnamon Dove")	70	1·00
802	2k. Silvery-cheeked hornbill	90	1·40
803	4k. Crowned eagle	1·25	2·00
804	10k. Anchieta's sunbird ("Red and Blue Sunbird")	10·00	11·00
804a	10k. As 10t.	5·00	2·25

1988. 300th Anniv of Lloyd's of London. Mult.

805	15t. Type **167a**	30	10
806	35t. Opening ceremony, Nkula Falls Hydro-electric Power Station (horiz)	60	20
807	50t. Air Malawi B.A.C. One Eleven airliner (horiz)	2·00	60
808	2k. "Seawise University" (formerly "Queen Elizabeth") on fire, Hong Kong, 1972	3·75	4·00

168 "Madonna in the Church" (Jan van Eyck)

1988. Christmas. Multicoloured.

809	15t. Type **168**	60	10
810	35t. "Virgin, Infant Jesus and St. Anna" (da Vinci)	90	25
811	50t. "Virgin and Angels" (Cimabue)	1·25	70
812	2k. "Virgin and Child" (Baldovinetti Apenio)	3·00	6·50

169 Robust Cichlid

1989. 50th Anniv of Malawi Angling Society. Multicoloured.

813	15t. Type **169**	60	20
814	35t. Small-scaled minnow ("Mpasa")	1·10	35
815	50t. Long-scaled yellowfish	1·50	1·40
816	2k. Tigerfish	4·00	9·50

170 Independence Arch, Blantyre

1989. 25th Anniv of Independence. Multicoloured.

817	15t. Type **170**	80	20
818	35t. Grain silos	1·50	35
819	50t. Capital Hill, Lilongwe	2·00	1·50
820	2k. Reserve Bank Headquarters	5·00	9·50

171 Blantyre Digital Telex Exchange

1989. 25th Anniv of African Development Bank. Multicoloured.

821	15t. Type **171**	80	20
822	40t. Dzalanyama steer	1·50	35
823	50t. Mikolongwe heifer	2·00	1·50
824	2k. Zebu bull	5·00	9·50

172 Rural House with Verandah

1989. 25th Anniv of Malawi–United Nations Co-operation. Multicoloured.

825	15t. Type **172**	80	20
826	40t. Rural house	1·50	35
827	50t. Traditional hut and modern houses	2·00	1·50
828	2k. Tea plantation	5·00	9·50

173 St. Michael and All Angels Church

1989. Christmas. Churches of Malawi. Mult.

829	15t. Type **173**	80	20
830	40t. Catholic Cathedral, Limbe	1·50	35
831	50t. C.C.A.P. Church, Nkhoma	2·00	1·50
832	2k. Cathedral, Likoma Island	5·00	9·50

174 Ford "Sedan", 1915

1990. Vintage Vehicles. Multicoloured.

833	15t. Type **174**	1·25	20
834	40t. Two-seater Ford, 1915	1·75	35
835	50t. Ford pick-up, 1915	2·00	1·50
836	1k. Chevrolet bus, 1930	5·00	9·50
MS837	120 × 85mm. Nos. 833/6	15·00	15·00

175 Player heading Ball into Net

1990. World Cup Football Championship, Italy. Multicoloured.

838	15t. Type **175**	1·00	20
839	40t. Player tackling	1·60	35
840	50t. Player scoring goal	2·00	1·50
841	2k. World Cup	5·50	10·00
MS842	88 × 118 mm. Nos. 838/41	9·50	11·00

176 Anniversary Emblem on Map

1990. 10th Anniv of Southern Africa Development Co-ordination Conference. Multicoloured.

843	15t. Type **176**	1·00	20
844	40t. Tilapia	1·00	40
845	50t. Cedar plantation	2·00	1·50
846	2k. Male nyala (antelope)	5·00	10·00
MS847	174 × 116 mm. Nos. 843/6	12·00	13·00

177 "Aerangis kotschyana"

178 "The Virgin and the Child Jesus" (Raphael)

1990. Orchids. Multicoloured.

848	15t. Type **177**	1·75	25
849	40t. "Angraecum eburneum"	2·75	80
850	50t. "Aerangis luteo-alba rhodostica"	2·75	1·60
851	2k. "Cyrtorchis arcuata whytei"	6·50	10·00
MS852	85 × 120 mm. Nos. 848/51	13·00	13·00

1990. Christmas. Paintings by Raphael. Mult.

853	15t. Type **178**	1·00	20
854	40t. "Transfiguration" (detail)	1·75	35
855	50t. "St. Catherine of Alexandrie" (detail)	1·75	90
856	2k. "Transfiguration"	5·50	11·00
MS857	85 × 120 mm. Nos. 853/6	12·00	13·00

179 Buffalo

1991. Wildlife. Multicoloured.

858	20t. Type **179**	1·00	25
859	60t. Cheetah	2·25	1·00
860	75t. Greater kudu	2·25	1·00
861	2k. Black rhinoceros	9·00	10·00
MS862	120 × 85 mm. Nos. 858/61	13·00	14·00

180 Chiromo Post Office, 1891

1991. Centenary of Postal Services. Mult.

863	20t. Type **180**	1·25	20
864	60t. Re-constructed mail exchange hut at Walala	2·00	85
865	75t. Mangochi post office	2·00	95
866	2k. Satellite Earth station	7·50	12·00
MS867	119 × 83 mm. Nos. 863/6	11·00	12·00

181 Red Locust

182 Child in a Manger

1991. Insects. Multicoloured.

868	20t. Type **181**	1·00	25
869	60t. Weevil	2·25	1·10
870	75t. Cotton stainer bug	2·25	1·40
871	2k. Pollen beetle	6·50	10·00

1991. Christmas. Multicoloured.

872	20t. Type **182**	80	20
873	60t. Adoration of the Kings and Shepherds	1·75	55
874	75t. Nativity	2·00	75
875	2k. Virgin and Child	4·75	11·00

183 Red Bishop

1992. Birds. Multicoloured.

876	75t. Type **183**	2·00	2·00
877	75t. Lesser striped swallow	2·00	2·00
878	75t. Long-crested eagle	2·00	2·00
879	75t. Lilac-breasted roller	2·00	2·00
880	75t. African paradise flycatcher	2·00	2·00
881	75t. White-fronted bee eater	2·00	2·00
882	75t. White-winged black tern	2·00	2·00
883	75t. African fire finch ("Brown-backed Fire-finch")	2·00	2·00
884	75t. White-browed robin chat	2·00	2·00
885	75t. African fish eagle	2·00	2·00
886	75t. Malachite kingfisher	2·00	2·00
887	75t. Lesser masked weaver ("Cabani's Masked Weaver")	2·00	2·00
888	75t. Barn owl ("African Barn Owl")	2·00	2·00
889	75t. Variable sunbird ("Yellow-bellied Sunbird")	2·00	2·00
890	75t. Lesser flamingo	2·00	2·00
891	75t. South African crowned crane ("Crowned Crane!")	2·00	2·00
892	75t. African pitta	2·00	2·00
893	75t. African darter	2·00	2·00
894	75t. White-faced whistling duck ("White-faced Tree-duck")	2·00	2·00
895	75t. African pied wagtail	2·00	2·00

184 Long Jumping

1992. Olympic Games, Barcelona. Multicoloured.

896	20t. Type **184**	80	20
897	60t. High jumping	1·25	60
898	75t. Javelin	1·50	90
899	2k. Running	3·50	6·50
MS900	110 × 100 mm. Nos. 896/9	6·50	8·00

185 "The Angel Gabriel" (detail, "The Annunciation") (Philippe de Champaigne)

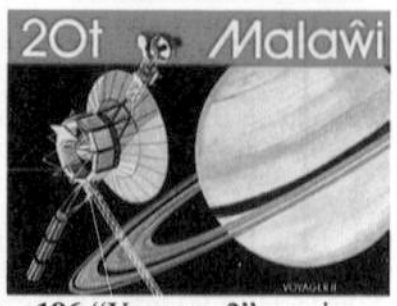

186 "Voyager 2" passing Saturn

1992. Christmas. Religious Paintings. Mult.

901	20t. Type **185**	70	20
902	75t. "Virgin and Child" (Bernandino Luini)	1·50	50
903	95t. "Virgin and Child" (Sassoferrato)	1·75	90
904	2k. "Virgin Mary" (detail, "The Annunciation") (De Champaigne)	4·50	8·50

1992. International Space Year. Multicoloured.

905	20t. Type **186**	1·00	30
906	75t. Centre of galaxy	2·00	90

907	95t. Kanjedza II Standard A Earth Station	2·00	1·00
908	2k. Communications satellite	4·50	7·50

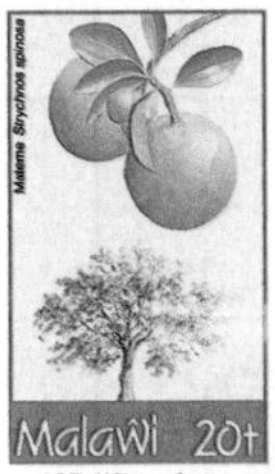

187 "Strychnos spinosa"

188 "Apaturopsis cleocharis"

1993. World Forestry Day. Indigenous Fruit Trees. Multicoloured.

909	20t. Type **187**	70	20
910	75t. "Adansonia digitata"	1·50	80
911	95t. "Ximenia caffra"	1·60	1·00
912	2k. "Uapaca kirkiana"	3·25	6·50

1993. Butterflies. Multicoloured.

913	20t. Type **188**	90	30
914	75t. "Euryphura achlys"	1·75	85
915	95t. "Cooksonia aliciae"	2·00	1·25
916	2k. "Charaxes protoclea azota"	3·00	5·50

189 The Holy Family

190 Kentrosaurus

1993. Christmas. Multicoloured.

917	20t. Type **189**	15	10
918	75t. Shepherds and star	30	20
919	95t. Three Kings	30	30
920	2k. Adoration of the Kings	75	2·50

1993. Prehistoric Animals. Multicoloured.

921	20t. Type **190**	55	30
922	75t. Stegosaurus	90	90
923	95t. Sauropod	1·00	1·00
MS924	157 × 97 mm. 2k. Tyrannosaurus; 2k. Dilophosaurus; 2k. Brachiosaurus; 2k. Gallimimus; 2k. Triceratops; 2k. Velociraptor	11·00	12·00

191 Socolof's Mbuna

1994. Fishes. Multicoloured.

925	20t. Type **191**	20	10
926	75t. Golden mbuna	50	30
927	95t. Lombardo's mbuna	55	35
928	1k. Scraper-mouthed mbuna	60	70
929	2k. Zebra mbuna	1·25	2·00
930	4k. Elongate mbuna	2·00	4·00

192 "Ilala II" (lake vessel)

1994. Ships of Lake Malawi. Multicoloured.

931	20t. Type **192**	25	10
932	75t. "Ufulu" (tanker)	35	25
933	95t. "Pioneer" (steam launch)	40	30
934	2k. "Dove" (paddle-steamer)	65	2·25
MS935	85 × 51 mm. 5k. "Monteith" (lake vessel)	3·00	4·00

193 "Virgin and Child" (detail) (Durer)

194 Pres. Bakili Muluzi (C.O.M.E.S.A. chairman, 1994–95)

1994. Christmas. Religious Paintings. Mult.

936	20t. Type **193**	30	10
937	75t. "Wise Men present Gifts" (Franco-Flemish Book of Hours)	60	15
938	95t. "The Nativity" (detail) (Fra Filippo Lippi) (horiz)	65	15
939	2k. "Nativity Scene with Wise Men" (Rogier van der Weyden) (horiz)	1·50	2·50

1995. Establishment of C.O.M.E.S.A. (Common Market for Eastern and Southern African States).

940	**194** 40t. multicoloured	15	10
941	1k.40 multicoloured	30	20
942	1k.80 multicoloured	30	55
943	2k. multicoloured	40	1·00

195 Telecommunications Training

1995. 50th Anniv of the United Nations. Mult.

944	40t. Type **195**	30	10
945	1k.40 Village women collecting water	60	25
946	1k.80 Mt. Mulanje	70	85
947	2k. Villagers in field	85	1·10
MS948	123 × 77 mm. Nos. 944/7	1·50	2·00

196 Teacher and Class

1995. Christmas. Multicoloured.

949	40t. Type **196**	15	10
950	1k.40 Dispensing medicine	40	25
951	1k.80 Crowd at water pump	45	60
952	2k. Refugees on ferries	65	85

197 "Precis tugela"

1996. Butterflies. Multicoloured.

953	60t. Type **197**	20	10
954	3k. "Papilio pelodorus"	45	35
955	4k. "Acrea acrita"	55	45
956	10k. "Melanitis leda"	1·00	2·25

198 Children's Party

199 Map of Malawi

1996. Christmas. Multicoloured.

957	10t. Type **198**	35	15
958	20t. Nativity play	55	15
959	30t. Children wearing party hats	65	20
960	60t. Mother and child	1·10	1·50

1997. 50th Death Anniv of Paul Harris (founder of Rotary International). Multicoloured.

961	60t. Type **199**	40	10
962	3k. African fish eagle	75	70
963	4k.40 Leopard	80	1·10
964	5k. Rotary International emblem	80	1·25

200 Mother and Child

201 The Nativity

1997. 50th Anniv of UNICEF. Multicoloured.

965	60t. Type **200**	25	10
966	3k. Children in class	55	35
967	4k.40 Boy with fish	1·00	1·10
968	5k. Nurse inoculating child	1·10	1·40

1997. Christmas. Multicoloured.

969	60t. Type **201**	15	10
970	3k. The Nativity (different)	45	20
971	4k.40 Adoration of the Magi	60	70
972	5k. The Holy Family	65	95

1998. Diana, Princess of Wales Commemoration. As T **91** of Kiribati. Multicoloured.

973	60t. Wearing red dress	20	10
974	6k. Wearing lilac jacket	40	35
975	7k. With head scarf	50	70
976	8k. Wearing blue evening dress	55	80
MS977	145 × 70 mm. Nos. 973/6	1·25	1·75

202 Tattooed Rock, Mwalawamphini, Cape Maclear

1998. Monuments. Multicoloured.

978	60t. Type **202**	15	10
979	6k. War Memorial Tower, Zomba	50	40
980	7k. Mtengatenga Postal Hut, Walala (horiz)	60	70
981	8k. P.I.M. Church, Chiradzulu (horiz)	75	90

No. 978 is inscribed "tatooed" and No. 979 "Memoral", both in error.

203 Woman voting

1998. 50th Anniv of Declaration of Human Rights. Multicoloured.

982	60t. Type **203**	15	10
983	6k. Books, pens and pencils ("Education")	50	40
984	7k. Man and woman on scales ("Justice")	60	70
985	8k. Person hugging house and land ("Property")	75	90

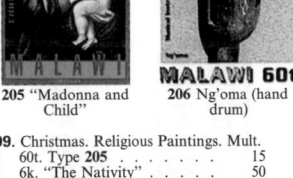

205 "Madonna and Child"

206 Ng'oma (hand drum)

1999. Christmas. Religious Paintings. Mult.

990	60t. Type **205**	15	10
991	6k. "The Nativity"	50	20
992	7k. "Adoration of the Magi"	60	50
993	8k. "Flight into Egypt"	75	85

2000. 50th Anniv of the Commonwealth. Musical Instruments. Multicoloured.

994	60t. Type **206**	15	10
995	6k. Kaligo (single stringed fiddle)	50	40
996	7k. Kalimba (thumb dulcitone)	60	70
997	8k. Chisekese (rattle)	75	85

207 Map of Africa and S.A.D.C. Emblem

208 "Madonna and Child"

2000. South African Development Community. Mult.

998	60t. Type **207**	25	10
999	6k. Bottles of Malambe fruit juice	50	40
1000	7k. *Ndunduma* (fisheries research ship) (horiz)	75	75
1001	8k. Class "Shire" diesel locomotive and goods train (horiz)	90	90

2000. Christmas. Religious Paintings. Mult.

1002	5k. Type **208**	20	10
1003	18k. "Adoration of the Shepherds"	80	90
1004	20k. "Madonna and Child"	80	90

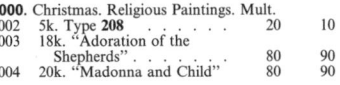

209 *Euxanthe wakefieldi*

2002. Butterflies. Multicoloured.

1005	1k. Type **209**	10	10
1006	2k. *Pseudacraea boisdurali*	10	10
1007	4k. *Catacroptera cloanthe*	10	10
1008	5k. *Myrina silenus ficedula*	10	10
1009	10k. *Cymothoe zombana*	10	15
1010	20k. *Charaxes castor*	20	25
1011	50k. *Charaxes pythoduras ventersi*	50	55
1012	100k. *Iolaus lalos*	1·00	1·10

210 Puku

2003. Endangered Species. Puku (*Kobus vardonii*). Multicoloured.

1013	50k. Type **210**	50	55
1014	50k. Two males	50	55
1015	50k. Male and female	50	55
1016	50k. Herd	50	55
MS1017	204 × 138 mm. Nos. 1013/16, each × 2	4·00	4·25

211 Hoopoe (*Upupa epops*)

2003. Fauna and Flora of Africa. Multicoloured.

MS1018 118 × 137 mm. 50k. Type **211**; 50k. Grey parrot (*Psittacus erithacus*); 50k. Bateleur (*Terathopius ecaudatus*) 50k. Martial eagle (*Polemaetus bellicosus*); 50k. Masked lovebird (*Agapornis personatus*); 50k. Pel's pishing owl (*Scotopelia peli*) . . 3·00 3·25

MS1019 113 × 138 mm. 50k. *Bebearia octogramma*; 50k. *Charaxes nobilis*; 50k. *Cymothoe beckeri*; 50k. *Salamis anteva*; 50k. *Charaxes xiphares*; 50k. *Bebearia arcadius Fabricius* (all horiz) . . 3·00 3·25

MS1020 137 × 117 mm. 50k. *Pleurotus ostreatus*; 50k. *Macrolepiota procera*; 50k. *Amanita vaginata*; 50k.*Cantharellus tubaeformis*; 50k. *Hydnum repandum*; 50k.*Trametes versicolor* (all horiz) . . . . . 3·00 3·25

MS1021 95 × 135 mm. 50k. *Angraecum eburneum*; 50k.*Ancistrochilus rothschildianus*; 50k. *Angraecum infundibulare*; 50k. *Ansellia Africana*; 50k. *Disa veitchii*; 50k.*Angraecum compactum* . . . . 3·00 3·25

MS1022 Four sheets. (a) 105 × 71 mm. 180k. Grey heron (*Arde cinerea*) (horiz). (b) 72 × 98 mm. 180k. *Carterocephalus palaemon* (horiz). (c) 68 × 94 mm. 180k. *Auricularia auricula*. (d) 93 × 66 mm. 180k. *Aerangis kotschyana* (horiz) Set of 4 . . 7·25 7·50

212 Vickers Vimy

2004. Centenary of Powered Flight. Multicoloured.

MS1023 174 × 97 mm. 75k. Type **212**; 75k. D.H.9A; 75k. Messerschmitt Bf; 75k. Mitsubishi A6M3 . . . . 3·00 3·25

MS1024 96 × 67 mm. 180k. Fiat CR.2 . . . . 1·80 2·00

213 Corvette Convertible (1965)

2004. 50th Anniv of the Corvette. Multicoloured.

MS1025 116 × 156 mm. 75k. Type **213**; 75k. Corvette Stingray (1965); 75k. Corvette (1979); 75k. Corvette (1998) . . . . 3·00 3·25

MS1026 110 × 83 mm. 180k. Corvette (1998) . . . . 1·80 2·00

214 Cadillac Eldorado (1959)

2004. Centenary of the Cadillac. Multicoloured.

MS1027 116 × 156 mm. 75k. Type **214**; 75k. Cadillac Series 62 (1962); 75k. Cadillac Sedan DeVille (1961); 75k. Cadillac V-16 (1930) . . . . 3·00 3·25

MS1028 110 × 85 mm. 180k. Cadillac Eldorado (1954) . . . . 1·80 2·00

215 Joop Zoetemelk (1980)

2004. Centenary of Tour de France Cycle Race. T **215** and similar vert designs showing winners. Multicoloured.

MS1029 157 × 96 mm. 75k. Type **215**; 75k. Bernard Hinault (1981); 75k. Bernard Hinault (1982); 75k. Laurent Fignon (1983) . . . . 3·00 3·25

MS1030 95 × 67 mm. 180k. Miguel Indurain (199–5) . . . . . . 1·80 1·80

POSTAGE DUE STAMPS

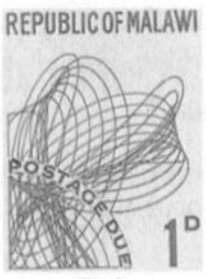

D 2

1967.

D 6	D 2	1d. red	15	3·75
D 7		2d. brown	20	3·75
D 8		4d. violet	25	4·00
D 9		6d. blue	25	4·25
D10		8d. green	35	4·75
D11		1s. black	45	5·00

1971. Values in tambalas. No accent over "W" of "MALAWI".

D12	D 2	2t. brown	30	4·50
D13		4t. mauve	50	3·00
D14		6t. blue	50	3·25
D15		8t. green	50	3·25
D16		10t. brown	60	3·25

1975. With circumflex over "W" of "MALAWI".

D27	D 2	2t. brown	1·75	2·50
D28		4t. purple	1·75	2·50
D29		6t. blue	1·75	2·50
D21		8t. green	1·50	3·25
D31		10t. black	2·00	2·50

MALAYA (BRITISH MILITARY ADMINISTRATION) Pt. 1

The following stamps were for use throughout the Malayan States and in Singapore during the period of the British Military Administration and were gradually replaced by individual issues for each state.

100 cents = 1 dollar.

1945. Straits Settlements stamps optd **B M A MALAYA**.

1a	58	1c. black	10	30
2a		2c. orange	20	10
4		3c. green	30	50
5		5c. brown	70	1·00
6a		6c. grey	30	20
7		8c. red	30	10
8a		10c. purple	50	10
10		12c. blue	1·75	6·50
12a		15c. blue	75	20
13a		25c. purple and red	1·40	30
14a		50c. black on green	75	10
15		$1 black and red	2·00	10
16		$2 green and red	2·75	75
17		$5 green and red on green	85·00	95·00
18		$5 purple and orange	3·75	3·00

For stamps inscribed "MALAYA" at top and with Arabic characters at foot see under Kelantan, Negri Sembilan, Pahang, Perak, Selangor or Trengganu.

MALAYA (JAPANESE OCCUPATION) Pt. 1

Japanese forces invaded Malaya on 8 December 1941 and the conquest of the Malay peninsula was completed by the capture of Singapore on 15 February.

The following stamps were used in Malaya until the defeat of Japan in 1945.

100 cents = 1 dollar.

(a) JOHORE

POSTAGE DUE STAMPS

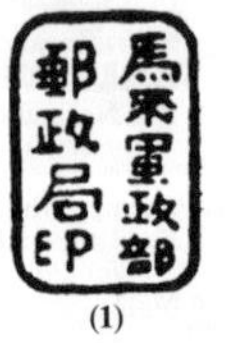

(1)

(2)

1942. Nos. D1/5 of Johore optd with T **1**.

JD1a	D 1	1c. red	20·00	70·00
JD2a		4c. green	65·00	80·00
JD3a		8c. orange	80·00	95·00
JD4a		10c. brown	16·00	50·00
JD5a		12c. purple	40·00	50·00

1943. Postage Due stamps of Johore optd with T **2**.

JD 6	D 1	1c. red	7·50	27·00
JD 7		4c. green	7·00	29·00
JD 8		8c. orange	8·50	29·00
JD 9		10c. brown	8·00	38·00
JD10		12c. purple	9·50	55·00

(b) KEDAH

1942. Stamps of Kedah optd **DAI NIPPON 2602**.

J 1	1	1c. black	5·50	8·50
J 2		2c. green	27·00	30·00
J 3		4c. violet	5·50	4·00
J 4		5c. yellow	5·50	4·25
J 5		6c. red	4·25	13·00
J 6		8c. black	4·25	2·25
J 7	6	10c. blue and brown	13·00	13·00
J 8		12c. black and violet	29·00	42·00
J 9		25c. blue and purple	9·50	14·00
J10		30c. green and red	70·00	80·00
J11		40c. black and purple	35·00	50·00
J12		50c. brown and blue	35·00	50·00
J13		$1 black and green	£140	£150
J14		$2 green and brown	£170	£170
J15		$5 black and red	65·00	90·00

(c) KELANTAN

(5) Sunagawa Seal

(6) Handa Seal

1942. Stamps of Kelantan surch. (a) With T **5**. (i) New value in **CENTS**.

J16	4	1c. on 50c. green and orange	£225	£180
J17		2c. on 40c. orange and green	£650	£300
J18		4c. on 30c. violet and red	£1700	£1200
J19		5c. on 12c. blue	£225	£190
J20		6c. on 25c. red and violet	£300	£190
J21		8c. on 5c. brown	£350	£140
J22		10c. on 6c. red	75·00	£120
J23		12c. on 8c. green	50·00	£110
J24		25c. on 10c. purple	£1200	£1300
J25		30c. on 4c. red	£1800	£2000
J26		40c. on 2c. green	60·00	85·00
J27		50c. on 1c. green and yellow	£1400	£1300
J28		$1 on 4c. black and red	50·00	80·00
J29		$2 on 5c. green & red on yell	50·00	80·00
J30		$5 on 6c. red	50·00	80·00

(ii) New Value in **Cents**.

J32	4	1c. on 50c. green and orange	£160	95·00
J33		2c. on 40c. orange and green	£140	£100
J34		5c. on 12c. blue	£140	£130
J35		8c. on 5c. brown	£120	75·00
J36		10c. on 6c. red	£325	£350

(b) With T **6** and new value.

J41	4	1c. on 50c. green and orange	£100	£150
J42		2c. on 40c. orange and green	£120	£160
J43		8c. on 5c. brown	65·00	£130
J44		10c. on 6c. red	85·00	£150
J31		12c. on 8c. green	£170	£225

(d) PENANG

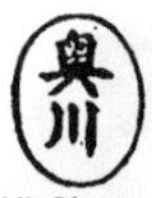

(11) Okugawa Seal

(12) Ochiburi Seal

1942. Straits Settlements stamps optd. (a) As T **11**.

J56	58	1c. black	9·50	11·00
J57		2c. orange	24·00	22·00
J58		3c. green	20·00	22·00
J59		5c. brown	24·00	25·00
J60		8c. grey	26·00	35·00
J61		10c. purple	50·00	50·00
J62		12c. blue	32·00	50·00
J63		15c. blue	50·00	50·00
J64		40c. red and purple	90·00	£110
J65		50c. black on green	£200	£225
J66		$1 black and red on blue	£200	£250
J67		$2 green and red	£650	£650
J68		$5 green and red on green	£1900	£1500

(b) With T **12**.

J69	58	1c. black	£140	£110
J70		2c. orange	£140	95·00
J71		3c. green	95·00	95·00
J72		5c. brown	£1800	£1800
J73		8c. grey	80·00	90·00
J74		10c. purple	£130	£140
J75		12c. blue	90·00	£110
J76		15c. blue	£100	£110

1942. Stamps of Straits Settlements optd **DAI NIPPON 2602 PENANG**.

J77	58	1c. black	4·50	3·00
J78		2c. orange	4·25	4·00
J79		3c. green	4·75	4·00
J80		5c. brown	2·75	7·00
J81		8c. grey	2·25	1·40
J82		10c. purple	1·50	2·25
J83		12c. blue	3·75	15·00
J84		15c. blue	1·75	3·25
J85		40c. red and purple	4·75	15·00
J86		50c. black on green	3·75	25·00
J87		$1 black and red on blue	6·00	35·00
J88		$2 green and red	50·00	80·00
J89		$5 green and red on green	£475	£550

(e) SELANGOR

1942. Agri-horticultural Exhibition. Stamps of Straits Settlements optd **SELANGOR EXHIBITION DAI NIPPON 2602 MALAYA**.

J90	58	2c. orange	12·00	24·00
J91		8c. grey	13·00	24·00

(f) SINGAPORE

(15) "Malay Military Government Division Postal Services Bureau Seal"

1942. Stamps of Straits Settlements optd with T **15**.

J92	58	1c. black	13·00	17·00
J93		2c. orange	13·00	13·00
J94		3c. green	50·00	70·00
J95		8c. grey	22·00	18·00
J96		15c. blue	15·00	15·00

(g) TRENGGANU

1942. Stamps of Trengganu optd with T **1**.

J 97	4	1c. black	90·00	90·00
J 98		2c. green	£140	£140
J 99		2c. on 5c. pur & yell (No. 59)	40·00	40·00
J100		3c. brown	85·00	80·00
J101		4c. red	£160	£140
J102		5c. purple on yellow	10·00	19·00
J103		6c. orange	9·00	25·00
J104		8c. grey	9·00	13·00
J105		8c. on 10c. blue (No. 60)	13·00	50·00
J106		10c. blue	23·00	40·00
J107		12c. blue	8·00	42·00
J108		20c. purple and orange	8·50	38·00
J109		25c. green and purple	7·50	45·00
J110		30c. purple and black	8·50	38·00
J111		35c. red on yellow	26·00	50·00
J112		50c. green and red	75·00	90·00
J113		$1 purple and blue on blue	£3000	£3000
J114		$3 green and red on green	60·00	£100
J115	–	$5 green and red on yellow (No. 31)	£160	£200
J116	–	$25 purple and blue (No. 40)	£1200	
J117	–	$50 green and yellow (No. 41)	£10000	
J118	–	$100 green and red (No. 42)	£1400	

1942. Stamps of Trengganu optd **DAI NIPPON 2602 MALAYA**.

J119	4	1c. black	12·00	12·00
J120		2c. green	£190	£200
J121		2c. on 5c. pur on yell (No. 59)	6·00	8·00
J122		3c. brown	12·00	24·00
J123		4c. red	13·00	11·00
J124		5c. purple on yellow	5·50	13·00
J125		6c. orange	5·00	13·00
J126		8c. grey	80·00	27·00
J127		8c. on 10c. blue (No. 60)	5·50	10·00
J128		12c. blue	5·00	26·00
J129		20c. purple and orange	14·00	15·00
J130		25c. green and purple	7·00	38·00
J131		30c. purple and black	7·50	30·00
J132		$3 green and red on green	75·00	£140

1942. Stamps of Trengganu optd with T **2**.

J133	4	1c. black	14·00	17·00
J134		2c. green	12·00	29·00
J135		2c. on 5c. pur on yell (No. 59)	8·50	21·00
J136		5c. purple on yellow	10·00	29·00
J137		6c. orange	12·00	35·00
J138		8c. grey	60·00	£100
J139		8c. on 10c. blue (No. 60)	24·00	50·00
J140		10c. blue	90·00	£225
J141		12c. blue	15·00	48·00
J142		20c. purple and orange	20·00	48·00
J143		25c. green and purple	16·00	50·00
J144		30c. purple and black	22·00	50·00
J145		35c. red on yellow	22·00	60·00

POSTAGE DUE STAMPS

1942. Postage Due stamps of Trengganu optd with T **2**.

JD17	D 1	1c. red	50·00	85·00
JD18a		4c. green	50·00	90·00
JD19		8c. yellow	14·00	50·00
JD20		10c. brown	14·00	50·00

(h) **GENERAL ISSUES**

1942. Stamps of various states optd with T **1**.
(a) Straits Settlements.

J146	**58**	1c. black	3·25	3·25
J147		2c. green	£2750	£1800
J148		2c. orange	3·00	2·25
J149		3c. green	2·75	2·25
J150		5c. brown	22·00	28·00
J151		8c. grey	4·00	2·25
J152		10c. purple	45·00	45·00
J153		12c. blue	75·00	£120
J154		15c. blue	4·25	3·75
J155		30c. purple and orange	£2000	£2000
J156		40c. red and purple	90·00	95·00
J157		50c. black and green	50·00	48·00
J158		$1 black and red on blue	75·00	75·00
J159		$2 green and red	£130	£160
J160		$5 green and red on green	£170	£190

There also exists a similar overprint with double-lined frame.

(b) Negri Sembilan.

J161b	**6**	1c. black	13·00	17·00
J162		2c. orange	27·00	19·00
J163		3c. green	35·00	20·00
J164c		5c. brown	15·00	11·00
J165		6c. grey	£140	£120
J166		8c. red	£120	£100
J167		10c. purple	£180	£180
J168		12c. blue	£1400	£1400
J169		15c. blue	22·00	8·00
J170		25c. purple and red	28·00	38·00
J171		30c. purple and orange	£200	£180
J172a		40c. red and purple	£850	£800
J173		50c. black on green	£850	£850
J174a		$1 black and red on blue	£170	£190
J175		$5 green and red on green	£500	£600

(c) Pahang.

J176	**15**	1c. black	50·00	45·00
J177a		3c. green	£250	£275
J178		5c. brown	14·00	12·00
J179		8c. grey	£800	£600
J180		8c. red	20·00	8·00
J181		10c. purple	£300	£140
J182a		12c. blue	£1200	£1200
J183		15c. blue	£140	£110
J184		25c. purple and red	21·00	29·00
J185		30c. purple and orange	12·00	28·00
J186		40c. red and purple	20·00	32·00
J187		50c. black on green	£750	£750
J188		$1 black and red on blue	£140	£150
J189		$5 green and red on green	£650	£800

(d) Perak.

J190	**51**	1c. black	55·00	35·00
J191		2c. orange	30·00	20·00
J192		3c. green	26·00	28·00
J193		5c. brown	7·00	6·00
J194		8c. grey	75·00	48·00
J195		8c. red	40·00	42·00
J196		10c. purple	26·00	24·00
J197		12c. blue	£225	£225
J198		15c. blue	24·00	32·00
J199		25c. purple and red	14·00	25·00
J200		30c. purple and orange	17·00	32·00
J201		40c. red and purple	£400	£350
J202		50c. black on green	40·00	50·00
J203		$1 black and red on blue	£425	£400
J204		$2 green and red	£3000	£3000
J205		$5 green and red on green	£475	

(e) Selangor.

J206	**46**	1c. black	12·00	24·00
J207		2c. green	£1400	£1100
J208		2c. orange	90·00	60·00
J210a		3c. green	18·00	15·00
J211		5c. brown	6·00	5·50
J212a		6c. red	£200	£250
J213		8c. grey	17·00	17·00
J214		10c. purple	13·00	21·00
J215		12c. blue	60·00	70·00
J216		15c. blue	16·00	22·00
J217a		25c. purple and red	60·00	80·00
J218		30c. purple and orange	11·00	24·00
J219		40c. red and purple	£140	£140
J220		50c. black on green	£140	£150
J221	**48**	$1 black and red on blue	30·00	45·00
J222		$2 green and red	35·00	60·00
J223		$5 green and red on green	65·00	90·00

1942. Various stamps optd **DAI NIPPON 2602 MALAYA**. (a) Stamps of Straits Settlements.

J224	**58**	2c. orange	2·00	60
J225		3c. green	50·00	65·00
J226		8c. grey	5·50	2·75
J227		15c. blue	14·00	9·00

(b) Stamps of Negri Sembilan.

J228	**6**	1c. black	2·50	60
J229		2c. orange	7·00	50
J230		3c. green	5·00	50
J231		5c. brown	1·75	2·75
J232		6c. grey	3·50	1·90
J233		8c. red	6·00	1·25
J234		10c. purple	3·00	2·50
J235		15c. blue	16·00	2·50
J236		25c. purple and red	4·50	4·00
J237		30c. purple and orange	7·50	3·00
J238		$1 black and red on blue	80·00	95·00

(c) Stamps of Pahang.

J239	**15**	1c. black	2·75	3·00
J240		5c. brown	1·25	70
J241		8c. red	25·00	2·75
J242		10c. purple	11·00	6·50
J243		12c. blue	12·00	14·00
J244		25c. purple and red	4·50	21·00
J245		30c. purple and orange	2·75	9·50

(d) Stamps of Perak.

J246	**51**	2c. orange	3·00	2·25
J247		3c. green	1·25	1·50
J248		8c. red	70	50
J249		10c. purple	14·00	6·00
J250		15c. blue	7·00	2·00
J251		50c. black on green	3·00	4·25
J252		$1 black and red on blue	£400	£450
J253		$5 green and red on green	38·00	70·00

(e) Stamps of Selangor.

J254	**46**	3c. green	1·75	3·25
J255		12c. blue	1·10	13·00
J256		15c. blue	6·00	1·50
J257		40c. red and purple	2·00	4·50
J258	**48**	$2 green and red	10·00	42·00

1942. No. 108 of Perak surch **DAI NIPPON 2602 MALAYA 2 Cents**.

J259	**88**	2c. on 5c. brown	1·25	3·00

1942. Stamps of Perak optd **DAI NIPPON YUBIN** ("Japanese Postal Service") or surch also in figures and words.

J260	**51**	1c. black	5·00	9·50
J261		2c. on 5c. brown	2·00	6·50
J262		8c. red	5·00	2·25

1943. Various stamps optd vert or horiz with T **2** or surch in figures and words. (a) Stamps of Straits Settlements.

J263	**58**	8c. grey	1·40	50
J264		12c. blue	1·25	10·00
J265		40c. red and purple	2·00	4·50

(b) Stamps of Negri Sembilan.

J266	**6**	1c. black	30	2·25
J267		2c. on 5c. brown	80	1·25
J268		6c. on 5c. brown	40	1·50
J269		25c. purple and red	1·10	15·00

(c) Stamp of Pahang.

J270	**7**	6c. on 5c. brown	50	75

(d) Stamps of Perak.

J272	**51**	1c. black	1·00	70
J274		2c. on 5c. brown	60	50
J275		5c. brown	55	65
J276		8c. red	55	1·75
J277		10c. purple	60	50
J278		30c. purple and orange	4·00	6·00
J279		50c. black on green	3·50	19·00
J280		$5 green and red on green	55·00	95·00

(e) Stamps of Selangor.

J288	**46**	1c. black	35	50
J289		2c. on 5c. brown	70	50
J282		3c. green	40	45
J290		3c. on 5c. brown	30	4·25
J291		5c. brown	1·40	4·25
J293		6c. on 5c. brown	30	70
J283		12c. blue	45	1·60
J284		15c. blue	3·50	3·25
J285	**48**	$1 black and red on blue	3·00	21·00
J295	**46**	$1 on 10c. purple	40	1·00
J296		$1.50 on 30c. purple and orange	40	1·00
J286	**48**	$2 green and red	10·00	45·00
J287		$5 green and red on green	22·00	80·00

25 Tapping Rubber

27 Japanese Shrine, Singapore

1943.

J297	**25**	1c. green	1·25	55
J298	–	2c. green	75	20
J299	**25**	3c. grey	30	20
J300	–	4c. red	2·00	20
J301	–	8c. blue	30	20
J302	–	10c. purple	30	20
J303	**27**	15c. violet	60	3·75
J304	–	30c. olive	1·00	35
J305	–	50c. blue	3·50	3·50
J306	–	70c. blue	16·00	10·00

DESIGNS—VERT: 2c. Fruit; 4c. Tin dredger; 8c. War Memorial, Bukit Batok, Singapore; 10c. Fishing village; 30c. Sago palms; 50c. Straits of Johore. HORIZ: 70c. Malay Mosque, Kuala Lumpur.

28 Ploughman

29 Rice-planting

1943. Savings Campaign.

J307	**28**	8c. violet	9·50	2·75
J308		15c. red	6·50	2·75

1944. "Re-birth of Malaya".

J309	**29**	8c. red	15·00	3·25
J310		15c. mauve	4·00	3·25

大日本

マライ郵便

50 セント

(30)

1944. Stamps intended for use on Red Cross letters. Surch with T **30**. (a) On Straits Settlements.

J311	**58**	50c. on 50c. black on grn	10·00	24·00
J312		$1 on $1 black & red on bl	20·00	35·00
J313		$1.50 on $2 green on red	30·00	70·00

(b) On Johore.

J314	**24**	50c. on 50c. purple & red	7·00	20·00
J315		$1.50 on $2 green and red	4·00	12·00

(c) On Selangor.

J316	**48**	$1 on $2 black & red on bl	3·50	14·00
J317		$1.50 on $2 green and red	5·00	20·00

POSTAGE DUE STAMPS

1942. Postage Due stamps of Malayan Postal Union optd with T **1**.

JD21	D **1**	1c. violet	12·00	25·00
JD22		3c. green	65·00	70·00
JD23		4c. green	50·00	35·00
JD24		8c. red	90·00	75·00
JD25		10c. orange	26·00	45·00
JD26		12c. blue	25·00	50·00
JD27		50c. black	60·00	80·00

1942. Postage Due stamps of Malayan Postal Union optd **DAI NIPPON 2602 MALAYA**.

JD28	D **1**	1c. violet	2·50	9·00
JD29		3c. green	15·00	21·00
JD30		4c. green	15·00	11·00
JD31		8c. red	21·00	18·00
JD32		10c. orange	1·75	15·00
JD33		12c. blue	1·75	29·00

1943. Postage Due stamps of Malayan Postal Union optd with T **2**.

JD34	D **1**	1c. violet	1·75	4·25
JD35		3c. green	1·75	4·25
JD36		4c. green	55·00	40·00
JD37		5c. red	1·50	4·50
JD38		9c. orange	80	7·50
JD39		10c. orange	1·75	8·00
JD40		12c. blue	1·75	15·00
JD41		15c. blue	2·00	8·00

MALAYA (THAI OCCUPATION) Pt. 1

Stamps issued for use in the four Malay states of Kedah, Kelantan, Perlis and Trengganu ceded by Japan to Thailand on 19 October 1943 and restored to British rule on the defeat of the Japanese.

100 cents = 1 dollar.

TM 1 War Memorial

1943.

TM1	TM **1**	1c. yellow	30·00	32·00
TM2		2c. brown	12·00	20·00
TM3		3c. green	20·00	38·00
TM4		4c. purple	14·00	28·00
TM5		8c. red	14·00	20·00
TM6		15c. blue	38·00	60·00

MALAYAN FEDERATION Pt. 1

An independent country within the British Commonwealth, comprising all the Malay States (except Singapore) and the Settlements of Malacca and Penang. The component units retained their individual stamps. In 1963 the Federation became part of Malaysia (q.v.).

100 cents (sen) = 1 Malayan dollar.

1 Tapping Rubber

1957.

1	**1**	6c. blue, red and yellow	50	10
2	–	12c. multicoloured	85	1·00
3	–	25c. multicoloured	2·75	20
4	–	30c. red and lake	1·00	20

DESIGNS—HORIZ: 12c. Federation coat of arms; 25c. Tin dredge. VERT: 30c. Map of the Federation.

5 Prime Minister Tunku Abdul Rahman and Populace greeting Independence

1957. Independence Day.

5	**5**	10c. brown	10	10

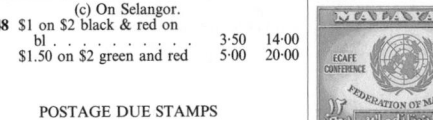

6 United Nations Emblem

8 Merdeka Stadium, Kuala Lumpur

1958. U.N. Economic Commission for Asia and Far East Conference, Kuala Lumpur.

6	**6**	12c. red	30	80
7	–	30c. purple	40	80

DESIGN: 30c. As Type **6** but vert.

1958. 1st Anniv of Independence.

8	**8**	10c. multicoloured	15	10
9	–	30c. multicoloured	40	70

DESIGN—VERT: 30c. Portrait of the Yang di-Pertuan Agong (Tuanku Abdul Rahman).

11 Malayan with "Torch of Freedom"

12 Mace and Malayan Peoples

1958. 10th Anniv of Declaration of Human Rights.

10	–	10c. multicoloured	15	10
11	**11**	30c. green	45	60

DESIGN—VERT: 10c. "Human Rights".

1959. Inauguration of Parliament.

12	**12**	4c. red	10	10
13		10c. violet	10	10
14		25c. green	75	20

14

15 Seedling Rubber Tree and Map

1960. World Refugee Year.

15	–	12c. purple	10	60
16	**14**	30c. green	10	10

DESIGN: 12c. As Type **14** but horiz.

1960. Natural Rubber Research Conf and 15th Int Rubber Study Group Meeting, Kuala Lumpur.

17	**15**	6c. multicoloured	20	1·25
18		30c. multicoloured	50	75

No. 18 is inscr "INTERNATIONAL RUBBER STUDY GROUP 15th MEETING KUALA LUMPUR" at foot.

16 The Yang di-Pertuan Agong (Tuanku Syed Putra)

1961. Installation of Yang di-Pertuan Agong, Tuanku Syed Putra.

19	**16**	10c. black and blue	10	10

17 Colombo Plan Emblem

18 Malaria Eradication Emblem

1961. Colombo Plan Conf, Kuala Lumpur.

20	**17**	12c. black and mauve	35	2·75
21		25c. black and green	80	2·25
22		30c. black and blue	70	1·00

1962. Malaria Eradication.

23	**18**	25c. brown	20	40
24		30c. lilac	20	15
25		50c. blue	40	80

19 Palmyra Palm Leaf

1962. National Language Month.
26 **19** 10c. brown and violet . . . 15 10
27 20c. brown and green . . . 50 1·25
28 50c. brown and mauve . . . 1·50 1·75

20 "Shadows of the Future"

1962. Introduction of Free Primary Education.
29 **20** 10c. purple 10 10
30 25c. ochre . . . . 50 1·25
31 30c. green . . . . 2·75 10

21 Harvester and Fisherman

1963. Freedom from Hunger.
32 **21** 25c. pink and green . . . . 2·25 3·00
33 30c. pink and lake . . . . 2·50 1·50
34 50c. pink and blue . . . . 2·50 3·00

22 Dam and Pylon

1963. Cameron Highlands Hydro-electric Scheme.
35 **22** 20c. green and violet 60 10
36 30c. turquoise and blue . . 1·00 1·50

MALAYAN POSTAL UNION Pt. 1

In 1936 postage due stamps were issued in Type D **1** for use in Negri Sembilan, Pahang, Perak, Selangor and Straits Settlements but later their use was extended to the whole of the Federation and Singapore, and from 1963 throughout Malaysia.

POSTAGE DUE STAMPS

D 1

1936.
D 7 D **1** 1c. purple . . . . 3·25 2·00
D14 1c. violet . . . . 70 1·60
D15 2c. slate . . . . 1·25 2·25
D 8 3c. green . . . . 6·00 5·00
D 2 4c. green . . . . 19·00 1·00
D17 4c. sepia . . . . 70 7·00
D 9 5c. red . . . . 6·00 3·50
D 3 8c. red . . . . 10·00 3·50
D19 8c. orange . . . . 2·25 4·50
D11 9c. orange . . . . 35·00 40·00
D 4 10c. orange . . . . . . 15·00 30
D 5 12c. blue . . . . 15·00 14·00
D20 12c. mauve . . . . 1·25 6·00
D12 15c. blue . . . . £110 28·00
D21 20c. blue . . . . 6·00 6·50
D 6 50c. black . . . . 28·00 6·00

1965. Surch **10 cents**.
D29 D **1** 10c. on 8c. orange . . . 60 2·75

MALAYSIA Pt. 1

Issues for use by the new Federation comprising the old Malayan Federation (Johore ("JOHOR"), Kedah, Kelantan, Malacca ("MELAKA"), Negri Sembilan ("NEGERI SEMBILAN"), Pahang, Penang ("PULAU PINANG"), Perak, Perlis, Selangor and Trengganu), Sabah (North Borneo), Sarawak and Singapore, until the latter became an independent state on 9 August 1965.

Stamps inscr "MALAYSIA" and state name are listed under the various states, as above.

100 cents (sen) = 1 Malaysian dollar.

A. NATIONAL SERIES

General issues for use throughout the Federation.

1 Federation Map

2 Bouquet of Orchids

1963. Inauguration of Federation.
1 **1** 10c. yellow and violet 40 10
2 12c. yellow and green . . . . 1·00 60
3 50c. yellow and brown . . . . 1·40 10

1963. 4th World Orchid Congress, Singapore.
4 **2** 6c. multicoloured . . . . . . 1·25 1·25
5 25c. multicoloured . . . . . . 1·25 25

4 Parliament House, Kuala Lumpur

1963. 9th Commonwealth Parliamentary Conf, Kuala Lumpur.
7 **4** 20c. mauve and gold . . . . 1·00 40
8 30c. green and gold . . . . . 1·00 15

5 "Flame of Freedom" and Emblems of Goodwill, Health and Charity

1964. Eleanor Roosevelt Commemoration.
9 **5** 25c. black, red and turquoise 20 10
10 30c. black, red and lilac . . . 20 15
11 50c. black, red and yellow . . 20 10

6 Microwave Tower and I.T.U. Emblem

1965. Centenary of I.T.U.
12 **6** 2c. multicoloured . . . . . . 15 1·25
13 25c. multicoloured . . . . . 1·25 60
14 50c. multicoloured . . . . . 1·75 10

7 National Mosque

1965. Opening of National Mosque, Kuala Lumpur.
15 **7** 6c. red 10 10
16 15c. brown 20 10
17 20c. green 20 15

8 Air Terminal

1965. Opening of Int Airport, Kuala Lumpur.
18 **8** 15c. black, green and blue . . 40 10
19 30c. black, green and mauve 60 20

9 Crested Wood Partridge

17 Sepak Raga (ball game) and Football

1965. Birds. Multicoloured.
20 25c. Type **9** 50 10
21 30c. Blue-backed fairy bluebird 60 10
22 50c. Black-naped oriole . . . 1·25 10
23 75c. Rhinoceros hornbill . . . 90 10
24 $1 Zebra dove . . . . 1·50 10
25 $2 Great argus pheasant . . . 4·25 30
26 $5 Asiatic paradise flycatcher 18·00 3·00
27 $10 Blue-tailed pitta . . . . . 48·00 13·00
For the lower values see the individual sets listed under each of the states which form Malaysia.

1965. 3rd South East Asian Peninsular Games.
28 **17** 25c. black and green . . . . 40 1·25
29 – 30c. black and purple . . . 40 20
30 – 50c. black and blue 70 30
DESIGNS: 30c. Running; 50c. Diving.

20 National Monument

21 The Yang di-Pertuan Agong (Tuanku Ismail Nasiruddin Shah)

1966. National Monument, Kuala Lumpur.
31 **20** 10c. multicoloured 30 10
32 20c. multicoloured 50 40

1966. Installation of Yang di-Pertuan Agong, Tuanku Ismail Nasiruddin Shah.
33 **21** 15c. black and yellow . . . 10 10
34 50c. black and blue 20 20

22 School Building

1966. 150th Anniv of Penang Free School.
35 **22** 20c. multicoloured 70 10
36 50c. multicoloured 90 10

23 "Agriculture"

1966. 1st Malaysia Plan. Multicoloured.
37 15c. Type **23** 20 10
38 15c. "Rural Health" 20 10
39 15c. "Communications" . . . 1·90 15
40 15c. "Education" 20 10
41 15c. "Irrigation" 20 10

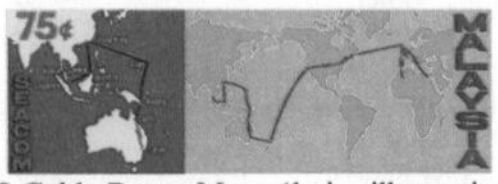

28 Cable Route Maps (½-size illustration)

1967. Completion of Malaysia–Hong Kong Link of SEACOM Telephone Cable.
42 **28** 30c. multicoloured 80 50
43 75c. multicoloured . . . . . 2·50 3·50

29 Hibiscus and Paramount Rulers

1967. 10th Anniv of Independence.
44 **29** 15c. multicoloured 20 10
45 50c. multicoloured . . . . . 1·25 80

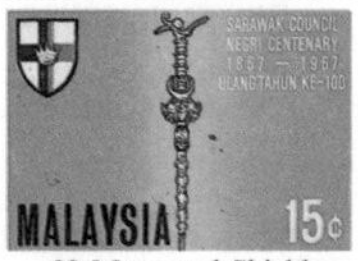

30 Mace and Shield

1967. Centenary of Sarawak Council.
46 **30** 15c. multicoloured 10 10
47 50c. multicoloured 30 60

31 Straits Settlements 1867 8c. Stamp and Malaysian 1965 25c. Stamp

1967. Stamp Centenary.
48 **31** 25c. multicoloured . . . . . 1·60 3·25
49 – 30c. multicoloured . . . . . 1·60 2·75
50 – 50c. multicoloured . . . . . 2·50 3·50
DESIGNS: 30c. Straits Settlements 1867 24c. stamp and Malaysian 1965 30c. stamp; 50c. Straits Settlements 1867 32c. stamp and Malaysian 1965 50c. stamp.

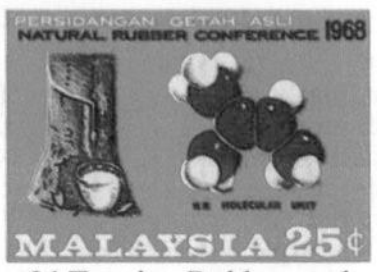

34 Tapping Rubber, and Molecular Unit

1968. Natural Rubber Conf, Kuala Lumpur. Mult.
51 25c. Type **34** 30 10
52 30c. Tapping rubber and export consignment 40 20
53 50c. Tapping rubber and aircraft tyres 40 10

37 Mexican Sombrero and Blanket with Olympic Rings

39 Tunku Abdul Rahman against background of Pandanus Weave

1968. Olympic Games, Mexico. Multicoloured.
54 30c. Type **37** 20 10
55 75c. Olympic Rings and Mexican embroidery 55 20

1969. Solidarity Week.
56 **39** 15c. multicoloured 15 10
57 – 20c. multicoloured . . . . . 45 1·75
58 – 50c. multicoloured 50 20
DESIGNS—VERT: 20c. As Type **39** (different). HORIZ: 50c. Tunku Abdul Rahman with pandanus pattern.

42 Peasant Girl with Sheaves of Paddy

1969. National Rice Year.
59 **42** 15c. multicoloured 15 10
60 75c. multicoloured . . . . . 55 1·50

43 Satellite-tracking Aerial

1970. Satellite Earth Station.
61 **43** 15c. drab, black and blue . . 1·00 15
62 – 30c. multicoloured . . . . . 1·00 2·50
63 – 30c. multicoloured . . . . . 1·00 2·50
DESIGN—40 × 27 mm: Nos. 62/3, "Intelstat III" in Orbit.
No. 62 has inscriptions and value in white and No. 63 has them in gold.

45 "Euploea leucostictus"

46 Emblem

1970. Butterflies. Multicoloured.
64 25c. Type **45** . . . . 1·00 10
65 30c. "Zeuxidia amethystus" . . 1·50 10
66 50c. "Polyura athamas" . . . 2·00 10
67 75c. "Papilio memnon" . . . 2·00 10
68 $1 "Appias nero" . . . . . . 2·50 10
69 $2 "Trogonoptera brookiana" 3·50 10
70 $5 "Narathura centaurus" . . 5·00 3·75
71 $10 "Terinos terpander" . . . 17·00 5·00
Lower values were issued for use in the individual States.

1970. 50th Anniv of Int Labour Organization.
72 **46** 30c. grey and blue 10 20
73 75c. pink and blue 20 30

47 U.N. Emblem encircled by Doves

50 The Yang di-Pertuan Agong (Tuanku Abdul Halim Shah)

1970. 25th Anniv of United Nations.
74 **47** 25c. gold, black and brown 35 40
75 – 30c. multicoloured 35 35
76 – 50c. black and green 40 75
DESIGNS: 30c. Line of doves and U.N. emblem; 50c. Doves looping U.N. emblem.

1971. Installation of Yang di-Pertuan Agong (Paramount Ruler of Malaysia).
77 **50** 10c. black, gold and yellow 20 30
78 15c. black, gold and mauve 20 30
79 50c. black, gold and blue . . 70 1·60

51 Bank Negara Complex

1971. Opening of Bank Negara Building.
80 **51** 25c. black and silver . . . . 2·25 2·50
81 50c. black and gold . . . . 1·75 1·25

52 Aerial View of Parliament Buildings

1971. 17th Commonwealth Parliamentary Association Conference, Kuala Lumpur. Multicoloured.
82 25c. Type **52** . . . . 1·25 50
83 75c. Ground view of Parliament Buildings (horiz, 73 × 23½ mm) . . . . 2·75 1·75

53 54 Malaysian Carnival 55

1971. Visit ASEAN Year.
84 **53** 30c. multicoloured . . . . . 1·60 55
85 **54** 30c. multicoloured . . . . . 1·60 55
86 **55** 30c. multicoloured . . . . . 1·60 55
ASEAN = Association of South East Asian Nations.
Nos. 84/6 form a composite design of a Malaysian Carnival, as illustrated.

56 Trees, Elephant and Tiger

1971. 25th Anniv of UNICEF. Multicoloured.
87 15c. Type **56** . . . . 2·50 60
88 15c. Cat and kittens . . . . . 2·50 60
89 15c. Sun, flower and bird (22 × 29 mm) . . . . 2·50 60
90 15c. Monkey, elephant and lion in jungle . . . . 2·50 60
91 15c. Spider and butterflies . . 2·50 60

57 Athletics

1971. 6th S.E.A.P. Games, Kuala Lumpur. Mult.
92 25c. Type **57** 45 40
93 30c. Sepak Raga players . . . 60 50
94 50c. Hockey . . . . 1·75 95
S.E.A.P. = South East Asian Peninsula.

58 59 Map and Tourist Attractions 60

1971. Pacific Area Tourist Association Conference.
95 **58** 30c. multicoloured . . . . . 3·00 1·50
96 **59** 30c. multicoloured . . . . . 3·00 1·50
97 **60** 30c. multicoloured . . . . . 3·00 1·50
Nos. 95/7 form a composite design of a map showing tourist attractions, as illustrated.

61 Kuala Lumpur City Hall

1972. City Status for Kuala Lumpur. Multicoloured.
98 25c. Type **61** . . . . 1·25 1·25
99 50c. City Hall in floodlights 2·00 1·25

62 SOCSO Emblem

64 Fireworks, National Flag and Flower

63 W.H.O. Emblem

1973. Social Security Organization.
100 **62** 10c. multicoloured 15 15
101 15c. multicoloured 15 10
102 50c. multicoloured . . . . 40 1·40

1973. 25th Anniv of W.H.O.
103 **63** 30c. multicoloured 50 25
104 – 75c. multicoloured . . . . 1·00 2·75
The 75c. is similar to Type **63**, but vertical.

1973. 10th Anniv of Malaysia.
105 **64** 10c. multicoloured 40 25
106 15c. multicoloured 55 15
107 50c. multicoloured . . . . 1·90 1·60

65 Emblems of Interpol and Royal Malaysian Police

1973. 50th Anniv of Interpol. Multicoloured.
108 25c. Type **65** . . . . 1·00 50
109 75c. Emblems within "50" . . 2·25 2·00

66 Boeing 737 and M.A.S. Emblem

1973. Foundation of Malaysian Airline System.
110 **66** 15c. multicoloured 35 10
111 30c. multicoloured 65 60
112 50c. multicoloured . . . . 95 1·60

67 Kuala Lumpur

1974. Establishment of Kuala Lumpur as Federal Territory.
113 **67** 25c. multicoloured 50 85
114 50c. multicoloured . . . . 1·00 1·75

68 Development Projects

1974. 7th Annual Meeting of Asian Development Bank's Board of Governors, Kuala Lumpur.
115 **68** 30c. multicoloured 25 50
116 75c. multicoloured . . . . 80 1·75

69 Scout Badge and Map

1974. Malaysian Scout Jamboree. Multicoloured.
117 10c. Type **69** . . . . 60 1·00
118 15c. Scouts saluting and flags (46 × 24 mm) 95 30
119 50c. Scout badge . . . . . . 1·75 3·00

70 Coat of Arms and Power Installations

1974. 25th Anniv of National Electricity Board. Multicoloured.
120 30c. Type **70** 30 50
121 75c. National Electricity Board building (37 × 27 mm) . . . . . . 1·00 2·50

71 U.P.U. and Post Office Emblems within "100"

1974. Centenary of U.P.U.
122 **71** 25c. green, yellow and red 20 35
123 30c. blue, yellow and red 25 35
124 75c. orange, yellow and red 65 1·75

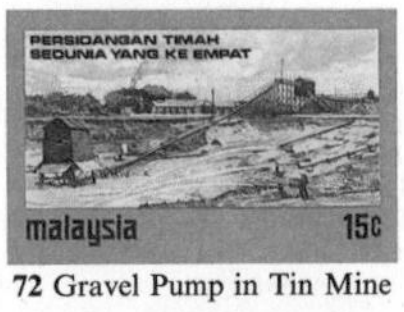

72 Gravel Pump in Tin Mine

1974. 4th World Tin Conf, Kuala Lumpur. Mult.
125 15c. Type **72** . . . . 1·75 20
126 20c. Open-cast mine . . . . 2·00 2·50
127 50c. Dredger within "ingot" 3·75 5·50

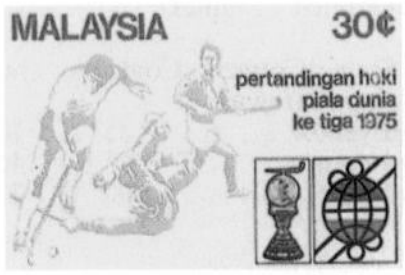

73 Hockey-players, World Cup and Federation Emblem

74 Congress Emblem

1975. 3rd World Cup Hockey Championships.
128 **73** 30c. multicoloured 90 60
129 75c. multicoloured . . . . 2·10 2·25

1975. 25th Anniv of Malaysian Trade Union Congress.
130 **74** 20c. multicoloured 15 25
131 25c. multicoloured 20 30
132 30c. multicoloured 65 60

75 Emblem of M.K.P.W. (Malayan Women's Organization)

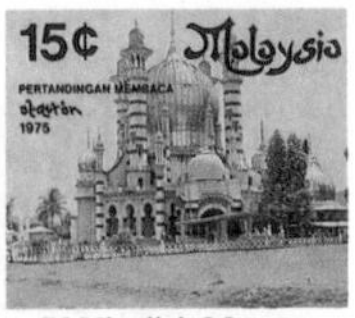

76 Ubudiah Mosque, Kuala Kangsar

1975. International Women's Year.
133 **75** 10c. multicoloured 15 25
134 15c. multicoloured 30 25
135 50c. multicoloured . . . . 1·25 2·25

1975. Koran Reading Competition. Multicoloured.
136 15c. Type **76** . . . . 1·75 60
137 15c. Zahir Mosque, Alor Star 1·75 60
138 15c. National Mosque, Kuala Lumpur . . . . 1·75 60
139 15c. Sultan Abu Bakar Mosque, Johore Bahru . . 1·75 60
140 15c. Kuching State Mosque, Sarawak . . . . 1·75 60

77 Plantation and Emblem

1975. 50th Anniv of Malaysian Rubber Research Institute. Multicoloured.
141 10c. Type **77** 40 15
142 30c. Latex cup and emblem 1·10 70
143 75c. Natural rubber in test-tubes . . . . 2·25 2·25

77a "Hebomoia glaucippe"

1976. Multicoloured.
144 10c. Type **77a** . . . . 2·75 7·00
145 15c. "Precis orithya" . . . . 2·75 7·00

78 Scrub Typhus

79 The Yang di-Pertuan Agong (Tuanku Yahya Petra)

1976. 75th Anniv of Institute of Medical Research. Multicoloured.
146 20c. Type **78** 25 15
147 25c. Malaria diagnosis . . . 40 20
148 $1 Beri-beri . . . . 1·60 2·50

1976. Installation of Yang di-Pertuan Agong.
149 **79** 10c. black, brown & yellow 25 10
150 15c. black, brown & mauve 40 10
151 50c. black, brown and blue 2·25 2·50

80 State Council Complex

1976. Opening of State Council Complex and Administrative Building, Sarawak.
152 **80** 15c. green and yellow . . . 35 10
153 20c. green and mauve . . . 45 40
154 50c. green and blue . . . . 1·00 1·40

81 E.P.F. Building

1976. 25th Anniv of Employees' Provident Fund. Multicoloured.
155 10c. Type **81** 15 10
156 25c. E.P.F. emblems (27 × 27 mm) 35 75
157 50c. E.P.F. Building at night 60 1·40

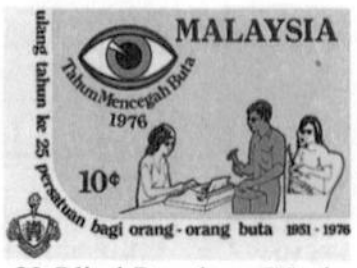

82 Blind People at Work

1976. 25th Anniv of Malayan Assn for the Blind. Multicoloured.
158 10c. Type **82** 15 15
159 75c. Blind man and shadow 1·25 2·75

83 Independence Celebrations, 1957

1977. 1st Death Anniv of Tun Abdul Razak (Prime Minister).
160 15c. Type **83** . . . . 1·50 60
161 15c. "Education" . . . . . . 1·50 60
162 15c. Tun Razak and map ("Development") . . . . . 1·50 60
163 15c. "Rukunegara" (National Philosophy) . . . . 1·50 60
164 15c. A.S.E.A.N. meeting . . 1·50 60

84 F.E.L.D.A. Village Scheme

1977. 21st Anniv of Federal Land Development Authority (F.E.L.D.A.). Multicoloured.
165 15c. Type **84** 30 10
166 30c. Oil palm settlement . . . 80 2·00

85 Figure "10" **86** Games Logos

1977. 10th Anniv of Association of South East Asian Nations (A.S.E.A.N.). Multicoloured.
167 10c. Type **85** 10 10
168 75c. Flags of members . . . 1·25 1·00

1977. 9th South East Asia Games, Kuala Lumpur. Multicoloured.
169 10c. Type **86** 15 15
170 20c. "Ball" 20 15
171 75c. Symbolic athletes . . . 75 1·75

87 Islamic Development Bank Emblem

1978. Islamic Development Bank Board of Governors' Meeting, Kuala Lumpur.
172 **87** 30c. multicoloured 25 15
173 75c. multicoloured 75 85

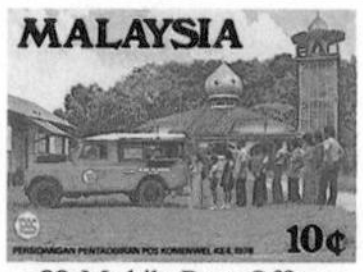

88 Mobile Post Office

1978. 4th Commonwealth Postal Administrations Conference, Kuala Lumpur. Multicoloured.
174 10c. Type **88** 30 10
175 25c. G.P.O., Kuala Lumpur 75 2·00
176 50c. Rural delivery by motorcycle . . . . 2·00 3·00

89 Boy Scout Emblem

1978. 4th Malaysian Scout Jamboree, Sarawak. Multicoloured.
177 15c. Type **89** 75 10
178 $1 Bees and honeycomb . . . 2·75 3·25

90 Dome of the Rock, Jerusalem

1978. Palestinian Welfare.
179 **90** 15c. multicoloured . . . . 1·00 25
180 30c. multicoloured . . . . 1·75 2·50

91 Globe and Emblems

1978. Global Eradication of Smallpox.
181 **91** 15c. black, red and blue . . 25 10
182 30c. black, red and green 40 30
183 50c. black, red and pink 70 95

92 "Seratus Tahun Getah Asli" and Tapping Knives Symbol

1978. Centenary of Rubber Industry.
184 **92** 10c. gold and green 10 10
185 – 20c. blue, brown and green 10 10
186 – 75c. gold and green . . . . 45 1·00
DESIGNS: 20c. Rubber tree seedling and part of "maxi stump"; 75c. Graphic design of rubber tree, latex cup and globe arranged to form "100".

93 Sultan of Selangor's New Palace

1978. Inauguration of Shah Alam New Town as State Capital of Selangor. Multicoloured.
187 10c. Type **93** 10 10
188 30c. Aerial view of Shah Alam 20 15
189 75c. Shah Alam . . . . . . 55 2·00

94 Tiger

1979. Animals. Multicoloured.
190 30c. Type **94** . . . . 1·75 10
191 40c. Malayan flying lemur . . 80 10
192 50c. Lesser Malay chevrotain 1·75 10
193 75c. Leathery pangolin . . . 1·00 10
194 $1 Malayan turtle . . . . . 1·50 10
195 $2 Malayan tapir . . . . . 1·50 10
196 $5 Gaur . . . . 4·50 2·00
197 $10 Orang-utang (vert) . . . 7·00 3·50

96 View of Central Bank of Malaysia **97** I.Y.C. Emblem

1979. 20th Anniv of Central Bank of Malaysia. Multicoloured.
198 10c. Type **96** 10 10
199 75c. Central Bank (vert) . . . 40 1·50

1979. International Year of the Child.
200 **97** 10c. gold, blue and salmon 35 20
201 – 15c. multicoloured 60 10
202 – $1 multicoloured . . . . . 3·00 4·00
DESIGNS: 15c. Children holding hands in front of globe; $1 Children playing.

98 Dam and Power Station

1979. Opening of Hydro-electric Power Station, Temengor.
203 **98** 15c. multicoloured 20 15
204 – 25c. multicoloured 35 70
205 – 50c. multicoloured . . . . 55 1·40
DESIGNS: 25c., 50c. Different views of dam.

99 Exhibition Emblem **100** Tuanku Haji Ahmad Shah

1979. 3rd World Telecommunications Exhibition, Geneva.
206 **99** 10c. orange, blue and silver 10 50
207 – 15c. multicoloured 15 10
208 – 50c. multicoloured . . . . 40 2·25
DESIGNS—34 × 24 mm: 15c. Telephone receiver joining the one half of World to the other. 39 × 28 mm: 50c. Communications equipment.

1980. Installation of Tuanku Haji Ahmad Shah as Yang di-Pertuan Agong.
209 **100** 10c. black, gold and yellow 10 40
210 15c. black, gold and purple 15 10
211 50c. black, gold and blue 55 2·00

101 Pahang and Sarawak Maps within Telephone Dials

1980. Kuantan–Kuching Submarine Cable Project. Multicoloured.
212 10c. Type **101** 10 40
213 15c. Kuantan and Kuching views within telephone dials 15 10
214 50c. Pahang and Sarawak maps within telephone receiver . . . . 35 1·75

102 Bangi Campus

1980. 10th Anniv of National University of Malaysia. Multicoloured.
215 10c. Type **102** 15 20
216 15c. Jalan Pantai Baru campus 20 10
217 75c. Great Hall . . . . . . 80 3·00

103 Mecca

1980. Moslem Year 1400 A.H. Commemoration.
218 **103** 15c. multicoloured 10 10
219 50c. multicoloured . . . . 30 1·50
No. 219 is inscribed in Roman lettering.

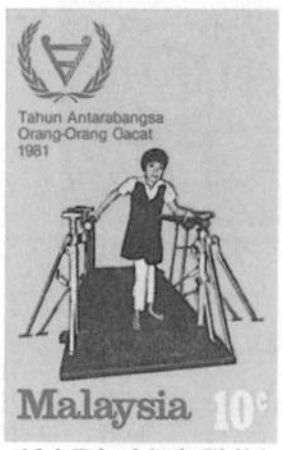

104 Disabled Child learning to Walk **105** Industrial Scene

1981. International Year for Disabled Persons. Multicoloured.
220 10c. Type **104** 30 30
221 15c. Girl sewing 55 10
222 75c. Disabled athlete . . . . 1·50 3·50

1981. Expo "81" Industrial Training Exposition, Kuala Lumpur and Seminar, Genting Highlands. Multicoloured.
223 10c. Type **105** 10 10
224 15c. Worker and bulldozer 15 10
225 30c. Workers at shipbuilding plant 25 35
226 75c. Agriculture and fishing produce, workers and machinery . . . . 65 2·25

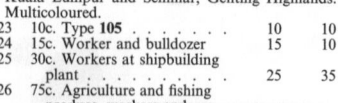

106 "25"

1981. 25th Anniv of Malaysian National Committee for World Energy Conferences. Multicoloured.
227 10c. Type **106** 20 20
228 15c. Drawings showing importance of energy sources in industry 45 10
229 75c. Symbols of various energy sources . . . . . . 2·25 3·50

107 Drawing showing development of Sabah from Village to Urbanized Area

1981. Centenary of Sabah. Multicoloured.
230 15c. Type **107** 50 15
231 80c. Drawing showing traditional and modern methods of agriculture . . 2·00 4·25

108 "Samanea saman"

1981. Trees. Multicoloured.
232 15c. Type **108** 55 10
233 50c. "Dyera costulata" (vert) 1·75 1·40
234 80c. "Dryobalanops aromatica" (vert) . . . . . 2·00 4·25

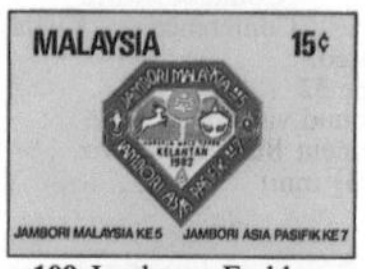

109 Jamboree Emblem

1982. 5th Malaysian/7th Asia–Pacific Boy Scout Jamboree. Multicoloured.
235 15c. Type **109** 35 10
236 50c. Malaysian flag and scout emblem 80 85
237 80c. Malaysian and Asia–Pacific scout emblem . . . 1·25 4·25

110 A.S.E.A.N. Building and Emblem

1982. 15th Anniv of Ministerial Meeting of A.S.E.A.N. (Association of South East Asian Nations). Multicoloured.
238 15c. Type **110** 15 10
239 $1 Flags of members . . . . 1·25 3·50

111 Dome of the Rock, Jerusalem

1982. "Freedom for Palestine".
240 **111** 15c. gold, green and black 1·00 15
241 $1 silver, green and black 3·25 4·75

112 Views of Kuala Lumpur in 1957 and 1982

1982. 25th Anniv of Independence. Multicoloured.
242 10c. Type **112** 10 10
243 15c. Malaysian industries . . 15 15
244 50c. Soldiers on parade . . . 40 55
245 80c. Independence ceremony 70 3·00
MS246a 120 × 190 mm. Nos. 242/5 10·00 10·00

113 Shadow Play

1982. Traditional Games. Multicoloured.
247 10c. Type **113** 55 30
248 15c. Cross top 55 15
249 75c. Kite flying . . . . . . 2·25 4·75

114 Sabah Hats

1982. Malaysian Handicrafts. Multicoloured.
250 10c. Type **114** 25 30
251 15c. Gold-threaded cloth . . 25 20
252 75c. Sarawak pottery . . . . 1·25 3·75

115 Gas Exploitation Logo

1983. Export of Liquefied Natural Gas from Bintulu Field, Sarawak. Multicoloured.
253 15c. Type **115** 75 15
254 20c. "Tenaga Satu" (liquid gas tanker) . . . . 1·50 70
255 $1 Gas drilling equipment . . 3·50 6·50

116 Flag of Malaysia

1983. Commonwealth Day. Multicoloured.
256 15c. Type **116** 20 10
257 20c. The King of Malaysia 20 20
258 40c. Oil palm tree and refinery 25 45
259 $1 Satellite view of Earth . . 60 2·75

117 Nile Mouthbrooder

1983. Freshwater Fishes. Multicoloured.
260 20c. Type **117** . . . . 1·25 2·00
261 20c. Common carp . . . . . 1·25 2·00
262 40c. Lampan barb . . . . . 1·75 2·75
263 40c. Grass carp . . . . . . 1·75 2·75

118 Lower Pergau River Bridge

1983. Opening of East–West Highway. Mult.
264 15c. Type **118** 80 15
265 20c. Perak river reservoir bridge . . . . 1·00 75
266 $1 Map showing East–West highway . . . . 3·75 6·50

119 Northrop Tiger II Fighter

1983. 50th Anniv of Malaysian Armed Forces. Multicoloured.
267 15c. Type **119** . . . . 1·25 15
268 20c. Missile boat . . . . . . 1·75 45
269 40c. Battle of Pasir Panjang 2·25 2·50
270 80c. Trooping the Colour . . 3·25 6·00
MS271 130 × 85 mm. Nos. 267/70 11·00 12·00

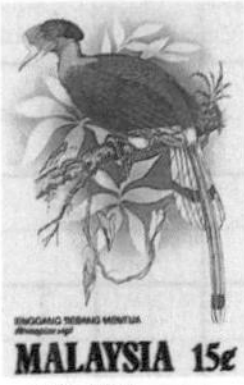

120 Helmeted Hornbill

122 Sky-scraper and Mosque, Kuala Lumpur

121 Bank Building, Ipoh

1983. Hornbills of Malaysia. Multicoloured.
280 15c. Type **120** . . . . 1·00 15
281 20c. Wrinkled hornbill . . . 1·25 50
282 50c. Long-crested hornbill . . 2·00 2·00
283 $1 Rhinoceros hornbill . . . 3·25 5·50

1984. 25th Anniv of Bank Negara. Multicoloured.
284 20c. Type **121** 40 30
285 $1 Bank building, Alor Setar 2·00 3·75

1984. 10th Anniv of Federal Territory of Kuala Lumpur. Multicoloured.
286 20c. Type **122** 80 20
287 40c. Aerial view . . . . . . 1·60 1·40
288 80c. Gardens and clock-tower (horiz) . . . . 2·50 6·50

123 Map showing Industries

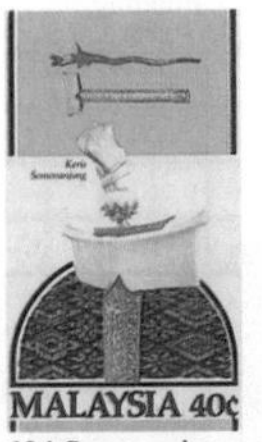

124 Semenanjung Keris

1984. Formation of Labuan Federal Territory. Multicoloured.
289 20c. Type **123** 75 25
290 $1 Flag and map of Labuan 3·75 6·00

1984. Traditional Malay Weapons. Multicoloured.
291 40c. Type **124** . . . . 1·25 2·10
292 40c. Pekakak keris . . . . . 1·25 2·10
293 40c. Jawa keris . . . . . . 1·25 2·10
294 40c. Lada tumbuk . . . . . 1·25 2·10

125 Map of World and Transmitter

1984. 20th Anniv of Asia–Pacific Broadcasting Union. Multicoloured.
295 20c. Type **125** 40 25
296 $1 Clasped hands within "20" . . . . 2·00 5·00

126 Facsimile Service

127 Yang di-Pertuan Agong (Tuanku Mahmood)

1984. Opening of New General Post Office, Kuala Lumpur. Multicoloured.
297 15c. Type **126** 35 20
298 20c. New G.P.O. building . . 45 45
299 $1 Mailbag conveyor . . . . 2·00 4·75

1984. Installation of Yang di-Pertuan Agong (Tuanku Mahmood).
300 **127** 15c. multicoloured 60 20
301 20c. multicoloured 65 20
302 – 40c. multicoloured . . . . 1·25 1·00
303 – 80c. multicoloured . . . . 2·50 5·00
DESIGN—HORIZ: 40c., 80c. Yang di-Pertuan Agong and federal crest.

128 White Hibiscus

129 Parliament Building

1984. Hibiscus. Multicoloured.
304 10c. Type **128** 50 30
305 20c. Red hibiscus . . . . . 1·00 20
306 40c. Pink hibiscus . . . . . 1·75 2·00
307 $1 Orange hibiscus . . . . . 2·75 5·75

1985. 25th Anniv of Federal Parliament. Mult.
308 20c. Type **129** 30 15
309 $1 Parliament Building (different) (horiz) . . . . . 1·75 3·50

130 Banded Linsang

1985. Protected Animals of Malaysia (1st series). Multicoloured.
310 10c. Type **130** 60 10
311 40c. Slow loris (vert) . . . . 2·00 1·40
312 $1 Spotted giant flying squirrel (vert) . . . . . . 4·00 6·50
See also Nos. 383/6.

131 Stylized Figures

1985. International Youth Year. Multicoloured.
313 20c. Type **131** 40 15
314 $1 Young workers . . . . . 3·50 5·50

132 Steam Locomotive No. 1, 1885

1985. Centenary of Malayan Railways.
315 **132** 15c. black, red and orange 1·60 50
316 – 20c. multicoloured . . . . 1·75 60
317 – $1 multicoloured . . . . 4·25 7·00
MS318 119 × 59 mm. 80c. multicoloured . . . . 8·00 9·00
DESIGNS—HORIZ: 20c. Class 20 diesel-electric locomotive, 1957; $1 Hitachi Class 23 diesel-electric locomotive, 1983. 48 × 31 mm: 80c. Class 56 steam locomotive No. 564.18, "Seletar", 1938.

133 Blue Proton "Saga 1.3s" Car

1985. Production of Proton "Saga" (Malaysian national car). Multicoloured.
319 20c. Type **133** 80 15
320 40c. White Proton "Saga 1.3s" . . . . 1·40 1·00
321 $1 Red Proton "Saga 1.5s" 2·50 6·50

134 Penang Bridge

135 Offshore Oil Rig

1985. Opening of Penang Bridge. Multicoloured.
322 20c. Type **134** 90 15
323 40c. Penang Bridge and location map . . . . . . 1·75 90
324 $1 Symbolic bridge linking Penang to mainland (40 × 24 mm) . . . . . . 3·50 6·00

1985. Malaysian Petroleum Production. Mult.
325 15c. Type **135** . . . . 1·25 20
326 20c. Malaysia's first oil refinery (horiz) . . . . . . 1·40 50
327 $1 Map of Malaysian offshore oil and gas fields (horiz) . . . . 3·75 6·00

136 Sultan Azlan Shah and Perak Royal Crest

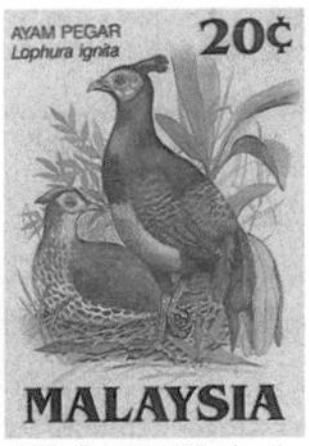

137 Crested Fireback Pheasant

1985. Installation of the Sultan of Perak.
328 **136** 15c. multicoloured 55 10
329 20c. multicoloured 60 25
330 $1 multicoloured . . . . 3·25 6·00

1986. Protected Birds of Malaysia (1st series). Multicoloured.
331 20c. Type **137** . . . . . . 2·50 3·25
332 20c. Malay peacock-pheasant . . . . 2·50 3·25
333b 40c. Bulwer's pheasant (horiz) . . . . 2·00 3·50
334b 40c. Great argus pheasant (horiz) . . . . 2·00 3·50
See also Nos. 394/7.

139 Two Kadazan Dancers, Sabah

140 Stylized Competitors

1986. Pacific Area Travel Association Conference, Malaysia. Multicoloured.
335 20c. Type **139** . . . . 85 1·25
336 20c. Dyak dancer and longhouse, Sarawak . . . 85 1·25
337 20c. Dancers and fortress, Malacca . . . . 85 1·25
338 40c. Malay dancer and Kuala Lumpur . . . . 1·25 1·50
339 40c. Chinese opera dancer and Penang Bridge . . . . 1·25 1·50
340 40c. Indian dancer and Batu Caves . . . . 1·25 1·50

1986. Malaysia Games. Multicoloured.
341 20c. Type **140** . . . . 1·25 20
342 40c. Games emblems (vert) 2·25 2·00
343 $1 National and state flags (vert) . . . . 7·00 7·75

141 Rambutan

142 Skull and Slogan "Drugs Can Kill"

1986. Fruits of Malaysia. Multicoloured.

344	40c. Type **141**	15	10
345	50c. Pineapple	15	10
346	80c. Durian	25	10
347	$1 Mangosteen	30	10
348	$2 Star fruit	65	10
349	$5 Banana	1·60	50
350	$10 Mango	3·25	1·25
351	$20 Papaya	6·50	3·25

1986. 10th Anniv of National Association for Prevention of Drug Addiction. Multicoloured.

352	20c. Type **142**	1·00	30
353	40c. Bird and slogan "Stay Free From Drugs"	1·40	1·10
354	$1 Addict and slogan "Drugs Can Destroy" (vert)	2·25	5·00

143 MAS Logo and Map showing Routes

144 Building Construction

1986. Inaugural Flight of Malaysian Airlines Kuala Lumpur–Los Angeles Service. Multicoloured.

355	20c. Type **143**	2·00	20
356	40c. Logo, stylized aircraft and route diagram	2·75	80
357	$1 Logo and stylized aircraft	3·75	4·25

1986. 20th Anniv of National Productivity Council and 25th Anniv of Asian Productivity Organization (40c., $1). Multicoloured.

358	20c. Type **144**	85	25
359	40c. Planning and design (horiz)	1·40	1·25
360	$1 Computer-controlled car assembly line (horiz)	3·75	6·50

145 Old Seri Menanti Palace, Negri Sembilan

1986. Historic Buildings of Malaysia (1st series). Multicoloured.

361	15c. Type **145**	1·00	20
362	20c. Old Kenangan Palace, Perak	1·10	20
363	40c. Old Town Hall, Malacca	2·00	80
364	$1 Astana, Kuching, Sarawak	3·50	5·00

See also Nos. 465/8.

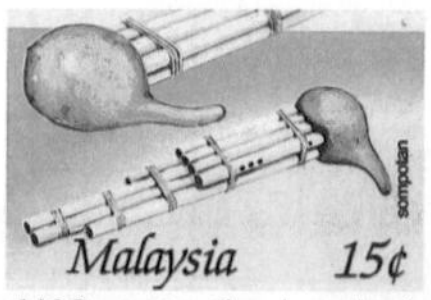

146 Sompotan (bamboo pipes)

1987. Malaysian Musical Instruments. Mult.

365	15c. Type **146**	1·00	10
366	20c. Sapih (four-stringed chordophone)	1·10	20
367	50c. Serunai (pipes) (vert)	2·25	40
368	80c. Rebab (three-stringed fiddle) (vert)	3·00	2·00

147 Modern Housing Estate

1987. International Year of Shelter for the Homeless. Multicoloured.

369	20c. Type **147**	1·00	15
370	$1 Stylized families and houses	2·50	1·50

148 Drug Addict and Family

1987. International Conference on Drug Abuse, Vienna. Multicoloured.

371	20c. Type **148**	1·75	1·40
372	20c. Hands holding drugs and damaged internal organs	1·75	1·40
373	40c. Healthy boy and broken drug capsule	2·50	1·60
374	40c. Drugs and healthy internal organs	2·50	1·60

Nos. 371/2 and 373/4 were printed together, se-tenant, forming composite designs.

149 Spillway and Power Station

1987. Opening of Sultan Mahmud Hydro-electric Scheme, Kenyir, Trengganu. Multicoloured.

375	20c. Type **149**	50	10
376	$1 Dam, spillway and reservoir	2·50	2·00

150 Crossed Maces and Parliament Building, Kuala Lumpur

1987. 33rd Commonwealth Parliamentary Conf. Multicoloured.

377	20c. Type **150**	25	10
378	$1 Parliament building and crossed mace emblem	1·25	1·25

151 Dish Aerial, Satellite and Globe

1987. Asia/Pacific Transport and Communications Decade. Multicoloured.

379	15c. Type **151**	50	10
380	20c. Diesel train and car	1·50	75
381	40c. Container ships and lorry	1·75	1·40
382	$1 Malaysian Airlines Boeing 747, Kuala Lumpur Airport	3·50	6·50

152 Temminck's Golden Cat

1987. Protected Animals of Malaysia (2nd series). Multicoloured.

383	15c. Type **152**	2·25	50
384	20c. Flatheaded cat	2·25	50
385	40c. Marbled cat	3·50	1·75
386	$1 Clouded leopard	6·50	7·50

153 Flags of Member Nations and "20"

1987. 20th Anniv of Association of South East Asian Nations. Multicoloured.

387	20c. Type **153**	35	10
388	$1 Flags of member nations and globe	1·25	1·50

154 Mosque and Portico

1988. Opening of Sultan Salahuddin Abdul Aziz Shah Mosque. Multicoloured.

389	15c. Type **154**	25	10
390	20c. Dome, minarets and Sultan of Selangor	25	20
391	$1 Interior and dome (vert)	1·25	2·50

155 Aerial View

1988. Sultan Ismail Hydro-electric Power Station, Paka, Trengganu. Multicoloured.

392	20c. Type **155**	30	10
393	$1 Power-station and pylons	1·10	1·25

156 Black-naped Blue Monarch

157 Outline Map and Products of Sabah

1988. Protected Birds of Malaysia (2nd series). Multicoloured.

394	20c. Type **156**	1·75	2·25
395	20c. Scarlet-backed flowerpecker	1·75	2·25
396	50c. Yellow-backed sunbird	2·50	3·00
397	50c. Black and red broadbill	2·50	3·00

1988. 25th Anniv of Sabah and Sarawak as States of Malaysia. Multicoloured.

398	20c. Type **157**	65	80
399	20c. Outline map and products of Sarawak	65	80
400	$1 Flags of Malaysia, Sabah and Sarawak (30 × 40 mm)	1·50	3·00

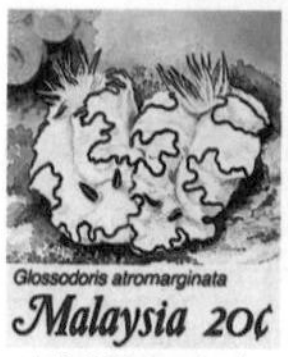

158 "Glossodoris atromarginata"

159 Sultan's Palace, Malacca

1988. Marine Life (1st series). Multicoloured.

401	20c. Type **158**	85	1·10
402	20c. Ocellate nudibranch	85	1·10
403	20c. "Chromodoris annae"	85	1·10
404	20c. "Flabellina macassarana"	85	1·10
405	20c. Ruppell's nudibranch	85	1·10
MS406	100 × 75 mm. $1 Blue-ringed angelfish (50 × 40 mm)	3·00	1·75

Nos. 401/5 were printed together, se-tenant, forming a composite background design.

See also Nos. 410/13, 450/3, 492/6 and 559/62.

1989. Declaration of Malacca as Historic City. Multicoloured.

407	20c. Type **159**	25	30
408	20c. Independence Memorial Building	25	30
409	$1 Porta De Santiago Fortress (vert)	1·25	2·00

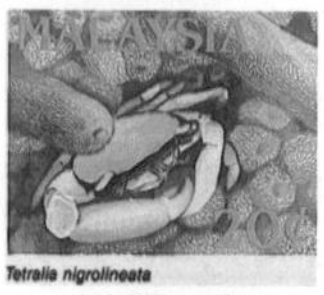

160 "Tetralia nigrolineata"

161 Map of Malaysia and Scout Badge

1989. Marine Life (2nd series). Crustaceans. Mult.

410	20c. Type **160**	45	90
411	20c. "Neopetrolisthes maculatus" (crab)	45	90
412	40c. "Periclimenes holthuisi" (shrimp)	55	1·10
413	40c. "Synalpheus neomeris" (shrimp)	55	1·10

1989. 7th National Scout Jamboree. Multicoloured.

414	10c. Type **161**	30	10
415	20c. Saluting national flag	60	25
416	80c. Scouts around camp fire (horiz)	1·40	2·75

162 Cycling

163 Sultan Azlan Shah

1989. 15th South East Asian Games, Kuala Lumpur. Multicoloured.

417	10c. Type **162**	75	40
418	20c. Athletics	40	20
419	50c. Swimming (vert)	75	85
420	$1 Torch bearer (vert)	1·25	3·25

1989. Installation of Sultan Azlan Shah as Yang di-Pertuan Agong.

421 **163**	20c. multicoloured	20	15
422	40c. multicoloured	35	35
423	$1 multicoloured	1·00	2·75

164 Putra World Trade Centre and Pan-Pacific Hotel

1989. Commonwealth Heads of Government Meeting, Kuala Lumpur. Multicoloured.

424	20c. Type **164**	20	10
425	50c. Traditional dancers (vert)	65	75
426	$1 National flag and map showing Commonwealth countries	1·25	3·00

165 Clock Tower, Kuala Lumpur City Hall and Big Ben

166 Sloth and Map of Park

1989. Inaugural Malaysia Airlines "747" Non-stop Flight to London. Each showing Malaysia Airlines Boeing "747-400". Multicoloured.

427	20c. Type **165**	1·75	2·00
428	20c. Parliament Buildings, Kuala Lumpur, and Palace of Westminster	1·75	2·00
429	$1 World map showing route	4·25	4·75

1989. 50th Anniv of National Park. Multicoloured.

430	20c. Type **166**	1·00	30
431	$1 Pair of crested argus	3·50	4·25

167 Outline Map of South-east Asia and Logo

168 "Dillenia suffruticosa"

1990. "Visit Malaysia Year". Multicoloured.

432	20c. Type **167**	65	15
433	50c. Traditional drums	85	1·00
434	$1 Scuba diving, windsurfing and yachting	1·75	3·00

1990. Wildflowers (1st series). Multicoloured.

435	15c. Type **168**	25	15
436	20c. "Mimosa pudica"	30	20
437	50c. "Ipmoea carnea"	60	90
438	$1 "Nymphaea pubescens"	80	2·75

See also Nos. 505/8.

169 Monument and Rainbow

171 Alor Setar

170 Seri Negara Building

1990. Kuala Lumpur, Garden City of Lights. Multicoloured.

439	20c. Type **169**	25	20
440	40c. Mosque and skyscrapers at night (horiz)	55	55
441	$1 Kuala Lumpur skyline (horiz)	1·40	3·00

1990. 1st Summit Meeting of South–South Consultation and Co-operation Group, Kuala Lumpur. Multicoloured.

442	20c. Type **170**	40	15
443	80c. Summit logo	1·40	2·25

1990. 250th Anniv of Alor Setar. Multicoloured.

444	20c. Type **171**	40	20
445	40c. Musicians and monument (vert)	50	40
446	$1 Zahir Mosque (vert)	1·25	3·25

172 Sign Language Letters

1990. International Literacy Year. Multicoloured.

447	20c. Type **172**	50	10
448	40c. People reading	70	40
449	$1 Symbolic person reading (vert)	1·75	3·25

173 Leatherback Turtle

1990. Marine Life (3rd series). Sea Turtles. Mult.

450	15c. Type **173**	60	10
451	20c. Common green turtle	60	15
452	40c. Olive Ridley turtle	1·25	80
453	$1 Hawksbill turtle	2·25	3·75

174 Safety Helmet, Dividers and Industrial Skyline

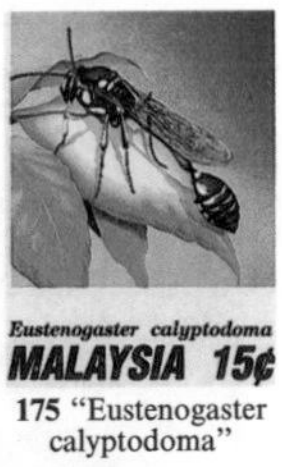

175 "Eustenogaster calyptodoma"

1991. 25th Anniv of MARA (Council of the Indigenous People). Multicoloured.

454	20c. Type **174**	15	10
455	40c. Documents and graph	30	35
456	$1 25th Anniversary logo	75	2·25

1991. Insects. Wasps. Multicoloured.

457	15c. Type **175**	25	30
458	20c. "Vespa affinis indonensis"	25	20
459	50c. "Sceliphorn javanum"	60	70
460	$1 "Ampulex compressa"	1·00	2·50
MS461	130 × 85 mm. Nos. 457/60	2·50	4·25

176 Tunku Abdul Rahman Putra and Independence Rally

1991. Former Prime Ministers of Malaysia. Multicoloured.

462	$1 Type **176**	70	1·25
463	$1 Tun Abdul Razak Hussein and jungle village	70	1·25
464	$1 Tun Hussein Onn and standard-bearers	70	1·25

177 Maziah Palace, Trengganu

1991. Historic Buildings of Malaysia (2nd series). Multicoloured.

465	15c. Type **177**	25	10
466	20c. Grand Palace, Johore	25	15
467	40c. Town Palace, Kuala Langat, Selangor	50	50
468	$1 Jahar Palace, Kelantan	1·00	2·75

178 Museum Building in 1891, Brass Lamp and Fabric

179 Rural Postman on Cycle

1991. Centenary of Sarawak Museum. Mult.

469	30c. Type **178**	20	15
470	$1 Museum building in 1991, vase and fabric	80	2·00

1992. Inauguration of Post Office Corporation. Multicoloured.

471	30c. Type **179**	60	85
472	30c. Urban postman on motorcycle	60	85
473	30c. Inner city post van	60	85
474	30c. Industrial post van	60	85
475	30c. Malaysian Airlines Boeing 747 and globe	60	85

180 Hill Forest and Jelutong Tree

1992. Tropical Forests. Multicoloured.

476	20c. Type **180**	35	10
477	50c. Mangrove swamp and Bakau Minyak tree	65	50
478	$1 Lowland forest and Chengal tree	1·10	2·50

181 Tuanku Ja'afar and Coat of Arms

182 Badminton Players

1992. 25th Anniv of Installation of Tuanku Ja'afar as Yang di-Pertuan Besar of Negri Sembilan. Multicoloured.

479	30c. Type **181**	20	20
480	$1 Palace, Negri Sembilan	80	2·25

1992. Malaysian Victory in Thomas Cup Badminton Championship. Multicoloured.

481	$1 Type **182**	70	1·25
482	$1 Thomas Cup and Malaysian flag	70	1·25
MS483	105 × 80 mm. $2 Winning team (76 × 28 mm)	1·75	2·75

183 Women in National Costumes

1992. 25th Anniv of A.S.E.A.N. (Association of South East Asian Nations). Multicoloured.

484	30c. Type **183**	40	30
485	50c. Regional flowers	65	75
486	$1 Traditional architecture	1·25	2·75

184 Straits Settlements 1867 1½c. and Malaysian Federation 1957 10c. Stamps

1992. 125th Anniv of Postage Stamps and "Kuala Lumpur '92" Int Stamp Exn. Multicoloured.

487	30c. Type **184**	45	90
488	30c. Straits Settlements 1867 2c. and Malaysia 1963 Federation Inauguration 12c.	45	90
489	50c. Straits Settlements 1868 4c. and Malaysia 1990 Kuala Lumpur 40c.	70	1·10
490	50c. Straits Settlements 1867 12c. and Malaysia "Kuala Lumpur '92" $2	70	1·10
MS491	120 × 92 mm. $2 "Kuala Lumpur '92" logo on Malaysian flag	1·75	2·75

185 "Acropora"

186 Girls smiling

1992. Marine Life (4th series). Corals. Mult.

492	30c. Type **185**	80	1·10
493	30c. "Dendronephthya"	80	1·10
494	30c. "Dendrophyllia"	80	1·10
495	30c. "Sinularia"	80	1·10
496	30c. "Melithaea"	80	1·10
MS497	100 × 70 mm. $2 "Subergorgia" (38 × 28 mm)	2·50	4·00

1993. 16th Asian–Pacific Dental Congress. Mult.

498	30c. Type **186**	50	75
499	30c. Girls smiling with koala bear	50	75
500	50c. Dentists with Japanese, Malaysian and South Korean flags	1·00	1·00
501	$1 Dentists with New Zealand, Thai, Chinese and Indonesian flags	1·25	2·00

187 View of Golf Course

188 "Alpinia rafflesiana"

1993. Cent of Royal Selangor Golf Club. Mult.

502	30c. Type **187**	60	20
503	50c. Old and new club houses	90	80
504	$1 Bunker on course (horiz)	1·75	3·25

1993. Wildflowers (2nd series). Gingers. Mult.

505	20c. Type **188**	40	10
506	30c. "Achasma megalocheilos"	50	20
507	50c. "Zingiber spectabile"	90	80
508	$1 "Costus speciosus"	1·75	3·00

189 Forest under Magnifying Glass

190 White-throated Kingfisher

1993. 14th Commonwealth Forestry Conference, Kuala Lumpur. Multicoloured.

509	30c. Type **189**	40	20
510	50c. Hand holding forest	65	70
511	$1 Forest in glass dome (vert)	1·40	2·75

1993. Kingfishers. Multicoloured.

512	30c. Type **190**	1·25	1·60
513	30c. Pair of blue-eared kingfishers	1·25	1·60
514	50c. Chestnut-collared kingfisher	1·40	1·75
515	50c. Pair of three-toed kingfishers	1·40	1·75

191 SME MD3-160m Light Aircraft

1993. Langkawi International Maritime and Aerospace Exhibition '93. Multicoloured.

516	30c. Type **191**	35	20
517	50c. Eagle X-TS light aircraft	65	75
518	$1 "Kasturi" (frigate)	1·25	2·50
MS519	120 × 80 mm. $2 Map of Langkawi	1·60	2·50

192 Jeriau Waterfalls

1994. Visit Malaysia. Multicoloured.

520	20c. Type **192**	50	10
521	30c. Flowers	50	25
522	50c. Turtle and fishes	75	65
523	$1 Orang-utan and other wildlife	1·60	2·50

193 Planetarium and Planets

1994. National Planetarium, Kuala Lumpur. Mult.

524	30c. Type **193**	50	25
525	50c. Static displays	65	80
526	$1 Planetarium auditorium	1·50	2·50

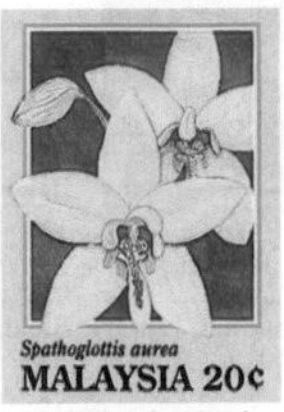

194 "Spathoglottis aurea"

195 Decorative Bowl

1994. Orchids. Multicoloured.

527	20c. Type **194**	40	15
528	30c. "Paphiopedilum barbatum"	50	25
529	50c. "Bulbophyllum lobbii"	85	90
530	$1 "Aerides odorata"	1·40	2·75
MS531	120 × 82 mm. $2 "Grammato-phyllum speciosum" (horiz)	2·50	4·00

No. **MS**531 also commemorates the "Hong Kong '94" International Stamp Exhibition.

1994. World Islamic Civilisation Festival '94, Kuala Lumpur. Multicoloured.

532	20c. Type **195**	15	10
533	30c. Celestial globe	25	20
534	50c. Dinar coins	40	65
535	$1 Decorative tile	75	2·00

196 Flock of Chickens and Vet examining Cat

197 Workers laying Electric Cable

1994. Centenary of Veterinary Services. Mult.

536	30c. Type **196**	50	25
537	50c. Vet in abattoir	70	55
538	$1 Herd of cows and veterinary equipment	1·00	2·25

1994. Centenary of Electricity Supply. Mult.

539	30c. Type **197**	40	65
540	30c. Illuminated city	40	65
541	$1 City of the future	1·00	2·00

198 Expressway from the Air

199 Sultan Tuanku Ja'afar

1994. Opening of North–South Expressway. Mult.
542 30c. Type **198** 30 20
543 50c. Expressway junction . . 45 50
544 $1 Expressway bridge . . . . 90 2·00

1994. Installation of Sultan Tuanku Ja'afar as Yang di-Pertuan Agong.
545 **199** 30c. multicoloured 20 20
546 50c. multicoloured 40 50
547 $1 multicoloured . . . . 80 2·00

200 Map of Malaysia and Logo

201 Tunku Abdul Rahman Putra and National Flag

1994. 16th Commonwealth Games, Kuala Lumpur (1998) (1st issue). Multicoloured.
548 $1 Type **200** . . . . 90 1·50
549 $1 Wira (games mascot) holding national flag . . . 90 1·50
See also Nos. 575/6, 627/30, 668/71, **MS**678, 693/708 and **MS**715/16.

1994. 5th Death Anniv of Tunku Abdul Rahman Putra (former Prime Minister). Multicoloured.
550 30c. Type **201** 25 20
551 $1 The Residency, Kuala Lumpur . . . . 75 1·75

202 Library Building

1994. Opening of New National Library Building. Multicoloured.
552 30c. Type **202** 20 25
553 50c. Computer plan on screen 45 50
554 $1 Ancient Koran . . . . . 1·00 2·00

203 "Microporus xanthopus"

1995. Fungi. Mult.
555 20c. Type **203** 15 10
556 30c. "Cookeina tricholoma" 25 20
557 50c. "Phallus indusiatus" ("Dictyophora phalloidea") 45 55
558 $1 "Ramaria sp." . . . . . 90 2·25

204 Seafans

1995. Marine Life (5th series). Corals. Mult.
559 20c. Type **204** . . . . 1·00 1·25
560 20c. Feather stars . . . . . 1·00 1·25
561 30c. Cup coral . . . . 1·00 1·25
562 30c. Soft coral . . . . 1·00 1·25

205 Clouded Leopard on Branch

1995. Endangered Species. Clouded Leopard. Mult.
563 20c. Type **205** 55 25
564 30c. With cubs 60 30
565 50c. Crouched on branch . . 80 70
566 $1 Climbing tree . . . . . . 1·25 2·00

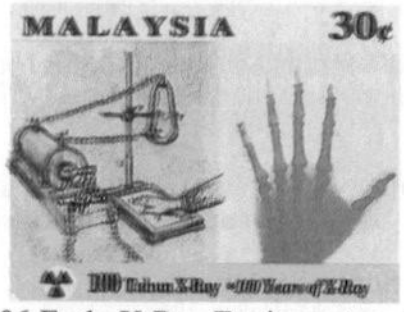

206 Early X-Ray Equipment and X-Ray of Hand

1995. Centenary of Discovery of X-Rays by Wilhelm Conrad Rontgen. Multicoloured.
567 30c. Type **206** 40 65
568 30c. Body scanner and brain scan 40 65
569 $1 Chest X-rays . . . . . . 1·00 1·75

207 Jembiah (curved dagger)

1995. "Singapore '95" International Stamp Exhibition. Traditional Malay Weapons. Mult.
570 20c. Type **207** 15 10
571 30c. Keris panjang (sword) 25 20
572 50c. Kerambit (curved dagger) 40 50
573 $1 Keris sundang (sword) . . 80 2·00
MS574 100 × 70 mm. $2 Ladig terus (dagger) . . . . 2·25 3·00

208 Badminton, Cricket, Shooting, Tennis, Hurdling, Hockey and Weightlifting

1995. 16th Commonwealth Games, Kuala Lumpur (1998) (2nd issue). Multicoloured.
575 $1 Type **208** . . . . 1·75 2·00
576 $1 Cycling, bowls, boxing, basketball, rugby, gymnastics and swimming 1·75 2·00

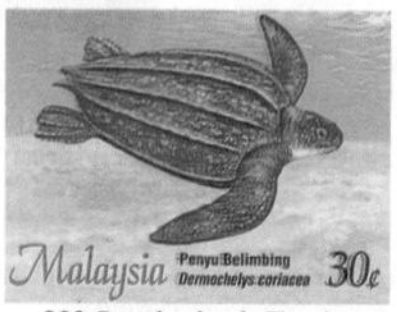

209 Leatherback Turtle ("Dermochelys coriacea")

1995. Turtles. Multicoloured.
577 30c. Type **209** . . . . 1·25 1·25
578 30c. Green turtle ("Chelonia mydas") . . . . 1·25 1·25

210 Anniversary Emblem and Symbolic People around Globe

1995. 50th Anniv of United Nations. Multicoloured.
579 30c. Type **210** 30 20
580 $1 United Nations emblem 70 1·50

211 Boeing 747, Globe, Emblem and Malaysian Scenes

212 Proton "Saga 1.5" Saloon, 1985

1995. 50th Anniv of International Air Transport Association. Designs each showing Boeing 747 and Globe. Multicoloured.
581 30c. Type **211** 40 60
582 30c. Asian and Australasian scenes 40 60
583 50c. European and African scenes 60 80
584 50c. North and South American scenes 60 80

1995. 10th Anniv of Proton Cars. Multicoloured.
585 30c. Type **212** 70 90
586 30c. "Iswara 1.5" aeroback, 1992 . . . . 70 90
587 30c. "Iswara 1.5" saloon, 1992 . . . . 70 90
588 30c. "Wira 1.6" saloon, 1993 70 90
589 30c. "Wira 1.6" aeroback, 1993 . . . . 70 90
590 30c. Proton rally car, 1994 70 90
591 30c. "Satria 1.6" hatchback, 1994 . . . . 70 90
592 30c. "Perdana 2.0" saloon, 1995 . . . . 70 90
593 30c. "Wira 1.6" aeroback, 1995 . . . . 70 90
594 30c. "Wira 1.8" saloon, 1995 70 90

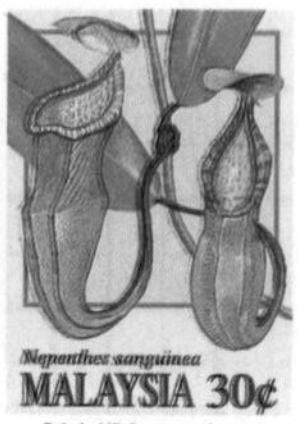

213 "Ariane 4" Launch Rocket

214 "Nepenthes sanguinea"

1996. Launch of MEASAT I (Malaysia East Asia Satellite). Multicoloured.
595 30c. Type **213** 25 20
596 50c. Satellite over Eastern Asia 40 45
597 $1 Satellite Earth station, Langkawi . . . . 90 2·00
MS598 100 × 70 mm. $5 Satellite orbiting Globe (hologram) (horiz) 5·50 6·00

1996. Pitcher Plants. Multicoloured.
599 30c. Type **214** 25 45
600 30c. "Nepenthes macfarlanei" 25 45
601 50c. "Nepenthes rajah" . . . 35 55
602 50c. "Nepenthes lowii" . . . 35 55

215 Brahminy Kite

1996. Birds of Prey. Multicoloured.
603 20c. Type **215** 25 15
604 30c. Crested serpent eagle . . 35 25
605 50c. White-bellied sea eagle 55 55
606 $1 Crested hawk eagle . . . 1·00 2·00
MS607 100 × 70 mm. $2 Blyth's Hawk Eagle (vert) . . . . . . 2·50 3·50
No. **MS**607 also includes the "CHINA '96" 9th Asian International Stamp Exhibition logo on the sheet margin.

216 Family, Globe and Burning Drugs

1996. International Day against Drug Abuse and Illicit Trafficking. Multicoloured.
608 30c. Type **216** 40 60
609 30c. Sporting activities . . . 40 60
610 $1 Family and rainbow . . . 75 1·50

217 "Graphium sarpedon"

218 Kuala Lumpur Tower

1996. "ISTANBUL '96" International Stamp Exhibition. Butterflies. Multicoloured.
611 30c. Type **217** . . . . 1·25 1·25
612 30c. "Terinos terpander" . . . 1·25 1·25
613 30c. "Melanocyma faunula" 1·25 1·25
614 30c. "Trogonoptera brookiana" . . . . 1·25 1·25
615 30c. "Delias hyparete" . . . 1·25 1·25

1996. Opening of Kuala Lumpur Telecommunications Tower. Multicoloured.
616 30c. Type **218** 20 20
617 50c. Diagram of top of tower 30 35
618 $1 Kuala Lumpur Tower at night . . . . 80 1·50
MS619 70 × 100 mm. $2 Top of Kuala Lumpur Tower (different) (vert) . . . . 1·50 2·50

219 C.A.P.A. Logo on Kite

1996. 14th Conference of the Confederation of Asian and Pacific Accountants. Multicoloured.
620 30c. Type **219** 25 20
621 $1 Globe and C.A.P.A. logo 75 1·40

1996. "TAIPEI '96" 10th Asian International Stamp Exhibition. As No. **MS**619, but with exhibition logo added to bottom right-hand corner of sheet.
MS622 70 × 100 mm. $2 Top of Kuala Lumpur Tower (vert) . . 1·50 2·25

220 Model of D.N.A. Molecule

1996. Opening of National Science Centre, Kuala Lumpur. Multicoloured.
623 30c. Type **220** 25 20
624 50c. Planetary model and Science Centre 40 40
625 $1 National Science Centre 90 1·50

221 Slow Loris

1996. Stamp Week. Wuildlife. Sheet 165 × 75 mm, containing T **221** and similar multicoloured designs.
MS626 20c. Type **221**; 30c. Prevost's squirrel; 50c. Atlas moth; $1 Rhinoceros hornbill (60 × 30 mm); $1 White-handed gibbon (30 × 60 mm); $2 Banded palm civet (60 × 30 mm) . . . . . . 3·25 4·00

222 Running

1996. 16th Commonwealth Games, Kuala Lumpur (1998) (3rd issue). Multicoloured.
627 30c. Type **222** 35 55
628 30c. Hurdling 35 55
629 50c. High jumping 45 65
630 50c. Javelin 45 65

223 Pygmy Blue Flycatcher

224 Transit Train leaving Station

1997. Highland Birds. Multicoloured.
631 20c. Type **223** 30 15
632 30c. Silver-eared mesia . . . 40 20
633 50c. Black-sided flower-pecker 55 55
634 $1 Scarlet sunbird . . . . . 85 1·50

1997. "HONG KONG '97" International Stamp Exhibition. As No. **MS**626, but with exhibition logo added to top sheet margin.
MS635 165 × 75 mm. 20c. Type **221**; 30c. Prevost's squirrel; 50c. Atlas moth; $1 Rhinoceros hornbill (60 × 30 mm); $1 White-handed gibbon (30 × 60 mm); $2 Banded palm civet (60 × 30 mm) . . . 4·00 5·00

1997. Opening of Kuala Lumpur Light Rail Transit System. Multicoloured.

636 30c. Type **224** . . . . 1·25 1·00
637 30c. Trains in central Kuala Lumpur . . . . 1·25 1·00

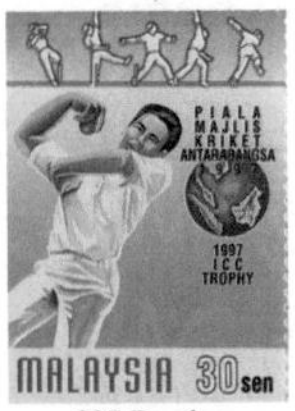
225 Bowler

1997. International Cricket Council Trophy, Kuala Lumpur. Multicoloured.

638 30c. Type **225** 35 15
639 50c. Batsman 50 45
640 $1 Wicket-keeper . . . . . . 90 1·50

226 Boeing 747-400 over World Map

1997. 50th Anniv of Aviation in Malaysia. Mult.

641 30c. Type **226** 65 15
642 50c. Boeing 747-400 over Kuala Lumpur 80 50
643 $1 Tail fins of four airliners 1·25 1·75

227 "Schima wallichii"

228 World Youth Football Championship Mascot

1997. Highland Flowers. Multicoloured.

644 30c. Type **227** 60 70
645 30c. "Aeschynanthus longicalyx" 60 70
646 30c. "Aeschynanthus speciosa" 60 70
647 30c. "Phyllagathis tuberculata" 60 70
648 30c. "Didymocarpus quinquevulnerus" 60 70

1997. 9th World Youth Football Championship, Malaysia. Multicoloured.

649 30c. Type **228** 25 10
650 50c. Football and players . . 40 35
651 $1 Map of Malaysia and football . . . . 75 1·60

229 Members of First Conference, 1897

1997. Centenary of Rulers' Conference. Mult.

652 30c. Type **229** 15 10
653 50c. State emblem 30 35
654 $1 Seal and press . . . . . 65 1·60

230 A.S.E.A.N. Logo and Ribbons

1997. 30th Anniv of Association of South-east Asian Nations. Multicoloured.

655 30c. Type **230** 50 10
656 50c. "30" enclosing logo . . 70 45
657 $1 Chevrons and logo . . . 1·25 1·75

231 "Tubastrea sp."

232 Women Athletes, Scientist and Politician

1997. International Year of the Coral Reefs. Multicoloured.

658 20c. Type **231** 20 10
659 30c. "Melithaea sp." 25 10
660 50c. "Aulostomus chinensis" 35 35
661 $1 "Symphillia sp." . . . . . 55 1·40
MS662 70 × 100 mm. $2 Green Turtle (horiz) . . . . 2·00 2·75

1997. 20th International Pan-Pacific and South-east Asia Women's Association Conference, Kuala Lumpur. Multicoloured.

663 30c. Type **232** 25 40
664 30c. Family and house . . . 25 40

233 1867 12c. on 4 anna with Malacca Postmark

1997. "Malpex '97" Stamp Exhibition, Kuala Lumpur. 50th Anniv of Organised Philately. Sheet 120 × 70 mm, containing T **233** and similar diamond-shaped designs. Multicoloured.

MS665 20c. Type **233**; 30c. 1997 Highland Birds set; 50c. 1996 Wildlife miniature sheet seen through magnifying glass; $1 1867 cover to Amoy . . . . 2·25 2·75

234 Group of 15 Emblem

1997. 7th Summit Conference of the Group of 15, Kuala Lumpur. Multicoloured.

666 30c. Type **234** 10 10
667 $1 Flags of member countries 90 1·25

235 Hockey

1997. 16th Commonwealth Games, Kuala Lumpur (1998) (4th issue). Multicoloured.

668 30c. Type **235** 60 60
669 30c. Netball 60 60
670 50c. Cricket 80 80
671 50c. Rugby 80 80

236 False Gharial

1997. Stamp Week '97. Endangered Wildlife. Sheet 165 × 75 mm, containing T **236** and similar multicoloured designs.

MS672 20c. Type **236**; 30c. Western tarsier (vert); 50c. Indian sambar (vert); $2 Crested wood partridge; $2 Malayan bony-tongue (fish) 2·50 3·25

1997. "INDEPEX '97" International Stamp Exhibition, New Delhi. As No. **MS**665, but with exhibition logo added to the sheet margin, in gold, at bottom right.

MS673 120 × 70 mm. 20c. Type **233**; 30c. 1997 Highlands Bird set; 50c. 1996 Wildlife miniature sheet seen through magnifying glass; $1 1867 cover to Amoy . . . . 1·25 2·00

237 Kundang

1998. Fruit. Multicoloured.

674 20c. Type **237** 15 10
675 30c. Sentul 20 10
676 50c. Pulasan 30 25
677 $1 Asam gelugur . . . . . . 70 1·60

238 Swimming Complex

1998. 16th Commonwealth Games, Kuala Lumpur (5th issue). Venues. Sheet 120 × 80 mm, containing T **238** and similar horiz designs. Multicoloured.

MS678 20c. Type **238**; 30c. Hockey Stadium; 50c. Indoor Stadium; $1 Main Stadium . . . . 1·25 2·00

239 Mas (coin) from Trengganu, 1793–1808

1998. Gold coins. Multicoloured.

679 20c. Type **239** 20 10
680 30c. Kupang from Kedah, 1661–1687 . . . . 25 10
681 50c. Kupang from Johore, 1597–1615 . . . . 45 35
682 $1 Kupang from Kelantan, 1400–1780 . . . . 60 1·50

240 Red Crescent Ambulance Boat and Emblem

1998. 50th Anniv of Malaysian Red Crescent Society. Multicoloured.

683 30c. Type **240** 25 10
684 $1 Ambulance and casualty 85 1·40

241 Transit Train and Boeing 747-400 at Airport

1998. Opening of Kuala Lumpur International Airport. Designs showing control tower. Mult.

685 30c. Type **241** 45 10
686 50c. Airport Terminals . . . 65 40
687 $1 Airliner in flight . . . . . 1·25 1·75
MS688 119 × 70 mm. $2 Globe and control tower (22 × 32 mm) . . 2·00 2·50

242 "Solanum torvum"

243 Weightlifting

1998. Medicinal Plants. Multicoloured.

689 20c. Type **242** 15 10
690 30c. "Tinospora crispa" . . . 20 10
691 50c. "Jatropha podagrica" . . 35 30
692 $1 "Hibiscus rosa-sinensis" 65 1·40

1998. 16th Commonwealth Games, Kuala Lumpur, Malaysia (5th issue). Sports. Multicoloured.

693 20c. Type **243** 25 40
694 20c. Badminton 25 40
695 20c. Netball 25 40
696 20c. Shooting 25 40
697 30c. Men's hockey 35 45
698 30c. Women's hockey 35 45
699 30c. Cycling 35 45
700 30c. Bowls 35 45
701 50c. Gymnastics 35 45
702 50c. Cricket 35 45
703 50c. Rugby 35 45
704 50c. Running 35 45
705 $1 Swimming 35 55
706 $1 Squash 35 55
707 $1 Boxing 35 55
708 $1 Ten-pin bowling 35 55

244 L.R.T. "Putra" Type Train

1998. Modern Kuala Lumpur Rail Transport. Multicoloured.

709b 30c. Type **244** 50 15
710b 50c. L.R.T. "Star" type train 35 25
711 $1 K.T.M. commuter train 40 1·25

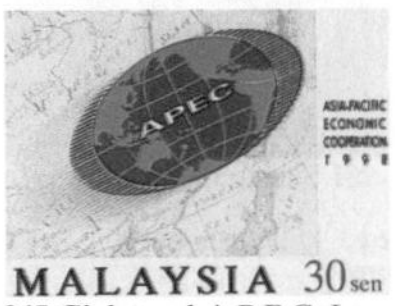
245 Globe and A.P.E.C. Logo

1998. Asia–Pacific Econmic Co-operation Conf. Multicoloured.

712b 30c. Type **245** 30 10
713 $1 Business meeting and computer office . . . . . 40 1·00

246 "Xylotrupes gideon"

247 Nural Hudda (Women's Air Rifle Shooting)

1998. Stamp Week '98. Malaysian Insects. Sheet 165 × 75 mm, containing T **246** and similar multicoloured designs.

MS714 20c. Type **246**; 30c. "Pomponia imperatoria"; 50c. "Phyllium pulchrifolium"; $2 "Hymenopus coronatus" (43 × 27 mm); $2 "Macrolyristes corporalis" (43 × 27 mm) . . . 2·25 3·00

1998. 16th Commonwealth Games, Kuala Lumpur (7th issue). Malaysian Gold Medal Winners. Two miniature sheets, each 160 × 125 mm, containing multicoloured designs as T **247**.

MS715 $2 Malaysian badminton team celebrating (128 × 80 mm) 2·75 3·25
MS716 30c. Type **247**; 30c. Sapok Biki (48kg Boxing); 30c. G. Saravanan (50km Walk); 30c. Muhamad Hidayat Hamidon (69kg Weightlifting); 50c. Kenny Ang and Ben Heng (Tenpin Bowling Men's Doubles); 50c. Kenny Ang (Tenpin Bowling Men's Singles); 50c. Choong Tan Fook and Lee Wan Wah (Badminton Men's Doubles); 50c. Wong Choon Hann (Badminton Men's Singles); $1 Women's Rhythmic Gymnastics team (63 × 26 mm) . . . . 6·00 7·50

248 Profile of Elderly Couple, World Map and Emblem

1999. International Year of the Older Person. Multicoloured.

717 $1 Type **248** 50 90
718 $1 Four silhouettes of elderly people, world map and emblem 50 90

249 "Syzygium malaccense"

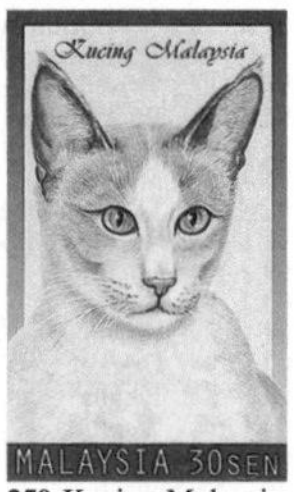

250 Kucing Malaysia Cat

1999. Rare Fruits of Malaysia. Multicoloured.

719	20c. Type **249**	20	15
720	30c. "Garcinia prainiana"	25	15
721	50c. "Mangifera caesia"	30	25
722	$1 "Salacca glabrescens"	60	1·00

1999. Malaysian Cats. Multicoloured.

727	30c. Type **250**	30	15
728	50c. Siamese	45	35
729	$1 Abyssinian	80	1·25
MS730	Two sheets, each 81 × 90 mm. (a) $1 British shorthair; $1 Scottish fold. (B) $1 Birman; $1 Persian Set of 2 sheets	2·00	2·50

251 Sumatran Rhinoceros

1999. Protected Mammals of Malaysia (1st series). Multicoloured.

731	20c. Type **251**	50	15
732	30c. Panther	20	15
733	50c. Sun bear	25	25
734	$1 Indian elephant	65	90
739	$2 Orang-utan	1·50	2·00
MS740	119 × 80 mm. $2 No. 739	1·50	2·00

See also Nos. 923/31.

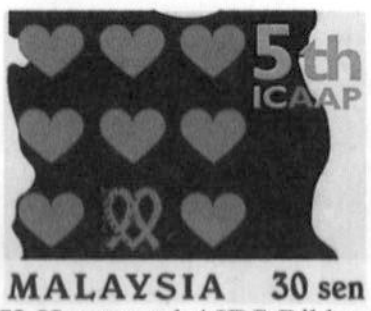

252 Hearts and AIDS Ribbons

1999. 5th International Conference on AIDS in Asia and the Pacific. Each red, blue and black.

741	30c. Type **252**	25	15
742	50c. Fragmenting and stylized AIDS ribbons	45	40
743	$1 Two AIDS ribbons	75	1·25

253 P. Ramlee in Traditional Dress

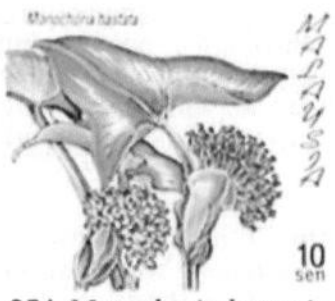

254 *Monochoria hastoria* (water plant)

1999. 70th Birth Anniv of P. Ramlee (actor and film director) Commemoration. (a) Multicoloured.

744	20c. Type **253**	45	15
745	30c. Receiving an award	55	15
746	50c. Playing part of soldier in film	75	45
747	$1 Using film camera	1·25	1·40
MS748a	Two sheets, each 100 × 70 mm. (a) $1 Wearing check shirt. (b) $1 In traditional dress Set of 2 sheets	14·00	14·00

(b) Each brown, light brown and black.

749	30c. In traditional dress	70	75
750	30c. With hands raised	70	75
751	30c. Singing into microphone	70	75
752	30c. Wearing army uniform	70	75

1999. Freshwater Fishes of Malaysia. Mult.

753	10c. Type **254**	20	30
754	10c. *Trichopsis vittatus*	20	30
755	15c. *Limnocharis flava* (water plant)	25	35
756	15c. *Betta imbellis*	25	35
757	25c. *Nymphaea pubescens* (water plant)	30	40
758	25c. *Trichogaster trichopterus*	30	40
759	50c. *Eichhornia crassipes* (water plant)	40	50
760	50c. *Sphaerichthys osphromenoides*	40	50
761	50c. *Ipomea aquatica* (water plant)	40	50
762	50c. *Helostoma temmincki*	40	50

No. 760 is inscribed "Sphaerichthys osphronemodies" in error.

255 *Lagerstroemia floribunda* (tree)

256 Petronas Twin Towers, Kuala Lumpur

1999. Trees of Malaysia. Multicoloured.

763	30c. Type **255**	60	60
764	30c. *Elateriospermum tapos*	60	60
765	30c. *Dryobalanops aromatica*	60	60
766	30c. *Alstonia angustiloba*	60	60
767	30c. *Fagraea fragrans*	60	60

1999. Completion of Petronas Twin Towers Building, Kuala Lumpur. Multicoloured (except 50c.).

768	30c. Type **256**	35	15
769	50c. Construction sketches (blue, violet and black)	45	35
770	$1 Twin Towers at night	80	1·00
MS771	100 × 75 mm. $5 Hologram of Twin Towers (30 × 50 mm)	3·50	3·75

257 Peace Hotel and Rickshaw

1999. 125th Anniv of Taiping, Perak. Mult.

772	20c. Type **257**	20	15
773	30c. Town Hall and 1930s car	20	15
774	50c. Railway Station	50	45
775	$1 Airport	1·00	1·25
MS776	120 × 69 mm. $2 Perak Museum and horse-drawn carriage	3·25	3·50

258 Power Station at Night

1999. 50th Anniv of Tenaga Nasional Berhad (electricity generating company). Multicoloured.

777	30c. Type **258**	25	15
778	50c. Control room and pylon	35	25
779	$1 Kuala Lumpur skyline at night	70	1·00
MS780	Two sheets, each 69 × 99 mm. (a) $1 Electric cart. (b) $1 Pylon Set of 2 sheets	1·25	1·75

259 New National Theatre and Traditional Characters

1999. Opening of New National Theatre, Kuala Lumpur. Multicoloured.

781	30c. Type **259**	25	15
782	50c. New National Theatre and horseman	40	30
783	$1 New National Theatre and traditional musician	75	1·00

260 New Yang di-Pertuan Agong and Malaysian Flag

1999. Installation of Sultan Salahuddin Abdul Aziz Shah of Selangor as Yang di-Pertuan Agong. (a) Horiz designs as T **260**. Multicoloured.

784	30c. Type **260**	20	15
785	50c. Yang di-Pertuan Agong and Palace	30	25
786	$1 Yang di-Pertuan Agong and Parliament Buildings	60	90

(b) Vert designs, 24 × 29 mm, showing portrait only.

787	(30c.) multicoloured (purple frame)	55	55
788	(30c.) multicoloured (yellow frame)	55	55
789	(30c.) multicoloured (blue frame)	55	55

Nos. 787/9 are inscribed "BAYARAN POS TEMPATAN HINGGA 20GM" and were valid on local mail weighing no more than 20 gm.

261 Motorway Junction outside Kuala Lumpur

1999. 21st World Road Congress, Kuala Lumpur. Mult.

790	30c. Type **261**	20	15
791	50c. Damansara Puchong Bridge at night	30	25
792	$1 Aerial view of motorway junction, Selatan	60	90

262 Driver's Helmet and Canopy Tower, Formula 1 Circuit, Sepang

1999. Malaysian Grand Prix, Sepang. Mult. (a) Designs including driver's helmet.

793	20c. Type **262**	25	15
794	30c. Central Grandstand	30	15
795	50c. Formula 1 racing car	45	35
796	$1 Formula 1 racing car from Red Bull team	70	90

(b) Scenes from Sepang Formula 1 Circuit.

797	20c. Canopy Tower and Central Grandstand	40	15
798	30c. Pit building	50	15
799	50c. Wheel-change in pits	65	50
800	$1 Race in progress	1·25	1·40

263 Sultan Haji Ahmad Shah and Flowers

1999. 25th Anniv of Installation of Sultan of Pahang. Multicoloured.

801	30c. Type **263**	35	40
802	30c. Butterfly and motorway	35	40
803	30c. Diver and beach	35	40
804	30c. Power station	35	40
805	30c. Mosque	35	40

264 World Cup

1999. World Cup Golf Championship, Mines Resort City. Multicoloured.

806	20c. Type **264**	25	10
807	30c. Emblem on golf ball	25	10
808	50c. Fairway	45	40
809	$1 First hole and club house	90	1·10

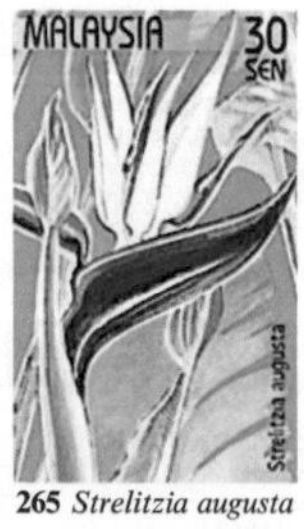

265 *Strelitzia augusta*

267 Fern, Pitcher Plant and Great Indian Hornbill

266 Letters and Computer Screen

1999. Stamp Week '99. Heliconias. Multicoloured.

814	30c. Type **265**	45	45
815	30c. *Heliconia rostrata*	45	45
816	30c. *Heliconia psittacorum* (yellow)	45	45
817	30c. *Heliconia stricta*	45	45
818	30c. *Musa violascens*	45	45
819	30c. *Strelitzia reginae*	45	45
820	30c. *Heliconia colganta*	45	45
821	30c. *Heliconia psittacorum* (white and pink)	45	45
822	30c. *Heliconia latispatha*	45	45
823	30c. *Phaeomeria speciosa*	45	45
MS824	198 × 136 mm. Nos. 814/23	4·00	4·25

1999. 125th Anniv of Universal Postal Union. Mult.

825	20c. Type **266**	20	10
826	30c. Globe and Malaysian stamps	25	10
827	50c. World map and mail plane	50	40
828	$1 POS Malaysia emblem	80	1·10

1999. New Millennium (1st issue). Land and History. Multicoloured (except No. **MS**839).

829	30c. Type **267**	45	45
830	30c. Ceramic pots and Mt. Kinabalu	45	45
831	30c. Frog and tualang (tree)	45	45
832	30c. Rolling rubber and palm trees	45	45
833	30c. Angelfish and sailing barge	45	45
834	30c. Mousedeer and traditional Malay building	45	45
835	30c. Ruler on elephant and Straits of Malacca	45	45
836	30c. Malay kris (sword) and junks	45	45
837	30c. Clock Tower, Kuala Lumpur, and A Famosa ruins	45	45
838	30c. Sailing boat and palm trees	45	45
MS839	120 × 80 mm. $1 Traditional Malay sailing ship (horiz) (black and red)	1·75	1·90

2000. New Millennium (2nd issue). People and Achievements. As T **267**. Multicoloured.

840	30c. Iban playing sape and traditional costumes from East Malaysia	40	45
841	30c. Hurricane lamp, shell and couple from fishing village	40	45
842	30c. Doctor with patient and toddler with mother	40	45
843	30c. Badminton player and young Malaysians	40	45
844	30c. Man with kite and traditional dancers	40	45
845	30c. Motor cycle, car and motorway	40	45
846	30c. Butterfly, Sepang motor racing circuit and airport	40	45
847	30c. High speed train and Kuala Lumpur skyline	40	45
848	30c. Computer operator and mosque	40	45
849	30c. Lorry and container port	40	45
MS850	120 × 80 mm. $1 Modern airliner (horiz)	1·75	1·90

268 Pottery Vase (New Stone Age)

2000. Chinese New Year ("Year of the Dragon"). Artefacts and Fish. Multicoloured.

851	30c. Type **268**	35	40
852	30c. Dragon eaves tile (Western Han Dynasty)	35	40
853	30c. Bronze knocker base (Tang Dynasty)	35	40
854	30c. Jade sword pommel (Western Han Dynasty)	35	40
855	30c. Dragon statue (Tang Dynasty)	35	40
856	30c. Arawana (*Osteoglossum bicirrhosum*)	35	40
857	30c. Spotted barramundi (*Scleropages leichardti*)	35	40
858	30c. Asian bonytongue (red) (Scleropages formosus)	35	40

859 30c. Black arawana (*Osteoglossum ferrerirai*) . . . 35 40
860 30c. Asian bonytongue (gold) (*Scleropages formosus*) . . 35 40
MS861 Two sheets, each 120 × 65 mm. (a) $1 Dragon dance (square). (b) $1 Dragon boat (square) Set of 2 sheets . . . . 1·75 2·25

269 Table Tennis Bats and Globe

2000. World Table Tennis Championships, Bukit Jalil. Multicoloured.
862 30c. Type **269** 20 10
863 50c. Mascot and logo 35 25
864 $1 Table tennis bats and ball 60 90
MS865 100 × 70 mm. $1 Mascot and table tennis table; $1 Bats and table tennis table . . . . . . 1·00 1·50

270 Malaysian Climbers on Mt. Everest

2000. New Millennium (3rd issue). Malaysian Triumphs. Two sheets, each 120 × 80 mm, containing T **270** and similar vert designs. Multicoloured.
MS866 (a) 50c. Type **270**; 50c. Hikers; 50c. Arctic expedition and Proton car. (B) 50c. Solo yachtsman Set of 2 sheets . . . 1·75 2·25

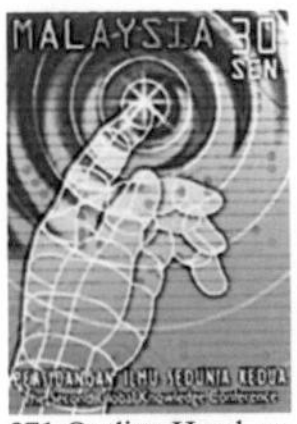

271 Outline Hand on Button

272 Internal Inverted Dome

2000. 2nd Global Knowledge Conference, Kuala Lumpur. Multicoloured.
867 30c. Type **271** 45 50
868 30c. Outline globe 45 50
869 50c. Woman's silhouette . . 65 70
870 50c. Man's silhouette 65 70

2000. Islamic Arts Museum, Kuala Lumpur. Mult.
871 20c. Type **272** 40 15
872 30c. Main dome of Museum 45 15
873 50c. Ottoman panel 65 45
874 $1 Ornate Mihrab . . . . . 1·25 1·50

273 Buatan Barat Prahu

274 Unit Trust Emblem and Women with Flags

2000. Traditional Malaysian Prahus (canoes). Mult.
875 30c. Type **273** 40 50
876 30c. Payang prahu (red and blue hull) 40 50
877 30c. Payang prahu (red, white and green hull) 40 50
878 30c. Burung prahu 40 50

2000. Unit Trust Week. Multicoloured.
879 30c. Type **274** 30 10
880 50c. City skyline and Malaysians in traditional costume 45 35
881 $1 Map of South East Asia and Malaysians in traditional costume . . . . 1·00 1·25

275 Badminton Player and Cup Logo

2000. Thomas Cup Badminton Championships, Bukit Jalil. Multicoloured.
882 30c. Type **275** 40 50
883 30c. Thomas Cup and flags 40 50
884 30c. Championship logo and mascot 40 50
885 30c. Uber Cup and flags . . 40 50
886 30c. Badminton player and mascot 40 50
MS887 120 × 80 mm. $1 Thomas Cup (vert) . . . . 1·50 1·60

276 Children playing Ting Ting

2000. Children's Traditional Games (1st series). Multicoloured.
888 30c. Type **276** 70 70
889 30c. Tarik Upih 70 70
890 30c. Kite flying 70 70
891 30c. Marbles 70 70
892 30c. Bicycle rim racing . . . 70 70

277 Aspects of Computer Technology

2000. 27th Islamic Foreign Ministers' Conference, Kuala Lumpur. Multicoloured.
898 30c. Type **277** 35 45
899 30c. Traditonal Islamic scrollwork 35 45
900 30c. Conference logo 35 45
901 30c. Early coin 35 45
902 30c. Pens and satellite photograph 35 45

278 Malaysian Family on Map

2000. Population and Housing Census. Mult.
903 30c. Type **278** 35 45
904 30c. Symbolic house 35 45
905 30c. People on pie-chart . . . 35 45
906 30c. Diplomas and workers 35 45
907 30c. Male and female symbols 35 45

279 Rothchild's Peacock-pheasant

2000. Pheasants and Partridges. Multicoloured.
908 20c. Type **279** 30 10
909 30c. Crested argus (female) 35 10
910 50c. Great argus pheasant . . 55 40
911 $1 Crestless fireback pheasant 1·00 1·25
MS912 100 × 40 mm. $2 Crested argus (male) (31 × 26mm) . . . 1·75 2·25

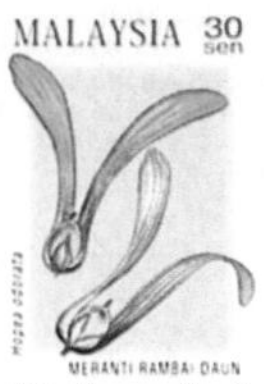

280 *Hopea odorata* (fruit)

282 Otter Civet

281 Institute in 1901, *Brugia malayi* and Beri-Beri

2000. International Union of Forestry Research Organisations Conference, Kuala Lumpur. Mult.
913 30c. Type **280** 60 60
914 30c. *Adenanthera pavonina* (seeds) 60 60
915 30c. *Shorea macrophylla* (seeds) 60 60
916 30c. *Dyera costulata* (fruits) 60 60
917 30c. *Alstonia angustiloba* (seeds) 60 60
MS918 Four sheets, each 92 × 71 mm. (a) Trees. 10c. *Fagraea fragrans*; 10c. *Dryobalanops aromatica*; 10c. *Terminalia catappa*; 10c. *Samanea saman*; 10c. *Dracontomelon dao*. (b) Leaves. 15c. *Heritiera javanica*; 15c. *Johannes-teijsmannia altifrons*; 15c. *Macaranga gigantea*; 15c. *Licuala grandis*; 15c. *Endospermum diadenum*. (c). Bark. 25c. *Pterocymbium javanicum*; 25c. *Dryobalanops aromatica*; 25c. *Dipterocarpus costulatus*; 25c. *Shorea leprosula*; 25c. *Ochanostachys amentacea*. (d) Forest fauna. 50c. Indian flycatcher; 50c. Slow loris; 50c. Marbled cat; 50c. Common carp; 50c. Pit viper Set of 4 sheets 5·00 5·50
No. MS918 contains four sheets each of five 18 × 22 mm designs, and a label showing the Conference logo.

2000. Centenary of Institute for Medical Research. Multicoloured.
919 30c. Type **281** 40 10
920 50c. Institute in 1953, bacteria and mosquito . . 65 50
921 $1 Institute in 1976, chromatogram and Eurycoma longifolia . . . 1·25 1·50
MS922 120 × 65 mm. $2 DNA molecule . . . . 2·00 2·25

2000. Protected Mammals of Malaysia (2nd series). Multicoloured.
923 20c. Type **282** 40 15
924 30c. Young otter civet . . . 45 50
927 30c. Hose's palm civet (*Hemigalus hosei*) 45 50
928 30c. Common palm civet (*Paradoxurus hermaphroditus*) 45 50
929 30c. Masked palm civet (Paguma larvata) 45 50
930 30c. Malay civet (Viverra tangalunga) 45 50
931 30c. Three-striped palm civet (*Arctogalidia trivirgata*) . . 45 50
925 50c. Binturong on bank . . . 65 45
926 $1 Head of binturong . . . . 1·25 1·40
MS932 140 × 80 mm. $1 Banded palm civet; $1 Banded linsang 2·00 2·25

283 Cogwheels

2000. 50th Anniv of RIDA-MARA (Rural and Industrial Development Authority – Council for Indigenous People). Multicoloured.
933 30c. Type **283** 30 10
934 50c. Compasses and stethoscope 45 40
935 $1 Computer disk, book and mouse . . . . 85 1·10

2000. Children's Traditional Games (2nd series). As T **276**. Multicoloured.
936 20c. Bailing tin 35 40
937 20c. Top-spinning 35 40
938 30c. Sepak Raga 50 60
939 30c. Letup-Letup 50 60

284 Cyclist and Pedestrians

285 *Rhododendron brookeanum*

2000. World Heart Day. Multicoloured.
940 30c. Type **284** 45 50
941 30c. Family at play 45 50
942 30c. Kite flying, football and no smoking sign 45 50
943 30c. Keep fit class 45 50
944 30c. Farmer, animals and food 45 50
Nos. 940/4 were printed together, se-tenant, with the backgrounds forming a composite design.

2000. Stamp Week 2000. Highland Flowers (2nd series). Multicoloured.
945 30c. Type **285** 30 35
946 30c. *Rhododendron jasminiflorum* 30 35
947 30c. *Rhododendron scortechinii* 30 35
948 30c. *Rhododendron pauciflorum* 30 35
949 30c. *Rhododendron crassifolium* 30 35
950 30c. *Rhododendron longiflorum* 30 35
951 30c. *Rhododendron javanicum* 30 35
952 30c. *Rhododendron variolosum* 30 35
953 30c. *Rhododendron acuminatum* 30 35
954 30c. *Rhododendron praetervisum* 30 35
955 30c. *Rhododendron himantodes* 30 35
956 30c. *Rhododendron maxwellii* 30 35
957 30c. *Rhododendron erocoides* 30 35
958 30c. *Rhododendron fallacinum* 30 35
MS959 55 × 90 mm. $1 *Rhododendron malayanum* . . . 1·00 1·25
No. 955 is inscribed "Rhodadendron", No. 957 "Ericoides", both in error.

286 *Neurobasis c. chinensis*

2000. Dragonflies and Damselflies. Multicoloured.
960 30c. Type **286** 30 35
961 30c. *Aristocypha fenestrella* (blue markings on tail) . . 30 35
962 30c. *Vestalis gracilis* 30 35
963 30c. *Nannophya pymaea* . . . 30 35
964 30c. *Aristocypha fenestrella* (white markings on tail) . . 30 35
965 30c. *Rhyothemis p. phyllis* . . 30 35
966 30c. *Crocothemis s. servilia* 30 35
967 30c. *Euphaea ochracea* (male) 30 35
968 30c. *Euphaea ochracea* (female) 30 35
969 30c. *Ceriagrion cerinorubellum* 30 35
970 (30c.) *Vestalis gracilis* 30 35
971 (30c.) *Crocothemis s. servilia* (male) 30 35
972 (30c.) *Trithemis aurora* . . . 30 35
973 (30c.) *Pseudothemis jorina* . . 30 35
974 (30c.) *Diplacodes nebulosa* . . 30 35
975 (30c.) *Crocothemis s. servilia* (female) 30 35
976 (30c.) *Neurobasis c. chinensis* (male) 30 35
977 (30c.) *Burmagomphus divaricatus* 30 35
978 (30c.) *Ictinogomphus d. melaenops* 30 35
979 (30c.) *Orthetrum testaceum* 30 35
980 (30c.) *Trithemis festiva* . . . 30 35
981 (30c.) *Brachythemis contaminata* 30 35
982 (30c.) *Neurobasis c. chinensis* (female) 30 35
983 (30c.) *Neurothemis fluctuans* 30 35
984 (30c.) *Acisoma panorpoides* 30 35
985 (30c.) *Orthetrum s. sabina* . . 30 35
986 (30c.) *Rhyothemis p. phyllis* 30 35
987 (30c.) *Rhyothemis obsolescens* 30 35
988 (30c.) *Neurothemis t. tulia* . . 30 35
989 (30c.) *Lathrecista a. asiatica* 30 35
990 (30c.) *Aethriamanta gracilis* 30 35
991 (30c.) *Diplacodes trivialis* . . 30 35
992 (30c.) *Neurothemis fulvia* . . 30 35
993 (30c.) *Rhyothemis triangularis* 30 35
994 (30c.) *Orthetrum glaucum* . . 30 35
Nos. 960/9 were issued togetther, se-tenant, and show the backgrounds forming a composite design.
Nos. 970/94 are inscribed "Bayaran Pos Tempatan Hingga 20gm". They were valid at 30c. for local mail up to 20 g.

287 Indian Blue Quail

2001. Quails and Partridges. Multicoloured.
995 30c. Type **287** 50 10
996 50c. Sumatran hill partridge 70 50
997 $1 Bustard quail . . . . . . 1·25 1·50
MS998 100 × 170 mm. $2 Chestnut-breasted tree partridge; $2 Crimson-headed wood partridge 3·00 3·00

288 Federal Government Administrative Centre

2001. Formation of Putrajaya Federal Territory. Multicoloured.
999 30c. Type **288** 35 10
1000 $1 Government buildings and motorway bridge . . 1·40 1·60

289 Sabah and Sarawak Beadwork

2001. Sabah and Sarawak Beadwork. Mult, background colours given.
1001 **289** 30c. green 40 50
1002 – 30c. blue 40 50
1003 – 30c. buff 40 50
1004 – 30c. red 40 50
DESIGN: Nos 1001/4 Showing different styles of beadwork

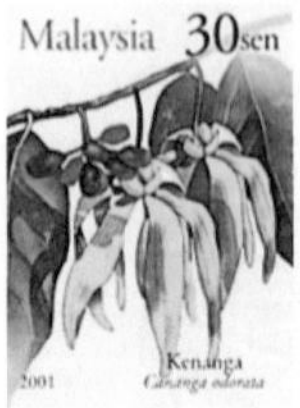

290 *Cananga odorata* **291** Raja Tuanku Syed Sirajuddin

2001. Scented Flowers. Multicoloured.
1005 30c. Type **290** 40 10
1006 50c. *Mimusops elengi* . . . 60 40
1007 $1 *Mesua ferrea* . . . . . . 1·10 1·50
MS1008 70 × 100mm. $2 *Muchelia champaca* . . . . 2·00 2·25

2001. Installation of Tuanku Syed Sirajuddin as Raja of Perlis.
1009 **291** 30c. multicoloured . . . 40 15
1010 50c. multicoloured . . . 60 40
1011 $1 multicoloured . . . . 1·10 1·50
MS1012 100 × 70 mm. $2 Raja Tuanku Syed Sirajuddin and Tengku Fauziah (horiz). Multicoloured . . . . 2·00 2·25

292 Beetlenut Leaf Arrangement

2001. Traditional Malaysian Artefacts. Mult.
1013 30c. Type **292** 35 40
1014 30c. Baby carrier 35 40
1015 50c. Quail trap 50 60
1016 50c. Ember container . . . 50 60

293 Perodua Kancil Car, 1995

2001. Malaysia-made Motor Vehicles. Mult.
1017 30c. Type **293** 45 50
1018 30c. Proton Tiara, 1995 . . 45 50
1019 30c. Perodua Rusa, 1995 . . 45 50
1020 30c. Proton Putra, 1997 . . 45 50
1021 30c. Inokom Permas, 1999 45 50
1022 30c. Perodua Kembara, 1999 . . . . 45 50
1023 30c. Proton GTI, 2000 . . . 45 50
1024 30c. TD 2000, 2000 . . . . 45 50
1025 30c. Perodua Kenari, 2000 45 50
1026 30c. Proton Waja, 2000 . . 45 50

294 Serama Bantam Cock **295** Diving

2001. Malaysian Bantams. Multicoloured.
1027 30c. Type **294** 45 15
1028 50c. Kapan bantam cock . . 65 45
1029 $1 Serama bantam hen . . . 1·25 1·50
MS1030 98 × 70 mm. $3 Red junglefowl hens and chicks (44 × 34 mm) . . . . 3·00 3·50

2001. 21st South East Asian Games, Kuala Lumpur. Mult.
1031 20c. Type **295** 25 10
1032 30c. Rhythmic gymnastics 30 15
1033 50c. Bowling 40 25
1034 $1 Weightlifting 75 65
1035 $2 Cycling . . . . 1·75 2·00
MS1036 110 × 90 mm. $5 Running 3·50 4·00

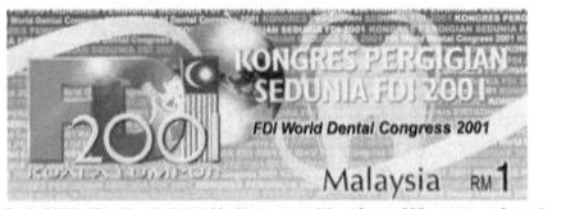

296 "F.D.I. 2001" Logo (½-size illustration)

2001. "F.D.I. 2001" World Dental Congress, Kuala Lumpur.
1037 **296** $1 multicoloured . . . . 1·00 1·25

297 K.W.S.P. Headquarters, Kuala Lumpur

2001. 50th Anniv of Employees' Provident Fund ("Kumpulan Wang Simpanan Pekerja"). Mult.
1038 30c. Type **297** 30 15
1039 50c. Column chart on coins and banknotes 45 40
1040 $1 Couple with K.W.S.P. logo . . . . 90 1·25

298 Satellite and Rainforest in Shape of Malaya Peninsula

2001. Centenary of Peninsular Malaysia Forestry Department. Multicoloured.
1041 30c. Type **298** 45 15
1042 50c. Cross-section through forest and soil 65 50
1043 $1 Newly-planted forest . . 1·25 1·75

299 *Tridacna gigas* (clam)

2001. Stamp Week. Endangered Marine Life. Multicoloured.
1044 20c. Type **299** 35 10
1045 30c. *Hippocampus sp.* (seahorse) 45 15
1046 50c. *Oreaster occidentalis* (starfish) 65 50
1047 $1 *Cassis cornu* (shell) . . . 1·25 1·75
MS1048 100 × 70 mm. $3 Dugong 2·50 2·75

300 Hockey Player in Orange **301** *Couroupita guianensis*

2002. 10th Hockey World Cup, Kuala Lumpur. Multicoloured.
1049 30c. Type **300** 40 15
1050 50c. Goalkeeper 60 50
1051 $1 Hockey player in yellow 1·25 1·25
MS1052 100 × 70 mm. $3 Hockey player in blue (30 × 40 mm) . . 2·25 2·25

2002. Malaysia–China Joint Issue. Rare Flowers. Multicoloured.
1053 30c. Type **301** 30 10
1054 $1 *Couroupita guianensis* . . 80 90
1055 $1 *Camellia nitidissima* . . . 80 90
MS1056 108 × 79 mm. $2 *Schima brevifolia* buds (horiz); $2 *Schima brevifolia* blossom . . . . . . 2·25 2·50

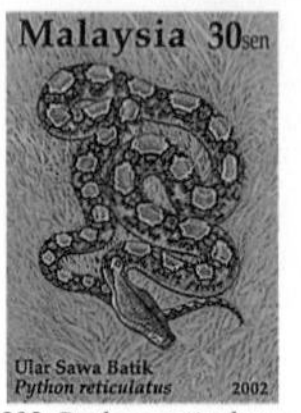

302 *Python reticulatus* **304** *Paraphalaenopsis labukensis*

303 Stesen Sentral Station, Kuala Lumpur

2002. Malaysian Snakes. Multicoloured.
1057 30c. Type **302** 50 20
1058 30c. *Gonyophis margaritatus* 50 20
1059 50c. *Bungarus candidus* . . . 75 50
1060 $1 *Maticora bivirgata* . . . 1·40 1·60
MS1061 108 × 78 mm. $2 *Ophiophagus hannah* (head of adult); $2 *Ophiophagus hannah* (juvenile) . . . . 3·00 3·00

2002. Express Rail Link from Central Kuala Lumpur to International Airport. Multicoloured.
1062 30c. Type **303** 65 20
1063 50c. Train and Central Station . . . . 1·10 1·25
1064 50c. Train and International Airport . . . . 1·10 1·25
MS1065 Two sheets, each 106 × 76 mm. (a) $1 KLIA Express and high speed train; $1 Express and local trains. (b) $2 KLIA Express Set of 2 sheets . . . . 4·00 4·50

2002. 17th World Orchid Conference. Multicoloured.
1066 30c. Type **304** 40 50
1067 30c. *Renanthera bella* . . . 40 50
1068 50c. *Paphiopedilum sanderianum* 75 25
1069 $1 *Coelogyne pandurata* . . 1·10 1·25
1070 $1 *Phalaenopsis amabilis* . . 1·10 1·25
MS1071 76 × 105 mm. $5 *Cleisocentron merillianum* (45 × 40 mm) . . . . 4·50 5·00

305 Raja Tuanku Syed Sirajuddin of Perlis **307** White-bellied Woodpecker (*Dryocopus javensis*)

306 *Cryptocoryne purpurea*

2002. Installation of Raja Tuanku Syed Sirajuddin as Yang di-Pertuan Agong.
1072 **305** 30c. multicoloured . . . 45 10
1073 50c. multicoloured . . . 65 40
1074 $1 multicoloured . . . . 1·25 1·40

2002. Aquatic Plants. Multicoloured.
1075 30c. Type **306** 45 10
1076 50c. *Barclaya kunstleri* . . . 65 25
1077 $1 *Neptunia oleracea* . . . . 1·25 1·40
1078 $1 *Monochoria hastata* . . . 1·25 1·40
MS1079 110 × 80 mm. $1 *Eichhornia crassipes* (vert); $2 *Nymphaea pubescens* . . . . 3·75 4·00

2002. Malaysia–Singapore Joint Issue. Birds. Multicoloured.
1080 30c. Type **307** 55 65
1081 30c. Black-naped oriole (*Oriolus chinensis*) 55 65
1082 $1 Red-throated sunbird (*Anthreptes rhodolaema*) 1·40 1·50
1083 $1 Asian fairy bluebird (*Irena puella*) . . . . . . 1·40 1·50
MS1084 99 × 70 mm. $5 Orange-bellied flowerpecker (*Dicaeum trigonostigma*) (60 × 40 mm) . . 4·50 5·00
Stamps with similar designs were issued by Singapore.

308 Sibu Island, Johore

2002. Tourist Beaches (1st series). Multicoloured.
1085 30c. Type **308** 50 50
1086 30c. Perhentian Islands, Trengganu 50 50
1087 50c. Manukan Island, Sabah 65 65
1088 50c. Tioman Island, Pahang 65 65
1089 $1 Singa Besar Island, Kedah . . . . 1·10 1·25
1090 $1 Pangkor Island, Perak 1·10 1·25
MS1091 110 × 80 mm. $1 Ferringhi Bay, Penang; $1 Port Dickson, Negri Sembilan . . . . 2·25 2·75
See also Nos. 1143/**MS**1153.

309 Ethnic Musicians and Dancers

2002. Malaysian Unity. Multicoloured.
1092 30c. Type **309** 40 40
1093 30c. Children playing mancala (game) 40 40
1094 50c. Children from different races (82 × 30 mm) 70 70
MS1095 68 × 99 mm. $1 Children playing tug-of-war . . . . . . 1·40 1·60

310 Zainal Abidin bin Ahmad ("Za'ba") as a Student

2002. 30th Death Anniv of Zainal Abidin bin Ahmad ("Za'ba") (2003) (scholar). Multicoloured.
1096 30c. Type **310** 40 10
1097 50c. Za'ba with typewriter 65 75
1098 50c. Za'ba and traditional Malay building 65 75
MS1099 100 × 70 mm. $1 Za'ba at desk (vert) . . . . 1·40 1·60

311 Green Kebaya, Nyonya **313** Leopard Cat with Kittens

312 Suluh Budiman Building, Sultan Idris University of Education

2002. The Kebaya Nyonya (traditional Malay women's blouse). Multicoloured.

1100 30c. Type **311** 45 30
1101 30c. Red kebaya nyonya . . 45 30
1102 50c. Yellow kebaya nyonya 75 75
1103 50c. Pink kebaya nyonya . . 75 75
MS1104 70 × 100 mm. $2 Kebaya nyonya and sarong (34 × 69 mm) 1·90 2·25

2002. 80th Anniv of Sultan Idris University of Education. Multicoloured.

1105 30c. Type **312** 45 10
1106 50c. Tadahan Selatan Building 65 75
1107 50c. Chancellery Building 65 75

No. 1107 is inscribed "Chancellory" in error.

2002. Stamp Week. Wild and Domesticated Animals. Multicoloured.

1108 30c. Type **313** 50 50
1109 30c. Domestic cat and kittens 50 50
1110 $1 Lesser sulphur-crested cockatoo . . . . 1·40 1·40
1111 $1 Malay fish owl . . . . . 1·40 1·40
MS1112 Two sheets, each 105 × 76 mm. (a) $1 Goldfish (horiz). $1 Porcupinefish (horiz); (b) $1 Giant squirrel; $1 Domestic rabbit with young Set of 2 sheets 3·25 3·50

314 Southern Serow

2003. Southern Serow. Multicoloured.

1113 30c. Type **314** 50 10
1114 50c. Southern serow lying down 75 80
1115 50c. Young southern serow 75 80

315 Peace Doves and Emblem

2003. 13th Conference of Heads of State or Government of the Non-Aligned Movement, Kuala Lumpur. Multicoloured.

1116 30c. Type **315** 35 35
1117 30c. Conference emblem in cupped hands 35 35
1118 50c. Emblem and outline map of Malaysia 65 70
1119 50c. "2003" with noughts containing Malaysian flag and emblem 65 70

Nos. 1116/17 and 1118/19 were each printed together, se-tenant, each pair forming a composite background design of a Malaysian flag and world map (Nos. 1116/17) or a globe (Nos. 1118/19).

316 Pale Pink Hybrid Tea Rose

2003. Roses in Malaysia. Multicoloured.

1120 30c. Type **316** 35 20
1121 30c. Red hybrid tea 35 20
1122 50c. Apricot hybrid tea . . 65 70
1123 50c. Pink and white striped floribunda 65 70
MS1124 70 × 100 mm. $1 Miniature floribunda (29 × 40 mm); $2 *Rosa centifolia* (29 × 81 mm) . . . . 1·75 2·00

317 Tunku Abdul Rahman **318** Sultan Sharafuddin Idris Shah

2003. Birth Centenary of Tunku Abdul Rahman (first Prime Minister of Federation of Malaya (1957–63) and of Malaysia (1963–70)). Multicoloured.

1125 30c. Type **317** 30 15
1126 50c. Tunku Abdul Rahman (different) 50 20
1127 $1 Tunku Abdul Rahman in ceremonial dress . . . . 85 1·00
1128 $1 Tunku Abdul Rahman wearing topi hat . . . . 85 1·00
MS1129 100 × 70 mm. $1 Tunku Abdul Rahman reading Proclamation of Independence, 1957 . . . . 1·00 1·25

2003. Coronation of Sultan of Selangor. Multicoloured.

1130 30c. Type **318** 35 15
1131 50c. Sultan in uniform . . . 55 30
1132 $1 Sultan of Selangor (wearing crown) . . . . . 1·00 1·10

319 Siamese Fighting Fish

2003. Siamese Fighting Fish (*Betta splendens*). Multicoloured.

1133 30c. Type **319** 35 15
1134 50c. Siamese Fighting fish (yellow) 55 20
1135 $1 Siamese Fighting fish (blue) . . . . 90 1·10
1136 $1 Siamese Fighting fish (red with fringed fins) . . 90 1·10
MS1137 99 × 70 mm. 50c. *Betta imbellis* (Local Fighting Fish) (33 × 28 mm); 50c. *Betta coccina* (Red Fighting Fish) (33 × 28 mm) 1·10 1·25

320 Christ Church Clock **321** Malaysian Flag and Sultan Tower, Malacca Abdul Samad Building, Kuala Lumpur

2003. Clock Towers. Multicoloured.

1138 30c. Type **320** 30 30
1139 30c. Jubilee Clock Tower, Penang 30 30
1140 30c. Sungai Petani Clock Tower, Jalan Ibrahim . . 30 30
1141 30c. Teluk Intan Clock Tower 30 30
1142 30c. Sarawak State Council Monument 30 30
MS1143 99 × 70 mm. $1 Sultan Abdul Samad Building; $1 Taiping Clock Tower, Perak . . . . . 1·75 2·00

2003. Islands and Beaches of Malaysia (2nd series). As T **308**. Multicoloured.

1149 30c. Aerial view of Ligitan Island 35 35
1150 30c. Outline map of Ligitan Island 35 35
1151 50c. Sipadan Island 55 60
1152 50c. Outline map of Sipadan Island 55 60
MS1153 70 × 100 mm. 50c. Aerial view of Sipadan Island (vert); 50c. Relief map of Ligitan Island (vert) 1·00 1·25

2003. 46th Independence Celebration.

1154 **321** 30c. multicoloured . . . 30 15
1155 – $1 multicoloured . . . . . 1·10 1·25
MS1156 70 × 100 mm. $1 black and grey . . . . 1·10 1·25

DESIGNS—59 × 40 mm No. 1155, Malaysian flag; No. **MS**1156, Independence delegation in motorcade, Malacca, 1956.

322 Modenas Jaguh 175

2003. Malaysian made Motorcycles and Scooters. Multicoloured.

1157 30c. Type **322** 30 15
1158 50c. Modenas Karisma 125 50 55
1159 50c. Modenas Kriss 1 . . . 50 55
1160 50c. Modenas Kriss 2 . . . 50 55
1161 50c. Modenas Kriss SG . . 50 55
MS1162 Four sheets, each 100 × 70 mm. (a) $1 Comel Turbulence RG125; $1 Comel Cyclone GP150. (b) $1 Demak Adventurer; $1 Demak Beetle. (c) $1 MZ 125SM; $1 MZ Perintis 120S Classic. (d) $1 Gagiva Momos 125R; $1 Nitro NE150 Windstar . . . . 3·75 4·25

323 Putrajaya Convention Centre

2003. 10th Session of Islamic Summit Conference, Putrajaya. Multicoloured.

1163 30c. Type **323** 30 30
1164 30c. Emblem 30 30
1165 50c. Putrajaya Mosque, modern Kuala Lumpur buildings and flag 50 50
1166 50c. Sultan Abdul Samad Building, Kuala Lumpur and Federal Government Administrative Centre, Putrajaya 50 50

Nos. 1165/6 were each printed together, se-tenant, forming a composite design.

2003. "Bangkok 2003" World Stamp Exhibition, Thailand. Nos. 1157/61 additionally inscr with "Bangkok" and exhibition logo.

1167 30c. Type **322** 30 15
1168 50c. Modenas Karisma 125 50 55
1169 50c. Modenas Kriss 1 . . . 50 55
1170 50c. Modenas Kriss 2 . . . 50 55
1171 50c. Modenas Kriss SG . . 50 55

324 Children in Circle and World Map

2003. 50th World Children's Day. Multicoloured.

1172 20c. Type **324** 20 10
1173 30c. Family outside their home 30 30
1174 30c. Girl flying kite and children with computer 30 30
1175 30c. "Sambutan 50 tahun Hari kanak-kanak Sedunia" in child's writing 30 30
1176 30c. Open book, house, Malaysian flag, rainbow, car and flower 30 30

Nos. 1173/4 were printed together, se-tenant, forming a composite design.

325 Red Leaf Monkey feeding **326** One Fathom Bank Lighthouse

2003. Stamp Week. Primates of Malaysia. Multicoloured.

1177 30c. Type **325** 30 30
1178 30c. Red leaf monkey sat on branch 30 30
1179 50c. Proboscis monkey . . . 50 50
1180 50c. Female proboscis monkey with baby . . . 50 50

2004. Lighthouses. Multicoloured.

1181 30c. Type **326** 40 40
1182 30c. Muka Head Lighthouse, Pulau Pinang 40 40
1183 30c. Pulau Undan Lighthouse, Melaka . . . 40 40
1184 30c. Althingsburg Lighthouse, Selangor . . 40 40
MS1185 70 × 100 mm. $1 Tanjung Tuan Lighthouse . . . . . . 1·50 1·50

327 Fauna at Seashore and in Forest

2004. 7th Conference of Convention on Biological Diversity and First Meeting of Cartagena Protocol on Biosafety. Multicoloured.

1186 30c. Type **327** 30 15
1187 50c. Conference logo . . . 50 50
1188 50c. DNA, leaf and test tube 50 50

328 Sultan of Kelantan

2004. Silver Jubilee of Sultan Ismail Petra Ibni Almarhum of Kelantan. Multicoloured.

1189 30c. Type **328** 30 15
1190 50c. Sultan and Istana Jahar, Museum of Royal Traditions and Customs 50 25
1191 $1 Sultan and Khota Bharu 90 1·10

329 Golf Ball, City Skyline and World Map

2004. 1st Commonwealth Tourism Ministers Meeting, Kuala Lumpur. Multicoloured.

1192 30c. Type **329** 40 20
1193 50c. World map and seashore 55 25
1194 $1 Logo and montage of images of Malaysia (vert) 90 1·10

330 Emblem **331** *Lanchara* (Malayan sailing ship)

2004. National Service Programme. Multicoloured.

1195 30s. Type **330** 10 15
1196 50s. Abseiling 15 20
1197 $1 Three youths with Malaysian flag 30 35
MS1198 70 × 100 mm. $2 Saluting 65 70

2004. 30th Anniv of Malaysia—China Diplomatic Relations. Multicoloured.

1199 30s. Type **331** 10 15
1200 30s. Chinese junk 10 15
1201 $1 Handshake and sailing ship 30 35
1202 $1 Sailing ship and flags of Malaysia and China . . . 30 35
MS1203 100 × 70 mm. $2 Niujie Mosque, Beijing and Kampung Hulu Mosque, Malacca (59 × 39 mm) 65 70

332 Banteng

2004. Wildlife in the Malaysian Forest. Multicoloured.

1204 30s. Type **332** 10 15
1205 30s. Gaur ("SELADANG") 10 15

1206	$1 Tiger	30	35
1207	$1 Indian elephant	30	35
MS1208	101 × 70 mm. $2 Malayan tapir (vert)	65	70

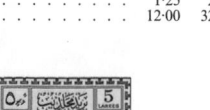

333 Multimedia Super Corridor Entrance

2004. Multimedia Super Corridor. Multicoloured.

1209	30s. Type **333**	10	15
1210	50s. Globe, binary code and Petronas Towers	15	20
1211	$1 ID card, computer terminals and brain linked to Multimedia Super Corridor	30	35
MS1212	70 × 100 mm. $2 Map of Multimedia Super Corridor	65	70

334 Johor

2004. Ports of Malaysia. Multicoloured.

1213	30c. Type **334**	10	15
1214	30c. Kota Kinabalu	10	15
1215	50c. Kuantan	15	20
1216	50c. Penang	15	20
1217	$1 Bintulu	30	35
MS1218	100 × 70 mm. $2 Northpor	65	70

335 Trishaw

2004. Traditional Transportation. Multicoloured.

1219	30s. Type **335**	10	15
1220	50s. Rickshaw	15	20
1221	$1 Padi horse	30	35
MS1222	100 × 70 mm. $2 Bullock cart (39 × 49 mm)	65	70

2004. World Stamp Championship, Singapore. As No. **MS**1203 but with exhibition logo and numbering added to the sheet margin.

MS1224	100 × 70 mm. $2 Niujie Mosque, Beijing and Kampung Hulu Mosque, Malacca (59 × 39 mm)	65	70

336 Long-tailed Macaque

2004. Centenary of Matang Mangroves, Perak. Multicoloured.

1225	30s. Type **336**	10	15
1226	30s. *Sonneratia ovata* (Mangrove apple) and moth	10	15
1227	$1 Fishing boat at jetty and cockle	30	35
1228	$1 Lesser adjutant stork and Brahminy kite	30	35
MS1229	100 × 69 mm. $2 Tall-stilted Mangrove	65	70

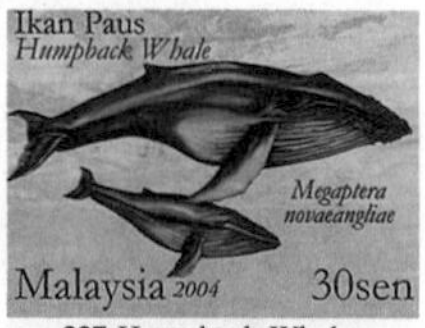

337 Humpback Whales

2004. Marine Life. Multicoloured.

1230	30s. Type **337**	10	15
1231	50s. Octopus	15	20
1232	$1 Bottlenose dolphins	30	35
MS1233	101 × 71 mm. $2 Thornback ray	65	70

338 Tongkat Ali

2004. Medicinal Plants. Multicoloured.

1234	30s. Type **338**	10	15
1235	50s. Kacip Fatimah	15	20
1236	$1 Kerdas	30	35
1237	$1 Buah Keras	30	35
MS1238	100 × 71 mm. $2 Mas Cotek	65	70

339 *Rhododendron stenophyllum*

2005. Rare Flowers. Multicoloured.

1239	30s. Type **339**	10	15
1240	30s. *Rhododendron nervulosum*	10	15
1241	50s. *Rhododendron rugosum*	15	20
1242	$1 *Rhododendron stapfianum*	30	35
MS1243	100 × 70 mm. $2 *Rhododendron lowii* (horiz)	65	70

340 Kuala Lumpur Skyline

2005. 5th Ministers Forum in the Asia Pacific. Multicoloured.

1244	30s. Type **340**	10	15
1245	50s. Putrajaya International Convention Centre and Parliament Building	30	35
1246	$1 Kuala Lumpur International Airport	30	35

341 Crested Honey Buzzard

2005. Migratory Birds. Multicoloured.

1247	30s. Type **341**	10	15
1248	50s. Purple heron	15	20
1249	$1 Lesser Crested tern	30	35
MS1250	70 × 100 mm. $2 Dunlin	65	70

342 Proton Gen. 2

2004. Proton Gen. 2. Multicoloured.

1251	30s. Type **342**	10	15
1252	50s. Proton Gen. 2 (blue)	15	20
1253	$2 Proton Gen. 2 (red)	30	35
MS1254	100 × 70 mm. $2 Proton Gen. 2 (purple) (vert)	65	70

343 Bharata Natyam and Kathak

2005. Traditional Dances. Multicoloured.

1255	30s. Type **343**	10	15
1256	50s. Kipas and Payung	15	20
1257	$1 Zapin and Asyik	30	35
MS1258	100 × 70 mm. $2 Datun julud and Sumazau	65	70

POSTAGE DUE STAMPS

Until 15 August 1966, the postage due stamps of Malaysian Postal Union were in use throughout Malaysia.

D 1

D 2

1966.

D 1	D 1	1c. red	20	4·00
D 2		2c. blue	25	2·75
D 3		4c. green	1·00	6·50
D18		8c. green	80	6·50
D19		10c. blue	80	3·00
D 6		12c. violet	60	4·50
D20		20c. brown	1·00	3·50
D21		50c. bistre	1·50	4·25

1986.

D22	D 2	5c. mauve and lilac	10	30
D23		10c. black and grey	15	30
D24		20c. red and brown	20	35
D25		50c. green and blue	30	50
D26		$1 blue and cobalt	55	90

B. FEDERAL TERRITORY ISSUES

For use in the Federal Territories of Kuala Lumpur, Labuan (from 1984) and Putrajaya (from 2001).

K 1 "Rafflesia hasseltii"

K 2 Coffee

1979. Flowers. Multicoloured.

K1	1c. Type K **1**	10	40
K2	2c. "Pterocarpus indicus"	10	40
K3	5c. "Lagerstroemia speciosa"	15	40
K4	10c. "Durio zibethinus"	15	10
K5	15c. "Hibiscus rosa-sinensis"	30	10
K6	20c. "Rhododendron scortechinii"	30	10
K7	25c. "Etlingera elatior" (inscr "Phaeomeria speciosa")	70	10

1986. Agricultural Products of Malaysia. Mult.

K15	1c. Type K **2**	10	10
K16	2c. Coconuts	10	10
K17	5c. Cocoa	15	10
K18	10c. Black pepper	15	10
K19	15c. Rubber	30	10
K20	20c. Oil palm	20	10
K21	30c. Rice	25	15

MALDIVE ISLANDS Pt. 1

A group of islands W. of Ceylon. A republic from 1 January 1953, but reverted to a sultanate in 1954. Became independent on 26 July 1965 and left the British Commonwealth, but was re-admitted as an Associate Member on 9 July 1982.

1906. 100 cents = 1 rupee.
1951. 100 larees = 1 rupee.

1906. Nos. 268, 277/9 and 283/4 of Ceylon optd **MALDIVES**.

1	44	2c. brown	15·00	40·00
2	48	3c. green	22·00	40·00
3		4c. orange and blue	38·00	80·00
4	–	5c. purple	4·00	6·50
5	48	15c. blue	75·00	£150
6		25c. brown	85·00	£160

2 Minaret, Juma Mosque, Male

5 Palm Tree and Dhow

1909.

7a	2	2c. brown	2·50	90
11A		2c. grey	2·75	2·00
8		3c. green	50	70
12A		3c. brown	70	2·75
9		5c. purple	50	35
15A		6c. red	1·50	5·50
10		10c. red	7·50	80
16A		10c. green	85	55
17A		15c. black	6·50	14·00
18A		25c. brown	6·50	14·00
19A		50c. purple	6·50	17·00
20B		1r. blue	15·00	3·25

1950.

21	5	2l. olive	2·25	1·50
22		3l. blue	10·00	50
23		5l. green	10·00	50
24		6l. brown	1·25	1·00
25		10l. red	1·25	70
26		15l. orange	1·25	70
27		25l. purple	1·25	1·25
28		50l. violet	1·25	2·00
29		1r. brown	12·00	32·00

8 Native Products

1952.

30	–	3l. blue (Fish)	2·00	60
31	8	5l. green	1·00	2·00

9 Male Harbour

10 Fort and Building

1956.

32	9	2l. purple	10	10
33		3l. slate	10	10
34		5l. brown	10	10
35		6l. violet	10	10
36		10l. green	10	10
37		15l. brown	10	85
38		25l. red	10	10
39		50l. orange	10	10
40	10	1r. green	15	10
41		5r. blue	1·25	30
42		10r. mauve	2·75	1·25

11 Cycling

1960. Olympic Games.

43	11	2l. purple and green	15	25
44		3l. slate and purple	15	25
45		5l. brown and blue	15	25
46		10l. green and brown	15	25
47		15l. sepia and blue	15	25
48	–	25l. red and olive	15	25
49	–	50l. orange and violet	20	40
50	–	1r. green and purple	40	1·25

DESIGN—VERT: 25l. to 1r. Basketball.

13 Tomb of Sultan

1960.

51	13	2l. purple	10	10
52	–	3l. green	10	10
53	–	5l. brown	3·50	3·50
54	–	6l. blue	10	10
55	–	10l. red	10	10
56	–	15l. sepia	10	10
57	–	25l. violet	10	10
58	–	50l. grey	10	10
59	–	1r. orange	15	10
60	–	5r. blue	5·50	60
61	–	10r. green	11·00	1·25

DESIGNS: 3l. Custom House; 5l. Cowrie shells; 6l. Old Royal Palace; 10l. Road to Juma Mosque, Male; 15l. Council House; 25l. New Government Secretariat; 50l. Prime Minister's Office; 1r. Old Ruler's Tomb; 5r. Old Ruler's Tomb (distant view); 10r. Maldivian port.

Higher values were also issued, intended mainly for fiscal use.

24 "Care of Refugees"

25 Coconuts

26 Map of Male

1960. World Refugee Year.

62	24	2l. violet, orange and green	10	10
63		3l. brown, green and red . .	10	10
64		5l. green, sepia and red . .	10	10
65		10l. green, violet and red . .	10	10
66		15l. violet, green and red . .	10	10
67		25l. blue, brown and green	10	10
68		50l. olive, red and blue . . .	10	10
69		1r. red, slate and violet . .	15	35

1961.

70	25	2l. brown and green	10	50
71		3l. brown and blue	10	50
72		5l. brown and mauve . . .	10	10
73		10l. brown and orange . . .	15	10
74		15l. brown and black . . .	20	15
75	26	25l. multicoloured	45	20
76		50l. multicoloured	45	40
77		1r. multicoloured	50	70

27 5c. Stamp of 1906

1961. 55th Anniv of First Maldivian Stamp.

78	27	2l. purple, blue and green	10	65
79		3l. purple, blue and green	10	65
80		5l. purple, blue and green	10	15
81		6l. purple, blue and green	10	80
82	–	10l. green, red and purple	10	15
83	–	15l. green, red and purple	15	15
84	–	20l. green, red and purple	15	20
85	–	25l. red, green and black . .	15	20
86	–	50l. red, green and black . .	25	80
87	–	1r. red, green and black . .	40	2·00
MS87a		114 × 88 mm. No. 87 (block of four). Imperf	1·50	5·50

DESIGNS: 10l. to 20l. Posthorn and 3c. stamp of 1906; 25l. to 1r. Olive sprig and 2c. stamp of 1906.

30 Malaria Eradication Emblem

31 Children of Europe and America

1962. Malaria Eradication.

88	30	2l. brown	10	75
89		3l. green	10	75
90		5l. turquoise	10	15
91		10l. red	10	15
92	–	15l. sepia	15	15
93	–	25l. blue	20	20
94	–	50l. myrtle	25	55
95	–	1r. purple	55	80

Nos. 92/5 are as Type **30**, but have English inscriptions at the side.

1962. 15th Anniv of UNICEF.

96	31	2l. multicoloured	10	75
97		6l. multicoloured	10	75
98		10l. multicoloured	10	10
99		15l. multicoloured	10	10
100	–	25l. multicoloured	15	10
101	–	50l. multicoloured	20	10
102	–	1r. multicoloured	25	20
103	–	5r. multicoloured	1·00	4·50

DESIGN: Nos. 100/3, Children of Middle East and Far East.

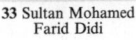

33 Sultan Mohamed Farid Didi

39 Fishes in Net

34 Royal Angelfish

1962. 9th Anniv of Enthronement of Sultan.

104	33	3l. brown and green . . .	10	65
105		5l. brown and blue	15	15
106		10l. brown and blue . . .	20	15
107		20l. brown and olive . . .	30	25
108		50l. brown and mauve . .	35	45
109		1r. brown and violet . . .	45	65

1963. Tropical Fish. Multicoloured.

110	2l. Type **34**	10	75
111	3l. Type **34**	10	75
112	5l. Type **34**	15	35
113	10l. Moorish idol (fish) . . .	25	35
114	25l. As 10l.	65	35
115	50l. Diadem soldierfish . . .	90	55
116	1r. Powder-blue surgeonfish	1·25	60
117	5r. Racoon butterflyfish . . .	6·25	10·00

1963. Freedom from Hunger.

118	39	2l. brown and green . . .	30	1·25
119	–	5l. brown and red	50	90
120	39	7l. brown and turquoise . .	70	90
121	–	10l. brown and blue . . .	85	90
122	39	25l. brown and red	2·50	3·50
123	–	50l. brown and violet . . .	3·75	8·00
124	39	1r. brown and mauve . . .	6·00	12·00

DESIGN—VERT: 5l., 10l., 50l. Handful of grain.

41 Centenary Emblem

42 Maldivian Scout Badge

1963. Centenary of Red Cross.

125	41	2l. red and purple	30	1·50
126		15l. red and green	65	80
127		50l. red and brown	1·25	1·75
128		1r. red and blue	1·75	2·00
129		4r. red and olive	4·00	21·00

1964. World Scout Jamboree, Marathon (1963).

130	42	2l. green and violet	10	65
131		3l. green and brown . . .	10	65
132		25l. green and blue	15	15
133		1r. green and red	55	1·50

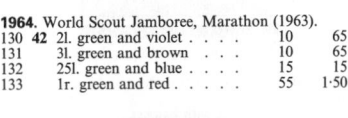

43 Mosque, Male

1964. "Maldives Embrace Islam".

134	43	2l. purple	10	60
135		3l. green	10	60
136		10l. red	10	10
137		40l. purple	30	25
138		60l. blue	50	40
139		85l. brown	60	60

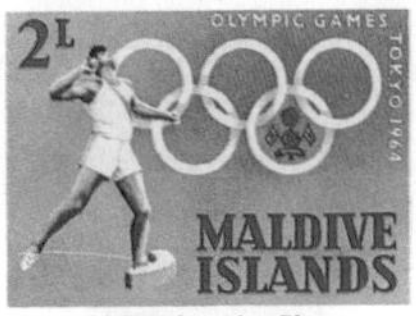

44 Putting the Shot

1964. Olympic Games, Tokyo.

140	44	2l. purple and blue	10	70
141		3l. red and brown	10	70
142		5l. bronze and green . . .	15	20
143		10l. violet and purple . . .	20	20
144	–	15l. sepia and brown . . .	30	20
145	–	25l. indigo and blue . . .	50	20
146	–	50l. bronze and olive . . .	75	35
147	–	1r. purple and grey	1·25	75
MS147a		126 × 140 mm. Nos. 145/7. Imperf	2·25	3·75

DESIGN: 15l. to 1r. Running.

46 Telecommunications Satellite

1965. International Quiet Sun Years.

148	46	5l. blue	15	65
149		10l. brown	20	65
150		25l. green	40	65
151		1r. mauve	90	1·00

47 Isis (wall carving, Abu Simbel)

49 "XX" and U.N. Flag

48 Pres. Kennedy and Doves

1965. Nubian Monuments Preservation.

152	47	2l. green and purple . . .	10	30
153	–	3l. lake and green	10	30
154	47	5l. green and purple . . .	15	10
155	–	10l. blue and orange . . .	20	10
156	47	15l. brown and violet . . .	35	15
157	–	25l. purple and blue . . .	60	15
158	47	50l. green and sepia . . .	75	35
159	–	1r. ochre and green	1·10	55

DESIGN: 3, 10, 25l., 1r. Rameses II on throne (wall carving, Abu Simbel).

1965. 2nd Death Anniv of Pres. Kennedy.

160	48	2l. black and mauve . . .	10	50
161		5l. brown and mauve . . .	10	10
162		25l. blue and mauve . . .	10	10
163	–	1r. purple, yellow and green	25	25
164	–	2r. bronze, yellow and green	40	70
MS164a		150 × 130 mm. No. 164 in block of four. Imperf	2·75	3·25

DESIGN: 1r., 2r. Pres. Kennedy and hands holding olive-branch.

1965. 20th Anniv of U.N.

165	49	3l. blue and brown	10	30
166		10l. blue and violet	20	10
167		1r. blue and green	1·10	35

50 I.C.Y. Emblem

1965. International Co-operation Year.

168	50	5l. brown and bistre . . .	15	20
169		15l. brown and lilac . . .	20	20
170		50l. brown and olive . . .	45	30
171		1r. brown and red	1·25	1·50
172		2r. brown and blue	1·75	3·50
MS173		101 × 126 mm. Nos. 170/2. Imperf	6·50	7·50

51 Princely Cone Shells

1966. Multicoloured.

174	2l. Type **51**	20	1·25
175	3l. Yellow flowers	20	1·25
176	5l. Reticulate distorsio and leopard shells	30	15
177	7l. Camellias	30	15
178	10l. Type **51**	1·00	15
179	15l. Crab plover and seagull	3·75	30
180	20l. As 3l.	80	30
181	30l. Type **51**	2·75	35
182	50l. As 15l.	6·00	55
183	1r. Type **51**	4·00	55
184	1r. As 7l.	3·50	55
185	1r.50 As 3l.	3·75	3·50
186	2r. As 7l.	5·00	4·00
187	5r. As 15l.	23·00	14·00
188	10r. As 5l.	23·00	20·00

The 3l., 7l., 20l., 1r. (No. 184), 1r.50 and 2r. are DIAMOND (43½ × 43½ mm).

52 Maldivian Flag

1966. 1st Anniv of Independence.

189	52	10l. green, red and turquoise	1·25	30
190		1r. multicoloured	3·75	70

53 "Luna 9" on Moon

1966. Space Rendezvous and Moon Landing.

191	53	10l. brown, indigo and blue	20	10
192	–	25l. green and red	30	10
193	53	50l. brown and green . . .	40	15
194	–	1r. turquoise and brown	70	35
195	–	2r. green and violet	1·50	65
196	–	5r. pink and turquoise . .	2·25	1·60
MS197		108 × 126 mm. Nos. 194/6. Imperf	3·50	4·50

DESIGNS: 25l., 1r., 5r. "Gemini 6" and "7" rendezvous in space; 2r. "Gemini" spaceship as seen from the other spaceship.

54 UNESCO Emblem and Owl on Book

1966. 20th Anniv of UNESCO. Multicoloured.

198	2l. Type **54**	20	1·25
199	3l. UNESCO emblem and globe and microscope . . .	20	1·25
200	5l. UNESCO emblem and mask, violin and palette . .	50	20
201	50l. Type **54**	3·00	55
202	1r. Design as 3l.	4·00	90
203	5r. Design as 5l.	13·00	17·00

55 Sir Winston Churchill and Cortege

1966. Churchill Commem. Flag in red and blue.

204	55	2l. brown	15	1·10
205	–	10l. turquoise	85	10
206	55	15l. green	1·60	10
207	–	25l. violet	2·25	15
208	–	1r. brown	6·50	75
209	55	2r.50 red	13·00	11·00

DESIGN: 10l., 25l., 1r. Churchill and catafalque.

56 Footballers and Jules Rimet Cup

1967. England's Victory in World Cup Football Championship. Multicoloured.

210	2l. Type **56**	15	80
211	3l. Player in red shirt kicking ball	15	80
212	5l. Scoring goal	15	10
213	25l. As 3l.	75	10
214	50l. Making a tackle	1·25	20
215	1r. Type **56**	2·25	55
216	2r. Emblem on Union Jack	3·75	3·50
MS217	100 × 121 mm. Nos. 214/16. Imperf	11·00	7·50

57 Ornate Butterflyfish

1967. Tropical Fishes. Multicoloured.

218	2l. Type **57**	10	60
219	3l. Black-saddled pufferfish	15	60
220	5l. Blue boxfish	20	10
221	6l. Picasso triggerfish . . .	20	20
222	50l. Semicircle angelfish . . .	3·25	30
223	1r. As 3l.	4·50	75
224	2r. As 50l.	8·50	8·00

58 Hawker Siddeley H.S.748 over Hulule Airport Building

1967. Inauguration of Hulule Airport.
225 **58** 2l. violet and olive 20 50
226 – 5l. green and lavender . . 25 10
227 **58** 10l. violet and green . . . 30 10
228 – 15l. green and ochre . . . 50 10
229 **58** 30l. ultramarine and blue 1·00 10
230 – 50l. brown and mauve . . 1·75 20
231 **58** 5r. blue and orange . . . . 5·50 5·50
232 – 10r. brown and blue . . . 7·50 9·00
DESIGN: 5, 15, 50l., 10r. Airport building and Hawker Siddeley H.S.748.

59 "Man and Music" Pavilion

1967. World Fair, Montreal. Multicoloured.
233 2l. Type **59** 10 60
234 5l. "Man and His Community" Pavilion . . . 10 10
235 10l. Type **59** 10 10
236 50l. As 5l. 40 30
237 1r. Type **59** 75 50
238 2r. As 5l. . . . . 1·75 1·75
MS239 102 × 137 mm. Nos. 237/8. Imperf . . . . 2·25 3·50

1968. International Tourist Year (1967). Nos. 225/32 optd **International Tourist Year 1967**.
240 **58** 2l. violet and olive 10 60
241 – 5l. green and lavender . . 15 15
242 **58** 10l. violet and green . . . 20 15
243 – 15l. green and ochre . . . 20 15
244 **58** 30l. ultramarine and blue 30 20
245 – 50l. brown and mauve . . 45 30
246 **58** 5r. blue and orange . . . . 3·50 4·00
247 – 10r. brown and blue . . . 5·00 6·50

61 Cub signalling and Lord Baden-Powell

63 Putting the Shot

62 French Satellite "A 1"

1968. Maldivian Scouts and Cubs.
248 **61** 2l. brown, green and yellow 10 80
249 – 3l. red, blue and light blue 10 80
250 **61** 25l. violet, lake and red . . 1·50 40
251 – 1r. green, brown and light green . . . . 3·50 1·60
DESIGN: 3l. and 1r. Scouts and Lord Baden-Powell.

1968. Space Martyrs.
252 **62** 2l. mauve and blue 10 40
253 – 3l. violet and brown . . . 10 40
254 – 7l. brown and lake 15 40
255 – 10l. blue, drab and black 15 15
256 – 25l. green and violet . . . 40 15
257 **62** 50l. blue and brown . . . 75 30
258 – 1r. purple and green . . . 1·10 50
259 – 2r. brown, blue and black 1·75 2·00
260 – 5r. mauve, drab and black 2·75 3·00
MS261 110 × 155 mm. Nos. 258/9. Imperf . . . . 4·50 4·75
DESIGNS: 3l., 25l. "Luna 10"; 7l., 1r. "Orbiter" and "Mariner"; 10l., 2r. Astronauts White, Grissom and Chaffee; 5r. Cosmonaut V. M. Komarov.

1968. Olympic Games, Mexico (1st Issue). Multicoloured.
262 2l. Type **63** 10 40
263 6l. Throwing the discus . . . 10 40
264 10l. Type **63** 15 10
265 25l. As 6l. 20 10
266 1r. Type **63** 60 35
267 2r.50 As 6l. . . . . 1·50 2·00
See also Nos. 294/7.

64 "Adriatic Seascape" (Bonington)

1968. Paintings. Multicoloured.
268 50l. Type **64** . . . . 1·75 30
269 1r. "Ulysses deriding Polyphemus" (Turner) . . 2·25 45
270 2r. "Sailing Boat at Argenteuil" (Monet) . . . 3·00 2·50
271 5r. "Fishing Boat at Les Saintes-Maries" (Van Gogh) . . . . 5·00 6·00

65 LZ-130 "Graf Zeppelin II" and Montgolfier's Balloon

1968. Development of Civil Aviation.
272 **65** 2l. brown, green and blue 15 50
273 – 3l. blue, violet and brown 15 50
274 – 5l. green, red and blue . . 15 15
275 – 7l. blue, purple and orange 90 60
276 **65** 10l. brown, blue and purple 35 15
277 – 50l. red, green and olive . . 1·50 20
278 – 1r. green, blue and red . . 2·25 50
279 – 2r. purple, bistre and blue 14·00 10·00
DESIGNS: 3l., 1r. Boeing 707-420 and Douglas DC-3; 5l., 50l. Wright Type A and Lilienthal's glider; 7l., 2r. Projected Boeing 733 and Concorde.

66 W.H.O. Building, Geneva

1968. 20th Anniv of World Health Organization.
280 **66** 10l. violet, turquoise & blue 60 10
281 25l. green, brown & yellow 1·00 15
282 1r. brown, emerald & green 3·25 90
283 2r. violet, purple and mauve . . . . 5·25 5·50

1968. 1st Anniv of Scout Jamboree, Idaho. Nos. 248/51 optd **International Boy Scout Jamboree, Farragut Park, Idaho, U.S.A. August 1–9, 1967**.
284 **61** 2l. brown, green and yellow 10 50
285 – 3l. red, blue and light blue 10 50
286 **61** 25l. violet, lake and red . . 1·50 40
287 – 1r. green, brown and light green . . . . 4·50 2·10

68 Curlew and Common Redshank

1968. Multicoloured.
288 2l. Type **68** 50 75
289 10l. Pacific grinning tun and Papal mitre shells . . . . 1·25 20
290 25l. Oriental angel wing and tapestry turban shells . . . 1·75 25
291 50l. Type **68** . . . . 7·00 1·10
292 1r. As 10l. . . . . 4·50 1·10
293 2r. As 25l. . . . . 5·00 4·75

69 Throwing the Discus

1968. Olympic Games, Mexico (2nd issue). Mult.
294 10l. Type **69** 10 10
295 50l. Running 20 10
296 1r. Cycling . . . . 3·75 60
297 2r. Basketball . . . . 4·75 2·50

70 Fishing Dhow

1968. Republic Day.
298 **70** 10l. brown, blue and green 75 30
299 – 1r. green, red and blue . . 6·25 1·40
DESIGN: 1r. National flag, crest and map.

71 "The Thinker" (Rodin)

1969. UNESCO. "Human Rights". Designs showing sculptures by Rodin. Multicoloured.
300 6l. Type **71** 30 15
301 10l. "Hands" 30 15
302 1r.50 "Eve" . . . . 2·00 2·25
303 2r.50 "Adam" . . . . 2·50 3·00
MS304 112 × 130 mm. Nos. 302/3. Imperf . . . . 8·50 8·50

72 Module nearing Moon's Surface

1969. 1st Man on the Moon. Multicoloured.
305 6l. Type **72** 15 15
306 10l. Astronaut with hatchet 15 15
307 1r.50 Astronaut and module 2·25 1·40
308 2r.50 Astronaut using camera 2·50 2·00
MS309 101 × 130 mm. Nos. 305/8. Imperf . . . . 3·50 4·50

1969. Gold Medal Winner, Olympic Games, Mexico (1968). Nos. 295/6 optd **Gold Medal Winner Mohamed Gammoudi 5000m. run Tunisia REPUBLIC OF MALDIVES** or similar opt.
310 50l. multicoloured 60 60
311 1r. multicoloured . . . . . . 1·40 90
The overprint on No. 310 honours P. Trentin (cycling, France).

74 Racoon Butterflyfish

1970. Tropical Fishes. Mult.
312 2l. Type **74** 40 70
313 5l. Clown triggerfish 65 40
314 25l. Broad-barred lionfish . . 2·25 40
315 50l. Long-nosed butterflyfish 3·00 1·00
316 1r. Emperor angelfish . . . . 4·00 1·00
317 2r. Royal angelfish . . . . . 5·50 6·50

75 Columbia Dauman Victoria, 1899

1970. "75 Years of the Automobile". Mult.
318 2l. Type **75** 20 50
319 5l. Duryea phaeton, 1902 . . 25 30
320 7l. Packard S-24, 1906 . . . 30 30
321 10l. Autocar Runabout, 1907 35 30
322 25l. Type **75** . . . . 1·50 30
323 50l. As 5l. . . . . 2·75 55

324 1r. As 7l. . . . . 3·50 90
325 2r. As 10l. . . . . 4·50 5·50
MS326 95 × 143 mm. Nos. 324/5 5·00 7·50

76 U.N. Headquarters, New York

1970. 25th Anniv of United Nations. Mult.
327 2l. Type **76** 10 75
328 10l. Surgical operation (W.H.O.) . . . . 1·50 25
329 25l. Student, actress and musician (UNESCO) . . . 2·50 40
330 50l. Children at work and play (UNICEF) . . . . . 2·00 70
331 1r. Fish, corn and farm animals (F.A.O.) . . . . . 2·00 1·00
332 2r. Miner hewing coal (I.L.O.) . . . . 6·00 6·50

77 Ship and Light Buoy

78 "Guitar-player and Masqueraders" (A. Watteau)

1970. 10th Anniv of I.M.C.O. Multicoloured.
333 50l. Type **77** 50 40
334 1r. Ship and lighthouse . . . 4·25 85

1970. Famous Paintings showing the Guitar. Multicoloured.
335 3l. Type **78** 15 80
336 7l. "Spanish Guitarist" (Manet) 25 80
337 50l. "Costumed Player" (Watteau) 85 40
338 1r. "Mandolin-player" (Roberti) . . . . 1·40 55
339 2r.50 "Guitar-player and Lady" (Watteau) . . . . . 3·00 3·50
340 5r. "Mandolin-player" (Frans Hals) . . . . 5·00 6·50
MS341 132 × 80 mm. Nos. 339/40 8·50 9·00

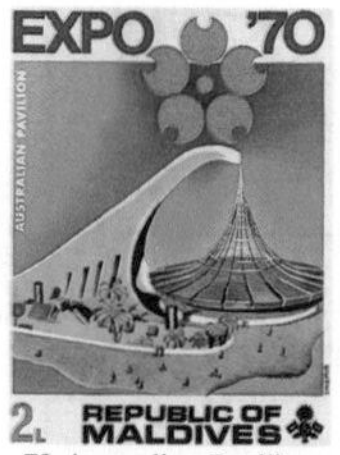

79 Australian Pavilion

82 Footballers

80 Learning the Alphabet

1970. "EXPO 70" World Fair, Osaka, Japan. Multicoloured.
342 2l. Type **79** 10 80
343 3l. West German Pavilion . . 10 80
344 10l. U.S. Pavilion 45 10
345 25l. British Pavilion . . . . 1·50 15
346 50l. Soviet Pavilion . . . . . 2·00 45
347 1r. Japanese Pavilion . . . . 2·50 65

1970. Int Education Year. Multicoloured.
348 5l. Type **80** 25 30
349 10l. Training teachers 30 15
350 25l. Geography lesson . . . 1·50 20
351 50l. School inspector . . . . 1·75 45
352 1r. Education by television 2·00 75

1970. "Philympia 1970" Stamp Exn, London. Nos. 306/8 optd **Philympia London 1970**.
353 10l. multicoloured 10 10
354 1r.50 multicoloured 65 75
355 2r.50 multicoloured . . . . 1·00 1·50
MS356 101 × 130 mm. Nos. 305/8 optd. Imperf . . . . 6·00 7·00

1970. World Cup Football Championship, Mexico.

357 **82**	3l. multicoloured	15	40
358 –	6l. multicoloured	20	40
359 –	7l. multicoloured	20	30
360 –	25l. multicoloured	90	20
361 –	1r. multicoloured	2·50	90

DESIGNS: 6l. to 1r. Different designs showing footballers in action.

83 Little Boy and UNICEF Flag

84 Astronauts Lovell, Haise and Swigert

1970. 25th Anniv of UNICEF. Multicoloured.

362	5l. Type **83**	10	15
363	10l. Little girl with UNICEF "balloon"	10	15
364	1r. Type **83**	1·75	85
365	2r. As 10l.	2·75	3·00

1971. Safe Return of "Apollo 13". Multicoloured.

366	5l. Type **84**	25	25
367	20l. Explosion in Space	55	15
368	1r. Splashdown	1·25	50

85 "Multiracial Flower"

86 "Mme. Charpentier and her Children" (Renoir)

1971. Racial Equality Year.

369 **85**	10l. multicoloured	10	15
370	25l. multicoloured	20	15

1971. Famous Paintings showing "Mother and Child". Multicoloured.

371	5l. Type **86**	25	20
372	7l. "Susanna van Collen and her Daughter" (Rembrandt)	30	20
373	10l. "Madonna nursing the Child" (Titian)	40	20
374	20l. "Baroness Belleli and her Children" (Degas)	1·00	20
375	25l. "The Cradle" (Morisot)	1·00	20
376	1r. "Helena Fourment and her Children" (Reubens)	3·00	85
377	3r. "On the Terrace" (Renoir)	5·50	6·50

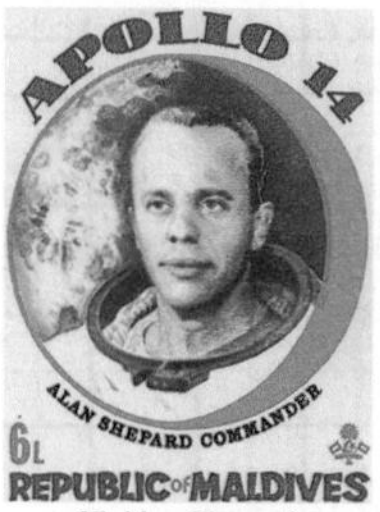

87 Alan Shepard

1971. Moon Flight of "Apollo 14". Multicoloured.

378	6l. Type **87**	40	40
379	10l. Stuart Roosa	45	30
380	1r.50 Edgar Mitchell	5·50	3·50
381	5r. Mission insignia	11·00	11·00

88 "Ballerina" (Degas)

1971. Famous Paintings showing "Dancers". Mult.

382	5l. Type **88**	20	20
383	10l. "Dancing Couple" (Renoir)	25	20
384	2r. "Spanish Dancer" (Manet)	2·75	2·50
385	5r. "Ballerinas" (Degas)	5·00	5·00
386	10r. "La Goulue at the Moulin Rouge" (Toulouse-Lautrec)	7·50	8·00

1972. Visit of Queen Elizabeth II and Prince Philip. Nos. 382/6 optd **ROYAL VISIT 1972**.

387 **88**	5l. multicoloured	15	10
388 –	10l. multicoloured	20	10
389 –	2r. multicoloured	4·50	4·00
390 –	5r. multicoloured	8·00	8·00
391 –	10r. multicoloured	9·50	10·00

90 Book Year Emblem

1972. International Book Year.

392 **90**	25l. multicoloured	15	10
393	5r. multicoloured	1·60	2·00

91 Scottish Costume

1972. National Costumes of the World. Mult.

394	10l. Type **91**	90	10
395	15l. Netherlands	1·00	15
396	25l. Norway	2·00	15
397	50l. Hungary	2·75	55
398	1r. Austria	3·25	80
399	2r. Spain	4·50	3·50

92 Stegosaurus

1972. Prehistoric Animals. Multicoloured.

400	2l. Type **92**	75	75
401	7l. Dimetrodon (inscr "Edaphosaurus")	1·50	60
402	25l. Diplodocus	2·25	50
403	50l. Triceratops	2·50	75
404	2r. Pteranodon	5·50	5·00
405	5r. Tyrannosaurus	9·50	9·50

93 Cross-country Skiing

1972. Winter Olympic Games, Sapporo, Japan. Multicoloured.

406	3l. Type **93**	10	50
407	6l. Bobsleighing	10	50
408	15l. Speed skating	20	20
409	50l. Ski jumping	1·00	45
410	1r. Figure skating (pair)	1·75	70
411	2r.50 Ice hockey	5·50	3·25

94 Scout Saluting

95 Cycling

1972. 13th Boy Scout Jamboree, Asagiri, Japan (1971). Multicoloured.

412	10l. Type **94**	75	20
413	15l. Scout signalling	95	20
414	50l. Scout blowing bugle	3·25	1·25
415	1r. Scout playing drum	4·50	2·25

1972. Olympic Games, Munich. Multicoloured.

416	5l. Type **95**	75	30
417	10l. Running	20	20
418	25l. Wrestling	30	20
419	50l. Hurdling	50	35
420	2r. Boxing	1·50	2·00
421	5r. Volleyball	3·00	3·75
MS422	92 × 120 mm. 3r. As 50l.; 4r. As 10l.	5·75	8·00

96 Globe and Conference Emblem

97 "Flowers" (Van Gogh)

1972. U.N. Environmental Conservation Conference, Stockholm.

423 **96**	2l. multicoloured	10	40
424	3l. multicoloured	10	40
425	15l. multicoloured	30	15
426	50l. multicoloured	75	45
427	2r.50 multicoloured	3·25	4·25

1973. Floral Paintings. Multicoloured.

428	1l. Type **97**	10	60
429	2l. "Flowers in Jug" (Renoir)	10	60
430	3l. "Chrysanthemums" (Renoir)	10	60
431	50l. "Mixed Bouquet" (Bosschaert)	1·50	30
432	1r. As 3l.	2·00	40
433	5r. As 2l.	4·25	5·50
MS434	120 × 94 mm. 2r. As 50l.; 3r. Type **97**	7·00	8·50

1973. Gold-medal Winners, Munich Olympic Games. Nos. 420/1 optd as listed below.

435	2r. multicoloured	3·25	2·50
436	5r. multicoloured	4·25	2·75
MS437	92 × 120 mm. 3r. multicoloured; 4r. multicoloured	7·50	8·50

OVERPRINTS: 2r. **LEMECHEV MIDDLE-WEIGHT GOLD MEDALLIST; 5r. JAPAN GOLD MEDAL WINNERS.** Miniature sheet: 3r. **EHRHARDT 100 METER HURDLES GOLD MEDALLIST**; 4r. **SHORTER MARATHON GOLD MEDALLIST.**

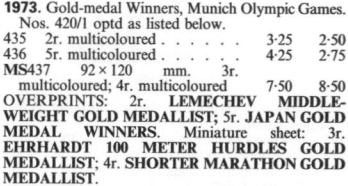

99 Animal Care

1973. International Scouting Congress, Nairobi and Addis Ababa. Multicoloured.

438	1l. Type **99**	10	30
439	2l. Lifesaving	10	30
440	3l. Agricultural training	10	30
441	4l. Carpentry	10	30
442	5l. Playing leapfrog	10	30
443	1r. As 2l.	2·75	75
444	2r. As 4l.	4·00	4·75
445	3r. Type **99**	4·50	7·00
MS446	101 × 79 mm. 5r. As 3l.	7·50	14·00

100 Blue Marlin

1973. Fishes. Multicoloured.

447	1l. Type **100**	10	40
448	2l. Skipjack tuna	10	40
449	3l. Blue-finned tuna	10	40
450	5l. Dolphin (fish)	10	40
451	60l. Humpbacked snapper	80	40
452	75l. As 60l.	1·00	40
453	1r.50 Yellow-edged lyretail	1·75	2·00
454	2r.50 As 5l.	2·25	3·00
455	3r. Spotted coral grouper	2·25	3·25
456	10r. Spanish mackerel	4·75	8·00
MS457	119 × 123 mm. 4r. As 2l. 5r. Type **100**	17·00	20·00

Nos. 451/2 are smaller, size 29 × 22 mm.

101 Golden-fronted Leafbird

1973. Fauna. Multicoloured.

458	1l. Type **101**	10	50
459	2l. Indian flying fox	10	50
460	3l. Land tortoise	10	50
461	4l. Butterfly ("Kallima inachus")	30	50
462	50l. As 3l.	60	40
463	2r. Type **101**	5·50	4·50
464	3r. As 2l.	3·50	4·50
MS465	66 × 74 mm. 5r. As 4l.	18·00	20·00

102 "Lantana camara"

1973. Flowers of the Maldive Islands. Mult.

466	1l. Type **102**	10	50
467	2l. "Nerium oleander"	10	50
468	3l. "Rosa polyantha"	10	50
469	4l. "Hibiscus manihot"	10	50
470	5l. "Bougainvillea glabra"	10	20
471	10l. "Plumera alba"	15	20
472	50l. "Poinsettia pulcherrima"	70	30
473	5r. "Ononis natrix"	3·75	5·50
MS474	110 × 100 mm. 2r. As 3l.; 3r. As 10l.	3·25	5·25

103 "Tiros" Weather Satellite

1974. Centenary of World Meteorological Organization. Multicoloured.

475	1l. Type **103**	10	30
476	2l. "Nimbus" satellite	10	30
477	3l. "Nomad" (weather ship)	10	30
478	4l. Scanner, A.P.T. Instant Weather Picture equipment	10	30
479	5l. Richard's wind-speed recorder	10	20
480	2r. Type **103**	3·50	3·75
481	3r. As 3l.	3·75	4·00
MS482	110 × 79 mm. 10r. As 2l.	8·50	14·00

104 "Apollo" Spacecraft and Pres. Kennedy

1974. American and Russian Space Exploration Projects. Multicoloured.

483	1l. Type **104**	10	35
484	2l. "Mercury" capsule and John Glenn	10	35
485	3l. "Vostok 1" and Yuri Gagarin	10	35
486	4l. "Vostok 6" and Valentina Tereshkova	10	35
487	5l. "Soyuz 11" and "Salyut" space-station	10	25
488	2r. "Skylab" space laboratory	3·75	3·75
489	3r. As 2l.	4·25	4·25
MS490	103 × 80 mm. 10r. Type **104**	12·00	14·00

105 Copernicus and "Skylab" Space Laboratory
106 "Maternity" (Picasso)

1974. 500th Birth Anniv of Nicholas Copernicus (astronomer). Multicoloured.

491	1l. Type **105**	10	35
492	2l. Orbital space-station of the future	10	35
493	3l. Proposed "Space-shuttle" craft	10	35
494	4l. "Mariner 2" Venus probe	10	35
495	5l. "Mariner 4" Mars probe	10	20
496	25l. Type **105**	1·25	20
497	1r.50 As 2l.	2·75	3·25
498	5r. As 3l.	4·50	11·00
MS499	106 × 80 mm. 10r. "Copernicus" orbital observatory	15·00	18·00

1974. Paintings by Picasso. Multicoloured.

500	1l. Type **106**	10	40
501	2l. "Harlequin and Friend"	10	40
502	3l. "Pierrot Sitting"	10	40
503	20l. "Three Musicians"	50	20
504	75l. "L'Aficionado"	1·25	80
505	5r. "Still Life"	4·75	6·50
MS506	100 × 101 mm. 2r. As 20l.; 3r. As 5r.	8·00	10·00

107 U.P.U. Emblem, Steam and Diesel Locomotives

1974. Cent of Universal Postal Union. Mult.

507	1l. Type **107**	10	30
508	2l. Paddle-steamer and modern mailboat	10	30
509	3l. Airship "Graf Zeppelin" and Boeing 747 airliner	10	30
510	1r.50 Mailcoach and motor van	1·10	1·10
511	2r.50 As 2l.	1·40	1·75
512	5r. Type **107**	2·00	3·25
MS513	126 × 105 mm. 4r. Type **107**	5·50	7·00

108 Footballers
109 "Capricorn"

1974. World Cup Football Championship, West Germany.

514	**108** 1l. multicoloured	15	20
515	– 2l. multicoloured	15	20
516	– 3l. multicoloured	15	20
517	– 4l. multicoloured	15	20
518	– 75l. multicoloured	1·25	75
519	– 4r. multicoloured	2·50	4·00
520	– 5r. multicoloured	2·50	4·00
MS521	88 × 95 mm. 10r. multicoloured	10·00	12·00

DESIGNS: Nos. 515/**MS**521 show football scenes similar to Type **108**.

1974. Signs of the Zodiac. Multicoloured.

522	1l. Type **109**	25	50
523	2l. "Aquarius"	25	50
524	3l. "Pisces"	25	50
525	4l. "Aries"	25	50
526	5l. "Taurus"	25	50
527	6l. "Gemini"	25	50
528	7l. "Cancer"	25	50
529	10l. "Leo"	40	50
530	15l. "Virgo"	40	50
531	20l. "Libra"	40	50
532	25l. "Scorpio"	40	50
533	5r. "Sagittarius"	6·50	12·00
MS534	119 × 99 mm. 10r. "The Sun" (49 × 37 mm)	19·00	21·00

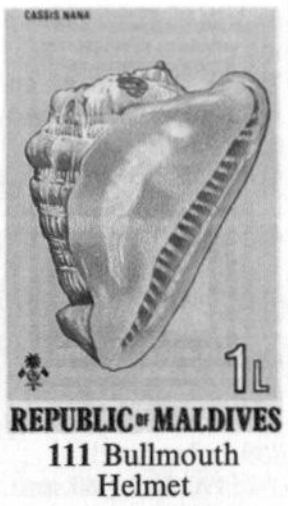

110 Churchill and Avro Type 683 Lancaster
111 Bullmouth Helmet

1974. Birth Cent of Sir Winston Churchill. Mult.

535	1l. Type **110**	20	50
536	2l. Churchill as pilot	20	50
537	3l. Churchill as First Lord of the Admiralty	25	50
538	4l. Churchill and H.M.S. "Eagle" (aircraft carrier)	25	50
539	5l. Churchill and De Havilland Mosquito bombers	25	30
540	60l. Churchill and anti-aircraft battery	3·00	1·75
541	75l. Churchill and tank in desert	3·25	1·75
542	5r. Churchill and Short S.25 Sunderland flying boat	12·00	13·00
MS543	113 × 83 mm. 10r. As 4l.	17·00	20·00

1975. Sea Shells and Cowries. Multicoloured.

544	1l. Type **111**	10	30
545	2l. Venus comb murex	10	30
546	3l. Common or major harp	10	30
547	4l. Chiragra spider conch	10	30
548	5l. Geography cone	10	30
549	60l. Dawn cowrie (22 × 30 mm)	3·00	2·00
550	75l. Purplish clanculus (22 × 30 mm)	3·50	2·00
551	5r. Ramose murex	8·50	11·00
MS552	152 × 126 mm. 2r. As 3l.; 3r. As 2l.	12·00	15·00

112 Royal Throne
113 Guavas

1975. Historical Relics and Monuments. Mult.

553	1l. Type **112**	10	40
554	10l. Candlesticks	10	10
555	25l. Lamp-tree	15	10
556	60l. Royal umbrellas	30	30
557	75l. Eid-Miskith Mosque (horiz)	35	35
558	3r. Tomb of Al-Hafiz Abu-al Barakath-al Barubari (horiz)	1·60	2·75

1975. Exotic Fruits. Multicoloured.

559	2l. Type **113**	10	40
560	4l. Maldive mulberry	15	40
561	5l. Mountain apples	15	40
562	10l. Bananas	20	15
563	20l. Mangoes	40	25
564	50l. Papaya	1·00	60
565	1r. Pomegranates	1·75	70
566	5r. Coconut	5·50	11·00
MS567	136 × 102 mm. 2r. As 10l.; 3r. As 2l.	10·00	14·00

114 "Phyllangia"

1975. Marine Life. Corals, Urchins and Sea Stars. Multicoloured.

568	1l. Type **114**	10	40
569	2l. "Madrepora oculata"	10	40
570	3l. "Acropora gravida"	10	40
571	4l. "Stylotella"	10	40
572	5l. "Acrophora cervicornis"	10	40
573	60l. "Strongylocentrotus purpuratus"	75	65
574	75l. "Pisaster ochraceus"	85	75
575	5r. "Marthasterias glacialis"	5·00	6·50
MS576	155 × 98 mm. 4r. As 1l. Imperf	11·00	14·00

115 Clock Tower and Customs Building within "10"

1975. 10th Anniv of Independence. Multicoloured.

577	4l. Type **115**	10	30
578	5l. Government offices	10	15
579	7l. Waterfront	10	20
580	15l. Mosque and minaret	10	15
581	10r. Sultan Park and museum	2·25	6·00

1975. "Nordjamb 75" World Scout Jamboree, Norway. Nos. 443/5 and **MS**446 optd **14th Boy Scout Jamboree July 29–August 7, 1975.**

582	– 1r. multicoloured	85	60
583	– 2r. multicoloured	1·25	80
584	**99** 3r. multicoloured	1·75	1·60
MS585	101 × 79 mm. 5r. multicoloured	7·00	8·00

117 Madura Prau

1975. Ships. Multicoloured.

586	1l. Type **117**	10	20
587	2l. Ganges patela	10	20
588	3l. Indian palla (vert)	10	20
589	4l. Odhi (dhow) (vert)	10	20
590	5l. Maldivian schooner	10	20
591	25l. "Cutty Sark" (British tea clipper)	90	40
592	1r. Maldivian baggala (vert)	1·50	70
593	5r. "Maldive Courage" (freighter)	3·00	6·00
MS594	99 × 85 mm. 10r. As 1r.	10·00	14·00

118 "Brahmophthalma wallichi" (moth)

1975. Butterflies and Moth. Multicoloured.

595	1l. Type **118**	15	30
596	2l. "Teinopalpus imperialis"	15	30
597	3l. "Cethosia biblis"	15	30
598	4l. "Idea jasonia"	15	30
599	5l. "Apatura ilia"	15	30
600	25l. "Kallima horsfieldi"	1·25	35
601	1r.50 "Hebomoia leucippe"	3·50	3·75
602	5r. "Papilio memnon"	8·00	10·00
MS603	134 × 97 mm. 10r. As 25l.	20·00	20·00

119 "The Dying Captive"
120 Beaker and Vase

1975. 500th Birth Anniv of Michelangelo. Mult.

604	1l. Type **119**	10	20
605	2l. Detail of "The Last Judgement"	10	20
606	3l. "Apollo"	10	20
607	4l. Detail of Sistine Chapel ceiling	10	20
608	5l. "Bacchus"	10	20
609	1r. Detail of "The Last Judgement" (different)	1·25	30
610	2r. "David"	1·50	2·00
611	5r. "Cumaean Sibyl"	2·25	5·00
MS612	123 × 113 mm. 10r. As 2r.	5·00	11·00

1975. Maldivian Lacquerware. Multicoloured.

613	2l. Type **120**	10	50
614	4l. Boxes	10	50
615	50l. Jar with lid	30	20
616	75l. Bowls with covers	40	30
617	1r. Craftsman at work	50	40

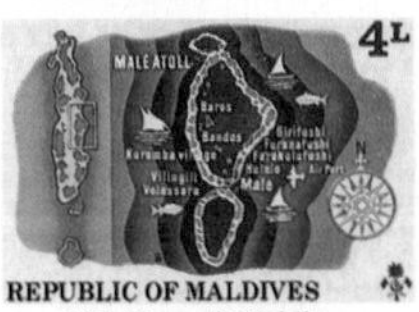

121 Map of Maldives

1975. Tourism. Multicoloured.

618	4l. Type **121**	30	40
619	5l. Motor launch and small craft	30	40
620	7l. Sailing-boats	30	40
621	15l. Underwater fishing	30	30
622	3r. Hulule Airport	4·50	3·00
623	10r. Motor cruisers	6·50	7·50

122 Cross-country Skiing
123 "General Burgoyne" (Reynolds)

1976. Winter Olympic Games, Innsbruck. Mult.

624	1l. Type **122**	10	20
625	2l. Speed-skating (pairs)	10	20
626	3l. Figure-skating (pairs)	10	20
627	4l. Four-man bobsleighing	10	20
628	5l. Ski-jumping	10	20
629	25l. Figure-skating (women's)	35	20
630	1r.15 Skiing (slalom)	90	1·25
631	4r. Ice-hockey	1·50	4·00
MS632	93 × 117 mm. 10r. Downhill Skiing	6·00	12·00

1976. Bicent of American Revolution. Mult.

633	1l. Type **123**	10	10
634	2l. "John Hancock" (Copley)	10	10
635	3l. "Death of Gen. Montgomery" (Trumbull) (horiz)	10	10
636	4l. "Paul Revere" (Copley)	10	10
637	5l. "Battle of Bunker Hill" (Trumbull) (horiz)	10	10
638	2r. "The Crossing of the Delaware" (Sully) (horiz)	2·00	2·50
639	3r. "Samuel Adams" (Copley)	2·50	3·00
640	5r. "Surrender of Cornwallis" (Trumbull) (horiz)	3·00	3·25
MS641	147 × 95 mm. 10r. "Washington at Dorchester Heights" (Stuart)	16·00	19·00

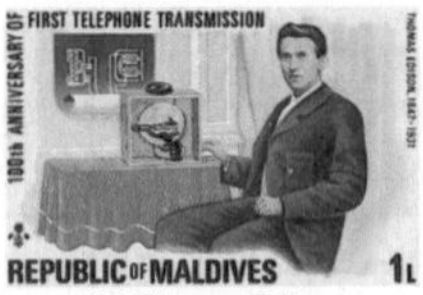

124 Thomas Edison

1976. Centenary of Telephone. Multicoloured.

642	1l. Type **124**	10	30
643	2l. Alexander Graham Bell	10	30
644	3l. Telephone of 1919, 1937 and 1972	10	30
645	10l. Cable entrance into station	20	20
646	20l. Equalizer circuit assembly	30	20
647	1r. "Salernum" (cable ship)	1·75	55
648	10r. "Intelsat IV-A" and Earth Station	4·75	7·50
MS649	156 × 105 mm. 4r. Early telephones	7·50	9·00

1976. "Interphil 76" International Stamp Exhibition, Philadelphia. Nos. 638/**MS**641 optd **MAY 29TH–JUNE 6TH "INTERPHIL" 1976.**

650	2r. multicoloured	1·50	1·75
651	3r. multicoloured	2·00	2·25
652	5r. multicoloured	2·50	2·75
MS653	147 × 95 mm. 10r. multicoloured	10·00	12·00

126 Wrestling
127 "Dolichos lablab"

1976. Olympic Games, Montreal. Multicoloured.

654	1l. Type **126**	10	20
655	2l. Putting the shot	10	20
656	3l. Hurdling	10	20
657	4l. Hockey	10	20
658	5l. Running	10	20
659	6l. Javelin-throwing	10	20
660	1r.50 Discus-throwing	1·25	1·75
661	5r. Volleyball	2·75	5·25
MS662	135 × 106 mm. 10r. Throwing the hammer	8·50	12·00

1976. Vegetables. Multicoloured.

663	2l. Type **127**	10	40
664	4l. "Moringa pterygosperma"	10	40
665	10l. "Solanum melongena"	15	15
666	20l. "Moringa pterygosperma"	2·75	2·25
667	50l. "Cucumis sativus"	50	65
668	75l. "Trichosanthes anguina"	55	75
669	1r. "Momordica charantia"	65	85
670	2r. "Trichosanthes anguina"	4·50	8·00

128 "Viking" approaching Mars

1977. "Viking" Space Mission. Multicoloured.

671	5r. Type **128**	2·25	2·75
MS672	121 × 89 mm. 20r. Landing module on Mars	10·00	14·00

129 Coronation Ceremony

1977. Silver Jubilee of Queen Elizabeth II. Mult.

673 1l. Type **129** 10 30
674 2l. Queen and Prince Philip 10 30
675 3l. Royal couple with Princes Andrew and Edward . . . 10 30
676 1r.15 Queen with Archbishops 65 35
677 3r. State coach in procession 1·25 75
678 4r. Royal couple with Prince Charles and Princess Anne 1·25 1·25
MS679 120 × 77 mm. 10r. Queen and Prince Charles . . . . 5·00 3·75

130 Beethoven and Organ

1977. 150th Death Anniv of Ludwig van Beethoven. Multicoloured.

680 1l. Type **130** 20 30
681 2l. Portrait and manuscript of "Moonlight Sonata" . . . 20 30
682 3l. With Goethe at Teplitz . . 20 30
683 4l. Beethoven and string instruments 20 30
684 5l. Beethoven's home, Heiligenstadt 20 20
685 25l. Hands and gold medals 1·25 20
686 2r. Portrait and "Missa solemnis" . . . . 3·75 3·75
687 5r. Composer's hearing-aids 6·00 7·00
MS688 121 × 92 mm. 4r. Death mask and room where composer died 8·50 10·00

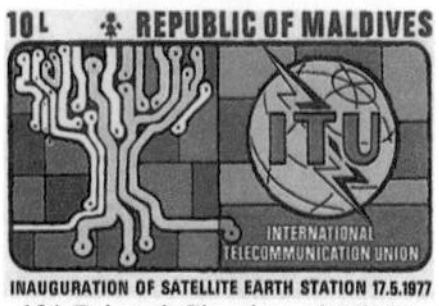

131 Printed Circuit and I.T.U. Emblem

1977. Inauguration of Satellite Earth Station. Mult.

689 10l. Type **131** 10 10
690 90l. Central Telegraph Office 45 45
691 10r. Satellite Earth Station 3·00 6·00
MS692 100 × 85 mm. 5r. "Intelsat IV-A" satellite over Maldives 4·50 5·50

132 "Miss Anne Ford" (Gainsborough)

133 Lesser Frigate Birds

1977. Artists' Birth Anniversaries. Multicoloured.

693 1l. Type **132** (250th anniv) . . 10 20
694 2l. Group painting by Rubens (400th anniv) . . . 10 20
695 3l. "Girl with Dog" (Titian) (500th Anniv) 10 20
696 4l. "Mrs. Thomas Graham" (Gainsborough) 10 20
697 5l. "Artist with Isabella Brant" (Rubens) 10 20
698 95l. Portrait by Titian . . . 1·00 30
699 1r. Portrait by Gainsborough 1·00 30
700 10r. "Isabella Brant" (Rubens) . . . . 3·75 7·00
MS701 152 × 116 mm. 5r. "Self-portrait" (Titian) . . . . . . 3·75 5·50

1977. Birds. Multicoloured.

702 1l. Type **133** 20 40
703 2l. Crab plover 20 40
704 3l. White-tailed tropic bird 20 40
705 4l. Wedge-tailed shearwater 20 40
706 5l. Grey heron 20 40
707 20l. White tern 90 30
708 95l. Cattle egret . . . . . . 2·25 1·60
709 1r.25 Black-naped tern . . . 2·50 2·50
710 5r. Pheasant coucal . . . . . 6·50 8·00
MS711 124 × 117 mm. 10r. Green-backed heron . . . . 25·00 25·00

134 Charles Lindbergh

136 Rheumatic Heart

135 Boat Building

1977. 50th Anniv of Lindbergh's Transatlantic Flight and 75th Anniv of First Navigable Airships. Multicoloured.

712 1l. Type **134** 20 30
713 2l. Lindbergh and "Spirit of St. Louis" 20 30
714 3l. Lindbergh's Miles Mohawk aircraft (horiz) . . 20 30
715 4l. Lebaudy-Juillot airship "Morning Post" (horiz) . . 20 30
716 5l. Airship "Graf Zeppelin" and portrait of Zeppelin 20 30
717 1r. Airship "Los Angeles" (horiz) . . . . 1·00 30
718 3r. Lindbergh and Henry Ford . . . . 1·75 2·00
719 10r. Vickers airship R-23 rigid airship . . . . . . 2·50 6·00
MS720 148 × 114 mm. 5r. Ryan NYP Special "Spirit of St. Louis", Statue of Liberty and Eiffel Tower; 7r.50, Airship L-31 over "Ostfriesland" (German battleship) . . . . 13·00 18·00
No. 715 is inscr "Lebaudy I built by H. Juillot 1902".

1977. Occupations. Multicoloured.

721 6l. Type **135** 50 45
722 15l. Fishing 85 20
723 20l. Cadjan weaving 90 20
724 90l. Mat-weaving . . . . . . 2·75 1·60
725 2r. Lace-making (vert) . . . 4·25 4·50

1977. World Rheumatism Year. Multicoloured.

726 1l. Type **136** 10 30
727 50l. Rheumatic shoulder . . 40 20
728 2r. Rheumatic hands . . . . 75 1·25
729 3r. Rheumatic knees . . . . 85 1·40

137 Lilienthal's Biplane Glider

1978. 75th Anniv of First Powered Aircraft. Multicoloured.

730 1l. Type **137** 20 40
731 2l. Chanute's glider 20 40
732 3l. Wright glider No. II, 1901 20 40
733 4l. A. V. Roe's Triplane I . . 20 40
734 5l. Wilbur Wright demonstrating Wright Type A for King Alfonso of Spain 30 40
735 10l. A. V. Roe's Avro Type D biplane 70 40
736 20l. Wright Brothers and A. G. Bell at Washington 2·00 40
737 95l. Hadley's triplane . . . . 5·00 2·25
738 5r. Royal Aircraft Factory B.E.2A biplanes at Upavon, 1914 . . . . . . 11·00 11·00
MS739 98 × 82 mm. 10r. Wright Brothers' Wright Type A . . . 14·00 16·00
No. 732 is wrongly dated "1900".

138 Newgate Prison

139 Television Set

1978. World Eradication of Smallpox. Mult.

740 15l. Foundling Hospital, London (horiz) 50 30
741 50l. Type **138** . . . . 1·25 60
742 2r. Edward Jenner (discoverer of smallpox vaccine) . . . 2·25 4·00

1978. Inaug of Television in Maldive Islands. Mult.

743 15l. Type **139** 40 30
744 25l. Television aerials 55 30
745 1r.50 Control desk (horiz) . . 2·25 2·75

140 Mas Odi

1978. Ships. Multicoloured.

746 1l. Type **140** 10 35
747 2l. Battela 10 35
748 3l. Bandu odi (vert) 10 35
749 5l. "Maldive Trader" (freighter) 20 35
750 1r. "Fath-hul Baaree" (brigantine) 65 30
751 1r.25 Mas dhoni . . . . . . 85 1·00
752 3r. Baggala (vert) . . . . . 1·10 1·75
753 4r. As 1r.25 . . . . 1·10 1·75
MS754 152 × 138 mm. 1r. As No. 747; 4r. As No. 751 . . . 2·50 3·75

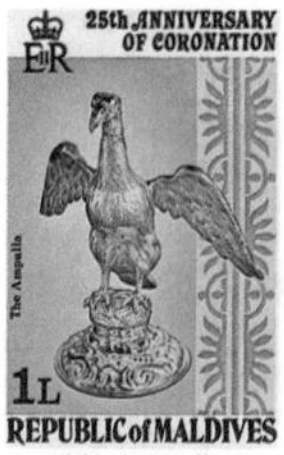

141 Ampulla

142 Capt. Cook

1978. 25th Anniv of Coronation. Multicoloured.

755 1l. Type **141** 10 20
756 2l. Sceptre with Dove 10 20
757 3l. Golden Orb 10 20
758 1r.15 St. Edward's Crown . . 35 20
759 2r. Sceptre with Cross . . . 50 35
760 5r. Queen Elizabeth II . . . 75 80
MS761 108 × 106 mm. 10r. Annointing spoon . . . . . . 1·75 2·25

1978. 250th Birth Anniv of Capt. James Cook and Bicent of Discovery of Hawaiian Islands. Mult.

762 1l. Type **142** 10 25
763 2l. Statue of Kamehameha I of Hawaii 10 25
764 3l. H.M.S. "Endeavour" . . . 10 25
765 25l. Route of third voyage . . 45 45
766 75l. H.M.S. "Discovery", H.M.S. "Resolution" and map of Hawaiian Islands (horiz) . . . . 1·25 1·25
767 1r.50 Cook meeting Hawaiian islanders (horiz) . . . . 2·00 2·25
768 10r. Death of Capt. Cook (horiz) . . . . 4·00 10·00
MS769 100 × 92 mm. 5r. H.M.S. "Endeavour" (different) . . . 15·00 20·00

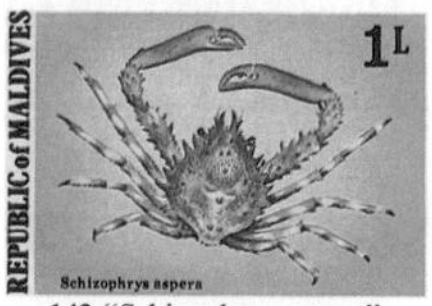

143 "Schizophrys aspera"

1978. Crustaceans. Multicoloured.

770 1l. Type **143** 10 25
771 2l. "Atergatis floridus" . . . 10 25
772 3l. "Perenon planissimum" . . 10 25
773 90l. "Portunus granulatus" . 50 40
774 1r. "Carpilius maculatus" . . 50 40
775 2r. "Huenia proteus" . . . . 1·00 1·40
776 25r. "Etisus laevimanus" . . 5·50 13·00
MS777 147 × 146 mm. 2r. "Panulirus longipes" (vert) . . . . 2·00 2·50

144 "Four Apostles"

145 T.V. Tower and Building

1978. 450th Death Anniv of Albrecht Durer (artist).

778 **144** 10l. multicoloured 10 10
779 – 20l. multicoloured 15 10
780 – 55l. multicoloured 20 20
781 – 1r. black, brown and buff 30 30
782 – 1r.80 multicoloured . . . 45 60
783 – 3r. multicoloured . . . . 70 1·25
MS784 141 × 122 mm. 10r. multicoloured . . . . 4·00 6·00

DESIGNS—VERT: 20l. "Self-portrait at 27"; 55l. "Madonna and Child with a Pear"; 1r.80, "Hare"; 3r. "Great Piece of Turf"; 10r. "Columbine". HORIZ: 1r. "Rhinoceros".

1978. 10th Anniv of Republic. Multicoloured.

785 1l. Fishing boat (horiz) . . . 10 50
786 5l. Montessori School (horiz) 10 30
787 10l. Type **145** 10 10
788 25l. Islet (horiz) 20 15
789 50l. Boeing 737 aircraft (horiz) 60 25
790 95l. Beach scene (horiz) . . . 60 30
791 1r.25 Dhow at night (horiz) 75 55
792 3r. President's residence (horiz) . . . . 80 1·25
793 5r. Masjidh Afeefuddin Mosque (horiz) . . . . . . 1·00 2·75
MS794 119 × 88 mm. 3r. Fisherman casting net . . . . 2·25 4·00

146 Human Rights Emblem

1978. 30th Anniv of Declaration of Human Rights.

795 **146** 30l. pink, lilac and green 15 15
796 90l. yellow, brown and green 40 60
797 1r.80 blue, deep blue and green . . . . 70 1·00

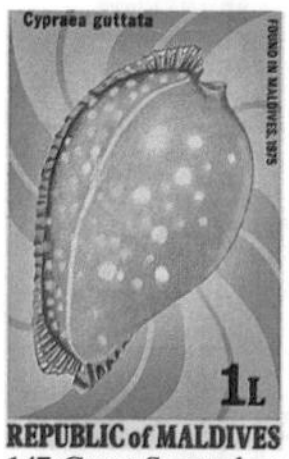

147 Great Spotted or Rare Spotted Cowrie

148 Delivery by Bellman

1979. Shells. Multicoloured.

798 1l. Type **147** 10 20
799 2l. Imperial cone 10 20
800 3l. Great green turban . . . 10 20
801 10l. Giant spider conch . . . 45 10
802 1r. White-toothed cowrie . . 2·00 40
803 1r.80 Fig cone . . . . 3·00 2·50
804 3r. Glory of the sea cone . . 4·50 3·75
MS805 141 × 110 mm. 5r. Common Pacific vase . . . . 12·00 12·00

1979. Death Cent of Sir Rowland Hill. Mult.

806 1l. Type **148** 10 20
807 2l. Mail coach, 1840 (horiz) 10 20
808 3l. First London letter box, 1855 . . . . 10 20
809 1r.55 Penny Black 40 50
810 5r. First Maldive Islands stamp . . . . 70 1·25
MS811 132 × 107 mm. 10r. Sir Rowland Hill . . . . 1·25 3·00

149 Girl with Teddy Bear

151 Sari with Overdress

150 "White Feathers"

1979. Int Year of the Child (1st issue). Mult.

812 5l. Type **149** 10 10
813 1r.25 Boy with sailing boat 40 50
814 2r. Boy with toy rocket . . . 45 55
815 3r. Boy with toy airship . . . 60 75
MS816 108 × 109 mm. 5r. Boy with toy train . . . . 1·25 2·00
See also Nos. 838/**MS**847.

1979. 25th Death Anniv of Henri Matisse (artist). Multicoloured.

817 20l. Type **150** 15 15
818 25l. "Joy of Life" 15 15
819 30l. "Eggplants" 15 15
820 1r.50 "Harmony in Red" . . 45 65
821 5r. "Still-life" . . . . 70 2·25
MS822 135 × 95 mm. 4r. "Water Pitcher" . . . . 4·00 4·50

1979. National Costumes. Multicoloured.

823	50l. Type **151**	20	15
824	75l. Sashed apron dress	25	20
825	90l. Serape	30	25
826	95l. Ankle-length printed dress	35	30

152 "Gloriosa superba"

1979. Flowers. Multicoloured.

827	1l. Type **152**	10	10
828	3l. "Hibiscus tiliaceus"	10	10
829	50l. "Barringtonia asiatica"	20	15
830	1r. "Abutilon indicum"	40	25
831	5r. "Guettarda speciosa"	1·00	2·00
MS832	94×85 mm. 4r. "Pandanus odoratissimus"	1·75	2·75

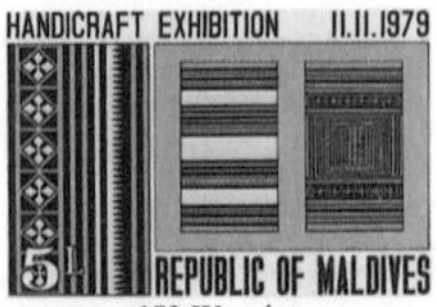

153 Weaving

1979. Handicraft Exhibition. Multicoloured.

833	5l. Type **153**	10	10
834	10l. Lacquerwork	10	10
835	1r.30 Tortoiseshell jewellery	50	55
836	2r. Carved woodwork	70	90
MS837	125×85 mm. 5r. Gold and silver jewellery	1·25	2·25

154 Mickey Mouse attacked by Bird

1979. International Year of the Child (2nd issue). Disney Characters. Multicoloured.

838	1l. Goofy delivering parcel on motor-scooter (vert)	10	10
839	2l. Type **154**	10	10
840	3l. Goofy half-covered with letters	10	10
841	4l. Pluto licking Minnie Mouse's envelopes	10	10
842	5l. Mickey Mouse delivering letters on roller skates (vert)	10	10
843	10l. Donald Duck placing letter in mail-box	10	10
844	15l. Chip and Dale carrying letter	10	10
845	1r.50 Donald Duck on monocycle (vert)	75	95
846	5r. Donald Duck with ostrich in crate (vert)	2·25	3·25
MS847	127×102 mm. 4r. Pluto putting parcel in mail-box	5·50	7·00

155 Post-Ramadan Dancing

1980. National Day. Multicoloured.

848	5l. Type **155**	10	10
849	15l. Musicians and dancer, Eeduu Festival	10	10
850	95l. Sultan's ceremonial band	35	30
851	2r. Dancer and drummers Circumcision Festival	60	85
MS852	131×99 mm. 5r. Swordsmen	1·90	2·50

156 Leatherback Turtle

1980. Turtle Conservation Campaign. Mult.

853	1l. Type **156**	10	30
854	2l. Flatback turtle	10	30
855	5l. Hawksbill turtle	15	30
856	10l. Loggerhead turtle	20	20
857	75l. Olive Ridley turtle	80	45
858	10r. Atlantic Ridley turtle	3·00	4·25
MS859	85×107 mm. 4r. Green turtle	2·00	2·75

157 Paul Harris (founder)

1980. 75th Anniv of Rotary Int. Mult.

860	75l. Type **157**	35	10
861	90l. Humanity	40	20
862	1r. Hunger	40	25
863	10r. Health	2·75	4·50
MS864	109×85 mm. 5r. Globe	1·50	2·50

1980. "London 1980" International Stamp Exhibition. Nos. 809/**MS**811 optd **LONDON 1980**.

865	1r.55 Penny Black	2·25	1·00
866	5r. First Maldives stamp	3·75	2·75
MS867	132×107 mm. 10r. Sir Rowland Hill	7·00	8·00

159 Swimming

1980. Olympic Games, Moscow. Multicoloured.

868	10l. Type **159**	10	10
869	50l. Running	20	20
870	3r. Putting the shot	70	1·10
871	4r. High jumping	80	1·40
MS872	105×85 mm. 5r. Weightlifting	1·25	2·25

160 White-tailed Tropic Bird

1980. Birds. Multicoloured.

873	75l. Type **160**	25	15
874	95l. Sooty tern	35	30
875	1r. Common noddy	35	30
876	1r.55 Curlew	50	70
877	2r. Wilson's storm petrel ("Wilson's Petrel")	60	85
878	4r. Caspian tern	1·10	1·60
MS879	124×85 mm. 5r. Red-footed booby and brown booby	8·00	9·00

161 Seal of Ibrahim II

1980. Seals of the Sultans.

880 **161**	1l. brown and black	10	10
881 –	2l. brown and black	10	10
882 –	5l. brown and black	10	10
883 –	1r. brown and black	30	30
884 –	2r. brown and black	50	70
MS885	131×95 mm. 3r. brown and black	85	1·60

DESIGNS: 2l. Mohammed Imadudeen II; 5l. Bin Haji Ali; 1r. Kuda Mohammed Rasgefaanu; 2r. Ibrahim Iskander I; 3r. Ibrahim Iskander I (different).

162 Queen Elizabeth the Queen Mother

1980. 80th Birthday of the Queen Mother.

886 **162**	4r. multicoloured	1·00	1·25
MS887	85×110 mm. **162** 5r. multicoloured	1·90	2·25

163 Munnaru

1980. 1400th Anniv of Hegira. Multicoloured.

888	5l. Type **163**	15	10
889	10l. Hukuru Miskiiy mosque	20	10
890	30l. Medhuziyaaraiy (shrine of saint)	25	30
891	55l. Writing tablets with verses of Koran	35	35
892	90l. Mother teaching child Koran	55	70
MS893	124×101 mm. 2r. Map of Maldives and coat of arms	80	1·60

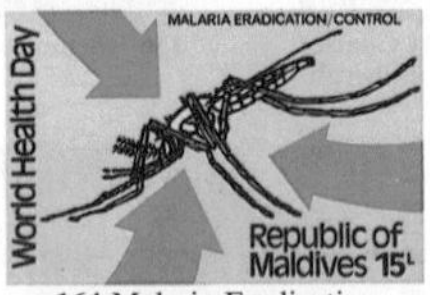

164 Malaria Eradication

1980. World Health Day.

894 **164**	15l. black, brown and red	10	10
895 –	25l. multicoloured	10	10
896 –	1r.50 brown, light brown and black	1·75	1·00
897 –	5r. multicoloured	3·00	3·00
MS898	68×85 mm. 4r. black, blue and light blue	1·25	2·50

DESIGNS: 25l. Nutrition; 1r.50, Dental health; 4, 5r. Clinics.

165 White Rabbit

1980. Walt Disney's "Alice in Wonderland". Multicoloured.

899	1l. Type **165**	10	10
900	2l. Alice falling into Wonderland	10	10
901	3l. Alice too big to go through door	10	10
902	4l. Alice with Tweedledum and Tweedledee	10	10
903	5l. Alice and caterpillar	10	10
904	10l. The Cheshire cat	10	10
905	15l. Alice painting the roses	10	10
906	2r.50 Alice and the Queen of Hearts	2·50	2·50
907	4r. Alice on trial	2·75	2·75
MS908	126×101 mm. 5r. Alice at the Mad Hatter's tea-party	4·50	6·50

166 Indian Ocean Ridley Turtle

1980. Marine Animals. Multicoloured.

909	90l. Type **166**	2·25	60
910	1r.25 Pennant coralfish	2·75	1·25
911	2r. Spiny lobster	3·25	1·75
MS912	140×94 mm. 4r. Oriental sweetlips and scarlet-finned squirrelfish	3·00	3·25

167 Pendant Lamp

168 Prince Charles and Lady Diana Spencer

1981. National Day. Multicoloured.

913	10l. Tomb of Ghaazee Muhammad Thakurufaan (horiz)	15	10
914	20l. Type **167**	20	10
915	30l. Chair used by Muhammad Thakurufaan	25	10
916	95l. Muhammad Thakurufaan's palace (horiz)	60	30
917	10r. Cushioned divan	2·75	4·50

1981. British Royal Wedding. Multicoloured.

918	1r. Type **168**	15	15
919	2r. Buckingham Palace	25	25
920	5r. Prince Charles, polo player	40	50
MS921	95×83 mm. 10r. State coach	75	1·10

169 First Majlis Chamber

1981. 50th Anniv of Citizens' Majlis (grievance rights). Multicoloured.

922	95l. Type **169**	30	30
923	1r. Sultan Muhammed Shamsuddin III	35	35
MS924	137×94 mm. 4r. First written constitution (horiz)	1·75	3·75

170 "Self-portrait with a Palette"

171 Airmail Envelope

1981. Birth Centenary of Pablo Picasso. Mult.

925	5l. Type **170**	15	10
926	10l. "Woman in Blue"	20	10
927	25l. "Boy with Pipe"	30	10
928	30l. "Card Player"	30	10
929	90l. "Sailor"	50	40
930	3r. "Self-portrait"	80	1·00
931	5r. "Harlequin"	1·00	1·25
MS932	106×130 mm. 10r. "Child holding a Dove". Imperf	2·50	3·50

1981. 75th Anniv of Postal Service.

933 **171**	25l. multicoloured	15	10
934	75l. multicoloured	25	25
935	5r. multicoloured	70	1·25

172 Boeing 737 taking off

1981. Male International Airport. Multicoloured.

936	5l. Type **172**	20	20
937	20l. Passengers leaving Boeing 737	40	20
938	1r.80 Refuelling	75	1·00
939	4r. Plan of airport	1·00	2·00
MS940	106×79 mm. 5r. Aerial view of airport	2·00	2·75

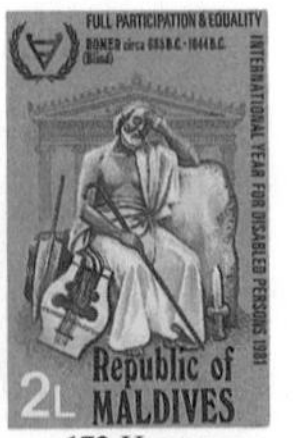

173 Homer

174 Preparation of Maldive Fish

1981. International Year of Disabled People. Multicoloured.

941	2l. Type **173**	10	10
942	5l. Miguel Cervantes	10	10
943	1r. Beethoven	2·00	85
944	5r. Van Gogh	3·00	5·00
MS945	116×91 mm. 4r. Helen Keller and Anne Sullivan	3·25	5·50

1981. Decade for Women. Multicoloured.

946	20l. Type **174**	10	10
947	90l. 16th-century Maldive women	25	25
948	1r. Farming	30	30
949	2r. Coir rope-making	55	1·10

175 Collecting Bait

1981. Fishermen's Day. Multicoloured.

950	5l. Type **175**	45	15
951	15l. Fishing boats	85	25
952	90l. Fisherman with catch	1·40	60
953	1r.30 Sorting fish	1·90	1·10
MS954	147×101 mm. 3r. Loading fish for export	1·50	2·50

176 Bread Fruit

1981. World Food Day. Multicoloured.
955 10l. Type **176** 40 10
956 25l. Hen with chicks 80 15
957 30l. Maize 80 20
958 75l. Skipjack tuna . . . . . 2·50 65
959 1r. Pumpkin . . . . 3·00 70
960 2r. Coconuts . . . . 3·25 3·25
MS961 110 × 85 mm. 5r. Eggplant 2·50 3·50

177 Pluto and Cat

1982. 50th Anniv of Pluto (Walt Disney Cartoon Character). Multicoloured.
962 4r. Type **177** . . . . 2·50 2·75
MS963 127 × 101 mm. 6r. Pluto (scene from "The Pointer") . . 3·25 4·00

178 Balmoral

180 Footballer

179 Scout saluting and Camp-site

1982. 21st Birthday of Princess of Wales. Mult.
964 95l. Type **178** 50 20
965 3r. Prince and Princess of Wales . . . . 1·00 65
966 5r. Princess on aircraft steps 1·75 95
MS967 103 × 75 mm. 8r. Princess of Wales . . . . 1·75 1·75

1983. 75th Anniv of Boy Scout Movement. Multicoloured.
968 1r.30 Type **179** 40 45
969 1r.80 Lighting a fire 50 60
970 4r. Life-saving . . . . 1·10 1·40
971 5r. Map-reading . . . . . . 1·40 1·75
MS972 128 × 66 mm. 10r. Scout emblem and flag of the Maldives 2·00 3·00

1982. World Cup Football Championship, Spain.
973 **180** 90l. multicoloured . . . . 1·50 60
974 – 1r.50 multicoloured . . . 2·00 1·10
975 – 3r. multicoloured . . . . 2·75 1·75
976 – 5r. multicoloured . . . . 3·25 2·50
MS977 94 × 63 mm. 10r. multicoloured . . . . 4·50 6·00
DESIGNS: 1r.50 to 10r. Various footballers.

1982. Birth of Prince William of Wales. Nos. 964/MS967 optd **ROYAL BABY 21.6.82.**
978 95l. Type **178** 30 20
979 3r. Prince and Princess of Wales . . . . 1·00 65
980 5r. Princess on aircraft steps 1·40 95
MS981 103 × 75 mm. 8r. Princess of Wales . . . . 3·00 2·50

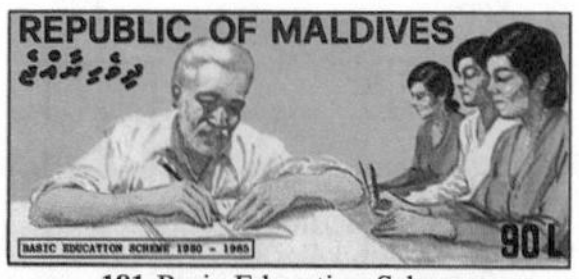
181 Basic Education Scheme

1983. National Education. Multicoloured.
982 90l. Type **181** 15 25
983 95l. Primary education . . . 15 25
984 1r.30 Teacher training . . . 20 30
985 2r.50 Printing educational material 40 60
MS986 100 × 70 mm. 6r. Thaana typewriter keyboard . . . . . 1·00 2·00

182 Koch isolates the Bacillus

183 Blohm and Voss Seaplane "Nordsee"

1983. Centenary of Robert Koch's Discovery of Tubercle Bacillus. Multicoloured.
987 5l. Type **182** 10 15
988 15l. Micro-organism and microscope 15 15
989 95l. Dr. Robert Koch in 1905 35 45
990 3r. Dr. Koch and plates from publication . . . . 85 1·50
MS991 77 × 61 mm. 5r. Koch in his laboratory (horiz) . . . . . . 1·00 2·00

1983. Bicentenary of Manned Flight. Mult.
992 90l. Type **183** . . . . 2·25 70
993 1r.45 Macchi Castoldi MC.72 seaplane . . . . 2·75 1·75
994 4r. Boeing F4B-3 biplane fighter . . . . 4·50 3·25
995 5r. Renard and Krebs airship "La France" . . . . . . 4·50 3·50
MS996 110 × 85 mm. 10r. Nadar's balloon "Le Geant" . . . . . 3·00 4·00

184 "Curved Dash" Oldsmobile, 1902

1983. Classic Motor Cars. Multicoloured.
997 5l. Type **184** 20 40
998 30l. Aston Martin "Tourer", 1932 . . . . 60 40
999 40l. Lamborghini "Muira", 1966 . . . . 60 45
1000 1r. Mercedes-Benz "300SL", 1945 . . . . 1·00 70
1001 1r.40 Stutz "Bearcat", 1913 1·25 2·00
1002 5r. Lotus "Elite", 1958 . . . 2·00 4·25
MS1003 132 × 103 mm. 10r. Grand Prix "Sunbeam", 1924 . . . . 6·00 10·00

185 Rough-toothed Dolphin

1983. Marine Mammals. Multicoloured.
1004 30l. Type **185** . . . . . . 1·60 60
1005 40l. Indo-Pacific hump-backed dolphin . . . . . 1·60 65
1006 4r. Finless porpoise . . . . 5·00 4·00
1007 6r. Pygmy sperm whale . . 10·00 7·00
MS1008 82 × 90 mm. 5r. Striped dolphin . . . . 6·50 5·50

186 Dish Aerial

1983. World Communications Year. Multicoloured.
1009 50l. Type **186** 40 20
1010 1r. Land, sea and air communications . . . . . 1·50 60
1011 2r. Ship-to-shore communications . . . . . 2·00 1·50
1012 10r. Air traffic controller . . 4·50 7·00
MS1013 91 × 76 mm. 20r. Telecommunications . . . . . 3·75 4·75

187 "La Donna Gravida"

1983. 500th Birth Anniv of Raphael. Mult.
1014 90l. Type **187** 25 25
1015 3r. "Giovanna d'Aragona" (detail) . . . . 75 1·60
1016 4r. "Woman with Unicorn" 75 2·25
1017 6r. "La Muta" . . . . . . 1·00 2·75
MS1018 121 × 97 mm. 10r. "The Knight's Dream" (detail) . . . 3·00 5·50

188 Refugee Camp

1983. Solidarity with the Palestinian People. Multicoloured.
1019 4r. Type **188** . . . . 1·75 2·00
1020 5r. Refugee holding dead child . . . . 1·90 2·00
1021 6r. Child carrying food . . 2·00 2·50

189 Education Facilities

1983. National Development Programme. Mult.
1022 7l. Type **189** 20 10
1023 10l. Health service and education 50 10
1024 5r. Growing more food . . 1·50 1·25
1025 6r. Fisheries development 2·25 1·50
MS1026 134 × 93 mm. 10r. Air transport . . . . 2·25 2·75

190 Baseball

194 Island Resort and Common Terns

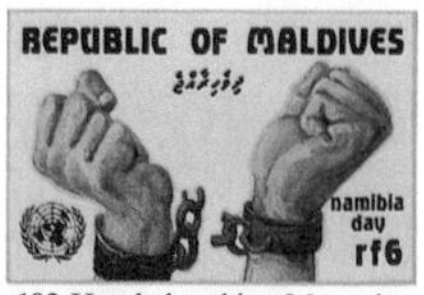
193 Hands breaking Manacles

1984. Olympic Games, Los Angeles. Multicoloured.
1027 50l. Type **190** 30 15
1028 1r.55 Backstroke swimming 65 40
1029 3r. Judo . . . . 1·40 90
1030 4r. Shot-putting . . . . . . 1·60 1·40
MS1031 85 × 105 mm. 10r. Team handball . . . . 2·40 2·75

1984. U.P.U. Congress, Hamburg. Nos. 994/**MS**996 optd **19th UPU CONGRESS HAMBURG.**
1032 4r. Boeing "F4B-3" . . . . 1·40 1·40
1033 5r. "La France" airship . . 1·60 1·60
MS1034 110 × 85 mm. 10r. Nadar's balloon "Le Geant" . . . . . 2·75 4·50

1984. Surch **Rf.1.45.** (a) Nos. 964/**MS**967.
1035 1r.45 on 95l. Type **178** . . 2·00 1·50
1036 1r.45 on 3r. Prince and Princess of Wales . . . . 2·00 1·50
1037 1r.45 on 5r. Princess on aircraft steps . . . . . . 2·00 1·50
MS1038 103 × 75 mm. 1r.45 on 8r. Princess of Wales . . . . . . 2·00 3·75

(b) Nos. 978/**MS**981.
1039 1r.45 on 95l. Type **178** . . 2·00 1·50
1040 1r.45 on 3r. Prince and Princess of Wales . . . . 2·00 1·50
1041 1r.45 on 5r. Princess on aircraft steps . . . . . . 2·00 1·50
MS1042 103 × 75 mm. 1r.45 on 8r. Princess of Wales . . . . . . 2·00 3·75

1984. Namibia Day. Multicoloured.
1043 6r. Type **193** . . . . 1·00 1·25
1044 8r. Namibian family . . . . 1·00 1·75
MS1045 129 × 104 mm. 10r. Map of Namibia . . . . 1·75 2·50

1984. Tourism. Multicoloured.
1046 7l. Type **194** . . . . 1·50 60
1047 15l. Dhow 80 15
1048 20l. Snorkelling 60 15
1049 2r. Wind-surfing . . . . . 2·00 50
1050 4r. Aqualung diving . . . . 2·50 1·10
1051 6r. Night fishing . . . . . 3·25 1·75
1052 8r. Game fishing . . . . . 3·50 2·00
1053 10r. Turtle on beach . . . . 3·75 2·25

195 Frangipani

1984. "Ausipex" International Stamp Exhibition, Melbourne. Multicoloured.
1054 5r. Type **195** . . . . 2·25 1·75
1055 10r. Cooktown orchid . . . 4·75 3·75
MS1056 105 × 77 mm. 15r. Sun orchid . . . . 10·00 5·50

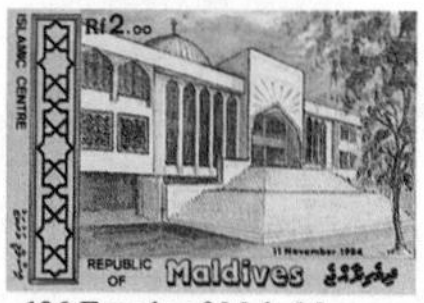
196 Facade of Male Mosque

1984. Opening of Islamic Centre. Multicoloured.
1057 2r. Type **196** 45 50
1058 5r. Male Mosque and minaret (vert) . . . . . . 1·10 1·25

197 Air Maldives Boeing 737

1984. 40th Anniv of I.C.A.O. Multicoloured.
1059 7l. Type **197** 70 35
1060 4r. Air Lanka Lockheed L-1011 TriStar . . . . . 3·00 1·75
1061 6r. Alitalia Douglas DC-10-30 . . . . 3·50 2·75
1062 8r. L.T.U. Lockheed L-1011 TriStar . . . . 3·75 3·50
MS1063 110 × 92 mm. 15r. Air Maldives Short S.7 Skyvan . . 3·75 4·00

198 Daisy Duck

1984. 50th Birthday of Donald Duck. Walt Disney Cartoon Characters. Multicoloured.
1064 3l. Type **198** 10 10
1065 4l. Huey, Dewey and Louie 10 10
1066 5l. Ludwig von Drake . . . 10 10
1067 10l. Gyro Gearloose 10 10
1068 15l. Uncle Scrooge painting self-portrait 15 10
1069 25l. Donald Duck with camera 15 10
1070 5r. Donald Duck and Gus Goose . . . . 2·25 1·25
1071 8r. Gladstone Gander . . . 2·50 2·00
1072 10r. Grandma Duck . . . . 3·00 2·50
MS1073 102 × 126 mm. 15r. Uncle Scrooge and Donald Duck in front of camera . . . . 4·75 5·00
MS1074 126 × 102 mm. 15r. Uncle Scrooge . . . . 4·75 5·00

199 "The Day" (detail)

200 "Edmond Iduranty" (Degas)

1984. 450th Death Anniv of Correggio (artist). Multicoloured.
1075 5r. Type **199** . . . . . . 1·00 1·50
1076 10r. "The Night" (detail) . . 1·50 1·75
MS1077 60 × 80 mm. 15r. "Portrait of a Man" . . . . 3·50 3·25

1984. 150th Birth Anniv of Edgar Degas (artist). Multicoloured.
1078 75l. Type **200** 20 20
1079 2r. "James Tissot" 50 50
1080 5r. "Achille de Gas in Uniform" . . . . 1·00 1·00
1081 10r. "Lady with Chrysanthemums" . . . . 1·75 2·00
MS1082 100 × 70 mm. 15r. "Self-portrait" . . . . 3·25 3·75

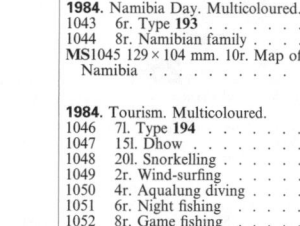

201 Pale-footed Shearwater ("Flest-footed Shearwater")

204 Queen Elizabeth the Queen Mother, 1981

202 Squad Drilling

1985. Birth Bicentenary of John J. Audubon (ornithologist) (1st issue). Designs showing original paintings. Multicoloured.

1083 3r. Type **201** 1·75 80
1084 3r.50 Little grebe (horiz) 2·00 90
1085 4r. Great cormorant 2·00 1·00
1086 4r.50 White-faced storm petrel (horiz) 2·00 1·10
MS1087 108 × 80 mm. 15r. Red-necked phalarope (horiz) 4·50 4·50

See also Nos. 1192/200.

1985. National Security Service. Multicoloured.

1088 15l. Type **202** 50 10
1089 20l. Combat patrol 50 10
1090 1r. Fire fighting 2·00 40
1091 2r. Coastguard cutter 2·50 1·00
1092 10r. Independence Day Parade (vert) 3·25 3·50
MS1093 128 × 85 mm. 10r. Cannon on saluting base and National Security Service badge 2·25 2·25

1985. Olympic Games Gold Medal Winners, Los Angeles. Nos. 1027/31 optd.

1094 50l. Type **190** (optd **JAPAN**) 30 10
1095 1r.55 Backstroke swimming (optd **GOLD MEDALIST THERESA ANDREWS USA**) 60 40
1096 3r. Judo (optd **GOLD MEDALIST FRANK WIENEKE USA**) 1·25 75
1097 4r. Shot-putting (optd **GOLD MEDALIST CLAUDIA LOCH WEST GERMANY**) 1·25 95
MS1098 85 × 105 mm. 10r. Team handball (optd **U.S.A.**) 1·90 2·00

1985. Life and Times of Queen Elizabeth the Queen Mother. Multicoloured.

1099 3r. Type **204** 45 60
1100 5r. Visiting the Middlesex Hospital (horiz) 65 1·00
1101 7r. The Queen Mother 85 1·25
MS1102 56 × 85 mm. 15r. With Prince Charles at Garter Ceremony 4·00 3·25

Stamps as Nos. 1099/1101 but with face values of 1r., 4r. and 10r. exist from additional sheetlets with changed background colours.

204a Lira da Braccio

1985. 300th Birth Anniversary of Johann Sebastian Bach (composer). Multicoloured (except No. **MS**1107).

1103 15l. Type **204a** 10 10
1104 2r. Tenor oboe 50 45
1105 4r. Serpent 90 85
1106 10r. Table organ 1·90 2·25
MS1107 104 × 75 mm. 15r. Johann Sebastian Bach (black and orange) 3·00 3·50

205 Mas Odi (fishing boat)

1985. Maldives Ships and Boats. Multicoloured.

1108 3l. Type **205** 10 20
1109 5l. Battela (dhow) 10 20
1110 10l. Addu odi (dhow) 10 20
1111 2r.60 Modern dhoni (fishing boat) 1·50 1·60
1112 2r.70 Mas dhoni (fishing boat) 1·50 1·60
1113 3r. Baththeli dhoni 1·60 1·60
1114 5r. "Inter I" (inter-island vessel) 2·50 2·75
1115 10r. Dhoni-style yacht 4·25 6·00

206 Windsurfing

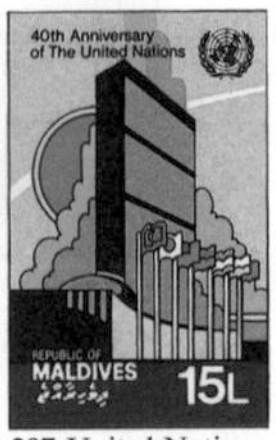

207 United Nations Building, New York

1985. 10th Anniv of World Tourism Organization. Multicoloured.

1116 6r. Type **206** 2·75 1·75
1117 8r. Scuba diving 3·00 2·00
MS1118 171 × 114 mm. 15r. Kuda Hithi Resort 2·75 3·00

1985. 40th Anniv of U.N.O. and International Peace Year. Multicoloured.

1119 15l. Type **207** 10 10
1120 2r. Hands releasing peace dove 40 45
1121 4r. U.N. Security Council meeting (horiz) 70 85
1122 10r. Lion and lamb 1·25 2·00
MS1123 76 × 92 mm. 15r. U.N. building and peace dove 2·25 2·75

208 Maldivian Delegate voting in U.N. General Assembly

1985. 20th Anniv of United Nations Membership. Multicoloured.

1124 20l. Type **208** 10 10
1125 15r. U.N. and Maldivian flags, and U.N. Building, New York 2·00 3·00

209 Youths playing Drums

1985. International Youth Year. Multicoloured.

1126 90l. Type **209** 15 20
1127 6r. Tug-of-war 80 1·10
1128 10r. Community service (vert) 1·25 2·00
MS1129 85 × 84 mm. 15r. Raising the flag at youth camp (vert) 2·25 3·00

210 Quotation and Flags of Member Nations

1985. 1st Summit Meeting of South Asian Association for Regional Co-operation, Dhaka, Bangladesh.

1130 **210** 3r. multicoloured 1·50 1·25

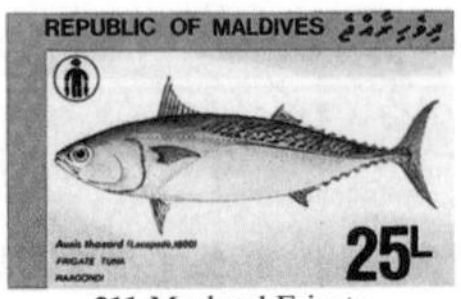

211 Mackerel Frigate

1985. Fishermen's Day. Species of Tuna. Mult.

1131 25l. Type **211** 35 10
1132 75l. Kawakawa ("Little tuna") 65 15
1133 3r. Dog-toothed tuna 2·00 75
1134 5r. Yellow-finned tuna 2·50 1·25
MS1135 130 × 90 mm. 15r. Skipjack tuna 3·50 3·50

1985. 150th Birth Anniv of Mark Twain. Designs as T **160a** of Lesotho, showing Walt Disney cartoon characters illustrating various Mark Twain quotations. Multicoloured.

1136 2l. Winnie the Pooh (vert) 10 10
1137 3l. Gepetto and Figaro the cat (vert) 10 10
1138 4l. Goofy and basket of broken eggs (vert) 10 10
1139 20l. Goofy as doctor scolding Donald Duck (vert) 25 10
1140 4r. Mowgli and King Louis (vert) 1·40 1·75
1141 13r. The wicked Queen and mirror (vert) 5·00 7·00
MS1142 126 × 101 mm. 15r. Mickey Mouse as Tom Sawyer on comet's tail 6·50 7·00

1985. Birth Bicentenaries of Grimm Brothers (folklorists). Designs as T **160b** of Lesotho, showing Walt Disney cartoon characters in scenes from "Dr. Knowall". Multicoloured.

1143 1l. Donald Duck as Crabb driving oxcart (horiz) 10 10
1144 5l. Donald Duck as Dr. Knowall (horiz) 10 10
1145 10l. Dr. Knowall in surgery (horiz) 10 10
1146 15l. Dr. Knowall with Uncle Scrooge as a lord (horiz) 10 10
1147 3r. Dr. and Mrs. Knowall in pony and trap (horiz) 1·10 1·50
1148 15r. Dr. Knowall and thief (horiz) 5·50 7·00
MS1149 126 × 101 mm. 15r. Donald and Daisy Duck as Dr. and Mrs. Knowall 6·50 7·00

211a Weapons on Road Sign

1986. World Disarmament Day. Multicoloured.

1149a 1r.50 Type **211a**
1149b 10r. Peace dove

1986. Appearance of Halley's Comet (1st issue). As T **162a** of Lesotho. Multicoloured.

1150 20l. N.A.S.A. space telescope and Comet 50 30
1151 1r.50 E.S.A. "Giotto" spacecraft and Comet 1·25 1·50
1152 2r. Japanese "Planet A" spacecraft and Comet 1·50 1·75
1153 4r. Edmond Halley and Stonehenge 2·25 3·00
1154 5r. Russian "Vega" spacecraft and Comet 2·25 3·00
MS1155 101 × 70 mm. 15r. Halley's Comet 8·00 9·50

See also Nos. 1206/11.

1986. Centenary of Statue of Liberty. Multicoloured. As T **163b** of Lesotho, showing the Statue of Liberty and immigrants to the U.S.A.

1156 50l. Walter Gropius (architect) 40 30
1157 70l. John Lennon (musician) 2·00 1·25
1158 1r. George Balanchine (choreographer) 2·00 1·25
1159 10r. Franz Werfel (writer) 4·00 7·00
MS1160 100 × 72 mm. 15r. Statue of Liberty (vert) 7·00 8·00

1986. "Ameripex" International Stamp Exhibition, Chicago. As T **163c** of Lesotho, showing Walt Disney cartoon characters and U.S.A. stamps. Multicoloured.

1161 3l. Johnny Appleseed and 1966 Johnny Appleseed stamp 10 10
1162 4l. Paul Bunyan and 1958 Forest Conservation stamp 10 10
1163 5l. Casey and 1969 Professional Baseball Centenary stamp 10 10
1164 10l. Ichabod Crane and 1974 "Legend of Sleepy Hollow" stamp 10 10
1165 15l. John Henry and 1944 75th Anniv of completion of First Transcontinental Railroad stamp 15 15
1166 20l. Windwagon Smith and 1954 Kansas Territory Centenary stamp 15 15
1167 13r. Mike Fink and 1970 Great Northwest stamp 7·00 7·00
1168 14r. Casey Jones and 1950 Railroad Engineers stamp 8·00 8·00
MS1169 Two sheets, each 127 × 101 mm. (a) 15r. Davy Crockett and 1967 Davy Crockett stamp. (b) 15r. Daisy Duck as Pocahontas saving Captain John Smith (Donald Duck) Set of 2 sheets 12·00 15·00

1986. 60th Birthday of Queen Elizabeth II. As T **163** of Lesotho.

1170 1r. black and yellow 30 25
1171 2r. multicoloured 40 55
1172 12r. multicoloured 1·50 2·50
MS1173 120 × 85 mm. 15r. black and brown 4·00 4·25

DESIGNS: 1r. Royal Family at Girl Guides Rally, 1938; 2r. Queen in Canada; 12r. At Sandringham, 1970; 15r. Princesses Elizabeth and Margaret at Royal Lodge, Windsor, 1940.

212 Player running with Ball

1986. World Cup Football Championship, Mexico. Multicoloured.

1174 15l. Type **212** 75 30
1175 2r. Player gaining control of ball 2·50 1·75
1176 4r. Two players competing for ball 4·00 3·50
1177 10r. Player bouncing ball on knee 7·50 8·00
MS1178 95 × 114 mm. 15r. Player kicking ball 5·00 6·00

1986. Royal Wedding. As T **170a** of Lesotho. Multicoloured.

1179 10l. Prince Andrew and Miss Sarah Ferguson 20 10
1180 2r. Prince Andrew 85 70
1181 12r. Prince Andrew in naval uniform 3·50 3·75
MS1182 88 × 88 mm. 15r. Prince Andrew and Miss Sarah Ferguson (different) 4·75 4·75

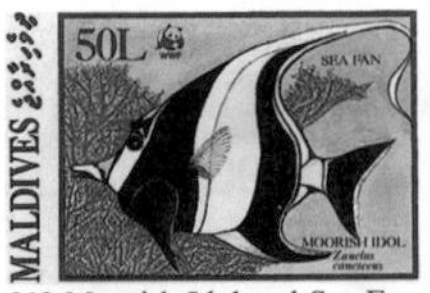

213 Moorish Idol and Sea Fan

(213b)

1986. Marine Wildlife. Multicoloured.

1183 50l. Type **213** 1·50 40
1184 90l. Regal angelfish 2·00 55
1185 1r. Maldive anemonefish 2·00 55
1186 2r. Tiger cowrie and stinging coral 2·50 1·60
1187 3r. Emperor angelfish and staghorn coral 2·50 2·00
1188 4r. Black-naped tern 3·00 3·00
1189 5r. Fiddler crab and staghorn coral 2·50 3·00
1190 10r. Hawksbill turtle 3·00 5·00
MS1191 Two sheets, each 107 × 76 mm. (a) 15r. Long-nosed butterflyfish. (b) 15r. Oriental trumpetfish Set of 2 sheets 12·00 15·00

1986. Birth Bicentenary (1985) of John J. Audubon (ornithologist) (2nd issue). As T **201** showing original paintings. Multicoloured.

1192 3l. Little blue heron (horiz) 40 60
1193 4l. White-tailed kite 40 60
1194 5l. Greater shearwater (horiz) 40 60
1195 10l. Magnificent frigate bird 45 40
1196 15l. Black-necked grebe ("Eared Grebe") 85 40
1197 20l. Goosander ("Common Merganser") 90 40
1198 13r. Peregrine falcon ("Great Footed Hawk") (horiz) 7·50 7·50
1199 14r. Prairie chicken ("Greater Prairie Chicken") (horiz) 7·50 7·50
MS1200 Two sheets, each 74 × 104 mm. (a) 15r. Fulmar ("Northern Fulmar"). (b) 15r. White-fronted goose (horiz) Set of 2 sheets 22·00 21·00

1986. World Cup Football Championship Winners, Mexico. Nos. 1174/7 optd **WINNERS Argentina 3 W. Germany 2.**

1201 15l. Type **212** 40 30
1202 2r. Player gaining control of ball 1·25 1·10
1203 4r. Two players competing for ball 2·00 2·00
1204 10r. Player bouncing ball on knee 3·25 4·25
MS1205 95 × 114 mm. 15r. Player kicking ball 3·00 4·25

1986. Appearance of Halley's Comet (2nd issue). Nos. 1150/4 optd with T **213b**.

1206 20l. N.A.S.A. space telescope and Comet 65 40
1207 1r.50 E.S.A. "Giotto" spacecraft and Comet 1·25 1·00
1208 2r. Japanese "Planet A" spacecraft and Comet 1·50 1·50
1209 4r. Edmond Halley and Stonehenge 2·00 2·25
1210 5r. Russia "Vega" spacecraft and Comet 2·00 2·25
MS1211 101 × 70 mm. 15r. Halley's Comet 6·00 6·50

214 Servicing Aircraft

216 Ixora

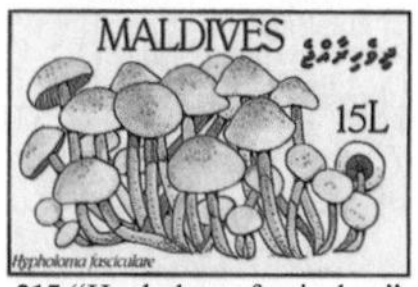

215 "Hypholoma fasciculare"

1986. 40th Anniv of UNESCO. Multicoloured.

1212	1r. Type **214**	80	30
1213	2r. Boat building	90	1·00
1214	3r. Children in classroom	1·00	1·40
1215	5r. Student in laboratory	1·10	2·50
MS1216	77 × 100 mm. 15r. Diving bell on sea bed	2·75	4·25

1986. Fungi of the Maldives. Multicoloured.

1217	15l. Type **215**	80	25
1218	50l. "Kuehneromyces mutabilis" (vert)	1·50	45
1219	1r. "Amanita muscaria" (vert)	1·75	60
1220	2r. "Agaricus campestris"	2·50	1·50
1221	3r. "Amanita pantherina" (vert)	2·50	1·75
1222	4r. "Coprinus comatus" (vert)	2·50	2·25
1223	5r. "Gymnopilus junonius" ("Pholiota spectabilis")	2·50	2·75
1224	10r. "Pluteus cervinus"	3·75	4·50
MS1225	Two sheets, each 100 × 70 mm. (a) 15r. "Armillaria mellea". (b) 15r. "Stropharia aeruginosa" (vert) Set of 2 sheets	15·00	14·00

1987. Flowers. Multicoloured.

1226	10l. Type **216**	10	10
1227	20l. Frangipani	10	10
1228	50l. Crinum	2·00	60
1229	2r. Pink rose	40	80
1230	4r. Flamboyant flower	60	1·50
1231	10r. Ground orchid	6·00	8·00
MS1232	Two sheets, each 100 × 70 mm. (a) 15r. Gardenia. (b) 15r. Oleander Set of 2 sheets	4·75	6·50

217 Guides studying Wild Flowers

1987. 75th Anniv (1985) of Girl Guide Movement. Multicoloured.

1233	15l. Type **217**	30	20
1234	2r. Guides with pet rabbits	60	80
1235	4r. Guide observing white spoonbill	3·00	2·25
1236	12r. Lady Baden-Powell and Guide flag	3·25	6·50
MS1237	104 × 78 mm. 15r. Guides in sailing dinghy	2·25	3·75

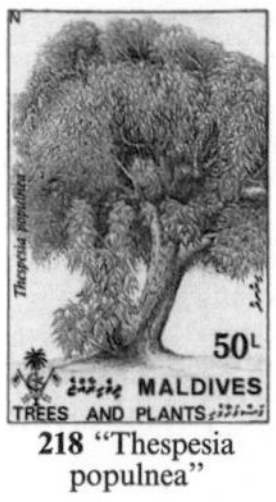

218 "Thespesia populnea"

219 "Precis octavia"

1987. Trees and Plants. Multicoloured.

1238	50l. Type **218**	15	10
1239	1r. "Cocos nucifera"	20	20
1240	2r. "Calophyllum mophyllum"	35	40
1241	3r. "Xanthosoma indica" (horiz)	55	65
1242	5r. "Ipomoea batatas" (horiz)	90	1·40
1243	7r. "Artocarpus altilis"	1·25	2·00
MS1244	75 × 109 mm. 15r. "Cocos nucifera" (different)	2·25	3·25

No. 1241 is inscr "Xanthosomaindica" in error.

1987. America's Cup Yachting Championship. As T **218a** of Lesotho. Multicoloured.

1245	15l. "Intrepid", 1970	10	10
1246	1r. "France II", 1974	20	20
1247	2r. "Gretel", 1962	40	60
1248	12r. "Volunteer", 1887	2·00	3·00
MS1249	113 × 83 mm. 15r. Helmsman and crew on deck of "Defender", 1895 (horiz)	2·25	3·25

1987. Butterflies. Multicoloured.

1250	15l. Type **219**	45	30
1251	20l. "Atrophaneura hector"	45	30
1252	50l. "Teinopalpus imperialis"	75	40
1253	1r. "Kallima horsfieldi"	1·00	45
1254	2r. "Cethosia biblis"	1·60	1·25
1255	4r. "Idea jasonia"	2·50	2·25
1256	7r. "Papilio memnon"	3·50	4·00
1257	10r. "Aeropetes tulbaghia"	4·00	5·00
MS1258	Two sheets, each 135 × 102 mm. (a) 15r. "Acraea violae". (b) 15r. "Hebomoia leucippe" Set of 2 sheets	9·00	11·00

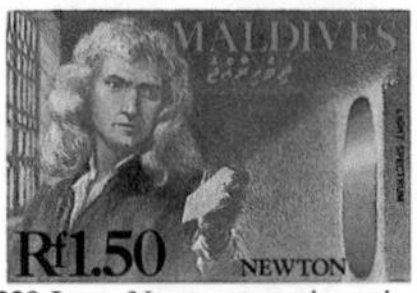

220 Isaac Newton experimenting with Spectrum

1988. Great Scientific Discoveries. Multicoloured.

1259	1r.50 Type **220**	1·25	1·00
1260	3r. Euclid composing "Principles of Geometry" (vert)	1·60	1·75
1261	4r. Mendel formulating theory of Genetic Evolution (vert)	1·75	2·00
1262	5r. Galileo and moons of Jupiter	3·00	3·00
MS1263	102 × 72 mm. 15r. "Apollo" lunar module (vert)	4·50	5·50

221 Donald Duck and Weather Satellite

1988. Space Exploration. Walt Disney cartoon characters. Multicoloured.

1264	3l. Type **221**	10	10
1265	4l. Minnie Mouse and navigation satellite	10	10
1266	5l. Mickey Mouse's nephews talking via communication satellite	10	10
1267	10l. Goofy in lunar rover (vert)	10	10
1268	20l. Minnie Mouse delivering pizza to flying saucer (vert)	10	10
1269	13r. Mickey Mouse directing spacecraft docking (vert)	5·00	5·00
1270	14r. Mickey Mouse and "Voyager 2"	5·00	5·00
MS1271	Two sheets, each 127 × 102 mm. (a) 15r. Mickey Mouse at first Moon landing, 1969. (b) 15r. Mickey Mouse and nephews in space station swimming pool (vert) Set of 2 sheets	13·00	13·00

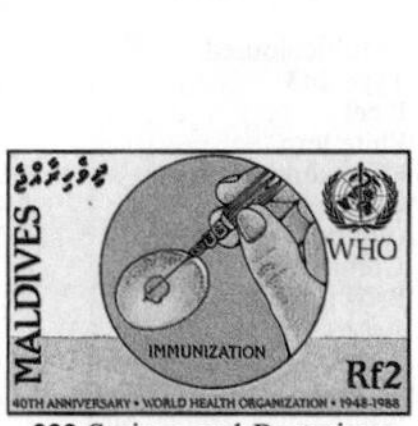

222 Syringe and Bacterium ("Immunization")

1988. 40th Anniv of W.H.O. Multicoloured.

1272	2r. Type **222**	40	40
1273	4r. Tap ("Clean Water")	60	85

223 Water Droplet and Atoll

1988. World Environment Day (1987). Mult.

1274	15l. Type **223**	10	10
1275	75l. Coral reef	20	40
1276	2r. Audubon's shearwaters in flight	85	1·40
MS1277	105 × 76 mm. 15r. Banyan tree (vert)	3·75	5·00

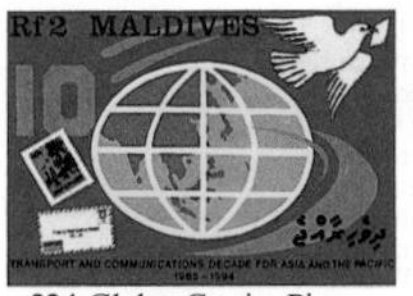

224 Globe, Carrier Pigeon and Letter

226 Discus-throwing

1988. Transport and Telecommunications Decade. Each showing central globe. Multicoloured.

1278	2r. Type **224**	60	65
1279	3r. Dish aerial and girl using telephone	1·00	1·10
1280	5r. Satellite, television, telephone and antenna tower	1·75	2·00
1281	10r. Car, ship and Lockheed TriStar airliner	9·50	6·50

1988. Royal Ruby Wedding. Nos. 1170/3 optd **40TH WEDDING ANNIVERSARY H.M. QUEEN ELIZABETH II H.R.H. THE DUKE OF EDINBURGH**.

1282	1r. black and yellow	45	25
1283	2r. multicoloured	60	60
1284	12r. multicoloured	2·75	3·50
MS1285	120 × 85 mm. 15r. black and brown	4·25	4·25

1988. Olympic Games, Seoul. Multicoloured.

1286	15l. Type **226**	10	10
1287	2r. 100 m race	40	40
1288	4r. Gymnastics (horiz)	70	80
1289	12r. Three-day equestrian event (horiz)	2·25	3·25
MS1290	106 × 76 mm. 20r. Tennis (horiz)	4·00	4·75

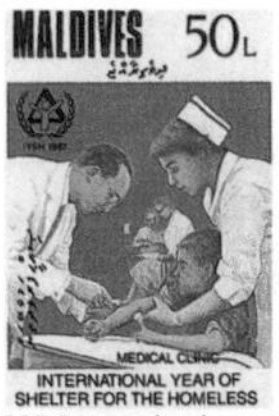

227 Immunization at Clinic

230 Pres. Kennedy and Launch of "Apollo" Spacecraft

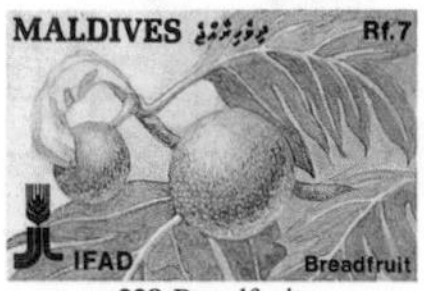

228 Breadfruit

1988. Int Year of Shelter for the Homeless. Mult.

1291	50l. Type **227**	30	30
1292	3r. Prefab housing estate	1·10	1·40
MS1293	63 × 105 mm. 15r. Building site	1·75	2·50

1988. 10th Anniv of International Fund for Agricultural Development. Multicoloured.

1294	7r. Type **228**	1·00	1·40
1295	10r. Mangoes (vert)	1·50	1·90
MS1296	103 × 74 mm. 15r. Coconut palm, fishing boat and yellowtail tuna	3·00	3·25

1988. World Aids Day. Nos. 1272/3 optd **WORLD AIDS DAY** and emblem.

1297	2r. Type **222**	35	45
1298	4r. "Tap" ("Clean Water")	65	80

1989. 25th Death Anniv (1988) of John F. Kennedy (American statesman). U.S. Space Achievements. Multicoloured.

1299	5r. Type **230**	2·25	2·50
1300	5r. Lunar module and astronaut on Moon	2·25	2·50
1301	5r. Astronaut and buggy on Moon	2·25	2·50
1302	5r. President Kennedy and spacecraft	2·25	2·50
MS1303	108 × 77 mm. 15r. President Kennedy making speech	4·00	4·75

1989. Olympic Medal Winners, Seoul. Nos. 1286/90 optd.

1304	15l. Type **226** (optd **J. SCHULT DDR**)	20	20
1305	2r. 100 m race (optd **C. LEWIS USA**)	65	65
1306	4r. Gymnastics (horiz) (optd **MEN'S ALL AROUND V. ARTEMOV USSR**)	1·40	1·40
1307	12r. Three-day equestrian event (horiz) (optd **TEAM SHOW JUMPING W. GERMANY**)	5·00	5·50
MS1308	106 × 76 mm. 20r. Tennis (horiz) (optd **OLYMPIC WINNERS MEN'S SINGLES GOLD M. MECIR CZECH SILVER T. MAYOTTE USA BRONZE B. GILBERT USA**)	6·50	7·50

On No. **MS**1308 the overprint appears on the sheet margin.

1989. 500th Birth Anniv of Titian (artist). As T **186a** of Lesotho, showing paintings. Multicoloured.

1309	15l. "Benedetto Varchi"	10	10
1310	1r. "Portrait of a Young Man"	20	15
1311	2r. "King Francis I of France"	40	40
1312	5r. "Pietro Aretino"	1·10	1·25
1313	15r. "The Bravo"	3·50	5·00
1314	20r. "The Concert" (detail)	3·50	6·00
MS1315	Two sheets. (a) 112 × 96 mm. 20r. "An Allegory of Prudence" (detail). (b) 96 × 110 mm. 20r. "Francesco Maria della Rovere" Set of 2 sheets	8·00	9·00

1989. 10th Anniversary of Asia–Pacific Telecommunity. Nos. 1279/80 optd **ASIA–PACIFIC TELECOMMUNITY 10 YEARS** and emblem. Multicoloured.

1316	3r. Dish aerial and girl using telephone	1·25	1·50
1317	5r. Satellite, television, telephone and antenna tower	1·75	2·00

1989. Japanese Art. Paintings by Hokusai. As T **187a** of Lesotho. Multicoloured.

1318	15l. "Fuji from Hodogaya" (horiz)	10	10
1319	50l. "Fuji from Lake Kawaguchi" (horiz)	15	15
1320	1r. "Fuji from Owari" (horiz)	25	15
1321	2r. "Fuji from Tsukudajima in Edo" (horiz)	50	40
1322	4r. "Fuji from a Teahouse at Yoshida" (horiz)	80	90
1323	6r. "Fuji from Tagonoura" (horiz)	90	1·25
1324	10r. "Fuji from Mishima-goe" (horiz)	2·25	2·75
1325	12r. "Fuji from the Sumida River in Edo" (horiz)	2·25	2·75
MS1326	Two sheets, each 101 × 77 mm. (a) 18r. "Fuji from Inume Pass". (b) 18r. "Fuji from Fukagawa in Edo" Set of 2 sheets	8·50	9·00

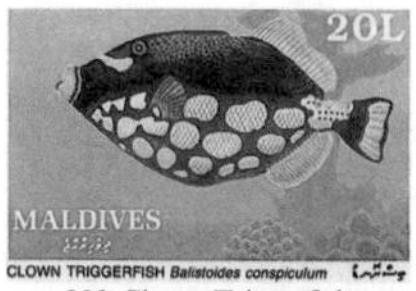

233 Clown Triggerfish

1989. Tropical Fishes. Multicoloured.

1327	20l. Type **233**	25	20
1328	50l. Blue-striped snapper	35	25
1329	1r. Powder-blue surgeonfish	45	30
1330	2r. Oriental sweetlips	75	65
1331	3r. Six-barred wrasse	1·00	85
1332	8r. Thread-finned butterflyfish	2·00	2·50
1333	10r. Bicoloured parrotfish	2·40	2·75
1334	12r. Scarlet-finned squirrelfish	2·40	2·75
MS1335	Two sheets, each 101 × 73 mm. (a) 15r. Butterfly perch. (b) 15r. Semicircle angelfish Set of 2 sheets	13·00	12·00

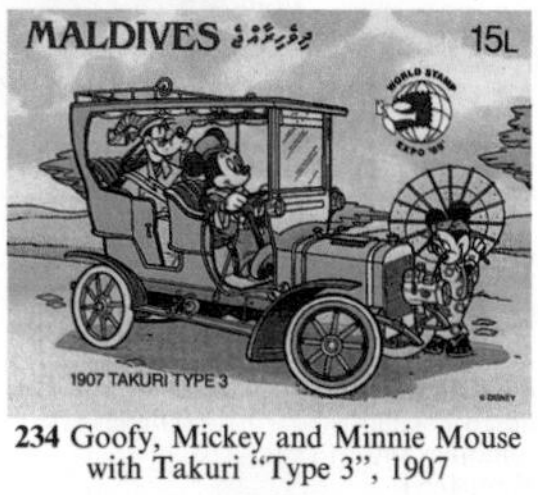

234 Goofy, Mickey and Minnie Mouse with Takuri "Type 3", 1907

1989. "World Stamp Expo '89" International Stamp Exhibition, Washington (1st issue). Designs showing Walt Disney cartoon characters with Japanese cars. Multicoloured.

1336	15l. Type **234**	20	15
1337	50l. Donald and Daisy Duck in Mitsubishi "Model A", 1917	40	30
1338	1r. Goofy in Datsun "Roadstar", 1935	70	50
1339	2r. Donald and Daisy Duck with Mazda, 1940	1·00	75

1340 4r. Donald Duck with Nissan "Bluebird 310", 1959 1·50 1·25
1341 6r. Donald and Daisy Duck with Subaru "360", 1958 1·75 1·75
1342 10r. Mickey Mouse and Pluto in Honda "5800", 1966 3·25 3·75
1343 12r. Mickey Mouse and Goofy in Daihatsu "Fellow", 1966 3·75 4·25
MS1344 Two sheets, each 127 × 102 mm. (a) 20r. Daisy Duck with Chip n'Dale and Isuzu "Trooper II", 1981. (b) 20r. Mickey Mouse with tortoise and Toyota "Supra", 1985 Set of 2 sheets 11·00 13·00

1989. "World Stamp Expo '89" International Stamp Exhibition, Washington (2nd issue). Landmarks of Washington. Sheet 62 × 78 mm, containing multicoloured designs as T **193a** of Lesotho, but vert.
MS1345 8r. Marine Corps Memorial, Arlington National Cemetery 2·25 2·75

235 Lunar Module "Eagle"

1989. 20th Anniv of First Manned Landing on Moon. Multicoloured.
1346 1r. Type **235** 30 20
1347 2r. Astronaut Aldrin collecting dust samples 50 60
1348 6r. Aldrin setting up seismometer 1·25 1·75
1349 10r. Pres. Nixon congratulating "Apollo 11" astronauts 1·90 2·50
MS1350 107 × 75 mm. 18r. Television picture of Armstrong about to step onto Moon (34 × 47 mm) 7·50 8·00

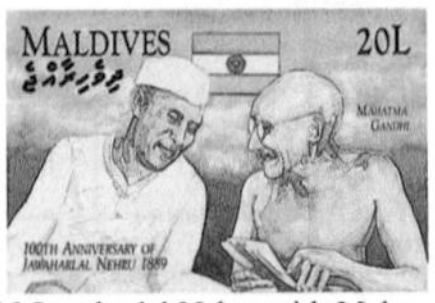

236 Jawaharlal Nehru with Mahatma Gandhi

1989. Anniversaries and Events. Multicoloured.
1351 20l. Type **236** (birth cent) 2·50 1·00
1352 50l. Opium poppies and logo (anti-drugs campaign) (vert) 1·50 45
1353 1r. William Shakespeare (425th birth anniv) 1·25 45
1354 2r. Storming the Bastille (bicent of French Revolution) (vert) 1·25 1·25
1355 3r. Concorde (20th anniv of first flight) 4·50 2·25
1356 8r. George Washington (bicent of inauguration) 2·00 3·00
1357 10r. William Bligh (bicent of mutiny on the "Bounty") 7·00 5·00
1358 12r. Hamburg harbour (800th anniv) (vert) 4·00 5·50
MS1359 Two sheets. (a) 115 × 85 mm. 18r. Baseball players (50th anniv of first televised game) (vert). (b) 110 × 80 mm. 18r. Franz von Taxis (500th anniv of regular European postal services) (vert) Set of 2 sheets 14·00 16·00

237 Sir William van Horne (Chairman of Canadian Pacific), Locomotive and Map, 1894

239 "Louis XVI in Coronation Robes" (Duplessis)

238 Bodu Thakurufaanu Memorial Centre, Utheemu

1989. Railway Pioneers. Multicoloured.
1360 10l. Type **237** 25 15
1361 25l. Matthew Murray (engineer) with Blenkinsop and Murray's rack locomotive, 1810 35 20
1362 50l. Louis Favre (railway engineer) and steam locomotive entering tunnel 40 25
1363 2r. George Stephenson (engineer) and "Locomotion", 1825 75 55
1364 6r. Richard Trevithick and "Catch-Me-Who-Can", 1808 1·50 1·50
1365 8r. George Nagelmackers and "Orient Express" dining car 1·75 1·75
1366 10r. William Jessop and horse-drawn wagon, Surrey Iron Railway, 1770 2·50 2·50
1367 12r. Isambard Brunel (engineer) and GWR steam locomotive, 1833 3·00 3·00
MS1368 Two sheets, each 71 × 103 mm. (a) 18r. George Pullman (inventor of sleeping cars), 1864. (b) 18r. Rudolf Diesel (engineer) and first oil engine Set of 2 sheets 9·50 10·50

1990. 25th Anniv of Independence. Multicoloured.
1369 20l. Type **238** 10 10
1370 25l. Islamic Centre, Male 10 10
1371 50l. National flag and logos of international organizations 10 10
1372 2r. Presidential Palace, Male 30 40
1373 5r. National Security Service 85 1·25
MS1374 128 × 90 mm. 10r. National emblem 4·00 4·25

1990. Bicentenary of French Revolution and "Philexfrance '89" International Stamp Exhibi-tion, Paris. French Paintings. Multicoloured.
1375 15l. Type **239** 15 15
1376 50l. "Monsieur Lavoisier and his Wife" (David) 35 25
1377 1r. "Madame Pastoret" (David) 55 35
1378 2r. "Oath of Lafayette, 14 July 1790" (anon) 90 70
1379 4r. "Madame Trudaine" (David) 1·50 1·50
1380 6r. "Chenard celebrating the Liberation of Savoy" (Boilly) 2·25 2·50
1381 10r. "An Officer swears Allegiance to the Constitution" (anon) 3·50 4·25
1382 12r. "Self Portrait" (David) 3·75 4·50
MS1383 Two sheets. (a) 104 × 79 mm. 20r. "The Oath of the Tennis Court, 20 June 1789" (David) (horiz). (b) 79 × 104 mm. 20r. "Rousseau and Symbols of the Revolution" (Jeaurat) Set of 2 sheets 12·00 13·00

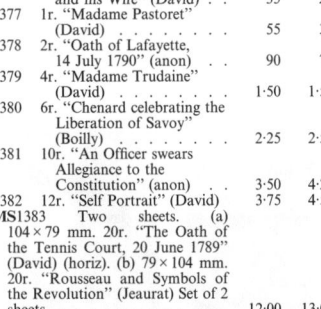

239a Donald Duck, Mickey Mouse and Goofy Playing Rugby

1990. "Stamp World London '90" International Stamp Exhibition. Walt Disney cartoon characters playing British sports. Multicoloured.
1384 15l. Type **239a** 30 15
1385 50l. Donald Duck and Chip-n-Dale curling 45 25
1386 1r. Goofy playing polo 65 40
1387 2r. Mickey Mouse and nephews playing soccer 90 70
1388 4r. Mickey Mouse playing cricket 1·75 1·50
1389 6r. Minnie and Mickey Mouse at Ascot races 2·25 1·90
1390 10r. Mickey Mouse and Goofy playing tennis 3·50 3·50
1391 12r. Donald Duck and Mickey Mouse playing bowls 3·50 3·50
MS1392 Two sheets, each 126 × 101 mm. (a) 20r. Minnie Mouse fox-hunting. (b) 20r. Mickey Mouse playing golf Set of 2 sheets 15·00 15·00

240 Silhouettes of Queen Elizabeth II and Queen Victoria

1990. 150th Anniv of the Penny Black.
1393 **240** 8r. black and green 2·75 2·75
1394 – 12r. black and blue 3·25 3·25
MS1395 109 × 84 mm. 18r. black and brown 5·50 6·50

DESIGN: 12r. As Type **240**, but with position of silhouettes reversed; 18r. Penny Black.

1990. 90th Birthday of Queen Elizabeth the Queen Mother. As T **198a** of Lesotho.
1396 6r. black, mauve and blue 1·10 1·40
1397 6r. black, mauve and blue 1·10 1·40
1398 6r. black, mauve and blue 1·10 1·40
MS1399 90 × 75 mm. 18r. multicoloured 3·25 3·50

DESIGNS: No. 1396, Lady Elizabeth Bowes-Lyon; 1397, Lady Elizabeth Bowes-Lyon wearing headband; 1398, Lady Elizabeth Bowes-Lyon leaving for her wedding; **MS**1399, Lady Elizabeth Bowes-Lyon wearing wedding dress.

241 Sultan's Tomb

1990. Islamic Heritage Year. Each black and blue.
1400 1r. Type **241** 35 45
1401 1r. Thakurufaan's Palace 35 45
1402 1r. Male Mosque 35 45
1403 2r. Veranda of Friday Mosque 45 55
1404 2r. Interior of Friday Mosque 45 55
1405 2r. Friday Mosque and Monument 45 55

242 Defence of Wake Island, 1941

1990. 50th Anniv of Second World War. Mult.
1406 15l. Type **242** 25 20
1407 25l. Stilwell's army in Burma, 1944 30 20
1408 50l. Normandy offensive, 1944 40 25
1409 1r. Capture of Saipan, 1944 55 40
1410 2r.50 D-Day landings, 1944 90 80
1411 3r.50 Allied landings in Norway, 1940 1·10 1·10
1412 4r. Lord Mountbatten, Head of Combined Operations, 1943 1·40 1·40
1413 6r. Japanese surrender, Tokyo Bay, 1945 1·75 2·00
1414 10r. Potsdam Conference, 1945 2·75 3·00
1415 12r. Allied invasion of Sicily, 1943 3·00 3·25
MS1416 115 × 87 mm. 18r. Atlantic convoy 5·50 6·50

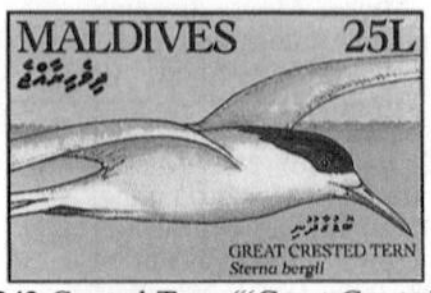

243 Crested Tern ("Great Crested Tern")

1990. Birds. Multicoloured.
1417 25l. Type **243** 15 15
1418 50l. Koel 25 25
1419 1r. White tern 35 35
1420 3r.50 Cinnamon bittern 90 1·00
1421 6r. Sooty tern 1·40 1·60
1422 8r. Audubon's shearwater 1·60 2·00
1423 12r. Common noddy ("Brown Noddy") 2·50 3·00
1424 15r. Lesser frigate bird 2·75 3·25
MS1425 Two sheets, each 100 × 69 mm. (a) 18r. Grey heron. (b) 18r. White-tailed tropic bird Set of 2 sheets 8·00 10·00

244 Emblem, Dish Aerial and Sailboards

245 "Spathoglottis plicata"

1990. 5th South Asian Association for Regional Co-operation Summit.
1426 **244** 75l. black and orange 25 25
1427 – 3r.50 multicoloured 1·50 1·25
MS1428 112 × 82 mm. 20r. multicoloured 4·50 5·50

DESIGN: 3r.50, Flags of member nations; 20r. Global warming diagram.

1990. "EXPO '90" International Garden and Greenery Exhibition, Osaka. Flowers. Mult.
1429 20l. Type **245** 1·25 40
1430 75l. "Hippeastrum puniceum" 1·50 50
1431 2r. "Tecoma stans" (horiz) 1·60 90
1432 3r.50 "Catharanthus roseus" (horiz) 1·60 1·60
1433 10r. "Ixora coccinea" (horiz) 3·00 3·25
1434 12r. "Clitorea ternatea" (horiz) 3·25 3·50
1435 15r. "Caesalpinia pulcherrima" 3·25 3·75
MS1436 Four sheets, each 111 × 79 mm. (a) 20r. "Plumeria obtusa" (horiz). (b) 20r. "Jasminum grandiflorum" (horiz). (c) 20r. "Rosa" sp (horiz). (d) 20r. "Hibiscus tiliaceous" (horiz) Set of 4 sheets 13·00 13·00

246 "The Hare and the Tortoise"

1990. International Literacy Year. Walt Disney cartoon characters illustrating fables by Aesop. Multicoloured.
1437 15l. Type **246** 30 15
1438 50l. "The Town Mouse and the Country Mouse" 50 25
1439 1r. "The Fox and the Crow" 80 35
1440 3r.50 "The Travellers and the Bear" 1·60 1·60
1441 4r. "The Fox and the Lion" 1·75 1·75
1442 6r. "The Mice Meeting" 2·25 2·25
1443 10r. "The Fox and the Goat" 2·75 3·00
1444 12r. "The Dog in the Manger" 2·75 3·25
MS1445 Two sheets, each 127 × 102 mm. (a) 20r. "The Miller, his Son and the Ass" (vert). (b) 20r. "The Miser's Gold" (vert) Set of 2 sheets 12·00 12·00

247 East African Railways Class 31 Steam Locomotive

248 Ruud Gullit of Holland

1990. Railway Steam Locomotives. Multicoloured.
1446 20l. Type **247** 75 30
1447 50l. Steam locomotive, Sudan 1·00 45
1448 1r. Class GM Garratt, South Africa 1·40 60
1449 3r. 7th Class, Rhodesia 2·25 2·00
1450 5r. Central Pacific Class No. 229, U.S.A. 2·50 2·25
1451 8r. Reading Railroad No. 415, U.S.A. 2·75 2·75
1452 10r. Porter narrow gauge, Canada 2·75 2·75
1453 12r. Great Northern Railway No. 515, U.S.A. 2·75 3·00
MS1454 Two sheets, each 90 × 65 mm. (a) 20r. 19th-century standard American locomotive No. 315. (b) 20r. East African Railways Garratt locomotive No. 5950 Set of 2 sheets 16·00 15·00

1990. World Cup Football Championship, Italy. Multicoloured.
1455 1r. Type **248** 1·50 50
1456 2r.50 Paul Gascoigne of England 2·25 1·25
1457 3r.50 Brazilian challenging Argentine player 2·25 1·60
1458 5r. Brazilian taking control of ball 2·50 2·00
1459 7r. Italian and Austrian jumping for header 3·25 3·25
1460 10r. Russian being chased by Turkish player 3·50 3·50
1461 15r. Andres Brehme of West Germany 4·00 4·25
MS1462 Four sheets, each 77 × 92 mm. (a) 18r. Head of an Austrian player (horiz). (b) 18r. Head of a South Korean player (horiz). (c) 20r. Diego Maradona of Argentina (horiz). (d) 20r. Schilacci of Italy (horiz) Set of 4 sheets 17·00 17·00

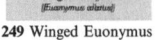

249 Winged Euonymus

251 Greek Messenger from Marathon, 490 B.C. (2480th Anniv)

250 "Summer" (Rubens)

1991. Bonsai Trees and Shrubs. Multicoloured.

1463	20l. Type **249**	50	20
1464	50l. Japanese black pine	65	35
1465	1r. Japanese five needle pine	90	55
1466	3r.50 Flowering quince	2·00	1·75
1467	5r. Chinese elm	2·50	2·50
1468	8r. Japanese persimmon	2·75	3·00
1469	10r. Japanese wisteria	2·75	3·00
1470	12r. Satsuki azalea	2·75	3·25
MS1471	Two sheets, each 89 × 88 mm. (a) 20r. Trident maple. (b) 20r. Sargent juniper Set of 2 sheets	12·00	14·00

1991. 350th Death Anniv of Rubens. Mult.

1472	20l. Type **250**	20	15
1473	50l. "Landscape with Rainbow" (detail)	35	25
1474	1r. "Wreck of Aeneas"	55	40
1475	2r.50 "Chateau de Steen" (detail)	1·00	1·00
1476	3r.50 "Landscape with Herd of Cows"	1·25	1·25
1477	7r. "Ruins on the Palantine"	2·00	2·50
1478	10r. "Landscape with Peasants and Cows"	2·25	2·50
1479	12r. "Wagon fording Stream"	2·50	3·00
MS1480	Four sheets, each 100 × 71 mm. (a) 20r. "Landscape at Sunset". (b) 20r. "Peasants with Cattle by a Stream". (c) 20r. "Shepherd with Flock". (d) 20r. "Wagon in Stream" Set of 4 sheets	15·00	16·00

1991. Anniversaries and Events (1990). Mult.

1481	50l. Type **251**	45	25
1482	1r. Anthony Fokker in Haarlem Spin monoplane (birth centenary)	80	45
1483	3r.50 "Early Bird" satellite (25th anniv)	1·50	1·50
1484	7r. Signing Reunification of Germany agreement (horiz)	1·75	2·50
1485	8r. King John signing Magna Carta (775th anniv)	2·25	2·50
1486	10r. Dwight D. Eisenhower (birth centenary)	2·25	2·50
1487	12r. Sir Winston Churchill (25th death anniv)	3·25	3·50
1488	15r. Pres. Reagan at Berlin Wall (German reunification) (horiz)	2·75	3·75
MS1489	Two sheets. (a) 180 × 81 mm. 20r. German Junkers Ju88 bomber (50th anniv of Battle of Britain) (horiz). (b) 160 × 73 mm. 20r. Brandenburg Gate (German reunification) (horiz) Set of 2 sheets	13·00	13·00

252 Arctic Iceberg and Maldives Dhoni

1991. Global Warming. Multicoloured.

1490	3r.50 Type **252**	1·50	1·25
1491	7r. Antarctic iceberg and "Maldive Trader" (freighter)	3·50	3·25

253 S.A.A.R.C. Emblem and Medal

1991. Year of the Girl Child.

1492	**253** 7r. multicoloured	1·75	1·75

254 Children on Beach

1991. Year of the Maldivian Child. Children's Paintings. Multicoloured.

1493	3r.50 Type **254**	2·25	1·40
1494	5r. Children in a park	2·75	2·25
1495	10r. Hungry child dreaming of food	3·75	4·00
1496	25r. Scuba diver	7·00	10·00

255 "Still Life: Japanese Vase with Roses and Anemones"

1991. Death Centenary (1990) of Vincent van Gogh (artist). Multicoloured.

1497	15l. Type **255**	50	25
1498	20l. "Still Life: Red Poppies and Daisies"	50	25
1499	2r. "Vincent's Bedroom in Arles" (horiz)	1·75	90
1500	3r.50 "The Mulberry Tree"	2·00	1·25
1501	7r. "Blossoming Chestnut Branches" (horiz)	3·00	3·00
1502	10r. "Peasant Couple going to Work" (horiz)	3·50	3·50
1503	12r. "Still Life: Pink Roses" (horiz)	3·75	4·00
1504	15r. "Child with Orange"	4·00	4·25
MS1505	Two sheets. (a) 77 × 101 mm. 25r. "Houses in Auvers" (70 × 94 mm). (b) 101 × 77 mm. 25r. "The Courtyard of the Hospital at Arles" (94 × 70 mm). Imperf Set of 2 sheets	12·00	13·00

1991. 65th Birthday of Queen Elizabeth II. As T **201** of Lesotho. Multicoloured.

1506	2r. Queen at Trooping the Colour, 1990	1·60	60
1507	5r. Queen with Queen Mother and Princess Margaret, 1973	2·75	1·75
1508	8r. Queen and Prince Philip in open carriage, 1986	3·25	3·00
1509	12r. Queen at Royal Estates Ball	3·50	3·75
MS1510	68 × 90 mm. 25r. Separate photographs of Queen and Prince Philip	5·75	6·50

1991. 10th Wedding Anniv of Prince and Princess of Wales. As T **210** of Lesotho. Multicoloured.

1511	1r. Prince and Princess skiing, 1986	80	20
1512	3r.50 Separate photographs of Prince, Princess and sons	1·75	1·10
1513	7r. Prince Henry in Christmas play and Prince William watching polo	2·00	2·00
1514	15r. Princess Diana at Ipswich, 1990, and Prince Charles playing polo	3·50	3·75
MS1515	68 × 90 mm. 25r. Prince and Princess of Wales in Hungary, and Princes William and Harry going to school	5·75	6·50

256 Boy painting

257 Class C57 Steam Locomotive

1991. Hummel Figurines. Multicoloured.

1516	10l. Type **256**	15	15
1517	25l. Boy reading at table	20	20
1518	50l. Boy with school satchel	30	30
1519	2r. Girl with basket	70	70
1520	3r.50 Boy reading	1·00	1·00
1521	8r. Girl and young child reading	2·25	2·50
1522	10r. School girls	2·25	2·50
1523	25r. School boys	4·75	6·50
MS1524	Two sheets, each 97 × 127 mm. (a) 5r. As No. 1519; 5r. As No. 1520; 5r. As No, 1521; 5r. As No. 1522. (b) 8r. As Type **256**; 8r. As No. 1517; 8r. As No. 1518; 8r. As No. 1523 Set of 2 sheets	9·00	11·00

1991. "Phila Nippon '91" International Stamp Exn, Tokyo. Japanese Steam Locomotives. Mult.

1525	15l. Type **257**	50	15
1526	25l. Class 6250 locomotive, 1915 (horiz)	65	25
1527	1r. Class D51 locomotive, 1936	1·25	40
1528	3r.50 Class 8620 locomotive, 1914 (horiz)	2·00	1·25
1529	5r. Class 10 locomotive, 1889 (horiz)	2·25	1·75
1530	7r. Class C61 locomotive, 1947	2·50	2·50
1531	10r. Class 9600 locomotive, 1913 (horiz)	2·50	2·75
1532	12r. Class D52 locomotive, 1943 (horiz)	2·75	3·50
MS1533	Two sheets, each 118 × 80 mm. (a) 20r. Class C56 locomotive, 1935 (horiz). (b) 20r. Class 1080 locomotive, 1925 (horiz) Set of 2 sheets	8·00	9·00

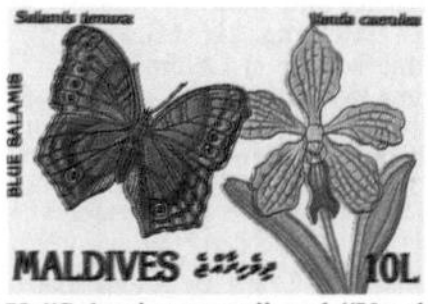

258 "Salamis temora" and "Vanda caerulea"

1991. Butterflies and Flowers. Multicoloured.

1534	10l. Type **258**	40	40
1535	25l. "Meneris tulbaghia" and "Incarvillea younghusbandii"	55	30
1536	50l. "Polyommatus icarus" and "Campsis grandiflora"	75	40
1537	2r. "Danaus plexippus" and "Thunbergia grandiflora"	1·25	90
1538	3r.50 "Colias interior" and "Medinilla magnifica"	1·75	1·75
1539	5r. "Ascalapha ordorata" and "Meconopsis horridula"	2·00	2·00
1540	8r. "Papilio memnon" and "Dillenia obovata"	2·50	3·00
1541	10r. "Precis octavia" and "Thespesia populnea"	2·50	3·00
MS1542	Two sheets, each 100 × 70 mm. (a) 20r. "Bombax ceiba" and "Plyciodes tharos". (b) 20r. "Amauris niavius" and "Bombax insigne" Set of 2 sheets	10·00	12·00

259 "H-II" Rocket

1991. Japanese Space Programme. Multicoloured.

1543	15l. Type **259**	40	20
1544	20l. Projected "H-II" orbiting plane	40	20
1545	2r. Satellite "GMS-5"	1·00	75
1546	3r.50 Satellite "MOMO-1"	1·40	1·40
1547	7r. Satellite "CS-3"	2·25	2·50
1548	10r. Satellite "BS-2a, 2b"	2·50	2·75
1549	12r. "H-I" Rocket (vert)	2·75	3·25
1550	15r. Space Flier unit and U.S. Space shuttle	2·75	3·25
MS1551	Two sheets. (a) 116 × 85 mm. 20r. Dish aerial, Katsura Tracking Station (vert). (b) 85 × 116 mm. 20r. "M-3SII" rocket (vert) Set of 2 sheets	12·00	12·00

260 Williams "FW-07"

1991. Formula 1 Racing Cars. Multicoloured.

1552	20l. Type **260**	30	20
1553	50l. Brabham/BMW "BT50" turbo	40	30
1554	1r. Williams/Honda "FW-11"	60	45
1555	3r.50 Ferrari "312 T3"	1·25	1·25
1556	5r. Lotus/Honda "99T"	1·75	1·75
1557	7r. Benetton/Ford "B188"	2·00	2·25
1558	10r. Tyrrell "P34" six-wheeler	2·25	2·50
1559	21r. Renault "RE-30B" turbo	4·00	5·00
MS1560	Two sheets, each 84 × 56 mm. (a) 25r. Brabham/BMW "BT50" turbo (different). (b) 25r. Ferrari "F189" Set of 2 sheets	16·00	13·00

261 "Testa Rossa", 1957

1991. Ferrari Cars. Multicoloured.

1561	5r. Type **261**	2·00	2·00
1562	5r. "275GTB", 1966	2·00	2·00
1563	5r. "Aspirarta", 1951	2·00	2·00
1564	5r. "Testarossa"	2·00	2·00
1565	5r. Enzo Ferrari	2·00	2·00
1566	5r. "Dino 246", 1958	2·00	2·00
1567	5r. "Type 375", 1952	2·00	2·00
1568	5r. Nigel Mansell's Formula 1 racing car	2·00	2·00
1569	5r. "312T", 1975	2·00	2·00

262 Franklin D. Roosevelt

1991. 50th Anniv of Japanese Attack on Pearl Harbor. American War Leaders. Multicoloured.

1570	3r.50 Type **262**	1·50	1·50
1571	3r.50 Douglas MacArthur and map of Philippines	1·50	1·50
1572	3r.50 Chester Nimitz and Pacific island	1·50	1·50
1573	3r.50 Jonathan Wainwright and barbed wire	1·50	1·50
1574	3r.50 Ernest King and U.S.S. "Hornet" (aircraft carrier)	1·50	1·50
1575	3r.50 Claire Chennault and Curtiss Tomahawk II fighters	1·50	1·50
1576	3r.50 William Halsey and U.S.S. "Enterprise" (aircraft carrier)	1·50	1·50
1577	3r.50 Marc Mitscher and U.S.S. "Hornet" (aircraft carrier)	1·50	1·50
1578	3r.50 James Doolittle and North American B-25 Mitchell bomber	1·50	1·50
1579	3r.50 Raymond Spruance and Douglas Dauntless dive bomber	1·50	1·50

263 Brandenburg Gate and Postcard Commemorating Berlin Wall

1992. Anniversaries and Events. Multicoloured.

1580	20l. Type **263**	15	10
1581	50l. Schwarzenburg Palace	80	40
1582	1r. Spa at Baden	1·10	50
1583	1r.75 Berlin Wall and man holding child	50	50
1584	2r. Royal Palace, Berlin	1·50	1·00
1585	4r. Demonstrator and border guards	1·10	1·25
1586	5r. Viennese masonic seal	3·25	2·25
1587	6r. De Gaulle and Normandy landings, 1944 (vert)	2·50	2·25
1588	6r. Lilienthal's signature and "Flugzeug Nr. 16"	2·50	2·25
1589	7r. St. Marx	3·25	2·25
1590	7r. Trans-Siberian Railway Class VL80T electric locomotive No. 1406 (vert)	3·25	2·25
1591	8r. Kurt Schwitters (artist) and Landesmuseum	2·50	2·50

1592 9r. Map of Switzerland and man in Uri traditional costume . . . . 2·50 2·50
1593 10r. De Gaulle in Madagascar, 1958 . . . . 2·50 2·50
1594 10r. Scouts exploring coral reef . . . . 2·50 2·50
1595 11r. Scout salute and badge (vert) . . . . 2·50 2·50
1596 12r. Trans-Siberian Railway steam locomotive . . . . 3·50 3·50
1597 15r. Imperial German badges . . . . 2·50 3·50
1598 20r. Josepsplatz, Vienna . . 4·00 4·00
MS1599 Eight sheets. (a) 76×116 mm. 15r. General de Gaulle during Second World War (vert). (b) 101×72 mm. 18r. Ancient German helmet. (c) 101×72 mm. 18r. 19th-century shako. (d) 101×72 mm. 18r. Helmet of 1939. (e) 90×117 mm. 18r. Postcard of Lord Baden-Powell carried by rocket, 1937 (grey, black and mauve) (vert). (f) 75×104 mm. 20r. Bust of Mozart (vert). (g) 115×85 mm. 20r. Trans-Siberian Railway Class P36 steam locomotive stopped at signal (57×43 mm). (h) 117×90 mm. 20r. Czechoslovakia 1918 10h. "Scout Post" stamp (vert) Set of 8 sheets . . . . 38·00 40·00

ANNIVERSARIES AND EVENTS: Nos. 1580, 1583, 1585, 1597, **MS**1599b/d, Bicentenary of Brandenburg Gate, Berlin; 1581/2, 1584, 1586, 1589, 1598, **MS**1599f, Death bicentenary of Mozart (1991); 1587, 1593, **MS**1599a, Birth centenary of Charles de Gaulle (French statesman) (1990); 1588, Centenary of Otto Lilienthal's first gliding experiments; 1590, 1596, **MS**1599g, Centenary of Trans-Siberian Railway; 1591, 750th anniv of Hannover; 1592, 700th anniv of Swiss Confederation; 1594/5, **MS**1599e,h, 17th World Scout Jamboree, Korea.

264 Mickey Mouse on Flying Carpet, Arabia

1992. Mickey's World Tour. Designs showing Walt Disney cartoon characters in different countries. Multicoloured.
1600 25l. Type **264** 45 20
1601 50l. Goofy and Big Ben, Great Britain 55 25
1602 1r. Mickey wearing clogs, Netherlands 75 35
1603 2r. Pluto eating pasta, Italy 1·25 75
1604 3r. Mickey and Donald doing Mexican hat dance 1·40 1·25
1605 3r.50 Mickey, Goofy and Donald as tiki, New Zealand . . . . 1·40 1·40
1606 5r. Goofy skiing in Austrian Alps . . . . 1·50 1·50
1607 7r. Mickey and city gate, Germany . . . . 1·75 2·00
1608 10r. Donald as samurai, Japan . . . . 2·00 2·25
1609 12r. Mickey as heroic statue, Russia . . . . 2·25 2·75
1610 15r. Mickey, Donald, Goofy and Pluto as German band . . . . 2·50 3·00
MS1611 Three sheets, each 83×104 mm. (a) 25r. Donald chasing leprechaun, Ireland (horiz). (b) 25r. Baby kangaroo surprising Pluto, Australia. (c) 25r. Mickey and globe Set of 3 sheets 13·00 14·00

265 Whimbrel

266 Powder-blue Surgeonfish

1992. Birds. Multicoloured.
1612 10l. Type **265** 50 60
1613 25l. Great egret 50 40
1614 50l. Grey heron 60 50
1615 2r. Shag . . . . 1·40 75
1616 3r.50 Roseate tern . . . . 1·50 85
1617 5r. Greater greenshank . . 1·75 1·10
1617a 6r.50+50l. Egyptian vulture 2·75 2·75
1618 8r. Hoopoe . . . . 2·25 2·25
1619 10r. Black-shouldered kite 2·25 2·25
1620 25r. Scarlet ibis . . . . . 2·75 3·00
1620a 30r. Peregrine falcon . . . 3·50 3·75
1620b 40r. Black kite . . . . . . 5·00 5·50
1621 50r. Grey plover . . . . . 5·00 6·00
1621a 100r. Common shoveler . . 11·00 12·00
Nos. 1617a, 1620a/b and 1621a are larger, 23×32 mm.

1992. 40th Anniv of Queen Elizabeth II's Accession. As T **214** of Lesotho. Multicoloured.
1622 1r. Palm trees on beach . . 50 25
1623 3r.50 Path leading to jetty 1·75 1·00
1624 7r. Tropical plant . . . . . 2·50 2·75
1625 10r. Palm trees on beach (different) . . . . 2·75 3·00
MS1626 Two sheets, each 74×97 mm. (a) 18r. Dhow. (b) 18r. Palm trees on beach (different) Set of 2 sheets . . . 12·00 11·00

1992. Fishes. Multicoloured.
1627 7l. Type **266** 30 20
1628 20l. Catalufa 40 25
1629 50l. Yellow-finned tuna . . 55 30
1630 1r. Twin-spotted red snapper 75 35
1631 3r.50 Hawaiian squirrelfish 1·50 1·25
1632 5r. Picasso triggerfish . . . 2·00 2·00
1633 8r. Bennet's butterflyfish . 2·25 2·50
1634 10r. Parrotfish . . . . . . 2·50 2·75
1635 12r. Coral hind . . . . . . 2·75 3·00
1636 15r. Skipjack tuna . . . . . 2·75 3·00
MS1637 Four sheets, each 116×76 mm. (a) 20r. Thread-finned butterflyfish. (b) 20r. Oriental sweetlips. (c) 20r. Two-banded anemonefish ("Clownfish"). (d) 20r. Clown triggerfish Set of 4 sheets . . . 13·00 15·00

1992. International Stamp Exhibitions. As T **215** of Lesotho showing Walt Disney cartoon characters. Multicoloured. (a) "Granada '92", Spain. The Alhambra.
1638 2r. Minnie Mouse in Court of the Lions 90 70
1639 5r. Goofy in Lions Fountain 1·75 1·75
1640 8r. Mickey Mouse at the Gate of Justice . . . . . 2·25 2·75
1641 12r. Donald Duck serenading Daisy at the Vermilion Towers . . . . 2·75 3·50
MS1642 127×102 mm. 25r. Goofy pushing Mickey in wheelbarrow 5·50 6·00

(b) "World Columbian Stamp Expo '92". Chicago Landmarks.
1643 1r. Mickey meeting Jean Baptiste du Sable (founder) . . . . 1·00 40
1644 3r.50 Donald Duck at Old Chicago Post Office . . . 2·00 1·25
1645 7r. Donald at Old Fort Dearborn . . . . 3·00 2·75
1646 15r. Goofy in Museum of Science and Industry . . 4·00 4·50
MS1647 127×102 mm. 25r. Mickey and Minnie Mouse at Columbian Exposition, 1893 (horiz) . . . 5·50 6·00
On No. 1646 the design is wrongly captioned as the Science and Industry Museum.

267 Coastguard Patrol Boats

1992. Cent of National Security Service. Mult.
1648 3r.50 Type **267** . . . . . . 2·25 1·25
1649 5r. Infantry in training . . . 2·25 1·75
1650 10r. Aakoatey fort . . . . 2·50 2·75
1651 15r. Fire Service . . . . . 8·50 8·50
MS1652 100×68 mm. 20r. Ceremonial procession, 1892 6·00 7·00

268 Flowers of the United States of America

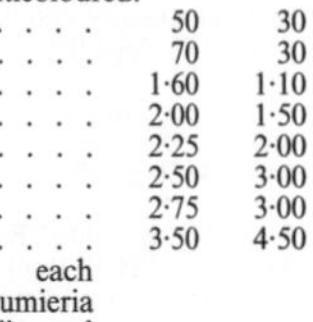

269 "Laetiporus sulphureus"

1992. National Flowers. Multicoloured.
1653 25l. Type **268** 50 30
1654 50l. Australia 70 30
1655 2r. England . . . . 1·60 1·10
1656 3r.50 Brazil . . . . 2·00 1·50
1657 5r. Holland . . . . 2·25 2·00
1658 8r. France . . . . 2·50 3·00
1659 10r. Japan . . . . 2·75 3·00
1660 15r. Africa . . . . 3·50 4·50
MS1661 Two sheets, each 114×85 mm. (a) 25r. "Plumieria rubra", "Classia fistula" and "Eugenia malaccensis" (57×43 mm). (b) 25r. "Bauhinia variegata", "Catharanthus roseus" and "Plumieria alba" (57×43 mm) Set of 2 sheets . . 9·00 10·00

1992. Fungi. Multicoloured.
1662 10l. Type **269** 30 30
1663 25l. "Coprinus atramentarius" 40 30
1664 50l. "Ganoderma lucidum" 60 40
1665 3r.50 "Russula aurata" . . 1·25 1·00
1666 5r. "Grifola umbellata" ("Polyporus umbellatus") 1·75 1·75
1667 8r. "Suillus grevillei" . . . 2·25 2·50
1668 10r. "Clavaria zollingeri" . . 2·50 2·50
1669 25r. "Boletus edulis" . . . 5·00 6·00
MS1670 Two sheets, each 100×70 mm. (a) 25r. "Marasmius oreades". (b) 25r. "Pycnoporus cinnabarinus" ("Trametes cinnabarina") Set of 2 sheets 12·00 13·00

1992. Olympic Games, Albertville and Barcelona (1st issue). As T **216** of Lesotho. Multicoloured.
1671 10l. Pole vault 20 10
1672 25l. Men's pommel horse (horiz) 25 15
1673 50l. Men's shot put 30 25
1674 1r. Men's horizontal bar (horiz) 35 30
1675 2r. Men's triple jump (horiz) 80 65
1676 3r.50 Table tennis . . . . . 1·10 1·10
1677 5r. Two-man bobsled . . . 1·40 1·40
1678 7r. Freestyle wrestling (horiz) . . . . 1·75 2·00
1679 8r. Freestyle ski-jump . . . 1·75 2·00
1680 9r. Baseball . . . . 2·00 2·25
1681 10r. Women's cross-country Nordic skiing . . . . . . 2·00 2·25
1682 12r. Men's 200 m backstroke (horiz) 2·00 2·25
MS1683 Three sheets. (a) 100×70 mm. 25r. Decathalon (horiz). (b) 100×70 mm. 25r. Women's slalom skiing (horiz). (c) 70×100 mm. 25r. Men's figure skating Set of 3 sheets . . . . 12·00 13·00
See also Nos. 1684/92.

270 Hurdling

271 Deinonychus

1992. Olympic Games, Barcelona (2nd issue). Multicoloured.
1684 10l. Type **270** 10 10
1685 1r. Boxing 30 30
1686 3r.50 Women's sprinting . . 80 70
1687 5r. Discus . . . . 1·25 1·25
1688 7r. Basketball . . . . 3·00 2·50
1689 10r. Long-distance running 2·25 2·50
1690 12r. Aerobic gymnastics . . 2·50 3·00
1691 20r. Fencing . . . . 3·25 4·00
MS1692 Two sheets, each 70×100 mm. (a) 25r. Olympic symbol and national flags. (b) 25r. Olympic symbol and flame Set of 2 sheets . . . . 8·50 9·00

1992. "Genova '92" International Thematic Stamp Exhibition. Prehistoric Animals. Multicoloured.
1693 5l. Type **271** 40 20
1694 10l. Styracosaurus 40 20
1695 25l. Mamenchisaurus . . . 50 30
1696 50l. Stenonychosaurus . . . 60 30
1697 1r. Parasaurolophus 75 40
1698 1r.25 Scelidosaurus 85 50
1699 1r.75 Tyrannosaurus . . . . 1·10 55
1700 2r. Stegosaurus . . . . . . 1·25 60
1701 3r.50 Iguanodon . . . . . 1·50 80
1702 4r. Anatosaurus . . . . . . 1·50 1·00
1703 5r. Monoclonius . . . . . . 1·60 1·10
1704 7r. Tenontosaurus . . . . . 1·90 1·90
1705 8r. Brachiosaurus . . . . . 1·90 1·90
1706 10r. Euoplocephalus . . . . 2·00 2·00
1707 25r. Triceratops . . . . . . 3·25 4·50
1708 50r. Apatosaurus . . . . . 6·00 8·00
MS1709 Four sheets, each 116×85 mm. (a) 25r. Hadrosaur hatchling. (b) 25r. Iguanodon fighting Allosaurus. (c) 25r. Tyrannosaurus attacking Triceratops. (d) 25r. Brachiosaurus and Iguanodons Set of 4 sheets . . . . . 14·00 15·00

1992. Postage Stamp Mega Event, New York. Sheet 100×70 mm, containing multicoloured design as T **219** of Lesotho, but horiz.
MS1710 20r. New York Public Library . . . . 2·50 3·25

272 Destruction of LZ-129 "Hindenburg" (airship), 1937

1992. Mysteries of the Universe. T **272** and similar multicoloured designs, each in separate miniature sheet.
MS1711 Sixteen sheets, each 100×71 mm. (a) 25r. Type **272**. (b) 25r. Loch Ness Monster. (c) 25r. Crystal skull. (d) 25r. Space craft in Black Hole. (e) 25r. Ghosts (vert). (f) 25r. Flying saucer, 1947 (vert). (g) 25r. Bust of Plato (Atlantis). (h) 25r. U.F.O., 1973. (i) 25r. Crop circles. (j) 25r. Mil Mi-26 Russian helicopter at Chernobyl nuclear explosion. (k) 25r. Figure from Plain of Nazca. (l) 25r. Stonehenge (vert). (m) 25r. Yeti footprint (vert). (n) 25r. The Pyramid of Giza. (o) 25r. "Marie Celeste" (brigantine) (vert). (p) 25r. American Grumman TBF Avenger fighter aircraft (Bermuda Triangle) Set of 16 sheets . . . 55·00 55·00

273 Zubin Mehta (musical director)

274 Friedrich Schmiedl

1992. 150th Anniv of New York Philharmonic Orchestra. Sheet 100×70 mm.
MS1712 **273** 20r. multicoloured 6·00 6·00

1992. 90th Birth Anniv of Friedrich Schmiedl (rocket mail pioneer). Sheet 104×69 mm.
MS1713 **274** 25r. multicoloured 5·50 6·00

275 Goofy in "Father's Weekend", 1953

1992. 60th Anniv of Goofy (Disney cartoon character). Goofy in various cartoon films. Multicoloured.
1714 10l. Type **275** 10 10
1715 50l. "Symphony Hour", 1942 . . . . 35 20
1716 75l. "Frank Duck Brings 'Em Back Alive", 1946 . . 45 20
1717 1r. "Crazy with the Heat", 1947 . . . . 45 20
1718 2r. "The Big Wash", 1948 70 60
1719 3r.50 "How to Ride a Horse", 1950 . . . . . . 1·25 1·25
1720 5r. "Two Gun Goofy", 1952 1·50 1·50
1721 8r. "Saludos Amigos", 1943 (vert) . . . . 2·00 2·25
1722 10r. "How to be a Detective", 1952 . . . . 2·00 2·25
1723 12r. "For Whom the Bulls Toil", 1953 . . . . . . 2·25 2·50
1724 15r. "Double Dribble", 1946 (vert) . . . . 2·25 2·50
MS1725 Three sheets, each 127×102 mm. (a) 20r. "Double Dribble", 1946 (different) (vert). (b) 20r. "The Goofy Success Story", 1955 (vert). (c) 20r. "Mickey and the Beanstalk", 1947 Set of 3 sheets . . . . 10·00 10·50

276 Minnie Mouse in "Le Missioner" (Toulouse-Lautrec)

1992. Opening of Euro-Disney Resort, France. Disney cartoon characters superimposed on Impressionist paintings. Multicoloured.
1726 5r. Type **276** . . . . 1·40 1·50
1727 5r. Goofy in "The Card Players" (Cezanne) . . . 1·40 1·50
1728 5r. Mickey and Minnie Mouse in "The Cafe Terrace, Place du Forum" (Van Gogh) . . . . . . 1·40 1·50
1729 5r. Mickey in "The Bridge at Langlois" (Van Gogh) 1·40 1·50
1730 5r. Goofy in "Chocolate Dancing" (Toulouse-Lautrec) . . . . 1·40 1·50
1731 5r. Mickey and Minnie in "The Seine at Asnieres" (Renoir) . . . . 1·40 1·50

1732 5r. Minnie in "Ball at the Moulin Rouge" (Toulouse-Lautrec) . . . 1·40 1·50
1733 5r. Mickey in "Wheatfield with Cypresses" (Van Gogh) . . . . 1·40 1·50
1734 5r. Minnie in "When will you Marry?" (Gauguin) 1·40 1·50
MS1735 Four sheets. (a) 128 × 100 mm. 20r. Minnie as can-can dancer. (b) 128 × 100 mm. 20r. Goofy as cyclist. (c) 100 × 128 mm. 20r. Mickey as artist. (d) 100 × 128 mm. 20r. Donald as Frenchman (vert) Set of 4 sheets 12·00 13·00

277 Rivers

1992. South Asian Association for Regional Co-operation Year of the Environment. Natural and Polluted Environments. Multicoloured.
1736 25l. Type **277** 15 10
1737 50l. Beaches 25 10
1738 5r. Oceans . . . . 80 1·00
1739 10r. Weather . . . . 1·50 2·00

278 Jurgen Klinsmann (Germany)

280 Elvis Presley

279 German Navy Airship L-13 bombing London, 1914–18

1993. World Cup Football Championship, U.S.A. (1994) (1st issue). German Players and Officials. Multicoloured.
1740 10l. Type **278** 40 20
1741 25l. Pierre Littbarski 45 20
1742 50l. Lothar Matthaus . . . 55 20
1743 1r. Rudi Voller 75 25
1744 2r. Thomas Hassler . . . . 1·25 60
1745 3r.50 Thomas Berthold . . 1·60 1·00
1746 4r. Jurgen Kohler . . . . . 1·75 1·25
1747 5r. Berti Vogts . . . . . . 1·90 1·40
1748 6r. Bodo Illgner . . . . . 2·25 2·25
1749 7r. Klaus Augenthaler . . . 2·25 2·25
1750 8r. Franz Beckenbauer . . . 2·25 2·25
1751 10r. Andreas Brehme . . . 2·50 2·75
1752 12r. Guido Buchwald . . . 2·50 3·25
MS1753 Two sheets, each 103 × 73 mm. (a) 35r. German players celebrating (horiz). (b) 35r. Rudi Voller (horiz) Set of 2 sheets 13·00 14·00
See also Nos. 1990/7 and 2089/2100.

1993. Anniversaries and Events. Multicoloured.
1754 1r. Type **279** 80 30
1755 3r.50 Radio telescope . . . 70 80
1756 3r.50 Chancellor Adenauer and Pres. de Gaulle . . . 70 80
1757 6r. Indian rhinoceros . . . 3·75 2·00
1758 6r. Columbus and globe . . 2·75 1·75
1759 7r. Conference emblems . . 1·50 1·75
1760 8r. Green seaturtle . . . . 1·75 1·75
1761 10r. "America" (yacht), 1851 . . . . 1·75 2·25
1762 10r. Melvin Jones (founder) and emblem . . . . . 1·75 2·25
1763 12r. Columbus landing on San Salvador . . . . . . 3·25 3·50
1764 15r. "Voyager I" approaching Saturn . . . 5·00 5·00
1765 15r. Adenauer, N.A.T.O. flag and Lockheed Starfighter aircraft . . . . 5·00 5·00
1766 20r. "Graf Zeppelin" over New York, 1929 . . . . 5·00 5·00
MS1767 Five sheets, each 111 × 80 mm. (a) 20r. Count Ferdinand von Zeppelin. (b) 20r. "Landsat" satellite. (c) 20r. Konrad Adenauer. (d) 20r. Scarlet macaw. (e) 20r. "Santa Maria" Set of 5 sheets . . . . 20·00 22·00
ANNIVERSARIES AND EVENTS: 1754, 1766, **MS**1767a, 75th death anniv of Count Ferdinand von Zeppelin; 1755, 1764, **MS**1767b, International Space Year; 1756, 1765, **MS**1767c, 25th death anniv of Konrad Adenauer; 1757, 1760, **MS**1767d, Earth Summit '92, Rio; 1758, 1763, **MS**1767e, 500th anniv of discovery of America by Columbus; 1759, International Conference on Nutrition, Rome; 1761, Americas Cup Yachting Championship; 1762, 75th anniv of International Association of Lions Clubs.

1993. 15th Death Anniv of Elvis Presley (singer). Multicoloured.
1768 3r.50 Type **280** 90 70
1769 3r.50 Elvis with guitar . . . 90 70
1770 3r.50 Elvis with microphone 90 70

1993. Bicentenary of the Louvre, Paris. As T **221a** of Lesotho. Multicoloured.
1771 8r. "The Study" (Fragonard) . . . . . . 90 1·10
1772 8r. "Denis Diderot" (Fragonard) . . . . . . 90 1·10
1773 8r. "Marie-Madelaine Guimard" (Fragonard) . . 90 1·10
1774 8r. "Inspiration" (Fragonard) . . . . . . 90 1·10
1775 8r. "Waterfalls, Tivoli" (Fragonard) . . . . . . 90 1·10
1776 8r. "The Music Lesson" (Fragonard) . . . . . . 90 1·10
1777 8r. "The Bolt" (Fragonard) 90 1·10
1778 8r. "Blind-man's Buff" (Fragonard) . . . . . . 90 1·10
1779 8r. "Self-portrait" (Corot) 90 1·10
1780 8r. "Woman in Blue" (Corot) . . . . 90 1·10
1781 8r. "Woman with a Pearl" (Corot) . . . . 90 1·10
1782 8r. "Young Girl at her Toilet" (Corot) . . . . 90 1·10
1783 8r. "Haydee" (Corot) . . . 90 1·10
1784 8r. "Chartres Cathedral" (Corot) . . . . 90 1·10
1785 8r. "The Belfry of Douai" (Corot) . . . . 90 1·10
1786 8r. "The Bridge of Mantes" (Corot) . . . . 90 1·10
1787 8r. "Madame Seriziat" (David) . . . . 90 1·10
1788 8r. "Pierre Seriziat" (David) 90 1·10
1789 8r. "Madame De Verninac" (David) . . . . 90 1·10
1790 8r. "Madame Recamier" (David) . . . . 90 1·10
1791 8r. "Self-portrait" (David) 90 1·10
1792 8r. "General Bonaparte" (David) . . . . 90 1·10
1793 8r. "The Lictors bringing Brutus his Son's Body" (David) (left detail) . . . 90 1·10
1794 8r. "The Lictors bringing Brutus his Son's Body" (David) (right detail) . . . 90 1·10
MS1795 Two sheets, each 100 × 70 mm. (a) 20r. "Gardens of the Villa D'Este, Tivoli" (Corot) (85 × 52 mm). (b) 20r. "Tiger Cub playing with its Mother" (Delacroix) (85 × 52 mm) Set of 2 sheets . . . . 8·50 8·50

281 James Stewart and Marlene Dietrich ("Destry Rides Again")

1993. Famous Western Films. Multicoloured.
1796 5r. Type **281** . . . . . . 1·40 1·10
1797 5r. Gary Cooper ("The Westerner") . . . . . . 1·40 1·10
1798 5r. Henry Fonda ("My Darling Clementine") . . 1·40 1·10
1799 5r. Alan Ladd ("Shane") . . 1·40 1·10
1800 5r. Kirk Douglas and Burt Lancaster ("Gunfight at the O.K. Corral") . . . . 1·40 1·10
1801 5r. Steve McQueen ("The Magnificent Seven") . . . 1·40 1·10
1802 5r. Robert Redford and Paul Newman ("Butch Cassidy and The Sundance Kid") . . . . . 1·40 1·10
1803 5r. Jack Nicholson and Randy Quaid ("The Missouri Breaks") . . . . 1·40 1·10
MS1804 Two sheets, each 134 × 120 mm. (a) 20r. John Wayne ("The Searchers") (French poster). (b) 20r. Clint Eastwood ("Pale Rider") (French poster) Set of 2 sheets . . . . 7·50 7·50

1993. 40th Anniv of Coronation. As T **224** of Lesotho.
1805 3r.50 multicoloured . . . . 1·00 1·10
1806 5r. multicoloured . . . . . 1·25 1·40
1807 10r. blue and black . . . . 1·50 1·75
1808 10r. blue and black . . . . 1·50 1·75
DESIGNS: No. 1805, Queen Elizabeth II at Coronation (photograph by Cecil Beaton); 1806, St. Edward's Crown; 1807, Guests in the Abbey; 1808, Queen Elizabeth II and Prince Philip.

282 Blue Goatfish

1993. Fishes. Multicoloured.
1809 3r.50 Type **282** 60 70
1810 3r.50 Emperor angelfish . . 60 70
1811 3r.50 Madagascar butterflyfish 60 70
1812 3r.50 Regal angelfish . . . 60 70
1813 3r.50 Forceps fish ("Longnose butterflyfish") 60 70
1814 3r.50 Racoon butterflyfish 60 70
1815 3r.50 Harlequin filefish . . . 60 70
1816 3r.50 Rectangle triggerfish 60 70
1817 3r.50 Yellow-tailed anemonefish 60 70
1818 3r.50 Clown triggerfish . . . 60 70
1819 3r.50 Zebra lionfish 60 70
1820 3r.50 Maldive anemonefish ("Clownfish") 60 70
1821 3r.50 Black-faced butterflyfish 60 70
1822 3r.50 Bird wrasse 60 70
1823 3r.50 Checkerboard wrasse 60 70
1824 3r.50 Yellow-faced angelfish 60 70
1825 3r.50 Masked bannerfish . . 60 70
1826 3r.50 Thread-finned butterflyfish 60 70
1827 3r.50 Painted triggerfish . . 60 70
1828 3r.50 Coral hind 60 70
1829 3r.50 Pennant coralfish . . . 60 70
1830 3r.50 Black-backed butterflyfish 60 70
1831 3r.50 Red-toothed triggerfish 60 70
1832 3r.50 Melon butterflyfish . . 60 70
MS1833 Two sheets. (a) 69 × 96 mm. 25r. Klein's butterflyfish (vert). (b) 96 × 69 mm. 25r. Brown anemonefish (vert) Set of 2 sheets 8·00 8·50
Nos. 1809/20 and 1821/32 were printed together, se-tenant, with the backgrounds forming composite designs.
Nos. 1810 and 1824 are both inscribed "Angelfish" in error.

283 Gull-billed Tern

1993. Birds. Multicoloured.
1834 3r.50 Type **283** 60 70
1835 3r.50 White-tailed tropic bird ("Long-tailed Tropicbird") 60 70
1836 3r.50 Great frigate bird ("Frigate Bird") 60 70
1837 3r.50 Wilson's storm petrel ("Wilson's Petrel") . . . 60 70
1838 3r.50 White tern 60 70
1839 3r.50 Brown booby 60 70
1840 3r.50 Marsh harrier 60 70
1841 3r.50 Common noddy . . . 60 70
1842 3r.50 Green-backed heron ("Little Heron") 60 70
1843 3r.50 Ruddy turnstone ("Turnstone") 60 70
1844 3r.50 Curlew 60 70
1845 3r.50 Crab plover 60 70
1846 3r.50 Pallid harrier (vert) . . 60 70
1847 3r.50 Cattle egret (vert) . . 60 70
1848 3r.50 Koel (vert) 60 70
1849 3r.50 Tree pipit (vert) . . . 60 70
1850 3r.50 Short-eared owl (vert) 60 70
1851 3r.50 Common kestrel ("European Kestrel") (vert) 60 70
1852 3r.50 Yellow wagtail (vert) 60 70
1853 3r.50 Grey heron ("Common Heron") (vert) 60 70
1854 3r.50 Black bittern (vert) . . 60 70
1855 3r.50 Common snipe (vert) 60 70
1856 3r.50 Little egret (vert) . . . 60 70
1857 3r.50 Little stint (vert) . . . 60 70
MS1858 Two sheets, each 105 × 75 mm. (a) 25r. Caspian tern. (b) 25r. Audubon's shearwater Set of 2 sheets . . . 8·50 9·00
Nos. 1834/45 and 1846/57 were printed together, se-tenant, with the backgrounds forming composite designs.

284 Precious Wentletrap

285 Sifaka Lemur

1993. Shells. Multicoloured.
1859 7l. Type **284** 30 30
1860 15l. Common purple janthina 35 30
1861 50l. Asiatic arabian cowrie 45 30
1862 3r.50 Common or major harp . . . . 1·50 1·00
1863 4r. Amplustre or royal paper bubble . . . . . 1·75 1·25
1864 5r. Sieve cowrie . . . . . 1·75 1·40
1865 6r. Episcopal mitre . . . . 2·00 2·00
1866 7r. Camp pitar venus . . . 2·00 2·25
1867 8r. Spotted or eyed auger 2·25 2·50
1868 10r. Exposed cowrie . . . . 2·50 2·50
1869 12r. Geographic map cowrie 2·75 3·50
1870 20r. Bramble murex . . . . 3·50 4·50
MS1871 Three sheets, each 104 × 75 mm. (a) 25r. Black-striped triton. 25r. Scorpion conch. (c) 25r. Bull-mouth helmet Set of 3 sheets . . . . 17·00 19·00

1993. Endangered Species. Multicoloured.
1872 7l. Type **285** 50 30
1873 10l. Snow leopard 50 30
1874 15l. Numbat 50 30
1875 25l. Gorilla 90 40
1876 2r. Koala . . . . 1·00 70
1877 3r.50 Cheetah . . . . . . 1·25 1·10
1878 5r. Yellow-footed rock wallaby . . . . 1·40 1·40
1879 7r. Orang-utan . . . . . . 2·25 2·25
1880 8r. Black lemur . . . . . . 2·25 2·25
1881 10r. Black rhinoceros . . . 2·75 2·75
1882 15r. Humpback whale . . . 3·00 3·50
1883 20r. Mauritius parakeet . . 3·25 3·75
MS1884 Three sheets, each 104 × 75 mm. (a) 25r. Giant panda. (b) 25r. Tiger. (c) 25r. Indian elephant Set of 3 sheets 16·00 17·00

286 Symbolic Heads and Arrows

287 Early Astronomical Equipment

1993. Productivity Year. Multicoloured.
1885 7r. Type **286** . . . . 1·25 1·40
1886 10r. Abstract . . . . 1·60 1·75

1993. Anniversaries and Events. Multicoloured.
1887 3r.50 Type **287** . . . . . . 1·00 1·00
1888 3r.50 "Still Life with Pitcher and Apples" (Picasso) . . 1·00 1·00
1889 3r.50 "Zolte Roze" (Menasze Seidenbeurel) 1·00 1·00
1890 3r.50 Prince Naruhito and engagement photographs (horiz) . . . . 1·00 1·00
1891 5r. "Bowls and Jug" (Picasso) . . . . 1·25 1·25
1892 5r. Krysztofory Palace, Cracow . . . . 1·25 1·25
1893 8r. "Jabtka i Kotara" (Waclaw Borowski) . . . 1·75 1·90
1894 8r. Marina Kiehl (Germany) (women's downhill skiing) 1·75 1·90
1895 10r. "Bowls of Fruit and Loaves on a Table" (Picasso) . . . . 1·90 2·00
1896 10r. Masako Owada and engagement photographs (horiz) . . . . 1·90 2·00
1897 15r. American astronaut in space . . . . 2·75 3·00
1898 15r. Vegard Ulvang (Norway) (30km cross-country skiing) . . . . . 2·75 3·00
MS1899 Five sheets. (a) 105 × 75 mm. (a) 20r. Copernicus. (b) 105 × 75 mm. 20r. "Green Still Life" (detail) (Picasso) (horiz). (c) 105 × 75 mm. 25r. "Pejzaz Morski-Port z Doplywajacym Ststkiem" (detail (Roman Sielski) (horiz). (d) 75 × 105 mm. 25r. Masako Owada. (e) 105 × 75 mm. 25r. Ice hockey goalkeeper Set of 5 sheets 21·00 23·00
ANNIVERSARIES AND EVENTS: Nos. 1887, 1897, **MS**1899a, 450th death anniv of Copernicus (astronomer); 1888, 1891, 1895, **MS**1899b, 20th death anniv of Picasso (artist); 1889, 1892/3, **MS**1899c, "Polska '93" International Stamp Exhibition, Poznan; 1890, 1896, **MS**1899d, Marriage of Crown Prince Naruhito of Japan; 1894, 1898, **MS**1899e, Winter Olympic Games '94, Lillehammer.

288 "Limenitis procris" and "Mussaenda"

1993. Butterflies and Flowers. Multicoloured.
1900 7l. Type **288** 30 20
1901 20l. "Danaus limniace" and "Thevetia neriifolia" . . . 45 20
1902 25l. "Amblypodia centaurus" and "Clitoria ternatea" 45 20

1903 50l. "Papilio crino" and "Crossandra infundibuliformis" 60 20
1904 5r. "Mycalesis patnia" and "Thespesia populnia" . . 1·75 1·40
1905 6r.50+50l. "Idea jasonia" and "Cassia glauca" . . . 2·00 2·25
1906 7r. "Catopsilia pomona" and "Calotropis" . . . . 2·00 2·25
1907 10r. "Precis orithyia" and "Thunbergia grandiflora" 2·25 2·50
1908 12r. "Vanessa cardui" and "Caesalpinia pulcherrima" 2·50 3·00
1909 15r. "Papilio polymnestor" and "Nerium oleander" 2·75 3·25
1910 18r. "Cirrochroa thais" and "Vinca rosea" . . . . . 3·00 3·50
1911 20r. "Pachliopta hector" and "Ixora coccinea" . . 3·00 3·50
MS1912 Three sheets, each 105 × 72 mm. (a) 25r. "Cheritra freja" and "Bauhinia purpurea" (vert). (b) 25r. "Rohana parisatis" and "Plumeria acutifolia" (vert). (c) 25r. "Hebomoia glaucippe" and "Punica granatum" (vert) Set of 3 sheets . . . . 15·00 17·00

289 Airship "Graf Zeppelin" in Searchlights

1993. Aviation Anniversaries. Multicoloured.
1913 3r.50 Type **289** . . . . . . 1·75 65
1914 5r. Homing pigeon and message from Santa Catalina mail service, 1894 . . . . 2·00 1·10
1915 10r. Eckener and airship "Graf Zeppelin" . . . . 2·50 2·50
1916 15r. Pilot's badge and loading Philadelphia–Washington mail, 1918 . . 3·50 4·00
1917 20r. U.S.S. "Macon" (airship) and mooring mast, 1933 . . . . 3·50 4·00
MS1918 Two sheets. (a) 70 × 100 mm. 25r. Santos Dumont's airship "Ballon No. 5" and Eiffel Tower, 1901. (b) 100 × 70 mm. 25r. Jean-Pierre Blanchard's balloon, 1793 (vert) Set of 2 sheets . . . . 6·50 7·50
ANNIVERSARIES: Nos. 1913, 1915, 1917, **MS**1918a, 125th birth anniv of Hugo Eckener (airship pioneer); 1914, 1916, **MS**1918b, Bicent of first airmail flight.

290 Ford Model "T"

1993. Centenaries of Henry Ford's First Petrol Engine (Nos. 1919/30) and Karl Benz's First Four-wheeled Car (others).
1919 **290** 3r.50 multicoloured . . . 90 1·00
1920 – 3r.50 multicoloured . . . 90 1·00
1921 – 3r.50 black and violet . . 90 1·00
1922 – 3r.50 multicoloured . . . 90 1·00
1923 – 3r.50 multicoloured . . . 90 1·00
1924 – 3r.50 multicoloured . . . 90 1·00
1925 – 3r.50 multicoloured . . . 90 1·00
1926 – 3r.50 multicoloured . . . 90 1·00
1927 – 3r.50 multicoloured . . . 90 1·00
1928 – 3r.50 multicoloured . . . 90 1·00
1929 – 3r.50 multicoloured . . . 90 1·00
1930 – 3r.50 black, brn & vio 90 1·00
1931 – 3r.50 multicoloured . . . 90 1·00
1932 – 3r.50 multicoloured . . . 90 1·00
1933 – 3r.50 green, blk & vio 90 1·00
1934 – 3r.50 multicoloured . . . 90 1·00
1935 – 3r.50 multicoloured . . . 90 1·00
1936 – 3r.50 multicoloured . . . 90 1·00
1937 – 3r.50 multicoloured . . . 90 1·00
1938 – 3r.50 multicoloured . . . 90 1·00
1939 – 3r.50 multicoloured . . . 90 1·00
1940 – 3r.50 multicoloured . . . 90 1·00
1941 – 3r.50 multicoloured . . . 90 1·00
1942 – 3r.50 black, brn and violet . . . . 90 1·00
MS1943 Two sheets, each 100 × 70 mm. (a) 25r. multicoloured. (b) 25r. multicoloured Set of 2 sheets 9·00 10·00
DESIGNS: No. 1920, Henry Ford; 1921, Plans of first petrol engine; 1922, Ford "Probe GT", 1993; 1923, Front of Ford "Sportsman", 1947; 1924, Back of Ford "Sportsman"; 1925, Advertisement of 1915; 1926, Ford "Thunderbird", 1955; 1927, Ford logo; 1928, Ford "Edsel Citation", 1958; 1929, Ford half-ton pickup, 1941; 1930, Silhouette of early Ford car; 1931, Daimler-Benz "Straight 8", 1937; 1932, Karl Benz; 1933, Mercedes-Benz poster; 1934, Mercedes "38-250SS", 1929; 1935, Benz "Viktoria", 1893; 1936, Benz logo; 1937, Plan of Mercedes engine; 1938, Mercedes-Benz "300SL Gullwing", 1952; 1939, Mercedes-Benz "SL", 1993; 1940, Front of Benz 4-cylinder car, 1906; 1941, Back of Benz 4-cylinder car and advertisement; 1942, Silhouette of early Benz car; **MS**1943a, Ford Model "Y", 1933; **MS**1943b, Mercedes "300S", 1955.
Nos. 1919/30 and 1931/42 were printed together, se-tenant, forming a composite design.

291 Ivan, Sonia, Sasha and Peter in the Snow

1993. "Peter and the Wolf". Scenes from Walt Disney's cartoon film. Multicoloured.
1944 7l. Type **291** 25 25
1945 15l. Grandpa and Peter . . 30 25
1946 20l. Peter on bridge 30 25
1947 25l. Yascha, Vladimir and Mischa 30 25
1948 50l. Sasha on lookout . . . 45 30
1949 1r. The wolf 60 35
1950 3r.50 Peter dreaming . . . 70 80
1951 3r.50 Peter taking gun . . . 70 80
1952 3r.50 Peter with gun in snow 70 80
1953 3r.50 Sasha and Peter . . . 70 80
1954 3r.50 Sonia and Peter . . . 70 80
1955 3r.50 Peter with Ivan and Sasha 70 80
1956 3r.50 Ivan warning Peter of the wolf 70 80
1957 3r.50 Ivan, Peter and Sasha in tree 70 80
1958 3r.50 Wolf below tree . . . 70 80
1959 3r.50 Wolf and Sonia . . . 70 80
1960 3r.50 Sasha attacking the wolf 70 80
1961 3r.50 Sasha walking into wolf's mouth 70 80
1962 3r.50 Peter firing pop gun at wolf 70 80
1963 3r.50 Wolf chasing Sonia . . 70 80
1964 3r.50 Ivan tying rope to wolf's tail 70 80
1965 3r.50 Peter and Ivan hoisting wolf 70 80
1966 3r.50 Sasha and the hunters 70 80
1967 3r.50 Ivan and Peter on wolf hanging from tree 70 80
MS1968 Two sheets. (a) 102 × 127 mm. 25r. Sonia as an angel. (b) 127 × 102 mm. 25r. Ivan looking proud Set of 2 sheets 8·00 8·50

292 "Girl with a Broom" (Rembrandt)

1994. Famous Paintings by Rembrandt and Matisse. Multicoloured.
1969 50l. Type **292** 40 25
1970 2r. "Girl with Tulips" (Matisse) 90 70
1971 3r.50 "Young Girl at half-open Door" (Rembrandt) 1·25 1·10
1972 3r.50 "Portrait of Greta Moll" (Matisse) . . . . . 1·25 1·10
1973 5r. "The Prophetess Hannah" (Rembrandt) . . 1·50 1·25
1974 6r.50 "The Idol" (Matisse) 1·75 1·75
1975 7r. "Woman with a Pink Flower" (Rembrandt) . . 1·75 1·75
1976 9r. "Mme Matisse in a Japanese Robe" (Matisse) 2·00 2·25
1977 10r. "Portrait of Mme Matisse" (Matisse) . . 2·00 2·25
1978 12r. "Lucretia" (Rembrandt) 2·25 2·50
1979 15r. "Lady with a Ostrich Feather Fan" (Rembrandt) . . . . . . 2·25 2·75
1980 15r. "The Woman with the Hat" (Matisse) . . . . . 2·25 2·75
MS1981 Three sheets. (a) 106 × 132 mm. 25r. "The Music-makers" (detail) (Rembrandt). (b) 132 × 106 mm. 25r. "Married Couple with Three Children" (detail) (Rembrandt) (horiz). (c) 132 × 106 mm. 25r. "The Painter's Family" (detail) (Matisse) Set of 3 sheets . . . . 15·00 15·00
No. 1979 is inscribed "The Lady with an Ostich Feather Fan" in error.

293 Hong Kong 1983 Space Museum Stamp and Moon-lantern Festival

1994. "Hong Kong '94" International Stamp Exn (1st issue). Multicoloured.
1982 4r. Type **293** 65 80
1983 4r. Maldive Islands 1976 5r. "Viking" space mission stamp and Moon-lantern festival 65 80
Nos. 1982/3 were printed together, se-tenant, forming a composite design.

294 Vase

295 Windischmann (U.S.A.) and Giannini (Italy)

1994. "Hong Kong '94" International Stamp Exhibition (2nd issue). Ching Dynasty Cloisonne Enamelware. Multicoloured.
1984 2r. Type **294** 85 85
1985 2r. Flower holder 85 85
1986 2r. Elephant with vase on back 85 85
1987 2r. Tibetan style lama's teapot 85 85
1988 2r. Fo-Dog 85 85
1989 2r. Teapot with swing handle 85 85

1994. World Cup Football Championship, U.S.A. (2nd issue). Multicoloured.
1990 7l. Type **295** 30 25
1991 20l. Carnevale (Italy) and Gascoigne (England) . . . 50 25
1992 25l. England players congratulating Platt . . . 50 25
1993 3r.50 Koeman (Holland) and Klinsmann (Germany) . . . . 1·25 80
1994 5r. Quinn (Ireland) and Maldini (Italy) . . . . . 1·40 1·00
1995 7r. Lineker (England) . . . 2·00 1·50
1996 15r. Hassam (Egypt) and Moran (Ireland) . . . . 3·00 3·50
1997 18r. Canniggia (Argentina) 3·25 3·50
MS1998 Two sheets, each 103 × 73 mm. 25r. Ogris (Austria). (b) 25r. Conejo (Costa Rica) (horiz) Set of 2 sheets . . . . 13·00 12·00

296 Humpback Whale

297 Dome of the Rock, Jerusalem

1994. Centenary (1992) of Sierra Club (environmental protection society). Endangered Species. Multicoloured.
1999 6r.50 Type **296** . . . . . . 1·60 1·60
2000 6r.50 Ocelot crouched in grass . . . . 1·60 1·60
2001 6r.50 Ocelot sitting . . . . 1·60 1·60
2002 6r.50 Snow monkey . . . . 1·60 1·60
2003 6r.50 Prairie dog . . . . . 1·60 1·60
2004 6r.50 Golden lion tamarin 1·60 1·60
2005 6r.50 Prairie dog eating (horiz) . . . . 1·60 1·60
2006 6r.50 Prairie dog outside burrow (horiz) . . . . . 1·60 1·60
2007 6r.50 Herd of woodland caribou (horiz) . . . . . 1·60 1·60
2008 6r.50 Woodland caribou facing left (horiz) . . . . 1·60 1·60
2009 6r.50 Woodland caribou facing right (horiz) . . . 1·60 1·60
2010 6r.50 Pair of Galapagos penguins (horiz) . . . . . 1·60 1·60
2011 6r.50 Galapagos penguin facing right . . . . 1·60 1·60
2012 6r.50 Galapagos penguin looking straight ahead . . 1·60 1·60
2013 6r.50 Bengal tiger looking straight ahead . . . . . 1·60 1·60
2014 6r.50 Bengal tiger looking right . . . . 1·60 1·60
2015 6r.50 Philippine tarsier with tree trunk at left . . . . 1·60 1·60
2016 6r.50 Philippine tarsier with tree trunk at right . . . . 1·60 1·60
2017 6r.50 Head of Philippine tarsier . . . . 1·60 1·60
2018 6r.50 Sierra Club centennial emblem (black, buff and green) . . . . 1·60 1·60
2019 6r.50 Golden lion tamarin between two branches (horiz) . . . . 1·60 1·60
2020 6r.50 Golden lion tamarin on tree trunk (horiz) . . . 1·60 1·60
2021 6r.50 Tail fin of humpback whale and coastline (horiz) . . . . 1·60 1·60
2022 6r.50 Tail fin of humpback whale at night (horiz) . . 1·60 1·60
2023 6r.50 Bengal tiger (horiz) . . 1·60 1·60
2024 5r.50 Ocelot (horiz) . . . . 1·60 1·60
2025 6r.50 Snow monkey in water climbing out of pool (horiz) . . . . 1·60 1·60
2026 6r.50 Snow monkey swimming (horiz) . . . . 1·60 1·60

1994. Solidarity with the Palestinians.
2027 **297** 8r. multicoloured . . . . 1·60 1·60

298 Elasmosaurus

1994. Prehistoric Animals. Multicoloured.
2028/59 25l., 50l., 1r., 3r. × 24, 5r., 8r., 10r., 15r., 20r. . . Set of 32 . . . . 30·00 28·00
MS2060 Two sheets, each 106 × 76 mm. (a) 25r. Gallimimus. (b) 25r. Plateosaurus (vert) Set of 2 sheets . . . . 8·00 8·50
Nos. 2031/42 and 2043/54 respectively were printed together, se-tenant, forming composite designs. The species depicted are, in addition to Type **298**, Dilophosaurus, Avimimus, Dimorphodon, Megalosaurus, Kuehneosaurus, Dryosaurus, Kentrosaurus, Baraposaurus, Tenontosaurus, Elaphrosaurus, Maiasaura, Huayangosaurus, Rutiodon, Pianitzkysaurus, Quetzalcoatlus, Daspletosaurus, Pleurocoelus, Baryonyx, Pentaceratops, Kritosaurus, Microvenator, Nodosaurus, Montanaceratops, Dromiceiomimus, Dryptosaurus, Parkosaurus, Chasmosaurus, Edmontonia, Anatosaurus, Velociraptor and Spinosaurus.

299 Mallet Steam Locomotive, Indonesia

1994. Railway Locomotives of Asia. Multicoloured.
2061 25l. Type **299** 20 20
2062 50l. Class C62 steam locomotive, Japan, 1948 25 20
2063 1r. Class D51 steam locomotive, Japan, 1936 (horiz) 30 20
2064 5r. Steam locomotive, India (horiz) 90 90
2065 6r.50+50l. Class W steam locomotive, India (horiz) 1·25 1·50
2066 6r.50+50l. Class C53 steam locomotive, Indonesia (horiz) . . . . 1·25 1·50
2067 6r.50+50l. Class C10 steam locomotive, Japan (horiz) 1·25 1·50
2068 6r.50+50l. Hanomag steam locomotive, India (horiz) 1·25 1·50
2069 6r.50+50l. "Hikari" express train, Japan (horiz) . . . 1·25 1·50
2070 6r.50+50l. Class C55 steam locomotive, Japan, 1935 (horiz) . . . . 1·25 1·50
2071 8r. Class 485 electric locomotive, Japan (horiz) 1·50 1·75
2072 10r. Class WP steam locomotive, India (horiz) 1·75 2·00
2073 15r. Class RM steam locomotive, China (horiz) 2·00 2·25
2074 20r. Class C57 steam locomotive, Japan, 1937 2·25 2·50
MS2075 Two sheets, each 110 × 80 mm. (a) 25r. Steam locomotive pulling goods train, Indonesia (horiz). (b) 25r. Class 8620 steam locomotive, Japan, 1914 (horiz) Set of 2 sheets . . 9·00 9·50
No. 2069 is inscribed "Hakari" in error.

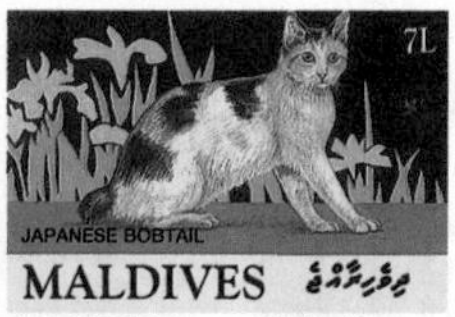

300 Japanese Bobtail

1994. Cats. Multicoloured.
2076 7l. Type **300** 20 20
2077 20l. Siamese (vert) 35 20
2078 25l. Persian longhair 35 20
2079 50l. Somali (vert) 40 20
2080 3r.50 Oriental shorthair . . 1·00 80
2081 5r. Burmese . . . . 1·25 1·00
2082 7r. Bombay carrying kitten 1·50 1·50
2083 10r. Turkish van (vert) . . . 1·50 1·75
2084 12r. Javanese (vert) . . . . 1·75 2·00
2085 15r. Singapura . . . . . . 2·00 2·50
2086 18r. Turkish angora (vert) 2·25 2·75
2087 20r. Egyptian mau (vert) . . 2·25 2·75
MS2088 Three sheets. (a) 70 × 100 mm. 25r. Birman (vert). (b) 70 × 100 mm. 25r. Korat (vert). (c) 100 × 70 mm. 25r. Abyssinian (vert) Set of 3 sheets . . . . . 13·00 15·00

301 Franco Baresi (Italy) and Stuart McCall (Scotland)

1994. World Cup Football Championship, U.S.A. (3rd issue). Multicoloured. (a) Horiz designs.
2089 10l. Type **301** 40 40
2090 25l. Mick McCarthy (Ireland) and Gary Lineker (England) 50 50
2091 50l. J. Helt (Denmark) and R. Gordillo (Spain) . . . 50 50
2092 5r. Martin Vasquez (Spain) and Enzo Scifo (Belgium) 1·25 1·00
2093 10r. Championship emblem 1·60 1·60
2094 12r. Tomas Brolin (Sweden) and Gordon Durie (Scotland) . . . . 1·75 1·75

(b) Vert designs.
2095 6r.50 Bebeto (Brazil) . . . . 1·25 1·25
2096 6r.50 Lothar Matthaus (Germany) . . . . 1·25 1·25
2097 6r.50 Diego Maradona (Argentina) . . . . 1·25 1·25
2098 6r.50 Stephane Chapuasti (Switzerland) . . . . . . 1·25 1·25
2099 6r.50 George Hagi (Rumania) . . . . 1·25 1·25
2100 6r.50 Carlos Valderama (Colombia) . . . . 1·25 1·25
MS2101 100 × 70 mm. 10r. Egyptian players . . . . 4·25 4·25

302 Crew of "Apollo 11"

1994. 25th Anniv of First Manned Moon Landing. Multicoloured.
2102 5r. Type **302** . . . . 1·00 1·00
2103 5r. "Apollo 11" mission logo . . . . 1·00 1·00
2104 5r. Edwin Aldrin (astronaut) and "Eagle" . . . . . . 1·00 1·00
2105 5r. Crew of "Apollo 12" . . 1·00 1·00
2106 5r. "Apollo 12" mission logo . . . . 1·00 1·00
2107 5r. Alan Bean (astronaut) and equipment . . . . . 1·00 1·00
2108 5r. Crew of "Apollo 16" . . 1·00 1·00
2109 5r. "Apollo 16" mission logo . . . . 1·00 1·00
2110 5r. Astronauts with U.S. flag . . . . 1·00 1·00
2111 5r. Crew of "Apollo 17" . . 1·00 1·00
2112 5r. "Apollo 17" mission logo . . . . 1·00 1·00
2113 5r. Launch of "Apollo 17" 1·00 1·00
MS2114 100 × 76 mm. 25r. Launch of Russian rocket from Baikonur (vert) . . . . 4·00 4·75

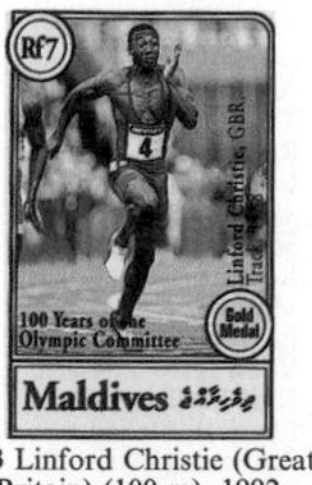

303 Linford Christie (Great Britain) (100 m), 1992

1994. Centenary of International Olympic Committee. Gold Medal Winners. Multicoloured.
2115 7r. Type **303** . . . . 1·50 1·25
2116 12r. Koji Gushiken (Japan) (gymnastics), 1984 . . . . 1·75 2·00
MS2117 106 × 71 mm. 25r. George Hackl (Germany) (single luge), 1994 . . . . 4·50 5·00

304 U.S. Amphibious DUKW

1994. 50th Anniv of D-Day. Multicoloured.
2118 2r. Type **304** 45 30
2119 4r. Tank landing craft unloading at Sword Beach 75 60
2120 18r. Infantry landing craft at Omaha Beach . . . . . 3·00 4·25
MS2121 105 × 76 mm. 25r. Landing craft with Canadian commandos 4·50 4·75

305 Duckpond, Suwan Folk Village

1994. "Philakorea '94" International Stamp Exn, Seoul. Multicoloured.
2122 50l. Type **305** 50 30
2123 3r. Pear-shaped bottle (vert) 60 70
2124 3r. Vase with dragon decoration (vert) 60 70
2125 3r. Vase with repaired lip (vert) 60 70
2126 3r. Stoneware vase with floral decoration (vert) . . 60 70
2127 3r. Celadon-glazed vase (vert) 60 70
2128 3r. Unglazed stone vase (vert) 60 70
2129 3r. Ritual water sprinkler (vert) 60 70
2130 3r. Long-necked celadon-glazed vase (vert) 60 70
2131 3r.50 Yongduson Park . . . 70 75
2132 20r. Ploughing with ox, Hahoe . . . . 3·50 4·50
MS2133 70 × 102 mm. 25r. "Hunting" (detail from eight-panel painted screen) (vert) . . 4·50 5·50

306 U.S. "Voyager 2" Satellite

1994. Space Exploration. Multicoloured.
2134 5r. Type **306** . . . . 1·50 1·25
2135 5r. Russian "Sputnik" satellite . . . . 1·50 1·25
2136 5r. "Apollo-Soyuz" mission 1·50 1·25
2137 5r. "Apollo 10" on parachutes . . . . 1·50 1·25
2138 5r. "Apollo 11" mission flag 1·50 1·25
2139 5r. Hubble space telescope 1·50 1·25
2140 5r. Edwin "Buzz" Aldrin (astronaut) . . . . . . 1·50 1·25
2141 5r. RCA lunar camera . . . 1·50 1·25
2142 5r. Lunar Rover (space buggy) . . . . 1·50 1·25
2143 5r. Jim Irwin (astronaut) . . 1·50 1·25
2144 5r. "Apollo 12" lunar module . . . . 1·50 1·25
2145 5r. Astronaut holding equipment . . . . 1·50 1·25
MS2146 Two sheets. (a) 70 × 100 mm. 25r. David Scott (astronaut) in open hatch of "Apollo 9". (b) 100 × 70 mm. 25r. Alan Shepherd Jr. (astronaut) (horiz) Set of 2 sheets . . . . 13·00 12·00

307 Mother, Child, Old Man and Town Skyline

1994. United Nations Development Programme. Multicoloured.
2147 1r. Type **307** 25 10
2148 8r. Fisherman with son and island . . . . 1·60 2·25

308 School Band

1994. 50th Anniv of Aminiya School. Children's Paintings. Multicoloured.
2149 15l. Type **308** 10 10
2150 50l. Classroom 20 15
2151 1r. School emblem and hand holding book (vert) . . . 30 15
2152 8r. School girls holding books (vert) . . . . . . 1·75 2·00
2153 10r. Sporting activities . . . 1·75 2·00
2154 11r. School girls holding crown (vert) . . . . . . 1·90 2·50
2155 13r. Science lesson . . . . 1·90 2·50

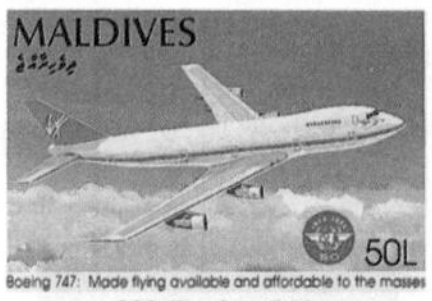

309 Boeing 747

1994. 50th Anniv of I.C.A.O. Multicoloured.
2156 50l. Type **309** 50 25
2157 1r. Hawker Siddeley ("de Havilland") Comet 4 . . 60 25
2158 2r. Male International Airport 85 55
2159 3r. Lockheed L.1649 Super Star . . . . 1·25 85
2160 8r. European Airbus . . . . 2·00 2·50
2161 10r. Dornier Do-228 . . . . 2·00 2·50
MS2162 100 × 70 mm. 25r. Concorde . . . . 4·50 5·00

310 Pintail ("Northern Pintail")

1995. Ducks. Multicoloured.
2163 5r. Type **310** . . . . 90 1·00
2164 5r. Comb duck . . . . . . 90 1·00
2165 5r. Ruddy shelduck . . . . 90 1·00
2166 5r. Garganey . . . . 90 1·00
2167 5r. Indian whistling duck ("Lesser Whistling Duck") 90 1·00
2168 5r. Green-winged teal . . . 90 1·00
2169 5r. Fulvous whistling duck 90 1·00
2170 5r. Common shoveler ("Northern Shoveler") . . 90 1·00
2171 5r. Cotton teal ("Cotton Pygmy Goose") . . . . . 90 1·00
2172 6r.50+50l. Common pochard ("Pochard") (vert) . . . 90 1·00
2173 6r.50+50l. Mallard (vert) . . 90 1·00
2174 6r.50+50l. European wigeon ("Wigeon") (vert) . . . . 90 1·00
2175 6r.50+50l. Common shoveler ("Northern Shoveler") (vert) . . . . 90 1·00
2176 6r.50+50l. Pintail ("Northern Pintail") (vert) 90 1·00
2177 6r.50+50l. Garganey (vert) 90 1·00
2178 6r.50+50l. Tufted duck (vert) . . . . 90 1·00
2179 6r.50+50l. Red-crested pochard ("Ferruginous Duck") (vert) . . . . . . 90 1·00
2180 6r.50+50l. Ferruginous duck ("Red-crested Pochard") (vert) . . . . 90 1·00
MS2181 Two sheets. (a) 100 × 71 mm. 25r. Spotbill duck ("Garganey"). (b) 73 × 100 mm. 25r. Cotton teal ("Cotton Pygmy Goose") (vert) Set of 2 sheets 7·50 8·50
Nos. 2163/71 and 2172/80 were printed together, se-tenant, forming composite designs.

311 Taj Mahal, India

1995. Famous Monuments of the World. Mult.
2182 7l. Type **311** 50 25
2183 10l. Washington Monument, U.S.A. 10 10
2184 15l. Mount Rushmore, U.S.A. 10 10
2185 25l. Arc de Triomphe, Paris (vert) 10 10
2186 50l. Sphinx, Egypt (vert) . . 50 20
2187 5r. El Castillo, Toltec pyramid, Yucatan 85 90
2188 8r. Toltec statue, Tula, Mexico (vert) . . . . . . 1·25 1·75
2189 12r. Victory Column, Berlin (vert) . . . . 1·60 2·25
MS2190 Two sheets, each 112 × 85 mm. (a) 25r. Easter Island statue (42 × 56 mm). (b) 25r. Stonehenge, Wiltshire (85 × 28 mm) Set of 2 sheets . . 7·50 8·50

312 Donald Duck driving Chariot

1995. History of Wheeled Transport. Scenes from Disney cartoon film "Donald and the Wheel". Multicoloured.
2191 3l. Type **312** 10 10
2192 4l. Donald with log 10 10
2193 5l. Donald driving Stephenson's "Rocket" . . 10 10
2194 10l. Donald pondering over circle (vert) 10 10
2195 20l. Donald in crashed car (vert) 10 10
2196 25l. Donald listening to early gramophone 10 10
2197 5r. Donald on mammoth . . 1·25 1·25
2198 20r. Donald pushing early car . . . . 3·75 4·75

313 Donald Duck playing Saxophone

1995. 60th Birthday of Donald Duck. Walt Disney cartoon characters. Multicoloured.
2199 5r. Type **313** 90 90
2200 5r. Moby Duck playing fiddle 90 90
2201 5r. Feathry Duck with banjo and drum 90 90
2202 5r. Daisy Duck playing harp 90 90
2203 5r. Gladstone Gander with clarinet 90 90
2204 5r. Huey, Dewey and Louie with bassoon 90 90
2205 5r. Gus Goose playing flute 90 90
2206 5r. Prof. Ludwig von Drake playing trombone 90 90
2207 5r. Daisy picking flowers . . 90 90
2208 5r. Donald with backpack 90 90
2209 5r. Grandma Duck with kitten 90 90
2210 5r. Gus Goose and pie . . . 90 90
2211 5r. Gyro Gearloose in space 90 90
2212 5r. Huey, Dewey and Louie photographing porcupine 90 90
2213 5r. Prof. Ludwig von Drake 90 90
2214 5r. Scrooge McDuck with money 90 90
MS2215 Four sheets. (a) 108 × 130 mm. 25r. Donald playing banjo. (b) 133 × 108 mm. 25r. Donald posing for photo. (c) 108 × 130 mm. 25r. Donald conducting (horiz). (d) 102 × 121 mm. 25r. Huey, Dewey and Louie (horiz) Set of 4 sheets 14·00 15·00

314 Islamic Centre, Male

1995. Eid Greetings. Multicoloured.
2216 1r. Type **314** 15 15
2217 1r. Rose 15 15

2218	8r. Orchid	1·50	1·50
2219	10r. Orchid (different)	1·50	1·50

315 Killer Whale

1995. "Singapore '95" International Stamp Exhibition (1st issue). Whales, Dolphins and Porpoises. Multicoloured.

2220	1r. Type **315**	40	30
2221	2r. Bottlenose dolphins	45	35
2222	3r. Right whale	60	70
2223	3r. Pair of killer whales	60	70
2224	3r. Humpback whale	60	70
2225	3r. Pair of belugas	60	70
2226	3r. Narwhal	60	70
2227	3r. Head of blue whale	60	70
2228	3r. Bowhead whale	60	70
2229	3r. Head of fin whale	60	70
2230	3r. Pair of pilot whales	60	70
2231	3r. Grey whale	60	70
2232	3r. Sperm whale	60	70
2233	3r. Pair of goosebeaked whales	60	70
2234	3r. Hourglass dolphin	60	70
2235	3r. Bottlenose dolphin (different)	60	70
2236	3r. Dusky dolphin	60	70
2237	3r. Spectacled porpoise	60	70
2238	3r. Fraser's dolphin	60	70
2239	3r. Camerson's dolphin	60	70
2240	3r. Pair of spinner dolphins	60	70
2241	3r. Pair of Dalls dolphins	60	70
2242	3r. Spotted dolphin	60	70
2243	3r. Indus River dolphin	60	70
2244	3r. Hector's dolphin	60	70
2245	3r. Amazon River dolphin	60	70
2246	8r. Humpback whale and calf	1·25	1·50
2247	10r. Common dolphin	1·40	1·60
MS2248	Two sheets, each 100 × 70 mm. (a) 25r. Sperm whale (different). (b) 25r. Pair of hourglass dolphins Set of 2 sheets	9·00	9·00

See also Nos. 2302/10.

316 Scout Camp and National Flag

1995. 18th World Scout Jamboree, Netherlands. Multicoloured.

2249	10r. Type **316**	1·75	2·00
2250	12r. Campfire cooking	1·90	2·25
2251	15r. Scouts erecting tent	2·00	2·40
MS2252	102 × 72 mm. 25r. Scouts around camp fire (vert)	3·50	4·00

Nos. 2249/51 were printed together, se-tenant, forming a composite design.

317 Soviet Heavy Howitzer Battery

1995. 50th Anniv of End of Second World War in Europe. Multicoloured.

2253	5r. Type **317**	85	85
2254	5r. Ruins of Berchtesgaden	85	85
2255	5r. U.S. Boeing B-17 Flying Fortress dropping food over the Netherlands	85	85
2256	5r. Soviet Ilyushin Il-1 bomber	85	85
2257	5r. Liberation of Belsen	85	85
2258	5r. Supermarine Spitfire and V-1 flying bomb	85	85
2259	5r. U.S. tanks advancing through Cologne	85	85
2260	5r. Reichstag in ruins	85	85
MS2261	107 × 76 mm. 25r. Soviet and U.S. troops celebrating	3·50	3·75

318 Asian Child and Dove

320 Asian Child eating Rice

319 United Nations Emblem

1995. 50th Anniv of United Nations (1st issue). Multicoloured.

2262	6r.50+50l. Type **318**	90	1·25
2263	8r. Globe and dove	1·00	1·40
2264	10r. African child and dove	1·10	1·50
MS2265	72 × 102 mm. 25r. United Nations emblem and dove	2·75	3·75

Nos. 2262/4 were printed together, se-tenant, forming a composite design.

1995. 50th Anniv of United Nations (2nd issue).

2266	**319** 30l. black, blue & grn	10	10
2267	– 8r. multicoloured	1·00	1·25
2268	– 11r. multicoloured	1·25	1·50
2269	– 13r. black, grey and red	1·60	1·90

DESIGNS: 8r. Symbolic women, flag and map; 11r. U.N. soldier and symbolic dove; 13r. Gun barrels, atomic explosion and bomb sight.

1995. 50th Anniv of F.A.O. (1st issue). Mult.

2270	6r.50+50l. Type **320**	90	1·10
2271	8r. F.A.O. emblem	1·00	1·25
2272	10r. African mother and child	1·10	1·40
MS2273	72 × 102 mm. 25r. African child and symbolic hand holding maize	2·75	3·75

See also Nos. 2311/12.

321 Queen Elizabeth the Queen Mother

1995. 95th Birthday of Queen Elizabeth the Queen Mother.

2274	**321** 5r. brown, lt brn & blk	1·00	1·10
2275	– 5r. multicoloured	1·00	1·10
2276	– 5r. multicoloured	1·00	1·10
2277	– 5r. multicoloured	1·00	1·10
MS2278	125 × 100 mm. 25r. multicoloured	5·00	5·50

DESIGNS: No. 2275, Without hat; 2276, At desk (oil painting); 2277, Queen Elizabeth the Queen Mother; MS2278, Wearing lilac hat and dress.

1995. 50th Anniv of End of Second World War in the Pacific. As T **317**. Multicoloured.

2279	6r.50+50l. Grumman F6F-3 Hellcat aircraft	1·50	1·50
2280	6r.50+50l. F4-U1 fighter aircraft attacking beach	1·50	1·50
2281	6r.50+50l. Douglas SBD Dauntless aircraft	1·50	1·50
2282	6r.50+50l. American troops in landing craft, Guadalcanal	1·50	1·50
2283	6r.50+50l. U.S. marines in Alligator tanks	1·50	1·50
2284	6r.50+50l. U.S. landing ship	1·50	1·50
MS2285	106 × 74 mm. 25r. F4-U1 fighter aircraft	4·00	4·50

322 Students using Library

1995. 50th Anniv of National Library. Mult.

2286	2r. Type **322**	25	25
2287	8r. Students using library (different)	1·00	1·50
MS2288	105 × 75 mm. 10r. Library entrance (100 × 70 mm). Imperf	1·40	1·60

323 Spur-thighed Tortoise

1995. Turtles and Tortoises. Multicoloured.

2289	3r. Type **323**	60	70
2290	3r. Aldabra turtle	60	70
2291	3r. Loggerhead turtle	60	70
2292	3r. Olive Ridley turtle	60	70
2293	3r. Leatherback turtle	60	70
2294	3r. Green turtle	60	70
2295	3r. Atlantic Ridley turtle	60	70
2296	3r. Hawksbill turtle	60	70
2297	10r. Hawksbill turtle on beach	1·40	1·60
2298	10r. Pair of hawksbill turtles	1·40	1·60
2299	10r. Hawksbill turtle climbing out of water	1·40	1·60
2300	10r. Hawksbill turtle swimming	1·40	1·60
MS2301	100 × 70 mm. 25r. Green turtle	3·75	4·50

Nos. 2289/96 were printed together, se-tenant, forming a composite design.

Nos. 2297/2300 include the W.W.F. Panda emblem.

324 "Russula aurata" (fungi) and "Papilio demodocus" (butterfly)

1995. "Singapore '95" International Stamp Exhibition. Butterflies and Fungi. Multicoloured.

2302	2r. Type **324**	75	75
2303	2r. "Lepista saeva" and "Kallimoides rumia"	75	75
2304	2r. "Lepista nuda" and "Hypolimnas salmacis"	75	75
2305	2r. "Xerocomus subtomentosus" ("Boletus subtomentosus" and "Precis octavia")	75	75
2306	5r. "Gyroporus castaneus" and "Hypolimnas salmacis"	1·10	1·10
2307	8r. "Gomphidius glutinosus" and "Papilio dardanus"	1·25	1·25
2308	10r. "Russula olivacea" and "Precis octavia"	1·40	1·40
2309	12r. "Boletus edulis" and "Prepona praeneste"	1·40	1·40
MS2310	Two sheets, each 105 × 76 mm. (a) 25r. "Amanita muscaria" and "Kallimoides rumia" (vert). (b) 25r. "Boletus rhodoxanthus" and "Hypolimnas salmacis" (vert) Set of 2 sheets	8·00	8·00

Nos. 2302/5 and 2306/9 respectively were printed together, se-tenant, forming composite designs.

No. 2304 is inscribed "Lapista" in error.

325 Planting Kaashi

1995. 50th Anniv of F.A.O. (2nd issue). Mult.

2311	7r. Type **325**	90	1·10
2312	8r. Fishing boat	1·10	1·25

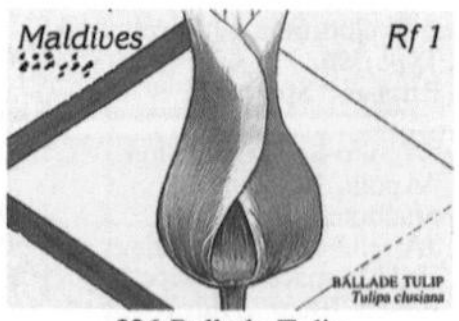

326 Ballade Tulip

1995. Flowers. Multicoloured.

2313	1r. Type **326**	20	15
2314	3r. White mallow	50	50
2315	5r. Regale trumpet lily	1·00	1·00
2316	5r. "Dendrobium Waipahu Beauty"	1·00	1·00
2317	5r. "Brassocattleya Jean Murray"	1·00	1·00
2318	5r. "Cymbidium Fort George"	1·00	1·00
2319	5r. "Paphiopedilum malipoense"	1·00	1·00
2320	5r. "Cycnoches chlorochilon"	1·00	1·00
2321	5r. "Rhyncholaelia digbgana"	1·00	1·00
2322	5r. "Lycaste deppei"	1·00	1·00
2323	5r. "Masdevallia constricta"	1·00	1·00
2324	5r. "Paphiopedilum Clair de Lune"	1·00	1·00
2325	7r. "Lilactime dahlia"	1·25	1·25
2326	8r. Blue ideal iris	1·25	1·25
2327	10r. Red crown imperial	1·40	1·40
MS2328	Two sheets, each 106 × 76mm. (a) 25r. "Encyclia cochleata" (vert). (b) 25r. "Psychopsis kramerina" (vert) Set of 2 sheets	8·00	9·50

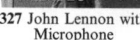

327 John Lennon with Microphone

329 Johannes van der Waals (1919 Physics)

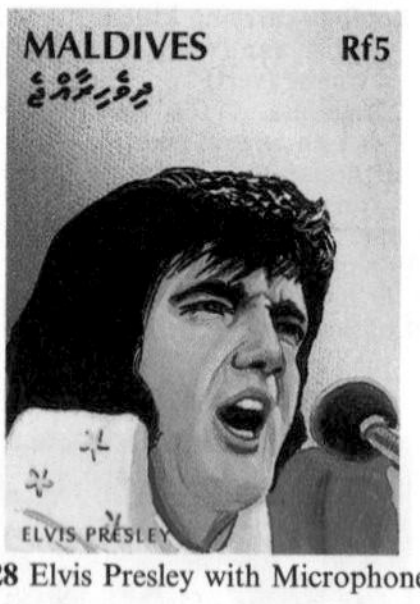

328 Elvis Presley with Microphone

1995. 15th Death Anniv of John Lennon (musician). Multicoloured.

2329	5r. Type **327**	1·40	1·25
2330	5r. With glasses and moustache	1·40	1·25
2331	5r. With guitar	1·40	1·25
2332	5r. With guitar and wearing glasses	1·40	1·25
2333	5r. Wearing sun glasses and red jacket	1·40	1·25
2334	5r. Wearing headphones	1·40	1·25
MS2335	88 × 117 mm. 2, 3, 8, 10r. Different portraits of John Lennon	5·50	5·50
MS2236	102 × 72 mm. 25r. John Lennon performing	5·50	5·50

1995. 60th Birth Anniv of Elvis Presley (entertainer). Multicoloured.

2337	5r. Type **328**	90	80
2338	5r. Wearing red jacket	90	80
2339	5r. Wearing blue jacket	90	80
2340	5r. With microphone and wearing blue jacket	90	80
2341	5r. In army uniform	90	80
2342	5r. Wearing yellow bow tie	90	80
2343	5r. In yellow shirt	90	80
2344	5r. In light blue shirt	90	80
2345	5r. Wearing red and white high-collared jacket	90	80
MS2346	80 × 110 mm. 25r. Elvis Presley (horiz)	4·25	4·50

1995. Cent of Nobel Prize Trust Fund. Mult.

2347/55 5r. × 9 (Type **329**; Charles Guillaume (1920 Physics); Sir James Chadwick (1935 Physics); Willem Einthoven (1924 Medicine); Henrik Dam (1943 Medicine); Sir Alexander Fleming (1945 Medicine); Hermann Muller (1946 Medicine); Rodney Porter (1972 Medicine); Werner Arber (1978 Medicine))

2356/64 5r. × 9 (Niels Bohr (1922 Physics); Ben Mottelson (1975 Physics); Patrick White (1973 Literature); Elias Canetti (1981 Literature); Theodor Kocher (1909 Medicine); August Krogh (1920 Medicine); William Murphy (1934 Medicine); John Northrop (1946 Chemistry); Luis Leloir (1970 Chemistry))

2365/73 5r. × 9 (Dag Hammarskjold (1961 Peace); Alva Myrdal (1982 Peace); Archbishop Desmond Tutu (1984 Peace); Rudolf Eucken (1908 Literature); Aleksandr Solzhenitsyn (1970 Literature); Gabriel Marquez (1982 Literature); Chen Yang (1957 Physics); Karl Muller (1987 Physics); Melvin Schwartz (1988 Physics))

2374/82 5r. × 9 (Robert Millikan (1923 Physics); Louis de Broglie (1929 Physics); Ernest Walton (1951 Physics); Richard Willstatter (1915 Chemistry); Lars Onsager (1968 Chemistry); Gerhard Herzberg (1971 Chemistry); William B. Yeats (1923 Literature); George Bernard Shaw (1925 Literature); Eugene O'Neill (1936 Literature)) . . . . .

2383/91 5r. × 9 (Bernardo Houssay (1947 Medicine); Paul Muller (1948 Medicine); Walter Hess (1949 Medicine); Sir MacFarlane Burnet (1960 Medicine); Baruch Blumberg (1976 Medicine); Daniel Nathans (1978 Medicine); Glenn Seaborg (1951 Chemistry); Ilya Prigogine (1977 Chemistry); Kenichi Fukui (1981 Chemistry)) . . . .

2392/2400 5r. × 9 (Carl Spitteler (1919 Literature); Henri Bergson (1927 Literature); Johannes Jensen (1944 Literature); Antoine-Henri Becquerel (1903 Physics); Sir William H. Bragg (1915 Physics); Sir William L. Bragg (1915 Physics); Frederik Bajer (1908 Peace); Leon Bourgeois (1920 Peace); Karl Benning (1921 Peace)) . . . .

Set of 54 . . . . 38·00 42·00

MS2401 Six sheets. (a) 80 × 110 mm. 25r. Konrad bloch (1964 Medicine). (b) 80 × 110 mm. 25r. Samuel Beckett (1969 Literature). (c) 80 × 110 mm. 25r. Otto Wallach (1910 Chemistry). (d) 110 × 80 mm. 25r. Hideki Yukawa (1949 Physics). (e) 110 × 80 mm. 25r. Eisaku Sato (1974 Peace). (f) 110 × 80 mm. 25r. Robert Koch (1905 Medicine) Set of 6 sheets 16·00 17·00

330 Rythmic Gymnast and Japanese Fan

1996. Olympic Games, Atlanta (1st issue). Mult.

2402	1r. Type **330**	25	10
2403	3r. Archer and Moscow Olympics logo	50	35
2404	5r. Diver and Swedish flag	80	85
2405	5r. Canadian Maple Leaf . .	80	85
2406	5r. Shot putting (decathlon)	80	85
2407	5r. Moscow Olympic medal and ribbon	80	85
2408	5r. Fencer	80	85
2409	5r. Gold medal	80	85
2410	5r. Equestrian competitor	80	85
2411	5r. Sydney Opera House . .	80	85
2412	5r. Athlete on starting blocks	80	85
2413	5r. South Korean flag . . .	80	85
2414	7r. High jumper and Tower Bridge, London	1·00	1·10
2415	10r. Athlete on starting blocks and Brandenburg Gate, Germany	1·40	1·60
2416	12r. Hurdler and Amsterdam Olympic logo	1·60	1·90

MS2417 Two sheets, each 113 × 80 mm. (a) 25r. Red Olympic Flame (vert). (b) 25r. Multicoloured Olympic Flame (vert) Set of 2 sheets . . . . . 8·00 9·00

See also Nos. 2469/87.

331 "Self Portrait" (Degas)

1996. 125th Anniv of Metropolitan Museum of Art, New York. Multicoloured.

2418/25 4r. × 8 ("Self-Portrait" (Degas); "Andromache and Astyanax" (Prud'hon); "Rene Grenier" (Toulouse-Lautrec); "The Banks of the Bievre near Bicetre" (Rousseau); "The Repast of the Lion" (Rousseau); "Portrait of Yves Gobillard-Morisot" (Degas); "Sunflowers" (Van Gogh); "The Singer in Green" (Degas)) . . . .

2426/33 4r. × 8 ("Still Life" (Fantin-Latour); "Portrait of a Lady in Grey" (Degas); "Apples and Grapes" (Monet); "The Englishman" (Toulouse-Lautrec); "Cypresses" (Van Gogh); "Flowers in a Chinese Vase" (Redon); "The Gardener" (Seurat); "Large Sunflowers I" (Nolde))

2434/41 4r. × 8 (All by Manet: "The Spanish Singer"; "Young Man in Costume of Majo"; "Mademoiselle Victorine"; "Boating"; "Peonies"; "Woman with a Parrot"; "George Moore"; "The Monet Family in their Garden") . . . . . .

2442/9 4r. × 8 ("Goldfish" (Matisse); "Spanish Woman: Harmony in Blue" (Matisse); "Nasturtiums and the "Dance" II" (Matisse); "The House behind Trees" (Braque); "Mada Primavesi" (Klimt); "Head of a Woman" (Picasso); "Woman in White" (Picasso); "Harlequin" (Picasso)) . . . . . .

2418/49 Set of 32 . . . . 25·00 27·00

MS2450 Four sheets, each 95 × 70 mm, containing horiz designs, 81 × 53 mm. (a) 25r. "Northeaster" (Homer). (b) 25r. "The Fortune Teller" (De La Tour). (c) 25r. "Santo (Sanzio), Ritratto de Andrea Navagero e Agostino Beazzano" (Raphael). (d) 25r. "Portrait of a Woman" (Rubens) Set of 4 sheets . . . 17·00 19·00

332 Mickey Mouse on Great Wall of China

1996. "CHINA '96" 9th Asian International Stamp Exhibition, Peking. Walt Disney cartoon characters in China. Multicoloured.

2451	2r. Type **332**	80	80
2452	2r. Pluto with temple guardian	80	80
2453	2r. Minnie Mouse with pandas	80	80
2454	2r. Mickey windsurfing near junks	80	80
2455	2r. Goofy cleaning grotto statue	80	80
2456	2r. Donald and Daisy Duck at Marble Boat	80	80
2457	2r. Mickey with terracotta warriors	80	80
2458	2r. Goofy with geese and masks	80	80
2459	2r. Donald and Goofy on traditional fishing boat . .	80	80
2460	2r. Mickey and Minnie in dragon boat	80	80
2461	2r. Donald at Peking opera	80	80
2462	2r. Mickey and Minnie in Chinese garden	80	80
2463	3r. Mickey and Minnie at the Ice Pagoda (vert) . .	1·00	1·00
2464	3r. Donald and Mickey flying Chinese kites (vert)	1·00	1·00
2465	3r. Goofy playing anyiwu (vert)	1·00	1·00
2466	3r. Paper cutouts of Mickey and Goofy (vert)	1·00	1·00
2467	3r. Donald and Mickey in dragon dance (vert) . . .	1·00	1·00

MS2468 Three sheets. (a) 108 × 133 mm. 5r. Mickey pointing. (b) 133 × 108 mm. 7r. Mickey and Minnie watching Moon. (c) 133 × 108 mm. 8r. Donald using chopsticks Set of 3 sheets . . . . 5·50 6·00

333 Stella Walsh (Poland) (100 m sprint, 1932) on Medal

1996. Olympic Games, Atlanta (2nd issue). Previous Gold Medal Winners. Multicoloured.

2469	1r. Type **333**	25	15
2470	3r. Emile Zatopek (Czechoslovakia) (10,000 m running, 1952) and Olympic torch (vert)	50	35
2471	5r. Yanko Rousseu (Bulgaria) (lightweight, 1980) (vert)	75	80
2472	5r. Peter Baczako (Hungary) (middle heavyweight, 1980) (vert)	75	80
2473	5r. Leonid Taranenko (Russia) (heavyweight, 1980) (vert)	75	80
2474	5r. Aleksandr Kurlovich (Russia) (heavyweight, 1988) (vert)	75	80
2475	5r. Assen Zlateu (Bulgaria) (middleweight, 1980) (vert)	75	80
2476	5r. Zeng Guoqiang (China) (flyweight, 1984) (vert) . .	75	80
2477	5r. Yurik Vardanyan (Russia) (heavyweight, 1980) (vert)	75	80
2478	5r. Sultan Rakhmanov (Russia) (super heavyweight, 1980) (vert)	75	80
2479	5r. Vassily Alexeev (Russia) (super heavyweight, 1972) (vert)	75	80
2480	5r. Ethel Catherwood (Canada) (high jump, 1928)	75	80
2481	5r. Mildred Didrikson (U.S.A.) (javelin, 1932) . .	75	80
2482	5r. Francina Blankers-Koen (Netherlands) (80 m hurdles, 1948) . . .	75	80
2483	5r. Tamara Press (Russia) (shot put, 1960)	75	80
2484	5r. Lia Manoliu (Rumania) (discus, 1968)	75	80
2485	5r. Rosa Mota (Portugal) (marathon, 1988)	75	80
2486	10r. Olga Fikotova (Czechoslovakia) (discus, 1956) on medal	1·40	1·60
2487	12r. Joan Benoit (U.S.A.) (marathon, 1984) on medal	1·60	1·90

MS2488 Two sheets. (a) 76 × 106 mm. 25r. Naeem Suleymanoglu (Turkey) (weightlifting, 1988) (vert). (b) 105 × 75 mm. 25r. Irena Szewinska (Poland) (400 m running, 1976) on medal Set of 2 sheets . . . . . 8·00 9·00

No. 2469 identifies the event as 10 metres in error.

334 Queen Elizabeth II

1996. 70th Birthday of Queen Elizabeth II. Mult.

2489	8r. Type **334**	1·60	1·75
2490	8r. Wearing hat	1·60	1·75
2491	8r. At desk	1·60	1·75

MS2492 125 × 103 mm. 25r. Queen Elizabeth and Queen Mother on Buckingham Palace balcony . . 5·50 5·50

335 African Child

1996. 50th Anniv of UNICEF. Multicoloured.

2493	5r. Type **335**	60	55
2494	7r. European girl	85	90
2495	7r. Maldivian boy	85	90
2496	10r. Asian girl	1·25	1·40

MS2497 114 × 74 mm. 25r. Baby with toy . . . . 3·50 4·00

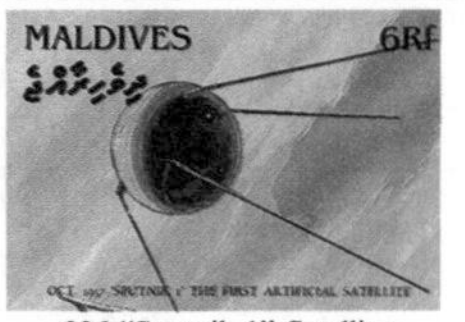

336 "Sputnik 1" Satellite

1996. Space Exploration. Multicoloured.

2498	6r. Type **336**	1·10	1·10
2499	6r. "Apollo 11" command module	1·10	1·10
2500	6r. "Skylab"	1·10	1·10
2501	6r. Astronaut Edward White walking in space	1·10	1·10
2502	6r. "Mariner 9"	1·10	1·10
2503	6r. "Apollo" and "Soyuz" docking	1·10	1·10

MS2504 104 × 74 mm. 25r. Launch of "Apollo 8" (vert) . . . . . 4·50 4·75

337 "Epiphora albida"

1996. Butterflies. Multicoloured.

2505	7r. Type **337**	1·10	1·10
2506	7r. "Satyrus dryas"	1·10	1·10
2507	7r. "Satyrus lena"	1·10	1·10
2508	7r. "Papilio tynderaeus" . .	1·10	1·10
2509	7r. "Urota suraka"	1·10	1·10
2510	7r. "Satyrus nercis"	1·10	1·10
2511	7r. "Papilio troilus" (vert)	1·10	1·10
2512	7r. "Papilio cresphontes" (vert)	1·10	1·10
2513	7r. Lime swallowtail caterpillar (vert)	1·10	1·10
2514	7r. "Cynthia virginiensis" (vert)	1·10	1·10
2515	7r. Monarch caterpillar (vert)	1·10	1·10
2516	7r. "Danaus plexippus" (vert)	1·10	1·10
2517	7r. Monarch caterpillar and pupa (vert)	1·10	1·10
2518	7r. "Chlosyne harrisii" (vert)	1·10	1·10
2519	7r. "Cymothoe coccinata" (vert)	1·10	1·10
2520	7r. "Morpho rhetenor" (vert)	1·10	1·10
2521	7r. "Callicore lidwina" (vert)	1·10	1·10
2522	7r. "Heliconius erato reductimacula" (vert) . .	1·10	1·10

MS2523 Two sheets, each 106 × 76 mm. (a) 25r. "Heliconius charitonius" (vert). (b) 25r. "Heliconius cydno" (vert) Set of 2 sheets . . . . 8·50 9·00

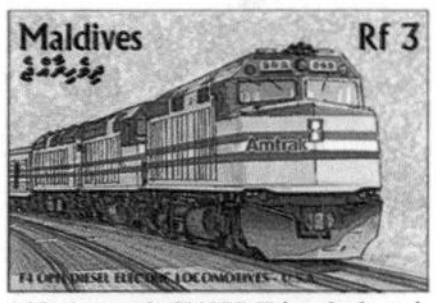

338 Amtrak F40H Diesel-electric Locomotive, U.S.A.

1996. Trains of the World. Multicoloured.

2524	3r. Type **338**	70	70
2525	3r. Stephenson's "Experiment"	70	70
2526	3r. Indian-Pacific Intercontinental, Australia	70	70
2527	3r. Stephenson's Killingworth type steam locomotive, 1815	70	70
2528	3r. George Stephenson . . .	70	70
2529	3r. Stephenson's "Rocket", 1829	70	70
2530	3r. High Speed Train 125, Great Britain	70	70
2531	3r. First rail passenger coach "Experiment", 1825	70	70
2532	3r. Union Pacific Class U25B diesel locomotive (inscr "Tofac"), U.S.A.	70	70
2533	3r. Southern Pacific's "Daylight" express, 1952, U.S.A.	70	70
2534	3r. Timothy Hackworth's "Sans Pareil", 1829 . . .	70	70
2535	3r. Chicago and North Western diesel locomotive, U.S.A.	70	70
2536	3r. Richard Trevithick's "Pen-y-Darren" locomotive, 1804	70	70
2537	3r. Isambard Kingdom Brunel	70	70
2538	3r. Great Western locomotive, 1838	70	70
2539	3r. Vistadome observation car, Canada	70	70
2540	3r. Mohawk and Hudson Railroad "Experiment", 1832	70	70
2541	3r. ICE high speed train, Germany	70	70
2542	3r. Electric container locomotive, Germany . .	70	70
2543	3r. John Blenkinsop's rack locomotive, 1811	70	70

2544 3r. Diesel-electric locomotive, Western Australia 70 70
2545 3r. Timothy Hackworth's "Royal George", 1827 . . 70 70
2546 3r. Robert Stephenson . . . 70 70
2547 3r. Trevithick's "Newcastle" 70 70
2548 3r. Deltic diesel-electric locomotive, Great Britain 70 70
2549 3r. Stockton and Darlington Railway locomotive No. 5 "Stockton", 1826 . . . . 70 70
2550 3r. Channel Tunnel "Le Shuttle" train 70 70
MS2551 Three sheets, each 96 × 91 mm. (a) 25r. Peter Cooper's "Tom Thumb", 1829. (b) 25r. John Jarvis's "De Witt Clinton", 1831. (c) 25r. William Hudson's "The General", 1855 Set of 3 sheets . . . . 13·00 13·00
No. 2524 is inscribed "F4 OPH" in error.

339 Bongo

1996. Wildlife of the World. Multicoloured.
2552 5r. Type **339** 90 90
2553 5r. Bushbuck 90 90
2554 5r. Namaqua dove 90 90
2555 5r. Hoopoe 90 90
2556 5r. African fish eagle . . . 90 90
2557 5r. Egyptian goose 90 90
2558 5r. Saddle-bill stork 90 90
2559 5r. Blue-breasted kingfisher 90 90
2560 5r. Yellow baboon 90 90
2561 5r. Banded duiker ("Zebra Duiker") 90 90
2562 5r. Yellow-backed duiker . . 90 90
2563 5r. Pygmy hippopotamus . . 90 90
2564 5r. Large-spotted genet . . . 90 90
2565 5r. African spoonbill . . . 90 90
2566 5r. White-faced whistling duck 90 90
2567 5r. Helmeted guineafowl . . 90 90
2568 7r. Cotton-headed tamarin (horiz) . . . . 1·25 1·25
2569 7r. European bison (horiz) 1·25 1·25
2570 7r. Tiger (horiz) . . . . . . 1·25 1·25
2571 7r. Western capercaillie (horiz) . . . . 1·25 1·25
2572 7r. Giant panda (horiz) . . 1·25 1·25
2573 7r. "Trogonoptera brookiana" (butterfly) (horiz) . . . . 1·25 1·25
2574 7r. American beaver (horiz) 1·25 1·25
2575 7r. "Leiopelma hamiltoni" (frog) (horiz) . . . . . 1·25 1·25
2576 7r. Manatee (horiz) . . . . 1·25 1·25
MS2577 106 × 76 mm. 25r. Chimpanzee (horiz) . . . . . 3·75 4·50
Nos. 2552/9, 2560/7 and 2568/76 respectively were printed together, se-tenant, with the backgrounds forming composite designs.
No. 2553 is inscribed "BUSHBACK" in error.

340 Giant Panda

1996. Endangered Species. Multicoloured.
2578 5r. Type **340** 90 90
2579 5r. Indian elephant 90 90
2580 5r. Arrow-poison frog . . . 90 90
2581 5r. Mandrill 90 90
2582 5r. Snow leopard 90 90
2583 5r. California condor . . . 90 90
2584 5r. Whale-headed stork ("Shoebill Stork") 90 90
2585 5r. Red-billed hornbill . . . 90 90
2586 5r. Hippopotamus 90 90
2587 5r. Gorilla 90 90
2588 5r. Lion 90 90
2589 5r. South African crowned crane ("Gray Crowned Crane") 90 90
MS2590 Two sheets, each 110 × 80 mm. (a) 25r. Tiger (vert). (b) 25r. Leopard Set of 2 sheets 8·50 9·00

341 Mickey Mouse climbing out of Puddle

1996. Centenary of the Cinema. Cartoon Frames from "The Little Whirlwind" (Nos. 2591/2607) or "Pluto and the Flypaper" (Nos. 2608/24). Mult.
2591 4r. Type **341** . . . . 1·25 1·25
2592 4r. Frame 2 . . . . 1·25 1·25
2593 4r. Frame 3 . . . . 1·25 1·25
2594 4r. Frame 4 . . . . 1·25 1·25
2595 4r. Frame 5 . . . . 1·25 1·25
2596 4r. Frame 6 . . . . 1·25 1·25
2597 4r. Frame 7 . . . . 1·25 1·25
2598 4r. Frame 8 . . . . 1·25 1·25
2599 4r. Frame 9 . . . . 1·25 1·25
2600 4r. Frame 10 . . . . . . 1·25 1·25
2601 4r. Frame 11 . . . . . . 1·25 1·25
2602 4r. Frame 12 . . . . . . 1·25 1·25
2603 4r. Frame 13 . . . . . . 1·25 1·25
2604 4r. Frame 14 . . . . . . 1·25 1·25
2605 4r. Frame 15 . . . . . . 1·25 1·25
2606 4r. Frame 16 (Mickey holding fish above head) 1·25 1·25
2607 4r. Frame 17 (Mickey throwing fish into pool) 1·25 1·25
2608 4r. Frame 1 (Pluto) . . . . 1·25 1·25
2609 4r. Frame 2 . . . . 1·25 1·25
2610 4r. Frame 3 . . . . 1·25 1·25
2611 4r. Frame 4 . . . . 1·25 1·25
2612 4r. Frame 5 . . . . 1·25 1·25
2613 4r. Frame 6 . . . . 1·25 1·25
2614 4r. Frame 7 . . . . 1·25 1·25
2615 4r. Frame 8 . . . . 1·25 1·25
2616 4r. Frame 9 . . . . 1·25 1·25
2617 4r. Frame 10 . . . . . . 1·25 1·25
2618 4r. Frame 11 . . . . . . 1·25 1·25
2619 4r. Frame 12 . . . . . . 1·25 1·25
2620 4r. Frame 13 . . . . . . 1·25 1·25
2621 4r. Frame 14 . . . . . . 1·25 1·25
2622 4r. Frame 15 . . . . . . 1·25 1·25
2623 4r. Frame 16 . . . . . . 1·25 1·25
2624 4r. Frame 17 . . . . . . 1·25 1·25
MS2625 Two sheets, 111 × 131 mm. (a) 25r. Frame 18 ("The Little Whirlwind"). (b) 25r. Frame 18 ("Pluto and the Flypaper") Set of 2 sheets . . . . 14·00 15·00

342 Letter "O" with Chinese Character

1997. "HONG KONG '97" International Stamp Exhibition. Multicoloured.
2626 5r. Letter "H" and Chinese couple 85 85
2627 5r. Type **342** 85 85
2628 5r. Letter "N" and Chinese dragon 85 85
2629 5r. Letter "G" and carnival dragon 85 85
2630 5r. Letter "K" and modern office block 85 85
2631 5r. Letter "O" and Chinese character (different) . . . 85 85
2632 5r. Letter "N" and Chinese fan cases 85 85
2633 5r. Letter "G" and Chinese junk 85 85
MS2634 106 × 125 mm. 25r. "HONG KONG" as on Nos. 2626/33 (76 × 38 mm) . . 3·75 4·50

343 California Condor **344** Ye Qiabo (China) (women's 500/1000 m speed skating, 1992)

1997. Birds of the World. Multicoloured.
2635 5r. Type **343** 90 90
2636 5r. Audouin's gull 90 90
2637 5r. Atlantic puffin 90 90
2638 5r. Resplendent quetzal . . 90 90
2639 5r. Puerto Rican amazon . . 90 90
2640 5r. Lesser bird of paradise 90 90
2641 5r. Japanese crested ibis . . 90 90
2642 5r. Mauritius kestrel 90 90
2643 5r. Kakapo 90 90
MS2644 76 × 106 mm. 25r. Ivory-billed woodpecker . . . . . . 4·50 5·00
Nos. 2635/43 were printed together, se-tenant, with the backgrounds forming a composite design.

1997. Winter Olympic Games, Nagano, Japan (1998). Multicoloured.
2645 2r. Type **344** 40 25
2646 3r. Leonhard Stock (Austria) (downhill skiing, 1980) 55 35
2647 5r. Herma von Szabo-Planck (Austria) (figure skating, 1924) 75 80
2648 5r. Katarina Witt (Germany) (figure skating, 1988) 75 80
2649 5r. Natalia Bestemianova and Andrei Bukin (Russia) (pairs ice dancing, 1988) 75 80
2650 5r. Jayne Torvill and Christopher Dean (Great Britain) (pairs ice dancing, 1984) 75 80
2651 8r. Bjorn Daehlie (Norway) (cross-country skiing, 1992) . . . . 1·25 1·40
2652 12r. Wolfgang Hoppe (Germany) (bobsleigh, 1984) . . . . 1·75 2·00
MS2653 Two sheets, each 76 × 106 mm. (a) 25r. Sonja Henie (Norway) (figure skating, 1924). (b) 25r. Andree Joly and Pierre Brunet (France) (pairs ice dancing, 1932) Set of 2 sheets . . . . . 8·00 9·00

345 Crowned Solitary Eagle

1997. Eagles. Multicoloured.
2654 1r. Type **345** 45 20
2655 2r. African hawk eagle (horiz) 60 30
2656 3r. Lesser spotted eagle . . 70 40
2657 5r. Stellar's sea eagle . . . 85 90
2658 5r. Bald eagle attacking . . 85 90
2659 5r. Bald eagle on branch . . 85 90
2660 5r. Bald eagle looking left 85 90
2661 5r. Bald eagle looking right 85 90
2662 5r. Bald eagle sitting on branch with leaves . . . 85 90
2663 5r. Bald eagle soaring . . . 85 90
2664 8r. Imperial eagle ("Spanish Imperial Eagle") (horiz) 1·40 1·50
2665 10r. Harpy eagle . . . . . 1·50 1·60
2666 12r. Crested serpent eagle (horiz) . . . . 1·75 1·90
MS2667 Two sheets. (a) 73 × 104 mm. 25r. Bald eagle. (b) 104 × 73 mm. 25r. American bald eagle (horiz) Set of 2 sheets . . 8·00 8·50

346 Blitzer Benz, 1911

1997. Classic Cars. Multicoloured.
2668 5r. Type **346** 80 85
2669 5r. Datsun, 1917 . . . . . 80 85
2670 5r. Auburn 8-120, 1929 . . 80 85
2671 5r. Mercedes-Benz C280, 1996 . . . . 80 85
2672 5r. Suzuki UR-1 . . . . . . 80 85
2673 5r. Chrysler Atlantic 80 85
2674 5r. Mercedes-Benz 190SL, 1961 . . . . 80 85
2675 5r. Kwaishinha D.A.T., 1916 . . . . 80 85
2676 5r. Rolls-Royce Roadster 20/25 . . . . 80 85
2677 5r. Mercedes-Benz SLK, 1997 . . . . 80 85
2678 5r. Toyota Camry, 1996 . . 80 85
2679 5r. Jaguar MK 2, 1959 . . . 80 85
MS2680 Two sheets, each 100 × 70 mm. (a) 25r. Volkswagen, 1939. (b) 25r. Mazda RX-01 Set of 2 sheets . . . . 7·50 8·50

347 "Patris II", Greece (1926)

1997. Passenger Ships. Multicoloured.
2681 1r. Type **347** 30 15
2682 2r. "Infanta Beatriz", Spain (1928) 40 25
2683 3r. "Vasilefs Constantinos", Greece (1914) 55 60
2684 3r. "Cunene", Portugal (1911) 55 60
2685 3r. "Selandia", Denmark (1912) 55 60
2686 3r. "President Harding", U.S.A. (1921) 55 60
2687 3r. "Ulster Monarch", Great Britain (1929) 55 60
2688 3r. "Matsonia", U.S.A. (1913) 55 60
2689 3r. "France", France (1911) 55 60
2690 3r. "Campania", Great Britain (1893) 55 60
2691 3r. "Klipfontein", Holland (1922) 55 60
2692 3r. "Eridan", France (1929) 55 60
2693 3r. "Mount Clinton", U.S.A. (1921) 55 60
2694 3r. "Infanta Isabel", Spain (1912) 55 60
2695 3r. "Suwa Maru", Japan (1914) 55 60
2696 3r. "Yorkshire", Great Britain (1920) 55 60
2697 3r. "Highland Chieftain", Great Britain (1929) . . . 55 60
2698 3r. "Sardinia", Norway (1920) 55 60
2699 3r. "San Guglielmo", Italy (1911) 55 60
2700 3r. "Avila", Great Britain (1927) 55 60
2701 8r. "Stavangerfjord", Norway (1918) . . . . . 1·25 1·40
2702 12r. "Baloeran", Netherlands (1929) . . . 1·75 1·90
MS2703 Four sheets. (a) 69 × 69 mm. 25r. "Mauritania", Great Britain (1907). (b) 69 × 69 mm. 25r. "United States", U.S.A. (1952). (c) 69 × 69 mm. 25r. "Queen Mary", Great Britain (1930). (d) 91 × 76 mm. 25r. Royal Yacht "Britannia" amd Chinese junk, Hong Kong (56 × 42 mm) Set of 4 sheets . . . . 15·00 15·00
No. **MS**2703d is inscribed "BRITTANIA" in error.

348 Prayer Wheels, Lhasa

1997. 50th Anniv of UNESCO. Multicoloured.
2704 1r. Type **348** 20 15
2705 2r. Ruins of Roman Temple of Diana, Portugal (horiz) 30 25
2706 3r. Santa Maria Cathedral, Hildesheim, Germany (horiz) 45 35
2707 5r. Vivunga National Park, Zaire 65 70
2708 5r. Valley of Mai Nature Reserve, Seychelles . . . 65 70
2709 5r. Kandy, Sri Lanka 65 70
2710 5r. Taj Mahal, India 65 70
2711 5r. Istanbul, Turkey 65 70
2712 5r. Sana'a, Yemen 65 70
2713 5r. Bleinheim Palace, England 65 70
2714 5r. Grand Canyon National Park, U.S.A. 65 70
2715 5r. Tombs, Gondar, Ethiopia 65 70
2716 5r. Bwindi National Park, Uganda 65 70
2717 5r. Bemaraha National Reserve, Madagascar . . 65 70
2718 5r. Buddhist ruins at Takht-I-Bahi, Pakistan 65 70
2719 5r. Anuradhapura, Sri Lanka 65 70
2720 5r. Cairo, Egypt 65 70
2721 5r. Ruins, Petra, Jordan . . 65 70
2722 5r. Volcano, Ujung Kulon National Park, Indonesia 65 70
2723 5r. Terrace, Mount Taishan, China 65 70
2724 5r. Temple, Mount Taishan, China 65 70
2725 5r. Temple turret, Mount Taishan, China 65 70
2726 5r. Standing stones, Mount Taishan, China 65 70
2727 5r. Courtyard, Mount Taishan, China 65 70
2728 5r. Staircase, Mount Taishan, China 65 70
2729 5r. Terracotta Warriors, China 65 70
2730 5r. Head of Terracota Warrior, China 65 70
2731 7r. Doorway, Abu Simbel, Egypt 90 95
2732 8r. Mandraki, Rhodes, Greece (horiz) . . . . . 1·10 1·25
2733 8r. Agios Stefanos Monastery, Meteora, Greece (horiz) . . . . . 1·10 1·25
2734 8r. Taj Mahal, India (horiz) 1·10 1·25
2735 8r. Cistercian Abbey of Fontenay, France (horiz) 1·10 1·25
2736 8r. Yarushima, Japan (horiz) 1·10 1·25
2737 8r. Cloisters, San Gonzalo Convent, Portugal (horiz) 1·10 1·25
2738 8r. Olympic National Park, U.S.A. (horiz) . . . . . 1·10 1·25

2739	8r. Waterfall, Nahanni National Park, Canada (horiz)	1·10	1·25
2740	8r. Mountains, National Park, Argentina (horiz)	1·10	1·25
2741	8r. Bonfin Salvador Church, Brazil (horiz)	1·10	1·25
2742	8r. Convent of the Companions of Jesus, Morelia, Mexico (horiz)	1·10	1·25
2743	8r. Two-storey temple, Horyu Temple, Japan (horiz)	1·10	1·25
2744	8r. Summer house, Horyu Temple, Japan (horiz)	1·10	1·25
2745	8r. Temple and cloister, Horyu Temple, Japan (horiz)	1·10	1·25
2746	8r. Single storey temple, Horyu Temple, Japan (horiz)	1·10	1·25
2747	8r. Well, Horyu Temple, Japan (horiz)	1·10	1·25
2748	10r. Scandola Nature Reserve, France (horiz)	1·25	1·40
2749	12r. Temple on the Lake, China (horiz)	1·50	1·75
MS2750	Four sheets, each 127×102 mm. (a) 25r. Fatehpur Sikri Monument, India (horiz). (b) 25r. Temple, Chengde, China (horiz). (c) 25r. Serengeti National Park, Tanzania (horiz). (d) 25r. Buddha, Anuradhapura, Sri Lanka (horiz) Set of 4 sheets	13·00	14·00

No. 2717 is inscribed "MADAGASGAR" and 2737 "COVENT", both in error.

349 White Doves and S.A.A.R.C. Logo

1997. 9th South Asian Association for Regional Cooperation Summit, Male. Multicoloured.

2751	3r. Type **349**	40	35
2752	5r. Flags of member countries	1·00	75

350 Queen Elizabeth II

1997. Golden Wedding of Queen Elizabeth and Prince Philip. Multicoloured.

2753	5r. Type **350**	90	90
2754	5r. Royal coat of arms	90	90
2755	5r. Queen Elizabeth and Prince Philip at opening of Parliament	90	90
2756	5r. Queen Elizabeth and Prince Philip with Prince Charles, 1948	90	90
2757	5r. Buckingham Palace from the garden	90	90
2758	5r. Prince Philip	90	90
MS2759	100×70 mm. 25r. Queen Elizabeth II	3·75	3·75

351 Early Indian Mail Messenger

1997. "Pacific '97" International Stamp Exhibition, San Francisco. Death Centenary of Heinrich von Stephan (founder of the U.P.U.).

2760	**351** 2r. green and black	50	60
2761	– 2r. brown and black	50	60
2762	– 2r. violet	50	60

DESIGNS: No. 2761, Von Stephan and Mercury; 2762, Autogyro, Washington.

352 "Dawn at Kanda Myojn Shrine"

1997. Birth Bicentenary of Hiroshige (Japanese painter). "One Hundred Famous Views of Edo". Multicoloured.

2763	8r. Type **352**	1·25	1·25
2764	8r. "Kiyomizu Hall and Shinobazu Pond at Ueno"	1·25	1·25
2765	8r. "Ueno Yamashita"	1·25	1·25
2766	8r. "Moon Pine, Ueno"	1·25	1·25
2767	8r. "Flower Pavilion, Dango Slope, Sendagi"	1·25	1·25
2768	8r. "Shitaya Hirokoji"	1·25	1·25
MS2769	Two sheets, each 102×127 mm. (a) 25r. "Hilltop View, Yushima Tenjin Shrine". (b) 25r "Seido and Kanda River from Shohei Bridge" Set of 2 sheets	7·50	8·50

353 Common Noddy

354 "Canarina eminii"

1997. Birds. Multicoloured.

2770	30l. Type **353**	20	30
2771	1r. Spectacled owl	45	25
2772	2r. Malay fish owl	60	35
2773	3r. Peregrine falcon	70	50
2774	5r. Golden eagle	90	70
2775	7r. Ruppell's parrot	1·00	1·10
2776	7r. Blue-headed parrot	1·00	1·10
2777	7r. St Vincent amazon ("St Vincent Parrot")	1·00	1·10
2778	7r. Grey parrot	1·00	1·10
2779	7r. Masked lovebird	1·00	1·10
2780	7r. Sun conure ("Sun Parakeet")	1·00	1·10
2781	8r. Bateleur	1·25	1·25
2782	10r. Whiskered tern with chicks	1·50	1·50
2783	10r. Common caracara	1·50	1·50
2784	15r. Red-footed booby	2·00	2·25
MS2785	Two sheets, each 67×98 mm. (a) 25r. American bald eagle. (b) 25r. Secretary bird Set of 2 sheets	8·00	8·50

1997. Flowers. Multicoloured.

2786	1r. Type **354**	25	15
2787	2r. "Delphinium macrocentron"	40	25
2788	3r. "Leucadendron discolor"	55	40
2789	5r. "Nymphaea caerulea"	75	60
2790	7r. "Rosa multiflora polyantha" (20×23 mm)	1·00	1·00
2791	8r. "Bulbophyllum barbigerum"	1·25	1·40
2792	8r. "Acacia seyal" (horiz)	1·25	1·40
2793	8r. "Gloriosa superba" (horiz)	1·25	1·40
2794	8r. "Gnidia subcordata" (horiz)	1·25	1·40
2795	8r. "Platycelyphium voense" (horiz)	1·25	1·40
2796	8r. "Aspilia mossambicensis" (horiz)	1·25	1·40
2797	8r. "Adenium obesum" (horiz)	1·25	1·40
2798	12r. "Hibiscus vitifolius"	2·00	2·25
MS2799	Two sheets, each 105×76 mm. (a) 25r. "Aerangis rhodosticta" (horiz). (b) 25r. "Dichrostachys cinerea" and two sailing boats (horiz) Set of 2 sheets	13·00	13·00

Nos. 2792/7 were printed together, se-tenant, with the backgrounds forming a composite design.

355 Archaeopteryx

1997. Prehistoric Animals. Multicoloured. (a) Horiz designs.

2800	5r. Type **355**	90	65
2801	7r. Diplodocus	1·00	1·00
2802	7r. Tyrannosaurus rex	1·00	1·00
2803	7r. Pteranodon	1·00	1·00
2804	7r. Montanceratops	1·00	1·00
2805	7r. Dromaeosaurus	1·00	1·00
2806	7r. Oviraptor	1·00	1·00
2807	8r. Mosasaurus	1·25	1·25
2808	12r. Deinonychus	1·60	1·75
2809	15r. Triceratops	1·75	2·00

(b) Square designs, 31×31 mm.

2810	7r. Troodon	1·00	1·00
2811	7r. Brachiosaurus	1·00	1·00
2812	7r. Saltasaurus	1·00	1·00
2813	7r. Oviraptor	1·00	1·00
2814	7r. Parasaurolophus	1·00	1·00
2815	7r. Psittacosaurus	1·00	1·00
2816	7r. Triceratops	1·00	1·00
2817	7r. Pachycephalosaurus	1·00	1·00
2818	7r. Iguanodon	1·00	1·00
2819	7r. Tyrannosaurus rex	1·00	1·00
2820	7r. Corythosaurus	1·00	1·00
2821	7r. Stegosaurus	1·00	1·00
2822	7r. Euophlocephalus	1·00	1·00
2823	7r. Compsognathus	1·00	1·00
2824	7r. Herrerasaurus	1·00	1·00
2825	7r. Styracosaurus	1·00	1·00
2826	7r. Baryonyx	1·00	1·00
2827	7r. Lesothosaurus	1·00	1·00
MS2828	Two sheets. (a) 99×79 mm. 25r. Tyrannosaurus rex (42×28 mm). (b) 73×104 mm. 25r. Archaeopteryx (31×31 mm) Set of 2 sheets	17·00	17·00

Nos. 2801/6, 2810/15, 2816/21 and 2822/7 respectively were printed together, se-tenant, with the backgrounds of Nos. 2801/6 and 2810/15 forming composite designs.

1997. World Cup Football Championship, France. As T **246** of Lesotho.

2829	1r. black	30	15
2830	2r. black	45	25
2831	3r. multicoloured	55	35
2832/39	3r. × 8 (black; black; multicoloured; multicoloured; black; multicoloured; black; multicoloured)	3·75	4·00
2840/47	3r. × 8 (multicoloured; multicoloured; black; black; black; multicoloured; multicoloured; black)	3·75	4·00
2848/55	3r. × 8 (multicoloured; multicoloured; multicoloured; black; black; multicoloured; multicoloured; multicoloured)	3·75	4·00
2856	7r. black	1·10	1·10
2857	8r. black	1·40	1·40
2858	10r. multicoloured	1·50	1·60
MS2859	Three sheets. (a) 103×128 mm. 25r. multicoloured. (b) 103×128 mm. 25r. multicoloured. (c) 128×103 mm. 25r. multicoloured Set of 3 sheets	12·00	13·00

DESIGNS—HORIZ: No. 2829, Brazilian team, 1994; 2830, German player, 1954; 2831, Maradona holding World Cup, 1986; 2832, Brazilian team, 1958; 2833, Luis Bellini, Brazil, 1958; 2834, Brazilian team, 1962; 2835, Carlos Alberto, Brazil, 1970; 2836, Mauro, Brazil, 1962; 2837, Brazilian team, 1970; 2838, Dunga, Brazil, 1994; 2839, Brazilian team, 1994; 2840, Paulo Rossi, Italy, 1982; 2841, Zoff and Gentile, Italy, 1982; 2842, Angelo Schavio, Italy; 2843, Italian team, 1934; 2844, Italian team with flag, 1934; 2845, Italian team, 1982; 2846, San Paolo Stadium, Italy; 2847, Italian team, 1938; 2848, English player with ball, 1966; 2849, Wembley Stadium, London; 2850, English player heading ball, 1966; 2851, English players celebrating, 1966; 2852, English and German players chasing ball, 1966; 2853, English player wearing No. 21 shirt, 1966; 2854, English team with Jules Rimet trophy, 1966; 2855, German player wearing No. 5 shirt, 1966; 2856, Argentine player holding trophy, 1978; 2857, English players with Jules Rimet trophy, 1966; 2858, Brazilian player with trophy, 1970; **MS**2859c, Klinsmann, Germany. VERT: No. **MS**2859a, Ronaldo, Brazil; **MS**2892b, Schmeichel, Denmark.

1998. Diana, Princess of Wales Commemoration. As T **249** of Lesotho. Multicoloured (except Nos. 2864, 2870, 2872, 2877 and **MS**2878b).

2860	7r. Laughing	80	85
2861	7r. With Prince William and Prince Harry	80	85
2862	7r. Carrying bouquets	80	85
2863	7r. In white evening dress	80	85
2864	7r. Wearing bow tie (brown and black)	80	85
2865	7r. Wearing black jacket	80	85
2866	7r. With Indian child on lap	80	85
2867	7r. Wearing blue evening dress	80	85
2868	7r. Wearing blue jacket and poppy	80	85
2869	7r. Wearing cream jacket	80	85
2870	7r. Wearing blouse and jacket (brown and black)	80	85
2871	7r. Wearing red jacket	80	85
2872	7r. Wearing hat (blue and black)	80	85
2873	7r. Wearing red evening dress	80	85
2874	7r. With Sir Richard Attenborough	80	85
2875	7r. Wearing jeans and white shirt	80	85
2876	7r. Wearing white jacket	80	85
2877	7r. Carrying bouquet (brown and black)	80	85
MS2878	Three sheets. (a) 100×70 mm. 25r. On ski-lift. (b) 100×70 mm. 25r. Wearing polkadot dress (brown and black). (c) 70×100 mm. 25r. Wearing garland of flowers Set of 3 sheets	9·50	11·00

356 Pres. Nelson Mandela

357 Pres. John F. Kennedy

1998. 80th Birthday of Nelson Mandela (President of South Africa).

2879	**356** 7r. multicoloured	1·00	1·10

1998. Pres. John F. Kennedy Commemoration. Multicoloured, background colours given.

2880	**357** 5r. green	75	80
2881	– 5r. green	75	80
2882	– 5r. brown (inscr at right)	75	80
2883	– 5r. yellow	75	80
2884	– 5r. violet	75	80
2885	– 5r. blue	75	80
2886	– 5r. grey	75	80
2887	– 5r. brown (inscr at left)	75	80
2888	– 5r. blue (value at bottom right)	75	80

DESIGNS: Nos. 2881/8, Various portraits.

358 Yakovlev Yak-18 (from 1947)

1998. Aircraft in Longest Continuous Production. Multicoloured.

2889	5r. Type **358**	85	85
2890	5r. Beechcraft Bonanza (from 1947)	85	85
2891	5r. Piper Cub (1937–82)	85	85
2892	5r. Tupolev Tu-95 (1954–90)	85	85
2893	5r. Lockheed C-130 Hercules (from 1954)	85	85
2894	5r. Piper PA-28 Cherokee (from 1961)	85	85
2895	5r. Mikoyan Gurevich MiG-21 (from 1959)	85	85
2896	5r. Pilatus PC-6 Turbo Porter (from 1960)	85	85
2897	5r. Antonov An-2 (from 1949)	85	85
MS2898	120×90 mm. 25r. Boeing KC-135E (from 1956) (84×28 mm)	3·75	4·00

359 White American Shorthair

1998. Cats. Multicoloured.

2899	5r. Type **359**	90	65
2900	7r. American curl and Maine coon (horiz)	1·00	1·00
2901	7r. Maine coon (horiz)	1·00	1·00
2902	7r. Siberian (horiz)	1·00	1·00
2903	7r. Somali (horiz)	1·00	1·00
2904	7r. European Burmese (horiz)	1·00	1·00
2905	7r. Nebelung (horiz)	1·00	1·00
2906	7r. Bicolour British shorthair (horiz)	1·00	1·00
2907	7r. Manx (horiz)	1·00	1·00
2908	7r. Tabby American shorthair (horiz)	1·00	1·00
2909	7r. Silver tabby Persian (horiz)	1·00	1·00
2910	7r. Oriental white (horiz)	1·00	1·00
2911	7r. Norwegian forest cat (horiz)	1·00	1·00
2912	8r. Sphynx cat	1·10	1·10
2913	10r. Tabby American shorthair	1·25	1·25
2914	12r. Scottish fold	1·40	1·60
MS2915	Two sheets, each 98×68 mm. (a) 30r. Norwegian forest cat. (b) 30r. Snowshoe Set of 2 sheets	8·50	9·00

Nos. 2900/5 and 2906/11 respectively were printed together, se-tenant, forming composite designs.

360 Boeing 737 HS

1998. Aircraft. Multicoloured.

2916	2r. Type **360**	45	30
2917	5r. CL-215 (flying boat)	75	80
2918	5r. Orion	75	80
2919	5r. Yakolev Yak-54	75	80
2920	5r. Cessna sea plane	75	80
2921	5r. CL-215 (amphibian)	75	80
2922	5r. CL-215 SAR (amphibian)	75	80
2923	5r. Twin Otter	75	80
2924	5r. Rockwell Quail	75	80
2925	5r. F.S.W. fighter	75	80
2926	5r. V-Jet II	75	80
2927	5r. Pilatus PC-12	75	80
2928	5r. Citation Exel	75	80
2929	5r. Stutz Bearcat	75	80
2930	5r. Cessna T-37 (B)	75	80
2931	5r. Peregrine Business Jet	75	80
2932	5r. Beech 58 Baron	75	80
2933	7r. Boeing 727	1·00	1·00

2934 8r. Boeing 747-400 . . . . 1·10 1·10
2935 10r. Boeing 737 . . . . . . 1·25 1·25
MS2936 Two sheets, each 98 × 68 mm. (a) 25r. Beechcraft Model 18. (b) 25r. Falcon Jet Set of 2 sheets . . . . 8·50 9·00

361 Captain Edward Smith's Cap

1998. "Titanic" Commemoration. Multicoloured.
2937 7r. Type **361** . . . . 1·10 1·10
2938 7r. Deck chair . . . . . . 1·10 1·10
2939 7r. Fifth Officer Harold Lowe's coat button . . . 1·10 1·10
2940 7r. Lifeboat . . . . 1·10 1·10
2941 7r. "Titanic's" wheel . . . . 1·10 1·10
2942 7r. Passenger's lifejacket . . 1·10 1·10
MS2943 110 × 85 mm. 25r. "Titanic" from newspaper picture . . . . 4·25 4·50

362 Guava Tree

1998. 20th Anniv of International Fund of Agriculture. Multicoloured.
2944 1r. Type **362** 20 15
2945 5r. Selection of fruit 75 75
2946 7r. Fishing boat 95 95
2947 8r. Papaya tree . . . . . . 1·00 1·10
2948 10r. Vegetable produce . . . 1·25 1·40

363 Thread-finned Butterflyfish

1998. Fish. Multicoloured.
2949 50l. Type **363** 15 15
2950 50l. Queen angelfish 15 15
2951 1r. Oriental sweetlips . . . 25 15
2952 3r. Mandarin fish 45 50
2953 3r. Copper-banded butterflyfish 45 50
2954 3r. Harlequin tuskfish . . . 45 50
2955 3r. Yellow-tailed demoiselle 45 50
2956 3r. Wimplefish 45 50
2957 3r. Red emperor snapper . . 45 50
2958 3r. Clown triggerfish 45 50
2959 3r. Common clown 45 50
2960 3r. Palette surgeonfish ("Regal Tang") 45 50
2961 5r. Emperor angelfish . . . 75 80
2962 5r. Common squirrelfish ("Diadem Squirrelfish") 75 80
2963 5r. Lemon-peel angelfish . . 75 80
2964 5r. Powder-blue surgeonfish 75 80
2965 5r. Moorish idol 75 80
2966 5r. Bicolor angelfish ("Bicolor Cherub") . . . 75 80
2967 5r. Dubouiay's angelfish ("Scribbled Angelfish") 75 80
2968 5r. Two-banded anemonefish 75 80
2969 5r. Yellow tang 75 80
2970 7r. Red-tailed surgeonfish ("Achilles Tang") 90 95
2971 7r. Bandit angelfish 90 95
2972 8r. Hooded butterflyfish ("Red-headed Butterflyfish") . . . . . 1·00 1·10
2973 50r. Blue-striped butterflyfish . . . . . 5·50 6·50
MS2974 Two sheets, each 110 × 85 mm. (a) 25r. Long-nosed butterflyfish. (b) 25r. Porkfish Set of 2 sheets . . . . 7·00 7·50

364 Baden-Powell inspecting Scouts, Amesbury, 1909

1998. 19th World Scout Jamboree, Chile. Multicoloured.
2975 12r. Type **364** . . . . . . 1·50 1·60
2976 12r. Sir Robert and Lady Baden-Powell with children, 1927 . . . . . 1·50 1·60
2977 12r. Sir Robert Baden-Powell awarding merit badges, Chicago, 1926 . . 1·50 1·60

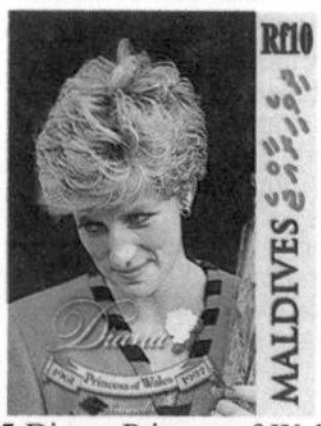

365 Diana, Princess of Wales

1998. 1st Death Anniv of Diana, Princess of Wales.
2978 **365** 10r. multicoloured . . . 1·25 1·50

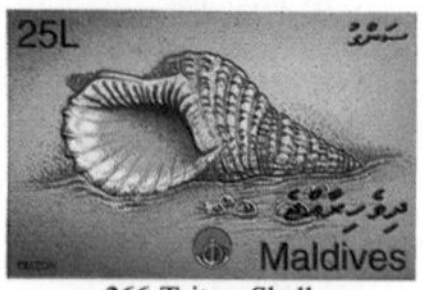

366 Triton Shell

1999. International Year of the Ocean. Marine Life. Multicoloured.
2979 25l. Type **366** 15 15
2980 50l. Napoleon wrasse . . . 15 15
2981 1r. Whale shark 25 15
2982 3r. Grey reef shark 45 40
2983 5r. Harp seal 75 80
2984 5r. Killer whale 75 80
2985 5r. Sea otter 75 80
2986 5r. Beluga 75 80
2987 5r. Narwhal 75 80
2988 5r. Walrus 75 80
2989 5r. Sea lion 75 80
2990 5r. Humpback salmon . . . 75 80
2991 5r. Emperor penguin . . . 75 80
2992 7r. Blue whale 95 95
2993 7r. Skipjack tuna 95 95
2994 8r. Ocean sunfish . . . . . 1·10 1·10
2995 8r. Opalescent squid . . . . 1·10 1·10
2996 8r. Electric ray . . . . . . 1·10 1·10
2997 8r. Corded neptune . . . . 1·10 1·10
MS2998 Three sheets, each 110 × 85 mm. (a) 25r. Horseshoe crab. (b) 25r. Blue whale. (c) 25r. Triton shell Set of 3 sheets . . 9·50 10·00
Nos. 2983/91 were printed together, se-tenant, with the backgrounds forming a composite design.

367 Broderip's Cowrie

1999. Marine Life. Multicoloured.
2999 30l. Type **367** 15 15
3000 1r. White tern ("Fairy Tern") 20 15
3001 3r. Green-backed heron ("Darker Maldivian Green Heron") 45 40
3002 5r. Manta ray 75 80
3003 5r. Green turtle 75 80
3004 5r. Spotted dolphins 75 80
3005 5r. Moorish idols 75 80
3006 5r. Threadfin anthias . . . 75 80
3007 5r. Goldbar wrasse 75 80
3008 5r. Palette surgeonfish . . . 75 80
3009 5r. Three-spotted angelfish 75 80
3010 5r. Oriental sweetlips . . . 75 80
3011 5r. Brown booby 75 80
3012 5r. Red-tailed tropic bird . . 75 80
3013 5r. Sooty tern 75 80
3014 5r. Striped dolphin 75 80
3015 5r. Spinner dolphin 75 80
3016 5r. Crab plover 75 80
3017 5r. Hawksbill turtle 75 80
3018 5r. Indo-Pacific sergeant . . 75 80
3019 5r. Yellow-finned tuna . . . 75 80
3020 7r. Blackflag sandperch . . 95 95
3021 8r. Coral hind . . . . . . 1·10 1·10
3022 10r. Olive Ridley turtle . . . 1·25 1·25
MS3023 Two sheets, each 110 × 85 mm. (a) 25r. Cinnamon bittern. (b) 25r. Blue-faced angelfish Set of 2 sheets . . . 7·50 8·00
Nos. 3002/10 and 3011/19 were each printed together, se-tenant, with the backgrounds forming composite designs.

368 Mickey Mouse

1999. 70th Anniv of Mickey Mouse (Disney cartoon character). Multicoloured.
3024/9 5r. × 6 (Mickey Mouse: Type **368**; laughing; looking tired; frowning; smiling; winking) . . .
3030/5 5r. × 6 (Minnie Mouse: facing left and smiling; with eyes closed; with hand on head; looking surprised; smiling; looking cross) . . . .
3036/41 7r. × 6 (Donald Duck: facing left and smiling; laughing; looking tired; looking cross; smiling; winking) . . . .
3042/7 7r. × 6 (Daisy Duck: with half closed eyes; laughing; looking shocked; looking cross; facing forwards; with head on one side) . . .
3048/53 7r. × 6 (Goofy: facing right and smiling; with eyes closed; with half closed eyes; looking shocked; looking puzzled; looking thoughtful) . . . . . .
3054/9 7r. × 6 (Pluto: looking shocked; with eyes closed; smiling; scowling; with tongue out (orange background); with tongue out (green background) . . . . .
3024/59 Set of 30 . . . . 32·00 32·00
MS3060 Six sheets, each 127 × 102 mm. (a) 25r. Minnie Mouse wearing necklace. (b) 25r. Mickey with hand on head. (c) 25r. Mickey wearing baseball hat. (d) 25r. Mickey facing right (horiz). (e) 25r. Minnie looking left (includes label showing Mickey with bouquet). (f) 25r. Minnie drinking through straw Set of 6 sheets . . . . 23·00 23·00

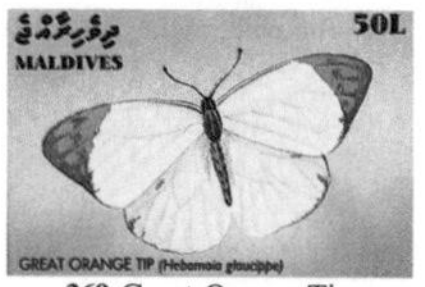

369 Great Orange Tip

1999. Butterflies. Multicoloured.
3061 50l. Type **369** 15 15
3062 1r. Large green aporandria 25 15
3063 2r. Common mormon . . . 40 30
3064 3r. African migrant 55 40
3065 5r. Common pierrot 85 60
3066 7r. Crimson tip (vert) . . . 95 1·00
3067 7r. Tawny rajah (vert) . . . 95 1·00
3068 7r. Leafwing butterfly (vert) 95 1·00
3069 7r. Great egg-fly (vert) . . . 95 1·00
3070 7r. Blue admiral (vert) . . . 95 1·00
3071 7r. African migrant (vert) 95 1·00
3072 7r. Common red flash (vert) 95 1·00
3073 7r. Burmese lascar (vert) . . 95 1·00
3074 7r. Common perriot (vert) 95 1·00
3075 7r. Baron (vert) . . . . . . 95 1·00
3076 7r. Leaf blue (vert) . . . . 95 1·00
3077 7r. Great orange tip (vert) 95 1·00
3078 10r. Giant red-eye . . . . . 1·25 1·40
MS3079 Two sheets, each 70 × 100 mm. (a) 25r. Crimson tip. (b) 25r. Large oak blue Set of 2 sheets . . . . 7·50 8·00
Nos. 3066/71 and 3072/7 were each printed together, se-tenant, with the backgrounds forming composite designs.

370 Scelidosaurus

1999. Prehistoric Animals. Multicoloured.
3080 1r. Type **370** 25 15
3081 3r. Yansudaurus 45 40
3082 5r. Ornitholestes 85 60
3083 7r. Dimorphodon (vert) . . 95 1·00
3084 7r. Rhamphorhynchus (vert) 95 1·00
3085 7r. Allosaurus (vert) . . . . 95 1·00
3086 7r. Leaellynasaura (vert) . . 95 1·00
3087 7r. Troodon (vert) . . . . . 95 1·00
3088 7r. Syntarsus (vert) . . . . 95 1·00
3089 7r. Anchisaurus (vert) . . . 95 1·00
3090 7r. Pterenodon (vert) . . . 95 1·00
3091 7r. Barosaurus (vert) . . . . 95 1·00
3092 7r. Iguanodon (vert) . . . . 95 1·00
3093 7r. Archaeopteryx (vert) . . 95 1·00
3094 7r. Ceratosaurus (vert) . . . 95 1·00
3095 7r. Stegosaurus . . . . . . 95 1·00
3096 7r. Corythosaurus . . . . . 95 1·00
3097 7r. Cetiosaurus . . . . . . 95 1·00
3098 7r. Avimimus . . . . 95 1·00
3099 7r. Styracosaurus . . . . . 95 1·00
3100 7r. Massospondylus . . . . 95 1·00
3101 8r. Astrodon . . . . 1·10 1·25
MS3102 Two sheets, each 116 × 81 mm. (a) 25r. Megalosaurus (vert). (b) 25r. Brachiosaurus (vert) Set of 2 sheets . . . . 7·50 8·00

Nos. 3083/8, 3089/94 and 3095/100 were each printed together, se-tenant, forming composite designs.

371 Express Locomotive, Egypt, 1856

1999. Trains of the World. Multicoloured.
3103 50l. Type **371** 20 15
3104 1r. Channel Tunnel Le Shuttle, France, 1994 . . 25 15
3105 2r. Gowan and Marx locomotive, U.S.A., 1839 . . 35 25
3106 3r. TGV train, France, 1981 45 35
3107 5r. "Ae 6/6" electric locomotive, Switzerland, 1954 85 60
3108 7r. Stephenson's long-boilered locomotive, Great Britain, 1846 (red livery) 95 1·00
3109 7r. "Cornwall", Great Britain, 1847 . . . . . . 95 1·00
3110 7r. First locomotive, Germany, 1848 . . . . . 95 1·00
3111 7r. Great Western locomotive, Great Britain, 1846 . . . . 95 1·00
3112 7r. Standard Stephenson locomotive, France, 1837 95 1·00
3113 7r. "Meteor", Great Britain, 1843 . . . . 95 1·00
3114 7r. Class 4T diesel-electric locomotive, Great Britain, 1940–65 . . . . 95 1·00
3115 7r. Mainline diesel-electric locomotive No. 20101, Malaya, 1940–65 . . . . 95 1·00
3116 7r. Class 7000 high-speed electric locomotive, France, 1949 . . . . . . 95 1·00
3117 7r. Diesel hydraulic express locomotive, Thailand, 1940–65 . . . . 95 1·00
3118 7r. Diesel hydraulic locomotive, Burma, 1940–65 . . . . 95 1·00
3119 7r. "Hikari" super express train, Japan, 1940–65 . . 95 1·00
3120 8r. Stephenson's long-boilered locomotive, Great Britain, 1846 (orange and green livery) . . . . . . 1·10 1·10
3121 10r. "Philadelphia", Austria, 1838 . . . . 1·25 1·25
3122 15r. S.E. and C.R. Class E steam locomotive, Great Britain, 1940 . . . . . . 1·60 1·75
MS3123 Two sheets, each 110 × 85 mm. (a) 25r. Passenger locomotive, France, 1846. (b) 25r. Southern Railway Class "King Arthur", steam locomotive, Great Britain, 1940 Set of 2 sheets . . 7·50 8·00

1999. "Queen Elizabeth the Queen Mother's Century". As T **267** of Lesotho.
3124 7r. black and gold . . . . . 1·25 1·25
3125 7r. black and gold . . . . . 1·25 1·25
3126 7r. multicoloured . . . . . 1·25 1·25
3127 7r. multicoloured . . . . . 1·25 1·25
MS3128 153 × 157 mm. 25r. multicoloured . . . . 5·00 5·00
DESIGNS: No. 3124, King George VI and Queen Elizabeth, 1936; 3125, Queen Elizabeth, 1941; 3126, Queen Elizabeth in evening dress, 1960; 3127, Queen Mother at Ascot, 1981. 37 × 50 mm: No. **MS**3128, Queen Mother in Garter robes.

1999. "iBRA '99" International Stamp Exhibition, Nuremberg. As T **262** of Lesotho. Multicoloured.
3129 12r. "Adler" (first German railway locomotive), 1833 2·00 2·25
3130 15r. "Drache" (Henshell and Sohn's first locomotive), 1848 . . . . 2·25 2·50
The captions on Nos. 3129/30 are transposed.

1999. 150th Death Anniv of Katsushika Hokusai (Japanese artist). As T **263** of Lesotho. Multicoloured (except No. 3133).
3131 7r. "Haunted House" . . . 1·00 1·10
3132 7r. "Juniso Shrine at Yotsuya" . . . . 1·00 1·10
3133 7r. Drawing of bird (black, green and gold) . . . . 1·00 1·10
3134 7r. Drawing of two women 1·00 1·10
3135 7r. "Lover in the Snow" . . 1·00 1·10
3136 7r. "Mountain Tea House" 1·00 1·10
3137 7r. "A Coastal View" . . . 1·00 1·10
3138 7r. "Bath House by a Lake" 1·00 1·10
3139 7r. Drawing of a horse . . . 1·00 1·10
3140 7r. Drawing of two birds on branch . . . . 1·00 1·10
3141 7r. "Evening Cool at Ryogoku" . . . . 1·00 1·10
3142 7r. "Girls boating" . . . . 1·00 1·10
MS3143 Two sheets, each 100 × 70 mm. (a) 25r. "Girls gathering Spring Herbs" (vert). (b) 25r. "Scene in the Yoshiwara" (vert) Set of 2 sheets . . . . . 7·50 8·00

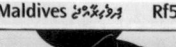

1999. 10th Anniv of United Nations Rights of the Child Convention. As T **264** of Lesotho. Mult.
3144 10r. Baby boy and young mother . . . . 1·40 1·60
3145 10r. Young girl laughing . . 1·40 1·60
3146 10r. Three children . . . . 1·40 1·60
MS3147 110 × 85 mm. 25r. Sir Peter Ustinov (Goodwill ambassador for UNICEF) . . . . 4·00 4·50

372 Standard Stephenson Railway Locomotive "Versailles", 1837

1999. "PhilexFrance '99" International Stamp Exhibition, Paris. Railway Locomotives. Two sheets, each 106 × 81 mm, containing T **372** and similar horiz design. Multicoloured.
MS3148 (a) 25r. Type **372**. (b) 25r. Stephenson long-boilered locomotive, 1841 Set of 2 sheets 7·50 8·00

373 Phobos and Demos (Martian Moons)

2000. Future Colonization of Mars. Multicoloured.
3149 5r. Type **373** 75 80
3150 5r. Improved Hubble Telescope 75 80
3151 5r. Passenger shuttle 75 80
3152 5r. Skyscrapers on Mars . . 75 80
3153 5r. Martian taxi 75 80
3154 5r. Martian landing facilities 75 80
3155 5r. Vegetation in Martian biosphere 75 80
3156 5r. Walking on Mars and biosphere 75 80
3157 5r. Mars rover 75 80
3158 5r. Russian Phobos 25 satellite 75 80
3159 5r. Earth and Moon 75 80
3160 5r. Space shuttle leaving Earth 75 80
3161 5r. Lighthouse on Mars . . 75 80
3162 5r. Mars excursion space liner 75 80
3163 5r. Mars shuttle and skyscrapers 75 80
3164 5r. Viking Lander 75 80
3165 5r. Mars air and water purification plant 75 80
3166 5r. Family picnic on Mars 75 80
MS3167 Two sheets, each 110 × 85 mm. (a) 25r. Astronaut with jet-pack. (b) 25r. Mars Set of 2 sheets . . . . 7·50 8·00
Nos. 3149/57 and 3158/66 were each printed together, se-tenant, with the backgrounds forming composite designs.

374 Coconuts

2000. "Destination 2000 – Maldives" Campaign. Multicoloured.
3168 7r. Type **374** . . . . 1·25 1·25
3169 7r. Shoal of skipjack tuna 1·25 1·25
3170 7r. Seaplane and traditional dhow . . . . 1·25 1·25
3171 7r. "Plumeria alba" . . . . 1·25 1·25
3172 7r. Lionfish . . . . 1·25 1·25
3173 7r. Windsurfers . . . . . . 1·25 1·25

2000. New Millennium. People and Events of Eighteenth Century (1750–1800). As T **268** of Lesotho. Multicoloured.
3174 3r. American bald eagle and American Declaration of Independence, 1776 . . . 50 55
3175 3r. Montgolfier brothers and first manned hot- air balloon flight, 1783 . . . 50 55
3176 3r. Napoleon and mob (French Revolution, 1789) 50 55
3177 3r. James Watt and drawing of steam engine, 1769 . . 50 55
3178 3r. Wolfgang Amadeus Mozart (born 1756) . . . 50 55
3179 3r. Front cover of The Dream of the Red Chamber (Chinese novel, published 1791) 50 55
3180 3r. Napoleon and pyramid (conquest of Egypt, 1798) 50 55
3181 3r. Empress Catherine the Great of Russia and St. Petersburg, 1762 . . . 50 55
3182 3r. Joseph Priestley (discovery of oxygen, 1774) 50 55
3183 3r. Benjamin Franklin (publication of work on electricity, 1751) 50 55
3184 3r. Edward Jenner (development of smallpox vaccine, 1796) 50 55
3185 3r. Death of General Wolfe, 1759 . . . . 50 55
3186 3r. "The Swing" (Jean Honore Fragonard), 1766 50 55
3187 3r. Ludwig von Beethoven (born 1770) 50 55
3188 3r. Marriage of Louis XVI of France and Marie Antoinette, 1770 . . . . 50 55
3189 3r. Captain James Cook (exploration of Australia, 1770) (59 × 39 mm) . . . 50 55
3190 3r. Luigi Galvani and frog (experiments into the effect of electricity on nerves and muscles, 1780) 50 55
The main design on No. 3184 may depict Sir William Jenner who undertook research into typhus.
On No. 3185 the uniforms are incorrectly shown as blue instead of red.

375 Sun and Moon over Forest

2000. Solar Eclipse Showing varying stages of eclipse as seen from Earth (Nos. 3191/6) or Space (Nos. 3197/202). Mult.
3191 7r. Type **375** . . . . 1·00 1·10
3192 7r. "Second Contact" . . . 1·00 1·10
3193 7r. "Totality" . . . . 1·00 1·10
3194 7r. "Third Contact" . . . . 1·00 1·10
3195 7r. "Fourth Contact" . . . 1·00 1·10
3196 7r. Observatory . . . . . . 1·00 1·10
3197 7r. "First Contact" . . . . 1·00 1·10
3198 7r. "Second Contact" . . . 1·00 1·10
3199 7r. "Totality" . . . . 1·00 1·10
3200 7r. "Third Contact" . . . . 1·00 1·10
3201 7r. "Fourth Contact" . . . 1·00 1·10
3202 7r. Solar and heliospheric observatory . . . . . . 1·00 1·10
Nos. 3191/6 and 3197/202 were each printed together, se-tenant, with the backgrounds forming composite designs.

376 Red Lacewing

2000. Butterflies of the Maldives. Multicoloured.
3203 5r. Type **376** 75 80
3204 5r. Large oak blue 75 80
3205 5r. Yellow coster 75 80
3206 5r. Great orange-tip 75 80
3207 5r. Common pierrot 75 80
3208 5r. Cruiser 75 80
3209 5r. Hedge blue 75 80
3210 5r. Common eggfly 75 80
3211 5r. Plain tiger 75 80
3212 5r. Common wall butterfly 75 80
3213 5r. Koh-i-Noor butterfly . . 75 80
3214 5r. Painted lady ("Indian Red Admiral") 75 80
3215 5r. Tawny rajah 75 80
3216 5r. Blue triangle 75 80
3217 5r. Orange albatross 75 80
3218 5r. Common rose swallowtail 75 80
3219 5r. Jewelled nawab 75 80
3220 5r. Striped blue crow . . . 75 80
MS3221 Two sheets. (a) 85 × 110 mm. 25r. Large tree nymph. (b) 110 × 85 mm. 25r. Blue pansy Set of 2 sheets . . . . . 7·50 8·00
Nos. 3203/11 and 3212/20 were each printed together, se-tenant, with the backgrounds forming composite designs.
No. 3219 is inscribed "JEWELED NAWAB" in error.

377 "Martin Rijckaert"

2000. 400th Birth Anniv of Sir Anthony Van Dyck (Flemish painter). Multicoloured.
3222 5r. Type **377** 75 80
3223 5r. "Frans Snyders" 75 80
3224 5r. "Quentin Simons" . . . 75 80
3225 5r. "Lucas van Uffel", 1632 75 80
3226 5r. "Nicolaes Rockox" . . . 75 80
3227 5r. "Nicholas Lamier" . . . 75 80
3228 5r. "Inigo Jones" 75 80
3229 5r. "Lucas van Uffel", c. 1622–25 . . . . 75 80
3230 5r. Detail of "Margaretha de Vos, Wife of Frans Snyders" 75 80
3231 5r. "Peter Brueghel the Younger" 75 80
3232 5r. "Cornelis van der Geest" 75 80
3233 5r. "Francois Langlois as a Savoyard" 75 80
3234 5r. "Portrait of a Family" 75 80
3235 5r. "Earl and Countess of Denby and Their Daughter" 75 80
3236 5r. "Family Portrait" . . . 75 80
3237 5r. "A Genoese Nobleman with his Children" . . . 75 80
3238 5r. "Thomas Howard, Earl of Arundel, and His Grandson" 75 80
3239 5r. "La dama d'oro" . . . 75 80
MS3240 Six sheets. (a) 102 × 127 mm. 25r. "The Painter Jan de Wael and his Wife Gertrude de Jode". (b) 102 × 127 mm. 25r. "John, Count of Nassau-Siegen, and His Family". (c) 102 × 127 mm. 25r. "The Lomellini Family". (d) 102 × 127 mm. 25r. "Lucas and Cornelis de Wael". (e) 127 × 102 mm. 25r. "Sir Kenelm and Lady Digby with their two Eldest Sons". (f) 127 × 102 mm. 25r. "Sir Philip Herbert, 4th Earl of Pembroke, and His Family" (horiz) Set of 6 sheets . . . . 19·00 21·00
No. 3230 is inscribed "Margaretha de Vos, Wife of Frans Snders" in error.

378 Japanese Railways "Shinkansen", High Speed Electric Train

2000. "The Stamp Show 2000" International Stamp Exhibition, London. Asian Railways. Mult.
3241 5r. Type **378** 85 60
3242 8r. Japanese Railways "Super Azusa", twelve-car train . . . . 1·10 1·10
3243 10r. Tobu Railway "Spacia", ten-car electric train, Japan . . . . . . 1·25 1·40
3244 10r. Shanghai-Nanking Railway passenger tank locomotive, China, 1909 1·25 1·40
3245 10r. Shanghai–Nanking Railway "Imperial Yellow" express mail locomotive, China, 1910 1·25 1·40
3246 10r. Manchurian Railway "Pacific" locomotive, China, 1914 . . . . . . 1·25 1·40
3247 10r. Hankow Line mixed traffic locomotive, China, 1934 . . . . 1·25 1·40
3248 10r. Chinese National Railway freight locomotive, 1949 . . . . 1·25 1·40
3249 10r. Chinese National Railway mixed traffic locomotive, 1949 . . . . 1·25 1·40
3250 10r. East Indian Railway passenger tank locomotive Fawn, 1856 . . . . . . 1·25 1·40
3251 10r. East Indian Railway express locomotive, 1893 1·25 1·40
3252 10r. Bengal–Nagpur Railway Atlantic Compound loco-motive, India, 1909 . . . . 1·25 1·40
3253 10r. Great Peninsular Railway passenger and mail locomotive, India, 1924 . . . . 1·25 1·40
3254 10r. North Western Class XS2 Pacific locomotive, India, 1932 . . . . 1·25 1·40
3255 10r. Indian National Railway Class YP Pacific locomotive, India, 1949–70 . . . . 1·25 1·40
3256 15r. Japanese Railway "Nozomi", high-speed electric train . . . . . . 1·60 1·75
MS3257 Two sheets, each 100 × 70 mm. (a) 25r. Indian National Railways Class WP locomotive (57 × 41 mm). (b) 25r. Chinese National Railway Class JS locomotive (57 × 41 mm) Set of 2 sheets . . . . 7·50 8·00

379 Republic Monument

2000. New Millennium (2nd issue). Multicoloured.
3258 10l. Type **379** 10 20
3259 30l. Bodu Thakurufaanu Memorial Centre 15 15
3260 1r. Modern medical facilities and new hospital 25 15
3261 7r. Male International Airport . . . . 1·10 1·25
3262 7r. Hukuru Miskiiy . . . . 1·10 1·25
3263 10r. Computer room, science lab and new school . . . 1·40 1·60
MS3264 Three sheets, each 106 × 77 mm. (a) 25r. Tourist resort and fish packing factory. (b) 25r. Islamic Centre. (c) 25r. People's Majlis (assembly) Set of 3 sheets . . . . 10·00 11·00

2000. 25th Anniv of "Apollo–Soyuz" Joint Project. As T **271** of Lesotho. Multicoloured.
3265 13r. "Apollo 18" and "Soyuz 19" docking (vert) 1·50 1·60
3266 13r. "Soyuz 19" (vert) . . . 1·50 1·60
3267 13r. "Apollo 18" (vert) . . . 1·50 1·60
MS3268 105 × 76 mm. 25r. "Soyuz 19" . . . . 3·75 4·00

380 George Stephenson and *Locomotion No. 1,* 1825

2000. 175th Anniv of Stockton and Darlington Line (first public railway). Multicoloured.
3269 10r. Type **380** . . . . . . 1·50 1·50
3270 10r. William Hedley's *Puffing Billy* locomotive 1·50 1·50

2000. Centenary of First Zeppelin Flight. As T **276** of Lesotho. Multicoloured.
3271 13r. LZ-127 *Graf Zeppelin*, 1928 . . . . 1·50 1·60
3272 13r. LZ-130 *Graf Zeppelin II*, 1938 . . . . 1·50 1·60
3273 13r. LZ-9 *Ersatz*, 1911 . . . 1·50 1·60
MS3274 115 × 80 mm. 25r. LZ-88 (L-40), 1917 (37 × 50 mm) . . . 3·75 4·00
No. 3272 is inscribed "LZ-127" in error.

2000. Olympic Games, Sydney. As T **277** of Lesotho. Multicoloured.
3275 10r. Suzanne Lenglen, (French tennis player), 1920 . . . . 1·40 1·40
3276 10r. Fencing . . . . 1·40 1·40
3277 10r. Olympic Stadium, Tokyo, 1964, and Japanese flag . . . . . . 1·40 1·40
3278 10r. Ancient Greek long jumping . . . . 1·40 1·40

381 White Tern

2000. Tropical Birds. Multicoloured.
3279 15l. Type **381** 10 20
3280 25l. Brown booby 15 20
3281 30l. White-collared kingfisher (vert) 15 20
3282 1r. Black-winged stilt (vert) 25 15
3283 10r. White-collared kingfisher (different) (vert) 1·25 1·40
3284 10r. Island thrush (vert) . . 1·25 1·40
3285 10r. Red-tailed tropic bird (vert) . . . . 1·25 1·40
3286 10r. Peregrine falcon (vert) 1·25 1·40
3287 10r. Black-crowned night heron ("Night Heron") (vert) . . . . 1·25 1·40
3288 10r. Great egret (vert) . . . 1·25 1·40
3289 10r. Great frigate bird . . . 1·25 1·40
3290 10r. Common noddy . . . 1·25 1·40
3291 10r. Common tern . . . . 1·25 1·40

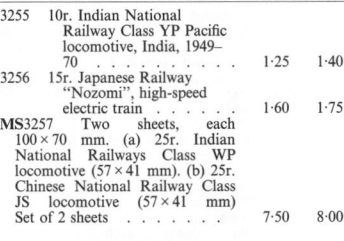

3292 10r. Red-footed booby ("Sula Sula") . . . . . . 1·25 1·40
3293 10r. Sooty tern . . . . . . 1·25 1·40
3294 10r. White-tailed tropic bird (*Phaethon lepturus*) . . . 1·25 1·40
3295 13r. Ringed plover . . . . 1·50 1·60
3296 13r. Ruddy turnstone ("Turnstone") . . . . . 1·50 1·60
3297 13r. Australian stone-curlew 1·50 1·60
3298 13r. Grey plover ("Black-bellied Plover") . . . . . 1·50 1·60
3299 13r. Crab lover . . . . . . 1·50 1·60
3300 13r. Western curlew ("Curlew") . . . . 1·50 1·60
MS3301 Two sheets, each 77 × 103 mm. (a) 25r. Great cormorant (vert). (b) 25r. Cattle egret (vert) Set of 2 sheets . . 7·50 8·00

Nos. 3283/8, 3289/4 and 3295/300 were each printed together, se-tenant, with the backgrounds forming composite designs.

No. 3294 is inscribed "Leturus" in error.

382 *Dendrobium crepidatum*

384 Corn Lily

383 Honda CB 750 Motorcycle, 1969

2000. Orchids. Multicoloured.
3302 50l. Type **382** 15 15
3303 1r. *Eulophia guineensis* . . 25 15
3304 2r.50 *Cymbidium finlaysonianum* 40 30
3305 3r.50 *Paphiopedilum druryi* 50 45
3306 10r. *Angraecum germinyanum* . . . . . . 1·25 1·40
3307 10r. *Phalaenopsis amabilis* 1·25 1·40
3308 10r. *Thrixspermum cantipeda* . . . . 1·25 1·40
3309 10r. *Phaius tankervilleae* . . 1·25 1·40
3310 10r. *Rhynchostylis gigantea* 1·25 1·40
3311 10r. *Papilionanthe teres* . . 1·25 1·40
3312 10r. Aerides odorata . . . . 1·25 1·40
3313 10r. *Dendrobium chrysotoxum* . . . . . . 1·25 1·40
3314 10r. *Dendrobium anosmum* 1·25 1·40
3315 10r. *Calypso bulbosa* . . . 1·25 1·40
3316 10r. *Paphiopedilum fairrieanum* . . . . . . 1·25 1·40
3317 10r. *Cynorkis fastigiata* . . 1·25 1·40
MS3318 Two sheets, each 96 × 72 mm. (a) 25r. *Cymbidium dayanum*. (b) 25r. *Spathoglottis plicata* Set of 2 sheets . . . . 7·50 8·00

Nos. 3306/11 and 3312/17 were each printed together, se-tenant, with the backgrounds forming composite designs.

2000. A Century of Motorcycles. Multicoloured.
3319 7r. Type **383** . . . . 1·00 1·10
3320 7r. Pioneer Harley Davidson, 1913 . . . . . 1·00 1·10
3321 7r. Bohmerland, 1925 . . . 1·00 1·10
3322 7r. American Indian, 1910 1·00 1·10
3323 7r. Triumph Trophy 1200, 1993 . . . . 1·00 1·10
3324 7r. Moto Guzzi 500S, 1928 1·00 1·10
3325 7r. Matchless, 1907 . . . . 1·00 1·10
3326 7r. Manch 4 1200 TTS, 1966 1·00 1·10
3327 7r. Lambretta LD-150, 1957 1·00 1·10
3328 7r. Yamaha XJP 1200, 1990's . . . . 1·00 1·10
3329 7r. Daimler, 1885 . . . . . 1·00 1·10
3330 7r. John Player Norton, 1950s–60's . . . . 1·00 1·10
MS3331 Two sheets, each 62 × 46 mm. (a) 25r. Harley Davidson, 1950. (b) 25r. Electra Glide, 1960 Set of 2 sheets . . 7·50 8·00

2000. Flowers of the Indian Ocean. Multicoloured.
3332 5r. Type **384** 85 90
3333 5r. Clivia 85 90
3334 5r. Red hot poker 85 90
3335 5r. Crown of Thorns . . . 85 90
3336 5r. Cape daisy 85 90
3337 5r. Geranium 85 90
3338 5r. Fringed hibiscus (horiz) 85 90
3339 5r. *Erica vestita* (horiz) . . . 85 90
3340 5r. Bird-of-paradise flower (horiz) 85 90
3341 5r. Peacock orchid (horiz) 85 90
3342 5r. Mesembryanthemums (horiz) 85 90
3343 5r. African violets (horiz) . . 85 90
MS3344 Two sheets, each 112 × 80 mm. (a) 25r. Gladiolus. (b) 25r. Calla lily (horiz) Set of 2 sheets . . . . 7·50 8·00

Nos. 3332/7 and 3338/43 were each printed together, se-tenant, with the backgrounds forming composite designs.

385 Racoon Butterflyfish (*Chaetodon lunula*)

2000. Marine Life of the Indian Ocean. Multicoloured.
3345 5r. Type **385** 75 80
3346 5r. Wrasse (*Stethojulis albovittata*) 75 80
3347 5r. Green turtle 75 80
3348 5r. Jobfish 75 80
3349 5r. Damsel fish 75 80
3350 5r. Meyer's butterflyfish (*Chaetodon meyeri*) . . . 75 80
3351 5r. Wrasse (*Cirrhilabrus exquisitus*) 75 80
3352 5r. Maldive anemonefish . . 75 80
3353 5r. Hind (*Cephalopholis* sp) 75 80
3354 5r. Regal angelfish (*Pygopolites diacanthus*) (red face value) 75 80
3355 5r. Forceps butterflyfish (*Forcipiger flavissimus*) . . 75 80
3356 5r. Goatfish 75 80
3357 5r. Trumpet fish 75 80
3358 5r. Butterfly perch (*Pseudanthias squamipinnis*) 75 80
3359 5r. Two-spined angelfish (*Centropyge bispinosus*) . . 75 80
3360 5r. Sweetlips 75 80
3361 5r. Twin-spotted wrasse (*Coris aygula*) 75 80
3362 5r. Snapper 75 80
3363 5r. Sea bass 75 80
3364 5r. Bennett's butterflyfish (*Chaetodon bennetti*) . . . 75 80
3365 5r. Pelagic snapper 75 80
3366 5r. Cardinalfish 75 80
3367 5r. Six-barred wrasse (*Thalassoma hardwicke*) 75 80
3368 5r. Surgeonfish 75 80
3369 5r. Longnosed filefish . . . 75 80
3370 5r. Hawaiian squirrelfish . . 75 80
3371 5r. Freckled hawkfish . . . 75 80
3372 5r. McCosker's flasher wrasse 75 80
3373 5r. Regal angelfish (*Pygoplites diacanthus*) (white face value) 75 80
3374 5r. Angelfish (*Parseentzopyge venusta*) 75 80
MS3375 Four sheets, each 108 × 80 mm. (a) 25r. Moray eel. (b) 25r. Yellow-bellied hamlet (*Hypoplectrus aberrans*). (c) 25r. Yellow-banded angelfish (*Pomacanthus maculosus*). (d) 25r. Spiny butterflyfish (*Pygoplites diacanthus*) Set of 4 sheets . . 13·00 14·00

Nos. 3345/52, 3353/60, 3361/8 and 3369/74 were each printed together, se-tenant, with the backgrounds forming composite designs.

385a "Nobleman with Golden Chain" (Tintoretto)

2000. "Espana 2000" International Stamp Exhibition, Madrid. Paintings from the Prado Museum. Multicoloured.
3376 7r. Type **385a** 85 90
3377 7r. "Triumphal Arch" (Domenichino) 85 90
3378 7r. "Don Garzia de'Medici" (Bronzino) 85 90
3379 7r. Man from "Micer Marsilio and his Wife" (Lorenzo Lotto) 85 90
3380 7r. "The Infanta Maria Antonieta Fernanda" (Jacopo Amigoni) 85 90
3381 7r. Woman from "Micer Marsilio and his Wife" . . 85 90
3382 7r. "Self-portrait" (Albrecht Durer) 85 90
3383 7r. "Woman and her Daughter" (Adriaen van Cronenburch) 85 90
3384 7r. "Portrait of a Man" (Albrecht Durer) 85 90
3385 7r. Wife and daughters from "The Artist and his Family" (Jacob Jordaens) 85 90
3386 7r. "Artemisia" (Rembrandt) 85 90
3387 7r. Man from "The Artist and his Family" 85 90
3388 7r. "The Painter Andrea Sacchi" (Carlo Maratta) 85 90
3389 7r. Two Turks from "The Turkish Embassy to the Court of Naples" (Giuseppe Bonito) 85 90
3390 7r. "Charles Cecil Roberts" (Pompeo Girolamo Batoni) 85 90
3391 7r. "Francesco Albani" (Andrea Sacchi) 85 90
3392 7r. Three Turks from "The Turkish Embassy to the Court of Naples" 85 90
3393 7r. "Sir William Hamilton" (Pompeo Girolamo Batoni) 85 90
3394 7r. Women from "Achilles amongst the Daughters of Lycomedes" (Rubens and Van Dyck) 85 90
3395 7r. Woman in red dress from "Achilles amongst the Daughters of Lycomedes" 85 90
3396 7r. Men from "Achilles amongst the Daughters of Lycomedes" 85 90
3397 7r. "The Duke of Lerma on Horseback" (Rubens) . . 85 90
3398 7r. "The Death of Seneca" (workshop of Rubens) . . 85 90
3399 7r. "Marie de' Medici" (Rubens) 85 90
3400 7r. "The Marquesa of Villafranca" (Goya) . . . 85 90
3401 7r. "Maria Ruthven" (Van Dyck) 85 90
3402 7r. "Cardinal-Infante Ferdinand" (Van Dyck) 85 90
3403 7r. "Prince Frederick Hendrick of Orange-Nassau" (Van Dyck) . . 85 90
3404 7r. Endymion Porter from "Self-portrait with Endymion Porter" (Van Dyck) 85 90
3405 7r. Van Dyck from "Self-portrait with Endymion Porter" 85 90
3406 7r. "King Philip V of Spain" (Hyacinthe Rigaud) 85 90
3407 7r. "King Louis XIV of France" (Hyacinthe Rigaud) 85 90
3408 7r. "Don Luis, Prince of Asturias" (Michel-Ange Houasse) 85 90
3409 7r. "Duke Carlo Emanuele II of Savoy with his Wife and Son" (Charles Dauphin) 85 90
3410 7r. "Kitchen Maid" (Charles-Francois Hutin) 85 90
3411 7r. "Hurdy-gurdy Player" (Georges de la Tour) . . 85 90
MS3412 Six sheets. (a) 110 × 90 mm. 25r. "The Devotion of Rudolf I" (Peter Paul Rubens and Jan Wildens) (horiz). (b) 110 × 90 mm. 25r. "The Artist and his Family" (Jacob Jordaens) (horiz). (c) 90 × 110 mm. 25r. "The Turkish Embassy to the Court of Naples" (Guiseppe Bonito). (d) 90 × 110 mm. 25r. "Camilla Gonzaga, Countess of San Segundo, with her Three Children" (Parmigianino). (e) 90 × 110 mm. 25r. "Elizabeth of Valois" (Sofonisba Anguisciola). (f) 110 × 90 mm. 25r. "Duke Carlo Emanuele II of Savoy with his Wife and Son" (Charles Dauphin) Set of 6 sheets . . . . 18·00 19·00

386 Steam Locomotive *Hiawatha*, 1935

2000. Milestones in Twentieth-century Transport. Multicoloured.
3413 2r. 50 Steam locomotive *Papyrus*, 1934 (vert) . . . 35 30
3414 3r. Type **386** 45 40
3415 5r. Thrust SSC rocket car, 1997 . . . . 75 80
3416 5r. Curtiss R3C-2 seaplane, 1925 . . . . 75 80
3417 5r. Steam locomotive *Rocket*, 1829 . . . . . . 75 80
3418 5r. BB-9004 electric train, 1955 . . . . 75 80
3419 5r. Steam locomotive *Mallard*, 1938 . . . . . 75 80
3420 5r. T.G.V. electric train, 1980 . . . . 75 80
3421 5r. Lockheed XP-80 aircraft, 1947 . . . . 75 80
3422 5r. Mikoyan Mig 23 Foxbat aircraft, 1965 . . . . . 75 80
3423 5r. Hawker Tempest aircraft, 1943 . . . . . . 75 80
3424 5r. *Bluebird* car, 1964 . . . 75 80
3425 5r. *Blue Flame* car, 1970 . . 75 80
3426 5r. *Thrust 2* car, 1983 . . . 75 80
3427 12r. Supermarine S.B.G. seaplane, 1931 . . . . . 1·50 1·75
3428 13r. MLX01 train, 1998 . . 1·50 1·75
MS3429 Two sheets. (a) 100 × 75 mm. 25r. Lockheed SR-71 Blackbird airplane, 1976 (vert). (b) 75 × 100 mm. 25r. Bell X-1 aircraft, 1947 Set of 2 sheets 7·50 8·00

Nos. 3415/20 and 3421/6 were each printed together, se-tenant, with the backgrounds forming composite designs.

387 Porsche 911S, 1966

2000. "The World of Porsche". Multicoloured.
3430 12r. Type **387** . . . . . . 1·50 1·60
3431 12r. Model 959, 1988 . . . 1·50 1·60
3432 12r. Model 993 Carrera, 1995 . . . . 1·50 1·60
3433 12r. Model 356 SC, 1963 . . 1·50 1·60
3434 12r. Model 911 Turbo, 1975 1·50 1·60
3435 12r. Contemporary model 1·50 1·60
MS3436 110 × 85 mm. 25r. Model Boxter, 2000 (56 × 42 mm) . . 3·75 4·00

388 Limited Edition Trans-Am, 1976

2000. "The World of the Pontiac". Multicolourd.
3437 12r. Type **388** . . . . . . 1·50 1·60
3438 12r. Trans-Am, 1988 . . . . 1·50 1·60
3439 12r. Trans-Am Coupe, 1988 1·50 1·60
3440 12r. Yellow Trans-Am, 1970–72 . . . . 1·50 1·60
3441 12r. 25th Anniv Trans-Am, 1989 . . . . 1·50 1·60
3442 12r. Trans-Am GT convertible, 1994 . . . . 1·50 1·60
MS3443 110 × 85 mm. 25r. Trans-Am model, 1999 (56 × 42 mm) 3·75 4·00

389 Pierce-Arrow

2000. Twentieth-century Classic Cars. Multicoloured.
3444 1r. Type **389** 25 15
3445 2r. Mercedes-Benz 540K (1938) 40 30
3446 7r. Auburn Convertible Sedan (1931) . . . . . . 1·00 1·10
3447 7r. Mercedes SSKL (1931) 1·00 1·10
3448 7r. Packard Roadster (1929) 1·00 1·10
3449 7r. Chevrolet (1940) . . . . 1·00 1·10
3450 7r. Mercer (1915) . . . . . 1·00 1·10
3451 7r. Packard Sedan (1941) . . 1·00 1·10
3452 7r. Chevrolet Roadster (1932) . . . . 1·00 1·10
3453 7r. Cadillac Fleetwood Roadster (1929) . . . . 1·00 1·10
3454 7r. Bentley Speed Six (1928) 1·00 1·10
3455 7r. Cadillac Fleetwood (1930) . . . . 1·00 1·10
3456 7r. Ford Convertible (1936) 1·00 1·10
3457 7r. Hudson Phaeton (1929) 1·00 1·10
3458 8r. Duesenberg J (1934) . . 1·10 1·25
3459 10r. Bugatti Royale (1931) 1·25 1·40
MS3460 Two sheets, each 106 × 81 mm. (a) 25r. Rolls Royce P-1 (1931). (b) 25r. Cord Brougham (1930) Set of 2 sheets 7·50 8·00

No. 3457 is inscribed "HUDSIN" in error.

390 *Cortinarius collinitus*

2001. Fungi. Multicoloured.
3461 30l. Type **390** 15 15
3462 50l. *Russula ochroleuca* . . . 15 15
3463 2r. *Lepiota acutesquamosa* 40 30
3464 3r. *Hebeloma radicosum* . . 45 35
3465 7r. *Tricholoma aurantium* . . 1·00 1·10
3466 7r. *Pholiota spectabilis* . . . 1·00 1·10
3467 7r. *Russula caerulea* . . . . 1·00 1·10
3468 7r. *Amanita phalloides* . . . 1·00 1·10
3469 7r. *Mycena strobilinoides* . . 1·00 1·10
3470 7r. *Boletus satanas* . . . . 1·00 1·10
3471 7r. *Amanita muscaria* . . . 1·00 1·10
3472 7r. *Mycena lilacifolia* . . . 1·00 1·10
3473 7r. *Coprinus comatus* . . . . 1·00 1·10
3474 7r. *Morchella crassipes* . . . 1·00 1·10
3475 7r. *Russula nigricans* . . . . 1·00 1·10

3476 7r. *Lepiota procera* . . . . 1·00 1·10
3477 13r. *Amanita echinocephala* 1·50 1·75
3478 15r. *Collybia iocephala* . . . 1·60 1·75
MS3479 Two sheets, each 112 × 82 mm. (a) 25r. *Tricholoma aurantium*. (b) 25r. *Lepiota procera* Set of 2 sheets . . . . 7·50 8·00

390a German Commanders looking across English Channel

2001. 60th Anniv of Battle of Britain. Multicoloured.
3480 5r. Type **390a** 75 80
3481 5r. Armourers with German bomber 75 80
3482 5r. German Stuka dive-bombers 75 80
3483 5r. Bombing the British coast 75 80
3484 5r. German bomber over Greenwich 75 80
3485 5r. St. Paul's Cathedral surrounded by fire 75 80
3486 5r. British fighter from German bomber 75 80
3487 5r. Spitfire on fire 75 80
3488 5r. Prime Minister Winston Churchill 75 80
3489 5r. British fighter pilots running to planes 75 80
3490 5r. R.A.F. planes taking off 75 80
3491 5r. British fighters in formation 75 80
3492 5r. German bomber crashing 75 80
3493 5r. British fighters attacking 75 80
3494 5r. German bomber in sea 75 80
3495 5r. Remains of German bomber in flames 75 80
MS3496 Two sheets, each 103 × 66 mm. (a) 25r. Hawker Hurricane. (b) 25r. Messerschmitt ME 109 Set of 2 sheets . . . . 7·50 8·00

390b Donkeys from "Donkey Ride on the Beach" (Isaac Lazarus Israels)

2001. Bicentenary of Rijksmuseum, Amsterdam. Dutch Paintings. Multicoloured.
3497 7r. Type **390b** 85 90
3498 7r. "The Paternal Admonition" (Gerard ter Borch) 85 90
3499 7r. "The Sick Woman" (Jan Havicksz Steen) 85 90
3500 7r. Girls from "Donkey Ride on the Beach" . . . 85 90
3501 7r. "Pompejus Occo" (Dick Jacobsz) 85 90
3502 7r. "The Pantry" (Pieter de Hooch) 85 90
3503 7r. Woman in doorway from "The Little Street" (Johannes Vermeer) . . . 85 90
3504 7r. Woman with maid from "The Love Letter" (Johannes Vermeer) . . . 85 90
3505 7r. "Woman in Blue Reading a Letter" (Johannes Vermeer) . . . 85 90
3506 7r. Woman from "The Love Letter" 85 90
3507 7r. "The Milkmaid" (Johannes Vermeer) . . . 85 90
3508 7r. Woman in alley from "The Little Street" . . . 85 90
3509 7r. "Rembrandt's Mother" (Gerard Dou) 85 90
3510 7r. "Girl dressed in Blue" (Johannes Verspronck) . . 85 90
3511 7r. "Old Woman at Prayer" (Nicolaes Maes) 85 90
3512 7r. "Feeding the Hungry" (De Meester van Alkmaar) 85 90
3513 7r. "The Threatened Swan" (Jan Asselyn) 85 90
3514 7r. "The Daydreamer" (Nicolaes Maes) 85 90
3515 7r. "The Holy Kinship" (Geertgen Tot Sint Jans) 85 90
3516 7r. "Sir Thomas Gresham" (Anthonis Mor Vas Dashorst) 85 90
3517 7r. "Self portrait as St. Paul" (Rembrandt) . . 85 90
3518 7r. "Cleopatra's Banquet" (Gerard Lairesse) 85 90
3519 7r. "Flowers in a Glass" (Jan Brueghel the elder) 85 90
3520 7r. "Nicolaes Hasselaer" (Frans Hals) 85 90
MS3521 Four sheets. (a) 118 × 78 mm. 25r. "The Syndics" (Rembrandt). (b) 88 × 118 mm. 25r. "Johannes Wtenbogaert" (Rembrandt). (c) 118 × 88 mm. 25r. "The Night Watch" (Rembrandt). (d) 118 × 88 mm. 25r. "Shipwreck on a Rocky Coast" (Wijnandus Johannes Nuyen) (horiz) Set of 4 sheets 13·00 14·00

391 *Windfall* (schooner), 1962

392 Roses

2001. Maritime Disasters. Multicoloured.
3522 5r. Type **391** 75 80
3523 5r. *Kobenhavn* (barque), 1928 . . . . 75 80
3524 5r. *Pearl* (schooner), 1874 75 80
3525 5r. H.M.S. *Bulwark* (battleship), 1914 . . . . 75 80
3526 5r. *Patriot* (brig), 1812 . . . 75 80
3527 5r. *Lusitania* (liner), 1915 . . 75 80
3528 5r. *Milton Iatrides* (coaster), 1970 . . . . 75 80
3529 5r. *Cyclops* (freighter), 1918 75 80
3530 5r. *Marine Sulphur Queen* (tanker), 1963 . . . . . 75 80
3531 5r. *Rosalie* (full-rigged ship), 1840 . . . . 75 80
3532 5r. *Mary Celeste* (sail merchantman), 1872 . . . 75 80
3533 5r. *Atlanta* (brig), 1880 . . . 75 80
MS3534 Two sheets, each 110 × 85 mm. (a) 25r. *L'Astrolabe* and *La Boussole* (La Perouse, 1789). (b) 25r. *Titanic* (liner), 1912 Set of 2 sheets . . . . 7·50 8·00

Nos. 3522/7 and 3528/33 were printed together, se-tenant, with the backgrounds forming composite designs.

No. 3530 is inscribed "SULPHER" and No. MS3517a "LA BAUSSOLE", both in error.

2001.
3535 **392** 10r. multicoloured . . . 1·25 1·25

393 Interior of Dharumavantha Rasgefaanu Mosque

2001. 848th Anniv of Introduction of Islam to the Maldives. Multicoloured (except Nos. 3537/8).
3536 10r. Type **393** . . . . . . 1·25 1·40
3537 10r. Plaque of Hukurumiskiiy (black and green) . . . . 1·25 1·40
3538 10r. Family studying the Holy Quran (black) . . 1·25 1·40
3539 10r. Class at Institute of Islamic Studies . . . . . 1·25 1·40
3540 10r. Centre for the Holy Quran . . . . 1·25 1·40
3541 10r. Islamic Centre, Male 1·25 1·40
MS3542 116 × 90 mm. 25r. Tomb of Sultan Abdul Barakaat . . . . 3·50 3·75

394 Emperor Angelfish

395 "Young Women in Mist"

2001. Fish. Multicoloured.
3543 10r. Type **394** . . . . . . 1·25 1·40
3544 10r. Indian Ocean lionfish ("*Pterois miles*") . . . . 1·25 1·40

2001. "Philanippon '01" International Stamp Exhibition, Tokyo. Japanese Art. Multicoloured.
3545 7r. Type **395** . . . . 90 1·00
3546 7r. "Woman with Parasol" 90 1·00
3547 7r. "Courtesan" . . . . . . 90 1·00
3548 7r. "Comparison of Beauties" . . . . 90 1·00
3549 7r. "Barber" . . . . 90 1·00
3550 7r. Ichikawa Danjuro V in black robes (20 × 81 mm) 90 1·00
3551 7r. Ichikawa Danjuro V in brown robes with sword (20 × 81 mm) . . . . . . 90 1·00
3552 7r. Ichikawa Danjuro V with arms folded (20 × 81 mm) . . . . . . 90 1·00
3553 7r. Ichikawa Danjuro V seated in brown robes (20 × 81 mm) . . . . . . 90 1·00
3554 7r. Otani Tomoeman I and Bando Mitsugaro I (53 × 81 mm) . . . . . . 90 1·00
MS3555 Two sheets, each 88 × 124 mm. (a) 25r. "Courtesan Hinazuru" (Kitagawa Utamaro). (b) 25r. "Tsutsui Jōmyō and the Priest Ichirai" (Torii Kiyomasu I) Set of 2 sheets . . . . 7·50 8·00

Nos. 3545/9 show paintings of women by Kitagawa Utamaro, and Nos. 3550/4 show famous actors by Katsukawa Shunsho.

395a Victoria as a Young Girl (face value bottom left)

2001. Death Centenary of Queen Victoria. Multicoloured.
3556 10r. Type **395a** . . . . . . 1·25 1·40
3557 10r. Victoria in old age . . 1·25 1·40
3558 10r. Victoria as a young girl (face value top right) . . 1·25 1·40
3559 10r. Queen Victoria in mourning . . . . 1·25 1·40
MS3560 125 × 87 mm. 25r. Young Queen Victoria in evening dress 3·75 4·00

395b Mao as a teenager (brown background)

2001. 25th Death Anniv of Mao Tse-tung (Chinese leader). Multicoloured.
3561 15r. Type **395b** . . . . . . 1·50 1·75
3562 15r. Mao as leader of Communist Party in 1930s (violet background) . . . 1·50 1·75
3563 15r. Mao in 1940s (grey background) . . . . . . 1·50 1·75
MS3564 139 × 132 mm. 25r. Mao as leader of China in 1960s . . . 3·50 3·75

395c Portrait in Garter robes

395d Alfred Piccaver (opera singer) after Annigoni as Duke of Mantua

2001. 75th Birthday of Queen Elizabeth II. Multicoloured.
3565 7r. Type **395c** . . . . 1·00 1·10
3566 7r. Queen at Coronation . . 1·00 1·10
3567 7r. In evening gown and tiara . . . . 1·00 1·10
3568 7r. In uniform for Trooping the Colour . . . . 1·00 1·10
3569 7r. In Garter robes and hat 1·00 1·10
3570 7r. Queen wearing cloak of kiwi feathers . . . . . . 1·00 1·10
MS3571 112 × 138 mm. 25r. Young Queen Elizabeth . . . . 3·75 4·00

2001. Death Centenary of Giuseppe Verdi (Italian composer). Multicoloured.
3572 10r. Type **395d** . . . . . . 1·40 1·40
3573 10r. Heinrich's costume from Rigoletto (opera) . . 1·40 1·40
3574 10r. Cologne's costume from Rigoletto . . . . 1·40 1·40
3575 10r. Cornell MacNeil (opera singer) as Rigoletto . . . 1·40 1·40
MS3576 79 × 119 mm. 25r. Matteo Manvgerri (opera singer) as Rigoletto . . . . 4·00 4·25

396 Adolfo Perez Esquivel (Peace Prize, 1980)

398 Eusebio and Portuguese Flag

397 Mercedes-Benz W165 Racing Car, 1939

2001. Centenary of Nobel Prizes. Prize Winners. Multicoloured.
3577 7r. Type **396** 85 90
3578 7r. Mikhail Gorbachev (Peace, 1990) 85 90
3579 7r. Betty Williams (Peace, 1976) 85 90
3580 7r. Alfonso Garcia Robles (Peace, 1982) 85 90
3581 7r. Paul d'Estournelles de Constant (Peace, 1909) . . 85 90
3582 7r. Louis Renault (Peace, 1907) 85 90
3583 7r. Ernesto Moneta (Peace, 1907) 85 90
3584 7r. Albert Luthuli (Peace, 1960) 85 90
3585 7r. Henri Dunant (Peace, 1901) 85 90
3586 7r. Albert Gobat (Peace, 1902) 85 90
3587 7r. Sean MacBride (Peace, 1974) 85 90
3588 7r. Elie Ducommun (Peace, 1902) 85 90
3589 7r. Simon Kuznets (Economics, 1971) 85 90
3590 7r. Wassily Leontief (Economics, 1973) 85 90
3591 7r. Lawrence Klein (Economics, 1980) 85 90
3592 7r. Friedrich von Hayek (Economics, 1974) 85 90
3593 7r. Leonid Kantorovich (Economics, 1975) 85 90
MS3594 Three sheets, each 108 × 127 mm. (a) 25r. Trygve Haavelmo (Economics, 1989). (b) 25r. Octavio Paz (Literature, 1990). (c) 25r. Vicente Aleixandre (Literature, 1977) Set of 3 sheets 9·50 10·00

2001. Centenary of Mercedes-Benz Cars. Multicoloured.
3595 2r.50 Type **397** 45 35
3596 5r. 460 Nurburg Sport-roadster, 1928 . . . . . 85 65
3597 7r. 680S racing car, 1927 . . 1·00 1·10
3598 7r. 150, 1934 . . . . 1·00 1·10
3599 7r. 540K Roadster, 1936 . . 1·00 1·10
3600 7r. 770 "Grosser Mercedes", 1932 . . . . 1·00 1·10
3601 7r. 220SE, 1958 . . . . . . 1·00 1·10
3602 7r. 500SL, 1990 . . . . . . 1·00 1·10
3603 7r. 290, 1933 . . . . 1·00 1·10
3604 7r. Model 680S, 1927 . . . 1·00 1·10
3605 7r. 300SL Coupe, 1953 . . . 1·00 1·10
3606 7r. Benz Victoria, 1911 . . . 1·00 1·10
3607 7r. 280SL, 1968 . . . . . . 1·00 1·10
3608 7r. W125 racing car, 1937 1·00 1·10
3609 8r. Boattail Speedster, 1938 1·10 1·25
3610 15r. "Blitzen Benz", 1909 1·60 1·75
MS3611 Two sheets, each 109 × 96 mm. (a) 25r. 370S, 1931. (b) 25r. 300SLR racing car, 1955 Set of 2 sheets . . . . 7·50 8·00

Nos. 3600 and 3606 are inscribed "GROBERMERCEDES" or "BENA", both in error.

2001. World Cup Football Championship, Japan and Korea (2002). Multicoloured.
3612 1r. Type **398** 20 15
3613 3r. Johan Cruyff and Dutch flag 45 35
3614 7r. Footballer and French flag 1·00 90
3615 10r. Footballer and Japanese flag 1·25 1·25
3616 12r. World Cup Stadium, Seoul, Korea (horiz) 1·50 1·60
3617 15r. Poster for first World Cup Championship, Uruguay, 1930 1·75 1·90
MS3618 70 × 100 mm. 25r. Gerd Muller, 1974 World Cup Final (43 × 57 mm) 3·75 4·00

399 *Cymothoe lucasi*

2001. Moths and Butterflies. Multicoloured.
3619 7r. Type **399** 90 95
3620 7r. *Milionia grandis* 90 95
3621 7r. *Ornithoptera croesus* 90 95
3622 7r. *Hyantis hodeva* 90 95
3623 7r. *Ammobiota festiva* 90 95
3624 7r. *Salamis temora* 90 95
3625 7r. *Zygaena occitanica* 90 95
3626 7r. *Campylotes desgodinsi* 90 95
3627 7r. *Bhutanitis thaidina* 90 95
3628 7r. *Helicopsis endymion* 90 95
3629 7r. *Parnassius charitonius* 90 95
3630 7r. *Acaca ecucogiap* 90 95
3631 10r. *Papilio dardanus* 1·25 1·40
3632 10r. *Baomisa hieroglyphica* 1·25 1·40
3633 10r. *Troides prattorum* 1·25 1·40
3634 10r. *Funonia rhadama* 1·25 1·40
MS3635 Two sheets. (a) 83 × 108 mm. 25r. *Hypolera cassotis*. (b) 108 × 83 mm. 25r. *Euphydryas maturna* (vert) 7·50 8·00
Nos. 3621 and 3629 are inscribed "eroesus" or "charltonius", both in error.

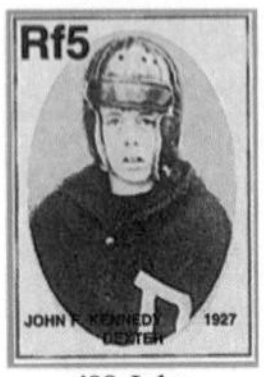

400 John F. Kennedy in American Football Kit, 1927 **401** Princess Diana wearing Pink Jacket

2001. John F. Kennedy (American President) Commemoration. Multicoloured.
3636 5r. Type **400** 75 80
3637 5r. John Kennedy at Harvard, 1935 75 80
3638 5r. As U.S. Navy officer, Solomon Islands, 1943 75 80
3639 5r. On wedding day, 1953 75 80
3640 5r. With brother, Robert, 1956 75 80
3641 5r. Presidential Inauguration, 1961 75 80
3642 5r. With First Secretary Nikita Khrushchev of U.S.S.R., 1961 75 80
3643 5r. With Prime Minister Harold MacMillan of Great Britain 75 80
3644 5r. With Pres. Charles de Gaulle of France, 1961 75 80
3645 5r. With Prime Minister Jawaharlal Nehru of India, 1962 75 80
3646 5r. With Chancellor Konrad Adenauer of West Germany, 1963 75 80
3647 5r. With Martin Luther King (Civil Rights campaigner) 1963 75 80
MS3648 Two sheets, each 82 × 112 mm. (a) 25r. John Kennedy. (b) 25r. With wife, Paris, 1961 7·50 8·00
No. 3642 is inscribed "PRIMIER" in error.

2001. 40th Birth Anniv of Diana, Princess of Wales. Multicoloured.
3649 10r. Type **401** 1·25 1·40
3650 10r. In evening dress with tiara 1·25 1·40
3651 10r. Wearing matching yellow hat and coat 1·25 1·40
3652 10r. In beige dress 1·25 1·40
MS3653 73 × 109 mm. 25r. Princess Diana wearing pearls 3·75 4·00

402 "Running Horse" (Xu Beihong) **404** Havana Brown

403 Swinhoe's Snipe

2001. Chinese New Year ("Year of the Horse"). Paintings by Xu Beihong. Multicoloured.
3654 5r. Type **402** 75 80
3655 5r. "Standing Horse" (from back, with head up) 75 80
3656 5r. "Running Horse" (different) 75 80
3657 5r. "Standing Horse" (with head down) 75 80
3658 5r. "Horse" (with head up, from front) 75 80
MS3659 110 × 70 mm. 15r. "Six Horses running" (57 × 37 mm) 1·75 1·90

2002. Birds. Multicoloured.
3660 1r. Type **403** 25 15
3661 2r. Oriental honey buzzard 40 30
3662 3r. Asian koel 50 35
3663 5r. Red-throated pipet 75 80
3664 5r. Cattle egret 75 80
3665 5r. Barn swallow 75 80
3666 5r. Osprey 75 80
3667 5r. Green-backed heron ("Little Heron") 75 80
3668 5r. Ruddy turnstone 75 80
3669 5r. Sooty tern 75 80
3670 5r. Lesser noddy 75 80
3671 5r. Roseate tern 75 80
3672 5r. Great frigate bird ("Frigate Minor") 75 80
3673 5r. Black-shafted tern ("Saunder's Tern") 75 80
3674 5r. White-bellied storm petrel 75 80
3675 5r. Red-footed booby 75 80
3676 7r. Rose-ringed parakeet 1·00 1·10
3677 7r. Common swift 1·00 1·10
3678 7r. Lesser kestrel 1·00 1·10
3679 7r. Golden oriole 1·00 1·10
3680 7r. Asian paradise flycatcher 1·00 1·10
3681 7r. Indian roller 1·00 1·10
3682 7r. Pallid harrier 1·00 1·10
3683 7r. Grey heron 1·00 1·10
3684 7r. Blue-tailed bee eater 1·00 1·10
3685 7r. White-breasted water hen 1·00 1·10
3686 7r. Cotton teal ("Cotton Pygmy Goose") 1·00 1·10
3687 7r. Maldivian pond heron 1·00 1·10
3688 7r. Short-eared owl 1·00 1·10
3689 10r. White spoonbill ("Eurasian Spoonbill") 1·25 1·40
3690 12r. Pied wheatear 1·50 1·75
3691 15r. Oriental pratincole 1·75 1·90
MS3692 Four sheets, each 114 × 57 mm. (a) 25r. White tern. (b) 25r. Greater flamingo. (c) 25r. Cinnamon bittern. (d) 25r. White-tailed tropicbird 14·00 15·00
Nos. 3664/9, 3670/5, 3676/81 and 3682/7 were each printed together, se-tenant, with the backgrounds forming composite designs.

2002. Cats. Multicoloured.
3693 3r. Type **404** 45 35
3694 5r. American wirehair 75 60
3695 7r. Persian (horiz) 90 1·00
3696 7r. Exotic shorthair (horiz) 90 1·00
3697 7r. Ragdoll (horiz) 90 1·00
3698 7r. Manx (horiz) 90 1·00
3699 7r. Tonkinese (horiz) 90 1·00
3700 7r. Scottish fold (horiz) 90 1·00
3701 7r. British blue 90 1·00
3702 7r. Red mackerel manx 90 1·00
3703 7r. Scottish fold 90 1·00
3704 7r. Somali 90 1·00
3705 7r. Balinese 90 1·00
3706 7r. Exotic shorthair 90 1·00
3707 8r. Norwegian forest cat 1·00 1·10
3708 10r. Seal point siamese 1·25 1·40
MS3709 110 × 85 mm. 25r. Blue mackerel tabby cornish rex 3·75 4·00

405 Queen Elizabeth with Princess Margaret

2002. Golden Jubilee. Multicoloured.
3710 10r. Type **405** 1·40 1·40
3711 10r. Princess Elizabeth wearing white hat and coat 1·40 1·40
3712 10r. Queen Elizabeth in evening dress 1·40 1·40
3713 10r. Queen Elizabeth on visit to Canada 1·40 1·40
MS3714 76 × 108 mm. 25r. Paying homage, at Coronation, 1953 3·75 4·00

406 Sivatherium

2002. Prehistoric Animals. Multicoloured.
3715 7r. Type **406** 1·00 1·10
3716 7r. Flat-headed peccary 1·00 1·10
3717 7r. Shasta ground sloth 1·00 1·10
3718 7r. Harlan's ground sloth 1·00 1·10
3719 7r. European woolly rhinoceros 1·00 1·10
3720 7r. Dwarf pronghorn 1·00 1·10
3721 7r. Macrauchenia 1·00 1·10
3722 7r. Glyptodon 1·00 1·10
3723 7r. Nesodon 1·00 1·10
3724 7r. Imperial tapir and calf 1·00 1·10
3725 7r. Short-faced bear 1·00 1·10
3726 7r. Mastodon 1·00 1·10
MS3727 Two sheets, each 94 × 67 mm. (a) 25r. Sabre-toothed cat. (b) 25r. Mammoth 7·50 8·00
Nos. 3715/20 and 3721/6 were each printed together, se-tenant, with the backgrounds forming composite designs.
Nos. 3722 and 3726 are inscribed "GIYPTODON" and "MAMMOTH", both in error.

2002. International Year of Mountains. As T **219** of Lesotho, but vert. Multicoloured.
3728 15r. Ama Dablam, Nepal 1·75 2·00
3729 15r. Mount Clements, U.S.A. 1·75 2·00
3730 15r. Mount Artesonraju, Peru 1·75 2·00
3731 15r. Mount Cholatse, Nepal 1·75 2·00
MS3732 96 × 65 mm. 25r. Mount Jefferson, U.S.A., and balloon 3·75 4·00

407 Downhill Skiing

2002. Winter Olympic Games, Salt Lake City. Multicoloured.
3733 12r. Type **407** 1·50 1·60
3734 12r. Ski jumping 1·50 1·60
MS3735 82 × 103 mm. Nos. 3733/4 3·50 3·75

2002. 20th World Scout Jamboree, Thailand. As T **295** of Lesotho. Multicoloured.
3736 15r. Buddhist pagoda, Thailand (vert) 1·75 2·00
3737 15r. Thai scout (vert) 1·75 2·00
3738 15r. Scout badges on Thai flag (vert) 1·75 2·00
MS3739 106 × 78 mm. 25r. Mountain-climbing badge and knot diagrams 3·50 3·75

408 Ship, Aircraft and W.C.O. Logo

2002. 50th Anniv of World Customs Organization. Sheet 135 × 155 mm.
MS3740 **408** 50r. multicoloured 6·50 7·00

409 Elvis Presley

2002. 25th Death Anniv of Elvis Presley (American entertainer).
3741 **409** 5r. multicoloured 75 75

410 *Morpho menelaus*

2002. Flora and Fauna. Multicoloured.
3742 7r. Type **410** 1·00 1·00
3743 7r. *Heliconius erato* 1·00 1·00
3744 7r. *Thecla coronata* 1·00 1·00
3745 7r. *Battus philenor* 1·00 1·00
3746 7r. *Ornithoptera priamus* 1·00 1·00
3747 7r. *Danaus gilippus berenice* 1·00 1·00
3748 7r. *Ipomoea tricolor* Morning Glory 1·00 1·00
3749 7r. *Anemone coronaria* Wedding Bell 1·00 1·00
3750 7r. *Narcissus* Barrett Browning 1·00 1·00
3751 7r. *Nigella* Persian Jewel 1·00 1·00
3752 7r. *Osteospermum* Whirligig Pink 1·00 1·00
3753 7r. *Iris* Brown Lasso 1·00 1·00
3754 7r. *Laelia gouldiana* 1·00 1·00
3755 7r. *Cattleya* Louise Georgiana 1·00 1·00
3756 7r. *Laeliocattleya* Christopher Gubler 1·00 1·00
3757 7r. *Miltoniopsis* Bert Field Crimson Glow 1·00 1·00
3758 7r. *Lemboglossum bictoniense* 1·00 1·00
3759 7r. *Derosara* Divine Victor 1·00 1·00
MS3760 Three sheets. (a) 72 × 50 mm. 25r. *Cymothoe lurida* (butterfly). (b) 66 × 45 mm. 25r. Perennial Aster Little Pink Beauty. (c) 50 × 72 mm. 25r. *Angraecum veitchii* (vert) 9·50 10·00
Nos. 3742/7 (butterflies), 3748/53 (flowers) and 3754/9 (orchids) were each printed together, se-tenant, with the backgrounds forming composite designs.
Nos. 3742 and 3748 are inscribed "Menelus" or "Impomoea", both in error.

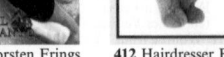

411 Torsten Frings (Germany) **412** Hairdresser Bear

2002. World Cup Football Championship, Japan and Korea. Multicoloured.
3761 7r. Type **411** 90 90
3762 7r. Roberto Carlos (Brazil) 90 90
3763 7r. Torsten Frings (Germany) (different) 90 90
3764 7r. Ronaldo (Brazil), with one finger raised 90 90
3765 7r. Oliver Neuville (Germany) 90 90
3766 7r. Ronaldo (Brazil), heading ball 90 90
3767 7r. Eul Yong Lee (South Korea) and Alpay Ozalan (Turkey) 90 90
3768 7r. Myung Bo Hong (South Korea) and Hakan Sukur (Turkey) 90 90
3769 7r. Chong Gug Song (South Korea) and Emre Belozoglu (Turkey) 90 90
3770 7r. Chong Gug Song (South Korea) and Ergun Penbe (Turkey) 90 90

3771 7r. Ki Hyeon Seol (South Korea) and Ergun Penbe (Turkey) 90 90
3772 7r. Chong Gug Song (South Korea) and Hakan Unsal (Turkey) 90 90
MS3773 Four sheets, each 82 × 82 mm. (a) 15r. Cafu (Brazil) and Oliver Neuville (Germany); 15r. World Cup Trophy. (b) 15r. Dietmar Hamann (Germany); 15r. Cafu (Brazil), holding Trophy. (c) 15r. Hakan Sukur (Turkey); 15r. Sang Chul Yoo (South Korea). (d) 15r. Ilhan Mansiz (Turkey); 15r. Young Pyo Lee (South Korea) 14·00 15·00

2002. Centenary of the Teddy Bear. Multicoloured.
3774 8r. Type **412** . . . . 1·00 1·10
3775 8r. Construction worker bear . . . . 1·00 1·10
3776 8r. Gardener bear . . . . . 1·00 1·10
3777 8r. Chef bear . . . . 1·00 1·10
3778 12r. Nurse bear . . . . . . 1·40 1·50
3779 12r. Doctor bear . . . . . 1·40 1·50
3780 12r. Dentist bear . . . . . 1·40 1·50
3781 12r. Bride ("MOTHER") bear . . . . 1·40 1·50
3782 12r. Brother and sister bears 1·40 1·50
3783 12r. Groom ("FATHER") bear . . . . 1·40 1·50
MS3784 Three sheets, each 110 × 105 mm. (a) 30r. Golfer bear. (b) 30r. Footballer bear. (c) 30r. Skier bear ("SNOW BOARDER") . . . . 11·00 12·00

413 Charles Lindbergh and *Spirit of St. Louis*

414 Princess Diana

2002. 75th Anniv of First Solo Transatlantic Flight. Multicoloured.
3785 12r. Type **413** . . . . . . 1·40 1·60
3786 12r. Lindbergh in flying helmet and *Spirit of St. Louis* . . . . 1·40 1·60
3787 12r. Lindbergh holding propeller . . . . 1·40 1·60
3788 12r. Lindbergh in overalls and *Spirit of St. Louis* . . 1·40 1·60
3789 12r. Donald Hall (designer) 1·40 1·60
3790 12r. Charles Lindbergh (pilot) . . . . 1·40 1·60
3791 12r. Lindbergh under wing of *Spirit of St. Louis* . . . 1·40 1·60
3792 12r. Lindbergh, Mahoney and Hall at Ryan Airlines 1·40 1·60

2002. 5th Death Anniv of Diana, Princess of Wales. Multicoloured.
3793 12r. Type **414** . . . . . . 1·40 1·60
3794 12r. In evening dress and tiara . . . . 1·40 1·60

415 Joseph Kennedy with Sons Joseph Jr. and John, 1919

2002. Presidents John F. Kennedy and Ronald Reagan Commemoration. Multicoloured.
3795 7r. Type **415** 90 95
3796 7r. John F. Kennedy aged 11 . . . . 90 95
3797 7r. Kennedy inspecting Boston waterfront, 1951 90 95
3798 7r. Kennedy in naval ensign uniform, 1941 . . . . . 90 95
3799 7r. With sister Kathleen in London, 1939 . . . . . 90 95
3800 7r. Talking to Eleanor Roosevelt, 1951 . . . . . 90 95
3801 12r. Ronald Reagan facing right . . . . 1·40 1·60
3802 12r. Ronald Reagan (full-face portrait) . . . . . . 1·40 1·60

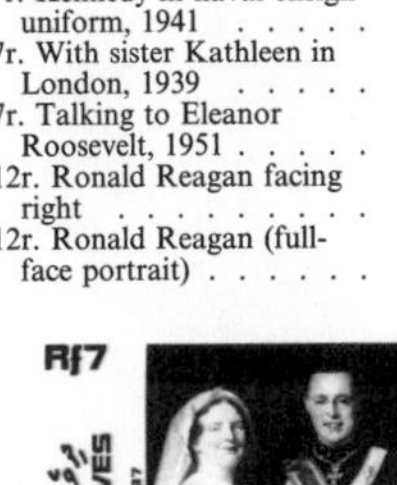

416 Wedding of Princess Juliana and Prince Bernhard, 1937

2002. "Amphilex '02" International Stamp Exhibition, Amsterdam. Dutch Royal Family.
3803 **416** 7r. blue and black . . . 90 95
3804 – 7r. brown and black . . . 90 95
3805 – 7r. red and black 90 95
3806 – 7r. brown and black . . . 90 95
3807 – 7r. violet and black . . . 90 95
3808 – 7r. green and black . . . 90 95
3809 – 7r. multicoloured 90 95
3810 – 7r. brown and black . . 90 95
3811 – 7r. multicoloured 90 95
3812 – 7r. multicoloured 90 95
3813 – 7r. multicoloured 90 95
3814 – 7r. multicoloured 90 95

DESIGNS: No. 3804, Princess Juliana and Prince Bernhard with baby Princess Beatrix, 1938; 3805, Princess Juliana with her daughters in Canada, 1940–45; 3806, Inauguration of Queen Juliana, 1948; 3807, Royal Family inspecting Zeeland floods, 1953; 3808, Queen Juliana and Prince Bernhard; 3809, "Princess Beatrix as a Baby" (Pauline Hille); 3810, "Princess Beatrix in Flying Helmet" (John Klinkenberg); 3811, "Princess Beatrix" (Beatrice Filius); 3812, "Princess Beatrix and Prince Claus" (Will Kellermann); 3813, "Queen Beatrix in Royal Robes" (Graswinkel); 3814, "Queen Beatrix" (Marjolijn Spreeuwenberg).

417 Flame Basslet

2002. Marine Life. Multicoloured.
3815 10l. Type **417** 10 10
3816 15l. Teardrop butterflyfish 10 10
3817 20l. White-tailed damselfish ("Hambug Damselfish") 10 10
3818 25l. Bridled tern (23 × 27 mm) 10 10
3819 50l. Clown surgeonfish ("Blue-lined Surgeonfish") 10 10
3820 1r. Common tern (23 × 27 mm) 15 15
3821 2r. Common noddy (23 × 27 mm) 25 25
3822 2r.50 Yellow-breasted wrasse 30 30
3823 2r.50 Blue shark (23 × 27 mm) 30 30
3824 4r. Harlequin filefish 50 50
3825 5r. Masked unicornfish ("Orangespine Unicornfish") 65 65
3826 10r. Emperor angelfish . . . 1·00 1·00
3827 12r. Catalufa ("Bullseye") 1·25 1·40
3828 20r. Scalloped hammerhead shark (23 × 27 mm) . . . 2·25 2·50

No. 3822 is inscribed "wrass" in error.

418 Atolls from the Air

2002. 30 Years of Maldives' Tourism Promotion. Multicoloured.
3829 12r. Type **418** . . . . . . 1·40 1·60
3830 12r. Island beach . . . . . 1·40 1·60
3831 12r. Surfing . . . . 1·40 1·60
3832 12r. Scuba diving . . . . . 1·40 1·60

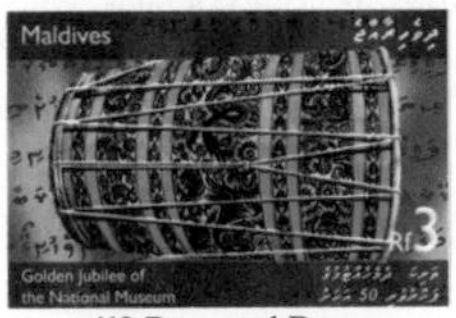

419 Decorated Drum

2003. 50th Anniv of National Museum. Multicoloured.
3835 3r. Type **419** 40 40
3836 3r.50 Carved covered bowl 50 50
3837 6r.50 Ceremonial sunshade 80 85
3838 22r. Ceremonial headdress 2·50 2·75

420 Popeye diving

2003. "Popeye" (cartoon character). Multicoloured. Summer sports.
3839 7r. Type **420** 85 95
3840 7r. Surfing 85 95
3841 7r. Sailboarding 85 95
3842 7r. Baseball 85 95
3843 7r. Hurdling 85 95
3844 7r. Tennis 85 95
MS3845 120 × 90 mm. 25r. Volleyball (horiz) . . . . . . 3·25 3·75

Nos. 3839/45 were printed together, se-tenant, with the backgrounds forming a composite design.

421 Father with Baby

2003. UNICEF. "First Steps" Campaign. Multicoloured.
3846 2r.50 Type **420** 40 35
3847 5r. Mother and baby . . . 75 75
3848 20r. Campaign emblem . . 2·50 2·75

422 *Cypraea caputserpentis* (Cowrie)

423 David Brown

2003. Sea Shells. Multicoloured.
3849 10r. Type **422** . . . . . . 1·25 1·40
3850 10r. *Trachycardium orbita* (Cardita clam) . . . . . 1·25 1·40
3851 10r. *Architectonica perspective* (Sundial shell) 1·25 1·40
3852 10r. *Conus capitaneus* (Corn shell) . . . . 1·25 1·40

2003. Columbia Space Shuttle Commemoration. Sheet 184 × 145 mm, containing T **423** and similar vert designs showing crew members. Multicoloured.
MS3853 7r. Type **423**; 7r. Commander Rick Husband; 7r. Laurel Clark; 7r. Kalpana Chawla; 7r. Michael Anderson; 7r. William McCool; 7r. Ilan Ramon 6·00 6·50

424 Queen wearing Polka Dot Jacket

425 Prince William as Toddler

2003. 50th Anniv of Coronation.
MS3854 147 × 85 mm.15r. Type **424**; 15r. Queen after Coronation wearing Imperial State Crown; 15r. Queen wearing tiara (all black, deep brown and brown) 4·50 4·75
MS3855 68 × 98 mm. 25r. Queen wearing tiara and blue sash (multicoloured) . . . . 3·25 3·50

2003. 21st Birthday of Prince William. Multicoloured.
MS3856 148 × 78 mm. 15r. Type **425**; 15r. As teenager (looking forward); 15r. As teenager (looking right) . . . . 4·50 4·75
MS3857 68 × 98 mm. 25r. As young boy, wearing school cap . . . 3·25 3·50

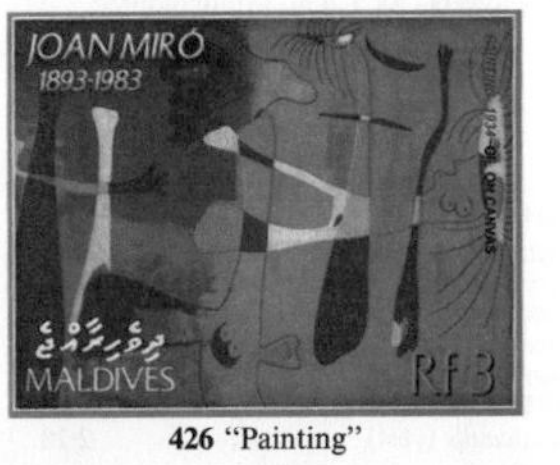

426 "Painting"

2003. 20th Death Anniv of Joan Miro (artist). Multicoloured.
3858 3r. Type **426** 45 35
3859 5r. "Hirondelle Amour" . . 75 60
3860 10r. "Two Women" . . . . 1·25 1·40
3861 15r. "Women listening to Music" . . . . 1·60 1·75
MS3862 176 × 134 mm. 12r. "Woman and Birds"; 12r. "Nocturne"; 12r. "Morning Star"; 12r. "The Escape Ladder" . . 5·00 5·50
MS3863 Two sheets, each 83 × 104 mm. (a) 25r. "Women encircled by the Flight of a Bird". (b) 25r. "Rhythmic Personages". Both imperf Set of 2 sheets . . 5·50 6·00

427 "Jabach Altarpiece" (detail of drummer and piper)

2003. 475th Death Anniv of Albrecht Dürer (artist). Multicoloured.
3864 3r. Type **427** 45 35
3865 5r. "Portrait of a Young Man" 75 60
3866 7r. "Wire-drawing Mill" (horiz) . . . . 1·00 1·00
3867 10r. "Innsbruck from the North" (horiz) . . . . . 1·25 1·40
MS3868 174 × 157 mm. 12r. "Portrait of Jacob Muffel"; 12r. "Portrait of Hieronymus Holzschuher"; 12r. "Portrait of Johannes Kleburger"; 12r. "Self-portrait" . . . . 5·00 5·50
MS3869 145 × 105 mm. 25r. "The Weiden Mill" . . . . 3·00 3·25

428 "The Actor Nakamura Sojuro as Mitsukuni" (detail) (Utagawa Yoshitaki)

429 Maurice Garin (1903)

2003. Japanese Art. Ghosts and Demons. Multicoloured.
3870 2r. Type **428** 35 30
3871 5r. "The Actor Nakamura Sojuro as Mitsukuni" (detail of ghosts) (Utagawa Yoshitaki) . . . 75 60
3872 7r. "The Ghost of Kohada Koheiji" (Shunkoosai Hokuei) . . . . 1·00 1·00
3873 15r. "Ariwara no Narihira as Seigen" (Utagawa Kunisada) . . . . 1·60 1·75
MS3874 149 × 145 mm. 10r. "The Ghost of Shikibunojo Mitsumune" (Utagawa Kunisada); 10r. "Fuwa Bansakui" (Tsukioka Yoshitoshi); 10r. "The Lantern Ghost of Oiwa" (Shunkosai Hokuei); 10r. "The Greedy Hag" (Tsukioka Yoshitoshi) . . . . 4·50 5·00
MS3875 116 × 86 mm. 25r. "The Spirit of Sakura Sogoro haunting Hotta Kozuke" (Utagawa Kuniyoshi) . . . . 3·00 3·25

2003. Centenary of Tour de France Cycle Race. Past winners. Multicoloured.
MS3876 160 × 100 mm. 10r. Type **429**; 10r. Henri Cornet (1904); 10r. Louis Trousselier (1905); 10r. Rene Pottier (1906) 4·50 5·00
MS3877 160 × 100 mm. 10r. Lucien Petit-Breton on cycle (1907); 10r. Close up of Lucien Petit-Breton (1907); 10r. Francois Faber (1909); 10r. Octave Lapize (1910) . . . 4·50 5·00
MS3878 160 × 100 mm. 10r. Eddy Merckx (1974); 10r. Bernard Thevenet (1975); 10r. Lucien van Impe (1976); 10r. Bernard Thevenet (1977) . . . . 4·50 5·00
MS3879 Three sheets, each 100 × 70 mm. (a) 25r. Start of first Tour De France at Le Reveil Matin cafe, Montgeron. (b) 25r. Henri Desgranges (editor of L'Auto). (c) 25r. Bernard Hinault (1979) Set of 3 sheets . . . . 8·50 9·00

430 Santos-Dumont Monoplane No. 20 Demoiselle on Ground, 1909

2003. Centenary of Powered Flight. Multicoloured.
MS3880 176 × 97 mm. 10r. Type **430**; 10r. Santos-Dumont monoplane No. 20 Demoiselle taking off, 1909; 10r. Voisin-Farman No. 1 biplane, 1908; 10r. Glenn Curtiss' *Gold Bug*, 1909 . . . . 4·50 5·00
MS3881 176 × 97 mm. 10r. Santos-Dumont's *Airship No. 1*; 10r. Santos-Dumont's *Airship No. 4*; 10r. Santos Dumont's *Ballon No. 14 and 14 bis* biplane, 1906; 10r. Santos-Dumont's *Airship No. 16* . . . . 4·50 5·00
MS3882 Two sheets, each 105 × 75 mm. (a) 25r. Santos-Dumont's *Ballon No. 6* circling Eiffel Tower, Paris, 1901. (b) 25r. Santos-Dumont's *14 bis* biplane,1906 Set of 2 sheets . . 6·00 7·00

431 "Near Taormina, Scirocco" (1924)

2003. Paul Klee (artist) Commemoration. Multicoloured.
MS3883 162 × 135 mm. 10r. Type **431**; 10r. "Small Town Among the Rocks" (1932);10r. "Still Life with Props" (1924); 10r. "North Room", (1932) . . . . 3·50 3·75
MS3884 70 × 103 mm. 25r. "Dame Demon" (1935) (vert) . . . . 2·20 2·30

432 Man Ice-skating

2003. 25th Death Anniv of Norman Rockwell (artist). Multicoloured.
MS3885 10r. Type **432**; 10r. Man lying on back and boy with dog; 10r. Man and boy going fishing; 10r. Man and boy sweeping leaves 3·50 3·75
MS3886 45 × 81 mm. 25r. Illustration for Hallmark Cards (1957). Imperf . . . . 2·20 2·30

433 "Portrait of Jaime Sabartes" (1901)

2003. 30th Death Anniv of Pablo Picasso (artist). Multicoloured.
MS3887 133 × 167 mm. 10r. Type **433**; 10r. "Portrait of the Artist's Wife (Olga)" (1923); 10r. "Portrait of Olga" (1923); 10r. "Portrait of Jaime Sabartes" (1904) . . . . 3·50 3·75
MS3888 67 × 100 mm. 30r. "The Tragedy" (1903). Imperf . . . 2·75 3·00

434 Ari Atoll

2003. International Year of Freshwater. Multicoloured.
MS3889 147 × 85 mm. 15r. Type **434**; 15r. Running tap; 15r. Desalination plant, Male . . . 4·00 4·25
MS3890 96 × 66 mm. 25r. Community rain water tank . . 2·20 2·30

435 Goldtail Demoiselle

2003. Marine Life. Sheet 147 × 105 mm containing T **435** and similar horiz designs. Multicoloured.
MS3891 4r. Type **435**; 4r. Queen coris; 4r. Eight-banded butterflyfish; 4r. Meyer's butterflyfish; 4r. Exquisite butterflyfish; 4r. Yellowstripe snapper; 4r. Yellowback anthias; 4r. Black-spotted moray; 4r. Clown anemonefish . . . . . 3·25 3·50

The stamps in No. **MS**3891 were printed together, se-tenant, with the backgrounds forming a composite design.

436 Clown Triggerfish

2003. Tropical Fish. Multicoloured.
3892 1r. Type **436** 10 10
3893 7r. Sixspot grouper 60 65
3894 10r. Long-nosed butterflyfish 90 95
3895 15r. Longfin bannerfish . . 1·30 1·40
MS3896 116 × 134 mm. 7r. Bluestreak cleaner wrasse; 7r. Threeband demoiselle; 7r. Palette surgeonfish; 7r. Emperor snapper; 7r. Bicolor angelfish; 7r. Picasso triggerfish . . . . 3·75 4·00
MS3897 72 × 102 mm. 25r. Chevron butterflyfish . . . . 2·20 2·30

2003. Tropical Butterflies. As T **436**. Multicoloured.
3898 3r. Yamfly (vert) 25 30
3899 5r. Striped blue crow (vert) 45 50
3900 8r. Indian red admiral (vert) 70 60
3901 15r. Great eggfly (vert) . . . 1·30 1·40
MS3902 116 × 134 mm. 7r. Blue triangle; 7r. Monarch; 7r. Broad-bordered grass yellow; 7r. Red lacewing; 7r. African migrant; 7r. Plain tiger . . . . 3·75 4·00
MS3903 102 × 72 mm. 25r. Beak butterfly (vert) . . . . . . 2·20 2·30

2003. Birds. As T **436**. Multicoloured.
3904 15l. Great frigate bird . . . 10 10
3905 20l. Ruddy turnstone . . . 10 10
3906 25l. Hoopoe 10 10
3907 1r. Cattle egret 10 10
MS3908 116 × 134 mm. 7r. Red-billed tropic bird; 7r. Red-footed booby; 7r. Common tern; 7r. Caspian tern; 7r. Western ("Common") curlew; 7r. Grey ("Black-bellied") plover . . . 3·75 4·00
MS3909 72 × 102 mm. 25r. Grey heron . . . . 2·20 2·30

2003. Flowers. As T **436**. Multicoloured.
3910 30l. *Coelogyne asperata* (vert) 10 10
3911 75l. *Calanthe rosea* (vert) . . 10 10
3912 2r. *Eria javanica* (vert) . . . 20 25
3913 10r. *Spathoglottis affinis* (vert) 90 95
MS3914 116 × 134 mm. 7r. *Strelitzia reginae*; 7r. *Anthurium andreanum*; 7r. *Alpinia Purpurata*; 7r. *Dendrobium phalaenopsis*; 7r. *Vanda tricolo*; 7r. *Hibiscus rosa-Sinensis* . . . . 3·75 4·00
MS3915 72 × 102 mm. 25r. *Ipomoea crassicaulis* (vert) . . . . . . 2·20 2·30

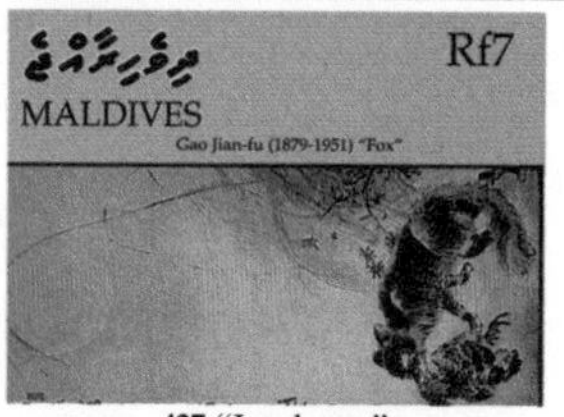

437 "Landscape"

2004. Hong Kong 2004 International Stamp Exhibition. 125th Birth Anniv of Gao Jian-fu (artist). T **437** and similar vert designs. Multicoloured.
MS3916 170 × 149 mm. 7r. Type **437**; 7r. "Moon Night"; 7r. "Fox"; 7r. Chinese ink and colour on paper (spider and web); 7r. Chinese ink and colour on paper (girl); 7r. Chinese ink and colour on paper (man) . . . . 3·75 4·00
MS3917 108 × 129 mm. 12r. "Eagle"; 12r. "Sunset" . . . . 2·20 2·30

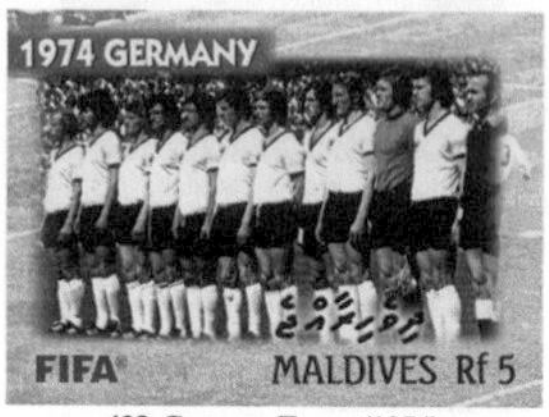

438 German Team (1974)

2004. Centenary of FIFA (Federation Internationale de Football Association). T **438** and similar horiz designs showing winning football teams. Multicoloured.
3918 5r. Type **438** 45 50
3919 5r. Argentina (1978) 45 50
3920 5r. Italy (1982) 45 50
3921 5r. Argentina (1986) 45 50
3922 5r. Germany (1990) 45 50
3923 5r. Brazil (1994) 45 50
3924 5r. France (1998) 45 50
3925 5r. Brazil (2002) 45 50

439 F-BVFD over Rio de Janeiro

2004. Last Flight of Concorde (2003). Multicoloured.
MS3926 147 × 150 mm. 1r. Type **439**; 1r. F-BVFC over New York; 1r. F-BTSD over Honolulu; 1r. F-BTDS over Lisbon; 1r. F-BVFA over Washington; 1r. F-BVFD over Dakar; 1r. G-BOAC over Singapore; 1r. G-BOAA over Sydney; 1r. G-BOAD over Hong Kong; 1r. G-BOAD over Amsterdam; 1r. G-BOAE over Tokyo; 1r. G-BOAF over Madrid 1·10 1·20
MS3927 Three sheets, each 70 × 100 mm. (a) 25r. G-BOAC against Union Jack. (b) 25r. G-BOAG over London. (c) 25r. G-BOAG against museum exhibits Set of 3 sheets . . . . 6·75 7·00

440 "Self Portrait" (Anthony van Dyck)

2004. 300th Anniv of St. Petersburg. "Treasures of the Hermitage". Multicoloured.
3928 1r. Type **440** 10 10
3929 3r. "Self Portrait" (Michael Sweets) 25 30
3930 7r. "Anna Dalkeith, Countess of Morton" (Anthony van Dyck) . . . 60 65
3931 12r. "Lady Anna Kirk" (Anthony van Dyck) . . . 1·10 1·20

MS3932 116 × 180 mm. 10r. "Portrait of Prince Alexander Kurakin" (Louis-Elisabeth Vigee-Lebrun); 10r. "Portrait of a Lady in Waiting to the Infanta Isabella" (Peter Paul Rubens); 10r. "Portrait of a Lady in Blue" (Thomas Gainsborough); 10r. "The Actor Pierre Jeliolte in the Role of Apollo" (Louis Tocque) . . . 3·50 3·75
MS3933 Two sheets, each 102 × 72 mm. (a) 25r. "A Scene from Corneille's Tragedy Le Comte d'Essex" (Nicolas Lancret) (horiz). (b) 25r. "The Stolen Kiss" (Jean-Honore Fragonard) (horiz) Set of 2 sheets . . . . 4·50 4·75

441 Major General Clarence Huebner

2004. 60th Anniv of D-Day Landings. Ten sheets containing T **441** and similar multicoloured designs.
MS3934 Five sheets. (a) 137 × 117 mm. 6r. Type **441**; 6r. Brig. General Anthony McAuliffe; 6r. Major General Leonard Gerow; 6r. General Adolf Galland; 6r. Brig. General W. M. Hoge; 6r. Major General Sir Percy Hobart. (b) 127 × 127 mm. 6r. Rear Admiral Kirk; 6r. General Field Marshal Erwin Rommel; 6r. General George Marshal; 6r. General Jan Smuts; 6r. General Lieutenant Gunther Blumentritt; 6r. Major General J. Lawton Collins. (c) 138 × 137 mm. 6r. Winston Churchill; 6r. Admiral Sir Bertram Ramsey; 6r. General Lieutenant Dietrich Kraiss; 6r. Major General Richard Gale; 6r. General George Patton; 6r. Major General Maxwell Taylor. (d) 138 × 137 mm. 6r. General Dwight Eisenhower; 6r. Field Marshal Guenther von Kluge; 6r. Air Marshal Sir Trafford Leigh-Mallory; 6r. Field Marshal Walter Model; 6r. Field Marshal Gerd von Rundstedt; 6r. Sir Arthur Tedder. (e) 137 × 127 mm. 6r. Lieutenant General Omar Bradley (horiz); 6r. Rear Admiral Hall (horiz); 6r. Major General Huebner (horiz); 6r. Grossadmiral Karl Donitz (horiz); 6r. Rear Admiral Wilkes (horiz); 6r. Capt. Chauncey Camp (horiz) Set of 10 sheets . . . . 5·25 5·50
MS3935 Five sheets. (a) 68 × 98 mm. 30r. Rear Admiral Donald Moon. (b) 68 × 98 mm. 30r. Lieutenant General Sir Frederick Morgan. (c) 68 × 98 mm. 30r. General Henry Arnold. (d) 69 × 99 mm. 30r. General Sir Bernard Montgomery. (e) 98 × 68 mm. 30r. Rear Admiral Carlton Bryant (horiz) Set of 5 sheets . . . . 13·00 14·00

MALI Pt. 6; Pt. 13

Federation of French Sudan and Senegal, formed in 1959 as an autonomous republic within the French Community. In August 1960 the Federation was split up and the French Sudan part became the independent Mali Republic.

100 centimes = 1 franc.

A. FEDERATION.

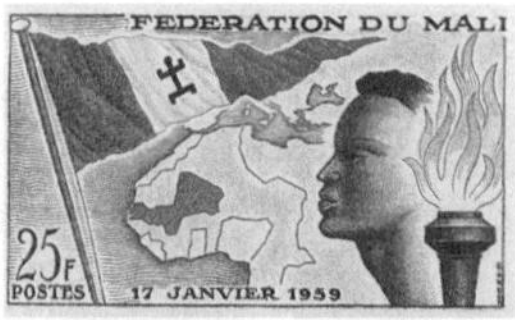

1 Map, Flag, Mali and Torch

1959. Establishment of Mali Federation.

1	**1**	25f. multicoloured	35	25

2

1959. Air. 300th Anniv of St. Louis, Senegal.

2	**2**	85f. multicoloured	50	40

3 West African Parrotfish

4 Violet Starling

1960. (a) Postage. Fish as T **3**.

3	**3**	5f. orange, blue and bronze	40	15
4	–	10f. black, brown and turquoise	40	25
5	–	15f. brown, slate and blue	55	25
6	–	20f. black, bistre and green	65	35
7	–	25f. yellow, sepia and green	80	40
8	–	30f. red, purple and blue	1·00	50
9	–	85f. red, blue and green	3·00	1·75

(b) Air. Birds as T **4**.

10	**4**	100f. multicoloured	5·50	1·25
11	–	200f. multicoloured	12·00	3·75
12	–	500f. multicoloured	32·00	11·50

DESIGNS—HORIZ: 10f. West African triggerfish; 15f. Guinean fingerfish; 20f. Threadfish; 25f. Shining butterflyfish; 30f. Monrovian surgeonfish; 85f. Pink dentex; 200f. Bateleur. VERT: 500f. Common gonolek.

1960. 10th Anniv of African Technical Co-operation Commission. As T **4** of Malagasy Republic.

13		25f. purple and violet	1·10	65

B. REPUBLIC.

1960. Nos. 6, 7, 9 and 10/12 optd **REPUBLIQUE DU MALI** and bar or bars or surch also.

14	20f. black, bistre and green (postage)	1·50	60
15	25f. red, purple and blue	2·00	60
16	85f. red, blue and green	3·75	1·50
17	100f. multicoloured (air)	5·50	1·50
18	200f. multicoloured	8·50	3·50
19	300f. on 500f. multicoloured	14·00	6·00
20	500f. multicoloured	28·00	17·00

7 Pres. Mamadou Konate

1961.

21	**7**	20f. sepia and green (postage)	25	15
22	–	25f. black and purple	35	15
23	**7**	200f. sepia and red (air)	3·00	1·00
24	–	300f. black and green	4·25	1·25

DESIGN: 25, 300f. President Keita. Nos. 23/4 are larger, 27 × 38 mm.

8 U.N. Emblem, Flag and Map

1961. Air. Proclamation of Independence and Admission into U.N.

25	**8**	100f. multicoloured	1·60	95

9 Sankore Mosque, Timbuktu

1961. Air.

26	**9**	100f. brown, blue and sepia	1·75	55
27	–	200f. brown, red and green	4·50	1·50
28	–	500f. green, brown and blue	13·00	3·25

DESIGN: 200f. View of Timbuktu; 500f. Arms and view of Bamako.

10 Africans learning Vowels

1961. 1st Anniv of Independence.

29	**10**	25f. multicoloured	60	30

11 Sheep at Pool

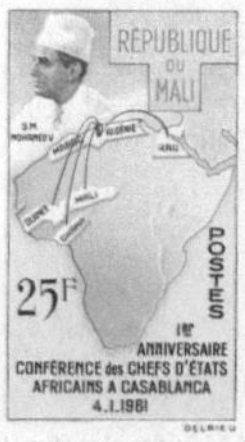

12 African Map and King Mohammed V of Morocco

1961.

30	**11**	50c. sepia, myrtle and red	15	15
31	A	1f. bistre, green and blue	15	15
32	B	2f. red, green and blue	15	15
33	C	3f. brown, green and blue	15	15
34	D	4f. blue, green and bistre	15	15
35	**11**	5f. purple, green and blue	20	15
36	A	10f. brown, myrtle and blue	20	15
37	B	15f. brown, green and blue	20	15
38	C	20f. red, green and blue	30	25
39	D	25f. brown and blue	40	20
40	**11**	30f. brown, green and violet	55	30
41	A	40f. brown, green and blue	1·25	30
42	B	50f. lake, green and blue	50	30
43	C	60f. brown, green and blue	15	15
44	D	85f. brown, bistre and blue	1·75	35

DESIGNS: A, Oxen at pool; B, House of Arts, Mali; C, Land tillage; D, Combine-harvester in rice field.

1962. 1st Anniv of African Conf, Casablanca.

45	**12**	25f. multicoloured	25	15
46		50f. multicoloured	50	20

13 Patrice Lumumba

1962. 1st Death Anniv of Patrice Lumumba (Congo leader).

47	**13**	25f. brown and bistre	20	20
48		100f. brown and green	75	50

1962. Malaria Eradication. As T **43** of Mauritania.

49	25f.+5f. blue	50	60

14 Pegasus and U.P.U. Emblem

1962. 1st Anniv of Admission into U.P.U.

50	**14**	85f. multicoloured	1·00	65

14a Posthorn on Map of Africa

15 Sansanding Dam

1962. African Postal Union Commem.

51	**14a**	25f. green and brown	25	20
52		85f. orange and green	75	50

1962.

53	**15**	25f. black, green and blue	40	20
54	–	45f. multicoloured	1·25	50

DESIGN—HORIZ: 45f. Cotton plant.

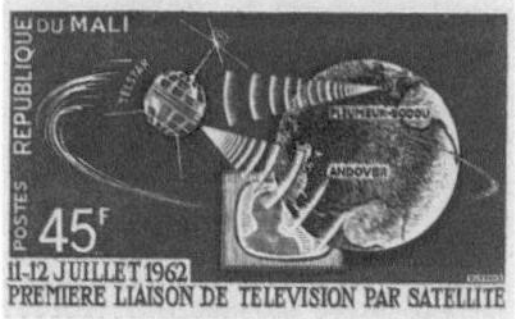

16 "Telstar" Satellite, Globe and Television Receiver

1962. 1st Trans-Atlantic Telecommunications Satellite Link.

55	**16**	45f. brown, violet and lake	80	40
56		55f. violet, olive and green	95	60

17 Soldier and Family

18 Bull's Head, Laboratory Equipment and Chicks

1962. Mali–Algerian Solidarity.

57	**17**	25f.+5f. multicoloured	30	30

1963. Zoological Research Centre, Sobuta.

58	**18**	25f. turq & brn (postage)	35	25
59	–	200f. turquoise, purple and bistre (air)	3·50	1·25

DESIGN: 200f. As Type **18** but horiz, 47 × 27 mm.

19 Tractor and Campaign Emblem

1963. Freedom from Hunger.

60	**19**	25f. purple, black and blue	45	20
61		45f. brown, green & turq	80	35

20 Balloon and W.M.O. Emblem

1963. Atmospheric Research.

62	**20**	25f. multicoloured	40	20
63		45f. multicoloured	70	35
64		60f. multicoloured	95	50

21 Race Winners

22 Centenary Emblem and Globe

1963. Youth Week. Multicoloured.

65	5f. Type **21**	15	10
66	10f. Type **21**	20	15
67	20f. Acrobatic dance (horiz)	35	20
68	85f. Football (horiz)	1·60	55

1963. Red Cross Centenary. Inscr in black.

69	**22**	5f. multicoloured	30	15
70		10f. red, yellow and grey	40	20
71		85f. red, yellow and grey	1·25	60

23 Stretcher case entering Aero 145 Ambulance Airplane

1963. Air.

72	**23**	25f. brown, blue and green	45	20
73	–	55f. blue, ochre and brown	1·25	40
74	–	100f. blue, brown and green	2·00	75

DESIGNS: 55f. Douglas DC-3 airliner on tarmac; 100f. Illyushin Il-18 airliner taking off.

24 South African Crowned Crane standing on Giant Tortoise

26 "Kaempferia aethiopica"

25 U.N. Emblem, Doves and Banner

1963. Air. Fauna Protection.

75	**24**	25f. brown, red and orange	1·50	50
76		200f. multicoloured	5·50	2·50

1963. Air. 15th Anniv of Declaration of Human Rights.

77	**25**	50f. yellow, red and green	75	40

1963. Tropical Flora. Multicoloured.

78	30f. Type **26**	60	25
79	70f. "Bombax costatum"	1·75	50
80	100f. "Adenium honghel"	3·00	65

27 Pharaoh and Cleopatra, Philae

28 Locust on Map of Africa

1964. Air. Nubian Monuments Preservation.

81	**27**	25f. brown and purple	75	25
82		55f. olive and purple	1·60	50

1964. Anti-locust Campaign.
83 **28** 5f. brown, green and purple 20 15
84 – 10f. brown, green and olive 30 20
85 – 20f. brown, green and bistre 75 25
DESIGNS—VERT: 10f. Locust and map. HORIZ: 20f. Air-spraying, locust and village.

29 Football

1964. Olympic Games, Tokyo.
86 **29** 5f. purple, green and red . . 15 10
87 – 10f. brown, blue and sepia 30 20
88 – 15f. red and violet 40 20
89 – 85f. green, brown and violet 1·25 70
DESIGNS—VERT: 10f. Boxing; 15f. Running and Olympic Flame. HORIZ: 85f. Hurdling. Each design has a stadium in the background.

30 Solar Flares **32** Map of Vietnam

31 President Kennedy

1964. International Quiet Sun Years.
90 **30** 45f. olive, red and blue . . 1·00 35

1964. Air. 1st Death Anniv of Pres. Kennedy.
91 **31** 100f. multicoloured . . . . 1·75 1·25

1964. Mali–South Vietnam Workers' Solidarity Campaign.
92 **32** 30f. multicoloured 30 20

33 Greater Turacos ("Touraco")

1965. Air. Birds.
93 **33** 100f. green, blue and red . . 5·00 95
94 – 200f. black, red and blue . . 13·00 1·75
95 – 300f. black, ochre and green 18·00 2·50
96 – 500f. red, brown and green 29·00 4·75
BIRDS—VERT: 200f. Abyssinian ground hornbills; 300f. Egyptian vultures. HORIZ: 500f. Goliath herons.

34 I.C.Y. Emblem and U.N. Headquarters **36** Abraham Lincoln

35 African Buffalo

1965. Air. International Co-operation Year.
97 **34** 55f. ochre, purple and blue 75 40

1965. Animals.
98 – 1f. brown, blue and green 10 10
99 **35** 5f. brown, orange and green 15 10
100 – 10f. brown, mauve & green 40 25
101 – 30f. brown, green and red 75 30
102 – 90f. brown, grey and green 2·50 95
ANIMALS—VERT: 1f. Waterbuck; 10f. Scimitar oryx; 90f. Giraffe. HORIZ: 30f. Leopard.

1965. Death Centenary of Abraham Lincoln.
103 **36** 45f. multicoloured 60 40
104 55f. multicoloured 65 50

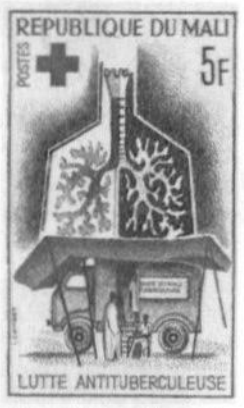

37 Hughes' Telegraph **38** "Lungs" and Mobile X-Ray Unit (Anti-T.B.)

1965. Centenary of I.T.U.
105 – 20f. black, blue and orange 30 25
106 **37** 30f. green, brown & orange 60 25
107 – 50f. green, brown & orange 90 45
DESIGNS—VERT: 20f. Denis's pneumatic tube; 50f. Lescurre's heliograph.

1965. Mali Health Service.
108 **38** 5f. violet, red and crimson 15 15
109 – 10f. green, bistre and red 25 15
110 – 25f. green and brown . . . 40 20
111 – 45f. green and brown . . . 75 40
DESIGNS: 10f. Mother and children (Maternal and Child Care); 25f. Examining patient (Marchoux Institute); 45f. Nurse (Biological Laboratory).

39 Diving

1965. 1st African Games, Brazzaville, Congo.
112 **39** 5f. red, brown and blue . . 25 10
113 – 15f. turquoise, brown and red (Judo) 75 30

40 Pope John XXIII

1965. Air. Pope John Commemoration.
114 **40** 100f. multicoloured . . . . 1·90 75

41 Sir Winston Churchill

1965. Air. Churchill Commemoration.
115 **41** 100f. blue and brown . . . 2·00 75

42 Dr. Schweitzer and Young African

1965. Air. Dr. Albert Schweitzer Commemoration.
116 **42** 100f. multicoloured . . . . 2·00 75

43 Leonov

1966. International Astronautic Conference, Athens (1965). Multicoloured.
117 100f. Type **43** . . . . 1·75 60
118 100f. White . . . . 1·75 60
119 300f. Cooper, Conrad, Leonov and Beliaiev (vert) 4·50 2·00

44 Vase, Quill and Cornet

1966. World Festival of Negro Arts, Dakar, Cameroun.
120 **44** 30f. black, red and ochre 30 20
121 – 55f. red, black and green 75 35
122 – 90f. brown, orange and blue . . . . 1·25 60
DESIGNS: 55f. Mask, brushes and palette, microphones; 90f. Dancers, mask and patterned cloth.

45 W.H.O. Building

1966. Inaug of W.H.O. Headquarters, Geneva.
123 **45** 30f. green, blue and yellow 40 20
124 45f. red, blue and yellow 60 35

46 Fisherman with Net

1966. River Fishing.
125 **46** 3f. brown and blue 15 15
126 – 4f. purple, blue and brown 20 15
127 – 20f. purple, green and blue 35 15
128 **46** 25f. purple, blue and green 75 20
129 – 60f. purple, lake and green 1·50 45
130 – 85f. plum, green and blue 1·50 50
DESIGNS: 4f., 60f. Collective shore fishing; 20f., 85f. Fishing pirogue.

47 Papal Arms, U.N. and Peace Emblems

1966. Air. Pope Paul's Visit to U.N.
131 **47** 200f. blue, green & turq . . 2·75 1·10

48 Initiation Ceremony **49** People and UNESCO Emblem

1966. Mali Pioneers. Multicoloured.
132 5f. Type **48** 25 15
133 25f. Pioneers dancing 75 20

1966. Air. 20th Anniv of UNESCO.
134 **49** 100f. red, green and blue 1·75 70

50 Footballers, Globe, Cup and Football

1966. Air. World Cup Football Championship, England.
135 **50** 100f. multicoloured . . . . 1·75 70

51 Cancer ("The Crab") **52** UNICEF Emblem and Children

1966. Air. 9th International Cancer Congress, Tokyo.
136 **51** 100f. multicoloured . . . . 1·75 55

1966. 20th Anniv of UNICEF.
137 **52** 45f. blue, purple and brown 60 25

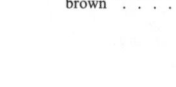

53 Inoculating Cattle **55** "Diamant" Rocket and Francesco de Lana-Terzis's "Aerial Ship"

54 Desert Vehicles in Pass

1967. Campaign for Preventing Cattle Plague.
138 **53** 10f. multicoloured 25 10
139 30f. multicoloured 50 20

1967. Air. Crossing of the Hoggar (1924).
140 **54** 200f. green, brown & violet 4·75 2·25

1967. Air. French Space Rockets and Satellites.
141 **55** 50f. blue, turquoise & pur 85 30
142 – 100f. lake, purple & turq 1·60 50
143 – 200f. purple, olive and blue 2·60 1·00
DESIGNS: 100f. Satellite "A 1" and Jules Verne's "rocket"; 200f. Satellite "D 1" and Da Vinci's "bird-powered" flying machine.

56 Ancient City

1967. International Tourist Year.
144 **56** 25f. orange, blue and violet 30 20

57 Amelia Earhart and Mail Route-map

1967. Air. 30th Anniv of Amelia Earhart's Flight, via Gao.
145 **57** 500f. multicoloured . . . . 7·50 3·25

58 "The Bird Cage"

1967. Air. Picasso Commemoration. Designs showing paintings. Multicoloured.
146 50f. Type **58** . . . . 1·25 30
147 100f. "Paul as Harlequin" . . 2·00 70
148 250f. "The Pipes of Pan" . . 4·00 1·50
See also Nos. 158/9 and 164/7.

59 Scout Emblems and Rope Knots

1967. Air. World Scout Jamboree, Idaho.
149 **59** 70f. red and green . . . . 1·00 30
150 – 100f. black, lake and green 1·25 45
DESIGN: 100f. Scout with "walkie-talkie" radio.

60 "Chelorrhina polyphemus"

61 School Class

1967. Insects.
151 **60** 5f. green, brown and blue 40 20
152 – 15f. purple, brown & green 75 25
153 – 50f. red, brown and green 1·25 55
INSECTS—HORIZ: 15f. "Ugada grandicollis"; 50f. "Phymateus cinctus".

1967. International Literacy Day.
154 **61** 50f. black, red and green 60 20

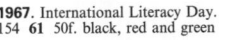

62 "Europafrique"

1967. Europafrique.
155 **62** 45f. multicoloured 85 25

63 Lions Emblem and Crocodile

65 Block of Flats, Grenoble

64 "Water Resources"

1967. 50th Anniv of Lions International.
156 **63** 90f. multicoloured . . . . 1·10 55

1967. International Hydrological Decade.
157 **64** 25f. black, blue and bistre 70 20

1967. Air. Toulouse-Lautrec Commemoration. Paintings as T **58**. Multicoloured.
158 100f. "Gazelle" (horse's head) (horiz) . . . . 2·50 1·10
159 300f. "Gig drawn by Cob" (vert) . . . . 5·50 2·25

1968. Air. Winter Olympic Games, Grenoble.
160 **65** 50f. brown, green and blue 85 35
161 – 150f. brown, blue and ultramarine . . . . . . 1·75 65
DESIGN: 150f. Bobsleigh course, Huez mountain.

66 W.H.O. Emblem

1968. 20th Anniv of W.H.O.
162 **66** 90f. blue, lake and green 85 30

67 Human Figures and Entwined Hearts

1968. World "Twin Towns" Day.
163 **67** 50f. red, violet and green 40 15

1968. Air. Flower Paintings. As T **58**. Mult.
164 50f. "Roses and Anemones" (Van Gogh) 75 25
165 150f. "Vase of Flowers" (Manet) . . . . 1·75 55
166 300f. "Bouquet of Flowers" (Delacroix) . . . . 3·25 1·10
167 500f. "Marguerites" (Millet) 5·00 2·00
SIZES: 50f., 300f. 40 × 41½ mm; 150f. 36 × 47½ mm; 500f. 50 × 36 mm.

68 Dr. Martin Luther King

69 "Draisienne" Bicycle, 1809

1968. Air. Martin Luther King Commemoration.
168 **68** 100f. black, pink and purple 85 35

1968. Veteran Bicycles and Motor Cars.
169 **69** 2f. brown, mauve and green (postage) 35 15
170 – 5f. red, blue and bistre . . 75 20
171 – 10f. blue, brown and green 1·25 25
172 – 45f. black, green and brown . . . . 2·00 40
173 – 50f. red, green & brn (air) 1·00 25
174 – 100f. blue, mauve and bistre . . . . 2·00 60
DESIGNS—HORIZ: 5f. De Dion-Bouton, 1894; 45f. Panhard-Levassor, 1914; 100f. Mercedes-Benz, 1927. VERT: 10f. Michaux Bicycle, 1861; 50f. "Bicyclette, 1918".

70 Books, Graph and A.D.B.A. Emblem

1968. 10th Anniv of International African Libraries and Archives Development Association.
175 **70** 100f. red, black and brown 65 30

71 Football

1968. Air. Olympic Games, Mexico. Multicoloured.
176 100f. Type **71** . . . . 1·00 40
177 150f. Long-jumping (vert) . . 1·50 60

1968. Air. "Philexafrique" Stamp Exhibition, Abidjan, Ivory Coast, 1969 (1st issue). As T **113a** of Mauritania. Multicoloured.
178 200f. "The Editors" (F. M. Granet) . . . . 2·00 1·50

1969. Air. "Philexafrique" Stamp Exn, Abidjan, Ivory Coast (2nd issue). As T **114a** of Mauritania.
179 100f. purple, red and violet 1·50 1·25
DESIGN: 100f. Carved animal and French Sudan stamp of 1931.

1969. Air. Birth Bicentenary of Napoleon Bonaparte. Multicoloured. As T **114b** of Mauritania.
180 150f. "Napoleon Bonaparte, First Consul" (Gros) . . . 2·50 1·25
181 200f. "The Bivouac – Battle of Austerlitz" (Lejeune) (horiz) . . . . 4·25 1·75

73 Montgolfier Balloon

1969. Air. Aviation History. Multicoloured.
182 50f. Type **73** 50 20
183 150f. Ferdinand Ferber's Glider No. 5 . . . . . . 1·75 40
184 300f. Concorde . . . . . . 3·50 1·40

74 African Tourist Emblem

1969. African Tourist Year.
185 **74** 50f. red, green and blue . . 25 20

75 "O.I.T." and I.L.O. Emblem

1969. 50th Anniv of I.L.O.
186 **75** 50f. violet, blue and green 30 20
187 60f. slate, red and brown 35 20

76 Panhard of 1897 and Model "24-CT"

1969. French Motor Industry.
188 **76** 25f. lake, black and bistre (postage) 50 20
189 – 30f. green and black . . . 75 20
190 – 55f. red, black and purple (air) . . . . 1·25 35
191 – 90f. blue, black and red . . 1·75 45
DESIGNS: 30f. Citroen of 1923 and Model "DS-21"; 55f. Renault of 1898 and Model "16"; 90f. Peugeot of 1893 and Model "404".

77 Clarke (Australia), 10,000 m (1965)

1969. Air. World Athletics Records.
192 **77** 60f. brown and blue . . . 30 25
193 – 90f. brown and red 45 25
194 – 120f. brown and green . . 55 35
195 – 140f. brown and slate . . . 70 35
196 – 150f. black and red 85 50
DESIGNS: 90f. Lusis (Russia), Javelin (1968); 120f. Miyake (Japan), Weightlifting (1967); 140f. Matson (U.S.A.), Shot-putting (1968); 150f. Keino (Kenya), 3,000 m (1965).

78 Hollow Blocks

1969. International Toy Fair, Nuremberg.
197 **78** 5f. red, yellow and grey . . 15 10
198 – 10f. multicoloured 15 10
199 – 15f. green, red and pink . . 30 10
200 – 20f. orange, blue and red 35 15
DESIGNS: 10f. Toy donkey on wheels; 15f. "Ducks"; 20f. Model car and race-track.

79 "Apollo 8", Earth and Moon

1969. Air. Moon Flight of "Apollo 8".
201 **79** 2,000f. gold . . . . 14·00 14·00
This stamp is embossed on gold foil.

1969. Air. 1st Man on the Moon. Nos. 182/4 optd **L'HOMME SUR LA LUNE JUILLET 1969** and Apollo 11.
202 50f. multicoloured 95 65
203 150f. multicoloured . . . . . 2·00 1·25
204 300f. multicoloured . . . . . 3·25 2·50

81 Sheep

1969. Domestic Animals.
205 **81** 1f. olive, brown and green 10 10
206 – 2f. brown, grey and red . . 10 10
207 – 10f. olive, brown and blue 20 10
208 – 35f. slate and red 60 30
209 – 90f. brown and blue . . . 1·25 55
ANIMALS: 2f. Goat; 10f. Donkey; 35f. Horse; 90f. Dromedary.

1969. 5th Anniv of African Development Bank. As T **122a** of Mauritania.
210 50f. brown, green and purple 25 20
211 90f. orange, green and brown 45 20

83 "Mona Lisa" (Leonardo da Vinci)

1969. Air. 450th Death Anniv of Leonardo da Vinci.
212 **83** 500f. multicoloured . . . . 4·50 3·25

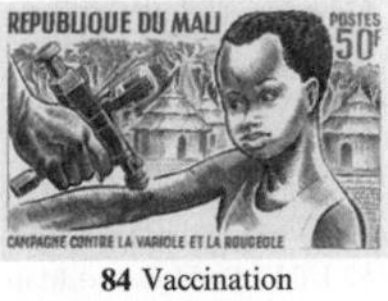

84 Vaccination

1969. Campaign against Smallpox and Measles.
213 **84** 50f. slate, brown and green 40 15

85 Mahatma Gandhi

1969. Air. Birth Centenary of Mahatma Gandhi.
214 **85** 150f. brown and green . . 1·75 55

1969. 10th Anniv of Aerial Navigation Security Agency for Africa and Madagascar (A.S.E.C.N.A.). As T **94a** of Niger.
215 100f. green 75 25

87 West African Map and Posthorns

1970. Air. 11th Anniv of West African Postal Union (C.A.P.T.E.A.O.).
216 **87** 100f. multicoloured 60 35

1970. Air. Religious Paintings. As T **83**. Mult.
217 100f. "Virgin and Child" (Van der Weydan School) 70 40
218 150f. "The Nativity" (The Master of Flamalle) . . . 1·10 65
219 250f. "Virgin, Child and St. John the Baptist" (Low Countries School) . . . . 2·40 1·40

89 Franklin D. Roosevelt

91 Lenin

90 Women of Mali and Japan

1970. Air. 25th Death Anniv of Franklin D. Roosevelt.
220 **89** 500f. black, red and blue 3·50 2·00

1970. "EXPO 70" World Fair, Osaka, Japan.
221 **90** 100f. orange, brown & blue 60 20
222 – 150f. red, green and yellow 80 30
DESIGN: 150f. Flags and maps of Mali and Japan.

1970. Air. Birth Centenary of Lenin.
223 **91** 300f. black, green and flesh 2·25 1·00

92 Verne and Moon Rockets

1970. Air. Jules Verne "Prophet of Space Travel". Multicoloured.
224 50f. Type **92** 75 25
225 150f. Moon orbit . . . . . . 1·75 50
226 300f. Splashdown . . . . . 2·50 1·10

93 I.T.U. Emblem and Map

1970. World Telecommunications Day.
227 **93** 90f. red, brown and sepia 75 25

1970. New U.P.U. Headquarters Building, Berne. As Type **81** of New Caledonia.
228 50f. brown, green and red . . 40 20
229 60f. brown, blue and mauve 60 20

1970. Air. Space Flight of "Apollo 13". Nos. 224/6 optd **APOLLO XIII EPOPEE SPATIALE 11-17 AVRIL 1970** in three lines.
230 50f. multicoloured 50 25
231 150f. multicoloured . . . . . 1·25 45
232 300f. multicoloured . . . . . 2·25 1·25

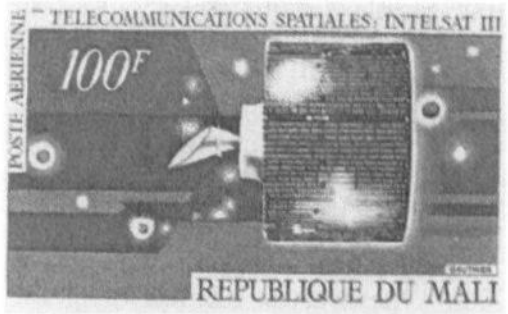

96 "Intelsat 3" Satellite

1970. Air. Space Telecommunications.
233 **96** 100f. indigo, blue & orange 75 35
234 – 200f. purple, grey and blue 1·40 50
235 – 300f. brown, orange & slate . . . . 2·50 1·10
236 – 500f. brown, blue & indigo 3·75 1·60
DESIGNS: 200f. "Molnya I" satellite; 300f. Dish aerial, Type PB 2; 500f. "Symphony Project" satellite.

97 Auguste and Louis Lumiere, Jean Harlow and Marilyn Monroe

1970. Air. Lumiere Brothers (inventors of the cine camera) Commemoration.
237 **97** 250f. multicoloured . . . . 2·50 1·25

98 Footballers

1970. Air. World Cup Football Championship, Mexico.
238 **98** 80f. green, brown and red 50 25
239 200f. red, brown and blue 1·25 55

99 Rotary Emblem, Map and Antelope

100 "Supporting United Nations"

1970. Air. Rotary International.
240 **99** 200f. multicoloured . . . . 1·75 60

1970. Air. 25th Anniv of U.N.O.
241 **100** 100f. blue, brown & violet 70 35

101 Page from 11th century Baghdad Koran

1970. Air. Ancient Muslim Art. Multicoloured.
242 50f. Type **101** 50 25
243 200f. "Tree and wild Animals" (Jordanian mosaic, c.730) . . . . . . 1·25 55
244 250f. "The Scribe" (Baghdad miniature, 1287) . . . . . 2·00 90

1970. Air. Moon Landing of "Luna 16". Nos. 234/5 surch **LUNA 16 PREMIERS PRELEVEMENTS AUTOMATIQUES SUR LA LUNE SEPTEMBRE 1970** and new values.
245 150f. on 200f. purple, grey and blue . . . . 1·25 40
246 250f. on 300f. brown, orange and grey . . . . 1·75 60

103 G.P.O., Bamako

1970. Public Buildings.
247 **103** 30f. olive, green and brown 20 20
248 – 40f. purple, brown & green 30 20
249 – 60f. grey, green and red 40 20
250 – 80f. brown, green and grey 50 25
BUILDINGS: 40f. Chamber of Commerce, Bamako; 60f. Ministry of Public Works, Bamako; 80f. Town Hall, Segou.

104 Pres. Nasser

106 Gallet Steam Locomotive, 1882

105 "The Nativity" (Antwerp School 1530)

1970. Air. Pres. Gamal Nasser of Egypt. Commemoration.
251 **104** 1000f. gold . . . . 7·50 7·50

1970. Air. Christmas. Paintings. Multicoloured.
252 100f. Type **105** 70 40
253 250f. "Adoration of the Shepherds" (Memling) . . 1·60 95
254 300f. "Adoration of the Magi" (17th-century Flemish school) . . . . . 2·25 1·25

1970. Mali Railway Locomotives from the Steam Era (1st series).
255 **106** 20f. black, red and green 1·60 1·40
256 – 40f. black, green & brown 2·40 1·75
257 – 50f. black, green & brown 2·75 2·10
258 – 80f. black, red and green 4·00 3·00
259 – 100f. black, green & brn 4·75 4·00
LOCOMOTIVES: 40f. Felou, 1882; 50f. Bechevel, 1882; 80f. Series 1100, 1930 (inscr "Type 23"); 100f. Class 40, 1927 (incr "Type 141" and "vers 1930").
See also Nos. 367/70.

107 Scouts crossing Log-bridge

108 Bambara de San Mask

1970. Scouting in Mali. Multicoloured.
260 5f. Type **107** 20 15
261 30f. Bugler and scout camp (vert) 35 15
262 100f. Scouts canoeing 90 35

1971. Mali Masks and Ideograms. Multicoloured.
263 20f. Type **108** 15 10
264 25f. Dogon de Bandiagara mask 20 10
265 50f. Kanaga ideogram . . . 45 15
266 80f. Bambara ideogram . . . 60 25

109 General De Gaulle

1971. Air. Charles De Gaulle Commem. Die-stamped on gold foil.
267 **109** 2000f. gold, red and blue 30·00 30·00

110 Alfred Nobel

111 Tennis Player (Davis Cup)

1971. Air. 75th Death Anniv of Alfred Nobel (philanthropist).
268 **110** 300f. red, brown and green . . . . 2·50 1·25

1971. Air. World Sporting Events.
269 **111** 100f. slate, purple and blue 75 25
270 – 150f. olive, brown & green . . . . 1·40 40
271 – 200f. brown, olive and blue . . . . 2·00 60
DESIGNS—HORIZ: 150f. Steeplechase (inscr "Derby at Epsom" but probably represents the Grand National). VERT: 200f. Yacht (Americas Cup).

112 Youth, Sun and Microscope

1971. 50th Anniv of 1st B.C.G. Vaccine Innoculation.
272 **112** 100f. brown, green and red 85 40

113 "The Thousand and One Nights"

1971. Air. "Tales of the Arabian Nights". Mult.
273 120f. Type **113** 70 30
274 180f. "Ali Baba and the Forty Thieves" . . . . 1·00 40
275 200f. "Aladdin's Lamp" . . . 1·40 50

114 Scouts, Japanese Horseman and Mt. Fuji

1971. 13th World Scout Jamboree, Asagiri, Japan.
276 **114** 80f. plum, green and blue 75 20

115 Rose between Hands

116 Rural Costume

1971. 25th Anniv of UNICEF.
277 **115** 50f. brown, red and orange 30 20
278 – 60f. blue, green and brown 40 20
DESIGN—VERT: 60f. Nurses and children.

1971. National Costumes. Multicoloured.
279 5f. Type **116** 15 10
280 10f. Rural costume (female) 20 15
281 15f. Tuareg 20 15
282 60f. Embroidered "boubou" 45 20
283 80f. Women's ceremonial costume 60 25

117 Olympic Rings and Events

1971. Air. Olympic Games Publicity.
284 **117** 80f. blue, purple and green 40 20

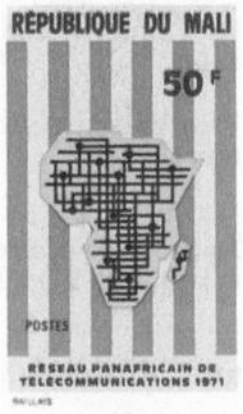

118 Telecommunications Map

1971. Pan-African Telecommunications Network Year.
285 **118** 50f. multicoloured 25 20

119 "Mariner 4" and Mars

1971. Air. Exploration of Outer Space.
286 **119** 200f. green, blue & brown 1·25 50
287 – 300f. blue, plum & purple 1·75 60
DESIGN: 300f. "Venera 5" and Venus.

120 "Santa Maria" (1492)

1971. Air. Famous Ships.
288 **120** 100f. brown, violet & blue 70 35
289 – 150f. violet, brown & grn 1·25 45
290 – 200f. green, blue and red 1·60 75
291 – 250f. red, blue and black 2·25 90
DESIGNS: 150f. "Mayflower" (1620); 200f. Battleship "Potemkin" (1905); 250f. Liner "Normandie" (1935).

121 "Hibiscus rosa-sinensis"

1971. Flowers. Multicoloured.
292 20f. Type **121** 20 10
293 50f. "Euphorbia pulcherrima" 55 15
294 60f. "Adenium obesum" . . 80 20
295 80f. "Allamanda cathartica" 1·25 25
296 100f. "Satanocrater berhautii" . . . . 1·50 35

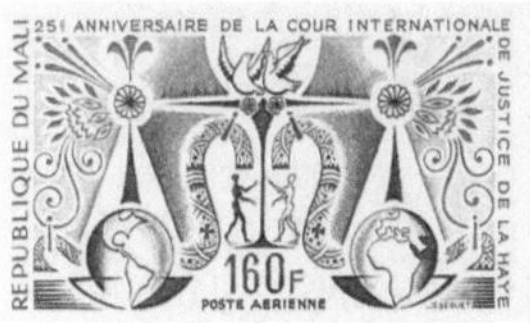

122 Allegory of Justice

1971. 25th Anniv of Int Court of Justice, The Hague.
297 **122** 160f. chocolate, red & brn 80 35

123 Nat King Cole

124 Statue of Olympic Zeus (by Pheidias)

1971. Air. Famous Negro Musicians. Multicoloured.
298 130f. Type **123** . . . . . . 1·25 25
299 150f. Erroll Garner . . . . . 1·25 30
300 270f. Louis Armstrong . . . 1·75 45

1971. Air. "The Seven Wonders of the Ancient World".
301 **124** 70f. blue, brown & purple 35 20
302 – 80f. black, brown and blue 40 20
303 – 100f. blue, red and violet 50 25
304 – 130f. black, purple & blue 75 30
305 – 150f. brown, green & blue 1·10 35
306 – 270f. blue, brown & pur 1·60 75
307 – 280f. blue, purple & brn 2·00 85
DESIGNS—VERT: 80f. Pyramid of Cheops, Egypt; 130f. Pharos of Alexandria; 270f. Mausoleum of Halicarnassos; 280f. Colossus of Rhodes. HORIZ: 100f. Temple of Artemis, Ephesus; 150f. Hanging Gardens of Babylon.

125 "Family Life" (carving)

1971. 15th Anniv of Social Security Service.
308 **125** 70f. brown, green and red 40 20

126 Slalom-skiing and Japanese Girl

1972. Air. Winter Olympic Games, Sapporo, Japan.
309 **126** 150f. brown, green & orge 1·00 35
310 – 200f. green, brown and red . . . . 1·50 55
DESIGN: 200f. Ice-hockey and Japanese actor.

127 "Santa Maria della Salute" (Caffi)

1972. Air. UNESCO "Save Venice" Campaign. Multicoloured.
312 130f. Type **127** 80 35
313 270f. "Rialto Bridge" . . . . 1·50 60
314 280f. "St. Mark's Square" (vert) . . . . 1·75 70

128 Hands clasping Flagpole

1972. Air. Int Scout Seminar, Cotonou, Dahomey.
315 **128** 200f. green, orange & brn 1·75 55

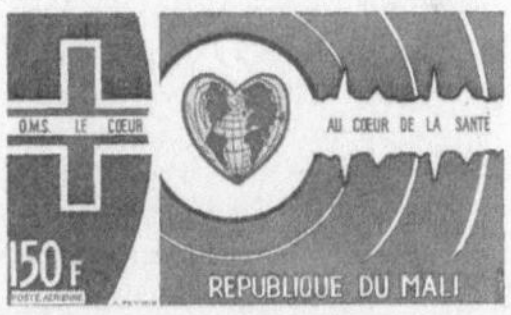

129 Heart and Red Cross Emblems

1972. Air. World Heart Month.
316 **129** 150f. red and blue . . . . 1·00 40

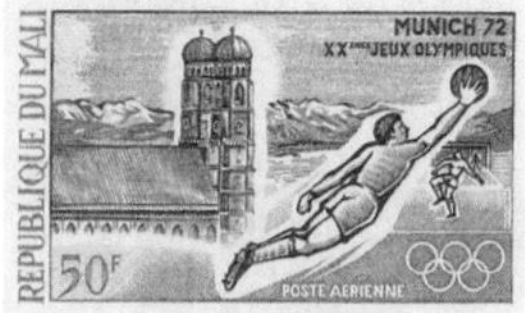

130 Football

1972. Air. Olympic Games, Munich (1st issue). Sports and Munich Buildings.
317 **130** 50f. blue, brown and green 25 20
318 – 150f. blue, brown & green 70 30
319 – 200f. blue, brown & green 80 50
320 – 300f. blue, brown & green 1·25 70
DESIGNS—VERT: 150f. Judo; 200f. Hurdling. HORIZ: 300f. Running.
See also Nos. 357/62.

131 "Apollo 15" and Lunar Rover

1972. Air. History of Transport Development.
322 **131** 150f. red, green and lake 80 40
323 – 250f. red, blue and green 2·00 1·00
DESIGN: 250f. Montgolfier's balloon and Cugnot's steam car.

132 "UIT" on T.V. Screen

1972. World Telecommunications Day.
324 **132** 70f. black, blue and red 40 20

133 Clay Funerary Statue

134 Samuel Morse and Early Telegraph

1972. Mali Archaeology. Multicoloured.
325 30f. Type **133** 20 15
326 40f. Female Figure (wood-carving) 30 20
327 50f. "Warrior" (stone-painting) 40 20
328 100f. Wrought-iron ritual figures . . . . 1·00 35

1972. Death Centenary of Samuel Morse (inventor of telegraph).
329 **134** 80f. purple, green and red 45 20

135 "Cinderella"

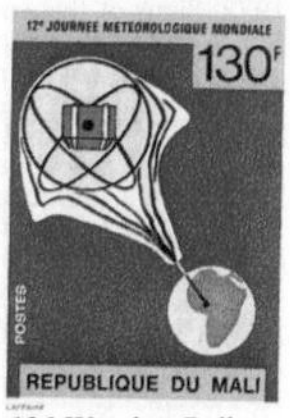

136 Weather Balloon

1972. Air. Charles Perrault's Fairy Tales.
330 **135** 70f. green, red and brown 45 20
331 – 80f. brown, red and green 50 25
332 – 150f. violet, purple & blue 1·10 35
DESIGNS: 80f. "Puss in Boots"; 150f. "The Sleeping Beauty".

1972. World Meteorological Day.
333 **136** 130f. multicoloured . . . 60 30

137 Astronauts and Lunar Rover

1972. Air. Moon Flight of "Apollo 16".
334 **137** 500f. brown, violet & grn 3·00 1·25

138 Book Year Emblem

1972. Air. International Book Year.
335 **138** 80f. gold, green and blue 40 25

139 Sarakole Dance, Kayes

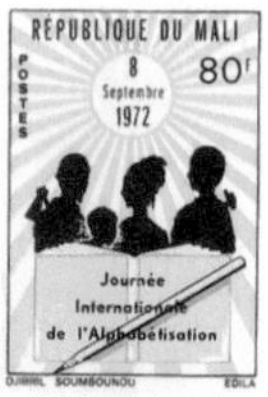

140 Learning the Alphabet

1972. Traditional Dances. Multicoloured.
336 10f. Type **139** 25 15
337 20f. Malinke dance, Bamako 30 15
338 50f. Hunter's dance, Bougouni 55 20
339 70f. Bambara dance, Segou 70 20
340 80f. Dogon dance, Sanga . . 80 30
341 120f. Targuie dance, Timbukto . . . . 1·40 45

1972. International Literacy Day.
342 **140** 80f. black and green . . . 40 15

141 Statue and Musical Instruments

142 Club Banner

1972. 1st Anthology of Mali Music.
343 **141** 100f. multicoloured . . . 85 30

1972. Air. 10th Anniv of Bamako Rotary Club.
344 **142** 170f. purple, blue and red 1·00 40

143 Aries the Ram

1972. Signs of the Zodiac.

345	**143**	15f. brown and purple	30	20
346	–	15f. black and brown	30	20
347	–	35f. blue and red	50	25
348	–	35f. red and green	50	25
349	–	40f. brown and blue	60	30
350	–	40f. brown and purple	60	30
351	–	45f. red and blue	70	35
352	–	45f. green and red	70	35
353	–	65f. blue and violet	1·00	35
354	–	65f. brown and violet	1·00	35
355	–	90f. blue and mauve	1·60	65
356	–	90f. green and mauve	1·60	65

DESIGNS: No. 346, Taurus the Bull; No. 347, Gemini the Twins; No. 348, Cancer the Crab; No. 349, Leo the Lion; No. 350, Virgo the Virgin; No. 351, Libra the Scales; No. 352, Scorpio the Scorpion; No. 353, Sagittarius the Archer; No. 354, Capricornus the Goat; No. 355, Aquarius the Water-carrier; No. 356, Pisces the Fish.

1972. Air. Olympic Games, Munich (2nd issue). Sports and Locations of Games since 1952. As Type **130**.

357	70f. blue, brown and red	1·75	40
358	90f. green, red and blue	35	20
359	140f. olive, green and brown	60	20
360	150f. brown, green and red	65	25
361	170f. blue, brown and purple	75	30
362	210f. blue, red and green	90	40

DESIGNS—VERT: 70f. Boxing, Helsinki Games (1952); 150f. Weightlifting, Tokyo Games (1964). HORIZ: 90f. Hurdling, Melbourne Games (1956); 140f. 200 metres, Rome Games (1960); 170f. Swimming, Mexico Games (1968); 210f. Throwing the javelin, Munich Games (1972).

1972. Medal Winners, Munich Olympic Games. Nos. 318/20 and 362 optd with events and names, etc.

363	150f. blue, brown and green	70	30
364	200f. blue, brown and green	90	40
365	210f. blue, red and green	90	40
366	300f. blue, brown and green	1·25	70

OVERPRINTS: 150f. **JUDO RUSKA 2 MEDAILLES D'OR**; 200f. **STEEPLE KEINO MEDAILLE D'OR**; 210f. **MEDAILLE D'OR 90m. 48**; 300f. **100m. - 200m. BORZOV 2 MEDAILLES D'OR**.

1972. Mali Locomotives (2nd series). As T **106**.

367	10f. blue, green and red	1·60	1·25
368	30f. blue, green and brown	3·25	2·50
369	60f. blue, brown and green	4·00	3·25
370	120f. purple, green and black	6·75	5·25

LOCOMOTIVES: 10f. First Locomotive to arrive at Bamako, 1906; 30f. Steam locomotive, Thies–Bamako line, 1920; 60f. Class 40 steam locomotive, Thies–Bamako line, 1927 (inscr "141");. 120f. Alsthom series BB 100 coupled diesel, Dakar–Bamako line, 1947.

146 Emperor Haile Selassie

1972. Air. 80th Birth Anniv of Emperor Haile Selassie.

371	**146**	70f. multicoloured	30	20

147 Balloon, Breguet 14T Biplane and Map

1972. Air. 1st Mali Airmail Flight by Balloon, Bamako to Timbuktu. Multicoloured.

372	200f. Type **147**	1·00	45
373	300f. Balloon, Concorde and map	1·40	60

148 High Jumping

1973. 2nd African Games, Lagos, Nigeria. Mult.

374	70f. Type **148**	30	20
375	270f. Throwing the discus	1·25	60
376	280f. Football	1·40	65

149 14th-century German Bishop **150** Interpol Headquarters, Paris

1973. Air. World Chess Championship, Reykjavik, Iceland.

377	**149**	100f. lt blue, blue & brown	1·25	35
378	–	200f. red, light red & black	2·50	75

DESIGN: 200f. 18th-century Indian knight (elephant).

1973. 50th Anniv of International Criminal Police Organization (Interpol).

379	**150**	80f. multicoloured	65	20

151 Emblem and Dove with letter **152** "Fauna Protection" Stamp of 1963

1973. 10th Anniv (1971) of African Postal Union.

380	**151**	70f. multicoloured	35	20

1973. Air. Stamp Day.

381	**152**	70f. orange, red and brown	1·10	65

153 Astronauts on Moon **155** Handicapped Africans

154 Copernicus

1973. Moon Mission of "Apollo" 17.

382	**153**	250f. brown and blue	1·75	65

1973. 500th Birth Anniv of Copernicus.

384	**154**	300f. purple and blue	2·25	1·10

1973. "Help the Handicapped".

385	**155**	70f. orange, black and red	35	20

156 Dr. G. A. Hansen

1973. Centenary of Hansen's Identification of the Leprosy Bacillus.

386	**156**	200f. green, black and red	1·60	60

157 Bentley and Alfa Romeo, 1930

1973. 50th Anniv of Le Mans 24-hour Endurance Race.

387	**157**	50f. green, orange and blue	50	15
388	–	100f. green, blue and red	1·00	25
389	–	200f. blue, green and red	2·00	50

DESIGNS: 100f. Jaguar and Talbot, 1953; 200f. Matra and Porsche, 1952.

158 Scouts around Campfire

1973. International Scouting Congress, Addis Ababa and Nairobi.

390	**158**	50f. brown, red and blue	30	15
391	–	70f. brown, red and blue	50	20
392	–	80f. red, brown and green	60	20
393	–	130f. green, blue & brown	85	30
394	–	270f. red, violet and grey	1·75	60

DESIGNS—VERT: 70f. Scouts saluting flag; 130f. Lord Baden-Powell. HORIZ: 80f. Standard-bearers; 270f. Map of Africa and Scouts and Guides in ring.

159 Swimming and National Flags

1973. 1st Afro-American Sports Meeting, Bamako.

395	**159**	70f. green, red and blue	30	20
396	–	80f. green, red and blue	35	25
397	–	330f. blue and red	1·50	70

DESIGNS—VERT: 80f. Throwing the discus and javelin. HORIZ: 330f. Running.

1973. Pan-African Drought Relief. No. 296 surch **SECHERESSE SOLIDARITE AFRICAINE** and value.

398	200f. on 100f. multicoloured	1·10	65

1973. Air. African Fortnight, Brussels. As T **168a** of Niger.

399	70f. violet, blue and brown	30	20

162 "Perseus" (Cellini)

1973. Air. Famous Sculptures.

400	**162**	100f. green and red	55	25
401	–	150f. purple and red	85	35
402	–	250f. green and red	1·50	65

DESIGNS: 150f. "Pieta" (Michelangelo); 250f. "Victory of Samothrace".

163 Stephenson's "Rocket" (1829) and French Buddicom Locomotive

1973. Air. Famous Locomotives.

403	**163**	100f. black, blue & brown	1·50	45
404	–	150f. multicoloured	1·90	50
405	–	200f. blue, slate and brown	3·25	80

DESIGNS: 150f. Union Pacific steam locomotive No. 119 (1890) and Santa Fe Railroad steam locomotive "Blue Goose" (1937), U.S.A.; 200f. "Mistral" express (France) and "Hikari" express train (Japan).

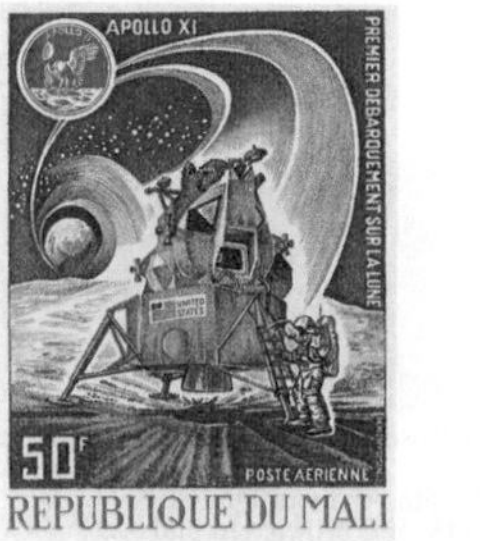

164 "Apollo 11" First Landing

1973. Conquest of the Moon.

406	**164**	50f. purple, red and brown	25	20
407	–	75f. grey, blue and red	30	20
408	–	100f. slate, brown and blue	75	30
409	–	280f. blue, green and red	1·40	65
410	–	300f. blue, red and green	1·75	80

DESIGNS: 75f. "Apollo 13" Recovery capsule; 100f. "Apollo 14" Lunar trolley; 280f. "Apollo 15" Lunar rover; 300f. "Apollo 17" lift off from Moon.

165 Picasso **166** Pres. John Kennedy

1973. Air. Pablo Picasso (artist). Commem.

411	**165**	500f. multicoloured	3·00	1·25

1973. Air. 10th Death Anniv of Pres. Kennedy.

412	**166**	500f. black, purple & gold	2·50	1·25

1973. Air. Christmas. As T **105** but dated "1973". Multicoloured.

413	100f. "The Annunciation" (V. Carpaccio) (horiz.)	50	25
414	200f. "Virgin of St. Simon" (F. Baroccio)	1·25	50
415	250f. "Flight into Egypt" (A. Solario)	1·60	70

167 Player and Football **168** Cora

1973. Air. World Football Cup Championship, West Germany.

416	**167**	150f. red, brown and green	90	35
417	–	250f. green, brown & violet	1·75	60

DESIGN: 250f. Goalkeeper and ball.

1973. Musical Instruments.

419	**168**	5f. brown, red and green	20	10
420	–	10f. brown and blue	25	10
421	–	15f. brown, red and yellow	35	15
422	–	20f. brown and red	40	15
423	–	25f. brown, red and yellow	45	15
424	–	30f. black and blue	60	20
425	–	35f. sepia, brown and red	70	20
426	–	40f. brown and red	75	30

DESIGNS—HORIZ: 10f. Balafon. VERT: 15f. Djembe; 20f. Guitar; 25f. N'Djarka; 30f. M'Bolon; 35f. Dozo N'Goni; 40f. N'Tamani.

169 "Musicians" (mosaic)

1974. Roman Frescoes and Mosaics from Pompeii.
427 **169** 150f. red, brown and grey . . . 75 35
428 – 250f. brown, red & orange . . 1·25 60
429 – 350f. brown, orange and olive . . . . 1·75 75
DESIGNS—VERT: 250f. "Alexander the Great" (mosaic); 350f. "Bacchante" (fresco).

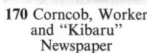

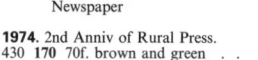

170 Corncob, Worker and "Kibaru" Newspaper
171 Sir Winston Churchill

1974. 2nd Anniv of Rural Press.
430 **170** 70f. brown and green . . 35 20

1974. Air. Birth Cent of Sir Winston Churchill.
431 **171** 500f. black . . . . 2·50 1·50

172 Chess-pieces on Board

1974. Air. 21st Chess Olympiad, Nice.
432 **172** 250f. indigo, red and blue 3·50 75

173 "The Crucifixion" (Alsace School c. 1380)

1974. Air. Easter. Multicoloured.
433 400f. Type **173** . . . . . . 1·60 1·00
434 500f. "The Entombment" (Titian) (horiz) . . . . . . 2·25 1·25

174 Lenin

1974. Air. 50th Death Anniv of Lenin.
435 **174** 150f. purple and violet . . 70 30

175 Goalkeeper and Globe
177 Full-rigged Sailing Ship and Modern Liner

176 Horse-jumping Scenes

1974. World Cup Football Championship, West Germany.
436 **175** 270f. red, green and lilac 1·25 80
437 – 280f. blue, brown and red 1·60 80
DESIGN: 280f. World Cup emblem on football.

1974. Air. World Equestrian Championships, La Baule.
438 **176** 130f. brown, lilac and blue . . . . 1·50 60

1974. Centenary of Universal Postal Union.
439 **177** 80f. purple, lilac & brown 55 25
440 – 90f. orange, grey and blue 40 30
441 – 270f. purple, olive & green . . . . 2·75 1·10
DESIGNS: 90f. Breguet 14T biplane and Douglas DC-8; 270f. Steam and electric mail trains.
See also Nos. 463/4.

178 "Skylab" over Africa

1974. Air. Survey of Africa by "Skylab" Space Station.
442 **178** 200f. indigo, blue & orge 1·00 40
443 – 250f. blue, purple & orge 1·25 60
DESIGN: 250f. Astronaut servicing cameras.

1974. Air. 11th Arab Scout Jamboree, Lebanon. Nos. 391/2 surch **130f. 11e JAMBOREE ARABE AOUT 1974 LIBAN** or **170f. CONGRES PAN-ARABE LIBAN AOUT 1974.**
444 130f. on 70f. brown, red & bl 70 40
445 170f. on 80f. blue, green & red 75 50

1974. Air. 5th Anniv of First Landing on Moon. Nos. 408/9 surch **130f. 1er DEBARQUEMENT SUR LA LUNE 20-VII-69** or **300f. 1er PAS SUR LA LUNE 21-VII-69.**
446 130f. on 100f. slate, brown and blue 70 45
447 300f. on 280f. blue, grn & red 1·40 70

1974. West Germany's Victory in World Cup Football Championship. Nos. 436/7 surch **R.F.A. 2 HOLLANDE 1** and value.
448 **175** 300f. on 270f. red, green and lilac . . . . 1·40 80
449 – 330f. on 280f. blue, brown and red . . . . 1·60 80

182 Weaver
183 River Niger near Gao

1974. Crafts and Craftsmen. Multicoloured.
450 50f. Type **182** 25 15
451 60f. Potter 30 15
452 70f. Smith 40 20
453 80f. Wood-carver 55 20

1974. Mali Views. Multicoloured.
454 10f. Type **183** 15 10
455 20f. "The Hand of Fatma" (rock formation, Hombori) (vert) 15 10
456 40f. Waterfall, Gouina . . . 35 15
457 70f. Hill-dwellings, Dogon (vert) 60 20

184 Class C No. 3 (1906) and Class P (1939) Steam Locomotives, France

1974. Air. Steam Locomotives.
458 **184** 90f. indigo, red and blue 1·25 50
459 – 120f. brown, orange & bl 1·40 60
460 – 210f. brown, orange & bl 2·75 90
461 – 330f. black, green and blue . . . . 4·00 1·90
DESIGNS: 120f. Baldwin (1870) and Pacific (1920) steam locomotives, U.S.A.; 210f. Class A1 (1925) and Buddicom (1847) steam locomotives; 330f. Hudson steam locomotive, 1938 (U.S.A.) and steam locomotive "Gironde", 1839.

185 Skiing

1974. Air. 50th Anniv of Winter Olympics.
462 **185** 300f. red, blue and green 1·40 80

1974. Berne Postal Convention. Cent, Nos. 439 and 441 surch **9 OCTOBRE 1974** and value.
463 **177** 250f. on 80f. purple, lilac and brown . . . . . . 1·40 80
464 – 300f. on 270f. purple, olive and green . . . . 3·00 1·25

187 Mao Tse-tung and Great Wall of China

1974. 25th Anniv of Chinese People's Republic.
465 **187** 100f. blue, red and green 50 30

188 "The Nativity" (Memling)

1974. Air. Christmas. Multicoloured.
466 290f. Type **188** . . . . . . 1·25 70
467 310f. "Virgin and Child" (Bourgogne School) . . . 1·50 75
468 400f. "Adoration of the Magi" (Schongauer) . . . 1·90 1·10

189 Raoul Follereau (missionary)
191 Dr. Schweitzer

190 Electric Train and Boeing 707

1974. Air. Raoul Follereau, "Apostle of the Lepers".
469 **189** 200f. blue . . . . 1·25 55
469a 200f. brown . . . . . . 1·75 1·10

1974. Air. Europafrique.
470 **190** 100f. green, brown & blue 2·75 70
471 110f. blue, violet & brown 3·00 70

1975. Birth Centenary of Dr Albert Schweitzer.
472 **191** 150f. turquoise, green & bl 90 40

192 Patients making Handicrafts and Lions International Emblem

1975. 5th Anniv of Samanko (Leprosy rehabilitation village). Multicoloured.
473 90f. Type **192** 50 20
474 100f. View of Samanko . . . 60 25

193 "The Pilgrims at Emmaus" (Champaigne)

1975. Air. Easter. Multicoloured.
475 200f. Type **193** 90 45
476 300f. "The Pilgrims at Emmaus" (Veronese) . . . 1·25 60
477 500f. "Christ in Majesty" (Limoges enamel) (vert) . . 2·25 1·25

194 "Journey to the Centre of the Earth"

1975. Air. 70th Death Anniv of Jules Verne.
478 **194** 100f. green, blue & brown 45 25
479 – 170f. brown, blue & lt brn 75 35
480 – 190f. blue, turquoise & brn . . . . 1·25 55
481 – 220f. brown, purple & blue . . . . 1·50 60
DESIGNS: 170f. Jules Verne and "From the Earth to the Moon"; 190f. Giant octopus–"Twenty Thousand Leagues Under the Sea"; 220f. "A Floating City".

195 Head of "Dawn" (Tomb of the Medici)

1975. Air. 500th Birth Anniv of Michelangelo (artist). Multicoloured.
482 400f. Type **195** . . . . . . 1·75 1·10
483 500f. "Moses" (marble statue, Rome) . . . . 2·25 1·25

196 Nile Pufferfish

1975. Fishes (1st series).
484 **196** 60f. brown, yellow & grn 80 25
485 – 70f. black, brown and grey 90 35
486 – 80f. multicoloured . . . . 1·10 40
487 – 90f. blue, grey and green 1·60 50
488 – 110f. black and blue . . . 2·25 70
DESIGNS: 70f. Electric catfish; 80f. Deep-sided citharinid; 90f. Lesser tigerfish; 110f. Nile perch.
See also Nos. 544/8.

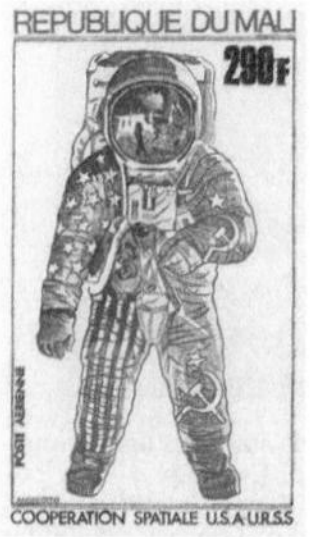

197 Astronaut

199 Woman with Bouquet

198 Einstein and Equation

1975. Air. Soviet–U.S. Space Co-operation.
489 **197** 290f. red, blue and black 1·10 50
490 – 300f. red, blue and black 1·10 60
491 – 370f. green, purple & black . . . . 1·40 80
DESIGNS: 300f. "America and Russia"; 370f. New York and Moscow landmarks.

1975. Air. 20th Death Anniv of Albert Einstein.
492 **198** 90f. blue, purple & brown 55 30
See also Nos. 504, 507 and 519.

1975. International Women's Year.
493 **199** 150f. red and green . . . 70 35

200 Morris "Oxford", 1913

1975. Early Motor-cars.
494 **200** 90f. violet, brown and blue 60 20
495 – 130f. red, grey and blue 95 25
496 – 190f. deep blue, green and blue . . . . 1·40 40
497 – 230f. brown, blue and red 1·75 45
DESIGNS—MOTOR-CARS: 130f. Franklin "E", 1907; 190f. Daimler, 1900; 230f. Panhard & Levassor, 1895.

201

1975. Air. "Nordjamb 75" World Scout Jamboree, Norway.
498 **201** 100f. blue, brown and lake 55 25
499 – 150f. green, brown & blue 75 30
500 – 290f. lake, brown and blue . . . . 1·40 75
DESIGNS: 150f., 290f. Scouts and emblem (different).

202 Lafayette and Battle Scene

1975. Air. Bicentenary of American Revolution. Mult.
501 290f. Type **202** . . . . . . 1·50 65
502 300f. Washington and battle scene . . . . 1·50 65
503 370f. De Grasse and Battle of the Chesapeake, 1781 . . . 1·90 95

1975. 20th Death Anniv of Sir Alexander Fleming (scientist). As T **198**.
504 150f. brown, purple and blue 80 35

204 Olympic Rings

1975. Air. "Pre-Olympic Year".
505 **204** 350f. violet and blue . . . 1·00 65
506 – 400f. blue . . . . 1·10 80
DESIGNS: 400f. Emblem of Montreal Olympics (1976).

1975. Birth Bicentenary of Andre-Marie Ampere. As T **198**.
507 90f. brown, red and violet . . 45 20

205 Tristater of Carthage

1975. Ancient Coins.
508 **205** 130f. black, blue & purple 50 25
509 – 170f. black, green & brn 70 35
510 – 190f. black, green and red 1·00 65
511 – 260f. black, blue & orange 1·75 1·25
COINS: 170f. Decadrachm of Syracuse; 190f. Tetradrachm of Acanthe; 260f. Didrachm of Eretrie.

1975. Air. "Apollo–Soyuz" Space Link. Nos. 489/91 optd **ARRIMAGE 17 Juil. 1975**.
512 **197** 290f. red, blue and black 1·25 65
513 – 300f. red, blue and black 1·25 65
514 – 370f. green, purple & black . . . . 1·50 95

207 U.N. Emblem and Names of Agencies forming "ONU"

1975. 30th Anniv of United Nations Charter.
515 **207** 200f. blue and green . . . 70 45

208 "The Visitation" (Ghirlandaio)

1975. Air. Christmas. Religious Paintings.
516 290f. Type **208** . . . . . . 1·40 55
517 300f. "Nativity" (Fra Filippo Lippi School) . . . . . . 1·40 65
518 370f. "Adoration of the Magi" (Velasquez) . . . . 1·60 1·10

1975. Air. 50th Death Anniv of Clement Ader (aviation pioneer). As T **198**.
519 100f. purple, red and blue . . 55 20

209 Concorde in Flight

1976. Air. Concorde's First Commercial Flight.
520 **209** 500f. multicoloured . . . 3·75 1·50

210 Figure-Skating

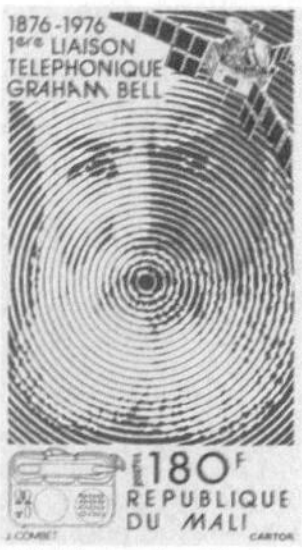

211 Alexander Graham Bell

1976. Air. Winter Olympic Games, Innsbruck. Multicoloured.
521 120f. Type **210** 50 25
522 420f. Ski-jumping . . . . . 1·50 65
523 430f. Skiing (slalom) . . . . 1·50 75

1976. Telephone Centenary.
524 **211** 180f. blue, brown and light brown 65 35

212 Chameleon

1976. Reptiles. Multicoloured.
525 20f. Type **212** 20 15
526 30f. Lizard 30 15
527 40f. Tortoise 35 20
528 90f. Python 75 25
529 120f. Crocodile . . . . . . 1·25 50

213 Nurse and Patient

1976. Air. World Health Day.
530 **213** 130f. multicoloured . . . 55 25

214 Dr. Adenauer and Cologne Cathedral

1976. Birth Centenary Dr. Konrad Adenauer.
531 **214** 180f. purple and brown 90 40

215 Constructing Orbital Space Station

1976. Air. "The Future in Space".
532 **215** 300f. deep blue, blue and orange . . . . 1·25 60
533 – 400f. blue, red and purple 1·90 90
DESIGN: 400f. Sun and space-ship with solar batteries.

216 American Bald Eagle and Liberty Bell

1976. Air. American Revolution Bicentenary and "Interphil '76" Int Stamp Exn, Philadelphia.
534 **216** 100f. blue, purple & black 70 20
535 – 400f. brown, blue & black 2·50 85
536 – 440f. violet, green & black 2·00 85
DESIGNS—HORIZ: 400f. Warships and American bald eagle. VERT: 440f. Red Indians and American bald eagle.

217 Running

1976. Air. Olympic Games, Montreal.
537 **217** 200f. black, brown and red 70 40
538 – 250f. brown, green & blue 80 50
539 – 300f. black, blue and green . . . . 1·25 60
540 – 400f. black, blue and green . . . . 1·60 90
DESIGNS: 250f. Swimming; 300f. Handball; 440f. Football.

218 Scouts marching

1976. Air. 1st All-African Scout Jamboree, Nigeria.
541 **218** 140f. brown, blue & green 70 35
542 – 180f. brown, green & grey 1·00 40
543 – 200f. violet and brown . . 1·10 50
DESIGNS—HORIZ: 180f. Scouts tending calf. VERT: 200f. Scout surveying camp at dusk.

1976. Fishes (2nd series). As T **196**.
544 100f. black and blue 80 25
545 120f. yellow, brown and green 90 35
546 130f. turquoise, brown & black . . . . 1·10 35
547 150f. yellow, drab and green 1·25 45
548 220f. black, green and brown 2·10 80
DESIGNS: 100f. African bonytongue; 120f. Budgett's upsidedown catfish; 130f. Double-dorsal catfish; 150f. Monod's tilapia; 220f. Big-scaled tetra.

220 Scenes from Children's Book

221 "Roi de L'Air"

1976. Literature for Children.
549 **220** 130f. grey, green and red 45 25

1976. 1st Issue of "L'Essor" Newspaper.
550 **221** 120f. multicoloured . . . 1·00 30

222 Fall from Scaffolding

1976. 20th Anniv of National Social Insurance.
551 **222** 120f. multicoloured . . . 35 25

223 Moenjodaro

1976. Air. UNESCO "Save Moenjodaro" (Pakistan) Campaign.
552 **223** 400f. purple, blue & black 1·75 80
553 – 500f. red, yellow and blue 2·00 1·25
DESIGN: 500f. Effigy, animals and remains.

224 Freighter, Vickers Viscount 800 and Map

1976. Air. Europafrique.
554 **224** 200f. purple and blue . . 1·10 45

225 Cascade of Letters

1976. 25th Anniv of U.N. Postal Administration.
555 **225** 120f. orange, green & lilac 45 25

226 Moto Guzzi "254" (Italy)

1976. Motorcycling.
556 **226** 90f. red, grey and brown 45 20
557 – 120f. violet, blue and black 55 25
558 – 130f. red, grey and green 70 25
559 – 140f. blue, green and grey 90 30
DESIGNS: 120f. B.M.W. "900" (Germany); 130f. Honda "Egli" (Japan); 140f. Motobecane "LT3" (France).

227 "The Nativity" (Taddeo Gaddi)

1976. Air. Christmas. Religious Paintings. Mult.
560 280f. Type **227** . . . . . . 1·25 50
561 300f. "Adoration of the Magi" (Hans Memling) . . 1·40 60
562 320f. "The Nativity" (Carlo Crivelli) . . . . 1·50 75

228 Muscat Fishing Boat

1976. Ships.
563 **228** 160f. purple, green & blue 75 30
564 – 180f. green, red and blue 75 35
565 – 190f. purple, blue & green 80 40
566 – 200f. green, red and blue 85 40
DESIGNS: 180f. Cochin Chinese junk; 190f. Dunkirk lightship "Ruytingen"; 200f. Nile felucca.

229 Rocket in Flight

1976. Air. Operation "Viking".
567 **229** 500f. blue, red and lake 1·75 1·25
568 – 1000f. lake, blue and deep blue . . . . 3·00 1·90
DESIGN: 1000f. Spacecraft on Mars.

230 Pres. Giscard d'Estaing and Sankore Mosque, Timbuktu

1977. Air. Visit of Pres. Giscard d'Estaing of France.
570 **230** 430f. multicoloured . . . 2·00 80

231 Rocket on Launch-pad, Newton and Apple

1977. Air. 250th Death Anniv of Isaac Newton.
571 **231** 400f. purple, red and green . . . . 2·00 75

232 Prince Philip and Queen Elizabeth II

1977. Air. "Personalities of Decolonization". Mult.
572 180f. Type **232** 65 35
573 200f. General De Gaulle (vert) . . . . 1·10 50
574 250f. Queen Wilhelmina of the Netherlands (vert) . . . 75 55
575 300f. King Baudouin and Queen Fabiola of Belgium 1·10 70
576 480f. Crowning of Queen Elizabeth II (vert) . . . . 2·00 1·25

233 Lindbergh and "Spirit of St. Louis"

1977. Air. 50th Anniv of Lindbergh's Transatlantic Flight.
577 **233** 420f. orange and violet . . 1·90 85
578 – 430f. blue, orange & green 1·90 85
DESIGN: 430f. "Spirit of St. Louis" crossing the Atlantic.

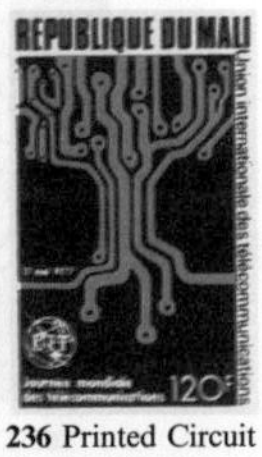

234 Village Indigobird **236** Printed Circuit

235 Louis Braille and Hands reading Book

1977. Mali Birds. Multicoloured.
579 15f. Type **234** 45 10
580 25f. Yellow-breasted barbet 75 10
581 30f. Vitelline masked weaver 75 25
582 40f. Carmine bee eater . . . 1·00 35
583 50f. Senegal parrot . . . . . 1·00 35

1977. 125th Death Anniv of Louis Braille (inventor of "Braille" system of reading and writing for the blind).
584 **235** 200f. blue, red and green 1·10 45

1977. World Telecommunications Day.
585 **236** 120f. red and brown . . . 35 20

236a Chateau Sassenage, Grenoble

1977. Air. 10th Anniv of International French Language Council.
586 **236a** 300f. multicoloured . . . 1·00 50

237 Airship LZ-1 over Lake Constance

1977. Air. History of the Zeppelin.
587 **237** 120f. green, brown & blue 55 25
588 – 130f. deep blue, brown and blue 65 25
589 – 350f. red, blue and deep blue . . . . 1·75 75
590 – 500f. deep blue, green and blue . . . . 2·50 95
DESIGNS: 130f. "Graf Zeppelin" over Atlantic; 350f. Burning of "Hindenburg" at Lakehurst; 500f. Count Ferdinand von Zeppelin and "Graf Zeppelin" at mooring mast.

238 "Anaz imperator"

1977. Insects. Multicoloured.
591 5f. Type **238** 20 15
592 10f. "Sphadromantis viridis" 25 15
593 20f. "Vespa tropica" 25 15
594 35f. "Melolontha melolantha" 30 15
595 60f. Stag beetle 55 20

239 Knight and Rook

1977. Chess Pieces.
596 **239** 120f. black, green & brn 1·10 30
597 – 130f. green, red and black 1·25 30
598 – 300f. green, red and blue 2·75 75
DESIGNS—VERT: 130f. Pawn and Bishop. HORIZ: 300f. King and Queen.

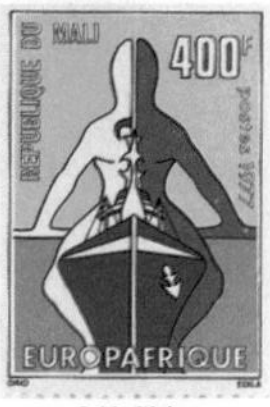

240 Henri Dunant **241** Ship

1977. Air. Nobel Peace Prize Winners. Multicoloured.
599 600f. Type **240** (founder of Red Cross) . . . . 2·00 1·00
600 700f. Martin Luther King . . 2·25 1·10

1977. Europafrique.
601 **241** 400f. multicoloured . . . 1·25 75

242 "Head of Horse"

1977. 525th Birth Anniv of Leonardo da Vinci.
602 **242** 200f. brown and black . . 75 50
603 – 300f. brown . . . . . . 1·10 60
604 – 500f. red . . . . 2·00 85
DESIGNS: 300f. "Head of Young Girl"; 500f. Self-portrait.

243 Footballers **245** Dome of the Rock

244 Friendship Hotel

1977. Air. Football Cup Elimination Rounds.
605 – 180f. brown, green & orge 50 30
606 **243** 200f. brown, green & orge 60 35
607 – 420f. grey, green and lilac 1·25 70
DESIGNS—HORIZ: 180f. Two footballers; 420f. Tackling.

1977. Inauguration of Friendship Hotel, Bamako.
608 **244** 120f. multicoloured . . . 35 25

1977. Palestinian Welfare.
609 **245** 120f. multicoloured . . . 55 20
610 180f. multicoloured . . . 70 30

246 Mao Tse-tung and "Comatex" Hall, Bamako

1977. Air. Mao Tse-tung Memorial.
611 **246** 300f. red . . . . 1·25 50

1977. Air. First Commercial Paris–New York Flight by Concorde. Optd **PARIS NEW - YORK 22.11.77.**
612 **209** 500f. multicoloured . . . 7·00 4·50

248 "Adoration of the Magi" (Rubens)

1977. Air. Christmas. Details from "Adoration of the Magi" by Rubens.
613 **248** 400f. multicoloured . . . 1·25 75
614 – 500f. multicoloured . . . 1·60 95
615 – 600f. multicoloured (horiz) 2·00 1·10

249 "Hercules and the Nemean Lion"

1978. 400th Birth Anniv of Peter Paul Rubens. Multicoloured.
616 200f. "Battle of the Amazons" (horiz) 70 35
617 300f. "Return from Labour in the Fields" (horiz) . . . 1·00 55
618 500f. Type **249** . . . . . . 1·75 95

250 Schubert and Mute Swans

1978. Air. 150th Death Anniv of Franz Schubert (composer). Multicoloured.
619 300f. Schubert and bars of music (vert) . . . . 1·75 60
620 420f. Type **250** . . . . . . 2·00 85

251 Cook and Shipboard Scene

1978. Air. 250th Birth Anniv of Captain James Cook.
621 **251** 200f. blue, red and violet 1·50 40
622 – 300f. brown, blue & green 3·00 70
DESIGN: 300f. Capt. Cook meeting natives.

252 African and Chained Building

1978. World Anti-Apartheid Year.
623 **252** 120f. violet, brown & blue 40 20
624 – 130f. violet, blue & orange 40 20
625 – 180f. brown, pur & orge 60 30
DESIGNS: 130f. Statue of Liberty and Africans walking to open door; 180f. African children and mule in fenced enclosure.

253 Players and Ball

1978. Air. World Cup Football Championship, Argentina.
626 **253** 150f. red, green and brown 60 30
627 – 250f. red, brown and green . . . . 1·25 45
628 – 300f. red, brown and blue 1·50 50
DESIGNS—VERT: 250f. HORIZ: 300f. Different football scenes.

254 "Head of Christ"

1978. Air. Easter. Works by Durer.
630 **254** 420f. green and brown . . 1·60 75
631 – 430f. blue and brown . . 1·60 75
DESIGN: 430f. "The Resurrection".

255 Red-cheeked Cordon-bleu

1978. Birds. Multicoloured.
632 20f. Type **255** 10 10
633 30f. Masked fire finch 45 10
634 50f. Red-billed fire finch . . . 55 20
635 70f. African collared dove . . 1·00 20
636 80f. White-billed buffalo weaver . . . . 1·40 35

256 C-3 "Trefle"

1978. Air. Birth Centenary of Andre Citroen (automobile pioneer).
637 **256** 120f. brown, lake & green 70 20
638 – 130f. grey, orange and blue 85 25
639 – 180f. blue, green and red 1·25 30
640 – 200f. black, red and lake 1·50 40
DESIGNS: 130f. B-2 "Croisiere Noir" track-laying vehicle, 1924; 180f. B-14 G Saloon, 1927; 200f. Model-11 front-wheel drive car, 1934.

1978. 20th Anniv of Bamako Lions Club. Nos. 473/4 surch **XXe ANNIVERSAIRE DU LIONS CLUB DE BAMAKO 1958-1978** and value.
641 120f. on 90f. Type **192** . . . 45 20
642 130f. on 100f. View of Samanko 55 30

258 Names of 1978 U.P.U. members forming Map of the World

1978. Centenary of U.P.U. Foundation Congress, Paris.
643 **258** 120f. green, orange & mve 45 20
644 – 130f. yellow, red and green 45 20
DESIGN: 130f. Names of 1878 member states across globe.

259 Desert Scene

1978. Campaign against Desertification.
645 **259** 200f. multicoloured . . . 70 35

260 Mahatma Gandhi

262 Dominoes

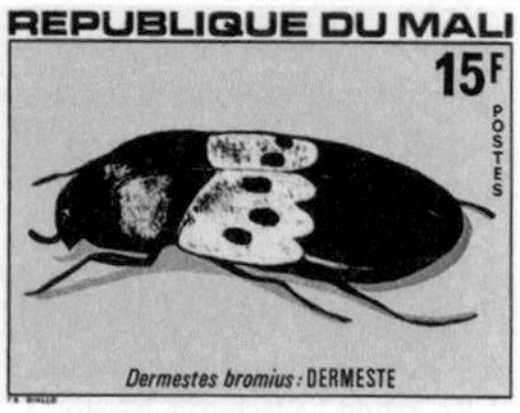

261 "Dermestes bromius"

1978. 30th Anniv of Gandhi's Assassination.
646 **260** 140f. brown, red and black 85 30

1978. Insects. Multicoloured.
647 15f. Type **261** 20 15
648 25f. "Calosoma sp." 25 15
649 90f. "Lopocerus variegatus" 45 20
650 120f. "Coccinella septempunctata" 55 25
651 140f. "Goliathus giganteus" 70 30

1978. Social Games.
652 **262** 100f. black, green and red 40 20
653 – 130f. red, black and blue 85 25
DESIGN: 130f. Bridge hand.

263 Ostrich on Nest (Syrian Manuscript)

1978. Air. Europafrique. Multicoloured.
654 100f. Type **263** 80 25
655 110f. Common zebra (Mansur miniature) 50 30

1978. Air. World Cup Football Championship Finalists. Nos. 626/8 optd with results.
656 **253** 150f. red, green and brown 60 25
657 – 250f. red, brown and green . . . . 1·00 45
658 – 300f. red, brown and blue 1·25 60
OPTS: 150f. **CHAMPION 1978 ARGENTINE**; 250f. **2e HOLLANDE**; 300f. **3e BRESIL 4e ITALIE**.

265 Coronation Coach

1978. Air. 25th Anniv of Coronation of Queen Elizabeth II. Multicoloured.
660 500f. Type **265** . . . . . . 1·50 70
661 1000f. Queen Elizabeth II . . 2·75 1·40

266 Aristotle and African Animals

1978. 2300th Death Anniv of Aristotle (Greek philosopher).
662 **266** 200f. brown, red and green 90 35

267 Douglas DC-3 and U.S.A. 1918 24c. stamp

1978. Air. History of Aviation.
663 **267** 80f. deep blue, red & blue 35 15
664 – 100f. multicoloured . . . 50 20
665 – 120f. black, blue and red 60 25
666 – 130f. green, red and black 65 30
667 – 320f. violet, blue and red 1·50 65
DESIGNS: 100f. Stampe and Renard SV-4 and Belgium Balloon stamp of 1932; 120f. Clement Ader's Avion III and France Concorde stamp of 1976; 130f. Junkers Ju-52/3m and Germany Biplane stamp of 1919; 320f. Mitsubishi A6M Zero-Sen and Japan Pagoda stamp of 1951.

268 "The Annunciation"

1978. Air. Christmas. Works by Durer.
668 **268** 420f. brown and black . . 1·25 60
669 – 430f. brown and green . . 1·25 60
670 – 500f. black and brown . . 1·60 75
DESIGNS: 430f. "Virgin and Child"; 500f. "Adoration of the Magi".

269 Launch of "Apollo 8" and Moon

1978. Air. 10th Anniv of First Manned Flight around the Moon.
671 **269** 200f. red, green and violet 60 30
672 – 300f. violet, green and red 1·10 50
DESIGN: 300f. "Apollo 8" in orbit around the Moon.

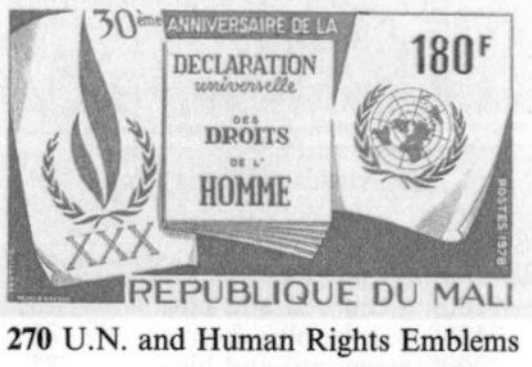

270 U.N. and Human Rights Emblems

1978. 30th Anniv of Declaration of Human Rights.
673 **270** 180f. red, blue and brown 60 35

271 Concorde and Clement Ader's "Eole"

1979. Air. 3rd Anniv of First Commercial Concorde Flight. Multicoloured.
674 120f. Type **271** 70 25
675 130f. Concorde and Wright Flyer I 85 30
676 200f. Concorde and "Spirit of St. Louis" . . . . 1·40 45

1979. Air. "Philexafrique" Stamp Exhibition, Libreville, Gabon (1st issue) and International Stamp Fair, Essen, West Germany. As T **262** of Niger. Multicoloured.
677 200f. Ruff (bird) and Lubeck 1859 ½s. stamp . . . . . . 2·00 90
678 200f. Dromedary and Mali 1965 200f. stamp . . . . . 3·00 1·75
See also Nos. 704/5.

1979. Air. Birth Centenary of Albert Einstein (physicist). No. 492 surch **"1879-1979" 130F**.
679 **198** 130f. on 90f. blue, purple and brown 55 30

273 "Christ carrying the Cross"

1979. Air. Easter. Works by Durer.
680 **273** 400f. black and turquoise 1·40 60
681 – 430f. black and red . . . 1·40 60
682 – 480f. black and blue . . . 1·60 1·00
DESIGNS: 430f. "Christ on the Cross"; 480f. "The Great Lamentation".

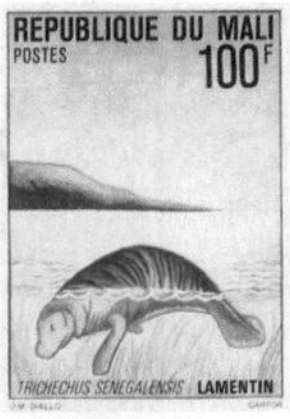

274 Basketball and St. Basil's Cathedral, Moscow **275** African Manatee

1979. Air. Pre-Olympic Year. Multicoloured.
683 420f. Type **274** . . . . . . 1·50 75
684 430f. Footballer and Kremlin 1·50 75

1979. Endangered Animals. Multicoloured.
685 100f. Type **275** 45 20
686 120f. Chimpanzee 65 30
687 130f. Topi 75 35
688 180f. Gemsbok 90 40
689 200f. Giant eland . . . . . 1·00 55

276 Child and I.Y.C. Emblem

1979. International Year of the Child.
690 **276** 120f. green, red and brown 40 20
691 – 200f. purple and green . . 70 35
692 – 300f. brown, mauve and deep brown . . . . . 1·00 50
DESIGNS: 200f. Girl and scout with birds; 300f. Children with calf.

277 Judo

1979. World Judo Championships, Paris.
693 **277** 200f. sepia, red and ochre 80 40

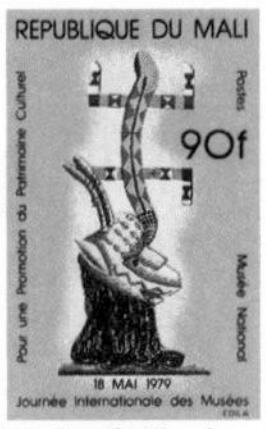

278 Wave Pattern and Human Figures **279** Goat's Head and Lizard Fetishes

1979. World Telecommunications Day.
694 **278** 120f. multicoloured . . . 35 20

1979. World Museums Day. Multicoloured.
695 90f. Type **279** 30 15
696 120f. Seated figures (wood carving) 40 20
697 130f. Two animal heads and figurine (wood carving) . . 50 25

280 Rowland Hill and Mali 1961 25f. stamp **281** Cora Players

1979. Death Centenary of Sir Rowland Hill.
698 **280** 120f. multicoloured . . . 40 20
699 – 130f. red, blue and green 40 20
700 – 180f. black, green and blue 60 30
701 – 200f. black, red and purple 70 35
702 – 300f. blue, deep blue and red . . . . 1·25 50
DESIGNS: 130f. Airship "Graf Zeppelin" and Saxony stamp of 1850; 180f. Concorde and France stamp of 1849; 200f. Stage coach and U.S.A. stamp of 1849; 300f. U.P.U. emblem and Penny Black.

1979.
703 **281** 200f. multicoloured . . . 1·00 40

282 Sankore Mosque and "Adenium obesum"

1979. "Philexafrique" Exhibition, Libreville, Gabon (2nd issue).
704 **282** 120f. multicoloured . . . 90 55
705 – 300f. red, blue and orange 1·90 1·25
DESIGN: 300f. Horseman and satellite.

283 Map of Mali showing Conquest of Desert

1979. Operation "Sahel Vert". Multicoloured.
706 200f. Type **283** 70 30
707 300f. Planting a tree . . . . 1·10 50

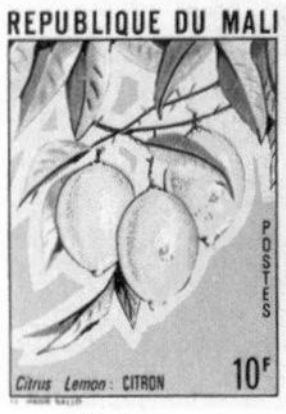

284 Lemons **285** Sigmund Freud

1979. Fruit (1st series). Multicoloured.
708 10f. Type **284** 15 10
709 60f. Pineapple 30 15
710 100f. Papaw 50 15
711 120f. Sweet-sops 55 20
712 130f. Mangoes 65 25
See also Nos. 777/81.

1979. 40th Death Anniv of Sigmund Freud (psychologist).
713 **285** 300f. sepia and violet . . 1·25 60

286 Caillie and Camel approaching Fort

1979. 180th Birth Anniv of Rene Caillie (explorer).
714 **286** 120f. sepia, brown & blue 50 20
715 – 130f. blue, green & brown 60 25
DESIGN: 130f. Rene Caillie and map of route across Sahara.

287 "Eurema brigitta"

1979. Butterflies and Moths (1st series). Mult.
716 100f. Type **287** 60 20
717 120f. "Papilio pylades" . . . 75 20
718 130f. "Melanitis leda satyridae" 90 40
719 180f. "Gonimbrasis belina occidentalis" . . . . 1·50 45
720 200f. "Bunaea alcinoe" . . . 1·75 50
See also Nos. 800/4.

288 Mali 1970 300f. Stamp and Modules orbiting Moon

1979. Air. 10th Anniv of First Moon Landing.
721 430f. Type **288** . . . . . . 1·40 60
722 500f. 1973 250f. stamp and rocket launch . . . . . . 1·60 95

289 Capt. Cook and H.M.S. "Resolution" off Kerguelen Islands

1979. Air. Death Bicent of Captain James Cook.
723 300f. Type **289** . . . . . . 1·75 80
724 400f. Capt. Cook and H.M.S. "Resolution" off Hawaii 2·50 1·10

290 Menaka Greyhound

1979. Dogs. Multicoloured.
725 20f. Type **290** 30 15
726 50f. Water spaniel 45 15
727 70f. Beagle 60 15
728 80f. Newfoundland 70 20
729 90f. Sheepdog 85 20

291 David Janowski

1979. Air. Chess Grand-masters.
730 **291** 100f. red and brown . . . 85 30
731 – 140f. red, brown and blue 1·25 30
732 – 200f. blue, violet and green . . . . 1·75 50
733 – 300f. brown, ochre and red . . . . 2·25 70
DESIGNS: 140f. Alexander Alekhine; 200f. Willi Schlage; 300f. Efim Bogoljubow.

292 "The Adoration of the Magi" 1511 (detail, Durer)

1979. Air. Christmas. Works by Durer.
734 **292** 300f. brown and orange 1·00 50
735 – 400f. brown and blue . . 1·25 75
736 – 500f. brown and green . . 1·60 95
DESIGNS: 400f. "Adoration of the Magi" (1503); 500f. "Adoration of the Magi" (1511, different).

1979. Air. 20th Anniv of ASECNA (African Air Safety Organization). As T **198** of Malagasy but 36 × 27 mm.
737 120f. multicoloured 40 20

293 Globe, Rotary Emblem and Diesel-electric Train

1980. Air. 75th Anniv of Rotary International. Multicoloured.
738 220f. Type **293** . . . . . . 2·75 80
739 250f. Globe, Rotary emblem and Douglas DC-10 airliner . . . . 1·00 45
740 430f. Bamako Rotary Club and emblem . . . . 1·40 75

294 African Ass **295** Speed Skating

1980. Protected Animals. Multicoloured.
741 90f. Type **294** 50 20
742 120f. Addax 60 20
743 130f. Cheetahs 75 35
744 140f. Barbary sheep 80 45
745 180f. African buffalo . . . . 1·00 50

1980. Air. Winter Olympic Games, Lake Placid. Multicoloured.

746	200f. Type **295**	70	30
747	300f. Ski jump	1·10	60

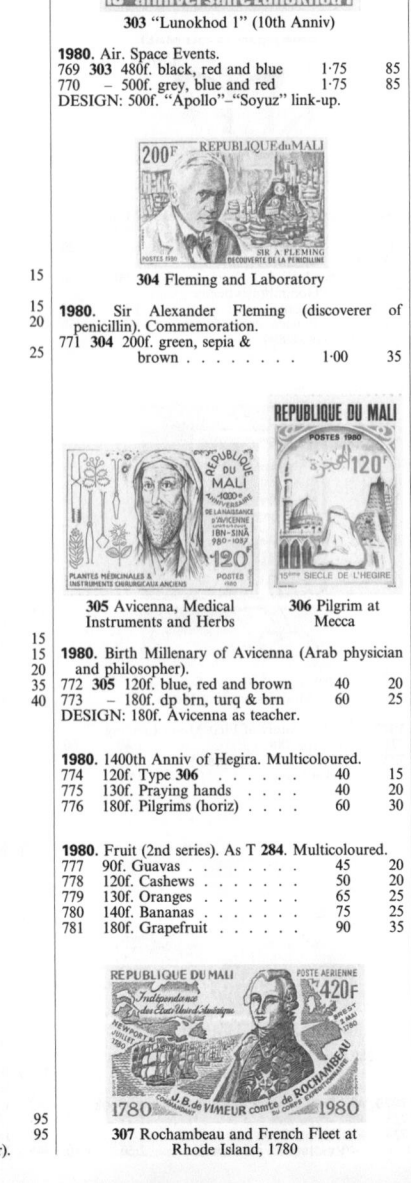

296 Stephenson's "Rocket" (1829) and Mali 30f. Stamp, 1972

1980. Air. 150th Anniv of Liverpool and Manchester Railway.

749 **296**	200f. blue, brown & green	1·25	45
750 –	300f. black, brown & turq	2·00	80

DESIGN: 300f. "Rocket" (1829) and Mali 50f. railway stamp, 1970.

297 Horse Jumping

1980. Air. Olympic Games, Moscow.

751 **297**	200f. green, brown & blue	70	30
752 –	300f. blue, brown & green	1·00	50
753 –	400f. red, green & lt green	1·50	75

DESIGN: 300f. Sailing. 400f. Football.

298 Solar Pumping Station, Koni

1980. Solar Energy. Multicoloured.

755	90f. Type **298**	30	15
756	100f. Solar capture tables, Dire	35	15
757	120f. Solar energy cooker	50	20
758	130f. Solar generating station, Dire	55	25

299 Nioro Horse

1980. Horses. Multicoloured.

759	100f. Mopti	50	15
760	120f. Type **299**	65	15
761	130f. Koro	75	20
762	180f. Lake zone horse	90	35
763	200f. Banamba	1·10	40

300 "Head of Christ" (Maurice Denis)

1980. Air. Easter.

764 **300**	480f. red and brown	1·60	95
765 –	500f. brown and red	1·60	95

DESIGN: 500f. "Christ before Pilate" (Durer).

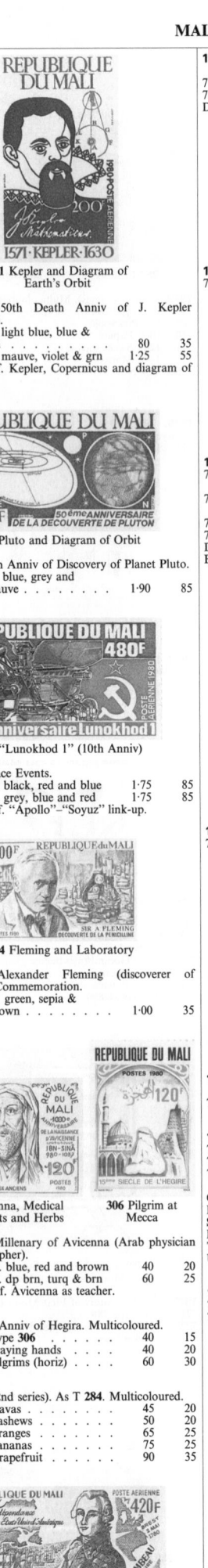

301 Kepler and Diagram of Earth's Orbit

1980. Air. 350th Death Anniv of J. Kepler (astronomer).

766 **301**	200f. light blue, blue & red	80	35
767 –	300f. mauve, violet & grn	1·25	55

DESIGN: 300f. Kepler, Copernicus and diagram of solar system.

302 Pluto and Diagram of Orbit

1980. Air. 50th Anniv of Discovery of Planet Pluto.

768 **302**	402f. blue, grey and mauve	1·90	85

303 "Lunokhod 1" (10th Anniv)

1980. Air. Space Events.

769 **303**	480f. black, red and blue	1·75	85
770 –	500f. grey, blue and red	1·75	85

DESIGN: 500f. "Apollo"–"Soyuz" link-up.

304 Fleming and Laboratory

1980. Sir Alexander Fleming (discoverer of penicillin). Commemoration.

771 **304**	200f. green, sepia & brown	1·00	35

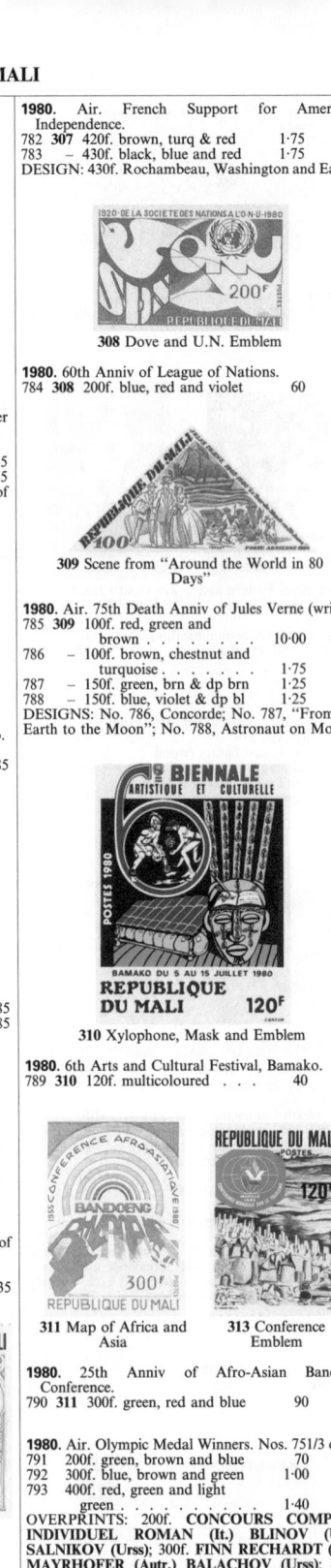

305 Avicenna, Medical Instruments and Herbs

306 Pilgrim at Mecca

1980. Birth Millenary of Avicenna (Arab physician and philosopher).

772 **305**	120f. blue, red and brown	40	20
773 –	180f. dp brn, turq & brn	60	25

DESIGN: 180f. Avicenna as teacher.

1980. 1400th Anniv of Hegira. Multicoloured.

774	120f. Type **306**	40	15
775	130f. Praying hands	40	20
776	180f. Pilgrims (horiz)	60	30

1980. Fruit (2nd series). As T **284**. Multicoloured.

777	90f. Guavas	45	20
778	120f. Cashews	50	20
779	130f. Oranges	65	25
780	140f. Bananas	75	25
781	180f. Grapefruit	90	35

307 Rochambeau and French Fleet at Rhode Island, 1780

1980. Air. French Support for American Independence.

782 **307**	420f. brown, turq & red	1·75	75
783 –	430f. black, blue and red	1·75	80

DESIGN: 430f. Rochambeau, Washington and Eagle.

308 Dove and U.N. Emblem

1980. 60th Anniv of League of Nations.

784 **308**	200f. blue, red and violet	60	35

309 Scene from "Around the World in 80 Days"

1980. Air. 75th Death Anniv of Jules Verne (writer).

785 **309**	100f. red, green and brown	10·00	2·75
786 –	100f. brown, chestnut and turquoise	1·75	30
787 –	150f. green, brn & dp brn	1·25	40
788 –	150f. blue, violet & dp bl	1·25	40

DESIGNS: No. 786, Concorde; No. 787, "From the Earth to the Moon"; No. 788, Astronaut on Moon.

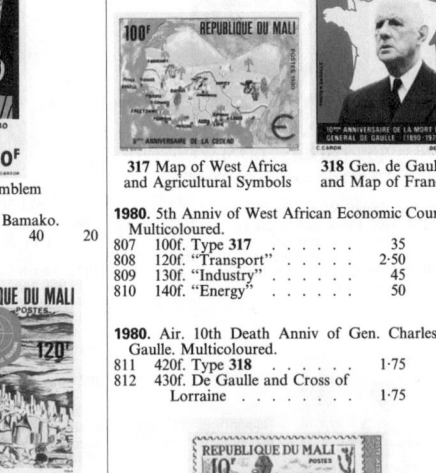

310 Xylophone, Mask and Emblem

1980. 6th Arts and Cultural Festival, Bamako.

789 **310**	120f. multicoloured	40	20

311 Map of Africa and Asia

313 Conference Emblem

1980. 25th Anniv of Afro-Asian Bandung Conference.

790 **311**	300f. green, red and blue	90	55

1980. Air. Olympic Medal Winners. Nos. 751/3 optd.

791	200f. green, brown and blue	70	35
792	300f. blue, brown and green	1·00	55
793	400f. red, green and light green	1·40	75

OVERPRINTS: 200f. **CONCOURS COMPLET INDIVIDUEL ROMAN (It.) BLINOV (Urss) SALNIKOV (Urss)**; 300f. **FINN RECHARDT (Fin.) MAYRHOFER (Autr.) BALACHOV (Urss)**; 400f. **TCHECOSLOVAQUIE ALLEMAGNE DE L'EST URSS**.

1980. World Tourism Conference, Manila. Mult.

795	120f. Type **313**	35	15
796	180f. Encampment outside fort and Conference emblem	50	30

314 Dam and Rural Scene

1980. 20th Anniv of Independence. Multicoloured.

797	100f. Type **314**	40	15
798	120f. National Assembly Building	40	20
799	130f. Independence Monument (vert)	45	25

1980. Butterflies. (2nd series). As T **287** but dated "1980". Multicoloured.

800	50f. "Uterheisa pulchella" (postage)	40	20
801	60f. "Mylothis chloris pieridae"	50	20
802	70f. "Hypolimnas mishippus"	60	20
803	80f. "Papilio demodocus"	75	20
804	420f. "Denaus chrysippus" (48 × 36 mm) (air)	2·50	1·25

315 Pistol firing Cigarette and Target over Lungs

1980. Anti-smoking Campaign.

805 **315**	200f. multicoloured	75	35

316 Electric Train, Boeing 737 and Globe

1980. Europafrique.

806 **316**	300f. multicoloured	3·75	85

317 Map of West Africa and Agricultural Symbols

318 Gen. de Gaulle and Map of France

1980. 5th Anniv of West African Economic Council. Multicoloured.

807	100f. Type **317**	35	15
808	120f. "Transport"	2·50	85
809	130f. "Industry"	45	25
810	140f. "Energy"	50	25

1980. Air. 10th Death Anniv of Gen. Charles de Gaulle. Multicoloured.

811	420f. Type **318**	1·75	75
812	430f. De Gaulle and Cross of Lorraine	1·75	75

319 "Hikari" Express Train (Japan) and Mali 1972 10f. Stamp

1980. Air. Locomotives.

813 **319**	120f. blue, green and red	95	20
814 –	130f. green, blue and red	1·25	25
815 –	200f. orange, black & grn	1·60	40
816 –	480f. black, red and green	4·25	95

DESIGNS—HORIZ: 130f. RTG train, U.S.A. and 20f. locomotive stamp of 1970; 200f. "Rembrandt" express, Germany, and 100f. locomotive stamp of 1970. VERT: 480f. TGV 001 turbotrain, France, and 80f. locomotive stamp of 1970.

320 "Flight into Egypt" (Rembrandt)

1980. Air. Christmas. Multicoloured.
817 300f. "St. Joseph showing the infant Jesus to St. Catherine" (Lorenzo Lotto) (horiz) . . . . . . 1·00 55
818 400f. Type **320** . . . . . . 1·40 80
819 500f. "Christmas Night" (Gauguin) (horiz) . . . . 1·60 90

1980. 5th Anniv of African Posts and Telecommunications Union. As T **292** of Niger.
820 130f. multicoloured 40 20

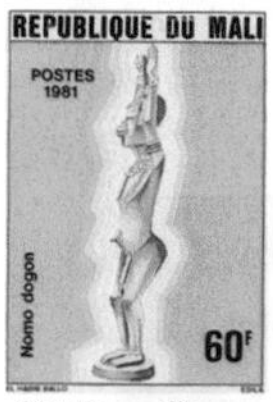

321 Nomo Dogon

323 Mambie Sidibe

322 "Self-portrait" (Blue Period)

1981. Statuettes. Multicoloured.
821 60f. Type **321** 20 15
822 70f. Senoufo fertility symbol 25 15
823 90f. Bamanan fertility statuette 35 15
824 100f. Senoufo captives snuff-box 40 15
825 120f. Dogon fertility statuette 50 20

1981. Birth Bicentenary of Pablo Picasso (artist).
826 **322** 1000f. multicoloured . . . 3·50 1·75

1981. Mali Thinkers and Savants.
827 **323** 120f. brown, buff and red 40 20
828 – 130f. brown, buff & black 40 25
DESIGN: 130f. Amadou Hampate Ba.

324 Mosque and Ka'aba **325** Tackle

1981. 1400th Anniv of Hejira.
829 **324** 120f. multicoloured . . . 40 20
830 180f. multicoloured . . . 60 30

1981. Air. World Cup Football Championship Eliminators. Multicoloured.
831 100f. Type **325** 40 20
832 200f. Heading the ball . . . 85 35
833 300f. Running for ball . . . 1·40 50

326 Kaarta Zebu **327** Crinum de Moore "Crinum moorei"

1981. Cattle. Multicoloured.
835 20f. Type **326** 15 15
836 30f. Peul du Macina sebu . . 15 15
837 40f. Maure zebu 25 15
838 80f. Touareg zebu 50 15
839 100f. N'Dama cow 60 20

1981. Flowers. Multicoloured.
840 50f. Type **327** 30 15
841 100f. Double rose hibiscus "Hibiscus rosa-sinensis" . . 80 15
842 120f. Pervenche "Catharanthus roseus" . . 90 20
843 130f. Frangipani "Plumeria rubra" 90 25
844 180f. Orgueil de Chine "Caesalpinia pulcherrima" 1·40 40

328 Mozart and Musical Instruments

1981. Air. 225th Birth Anniv of Mozart. Mult.
845 420f. Type **328** . . . . . . 2·00 85
846 430f. Mozart and musical instruments (different) . . 2·00 85

329 "The Fall on the Way to Calvary" (Raphael)

1981. Air. Easter.
847 500f. Type **329** . . . . . . 1·50 85
848 600f. "Ecce Homo" (Rembrandt) . . . . . . 2·00 1·25

330 Yuri Gagarin

1981. Air. Space Anniversaries and Events.
849 **330** 200f. blue, black and red 85 30
850 – 200f. blue, black & lt blue 85 30
851 – 380f. multicoloured . . . 1·40 55
852 – 430f. violet, black and blue . . . . 1·60 70
DESIGNS—VERT: No. 849, Type **330**: first man in space (20th anniv); No. 850, Alan Shepard, first American in space (20th anniv); No. 851, Saturn and moons (exploration of Saturn). HORIZ: No. 852, Sir William Herschel, and diagram of Uranus (discovery bicentenary).

331 Blind and Sighted Faces **332** Caduceus (Telecommunications and Health)

1981. International Year of Disabled People.
853 **331** 100f. light brown, brown and green 35 15
854 – 120f. violet, blue and purple 45 20
DESIGN: 120f. Mechanical hand and human hand with spanner.

1981. World Telecommunications Day.
855 **332** 130f. multicoloured . . . 40 25

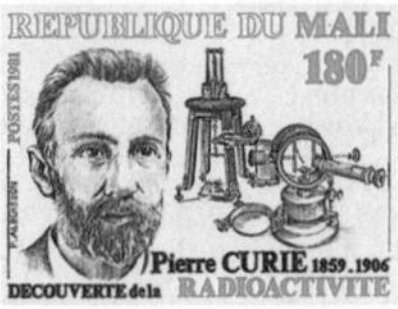

333 Pierre Curie and Instruments

1981. 75th Death Anniv of Pierre Curie (discoverer of radioactivity).
856 **333** 180f. blue, black & orange 90 30

334 Scouts at Well and Dorcas Gazelle

1981. 4th African Scouting Conference, Abidjan. Multicoloured.
857 110f. Type **334** 70 30
858 160f. Scouts signalling and patas monkey . . . . . . 1·25 60
859 300f. Scouts saluting and cheetah (vert) . . . . . . 1·75 85

1981. Air. World Railway Speed Record. No. 816 optd **26 fevrier 1981 Record du monde de vitesse–380 km/h.**
861 480f. black, red and blue . . 3·00 90

336 Columbus, Fleet and U.S. Columbus Stamp of 1892

1981. Air. 475th Death Anniv of Christopher Columbus.
862 **336** 180f. brown, black & blue 90 40
863 – 200f. green, blue & brown 1·10 40
864 – 260f. black, violet and red 1·60 60
865 – 300f. lilac, red and green 1·75 70
DESIGNS—VERT: 200f. "Nina" and 1c. Columbus stamp of Spain; 260f. "Pinta" and 5c. Columbus stamp of Spain. HORIZ: 300f. "Santa Maria" and U.S. 3c. Columbus stamp.

1981. 23rd World Scouting Conference, Dakar. Nos. 857/9 optd **DAKAR 8 AOUT 1981 28e CONFERENCE MONDIALE DU SCOUTISME.**
866 **334** 110f. multicoloured . . . 40 20
867 – 160f. multicoloured . . . 50 30
868 – 300f. multicoloured . . . 1·25 55

338 Space Shuttle after Launching

1981. Air. Space Shuttle. Multicoloured.
870 200f. Type **338** 90 30
871 500f. Space Shuttle in orbit 2·25 75
872 600f. Space Shuttle landing 2·50 1·25

339 "Harlequin on a Horse"

1981. Air. Birth Centenary of Pablo Picasso. Mult.
874 600f. Type **339** . . . . . . 2·75 1·25
875 750f. "Child with Pigeon" . . 3·25 1·40

340 Prince Charles, Lady Diana Spencer and St. Paul's Cathedral

1981. Air. British Royal Wedding. Multicoloured.
876 500f. Type **340** . . . . . . 1·25 75
877 700f. Prince Charles, Lady Diana Spencer and coach 1·75 1·10

342 Maure Sheep

1981. Sheep. Multicoloured.
886 10f. Type **342** 15 10
887 25f. Peul sheep 20 10
888 140f. Sahael sheep 50 25
889 180f. Touareg sheep 75 35
890 200f. Djallonke ram 85 35

343 Heinrich von Stephan (founder of U.P.U.), Latecoere 28 and Concorde

1981. Universal Postal Union Day.
891 **343** 400f. red and green . . . 1·60 70

344 Woman drinking from Bowl

1981. World Food Day.
892 **344** 200f. brown, orge & mve 65 30

345 "The Incarnation of the Son of God" (detail, Grunewald)

1981. Air. Christmas. Multicoloured.
893 500f. Type **345** . . . . . . 1·75 75
894 700f. "The Campori Madonna" (Correggio) . . 2·25 1·25

347 Transport and Hands holding Map of Europe and Africa

1981. Europafrique.
896 **347** 700f. blue, brown & orge 4·75 1·40

348 Guerin, Calmette, Syringe and Bacillus

1981. 60th Anniv of First B.C.G. Inoculation.
897 **348** 200f. brown, violet & blk 85 40

1982. Air. World Chess Championship, Merano. Nos. 731 and 733 optd.
898 140f. red, brown and blue . . 1·25 50
899 300f. brown, ochre and red 2·25 75
OPTS: 140f. **ANATOLI KARPOV VICTOR KORTCHNOI MERANO (ITALIE) Octobre-Novembre 1981**; 300f. **Octobre-Novembre 1981 ANATOLI KARPOV Champion du Monde 1981.**

350 "Nymphaea lotus"

1982. Flowers. Multicoloured.

900	170f. Type **350**	85	35
901	180f. "Bombax costatum"	90	35
902	200f. "Parkia biglobosa"	1·00	40
903	220f. "Gloriosa simplex"	1·25	45
904	270f. "Satanocrater berhautii"	1·40	50

351 Lewis Carroll and Characters from "Alice" Books

1982. Air. 150th Birth Anniv of Lewis Carroll (Revd. Charles Dodgson).

905	110f. Type **351**	1·00	25
906	130f. Characters from "Alice" books	75	30
907	140f. Characters from "Alice" books (different)	90	30

352 "George Washington" (Gilbert Stuart)

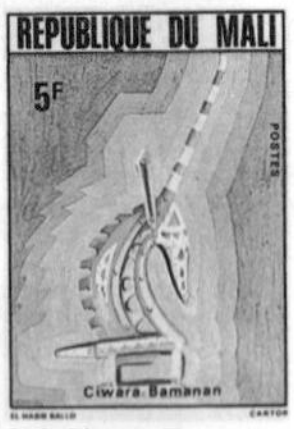

353 Ciwara Bamanan

1982. Air. 250th Birth Anniv of George Washington.

908 **352**	700f. multicoloured	2·00	1·25

1982. Masks. Multicoloured.

909	5f. Type **353**	10	10
910	35f. Kanga Dogon	15	10
911	180f. N Domo Bamanan	1·00	40
912	200f. Cimier (Sogoninkum Bamanan)	1·00	40
913	250f. Kpelie Senoufo	1·10	45

354 Football

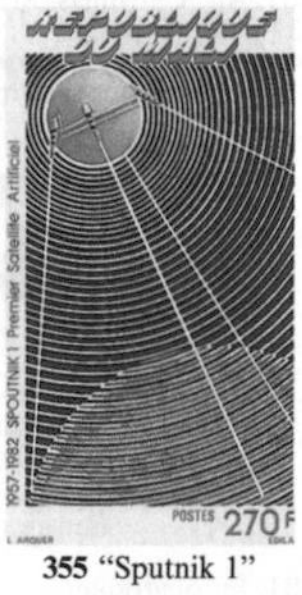

355 "Sputnik 1"

1982. Air. World Cup Football Championship, Spain.

914 **354**	220f. multicoloured	80	45
915 –	420f. multicoloured	1·50	90
916 –	500f. multicoloured	1·75	90

DESIGNS: 420f., 500f. Football scenes.

1982. 25th Anniv of First Artificial Satellite.

918 **355**	270f. violet, blue and red	1·25	50

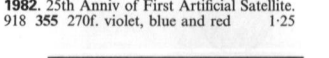

356 Lord Baden-Powell, Tent and Scout Badge

1982. Air. 125th Birth Anniv of Lord Baden-Powell.

919	300f. Type **356**	1·50	50
920	500f. Saluting scout	2·25	90

357 "The Transfiguration" (Fra Angelico)

1982. Air. Easter. Multicoloured.

921	680f. Type **357**	2·00	1·25
922	1000f. "Pieta" (Giovanni Bellini)	3·00	1·90

358 Doctor giving Child Oral Vaccine

360 "En Bon Ami" (N'Teri)

359 Lions Emblem and Blind Person

1982. Anti-polio Campaign.

923 **358**	180f. multicoloured	80	35

1982. Lions Club Blind Day.

924 **359**	260f. orange, blue and red	1·25	50

1982. Hairstyles. Multicoloured.

925	140f. Type **360**	35	30
926	150f. Tucked-in pony tail	60	35
927	160f. "Pour l'Art"	70	45
928	180f. "Bozo Kun"	75	50
929	270f. "Fulaw Kun"	1·25	60

361 Arms Stamp of Mali and France

1982. Air. "Philexfrance 82" International Stamp Exhibition, Paris. Multicoloured.

930	180f. Type **361**	60	35
931	200f. Dromedary caravan and 1979 "Philexafrique II" stamp	1·00	40

362 Fire-engine, 1850

1982. Fire-engines. Multicoloured.

932	180f. Type **362**	95	35
933	200f. Fire-engine, 1921	1·40	40
934	270f. Fire-engine, 1982	1·60	50

363 Gobra

1982. Zebu Cattle. Multicoloured.

935	10f. Type **363**	10	10
936	60f. Azaouak	25	15
937	110f. Maure	35	25
938	180f. Toronke	65	35
939	200f. Peul Sambourou	75	40

1982. Air. World Cup Football Championship Winners. Nos. 914/16 optd.

940 **354**	220f. multicoloured	75	45
941 –	420f. multicoloured	1·50	90
942 –	500f. multicoloured	1·75	90

OPTS: 220f. **1 ITALIE 2 RFA 3 POLOGNE**; 420f. **POLOGNE FRANCE 3-2**; 500f. **ITALIE RFA 3-1**.

365 "Urchin with Cherries"

1982. Air. 150th Birth Anniv of Edouard Manet (painter).

944 **365**	680f. multicoloured	2·75	1·25

366 "Virgin and Child" (detail) (Titian)

1982. Air. Christmas. Multicoloured.

945	500f. Type **366**	1·50	90
946	1000f. "Virgin and Child" (Giovanni Bellini)	2·75	1·90

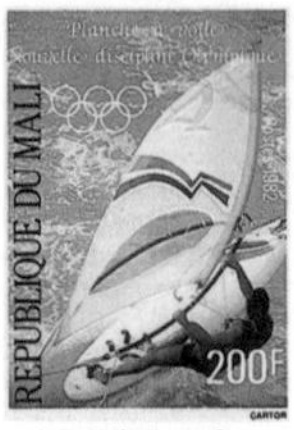

367 Wind-surfing

368 Goethe

1982. Introduction of Wind-surfing as Olympic Event. Multicoloured.

947	200f. Type **367**	80	45
948	270f. Wind-surfer	1·25	55
949	300f. Wind-surfer (different)	1·40	55

1982. Air. 150th Death Anniv of Goethe (poet).

950 **368**	500f. brown, light brown and black	2·00	90

369 Valentina Tereshkova

370 Transatlantic Balloon "Double Eagle II"

1983. Air. 20th Anniv of Launching of Vostok VI.

951 **369**	400f. multicoloured	1·25	75

1983. Air. Bicentenary of Manned Flight. Mult.

952	500f. Type **370**	2·00	90
953	700f. Montgolfier balloon	2·50	1·25

371 Football

1983. Air. Olympic Games, Los Angeles. Mult.

954	180f. Type **371**	50	30
955	270f. Hurdles	75	40
956	300f. Windsurfing	1·10	55

372 "The Transfiguration" (detail)

1983. Air. Easter. Multicoloured.

957	400f. Type **372**	1·25	75
958	600f. "The Entombment" (detail from Baglioni Retable)	2·00	1·10

373 Martin Luther King

374 Oua Hairstyle

1983. Celebrities.

959 **373**	800f. brown, blue & pur	2·50	1·40
960 –	800f. brown, red & dp red	3·00	1·25

DESIGN: No. 960, President Kennedy.

1983. Hairstyles. Multicoloured.

961	180f. Type **374**	60	30
962	200f. Nation (Diamani)	70	30
963	270f. Rond Point	90	40
964	300f. Naamu-Naamu	1·00	45
965	500f. Bamba-Bamba	2·50	1·40

375 "Family of Acrobats with Monkey"

1983. Air. 10th Death Anniv of Picasso.

966 **375**	680f. multicoloured	2·00	1·25

376 Lions Club Emblem and Lions

1983. Air. Lions and Rotary Clubs. Mult.

967	700f. Type **376**	2·25	2·00
968	700f. Rotary Club emblem, container ship, diesel railcar and Boeing 737 airliner	6·75	2·25

377 Satellite, Antenna and Telephone

1983. World Communications Year.
969 **377** 180f. multicoloured . . . 55 30

378 Lavoisier and Apparatus
379 Banzoumana Sissoko

1983. Bicent of Lavoisier's Analysis of Water.
970 **378** 300f. green, brown & blue 1·10 50

1983. Mali Musicians. Multicoloured.
971 200f. Type **379** . . . . . . 1·00 30
972 300f. Batourou Sekou Kouyate . . . . 1·50 45

380 Nicephore Niepce and Camera
381 Space Shuttle "Challenger"

1983. 150th Death Anniv of Nicephore Niepce (pioneer of photography).
973 **380** 400f. blue, green & dp grn 1·75 65

1983. Air. Space Shuttle.
974 **381** 1000f. multicoloured . . . 3·25 1·75

382 Young People and Map of Africa

1983. 2nd Pan-African Youth Festival. Mult.
975 240f. Type **382** 75 40
976 270f. Hands reaching for map of Africa 75 40

383 Mercedes, 1914

1983. Air. Paris–Dakar Rally. Multicoloured.
977 240f. Type **383** . . . . . . 1·40 40
978 270f. Mercedes SSK, 1929 . . 1·50 50
979 500f. Mercedes W 196, 1954 2·50 80

384 Liner and U.P.U. Emblem
385 Pawn and Bishop

1983. U.P.U. Day.
981 **384** 240f. red, black and blue 1·50 50

1983. Air. Chess Pieces.
982 **385** 300f. grey, violet and green . . . . 2·00 60
983 – 420f. green, pink and grey 2·50 85
984 – 500f. blue, dp blue & green . . . . 3·25 1·00
DESIGNS: 420f. Rook and knight; 500f. King and queen.

386 "Canigiani Madonna"

1983. Air. Christmas. 500th Birth Anniv of Raphael. Multicoloured.
986 700f. Type **386** . . . . . . 2·00 1·00
987 800f. "Madonna of the Lamb" . . . . 2·25 1·25

387 Sahara Goat

1984. Goats. Multicoloured.
988 20f. Type **387** 15 10
989 30f. Billy goat 20 10
990 50f. Billy goat (different) . . 25 15
991 240f. Kaarta goat . . . . . 1·00 40
992 350f. Southern goat . . . . 1·40 75

388 "Leopold Zborowski" (Modigliani)

1984. Air. Birth Centenary of Modigliani (painter).
993 **388** 700f. multicoloured . . . 2·75 1·25

389 Henri Dunant (founder of Red Cross)
390 Sidney Bechet

1984. Air. Celebrities.
994 **389** 400f. deep blue, red & blue . . . . 1·50 65
995 – 540f. deep blue, red & blue . . . . 1·60 85
DESIGN: 540f. Abraham Lincoln.

1984. Air. Jazz Musicians. Multicoloured.
996 470f. Type **390** . . . . . . 2·50 75
997 500f. Duke Ellington . . . . 2·50 80

391 Microlight Aircraft

1984. Air. Microlight Aircraft. Multicoloured.
998 270f. Type **391** . . . . . . 1·10 40
999 350f. Lazor Gemini motorized hang-glider . . . 1·40 55

392 Weightlifting

1984. Air. Olympic Games, Los Angeles. Multicoloured.
1000 265f. Type **392** 75 40
1001 440f. Show jumping 90 70
1002 500f. Hurdles . . . . 1·10 80

393 "Crucifixion" (Rubens)

1984. Air. Easter.
1004 **393** 940f. brown & dp brown 3·00 1·50
1005 – 970f. brown and red . . 3·00 1·50
DESIGN—HORIZ: 970f. "The Resurrection" (Mantegna).

1984. Currency revaluation. Various stamps surch. (i) U.P.U. Day (No. 981).
1006 **384** 120f. on 240f. red, black and blue (postage) . . 1·10 50
(ii) Goats (Nos. 988/92)
1007 **387** 10f. on 20f. mult 10 10
1008 – 15f. on 30f. mult 15 10
1009 – 25f. on 50f. mult 20 15
1010 – 125f. on 240f. mult . . . 95 40
1011 – 175f. on 350f. mult . . . 1·75 65
(iii) Paris–Dakar Rally (No. 977)
1012 **383** 120f. on 240f. mult (air) 1·25 40

395 Mercedes "Simplex"

1984. Air. 150th Birth Anniv of Gottlieb Daimler (motor car designer).
1035 **395** 350f. olive, blue and mauve . . . . 2·50 1·10
1036 – 470f. green, violet and plum . . . . 3·25 1·50
1037 – 485f. blue, violet and plum . . . . 3·50 1·75
DESIGNS: 470f. Mercedes-Benz Type "370 S"; 485f. Mercedes-Benz "500 S EC".

396 Farm Workers

1984. Progress in Countryside and Protected Essences. Multicoloured.
1038 5f. Type **396** 10 10
1039 90f. Carpentry 60 30
1040 100f. Tapestry making . . . 70 35
1041 135f. Metal work 80 40
1042 515f. "Borassus flabelifer" 3·25 1·90
1043 1225f. "Vitelaria paradoxa" 7·50 3·75

397 Emblem and Child

1984. United Nations Children's Fund.
1044 **397** 120f. red, brown and green 80 40
1045 – 135f. red, blue and brown 90 50
DESIGN: 135f. Emblem and two children.

398 U.P.U. Emblem, Anchor and Hamburg

1984. Universal Postal Union Congress, Hamburg.
1046 **398** 135f. mauve, green and blue 80 40

1984. Air. Olympic Winners, Los Angeles. No. 1000/1002 optd.
1047 135f. on 265f. Optd **HALTERES 56 KGS / 1. WU (CHINE). 2. LAI (CHINE). 3. KOTAKA (JAPON)** 80 40
1048 220f. on 440f. Optd **DRESSAGE / PAR EQUIPES / 1. RFA 2. SUISSE / 3. SUEDE** . . 1·10 75
1049 250f. on 500f. Optd **ATHLETISME 3000 METRES STEEPLE / 1. KORIR (KENYA). / 2. MAHMOUD (FRANCE). / 3. DIEMER (E-U)** . . 1·40 1·00

400 Emblem

1984. 10th Anniv of Economic Community of West Africa.
1051 **400** 350f. multicoloured . . . 1·75 1·10

401 Dimetrodon

1984. Prehistoric Animals. Multicoloured.
1052 10f. Type **401** 15 15
1053 25f. Iguanodon (vert) . . . 25 15
1054 30f. Archaeopteryx (vert) . . 35 10
1055 120f. Type **401** . . . . . . 1·50 45
1056 175f. As No. 1053 . . . . . 1·75 70
1057 350f. As No. 1054 . . . . . 3·25 95
1058 470f. Triceratops . . . . . 5·00 2·50

402 "Virgin and Child between St. Joseph and St. Jerome" (detail, Lorenzo Lotto)

1984. Air. Christmas.
1059 **402** 500f. multicoloured . . . 3·00 1·60

1984. Drought Aid. No. 758 surch.
1060 **298** 470f. on 130f. mult . . . 2·75 1·75

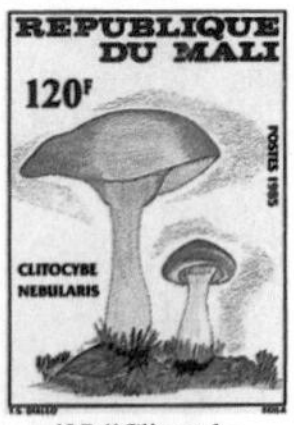

404 Horse Galloping
405 "Clitocybe nebularis"

1985. Horses. Multicoloured.
1061 90f. Type **404** 70 35
1062 135f. Beledougou horse . . 1·25 40
1063 190f. Nara horse . . . . . 1·50 70
1064 530f. Trait horse . . . . . 4·50 2·00

1985. Fungi. Multicoloured.
1065 120f. Type **405** . . . . . . 1·75 65
1066 200f. "Lepiota cortinarius" 2·40 1·00
1067 485f. "Agaricus semotus" 6·00 2·40
1068 525f. "Lepiota procera" . . 6·50 2·75

406 Emile Marchoux and Marchoux Institute

1985. Health. Multicoloured.
1069 120f. Type **406** (World Lepers' Day and 40th anniv of Marchoux Institute) (postage) . . . 80 30
1070 135f. Lions' emblem and Samanto Village (15th anniv) 85 35
1071 470f. Laboratory technicians and polio victim (anti-polio campaign) (air) . . 3·50 1·50

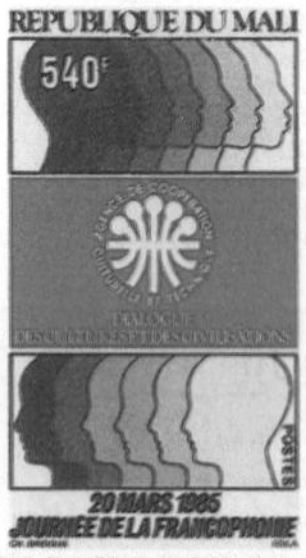

407 Profiles and Emblem

1985. 15th Anniv of Technical and Cultural Co-operation Agency.
1072 **407** 540f. green and brown 3·50 1·90

408 River Kingfisher

1985. Air. Birth Bicentenary of John J. Audubon (ornithologist). Multicoloured.
1073 180f. Type **408** . . . . . . 1·50 55
1074 300f. Great bustard (vert) 2·50 90
1075 470f. Ostrich (vert) . . . . 4·25 1·50
1076 540f. Ruppell's griffon . . . 4·50 2·00

409 National Pioneers Movement Emblem

1985. International Youth Year. Multicoloured.
1077 120f. Type **409** 80 40
1078 190f. Boy leading oxen . . . 1·40 70
1079 500f. Sports motifs and I.Y.Y. emblem . . . . . 3·50 1·75

410 Sud Aviation Caravelle, Boeing 727-200 and Agency Emblem

1985. Air. 25th Anniv of Aerial Navigation Security Agency for Africa and Madagascar (ASECNA).
1080 **410** 700f. multicoloured . . . 4·50 2·50

411 Lion, and Scouts collecting Wood

1985. Air. "Philexafrique" Stamp Exhibition, Lome. Multicoloured.
1081 200f. Type **411** . . . . . . 1·75 1·25
1082 200f. Satellite, dish aerial and globe . . . . 1·75 1·25

412 U.P.U. Emblem, Computer and Reservoir (Development)

1985. "Philexafrique" Stamp Exhibition, Lome, Togo (2nd issue). Multicoloured.
1083 250f. Type **412** . . . . . . 1·75 1·25
1084 250f. Satellite, girls writing and children learning from television (Youth) 1·75 1·25

413 Grey Cat

1986. Cats. Multicoloured.
1085 150f. Type **413** . . . . . . 1·50 60
1086 200f. White cat . . . . . . 2·25 80
1087 300f. Tabby cat . . . . . . 2·50 1·10

414 Hands releasing Doves and Globe

1986. Anti-apartheid Campaign. Multicoloured.
1088 100f. Type **414** 65 40
1089 120f. People breaking chain around world 85 50

415 Comet and Diagram of Orbit

1986. Air. Appearance of Halley's Comet.
1090 **415** 300f. multicoloured . . . 2·25 1·25

416 Internal Combustion Engine

1986. Air. Centenaries of First Motor Car with Internal Combustion Engine and Statue of Liberty. Multicoloured.
1091 400f. Type **416** . . . . . . 3·00 1·50
1092 600f. Head of statue, and French and American flags . . . . 4·00 2·25

417 Robeson

1986. Air. 10th Death Anniv of Paul Robeson (singer).
1093 **417** 500f. multicoloured . . . 4·00 2·00

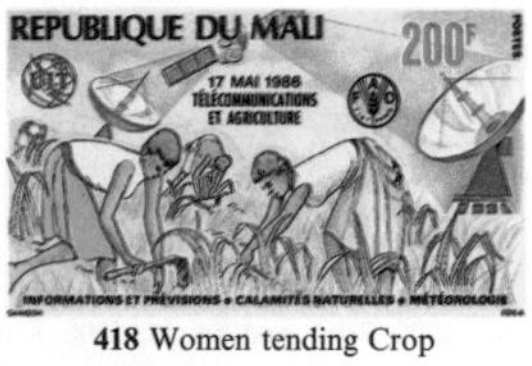

418 Women tending Crop

1986. World Communications Day.
1094 **418** 200f. multicoloured . . . 1·50 80

419 Players

1986. World Cup Football Championship, Mexico. Multicoloured.
1095 160f. Type **419** . . . . . . 1·40 65
1096 225f. Player capturing ball 1·90 90

420 Watt

1986. 250th Birth Anniv of James Watt (inventor).
1098 **420** 110f. multicoloured . . . 8·00 3·50

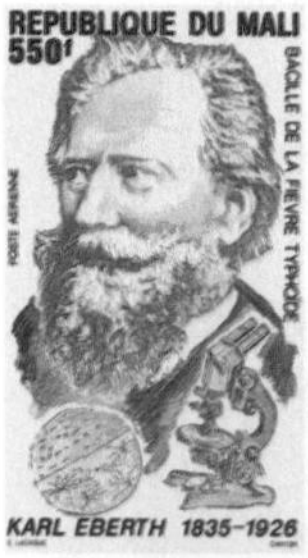

421 Eberth and Microscope **422** Chess Pieces on Board

1986. Air. 60th Death Anniv of Karl Eberth (discoverer of typhoid bacillus).
1099 **421** 550f. multicoloured . . . 4·00 1·90

1986. Air. World Chess Championship, London and Leningrad. Multicoloured.
1100 400f. Type **422** . . . . . . 3·75 1·75
1101 500f. Knight and board . . 4·75 2·25

1986. World Cup Winners. Nos. 1095/6 optd **ARGENTINE 3 R.F.A. 2.**
1102 160f. multicoloured . . . . 1·25 85
1103 225f. multicoloured . . . . 1·60 1·00

424 Head

1986. Endangered Animals. Giant Eland. Mult.
1105 5f. Type **424** 20 10
1106 20f. Standing by dead tree 40 10
1107 25f. Stepping over fallen branch 40 10
1108 200f. Mother and calf . . . 2·25 95

425 Mermoz and "Croix du Sud"

1986. Air. 50th Anniv of Disappearance of Jean Mermoz (aviator). Multicoloured.
1109 150f. Type **425** . . . . . . 1·25 60
1110 600f. CAMS 53 flying boat and monoplane . . . . . 4·25 2·25
1111 625f. Map and seaplane "Comte de la Vaulx" . . 4·50 2·50

1986. 10th Anniv of Concorde's First Commercial Flight. Nos. 674/6 surch **1986–10e Anniversaire du 1er Vol Commercial Supersonique.**
1112 175f. on 120f. Type **271** . . 1·40 80
1113 225f. on 130f. Concorde and Wright Flyer I . . . . . 1·75 1·00
1114 300f. on 200f. Concorde and Lindbergh's "Spirit of St. Louis" . . . . 2·75 1·50

427 Hansen and Follereau

1987. Air. 75th Death Anniv of Gerhard Hansen (discoverer of bacillus) and 10th Death Anniv of Raoul Follereau (leprosy pioneer).
1115 **427** 500f. multicoloured . . . 3·50 1·90

428 Model "A", 1903

1987. 40th Death Anniv of Henry Ford (motor car manufacturer). Multicoloured.
1116 150f. Type **428** . . . . . . 1·50 55
1117 200f. Model "T", 1923 . . . 2·00 75
1118 225f. "Thunderbird", 1968 2·00 95
1119 300f. "Continental", 1963 2·25 1·25

429 Konrad Adenauer **431** Scenes from "The Jazz Singer"

430 Runners and Buddha's Head

1987. Air. 20th Death Anniv of Konrad Adenauer (German statesman).
1120 **429** 625f. stone, brown and red . . . . 4·00 2·25

1987. Air. Olympic Games, Seoul (1988) (1st issue).
1121 **430** 400f. black and brown 2·00 1·40
1122 – 500f. dp green, grn & red . . . . 2·75 1·75
DESIGN: 500f. Footballers.
See also Nos. 1133/4.

1987. Air. 60th Anniv of First Talking Picture.
1123 **431** 550f. red, brn & dp brn 4·00 2·25

432 "Apis florea"

1987. Bees. Multicoloured.
1124 100f. Type **432** 80 50
1125 150f. "Apis dorsata" . . . 1·40 70
1126 175f. "Apis adonsonii" . . . 1·60 80
1127 200f. "Apis mellifera" . . . 1·75 1·00

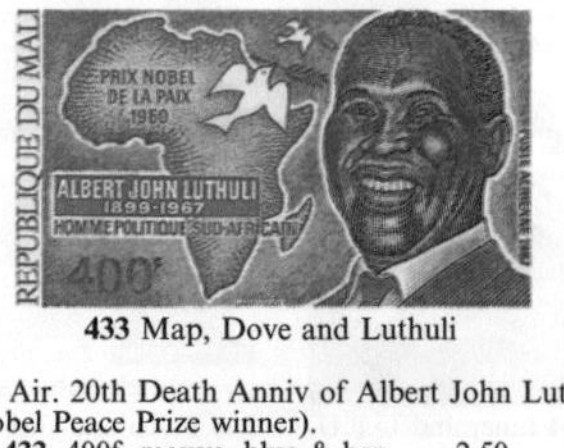

433 Map, Dove and Luthuli

1987. Air. 20th Death Anniv of Albert John Luthuli (Nobel Peace Prize winner).
1128 **433** 400f. mauve, blue & brn 2·50 1·50

434 Profiles and Lions Emblem

1987. Air. Lions International and Rotary International. Multicoloured.
1129 500f. Type **434** . . . . . . 3·00 1·75
1130 500f. Clasped hands and Rotary emblem . . . . . 3·00 1·75

435 Anniversary Emblem and Symbols of Activities

1988. 30th Anniv of Lions International in Mali.
1131 **435** 200f. multicoloured . . . 1·25 75

436 Emblem and Doctor examining Boy

1988. 40th Anniv of W.H.O.
1132 **436** 150f. multicoloured . . . 1·10 60

437 Coubertin and Ancient and Modern Athletes

1988. Air. Olympic Games, Seoul (2nd issue). 125th Birth Anniv of Pierre de Coubertin (founder of modern games). Multicoloured.
1133 240f. Type **437** . . . . . . 1·10 90
1134 400f. Stadium, Olympic rings and sports pictograms . . . . 1·90 1·40

438 "Harlequin"

1988. Air. 15th Death Anniv of Pablo Picasso (painter).
1135 **438** 600f. multicoloured . . . 4·25 2·25

439 Concorde and Globe

1988. Air. 15th Anniv of First North Atlantic Crossing by Concorde.
1136 **439** 500f. multicoloured . . . 4·00 2·00

440 Pres. Kennedy

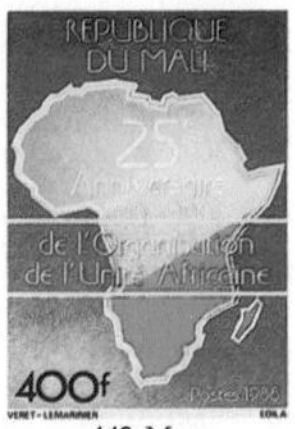

442 Map

1988. 25th Death Anniv of John Fitzgerald Kennedy (American President).
1137 **440** 640f. multicoloured . . . 4·00 2·40

1988. Mali Mission Hospital, Mopti. No. 1132 surch **MISSION MALI HOPITAL de MOPTI 300F** and **MEDECINS DU MONDE** emblem.
1138 **436** 300f. on 150f. mult . . . 2·40 1·75

1988. 25th Anniv of Organization of African Unity.
1139 **442** 400f. multicoloured . . . 2·50 1·25

443 Map, Leaf and Stove

1989. Air. "Improved Stoves: For a Green Mali". Multicoloured.
1140 5f. Type **443** 10 10
1141 10f. Tree and stove 10 10
1142 25f. Type **443** 15 10
1143 100f. As No. 1141 . . . . . 60 35

444 Astronauts on Moon

1989. Air. 20th Anniv of First Manned Moon Landing.
1144 **444** 300f. blue, purple & grn 2·00 1·25
1145 – 500f. purple, blue & brn 3·25 1·75
DESIGN: 500f. Astronauts on Moon (different).

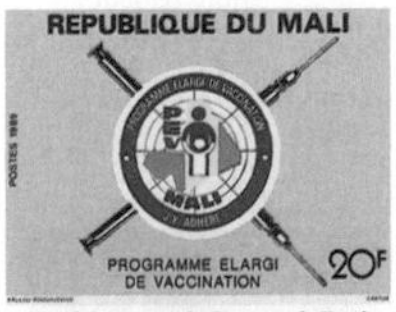

445 Emblem and Crossed Syringes

1989. Vaccination Programme. Multicoloured.
1146 20f. Type **445** 15 10
1147 30f. Doctor vaccinating woman 20 10
1148 50f. Emblem and syringes 40 15
1149 175f. Doctor vaccinating child . . . . 1·40 65

446 Emblem

1989. 25th Anniv of International Law Institute of French-speaking Countries.
1150 **446** 150f. multicoloured . . . 1·10 55
1151 200f. multicoloured . . . 1·40 70

447 Crowd

448 U.P.U. Emblem and Hands holding Envelopes

1989. Air. Bicentenary of French Revolution and "Philexfrance 89" International Stamp Exn, Paris.
1152 **447** 400f. red, blue and purple . . . . . . 2·50 1·25
1153 – 600f. violet, pur & mve 3·50 2·00
DESIGN: 600f. Marianne and Storming of Bastille.

1989. World Post Day.
1154 **448** 625f. multicoloured . . . 3·50 2·25

449 Pope and Cathedral

1990. Visit of Pope John Paul II.
1155 **449** 200f. multicoloured . . . 1·60 80

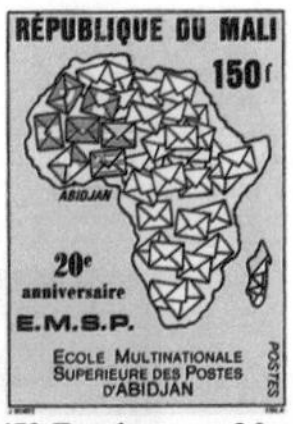

450 Envelopes on Map

1990. 20th Anniv of Multinational Postal Training School, Abidjan.
1156 **450** 150f. multicoloured . . . 1·25 55

451 Footballers

1990. Air. World Cup Football Championship, Italy. Multicoloured.
1157 200f. Type **451** . . . . . . 1·50 75
1158 225f. Footballers (different) 1·75 85

1990. World Cup Result. Nos. 1157/8 optd. Mult.
1160 200f. **ITALIE : 2 / ANGLETERRE : 1** . . . 1·50 85
1161 225f. **R.F.A. : 1 / ARGENTINE : 0** . . . . 1·75 85

453 Pres. Moussa Traore and Bamako Bridge

1990. 30th Anniv of Independence.
1163 **453** 400f. multicoloured . . . 2·50 1·50

454 Man writing and Adults learning to Read

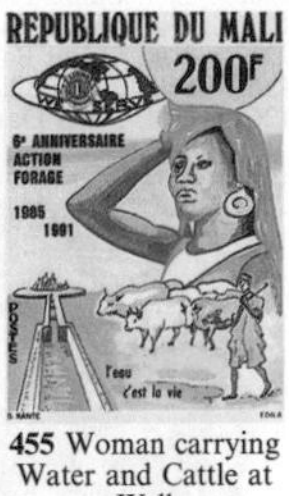

455 Woman carrying Water and Cattle at Well

1990. International Literacy Year.
1164 **454** 150f. multicoloured . . . 1·25 55
1165 200f. multicoloured . . . 1·50 75

1991. Lions Club (1166) and Rotary International (1167) Projects. Multicoloured.
1166 200f. Type **455** (6th anniv of wells project) . . . . . . 1·40 75
1167 200f. Bamako branch emblem and hand (30th anniv of anti-polio campaign) . . . . 1·40 75

456 Sonrai Dance, Takamba

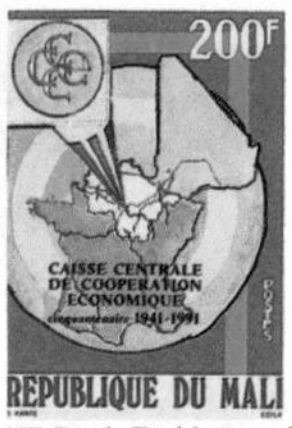

457 Bank Emblem and Map of France

1991. Dances. Multicoloured.
1168 50f. Type **456** 30 15
1169 100f. Malinke dance, Mandiani 60 30
1170 150f. Bamanan dance, Kono 90 50
1171 200f. Dogon dance, Songho 1·10 75

1991. 50th Anniv of Central Economic Co-operation Bank.
1172 **457** 200f. multicoloured . . . 1·25 75

458 Women with Torch and Banner

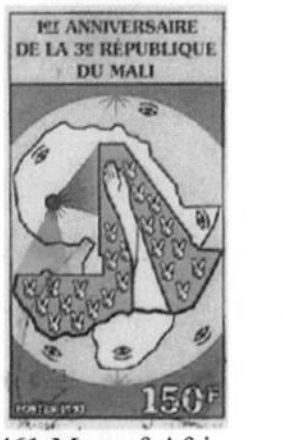

461 Map of Africa

1992. National Women's Movement for the Safeguarding of Peace and National Unity.
1173 **458** 150f. multicoloured . . . 75 40

1992. Various stamps surch.
1174 – 25f. on 470f. mult (No. 1058) (postage) 15 10
1175 **420** 30f. on 110f. mult . . . 18·00 4·50
1176 – 50f. on 300f. mult (No. 1087) 25 15
1177 – 50f. on 1225f. mult (No. 1043) 25 15
1178 – 150f. on 135f. mult (No. 1070) 75 40
1179 – 150f. on 190f. mult (No. 1063) 75 40
1180 – 150f. on 190f. mult (No. 1078) 75 40
1181 **400** 150f. on 350f. mult . . . 75 40
1182 – 150f. on 485f. mult (No. 1067) . . . . . 1·25 50
1183 – 150f. on 525f. mult (No. 1068) . . . . . 1·25 50
1184 – 150f. on 530f. mult (No. 1064) 75 40
1185 **440** 200f. on 640f. mult . . . 1·00 50
1186 – 240f. on 350f. mult (No. 1057) . . . . . 1·90 1·40
1187 **448** 240f. on 625f. mult . . . 1·25 65
1188 **410** 20f. on 700f. mult (air) 10 10
1189 **415** 20f. on 300f. mult . . . 10 10
1190 – 25f. on 470f. mult (No. 1071) 15 10
1191 **408** 30f. on 180f. mult . . . 15 10
1192 – 30f. on 500f. purple, blue and brown (No. 1145) 25 10
1193 – 100f. on 540f. mult (No. 1076) 80 50
1194 **438** 100f. on 600f. mult . . . 50 25
1195 **444** 150f. on 300f. blue, purple and green . . . 75 40
1196 **447** 150f. on 400f. red, blue and purple 75 40
1197 – 200f. on 300f. mult (No. 1074) . . . . . 1·60 1·00
1198 – 240f. on 600f. violet, purple and mauve (No. 1153) . . . . . 1·25 65

1992. (a) Postage. No. 1095 surch **150 f "Euro 92"**.
1199 **419** 150f. on 160f. mult . . . 75 40

(b) Air. No. 1134 surch **150F "Barcelone 92"**.
1200 150f. on 400f. multicoloured 75 40

1993. 1st Anniv of Third Republic.
1201 **461** 150f. multicoloured . . . 2·00 80

462 Blood, Memorial and Martyrs

463 Polio Victims

1993. 2nd Anniv of Martyrs' Day.
1203 **462** 150f. multicoloured . . . 70 35
1204 160f. multicoloured . . . 75 40

1993. Vaccination Campaign.
1205 **463** 150f. multicoloured . . . 2·00 1·00

464 Lecture on Problem Issues

1993. 35th Anniv of Lions International in Mali.

1207	**464**	200f. multicoloured	90	45
1208		225f. multicoloured	1·00	50

465 Place de la Liberte

466 Figure Skating

1993. Multicoloured, background colour of top panel given.

1209	**465**	20f. blue	10	10
1210		25f. yellow	10	10
1211		50f. pink	35	20
1212		100f. grey	65	20
1213		110f. yellow	65	35
1214		150f. green	90	35
1215		200f. yellow	1·40	55
1216		225f. flesh	1·40	65
1217		240f. lilac	1·75	65
1218		260f. lilac	1·75	65

1994. Winter Olympic Games, Lillehammer. Multicoloured.

1219	150f. Type **466**	35	20
1220	200f. Giant slalom	50	25
1221	225f. Ski jumping	55	30
1222	750f. Speed skating	1·75	90

467 Juan Schiaffino (Uruguay)

468 Scaphonyx

1994. World Cup Football Championship, U.S.A. Players from Different Teams. Multicoloured.

1224	200f. Type **467**	50	25
1225	240f. Diego Maradona (Argentine Republic)	60	30
1226	260f. Paolo Rossi (Italy)	65	35
1227	1000f. Franz Beckenbauer (Germany)	2·40	1·25

1994. Prehistoric Animals. Multicoloured.

1229	5f. Type **468**	10	10
1230	10f. Cynognathus	10	10
1231	15f. Lesothosaurus	10	10
1232	20f. Scutellosaurus	10	10
1233	25f. Ceratosaurus	10	10
1234	30f. Dilophosaurus	10	10
1235	40f. Dryosaurus	10	10
1236	50f. Heterodontosaurus	10	10
1237	60f. Anatosaurus	15	10
1238	70f. Saurornithoides	15	10
1239	80f. Avimimus	20	10
1240	90f. Saltasaurus	20	10
1241	300f. Dromaeosaurus	75	40
1242	400f. Tsintaosaurus	95	50
1243	600f. Velociraptor	1·50	75
1244	700f. Ouranosaurus	1·75	90

Nos. 1229/44 were issued together, se-tenant, forming a composite design.

469 "Sternuera castanea"

1994. Insects. Multicoloured.

1246	40f. Type **469**	20	10
1247	50f. "Eudicella gralli" (horiz)	20	10
1248	100f. "Homoderus mellyi"	35	15
1249	200f. "Kraussaria angulifera" (horiz)	60	25

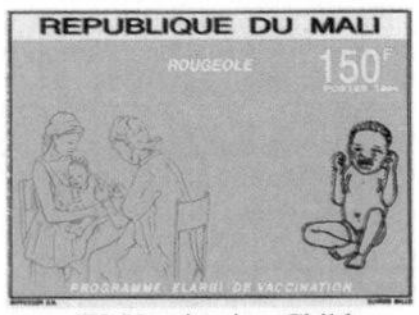

470 Vaccinating Child

1994. Vaccination Campaign.

1250	**470**	150f. green and black	35	20
1251		200f. blue and black	50	25

471 Feral Rock Pigeons

1994. Birds. Multicoloured.

1252	25f. Type **471**	10	10
1253	30f. Helmeted guineafowl	10	10
1254	150f. South African crowned cranes (vert)	35	20
1255	200f. Red junglefowl (vert)	50	25

472 Family

473 Kirk Douglas in "Spartacus"

1994. International Year of the Family.

1256	**472**	200f. multicoloured	50	25

1994. Film Stars. Multicoloured.

1257	100f. Type **473** (postage)	50	15
1258	150f. Elizabeth Taylor in "Cleopatra"	70	20
1259	225f. Marilyn Monroe in "The River of No Return"	1·10	30
1260	500f. Arnold Swarzenegger in "Conan the Barbarian"	2·50	65
1261	1000f. Elvis Presley in "Loving You"	5·25	1·25
1263	200f. Clint Eastwood in "A Mule for Sister Sara" (inscr "SIERRA TORRIDE") (air)	1·00	25

474 Ella Fitzgerald

1994. Jazz Singers. Multicoloured.

1264	200f. Type **474**	50	25
1265	225f. Lionel Hampton	65	30
1266	240f. Sarah Vaughan	75	30
1267	300f. Count Basie	90	40
1268	400f. Duke Ellington	1·10	50
1269	600f. Miles Davis	1·75	75

475 Soldiers caught in Explosion

1994. 50th Anniv of Second World War D-Day Landings. Multicoloured. (a) Villers-Bocage.

1271	200f. Type **475**	75	50
1272	200f. Tank (29 × 47 mm)	75	50
1273	200f. Troops beside tank	75	50

(b) Beaumont-sur-Sarthe.

1274	300f. Bombers and troops under fire	1·25	75
1275	300f. Bombers and tanks (29 × 47 mm)	1·25	75
1276	300f. Tank and soldier with machine gun	1·25	75

(c) Utah Beach (wrongly inscr "Utha").

1277	300f. Wounded troops and bow of boat	1·25	75
1278	300f. Troops in boat (29 × 47 mm)	1·25	75
1279	300f. Troops in boats	1·25	75

(d) Air Battle.

1280	400f. Bombers	1·25	75
1281	400f. Aircraft (29 × 47 mm)	1·25	75
1282	400f. Airplane on fire	1·25	75

(e) Sainte-Mere-Eglise.

1283	400f. Troops firing at paratrooper	1·25	75
1284	400f. Church and soldier (29 × 47 mm)	1·25	75
1285	400f. Paratroopers and German troops	1·25	75

Nos. 1271/3, 1274/6, 1277/9, 1280/2 and 1283/5 respectively were issued together, se-tenant, forming composite designs.

476 Olympic Rings on National Flag

1994. Centenary of International Olympic Committee (1st issue).

1286	**476**	150f. multicoloured	75	20
1287		200f. multicoloured	1·25	25

See also Nos. 1342/5.

477 Couple holding Condoms

1994. Anti-AIDS Campaign. Multicoloured.

1288	150f. Type **477**	50	20
1289	225f. Nurse treating patient and laboratory worker	75	30

478 "Venus of Brassempoury"

1994. Ancient Art. Multicoloured.

1290	15f. Type **478**	10	10
1291	25f. Cave paintings, Tanum	10	10
1292	45f. Prehistoric men painting mural	10	10
1293	50f. Cave paintings, Lascaux (horiz)	10	10
1294	55f. Painting from tomb of Amonherkhopeshef	15	10
1295	65f. God Anubis laying out Pharaoh (horiz)	15	10
1296	75f. Sphinx and pyramid, Mycerinus (horiz)	20	10
1297	85f. Bust of Nefertiti	20	10
1298	95f. Statue of Shibum	25	15
1299	100f. Cavalry of Ur (horiz)	25	15
1300	130f. Head of Mesopotamian harp	30	15
1301	135f. Mesopotamian tablet (horiz)	35	20
1302	140f. Assyrian dignitary	35	20
1303	180f. Enamel relief from Babylon (horiz)	45	25
1304	190f. Assyrians hunting	45	25
1305	200f. "Mona Lisa of Nimrod"	60	25
1306	225f. Phoenician coins (horiz)	65	30
1307	250f. Phoenician sphinx	70	30
1308	275f. Persian archer	75	35
1309	280f. Glass paste mask	80	35

479 "Polyptychus roseus"

1994. Multicoloured. (a) Butterflies and Moths.

1310	20f. Type **479**	10	10
1311	30f. "Elymniopsis bammakoo"	10	10
1312	40f. Silver-striped hawk moth	20	10
1313	150f. Crimson-speckled moth	50	20
1314	180f. Foxy charaxes	60	25
1315	200f. Common dotted border	75	25

(b) Plants.

1316	25f. "Disa kewensis"	10	10
1317	50f. "Angraecum eburneum"	10	10
1318	100f. "Ansellia africana"	25	15
1319	140f. Sorghum	35	20
1320	150f. Onion	35	20
1321	190f. Maize	45	25
1322	200f. Clouded agaric	70	25
1323	225f. Parasol mushroom	75	30
1324	500f. "Lepiota aspera"	1·40	65

(c) Insects.

1325	225f. Goliath beetle	70	30
1326	240f. Cricket	75	30
1327	350f. Praying mantis	1·00	45

1994. Winter Olympic Games Medal Winners, Lillehammer. Nos. 1219/22 optd.

1328	150f. **O GRISHSHUK Y. PLATOV RUSSIE**	35	20
1329	150f. **Y. GORDEYEVA S. GRINKOV RUSSIE**	35	20
1330	200f. **M. WASMEIER ALLEMAGNE**	50	25
1331	200f. **D. COMPAGNONI ITALIE**	50	25
1332	225f. **T. WEISSFLOG ALLEMAGNE**	55	30
1333	225f. **E. BREDESEN NORVEGE**	55	30
1334	750f. **J.O. KOSS NORVEGE**	1·75	90
1335	750f. **B. BLAIR U.S.A.**	1·75	90

A sheetlet also exists containing Nos. 1219/22 each optd with both of the inscriptions for that value.

1994. Results of World Cup Football Championship. Nos. 1224/27 optd **1. BRESIL 2. ITALIE 3. SUEDE.**

1337	200f. multicoloured	80	25
1338	240f. multicoloured	90	30
1339	260f. multicoloured	95	35
1340	1000f. multicoloured	3·00	1·25

482 Pierre de Coubertin (founder) and Torchbearer

483 Statue and Village

1994. Centenary of International Olympic Committee (2nd issue). Multicoloured.

1342	225f. Type **482**	1·00	30
1343	240f. Coubertin designing Olympic rings	1·10	30
1344	300f. Athlete bearing torch and Coubertin (horiz)	1·40	40
1345	500f. Olympic rings and Coubertin at desk (horiz)	2·00	65

1994. 20th International Tourism Day. Multicoloured.

1347	150f. Type **483**	75	20
1348	200f. Sphinx, pyramids and Abu Simbel temple (horiz)	1·00	25

484 Reiner Klimker (dressage)

1995. Olympic Games, Atlanta (1996). Multicoloured.

1349	25f. Type **484**	10	10
1350	50f. Kristin Otto (swimming)	10	10
1351	100f. Gunther Winkler (show jumping)	30	10

1352 150f. Birgit Fischer-Schmidt (single kayak) 40 10
1353 200f. Nicole Uphoff (dressage) (vert) 60 20
1354 225f. Renate Stecher (athletics) (vert) 60 20
1355 230f. Michael Gross (swimming) 70 20
1356 240f. Karin Janz (gymnastics) 85 20
1357 550f. Anja Fichtel (fencing) (vert) . . . . 2·00 50
1358 700f. Heide Rosendahl-Ecker (long jump) (vert) 2·50 80

485 Ernst Opik, "Galileo" Probe, Shoemaker-Levy Comet and Jupiter

1995. Anniversaries and Events. Multicoloured.
1359 150f. Type **485** 40 10
1360 200f. Clyde Tombaugh (discoverer of Pluto, 1930) and "Pluto" probe . . . 75 20
1361 500f. Henri Dunant (founder of Red Cross) . . . . . 1·50 40
1362 650f. Astronauts and lunar rover (first manned moon landing, 1969) . . . . . 2·00 40
1363 700f. Emblems of Lions International and Rotary International and child drinking from pump . . . 3·00 40
1364 800f. Gary Kasparov (world chess champion, 1993) . . 4·50 50

486 Agriculture and Fishing (regional integration)

1995. 20th Anniv of Economic Community of West African States. Multicoloured.
1365 150f. Type **486** 50 20
1366 200f. Emblem and handshake (co-operation) (vert) 75 20
1367 220f. Emblem and banknotes (proposed common currency) . . . 90 30
1368 225f. Emblem and doves (peace and security) . . . 1·10 30

487 Emblems of Alliance for Democracy in Mali and Sudanese Union-RDA

1995. 3rd Anniv of New Constitution. Multicoloured.
1369 150f. Type **487** (second round of Presidential election) 40 20
1370 200f. President Alpha Oumar Konare (vert) . . 50 20
1371 225f. Emblems of competing parties (first round of Presidential election) . . . 60 30
1372 240f. Map, flag and initials of parties (multi-party democracy) (vert) 70 30

488 Scout and Viennese Emperor Moth

1995. Scout Jamboree, Netherlands. Designs showing scouts and insects or fungi. Multicoloured.
1373 150f. Type **488** 40 10
1374 225f. Brimstone 60 20
1375 240f. Fig-tree blue 70 20
1376 500f. Clouded agaric . . . . 1·75 40
1377 650f. "Agaricus semotus" . . 2·00 50
1378 725f. Parasol mushroom . . 2·25 60

489 Paul Harris (founder) and Emblem

490 Imperial Woodpecker ("Campephilus imperialis")

1995. 90th Anniv of Rotary International.
1380 **489** 1000f. multicoloured . . 5·00 1·25

1995. Birds and Butterflies. Multicoloured.
1382 50f. Type **490** 10 10
1383 50f. Blue-crowned motmot ("Momotus momota") . . 10 10
1384 50f. Keel-billed toucan ("Ramphastos sulfuratus") 10 10
1385 50f. Blue-breasted kingfisher ("Halycon malimbica") 10 10
1386 50f. Streamertail ("Trochilus polytmus") 10 10
1387 50f. Common cardinal ("Cardinalis cardinalis") 10 10
1388 50f. Resplendent quetzal ("Pharomachrus mocinno") 10 10
1389 50f. Sun conure ("Aratinga solstitialis") 10 10
1390 50f. Red-necked amazon ("Amazona arausiaca") 10 10
1391 50f. Scarlet ibis ("Eudocimus ruber") . . 10 10
1392 50f. Red siskin ("Carduelis cucullatus") 10 10
1393 50f. Hyacinth macaw ("Anodorhynchus hyacinthinus") 10 10
1394 50f. Orange-breasted bunting ("Passerina leclancherii") 10 10
1395 50f. Red-capped manakin ("Pipra mentalis") 10 10
1396 50f. Guianan cock of the rock ("Rupicola rupicola") 10 10
1397 50f. Saffron finch ("Sicalis flaveola") 10 10
1398 100f. Black-spotted barbet ("Capito niger") 40 10
1399 100f. Amazon kingfisher ("Chloroceryle amazona") 40 10
1400 100f. Swallow tanager ("Tersina viridis") 40 10
1401 100f. Blue-crowned motmot ("Momotus momota") . . 40 10
1402 100f. Crimson-crested woodpecker ("Campephilus melanoleucos") 40 10
1403 100f. Red-breasted blackbird ("Leistes militaris") . . . 40 10
1404 100f. King vulture ("Sarcorhamphus papa") 40 10
1405 100f. Capped heron ("Pilherodius pileatus") 40 10
1406 100f. Black-tailed tityra ("Tityra cayana") 40 10
1407 100f. Paradise tanager ("Tangara chilensis") . . 40 10
1408 100f. Yellow-crowned amazon ("Amazona ochrocephala") 40 10
1409 100f. Buff-throated saltator ("Saltator maximus") . . 40 10
1410 100f. Red-cowled cardinal ("Paroaria dominicana") 40 10
1411 100f. Louisiana heron ("Egretta tricolor") . . . 40 10
1412 100f. Black-bellied cuckoo ("Piaya melanogaster") 40 10
1413 100f. Barred antshrike ("Thamnophilus doliatus") 40 10
1414 150f. Paradise whydah . . . 70 10
1415 150f. Red-necked spurfowl ("Red-necked Francolin") 70 10
1416 150f. Whale-headed stork (inscr "Shoebill") 70 10
1417 150f. Ruff 70 10
1418 150f. Marabou stork 70 10
1419 150f. Eastern white pelican ("White Pelican") 70 10
1420 150f. Western curlew . . . 70 10
1421 150f. Scarlet ibis 70 10
1422 150f. Great crested grebe . . 70 10
1423 150f. White spoonbill . . . 70 10
1424 150f. African jacana 70 10
1425 150f. African pygmy goose 70 10
1426 200f. Ruby-throated hummingbird 85 15
1427 200f. Grape shoemaker and blue morpho butterflies 85 15
1428 200f. Northern hobby . . . 85 15
1429 200f. Black-mandibled toucan ("Cuvier Toucan") 85 15
1430 200f. Black-necked red cotinga and green-winged macaw 85 15
1431 200f. Green-winged macaws and blue and yellow macaw 85 15
1432 200f. Greater flamingo ("Flamingo") 85 15
1433 200f. Malachite kingfisher 85 15
1434 200f. Bushy-crested hornbill 85 15
1435 200f. Purple swamphen . . 85 15
1436 200f. Striped body 85 15
1437 200f. Painted lady 85 15

Stamps of the same value were issued together, in se-tenant sheetlets, each sheetlet forming a composite design.

491 Emblem and Scales of Justice

1995. 50th Anniv of U.N.O. Multicoloured.
1439 20f. Type **491** 10 10
1440 170f. Type **491** 70 30
1441 225f. Emblem, doves and men with linked arms (horiz) 80 30
1442 240f. As No. 1441 . . . . . 1·00 50

492 Food Jar

1995. Cooking Utensils. Multicoloured.
1443 5f. Type **492** 20 10
1444 50f. Pestle and mortar . . . 20 10
1445 150f. Bowl (horiz) . . . . . 1·00 10
1446 200f. Grain sack . . . . . 1·10 15

493 Lennon

1995. 15th Death Anniv of John Lennon (musician).
1448 **493** 150f. multicoloured . . . 2·50 10

494 Justus Barnes

1995. 40th Anniv of Rock Music (1461/6) and Centenary of Motion Pictures (others). Multicoloured. (a) Actors in Western Films.
1449 150f. Type **494** 80 40
1450 150f. William S. Hart . . . 80 40
1451 150f. Tom Mix 80 40
1452 150f. Wallace Beery 80 40
1453 150f. Gary Cooper 80 40
1454 150f. John Wayne 80 40

(b) Leading Ladies and their Directors.
1455 200f. Marlene Dietrich and Josef von Sternberg ("The Blue Angel") . . . . . . 1·00 70
1456 200f. Jean Harlow and George Cukor ("Dinner at Eight") . . . . 1·00 70
1457 200f. Mary Astor and John Houston ("The Maltese Falcon") . . . . 1·00 70
1458 200f. Ingrid Bergman and Alfred Hitchcock ("Spellbound") . . . . . . 1·00 70
1459 200f. Claudette Colbert and Cecil B. de Mille ("Cleopatra") . . . . . . 1·00 70
1460 200f. Marilyn Monroe and Billy Wilder ("Some Like it Hot") . . . . 1·00 70

(c) Female Singers.
1461 225f. Connie Francis . . . 1·25 70
1462 225f. The Ronettes . . . . 1·25 70
1463 225f. Janis Joplin . . . . . 1·25 70
1464 225f. Debbie Harry . . . . 1·25 70
1465 225f. Cyndi Lauper . . . . 1·25 70
1466 225f. Carly Simon . . . . . 1·25 70

(d) Musicals.
1467 240f. Gene Kelly in "Singin' in the Rain" . . . . . . 1·25 70
1468 240f. Cyd Charisse and Fred Astaire in "The Bandwagon" . . . . . . 1·25 70
1469 240f. Liza Minelli in "Cabaret" . . . . 1·25 70
1470 240f. Julie Andrews in "The Sound of Music" . . . . 1·25 70
1471 240f. Ginger Rogers and Fred Astaire in "Top Hat" . . . . 1·25 70
1472 240f. John Travolta and Karen Lynn Gorney in "Saturday Night Fever" 1·25 70

No. 1449 is wrongly inscribed George Barnes.

495 Charles de Gaulle (French statesman, 25th death anniv)

1995. Anniversaries. Multicoloured.
1474 150f. Type **495** 50 20
1475 200f. General de Gaulle (50th anniv of liberation of France) 70 20
1476 240f. Enzo Ferrari (car designer, 7th death anniv) 75 30
1477 500f. Ayrton Senna (racing driver, 1st death anniv) 1·50 20
1478 650f. Paul Emile Victor (explorer, 88th birthday) 2·25 30
1479 725f. Paul Harris (founder, 90th anniv of Rotary International) . . . . . . 3·50 40
1480 740f. Michael Schumacher (racing driver, 26th birth anniv) (wrongly dated "1970") . . . . 3·50 40
1481 1000f. Jerry Garcia (popular singer, death commemoration) . . . . 4·00 50

OFFICIAL STAMPS

O 9 Dogon Mask

O 30 Mali Flag and Emblems

1961.
O26 **O 9** 1f. violet 10 10
O27 2f. red 10 10
O28 3f. slate 10 10
O29 5f. turquoise 15 15
O30 10f. brown 20 15
O31 25f. blue 35 15
O32 30f. red 40 20
O33 50f. myrtle 70 25
O34 85f. purple . . . . . . 1·10 65
O35 100f. green . . . . . . 1·40 65
O36 200f. purple . . . . . . 2·75 1·40

1964. Centre and flag mult; frame colour given.
O 90 **O 30** 1f. green 10 10
O 91 2f. lavender 10 10
O 92 3f. slate 10 10
O 93 5f. purple 10 10
O 94 10f. blue 15 10
O 95 25f. ochre 20 15
O 96 30f. green 25 15
O 97 50f. orange 35 15
O 98 85f. brown 50 20
O 99 100f. red 65 30
O100 200f. blue . . . . . . 1·50 60

O 341 Arms of Gao

1981. Town Arms. Multicoloured.
O878 5f. Type **O 341** 10 10
O879 15f. Tombouctou 10 10
O880 50f. Mopti 20 10
O881 180f. Segou 60 30
O882 200f. Sikasso 80 30
O883 680f. Koulikoro . . . . . 2·50 95
O884 700f. Kayes . . . . 2·75 1·25
O885 1000f. Bamako . . . . . . 4·00 1·50

1984. Nos. O878/85 surch.

O1013		15f. on 5f. Type O **341**	15	10
O1014		50f. on 15f. Tombouctou	30	15
O1015		120f. on 50f. Mopti	70	25
O1016		295f. on 180f. Segou	2·00	90
O1017		470f. on 200f. Sikasso	3·00	1·50
O1018		515f. on 680f. Koulikoro	3·50	1·90
O1019		845f. on 700f. Kayes	6·00	2·50
O1020		1225f. on 1000f. Bamako	7·50	3·75

POSTAGE DUE STAMPS

D **9** Bambara Mask

1961.

D26	D **9**	1f. black	10	10
D27		2f. blue	10	10
D28		5f. mauve	20	10
D29		10f. orange	25	15
D30		20f. turquoise	50	25
D31		25f. purple	65	30

D **28** "Polyptychus roseus"

1964. Butterflies and Moths. Multicoloured.

D83		1f. Type D **28**	10	10
D84		1f. "Deilephila nerii"	10	10
D85		2f. "Bunaea alcinoe"	15	15
D86		2f. "Gynanisa maja"	15	15
D87		3f. "Teracolus eris"	35	30
D88		3f. "Colotis antevippe"	35	30
D89		5f. "Manatha microcera"	35	30
D90		5f. "Charaxes epijasius"	35	30
D91		10f. "Hypokopelates otraeda"	45	35
D92		10f. "Lipaphnaeus leonina"	45	35
D93		20f. "Lobobunaea christyi"	75	70
D94		20f. "Gonimbrasia hecate"	75	70
D95		25f. "Hypolimnas misippus"	1·10	90
D96		25f. "Castopsilia florella"	1·10	90

1984. Nos. D83/96 surch.

D1021		5f. on 1f. Type D **28**	10	10
D1022		5f. on 1f. "Deilephila nerii"	10	10
D1023		10f. on 2f. "Bunaea alcinoe"	10	10
D1024		10f. on 2f. "Gynanisa maja"	10	10
D1025		15f. on 3f. "Teracolus eris"	15	10
D1026		15f. on 3f. "Colotis antevippe"	15	10
D1027		25f. on 5f. "Manatha microcera"	15	15
D1028		25f. on 5f. "Charaxes epijasius"	15	15
D1029		50f. on 10f. "Hypokopelates otraeda"	30	30
D1030		50f. on 10f. "Lipaphnaeus leonina"	30	30
D1031		100f. on 20f. "Lobobunaea christyi"	60	60
D1032		100f. on 20f. "Gonimbrasia hecate"	60	60
D1033		125f. on 25f. "Hypolimnas misippus"	75	75
D1034		125f. on 25f. "Catopsilia florella"	75	75

APPENDIX

The following stamps have either been issued in excess of postal needs or have not been available to the public in reasonable quantities at face value. Such stamps may later be given full listing if there is evidence of regular postal use.

All on gold foil.

1994.

World Cup Football Championship, U.S.A. Air. 3000f.

Film Stars. Air 3000f.

MALTA Pt. 1

An island in the Mediterranean Sea, south of Italy. After a period of self-government under various Constitutions, independence was attained on 21 September 1964. The island became a republic on 13 December 1974.

1860. 12 pence = 1 shilling;
20 shillings = 1 pound.
1972. 10 mils = 1 cent;
100 cents = M£1.

1

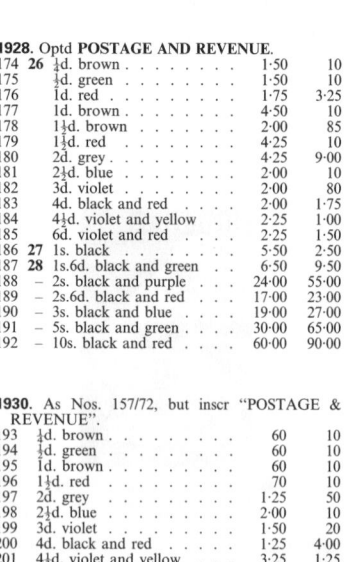

5

1860. Various frames.

18	**1**	½d. yellow	35·00	35·00
20		½d. green	2·50	50
22	–	1d. red	4·50	35
23	–	2d. grey	5·50	1·50
26	–	2½d. blue	38·00	1·00
27	–	4d. brown	11·00	3·00
28	–	1s. violet	35·00	9·00
30	**5**	5s. red	£110	80·00

6 Harbour of Valletta

7 Gozo Fishing Boat

8 Ancient Maltese Galley

9 Emblematic Figure of Malta

10 Shipwreck of St. Paul

12

1899.

31a	**6**	¼d. brown	1·50	40
79		¼d. black	15·00	3·50
32	**7**	4½d. brown	18·00	12·00
58		4½d. orange	4·50	3·50
59	**8**	5d. red	27·00	5·00
60		5d. green	4·25	3·50
34	**9**	2s.6d. olive	40·00	12·00
35	**10**	10s. black	90·00	65·00

1902. No. 26 surch **One Penny**.

36		1d. on 2½d. blue	1·00	1·40

1903.

47b	**12**	½d. green	4·50	10
48		1d. black and red	18·00	20
49		1d. red	2·50	10
50		2d. purple and grey	9·00	2·25
51		2d. grey	3·25	5·50
52		2½d. purple and blue	20·00	60
53		2½d. blue	5·50	3·00
42		3d. grey and purple	1·75	50
54		4d. black and brown	11·00	5·50
55		4d. black and red on yellow	4·00	3·50
44		1s. grey and violet	17·00	7·00
62		1s. black on green	7·50	3·00
63		5s. green and red on yellow	65·00	75·00

13

15

17

18

1914.

69	**13**	¼d. brown	1·00	10
71		½d. green	2·25	30
73		1d. red	1·50	10
75		2d. grey	9·50	3·75
77		2½d. blue	2·25	50
78		3d. purple on yellow	2·50	9·00
80		6d. purple	11·00	18·00
81a		1s. black on green	12·00	16·00
86	**15**	2s. purple and blue on blue	50·00	30·00
88		5s. green and red on yellow	85·00	£100
104	**17**	10s. black	£350	£700

1918. Optd **WAR TAX**.

92	**13**	½d. green	1·50	15
93	**12**	3d. grey and purple	1·75	8·50

1921.

100	**18**	2d. grey	4·50	1·75

1922. Optd **SELF-GOVERNMENT**.

114	**13**	¼d. brown	30	75
106		½d. green	1·00	1·75
116		1d. red	1·00	20
117	**18**	2d. grey	2·25	45
118	**13**	2½d. blue	1·10	1·00
108		3d. purple on yellow	3·50	18·00
109		6d. purple	2·75	17·00
110		1s. black on green	3·50	17·00
120	**15**	2s. purple and blue on blue	40·00	85·00
112	**9**	2s.6d. olive	22·00	45·00
113	**15**	5s. green and red on yellow	50·00	80·00
105	**10**	10s. black	£190	£350
121	**17**	10s. black	£140	£325

1922. Surch **One Farthing**.

122	**18**	¼d. on 2d. grey	85	30

22

23

1922.

123	**22**	¼d. brown	2·50	60
124		½d. green	2·50	15
125		1d. orange and purple	3·25	20
126		1d. violet	3·25	80
127		1½d. red	4·25	15
128		2d. brown and blue	2·75	1·25
129		2½d. blue	3·00	7·50
130		3d. blue	4·00	1·50
131		3d. black on yellow	3·50	13·00
132		4d. yellow and blue	2·00	2·75
133		6d. green and violet	3·25	2·50
134	**23**	1s. blue and brown	7·50	2·50
135		2s. brown and blue	11·00	11·00
136		2s.6d. purple and black	11·00	15·00
137		5s. orange and blue	21·00	45·00
138		10s. grey and brown	60·00	£150
140	**22**	£1 black and red	£100	30·00

1925. Surch **Two pence halfpenny**.

141	**22**	2½d. on 3d. blue	1·75	3·75

1926. Optd **POSTAGE**.

143	**22**	¼d. brown	70	4·00
144		½d. green	70	15
145		1d. violet	1·00	25
146		1½d. red	1·00	60
147		2d. brown and blue	75	1·00
148		2½d. blue	1·25	80
149		3d. black on yellow	75	80
150		4d. yellow and blue	7·50	18·00
151		6d. green and violet	2·75	3·75
152	**23**	1s. blue and brown	5·50	12·00
153		2s. brown and blue	50·00	£140
154		2s.6d. purple and black	14·00	38·00
155		5s. orange and blue	9·00	38·00
156		10s. grey and brown	7·00	18·00

26

27 Valletta Harbour

28 St. Publius

1926. Inscr "POSTAGE".

157	**26**	¼d. brown	80	15
158		½d. green	60	15
159		1d. red	3·00	1·00
160		1½d. brown	2·00	10
161		2d. grey	4·50	10·00
162		2½d. blue	4·00	1·25
162a		3d. violet	4·25	2·75
163		4d. black and red	3·25	10·00
164		4½d. violet and yellow	3·50	3·00
165		6d. violet and red	4·25	4·00
166	**27**	1s. black	6·50	4·75
167	**28**	1s.6d. black and green	6·50	14·00
168	–	2s. black and purple	6·50	16·00
169	–	2s.6d. black and red	15·00	48·00
170	–	3s. black and blue	17·00	30·00
171	–	5s. black and green	22·00	60·00
172	–	10s. black and red	55·00	£100

DESIGNS—As Type **27**: 2s. Mdina (Notabile); 5s. Neolithic temple, Mnajdra. As Type **28**: 2s.6d. Gozo boat; 3s. Neptune; 10s. St. Paul.

1928. Air. Optd **AIR MAIL**.

173	**26**	6d. violet and red	1·75	1·00

1928. Optd **POSTAGE AND REVENUE**.

174	**26**	¼d. brown	1·50	10
175		½d. green	1·50	10
176		1d. red	1·75	3·25
177		1d. brown	4·50	10
178		1½d. brown	2·00	85
179		1½d. red	4·25	10
180		2d. grey	4·25	9·00
181		2½d. blue	2·00	10
182		3d. violet	2·00	80
183		4d. black and red	2·00	1·75
184		4½d. violet and yellow	2·25	1·00
185		6d. violet and red	2·25	1·50
186	**27**	1s. black	5·50	2·50
187	**28**	1s.6d. black and green	6·50	9·50
188	–	2s. black and purple	24·00	55·00
189	–	2s.6d. black and red	17·00	23·00
190	–	3s. black and blue	19·00	27·00
191	–	5s. black and green	30·00	65·00
192	–	10s. black and red	60·00	90·00

1930. As Nos. 157/72, but inscr "POSTAGE & REVENUE".

193		¼d. brown	60	10
194		½d. green	60	10
195		1d. brown	60	10
196		1½d. red	70	10
197		2d. grey	1·25	50
198		2½d. blue	2·00	10
199		3d. violet	1·50	20
200		4d. black and red	1·25	4·00
201		4½d. violet and yellow	3·25	1·25
202		6d. violet and red	2·75	1·25
203		1s. black	10·00	14·00
204		1s.6d. black and green	8·50	19·00
205		2s. black and purple	10·00	20·00
206		2s.6d. black and red	17·00	48·00
207		3s. black and blue	28·00	55·00
208		5s. black and green	35·00	65·00
209		10s. black and red	80·00	£170

1935. Silver Jubilee. As T **14a** of Kenya, Uganda and Tanganyika.

210		½d. black and green	50	60
211		2½d. brown and blue	2·50	4·50
212		6d. blue and olive	7·00	5·00
213		1s. grey and purple	11·00	17·00

1937. Coronation. As T **14b** of Kenya, Uganda and Tanganyika.

214		½d. green	10	20
215		1½d. red	1·25	65
216		2½d. blue	1·00	80

37 Grand Harbour, Valletta

38 H.M.S. "St. Angelo"

39 Verdala Palace

1938. Various designs with medallion King George VI.

217	**37**	¼d. brown	10	10
218	**38**	½d. green	2·00	30
218a		½d. brown	55	30
219	**39**	1d. brown	4·25	40
219a		1d. green	60	10
220	–	1½d. red	1·00	30
220b	–	1½d. black	30	15
221	–	2d. black	40	2·00
221a	–	2d. red	40	30
222	–	2½d. blue	75	60
222a	–	2½d. violet	60	10
223	–	3d. violet	55	80
223a	–	3d. blue	30	20
224	–	4½d. olive and brown	50	30
225	–	6d. olive and red	1·00	30
226	–	1s. black	1·00	30
227	–	1s.6d. black and olive	7·00	4·00
228	–	2s. green and blue	4·50	4·00
229	–	2s.6d. black and red	8·50	5·50
230	–	5s. black and green	4·50	6·50
231	–	10s. black and red	17·00	16·00

DESIGNS—As Types **38/9**. VERT: 1½d. Hypogeum, Hal Saflieni; 3d. St. John's Co-Cathedral; 6d. Statue of Manoel de Vilhena; 1s. Maltese girl wearing faldetta; 5s. Palace Square, Valletta; 10s. St. Paul. HORIZ: 2d. Victoria and Citadel, Gozo; 2½d. De l'Isle Adam entering Mdina; 4½d. Ruins at Mnajdra; 1s.6d. St. Publius; 2s. Mdina Cathedral; 2s.6d. Statue of Neptune.

1946. Victory. As T **60** of Jamaica.

232		1d. green	15	10
233		3d. blue	40	1·00

1948. Self-government. As 1938 issue optd **SELF-GOVERNMENT 1947**.

234	¼d. brown	30	20
235	½d. brown	30	10
236	1d. green	30	10
236a	1d. grey	30	10
237	1½d. black	1·25	10
237b	1½d. green	30	10
238	2d. red	1·25	10
238b	2d. yellow	30	10
239	2½d. violet	80	10
239a	2½d. red	50	1·50
240	3d. blue	1·25	15
240a	3d. violet	50	15
241	4½d. olive and brown	2·00	1·50
241a	4½d. olive and blue	50	90
242	6d. olive and red	3·25	15
243	1s. black	3·00	40
244	1s.6d. black and olive	2·50	50
245	2s. green and blue	5·00	2·50
246	2s.6d. black and red	12·00	2·50
247	5s. black and green	21·00	3·50
248	10s. black and red	21·00	22·00

1949. Silver Wedding. As T **61/2** of Jamaica.

249	1d. green	50	10
250	£1 blue	38·00	35·00

1949. U.P.U. As T **63/6** of Jamaica.

251	2½d. violet	30	10
252	3d. blue	3·00	1·00
253	6d. red	60	1·00
254	1s. black	60	2·50

53 Queen Elizabeth II when Princess

54 "Our Lady of Mount Carmel" (attrib Palladino)

1950. Visit of Princess Elizabeth.

255	**53**	1d. green	10	15
256		3d. blue	20	20
257		1s. black	65	1·25

1951. 7th Centenary of the Scapular.

258	**54**	1d. green	15	15
259		3d. violet	50	10
260		1s. black	1·10	85

1953. Coronation. As T **71** of Jamaica.

261	1½d. black and green	50	10

55 St. John's Co-Cathedral

56 "Immaculate Conception" (Caruana) (altar-piece, Cospicua)

1954. Royal Visit.

262	**55**	3d. violet	30	10

1954. Centenary of Dogma of the Immaculate Conception.

263	**56**	1½d. green	10	10
264		3d. blue	10	10
265		1s. grey	35	20

57 Monument of the Great Siege, 1565

74 "Defence of Malta"

1956.

266	**57**	¼d. violet	20	10
267	–	½d. orange	50	10
314	–	1d. black	50	30
269	–	1½d. green	30	10
270	–	2d. sepia	1·50	10
271	–	2½d. brown	1·50	30
272	–	3d. red	1·50	10
273	–	4½d. blue	2·50	20
274	–	6d. indigo	75	10
275	–	8d. ochre	3·50	1·00
276	–	1s. violet	1·00	10
277	–	1s.6d. turquoise	12·00	20
278	–	2s. olive	12·00	2·50
279	–	2s.6d. brown	9·00	2·50
280	–	5s. green	15·00	2·75
281	–	10s. red	38·00	13·00
282	–	£1 brown	38·00	26·00

DESIGNS—VERT: ½d. Wignacourt aqueduct horsetrough; 1d. Victory church; 1½d. Second World War memorial; 2d. Mosta Church; 3d. The King's Scroll; 4½d. Roosevelt's Scroll; 8d. Vedette (tower); 1s. Mdina Gate; 1s.6d. "Les Gavroches" (statue); 2s. Monument of Christ the King; 2s.6d. Monument of Grand Master Cottoner; 5s. Grand Master Perellos's monument; 10s. St. Paul (statue); £1 Baptism of Christ (statue). HORIZ: 2½d. Auberge de Castile; 6d. Neolithic Temples at Tarxien.

1957. George Cross Commem. Cross in Silver.

283	**74**	1½d. green	15	10
284	–	3d. red	15	10
285	–	1s. brown	15	10

DESIGNS—HORIZ: 3d. Searchlights over Malta. VERT: 1s. Bombed buildings.

77 Design

81 Sea Raid on Grand Harbour, Valletta

1958. Technical Education in Malta. Inscr "TECHNICAL EDUCATION".

286	**77**	1½d. black and green	10	10
287	–	3d. black, red and grey	10	10
288	–	1s. grey, purple and black	15	10

DESIGNS—VERT: 3d. "Construction". HORIZ: 1s. Technical School, Paola.

1958. George Cross Commem. Cross in first colour outlined in silver.

289	–	1½d. green and black	15	10
290	**81**	3d. red and black	15	10
291	–	1s. mauve and black	15	10

DESIGNS—HORIZ: 1½d. Bombed-out family; 1s. Searchlight crew.

83 Air Raid Casualties

86 Shipwreck of St. Paul (after Palombi)

87 Statue of St. Paul, Rabat, Malta

1959. George Cross Commemoration.

292	**83**	1½d. green, black and gold	25	10
293	–	3d. mauve, black and gold	25	10
294	–	1s. grey, black and gold	85	95

DESIGNS—HORIZ: 3d. "For Gallantry". VERT: 1s. Maltese under bombardment.

1960. 19th Centenary of the Shipwreck of St. Paul. Inscr as in T **86/7**.

295	**86**	1½d. blue, gold and brown	15	10
296	–	3d. purple, gold and blue	15	10
297	–	6d. red, gold and grey	25	10
298	**87**	8d. black and gold	30	50
299	–	1s. purple and gold	25	10
300	–	2s.6d. blue, green and gold	1·00	2·00

DESIGNS—As Type **88**: 3d. Consecration of St. Publius, First Bishop of Malta; 6d. Departure of St. Paul (after Palombi). As Type **87**: 1s. Angel with the "Acts of the Apostles"; 2s.6d. St. Paul with the "Second Epistle to the Corinthians".

92 Stamp of 1860

1960. Centenary of Malta Stamps. Stamp in buff and blue.

301	**92**	1½d. green	25	10
302		3d. red	30	10
303		6d. blue	40	1·00

93 George Cross

1961. George Cross Commemoration.

304	**93**	1½d. black, cream and bistre	15	10
305	–	3d. brown and blue	30	10
306	–	1s. green, lilac and violet	75	1·75

DESIGNS: 3d. and 1s. show George Cross as Type **93** over backgrounds with different patterns.

96 "Madonna Damascena"

100 Bruce, Zammit and Microscope

1962. Great Siege Commemoration.

307	**96**	2d. blue	10	10
308	–	3d. red	10	10
309	–	6d. bronze	25	10
310	–	1s. purple	25	40

DESIGNS: 3d. Great Siege Monument; 6d. Grand Master La Valette; 1s. Assault on Fort St. Elmo.

1963. Freedom from Hunger. As T **20a** of Pitcairn Islands.

311	1s.6d. sepia	1·75	2·50

1963. Cent of Red Cross. As T **20b** of Pitcairn Islands.

312	2d. red on black	25	15
313	1s.6d. red and blue	1·75	4·25

1964. Anti-brucellosis Congress.

316	**100**	2d. brown, black and green	10	10
317	–	1s.6d. black and purple	90	90

DESIGN: 1s.6d. Goat and laboratory equipment.

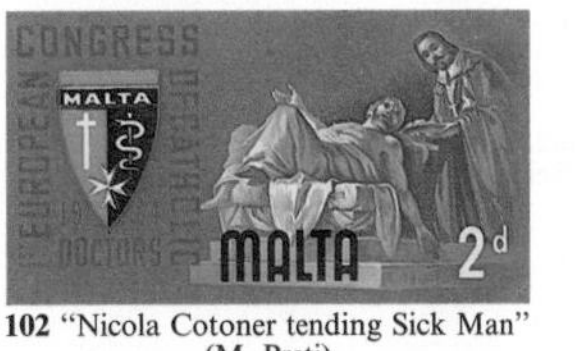

102 "Nicola Cotoner tending Sick Man" (M. Preti)

1964. 1st European Catholic Doctors' Congress, Valletta. Multicoloured.

318	2d. Type **102**	20	10
319	6d. St. Luke and hospital	50	15
320	1s.6d. Sacra Infermeria, Valletta	1·10	1·90

106 Dove and British Crown

110 Neolithic Era

109 "The Nativity"

1964. Independence.

321	**106**	2d. olive, red and gold	30	10
322	–	3d. brown, red and gold	30	10
323	–	6d. slate, red and gold	70	15
324	**106**	1s. blue, red and gold	70	15
325	–	1s.6d. blue, red and gold	1·50	1·00
326	–	2s.6d. blue, red and gold	1·50	2·25

DESIGNS: 3d., 1s.6d. Dove and Pope's tiara; 6d., 2s.6d. Dove and U.N. emblem.

1964. Christmas.

327	**109**	2d. purple and gold	10	10
328		4d. blue and gold	20	15
329		8d. green and gold	45	45

1965. Multicoloured.

330	½d. Type **110**	10	10
331	1d. Punic era	10	10
332	1½d. Roman era	30	10
333	2d. Proto Christian era	10	10
334	2½d. Saracenic era	80	10
335	3d. Siculo Norman era	10	10
336	4d. Knights of Malta	1·00	10
337	4½d. Maltese Navy	1·50	75
337b	5d. Fortifications	30	20
338	6d. French occupation	30	10
339	8d. British rule	70	10
339c	10d. Naval Arsenal	50	1·90
340	1s. Maltese Corps of the British Army	30	10
341	1s.3d. International Eucharistic Congress, 1913	2·00	1·40
342	1s.6d. Self-government, 1921	60	20
343	2s. Gozo Civic Council	70	10
344	2s.6d. State of Malta	70	50
345	3s. Independence, 1964	1·75	75
346	5s. HAFMED (Allied Forces, Mediterranean)	6·00	1·00
347	10s. The Maltese Islands (map)	3·00	4·00
348	£1 Patron Saints	3·75	5·00

Nos. 339/48 are larger, 41 × 29 mm from perf to perf, and include portrait of Queen Elizabeth II.

129 "Dante" (Raphael)

131 Turkish Fleet

1965. 700th Birth Anniv of Dante.

349	**129**	2d. blue	10	10
350		6d. green	25	10
351		2s. brown	1·10	1·50

1965. 400th Anniv of Great Siege. Multicoloured.

352	2d. Turkish camp	30	10
353	3d. Battle scene	30	10
354	6d. Type **131**	40	10
355	8d. Arrival of relief force	70	90
356	1s. Grand Master J. de La Valette's arms	40	10
357	1s.6d. "Allegory of Victory" (from mural by M. Preti)	75	30
358	2s.6d. Victory medal	1·25	3·25

SIZES—As Type **131**: 1s. SQUARE (32½ × 32½ mm): others.

137 "The Three Kings"

1965. Christmas.

359	**137**	1d. purple and red	10	10
360		4d. purple and blue	30	25
361		1s.3d. slate and purple	30	30

138 Sir Winston Churchill

1966. Churchill Commemoration.

362	**138**	2d. black, red and gold	20	10
363	–	3d. green, olive and gold	20	10
364	**138**	1s. purple, red and gold	30	10
365	–	1s.6d. blue, ultram & gold	40	1·10

DESIGN : 3d., 1s.6d. Sir Winston Churchill and George Cross.

140 Grand Master La Valette

145 Pres. Kennedy and Memorial

1966. 400th Anniv of Valletta. Multicoloured.

366	2d. Type **140**	10	10
367	3d. Pope Pius V	10	10
368	6d. Map of Valletta	15	10
369	1s. F. Laparelli (architect)	15	10
370	2s.6d. G. Cassar (architect)	35	50

1966. Pres. Kennedy Commemoration.
371 **145** 3d. olive, gold and black 10 10
372 1s.6d. blue, gold and black 10 10

146 "Trade"

147 "The Child in the Manger"

1966. 10th Malta Trade Fair.
373 **146** 2d. multicoloured 10 10
374 8d. multicoloured 30 50
375 2s.6d. multicoloured . . . 30 50

1966. Christmas.
376 **147** 1d. multicoloured 10 10
377 4d. multicoloured 10 10
378 1s.3d. multicoloured . . . 10 10

148 George Cross

149 Crucifixion of St. Peter

1967. 25th Anniv of George Cross Award to Malta.
379 **148** 2d. multicoloured 10 10
380 4d. multicoloured 10 10
381 3s. multicoloured 15 15

1967. 1900th Anniv of Martyrdom of Saints Peter and Paul.
382 **149** 2d. brown, orange & black 10 10
383 – 8d. olive, gold and black 15 10
384 – 3s. blue and black 20 15
DESIGNS—As Type **149**: 3s. Beheading of St. Paul. HORIZ (47 × 25 mm): 8d. Open Bible and episcopal emblems.

152 "St. Catherine of Siena"

156 Temple Ruins, Tarxien

1967. 300th Death Anniv of Melchior Gafa (sculptor). Multicoloured.
385 2d. Type **152** 10 10
386 4d. "St. Thomas of Villanova" 10 10
387 1s.6d. "Baptism of Christ" (detail) 15 10
388 2s.6d. "St. John the Baptist" (from "Baptism of Christ") 15 10

1967. 15th International Historical Architecture Congress, Valletta. Multicoloured.
389 2d. Type **156** 10 10
390 6d. Facade of Palazzo Falzon, Notabile 10 10
391 1s. Parish Church, Birkirkara 10 10
392 3s. Portal, Auberge de Castille 25 25

160 "Angels"

166 Human Rights Emblem and People

163 Queen Elizabeth II and Arms of Malta

1967. Christmas. Multicoloured.
393 1d. Type **160** 10 10
394 8d. "Crib" 20 10
395 1s.4d. "Angels" 20 10

1967. Royal Visit.
396 **163** 2d. multicoloured 10 10
397 – 4d. black, purple and gold 10 10
398 – 3s. multicoloured 20 25
DESIGNS—VERT: 4d. Queen in Robes of Order of St. Michael and St. George. HORIZ: 3s. Queen and outline of Malta.

1968. Human Rights Year. Multicoloured.
399 2d. Type **166** 10 10
400 6d. Human Rights emblem and people (different) . . . 10 10
401 2s. Type **166** (reversed) . . . 10 10

169 Fair "Products"

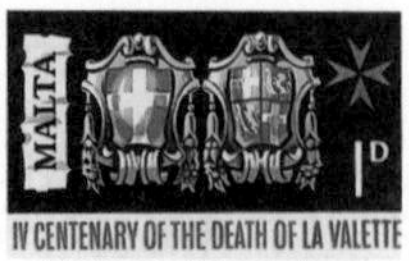

170 Arms of the Order of St. John and La Valette

1968. Malta International Trade Fair.
402 **169** 4d. multicoloured 10 10
403 8d. multicoloured 10 10
404 3s. multicoloured 15 10

1968. 4th Death Cent of Grand Master La Valette. Multicoloured.
405 1d. Type **170** 10 10
406 8d. "La Valette" (A. de Favray) (vert) 15 10
407 1s.6d. La Valette's tomb (28 × 23 mm) 15 10
408 2s.6d. Angels and scroll bearing date of death (vert) 20 20

174 Star of Bethlehem and Angel waking Shepherds

177 "Agriculture"

1968. Christmas. Multicoloured.
409 1d. Type **174** 10 10
410 8d. Mary and Joseph with shepherd watching over Cradle 15 10
411 1s.4d. Three Wise Men and Star of Bethlehem 15 20

1968. 6th Food and Agricultural Organization Regional Conference for Europe. Mult.
412 4d. Type **177** 10 10
413 1s. F.A.O. emblem and coin 10 10
414 2s.6d. "Agriculture" sowing Seeds 10 15

180 Mahatma Gandhi

181 ILO Emblem

1969. Birth Centenary of Mahatma Gandhi.
415 **180** 1s.6d. brown, black & gold 15 10

1969. 50th Anniv of Int Labour Organization.
416 **181** 2d. blue, gold & turquoise 10 10
417 6d. sepia, gold and brown 10 10

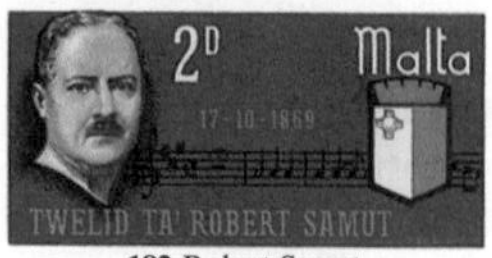

182 Robert Samut

1969. Birth Centenary of Robert Samut (composer of Maltese National Anthem).
418 **182** 2d. multicoloured 10 10

183 Dove of Peace, U.N. Emblem and Sea-bed

1969. United Nations Resolution on Oceanic Resources.
419 **183** 5d. multicoloured 10 10

184 "Swallows" returning to Malta

1969. Maltese Migrants' Convention.
420 **184** 10d. black, gold and olive 10 10

185 University Arms and Grand Master de Fonseca (founder)

1969. Bicentenary of University of Malta.
421 **185** 2s. multicoloured 15 20

187 Flag of Malta and Birds

1969. 5th Anniv of Independence.
422 – 2d. multicoloured 10 10
423 **187** 5d. black, red and gold 10 10
424 – 10d. black, blue and gold 10 10
425 – 1s.6d. multicoloured . . . 20 40
426 – 2s.6d. black, brown & gold 25 50
DESIGNS—SQUARE (31 × 31 mm): 2d. 1919 War Monument. VERT: 10d. "Tourism"; 1s.6d. U.N. and Council of Europe emblems; 2s.6d. "Trade and Industry".

191 Peasants playing Tambourine and Bagpipes

1969. Christmas. Children's Welfare Fund. Multicoloured.
427 1d.+1d. Type **191** 10 20
428 5d.+1d. Angels playing trumpet and harp 15 20
429 1s.6d.+3d. Choir boys singing 15 45

194 "The Beheading of St. John" (Caravaggio)

1970. 13th Council of Europe Art Exn. Mult.
430 1d. Type **194** 10 10
431 2d. "St. John the Baptist" (M. Preti) 10 10
432 5d. Interior of St. John's Co-Cathedral, Valletta 10 10
433 6d. "Allegory of the Order" (Neapolitan school) 10 10
434 8d. "St. Jerome" (Caravaggio) 15 50
435 10d. Articles from the Order of St. John in Malta . . . 15 10
436 1s.6d. "The Blessed Gerard receiving Godfrey de Bouillon" (A. de Favray) 20 40
437 2s. Cape and Stolone (16th cent) 20 55
SIZES—HORIZ: 1d., 8d. 56 × 30 mm; 2d., 6d. 45 × 32 mm; 10d., 2s. 63 × 21 mm; 1s.6d. 45 × 34 mm. SQUARE: 5d. 39 × 39 mm.

202 Artist's Impression of Fujiyama

1970. World Fair, Osaka.
438 **202** 2d. multicoloured 10 10
439 5d. multicoloured 10 10
440 3s. multicoloured 15 15

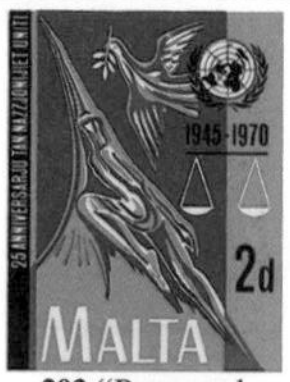

203 "Peace and Justice"

204 Carol-singers, Church and Star

1970. 25th Anniv of United Nations.
441 **203** 2d. multicoloured 10 10
442 5d. multicoloured 10 10
443 2s.6d. multicoloured . . . 15 15

1970. Christmas. Multicoloured.
444 1d.+½d. Type **204** 10 10
445 10d.+2d. Church, star and angels with Infant 15 20
446 1s.6d.+3d. Church, star and nativity scene 20 35

207 Books and Quill

1971. Literary Anniversaries. Multicoloured.
447 1s.6d. Type **207** (De Soldanis (historian) death bicent) . . 10 10
448 2s. Dun Karm (poet), books, pens and lamp (birth cent) 10 15

209 Europa "Chain"

211 "Centaurea spathulata"

210 "St. Joseph, Patron of the Universal Church" (G. Cali)

1971. Europa.
449 **209** 2d. orange, black and olive 10 10
450 5d. orange, black and red 10 10
451 1s.6d. orange, blk & slate 60 90

1971. Centenary of Proclamation of St. Joseph as Patron Saint of Catholic Church, and 50th Anniv of Coronation of the Statue of "Our Lady of Victories". Multicoloured.
452 2d. Type **210** 10 10
453 5d. Statue of "Our Lady of Victories" and galley . . . 10 10
454 10d. Type **210** 15 10
455 1s.6d. As 5d. 30 40

1971. National Plant and Bird of Malta. Multicoloured.
456 2s. Type **211** 10 10
457 5d. Blue rock thrush (horiz) 20 10
458 10d. As 5d. 30 15
459 1s.6d. Type **211** . . . . . 30 1·25

212 Angel

1971. Christmas. Multicoloured.
460 1d.+½d. Type **212** 10 10
461 10d.+2d. Mary and the Child Jesus 15 25
462 1s.6d.+3d. Joseph lying awake 20 40
MS463 131 × 113 mm. Nos. 460/2 75 2·50

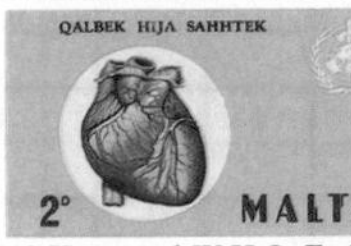

213 Heart and W.H.O. Emblem

1972. World Health Day.
464 **213** 2d. multicoloured 10 10
465 10d. multicoloured . . . 15 10
466 2s.6d. multicoloured . . . 40 80

214 Maltese Cross

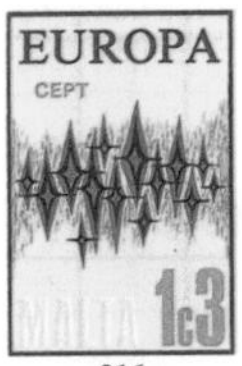

216 "Communications"

1972. Decimal Currency. Coins. Multicoloured.
467 2m. Type **214** 10 10
468 3m. Bee on honeycomb . . . 10 10
469 5m. Earthen lampstand . . . 10 10
470 1c. George Cross 10 10
471 2c. Classical head 10 10
472 5c. Ritual altar 10 10
473 10c. Grandmaster's galley . . 20 10
474 50c. Great Siege Monument 1·25 1·25
SIZES: 3m., 2c. As Type **214**: 5m., 1c., 5c. 25 × 30 mm; 10c., 50c. 31 × 38 mm.

1972. Nos. 337a, 339 and 341 surch.
475 1c.3 on 5d. multicoloured . . 10 10
476 3c. on 8d. multicoloured . . 15 10
477 5c. on 1s.3d. multicoloured 15 20

1972. Europa.
478 **216** 1c.3 multicoloured 10 10
479 3c. multicoloured 10 10
480 5c. multicoloured 15 35
481 7c.5 multicoloured 20 75

217 Angel

1972. Christmas.
482 **217** 8m.+2m. brown, grey and gold 10 10
483 – 3c.+1c. purple, violet and gold 15 40
484 – 7c.5+1c.5 indigo, blue and gold 20 50
MS485 137 × 113 mm. Nos. 482/4 1·75 4·50
DESIGNS: No. 483, Angel with tambourine; No. 484, Singing angel.
See also Nos. 507/9.

218 Archaeology

219 Europa "Posthorn"

1973. Multicoloured.
486 2m. Type **218** 10 10
487 4m. History 10 10
488 5m. Folklore 10 10
489 8m. Industry 10 10
490 1c. Fishing industry 10 10
491 1c.3 Pottery 10 10
492 2c. Agriculture 10 10
493 3c. Sport 10 10
494 4c. Yacht marina 15 10
495 5c. Fiesta 15 10
496 7c.5 Regatta 25 10
497 10c. Voluntary service . . . 25 10
498 50c. Education . . . . . . 1·25 50
499 £1 Religion . . . . 2·75 2·00
500 £2 Coat of arms (32 × 27 mm) . . . . . . 14·00 17·00
500b £2 National Emblem (32 × 27 mm) . . . . . . 9·00 14·00

1973. Europa.
501 **219** 3c. multicoloured 15 10
502 5c. multicoloured 15 35
503 7c.5 multicoloured 25 65

220 Emblem, and Woman holding Corn

221 Girolamo Cassar (architect)

1973. Anniversaries.
504 **220** 1c.3 multicoloured 10 10
505 – 7c.5 multicoloured 25 40
506 – 10c. multicoloured 30 50
ANNIVERSARIES: 1c.3, 10th anniv of World Food Programme; 7c.5, 25th anniv of W.H.O.; 10c. 25th anniv of Universal Declaration of Human Rights.

1973. Christmas. As T **217**. Multicoloured.
507 8m.+2m. Angels and organ pipes 15 10
508 3c.+1c. Madonna and Child 25 60
509 7c.5+1c.5 Buildings and Star 45 1·50
MS510 137 × 112 mm. Nos. 507/9 4·75 7·50

1973. Prominent Maltese.
511 **221** 1c.3 deep green, green and gold 10 10
512 – 3c. green, blue and gold 15 10
513 – 5c. brown, green and gold 20 15
514 – 7c.5 blue, lt blue & gold 20 30
515 – 10c. deep purple, purple and gold 20 40
DESIGNS: 3c. Giuseppe Barth (ophthalmologist); 5c. Nicolo' Isouard (composer); 7c.5, John Borg (botanist); 10c. Antonio Sciortino (sculptor).

222 "Air Malta" Emblem

1974. Air. Multicoloured.
516 3c. Type **222** 15 10
517 4c. Boeing 720B 15 10
518 5c. Type **222** 15 10
519 7c.5 As 4c. 20 10
520 20c. Type **222** 35 60
521 25c. As 4c. 35 60
522 35c. Type **222** . . . . 45 1·40

223 Prehistoric Sculpture

1974. Europa.
523 **223** 1c.3 blue, black and gold 15 10
524 – 3c. brown, black and gold 20 15
525 – 5c. purple, black and gold 25 50
526 – 7c.5 green, black and gold 35 1·00
DESIGNS—VERT: 3c. Old Cathedral Door, Mdina; 7c.5, "Vetlina" (sculpture by A. Sciortino). HORIZ: 5c. Silver monstrance.

224 Heinrich von Stephan (founder) and Land Transport

225 Decorative Star and Nativity Scene

1974. Centenary of U.P.U.
527 **224** 1c.3 green, blue & orange 30 10
528 – 5c. brown, red and green 30 10
529 – 7c.5 blue, violet and green 35 20
530 – 50c. purple, red and orange . . . . 1·00 1·25
MS531 126 × 91 mm. Nos. 527/30 4·50 7·50
DESIGNS (each containing portrait as Type **224**): 5c. "Washington" (paddle-steamer) and "Royal Viking Star" (liner); 7c.5, Balloon and Boeing 747-100; 50c. U.P.U. Buildings, 1874 and 1974.

1974. Christmas. Multicoloured.
532 8m.+2m. Type **225** 10 10
533 3c.+1c. "Shepherds" 15 20
534 5c.+1c. "Shepherds with gifts" 20 35
535 7c.5+1c.5 "The Magi" . . . 30 45

226 Swearing-in of Prime Minister

1975. Inauguration of Republic.
536 **226** 1c.3 multicoloured 10 10
537 – 5c. red and black 20 10
538 – 25c. multicoloured . . . . 60 1·00
DESIGNS: 5c. National flag; 25c. Minister of Justice, President and Prime Minister.

227 Mother and Child ("Family Life")

1975. International Women's Year.
539 **227** 1c.3 violet and gold . . . 15 10
540 – 3c. blue and gold 15 10
541 **227** 5c. brown and gold . . . 25 15
542 – 20c. brown and gold . . . 80 2·50
DESIGN: 3c., 20c. Office secretary ("Public Life").

228 "Allegory of Malta" (Francesco de Mura)

1975. Europa. Multicoloured.
543 5c. Type **228** 30 10
544 15c. "Judith and Holofernes" (Valentin de Boulogne) . . 50 75
The 15c. is smaller, 47 × 23 mm.

229 Plan of Ggantija Temple

1975. European Architectural Heritage Year.
545 **229** 1c.3 black and red 10 10
546 – 3c. purple, red and brown 20 10
547 – 5c. brown and red 30 25
548 – 25c. green, red and black 1·10 3·00
DESIGNS: 3c. Mdina skyline; 5c. View of Victoria, Gozo; 25c. Silhouette of Fort St. Angelo.

230 Farm Animals

231 "The Right to Work"

1975. Christmas. Multicoloured.
549 8m.+2m. Type **230** 25 25
550 3c.+1c. Nativity scene (50 × 23 mm) 40 75
551 7c.5+1c.5 Approach of the Magi . . . . 45 1·40

1975. 1st Anniv of Republic.
552 **231** 1c.3 multicoloured 10 10
553 – 5c. multicoloured 20 10
554 – 25c. red, blue and black 70 1·10
DESIGNS: 5c. "Safeguarding the Environment"; 25c. National flag.

232 "Festa Tar-Rahal"

233 Water Polo

1976. Maltese Folklore. Multicoloured.
555 1c.3 Type **232** 10 10
556 5c. "L-Imnarja" (horiz) . . . 15 10
557 7c.5 "Il-Karnival" (horiz) . . 35 70
558 10c. "Il-Gimgha L-Kbira" . . 55 1·40

1976. Olympic Games, Montreal. Multicoloured.
559 1c.7 Type **233** 10 10
560 5c. Sailing 25 10
561 30c. Athletics . . . . 85 1·50

234 Lace-making

1976. Europa. Multicoloured.
562 7c. Type **234** 20 35
563 15c. Stone carving 25 60

235 Nicola Cotoner

1976. 300th Anniv of School of Anatomy and Surgery. Multicoloured.
564 2c. Type **235** 10 10
565 5c. Arm 15 10
566 7c. Giuseppe Zammit 20 10
567 11c. Sacra Infermeria 35 65

236 St. John the Baptist and St. Michael

237 Jean de la Valette's Armour

1976. Christmas. Multicoloured.
568 1c.+5m. Type **236** 10 20
569 5c.+1c. Madonna and Child 15 60
570 7c.+1c.5 St. Christopher and St. Nicholas 20 80
571 10c.+2c. Complete painting (32 × 27 mm) . . . . . . 30 1·25
Nos. 568/71 show portions of "Madonna and Saints" by Domenico di Michelino.

1977. Suits of Armour. Multicoloured.
572 2c. Type **237** 10 10
573 7c. Aloph de Wignacourt's armour 20 10
574 11c. Jean Jacques de Verdelin's armour 25 50

1977. No. 336 surch **1c7**.
575 1c.7 on 4d. multicoloured . . 25 25

239 "Annunciation"

1977. 400th Birth Anniv of Rubens. Flemish Tapestries. Multicoloured.
576 2c. Type **239** 10 10
577 7c. "Four Evangelists" . . . 25 10
578 11c. "Nativity" 45 45
579 20c. "Adoration of the Magi" 80 1·00
See also Nos. 592/5, 615/18 and 638/9.

240 Map and Radio Aerial

242 "Aid to Handicapped Workers" (detail from Workers' Monument)

241 Ta' L-Isperanza

1977. World Telecommunications Day.
580 **240** 1c. black, green and red 10 10
581 6c. black, blue and red . . 20 10
582 – 8c. black, brown and red 30 10
583 – 17c. black, mauve and red 60 40
DESIGN—HORIZ: 8, 17c. Map, aerial and airplane tail-fin.

1977. Europa. Multicoloured.
584 7c. Type **241** 30 15
585 20c. Is-Salini . . . . 35 1·00

1977. Maltese Worker Commemoration.
586 **242** 2c. orange and brown . . 10 10
587 – 7c. light brown and brown 15 10
588 – 20c. multicoloured 40 60
DESIGNS—VERT: 7c. "Stoneworker, modern industry and ship-building" (monument detail). HORIZ: 20c. "Mother with Dead Son" and Service Medal.

243 The Shepherds

1977. Christmas. Multicoloured.
589 1c.+5m. Type **243** 10 35
590 7c.+1c. The Nativity 15 55
591 11c.+1c.5 The Flight into Egypt 20 70

1978. Flemish Tapestries. (2nd series). As T **239**. Multicoloured.
592 2c. "The Entry into Jerusalem" 10 10
593 7c. "The Last Supper" (after Poussin) 25 10
594 11c. "The Raising of the Cross" (after Rubens) 30 25
595 25c. "The Resurrection" (after Rubens) 70 80

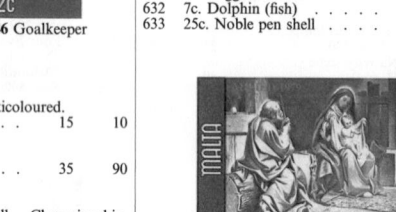

244 "Young Lady on Horseback and Trooper"

1978. 450th Death Anniv of Albrecht Durer.
596 **244** 1c.7 black, red and blue 10 10
597 – 8c. black, red and grey 15 10
598 – 17c. black, red and grey 40 45
DESIGNS: 8c. "The Bagpiper"; 17c. "The Virgin and Child with a Monkey".

245 Monument to Grand Master Nicola Cotoner (Foggini)
246 Goalkeeper

1978. Europa. Monuments. Multicoloured.
599 7c. Type **245** 15 10
600 25c. Monument to Grand Master Ramon Perellos (Mazzuoli) 35 90

1978. World Cup Football Championship, Argentina. Multicoloured.
601 2c. Type **246** 10 10
602 11c. Players heading ball 15 10
603 15c. Tackling 25 35
MS604 125 × 90 mm. Nos. 601/3 2·00 3·25

247 Boeing 707 over Megalithic Temple

1978. Air. Multicoloured.
605 5c. Type **247** 20 10
606 7c. Air Malta Boeing 720B 20 10
607 11c. Boeing 747 taking off from Luqa Airport 25 10
608 17c. Type **247** 35 30
609 20c. As 7c. 40 40
610 75c. As 11c. 1·25 2·75

248 Folk Musicians and Village Church
249 Fishing Boat and Aircraft Carrier

1978. Christmas. Multicoloured.
611 1c.+5m. Type **248** 10 10
612 5c.+1c. Choir of Angels 15 20
613 7c.+1c.5 Carol singers 20 35
614 11c.+3c. Folk musicians, church, angels and carol singers (58 × 22 mm) 25 45

1979. Flemish Tapestries (3rd series) showing paintings by Rubens. As T **239**. Multicoloured.
615 2c. "The Triumph of the Catholic Church" 10 10
616 7c. "The Triumph of Charity" 20 10
617 11c. "The Triumph of Faith" 30 25
618 25c. "The Triumph of Truth" 95 80

1979. End of Military Facilities Agreement. Multicoloured.
619 2c. Type **249** 10 10
620 5c. Raising the flag ceremony 10 10
621 7c. Departing soldier and olive sprig 15 10
622 8c. Type **249** 40 40
623 17c. As 5c. 55 60
624 20c. As 7c. 55 60

250 Speronara (fishing boat) and Tail of Air Malta Airliner
251 Children on Globe

1979. Europa. Communications. Multicoloured.
625 7c. Type **250** 20 10
626 25c. Coastal watch tower and radio link towers 40 75

1979. International Year of the Child. Multicoloured.
627 2c. Type **251** 10 10
628 7c. Children flying kites (27 × 33 mm) 15 10
629 11c. Children in circle (27 × 33 mm) 20 35

252 Shells

1979. Marine Life. Multicoloured.
630 2c. Type **252** 10 10
631 5c. Loggerhead turtle 20 10
632 7c. Dolphin (fish) 25 10
633 25c. Noble pen shell 90 1·25

253 "The Nativity" (detail)

1979. Christmas. Paintings by Giuseppe Cali. Multicoloured.
634 1c.+5m. Type **253** 10 10
635 5c.+1c. "The Flight into Egypt" (detail) 10 15
636 7c.+1c.5 "The Nativity" 15 20
637 11c.+3c. "The Flight into Egypt" 25 50

1980. Flemish Tapestries (4th series). As T **239**. Multicoloured.
638 2c. "The Institution of Corpus Domini" (Rubens) 10 10
639 8c. "The Destruction of Idolatry" (Rubens) 20 20
MS640 114 × 86 mm. 50c. "Grand Master Perelles with St. Jude and St. Simon (unknown Maltese artist) (vert) 80 1·60

254 Hal Saflieni Hypogeum, Paola
255 Dun Gorg Preca

1980. Int Restoration of Monuments Campaign. Multicoloured.
641 2c.5 Type **254** 10 15
642 6c. Vilhena Palace, Mdina 15 20
643 8c. Citadel of Victoria, Gozo (horiz) 20 40
644 12c. Fort St. Elmo, Valletta (horiz) 30 60

1980. Birth Centenary of Dun Gorg Preca (founder of Society of Christian Doctrine).
645 **255** 2c. 5 grey and black 10 10

256 Ruzar Briffa (poet)

1980. Europa.
646 **256** 8c. yellow, brown & green 20 10
647 – 30c. green, brown and lake 55 1·25
DESIGN: 30c. Nikiol Anton Vassalli (scholar and patriot).

257 "Annunciation"
258 Rook and Pawn

1980. Christmas. Paintings by A. Inglott. Multicoloured.
648 2c.+5m. Type **257** 10 10
649 6c.+1c. "Conception" 20 20
650 8c.+1c.5 "Nativity" 25 40
651 12c.+3c. "Annunciation", "Conception" and "Nativity" (47 × 38 mm) 30 70

1980. 24th Chess Olympiad and International Chess Federation Congress. Multicoloured.
652 2c.5 Type **258** 25 20
653 8c. Bishop and pawn 65 20
654 30c. King, queen and pawn (vert) 1·00 1·50

259 Barn Owl
260 Traditional Horse Race

1981. Birds. Multicoloured.
655 3c. Type **259** 30 25
656 8c. Sardinian warbler 50 25
657 12c. Woodchat shrike 60 80
658 23c. British storm petrel 1·10 1·75

1981. Europa. Folklore. Multicoloured.
659 8c. Type **260** 20 10
660 30c. Attempting to retrieve flag from end of "gostra" (greasy pole) 40 65

261 Stylized "25"
262 Disabled Artist at Work

1981. 25th Maltese International Trade Fair.
661 **261** 4c. multicoloured 15 15
662 25c. multicoloured 50 60

1981. International Year for Disabled Persons. Multicoloured.
663 3c. Type **262** 20 10
664 35c. Disabled child playing football 90 75

263 Wheat Ear in Conical Flask
264 Megalithic Building

1981. World Food Day.
665 **263** 8c. multicoloured 15 15
666 23c. multicoloured 60 50

1981. History of Maltese Industry. Multicoloured.
667 5m. Type **264** 10 85
668 1c. Cotton production 10 10
669 2c. Early ship-building 85 10
670 3c. Currency minting 30 10
671 5c. "Art" 30 25
672 6c. Fishing 1·25 25
673 7c. Agriculture 30 1·50
674 8c. Stone quarrying 1·00 35
675 10c. Grape pressing 35 50
676 12c. Modern ship-building 2·00 2·25
677 15c. Energy 70 2·00
678 20c. Telecommunications 70 75
679 25c. "Industry" 1·00 2·00
680 50c. Drilling for Water 2·50 2·75
681 £1 Sea transport 7·00 7·50
682 £3 Air transport 12·00 18·00

265 Children and Nativity Scene
266 Shipbuilding

1981. Christmas. Multicoloured.
683 2c.+1c. Type **265** 25 10
684 8c.+2c. Christmas Eve procession (horiz) 35 20
685 20c.+3c. Preaching midnight sermon 75 1·10

1982. Shipbuilding Industry.
686 **266** 3c. multicoloured 15 10
687 – 8c. multicoloured 30 30
688 – 13c. multicoloured 55 55
689 – 27c. multicoloured 1·25 1·25
DESIGNS: 8c. to 27c. Differing shipyard scenes.

267 Elderly Man and Has-Serh (home for elderly)

1982. Care of Elderly. Multicoloured.
690 8c. Type **267** 40 20
691 30c. Elderly woman and Has-Zmien (hospital for elderly) 1·40 1·40

268 Redemption of Islands by Maltese, 1428

1982. Europa. Historical Events. Multicoloured.
692 8c. Type **268** 40 20
693 30c. Declaration of rights by Maltese, 1802 1·00 1·40

269 Stylized Footballer

1982. World Cup Football Championship, Spain.
694 **269** 3c. multicoloured 20 10
695 – 12c. multicoloured 60 55
696 – 15c. multicoloured 70 65
MS697 125 × 90 mm. Nos. 694/6 3·50 4·50
DESIGNS: 12c., 15c. Various stylized footballers.

270 Angel appearing to Shepherds

1982. Christmas. Multicoloured.
698 2c.+1c. Type **270** 15 20
699 8c.+2c. Nativity and Three Wise Men bearing gifts 50 60
700 20c.+3c. Nativity scene (45 × 37 mm) 1·00 1·25

271 "Ta Salvo Serafino" (oared brigantine), 1531

1982. Maltese Ships (1st series). Multicoloured.
701 3c. Type **271** 30 10
702 8c. "La Madonna del Rosaria" (tartane), 1740 . . 60 30
703 12c. "San Paulo" (xebec), 1743 . . . . 85 55
704 20c. "Ta' Pietro Saliba" (xprunara), 1798 . . . . . 1·10 90
See also Nos. 725/8, 772/5, 792/5 and 809/12.

272 Locomotive "Manning Wardle", 1883

1983. Centenary of Malta Railway. Multicoloured.
705 3c. Type **272** 45 15
706 13c. Locomotive "Black Hawthorn", 1884 . . . . 1·00 1·00
707 27c. Beyer Peacock locomotive, 1895 . . . . . 2·00 3·25

273 Peace Doves leaving Malta

1983. Commonwealth Day. Multicoloured.
708 8c. Type **273** 20 30
709 12c. Tourist landmarks . . . 30 60
710 15c. Holiday beach (vert) . . 35 75
711 23c. Ship-building (vert) . . . 55 1·00

274 Ggantija Megalithic Temples, Gozo

1983. Europa. Multicoloured.
712 8c. Type **274** 40 40
713 30c. Fort St. Angelo . . . . 1·00 2·40

275 Dish Aerials (World Communications Year)

1983. Anniversaries and Events. Multicoloured.
714 3c. Type **275** 45 15
715 7c. Ships' prows and badge (25th anniv of I.M.O. Convention) 70 55
716 13c. Container lorries and badge (30th anniv of Customs Co-operation Council) 90 90
717 20c. Stadium and emblem (9th Mediterranean Games) 1·00 2·25

276 Monsignor Giuseppe de Piro

277 Annunciation

1983. 50th Death Anniv of Monsignor Giuseppe de Piro.
718 **276** 3c. multicoloured 15 15

1983. Christmas. Multicoloured.
719 2c.+1c. Type **277** 35 15
720 8c.+2c. The Nativity 85 60
721 20c.+3c. Adoration of the Magi . . . . 1·60 2·25

278 Workers at Meeting

1983. 40th Anniv of General Workers' Union. Multicoloured.
722 3c. Type **278** 30 10
723 8c. Worker with family . . . 60 40
724 27c. Union H.Q. Building . . 1·60 1·75

1983. Maltese Ships (2nd series). As T **271**. Multicoloured.
725 2c. "Strangier" (full-rigged ship), 1813 . . . . 30 25
726 12c. "Tigre" (topsail schooner), 1839 . . . . . 80 1·25
727 13c. "La Speranza" (brig), 1844 . . . . 80 1·25
728 20c. "Wignacourt" (barque), 1844 . . . . 1·25 2·75

279 Boeing 737

1984. Air. Multicoloured.
729 7c. Type **279** 50 30
730 8c. Boeing 720B 60 35
731 16c. Vickers Vanguard . . . 1·25 70
732 23c. Vickers Viscount . . . . 1·50 70
733 27c. Douglas DC-3 . . . . . 1·75 80
734 38c. Armstrong Whitworth Atalanta "Artemis" . . . 2·25 2·75
735 75c. "Marina" Fiat MF.5 flying boat . . . . 3·25 5·00

280 Bridge

1984. Europa. 25th Anniv of C.E.P.T.
736 **280** 8c. green, black and yellow 35 35
737 30c. red, black and yellow 1·25 1·25

281 Early Policeman

282 Running

1984. 170th Anniv of Malta Police Force. Multicoloured.
738 3c. Type **281** 65 15
739 8c. Mounted police . . . . . 1·50 65
740 11c. Motorcycle policeman 1·75 2·00
741 25c. Policeman and firemen 2·75 3·75

1984. Olympic Games, Los Angeles. Multicoloured.
742 7c. Type **282** 25 30
743 12c. Gymnastics 50 70
744 23c. Swimming . . . . . . 85 1·25

283 "The Visitation" (Pietru Caruana)

284 Dove on Map

1984. Christmas. Paintings from Church of Our Lady of Porto Salvo, Valletta. Multicoloured.
745 2c.+1c. Type **283** 55 65
746 8c.+2c. "The Epiphany" (Rafel Caruana) (horiz) . . 1·00 1·40
747 20c.+3c. "Jesus among the Doctors" (Rafel Caruana) (horiz) . . . . 2·00 4·00

1984. 10th Anniv of Republic. Multicoloured.
748 3c. Type **284** 40 20
749 8c. Fort St. Angelo 75 65
750 30c. Hands . . . . 2·50 4·75

285 1885 ½d. Green Stamp

287 Nicolo Baldacchino (tenor)

286 Boy, and Hands planting Vine

1985. Centenary of Malta Post Office. Mult.
751 3c. Type **285** 45 15
752 8c. 1885 1d. rose 65 45
753 12c. 1885 2½d. blue . . . . . 90 1·40
754 20c. 1885 4d. brown . . . . 1·40 3·00
MS755 165 × 90 mm. Nos. 751/4 3·75 6·50

1985. International Youth Year. Multicoloured.
756 2c. Type **286** 15 15
757 13c. Young people and flowers (vert) 85 60
758 27c. Girl holding flame in hand . . . . 1·75 1·40

1985. Europa. European Music Year. Mult.
759 8c. Type **287** . . . . 1·50 50
760 30c. Francesco Azopardi (composer) . . . . 2·75 5·00

288 Guzeppi Bajada and Manwel Attard (victims)

1985. 66th Anniv of 7 June 1919 Demonstrations. Multicoloured.
761 3c. Type **288** 35 15
762 7c. Karmnu Abela and Wenzu Dyer (victims) . . . 75 40
763 35c. Model of projected Demonstration monument by Anton Agius (vert) . . 2·50 2·75

289 Stylized Birds

1985. 40th Anniv of United Nations Organization. Multicoloured.
764 4c. Type **289** 25 15
765 11c. Arrow-headed ribbons 60 1·25
766 31c. Stylized figures . . . . 1·40 3·25

290 Giorgio Mitrovich (nationalist) (death centenary)

291 The Three Wise Men

1985. Celebrities' Anniversaries. Multicoloured.
767 8c. Type **290** . . . . 1·00 35
768 12c. Pietru Caxaru (poet and administrator) (400th death anniversary) . . . . 1·75 2·50

1985. Christmas. Designs showing details of terracotta relief by Ganni Bonnici. Multicoloured.
769 2c.+1c. Type **291** 55 75
770 8c.+2c. Virgin and Child . . 1·25 1·75
771 20c.+3c. Angels . . . . . . 2·50 4·00

1985. Maltese Ships (3rd series). Steamships. As T **271**. Multicoloured.
772 3c. "Scotia" (paddle-steamer), 1844 . . . . 85 20
773 7c. "Tagliaferro" (screw-steamer), 1822 . . . . . 1·50 1·00
774 15c. "Gleneagles" (screw-steamer), 1885 . . . . . 2·25 3·50
775 23c. "L'Isle Adam" (screw-steamer), 1886 . . . . . 2·75 4·25

292 John XXIII Peace Laboratory and Statue of St. Francis of Assisi

1986. International Peace Year. Multicoloured.
776 8c. Type **292** . . . . 1·25 50
777 11c. Dove and hands holding olive branch (40 × 19 mm) 1·50 2·50
778 27c. Map of Africa, dove and two heads . . . . 3·25 4·75

293 Symbolic Plant and "Cynthia cardui", "Vanessa atalanta" and "Polyommatus icarus"

294 Heading the Ball

1986. Europa. Environmental Conservation. Multicoloured.
779 8c. Type **293** . . . . 1·50 50
780 35c. Island, Neolithic frieze, sea and sun . . . . 2·75 6·00

1986. World Cup Football Championship, Mexico. Multicoloured.
781 3c. Type **294** 60 20
782 7c. Saving a goal . . . . . . 1·25 1·00
783 23c. Controlling the ball . . 4·00 6·50
MS784 125 × 90 mm. Nos. 781/3 7·00 8·50

295 Father Diegu

1986. Maltese Philanthropists. Multicoloured.
785 2c. Type **295** 40 30
786 3c. Adelaide Cini 50 30
787 8c. Alfonso Maria Galea . . 1·25 60
788 27c. Vincenzo Bugeja . . . . 3·25 6·00

296 "Nativity"

1986. Christmas. Paintings by Giuseppe D'Arena. Multicoloured.
789 2c.+1c. Type **296** . . . . . 1·50 1·75
790 8c.+2c. "Nativity" (detail) (vert) . . . . 3·25 3·50
791 20c.+3c. "Epiphany" . . . . 4·75 7·00

1986. Maltese Ships (4th series). As T **271**. Multicoloured.
792 7c. "San Paul" (freighter), 1921 . . . . 1·00 50
793 10c. "Knight of Malta" (mail steamer), 1930 . . . . . . 1·25 1·75
794 12c. "Valetta City" (freighter), 1948 . . . . . 1·50 2·75
795 20c. "Saver" (freighter), 1959 2·25 4·50

297 European Robin

1987. 25th Anniv of Malta Ornithological Society. Multicoloured.

796	3c. Type **297**	1·25	50
797	8c. Peregrine falcon (vert)	2·50	1·00
798	13c. Hoopoe (vert)	3·25	4·00
799	23c. Cory's shearwater	3·75	6·00

298 Aquasun Lido

299 16th-century Pikeman

1987. Europa. Modern Architecture. Multicoloured.

800	8c. Type **298**	1·25	75
801	35c. Church of St. Joseph, Manikata	3·50	6·25

1987. Maltese Uniforms (1st series). Multicoloured.

802	3c. Type **299**	75	40
803	7c. 16th-century officer	1·40	90
804	10c. 18th-century standard bearer	1·60	2·25
805	27c. 18th-century General of the Galleys	3·50	4·75

See also Nos. 832/5, 851/4, 880/3 and 893/6.

300 Maltese Scenes, Wheat Ears and Sun

1987. Anniversaries and Events. Multicoloured.

806	5c. Type **300** (European Environment Year)	1·25	50
807	8c. Esperanto star as comet (Centenary of Esperanto)	2·00	60
808	23c. Family at house door (International Year of Shelter for the Homeless)	3·00	3·00

1987. Maltese Ships (5th series). As T **271**. Multicoloured.

809	2c. "Medina" (freighter), 1969	70	60
810	11c. "Rabat" (container ship), 1974	2·50	2·50
811	13c. "Ghawdex" (passenger ferry), 1979	2·75	2·75
812	20c. "Pinto" (car ferry), 1987	3·75	4·00

301 "The Visitation"

1987. Christmas. Illuminated illustrations, score and text from 16th-century choral manuscript. Multicoloured.

813	2c.+1c. Type **301**	65	65
814	8c.+2c. "The Nativity"	2·25	3·00
815	20c.+3c. "The Adoration of the Magi"	3·75	5·00

302 Dr. Arvid Pardo (U.N. representative)

1987. 20th Anniv of United Nations Resolution on Peaceful Use of the Seabed. Multicoloured.

816	8c. Type **302**	1·00	75
817	12c. U.N. emblem and sea	1·75	3·00
MS818	125 × 90 mm. Nos. 816/17	3·75	4·50

303 Ven. Nazju Falzon (Catholic catechist)

304 "St. John Bosco with Youth" (statue)

1988. Maltese Personalities. Multicoloured.

819	2c. Type **303**	25	30
820	3c. Mgr. Sidor Formosa (philanthropist)	25	30
821	4c. Sir Luigi Preziosi (ophthalmologist)	40	30
822	10c. Fr. Anastasju Cuschieri (poet)	80	85
823	25c. Mgr. Pietru Pawl Saydon (Bible translator)	2·25	3·25

1988. Religious Anniversaries. Multicoloured.

824	10c. Type **304** (death centenary)	1·00	1·00
825	12c. "Assumption of Our Lady" (altarpiece by Perugino, Ta' Pinu, Gozo) (Marian Year)	1·25	1·50
826	14c. "Christ the King" (statue by Sciortino) (75th anniv of International Eucharistic Congress, Valletta)	1·75	2·50

305 Bus, Ferry and Aircraft

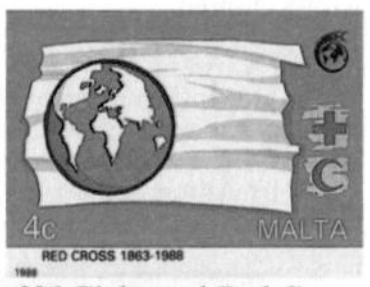

306 Globe and Red Cross Emblems

1988. Europa. Transport and Communications. Multicoloured.

827	10c. Type **305**	1·25	75
828	35c. Control panel, dish aerial and pylons	2·75	4·50

1988. Anniversaries and Events. Multicoloured.

829	4c. Type **306** (125th anniv of Int Red Cross)	75	50
830	18c. Divided globe (Campaign for North–South Interdependence and Solidarity)	2·00	3·00
831	19c. Globe and symbol (40th anniv of W.H.O.)	2·00	3·00

1988. Maltese Uniforms (2nd series). As T **299**. Multicoloured.

832	3c. Private, Maltese Light Infantry, 1800	40	30
833	4c. Gunner, Malta Coast Artillery, 1802	45	35
834	10c. Field Officer, 1st Maltese Provincial Battalion, 1805	1·10	1·25
835	25c. Subaltern, Royal Malta Regiment, 1809	2·50	4·25

307 Athletics

308 Shepherd with Flock

1988. Olympic Games, Seoul. Multicoloured.

836	4c. Type **307**	30	30
837	10c. Diving	70	80
838	35c. Basketball	2·00	3·00

1988. Christmas. Multicoloured.

839	3c.+1c. Type **308**	30	30
840	10c.+2c. The Nativity	85	1·25
841	25c.+3c. Three Wise Men	2·00	2·75

309 Commonwealth Emblem

311 Two Boys flying Kite

310 New State Arms

1989. 25th Anniv of Independence. Multicoloured.

842	2c. Type **309**	25	35
843	3c. Council of Europe flag	25	35
844	4c. U.N. flag	30	35
845	10c. Workers, hands gripping ring and national flag	75	95
846	12c. Scales and allegorical figure of Justice	90	1·40
847	25c. Prime Minister Borg Olivier with Independence constitution (42 × 28 mm)	1·90	3·25

1989.

848	**310** £1 multicoloured	4·00	4·50

1989. Europa. Children's Games. Multicoloured.

849	10c. Type **311**	1·25	75
850	35c. Two girls with dolls	3·25	4·50

1989. Maltese Uniforms (3rd series). As T **299**. Multicoloured.

851	3c. Officer, Maltese Veterans, 1815	45	45
852	4c. Subaltern, Royal Malta Fencibles, 1839	50	50
853	10c. Private, Malta Militia, 1856	1·50	1·50
854	25c. Colonel, Royal Malta Fencible Artillery, 1875	2·75	3·75

312 Human Figures and Buildings

1989. Anniversaries and Commemorations. Designs showing logo and stylized human figures. Multicoloured.

855	3c. Type **312** (20th anniv of U.N. Declaration on Social Progress and Development)	30	30
856	4c. Workers and figure in wheelchair (Malta's Ratification of European Social Charter)	35	35
857	10c. Family (40th anniv of Council of Europe)	80	1·25
858	14c. Teacher and children (70th anniv of Malta Union of Teachers)	1·00	1·75
859	25c. Symbolic knights (Knights of the Sovereign Military Order of Malta Assembly)	2·25	3·50

313 Angel and Cherub

315 General Post Office, Auberge d'Italie, Valletta

314 Presidents George H. Bush and Mikhail Gorbachev

1989. Christmas. Vault paintings by Mattia Preti from St. John's Co-Cathedral, Valletta.

860	3c.+1c. Type **313**	80	70
861	10c.+2c. Two angels	2·00	2·25
862	20c.+3c. Angel blowing trumpet	2·75	4·00

1989. U.S.A.–U.S.S.R. Summit Meeting, Malta.

863	**314** 10c. multicoloured	1·00	1·25

1990. Europa. Post Office Buildings. Multicoloured.

864	10c. Type **315**	1·00	50
865	35c. Branch Post Office, Zebbug (horiz)	2·50	3·75

316 Open Book and Letters from Different Alphabets (International Literacy Year)

318 St. Paul

317 Samuel Taylor Coleridge (poet) and Government House

1990. Anniversaries and Events. Multicoloured.

866	3c. Type **316**	25	25
867	4c. Count Roger of Sicily and Norman soldiers (900th anniv of Sicilian rule) (horiz)	60	30
868	19c. Communications satellite (25th anniv of I.T.U.) (horiz)	2·25	2·50
869	20c. Football and map of Malta (Union of European Football Association 20th Ordinary Congress, Malta)	2·25	2·50

1990. British Authors. Multicoloured.

870	4c. Type **317**	50	30
871	10c. Lord Byron (poet) and map of Valletta	90	70
872	12c. Sir Walter Scott (novelist) and Great Siege	1·00	95
873	25c. William Makepeace Thackeray (novelist) and Naval Arsenal	2·00	2·25

1990. Visit of Pope John Paul II. Bronze Bas-reliefs.

874	**318** 4c. black, flesh and red	50	1·50
875	– 25c. black, flesh and red	1·50	1·75

DESIGN: 25c. Pope John Paul II.

319 Flags and Football

320 Innkeeper

1990. World Cup Football Championship, Italy. Multicoloured.

876	5c. Type **319**	35	30
877	10c. Football in net	65	1·00
878	14c. Scoreboard and football	1·00	1·75
MS879	123 × 90 mm. Nos. 876/8	3·00	4·00

1990. Maltese Uniforms (4th series). As T **299**. Multicoloured.

880	3c. Captain, Royal Malta Militia, 1889	1·25	55
881	4c. Field officer, Royal Malta Artillery, 1905	1·40	60
882	10c. Labourer, Malta Labour Corps, 1915	2·50	1·50
883	25c. Lieutenant, King's Own Malta Regiment of Militia, 1918	3·75	4·50

1990. Christmas. Figures from Crib by Austin Galea, Marco Bartolo and Rosario Zammit. Multicoloured.

884	3c.+1c. Type **320**	30	50
885	10c.+2c. Nativity (41 × 28 mm)	70	1·25
886	25c.+3c. Shepherd with sheep	1·60	2·50

321 1919 10s. Stamp under Magnifying Glass

1991. 25th Anniv of Philatelic Society of Malta.
887 **321** 10c. multicoloured 60 70

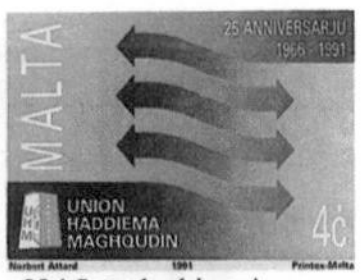

322 "Eurostar" Satellite and V.D.U. Screen **324** Interlocking Arrows

323 St. Ignatius Loyola (founder of Jesuits) (500th birth anniv)

1991. Europa. Europe in Space. Multicoloured.
888 10c. Type **322** . . . . 1·00 70
889 35c. "Ariane 4" rocket and projected HOTOL aerospace-plane . . . . . 2·00 2·75

1991. Religious Commemorations. Multicoloured.
890 3c. Type **323** 30 20
891 4c. Abbess Venerable Maria Adeodata Pisani (185th birth anniversary) (vert) . . 35 25
892 30c. St. John of the Cross (400th death anniversary) 2·00 2·75

1991. Maltese Uniforms (5th series). As T **299**. Multicoloured.
893 3c. Officer with colour, Royal Malta Fencibles, 1860 . . 30 25
894 10c. Officer with colour, Royal Malta Regiment of Militia, 1903 . . . . . . 70 60
895 19c. Officer with Queen's colour, King's Own Malta Regiment, 1968 . . . . . 1·40 1·75
896 25c. Officer with colour, Malta Armed Forces, 1991 1·75 2·00

1991. 25th Anniv of Union Haddiema Maghqudin (public services union).
897 **324** 4c. multicoloured 30 30

325 Western Honey Buzzard **326** Three Wise Men

1991. Endangered Species. Birds. Multicoloured.
898 4c. Type **325** . . . . 1·75 2·00
899 4c. Marsh harrier . . . . . . 1·75 2·00
900 10c. Eleonora's falcon . . . 1·75 2·00
901 10c. Lesser kestrel . . . . . 1·75 2·00

1991. Christmas. Multicoloured.
902 3c.+1c. Type **326** 45 50
903 10c.+2c. Holy Family . . . . 1·00 1·25
904 25c.+3c. Two shepherds . . . 2·00 3·00

327 Ta' Hagrat Neolithic Temple

1991. National Heritage of the Maltese Islands. Multicoloured.
905 1c. Type **327** 25 50
906 2c. Cottoner Gate 25 50
907 3c. St. Michael's Bastion, Valletta 25 50
908 4c. Spinola Palace, St. Julian's 25 15
909 5c. Birkirkara Church . . . 30 20
910 10c. Mellieha Bay 60 35
911 12c. Wied iz-Zurrieq 65 40
912 14c. Mgarr harbour, Gozo 75 45
913 20c. Yacht marina . . . . . 1·10 65
914 50c. Gozo Channel . . . . . 2·00 1·60
915 £1 "Arab Horses" (sculpture by Antonio Sciortino) . . . 4·25 3·25
916 £2 Independence Monument (Ganni Bonnici) (vert) . . 8·50 7·00

328 Aircraft Tailfins and Terminal

1992. Opening of Int Air Terminal. Mult.
917 4c. Type **328** 75 30
918 10c. National flags and terminal . . . . 1·25 70

329 Ships of Columbus

1992. Europa. 500th Anniv of Discovery of America by Columbus. Multicoloured.
919 10c. Type **329** . . . . 1·25 55
920 35c. Columbus and map of Americas . . . . 2·50 2·25

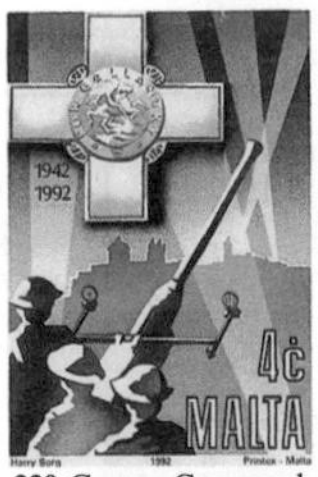

330 George Cross and Anti-aircraft Gun Crew **332** Church of the Flight into Egypt

331 Running

1992. 50th Anniv of Award of George Cross to Malta. Multicoloured.
921 4c. Type **330** . . . . 1·00 30
922 10c. George Cross and memorial bell . . . . . . 1·50 1·00
923 50c. Tanker "Ohio" entering Grand Harbour . . . . . 7·00 8·50

1992. Olympic Games, Barcelona. Multicoloured.
924 3c. Type **331** 65 20
925 10c. High jumping . . . . . 1·25 1·00
926 30c. Swimming . . . . . . 2·50 4·50

1992. Rehabilitation of Historical Buildings.
927 **332** 3c. black, stone and grey 55 30
928 – 4c. black, stone and pink 60 30
929 – 19c. black, stone and lilac 2·50 3·50
930 – 25c. black, stone and green . . . . 2·75 3·50
DESIGNS—HORIZ: 4c. St. John's Co-Cathedral; 25c. Auberge de Provence. VERT: 19c. Church of Madonna del Pillar.

333 "The Nativity" (Giuseppe Cali)

1992. Christmas. Religious Paintings by Giuseppe Cali from Mosta Church. Multicoloured.
931 3c.+1c. Type **333** . . . . . 1·00 1·10
932 10c.+2c. "Adoration of the Magi" . . . . 2·25 2·50
933 25c.+3c. "Christ with the Elders in the Temple" . . 3·75 4·50

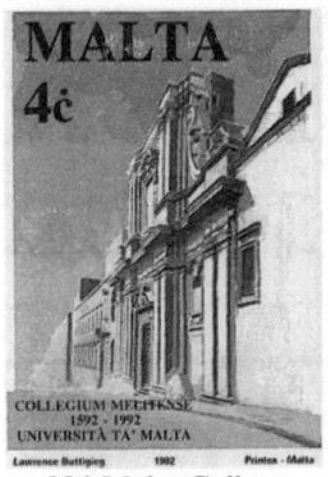

334 Malta College Building, Valletta **335** Lions Club Emblem

1992. 400th Anniv of University of Malta. Multicoloured.
934 4c. Type **334** 75 25
935 30c. Modern University complex, Tal-Qroqq (horiz) 2·75 4·00

1993. 75th Anniv of International Association of Lions Club. Multicoloured.
936 4c. Type **335** 50 25
937 50c. Eye (Sight First Campaign) . . . . 2·75 4·00

336 Untitled Painting by Paul Carbonaro

1993. Europa. Contemporary Art. Mult.
938 10c. Type **336** . . . . 1·00 50
939 35c. Untitled painting by Alfred Chircop (horiz) . . 2·50 4·25

337 Mascot holding Flame

1993. 5th Small States of Europe Games. Multicoloured.
940 3c. Type **337** 20 20
941 4c. Cycling 80 30
942 10c. Tennis . . . . 1·50 1·00
943 35c. Yachting . . . . 2·75 3·50
MS944 120 × 80 mm. Nos. 940/3 4·00 4·00

338 Learning First Aid **339** "Papilio machaon"

1993. 50th Anniv of Award of Bronze Cross to Maltese Scouts and Guides. Multicoloured.
945 3c. Type **338** 40 15
946 4c. Bronze Cross 40 20
947 10c. Scout building camp fire 90 90
948 35c. Governor Lord Gort presenting Bronze Cross, 1943 . . . . 2·50 3·50

1993. European Year of the Elderly. Butterflies. Multicoloured.
949 5c. Type **339** 35 20
950 35c. "Vanessa atalanta" . . . 1·75 2·25

340 G.W.U. Badge and Interlocking "50" **341** Child Jesus and Star

1993. 50th Anniv of General Workers Union.
951 **340** 4c. multicoloured 35 40

1993. Christmas. Multicoloured.
952 3c.+1c. Type **341** 30 35
953 10c.+2c. Christmas tree . . . 85 1·10
954 25c.+3c. Star in traditional window . . . . 1·60 2·50

342 Council Arms (face value top left)

1993. Inauguration of Local Community Councils. Sheet 110 × 93 mm, containing T **342** and similar horiz designs showing different Council Arms. Multicoloured.
MS955 5c. Type **342**; 5c. Face value top right; 5c. Face value bottom left; 5c. Face value bottom right 1·50 2·25

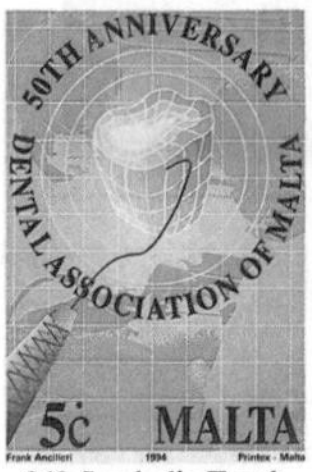

343 Symbolic Tooth and Probe **344** Sir Themistocles Zammit (discoverer of Brucella microbe)

1994. 50th Anniv of Maltese Dental Association. Multicoloured.
956 5c. Type **343** 35 30
957 44c. Symbolic mouth and dental mirror . . . . . . 3·00 3·00

1994. Europa. Discoveries. Multicoloured.
958 14c. Type **344** 50 30
959 30c. Bilingually inscribed candelabrum of 2nd century B.C. (deciphering of ancient Phoenician language) . . . . 1·90 3·25

345 Family in Silhouette (International Year of the Family) **346** Football and Map

1994. Anniversaries and Events. Multicoloured.
960 5c. Type **345** 30 20
961 9c. Stylized Red Cross (International recognition of Malta Red Cross Society) 60 50
962 14c. Animals and crops (150th anniv of Agrarian Society) 90 80
963 20c. Worker in silhouette (75th anniv of I.L.O.) . . . 1·25 1·60
964 25c. St. Paul's Anglican Cathedral (155th anniv) (vert) . . . . 1·40 1·75

1994. World Cup Football Championship, U.S.A. Multicoloured.
965 5c. Type **346** 40 20
966 14c. Ball and goal . . . . . 1·00 80
967 30c. Ball and pitch superimposed on map . . 2·50 4·25
MS968 123 × 88 mm. Nos. 965/7 3·75 4·00

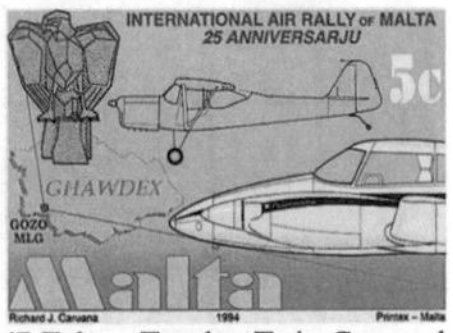

347 Falcon Trophy, Twin Comanche and Auster (25th anniv of Malta International Rally)

1994. Aviation Anniversaries and Events. Multicoloured.
969 5c. Type **347** 50 20
970 14c. Alouette helicopter, display teams and logo (Malta International Airshow) . . . . 1·75 85

971 20c. De Havilland Dove "City of Valetta" and Avro York aircraft with logo (50th anniv of I.C.A.O.) . . . 1·90 1·75
972 25c. Airbus 320 "Nicolas Cottoner" and De Havilland Comet aircraft with logo (50th anniv of I.C.A.O.) . . . . 1·90 1·90

348 National Flags and Astronaut on Moon

350 Helmet-shaped Ewer

349 Virgin Mary and Child with Angels

1994. 25th Anniv of First Manned Moon Landing.
973 **348** 14c. multicoloured . . . . 1·10 1·25

1994. Christmas. Multicoloured.
974 5c. Type **349** 25 10
975 9c.+2c. Angel in pink (vert) 65 70
976 14c.+3c. Virgin Mary and Child (vert) . . . . 90 1·25
977 20c.+3c. Angel in green (vert) 1·60 2·50
Nos. 975/7 are larger, 28 × 41 mm, and depict details from Type **349**.

1994. Maltese Antique Silver Exhibition. Multicoloured.
978 5c. Type **350** 40 20
979 14c. Balsamina 90 80
980 20c. Coffee pot . . . . . . 1·60 1·90
981 25c. Sugar box . . . . 1·90 2·50

351 "60 plus" and Hands touching

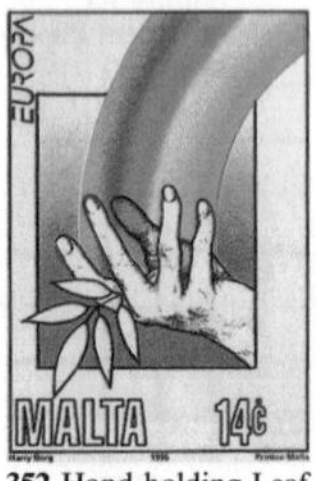

352 Hand holding Leaf and Rainbow

1995. Anniversaries and Events. Multicoloured.
982 2c. Type **351** (25th anniv of National Association of Pensioners) 15 15
983 5c. Child's drawing (10th anniv of National Youth Council) 25 20
984 14c. Conference emblem (4th World Conference on Women, Peking, China) . . 70 80
985 20c. Nurse and thermometer (50th anniv of Malta Memorial District Nursing Association) . . . . 1·25 1·40
986 25c. Louis Pasteur (biologist) (death centenary) . . . . . 1·50 1·75

1995. Europa. Peace and Freedom. Multicoloured.
987 14c. Type **352** . . . . 1·00 55
988 30c. Peace doves (horiz) . . . 1·75 2·50

353 Junkers Ju 87B "Stuka" Dive Bombers over Valletta and Anti-aircraft Gun

1995. Anniversaries. Multicoloured.
989 5c. Type **353** (50th anniv of end of Second World War) 25 25
990 14c. Silhouetted people holding hands (50th anniv of United Nations) 70 80
991 35c. Hands holding bowl of wheat (50th anniv of F.A.O.) (vert) . . . . . . 2·00 2·25

354 Light Bulb

356 Pinto's Turret Clock

355 Rock Wall and Girna

1995. Maltese Electricity and Telecommunications. Multicoloured.
992 2c. Type **354** 15 15
993 5c. Symbolic owl and binary codes 25 25
994 9c. Dish aerial 45 50
995 14c. Sun and rainbow over trees 70 80
996 20c. Early telephone, satellite and Moon's surface . . . 1·25 1·50

1995. European Nature Conservation Year. Multicoloured.
997 5c. Type **355** 75 25
998 14c. Maltese wall lizards . . 2·25 80
999 44c. Aleppo pine . . . . . . 3·50 3·00

1995. Treasures of Malta. Antique Maltese Clocks. Multicoloured.
1000 1c. Type **356** 15 60
1001 5c. Michelangelo Sapiano (horologist) and clocks . . 50 25
1002 14c. Arlogg tal-lira clock . . 1·50 80
1003 25c. Sundials . . . . 2·50 3·50

357 Children's Christmas Eve Procession

1995. Christmas. Multicoloured.
1004 5c. Type **357** 25 10
1005 5c.+2c. Children with crib (vert) 30 50
1006 14c.+3c. Children with lanterns (vert) . . . . . 1·00 1·25
1007 25c.+3c. Boy with lantern and balustrade (vert) . . 1·75 2·75
Nos. 1005/7 are 27 × 32 mm and depict details from Type **357**.

358 Silhouetted Children and President's Palace, San Anton

1996. Anniversaries. Multicoloured.
1008 5c. Type **358** (35th anniv of the President's Award) . . 25 25
1009 14c. Nazzareno Camilleri (priest) and St. Patrick's Church, Salesjani (90th birth anniv) 65 65
1010 20c. St. Mary Euphrasia and convent (birth bicentenary) . . . . . . 1·00 1·10
1011 25c. Silhouetted children and fountain (50th anniv of UNICEF) . . . . . . 1·25 1·40

359 Carved Figures from Skorba

1996. Maltese Prehistoric Art Exhibition. Multicoloured.
1012 5c. Type **359** 30 20
1013 14c. Temple carving, Gozo 80 85
1014 20c. Carved figure of a woman, Skorba (vert) . . 1·10 1·25
1015 35c. Ghar Dalam pot (vert) 1·90 2·50

360 Mabel Strickland (politician and journalist)

361 Face and Emblem (United Nations Decade against Drug Abuse)

1996. Europa. Famous Women. Multicoloured.
1016 14c. Type **360** 75 55
1017 30c. Inez Soler (artist, musician and writer) . . . 2·00 2·00

1996. Anniversaries and Events. Multicoloured.
1018 5c. Type **361** 25 25
1019 5c. "Fi" and emblem (50th anniv of Malta Federation of Industry) 25 25
1020 14c. Commemorative plaque and national flag (75th anniv of self-government) 80 80
1021 44c. Guglielmo Marconi and early radio equipment (centenary of radio) . . . 2·25 2·50

362 Judo

1996. Olympic Games, Atlanta. Multicoloured.
1022 2c. Type **362** 10 10
1023 5c. Athletics 30 25
1024 14c. Diving 80 80
1025 25c. Rifle-shooting . . . . 1·40 1·60

363 "Harvest Time" (Cali)

1996. 150th Birth Anniv of Guiseppe Cali (painter). Multicoloured.
1026 5c. Type **363** 30 25
1027 14c. "Dog" (Cali) 80 70
1028 20c. "Countrywoman in a Field" (Cali) (vert) . . . 1·10 1·10
1029 25c. "Cali at his Easel" (Edward Dingli) (vert) . . 1·25 1·25

364 Bus No. 1990 "Diamond Star", 1920s

1996. Buses. Multicoloured.
1030 2c. Type **364** 30 10
1031 5c. No. 434 "Tom Mix", 1930s 60 25
1032 14c. No. 1764 "Verdala", 1940s . . . . 1·25 80
1033 30c. No. 3495, 1960s . . . 1·75 2·00

365 Stained Glass Window

1996. Christmas. Multicoloured.
1034 5c. Type **365** 35 10
1035 5c.+2c. Madonna and Child (29 × 35 mm) 40 60
1036 14c.+3c. Angel facing right (29 × 35 mm) . . . . . . 80 1·40
1037 25c.+3c. Angel facing left (29 × 35 mm) . . . . . . 1·25 2·50
Nos. 1035/7 show details from Type **365**.

366 Hompesch Arch and Arms, Zabbar

368 Gahan carrying Door

367 Captain-General of the Galleys' Sedan Chair

1997. Bicentenary of Maltese Cities. Multicoloured.
1038 6c. Type **366** 30 25
1039 16c. Statue, church and arms, Siggiewi 70 70
1040 26c. Seated statue and arms, Zejtun . . . . 1·10 1·10
MS1041 125 × 90 mm. Nos. 1038/40 3·50 3·50

1997. Treasures of Malta. Sedan Chairs. Multicoloured.
1042 2c. Type **367** 15 15
1043 6c. Cotoner Grandmasters' chair 30 30
1044 16c. Chair from Cathedral Museum, Mdina (vert) . . 70 70
1045 27c. Chevalier D'Arezzo's chair (vert) . . . . 1·10 1·10

1997. Europa. Tales and Legends. Multicoloured.
1046 16c. Type **368** . . . . . . 1·25 75
1047 35c. St. Dimitrius appearing from painting . . . . . . 2·00 1·50

369 Modern Sculpture (Antonio Sciortino)

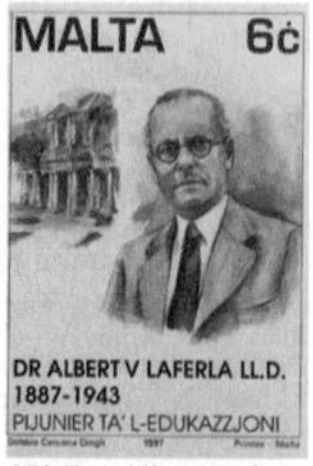

370 Dr. Albert Laferla

1997. Anniversaries. Multicoloured.
1048 1c. Type **369** 10 15
1049 6c. Joseph Calleia and film reel (horiz) 40 40
1050 6c. Gozo Cathedral (horiz) 40 40
1051 11c. City of Gozo (horiz) . . 60 50
1052 16c. Sculpture of head (Sciortino) 80 70
1053 22c. Joseph Calleia and film camera (horiz) . . . . . 1·00 1·00
ANNIVERSARIES: 1, 16c. 50th death anniv of Antonio Sciortino (sculptor); 6 (No. 1049), 22c. Birth centenary of Joseph Calleia (actor); 6 (No. 1050), 11c. 300th anniv of construction of Gozo Cathedral.

1997. Pioneers of Education. Multicoloured.
1054 6c. Type **370** 30 25
1055 16c. Sister Emilie de Vialar 70 70
1056 19c. Mgr. Paolo Pullicino 80 80
1057 26c. Mgr. Tommaso Gargallo . . . . 1·00 1·10

371 The Nativity

1997. Christmas. Multicoloured.
1058 6c. Type **371** 30 10
1059 6c.+2c. Mary and baby Jesus (vert) 35 50
1060 16c.+3c. Joseph with donkey (vert) . . . . 1·00 1·40
1061 26c.+3c. Shepherd with lamb (vert) . . . . 1·50 2·50
Nos. 1059/61 show details from Type **371**.

372 Plan of Fort and Soldiers in Victoria Lines

1997. Anniversaries. Multicoloured (except 6c.).
1062 2c. Type **372** 20 10
1063 6c. Sir Paul Boffa making speech (black and red) . . 30 25
1064 16c. Plan of fort and gun crew 90 65
1065 37c. Queue of voters . . . . 1·50 2·00
ANNIVERSARIES: 2, 16c. Centenary of Victoria Lines; 6, 37c. 50th anniv of 1947 Self-government Constitution.

373 "Maria Amelia Grognet" (Antonine de Favray)

1998. Treasures of Malta. Costumes and Paintings.
1066 6c. Type **373** 80 50
1067 6c. Gentleman's waistcoat, c.1790–1810 . . . . 80 50
1068 16c. Lady's dinner dress, c.1880 . . . . 1·10 90
1069 16c. "Veneranda, Baroness Abela, and her Grandson" (De Favray) 1·10 90
MS1070 123 × 88 mm. 26c. City of Valletta from old print (39 × 47 mm) . . . . 1·60 1·60

374 Grand Master Ferdinand von Hompesch

1998. Bicentenary of Napoleon's Capture of Malta. Multicoloured.
1071 6c. Type **374** 60 70
1072 6c. French fleet 60 70
1073 16c. French landing . . . . 1·10 1·40
1074 16c. General Napoleon Bonaparte . . . . 1·10 1·40

375 Racing Two-man Luzzus **376** Dolphin and Diver

1998. Europa. Sailing Regatta, Grand Harbour. Multicoloured.
1075 16c. Type **375** . . . . . . 1·40 55
1076 35c. Racing four-man luzzus 1·90 2·50

1998. International Year of the Ocean. Multicoloured.
1077 2c. Type **376** 40 25
1078 6c. Diver and sea-urchin . . 65 25
1079 16c. Jacques Cousteau and diver (horiz) . . . . . . 1·60 80
1080 27c. Two divers (horiz) . . 2·00 2·25

377 Goalkeeper saving Goal **378** Ships' Wheels (50th anniv of Int Maritime Organization)

1998. World Cup Football Championship, France. Players and flags. Multicoloured.
1081 6c. Type **377** 70 25
1082 16c. Two players and referee 1·40 70
1083 22c. Two footballers . . . . 1·60 2·00
MS1084 122 × 87 mm. Nos. 1081/3 3·25 3·25

1998. Anniversaries. Multicoloured.
1085 1c. Type **378** 10 30
1086 6c. Symbolic family (50th anniv of Universal Declaration of Human Rights) 40 25
1087 11c. "GRTU" and cogwheels (50th anniv of General Retailers and Traders Union) 70 40
1088 19c. Mercury (50th anniv of Chamber of Commerce) 1·10 1·40
1089 26c. Aircraft tailfins (25th anniv of Air Malta) . . . 2·40 2·50

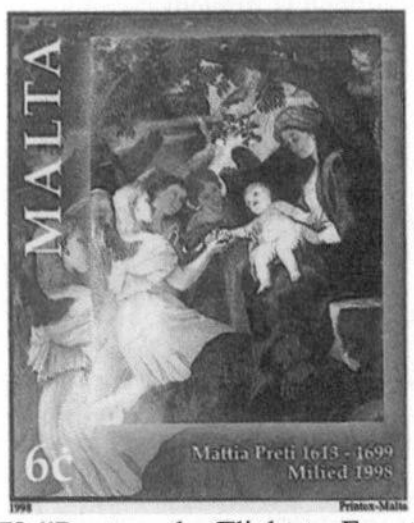

379 "Rest on the Flight to Egypt"

1998. Christmas. Paintings by Mattia Preti. Mult.
1090 6c. Type **379** 40 10
1091 6c.+2c. "Virgin and Child with Sts. Anthony and John the Baptist" 50 70
1092 16c.+3c. "Virgin and Child with Sts. Raphael, Nicholas and Gregory" 1·25 1·75
1093 26c.+3c. "Virgin and Child with Sts. John the Baptist and Nicholas" . . . . . 1·75 2·75

380 Fort St. Angelo

1999. 900th Anniv of the Sovereign Military Order of Malta. Multicoloured.
1094 2c. Type **380** 30 10
1095 6c. Grand Master De l'Isle Adam (vert) 60 25
1096 16c. Grand Master La Valette (vert) . . . . . . 1·10 55
1097 27c. Auberge de Castille et Leon . . . . 1·75 1·60

381 Little Ringed Plover, Ghadira Nature Reserve

1999. Europa. Parks and Gardens. Multicoloured.
1098 16c. Type **381** . . . . . . 2·00 55
1099 35c. River kingfisher, Simar Nature Reserve . . . . . 2·50 3·00

382 Council of Europe Assembly

1999. 50th Anniv of Council of Europe. Mult.
1100 6c. Type **382** 75 25
1101 16c. Council of Europe Headquarters, Strasbourg 1·25 1·25

383 U.P.U. Emblem and Marsamxett Harbour, Valletta

1999. 125th Anniv of Universal Postal Union. Multicoloured.
1102 6c. Type **383** . . . . 1·25 1·40
1103 16c. Nuremberg and "iBRA '99" International Stamp Exhibition emblem . . . 1·50 1·60
1104 22c. Paris and "Philexfrance '99" International Stamp Exhibition emblem . . . 1·60 1·75
1105 27c. Peking and "China '99" International Stamp Exhibition emblem . . . 1·75 1·90
1106 37c. Melbourne and "Australia '99" International Stamp Exhibition emblem . . . 1·90 2·25

384 Couple in Luzzu

1999. Tourism. Multicoloured.
1107 6c. Type **384** 50 25
1108 16c. Tourist taking photograph 95 55
1109 22c. Man sunbathing (horiz) 1·25 1·00
1110 27c. Couple with horse-drawn carriage (horiz) . . 1·90 1·25
1111 37c. Caveman at Ta' Hagrat Neolithic temple (horiz) 2·50 2·75

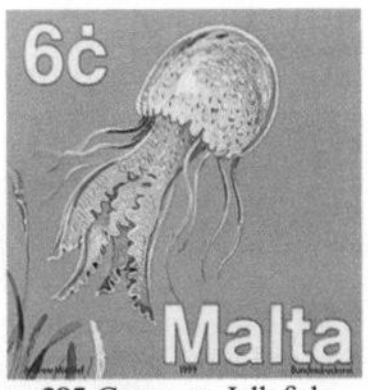

385 Common Jellyfish

1999. Marine Life of the Mediterranean. Mult.
1112 6c. Type **385** 65 65
1113 6c. Peacock wrasse 65 65
1114 6c. Common cuttlefish . . . 65 65
1115 6c. Violet sea-urchin 65 65
1116 6c. Dusky grouper 65 65
1117 6c. Common two-banded seabream 65 65
1118 6c. Star-coral 65 65
1119 6c. Spiny spider crab . . . 65 65
1120 6c. Rainbow wrasse 65 65
1121 6c. Octopus 65 65
1122 6c. Atlantic trumpet triton 65 65
1123 6c. Mediterranean parrotfish 65 65
1124 6c. Long-snouted seahorse 65 65
1125 6c. Deep-water hermit crab 65 65
1126 6c. Mediterranean moray . . 65 65
1127 6c. Common starfish 65 65
Nos. 1112/27 were printed together, se-tenant, forming a composite design.

386 Father Mikiel Scerri

1999. Bicentenary of Maltese Uprising against the French. Multicoloured.
1128 6c. Type **386** 70 70
1129 6c. "L-Eroj Maltin" (statue) 70 70
1130 16c. General Belgrand de Vaubois (French commander) . . . . . . 1·25 1·25
1131 16c. Captain Alexander Ball R.N. . . . . 1·25 1·25

387 "Wolfgang Philip Guttenberg interceding with The Virgin" (votive painting)

1999. Mellieha Sanctuary Commemoration. Mult.
1132 **387** 35c. multicoloured . . . 2·25 2·25
MS1133 123 × 88 mm. 6c. "Mellieha Virgin and Child" (rock painting) (vert) . . . . 1·00 1·10

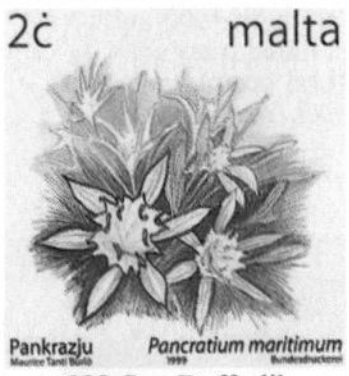

388 Sea Daffodil

1999. Maltese Flowers. Multicoloured.
1134 1c. *Helichrysum melitense* 10 10
1135 2c. Type **388** 10 10
1136 3c. *Cistus creticus* 10 15
1137 4c. Southern dwarf iris . . 10 15
1138 5c. *Papaver rhoeas* 15 20
1139 6c. French daffodil 20 25
1139a 7c. *Vitex angus-castus* . . . 20 25
1140 10c. *Rosa sempervirens* . . 30 35
1141 11c. *Silene colorata* . . . 35 40
1142 12c. *Cynara cardunculus* 40 45
1143 16c. Yellow-throated crocus 50 55
1144 19c. *Anthemis arvensis* . . 60 65
1145 20c. *Anacamptis pyramidalis* 65 70
1145a 22c. *Spartium junceum* . . 70 75
1146 25c. Large Star of Bethlehem 80 85
1147 27c. *Borago officinalis* . . 85 90
1147a 28c. *Crataegus azalorus* . . 90 95
1147b 37c. *Cercis siliquastrum* . . 1·10 1·20
1147c 45c. *Myrtus communis* . . 1·40 1·50
1148 46c. Wild tulip . . . . . . 1·40 1·50
1149 50c. *Chrysanthemum coronarium* . . . . . . 1·60 1·70
1149a 76c. *Pistacia lentiscus* . . . 2·40 2·50
1150 £1 *Malva sylvestris* . . . 3·25 3·50
1151 £2 *Adonis microcarpa* . . 6·25 6·50

389 Madonna and Child

1999. Christmas. Multicoloured.
1152 6c. Type **389** 50 10
1153 6c.+3c. Carol singers . . . 55 65
1154 16c.+3c. Santa Claus . . . 1·40 1·75
1155 26c.+3c. Christmas decorations . . . . 1·75 2·50

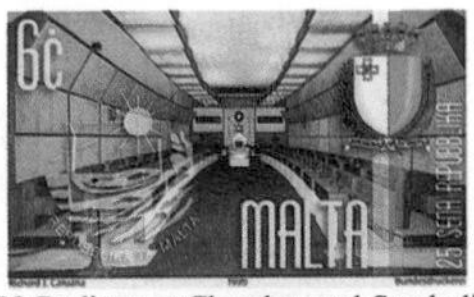

390 Parliament Chamber and Symbolic Luzzu

1999. 25th Anniv of Republic. Multicoloured.
1156 6c. Type **390** 40 25
1157 11c. Parliament in session and Council of Europe emblem 60 35
1158 16c. Church and Central Bank of Malta building 80 55
1159 19c. Aerial view of Gozo and emblems . . . . . . 1·10 1·00
1160 26c. Computer and shipyard 1·40 1·60

391 Gift and Flowers

2000. Greetings Stamps. Multicoloured.
1161 3c. Type **391** 30 15
1162 6c. Photograph, envelope and rose 50 25
1163 16c. Flowers and silver heart 90 55
1164 20c. Champagne and pocket watch . . . . 1·10 1·00
1165 22c. Wedding rings and roses . . . . 1·25 1·40

392 Luzzu and Cruise Liner

2000. Malta during the 20th Century. Multicoloured.
1166 6c. Type **392** 50 25
1167 16c. Street musicians and modern street carnival . . 90 55

1168 22c. Family in 1900 and illuminated quayside . . . 1·25 85
1169 27c. Rural occupations and Citadel, Victoria . . . . 1·75 1·75

393 Footballers and Trophy (Centenary of Malta Football Association)

2000. Sporting Events. Multicoloured.
1170 6c. Type **393** 55 25
1171 16c. Swimming and sailing (Olympic Games, Sydney) 85 55
1172 26c. Judo, shooting and running (Olympic Games, Sydney) . . . . 1·40 1·10
1173 37c. Football (European Championship) . . . . . 1·75 2·50

394 "Building Europe"

2000. Europa.
1174 **394** 16c. multicoloured . . . 1·25 65
1175 46c. multicoloured . . . 2·75 2·75

395 D.H.66 Hercules, 1928

2000. Century of Air Transport, 1900–2000. Mult.
1176 6c. Type **395** 85 85
1177 6c. LZ 127 *Graf Zeppelin*, 1933 . . . . 85 85
1178 16c. Douglas DC-3 Dakota of Air Malta Ltd, 1949 1·60 1·60
1179 16c. Airbus A320 of Air Malta . . . . 1·60 1·60
MS1180 122 × 87 mm. Nos. 1176/9 4·25 4·25

Nos. 1176/7 and 1178/9 were each printed together, se-tenant, with the backgrounds forming composite designs.

396 Catherine Wheel and Fireworks

2000. Fireworks. Multicoloured.
1181 2c. Type **396** 30 10
1182 6c. Exploding multicoloured fireworks 65 25
1183 16c. Catherine wheel . . . . 1·25 55
1184 20c. Exploding green fireworks . . . . 1·40 1·00
1185 50c. Numbered rockets in rack . . . . 3·00 4·00

397 "Boy walking Dog" (Jean Paul Zammit)

2000. "Stampin' the Future" (Children's stamp design competition winners). Multicoloured.
1186 6c. Type **397** 55 55
1187 6c. "Stars and Woman in Megalithic Temple" (Chiara Borg) 55 55
1188 6c. "Sunny Day" (Bettina Paris) 55 55
1189 6c. "Hands holding Heart" (Roxana Caruana) . . . 55 55

398 Boy's Sermon, Nativity Play and Girl with Doll

2000. Christmas. Multicoloured.
1190 6c. Type **398** 45 10
1191 6c.+3c. Three Wise Men (23 × 27 mm) 55 65
1192 16c.+3c. Family with Father Christmas . . . . 1·25 1·75
1193 26c.+3c. Christmas tree, church and family . . . . 1·75 2·50
MS1194 174 × 45 mm. Nos. 1190/3 3·50 4·50

399 Crocodile Float

2001. Maltese Carnival. Multicoloured.
1195 6c. Type **399** 50 25
1196 11c. King Karnival in procession (vert) 75 40
1197 16c. Woman and children in costumes (vert) 90 55
1198 19c. Horseman carnival float (vert) . . . . 1·10 1·25
1199 27c. Carnival procession . . 1·50 1·75
MS1200 127 × 92 mm. 12c. Old-fashioned clowns; 37c. Women dressed as clowns (both 32 × 32 mm) . . . . 2·50 3·00

400 St. Elmo Lighthouse

401 "The Chicken Seller" (E. Caruana Dingli)

2001. Maltese Lighthouses. Multicoloured.
1201 6c. Type **400** 65 25
1202 16c. Gurdan Lighthouse . . 1·25 70
1203 22c. Delimara Lighthouse 1·75 2·00

2001. Edward Caruana Dingli (painter) Commemoration. Multicoloured.
1204 2c. Type **401** 20 15
1205 4c. "The Village Beau" . . 35 15
1206 6c. "The Faldetta" 50 25
1207 10c. "The Guitar Player" . . 80 60
1208 26c. "Wayside Orange Seller" . . . . 2·00 2·50

402 Nazju Falzon, Gorg Preca and Adeodata Pisani (candidates for Beatification)

2001. Visit of Pope John Paul II. Multicoloured.
1209 6c. Type **402** 85 25
1210 16c. Pope John Paul II and statue of St. Paul . . . . 1·40 1·00
MS1211 123 × 87 mm. 75c. Pope John Paul with Nazju Falzon, Gorg Preca and Adeodata Pisani 3·50 3·50

403 Painted Frog

2001. Europa. Pond Life. Multicoloured.
1212 16c. Type **403** . . . . . . 1·25 65
1213 46c. Red-veined darter (dragonfly) . . . . 2·25 2·75

404 Herring Gull ("Yellow-legged Gull") (*Larus cachinnans*)

2001. Maltese Birds. Multicoloured.
1214 6c. Type **404** 60 60
1215 6c. Common kestrel (*Falco tinnunculus*) 60 60
1216 6c. Golden oriole (*Oriolus oriolus*) 60 60
1217 6c. Chaffinch (*Fringilla coelebs*) and Eurasian goldfinch (*Carduelis carduelis*) 60 60
1218 6c. Blue rock thrush (*Monticola solitarius*) . . 60 60
1219 6c. European bee-eater (*Merops apiaster*) 60 60
1220 6c. House martin (*Delichon urbica*) and barn swallow (*Hirundo rustica*) 60 60
1221 6c. Spanish sparrow (*Passer hispaniolensis*) 60 60
1222 6c. Spectacled warbler (*Sylvia conspicillata*) . . . 60 60
1223 6c. Turtle dove (*Streptopelia turtur*) 60 60
1224 6c. Northern pintail (*Anas acuta*) 60 60
1225 6c. Little bittern (*Ixobrychus minutus*) 60 60
1226 6c. Eurasian woodcock (*Scolopax rusticola*) . . . 60 60
1227 6c. Short-eared owl (*Asio flammeus*) 60 60
1228 6c. Northern lapwing (*Vanellus vanellus*) 60 60
1229 6c. Moorhen (*Gallinula chloropus*) 60 60

Nos 1214/29 were printed together, se-tenant, with the backgrounds forming a composite design.

405 Whistle Flute

407 Man with Net chasing Star

406 Kelb tal-Fenek (Pharaoh Hound)

2001. Traditional Maltese Musical Instruments. Multicoloured.
1230 1c. Type **405** 15 50
1231 3c. Reed pipe 30 40
1232 14c. Maltese bagpipe . . . 85 50
1233 20c. Friction drum . . . . 1·25 1·40
1234 25c. Frame drum . . . . . 1·50 1·75

2001. Maltese Dogs. Multicoloured.
1235 6c. Type **406** 60 25
1236 16c. Kelb tal-Kacca . . . . 1·25 55
1237 19c. Maltese . . . . 1·25 1·10
1238 35c. Kelb tal-But . . . . . 2·00 2·75

2001. Christmas. Multicoloured.
1239 6c.+2c. Type **407** 60 40
1240 15c.+2c. Father and children 1·25 1·40
1241 16c.+2c. Mother and daughter . . . . 1·25 1·40
1242 19c.+3c. Young woman with shopping bags . . . . . 1·40 1·75

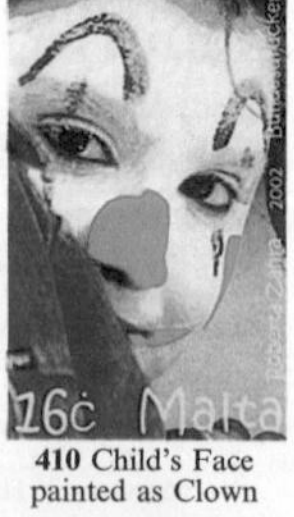

408 *Hippocampus guttulatus*

410 Child's Face painted as Clown

409 Sideboard

2002. Endangered Species. Mediterranean Seahorses. Multicoloured.
1243 6c. Type **408** 60 60
1244 6c. *Hippocampus hippocampus* 60 60
1245 16c. Close-up of *Hippocampus guttulatus* 1·25 1·25
1246 16c. *Hippocampus hippocampus* on seabed . . 1·25 1·25

2002. Antique Furniture. Multicoloured.
1247 2c. Type **409** 25 40
1248 4c. Bureau (vert) 45 30
1249 11c. Inlaid table (vert) . . . 85 40
1250 26c. Cabinet (vert) . . . . 1·50 85
1251 60c. Carved chest . . . . . 3·00 4·00

2002. Europa. Circus.
1252 **410** 16c. multicoloured . . . 1·25 1·00

411 *Hyles sammuti*

2002. Moths and Butterflies. Multicoloured.
1253 6c. Type **411** 50 50
1254 6c. *Utetheisa pulchella* . . . 50 50
1255 6c. *Ophiusa tirhaca* 50 50
1256 6c. *Phragmatobia fulginosa melitensis* 50 50
1257 6c. *Vanessa cardui* 50 50
1258 6c. *Polyommatus icarus* . . 50 50
1259 6c. *Gonepteryx cleopatra* . . 50 50
1260 6c. *Vanessa atlanta* 50 50
1261 6c. *Eucrostes indigenata* . . 50 50
1262 6c. *Macroglossum stellatarum* 50 50
1263 6c. *Lasiocampa quercus* . . 50 50
1264 6c. *Catocala electa* 50 50
1265 6c. *Maniola jurtina hyperhispulla* 50 50
1266 6c. *Pieris brassicaei* 50 50
1267 6c. *Papilio machaon melitensis* 50 50
1268 6c. *Dainaus chrysippus* . . . 50 50

No. 1260 is inscribed "atalania" and 1264 "elocata", both in error.

412 "Kusksu Bil-ful" (bean stew)

2002. Maltese Cookery. Multicoloured.
1269 7c. Type **412** 60 25
1270 12c. "Qaqocc mimli" (stuffed artichoke) . . . . 1·00 50
1271 16c. "Lampuki" (dorada with aubergines) . . . . 1·10 65
1272 27c. "Qaghqd Tal-kavatelli" (chestnut dessert) . . . . 2·00 2·50
MS1273 125 × 90 mm. 75c. "Stuffat Tal-fenek" (rabbit stew) . . . 4·50 5·00

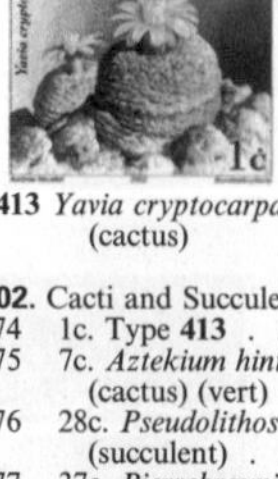

413 *Yavia cryptocarpa* (cactus)

414 Chief Justice Adrian Dingli,

2002. Cacti and Succulents. Multicoloured.
1274 1c. Type **413** 15 50
1275 7c. *Aztekium hintonii* (cactus) (vert) 65 25
1276 28c. *Pseudolithos migiurtinus* (succulent) . . . . 1·75 70
1277 37c. *Pierrebraunia brauniorum* (cactus) (vert) 2·25 1·50
1278 76c. *Euphorbia turbiniformis* (succulent) . . . . 4·00 5·00

2002. Personalities.
1279 **414** 3c. green and black . . . 30 40
1280 – 7c. green and black . . . 60 25

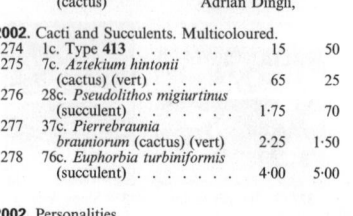

1281 – 15c. brown and agate . . 1·00 60
1282 – 35c. brown and sepia . . 2·00 1·75
1283 – 50c. light blue and blue 2·50 3·00
DESIGNS: 7c. Oreste Kirkop (opera singer); 15c. Athanasius Kircher (Jesuit scholar); 35c. Archpriest Saverio Cassar; 50c. Emmanuele Vitali (notary).

415 Mary and Joseph in Donkey Cart

2002. Christmas. Multicoloured.
1284 7c. Type **415** 70 25
1285 16c. Shepherds and Kings on a bus . . . . 1·25 55
1286 22c. Holy Family and angels in luzzu (boat) . . . . . 1·60 75
1287 37c. Holy Family in horse-drawn carriage . . . . . 2·00 1·50
1288 75c. Nativity on Maltese fishing boat . . . . . . 3·75 5·00

416 Vanden Plas Princess Landaulette, 1965

2003. Vintage Cars. Multicoloured.
1289 2c. Type **416** 25 45
1290 7c. Allard "M" type, 1948 65 25
1291 10c. Cadillac Model "B", 1904 . . . . 85 35
1292 26c. Fiat Cinquecento Model "A" Topolino, 1936 . . . . 1·60 1·50
1293 35c. Ford Anglia Super, 1965 . . . . 2·25 2·50

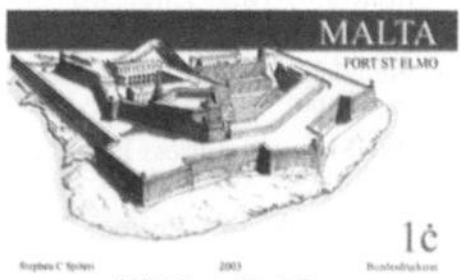

417 Fort St. Elmo

2003. Maltese Military Architecture. Multicoloured.
1294 1c. Type **417** 15 40
1295 4c. Rinella Battery 40 30
1296 11c. Fort St. Angelo 85 40
1297 16c. Section through Reserve Post R15 . . . . 1·25 60
1298 44c. Fort Tigne . . . . . . 2·75 3·50

418 St. George on Horseback **419** "CISKBEER"

2003. Paintings of St. George.
1299 **418** 3c. multicoloured 30 30
1300 – 7c. multicoloured 60 30
1301 – 14c. multicoloured . . . 95 60
1302 – 19c. multicoloured . . . 1·40 1·25
1303 – 27c. multicoloured . . . 1·75 1·90
DESIGNS: 7c. to 27c. Various paintings of St. George.

2003. Europa. Poster Art. Multicoloured.
1304 16c. Type **419** . . . . . . 1·10 55
1305 46c. "CARNIVAL 1939" 2·75 2·75

420 Games Mascot with Javelin

2003. Games of Small European States, Malta. Multicoloured.
1306 25c. Type **420** . . . . . . 1·25 85
1307 50c. Mascot with gun . . . 2·25 1·75
1308 75c. Mascot with ball and net . . . . 3·75 2·75
1309 £3 Mascot with rubber ring at poolside . . . . 14·00 15·00

421 Princess Elizabeth in Malta, c. 1950

2003. 50th Anniv of Coronation. Multicoloured (except No. 1312).
1310 – 12c. black, grey and cinnamon 70 45
1311 – 15c. multicoloured 75 50
1312 – 22c. black, deep grey and grey . . . . 1·00 90
1313 – 60c. black, grey and deep ultramarine . . . . . . 2·50 3·00
MS1314 100 × 72 mm. £1 multicoloured . . . . 4·25 4·75
DESIGNS: 15c. Princess Elizabeth with crowd of children, Malta, c. 1950; 22c. Queen Elizabeth II in evening dress with Duke of Edinburgh, Malta; 60c. Queen Elizabeth II (receiving book) and Duke of Edinburgh, Malta; £1 Queen on walkabout with crowd.

422 Valletta Bastions at Night

2003. Elton John, The Granaries, Floriana. Sheet 125 × 90 mm.
MS1315 **422** £1.50 multicoloured 6·25 6·75
No. **MS**1315 also contains four labels showing different portraits of Elton John.

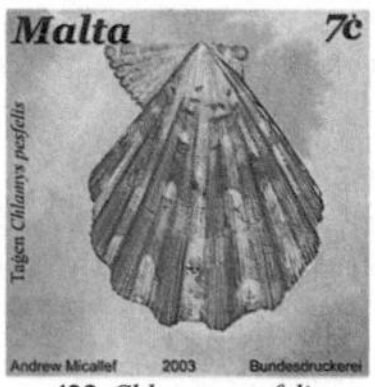

423 *Chlamys pesfelis*

2003. Sea Shells. Multicoloured.
1316 7c. Type **423** 40 45
1317 7c. *Gyroscala lamellose* . . . 40 45
1318 7c. *Phalium granulatum* . . 40 45
1319 7c. *Fusiturris similes* 40 45
1320 7c. *uria lurida* 40 45
1321 7c. *Bolinus brandaris* 40 45
1322 7c. *Charonia tritonis variegate* 40 45
1323 7c. *Clanculus corallinus* . . . 40 45
1324 7c. *Fusinus syracusanus* . . . 40 45
1325 7c. *Pinna nobilis* 40 45
1326 7c. *Acanthocardia tuberculata* 40 45
1327 7c. *Aporrhais pespelecani* . . 40 45
1328 7c. *Haliotis tuberculata lamellose* 40 45
1329 7c. *Tonna galea* 40 45
1330 7c. *Spondylus gaederopus* . . 40 45
1331 7c. *Mitra zonata* 40 45

424 Racing Yachts, Malta–Syracuse Race

2003. Yachting. Multicoloured.
1332 8c. Type **424** 40 30
1333 22c. Yacht, Middle Sea Race (vert) . . . . 1·00 90
1334 35c. Racing yachts, Royal Malta Yacht Club (vert) 1·50 1·75

2003. As Nos. 1139a and 1143 but smaller, 23 × 23 mm. Self-adhesive.
1335 7c. *Vitex agnus-castus* . . . 30 25
1336 16c. *Crocus longiflorus* . . . 70 65

425 Is-Sur ta' San Mikiel, Valletta

2003. Windmills. Each black.
1337 11c. Type **425** 50 40
1338 27c. Ta' Kola, Xaghra (vert) 1·25 1·00
1339 45c. Tax-Xarolla, Zurrieq (vert) . . . . 1·90 2·00

426 The Annunciation

2003. Christmas. Multicoloured.
1340 7c. Type **426** 50 30
1341 16c. Holy Family 70 35
1342 22c. The Shepherds following the Star (horiz) 1·00 75
1343 50c. The Three Kings with gifts (horiz) . . . . 2·25 2·75

427 Pillar Box on Seafront

2004. Letter Boxes. Multicoloured.
1344 1c. Type **427** 10 10
1345 16c. Pillar box on pavement 50 55
1346 22c. Wall pillar boxes . . . 70 75
1347 37c. Pillar box inside post office . . . . 1·10 1·20
1348 76c. Square pillar box and statue . . . . 2·40 2·50

428 Tortoiseshell Cat

2004. Cats. Multicoloured.
1349 7c. Type **428** 20 25
1350 27c. Tabby 85 90
1351 28c. Silver tabby 90 95
1352 50c. Ginger tabby . . . . . 1·60 1·70
1353 60c. Black and white cat . . 1·90 1·90

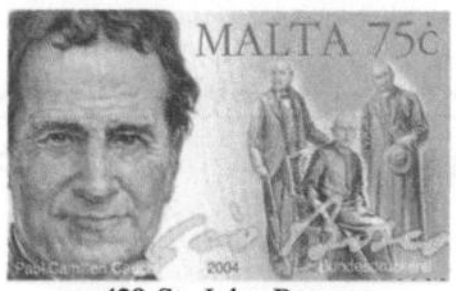

429 St. John Bosco

2004. Centenary of Salesians in Malta. Sheet 124 × 89 mm.
MS1354 **429** 75c. multicoloured 2·40 2·50

430 Pipistrelle (*Pipistrellus pygmaeus*)

2004. Mammals and Reptiles. Multicoloured.
1355 16c. Type **430** 50 55
1356 16c. Lesser mouse-eared bat (*Myotis blythi punicus*) . . 50 55
1357 16c. Weasel (*Mustela nivalis*) 50 55
1358 16c. Algerian hedgehog (*Atelerix algirus fallax*) . . 50 55
1359 16c. Mediterranean chameleon (*Chamaeleo chamaeleon*) 50 55
1360 16c. Sicilian shrew (*Crocidura sicula*) 50 55
1361 16c. Ocellated skink (*Chalcides ocellatus*) . . . 50 55
1362 16c. Filfla Maltese wall lizard (*Podarcis filfolensis filfolensis*) 50 55
1363 16c. Moorish gecko (*Tarentola mauritanica*) 50 55
1364 16c. Turkish gecko (*Hemidactylus turcicus*) . . 50 55
1365 16c. Leopard snake (*Elaphe situla*) 50 55
1366 16c. Western whip snake (*Coluber viridiflavus*) . . . 50 55
1367 16c. Common dolphin (*Delphinus delphis*) 50 55
1368 16c. Striped dolphin (*Stenella coeruleoalba*) . . 50 55
1369 16c. Mediterranean donk seal (*Monachus monachus*) 50 55
1370 16c. Green turtle (*Chelonia mydas*) 50 55
Nos. 1355/70 were printed together, se-tenant, in sheetlets of 16 with the background of each horizontal pair (1355/6, 1357/8, 1359/60, 1361/2, 1363/4, 1365/6, 1367/8 and 1369/70) forming a composite design.

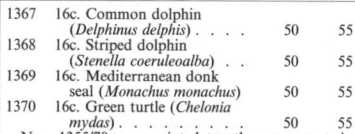

431 New Members Flags inside E.U. Stars

2004. Accession to European Union. Multicoloured.
1371 16c. Type **431** 50 55
1372 28c. Former Prime Minister Eddie Fenech Adami and former Foreign Minister Joe Borg signing Accession Treaty 90 95

432 Children Jumping into Water

2004. Europa. Holidays. Multicoloured.
1373 16c. Type **432** 50 55
1374 51c. Hagar Qim prehistoric temples . . . . 1·90 2·00

433 Hal Millieri Chapel, Zurrieq

2004. Chapels. Multicoloured.
1375 3c. Type **433** 10 10
1376 7c. San Basilju, Mqabba . . 20 25
1377 39c. San Cir, Rabat . . . . 1·20 1·30
1378 48c. Santa Lucija, Mtarfa 1·50 1·60
1379 66c. Ta' Santa Marija, Kemmuna . . . . 2·10 2·20

434 Tram

2004. Trams.
1380 **434** 19c. green and black . . 60 65
1381 – 37c. orange and black (25 × 42 mm) . . . . 1·10 1·20
1382 – 50c. yellow and black (25 × 42 mm) . . . . 1·60 1·70
1383 – 75c. blue and black . . . 2·40 2·50
DESIGNS: 19c. Type **434**; 37c. Tram driver; 50c. Ticket; 75c. Tram under bridge.

435 Discus Thrower

2004. Olympic Games, Athens. Multicoloured.
1384 11c. Type **435** 35 40
1385 16c. Greek column and laurel wreath 50 55
1386 76c. Javelin thrower . . . . 2·40 2·50

436 Children playing on Ascension Day (Luigi Brocktorff painting) (Lapsi)

2004. Festivals. Multicoloured.

1387	5c. Type **436**	15	20
1388	15c. Votive Penitentiary General Procession, Zejtun (San Girgor)	45	50
1389	27c. Pilgrimage in front of the Sanctuary of Our Lady of Graces, Zabbar (painting, Italo Horatio Serge) (Hadd In-Nies)	85	90
1390	51c. Children with St. Martin's Bags of nuts (Michele Bellanti lithograph) (San Martin) (vert)	1·90	2·00
1391	£1 Peasants in traditional costumes singing and dancing (painting, Antoine Favray) (Mnarja) (vert)	3·25	3·50

437 Church of St. Mary, Attard

2004. Art. Multicoloured.

1392	2c. Type **437**	10	10
1393	20c. Mdina Cathedral organ and music score (vert)	65	70
1394	57c. Statue of St. Agatha (vert)	1·70	1·80
1395	62c. Il-Gifen Tork (poem) and books (vert)	2·00	2·10
MS1396	93 × 100 mm. 72c. Medieval painting of St. Paul (vert)	2·30	2·40

438 Papier mache Bambino on rocks, Lecce

2004. Christmas. Bambino Models. Multicoloured.

1397	7c. Type **438**	20	25
1398	16c. Wax Bambino inside glass dome (vert)	50	55
1399	22c. Wax Bambino on back, Lija (vert)	70	75
1400	50c. Beeswax Bambino under tree (vert)	1·50	1·70

439 Quintinus Map

2005. Old Maps.

1401	**439**	1c. black and scarlet	10	10
1402	–	12c. multicoloured	40	45
1403	–	37c. multicoloured	1·10	1·20
1404	–	£1 multicoloured	3·25	3·50

DESIGNS: 1c. Type **439**; 12c. Copper-engraved map; 37c. Fresco map; £1 Map of Gozo.

440 Dar il-Kaptan (Respite Home)

2005. Centenary of Rotary International (humanitarian organisation). Multicoloured.

1405	27c. Type **440**	85	90
1406	76c. Outline of Malta and Gozo and "CELEBRATE ROTARY"	2·40	2·50

441 Hans Christian Andersen

2005. Birth Bicentenary of Hans Christian Andersen (artist and children's writer).

1407	**441**	7c. black and silver	20	25
1408	–	22c. multicoloured	70	75
1409	–	60c. multicoloured	1·90	2·00
1410	–	75c. multicoloured	2·40	2·50

DESIGNS: 7c. Type **441**; 20 × 38 mm—22c. Scissors and paper cutting; 60c. Ugly Duckling, pen and inkwell; 75c. Moroccan travelling boots and drawing of Villa Borghese, Rome.

POSTAGE DUE STAMPS

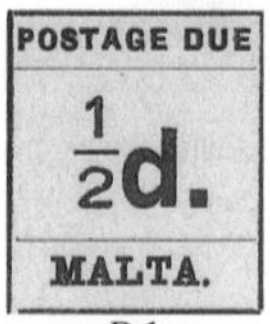

D 1

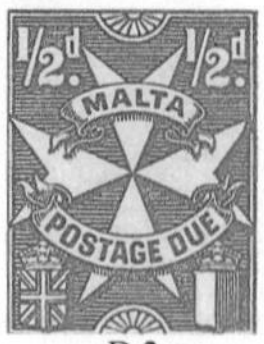

D 2

1925. Imperf.

D 1	D 1	½d. black	1·25	7·50
D 2		1d. black	3·25	3·00
D 3		1½d. black	3·00	3·75
D 4		2d. black	8·00	14·00
D 5		2½d. black	2·75	2·75
D 6		3d. black on grey	9·00	15·00
D 7		4d. black on yellow	5·00	9·50
D 8		6d. black on yellow	5·00	17·00
D 9		1s. black on yellow	7·50	21·00
D10		1s. 6d. black on yellow	14·00	55·00

1925. Perf.

D11	D 2	½d. green	1·25	60
D12		1d. violet	1·25	45
D13		1½d. brown	1·50	80
D14		2d. grey	11·00	1·00
D35		2d. brown	85	70
D36		2½d. orange	60	70
D37		3d. blue	60	60
D38		4d. green	1·00	80
D39		6d. purple	75	1·50
D40		1s. black	90	1·50
D41		1s.6d. red	2·25	7·00

D 3 Maltese Lace

D 4

1973.

D42	D 3	2m. brown and red	10	10
D43		3m. orange and red	10	15
D44		5m. pink and red	15	20
D45		1c. blue and green	30	35
D46		2c. grey and black	40	35
D47		3c. light brown & brown	40	35
D48		5c. dull blue and blue	65	70
D49		10c. lilac and plum	85	1·00

1993.

D50	D 4	1c. magenta and mauve	15	30
D51		2c. blue and light blue	20	40
D52		5c. green and turquoise	30	45
D53		10c. orange and yellow	45	55

MANAMA Pt. 19

A dependency of Ajman.

100 dirhams = 1 riyal.

1966. Nos. 10, 12, 14 and 18 of Ajman surch **Manama** in English and Arabic and new value.

1	40d. on 40n.p. multicoloured	50	50
2	70d. on 70n.p. multicoloured	50	50
3	1r.50 on 1r.50 multicoloured	1·50	95
4	10r. on 10r. multicoloured	6·50	6·50

1967. Nos. 140/8 of Ajman optd **MANAMA** in English and Arabic. (a) Postage.

5	15d. blue and brown	10	10
6	30d. brown and black	20	20
7	50d. black and brown	40	40
8	70d. violet and black	40	40

(b) Air.

9	1r. green and brown	55	55
10	2r. mauve and black	1·10	75
11	3r. black and brown	1·60	1·10
12	5r. brown and black	3·50	3·50
13	10r. blue and brown	6·25	6·25

APPENDIX

The following stamps have either been issued in excess of postal needs or have not been available to the public in reasonable quantities at face value. Such stamps may later be given full listing if there is evidence of regular postal use.

1966. New Currency Surcharges. Stamps of Ajman surch **Manama** in English and Arabic and new value.

(a) Nos. 19/20 and 22/4 (Kennedy). 10d. on 10n.p., 15d. on 15n.p., 1r. on 1r., 2r. on 2r., 3r. on 3r.

(b) Nos. 27, 30 and 35/6 (Olympics). 5d. on 5n.p., 25d. on 25n.p., 3r. on 3r., 5r. on 5r.

(c) Nos. 80/2 and 85 (Churchill). 50d. on 50n.p., 75d. on 75n.p., 1r. on 1r., 5r. on 5r.

(d) Nos. 95/8 (Space). Air 50d. on 50n.p., 1r. on 1r., 3r. on 3r., 5r. on 5r.

1967.

World Scout Jamboree, Idaho. Postage 30, 70d., 1r.; Air 2, 3, 4r.

Olympic Games, Mexico (1968). Postage 35, 65, 75d., 1r.; Air 1r.25, 2, 3, 4r.

Winter Olympic Games, Grenoble (1968). Postage 5, 35, 60, 75d.; Air 1, 1r.25, 2, 3r.

Paintings by Renoir and Terbrugghen. Air 35, 65d., 1, 2r. × 3.

1968.

Paintings by Velazquez. Air 1r. × 2, 2r. × 2.

Costumes. Air 30d. × 2, 70d. × 2, 1r. × 2, 2r. × 2.

Olympic Games, Mexico. Postage 1r. × 4; Air 2r. × 4.

Satellites and Spacecraft. Air 30d. × 2, 70d. × 2, 1r. × 2, 2r. × 2, 3r. × 2.

Human Rights Year. Kennedy Brothers and Martin Luther King. Air 1r. × 3, 2r. × 3.

Sports Champions, Famous Footballers. Postage 15, 20, 50, 75d., 1r.; Air 10r.

Heroes of Humanity. Circular designs on gold or silver foil. 60d. × 12.

Olympic Games, Mexico. Circular designs on gold or silver foil. Air 3r. × 8.

Mothers' Day. Paintings. Postage 1r. × 6.

Kennedy Brothers Commem. Postage 2r.; Air 5r.

Cats (1st series). Postage 1, 2, 3d.; Air 2, 3r.

5th Death Anniv of Pres. Kennedy. Air 10r.

Space Exploration. Postage 5, 10, 15, 20, 25d.; Air 15r.

Olympic Games, Mexico. Gold Medals. Postage 2r. × 4; Air 5r. × 4.

Christmas. Air 5r.

1969.

Sports Champions. Cyclists. Postage 1, 2, 5, 10, 15, 20d.; Air 12r.

Sports Champions. German Footballers. Postage 5, 10, 15, 20, 25d.; Air 10r.

Sports Champions. Motor-racing Drivers. Postage 1, 5, 10, 15, 25d.; Air 10r.

Motor-racing Cars. Postage 1, 5, 10, 15, 25d.; Air 10r.

Sports Champions. Boxers. Postage 5, 10, 15, 20d.; Air 10r.

Sports Champions. Baseball Players. Postage 1, 2, 5, 10, 15d.; Air 10r.

Birds. Air 1r. × 11.

Roses. Postage 1r. × 6.

Animals. Air 1r. × 6.

Paintings by Italian Artists. 5, 10, 15, 20d., 10r.

Great Composers. Air 5, 10, 25d., 10r.

Paintings by French Artists. 1r. × 4.

Nude Paintings. Air 2r. × 4.

Kennedy Brothers. Air 2, 3, 10r.

Olympic Games, Mexico. Gold Medal Winners. Postage 1, 2d., 10r.; Air 10d., 5, 10r.

Paintings of the Madonna. Postage 10d.; Air 10r.

Space Flight of "Apollo 9". Optd on 1968 Space Exploration issue. Air 15r.

Space Flight of "Apollo 10". Optd on 1968 Space Exploration issue. Air 15r.

1st Death Anniv of Gagarin. Optd on 1968 Space Exploration issue. 5d.

2nd Death Anniv of Edward White (astronaut). Optd on 1968 Space Exploration issue. 10d.

1st Death Anniv of Robert Kennedy. Optd on 1969 Kennedy Brothers issue. Air 2r.

Olympic Games, Munich (1972). Optd on 1969 Mexico Gold Medal Winners issue. Air 10d., 5, 10r.

Moon Mission of "Apollo 11". Air 1, 2, 3r.

Christmas. Paintings by Brueghel. Postage 1, 2, 4, 5, 10d.; Air 6r.

1970.

"Soyuz" and "Apollo" Space Programmes. Postage 1, 2, 4, 5, 10d.; Air 3, 5r.

Kennedy and Eisenhower Commem. Embossed on gold foil. Air 20r.

Lord Baden-Powell Commem. Embossed on gold foil. Air 20r.

World Cup Football Championship, Mexico. Postage 20, 40, 60, 80d., 1r.; Air 3r.

Brazil's Victory in World Cup Football Championship. Optd on 1970 World Cup issue. Postage 20, 40, 60, 80d., 1r.; Air 3r.

Paintings by Michelangelo. Postage 1, 2, 4, 5, 10d.; Air 6r.

World Fair "Expo 70", Osaka, Japan. Air 25, 50, 75d., 1, 2, 3, 12r.

Paintings by Renoir. Postage 1, 2, 5, 6, 10d.; Air 5, 12r.

Olympic Games, Rome, Tokyo, Mexico and Munich. Postage 15, 30, 50, 70d.; Air 2, 5r.

Winter Olympic Games, Sapporo (1972) (1st issue). Postage 2, 3, 4, 10d.; Air 2, 5r.

Christmas. Flower Paintings by Brueghel. Postage 5, 20, 25, 30, 50d.; Air 60d., 1, 2r.

1971.

Winter Olympic Games, Sapporo (2nd issue). Postage 1, 2, 3, 4, 5, 6, 8, 10, 12, 15, 20, 25, 30, 35, 40, 50d.; Air 75 d, 1, 2, 2r.50.

Roses. Postage 5, 20, 25, 30, 50d.; Air 60d., 1, 2r.

Birds. Postage 5, 20, 25, 30, 50d.; Air 60d., 1, 2r.

Paintings by Modigliani. Air 25, 50, 60, 75d., 1r.50, 3r.

Paintings by Rubens. Postage 1, 2, 3, 4, 5, 10d.; Air 2, 3r.

"Philatokyo '71" Stamp Exhibition, Paintings by Hokusai and Hiroshige. Postage 10, 15, 20, 25, 50, 75d.; Air 1, 2r.

25th Anniv of United Nations. Optd on 1970 Christmas issue. Postage 5, 20, 25, 30, 50d.; Air 60d., 1, 2r.

British Military Uniforms. Postage 5, 20, 25, 30, 50d.; Air 60d., 1, 2r.

Space Flight of "Apollo 14". Postage 15, 25, 50, 60, 70d.; Air 5r.

Space Flight of "Apollo 15". Postage 25, 40, 50, 60d.; Air 1, 6r.

13th World Scout Jamboree, Asagiri, Japan (1st issue). Postage 1, 2, 3, 5, 7, 10, 12, 15, 20, 25, 30, 35, 40, 50, 65, 80d.; Air 1, 1r.25, 1r.50, 2r.

World Wild Life Conservation. Postage 1, 2, 3, 5, 7, 10, 12, 15, 20, 25, 30, 35, 40, 50, 65, 80d.; Air 1r., 1r.25, 1r.50, 2r.

13th World Scout Jamboree, Asagiri, Japan (2nd issue). Stamps. Postage 10, 15, 20, 25, 50, 75d.; Air 1, 2r.

Winter Olympic Games, Sapporo (3rd issue). Postage 1, 2, 3, 4, 5, 10d.; Air 2, 3r.

Cats (2nd series). Postage 15, 25, 40, 60d.; Air 3, 10r.

Lions International Clubs. Optd on 1971 Uniforms issue. Postage 5, 20, 25, 30, 50d.; Air 60d., 1, 2r.

Paintings of Ships. Postage 15, 20, 25, 30, 50d.; Air 60d., 1, 2r.

Great Olympic Champions. Postage 25, 50, 75d., 1r.; Air 5r.

Prehistoric Animals. Postage 15, 20, 25, 30, 50, 60d.; Air 1, 2r.

Footballers. Postage 5, 10, 15, 20, 40d.; Air 5r.

Royal Visit of Queen Elizabeth II to Japan. Postage 10, 20, 30, 40, 50d.; Air 2, 3r.

Fairy Tales. Stories by Hans Andersen. Postage 1, 2, 4, 5, 10d.; Air 3r.

World Fair, Philadelphia (1976). American Paintings. Postage 20, 25, 50, 60, 75d.; Air 3r.

Fairy Tales. Well-known stories. Postage 1, 2, 4, 5, 10d.; Air 3r.

Space Flight of "Apollo 16". Postage 20, 30, 40, 50, 60d.; Air 3, 4r.

Tropical Fishes. Postage 1, 2, 3, 4, 5, 10d.; Air 2, 3r.

European Tour of Emperor Hirohito of Japan. Postage 1, 2, 4, 5, 10d.; Air 6r.

Meeting of Pres. Nixon and Emperor Hirohito of Japan in Alaska. Optd on 1971 Emperor's Tour issue. Air 6r.

2500th Anniv of Persian Empire. Postage 10, 20, 30, 40, 50d.; Air 3r.

Space Flight of "Apollo 15" and Future Developments in Space. Postage 10, 15, 20, 25, 50d.; Air 1, 2r.

1972.

150th Death Anniv (1971) of Napoleon. Postage 10, 20, 30, 40d.; Air 1, 2, 3, 4r.

1st Death Anniv of Gen. de Gaulle. Postage 10, 20, 30, 40d.; Air 1, 2, 3, 4r.

Paintings from the "Alte Pinakothek", Munich. Postage 5, 10, 15, 20, 25d.; Air 5r.

"Tour de France" Cycle Race. Postage 5, 10, 15, 20, 25, 30, 35, 40, 45, 50, 55, 60d.; Air 65, 70, 75, 80, 85, 90, 95d., 1r.

Cats and Dogs. Postage 10, 20, 30, 40, 50d.; Air 1r.

25th Anniv of U.N.I.C.E.F. Optd on 1971 World Scout Jamboree, Asagiri (2nd issue). Postage 10, 15, 20, 25, 50, 75d.; Air 1, 2r.

Past and Present Motorcars. Postage 10, 20, 30, 40, 50d.; Air 1r.

Military Uniforms. 1r. × 11.

The United Arab Emirates Ministry of Communications took over the Manama postal service on 1 August 1972. Further stamps inscribed "Manama" issued after that date were released without authority and had no validity.

MANCHUKUO Pt. 17

Issues for the Japanese puppet Government set up in 1932 under President (later Emperor) Pu Yi.

100 fen = 1 yuan.

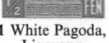

1 White Pagoda, Liaoyang

2 Pu Yi, later Emperor Kang-teh

1932. (a) With five characters in top panel as T **1** and **2**.

1	1	½f. brown	75	25
2		1f. red	75	10
24		1f. brown	75	10
25		1½f. violet	1·50	75
4		2f. grey	2·25	20
26		2f. blue	3·50	50
27		3f. brown	2·50	10
6		4f. green	50	10
28		4f. brown	18·00	75
7		5f. green	75	15
8		6f. red	3·50	40
9		7f. grey	1·25	20
10		8f. brown	9·00	6·00
11		10f. orange	1·50	15
12	2	13f. brown	4·50	4·25
13		15f. red	15·00	75
14		16f. blue	14·00	2·25
15		20f. brown	2·75	40
16		30f. orange	3·25	1·25
17		50f. green	3·75	70
31		1y. violet	8·00	5·50

(b) With six characters in top panel.

40	1	½f. brown	25	10
41		1f. brown	25	10
42		1½f. violet	65	40
43		3f. brown	40	10
44		5f. blue	8·50	60
45		5f. slate	3·50	40
46		6f. red	1·00	15
47		7f. grey	1·25	40
48		9f. orange	1·25	20
55		10f. blue	4·25	10
56	2	13f. brown	3·75	4·25
49		15f. red	2·00	25
50		18f. green	12·00	3·50
51		20f. brown	2·25	20
52		30f. brown	3·35	35
53		50f. green	3·75	30
54		1y. violet	10·00	3·50

3 Map and Flags

6 Emperor's Palace

1933. 1st Anniv of Republic.

19	3	1f. orange	1·25	1·00
20	–	2f. green	8·50	7·50
21	3	4f. red	1·25	50
22	–	10f. blue	13·00	11·00

DESIGN: 2, 10f. Council Hall, Hsinking.

1934. Enthronement of Emperor.

32	6	1½f. brown	1·25	40
33	–	3f. red	1·75	20
34	6	6f. green	5·00	3·75
35	–	10f. blue	7·50	3·75

DESIGN: 3f., 10f. Phoenixes.

1934. Stamps of 1932 surch with four Japanese characters.

36	1	1f. on 4f. green (No. 6)	3·50	2·25
37		3f. on 4f. green	22·00	18·00
38		3f. on 4f. brown (No. 28)	4·25	2·50
39	2	3f. on 16f. blue (No. 14)	6·50	6·50

In No. 38 the left hand upper character of the surcharge consists of three horizontal lines.

12 Orchid Crest of Manchukuo

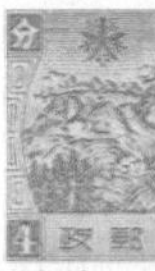
13 Changpai Mountain and Sacred Lake

1935. China Mail.

64	12	2f. green	45	15
65		2½f. violet	35	15
66	13	4f. green	1·00	30
67		5f. blue	25	10
68	12	8f. yellow	2·25	30
60	13	12f. red	4·50	2·25
70		13f. brown	50	15

15 Mt. Fuji

16 Phoenixes

1935. Visit of Emperor Kang-teh to Japan.

71	15	1½f. green	1·00	80
72	16	3f. orange	1·50	25
73	15	6f. red	3·25	3·25
74	16	10f. blue	5·00	2·50

17 Symbolic of Accord

19 State Council Building, Hsinking

20 Chengte Palace, Jehol

1936. Japan–Manchukuo Postal Agreement.

75	17	1½f. brown	1·75	1·50
76	–	3f. purple	1·50	25
77	17	6f. red	6·50	6·50
78	–	10f. blue	5·50	3·50

DESIGN—HORIZ: 3f., 10f. Department of Communications.

1936.

79	19	½f. brown	25	15
80		1f. red	25	10
81		1½f. lilac	2·50	2·00
82	A	2f. green	20	10
83	19	3f. brown	25	15
84	B	4f. green	20	10
149	19	5f. black	10	1·00
86	A	6f. red	75	10
87	B	7f. black	1·00	10
88		9f. red	75	20
89	20	10f. blue	40	10
90	B	12f. orange	25	10
91		13f. brown	10·00	20·00
92		15f. red	1·25	30
93	C	18f. green	7·50	7·50
94		19f. green	3·50	1·50
95	A	20f. brown	1·50	35
96	20	30f. brown	1·75	30
97	D	38f. blue	13·00	14·00
98		39f. blue	1·00	1·00
99	A	50f. green	2·25	30
154	20	1y. purple	45	2·75

DESIGNS: A, Carting soya-beans; B, Peiling Mausoleum; C, Airplane and grazing sheep (domestic and China air mail); D, Nakajima-built Fokker F.VIIb/3m airplane over Sungari River railway bridge (air mail to Japan).

21 Sun rising over Fields

22 Shadowgraph of old and new Hsinking

1937. 5th Anniv of Founding of State.

101	21	1½f. red	5·00	6·00
102	22	3f. green	1·50	1·75

1937. China Mail. Surch in Chinese characters.

108	12	2½f. on 2f. green	2·75	2·00
110	13	5f. on 4f. green	2·75	2·50
111		13f. on 12f. brown	9·50	7·00

27 Pouter Pigeon and Hsinking

1937. Completion of Five Year Reconstruction Plan for Hsinking.

112	27	2f. purple	2·00	1·00
113	–	4f. red	2·00	25
114	27	10f. green	6·50	4·00
115	–	20f. blue	7·50	5·00

DESIGN: 4, 20f. Flag over Imperial Palace.

29 Manchukuo

30 Japanese Residents Assn. Building

1937. Japan's Relinquishment of Extra-territorial Rights.

116	29	2f. red	1·00	25
117	30	4f. green	2·75	75
118		8f. orange	3·25	2·00
119	–	10f. blue	2·75	50
120	–	12f. violet	3·50	3·00
121	–	20f. brown	4·75	2·75

DESIGNS—As Type **30**: 10, 20f. Dept. of Communications Bldg. HORIZ: 12f. Ministry of Justice.

32 "Twofold Happiness"

33 Red Cross on Map and Globe

1937. New Year's Greetings.

122	32	2f. red and blue	3·00	30

1938. Inaug of Manchukuo Red Cross Society.

123	33	2f. red	1·00	1·25
124		4f. green	1·00	25

34 Map of Railway Lines

35 "Asia" Express

1939. Completion of 10,000 Kilometres of Manchurian Railways.

125	34	2f. blue and orange	2·75	1·60
126	35	4f. deep blue and blue	2·75	1·90

36 Manchurian Cranes over Shipmast

37 Census Official and Manchukuo

38 Census Slogans in Chinese and Mongolian

1940. 2nd Visit of Emperor Kang-teh to Japan.

127	36	2f. purple	65	35
128		4f. green	95	50

1940. National Census.

129	37	2f. brown and yellow	60	1·50
130	38	4f. deep green and green	60	1·50

39 Message of Congratulation

40 Dragon Dance

1940. 2600th Anniv of Founding of Japanese Empire.

131	39	2f. red	15	1·50
132	40	4f. blue	15	1·50

41 Recruit

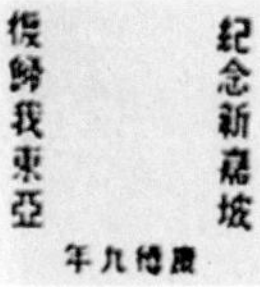
(42)

1941. Enactment of Conscription Law.

133	41	2f. red	75	1·50
134		4f. blue	75	1·50

1942. Fall of Singapore. Stamps of 1936 optd with T **42**.

135	A	2f. green	1·00	2·00
136	B	4f. green	1·00	2·00

43 Kenkoku Shrine

44 Achievement of Fine Crops

45 Women of Five Races Dancing

46 Map of Manchukuo

1942. 10th Anniv of Founding of State.

137	43	2f. red	25	75
138	44	3f. orange	2·25	2·25
139	43	4f. lilac	40	75
140	45	6f. green	2·25	2·50
141	46	10f. red on yellow	75	1·50
142	–	20f. blue on yellow	1·00	1·50

DESIGN—HORIZ: 20f. Flag of Manchukuo.

1942. 1st Anniv of "Greater East Asia War". Stamps of 1936 optd with native characters above date **8.12.8**.

143	19	3f. brown	1·00	1·75
144	A	6f. red	1·00	1·75

1943. Labour Service Law Proclamation. Stamps of 1936 optd with native characters above heads of pick and shovel.

145	19	3f. brown	1·00	1·75
146	A	6f. red	1·00	1·75

49 Nurse and Stretcher

50 Furnace at Anshan Plant

1943. 5th Anniv of Manchukuo Red Cross Society.

147	49	6f. green	75	2·50

1943. 2nd Anniv of "Greater East Asia War".

148	50	6f. red	75	2·50

51 Chinese characters

52 Japanese characters

53 "One Heart One Soul"

1944. Friendship with Japan. (a) Chinese characters.

155	51	10f. red	25	75
156		40f. green	75	1·00

(b) Japanese characters.

157	52	10f. red	25	75
158		40f. green	75	1·00

1945. 10th Anniv of Emperor's Edict.

159	53	10f. red	1·25	4·50

MARIANA ISLANDS Pt. 7

A group of Spanish islands in the Pacific Ocean of which Guam was ceded to the U.S.A. and the others to Germany. The latter are now under U.S. Trusteeship.

100 pfennig = 1 mark.

1899. German stamps optd **Marianen**.

7	8	3pf. brown	13·00	30·00
8		5pf. green	15·00	34·00
9	9	10pf. red	19·00	47·00
10		20pf. blue	26·00	£130
11		25pf. orange	65·00	£170
12		50pf. brown	65·00	£225

1901. "Yacht" key-type inscr "MARIANEN".

13	N	3pf. brown	1·10	1·50
14		5pf. green	1·10	1·50
15		10pf. red	1·10	3·75
16		20pf. blue	1·10	6·75
17		25pf. black & red on yellow	1·70	13·00
18		30pf. black & orge on buff	1·70	13·00
19		40pf. black and red	1·70	13·00
20		50pf. black & pur on buff	1·90	15·00
21		80pf. black and red on rose	2·50	26·00
22	O	1m. red	3·00	70·00
23		2m. blue	5·00	95·00
24		3m. black	6·75	£130
25		5m. red and black	£130	£500

MARIENWERDER Pt. 7

A district of E. Prussia where a plebiscite was held in 1920. As a result the district remained part of Germany. After the War of 1939–45 it was returned to Poland and reverted to its original name of Kwidzyn.

100 pfennig = 1 mark.

1

1920.

1	1	5pf. green	60	1·10
2		10pf. red	50	80
3		15pf. grey	50	65
4		20pf. brown	60	80
5		25pf. blue	60	80
6		30pf. orange	1·00	90
7		40pf. brown	65	80
8		50pf. violet	70	1·00
9		60pf. brown	4·25	2·75
10		75pf. brown	95	1·00
11		1m. brown and green	75	80
12		2m. purple	2·30	3·25
13		3m. red	5·00	4·50
14		5m. blue and red	24·00	22·00

1920. Stamps of Germany inscr "DEUTSCHES REICH" optd or surch **Commission Interalliee Marienwerder**.

15	10	5pf. green	16·00	29·00
16		20pf. blue	6·50	23·00
17		50pf. black & purple on buff	£400	£900
18		75pf. black and green	4·00	6·75
19		80pf. black and red on rose	85·00	£120
25	12	1m. red	2·75	4·25
21	24	1m. on 2pf. grey	24·00	49·00
26	12	1m.25 green	3·50	5·00
27		1m.50 brown	4·75	6·75
22	24	2m. on 2½pf. grey	10·00	18·00
28	13	2m.50 purple	3·00	5·00
23	10	3m. on 3pf. brown	13·00	19·00
24	24	5m. on 7½pf. orange	10·00	22·00

1920. As T **1**, with inscription at top changed to "PLEBISCITE".

29	5pf. green	2·50	1·70
30	10pf. red	2·50	1·70
31	15pf. grey	11·50	10·00
32	20pf. brown	1·30	1·70
33	25pf. blue	13·50	17·00
34	30pf. orange	1·10	80
35	40pf. brown	80	70
36	50pf. violet	1·50	1·00
37	60pf. brown	5·25	3·50
38	75pf. brown	6·25	5·00
39	1m. brown and green	90	70
40	2m. purple	1·20	80
41	3m. red	1·90	1·00
42	5m. blue and red	2·75	1·20

MARSHALL ISLANDS Pts. 7, 22

A group of islands in the Pacific Ocean, a German protectorate from 1885. From 1920 to 1947 it was a Japanese mandated territory and from 1947 part of the United States Trust Territory of the Pacific Islands, using United States stamps. In 1984 it assumed control of its postal services.

A. GERMAN PROTECTORATE

100 pfennig = 1 mark.

1897. Stamps of Germany (a) optd **Marschall-Inseln**.

G1	8	3pf. brown	£4000	£700
G2		5pf. green	£550	£475
G3	9	10pf. red	44·00	85·00
G4		20pf. blue	44·00	90·00

(b) optd **Marshall-Inseln**.

G 5	8	3pf. brown	3·50	5·75
G 6		5pf. green	8·75	11·00
G 7	9	10pf. red	11·00	18·00
G 8		20pf. blue	16·00	27·00
G 9		25pf. orange	20·00	44·00
G10		50pf. brown	31·00	49·00

1901. "Yacht" key-type inscr "MARSHALL INSELN".

G11	N	3pf. brown	65	1·60
G12		5pf. green	65	1·60
G13		10pf. red	65	4·50
G14		20pf. blue	90	8·75
G15		25pf. black & red on yell	1·10	18·00
G16		30pf. black & orge on buff	1·10	18·00
G17		40pf. black and red	1·10	18·00
G18		50pf. black & pur on buff	1·60	24·00
G19		80pf. black & red on rose	2·75	35·00
G20	O	1m. red	3·75	85·00
G21		2m. blue	5·25	£120
G22		3m. black	8·75	£200
G23		5m. red and black	£130	£550

B. REPUBLIC

100 cents = 1 dollar.

1 Canoe

1984. Inauguration of Postal Independence. Multicoloured.

1	20c. Type **1**	55	30
2	20c. Fishes and net	55	30
3	20c. Navigational stick-chart	55	30
4	20c. Islet with coconut palms	55	30

2 Mili Atoll

3 German Marshall Islands 1900 3pf. Optd Stamp

1984. Maps. Multicoloured.

5	1c. Type **2**	10	10
6	3c. Likiep Atoll	10	10
7	5c. Ebon Atoll	15	10
8	10c. Jaluit Atoll	15	10
9	13c. Ailinginae Atoll	25	15
10	14c. Wotho Atoll	25	15
11	20c. Kwajalein and Ebeye Atolls	30	20
12	22c. Enewetak Atoll	30	20
13	28c. Ailinglaplap Atoll	45	35
14	30c. Majuro Atoll	45	25
15	33c. Namu Atoll	50	40
16	37c. Rongelap Atoll	55	45
16a	39c. Taka and Utirik Atolls	55	45
16b	44c. Ujelang Atoll	65	50
16c	50c. Aur and Maloclap Atolls	80	65
17	$1 Arno Atoll	1·75	75
18	$2 Wotje and Erikub Atolls	3·25	2·50
19	$5 Bikini Atoll	7·50	6·50
20	$10 Mashallese stick chart (31 × 31 mm)	12·00	10·50

1984. 19th Universal Postal Union Congress Philatelic Salon, Hamburg.

21	3	40c. brown, black and yellow	70	50
22	–	40c. brown, black and yellow	70	50
23	–	40c. blue, black and yellow	70	50
24	–	40c. multicoloured	70	50

DESIGNS: No. 22, German Marshall Islands 1901 3pf. "Yacht" stamp; 23, German Marshall Islands 1897 20pf. stamp; 24, German Marshall Islands 1901 5m. "Yacht" stamp.

4 Common Dolphin

1984. "Ausipex 84" International Stamp Exhibition, Melbourne. Dolphins. Multicoloured.

25	20c. Type **4**	50	35
26	20c. Risso's dolphin	50	35
27	20c. Spotter dolphins	50	35
28	20c. Bottle-nosed dolphin	50	35

5 Star over Bethlehem and Text

6 Traditional Chief and German and Marshallese Flags

1984. Christmas. Multicoloured.

29	20c. Type **5**	50	30
30	20c. Desert landscape	50	30
31	20c. Two kings on camels	50	30
32	20c. Third king on camel	50	30

1984. 5th Anniv of Constitution. Multicoloured.

33	20c. Type **6**	50	30
34	20c. Pres. Amata Kabua and American and Marshallese flags	50	30
35	20c. Admiral Chester W. Nimitz and Japanese and Marshallese flags	50	30
36	20c. Trygve H. Lie (first Secretary-General of United Nations) and U.N. and Marshallese flags	50	30

7 Leach's Storm Petrel ("Forked-tailed Petrel")

1985. Birth Bicentenary of John J. Audubon (ornithologist). Multicoloured.

37	22c. Type **7** (postage)	85	85
38	22c. Pectoral sandpiper	85	85
39	44c. Brown booby ("Booby Gannet") (air)	1·50	1·50
40	44c. Whimbrel ("Great Esquimaux Curlew")	1·50	1·50

8 Black-spotted Triton

1985. Sea Shells (1st series). Multicoloured.

41	22c. Type **8**	50	35
42	22c. Monodon murex	50	35
43	22c. Diana conch	50	35
44	22c. Great green turban	50	35
45	22c. Rose-branch murex	50	35

See also Nos. 85/9, 131/5 and 220/4.

9 Woman as Encourager and Drum

1985. International Decade for Women. Mult.

46	22c. Type **9**	40	30
47	22c. Woman as Peacemaker and palm branches	40	30
48	22c. Woman as Nurturer and pounding stone	40	30
49	22c. Woman as Benefactress and lesser frigate bird	65	65

Nos. 46/9 were printed together in se-tenant blocks of four within the sheet, each block forming a composite design.

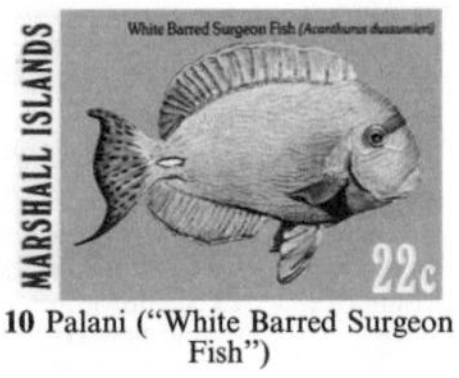

10 Palani ("White Barred Surgeon Fish")

1985. Lagoon Fishes. Multicoloured.

50	22c. Type **10**	60	40
51	22c. Silver-spotted squirrelfish ("White Blotched Squirrel Fish")	60	40
52	22c. Spotted boxfish	60	40
53	22c. Saddle butterflyfish	60	40

11 Basketball

1985. International Youth Year. Multicoloured.

54	22c. Type **11**	40	30
55	22c. Elderly woman recording for oral history project	40	30
56	22c. Islander explaining navigational stick charts	40	30
57	22c. Dancers at inter-atoll music and dance competition	40	30

12 American Board of Commissions for Foreign Missions Stock Certificate

1985. Christmas. "Morning Star I" (first Christian missionary ship to visit Marshall Islands). Multicoloured.

58	14c. Type **12**	15	30
59	22c. Launching of "Morning Star I", 1856	45	30
60	33c. Departure from Honolulu, 1857	70	50
61	44c. Entering Ebon Lagoon, 1857	80	60

13 "Giotto" and Section of Comet Tail

1985. Appearance of Halley's Comet. Designs showing comet over Roi-Namur Island. Multicoloured.

62	22c. Space shuttle and comet	1·00	55
63	22c. "Planet A" space probe and dish aerial	1·00	55
64	22c. Type **13**	1·00	55
65	22c. "Vega" satellite and buildings on island	1·00	55
66	22c. Sir Edmund Halley, satellite communications ship and airplane	1·00	55

Nos. 62/6 were printed together, se-tenant, forming a composite design.

14 Mallow

1985. Medicinal Plants. Multicoloured.

67	22c. Type **14**	45	35
68	22c. Half-flower	45	35
69	22c. "Guettarda speciosa"	45	35
70	22c. Love-vine	45	35

15 Trumpet Triton

1986. World Wildlife Fund. Marine Life. Mult.

71	14c. Type **15**	40	30
72	14c. Giant clam	40	30
73	14c. Small giant clam	40	30
74	14c. Coconut crab	40	30

16 Consolidated PBY-5A Catalina Amphibian

1986. Air. "Ameripex 86" International Stamp Exhibition, Chicago. Mail Planes. Multicoloured.

75	44c. Type **16**	85	65
76	44c. Grumman SA-16 Albatross	85	65
77	44c. Douglas DC-6B	85	65
78	44c. Boeing 727-100	85	65

17 Islanders in Outrigger Canoe

1986. 40th Anniv of Operation Crossroads (atomic bomb tests on Bikini Atoll). Multicoloured.

80	22c. Type **17**	55	35
81	22c. Advance landing of amphibious DUKW from U.S.S. "Sumner"	55	35
82	22c. Loading "L.S.T. 1108" (tank landing ship) for islanders' departure	55	35
83	22c. Man planting coconuts as part of reclamation programme	55	35

1986. Sea Shells (2nd series). As T **8**. Multicoloured.

85	22c. Ramose ("Rose") murex	50	35
86	22c. Orange spider conch	50	35

87 22c. Red-mouth frog shell . . 50 35
88 22c. Laciniate conch 50 35
89 22c. Giant frog shell 50 35

18 Blue Marlin

1986. Game Fishes. Multicoloured.
90 22c. Type **18** 50 40
91 22c. Wahoo 50 40
92 22c. Dolphin 50 40
93 22c. Yellow-finned tuna . . . 50 40

19 Flowers (top left)

1986. International Peace Year. Multicoloured.
94 22c. Type **19** (Christmas) (postage) 50 35
95 22c. Flowers (top right) . . . 50 35
96 22c. Flowers (bottom left) . . 50 35
97 22c. Flowers (bottom right) . . 50 35
98 44c. Head of Statue crowned with flowers (24 × 39 mm) (cent of Statue of Liberty) (air) . . . . 1·00 70

Nos. 94/7 were issued together, se-tenant, in blocks of four within the sheet, each block forming a composite design of mixed flower arrangement.

20 Girl Scout giving Plant to Patient

1986. Air. 20th Anniv of Marshall Island Girl Scouts and 75th Anniv (1987) of United States Girl Scout Movement. Multicoloured.
99 44c. Type **20** 75 55
100 44c. Giving salute 75 55
101 44c. Girl scouts holding hands in circle 75 55
102 44c. Weaving pandana and palm branch mats 75 55

21 Wedge-tailed Shearwater

1987. Air. Sea Birds. Multicoloured.
103 44c. Type **21** . . . . 1·10 1·10
104 44c. Red-footed booby . . . 1·10 1·10
105 44c. Red-tailed tropic bird . . 1·10 1·10
106 44c. Lesser frigate bird ("Great Frigatebird") . . . 1·10 1·00

22 "James T. Arnold", 1854

1987. Whaling Ships. Multicoloured.
107 22c. Type **22** 60 45
108 22c. "General Scott", 1859 60 45
109 22c. "Charles W. Morgan", 1865 . . . . 60 45
110 22c. "Lucretia", 1884 . . . . 60 45

23 Lindbergh's "Spirit of St. Louis" and Congressional Medal of Honour, 1927

1987. Aviators. Multicoloured.
111 33c. Type **23** 70 45
112 33c. Charles Lindbergh and Chance Vought F4U Corsair fighter, Marshall Islands, 1944 . . . . . . 70 45
113 39c. William Bridgeman and Consolidated B-24 Liberator bomber, Kwajalein, 1944 . . . . . 80 60
114 39c. Bridgeman and Douglas Skyrocket, 1951 . . . . . 80 60
115 44c. John Glenn and Chance Vought F4U Corsair fighters, Marshall Islands, 1944 . . . . 1·00 75
116 44c. Glenn and "Friendship 7" space capsule . . . . . 1·00 75

24 Earhart's Lockheed 10E Electra taking off from Lae, New Guinea

1987. Air. "Capex '87" International Stamp Exhibition, Toronto. 50th Anniv of Amelia Earhart's Round the World Flight Attempt. Multicoloured.
117 44c. Type **24** 90 65
118 44c. U.S. Coastguard cutter "Itasca" waiting off Howland Island for Electra 90 65
119 44c. Islanders and crashed Electra on Mili Atoll . . . 90 65
120 44c. Japanese patrol boat "Koshu" recovering Electra 90 65

25 "We, the people of the Marshall Islands ..."

1987. Bicentenary of United States of America Constitution. Multicoloured.
122 14c. Type **25** 30 25
123 14c. Marshall Is. and U.S.A. emblems 30 25
124 14c. "We the people of the United States ..." 30 25
125 22c. "All we have and are today as a people ..." . . . 45 25
126 22c. Marshall Is. and U.S.A. flags 45 25
127 22c. "... to establish Justice ..." 45 25
128 44c. "With this Constitution ..." 85 75
129 44c. Marshall Is. stick chart and U.S. Liberty Bell . . . 85 75
130 44c. "... to promote the general Welfare ..." 85 75

The three designs of each value were printed together, se-tenant, the left hand stamp of each strip bearing quotations from the preamble to the Marshall Islands Constitution and the right hand stamp, quotations from the United States Constitution preamble.

1987. Sea Shells (3rd series). As T **8**. Multicoloured.
131 22c. Magnificent cone 50 35
132 22c. Pacific partridge tun . . 50 35
133 22c. Scorpion spider conch 50 35
134 22c. Common hairy triton . . 50 35
135 22c. Arthritic ("Chiragra") spider conch 50 35

26 Planting Coconut

1987. Copra Industry. Multicoloured.
136 44c. Type **26** 70 55
137 44c. Making copra 70 55
138 44c. Bottling extracted coconut oil 70 55

27 "We have seen his star in the east ..."

1987. Christmas. Multicoloured.
139 14c. Type **27** 30 25
140 22c. "Glory to God in the highest; ..." 40 30
141 33c. "Sing unto the Lord a new song ..." 60 40
142 44c. "Praise him in the cymbals and dances; ..." 80 65

28 Reef Heron ("Pacific Reef Heron")

1988. Shore and Water Birds. Multicoloured.
143 44c. Type **28** . . . . 1·10 1·00
144 44c. Bar-tailed godwit . . . 1·10 1·00
145 44c. Blue-faced booby ("Masked Booby") . . . . 1·10 1·00
146 44c. Northern shoveler . . . 1·10 1·00

29 Maroon Anemonefish ("Damselfish")

30 Javelin Thrower

1988. Fishes. Multicoloured.
147 1c. Type **29** 10 10
148 3c. Black-faced butterflyfish 10 10
149 14c. Stocky hawkfish 20 10
150 15c. White-spotted puffer ("Balloonfish") 20 10
151 17c. Starry pufferfish ("Trunk Fish") 25 15
152 22c. Moon ("Lyretail") wrasse 30 20
153 25c. Six-banded parrotfish . . 30 20
154 33c. Spotted ("White-spotted") boxfish 40 25
155 36c. Yellow ("Spotted") boxfish 45 30
156 39c. Red-tailed surgeonfish 50 40
157 44c. Forceps ("Long-snouted") butterflyfish . . 55 45
158 45c. Oriental trumpetfish . . 55 45
159 56c. False-eyed pufferfish ("Sharp-nosed Puffer") . . 70 50
160 $1 Yellow seahorse . . . . . 1·50 70
161 $2 Ghost pipefish . . . . . 3·50 1·50
162 $5 Clown triggerfish ("Big-spotted Triggerfish") . . . 7·50 5·50
163 $10 Blue-finned trevally ("Blue Jack") (50 × 28 mm) 15·00 11·00

1988. Olympic Games, Seoul. Multicoloured.
166 15c. Type **30** 35 15
167 15c. Drawing javelin back and star 35 15
168 15c. Javelin drawn back fully (value at left) 35 15
169 15c. Commencing throw (value at right) 35 15
170 15c. Releasing javelin 35 15
171 25c. Runner and star (left half) 45 25
172 25c. Runner and star (right half) 45 25
173 25c. Runner (value at left) . . 45 25
174 25c. Runner (value at right) 45 25
175 25c. Finish of race 45 25

Nos. 166/70 were printed together, se-tenant, forming a composite design of a javelin throw with background of the Marshallese flag. Nos. 171/5 were similarly arranged forming a composite design of a runner and flag.

31 "Casco" sailing through Golden Gate of San Francisco

1988. Centenary of Robert Louis Stevenson's Pacific Voyages. Multicoloured.
176 25c. Type **31** 60 60
177 25c. "Casco" at the Needles of Ua-Pu, Marquesas . . . 60 40
178 25c. "Equator" leaving Honolulu 60 40
179 25c. Chieftain's canoe, Majuro Lagoon 60 40
180 25c. Bronze medallion depicting Stevenson by Augustus St. Gaudens, 1887 . . . . 60 40
181 25c. "Janet Nicoll" (inter-island steamer), Majuro Lagoon 60 40
182 25c. Stevenson's visit to maniap of King Tembinoka of Gilbert Islands 60 40
183 25c. Stevenson in Samoan canoe, Apia Harbour . . . 60 40
184 25c. Stevenson on horse Jack at Valima (Samoan home) 60 40

32 Spanish Ragged Cross Ensign (1516–1785) and Magellan's Ship "Vitoria"

1988. Exploration Ships and Flags. Multicoloured.
185 25c. Type **32** 50 35
186 25c. British red ensign (1707–1800), "Charlotte" and "Scarborough" (transports) 50 35
187 25c. American flag and ensign (1837–45), U.S.S. "Flying Fish" (schooner) and U.S.S. "Peacock" (sloop) 50 35
188 25c. German flag and ensign (1867–1919) and "Planet" (auxiliary schooner) . . . 50 35

33 Father Christmas in Sleigh

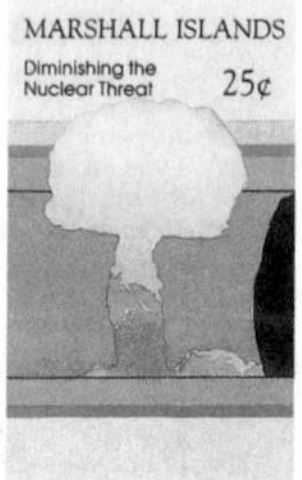

34 Nuclear Test on Bikini Atoll

1988. Christmas. Multicoloured.
189 25c. Type **33** 45 30
190 25c. Reindeer over island with palm huts and trees 45 30
191 25c. Reindeer over island with palm trees 45 30
192 25c. Reindeer and billfish . . 45 30
193 25c. Reindeer over island with outrigger canoe . . . 45 30

1988. 25th Anniv of Assassination of John F. Kennedy (American President). Multicoloured.
194 25c. Type **34** 50 30
195 25c. Kennedy signing Test Ban Treaty 50 30
196 25c. Kennedy 50 30
197 25c. Kennedy using hot-line between Washington and Moscow 50 30
198 25c. Peace Corps volunteers 50 30

35 "SV-5D PRIME" Vehicle Launch from Vandenberg Air Force Base

1988. Kwajalein Space Shuttle Tracking Station. Multicoloured.
199 25c. Type **35** (postage) . . . 45 30
200 25c. Re-entry of "SV-5D" . . 45 30
201 25c. Recovery of "SV-5D" off Kwajalein 45 30
202 25c. Space shuttle "Discovery" over Kwajalein 45 30
203 45c. Shuttle and astronaut over Rongelap (air) 75 55

Nos. 199/202 were printed together, se-tenant, forming a composite design.

36 1918 Typhoon Monument, Majuro

1989. Links with Japan. Multicoloured.
204 45c. Type **36** 80 55
205 45c. Japanese seaplane base and railway, Djarret Islet, 1940s . . . . 1·25 90

206 45c. Japanese fishing boats 1·25 90
207 45c. Japanese skin-divers . . 80 55

37 "Island Woman"

1989. Links with Alaska. Oil Paintings by Claire Fejes. Multicoloured.
208 45c. Type **37** 75 55
209 45c. "Kotzebue, Alaska" . . 75 55
210 45c. "Marshallese Madonna" 75 55

38 Dornier Do-228

1989. Air. Airplanes. Multicoloured.
211 12c. Type **38** 30 20
212 36c. Boeing 737 . . . . . . 55 40
213 39c. Hawker Siddeley H.S. 748 . . . . 65 45
214 45c. Boeing 727 . . . . . . 75 55

1989. Sea Shells (4th series). As T **8**. Mult.
220 25c. Pontifical mitre 55 35
221 25c. Tapestry turban 55 35
222 25c. Flame mouthed ("Bull-mouth") helmet 55 35
223 25c. Prickly Pacific drupe . . 55 35
224 25c. Blood-mouth conch . . 55 35

40 Wandering Tattler

1989. Birds. Multicoloured.
226 45c. Type **40** . . . . 1·10 95
227 45c. Ruddy turnstone . . . . 1·10 95
228 45c. Pacific golden plover . . 1·10 95
229 45c. Sanderling . . . . . . 1·10 95

41 "Bussard" (German cruiser) and 1897 Ship's Post Cancellation

1989. "Philexfrance 89" International Stamp Exhibition, Paris. Marshall Islands Postal History. Multicoloured.
230 25c. Type **41** . . . . 1·50 50
231 25c. First day cover bearing first Marshall Islands stamps and U.S. 10c. stamp . . . . 1·50 50
232 25c. Consolidated PBY-5 Catalina flying boats, floating Fleet Post Office ("L.S.T. 119"), Majuro, and 1944 U.S. Navy cancellation . . . . 1·50 50
233 25c. Nakajima A6M2 "Rufe" seaplane, mailboat off Mili Island and Japanese cancellation . . . . 1·50 50
234 25c. Majuro Post Office . . . 1·50 50
235 25c. Consolidated PBY-5A Catalina amphibian, outrigger canoe and 1951 U.S. civilian mail cancellation . . . . 1·50 50
236 45c. "Morning Star V" (missionary ship) and 1905 Jaluit cancellation . . . . 1·75 55
237 45c. 1906 registered cover with Jaluit cancellation . . 1·75 55
238 45c. "Prinz Eitel Freiderich" (auxiliary cruiser) and 1914 German ship's post cancellation . . . . 1·75 55
239 45c. "Scharnhorst" (cruiser) leading German Asiatic Squadron and 1914 ship's post cancellation . . . . . 1·75 55

Nos. 230/5 were printed together, se-tenant, Nos. 231 and 234 forming a composite design to commemorate the 5th anniversary of Marshall Islands Independent Postal Service.

42 Launch of Apollo "11"

1989. 20th Anniv of First Manned Moon Landing. Multicoloured.
241 25c. Type **42** . . . . 1·00 75
242 25c. Neil Armstrong . . . . 1·00 75
243 25c. Descent of lunar module to moon's surface . . . . 1·00 75
244 25c. Michael Collins . . . . 1·00 75
245 25c. Planting flag on Moon 1·00 75
246 25c. Edwin "Buzz" Aldrin . . 1·00 75

43 Polish Cavalry and German Tanks

1989. History of Second World War. Multicoloured.
(a) 1st issue. Invasion of Poland, 1939.
248 25c. Type **43** 45 35

(b) 2nd issue. Sinking of H.M.S. "Royal Oak", 1939.
249 45c. U-boat and burning battleship 75 55

(c) 3rd issue. Invasion of Finland, 1939.
250 45c. Troops on skis and tanks 75 55

(d) 4th issue. Battle of the River Plate, 1939.
251 45c. H.M.S. "Exeter" (cruiser) 75 55
252 45c. H.M.S. "Ajax" (cruiser) 75 55
253 45c. "Admiral Graf Spee" (German battleship) . . . 75 55
254 45c. H.M.N.Z.S. "Achilles" (cruiser) 75 55

See also Nos. 320/44, 359/84, 409/40, 458/77, 523/48 and 575/95.

44 Angel with Horn

45 Dr. Robert Goddard

1989. Christmas. Multicoloured.
255 25c. Type **44** 70 50
256 25c. Angel singing 70 50
257 25c. Angel with lute 70 50
258 25c. Angel with lyre 70 50

1989. Milestones in Space Exploration. Multicoloured.
259 45c. Type **45** (first liquid fuel rocket launch, 1926) . . . 90 55
260 45c. "Sputnik 1" (first man-made satellite, 1957) . . . 90 55
261 45c. Rocket lifting off (first American satellite, 1958) 90 55
262 45c. Yuri Gagarin (first man in space, 1961) 90 55
263 45c. John Glenn (first American in Earth orbit, 1962) 90 55
264 45c. Valentina Tereshkova (first woman in space, 1963) 90 55
265 45c. Aleksei Leonov (first space walk, 1965) 90 55
266 45c. Edward White (first American space walk, 1965) 90 55
267 45c. "Gemini 6" and "7" (first rendezvous in space, 1965) 90 55
268 45c. "Luna 9" (first soft landing on the Moon, 1966) 90 55
269 45c. "Gemini 8" (first docking in space, 1966) . . 90 55
270 45c. "Venera 4" (first successful Venus probe, 1967) 90 55
271 45c. Moon seen from "Apollo 8" (first manned orbit of Moon, 1968) . . . 90 55
272 45c. Neil Armstrong and U.S. flag (first man on Moon, 1969) 90 55
273 45c. "Soyuz 11" and "Salyut 1" space station (first space station crew, 1971) 90 55
274 45c. Lunar rover of "Apollo 15" (first manned lunar vehicle, 1971) 90 55
275 45c. "Skylab 1" (first American space station, 1973) 90 55
276 45c. "Pioneer 10" and Jupiter (first flight past Jupiter, 1973) 90 55
277 45c. "Apollo" and "Soyuz" craft approaching each other (first international joint space flight, 1975) . . 90 55
278 45c. "Viking 1" on Mars (first landing on Mars, 1976) 90 55
279 45c. "Voyager 1" and Saturn's rings (first flight past Saturn, 1979) 90 55
280 45c. "Columbia" (first space shuttle flight, 1981) 90 55
281 45c. Satellite in outer space (first probe beyond the solar system, 1983) 90 55
282 45c. Astronaut (first untethered space walk, 1984) 90 55
283 45c. Launch of space shuttle "Discovery", 1988 . . . . 90 55

46 White-capped Noddy ("Black Noddy")

1990. Birds. Multicoloured.
284 1c. Type **46** 20 20
285 5c. Red-tailed tropic bird . . 20 20
286 9c. Whimbrel 20 20
287 10c. Sanderling 25 25
288 12c. Black-naped tern 25 25
289 15c. Wandering tattler . . . 30 30
290 20c. Bristle-thighed curlew . . 35 35
291 22c. Greater scaup 40 40
292 23c. Common (inscr "Northern") shoveler . . . 40 40
293 25c. Common (inscr "Brown") noddy 50 50
294 27c. Sooty tern 50 50
295 28c. Sharp-tailed sandpiper 50 50
296 29c. Wedge-tailed shearwater 55 50
297 30c. Pacific golden plover . . 55 55
298 35c. Brown booby 60 60
299 36c. Red-footed booby 65 65
300 40c. White tern 75 75
301 45c. Green-winged (inscr "Common") teal 85 85
302 50c. Great frigate bird . . . 95 95
303 52c. Crested tern (inscr "Great Crested Tern") . . 1·10 1·10
304 65c. Lesser sand plover . . . 1·25 1·25
305 75c. Little tern . . . . 1·50 1·50
306 $1 Reef heron (inscr "Pacific") . . . . 2·25 2·25
307 $2 Blue-faced (inscr "Masked") booby . . . . 4·50 4·50

47 Lodidean (coconut-palm leaf windmill)

1990. Children's Games. Multicoloured.
309 25c. Type **47** 70 55
310 25c. Lejonjon (juggling green coconuts) 70 55
311 25c. Etobobo (coconut leaf musical instrument) 70 55
312 25c. Didmakol (pandanus leaf flying-toy) 70 55

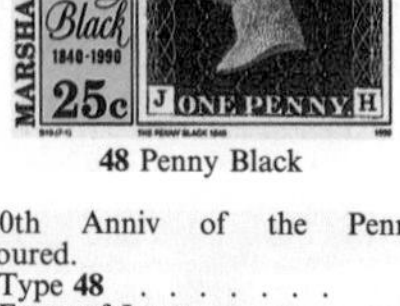

48 Penny Black

1990. 150th Anniv of the Penny Black. Multicoloured.
313 25c. Type **48** 75 75
314 25c. Essay of James Chalmers's cancellation . . 75 75
315 25c. Stamp essay by Robert Sievier 75 75
316 25c. Stamp essay by Charles Whiting 75 75
317 25c. Stamp essay by George Dickinson 75 75
318 25c. "City" medal by William Wyon (struck to commemorate Queen Victoria's first visit to City of London) 75 75

1990. History of Second World War. As T **43**. Multicoloured. (a) 5th issue. Invasions of Denmark and Norway, 1940.
320 25c. German soldier and "Stuka" dive bombers in Copenhagen 45 35
321 25c. Norwegian soldiers, burning building and German column 45 35

(b) 6th issue. Katyn Forest Massacre of Polish Prisoners, 1940.
322 25c. Bound hands and grave (vert) 45 35

(c) 7th issue. Appointment of Winston Churchill as Prime Minister of Great Britain, 1940.
323 45c. Union Jack, Churchill and war scenes 70 50

(d) 8th issue. Invasion of Low Countries, 1940.
324 25c. Bombing of Rotterdam 45 35
325 25c. Invasion of Belgium . . 45 35

(e) 9th issue. Evacuation at Dunkirk, 1940.
326 45c. British bren-gunner on beach 70 50
327 45c. Soldiers queueing for boats 70 50

Nos. 326/7 were issued together, se-tenant, forming a composite design.

(f) 10th issue. German Occupation of Paris, 1940.
328 45c. German soldiers marching through Arc de Triomphe (vert) 70 50

(g) 11th issue. Battle of Mers-el-Kebir, 1940.
329 25c. Vice-Admiral Sir James Somerville, Vice-Admiral Marcel Gensoul and British and French battleships . . 45 35

(h) 12th issue. The Burma Road, 1940.
330 25c. Allied and Japanese forces (vert) 45 35

(i) 13th issue. British Bases and American Destroyers Lend-lease Agreement, 1940.
331 45c. H.M.S. "Georgetown" (formerly U.S.S. "Maddox") 70 50
332 45c. H.M.S. "Banff" (formerly U.S.C.G.C. "Saranac") 70 50
333 45c. H.M.S. "Buxton" (formerly U.S.S. "Edwards") 70 50
334 45c. H.M.S. "Rockingham" (formerly U.S.S. "Swasey") 70 50

(j) 14th issue. Battle of Britain, 1940.
335 45c. Supermarine Spitfire Mk 1A fighters 70 50
336 45c. Hawker Hurricane Mk 1 and Spitfire fighters 70 50
337 45c. Messerschmitt Bf 109E fighters 70 50
338 45c. Junkers Ju 87B-2 "Stuka" dive bomber . . . 70 50

Nos. 335/8 were issued together, se-tenant, forming a composite design.

(k) 15th issue. Tripartite Pact, 1940.
339 45c. Officers' caps of Germany, Italy and Japan (vert) 70 50

(l) 16th issue. Election of Franklin D. Roosevelt for Third United States Presidential Term, 1940.
340 25c. Roosevelt (vert) 45 35

(m) 17th issue. Battle of Taranto, 1940.
341 25c. H.M.S. "Illustrious" (aircraft carrier) 45 35
342 25c. Fairey Swordfish bomber 45 35
343 25c. "Andrea Doria" (Italian battleship) 45 35
344 25c. "Conte di Cavour" (Italian battleship) 45 35

Nos. 341/4 were issued together, se-tenant, forming a composite design.

49 Pacific Green Turtles

1990. Endangered Turtles. Multicoloured.
345 25c. Type **49** . . . . 1·10 75
346 25c. Pacific green turtle swimming . . . . 1·10 75
347 25c. Hawksbill turtle hatching 1·10 75
348 25c. Hawksbill turtle swimming . . . . 1·10 75

50 Stick Chart, Outrigger Canoe and Flag

1990. 4th Anniv of Ratification of Compact of Free Association with United States.
349 **50** 25c. multicoloured 75 45

51 Brandenburg Gate, Berlin

1990. Re-unification of Germany.
350 **51** 45c. multicoloured . . . . 1·00 70

52 Outrigger Canoe and Stick Chart

1990. Christmas. Multicoloured.
351 25c. Type **52** 70 50
352 25c. Missionary preaching and "Morning Star" (missionary ship) 70 50
353 25c. British sailors dancing 70 50
354 25c. Electric guitar and couple dancing 70 50

53 Harvesting Breadfruit

1990. Breadfruit. Multicoloured.
355 25c. Type **53** 70 50
356 25c. Peeling breadfruit . . . 70 50
357 25c. Soaking breadfruit . . . 70 50
358 25c. Kneading dough 70 50

1991. History of Second World War. As T **43**. Multicoloured. (a) 18th issue. Four Freedoms Speech to U.S. Congress by President Franklin Roosevelt, 1941.
359 30c. Freedom of Speech . . . 50 40
360 30c. Freedom from Want . . 50 40
361 30c. Freedom of Worship . . 50 40
362 30c. Freedom from Fear . . 50 40

(b) 19th issue. Battle of Beda Fomm, 1941.
363 30c. Tank battle 50 40

(c) 20th issue. German Invasion of Balkans, 1941.
364 29c. German Dornier DO-17Z bombers over Acropolis, Athens (Greece) (vert) 50 40
365 29c. German tank and Yugoslavian Parliament building (vert) 50 40

(d) 21st issue. Sinking of the "Bismarck" (German battleship), 1941.
366 50c. H.M.S. "Prince of Wales" (battleship) 75 60
367 50c. H.M.S. "Hood" (battle cruiser) 75 60
368 50c. "Bismarck" 75 60
369 50c. Fairey Swordfish torpedo bombers 75 60

(e) 22nd issue. German Invasion of Russia, 1941.
370 30c. German tanks 50 40

(f) 23rd issue. Declaration of Atlantic Charter by United States and Great Britain, 1941.
371 29c. U.S.S. "Augusta" (cruiser) and Pres. Roosevelt of United States (vert) 50 40
372 29c. H.M.S. "Prince of Wales" (battleship) and Winston Churchill (vert) 50 40

Nos. 371/2 were issued together, se-tenant, forming a composite design.

(g) 24th issue. Siege of Moscow, 1941.
373 29c. German tanks crossing snow-covered plain 50 40

(h) 25th issue. Sinking of U.S.S. "Reuben James", 1941.
374 30c. U.S.S. "Reuben James" (destroyer) 50 40
375 30c. German U-boat 562 (submarine) 50 40

Nos. 374/5 were issued together, se-tenant, forming a composite design.

(i) 26th issue. Japanese Attack on Pearl Harbor, 1941.
376 50c. American airplanes (inscr "Peal Harbor") (vert) 75 60
376b As No. 376 but inscr "Pearl Harbor" 75 60
377 50c. Japanese dive bombers (vert) 75 60
378 50c. U.S.S. "Arizona" (battleship) (vert) 75 60
379 50c. "Akagi" (Japanese aircraft carrier) (vert) . . 75 60

Nos. 376/9 were issued together, se-tenant, forming a composite design.

(j) 27th issue. Japanese Capture of Guam, 1941.
380 29c. Japanese troops (vert) 50 40

(k) 28th issue. Fall of Singapore to Japan, 1941.
381 29c. Japanese soldiers with Japanese flag, Union Jack and white flag 50 40

(l) 29th issue. Formation of "Flying Tigers" (American volunteer group), 1941.
382 50c. American Curtiss Tomahawk fighters 75 60
383 50c. Japanese Mitsubishi Ki-21 "Sally" bombers . . 75 60

Nos. 382/3 were issued together, se-tenant, forming a composite design.

(m) 30th issue. Fall of Wake Island to Japan, 1941.
384 29c. American Grumman Wildcat fighters and Japanese Mitsubishi G3M "Nell" bombers over Wake Island 50 40

54 Boeing 747 carrying "Columbia" to Launch Site

1991. Ten Years of Space Shuttle Flights. Multicoloured.
385 50c. Type **54** 90 70
386 50c. Orbital release of Long Duration Exposure Facility from "Challenger", 1984 90 70
387 50c. Shuttle launch at Cape Canaveral 90 70
388 50c. Shuttle landing at Edwards Air Force Base 90 70

Nos. 385/8 were issued together, se-tenant, the backgrounds forming a composite design.

55 "Ixora carolinensis"

1991. Native Flowers. Multicoloured.
389 52c. Type **55** 90 70
390 52c. Glory-bower ("Clerodendum inerme") 90 70
391 52c. "Messerschmidia argentea" 90 70
392 52c. "Vigna marina" 90 70

56 American Bald Eagle and Marshall Islands and U.S. Flags

1991. United States Participation in Operation Desert Storm (campaign to liberate Kuwait).
394 **56** 29c. multicoloured 60 45

57 Red-footed Booby

1991. Birds. Multicoloured.
395 29c. Type **57** 90 40
396 29c. Great frigate bird (facing right) 90 40
397 29c. Brown booby 90 40
398 29c. White tern 90 40
399 29c. Great frigate bird (facing left) 90 40
400 29c. White-capped noddy ("Black Noddy") 90 40

58 Dornier Do-228

1991. Passenger Aircraft. Multicoloured.
402 12c. Type **58** 35 20
403 29c. Douglas DC-8 jetliner 75 50
404 50c. Hawker Siddeley H.S. 748 airliner . . . . 1·25 90
405 50c. Saab 2000 . . . . . . 1·25 90

59 U.N. and State Emblems and Outrigger Canoe

1991. Admission of Marshall Islands to the United Nations.
406 **59** 29c. multicoloured 60 45

60 Dove and Glory-bower Flowers

1991. Christmas.
407 **60** 30c. multicoloured 65 50

61 State Flag and Dove

1991. 25th Anniv of Peace Corps in Marshall Islands.
408 **61** 29c. multicoloured 55 45

1992. History of Second World War. As T **43**. Multicoloured. (a) 31st issue. Arcadia Conference, Washington D.C., 1942.
409 29c. Pres. Franklin Roosevelt of U.S.A., Winston Churchill of Great Britain, White House and United Nations emblem 50 40

(b) 32nd issue. Fall of Manila to Japan, 1942.
410 50c. Japanese tank moving through Manila 75 60

(c) 33rd issue. Capture of Rabaul by Japan, 1942.
411 29c. Japanese flag, Admiral Yamamoto, General Douglas MacArthur and U.S. flag 50 40

(d) 34th issue. Battle of the Java Sea, 1942.
412 29c. Sinking of the "De Ruyter" (Dutch cruiser) . . 50 40

(e) 35th issue. Capture of Rangoon by Japan, 1942.
413 50c. Japanese tank and soldiers in Rangoon (vert) 75 60

(f) 36th issue. Japanese Landing on New Guinea, 1942.
414 29c. Japanese soldiers coming ashore 50 40

(g) 37th issue. Evacuation of General Douglas MacArthur from Corregidor, 1942.
415 29c. MacArthur 50 40

(h) 38th issue. British Raid on Saint Nazaire, 1942.
416 29c. H.M.S. "Campbeltown" (destroyer) and motor torpedo boat 50 40

(i) 39th issue. Surrender of Bataan, 1942.
417 29c. Prisoners on "death" march (vert) 50 40

(j) 40th issue. Doolittle Raid on Tokyo, 1942.
418 50c. North American B-25 Mitchell bomber taking off from U.S.S. "Hornet" (aircraft carrier) (vert) . . 75 60

(k) 41st issue. Fall of Corregidor to Japan, 1942.
419 29c. Lt.-Gen. Jonathan Wainwright 50 40

(l) 42nd issue. Battle of the Coral Sea, 1942.
420 50c. U.S.S. "Lexington" (aircraft carrier) and Grumman F4F-3 Wildcat fighter (inscr "U.S.S. Lexington") 75 60
420b As No. 420 but additionally inscr with aircraft name 75 60
421 50c. Japanese Aichi D3A 1 "Val" and Nakajima B5N2 "Kate" dive bombers (wrongly inscr 'Mitsubishi A6M2 "Zero" ') 75 60
421a As No. 421 but inscr corrected 75 60
422 50c. American Douglas TBD-1 Devastator torpedo bombers (wrongly inscr "U.S. Douglas SBD Dauntless") 75 60
422a As No. 422 but with inscr corrected 75 60
423 50c. "Shoho" (Japanese aircraft carrier) and Mitsubishi A6M2 Zero-Sen fighters (inscr "Japanese carrier Shoho") 75 60
423a As No. 423 but additionally inscr with aircraft name 75 60

The four designs were issued together, se-tenant, each pair forming a composite design.

(m) 43rd issue. Battle of Midway, 1942.
424 50c. "Akagi" (Japanese aircraft carrier) 75 60
425 50c. U.S.S. "Yorktown" (aircraft carrier) 75 60
426 50c. American Douglas SBD Dauntless dive bombers . . 75 60
427 50c. Japanese Nakajima B5N2 "Kate" dive bombers 75 60

Nos. 424/7 were issued together, se-tenant, forming a composite design.

(n) 44th issue. Destruction of Lidice (Czechoslovakian village), 1942.
428 29c. Cross and memorial at Lidice 50 40

(o) 45th issue. German Capture of Sevastopol, 1942.
429 29c. German siege gun "Dora" (vert) 50 40

(p) 46th issue. Destruction of Convoy PQ-17, 1942.
430 29c. British merchant ship . . 50 40
431 29c. German U-boat 50 40

(q) 47th issue. Marine Landing on Guadalcanal, 1942.
432 29c. American marines landing on beach 50 40

(r) 48th issue. Battle of Savo Island, 1942.
433 29c. Admiral Mikawa of Japan (vert) 50 40

(s) 49th issue. Dieppe Raid, 1942.
434 29c. Soldiers landing at Dieppe 50 40

(t) 50th issue. Battle of Stalingrad, 1942.
435 50c. Heroes monument and burning buildings (vert) . . 75 60

(u) 51st issue. Battle of Eastern Solomon Islands, 1942.
436 29c. Aircraft over U.S.S. "Enterprise" (aircraft carrier) 50 40

(v) 52nd issue. Battle of Cape Esperance, 1942.
437 50c. American cruiser firing guns at night 75 60

(w) 53rd issue. Battle of El Alamein, 1942.
438 29c. Gen. Bernard Montgomery of Great Britain and Gen. Erwin Rommel of Germany . . . 50 40

(x) 54th issue. Battle of Barents Sea, 1942.
439 29c. H.M.S. "Sheffield" (cruiser) 50 40
440 29c. "Admiral Hipper" (German cruiser) 50 40

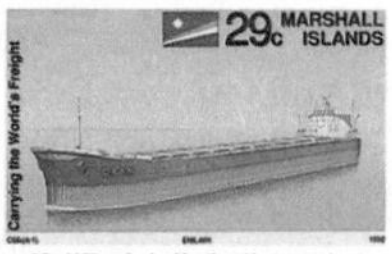

62 "Emlain" (bulk carrier)

63 Northern Pintail

1992. Ships flying the Marshall Islands Flag. Multicoloured.
441 29c. Type **62** 70 50
442 29c. "CSK Valiant" (tanker) 70 50
443 29c. "Ionmeto" (fisheries protection vessel) 70 50
444 29c. "Micro Pilot" (inter-island freighter) 70 50

1992. Nature Protection.
445 **63** 29c. multicoloured 60 45

64 Tipnol (outrigger canoe)

65 Basket Making

1992. Legends of Discovery. Multicoloured.
446 50c. Type **64** 75 75
447 50c. "Santa Maria" (reconstruction of Columbus's flagship) . . . 75 75
448 50c. Constellation Argo Navis 75 75
449 50c. Sailor and tipnol 75 75
450 50c. Christopher Columbus and "Santa Maria" 75 75
451 50c. Astronaut and Argo Navis constellation 75 75

1992. Handicrafts. Multicoloured.
453 29c. Type **65** 50 40
454 29c. Boy holding model outrigger canoe 50 40
455 29c. Man carving boat . . . 50 40
456 29c. Fan making 50 40

66 Christmas Offering

1992. Christmas.
457 **66** 29c. multicoloured 50 40

1993. History of Second World War. As T **43**. Multicoloured. (a) 55th issue. Casablanca Conference, 1943.
458 29c. Pres. Franklin Roosevelt and Winston Churchill . . 50 40
(b) 56th issue. Liberation of Kharkov, 1943.
459 29c. Russian tank in Kharkov 50 40
(c) 57th issue. Battle of the Bismarck Sea, 1943.
460 50c. Japanese Mitsubishi A6M Zero-Sen fighters and "Arashio" (Japanese destroyer) 75 60
461 50c. American Lockheed P-38 Lightnings and Australian Bristol Beaufighter fighters 75 60
462 50c. "Shirayuki" (Japanese destroyer) 75 60
463 50c. American A-20 Havoc and North American B-52 Mitchell bombers 75 60
Nos 460/63 were issued together, se-tenant, forming a composite design.
(d) 58th issue. Interception of Yamamoto, 1943.
464 50c. Admiral Yamamoto . . 75 60
(e) 59th issue. Battle of Kursk, 1943.
465 29c. German "Tiger 1" tank 50 40
466 29c. Soviet "T-34" tank . . . 50 40
Nos. 465/6 were issued together, se-tenant, forming a composite design.
(f) 60th issue. Allied Invasion of Sicily, 1943.
467 52c. Gen. George Patton, Jr 85 60
468 52c. Gen. Bernard Montgomery 85 65
469 52c. Americans landing at Licata 85 65
470 52c. British landing south of Syracuse 85 65
(g) 61st issue. Raids on Schweinfurt, 1943.
471 50c. American Boeing B-17F Flying Fortress bombers and German Messerschmitt Bf 109 fighter 75 60
(h) 62nd issue. Liberation of Smolensk, 1943.
472 29c. Russian soldier and burning buildings (vert) . . 50 40
(i) 63rd issue. Landing at Bougainville, 1943.
473 29c. American Marines on beach at Empress Augusta Bay 50 40
(j) 64th issue. U.S. Invasion of Tarawa, 1943.
474 50c. American Marines . . . 75 60
(k) 65th issue. Teheran Allied Conference, 1943.
475 52c. Winston Churchill of Great Britain, Pres. Franklin Roosevelt of U.S.A. and Josef Stalin of Russia (vert) 85 65
(l) 66th issue. Battle of North Cape, 1943.
476 29c. H.M.S. "Duke of York" (British battleship) 50 40
477 29c. "Scharnhorst" (German battleship) 50 40

67 Atoll Butterflyfish

1993. Reef Life. Multicoloured.
478 50c. Type **67** 90 60
479 50c. Brick soldierfish 90 60
480 50c. Caerulean damselfish . . 90 60
481 50c. Japanese inflator-filefish 90 60
482 50c. Arc-eyed hawkfish . . . 90 60
483 50c. Powder-blue surgeonfish 90 60

68 "Britannia" (full-rigged ship)

1993. Ships. Multicoloured. (a) Size 35 × 20 mm.
485 10c. "San Jeronimo" (Spanish galleon) 10 10
486 14c. U.S.C.G. "Cape Corwin" (fisheries patrol vessel) 15 10
487 15c. Type **68** 20 15
488 19c. "Micro Palm" (inter-island freighter) 25 15
489 20c. "Eendracht" (Dirk Hartog's ship) 30 15
490 23c. H.M.S "Cornwallis" (sail frigate) 35 20
491 24c. U.S.S. "Dolphin" (schooner) 40 20
492 29c. "Morning Star I" (missionary brigantine) . . 45 25
493 30c. "Rurik" (Otto von Kotzebue's brig) (inscr "Rurick") 50 25
494 32c. "Vitoria" (Magellan's flagship) 55 25
669 32c. As Type **68** 50 40
670 32c. U.S.S. "Dolphin" (schooner) 50 40
671 32c. "Morning Star I" (missionary brigantine) . . 50 40
672 32c. U.S.S. "Lexington" (aircraft carrier) 50 40
673 32c. "Micro Palm" (inter-island freighter) 50 40
674 32c. H.M.S. "Cornwallis" (sail frigate) 50 40
675 32c. H.M.S. "Serpent" (brig) 50 40
676 32c. "Scarborough" (transport) 50 40
677 32c. "San Jeronimo" (Spanish galleon) 50 40
678 32c. "Rurik" (Otto van Kotzebue's brig) (inscr "Rurick") 50 40
679 32c. "Nautilus" (German gunboat) 50 40
680 32c. Fishing vessels 50 40
681 32c. Malmel outrigger canoe 50 40
682 32c. "Eendracht" (Dirk Hartog's ship) 50 40
683 32c. "Nautilus" (brig) 50 40
684 32c. "Nagara" and "Isuzu" (Japanese cruisers) 50 40
685 32c. "Potomac" (whaling ship) 50 40
687 32c. U.S.C.G. "Assateague" (cutter) 50 40
688 32c. "Charles W. Morgan" (whaling ship) 50 40
689 32c. "Victoria" (whaling ship) 50 40
690 32c. U.S.C.G. "Cape Corwin" (fisheries patrol vessel) 50 40
691 32c. "Equator" (schooner) . . 50 40
692 32c. "Tanager" (inter-island steamer) 50 40
693 32c. "Tole Mour" (hospital schooner) 50 40
495 35c. "Nautilus" (German gunboat) 60 30
496 40c. "Nautilus" (British brig) 65 30
497 45c. "Nagara" and "Isuzu" (Japanese cruisers) 70 35
498 46c. "Equator" (schooner) . . 75 35
499 50c. U.S.S. "Lexington" (aircraft carrier) 80 40
500 52c. H.M.S. "Serpent" (brig) 85 45
501 55c. "Potomac" (whaling ship) 90 50
502 60c. U.S.C.G. "Assateague" (cutter) . . . . 1·00 70
503 75c. "Scarborough" (transport) . . . . 1·10 75
504 78c. "Charles W. Morgan" (whaling ship) . . . . . 1·25 90
505 95c. "Tanager" (inter-island steamer) . . . . 1·40 1·00
506 $1 "Tole Mour" (hospital schooner) . . . . 1·50 1·10
507 $2.90 Fishing vessels . . . . 4·25 2·75
508 $3.00 "Victoria" (whaling ship) . . . . 4·50 3·00
(b) Size 46 × 26 mm.
509 $1 Enewetak outrigger canoe 1·50 1·00
510 $2 Jaluit outrigger canoe . . 4·00 3·00
511 $5 Ailuk outrigger canoe . . 7·00 5·00
512 $10 Racing outrigger canoes 14·00 10·00

69 Capitol Complex

1993. Inauguration of New Capitol Complex, Majuro. Multicoloured.
513 29c. Type **69** 40 25
514 29c. Parliament building . . 40 25
515 29c. National seal (vert) . . . 40 25
516 29c. National flag (vert) . . . 40 25

71 Woman with Breadfruit

1993. Marshallese Life in the 1800s. Designs adapted from sketches by Louis Choris. Multicoloured.
518 29c. Type **71** 50 35
519 29c. Canoes and warrior . . 50 35
520 29c. Chief and islanders . . . 50 35
521 29c. Drummer and dancers 50 35

72 Singing Silent Night

1993. Christmas.
522 **72** 29c. multicoloured 50 35

1994. History of Second World War. As T **43**. Multicoloured. (a) 67th issue. Appointment of Gen. Dwight D. Eisenhower as Commander of Supreme Headquarters, Allied Expeditionary Force, 1944.
523 29c. Eisenhower 50 40
(b) 68th issue. Invasion of Anzio, 1944.
524 50c. Troops landing 70 60
(c) 69th issue. Lifting of Siege of Leningrad, 1944.
525 52c. St. Isaac's Cathedral and soldier with Soviet flag . . 85 65
(d) 70th issue. U.S. Liberation of Marshall Islands, 1944.
526 29c. Douglas SBD Dauntless dive bombers 50 40
(e) 71st issue. Japanese Defeat at Truk, 1944.
527 29c. Admirals Spruance and Marc Mitscher (vert) . . . 50 40
(f) 72nd issue. U.S. Bombing of Germany, 1944.
528 52c. Boeing B-17 Flying Fortress bombers 85 65
(g) 73rd issue. Allied Liberation of Rome, 1944.
529 50c. Lt.-Gen. Mark Clark and flowers in gun barrel (vert) 75 60
(h) 74th issue. Allied Landings in Normandy, 1944.
530 75c. Airspeed A.S.51 Horsa gliders (inscr "Horsa Gliders") . . . . 1·10 80
530b As No. 530 but inscr "Horsa Gliders, Parachute Troops" . . . . 1·10 80
531 75c. Hawker Typhoon 1B and North American P-51B Mustang fighters (wrongly inscr "U.S. P51B Mustangs, British Hurricanes") . . . . . . 1·10 80
531a As No. 531 but inscr corrected . . . . 1·10 80
532 75c. German gun defences (inscr "German Gun Defenses") . . . . 1·10 80
532a As No. 523 but inscr "German Gun Defenses, Pointe du Hoc" . . . . . 1·10 80
533 75c. Allied amphibious landing . . . . 1·10 80
The four designs were issued together, se-tenant, forming a composite design.
(i) 75th issue. V-1 Bombardment of England, 1944.
534 50c. V-1 flying bomb over River Thames 75 60
(j) 76th issue. U.S. Marines Land on Saipan, 1944.
535 29c. U.S. and Japanese troops 50 40
(k) 77th issue. First Battle of the Philippine Sea, 1944.
536 50c. Grumman F6F-3 Hellcat fighter 75 60
(l) 78th issue. U.S. Liberation of Guam, 1944.
537 29c. Naval bombardment . . 50 40
(m) 79th issue. Warsaw Uprising, 1944.
538 50c. Polish Home Army fighter 75 60
(n) 80th issue. Liberation of Paris, 1944.
539 50c. Allied troops marching along Champs Elysee . . . 75 60
(o) 81st issue. U.S. Marines Land on Peleliu, 1944.
540 29c. Amphibious armoured tracked vehicle 50 40
(p) 82nd issue. General Douglas MacArthur's Return to Philippines, 1944.
541 52c. McArthur and soldiers 85 65
(q) 83rd issue. Battle of Leyte Gulf, 1944.
542 52c. American motor torpedo boat and Japanese warships 85 65
(r) 84th issue. Sinking of the "Tirpitz" (German battleship), 1944.
543 50c. Avro Lancaster bombers 75 60
544 50c. Tirpitz burning 75 60
(s) 85th issue. Battle of the Bulge, 1944.
545 50c. Infantrymen 75 60
546 50c. Tank driver and tanks 75 60
547 50c. Pilot and aircraft 75 60
548 50c. Lt.-Col. Creighton Abrams and Brig.-Gen. Anthony McAuliffe shaking hands 75 60

75 Footballers

76 Neil Armstrong stepping onto Moon

1994. World Cup Football Championship, U.S.A. Multicoloured.
552 50c. Type **75** . . . . 1·40 60
553 50c. Footballers (different) 1·40 60
Nos. 552/53 were issued together, se-tenant, forming a composite design.

1994. 25th Anniv of First Manned Moon Landing. Multicoloured.
554 75c. Type **76** 95 70
555 75c. Planting U.S. flag on Moon 95 70
556 75c. Astronauts saluting . . . 95 70
557 75c. Pres. John F. Kennedy and Armstrong 95 70

77 Solar System

1994. The Solar System. Multicoloured.
559 50c. Type **77** 85 65
560 50c. Sun 85 65
561 50c. Moon 85 65
562 50c. Mercury 85 65
563 50c. Venus 85 65
564 50c. Earth 85 65
565 50c. Mars 85 65
566 50c. Jupiter 85 65
567 50c. Saturn 85 65
568 50c. Uranus 85 65
569 50c. Neptune 85 65
570 50c. Pluto 85 65

79 Church and Christmas Tree (Ringo Baso)

1994. Christmas.
573 **79** 29c. multicoloured 50 40

1995. History of Second World War. As T **43**. Multicoloured. (a) 86th issue. Yalta Conference, 1945.
575 32c. Josef Stalin of U.S.S.R., Winston Churchill of Great Britain and Franklin Roosevelt of U.S.A. (vert) 55 45
(b) 87th issue. Allied Bombing of Dresden, 1945.
576 55c. "Europe" (Meissen porcelain statuette), flames and bombers (vert) 90 70
(c) 88th issue. U.S. Marine Invasion of Iwo Jima, 1945.
577 $1 Marines planting flag on Mt. Suribachi (vert) . . . 1·60 1·25
(d) 89th issue. U.S. Capture of Remagen Bridge, Germany, 1945.
578 32c. Troops and tanks crossing bridge (vert) . . . 55 45
(e) 90th issue. U.S. Invasion of Okinawa, 1945.
579 55c. Soldiers throwing grenades (vert) 90 70
(f) 91st issue. Death of Franklin D. Roosevelt, 1945.
580 50c. Funeral cortege 75 60
(g) 92nd issue. U.S. and U.S.S.R. Troops meet at Elbe, 1945.
581 32c. American and Soviet troops 55 45
(h) 93rd issue. Capture of Berlin by Soviet Troops, 1945.
582 60c. Soviet Marshal Georgi Zhukov and Berlin landmarks 95 75

(i) 94th issue. Allied Liberation of Concentration Camps, 1945.

583	55c. Inmates and soldier cutting barbed-wire fence	90	70

(j) 95th issue. V-E (Victory in Europe) Day, 1945.

584	75c. Signing of German surrender, Rheims	1·10	80
585	75c. Soldier kissing girl, Times Square, New York	1·10	80
586	75c. Victory Parade, Red Square, Moscow	1·10	80
587	75c. Royal Family and Churchill on balcony of Buckingham Palace, London	1·10	80

(k) 96th issue. Signing of United Nations Charter, 1945.

588	32c. U.S. President Harry S. Truman and Veterans' Memorial Hall, San Francisco	55	45

(l) 97th issue. Potsdam Conference, 1945.

589	55c. Pres. Harry S. Truman of U.S.A., Winston Churchill and Clement Attlee of Great Britain and Josef Stalin of U.S.S.R.	90	70

(m) 98th issue. Resignation of Winston Churchill, 1945.

590	60c. Churchill leaving 10 Downing Street (vert)	95	75

(n) 99th issue. Dropping of Atomic Bomb on Hiroshima, 1945.

591	$1 Boeing B-29 Superfortress bomber "Enola Gay" and mushroom cloud	1·60	1·25

(o) 100th issue. V-J (Victory in Japan) Day, 1945.

592	75c. Mount Fuji and warships in Tokyo Bay	1·10	80
593	75c. U.S.S. "Missouri" (battleship)	1·10	80
594	75c. Admiral Chester Nimitz signing Japanese surrender watched by Gen. Douglas MacArthur and Admirals William Halsey and Forest Sherman	1·10	80
595	75c. Japanese Foreign Minister Shigemitsu, General Umezu and delegation	1·10	80

Nos. 592/5 were issued together, se-tenant, each pair forming a composite design.

81 Scuba Diver, Meyer's Butterflyfish and Red-tailed Surgeonfish ("Achilles Tang")

1995. Undersea World (1st series). Multicoloured.

596	55c. Type **81**	90	70
597	55c. Moorish idols and scuba diver	90	70
598	55c. Pacific green turtle and anthias ("Fairy Basslet")	90	70
599	55c. Anthias ("Fairy Basslet"), emperor angelfish and orange-finned anemonefish	90	70

Nos. 596/9 were issued together, se-tenant, forming a composite design.

See also Nos. 865/8.

82 U.S.S. "PT 109" (motor torpedo boat)

83 Marilyn Monroe

1995. 35th Anniv of Election of John F. Kennedy as U.S. President. Multicoloured.

600	55c. Type **82** (Second World War command)	80	65
601	55c. Presidential inauguration	80	65
602	55c. Peace corps on agricultural project in Marshall Islands	80	65
603	55c. U.S. airplane and warships superintending removal of Soviet missiles from Cuba	80	65
604	55c. Kennedy signing Nuclear Test Ban Treaty, 1963	80	65
605	55c. Eternal flame on Kennedy's grave, Arlington National Cemetery, Washington D.C.	80	65

1995. 69th Birth Anniv of Marilyn Monroe (actress). Multicoloured.

606	75c. Type **83**	1·10	80
607	75c. Monroe (face value top right)	1·10	80
608	75c. Monroe (face value bottom left)	1·10	80
609	75c. Monroe (face value bottom right)	1·10	80

85 "Mir" (Soviet space station)

86 Siamese and Exotic Shorthair

1995. Docking of Atlantis with "Mir" Space Station (611/12) and 20th Anniv of "Apollo"–"Soyuz" Space Link (613/14). Multicoloured.

611	75c. Type **85**	1·10	80
612	75c. "Atlantis" (U.S. space shuttle)	1·10	80
613	75c. "Apollo" (U.S. spacecraft)	1·10	80
614	75c. "Soyuz" (Soviet spacecraft)	1·10	80

Nos. 611/14 were issued together, se-tenant, forming a composite design.

1995. Cats. Multicoloured.

615	32c. Type **86**	55	45
616	32c. American shorthair tabby and red Persian	55	45
617	32c. Maine coon and Burmese	55	45
618	32c. Himalayan and Abyssinian	55	45

87 Sailfish and Tuna

1995. Pacific Game Fish. Multicoloured.

619	60c. Type **87**	1·00	75
620	60c. Albacores	1·00	75
621	60c. Wahoo	1·00	75
622	60c. Blue marlin	1·00	75
623	60c. Yellow-finned tunas	1·00	75
624	60c. Giant trevally	1·00	75
625	60c. Dolphin (fish)	1·00	75
626	60c. Short-finned mako	1·00	75

Nos. 619/26 were issued together, se-tenant, forming a composite design.

88 Inedel's Magic Kite

91 Shepherds gazing at Sky

1995. Folk Legends (1st series). Multicoloured.

627	32c. Type **88**	60	45
628	32c. Lijebake rescues her granddaughter	60	45
629	32c. Jebro's mother invents the sail	60	45
630	32c. Limajnon escapes to the moon	60	45

See also Nos. 727/30 and 861/4.

1995. Christmas.

633 **91**	32c. multicoloured	45	25

92 Messerschmit Me 262-Ia Schwalbe

93 Rabin

1995. Jet Fighters. Multicoloured.

634	32c. Type **92**	50	40
635	32c. Gloster Meteor F Mk 8	50	40
636	32c. Lockheed F-80 Shooting Star	50	40
637	32c. North American F-86 Sabre	50	40
638	32c. F9F-2 Panther	50	40
639	32c. Mikoyan Gurevich MiG-15	50	40
640	32c. North American F-100 Super Sabre	50	40
641	32c. Convair TF-102A Delta Dagger	50	40
642	32c. Lockheed F-104 Starfighter	50	40
643	32c. Mikoyan Gurevich MiG-21 MT	50	40
644	32c. F8U Crusader	50	40
645	32c. Republic F-105 Thunderchief	50	40
646	32c. Saab J35 Draken	50	40
647	32c. Fiat G-91Y	50	40
648	32c. McDonnell Douglas F-4 Phantom II	50	40
649	32c. Saab JA 37 Viggen	50	40
650	32c. Dassault Mirage F1C	50	40
651	32c. Grumman F-14 Tomcat	50	40
652	32c. F-15 Eagle	50	40
653	32c. General Dynamics F-16 Fighting Falcon	50	40
654	32c. Panavia Tornado F Mk 3	50	40
655	32c. Sukhoi Su-27UB	50	40
656	32c. Dassault Mirage 2000C	50	40
657	32c. Hawker Siddeley Sea Harrier FRS.MK1	50	40
658	32c. F-117 Nighthawk	50	40

1995. Yitzhak Rabin (Israeli Prime Minister) Commemoration.

659 **93**	32c. multicoloured	45	35

95 Blue-grey Noddy

1996. Birds. Multicoloured.

661	32c. Type **95**	70	55
662	32c. Spectacled tern ("Gray-backed Tern")	70	55
663	32c. Blue-faced booby ("Masked Booby")	70	55
664	32c. Black-footed albatross	70	55

96 Cheetah

1996. Big Cats. Multicoloured.

665	55c. Type **96**	90	70
666	55c. Tiger	90	70
667	55c. Lion	90	70
668	55c. Jaguar	90	70

97 5l. Stamp

1996. Centenary of Modern Olympic Games. Designs reproducing 1896 Greek Olympic stamps. Multicoloured.

694	60c. Type **97**	90	70
695	60c. 60l. stamp	90	70
696	60c. 40l. stamp	90	70
697	60c. 1d. stamp	90	70

98 Undersea Eruptions form Islands

99 Presley

1996. History of Marshall Islands. Multicoloured.

698	55c. Type **98**	75	60
699	55c. Coral reefs grow around islands	75	60
700	55c. Storm-driven birds carry seeds to atolls	75	60
701	55c. First human inhabitants arrive, 1500 B.C.	75	60
702	55c. Spanish explorers discover islands, 1527	75	60
703	55c. John Marshall charts islands, 1788	75	60
704	55c. German Protectorate, 1885	75	60
705	55c. Japanese soldier on beach, 1914	75	60
706	55c. American soldiers liberate islands, 1944	75	60
707	55c. Evacuation of Bikini Atoll for nuclear testing, 1946	75	60
708	55c. Marshall Islands becomes United Nations Trust Territory, 1947	75	60
709	55c. People and national flag (independence, 1986)	75	60

1996. 40th Anniv of Elvis Presley's First Number One Hit Record "Heartbreak Hotel".

710 **99**	32c. multicoloured	50	40

101 Dean

102 1896 Quadricycle

1996. 65th Birth Anniv of James Dean (actor).

712 **101**	32c. multicoloured	50	40

1996. Centenary of Ford Motor Vehicle Production. Multicoloured.

713	60c. Type **102**	80	60
714	60c. 1903 Model A Roadster	80	60
715	60c. 1909 Model T touring car	80	60
716	60c. 1929 Model A station wagon	80	60
717	60c. 1955 "Thunderbird"	80	60
718	60c. 1964 "Mustang" convertible	80	60
719	60c. 1995 "Explorer"	80	60
720	60c. 1996 "Taurus"	80	60

103 Evacuees boarding "L.S.T. 1108" (tank landing ship)

1996. 50th Anniv of Operation Crossroads (nuclear testing) at Bikini Atoll. Multicoloured.

721	32c.+8c. Type **103**	60	60
722	32c.+8c. U.S. Navy preparation of site	60	60
723	32c.+8c. Explosion of "Able" (first test)	60	60
724	32c.+8c. Explosion of "Baker" (first underwater test)	60	60
725	32c.+8c. Ghost fleet (targets)	60	60
726	32c.+8c. Bikinian family	60	60

1996. Folk Legends (2nd series). As T **88**. Multicoloured.

727	32c. Letao gives gift of fire	50	40
728	32c. Mennin Jobwodda flying on giant bird	50	40
729	32c. Koko chasing Letao in canoe	50	40
730	32c. Mother and girl catching Kouj (octopus) to cook	50	40

104 Pennsylvania Railroad Class K4, U.S.A.

1996. Steam Railway Locomotives. Multicoloured.

731	55c. Type **104**	75	75
732	55c. Big Boy, U.S.A.	75	75
733	55c. Class A4 "Mallard", Great Britain	75	75
734	55c. Class 242, Spain	75	75
735	55c. Class 01 No. 052, Germany	75	75
736	55c. Class 691 No. 031, Italy	75	75
737	55c. "Royal Hudson", Canada	75	75
738	55c. "Evening Star", Great Britain	75	75
739	55c. Class 520, South Australia	75	75
740	55c. Class 232.U.2, France	75	75
741	55c. Class QJ "Advance Forward", China	75	75
742	55c. Class C62 "Swallow", Japan	75	75

105 Stick Chart, Outrigger Canoe and Flag

1996. 10th Anniv of Ratification of Compact of Free Association with U.S.A.

744	**105** $3 multicoloured	4·50	3·50

106 "Madonna and Child with Four Saints" (detail, Rosso Fiorentino)

1996. Christmas.

745	**106** 32c. multicoloured	50	40

107 Curtiss JN-4 "Jenny"

1996. Biplanes. Multicoloured.

746	32c. Type **107**	50	40
747	32c. SPAD XIII	50	40
748	32c. Albatros	50	40
749	32c. De Havilland D.H.4 Liberty	50	40
750	32c. Fokker Dr-1	50	40
751	32c. Sopwith Camel	50	40
752	32c. Martin MB-2	50	40
753	32c. Martin MB-3A Tommy	50	40
754	32c. Curtiss TS-1	50	40
755	32c. P-1 Hawk	50	40
756	32c. Boeing PW-9	50	40
757	32c. Douglas O-2-H	50	40
758	32c. LB-5 Pirate	50	40
759	32c. O2U-1 Corsair	50	40
760	32c. Curtiss F8C Helldiver	50	40
761	32c. Boeing F4B-4	50	40
762	32c. J6B Gerfalcon	50	40
763	32c. Martin BM	50	40
764	32c. FF-1 Fifi	50	40
765	32c. C.R.32 Cricket	50	40
766	32c. Polikarpov I-15 Gull . .	50	40
767	32c. Fairey Swordfish	50	40
768	32c. Aichi D1A2	50	40
769	32c. Grumman F3F	50	40
770	32c. SOC-3 Seagull	50	40

108 Fan-making

1996. Traditional Crafts. Multicoloured. Self-adhesive gum (780, 782); ordinary or self-adhesive gum (others).

771	32c. Type **108**	50	40
772	32c. Boys sailing model outrigger canoes (country name at right)	50	40
773	32c. Carving canoes	50	40
774	32c. Weaving baskets (country name at right) . .	50	40
780	32c. As No. 772 but with country name at left . . .	55	45
782	32c. As No. 774 but with country name at left . . .	55	45

110 "Rocking '50s"

1997. 20th Death Anniv of Elvis Presley (entertainer). Different portraits. Multicoloured.

784	32c. Type **110**	55	45
785	32c. "Soaring '60s"	55	45
786	32c. "Sensational '70s" . . .	55	45

111 Kabua **113** St. Andrew

1997. President Amata Kabua Commemoration. Multicoloured.

787	32c. Type **111**	50	40
788	60c. As Type **111** but inscr in English at left and right and in Marshallese at foot	1·00	75

1997. Easter. 140th Anniv of Introduction of Christianity to the Marshall Islands. The Twelve Disciples. Multicoloured.

790	60c. Type **113**	90	70
791	60c. St. Matthew	90	70
792	60c. St. Philip	90	70
793	60c. St. Simon	90	70
794	60c. St. Thaddeus	90	70
795	60c. St. Thomas	90	70
796	60c. St. Bartholomew	90	70
797	60c. St. John	90	70
798	60c. St. James the Lesser . .	90	70
799	60c. St. James the Greater . .	90	70
800	60c. St. Paul	90	70
801	60c. St. Peter	90	70

114 Immigrants arriving at Ellis Island, New York, 1900

1997. The Twentieth Century (1st series). "Decade of New Possibilities, 1900–1909". Multicoloured.

803	60c. Type **114**	90	70
804	60c. Chinese and Dowager Empress Ci Xi, 1900 (Boxer Rebellion)	90	70
805	60c. George Eastman (inventor of box camera) photographing family, 1900	90	70
806	60c. Walter Reed (discoverer of yellow fever transmission by mosquito), 1900	90	70
807	60c. Sigmund Freud (pioneer of psychoanalysis) (publication of "Interpretation of Dreams", 1900)	90	70
808	60c. Guglielmo Marconi sending first transatlantic wireless message, 1901 . .	90	70
809	60c. Enrico Caruso (opera singer) (first award of Gold Disc for one million record sales, 1903)	90	70
810	60c. Wright Brothers' Flyer I (first powered flight, Kitty Hawk, 1903)	90	70
811	60c. Albert Einstein and formula (development of Theory of Relativity, 1905)	90	70
812	60c. White ensign and H.M.S. "Dreadnought" (battleship), 1906	90	70
813	60c. San Francisco earthquake, 1906	90	70
814	60c. Mohandas Gandhi and protestors, Johannesburg, South Africa, 1906	90	70
815	60c. Pablo Picasso and "Les Demoiselles d'Avignon", 1907	90	70
816	60c. First Paris–Peking motor car race, 1907	90	70
817	60c. Masjik-i-Salaman oil field, Persia, 1908	90	70

See also Nos. 872/86, 948/62, 975//89, 1067/81, 1165/79, 1218/32, 1239/55, 1256/70 and 1303/17.

115 Deng Xiaoping

1997. Deng Xiaoping (Chinese statesman) Commemoration.

818	**115** 60c. multicoloured	85	65

116 German Marshall Islands 1899 3pf. Stamp

1997. "Pacific 97" International Stamp Exhibition, San Francisco. Centenary of Marshall Islands Postage Stamps. Multicoloured.

819	50c. Type **116**	70	70
820	50c. German Marshall Islands 1899 5pf. stamp . .	70	70
821	50c. German Marshall Islands 1897 10pf. stamp	70	70
822	50c. German Marshall Islands 1897 20pf. stamp	70	70
823	50c. Unissued German Marshall Islands 25pf. stamp	70	70
824	50c. Unissued German Marshall Islands 50pf. stamp	70	70

117 Curlew on Seashore

1997. The Bristle-thighed Curlew. Multicoloured.

826	16c. Type **117**	30	20
827	16c. Flying	30	20
828	16c. Running	30	20
829	16c. Standing on branch . .	30	20

119 Pacific Arts Festival Canoe, Enewetak

1997. Traditional Outrigger Canoes. Multicoloured.

831	32c. Type **119**	55	45
832	32c. Kor Kor racing canoes	55	45
833	32c. Large voyaging canoe, Jaluit	55	45
834	32c. Sailing canoe, Ailuk . .	55	45

120 Douglas C-54 Skymaster Transport

1997. Aircraft of United States Air Force (1st series). Multicoloured.

835	32c. Type **120**	50	40
836	32c. Boeing B-36 Peacemaker	50	40
837	32c. North American F-86 Sabre jet fighter	50	40
838	32c. Boeing B-47 Stratojet jet bomber	50	40
839	32c. Douglas C-124 Globemaster II transport	50	40
840	32c. Lockheed C-121 Constellation	50	40
841	32c. Boeing B-52 Stratofortress jet bomber	50	40
842	32c. North American F-100 Super Sabre jet fighter . .	50	40
843	32c. Lockheed F-104 Starfighter jet fighter . . .	50	40
844	32c. Lockheed C-130 Hercules transport	50	40
845	32c. Republic F-105 Thunderchief jet fighter . .	50	40
846	32c. KC-135 Stratotanker . .	50	40
847	32c. Convair B-58 Hustler jet bomber	50	40
848	32c. McDonnell Douglas F-4 Phantom II jet fighter . . .	50	40
849	32c. Northrop T-38 Talon trainer	50	40
850	32c. Lockheed C-141 StarLifter jet transport . .	50	40
851	32c. General Dynamics F-111 Aardvark jet fighter . .	50	40
852	32c. SR-71 "Blackbird" . . .	50	40
853	32c. Lockheed C-5 Galaxy jet transport	50	40
854	32c. A-10 Thunderbolt II bomber	50	40
855	32c. F-15 Eagle fighter . . .	50	40
856	32c. General Dynamics F-16 Fighting Falcon jet fighter	50	40
857	32c. Lockheed F-117 "Nighthawk" Stealth bomber	50	40
858	32c. B-2 Spirit	50	40
859	32c. C-17 Globemaster III transport	50	40

See also Nos. 1272/96.

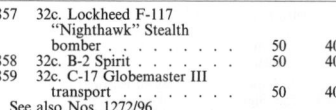

121 U.S.S. "Constitution"

1997. Bicentenary of Launch of U.S.S. "Constitution" (frigate).

860	**121** 32c. multicoloured	50	40

1997. Folk Legends (3rd series). As T **88**. Multicoloured.

861	32c. The Large Pool of Mejit	55	45
862	32c. The Beautiful Woman of Kwajalein	55	45
863	32c. Sharks and Lowakalle Reef	55	45
864	32c. The Demon of Adrie . .	55	45

1997. Undersea World (2nd series). As T **81**. Multicoloured.

865	60c. Watanabe's angelfish, blue-finned trevallys ("Bluefin Jack"), grey reef shark and scuba diver . .	95	75
866	60c. Scuba diver, anchor and racoon butterflyfish	95	75
867	60c. Lionfish and flame angelfish	95	75
868	60c. Square-spotted anthias ("Fairy Basslet"), anchor, scuba diver with torch and orange-finned anemonefish	95	75

Nos. 865/8 were issued together, se-tenant, forming a composite design.

122 Diana, Princess of Wales, aged 20

1997. Diana, Princess of Wales Commemoration. Multicoloured.

869	60c. Type **122**	1·00	75
870	60c. Wearing pearl drop earrings (aged 27)	1·00	75
871	60c. Wearing pearl choker (aged 36)	1·00	75

123 Flags and Suffragettes

1997. The Twentieth Century (2nd series). "Decade of Revolution and Great War, 1910–1919". Mult.

872	60c. Type **123**	75	55
873	60c. Nobel Prize medal, Ernest Rutherford and diagram of atom, 1911 . .	75	55
874	60c. Sun Yat-Sen (Chinese Revolution, 1911–12) . . .	75	55
875	60c. Sinking of the "Titanic" (liner), 1912	75	55
876	60c. Igor Stravinsky (composer) and score of "The Rite of Spring", 1913	75	55
877	60c. Building motor car (introduction of assembly line construction of motor vehicles by Ford Motor Company), 1913	75	55
878	60c. Countess Sophie Chotek and Archduke Franz Ferdinand of Austria, 1914 (assassination in Sarajevo leads to First World War)	75	55
879	60c. Torpedo striking "Lusitania" (liner), 1915	75	55
880	60c. Battle of Verdun, 1916	75	55
881	60c. Patrick Pearse and proclamation of Irish Republic (Easter Rebellion, 1916)	75	55
882	60c. Western wall, Jerusalem (Balfour Declaration of Jewish Homeland, 1917)	75	55
883	60c. "Aurora" (cruiser) signals start of Russian Revolution, 1917	75	55

884 60c. Biplanes and "Red" Baron Manfred von Richthofen (fighter pilot), 1918 . . . . 75 55
885 60c. Armed revolutionaries, Berlin, 1918 . . . . 75 55
886 60c. Meeting of heads of state (Treaty of Versailles, 1919) 75 55

124 Cherub

1997. Christmas. Details of "Sistine Madonna" by Raphael. Multicoloured.
887 32c. Type **124** 45 35
888 32c. Cherub resting head on folded arms 45 35

125 U.S.S. "Alabama" (battleship), 1942

1997. Ships named after U.S. States. Multicoloured.
889 20c. Type **125** 30 20
890 20c. U.S.S. "Alaska" (cruiser), 1869, and junk 30 20
891 20c. U.S.S. "Arizona" (battleship), 1916 . . . . . 30 20
892 20c. U.S.S. "Arkansas" (battleship), 1912 . . . . . 30 20
893 20c. U.S.S. "California" (cruiser), 1974 . . . . . . 30 20
894 20c. U.S.S. "Colorado" (battleship), 1921, and landing craft 30 20
895 20c. U.S.S. "Connecticut" (gunboat), 1776, with fleet 30 20
896 20c. U.S.S. "Delaware" (ship of the line), 1828 . . . . . 30 20
897 20c. U.S.S. "Florida" (cruiser), 1967 . . . . . . 30 20
898 20c. U.S.S. "Georgia" (battleship), 1906 . . . . . 30 20
899 20c. U.S.S. "Honolulu" (cruiser), 1938 . . . . . . 30 20
900 20c. U.S.S. "Idaho" (battleship), 1919 . . . . . 30 20
901 20c. U.S.S. "Illinois" (battleship), 1901 . . . . . 30 20
902 20c. U.S.S. "Indiana" (battleship), 1895 . . . . . 30 20
903 20c. U.S.S. "Iowa" (battleship), 1943 . . . . . 30 20
904 20c. U.S.S. "Kansas" (battleship), 1907 . . . . . 30 20
905 20c. U.S.S. "Kentucky" (battleship), 1900 . . . . . 30 20
906 20c. U.S.S. "Louisiana" (frigate), 1812 . . . . . . 30 20
907 20c. U.S.S. "Maine" (battleship), 1895 . . . . . 30 20
908 20c. U.S.S. "Maryland" (frigate), 1799 . . . . . . 30 20
909 20c. U.S.S. "Massachusetts" (battleship), 1942 . . . . . 30 20
910 20c. U.S.S. "Michigan" (paddle gunboat), 1843 . . 30 20
911 20c. U.S.S. "Minnesota" (corvette), 1857 . . . . . 30 20
912 20c. U.S.S. "Mississippi" (paddle gunboat), 1841, and junk 30 20
913 20c. U.S.S. "Missouri" (battleship), 1944, in Tokyo Bay 30 20
914 20c. U.S.S. "Montana" (battleship), 1908 . . . . . 30 20
915 20c. U.S.S. "Nebraska" (battleship), 1907 . . . . . 30 20
916 20c. U.S.S. "Nevada" (battleship), 1916, at Pearl Harbor 30 20
917 20c. U.S.S. "New Hampshire" (battleship), 1908, and Statue of Liberty 30 20
918 20c. U.S.S. "New Jersey" (battleship), 1943 . . . . . 30 20
919 20c. U.S.S. "New Mexico" (battleship), 1918, in Tokyo Bay 30 20
920 20c. U.S.S. "New York" (frigate), 1800, and felucca 30 20
921 20c. U.S.S. "North Carolina" (battleship), 1941 . . . . . 30 20
922 20c. U.S.S. "North Dakota" (battleship), 1910 . . . . . 30 20
923 20c. U.S.S. "Ohio" (ship of the line), 1838 . . . . . . 30 20
924 20c. U.S.S. "Oklahoma" (battleship), 1916 . . . . . 30 20
925 20c. U.S.S. "Oregon" (battleship), 1896 . . . . . 30 20
926 20c. U.S.S. "Pennsylvania" (battleship), 1905 . . . . . 30 20
927 20c. U.S.S. "Rhode Island" (paddle gunboat), 1861 . . 30 20
928 20c. U.S.S. "South Carolina" (frigate), 1783 . . . . . . 30 20
929 20c. U.S.S. "South Dakota" (battleship), 1942 . . . . . 30 20
930 20c. U.S.S. "Tennessee" (battleship), 1906 . . . . . 30 20
931 20c. U.S.S. "Texas" (battleship), 1914 . . . . . 30 20
932 20c. U.S.S. "Utah" (battleship), 1911 . . . . . 30 20
933 20c. U.S.S. "Vermont" (battleship), 1907 . . . . . 30 20
934 20c. U.S.S. "Virginia" (schooner), 1798 . . . . . 30 20
935 20c. U.S.S. "Washington" (battleship), 1941 . . . . . 30 20
936 20c. U.S.S. "West Virginia" (battleship), 1923 . . . . . 30 20
937 20c. U.S.S. "Wisconsin" (battleship), 1944 . . . . . 30 20
938 20c. U.S.S. "Wyoming" (monitor), 1902 . . . . . 30 20

Dates given are those of either launch or commission.

128 Presley

1998. 30th Anniv of First Television Special by Elvis Presley (entertainer). Multicoloured.
941 32c. Type **128** 45 35
942 32c. Presley in black leather jacket 45 35
943 32c. Presley in white suit in front of "ELVIS" in lights 45 35

129 Chiragra Spider Conch ("Lambis chiragra")

1998. Sea Shells. Multicoloured.
944 32c. Type **129** 50 40
945 32c. Fluted giant clam ("Tridacna squamosa") . . 50 40
946 32c. Adusta murex ("Chicoreus brunneus") . . 50 40
947 32c. Golden cowrie ("Cypraea aurantium") . . 50 40

130 Family listening to Radio

1998. The Twentieth Century (3rd series). "Decade of Optimism and Disillusionment, 1920–1929". Multicoloured.
948 60c. Type **130** 75 55
949 60c. Leaders from Japan, United States, France, Great Britain and Italy (Washington Conference, 1920) 75 55
950 60c. Ludwig Mies van der Rohe (architect), 1922 . . 75 55
951 60c. Mummiform coffin of Tutankhamun (discovery of tomb, 1922) 75 55
952 60c. Workers from U.S.S.R., 1923 (emergence of U.S.S.R. as communist state) 75 55
953 60c. Kemal Ataturk (first president of modern Turkey, 1923) (break-up of Turkish Empire) 75 55
954 60c. Bix Beiderbecke (trumpeter) and flappers (dancers), 1924 (Jazz Age) 75 55
955 60c. Robert Goddard demonstrates first liquid-propelled rocket, 1926 . . 75 55
956 60c. Poster for "The Jazz Singer" (second talking picture, 1926) 75 55
957 60c. Benito Mussolini assumes total power in Italy, 1926 . . . . 75 55
958 60c. Explosive glare and Leonardo da Vinci's "Proportion of Man" (Big Bang Theory of beginning of Universe, 1927) 75 55
959 60c. Sir Alexander Fleming discovers penicillin, 1928 75 55
960 60c. John Logie Baird invents television, 1926 . . . . . 75 55
961 60c. Airship "Graf Zeppelin" above Mt. Fuji, Japan (first round the world flight, 1929) 75 55
962 60c. U.S. stock market crash, 1929 (economic depression) 75 55

131 Pahi Sailing Canoe, Tuamotu Archipelago

1998. Canoes of the Pacific. Multicoloured.
963 32c. Type **131** 45 35
964 32c. Maori war canoe, New Zealand 45 35
965 32c. Wa'a Kaukahi fishing canoe, Hawaii 45 35
966 32c. Amatasi sailing canoe, Samoa 45 35
967 32c. Ndrua sailing canoe, Fiji Islands 45 35
968 32c. Tongiaki voyaging canoe, Tonga 45 35
969 32c. Tipairua travelling canoe, Tahiti 45 35
970 32c. Walap sailing canoe, Marshall Islands 45 35

132 Douglas C-54 Skymaster Transport

1998. 50th Anniv of Berlin Airlift (relief of Berlin during Soviet blockade). Multicoloured.
971 60c. Type **132** 75 55
972 60c. Avro Type 685 York transport 75 55
973 60c. Crowd and building . . 75 55
974 60c. Crowd 75 55

Nos. 971/4 were issued together, se-tenant, forming a composite design.

133 Soup Kitchens, 1930 (depression)

1998. The Twentieth Century (4th series). "Decade of the Great Depression, 1930–1939". Multicoloured.
975 60c. Type **133** 75 55
976 60c. Ernest Lawrence and first cyclotron, 1931 (splitting of atom) 75 55
977 60c. Forced collectivization of farms in Soviet Union, 1932 (Stalin era) 75 55
978 60c. Torchlight Parade celebrates rise of Hitler to power, 1933 (fascism) . . . 75 55
979 60c. Dneproges Dam on Dnepr River, 1933 (harnessing of nature) . . . 75 55
980 60c. Streamlined locomotive "Zephyr" (record-breaking run, Denver to Chicago, 1934) 75 55
981 60c. Douglas DC-3 airliner (first all-metal airliner, 1936) 75 55
982 60c. Pablo Picasso (artist) and "Guernica" (German bombing during Spanish Civil War, 1937) 75 55
983 60c. "Hindenburg" (airship disaster), 1937 (media reporting) 75 55
984 60c. Families fleeing ruins (Japanese assault on Nanjing, 1937) 75 55
985 60c. Neville Chamberlain declares "Peace in our Time", 1938 (appeasement) 75 55
986 60c. Chester Carlson (invention of xerography, 1938) 75 55
987 60c. Jew and Star of David (Kristallnacht (Nazi violence against Jews), 1938) 75 55
988 60c. Junkers "Stuka" bombers over Poland, 1939 (start of Second World War) 75 55
989 60c. Audience (premiere of "Gone with the Wind", 1939) (movies) 75 55

134 Coronation of Tsar Nicholas II, 1896

1998. 80th Death Anniv of Tsar Nicholas II and his Family. Multicoloured.
990 60c. Type **134** 75 55
991 60c. "Varyag" (cruiser) and Tsar (Russo-Japanese war, 1904–05) 75 55
992 60c. Troops firing on crowd, Tsar and October manifesto, 1905 . . . . . 75 55
993 60c. Peasant sowing, Tsar and Rasputin, 1905 . . . . 75 55
994 60c. Mounted troops, Tsar and Nicholas II at strategy meeting, 1915 . . . . . . 75 55
995 60c. Abdication, Tsar and Ipateva House, Ekaterinburg, 1917 . . . . 75 55

135 Babe Ruth

1998. 50th Death Anniv of Babe Ruth (baseball player).
997 **135** 132c. multicoloured . . . 50 40

136 NC-4

1998. Aircraft of United States Navy. Mult.
998 32c. Type **136** 45 35
999 32c. Consolidated PBY-5 Catalina flying boat . . . 45 35
1000 32c. TBD Devastator . . . 45 35
1001 32c. SB2U Vindicator . . . 45 35
1002 32c. Grumman F4F Wildcat fighter 45 35
1003 32c. Vought-Sikorsky OS2U Kingfisher seaplane . . . 45 35
1004 32c. Douglas SBD Dauntless bomber 45 35
1005 32c. Chance Vought F4U Corsair fighter 45 35
1006 32c. Curtiss SB2C Helldiver bomber 45 35
1007 32c. Lockheed PV-1 Ventura bomber 45 35
1008 32c. Grumman TBM Avenger bomber 45 35
1009 32c. Grumman F6F Hellcat fighter 45 35
1010 32c. PB4Y-2 Privateer . . . 45 35
1011 32c. A-1J Skyraider 45 35
1012 32c. McDonnell F2H-2P Banshee 45 35
1013 32c. F9F-2B Panther . . . 45 35
1014 32c. P5M Marlin 45 35
1015 32c. F-8 Crusader 45 35
1016 32c. McDonnell Douglas F-4 Phantom II fighter . . 45 35
1017 32c. A-6 Intruder 45 35
1018 32c. Lockheed P-3 Orion reconnaissance 45 35
1019 32c. Vought A-70 Corsair II 45 35
1020 32c. Douglas A-4 Skyhawk bomber 45 35
1021 32c. S-3 Viking 45 35
1022 32c. F/A-18 Hornet 45 35

137 Classic Six, 1912

1998. Chevrolet Vehicles. Multicoloured.
1023 60c. Type **137** 75 55
1024 60c. Sport Roadster, 1931 75 55
1025 60c. Special Deluxe, 1941 75 55
1026 60c. Cameo Carrier Fleetside, 1955 . . . . . 75 55
1027 60c. Corvette, 1957 . . . . 75 55
1028 60c. Bel Air, 1957 . . . . . 75 55
1029 60c. Camaro, 1967 . . . . 75 55
1030 60c. Chevelle SS 454, 1970 75 55

138 Letter "A" and Pres. Amata Kabua

1998. Marshallese Alphabet and Language. Mult.

1031 33c. Type **138** 45 35
1032 33c. Letter "A" and woman weaving 45 35
1033 33c. Letter "B" and butterfly 45 35
1034 33c. Letter "D" and woman wearing garland of flowers 45 35
1035 33c. Letter "E" and fish 45 35
1036 33c. Letter "I" and couple in front of rainbow 45 35
1037 33c. Letter "J" and woven mat 45 35
1038 33c. Letter "K" and Government House 45 35
1039 33c. Letter "L" and night sky 45 35
1040 33c. Letter "L" and red-tailed tropicbird 45 35
1041 33c. Letter "M" and breadfruit 45 35
1042 33c. Letter "M" and arrowroot plant 45 35
1043 33c. Letter "N" and coconut tree 45 35
1044 33c. Letter "N" and wave 45 35
1045 33c. Letter "N" and shark 45 35
1046 33c. Letter "O" and fisherman 45 35
1047 33c. Letter "O" and tattooed woman 45 35
1048 33c. Letter "O" and lionfish 45 35
1049 33c. Letter "P" and visitor's hut 45 35
1050 33c. Letter "R" and whale 45 35
1051 33c. Letter "T" and outrigger sailing canoe 45 35
1052 33c. Letter "U" and fire 45 35
1053 33c. Letter "U" and whale's fin 45 35
1054 33c. Letter "W" and woven leaf sail 45 35

139 Trust Company of the Marshall Islands Offices, 1998

1998. New Buildings. Multicoloured.

1055 33c. Type **139** 45 35
1056 33c. Embassy of the People's Republic of China, 1996 45 35
1057 33c. Outrigger Marshall Islands Resort, 1996 45 35

140 Midnight Angel

1998. Christmas.

1058 **140** 33c. multicoloured 45 35

141 Launch of "Friendship 7", 1962

1998. John Glenn's (astronaut) Return to Space. Multicoloured.

1059 60c. Type **141** 75 55
1060 60c. John Glenn, 1962, and Earth 75 55
1061 60c. "Friendship 7" orbiting Earth 75 55
1062 60c. Launch of space shuttle "Discovery", 1998 75 55
1063 60c. John Glenn, 1998, and flag 75 55
1064 60c. "Discovery" orbiting Earth, 1998 75 55

143 British and German Planes over St. Paul's Cathedral (Battle of Britain, 1940)

1998. The Twentieth Century (5th series). "Decade of War and Peace, 1940–1949". Multicoloured.

1067 60c. Type **143** 75 55
1068 60c. Japanese aircraft attack American battleship (Pearl Harbor, 1941) (global warfare) 75 55
1069 60c. Wernher von Braun and missiles (first surface to surface guided missile, 1942) 75 55
1070 60c. The Dorsey Brothers (Big Bands, 1942) 75 55
1071 60c. Soviet worker building weaponry (fight for survival against Germans, 1943) 75 55
1072 60c. Concentration camp prisoners (the Holocaust, 1945) 75 55
1073 60c. Mushroom cloud and skull (first atomic bomb tested, Alamogordo, New Mexico, 1945) 75 55
1074 60c. Families reunited (end of war, 1945) 75 55
1075 60c. Eniac computer and worker (first electronic digital computer goes into operation, 1946) 75 55
1076 60c. American delegate (United Nations, 1946) 75 55
1077 60c. Nuremberg Tribunal (trials of Germans for war crimes 1946) 75 55
1078 60c. George Marshall (U.S. Secretary of State) and Europeans (Marshall Plan, 1947) 75 55
1079 60c. William Shockley, John Bardeen and Walter Brattain (development of transistor, 1948) 75 55
1080 60c. Berlin Airlift, 1948–49 (Cold War) 75 55
1081 60c. Mao Tse-tung proclaiming People's Republic of China, 1949 75 55

144 Trireme

1998. Warships. Multicoloured.

1082 33c. Type **144** 45 35
1083 33c. Roman galley ("Trireme Romano") 45 35
1084 33c. Viking longship 45 35
1085 33c. Ming treasure ship 45 35
1086 33c. "Mary Rose" (English galleon) 45 35
1087 33c. "Nuestra Senora del Rosario" (Spanish galleon) 45 35
1088 33c. Korean "turtle" ship 45 35
1089 33c. "Brederode" (Dutch ship of the line) 45 35
1090 33c. Venetian galley 45 35
1091 33c. "Santissima Trinidad" (Spanish ship of the line) 45 35
1092 33c. "Ville de Paris" (French ship of the line) 45 35
1093 33c. H.M.S. "Victory" (ship of the line) 45 35
1094 33c. "Bonhomme Richard" (American sail frigate) 45 35
1095 33c. U.S.S. "Constellation" (sail frigate) 45 35
1096 33c. U.S.S. "Hartford" (steam frigate) 45 35
1097 33c. Fijian Ndrua canoe 45 35
1098 33c. H.M.S. "Dreadnought" (battleship) 45 35
1099 33c. H.M.A.S. "Australia" (battle cruiser) 45 35
1100 33c. H.M.S. "Dorsetshire" (cruiser) 45 35
1101 33c. "Admiral Graf Spee" (German battleship) 45 35
1102 33c. "Yamato" (Japanese battleship) 45 35
1103 33c. U.S.S. "Tautog" (submarine) 45 35
1104 33c. "Bismarck" (German battleship) 45 35
1105 33c. U.S.S. "Hornet" (aircraft carrier) 45 35
1106 33c. U.S.S. "Missouri" (battleship) 45 35

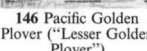

146 Pacific Golden Plover ("Lesser Golden Plover") **147** Tecumseh

1999. Birds. Multicoloured.

1108 1c. Type **146** 10 10
1109 3c. Grey-rumped sandpiper ("Siberian (gray-tailed) Tattler") 10 10
1110 5c. Black-tailed godwit 10 10
1113 20c. Common noddy ("Brown Noddy") 25 20
1114 22c. White tern ("Common Fairy Tern") 30 25
1116 33c. Micronesian pigeon 40 30
1117 40c. Franklin's gull 50 40
1118 45c. Rufous-necked sandpiper ("Rufous-necked Stint") 55 40
1119 55c. Long-tailed koel ("Long-tailed Cuckoo") 70 55
1121 75c. Kermadec petrel 95 70
1122 $1 Christmas Island shearwater ("Christmas Shearwater") 1·25 95
1123 $1.20 Purple-capped fruit dove 1·50 1·25
1124 $2 Lesser sand plover ("Mongolian Plover") 2·50 1·90
1125 $3.20 Cattle egret 4·00 3·00
1127 $5 Dunlin 6·25 4·75
1129 $10 Eurasian tree sparrow 12·50 9·50

1999. Canoes of the Pacific. Multicoloured. (a) Size 49 × 30 mm.

1130 33c. Type **131** 40 30
1131 33c. As No. 964 40 30
1132 33c. As No. 965 40 30
1133 33c. As No. 966 but inscr changed to "Tongiaki voyaging canoe, Tonga" 40 30
1134 33c. As No. 967 40 30
1135 33c. As No. 968 but inscr changed to "Amatasi sailing canoe, Samoa" 40 30
1136 33c. As No. 969 40 30
1137 33c. As No. 970 40 30

(b) Size 39 × 24 mm.

1138 33c. Type **131** 40 30
1139 33c. As No. 1131 40 30
1140 33c. As No. 1132 40 30
1141 33c. As No. 1133 40 30
1142 33c. As No. 1134 40 30
1143 33c. As No. 1135 40 30
1144 33c. As No. 1136 40 30
1145 33c. As No. 1137 40 30

Nos. 1138/45 were self-adhesive.

1999. Great American Indian Chiefs. Multicoloured.

1146 60c. Type **147** 75 55
1147 60c. Powhatan 75 55
1148 60c. Hiawatha 75 55
1149 60c. Dull Knife 75 55
1150 60c. Sequoyah 75 55
1151 60c. Sitting Bull 75 55
1152 60c. Cochise 75 55
1153 60c. Red Cloud 75 55
1154 60c. Geronimo 75 55
1155 60c. Chief Joseph 75 55
1156 60c. Pontiac 75 55
1157 60c. Crazy Horse 75 55

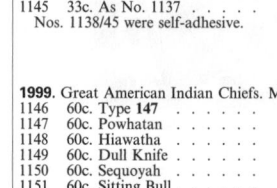

148 State Flag

1999.

1158 **148** 33c. multicoloured 40 30

149 Plumeria

1999. Flowers of the Pacific. Multicoloured.

1159 33c. Type **149** 40 30
1160 33c. Vanda 40 30
1161 33c. Ilima 40 30
1162 33c. Tiare 40 30
1163 33c. White ginger 40 30
1164 33c. Hibiscus 40 30

150 Family watching Television

1999. The Twentieth Century (6th series). "Decade of Peril and Progress, 1950–1959". Multicoloured.

1165 60c. Type **150** 75 55
1166 60c. U.N. landing at Inchon, Korea, 1950 (Cold War) 75 55
1167 60c. Vaccination against polio, 1952 75 55
1168 60c. American hydrogen bomb test, Enewetak Atoll, 1952 (Arms race) 75 55
1169 60c. James Watson and Francis Crick (scientists) and DNA double helix, 1953 (unravelling of genetic code) 75 55
1170 60c. Sir Edmund Hillary, Tenzing Norgay and Mt. Everest, 1953 75 55
1171 60c. Coronation of Queen Elizabeth II, Westminster Abbey, 1953 75 55
1172 60c. Singer and dancers, 1954 (rock 'n' roll music) 75 55
1173 60c. Ho Chi Minh and Vietnamese troops celebrating victory over French garrison at Dien Bien Phu, 1954 (end of colonial empires) 75 55
1174 60c. People of different races on bus, 1955 (condemnation of racial discrimination) 75 55
1175 60c. Hungarians firing on Russian tanks, Budapest, 1956 (challenge to Communism) 75 55
1176 60c. Signing of Treaty of Rome, 1957 (European union) 75 55
1177 60c. Launch of Russian sputnik, 1957 (space race) 75 55
1178 60c. De Havilland Comet (first commercial jet airline service, 1958) 75 55
1179 60c. Jack Kilby (inventor) and first microchip, 1959 75 55

152 Presley

1999. Elvis Presley, "Artist of the Century".

1181 **152** 33c. multicoloured 40 30

153 5m. Stamp

1999. "iBRA '99" International Stamp Exhibition, Nuremberg, Germany. Multicoloured.

1182 60c. Type **153** 75 55
1183 60c. 3m. stamp 75 55
1184 60c. 2m. stamp 75 55
1185 60c. 1m. stamp 75 55

154 Magnifying Glass over Committee Members

1999. 20th Anniv of Marshall Islands Constitution.

1186 **154** 33c. multicoloured 40 30

155 Marshall Island Stamps

1999. 15th Anniv of Marshall Islands Postal Service. Multicoloured.

1187 33c. Type **155** 40 30
1188 33c. Butterfly, fish, canoe and flower stamps 40 30
1189 33c. Pres. Amata Kabua, flower and legend stamps 40 30
1190 33c. Stamps and magnifying glass 40 30

Nos. 1187/90 were issued together, se-tenant, forming a composite design.

156 B-10 B

1999. Legendary Aircraft. Multicoloured.

1191 33c. Type **156** 40 30
1192 33c. A-17A Nomad 40 30
1193 33c. Douglas B-18 Bolo bomber 40 30
1194 33c. Boeing B-17F Flying Fortress bomber 40 30
1195 33c. A-20 Havoc 40 30
1196 33c. North American B-25B Mitchell bomber 40 30
1197 33c. Consolidated B-24D Liberator bomber 40 30
1198 33c. North American P-51B Mustang fighter 40 30
1199 33c. Martin B-26 Marauder bomber 40 30
1200 33c. A-26B Invader 40 30
1201 33c. P-59 Airacomet 40 30
1202 33c. KC-97 Stratofreighter 40 30
1203 33c. A-1J Skyraider 40 30
1204 33c. P2V-7 Neptune 40 30
1205 33c. B-45 Tornado 40 30
1206 33c. Boeing B-50 Superfortress 40 30
1207 33c. AJ-2 Savage 40 30
1208 33c. F9F Cougar 40 30
1209 33c. Douglas A-3 Skywarrior jet bomber . . 40 30
1210 33c. English Electric B-57E Canberra jet bomber . . 40 30
1211 33c. EB-66 Destroyer . . . 40 30
1212 33c. E-2A Hawkeye 40 30
1213 33c. Northrop F-5E Tiger II jet fighter 40 30
1214 33c. AV-8B Harrier II . . . 40 30
1215 33c. B-1B Lancer 40 30

159 T. H. Maiman and Ruby Crystal Laser, 1960

1999. The Twentieth Century (7th series). "Decade of Upheaval and Exploration 1960–1969". Mult.

1218 60c. Type **159** 75 55
1219 60c. Young couple (birth control pill, 1960) 75 55
1220 60c. Yuri Gagarin (first man in space, 1961) 75 55
1221 60c. John F. Kennedy (President of U.S.A., 1960–63) making speech in Berlin, 1961 (failures of Communism) 75 55
1222 60c. Rachel Carson and endangered species (publication of "Silent Spring", 1962) 75 55
1223 60c. John F. Kennedy and Russian President Nikita Khrushchev (Cuban missile crisis, 1962) . . . 75 55
1224 60c. Pope John XXIII and crowds (Spirit of Ecumenism) 75 55
1225 60c. "Hikari" express train, Japan (new railway record speeds, 1964) 75 55
1226 60c. Chinese workers waving banners (Chinese cultural revolution, 1965) 75 55
1227 60c. Soldier with gun (Arab–Israeli six-day war, 1967) 75 55
1228 60c. Surgeons (first human heart transplants, 1967) 75 55
1229 60c. American soldiers in jungle (Vietnam war) . . 75 55
1230 60c. Robert F. Kennedy (U.S. presidential candidate) and statue of Abraham Lincoln (political assassinations) 75 55
1231 60c. British Aerospace/ Aerospatiale Concorde supersonic jetliner (maiden flight, 1969) 75 55
1232 60c. Neil Armstrong and Buzz Aldrin planting American flag (first men on Moon, 1969) 75 55

161 "Los Reyes" (Alvarao de Menana de Neyra's galleon, 1568)

1999. European Exploration of Marshall Islands. Multicoloured.

1234 33c. Type **161** 40 30
1235 33c. H.M.S. "Dolphin" (Samuel Wallis's frigate, 1767) 40 30
1236 33c. "Scarborough" (John Marshall's transport, 1788) 40 30
1237 33c. "Rurik" (Otto van Kotzebue's brig, 1817) . . 40 30

No. 1236 is wrongly inscribed "Scarsborough" and No. 1237 "Rurick".

162 Nativity

164 Earth in Darkness, December 31, 1999

163 First Scheduled Transatlantic Flight of Boeing 747 Jetliner, 1970

1999. Christmas.

1238 **162** 33c. multicoloured . . . 40 30

1999. The Twentieth Century (8th series). "Decade of Detente and Discovery 1970–1979". Multicoloured.

1239 60c. Type **163** 75 55
1240 60c. Mao Tse Tung and U.S. President Richard Nixon (visit to China, 1972) 75 55
1241 60c. Terrorist with gun (murder of Israeli athletes at Munich Olympics, 1972) 75 55
1242 60c. U.S. "Skylab" and U.S.S.R. "Salyut" space stations orbiting Earth . . 75 55
1243 60c. Cars queueing for petrol (oil crisis, 1973) . . 75 55
1244 60c. Terracotta warriors (discovery of Qin Shi Huang's tomb at Xian, China, 1974) 75 55
1245 60c. Skulls and Cambodians in paddy fields 75 55
1246 60c. "Apollo"–"Soyuz" link-up, 1975 (era of detente) 75 55
1247 60c. "Eagle" (cadet ship) in New York Harbour (bicentenary of U.S. Independence, 1976) . . . 75 55
1248 60c. Computer and family (personal computers reach markets, 1977) 75 55
1249 60c. Scanner and scanned images (diagnostic tools revolutionize medicine, 1977) 75 55
1250 60c. Volkswagen Beetle motor car, 1978 . . . . . 75 55
1251 60c. Pres. Anwar Sadat of Egypt, U.S. President Jimmy Carter and Israeli Prime Minister Menachim Begin, 1978 (peace in Middle East) 75 55
1252 60c. Compact disc, 1979 . . 75 55
1253 60c. Ayatollah Khomeini becomes Iran's leader, 1979 . . . . 75 55

1999. Year 2000. Multicoloured.

1254 33c. Type **164** 40 30
1255 33c. Earth in sunlight, 1 January 2000 . . . . . 40 30

Nos. 1254/5 were issued together, se-tenant, forming a composite design.

165 Lech Walesa and Protestors at Gdansk Shipyard, Poland, 1980

2000. The Twentieth Century (9th series). "Decade of People and Democracy, 1980–1989". Multicoloured.

1256 60c. Type **165** 85 65
1257 60c. Doctor treating AIDS patient, 1981 . . . . . . 85 65
1258 60c. Prince and Princess of Wales (Royal wedding, 1981) 85 65
1259 60c. Man and computer (IBM personal computers introduced 1981) 85 65
1260 60c. British jet fighter and warships (Falkland Islands war, 1982) 85 65
1261 60c. Man using mobile phone (first commercial wireless cellular system, Chicago, 1983) 85 65
1262 60c. Girl playing football (camcorders, 1983) . . . 85 65
1263 60c. Astronauts (space shuttle *Challenger* explodes, 1986) 85 65
1264 60c. Power station and man wearing protective clothing (Chernobyl Nuclear Power Station disaster, 1986) 85 65
1265 60c. Mikhail Gorbachev and workers (era of Glasnost (openness) and Perestroika (restructuring) in U.S.S.R., 1987) 85 65
1266 60c. American B-2 stealth bomber, 1988 . . . . . . 85 65
1267 60c. Aircraft wreckage (bombing of Pan-American flight 103 over Lockerbie, Scotland, 1988) 85 65
1268 60c. *Exxon Valdez* (oil-tanker) and whales (oil spill off Alaskan Coast, 1989) 85 65
1269 60c. Student demonstrators and police in Tiananmen Square, China, 1989 . . . 85 65
1270 60c. German breaking down wall (dismantling of Berlin Wall, 1989) 85 65

167 Boeing P-26A "Peashooter" fighter

2000. Legendary Aircraft (2nd series). Multicoloured.

1272 33c. Type **167** 45 35
1273 33c. Stearman N2S-1 Kaydett biplane 45 35
1274 33c. Seversky P-35A 45 35
1275 33c. Curtiss P-36A Hawk 45 35
1276 33c. Curtiss P-40B Warhawk fighter 45 35
1277 33c. Lockheed P-38 Lightning fighter 45 35
1278 33c. Bell P-39D Airacobra fighter 45 35
1279 33c. Curtiss C-46 Commando airliner . . . 45 35
1280 33c. Republic P-47D Thunderbolt fighter . . . 45 35
1281 33c. Northrop P-61A Black Widow 45 35
1282 33c. Boeing B-29 Superfortress bomber . . 45 35
1283 33c. Grumman F7F-3N Tigercat 45 35
1284 33c. Grumman F8F-2 Bearcat 45 35
1285 33c. North American F-82 Twin Mustang 45 35
1286 33c. Republic F-84G Thunderjet jet fighter . . 45 35
1287 33c. North American FJ-1 Fury 45 35
1288 33c. Fairchild C-119C Flying Boxcar 45 35
1289 33c. Douglas F3D-2 Skynight 45 35
1290 33c. Northrop F-89D Scorpion 45 35
1291 33c. Lockheed F-94B Starfire 45 35
1292 33c. Douglas F4D Skyray 45 35
1293 33c. McDonnell F3H-2 Demon 45 35
1294 33c. McDonnell RF-101A/C Voodoo 45 35
1295 33c. Lockheed U-2F Dragon Lady 45 35
1296 33c. Rockwell OV-10 Bronco 45 35

168 "Masquerade"

2000. Garden Roses. Multicoloured.

1297 33c. Type **168** 45 35
1298 33c. "Tuscany Superb" . . 45 35
1299 33c. "Frau Dagmar Hastrup" 45 35
1300 33c. "Ivory Fashion" . . . 45 35
1301 33c. "Charles de Mills" . . . 45 35
1302 33c. "Peace" 45 35

169 Container Ships (political reform in Poland, 1990)

2000. The Twentieth Century (10th series). "Decade of Globalization and Hope, 1990–1999". Multicoloured.

1303 60c. Type **169** 85 65
1304 60c. Fighter planes over burning oil wells, 1991 . . 85 65
1305 60c. Nelson Mandela and F. W. de Klerk (abolition of apartheid, 1991) . . . 85 65
1306 60c. Tim Berners-Lee and computer (creator of World Wide Web, 1991) 85 65
1307 60c. Boris Yeltsin (President of Russian Federation, 1991) 85 65
1308 60c. Yitzhak Rabin, Bill Clinton and Yasir Arafat (signing of Middle East Peace Accord, Washington D.C., 1993) 85 65
1309 60c. High-speed train (inauguration of the "Channel Tunnel" between United Kingdom and France, 1994) 85 65
1310 60c. Family (Bosnian civil war, 1995) 85 65
1311 60c. Athletes (Atlanta Olympic Games, 1996) . . 85 65
1312 60c. Sheep (researchers clone Dolly, 1997) 85 65
1313 60c. Hong Kong and Chinese flag (return of Hong Kong to Chinese rule, 1997) 85 65
1314 60c. Sojourner (roving vehicle) (Mars "Pathfinder" mission, 1997) 85 65
1315 60c. Deaths of Diana, Princess of Wales and Mother Teresa, 1997 . . . 85 65
1316 60c. Rebuilding of German Reichstag, 1999 . . . . . 85 65
1317 60c. People of different races (birth of World's sixth billionth inhabitant, 1999) 85 65

170 Panda

2000. Giant Pandas. Multicoloured.

1318 33c. Type **170** 45 35
1319 33c. Adult facing cub . . . 45 35
1320 33c. Adult holding cub . . . 45 35
1321 33c. Two adults 45 35
1322 33c. Moving rock 45 35
1323 33c. Cub beside adult eating bamboo 45 35

171 George Washington

2000. American Presidents. Multicoloured.

1324 1c. Type **171** 10 10
1325 2c. John Adams 10 10
1326 3c. Thomas Jefferson . . . 10 10
1327 4c. James Madison 10 10

1328	5c. James Monroe	10	10
1329	6c. John Quincy Adams	10	10
1330	7c. Andrew Jackson	10	10
1331	8c. Martin van Buren	10	10
1332	9c. William Henry Harrison	10	10
1333	10c. John Tyler	15	10
1334	11c. James K. Polk	15	10
1335	12c. Zachary Taylor	15	10
1336	13c. Millard Filmore	20	15
1337	14c. Franklin Pierce	20	15
1338	15c. James Buchanan	20	15
1339	16c. Abraham Lincoln	20	15
1340	17c. Andrew Johnson	25	20
1341	18c. Ulysses S. Grant	25	20
1342	19c. Rutherford B. Hayes	25	20
1343	20c. James A. Garfield	30	25
1344	21c. Chester A. Arthur	30	25
1345	22c. Grover Cleveland	30	25
1346	23c. Benjamin Harrison	30	25
1347	24c. The White House	30	25
1348	25c. William McKinley	35	25
1349	26c. Theodore Roosevelt	35	25
1350	27c. William H. Taft	35	25
1351	28c. Woodrow Wilson	40	30
1352	29c. Warren G. Harding	40	30
1353	30c. Calvin Coolidge	40	30
1354	31c. Herbert C. Hoover	40	30
1355	32c. Franklin D. Roosevelt	45	35
1356	33c. Harry S. Truman	45	35
1357	34c. Dwight D. Eisenhower	45	35
1358	35c. John F. Kennedy	50	40
1359	36c. Lyndon B. Johnson	50	40
1360	37c. Richard M. Nixon	50	40
1361	38c. Gerald R. Ford	50	40
1362	39c. James E. Carter	50	40
1363	40c. Ronald W. Reagan	55	45
1364	41c. George H. Bush	55	45
1365	42c. William J. Clinton	60	45

172 LZ-1 (first Zeppelin airship), 1900

2000. Centenary of Zeppelin Airships. Multicoloured.

1366	33c. Type **172**	45	35
1367	33c. *Graf Zeppelin I*, 1928	45	35
1368	33c. *Hindenburg*, 1936	45	35
1369	33c. *Graf Zeppelin II*, 1937	45	35

173 Churchill in South Africa as War Correspondent, 1899–1900

2000. 35th Death Anniv of Winston Churchill (British Prime Minister, 1940–45 and 1951–55). Multicoloured.

1370	60c. Type **173**	85	65
1371	60c. Churchill and Clementine Hozier on wedding day, 1908	85	65
1372	60c. Kaiser Wilhelm II, Churchill and clock tower, Houses of Parliament	85	65
1373	60c. Various portraits of Churchill between 1898 and 1960	85	65
1374	60c. Wearing naval cap (First Lord of the Admiralty, 1939–40)	85	65
1375	60c. Churchill giving "Victory" sign and St. Paul's Cathedral (Prime Minister, 1940–45)	85	65

174 Cannon, Flag and Soldier preparing to Fire (Army)

2000. 225th Anniv of United States Military Forces. Multicoloured.

1377	33c. Type **174**	45	35
1378	33c. Ship, flag and officer looking through telescope (Navy)	45	35
1379	33c. Ship, cannon and mariner drawing sword (Marines)	45	35

175 Nitijela (elected lower house) Complex

2000. Multicoloured.

1380	33c. Type **175**	45	35
1381	33c. Capitol building	45	35
1382	33c. National Seal and Nitijela Complex (vert)	45	35
1383	33c. National Flag and Nitijela Complex (vert)	45	35

176 *Half Moon* (Hudson)

2000. Sailing Ships. Multicoloured.

1384	60c. Type **176**	85	65
1385	60c. *Grande Hermine* (Cartier)	85	65
1386	60c. *Golden Hind* (Drake)	85	65
1387	60c. *Matthew* (Cabot) (wrongly inscr "Mathew")	85	65
1388	60c. *Vitoria* (Magellan) (inscr "Victoria")	85	65
1389	60c. *Sao Gabriel* (Vasco da Gama)	85	65

177 As a Young Girl, 1904

2000. "Queen Elizabeth the Queen Mother's Century". Multicoloured.

1390	60c. Type **177**	85	65
1391	60c. Wearing a turquoise hat, 1923	85	65
1392	60c. Wearing pearl necklace, 1940	85	65
1393	60c. Wearing purple hat, 1990	85	65

178 Green Sea Turtle

2000. Marine Life. Multicoloured.

1394	33c. Type **178**	45	35
1395	33c. Blue-girdled angelfish	45	35
1396	33c. Clown triggerfish	45	35
1397	33c. Harlequin tuskfish	45	35
1398	33c. Lined butterflyfishes	45	35
1399	33c. Whitebonnet anemonefish	45	35
1400	33c. Long-nose filefish	45	35
1401	33c. Emperor angelfish	45	35

Nos. 1394/1401 were issued together, se-tenant, forming the composite design of the reef.

179 Holly Blue Butterfly

2000. Butterflies. Multicoloured.

1402	60c. Type **179**	85	65
1403	60c. Swallowtail butterfly	85	65
1404	60c. Clouded yellow butterfly	85	65
1405	60c. Small tortoiseshell butterfly	85	65
1406	60c. Nettle-tree butterfly	85	65
1407	60c. Long tailed blue butterfly	85	65
1408	60c. Cranberry blue butterfly	85	65
1409	60c. Small heath butterfly	85	65
1410	60c. Pontic blue butterfly	85	65
1411	60c. Lapland fritillary butterfly	85	65
1412	60c. Large blue butterfly	85	65
1413	60c. Monarch butterfly	85	65

180 Brandenburg Gate, Berlin and Flag

182 Decorated Trees

181 S-44 Submarine, 1925 (½ size illustration)

2000. 10th Anniv of Reunification of Germany.

1414	**180** 33c. multicoloured	45	35

2000. Centenary of United States Submarine Fleet. Multicoloured.

1415	33c. Type **181**	45	35
1416	33c. Gato, 1941	45	35
1417	33c. Wyoming, 1996	45	35
1418	33c. Cheyenne, 1997	45	35

2000. Christmas.

1419	**182** 33c. multicoloured	45	35

183 Sun Yat-sen as Young Boy, 1866

2000. 75th Death Anniv of Dr. Sun Yat-sen (President of Republic of China, 1912–25). Multicoloured.

1420	60c. Type **183**	85	65
1421	60c. With family in Honolulu, 1879 and amongst other students in Hong Kong	85	65
1422	60c. As President of Tong Meng Hui, 1905	85	65
1423	60c. Empress Dowager (Revolution, 1911)	85	65
1424	60c. As President of Republic of China, 1912	85	65
1425	60c. Flag and various portraits of Sun Yat-sen	85	65

184 Snake (½-size illustration)

2001. New Year. Year of the Snake. Sheet 111 × 88 mm.

1427	**184** 80c. multicoloured	95	55

185 Carnations

2001. Flowers. Multicoloured.

1428	34c. Type **185**	40	25
1429	34c. Violet	40	25
1430	34c. Jonquil	40	25
1431	34c. Sweet pea	40	25
1432	34c. Lily of the valley	40	25
1433	34c. Rose	40	25
1434	34c. Larkspur	40	25
1435	34c. Poppy	40	25
1436	34c. Aster	40	25
1437	34c. Marigold	40	25
1438	34c. Chrysanthemum	40	25
1439	34c. Poinsettia	40	25

186 Walap (canoe), Jaluitt

187 Amata Kabua (first President)

2001. Sailing Canoes.

1440	**186** $5 green	6·00	3·50
1441	– $10 blue	12·00	7·25

DESIGN: $10 Walap, Enewetak.

2001. Personalities. Multicoloured.

1442	34c. Type **187**	40	25
1442a	37c. Oscar Debrum (statesman)	45	30
1443	55c. Robert Reimers (entrepreneur)	65	40
1444	57c. Atlan Anien (legislator)	70	45
1445	80c. Father Leonard Hacker (humanitarian)	95	55
1446	$1 Dwight Heine (educator)	1·25	75
1447	$3.85 Tipne Philippo (senator)	4·75	2·75
1448	$13.65 Henchi Balos (senator)	17·00	10·00

188 Red Admiral

2001. Butterflies (1st series). Multicoloured.

1450	80c. Type **188**	95	55
1451	80c. Moroccan orange tip	95	55
1452	80c. Silver-studded blue	95	55
1453	80c. Marbled white	95	55
1454	80c. False Apollo	95	55
1455	80c. Ringlet	95	55
1456	80c. Map	95	55
1457	80c. Fenton's wood white	95	55
1458	80c. Grecian copper	95	55
1459	80c. Pale Arctic clouded yellow	95	55
1460	80c. Great banded greyling	95	55
1461	80c. Cardinal	95	55

See also Nos. 1565/76 and 1698/1709.

189 *Tom Thumb*

2001. Fairytales. Multicoloured.

1462	34c. Type **189**	40	25
1463	34c. *Three Little Pigs*	40	25
1464	34c. *Gulliver's Travels*	40	25
1465	34c. *Cinderella*	40	25
1466	34c. *Gallant John*	40	25
1467	34c. *The Ugly Duckling*	40	25
1468	34c. *Fisher and the Goldfish*	40	25

190 Pirogues

2001. Racing Watercraft. Multicoloured.

1469	34c. Type **190**	35	20
1470	34c. Windsurfers	35	20
1471	34c. Yachts	35	20
1472	34c. Sailing dinghies	35	20

191 Yuri Alekseyevich Gagarin

2001. 40th Anniv of First Manned Space Flight. Multicoloured.

1473	80c. Type **191**	85	50
1474	80c. Alan Bartlett Shepard	85	50

1475	80c. Virgil Ivan (Gus) Grissom	85	50
1476	80c. Gherman Stepanovich Titov	85	50

192 2000–1 Marshall Island Stamps

2001. Stamp Day.

1477 **192**	34c. multicoloured	35	20

193 Friendship 7 Spacecraft and John Glenn (first USA manned orbit of Earth, 1962)

2001. Space Exploration. Multicoloured.

1478	80c. Type **193**	85	50
1479	80c. First space walk, 1965	85	50
1480	80c. First man on moon, 1969	85	50
1481	80c. First space shuttle voyage, 1977	85	50

194 Longnose Butterflyfish, Star Puffer and Star Fish

2001. Coral Reef Fauna. Multicoloured.

1482	34c. Type **194**	40	25
1483	34c. Nautilus	40	25
1484	34c. Raccoon butterflyfish	40	25
1485	34c. Porkfish and grouper	40	25

195 Basketball

2001. Sport. Multicoloured.

1486	34c. Type **195**	40	25
1487	34c. Bowling	40	25
1488	34c. Table tennis	40	25
1489	34c. Kayaking	40	25

196 Aries

2001. Signs of the Zodiac. Multicoloured.

1490	34c. Type **196**	40	25
1491	34c. Taurus	40	25
1492	34c. Gemini	40	25
1493	34c. Cancer	40	25
1494	34c. Leo	40	25
1495	34c. Virgo	40	25
1496	34c. Libra	40	25
1497	34c. Scorpio	40	25
1498	34c. Sagittarius	40	25
1499	34c. Capricorn	40	25
1500	34c. Aquarius	40	25
1501	34c. Pisces	40	25

197 Black Cat (Tan Axi)

2001. Philanippon 2001 International Stamp Exhibition. Children's Paintings. Multicoloured.

1502	34c. Type **197**	40	25
1503	34c. Brown cat (Tan Axi)	40	25
1504	34c. Cliffs (Wang Xihai)	40	25
1505	34c. Boat and bridge (Li Yan)	40	25
1506	34c. Rooster (Wang Xinlan)	40	25
1507	34c. Great Wall of China (Lui Zhong)	40	25
1508	34c. Crane (Wang Lynn)	40	25
1509	34c. Baboon with basket (Wang Yani)	40	25
1510	34c. Baboon in tree (Wang Yani)	40	25
1511	34c. Umbrella (Sun Yuan)	40	25
1512	34c. Baboon with fruit (Wang Yani)	40	25
1513	34c. Baboon riding ox (Wang Yani)	40	25

198 Raymond Spruance (head of Cruiser Division 5)

199 Stutz Bearcat (1916)

2001. Naval Heroes of World War II in the Pacific. Sheet 117 × 144 mm containing T **198** and similar vert designs. Multicoloured.

MS1514 80c. × 9, Type **198**; Arleigh Burke (destroyer fleet commander); Ernest King (Commander in Chief of the USA Fleet); Richmond Turner (Amphibious Forces commander); Marc Mitscher (Fleet Air commander, Solomon Islands); Chester Nimitz (Pacific Fleet commander); Edward O'Hare (naval pilot); William Halsey Jr. (Guadalcanal campaign commander); Albert, Francis, George, Joseph and Madison Sullivan (brothers) . . . 8·50 8·50

2001. Vintage Cars (1st series). Multicoloured.

1515	34c. Type **199**	40	25
1516	34c. Stanley Steamer (1909)	40	25
1517	34c. Citroen 7CV (1934)	40	25
1518	34c. Rolls-Royce Silver Ghost (1910)	40	25
1519	34c. Daimler (1927)	40	25
1520	34c. Hispano Suiza (1935)	40	25
1521	34c. Lancia Lambda V4 (1928)	40	25
1522	34c. Volvo OV4 (1927)	40	25

See also Nos. 1553/60, 1660/8, 1720/7 and 1744/51.

200 USA Flag and "Blessed are those who mourn for they shall be comforted"

2001. Support for Victims of Attack on World Trade Centre, New York (1st issue). Multicoloured.

1523	34c. Type **200**	40	25
1524	34c. Statue of Liberty, New York and script	40	25
1525	34c. "An attack on freedom anywhere is an attack on freedom everywhere"	40	25
1526	34c. "In the great struggle of good versus evil good will prevail"	40	25
1527	34c. Statue of Freedom, Washington and script	40	25
1528	34c. "In the face of terrorism we remain one nation under God indivisible"	40	25
1529	$1 Rescue workers, service personnel and New York citizens (75 × 34 mm)	1·25	75

See also No. 1552.

201 Adoration of the Shepherds

2001. Christmas. Multicoloured.

1530	34c. Type **201**	40	25
1531	34c. Angel on high	40	25
1532	34c. Adoration of the Magi	40	25
1533	34c. Nativity	40	25

202 Supermarine Sea Eagle

2001. Classic Aircraft. Multicoloured.

1534	80c. Type **202**	95	55
1535	80c. Gloster Sea Gladiator	95	55
1536	80c. De Havilland DHC-6 Twin Otter	95	55
1537	80c. Shorts 330 airliner	95	55
1538	80c. Sandringham Flying Boat	95	55
1539	80c. De Havilland DHC-7	95	55
1540	80c. Beech Duke B60	95	55
1541	80c. Fokker/Fairchild Friendship F27	95	55
1542	80c. Consolidated B-24J Liberator	95	55
1543	80c. Vickers 953C Merchantman	95	55

203 Decorated Horse (½-size illustration)

2002. New Year. "Year of the Horse". Sheet 110 × 86 mm.

1544 **203**	80c. multicoloured	85	55

204 Frilled Dog Winkle (*Nucella lamellose*)

2002. Sea Shells. Multicoloured.

1545	34c. Type **204**	40	25
1546	34c. Reticulated cowrie-helmet (*Cypraecassis testiculus*)	40	25
1547	34c. New England neptune (*Neptunea decemcostata*)	40	25
1548	34c. Calico scallop (*Argopecten gibbus*)	40	25
1549	34c. Lightning whelk (*Busycon contrarium*)	40	25
1550	34c. Hawk-wing conch (*Strombus raninus*) (inscr "ranius")	40	25

205 Queen Elizabeth II (½-size illustration)

2002. Golden Jubilee. 50th Anniv of Queen Elizabeth II's Accession to the Throne. Sheet 110 × 87 mm.

MS1551 **205** 80c. multicoloured . . . 95 55

206 Rescue Workers, Service Personnel and New York Citizens

207 Mixed Coral

2002. Support for Victims of Attack on World Trade Centre, New York (2nd issue).

1552 **206**	34c. multicoloured	40	25

2002. Vintage Cars (2nd series). As T **199**. Multicoloured.

1553	34c. Le Zebre (1909)	40	25
1554	34c. Hammel (1886)	40	25
1555	34c. Wolseley (1902)	40	25
1556	34c. Eysink (1899)	40	25
1557	34c. Dansk (1903)	40	25
1558	34c. Spyker (1907)	40	25
1559	34c. Fiat Zero (1913)	40	25
1560	34c. Weber (1902)	40	25

2002. Marine Life (1st series). Showing corals and fish. Multicoloured.

1561	34c. Type **207**	40	25
1562	34c. Chalice coral	40	25
1563	34c. Elkhorn coral	40	25
1564	34c. Finger coral	40	25

See also Nos. 1763/4.

2002. Butterflies (2nd series). As T **88**. Multicoloured.

1565	80c. Grayling	95	55
1566	80c. Eastern festoon	95	55
1567	80c. Speckled wood	95	55
1568	80c. Cranberry fritillary	95	55
1569	80c. Bath white	95	55
1570	80c. Meadow brown	95	55
1571	80c. Two-tailed pasha	95	55
1572	80c. Scarce swallowtail	95	55
1573	80c. Dusky grizzled skipper	95	55
1574	80c. Provencal short-tailed blue	95	55
1575	80c. The dryal	95	55
1576	80c. Comma	95	55

208 "Horses" (Giorgio de Chiroco)

2002. Horse Paintings. Multicoloured.

1577	34c. Type **208**	40	25
1578	34c. "Tartar Envoys giving Horse to Qianlong" (Guiseppe Castiglione)	40	25
1579	34c. "Gathering Seaweed" (Anton Mauve)	40	25
1580	34c. "Mares and Foals" (George Stubbs)	40	25
1581	34c. "Mare and Foal in spring Meadow" (Wilson Hepple)	40	25
1582	34c. "Horse with Child and Dog" (Natale Attanasio)	40	25
1583	34c. "The Horse" (Waterhouse Hawkins)	40	25
1584	34c. "Attendants and Horse" (Edgar Degas)	40	25
1585	34c. "Mares and Foals in Landscape" (George Stubbs)	40	25
1586	34c. "The Horse" (Guliemo Clardi)	40	25
1587	34c. "Little Blue Horse" (Franz Marc)	40	25
1588	34c. Sketch for "Firebird" (ballet) (Pavel Kuznetsov)	40	25

MS1589 110 × 87 mm. 80c. "Emperor Qianlong leaving for his Summer Residence" (Guiseppe Castiglione) (inscr "Casiglione") . . . 95 55

209 Ivan and his Brothers shoot Arrows

2002. "The Frog Princess" (fairytale). Multicoloured.

1590	37c. Type **209**	40	25
1591	37c. First brother finds a wife	40	25
1592	37c. Second brother finds a wife	40	25
1593	37c. Ivan and the frog princess	40	25
1594	37c. Ivan presents shirt to king	40	25
1595	37c. Ivan presents bread to king	40	25
1596	37c. Princess arrives at ball	40	25
1597	37c. Princess dances for king	40	25
1598	37c. Princess says goodbye to Ivan	40	25
1599	37c. Ivan and little hut	40	25
1600	37c. Ivan and princess re-united	40	25
1601	37c. Ivan and princess on magic carpet	40	25

210 Armoured Horse and Rabbit — **211** Lesser Golden Plover

2002. Carousel Animals. Multicoloured.
1602 80c. Type **210** 95 55
1603 80c. Zebra and camel 95 55
1604 80c. Horse, angel and reindeer 95 55
1605 80c. Horse, frog and tiger 95 55

2002. Birds. Multicoloured.
1606 37c. Type **211** 40 25
1607 37c. Siberian tattler 40 25
1608 37c. Brown noddy 40 25
1609 37c. Fairy tern 40 25
1610 37c. Micronesian pigeon 40 25
1611 37c. Long-tailed cuckoo 40 25
1612 37c. Christmas shearwater 40 25
1613 37c. Eurasian tree sparrow 40 25
1614 37c. Black-tailed godwit 40 25
1615 37c. Franklin's gull 40 25
1616 37c. Rufous-necked stint 40 25
1617 37c. Kermadec petrel 40 25
1618 37c. Purple-capped fruit dove 40 25
1619 37c. Mongolian plover 40 25
1620 37c. Cattle egret 40 25
1621 37c. Dunlin 40 25

212 Benjamin Franklin, Inventor (Gherman Komlev)

2002. Benjamin Franklin, Commemoration. Multicoloured.
1622 80c. Type **212** 95 55
1623 80c. Benjamin Franklin, scholar (David Martin) 95 55

213 Loggerhead Turtle

2002. Sea Turtles. Multicoloured.
1624 37c. Type **213** 40 25
1625 37c. Leatherback 40 25
1626 37c. Hawksbill 40 25
1627 37c. Green 40 25

214 "The Stamp Collector"

2002. 50th Anniv of International Federation of Stamp Dealers' Association (IFSDA). Paintings by Lyle Tayson. Multicoloured.
1628 80c. Type **214** 95 55
1629 80c. "The First Day of Issue" 95 55
1630 80c. "Father and Daughter Collectors" 95 55
1631 80c. "The Young Collector" 95 55
1632 80c. "Sharing Dad's Stamp Collection" 95 55
1633 80c. "The New Generation" 95 55

215 *Hartford* — **216** Black Widow Spider

2002. USA Naval Sail Ships. Multicoloured.
1634 37c. Type **215** 40 25
1635 37c. *Bon Homme Richard* 40 25
1636 37c. *Prince de Neufchatel* 40 25
1637 37c. *Ohio* 40 25
1638 37c. *Onkahye* 40 25
1639 37c. *Oneida* 40 25

2002. Insects. Multicoloured.
1640 23c. Type **216** 25 10
1641 23c. Elderberry longhorn 25 10
1642 23c. Lady beetle 25 10
1643 23c. Yellow garden spider 25 10
1644 23c. Dogbane beetle 25 10
1645 23c. Flower fly 25 10
1646 23c. Assassin bug 25 10
1647 23c. Ebony jewel wing 25 10
1648 23c. Velvet ant 25 10
1649 23c. Monarch caterpillar 25 10
1650 23c. Monarch butterfly 25 10
1651 23c. Eastern Hercules beetle 25 10
1652 23c. Bombardier beetle 25 10
1653 23c. Dung beetle 25 10
1654 23c. Spotted water beetle 25 10
1655 23c. True katydid 25 10
1656 23c. Spiny-backed spider 25 10
1657 23c. Periodical cicada 25 10
1658 23c. Scorpion fly 25 10
1659 23c. Jumping spider 25 10

2002. Vintage Cars (3rd series). As T **199**. Multicoloured.
1660 34c. Hotchkiss (1934) 40 25
1661 34c. De Dion Bouton (1909) 40 25
1662 34c. Renault (1922) 40 25
1663 34c. Amilcar "Surbaisse" (1927) 40 25
1664 34c. Austin (1943) 40 25
1665 34c. Peugeot "Bebe" (1927) 40 25
1666 34c. O.M. "Superba" (1913) 40 25
1668 34c. Elizade-Tipo (1922) 40 25

218 Elizabeth Bowes-Lyon (1904)

2002. Queen Elizabeth the Queen Mother Commemoration. Multicoloured.
1669 80c. Type **218** 95 55
1670 80c. Duchess of York (1923) 95 55
1671 80c. Queen Elizabeth wearing pearl necklace (1940) 95 55
1672 80c. Queen Elizabeth the Queen Mother wearing blue outfit (1990) 95 55

219 *Regal Princess* (cruise liner), Majuro Lagoon, Marshall Islands (½-size illustration)

2002. World War II Veterans Visit Sites in the South Pacific. Sheet 110 × 88 mm.
MS1673 **219** 80c. multicoloured 95 55

220 William Sims (commander USA Navy in Europe)

2002. World War I Military Heroes. Multicoloured.
1674 80c. Type **220** 95 55
1675 80c. William Mitchell (senior aviation officer) 95 55
1676 80c. Freddie Stowers (posthumous Medal of Honor) 95 55
1677 80c. Smedley Butler (United States Marine Corps) 95 55
1678 80c. Edward Rickenbacker (USA flying ace) 95 55
1679 80c. Alvin York (French Medaille Militaire, Croix de Guerre, Italian Groce de Guerra and Medal of Honor) 95 55
1680 80c. John Lejeune (division commander) 95 55
1681 80c. John Pershing (Commander-in-Chief American expeditionary force in Europe) 95 55

221 Snowman Cookie — **223** Indel's Magic Kite

222 Decorated Ram (½-size illustration)

2002. Christmas. Multicoloured.
1682 37c. Type **221** 40 25
1683 37c. Snowman cookie wearing hat 40 25

2003. New Year. "Year of the Ram".
1684 **222** 80c. multicoloured 95 55

2003. Folktales. Multicoloured.
1685 50c. Type **223** 55 30
1686 50c. Lijebake rescues her Granddaughter 55 30
1687 50c. Jebro's Mother invents the Sail 55 30
1688 50c. Limajnon escapes to the Moon 55 30

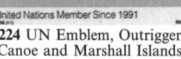

224 UN Emblem, Outrigger Canoe and Marshall Islands Emblem — **225** Lagajimi (Franz Hernsheim)

2003. 12th Anniv of Marshall Islands' Membership of United Nations.
1689 **224** 60c. multicoloured 85 65

2003. Cultural Heritage (1st issue). Multicoloured.
1690 37c. Type **225** 40 25
1691 37c. Traditional house (50 × 42 mm) 40 25
1692 37c. Lake, Jabwor, Jaluit Atoll (50 × 42 mm) 40 25
1693 37c. Kabua (Franz Hernsheim) 40 25
1694 37c. Children wearing traditional dress 40 25
1695 37c. Jaluit Pass (Franz Hernsheim) (50 × 42 mm) 40 25
1696 37c. Traditional Canoe (Franz Hernsheim) (50 × 42 mm) 40 25
1697 37c. Fisherman 40 25
See also Nos. 1728/35.

2003. Butterflies (3rd series). As T **188**. Multicoloured.
1698 80c. False grayling 95 55
1699 80c. Green hairstreak 95 55
1700 80c. Purple-shot copper 95 55
1701 80c. Black-veined white 95 55
1702 80c. Arctic grayling 95 55
1703 80c. Greek clouded yellow 95 55
1704 80c. American painted lady 95 55
1705 80c. Wall brown 95 55
1706 80c. Polar fritillary 95 55
1707 80c. Mountain clouded yellow 95 55
1708 80c. Camberwell beauty 95 55
1709 80c. Large white 95 55

226 *Wright Flyer I* — **227** Bauble containing Snow Scene

2003. Centenary of Powered Flight. Multicoloured.
1710 37c. Type **226** 40 25
1711 37c. Curtiss JN-3 40 25
1712 37c. Douglas World Cruiser 40 25
1713 37c. Ryan NYP *Spirit of St Louis* 40 25
1714 37c. Lockheed Vega 40 25
1715 37c. Boeing 314 Clipper 40 25
1716 37c. Douglas C-47 Skytrain 40 25
1717 37c. Boeing B-50 Superfortress 40 25
1718 37c. Antonov An-225 Mriya 40 25
1719 37c. B-2 Spirit 40 25

2003. Vintage Cars (4th series). As T **199**. Multicoloured.
1720 37c. Alfa Romeo (1927) 40 25
1721 37c. Austro-Daimler "Prince Henry" (1912) 40 25
1722 37c. Mors 14/20 Tourer (1923) 40 25
1723 37c. AC Tourer (1926) 40 25
1724 37c. Scania (1903) and Vabis (1897) 40 25
1725 37c. Graf und Stift (1914) 40 25
1726 37c. Pic-Pic (1919) 40 25
1727 37c. Hispano Suiza-Alfonso XIII (1911) 40 25

2003. Cultural Heritage (2nd issue) As T **225**. Multicoloured.
1728 37c. Kabua's daughter 40 25
1729 37c. Walap (50 × 42 mm) 40 25
1730 37c. Jabwor, Jaluit Atoll (50 × 42 mm) 40 25
1731 37c. Traditional and modern dress 40 25
1732 37c. Nemedj 40 25
1733 37c. Typhoon damage, 1905 (50 × 42 mm) 40 25
1734 37c. Marshallese kor kor (50 × 42 mm) 40 25
1735 37c. Grandfather 40 25

2003. Christmas. Multicoloured.
1736 37c. Type **227** 40 25
1737 37c. Jack-in-the-box 40 25
1738 37c. Toy soldier 40 25
1739 37c. Reindeer 40 25

228 Decorated Monkey (½-size illustration)

2004. New Year. "Year of the Monkey".
MS1740 **228** 80c. multicoloured 95 55

229 *Bonhomme Richard* — **230** "THANK YOU"

2004. 225th Anniversaries. Multicoloured.
1741 37c. Type **229** (American revolution sea battle) 40 25
1742 37c. HMS *Resolution* (Captain Cook's final voyages) 40 25
1743 37c. HMS *Resolution* (different) (Captain Cook's final voyages) 40 25

2004. Vintage Cars (5th series). As T **199**. Multicoloured.
1744 37c. Wolseley-Siddeley (1906) 40 25
1745 37c. Mors (1901) 40 45
1746 37c. Hutton (1908) 40 25
1747 37c. Metallurgique (1907) 40 25
1748 37c. Benz (1902) 40 25
1749 37c. Cudell (1900) 40 25
1750 37c. Peugeot (1906) 40 25
1751 37c. Inscr "The 60 Mercedes" 40 25

2004. Greetings Stamps. Sheet 148 × 104 mm containing T **230** and similar vert designs. Multicoloured.
MS1752 37c. × 8, Type **230**; "CONGRATULATIONS"; "HAPPY BIRTHDAY"; "Best Wishes"; "Get Well Soon"; "LOVE YOU DAD"; "Love you Mom"; Bouquet of greetings 3·25 3·25

231 Runner and Outrigger Canoe

2004. 20th Anniv of Marshall Islands Postal Service.
1753 **231** 37c. multicoloured . . . 40 25
1754 60c. multicoloured . . . 85 65
1755 $2.30 multicoloured . . 2·50 1·50
No. 1753 was for use on first class mail, No. 1754 was for use on international mail and No. 1755 was for use on certified mail.

232 Expeditionary Corps aboard Boat

2004. Bicentenary of Meriwether Lewis and William Clark's Expedition to Explore the West Coast of America (1st issue). Multicoloured.
1756 37c. Type **232** 40 25
1757 37c. Clark and Sacagawea (Shoshone guide) 40 25
1758 37c. Lewis and Clark and bison herd 40 25
See also Nos. 1832/4 and 1839/41.

233 Horsa Gliders and Parachute Troops

2004. 60th Anniv of D-Day (invasion of German occupied French coast). Multicoloured.
1759 37c. Type **233** 40 25
1760 37c. Typhoon-1B and P518 Mustangs 40 25
1761 37c. Gun emplacements . . 40 25
1762 37c. Allied craft and soldiers landing 40 25
Nos. 1759/62 were issued together, se-tenant, forming a composite design.

234 Chambered Nautilus, Map Cowrie and Trumpet Triton

2004. Marine Life (2nd series). Multicoloured.
1763 37c. Type **234** 40 25
1764 37c. Marlin spike, turban shell and Toulerei's cowrie 40 25

235 Ronald Reagan

2004. Ronald Reagan (president of USA, 1980–88) Commemoration.
1765 **235** 60c. multicoloured . . . 85 65

236 Astronaut in Space

2004. 35th Anniv of First Moon Walk. Multicoloured.
1766 37c. Type **236** 40 25
1767 37c. Astronaut and Saturn 40 25
1768 37c. Astronaut and Space Shuttle 40 25
1769 37c. Two astronauts 40 25

237 Making Fans

2004. Festival of Pacific Arts, Koror, Palau. Multicoloured.
1770 37c. Type **237** 40 25
1771 37c. Basket makers 40 25
1772 37c. Carving canoes 40 25
1773 37c. Boys and toy outrigger canoes 40 25
1774 37c. Older woman and white ginger flowers 40 25
1775 37c. Boy and vandal flower 40 25
1776 37c. Man and tiare flower 40 25
1777 37c. Young woman and hibiscus flower 40 25
1778 37c. Woman carrying breadfruit 40 25
1779 37c. Canoes and tattooed man 40 25
1780 37c. Men in traditional dress 40 25
1781 37c. Drummer and dancers 40 25

238 *Wright Flyer I*

239 John Wayne

2004. Aircraft. Multicoloured.
1782 23c. Type **238** 25 10
1783 23c. Bleriot XI 25 10
1784 23c. Curtiss Golden Flyer 25 10
1785 23c. Curtiss Flying Boat . . 25 10
1786 23c. Deperdussin Racer . . 25 10
1787 23c. Sikorsky Ilya Muromets 25 10
1788 23c. Fokker E I 25 10
1789 23c. Junkers JI 25 10
1790 23c. S. E. 5A 25 10
1791 23c. Handley Page O/400 . . 25 10
1792 23c. Fokker D VII 25 10
1793 23c. Junkers F 13 . . . . . 25 10
1794 23c. Lockheed Vega 25 10
1795 23c. M-130 Pan Am Clipper 25 10
1796 23c. Messerschmitt BF 109 25 10
1797 23c. Spitfire 25 10
1798 23c. Junkers JU 88 . . . . 25 10
1799 23c. A6M Zero 25 10
1800 23c. Ilyushin Il-2 . . . . . 25 10
1801 23c. Heinkel HE 178 . . . 25 10
1802 23c. C-47 Skytrain 25 10
1803 23c. Piper Cub 25 10
1804 23c. Avro Lancaster 25 10
1805 23c. B-17F Flying Fortress 25 10
1806 23c. Messrschmitt ME-262 25 10
1807 23c. B-29 Superfortress . . 25 10
1808 23c. P-51 Mustang 25 10
1809 23c. Yak 9 . . . . 25 10
1810 23c. Bell Model 47 . . . . 25 10
1811 23c. Bell X-1 . . . . 25 10
1812 23c. Beechcraft Bonanza . . 25 10
1813 23c. AN-225 Mriya 25 10
1814 23c. B-47 Stratojet 25 10
1815 23c. MIG-15 . . . . 25 10
1816 23c. Saab J35 Draken . . . 25 10
1817 23c. B-52 Stratofortress . . 25 10
1818 23c. Boeing 367-80 . . . . 25 10
1819 23c. U-2 . . . . 25 10
1820 23c. C-130 Hercules 25 10
1821 23c. F-4 Phantom II 25 10
1822 23c. North American X-15 25 10
1823 23c. Sikorsky S-61 helicopter 25 10
1824 23c. Learjet 23 . . . . . . 25 10
1825 23c. SR-71 Blackbird . . . 25 10
1826 23c. Boeing 747 . . . . . . 25 10
1827 23c. Concorde 25 10
1828 23c. Airbus A300 . . . . . 25 10
1829 23c. MIG-29 . . . . 25 10
1830 23c. F-117A Nighthawk . . 25 10
1831 23c. F/A-22 Raptor 25 10

2004. Bicentenary of Meriwether Lewis and William Clark's Expedition to Explore the West Coast of America (2nd issue). As T **232**. Multicoloured.
1832 37c. Celebrating July 4th . . 40 25
1833 37c. Corps surrounding flag (burial of Charles Floyd) 40 25
1834 37c. Smoking peace pipe . . 40 25

2004. 25th Death Anniv of John Wayne (actor).
1835 **239** 37c. multicoloured . . . 40 25

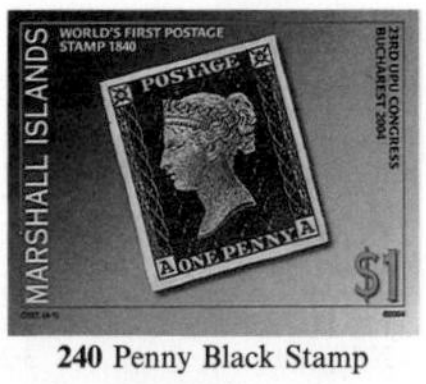

240 Penny Black Stamp

2004. 23rd Universal Postal Union Congress, Bucharest. Sheet 100 × 92 mm containing T **240** and similar horiz designs. Multicoloured.
MS1836 $1 ×4, Type **240** (first postage stamp); First Romanian stamp (1858); First Marshall Islands' stamp (1897); First Republic of Marshall Islands' stamp (1984) . . . . 2·20 2·20

241 Emperor Angelfish

243 Infantryman

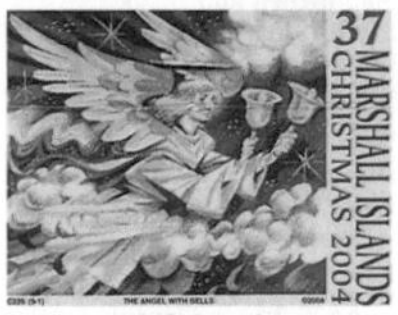

242 Angel

2004. Pacific Coral Reef. Sheet 179 × 104 mm containing T **241** and similar vert designs. Multicoloured.
MS1837 37c. ×10, Type **241**; Pink anemone fish; Humphead wrasse and moorish idol; Black-spotted puffer; Snowflake moray eel; Lionfish; Bumphead parrotfish and threadfin butterfly fish; Hawksbill turtle; Triton's trumpet; Oriental sweetlips. . . . . . . 3·25 3·25

2004. Christmas. Sheet 144 × 118 mm containing T **242** and similar horiz designs. Multicoloured.
MS1838 37c. ×9, Type **242**; God crowned; Adoration of the kings; Three wise men; Procession of poor people; Shepherds; Flight into Egypt; Nativity; Jesus and animals . . . . 3·00 3·00

2004. Bicentenary of Meriwether Lewis and William Clark's Expedition to Explore the West Coast of America (3rd issue). As T **232**. Multicoloured.
1839 37c. Interpreters 40 25
1840 37c. Hunting bison 40 25
1841 37c. Attack by Sioux . . . 40 25

2004. 60th Anniv of Battle of the Bulge. Multicoloured.
1842 37c. Type **243** 40 25
1843 37c. Tank division soldier 40 25
1844 37c. Aviator 40 25
1845 37c. Lt. Colonel Creighton Abrams and General Anthony McAuliffe (inscr "Anathony") 40 25

MARTINIQUE Pt. 6

An island in the West Indies, now an overseas department using the stamps of France.

100 centimes = 1 franc.

1886. Stamp of French Colonies, "Commerce" type. (a) Surch **MARTINIQUE** and new value.
3 J 01 on 20c. red on green . . . 10·00 13·50
1 5 on 20c. red on green . . . . 38·00 45·00
4 05 on 20c. red on green . . . 8·25 7·75
2 5c. on 20c. red on green . . . £11000 £11000
6 015 on 20c. red on green . . . 42·00 55·00
5 15 on 20c. red on green . . . £140 £120

(b) Surch **MQE 15 c.**
7 J 15c. on 20c. red on green . . . 65·00 65·00

1888. Stamps of French Colonies, "Commerce" type, surch **MARTINIQUE** and value, thus **01 c.**
10 01c. on 4c. brown on grey . . 8·25 3·00
11 05c. on 4c. brown on grey . . £950 £800
12 05c. on 10c. black and lilac . . 85·00 38·00
13 05c. on 20c. red on green . . 20·00 16·00
14 05c. on 30c. brown on drab 16·00 21·00
15 05c. on 35c. black on yellow 18·00 11·50
16 05c. on 40c. red on yellow . . 50·00 32·00
17 15c. on 4c. brown on grey . . £7250 £6750
18 15c. on 20c. red on green . . £110 60·00
19 15c. on 25c. black on pink . . 10·00 7·25
20 15c. on 75c. red on pink . . . £130 £120

1891. Postage Due stamps of French Colonies surch **TIMBRE-POSTE MARTINIQUE** and value in figures.
21 U 05c. on 5c. black . . . . . 10·00 12·00
25 05c. on 10c. black . . . . . 5·25 5·75
22 05c. on 15c. black . . . . . 6·50 6·00
23 15c. on 20c. black . . . . . 13·00 9·25
24 15c. on 30c. black . . . . . 17·00 9·25

1891. Stamp of French Colonies, "Commerce" type, surch **TIMBRE-POSTE 01c. MARTINIQUE**.
9 01c. on 2c. brown on buff . . . 80 1·00

1892. Stamp of French Colonies, "Commerce" type, surch **1892 MARTINIQUE** and new value.
31 15c. on 25c. black on pink . . 20·00 20·00

1892. "Tablet" key-type inscr "MARTINIQUE", in red (1, 5, 15, 25, 75c., 1f.) or blue (others).
33 D 1c. black on blue . . . . . 1·00 1·00
34 2c. brown on buff . . . . . 1·25 1·40
35 4c. brown on grey . . . . . 1·60 1·75
36 5c. green on green . . . . . 3·50 50
37 10c. black on lilac . . . . . 8·50 70
47 10c. red . . . . 3·75 30
38 15c. blue . . . . 34·00 2·25
48 15c. grey . . . . 11·50 75
39 20c. red on green . . . . . 17·00 7·75
40 25c. black on pink . . . . . 12·00 1·00
49 25c. blue . . . . 14·00 19·00
41 30c. brown on drab . . . . 17·00 12·50
50 35c. black on yellow . . . . 16·00 5·50
42 40c. red on yellow . . . . . 30·00 13·00
43 50c. red on pink . . . . . . 25·00 14·00
51 50c. brown on blue . . . . 16·00 28·00
44 75c. brown on orange . . . 25·00 17·00
45 1f. green . . . . 24·00 16·00
52 2f. violet on pink . . . . . 80·00 65·00
53 5f. mauve on lilac . . . . . 85·00 80·00

1903. Postage Due stamp of French Colonies surch **TIMBRE POSTE 5 F. MARTINIQUE COLIS POSTAUX**.
53a U 5f. on 60c. brown on buff £450 £475
Despite the surcharge No. 53a was for use on letters as well as parcels.

1904. Nos. 41 and 43 surch **10 c.**
54 10c. on 30c. brown and drab 9·25 12·00
55 10c. on 5f. mauve on lilac . . 8·75 15·00

1904. Surch **1904 0f10**.
56 0f.10 on 30c. brown on drab 14·50 18·00
57 0f.10 on 40c. red on yellow . . 15·00 18·00
58 0f.10 on 50c. red on pink . . 14·50 18·00
59 0f.10 on 75c. brown on orange 11·50 17·00
60 0f.10 on 1f. green . . . . . . 17·00 18·00
61 0f.10 on 5f. mauve on lilac . . £150 £150

13 Martinique Woman

15 Woman and Sugar Cane

14 Fort-de-France

1908.
62 **13** 1c. chocolate and brown 15 20
63 2c. brown and green . . . 15 45
64 4c. brown and purple . . . 40 65
65 5c. brown and green . . . 50 15
87 5c. brown and orange . . . 15 15
66 10c. brown and red . . . . 2·75 15
88 10c. olive and green . . . 1·60 1·00
89 10c. red and purple . . . . 1·25 60
67 15c. red and purple . . . . 1·00 1·10
90 15c. olive and green . . . 15 20
91 15c. red and blue . . . . 2·00 95
68 20c. brown and lilac . . . 2·50 1·40
69 **14** 25c. brown and blue . . . 3·00 45
92 25c. brown and orange . . 35 15
93 30c. brown and red . . . . 2·25 2·75
94 30c. red and carmine . . . 55 2·75
95 30c. brown and light brown . . . . 40 1·00
96 30c. green and blue . . . . 3·00 1·25
71 35c. brown and lilac . . . 1·00 1·50
72 40c. brown and green . . . 1·25 45
73 45c. chocolate and brown 2·25 2·50
74 50c. brown and red . . . . 2·75 3·00
97 50c. brown and blue . . . 1·90 2·50
98 50c. green and red . . . . 1·75 20
99 60c. pink and blue . . . . 85 2·75
100 65c. brown and violet . . . 3·00 3·50
75 75c. brown and black . . . 85 3·25
101 75c. blue and deep blue . . 2·00 2·25
102 75c. blue and brown . . . 3·75 3·50
103 90c. carmine and red . . . 7·00 8·50
76 **15** 1f. brown and red . . . . 2·50 3·00
104 1f. blue . . . . 2·25 2·25
105 1f. green and red . . . . . 2·50 2·00
106 1f.10 brown and violet . . . 4·50 6·00
107 1f.50 light blue and blue 8·00 8·75
77 2f. brown and grey . . . . 4·00 3·25
108 3f. mauve on pink . . . . 12·00 14·00
78 5f. brown and red . . . . 12·00 15·00

1912. Stamps of 1892 surch.
79 05 on 15c. grey 30 25
80 05 on 25c. black on pink . . . 45 3·00
81 10 on 40c. red on yellow . . . 2·25 2·50
82 10 on 5f. mauve on lilac . . . 2·75 4·00

1915. Surch **5c** and red cross.
83 **13** 10c.+5c. brown and red . . 1·90 2·00

1920. Surch in figures.

115	13	0,01 on 2c. brown & green	3·00	4·25
109		0,01 on 15c. red and purple	45	30
110		0,02 on 15c. red and purple	45	2·75
84		05 on 1c. chocolate & brn	3·50	3·25
111		0,05 on 15c. red and purple	15	2·75
116		0,05 on 20c. brown and lilac	3·50	4·25
85		10 on 2c. brown and green	85	80
117	14	0,15 on 30c. brown and red	3·50	18·00
86	13	25 on 15c. red and purple	2·50	2·75
121		25c. on 15c. red and purple	15	2·75
119	14	0,25 on 50c. brown and red	£200	£200
120		0,25 on 50c. brown and blue	4·25	5·00
122	15	25c. on 2f. brown and grey	50	2·75
123		25c. on 5f. brown and red	2·00	3·25
112	14	60 on 75c. pink and blue	10	40
113		65 on 45c. brown & lt brn	1·75	3·25
114		85 on 75c. brown and black	2·25	3·50
124		90c. on 75c. carmine and red	2·75	4·50
125	15	1f.25 on 1f. blue	75	2·50
126		1f.50 on 1f. ultram & bl	2·50	1·75
127		3f. on 5f. green and red	3·00	2·50
128		10f. on 5f. red and green	10·50	14·50
129		20f. on 5f. violet & brown	17·00	21·00

1931. "Colonial Exhibition" key-types inscr "MARTINIQUE".

130	E	40c. black and green	4·50	5·50
131	F	50c. black and mauve	4·00	3·00
132	G	90c. black and red	4·50	5·50
133	H	1f.50 black and blue	4·75	5·25

26 Basse Pointe Village

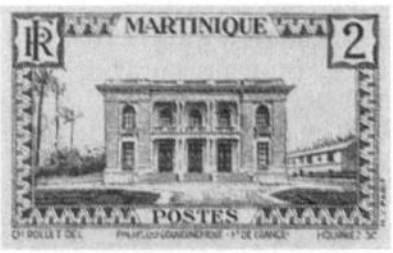

27 Government House, Fort-de-France

28 Martinique Woman

1933.

134	26	1c. red on pink	15	2·00
135	27	2c. blue	15	2·50
136		3c. purple	30	2·75
137	26	4c. green	15	2·75
138	27	5c. purple	15	35
139	26	10c. black on pink	15	30
140	27	15c. black on red	15	30
141	28	20c. brown	15	30
142	26	25c. purple	40	30
143	27	30c. green	55	30
144		30c. blue	45	2·75
145	28	35c. green	60	1·40
146		40c. brown	15	70
147	27	45c. brown	2·75	3·50
148		45c. green	70	2·25
149		50c. red	70	35
150	26	55c. red	1·50	2·25
151		60c. blue	40	2·75
152	28	65c. red on blue	1·00	1·75
153		70c. purple	1·25	2·25
154	26	75c. brown	2·00	2·00
155	27	80c. violet	1·10	1·75
156	26	90c. red	3·00	80
157		90c. purple	1·60	1·75
158	27	1f. black on green	1·75	1·10
159		1f. red	90	2·10
160	28	1f.25 violet	2·50	2·50
161		1f.25 red	2·00	2·50
162		1f.40 blue	1·90	2·25
163	27	1f.50 blue	95	75
164		1f.60 brown	2·00	2·25
165	28	1f.75 green	12·00	6·00
166		1f.75 blue	2·00	1·60
167	26	2f. blue on green	2·50	1·00
168	28	2f.25 blue	2·50	3·00
169	26	2f.50 purple	2·00	2·50
170	28	3f. purple	2·25	1·50
171		5f. red on pink	2·50	1·50
172	26	10f. blue on blue	1·75	1·50
173	27	20f. red on yellow	2·25	2·00

30 Belain d'Esnambuc, 1635

31 Schoelcher and Abolition of Slavery, 1848

1935. West Indies Tercentenary.

174	30	40c. brown	3·75	3·50
175		50c. red	3·75	3·75
176		1f.50 blue	13·00	16·00
177	31	1f.75 red	16·00	13·00
178		5f. brown	14·50	16·00
179		10f. green	11·00	9·75

1937. International Exhibition, Paris. As T **16** of Mauritania.

180	20c. violet	80	2·75
181	30c. green	1·10	2·75
182	40c. red	45	2·25
183	50c. brown and agate	45	1·60
184	90c. red	60	3·25
185	1f.50 blue	75	2·25
MS185a	120×100 mm. 3f. green (as T **16**) Imperf	7·75	13·50

1938. Int Anti-cancer Fund. As T **22** of Mauritania.

186	1f.75+50c. blue	7·00	14·00

1939. New York World's Fair. As T **28** of Mauritania.

187	1f.25 red	2·00	3·25
188	2f.25 blue	2·25	3·25

1939. 150th Anniv of French Revolution. As T **29** of Mauritania.

189	45c.+25c. green and black	7·50	11·00
190	70c.+30c. brown and black	7·50	11·00
191	90c.+35c. orange and black	6·75	11·00
192	1f.25+1f. red and black	6·75	11·00
193	2f.25+2f. blue and black	6·75	11·00

1944. Mutual Aid and Red Cross Funds. As T **19b** of Oceanic Settlements.

194	5f.+20f. violet	90	3·50

1945. Eboue. As T **20a** of Oceanic Settlements.

195	2f. black	10	40
196	25f. green	1·10	2·50

1945. Surch.

197	27	1f. on 2c. blue	2·50	1·25
198	26	2f. on 4c. olive	50	1·40
199	27	3f. on 2c. blue	2·25	90
200	28	5f. on 65c. red on blue	70	2·00
201		10f. (DIX f.) on 65c. red on blue	2·50	2·00
202	27	20f. (VINGT f.) on 3c. pur	2·50	2·75

33 Victor Schoelcher

1945.

203	33	10c. blue and violet	15	2·75
204		30c. brown and red	20	2·00
205		40c. blue and light blue	40	2·25
206		50c. red and purple	40	2·50
207		60c. orange and yellow	30	1·75
208		70c. purple and brown	95	3·00
209		80c. green and light green	95	2·75
210		1f. blue and light blue	30	1·60
211		1f.20 violet and purple	90	3·00
212		1f.50 red and orange	55	1·40
213		2f. black and grey	60	1·25
214		2f.40 red and pink	1·10	3·25
215		3f. pink and light pink	85	1·00
216		4f. ultramarine and blue	70	2·00
217		4f.50 turquoise and green	85	1·25
218		5f. light brown and brown	95	1·50
219		10f. purple and mauve	1·10	1·25
220		15f. red and pink	90	1·50
221		20f. olive and green	60	1·60

1945. Air. As No. 299 of New Caledonia.

222	50f. green	60	1·75
223	100f. red	55	2·75

1946. Air. Victory. As T **20b** of Oceanic Settlements.

224	8f. blue	25	3·25

1946. Air. From Chad to the Rhine. As T **25a** of Madagascar.

225	5f. orange	80	2·75
226	10f. green	40	2·75
227	15f. red	80	3·25
228	20f. brown	1·00	2·50
229	25f. blue	55	3·25
230	50f. grey	1·10	2·25

34 Martinique Woman

39 Mountains and Palms

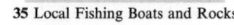

35 Local Fishing Boats and Rocks

40 West Indians and Latecoere 611 (flying boat)

1947.

231	34	10c. lake (postage)	20	2·50
232		30c. blue	15	2·50
233		50c. brown	15	2·75
234	35	60c. green	30	2·75
235		1f. lake	30	1·00
236		1f.50 violet	45	2·75
237	–	2f. green	80	2·25
238	–	2f.50 brown	80	3·00
239	–	3f. blue	95	1·50
240	–	4f. brown	80	2·00
241	–	5f. green	75	1·50
242	–	6f. mauve	90	50
243	–	10f. blue	2·00	1·75
244	–	15f. lake	2·25	2·00
245	–	20f. brown	1·75	1·90
246	39	25f. violet	1·90	2·00
247		40f. green	1·90	3·50
248	40	50f. purple (air)	4·50	4·00
249	–	100f. green	5·50	6·25
250	–	200f. violet	32·00	22·00

DESIGNS—HORIZ: As Type **35**: 2f. to 3f. Gathering sugar cane; 4f. to 6f. Mount Pele; 10f. to 20f. Fruit products. As Type **40**—VERT: 100f. Aeroplane over landscape. HORIZ: 200f. Wandering albatross in flight.

POSTAGE DUE STAMPS

1927. Postage Due stamps of France optd **MARTINIQUE**.

D130	D 11	5c. blue	25	3·25
D131		10c. brown	40	3·75
D132		20c. olive	65	3·75
D133		25c. red	1·00	4·25
D134		30c. red	1·25	4·50
D135		45c. green	1·75	4·75
D136		50c. purple	2·25	9·00
D137		60c. green	3·25	9·75
D138		1f. red on yellow	4·75	12·00
D139		2f. mauve	6·75	18·00
D140		3f. red	6·25	21·00

D 29 Fruit

D 43 Map of Martinique

1933.

D174	D 29	5c. blue on green	35	1·60
D175		10c. brown	15	2·75
D176		20c. blue	95	3·00
D177		25c. red on pink	65	3·00
D178		30c. purple	65	2·75
D179		45c. red on yellow	85	2·50
D180		50c. brown	50	3·25
D181		60c. green	1·00	3·25
D182		1f. black on red	85	3·75
D183		2f. purple	90	3·50
D184		3f. blue on blue	1·25	3·75

1947.

D251	D 43	10c. blue	15	2·75
D252		30c. green	15	2·75
D253		50c. blue	15	3·00
D254		1f. orange	15	3·00
D255		2f. purple	1·25	3·25
D256		3f. purple	1·25	3·25
D257		4f. brown	2·25	3·50
D258		5f. red	2·25	3·00
D259		10f. black	2·50	4·25
D260		20f. green	3·25	4·25

MAURITANIA Pt. 6; Pt. 13

A French colony extending inland to the Sahara, incorporated in French West Africa from 1945 to 1959. In 1960 Mauritania became an independent Islamic republic.

1906. 100 centimes = 1 franc.
1973. 100 cents = 1 ouguiya (um).

1906. "Faidherbe", "Palms" and "Balay" key-types inscr "MAURITANIE" in blue (10, 40c., 5f.) or red (others).

1	I	1c. grey	90	80
2		2c. brown	80	1·00
3		4c. brown on blue	2·50	2·25
4		5c. green	2·75	2·25
5		10c. pink	10·00	7·00
6	J	20c. black on blue	17·00	18·00
7		25c. blue	9·00	7·50
8		30c. brown on pink	£100	60·00
9		35c. black on yellow	5·75	6·00
10		40c. red on blue	8·50	8·25
11		45c. brown on green	8·25	8·25
12		50c. violet	8·75	8·00
13		75c. green on orange	8·00	6·75
14	K	1f. black on blue	21·00	19·00
15		2f. blue on pink	55·00	70·00
16		5f. red on yellow	£130	£110

6 Merchants crossing Desert

1913.

18	6	1c. brown and lilac	10	20
19		2c. blue and black	10	1·25
20		4c. black and violet	10	1·50
21		5c. green and light green	1·75	2·25
37		5c. red and purple	30	2·50
22		10c. orange and pink	2·50	2·75
38		10c. green and light green	10	2·50
39		10c. pink on blue	15	2·75
23		15c. black and brown	95	2·75
24		20c. orange and brown	2·00	3·00
25		25c. ultramarine and blue	3·00	3·25
40		25c. red and green	1·75	2·25
26		30c. pink and green	2·50	3·25
41		30c. orange and red	2·25	2·50
42		30c. yellow and black	15	2·50
43		30c. light green and green	2·75	3·75
27		35c. violet and brown	1·25	3·25
44		35c. light green and green	1·00	3·00
28		40c. green and brown	2·50	3·50
29		45c. brown and orange	1·60	2·75
30		50c. pink and lilac	75	3·25
45		50c. ultramarine and blue	1·10	2·75
46		50c. blue and green	1·90	2·75
47		60c. violet on pink	1·50	2·75
48		65c. blue and brown	2·25	3·25
31		75c. brown and blue	1·50	3·25
49		85c. brown and green	45	3·00
50		90c. pink and red	3·00	3·75
32		1f. black and red	1·60	2·50
51		1f.10 red and mauve	9·50	15·00
52		1f.25 brown and blue	3·50	4·00
53		1f.50 blue and light blue	1·75	3·00
54		1f.75 red and green	2·50	3·25
55		1f.75 ultramarine and blue	1·25	3·25
33		2f. violet and orange	1·60	3·75
56		3f. mauve on pink	1·90	3·75
34		5f. blue and violet	3·00	4·25

1915. Surch **5c** and red cross.

35	6	10c.+5c. orange and pink	1·25	2·25
36		15c.+5c. black and brown	95	3·25

1922. Surch in figures and bars (some colours changed).

60	6	25c. on 2f. violet and orange	2·75	3·25
57		60 on 75c. violet on pink	1·60	2·75
58		65 on 15c. black and brown	3·00	4·25
59		85 on 75c. brown and blue	2·00	4·00
61		90c. on 75c. pink and red	3·00	4·00
62		1f.25 on 1f. ultram & blue	2·00	3·25
63		1f.50 on 1f. blue & light blue	1·25	3·00
64		3f. on 5f. mauve and brown	9·75	12·00
65		10f. on 5f. green and mauve	9·00	10·50
66		20f. on 5f. orange and blue	5·75	11·00

1931. "Colonial Exhibition" key-types inscr "MAURITANIE".

67	E	40c. green and black	9·25	13·00
68	F	50c. purple and black	5·00	6·00
69	G	90c. red and black	5·00	6·50
70	H	1f.50 blue and black	5·00	6·50

16 Commerce

22 Pierre and Marie Curie

1937. International Exhibition, Paris.

71	16	20c. violet	45	2·50
72		30c. green	80	3·25
73		40c. red	40	3·00
74		50c. brown	35	1·40
75		90c. red	30	2·00
76		1f.50 blue	35	3·25
MS76a		120× 100 mm. **18** 3f. blue. Imperf	8·25	10·00

1938. International Anti-cancer Fund.

76b	22	1f.75+50c. blue	3·00	12·50

23 Man on Camel **24** Warriors

25 Encampment **26** Mauritanians

1938.

77	23	2c. purple	15	2·50
78		3c. blue	10	2·25
79		4c. lilac	45	2·50
80		5c. red	10	2·00
81		10c. red	80	3·00
82		15c. violet	1·10	2·50
83	24	20c. red	35	80
84		25c. blue	80	2·25
85		30c. purple	75	2·50
86		35c. green	60	2·75
87		40c. red	90	3·00
88		45c. green	1·75	3·00
89		50c. violet	55	3·25
90	25	55c. lilac	55	2·50
91		60c. violet	2·00	3·00
92		65c. green	45	3·00
93		70c. red	2·00	3·25
94		80c. blue	1·50	4·00
95		90c. lilac	1·10	2·75
96		1f. red	70	3·50
97		1f. green	10	2·50
98		1f.25 red	1·60	3·50
99		1f.40 blue	2·25	3·25
100		1f.50 violet	1·25	3·00
100a		1f.50 red	£110	£100
101		1f.60 brown	3·00	3·50
102	26	1f.75 blue	95	2·00
103		2f. lilac	85	3·00
104		2f.25 blue	2·00	3·25
105		2f.50 brown	2·00	3·00
106		3f. green	75	3·50
107		5f. red	2·00	3·25
108		10f. purple	1·25	4·00
109		20f. red	1·50	3·25

27 Rene Caillie (explorer)

1939. Death Centenary of Caillie.

110	27	90c. orange	30	2·75
111		2f. violet	40	2·00
112		2f.25 blue	50	3·50

28

1939. New York World's Fair.

113	28	1f.25 red	1·00	3·25
114		2f.25 blue	1·10	3·25

29 Storming the Bastille

1939. 150th Anniv of French Revolution.

115	29	45c.+25c. green and black	7·75	13·00
116		70c.+30c. brown and black	7·75	13·00
117		90c.+35c. orange and black	7·75	13·00
118		1f.25+1f. red and black	8·00	13·00
119		2f.25+2f. blue and black	7·75	13·00

30 Twin-engine Airliner over Jungle

1940. Air.

120	30	1f.90 blue	85	2·75
121		2f.90 red	35	3·25
122		4f.50 green	45	3·00
123		4f.90 olive	1·25	2·25
124		6f.90 orange	80	2·75

1941. National Defence Fund. Surch **SECOURS NATIONAL** and value.

124a	+1f. on 50c. (No. 89)	4·75	4·75
124b	+2f. on 80c. (No. 94)	8·50	9·50
124c	+2f. on 1f.50 (No. 100)	8·25	9·50
124d	+3f. on 2f. (No. 103)	8·50	9·50

31a Ox Caravan

1942. Marshal Petain issue.

124e	31a	1f. green	60	4·00
124f		2f.50 blue	15	4·00

1942. Air. Colonial Child Welfare Fund. As Nos. 98g/i of Niger.

124g	1f.50+3f.50 green	15	3·25
124h	2f.+6f. brown	15	3·25
124i	3f.+9f. red	15	3·25

1942. Air. Imperial Fortnight. As No. 98j of Niger.

124j	1f.20+1f.80 blue and red	50	3·25

32 Twin-engine Airliner over Camel Caravan

1942. Air. T **32** inscr "MAURITANIE" at foot.

124k	32	50f. orange and yellow	2·00	3·50

1944. Surch.

125	25	3f.50 on 65c. green	10	15
126		4f. on 65c. green	15	35
127		5f. on 65c. green	20	65
128		10f. on 65c. green	25	40
129	27	15f. on 90c. orange	75	1·25

ISLAMIC REPUBLIC

35 Flag of Republic **37** Well

38 Slender-billed Gull

1960. Inauguration of Islamic Republic.

130	35	25f. bistre, grn & brn on rose	2·00	2·00

1960. 10th Anniv of African Technical Co-operation Commission. As T **4** of Malagasy Republic.

131	25f. blue and turquoise	2·00	2·00

1960.

132	37	50c. purple & brn (postage)	10	10
133	–	1f. bistre, brown and green	10	10
134	–	2f. brown, green and blue	15	10
135	–	3f. red, sepia and turquoise	20	20
136	–	4f. buff and green	20	20
137	–	5f. chocolate, brown and red	15	10
138	–	10f. blue, black and brown	20	15
139	–	15f. multicoloured	40	15
140	–	20f. brown and green	30	15
141	–	25f. blue and green	50	15
142	–	30f. blue, violet and bistre	50	15
143	–	50f. brown and green	80	40
144	–	60f. purple, red and green	1·25	40
145	–	85f. brown, sepia and blue	3·50	1·50
146	–	100f. brn, choc & bl (air)	6·75	2·40
147	–	200f. myrtle, brown & sepia	14·00	4·25
148	38	500f. sepia, blue and brown	32·00	8·75

DESIGNS—VERT: (As Type **37**) 2f. Harvesting dates; 5f. Harvesting millet; 25, 30f. Seated dance; 50f. "Telmidi" (symbolic figure); 60f. Metalsmith; 85f. Scimitar oryx; 100f. Greater flamingo; 200f. African spoonbill. HORIZ: 3f. Barbary sheep; 4f. Fennec foxes; 10f. Cordwainer; 15f. Fishing-boat; 20f. Nomad school.

39 Flag and Map **43** Campaign Emblem

42 European, African and Boeing 707 Airliners

1960. Proclamation of Independence.

149	39	25f. green, brown & chest	50	50

1962. Air. Air Afrique Airline.

150	42	100f. green, brown & bistre	1·75	1·10

1962. Malaria Eradication.

151	43	25f.+5f. olive	50	50

44 U.N. Headquarters and View of Nouakchott

1962. Admission to U.N.O.

152	44	15f. brown, black and blue	20	20
153		25f. brown, myrtle and blue	35	35
154		85f. brown, purple and blue	1·00	1·00

45 Union Flag

1962. 1st Anniv of Union of African and Malagasy States.

155	45	30f. blue	45	45

46 Eagle and Crescent over Nouakchott

1962. 8th Endemic Diseases Eradication Conference, Nouakchott.

156	46	30f. green, brown and blue	45	35

47 Diesel Mineral Train

1962.

157	47	50f. multicoloured	3·75	1·25

1962. Air. 1st Anniv of Admission to U.N.O. As T **44** but views from different angles and inscr "1 er ANNIVERSAIRE 27 OCTOBRE 1962".

158	100f. blue, brown & turquoise	1·10	90

49 Map and Agriculture

1962. 2nd Anniv of Independence.

159	49	30f. green and purple	45	30

50 Congress Representatives

1962. 1st Anniv of Unity Congress.

160	50	25f. brown, myrtle and blue	45	40

51 Globe and Emblem

1962. Freedom from Hunger.

161	51	25f.+5f. blue, brown & pur	55	55

52 Douglas DC-3 Airliner over Nouakchott Airport

1963. Air. Creation of National Airline.

162	52	500f. myrtle, brown & blue	12·00	4·50

53 Open-cast Mining, Zouerate

1963. Air. Mining Development. Multicoloured.

163	100f. Type **53**	2·50	60
164	200f. Port-Etienne	5·25	2·50

54 Striped Hyena **56** "Posts and Telecommunications"

1963. Animals.

165	54	50c. black, brown & myrtle	10	10
166	–	1f. black, blue and buff	10	10
167	–	1f.50 brown, olive & pur	20	15
168	–	2f. purple, green and red	15	15
169	–	5f. bistre, blue and ochre	25	20
170	–	10f. black and ochre	50	20
171	–	15f. purple and blue	50	20
172	–	20f. bistre, purple and blue	60	20
173	–	25f. ochre, brown & turq	85	25
174	–	30f. bistre, brown and blue	1·50	30

175 – 50f. bistre, brown and green . . . . 2·00 60
176 – 60f. bistre, brown & turq 2·50 90
ANIMALS—HORIZ: 1f. Spotted hyena; 2f. Guinea baboons; 10f. Leopard; 15f. Bongos; 20f. Aardvark; 30f. North African crested porcupine; 60f. Chameleon. VERT: 1f.50, Cheetah; 5f. Dromedaries; 25f. Patas monkeys; 50f. Dorcas gazelle.

1963. Air. African and Malagasy Posts and Telecommunications Union.
177 **56** 85f. multicoloured . . . . 1·00 65

57 "Telstar" Satellite

1963. Air. Space Telecommunications.
178 **57** 50f. brown, purple & green 65 45
179 – 100f. blue, brown and red 1·25 80
180 – 150f. turquoise and brown 2·25 1·50
DESIGNS: 100f. "Syncom" satellite; 150f. "Relay" satellite.

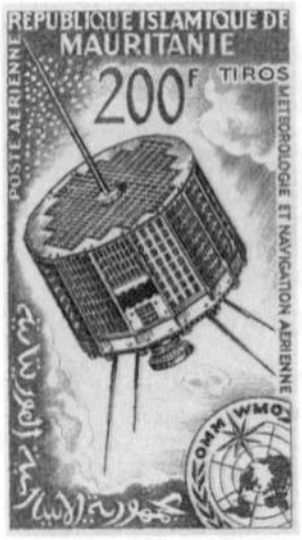

58 "Tiros" Satellite **60** U.N. Emblem, Sun and Birds

59 Airline Emblem

1963. Air. World Meteorological Day.
181 **58** 200f. brown, blue and green . . . . 3·50 1·75

1963. Air. 1st Anniv of "Air Afrique" and DC-8 Service Inauguration.
182 **59** 25f. multicoloured 50 25

1963. Air. 15th Anniv of Declaration of Human Rights.
183 **60** 100f. blue, violet and purple . . . . 1·25 85

61 Cogwheels and Wheat **62** Lichtenstein's Sandgrouse

1964. Air. European-African Economic Convention.
184 **61** 50f. multicoloured . . . . 1·10 70

1964. Air. Birds.
185 **62** 100f. ochre, brown & green 8·50 1·00
186 – 200f. black, brown and blue . . . . 12·00 2·50
187 – 500f. slate, red and green 29·00 7·00
DESIGNS: 200f. Reed cormorant; 500f. Dark chanting goshawk.

63 Temple, Philae

1964. Air. Nubian Monuments Preservation.
188 **63** 10f. brown, black and blue 45 30
189 25f. slate, brown and blue 70 60
190 60f. chocolate, brown & bl 1·50 1·10

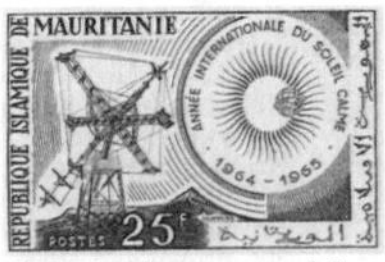

64 W.M.O. Emblem. Sun and Lightning **65** Radar Antennae and Sun Emblem

1964. World Meteorological Day.
191 **64** 85f. blue, orange and brown . . . . 1·25 80

1964. International Quiet Sun Years.
192 **65** 25f. red, green and blue . . 35 25

66 Bowl depicting Horse-racing

1964. Air. Olympic Games, Tokyo.
193 **66** 15f. brown and bistre . . . 30 25
194 – 50f. brown and blue . . . 60 50
195 – 85f. brown and red . . . . 1·10 1·00
196 – 100f. brown and green . . 1·50 1·25
DESIGNS—VERT: 50f. Running (vase); 85f. Wrestling (vase). HORIZ: 100f. Chariot-racing (bowl).

67 Flat-headed Grey Mullet

1964. Marine Fauna.
197 **67** 1f. green, blue and brown 25 15
198 – 5f. purple, green and brown 40 15
199 – 10f. green, ochre and blue 50 20
200 – 60f. slate, green and brown 3·50 1·10
DESIGNS—VERT: 5f. Lobster ("Panulirus mauritanicus"); 10f. Lobster ("Panulirus regius"). HORIZ: 60f. Meagre.

68 "Co-operation" **69** Pres. Kennedy

1964. French, African and Malagasy Co-operation.
201 **68** 25f. brown, green & mauve 40 30

1964. Air. 1st Death Anniv of Pres. Kennedy.
202 **69** 100f. multicoloured . . . . 1·75 1·00

70 "Nymphaea lotus"

1965. Mauritanian Flowers.
203 **70** 5f. green, red and blue . . 25 15
204 – 10f. green, ochre and purple 40 15
205 – 20f. brown, red and sepia 60 20
206 – 45f. turquoise, purple & grn . . . . 1·25 60
FLOWERS—VERT: 10f. "Acacia gommier"; 45f. "Caralluma retrospiciens". HORIZ: 20f. "Adenium obesum".

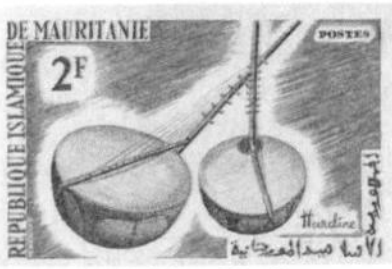

71 "Hardine" **72** Abraham Lincoln

1965. Musical Instruments and Musicians.
207 **71** 2f. brown, bistre and blue 25 15
208 – 8f. brown, bistre and red 50 15
209 – 25f. brown, black and green 85 20
210 – 40f. black, blue and violet 1·10 35
DESIGNS: 8f. "Tobol" (drums); 25f. "Tidinit" ("Violins"); 40f. Native band.

1965. Death Centenary of Abraham Lincoln.
211 **72** 50f. multicoloured 70 35

73 Early Telegraph and Relay Satellite

1965. Air. Centenary of I.T.U.
212 **73** 250f. green, mauve and blue . . . . 4·25 3·25

74 Palms in the Adrar

1965. "Tourism and Archaeology" (1st series).
213 **74** 1f. green, brown and blue 10 10
214 – 4f. brown, red and blue . . 15 10
215 – 15f. multicoloured 30 20
216 – 60f. sepia, brown and green 90 45
DESIGNS—VERT: 4f. Chinguetti Mosque. HORIZ: 15f. Clay-pits; 60f. Carved doorway, Qualata.
See also Nos. 255/8.

75 "Attack on Cancer" (the Crab)

1965. Air. Campaign against Cancer.
217 **75** 100f. red, blue and ochre 1·50 60

76 Wooden Tea Service

1965. Native Handicrafts.
218 **76** 3f. brown, ochre and slate 15 15
219 – 7f. purple, orange and blue 20 20
220 – 25f. brown, black and red 35 20
221 – 50f. red, green and orange 75 35
DESIGNS—VERT: 7f. Snuff-box and pipe; 25f. Damasquine dagger. HORIZ: 50f. Mederdra chest.

77 Nouakchott Wharf **78** Sir Winston Churchill

1965. Mauritanian Development.
222 – 5f. green and brown . . . 1·75 90
223 **77** 10f. red, turquoise and blue 15 10
224 – 30f. red, brown and purple 3·50 1·10
225 – 85f. violet, lake and blue 1·25 55
DESIGNS—VERT: 5f., 30f. Choum Tunnel. HORIZ: 85f. Nouakchott Hospital.

1965. Air. Churchill Commem.
226 **78** 200f. multicoloured . . . . 2·50 1·25

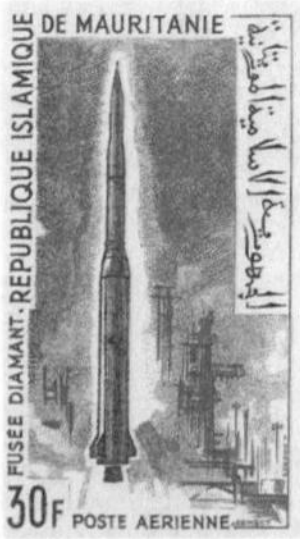

79 Rocket "Diamant"

1966. Air. French Satellites.
227 **79** 30f. green, red and blue . . 50 25
228 – 60f. purple, blue & turquoise . . . . 1·00 45
229 – 90f. lake, violet and blue 1·50 75
DESIGNS—HORIZ: 60f. Satellite "A 1" and Globe; 90f. Rocket "Scout" and satellite "FR 1".

80 Dr. Schweitzer and Hospital Scene

1966. Air. Schweitzer Commem.
230 **80** 50f. multicoloured . . . . 1·10 50

81 Stafford, Schirra and "Gemini 6"

1966. Air. Space Flights. Multicoloured.
231 50f. Type **81** 60 25
232 100f. Borman, Lovell and "Gemini 7" . . . . 1·25 60
233 200f. Beliaiev, Leonov and "Voskhod 2" . . . . . . 2·50 1·25

82 African Woman and Carved Head

1966. World Festival of Negro Arts, Dakar.
234 **82** 10f. black, brown and green 20 10
235 – 30f. purple, black and blue 35 20
236 – 60f. purple, red and orange 75 45
DESIGNS: 30f. Dancers and hands playing cornet; 60f. Cine-camera and village huts.

83 "Dove" over Map of Africa **84** Satellite "D 1"

1966. Air. Organization of African Unity (O.A.U.).
237 **83** 100f. multicoloured . . . . 1·00 50

1966. Air. Launching of Satellite "D 1".
238 **84** 100f. plum, brown and blue . . . . 1·10 75

85 Breguet 14T2 Salon

1966. Air. Early Aircraft.
239 **85** 50f. indigo, blue and bistre . . 1·00 25
240 – 100f. green, purple and blue . . . . 2·00 50
241 – 150f. turquoise, brown & bl . . . . 3·00 75
242 – 200f. indigo, blue & purple 4·00 1·25
AIRCRAFT: 100f. Farman Goliath; 150f. Couzinet "Arc en Ciel"; 200f. Latecoere 28-3 seaplane "Comte de la Vaulx".

86 "Acacia ehrenbergiana"

1966. Mauritanian Flowers. Multicoloured.
243 10f. Type **86** 25 15
244 15f. "Schouwia purpurea" . . 50 15
245 20f. "Ipomaea asarifolia" . . 65 20
246 25f. "Grewia bicolor" 75 25
247 30f. "Pancratium trianthum" 1·10 25
248 60f. "Blepharis linariifolia" 1·75 55

87 DC-8F and "Air Afrique" Emblem

1966. Air. Inauguration of Douglas DC-8F Air Services.
249 **87** 30f. grey, black and red . . 75 15

88 "Raft of the Medusa" (after Gericault)

1966. Air. 150th Anniv of Shipwreck of the "Medusa".
250 **88** 500f. multicoloured . . . . 9·00 6·50

89 "Myrina silenus"

90 "Hunting" (petroglyph from Tenses, Adrar)

1966. Butterflies. Multicoloured.
251 5f. Type **89** 50 20
252 30f. "Colotis danae" . . . . 1·25 40
253 45f. "Hypolimnas misippus" 2·00 60
254 60f. "Danaus chrysippus" . . 2·75 85

1966. Tourism and Archaeology (2nd series).
255 **90** 2f. chestnut and brown . . 15 15
256 – 3f. brown and blue 20 20
257 – 30f. green and red 55 25
258 – 50f. brown, green & purple 1·25 80
DESIGNS: 3f. "Fighting" (petroglyph from Tenses, Adrar); 30f. Copper jug (from Le Meyer, Adrar); 50f. Camel and caravan.

91 Cogwheels and Ears of Wheat

1966. Air. Europafrique.
259 **91** 50f. multicoloured 70 40

92 UNESCO Emblem

1966. 20th Anniv of UNESCO.
260 **92** 30f. multicoloured 45 20

93 Olympic Village, Grenoble

1967. Publicity for Olympic Games (1968).
261 – 20f. brown, blue and green 30 20
262 **93** 30f. brown, green and blue 40 30
263 – 40f. brown, purple and blue 60 40
264 – 100f. brown, green & black 1·10 70
DESIGNS—VERT: 20f. Old and new buildings, Mexico City; 40f. Ice rink, Grenoble and Olympic torch. HORIZ: 100f. Olympic stadium, Mexico City.

94 South African Crowned Crane

95 Globe, Rockets and Eye

1967. Air. Birds. Multicoloured.
265 100f. Type **94** . . . . 3·75 1·10
266 200f. Great egret . . . . . . 8·00 1·50
267 500f. Ostrich . . . . 18·00 5·25

1967. Air. World Fair, Montreal.
268 **95** 250f. brown, blue and black . . . . 2·25 1·25

96 Prosopis

97 Jamboree Emblem and Scout Kit

1967. Trees.
269 **96** 10f. green, blue and brown 20 10
270 – 15f. green, blue and purple 25 15
271 – 20f. green, purple and blue 30 15
272 – 25f. brown and green . . . 40 20
273 – 30f. brown, green and red 55 25
TREES: 15f. Jujube; 20f. Date palm; 25f. Peltophorum; 30f. Baobab.

1967. World Scout Jamboree, Idaho.
274 **97** 60f. blue, green and brown 85 35
275 – 90f. blue, green and red . . 1·40 50
DESIGN—HORIZ: 90f. Jamboree emblem and scouts.

98 Weaving

99 Atomic Symbol

1967. Advancement of Mauritanian Women.
276 **98** 5f. red, black and violet . . 15 10
277 – 10f. black, violet and green 20 10
278 – 20f. black, purple and blue 35 15
279 – 30f. blue, black and brown 45 25
280 – 50f. black, violet and indigo 70 30

DESIGNS—VERT: 10f. Needlework; 30f. Laundering. HORIZ: 20f. Nursing; 50f. Sewing (with machines).

1967. Air. International Atomic Energy Agency.
281 **99** 200f. blue, green and red 2·25 1·10

100 Cattle

1967. Campaign for Prevention of Cattle Plague.
282 **100** 30f. red, blue and green 35 25

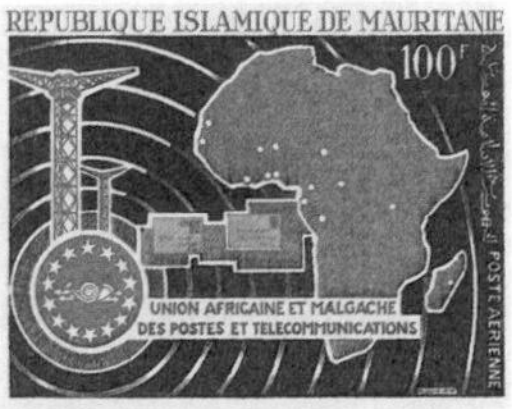

101 Map of Africa, Letters and Pylons

1967. Air. 5th Anniv of U.A.M.P.T.
283 **101** 100f. green, brown & pur 1·00 60

102 "Francois of Rimini" (Ingres)

103 Currency Tokens

1967. Air. Death Centenary of Jean Ingres (painter). Multicoloured.
284 90f. Type **102** . . . . 1·25 60
285 200f. "Ingres in his Studio" (Alaux) . . . . 2·50 1·25
See also Nos. 306/8.

1967. 5th Anniv of West African Monetary Union.
286 **103** 30f. grey and orange . . . 35 15

104 "Hyphaene thebaica"

105 Human Rights Emblem

1967. Mauritanian Fruits.
287 **104** 1f. brown, green & purple 15 10
288 – 2f. yellow, green & brown 15 10
289 – 3f. olive, green and violet 15 10
290 – 4f. red, green and brown 15 10
291 – 5f. orange, brown & green 20 10
FRUITS—HORIZ: 2f. "Balanites aegyptiaca"; 4f. "Ziziphus lotus". VERT: 3f. "Adansonia digitata"; 5f. "Phoenix dactylifera".

1968. Human Rights Year.
292 **105** 30f. yellow, green & black 30 20
293 50f. yellow, brown & black 55 35

106 Chancellor Adenauer

108 Mosque, Nouakchott

107 Skiing

1968. Air. Adenauer Commemoration.
294 **106** 100f. sepia, brown & blue 1·25 60

1968. Air. Olympic Games, Grenoble and Mexico.
296 **107** 20f. purple, indigo & blue 30 10
297 – 30f. brown, green & plum 35 15
298 – 50f. green, blue and ochre 55 25
299 – 100f. green, red and brown . . . . 1·00 50
DESIGNS—VERT: 30f. Horse-vaulting; 50f. Ski-jumping. HORIZ: 100f. Hurdling.

1968. Tourism. Multicoloured.
300 30f. Type **108** 25 20
301 45f. Amogjar Pass 35 20
302 90f. Cavaliers' Tower, Boutilimit 65 35

109 Man and W.H.O. Emblem

1968. Air. 20th Anniv of W.H.O.
303 **109** 150f. blue, purple & brown . . . . 1·50 75

110 UNESCO Emblem and "Movement of Water"

1968. International Hydrological Decade.
304 **110** 90f. green and lake . . . 70 40

111 U.P.U. Building, Berne

1968. Admission of Mauritania to U.P.U.
305 **111** 30f. brown and red . . . 35 20

1968. Air. Paintings by Ingres. As T **102**. Mult.
306 100f. "Man's Torso" . . . . 1·10 65
307 150f. "The Iliad" . . . . . . 1·75 95
308 250f. "The Odyssey" . . . . 2·75 1·60

112 Land-yachts crossing Desert

113 Dr. Martin Luther King

1968. Land-yacht Racing.
309 **112** 30f. blue, yellow & orange 45 25
310 – 40f. purple, blue & orange 55 30
311 – 60f. green, yellow & orange 85 50
DESIGNS—HORIZ: 40f. Racing on shore. VERT: 60f. Crew making repairs.

1968. Air. "Apostles of Peace".
312 **113** 50f. brown, blue and olive 1·00 40
313 – 50f. brown and blue . . . 60 25
DESIGN: No. 313, Mahatma Gandhi.

113a "Surprise Letter" (C. A. Coypel) **114** Donkey and Foal

1968. Air. "Philexafrique" Stamp Exn, Abidjan, Ivory Coast (1969) (1st issue).
315 **113a** 100f. multicoloured . . . 1·75 1·75

1968. Domestic Animals. Multicoloured.
316 5f. Type **114** 15 10
317 10f. Ewe and lamb 20 15
318 15f. Dromedary and calf . . 25 15
319 30f. Mare and foal 45 25
320 50f. Cow and calf 70 35
321 90f. Goat and kid . . . . . 1·40 50

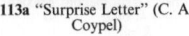

114a Forest Scene and Stamp of 1938

1969. Air. "Philexafrique" Stamp Exhibition, Abidjan, Ivory Coast (2nd issue).
322 **114a** 50f. purple, green & brown . . . . 1·10 1·10

114b "Napoleon at Council of Five Hundred" (Bouchot) **115** Map and I.L.O. Emblem

1969. Air. Birth Bicentenary of Napoleon Bonaparte. Multicoloured.
323 50f. **114b** . . . . 1·50 90
324 90f. "Napoleon's Installation by the Council of State" (Conder) . . . . 2·00 1·25
325 250f. "The Farewell of Fontainebleau" (Vernet) . . 5·00 3·25

1969. 50th Anniv of I.L.O.
326 **115** 50f. multicoloured 50 25

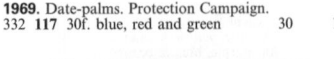

116 Monitor Lizard **117** Date Palm, "Parlatoria blanchardi" and "Pharoscymus anchorage"

1969. Reptiles. Multicoloured.
327 5f. Type **116** 35 20
328 10f. Horned viper 55 30
329 30f. Black-collared cobra . . 1·25 35
330 60f. Rock python . . . . . 2·00 1·10
331 85f. Nile crocodile . . . . . 3·00 1·40

1969. Date-palms. Protection Campaign.
332 **117** 30f. blue, red and green 30 15

118 Camel and Emblem

1969. Air. African Tourist Year.
333 **118** 50f. purple, blue & orange 85 35

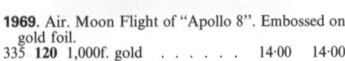

119 Dancers and Baalbek Columns

1969. Baalbek Festival, Lebanon.
334 **119** 100f. brown, red and blue 1·50 55

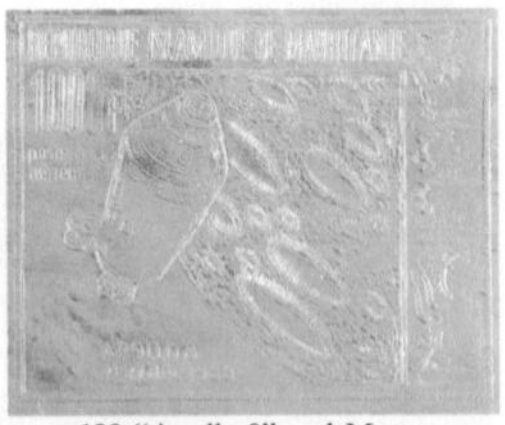

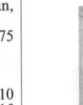

120 "Apollo 8" and Moon

1969. Air. Moon Flight of "Apollo 8". Embossed on gold foil.
335 **120** 1,000f. gold . . . . . . 14·00 14·00

121 Wolde (marathon) **122a** Bank Emblem

122 London-Istanbul Route-Map

1969. Air. Gold Medal Winners, Mexico Olympic Games.
336 **121** 30f. red, brown and blue 25 15
337 – 70f. red, brown and green 50 30
338 – 150f. green, bistre and red 1·25 70
DESIGNS: 70f. Beamon (athletics); 150f. Vera Caslavska (gymnastics).

1969. Air. London–Sydney Motor Rally.
339 **122** 10f. brown, blue & purple 25 10
340 – 20f. brown, blue & purple 50 15
341 – 50f. brown, blue & purple 85 25
342 – 70f. brown, blue & purple 1·10 30
ROUTE—MAPS: 20f. Ankara–Teheran; 50f. Kandahar–Bombay; 70f. Perth–Sydney.

1969. 5th Anniv of African Development Bank. Multicoloured.
344 **122a** 30f. brown, green & blue 30 15

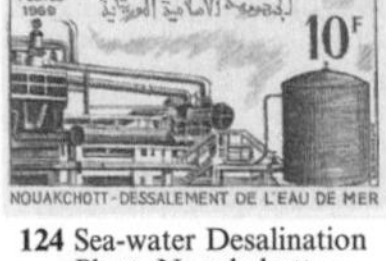

123 Pendant **124** Sea-water Desalination Plant, Nouakchott

1969. Native Handicrafts.
345 **123** 10f. brown and purple . . 20 15
346 – 20f. red, black and blue 40 20
DESIGN—HORIZ: 20f. Rahla headdress.

1969. Economic Development.
347 **124** 10f. blue, purple and red 20 15
348 – 15f. black, lake and blue 25 15
349 – 30f. black, purple and blue 30 20
DESIGNS: 15f. Fishing quay, Nouadhibou; 30f. Meat-processing plant, Kaedi.

125 Lenin **126** "Sternocera interrupta"

1970. Birth Centenary of Lenin.
350 **125** 30f. black, red and blue 30 20

1970. Insects.
351 **126** 5f. black, buff and brown 25 15
352 – 10f. brown, yellow & lake 35 15
353 – 20f. olive, purple & brown 50 25
354 – 30f. violet, green & brown 80 45
355 – 40f. brown, blue and lake 1·50 70
INSECTS: 10f. "Anoplocnemis curvipes"; 20f. "Julodis aequinoctialis"; 30f. "Thermophilum sexmaculatum marginatum"; 40f. "Plocaederus denticornis".

127 Footballers and Hemispheres **128** Japanese Musician, Emblem and Map on Palette

1970. World Cup Football Championship, Mexico.
356 **127** 25f. multicoloured 30 20
357 – 30f. multicoloured 35 20
358 – 70f. multicoloured 70 30
359 – 150f. multicoloured . . . 1·60 75
DESIGNS: 30, 70, 150f. As Type **127**, but with different players.

1970. New U.P.U. Headquarters Building. As T **81** of New Caledonia.
360 30f. red, brown and green . . 35 20

1970. Air. "EXPO 70" World Fair, Osaka, Japan. Multicoloured.
361 50f. Type **128** 50 20
362 75f. Japanese fan 75 35
363 150f. Stylised bird, map and boat . . . . 1·40 80

129 U.N. Emblem and Examples of Progress

1970. Air. 25th Anniv of U.N.O.
364 **129** 100f. green, brown & blue 1·25 60

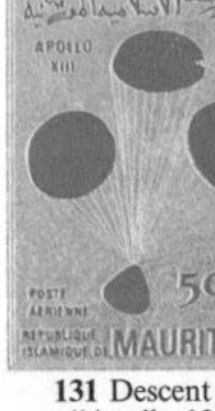

130 Vladimir Komarov **131** Descent of "Apollo 13"

1970. Air. "Lost Heroes of Space" (1st series).
365 **130** 150f. brown, orge & slate 1·50 70
366 – 150f. brown, blue and slate . . . . 1·50 70
367 – 150f. brown, orge & slate 1·50 70
HEROES: No. 366, Elliott See; 367, Yuri Gagarin. See also Nos. 376/8.

1970. Air. Space Flight of "Apollo 13".
369 **131** 500f. red, blue and gold 5·00 5·00

132 Woman in Traditional Costume **133** Arms and State House

1970. Traditional Costumes. As T **132**.
370 **132** 10f. orange and brown . . 20 15
371 – 30f. blue, red and brown 40 20
372 – 40f. brown, purple and red 50 30
373 – 50f. blue and brown . . . 70 35
374 – 70f. brown, choc & bl . . 90 45

1970. Air. 10th Anniv of Independence.
375 **133** 100f. multicoloured . . . 1·00 45

1970. Air. "Lost Heroes of Space" (2nd series). As T **130**.
376 150f. brown, blue & turquoise 1·50 70
377 150f. brown, blue & turquoise 1·50 70
378 150f. brown, blue and orange 1·50 70
HEROES: No. 376, Roger Chaffee; No. 377, Virgil Grissom; No. 378, Edward White.

134 Greek Wrestling

1971. Air. "Pre-Olympics Year".
380 **134** 100f. brown, purple & blue . . . . 1·10 75

135 People of Different Races

1971. Racial Equality Year.
381 **135** 30f. plum, blue and brown 30 15
382 – 40f. black, red and blue 35 20
DESIGN—VERT: 40f. European and African hands.

136 Pres. Nasser

1971. Air. Pres. Gamal Nasser of Egypt Commemoration.
383 **136** 100f. multicoloured . . . 85 40

137 Gen. De Gaulle in Uniform

1971. De Gaulle Commem. Multicoloured.
384 40f. Type **137** . . . . 1·25 60
385 100f. De Gaulle as President of France . . . . 2·75 1·40

138 Scout Badge, Scout and Map

1971. Air. 13th World Scout Jamboree, Asagiri, Japan.
387 **138** 35f. multicoloured 40 20
388 40f. multicoloured 50 20
389 100f. multicoloured . . . 1·25 45

139 Diesel Locomotive

1971. Miferma Iron-ore Mines. Multicoloured.
390 35f. Iron ore train . . . . . 2·25 1·00
391 100f. Type **139** . . . . . . 5·00 2·50
Nos. 390/1 were issued together, se-tenent, forming a composite design.

139a Headquarters, Brazzaville, and Ardin Musicians

1971. Air. 10th Anniv of African and Malagasy Posts and Telecommunications Union.
392 **139a** 100f. multicoloured . . . 1·10 60

140 A.P.U. Emblem and Airmail Envelope

1971. Air. 10th Anniv of African Postal Union.
393 **140** 35f. multicoloured 40 25

141 UNICEF Emblem and Child

1971. 25th Anniv of UNICEF.
394 **141** 35f. black, brown and blue 35 20

142 "Moslem King" (c. 1218)

1972. Air. Moslem Miniatures. Multicoloured.
395 35f. Type **142** 45 20
396 40f. "Enthroned Prince" (Egypt, c. 1334) 60 25
397 100f. "Pilgrims' Caravan" (Maquamat, Baghdad, 1237) . . . . 1·50 70

1972. Air. UNESCO "Save Venice" Campaign. As T **127** of Mali. Multicoloured.
398 45f. "Quay and Ducal Palace" (Carlevaris) (vert) 60 25
399 100f. "Grand Canal" (Canaletto) . . . . 1·40 60
400 250f. "Santa Maria della Salute" (Canaletto) . . . . 3·00 1·50

143 Hurdling

1972. Air. Olympic Games, Munich.
401 **143** 75f. purple, orange & grn 55 30
402 100f. purple, blue & brn 75 40
403 200f. purple, lake & green 1·60 70

144 Nurse tending Baby

1972. Mauritanian Red Crescent Fund.
405 **144** 35f.+5f. multicoloured . . 60 60

145 Samuel Morse and Morse Key

1972. World Telecommunications Day. Mult.
406 35f. Type **145** 35 20
407 40f. "Relay" satellite and hemispheres 45 20
408 75f. Alexander Graham Bell and early telephone 70 35

146 Spirifer Shell

1972. Fossil Shells. Multicoloured.
409 25f. Type **146** . . . . 1·00 35
410 75f. Trilobite . . . . 2·75 1·10

147 "Luna 16" and Moon Probe

151 Mediterranean Monk Seal with Young

149 Africans and 500f. Coin

1972. Air. Russian Exploration of the Moon.
411 **147** 75f. brown, blue and green 60 30
412 – 100f. brown, grey & violet 90 50
DESIGN—HORIZ: 100f. "Lunokhod 1".

1972. Air. Gold Medal Winners, Munich. Nos. 401/3 optd as listed below.
413 **143** 75f. purple, orange & grn 60 30
414 100f. purple, blue & brn 80 50
415 200f. purple, lake & green 1·60 1·00
OVERPRINTS: 75f. **110m. HAIES MILBURN MEDAILLE D'OR**; 100f. **400m. HAIES AKII-BUA MEDAILLE D'OR**; 200f. **3,000m. STEEPLE KEINO MEDAILLE D'OR**.

1972. 10th Anniv of West African Monetary Union.
416 **149** 35f. grey, brown and green 30 20

1973. Air. Moon Flight of "Apollo 17". No. 267 surch **Apollo XVII Decembre 1972** and value.
417 250f. on 500f. multicoloured 4·00 2·00

1973. Seals. Multicoloured.
418 40f. Type **151** (postage) . . . 1·50 50
419 135f. Head of Mediterranean monk seal (air) . . . . . 3·00 1·60

152 "Lion and Crocodile" (Delacroix)

1973. Air. Paintings by Delacroix. Mult.
420 100f. Type **152** . . . . . . 1·50 75
421 250f. "Lion attacking Forest Hog" . . . . 3·25 2·00

153 "Horns of Plenty"

1973. 10th Anniv of World Food Programme.
422 **153** 35f. multicoloured 30 20

154 U.P.U. Monument, Berne, and Globe

1973. World U.P.U. Day.
423 **154** 100f. blue, orange & green 1·00 65

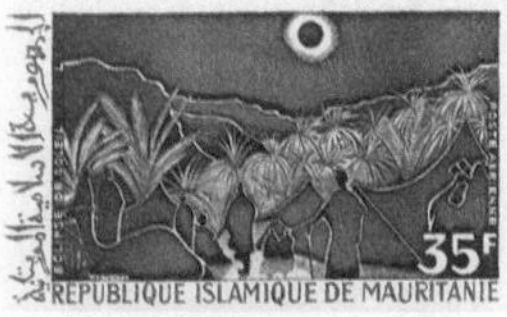

155 Nomad Encampment and Eclipse

1973. Total Eclipse of the Sun.
424 **155** 35f. purple and green . . 35 20
425 – 40f. purple, red and blue 45 20
426 – 140f. purple and red . . . 1·60 75
DESIGNS—VERT: 40f. Rocket and Concorde. HORIZ: 140f. Observation team.

1973. "Drought Relief". African Solidarity. No. 320 surch **SECHERESSE SOLIDARITE AFRICAINE** and value.
428 20um. on 50f. multicoloured 65 45

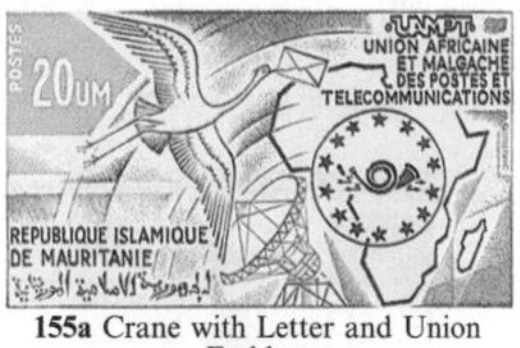

155a Crane with Letter and Union Emblem

1973. 12th Anniv of African and Malagasy Posts and Telecommunications Union.
429 **155a** 20um. brown, lt brn & orge . . . . 1·00 45

157 Detective making Arrest and Fingerprint

1973. 50th Anniv of International Criminal Police Organization (Interpol).
430 **157** 15um. violet, red & brown 1·10 45

1974. Various stamps surch with values in new currency. (a) Postage. (i) Nos. 345/6.
431 **123** 27um. on 10f. brn & pur 1·50 70
432 – 28um. on 20f. red, blk & bl . . . . 1·75 90

(ii) Nos. 351/5.
433 **126** 5um. on 5f. black, buff and brown 70 50
434 – 7um. on 10f. brown, yellow and lake 60 30
435 – 8um. on 20f. olive, purple and brown 70 35
436 – 10um. on 30f. violet, purple and brown . . . 1·00 45
437 – 20um. on 40f. brown, blue and lake . . . . 2·00 1·10

(iii) Nos. 409/10.
438 **146** 5um. on 25f. multicoloured 60 40
439 – 15um. on 75f. mult . . . 1·75 1·00

(iv) No. 418.
440 **151** 8um. on 40f. multicoloured 90 45

(b) Air. (i) Nos. 395/7.
441 **142** 7um. on 35f. mult 40 20
442 – 8um. on 40f. mult 40 20
443 – 20um. on 100f. mult . . . 1·50 70

(ii) No. 419.
444 – 27um. on 135f. mult . . . . 2·25 85

(iii) Nos. 420/1.
445 **152** 20um. on 100f. mult . . . 1·60 70
446 – 50um. on 250f. mult . . . 3·75 2·00

(iv) Nos. 424/6.
447 **155** 7um. on 35f. purple & grn 45 20
448 – 8um. on 40f. pur, red & bl 45 20
449 – 28um. on 140f. pur & red 1·90 70

159 Footballers

161 Sir Winston Churchill

160 Jules Verne and Scenes from Books

1974. Air. World Cup Football Championship, West Germany.
450 **159** 7um. multicoloured . . . 40 20
451 8um. multicoloured . . . 40 20
452 20um. multicoloured . . . 1·10 50

1974. Air. Jules Verne "Prophet of Space Travel" and "Skylab" Flights Commemoration.
454 **160** 70um. silver . . . . . . 4·50 4·50
455 – 70um. silver . . . . . . 4·50 4·50
456 **160** 250um. gold . . . . . . 12·00 12·00
457 – 250um. gold . . . . . . 12·00 12·00
DESIGNS: Nos. 455, 457, "Skylab" in Space.

1974. Air. Birth Centenary of Sir Winston Churchill.
458 **161** 40um. red and purple . . 1·75 95

162 U.P.U. Monument and Globes

1974. Centenary of U.P.U.
459 **162** 30um. red, green & dp grn . . . . 1·25 75
460 50um. red, lt blue & blue 2·00 1·25

163 5 Ouguiya Coin and Banknote

1974. 1st Anniv of Introduction of Ouguiya Currency.
461 **163** 7um. black, green and blue 35 20
462 – 8um. black, mauve and green 40 20
463 – 20um. black, blue and red 1·00 50

DESIGNS: 8um. 10 ouguiya coin and banknote; 20um. 20 ouguiya coin and banknote.

164 Lenin

166 Two Hunters

1974. Air. 50th Death Anniv of Lenin.
464 **164** 40um. green and red . . . 2·00 95

1974. Treaty of Berne Centenary. Nos. 459/60 optd **9 OCTOBRE 100 ANS D'UNION POSTALE INTERNATIONALE**.
465 **162** 30um. red, green and deep green . . . . 1·60 80
466 50um. red, light blue and blue . . . . 2·00 1·25

1975. Nos. 287/91 surch in new currency.
467 – 1um. on 5f. orange, brown and green . . . 10 10
468 – 2um. on 4f. red, green and brown 15 15
469 – 3um. on 2f. yellow, green and brown 20 15
470 **104** 10um. on 1f. brown, green and purple 60 20
471 – 12um. on 3f. olive, green and violet 75 30

1975. Rock-carvings, Zemmour.
472 **166** 4um. red and brown . . . 40 15
473 – 5um. purple 45 25
474 – 10um. blue and light blue 80 35
DESIGNS—VERT: 5um. Ostrich. HORIZ: 10um. Elephant.

167 Mauritanian Women

1975. Air. International Women's Year.
475 **167** 12um. purple, brown & bl 50 25
476 – 40um. purple, brown & bl 1·75 85
DESIGNS: 40um. Head of Mauritanian woman.

168 Combined European and African Heads

169 Dr. Schweitzer

1975. Europafrique.
477 **168** 40um. brown, red & bistre 1·60 95

1975. Birth Centenary of Dr. Albert Schweitzer.
478 **169** 60um. olive, brown & green . . . . 2·50 1·50

1975. Pan-African Drought Relief. Nos. 301/2 surch **SECHERESSE SOLIDARITE AFRICAINE** and value.
479 15um. on 45f. multicoloured 1·00 50
480 25um. on 90f. multicoloured 1·40 75

171 Akoujt Plant and Man with Camel

172 Fair Emblem

1975. Mining Industry.
481 **171** 10um. brown, blue & orge 1·25 30
482 – 12um. blue, red and brown . . . . 1·50 40
DESIGN: 12um. Mining operations.

1975. Nouakchott National Fair.
483 **172** 10um. multicoloured . . . 40 25

173 Throwing the Javelin

1975. Air. "Pre-Olympic Year". Olympic Games, Montreal (1976).
484 **173** 50um. red, green & brown 1·60 1·40
485 – 52um. blue, brown and red . . . . 1·75 1·40
DESIGN: 52um. Running.

174 Commemorative Medal

1975. 15th Anniv of Independence. Multicoloured.
486 10um. Type **174** 50 30
487 12um. Map of Mauritania . . 1·60 60

175 "Soyuz" Cosmonauts Leonov and Kubasov

1975. "Apollo–Soyuz" Space Link. Multicoloured.
488 8um. Type **175** (postage) . . 45 20
489 10um. "Soyuz" on launch-pad 55 25
490 20um. "Apollo" on launch-pad (air) 70 45
491 50um. Cosmonauts meeting astronauts . . . . 2·00 1·00
492 60um. Parachute splashdown 2·25 1·25

176 Foot-soldier of Lauzun's Legion

1976. Bicentenary of American Independence. Mult.
494 8um. Type **176** (postage) . . 60 20
495 10um. "Green Mountain" infantryman 70 20
496 20um. Lauzun Hussars officer (air) 90 40
497 50um. Artillery officer of 3rd Continental Regiment . . . 2·40 1·00
498 60um. Grenadier of Gatinais' Regiment . . . . 3·00 1·25

1976. 10th Anniv of Arab Labour Charter. No. 408 surch **10e ANNIVERSAIRE DE LA CHARTE ARABE DU TRAVAIL** in French and Arabic.
500 12um. on 75f. blue, blk & grn 55 30

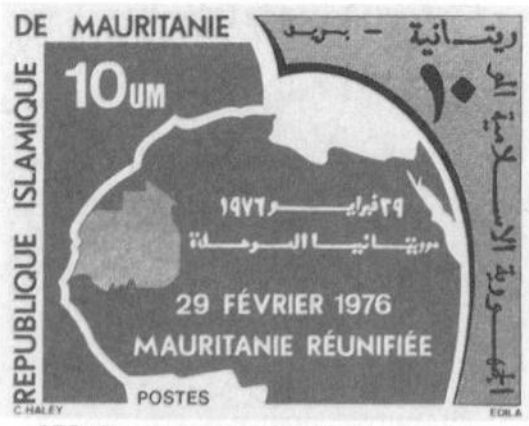

178 Commemorative Text on Map

1976. Reunification of Mauritania.
501 **178** 10um. green, lilac and deep green 45 30

181 Running

1976. Air. Olympic Games, Montreal.
514 **181** 10um. brown, green and violet 40 25
515 – 12um. brown, green and violet 50 35
516 – 52um. brown, green and violet . . . . 1·75 1·25
DESIGNS: 12um. Vaulting (gymnastics); 52um. Fencing.

182 LZ-4 at Friedrichshafen

1976. 75th Anniv of Zeppelin Airship. Mult.
517 5um. Type **182** (postage) . . 25 15
518 10um. "Schwaben" over German Landscape 40 20
519 12um. "Hansa" over Heligoland 50 25
520 20um. "Bodensee" and Doctor H. Durr . . . . . 1·10 50
521 50um. "Graf Zeppelin" over Capitol, Washington (air) 2·25 90
522 60um. "Graf Zeppelin II" crossing Swiss Alps . . . . 3·00 1·25

183 Temple and Bas-relief

1976. UNESCO "Save Moenjodaro" (Pakistan) Campaign.
524 **183** 15um. multicoloured . . . 80 40

184 Sacred Ibis and Yellow-billed Stork

1976. Air. Mauritanian Birds. Multicoloured.
525 50um. Type **184** . . . . . . 5·00 1·25
526 100um. Marabou storks (horiz) . . . . 8·50 2·75
527 200um. Long-crested and Martial eagles . . . . . . 18·00 5·00

185 Alexander Graham Bell, Early Telephone and Satellite

1976. Telephone Centenary.
528 **185** 10um. blue, lake and red 50 25

186 Mohammed Ali Jinnah

1976. Birth Centenary of Mohammed Ali Jinnah (first Governor-General of Pakistan).
529 **186** 10um. multicoloured . . . 35 20

187 Capsule Assembly

1977. "Viking" Space Mission. Multicoloured.
530 10um. Misson Control (horiz) (postage) 50 15
531 12um. Type **187** 55 20
532 20um. "Viking" in flight (horiz) (air) 80 25
533 50um. "Viking" over Mars (horiz) . . . . 2·00 60
534 60um. Parachute descent . . 2·25 65

188 Bush Hare

1977. Mauritanian Animals. Multicoloured.
536 5um. Type **188** 30 15
537 10um. Golden jackals 65 30
538 12um. Warthogs 90 40
539 14um. Lion and lioness . . . 1·00 50
540 15um. African elephants . . 1·90 80

189 Frederic and Irene Joliot-Curie (Chemistry, 1935)

1977. Nobel Prize-winners. Multicoloured.
541 12um. Type **189** (postage) . . 75 15
542 15um. Emil von Behring and nurse inoculating patient (1901) 75 20
543 14um. George Bernard Shaw and scene from "Androcles and the Lion" (1925) (air) 75 30
544 55um. Thomas Mann and scene from "Joseph and his Brethren" (1929) . . . . . 1·90 60
545 60um. International Red Cross and scene on Western Front (Peace Prize) (1917) . . . . 2·25 70

190 A.P.U. Emblem

1977. 25th Anniv of Arab Postal Union.
547 **190** 12um. multicoloured . . . 45 30

191 Oil Lamp

1977. Pottery from Tegdaoust.
548 **191** 1um. olive, brown and blue 10 10
549 – 2um. mauve, brown & blue 15 10
550 – 5um. orange, brown & blue 25 10
551 – 12um. brown, green and red 55 20
DESIGNS: 2um. Four-handled tureen; 5um. Large jar; 12um. Narrow-necked jug.

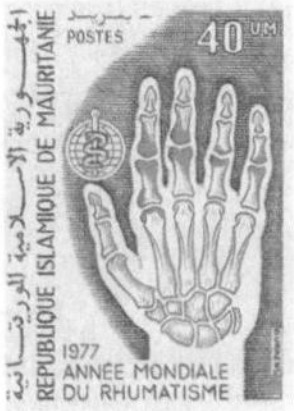

192 Skeleton of Hand

1977. World Rheumatism Year.
552 **192** 40um. orange, brown & grn . . . . 2·00 1·25

193 Holy Kaaba, Mecca

1977. Air. Pilgrimage to Mecca.
553 **193** 12um. multicoloured . . . 60 40

194 Charles Lindbergh and "Spirit of St. Louis"

1977. History of Aviation. Multicoloured.
554 12um. Type **194** 60 15
555 14um. Clement Ader and "Eole" 70 25
556 15um. Louis Bleriot and Bleriot XI 85 25
557 55um. General Italo Balbo and Savoia Marchetti S-55X flying boats . . . . 2·50 70
558 60um. Concorde . . . . . . 2·75 85

195 Dome of the Rock

1977. Palestinian Welfare.
560 **195** 12um. multicoloured . . . 70 30
561 14um. multicoloured . . . 80 35

196 Two Players

1977. World Cup Football Championship—Elimination Rounds. Multicoloured.
562 12um. Type **196** (postage) . . 40 15
563 14um. Sir Alf Ramsey and Wembley Stadium 50 20
564 15um. A "throw-in" 60 20
565 50um. Football and emblems (air) . . . . 2·00 60
566 60um. Eusebio Ferreira . . . 2·40 1·00

197 "Helene Fourment and Her Children" (Rubens)

1977. 400th Birth Anniv of Rubens. Paintings. Multicoloured.
568 12um. Type **197** 50 15
569 14um. "The Marquis of Spinola" 60 20
570 67um. "The Four Philosophers" . . . . . . 2·25 75
571 69um. "Steen Castle and Park" (horiz) . . . . . . 2·50 85

198 Addra Gazelles

1978. Endangered Animals. Multicoloured.
573 5um. Scimitar oryx (horiz) . . 35 15
574 12um. Type **198** 65 25
575 14um. African manatee (horiz) 80 35
576 55um. Barbary sheep . . . . 3·00 1·00
577 60um. African elephant (horiz) . . . . 3·25 1·25
578 100um. Ostrich . . . . . . 4·50 1·75

199 Clasped Hands and President Giscard d'Estaing of France

1978. Air. Franco-African Co-operation. Embossed on foil.
579 **199** 250um. silver . . . . . . 7·00 7·00
580 500um. gold . . . . . . 14·00 14·00

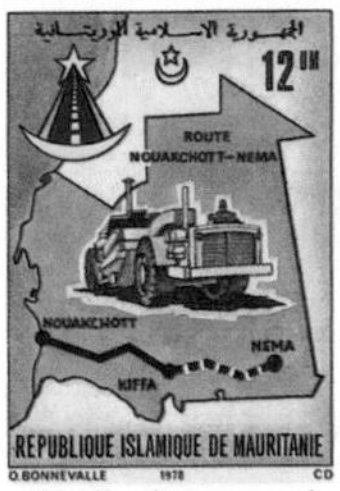

199a Earth-mover and Route Map

200 Footballers

1978. Nouakchott–Nema Highway. Mult.
580a 12um. Type **199a** . . . . . 2·00 1·50
580b 14um. Bulldozer and route map . . . . 2·25 1·75

1978. World Cup Football Championship, Argentina. Multicoloured.
581 12um. Type **200** 40 20
582 14um. World Cup 50 25
583 20um. F.I.F.A. flag and football 85 35

201 Raoul Follereau and St. George fighting Dragon

1978. 25th Anniv of Raoul Follereau Foundation.
585 **201** 12um. brown and green 70 40

202 Emblem and People holding Hands

1978. International Anti-Apartheid Year.
586 – 25um. brown, blue and red 90 60
587 **202** 30um. brown, blue & green . . . . 1·10 70
DESIGN—HORIZ: 25um. Emblem and people behind fence.

203 Charles de Gaulle

1978. Personalities. Multicoloured.
588 12um. Type **203** 90 30
589 14um. King Baudouin of Belgium 90 30
590 55um. Queen Elizabeth II (25th anniv of Coronation) 2·00 90

1978. Air. "Philexafrique" Stamp Exhibition, Libreville (Gabon) (1st issue), and 2nd International Stamp Fair, Essen (West Germany). As T **262** of Niger. Multicoloured.
591 20um. Water rail and Hamburg 1859 ½s. stamp 2·10 1·50
592 20um. Spotted hyena and Mauritania 1967 100f. South African crowned crane stamp . . . . 2·10 1·50
See also Nos. 619/20.

1978. Argentina's Victory in World Cup Football Championship. Nos. 562/6 optd **ARGENTINE–PAYS BAS 3-1** in English and Arabic.
593 **196** 12um. mult (postage) . . 50 25
594 – 14um. multicoloured . . . 55 30
595 – 15um. multicoloured . . . 65 30
596 – 50um. multicoloured (air) 1·75 1·10
597 – 60um. multicoloured . . . 2·25 1·40

205 View of Nouakchott

1978. 20th Anniv of Nouakchott.
599 **205** 12um. multicoloured . . . 45 30

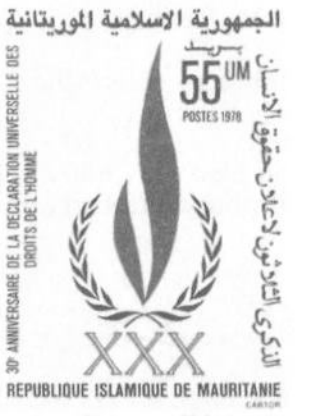

206 Human Rights Emblem

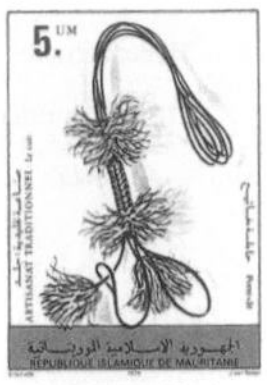

208 Key Chain

207 Wright Flyer I and Clement Ader's Avion III

1978. 30th Anniv of Declaration of Human Rights.
600 **206** 55um. red and blue . . . 1·60 1·25

1979. Air. 75th Anniv of First Powered Flight.
601 **207** 15um. grey, red and blue 1·00 35
602 – 40um. violet, blue & brn 2·00 1·10
DESIGN: 40um. Concorde and Wright Flyer I.

1979. Handicrafts. Multicoloured.
603 5um. Type **208** 25 15
604 7um. Tooth-brush case . . . 30 20
605 10um. Knife sheath 45 25

209 "Market Peasant and Wife"

210 Seated Buddha, Temple of Borobudur

1979. 450th Birth Anniv of Albrecht Durer (artist).
606 **209** 12um. black and red . . . 70 30
607 – 14um. black and red . . . 60 25
608 – 55um. black and red . . . 1·60 75
609 – 60um. black and red . . . 1·90 1·00
DESIGNS: 14um. "Young Peasant and his Wife"; 55um. "Mercenary with Banner"; 60um. "St. George and the Dragon".

1979. UNESCO Campaign for Preservation of Historic Monuments. Multicoloured.
611 12um. Type **210** 50 30
612 14um. Carthaginian warrior and hunting dog 60 30
613 55um. Erechtheum Caryatid, Acropolis . . . . 1·75 1·25

211 Rowland Hill and Paddle-steamer "Sirius"

1979. Death Centenary of Sir Rowland Hill. Multicoloured.
614 12um. Type **211** 50 25
615 14um. Hill and "Great Republic" (paddle-steamer) 65 25
616 55um. Hill and "Mauretania I" (liner) . . . . 2·00 60
617 60um. Hill and "Stirling Castle" (liner) . . . . . . 2·50 85

212 Satellite over Earth

1979. "Philexafrique" Exhibition, Libreville (2nd issue).
619 – 12um. multicoloured . . . 60 50
620 **212** 30um. red, blue and lilac 1·40 1·25
DESIGN—HORIZ: 12um. Embossed leather cushion cover.

213 Mother and Children **215** Sprinter on Starting-blocks

1979. International Year of the Child. Multicoloured.
621 12um. Type **213** 45 25
622 14um. Mother with sleeping baby 55 35
623 40um. Children playing with ball . . . . 1·50 90

1979. 10th Anniv of "Apollo 11" Moon Landing. Nos. 530/4 optd **ALUNISSAGE APOLLO XI JUILLET 1969**, with Lunar module, or surch also.
624 10um. Mission Control (horiz) (postage) 40 25
625 12um. Type **187** 45 30
626 14um. on 20um. "Viking" in flight (horiz) (air) 60 25
627 50um. "Viking" over Mars (horiz) . . . . 1·60 1·00
628 60um. Parachute descent . . 1·90 1·10

1979. Pre-Olympic Year. Multicoloured.
630 12um. Type **215** 35 15
631 14um. Female runner 40 15
632 55um. Male runner leaving start . . . . 1·50 60
633 60um. Hurdling . . . . . . 1·60 60

215a Skipper

1979. Fishes. Multicoloured.
634a 1um. Type **215a** 10 10
634b 2um. Swordfish 25 15
634c 5um. Tub gurnard 40 20

216 Ice Hockey

1979. Winter Olympic Games, Lake Placid (1980). Ice Hockey. Multicoloured.
635 10um. Type **216** 40 20
636 12um. Saving a goal 45 25
637 14um. Goalkeeper and player 55 25
638 55um. Two players . . . . . 2·00 60
639 60um. Goalkeeper . . . . . 2·25 65
640 100um. Tackle . . . . 3·50 1·25

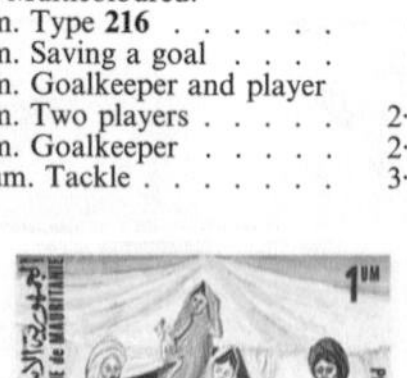

217 Woman pouring out Tea

1980. Taking Tea.
641 **217** 1um. multicoloured . . . 10 10
642 5um. multicoloured . . . 20 10
643 12um. multicoloured . . . 45 20

218 Koran, World Map and Symbols of Arab Achievements

1980. The Arabs.
644 **218** 12um. multicoloured . . . 40 25
645 15um. multicoloured . . . 50 30

1980. Winter Olympics Medal Winners. Nos. 635/40 optd.
646 10um. **Medaille de bronze SUEDE** 35 20
647 12um. **MEDAILLE DE BRONZE SUEDE** . . . 40 20
648 14um. **Medaille d'argent U.R.S.S.** 45 25
649 55um. **MEDAILLE D'ARGENT U.R.S.S.** . . 1·50 80
650 60um. **MEDAILLE D'OR ETATS-UNIS** . . . . . 1·75 90
651 100um. **Medaille d'or ETATS-UNIS** . . . . . 3·00 1·50

220 Holy Kaaba, Mecca **221** Mother and Child

1980. Pilgrimage to Mecca. Multicoloured.
652 10um. Type **220** 40 20
653 50um. Pilgrims outside Mosque . . . . 1·60 1·10

1980. World Red Cross Societies Day.
654 **221** 20um. multicoloured . . . 70 40

222 Crowd greeting Armed Forces

1980. Armed Forces Festival.
655 **222** 12um. multicoloured . . . 35 20
656 14um. multicoloured . . . 40 25

223 Horse jumping Bar **224** Trees on Map of Mauritania

1980. Olympic Games, Moscow. Multicoloured.
657 10um. Type **223** 30 20
658 20um. Water polo 55 30
659 50um. Horse jumping brick wall (horiz) . . . . 1·40 55
660 70um. Horse jumping stone wall . . . . 1·90 75

1980. Tree Day.
662 **224** 12um. multicoloured . . . 35 20

225 "Rembrandt's Mother"

1980. Paintings by Rembrandt. Multicoloured.
663 10um. "Self-portrait" 30 20
664 20um. Type **225** 75 30
665 50um. "Portrait of a Man in Oriental Costume" . . . . 1·75 55
666 70um. "Titus Lisant" . . . . 2·25 75

226 Footballers

1980. Air. World Cup Football Championship, Spain (1982). Multicoloured.
668 10um. Type **226** 30 20
669 12um. Goalkeeper and players 35 20
670 14um. Goalkeeper catching ball 40 25
671 20um. Fighting for possession 55 30
672 67um. Tackle . . . . 1·90 75

1980. Olympic Medal Winners. Nos. 657/60 optd.
674 10um. **VAINQUEUR KOWALLZYK (POL)** . . 30 20
675 20um. **VAINQUEUR THEURER (AUTR)** . . . 55 30
676 50um. **VAINQUEUR URSS** 1·40 55
677 70um. **VAINQUEUR ROMAN (IT)** . . . . . . 1·90 75

228 "Mastodonte del Giovi", 1853, Italy

1980. Steam Locomotives. Multicoloured.
679 10um. Type **228** 55 15
680 12um. Diesel ore train . . . 60 15
681 14um. Chicago, Milwaukee and St. Paul Railway locomotive No. 810, U.S.A. 75 20
682 20um. Bury steam locomotive, 1837, Great Britain . . . . 1·00 25
683 67um. Locomotive No. 170, France . . . . 3·50 55
684 100um. Berlin–Potsdam line, Germany . . . . 5·25 95

229 Palm Tree, Crescent and Star, Maize and Map

1980. 20th Anniv of Independence.
685 **229** 12um. multicoloured . . . 40 20
686 15um. multicoloured . . . 50 30

230 El Haram Mosque

1981. 15th Century of Hegira. Multicoloured.
687 2um. Type **230** 10 10
688 12um. Medine Mosque . . . 40 20
689 14um. Chinguetti Mosque . . 50 30

231 Space Shuttle in Orbit

1981. Air. Space Shuttle. Multicoloured.
690 12um. Type **231** 40 20
691 20um. Shuttle and space station 85 30
692 50um. Shuttle performing experiment . . . . 1·75 75
693 70um. Shuttle landing . . . . 2·50 1·00

232 "The Harlequin"

1981. Air. Birth Centenary of Pablo Picasso. Multicoloured.
695 12um. Type **232** 50 20
696 20um. "Vase of Flowers" . . 75 30
697 50um. "Three Women at a Fountain" (horiz) . . . . 1·40 75
698 70um. "Dinard Landscape" (horiz) . . . . 2·25 1·00
699 100um. "Le Dejeuner sur l'Herbe" (horiz) . . . . . 3·00 1·50

233 I.Y.D.P. Emblem

1981. International Year of Disabled People.
700 **233** 12um. violet, gold and blue 45 30

234 Open Landau

1981. British Royal Wedding. Multicoloured.
701 14um. Type **234** 40 20
702 18um. Light carriage 45 20
703 77um. Closed coupe . . . . 1·40 1·10

235 George Washington

1981. Bicentenary of Battles of Yorktown and Chesapeake Bay. Multicoloured.
705 14um. Type **235** 45 25
706 18um. Admiral de Grasse . . 55 25
707 63um. Surrender of Cornwallis at Yorktown (horiz) . . . . 1·75 95
708 81um. Battle of Chesapeake Bay (horiz) . . . . 2·25 1·50

236 Columbus and "Pinta"

1981. 450th Death Anniv of Christopher Columbus. Multicoloured.
709 19um. Type **236** . . . . . . 1·00 40
710 55um. Columbus and "Santa Maria" . . . . 2·75 1·10

237 Wheat and F.A.O. Emblem

238 Kemal Ataturk

1981. World Food Day.
711 **237** 19um. multicoloured . . . 60 40

1981. Birth Centenary of Kemal Ataturk (Turkish statesman).
712 **238** 63um. multicoloured . . . 2·00 1·25

239 Eastern White Pelicans

1981. Birds of the Arguin. Multicoloured.
713 2um. Type **239** 40 15
714 18um. Greater flamingoes . . 1·75 80

240 Hand holding Torn Flag

1981. Battle of Karameh Commemoration.
715 **240** 14um. multicoloured . . . 45 30

241 "Dermochelys coiacer"

1981. Turtles. Multicoloured.
716 1um. Type **241** 30 15
717 3um. "Chelonia mydas" . . . 40 15
718 4um. "Eretmochelys imbricata" 50 15

242 Sea Scouts

1982. 75th Anniv of Boy Scout Movement. Multicoloured.
719 14um. Type **242** 55 25
720 19um. Scouts boarding rowing boat 90 35
721 22um. Scouts in rowing boat 1·00 40
722 92um. Scouts in yacht . . . 3·00 1·25

243 Deusenberg, 1921

1982. 75th Anniv of French Grand Prix Motor Race. Multicoloured.
724 7um. Type **243** 50 20
725 12um. Alfa Romeo, 1932 . . 60 20
726 14um. Juan Fangio 75 35
727 18um. Renault, 1979 . . . . 1·00 40
728 19um. Niki Lauda . . . . . 1·00 45

244 A.P.U. Emblem

245 Hexagonal Pattern

1982. 30th Anniv of Arab Postal Union.
730 **244** 14um. orange and brown 45 30

1982. World Telecommunications Day.
731 **245** 21um. multicoloured . . . 65 45

246 Environmental Emblem on Map

1982. 10th Anniv of U.N. Environmental Programme.
732 **246** 14um. blue and light blue 45 30

247 Princess of Wales

1982. 21st Birthday of Princess of Wales. Mult.
733 21um. Type **247** 75 35
734 77um. Princess of Wales (different) . . . . 2·40 1·10

248 Straw Hut

1982. Traditional Houses. Multicoloured.
736 14um. Type **248** 45 30
737 18um. Thatched hut 55 45
738 19um. Tent 60 45

1982. Birth of Prince William of Wales. Nos. 701/3 surch **NAISSANCE ROYALE 1982**.
739 14um. Type **234** 45 35
740 18um. Light carriage 55 40
741 77um. Closed coupe . . . . 2·40 1·25

1982. Air. World Cup Football Championship Results. Nos. 668/72 optd **ITALIE 3 ALLEMAGNE (R.F.A.) 1**.
743 10um. Type **226** 40 25
744 12um. Goalkeeper punching ball 40 30
745 14um. Goalkeeper catching ball 45 30
746 20um. Three players 70 40
747 67um. Tackle . . . . 2·25 1·40

251 Cattle at Collinaire Dam, Hodh El Gharbi

1982. Agricultural Development.
749 14um. Type **251** . . . . . . 1·25 1·10
750 18um. Irrigation canal, Gorgol . . . . 1·75 1·25

252 Desert Rose

1982. Desert Rose.
751 **252** 21um. multicoloured . . . 1·50 1·00

253 Montgolfier Balloon, 1783

1983. Bicent of Manned Flight. Multicoloured.
752 14um. Type **253** 65 20
753 18um. Charles's hydrogen balloon ascent, 1783 (horiz) 65 30
754 19um. Goodyear Aerospace airship 65 30
755 55um. Nieuport 11 "Bebe" biplane (horiz) . . . . . . 1·75 70
756 63um. Concorde (horiz) . . . 3·00 1·00
757 77um. "Apollo 11" on Moon 2·50 1·00
No. 754 is wrongly inscribed "Zeppelin".

254 Ouadane

1983. Protection of Ancient Sites. Multicoloured.
758 14um. Type **254** 40 25
759 18um. Chinguetti 50 30
760 24um. Oualata 70 45
761 30um. Tichitt . . . . 1·00 55

255 Manuscript

256 I.M.O. Emblem

1983. Ancient Manuscripts. Multicoloured.
762 2um. Type **255** 10 10
763 5um. Decorated manuscript 15 15
764 7um. Shield-shaped patterned manuscript 25 20

1983. 25th Anniv of I.M.O.
765 **256** 18um. multicoloured . . . 50 30

257 W.C.Y. Emblem

1983. World Communications Year.
766 **257** 14um. multicoloured . . . 55 30

258 Customs Emblems

1983. 30th Anniv of Customs Co-operation Council.
767 **258** 14um. multicoloured . . . 45 30

259 Pilatre de Rozier and Montgolfier Balloon

260 Grinding Stone

1983. Bicentenary of Manned Flight. Mult.
768 10um. Type **259** (postage) . . 40 20
769 14um. John Wise and balloon "Atlantic" 50 30
770 25um. Charles Renard and Renard and Krebs' airship "La France" (horiz) . . . 85 35
771 100um. Henri Juillot and Lebaudy-Juillot airship "Patrie" (horiz) (air) . . . 3·75 1·25

1983. Prehistoric Grindstones. Multicoloured.
773 10um. Type **260** 50 30
774 14um. Pestle and mortar . . 75 40
775 18um. Grinding dish . . . . 1·00 60

261 Basketball

1983. Pre-Olympic Year. Multicoloured.
776 1um. Type **261** (postage) . . 10 10
777 20um. Wrestling 60 25
778 50um. Show-jumping . . . . 1·50 80
779 77um. Running (air) . . . . 2·25 1·25

262 Lord Baden-Powell (founder of Scout Movement)

1984. Celebrities. Multicoloured.
781 5um. Type **262** (postage) . . 15 10
782 14um. Goethe (poet) 45 20
783 25um. Rubens and detail of painting "The Virgin and Child" 75 45
784 100um. P. Harris (founder of Rotary International) (air) 3·00 1·40

263 Blue-finned Tuna

1984. Fishing Resources. Multicoloured.
786 1um. Type **263** 10 10
787 2um. Atlantic mackerel . . . 15 10
788 5um. European hake 40 15
789 14um. Atlantic horse-mackerel . . . . 1·10 45
790 18um. Building a fishing boat 1·25 55

264 Durer and "Madonna and Child"

1984. Multicoloured.
791 10um. Type **264** (postage) . . 35 20
792 12um. "Apollo 11" and astronaut (15th anniv of first manned Moon landing) 40 25
793 50um. Chess pieces and globe 2·00 80
794 77um. Prince and Princess of Wales (air) . . . . 2·25 1·40

265 Start of Race

1984. Olympic Games, Los Angeles. Multicoloured.
796 14um. Type **265** 40 25
797 18um. Putting the shot (vert) 55 25
798 19um. Hurdling (vert) . . . 55 25
799 44um. Throwing the javelin (vert) . . . . 1·25 65
800 77um. High jumping . . . . 2·00 1·25

266 Feeding Dehydrated Child from Glass

1984. Infant Survival Campaign. Multicoloured.
802 1um. Type **266** 10 10
803 4um. Breast-feeding baby . . 15 10
804 10um. Vaccinating baby . . . 30 20
805 14um. Weighing baby 45 30

267 Aerial View of Complex

1984. Nouakchott Olympic Complex.
806 **267** 14um. multicoloured . . . 50 40

268 Tents and Mosque Courtyard

1984. Pilgrimage to Mecca. Multicoloured.
807 14um. Type **268** 50 30
808 18um. Tents and courtyard (different) 75 40

269 Emblem

1984. 10th Anniv of West African Economic Community.
809 **269** 14um. multicoloured . . . 45 30

270 S. van den Berg (windsurfing)

1984. Air. Olympic Games Sailing Gold Medallists. Multicoloured.
810 14um. Type **270** 55 25
811 18um. R. Coutts ("Finn" class) 75 25
812 19um. Spain ("470" class) . . 1·00 25
813 44um. U.S.A. ("Soling" class) 1·90 60

1984. Drought Relief. No. 537 surch **Aide au Sahel 84**.
815 18um. on 10um. multicoloured 70 50

272 Profiles and Emblem

1985. 15th Anniv of Technical and Cultural Co-operation Agency.
816 **272** 18um. blue, deep blue and red 60 45

273 Animal drinking in Water Droplet and Skeletons

1985. Campaign against Drought. Multicoloured.
817 14um. Type **273** . . . . . . 1·10 50
818 18um. Lush trees by river in water droplet and dead trees . . . . 1·10 50

274 Replanting Trees

1985. Anti-desertification Campaign. Multicoloured.
819 10um. Type **274** 35 25
820 14um. Animals fleeing from forest fire . . . . 1·60 85
821 18um. Planting grass to hold sand dunes 65 50

275 Emblem

1985. 30th Anniv (1984) of Arab League.
822 **275** 14um. green and black . . 45 30

276 Map, I.Y.Y. Emblem and Youths

1985. Air. "Philexafrique" Stamp Exhibition, Lome. Multicoloured.
823 40um. Type **276** (International Youth Year) 1·50 1·25
824 40um. Nouadhibou oil refinery . . . . 1·50 1·25

277 Bonaparte's Gulls

1985. Air. Birth Bicentenary of John J. Audubon (ornithologist). Multicoloured.
825 14um. Wester tanager and scarlet tanager . . . . . . 1·25 20
826 18um. Type **277** . . . . . . 1·50 25
827 19um. Blue jays . . . . . . 1·75 35
828 44um. Black skimmer . . . . 4·50 1·40

278 Locomotive "Adler", 1835

1985. Anniversaries. Multicoloured.
830 12um. Type **278** (150th anniv of German railways) . . . 2·25 60
831 18um. Class 10 steam locomotive, 1956 (150th anniv of German railways) 2·50 60
832 44um. Johann Sebastian Bach (composer, 300th birth anniv European Music Year) . . . . 1·60 70
833 77um. Georg Frederick Handel (composer, 300th birth anniv European Music Year) . . . . 2·75 1·25
834 90um. Statue of Liberty (centenary) (vert) . . . . . 2·75 1·40

279 Globe and Emblem

1985. World Food Day.
836 **279** 18um. multicoloured . . . 55 35

280 Tending Sheep and reading Book

1985. Air. "Philexafrique" Stamp Exhibition, Lome, Togo (2nd issue). Multicoloured.
837 50um. Type **280** . . . . . . 2·00 1·50
838 50um. Dock, iron ore mine and diesel train . . . . . 3·50 90

281 Map showing Industries

1985. 25th Anniv of Independence.
839 **281** 18um. multicoloured . . . 60 40

282 Development

1986. International Youth Year. Multicoloured.
840 18um. Type **282** 60 30
841 22um. Re-afforestation (voluntary work) 70 40
842 25um. Hands reaching from globe to dove (peace) (vert) 75 50

283 Latecoere Seaplane "Comte de la Vaulx" and Map

1986. Air. 55th Anniv (1985) of First Commercial South Atlantic Flight. Multicoloured.
843 18um. Type **283** 75 35
844 50um. Piper Twin Commanche airplanes crossing between maps of Africa and South America 2·00 1·25

284 Toujounine Earth Receiving Station

1986.
845 **284** 25um. multicoloured . . . 90 50

285 Heads of Mother and Pup

1986. World Wildlife Fund. Mediterranean Monk Seal. Multicoloured.
846 2um. Type **285** 50 30
847 5um. Mother and pup on land 75 50
848 10um. Mother and pup swimming . . . . 1·00 75
849 18um. Seal family . . . . . 2·00 1·00

286 Player and 1970 25f. Stamp

1986. Air. World Cup Football Championship, Mexico. Multicoloured.
851 8um. Type **286** 25 10
852 18um. Player and 1970 30f. stamp 60 20
853 22um. Player and 1970 70f. stamp 70 30
854 25um. Player and 1970 150f. stamp 85 35
855 40um. Player and World Cup trophy on "stamp" . . . . 1·25 60

287 Weaving

1986.
857 **287** 18um. multicoloured . . . 60 35

288 Emblem, Boeing 737, Douglas DC-10 and Map

1986. Air. 25th Anniv of Air Afrique.
858 **288** 26um. multicoloured . . . 1·00 40

289 Indian, "Santa Maria" and Route Map

1986. 500th Anniv (1992) of Discovery of America by Christopher Columbus. Multicoloured.
859 2um. Type **289** (postage) . . 10 10
860 22um. Indian, "Nina" and map 65 30
861 35um. Indian, "Pinta" and map . . . . 1·10 50
862 150um. Indian, map and Christopher Columbus (air) 4·50 1·60

290 J. H. Dort, Comet Picture and Space Probe "Giotto"

1986. Appearance of Halley's Comet. Multicoloured.
864 5um. Type **290** (postage) . . 15 10
865 18um. William Huggins (astronomer) and "Ariane" space rocket 60 20
866 26um. E. J. Opik and space probes "Giotto" and "Vega" 80 30
867 80um. F. L. Whipple and "Planet A" space probe (air) . . . . 2·75 1·25

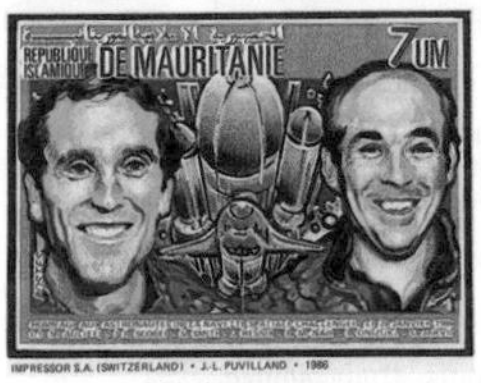

291 Astronauts

1986. "Challenger" Astronauts Commemoration. Multicoloured.
869 7um. Type **291** (postage) . . 20 10
870 22um. Judith Resnik and astronaut 60 30
871 32um. Ellison Onizuka and Ronald McNair . . . . . 1·00 45
872 43um. Christa Corrigan McAuliffe (air) . . . . . 1·50 60

292 Red Seabream

1986. Fishes and Birds. Multicoloured.
874 4um. Type **292** 30 15
875 22um. White spoonbills . . . 1·75 65
876 32um. Bridled terns . . . . . 2·00 1·00
877 98um. Sea-trout . . . . . . 5·50 3·00
See also Nos. 896/900.

293 Arrow through Victim
294 Fisherman

1986. 4th Anniv of Massacre of Palestinian Refugees in Sabra and Shatila Camps, Lebanon.
878 **293** 22um. black, gold and red 80 40

1986. World Food Day.
879 **294** 22um. multicoloured . . . 1·25 40

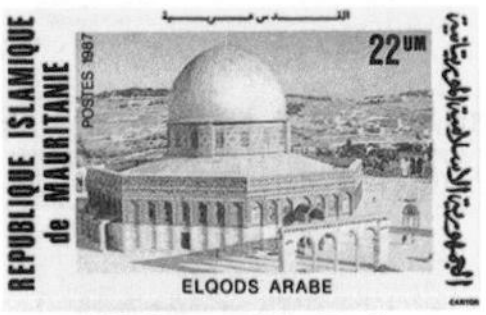

295 Dome of the Rock

1987. "Arab Jerusalem".
880 **295** 22um. multicoloured . . . 80 40

296 Boxing

1987. Air. Olympic Games, Seoul (1988) (1st issue). Multicoloured.
881 30um. Type **296** 80 40
882 40um. Judo . . . . 1·00 55
883 50um. Fencing . . . . 1·25 70
884 75um. Wrestling . . . . . . 2·00 1·10
See also Nos. 902/5.

297 Cordoue Mosque

1987. 1200th Anniv of Cordoue Mosque.
886 **297** 30um. multicoloured . . . 1·00 50

298 Women's Slalom

1987. Air. Winter Olympic Games, Calgary (1988). Multicoloured.
887 30um. Type **298** . . . . . . 1·10 40
888 40um. Men's speed skating . . 1·40 55
889 50um. Ice hockey . . . . . 1·60 75
890 75um. Women's downhill skiing . . . . 2·50 1·10

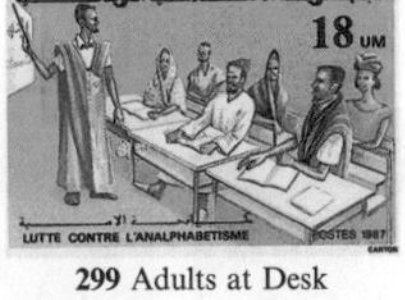

299 Adults at Desk

1987. Literacy Campaign. Multicoloured.
892 18um. Type **299** 60 40
893 20um. Adults and children reading 80 50

300 People queueing for Treatment

1987. World Health Day.
894 **300** 18um. multicoloured . . . 70 40

301 Map within Circle

1988. National Population and Housing Census.
895 **301** 20um. multicoloured . . . 60 35

1988. Fishes and Birds. Horiz designs as T **292**. Multicoloured.
896 1um. Small-horned blenny . . 10 10
897 7um. Grey triggerfish 40 15
898 15um. Skipjack tuna 70 30
899 18um. Great cormorants . . 95 65
900 80um. Royal terns . . . . . 4·00 2·75

302 People with Candles
303 Hammer Throwing

1988. 40th Anniv of W.H.O.
901 **302** 30um. multicoloured . . . 1·00 40

1988. Air. Olympic Games, Seoul (2nd issue). Multicoloured.
902 20um. Type **303** 50 25
903 24um. Discus 60 30
904 30um. Putting the shot . . . 80 40
905 150um. Javelin throwing . . 4·00 2·10

1988. Winter Olympic Games Gold Medal Winners. Nos. 887/90 optd.
907 30um. Optd **Medaille d'or Vreni Schneider (Suisse)** 1·00 50
908 40um. Optd **Medaille d'or 1500m. Andre Hoffman (R.D.A.)** . . . . 1·10 75
909 50um. Optd **Medaille d'or U.R.S.S.** . . . . 1·50 1·00
910 75um. Optd **Medaille d'or Marina Kiehl (R.F.A.)** . . 2·25 1·50

305 Flags and Globe

1988. 75th Anniv of Arab Scout Movement.
912 **305** 35um. multicoloured . . . 1·50 55

306 Men at Ballot Box

1988. 1st Municipal Elections. Multicoloured.
913 20um. Type **306** 60 30
914 24um. Woman at ballot box 80 40

307 Emblem
308 Ploughing with Oxen

1988. 25th Anniv of Organization of African Unity.
915 **307** 40um. multicoloured . . . 1·25 60

1988. 10th Anniv of International Agricultural Development Fund.
916 **308** 35um. multicoloured . . . 1·10 70

309 Port Activities

1989. 1st Anniv of Nouakchott Free Port.
917 **309** 24um. multicoloured . . . 1·25 65

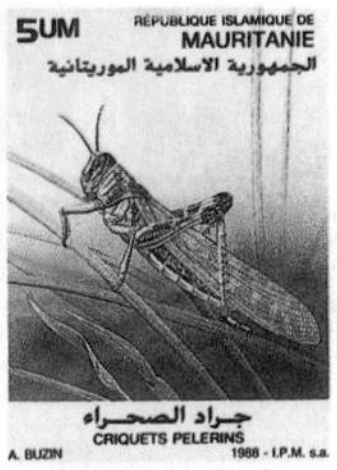

310 "Heliothis armigera"
311 "Nomadacris septemfasciata"

1989. Plant Pests. Multicoloured.
918 2um. Type **310** 15 15
919 6um. "Aphis gossypii" . . . 20 15
920 10um. "Agrotis ypsilon" . . . 35 15
921 20um. "Chilo" sp. 75 30
922 24um. "Plitella xylostella" . . 85 40
923 30um. "Henosepilachna elaterii" . . . . 1·25 55
924 42um. "Trichoplusia ni" . . 1·50 70

1989. Locusts. Multicoloured.
925 5um. Type **311** 15 10
926 20um. Locusts mating . . . 60 30
927 24um. Locusts emerging from chrysallis 70 40
928 40um. Locusts flying . . . . 1·25 75
929 88um. Locust (different) . . . 3·00 1·25

312 Men of Different Races embracing
313 Footballers

1989. "Philexfrance '89" Int Stamp Exn, Paris, and Bicent of French Revolution.
930 **312** 35um. multicoloured . . . 1·10 60

1989. World Cup Football Championship, Italy (1990) (1st issue).
931 **313** 20um. multicoloured . . . 1·00 40
See also Nos. 937/41.

314 Attan'eem Migat, Mecca

1989. Pilgrimage to Mecca.
932 **314** 20um. multicoloured . . . 75 30

315 Emblem

317 Youths

316 Carpet

1989. 25th Anniv of African Development Bank.
933 **315** 37um. black and mauve . . . 1·00 50

1989.
934 **316** 50um. multicoloured . . . 1·50 80

1989. 2nd Anniv of Palestinian "Intifada" Movement.
935 **317** 35um. multicoloured . . . 1·25 50

318 Member Countries' Leaders (½-size illustration)

1990. 1st Anniv of Arab Maghreb Union.
936 **318** 50um. multicoloured . . . 1·50 70

319 Players

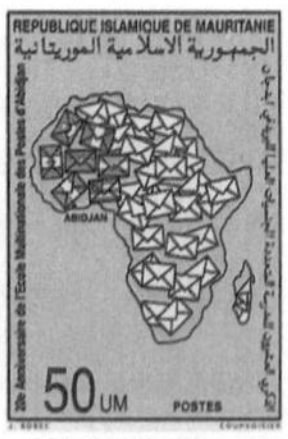

320 Envelopes on Map

1990. Air. World Cup Football Championship, Italy (2nd issue).
937 **319** 50um. multicoloured . . . 1·50 50
938 – 60um. multicoloured . . . 1·90 60
939 – 70um. multicoloured . . . 2·00 75
940 – 90um. multicoloured . . . 2·75 75
941 – 150um. multicoloured . . 4·50 1·25
DESIGNS: 60 to 150um. Show footballers.

1990. 20th Anniv of Multinational Postal Training School, Abidjan.
942 **320** 50um. multicoloured . . . 1·10 50

321 Books and Desk

1990. International Literacy Year.
943 **321** 60um. multicoloured . . . 1·75 1·00

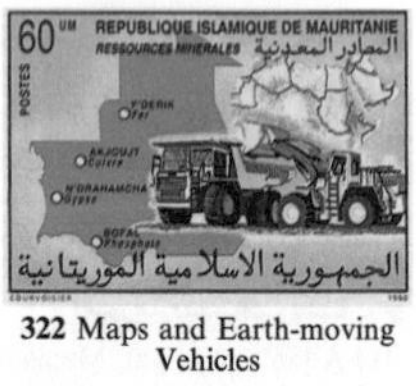

322 Maps and Earth-moving Vehicles

1990. Mineral Resources.
944 **322** 60um. multicoloured . . . 2·75 1·25

323 Dressage

324 Emblem

1990. Olympic Games, Barcelona (1992). Mult.
945 5um. Type **323** (postage) . . 20 15
946 50um. Archery . . . . 1·40 40
947 60um. Throwing the hammer 1·50 50
948 75um. Football . . . . . . 2·00 50
949 90um. Basketball . . . . . . 2·75 65
950 220um. Table tennis (air) . . 6·00 1·40

1990. 2nd Anniv of Declaration of State of Palestine.
952 **324** 85um. multicoloured . . . 1·75 1·10

325 Camp

1990. Integration of Repatriates from Senegal. Multicoloured.
953 50um. Type **325** 90 60
954 75um. Women's sewing group 1·25 1·00
955 85um. Water collection . . . 1·40 1·00

326 Map, Dove and Mandela

1990. Release from South African Prison of Nelson Mandela.
956 **326** 85um. multicoloured . . . 1·60 1·10

327 Downhill skiing

1990. Winter Olympic Games, Albertville (1992). Multicoloured.
957 60um. Type **327** (postage) . . 1·00 60
958 75um. Cross-country skiing 1·50 75
959 90um. Ice hockey . . . . . 1·75 95
960 220um. Figure skating (pairs) (air) . . . . 3·75 2·25

328 Blue Leg

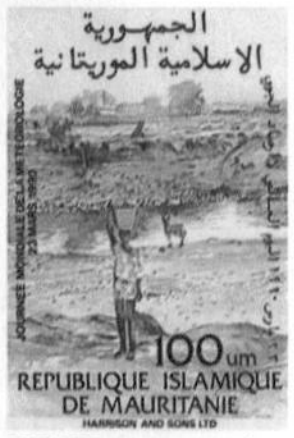

330 Woman carrying Bucket of Water

329 Dish Aerials and Transmitting Tower

1991. Scouts, Fungi and Butterflies. Multicoloured.
962 5um. Type **328** (postage) . . 40 20
963 50um. "Agaricus bitorquis edulis" . . . . 2·50 80
964 60um. "Bunea alcinoe" (butterfly) . . . . 2·25 75
965 90um. "Salamis cytora" (butterfly) . . . . 2·75 1·10
966 220um. "Bronze boletus" . . 6·50 3·00
967 75um. "Cyrestis camillus" (butterfly) (air) . . . . . . 2·50 85

1991. 30th Anniv of Independence. Multicoloured.
968 50um. Type **329** . . . . . . 1·00 65
969 60um. Container ship in dock 2·00 85
970 100um. Workers in field . . . 1·75 1·00

1991. World Meteorological Day.
972 **330** 100um. multicoloured . . 1·75 1·10

331 Health Centre

1991. 20th Anniv of Medecins sans Frontieres (international medical relief organization).
973 **331** 60um. multicoloured . . . 70 45

332 Cats

1991. Domestic Animals. Multicoloured.
974 50um. Type **332** 75 35
975 60um. Basenji dog . . . . . 1·00 45

333 Globe and Stylized Figures

1991. World Population Day.
976 **333** 90um. multicoloured . . . 1·00 60

334 Blind Woman with Sight restored

1991. Anti-blindness Campaign.
977 **334** 50um. multicoloured . . . 55 35

335 Nouakchott Electricity Station

1991. 2nd Anniv of Nouakchott Electricity Station.
978 **335** 50um. multicoloured . . . 55 35

336 Quarrying

1993. Mineral Exploitation, Haoudat. Multicoloured.
979 50um. Type **336** 75 35
980 60um. Dry land 85 40

337 Camel Train

338 Palestinians

1993.
981 **337** 50um. multicoloured . . . 55 35
982 60um. multicoloured . . . 65 40

1993. Palestinian "Intifada" Movement. Multicoloured.
983 50um. Type **338** 55 35
984 60um. Palestinian children by fire (horiz) 65 40

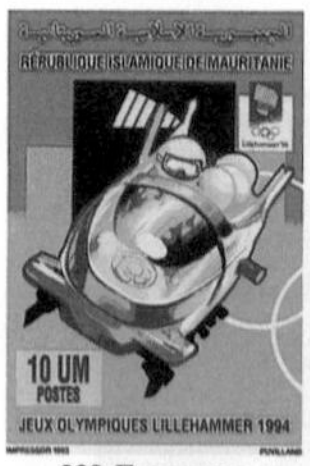

339 Four-man Bobsleighing

340 Soldier Field, Chicago

1993. Winter Olympic Games, Lillehammer. Multicoloured.
985 10um. Type **339** 10 10
986 50um. Luge 55 35
987 60um. Figure skating 65 40
988 80um. Skiing 85 55
989 220um. Cross-country skiing 2·40 1·50

1994. World Cup Football Championship, U.S.A. Players and Stadiums. Multicoloured.
991 10um. Type **340** 10 10
992 50um. Foxboro Stadium, Boston 50 30
993 60um. Robert F. Kennedy Stadium, Washington D.C. 65 40
994 90um. Stanford Stadium, San Francisco 95 60
995 220um. Giant Stadium, New York . . . . 2·25 1·40

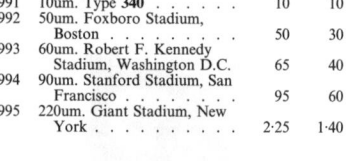

341 Anniversary Emblem and 1962 15f. Stamp

1995. 50th Anniv of U.N.O.
997 **341** 60um. multicoloured . . . 60 40

342 Stabilizing Desert

345 Weaving

1995. 50th Anniv of F.A.O. Multicoloured.
998 50um. Type **342** 50 30
999 60um. Fishermen launching boat 60 40
1000 90um. Planting crops . . . 85 55

1995. Crafts. Multicoloured.
1006 50um. Type **345** 30 15
1007 60um. Metalwork 35 20

346 Door

347 Start of Race

1995. Tourism. Re-vitalization of Ancient Towns. Multicoloured.
1008 10um. Type **346** 10 10
1009 20um. Arch and rubble . . 10 10
1010 40um. Town in desert . . . 25 15
1011 50um. Door in ornate wall 30 15

1996. Olympic Games, Atlanta, U.S.A. Mult.
1012 20um. Type **347** 10 10
1013 30um. Start of race (horiz) 15 10
1014 40um. Running in lane . . . 25 15
1015 50um. Long-distance race (horiz) 30 15

348 Beaded Locks and Headdress

349 Ball-in-Pot Game

1996. Traditional Hairstyles. Multicoloured.

1016		50um. Type **348**	30	15
1017		60um. Woman with hair adornments	35	20

1996. Traditional Games. Multicoloured.

1018		50um. Type **349**	30	15
1019		60um. Strategy game with spherical and conical pieces (horiz)	35	20
1020		90um. Pegs-in-board game (horiz)	50	30

350 Family

1996. 50th Anniv of United Nations Children's Fund. The Rights of the Child. Showing children's drawings. Multicoloured.

1021		50um. Type **350**	30	15
1022		60um. Boy in wheelchair	35	20

OFFICIAL STAMPS

O 41 Cross of Trarza

O 179

1961.

O150	O 41	1f. purple and blue	10	10
O151		3f. myrtle and red	10	10
O152		5f. brown and green	10	10
O153		10f. blue and turquoise	20	10
O154		15f. orange and blue	30	15
O155		20f. green and myrtle	35	20
O156		25f. red and orange	40	30
O157		30f. green and purple	45	30
O158		50f. sepia and red	1·00	45
O159		100f. blue and orange	1·60	75
O160		200f. red and green	3·00	1·60

1976.

O502	O 179	1um. multicoloured	10	10
O503		2um. multicoloured	15	10
O504		5um. multicoloured	20	15
O505		10um. multicoloured	40	20
O506		12um. multicoloured	55	30
O507		40um. multicoloured	1·75	1·00
O508		50um. multicoloured	2·25	1·25

POSTAGE DUE STAMPS

1906. Stamps of 1906 optd **T** in a triangle.

D18	I	5c. green and red	—	32·00
D19		10c. pink and blue	—	32·00
D20	J	20c. black and red on blue	—	52·00
D21		25c. blue and red	—	52·00
D22		30c. brown & red on pink	—	£120
D23		40c. red on blue	—	£500
D24		50c. violet and red	—	£120
D25	K	1f. black and red on blue	—	£180

1906. "Natives" key-type inscr "MAURITANIE" in blue (10, 30c.) or red (others).

D25	L	5c. green	1·25	1·10
D26		10c. purple	2·00	1·90
D27		15c. blue on blue	4·00	2·50
D28		20c. black on yellow	4·75	7·75
D29		30c. red on cream	6·75	14·50
D30		50c. violet	10·00	21·00
D31		60c. black on buff	7·25	11·50
D32		1f. black on pink	14·00	23·00

1914. "Figure" key-type inscr "MAURITANIE".

D35	M	5c. green	10	65
D36		10c. red	15	25
D37		15c. grey	15	1·75
D38		20c. brown	15	2·25
D39		30c. blue	30	2·50
D40		50c. black	30	2·25
D41		60c. orange	20	1·90
D42		1f. violet	35	2·25

1927. Surch in figures.

D67	M	2f. on 1f. purple	70	4·25
D68		3f. on 1f. brown	65	4·50

D 40 Qualata Motif

D 180

D 55 Ruppell's Griffon

1961.

D150	D 40	1f. yellow and purple	10	10
D151		2f. grey and red	10	10
D152		5f. pink and red	20	15
D153		10f. green and myrtle	25	15
D154		15f. brown and drab	30	15
D155		20f. blue and red	35	20
D156		25f. red and green	55	35

1963. Birds. Multicoloured.

D177		50c. Type D **55**	45	15
D178		50c. Common crane	45	15
D179		1f. Eastern white pelican	55	20
D180		1f. Garganey	55	20
D181		2f. Golden oriole	80	25
D182		2f. Variable sunbird	80	25
D183		5f. Great snipe	85	45
D184		5f. Common shoveler	85	45
D185		10f. Vulturine guineafowl	1·40	80
D186		10f. Black stork	1·40	80
D187		15f. Grey heron	1·60	1·25
D188		15f. White stork	1·60	1·25
D189		20f. Paradise whydah	2·10	1·40
D190		20f. Red-legged partridge	2·10	1·40
D191		25f. Little stint	2·75	1·75
D192		25f. Arabian bustard	2·75	1·75

1976.

D509	D 180	1um. multicoloured	10	10
D510		3um. multicoloured	15	15
D511		10um. multicoloured	35	35
D512		12um. multicoloured	40	40
D513		20um. multicoloured	70	70

APPENDIX

The following stamps have either been issued in excess of postal needs or have not been available to the public in a reasonable quantities at face value. Such stamps may later be given full listing if there is evidence of regular postal use.

1962.

World Refugee Year (1960). Optd on 1960 Definitive issue, 30, 50, 60f.

Olympic Games in Rome (1960) and Tokyo (1964). Surch on 1960 Definitive issue 75f. on 15f., 75f. on 20f.

European Steel and Coal Community and Exploration of Iron-ore in Mauritania. Optd on 1960 Definitive issue. Air 500f.

Malaria Eradication. Optd on 1960 Definitive issue. Air. 100, 200f.

MAURITIUS Pt. 1

An island in the Indian Ocean, east of Madagascar. Attained self-government on 1 September 1967, and became independent on 12 March 1968.

1847. 12 pence = 1 shilling;
20 shillings = 1 pound.
1878. 100 cents = 1 rupee.

1 ("POST OFFICE")

2 ("POST PAID")

1847. Imperf.

1	1	1d. red	—	£450000
2		2d. blue	—	£550000

1848. Imperf.

23	2	1d. red	£1900	£425
25		2d. blue	£2500	£650

3

5

1854. Surch **FOUR-PENCE**. Imperf.

26	3	4d. green	£1100	£425

1858. No value on stamps. Imperf.

27	3	(4d.) green	£425	£200
28		(6d.) red	35·00	65·00
29		(9d.) purple	£600	£200

1859. Imperf.

32	5	6d. blue	£600	40·00
33		6d. black	23·00	45·00
34		1s. red	£2000	45·00
35		1s. green	£550	£120

6

8

1859. Imperf.

39	6	2d. blue	£1500	£475

1859. Imperf.

42	8	1d. red	£4000	£850
44		2d. blue	£2250	£475

9

10

1860.

56	9	1d. purple	70·00	12·00
57		1d. brown	90·00	7·50
60		2d. blue	80·00	8·50
61a		3d. red	55·00	12·00
62		4d. red	80·00	3·25
65		6d. green	£140	5·00
50		6d. grey	£275	95·00
63		6d. violet	£225	28·00
51		9d. purple	£120	40·00
66		9d. green	£140	£225
67	10	10d. red	£275	38·00
70	9	1s. yellow	£190	12·00
53		1s. green	£600	£160
69		1s. blue	£130	22·00
71		5s. mauve	£180	55·00

1862. Perf.

54	5	6d. black	22·00	65·00
55		1s. green	£2000	£325

HALF PENNY (11)

HALF PENNY (13)

1876. Surcharged with T **11**.

76	9	½d. on 9d. purple	9·00	14·00
77	10	½d. on 10d. red	1·75	19·00

1877. Surch with T **13**.

79	10	½d. on 10d. red	4·50	30·00

1877. Surch in words.

80	9	1d. on 4d. red	9·50	15·00
82		1s. on 5s. mauve	£225	£110

1878. Surch.

83	10	2c. red	8·00	5·50
84	9	4c. on 1d. brown	15·00	5·50
85		8c. on 2d. blue	70·00	2·00
86		13c. on 3d. red	13·00	28·00
87		17c. on 4d. red	£150	2·75
88		25c. on 6d. blue	£200	5·50
89		38c. on 9d. purple	22·00	65·00
90		50c. on 1s. green	85·00	3·00
91		2r.50 on 5s. mauve	14·00	17·00

18

19

1879. Various frames.

101	18	1c. violet	1·75	50
102		2c. red	30·00	4·75
103		2c. green	2·25	60
104	19	4c. orange	70·00	3·25
105		4c. red	2·75	80
106	–	8c. blue	2·00	1·25
95	–	13c. grey	£130	£170
107	–	15c. brown	4·25	1·25
108	–	15c. blue	5·50	1·00
109	–	16c. brown	4·25	1·50
96	–	17c. red	60·00	5·50
110	–	25c. olive	5·50	2·25
98	–	38c. purple	£160	£250
99	–	50c. green	3·75	3·00
111	–	50c. orange	29·00	9·50
100	–	2r.50 purple	38·00	60·00

1883. No. 96 surch **16 CENTS**.

112		16c. on 17c. red	£140	50·00

1883. No. 96 surch **SIXTEEN CENTS**.

115		16c. on 17c. red	80·00	1·75

1885. No. 98 surch **2 CENTS** with bar.

116		2c. on 38c. purple	£110	35·00

1887. No. 95 surch **2 CENTS** without bar.

117		2c. on 13c. grey	50·00	90·00

1891. Surch in words with or without bar.

123	18	1c. on 2c. violet	1·50	50
124	–	1c. on 16c. brown (No. 109)	1·50	2·75
118	19	2c. on 4c. red	1·50	60
119	–	2c. on 17c. red (No. 96)	£100	£110
120	9	2c. on 38c. on 9d. purple (No. 89)	3·50	4·00
121	–	2c. on 38c. purple (No. 98)	4·50	5·50

36

37

1895.

127	36	1c. purple and blue	75	1·50
128		2c. purple and orange	3·50	50
129		3c. purple	70	50
130		4c. purple and green	3·75	50
131		6c. green and red	4·50	4·00
132		18c. green and blue	11·00	3·50

1898. Diamond Jubilee.

133	37	36c. orange and blue	11·00	19·00

1899. Surch in figures and words.

137	–	4c. on 16c. brown (No. 109)	3·75	14·00
134	36	6c. on 18c. (No. 132)	1·00	1·00
156		12c. on 18c. (No. 132)	2·00	5·00
163	37	12c. on 36c. (No. 133)	1·25	1·25
135		15c. on 36c. (No. 133)	1·40	1·75

40 Admiral Mahe de Labourdonnais, Governor of Mauritius 1735–46

42

1899. Birth Bicentenary of Labourdonnais.

136	40	15c. blue	13·00	3·75

1900.

138	36	1c. grey and black	50	10
139		2c. purple	75	20
140		3c. green & red on yellow	3·75	1·25
141		4c. purple & red on yellow	1·50	40
142		4c. green and violet	75	2·00
167a		4c. black and red on blue	4·50	10
144		5c. purple on buff	6·50	50·00
145		5c. purple & black on buff	2·50	2·50
168a		6c. purple and red on red	5·00	10
147		8c. green & black on buff	2·00	7·50
148		12c. black and red	1·75	2·25
149		15c. green and orange	13·00	6·00
171		15c. black & blue on blue	4·00	35
151a		25c. green & red on green	3·50	14·00
174		50c. green on yellow	2·00	2·50
175	42	1r. grey and red	25·00	45·00
154		2r.50 green & blk on blue	18·00	85·00
155		5r. purple and red on red	65·00	85·00

1902. Optd **Postage & Revenue**.

157	36	4c. purple and red on yellow	1·25	20
158		6c. green and red	1·25	2·75
159		15c. green and orange	3·00	75
160	–	25c. olive (No. 110)	3·75	2·75
161	–	50c. green (No. 99)	5·00	3·25
162	–	2r.50 purple (No. 100)	90·00	£140

46

47

1910.

205	46	1c. black	1·00	1·00
206		2c. brown	1·00	10
207		2c. purple on yellow	1·00	30
183		3c. green	3·00	10
184		4c. green and red	3·50	10
210		4c. green	1·00	10
211		4c. brown	2·75	1·50
186		6c. red	2·25	20
213		6c. mauve	1·25	10
187		8c. orange	3·00	1·25
215		10c. grey	2·00	3·25
216		10c. red	4·50	1·75
217		12c. red	1·50	40
218		12c. grey	1·75	3·50
219b		15c. blue	75	25
220		20c. blue	2·00	80
221		20c. purple	8·50	10·00

1910.

185	47	5c. grey and red	2·75	3·00
188		12c. grey	2·25	2·75
190		25c. black & red on yellow	2·00	12·00
191		50c. purple and black	2·25	18·00
192		1r. black on green	7·00	12·00
193		2r.50 black and red on blue	14·00	70·00
194		5r. green and red on yellow	26·00	95·00
195		10r. green and red on green	£100	£180

48

51

1913.

223	48	1c. black	1·00	1·50
224		2c. brown	70	10
225		3c. green	70	40
226		4c. green and red	80	30
226c		4c. green	6·00	45
227		5c. grey and red	90	10
228		6c. brown	2·00	60
229		8c. orange	75	10·00
230		10c. red	1·50	20
232		12c. red	30	3·50
232b		12c. grey	6·00	20
233		15c. blue	1·50	20
234		20c. purple	85	40
235		20c. blue	9·50	90
236		25c. black & red on yellow	70	15
237		50c. purple and black	7·50	3·50
238		1r. black on green	3·50	50
239		2r.50 black & red on blue	20·00	7·50
240		5r. green and red on yellow	28·00	75·00
204d		10r. green & red on green	28·00	£120

1924. As T **42** but Arms similar to T **46**.

222		50r. purple and green	£700	£1800

1925. Surch with figures, words and bar.

242	46	3c. on 4c. green	3·25	3·75
243		10c. on 12c. red	35	50
244		15c. on 20c. blue	55	20

1935. Silver Jubilee. As T **14a** of Kenya, Uganda and Tanganyika.

245		5c. blue and grey	50	10
246		12c. green and blue	4·50	10
247		20c. brown and blue	5·50	20
248		1r. grey and purple	29·00	42·00

1937. Coronation. As T **14b** of Kenya, Uganda and Tanganyika.

249		5c. violet	40	10
250		12c. red	50	2·25
251		20c. blue	85	10

1938.

252	51	2c. grey	30	10
253		3c. purple and red	2·00	2·00
254b		4c. green	2·00	2·00
255a		5c. violet	3·25	20
256b		10c. red	2·50	20
257		12c. orange	1·00	20
258		20c. blue	1·00	10
259b		25c. purple	6·00	10
260b		1r. brown	19·00	1·25
261a		2r.50 violet	30·00	13·00
262a		5r. olive	27·00	25·00
263a		10r. purple	12·00	25·00

1946. Victory. As T **60** of Jamaica.

264		5c. violet	10	60
265		20c. blue	20	25

52 1d. "Post Office" Mauritius and King George VI

1948. Cent of First British Colonial Stamp.

266	52	5c. orange and mauve	10	50
267		12c. orange and green	15	25
268	–	20c. blue	15	10
269	–	1r. blue and brown	25	30

DESIGN: 20c., 1r. As Type **52**, but showing 2d. "Post Office" Mauritius.

1948. Silver Wedding. As T **61/2** of Jamaica.

270		5c. violet	10	10
271		10r. mauve	11·00	25·00

1949. U.P.U. As T **63/6** of Jamaica.

272		12c. red	50	1·50
273		20c. blue	2·25	2·50
274		35c. purple	60	1·50
275		1r. brown	50	20

55 Aloe Plant

60 Legend of Paul and Virginie

67 Arms of Mauritius

69 Historical Museum, Mahebourg

1950.

276	–	1c. purple	10	50
277	–	2c. red	15	10
278	55	3c. green	60	2·75
279	–	4c. green	20	1·75
280	–	5c. blue	15	10
281	–	10c. red	30	75
282	–	12c. green	1·50	2·50
283	60	20c. blue	1·00	15
284	–	25c. red	1·75	40
285	–	35c. violet	30	10
286	–	50c. green	2·75	50
287	–	1r. brown	5·50	10
288	–	2r.50 orange	12·00	11·00
289	–	5r. brown	14·00	15·00
290	67	10r. blue	15·00	23·00

DESIGNS—HORIZ: 1c. Labourdonnais sugar factory; 2c. Grand Port; 5c. Rempart Mountain; 10c. Transporting cane; 12c. Mauritius dodo and map; 35c. Government House, Reduit; 1r. Timor deer; 2r.50, Port Louis; 5r. Beach scene. VERT: 4c. Tamarind Falls; 25c. Labourdonnais statue; 50c. Pieter Both Mountain.

1953. Coronation. As T **71** of Jamaica.

291		10c. black and green	1·25	15

1953. As 1950 but portrait of Queen Elizabeth II. Designs as for corresponding values except where stated.

293	–	2c. red	10	10
294	–	3c. green	30	40
295	–	4c. purple (as 1c.)	10	1·00
296	–	5c. blue	10	10
314	–	10c. green (as 4c.)	15	10
298	69	15c. red	10	10
299	–	20c. red (as 25c.)	15	20
300	–	25c. blue (as 20c.)	1·50	10
301	–	35c. violet	20	10
302	–	50c. green	55	85
315	–	60c. green (as 12c.)	1·75	10
303	–	1r. sepia	30	10
316	–	2r.50 orange	8·00	8·50
305	–	5r. brown	14·00	10·00
306	–	10r. blue	13·00	2·00

70 Queen Elizabeth II and King George III (after Lawrence)

1961. 150th Anniv of British Post Office in Mauritius.

307	70	10c. black and red	10	10
308		20c. ultramarine and blue	30	35
309		35c. black and yellow	40	35
310		1r. purple and green	60	30

1963. Freedom from Hunger. As T **97** of Malta.

311		60c. violet	40	10

1963. Cent of Red Cross. As T **20b** of Pitcairn Islands.

312		10c. red and black	15	10
313		60c. red and blue	60	20

71 Bourbon White-eye

1965. Birds. Multicoloured.

317		2c. Type **71** (yellow background)	40	15
318		3c. Rodriguez fody ("Rodrigues Fody") (brown background)	1·00	15
319		4c. Mauritius olive white-eye ("Olive White-Eye")	30	15
340		5c. Mascarene paradise flycatcher ("Paradise Flycatcher")	70	15
321		10c. Mauritius fody	30	10
322		15c. Mauritius parakeet ("Parrakeet") (grey background)	2·00	40
323		20c. Mauritius greybird ("Cuckoo-Shrike") (yellow background)	2·00	10
324		25c. Mauritius kestrel ("Kestrel")	2·00	30
341		35c. Pink pigeon	30	15
326		50c. Reunion bulbul ("Mascarene Bul-Bul")	50	40
327		60c. Mauritius blue pigeon (extinct) ("Dutch Pigeon") (yellow background)	60	10
328		1r. Mauritius dodo (extinct) (olive background)	5·50	10
329		2r.50 Rodriguez solitaire (extinct) ("Rodrigues Solitaire")	5·00	6·00
330		5r. Mauritius red rail (extinct) ("Red Rail")	14·00	13·00
331		10r. Broad-billed parrot (extinct)	29·00	26·00

For some values with background colours changed see Nos. 370/5.

1965. Centenary of I.T.U. As T **24a** of Pitcairn Islands.

332		10c. orange and green	20	10
333		60c. yellow and violet	70	20

1965. I.C.Y. As T **24b** of Pitcairn Islands.

334		10c. purple and turquoise	15	10
335		60c. green and violet	30	20

1966. Churchill Commemoration. As T **24c** of Pitcairn Islands.

336		2c. blue	10	3·00
337		10c. green	25	10
338		60c. brown	1·10	20
339		1r. violet	1·25	20

1966. 20th Anniv of UNESCO. As T **25b/d** of Pitcairn Islands.

342		5c. multicoloured	25	30
343		10c. yellow, violet and green	30	10
344		60c. black, purple and orange	1·40	15

86 Red-tailed Tropic Bird

1967. Self-Government. Multicoloured.

345		2c. Type **86**	20	2·00
346		10c. Rodriguez brush warbler	60	10
347		60c. Rose-ringed parakeet (extinct) ("Rodrigues Parakeet")	70	10
348		1r. Grey-rumped swiftlet ("Mauritius Swiftlet")	70	10

1967. Self-Government. Nos. 317/31 optd **SELF GOVERNMENT 1967**.

349	71	2c. multicoloured	10	50
350	–	3c. multicoloured	10	50
351	–	4c. multicoloured	10	50
352	–	5c. multicoloured	10	10
353	–	10c. multicoloured	10	10
354	–	15c. multicoloured	10	30
355	–	20c. multicoloured	15	10
356	–	25c. multicoloured	15	10
357	–	35c. multicoloured	20	10
358	–	50c. multicoloured	30	15
359	–	60c. multicoloured	30	10
360	–	1r. multicoloured	1·50	10
361	–	2r.50 multicoloured	1·00	2·25
362	–	5r. multicoloured	6·00	3·25
363	–	10r. multicoloured	8·00	15·00

91 Flag of Mauritius

1968. Independence. Multicoloured.

364		2c. Type **91**	10	1·50
365		3c. Arms and Mauritius dodo emblem	15	1·50
366		15c. Type **91**	20	10
367		20c. As 3c.	50	10
368		60c. Type **91**	60	10
369		1r. As 3c.	95	10

1968. As Nos. 317/8, 322/3 and 327/8 but background colours changed as below.

370	71	2c. olive	20	3·00
371	–	3c. blue	1·75	6·00
372	–	15c. brown	55	20
373	–	20c. buff	3·50	4·00
374	–	60c. red	1·50	15
375	–	1r. purple	3·25	1·50

93 Dominique rescues Paul and Virginie

1968. Bicentenary of Bernardin de St. Pierre's Visit to Mauritius. Multicoloured.

376		2c. Type **93**	10	1·25
377		15c. Paul and Virginie crossing the river (vert)	35	10
378		50c. Visit of Labourdonnais to Madame de la Tour	50	10
379		60c. Meeting of Paul and Virginie in Confidence (vert)	50	10
380		1r. Departure of Virginie for Europe	50	20
381		2r.50 Bernardin de St. Pierre (vert)	1·50	3·75

99 Black-spotted Emperor

1969. Multicoloured (except 10, 15, 25, 60c.).

382		2c. Type **99**	10	2·75
383		3c. Red reef crab	10	3·50
384		4c. Episcopal mitre	2·00	3·75
385		5c. Black-saddled pufferfish ("Bourse")	30	10
386		10c. Starfish (red, black and flesh)	2·00	10
387		15c. Sea urchin (brown, black and blue)	30	10
480		20c. Fiddler crab	1·25	30
389		25c. Spiny shrimp (red, black and green)	30	3·50
390		30c. Single harp shells and double harp shell	1·50	1·75
483		35c. Common paper nautilus	1·75	15
484		40c. Spanish dancer	1·00	60
448		50c. Orange spider conch and violet spider conch	45	10
449b		60c. Blue marlin (black, pink and blue)	65	10
487		75c. "Conus clytospira"	1·25	1·50
396		1r. Dolphin (fish)	60	10
452		2r.50 Spiny lobster	2·00	4·50
453		5r. Ruby snapper ("Sacre chien rouge")	2·50	2·00
399w		10r. Yellow-edged lyretail ("Croissant queue jaune")	1·50	1·50

117 Gandhi as Law Student

1969. Birth Cent of Mahatma Gandhi. Mult.

400		2c. Type **117**	10	20
401		15c. Gandhi as stretcher-bearer during Zulu Revolt	20	10
402		50c. Gandhi as Satyagrahi in South Africa	20	50
403		60c. Gandhi at No. 10 Downing Street, London	20	10
404		1r. Gandhi in Mauritius, 1901	20	10
405		2r.50 Gandhi, the "Apostle of Truth and Non-Violence"	45	2·00
MS406		153 × 153 mm. Nos. 400/5	2·00	7·50

124 Frangourinier Cane-crusher (18th cent)

1969. 150th Anniv of Telfair's Improvements to the Sugar Industry. Multicoloured.

407		2c. Three-roller Vertical Mill	10	20
408		15c. Type **124**	10	10
409		60c. Beau Rivage Factory, 1867	10	10
410		1r. Mon Desert-Alma Factory, 1969	10	10
411		2r.50 Dr. Charles Telfair (vert)	25	1·25
MS412		159 × 88 mm. Nos. 407/11	1·25	2·25

1970. Expo '70. Nos. 394 and 396 optd **EXPO '70' OSAKA**.

413		60c. black, red and blue	10	10
414		1r. multicoloured	10	10

129 Morne Plage, Mountain and Boeing 707

1970. Inauguration of Lufthansa Flight, Mauritius–Frankfurt. Multicoloured.
415 25c. Type **129** 10 10
416 50c. Boeing 707 and map (vert) 10 10

131 Lenin as a Student

1970. Birth Centenary of Lenin.
417 **131** 15c. green and silver . . . 10 10
418 – 75c. brown 20 20
DESIGN: 75c. Lenin as founder of U.S.S.R.

133 2d. "Post Office" Mauritius and original Post Office

1970. Port Louis, Old and New. Multicoloured.
419 5c. Type **133** 10 10
420 15c. G.P.O. Building (built 1870) 10 10
421 50c. Mail coach (c. 1870) . . 40 10
422 75c. Port Louis Harbour (1970) 55 10
423 2r.50 Arrival of Pierre A. de Suffren (1783) 70 70
MS424 165 × 95 mm. Nos. 419/23 2·75 7·50

138 U.N. Emblem and Symbols

1970. 25th Anniv of U.N.
425 **138** 10c. multicoloured 10 10
426 60c. multicoloured 40 10

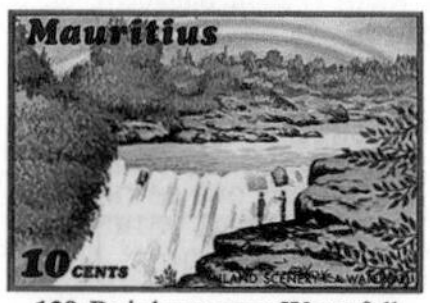

139 Rainbow over Waterfall

1971. Tourism. Multicoloured.
427 10c. Type **139** 25 10
428 15c. Trois Mamelles Mountains 25 10
429 60c. Beach scene 35 10
430 2r.50 Marine life . . . . . . 50 1·50
Nos. 427/30 have inscriptions on the reverse.

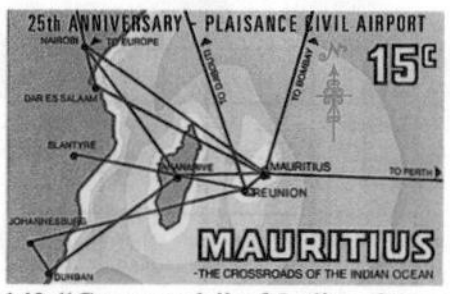

140 "Crossroads" of Indian Ocean

1971. 25th Anniv of Plaisance Airport. Multicoloured.
431 15c. Type **140** 35 10
432 60c. Boeing 707 and Terminal buildings 60 10
433 1r. Air hostesses on gangway 65 10
434 2r.50 Farman F.190, "Roland Garros" airplane, Choisy Airfield, 1937 . . . . . . 2·00 4·50

141 Princess Margaret Orthopaedic Centre

1971. 3rd Commonwealth Medical Conference. Multicoloured.
435 10c. Type **141** 10 10
436 75c. Operating theatre in National Hospital 20 20

142 Queen Elizabeth II and Prince Philip

1972. Royal Visit. Multicoloured.
455 15c. Type **142** 15 10
456 2r.50 Queen Elizabeth II (vert) . . . . 2·00 2·00

143 Theatre Facade

1972. 150th Anniv of Port Louis Theatre. Multicoloured.
457 10c. Type **143** 10 10
458 1r. Theatre auditorium . . . 40 20

144 Pirate Dhow

1972. Pirates and Privateers. Multicoloured.
459 15c. Type **144** 65 15
460 60c. Treasure chest (vert) . . 1·00 20
461 1r. Lemene and "L'Hirondelle" (vert) . . . 1·25 20
462 2r.50 Robert Surcouf . . . . 4·50 8·00

145 Mauritius University

1973. 5th Anniv of Independence. Multicoloured.
463 15c. Type **145** 10 10
464 60c. Tea development 15 15
465 1r. Bank of Mauritius . . . 15 15

146 Map and Hands

1973. O.C.A.M. Conference. Multicoloured.
466 10c. O.C.A.M. emblem (horiz) 10 10
467 2r.50 Type **146** 40 45
O.C.A.M. = Organisation Commune Africaine Malgache et Mauricienne.

147 W.H.O. Emblem

1973. 25th Anniv of W.H.O.
468 **147** 1r. multicoloured 10 10

148 Meteorological Station, Vacoas

1973. Centenary of I.M.O./W.M.O.
469 **148** 75c. multicoloured 30 70

149 Capture of the "Kent" 1800

1973. Birth Bicentenary of Robert Surcouf (privateer).
470 **149** 60c. multicoloured 50 85

150 P. Commerson

1974. Death Bicentenary (1973) of Philibert Commerson (naturalist).
471 **150** 2r.50 multicoloured . . . 30 40

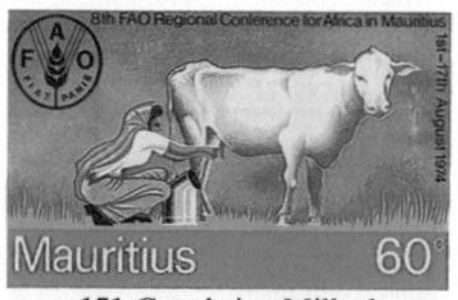

151 Cow being Milked

1974. 8th F.A.O. Regional Conf for Africa, Mauritius.
472 **151** 60c. multicoloured 20 20

152 Mail Train

1974. Centenary of U.P.U. Multicoloured.
473 15c. Type **152** 40 15
474 1r. New G.P.O., Port Louis 40 20

153 "Cottage Life" (F. Leroy)

1975. Aspects of Mauritian Life. Paintings. Mult.
493 15c. Type **153** 10 10
494 60c. "Milk Seller" (A. Richard) (vert) 25 10
495 1r. "Entrance of Port Louis Market" (Thuillier) 25 10
496 2r.50 "Washerwoman" (Max Boullee) (vert) 80 80

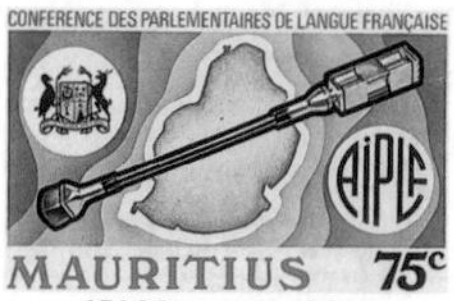

154 Mace across Map

1975. French-speaking Parliamentary Assemblies Conference, Port Louis.
497 **154** 75c. multicoloured . . . . 30 1·25

155 Woman with Lamp ("The Light of the World")

1976. International Women's Year.
498 **155** 2r.50 multicoloured . . . 35 2·00

156 Parched Landscape

1976. Drought in Africa. Multicoloured.
499 50c. Type **156** 15 30
500 60c. Map of Africa and carcass (vert) 15 30

157 "Pierre Loti", 1953–70

1976. Mail Carriers to Mauritius. Multicoloured.
501 10c. Type **157** 70 10
502 15c. "Secunder", 1907 . . . 95 10
503 50c. "Hindoostan", 1842 . . 1·60 15
504 60c. "St. Geran", 1740 . . . 1·75 15
505 2r.50 "Maen", 1638 . . . . 4·00 7·50
MS506 115 × 138 mm. Nos. 501/5 9·00 12·00

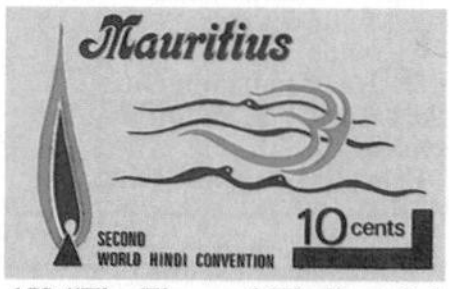

158 "The Flame of Hindi carried across the Seas"

1976. 2nd World Hindi Convention. Multicoloured.
507 10c. Type **158** 10 10
508 75c. Type **158** 10 30
509 1r.20 Hindi script . . . . . 20 1·25

159 Conference Logo and Map of Mauritius
160 King Priest and Breastplate

1976. 22nd Commonwealth Parliamentary Association Conference. Multicoloured.
510 1r. Type **159** 25 10
511 2r.50 Conference logo . . . 50 1·75

1976. Moenjodaro Excavations, Pakistan. Mult.
512 60c. Type **160** 50 10
513 1r. House with well and goblet 65 10
514 2r.50 Terracotta figurine and necklace . . . . 1·75 1·00

161 Sega Scene

1977. 2nd World Black and African Festival of Arts and Culture, Nigeria.
515 **161** 1r. multicoloured 30 15

162 The Queen with Sceptre and Rod

1977. Silver Jubilee. Multicoloured.

516 50c. The Queen at Mauritius Legislative Assembly, 1972 . . . 15 10
517 75c. Type **162** 20 10
518 5r. Presentation of Sceptre and Rod 55 75

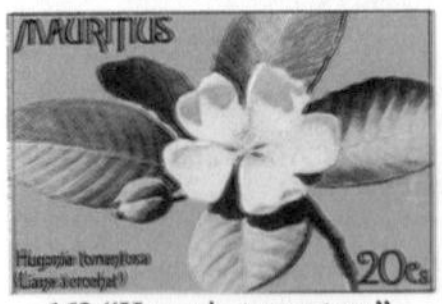

163 "Hugonia tomentosa"

1977. Indigenous Flowers. Multicoloured.

519 20c. Type **163** 25 10
520 1r. "Ochna mauritiana" (vert) 45 10
521 1r.50 "Dombeya acutangula" 60 20
522 5r. "Trochetia blackburniana" (vert) . . . 1·25 1·50
MS523 130 × 130 mm. Nos. 519/22 3·75 7·50

164 De Havilland Twin Otter 200/300

1977. Inaugural International Flight of Air Mauritius. Multicoloured.

524 25c. Type **164** 60 10
525 50c. De Havilland Twin Otter 200/300 and Air Mauritius emblem 80 10
526 75c. Piper Navajo and Boeing 747-100 . . . . 95 20
527 5r. Boeing 707 . . . . 3·00 3·75
MS528 110 × 152 mm. Nos. 524/7 8·00 8·00

165 Portuguese Map of Mauritius, 1519 — 166 Mauritius Dodo

1978.

529B **165** 10c. multicoloured . . . 75 1·25
530A – 15c. multicoloured . . . 1·50 2·75
531A – 20c. multicoloured . . . 80 2·75
532A – 25c. multicoloured . . . 60 2·00
533B – 35c. multicoloured . . . 1·00 20
534A – 50c. multicoloured . . . 50 75
535A – 60c. multicoloured . . . 60 2·75
536A – 70c. multicoloured . . . 2·75 4·00
537B – 75c. multicoloured . . . 1·75 3·50
538A – 90c. multicoloured . . . 4·00 4·25
539A – 1r. multicoloured . . . 60 50
540A – 1r.20 multicoloured . . 1·75 4·00
541B – 1r.25 multicoloured . . 1·50 20
542A – 1r.50 multicoloured . . 1·00 2·75
543A – 2r. multicoloured . . . 60 70
544A – 3r. multicoloured . . . 60 50
545A – 5r. multicoloured . . . 60 1·75
546A – 10r. multicoloured . . . 1·00 1·00
547A – 15r. multicoloured . . . 1·50 3·00
548A – 25r. green, black & brn 2·00 3·25

DESIGNS—HORIZ: 15c. Dutch Occupation, 1638–1710; 20c. Map by Van Keulen, c. 1700; 50c. Construction of Port Louis, c. 1736; 70c. Map by Bellin, 1763; 90c. Battle of Grand Port, 1810; 1r. Landing of the British, 1810; 1r.20, Government House, c. 1840; 1r.50, Indian immigration, 1835; 2r. Race Course, c. 1870; 3r. Place d'Armes, c. 1880; 5r. Royal Visit postcard, 1901; 10r. Royal College, 1914; 25r. First Mauritian Governor-General and Prime Minister. VERT: 25c. Settlement on Rodriguez, 1691; 35c. French settlers Charter, 1715; 60c. Pierre Poivre, c. 1767; 75c. First coinage, 1794; 1r.25 Lady Gomm's Ball, 1847; 15r. Unfurling of Mauritian flag.

1978. 25th Anniv of Coronation.

549 – 3r. grey, black and blue 25 45
550 – 3r. multicoloured 25 45
551 **166** 3r. grey, black and blue 25 45

DESIGNS: No. 549, Antelope of Bohun; No. 550, Queen Elizabeth II.

167 Problem of Infection, World War I

1978. 50th Anniv of Discovery of Penicillin.

552 **167** 20c. multicoloured 85 10
553 – 1r. multicoloured . . . . 1·75 10
554 – 1r.50 black, brown & grn 2·50 1·40
555 – 5r. multicoloured . . . . 3·25 6·00
MS556 150 × 90 mm. Nos. 552/5 9·50 11·00

DESIGNS: 1r. First mould growth, 1928; 1r.50, "Penicillium chrysogenum" ("notatum"); 5r. Sir Alexander Fleming.

168 "Papilio manlius" (butterfly)

1978. Endangered Species. Multicoloured.

557 20c. Type **168** . . . . 2·00 30
558 1r. Geckos . . . . 1·00 10
559 1r.50 Greater Mascarene flying fox . . . . 1·25 1·00
560 5r. Mauritius kestrel . . . . 14·00 9·00
MS561 154 × 148 mm. Nos. 557/60 45·00 18·00

169 Ornate Table — 171 Father Laval and Crucifix

170 Whitcomb Diesel Locomotive 65H.P., 1949

1978. Bicentenary of Reconstruction of Chateau Le Reduit. Multicoloured.

562 15c. Type **169** 10 10
563 75c. Chateau Le Reduit . . . 10 10
564 3r. Le Reduit gardens 40 45

1979. Railway Locomotives. Multicoloured.

565 20c. Type **170** 20 10
566 1r. "Sir William", 1922 . . . 40 10
567 1r.50 Kitson type 1930 . . . 60 45
568 2r. Garratt type, 1927 . . . . 75 85
MS569 128 × 128 mm. Nos. 565/8 2·00 4·00

1979. Beatification of Father Laval (missionary). Multicoloured.

570 20c. Type **171** 10 10
571 1r.50 Father Laval 10 10
572 5r. Father Laval's tomb (horiz) 35 50
MS573 150 × 96 mm. Nos. 570/2 2·50 3·25

172 Astronaut descending from Lunar Module — 173 Great Britain 1855 4d. Stamp and Sir Rowland Hill

1979. 10th Anniv of Moon Landing. Multicoloured. Self-adhesive.

574 20c. Type **172** 40 50
575 3r. Astronaut performing experiment on Moon . . . 90 1·25
576 5r. Astronaut on Moon . . . 3·50 6·50

1979. Death Cent of Sir Rowland Hill. Mult.

577 25c. Type **173** 10 10
578 2r. 1954 60c. definitive . . . 55 55
579 5r. 1847 1d. "POST OFFICE" . . . . 1·00 1·75
MS580 120 × 89 mm. 3r. 1847 2d. "POST OFFICE" . . . . . . 1·10 1·75

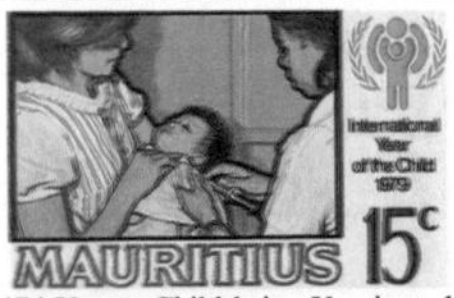

174 Young Child being Vaccinated

1979. International Year of the Child.

581 **174** 15c. multicoloured 10 10
582 – 25c. multicoloured 10 10
583 – 1r. black, blue and light blue 15 10
584 – 1r.50 multicoloured . . . 30 35
585 – 3r. multicoloured . . . . 50 1·10

DESIGNS—HORIZ: 25c. Children playing; 1r.50, Girls in chemistry laboratory; 3r. Boy operating lathe. VERT: 1r. I.Y.C. emblem.

175 The Lienard Obelisk

1980. Pamplemousses Botanical Gardens. Multicoloured.

586 20c. Type **175** 15 10
587 25c. Poivre Avenue 15 10
588 1r. Varieties of Vacoas . . . 25 10
589 2r. Giant water lilies 50 55
590 5r. Mon Plaisir (mansion) . . 85 3·00
MS591 152 × 105 mm. Nos. 586/90 3·50 5·00

176 "Emirne" (French steam packet)

1980. "London 1980" International Stamp Exhibition. Mail-carrying Ships. Multicoloured.

592 25c. Type **176** 25 10
593 1r. "Boissevain" (cargo liner) 40 10
594 2r. "La Boudeuse" (Bougainville's ship) . . . 60 70
595 5r. "Sea Breeze" (English clipper) . . . . 70 2·50

177 Blind Person Basket-making — 178 Prime Minister Sir Seewoosagur Ramgoolam

1980. Birth Centenary of Helen Keller (campaigner for the handicapped). Multicoloured.

596 25c. Type **177** 20 10
597 1r. Deaf child under instruction 45 10
598 2r.50 Helen reading braille 70 35
599 5r. Helen at graduation, 1904 1·25 1·25

1980. 80th Birthday and 40th Year in Parliament of Prime Minister Sir Seewoosagur Ramgoolam.

600 **178** 15r. multicoloured . . . . 1·00 1·40

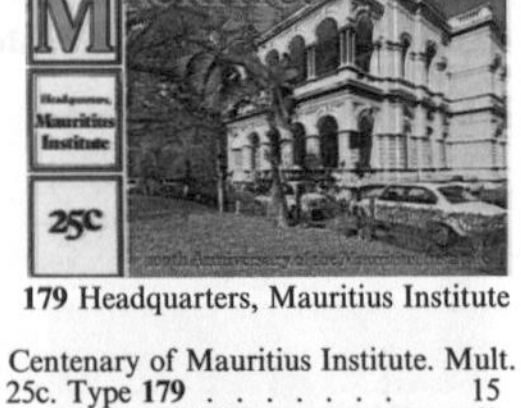

179 Headquarters, Mauritius Institute

1980. Centenary of Mauritius Institute. Mult.

601 25c. Type **179** 15 10
602 2r. Rare copy of Veda . . . 40 20
603 2r.50 Glory of India cone shell 55 25
604 5r. "Le Torrent" (painting by Harpignies) . . . . 65 1·50

180 "Hibiscus liliiflorus" — 181 Beau-Bassin/Rose Hill

1981. Flowers. Multicoloured.

605 25c. Type **180** 20 10
606 2r. "Erythrospermum monticolum" 60 65
607 2r.50 "Chasalia boryana" . . 65 1·25
608 5r. "Hibiscus columnaris" . . 1·00 3·25

1981. Coats of Arms of Mauritius Towns. Multicoloured.

609 25c. Type **181** 10 10
610 1r.50 Curepipe 25 20
611 2r. Quatre-Bornes 30 25
612 2r.50 Vacoas/Phoenix 35 30
613 5r. Port Louis 55 75
MS614 130 × 130 mm. Nos. 609/13 1·75 5·50

182 Prince Charles as Colonel-in-Chief, Royal Regiment of Wales — 184 Drummer and Piper

183 Emmanuel Anquetil and Guy Rozemont

1981. Royal Wedding. Multicoloured.

615 25c. Wedding bouquet from Mauritius 10 10
616 2r.50 Type **182** 40 15
617 10r. Prince Charles and Lady Diana Spencer 80 90

1981. Famous Politicians and Physician.

618 **183** 20c. black and red 10 10
619 – 25c. black and yellow . . . 10 10
620 – 1r.25 black and green . . 30 30
621 – 1r.50 black and red . . . 35 15
622 – 2r. black and blue 45 20
623 – 2r.50 black and brown . . 50 70
624 – 5r. black and blue . . . . 1·75 1·75

DESIGNS: 25c. Remy Ollier and Sookdeo Bissoondoyal; 1r.25, Maurice Cure and Barthelemy Ohsan; 1r.50, Sir Guy Forget and Renganaden Seeneevassen; 2r. Sir Abdul Razak Mohamed and Jules Koenig; 2r.50, Abdoollatiff Mahomed Osman and Dazzi Rama (Pandit Sahadeo); 5r. Sir Thomas Lewis (physician) and electrocardiogram.

1981. Religion and Culture. Multicoloured.

625 20c. Type **184** 10 10
626 2r. Swami Sivananda (vert) 1·00 1·00
627 5r. Chinese Pagoda . . . . . 1·25 3·25

The 20c. value commemorates the World Tamil Culture Conference (1980).

185 "Skills" — 186 Ka'aba (sacred shrine, Great Mosque of Mecca)

1981. 25th Anniv of Duke of Edinburgh Award Scheme. Multicoloured.

628 25c. Type **185** 10 10
629 1r.25 "Service" 10 10
630 5r. "Expeditions" 20 30
631 10r. Duke of Edinburgh . . . 40 70

1981. Moslem Year 1400 A.H. Commemoration. Multicoloured.

632 25c. Type **186** 30 10
633 2r. Mecca 80 80
634 5r. Mecca and Ka'aba . . . 1·40 2·75

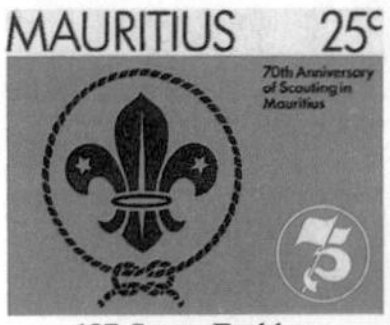

187 Scout Emblem

189 Bride and Groom at Buckingham Palace

188 Charles Darwin

1982. 75th Anniv of Boy Scout Movement and 70th Anniv of Scouting in Mauritius.
635 **187** 25c. lilac and green . . . 10 10
636 – 2r. brown and ochre . . . 40 30
637 – 5r. green and olive . . . 85 1·00
638 – 10r. green and blue . . . 1·25 2·00
DESIGNS: 2r. Lord Baden-Powell and Baden-Powell House; 5r. Grand Howl; 10r. Ascent of Pieter Both.

1982. 150th Anniv of Charles Darwin's Voyage. Multicoloured.
639 25c. Type **188** 20 10
640 2r. Darwin's telescope . . . 40 45
641 2r.50 Darwin's elephant ride 1·00 55
642 10r. H.M.S. "Beagle" beached for repairs . . . . 1·50 2·75

1982. 21st Birthday of Princess of Wales. Mult.
643 25c. Mauritius coat of arms 10 10
644 2r.50 Princess Diana in Chesterfield, November 1981 . . . . 60 45
645 5r. Type **189** . . . . 75 1·25
646 10r. Formal portrait . . . . 2·75 3·00

190 Prince and Princess of Wales with Prince William

1982. Birth of Prince William of Wales.
647 **190** 2r.50 multicoloured . . . 1·00 50

191 Bois Fandamane Plant

193 Early Wall-mounted Telephone

192 Arms and Flag of Mauritius

1982. Centenary of Robert Koch's Discovery of Tubercle Bacillus. Multicoloured.
648 25c. Type **191** 10 10
649 1r.25 Central market, Port Louis 35 40
650 2r. Bois Banane plant 50 75
651 5r. Platte de Lezard plant . . 60 2·25
652 10r. Dr. Robert Koch . . . 90 3·75

1983. Commonwealth Day. Multicoloured.
653 25c. Type **192** 10 10
654 2r.50 Satellite view of Mauritius 20 30
655 5r. Harvesting sugar cane . . 30 75
656 10r. Port Louis harbour . . . 95 1·50

1983. World Communications Year. Mult.
657 25c. Type **193** 10 10
658 1r.25 Early telegraph apparatus (horiz.) 35 20
659 2r. Earth satellite station . . 45 50
660 10r. First hot-air balloon in Mauritius, 1784 (horiz) . . 80 2·75

194 Map of Namibia

195 Fish Trap

1983. Namibia Day. Multicoloured.
661 25c. Type **194** 45 10
662 2r.50 Hand breaking chains 1·50 75
663 5r. Family and settlement . . 2·00 2·25
664 10r. Diamond mining . . . . 4·75 3·75

1983. Fishery Resources. Multicoloured.
665 25c. Type **195** 15 10
666 1r. Fishing boat (horiz) . . . 30 15
667 5r. Game fishing . . . . . . 55 2·25
668 10r. Octopus drying (horiz) 80 4·00

196 Swami Dayananda

197 Adolf von Plevitz

1983. Death Centenary of Swami Dayananda. Multicoloured.
669 25c. Type **196** 10 10
670 35c. Last meeting with father 10 10
671 2r. Receiving religious instruction 50 65
672 5r. Swami demonstrating strength . . . . 70 2·50
673 10r. At a religious gathering 1·00 3·75

1983. 125th Anniv of Arrival in Mauritius of Adolf von Plevitz (social reformer). Multicoloured.
674 25c. Type **197** 10 10
675 1r.25 La Laura, Government school 30 30
676 5r. Von Plevitz addressing Commission of Enquiry, 1872 . . . . 1·00 2·50
677 10r. Von Plevitz with Indian farm workers . . . . . . 1·75 3·75

198 Courtship Chase

1984. The Mauritius Kestrel. Multicoloured.
678 25c. Type **198** 85 30
679 2r. Kestrel in tree (vert) . . . 2·00 1·25
680 2r.50 Young kestrel . . . . 2·25 2·25
681 10r. Head (vert) . . . . . . 3·25 8·50

199 Wreck of S.S. "Tayeb"

200 Blue Latan Palm

1984. 250th Anniv of "Lloyd's List" (newspaper). Multicoloured.
682 25c. Type **199** 30 10
683 1r. S.S. "Taher" 95 15
684 5r. East Indiaman "Triton" 3·00 3·25
685 10r. M.S. "Astor" . . . . . 3·50 6·50

1984. Palm Trees. Multicoloured.
686 25c. Type **200** 10 10
687 50c. "Hyophorbe vaughanii" 20 20
688 2r.50 "Tectiphiala ferox" . . 1·50 1·75
689 5r. Round Island bottle-palm 2·25 3·50
690 10r. "Hyophorbe amaricaulis" . . . . 3·50 7·00

201 Slave Girl

203 The Queen Mother on Clarence House Balcony, 1980

202 75th Anniversary Production of "Faust" and Leoville L'Homme

1984. 150th Anniv of Abolition of Slavery and Introduction of Indian Immigrants.
691 **201** 25c. purple, lilac and brown 15 10
692 – 1r. purple, lilac and brown 70 10
693 – 2r. purple and lilac . . . 1·50 1·00
694 – 10r. purple and lilac . . . 7·00 11·00
DESIGNS—VERT: 1r. Slave market. HORIZ: 2r. Indian immigrant family; 10r. Arrival of Indian immigrants.

1984. Centenary of Alliance Francaise (cultural organization). Multicoloured.
695 25c. Type **202** 20 10
696 1r.25 Prize-giving ceremony and Aunauth Beejadbur . . 70 50
697 5r. First headquarters and Hector Clarenc . . . . . 2·00 3·00
698 10r. Lion Mountain and Labourdonnais . . . . . 2·50 5·50

1985. Life and Times of Queen Elizabeth the Queen Mother. Multicoloured.
699 25c. The Queen Mother in 1926 . . . . 60 10
700 2r. With Princess Margaret at Trooping the Colour . . . 1·50 45
701 5r. Type **203** . . . . 1·60 1·60
702 10r. With Prince Henry at his christening (from photo by Lord Snowdon) . . . . . 1·90 4·00
MS703 91 × 73 mm. 15r. Reopening the Stratford Canal, 1964 . . . 6·00 4·25

204 High Jumping

205 Adult and Fledgling Pink Pigeons

1985. 2nd Indian Ocean Islands Games. Multicoloured.
704 25c. Type **204** 40 10
705 50c. Javelin-throwing 70 30
706 1r.25 Cycling . . . . 4·50 2·00
707 10r. Wind surfing . . . . . 7·50 13·00

1985. Pink Pigeon. Multicoloured.
708 25c. Type **205** . . . . 3·00 50
709 2r. Pink pigeon displaying at nest . . . . 7·00 1·75
710 2r.50 On nest . . . . 7·50 3·75
711 5r. Pair preening . . . . . . 12·00 12·00

10TH ANNIVERSARY OF THE WORLD TOURISM ORGANISATION
25c
MAURITIUS

206 Caverne Patates, Rodrigues

1985. 10th Anniv of World Tourism Organization. Multicoloured.
712 25c. Type **206** 50 10
713 35c. Coloured soils, Chamarel 50 40
714 5r. Serpent Island . . . . . 5·00 5·50
715 10r. Coin de Mire Island . . 7·00 11·00

207 Old Town Hall, Port Louis

1985. 250th Anniv of Port Louis. Multicoloured.
716 25c. Type **207** 10 10
717 1r. Al-Aqsa Mosque (180th anniv) . . . . 1·50 10
718 2r.50 Vase and trees (250th anniv of settlement of Tamil-speaking Indians) . . 1·25 1·75
719 10r. Port Louis Harbour . . 7·00 12·00

208 Edmond Halley and Diagram

1986. Appearance of Halley's Comet. Mult.
720 25c. Type **208** 40 10
721 1r.25 Halley's Comet (1682) and Newton's Reflector . . 1·10 50
722 3r. Halley's Comet passing Earth . . . . 1·60 2·25
723 10r. "Giotto" spacecraft . . 3·50 7·00

1986. 60th Birthday of Queen Elizabeth II. As T **246a** of Papua New Guinea. Multicoloured.
724 25c. Princess Elizabeth wearing badge of Grenadier Guards, 1942 . . 10 10
725 75c. Investiture of Prince of Wales, 1969 . . . . 10 10
726 2r. With Prime Minister of Mauritius, 1972 . . . . . 20 25
727 3r. In Germany, 1978 . . . . 30 40
728 15r. At Crown Agents Head Office, London, 1983 . . . 1·25 2·00

209 Maize (World Food Day)

210 "Cryptopus elatus"

1986. International Events. Multicoloured.
729 25c. Type **209** 10 10
730 1r. African Regional Industrial Property Organization emblem (10th anniv) 30 10
731 1r.25 International Peace Year emblem 65 50
732 10r. Footballer and Mauritius Football Association emblem (World Cup Football Championship, Mexico) . . . . 5·50 10·00

1986. Orchids. Multicoloured.
733 25c. Type **210** 50 10
734 2r. "Jumellea recta" . . . . 1·25 45
735 2r.50 "Angraecum mauritianum" . . . . 1·40 60
736 10r. "Bulbophyllum longiflorum" . . . . . . 2·25 4·50

211 Hesketh Bell Bridge

1987. Mauritius Bridges. Multicoloured.
758 25c. Type **211** 25 10
759 50c. Sir Colville Deverell Bridge 35 20
760 2r.50 Cavendish Bridge . . . 70 75
761 5r. Tamarin Bridge . . . . . 90 2·00
762 10r. Grand River North West Bridge . . . . 1·25 2·50

212 Supreme Court, Port Louis

213 Mauritius Dodo Mascot

1987. Bicentenary of the Mauritius Bar. Mult.
763 25c. Type **212** 10 10
764 1r. District Court, Flacq . . 40 10
765 1r.25 Statue of Justice . . . 50 20
766 10r. Barristers of 1787 and 1987 . . . . 2·00 2·25

1987. International Festival of the Sea. Mult.

767	25c. Type **213**	60	10
768	1r.50 Yacht regatta (horiz)	2·00	1·00
769	3r. Water skiing (horiz)	3·00	3·75
770	5r. "Svanen" (barquentine)	3·50	8·00

214 Toys

1987. Industrialization. Multicoloured.

771	20c. Type **214**	10	10
772	35c. Spinning factory	10	10
773	50c. Rattan furniture	10	10
774	2r.50 Spectacle factory	85	80
775	10r. Stone carving	2·50	2·75

215 Maison Ouvriere (Int Year of Shelter for the Homeless)

1987. Art and Architecture.

776 **215**	25c. multicoloured	10	10
777 –	1r. black and grey	25	10
778 –	1r.25 multicoloured	30	30
779 –	2r. multicoloured	55	55
780 –	5r. multicoloured	1·00	1·25

DESIGNS: 1r. "Paul et Virginie" (lithograph); 1r.25, Chateau de Rosnay; 2r. "Vieille Ferme" (Boulle); 5r. "Trois Mamelles".

216 University of Mauritius

1988. 20th Anniv of Independence. Mult.

781	25c. Type **216**	10	10
782	75c. Anniversary gymnastic display	20	10
783	2r.50 Hurdlers and aerial view of Sir Maurice Rault Stadium	70	55
784	5r. Air Mauritius aircraft at Sir Seewoosagur Ramgoolam International Airport	1·40	1·60
785	10r. Governor-General Sir Veerasamy Ringadoo and Prime Minister Aneerood Jugnauth	2·25	2·75

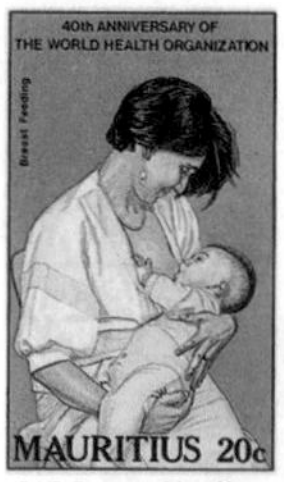

217 Breast Feeding

218 Modern Bank Building

1988. 40th Anniv of W.H.O. Multicoloured.

786	20c. Type **217**	15	10
787	2r. Baby under vaccination umbrella and germ droplets	1·25	70
788	3r. Nutritious food	1·40	1·25
789	10r. W.H.O. logo	2·75	3·75

1988. 150th Anniv of Mauritius Commercial Bank Ltd.

790 **218**	25c. black, green and blue	10	10
791 –	1r. black and red	20	10
792 –	1r.25 multicoloured	40	30
793 –	25r. multicoloured	6·50	8·50

DESIGNS—HORIZ: 1r. Mauritius Commercial Bank, 1897; 25r. Fifteen dollar bank note of 1838. VERT: 1r.25, Bank arms.

219 Olympic Rings and Athlete

1988. Olympic Games, Seoul. Multicoloured.

794	25c. Type **219**	10	10
795	35c. Wrestling	15	15
796	1r.50 Long distance running	75	60
797	10r. Swimming	2·50	4·00

220 Nature Park

1989. Protection of the Environment. Mult.

798B	15c. Underwater view	15	1·25
799B	20c. As 15c.	15	1·25
800B	30c. Common greenshank ("Greenshank")	1·75	1·25
801B	40c. Type **220**	15	60
810A	50c. Round Island (vert)	15	10
801cB	60c. As 50c.	20	10
811A	75c. Bassin Blanc	20	10
812A	1r. Mangrove (vert)	20	10
802A	1r.50 Whimbrel	1·00	35
813A	2r. Le Morne	30	20
803A	3r. Marine life	50	20
804B	4r. Fern tree (vert)	50	70
814A	5r. Riviere du Poste estuary	60	50
805A	6r. Ecological scenery (vert)	60	50
806B	10r. "Phelsuma ornata" (gecko) on plant (vert)	85	1·40
806aB	15r. Benares waves	1·50	2·50
807B	25r. Migratory birds and map (vert)	3·50	4·00

221 La Tour Sumeire, Port Louis

222 Cardinal Jean Margeot

1989. Bicentenary of the French Revolution.

818 **221**	30c. black, green & yellow	10	10
819 –	1r. black, brown and light brown	25	10
820 –	8r. multicoloured	2·25	2·50
821 –	15r. multicoloured	3·00	4·00

DESIGNS: 1r. Salle de Spectacle du Jardin; 8r. Portrait of Comte de Malartic; 15r. Bicentenary logo.

1989. Visit of Pope John Paul II. Multicoloured.

822	30c. Type **222**	30	10
823	40c. Pope John Paul II and Prime Minister Jugnauth, Vatican, 1988	1·00	25
824	3r. Mere Marie Magdeleine de la Croix and Chapelle des Filles de Marie, Port Louis, 1864	1·50	1·25
825	6r. St. Francois d'Assise Church, Pamplemousses, 1756	2·25	2·50
826	10r. Pope John Paul II	6·00	7·00

223 Nehru

1989. Birth Centenary of Jawaharlal Nehru (Indian statesman). Multicoloured.

827	40c. Type **223**	1·25	20
828	1r.50 Nehru with daughter, Indira, and grandsons	2·75	85
829	3r. Nehru and Gandhi	4·50	2·75
830	4r. Nehru with Presidents Nasser and Tito	3·25	3·00
831	10r. Nehru with children	6·00	10·00

224 Cane Cutting

1990. 350th Anniv of Introduction of Sugar Cane to Mauritius. Multicoloured.

832	30c. Type **224**	15	10
833	40c. Sugar factory, 1867	20	10
834	1r. Mechanical loading of cane	40	10
835	25r. Modern sugar factory	11·00	13·00

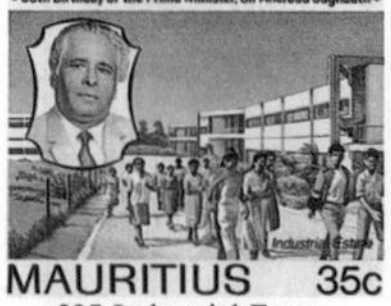

225 Industrial Estate

226 Desjardins (naturalist) (150th death anniv)

1990. 60th Birthday of Prime Minister Sir Anerood Jugnauth. Multicoloured.

836	35c. Type **225**	10	10
837	40c. Sir Anerood Jugnauth at desk	10	10
838	1r.50 Mauritius Stock Exchange symbol	40	30
839	4r. Jugnauth with Governor-General Sir Seewoosagur Ramgoolam	1·50	2·25
840	10r. Jugnauth greeting Pope John Paul II	11·00	12·00

1990. Anniversaries. Multicoloured.

841	30c. Type **226**	30	10
842	35c. Logo on TV screen (25th anniv of Mauritius Broadcasting Corporation) (horiz)	30	10
843	6r. Line Barracks (now Police Headquarters) (250th anniv)	4·50	4·75
844	8r. Town Hall, Curepipe (centenary of municipality) (horiz)	3·50	5·50

227 Letters from Alphabets

1990. International Literacy Year. Multicoloured.

845	30c. Type **227**	25	10
846	1r. Blind child reading Braille	1·75	15
847	3r. Open book and globe	3·25	2·25
848	10r. Book showing world map with quill pen	11·00	12·00

1991. 65th Birthday of Queen Elizabeth II and 70th Birthday of Prince Philip. As T **58** of Kiribati. Multicoloured.

849	8r. Queen Elizabeth II	1·75	2·75
850	8r. Prince Philip in Grenadier Guards ceremonial uniform	1·75	2·75

228 City Hall, Port Louis (25th anniv of City status)

1991. Anniversaries and Events. Multicoloured.

851	40c. Type **228**	10	10
852	4r. Colonel Draper (race course founder) (150th death anniv) (vert)	1·75	2·00
853	6r. Joseph Barnard (engraver) and "POST PAID" 2d. stamp (175th birth anniv) (vert)	2·00	2·75
854	10r. Supermarine Spitfire "Mauritius II" (50th anniv of Second World War)	4·50	8·00

229 "Euploea euphon"

1991. "Phila Nippon '91" International Stamp Exn, Tokyo. Butterflies. Multicoloured.

855	40c. Type **229**	60	20
856	3r. "Hypolimnas misippus" (female)	1·90	1·00
857	8r. "Papilio manlius"	3·50	4·25
858	10r. "Hypolimnas misippus" (male)	3·50	4·50

230 Green Turtle, Tromelin

1991. Indian Ocean Islands. Multicoloured.

859	40c. Type **230**	50	20
860	1r. Glossy ibis ("Ibis"), Agalega	1·50	40
861	2r. Takamaka flowers, Chagos Archipelago	1·60	1·10
862	15r. Violet spider conch sea shell, St. Brandon	7·00	9·50

231 Pres. Veerasamy Ringadoo and President's Residence

1992. Proclamation of Republic. Multicoloured.

863	40c. Type **231**	10	10
864	4r. Prime Minister Anerood Jugnauth and Government House	1·00	1·25
865	8r. Children and rainbow	2·25	3·75
866	10r. Presidential flag	5·50	6·00

232 Ticolo (mascot)

233 Bouquet (25th anniv of Fleurir Maurice)

1992. 8th African Athletics Championships, Port Louis. Multicoloured.

867	40c. Type **232**	10	10
868	4r. Sir Anerood Jugnauth Stadium (horiz)	75	1·25
869	5r. High jumping (horiz)	90	1·40
870	6r. Championships emblem	1·25	1·90

1992. Local Events and Anniversaries. Mult.

871	40c. Type **233**	15	10
872	1r. Swami Krishnanandji Maharaj (25th anniv of arrival)	50	10
873	2r. Boy with dog (humane education) (horiz)	1·40	75
874	3r. Commission Headquarters (10th anniv of Indian Ocean Commission) (horiz)	1·25	1·00
875	15r. Radio telescope antenna, Bras d'Eau (project inauguration) (horiz)	4·50	7·50

234 Bank of Mauritius Headquarters

235 Housing Development

1992. 25th Anniv of Bank of Mauritius. Mult.

876	40c. Type **234**	10	10
877	4r. Dodo gold coin (horiz)	1·75	1·10
878	8r. First bank note issue (horiz)	2·50	3·25
879	15r. Graph of foreign exchange reserves, 1967–92 (horiz)	4·50	7·50

1993. 25th Anniv of National Day. Multicoloured.

880	30c. Type **235**	10	10
881	40c. Gross domestic product graph on computer screen	10	10
882	3r. National colours on map of Mauritius	40	60
883	4r. Ballot box	45	75
884	15r. Grand Commander's insignia for Order of Star and Key of the Indian Ocean	2·00	5·00

236 Bell 206 B JetRanger Helicopter

1993. 25th Anniv of Air Mauritius Ltd. Mult.

885	40c. Type **236**	1·00	40
886	3r. Boeing 747SP	1·50	1·25

887 4r. Aerospatiale/Aeritalia ATR 42 . . . . 1·75 1·75
888 10r. Boeing 767-200ER . . . 4·50 7·00
MS889 150 × 91 mm. Nos. 885/8 10·00 12·00

1993. No. 811 surch **40cs**.
890 40c. on 75c. Bassin Blanc . . 1·00 60

238 French Royal Charter, 1715, and Act of Capitulation, 1810

239 "Scotia" (cable ship) and Map of Cable Route

1993. 5th Summit of French-speaking Nations. Multicoloured.
891 1r. Type **238** 90 10
892 5r. Road signs . . . . 3·00 2·50
893 6r. Code Napoleon . . . . . 3·00 3·25
894 7r. Early Mauritius newspapers . . . . 3·00 3·50

1993. Centenary of Telecommunications. Mult.
895 40c. Type **239** . . . . 1·00 30
896 3r. Morse key and code . . . 1·50 1·00
897 4r. Signal Mountain Earth station . . . . 1·75 1·75
898 8r. Communications satellite 3·25 6·00

240 Indian Mongoose

1994. Mammals. Multicoloured.
899 40c. Type **240** 40 10
900 2r. Indian black-naped hare 1·25 40
901 8r. Pair of crab-eating macaques . . . . 3·25 4·00
902 10r. Adult and infant common tenrec . . . . . 3·50 4·50

241 Dr Edouard Brown-Sequard (physiologist) (death cent)

1994. Anniversaries and Events. Multicoloured.
903 40c. Type **241** 15 10
904 4r. Family in silhouette (International Year of the Family) 45 55
905 8r. World Cup and map of U.S.A. (World Cup Football Championship, U.S.A.) . . . . 1·25 2·25
906 10r. Control tower, SSR International Airport (50th anniv of Civil Aviation Organization) . . . . . . 1·50 2·50

242 "St. Geran" leaving L'Orient for Isle de France, 1744

1994. 250th Anniv of Wreck of "St. Geran" (sailing packet). Multicoloured.
907 40c. Type **242** 25 10
908 5r. In rough seas off Isle de France 75 80
909 6r. Bell and main mast . . . 85 1·25
910 10r. Artifacts from wreck . . 1·40 3·00
MS911 119 × 89 mm. 15r. "St. Geran" leaving L'Orient (vert) . . . . 4·00 5·00

243 Ring-a-ring-a-roses

1994. Children's Games and Pastimes. Children's paintings. Multicoloured.
912 30c. Type **243** 10 10
913 40c. Skipping and ball games 10 10
914 8r. Water sports . . . . . . 1·40 2·25
915 10r. Blind man's buff . . . . 1·40 2·25

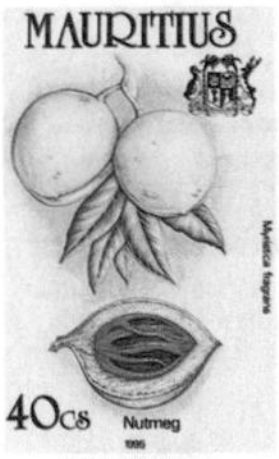

244 Nutmeg

245 Mare Longue Reservoir

1995. Spices. Multicoloured.
916 40c. Type **244** 10 10
917 4r. Coriander 55 65
918 5r. Cloves 65 80
919 10r. Cardamom . . . . . . 1·25 2·50

1995. 50th Anniv of End of Second World War. As T **75** of Kiribati, but 35 × 28 mm. Mult.
920 5r. H.M.S. "Mauritius" (cruiser) . . . . 1·75 2·25
921 5r. Mauritian soldiers and map of North Africa . . . 1·75 2·25
922 5r. Consolidated PBY-5 Catalina flying boat, Tombeau Bay . . . . . . 1·75 2·25

1995. Anniversaries. Multicoloured.
923 40c. Type **245** (50th anniv of construction) 15 10
924 4r. Mahebourg to Curepipe road (bicentenary of construction) . . . . . . 1·25 1·40
925 10r. Buildings on fire (centenary of Great Fire of Port Louis) . . . . 2·50 3·25

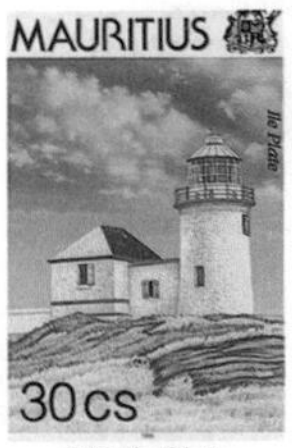

246 Ile Plate Lighthouse

247 Symbolic Children under UNICEF Umbrella

1995. Lighthouses. Multicoloured.
926 30c. Type **246** 85 20
927 40c. Pointe aux Caves . . . 85 20
928 8r. Ile aux Fouquets . . . . 3·00 3·25
929 10r. Pointe aux Canonniers 3·50 3·75
MS930 130 × 100 mm. Nos. 926/9 9·00 9·50

1995. 50th Anniv of United Nations. Multicoloured.
931 40c. Type **247** 10 10
932 4r. Hard hat and building construction (I.L.O.) . . . 40 55
933 8r. Satellite picture of cyclone (W.M.O.) . . . . 85 1·40
934 10r. Bread and grain (F.A.O.) 1·00 1·60

248 C.O.M.E.S.A. Emblem

1995. Inauguration of Common Market for Eastern and Southern Africa.
935 **248** 60c. black and pink . . . 15 10
936 4r. black and blue 55 60
937 8r. black and yellow . . . 1·10 1·60
938 10r. black and green . . . 1·40 1·90

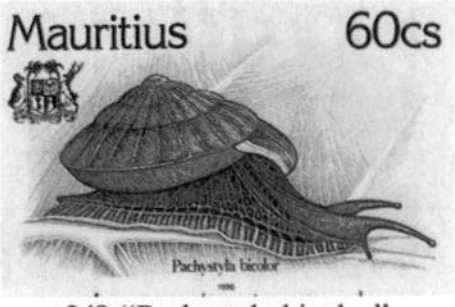

249 "Pachystyla bicolor"

1996. Snails. Multicoloured.
939 60c. Type **249** 15 10
940 4r. "Gonidomus pagodus" 65 55
941 5r. "Harmogenanina implicata" 65 65
942 10r. "Tropidophora eugeniae" . . . . 1·10 1·75

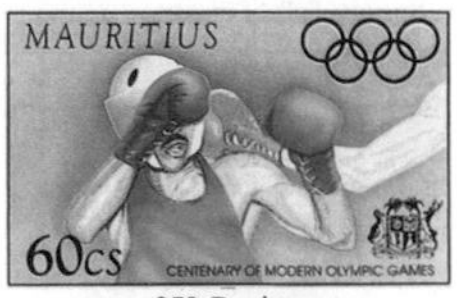

250 Boxing

1996. Centenary of Modern Olympic Games. Mult.
943 60c. Type **250** 10 10
944 4r. Badminton 50 50
945 5r. Basketball 80 80
946 10r. Table tennis . . . . . . 1·25 2·00

251 "Zambezia" (freighter)

1996. Ships. Multicoloured.
947 60c. Type **251** 20 10
948 4r. "Sir Jules" (coastal freighter) 65 55
949 5r. "Mauritius" (cargo liner) 75 85
950 10r. "Mauritius Pride" (container ship) . . . . . 1·50 2·50
MS951 125 × 91 mm. Nos. 947/50 3·00 4·50

252 Posting a Letter

1996. 150th Anniv of the Post Office Ordinance. Multicoloured.
952 60c. Type **252** 15 10
953 4r. "B53" duplex postmark 55 55
954 5r. Modern mobile post office 65 65
955 10r. Carriole (19th-century horse-drawn postal carriage) . . . . 1·50 2·00

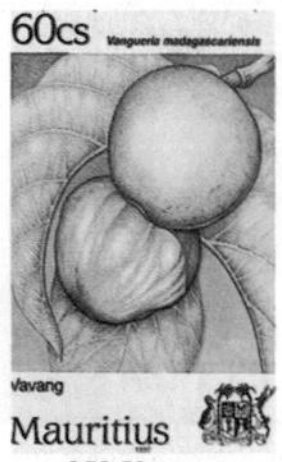

253 Vavang

1997. Fruits. Multicoloured.
956 60c. Type **253** 10 10
957 4r. Pom zako 45 50
958 5r. Zambos 55 65
959 10r. Sapot negro . . . . . . 1·00 1·75

254 Governor Mahe de la Bourdonnais and Map

1997. Aspects of Mauritius History. Multicoloured.
960 60c. Type **254** 50 20
961 1r. La Perouse and map of Pacific 65 20
962 4r. Governor Sir William Gomm and Lady Gomm's Ball, 1847 . . . . 1·10 70
963 6r. George Clark discovering skeleton of dodo, 1865 . . 1·60 1·60
964 10r. Professor Brian Abel-Smith and Social Policies report of 1960 . . . . . . 1·50 2·50

255 1d. "POST OFFICE" Mauritius

1997. 150th Anniv of "POST OFFICE" Stamps. Multicoloured.
965 60c. Type **255** 30 10
966 4r.2d. "POST OFFICE" Mauritius 80 60
967 5r. "POST OFFICE" 1d. and 2d. on gold background . . 1·10 1·25
968 10r. "POST OFFICE" 2d. and 1d. on silver background . . . . 2·00 3·00
MS969 127 × 90 mm. 20r. "POST OFFICE" stamps on cover to Bordeaux . . . . 3·50 4·50

256 Wheelwright

1997. Small Businesses. Multicoloured.
970 60c. Type **256** 10 10
971 4r. Laundryman 40 40
972 5r. Shipwright 80 80
973 15r. Quarryman . . . . . . 3·00 4·00

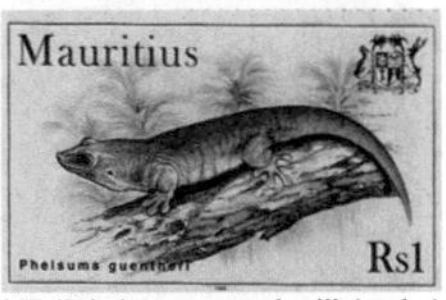

257 "Phelsuma guentheri" (gecko)

1998. Geckos. Multicoloured.
974 1r. Type **257** 20 10
975 6r. "Nactus serpensinsula durrelli" 55 65
976 7r. "Nactus coindemirensis" 65 1·25
977 8r. "Phelsuma edwardnewtonii" . . . . . 75 1·25

258 Steam Train on Viaduct

1998. Inland Transport. Multicoloured.
978 40c. Type **258** 35 10
979 5r. Early lorry 75 55
980 6r. Bus in town street 90 90
981 10r. Sailing barge at wharf 1·75 2·75

259 President Nelson Mandela

1998. State Visit of President Nelson Mandela of South Africa.
982 **259** 25r. multicoloured . . . . 2·75 3·50

260 Count Maurice of Nassau and Dutch Landing

1998. 400th Anniv of Dutch Landing on Mauritius. Multicoloured.
983 50c. Type **260** 30 15
984 1r. Fort Frederik Hendrik and sugar cane 30 15
985 7r. Dutch map of Mauritius (1670) . . . . 1·75 1·75
986 8r. Diagram of landing . . . 1·75 1·75
MS987 105 × 80 mm. 25r. Two Dutch ships . . . . 3·50 4·00

261 Cascade Balfour

1998. Waterfalls. Multicoloured.
988 1r. Type **261** 35 10
989 5r. Rochester Falls 90 65
990 6r. Cascade G.R.S.E. (vert) 1·00 90
991 10r. 500ft. Cascade (vert) . . 2·00 2·50

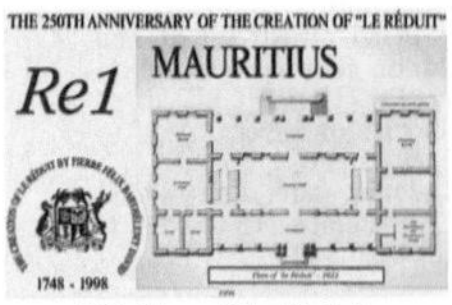

262 Plan of Le Reduit

1998. 250th Anniv of Chateau Le Reduit. Multicoloured.
992 1r. Type **262** 25 10
993 4r. "Le Chateau du Reduit, 1814" (P. Thuillier) 65 60
994 5r. "Le Reduit, 1998" (Hassen Edun) 75 75
995 15r. Commemorative monument . . . . 2·25 3·25

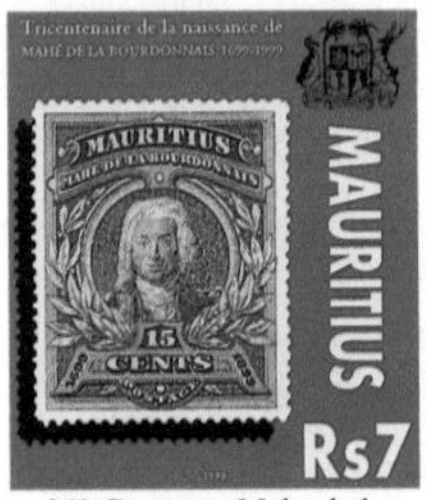

263 Governor Mahe de la Bourdonnais on 15c. Stamp of 1899

1999. 300th Birth Anniv of Governor Mahe de la Bourdonnais.
996 **263** 7r. blue, black and red . . 1·00 1·25

264 "Clerodendron laciniatum"

1999. Local Plants. Multicoloured.
997 1r. Type **264** 10 10
998 2r. "Senecio lamarckianus" 15 15
999 5r. "Cylindrocline commersonii" 40 60
1000 9r. "Psiadia pollicina" . . . 75 1·75

265 "The Washerwomen" (Herve Masson)

1999. Mauritius through Local Artists' Eyes. Multicoloured.
1001 1r. Type **265** 20 10
1002 3r. "The Casino" (Gaetan de Rosnay) 55 45
1003 4r. "The Four Elements" (Andree Poilly) 65 60
1004 6r. "Going to Mass" (Xavier Le Juge de Segrais) . . . . 95 1·40

266 Old Chimney, Alma

1999. Old Sugar Mill Chimneys. Multicoloured.
1005 1r. Type **266** 20 10
1006 2r. Antoinette 40 15
1007 5r. Belle Mare 75 75
1008 7r. Grande Rosalie . . . . 1·00 1·50
MS1009 132 × 100 mm. Nos. 1005/8 2·10 2·50

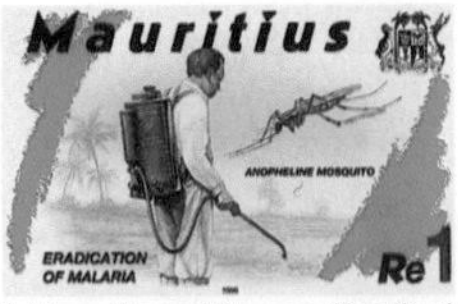

267 Mosquito and Sprayer (Eradication of Malaria)

1999. 20th-century Achievements. Multicoloured.
1010 1r. Type **267** 35 10
1011 2r. Judge's robes, silhouette and airliner (emancipation of women) 70 20
1012 5r. Conference room (international conference centre) 90 80
1013 9r. Spoons full of sugar (development of sugar industry) . . . . 1·75 2·25

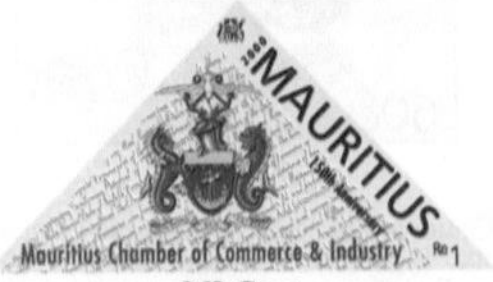

268 Crest

2000. 150th Anniv of Mauritius Chamber of Commerce and Industry. Multicoloured.
1014 1r. Type **268** 30 15
1015 2r. Unity, Vision and Service logos 55 25
1016 7r. Francis Channell (First Secretary, 1850–72) . . . 1·25 1·40
1017 15r. Louis Lechelle (First President, 1850) . . . . . 2·25 3·50

269 "Cratopus striga" (beetle)

2000. Beetles. Multicoloured.
1018 1r. Type **269** 20 10
1019 2r. "Cratopus armatus" . . 30 15
1020 3r. "Cratopus chrysochlorus" 50 30
1021 15r. "Cratopus nigrogranatus" . . . . . 2·00 2·50
MS1022 130 × 100 mm. Nos. 1018/21 . . . . 2·50 2·75

270 Handball

2000. Olympic Games, Sydney. Multicoloured.
1023 1r. Type **270** 25 10
1024 2r. Archery 50 15
1025 5r. Sailing 85 70
1026 15r. Judo . . . . 2·00 2·50

271 Sir Seewoosagur Ramgoolam greeting Mother Teresa, 1984

2000. Birth Centenary of Sir Seewoosagur Ramgoolam (former Prime Minister). Multicoloured.
1027 1r. Type **271** 90 15
1028 2r. Election as member of Legislative Council, 1948 (vert) 35 15
1029 5r. As a student, 1926 (vert) 80 70
1030 15r. As Prime Minister, 1968 (vert) . . . . 2·00 2·50

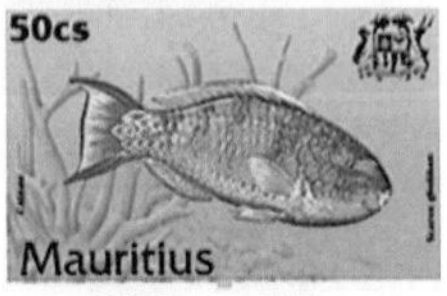

272 *Scarus ghobban*

2000. Fish. Multicoloured.
1031 50c. Type **272** 10 10
1032 1r. *Cephalopholis sonnerati* 10 10
1033 2r. *Naso brevirostris* 15 10
1034 3r. *Lethrinus nebulosus* . . . 25 15
1035 4r. *Centropyge debelius* . . . 30 20
1036 5r. *Amphiprion chrysogaster* 35 25
1037 6r. *Forcipiger flavissimus* . . 40 30
1038 7r. *Acanthurus leucosternon* 50 35
1039 8r. *Pterois volitans* 55 35
1040 10r. *Siderea grisea* 70 55
1041 15r. *Carcharhinus wheeleri* 1·10 1·10
1042 25r. *Istiophrous platypterus* 1·50 1·60
MS1043 Three sheets, each 132 × 102 mm. (a) Nos. 1031/3 and 1042. (b) Nos. 1035 and 1038/40. (c) Nos. 1034, 1036/7 and 1041 Set of 3 sheets . . . . 6·50 8·00

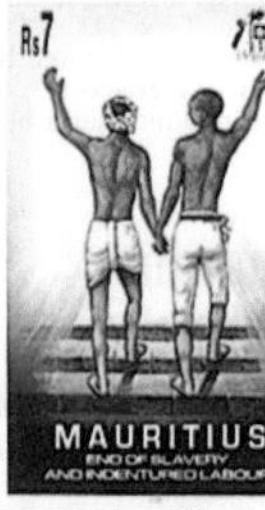

273 Affan Tank Wen **275** African Slave and Indian Indentured Labourer

274 Finished Pullover

2000. Famous Mauritians. Multicoloured.
1044 1r. Type **273** 30 10
1045 5r. Alphonse Ravatoni . . . 75 50
1046 7r. Dr. Idrice Goumany . . 1·10 1·25
1047 9r. Anjalay Coopen . . . . 1·40 1·60

2001. Textile Industry. Multicoloured.
1048 1r. Type **274** 30 10
1049 3r. Computer-aided machinery 55 50
1050 6r. T-shirt folding . . . . . 1·00 1·00
1051 10r. Embroidery machine . . 1·50 2·00

2001. Anti-slavery and Indentured Labour Campaign Commemoration.
1052 **275** 7r. multicoloured . . . . 1·25 1·40

276 *Foetidia mauritiana*

2001. Trees. Multicoloured.
1053 1r. Type **276** 30 10
1054 3r. *Diospyros tessellaria* . . 60 20
1055 5r. *Sideroxylon puberulum* 80 70
1056 15r. *Gastonia mauritiana* . . 2·00 2·50

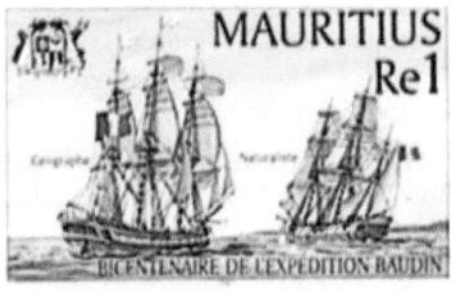

277 *Geographe* and *Naturaliste* (French corvettes)

2001. Bicentenary of Baudin's Expedition to New Holland (Australia). Multicoloured.
1057 1r. Type **277** 40 15
1058 4r. Capt. Nicholas Baudin and map of voyage . . . 80 45
1059 6r. Mascarene martin (bird) 1·25 1·10
1060 10r. M. F. Peron and title page of book (vert) . . . 1·75 2·25

278 Hotel School

2001. Mauritius Economic Achievements during the 20th Century. Multicoloured.
1061 2r. Type **278** 30 15
1062 3r. Steel bar milling 35 20
1063 6r. Solar energy panels, Agalega 75 75
1064 10r. Indian Ocean Rim Association for Regional Co-operation . . . . . . 1·50 2·00

279 Gandhi on Mauritius Stamp of 1969 **280** De-husking Coconuts

2001. Centenary of Gandhi's Visit to Mauritius.
1065 **279** 15r. multicoloured . . . 2·00 2·25

2001. Coconut Industry. Multicoloured.
1066 1r. Type **280** 25 10
1067 5r. Shelling coconuts (horiz) 70 45
1068 6r. Drying copra (horiz) . . 80 75
1069 10r. Extracting coconut oil 1·50 1·75

281 New Container Port

2002. 10th Anniv of Republic. Multicoloured.
1070 1r. Type **281** 30 15
1071 4r. Symbols of Mauritius stock exchange 60 45
1072 5r. New reservoir under construction 70 65
1073 9r. Motorway junction . . . 1·40 1·75

282 *Abricta* **284** Constellation of Orion

283 Map by Alberto Cantino, 1502

2002. Cicadas. Multicoloured.
1074 1r. Type **282** 25 15
1075 6r. *Fractuosella darwini* . . 75 65
1076 7r. *Distantada thomaseti* . . 85 85
1077 8r. *Dinarobia claudeae* . . . 95 1·10
MS1078 130 × 100 mm. Nos. 1074/7 2·50 2·75

2002. 16th-century Maps of the South-west Indian Ocean. Multicoloured.
1079 1r. Type **283** 30 15
1080 3r. Map by Jorge Reinel, 1520 . . . . 75 40
1081 4r. Map by Diogo Ribeiro, 1529 . . . . 85 65
1082 10r. Map by Gerard Mercator, 1569 . . . . . 2·00 2·25

2002. Constellations. Multicoloured.
1083 1r. Type **284** 30 15
1084 7r. Sagittarius 80 80
1085 8r. Scorpius . . . . 90 1·00
1086 9r. Southern Cross . . . . 1·00 1·25

285 African Growth and Opportunity Act Logo **286** Echo Parakeet Chick

2003. 2nd United States/Sub-Saharan Africa Trade and Economic Co-operation Forum.
1087 **285** 1r. red, blue and yellow 25 10
1088 25r. red, ultramarine and blue . . . . 2·75 3·25

2003. Endangered Species. Echo Parakeet. Multicoloured.
1089 1r. Type **286** 30 15
1090 2r. Fledgling 55 25
1091 5r. Female parakeet . . . . 1·00 70
1092 15r. Male parakeet . . . . 2·25 2·50

287 *Trochetia boutoniana*

2003. Trochetias. Multicoloured.
1093 1r. Type **287** 25 10
1094 4r. *Trochetia uniflora* . . . 50 30
1095 7r. *Trochetia triflora* 85 90
1096 9r. *Trochetia parviflora* . . . 1·10 1·25

288 Dolphin Emblem (Sixth Indian Ocean Games, Mauritius)

2003. Anniversaries and Events. Multicoloured.
1097 2r. Type **288** 30 15
1098 6r. Crop in field and emblem (150th anniv of Mauritius Chamber of Agriculture) 65 50
1099 9r. Journal of voyage of Bonne-Esperance (250th anniv of visit of Abbe de la Caille) . . . . 1·10 1·25
1100 10r. Sugar cane and emblem (50th anniv of Mauritius Sugar Industry Research Institute) . . . . 1·10 1·25

289 Batterie de la Pointe du Diable

2003. Fortifications. Multicoloured.
1101 2r. Type **289** 25 15
1102 5r. Donjon St. Louis . . . 55 40
1103 6r. Martello Tower 65 50
1104 12r. Fort Adelaide . . . . 1·25 1·40

290 Emblem

2004. 20th Anniv of the Indian Ocean Commission.
1105 **290** 10r. multicoloured . . . 40 45

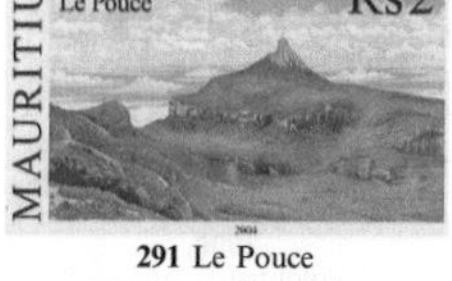
291 Le Pouce

2004. Mountains. Multicoloured.
1106 2r. Type **291** 10 10
1107 7r. Corps de Garde 30 35
1108 8r. Le Chat et La Souris . . 30 35
1109 25r. Piton du Milieu . . . . 1·00 1·10

292 Tinman

2004. Traditional Trades. Multicoloured.
1110 2r. Type **292** 10 10
1111 7r. Shoe maker 30 35
1112 9r. Blacksmith 45 50
1113 15r. Basket maker 60 65

293 Work Station, Emblem and SADC Head Quarters

2004. 24th Southern African Development Community Summit. Multicoloured.
1114 2r. Type **293** 10 10
1115 50r. As Type **293** but with "24th SADC Summit" in bright purple banner . . . 2·00 2·10

294 Plaine Corail Airport

2004. Rodrigues Regional Assembly. Multicoloured.
1116 2r. Type **294** 10 10
1117 7r. Eco Tourism 30 35
1118 8r. Agricultural products . . 30 35

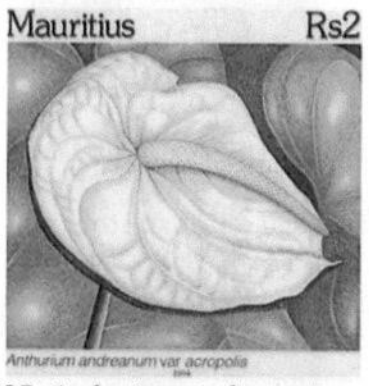
295 *Anthurium andreanum var acropolis*

2004. Anthurium Species. Multicoloured.
1120 2r. Type **295** 10 10
1121 8r. *Anthurium andreanum var tropical* 30 35
1122 10r. *Anthurium andreanum var paradisio* 40 45
1123 25r. *Anthurium andreanum var fantasia* . . . . 1·00 1·10

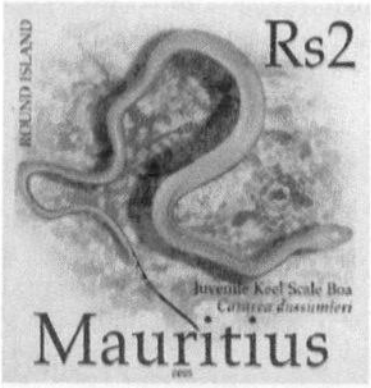
296 Juvenile Keel Scale Boa

2005. Round Island. Multicoloured.
1124 2r. Type **296** 10 10
1125 8r. Hurricane palm 30 35
1126 9r. Round Island petrel . . 45 50
1127 25r. Mazambron . . . . . 1·00 1·10

EXPRESS DELIVERY STAMPS

1903. No. 136 surch **EXPRESS DELIVERY 15c.**
E1 **40** 15c. on 15c. blue . . . . . 9·00 24·00

1903. No. 136 surch **EXPRESS DELIVERY (INLAND) 15c.**
E3 **40** 15c. on 15c. blue . . . . . 7·50 3·00

1904. T **42** without value in label. (a) Surch **(FOREIGN) EXPRESS DELIVERY 18 CENTS.**
E5 **42** 18c. green . . . . 1·75 25·00

(b) Surch **EXPRESS DELIVERY (INLAND) 15c.**
E6 **42** 15c. green . . . . 4·50 4·50

POSTAGE DUE STAMPS

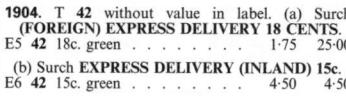

D 1

1933.
D 1 D 1 2c. black . . . . 1·25 50
D 2 4c. violet 50 65
D 3 6c. red 60 80
D 4 10c. green . . . . 70 1·25
D 5 20c. blue . . . . 50 1·50
D13 50c. purple . . . . 75 12·00
D 7 1r. orange . . . . 70 16·00

1982. Nos. 530/1, 535, 540, 542 and 547 surch **POSTAGE DUE** and value.
D14 10c. on 15c. Dutch Occupation, 1638–1710 . . 20 50
D15 20c. on 20c. Van Keulen's map, c. 1700 . . . . . 30 50
D16 50c. on 60c. Pierre Poivre, c. 1767 (vert) . . . 30 30
D17 1r. on 1r.20 Government House, c. 1840 . . . . . 40 30
D18 1r.50 on 1r.50 Indian immigration, 1835 . . . . 50 75
D19 5r. on 15r. Unfurling Mauritian flag, 1968 . . . 1·00 2·25

MAYOTTE Pt. 6

One of the Comoro Islands adjacent to Madagascar.

In 1974 (when the other islands became an independent state) Mayotte was made an Overseas Department of France, using French stamps. From 1997 it again had its own issues.

100 centimes = 1 franc.

1892. "Tablet" key-type inscr "MAYOTTE".
1 D 1c. black and red on blue . . 1·25 75
2 2c. brown and blue on buff 1·75 1·90
3 4c. brown and blue on grey 2·25 2·25
4 5c. green and red on green 2·50 2·75
5 10c. black and blue on lilac 4·75 4·50
15 10c. red and blue . . . . . 30·00 45·00
6 15c. blue and red . . . . . 10·50 9·50
16 15c. grey and red . . . . . 90·00 75·00
7 20c. red and blue on green 11·00 11·00
8 25c. black and red on pink 6·50 5·50
17 25c. blue and red . . . . . 7·00 8·50
9 30c. brown and blue on drab 14·50 14·50
18 35c. black and red on yellow 4·50 4·00
10 40c. red and blue on yellow 13·50 13·00
19 45c. black on green . . . . 14·00 14·00
11 50c. red and blue on pink 22·00 18·00
20 50c. brown and red on blue 10·50 20·00
12 75c. brown & red on orange 19·00 22·00
13 1f. green and red . . . . 15·00 19·00
14 5f. mauve and blue on lilac 95·00 10·00

1912. Surch in figures.
21 D 05 on 20c. brown and blue on buff . . . . 1·10 3·75
22 05 on 4c. brown and blue on grey . . . . 1·60 2·25
23 05 on 15c. blue and red . . 1·60 2·00
24 05 on 20c. red and blue on green . . . . 1·50 2·75
25 05 on 25c. black and red on pink . . . . 1·25 2·75
26 05 on 30c. brown and blue on drab . . . . 1·40 3·00
27 10 on 40c. red and blue on yellow . . . . 1·00 2·75
28 10 on 45c. black and red on green . . . . 1·50 1·40
29 10 on 50c. red and blue on pink . . . . 2·75 4·75
30 10 on 75c. brown and red on orange . . . . 1·90 3·75
31 10 on 1f. green and red . . 2·75 3·25

1997. Stamps of France optd **MAYOTTE**. (a) Nos. 2907/10, 2912, 2917, 2924 and 2929/30.
40 **1118** 10c. brown 15 10
41 20c. green 15 10
42 50c. violet 15 10
43 1f. orange 35 15
44 2f. blue 60 35
45 2f.70 green 80 45
46 3f.80 blue . . . . 1·00 55
47 5f. blue . . . . 1·75 70
48 10f. violet . . . . 3·50 1·50

(b) No. 3121. No value expressed.
49 **1118** (–) red 75 55
No. 49 was sold at 3f.

6 Ylang-ylang

1997.
50 **6** 2f.70 multicoloured 85 50

7 Arms

1997.
51 **7** 3f. multicoloured 70 40

8 Terminal Building and Airplane

1997. Air. Inauguration of New Airport.
52 **8** 20f. indigo, red and blue . . 6·00 2·75

9 Le Banga

1997.
53 **9** 3f.80 multicoloured 95 55

10 Dzen-dze (musical instrument)

1997.
54 **10** 5f.20 multicoloured . . . . 1·40 70

1997. Stamps of France optd **MAYOTTE**. (a) On Nos. 3415/20, 3425, 3430 and 3432.
55 **1318** 10c. brown 15 10
56 20c. green 15 10
57 50c. violet 15 10
58 1f. orange 30 15
59 2f. blue 50 35
60 2f.70 green 55 40
62 3f.80 blue 80 55
66 5f. blue . . . . 1·10 65
68 10f. violet . . . . 2·40 1·25

(b) On No. 3407. No value expressed. Ordinary or self-adhesive gum.
69 **1318** (3f.) red 75 35

11 Lemur

1997.
71 **11** 3f. brown and red 80 45

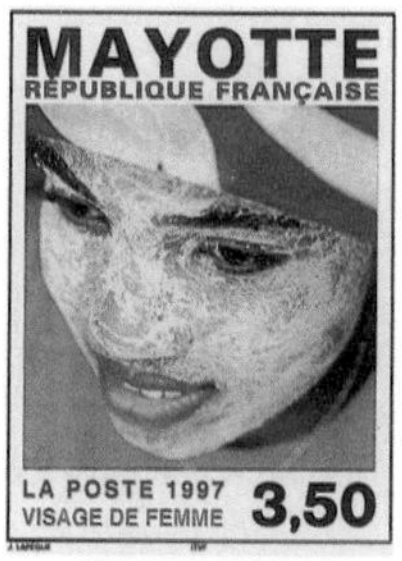
12 Woman's Face

1997.
72 **12** 3f.50 multicoloured 85 55

13 Fishes and Corals

1997. Marine Life.
73 **13** 3f. multicoloured 75 45

14 Reunion, Maps and Airplane

1997. Air. 20th Anniv of First Mayotte–Reunion Air Flight.
74 **14** 5f. black, blue and green . . 1·25 75

15 Longoni Port

1998.
75 **15** 2f.70 multicoloured 70 40

16 Indian Ocean Green Turtle

1998.
76 **16** 3f. multicoloured 75 45

17 Family on Island

18 Cattle Egret on Zebu's Head

1998. Family Planning.
77 **17** 1f. multicoloured 25 10

1998. Air.
78 **18** 30f. multicoloured . . . . . 7·50 3·75

19 Children in Costume

1998. Children's Carnival.
79 **19** 3f. multicoloured 75 40

20 "Salama Djema II" (ferry)

1998. Mamoudzou–Dzaoudzi Ferry.
80 **20** 3f.80 multicoloured 90 50

21 Tsingoni Mosque

22 Mariama Salim

1998.
81 **21** 3f. multicoloured 75 40

1998. 2nd Death Anniv of Mariama Salim (women's rights activist).
82 **22** 2f.70 multicoloured 65 35

23 Spreading Nets

1998. Traditional Fishing, Djarifa.
83 **23** 2f. multicoloured 50 25

24 Emperor Angelfish

1998.
84 **24** 3f. multicoloured 70 40

25 Chombos and Workers

1998. The Chombo (agricultural tool).
85 **25** 3f. multicoloured 65 40

26 Map of Mayotte

1999.
86 **26** 3f. multicoloured 65 40

27 Reservoir, Combani

1999.
87 **27** 8f. multicoloured . . . . . 1·90 1·00

28 Coral Hind

1999. Lagoon Fishes. Multicoloured.
88 2f.70 Type **28** 60 30
89 3f. Lionfish (horiz) 70 35
90 5f.20 Regal angelfish (horiz) 1·00 60
91 10f. Powder-blue surgeonfish (horiz) . . . . 2·25 1·10

1999. The Euro (European currency). No. 3553 of France optd **MAYOTTE**.
92 3f. red and blue 75 35

29 Genet

1999.
93 **29** 5f.40 orange, black & stone 1·40 70

30 Baobab Tree

1999.
94 **30** 8f. multicoloured . . . . . 1·90 1·00

1999. "Philexfrance 99" International Stamp Exhibition, Paris. Sheet 150 × 120 mm.
MS95 No. 51 × 4, multicoloured 3·00 3·00

31 Prefecture Building

1999. Dzaoudzi Prefecture.
96 **31** 3f. multicoloured 70 40

32 Pirogues

1999. Pirogues. Sheet 163 × 84 mm containing T **32** and similar multicoloured designs.
MS97 5f. Type **32**; 5f. Two pirogues (vert); 5f. Three pirogues . . . 3·50 3·50

33 Vanilla

1999.
98 **33** 4f.50 multicoloured 95 50

34 "Le Deba"

1999. Air.
99 **34** 10f. multicoloured . . . . . 2·10 1·10

35 Map of Mayotte, Arrow and "2000"

1999. Year 2000.
100 **35** 3f. multicoloured 65 40

36 Soulou Waterfall

1999.
101 **36** 10f. multicoloured . . . . 2·00 1·10

37 Sailing Boat

2000. Indian Ocean.
102 **37** 3f. multicoloured 65 40

38 Two Whales

2000. Whales.
103 **38** 5f.20 multicoloured . . . . 1·10 60

39 Emblem

2000. District 920 of Inner Wheel (women's section of Rotary International).
104 **39** 5f.20 multicoloured . . . . 1·00 60

40 L'île au Lagon

2000.
105 **40** 3f. multicoloured 65 40

41 Woman wearing Traditional Clothes

2000. Women of Mayotte. Sheet 90 × 70 mm containing T **41** and similar vert design. Multicoloured.
MS106 3f. Type **41**; 5f.20, Women wearing modern clothes . . . 1·60 1·60

42 Tyre Race

2000.
107 **42** 3f. multicoloured 65 40

43 Sultan Andriantsouli's Tomb

2000.
108 **43** 5f.40 multicoloured . . . . 1·00 60

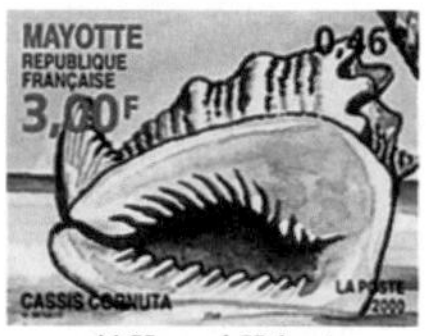

44 Horned Helmet

2000. Shells. Multicoloured.
109 3f. Type **44** 65 40
110 3f. Trumpet triton (*Charonia tritonis*) 65 40
111 3f. Bullmouth helmet (*Cypraecassis rufa*) 65 40
112 3f. Humpback cowrie (*Cyprae mauritiana*) (wrongly inscr "mauritania") and tiger cowrie (*Cyprae tigris*) . . . 65 40
Nos. 109/12 were issued together, se-tenant, with the backgrounds forming a composite design of a beach.

45 M'Dere

2000. 1st Death Anniv of Zena M'Dere.
113 **45** 3f. multicoloured 65 40

46 Distillery

2000. Ylang-ylang Distillery.
114 **46** 2f.70 multicoloured 60 35

47 Building

48 Map of Mayotte

2000. New Hospital.
115 **47** 10f. multicoloured . . . . 2·00 1·10

2001.
116 **48** 2f.70 black and green . . . 60 35

2001. No value expressed. As T **48**.
120 **48** (3f.) black and red 65 40

49 Mother breast-feeding

2001. Breast-feeding.
130 **49** 3f. multicoloured 65 40

50 Pilgrims

2001. Pilgrimage to Mecca.
131 **50** 2f.70 multicoloured 60 35

51 Bush Taxi

2001.
132 **51** 3f. multicoloured 65 40

52 Children playing Football

2001.
133 **52** 3f. multicoloured 60 35

53 Pyjama Cardinalfish

2001.
134 **53** 10f. multicoloured . . . . 2·00 1·25

54 Legionnaire, Map and Market Scene

2001. 25th Anniv of Mayotte Foreign Legion Detachment.
135 **54** 5f.20 multicoloured . . . . 1·00 60

55 Bats in Tree

2001. The Comoro Roussette. Sheet 65 × 90 mm containing T **55** and similar horiz design. Multicoloured.
MS136 3f. Type **55**; 5f.20, Bat in flight . . . . 1·60 1·60

56 Airplanes and Club House

2001. Air. Dzaoudzi Flying Club.
137 **56** 20f. multicoloured . . . . 4·00 2·40

57 Military Personnel and Building

2001. 1st Anniv of Adapted Military Service Units.
138 **57** 3f. multicoloured 60 35

58 *Protea* sp.

2001. Flower and Fruit. Multicoloured.
139 3f. Type **58** 60 35
140 5f.40 Selection of fruit . . . 1·00 60

59 Dziani Dzaha Lake

2001.
141 **59** 5f.20 multicoloured . . . . 1·00 60

60 Mayotte Post Office

2001.
142 **60** 10f. multicoloured . . . . 2·00 1·25

2002. Stamps of France optd **MAYOTTE**. (a) Nos. 3770/85.
143 **1318** 1c. yellow 10 10
144 2c. brown 10 10
145 5c. green 10 10
146 10c. violet 15 10
147 20c. orange 30 15
148 41c. green 55 35
149 50c. blue 70 40
150 53c. green 75 45
151 58c. blue 80 50
152 64c. orange 90 55
153 67c. blue 95 60
154 69c. mauve 95 60
155 €1 turquoise . . . . . 1·40 85
156 €1.02 green . . . . . . 1·40 85
157 €2 violet . . . . 2·75 1·60

(b) No value expressed. No. 3752.
166 41e. red 55 35
No. 166 was sold at the rate for inland letters up to 20 grammes.

61 Arms

2002. Attainment of Department Status within France (11 July 2001).
167 **61** 46c. multicoloured 65 40

62 Runners

2002. Athletics.
168 **62** 41c. multicoloured 55 35

63 Mangroves, Kaweni Basin

2002.
169 **63** €1.52 multicoloured . . . 2·10 1·60

64 Building Facade

66 House and People

65 Women processing Salt (½-size illustration)

2002. 25th Anniv of Mayotte Commune.
170 **64** 46c. multicoloured 65 40

2002. Salt Production at Bandrele.
171 **65** 79c. multicoloured . . . . 1·10 65

2002. National Census.
172 **66** 46c. multicoloured 65 40

67 Sunbird (inscr "Souimanga")

2002. Birds. Sheet 61 × 141 mm containing T **67** and similar horiz designs. Multicoloured.
MS173 46c. Type **67**; 46c. Drongo; 46c. Olive white eye (inscr "Oiseau-lunette"); 46c. Red-headed fody (inscr "Foudy") 2·40 2·40

68 Processing Machinery

2002. Remains of the Sugar Industry.
174 **68** 82c. multicoloured . . . . 1·10 65

69 Mount Choungui

70 Jack Fruit (inscr "Le Jaquier")

2002.
175 **69** 46c. multicoloured 60 35

2002.
176 **70** €1.22 multicoloured . . . 80 50

71 Museum Buildings

2003. Vanilla and Ylang Ylang Eco-museum.

177	**71**	46c. multicoloured	60	35

72 Bananas

2003.

178	**72**	79c. multicoloured	1·00	60

73 Woman with Painted Face

2003. Festival Masks.

179	**73**	46c. multicoloured	60	35

74 Sailfish

2003.

180	**74**	79c. multicoloured	1·00	60

75 Gecko

2003.

181	**75**	50c. multicoloured	65	40

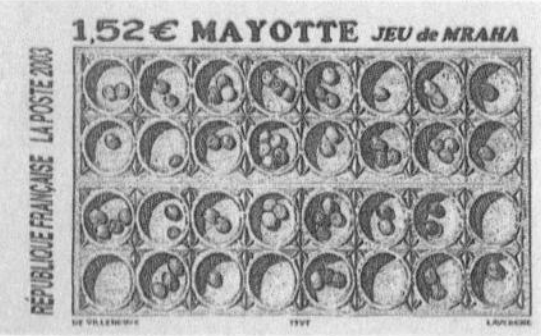

76 Mraha Board and Counters (game)

2003.

182	**76**	€1.52 brown and mauve	2·00	1·20

77 Mtzamboro College

2003.

183	**77**	45c. multicoloured	60	35

78 Ziyara de Pole

2003.

184	**78**	82c. multicoloured	1·10	65

79 Players, Ball and Basket

2003. Basketball.

185	**79**	50c. multicoloured	65	40

80 Dzaoudzi Islet(½-size illustration)

2003.

186	**80**	$1.50 multicoloured . . .	2·00	1·20

81 Women Dancing ("Le Wadaha")

2004.

187	**81**	50c. multicoloured	65	40

2004. Map. As T **48** but new currency.

188	**48**	1c. yellow and black . . .	10	10
189		2c. grey and black	10	10
190		5c. green and black	10	10
191		10c. mauve and black . . .	15	10
192		20c. orange and black . .	25	15
193		45c. blue green and black	60	35
194		50c. ultramarine and black	80	50
195		€1 green and black . . .	1·30	80
196		€2 violet and black . . .	2·70	1·70

82 Blue Argus (*Junonia* (Precis) *rhadama*)

2004. Butterflies. Sheet 100 × 80 mm containing T **82** and similar horiz designs. Multicoloured.
MS200 50c. × 4 Type **82**; Citrus butterfly (*Papilio demodocus*); *Acraea ranavalona*; *Danaus chrysippus* . . . . 2·70 2·70

83 Sada Bay

2004.

201	**83**	90c. multicoloured	1·20	70

84 Papaya Tree and Fruit

2004.

202	**84**	50c. multicoloured	80	50

85 Filigree Jewellery

2004.

203	**85**	€2.40 ultramarine, black and gold	3·25	2·00

86 Bridge over Kwale River

2004.

204	**86**	50c. multicoloured	80	50

87 Maki (monkey) and Young

2004.

205	**87**	75c. multicoloured	1·00	60

88 Mamas Brochettis (street vendor)

2004.

206	**88**	45c. multicoloured	60	35

89 Playing Dominoes

2004.

207	**89**	75c. multicoloured	1·00	60

90 Ylang-ylang

2005.

208	**90**	50c. multicoloured	70	40

91 Two Women

2005. Women's Traditional Costume.

209	**91**	53c. multicoloured	70	40

92 Breadfruit Tree and Fruit

2005.

210	**92**	64c. multicoloured	85	50

MECKLENBURG-SCHWERIN Pt. 7

In northern Germany. Formerly a Grand Duchy, Mecklenburg-Schwerin joined the North German Confederation in 1868.

48 schilling = 1 thaler.

1

2

1856. Imperf.

1a	**1**	¼s. red	†	£225
1		¼s. red	£140	£130
2	**2**	3s. yellow	£100	55·00
4		5s. blue	£250	£300

See note below No. 7.

1864. Roul.

5a	**1**	¼s. red	†	£1700
6a		¼s. red	†	£190
5		¼s. red	£3000	£1900
6		¼s. red	£425	75·00
11	**2**	2s. purple	£250	£250
9		3s. yellow	£170	£130
7		5s. bistre	£150	£250

Nos. 1, 1a, 5, 5a have a dotted background, Nos. 6 and 6a a plain background. Prices for Nos. 1a, 5a and 6a are for quarter stamps; prices for Nos. 1, 5 and 6 are for the complete on cover stamp (four quarters) as illustrated in Type **1**.

MECKLENBURG-STRELITZ Pt. 7

In northern Germany. Formerly a Grand Duchy, Mecklenburg-Strelitz joined the North German Confederation in 1868.

30 silbergroschen = 1 thaler.

1

2

1864. Roul. Various frames.

2	**1**	¼sgr. orange	£190	£2500
3		⅓sgr. green	85·00	£1500
6		1sch. mauve	£300	£3500
7	**2**	1sgr. red	£160	£200
9		2sgr. blue	37·00	£850
11		3sgr. bistre	34·00	£1400

MEMEL Pt. 7

A seaport and district on the Baltic Sea, formerly part of Germany. Under Allied control after the 1914–18 war, it was captured and absorbed by Lithuania in 1923 and returned to Germany in 1939. From 1945 the area has been part of Lithuania.

1920. 100 pfennig = 1 mark.
1923. 100 centu = 1 litas.

1920. Stamps of France surch **MEMEL** and **pfennig** or **mark** with figure of value.

1	18	5pf. on 5c. green	35	1·00
2		10pf. on 10c. red	40	75
3		20pf. on 25c. blue	45	60
4		30pf. on 30c. orange	45	70
19		40pf. on 20c. brown	15	35
5		50pf. on 35c. violet	80	55
6	13	60pf. on 40c. red and blue	65	1·10
7		80pf. on 45c. green and blue	90	1·20
8		1m. on 50c. brown and lilac	60	85
9		1m.25 on 60c. violet & blue	1·20	2·00
10		2m. on 1f. red and green	50	65
11		3m. on 2f. orange and green	13·00	36·00
12		3m. on 5f. blue and buff	20·00	36·00
13		4m. on 2f. orange and green	1·10	1·30
14		10m. on 5f. blue and buff	2·00	6·50
15		20m. on 5f. blue and buff	39·00	90·00

1920. Stamps of Germany inscr "DEUTSCHES REICH" optd **Memel- gebiet** or **Memelgebiet**.

25	10	5pf. green	45	2·10
26		10pf. red	2·40	9·25
27		10pf. orange	40	3·00
28	24	15pf. brown	2·50	7·75
29	10	20pf. blue	40	1·60
30		30pf. black & orange on buff	4·75	10·50
31		30pf. blue	30	4·00
32		40pf. black and red	35	2·75
33		50pf. black & purple on buff	25	95
34		60pf. green	70	1·80
35		75pf. black and green	2·20	6·75
36		80pf. blue	1·30	2·50
37	12	1m. red	70	1·40
38		1m.25 green	11·50	43·00
39		1m.50 brown	4·25	13·00
40	13	2m. blue	1·90	4·75
41		2m.50 purple	12·50	30·00

1921. Nos. 2/3, 5, 8, 10, 19 and 49 further surch in large figures.

42	18	15 on 10pf. on 10c. red	35	85
43		15 on 20pf. on 25c. blue	35	85
44		15 on 50pf. on 35c. violet	25	65
45		60 on 40pf. on 20c. brown	50	75
46	13	75 on 60pf. on 40c. red and blue (49)	1·00	1·40
47		1,25 on 1m. on 50c. brown and lilac	30	95
48		5,00 on 2m. on 1f. red and green	1·00	2·00

1921. Surch **MEMEL** and **Pfennig** or **Mark** with figure of value.

60	18	5pf. on 5c. orange	25	65
61		10pf. on 10c. red	1·00	3·75
62		10pf. on 10c. green	35	55
63		15pf. on 10c. green	30	90
64		20pf. on 20c. brown	6·00	26·00
65		20pf. on 25c. blue	6·00	26·00
66		25pf. on 5c. orange	10	50
67		30pf. on 30c. red	75	3·75
68		35pf. on 35c. violet	30	55
77	13	40pf. on 40c. red and blue	25	70
69	15	50pf. on 50c. blue	25	70
49	13	60pf. on 40c. red and blue	3·50	10·50
71	15	75pf. on 15c. green	20	70
70	18	75pf. on 35c. violet	20	40
78	13	80pf. on 45c. green & blue	15	65
72	18	1m. on 25c. blue	25	70
79	13	1m. on 40c. red and blue	15	45
73	18	1½m. on 30c. red	25	60
80	13	1m.25 on 60c. violet & bl	30	45
81		1m.50 on 45c. green & bl	25	70
82		2m. on 45c. green and blue	40	55
83		2m. on 1f. red and green	20	45
84		2¼m. on 40c. red and blue	40	60
85		2½m. on 60c. violet and blue	45	95
74	18	3m. on 5c. orange	15	1·50
86	13	3m. on 60c. violet and blue	65	1·20
87		4m. on 45c. green and blue	20	75
88		5m. on 1f. red and green	40	75
75	15	6m. on 15c. green	20	1·30
89	13	6m. on 60c. violet and blue	70	75
90		6m. on 2f. orange & green	40	70
76	18	8m. on 30c. red	45	6·75
91	13	9m. on 1f. red and green	35	70
92		9m. on 5f. blue and buff	40	1·70
93		10m. on 45c. green & blue	45	1·50
51		10m. on 5f. blue and buff	85	2·10
94		12m. on 40c. red and blue	25	85
95		20m. on 40c. red and blue	70	2·10
52		20m. on 45c. green & blue	3·75	12·50
96		20m. on 2f. orange & green	40	80
97		30m. on 60c. violet & blue	50	1·90
98		30m. on 5f. blue and buff	3·25	10·50
99		40m. on 1f. red and green	45	1·00
100		50m. on 2f. orange & green	9·25	23·00
101		80m. on 2f. orange & green	55	1·90
102		100m. on 5f. blue and buff	1·00	4·75

1921. Air. Nos. 6/8, 10, 13 and 49/50 optd **FLUGPOST** in double-lined letters.

53	13	60pf. on 40c. red and blue	32·00	70·00
54		60pf. on 40c. red and blue (No. 49)	3·50	7·25
55		80pf. on 45c. green and blue	2·50	6·00
56		1m. on 50c. brown and lilac	2·10	4·75
57		2m. on 1f. red and green	2·50	6·00
58		3m. on 60c. violet and blue (No. 50)	3·00	8·50
59		4m. on 2f. orange and green	3·75	10·50

1922. Air. Nos. 13, 50, 77/81, 83, 86, 88, 90 and 92 further optd **Flugpost** in script letters.

103	13	40pf. on 40c. red and blue (No. 77)	1·00	1·70
104		80pf. on 45c. green and blue (No. 78)	1·00	1·70
105		1m. on 40c. red and blue (No. 68)	1·00	1·70
106		1m.25 on 60c. violet and blue (No. 80)	1·50	2·30
107		1m.50 on 45c. green and blue (No. 81)	1·50	2·30
108		2m. on 1f. red and green (No. 83)	1·50	2·30
110		3m. on 60c. violet and blue (No. 86)	1·50	2·30
111		4m. on 2f. orange and green (No. 13)	1·70	2·30
112		5m. on 1f. red and green (No. 88)	1·70	2·30
113		6m. on 2f. orange and green (No. 90)	1·70	2·30
114		9m. on 5f. blue and buff (No. 92)	1·70	2·30

1922. Air. Surch as in 1921 and optd **FLUGPOST** in ordinary capitals.

115	13	40pf. on 40c. red and blue	1·40	7·75
116		1m. on 40c. red and blue	1·40	7·75
117		1m.25 on 60c. violet and blue	1·40	7·75
118		1m.50 on 45c. green and blue	1·40	7·75
119		2m. on 1f. red and green	1·40	7·75
120		3m. on 60c. violet and blue	1·40	7·75
121		4m. on 2f. orange & green	1·40	7·75
122		5m. on 1f. red and green	1·40	7·75
123		6m. on 2f. orange & green	1·40	7·75
124		9m. on 5f. blue and buff	1·40	7·75

1922. Nos. 62, 64 and 69 further surch as in 1921 but with additional surch **Mark** obliterating **Pfennig**.

125	18	10m. on 10pf. on 10c. green (No. 62)	70	4·25
126		20m. on 20pf. on 20c. brown (No. 64)	50	1·10
127	15	50m. on 50pf. on 50c. blue (No. 69)	1·70	7·75

1923. Nos. 77 and 80 with additional surch.

128	13	40m. on 40pf. on 40c. red and blue	85	1·90
129		80m. on 1m.25 on 60c. violet and blue	85	3·50

1923. Nos. 72 and 82 surch with large figures.

130	13	10m. on 2m. on 45c. green and blue	1·70	7·75
131	18	25m. on 1m. on 25c. blue	1·70	7·75

LITHUANIAN OCCUPATION

The port and district of Memel was captured by Lithuanian forces in 1923 and incorporated in Lithuania.

1

5

1923. (a) Surch **KLAIPEDA (MEMEL)** and value over curved line and **MARKIU**.

1	1	10m. on 5c. blue	45	1·50
2		25m. on 5c. blue	45	1·50
3		50m. on 25c. red	45	1·50
4		100m. on 25c. red	65	2·10
5		400m. on 1l. brown	1·30	3·75

(b) Surch **Klaipeda (Memel)** and value over two straight lines and **Markiu**.

6	1	10m. on 5c. blue	85	3·50
7		25m. on 5c. blue	85	3·50
8		50m. on 25c. red	85	3·50
9		100m. on 25c. red	85	3·50
10		400m. on 1l. brown	1·10	4·50
11		500m. on 1l. brown	1·10	4·50

(c) Surch **KLAIPEDA (Memel)** and value over four stars and **MARKIU**.

12	1	10m. on 5c. blue	1·50	5·50
13		20m. on 5c. blue	1·50	5·50
14		25m. on 25c. red	1·50	6·50
15		50m. on 25c. red	2·10	7·25
16		100m. on 1l. brown	2·75	8·50
17		200m. on 1l. brown	3·25	8·50

1923.

18	5	10m. brown	35	65
19		20m. yellow	35	65
20		25m. orange	35	65
21		40m. violet	35	65
22		50m. green	70	1·30
23		100m. red	55	65
24		300m. green	5·00	75·00
25		400m. brown	55	85
26		500m. purple	5·00	75·00
27		1000m. blue	85	2·10

7 Liner, Memel Port

8 Memel Arms

9 Memel Lighthouse

1923. Uniting of Memel with Lithuania and Amalgamation of Memel Harbours.

28	7	40m. green	3·25	17·00
29		50m. brown	3·25	17·00
30		80m. green	3·25	17·00
31		100m. red	3·25	17·00
32	8	200m. blue	3·25	17·00
33		300m. brown	3·25	17·00
34		400m. purple	3·25	17·00
35		500m. orange	3·25	17·00
36		600m. green	3·25	17·00
37	9	800m. blue	3·25	17·00
38		1000m. purple	3·25	17·00
39		2000m. red	3·25	17·00
40		3000m. green	3·25	17·00

1923. No. 123 of Memel surch **Klaipeda**, value and large **M** between bars, sideways.

41		100m. on 80 on 1m.25 on 60c.	4·75	17·00
42		400m. on 80 on 1m.25 on 60c.	4·75	17·00
43		500m. on 80 on 1m.25 on 60c.	4·75	17·00

1923. Surch in **CENTU**.

44	5	2c. on 300m. green	6·50	8·50
45		3c. on 300m. green	6·75	10·50
46		10c. on 25m. orange	8·50	8·50
47		15c. on 25m. orange	8·50	8·50
48		20c. on 500m. purple	10·00	19·00
49		30c. on 500m. purple	8·50	8·50
50		50c. on 500m. purple	13·00	23·00

1923. Surch (thin or thick figures) in **CENT.** or **LITAS**.

60	5	2c. on 10m. brown	1·70	6·75
51		2c. on 20m. yellow	3·50	13·00
52		2c. on 50m. green	3·50	10·50
63		3c. on 10m. brown	2·75	8·50
53		3c. on 40m. violet	4·25	10·50
54		3c. on 300m. green	3·00	5·00
55		5c. on 100m. red	3·75	5·00
56		5c. on 300m. green	4·25	10·50
57		10c. on 400m. brown	8·50	15·00
67		15c. on 25m. orange	95·00	£500
58		30c. on 500m. purple	8·50	8·50
68		50c. on 1000m. blue	2·30	8·50
69		1l. on 1000m. blue	4·75	15·00

1923. Surch in **CENT.** or **LITAS**.

70	7	15c. on 40m. green	4·75	16·00
71		30c. on 50m. brown	4·75	8·00
72		30c. on 80m. green	4·75	19·00
73		30c. on 100m. red	4·75	8·00
74	8	50c. on 200m. blue	4·75	16·00
75		50c. on 300m. brown	4·75	8·00
76		50c. on 400m. purple	4·75	14·00
77		50c. on 500m. orange	4·75	8·00
78		1l. on 600m. green	5·50	16·00
79	9	1l. on 800m. blue	5·50	16·00
80		1l. on 1000m. purple	5·50	16·00
81		1l. on 2000m. red	5·50	17·00
82		1l. on 3000m. green	5·50	16·00

1923. Surch in large figures and **Centu** and bars reading upwards.

83	1	10c. on 25m. on 5c. blue (No. 2)	23·00	47·00
84		15c. on 100m. on 25c. red (No. 4)	23·00	£160
85		30c. on 400m. on 1l. brown (No. 5)	8·50	30·00
86		60c. on 50m. on 25c. red (No. 8)	23·00	£190

1923. Surch in large figures and **CENT.** and bars.

87	7	15c. on 50m. brown	£190	£2250
88		25c. on 100m. red	70·00	£1300
89	8	30c. on 300m. brown	£150	£1400
90		60c. on 500m. orange	70·00	£1300

1923. Surch in **Centu** or **Centai** (25c.) between bars.

91	5	15c. on 10m. brown	6·50	28·00
92		15c. on 20m. yellow	3·25	15·00
93		15c. on 25m. orange	3·25	17·00
94		15c. on 40m. violet	3·25	15·00
95		15c. on 50m. green	2·30	13·00
96		15c. on 100m. red	2·30	13·00
97		15c. on 400m. brown	2·10	10·50
98		15c. on 1000m. blue	65·00	£325
99		25c. on 10m. brown	3·75	23·00
100		25c. on 20m. yellow	3·25	15·00
101		25c. on 25m. orange	3·25	17·00
102		25c. on 40m. violet	3·75	23·00
103		25c. on 50m. green	2·30	11·50
104		25c. on 100m. red	2·10	11·50
105		25c. on 400m. brown	2·10	11·50
106		25c. on 1000m. blue	65·00	£375
107		30c. on 10m. brown	6·50	30·00
108		30c. on 20m. yellow	3·25	19·00
109		30c. on 25m. orange	4·25	23·00
110		30c. on 40m. violet	3·50	17·00
111		30c. on 50m. green	2·30	13·00
112		30c. on 100m. red	2·30	13·00
113		30c. on 400m. brown	2·30	13·00
114		30c. on 1000m. blue	65·00	£350

MEXICO Pt. 15

A republic of Central America. From 1864–67 an Empire under Maximilian of Austria.

8 reales = 100 centavos = 1 peso.

1 Miguel Hidalgo y Costilla

2

1856. With or without optd district name. Imperf.

1c	1	½r. blue	12·50	14·00
8c		½r. black on buff	12·50	17·00
6		1r. orange	11·00	1·60
9b		1r. black on green	2·50	2·75
7b		2r. green	10·50	1·60
10c		2r. black on red	1·40	3·25
4b		4r. red	55·00	75·00
11b		4r. black on yellow	22·00	35·00
12a		4r. red on yellow	50·00	60·00
5c		8r. lilac	75·00	95·00
13a		8r. black on brown	48·00	95·00
14a		8r. green on brown	60·00	80·00

1864. Perf.

15a	2	1r. red	10	
16a		2r. blue	15	
17a		4r. brown	25	
18a		1p. black	95	

3 Arms of Mexico

4 Emperor Maximilian

1864. Imperf.

30	3	3c. brown	£600	£1200
19a		½r. brown	85·00	£225
31		½r. purple	35·00	28·00
31c		½r. grey	40·00	40·00
32b		1r. blue	8·25	5·00
33		2r. orange	2·50	1·60
34		4r. green	55·00	32·00
35b		8r. red	80·00	48·00

1864. Imperf.

40	4	7c. purple	£225	£2500
36c		7c. grey	32·00	60·00
41		13c. blue	3·75	5·50
42		25c. orange	3·25	5·00
39c		50c. green	11·50	11·50

7 Hidalgo

8 Hidalgo

9 Hidalgo

10 Hidalgo

15 Benito Juarez

16

1868. Imperf or perf.

67	7	6c. black on brown	4·50	2·50
68		12c. black on green	1·90	60
69		25c. blue on pink	3·50	45
70b		50c. black on yellow	60·00	7·50
71		100c. black on brown	60·00	22·00
76		100c. brown on brown	95·00	28·00

1872. Imperf or perf.

87	8	6c. green	6·25	6·25
88		12c. blue	80	65
94		25c. red	3·50	75
90		50c. yellow	70·00	16·00
91		100c. lilac	48·00	25·00

1874. Various frames. Perf.

102a	9	4c. orange	3·50	6·25
97	10	5c. brown	2·10	1·40
98	9	10c. black	85	50
105		10c. orange	85	50
99	10	25c. blue	35	30
107	9	50c. green	7·00	6·25
108		100c. red	9·50	8·25

1879.

115	15	1c. brown	1·90	1·75
116		2c. violet	1·75	1·50
117		5c. orange	1·25	60
118		10c. blue	1·60	1·25
127a		10c. brown	1·25	
128		12c. brown	3·25	3·25
129		18c. brown	3·75	3·25
130		24c. mauve	3·75	3·25
119		25c. red	4·00	4·75
132		25c. brown	2·10	
120		50c. green	6·25	6·00
134		50c. yellow	35·00	38·00
121		85c. violet	11·00	9·50
122		100c. black	12·50	11·00
137		100c. orange	40·00	48·00

1882.

138	**16**	2c. green	3·25	2·50
139		3c. red	3·25	2·50
140		6c. blue	2·50	1·90

17 Hidalgo

18

1884.

141	**17**	1c. green	1·25	15
142		2c. green	1·90	25
157		2c. red	6·25	1·40
143		3c. green	3·75	80
158		3c. brown	8·75	2·50
144		4c. green	5·00	80
159		4c. red	12·50	7·50
145		5c. green	5·00	60
160		5c. blue	8·75	1·60
146		6c. green	4·50	45
161		6c. brown	10·00	2·50
147		10c. green	4·75	15
162		10c. orange	7·50	45
148		12c. green	8·75	1·25
163		12c. brown	16·00	3·75
149		20c. green	25·00	95
150		25c. green	45·00	1·90
164		25c. blue	55·00	8·75
151		50c. green	40	1·25
152		1p. blue	40	4·75
153		2p. blue	40	8·75
154		5p. blue	£120	80·00
155		10p. blue	£170	95·00

1886.

196	**18**	1c. green	30	10
209		2c. red	35	10
167		3c. lilac	2·50	1·25
189		3c. red	30	10
198		3c. orange	95	35
168		4c. lilac	4·50	95
211		4c. red	75	50
199		4c. orange	1·10	50
191		5c. blue	20	10
170		6c. lilac	5·00	60
213		6c. red	95	60
200		6c. orange	1·40	35
171		10c. lilac	5·00	15
193		10c. red	10	10
185a		10c. brown	8·75	1·90
201		10c. orange	7·50	35
172		12c. lilac	5·00	3·25
215		12c. red	3·25	3·75
173		20c. lilac	40·00	22·00
194		20c. red	50	20
202		20c. orange	12·50	1·60
174		25c. lilac	16·00	3·75
217		25c. red	95	25
203		25c. orange	4·00	1·10
206		5p. red	£350	£225
207		10p. red	£550	£350

19 Foot Postman

20 Mounted Postman and Pack Mules

21 Statue of Cuauhtemoc

22 Mailcoach

23 Steam Mail Train

1895.

253	**19**	1c. green	20	10
219		2c. red	30	10
220		3c. brown	30	10
221	**20**	4c. orange	1·50	25
257	**21**	5c. blue	35	10
223	**22**	10c. purple	50	10
224	**20**	12c. olive	8·25	3·75
225	**22**	15c. blue	4·00	80
226		20c. red	4·00	40
227		50c. mauve	12·00	4·75
228	**23**	1p. brown	32·00	10·00
229		5p. red	£150	60·00
230		10p. blue	£190	90·00

27

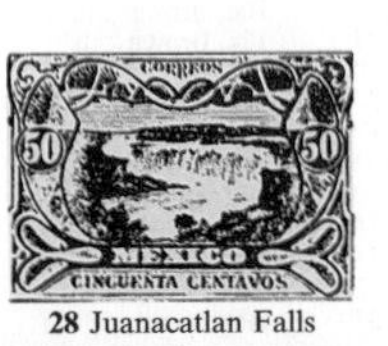
28 Juanacatlan Falls

29 Popocatepetl

30 Cathedral, Mexico

1899. Various frames for T **27**.

266	**27**	1c. green	80	10
276		1c. purple	60	10
267		2c. red	2·40	10
277		2c. green	80	10
268		3c. brown	1·60	10
278		4c. red	2·50	20
269		5c. blue	2·50	10
279		5c. orange	45	10
270		10c. brown and purple	3·25	15
280		10c. orange and blue	2·50	10
271		15c. purple and lavender	4·25	10
272		20c. blue and red	4·75	15
273a	**28**	50c. black and purple	19·00	1·25
281		50c. black and red	40·00	3·50
274	**29**	1p. black and blue	42·00	1·90
275	**30**	5p. black and red	£130	6·25

32 Josefa Ortiz

40 Hidalgo at Dolores

1910. Centenary of First Independence Movement.

282	**32**	1c. purple	10	10
283	–	2c. green	10	10
284	–	3c. brown	25	10
285	–	4c. red	1·25	20
286	–	5c. orange	10	10
287	–	10c. orange and blue	80	10
288	–	15c. lake and slate	4·50	20
289	–	20c. blue and lake	2·50	10
290	**40**	50c. black and brown	6·25	95
291	–	1p. black and blue	7·50	1·10
292	–	5p. black and red	28·00	2·75

DESIGNS: As Type **32**: 2c. L. Vicario; 3c. L. Rayon; 4c. J. Aldama; 5c. M. Hidalgo; 10c. I. Allende; 15c. E. Gonzalez; 20c. M. Abasolo. As Type **40**: 1p. Mass on Mt. of Crosses; 5p. Capture of Granaditas.

REVOLUTIONARY PROVISIONALS

For full list of the provisional issues made during the Civil War from 1913 onwards, see the Stanley Gibbons Part 15 (Central America) Catalogue.

CONSTITUTIONALIST GENERAL ISSUES

CT 1

1914. "Transitorio".

CT1	CT **1**	1c. blue	20	15
CT2		2c. green	30	15
CT3		4c. blue	7·00	1·60
CT4		5c. green	7·00	1·90
CT9		5c. green	10	10
CT5		10c. red	15	15
CT6		20c. brown	25	25
CT7		50c. red	1·60	2·10
CT8		1p. violet	8·75	10·00

The words of value on No. CT4 are 2 × 14 mm and on No. CT9 are 2½ × 16 mm.

1914. Victory of Torreon. Nos. CT1/7 optd **Victoria de TORREON ABRIL 2-1914.**

CT10	CT **1**	1c. blue	95·00	80·00
CT11		2c. green	£110	95·00
CT12		4c. blue	£130	£160
CT13		5c. green	11·50	12·50
CT14		10c. red	60·00	60·00
CT15		20c. brown	£1100	£1100
CT16		50c. red	£1200	£1200

CT 3

CT 4

1914. Handstamped with Type CT **3**. (a) Nos. D282/6.

CT17	D **32**	1c. blue	8·75	10·00
CT18		2c. blue	8·75	10·00
CT19		4c. blue	8·75	10·00
CT20		5c. blue	8·75	10·00
CT21		10c. blue	8·75	10·00

(b) Nos. 282/92.

CT22	**32**	1c. purple	35	30
CT23	–	2c. green	95	80
CT24	–	3c. brown	95	80
CT25	–	4c. red	1·60	1·25
CT26	–	5c. orange	20	10
CT27	–	10c. orange and blue	1·90	1·25
CT28	–	15c. lake and slate	3·25	1·90
CT29	–	20c. blue and lake	6·25	3·75
CT30	**40**	50c. black and brown	7·50	5·00
CT31	–	1p. black and blue	16·00	6·25
CT32	–	5p. black and red	£100	95·00

1914.

CT33	CT **4**	1c. pink	80	12·50
CT34		2c. green	80	11·50
CT35		3c. orange	80	12·50
CT36		5c. red	60	5·00
CT37		10c. green	60	22·00
CT38		25c. blue	10·00	

CT 5

1914. "Denver" issue.

CT39	CT **5**	1c. blue	15	20
CT40		2c. green	15	15
CT41		3c. orange	25	15
CT42		5c. red	25	15
CT43		10c. red	35	40
CT44		15c. mauve	60	1·10
CT45		50c. yellow	1·25	1·60
CT46		1p. violet	5·25	7·50

1914. Optd **GOBIERNO CONSTITUCIONALISTA**. (a) Nos. 279 and 271/2.

CT50	–	5c. orange	48·00	35·00
CT51	–	15c. purple and lavender	95·00	95·00
CT52	–	20c. blue and red	£300	£250

(b) Nos. D282/6.

CT53	D **32**	1c. blue	1·10	1·10
CT54		2c. blue	1·25	1·25
CT55		4c. blue	9·50	9·50
CT56		5c. blue	9·50	9·50
CT57		10c. blue	1·60	1·60

(c) Nos. 282/92.

CT58	**32**	1c. purple	10	10
CT59	–	2c. green	10	10
CT60	–	3c. brown	20	20
CT61	–	4c. red	25	25
CT62	–	5c. orange	10	10
CT63	–	10c. orange and blue	10	10
CT64	–	15c. lake and slate	35	30
CT65	–	20c. blue and lake	35	35
CT66	**40**	50c. black and brown	1·10	75
CT67	–	1p. black and blue	4·75	3·25
CT68	–	5p. black and red	25·00	19·00

CONVENTIONIST ISSUES

(CV 1) Villa–Zapata Monogram

1914. Optd with Type CV **1**. (a) Nos. 266/75.

CV 1	**27**	1c. green	60·00
CV 2		2c. red	60·00
CV 3		3c. brown	32·00
CV 4		5c. blue	60·00
CV 5		10c. brown and purple	60·00
CV 6		15c. purple and lavender	60·00
CV 7		20c. blue and red	60·00
CV 8	**28**	50c. black and red	£160
CV 9	**29**	1p. black and blue	£160
CV10	**30**	5p. black and red	£300

(b) Nos. 276/80.

CV11	**27**	1c. purple	60·00
CV12		2c. green	60·00
CV13		4c. red	60·00
CV14		5c. orange	7·75
CV15		10c. orange and blue	48·00

(c) Nos. D282/6.

CV16	D **32**	1c. blue	6·00	6·25
CV17		2c. blue	6·00	6·25
CV18		4c. blue	6·00	6·25
CV19		5c. blue	6·00	6·25
CV20		10c. blue	60·00	6·25

(d) Nos. 282/92.

CV21	**32**	1c. purple	40	40
CV22	–	2c. green	45	20
CV23	–	3c. brown	30	30
CV24	–	4c. red	1·25	1·25
CV25	–	5c. orange	10	10
CV26	–	10c. orange and blue	95	95
CV27	–	15c. lake and slate	95	95
CV28	–	20c. blue and lake	95	95
CV29	**40**	50c. black and brown	6·25	6·25
CV30	–	1p. black and blue	9·50	9·50
CV31	–	5p. black and red	95·00	95·00

CONSTITUTIONALIST PROVISIONAL ISSUES

CT 10

CT 11 Carranza Monogram

1914. Nos. 282/92 handstamped with Type CT **10**.

CT69	**32**	1c. purple	6·00	5·50
CT70	–	2c. green	6·00	5·50
CT71	–	3c. brown	6·00	5·50
CT72	–	4c. red	7·50	7·00
CT73	–	5c. orange	90	90
CT74	–	10c. orange and blue	7·00	6·25
CT75	–	15c. lake and slate	7·00	6·25
CT76	–	20c. blue and lake	8·75	5·75
CT77	**40**	50c. black and brown	19·00	19·00
CT78	–	1p. black and blue	28·00	
CT79	–	5p. black and red	£100	

1915. Optd with Type CT **11**. (a) No. 271.

CT80	–	15c. purple and lavender	50·00	50·00

(b) No. 279.

CT81	–	5c. orange	12·50	12·50

(c) Nos. D282/6.

CT82	D **32**	1c. blue	7·00
CT83		2c. blue	7·00
CT84		4c. blue	7·00
CT85		5c. blue	7·00
CT86		10c. blue	7·00

(d) Nos. 282/92.

CT87	**32**	1c. purple	35	35
CT88	–	2c. green	35	30
CT89	–	3c. brown	35	35
CT90	–	4c. red	1·25	1·25
CT91	–	5c. orange	10	10
CT92	–	10c. orange and blue	75	75
CT93	–	15c. lake and slate	75	75
CT94	–	20c. blue and lake	75	75
CT95	**40**	50c. black and brown	6·25	6·25
CT96	–	1p. black and blue	9·50	9·50
CT97	–	5p. black and red	95·00	95·00

GENERAL ISSUES.

43 Coat of Arms

44 Statue of Cuauhtemoc

45 Ignacio Zaragoza

1915. Portraits as T **45**. Roul or perf.

293	**43**	1c. violet	10	10
294	**44**	2c. green	20	15
304	**45**	3c. brown	20	15
305		4c. red (Morelos)	20	20
306		5c. orange (Madero)	25	15
307		10c. blue (Juarez)	15	10

46 Map of Mexico

47 Lighthouse, Veracruz

48 Post Office, Mexico City

1915.

299	**46**	40c. grey	2·25	70
433		40c. mauve	1·75	25
300	**47**	1p. grey and brown	35	60
411		1p. grey and blue	22·00	60
301	**48**	5p. blue and lake	5·00	5·50
412		5p. grey and green	1·25	1·50

(49)

50 V. Carranza

1916. Silver Currency. Optd with T **49**. (a) No. 271.

309	–	15c. purple and lavender	£250	£250

(b) No. 279.

309a	–	5c. orange	55·00	55·00

(c) Nos. 282/92.

310	**32**	1c. purple	2·10	3·25
311	–	2c. green	25	15
312	–	3c. brown	25	15
313	–	4c. red	3·75	5·00
314	–	5c. orange	10	10
315	–	10c. orange and blue	60	95
316	–	15c. lake and slate	1·10	1·90
317	–	20c. blue and lake	1·10	1·90
318	**40**	50c. black and brown	5·25	3·25
319	–	1p. black and blue	9·50	4·00
320	–	5p. black and red	95·00	80·00

(d) Nos. CT1/3 and CT5/8.

320b	CT **1**	1c. blue	15·00
320c		2c. green	7·50
320d		4c. blue	£160
320e		10c. red	1·40
320f		20c. brown	1·90
320g		50c. red	9·50
320h		1p. violet	15·00

(e) Nos. CT39/46.
321 CT 5 1c. blue . . . . 2·40 12·00
322 2c. green . . . . 2·40 7·00
323 3c. orange . . . . . . 45 7·00
324 5c. red . . . . 45 7·00
325 10c. red . . . . 45 3·25
326 15c. mauve . . . . . 45 7·00
327 50c. yellow . . . . . 70 8·00
328 1p. violet . . . . 6·00 15·00

(f) Nos. CT58/68.
329 **32** 1c. purple . . . . 1·60 2·50
330 – 2c. green 35 30
331 – 3c. brown 30 30
332 – 4c. red 30 30
333 – 5c. orange 50 15
334 – 10c. orange and blue . . . 35 30
335 – 15c. lake and slate . . . 40 40
336 – 20c. blue and lake 40 40
337 **40** 50c. black and brown . . . 4·75 3·75
338 – 1p. black and blue . . . . 10·00 10·00
339 – 5p. black and red . . . . 95·00 85·00

(g) Nos. CV22/9.
340 **32** 1c. purple . . . . 7·00 9·50
341 – 2c. green 75 45
342 – 3c. brown . . . . 2·00 2·75
343 – 4c. red . . . . 8·25 9·50
344 – 5c. orange . . . . 2·75 3·75
345 – 10c. orange and blue . . . 7·50 8·75
346 – 15c. lake and slate . . . 7·50 8·75
347 – 20c. blue and lake . . . . 7·50 8·75

(h) Nos. CT87/97.
348 **32** 1c. purple . . . . 1·60 2·10
349 – 2c. green 30 30
350 – 3c. brown 25 20
351 – 4c. red . . . . 3·25 3·75
352 – 5c. orange 40 10
353 – 10c. orange and blue . . . 75 1·25
354 – 15c. lake and slate . . . 60 30
355 – 20c. blue and red 60 55
356 **40** 50c. black and brown . . . 4·75 5·50
357 – 1p. black and blue . . . . 7·00 7·50

1916. Carranza's Triumphal Entry into Mexico City.
358 **50** 10c. brown . . . . 7·50 8·25
359 10c. blue 60 30

(51)

1916. Optd with T **51**. (a) Nos. D282/6.
360 D **32** 5c. on 1c. blue . . . . 1·60 1·60
361 10c. on 2c. blue . . . . 1·60 1·60
362 20c. on 4c. blue . . . . 1·60 1·60
363 25c. on 5c. blue . . . . 1·60 1·60
364 60c. on 10c. blue 75 75
365 1p. on 1c. blue 75 75
366 1p. on 2c. blue 75 75
367 1p. on 4c. blue 40 40
368 1p. on 5c. blue . . . . 1·60 1·60
369 1p. on 10c. blue . . . . 1·60 1·60

(b) Nos. 282, 286 and 283.
370 **32** 5c. on 1c. purple 10 10
371 10c. on 1c. purple 10 10
372 – 20c. on 5c. orange 10 10
373 – 25c. on 5c. orange 15 15
374 – 60c. on 2c. green . . . . . 10·50 12·50

(c) Nos. CT39/40.
375 CT 5 60c. on 1c. blue . . . . 1·90 3·75
376 60c. on 2c. green . . . 1·90 3·75

(d) Nos. CT58, CT62 and CT59.
377 **32** 5c. on 1c. purple 10 10
378 – 10c. on 1c. purple 60 60
379 – 25c. on 5c. purple 15 15
380 – 60c. on 2c. green £130 £170

(e) No. CV25.
381 – 25c. on 5c. orange 15 10

(f) Nos. CT87, CT91 and CT88.
382 **32** 5c. on 1c. purple . . . . . 9·50 12·50
383 – 10c. on 1c. purple . . . . 3·25 4·75
385 – 25c. on 5c. orange 50 95
386 – 60c. on 2c. green £140

1916. Nos. D282/6 surch **GPM** and value.
387 D **32** $2.50 on 1c. blue . . . 60 60
388 $2.50 on 2c. blue . . . 6·25 6·25
389 $2.50 on 4c. blue . . . 6·25 6·25
390 $2.50 on 5c. blue . . . 6·25 6·25
391 $2.50 on 10c. blue . . . 6·25 6·25

52a Arms

53 Zaragoza

1916.
392 **52a** 1c. purple 15 15

1917. Portraits. Roul or perf.
393 **53** 1c. violet 25 10
393a 1c. grey 70 20
394 – 2c. green (Vazquez) . . . 35 10
395 – 3c. brown (Suarez) . . . 35 10
396 – 4c. red (Carranza) 60 20
397 – 5c. blue (Herrera) 85 10
398 – 10c. blue (Madero) . . . 1·40 10
399 – 20c. lake (Dominguez) . . 14·00 35
400 – 30c. purple (Serdan) . . . 38·00 60
401 – 30c. black (Serdan) . . . 45·00 60

1919. Red Cross Fund. Surch with cross and premium.
413 5c.+3c. blue (No. 397) . . . 9·00 9·50
414 10c.+5c. blue (No. 398) . . . 11·00 9·50

56 Meeting of Iturbide and Guerrero

1921. Centenary of Declaration of Independence.
415 **56** 10c. brown and blue . . . 9·50 1·90
416 – 10p. black and brown . . . 9·50 22·00
DESIGN: 10p. Entry into Mexico City.

58 Golden Eagle

1922. Air.
454 **58** 25c. sepia and lake 50 25
455 25c. sepia and green . . . 55 30
456 50c. red and blue 70 40

59 Morelos Monument

60 Fountain and Aqueduct

61 Pyramid of the Sun, Teotihuacan

62 Castle of Chapultepec

63 Columbus Monument

74 Benito Juarez

64 Juarez Colonnade

65 Monument to Dona Josefa Ortiz de Dominguez

66 Cuauhtemoc Monument

68 Ministry of Communications

69 National Theatre and Palace of Fine Arts

1923. Roul or perf.
436 **59** 1c. brown 25 10
437 **60** 2c. red 15 10
438 **61** 3c. brown 10 10
429 **62** 4c. green 60 10
440 **63** 4c. green 15 10
441 5c. orange 10 10
453 **74** 8c. orange 15 10
423 **64** 10c. brown . . . . 4·75 10
442 **66** 10c. lake 15 10
443 **65** 20c. blue 35 10
426 **66** 30c. green . . . . 35·00 2·50
432 **64** 30c. green 45 10
434 **68** 50c. brown 30 10
435 **69** 1p. blue and lake 50 25

70

72 Sr. Francisco Garcia y Santos

73 Post Office, Mexico City

1926. 2nd Pan-American Postal Congress. Inscr as in T **70/3**.
445 **70** 2c. red . . . . 1·25 35
446 – 4c. green . . . . 1·25 40
447 **70** 5c. orange . . . . 1·25 25
448 – 10c. red . . . . 1·90 25
449 **72** 20c. blue . . . . 1·90 50
450 30c. green . . . . 3·25 1·90
451 40c. mauve . . . . 6·25 1·60
452 **73** 1p. blue and brown . . . . 17·00 3·75
DESIGN—As Type **70**: 4c., 10c. Map of North and South America.

1929. Child Welfare. Optd **Proteccion a la Infancia**.
457 **59** 1c. brown 25 15

77

79 Capt. Emilio Carranza

1929. Obligatory Tax. Child Welfare.
459 **77** 1c. violet 10 10
461 2c. green 20 10
462 5c. brown 15 10

1929. Air. 1st Death Anniv of Carranza (airman).
463 **79** 5c. sepia and green 55 30
464 10c. red and sepia 65 35
465 15c. green and violet . . . 1·90 60
466 20c. black and sepia . . . 60 35
467 50c. black and red . . . . 3·75 1·25
468 1p. sepia and black . . . . 7·75 1·75

80

1929. Air. Perf or roul (10, 15, 20, 50c.), roul (5, 25c.), perf (others).
476a **80** 5c. blue 10 10
477 10c. violet 10 10
478 15c. red 15 10
479 20c. brown 75 10
480 25c. purple 45 40
472 30c. black 10 10
473 35c. blue 15 10
481 50c. red 45 35
474 1p. blue and black . . . 60 30
475 5p. blue and red . . . . 2·50 2·10
476 10p. brown and violet . . 3·75 4·50

81

87

1929. Air. Aviation Week.
482 **81** 20c. violet 60 50
483 40c. green . . . . 55·00 48·00

1930. 2nd Pan-American Postal Congress issue optd **HABILITADO 1930**.
484 **70** 2c. red . . . . 2·10 1·40
485 – 4c. green . . . . 2·10 1·25
486 **70** 5c. orange . . . . 2·10 1·10
487 – 10c. red . . . . 3·75 1·25
488 **72** 20c. blue . . . . 5·00 1·90
489 30c. green . . . . 4·50 2·10
490 40c. mauve . . . . 6·25 4·50
491 **73** 1p. blue and brown . . . . 5·50 3·75

1930. Air. National Tourist Congress. Optd **Primer Congreso Nacional de Turismo. Mexico. Abril 20-27 de 1930.**
492 **80** 10c. violet (No. 477) . . . 1·25 60

1930. Obligatory Tax. Child Welfare. Surch **HABILITADO $0.01.**
494 **77** 1c. on 2c. green 30 15
495 1c. on 5c. brown 60 15

1930. Air. Optd **HABILITADO 1930.**
496 **79** 5c. sepia and green . . . . 3·50 2·75
497 15c. green and violet . . . 5·50 4·75

1930. Air. Optd **HABILITADO Aereo 1930-1931.**
498 **79** 5c. sepia and green . . . . 3·75 4·00
499 10c. red and sepia . . . . 2·10 2·50
500 15c. green and violet . . . 4·00 4·50
501 20c. black and sepia . . . 4·50 3·50
502 50c. black and red . . . . 8·75 6·25
503 1p. sepia and black . . . . 2·50 1·75

1931. Obligatory Tax. Child Welfare. No. CT58 optd **PRO INFANCIA.**
504 **32** 1c. purple 20 15

1931. Fourth Centenary of Puebla.
505 **87** 10c. brown and blue . . . 1·60 25

88

1931. Air. Aeronautic Exhibition.
506 **88** 25c. lake . . . . 2·00 1·60

1931. Nos. 446/52 optd **HABILITADO 1931.**
508 – 4c. green . . . . 35·00
509 **70** 5c. orange . . . . 6·25
510 – 10c. red . . . . 6·25
511 **72** 20c. blue . . . . 6·25
512 30c. green . . . . 11·00
513 40c. mauve . . . . 16·00
514 **73** 1p. blue and brown . . . . 19·00

1931. Air. Surch **HABILITADO Quince centavos.** Perf or rouletted.
516 **80** 15c. on 20c. sepia 20 10

1932. Air. Surch in words and figures. Perf. or roul.
517 **88** 20c. on 25c. lake 30 15
521 **80** 30c. on 20c. sepia 15 10
519 **58** 40c. on 25c. sepia and lake 2·10 1·10
520 40c. on 25c. sepia & green 40·00 40·00
522 **80** 80c. on 25c. (No. 480) . . 90 60

1932. Air. 4th Death Anniv of Emilio Carranza. Optd **HABILITADO AEREO-1932.**
523 **79** 5c. sepia and green . . . . 3·75 3·25
524 10c. red and sepia . . . . 3·25 1·90
525 15c. green and violet . . . 3·75 2·50
526 20c. black and sepia . . . 3·25 1·75
527 50c. black and red . . . . 22·00 22·00

92 Fray Bartolome de las Casas

1933. Roul.
528 **92** 15c. blue 15 10

93 Mexican Geographical and Statistical Society's Arms

94 National Theatre and Palace of Fine Arts

1933. 21st Int Statistical Congress and Centenary of Mexican Geographical and Statistical Society.
529 **93** 2c. green (postage) 75 20
530 5c. brown . . . . 1·10 25
531 10c. blue 35 10
532 1p. violet . . . . 32·00 38·00
533 **94** 20c. violet and red (air) . . 2·10 85
534 30c. violet and brown . . . 4·25 3·75
535 1p. violet and green . . . 42·00 45·00

95 Mother and Child

98 Nevada de Toluca

1934. National University. Inscr "PRO-UNIVERSIDAD".
543 **95** 1c. orange (postage) . . . 10 10
544 – 5c. green . . . . 1·00 15
545 – 10c. lake . . . . 1·25 30
546 – 20c. blue . . . . 5·00 3·25
547 – 30c. black . . . . 8·75 7·50
548 – 40c. brown . . . . 15·00 10·00
549 – 50c. blue . . . . 28·00 32·00
550 – 1p. black and red . . . . 32·00 30·00

551 – 5p. brown and black . . . £120 £160
552 – 10p. violet and brown . . £500 £650
DESIGNS: 5c. Archer; 10c. Festive headdress; 20c. Woman decorating pot; 30c. Indian and Inca Lily; 40c. Potter; 50c. Sculptor; 1p. Gold craftsman; 5p. Girl offering fruit; 10p. Youth burning incense.

553 **98** 20c. orange (air) . . . . . 1·75 1·75
554 – 30c. purple and mauve . . 3·50 4·25
555 – 50c. brown and green . . . 4·00 6·25
556 – 75c. green and black . . . 4·75 8·75
557 – 1p. blue and green . . . . 5·00 6·25
558 – 5p. blue and brown . . . . 26·00 60·00
559 – 10p. red and blue . . . . 80·00 £130
560 – 20p. red and brown . . . £475 £750
DESIGNS—Airplane over: 30c. Pyramids of the Sun and Moon, Teotihuacan; 50c. Mt. Ajusco; 75c. Mts. Ixtaccihuatl and Popocatepetl; 1p. Bridge over R. Papagallo; 5p. Chapultepec Castle entrance; 10p. Orizaba Peak, Mt. Citlaltepetl; 20p. Girl and Aztec calendar stone.

101 Zapoteca Indian Woman

110 Coat of Arms

1934. Pres. Cardenas' Assumption of Office. Designs as Type **101** and **110**. Imprint "OFICINA IMPRESORA DE HACIENDA-MEXICO" at foot of stamp. (a) Postage.
561 – 1c. orange 30 10
562 **101** 2c. green 30 10
563 – 4c. red 45 15
564 – 5c. brown 30 10
565 – 10c. blue 40 10
565a – 10c. violet 80 10
566 – 15c. blue . . . . 2·50 15
567 – 20c. green . . . . 1·25 10
567a – 20c. blue 85 10
568 – 30c. red 35 10
653 – 30c. blue 40 10
569 – 40c. brown 40 10
570 – 50c. black 45 10
571 **110** 1p. red and brown . . . 1·60 10
572 – 5p. violet and orange . . 4·75 55
DESIGNS: 1c. Yalalteca Indian; 4c. Revolution Monument; 5c. Los Remedios Tower; 10c. Cross of Palenque; 15c. Independence Monument, Mexico City; 20c. Independence Monument, Puebla; 30c. "Heroic Children" Monument, Mexico City; 40c. Sacrificial Stone; 50c. Ruins of Mitla, Oaxaca; 5p. Mexican "Charro" (Horseman).

112 Mictlantecuhtli

120 "Peasant admiration"

(b) Air.
573 **112** 5c. black 20 10
574 – 10c. brown 45 10
575 – 15c. green 90 10
576 – 20c. red . . . . 1·90 10
577 – 30c. olive 35 10
577a – 40c. blue 60 10
578 – 50c. green . . . . . . 1·60 10
579 – 1p. red and green . . . 2·50 10
580 **120** 5p. black and red . . . 4·50 25
DESIGNS—HORIZ: 10c. Temple at Quetzalcoatl; 15c. Aeroplane over Citlaltepetl; 20c. Popocatepetl; 30c. Pegasus; 50c. Uruapan pottery; 1p. "Warrior Eagle". VERT: 40c. Aztec idol.

121 Tractor

122 Arms of Chiapas

1935. Industrial Census.
581 **121** 10c. violet . . . . 2·50 25

1935. Air. Amelia Earhart Flight to Mexico. No. 576 optd **AMELIA EARHART VUELO DE BUENA VOLUNTAD MEXICO 1935**.
581a 20c. red £1900 £2500

1935. Annexation of Chiapas Centenary.
582 **122** 10c. blue 35 15

123 E. Zapata

124 Francisco Madero

1935. 25th Anniv of Revolutionary Plans of Ayala and San Luis Potosi.
583 **123** 10c. violet (postage) . . . 35 10
584 **124** 20c. red (air) 20 10

129 Nuevo Laredo Road

131 Rio Corona Bridge

1936. Opening of Nuevo Laredo Highway (Mexico City–U.S.A.).
591 – 5c. red and green (postage) 15 10
592 – 10c. grey 25 10
593 **129** 20c. green and brown . . 75 50
DESIGNS: As Type **129**: 5c. Symbolical Map of Mexico–U.S.A. road; 10c. Matalote Bridge.

594 – 10c. blue (air) 30 10
595 **131** 20c. orange and violet . . 30 10
596 – 40c. green and blue . . . 40 30
DESIGNS: As Type **131**: 10c. Tasquillo Bridge over Rio Tula; 40c. Guayalejo Bridge.

1936. 1st Congress of Industrial Medicine and Hygiene. Optd **PRIMER CONGRESO NAL. DE HIGIENE Y. MED. DEL TRABAJO**.
597 – 10c. violet (No. 565a) . . . 30 20

1937. As Nos. 561/4, 565a and 576, but smaller. Imprint at foot changed to "TALLERES DE IMP.(RESION) DE EST. (AMPILLAS) Y VALORES-MEXICO".
708 1c. orange (postage) 25 10
709 2c. green 25 10
600 4c. red 40 10
601 5c. brown 35 10
602 10c. violet 25 10
603 20c. red (air) 80 10

134 Blacksmith

1938. Carranza's "Plan of Guadelupe". 25th Anniv. Inscr "CONMEMORATIVO PLAN DE GUADALUPE", etc.
604 **134** 5c. brown & blk (postage) 30 10
605 – 10c. brown 10 10
606 – 20c. orange and brown . . 3·25 50
607 – 20c. blue and red (air) . . 20 10
608 – 40c. red and blue 45 15
609 – 1p. blue and yellow . . . 3·00 1·40
DESIGNS—VERT: 10c. Peasant revolutionary; 20c. Preaching revolt. HORIZ: 20c. Horseman; 40c. Biplane; 1p. Mounted horseman.

140 Arch of the Revolution

141 Cathedral and Constitution Square

1938. 16th International Town Planning and Housing Congress, Mexico City. Inscr as in T **140/1**.
610 **140** 5c. brown (postage) . . . 80 30
611 – 5c. olive . . . . 1·60 1·40
612 – 10c. orange . . . . . . 8·75 7·00
613 – 10c. brown 30 10
614 – 20c. black . . . . 2·10 2·50
615 – 20c. lake . . . . 11·50 9·50
DESIGNS: As Type **140**: 10c. National Theatre; 20c. Independence Column.

616 **141** 20c. red (air) 15 10
617 – 20c. violet . . . . 8·75 6·25
619 – 40c. green . . . . 4·50 3·25
620 – 1p. slate . . . . 4·50 3·25
621 – 1p. light blue . . . . . 4·50 3·25

DESIGNS: As Type **141**: 40c. Chichen Itza Ruins (Yucatan); 1p. Acapulco Beach.

142 Mosquito and Malaria Victim

1939. Obligatory Tax. Anti-malaria Campaign.
622 **142** 1c. blue 95 10

143 Statue of an Indian

144 Statue of Woman Pioneer and Child

1939. Tulsa Philatelic Convention, Oklahoma.
623 **143** 10c. red (postage) 20 10
624 **144** 20c. brown (air) 50 20
625 40c. green . . . . 1·25 60
626 1p. violet 80 45

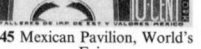

145 Mexican Pavilion, World's Fair

146 Morelos Statue on Mexican Pavilion

1939. Air. F. Sarabia non-stop Flight to New York. Optd **SARABIA Vuelo MEXICO-NUEVA YORK**.
626a **146** 20c. blue and red £160 £300

1939. New York World's Fair.
627 **145** 10c. green & blue (postage) 30 10
628 **146** 20c. green (air) 60 25
629 40c. purple . . . . 1·60 60
630 1p. brown and red . . . 1·00 50

147 J. de Zumarraga

152 "Building"

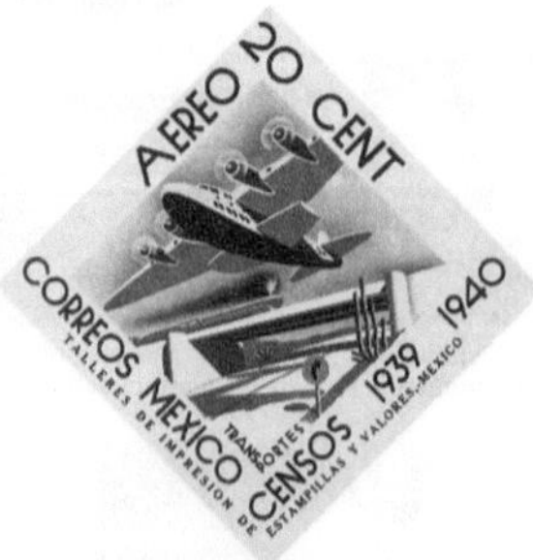
154 "Transport"

1939. 400th Anniv of Printing in Mexico.
631 **147** 2c. black (postage) . . . 35 10
632 – 5c. green 35 10
633 – 10c. red 10 10
634 – 20c. blue (air) 10 10
635 – 40c. green 30 10
636 – 1p. red and brown . . . 55 35
DESIGNS: 5c. First printing works in Mexico; 10c. Antonio D. Mendoza; 20c. Book frontispiece; 40c. Title page of first law book printed in America; 1p. Oldest Mexican Colophon.

1939. National Census. Inscr "CENSOS 1939 1940".
637 **152** 2c. red (postage) 60 10
638 – 5c. green 10 10
639 – 10c. brown 10 10
640 **154** 20c. blue (air) . . . . . . 2·50 40
641 – 40c. orange 35 10
642 – 1p. violet and blue . . . 1·75 35

DESIGNS: As Type **152**: 5c. "Agriculture"; 10c. "Commerce". As Type **154**: 40c. "Industry"; 1p. "Seven Censuses".

155 "Penny Black"

156 Roadside Monument

1940. Centenary of First Adhesive Postage Stamps.
643 **155** 5c. yellow & black (postage) 45 25
644 10c. purple 10 10
645 20c. red and blue 15 10
646 1p. red and grey . . . . 4·50 2·50
647 5p. blue and black . . . 23·00 19·00
648 5c. green and black (air) 45 30
649 10c. blue and brown . . . 35 10
650 20c. violet and red . . . 25 10
651 1p. brown and red . . . 2·10 3·25
652 5p. brown and green . . . 25·00 35·00

1940. Opening of Highway from Mexico City to Guadalajara.
654 **156** 6c. green 35 10

159 Original College at Patzcuaro

1940. 4th Centenary of National College of St. Nicholas de Hidalgo.
655 – 2c. violet (postage) . . . 65 25
656 – 5c. red 40 10
657 – 10c. olive 40 10
658 **159** 20c. green (air) 20 10
659 – 40c. orange 25 10
660 – 1p. violet, brown & orange 60 45
DESIGNS—VERT: 2c. V. de Quiroga; 5c. M. Ocampo; 10c. St. Nicholas College Arms; 40c. Former College at Morelia. HORIZ: 1p. Present College at Morelia.

163 Pirate Galleon

1940. 400th Anniv of Campeche. Inscr as in T **163**.
661 – 10c. red & brown (postage) . . . . 1·90 60
662 **163** 20c. brown and red (air) 90 35
663 – 40c. green and black . . . 75 25
664 – 1p. black and blue . . . 3·25 1·90
DESIGNS: 10c. Campeche City Arms; 40c. St. Miguel Castel; 1p. Temple of San Francisco.

165 Helmsman

166 Miguel Hidalgo y Costilla

1940. Inauguration of Pres. Camacho.
665 **165** 2c. orange & black (postage) . . . . 1·00 30
666 5c. blue and brown . . . 3·75 2·10
667 10c. olive and brown . . 1·40 40
668 20c. grey and orange (air) 1·25 60
669 40c. brown and green . . 1·25 95
670 1p. purple and red . . . 2·10 1·25

1940. Compulsory Tax. Dolores Hidalgo Memorial Fund.
671 **166** 1c. red 30 10

168 Javelin throwing

169 Dark Nebula in Orion

1941. National Athletic Meeting.

675	**168**	10c. green	2·10	25

1942. Inauguration of Astro-physical Observatory at Tonanzintla, Puebla.

676	**169**	2c. blue & violet (postage)	80	50
677	–	5c. blue	5·50	1·25
678	–	10c. blue and orange	5·50	25
679	–	20c. blue and green (air)	7·75	1·90
680	–	40c. blue and red	7·00	2·50
681	–	1p. black and orange	7·00	2·75

DESIGNS: 5c. Solar Eclipse; 10c. Spiral Galaxy of the "Hunting Dog"; 20c. Extra-Galactic Nebula in Virgo; 40c. Ring Nebula in Lyra; 1p. Russell Diagram.

171 Ruins of Chichen-Itza

172 Merida Nunnery

1942. 400th Anniv of Merida. Inscr as in T **171/2**.

682	**171**	2c. brown (postage)	70	30
683	–	5c. red	1·40	30
684	–	10c. violet	80	10
685	**172**	20c. blue (air)	95	25
686	–	40c. green	1·40	1·25
687	–	1p. red	1·60	1·25

DESIGNS–VERT: 5c. Mayan sculpture; 10c. Arms of Merida; 40c. Montejo University Gateway. HORIZ: 1p. Campanile of Merida Cathedral

173 "Mother Earth"

175 Hidalgo Monument

1942. 2nd Inter-American Agricultural Conference.

688	**173**	2c. brown (postage)	40	20
689	–	5c. blue	1·90	55
690	–	10c. orange	60	25
691	–	20c. green (air)	1·25	25
692	–	40c. brown	75	25
693	–	1p. violet	1·60	1·25

DESIGNS: 5c. Sowing wheat; 10c. Western Hemisphere carrying torch; 20c. Corn; 40c. Coffee; 1p. Bananas.

1942. 400th Anniv of Guadalajara.

694	**175**	2c. brown & blue (postage)	15	15
695	–	5c. red and black	60	25
696	–	10c. blue and red	60	20
697	–	20c. black and green (air)	80	35
698	–	40c. green and olive	1·10	50
699	–	1p. violet and brown	80	60

DESIGNS—VERT: 5c. Government Palace; 10c. Guadalajara. HORIZ: 20c. St. Paul's Church, Zapopan; 40c. Sanctuary of Our Lady of Guadalupe; 1p. Arms of Guadalajara.

186 Saltillo Athenaeum, Coahuila

1942. 75th Anniv of Saltillo Athenaeum.

700	**186**	10c. black	90	20

189 Birthplace of Allende

190 "Liberty"

1943. 400th Anniv of San Miguel de Allende.

701	–	2c. blue (postage)	50	15
702	–	5c. brown	55	15
703	–	10c. black	2·10	50
704	–	20c. green (air)	45	30
705	**189**	40c. purple	60	30
706	–	1p. red	1·75	1·60

DESIGNS—VERT: 2c. Cupola de las Monjas; 5c. Gothic Church; 10c. Gen. de Allende. HORIZ: 20c. San Miguel de Allende; 1p. Church seen through cloisters.

1944.

707	**190**	12c. brown	20	10

192 Dr. de Castorena

194 "Flight"

1944. 3rd National Book Fair.

732	**192**	12c. brown (postage)	40	10
733	–	25c. green (air)	45	10

DESIGN: 25c. Microphone, book and camera.

1944. Air.

734	**194**	25c. brown	30	10

195 Hands clasping Globe

1945. Inter-American Conference.

735	**195**	12c. red (postage)	25	10
736		1p. green	45	10
737		5p. brown	3·50	2·75
738		10p. black	6·25	5·00
739		25c. orange (air)	10	10
740		1p. green	15	10
741		5p. blue	1·50	1·10
742		10p. red	4·00	3·25
743		20p. blue	8·75	8·00

196 La Paz Theatre, San Luis Potosi

1945. Reconstruction of La Paz Theatre, San Luis Potosi.

744	**196**	12c. pur & blk (postage)	20	10
745		1p. blue and black	30	10
746		5p. red and black	3·75	3·25
747		10p. green and black	8·25	7·50
748		30c. green (air)	10	10
749		1p. purple and green	15	10
750		5p. black and green	1·40	1·25
751		10p. blue and green	2·75	2·10
752		20p. green and black	6·00	5·25

197 Fountain of Diana the Huntress

198 Removing Bandage

1945.

753	**197**	3c. violet	40	10

1945. Literacy Campaign.

754	**198**	2c. blue (postage)	15	10
755		6c. orange	20	10
756		12c. blue	20	10
757		1p. olive	25	10
758		5p. red and black	2·40	1·90
759		10p. green and blue	13·00	12·50
760		30c. green (air)	10	10
761		1p. red	15	10
762		5p. blue	1·60	1·40
763		10p. red	2·75	2·75
764		20p. brown and green	13·00	12·50

199 Founder of National Post Office

200 O.N.U., Olive Branch and Globe

201 O.N.U. and Flags of United Nations

1946. Foundation of Posts in Mexico in 1580.

765	**199**	8c. black	60	10

1946. United Nations.

766	**200**	2c. olive (postage)	15	10
767		6c. brown	15	10
768		12c. blue	10	10
769		1p. green	30	10
770		5p. red	3·25	3·25
771		10p. blue	14·00	12·50
772	**201**	3c. brown (air)	10	10
773		1p. grey	10	10
774		5p. green and brown	70	50
775		10p. brown and sepia	2·75	2·50
776		20p. red and slate	6·75	4·75

202 Zacatecas City Arms

205 Don Genaro Codina and Zacatecas

1946. 400th Anniv of Zacatecas.

777	**202**	2c. brown (postage)	25	10
778	–	12c. blue	15	10
779	–	1p. mauve	30	10
780	–	5p. red	3·50	1·90
781	–	10p. black and blue	20·00	6·25

DESIGNS: 1p. Statue of Gen. Ortega; 5p. R. L. Velarde (poet); 10p. F. G. Salinas.

782	–	30c. grey (air)	10	10
783	**205**	1p. green and brown	15	10
784	–	5p. green and red	1·90	1·60
785	–	10p. brown and green	7·50	2·75

PORTRAITS: 30c. Fr. Margil de Jesus; 5p. Gen. Enrique Estrada; 10p. D. Fernando Villalpando.

207 Learning Vowels

208 Postman

1946. Education Plan.

786	**207**	1c. sepia	20	10

1947.

787	**208**	15c. blue	15	10

209 Roosevelt and First Mexican Stamp

210 10c. U.S.A. 1847 and Mexican Eagle

1947. U.S.A. Postage Stamp Centenary.

788	**209**	10c. brown (postage)	1·10	60
789	–	15c. green	10	10
790	–	25c. blue (air)	35	20
791	**210**	30c. black	25	10
792	–	1p. blue and red	80	15

DESIGNS: 15c. as Type **209** but vert; 25c., 1p. as Type **210** but horiz.

213 Justo Sierra

214 Ministry of Communications

212 Douglas DC-4

1947.

795	**213**	10p. green and brown (postage)	65·00	8·50
796	**214**	20p. mauve and green	1·10	90
793	–	10p. red and brown (air)	75	80
794	**212**	20p. red and blue	1·50	1·25

DESIGN—HORIZ: 10p. E. Carranza.

215 Manuel Rincon

217 Vicente Suarez

1947. Battle Centenaries. Portraits of "Child Heroes" etc. Inscr "1er CENTENARIO CHAPULTEPEC ("CHURUBUSCO" or "MOLINO DEL REY") 1847 1947".

797	–	2c. black (postage)	30	10
798	–	5c. red	15	10
799	–	10c. brown	15	10
800	–	15c. green	15	10
801	**215**	30c. olive	20	10
802	–	1p. blue	30	15
803	–	5p. red and blue	1·25	1·25

DESIGNS—VERT: 2c. Francisco Marquez; 5c. Fernando Montes de Oca; 10c. Juan Escutin; 15c. Agustin Melgar; 1p. Lucas Balderas; 5p. Flag of San Blas Battalion.

804	**217**	25c. violet (air)	15	10
805	–	30c. blue	15	10
806	–	50c. green	25	10
807	–	1p. violet	30	10
808	–	5p. brown and blue	1·25	1·25

DESIGNS—HORIZ: 30c. Juan de la Barrera; 50c. Military Academy; 1p. Pedro Maria Anaya; 5p. Antonio de Leon.

218 Puebla Cathedral

221 Dance of the Half Moons, Puebla

1950. (a) Postage. As T **218**.

835	–	3c. blue	15	10
874	–	5c. brown	25	10
875a	–	10c. green	40	10
876a	–	15c. green	20	10
877e	**218**	20c. blue	30	10
840	–	30c. red	25	10
879	–	30c. brown	35	10
880b	–	40c. orange	95	10
1346b	–	50c. blue	10	10
1327b	–	80c. green	35	10
843	–	1p. brown	2·75	10
1346f	–	1p. green	10	10

1011ab – 1p. grey 30 10
1327d – 3p. red 55 10
1012a – 5p. blue and green . . 1·50 60
1013ab – 10p. black and blue 2·50 1·25
846 – 20p. violet and green 6·25 6·25
1014 – 20p. violet and black 5·75 4·50
1327e – 50p. orange and green 6·25 4·75
DESIGNS: 3 c, 3p. La Purisima Church, Monterrey; 5c. Modern building, Mexico City; 10c. Convent of the Nativity, Tepoztlan; 15 c, 50p. Benito Juarez; 30c., 80c. Indian dancer, Michoacan; 40c. Sculpture, Tabasco; 50c. Carved head, Veracruz; 1p. Actopan Convent and carved head; 5p. Galleon, Campeche; 10p. Francisco Madero; 20p. Modern building, Mexico City.

(b) Air. As T **221**.
897 – 5c. blue 15 10
898a – 10c. brown 25 15
899a – 20c. red 35 10
850 – 25c. brown 60 10
851 – 30c. olive 15 10
902 – 35c. violet 55 10
1327f – 40c. blue 10 10
904c – 50c. green 35 10
1056 – 80c. red 60 70
906a **221** 1p. grey 45 10
1327h – 1p.60 red 60 10
1327i – 1p.90 red 35 10
907ab – 2p. brown 65 25
908 – 2p.25 purple 60 45
1327j – 4p.30 blue 45 10
1017a – 5p. orange and brown 2·75 35
1327k – 5p.20 lilac 70 25
1327l – 5p.60 green . . . . . 1·40 30
895 – 10p. blue and black 3·75 60
859a – 20p. blue and red . . 5·25 5·75
DESIGNS: 5c., 1p.90 Bay of Acapulco; 10c., 4p.30, Dance of the Plumes, Oaxaca; 20c. Mayan frescoes, Chiapas; 25c., 2p.25, 5p.60, Masks, Michoacan; 30c. Cuauhtemoc; 35c., 2p., 5p.20, Taxco, Guerrero; 40c. Sculpture, San Luis Potosi; 50c., 1p.60, Ancient carvings, Chiapas; 80c. University City, Mexico City; 5p. Architecture, Queretaro; 10p. Hidalgo; 20p. National Music Conservatoire, Mexico City.

222 Arterial Road

224 Diesel Locomotive and Map

1950. Opening of Mexican Section of Pan-American Highway. Inscr "CARRETERA INTERNACIONAL 1950".
860 – 15c. violet (postage) . . . 30 10
861 **222** 20c. blue 20 10
862 – 25c. pink (air) . . . . . 1·60 20
863 – 35c. green 10 10
DESIGNS—HORIZ: 15c. Bridge; 25c. Pres. M. Aleman, bridge and map; 35c. B. Juarez and map.

1950. Inauguration of Mexico–Yucatan Railway.
864 – 15c. purple (postage) . . 1·75 30
865 **224** 20c. red 70 35
866 – 25c. green (air) 70 35
867 – 35c. blue 70 40
DESIGNS—VERT: 15c. Rail-laying. HORIZ: 25c. Diesel trains crossing Isthmus of Tehuantepac; 35c. M. Aleman and railway bridge at Coatzacoalcos.

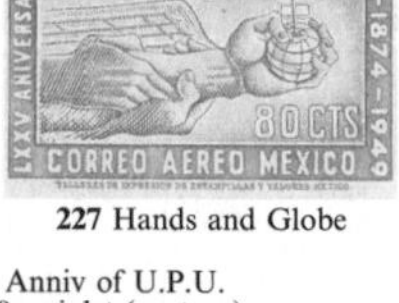
227 Hands and Globe

1950. 75th Anniv of U.P.U.
868 – 50c. violet (postage) . . . 25 10
869 – 25c. red (air) 55 25
870 **227** 80c. blue 30 20
DESIGNS—HORIZ: 25c. Aztec runner. VERT: 50c. Letters "U.P.U.".

228 Miguel Hidalgo

229

1953. Birth Bicentenary of Hidalgo.
871 **228** 20c. sepia & blue (postage) . . . . 1·10 10
872 – 25c. lake and blue (air) 35 10
873 **229** 35c. green 35 10
DESIGN: As Type **229**: 25c. Full face portrait.

231 Aztec Athlete

232 View and Mayan Bas-relief

1954. 7th Central American and Caribbean Games.
918 **231** 20c. blue & pink (postage) 55 10
919 **232** 25c. brown and green (air) 35 15
920 – 35c. turquoise and purple 30 10
DESIGN: 35c. Stadium.

233

234

1954. Mexican National Anthem Centenary.
921 **233** 5c. lilac and blue (postage) 45 15
922 20c. brown and purple . . 55 10
923 1p. green and red 30 20
924 **234** 25c. blue and lake (air) 45 15
925 35c. purple and blue . . . 20 10
926 80c. green and blue . . . 25 15

235 Torchbearer and Stadium

236 Aztec God and Map

1955. 2nd Pan-American Games, Mexico City. Inscr "II JUEGOS DEPORTIVOS PANAMERICANOS".
927 **235** 20c. green & brn (postage) 40 10
928 **236** 25c. blue and brown (air) 30 10
929 – 35c. brown and red . . . 30 10
DESIGN: As Type **236**: 35c. Stadium and map.

237 Olin Design

238 Feathered Serpent and Mask

1956. Mexican Stamp Centenary.
930 **237** 5c. green & brn (postage) 30 10
931 – 10c. blue and grey 30 10
932 – 30c. purple and red . . . 20 10
933 – 50c. brown and blue . . . 25 10
934 – 1p. black and green . . . 35 10
935 – 5p. sepia and bistre . . . 1·60 1·40
DESIGNS: As Type **237**: 10c. Tohtli bird; 30c. Zochitl flower; 50c. Centli corn; 1p. Mazatl deer; 5p. Teheutli man's head.

937 **238** 5c. black (air) 15 10
938 – 10c. blue 15 10
939 – 50c. purple 10 10
940 – 1p. violet 15 10
941 – 1p.20 mauve 15 10
942 – 5p. turquoise 80 80
DESIGNS: As Type **238**: 10c. Bell tower, coach and Viceroy Enriquez de Almanza; 50c. Morelos and cannon; 1p. Mother, child and mounted horseman; 1p.20, Sombrero and spurs; 5p. Emblems of food and education and pointing hand.

239 Stamp of 1856

1956. Centenary Int Philatelic Exn, Mexico City.
944 **239** 30c. blue and brown . . . 45 15

240 F. Zarco

241 V. Gomez Farias and M. Ocampo

1956. Inscr "CONSTITUYENTE(S) DE 1857".
945 – 25c. brown (postage) 35 10
946 – 45c. blue 15 10
947 – 60c. purple 15 10
1346d **240** 70c. blue 20 10
1327c – 2p.30 blue 55 10
949 **241** 15c. blue (air) 20 10
1327g – 60c. green 15 15
950 – 1p.20 violet and green 35 15
951 **241** 2p.75 purple 50 30
PORTRAITS: As T **240** (postage): 25, 45c., 2p.30, G. Prieto; 60c. P. Arriaga. As T **41** (air): 60c., 1p.20, L. Guzman and I. Ramirez.

242 Paricutin Volcano

1956. Air. 20th International Geological Congress.
952 **242** 50c. violet 30 10

243 Map of Central America and the Caribbean

1956. Air. 4th Inter-American Congress of Caribbean Tourism.
953 **243** 25c. blue and grey 20 10

244 Assembly of 1857

245 Mexican Eagle and Scales

1957. Centenary of 1857 Constitution.
958 – 30c. gold & lake (postage) 35 10
959 **244** 1p. green and sepia . . . 25 10
960 **245** 50c. brown and green (air) 20 10
961 – 1p. lilac and blue 30 15
DESIGNS—VERT: 30c. Emblem of Constitution. HORIZ: 1p. (Air), "Mexico" drafting the Constitution.

246 Globe, Weights and Dials

1957. Air. Centenary of Adoption of Metric System in Mexico.
962 **246** 50c. black and silver . . . 30 10

247 Train Disaster

248 Oil Derrick

1957. Air. 50th Anniv of Heroic Death of Jesus Garcia (engine driver) at Nacozari.
963 **247** 50c. purple and red . . . 90 25

1958. 20th Anniv of Nationalization of Oil Industry.
964 **248** 30c. black & blue (postage) 25 10
965 – 5p. red and blue . . . . 3·50 2·50
966 – 50c. green and black (air) 10 10
967 – 1p. black and red 20 10
DESIGNS—HORIZ: 50c. Oil storage tank and "AL SERVICIO DE LA PATRIA" ("At the service of the Fatherland"); 1p. Oil refinery at night. VERT: 5p. Map of Mexico and silhouette of oil refinery.

249 Angel, Independence Monument, Mexico City

250 UNESCO Headquarters, Paris

1958. Air. 10th Anniv of Declaration of Human Rights.
968 **249** 50c. blue 20 10

1959. Inauguration of UNESCO Headquarters Building, Paris.
969 **250** 30c. black and purple . . 30 10

251 U.N. Headquarters, New York

252 President Carranza

1959. U.N. Economic and Social Council Meeting, Mexico City.
970 **251** 30c. blue and yellow . . . 30 10

1960. "President Carranza Year" (1959) and his Birth Centenary.
971 **252** 30c. pur & grn (postage) 20 10
972 – 50c. violet and salmon (air) 20 10
DESIGN—HORIZ: 50c. Inscription "Plan de Guadalupe Constitucion de 1917" and portrait as Type **252**.

253 Alexander von Humboldt (statue)

254 Alberto Braniff's Voisin "Boxkite" and Bristol Britannia

1960. Death Centenary of Alexander von Humboldt (naturalist).
973 **253** 40c. green and brown . . 20 10

1960. Air. 50th Anniv of Mexican Aviation.
974 **254** 50c. brown and violet . . 40 10
975 1p. brown and green . . . 40 15

255 Francisco I. Madero

257 Dolores Bell

1960. Visit to Mexico of Members of Elmhurst Philatelic Society (American Society of Mexican Specialists). Inscr "HOMENAJE AL COLECCIONISTA".
976 **255** 10p. sepia, green and purple (postage) . . . . 27·00 45·00
977 – 20p. sepia, green and purple (air) . . . . . . 38·00 50·00
DESIGN: As No. 1019a 20p. National Music Conservatoire inscr "MEX. D.F.".

1960. 150th Anniv of Independence.
978 **257** 30c. red & green (postage) 60 10
979 – 1p. sepia and green . . . 25 10
980 – 5p. blue and purple . . . 3·25 3·25
981 – 50c. red and green (air) 15 10
982 – 1p.20 sepia and blue . . . 20 10
983 – 5p. sepia and green . . . 3·50 1·40
DESIGNS—VERT: No. 979, Independence Column; 980, Hidalgo, Dolores Bell and Mexican Eagle. HORIZ: No. 981, Mexican Flag; 982, Eagle breaking chain and bell tolling; 983, Dolores Church.

259 Children at Desk, University and School Buildings

261 Count S. de Revillagigedo

1960. 50th Anniv of Mexican Revolution.
984 – 10c. multicoloured (postage) 30 10
985 – 15c. brown and green . . 1·75 10
986 – 20c. blue and brown . . . 50 10
987 – 30c. violet and sepia . . . 20 10
988 **259** 1p. slate and purple . . . 25 10
989 – 5p. grey and purple . . . 2·10 2·10
990 – 50c. black and blue (air) 20 10
991 – 1p. green and red 20 10
992 – 1p.20 sepia and green . . 20 10
993 – 5p. lt blue, blue & mauve 2·00 90
DESIGNS: No. 984, Pastoral scene (35½ × 45½ mm). As Type **259** VERT: No. 985, Worker and hospital buildings; 986, Peasant, soldier and marine; 987, Power lines and pylons; 989, Coins, banknotes and bank entrance. HORIZ: No. 990, Douglas DC-8 airliner; 991, Riggers on oil derrick; 992, Main highway and map; 993, Barrage.

1960. Air. National Census.
994 **261** 60c. black and lake . . . 35 10

262 Railway Tunnel

263 Mosquito Globe and Instruments

1961. Opening of Chihuahua State Railway.
995 **262** 40c. black & grn (postage) 75 30
996 – 60c. blue and black (air) 75 30
997 – 70c. black and blue . . . 75 30
DESIGNS—HORIZ: 60c. Railway tracks and map of railway; 70c. Railway viaduct.

1962. Malaria Eradication.
998 **263** 40c. brown and blue . . . 25 10

264 Pres. Goulart of Brazil

265 Soldier and Memorial Stone

1962. Visit of President of Brazil.
999 **264** 40c. bistre 65 10

1962. Centenary of Battle of Puebla.
1000 **265** 40c. sepia and green (postage) 25 10
1001 – 1p. olive and green (air) 35 10
DESIGN—HORIZ: 1p. Statue of Gen. Zaragoza.

266 Draughtsman and Surveyor

267 Plumb-line

1962. 25th Anniv of National Polytechnic Institute.
1002 **266** 40c. turquoise and blue (postage) 65 10
1003 – 1p. olive and blue (air) 35 10
DESIGN—HORIZ: 1p. Scientist and laboratory assistant.

1962. Mental Health.
1004 **267** 20c. blue and black . . . 90 15

268 Pres. J. F. Kennedy

269 Tower and Cogwheels

1962. Air. Visit of U.S. President.
1005 **268** 80c. blue and red . . . . 1·00 15

1962. "Century 21" Exn ("World's Fair"), Seattle.
1006 **269** 40c. black and green . . 35 10

270 Globe and O.E.A. Emblem

271 Pres. Alessandri of Chile

1962. Inter-American Economic and Social Council.
1007 **270** 40c. sepia and grey (postage) 25 10
1008 – 1p.20 sepia & violet (air) 35 15
DESIGN—HORIZ: 1p.20, Globe, Scroll and O.E.A. emblem.

1962. Visit of President of Chile.
1009 **271** 20c. brown 45 10

272 Balloon over Mexico City

273 "ALALC" Emblem

1962. Air. 1st Mexican Balloon Flight Centenary.
1010 **272** 80c. black and blue . . . 90 25

1963. Air. 2nd "ALALC" Session.
1023 **273** 80c. purple and orange 65 20

274 Pres. Betancourt of Venezuela

275 Petroleum Refinery

1963. Visit of President of Venezuela.
1024 **274** 20c. blue 35 10

1963. Air. 25th Anniv of Nationalization of Mexican Petroleum Industry.
1025 **275** 80c. slate and orange . . 35 10

276 Congress Emblem

277 Campaign Emblem

1963. 19th International Chamber of Commerce Congress, Mexico City.
1026 **276** 40c. brown and black (postage) 45 10
1027 – 80c. black and blue (air) 55 20
DESIGN—HORIZ: 80c. World map and "C.I.C." emblem.

1963. Freedom from Hunger.
1028 **277** 40c. red and blue 45 15

278 Arms and Mountain

279 B. Dominguez

1963. 4th Centenary of Durango.
1029 **278** 20c. brown and blue . . 45 15

1963. Birth Centenary of B. Dominguez (revolutionary).
1030 **279** 20c. olive and green . . 45 15

280 Exhibition Stamp of 1956

281 Pres. Tito

1963. 77th American Philatelic Society Convention, Mexico City.
1031 **280** 1p. brown & bl (postage) 60 45
1032 – 5p. red (air) . . . . . . 1·40 1·00
DESIGN—HORIZ: 5p. EXMEX "stamp" and "postmark".

1963. Air. Visit of President of Yugoslavia.
1033 **281** 2p. green and violet . . 1·10 30

283 Part of U.I.A. Building

284 Red Cross on Tree

1963. Air. International Architects' Day.
1034 **283** 80c. grey and blue . . . 45 15

1963. Red Cross Centenary.
1035 **284** 20c. red & grn (postage) 30 15
1036 – 80c. red and green (air) 70 25
DESIGN—HORIZ: 80c. Red Cross on dove.

285 Pres. Estenssoro

286 Jose Morelos

1963. Visit of President of Bolivia.
1037 **285** 40c. purple and brown 45 15

1963. 150th Anniv of First Anahuac Congress.
1038 **286** 40c. bronze and green 40 15

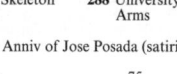

287 Don Quixote as Skeleton

288 University Arms

1963. Air. 50th Death Anniv of Jose Posada (satirical artist).
1039 **287** 1p.20 black 75 20

1963. 90th Anniv of Sinaloa University.
1040 **288** 40c. bistre and green . . 45 15

289 Diesel-electric Train

290 "F.S.T.S.E." Emblem

1963. 11th Pan-American Railways Congress, Mexico City.
1041 **289** 20c. brn & blk (postage) 1·25 70
1042 – 1p.20 blue and violet (air) . . . . 1·25 55
DESIGN: 1p.20, Steam and diesel-electric locomotives and horse-drawn tramcar.

1964. 25th Anniv of Workers' Statute.
1075 **290** 20c. sepia and orange . . 30 10

291 Mrs. Roosevelt, Flame and U.N. Emblem

1964. Air. 15th Anniv of Declaration of Human Rights.
1076 **291** 80c. blue and orange . . 50 10

292 Pres. De Gaulle

1964. Air. Visit of President of France.
1077 **292** 2p. blue and brown . . . 1·25 35

293 Pres. Kennedy and Pres. A. Lopez Mateos

1964. Air. Ratification of Chamizal Treaty (1963).
1078 **293** 80c. black and blue . . . 55 15

294 Queen Juliana and Arms

295 Academy Emblem

1964. Air. Visit of Queen Juliana of the Netherlands.
1079 **294** 20c. bistre and blue . . . 70 15

1964. Centenary of National Academy of Medicine.
1080 **295** 20c. gold and black . . . 30 10

296 Lieut. Jose Azueto and Cadet Virgillo Uribe

1964. Air. 50th Anniv of Heroic Defence of Veracruz.
1081 **296** 40c. green and brown . . 30 10

297 Arms and World Map

298 Colonel G. Mendez

1964. Air. International Bar Assn Conf, Mexico City.
1082 **297** 40c. blue and brown . . 45 10

1964. Centenary of Battle of the Jahuactal Tabasco.
1083 **298** 40c. olive and brown . . 35 10

299 Dr. Jose Rizal

300 Zacatecas

1964. 400 Years of Mexican–Philippine Friendship. Inscr "1564 AMISTAD MEXICANO–FILIPINA 1964".
1084 **299** 20c. blue & grn (postage) 35 10
1085 – 40c. blue and violet . . . 40 10
1086 – 80c. blue & lt blue (air) 1·75 25
1087 – 2p.75 black and yellow 1·75 70
DESIGNS—As Type **299**: VERT: 40c. Legaspi. HORIZ: 80c. "San Pedro" (16th-century Spanish galleon). LARGER (44 × 36 mm): 2p.75, Ancient map of Pacific Ocean.

1964. 50th Anniv of Conquest of Zacatecas.
1088 **300** 40c. green and red . . . 40 10

301 Morelos Theatre, Aguascalientes

302 Andres Manuel del Rio

1965. 50th Anniv of Aguascalientes Convention.
1089 **301** 20c. purple and grey . . 30 10

1965. Andres M. del Rio Commemoration.
1090 **302** 30c. black 35 10

303 Netzahualcoyotl Dam

304 J. Morelos (statue)

1965. Air. Inauguration of Netzahualcoyotl Dam.
1091 **303** 80c. slate and purple . . 30 10

1965. 150th Anniv (1964) of First Constitution.
1092 **304** 40c. brown and green . . 40 10

305 Microwave Tower

306 Fir Trees

1965. Air. Centenary of I.T.U.
1093 **305** 80c. blue and indigo . . 40 20
1094 – 1p.20 green and black 45 20
DESIGN: 1p.20, Radio-electric station.

1965. Forest Conservation.
1095 **306** 20c. green and blue . . . 30 10
The inscription "¡CUIDALOS!" means "CARE FOR THEM!".

307 I.C.Y. Emblem

1965. International Co-operation Year.
1096 **307** 40c. brown and green . . 25 10

308 Camp Fire and Tent

1965. Air. World Scout Conference, Mexico City.
1097 **308** 30c. ultramarine and blue 40 20

309 King Baudouin and Queen Fabiola

1965. Air. Visit of Belgian King and Queen.
1098 **309** 2p. blue and green . . . 75 20

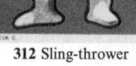

310 Mexican Antiquities and Unisphere

311 Dante (after R. Sanzio)

1965. Air. New York World's Fair.
1099 **310** 80c. green and yellow . . 30 15

1965. Air. Dante's 700th Birth Anniv.
1100 **311** 2p. red . . . . 1·00 55

312 Sling-thrower

313 Jose M. Morelos y Pavon (leader of independence movement)

1965. Olympic Games (1968) Propaganda (1st series). Museum pieces.
1101 **312** 20c. blue & olive (postage) 45 10
1102 – 40c. sepia and red . . . 15 10
1103 – 80c. slate and red (air) 35 10
1104 – 1p.20 indigo and blue . . 45 15
1105 – 2p. brown and blue . . . 35 10
DESIGNS—As Type **312**: VERT: 40c. Batsman. HORIZ: 2p. Ball game. HORIZ (36 × 20 mm): 80c. Fieldsman. 1p.20, Scoreboard.

1965. 150th Anniv of Morelos's Execution.
1108 **313** 20c. black and blue . . . 30 10

314 Agricultural Produce

315 Ruben Dario

1966. Centenary of Agrarian Reform Law.
1109 **314** 20c. red 30 10
1110 – 40c. black 40 10
DESIGN: 40c. Emilio Zapata, pioneer of agrarian reform.

1966. Air. 50th Death Anniv of Ruben Dario (Nicaraguan poet).
1111 **315** 1p.20 sepia 55 20

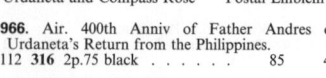

316 Father Andres de Urdaneta and Compass Rose

317 Flag and Postal Emblem

1966. Air. 400th Anniv of Father Andres de Urdaneta's Return from the Philippines.
1112 **316** 2p.75 black 85 45

1966. 9th Postal Union of Americas and Spain Congress (U.P.A.E.), Mexico City.
1113 **317** 40c. blk & grn (postage) 35 10
1114 – 80c. black & mauve (air) 30 15
1115 – 1p.20 black and blue . . 35 15
DESIGNS—VERT: 80c. Flag and posthorn. HORIZ: 1p.20, U.P.A.E. emblem and flag.

318 Friar B. de Las Casas

319 E.S.I.M.E. Emblem and Diagram

1966. 400th Death Anniv of Friar Bartolome de Las Casas ("Apostle of the Indies").
1116 **318** 20c. black on buff . . . 35 10

1966. 50th Anniv of Higher School of Mechanical and Electrical Engineering.
1117 **319** 20c. green and grey . . . 30 10

320 U Thant and U.N. Emblem

321 "1966 Friendship Year"

1966. Air. U.N. Secretary-General U Thant's Visit to Mexico.
1118 **320** 80c. black and blue . . . 30 15

1966. Air. "Year of Friendship" with Central American States.
1119 **321** 80c. green and red . . . 25 10

322 F.A.O. Emblem

323 Running and Jumping

1966. International Rice Year.
1120 **322** 40c. green 30 10

1966. Olympic Games (1968) Propaganda (2nd series).
1121 **323** 20c. black & bl (postage) 55 10
1122 – 40c. black and lake . . . 25 10
1124 – 80c. black & brown (air) 35 10
1125 – 2p.25 black and green 55 25
1126 – 2p.75 black and violet 60 35
DESIGNS: 40c. Wrestling. LARGER (57 × 20 mm): 80c. Obstacle race; 2p.25, American football; 2p.75, Lighting Olympic flame.

324 UNESCO Emblem

325 Constitution of 1917

1966. Air. 20th Anniv of UNESCO.
1128 **324** 80c. multicoloured . . . 30 10

1967. 50th Anniv of Mexican Constitution.
1129 **325** 40c. black (postage) . . 45 10
1130 – 80c. brown & ochre (air) 35 10
DESIGN: 80c. President V. Carranza.

326 Earth and Satellite

327 Oil Refinery

1967. Air. World Meteorological Day.
1131 **326** 80c. blue and black . . . 30 20

1967. 7th World Petroleum Congress, Mexico City.
1132 **327** 40c. black and blue . . . 30 10

328 Nayarit Indian

329 Degollado Theatre

1967. 50th Anniv of Nayarit State.
1133 **328** 20c. black and green . . 30 10

1967. Cent of Degollado Theatre, Guadalajara.
1134 **329** 40c. brown and mauve 10 10

330 Mexican Eagle and Crown

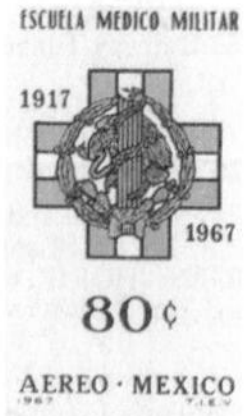

331 School Emblem

1967. Centenary of Triumph over the Empire.
1135 **330** 20c. black and ochre . . 30 10

1967. Air. 50th Anniv of Military Medical School.
1136 **331** 80c. green and yellow . . 35 15

332 Capt. H. Ruiz Gavino

333 Marco Polo

1967. Air. 50th Anniv of 1st Mexican Airmail Flight, Pachuca–Mexico City.
1137 **332** 80c. brown and black . . 30 10
1138 – 2p. brown and black . . 70 20
DESIGN—HORIZ: 2p. De Havilland D.H.6A biplane.

1967. Air. International Tourist Year.
1139 **333** 80c. red and black . . . 20 10

334 Canoeing

335 A. del Valle-Arizpe (writer)

1967. Olympic Games (1968) Propaganda (3rd series).
1140 **334** 20c. black & bl (postage) 20 10
1141 – 40c. black and red . . . 15 10
1142 – 50c. black and green . . 15 10
1143 – 80c. black and violet . . 25 10

1144 – 2p. black and orange . . 40 15
1146 – 80c. black & mauve (air) 15 10
1147 – 1p.20 black and green 15 10
1148 – 2p. black and lemon . . 60 20
1149 – 5p. black and yellow . . 1·00 35
DESIGNS: 40c. Basketball; 50c. Hockey; 80c. (No. 1143), Cycling; 80c. (No. 1146), Diving; 1p.20, Running; 2p. (No. 1144), Fencing; 2p. (No. 1148), Weightlifting; 5p. Football.

1967. Centenary of Fuente Athenaeum, Saltillo.
1151 **335** 20c. slate and brown . . 30 10

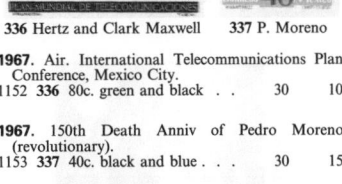

336 Hertz and Clark Maxwell

337 P. Moreno

1967. Air. International Telecommunications Plan Conference, Mexico City.
1152 **336** 80c. green and black . . 30 10

1967. 150th Death Anniv of Pedro Moreno (revolutionary).
1153 **337** 40c. black and blue . . . 30 15

338 Gabino Berreda (founder of Preparatory School)

339 Exhibition Emblem

1968. Centenary of National Preparatory and Engineering Schools.
1154 **338** 40c. red and blue 35 10
1155 – 40c. blue and black 35 10
DESIGN: No. 1155, Staircase, Palace of Mining.

1968. Air. "Efimex '68" International Stamp Exn, Mexico City.
1156 **339** 80c. green and black . . 25 30
1157 – 2p. red and black . . . 25 30
The emblem reproduces the "Hidalgo" Official stamp design of 1884.

1968. Olympic Games (1968) Propaganda (4th series). Designs as T **334**, but inscr "1968".
1158 20c. black and olive (postage) 25 10
1159 40c. black and purple . . . 25 10
1160 50c. black and green 25 10
1161 80c. black and mauve 25 10
1162 1p. black and brown . . . . 1·50 25
1163 2p. black and grey . . . . 1·75 95
1165 80c. black and blue (air) . . 30 10
1166 1p. black and turquoise . . 35 15
1167 2p. black and yellow 35 20
1168 5p. black and brown 80 70
DESIGNS: 20c. Wrestling; 40c. Various sports; 50c. Water-polo; 80c. (No. 1161), Gymnastics; 80c. (No. 1165), Yachting; 1p. (No. 1162), Boxing; 1p. (No. 1166), Rowing; 2p. (No. 1163), Pistol-shooting; 2p. (No. 1167), Volleyball; 5p. Horse-racing.

340 Dr. Martin Luther King

1968. Air. Martin Luther King Commemorative.
1170 **340** 80c. black and grey . . . 35 15

341 Olympic Flame

342 Emblems of Games

1968. Olympic Games, Mexico. (i) Inaug Issue.
1171 **341** 10p. multicoloured . . . 2·00 1·25

(ii) Games Issue. Multicoloured designs as T **341** (20, 40, 50c. postage and 80c., 1, 2p. air) or as T **342** (others).
1172 20c. Dove of Peace on map (postage) 25 10
1173 40c. Stadium 30 10
1174 50c. Telecommunications Tower, Mexico City . . . 30 10
1175 2p. Palace of Sport, Mexico City . . . . 1·40 25
1176 5p. Cultural symbols of Games . . . . 2·75 80
1178 80c. Dove and Olympic rings (air) 15 10
1179 1p. "The Discus-thrower" 15 10
1180 2p. Olympic medals 45 25
1181 5p. Type **342** . . . . 1·75 85
1182 10p. Line-pattern based on "Mexico 68" and rings . . 1·50 95

343 Arms of Vera Cruz

344 "Father Palou" (M. Guerrero)

1969. 450th Anniv of Vera Cruz.
1185 **343** 40c. multicoloured . . . 30 10

1969. Air. 220th Anniv of Arrival in Mexico of Father Serra (colonizer of California).
1186 **344** 80c. multicoloured . . . 35 10
It was intended to depict Father Serra in this design, but the wrong detail of the painting by Guerrero, which showed both priests, was used.

345 Football and Spectators

1969. Air. World Cup Football Championship (1st issue). Multicoloured.
1187 80c. Type **345** 25 10
1188 2p. Foot kicking ball . . . 35 10
See also Nos. 1209/10.

346 Underground Train

1969. Inauguration of Mexico City Underground Railway System.
1189 **346** 40c. multicoloured . . . 60 20

347 Mahatma Gandhi

348 Footprint on Moon

1969. Air. Birth Centenary of Mahatma Gandhi.
1190 **347** 80c. multicoloured . . . 30 10

1969. Air. 1st Man on the Moon.
1191 **348** 2p. black 30 25

349 Bee and Honeycomb

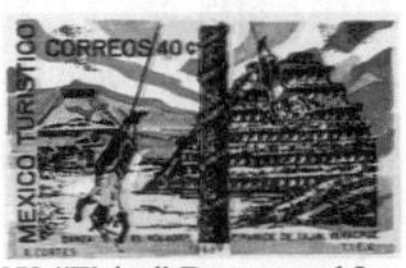

350 "Flying" Dancers and Los Nichos Pyramid, El Tajin

1969. 50th Anniv of I.L.O.
1192 **349** 40c. brown, blue & yell 20 10

1969. Tourism (1st series). Multicoloured.
1193 40c. Type **350**(postage) . . 25 10
1193a 40c. Puerto Vallarta, Jalisco (vert) 25 10
1194 80c. Acapulco (air) 80 15
1195 80c. Pyramid, Teotihuacan 60 15
1196 80c. "El Caracol" (Maya ruin), Yucatan 60 15
See also Nos. 1200/2 and 1274/7.

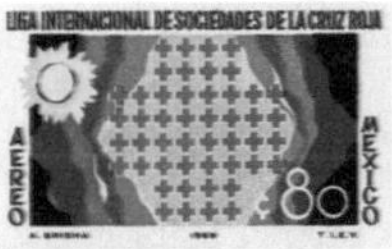

351 Red Crosses and Sun

352 "General Allende" (D. Rivera)

1969. Air. 50th Anniv of League of Red Cross Societies.
1197 **351** 80c. multicoloured . . . 30 10

1969. Birth Bicentenary of General Ignacio Allende ("Father of Mexican Independence").
1198 **352** 40c. multicoloured . . . 20 10

353 Dish Aerial

354 Question Marks

1969. Air. Inauguration of Satellite Communications Station, Tulancingo.
1199 **353** 80c. multicoloured . . . 35 10

1969. Tourism (2nd series). As T **350** but dated "1970". Multicoloured.
1200 40c. Puebla Cathedral . . . 40 10
1201 40c. Anthropological Museum, Mexico City . . 40 10
1202 40c. Belaunzaran Street, Guanajuato 40 10

1970. 9th National and 5th Agricultural Census. Multicoloured.
1204 20c. Type **354** 30 10
1205 40c. Horse's head and agricultural symbols . . . 25 10

355 Diagram of Human Eye

1970. 21st International Ophthalmological Congress, Mexico City.
1206 **355** 40c. multicoloured . . . 25 10

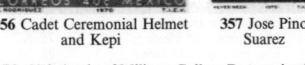

356 Cadet Ceremonial Helmet and Kepi

357 Jose Pino Suarez

1970. 50th Anniv of Military College Reorganization.
1207 **356** 40c. multicoloured . . . 20 10

1970. Birth Centenary (1969) of Jose Maria Pino Suarez (statesman).
1208 **357** 40c. multicoloured . . . 20 10

358 Football and Masks

361 Arms of Celaya

360 Composition by Beethoven

1970. Air. World Cup Football Championship (2nd issue). Multicoloured.
1209 80c. Type **358** 30 15
1210 2p. Football and Mexican idols 25 25

1970. Air. Birth Bicentenary of Beethoven.
1212 **360** 2p. multicoloured . . . 50 25

1970. 400th Anniv of Celaya.
1213 **361** 40c. multicoloured . . . 20 10

362 "General Assembly"

1970. Air. 25th Anniv of U.N.O.
1214 **362** 80c. multicoloured . . . 30 10

363 "Eclipse de Sol"

364 "Galileo" (Susterman)

1970. Total Eclipse of the Sun.
1215 **363** 40c. black 20 10

1971. Air. Conquest of Space. Early Astronomers. Multicoloured.
1216 2p. Type **364** 25 10
1217 2p. "Kepler" (unknown artist) 25 10
1218 2p. "Sir Isaac Newton" (Kneller) 25 10

365 "Sister Juana" (M. Cabrera)

1971. Air. Mexican Arts and Sciences (1st series). Paintings. Multicoloured.
1219 80c. Type **365** 40 15
1220 80c. "El Paricutin" (volcano) (G. Murillo) . . 40 15
1221 80c. "Men of Flames" (J. C. Orozco) 40 15
1222 80c. "Self-portrait" (J. M. Velasco) 40 15
1223 80c. "Mayan Warriors" ("Dresden Codex") . . . 40 15
See also Nos. 1243/7, 1284/8, 1323/7, 1351/5, 1390/4, 1417/21, 1523/7, 1540/4, 1650/4, 1688/92, 1834 and 1845.

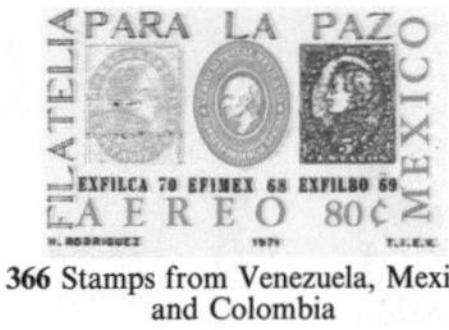

366 Stamps from Venezuela, Mexico and Colombia

1971. Air. "Philately for Peace". Latin-American Stamp Exhibitions.
1224 **366** 80c. multicoloured . . . 35 15

367 Lottery Balls

1971. Bicentenary of National Lottery.
1225 **367** 40c. black and green . . 25 10

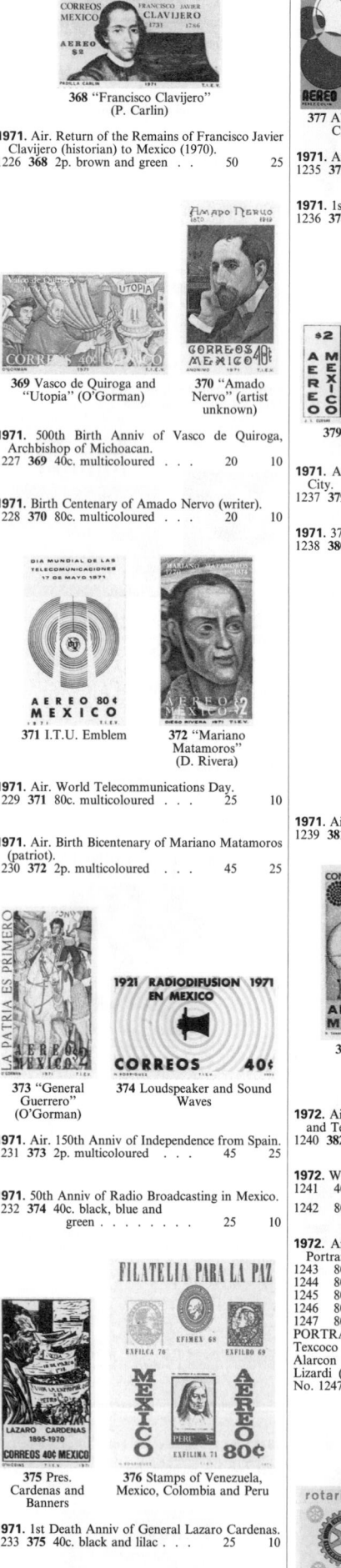

368 "Francisco Clavijero" (P. Carlin)

1971. Air. Return of the Remains of Francisco Javier Clavijero (historian) to Mexico (1970).
1226 **368** 2p. brown and green . . 50 25

369 Vasco de Quiroga and "Utopia" (O'Gorman)
370 "Amado Nervo" (artist unknown)

1971. 500th Birth Anniv of Vasco de Quiroga, Archbishop of Michoacan.
1227 **369** 40c. multicoloured . . . 20 10

1971. Birth Centenary of Amado Nervo (writer).
1228 **370** 80c. multicoloured . . . 20 10

371 I.T.U. Emblem
372 "Mariano Matamoros" (D. Rivera)

1971. Air. World Telecommunications Day.
1229 **371** 80c. multicoloured . . . 25 10

1971. Air. Birth Bicentenary of Mariano Matamoros (patriot).
1230 **372** 2p. multicoloured . . . 45 25

373 "General Guerrero" (O'Gorman)
374 Loudspeaker and Sound Waves

1971. Air. 150th Anniv of Independence from Spain.
1231 **373** 2p. multicoloured . . . 45 25

1971. 50th Anniv of Radio Broadcasting in Mexico.
1232 **374** 40c. black, blue and green 25 10

375 Pres. Cardenas and Banners
376 Stamps of Venezuela, Mexico, Colombia and Peru

1971. 1st Death Anniv of General Lazaro Cardenas.
1233 **375** 40c. black and lilac . . . 25 10

1971. Air. "EXFILIMA 71" Stamp Exhibition Lima, Peru.
1234 **376** 80c. multicoloured . . . 45 15

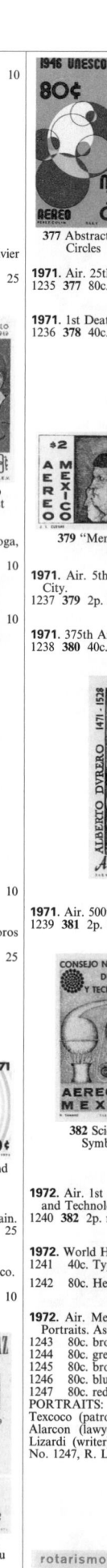

377 Abstract of Circles
378 Piano Keyboard

1971. Air. 25th Anniv of UNESCO.
1235 **377** 80c. multicoloured . . . 30 15

1971. 1st Death Anniv of Agustin Lara (composer).
1236 **378** 40c. black, blue & yellow 30 10

379 "Mental Patients"
380 City Arms of Monterrey

1971. Air. 5th World Psychiatric Congress, Mexico City.
1237 **379** 2p. multicoloured . . . 25 20

1971. 375th Anniv of Monterrey.
1238 **380** 40c. multicoloured . . . 10 10

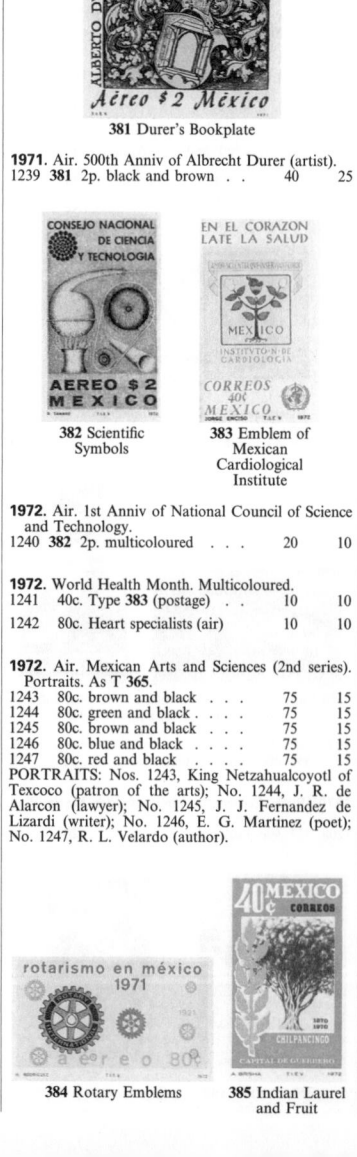

381 Durer's Bookplate

1971. Air. 500th Anniv of Albrecht Durer (artist).
1239 **381** 2p. black and brown . . 40 25

382 Scientific Symbols
383 Emblem of Mexican Cardiological Institute

1972. Air. 1st Anniv of National Council of Science and Technology.
1240 **382** 2p. multicoloured . . . 20 10

1972. World Health Month. Multicoloured.
1241 40c. Type **383** (postage) . . 10 10
1242 80c. Heart specialists (air) 10 10

1972. Air. Mexican Arts and Sciences (2nd series). Portraits. As T **365**.
1243 80c. brown and black . . . 75 15
1244 80c. green and black . . . 75 15
1245 80c. brown and black . . . 75 15
1246 80c. blue and black . . . 75 15
1247 80c. red and black . . . 75 15
PORTRAITS: Nos. 1243, King Netzahualcoyotl of Texcoco (patron of the arts); No. 1244, J. R. de Alarcon (lawyer); No. 1245, J. J. Fernandez de Lizardi (writer); No. 1246, E. G. Martinez (poet); No. 1247, R. L. Velardo (author).

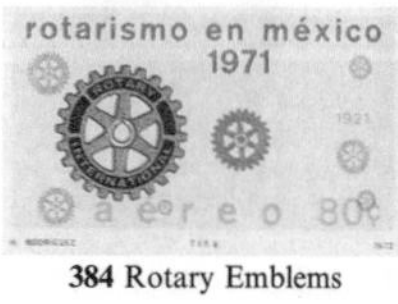

384 Rotary Emblems
385 Indian Laurel and Fruit

1972. Air. 50th Anniv of Rotary Movement in Mexico.
1248 **384** 80c. multicoloured . . . 10 10

1972. Centenary of Chilpancingo as Capital of Guerrero State.
1249 **385** 40c. black, gold and green 10 10

386 Track of Car Tyre

1972. Air. 74th Assembly of International Tourist Alliance, Mexico City.
1250 **386** 80c. black and grey . . . 10 10

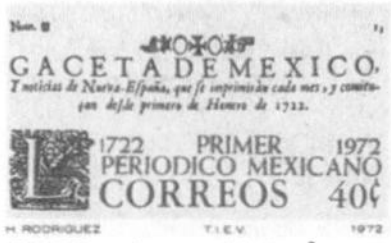

387 First issue of "Gaceta De Mexico"
388 Emblem of Lions Organization

1972. 250th Anniv of Publication of "Gaceta De Mexico" (1st newspaper to be published in Latin America).
1251 **387** 40c. multicoloured . . . 10 10

1972. Lions' Clubs Convention, Mexico City.
1252 **388** 40c. multicoloured . . . 10 10

389 "Zaragoza" (cadet sail corvette)
390 "Margarita Maza de Juarez" (artist unknown)

1972. 75th Anniv of Naval Academy, Veracruz.
1253 **389** 40c. multicoloured . . . 60 10

1972. Death Centenary of Pres. Benito Juarez.
1254 **390** 20c. mult (postage) . . . 35 10
1255 – 40c. multicoloured . . . 35 10
1256 – 80c. black and blue (air) 10 10
1257 – 1p.20 multicoloured . . 15 10
1258 – 2p. multicoloured . . . 20 10
DESIGNS: 40c. "Benito Juarez" (D. Rivera); 80c. Page of Civil Register with Juarez signature; 1p.20, "Benito Juarez" (P. Clave); 2p. "Benito Juarez" (J. C. Orozco).

391 "Emperor Justinian I" (mosaic)
392 Atomic Emblem

1972. 50th Anniv of Mexican Bar Association.
1259 **391** 40c. multicoloured . . . 55 10

1972. Air. 16th General Conference of Int Atomic Energy Organization, Mexico City.
1260 **392** 2p. black, blue and grey 15 10

393 Caravel on "Stamp"
394 "Sobre las Olas" (sheet-music cover by O'Brandstetter)

1972. Stamp Day of the Americas.
1261 **393** 80c. violet and brown . . 15 10

1972. Air. 28th International Authors' and Composers' Society Congress, Mexico City.
1262 **394** 80c. brown 15 10

395 "Mother and Child" (G. Galvin)

1972. Air. 25th Anniv of UNICEF.
1263 **395** 80c. multicoloured . . . 50 10

396 "Father Pedro de Gante" (Rodriguez y Arangorti)
397 Olympic Emblems

1972. Air. 400th Death Anniv of Father Pedro de Gante (founder of first school in Mexico).
1264 **396** 2p. multicoloured . . . 25 10

1972. Olympic Games, Munich.
1265 **397** 40c. multicoloured (postage) 10 10
1266 – 80c. multicoloured (air) 15 10
1267 – 2p. black, green and blue 25 10
DESIGNS—HORIZ: 80c. "Football". VERT: 2p. Similar to Type **397**.

398 Books on Shelves
400 "Footprints on the Americas"

399 Common Snook ("Pure Water")

1972. International Book Year.
1268 **398** 40c. multicoloured . . . 10 10

1972. Anti-pollution Campaign.
1269 **399** 40c. black & bl (postage) 20 10
1270 – 80c. black and blue (air) 15 10
DESIGN—VERT: 80c. Pigeon on cornice ("Pure Air").

1972. Air. Tourist Year of the Americas.
1271 **400** 80c. multicoloured . . . 15 10

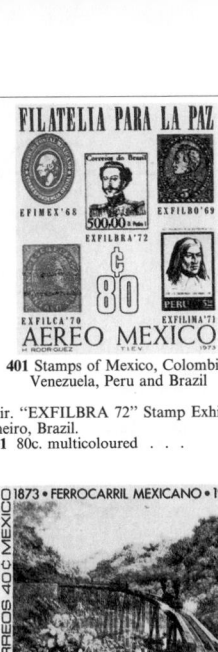

401 Stamps of Mexico, Colombia, Venezuela, Peru and Brazil

1973. Air. "EXFILBRA 72" Stamp Exhibition, Rio de Janeiro, Brazil.
1272 **401** 80c. multicoloured . . . 15 10

402 "Metlac Viaduct" (J. M. Velasco)

1973. Centenary of Mexican Railways.
1273 **402** 40c. multicoloured . . . 1·25 25

403 Ocotlan Abbey

1973. Tourism (3rd series). Multicoloured.
1274 40c. Type **403** (postage) . . 20 10
1275 40c. Indian hunting dance, Sonora (vert) 20 10
1276 80c. Girl in local costume (vert) (air) 35 15
1277 80c. Sport fishing, Lower California 35 10

404 "God of the Winds"

1973. Air. Centenary of W.M.O.
1278 **404** 80c. black, blue & mauve 35 10

405 Copernicus

406 Cadet

1973. Air. 500th Birth Anniv of Copernicus (astronomer).
1279 **405** 80c. green 15 10

1973. 150th Anniv of Military College.
1280 **406** 40c. multicoloured . . . 10 10

407 "Francisco Madero" (D. Rivera)

408 Antonio Narro (founder)

1973. Birth Centenary of Pres. Francisco Madero.
1281 **407** 40c. multicoloured . . . 10 10

1973. 50th Anniv of "Antonio Narro" Agricultural School, Saltillo.
1282 **408** 40c. grey 10 10

409 San Martin Statue

410 Caryon Molecules

1973. Air. Argentina's Gift of San Martin Statue to Mexico City.
1283 **409** 80c. multicoloured . . . 15 10

1973. Air. "Mexican Arts and Sciences" (3rd series). Astronomers. As T **365** but dated "1973".
1284 80c. green and red 10 10
1285 80c. multicoloured 10 10
1286 80c. multicoloured 10 10
1287 80c. multicoloured 10 10
1288 80c. multicoloured 10 10
DESIGNS: No. 1284, Aztec "Sun" stone; No. 1285, Carlos de Siguenza y Gongora; No. 1286, Francisco Diaz Covarrubias; No. 1287, Joaquin Gallo; No. 1288, Luis Enrique Erro.

1973. 25th Anniv of Chemical Engineering School.
1289 **410** 40c. black, yellow and red 10 10

411 Fist with Pointing Finger

412 "EXMEX 73" Emblem

1974. Promotion of Exports.
1294 **411** 40c. black and green . . 10 10

1974. "EXMEX 73" National Stamp Exhibition, Cuernavaca.
1295 **412** 40c. black (postage) . . 10 10
1296 – 80c. multicoloured (air) 15 10
DESIGN: 80c. Cortes' Palace, Cuernavaca.

413 Manuel Ponce

1974. 25th Death Anniv (1973) of Manuel M. Ponce (composer).
1297 **413** 40c. multicoloured . . . 10 10

414 Gold Brooch, Mochica Culture

1974. Air. Exhibition of Peruvian Gold Treasures, Mexico City.
1298 **414** 80c. multicoloured . . . 15 10

415 C.E.P.A.L. Emblem and Flags

416 Baggage

1974. Air. 25th Anniv of U.N. Economic Commission for Latin America (C.E.P.A.L.).
1299 **415** 80c. multicoloured . . . 15 10

1974. Air. 16th Confederation of Latin American Tourist Organizations (C.O.T.A.L.) Convention, Acapulco.
1300 **416** 80c. multicoloured . . . 15 10

417 Silver Statuette

419 "Dancing Dogs" (Indian statuette)

418 "The Enamelled Saucepan" (Picasso)

1974. 1st International Silver Fair, Mexico City.
1301 **417** 40c. multicoloured . . . 10 10

1974. Air. 1st Death Anniv of Pablo Picasso (artist).
1302 **418** 80c. multicoloured . . . 15 10

1974. 6th Season of Dog Shows.
1303 **419** 40c. multicoloured . . . 10 10

420 Mariano Azuela

1974. Birth Cent (1973) of Mariano Azuela (writer).
1304 **420** 40c. multicoloured . . . 10 10

421 Tepotzotlan Viaduct

1974. National Engineers' Day.
1305 **421** 40c. black and blue . . . 55 15

422 R. Robles (surgeon)

1974. 25th Anniv of W.H.O.
1306 **422** 40c. brown and green . . 10 10

423 U.P.U. Emblem

1974. "Exfilmex 74" Inter-American Stamp Exhibition, Mexico City.
1307 **423** 40c. black and green on yellow (postage) . . . 10 10
1308 80c. black and brown on yellow (air) 15 10

424 Demosthenes

426 Map and Indian Head

425 Lincoln Standard Biplane

1974. 2nd Spanish-American Reading and Writing Studies Congress, Mexico City.
1309 **424** 20c. green and brown . . 35 10

1974. Air. 50th Anniv of "Mexicana" (Mexican Airlines). Multicoloured.
1310 80c. Type **425** 15 10
1311 2p. Boeing 727-200 jetliner 40 10

1974. 150th Anniv of Union with Chiapas.
1312 **426** 20c. green and brown . . 10 10

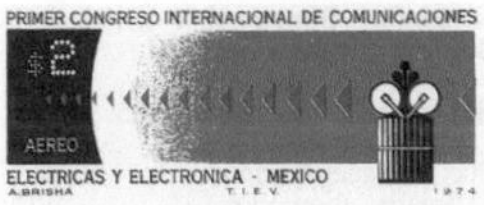

427 "Sonar Waves"

1974. Air. 1st International Electrical and Electronic Communications Congress, Mexico City.
1313 **427** 2p. multicoloured . . . 15 10

428 S. Lerdo de Tejada

429 Manuscript of Constitution

1974. Centenary of Restoration of Senate.
1314 **428** 40c. black and blue . . . 10 10

1974. 150th Anniv of Federal Republic.
1315 **429** 40c. black and green . . 10 10

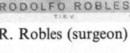

430 Ball in Play

1974. Air. 8th World Volleyball Championships, Mexico City.
1316 **430** 2p. black, brown & orge 15 10

432 F. C. Puerto

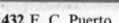

433 Mask, Bat and Catcher's Glove

1974. Air. Birth Centenary of Felipe Carrillo Puerto (politician and journalist).
1318 **432** 80c. brown and green . . 10 10

1974. Air. 50th Anniv of Mexican Baseball League.
1319 **433** 80c. brown and green . . 10 10

434 U.P.U. Monument

1974. Centenary of U.P.U.
1320 **434** 40c. brown and blue (postage) 10 10
1321 – 80c. multicoloured (air) 10 10
1322 – 2p. brown and green . . 20 10
DESIGNS: 80c. Man's face as letter-box, Colonial period; 2p. Heinrich von Stephan, founder of U.P.U.

1974. Air. Mexican Arts and Sciences (4th series). Music and Musicians. As T **365** but dated "1974". Multicoloured.
1323 80c. "Musicians" – Mayan painting, Bonampak . . . 15 10
1324 80c. First Mexican-printed score, 1556 . . . . 15 10
1325 80c. Angela Peralta (soprano and composer) 15 10
1326 80c. "Miguel Lerdo de Tejada" (composer) . . . 15 10
1327 80c. "Silvestre Revueltas" (composer) (bronze by Carlos Bracho) 15 10

435 I.W.Y. Emblem

436 Economic Charter

1975. Air. International Women's Year.
1328 **435** 1p.60 black and red . . 15 10

1975. Air. U.N. Declaration of Nations' Economic Rights and Duties.
1329 **436** 1p.60 multicoloured . . 15 10

437 Jose Maria Mora

439 Dr. M. Jimenez

438 Trans-Atlantic Balsa Raft "Acali"

1975. 150th Anniv of Federal Republic.
1330 **437** 20c. multicoloured . . . 10 10

1975. Air. Trans-Atlantic Voyage of "Acali", Canary Islands to Yucatan (1973).
1331 **438** 80c. multicoloured . . . 50 10

1975. Air. 5th World Gastroenterological Congress.
1332 **439** 2p. multicoloured . . . 15 10

440 Aztec Merchants with Goods ("Codex Florentino")

1975. Centenary (1974) of Mexican Chamber of Commerce.
1333 **440** 80c. multicoloured . . . 10 10

441 Miguel de Cervantes Saavedra (Spanish author)

443 Salvador Novo

442 4-reales Coin of 1675

1975. Air. 3rd International Cervantes Festival, Guanajuato.
1334 **441** 1p.60 red and black . . 15 10

1975. Air. International Numismatics Convention "Mexico 74".
1335 **442** 1p.60 bronze and blue 15 10

1975. Air. 1st Death Anniv of Salvador Novo (poet and writer).
1336 **443** 1p.60 multicoloured . . 15 10

444 "Self-portrait" (Siqueiros)

1975. Air. 1st Death Anniv of David Alfaro Siqueiros (painter).
1337 **444** 1p.60 multicoloured . . 15 10

445 General Juan Aldama (detail from mural by Diego Rivera)

1975. Birth Bicentenary (1974) of General Aldama.
1338 **445** 80c. multicoloured . . . 10 10

446 U.N. and I.W.Y. Emblems

1975. Air. International Women's Year and World Conference.
1339 **446** 1p.60 blue and pink . . 15 10

447 Eagle and Snake ("Codex Duran")

1975. 650th Anniv of Tenochtitlan (now Mexico City). Multicoloured.
1340 80c. Type **447** (postage) . . 10 10
1341 1p.60 Arms of Mexico City (air) 15 10

448 Domingo F. Sarmiento (educator and statesman)

449 Teachers' Monument, Mexico City

1975. Air. 1st International Congress of "Third World" Educators, Acapulco.
1342 **448** 1p.60 green and brown 15 10

1975. Air. Mexican–Lebanese Friendship.
1343 **449** 4p.30 green and brown 25 10

450 Games' Emblem

1975. Air. 7th Pan-American Games, Mexico City.
1344 **450** 1p.60 multicoloured . . 15 10

451 Julian Carrillo (composer)

452 Academy Emblem

1975. Birth Centenary of J. Carrillo.
1345 **451** 80c. brown and green . . 10 10

1975. Cent of Mexican Languages Academy.
1346 **452** 80c. yellow and brown 10 10

453 University Building

1975. 50th Anniv of Guadalajara University.
1347 **453** 80c. black, brown & pink 10 10

454 Dr. Atl

455 Road Builders

1975. Air. Atl (Gerardo Murillo, painter and writer). Birth Centenary.
1348 **454** 4p.30 multicoloured . . 25 10

1975. "50 Years of Road Construction" and 15th World Road Congress, Mexico City.
1349 **455** 80c. black & grn (postage) 10 10
1350 – 1p.60 black & blue (air) 15 10
DESIGN: 1p.60, Congress emblem.

1975. Air. Mexican Arts and Sciences (5th series). As T **365**, but dated "1975". Multicoloured.
1351 1p.60 Title page, F. Hernandez' "History of New Spain" 15 10
1352 1p.60 A. L. Herrera (naturalist) 15 10
1353 1p.60 Page from "Badiano Codex" (Aztec herbal) . . 15 10
1354 1p.60 A. Rosenblueth Stearns (neurophysiologist) . . . 15 10
1355 1p.60 A. A. Duges (botanist and zoologist) 15 10

456 Car Engine Parts

457 Aguascalientes Cathedral

1975. Mexican Exports. Multicoloured.

1356	–	5c. blue (postage) . .	35	10
1471	–	20c. black	35	10
1356b	–	40c. brown	30	10
1356c	456	50c. blue	35	10
1472		50c. black	10	10
1473	–	80c. red	10	10
1474	–	1p. violet and yellow	10	10
1358a	–	1p. black and orange	10	10
1475	–	2p. blue and turquoise	55	10
1476	–	3p. brown	25	10
1359b	–	4p. red and brown . .	25	10
1359e	–	5p. brown	10	10
1359ed	–	6p. red	10	10
1359ee	–	6p. grey	10	10
1359f	–	7p. blue	10	10
1359g	–	8p. brown	10	10
1359h	–	9p. blue	10	10
1479	–	10p. lt green & green	95	45
1360ac	–	10p. red	10	10
1360ad	–	15p. orange and brown	15	10
1360b	–	20p. black	15	10
1360bc	–	20p. black and red . .	10	10
1360be	–	25p. brown	25	10
1360bh	–	35p. yellow and mauve	25	10

1360bk	–	40p. yellow and brown	25	10
1360bl	–	40p. gold and green	25	10
1360bm	–	40p. black	10	10
1360c	–	50p. multicoloured	1·25	35
1360d	–	50p. yellow and blue	35	20
1360da	–	50p. red and green	35	20
1360db	–	60p. brown	30	15
1360dc	–	70p. brown	35	20
1360de	–	80p. gold and mauve	20	50
1360df	–	80p. blue	80	50
1360dg	–	90p. blue and green	1·25	55
1360e	–	100p. red, green and grey	70	35
1360ea	–	100p. brown	10	10
1360f	–	200p. yellow, green and grey	1·90	30
1360fb	–	200p. yellow and green	10	10
1360g	–	300p. blue, red and grey	60	60
1360gb	–	300p. blue and red	15	10
1360h	–	400p. bistre, brown and grey	95	35
1360hb	–	450p. brown and mauve	20	10
1360i	–	500p. green, orange and grey	1·90	30
1360ib	–	500p. grey and blue	20	10
1360j	–	600p. multicoloured	30	10
1360k	–	700p. black, red and green	35	10
1360kb	–	750p. black, red and green	30	10
1360l	–	800p. brown & dp brown	40	10
1360m	456	900p. black	50	10
1360n		950p. blue	40	20
1481a	–	1000p. black, red and grey	50	20
1360pa	–	1000p. red and black	40	10
1360q	–	1100p. grey	60	30
1360r	–	1300p. red, green and grey	60	30
1360rb	–	1300p. red and green	50	25
1360rg	–	1400p. black	50	20
1360s	–	1500p. brown	55	45
1360t	–	1600p. orange	65	30
1360u	–	1700p. green and deep green	70	30
1360w	–	1900p. blue and green	2·25	75
1481b	–	2000p. black and grey	1·25	50
1360xa	–	2000p. black	80	55
1360y	–	2100p. black, orange and grey	80	55
1360ya	–	2100p. black and red	80	55
1360yb	–	2200p. red	90	60
1360z	–	2500p. blue and grey	95	65
1360za	–	2500p. blue	95	65
1630zc	–	2800p. black	1·10	75
1481c	–	3000p. green, grey and orange	1·75	75
1360zf	456	3600p. black and grey	1·50	1·00
1360zg	–	3900p. grey and blue	1·60	1·10
1481d	–	4000p. yellow, grey and red	2·40	1·25
1360zj	–	4800p. red, green and grey	1·90	1·25
1481e	–	5000p. grey, green and orange	3·00	1·50
1360zn	–	6000p. green, yellow and grey	2·40	1·60
1360zq	–	7200p. multicoloured	3·00	2·00
1361	–	30c. bronze (air)	30	10
1482	–	50c. green and brown	10	10
1361a	–	80c. blue	10	10
1483	–	1p.60 black and orange	10	10
1484	–	1p.90 red and green	15	10
1361d	–	2p. gold and blue	25	10
1485	–	2p.50 red and green	10	10
1361e	–	4p. yellow and brown	25	10
1361f	–	4p.30 mauve and green	10	20
1361g	–	5p. blue and yellow	95	20
1361h	–	5p.20 black and red	25	25
1361i	–	5p.60 green and yellow	10	30
1488	–	10p. green and light green	55	40
1361j	–	20p. black, red and green	2·75	85
1361k	–	50p. multicoloured	1·60	95

DESIGNS—POSTAGE. 5c., 6, 1600p. Steel tubes; 20c., 40 (1360bm), 1400, 2800p. Laboratory flasks; 40c., 100p. (1360ea) Cup of coffee; 80c., 10 (1360ac), 2200p. Steer marked with beef cuts; 1, 3000p. Electric cable; 2, 90, 1900p. Abalone shell; 3, 60p. Men's shoes; 4p. Ceramic tiles; 5, 1100p. Chemical formulae; 7, 8, 9, 80 (1360df), 2500p. Textiles; 10 (1479), 1700p. Tequila; 15p. Honeycomb; 20 (1360b), 2000p. Wrought iron; 20 (1360bc), 2100p. Bicycles; 25, 70, 1500p. Hammered copper vase; 35, 40 (1360bk/bl), 50 (1360d), 80p. (1360de) Books; 50 (1360c), 600p. Jewellery; 50 (1360da), 4800p. Tomato; 100 (1360e), 1300p. Strawberries; 200, 6000p. Citrus fruit; 300p. Motor vehicles; 400, 450p. Printed circuit; 500 (1360i), 5000p. Cotton boll; 500 (1360ib), 3900p. Valves (petroleum) industry; 700, 750, 7200p. Film; 800p. Construction materials; 1000p. Farm machinery; 4000p. Bee and honeycomb. AIR. 30c. Hammered copper vase; 50c. Electronic components; 80c. Textiles; 1p.60, Bicycles; 1p.90, Valves (petroleum) industry; 2p. Books; 2p.50, Tomato; 4p. Bee and honeycomb; 4p.30, Strawberry; 5p. Motor vehicles; 5p.20, Farm machinery; 5p.60, Cotton boll; 10p. Citrus fruit; 20p. Film; 50p. Cotton.

1975. 400th Anniv of Aguascalientes.
1362 **457** 50c. black and green . . 35 10

458 J. T. Bodet

460 "Death of Cuautemoc" (Chavez Morado)

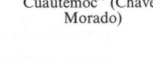

459 "Fresco" (J. C. Orozco)

1975. 1st Death Anniv of Jaime T. Bodet (author and late Director-General of UNESCO).
1363 **458** 80c. brown and blue . . 10 10

1975. 150th Anniv of Mexican Supreme Court of Justice.
1364 **459** 80c. multicoloured . . . 10 10

1975. 450th Death Anniv of Emperor Cuautemoc.
1365 **460** 80c. multicoloured . . . 10 10

461 Allegory of Irrigation

1976. 50th Anniv of Nat Irrigation Commission.
1366 **461** 80c. deep blue and blue 10 10

462 City Gateway

1976. 400th Anniv of Leon de los Aldamas, Guanajuato.
1367 **462** 80c. yellow and purple 10 10

463 Early Telephone

464 Gold Coin

1976. Air. Telephone Centenary.
1368 **463** 1p.60 black and grey . . 10 10

1976. Air. 4th Int Numismatics Convention.
1369 **464** 1p.60 gold, brown & blk 10 10

465 Tlaloc (Aztec god of rain) and Calles Dam

1976. Air. 12th Int Great Dams Congress.
1370 **465** 1p.60 purple and green 20 10

466 Perforation Gauge

1976. Air. "Interphil '76" International Stamp Exhibition, Philadelphia.
1371 **466** 1p.60 black, red and blue 20 10

467 Rainbow over Industrial Skyline

470 Liberty Bell

1976. Air. U.N. Conf on Human Settlements.
1372 **467** 1p.60 multicoloured . . 20 10

1976. Air. Bicentenary of American War of Independence.
1378 **470** 1p.60 blue and mauve 20 10

471 Forest Fire

1976. Fire Prevention Campaign.
1379 **471** 80c. multicoloured . . . 10 10

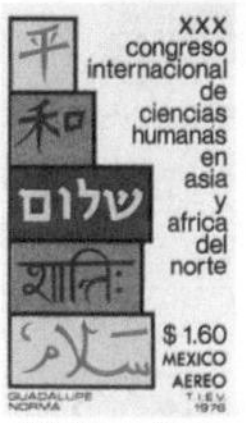

472 Peace Texts

473 Children on TV Screen

1976. Air. 30th International Asian and North American Science and Humanities Congress, Mexico City.
1380 **472** 1p.60 multicoloured . . 15 10

1976. Air. 1st Latin-American Forum on Children's Television.
1381 **473** 1p.60 multicoloured . . 20 10

474 Scout's Hat

475 Exhibition Emblem

1976. 50th Anniv of Mexican Boy Scout Movement.
1382 **474** 80c. olive and brown . . 10 10

1976. "Mexico Today and Tomorrow" Exhibition.
1383 **475** 80c. black, red & turq 10 10

476 New Buildings

477 Dr. R. Vertiz

1976. Inaug of New Military College Buildings.
1384 **476** 50c. brown and ochre . . 10 10

1976. Centenary of Ophthalmological Hospital of Our Lady of the Light.
1385 **477** 80c. brown and black . . 10 10

478 Guadalupe Basilica

1976. Inauguration of Guadalupe Basilica.
1386 **478** 50c. bistre and black . . 10 10

479 "40" and Emblem

1976. 40th Anniv of National Polytechnic Institute.
1387 **479** 80c. black, red and green 10 10

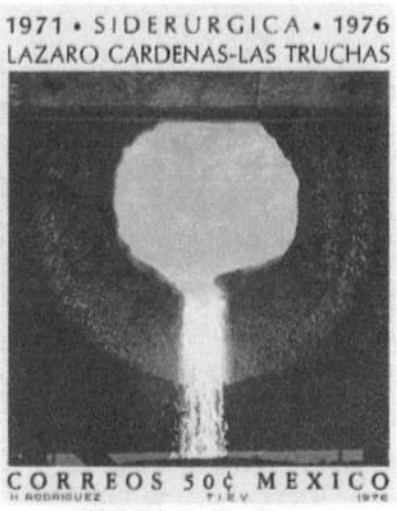

480 Blast Furnace

1976. Inauguration of Lazaro Cardenas Steel Mill, Las Truchas.
1388 **480** 50c. multicoloured . . . 10 10

481 Natural Elements

1976. Air. World Urbanization Day.
1389 **481** 1p.60 multicoloured . . 10 10

1976. Air. Mexican Arts and Sciences (6th series). As T **365** but dated "1976". Multicoloured.

1390	1p.60 black and red	10	10
1391	1p.60 multicoloured	10	10
1392	1p.60 black and yellow	10	10
1393	1p.60 multicoloured	10	10
1394	1p.60 brown and black	10	10

DESIGNS: No. 1390, "The Signal" (Angela Gurria); No. 1391, "The God of Today" (L. Ortiz Monasterio); No. 1392, "The God Coatlicue" (traditional Mexican sculpture); No. 1393, "Tiahuicole" (Manuel Vilar); No. 1394, "The Horseman" (Manuel Tolsa).

482 Score of "El Pesebre"

1977. Air. Birth Centenary of Pablo Casals (cellist).
1395 **482** 4p.30 blue and brown . . 15 10

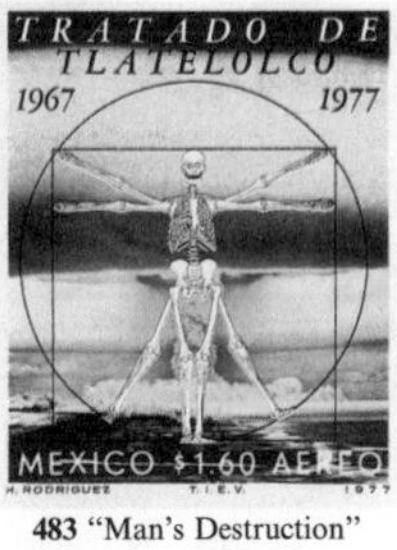

483 "Man's Destruction"

1977. Air. 10th Anniv of Treaty of Tlatelolco.
1396 **483** 1p.60 multicoloured . . 10 10

484 Saltillo Cathedral

485 Light Switch, Pylon and Engineers

1977. 400th Anniv of Founding of Saltillo.
1397 **484** 80c. brown and yellow 10 10

1977. 40 Years of Development in Mexico. Federal Electricity Commission.
1398 **485** 80c. multicoloured . . . 10 10

486 Footballers

1977. Air. 50th Anniv of Mexican Football Federation.
1399 **486** 1p.60 multicoloured . . 10 10
1400 – 4p.30 yellow, blue & blk 15 10
DESIGN: 4p.30, Football emblem.

487 Hands and Scales

1977. Air. 50th Anniv of Federal Council of Reconciliation and Arbitration.
1401 **487** 1p.60 orange, brn & blk 10 10

488 Flags of Spain and Mexico

489 Tlaloc (weather god)

1977. Resumption of Diplomatic Relations with Spain.
1402 **488** 50c. multicoloured (postage) 10 10
1403 80c. multicoloured . . . 10 10
1404 – 1p.60 black and grey (air) 10 10
1405 – 1p.90 red, green & lt grn 10 10
1406 – 4p.30 grey, brown & grn 15 10
DESIGNS: 1p.60, Arms of Mexico and Spain; 1p.90, Maps of Mexico and Spain; 4p.30, President Jose Lopez Portillo and King Juan Carlos.

1977. Air. Centenary of Central Meterological Observatory.
1407 **489** 1p.60 multicoloured . . 10 10

490 Ludwig van Beethoven

491 A. Serdan

1977. Air. 150th Death Anniv of Beethoven.
1408 **490** 1p.60 green and brown 10 10
1409 4p.30 red and blue . . . 15 10

1977. Birth Centenary of Aquiles Serdan (revolutionary martyr).
1410 **491** 80c. black, turq & grn 10 10

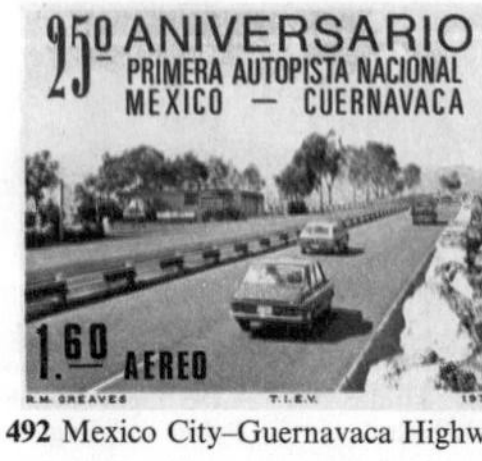

492 Mexico City–Guernavaca Highway

1977. Air. 25th Anniv of First National Highway.
1411 **492** 1p.60 multicoloured . . 10 10

493 Poinsettia

494 Arms of Campeche

1977. Christmas.
1412 **493** 50c. multicoloured . . . 10 10

1977. Air. Bicentenary of Naming of Campeche.
1413 **494** 1p.60 multicoloured . . 10 10

495 Tractor and Dam

1977. Air. U.N. Desertification Conference, Mexico City.
1414 **495** 1p.60 multicoloured . . 10 10

496 Congress Emblem

1977. Air. 20th World Education, Hygiene and Recreation Congress.
1415 **496** 1p.60 multicoloured . . 10 10

497 Freighter "Rio Yaqui"

498 Mayan Dancer

1977. Air. 60th Anniv of National Merchant Marine.
1416 **497** 1p.60 multicoloured . . 60 10

1977. Air. Mexican Arts and Sciences (7th series). Pre-colonial statuettes.
1417 **498** 1p.60 red, black and pink 10 10
1418 – 1p.60 blue, black and light blue 10 10
1419 – 1p.60 grey, black and yellow 10 10
1420 – 1p.60 green, black and turquoise 10 10
1421 – 1p.60 red, black and grey 10 10
DESIGNS: No. 1418, Aztec god of dance; No. 1419, Snake dance; No. 1420, Dancer, Monte Alban; No. 1421, Dancer, Totonaca.

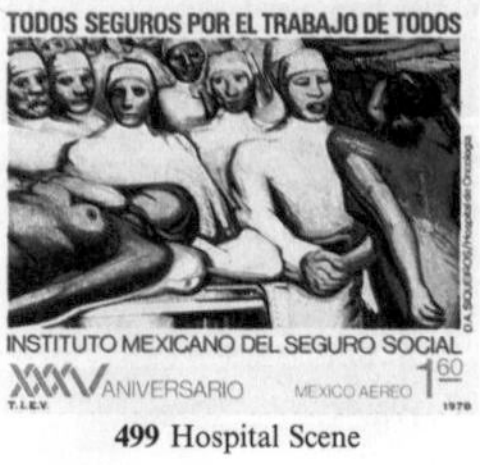

499 Hospital Scene

1978. Air. 35th Anniv of Mexican Social Insurance Institute. Multicoloured.
1422 1p.60 Type **499** 10 10
1423 4p.30 Workers drawing benefits 15 10

500 Moorish Fountain

1978. Air. 450th Anniv of Chiapa de Corzo, Chiapas.
1424 **500** 1p.60 multicoloured . . 10 10

501 Telephones, 1878 and 1978

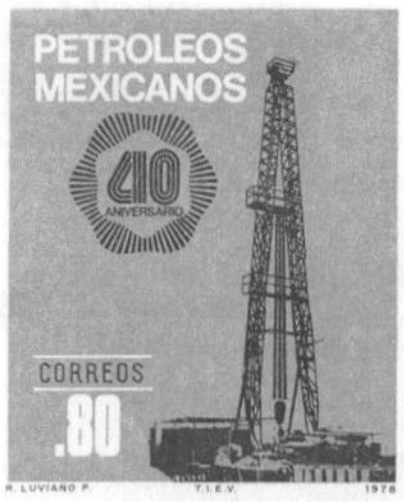

502 Oilwell

1978. Centenary of Mexican Telephone.
1425 **501** 80c. red and salmon . . 10 10

1978. 40th Anniv of Nationalization of Oil Resources.
1426 **502** 80c. red and salmon (postage) 10 10
1427 – 1p.60 blue and red (air) 10 10
1428 – 4p.30 black, light blue and blue 55 20
DESIGNS: 1p.60, General I. Cardenas (President, 1938); 4p.30, Oil rig, Gulf of Mexico.

503 Arms of San Cristobal de las Casas

1978. Air. 450th Anniv of San Cristobal de las Casas, Chiapas.
1429 **503** 1p.60 purple, pink and black 10 10

504 Fairchild FC-71 Mail Plane

506 Blood Pressure Gauge and Map of Mexico

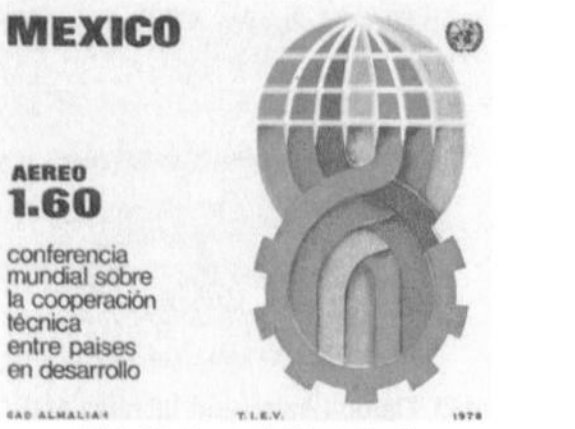

505 Globe and Cogwheel

1978. Air. 50th Anniv of First Mexican Airmail Route.
1430 **504** 1p.60 multicoloured . . 20 10
1431 4p.30 multicoloured . . 30 10

1978. Air. World Conference on Technical Co-operation between Underdeveloped Countries. Multicoloured.
1432 1p.60 Type **505** 10 10
1433 4p.30 Globe and cogwheel joined by flags 15 10

1978. Air. World Hypertension Month and World Health Day.
1434 **506** 1p.60 blue and red . . . 10 10
1435 – 4p.30 salmon and blue 15 10
DESIGN: 4p.30, Hand with stethoscope.

507 Kicking Ball

508 Francisco (Pancho) Villa

1978. Air. World Cup Football Championship, Argentina.
1436 **507** 1p.60 bl, lt orge & orge 10 10
1437 – 1p.90 blue, brn & orge 10 10
1438 – 4p.30 blue, grn & orge 15 10
DESIGNS: 1p.90, Saving a goal; 4p.30, Footballer.

1978. Air. Birth Centenary of Francisco Villa (revolutionary leader).
1439 **508** 1p.60 multicoloured . . 10 10

509 Emilio Carranza Stamp of 1929

510 Woman and Calendar Stone

1978. Air. 50th Anniv of Mexico–Washington Flight by Emilio Carranza.
1440 **509** 1p.60 red and brown . . 10 10

1978. Air. Miss Universe Contest, Acapulco.
1441 **510** 1p.60 black, brn & red 10 10
1442 1p.90 black, brn & grn 10 10
1443 4p.30 black, brn & red 15 10

511 Alvaro Obregon (J. Romero)

1978. Air. 50th Death Anniv of Alvaro Obregon (statesman).
1444 **511** 1p.60 multicoloured . . 10 10

512 Institute Emblem

1978. 50th Anniv of Pan-American Institute for Geography and History.
1445 **512** 80c. blue and black (postage) 10 10
1446 – 1p.60 green and black (air) 10 10
1447 – 4p.30 brown and black 15 10
DESIGNS: 1p.60, 4p.30, Designs as Type **512**, showing emblem.

513 Sun rising over Ciudad Obregon

514 Mayan Statue, Rook and Pawn

1978. Air. 50th Anniv of Ciudad Obregon.
1448 **513** 1p.60 multicoloured . . 10 10

1978. Air. World Youth Team Chess Championship, Mexico City.
1449 **514** 1p.60 multicoloured . . 10 10
1450 4p.30 multicoloured . . 20 10

515 Aristotle

516 Mule Deer

1978. Air. 2300th Death Anniv of Aristotle.

1451 **515** 1p.60 grey, blue and yellow 10 10
1452 – 4p.30 grey, red and yellow 20 10

DESIGN: 4p.30, Statue of Aristotle.

1978. Air. World Youth Team Chess Championship, Mexico City.

1453 1p.60 Type **516** 20 10
1454 1p.60 Ocelot 20 10

See also Nos. 1548/9, 1591/2, 1638/9 and 1683/4.

517 Man's Head and Dove

518 "Dahlia coccinea". ("Dalia" on stamp)

1978. Air. International Anti-Apartheid Year.

1455 **517** 1p.60 grey, red and black 10 10
1456 – 4p.30 grey, lilac and black 15 10

DESIGN: 4p.30, Woman's head and dove.

1978. Mexican Flowers (1st series). Multicoloured.

1457 50c. Type **518** 10 10
1458 80c. "Plumeria rubra" . . . 10 10

See also Nos. 1550/1, 1593/4, 1645/6, 1681/2, 1791/2 and 1913/14.

519 Emblem

520 Dr. Rafael Lucio

1978. Air. 12th World Architects' Congress.

1459 **519** 1p.60 red, black and orange 10 10

1978. Air. 11th International Leprosy Congress.

1460 **520** 1p.60 green 10 10

521 Franz Schubert and "Death and the Maiden"

522 Decorations and Candles

1978. Air. 150th Death Anniv of Franz Schubert (composer).

1461 **521** 4p.30 brown, black and green 15 10

1978. Christmas. Multicoloured.

1462 50c. Type **522** (postage) . . 10 10
1463 1p.60 Children and decoration (air) 10 10

523 Antonio Vivaldi

524 Wright Flyer III

1978. Air. 300th Birth Anniv of Antonio Vivaldi (composer).

1464 **523** 4p.30 red, stone and brown 15 10

1978. Air. 75th Anniv of First Powered Flight.

1465 **524** 1p.60 orange, yell & mve 15 10
1466 – 4p.30 yellow, red & flesh 30 10

DESIGN: 4p.30, Side view of Wright Flyer I.

525 Albert Einstein and Equation

1979. Air. Birth Centenary of Albert Einstein (physicist).

1467 **525** 1p.60 multicoloured . . 10 10

526 Arms of Hermosillo

527 Sir Rowland Hill

1979. Centenary of Hermosillo, Sonora.

1468 **526** 80c. multicoloured . . . 10 10

1979. Air. Death Centenary of Sir Rowland Hill.

1469 **527** 1p.60 multicoloured . . 10 10

528 "Children" (Adriana Blas Casas)

1979. Air. International Year of the Child.

1470 **528** 1p.60 multicoloured . . 10 10

529 Registered Letter from Mexico to Rome, 1880

1979. Air. "Mepsipex 79", Third International Exhibition of Elmhurst Philatelic Society, Mexico City.

1499 **529** 1p.60 multicoloured . . 10 10

530 Football

531 Josefa Ortiz de Dominguez

1979. "Universiada 79", 10th World University Games, Mexico City (1st issue).

1500 **530** 50c. grey, black and blue (postage) 10 10
1501 – 80c. multicoloured . . . 10 10
1502 – 1p. multicoloured . . . 10 10
1504 – 1p.60 multicoloured (air) 10 10
1505 – 4p.30 multicoloured . . . 15 10

DESIGNS—VERT: 80c. Aztec ball player; 1p. Wall painting of athletes; 1p.60, Games emblem; 4p.30, Flame and doves.

See also Nos. 1514/19.

1979. 150th Death Anniv of Josefa Ortiz de Dominguez (Mayor of Queretaro).

1507 **531** 80c. pink, black and bright pink 10 10

532 "Allegory of National Culture" (Alfaro Siqueiros)

1979. 50th Anniv of National University's Autonomy. Multicoloured.

1508 80c. Type **532** (postage) . . 10 10
1509 3p. "The Conquest of Energy" (Chavez Morado) 20 10
1510 1p.60 "The Return of Quetzalcoati" (Chavez Morado) (air) 10 10
1511 4p.30 "Students reaching for Culture" (Alfaro Siqueiros) 15 10

533 Messenger and U.P.U. Emblem

534 Emiliano Zapata (after Diego Rivera)

1979. Air. Centenary of Mexico's Admission to U.P.U.

1512 **533** 1p.60 yellow, black and brown 10 10

1979. Birth Centenary of Emiliano Zapata (revolutionary).

1513 **534** 80c. multicoloured . . . 10 10

535 Football

536 Tepoztlan, Morelos

1979. "Universiada '79", 10th World University Games, Mexico City (2nd issue). Multicoloured.

1514 50c. Type **535** (postage) . . 10 10
1515 80c. Volleyball 10 10
1516 1p. Basketball 10 10
1518 1p.60 Tennis (air) 10 10
1519 5p.50 Swimming 30 20

1979. Tourism (1st series). Multicoloured.

1526 80c. Type **536** (postage) . . 10 10
1527 80c. Mexacaltitan, Nayarit 10 10
1528 1p.60 Agua Azul waterfall, Chipas (air) 10 10
1529 1p.60 King Coliman statue, Colima 10 10

See also Nos. 1631/4 and 1675/8.

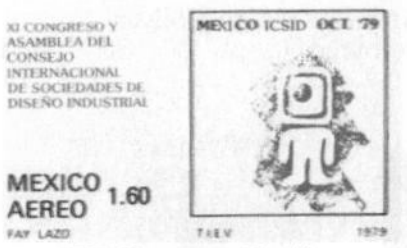

537 Congress Emblem

538 Edison Lamp

1979. Air. 11th Congress and Assembly of International Industrial Design Council.

1530 **537** 1p.60 black, mauve and turquoise 10 10

1979. Air. Centenary of Electric Light.

1531 **538** 1p.60 multicoloured . . 10 10

539 Martin de Olivares (postmaster)

540 Assembly Emblem

1979. 400th Anniv of Royal Proclamation of Mail Services in the New World. Multicoloured.

1532 80c. Type **539** (postage) . . 10 10
1533 1p.60 Martin Enriquez de Almanza (viceroy of New Spain) (air) 10 10
1534 5p.50 King Philip II of Spain 35 20

1979. Air. 8th General Assembly of Latin American Universities Union.

1536 **540** 1p.60 multicoloured . . 10 10

541 Shepherd

542 Moon Symbol from Mexican Codex

1979. Christmas. Multicoloured.

1537 50c. Type **541** (postage) . . 10 10
1538 1p.60 Girl and Christmas tree (air) 10 10

1979. Air. 10th Anniv of First Man on Moon.

1539 **542** 2p.50 multicoloured . . 15 10

543 Church, Yanhuitlan

1980. Air. Mexican Arts and Sciences (8th series). Multicoloured.

1540 1p.60 Type **543** 10 10
1541 1p.60 Monastery, Yuriria . . 10 10
1542 1p.60 Church, Tlayacapan 10 10
1543 1p.60 Church, Actopan . . 10 10
1544 1p.60 Church, Acolman . . 10 10

544 Steps and Snake's Head

1980. National Pre-Hispanic Monuments (1st series). Multicoloured.

1545 80c. Type **544** (postage) . . 10 10
1546 1p.60 Doble Tlaloc (rain god) (air) 10 10
1547 5p.50 Coyolzauhqui (moon goddess) 35 20

See also Nos. 1565/7 and 1605/7.

1980. Mexican Fauna (2nd series). As T **516**. Multicoloured.

1548 80c. Common turkey (postage) 90 15
1549 1p.60 Greater flamingo (air) 90 40

1980. Mexican Flowers (2nd series). As T **518**. Multicoloured.
1550 80c. "Tajetes erecta" (postage) 15 10
1551 1p.60 "Vanilla planifolia" (air) 25 10

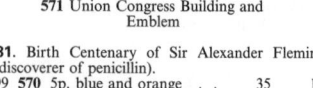

545 Jules Verne

1980. Air. 75th Death Anniv of Jules Verne (author).
1552 **545** 5p.50 brown and black 35 20

546 Skeleton smoking Cigar (after Guadalupe Posada) **547** China Poblana, Puebla

1980. Air. World Health Day. Anti-smoking Campaign.
1553 **546** 1p.60 purple, blue & red 10 10

1980. National Costumes (1st series). Multicoloured.
1554 50c. Type **547** (postage) . . 10 10
1555 80c. Jarocha, Veracruz . . . 10 10
1556 1p.60 Chiapaneca, Chiapas (air) 10 10
See also Nos. 1588/90.

548 Family **549** Cuauhtemoc (last Aztec Emperor)

1980. 10th Population and Housing Census.
1557 **548** 3p. black and silver . . . 20 10

1980. Pre-Hispanic Personalities (1st series). Multicoloured.
1558 80c. Type **549** 10 10
1559 1p.60 Nezahualcoyotl (governor of Tetzcoco) . . 10 10
1560 5p.50 Eight Deer Tiger's Claw (11th Mixtec king) 35 20
See also Nos. 1642/4 and 1846/8.

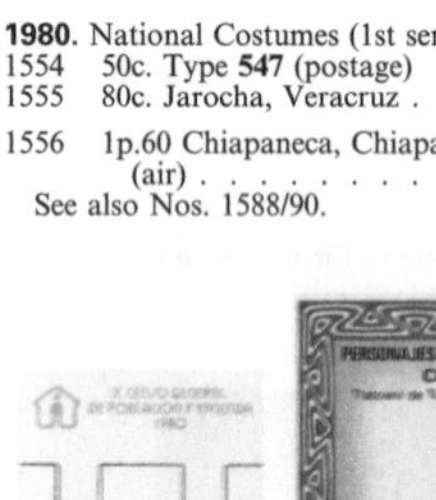

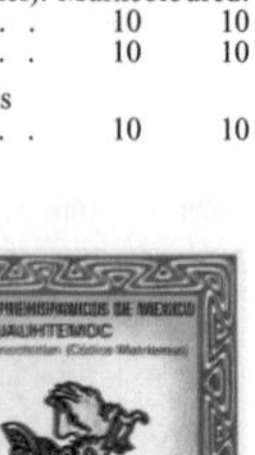

550 Xipe (Aztec god of medicine) **551** Bronze Medal

1980. 22nd World Biennial Congress of International College of Surgeons, Mexico City.
1561 **550** 1p.60 multicoloured . . 10 10

1980. Olympic Games, Moscow.
1562 **551** 1p.60 bronze, black and turquoise 10 10
1563 – 3p. silver, black and blue 20 10
1564 – 5p.50 gold, black and red 35 20
DESIGNS: 3p. Silver medal; 5p.50, Gold medal.

1980. National Pre-Hispanic Monuments (2nd series). As T **554**. Multicoloured.
1565 80c. Sacred glass 10 10
1566 1p.60 Stone snail 10 10
1567 5p.50 Chac Mool (god) . . 35 20

552 Sacromonte Sanctuary, Amecameca

1980. Colonial Architecture (1st series).
1568 **552** 2p.50 grey and black . . 20 10
1569 – 2p.50 grey and black . . 20 10
1570 – 3p. grey and black . . . 25 10
1571 – 3p. grey and black . . . 25 10
DESIGNS—HORIZ: No. 1552, St. Catherine's Convent, Patzcuaro; No. 1554, Hermitage, Cuernavaca. VERT: No. 1553, Basilica, Culiapan.
See also Nos. 1617/20, 1660/3, 1695/8 and 1784/7.

553 Quetzalcoatl (god) **554** Arms of Sinaloa

1980. World Tourism Conference, Manila, Philippines.
1572 **553** 2p.50 multicoloured . . 15 10

1980. 150th Anniv of Sinaloa State.
1573 **554** 1p.60 multicoloured . . 10 10

555 Straw Angel **556** Congress Emblem

1980. Christmas. Multicoloured.
1574 50c. Type **555** 10 10
1575 1p.60 Poinsettia in a jug . . 10 10

1980. 4th International Civil Justice Congress.
1576 **556** 1p.60 multicoloured . . 10 10

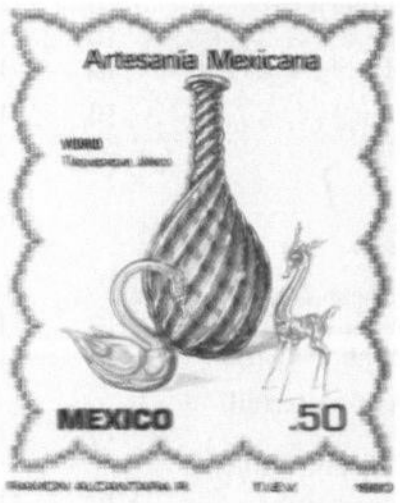

557 Glass Demijohn and Animals **558** "Simon Bolivar" (after Paulin Guerin)

1980. Mexican Crafts (1st series). Multicoloured.
1577 50c. Type **557** 10 10
1578 1p. Poncho 10 10
1579 3p. Wooden mask 20 15
See also Nos. 1624/6.

1980. 150th Death Anniv of Simon Bolivar.
1580 **558** 4p. multicoloured . . . 30 20

559 Vicente Guerrero **560** Valentin Gomez Farias

1981. 150th Death Anniv of Vicente Guerrero (liberator).
1581 **559** 80c. multicoloured . . . 10 10

1981. Birth Bicentenary of Valentin Gomez Farias.
1582 **560** 80c. black and green . . 10 10

561 Table Tennis Balls in Flight

1981. 1st Latin-American Table Tennis Cup.
1583 **561** 4p. multicoloured . . . 30 20

562 Jesus Gonzalez Ortega **563** Gabino Barreda

1981. Death Centenary of Jesus Gonzalez Ortega.
1584 **562** 80c. light brown & brown 10 10

1981. Death Centenary of Gabino Barreda (politician).
1585 **563** 80c. pink, black and green 10 10

564 Benito Juarez **565** Foundation Monument

1981. 175th Birth Anniv of Benito Juarez (patriot).
1586 **564** 1p.60 green, brn & lt brn 15 10

1981. 450th Anniv of Puebla City.
1587 **565** 80c. multicoloured . . . 10 10

1981. National Costumes (2nd series). Vert designs as T **547**. Multicoloured.
1588 50c. Purepecha, Michoacan 10 10
1589 80c. Charra, Jalisco 10 10
1590 1p.60 Mestiza, Yucatan . . 15 10

1981. Mexican Fauna (3rd series). Vert designs as T **516**. Multicoloured.
1591 80c. Northern mockingbird 65 20
1592 1p.60 Mexican trogon . . . 1·25 40

1981. Mexican Flowers (3rd series). Vert designs as T **518**. Multicoloured.
1593 80c. Avocado 10 10
1594 1p.60 Cacao 15 10

566 "Martyrs of Cananea" (David A. Siqueiros)

1981. 75th Anniv of Martyrs of Cananea.
1595 **566** 1p.60 multicoloured . . 15 10

567 Toy Drummer with One Arm **568** Arms of Queretaro

1981. International Year of Disabled People.
1596 **567** 4p. multicoloured . . . 30 20

1981. 450th Anniv of Queretaro City.
1597 **568** 80c. multicoloured . . . 10 10

569 Mexican Stamp of 1856 and Postal Service Emblem

1981. 125th Anniv of First Mexican Stamp.
1598 **569** 4p. multicoloured . . . 30 20

570 Sir Alexander Fleming **572** St. Francisco Xavier Claver

571 Union Congress Building and Emblem

1981. Birth Centenary of Sir Alexander Fleming (discoverer of penicillin).
1599 **570** 5p. blue and orange . . 35 10

1981. Opening of New Union Congress Building.
1600 **571** 1p.60 green and red . . 10 10

1981. 250th Birth Anniv of St. Francis Xavier Claver.
1601 **572** 80c. multicoloured . . . 10 10

573 "Desislava" (detail of Bulgarian Fresco)

1981. 1300th Anniv of Bulgarian State. Mult.
1602 1p.60 Type **573** 10 10
1603 4p. Horse-headed cup from Thrace 25 20
1604 7p. Madara Horseman (relief) 45 30

1981. Pre-Hispanic Monuments. As T **544**. Multicoloured.
1605 80c. Seated God 10 10
1606 1p.60 Alabaster deer's head 15 10
1607 4p. Jade fish 45 20

574 Pablo Picasso

1981. Birth Centenary of Pablo Picasso (artist).
1608 **574** 5p. deep green and green 35 20

575 Shepherd **576** Wheatsheaf

1981. Christmas. Multicoloured.
1609 50c. Type **575** 10 10
1610 1p.60 Praying girl 15 10

1981. World Food Day.
1611 **576** 4p. multicoloured . . . 25 15

577 Thomas Edison, Lightbulb and Gramophone

1981. 50th Death Anniv of Thomas Edison (inventor).
1612 **577** 4p. stone, brown & green 25 15

578 Co-operation Emblem and Wheat

1981. International Meeting on Co-operation and Development, Cancun.
1613 **578** 4p. blue, grey and black 25 20

579 Globe and Diesel Locomotive

1981. 15th Pan-American Railway Congress.
1614 **579** 1p.60 multicoloured . . 50 25

580 Film Frame

1981. 50th Anniv of Mexican Sound Movies.
1615 **580** 4p. grey, black and green 25 20

581 Postcode and Bird delivering Letter

1981. Inauguration of Postcodes.
1616 **581** 80c. multicoloured . . . 10 10

1981. Colonial Architecture (2nd series). As T **552**. Multicoloured.
1617 4p. Mascarones House . . . 25 15
1618 4p. La Merced Convent . . 25 15
1619 5p. Chapel of the Third Order, Texcoco 30 20
1620 5p. Father Tembleque Aqueduct, Otumba . . . 30 20

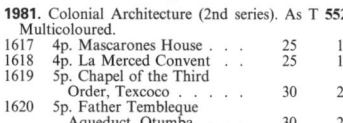

582 "Martyrs of Rio Blanco" (Orozco)

1982. 75th Anniv of Martyrs of Rio Blanco.
1621 **582** 80c. multicoloured . . . 10 10

583 Ignacio Lopez Rayon

1982. 150th Death Anniv of Ignacio Lopez Rayon.
1622 **583** 1p.60 green, red & black 10 10

584 Postal Headquarters

1982. 75th Anniv of Postal Headquarters.
1623 **584** 4p. pink and green . . . 25 20

1982. Mexican Crafts (2nd series). As T **557**. Multicoloured.
1624 50c. "God's Eye" (Huichol art) 10 10
1625 1p. Ceramic snail 10 10
1626 3p. Tiger mask 20 15

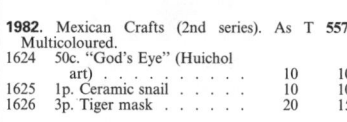

585 Postcoded Letter and Bird

1982. Postcode Publicity.
1627 **585** 80c. multicoloured . . . 10 10

586 Dr. Robert Koch and Cross of Lorraine

1982. Centenary of Discovery of Tubercle Bacillus.
1628 **586** 4p. multicoloured . . . 15 10

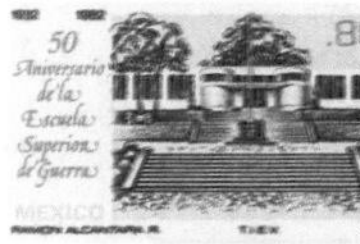

587 Military Academy **588** Arms of Oaxaca

1982. 50th Anniv of Military Academy.
1629 **587** 80c. yellow, black & gold 10 10

1982. 450th Anniv of Oaxaca City.
1630 **588** 1p.60 multicoloured . . 10 10

1982. Tourism (2nd series). As T **563**. Multicoloured.
1631 80c. Basaseachic Falls, Chihuahua 10 10
1632 80c. Natural rock formation, Pueblo Nuevo, Durango 10 10
1633 1p.60 Mayan City of Edzna, Campeche 10 10
1634 1p.60 La Venta (Olmeca sculpture, Tabasco) . . . 10 10

589 Footballers

1982. World Cup Football Championship, Spain. Multicoloured.
1635 1p.60 Type **589** 10 10
1636 4p. Dribbling 15 10
1637 7p. Tackling 25 15

590 Hawksbill Turtles

1982. Mexican Fauna. Multicoloured.
1638 1p.60 Type **590** 10 10
1639 4p. Grey Whales 15 30

591 Vicente Guerrero

1982. Birth Bicentenary of Vicente Guerrero (independence fighter).
1640 **591** 80c. multicoloured . . . 10 10

592 Symbols of Peace and Communication

1982. Second U.N. Conference on the Exploration and Peaceful Uses of Outer Space, Vienna.
1641 **592** 4p. multicoloured . . . 10 10

1982. Pre-Hispanic Personalities (2nd series). As T **549**. Multicoloured.
1642 80c. Tariacuri 10 10
1643 1p.60 Acamapichtli 10 10
1644 4p. Ten Deer Tiger's breastplate 10 10

593 Pawpaw ("Carica papaya")

1982. Mexican Flora. Multicoloured.
1645 80c. Type **593** 10 10
1646 1p.60 Maize ("Zea mays") 10 10

594 Astrologer

1982. Native Mexican Codices. Florentine Codex. Multicoloured.
1647 80c. Type **594** 10 10
1648 1p.60 Arriving at School . . 10 10
1649 4p. Musicians 10 10

595 Manuel Gamio (anthropologist)

1982. Mexican Arts and Scientists. Multicoloured.
1650 1p.60 Type **595** 10 10
1651 1p.60 Isaac Ochoterena (biologist) 10 10
1652 1p.60 Angel Maria Garibay (philologist) 10 10
1653 1p.60 Manuel Sandoval Vallarta (nuclear physicist) 10 10
1654 1p.60 Guillermo Gonzalez Camarena (electronics engineer) 10 10

596 State Archives Building

1982. Inaug of State Archives Building.
1655 **596** 1p.60 black and green 10 10

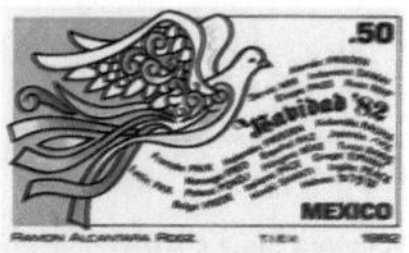

597 Dove and Peace Text

1982. Christmas. Multicoloured.
1656 50c. Type **597** 10 10
1657 1p.60 Dove and Peace text (different) 10 10

598 Hands holding Food

1982. Mexican Food System.
1658 **598** 1p.60 multicoloured . . 20 10

599 "Revolutionary Mexico" Stamp, 1956

1982. Inauguration of Revolution Museum, Chihuahua.
1659 **599** 1p.60 grey and green . . 10 10

1982. Colonial Architecture (3rd series). As T **552**. Multicoloured.
1660 1p.60 College of Sts. Peter and Paul, Mexico City . . 10 10
1661 8p. Convent of Jesus Maria, Mexico City 15 10
1662 10p. Open Chapel, Tlalmanalco 20 15
1663 14p. Convent, Actopan . . 25 20

600 Alfonso Garcia Robles and Laurel 601 Jose Vasconcelos

1982. Alfonso Garcia Robles (Nobel Peace Prize Winner) Commemoration.
1664 **600** 1p.60 grey, black & gold 10 10
1665 – 14p. pink, black and gold 25 20
DESIGN: 14p. Robles and medal.

1982. Birth Centenary of Jose Vasconcelos (philosopher).
1666 **601** 1p.60 black and blue . . 10 10

602 W.C.Y. Emblem and Methods of Communication

1983. World Communications Year.
1667 **602** 16p. multicoloured . . . 20 15

603 Sonora State Civil War Stamp, 1913

1983. "Herfilex 83" Mexican Revolution Stamp Exhibition.
1668 **603** 6p. brown, black & green 10 10

604 "Nauticas Mexico" (container ship), World Map and I.M.O. Emblem

1983. 25th Anniv of International Maritime Organization.
1669 **604** 16p. multicoloured . . . 1·25 30

605 Doctor treating Patient

1983. Constitutional Right to Health Protection.
1670 **605** 6p. green and red . . . 10 10

606 Valentin Gomez Farias (founder) and Arms of Society

1983. 150th Anniv of Mexican Geographical and Statistical Society.
1671 **606** 6p. multicoloured . . . 10 10

607 Football

1983. 2nd World Youth Football Championship, Mexico.
1672 **607** 6p. black and green . . 10 10
1673 13p. black and red . . . 15 10
1674 14p. black and blue . . 20 15

1983. Tourism. As T **536**. Multicoloured.
1675 6p. Federal Palace, Queretaro 10 10
1676 6p. Water tank, San Luis Potosi 10 10
1677 13p. Cable car, Zacatecas 15 10
1678 14p. Carved head of Kohunlich, Quintana Roo 20 15

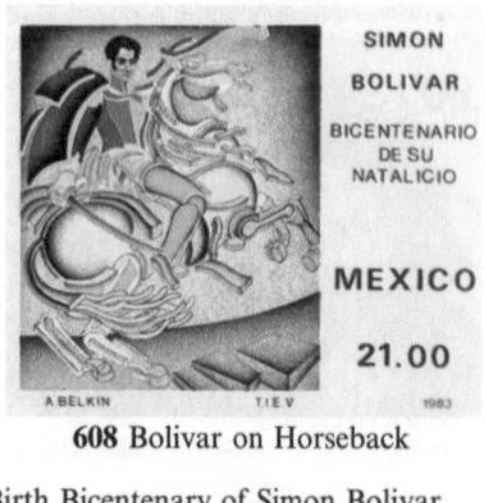

608 Bolivar on Horseback

1983. Birth Bicentenary of Simon Bolivar.
1679 **608** 21p. multicoloured . . . 25 15

609 Angela Peralta 610 Agave

1983. Death Centenary of Angela Peralta (opera singer).
1680 **609** 9p. light brown & brown 10 10

1983. Mexican Flora and Fauna (5th series). Multicoloured.
1681 9p. Type **610** 10 10
1682 9p. Sapodilla 10 10
1683 9p. Swallowtail 30 10
1684 9p. Boa constrictor 10 10

611 Two Candles

1983. Christmas. Multicoloured.
1685 9p. Type **611** 10 10
1686 20p. Three candles 25 15

612 S.C.T. Emblem

1983. Integral Communications and Transport System.
1687 **612** 13p. blue and black . . 15 10

613 Carlos Chavez (musician)

1983. Mexican Arts and Sciences (10th series). Contemporary Artists. Multicoloured.
1688 **613** 9p. brown, light brown and deep brown . . . 10 10
1689 – 9p. brown, light brown and deep brown . . . 10 10
1690 – 9p. deep brown, light brown and brown . . 10 10
1691 – 9p. light brown, deep brown and brown . . 10 10
1692 – 9p. deep brown, stone and brown 10 10
DESIGNS: No. 1689, Francisco Goitia (painter); No. 1690, S. Diaz Miron (poet); No. 1691, Carlos Bracho (sculptor); No. 1692, Fanny Anitua (singer).

614 Orozco (self-portrait)

1983. Birth Centenary of Jose Clemente Orozco (artist).
1693 **614** 9p. multicoloured . . . 10 10

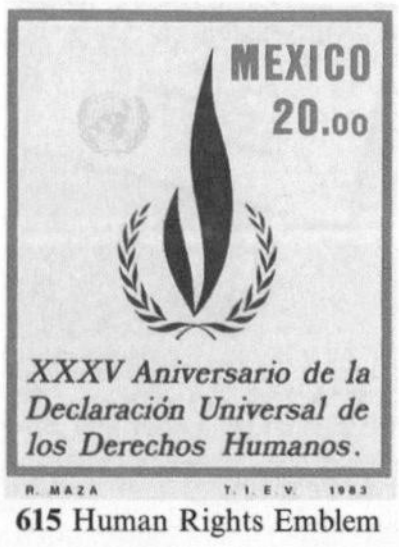

615 Human Rights Emblem

1983. 35th Anniv of Human Rights Declaration.
1694 **615** 20p. deep blue, yellow and blue 25 15

1983. Colonial Architecture (4th series). As T **552**. Each grey and black.
1695 9p. Convent, Malinalco . . 10 10
1696 20p. Cathedral, Cuernavaca 25 15
1697 21p. Convent, Tepeji del Rio 25 15
1698 24p. Convent, Atlatlahucan 30 20

616 Antonio Caso and Books

1983. Birth Centenary of Antonio Caso (philospher).
1699 **616** 9p. blue, lilac and red . . 10 10

617 Joaquin Velazquez

1983. Bicentenary of Royal Legislation on Mining.
1700 **617** 9p. multicoloured . . . 10 10

618 Book and Envelopes

1984. Centenary of First Postal Laws.
1701 **618** 12p. multicoloured . . . 15 10

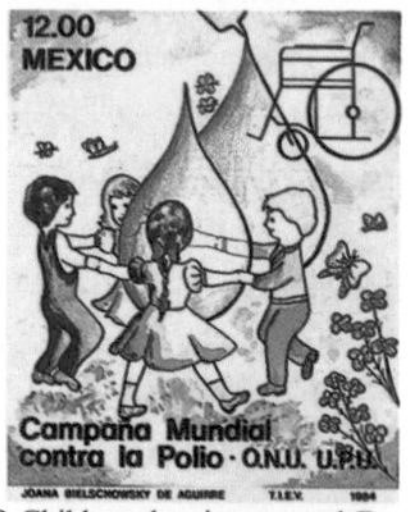

619 Children dancing around Drops of Anti-Polio Serum

1984. World Anti-polio Campaign.
1702 **619** 12p. multicoloured . . . 15 10

620 Muscovy Duck

1984. Mexican Fauna (6th series). Multicoloured.
1703 12p. Type **620** 70 65
1704 20p. Red-billed whistling duck . . . . 1·40 1·25

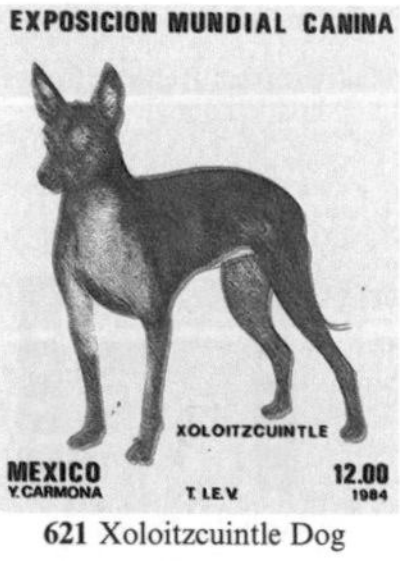

621 Xoloitzcuintle Dog

1984. World Dog Show.
1705 **621** 12p. multicoloured . . . 15 10

622 Bank Headquarters

1984. Centenary of National Bank.
1706 **622** 12p. multicoloured . . . 15 10

623 Hands holding Trees

624 Putting the Shot

1984. Protection of Forest Resources.
1707 **623** 20p. multicoloured . . . 20 15

1984. Olympic Games, Los Angeles. Multicoloured.
1708 14p. Type **624** 15 15
1709 20p. Show jumping 20 15
1710 23p. Gymnastics (floor exercise) 25 20
1711 24p. Diving 25 20
1712 25p. Boxing 25 20
1713 26p. Fencing 25 20

625 Mexican and Russian Flags

1984. 60th Anniv of Diplomatic Relations with U.S.S.R.
1715 **625** 23p. multicoloured . . . 25 20

626 Hand holding U.N. emblem

1984. International Population Conference.
1716 **626** 20p. multicoloured . . . 20 15

627 Gen. Mugica

1984. Birth Centenary of General Francisco Mugica (politician).
1717 **627** 14p. brown and black . . 15 15

628 Emblem and Dates

629 Airline Emblem

1984. 50th Anniv of Economic Culture Fund.
1718 **628** 14p. brown, black and red 15 15

1984. 50th Anniv of Aeromexico (state airline).
1719 – 14p. multicoloured . . . 15 15
1720 **629** 20p. black and red . . . 20 15
DESIGN—36 × 44 mm: 14p. "Red Cactus" (sculpture, Sebastian).

630 Palace of Fine Arts

1984. 50th Anniv of Palace of Fine Arts.
1721 **630** 14p. blue, black and brown 15 15

631 Metropolitan Cathedral (detail of facade)

633 Dove and Hand holding Flame

632 Coatzacoalcos Bridge

1984. 275th Anniv of Chihuahua City.
1722 **631** 14p. brown and black . . 15 15

1984. Inaug of Coatzacoalcos Bridge.
1723 **632** 14p. multicoloured . . . 15 15

1984. World Disarmament Week.
1724 **633** 20p. multicoloured . . . 20 15

634 Christmas Tree and Toy Train

1984. Christmas. Multicoloured.
1725 14p. Type **634** 50 25
1726 20p. Breaking the pinata (balloon filled with gifts) (vert) 20 15

635 Ignacio Manuel Altamirano

1984. 150th Birth Anniv of Ignacio Manuel Altamirano (politician and journalist).
1727 **635** 14p. red and black . . . 15 15

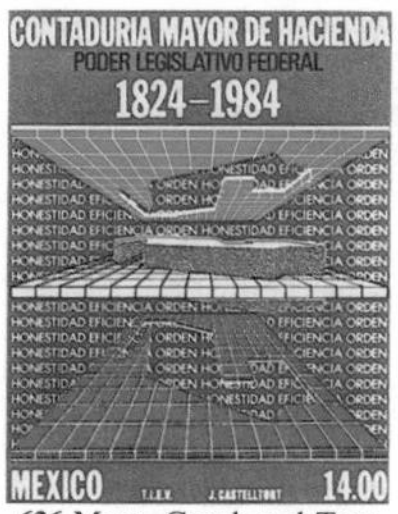

636 Maps, Graph and Text

1984. 160th Anniv of State Audit Office.
1728 **636** 14p. multicoloured . . . 15 15

637 Half a Football and Mexican Colours

1984. Mexico, Site of 1986 World Cup Football Championship. Multicoloured.
1729 20p. Type **637** 20 15
1730 24p. Football and Mexican colours 25 20

638 Romulo Gallegos

639 State Arms and Open Register

1984. Birth Centenary of Romulo Gallegos.
1731 **638** 20p. black and blue . . 20 15

1984. 125th Anniv of Mexican Civil Register.
1732 **639** 24p. blue 25 20

640 Mexican Flag

641 Johann Sebastian Bach

1985. 50th Anniv of National Flag.
1733 **640** 22p. multicoloured . . . 25 20

1985. 300th Birth Anniv of Johann Sebastian Bach (composer).
1734 **641** 35p. red and black . . . 15 30

642 I.Y.Y. Emblem

643 Children and Fruit within Book

1985. International Youth Year.
1735 **642** 35p. purple, gold and black 15 30

1985. Child Survival Campaign.
1736 **643** 36p. multicoloured . . . 15 10

644 Commemorative Medallion

1985. 450th Anniv of State Mint.
1737 **644** 35p. gold, mauve & blue 15 10

645 Victor Hugo, Text and Gateway

1985. Death Centenary of Victor Hugo (novelist).
1738 **645** 35p. grey 15 10

646 Hidalgo 8r. Stamp, 1856

1985. "Mexifil 85" Stamp Exhibition.
1739 **646** 22p. grey, black and purple 10 10
1740 – 35p. grey, black and blue 15 10
1741 – 36p. multicoloured . . . 15 10
DESIGNS: 35p. Carranza 10c. stamp, 1916; 36p. Juarez 50p. stamp, 1975.

647 Rockets, Satellite, Nurse and Computer Operator

1985. Launching of First Morelos Satellite. Mult.
1743 22p. Type **647** 10 10
1744 36p. Camera, dish aerial, satellite and computers . . 15 10
1745 90p. Camera, dish aerial, satellite, television and couple telephoning . . . 25 20
Nos. 1743/5 were printed together, se-tenant, forming a composite design.

648 Conifer

1985. 9th World Forestry Congress, Mexico.
1747 **648** 22p. brown, black and green 10 10
1748 – 35p. brown, black and green 15 10
1749 – 36p. brown, black and green 15 10
DESIGNS: 35p. Silk-cotton trees; 36p. Mahogany tree.

649 Martin Luis Guzman

1985. Mexican Arts and Sciences (11th series). Contemporary Writers.
1750 **649** 22p. grey and blue . . . 10 10
1751 – 22p. grey and blue . . . 10 10
1752 – 22p. grey and blue . . . 10 10
1753 – 22p. grey and blue . . . 10 10
1754 – 22p. grey and blue . . . 10 10
DESIGNS: No. 1751, Augustin Yanez; 1752, Alfonso Reyes; 1753, Jose Ruben Romero; 1754, Artemio de Valle-Arizpe.

650 Miguel Hidalgo

1985. 175th Anniv of Independence Movement. Each green, black and red.
1755 22p. Type **650** 10 10
1756 35p. Jose Ma. Morelos . . . 10 10
1757 35p. Ignacio Allende 10 10
1758 36p. Leona Vigario 10 10
1759 110p. Vicente Guerrero . . 20 15

651 San Ildefonso

1985. 75th Anniv of National University. Mult.
1761 26p. Type **651** 10 10
1762 26p. Emblem 10 10
1763 40p. Modern building . . . 10 10
1764 45p. 1910 crest and Justo Sierra (founder) 10 10
1765 90p. University crest 15 10

652 Rural and Industrial Landscapes

1985. 25th Anniv of Inter-American Development Bank.
1766 **652** 26p. multicoloured . . . 10 10

653 Guns and Doves

654 Hands and Dove

1985. United Nations Disarmament Week.
1767 **653** 36p. multicoloured . . . 10 10

1985. 40th Anniv of U.N.O.
1768 **654** 26p. multicoloured . . . 10 10

655 "Girls Skipping" (Mishinoya K. Maki)

1985. Christmas. Children's Paintings. Mult.
1769 26p. Disabled and able-bodied children playing (Margarita Salazar) . . . 10 10
1770 35p. Type **655** 10 10

656 Soldadera

1985. 75th Anniv of 1910 Revolution. Each red, black and green.
1771 26p. Type **656** 10 10
1772 35p. Pancho Villa 10 10
1773 40p. Emiliano Zapata . . . 10 10
1774 45p. Venustiano Carranza 10 10
1775 110p. Francisco Madero . . 20 15

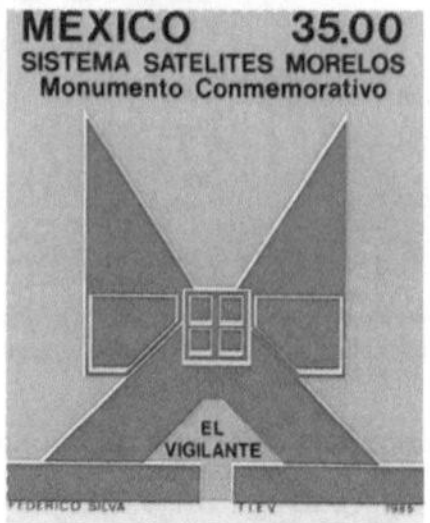

657 "Vigilante" (Federico Silva)

1985. 2nd "Morelos" Telecommunications Satellite Launch.
1777 – 26p. black and blue . . 10 10
1778 **657** 35p. grey, pink and black 10 10
1779 – 45p. multicoloured . . . 10 10
DESIGNS—VERT: 26p. "Cosmonaut" (sculpture by Sebastian). HORIZ: 45p. "Mexican Astronaut" (painting by Cauduro).

658 "Mexico" holding Book

1985. 25th Anniv of Free Textbooks National Commission.
1781 **658** 26p. multicoloured . . . 10 10

659 Olympic Stadium, University City

1985. World Cup Football Championship, Mexico. Each grey and black.
1782 26p. Type **659** 10 10
1783 45p. Azteca Stadium 10 10

1985. Colonial Architecture (5th series). Vert designs as T **552**. Each brown and black.
1784 26p. Vizcayan College, Mexico City 10 10
1785 35p. Counts of Heras y Soto Palace, Mexico City . . . 10 10
1786 40p. Counts of Calimaya Palace, Mexico City . . . 10 10
1787 45p. St. Carlos Academy, Mexico City 10 10

661 Luis Enrique Erro Planetarium

1986. 50th Anniv of National Polytechnic Institute. Multicoloured.
1788 40p. Type **661** 10 10
1789 65p. National School of Arts and Crafts 10 10
1790 75p. Founders, emblem and "50" 10 10

1986. Mexican Flowers (6th series). As T **518**. Multicoloured.
1791 40p. Calabash 10 10
1792 65p. "Nopalea coccinellifera" (cactus) . . 10 10

663 Doll

1986. World Health Day.
1793 **663** 65p. multicoloured . . . 10 10

664 Halley and Comet

1986. Appearance of Halley's Comet.
1794 **664** 90p. multicoloured . . . 15 10

665 Emblem

1986. Centenary of Geological Institute.
1795 **665** 40p. multicoloured . . . 10 10

666 "Three Footballers with Berets"

1986. World Cup Football Championship, Mexico (2nd issue). Paintings by Angel Zarraga. Multicoloured.
1796 30p. Type **666** 10 10
1797 40p. "Portrait of Ramon Novaro" 10 10
1798 65p. "Sunday" 10 10
1799 70p. "Portrait of Ernest Charles Gimpel" 10 10
1800 90p. "Three Footballers" . . 15 10

667 Ignacio Allende

1986. 175th Death Annivs of Independence Heroes. Multicoloured.
1802 40p. Type **667** 10 10
1803 40p. Miguel Hidalgo (after J. C. Orozco) 10 10
1804 65p. Juan Aldama 10 10
1805 75p. Mariano Jimenez . . . 10 10

668 Mexican Arms over "FTF"

669 Nicolas Bravo

1986. 50th Anniv of Fiscal Tribunal.
1806 **668** 40p. black, blue and grey 10 10

1986. Birth Bicentenary of Nicolas Bravo (independence fighter).
1807 **669** 40p. multicoloured . . . 10 10

670 "Zapata Landscape"

1986. Paintings by Diego Rivera. Multicoloured.
1808 50p. Type **670** 10 10
1809 80p. "Nude with Arum Lilies" 10 10
1810 110p. "Vision of a Sunday Afternoon Walk on Central Avenue" (horiz) 20 15

671 Guadalupe Victoria

1986. Birth Bicentenary of Guadalupe Victoria (first President).
1811 **671** 50p. multicoloured . . . 10 10

672 People depositing Produce

1986. 50th Anniv of National Depositories.
1812 **672** 40p. multicoloured . . . 10 10

673 Pigeon above Hands holding Posthorn

674 Emblem

1986. World Post Day.
1813 **673** 120p. multicoloured . . 20 15

1986. Foundation of National Commission to Mark 500th Anniv (1992) of Discovery of America.
1814 **674** 50p. black and red . . . 10 10

675 Ministry of Mines 676 Liszt

1986. 15th Pan-American Roads Congress.
1815 **675** 80p. grey and black . . 10 10

1986. 175th Birth Anniv of Franz Liszt (composer).
1816 **676** 100p. brown and black 15 10

677 U.N. and "Pax Cultura" Emblems

1986. International Peace Year.
1817 **677** 80p. blue, red and black 10 10

678 Jose Maria Pino Suarez (1st Vice-President of Revolutionary Govt.)

1986. Famous Mexicans buried in The Rotunda of Illustrious Men (1st series).
1818 **678** 50p. multicoloured . . . 10 10
See also Nos. 1823/4, 1838 and 1899.

679 King 680 "Self-portrait"

1986. Christmas. Multicoloured.
1819 50p. Type **679** 10 10
1820 80p. Angel 10 10

1986. Birth Centenary of Diego Rivera (artist).
1821 **680** 80p. multicoloured . . . 10 10

681 Baby receiving Vaccination 682 Perez de Leon College

1987. National Days for Poliomyelitis Vaccination.
1822 **681** 50p. multicoloured . . . 10 10

1987. Famous Mexicans buried in The Rotunda of Illustrious Men (2nd series). As T **678**. Mult.
1823 100p. Jose Maria Iglesias . . 10 10
1824 100p. Pedro Sainz de Baranda 10 10

1987. Centenary of Higher Education.
1825 **682** 100p. multicoloured . . 10 10

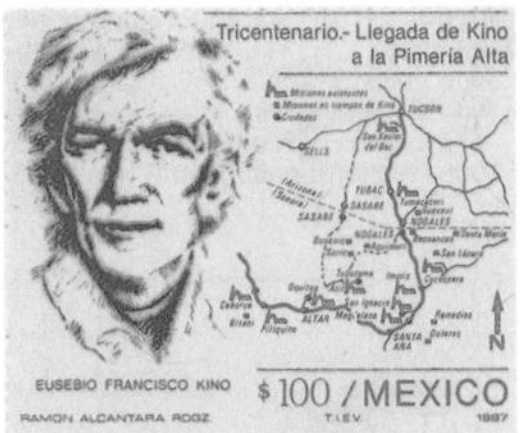

683 Kino and Map

1987. 300th Anniv of Father Eusebio Francisco Kino's Mission to Pimeria Alta.
1826 **683** 100p. multicoloured . . 10 10

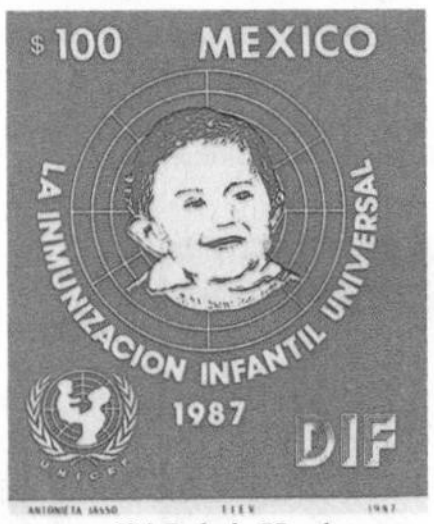

684 Baby's Head

1987. Child Immunization Campaign.
1827 **684** 100p. deep blue and blue 10 10

685 Staircase 686 "5th of May, 1862, and the Siege of Puebla" Exhibition Poster, 1887

1987. 50th Anniv of Puebla Independent University.
1828 **685** 200p. grey, pink and black 10 10

1987. 125th Anniv of Battle of Puebla.
1829 **686** 100p. multicoloured . . 10 10

687 Stylized City

1987. "Metropolis 87" World Association of Large Cities Congress.
1830 **687** 310p. red, black and green 45 30

688 Lacquerware Tray, Uruapan, Michoacan 689 Genaro Estrada (author and pioneer of democracy)

1987. Handicrafts. Multicoloured.
1831 100p. Type **688** 10 10
1832 200p. Woven blanket, Santa Ana Chiautempan, Tlaxcala 10 10
1833 230p. Ceramic jar with lid, Puebla, Puebla 15 10

1987. Mexican Arts and Sciences (12th series).
1834 **689** 100p. brown, black and pink 10 10
See also Nos. 1845, 1880 and 1904/5.

690 "Native Traders" (mural, P. O'Higgins)

1987. 50th Anniv of National Foreign Trade Bank.
1835 **690** 100p. multicoloured . . 10 10

691 Diagram of Longitudinal Section through Ship's Hull

1987. 400th Anniv of Publication of First Shipbuilding Manual in America, Diego Garcia de Palacio's "Instrucion Nautica".
1836 **691** 100p. green, blue & brn 10 10

692 Man carrying Sack of Maize Flour

1987. 50th Anniv of National Food Programme.
1837 **692** 100p. multicoloured . . 10 10

1987. Mexicans in Rotunda of Illustrious Men (3rd series). As T **678**. Multicoloured.
1838 100p. Leandro Valle 10 10

693 "Self-portrait with Skull"

1987. Paintings by Saturnino Herran.
1839 **693** 100p. brown and black 15 10
1840 – 100p. multicoloured . . 15 10
1841 – 400p. multicoloured . . 60 50
DESIGNS: No. 1840, "The Offering"; 1841, "Creole with Shawl".

694 Flags of Competing Countries

1987. 10th Pan-American Games, Indianapolis.
1842 **694** 100p. multicoloured . . 10 10
1843 – 200p. black, red and green 10 10
DESIGN: 200p. Running.

695 Electricity Pylon

1987. 50th Anniv of Federal Electricity Commission.
1844 **695** 200p. multicoloured . . 10 10

1987. Mexican Arts and Sciences (13th series). As T **689**. Multicoloured.
1845 100p. J. E. Hernandez y Davalos (author) 10 10

1987. Pre-Hispanic Personalities (3rd series). As T **549**. Multicoloured.
1846 100p. Xolotl (Chichimeca commander) 10 10
1847 200p. Nezahualpilli (leader of Tezcoco tribe) 10 10
1848 400p. Motecuhzoma Ilhuicamina (leader of Tenochtitlan tribe) . . . 45 10

696 Stylized Racing Car

1987. Mexico Formula One Grand Prix.
1849 **696** 100p. multicoloured . . 10 10

697 Mexican Cultural Centre, Mexico City 698 "Santa Maria" and 1922 Mexican Festival Emblem

1987. Mexican Tourism.
1850 **697** 100p. multicoloured . . 10 10

1987. 500th Anniv of "Meeting of Two Worlds" (discovery of America by Columbus) (1st issue).
1851 **698** 150p. multicoloured . . 65 20
See also Nos. 1902, 1941, 1979, 2038 and 2062/6.

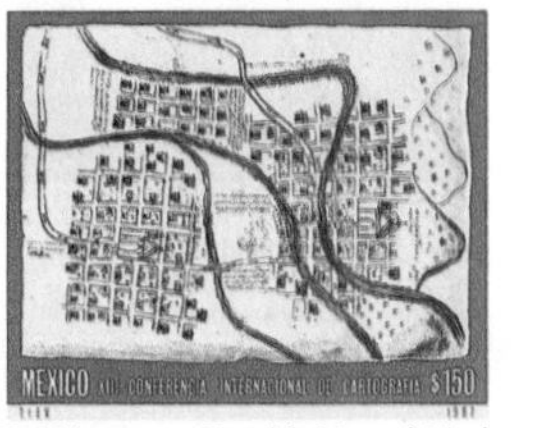

699 16th-century Spanish Map of Mexico City

1987. 13th International Cartography Conference.
1852 **699** 150p. multicoloured . . 10 10

1987. Mexican Tourism. As T **697**. Multicoloured.
1853 150p. Michoacan 30 10
1854 150p. Garcia Caves, Nuevo Leon 10 10
1855 150p. View of Mazatlan, Sinaloa 10 10

700 Pre-Hispanic Wedding Ceremony

1987. Native Codices. Mendocino Codex. Mult.
1856 150p. Type **700** 10 10
1857 150p. Moctezuma's council chamber 10 10
1858 150p. Foundation of Tenochtitlan 10 10

701 Dove with Olive Twig

1987. Christmas.
1859 **701** 150p. mauve 10 10
1860 – 150p. blue 10 10
DESIGN: No. 1860, As T **701** but dove facing left.

702 "Royal Ordinance for the Carriage of Maritime Mail" Title Page

1987. World Post Day.
1861 **702** 150p. green and grey . . 10 10

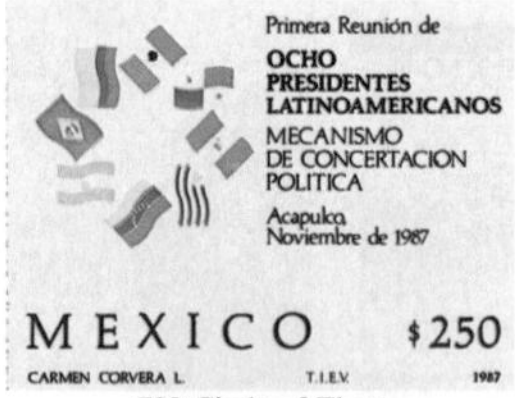

703 Circle of Flags

1987. 1st Meeting of Eight Latin-American Presidents, Acapulco. Multicoloured.
1863 250p. Type **703** 10 10
1864 500p. Flags and doves . . . 25 10

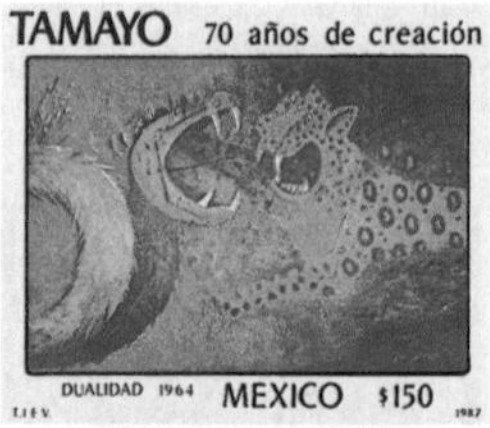

704 "Dualidad 1964"

1987. Rufino Tamayo (painter). "70 Years of Creativity".
1865 **704** 150p. multicoloured . . 10 10

705 Train on Metlac Viaduct

1987. 50th Anniv of Railway Nationalization.
1866 **705** 150p. multicoloured . . 40 15

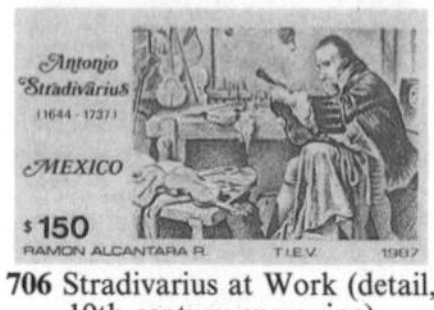

706 Stradivarius at Work (detail, 19th-century engraving)

1987. 250th Death Anniv of Antonio Stradivarius (violin-maker).
1867 **706** 150p. light violet and violet 10 10

707 Statue of Manuel Crescencio Rejon (promulgator of Yucatan State Constitution)

1988. Constitutional Tribunal, Supreme Court of Justice.
1868 **707** 300p. multicoloured . . 15 10

708 American Manatee

1988. Animals. Multicoloured.
1869 300p. Type **708** 15 10
1870 300p. Mexican mole salamander 15 10

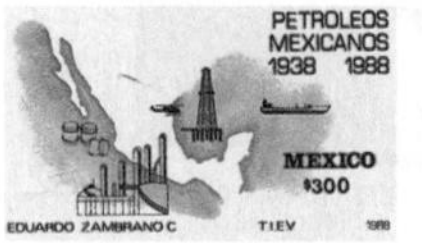

709 Map and Oil Industry Symbols **710** "The Vaccination"

1988. 50th Anniv of Pemex (Nationalized Petroleum Industry).
1871 **709** 300p. blue and black . . 40 10
1872 – 300p. multicoloured . . 15 10
1873 – 500p. multicoloured . . 25 10
DESIGNS:—36 × 43 mm: No. 1872, PEMEX emblem. 43 × 36 mm: No. 1873, "50" and oil exploration platform.

1988. World Health Day (1874) and 40th Anniv of W.H.O. (1875). Paintings by Diego Rivera.
1874 **710** 300p. brown and green 15 10
1875 – 300p. multicoloured . . 15 10
DESIGN:—43 × 36 mm: No. 1875, "The People demand Health".

711 "Death Portrait" (Victor Delfin)

1988. 50th Death Anniv of Cesar Vallejo (painter and poet). Multicoloured.
1876 300p. Type **711** 15 10
1877 300p. Portrait by Arnold Belkin and "Hoy me palpo ..." 15 10
1878 300p. Portrait as in T **711** but larger (30 × 35 mm) 15 10
1879 300p. Portrait as in No. 1877 but larger (23 × 35 mm) 15 10

1988. Mexican Arts and Sciences (14th series). As T **689**.
1880 300p. brown, black and violet 15 10
DESIGN: 300p. Carlos Pellicer (poet).

712 Girl and Boy holding Stamp in Tweezers

1988. "Mepsirrey '88" Stamp Exhibition, Monterrey. Multicoloured.
1881 300p. Type **712** 15 10
1882 300p. Envelope with "Monterrey" handstamp 15 10
1883 500p. Exhibition emblem . . 25 10

713 Hernandos Rodriguez Racing Circuit, Mexico City

1988. Mexico Formula One Grand Prix.
1884 **713** 500p. multicoloured . . 25 10

714 Lopez Verlarde and Rose **715** Emblem

1988. Birth Centenary of Ramon Lopez Verlarde (poet). Multicoloured.
1885 300p. Type **714** 15 10
1886 300p. Abstract 15 10

1988. 50th Anniv of Military Sports.
1887 **715** 300p. multicoloured . . 15 10

716 Chrysanthemum, Container Ship and Flags

1988. Centenary of Mexico–Japan Friendship, Trade and Navigation Treaty.
1888 **716** 500p. multicoloured . . 45 10

717 Map

1988. Oceanographical Assembly.
1889 **717** 500p. multicoloured . . 25 10

718 Runners **719** Boxer and Flags

1988. Olympic Games, Seoul.
1890 **718** 500p. multicoloured . . 25 10

1988. 25th Anniv of World Boxing Council.
1892 **719** 500p. multicoloured . . 25 10

720 Hospital and Emblem

1988. 125th Anniv of Red Cross.
1893 **720** 300p. grey, red and black 15 10

721 Posada

1988. 75th Death Anniv of Jose Guadalupe Posada (painter).
1894 **721** 300p. black and silver . . 15 10

722 "Danaus plexippus"

1988. Endangered Insects. The Monarch Butterfly. Multicoloured.
1895 300p. Type **722** . . . . . 1·00 10
1896 300p. Butterflies on wall . . 1·00 10
1897 300p. Butterflies on leaves 1·00 10
1898 300p. Caterpillar, butterfly and chrysalis . . . . . . 1·00 10

1988. Mexicans in Rotunda of Illustrious Persons (4th series). As T **678**. Multicoloured.
1899 300p. Manuel Sandoval Vallarta 15 10

723 Envelopes forming Map

1988. World Post Day.
1900 **723** 500p. black and blue . . 20 10

724 Indian and Monk writing

1988. 500th Anniv of "Meeting of Two Worlds" (2nd issue). Yanhuitian Codex.
1902 **724** 500p. multicoloured . . 20 10

725 Man watering Plant

1988. World Food Day. "Rural Youth".
1903 **725** 500p. multicoloured . . 20 10

1988. Mexican Arts and Sciences (15th series). As T **689**.
1904 300p. black and grey . . . 15 10
1905 300p. brown, black & yellow 15 10
DESIGNS: No. 1904, Alfonso Caso; 1905, Vito Alessio Robles.

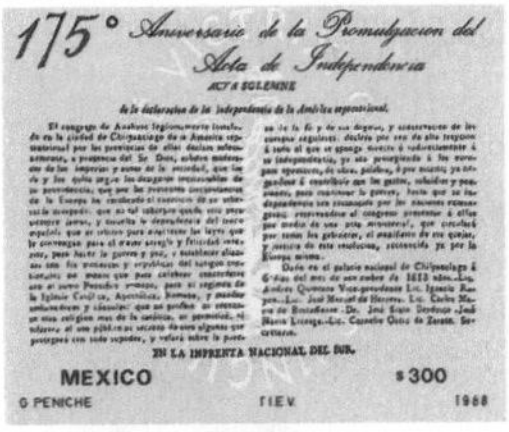

726 Act

1988. 175th Anniv of Promulgation of Act of Independence.
1906 **726** 300p. flesh and brown 15 10

727 "Self-portrait 1925" 728 Children and Kites

1988. 25th Death Anniv of Antonio Ruiz (painter). Multicoloured.
1907 300p. Type **727** 15 10
1908 300p. "La Malinche" . . . 15 10
1909 300p. "March Past" 15 10

1988. Christmas. Multicoloured.
1910 300p. Type **728** 15 10
1911 300p. Food (horiz) 15 10

729 Emblem

1988. 50th Anniv of Municipal Workers Trade Union.
1912 **729** 300p. black and brown 15 10

1988. Mexican Flowers (7th series). As T **518**. Multicoloured.
1913 300p. "Mimosa tenuiflora" 15 10
1914 300p. "Ustilago maydis" . . 30 10

731 "50" and Emblem

1989. 50th Anniv of State Printing Works.
1915 **731** 450p. brown, grey and red 20 10

732 Arms and Score of National Anthem

1989. 145th Anniv of Dominican Independence.
1916 **732** 450p. multicoloured . . 20 10

733 Emblem

1989. Centenary of International Boundary and Water Commission.
1917 **733** 1100p. multicoloured . . 50 50

734 Emblem

1989. 10th International Book Fair, Mineria.
1918 **734** 450p. multicoloured . . 20 10

735 Composer at Work

1989. 25th Anniv of Society of Authors and Composers.
1919 **735** 450p. multicoloured . . 20 10

736 People

1989. Anti-AIDS Campaign.
1920 **736** 450p. multicoloured . . 20 10

737 Vicario 738 Statue of Reyes

1989. Birth Bicentenary of Leona Vicario (Independence fighter).
1921 **737** 450p. brown, deep brown and black . . . 20 10

1989. Birth Centenary of Alfonso Reyes (writer).
1922 **738** 450p. multicoloured . . 20 10

739 Speeding Cars

1989. Mexico Formula One Grand Prix.
1923 **739** 450p. multicoloured . . 20 10

740 Sea and Mountains 741 Huehuetcotl (god)

1989. 14th Travel Agents' Meeting, Acapulco.
1924 **740** 1100p. multicoloured . . 50 50

1989. 14th International Congress on Ageing.
1925 **741** 450p. pink, black and stone 20 10

742 Revolutionary and Battle Site

1989. 75th Anniv of Battle of Zacatecas.
1926 **742** 450p. black 20 10

743 Catchers

1989. Baseball Professionals' Hall of Fame. Multicoloured.
1927 550p. Type **743** 20 10
1928 550p. Striker 20 10
Nos. 1927/8 were printed together, se-tenant, forming a composite design.

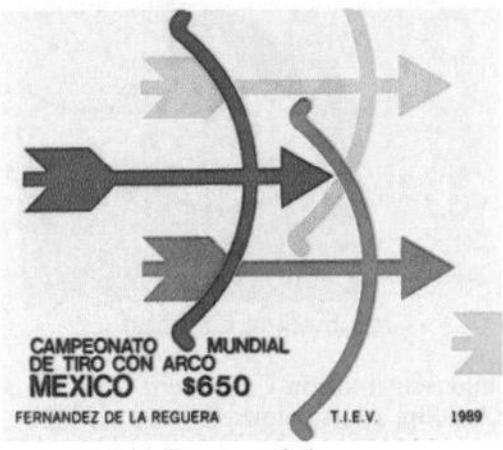

744 Bows and Arrows

1989. World Archery Championships, Switzerland. Multicoloured.
1929 650p. Type **744** 25 10
1920 650p. Arrows and target . . 25 10
Nos. 1929/30 were printed together, se-tenant, forming a composite design.

745 Arms

1989. Centenary of Tijuana.
1931 **745** 1100p. multicoloured . . 50 20

746 Storming the Bastille

1989. Bicentenary of French Revolution.
1932 **746** 1300p. multicoloured . . 60 50

747 Mina

1989. Birth Bicentenary of Francisco Xavier Mina (independence fighter).
1933 **747** 450p. multicoloured . . 20 10

748 Cave Paintings

1989. 25th Anniv of National Anthropological Museum, Chapultepec.
1934 **748** 450p. multicoloured . . 20 10

749 Runners

1989. 7th Mexico City Marathon.
1935 **749** 450p. multicoloured . . 20 10

750 Printed Page

1989. 450th Anniv of First American and Mexican Printed Work.
1936 **750** 450p. multicoloured . . 20 10

751 Posthorn and Cancellations

1989. World Post Day.
1937 **751** 1100p. multicoloured . . 50 20

752 "Aguascalientes in History" (Osvaldo Barra)

1989. 75th Anniv of Aguascalientes Revolutionary Convention.
1936 **752** 450p. multicoloured . . 20 10

753 Patterns

1989. America. Pre-Columbian Culture.
1939 450p. Type **753** 20 10
1940 450p. Traditional writing . . 20 10

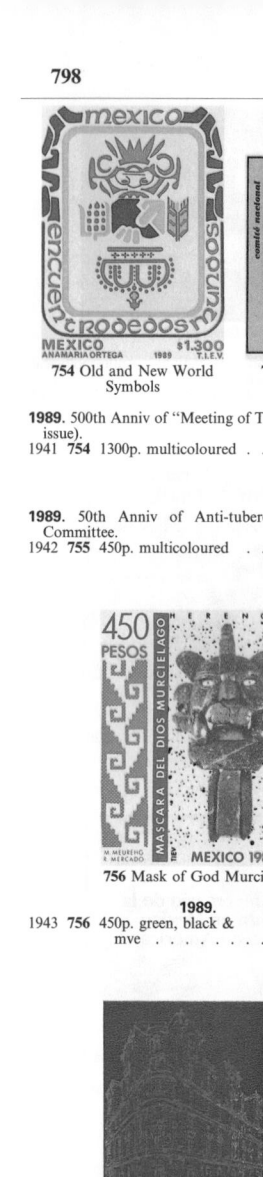

754 Old and New World Symbols

755 Cross of Lorraine

1989. 500th Anniv of "Meeting of Two Worlds" (3rd issue).
1941 **754** 1300p. multicoloured . . 60 25

1989. 50th Anniv of Anti-tuberculosis National Committee.
1942 **755** 450p. multicoloured . . 20 10

756 Mask of God Murcielago

1989.
1943 **756** 450p. green, black & mve 20 10

757 Bank

1989. 125th Anniv of Serfin Commercial Bank.
1944 **757** 450p. blue, gold and black 20 10

758 Cortines

759 Man with Sparkler

1989. Birth Centenary of Adolfo Ruiz Cortines (President, 1952–58).
1945 **758** 450p. multicoloured . . 20 10

1989. Christmas. Multicoloured.
1946 450p. Type **759** 20 10
1947 450p. People holding candles (horiz) 20 10

760 Emblem

1989. 50th Anniv of National Institute of Anthropology and History.
1948 **760** 450p. gold, red and black 20 10

761 Steam Locomotive, Diesel Train and Felipe Pescador

1989. 80th Anniv of Nationalization of Railways.
1949 **761** 450p. multicoloured . . 50 15

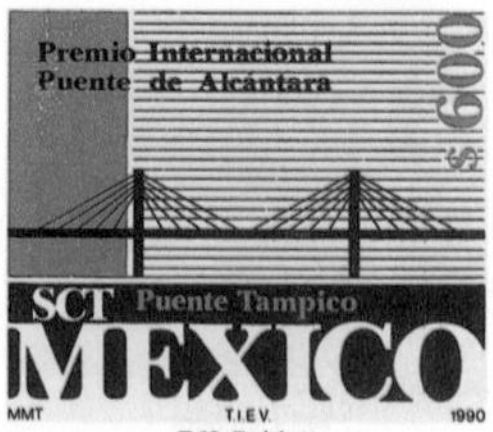

762 Bridge

1990. Opening of Tampico Bridge.
1950 **762** 600p. black, gold and red 20 10

763 Smiling Children

1990. Child Vaccination Campaign.
1951 **763** 700p. multicoloured . . 25 10

764 People in Houses

1990. 11th General Population and Housing Census.
1952 **764** 700p. green, yell & lt grn 25 10

765 Stamp under Magnifying Glass

1990. 10th Anniv of Mexican Philatelic Association.
1953 **765** 700p. multicoloured . . 25 10

766 Archive

1990. Bicentenary of National Archive.
1954 **766** 700p. blue 25 10

767 Emblem and "90"

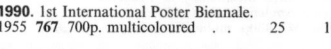

1990. 1st International Poster Biennale.
1955 **767** 700p. multicoloured . . 25 10

768 Messenger, 1790

1990. "Stamp World London 90" International Stamp Exhibition.
1956 **768** 700p. yellow, red & black 25 10

769 Penny Black

1990. 150th Anniv of the Penny Black.
1957 **769** 700p. black, red and gold 25 10

770 National Colours and Pope John Paul II

1990. Papal Visit.
1958 **770** 700p. multicoloured . . 25 10

771 Church

772 Mother and Child

1990. 15th Travel Agents' Congress.
1959 **771** 700p. multicoloured . . 25 10

1990. Mother and Child Health Campaign.
1960 **772** 700p. multicoloured . . 25 10

773 Smoke Rings forming Birds

774 Globe as Tree

1990. World Anti-Smoking Day.
1961 **773** 700p. multicoloured . . 25 10

1990. World Environment Day.
1962 **774** 700p. multicoloured . . 25 10

775 Racing Car and Chequered Flag

1990. Mexico Formula One Grand Prix.
1963 **775** 700p. black, red and green 25 10

776 Aircraft Tailfin

1990. 25th Anniv of Airports and Auxiliary Services.
1964 **776** 700p. multicoloured . . 25 10

777 Family

1990. United Nations Anti-drugs Decade.
1965 **777** 700p. multicoloured . . 25 10

778 Tree Trunk

1990. Forest Conservation.
1966 **778** 700p. multicoloured . . 25 10

779 Emblem

1990. "Solidarity".
1967 **779** 700p. multicoloured . . 25 10
See also No. 2047.

780 Columns and Native Decoration

1990. World Heritage Site. Oaxaca.
1968 **780** 700p. multicoloured . . 25 10

781 Elegant Tern

1990. Conservation of Rasa Island, Gulf of California.
1969 **781** 700p. grey, black and red 1·10 40

782 Institute Activities

1990. 25th Anniv of Mexican Petroleum Institute.
1970 **782** 700p. blue and black . . 25 10

783 National Colours, City Monuments and Runners

1990. 18th International Mexico City Marathon.
1971 **783** 700p. black, red & green 25 10

784 Facade

1990. 50th Anniv of Colima University.
1972 **784** 700p. multicoloured . . 25 10

785 Abstract

1990. Mexico City Consultative Council.
1973 **785** 700p. multicoloured . . 25 10

786 Electricity Worker

1990. 30th Anniv of Nationalization of Electricity Industry.
1974 **786** 700p. multicoloured . . 25 10

787 Violin and Bow

1990. 50th Death Anniv of Silvestre Revueltas (violinist).
1975 **787** 700p. multicoloured . . 25 10

788 Building

1990. 450th Anniv of Campeche.
1976 **788** 700p. multicoloured . . 25 15

789 Crossed Rifle and Pen 790 Emblem

1990. 80th Anniv of San Luis Plan.
1977 **789** 700p. multicoloured . . 25 15

1990. 14th World Supreme Councils Conference.
1978 **790** 1500p. multicoloured . . 55 35

791 Spanish Tower and Mexican Pyramid

1990. 500th Anniv of "Meeting of Two Worlds" (4th issue).
1979 **791** 700p. multicoloured . . 25 15

792 Glass of Beer, Ear of Barley and Hop 793 Carving

1990. Centenary of Brewing Industry.
1980 **792** 700p. multicoloured . . 25 15

1990. Bicentenary of Archaeology in Mexico.
1981 **793** 1500p. multicoloured . . 55 35

794 Ball-game Field 795 Globe and Poinsettia

1990. 16th Central American and Caribbean Games. Multicoloured.
1982 750p. Type **794** . . . . . 1·10 20
1983 750p. Amerindian ball-game player . . . . 1·10 20
1984 750p. Amerindian ball-game player (different) (horiz) 1·10 20
1985 750p. Yutsil and Balam (mascots) (horiz) . . . . 1·10 20

1990. Christmas. Multicoloured.
1986 700p. Type **795** 25 15
1987 700p. Fireworks and candles 25 15

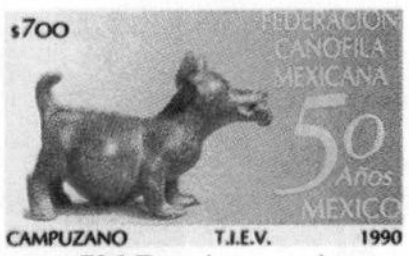

796 Dog (statuette)

1990. 50th Anniv of Mexican Canine Federation.
1988 **796** 700p. multicoloured . . 25 15

797 Microscope, Dolphin and Hand holding Map

1991. 50th Anniv of Naval Secretariat.
1989 **797** 1000p. gold, black & blue 40 25

798 Means of Transport

1991. Accident Prevention.
1990 **798** 700p. multicoloured . . 65 20

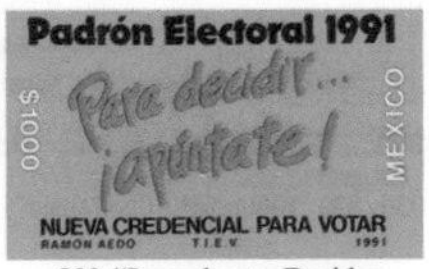

799 Products in Bags 800 "In order to Decide, Register"

1991. 15th Anniv of National Consumer Institute.
1991 **799** 1000p. multicoloured . . 40 25

1991. Electoral Register.
1992 **800** 1000p. orange, grn & blk 40 25

801 Basketball Player 802 Flowers and Caravel

1991. Olympic Games, Barcelona (1992) (1st issue).
1993 **801** 1000p. black and yellow 40 25
See also Nos. 2050, 2057 and 2080/9.

1991. America (1990). Natural World. Mult.
1994 700p. Type **802** 75 20
1995 700p. Right half of caravel, blue and yellow macaw and flowers 75 40
Nos. 1994/5 were issued together, se-tenant, forming a composite design.

803 Children in Droplet

1991. Children's Month. Vaccination Campaign.
1996 **803** 1000p. multicoloured . . 40 25

804 Map 805 Dove and Children

1991. World Post Day (1990).
1997 **804** 1500p. multicoloured . . 55 35

1991. Children's Days for Peace and Development.
1998 **805** 1000p. multicoloured . . 40 25

806 Dove 807 Mining

1991. Family Health and Unity.
1999 **806** 1000p. multicoloured . . 40 25

1991. 500th Anniv of Mining.
2000 **807** 1000p. multicoloured . . 40 25

808 Mother feeding Baby 809 Emblem

1991. Breastfeeding Campaign.
2001 **808** 1000p. buff, blue & brn 40 25

1991. 16th Tourism Fair, Acapulco.
2002 **809** 1000p. green & dp green 40 25

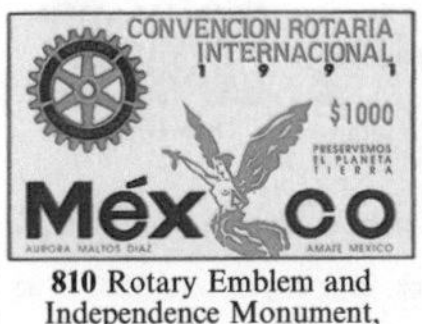

810 Rotary Emblem and Independence Monument, Mexico City 811 "Communication"

1991. Rotary International Convention. "Let us Preserve the Planet Earth".
2003 **810** 1000p. gold and blue . . 40 25

1991. Centenary of Ministry of Transport and Communications (S.C.T.). Multicoloured.

2004 1000p. Type **811** . . . . . 1·25 50
2005 1000p. Boeing 737 landing 65 25
2006 1000p. Facsimile machine 65 25
2007 1000p. Van 65 25
2008 1000p. Satellites and Earth 65 25
2009 1000p. Railway freight wagons on bridge . . . . 1·25 35
2010 1000p. Telephone users . . 65 25
2011 1000p. Road bridge over road 65 25
2012 1000p. Road bridge and cliffs 65 25
2013 1000p. Stern of container ship and dockyard . . . 1·25 35
2014 1000p. Television camera and presenter 65 25
2015 1000p. Front of truck at toll gate 65 25
2016 1000p. Roadbuilding ("Solidarity") 65 25
2017 1500p. Boeing 737 and control tower 80 35
2018 1500p. Part of fax machine, transmitters and dish aerials on S.C.T. building 80 35
2019 1500p. Satellite (horiz) . . . 80 35
2020 1500p. Diesel and electric trains . . . . 1·25 50
2021 1500p. S.C.T. building . . . 80 35
2022 1500p. Road bridge over ravine 80 35
2023 1500p. Bow of container ship and dockyard . . . 1·25 50
2024 1500p. Bus at toll gate . . . 80 35
2025 1500p. Rear of truck and trailer at toll gate 80 35

Nos. 2005/25 were issued together, se-tenant, each block containing several composite designs.

812 Jaguar

1991. Lacandona Jungle Conservation.
2026 **812** 1000p. black, orge & red 40 25

813 Driver and Car

814 Emblem and Left-hand Sections of Sun and Earth

1991. Mexico Formula 1 Grand Prix.
2027 **813** 1000p. multicoloured . . 40 25

1991. Total Eclipse of the Sun. Multicoloured.
2028 1000p. Type **814** . . . . . 1·00 25
2029 1000p. Emblem and right-hand sections of sun and Earth . . . . 1·00 25
2030 1500p. Emblem and centre of sun and Earth showing north and central America 1·50 35

Nos. 2028/30 were issued together, se-tenant, forming a composite design.

815 "Solidarity" (Rufino Tamayo)

816 Bridge

1991. 1st Latin American Presidential Summit, Guadalajara.
2031 **815** 1500p. black, orge & yell 55 35

1991. Solidarity between Nuevo Leon and Texas.
2032 **816** 2000p. multicoloured . . 1·10 75

817 Runners

819 Emblem

818 Cogwheel

1991. 9th Mexico City Marathon.
2033 **817** 1000p. multicoloured . . 40 25

1991. 50th Anniv (1990) of National Chambers of Industry and Commerce.
2034 **818** 1500p. multicoloured . . 55 35

1991. 55th Anniv of Federation Fiscal Tribunal.
2035 **819** 1000p. silver and blue . . 40 25

820 National Colours forming Emblem

1991. "Solidarity—Let us Unite in order to Progress".
2036 **820** 1000p. multicoloured . . 40 25

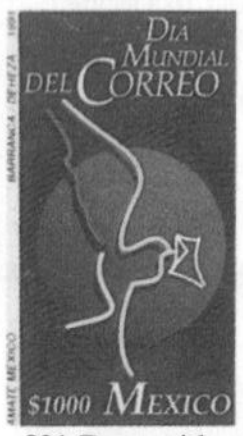

821 Dove with Letter

822 World Map

1991. World Post Day.
2037 **821** 1000p. multicoloured . . 40 25

1991. 500th Anniv of "Meeting of Two Worlds" (5th issue).
2038 **822** 1000p. multicoloured . . 95 25

823 Caravel, Sun and Trees

1991. America. Voyages of Discovery. Mult.
2039 1000p. Type **823** 75 25
2040 1000p. Storm cloud, caravel and broken snake 75 25

824 Flowers and Pots

1991. Christmas. Multicoloured.
2041 1000p. Type **824** 40 25
2042 1000p. Children with decoration 40 25

825 Abstract

1991. Carlos Merida (artist) Commemoration.
2043 **825** 1000p. multicoloured . . 40 25

826 Score and Portrait

1991. Death Bicentenary of Wolfgang Amadeus Mozart (composer).
2044 **826** 1000p. multicoloured . . 40 25

827 Kidney Beans and Maize

1991. Self-sufficiency in Kidney Beans and Maize.
2045 **827** 1000p. multicoloured . . 40 25

828 City Plan

1991. 450th Anniv of Morelia.
2046 **828** 1000p. brown, stone and red 40 25

1991. "Solidarity". As No. 1967 but new value.
2047 **779** 1000p. multicoloured . . 40 25

829 Merida

1992. 450th Anniv of Merida.
2048 **829** 1300p. multicoloured . . 60 40

830 Colonnade

1992. Bicentenary of Engineering Training in Mexico.
2049 **830** 1300p. blue and red . . 60 40

831 Horse Rider

1992. Olympic Games, Barcelona (2nd issue).
2050 **831** 2000p. multicoloured . . 90 60

832 City Arms

1992. 450th Anniv of Guadalajara. Multicoloured.
2051 1300p. Type **832** . . . . . 1·10 40
2052 1300p. "Guadalajara Town Hall" (Jorge Navarro) . . 1·10 40
2053 1300p. "Guadalajara Cathedral" (Gabriel Flores) . . . . 1·10 40
2054 1900p. "Founding of Guadalajara" (Rafael Zamarripa) . . . . 1·60 55
2055 1900p. Anniversary emblem (Ignacio Vazquez) . . . . 1·60 55

833 Children and Height Gauge

834 Olympic Torch and Rings

1992. Child Health Campaign.
2056 **833** 2000p. multicoloured . . 90 60

1992. Olympic Games, Barcelona (3rd issue).
2057 **834** 2000p. multicoloured . . 90 60

835 Horse and Racing Car

1992. "500th Anniv of the Wheel and the Horse in America". Mexico Formula 1 Grand Prix.
2058 **835** 1300p. multicoloured . . 60 40

836 Satellite and Map of Americas

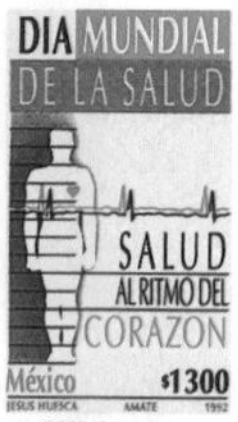

837 Human Figure and Cardiograph

1992. "Americas Telecom '92" Telecommunications Exhibition.
2059 **836** 1300p. multicoloured . . 60 40

1992. World Health Day.
2060 **837** 1300p. black, red and blue 60 40

838 Emblem

1992. 60th Anniv of Military Academy.
2061 **838** 1300p. red, yellow & blk 60 40

839 "Inspiration of Christopher Columbus" (Jose Maria Obregon)

840 Complex

1992. 500th Anniv of "Meeting of Two Worlds" (6th issue). "Granada 92" International Stamp Exhibition.
2062 1300p. Type **839** . . . . . 1·00 40
2063 1300p. "Racial Encounter" (Jorge Gonazalez Camarena) . . . . 1·00 40
2064 2000p. "Origin of the Sky" (Selden Codex) . . . . . 1·75 60
2065 2000p. "Quetzalcoatl and Tezcatlipoca" (Borhomico Codex) . . . . 1·75 60
2066 2000p. "From Spaniard and Indian, mestizo" . . . . 1·75 60

1992. National Medical Centre.
2068 **840** 1300p. multicoloured . . 60 40

841 Children, Dove and Globe

842 New-born Baby

1992. Children's Rights.

2069	**841**	1300p. multicoloured . .	60	40

1992. Traditional Childbirth.

2070	**842**	1300p. multicoloured . .	60	40

1992. "World Columbian Stamp Expo '92", Chicago. Nos. 2062/6 optd **WORLD COLUMBIAN STAMP EXPO '92 MAY 22-31, 1992 - CHICAGO** and emblem.

2071	1300p. mult (No. 2062) . .	2·00	2·00
2072	1300p. mult (No. 2063) . .	2·00	2·00
2073	2000p. mult (No. 2064) . .	5·00	5·00
2074	2000p. mult (No. 2065) . .	5·00	5·00
2075	2000p. mult (No. 2066) . .	5·00	5·00

845 Arms of Colleges

1992. Bicentenary of Mexico Notary College.

2078	**845**	1300p. multicoloured . .	50	35

846 Trees and Cacti

1992. Tree Day.

2079	**846**	1300p. multicoloured . .	50	35

847 Boxing

848 Athlete

1992. Olympic Games, Barcelona (4th issue). Mult.

2080	1300p. Type **847**	80	35
2081	1300p. High jumping . . .	80	35
2082	1300p. Fencing	80	35
2083	1300p. Shooting	80	35
2084	1300p. Gymnastics	80	35
2085	1900p. Rowing	1·60	50
2086	1900p. Running	1·60	50
2087	1900p. Football	1·60	50
2088	1900p. Swimming	1·60	50
2089	2000p. Equestrian	1·60	55

1992. 10th Mexico City Marathon.

2091	**848**	1300p. multicoloured . .	50	35

849 Emblem

1992. "Solidarity".

2092	**849**	1300p. multicoloured . .	50	35

851 Television, Map and Radio

1992. 50th Anniv of National Chamber of Television and Radio Industry.

2094	**851**	1300p. multicoloured . .	50	35

852 Letter orbiting Globe

1992. World Post Day.

2095	**852**	1300p. multicoloured . .	50	35

853 Satellite above South and Central America and Flags

1992. American Cadena Communications System.

2096	**853**	2000p. multicoloured . .	1·10	55

854 Gold Compass Rose

1992. America. 500th Anniv of Discovery of America by Columbus. Multicoloured.

2097	2000p. Type **854**	1·25	55
2098	2000p. Compass rose (different) and fish . . .	1·25	55

Nos. 2097/8 were issued together, se-tenant, forming a composite design.

855 Scroll

1992. 400th Anniv of San Luis Potosi.

2099	**855**	1300p. black and mauve	50	35

856 Berrendos Deer

1992. Conservation.

2100	**856**	1300p. multicoloured . .	50	35

857 Schooner, Landing Ship, Emblem and Sailors

858 Christmas Tree, Children and Crib

1992. Navy Day.

2101	**857**	1300p. multicoloured . .	50	35

1992. Christmas. Children's Drawings. Mult.

2102	1300p. Type **858**	50	35
2103	2000p. Street celebration (horiz)	1·25	55

Currency Reform. 1 (new) peso = 1000 (old) pesos.

859 Anniversary Emblem

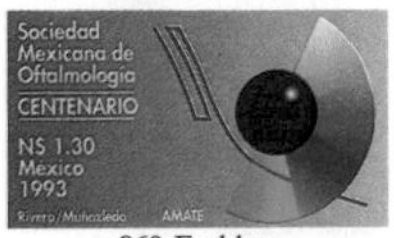
860 Emblem

1993. 50th Anniv of Mexican Social Security Institute (1st issue).

2104	**859**	1p.50 green, gold & blk	60	40

See also Nos. 2110 and 2152/3.

1993. Centenary of Mexican Ophthalmological Society.

2105	**860**	1p.30 multicoloured . .	50	35

861 Children

862 Society Arms and Founders

1993. Children's Month.

2106	**861**	1p.30 multicoloured . .	50	35

1993. 160th Anniv of Mexican Geographical and Statistical Society.

2107	**862**	1p.30 multicoloured . .	50	35

863 1824 Constitution

864 Gomez, Children and Hospital

1993. 150th Death Anniv of Miguel Ramos Arizpe, "Father of Federalism".

2108	**863**	1p.30 multicoloured . .	50	35

1993. 50th Anniv of Federico Gomez Children's Hospital.

2109	**864**	1p.30 multicoloured . .	50	35

865 Doctor with Child

1993. 50th Anniv of Mexican Social Security Institute (2nd issue). Medical Services.

2110	**865**	1p.30 multicoloured . .	50	35

866 Mother feeding Baby

1993. "Health begins at Home".

2111	**866**	1p.30 multicoloured . .	50	35

867 Seal and Map

1993. Upper Gulf of California Nature Reserve.

2112	**867**	1p.30 multicoloured . .	50	35

868 Cantinflas

1993. Mexican Film Stars. Mario Moreno (Cantinflas).

2113	**868**	1p.30 black and blue . .	50	35

See also Nos. 2156/60.

869 Campeche

1993. Tourism. Value expressed as "NS". Mult.

2114	90c. Type **869**	65	25
2115	1p. Guanajuato	70	25
2263	1p.10 As No. 2115	70	10
2116	1p.30 Colima	80	35
2264	1p.80 As No. 2124	55	20
2265	1p.80 As No. 2118	65	20
2266	1p.80 As No. 2116	55	20
2267	1p.80 As Type **869**	55	20
2117	1p.90 Michoacan (vert) . .	1·25	50
2118	2p. Coahuila	1·25	55
2269	2p. As No. 2266	90	20
2119	2p.20 Queretaro	1·60	60
2271	2p.30 As No. 2122	70	25
2272	2p.40 As No. 2123	80	25
2120	2p.50 Sonora	2·00	65
2274	2p.70 As No. 2145	1·25	25
2121	2p.80 Zacatecas (vert) . . .	2·25	75
2276	3p. Type **869**	1·40	30
2278	3p.40 As No. 2271	1·40	35
2122	3p.70 Sinaloa	3·25	1·25
2280	3p.80 As No. 2272	1·25	40
2123	4p.40 Yucatan	3·50	1·50
2124	4p.80 Chiapas	3·75	1·60
2145	6p. Mexico City	4·00	2·00
2290	6p.80 As No. 2120	2·50	90

See also Nos. 2410/29.

870 Dr. Maximiliano Ruiz Castaneda

1993. 50th Anniv of Health Service. Multicoloured.

2126	1p.30 Type **870**	50	35
2127	1p.30 Dr. Bernardo Sepulveda Gutierrez . . .	50	35
2128	1p.30 Dr. Ignacio Chavez Sanchez	50	35
2129	1p.30 Dr. Mario Salazar Mallen	50	35
2130	1p.30 Dr. Gustavo Baz Prada	50	35

871 Brazil 30r. "Bull's Eye" Stamp

872 Runners

1993. 150th Anniv of First Brazilian Stamps.

2131	**871**	2p. multicoloured . . .	80	55

1993. 11th Mexico City Marathon.

2132	**872**	1p.30 multicoloured . .	1·40	55

873 Emblem

874 Open Book and Symbols

1993. "Solidarity".

2133	**873**	1p.30 multicoloured . .	50	35

1993. 50th Anniv of Monterrey Institute of Technology and Higher Education. Multicoloured.
2134 1p.30 Type **874** 50 35
2135 2p. Buildings and mountains 80 55
Nos. 2134/5 were issued together, se-tenant, forming a composite design.

875 Cogwheels and Emblem

876 Torreon

1993. 75th Anniv of Concamin.
2136 **875** 1p.30 multicoloured . . 50 35

1993. Centenary of Torreon.
2137 **876** 1p.30 multicoloured . . 50 35

877 Emblem

1993. "Europalia 93 Mexico" Festival.
2138 **877** 2p. multicoloured . . . 80 55

878 Globe in Envelope

879 Gen. Guadalupe Victoria

1993. World Post Day.
2139 **878** 2p. multicoloured . . . 80 55

1993. 150th Death Anniv of General Manuel Guadalupe Victoria (first President, 1824–28).
2140 **879** 1p.30 multicoloured . . 50 35

880 Emblem

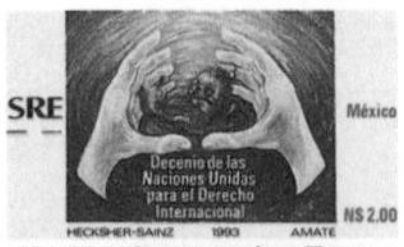
881 Hands protecting Foetus

1993. National Civil Protection System and International Day for Reduction of Natural Disasters.
2141 **880** 1p.30 red, black & yell 50 35

1993. United Nations Decade of International Law.
2142 **881** 2p. multicoloured . . . 80 55

882 Torch Carrier

1993. 20th National Wheelchair Games.
2143 **882** 1p.30 multicoloured . . 50 35

883 Peon y Contreras

1993. 150th Birth Anniv of Jose Peon y Contreras (poet, dramatist and founder of National Romantic Theatre).
2144 **883** 1p.30 violet and black 50 35

884 Horned Guan

885 Presents around Trees

1993. America. Endangered Birds. Multicoloured.
2145 2p. Type **884** . . . . . . 2·50 1·25
2146 2p. Resplendent quetzal on branch (horiz) . . . . . 2·50 1·25

1993. Christmas. Multicoloured.
2147 1p.30 Type **885** 50 35
2148 1p.30 Three wise men (horiz) 50 35

886 Satellites orbiting Earth

1993. "Solidarity".
2149 **886** 1p.30 multicoloured . . 50 35

887 School and Arms

1993. 125th Anniv of National Preparatory School.
2150 **887** 1p.30 multicoloured . . 50 35

888 Emblem on Map

1993. 55th Anniv of Municipal Workers Trade Union.
2151 **888** 1p.30 multicoloured . . 50 35

889 Hands

1993. 50th Anniv of Mexican Social Security Institute (3rd issue). Multicoloured.
2152 1p.30 Type **889** (social security) 50 35
2153 1p.30 Ball, building blocks, child's painting and dummy (day nurseries) . . 50 35

890 Mezcala Solidarity Bridge

1993. Tourism. Multicoloured.
2154 1p.30 Type **890** 50 35
2155 1p.30 Mexico City–Acapulco motorway 50 35

1993. Mexican Film Stars. As T **868**.
2156 1p.30 black and blue . . . 50 35
2157 1p.30 black and orange . . 50 35
2158 1p.30 black and green . . 50 35
2159 1p.30 black and violet . . . 50 35
2160 1p.30 black and pink . . . 50 35
DESIGNS:—No, 2156, Pedro Armendariz in "Juan Charrasqueado"; 2157, Maria Felix in "The Lover"; 2158, Pedro Infante in "Necesito dinero"; 2159, Jorge Negrete in "It is not enough to be a Peasant"; 2160, Dolores del Rio in "Flor Silvestre".

891 Estefania Castaneda Nunez

1994. 72nd Anniv of Secretariat of Public Education. Educationists. Multicoloured.
2161 1p.30 Type **891** 50 35
2162 1p.30 Lauro Aguirre Espinosa 50 35
2163 1p.30 Rafael Ramirez Castaneda 50 35
2164 1p.30 Moises Saenz Garza 50 35
2165 1p.30 Gregorio Torres Quintero 50 35
2166 1p.30 Jose Vasconcelos . . 50 35
2167 1p.30 Rosaura Zapato Cano 50 35

892 Zapata (after H. Velarde)

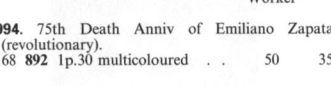

893 Emblem and Worker

1994. 75th Death Anniv of Emiliano Zapata (revolutionary).
2168 **892** 1p.30 multicoloured . . 50 35

1994. 75th Anniv of I.L.O.
2169 **893** 2p. multicoloured . . . 80 50

894 Map and Emblem

895 "Earth and Communication" (frieze, detail)

1994. 50th Anniv of National Schools Building Programme Committee.
2170 **894** 1p.30 multicoloured . . 50 35

1994. 3rd Death Anniv of Francisco Zuniga (sculptor).
2171 **895** 1p.30 multicoloured . . 50 35

896 Flower and Children

1994. Children's Organization for Peace and Development.
2172 **896** 1p.30 multicoloured . . 50 35

897 Greater Flamingo

1994. DUMAC Nature Protection Organization.
2173 **897** 1p.30 multicoloured . . 1·50 85

898 Children and Silhouette of Absentee

1994. Care and Control of Minors.
2174 **898** 1p.30 black and green 50 35

899 Man and Letters

900 Route Map

1994. 34th World Advertising Congress, Cancun.
2175 **899** 2p. multicoloured . . . 80 35

1994. 50th Anniv of National Association of Importers and Exporters.
2176 **900** 1p.30 multicoloured . . 50 35

901 Head and Emblem

1994. International Telecommunications Day.
2177 **901** 2p. multicoloured . . . 80 55

902 Animals

1994. Yumka Wildlife Centre, Villahermosa.
2178 **902** 1p.30 multicoloured . . 1·25 85

903 Town Centre

904 Mother and Baby

1994. UNESCO World Heritage Site, Zacatecas.
2179 **903** 1p.30 multicoloured . . 50 35

1994. Friendship Hospital. Mother and Child Health Month.
2180 **904** 1p.30 multicoloured . . 55 45

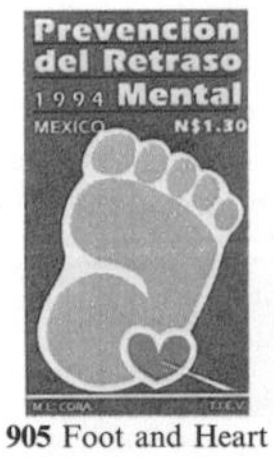
905 Foot and Heart

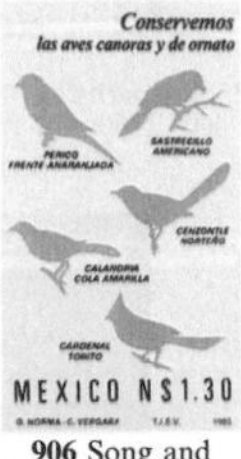
906 Song and Ornamental Birds

1994. Prevention of Mental Retardation.
2181 **905** 1p.30 multicoloured . . 55 45

1994. Nature Conservation. Multicoloured.

2182 1p.30 Type **906** . . . . . 1·25 85
2183 1p.30 Game birds (silhouettes) . . . . . . 1·25 85
2184 1p.30 Threatened animals (silhouettes) . . . . . . 1·25 85
2185 1p.30 Animals in danger of extinction (silhouettes) . . 1·25 85
2186 1p.30 Orange-fronted conures . . . . 1·25 85
2187 1p.30 Yellow-tailed oriole 1·25 85
2188 1p.30 Pyrrhuloxias . . . . 1·25 85
2189 1p.30 Loggerhead shrike . . 1·25 85
2190 1p.30 Northern mockingbird 1·25 85
2191 1p.30 Common turkey . . . 1·25 85
2192 1p.30 White-winged dove . . 1·25 85
2193 1p.30 Red-billed whistling duck . . . . 1·25 85
2194 1p.30 Snow goose . . . . . 1·25 85
2195 1p.30 Gambel's quail . . . 1·25 85
2196 1p.30 Peregrine falcon . . . 1·25 85
2197 1p.30 Jaguar 80 50
2198 1p.30 Jaguarundi 80 50
2199 1p.30 Mantled howler monkey 80 50
2200 1p.30 Californian sealions 80 50
2201 1p.30 Pronghorn 80 50
2202 1p.30 Scarlet macaw . . . . 1·25 85
2203 1p.30 Mexican prairie dogs 80 50
2204 1p.30 Wolf 80 50
2205 1p.30 American manatee . . 80 50

907 Player

908 Fish

1994. World Cup Football Championship, U.S.A. Multicoloured.

2206 2p. Type **907** . . . . . . 1·00 70
2207 2p. Goalkeeper . . . . . . 1·00 70

Nos. 2206/7 were issued together, se-tenant, forming a composite design.

1994. International Fishing Festival, Veracruz.

2208 **908** 1p.30 multicoloured . . 55 45

909 Stylized Figure and Emblem

910 "Butterflies" (Carmen Parra)

1994. 25th Anniv of Juvenile Integration Centres.

2209 **909** 1p.30 multicoloured . . 55 45

1994. 50th Anniv of Diplomatic Relations with Canada.

2210 **910** 2p. multicoloured . . . 90 65

911 Emblems

912 Emblem and Family

1994. 20th Anniv of National Population Council.

2211 **911** 1p.30 multicoloured . . 55 45

1994. International Year of the Family.

2212 **912** 2p. multicoloured . . . 90 60

913 Runner breasting Tape

914 Giant Panda

1994. 12th Mexico City International Marathon.

2213 **913** 1p.30 multicoloured . . 55 45

1994. Chapultepec Zoo.

2214 **914** 1p.30 multicoloured . . 80 45

915 Tree

916 Anniversary Emblem

1994. Tree Day.

2215 **915** 1p.30 brown and green 55 45

1994. 60th Anniv of Economic Culture Fund.

2216 **916** 1p.30 multicoloured . . 55 45

917 Statue and Light Rail Transit Train

918 Cathedral and Gardens

1994. 25th Anniv of Mexico City Transport System.

2217 **917** 1p.30 multicoloured . . 65 45

1994. 350th Anniv of Salvatierra City, Guanajuato.

2218 **918** 1p.30 purple, grey and black 55 45

919 State Flag and National Anthem

1994. National Symbols Week.

2219 **919** 1p.30 multicoloured . . 55 45

920 Building and Anniversary Emblem

921 Figures with Flags

1994. 40th Anniv of University City.

2220 **920** 1p.30 multicoloured . . 55 45

1994. 5th Solidarity Week.

2221 **921** 1p.30 black, red and green 55 45

922 Lopez Mateos

923 Palace Facade

1994. 25th Death Anniv of Adolfo Lopez Mateos (President, 1958–64).

2222 **922** 1p.30 multicoloured . . 55 45

1994. 60th Anniv of Palace of Fine Arts.

2223 **923** 1p.30 black and grey . . 55 45

924 Rings and "100"

1994. Centenary of International Olympic Committee.

2224 **924** 2p. multicoloured . . . 90 60

925 Quarter Horse (Juan Rayas)

1994. Horses. Paintings by artists named. Multicoloured.

2225 1p.30 Aztec horse (Heladio Velarde) 80 45
2226 1p.30 Type **925** 80 45
2227 1p.30 Quarter horse (Rayas) (different) 80 45
2228 1p.30 Vaquero on horseback (Velarde) 80 45
2229 1p.30 Aztec horse (Velarde) 80 45
2230 1p.30 Rider with lance (Velarde) 80 45

926 Emblem

927 Saint-Exupery and The Little Prince (book character)

1994. Inauguration of 20 November National Medical Centre.

2231 **926** 1p.30 multicoloured . . 55 45

1994. 50th Death Anniv of Antoine de Saint-Exupery (pilot and writer).

2232 **927** 2p. multicoloured . . . 90 60

928 Man writing Letters to Woman

929 Urban Postman on Bicycle

1994. World Post Day.

2233 **928** 2p. multicoloured . . . 90 60

1994. America. Postal Transport. Multicoloured.

2234 2p. Type **929** 85 50
2235 2p. Rural postman on rail tricycle . . . . 1·40 75

Nos. 2234/5 were issued together, se-tenant, forming a composite design.

930 Couple (Sofia Bassi)

1994. Ancestors' Day.

2236 **930** 1p.30 multicoloured . . 55 45

931 Water Drop and Hand

932 Dr. Mora

1994. National Clean Water Programme.

2237 **931** 1p.30 multicoloured . . 55 45

1994. Birth Bicentenary of Dr. Jose Maria Luis Mora (journalist and politician).

2238 **932** 1p.30 multicoloured . . 55 45

933 Theatre and Soler (actor)

1994. 15th Anniv of Fernando Soler Theatre, Saltillo, Coahuila.

2239 **933** 1p.30 multicoloured . . 55 45

934 Allegory of Flight

935 Museum's Central Pillar

1994. 50th Anniv of I.C.A.O.

2240 **934** 2p. multicoloured . . . 1·10 60

1994. 30th Anniv of National Anthropological Museum.

2241 **935** 1p.30 multicoloured . . 55 45

936 Theatrical Masks

937 Allende

1994. 60th Anniv of National Association of Actors.

2242 **936** 1p.30 multicoloured . . 55 45

1994. 225th Birth Anniv of Ignacio Allende (independence hero).

2243 **937** 1p.30 multicoloured . . 55 45

938 Chapultepec Castle

1994. 50th Anniv of National History Museum.

2244 **938** 1p.30 multicoloured . . 55 45

939 Dome

940 Anniversary Emblem

1994. Centenary of Coahuila School.

2245 **939** 1p.30 multicoloured . . 55 45

1994. 40th Anniv of Pumas University Football Club.

2246 **940** 1p.30 blue and gold . . 55 45

941 Decorated Tree

942 Valley

1994. Christmas. Multicoloured.

2247 2p. Type **941** 80 60
2248 2p. Couple watching shooting star (horiz) . . . 80 60

1994. "Solidarity". Chalco Valley.
2249 **942** 1p.30 multicoloured . . 20 15

943 Ines de la Cruz (after Miguel de Cabrera)
944 X-Ray of Hand and Rontgen

1995. 300th Birth Anniv of Juana Ines de la Cruz (mystic poet).
2250 **943** 1p.80 multicoloured . . 30 20

1995. Centenary of Discovery of X-Rays by Wilhelm Rontgen.
2251 **944** 2p. multicoloured . . . 35 25

945 Ignacio Altamirano
946 Emblem

1995. Teachers' Day.
2252 **945** 1p.80 black, green & bl 30 20

1995. World Telecommunications Day. "Telecommunications and the Environment".
2253 **946** 2p.70 multicoloured . . 70 55

947 Anniversary Emblem
948 Marti

1995. 40th Anniv of National Institute of Public Administration.
2254 **947** 1p.80 green, mve & lilac 30 20

1995. Death Centenary of Jose Marti (Cuban writer and revolutionary).
2255 **948** 2p.70 multicoloured . . 70 55

949 Carranza
950 Kite

1995. 75th Death Anniv of Venustiano Carranza (President 1914–20).
2256 **949** 1p.80 multicoloured . . 30 20

1995. 20th Anniv of National Tourist Organization.
2257 **950** 2p.70 multicoloured . . 70 55

951 Drugs, Skull and Unhappy Face
952 Cardenas del Rio

1995. International Day against Drug Abuse and Trafficking. Multicoloured.
2258 1p.80 Type **951** 85 20
2259 1p.80 Drug addict on swing 85 20
2260 1p.80 Faces behind bars . . 85 20

1995. Birth Centenary of Gen. Lazaro Cardenas del Rio (President 1934–40).
2261 **952** 1p.80 black 30 20

953 Man with White Stick and Hand reading Braille

1995. 125th Anniv of National Blind School. Mult.
2262 **953** 1p.30 brown and black 20 15

954 Northern Pintails

1995. Animals. Multicoloured.
2295 2p.70 Type **954** 90 50
2296 2p.70 Belted kingfisher . . . 90 50
2297 2p.70 Orange tiger 90 50
2298 2p.70 Hoary bat 90 50

955 Runners
956 Envelopes

1995. 13th International Marathon, Mexico City.
2299 **955** 2p.70 multicoloured . . 40 25

1995. 16th Congress of Postal Union of the Americas, Spain and Portugal, Mexico City.
2300 **956** 2p.70 multicoloured . . 40 25

957 Pasteur
958 Hands holding Envelopes

1995. Death Centenary of Louis Pasteur (chemist).
2301 **957** 2p.70 blue, black and green 40 25

1995. World Post Day.
2302 **958** 2p.70 multicoloured . . 40 25

959 Basket of Shopping
960 Anniversary Emblem

1995. World Food Day.
2303 **959** 1p.80 multicoloured . . 30 20

1995. 50th Anniv of F.A.O.
2304 **960** 2p.70 multicoloured . . 40 25

961 Elias Calles
962 Cuauhtemoc

1995. 50th Death Anniv of General Plutarco Elias Calles (President 1924–28).
2305 **961** 1p.80 multicoloured . . 30 20

1995. 500th Birth Anniv of Cuauhtemoc (Aztec Emperor of Tenochtitlan).
2306 **962** 1p.80 multicoloured . . 30 20

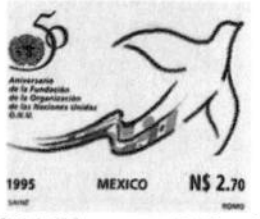

963 National Flag, National Anthem and Constitution
964 Flags as Tail of Dove

1995. National Constitution and Patriotic Symbols Day.
2307 **963** 1p.80 multicoloured . . 30 20

1995. 50th Anniv of U.N.O.
2308 **964** 2p.70 multicoloured . . 40 25

965 Airplane, Streamlined Train and Motor Vehicle

1995. International Passenger Travel Year.
2309 **965** 2p.70 multicoloured . . 80 25

966 "The Holy Family" (Andres de Concha)

1995. 30th Anniv of Museum of Mexican Art in the Vice-regency Period.
2310 **966** 1p.80 multicoloured . . 30 20

967 Pedro Maria Anaya

1995. Generals in Mexican History. Each black, yellow and gold.
2311 1p.80 Type **967** 30 20
2312 1p.80 Felipe Berriozabal . . 30 20
2313 1p.80 Santos Degollado . . 30 20
2314 1p.80 Sostenes Rocha . . . 30 20
2315 1p.80 Leandro Valle 30 20
2316 1p.80 Ignacio Zaragoza . . 30 20

968 Children playing in Garden (Pablo Osorio Gomez)
969 Emblem

1995. Christmas. Children's Drawings. Multicoloured.
2317 1p.80 Type **968** 30 20
2318 2p.70 Adoration of the Wise Men (Oscar Enrique Carrillo) 40 25

1995. 10th Anniv of Mexican Health Foundation.
2319 **969** 1p.80 multicoloured . . 30 20

970 Ocelot
971 Louis Lumiere and Cine-camera

1995. Nature Conservation.
2320 **970** 1p.80 multicoloured . . 30 20

1995. Centenary of Motion Pictures.
2321 **971** 1p.80 black, mauve and blue 30 20

972 Library

1995. National Education Library, Mexico City.
2322 **972** 1p.80 green, blue and yellow 30 20

973 "Proportions of Man" (Leonardo da Vinci)
974 Pedro Vargas

1995. 50th Anniv of National Science and Arts Prize.
2323 **973** 1p.80 multicoloured . . 30 20

1995. Radio Personalities. Multicoloured.
2324 1p.80 Type **974** 85 20
2325 1p.80 Agustin Lara 85 20
2326 1p.80 Aguila Sisters 85 20
2327 1p.80 Tona "La Negra" . . 85 20
2328 1p.80 F. Gabilondo Soler "Cri-Cri" 85 20
2329 1p.80 Emilio Teuro 85 20
2330 1p.80 Gonzalo Curiel . . . 85 20
2331 1p.80 Lola Beltran 85 20

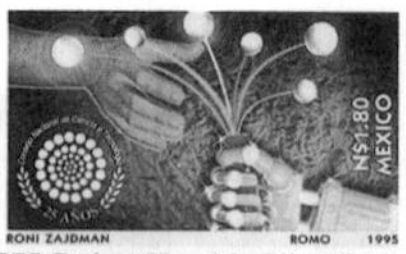

975 Robot Hand holding Optic Fibres

1995. 25th Anniv of Science and Technology Council.
2332 **975** 1p.80 multicoloured . . 30 20

976 Airplane

1996. National Aviation Day. Multicoloured.
2333 1p.80 Type **976** 70 20
2334 1p.80 Squadron 201, 1945 70 20
2335 2p.70 Ley Airport 90 25
2336 2p.70 Modern jetliner and biplane 90 25

977 Child and Caso

1996. Birth Centenary of Dr. Alfonso Caso (anthropologist).
2337 **977** 1p.80 multicoloured . . 30 20

978 Silverio Perez, Carlos Arruza and Manolo Martinez

1996. 50th Anniv of Plaza Mexico (bullring). Matadors. Multicoloured.
2338 1p.80 Type **978** 30 20
2339 2p.70 Roldolfo Gaona, Fermin Espinosa and Lorenzo Garza 40 25

Nos. 2338/9 were issued together, se-tenant, forming a composite design of the bullring.

979 Bag of Groceries

1996. 20th Anniv of Federal Consumer Council.
2340 **979** 1p.80 multicoloured . . 30 20

980 "Treatment of Fracture" (from Sahagun Codex)

1996. 50th Anniv of Mexican Society of Orthopaedics.
2341 **980** 1p.80 multicoloured . . 30 20

981 Rulfo

1996. 10th Death Anniv of Juan Rulfo (writer).
2342 **981** 1p.80 multicoloured . . 30 20

982 Anniversary Emblem and Map of Mexico

983 Healthy Hand reaching for Sick Hand

1996. 60th Anniv of National Polytechnic Institute.
2343 **982** 1p.80 grey, black and red 30 20

1996. United Nations Decade against the Abuse and Illicit Trafficking of Drugs. Multicoloured.
2344 1p.80 Type **983** 60 15
2345 1p.80 Man helping addict out of dark hole 60 15
2346 2p.70 Stylized figures . . . 90 25

984 Gymnastics

985 Cameraman and Film Frames of Couples

1996. Olympic Games, Atlanta, U.S.A. Multicoloured.
2347 1p.80 Type **984** 45 15
2348 1p.80 Hurdling 45 15
2349 2p.70 Football 65 25
2350 2p.70 Running 65 25
2351 2p.70 Show jumping 65 25

1996. Centenary of Mexican Films. Multicoloured.
2352 1p.80 Type **985** 25 15
2353 1p.80 Camera and film frames of individuals . . 25 15

986 Scales

1996. 60th Anniv of Fiscal Tribunal.
2354 **986** 1p.80 multicoloured . . 25 15

987 Runners' Feet

1996. 14th Mexico City International Marathon.
2355 **987** 2p.70 multicoloured . . 40 25

988 Flask, Open Books, Atomic Model and Microscope

1996. Science.
2356 **988** 1p.80 multicoloured . . 25 15

989 "Allegory of Foundation of Zacatecas" (anon)

1996. 450th Anniv of Zacatecas.
2357 **989** 1p.80 multicoloured . . 25 15

990 Rural Education

992 Emblem

1996. 25th Anniv of National Council for the Improvement of Education.
2358 **990** 1p.80 multicoloured . . 25 15

1996. Family Planning Month.
2360 **992** 1p.80 green, mauve and blue 25 15

993 Flag of the "Three Guarantees", 1821

1996. 175th Anniv of Declaration of Independence.
2361 **993** 1p.80 multicoloured . . 25 15

994 Blue Morpho, Monkey, Harpy Eagle and other Birds

1996. Nature Conservation. Multicoloured.
2362 1p.80 Type **994** 55 15
2363 1p.80 Turtle dove, yellow grosbeak with chicks in nest, trogon and hummingbird 55 15
2364 1p.80 Mountains, monarchs (butterflies) in air and American black bear with cub 55 15
2365 1p.80 Fishing buzzard, mule deer, lupins and monarchs (butterflies) on plant . . . 55 15
2366 1p.80 Scarlet macaws, monarchs, toucan, peafowl and spider monkey hanging from tree 55 15
2367 1p.80 Resplendent quetzal, emerald toucanet, bromeliads and tiger-cat 55 15
2368 1p.80 Parrots, white-tailed deer and rabbit by river 55 15
2369 1p.80 Snake, wolf, puma and lizard on rock and blue-capped bird 55 15
2370 1p.80 Coyote, prairie dogs at burrow, quail on branch, deer, horned viper and caracara on cactus . . 55 15
2371 1p.80 Jaguar, euphonias, long-tailed bird, crested bird and bat 55 15
2372 1p.80 "Martucha", peacock, porcupine, butterfly and green snake 55 15
2373 1p.80 Blue magpie, green-headed bird, owl, woodpecker and hummingbird by river . . 55 15
2374 1p.80 Cinnamon cuckoo in tree, fox by river and green macaws in tree . . 55 15
2375 1p.80 Wild sheep by rocks, bird on ocotillo plant, bats, owl, lynx and woodpecker on cactus . . 55 15
2376 1p.80 Ant-eater climbing sloping tree, jaguarundi, bat, orchid and ocellated turkey in undergrowth . . 55 15
2377 1p.80 Ocelot, "grison", coral snake, "temazate", paca and otter by river 55 15
2378 1p.80 Grey squirrel in tree, salamander, beaver, bird, shrew-mole, mountain hen and racoon by river . . . 55 15
2379 1p.80 Butterfly, trogon in red tree, "chachalaca", crested magpie and "tejon" 55 15
2380 1p.80 Bat, "tlalcoyote", "rata neotoma", "chichimoco", hare, cardinal (bird), lizard, kangaroo rat and tortoise 55 15
2381 1p.80 Beetle on leaf, tapir, tree frog and "tunpache" 55 15
2382 1p.80 Crocodile, insect, cup fungus, boa constrictor and butterfly 55 15
2383 1p.80 Armadillo, "tlacuache", iguana, turkey and butterfly . . . 55 15
2384 1p.80 Turkey, collared peccary, zorilla, lizard, rattlesnake and mouse . . 55 15
2385 1p.80 Cacomistle, "matraca", lark, collared lizard and cacti 55 15

Nos. 2362/85 were issued together, se-tenant, forming a composite design of habitats and wildlife under threat.

995 Bird with Letter in Beak

996 Institute

1996. World Post Day.
2386 **995** 2p.70 multicoloured . . 40 25

1996. 50th Anniv of Salvador Zubiran National Nutrition Institute.
2387 **996** 1p.80 multicoloured . . 25 15

997 Constantino de Tarnava

998 "Portrait of a Woman" (Baltasar de Echave Ibia)

1996. 75th Anniv of Radio Broadcasting in Mexico.
2388 **997** 1p.80 multicoloured . . 25 15

1996. Virreinal Art Gallery. Multicoloured.
2389 1p.80 Type **998** 50 15
2390 1p.80 "Portrait of the Child Joaquin Manuel Fernandez de Santa Cruz" (Nicolas Rodriguez Xuarez) 50 15
2391 1p.80 "Portrait of Dona Maria Luisa Gonzaga Foncerrada y Labarrieta" (Jose Maria Vazquez) . . 50 15
2392 1p.80 "Archangel Michael" (Luis Juarez) 50 15
2393 2p.70 "Virgin of the Apocalypse" (Miguel Cabrera) 65 25

999 Isidro Fabela and Genaro Estrada

1000 Maize

1996. "Precursors of Foreign Policy".
2394 **999** 1p.80 multicoloured . . 25 15

1996. World Food Day.
2395 **1000** 2p.70 multicoloured . . 40 25

1001 Underground Train around Globe

1996. International Metros Conference.
2396 **1001** 2p.70 multicoloured . . 40 25

1002 Star (Elias Martin del Campo)

1996. Christmas. Multicoloured.
2397 1p. Type **1002** 15 10
2398 1p.80 Man with star-shaped bundles on stick (Ehecatl Cabrera Franco) (vert) . . 25 15

1003 Henestrosa

1996. Andres Henestrosa (writer) Commemoration.
2399 **1003** 1p.80 multicoloured . . 25 15

1004 Old and New Institute Buildings

1005 Emblem

1996. 50th Anniv of National Cancer Institute.
2400 **1004** 1p.80 multicoloured . . 25 15

1996. Paisano Programme.
2401 **1005** 2p.70 multicoloured . . 40 25

1006 Painting

1996. Birth Centenary of David Alfaro Siqueiros (painter).
2402 **1006** 1p.80 multicoloured . . 25 15

1007 Dr. Jose Maria Barcelo de Villagran

1996. 32nd National Assembly of Surgeons.
2403 **1007** 1p.80 multicoloured . . 25 15

1008 Black Bears

1996. Nature Conservation.
2404 **1008** 1p.80 multicoloured . . 25 15

1009 Smiling Sun

1010 Library

1996. 50th Anniv of UNICEF.
2405 **1009** 1p.80 multicoloured . . 25 15

1996. 350th Anniv of Palafoxiana Library, Puebla.
2406 **1010** 1p.80 multicoloured . . 25 15

1011 Sphere and Atomic Symbol

1012 Sun's Rays and Earth

1996. National Institute for Nuclear Research.
2407 **1011** 1p.80 multicoloured . . 25 15

1996. World Day for the Preservation of the Ozone Layer.
2408 **1012** 1p.80 multicoloured . . 25 15

1013 Sculpture

1014 Pellicer (after D. Rivera)

1996. 30 Years of Work by Sebastian (sculptor).
2409 **1013** 1p.80 multicoloured . . 25 15

1997. Tourism. As Nos. 2263 etc but with value expressed as "$".

2410	1p. Colima	15	10
2411	1p.80 Chiapas	25	15
2412	2p. Colima	30	20
2413	2p. Guanajuato	30	20
2413a	2p. Coahiula	30	20
2414	2p.30 Chiapas	35	25
2415	2p.50 Quretaro	35	25
2415a	2p.50 Yucatan	35	25
2416	2p.60 Colima	40	25
2417	2p.70 Mexico City	40	25
2418	3p. Type **869**	45	30
2419	3p.10 Coahuila	45	30
2420	3p.40 Sinaloa	50	35
2421	3p.50 Mexico City	50	35
2421a	3p.60 Sonora	50	35
2421b	3p.60 Coahuila	50	35
2421c	3p.70 Campeche	50	35
2422	4p. Michoacan (vert)	60	40
2422a	4p.20 Guanajuato	55	35
2423	4p.40 Yucatan	65	45
2424	4p.90 Sonora	70	45
2425	5p. Queretaro	70	45
2426	5p. Colima	65	45
2426a	5p.30 Michoacan (vert)	70	45
2426b	5p.90 Queretaro	80	55
2427	6p. Zacatacas (vert)	85	55
2427a	6p. Sinaloa	85	55
2427b	6p.50 Sinaloa	85	50
2428	7p. Sonora	1·00	65
2428a	8p. Zacatecas (vert)	1·10	75
2429	8p.50 Mexico City	1·25	85
2433	10p. Campeche	1·40	1·10

1997. Birth Centenary of Carlos Pellicer (lyricist).
2435 **1014** 2p.30 multicoloured . . 35 25

1015 Eloy Blanco (after Oswaldo)

1997. Birth Centenary (1996) of Andres Eloy Blanco (poet).
2436 **1015** 3p.40 multicoloured . . 50 35

1016 Book, Inkwell and Pencil

1017 Tree, Globe and Atomic Cloud

1997. Confederation of American Educationalists' International Summit Conference.
2437 **1016** 3p.40 multicoloured . . 50 35

1997. 30th Anniv of Tlatelolco Treaty (Latin American and Caribbean treaty banning nuclear weapons).
2438 **1017** 3p.40 multicoloured . . 50 35

1019 Felipe Angeles

1020 Woman dancing

1997. Noted Generals. Multicoloured.

2440	2p.30 Type **1019**	35	25
2441	2p.30 Joaquin Amaro Dominguez	35	25
2442	2p.30 Mariano Escobedo	35	25
2443	2p.30 Jacinto Trevino Glez	35	25
2444	2p.30 Candido Aguilar Vargas	35	25
2445	2p.30 Francisco Urquizo	35	25

1997. International Women's Day.
2446 **1020** 2p.30 multicoloured . . 35 25

1021 "Grammar" (Juan Correa)

1997. 1st International Spanish Language Congress.
2447 **1021** 3p.40 multicoloured . . 50 35

1022 Chavez

1997. Birth Centenary of Dr. Ignacio Chavez.
2448 **1022** 2p.30 multicoloured . . 35 25

1023 State Emblem and Venustiano Carranza (President 1915–20)

1997. 80th Anniv of 1917 Constitution.
2449 **1023** 2p.30 multicoloured . . 35 25

1024 Yanez

1997. 50th Anniv of First Edition of "At the Water's Edge" by Agustin Yanez.
2450 **1024** 2p.30 multicoloured . . 35 25

1025 Mexican Mythological Figures (Luis Nishizawa)

1997. Centenary of Japanese Immigration.
2451 **1025** 3p.40 red, gold and black 50 35

1026 Rafael Ramirez

1027 University

1997. Teachers' Day.
2452 **1026** 2p.30 green and black 35 25

1997. 40th Anniv of Autonomous University of Lower California.
2453 **1027** 2p.30 multicoloured . . 35 25

1028 Dove flying Free

1029 Freud

1997. International Day against Illegal Use and Illicit Trafficking of Drugs. Multicoloured.

2454	2p.30 Type **1028**	35	25
2455	3p.40 Dove imprisoned behind bars	50	35
2456	3p.40 Man opening cage	50	35

Nos. 2454/6 were issued together, se-tenant, forming a composite design.

1997. 58th Death Anniv of Sigmund Freud (pioneer of psychoanalysis).
2457 **1029** 2p.30 blue, green and violet 35 25

1030 School Arms

1031 Emblem

1997. Centenary of Naval School.
2458 **1030** 2p.30 multicoloured . . 35 25

1997. Introduction of New Social Security Law.
2459 **1031** 2p.30 multicoloured . . 30 20

1032 Globes and Anniversary Emblem

1997. 60th Anniv of National Bank of Foreign Commerce.
2460 **1032** 3p.40 multicoloured . . 40 25

1033 Common Porpoises

1997. Nature Conservation.
2461 **1033** 2p.30 multicoloured . . 30 20

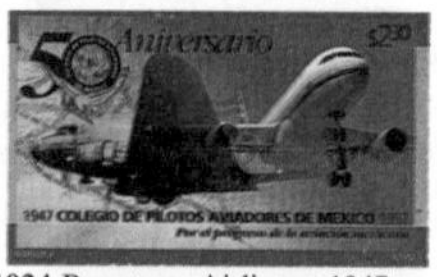
1034 Passenger Airliners, 1947 and 1997

1997. 50th Anniv of Mexican Air Pilots' College.
2462 **1034** 2p.30 multicoloured . . 30 20

1035 Runners

1997. 15th Mexico City Marathon.
2463 **1035** 3p.40 multicoloured . . 40 25

1036 Hospital Entrance

1997. 150th Anniv of Juarez Hospital.
2464 **1036** 2p.30 multicoloured . . 30 20

1037 Battle of Padierna

1997. 150th Anniversaries of Battles. Multicoloured.

2465	2p.30 Type **1037**	30	20
2466	2p.30 Battle of Churubusco	30	20
2467	2p.30 Battle of Molino del Rey	30	20
2468	2p.30 Defence of Chapultepec Fort	30	20

1038 Prieto

1039 Commemorative Cross

1997. Death Centenary of Guillermo Prieto (writer).
2469 **1038** 2p.30 blue 30 20

1997. 150th Anniv of Mexican St. Patrick's Battalion.
2470 **1039** 3p.40 multicoloured . . 40 25

1040 Emblem

1041 Bird carrying Letter

1997. Adolescent Reproductive Health Month.
2471 **1040** 2p.30 multicoloured . . 30 20

1997. World Post Day. Multicoloured.
2472 3p.40 Type **1041** 40 25
2473 3p.40 Heinrich von Stephan (founder of U.P.U.) (horiz) 40 25

1042 Gomez Morin

1043 Hospital

1997. Birth Centenary of Manuel Gomez Morin (politician).
2474 **1042** 2p.30 multicoloured . . 30 20

1997. 50th Anniv of Dr. Manuel Gea Gonzalez General Hospital.
2475 **1043** 2p.30 multicoloured . . 30 20

1044 Emblem

1045 Children celebrating Christmas (Ana Botello)

1997. 75th Anniv of Mexican Bar College of Law.
2476 **1044** 2p.30 red and black . . 30 20

1997. Christmas. Children's Paintings. Multicoloured.
2477 2p.30 Type **1045** 30 20
2478 2p.30 Children playing blind-man's-buff (Adrian Laris) 30 20

1046 Emblem and Hospital Facade

1997. Centenary of Central University Hospital, Chihuahua.
2479 **1046** 2p.30 multicoloured . . 30 20

1047 Molina and Nobel Medal

1997. Dr. Mario Molina (winner of Nobel Prize for Chemistry, 1995).
2480 **1047** 3p.40 multicoloured . . 40 25

1048 Products and Storage Shelves

1049 "Buildings" (Jose Chavez Morado)

1997. National Chamber of Baking Industry. Multicoloured.
2481 2p.30 Type **1048** 30 20
2482 2p.30 Baker putting loaves in oven 30 20
2483 2p.30 Wedding cake, ingredients and baker . . 30 20
Nos. 2481/3 were issued together, se-tenant, forming a composite design.

1997. 25th Cervantes Festival, Guanajuato.
2484 **1049** 2p.30 multicoloured . . 30 20

1050 Galleon and Map of Loreto, California

1051 Sword and Rifle

1997. 300th Anniv of Loreto.
2485 **1050** 2p.30 multicoloured . . 30 20

1998. 50th Anniv of Military Academy, Puebla.
2486 **1051** 2p.30 multicoloured . . 30 20

1052 Hands holding Children on Heart

1053 Dancers (5th of May Festival)

1998. International Women's Day.
2487 **1052** 2p.30 multicoloured . . 30 20

1998. Festivals.
2488 **1053** 3p.50 multicoloured . . 45 30

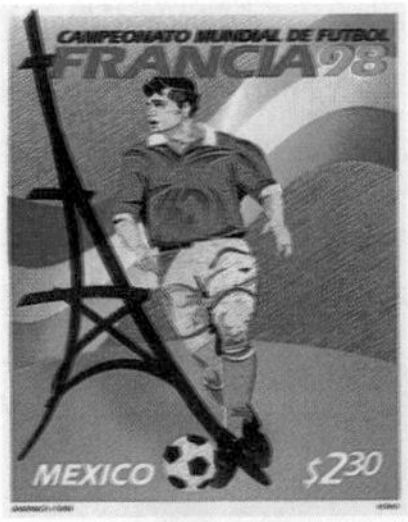

1054 Eiffel Tower, Player and Flag

1055 Sierra

1998. World Cup Football Championship, France. Multicoloured.
2489 2p.30 Type **1054** 30 20
2490 2p.30 Mascot, Eiffel Tower and flag 30 20

1998. 150th Birth Anniv of Justo Sierra (educationist).
2492 **1055** 2p.30 multicoloured . . 30 20

1056 Zubiran

1998. Birth Centenary of Salvador Zubiran (physician).
2493 **1056** 2p.30 multicoloured . . 30 20

1057 Emblem

1998. 50th Anniv of Organization of American States.
2494 **1057** 3p.40 multicoloured . . 40 25

1058 University Emblem

1059 Soledad Anaya Solorzano

1998. 25th Anniv of People's Autonomous University of Puebla State.
2495 **1058** 2p.30 red, silver and black 30 20

1998. Teachers' Day.
2496 **1059** 2p.30 bistre, black and cream 30 20

1060 Crops

1998. 250th Anniv of Tamaulipas (formerly New Santander) (1st issue).
2497 **1060** 2p.30 multicoloured . . 30 20
See also Nos. 2548.

1061 Macuilxochitl

1998. 20th Anniv of Sports Lottery.
2498 **1061** 2p.30 multicoloured . . 30 20

1062 Manila Galleon

1998. Centenary of Philippine Independence.
2499 **1062** 3p.40 multicoloured . . 45 30

1063 Garcia Lorca

1998. Birth Centenary of Federico Garcia Lorca (poet).
2501 **1063** 3p.40 multicoloured . . 40 25

1064 Emblems

1998. 50th Anniv of Universal Declaration of Human Rights.
2502 **1064** 3p.40 green and black 45 30

1065 Open Book and Dove

1067 Tree

1066 Alfonso Herrera (founder) and Leopard

1998. International Day against the Use and Illegal Trafficking of Drugs.
2503 **1065** 2p.30 multicoloured . . 30 20

1998. 75th Anniv of Chapultepec Zoo.
2504 **1066** 2p.30 multicoloured . . 30 20

1998. Tree Day.
2505 **1067** 2p.30 multicoloured . . 30 20

1068 St. Peter and St. Paul's Monastery, Teposcolula

1998. Inauguration of Philatelic Museum, Oaxaca. Multicoloured.
2506 2p.30 Type **1068** 30 20
2507 2p.30 Clay pot, San Bartolo Coyotepec 30 20
2508 2p.30 "The Road" (painting, Francisco Toledo) 30 20
2509 2p.30 Gold pectoral from Tomb 7, Monte Alban . . 30 20

1069 Juarez

1998. 126th Death Anniv of Benito Juarez (President 1859–64 and 1867–72).
2510 **1069** 2p.30 stone, black and brown 30 20

1070 Cultural Museum

1998. St. Dominic's Cultural Centre, Oaxaca. Multicoloured.
2511 2p.30 Type **1070** 30 20
2512 2p.30 Francisco de Burgoa Library 30 20
2513 2p.30 Historical botanic garden 30 20
2514 3p.40 St. Dominic's Monastery (after Teodoro Velasco) 45 30

1071 Frigate Bird, Blue-footed Booby, Whales and Cacti

1998. Marine Life. Multicoloured.
2515 2p.30 Type **1071** 30 20
2516 2p.30 Albatross, humpback whale and seagulls . . . 30 20
2517 2p.30 Tail of whale and swordfish 30 20
2518 2p.30 Fish eagle, flamingo, herons and dolphins . . . 30 20
2519 2p.30 Turtles, flamingoes, cormorant and palm tree 30 20
2520 2p.30 Oystercatcher, turnstone, elephant seal and sealions 30 20
2521 2p.30 Dolphin, turtle, seagulls and swallows . . 30 20
2522 2p.30 Killer whale, dolphins and ray 30 20
2523 2p.30 Flamingoes, pelican, kingfishers and spider . . 30 20
2524 2p.30 Crocodile, roseate spoonbill and tiger heron 30 20
2525 2p.30 Schools of sardines and anchovies 30 20
2526 2p.30 Turtle, squid, gold-finned tunnyfish and shark 30 20
2527 2p.30 Jellyfish, dolphins and fishes 30 20
2528 2p.30 Dolphin (fish), barracudas and haddock 30 20
2529 2p.30 Manatee, fishes, anemone and coral . . . 30 20
2530 2p.30 Seaweed, starfish, coral and fishes 30 20

2531 2p.30 Hammerhead shark, angelfish, gudgeon, eels and coral 30 20
2532 2p.30 Shrimps, ray and other fishes 30 20
2533 2p.30 Octopus, bass, crayfish and other fishes 30 20
2534 2p.30 Turtle, porcupinefish, coral, angelfish and other fishes 30 20
2535 2p.30 Abalone, clams, razor clam, crayfish and anemone 30 20
2536 2p.30 Seahorses, angelfishes, coral and shells 30 20
2537 2p.30 Octopus, turtle, crab and moray eel 30 20
2538 2p.30 Butterflyfishes and other fishes 30 20
2539 2p.30 Reef shark, angelfish and corals 30 20

Nos. 2515/39 were issued together, se-tenant, forming a composite design.

1072 Runners

1998. 16th International Marathon, Mexico City.
2540 **1072** 3p.40 multicoloured . . 45 30

1073 Aztec Deity

1998. World Tourism Day.
2541 **1073** 3p.40 multicoloured . . 45 30

1074 Lucas Alaman (founder)

1998. 175th Anniv of National Archives.
2542 **1074** 2p.30 green, red and black 30 20

1075 Emblem

1076 Stylized Couple

1998. 75th Anniv of Interpol.
2543 **1075** 3p.40 multicoloured . . 45 30

1998. Healthy Pregnancy Month.
2544 **1076** 2p.30 multicoloured . . 30 20

1077 Painting by Luis Nishizawa

1998.
2545 **1077** 2p.30 multicoloured . . 30 20

1078 Key and Globe

1998. World Post Day.
2546 **1078** 3p.40 multicoloured . . 45 30

1079 College Campus

1998. 175th Anniv of Military College.
2547 **1079** 2p.30 multicoloured . . 30 20

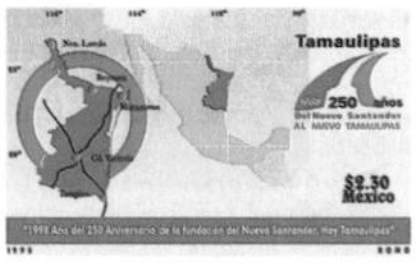
1080 Map

1998. 250th Anniv of Tamaulipas (formerly New Santander) (2nd issue).
2548 **1080** 2p.30 multicoloured . . 30 20

1081 Golden Eagle

1998. Nature Conservation.
2549 **1081** 2p.30 multicoloured . . 30 20

1082 Woman and Potatoes

1998. World Food Day.
2550 **1082** 3p.30 multicoloured . . 45 30

1083 Mexico arrowed on Globe

1998. National Migration Week.
2551 **1083** 2p.30 multicoloured . . 30 20

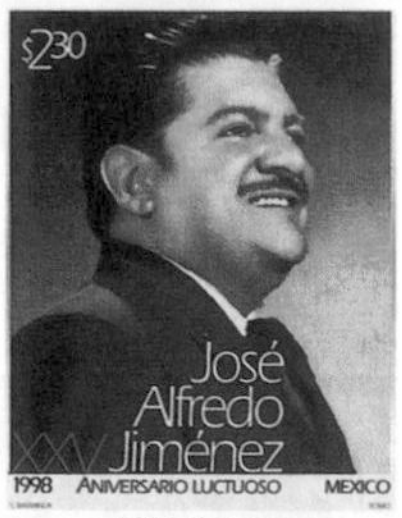
1084 Jimenez

1998. 25th Death Anniv of Jose Alfredo Jimenez (writer).
2552 **1084** 2p.30 multicoloured . . 30 20

1085 Oil Rig and Emblem

1087 Franciscan Monastery, Colima

1086 Mexican Stone Carving and Eiffel Tower

1998. 25th Anniv of Mexican Petroleum Engineers' Association.
2553 **1085** 3p.40 multicoloured . . 45 30

1998. Mexican–French Economic and Cultural Co-operation.
2554 **1086** 3p.40 multicoloured . . 45 30

1998. 475th Anniv of Colima.
2555 **1087** 2p.30 multicoloured . . 30 20

1088 Wise Men approaching Stable

1998. Christmas. Multicoloured. Self-adhesive.
2556 2p.30 Type **1088** 30 20
2557 3p.40 Decorations and pot (vert) 45 30

1089 Woman with Baby

1998. 50th Anniv of National Institute of Indigenous Peoples.
2558 **1089** 2p.30 multicoloured . . 30 20

1090 Eagle holding Statute

1998. 60th Anniv of Federation of Civil Servants' Trade Unions.
2559 **1090** 2p.30 multicoloured . . 30 20

1091 Airplane and Aztec Bird-man

1092 University Arms

1998. 25th Anniv of Latin-American Civil Aviation Commission.
2560 **1091** 3p.40 multicoloured . . 45 30

1998. 125th Anniv of Sinaloa Autonomous University.
2561 **1092** 2p.30 multicoloured . . 30 20

1094 "Satmex 5" and Earth

1999. Launch of "Satmex 5" Satellite.
2563 **1094** 3p. multicoloured . . . 40 25

1095 Maracas Player and Streamers

1096 Couple in Hammock

1999. Veracruz Carnival.
2564 **1095** 3p. multicoloured . . . 40 25

1999. Bicentenary of Acapulco, Guerrero. Mult.
2565 3p. Type **1096** 40 25
2566 4p.20 Diving from cliff . . . 55 30

Nos. 2565/6 were issued together, se-tenant, forming a composite design.

1097 Internet Website

1999. International Women's Day.
2567 **1097** 4p.20 multicoloured . . 55 30

1098 "Mexico" (Jorge Gonzalez Camarena)

1999. 40th Anniv of National Commission for Free Textbooks.
2568 **1098** 3p. multicoloured . . . 40 25

1099 Family Members

1999. 25th Anniv of National Population Council.
2569 **1099** 3p. multicoloured . . . 40 25

1101 Guadalupe Ceniceros de Perez

1999. Teachers' Day.
2571 **1101** 3p. multicoloured . . . 40 25

1102 Pitcher

1999. 75th Anniv of Mexican Baseball League. Each black and grey.
2572 3p. Type **1102** 40 25
2573 3p. Catcher 40 25
2574 3p. Skeletal pitcher 40 25
2575 3p. Pitcher (different) . . . 40 25

1103 10p. Banknote

1999. 115th Anniv of National Bank of Mexico. Multicoloured.
2576 3p. Type **1103** 40 25
2577 3p. Former and current headquarters 40 25

1105 Couple holding Hands

1106 Skyscraper

1999. International Day against Illegal Use and Illicit Trafficking of Drugs.
2579 **1105** 4p.20 multicoloured . . 60 40

1999. 65th Anniv of National Financial Institute.
2580 **1106** 3p. multicoloured . . . 45 30

1107 Tree

1999. Tree Day.
2581 **1107** 3p. multicoloured . . . 45 30

1108 Registration Documents and Fingerprint

1999. 140th Anniv of National Civil Register.
2582 **1108** 3p. multicoloured . . . 45 30

1109 Runner's Feet

1999. 17th International Marathon, Mexico City.
2583 **1109** 4p.20 multicoloured . . 60 40

1110 Children, Flag and Book on Island ("Conoce nuestra Constitucion")

1999. 40th Anniv of National Commission for Free Textbooks (2nd issue). Multicoloured.
2584 3p. Type **1110** 45 30
2585 3p. Children dancing ("Tsuni tsame") 45 30
2586 3p. Bird on flower ("Ciencias naturales") . . 45 30

1111 "Self-portrait"

1999. Birth Centenary of Rufino Tamayo (artist).
2587 **1111** 3p. multicoloured . . . 45 30

1112 Building

1999. Bicentenary of Toluca City.
2588 **1112** 3p. black and copper 45 30

1113 State Arms, Model Figures and Signature

1999. 175th Anniv of State of Mexico.
2589 **1113** 3p. multicoloured . . . 45 30

1114 "50" and Map of Americas

1999. 50th Anniv of Union of Universities of Latin America.
2590 **1114** 4p.20 multicoloured . . 60 40

1115 Emblem

1999. 40th Anniv of Institute of Security and Social Services of State Workers (I.S.S.S.T.E.).
2591 **1115** 3p. multicoloured . . . 45 30

1116 Map and State Emblem

1999. 25th Anniv of State of Baja California Sur.
2592 **1116** 3p. multicoloured . . . 45 30

1117 Emblem, "25" and Map

1999. 25th Anniv of Mexican Family Planning.
2593 **1117** 3p. multicoloured . . . 45 30

1118 Harpy Eagle

1999. Nature Conservation.
2594 **1118** 3p. multicoloured . . . 45 30

1119 Stone Carving and Arms

1120 U.P.U. Messengers

1999. 25th Anniv of State of Quintana Roo.
2595 **1119** 3p. multicoloured . . . 45 30

1999. 125th Anniv of Universal Postal Union.
2596 **1120** 4p.20 multicoloured . . 60 40

1121 Globe and Stamps

1999. World Post Day.
2597 **1121** 4p.20 multicoloured . . 60 40

1122 Emblem and Monument

1999. 12th General Assembly of International Council on Monuments and Sites.
2598 **1122** 4p.20 silver, blue and black 60 40

1123 Chavez and Revueltas

1999. Birth Centenaries of Carlos Chavez and Silvestre Revueltas (composers).
2599 **1123** 3p. multicoloured . . . 45 30

1124 Emblem

1126 "Mexico 1999" in Star and Children (Alfredo Carciarreal)

1125 Map, Cave Painting and State Arms

1999. 25th Anniv of Autonomous Metropolitan University.
2600 **1124** 3p. multicoloured . . . 45 30

1999. 150th Anniv of State of Guerrero.
2601 **1125** 3p. multicoloured . . . 45 30

1999. Christmas. Children's Drawings. Multicoloured.
2602 3p. Type **1126** 45 30
2603 4p.20 Christmas decorations (Rodrigo Santiago Salazar) 60 40

1127 Anniversary Emblem

1999. 20th Anniv of National Commission on Professional Education.
2604 **1127** 3p. green, ultramarine and black 45 30

1128 Humboldt (naturalist)

1999. Bicentenary of Alexander von Humboldt's Exploration of South America.
2605 **1128** 3p. multicoloured . . . 45 30

1130 Emblem and Crowd

1131 Woman ascending Stairs

2000. Census.
2607 **1130** 3p. multicoloured . . . 45 30

2000. International Women's Day.
2608 **1131** 4p.20 multicoloured . . 60 40

1134 Totonaca Temple, El Tajin

2000.
2611 **1134** 3p. multicoloured . . . 45 30

1135 Emblem, Books and Keyboard

2000. 50th Anniv of National Association of Universities and Institutes of Higher Education.
2612 **1135** 3p. multicoloured . . . 45 30

1136 Emblem

2000. 25th Tourism Fair, Acapulco.
2613 **1136** 4p.20 multicoloured . . 60 40

1137 Men in Canoe and Sailing Ship

2000. 500th Anniv of the Discovery of Brazil.
2614 **1137** 4p.20 multicoloured . . 60 40

1138 Luis Alvarez Barret

2000. Teachers' Day.
2615 **1138** 3p. multicoloured . . . 45 30

1139 Flying Cars and Boy with Dog (Alejandro Guerra Millan)

2000. "Stampin the Future". Winning Entries in Children's International Painting Competition. Mult.
2616 3p. Type **1139** 45 30
2617 4p.20 Houses and space ships (Carlos Hernandez Garcia) 60 40

1140 Emblem

2000. 4th Asian–Pacific Telecommunications and Information Industry Economic Co-operation Forum.
2618 **1140** 4p.20 multicoloured . . 60 40

1141 Young Children

1144 Pictograms

2000. International Anti-drugs Day.
2619 **1141** 4p.20 multicoloured . . 60 40

2000. Convive (disabled persons' organization).
2622 **1144** 3p. multicoloured . . . 45 25

1145 Globe and Member Flags

1146 Emblem

2000. 20th Anniv of Association of Latin American Integration.
2623 **1145** 4p.20 multicoloured . . 65 40

2000. 125th Anniv of Restoration of Senate.
2624 **1146** 3p. multicoloured . . . 45 25

1149 Runners crossing Finishing Line

2000. 18th International Marathon, Mexico City.
2627 **1149** 4p.20 multicoloured . . 65 40

1150 Athletes and Sydney Opera House

2000. Olympic Games, Sydney.
2628 **1150** 4p.20 multicoloured . . 65 40

1151 Emblem and Family

2000. Paisano Programme (support for Mexicans returning home from abroad).
2629 **1151** 4p.20 multicoloured . . 65 40

1152 Emblem

2000. 2nd International UNESCO World Conference, Colima.
2630 **1152** 4p.20 multicoloured . . 65 40

1153 Profiles

1155 Bird holding Letter

1154 Building and Emblem

2000. Women's Health Month.
2631 **1153** 3p. multicoloured . . . 35 20

2000. 250th Anniv of Ciudad Victoria, Tamaulipas.
2632 **1154** 3p. multicoloured . . . 35 20

2000. World Post Day.
2633 **1155** 4p.20 multicoloured . . 50 30

1156 Emblem

2000. 50th Anniv of National Human Rights Commission.
2634 **1156** 3p. silver and blue . . . 35 20

1157 Doctors and Ambulance

2000. New Millennium. Sheet 223 × 135 mm in shape of flag, containing T **1157** and similar multicoloured designs.
MS2635 3p. Type **1157**; 3p. Posters, doctors and globe (79 × 25 mm); 3p. Children receiving injections; 3p. Poster showing tractor and crowd demonstrating (79 × 25 mm); 4p.20, Modern medical technology (oval- shaped, 39 × 49 mm) . . . . 2·00 1·25

1158 Clouds and Emblem

2000. 50th Anniv of World Meteorological Organization.
2636 **1158** 3p. multicoloured . . . 35 20

1159 Emblem

2000. 50th Anniv of International Diabetes Federation.
2637 **1159** 4p.20 gold and red . . 50 30

1160 Contemporary Art with Sculpture (½-size illustration)

2000. Art. Sheet 223 × 39 mm in shape of flag, containing T **1160** and similar multicoloured designs.
MS2638 3p. Type **1160**; 3p. Photographs (39 × 25 mm); 3p. Opera singer and movie actors; 3p. Dancers (39 × 25 mm); 4p.20 Ballet dancers and musicians (oval-shaped, 39 × 49 mm) . . 2·00 1·25

1161 Samuel Morse, Juan de la Granja and Telegraph Apparatus

2000. 150th Anniv of Telegraph in Mexico.
2639 **1161** 3p. multicoloured . . . 35 20
Samuel Morse invented the telegraph and Morse code system and Juan de la Granja introduced the telegraph to Mexico.

1162 Bunuel

2000. Birth Centenary of Luis Bunuel (film director).
2640 **1162** 3p. silver, black and red 35 20

1163 Lightning

2000. 25th Anniv of Electric Investigation Institute.
2641 **1163** 3p. multicoloured . . . 35 20

1164 Building Customs House, and Bridge

2000. Centenary of Customs.
2642 **1164** 3p. multicoloured . . . 35 20

1165 Star and Girl (Maria Carina Lona Martinez)

2000. Christmas. Children's paintings. Multicoloured.
2643 3p. Type **1165** 35 20
2644 4p.20 Poinsettia (Daniela Escamilla Rodriguez) . . 50 30

1166 Television Set and Emblem

2000. 50th Anniv of Television in Mexico.
2645 **1166** 3p. multicoloured . . . 35 20

1167 Adamo Boari (architect)

2000. Centenary of Commencement of Construction of Postal Headquarters, Mexico City. Sheet 92 × 100 mm, containing T **1167** and similar designs. Multicoloured.
MS2646 3p. multicoloured; 3p. black, brown and red; 3p. multicoloured; 10p. black, brown and red (71 × 39 mm) . . . . 2·10 1·25
DESIGNS: As Type **1167**—3p. Building facade; 3p. Gonzalo Garita y Frontera (engineer). 71 × 39 mm—10p. Completed building.

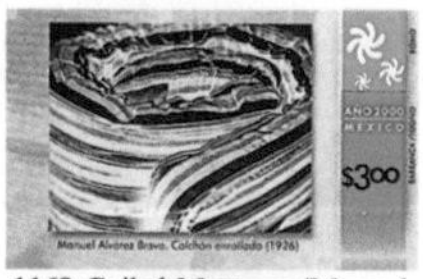

1168 Coiled Mattress (Manuel Alvarez Bravo)

2000. Photography. Sheet 223 × 135 mm in shape of flag, containing T **1168** and similar multicoloured designs.
MS2647 3p. Type **1168**; 3p. Various portraits (79 × 25 mm); 3p. Roses (Tina Modotti); 3p. Various photographs including a lift, a lake, a 1925 car, a helicopter, a ruined building, a street scene, men in costume and boot heels (79 × 25 mm); 4p.20 Men in gas masks (oval-shaped, 39 × 49 mm) 2·00 1·25

1169 Pyramid of the Niches

2000. El Tajin.
2648 **1169** 3p. multicoloured . . . 35 20

1170 Manatee

2000. Nature Conservation.
2649 **1170** 3p. multicoloured . . . 35 20

1171 Sarabia

2000. Birth Centenary of Francisco Sarabia (aviator).
2650 **1171** 3p. multicoloured . . . 35 20

1172 Telephone Exchange and Fabric Shops (½-size illustration)

2000. Industry. Sheet 223 × 135 mm in shape of flag, containing T **1172** and similar multicoloured designs.
MS2651 3p. Type **1172**; 3p. Tractor and modern farming (39 × 25 mm); 3p. Traditional farming methods and car; 3p. Manufacturing and industrial plant (39 × 25 mm); 4p.20 Globe and industries (oval-shaped, 39 × 49 mm) . . . . 2·00 1·60

1173 Stamps and Post Collection (½-size illustration)

2000. Forms of Communication. Sheet 223 × 135 mm in shape of flag, containing T **1173** and similar multicoloured designs.
MS2652 3p. Type **1173**; 3p. Telephone operators and telegraph clerk (39 × 25 mm); 3p. Old and modern train and station; 3p. Motorway (39 × 25 mm); 4p.20 Globe and satellite and satellite dish (oval-shaped, 39 × 49 mm) 2·00 1·60

2001. Tourism. As Nos. 2410 etc but with face value changed.
2658 6p.50 Queretaro 75 45

1174 Chiapas

2001. Tourism.
2670 **1174** 1p.50 multicoloured . . 20 15
2673 8p.50 multicoloured . . 1·00 60

1175 Emblem, Book and Building

2001. 50th Anniv of National Autonomous University.
2680 **1175** 3p. multicoloured . . . 35 20

1176 Woman

2001. International Women's Day.
2681 **1176** 4p.20 multicoloured . . 50 30

1177 Cement Factory

2001. 53rd Anniv of National Cement Chamber.
2682 **1177** 3p. multicoloured . . . 35 20

1178 Vasconcelos and Ink Pen **1179** People Running and Flames

2001. 42nd Death Anniv of Jose Vasconcelos (lawyer).
2683 **1178** 3p. multicoloured . . . 35 20

2001. 50th Anniv of United Nations High Commissioner for Refugees.
2684 **1179** 4p.20 multicoloured . . 50 30

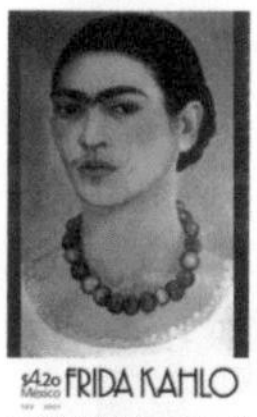

1180 "Self-portrait wearing Jade Necklace" **1181** Stylized Bird

2001. Frida Kahlo (artist) Commemoration.
2685 **1180** 4p.20 multicoloured . . 50 30
A stamp of similar design was issued by the United States of America.

2001. Anti-drugs Campaign.
2686 **1181** 4p.20 multicoloured . . 50 30

1182 De la Cueva

2001. Birth Centenary of Mario de la Cueva (university director).
2687 **1182** 3p. blue and gold . . . 35 20

1183 Emblem

2001. International Year of Volunteers.
2688 **1183** 4p.20 multicoloured . . 50 30

1184 Women and Flowers (painting)

2001. Rodolfo Morales (artist) Commemoration. Sheet 121 × 60 mm.
MS2689 **1184** 10p. multicoloured 1·10 65

1185 Owl

2001. 65th Anniv of Federal Justice Tribunal.
2690 **1185** 3p. multicoloured . . . 30 20

1186 Emblems and Building

2001. 450th Anniv of University of Mexico.
2691 **1186** 3p. multicoloured . . . 30 20

1187 Adela Formoso **1188** Daniel Villegas

2001. 20th Death Anniv of Adela Formoso de Obregon Santalla (women's rights activist).
2692 **1187** 3p. multicoloured . . . 30 20

2001. 25th Death Anniv of Daniel Cosío Villegas (historian).
2693 **1188** 3p. multicoloured . . . 30 20

1189 Past and Present Pharmaceutical Drugs

2001.
2694 **1189** 3p. multicoloured . . . 30 20

1190 Girl with Grandfather

2001. Grandparents Day.
2695 **1190** 3p. multicoloured . . . 30 20

1191 Children encircling Globe **1193** Lily

1192 Envelope as Bicycle

2001. United Nations Year of Dialogue among Civilizations.
2696 **1191** 3p. multicoloured . . . 30 20

2001. Stamp Day.
2697 **1192** 3p. yellow, red and blue 30 20

2001. Women's Health Day.
2698 **1193** 3p. multicoloured . . . 30 20

1194 Eye and People

2001. 25th Anniv of Ophthalmic Institute.
2699 **1194** 4p.20 multicoloured . . 40 25

1195 Tufted Jay (*Cyanocorax dickeyi*)

2001. Endangered Species.
2700 **1195** 5p.30 multicoloured . . 50 30

1196 Children (Eunice Gonzalez)

2001. Christmas. Children's Paintings. Multicoloured.
2701 3p. Type **1196** 30 20
2702 4p.20 Candles (Javier Nunez) 40 25

1197 Nurse and Children

2001. Educational Scholarship Fund for Indigenous Children. Sheet 101 × 72 mm. P 14.
MS2703 1197 3p. multicoloured 30 30

1198 Technicians

2001. National Fund for Education. Sheet 101 × 72 mm.
MS2704 1198 3p. multicoloured 30 30

1199 Boy and Girl **1200** Apple

2001. Children's Accident Prevention Campaign.
2705 **1199** 3p. multicoloured . . . 30 20

2001. World Food Day.
2706 **1200** 3p. multicoloured . . . 30 20

1201 Wild Sheep

2002. Endangered Species.
2707 **1201** 6p. multicoloured . . . 60 30

1202 Squash and Snail

2002. Birth Centenary of Manuel Alvarez Bravo (photographer).
2708 **1202** 6p. black 60 30

1203 Chinese Dragon and Quetzalcoatl

2002. 30th Anniv of China—Mexico Diplomatic Relations.
2709 **1203** 6p. multicoloured . . . 60 30

1204 Mangroves

2002. Conservation. Multicoloured.

2710	50c. Type **1204**	10	10
2711	1p. Rivers	10	10
2712	1p. Forests	15	10
2713	1p.50 Terrestrial mammals	15	10
2714	2p. Cacti	20	10
2715	2p. Cloud forest	20	10
2716	2p.50 No. 2715	25	15
2717	2p.50 No. 2713	25	15
2718	4p.50 Birds	45	25
2719	5p. Reptiles	50	25
2720	5p. Marine turtles	50	25
2721	6p. Birds of prey	60	30
2722	6p. Butterflies	60	30
2723	7p. Reefs	70	35
2724	8p.50 Tropical forests . . .	85	40
2725	10p. Marine mammals . . .	1·00	50
2726	10p. No. 2713	1·00	50
2727	10p.50 Wild cats	1·00	50
2728	10p.50 Orchids	1·00	50
2729	11p.50 Seas	1·10	55
2730	11p.50 Coastal birds	1·10	55
2731	12p. No. 2724	1·10	55
2732	30p. Deserts	2·75	1·40
2733	30p. Lakes and lagoons . .	2·75	1·40

1205 Emblems

2002. Olympic Games, Salt Lake City, USA.
2760 **1205** 8p.50 multicoloured . . 85 40

1206 Stylized Ship

2002. Centenary of Modernization of Veracruz Artificial Port.
2761 **1206** 6p. multicoloured . . . 60 30

1207 Mayan Head and Korean Symbol

2002. 40th Anniv of Korea—Mexico Diplomatic Relations.
2762 **1207** 8p.50 multicoloured . . 85 40

1208 Mexico City Buildings

2002. Consultative Council for the Restoration of Historic Buildings.
2763 **1208** 6p. multicoloured . . . 60 30

1209 Emblem **1210** "La Despedida del Revolucionario"

2002. International Women's Day. National Women's Institute.
2764 **1209** 8p.50 blue and vermilion 85 40

2002. 150th Birth Anniv of Jose Guadalupe Posada (artist).
2765 **1210** 6p. black and olive . . 60 30

1211 Jose Sierra Mendez

2002. 90th Death Anniv of Jose Sierra Mendez (writer).
2766 **1211** 6p. multicoloured . . . 60 30

1212 "Esteban and the Striped Cat" (Abel Quezada)

2002. United Nations Special Session for Children.
2767 **1212** 6p. multicoloured . . . 60 30

1213 Alberto Lhuillier (discoverer), Ruins and Mayan Head

2002. 50th Anniv of Discovery of Tumba de Pakal (Mayan archaeological site).
2768 **1213** 6p. multicoloured . . . 60 30

1214 Players at Goalmouth

2002. World Cup Football Championship, Japan and South Korea.
2769 **1214** 8p.50 multicoloured . . 85 40

1215 Pot with Map of Americas holding People as Tree **1216** Stylized Map of Americas

2002. International Day against Drug Abuse.
2770 **1215** 6p. multicoloured . . . 60 30

2002. 5th Mexico—Central American Summit.
2771 **1216** 6p. multicoloured . . . 60 30

1217 Mountain

2002. International Year of Mountains.
2772 **1217** 6p. multicoloured . . . 60 30

1218 Boy wearing Traditional Costume

2002. International Day of Indigenous Peoples.
2773 **1218** 6p. multicoloured . . . 60 30

1219 High Tension Power Lines

2002. Federal Commission of Electricity.
2774 **1219** 6p. multicoloured . . . 60 30

1220 Face enclosed in Blood Droplet **1222** Scales and Code

1221 Apple and Map of Mexico

2002. National Blood Donors' Day.
2775 **1220** 6p. multicoloured . . . 60 30

2002. Administrative Secretariat for Development Control (SECODAM).
2776 **1221** 6p. multicoloured . . . 60 30

2002. Code of Practise for Public Administrations.
2777 **1222** 6p. multicoloured . . . 60 30

1223 Clasped Hands

2002. International Day of Tourism.
2778 **1223** 8p.50 purple, black and lemon 85 40

1224 Torso, Electrocardiogram Diagram and Watch

2002. National Organ Donation Week.
2779 **1224** 6p. multicoloured . . . 60 30

1225 Birds and Envelopes

2002. Stamp Day.
2780 **1225** 8p.50 multicoloured . . 85 40

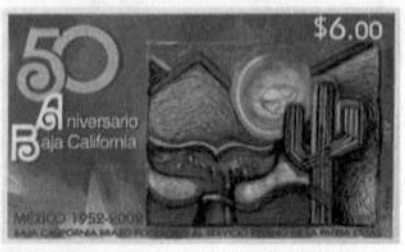

1226 Mountains, Whale Tail, Sun and Cactus

2002. 50th Anniv of Baja California Peninsula.
2781 **1226** 6p. multicoloured . . . 60 30

1227 Stairs

2002. Birth Centenary of Luis Barragan (architect).
2782 **1227** 6p. multicoloured . . . 60 30

1228 "Man's Conquest of the Air" (detail) (Juan O'Gorman) (⅔-size illustration)

2002. 50th Anniv of Mexico City Airport. Details from "Man's Conquest of the Air" by Juan O'Gorman. Multicoloured.
2783 6p. Type **1228** 60 30
2784 6p. Early aviators, parachutist and man wearing protective suit . . 60 30
2785 8p.50 Mexico city and aviators 85 40
Nos. 2783/5 were issued together, se-tenant, forming a composite design.

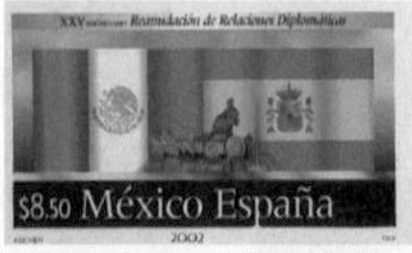

1229 Mexican and Spanish Flags

2002. 25th Anniv of Renewal of Spain—Mexico Diplomatic Relations.
2786 **1229** 8p.50 multicoloured . . 85 40

1230 Globe, "e" and Binary Codes **1231** Anniversary Emblem

2002. 75th Anniv of the Development of Information Technology in Mexico.
2787 **1230** 6p. violet, vermilion and black 60 30

2002. Centenary of Pan American Health Organization.
2788 **1231** 8p.50 multicoloured . . 85 40

1232 Nezahualcoyotl

2002. 600th Birth Anniv of Nezahualcoyotl (King of the Texcoco).
2789 **1232** 6p. multicoloured . . . 60 30

1233 Nativity (Sara Elisa Miranda Alcaraz)

2002. Christmas. Children's Paintings. Multicoloured.
2790 6p. Type **1233** 60 30
2791 8p.50 Nativity (Alejandro Ruiz Sampedro) 85 40

1234 Emblem

2002. "Life without Violence" Campaign.
2792 **1234** 8p.50 multicoloured . . 85 40

1235 Early Bi-plane

2003. Centenary of Powered Flight. Phosphorescent markings.
2793 **1235** 8p.50 multicoloured . . 85 60

1236 Emblem **1237** Woman

2003. 60th Anniv of Iberoamericana University, Mexico City.
2794 **1236** 6p. multicoloured . . . 60 30

2003. International Woman's Day.
2795 **1237** 8p.50 multicoloured . . 85 60

1238 City Arms and Buildings

2003. Centenary of Mexicali City.
2796 **1238** 6p. multicoloured . . . 60 30

1239 Dam and Crane

2003. 50th Anniv of Industry and Construction (cmic).
2797 **1239** 6p. multicoloured . . . 60 30

1240 Emblem and Children

2003. 60th Anniv of Frederico Gomez Children's Hospital.
2798 **1240** 6p. multicoloured . . . 60 30

1241 Miguel Hildago y Costilla

1242 Gregorio Torres Quintero

2003. 250th Birth Anniv of Miguel Hildago y Costilla (social reformer and independence pioneer).
2799 **1241** 6p. multicoloured . . . 60 30

2003. Teacher's Day. Gregorio Torres Quintero (writer) Commemoration.
2800 **1242** 6p. multicoloured . . . 60 30

1243 Telescope, Planets and Eclipse

1244 Film, Cigarette and Stop Sign

2003. 125th Anniv of National Astronomical Observatory.
2801 **1243** 6p. multicoloured . . . 60 30

2003. International No-Smoking Day. Smoking-free Cinemas Campaign.
2802 **1244** 8p.50 multicoloured . . 85 60

1245 Map

1247 Baseball and Bat

1246 Hands enclosing Globe

2003. 1st Satellite Network.
2803 **1245** 6p. multicoloured . . . 60 30

2003. International Day against Drug Abuse.
2804 **1246** 8p.50 multicoloured . . 85 60

2003. 30th Anniv of Professional Baseball Hall of Fame.
2805 **1247** 6p. multicoloured . . . 85 60

1248 Xavier Villaurrutia

2003. Birth Centenary of Xavier Villaurrutia (writer).
2806 **1248** 6p. multicoloured . . . 60 30

1249 Early Vet and Modern Veterinary Surgery

1250 University Building

2003. 150th Anniv of Veterinary Education in Mexico and America.
2807 **1249** 6p. multicoloured . . . 60 30

2003. 25th Anniv of National Teachers' University.
2808 **1250** 6p. multicoloured . . . 60 30

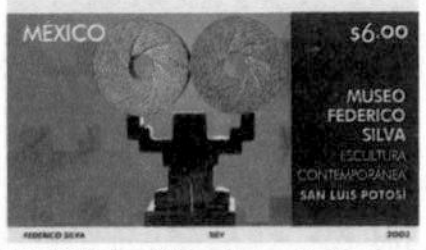

1251 "Tlaloc" (sculpture) (Federico Silva)

2003. Museo Federico Silva (contemporary culture museum), San Luis Potosí.
2809 **1251** 6p. multicoloured . . . 60 30

1252 Family

1253 Bird carrying Envelope

2003. National Seminar on Organ Donation.
2810 **1252** 6p. multicoloured . . . 60 30

2003. Stamp Day.
2811 **1253** 8p.50 multicoloured . . 85 60

1254 Voting Slip, Ballot Box and Women

1255 Secretariat Building

2003. 50th Anniv of Vote for Women.
2812 **1254** 6p. multicoloured . . . 60 30

2003. 60th Anniv of Health Secretariat.
2813 **1255** 6p. multicoloured . . . 60 30

1256 Auditorium

1257 Emblem

2003. Centenary of Juarez Theatre, Guanajuato City.
2814 **1256** 6p. multicoloured . . . 60 30

2003. 450th Anniv of First Chair of Law in America.
2815 **1257** 8p.50 multicoloured . . 85 60

1258 "Development and Impact of the Electricity" (German Reyes Retana)

2003. Centenary of Centralized Light and Power.
2816 **1258** 6p. multicoloured . . . 60 30

1259 The Nativity (Valeria Baez)

1260 Laughing Child

2003. Christmas. Children's Paintings. Multicoloured.
2817 6p. Type **1259** 60 30
2818 8p.50 Nativity (Octavio Aleman) 85 60

2003. Rights of the Child.
2819 **1260** 6p. multicoloured . . . 60 30

1261 Globe as Heart and Leaves

1262 College Facade and Students

2003. International Day of Freshwater.
2820 **1261** 8p.50 multicoloured . . 85 60

2003. 25th Anniv of Professional Technical College (CONALEP).
2821 **1262** 6p. multicoloured . . . 60 30

1263 John Paul II

2004. 25th Anniv of Pope John Paul II's First Visit to Mexico.
2822 **1263** 6p. multicoloured . . . 60 30

1264 Agustin Yanez

1265 Enrique Aguilar Gonzalez

2004. Birth Centenary of Agustin Yanez (writer and politician).
2823 **1264** 8p.50 multicoloured . . 85 60

2004. Teachers' Day. Enrique Aguilar Gonzalez Commemoration.
2824 **1265** 8p.50 blue 85 60

1266 Satellite, Cable and Globe

2004. 50th Anniv of Cable Television.
2825 **1266** 6p. multicoloured . . . 60 30

1267 Quartz and Society Emblem

2004. Centenary of Geological Society.
2826 **1267** 8p.50 multicoloured . . 85 60

1268 Stylized Figures

2004. International Day against Drug Abuse.
2827 **1268** 8p.50 multicoloured . . 85 60

EXPRESS LETTER STAMPS

E 55 Express Service Messenger

1919.
E445 E **55** 20c. black and red . . 35 15

E 95

1934.
E536 E **95** 10c. blue and red . . . 15 30

E 121 Indian Archer

E 222

1934. New President's Assumption of Office. Imprint "OFICINA IMPRESORA DE HACIENDA–MEXICO".
E581 E **121** 10c. violet . . . . . 1·00 20

1938. Imprint "TALLERES DE IMP. DE EST. Y VALORES-MEXICO".
E610 E **121** 10c. violet 55 20
E731 20c. orange 25 30

1940. Optd **1940**.
E665 E **55** 20c. black and red . . 20 15

1950.
E860 E **222** 25c. orange 20 10
E910 – 60c. green . . . . . 1·10 35
DESIGN: 60c. Hands and letter.

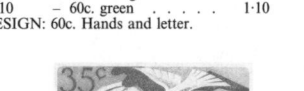

E 244

E 245

1956.
E 954 E **244** 35c. purple 25 10
E1065 50c. green 45 10
E 956 E **245** 80c. red 50 80
E1066 1p.20 lilac 1·50 75
E1346p E **244** 2p. orange 20 15
E1346q E **245** 5p. blue 20 60

E **468** Watch Face

1979.
E1373 E **468** 2p. black and orange 10 60

INSURED LETTER STAMPS

IN **125** Safe IN **222** P.O. Treasury Vault

1935. Inscr as in Type IN **125**.
IN583 – 10c. red 1·10 30
IN733 – 50c. blue 75 25
IN734 IN **125** 1p. green 75 35
DESIGNS: 10c. Bundle of insured letters; 50c. Registered mailbag.

1950.
IN911 IN **222** 20c. blue 15 10
IN912 40c. purple 15 10
IN913 1p. green 20 10
IN914 5p. green and blue 65 60
IN915 10p. blue and red 3·00 1·50

IN **469** Padlock

1976.
IN1374 IN **469** 40c. black & turq 10 10
IN1522 1p. black & turq 10 10
IN1376 2p. black and blue 10 10
IN1380 5p. black & turq 10 10
IN1524 10p. black & turq 10 10
IN1525 20p. black & turq 10 10
IN1383 50p. black & turq 95 95
IN1384 100p. black & turq 60 60
The 5, 10, 20p. exist with the padlock either 31 or 32½ mm high.

OFFICIAL STAMPS

O **18** Hidalgo

1884. No value shown.
O156 O **18** Red 30 20
O157 Brown 15 10
O158 Orange 80 15
O159 Green 30 15
O160 Blue 45 35

1894. Stamps of 1895 handstamped **OFICIAL**.
O231 **19** 1c. green 3·75 1·25
O232 2c. red 4·50 1·25
O233 3c. brown 3·75 1·25
O234 **20** 4c. orange 5·50 2·50
O235 **21** 5c. blue 7·50 2·50
O236 **22** 10c. purple 7·00 50
O237 **20** 12c. olive 15·00 6·25
O238 **22** 15c. blue 8·75 3·75
O239 20c. red 8·75 3·75
O240 50c. mauve 19·00 9·50
O241 **23** 1p. brown 48·00 19·00
O242 5p. red £200 95·00
O243 10p. blue £275 £150

1899. Stamps of 1899 handstamped **OFICIAL**.
O276 **27** 1c. green 9·50 60
O286 1c. purple 8·75 95
O277 2c. red 12·50 95
O287 2c. green 8·75 95
O278 3c. brown 12·50 60
O288 4c. red 16·00 45
O279 5c. blue 12·50 1·10
O289 5c. orange 16·00 3·25
O280 10c. brown and purple 16·00 1·40
O290 10c. orange and blue 19·00 95
O281 15c. purple and lavender 16·00 1·40
O282 20c. blue and red 19·00 45
O283 **28** 50c. black and purple 38·00 6·25
O291 50c. black and red 48·00 6·25
O284 **29** 1p. black and blue 80·00 6·25
O285 **30** 5p. black and red 50·00 19·00

1911. Independence stamps optd **OFICIAL**.
O301 **32** 1c. purple 1·25 1·25
O302 – 2c. green 75 45
O303 – 3c. brown 1·25 45
O304 – 4c. red 1·90 45
O305 – 5c. orange 3·25 1·75
O306 – 10c. orange and blue 1·90 45
O307 – 15c. lake and slate 3·25 2·00
O308 – 20c. blue and lake 2·50 45
O309 **40** 50c. black and brown 8·75 3·75
O310 – 1p. black and blue 15·00 6·25
O311 – 5p. black and red 55·00 32·00

1915. Stamps of 1915 optd **OFICIAL**.
O321 **43** 1c. violet 30 55
O322 **44** 2c. green 30 55
O323 **45** 3c. brown 30 55
O324 4c. red 30 55
O325 5c. orange 30 55
O326 10c. blue 30 55

1915. Stamps of 1915 optd **OFICIAL**.
O318 **46** 40c. grey 4·75 3·25
O455 40c. mauve 3·75 1·90
O319 **47** 1p. grey and brown 3·25 3·75
O456 1p. grey and blue 9·50 6·25
O320 **48** 5p. blue and lake 19·00 16·00
O457 5p. grey and green 55·00 95·00

1916. Nos. O301/11 optd with T **49**.
O358 **32** 1c. purple 1·90
O359 – 2c. green 30
O360 – 3c. brown 35
O361 – 4c. red 2·00
O362 – 5c. orange 35
O363 – 10c. orange and blue 35
O364 – 15c. lake and slate 35
O365 – 20c. blue and lake 40
O366 **40** 50c. black and brown 55·00
O367 – 1p. black and blue 3·25
O368 – 5p. black and red £1600

1918. Stamps of 1917 optd **OFICIAL**.
O424 **53** 1c. violet 1·25 60
O446 1c. grey 30 20
O447 – 2c. green 20 20
O448 – 3c. brown 25 20
O449 – 4c. red 3·75 45
O450 – 5c. blue 20 20
O451 – 10c. blue 30 15
O452 – 20c. lake 2·50 2·50
O454 – 30c. black 3·75 1·40

1923. No. 416 optd **OFICIAL**.
O485 10p. black and brown 60·00 95·00

1923. Stamps of 1923 optd **OFICIAL**.
O471 **59** 1c. brown 20 20
O473 **60** 2c. red 25 25
O475 **61** 3c. brown 55 40
O461 **62** 4c. green 1·90 1·90
O476 **63** 4c. green 40 40
O477 5c. orange 70 65
O489 **74** 8c. orange 3·75 2·50
O479 **66** 10c. lake 55 55
O480 **65** 20c. blue 3·25 2·50
O464 **64** 30c. green 35 25
O467 **68** 50c. brown 55 55
O469 **69** 1p. blue and lake 4·75 4·75

1929. Air. Optd **OFICIAL**.
O501 **80** 5c. blue (roul) 45 25
O502 **81** 20c. violet 55 55
O492 **58** 25c. sepia and lake 6·50 7·50
O490 25c. sepia and green 2·50 3·00

1929. Air. As 1926 Postal Congress stamp optd **HABILITADO Servicio Oficial Aereo**.
O493 **70** 2c. black 26·00 26·00
O494 – 4c. black 26·00 26·00
O495 **70** 5c. black 26·00 26·00
O496 – 10c. black 26·00 26·00
O497 **72** 20c. black 26·00 26·00
O498 30c. black 26·00 26·00
O499 40c. black 26·00 26·00
O500 **73** 1p. black £950 £950

O **85**

1930. Air.
O503 O **85** 20c. grey 2·75 2·75
O504 35c. violet 40 95
O505 40c. blue and brown 50 90
O506 70c. sepia and violet 50 95

1931. Air. Surch **HABILITADO Quince centavos**.
O515 O **85** 15c. on 20c. grey 45 45

1932. Air. Optd **SERVICIO OFICIAL** in one line.
O532 **80** 10c. violet (perf or roul) 30 30
O533 15c. red (perf or roul) 85 85
O534 20c. sepia (roul) 85 85
O531 **58** 50c. red and blue 1·25 1·25

1932. Stamps of 1923 optd **SERVICIO OFICIAL** in two lines.
O535 **59** 1c. brown 15 15
O536 **60** 2c. red 10 10
O537 **61** 3c. brown 95 95
O538 **63** 4c. green 3·25 2·50
O539 5c. red 3·75 2·50
O540 **66** 10c. lake 1·10 75
O541 **65** 20c. blue 4·75 3·25
O544 **64** 30c. green 2·50 95
O545 **46** 40c. mauve 4·75 3·25
O546 **68** 50c. brown 80 95
O547 **69** 1p. blue and lake 95 95

1933. Air. Optd **SERVICIO OFICIAL** in two lines.
O553 **58** 50c. red and blue 1·40 1·25

1933. Air. Optd **SERVICIO OFICIAL** in two lines.
O548 **80** 5c. blue (No. 476a) 30 30
O549 10c. violet (No. 477) 30 30
O550 20c. sepia (No. 479) 30 60
O551 50c. lake (No. 481) 40 95

1934. Optd **OFICIAL**.
O565 **92** 15c. blue 35 35

1938. Nos. 561/71 optd **OFICIAL**.
O622 1c. orange 70 1·25
O623 2c. green 45 45
O624 4c. red 45 45
O625 10c. violet 45 80
O626 20c. blue 55 80
O627 30c. red 70 1·25
O628 40c. brown 70 1·25
O629 50c. black 1·00 1·00
O630 1p. red and brown 2·50 3·75

PARCEL POST STAMPS

P **167** Steam Mail Train

1941.
P732 P **167** 10c. red 2·25 55
P733 20c. violet 2·75 70

P **228** Class DE-10 Diesel-electric Locomotive

1951.
P916 P **228** 10c. pink 1·50 20
P917 20c. violet 2·00 40

POSTAGE DUE STAMPS

D **32**

1908.
D282 D **32** 1c. blue 1·00 1·00
D283 2c. blue 1·00 1·00
D284 4c. blue 1·00 1·00
D285 5c. blue 1·00 1·00
D286 10c. blue 1·00 1·00

MICRONESIA Pt. 22

A group of islands in the Pacific, from 1899 to 1914 part of the German Caroline Islands. Occupied by the Japanese in 1914 the islands were from 1920 a Japanese mandated territory, and from 1947 part of the United States Trust Territory of the Pacific Islands, using United States stamps. Micronesia assumed control of its postal services in 1984.

100 cents = 1 dollar.

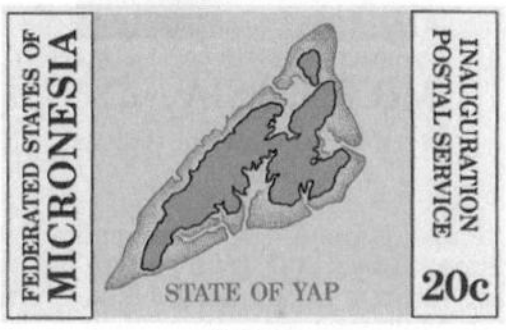

1 Yap

1984. Inauguration of Postal Independence. Maps. Multicoloured.

1	20c. Type **1**	50	40
2	20c. Truk	50	40
3	20c. Pohnpei	50	40
4	20c. Kosrae	50	40

2 Fernandez de Quiros

3 Boeing 727-100

1984.

5	2	1c. blue	10	10
6	–	2c. brown	10	10
7	–	3c. blue	10	10
8	–	4c. green	10	10
9	–	5c. brown and olive	10	10
10	–	10c. purple	15	10
11	–	13c. blue	20	10
11a	–	15c. red	20	10
12	–	17c. brown	25	10
13	2	19c. purple	30	10
14	–	20c. green	30	10
14a	–	22c. green	30	15
14b	–	25c. orange	30	15
15	–	30c. red	45	15
15a	–	36c. blue	50	20
16	–	37c. violet	50	20
16a	–	45c. green	60	30
17	–	50c. brown and sepia	80	35
18	–	$1 olive	1·25	85
19	–	$2 blue	2·50	1·50
20	–	$5 brown	6·00	4·50
20a	–	$10 blue	12·50	11·00

DESIGNS: 2, 20c. Louis Duperrey; 3, 30c. Fyodor Lutke; 4, 37c. Jules Dumont d'Urville; 5c. Men's house, Yap; 10, 45c. Sleeping Lady (mountains), Kosrae; 13, 15c. Liduduhriap waterfall, Pohnpei; 17, 25c. Tonachau Peak, Truk; 22, 36c. "Senyavin" (full-rigged sailing ship); 50c. Devil mask, Truk; $1 Sokehs Rock, Pohnpei; $2 Outrigger canoes, Kosrae; $5 Stone money, Yap; $10 Official seal.

1984. Air. Multicoloured.

21	28c. Type **3**	55	30
22	35c. Grumman SA-16 Albatros flying boat	70	50
23	40c. Consolidated PBY-5A Catalina amphibian	95	60

4 Truk Post Office

1984. "Ausipex 84" International Stamp Exhibition, Melbourne. Multicoloured.

24	20c. Type **4** (postage)	50	20
25	28c. German Caroline Islands 1919 3pf. yacht stamp (air)	60	40
26	35c. German 1900 20pf. stamp optd for Caroline Islands	70	50
27	40c. German Caroline Islands 1915 5m. yacht stamp	80	65

5 Baby in Basket

1984. Christmas. Multicoloured.

28	20c. Type **5** (postage)	55	25
29	28c. Open book showing Christmas scenes (air)	65	40
30	35c. Palm tree decorated with lights	85	50
31	40c. Women preparing food	1·00	65

6 U.S.S. "Jamestown" (warship)

1985. Ships.

32	6	22c. black & brown (postage)	65	35
33	–	33c. black and lilac (air)	85	50
34	–	39c. black and green	1·00	75
35	–	44c. black and red	1·40	90

DESIGNS: 33c. "L'Astrolabe" (D'Urville's ship); 39c. "La Coquille" (Duperrey's ship); 44c. "Shenandoah" (Confederate warship).

7 Lelu Protestant Church, Kosrae

1985. Christmas.

36	7	22c. black and orange (postage)	55	30
37	–	33c. black and violet (air)	80	50
38	–	44c. black and green	1·10	70

DESIGNS: 33c. Dublon Protestant Church; 44c. Pohnpei Catholic Church.

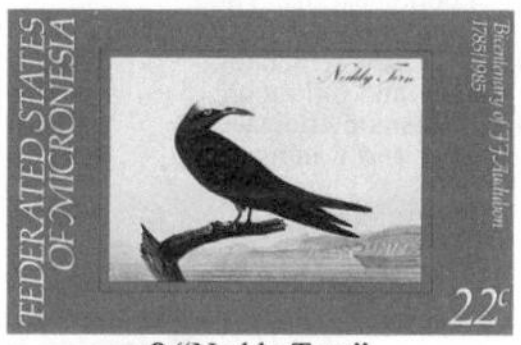

8 "Noddy Tern"

1985. Birth Bicentenary of John J. Audubon (ornithologist). Multicoloured.

39	22c. Type **8** (postage)	80	80
40	22c. "Turnstone"	80	80
41	22c. "Golden Plover"	80	80
42	22c. "Black-bellied Plover"	80	80
43	44c. "Sooty Tern" (air)	1·50	1·50

9 Land of Sacred Masonry

1985. Nan Madol, Pohnpei. Multicoloured.

44	22c. Type **9** (postage)	45	25
45	33c. Nan Tauas inner courtyard (air)	60	45
46	39c. Nan Tauas outer wall	75	60
47	44c. Nan Tauas burial vault	90	70

10 Doves, "LOVE" and Hands

12 Bully Hayes

1986. Anniversaries and Events. Multicoloured.

48	22c. Type **10** (International Peace Year)	50	35
49	44c. Halley's comet	1·25	80
50	44c. "Trienza" (cargo liner) arriving at jetty (40th anniv of return of Nauruans from Truk)	1·25	80

1986. Nos. 1/4 surch.

51	22c. on 20c. Type **1**	45	45
52	22c. on 20c. Truk	45	45
53	22c. on 20c. Pohnpei	45	45
54	22c. on 20c. Kosrae	45	45

1986. "Ameripex 86" International Stamp Exhibition, Chicago. Bully Hayes (buccaneer). Multicoloured.

55	22c. Type **12** (postage)	50	30
56	33c. Angelo (crew member) forging Hawaii 5c. blue stamp (air)	65	50
57	39c. "Leonora" sinking off Kosrae	75	60
58	44c. Hayes escaping capture on Kosrae	95	75
59	75c. Cover of book "Bully Hayes, Buccaneer" by Louis Becke	1·50	1·25

13 "Madonna and Child"

1986. Christmas. "Madonna and Child" Paintings.

61	–	5c. multicoloured (postage)	15	10
62	–	22c. multicoloured	70	30
63	–	33c. multicoloured (air)	95	65
64	13	44c. multicoloured	1·25	1·00

14 Passports on Globe

1986. 1st Micronesian Passport.

65	14	22c. blue, black and yellow	50	35

15 Emblem (International Year of Shelter for the Homeless)

1987. Anniversaries and Events.

66	15	22c. blue, red and black (postage)	50	40
67	–	33c. green, red and black (air)	75	50
68	–	39c. blue, black and red	90	60
69	–	44c. blue, red and black	1·25	75

DESIGNS: 33c. Dollar sign (bicentenary of dollar currency); 39c. Space capsule (25th anniv of first American to orbit Earth); 44c. "200 USA" (bicentenary of US constitution).

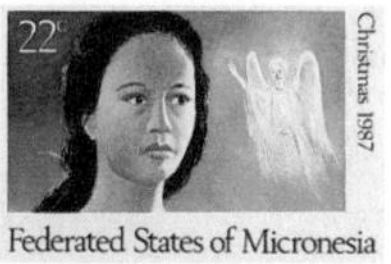

16 Archangel Gabriel appearing to Mary

1987. Christmas. Multicoloured.

71	22c. Type **16** (postage)	40	30
72	33c. Joseph praying and Mary with baby Jesus (air)	60	45
73	39c. Shepherds with their sheep	75	60
74	44c. Wise men	90	75

17 Spanish Missionary and Flag

1988. Micronesian History. Multicoloured.

75	22c. Type **17** (postage)	50	35
76	22c. Natives producing copra and German flag	50	35
77	22c. School pupils and Japanese flag	50	35
78	22c. General store and U.S. flag	50	35
79	44c. Traditional boatbuilding and fishing skills (air)	1·00	75
80	44c. Welcoming tourists from Douglas DC-10 airliner and divers investigating World War II wreckage	1·00	75

18 Ponape White Eye

19 Marathon

1988. Birds. Multicoloured.

81	3c. Type **18** (postage)	10	10
82	14c. Truk monarch	25	10
83	22c. Ponape starling	35	20
84	33c. Truk white eye (air)	55	35
85	44c. Blue-faced parrot finch	75	65
86	$1 Yap monarch	1·50	1·40

1988. Olympic Games, Seoul. Multicoloured.

87	25c. Type **19**	45	25
88	25c. Hurdling	45	25
89	45c. Basketball	70	55
90	45c. Volleyball	70	55

20 Girls decorating Tree

1988. Christmas. Multicoloured.

91	25c. Type **20**	45	30
92	25c. Dove with mistletoe in beak and children holding decorations	45	30
93	25c. Boy in native clothing and girl in floral dress sitting at base of tree	45	30
94	25c. Boy in T-shirt and shorts and girl in native clothing sitting at base of tree	45	30

Nos. 91/4 were printed together in blocks of four, se-tenant, forming a composite design.

21 Blue-girdled Angelfish

1988. Truk Lagoon, "Micronesia's Living War Memorial". Multicoloured.

95	25c. Type **21**	50	40
96	25c. Jellyfish and shoal of small fishes	50	40
97	25c. Snorkel divers	50	40
98	25c. Two golden trevally (black-striped fishes facing left)	50	40
99	25c. Blackfinned reef shark	50	40
100	25c. Deck railings of wreck and fishes	50	40
101	25c. Soldierfish (red fish) and damselfish	50	40
102	25c. Damselfish, narrow-banded batfish and aircraft cockpit	50	40
103	25c. Three Moorish idols (fishes with long dorsal fins)	50	40
104	25c. Four pickhandle barracuda and shoal	50	40
105	25c. Spot-banded butterflyfish and damselfish (facing alternate directions)	50	40
106	25c. Three-spotted dascyllus and aircraft propeller	50	40
107	25c. Fox-faced rabbitfish and shoal	50	40
108	25c. Lionfish (fish with spines)	50	40
109	25c. Scuba diver and white-tailed damselfish	50	40
110	25c. Tubular corals	50	40
111	25c. White-tailed damselfish, ornate butterflyfish and brain coral	50	40
112	25c. Pink anemonefish, giant clam and sea plants	50	40

Nos. 95/112 were printed together, se-tenant, in sheetlets of 18 stamps, the backgrounds of the stamps forming an overall design of the remains of a Japanese ship and "Zero" fighter plane on the Lagoon bed colonized by marine life.

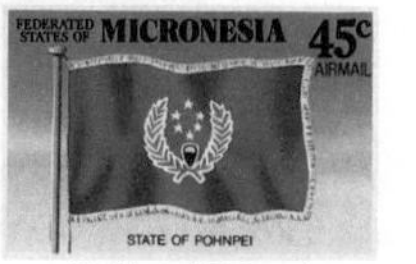

22 Flag of Pohnpei

1989. Air. State Flags. Multicoloured.

113	45c. Type **22**	65	50
114	45c. Truk	65	50
115	45c. Kosrae	65	50
116	45c. Yap	65	50

23 Plumeria and Headdress

1989. Mwarmwarms (floral decorations). Mult.

117	45c. Type **23**	65	50
118	45c. Hibiscus and lei	65	50

119	45c. Jasmine and Yap religious mwarmwarm	65	50
120	45c. Bougainvillea and Truk dance mwarmwarm	65	50

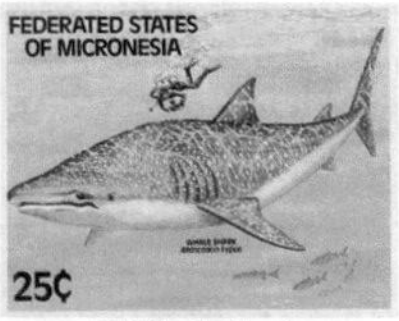

24 Whale Shark

1989. Sharks. Multicoloured.

121	25c. Type **24**	70	40
122	25c. Smooth hammerhead	70	40
123	45c. Tiger shark (vert)	1·10	75
124	45c. Great white shark (vert)	1·10	75

26 "Explorer 1" Satellite over North America

1989. 20th Anniv of First Manned Landing on the Moon. Multicoloured.

126	25c. Bell XS-15 rocket plane	40	30
127	25c. Type **26**	40	30
128	25c. Ed White on space walk during "Gemini 4" mission	40	30
129	25c. "Apollo 18" spacecraft	40	30
130	25c. "Gemini 4" space capsule over South America	40	30
131	25c. Space Shuttle "Challenger"	40	30
132	25c. Italian "San Marco 2" satellite	40	30
133	25c. Russian "Soyuz 19" spacecraft	40	30
134	25c. Neil Armstrong descending ladder to Moon's surface during "Apollo 11" mission	40	30
135	$2.40 Lunar module "Eagle" on Moon (34 × 46 mm)	3·50	2·75

Nos. 126/34 were printed together in se-tenant sheetlets of nine stamps, the backgrounds of the stamps forming an overall design of Earth as viewed from the Moon.

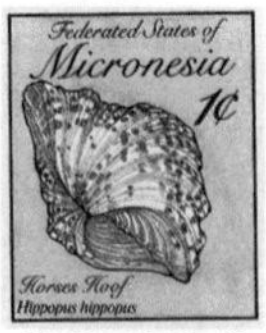

27 Horse's Hoof

1989. Sea Shells. Multicoloured.

136	1c. Type **27**	10	10
137	3c. Rare spotted cowrie	10	10
138	15c. Commercial trochus	20	10
139	20c. General cone	25	10
140	25c. Trumpet triton	30	20
141	30c. Laciniate conch	35	25
142	36c. Red-mouth olive	45	35
143	45c. All-red map cowrie	55	45
144	50c. Textile cone	60	50
145	$1 Orange spider conch	1·40	1·00
146	$2 Golden cowrie	2·75	2·00
147	$5 Episcopal mitre	6·50	4·50

28 Oranges

1989. "World Stamp Expo '89" International Stamp Exhibition, Washington D.C. "Kosrae–The Garden State". Multicoloured.

155	25c. Type **28**	40	30
156	25c. Limes	40	30
157	25c. Tangerines	40	30
158	25c. Mangoes	40	30
159	25c. Coconuts	40	30
160	25c. Breadfruit	40	30
161	25c. Sugar cane	40	30
162	25c. Kosrae house	40	30
163	25c. Bananas	40	30
164	25c. Children with fruit and flowers	40	30
165	25c. Pineapples	40	30
166	25c. Taro	40	30
167	25c. Hibiscus	40	30
168	25c. Ylang ylang	40	30
169	25c. White ginger	40	30
170	25c. Plumeria	40	30
171	25c. Royal poinciana	40	30
172	25c. Yellow allamanda	40	30

29 Angel over Micronesian Village

1989. Christmas. Multicoloured.

173	25c. Type **29**	30	20
174	45c. Truk children dressed as Three Kings	65	50

30 Young Kingfisher and Sokehs Rock, Pohnpei

1990. Endangered Species. Micronesian Kingfisher and Micronesian Pigeon.

175	10c. Type **30**	35	25
176	15c. Adult kingfisher and rain forest, Pohnpei	55	35
177	20c. Pigeon flying over lake at Sleeping Lady, Kosrae	90	65
178	25c. Pigeon perched on leaf, Tol Island, Truk	1·25	1·10

31 Wooden Whale Stamp and "Lyra"

1990. "Stamp World London 90" International Stamp Exhibition. 19th-century British Whaling Ships. Multicoloured.

179	45c. Type **31**	65	45
180	45c. Harpoon heads and "Prudent"	65	45
181	45c. Carved whale bone and "Rhone"	65	45
182	45c. Carved whale tooth and "Sussex"	65	45

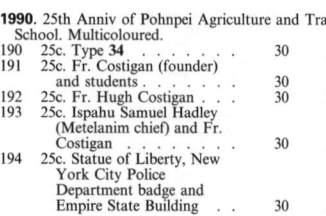

33 Beech 18 over Kosrae Airport

34 School Building

1990. Air. Aircraft. Multicoloured.

185	22c. Type **33**	30	15
186	36c. Boeing 727 landing at Truk	50	30
187	39c. Britten Norman Islander over Pohnpei	50	30
188	45c. Beech Queen Air over Yap	60	35

1990. 25th Anniv of Pohnpei Agriculture and Trade School. Multicoloured.

190	25c. Type **34**	30	20
191	25c. Fr. Costigan (founder) and students	30	20
192	25c. Fr. Hugh Costigan	30	20
193	25c. Ispahu Samuel Hadley (Metelanim chief) and Fr. Costigan	30	20
194	25c. Statue of Liberty, New York City Police Department badge and Empire State Building	30	20

36 Loading Mail Plane at Pohnpei Airport

1990. Pacific Postal Transport. Multicoloured.

196	25c. Type **36**	35	20
197	45c. Launch meeting "Nantaku" (inter-island freighter) in Truk Lagoon to exchange mail, 1940	65	40

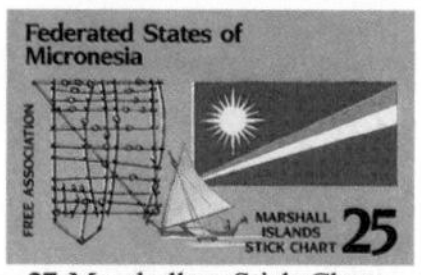

37 Marshallese Stick Chart, Outrigger Canoe and Flag

1990. 4th Anniv of Ratification of Micronesia and Marshall Islands Compacts of Free Association. Multicoloured.

198	25c. Type **37**	45	20
199	25c. Great frigate bird, U.S.S. "Constitution" (frigate), U.S. flag and American bald eagle	55	55
200	25c. Micronesian outrigger canoe and flag	45	20

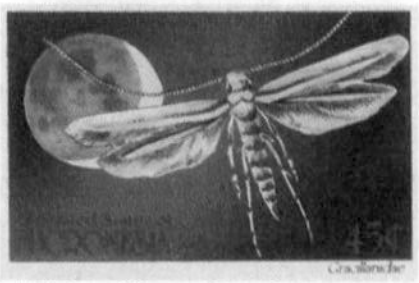

38 "Caloptilia sp." and New Moon

1990. Moths. Multicoloured.

201	45c. Type **38**	60	50
202	45c. "Anticrates sp." (inscr "Yponomeatidae") and waxing moon	60	50
203	45c. "Cosmopterigidae" family and full moon	60	50
204	45c. "Cosmopteridigae" family and waning moon	60	50

39 Cherub above Roof

41 Hawksbill Turtle returning to Sea

1990. Christmas. "Micronesian Holy Night". Multicoloured.

205	25c. Type **39**	30	20
206	25c. Two cherubs and Star of Bethlehem	30	20
207	25c. Cherub blowing horn	30	20
208	25c. Lambs, goat, pig and chickens	30	20
209	25c. Native wise men offering gifts to Child	30	20
210	25c. Children and dog beside lake	30	20
211	25c. Man blowing trumpet triton	30	20
212	25c. Adults and children on path	30	20
213	25c. Man and children carrying gifts	30	20

Nos. 205/13 were printed together, se-tenant, forming a composite design.

1991. Sea Turtles. Multicoloured.

215	29c. Type **41**	50	30
216	29c. Green turtles swimming underwater	50	30
217	50c. Hawksbill turtle swimming underwater	90	50
218	50c. Leatherback turtle swimming underwater	90	50

42 Boeing E-3 Sentry

1991. Operations Desert Shield and Desert Storm (liberation of Kuwait). Multicoloured.

219	29c. Type **42**	40	25
220	29c. Grumman F-14 Tomcat fighter	40	25
221	29c. U.S.S. "Missouri" (battleship)	40	25
222	29c. Multiple Launch Rocket System	40	25
223	$2.90 Great frigate bird with yellow ribbon and flag of Micronesia (50 × 37 mm)	5·50	5·50

43 "Evening Flowers, Toloas, Truk"

1991. "Phila Nippon '91" International Stamp Exhibition, Tokyo. 90th Birth Anniv (1992) of Paul Jacoulet (artist). Micronesian Ukiyo-e Prints by Jacoulet. Multicoloured.

225	29c. Type **43**	40	25
226	29c. "The Chief's Daughter, Mogomog"	40	25
227	29c. "Yagourouh and Mio, Yap"	40	25
228	50c. "Yap Beauty and Orchids"	70	45
229	50c. "The Yellow-Eyed Boys, Ohlol"	70	45
230	50c. "Violet Flowers, Tomil, Yap"	70	45

44 Sheep and Holy Family

1991. Christmas. Shell Cribs. Multicoloured.

232	29c. Type **44**	40	25
233	40c. Three Kings arriving at Bethlehem	55	35
234	50c. Sheep around manger	65	45

45 Pohnpei Fruit Bat

1991. Pohnpei Rain Forest. Multicoloured.

235	29c. Type **45**	55	55
236	29c. Purple-capped fruit dove	55	55
237	29c. Micronesian kingfisher	55	55
238	29c. Birdnest fern	55	55
239	29c. Caroline swiftlets ("Island Swiftlet")	55	55
240	29c. Ponape white-eye ("Long-billed White-eye")	55	55
241	29c. Common noddy ("Brown Noddy")	55	55
242	29c. Ponape lory ("Pohnpei Lory")	55	55
243	29c. Micronesian flycatcher ("Pohnpei Flycatcher")	55	55
244	29c. Truk Island ground dove ("Caroline Ground-Dove")	55	55
245	29c. White-tailed tropic bird	55	55
246	29c. Cardinal honeyeater ("Micronesian Honeyeater")	55	55
247	29c. Ixora	55	55
248	29c. Rufous fantail ("Pohnpei Fantail")	55	55
249	29c. Grey-brown white-eye ("Grey White-eye")	55	55
250	29c. Blue-faced parrot finch	55	55
251	29c. Common Cicadabird ("Cicadabird")	55	55
252	29c. Green skink	55	55

Nos. 235/52 were issued together, se-tenant, forming a composite design.

46 Britten Norman Islander and Outrigger Canoe

47 Volunteers learning Crop Planting

1992. Air. Multicoloured.

253	40c. Type **46**	55	35
254	50c. Boeing 727-200 airliner and outrigger canoe (different)	65	45

1992. 25th Anniv of Presence of United States Peace Corps in Micronesia. Multicoloured.

255	29c. Type **47**	40	25
256	29c. Education	40	25
257	29c. Pres. John Kennedy announcing formation of Peace Corps	40	25
258	29c. Public health nurses	40	25
259	29c. Recreation	40	25

48 Queen Isabella of Spain

1992. 500th Anniv of Discovery of America by Christopher Columbus. Multicoloured.

260	29c. Type **48**	1·10	50
261	29c. "Santa Maria"	1·10	50
262	29c. Christopher Columbus	1·10	50

49 Flags

1992. 1st Anniv of U.N. Membership.

264	**49** 29c. multicoloured	40	25
265	50c. multicoloured	65	45

50 Bouquet

1992. Christmas.

266	**50** 29c. multicoloured	40	25

51 Edward Rickenbacker (fighter pilot)

1993. Pioneers of Flight (1st series). Pioneers and aircraft. Multicoloured.

267	29c. Type **51**	45	30
268	29c. Manfred von Richthofen (fighter pilot)	45	30
269	29c. Andrei Tupolev (aeronautical engineer)	45	30
270	29c. John Macready (first non-stop crossing of U.S.A.)	45	30
271	29c. Sir Charles Kingsford-Smith (first trans-Pacific flight)	45	30
272	29c. Igor Sikorsky (aeronautical engineer)	45	30
273	29c. Lord Trenchard ("Father of the Royal Air Force")	45	30
274	29c. Glenn Curtiss (builder of U.S. Navy's first aircraft)	45	30

See also Nos. 322/9, 364/71, 395/402, 418/25, 441/8, 453/60 and 514/21.

52 Big-scaled Soldierfish

1993. Fishes. Multicoloured.

275	10c. Type **52**	15	10
276	19c. Bennett's butterflyfish	25	15
277	20c. Peacock hind ("Peacock Grouper")	25	15
278	22c. Great barracuda	30	20
278a	23c. Yellow-finned tuna	30	20
279	25c. Coral hind ("Coral Grouper")	30	20
280	29c. Regal angelfish	40	25
281	30c. Bleeker's parrotfish	40	25
282	32c. Saddle butterflyfish (dated "1995")	40	25
283	35c. Picasso triggerfish ("Picassofish")	45	30
284	40c. Mandarin fish	50	35
285	45c. Clown ("Bluebanded") surgeonfish	60	40
285a	46c. Red-tailed surgeonfish ("Achilles Tang")	60	40
286	50c. Undulate ("Orange-striped") triggerfish	65	45
287	52c. Palette surgeonfish	70	45
288	55c. Moorish idol	70	45
288a	60c. Skipjack tuna	80	55
289	75c. Oriental sweetlips	95	65
290	78c. Square-spotted anthias ("Square-spot Fairy Basslet")	1·00	65
290a	95c. Blue-striped ("Blue-lined") snapper	1·25	85
291	$1 Zebra moray	1·25	85
292	$2 Fox-faced rabbitfish	2·50	1·60
293	$2.90 Masked ("Orangespine") unicornfish	3·75	2·50
294	$3 Flame angelfish	3·75	2·50
295	$5 Six-blotched hind ("Cave Grouper")	6·50	4·25

See also Nos. 465/89 and 522/5.

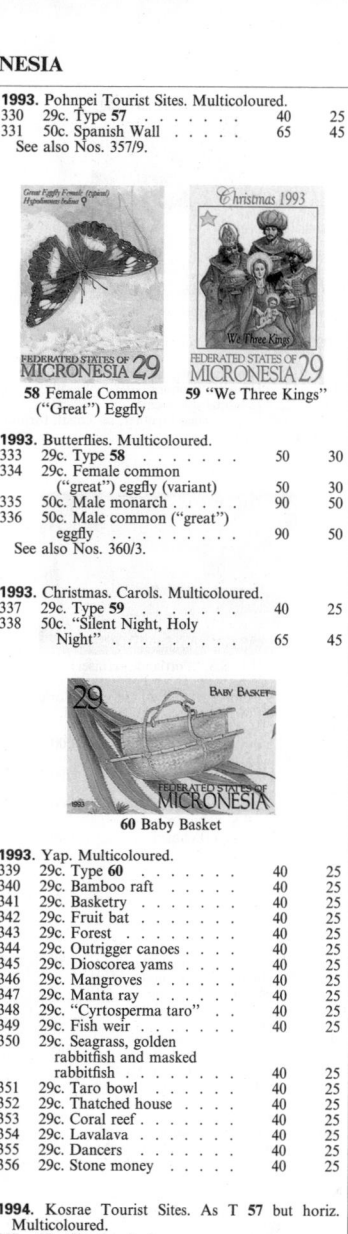

53 "Great Republic"

54 Jefferson

1993. American Clipper Ships. Multicoloured.

301	29c. Type **53**	50	35
302	29c. "Benjamin F. Packard"	50	35
303	29c. "Stag Hound"	50	35
304	29c. "Herald of the Morning"	50	35
305	29c. "Rainbow" and junk	50	35
306	29c. "Flying Cloud"	50	35
307	29c. "Lightning"	50	35
308	29c. "Sea Witch"	50	35
309	29c. "Columbia"	50	35
310	29c. "New World"	50	35
311	29c. "Young America"	50	35
312	29c. "Courier"	50	35

1993. 250th Birth Anniv of Thomas Jefferson (U.S. President, 1801–09).

313	**54** 29c. multicoloured	45	25

55 Yap Outrigger Canoe

1993. Traditional Canoes. Multicoloured.

314	29c. Type **55**	50	35
315	29c. Kosrae outrigger canoe	50	35
316	29c. Pohnpei lagoon outrigger canoe	50	35
317	29c. Chuuk war canoe	50	35

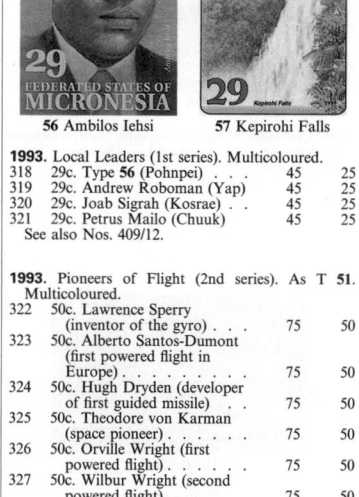

56 Ambilos Iehsi

57 Kepirohi Falls

1993. Local Leaders (1st series). Multicoloured.

318	29c. Type **56** (Pohnpei)	45	25
319	29c. Andrew Roboman (Yap)	45	25
320	29c. Joab Sigrah (Kosrae)	45	25
321	29c. Petrus Mailo (Chuuk)	45	25

See also Nos. 409/12.

1993. Pioneers of Flight (2nd series). As T **51**. Multicoloured.

322	50c. Lawrence Sperry (inventor of the gyro)	75	50
323	50c. Alberto Santos-Dumont (first powered flight in Europe)	75	50
324	50c. Hugh Dryden (developer of first guided missile)	75	50
325	50c. Theodore von Karman (space pioneer)	75	50
326	50c. Orville Wright (first powered flight)	75	50
327	50c. Wilbur Wright (second powered flight)	75	50
328	50c. Otto Lilienthal (first heavier-than-air flight)	75	50
329	50c. Sir Thomas Sopwith (aircraft designer)	75	50

1993. Pohnpei Tourist Sites. Multicoloured.

330	29c. Type **57**	40	25
331	50c. Spanish Wall	65	45

See also Nos. 357/9.

58 Female Common ("Great") Eggfly

59 "We Three Kings"

1993. Butterflies. Multicoloured.

333	29c. Type **58**	50	30
334	29c. Female common ("great") eggfly (variant)	50	30
335	50c. Male monarch	90	50
336	50c. Male common ("great") eggfly	90	50

See also Nos. 360/3.

1993. Christmas. Carols. Multicoloured.

337	29c. Type **59**	40	25
338	50c. "Silent Night, Holy Night"	65	45

60 Baby Basket

1993. Yap. Multicoloured.

339	29c. Type **60**	40	25
340	29c. Bamboo raft	40	25
341	29c. Basketry	40	25
342	29c. Fruit bat	40	25
343	29c. Forest	40	25
344	29c. Outrigger canoes	40	25
345	29c. Dioscorea yams	40	25
346	29c. Mangroves	40	25
347	29c. Manta ray	40	25
348	29c. "Cyrtosperma taro"	40	25
349	29c. Fish weir	40	25
350	29c. Seagrass, golden rabbitfish and masked rabbitfish	40	25
351	29c. Taro bowl	40	25
352	29c. Thatched house	40	25
353	29c. Coral reef	40	25
354	29c. Lavalava	40	25
355	29c. Dancers	40	25
356	29c. Stone money	40	25

1994. Kosrae Tourist Sites. As T **57** but horiz. Multicoloured.

357	29c. Sleeping Lady (mountains)	40	25
358	40c. Walung	50	35
359	50c. Lelu Ruins	65	45

1994. "Hong Kong '94" International Stamp Exhibition. Designs as Nos. 333/6 but with inscriptions in brown and additionally inscribed "Hong Kong '94 Stamp Exhibition" in English (361/2) or Chinese (others).

360	29c. As No. 333	50	25
361	29c. As No. 334	50	25
362	50c. As No. 335	75	50
363	50c. As No. 336	75	50

1994. Pioneers of Flight (3rd series). As T **51**. Multicoloured.

364	29c. Octave Chanute (early glider designer)	45	25
365	29c. T. Claude Ryan (founder of first commercial airline)	45	25
366	29c. Edwin (Buzz) Aldrin ("Apollo 11" crew member and second man to step onto moon)	45	25
367	29c. Neil Armstrong (commander of "Apollo 11" and first man on moon)	45	25
368	29c. Frank Whittle (developer of jet engine)	45	25
369	29c. Waldo Waterman (aircraft designer)	45	25
370	29c. Michael Collins ("Apollo 11" crew member)	45	25
371	29c. Wernher von Braun (rocket designer)	45	25

61 Spearfishing

1994. 3rd Micronesian Games. Multicoloured.

372	29c. Type **61**	45	25
373	29c. Basketball	45	25
374	29c. Coconut husking	45	25
375	29c. Tree climbing	45	25

62 Pohnpei

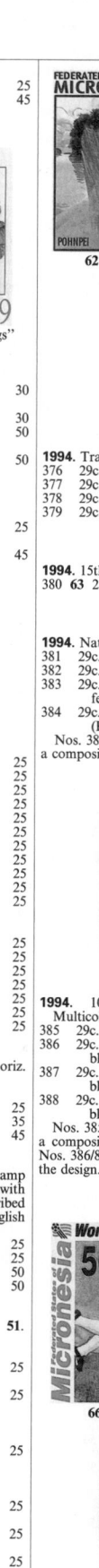

64 "Fagraea berteriana" (Kosrae)

63 People

1994. Traditional Costumes. Multicoloured.

376	29c. Type **62**	45	25
377	29c. Kosrae	45	25
378	29c. Chuuk	45	25
379	29c. Yap	45	25

1994. 15th Anniv of Constitution.

380	**63** 29c. multicoloured	45	25

1994. Native Flowers. Multicoloured.

381	29c. Type **64**	45	25
382	29c. "Pangium edule" (Yap)	45	25
383	29c. "Pittosporum ferrugineum" (Chuuk)	45	25
384	29c. "Sonneratia caseolaris" (Pohnpei)	45	25

Nos. 381/4 were issued together, se-tenant, forming a composite design.

65 1985 $10 Definitive under Magnifying Glass

1994. 10th Anniv of Postal Independence. Multicoloured.

385	29c. Type **65**	50	30
386	29c. 1993 traditional canoes block	50	30
387	29c. 1984 postal independence block	50	30
388	29c. 1994 native costumes block	50	30

Nos. 385/8 were issued together, se-tenant, forming a composite design of various Micronesian stamps. Nos. 386/8 are identified by the block in the centre of the design.

66 Players

69 Oriental Cuckoo

68 Iguanodons

1994. World Cup Football Championship, U.S.A. Multicoloured.

389	50c. Type **66**	70	45
390	50c. Ball and players	70	45

Nos. 389/90 were issued together, se-tenant, forming a composite design.

1994. "Philakorea 1994" International Stamp Exhibition, Seoul. Prehistoric Animals. Multicoloured.

392	29c. Type **68**	50	30
393	52c. Iguanodons and coelurosaurs	1·00	1·00
394	$1 Camarasaurus	1·60	1·00

Nos. 392/4 were issued together, se-tenant, forming a composite design.

1994. Pioneers of Flight (4th series). As T **51**. Multicoloured.

395	50c. Yuri Gagarin (first man in space)	75	50
396	50c. Alan Shepard Jr. (first American in space)	75	50
397	50c. William Bishop (fighter pilot)	75	50
398	50c. "Atlas" (first U.S. intercontinental ballistic missile) and Karel Bossart (aerospace engineer)	75	50
399	50c. John Towers (world endurance record, 1912)	75	50
400	50c. Hermann Oberth (space flight pioneer)	75	50
401	50c. Marcel Dassault (aircraft producer)	75	50
402	50c. Geoffrey de Havilland (aircraft designer)	75	50

1994. Migratory Birds. Multicoloured.

403	29c. Type **69**	65	65
404	29c. Long-tailed koel ("Long-tailed Cuckoo")	65	65
405	29c. Short-eared owl	65	65
406	29c. Eastern broad-billed roller ("Dollarbird")	65	65

70 Doves

1994. Christmas. Multicoloured.

407	29c. Type **70**	50	30
408	50c. Angels	90	60

1994. Local Leaders (2nd series). As T **56**. Mult.

409	32c. Anron Ring Buas	55	35
410	32c. Belarmino Hatheylul	55	35
411	32c. Johnny Moses	55	35
412	32c. Paliknoa Sigrah (King John)	55	35

72 Diver, Coral, Clown Triggerfish and Black-backed Butterflyfish

1995. Chuuk Lagoon. Multicoloured.

414	32c. Type **72**	55	35
415	32c. Black-backed butterflyfish, lionfish, regal angelfish and damselfishes	55	35
416	32c. Diver, thread-finned butterflyfish and damselfishes	55	35
417	32c. Pink anemonefish and damselfishes amongst anemone tentacles	55	35

Nos. 414/17 were issued together, se-tenant, forming a composite design.

1995. Pioneers of Flight (5th series). As T **51**. Multicoloured.

418	32c. Robert Goddard (first liquid-fuelled rocket)	50	30
419	32c. Leroy Grumman (first fighter with retractable landing gear)	50	30
420	32c. Louis-Charles Breguet (aeronautics engineer)	50	30
421	32c. Juan de la Cierva (inventor of autogyro)	50	30
422	32c. Hugo Junkers (aircraft engineer)	50	30
423	32c. James Lovell Jr. (astronaut)	50	30
424	32c. Donald Douglas (aircraft designer)	50	30
425	32c. Reginald Mitchell (designer of Spitfire fighter)	50	30

73 West Highland White Terrier

1995. Dogs. Multicoloured.

426	32c. Type **73**	55	35
427	32c. Welsh springer spaniel	55	35
428	32c. Irish setter	55	35
429	32c. Old English sheepdog	55	35

74 "Hibiscus tiliaceus"

1995. Hibiscus. Multicoloured.

430	32c. Type **74**	50	30
431	32c. "Hibiscus huegelii"	50	30
432	32c. "Hibiscus trionum"	50	30
433	32c. "Hibiscus splendens"	50	30

Nos. 430/3 were issued together, se-tenant, forming a composite design.

77 U.S.S. "Portland" (cruiser)

1995. 50th Anniv of End of Second World War. Liberation of Micronesia. Multicoloured.

436	60c. Type **77** (liberation of Chuuk)	1·00	70
437	60c. U.S.S. "Tillman" (destroyer) (Yap)	1·00	70
438	60c. U.S.S. "Soley" (destroyer) (Kosrae)	1·00	70
439	60c. U.S.S. "Hyman" (destroyer) (Pohnpei)	1·00	70

1995. Pioneers of Flight (6th series). As T **51**. Multicoloured.

441	60c. Frederick Rohr (developer of mass-production techniques)	90	60
442	60c. Juan Trippe (founder of Pan-American Airways)	90	60
443	60c. Konstantin Tsiolkovsky (rocket pioneer)	90	60
444	60c. Count Ferdinand von Zeppelin (airship inventor)	90	60
445	60c. Air Chief Marshal Hugh Dowding (commander of R.A.F. Fighter Command, 1940)	90	60
446	60c. William Mitchell (pioneer of aerial bombing)	90	60
447	60c. John Northrop (aircraft designer)	90	60
448	60c. Frederick Handley Page (producer of first twin-engine bomber)	90	60

79 Poinsettia

80 Rabin

1995. Christmas.

449	**79**	32c. multicoloured	40	25
450		60c. multicoloured	80	55

1995. Yitzhak Rabin (Israeli Prime Minister) Commemoration.

451	**80**	32c. multicoloured	55	35

1995. Pioneers of Flight (7th series). As T **51**. Multicoloured.

453	32c. James Doolittle (leader of America's Second World War bomb raid on Japan)	50	30
454	32c. Claude Dornier (aircraft designer)	50	30
455	32c. Ira Eaker (leader of air effort against occupied Europe during Second World War)	50	30
456	32c. Jacob Ellehammer (first European manned flight)	50	30
457	32c. Henry Arnold (Commander of U.S. air operations during Second World War)	50	30
458	32c. Louis Bleriot (first flight across the English Channel)	50	30
459	32c. William Boeing (founder of Boeing Corporation)	50	30
460	32c. Sydney Camm (aircraft designer)	50	30

82 Meeting House

1995. Tourism in Yap. Multicoloured.

461	32c. Type **82**	50	30
462	32c. Stone money	50	30
463	32c. Churu dancing	50	30
464	32c. Traditional canoe	50	30

1995. Fishes. As Nos. 275/95 but face values changed. Multicoloured.

465	32c. Bennett's butterflyfish	55	25
466	32c. Regal angelfish	55	25
467	32c. Undulate ("Orange-striped") triggerfish	55	25
468	32c. Zebra moray	55	25
469	32c. Great barracuda	55	25
470	32c. Bleeker's parrotfish	55	25
471	32c. Mandarin fish	55	25
472	32c. Clown ("Blue-banded") surgeonfish	55	25
473	32c. Big-scaled soldierfish	55	25
474	32c. Peacock hind ("Peacock Grouper")	55	25
475	32c. Picasso triggerfish ("Picassofish")	55	25
476	32c. Masked ("Orangespine") unicornfish	55	25
477	32c. Red-tailed surgeonfish	55	25
478	32c. Coral hind ("Coral Grouper")	55	25
479	32c. Palette surgeonfish	55	25
480	32c. Oriental sweetlips	55	25
481	32c. Fox-faced rabbitfish	55	25
482	32c. Saddle butterflyfish (dated "1996")	55	25
483	32c. Moorish idol	55	25
484	32c. Square-spotted anthias ("Square-spot Fairy Basslet")	55	25
485	32c. Flame angelfish	55	25
486	32c. Yellow-finned tuna	55	25
487	32c. Skipjack tuna	55	25
488	32c. Blue-striped ("Blue-lined") snapper	55	25
489	32c. Six-blotched hind ("Cave Grouper")	55	25

See also Nos. 522/5.

83 Necklace Sea Star

1996. Starfishes. Multicoloured.

490	55c. Type **83**	85	55
491	55c. Rhinoceros sea star	85	55
492	55c. Blue sea star	85	55
493	55c. Thick-skinned sea star	85	55

Nos. 490/3 were issued together, se-tenant, forming a composite design.

84 10l. Stamp

1996. Centenary of Modern Olympic Games. Designs reproducing 1896 Greek Olympic Issue. Multicoloured.

494	60c. Type **84**	1·10	70
495	60c. 25l. stamp	1·10	70
496	60c. 20l. stamp	1·10	70
497	60c. 10d. stamp	1·10	70

85 "Palikir"

1996. Patrol Boats. Multicoloured.

498	32c. Type **85**	45	25
499	32c. "Micronesia"	45	25

Nos. 498/9 were issued together, se-tenant, forming a composite design.

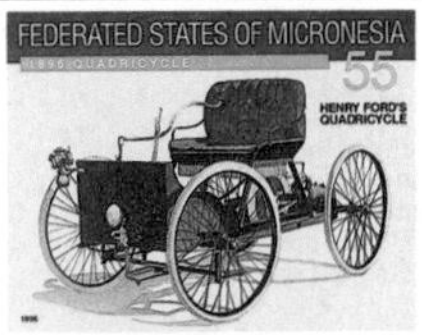

87 1896 Quadricycle

1996. Centenary of Ford Motor Vehicle Production. Multicoloured.

501	55c. Type **87**	90	60
502	55c. 1917 Model T Truck	90	60
503	55c. 1928 Model A Tudor Sedan	90	60
504	55c. 1932 V-8 Sport Roadster	90	60
505	55c. 1941 Lincoln Continental	90	60
506	55c. 1953 F-100 Truck	90	60
507	55c. 1958 Thunderbird convertible	90	60
508	55c. 1996 Mercury Sable	90	60

88 Reza

89 Oranges

1996. Reza (National Police Drug Enforcement Unit's dog).

509	**88**	32c. multicoloured	50	30

1996. Citrus Fruits. Multicoloured.

510	50c. Type **89**	90	60
511	50c. Limes	90	60
512	50c. Lemons	90	60
513	50c. Tangerines	90	60

Nos. 510/13 were issued together, se-tenant, forming a composite design.

1996. Pioneers of Flight (8th series). As T **51**. Multicoloured.

514	60c. Curtis LeMay (commander of Strategic Air Command)	90	60
515	60c. Grover Loening (first American graduate in aeronautical engineering)	90	60
516	60c. Gianni Caproni (aircraft producer)	90	60
517	60c. Henri Farman (founder of Farman Airlines)	90	60
518	60c. Glenn Martin (aircraft producer)	90	60
519	60c. Alliot Verdon Roe (aircraft designer)	90	60
520	60c. Sergei Korolyov (rocket scientist)	90	60
521	60c. Isaac Laddon (aircraft designer)	90	60

1996. 10th Asian International Stamp Exhibition, Taipeh. Fishes. As previous designs but additionally inscr for the exhibition in English (522, 525) or Chinese (523/4).

522	32c. As No. 465	55	35
523	32c. As No. 468	55	35
524	32c. As No. 475	55	35
525	32c. As No. 483	55	35

90 Wise Men following Star

1996. Christmas.

526	**90**	32c. multicoloured	50	35
527		60c. multicoloured	90	60

91 Outrigger Canoe and State Flag

1996. 10th Anniv of Ratification of Compact of Free Association with U.S.A.

528	**91**	$3 multicoloured	4·50	3·25

92 Water Buffalo

1997. New Year. Year of the Ox.
529 **92** 32c. multicoloured 50 35

93 Walutahanga, Melanesia
94 Deng Xiaoping

1997. "Pacific 97" International Stamp Exhibition, San Francisco. Sea Goddesses of the Pacific. Multicoloured.
531 32c. Type **93** 50 30
532 32c. Tien-Hou holding lantern, China 50 30
533 32c. Lorop diving in ocean, Micronesia 50 30
534 32c. Oto-Hime with fisherman, Japan 50 30
535 32c. Nomoi holding shell, Micronesia 50 30
536 32c. Junkgowa Sisters in canoe, Australia 50 30

1997. Deng Xiaoping (Chinese statesman) Commemoration. Multicoloured.
537 60c. Type **94** 85 50
538 60c. Facing left (bare-headed) 85 50
539 60c. Facing right 85 50
540 60c. Facing left wearing cap 85 50

95 "Melia azedarach"

1997. Return of Hong Kong to China. Multicoloured.
542 60c. Type **95** 85 50
543 60c. Victoria Peak 85 50
544 60c. "Dendrobium chrysotoxum" 85 50
545 60c. "Bauhinia blakeana" . . 85 50
546 60c. "Cassia surattensis" . . 85 50
547 60c. Sacred lotus ("Nelumbo nucifera") 85 50

96 Tennis

1997. 2nd National Games. Multicoloured.
549 32c. Type **96** 50 30
550 32c. Throwing the discus . . 50 30
551 32c. Swimming 50 30
552 32c. Canoeing 50 30

97 Rapids

1997. Birth Bicentenary of Hiroshige Ando (painter). Designs depicting details from "Whirlpools at Naruto in Awa Province" (Nos. 553/5), "Tail of Genji: Viewing the Plum Blossoms" (Nos. 556/8) and "Snow on the Sumida River" (Nos. 559/61). Multicoloured.
553 20c. Type **97** 30 20
554 20c. Whirlpools (rocky island at left) 30 20
555 20c. Whirlpools (rocky island at right) 30 20
556 50c. Woman on stepping stones 65 40
557 50c. Woman 65 40
558 50c. Woman on balcony of house 65 40
559 60c. House and junks . . . . 1·00 60
560 60c. Two women . . . . . . 1·00 60
561 60c. Woman alighting from junk . . . . 1·00 60
Nos. 553/5, 556/8 and 559/61 respectively, were issued, se-tenant, forming composite designs of the paintings depicted.

98 Presley from High School Graduation Yearbook

1997. 20th Death Anniv of Elvis Presley (entertainer). Multicoloured.
563 50c. Type **98** 85 55
564 50c. With hound dog Nipper (R.C.A. Records mascot) 85 55
565 50c. Wearing red striped shirt in publicity photograph for "Loving You" (film), 1957 85 55
566 50c. Wearing sailor's cap in scene from "Girls, Girls, Girls!" (film), 1963 . . . . 85 55
567 50c. Wearing knitted jacket with collar turned up, 1957 85 55
568 50c. Wearing stetson in scene from "Flaming Star" (film), 1960 . . . . 85 55

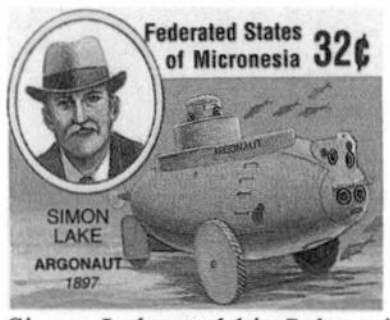

99 Simon Lake and his Submarine "Argonaut", 1897

1997. Ocean Exploration: Pioneers of the Deep. Multicoloured.
569 32c. Type **99** 40 25
570 32c. William Beebe and Otis Barton's bathysphere (record depth, 1934) . . . 40 25
571 32c. Auguste Piccard and his bathyscaphe, 1954 . . . . 40 25
572 32c. Harold Edgerton and his deep sea camera, 1954 . . 40 25
573 32c. Jacques Piccard and U.S. Navy bathyscaphe "Trieste" (designed by Auguste Piccard) (record depth with Don Walsh, 1960) 40 25
574 32c. Edwin Link and diving chamber ("Man-in-Sea" projects, 1962) 40 25
575 32c. Melvin Fisher and diver (discovery of "Atocha" and "Santa Margarita" (Spanish galleons), 1971) 40 25
576 32c. Robert Ballard and submersible "Alvin", 1978 40 25
577 32c. Sylvia Earle and submersible "Deep Rover" (record dive in armoured suit, 1979) 40 25

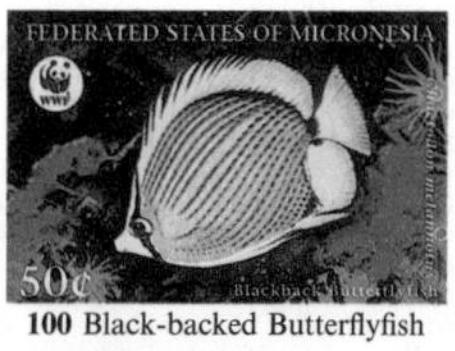

100 Black-backed Butterflyfish

1997. Butterflyfishes. Multicoloured.
579 50c. Type **100** 75 50
580 50c. Saddle butterflyfish . . . 75 50
581 50c. Thread-finned butterflyfish 75 50
582 50c. Bennett's butterflyfish . . 75 50

101 "Christ Glorified in the Court of Heaven" (Fra Angelico) (left detail)
102 Diana, Princess of Wales

1997. Christmas. Multicoloured.
583 32c. Type **101** 50 35
584 32c. "Christ Glorified in the Court of Heaven" (right detail) 50 35
585 60c . "A Choir of Angels" (detail, Simon Marmion) 75 50
586 60c. "A Choir of Angels" (different detail) 75 50

1997. Diana, Princess of Wales Commemoration.
587 **102** 60c. multicoloured 75 50

105 Rabbit

1998. Children's Libraries. The Hundred Acre Wood. Featuring characters from the Winnie the Pooh children's books. Multicoloured.
590 32c. Type **105** 55 35
591 32c. Owl 55 35
592 32c. Eeyore 55 35
593 32c. Kanga and Roo 55 35
594 32c. Piglet 55 35
595 32c. Tigger 55 35
596 32c. Pooh 55 35
597 32c. Christopher Robin . . . 55 35
Nos. 590/7 were issued together, se-tenant, forming a composite design.

106 Player celebrating Goal

1998. World Cup Football Championship, France. Multicoloured.
599 32c. Type **106** 50 30
600 32c. Player in green shirt kicking ball 50 30
601 32c. Player in yellow shirt tackling another player . . 50 30
602 32c. Goalkeeper throwing ball 50 30
603 32c. Player in yellow shirt kicking ball overhead . . . 50 30
604 32c. Goalkeeper in red shirt 50 30
605 32c. Player in yellow shirt with ball between legs . . 50 30
606 32c. Player in red shirt and player on ground 50 30
Nos. 599/606 were issued together, se-tenant, forming a composite design of a pitch.

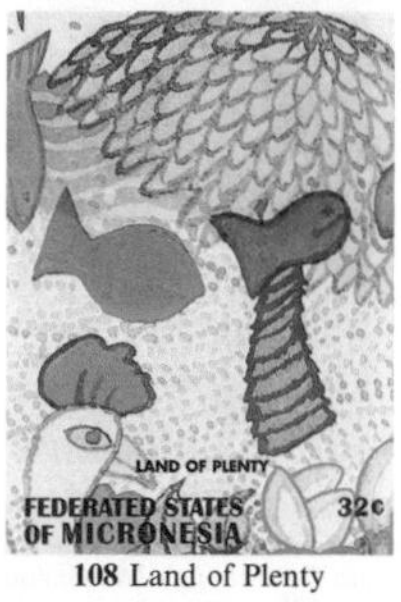

108 Land of Plenty

1998. Old Testament Stories. Multicoloured.
609 32c. Type **108** 50 30
610 32c. Adam and Eve 50 30
611 32c. Serpent of Temptation 50 30
612 40c. Three of Joseph's brothers 60 40
613 40c. Joseph and merchants 60 40
614 40c. Ishmaelites 60 40
615 60c. Rebekah in front of well 80 50
616 60c. Eliezer, Abraham's servant 80 50
617 60c. Angel 80 50

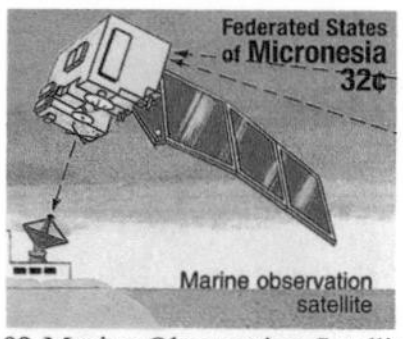

109 Marine Observation Satellite

1998. International Year of the Ocean. Deep Sea Research. Multicoloured.
619 32c. Type **109** 55 35
620 32c. "Natsushima" (support vessel) 55 35
621 32c. "Kaiyo" (research vessel) 55 35
622 32c. Anemone 55 35
623 32c. "Shinkai 2000" (deep-sea research vessel) 55 35
624 32c. Deep-towed research vessel 55 35
625 32c. Tripod fish 55 35
626 32c. Towed deep-survey system 55 35
627 32c. Black smokers 55 35
Nos. 619/27 were issued together, se-tenant, forming a composite design.

110 Grey-brown White-Eye ("Kosrae White-eye")
111 Ribbon-striped ("White-tipped") Soldierfish

1998. Birds. Multicoloured.
629 50c. Type **110** 60 40
630 50c. Truk monarch ("Chuuk Monarch") 60 40
631 50c. Yap monarch 60 40
632 50c. Pohnpei starling 60 40

1998. Fishes. Multicoloured.
634 1c. Type **111** 10 10
635 2c. Red-breasted wrasse . . . 10 10
636 3c. Bicoloured ("Bicolor") angelfish 10 10
637 4c. Falco hawkfish 10 10
638 5c. Convict tang 10 10
639 10c. Square-spotted anthias ("Square-spot Fairy Basslet") 10 10
640 13c. Orange-spotted ("Orangeband") surgeonfish 15 10
641 15c. Multibarred goatfish . . 20 15
642 17c. Masked rabbitfish . . . 20 15
643 20c. White-spotted surgeonfish 25 15
644 22c. Blue-girdled angelfish . . 30 20
645 32c. Rectangle triggerfish ("Wedge Picassofish") . . 40 25
646 33c. Black jack 40 25
647 39c. Red parrotfish 50 35
648 40c. Lemon-peel angelfish . . 50 35
649 50c. White-cheeked ("Whitecheek") surgeonfish 60 40
650 55c. Scarlet-finned ("Long-jawed") squirrelfish 65 45
651 60c. Hump-headed ("Humphead") wrasse . . . 75 50
652 77c. Onespot snapper 95 65
653 78c. Blue ("Sapphire") damselfish 95 65
654 $1 Blue-finned ("Bluefin") trevally . . . . 1·25 85
655 $3 Whitespot hawkfish . . . 3·75 2·25
656 $3.20 Tan-faced parrotfish . . 4·00 2·75
657 $5 Spotted boxfish ("Trunkfish") . . . . . . 6·25 4·25
658 $10.75 Pink-tailed ("Pinktail") triggerfish . . 13·50 9·00
659 $11.75 Yellow-faced angelfish (48 × 25 mm) . . . . . . 14·50 9·75

112 Fala being stroked

1998. Fala (Scottish terrier owned by Franklin D. Roosevelt). Multicoloured.
665 32c. Type **112** 40 25
666 32c. Fala and left half of wireless 40 25
667 32c. Fala and right half of wireless 40 25
668 32c. Fala and Roosevelt in car 40 25
669 32c. Fala's seal 40 25
670 32c. Fala 40 25

113 "Eskimo Madonna" (Claire Fejes)

1998. Christmas. Works of Art. Multicoloured.

671	32c. Type **113**	40	25
672	32c. "Madonna" (Man Ray)	40	25
673	32c. "Peasant Mother" (David Siquerios)	40	25
674	60c. "Mother and Child" (Pablo Picasso)	40	25
675	60c. "Gypsy Woman with Baby" (Amedeo Modigliani)	40	25
676	60c. "Mother and Child" (Jose Orozco)	40	25

114 Glenn

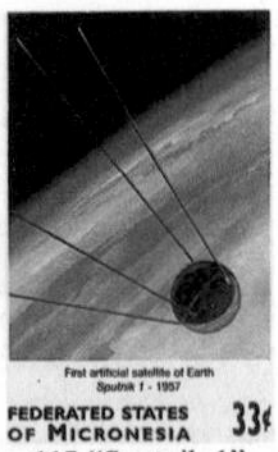

115 "Sputnik 1"

1998. John Glenn's (first American to orbit Earth) Return to Space. Multicoloured.

678	60c. Type **114**	75	50
679	60c. Launch of "Friendship 7"	75	50
680	60c. Glenn (bare-headed and in spacesuit) and United States flag on spaceship	75	50
681	60c. Glenn (in spacesuit) and "Friendship" space capsule	75	50
682	60c. Glenn (in spacesuit) and United States flag on pole	75	50
683	60c. Head and shoulders of Glenn in civilian clothes and stars (dated "1992")	75	50
684	60c. "Friendship 7"	75	50
685	60c. John Glenn with President Kennedy	75	50
686	60c. Glenn in overalls	75	50
687	60c. Launch of "Discovery" (space shuttle)	75	50
688	60c. Glenn in cockpit	75	50
689	60c. Head of Glenn in civilian suit	75	50
690	60c. Glenn fastening inner helmet	75	50
691	60c. Glenn with full helmet on	75	50
692	60c. Model of "Discovery"	75	50
693	60c. Head of Glenn smiling (bare-headed) in spacesuit	75	50

1999. Exploration of the Solar System. Multicoloured. (a) Space Achievements of Russia.

695	33c. Type **115** (first artificial satellite, 1957)	40	25
696	33c. Space dog Laika (first animal in space, 1957) (wrongly inscr "Leika")	40	25
697	33c. "Luna 1", 1959	40	25
698	33c. "Luna 3", 1959	40	25
699	33c. Yuri Gagarin (first man in space, 1961)	40	25
700	33c. "Venera 1" probe, 1961	40	25
701	33c. "Mars 1" probe, 1962	40	25
702	33c. Valentina Tereshkova (first woman in space, 1963)	40	25
703	33c. "Voskhod 1", 1964	40	25
704	33c. Aleksei Leonov and "Voskhod 2" (first space walk, 1965)	40	25
705	33c. "Venera 3" probe, 1966	40	25
706	33c. "Luna 10", 1966	40	25
707	33c. "Luna 9" (first landing on moon, 1966)	40	25
708	33c. "Lunokhod 1" moon-vehicle from "Luna 17" (first roving vehicle on Moon, 1970) (wrongly inscr "First robot mission ... Luna 16")	40	25
709	33c. "Luna 16" on Moon's surface (first robot mission, 1970) (wrongly inscr "First roving vehicle ... Luna 17")	40	25
710	33c. "Mars 3", 1971	40	25
711	33c. Leonid Popov, "Soyuz 35" and Valery Ryumin (first long manned space mission, 1980)	40	25
712	33c. Balloon ("Vega 1" Venus-Halley's Comet probe, 1985–86)	40	25
713	33c. "Vega 1" and Halley's Comet, 1986	40	25
714	33c. "Mir" space station	40	25

(b) Achievements of the United States of America

715	33c. "Explorer 1", 1958	40	25
716	33c. Space observatory "OSO-1", 1962	40	25
717	33c. "Mariner 2" Venus probe, 1962 (first scientifically successful planetary mission)	40	25
718	33c. "Mariner 2" Venus probe, 1962 (first scientific interplanetary space discovery)	40	25
719	33c. "Apollo 8" above Moon's surface	40	25
720	33c. Astronaut descending ladder on "Apollo 11" mission (first manned Moon landing, 1969)	40	25
721	33c. Astronaut taking Moon samples, 1969	40	25
722	33c. Lunar Rover of "Apollo 15", 1971	40	25
723	33c. "Mariner 9" Mars probe, 1971	40	25
724	33c. "Pioneer 10" passing Jupiter, 1973	40	25
725	33c. "Mariner 10" passing Mercury, 1974	40	25
726	33c. "Viking 1" on Mars, 1976	40	25
727	33c. "Pioneer 11" passing Saturn, 1979	40	25
728	33c. "STS-1" (first re-usable spacecraft, 1981)	40	25
729	33c. "Pioneer 10" (first man-made object to leave solar system, 1983)	40	25
730	33c. Solar Maximum Mission, 1984	40	25
731	33c. "Cometary Explorer", 1985	40	25
732	33c. "Voyager 2" passing Neptune, 1989	40	25
733	33c. "Galileo" space probe, 1992	40	25
734	33c. "Sojourner" (Mars rover), 1997	40	25

116 Map of the Pacific Ocean

1999. Voyages of the Pacific. Multicoloured.

736	33c. Type **116**	40	25
737	33c. Black-fronted parakeet	40	25
738	33c. Red-tailed tropic bird	40	25
739	33c. Plan of ship's hull	40	25
740	33c. Sketches of winches	40	25
741	33c. Yellow flowers	40	25
742	33c. Full-rigged sailing ship	40	25
743	33c. Three flowers growing from seeds and top of compass rose	40	25
744	33c. Fish (background of ship's planking)	40	25
745	33c. Flag of Yap	40	25
746	33c. Flag of Truk (palm tree)	40	25
747	33c. Flag of Kosrae (four stars) and bottom of compass rose	40	25
748	33c. Sketches of fruit	40	25
749	33c. Three plants and leaves	40	25
750	33c. Fish (leaves at left)	40	25
751	33c. Flag of Pohnpei and equator	40	25
752	33c. Sextant	40	25
753	33c. Red plant	40	25
754	33c. Fish and left side of compass rose	40	25
755	33c. Right side of compass rose and full-rigged sailing ship	40	25

Nos. 736/55 were issued together, se-tenant, forming a composite design.

117 Couple Meeting

1999. "Romance of the Three Kingdoms" (Chinese novel by Luo Guanzhong). Multicoloured.

756	33c. Type **117**	40	25
757	33c. Four men (one with lance) in room	40	25
758	33c. Two riders in combat	40	25
759	33c. Four men watching fifth man walking through room	40	25
760	33c. Captives before man on wheeled throne	40	25
761	50c. Riders approaching castle	40	25
762	50c. Warrior pointing at fire	40	25
763	50c. Opposing warriors riding through thick smoke	40	25
764	50c. Couple kneeling before man on dais	40	25
765	50c. Cauldron on fire	40	25

118 Carriage of Leipzig–Dresden Railway and Caroline Islands 1900 20pf. Stamp

1999. "iBRA" International Stamp Fair, Nuremberg, Germany. Multicoloured.

767	55c. Type **118**	65	45
768	55c. Golsdorf steam railway locomotive and Caroline Islands 1m. "Yacht" stamp	65	45

119 Black Rhinoceros

121 Deep-drilling for Brine Salt

120 "Ghost of O-Iwa"

1999. Earth Day. Multicoloured.

770	33c. Type **119**	40	25
771	33c. Cheetah	40	25
772	33c. Jackass penguin	40	25
773	33c. Blue whale	40	25
774	33c. Red-headed woodpecker	40	25
775	33c. African elephant	40	25
776	33c. Aurrochs	40	25
777	33c. Dodo	40	25
778	33c. Tasmanian wolf	40	25
779	33c. Giant lemur	40	25
780	33c. Quagga	40	25
781	33c. Steller's sea cow	40	25
782	33c. Pteranodon	40	25
783	33c. Shonisaurus	40	25
784	33c. Stegosaurus	40	25
785	33c. Gallimimus	40	25
786	33c. Tyrannosaurus	40	25
787	33c. Archelon	40	25
788	33c. Brachiosaurus	40	25
789	33c. Triceratops	40	25

1999. 150th Death Anniv of Hokusai Katsushika (Japanese artist). Multicoloured.

791	33c. Type **120**	40	25
792	33c. Spotted horse with head lowered	40	25
793	33c. "Abe Nakamaro"	40	25
794	33c. "Ghost of Kasane"	40	25
795	33c. Bay horse with head held up	40	25
796	33c. "The Ghost of Kiku and the Priest Mitazuki"	40	25
797	33c. "Belly Band Float"	40	25
798	33c. Woman washing herself	40	25
799	33c. "Swimmers"	40	25
800	33c. "Eel Climb"	40	25
801	33c. Woman playing lute	40	25
802	33c. "Kimo Ga Imo ni Naru"	40	25

Nos. 792 and 795 are inscribed "Hores Drawings".

1999. New Millennium. Multicoloured. (a) Science and Technology of Ancient China.

804	33c. Type **121**	40	25
805	33c. Chain pump	40	25
806	33c. Magic lantern	40	25
807	33c. Chang Heng's seismograph	40	25
808	33c. Dial and pointer devices	40	25
809	33c. Page of Lui Hui's mathematics treatise (value of Pi)	40	25
810	33c. Porcelain production	40	25
811	33c. Water mill	40	25
812	33c. Relief of horse from tomb of Tang Tai-Tsung (the stirrup)	40	25
813	33c. Page of Lu Yu's tea treatise and detail of Liu Songnian's painting of tea-making	40	25
814	33c. Umbrella	40	25
815	33c. Brandy and whisky production	40	25
816	33c. Page from oldest surviving printed book, woodblock and its print (printing)	40	25
817	33c. Copper plate and its print (paper money)	40	25
818	33c. Woodcut showing gunpowder demonstration	40	25
819	33c. Anji Bridge (segmented arch) (56½ × 36 mm)	40	25
820	33c. Mercator's star map and star diagram on bronze mirror	40	25

(b) People and Events of the Twelfth Century (1100–1150)

821	20c. Holy Roman Emperor Henry IV (death, 1106)	30	20
822	20c. Chastisement of monks of Enryakuji Temple, Kyoto, 1108	30	20
823	20c. Founding of Knights of the Hospital of St. John, 1113	30	20
824	20c. Invention of nautical compass, 1117	30	20
825	20c. Drowning of Prince William, heir of King Henry I of England, 1120	30	20
826	20c. Pope Callixtus II (Treaty of Worms, 1122, between Papacy and Holy Roman Emperor Henry V)	30	20
827	20c. Death of Omar Khayyam (Persian poet), 1126	30	20
828	20c. Death of Duke Guilhem IX, Count of Poitiers and Duke of Aquitaine (earliest known troubadour, 1127)	30	20
829	20c. Coronation of King Roger II of Sicily, 1130	30	20
830	20c. King Stephen and Queen Matilda (start of English civil war, 1135)	30	20
831	20c. Moses Maimonides (philosopher, birth, 1138)	30	20
832	20c. Abelard and Heloise (Church's censure of Abelard, 1140)	30	20
833	20c. Defeat of French and German crusaders at Damascus, 1148	30	20
834	20c. Fall of Mexican city of Tula, 1150s	30	20
835	20c. Completion of Angkor Vat, Cambodia, 1150	30	20
836	20c. Rise of Kingdom of Chimu, Peru, 1150s (56½ × 36 mm)	30	20
837	20c. Honen (Buddhist monk) becomes hermit, 1150	30	20

122 Flowers

1999. Faces of the Millennium: Diana, Princess of Wales. Showing collage of miniature flower photographs. Multicoloured, country panel at left (a) or right (b).

838	50c. Deep red shades (a)	60	40
839	50c. Deep red shades (b)	60	40
840	50c. Deep red shades with violet shades at bottom left (a)	60	40
841	50c. Blackish shades in bottom left corner (b)	40	60
842	50c. Violet shades at left and bottom, pinkish shades at right (a)	60	40
843	50c. Lemon and pink shades (b)	60	40
844	50c. Violet shades (a)	60	40
845	50c. Type **122** (rose in bottom row) (b)	60	40

Nos. 838/45 were issued together, se-tenant, and when viewed as a whole, form a portrait of Diana, Princess of Wales.

123 Face of Woman

1999. Costumes of the World. Multicoloured.

846	33c. Type **123**	30	20
847	33c. Tools for fabric making	30	20
848	33c. Head of African Masai warrior and textile pattern	30	20
849	33c. Head of woman and textile pattern (inscr "French Renaissance costume")	30	20
850	33c. Head of woman in hat with black feathers ("French princess gown 1900–1910")	30	20

851 33c. Head of Micronesian woman in wedding costume 30 20
852 33c. Body of African Masai warrior and head of woman 30 20
853 33c. Body of woman ("Textile patterns of French Renaissance costume") 30 20
854 33c. Body of woman ("1900–1910 French princess gown") 30 20
855 33c. Body and head of two Micronesian women in wedding costumes 30 20
856 33c. Hem of costume and body of woman ("Details of woman costume from African fabrics") 30 20
857 33c. Lower part of dress and head of woman ("French Renaissance costume") 30 20
858 33c. Hem of dress and furled umbrella 30 20
859 33c. Body and legs of two Micronesian women in wedding costumes 30 20
860 33c. Head of woman in Japanese Kabuki costume 30 20
861 33c. Rulers for tailoring 30 20
862 33c. Scissors 30 20
863 33c. Japanese fabrics 30 20
864 33c. Head and body of two women in Japanese Kabuki costumes 30 20
865 33c. Iron 30 20

Nos. 846/65 were issued together, se-tenant, forming several composite designs.

124 "Holy Family with St. John"

1999. Christmas. Paintings by Anthony van Dyck. Multicoloured.
866 33c. Type **124** 30 20
867 60c. "Madonna and Child" 75 50
868 $2 "Virgin and Child with Two Donors" (detail) 2·50 1·60

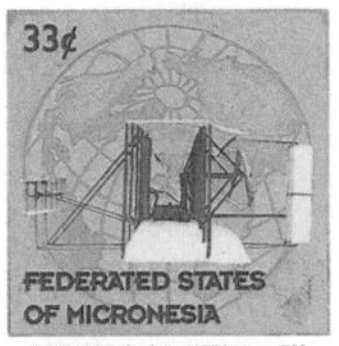

125 Wright "Flyer I"

1999. Man's First Century of Flight. Multicoloured.
870 33c. Type **125** 30 20
871 33c. Bleriot XI and Notre Dame Cathedral, Paris 30 20
872 33c. Fokker D.VII biplane and Brandenburg Gate, Berlin 30 20
873 33c. Dornier Komet I (numbered B 240) and Amsterdam 30 20
874 33c. Charles Lindbergh's Ryan NYP Special "Spirit of St. Louis" and steeple 30 20
875 33c. Mitsubishi A6M Zero-Sen fighter and Mt. Fuji 30 20
876 33c. Boeing B-29 Superfortress bomber and roof of building 30 20
877 33c. Messerschmitt Me 262A jet fighter (swastika on tail) 30 20
878 33c. Chuck Yeager's Bell X-1 rocket plane and Grand Canyon 30 20
879 33c. Mikoyan Gurevich MiG-19 over Russian church 30 20
880 33c. Lockheed U-2 reconnaissance plane over building at night 30 20
881 33c. Boeing 707 jetliner and head of Statue of Liberty, New York 30 20
882 33c. British Aerospace/Aerospatiale Concorde supersonic jetliner and top of Eiffel Tower, Paris 30 20
883 33c. McDonnell Douglas DC-10 jetliner and Sydney Opera House 30 20
884 33c. B-2 Spirit stealth bomber and globe 30 20

Nos. 870/84 were issued together, se-tenant, forming a composite design of the globe.

126 *Oncidium obryzatum*

127 Martin Luther King (civil rights leader)

2000. Orchids. Multicoloured.
886 33c. Type **126** 45 30
887 33c. *Oncidium phalaenopsis* 45 30
888 33c. *Oncidium pulvinatum* 45 30
889 33c. *Paphiodedilum armeniacum* 45 30
890 33c. *Paphiopedilum dayanum* 45 30
891 33c. *Paphiopedilum druryi* 45 30
892 33c. *Baptistonia echinata* 45 30
893 33c. *Bulbophyllum lobbii* 45 30
894 33c. *Cattleya bicolor* 45 30
895 33c. *Cischweinfia dasyandra* 45 30
896 33c. *Cochleanthes discolor* 45 30
897 33c. *Dendrobium bellatulum* 45 30
898 33c. *Esmeralda clarkei* 45 30
899 33c. *Gomesa crispa* 45 30
900 33c. *Masdevallia elephanticeps* 45 30
901 33c. *Maxillaria variabilis* 45 30
902 33c. *Mitoniopsis roezlii* 45 30
903 33c. *Oncidium cavendishianum* 45 30

2000. Personalities of the Twentieth Century. Multicoloured.
905 33c. Type **127** 45 30
906 33c. Dr. Albert Schweitzer (philosopher and missionary) 45 30
907 33c. Pope John Paul II 45 30
908 33c. Sarvepalli Radhakrishnan (philosopher and Indian statesman) 45 30
909 33c. Toyohiko Kagawa (social reformer) 45 30
910 33c. Mahatma Gandhi (Indian leader) 45 30
911 33c. Mother Teresa (nun and missionary) 45 30
912 33c. Khyentse Rinpoche (poet and philosopher) 45 30
913 33c. Desmond Tutu (religious leader) 45 30
914 33c. Chiara Lubich (founder of Focolare movement) 45 30
915 33c. Dalai Lama (religious leader) 45 30
916 33c. Abraham Heschel (theologian) 45 30

129 Mother-of-Pearl (*Salamis parhassus*)

2000. Butterflies. Multicoloured.
918 20c. Type **129** 30 20
919 20c. Blue morpho (*Morpho rhetenor*) 30 20
920 20c. Monarch (*Danaus plexippus*) 30 20
921 20c. *Phyciodes actinote* 30 20
922 20c. *Idea leuconoe* 30 20
923 20c. *Actinote negra sobrina* 30 20
924 55c. Blue triangle (*Graphium sarpedon*) 80 50
925 55c. Swallowtail (*Papilio machaon*) 80 50
926 55c. Cairn's birdwing (*Ornithoptera priamus*) 80 50
927 55c. *Ornithoptera chimaera* 80 50
928 55c. Five-bar swallowtail (*Graphium antiphates*) 80 50
929 55c. *Pachliopta aristolochiae* 80 50

130 Mahatma Gandhi (Indian leader)

131 Mikhail Gorbachev (statesman)

2000. New Millennium. Multicoloured.
931 20c. Type **130** 30 20
932 20c. Poster (Dada Art fair, Berlin, 1920) 30 20
933 20c. Women with American flags (female suffrage, 1930) 30 20
934 20c. Nicola Sacco and Bartolomeo Vanzetti (anarchists) (international controversy over murder conviction, 1921) 30 20
935 20c. Hermann Rorschach (psychiatrist and neurologist) (developed inkblot test, 1921) 30 20
936 20c. George W. Watson (incorporation of I.B.M., 1924) 30 20
937 20c. Leica camera (first commercial 35 mm camera, 1925) 30 20
938 20c. Scientists and John Thomas Scopes (brought to trial for teaching Darwin's theory of evolution, 1925) 30 20
939 20c. Charles Lindbergh (aviator) and Ryan NYP Special Spirit of St. Louis (first solo transatlantic flight, 1927) 30 20
940 20c. "Big Bang" (George Henri Lemaître) (astrophysicist and cosmologist) (formulated "Big Bang" theory, 1927) 30 20
941 20c. Chiang Kai-Shek (Chinese nationalist leader)
942 20c. Werner Heisenberg (theoretical physicist) developed "Uncertainty Principle", 1927 30 20
943 20c. Sir Alexander Fleming (bacteriologist) and microscope (discovery of penicillin, 1928) 30 20
944 20c. Emperor Hirohito of Japan 30 20
945 20c. Car and man (U.S. Stock Market crash causes Great Depression) 30 20
946 20c. Douglas World Cruiser seaplanes and men (round-the-world formation flight, 1924) (59 × 39 mm) 30 20
947 20c. *All Quiet on the Western Front* (novel by Erich Maria Remarque published 1929) 30 20

2000. International Relations in the Twentieth Century. Multicoloured.
948 33c. Type **131** 45 30
949 33c. U.S.S.R. and U.S. flags, Gorbachev and Reagan (end of Cold War) 45 30
950 33c. Ronald Reagan (U.S. President, 1980–88) 45 30
951 33c. Le Duc Tho (Vietnamese politician) 45 30
952 33c. Le Duc Tho and Henry Kissinger (resolution to Vietnam conflict) 45 30
953 33c. Henry Kissinger (U.S. Secretary of State) 45 30
954 33c. Linus Pauling (chemist) 45 30
955 33c. Pauling at protest against nuclear weapons 45 30
956 33c. Peter Benenson (founder of Amnesty International, 1961) 45 30
957 33c. Amnesty International emblem and prisoners 45 30
958 33c. Mahatma Gandhi (Indian leader) 45 30
959 33c. Gandhi fasting 45 30
960 33c. John F. Kennedy (U.S. President, 1960–3) making speech initiating Peace Corps 45 30
961 33c. President Kennedy 45 30
962 33c. Dalai Lama (Tibetan religious leader) praying 45 30
963 33c. Dalai Lama 45 30
964 33c. United Nations Headquarters, New York 45 30
965 33c. Cordell Hull (U.S. Secretary of State 1933–44) (active in creation of United Nations) 45 30
966 33c. Frederick Willem de Klerk (South African politician) 45 30
967 33c. De Klerk and Nelson Mandela (end of Apartheid) 45 30
968 33c. Nelson Mandela 45 30
969 33c. Franklin D. Roosevelt (U.S. President) 45 30
970 33c. Winston Churchill, Roosevelt and Josef Stalin (Soviet leader) (Yalta Conference, 1945) 45 30
971 33c. Winston Churchill (British Prime Minister) 45 30

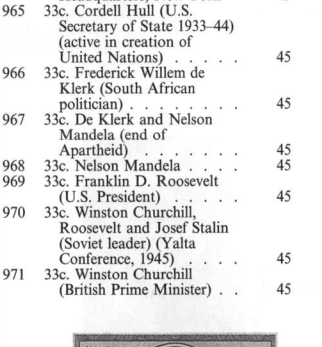

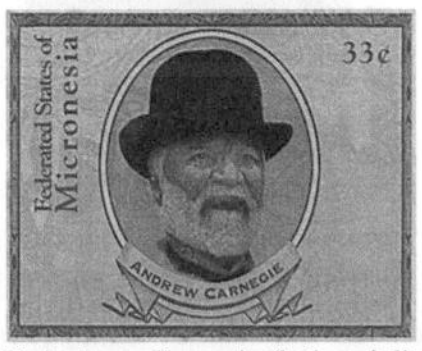

132 Andrew Carnegie (industrialist)

2000. Philanthropists of the Twentieth Century. Multicoloured.
972 33c. Type **132** 45 30
973 33c. John D. Rockefeller (oil magnate) 45 30
974 33c. Henry Ford (motor manufacturer) 45 30
975 33c. C. J. Walker 45 30
976 33c. James B. Duke 45 30
977 33c. Andrew Mellon (financier) 45 30
978 33c. Charles F. Kettering (engineer) 45 30
979 33c. R. W. Woodruff 45 30
980 33c. Brooke Astor 45 30
981 33c. Howard Hughes (businessman and aviator) 45 30
982 33c. Jesse H. Jones 45 30
983 33c. Paul Mellon 45 30
984 33c. Jean Paul Getty (oil exectutive) 45 30
985 33c. George Soros 45 30
986 33c. Phyllis Wattis 45 30
987 33c. Ted (Robert Edward) Turner (entrepreneur) 45 30

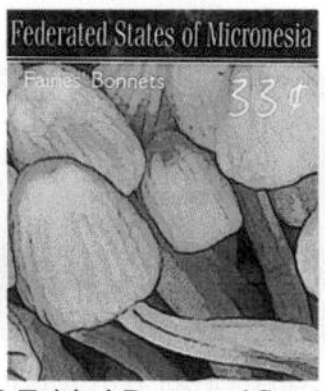

133 Fairies' Bonnets (*Coprinus disseminatus*)

2000. Fungi. Multicoloured.
988 33c. Type **133** 45 30
989 33c. Black Bulgar (*Bulgaria inquinans*) 45 30
990 33c. Amethyst deceiver (*Laccaria amethystina*) (inscr "amethystea") 45 30
991 33c. Common morel (*Morchella esculenta*) 45 30
992 33c. Common bird's nest (*Crucibulum laeve*) 45 30
993 33c. Trumpet agaric (*Clitocybe geotropa*) 45 30
994 33c. Bonnet mycena (*Mycena galericulata*) 45 30
995 33c. Underside of horse mushroom (*Agaricus arvensis*) 45 30
996 33c. Part of *Boletus subtomento* 45 30
997 33c. Oyster mushroom (*Pleurotus ostreatus*) 45 30
998 33c. Fly agaric (*Amanita muscaria*) 45 30
999 33c. Aztec mushroom mandala design 45 30

134 *Freycinetia arborea*

2000. Flowers. Multicoloured.
1001 33c. Type **134** 40 25
1002 33c. Mount Cook lily (*Ranunculus lyallii*) (inscr "lyalli") 40 25
1003 33c. Sun orchid (*Thelymitra nuda*) 40 25
1004 33c. *Bossiaea ensata* 40 25
1005 33c. Swamp hibiscus (*Hibiscus diversifolius*) 40 25
1006 33c. *Gardenia brighamii* 40 25
1007 33c. Elegant brodiaea (Brodiaea elegans) 40 25
1008 33c. Skyrocket (*Ipomopsis aggregata*) 40 25
1009 33c. Hedge bindweed (*Convovulus sepium*) 40 25
1010 33c. Woods' rose (*Rosa woodsii*) 40 25
1011 33c. Swamp rose (*Rosa palustris*) 40 25
1012 33c. Wake robin (*Trillium erectum*) 40 25
MS1013 Two sheets. (a) 95 × 80 mm. $2 Black-eyed susan (*Tetratheca juncea*). (b) 108 × 80 mm. $2 Yellow meadow lily (*Lilium canadense*) Set of 2 sheets 4·75 2·75

135 Two Siamese Cats

2000. Cats and Dogs. Multicoloured.
1014 33c. Type **135** 40 25
1015 33c. Red mackerel tabbies 40 25
1016 33c. British shorthair 40 25
1017 33c. Red Persian 40 25
1018 33c. Turkish angora 40 25

1019 33c. Calico 40 25
1020 33c. Afghan hounds 40 25
1021 33c. Yellow labrador retriever 40 25
1022 33c. Greyhound 40 25
1023 33c. German shepherd 40 25
1024 33c. King Charles spaniel 40 25
1025 33c. Jack Russell terrier 40 25
MS1026 Two sheets, each 85 × 110 mm. (a) $2 Tortoiseshell and white cat watching bird. (b) $2 Setter and trees Set of 2 sheets 4·75 2·75

Nos. 1014/19 (cats) and 1020/5 (dogs) respectively were issued together, se-tenant, each sheetlet forming a composite design.

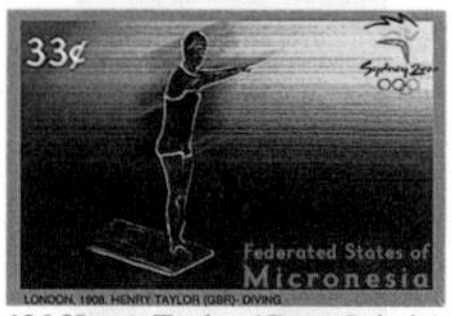

136 Henry Taylor (Great Britain) preparing to Dive, 1908, London

2000. Olympic Games, Sydney. Multicoloured.
1027 33c. Type **136** 40 25
1028 33c. Cyclist 40 25
1029 33c. Munich stadium and flag, West Germany 40 25
1030 33c. Ancient Greek wrestlers 40 25

137 Zodiac Airship *Capitaine Ferber*

2000. Centenary of First Zeppelin Flight and Airship Development. Multicoloured.
1031 33c. Type **137** 40 25
1032 33c. Astra airship *Adjutant Reau* 40 25
1033 33c. Airship 1A, Italy 40 25
1034 33c. Astra-Torres No. 14 40 25
1035 33c. Front of Astra-Torres No. 14, Schuttle-Lanz SL3 and front of Siemens-Schukert airship 40 25
1036 33c. Siemens-Schukert airship 40 25
MS1037 Two sheets, each 110 × 85 mm. (a) $2 LZ-130 *Graf Zeppelin II*. (b) $2 Dupuy de Lome airship Set of 2 sheets 4·75 2·75

Nos. 1031/6 were issued together, se-tenant, forming a composite design.

138 Top of Head

2000. 100th Birthday of Queen Elizabeth the Queen Mother. T **138** and similar vert designs showing collage of miniature flower photographs. Multicoloured, country inscription and face value at left (a) or right (b).
1038 33c. Type **138** 40 25
1039 33c. Top of head (b) 40 25
1040 33c. Eye and temple (a) 40 25
1041 33c. Temple (b) 40 25
1042 33c. Cheek (a) 40 25
1043 33c. Cheek (b) 40 25
1044 33c. Chin (a) 40 25
1045 33c. Chin and neck (b) 40 25

Nos. 1038/45 were issued together in se-tenant sheetlets of eight with the stamps arranged in two vertical columns separated by a gutter also containing miniature photographs. When viewed as a whole, the sheetlet forms a portrait of Queen Elizabeth the Queen Mother.

139 Woman Weightlifter and Traditional Cloth

2000. "OLYMPHILEX 2000" International Olympic Stamp Exhibition, Sydney. Sheet 137 × 82 mm, containing T **139** and similar vert designs. Multicoloured.
MS1046 33c. Type **139**; 33c. Woman playing basketball; $1 Male weightlifter 2·00 1·25

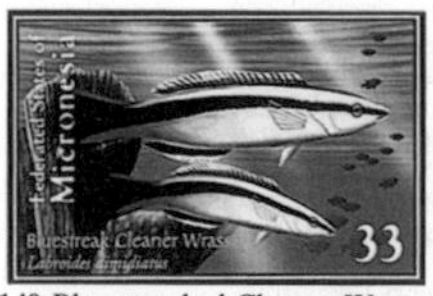

140 Blue-streaked Cleaner Wrasse (*Labroides dimidiatus*)

2000. Coral Reef. Multicoloured.
1047 33c. Type **140** 40 25
1048 33c. Pennant coralfish (*Heniochus acuminatus*) 40 25
1049 33c. Chevron butterflyfish (*Chaetodon trifascialis*) 40 25
1050 33c. Rock beauty (*Holacanthus tricolor*) 40 25
1051 33c. Mandarin fish (*Synchiropus splendidus*) 40 25
1052 33c. Emperor snapper (*Lutjanus sebae*) (wrongly inscr "timorensis") 40 25
1053 33c. Copper-banded butterflyfish (*rostratus*) 40 25
1054 33c. Chevron butterflyfish (*Chaetodon trifascialis*) (different) 40 25
1055 33c. Lemon-peel angelfish (*Centropyge flavissimus*) 40 25
1056 33c. Lemon-peel angelfish and harlequin tuskfish (*Choerodon fasciatus*) 40 25
1057 33c. Crown triggerfish (*Balistoides conspicillum*) 40 25
1058 33c. Coral hind (*Cephalopholis miniata*) 40 25
1059 33c. Pennant coralfish (*Heniochus acuminatus*) (different) 40 25
1060 33c. Scuba diver and six-blotched hind (*Cephalopholis sexmaculata*) 40 25
1061 33c. Common jellyfish (*Aurelia aurita*) 40 25
1062 33c. Palette surgeonfish (*Paracanthurus hepatus*) and common jellyfish 40 25
1063 33c. Bicoloured angelfish (*Centropyge bicolor*) 40 25
1064 33c. Thread-finned butterflyfish (*Chaetodon auriga*) and clown anemonefish 40 25
1065 33c. Clown anemonefish (*Amphiprion percula*) 40 25
1066 33c. Three-banded damselfish (*Chrysiptera tricincta*) 40 25
1067 33c. Three-banded damselfish and grey reef shark (*Carcharhinus amblyrhynchs*) (inscr "amblyrhynchos") 40 25
1068 33c. Tail of grey reef shark and starfish (*Luidia ciliaris*) 40 25
MS1069 Two sheets, each 98 × 68 mm. (a) $2 Forceps butterflyfish (*Forcipiger flavissimus*). (b) $2 Emperor angelfish (*Pomacanthus imperator*) Set of 2 sheets 4·75 2·75

Nos. 1051/59 and 1060/8 respectively were issued, se-tenant, forming a composite design.

141 Back of Head

2000. 80th Birthday of Pope John Paul II. T **141** and similar vert designs showing collage of miniature religious photographs. Multicoloured, country Inscription and face value at left (a) or right (b).
1070 50c. Type **141** 60 35
1071 50c. Forehead (b) 60 35
1072 50c. Ear (a) 60 35
1073 50c. Forehead and eye (b) 60 35
1074 50c. Neck and collar (a) 60 35
1075 50c. Nose and cheek (b) 60 35
1076 50c. Shoulder (a) 60 35
1077 50c. Hands (b) 60 35

Nos. 1070/7 were issued together in se-tenant sheetlets of eight with the stamps arranged in two vertical columns separated by a gutter also containing miniature photographs. When viewed as a whole, the sheetlet forms a portrait of Pope John Paul II.

142 "The Holy Trinity" (Titian)

2000. Christmas. Multicoloured.
1078 20c. Type **142** 25 10
1079 33c. "Adoration of the Magi" (Diego de Silva y Velasquez) 40 25
1080 60c. "Holy Nereus" (Peter Paul Rubens) 75 45
1081 $3.20 "St. Gregory, St. Maurus, St. Papianus and St. Domitilla" (Rubens) 4·00 2·40

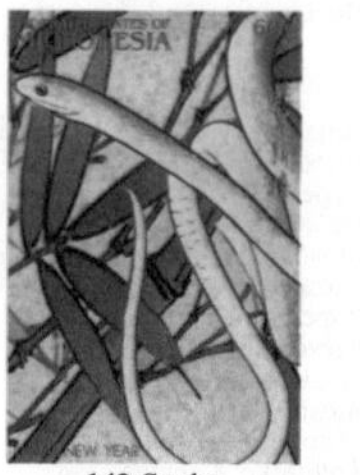
143 Snake

2001. New Year. Year of the Snake. Two sheets, each 72 × 101 mm, containing horiz design as T **143**. Multicoloured.
MS1082 (a) 60c. Type **143**. (b) 60c. Brown snake 1·50 90

144 Weepinbell

2001. Pokemon (children's computer game). Showing various Pokemon characters. Multicoloured.
1083 50c. Type **144** 60 35
1084 50c. Snorlax 60 35
1085 50c. Seel 60 35
1086 50c. Hitmonchan 60 35
1087 50c. Jynx 60 35
1088 50c. Pontya 60 35
MS1089 74 × 114 mm. $2 Farfetch'd (37 × 50 mm) 2·50 1·40

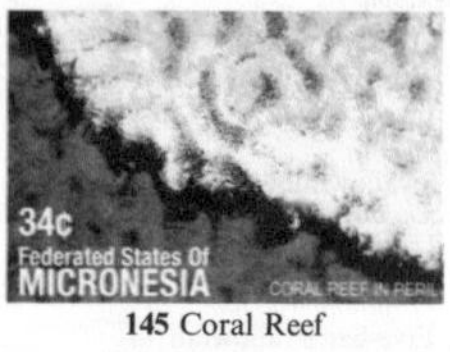

145 Coral Reef

2001. Environmental Protection. Multicoloured.
1090 34c. Type **145** 40 25
1091 34c. Galapagos turtle 40 25
1092 34c. Tasmanian tiger 40 25
1093 34c. Yanomami 40 25
1094 34c. Pelican and Florida Keys 40 25
1095 34c. Bird of prey 40 25
1096 60c. Factory chimneys (Pollution) 75 45
1097 60c. Desert and tree stump (Deforestation) 75 45
1098 60c. Forest (Acid rain) 75 45
1099 60c. Horse, mother and child, tree and Globe (Greenhouse effect) 75 45
MS1100 Two sheets each 110 × 77 mm. (a) $2 Sea bird (visit by Jacques Cousteau); (b) $2 Chimpanzee (Jane Goodall Institute) Set of 2 sheets 4·75 2·75

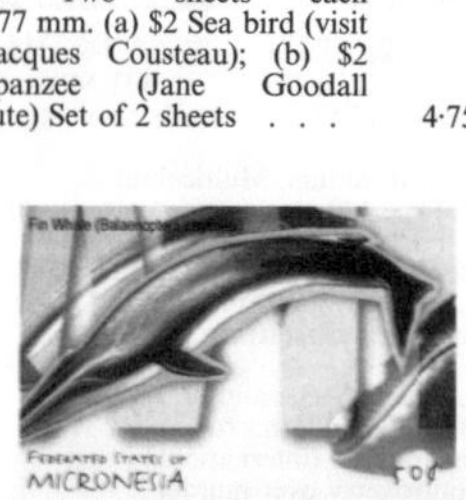

146 Fin Whale (*Balaenoptera physalus*)

2001. Whales of the Pacific. Multicoloured.
1101 50c. Type **146** 60 35
1102 50c. Right whale (*Balaena galacials*) 60 35
1103 50c. Pygmy right whale (*Caperea marginata*) 60 35
1104 50c. Humpback whale (*Megaptera novaeangliae*) (inscr "novaeangliae") 60 35
1105 50c. Blue whale (*Balaenoptera musculus*) 60 35
1106 50c. Bowhead whale (*Balaena mysticetus*) 60 35
1107 60c. True's beaked whale (*Mesoplodon mirus*) 75 45
1108 60c. Cuvier's beaked whale (*Ziphius cavirostris*) 75 45
1109 60c. Shepherd's beaked whale (*Tasmacetus shepherdi*) 75 45
1110 60c. Baird's beaked whale (*Berardius bairdii*) 75 45
1111 60c. Northern bottlenose whale (*Hyperodon ampullatus*) 75 45
1112 60c. Pygmy sperm whale (*Kogia breviceps*) 75 45
MS1113 Two sheets each 100 × 70 mm. (a) $2 Killer whale (*Orcinus orca*); (b) $2 Sperm whale (*Physeter macrocephalus*) Set of 2 sheets 4·75 2·75

Nos. 1101/6 and 1107/12 respectively were issued together, se-tenant, forming a composite design.

147 Three-spotted ("Yellow") Damselfish (*Stegastes planifrons*)

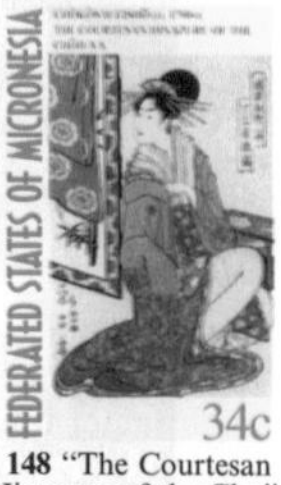

148 "The Courtesan Hinazuru of the Choji-ya" (Chokosai Eisho)

2001. Fishes. Multicoloured.
1114 11c. Type **147** 10 10
1115 34c. Rainbow runner (*Elegatis bipinnulatus*) 40 25
1118 70c. Whitelined grouper (*Anyperodon leucogrammicus*) 80 50
1119 80c. Purple queen anthias (*Pseudanthias pascalus*) 85 55
1123 $3.50 Eibl's angelfish (*Centropye eibli*) 4·25 2·50
1127 $12.25 Spotted ("Blue-spotted") boxfish (*Ostracion meleagris*) 14·00 6·00

2001. "PHILANIPPON '01" International Stamp Exhibition, Tokyo. Japanese Art. Multicoloured.
1130 34c. Type **148** 40 25
1131 34c. "The Iris Garden" (Torii Kiyonaga) 40 25
1132 34c. "Girl tying her Hair Ribbon" (Tori Kiyomine) 40 25
1133 34c. "The Courtesan of the Mayuzumi of the Daimonji-ya" (Katsukawa Shuncho) 40 25
1134 34c. "Parody of the Allegory of the Sage Chin Kao Riding a Carp" (Suzuki Harunobo) 40 25
1135 34c. "Bath-house Scene" (Utagawa Toyokuni) 40 25
1136 34c. "Dance of Kamisha" (Kitagawa Utamaro) 40 25
1137 34c. "The Courtesan Hinazura at the Keizetsuro" (Kitagawa Utamaro) 40 25
1138 34c. "Toilet Scene" (Kitagawa Utamaro) 40 25
1139 34c. "Applying Lip Rouge" (Kitagawa Utamaro) 40 25
1140 34c. "Beauty reading a Letter" (Kitagawa Utamaro) 40 25
1141 34c. "The Geisha Kamekichi" (Kitagawa Utamaro) 40 25
MS1142 Two sheets each 118 × 88 mm. (a) $2 "Girl seated by a Brook at Sunset" (Suzuki Harunobu). Imperf; (b) $2 "Allegory of Ariwara No Narihira" (Kikugawa Eizan). Imperf Set of 2 sheets 4·75 2·75

149 "Oscar Wilde"

2001. Death Centenary of Henri de Toulouse-Lautrec (artist). Multicoloured.

1143	60c. Type **149**	75	45
1144	60c. "Doctor Tapié in a Theatre Corridor"	75	45
1145	60c. "Monsieur Delaporte"	75	45
MS1146	54 × 84 mm. $2 "The Clowness Cha-U-Kao"	2·40	1·40

150 Queen Victoria **151** Queen Elizabeth

2001. Death Centenary of Queen Victoria. Each black (except **MS**1151 multicoloured).

1147	60c. Type **150**	75	45
1148	60c. Facing right	75	45
1149	60c. Facing left wearing black decorated hat	75	45
1150	60c. Facing forwards	75	45
1151	60c. Holding baby	75	45
1152	60c. Facing left wearing lace headdress	75	45
MS1153	84 × 110 mm. $2 Queen Victoria (37 × 50 mm)	2·40	1·40

2001. 75th Birthday of Queen Elizabeth II. Each black (except No. 1153 and **MS**1158 multicoloured).

1154	60c. Type **151**	75	45
1155	60c. Wearing blue jacket	75	45
1156	60c. As young girl	75	45
1157	60c. As infant	75	45
1158	60c. With dog	75	45
1159	60c. In profile	75	45
MS1160	78 × 108 mm. $2 Princess Elizabeth	2·40	1·40

152 Striped Dolphin

2001. Marine Life. Four sheets containing T **152** and similar multicoloured designs.

MS1161 (a) 162 × 153 mm. 60c. × 6, Type **152**; Olive ridley turtle; Goldrim tang; Blue shark; Picasso triggerfish; Polka dot grouper; (b) 152 × 164 mm. 60c. × 6, Loggerhead turtle; Striped marlin; Bicolor cherub; Clown wrasse (*Coris gaimard*) (inscr "gaimardi"); Clown triggerfish; Japanese tang; (c) 96 × 68 mm. $2 Harlequin tusk (50 × 38 mm); (d) 70 × 100 mm. $2 Emperor angelfish (38 × 50 mm) . . . . 17·00 17·00

153 Triceratops

2001. Dinosaurs. Multicoloured.

1162	60c. Type **153**	65	40
1163	60c. Psittacosaurus	65	40
1164	60c. Two Archaeopteryx	65	40
1165	60c. Head of Allosaurus	65	40

MS1166 Four sheets (a) 103 × 124 mm. 60c. × 6, Tyrannosaurus; Pteranodon; Brachiosaurus; Spinosaurus; Deinonychus; Teratosaurus;(b) 104 × 123 mm. 60c. × 6, Parasaurolophus; Plateosaurus; Archaeopteryx in flight; Allosaurus (different); Torosaurus; Euoplocephalus; (c)68 × 98 mm. $2 Tyrannosaurus (different); (d) 68 × 98 mm. $2 Parasaurolophus (different) (horiz) . . . . . . 17·00 17·00

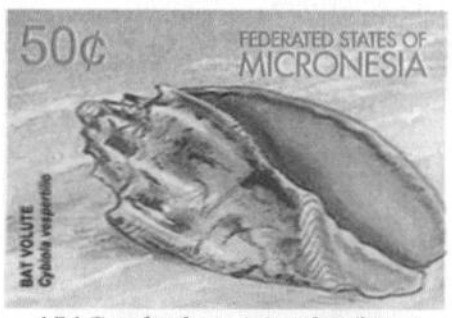

154 *Cymbiola vespertilio* (inscr "Cybiola")

2001. Shells. Four sheets containing T **154** and similar multicoloured designs.

MS1167 (a) 152 × 107 mm. 50c. × 6, Type **154**; Cassis cornuta; *Murex troscheli*; *Cymatium lotorium* (incr "lortrium"); Oliva sericea; *Phos senticosus*; (b) 111 × 145 mm. 50c. × 6; *Oblique nutmeg* (vert); *Cymbiola imperialis* (vert); Pontifical mitre (vert); *Conus eburneus Hwass in Bruguiere* (vert); *Heliacus areola* (inscr "variegated gmelin") (vert); *Corculum cardissa* (vert); (c) 76 × 59 mm. $2 Eyed auger; (d) 76 × 59 mm. $2 Geography cone . . . . 14·50 14·50

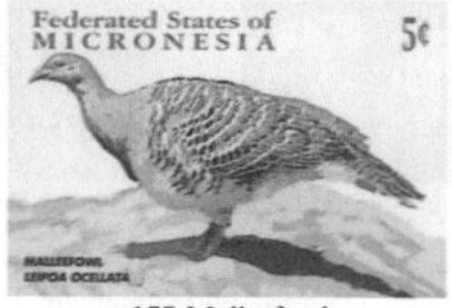

155 Malleefowl

2001. Birds. Multicoloured.

1168	5c. Type **155**	10	10
1169	22c. Corncrake	25	15
1170	23c. Hooded merganser	25	15
1171	$2.10 Purple gallinule	2·40	1·40

MS1172 Four sheets. (a) 146 × 167 mm. 60c. × 6, Fairy wren; Golden crowned kinglet (*Regulus satrapa*) (inscr " Bebrornis rodericanus"); Flame tempered babbler; Golden headed cisticola (*Cisticola exilis*) (inscr" Orthotomus moreauii"); White browed babbler; White throated dipper (inscr "breasted"); (b) 146 × 167 mm. Logrunner; Common tree creeper (inscr "Eurasian"); Chaffinch (inscr "Goldfinch"); Rufous fantail; Orange bellied flower pecker (inscr "billed"); Goldfinch (inscr "American goldfinch"); (c) 79 × 109 mm. $2 Emperor bird of paradise; (d) 79 × 109 mm. $2 Yellow eyed cuckoo shrike (vert) Set of 4 sheets . . . . 17·00 17·00

156 Alexis Carrel, 1912 (Physiology and Medicine)

2001. Centenary of First Nobel Prize. Four sheets containing T **156** and similar vert designs. Multicoloured.

MS1173 (a) 183 × 29 mm. 60c. × 6, Type **156**; Max Theiler, 1951 (Physiology and Medicine); Niels Finsen, 1903 (Physiology and Medicine); Philip S. Hench, 1950 (Physiology and Medicine); Sune Bergstrom, 1982 (Physiology and Medicine); JohnVane, 1982 (Physiology and Medicine) (b) 183 × 129 mm. 60c. × 6, Bengt Samuelsson, 1982 (Physiology and Medicine); Johannes Fibiger, 1926 (Physiology and Medicine); Theodore Richards, 1914 (Chemistry); Tadeus Reichstein, 1950 (Physiology and Medicine); Frederick Soddy, 1921 (Chemistry)bert Szent-Gyorgi von Nagyrapolt, 1937 (Physiology and Medicine) (c) 106 × 75 mm. Irving Langmuir, 1932 (Chemistry); (d) 106 × 5 mm. Artturi Ilmari Virtanen, 1945 (Chemistry) . . . . 17·00 17·00

157 Sinking of USS *Oklahoma*

2001. 60th Anniv of Attack on Pearl Harbour. Four sheets containing T **157** and similar horiz designs. Multicoloured.

MS1174 (a) 149 × 161 mm. 60c. × 6, Type **157**; Attack on Wheeler airfield; Japanese bomber; USS *Ward* sinking submarine; Bombing of USS *Arizona*; Attack on EWA marine base (b) 149 × 161 mm. 60c. × 6, "Remember Pearl Harbour" poster; Hideki Tojo (Japanese prime minister); Rescuing wounded, Bellows Field; Rescuing crew of USS *Arizona*; Isoroku Yamamoto (Japanese admiral); "Remember Pearl Harbour" poster (different) (c) 80 × 110 mm.; USS*Arizona Memorial*, Hawaii (d) 80 × 110 mm. President F. D. Roosevelt . . . . 17·00 17·00

158 Santa Claus riding Cat

2001. Christmas. Santa Claus. Multicoloured.

1175	22c. Type **158**	25	15
1176	34c. Between decorated trees	35	20
1177	60c. Flying in sleigh	65	40
1178	$1 Riding dog	1·20	70
MS1179	78 × 111 mm. $2 Climbing into chimney (vert)	2·25	2·25

159 Horse

2002. Year of the Horse. Sheet containing T **159** and similar vert designs. Each black.

MS1180 60c. × 6, Type **159**; Two horses; Two horses (different); Two horses' heads; Galloping horse . . . . 4·00 4·00

No. **MS**1180 forms a composite design of a herd of horses.

160 Queen Elizabeth II

2002. Golden Jubilee. 50th Anniv of Queen Elizabeth II's Accession to the Throne. Two sheets containing T **160** and similar square designs. Multicoloured.

MS1181 (a) 132 × 100 mm. 80c. × 4, Type **160**; Prince Phillip; Queen Elizabeth wearing white hat; Queen Elizabeth and children; (b) 76 × 109 mm. $2 Queen Elizabeth wearing headscarf . . . . . . 5·75 5·75

161 Statue of Liberty and American Flag

2002. "United We Stand".

1182	**161** $1 multicoloured	1·20	70

162 Luge Racer

2002. Winter Olympic Games, Salt Lake City (1st issue). Multicoloured.

1183	$1 Type **162**	1·10	65
1184	$1 Ice hockey player	1·10	65
MS1185	88 × 119 mm. Nos. 1183/4	2·20	2·20

See also Nos. 1191/**MS**1193.

163 Sun, Bird and Flowering Tree (January) **164** John F. Kennedy

2002. Japanese Art. "Birds and Flowers of Months of Year" (Nos. **MS**1186a/b). Four sheets containing T **163** and similar vert designs. Multicoloured.

MS1186 Two sheets (a/b), each 135 × 210 mm. (a) 60c. × 6, Type **163**; February; March; April; May; June. (b) 60c. × 6, July; August; September; October; November; December. Two sheets (c/d), each 100 × 69 mm. (c) $2 "Seashells and Plums" (Suzuki Kitsu). Imperf. (d) "Peacock and Peonies" (Nagasawa Rosetsu). Imperf Set of 4 sheets . . . . 8·00 8·25

2002. 85th Birth Anniv of John Fitzgerald Kennedy (USA president 1961–3) (**MS**1187a/b). Fifth Death Anniv of Diana, Princess of Wales (**MS**1187b/c). Four sheets containing T **164** and similar vert designs. Multicoloured.

MS1187 (a) 132 × 136 mm. 60c. × 4, Type **164**; Facing left; Looking left; Facing front. (b) 80 × 112 mm. $2 Facing right. (c) 114 × 133 mm. 60c. × 6, Princess Diana as bride; Wearing tiara; Wearing hat; Wearing scarf; Wearing pearl earrings; Wearing tiara facing left. (d) 87 × 60 mm. $2 Wearing wide-brimmed hat Set of 4 sheets . . 6·25 6·25

165 The Matterhorn, Switzerland

2002. International Year of Mountains. Two sheets containing T **165** and similar vert designs.
MS1188 (a) 136×95 mm. 80c.×4, Type **165**; Maroon Bells, USA; Wetterhorn, Switzerland; Mount Tasaranoro, Africa (inscr "Tasaranora"). (b) 96×62 mm. $2 Cerro Fitzroy, South America . . . 5·25 5·25

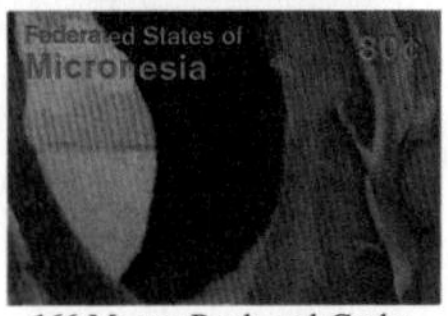

166 Money Rock and Gecko

2002. International Year of Eco Tourism. Two sheets containing T **166** and similar horiz designs. Multicoloured.
MS1189 (a) 138×99 mm. 80c.×6, Type **166**; Outrigger canoe; Tribal meeting house; Children wearing ceremonial costumes; Girl wearing lei; Two boys. (b) 85×55 mm. $2 Fishermen . . . . 4·00 4·00

167 Pagoda 168 Luge Racer

2002. World Scout Jamboree, Thailand. Multicoloured.
MS1190 (a) 161×68 mm. $1×3, Type **167**; American eagle; Scout cap. (b) 97×67 mm. $2 Scout badges . . . . 8·50 8·50

2002. Winter Olympic Games, Salt Lake City (2nd issue). Multicoloured.

1191	$1 Type **168**	1·10	65
1192	$1 Ice hockey player	1·10	65
MS1193	88×119 mm. Nos. 1191/2	2·20	2·20

Nos. 1191/MS1193 differ from the issue of 18 March in the design of the Olympic rings.

169 School Buildings

2002. 50th Anniv of Xavier High School, Sapwuk, Weno Island.
1194 **169** 37c. multicoloured . . . 40 25

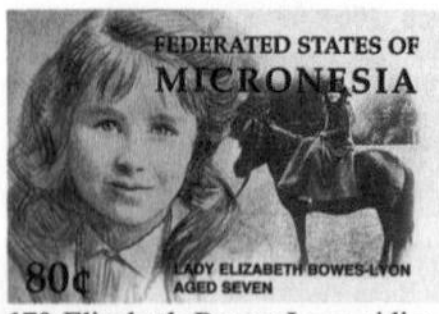

170 Elizabeth Bowes-Lyon riding Pony

2002. Queen Elizabeth the Queen Mother Commemoration. Two sheets containing T **170** and similar multicoloured designs.
MS1195 (a) 176×126 mm. 80c.×4, Type **170**; Wedding of Duke and Duchess of York; Holding Princess Elizabeth; Coronation of George VI and Queen Elizabeth. (b) 76×106 mm. $2 Queen Elizabeth the Queen Mother wearing hat with veil (vert) . . 5·50 5·50

171 Teddy Bear dressed as Burglar 173 "Madonna and Child" (detail) (Agnolo Bronzino)

172 Elvis Presley

2002. Centenary of the Teddy Bear. Sheet 141×145 mm containing T **171** and similar vert designs.
MS1196 80c.×4, Type **171**; Girl bear holding heart; Blue bear holding flowers; Boy bear holding heart . . . .

2002. 25th Death Anniv of Elvis Presley (entertainer). Sheet 214×163 mm containing T **172** and similar vert designs. Multicoloured.
MS1197 37c.×6, Type **172**; Kissing guitar; Wearing hat; Wearing checked shirt; With raised arms; Holding microphone . . . . . 2·40 2·40

2002. Christmas. Multicoloured.

1198	21c. Type **173**	20	10
1199	37c. "Madonna And Child" (Giovanni Bellini)	40	25
1200	70c. "Madonna and Child between St. Stephen and St. Ladislaus" (Simone Martini) (horiz)	75	45
1201	80c. "Holy Family" (Angola Bronzino)	90	55
1202	$2 "Holy Family" (Simone Martini)	2·10	1·30
MS1203	102×76 mm. $2 "Sacred Conversation" (Giovanni Bellini) (inscr "Giovanna")	2·10	2·10

174 Hyles lineate 175 Greater Flame-backed Woodpecker (*Chrysocolaptes lucidas*)

2002. Flora and Fauna. Ten sheets containing T **174** and similar multicoloured designs.
MS1204 Five sheets (a/e), each 127×157 mm. (a) Moths. 37c.×6, Type **174**; *Othreis fullonia*; Inscr "Dysphania cuprina"; *Agarista agricola*; *Actias elene*; Inscr "Rhodogastria crokeri". (b) Fungi. 55c.×6, *Phellinus robustus*; Inscr "Collybia iocephala"; *Leucocoprinus rachodes*; *Boletus edulis*; *Boletus crocipodius*; *Lepiota acutesquamosa*. (c) Butterflies. 60c.×6, *Junonia villida*; *Ornithoptera priamus*; *Danis danis*; *Libythea geoffroyi*; Inscr "Elyminas agondas"; *Eurema brigiitta*. (d) Orchids. 60c.×6, *Eria javanica*; *Cymbidium finlaysonianum*; *Coelogyne asperata*; *Spathoglottis affinis*; *Vanda tricolour*; *Calanthe rosea*. (e) Insects. Inscr "Pseudolucanus capreolus"; Honey bee (*Apis mellifera*); Black widow spider (*Latrodectus mactans*); Mosquito (*Anopheles*); Black ant (*Monomorium minimum*); Cicada (*Tibicen septendecim*). Five sheets (f/j), each 82×113 mm. (f) $2 *Alcides zodiaca*. (g) $2 *Lepiota acutesquamosa*. (h) $2 *Loxura atymnus*. (i) $2 *Dendrobium phalaenopsis*. (j) $2 *Anax junius* (horiz) . . . . 11·00 11·00
The stamps and margins of MS1204a/j form composite designs.

2002. Birds. Multicoloured.

1205	3c. Type **175**	10	10
1206	5c. Red-tailed tropicbird (*Phaethon rubricauda*) . .	10	10
1207	21c. Hair-crested drongo (*Dicrurus hottentottus*) (inscr "forficatus") . . .	20	10
1208	22c. *Zosterops citronella* . .	20	10
1209	23c. *Lonchura striata* . . .	25	15
1210	37c. Yap monarch (*Monarcha godeffroyi*) . .	40	25
1211	60c. Eclectus parrot (*Eclectus roratus*)	65	40
1212	70c. Sulphur-crested cockatoo (*Cacatua galerita*)	75	45
1213	80c. Inscr "Magazosterops palauensis"	85	50
1214	$2 Green magpie (*Cissa chinensis*)	2·10	1·30
1215	$3.85 Eastern broad-billed roller (inscr "Dollarbird") (*Eurystomus orientalis*) . .	4·00	2·40
1216	$5 Great frigate bird (*Fregata minor*)	5·50	3·50
1217	$13.65 Micronesian pigeon (*Ducula oceanica*)	14·00	8·50

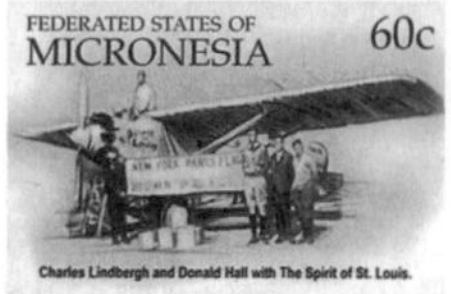

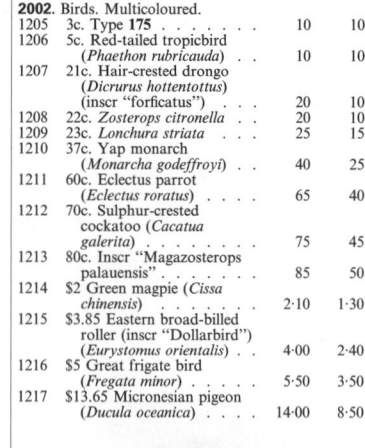

176 Charles Lindbergh, Donald Hall and *Spirit of St. Louis*

2003. 75th Anniv of First Transatlantic Flight. Sheet 135×118 mm containing T **176** and similar horiz designs. Multicoloured.
MS1218 60c.×6, Type **176**; *Spirit of St. Louis*; *Spirit of St. Louis* on Curtis Field; *Spirit of St. Louis* airborne; Arriving in Paris; Ticker tape parade, New York . . . 2·10 2·10

177 Long-haired Goat 178 David Brown

2003. New Year. "Year of the Ram" (stamps show goats). Sheet 110×121 mm containing T **177** and similar vert designs. Multicoloured.
MS1219 37c.×6, Type **177**×2; Angora goat×2; Dark-coloured goat×2 . . . . 2·40 2·40

2003. *Colombia* Space Shuttle Disaster, 1 February 2003. Crew Members. Sheet 184×146 mm containing T **178** and similar vert designs. Multicoloured.
MS1220 37c.×7, Type **178**; Rick Husband; Laurel Blair; Kalpana Chawla; Michael Anderson; William McCool; Ilan Ramon . . . 2·75 2·75

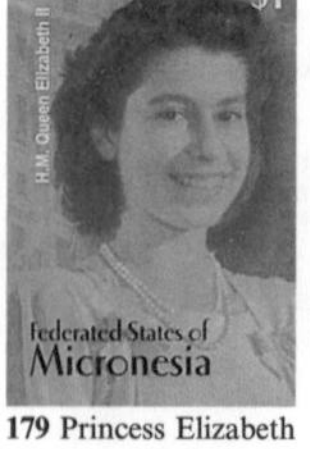

179 Princess Elizabeth 181 Prince William as Small Boy

180 Boeing B-52 Bomber

2003. 50th Anniv (2002) of Coronation of Queen Elizabeth. Two sheets containing T **179** and similar vert designs. Multicoloured.
MS1221 (a) 147×85 mm. $1×3, Type **179**; Wearing tiara; Wearing robe. (b) 68×98 mm. $2 Wearing state crown . . . . 5·50 5·50

2003. Military Operations in Iraq. Two sheets, each 136×136 mm containing T **180** and similar horiz designs. Multicoloured.
MS1222 (a) 37c.×5, Type **180**; General Dynamics F-16 Fighting Falcon; Bell Cobra helicopter; Hughes AH Apache helicopter; T8,000 Tow missile; US M3A2 Bradley tank. (b) 37c.×6, Stealth aircraft; Lockheed AC-130; Sikorsky MH-53j Pave Low II helicopter; General Atomics RQ-1 Predator; Vickers Challenger Two tank; Aegis cruiser . . . . . . 4·25 4·25

2003. 21st Birthday of Prince William. Two sheets containing T **181** and similar vert designs. Multicoloured.
MS1223 (a) 148×78 mm. $1×3, Type **181**; As schoolboy; As young man. (b) 98×68 mm. $2 As boy 5·50 5·50

182 Greg Lemond (1990) 183 Kosrae Mangroves

2003. Centenary of Tour de France Cycle Race. Two sheets containing T **182** and similar vert designs. Multicoloured. Litho. P 14.
MS1224 (a) 161×100 mm. 60c.×4, Type **182**; Miguel Indurain (1991); Miguel Indurain (1992); Miguel Indurain (1993). (b) 101×70 mm. $2 Marco Pantani (1998) . . . 4·75 4·75

2003. International Year of Freshwater. Two sheets containing T **183** and similar vert designs. Multicoloured.
MS1225 (a) 150×88 mm. $1×3, Type **183**; Chuuk lagoon; Pohnpei waterfalls. (b) 101×70 mm. $2 Pohnpei lagoon . . . . 5·50 5·50

184 Concorde

2003. Centenary of Powered Flight. Two sheets containing T **184** and similar horiz designs. Multicoloured.
MS1226 (a) 117×175 mm. 55c.×6, Type **184**; Boeing 757; Junkers F13a; Martin M-130 China Clipper; Handley Page HP 42W; *Wright Flyer II*. (b) 106×76 mm. $2 Boeing 747 . . . . 5·50 5·50

185 Glen Little 186 Scout wearing Tartan Scarf

2003. Centenary of Circus. Two sheets containing T **185** and similar vert designs. Multicoloured.
MS1227 (a) 118×200 mm. Clowns. 80c.×4, Type **185**; Joseph Grimaldi; Beverley Rebo Bergerson; Coco Michael Polakov. (b) 146×219 mm. Performers. 80c.×4, Jane Mandana (animal entertainer); Maxim Papazov (acrobat); Harry Keaton (illusionist); Giraffe . . . . . 6·75 6·75

2003. 25th Death Anniv of Norman Rockwell (illustrator). Two sheets containing T **186** and similar vert designs. Multicoloured.
MS1228 (a) 152×190 mm. 80c.×4, Type **186**; Scout carrying child; Scoutmaster. (b) 66×84 mm. $2 Boys and dog running away ("No Swimming"). Imperf . . . . . 5·25 5·25

187 "Vahine No Te Tiare"

2003. Death Centenary of Paul Gauguin (artist). Two sheets containing T **187** and similar horiz designs. Multicoloured.

MS1229		(a) 140×127 mm. 80c.×4, Type **187**; "Les Amants"; "Trois Tahitiens Conversation"; "Arearea". (b) 79×64 mm. $2 "Ta Matete". Imperf	5·25	5·25

188 "Blue and Silver Blue Wave, Biaritz"

2003. Death Centenary of James Whistler (artist). Multicoloured.

1230		37c. Type **188**	40	25
1231		55c. "Brown and Silver: Old Battersea Bridge"	60	35
1232		60c. "Nocturne in Blue and Silver: The Lagoon, Venice"	65	40
1233		80c. "Crepuscule In Flesh Colour and Green: Valparaiso"	85	50
MS1234		(a) 193×117 mm. $1×3, "Symphony in White No. 2: The Little White Girl" (38×51 mm); "At the Piano" (76×51 mm); "Symphony in White No. 1: The White Girl" (38×51 mm) . (b) 83×104 mm. $2 "Portrait of Thomas Carlyle" Imperf	5·50	5·50

189 "Madonna of the Carnation" (Leonardo da Vinci)

2003. Christmas. Multicoloured.

1235		37c. Type **189**	40	25
1236		60c. "Madonna with Yarn Winder"	65	40
1237		80c. "Litta Madonna"	85	50
1238		$1 "Madonna of the grand Duke" (Raphael)	1·10	65
MS1239		78×103 mm. $2 "The Adoration of the Magi" (Giambattista Tiepolo)	2·20	2·20

190 Green-winged Macaw

2003. Birds. Two sheets containing T **190** and similar multicoloured designs.

MS1240		(a) 179×155 mm. 80c.×4, Type **190**; Greater flamingo (inscr "American flamingo"); Blue and gold macaw; Abyssinian ground hornbill. (b) 62×76 mm. $2 Greater flamingo (inscr "American flamingo") (vert)	5·75	5·75

191 Leopard gecko

2003. Reptiles. Two sheets containing T **191** and similar horiz designs. Multicoloured.

MS1241		(a) 103×81 mm. 80c.×4, Type **191**; Red-eyed tree frog; Panther chameleon; Green and black poison frog. (b) 96×66 mm. $2 Madagascan chameleon	5·75	5·75

192 Australian Shepherd Dog

2003. Dogs and Cats. Four sheets containing T **192** and similar vert designs. Multicoloured.

MS1242		(a) 89×120 mm. 80c.×4, Type **192**; Greyhound; Bulldog; Schnauzer. (b) 96×67 mm. $2 Poodle. (c) 140×164 mm. 80c.×4, Ragdoll; Calico shorthair; Exotic shorthair; Dilute calico. (d) 66×96 mm. $2 Colour point shorthair	11·50	11·50

MIDDLE CONGO Pt. 6

One of three colonies into which Fr. Congo was divided in 1906. Became part of Fr. Equatorial Africa in 1937. Became part of the Congo Republic within the French Community on 28 November 1958.

100 centimes = 1 franc.

1 Leopard in Ambush

2 Bakalois Woman

3 Coconut Palms, Libreville

1907.

1	**1**	1c. olive and brown	50	25
2		2c. violet and brown	55	55
3		4c. blue and brown	1·00	1·60
4		5c. green and blue	1·25	50
21		5c. yellow and blue	1·60	3·00
5		10c. red and blue	1·10	80
22		10c. green and light green	3·25	4·25
6		15c. purple and pink	65	2·25
7		20c. brown and blue	3·00	4·25
8	**2**	25c. blue and green	2·50	85
23		25c. green and grey	2·50	3·25
9		30c. pink and green	1·50	3·25
24		30c. red	95	3·00
10		35c. brown and blue	2·25	2·50
11		40c. green and brown	2·75	3·25
12		45c. violet and orange	4·25	6·25
13		50c. green and orange	2·50	3·50
25		50c. blue and green	1·60	2·75
14		75c. brown and blue	6·00	8·00
15	**3**	1f. green and violet	9·00	11·00
16		2f. violet and green	6·50	10·50
17		5f. blue and pink	38·00	35·00

1916. Surch **5c** and red cross.

20	**1**	10c.+5c. red and blue	60	2·50

1924. Surch **AFRIQUE EQUATORIALE FRANCAISE** and new value.

26	**3**	25c. on 2f. green and violet	70	2·75
27		25c. on 5f. pink and blue	45	80
28		65 on 1f. brown and orange	50	3·00
29		85 on 1f. brown and orange	80	3·00
30	**2**	90 on 75c. scarlet and red	2·50	3·00
31		1f.25 on 1f. ultramarine & bl	80	2·50
32		1f.50 on 1f. blue & ultram	1·75	2·75
33		3f. on 5f. pink and brown	4·00	3·75
34		10f. on 5f. green and red	10·00	12·50
35		20f. on 5f. purple and brown	17·00	10·50

1924. Optd **AFRIQUE EQUATORIALE FRANCAISE.**

36	**1**	1c. olive and brown	15	2·25
37		2c. violet and brown	20	2·25
38		4c. blue and brown	20	2·25
39		5c. yellow and blue	40	2·25
40		10c. green and light green	80	2·75
41		10c. red and grey	55	2·25
42		15c. purple and pink	1·10	2·25
43		20c. brown and blue	25	2·75
44		20c. green and light green	40	2·75
45		20c. brown and mauve	2·50	2·75
46	**2**	25c. green and grey	50	50
47		30c. red	55	3·25
48		30c. grey and mauve	60	1·00
49		30c. deep green and green	2·25	3·25
50		35c. brown and blue	40	3·00
51		40c. green and brown	55	2·75
52		45c. violet and orange	35	3·00
53		50c. blue and green	60	1·25
54		50c. yellow and black	85	30
55		65c. brown and blue	2·75	4·00
56		75c. brown and blue	1·25	2·75
57		90c. red and pink	3·75	5·00
58	**3**	1f. green and violet	1·60	1·75
59		1f.10 mauve and brown	4·00	5·00
60		1f.50 ultramarine and blue	7·25	7·75
61		2f. violet and green	1·75	2·25
62		3f. mauve on pink	7·50	6·00
63		5f. blue and pink	2·00	2·50

1931. "Colonial Exhibition" key-types inscr "MOYEN CONGO".

65	E	40c. green and black	4·50	5·50
66	F	50c. mauve and black	2·75	3·75
67	G	90c. red and black	2·00	4·00
68	H	1f.50 blue and black	5·00	4·25

15 Mindouli Viaduct

1933.

69	**15**	1c. brown	10	2·25
70		2c. blue	10	2·50
71		4c. olive	20	50
72		5c. red	50	1·75
73		10c. green	1·60	2·50
74		15c. purple	2·00	2·75
75		20c. red on rose	7·75	8·00
76		25c. orange	1·90	2·75
77		30c. green	2·50	2·50
78	–	40c. brown	2·75	3·75
79	–	45c. black on green	2·75	3·50
80	–	50c. purple	2·25	45
81	–	65c. red on green	2·75	3·25
82	–	75c. black on red	10·00	8·50
83	–	90c. red	2·75	3·25
84	–	1f. red	1·75	1·50
85	–	1f.25 green	2·50	2·25
86	–	1f.50 blue	6·75	3·75
87	–	1f.75 violet	3·00	2·50
88	–	2f. olive	2·50	2·25
89	–	3f. black on red	4·00	3·00
90	–	5f. grey	15·00	16·00
91	–	10f. black	50·00	26·00
92	–	20f. brown	30·00	17·00

DESIGNS: 40c. to 1f.50 Pasteur Institute, Brazzaville; 1f.75 to 20f. Government Building, Brazzaville.

POSTAGE DUE STAMPS

1928. Postage Due type of France optd **MOYEN-CONGO A. E. F.**

D64	D **11**	5c. blue	20	2·50
D65		10c. brown	45	2·75
D66		20c. olive	45	3·00
D67		25c. red	85	3·25
D68		30c. red	50	3·00
D69		45c. green	60	3·00
D70		50c. purple	70	3·75
D71		60c. brown on cream	95	4·00
D72		1f. red on cream	1·25	3·75
D73		2f. red	1·60	5·00
D74		3f. violet	2·75	8·75

D 13 Village

1930.

D75	D **13**	5c. olive and blue	65	2·50
D76		10c. brown and red	65	3·00
D77		20c. brown and green	2·25	4·25
D78		25c. brown and blue	2·50	4·50
D79		30c. green and brown	1·75	7·75
D80		45c. olive and green	3·00	6·75
D81		50c. brown and mauve	3·50	7·75
D82		60c. black and violet	4·00	8·00
D83	–	1f. black and brown	11·00	16·00
D84	–	2f. brown and mauve	9·50	18·00
D85	–	3f. brown and red	8·75	16·00

DESIGN: 1 to 3f. "William Guinet" (steamer) on the River Congo.

D 17 "Le Djoue"

1933.

D 93	D **17**	5c. green	25	2·75
D 94		10c. blue on blue	1·25	2·75
D 95		20c. red on yellow	2·00	3·00
D 96		25c. red	2·25	3·25
D 97		30c. red	2·00	3·50
D 98		45c. purple	2·25	3·50
D 99		50c. black	2·50	4·50
D100		60c. black on red	3·00	5·50
D101		1f. red	2·75	7·25
D102		2f. orange	6·75	11·00
D103		3f. blue	11·50	15·00

For later issues see **FRENCH EQUATORIAL AFRICA**.

MODENA Pt. 8

A state in Upper Italy, formerly a duchy and now part of Italy. Used stamps of Sardinia after the cessation of its own issues in 1860. Now uses Italian stamps.

100 centesimi = 1 lira.

1 Arms of Este

5 Cross of Savoy

1852. Imperf.

9	**1**	5c. black on green	25·00	44·00
3		10c. black on pink	£325	65·00
4		15c. black on yellow	40·00	25·00
5		25c. black on buff	42·00	29·00
12		40c. black on blue	40·00	£120
13		1l. black on white	55·00	£2250

1859. Imperf.

18	**5**	5c. green	£1300	£600
19		15c. brown	£2500	£3500
20		15c. grey	£300	
21		20c. black	£1800	£150
22		20c. lilac	60·00	£1000
23		40c. red	£180	£1200
24		80c. brown	£180	£19000

NEWSPAPER STAMPS

1853. As T **1** but in the value tablet inscr "B.G. CEN" and value. Imperf.

N15	**1**	9c. black on mauve	£600	75·00
N16		10c. black on lilac	55·00	£275

N 4

1859. Imperf.

N17	N **4**	10c. black	£1000	£2000

MOHELI Pt. 6

An island in the Comoro Archipelago adjacent to Madagascar. A separate French dependency until 1914 when the whole archipelago was placed under Madagascar whose stamps were used until 1950. Now part of the Comoro Islands.

100 centimes = 1 franc.

1906. "Tablet" key-type inscr "MOHELI" in blue (2, 4, 10, 20, 30, 40c., 5f.) or red (others).

1	D	1c. black on blue	2·25	2·00
2		2c. brown on buff	1·25	2·00
3		4c. brown on grey	2·25	3·25
4		5c. green	3·00	2·50
5		10c. red	2·75	1·90
6		20c. red on green	9·75	9·25
7		25c. blue	9·25	5·25
8		30c. brown on drab	17·00	7·00
9		35c. black on yellow	7·00	2·75
10		40c. red on yellow	13·50	10·50
11		45c. black on green	55·00	52·00
12		50c. brown on blue	23·00	14·00
13		75c. brown on orange	30·00	29·00
14		1f. green	15·00	20·00
15		2f. violet on pink	32·00	42·00
16		5f. mauve on lilac	£110	£120

1912. Surch in figures.

17	D	05 on 4c. brown & bl on grey	2·00	3·25
18		05 on 20c. red & blue on grn	1·90	5·00
19		05 on 30c. brn & bl on drab	1·75	3·75
20		10 on 40c. red & blue on yell	1·90	3·50
21		10 on 45c. blk & red on grn	1·10	2·50
22		10 on 50c. brown & red on bl	1·75	4·00

MOLDOVA Pt. 10

Formerly Moldavia, a constituent republic of the Soviet Union. Moldova declared its sovereignty within the Union in 1990 and became independent in 1991.

1991. 100 kopeks = 1 rouble.
1993. Kupon (temporary currency).
1993. 100 bani = 1 leu.

1 Arms

2 Codrii Nature Reserve

1991. 1st Anniv of Declaration of Sovereignty. Multicoloured. Imperf.

1		7k. Type **1**	10	10
2		13k. Type **1**	10	10
3		30k. Flag (35 × 23 mm)	15	10

1992.

4	**2**	25k. multicoloured	55	25

3 Arms

4 Tupolev Tu-144

1992.

5	**3**	35k. green	10	10
6		50k. red	10	10
7		65k. brown	10	10
8		1r. purple	15	10
9		1r.50 blue	25	10

1992. Air.

15	**4**	1r.75 red	10	10
16		2r.50 mauve	15	10
17		7r.75 violet	60	30
18		8r.50 green	80	40

See also Nos. 70/3.

5 European Bee Eater

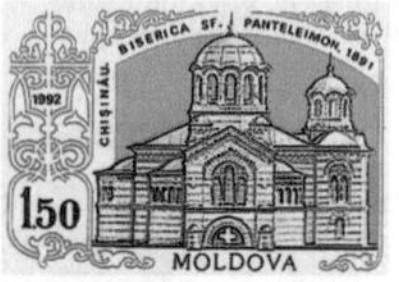
6 St. Panteleimon's Church

1992. Birds. Multicoloured.

19		50k. Type **5**	20	20
20		65k. Golden oriole	20	20
21		2r.50 Green woodpecker	40	40
22		6r. European roller	1·00	1·00
23		7r.50 Hoopoe	1·25	1·25
24		15r. European cuckoo	2·75	2·75

See also Nos. 63/9.

1992. Centenary (1991) of St. Panteleimon's Church, Chisinau.

25	**6**	1r.50 multicoloured	15	10

7 Wolf suckling Romulus and Remus

9 High Jumping

1992. Trajan Memorial, Chisinau.

26	**7**	5r. multicoloured	15	10

1992. Various stamps of Russia surch **MOLDOVA** and value.

27		2r.50 on 4k. red (No. 4672)	10	10
28		6r. on 3k. red (No. 4671)	10	10
29		8r.50 on 4k. red (No. 4672)	30	15
30		10r. on 3k. green (No. 6074)	50	25

1992. Olympic Games, Barcelona. Multicoloured.

31		35k. Type **9**	10	10
32		65k. Wrestling	10	10
33		1r. Archery	10	10
34		2r.50 Swimming	30	15
35		10r. Show jumping	1·10	55

1992. Nos. 4669/71 of Russia surch **MOLDOVA**, new value and bunch of grapes.

37		45k. on 2k. mauve	10	10
38		46k. on 2k. mauve	10	10
39		63k. on 1k. green	10	10
40		63k. on 3k. red	10	10
41		70k. on 1k. green	10	10
42		4r. on 1k. green	30	15

1992. Moldovan Olympic Games Medal Winners. Nos. 33/4 optd.

43		1r. Archery (optd **NATALIA VALEEV bronz** and emblem)	40	20
44		2r.50 Swimming (optd **IURIE BASCATOV argint** and emblem)	1·10	55

13 Moldovan Flag, Statue of Liberty and U.N. Emblem and Building

1992. Admission of Moldova to U.N.O. Mult.

46		1r.30 Type **13**	10	10
47		12r. As Type **13** but with motifs differently arranged	40	20

14 Moldovan Flag and Prague Castle

1992. Admission of Moldova to European Security and Co-operation Conference. Multicoloured.

48		2r.50 Type **14**	15	10
49		25r. Helsinki Cathedral and Moldovan flag	50	25

15 Carpet and Pottery

16 Galleon

1992. Folk Art.

50	**15**	7r.50 multicoloured	25	15

1992. 500th Anniv of Discovery of America by Columbus. Multicoloured.

51		1r. Type **16**	15	10
52		6r. Carrack	80	40
53		6r. Caravel	80	40
MS54		89 × 69 mm. 25r. Christopher Columbus	3·00	3·00

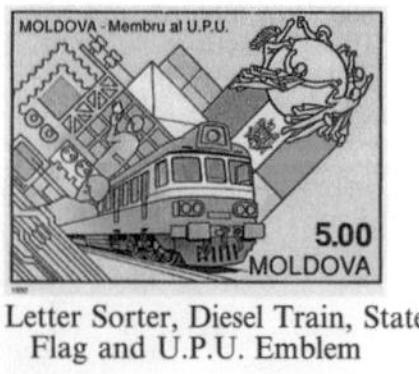
17 Letter Sorter, Diesel Train, State Flag and U.P.U. Emblem

1992. Admission to U.P.U. Multicoloured.

55		5r. Type **17**	75	40
56		10r. Douglas DC-10 jetliner, computerized letter sorting equipment, state flag and U.P.U. emblem	95	50

18 Aesculapius Snake

1993. Protected Animals. Snakes. Multicoloured.

57		3r. Type **18**	20	10
58		3r. Aesculapius in tree	20	10
59		3r. Aesculapius on path	20	10
60		3r. Aesculapius on rock	20	10
61		15r. Grass snake	75	40
62		25r. Adder	1·25	60

Nos. 57/60 were issued together, se-tenant, forming a composite design.

1993. Birds. As Nos. 19/24 but with values changed and additional design. Multicoloured.

63		2r. Type **5**	20	20
64		3r. As No. 20	20	20
65		5r. As No. 21	20	20
66		10r. As No. 22	30	20
67		15r. As No. 23	40	30
68		50r. As No. 24	1·50	1·40
69		100r. Barn swallow	3·25	2·75

1993. Air.

70	**4**	25r. red	20	10
71		45r. brown	35	20
72		50r. green	40	20
73		90r. blue	70	35

19 Arms

20 Arms

1993.

74	**19**	2k. blue	10	10
75		3k. purple	10	10
76		6k. green	10	10
77	–	10k. violet and green	10	10
78	–	15k. violet and green	10	10
79	–	20k. violet and grey	10	10
80	–	30k. violet and yellow	15	10
81	–	50k. violet and red	20	10
82	**20**	100k. multicoloured	40	20
83		250k. multicoloured	90	45

DESIGN: 10 to 50k. Similar to Type **19** but with inscription and value at foot differently arranged.

21 Red Admiral

22 "Tulipa bibersteiniana"

1993. Butterflies and Moths. Multicoloured.

94		6b. Type **21**	10	10
95		10b. Swallowtail	10	10
96		50b. Peacock	35	20
97		250b. Emperor moth	1·90	80

1993. Flowers. Multicoloured.

98		6b. Type **22**	10	10
99		15b. Lily of the valley	10	10
100		25b. Snowdrop	15	10
101		30b. Peony	20	10
102		50b. Snowdrop	30	15
103		90b. Pasque flower	60	30
MS104		88 × 68 mm. 250b. Lady's Slipper (*Cypripedium caleolus*) (44 × 29 mm)	1·40	1·40

23 Dragos Voda (1352–53)

24 "Story of One Life" (M. Grecu)

1993. 14th-century Princes of Moldavia. Mult.

105		6b. Type **23**	10	10
106		25b. Bogdan Voda I (1359–65)	10	10
107		50b. Latcu Voda (1365–75)	20	10
108		100b. Petru I Musat (1375–91)	45	25
109		150b. Roman Voda Musat (1391–94)	65	35
110		200b. Stefan I (1394–99)	90	45

1993. Europa. Contemporary Art. Multicoloured.

111		3b. Type **24**	10	10
112		150b. "Coming of Spring" (I. Vieru)	1·60	80

25 Biathletes

27 State Arms

1994. Winter Olympic Games, Lillehammer, Norway. Multicoloured.

113		3b. Type **25**	10	10
114		150b. Close-up of biathlete shooting	1·25	60

1994. No. 4669 of Russia surch **MOLDOVA**, grapes and value.

115		3b. on 1k. green	10	10
116		25b. on 1k. green	10	10
117		50b. on 1k. green	15	10

1994.

118	**27**	1b. multicoloured	10	10
119		10b. multicoloured	10	10
120		30b. multicoloured	10	10
121		38b. multicoloured	15	10
122		45b. multicoloured	15	10
123		75b. multicoloured	30	15
124		1l.50 multicoloured	60	30
125		1l.80 multicoloured	70	35
126		2l.50 mult (24 × 29 mm)	95	50
127		4l.50 multicoloured	1·75	1·25
128		5l.40 multicoloured	2·00	1·40
129		6l.90 multicoloured	2·50	1·50
130		7l.20 mult (24 × 29 mm)	2·75	1·75
131		13l. mult (24 × 29 mm)	5·25	3·50
132		24l. mult (24 × 29 mm)	9·25	6·00

28 Launch of "Titan II" Rocket

29 Maria Cibotari (singer)

1994. Europa. Inventions and Discoveries. 25th Anniv of First Manned Moon Landing. Multicoloured.

136		1b. Type **28**	10	10
137		45b. Ed White (astronaut) on space walk ("Gemini 4" flight, 1965)	65	35
138		2l.50 Lunar module landing, 1969	2·25	1·25

1994. Entertainers' Death Anniversaries. Mult.

139		3b. Type **29** (45th)	10	10
140		90b. Dumitru Caraciobanu (actor, 14th)	40	20
141		150b. Eugeniu Coca (composer, 40th)	70	35
142		250b. Igor Vieru (actor, 11th)	1·10	55

30 Preparing Stamp Design

1994. Stamp Day.

143	**30**	10b. black, blue and mauve	10	10
144	–	45b. black, mauve and yellow	30	15
145	–	2l. multicoloured	1·25	65

DESIGNS: 45b. Printing stamps; 2l. Checking finished sheets.

31 Pierre de Coubertin (founder)

32 Map

1994. Centenary of International Olympic Committee. Multicoloured.

146		60b. Type **31**	20	10
147		1l.50 Rings and "Paris 1994" centenary congress emblem	65	35

1994. Partnership for Peace Programme (co-operation of N.A.T.O. and Warsaw Pact members).

148	–	60b. black, ultram and bl	20	20
149	**32**	2l.50 multicoloured	30	30

DESIGN: 60b. Manfred Worner (Secretary-General of N.A.T.O.) and President Mircea Snegur of Moldova.

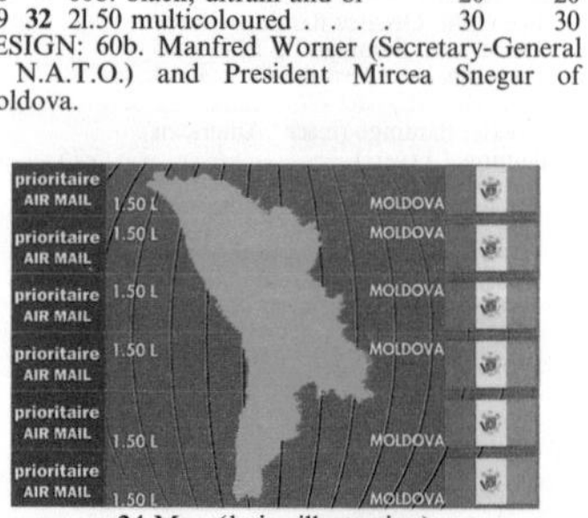
34 Map (½-size illustration)

1994. Air. Self-adhesive. Roul.
152 **34** 1l.50 multicoloured 50 25
153 4l.50 multicoloured . . . . 1·50 75

The individual stamps are peeled directly from the card backing. Each card contains six different designs with the same face value forming the composite design illustrated. Each stamp is a horizontal strip with a label indicating the main class of mail covered by the rate at the left, separated by a vertical line of rouletting. The outer edges of the cards are imperforate.

35 Family

36 Handshake

1994. International Year of the Family. Multicoloured.
154 30b. Type **35** 20 10
155 60b. Mother breast-feeding baby 40 20
156 1l.50 Child drawing . . . . 1·50 90

1994. Preliminary Rounds of European Football Championship, England (1996). Multicoloured.
157 10b. Type **36** 10 10
158 40b. Players competing for ball 25 15
159 2l.40 Goalkeeper making save 1·50 90
MS160 140 × 105 mm. 1l.10 Moldovan and German pennants; 2l.20, German and Moldovan shields on ball; 2l.40, Players 3·00 3·00

37 "Birth of Jesus Christ" (anon)

38 Cracked Green Russula

1994. Christmas. Multicoloured.
161 20b. Type **37** 15 10
162 3l.60 "Birth of Jesus Christ" (Gherasim) . . . . 1·90 1·00

1995. Fungi. Multicoloured.
163 4b. Type **38** 10 10
164 10b. Oak mushroom 25 15
165 20b. Chanterelle 45 25
166 90b. Red-capped scaber stalk 2·10 1·10
167 1l.80 "Leccinum duriusculum" . . . . . . 4·25 2·25

39 Booted Eagle

1995. European Nature Conservation Year. Multicoloured.
168 4b. Type **39** 15 15
169 45b. Roe deer . . . . 1·00 50
170 90b. Wild boar . . . . . . 2·00 1·10

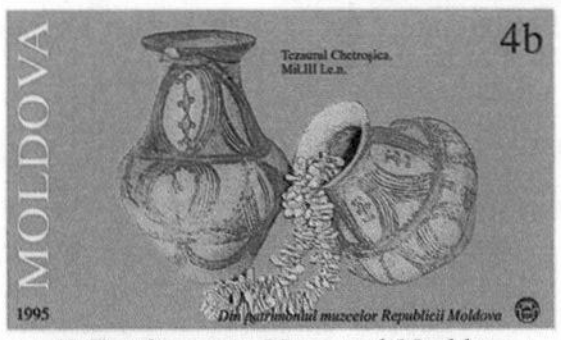

40 Earthenware Urns and Necklace

1995. National Museum Exhibits. Multicoloured.
171 4b. Type **40** 10 10
172 10b.+2b. Representation and skeleton of "Dinotherium gigantissimum" 25 15
173 1l.80+30b. Silver coins . . . 2·75 1·75

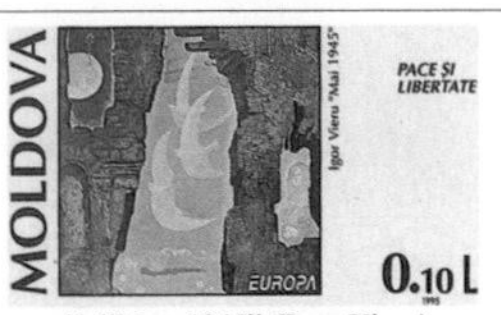

41 "May 1945" (Igor Vieru)

1995. Europa. Peace and Freedom. Paintings. Multicoloured.
174 10b. Type **41** 15 10
175 40b. "Peace" (Sergiu Cuciuc) 35 20
176 2l.20 "Spring 1944" (Cuciuc) 2·00 1·10

42 Constantin Stere (writer, 130th birth)

43 Alexandru cel Bun (1400–32)

1995. Anniversaries.
177 **42** 9b. brown and grey . . . 15 10
178 – 10b. purple and grey . . . 15 10
179 – 40b. lilac and grey 55 30
180 – 1l.80 green and grey . . . 2·50 1·50
DESIGNS: 10b. Tamara Ceban (singer, 5th death); 40b. Alexandru Plamadeala (sculptor, 55th death); 1l.80, Lucian Blaga (philosopher, birth centenary).

1995. 15th and 16th-century Princes of Moldavia. Multicoloured.
181 10b. Type **43** 15 10
182 10b. Petru Aron (1451–52 and 1454–57) 15 10
183 10b. Stefan cel Mare (1457–1504) 15 10
184 45b. Petru Rares (1527–38 and 1541–46) 65 35
185 90b. Alexandru Lapusneanu (1552–61 and 1564–68) . . 1·40 70
186 1l.80 Ioan Voda cel Cumplit (1572–74) . . . . 3·00 1·50
MS187 83 × 66 mm. 5l. Stefan del Mare (1457–1504) (24 × 29 mm) 1·40 1·40

44 Soroca Castle

1995. Castles. Multicoloured.
188 10b. Type **44** 15 10
189 20b. Tighina Castle 35 15
190 60b. Alba Castle . . . . . . 1·00 60
191 1l.30 Hotin Castle . . . . . 2·40 1·60

45 Seal in Eye

46 "50" and Emblem

1995. 50th Anniv of U.N.O. Multicoloured.
(a) Ordinary gum. Perf.
192 10b. Type **45** 20 10
193 10b. Airplane in eye 20 10
194 1l.50 Child's face and barbed wire in eye . . . . 3·25 2·00

(b) Self-adhesive. Rouletted.
195 90b. Type **46** 30 15
196 1l.50 Type **46** 45 25

47 "Last Moon of Autumn"

48 Fly Agaric

1995. Centenary of Motion Pictures.
197 **47** 10b. red and black 15 10
198 – 40b. green and black . . . 50 25
199 – 2l.40 blue and black . . . 3·00 2·00

DESIGNS: 40b. "Lautarii"; 2l.40, "Dimitrie Cantemir".

1996. Fungi. Multicoloured.
200 10b. Type **48** 10 10
201 10b. Satan's mushroom . . . 10 10
202 65b. Death cap 65 35
203 1l.30 Clustered woodlover . . 1·25 70
204 2l.40 Destroying angel . . . 2·40 1·25

49 Weightlifting

50 Rudi Monastery

1996. Olympic Games, Atlanta, U.S.A. Mult.
205 10b. Type **49** 10 10
206 20b.+5b. Judo 35 15
207 45b.+10b. Running 65 35
208 2l.40+30b. Kayaking . . . . 3·00 1·75

1996. Monasteries. Multicoloured.
210 10b. Type **50** 10 10
211 90b. Japca 40 20
212 1l.30 Curchi 60 30
213 2l.80 Saharna . . . . 1·25 70
214 4l.40 Capriana . . . . 2·10 1·25

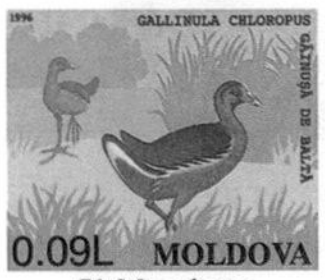

51 Moorhens

52 Elena Alistar (president of Women's League)

1996. Birds. Multicoloured.
215 9b. Type **51** 15 10
216 10b. Greylag geese 15 10
217 2l.20 Turtle doves . . . . . 1·75 1·10
218 4l.40 Mallard . . . . 3·50 2·10
MS219 82 × 65 mm. 2l.20 Ring-necked pheasant (*Phasianus colchicus*) . . . . 1·50 1·50

1996. Europa. Famous Women. Multicoloured.
220 10b. Type **52** 15 10
221 3l.70 Marie Sklodowska-Curie (physicist) . . . . . 2·75 1·90
MS222 94 × 104 mm. 2l.20 Iulia Hasdeu (writer) . . . . 1·60 1·60

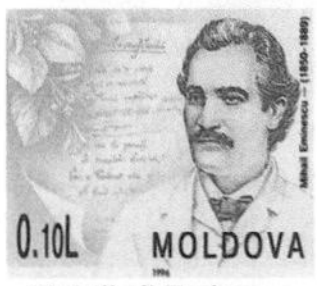

53 Mihail Eminescu (poet) (146th birth anniv)

54 Town Hall

1996. Birth Anniversaries.
223 **53** 10b. brown and deep brown 10 10
224 – 10b. sepia and brown . . . 10 10
225 – 2l.20 green and brown . . 90 45
226 – 3l.30 green and deep brown 1·40 75
227 – 5l.40 brown and deep brown . . . . 2·25 1·40
MS228 96 × 66 mm. 1l.80 brown 75 75
DESIGNS—HORIZ: 10b. Gavriil Banulescu-Bodoni (Metropolitan of Chisinau, 250th); 2l.20, Ion Creanga (writer, 159th); 3l.30, Vasile Alecsandri (writer, 172nd); 5l.40, Petru Movila and printing press (400th). VERT—1l.80, Mihail Eminesai (different).

1996. 560th Anniv of Chisinau. Multicoloured.
229 10b. Type **54** 10 10
230 1l.30 Cultural Palace . . . . 1·25 60
231 2l.40 Mazarache Church . . 2·25 1·40

55 Carol Singers with Star

57 Feteasca

1996. Christmas. Multicoloured.
232 10b. Type **55** 10 10
233 2l.20+30b. Mother and child at centre of star . . . . . 1·25 60
234 2l.80+50b. Children decorating Christmas tree 1·60 1·00

1996. Moldovan Olympic Games Medal Winners. No. **MS**209 optd **Nicolae JURAVSCHI Victor RENEISCHI – canoe, argint -, Serghei MUREICO – lupt Greco-romame, bronz**.
MS235 123 × 75 mm. 2l.20 mult 2·10 1·40

1997. Moldovan Wines. Each showing a grape variety and bottle of wine. Multicoloured.
236 10b. Type **57** 10 10
237 45b. Cabernet Sauvignon . . 30 15
238 65b. Sauvignon 45 25
239 3l.70 Rara Neagra . . . . . 2·50 1·50

58 Franz Schubert

1997. Composers. Each green and grey.
240 10b. Type **58** (birth bicentenary) 10 10
241 10b. Gavriil Musicescu (150th birth anniv) 10 10
242 45b. Sergei Rachmaninov . . 40 20
243 4l.40 Georges Enesco . . . . 3·75 2·40

59 Girl with Eggs

1997. Easter. Multicoloured.
244 10b. Type **59** 10 10
245 3l.30 Easter dish . . . . . . 1·75 1·10
MS246 87 × 70 mm. 5l. Easter basket with bread and eggs . . . . . 2·75 1·50

60 White Stork flying over Battlements

61 Praying Mantis

1997. Europa. Tales and Legends. Multicoloured.
247 10b. Type **60** 10 10
248 2l.80 Master Manole . . . . 1·25 75
MS249 90 × 70 mm. 5l. The Spring Fairy . . . . 2·75 1·50

1997. Insects in the Red Book. Multicoloured.
250 25b. Type **61** 10 10
251 80b. "Ascalaphus macaronius" (owl-fly) . . . 45 20
252 1l. Searcher 55 30
253 2l.20 "Liometopum microcephalum" (ant) . . . 1·25 70
MS254 84 × 67 mm. 5l. *Scolia maculata* (dagger wasp) . . . . 2·75 2·75

62 Post Office No. 12, Chisinau

63 Nicolai Zelinski School, Tiraspol

1997. World Post Day.
255 **62** 10b. green and olive . . . 10 10
256 – 2l.20 green and brown . . 1·60 80
257 – 3l.30 olive and green . . . 2·40 1·40
DESIGNS—HORIZ: 2l.20, District Head Post and Telegraph Office, Chisinau. VERT: 3l.30, Heinrich von Stephan (founder of U.P.U.) (death centenary).

1997. Protection of Buildings.
258 **63** 7b. black and violet . . . 10 10
259 – 10b. black and purple . . . 10 10
260 – 10b. black and blue . . . 10 10
261 – 90b. black and yellow . . . 50 25
262 – 1l.30 black and blue . . . 75 40
263 – 3l.30 black and grey . . . 1·90 90
DESIGNS: No. 259, Railway station, Tighina; 260, Sts. Constantine and Elena Cathedral, Balti; 261, Church, Causeni; 262, Archangel Michael Cathedral, Cahul; 263, Academy of Art, Chisinau.

64 Noul Neamt Monastery, Chitcani

65 Petru Schiopul (1574–77, 1578–79 and 1582–91)

1997. Christmas. Multicoloured.
264 10b. Type **64** 10 10
265 45b. "Birth of Our Lord Jesus Christ" 25 15
266 5l. "Birth of Jesus Christ" (different) . . . . 2·75 1·75

1997. 16th and 17th-century Princes of Moldavia. Multicoloured.
267 10b. Type **65** 10 10
268 10b. Ieremia Movila (1595–1606) 10 10
269 45b. Stefan Tomsa (1611–15 and 1621–23) 25 15
270 1l.80 Radu Mihnea (1616–19 and 1623–26) 95 55
271 2l.20 Miron Barnovschi Movila (1626–29 and 1633) 1·10 70
272 2l.80 Bogdan Orbul (1504–1517) . . . . 1·50 90
MS273 93 × 75 mm. 5l. Mihai Viteazul (May--Sept 1600) (25 × 30 mm) . . . . 2·00 2·00

66 Skiing

1998. Winter Olympic Games, Nagano, Japan. Multicoloured.
274 10b. Type **66** 10 10
275 45b. Pairs figure skating . . . 35 15
276 2l.20 Biathlon . . . . 1·75 1·10

67 Alexei Mateeici

68 Statue of Stefan cel Mare (Alexandru Plamadeala), Chisinau

1998. Anniversaries. Multicoloured.
277 10b. Type **67** (110th birth anniv) 10 10
278 40b. Pantelimon Halippa (115th birth anniv) 20 10
279 60b. Stefan Ciobanu (115th birth anniv) 35 20
280 2l. Constantin Stamati-Ciurea (death centenary) 90 45
MS281 100 × 80 mm. 5l. Nicolae Milescu-Spatarul (290th death anniv) . . . . 2·25 2·25

1998. Art. Multicoloured.
282 10b. Type **68** 10 10
283 60b. "The Resurrection of Christ" (icon) 35 20
284 1l. Modern sculpture (Constantin Brancusi), Targu-Jiu 55 30
285 2l.60 Trajan's Column, Rome 1·25 65

69 Masks and Eye

70 Cherries

1998. Europa. National Festivals. Multicoloured.
286 10b. Type **69** (Eugene Ionescu Theatre Festival) 10 10
287 2l.20 Medallion showing potter (Cermanics Fair) . . 1·10 55
MS288 70 × 58 mm. 5l. Bar of music (Martisor International Music Festival) . . . . 2·25 2·25

1998. Fruits. Multicoloured.
289 7b. Type **70** 10 10
290 10b. Plums 10 10
291 1l. Apples 55 30
292 2l. Pears 90 45

71 Diana, Princess of Wales

1998. Diana, Princess of Wales Commemoration. Sheet 144 × 116 mm containing T **71** and similar horiz designs. Multicoloured.
MS293 10d. Type **71**; 90b. Wearing orange jacket; 1l.80, Wearing burgundy jacket; 2l.20 Wearing jacket with white collar; 5l. Wearing jacket with velvet collar 4·50 4·50

72 Chilia

1998. Medieval Towns.
294 **72** 10b. grey and black . . . 10 10
295 – 60b. brown and black . . . 35 20
296 – 1l. red and black 50 25
297 – 2l. blue and black 95 50
DESIGNS: 60b. Orhei; 1l. Suceava; 2l. Ismail.

73 1858 Moldavia Stamps

1998. 140th Anniv of Stamp Issues for Moldavia. Multicoloured.
298 10b. Type **73** 10 10
299 90b. 1858 Moldavia 54p. and 1928 Rumania 1 and 5l. stamps 40 20
300 2l.20 1858 Moldavia 81p. and Russian stamps . . . . . 1·10 55
301 2l.40 1858 Moldavia 108p. and Moldova 1996 10b. and 1994 45b. stamps . . . 1·25 65

74 Northern Eagle Owl

75 Couple from Vara

1998. Birds. Multicoloured.
302 25b. Type **74** 30 15
303 2l. Demoiselle crane (horiz) 1·25 65

1998. Regional Costumes. Multicoloured.
304 25b. Type **75** 15 10
305 90b. Couple from Vara (different) 60 30
306 1l.80 Couple from Iarna . . 1·25 65
307 2l. Couple from Iarna (different) . . . . 1·40 70

76 Anniversary Emblem and "Proportions of Man" (Leonardo da Vinci)

1998. 50th Anniv of Universal Declaration of Human Rights.
308 **76** 2l.40 multicoloured . . . . 1·60 80

77 Conference Members

1998. 80th Anniv of Union of Bessarabia and Rumania.
309 **77** 90b. brown, blue and black 60 30

78 Mail Coach

1999. Anniversaries. Multicoloured.
310 25b. Type **78** (125th anniv of U.P.U.) 15 10
311 2l.20 Map of Europe and Council of Europe emblem (50th anniv) . . . . 1·50 75

79 Prutul de Jos Park

1999. Europa. Parks and Gardens. Multicoloured.
312 25b. Type **79** 15 10
313 2l.40 Padurea Domneasca Park . . . . 1·60 80
MS314 84 × 65 mm. 5l. Codru Park 3·25 3·25

80 Balzac

81 "Aleksandr Pushkin and Constantin Stamati" (B. Lebedev)

1999. Birth Bicent of Honore de Balzac (writer).
315 **80** 90b. multicoloured 60 30

1999. Birth Bicentenary of Aleksandr Pushkin (poet).
316 **81** 65b. brown, deep brown and black 45 25

82 Tranta

1999. National Sports.
317 **82** 25b. green and light green 15 10
318 – 1l.80 green and yellow . . 1·25 60
DESIGN: 1l.80, Oina.

83 Neil Armstrong (first man on Moon)

1999. 30th Anniv of First Manned Moon Landing. Multicoloured.
319 25b. Type **83** 15 10
320 25b. Michael Collins (pilot of Command Module) 15 10
321 5l. Edwin Aldrin (pilot of Lunar Module) . . . . . 3·25 1·75

84 Military Merit

85 Embroidered Shirt

1999. Orders and Medals. Multicoloured.
322 25b. Type **84** 15 10
323 25b. For Valour 15 10
324 25b. Civil Merit 15 10
325 90b. Mihai Eminescu Medal 60 30
326 1l.10 Order of Gloria Muncii 75 40
327 2l.40 Order of Stefan al Mare 1·60 80
MS328 70 × 50 mm. 5l. Order of the Republic . . . . 3·25 3·25

1999. Crafts. Multicoloured.
329 5b. Inlaid wine flask 10 10
330 25b. Type **85** 15 10
331 95b. Ceramic jugs 60 30
332 1l.80 Wicker table and chairs 1·25 60

86 Goethe

1999. 250th Birth Anniv of Johann Wolfgang von Goethe (poet).
333 **86** 1l.10 multicoloured 40 20

87 Emblem

88 Metropolitan Varlaam

1999. 10th Anniv of Adoption of Latin Alphabet.
334 **87** 25b. multicoloured 10 10

1999. Patriarchs of the Orthodox Church. Mult.
335 25b. Type **88** 10 10
336 2l.40 Metropolitan Gurie Grosu 80 40

89 Bogdan II (1449–51)

91 Player and Chessboard

90 European Otter ("Lutra lutra")

1999. 15th to 17th-century Princes of Moldavia. Multicoloured.
337 25b. Type **89** 10 10
338 25b. Bogdan IV (1568–72) . . 10 10
339 25b. Constantin Cantemir (1685–93) 10 10
340 1l.50 Simon Movila (1606–07) 55 25
341 3l. Gheorghe III Duca (1665–66, 1668–72 and 1678–84) 1·00 50
342 3l.90 Ilias Alexandru (1666–68) . . . . 1·25 65
MS343 97 × 78 mm. 5l. Vasile Lupu (1634–53) (25 × 30 mm) . . . . 3·25 3·25

1999. Animals in the Red Book. Multicoloured.
344 25b. Type **90** 10 10
345 1l.80 Beluga ("Huso huso") 65 30
346 3l.60 Greater horseshoe bat ("Rhinolophus ferrumequinum") . . . . . 1·10 55

1999. World Women's Chess Championship, Chisinau. Multicoloured.
347 25b. Type **91** 10 10
348 2l.20+30b. Championship venue and emblem 85 40

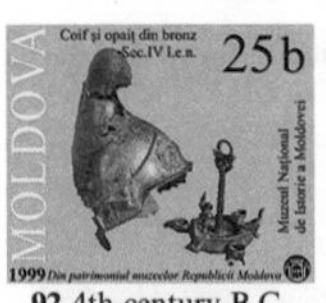
92 4th-century B.C. Bronze Helmet and Candle Holder

93 Raluca Eminovici

1999. National History Museum Exhibits. Mult.
349 25b. Type **92** 10 10
350 1l.80 10th-century B.C. ceramic pot 65 30
351 3l.60 Gospel, 1855 . . . . . 1·10 55

2000. 150th Birth Anniv of Mihail Eminescu (poet). Sheet 141 × 111 mm containing T **93** and similar vert designs. Multicoloured.
MS352 20b. Type **93**; 25b. Gheorghe Eminovici; 1l.50 Iosif Vulcan; 3l. Veronica Micle; 5l. Mihail Eminescu . . . . 3·25 3·25

94 Ileana Cosinzeana

2000. Folk Heroes. Multicoloured.
353 25b. Type **94** 10 10
354 1l.50 Fat-Frumos 55 25
355 1l.80 Harap Alb 65 30

95 Henri Coanda (aeronautical engineer)

2000. Birth Anniversaries. Each pink and black.
356 25b. Type **95** (114th anniv) 10 10
357 25b. Toma Ciorba (physician, 136th) 10 10
358 2l. Guglielmo Marconi (physicist, 126th) 70 35
359 3l.60 Norbert Wiener (mathematician, 106th) . . 1·10 55

96 Globe in Palm and Astronaut on Moon **97** "Resurrection" (anon)

2000. The Twentieth Century. Multicoloured.
360 25b. Type **96** (first manned moon landing, 1969) . . . 10 10
361 1l. Model of nuclear fission and hand (use of nuclear energy) 10 10
362 3l. Computer and mouse (development of electronic data processing) 35 15
363 3l.90 P. F. Teoctist (patriarch) and Pope John Paul II (consultation between Eastern and Roman churches) (horiz) 45 20

2000. Easter. Paintings in the National Gallery. Multicoloured.
364 25b. Type **97** 10 10
365 3l. "Resurrection" (anon) . . 35 15

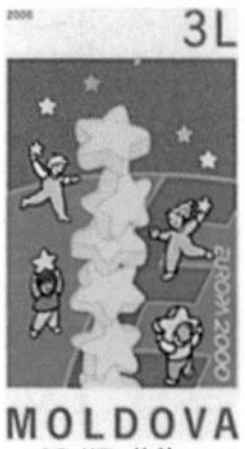

98 "Building Europe" **99** Emblem and Profiles

2000. Europa.
366 **98** 3l. multicoloured 35 15

2000. "EXPO 2000" World's Fair, Hanover, Germany (367) and "WIPA 2000" International Stamp Exhibition, Vienna, Austria (368). Mult.
367 25b. Type **99** 10 10
368 3l.60+30b. Hands holding tweezers and 1994 1b. State Arms stamp 20 10

100 Monastery, Tipova

2000. Churches and Monasteries. Multicoloured.
369 25b. Type **100** 10 10
370 1l.50 St. Nicolas's Church (vert) 15 10
371 1l.80 Palanca Church (vert) 20 10
372 3l. Butucheni Monastery . . 35 15

101 Judo

2000. Olympic Games, Sydney. Multicoloured.
373 25b. Type **101** 10 10
374 1l.80 Wrestling 20 10
375 5l. Weightlifting 55 25

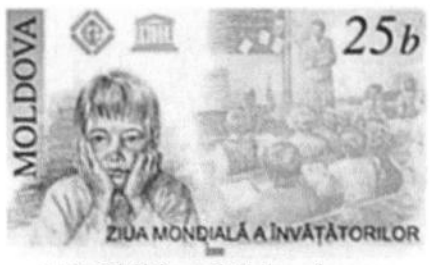

102 Child and Schoolroom

2000. International Teachers' Day.
376 **102** 25b. grey and green . . . 10 10
377 – 3l.60 blue and lilac . . . 40 20
DESIGN: 3l.60, Teacher holding book.

103 Adoration of the Shepherds (icon)

2000. Christmas. Multicoloured.
378 25b. Type **103** 10 10
379 1l.50 The Nativity (icon) . . 15 10
MS380 84 × 66 mm. 5l. Mary and Baby Jesus (icon) (27 × 32 mm) 3·25 3·25

104 Mother and Child

2001. 50th Anniv of United Nations High Commissioner for Refugees.
381 **104** 3l. multicoloured 30 15

105 Corncrake

2001. Endangered Species. The Corncrake. Multicoloured.
382 3l. Type **105** 30 15
383 3l. Singing 30 15
384 3l. In reeds 30 15
385 3l. With chicks 30 15
Nos. 382/5 were issued together, se-tenant, forming a composite design.

106 Yuri Gagarin and *Vostok* (spacecraft)

2001. 40th Anniv of First Manned Space Flight.
386 **106** 1l.80 multicoloured . . . 20 10

107 Maria Dragan

2001. Anniversaries. Multicoloured.
387 25b. Type **107** (singer, 15th death anniv) 10 10
388 1l. Marlene Dietrich (actress, birth centenary) 10 10
389 2l. Ruxandra Lupu (314th death anniv) 20 10
390 3l. Lidia Lipkovski (opera singer, 43rd death anniv) 30 15

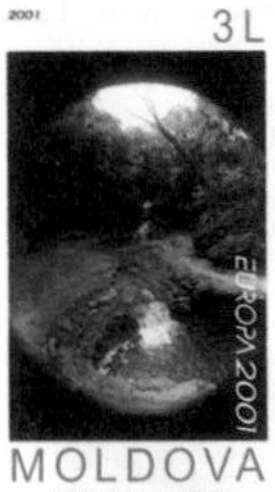

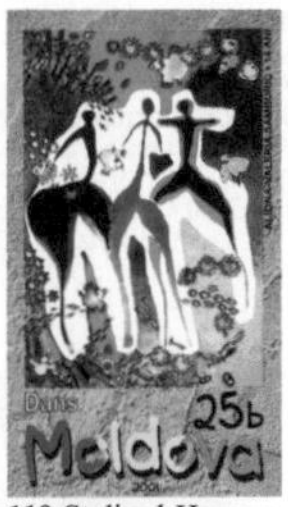

108 Waterfall **110** Stylized Humans (Aliona Valeria Samburic)

109 Prunariu

2001. Europa. Water Resources.
391 **108** 3l. multicoloured 25 15

2001. 20th Anniv of Space Flight by Dumitru Prunariu (first Rumanian cosmonaut).
392 **109** 1l.80 multicoloured . . . 15 10

2001. Winning Entries in Children's Painting Competition. Designs by named artist. Multicoloured.
393 25b. Type **110** 10 10
394 25b. Cars inside house and sun (Ion Sestacovschi) . . 10 10
395 25b. House, balloons and sun (Cristina Mereacre) 10 10
396 1l.80 Abstract painting (Andrei Sestacovschi) . . . 15 10

111 1991 7k. Arms Stamp **112** Tiger (*Panthera tigris*)

2001. 10th Anniv of First Moldovan Stamps. Sheet 100 × 74 mm, containing T **111** and similar multicoloured designs.
MS397 40b. Type **111**; 2l. 1991 13k. Arms stamp; 3l. 30k. 1991 Flag stamp (42 × 25 mm) 45 25

2001. Chisinau Zoo. Multicoloured.
398 40b. Type **112** 10 10
399 1l. Quagga (*Equus quagga*) 10 10
400 1l.50 Brown bear (*Ursus arctos*) 15 10
401 3l. + 30b. *Antilopa nilgau* . . 30 15
MS402 84 × 70 mm. 5l. Lion (*Panthera leo*) 45 25

113 Flag and Buildings

2001. 10th Anniv of Independence.
403 **113** 1l. multicoloured 10 10

114 Cimpoi **116** Nicolai Mavrocordat (1711–15)

115 Women's Profiles and Space Ship

2001. Musical Instruments. Multicoloured.
404 40b. Type **114** 10 10
405 1l. Fluier 10 10
406 1l.80 Nai 15 10
407 3l. Tar'agot 25 15

2001. United Nations Year of Dialogue among Civilizations. Multicoloured.
408 40b. Type **115** 10 10
409 3l.60 Children encircling globe (vert) 30 15

2001. Rulers. Multicoloured (except **MS**416).
410 40b. Type **116** 10 10
411 40b. Mihai Racovita (1716–26) 10 10
412 40b. Constantin Mavrocordat (1748–49) 10 10
413 40b. Grigore Callimachi (1767–69) 10 10
414 1l. Grigore Alexandru Gnica (1774–77) 10 10
415 3l. Anton Cantemir (1705–7) 25 15
MS416 61 × 88 mm. 5l. Dimitrie Cantemir (1710–11) (black, yellow and red) (horiz) 45 25

117 St. Treime Basilica, Manastirea Saharna

2001. Christmas. Multicoloured.
417 40b. Type **117** 10 10
418 1l. Adormirea Maicii Domnului Basilica, Manastirea Hancu 10 10
419 3l. St. Dumitru Basilica, Orhei 25 15
420 3l.90 Nasterea Domnului Cathedral, Chisinau . . . 35 20

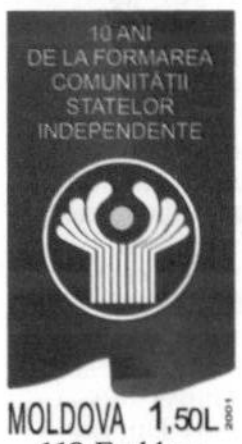

118 Emblem

2001. 10th Anniv of Union of Independent States.
421 **118** 1l.50 multicoloured . . . 15 10

119 Cross Country Sking

2002. Winter Olympic Games, Salt Lake City. Multicoloured.
422 40b. Type **119** 10 10
423 5l. Biathlon 45 25

120 Hora

2002. Traditional Dances. Multicoloured.
424 40b. Type **120** 10 10
425 1l.50 Sirba 15 10

121 "Fetele din Ceadir-lunga" (Mihai Grecu)

2002. Art. Multicoloured.
426 40b. Type **121** 10 10
427 40b. "Meleag Natal" (Eleonora Romanescu) . . 10 10
428 1l.50 "Fata la Fereastra" (Valentina Rusu-Ciobanu) 15 10
429 3l. "In Doi" (Igor Vieru) . . 30 20

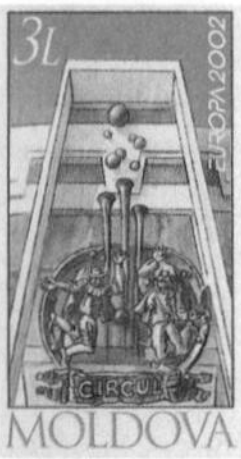

122 Entrance to Kishinev Circus
123 Rose

2002. Europa. Circus.
430 **122** 3l. multicoloured 30 20

2002. Botanical Gardens, Kishinev. Sheet 130 × 85 mm containing T **123** and similar vert designs. Multicoloured.
MS431 40b. Type **123**; 40b. Peony; 1l.50 Aster; 3l. Iris 50 30

124 Portrait of Cecilia Gallerani (Lady with an Ermine)
125 Ion Neculce (chronicler)

2002. 550th Birth Anniv of Leonardo da Vinci (artist). Sheet 129 × 85 mm containing T **124** and similar vert designs. Multicoloured.
MS432 40b. Type **124**; 1l.50 The Virgin and Child with St. Anne; 3l. Mona Lisa (La Gioconda) . . 50 30

2002. Personalities. All sepia.
433 40b. Type **125** 10 10
434 40b. Nicolae Costin (chronicler) 10 10
435 40b. Grigore Ureche (chronicler) 10 10
436 40b. Nicolae Testemiteanu (rector, Faculty of Medicine, Chisnau University) 10 10
437 1l.50 Sergiu Radautan (rector, Technical Faculty, Chisnau University) . . . 15 10
438 3l.90 Alexandre Dumas (writer) 35 20

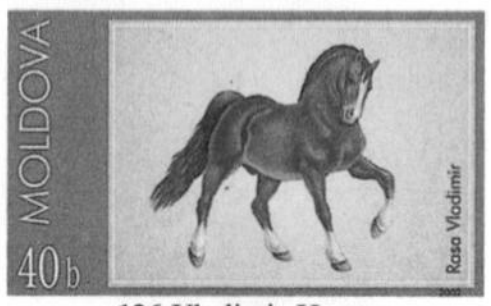

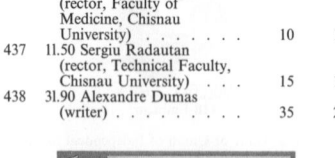

126 Vladimir Horse

2002. Horses. Showing horse breeds. Multicoloured.
439 40b. Type **126** 10 10
440 1l.50 Orlov 15 10
441 3l. Arab 30 20

127 Stork, Houses and Man carrying Grapes (Alexandru Catranji)
128 Union Emblem, Member States Presidents and Flags

2002. Children's Paintings. The Post. Multicoloured.
442 40b. Type **127** 10 10
443 1l.50 Birds, flower and globe 15 10
444 2l. Postman and globe . . . 20 15

2002. Union of Independent States Conference, Chisnau. Multicoloured.
445 1l.50 Type **128** 15 10
446 3l.60 Emblem and handshake 35 20

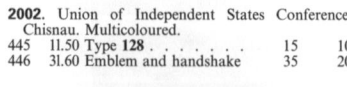

129 Entrance to Underground Warehouse

2002. 50th Anniv of Cricova Wine Factory. Multicoloured.
447 40b. Type **129** 10 10
448 40b. Barrels in warehouse . . 10 10
449 1l.50 Dining hall (vert) . . . 15 10
450 2l. Interior of warehouse . . 20 15
451 3l.60 Glasses and bottles of wine (vert) 35 20

130 Tissandier Brothers' Airship (1883)

2003. Airships. Multicoloured.
452 40b. Type **130** 10 10
453 2l. "Uchebny" (Training Craft) (1908) 20 15
454 5l. LZ 127 "Graf Zeppelin" (1928) (inscr "Count Zeppelin") 50 30

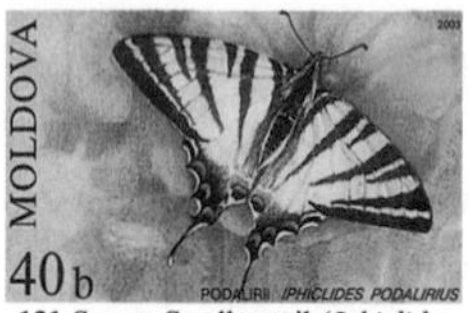

131 Scarce Swallowtail (*Iphiclides podalirius*)

2003. Butterflies and Moths. Multicoloured.
455 40b. Type **131** 10 10
456 2l. Jersey tiger moth (*Callimorpha quadripunctaria*) 20 15
457 3l. Oak hawk moth (*Marumba quercus*) 30 20
458 5l. Meleager's Blue (*Polyommatus daphnis*) . . 50 30
MS459 127 × 82 mm. Nos. 455/8 1·10 1·10

132 Rural Landscape

2003. 10th Anniv of Europa Stamps. Sheet 130 × 85 mm containing T **132** and similar horiz design. Multicoloured.
MS460 1l.50 Type **132**; 5l. Chisinau 60 60

133 Folk Ensemble "JOC"
135 Runner

134 Emblem and Flag

2003. Europa. Poster Art. Multicoloured.
461 3l. Type **133** 30 20
462 5l. Exhibition poster (Mihai Eminescu, 150th birth anniv (Rumanian writer)) 50 30

2003. Red Cross Society of Moldova. Multicoloured.
463 40b. Type **134** 10 10
464 5l. Damaged buildings and Red Cross workers 50 30

2003. European Youth Olympics Festival, Paris. Multicoloured.
465 40b. Type **135** 10 10
466 3l. Cyclists 30 20
467 5l. Gymnast 50 30

136 "Luminari" (A. Akhlupin)

2003. "World without Terror". Multicoloured.
468 40b. Type **136** 10 10
469 3l.90 "Pax Cultura" (N. Roerich) 35 20

137 Dimitrie Cantemir

2003. 340th Birth Anniv of Dimitrie Cantemir (linguist and scholar).
470 **137** 3l.60 multicoloured . . . 30 20

138 Vladimir Voronin (president of Moldova)

2003. Moldova—Chairman, Council of Europe Committee of Ministers, May–November 2003.
471 **138** 3l. multicoloured 25 15

139 Nicolae Donici

2003. Personalities. Multicoloured.
472 40b. Type **139** (astronomer) 10 10
473 1l.50 Nicolae Dimo (soil scientist) 10 10
474 2l. Nicolai Costenco (writer) 20 15
475 3l.90 Milestone Lewis (Lev Milstein) (film director) . . 35 20
476 5l. Vincent van Gogh (artist) 40 25

140 Mute Swan (*Cygnus olor*)

2003. Birds. Multicoloured.
477 40b. Type **140** 10 10
478 2l. Great egret (*Egretta alba*) 20 15
479 3l. Tawny eagle (*Aquila rapax*) (vert) 25 15
480 5l. Little bustard (*Tetrax tetrax*) (vert) 40 25
MS481 131 × 86 mm. Nos. 477/80 95 95

141 Natalie Gheorghiu

2004. Personalities. Multicoloured.
482 40b. Type **141** (doctor) . . . 10 10
483 1l.50 Metropolitan Dosoftei (scholar) 10 10

142 Archaeological Dig

2004. Europa. Holidays. Multicoloured.
484 40b. Type **142** 10 10
485 4l.40 Winemaking 40 25

143 Stefan III holding Sword
144 Goalkeeper and Ball

2004. 500th Death Anniv of Stefan III (Stefan cel Mare) (Moldavian ruler). Multicoloured.
486 40b. Type **143** 10 10
487 2l. Kneeling holding church 20 15
MS488 110 × 92 mm. 4l.40 Head and shoulders of Stefan III 40 40

2004. Centenary of FIFA (Federation Internationale de Football Association). Multicoloured.
489 2l. Type **144** 20 15
490 4l.40 Player and ball 40 25

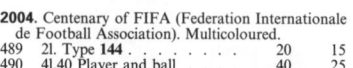

145 Memorial

2004. 60th Anniv of Iasi-Chisinau Battle. Sheet 81 × 62 mm.
MS491 **145** 2l. multicoloured . . 20 20

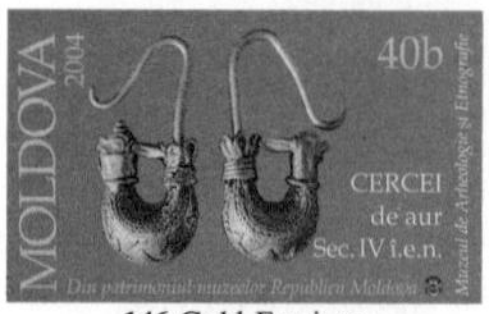

146 Gold Earrings

2004. Ancient Jewellery. Multicoloured.
492 40b. Type **146** 10 10
493 1l. Gold torque 10 10
494 1l.50 Silver earrings 10 10
495 2l. Bronze bracelet 20 15

147 Boxers

2004. Olympic Games, Athens. Multicoloured.
496 40b. Type **147** 10 10
497 4l.40 Weightlifter 40 25

148 *Ephedra distachya*

2004. Plants. Multicoloured.
498 40b. Type **148** 10 10
499 1l.50 *Pyrus elaeagrifolia* . . . 10 10
500 2l. *Padus avium* 20 15
501 2l. *Crataegus pentagyna* . . . 20 15

POSTAGE DUE STAMPS

D 33 Postal Emblems

1994.

D150	D 33	30b. brown and green	50	50
D151		40b. green and lilac . .	65	65

One stamp in the pair was put on insufficiently franked mail, the other stamp on associated documents.

MONACO Pt. 6

A principality on the S. coast of France including the town of Monte Carlo.

1885. 100 centimes = 1 French franc.
2002. 100 cents = 1 euro.

1 Prince Charles III

2 Prince Albert

4 War Widow and Monaco

1885.

1	1	1c. olive	22·00	13·00
2		2c. lilac	42·00	19·00
3		5c. blue	50·00	26·00
4		10c. brown on yellow	65·00	26·00
5		15c. red	£275	8·50
6		25c. green	£500	48·00
7		40c. blue on red	60·00	35·00
8		75c. black on red	£225	85·00
9		1f. black on yellow	£1400	£400
10		5f. red on green	£2500	£1700

1891.

11	2	1c. green	50	50
12		2c. purple	55	60
13		5c. blue	38·00	4·25
22		5c. green	35	30
14		10c. brown on yellow . . .	85·00	9·50
23		10c. red	2·50	40
15a		15c. pink	£150	6·50
24		15c. brown on yellow . . .	2·50	70
25		15c. green	1·50	2·10
16		25c. green	£225	19·00
26		25c. blue	14·00	3·00
17		40c. black on pink	2·50	1·90
18		50c. brown on orange . . .	5·25	3·25
19a		75c. brown on buff	24·00	15·00
20		1f. black on yellow	15·00	8·50
21		5f. red on green	£100	70·00
28		5f. mauve	£200	£200
29		5f. green	18·00	22·00

1914. Surcharged **+5c.**

30	2	10c.+5c. red	5·50	5·00

1919. War Orphans Fund.

31	4	2c.+3c. mauve	27·00	23·00
32		5c.+5c. green	15·00	13·00
33		15c.+10c. red	15·00	13·00
34		25c.+15c. blue	32·00	29·00
35		50c.+50c. brown on orange	£150	£130
36		1f.+1f. black on yellow . . .	£275	£275
37		5f.+5f. red	£850	£950

1920. Princess Charlotte's Marriage. Nos. 33/7 optd **20 mars 1920** or surch also.

38	4	2c.+3c. on 15c.+10c. red . .	35·00	35·00
39		2c.+3c. on 25c.+15c. blue . .	35·00	35·00
40		2c.+3c. on 50c.+50c. brown on orange	35·00	35·00
41		5c.+5c. on 1f.+1f. black on yellow	35·00	35·00
42		5c.+5c.on 5f.+ 5f. red	35·00	35·00
43		15c.+10c. red	22·00	22·00
44		25c.+15c. blue	11·00	10·50
45		50c.+50c. brown on orange	45·00	45·00
46		1f.+1f. black on yellow . . .	60·00	60·00
47		5f.+5f. red	£5500	£5500

1921. Princess Antoinette's Baptism. Optd **28 DECEMBRE 1920** or surch also.

48	2	5c. green	55	55
49		75c. brown on buff	4·00	5·00
50		2f. on 5f. mauve	30·00	38·00

1922. Surch.

51	2	20c. on 15c. green	1·00	1·50
52		25c. on 10c. red	60	80
53		50c. on 1f. black on yellow	4·50	8·00

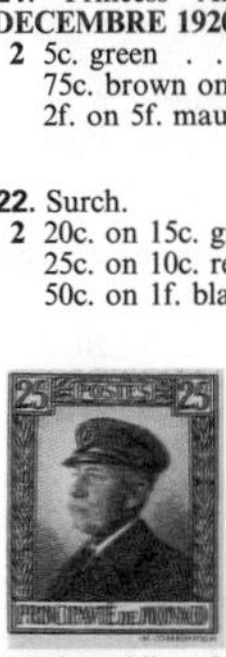
8 Prince Albert I

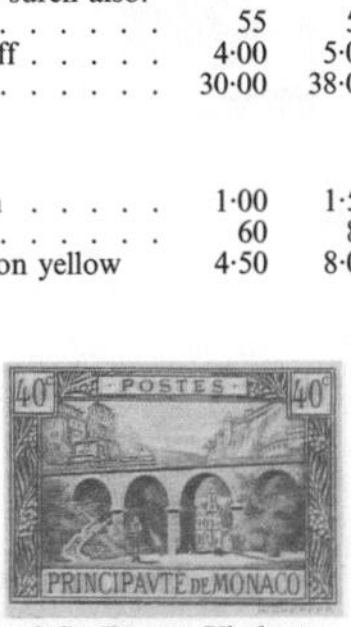
9 St. Devote Viaduct

1922.

54	8	25c. brown	3·00	3·50
55	–	30c. green	85	1·40
56	–	30c. red	40	40
57	9	40c. brown	45	55
58	–	50c. blue	3·50	3·25
59	–	60c. grey	35	30
60	–	1f. black on yellow	25	20
61a	–	2f. red	45	40
62	–	5f. brown	28·00	30·00
63	–	5f. green on blue	8·00	8·00
64	–	10f. red	11·00	12·50

DESIGNS:—As Type **9**: 30, 50c. Oceanographic Museum; 60c., 1, 2f. The Rock; 5, 10f. Prince's Palace, Monaco.

12 Prince Louis

13 Prince Louis and Palace

1923.

65	12	10c. green	35	45
66		15c. red	50	60
67		20c. brown	30	45
68		25c. purple	25	45
69	13	50c. blue	25	45

1924. Surch with new value and bars.

70	2	45c. on 50c. brown on orange	50	65
71		75c. on 1f. black on yellow	45	45
72		85c. on 5f. green	30	45

14

15

16

17 St. Devote Viaduct

1924.

73	14	1c. grey	10	10
74		2c. brown	10	10
75		3c. mauve	1·90	1·90
76		5c. orange	30	20
77		10c. blue	10	10
78	15	15c. green	10	10
79		15c. violet	1·90	1·40
80		20c. mauve	15	10
81		20c. pink	20	10
82		25c. pink	10	10
83		25c. red on yellow	15	15
84		30c. orange	10	10
85		40c. brown	15	10
86		40c. blue on blue	25	20
87		45c. black	50	30
88	16	50c. green	15	20
89	15	50c. brown on yellow . . .	10	10
90	16	60c. brown	10	20
91	15	60c. green on green	10	20
92		75c. green on green	20	20
93		75c. red on yellow	30	15
94		75c. black	60	30
95		80c. red on yellow	30	20
96		90c. red on yellow	1·25	95
97	17	1f. black on yellow	30	25
98		1f.05 mauve	30	25
99		1f.10 green	7·50	5·25
100	15	1f.25 blue on blue	10	25
101		1f.50 blue on blue	3·50	1·25
102	–	2f. brown and mauve . . .	95	60
103	–	3f. lilac and red on yellow	16·00	7·75
104	–	5f. red and green	5·75	4·00
105	–	10f. blue and brown . . .	16·00	15·00

DESIGN—As Type **17**: 2f. to 10f. Monaco.

1926. Surch.

106	15	30c. on 25c. pink	25	20
107		50c. on 60c. green on green	90	25
108	17	50c. on 1f.05 mauve	70	65
109		50c. on 1f.10 green	9·25	5·00
110	15	50c. on 1f.25 blue on blue	90	40
111		1f.25 on 1f. blue on blue	45	40
112	–	1f.50 on 2f. brown and mauve (No. 102)	3·75	3·25

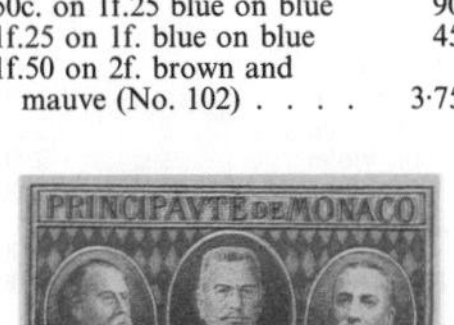
20 Prince Charles III, Louis II and Albert I

1928. International Philatelic Exn, Monte Carlo.

113	20	50c. red	1·75	3·75
114		1f.50 blue	1·75	3·75
115		3f. violet	1·75	3·75

20a

21 Palace Entrance

22 St. Devote's Church

23 Prince Louis II

1933.

116	20a	1c. plum	10	10
117		2c. green	10	10
118		3c. purple	10	10
119		5c. red	10	10
120		10c. blue	10	10
121		15c. violet	70	1·10
122	21	15c. red	75	25
123		20c. brown	75	25
124	A	25c. sepia	1·10	35
125	22	30c. green	1·25	35
126	23	40c. sepia	2·50	1·50
127	B	45c. brown	2·25	1·40
128	23	50c. violet	2·10	85
129	C	65c. green	2·50	60
130	D	75c. blue	3·00	1·60
131	23	90c. red	5·25	2·40
132	22	1f. brown	21·00	5·75
133	D	1f.25 red	5·00	3·00
134	23	1f.50 blue	29·00	7·00
135	A	1f.75 claret	27·00	6·75
136		1f.75 carmine	17·00	9·50
137	B	2f. blue	9·50	3·25
138	21	3f. violet	14·50	5·50
139	A	3f.50 orange	38·00	28·00
140	22	5f. purple	19·00	11·00
141	A	10f. blue	£100	60·00
142	C	20f. black	£275	£110

DESIGNS—HORIZ (as Type **21**): A, The Prince's Residence; B, The Rock of Monaco; C, Palace Gardens; D, Fortifications nd Harbour.

For other stamps in Type **20a** see Nos. 249, etc.

1933. Air. Surch with Bleriot XI airplane and **1f50.**

143		1f.50 on 5f. red & grn (No. 104)	21·00	19·00

28 Palace Gardens

1937. Charity.

144	28	50c.+50c. green	2·25	2·00
145	–	90c.+90c. red	2·25	2·00
146	–	1f.50+1f.50 blue	5·50	7·50
147	–	2f.+2f. violet	6·50	9·50
148	–	5f.+5f. red	95·00	90·00

DESIGNS—HORIZ: 90c. Exotic gardens; 1f.50, The Bay of Monaco. VERT: 2, 5f. Prince Louis II.

1937. Postage Due stamps optd **POSTES** or surch also.

149	D 18	5 on 10c. violet	80	1·00
150		10c. violet	80	1·00
151		15 on 30c. bistre	80	1·00
152		20 on 30c. bistre	80	1·00
153		25 on 60c. red	1·00	1·25
154		30c. bistre	2·00	2·25
155		40 on 60c. red	1·75	1·75
156		50 on 60c. red	2·50	3·25
157		65 on 1f. blue	1·90	2·25
158		85 on 1f. blue	4·50	5·00
159		1f. blue	6·00	6·50
160		2f.15 on 2f. red	6·00	6·50
161		2f.25 on 2f. red	15·00	16·00
162		2f.50 on 2f. red	21·00	25·00

30a Prince Louis II

31

1938. National Fete Day. Sheet 100 × 120 mm.

MS163	30a	10f. purple	50·00	70·00

1938.

164	31	55c. brown	4·50	1·75
165		65c. violet	21·00	17·00
166		70c. brown	15	15
167		90c. violet	15	15
168		1f. red	13·00	6·00
169		1f.25 red	20	20
170		1f.75 blue	13·00	7·75
171		2f.25 blue	20	15

33 Monaco Hospital

1938. Anti-cancer Fund. 40th Anniv of Discovery of Radium.

172	–	65c.+25c. green	8·50	7·75
173	33	1f.75+50c. blue	8·50	9·50

DESIGN—VERT: 65c. Pierre and Marie Curie.

34 The Cathedral

38 Monaco Harbour

1939.

174	34	20c. mauve	15	15
175	–	25c. brown	30	20
176	–	30c. green	20	20
177	–	40c. red	20	20
178	–	45c. purple	35	20
179	–	50c. green	25	15
180	–	60c. red	20	20
181	–	60c. green	20	50
182	38	70c. lilac	35	20
183		75c. green	35	20
184	–	1f. black	20	20
185	–	1f.30 brown	20	20
186	–	2f. purple	20	20
187	–	2f.50 red	18·00	19·00
188	–	2f.50 blue	1·25	1·10
189	38	3f. red	40	20
190	34	5f. blue	2·25	2·75
191	–	10f. green	95	1·10
192	–	20f. blue	1·10	1·10

DESIGNS—VERT: 25, 40c., 2f. Place St. Nicholas; 30, 60c., 20f. Palace Gateway; 50c., 1f., 1f.30, Palace of Monaco. HORIZ: 45c., 2f.50, 10f. Aerial view of Monaco.

40 Louis II Stadium

41 Lucien

1939. Inauguration of Louis II Stadium, Monaco.

198	40	10f. green	80·00	90·00

1939. National Relief. 16th–18th-century portrait designs and view.

199	41	5c.+5c. black	1·50	1·00
200	–	10c.+10c. purple	1·50	1·00
201	–	45c.+15c. green	5·75	5·00
202	–	70c.+30c. mauve	8·75	7·75
203	–	90c.+35c. violet	8·75	7·75
204	–	1f.+1f. blue	22·00	22·00
205	–	2f.+2f. red	22·00	22·00
206	–	2f.25+1f.25 blue	25·00	29·00
207	–	3f.+3f. red	32·00	42·00
208	–	5f.+5f. red	55·00	80·00

DESIGNS—VERT: 10c. Honore II; 45c. Louis I; 70c. Charlotte de Gramont; 90c. Antoine I; 1f. Marie de Lorraine; 2f. Jacques I; 2f.25, Louise-Hippolyte; 3f. Honore III. HORIZ: 5f. The Rock of Monaco.

1939. 8th International University Games. As T **40** but inscr "VIIIeme JEUX UNIVERSITAIRES INTERNATIONAUX 1939".

209		40c. green	90	1·25
210		70c. brown	1·25	1·50
211		90c. violet	1·40	2·25
212		1f.25 red	2·10	3·00
213		2f.25 blue	3·00	4·50

1940. Red Cross Ambulance Fund. As Nos. 174/92 in new colours surch with Red Cross and premium.

214	34	20c.+1f. violet	2·75	2·75
215	–	25c.+1f. green	2·75	2·75
216	–	30c.+1f. red	2·75	2·75
217	–	40c.+1f. blue	2·75	2·75
218	–	45c.+1f. red	3·00	3·00
219	–	50c.+1f. brown	3·00	3·00
220	–	60c.+1f. green	3·00	3·00
221	38	75c.+1f. black	3·50	3·50
222	–	1f.+1f. red	4·00	4·25
223	–	2f.+1f. slate	4·00	4·75
224	–	2f.50+1f. green	9·00	10·50
225	38	3f.+1f. blue	11·00	11·00
226	34	5f.+1f. black	12·00	13·00
227	–	10f.+5f. blue	24·00	22·00
228	–	20f.+5f. purple	24·00	33·00

44 Prince Louis II

1941.

229	44	40c. red	40	40
230		80c. green	40	40
231		1f. violet	10	10
232		1f.20 green	10	10
233		1f.50 red	10	10
234		1f.50 violet	10	10
235		2f. green	10	10
236		2f.40 red	10	10
237		2f.50 blue	70	70
238		4f. blue	10	10

45

46

1941. National Relief Fund.

239	45	25c.+25c. purple	60	1·10
240	46	50c.+25c. brown	60	1·10
241		75c.+50c. purple	1·60	1·50
242	45	1f.+1f. blue	1·60	1·50
243	46	1f.50+1f.50 red	1·75	2·75
244	45	2f.+2f. green	1·75	2·75
245	46	2f.50+2f. blue	2·25	3·50
246	45	3f.+3f. brown	2·25	3·50
247	46	5f.+5f. green	6·25	7·00
248	45	10f.+8f. sepia	13·50	14·00

1941. New values and colours.

249	20a	10c. black	10	10
250	–	30c. red (as No. 176)	20	25
251	20a	30c. green	10	10
252		40c. red	10	10
253		50c. violet	10	10
362	34	50c. brown	15	25
254	20a	60c. blue	10	10
363	–	60c. pink (as No. 175)	15	25
255	20a	70c. brown	10	10
256	34	80c. green	10	20
257	–	1f. brown (as Nos. 178)	10	10
258	38	1f.20 blue	15	15
259	–	1f.50 blue (as Nos. 175)	20	20
260	38	2f. blue	10	10
261	–	2f. green (as No. 179)	20	20
262	–	3f. black (as No. 175)	10	10
364	–	3f. purple (as No. 176)	40	30
391	–	3f. green (as No. 175)	1·25	90
263	34	4f. purple	20	40
365	–	4f. green (as No. 175)	40	30
264	–	4f.50 violet (as No. 179)	10	25
265	–	5f. green (as No. 176)	10	25
392	–	5f. green (as No. 178)	30	10
393	–	5f. red (as No. 176)	50	40
266	–	6f. violet (as No. 179)	60	30
368	–	8f. brown (as No. 179)	1·50	1·75
267	34	10f. blue	10	25
370	–	10f. brown (as No. 179)	2·00	1·25
394	38	10f. yellow	80	35
268		15f. red	20	25
269	–	20f. brown (as No. 178)	40	25
373	–	20f. red (as No. 178)	80	50
270	38	25f. green	1·25	85
374		25f. black	20·00	12·50
397	–	25f. blue (as No. 176)	32·00	12·50
398	–	25f. red (as No. 179)	2·00	2·25
399	–	30f. blue (as No. 176)	6·00	3·25
400	–	35f. blue (as No. 179)	6·50	3·00
401	34	40f. red	6·00	4·00
402		50f. violet	3·50	85
403	–	65f. violet (as No. 178)	12·00	6·00
404	34	70f. yellow	8·75	6·00
405	–	75f. green (as No. 175)	20·00	8·00
406	–	85f. red (as No. 175)	12·50	5·00
407	–	100f. turquoise (as No. 178)	12·00	5·50

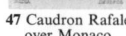

47 Caudron Rafale over Monaco

48 Propeller and Palace

49 Arms, Airplane and Globe

50 Charles II

1942. Air.

271	47	5f. green	30	30
272		10f. blue	30	30
273	48	15f. brown	40	60
274	–	20f. brown	50	90
275	–	50f. purple	2·40	3·00
276	49	100f. red and purple	2·40	3·00

DESIGNS—VERT: 20f. Pegasus. HORIZ: 50f. Mew gull over Bay of Monaco.

1942. National Relief Fund. Royal Personages.

277	–	2c.+3c. blue	20	30
278	50	5c.+5c. red	20	30
279	–	10c.+5c. black	20	30
280	–	20c.+10c. green	20	30
281	–	30c.+30c. purple	20	30
282	–	40c.+40c. red	20	30
283	–	50c.+50c. violet	20	30
284	–	75c.+75c. purple	20	30
285	–	1f.+1f. green	20	30
286	–	1f.50+1f. red	20	30
287	–	2f.50+2f.50 violet	1·90	3·75
288	–	3f.+3f. blue	1·90	3·75
289	–	5f.+5f. sepia	2·50	5·25
290	–	10f.+5f. purple	3·00	5·25
291	–	20f.+5f. blue	3·00	6·00

PORTRAITS: 2c. Rainier Grimaldi; 10c. Jeanne Grimaldi; 20c. Charles Auguste, Goyon de Matignon; 30c. Jacques I; 40c. Louise-Hippolyte; 50c. Charlotte Grimaldi; 75c. Marie Charles Grimaldi; 1f. Honore III; 1f.50, Honore IV; 2f.50, Honore V; 3f. Florestan I; 5f. Charles III; 10f. Albert I; 20f. Princess Marie-Victoire.

52 Prince Louis II

1943.

292	52	50f. violet	45	75

53 St. Devote

54 Blessing the Sea

55 Arrival of St. Devote at Monaco

1944. Charity. Festival of St. Devote.

293	53	50c.+50c. brown	20	20
294	–	70c.+80c. blue	20	20
295	–	80c.+70c. green	20	20
296	–	1f.+1f. purple	20	20
297	–	1f.50+1f.50 red	30	45
298	54	2f.+2f. purple	40	60
299	–	5f.+2f. violet	45	60
300	–	10f.+40f. blue	45	60
301	55	20f.+60f. blue	3·00	5·50

DESIGNS—VERT: 70c., 1f. Various processional scenes; 1f.50, Burning the boat; 10f. Trial scene. HORIZ: 80c. Procession; 5f. St. Devote's Church.

1945. Air. For War Dead and Deported Workers. As Nos. 272/6 (colours changed) surch.

302	1f.+4f. on 10f. red	50	45
303	1f.+4f. on 15f. brown	50	45
304	1f.+4f. on 20f. brown	50	45
305	1f.+4f. on 50f. blue	50	45
306	1f.+4f. on 100f. purple	50	45

57 Prince Louis II

58 Prince Louis II

1946.

361	57	30c. black	15	10
389		50c. olive	15	25
390		1f. violet	20	10
307		2f.50 green	30	30
308		3f. mauve	30	30
366		5f. brown	40	30
309		6f. red	30	30
367		6f. purple	3·50	1·75
310		10f. blue	30	30
369		10f. orange	40	25
371		12f. red	4·00	2·10
395		12f. slate	6·00	5·00
396		15f. lake	6·00	3·50
372		18f. blue	7·00	5·50
311	58	50f. grey	2·50	1·50
312		100f. red	3·50	2·25

59 Child Praying

60 Nurse and Baby

1946. Child Welfare Fund.

313	59	1f.+3f. green	30	30
314		2f.+4f. red	30	30
315		4f.+6f. blue	30	30
316		5f.+40f. mauve	80	75
317		10f.+60f. red	80	75
318		15f.+100f. blue	1·25	1·25

1946. Anti-tuberculosis Fund.

319	60	2f.+8f. blue	40	65

1946. Air. Optd **POSTE AERIENNE** over Sud Ouest Cassiopees airplane.

320	58	50f. grey	3·00	4·00
321		100f. red	4·75	3·25

62 Steamship and Chart

1946. Stamp Day.

322	62	3f.+2f. blue	30	40

63

1946. Air.

323	63	40f. red	60	75
324		50f. brown	1·50	90
325		100f. green	2·50	1·75
326		200f. violet	2·50	2·00
326a		300f. blue and ultramarine	55·00	50·00
326b		500f. green and deep green	35·00	30·00
326c		1000f. violet and brown	60·00	55·00

64 Pres. Roosevelt and Palace of Monaco

66 Pres. Roosevelt

1946. President Roosevelt Commemoration.

327	66	10c. mauve (postage)	30	25
328	–	30c. blue	30	15
329	64	60c. green	30	25
330	–	1f. sepia	80	85
331	–	2f.+3f. green	80	95
332	–	3f. violet	1·25	1·25
333	–	5f. red (air)	40	50
334	–	10f. black	70	45
335	66	15f.+10f. orange	1·50	1·25

DESIGNS—HORIZ: 30c., 5f. Rock of Monaco; 2f. Viaduct and St. Devote. VERT: 1, 3, 10f. Map of Monaco.

67 Prince Louis II

68 Pres. Roosevelt as a Philatelist

69 Statue of Liberty and New York Harbour

1947. Participation in the Centenary International Philatelic Exhibition, New York. (a) Postage.

336	67	10f. blue	3·25	3·25

(b) Air. Dated "1847 1947"

337	68	50c. violet	80	90
338	–	1f.50 mauve	30	40
339	–	3f. orange	40	45
340	–	10f. blue	2·75	2·75
341	69	15f. red	4·50	4·50

DESIGNS—HORIZ: As Type **68**: 1f.50, G.P.O., New York; 3f. Oceanographic Museum, Monte Carlo. As Type **69**: 10f. Bay of Monaco.

1947. Twenty-fifth Year of Reign of Prince Louis II. Sheet 85 × 98 mm.

MS341a	200f.+300f. brown	22·00	15·00

70 Prince Charles III

1948. Stamp Day.

342	70	6f.+4f. green on blue	40	40

71 Diving

72 Tennis

1948. Olympic Games, Wembley. Inscr "JEUX OLYMPIQUES 1948".

343	–	50c. green (postage)	20	20
344	–	1f. red	20	20
345	–	2f. blue	70	55
346	–	2f.50 red	1·75	3·50
347	71	4f. slate	1·90	1·75
348	–	5f.+5f. brown (air)	7·25	7·25
349	–	6f.+9f. violet	12·00	10·00
350	72	10f.+15f. red	20·00	18·00
351	–	15f.+25f. blue	24·00	25·00

DESIGNS—HORIZ: 50c. Hurdling; 15f. Yachting. VERT: 1f. Running; 2f. Throwing the discus; 2f.50, Basketball; 5f. Rowing; 6f. Skiing.

75 The Salmacis Nymph **77** F. J. Bosio (wrongly inscr "J. F.")

1948. Death Centenary of Francois Joseph Bosio (sculptor).

352	**75**	50c. green (postage)	40	25
353	–	1f. red	40	25
354	–	2f. blue	80	55
355	–	2f.50 violet	2·25	1·60
356	**77**	4f. mauve	2·25	1·90
357	–	5f.+5f. blue (air)	12·00	14·00
358	–	6f.+9f. green	12·00	14·00
359	–	10f.+15f. red	13·00	14·00
360	–	15f.+25f. brown	16·00	18·00

DESIGNS—VERT: 1, 5f. Hercules struggling with Achelous; 2, 6f. Aristaeus (Garden God); 15f. The Salmacis Nymph (36 × 48 mm). HORIZ: 2f.50, 10f. Hyacinthus awaiting his turn to throw a quoit.

79 Exotic Gardens **80** "Princess Alice II"

1949. Birth Centenary of Prince Albert I.

375	–	2f. blue (postage)	20	20
376	**79**	3f. green	20	20
377	–	4f. brown and blue	30	25
378	**80**	5f. red	80	85
379	–	6f. violet	50	55
380	–	10f. sepia	70	1·85
381	–	12f. pink	1·40	1·40
382	–	18f. orange and brown	2·50	2·75
383	–	20f. brown (air)	50	65
384	–	25f. blue	50	65
385	–	40f. green	95	1·40
386	–	50f. green, brown and black	1·50	1·75
387	–	100f. red	5·75	6·50
388	–	200f. orange	11·00	10·50

DESIGNS—HORIZ: 2f. Yacht "Hirondelle I" (1870); 4f. Oceanographic Museum, Monaco; 10f. "Hirondelle II" (1914); 12f. Albert harpooning whale; 18f. Buffalo (Palaeolithic mural); 20f. Constitution Day, 1911; 25f. Paris Institute of Palaeontology; 200f. Coin with effigy of Albert. VERT: 6f. Statue of Albert at tiller; 40f. Anthropological Museum; 50f. Prince Albert I; 100f. Oceanographic Institute, Paris.

82a Princess Charlotte **83** Palace of Monaco and Globe

1949. Red Cross Fund. Sheet 150 × 172½ mm, containing vert portraits as T **82a**.

MS408	10f.+5f. brown and red; 40f.+5f. green and red; 15f.+5f. red and 25f.+5f. blue and red. Each × 4	£300	£300
MS409	As **MS**408 but imperf	£300	£300

DESIGNS: 10, 40f. T **82a**; 15, 25f, Prince Rainier.

1949. 75th Anniv of U.P.U.

410	**83**	5f. green (postage)	30	35
411		10f. orange	3·50	4·00
412		15f. red	45	55
413		25f. blue (air)	50	55
414		40f. sepia and brown	1·50	1·60
415		50f. blue and green	2·50	2·75
416		100f. blue and red	3·50	4·00

84 Prince Rainier III and Monaco Palace **85** Prince Rainier III

1950. Accession of Prince Rainier III.

417	**84**	10c. purple & red (postage)	10	10
418		50c. brown, lt brn & orge	10	10
419		1f. violet	20	25
420		5f. deep green and green	1·60	1·40
421		15f. carmine and red	3·00	3·00
422		25f. blue, green & ultram	3·00	3·75
423		50f. brown and black (air)	4·75	5·25
424		100f. blue, dp brn & brn	7·75	6·75

1950.

425	**85**	50c. violet	20	10
426		1f. brown	20	10
434		5f. green	6·75	3·75
427		6f. green	95	60
428		8f. green	4·50	1·75
429		8f. orange	1·10	70
435		10f. orange	10·50	5·50
430		12f. blue	1·10	30
431		15f. red	2·00	50
432		15f. blue	1·40	40
433		18f. red	3·50	1·10

86 Prince Albert I **87** Edmond and Jules de Goncourt

1951. Unveiling of Prince Albert Statue.

436	**86**	15f. blue	5·75	5·75

1951. 50th Anniv of Goncourt Academy.

437	**87**	15f. purple	5·75	5·25

88 St. Vincent de Paul **90** St. Peter's Keys and Papal Bull

89 Judgement of St. Devote

1951. Holy Year.

438	**88**	10c. blue, ultramarine & red	20	20
439	–	50c. violet and red	20	20
440	**89**	1f. green and brown	20	25
441	**90**	2f. red and purple	30	45
442	–	5f. green	30	30
443	–	12f. violet	40	45
444	–	15f. red	3·00	3·00
445	–	20f. brown	4·50	5·25
446	–	25f. blue	5·75	7·25
447	–	40f. violet and mauve	7·75	8·25
448	–	50f. brown and olive	9·50	11·00
449	–	100f. brown	20·00	22·00

DESIGNS—TRIANGULAR: 50c. Pope Pius XII. HORIZ (as Type **90**): 5f. Mosaic. VERT (as Type **90**): 12f. Prince Rainier III in St. Peter's; 15f. St. Nicholas of Patara; 20f. St. Romain; 25f. St. Charles Borromeo; 40f. Coliseum; 50f. Chapel of St. Devote. VERT (as Type **89**): 100f. Rainier of Westphalia.

93 Wireless Mast and Monaco **94** Seal of Prince Rainier III

1951. Monte Carlo Radio Station.

450	**93**	1f. orange, red and blue	50	25
451		15f. purple, red and violet	2·50	80
452		30f. brown and blue	11·50	4·50

1951.

453	**94**	1f. violet	60	50
454		5f. black	2·10	1·40
512		5f. violet	3·00	70
513		6f. red	3·50	1·10
455		8f. red	5·25	3·00
514		8f. brown	4·00	2·75
456		15f. green	7·75	5·75
515		15f. blue	11·50	3·50
457		30f. blue	15·00	11·50
516		30f. green	14·50	11·00

1951. Nos. **MS**408/9 surch **1f. on 10f.+5f., 3f. on 15f.+5f., 5f. on 25f. + 5f., 6f. on 40f.+5f.**

MS458	As above	£300	£180
MS459	As above imperf	£300	£180

95 Gallery of Hercules

1952. Monaco Postal Museum.

460	**95**	5f. chestnut and brown	30	35
461		15f. violet and purple	60	35
462		30f. indigo and blue	1·10	40

96 Football

1953. 15th Olympic Games, Helsinki. Inscr "HELSINKI 1952".

463	–	1f. mauve & violet (postage)	20	25
464	**96**	2f. blue and green	20	25
465	–	3f. pale and deep blue	20	25
466	–	5f. green and brown	60	30
467	–	8f. red and lake	1·50	85
468	–	15f. brown, green and blue	80	70
469	–	40f. black (air)	7·75	6·75
470	–	50f. violet	9·00	6·75
471	–	100f. green	13·00	11·00
472	–	200f. red	17·00	11·50

DESIGNS: 1f. Basketball; 3f. Sailing; 5f. Cycling; 8f. Gymnastics; 15f. Louis II Stadium, Monaco; 40f. Running; 50f. Fencing; 100f. Rifle target and Arms of Monaco; 200f. Olympic torch.

97 "Journal Inedit"

1953. Centenary of Publication of Journal by E. and J. de Goncourt.

473	**97**	5f. green	50	35
474		15f. brown	2·25	1·25

98 Physalia, Yacht "Princess Alice", Prince Albert, Richet and Portier

1953. 50th Anniv of Discovery of Anaphylaxis.

475	**98**	2f. violet, green and brown	20	20
476		5f. red, lake and green	50	20
477		15f. lilac, blue and green	2·25	1·25

99 F. Ozanam **100** St. Jean-Baptiste de la Salle

1954. Death Centenary of Ozanam (founder of St. Vincent de Paul Conferences).

478	**99**	1f. red	20	25
479	–	5f. blue	30	35
480	**99**	15f. black	1·50	1·25

DESIGN: 5f. Outline drawing of Sister of Charity.

1954. St. J.-B. de la Salle (educationist).

481	**100**	1f. red	20	25
482	–	5f. sepia	30	45
483	**100**	15f. blue	1·50	1·25

DESIGN: 5f. Outline drawing of De la Salle and two children.

101 **102** **103**

1954. Arms.

484	–	50c. red, black and mauve	10	10
485	–	70c. red, black and blue	10	10
486	**101**	80c. red, black and green	10	10
487	–	1f. red, black and blue	10	10
488	**102**	2f. red, black and orange	10	10
489	–	3f. red, black and green	10	10
490	**103**	5f. multicoloured	20	25

DESIGNS—HORIZ: 50c. as Type **101**. VERT: 70c., 1, 3f. as Type **102**.

104 Seal of Prince Rainier III **105** Lambarene

106 Dr. Albert Schweitzer

1954. Precancelled.

491	**104**	4f. red	1·25	60
492		5f. blue	30	20
493		8f. green	1·25	80
494		8f. purple	80	45
495		10f. green	20	20
496		12f. violet	4·00	2·75
497		15f. orange	80	60
498		20f. green	1·25	80
499		24f. brown	6·75	3·25
500		30f. blue	1·40	95
501		40f. brown	2·00	1·60
502		45f. red	2·00	1·25
503		55f. blue	5·00	3·50

See also Nos. 680/3.

1955. 80th Birthday of Dr. Schweitzer (humanitarian).

504	**105**	2f. grn, turq & bl (postage)	20	20
505	**106**	5f. blue and green	70	95
506	–	15f. purple, black and green	2·10	2·00
507	–	200f. slate, grn & bl (air)	22·00	25·00

DESIGNS—As Type **106**: 15f. Lambarene Hospital. HORIZ (48 × 27 mm): 200f. Schweitzer and jungle scene.

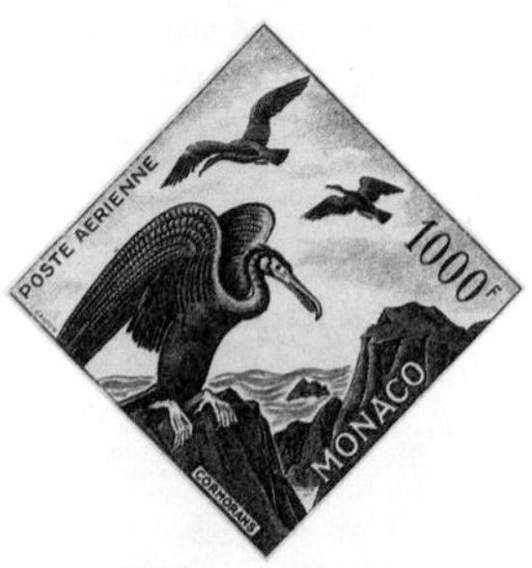

107 Great Cormorants

1955. Air.

508a	–	100f. indigo and blue	15·00	15·00
509	–	200f. black and blue	17·00	9·50
510	–	500f. grey and green	29·00	20·00
511a	**107**	1,000f. black, turq & grn	70·00	50·00

DESIGNS—As Type **107**: 100f. Roseate tern; 200f. Herring gull; 500f. Wandering albatrosses.

108 Eight Starting Points

109 Prince Rainier III

1955. 25th Monte Carlo Car Rally.
517 **108** 100f. red and brown . . . 60·00 60·00

1955.
518 **109** 6f. purple and green . . . 30 25
519 8f. violet and red 30 25
520 12f. green and red 30 25
521 15f. blue and purple . . . 70 25
522 18f. blue and orange . . . 3·00 25
523 20f. turquoise . . . . . . 1·40 45
524 25f. black and orange . . 70 40
525 30f. black and blue . . . 9·75 5·00
526 30f. violet . . . . 3·00 1·75
527 35f. brown . . . . 2·50 1·90
528 50f. lake and green . . . 3·50 1·25
See also Nos. 627/41.

110 "La Maison a Vapeur"

111 "The 500 Millions of the Begum"

113 U.S.S. "Nautilus"

112 "Round the World in Eighty Days"

1955. 50th Death Anniv of Jules Verne (author). Designs illustrating his works.
529 – 1f. blue & brown (postage) 10 10
530 – 2f. sepia, indigo and blue 10 10
531 **110** 3f. blue, black and brown 30 30
532 – 5f. sepia and red 30 30
533 **111** 6f. grey and sepia 70 60
534 – 8f. turquoise and olive . . 30 30
535 – 10f. sepia, turquoise & ind 70 60
536 **112** 15f. red and brown . . . 60 50
537 – 25f. black and green . . . 1·75 1·25
538 **113** 30f. black, purple & turq 4·00 3·25

539 – 200f. indigo and blue (air) 21·00 20·00
DESIGNS—VERT (as Type **111**): 1f. "Five Weeks in a Balloon". HORIZ (as Type **110**): 2f. "A Floating Island"; 10f. "Journey to the Centre of the Earth"; 25f. "20,000 Leagues under the Sea"; 200f. "From the Earth to the Moon". (as Type **111**): 5f. "Michael Strogoff"; 8f. "Le Superbe Orenoque".

114 "The Immaculate Virgin" (F. Brea)

1955. Marian Year.
540 **114** 5f. green, grey and brown 20 20
541 – 10f. green, grey and brown 30 30
542 – 15f. brown and sepia . . 40 40
DESIGNS—As Type **114**: 10f. "Madonna" (L. Brea). As Type **113**: 15f. Bienheureux Rainier.

115 Rotary Emblem

1955. 50th Anniv of Rotary International.
543 **115** 30f. blue and yellow . . . 70 85

116 George Washington **118** President Eisenhower

117 Abraham Lincoln

1956. 5th International Stamp Exhibition, New York.
544 **116** 1f. violet and lilac 10 10
545 – 2f. lilac and purple . . . 20 20
546 **117** 3f. blue and violet 20 20
547 **118** 5f. red 20 20
548 – 15f. brown and chocolate 50 40
549 – 30f. black, indigo and blue . . . . 2·25 1·25
550 – 40f. brown . . . . 3·00 1·50
551 – 50f. red . . . . 3·50 1·50
552 – 100f. green . . . . 3·50 2·50
DESIGNS—As Type **117**: 2f. F. D. Roosevelt. HORIZ (as Type **116**): 15f. Monaco Palace in the 18th century; 30f. Landing of Columbus. (48 × 36 mm): 50f. Aerial view of Monaco Palace in the 18th century; 100f. Louisiana landscape in 18th century. VERT (as Type **118**): 40f. Prince Rainier III.

120

1956. 7th Winter Olympic Games, Cortina d'Ampezzo and 16th Olympic Games, Melbourne.
553 – 15f. brown, green & pur 80 60
554 **120** 30f. red . . . . 1·40 1·40
DESIGN: 15f. "Italia" ski-jump.

1956. Nos. D482/95 with "TIMBRE TAXE" barred out and some surch also. (a) Postage.
555 2f. on 4f. slate and brown . . 30 30
556 2f. on 4f. brown and slate . . 30 30
557 3f. lake and green 30 30
558 3f. green and lake 30 30
559 5f. on 4f. slate and brown . . 50 40
560 5f. on 4f. brown and slate . . 50 40
561 10f. on 4f. slate and brown 70 60
562 10f. on 4f. brown and slate 70 60
563 15f. on 5f. violet and blue . . 1·10 1·40
564 15f. on 5f. blue and violet . . 1·10 1·40
565 20f. violet and blue . . . . . 1·75 2·25
566 20f. blue and violet . . . . . 1·75 2·25
567 25f. on 20f. violet and blue 3·50 2·50
568 25f. on 20f. blue and violet 3·50 2·50
569 30f. on 10f. indigo and blue 5·50 4·00
570 30f. on 10f. blue and indigo 5·50 4·00
571 40f. on 50f. brown and red 7·75 6·00
572 40f. on 50f. red and brown 7·75 6·00
573 50f. on 100f. green and purple . . . . 11·00 8·75
574 50f. on 100f. purple and green . . . . 11·00 8·75

(b) Air. Optd **POSTE AERIENNE** also.
575 100f. on 20f. violet and blue 6·75 7·75
576 100f. on 20f. blue and violet 6·75 7·75

121 Route Map from Glasgow

1956. 26th Monte Carlo Car Rally.
577 **121** 100f. brown and red . . . 17·00 19·00

122 Princess Grace and Prince Rainier III

1956. Royal Wedding.
578 **122** 1f. black & grn (postage) 10 10
579 2f. black and red 10 10
580 3f. black and blue 10 20
581 5f. black and green . . . 20 25
582 15f. black and brown . . 20 40

583 100f. brown & purple (air) 60 40
584 200f. brown and red . . . 60 40
585 500f. brown and grey . . 2·00 1·60

123 Princess Grace **124** Princess Grace with Princess Caroline

1957. Birth of Princess Caroline.
586 **123** 1f. grey 10 10
587 2f. olive 10 10
588 3f. brown 10 10
589 5f. red 20 20
590 15f. pink 20 25
591 25f. blue 60 55
592 30f. violet 60 55
593 50f. red . . . . 1·10 65
594 75f. orange . . . . 2·00 1·60

1958. Birth of Prince Albert.
595 **124** 100f. black . . . . 5·50 4·00

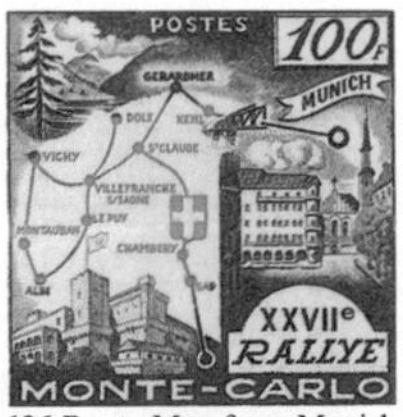

125 Order of St. Charles **126** Route Map from Munich

1958. Centenary of Creation of National Order of St. Charles.
596 **125** 100f. multicoloured . . . 1·50 1·60

1958. 27th Monte Carlo Rally.
597 **126** 100f. multicoloured . . . 5·00 5·50

127 Statue of the Holy Virgin and Popes Pius IX and Pius XII

1958. Centenary of Apparition of Virgin Mary at Lourdes.
598 **127** 1f. grey & brown (postage) 10 10
599 – 2f. violet and blue 10 10
600 – 3f. sepia and green . . . 10 10
601 – 5f. blue and sepia 10 10
602 – 8f. multicoloured 20 25
603 – 10f. multicoloured 20 20
604 – 12f. multicoloured 30 25
605 – 20f. myrtle and purple . . 30 25
606 – 35f. myrtle, bistre and brown 40 35
607 – 50f. blue, green and lake 60 55
608 – 65f. turquoise and blue 80 70

609 – 100f. grey, myrtle and blue (air) . . . . 1·40 1·10
610 – 200f. brown and chestnut 1·90 1·75
DESIGNS—VERT (26½ × 36 mm): 2f. St. Bernadette; 3f. St. Bernadette at Bartres; 5f. The Miracle of Bourriette; 20f. St. Bernadette at prayer; 35f. St. Bernadette's canonization. (22 × 36 mm): 8f. Stained-glass window. As Type **127**: 50f. St. Bernadette, Pope Pius XI, Mgr. Laurence and Abbe Peyramale. HORIZ (48 × 36 mm): 10f. Lourdes grotto; 12f. Interior of Lourdes grotto. (36 × 26½ mm): 65f. Shrine of St. Bernadette; (48 × 27 mm): 100f. Lourdes Basilica; 200f. Pope Pius X and subterranean interior of Basilica.

128 Princess Grace and Clinic

1959. Opening of new Hospital Block in "Princess Grace" Clinic, Monaco.
611 **128** 100f. grey, brown & green 2·50 1·50

129 UNESCO Headquarters, Paris, and Cultural Emblems

1959. Inaug of UNESCO Headquarters Building.
612 **129** 25f. multicoloured 20 20
613 – 50f. turquoise, black & ol 30 35
DESIGN: 50f. As Type **129** but with heads of children and letters of various alphabets in place of the emblems.

130 Route Map from Athens

1959. 28th Monte Carlo Rally.
614 **130** 100f. blue, red & grn on bl . . . . 4·50 3·50

131 Prince Rainier and Princess Grace

1959. Air.

615	**131**	300f. violet	9·50	6·75
616		500f. blue	14·50	12·50

See also Nos. 642/3.

132 "Princess Caroline" Carnation

1959. Flowers.

617	**132**	5f. mauve, green & brown	10	10
618	–	10f. on 3f. pink, green and brown	10	10
619	–	15f. on 1f. yellow & green	20	25
620	–	20f. purple and green	50	40
621	–	25f. on 6f. red, yellow and green	70	65
622	–	35f. pink and green	1·40	1·60
623	–	50f. green and sepia	2·25	1·75
624	–	85f. on 65f. lavender, bronze and green	2·75	2·00
625	–	100f. red and green	4·50	3·00

FLOWERS—As Type **132**: 10f. "Princess Grace" carnation; 100f. "Grace of Monaco" rose. VERT (22 × 36 mm): 15f. Mimosa; 25f. Geranium. HORIZ (36 × 22 mm): 20f. Bougainvillea; 35f. "Laurier" rose; 50f. Jasmine; 85f. Lavender.

(New currency. 100 (old) francs = 1 (new franc.)

133 "Uprooted Tree" **134** Oceanographic Museum

1960. World Refugee Year.

626	**133**	25c. green, blue and black	20	25

1960. Prince Rainier types with values in new currency.

627	**109**	25c. blk & orge (postage)	30	10
628		30c. violet	40	10
629		40c. red and brown	40	20
630		45c. brown and grey	40	20
631		50c. red and green	50	25
632		50c. red and brown	50	30
633		60c. brown and green	1·25	40
634		60c. brown and purple	1·60	55
635		65c. blue and brown	9·25	4·00
636		70c. blue and plum	1·00	55
637		85c. green and violet	1·40	90
638		95c. blue	95	85
639		1f.10 blue and brown	2·00	1·60
640		1f.30 brown and red	2·40	1·75
641		2f.30 purple and orange	2·00	65
642	**131**	3f. violet (air)	35·00	14·00
643		5f. blue	35·00	20·00

1960.

644	–	5c. green, black and blue	15	15
645	**134**	10c. brown and blue	30	25
646	–	10c. blue, violet and green	15	10
647	–	40c. purple, grn & dp grn	55	20
648	–	45c. brown, green and blue	4·50	60
649	–	70c. brown, red and green	40	30
650	–	80c. red, green and blue	1·40	60
651	–	85c. black, brown and grey	6·00	1·90
652	–	90c. red, blue and black	1·50	65
653	–	1f. multicoloured	1·25	30
654	–	1f.15 black, red and blue	2·10	1·25
655	–	1f.30 brown, green & blue	75	55
656	–	1f.40 orange, green & vio	2·25	1·90

DESIGNS—HORIZ: 5c. Palace of Monaco; 10c. (No. 646), Aquatic Stadium; 40, 45, 80c., 1f.40, Aerial view of Palace; 70, 85, 90c., 1f.15, 1f.30, Court of Honour, Monaco Palace; 1f. Palace floodlit.

134a St. Devote

1960. Air.

668	**134a**	2f. violet, blue and green	1·25	90
669		3f. brown, green and blue	1·90	1·25
670		5f. red	3·50	1·75
671		10f. brown, grey and green	5·00	3·25

135 Long-snouted Seahorse **136** Route Map from Lisbon

1960. Marine Life and Plants. (a) Marine Life.

672	–	1c. red and turquoise	10	10
673	–	12c. brown and blue	35	20
674	**135**	15c. green and red	45	20
675	–	20c. multicoloured	55	20

DESIGNS—HORIZ: 1c. "Macrocheira kampferi" (crab); 20c. Lionfish. VERT: 12c. Trapezium horse conch.

(b) Plants.

676	–	2c. multicoloured	25	10
677	–	15c. orange, brown and olive	60	10
678	–	18c. multicoloured	45	10
679	–	20c. red, olive and brown	45	20

PLANTS—VERT: 2c. "Selenicereus sp."; 15c. "Cereus sp."; 18c. "Aloe ciliaris"; 20c. "Nopalea dejecta".

1960. Prince Rainier Seal type with values in new currency. Precancelled.

680	**104**	8c. purple	1·40	70
681		20c. green	1·75	85
682		40c. brown	3·50	1·40
683		55c. blue	5·00	2·75

1960. 29th Monte Carlo Rally.

684	**136**	25c. black, red & bl on bl	1·50	1·50

137 Stamps of Monaco 1885, France and Sardinia, 1860

1960. 75th Anniv of First Monaco Stamp.

685	**137**	25c. bistre, blue and violet	70	75

138 Aquarium

1960. 50th Anniv of Oceanographic Museum, Monaco.

686	–	5c. black, blue and purple	30	25
687	**138**	10c. grey, brown and green	40	30
688	–	15c. black, bistre and blue	40	30
689	–	20c. black, blue and mauve	70	40
690	–	25c. turquoise	1·50	1·00
691	–	50c. brown and blue	1·75	1·75

DESIGNS—VERT: 5c. Oceanographic Museum (similar to Type **134**). HORIZ: 15c. Conference Hall; 20c. Hauling-in catch; 25c. Museum, aquarium and underwater research equipment; 50c. Prince Albert, "Hirondelle I" (schooner) and "Princess Alice" (steam yacht).

139 Horse-jumping

1960. Olympic Games.

692	**139**	5c. brown, red and green	10	10
693	–	10c. brown, blue and green	20	25
694	–	15c. red, brown and purple	20	25
695	–	20c. black, blue and green	2·00	2·25
696	–	25c. purple, turq & grn	70	60
697	–	50c. purple, blue & turq	1·10	90

DESIGNS: 10c. Swimming; 15c. Long-jumping; 20c. Throwing the javelin; 25c. Free-skating; 50c. Skiing.

140 Rally Badge, Old and Modern Cars

1961. 50th Anniv of Monte Carlo Rally.

698	**140**	1f. violet, red and brown	1·40	1·40

141 Route Map from Stockholm **142** Marine Life

1961. 30th Monte Carlo Rally.

699	**141**	1f. multicoloured	80	90

1961. World Aquariological Congress. Orange network background.

700	**142**	25c. red, sepia and violet	20	25

143 Leper in Town of Middle Ages **145** Insect within Protective Hand

144 Semi-submerged Sphinx of Ouadi-es-Saboua

1961. Sovereign Order of Malta.

701	**143**	25c. black, red and brown	20	25

1961. UNESCO Campaign for Preservation of Nubian Monuments.

702	**144**	50c. purple, blue & brown	70	75

1962. Nature Preservation.

703	**145**	25c. mauve and purple	20	25

146 Chevrolet, 1912

1961. Veteran Motor Cars.

704	**146**	1c. brown, green and chestnut	10	10
705	–	2c. blue, purple and red	10	10
706	–	3c. purple, black and mauve	10	10
707	–	4c. blue, brown and violet	10	10
708	–	5c. green, red and olive	10	10
709	–	10c. brown, red and blue	10	10
710	–	15c. green and turquoise	20	25
711	–	20c. brown, red and violet	20	25
712	–	25c. violet, red and brown	30	35
713	–	30c. lilac and green	70	80
714	–	45c. green, purple and brown	1·50	1·90
715	–	50c. blue, red and brown	1·50	1·90
716	–	65c. brown, red and grey	2·25	1·75
717	–	1f. blue, red and violet	2·50	2·75

MOTOR CARS: 2c. Peugeot, 1898; 3c. Fiat, 1901; 4c. Mercedes, 1901; 5c. Rolls Royce, 1903;. 10c. Panhard-Lavassor, 1899; 15c. Renault, 1898; 20c. Ford "N", 1906 (wrongly inscr "FORD-S-1908"); 25c. Rochet-Schneider, 1894; 30c. FN-Herstal, 1901; 45c. De Dion Bouton, 1900; 50c. Buick, 1910; 65c. Delahaye, 1901; 1f. Cadillac, 1906.

147 Racing Car and Race Route

1962. 20th Monaco Motor Grand Prix.

718	**147**	1f. purple	1·25	90

148 Route Map from Oslo

1962. 31st Monte Carlo Rally.

719	**148**	1f. multicoloured	95	80

149 Louis XII and Lucien Grimaldi

1962. 450th Anniv of Recognition of Monegasque Sovereignty by Louis XII.

720	**149**	25c. black, red and blue	20	25
721	–	50c. brown, lake and blue	30	30
722	–	1f. red, green and brown	50	55

DESIGNS: 50c. Parchment bearing declaration of sovereignty; 1f. Seals of two Sovereigns.

150 Mosquito and Swamp

1962. Malaria Eradication.

723	**150**	1f. green and olive	40	45

151 Sun, Bouquet and "Hope Chest"

1962. National Multiple Sclerosis Society, New York.

724	**151**	20c. multicoloured	20	20

152 Harvest Scene

1962. Europa.
725 **152** 25c. brown, green and blue (postage) 10 10
726 50c. olive and turquoise 20 25
727 1f. olive and purple . . . 40 50
728 – 2f. slate, brown & green (air) 90 90
DESIGN: 2f. Mercury in flight over Europe.

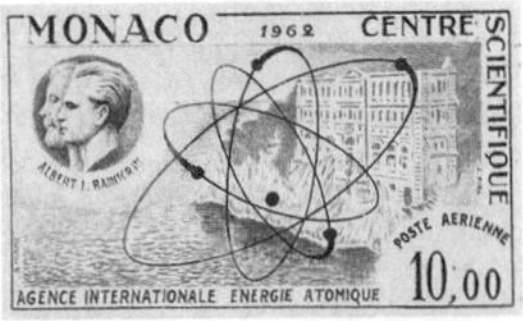

153 Atomic Symbol and Scientific Centre, Monaco

1962. Air. Scientific Centre, Monaco.
729 **153** 10f. violet, brown and blue . . . . 4·75 4·75

154 Yellow Wagtails **155** Galeazzi's Diving Turret

1962. Protection of Birds useful to Agriculture.
730 **154** 5c. yellow, brown & green 10 20
731 – 10c. red, bistre and purple 10 20
732 – 15c. multicoloured 25 20
733 – 20c. sepia, green & mauve 30 30
734 – 25c. multicoloured 40 35
735 – 30c. brown, blue & myrtle 55 45
736 – 45c. brown and violet . . 95 90
737 – 50c. black, olive & turq 1·25 1·10
738 – 85c. multicoloured . . . . 1·75 1·50
739 – 1f. sepia, red and green 2·00 1·75
BIRDS: 10c. European robins; 15c. Eurasian goldfinches; 20c. Blackcaps; 25c. Greater spotted woodpeckers; 30c. Nightingale; 45c. Barn owls; 50c. Common starlings; 85c. Red crossbills; 1f. White storks.

1962. Underwater Exploration.
740 – 5c. black, violet and blue 10 10
741 **155** 10c. blue, violet and brown 10 10
742 – 25c. bistre, green and blue 10 10
743 – 45c. black, blue and green 30 35
744 – 50c. green, bistre and blue 50 55
745 – 85c. blue and turquoise 80 85
746 – 1f. brown, green and blue 1·40 1·25
DESIGNS—HORIZ: 5c. Divers; 25c. Williamson's photosphere (1914) and bathyscaphe "Trieste"; 45c. Klingert's diving-suit (1797) and modern diving-suit; 50c. Diving saucer; 85c. Fulton's "Nautilus" (1800) and modern submarine; 1f. Alexander the Great's diving bell and Beebe's bathysphere.

156 Donor's Arm and Globe **158** Feeding Chicks in Nest

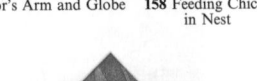

157 "Ring-a-ring o' Roses"

1962. 3rd Int Blood Donors' Congress Monaco.
747 **156** 1f. red, sepia and orange 50 65

1963. U.N. Children's Charter.
748 **157** 5c. red, blue and ochre . . 10 10
749 **158** 10c. green, sepia and blue 10 10
750 – 15c. blue, red and green 10 20
751 – 20c. multicoloured 10 20
752 – 25c. blue, purple & brown 25 25
753 – 50c. multicoloured 50 35
754 – 95c. multicoloured 80 55
755 – 1f. purple, red & turquoise . . . . . . 1·75 1·10
DESIGNS—As Type **157**: 1f. Prince Albert and Princess Caroline; Children's paintings as Type **158**: HORIZ: 15c. Children on scales; 50c. House and child. VERT: 20c. Sun's rays and children of three races; 25c. Mother and child; 95c. Negress and child.

159 Ship's Figurehead

1963. International Red Cross Centenary.
756 **159** 50c. red, brown & turquoise 30 35
757 – 1f. multicoloured 55 60
DESIGN—HORIZ: 1f. Moynier, Dunant and Dufour.

160 Racing Cars

1963. European Motor Grand Prix.
758 **160** 50c. multicoloured 55 40

161 Emblem and Charter

1963. Founding of Lions Club of Monaco.
759 **161** 50c. blue, bistre and violet 80 65

162 Hotel des Postes and U.P.U. Monument, Berne

1963. Paris Postal Conference Centenary.
760 **162** 50c. lake, green and yellow 30 45

163 "Telstar" Satellite and Globe

1963. 1st Link Trans-Atlantic T.V. Satellite.
761 **163** 50c. brown, green & purple 45 45

164 Route Map from Warsaw

1963. 32nd Monte Carlo Rally.
762 **164** 1f. multicoloured . . . . 1·00 1·10

165 Feeding Chicks

1963. Freedom from Hunger.
763 **165** 1f. multicoloured 50 50

166 Allegory

1963. 2nd Ecumenical Council, Vatican City.
764 **166** 1f. turquoise, green and red 45 45

167 Henry Ford and Ford "A" Car of 1903

1963. Birth Centenary of Henry Ford (motor pioneer).
765 **167** 20c. green and purple . . 25 25

168 H. Garin (winner of 1903 race) cycling through Village

1963. 50th "Tour de France" Cycle Race.
766 **168** 25c. green, brown and blue 30 30
767 – 50c. sepia, green and blue 30 35
DESIGN: 50c. Cyclist passing Desgrange Monument, Col du Galibier, 1963.

169 P. de Coubertin and Discus-thrower

1963. Birth Centenary of Pierre de Coubertin (reviver of Olympic Games).
768 **169** 1f. brown, red and lake 40 60

170 Roland Garros and Morane Saulnier Type I

1963. Air. 50th Anniv of 1st Aerial Crossing of Mediterranean Sea.
769 **170** 2f. sepia and blue . . . . 1·25 90

171 Route Map from Paris **173** "Europa"

172 Children with Stamp Album

1963. 33rd Monte Carlo Rally.
770 **171** 1f. red, turquoise and blue 80 70

1963. "Scolatex" International Stamp Exn, Monaco.
771 **172** 50c. blue, violet and red 20 25

1963. Europa.
772 **173** 25c. brown, red and green 30 25
773 50c. sepia, red and blue 50 50

174 Wembley Stadium

1963. Cent of (English) Football Association.
774 **174** 1c. violet, green and red 10 10
775 – 2c. red, black and green 10 10
776 – 3c. orange, olive and red 10 10
777 – 4c. multicoloured 10 10
Multicoloured horiz designs depicting (a) "Football through the Centuries".
778 10c. "Calcio", Florence (16th cent) 10 10
779 15c. "Soule", Brittany (19th cent) 10 10
780 20c. English military college (after Cruickshank, 1827) 10 10
781 25c. English game (after Overend, 1890) 10 10
(b) "Modern Football".
782 30c. Tackling 20 20
783 50c. Saving goal 50 50
784 95c. Heading ball 70 70
785 1f. Corner kick . . . . . . 1·00 1·00
DESIGNS—As Type **174**: 4c. Louis II Stadium, Monaco. This stamp is optd in commemoration of the Association Sportive de Monaco football teams in the French Championships and in the Coupe de France, 1962–63. HORIZ (36×22 mm): 2c. Footballer making return kick; 3c. Goalkeeper saving ball.
Nos. 778/81 and 782/5 were respectively issued together in sheets and arranged in blocks of 4 with a football in the centre of each block.

175 Communications in Ancient Egypt, and Rocket

1964. "PHILATEC 1964" Int Stamp Exn, Paris.
786 **175** 1f. brown, indigo and blue 40 40

176 Reproduction of Rally Postcard Design

1964. 50th Anniv of 1st Aerial Rally, Monte Carlo.
787 **176** 1c. olive, blue & grn (postage) 10 10
788 – 2c. bistre, brown and blue 10 10
789 – 3c. brown, blue and green 10 10
790 – 4c. red, turquoise and blue 10 10
791 – 5c. brown, red and violet 10 10
792 – 10c. violet, brown and blue 10 10
793 – 15c. orange, brown and blue 10 10
794 – 20c. sepia, green and blue 20 10
795 – 25c. brown, blue and red 30 10
796 – 30c. myrtle, purple and blue 40 20
797 – 45c. sepia, turquoise and brown 70 30
798 – 50c. ochre, olive and violet 70 45
799 – 65c. red, slate and turquoise 70 85
800 – 95c. turquoise, red and bistre . . . . 1·25 95
801 – 1f. brown, blue and turquoise . . . . . . 1·60 1·25

802 – 5f. sepia, blue and brown (air) . . . . 2·40 2·40

DESIGNS: 48 × 27 mm—Rally planes: 2c. Renaux's Farman M.F.7 floatplane; 3c. Espanet's Nieuport 4 seaplane; 4c. Moineau's Breguet HU-3 seaplane; 5c. Roland Garros' Morane Saulnier Type I seaplane; 10c. Hirth's WDD Albatros seaplane; 15c. Prevost's Deperdussin Monocoque Racer. Famous planes and flights: 20c. Vickers-Vimy (Ross Smith: London–Port Darwin, 1919); 25c. Douglas World Cruiser seaplane (U.S. World Flight, 1924); 30c. Savoia Marchetti S-55M flying boat "Santa Maria" (De Pinedo's World Flight, 1925); 45c. Fokker F. VIIa/3m "Josephine Ford" (Flight over North Pole, Byrd and Bennett, 1925); 50c. Ryan NYP Special "Spirit of St. Louis" (1st solo crossing of N. Atlantic, Lindbergh, 1927); 65c. Breguet 19 "Point d'Interrogation" (Paris–New York, Coste and Bellonte, 1930); 95c. Latecoere 28-3 seaplane "Comte de la Vaulx" (Dakar–Natal, first S. Atlantic airmail flight, Mermoz, 1930); 1f. Dornier Do-X flying boat (Germany–Rio de Janeiro, Christiansen, 1930); 5f. Convair B-58 Hustler (New York–Paris in 3 hours, 19' 41' Major Payne, U.S.A.F., 1961).

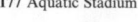

177 Aquatic Stadium

178 Europa "Flower"

1964. Precancelled.

803	177	10c. multicoloured . . .	1·40	90
803a		15c. multicoloured . . .	70	50
804		25c. turquoise, blue & blk	70	50
805		50c. violet, turq & blk	1·40	70

The "1962" date has been obliterated with two bars.

See also Nos. 949/51a and 1227/30.

1964. Europa.

806	178	25c. red, green and blue	20	25
807		50c. brown, bistre and blue	35	50

179 Weightlifting

1964. Olympic Games, Tokyo and Innsbruck.

808	179	1c. red, brown and blue (postage)	10	10
809	–	2c. red, green and olive	10	10
810	–	3c. blue, brown and red	10	10
811	–	4c. green, olive and red	10	10
812	–	5f. red, brown and blue (air)	2·00	1·90

DESIGNS: 2c. Judo; 3c. Pole vaulting; 4c. Archery; 5f. Bobsleighing.

180 Pres. Kennedy and Space Capsule

1964. Pres. Kennedy Commemoration.

813 180 50c. indigo and blue . . . 40 50

181 Monaco and Television Set

1964. 5th Int Television Festival, Monte Carlo.

814 181 50c. brown, blue and red 30 40

182 F. Mistral and Statue

1964. 50th Death Anniv of Frederic Mistral (poet).

815 182 1f. brown and olive . . . 40 50

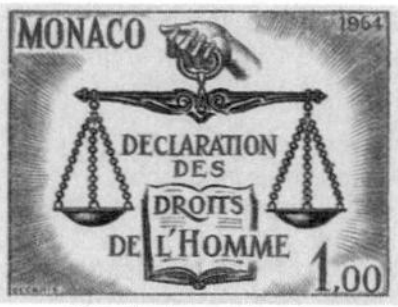

183 Scales of Justice

1964. 15th Anniv of Declaration of Human Rights.

816 183 1f. green and brown . . . 40 50

184 Route Map from Minsk

1964. 34th Monte Carlo Rally.

817 184 1f. brown, turq & ochre 70 70

185 FIFA Emblem

1964. 60th Anniv of Federation Internationale de Football Association (FIFA).

818 185 1f. bistre, blue and red . . 60 65

186 "Syncom 2" and Globe

1965. Centenary of I.T.U.

819	186	5c. grn & ultram (postage)	10	10
820	–	10c. chestnut, brown & bl	10	10
821	–	12c. purple, red and grey	10	10
822	–	18c. blue, red and purple	10	20
823	–	25c. violet, bistre & purple	10	20
824	–	30c. bistre, brown & sepia	20	25
825	–	50c. blue and green . . .	30	35
826	–	60c. blue and brown . . .	40	45
827	–	70c. sepia, orange and blue	60	60
828	–	95c. black, indigo and blue	80	80
829	–	1f. brown and blue . . .	95	90
830	–	10f. green, bl & brn (air)	1·60	2·50

DESIGNS—HORIZ (as Type **186**): 10c. "Echo 2"; 18c. "Lunik 3"; 30c. A. G. Bell and telephone; 50c. S. Morse and telegraph; 60c. E. Belin and "belinograph". (48½ × 27 mm): 25c. "Telstar" and Pleumeur-Bodou Station; 70c. Roman beacon and Chappe's telegraph; 95c. Cable ships "Great Eastern" and "Alsace"; 1f. E. Branly, G. Marconi and English Channel. VERT (as Type **186**): 12c. "Relay"; 10f. Monte Carlo television transmitter.

187 Europa "Sprig"

1965. Europa.

831	187	30c. brown and green . .	35	25
832		60c. violet and red . . .	1·00	45

188 Monaco Palace (18th cent)

1966. 750th Anniv of Monaco Palace.

833	188	10c. violet, green and blue	10	10
834	–	12c. bistre, blue and black	10	10
835	–	18c. green, black and blue	10	10
836	–	30c. brown, black and blue	30	30
837	–	60c. green, blue and bistre	40	55
838	–	1f.30 brown and green . .	90	1·10

DESIGNS (Different views of Palace): 12c. 17th century; 18c. 18th century; 30c. 19th century; 60c. 19th century; 1f.30, 20th century.

189 Dante

1966. 700th Anniv of Dante's Birth.

839	189	30c. green, deep green and red	20	25
840	–	60c. blue, turquoise & grn	40	50
841	–	70c. black, green and red	50	60
842	–	95c. blue, violet and purple	70	80
843	–	1f. turquoise, blue & dp bl	70	85

DESIGNS (Scenes from Dante's works): 60c. Dante harassed by the panther (envy); 70c. Crossing the 5th circle; 95c. Punishment of the arrogant; 1f. Invocation of St. Bernard.

190 "The Nativity"

1966. World Association of Children's Friends (A.M.A.D.E.).

844 190 30c. brown 20 25

191 Route Map from London

1966. 35th Monte Carlo Rally.

845 191 1f. blue, purple and red 60 70

192 Princess Grace with Children

1966. Air. Princess Stephanie's 1st Birthday.

846 192 3f. brown, blue and violet 2·00 2·00

193 Casino in 19th Century

194 Europa "Ship"

1966. Centenary of Monte Carlo.

847	–	12c. black, red and blue (postage)	10	10
848	193	25c. multicoloured	10	10
849	–	30c. multicoloured	10	10
850	–	40c. multicoloured	25	25
851	–	60c. multicoloured	30	25
852	–	70c. blue and lake	30	35
853	–	95c. black and purple . .	60	60
854	–	1f.30 purple, brown and chestnut	95	80
855	–	5f. lake, ochre and blue (air)	2·00	2·00

DESIGNS—VERT: 12c. Prince Charles III. HORIZ (as Type **143**): 40c. Charles III Monument; 95c. Massenet and Saint-Saens; 1f.30, Faure and Ravel. (48 × 27 mm): 30c. F. Blanc, originator of Monte Carlo, and view of 1860; 60c. Prince Rainier III and projected esplanade; 70c. Rene Blum and Diaghilev, ballet character from "Petrouchka". (36 × 36 mm): 5f. Interior of Opera House, 1879.

1966. Europa.

856	194	30c. orange	20	25
857		60c. green	30	35

195 Prince Rainier and Princess Grace

197 "Learning to Write"

196 Prince Albert I and Yachts "Hirondelle I" and "Princess Alice"

1966. Air.

858	195	2f. slate and red	85	40
859		3f. slate and green . . .	1·75	65
860		5f. slate and blue	2·25	1·00
860a		10f. slate and bistre . .	4·50	2·75
860b		20f. brown and orange	48·00	27·00

1966. 1st International Oceanographic History Congress, Monaco.

861 196 1f. lilac and blue 50 60

1966. 20th Anniv of UNESCO.

862	197	30c. purple and mauve . .	10	10
863		60c. brown and blue . . .	30	30

198 T.V. Screen, Cross and Monaco Harbour

1966. 10th Meeting of International Catholic Television Association (U.N.D.A.), Monaco.

864 198 60c. red, purple & crimson 20 25

199 "Precontinent III"

1966. 1st Anniv of Underwater Research Craft "Precontinent III".

865 199 1f. yellow, brown and blue 40 35

200 W.H.O. Building

1966. Inaug of W.H.O. Headquarters, Geneva.
866 **200** 30c. brown, green and blue 15 15
867 60c. brown, red and green 20 15

201 Bugatti, 1931

202 Dog (Egyptian bronze)

1967. 25th Motor Grand Prix, Monaco. Multicoloured. (a) Postage.
868 1c. Type **201** 10 10
869 2c. Alfa-Romeo, 1932 . . . . 10 10
870 5c. Mercedes, 1936 . . . . 10 10
871 10c. Maserati, 1948 . . . . 10 10
872 18c. Ferrari, 1955 . . . . 20 20
873 20c. Alfa-Romeo, 1950 . . . 10 10
874 25c. Maserati, 1957 . . . . 20 10
875 30c. Cooper-Climax, 1958 . . 30 20
876 40c. Lotus-Climax, 1960 . . 30 30
877 50c. Lotus-Climax, 1961 . . 50 45
878 60c. Cooper-Climax, 1962 . . 80 45
879 70c. B.R.M., 1963–6 . . . 90 70
880 1f. Walter Christie, 1907 . . 1·10 90
881 2f.30 Peugeot, 1910 . . . . 2·00 1·60

(b) Air. Diamond. 50 × 50 mm.
882 3f. black and blue . . . . 1·40 1·75
DESIGN: 3f. Panhard-Phenix, 1895.

1967. Int Cynological Federation Congress, Monaco.
883 **202** 30c. black, purple & green 35 35

203 View of Monte Carlo

1967. International Tourist Year.
884 **203** 30c. brown, green and blue 20 25

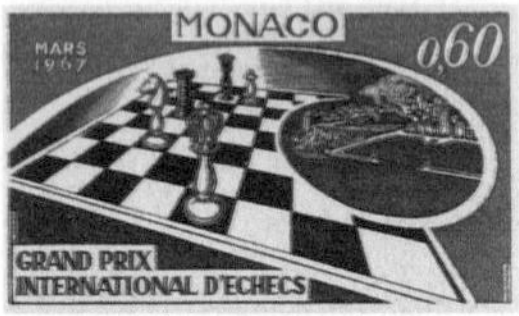

204 Pieces on Chessboard

1967. Int Chess Grand Prix, Monaco.
885 **204** 60c. black, plum and blue 50 40

205 Melvin Jones (founder), Lions Emblem and Monte Carlo

1967. 50th Anniv of Lions International.
886 **205** 60c. blue, ultramarine and brown 30 30

206 Rotary Emblem and Monte Carlo

1967. Rotary International Convention.
887 **206** 1f. bistre, blue and green 40 30

207 Fair Buildings

1967. World Fair, Montreal.
888 **207** 1f. red, slate and blue . . 40 45

208 Squiggle on Map of Europe

1967. European Migration Committee (C.I.M.E.).
889 **208** 1f. brown, bistre and blue 40 30

209 Cogwheels

1967. Europa.
890 **209** 30c. violet, purple and red 30 25
891 60c. green, turq & emer 50 35

210 Dredger and Coastal Chart

1967. 9th Int Hydrographic Congress, Monaco.
892 **210** 1f. brown, blue and green 40 35

211 Marie Curie and Scientific Equipment

1967. Birth Centenary of Marie Curie.
893 **211** 1f. blue, olive and brown 50 40

212 Skiing

1967. Winter Olympic Games, Grenoble.
894 **212** 2f.30 brown, blue & slate 90 90

213 "Prince Rainier I" (E. Charpentier)

1967. Paintings. "Princes and Princesses of Monaco". Multicoloured.
895 1f. Type **213** 40 40
896 1f. "Lucien Grimaldi" (A. di Predis) 55 55

See also Nos. 932/3, 958/9, 1005/6, 1023/4, 1070/1, 1108/9, 1213/14, 1271/2, 1325, 1380/1, 1405/6, 1460/1 and 1531/2.

214 Putting the Shot

1968. Olympic Games, Mexico.
897 **214** 20c. blue, brown and green (postage) 10 10
898 – 30c. brown, blue and plum 10 10
899 – 60c. blue, purple and red 20 25
900 – 70c. red, blue and ochre 30 30
901 – 1f. blue, brown and orange 50 50
902 – 2f.30 olive, blue and lake 1·00 1·25

903 – 3f. blue, violet & grn (air) 1·40 1·25
DESIGNS: 30c. High-jumping; 60c. Gymnastics; 70c. Water-polo; 1f. Greco-Roman wrestling; 2f.30, Gymnastics (different); 3f. Hockey.

215 "St. Martin"

1968. 20th Anniv of Monaco Red Cross.
904 **215** 2f.30 blue and brown . . 80 90

216 "Anemones" (after Raoul Dufy)

217 Insignia of Prince Charles III and Pope Pius IX

1968. Monte Carlo Floral Exhibitions.
905 **216** 1f. multicoloured 50 50

1968. Centenary of "Nullius Diocesis" Abbey.
906 **217** 10c. brown and red . . . 10 10
907 – 20c. red, green and brown 10 10
908 – 30c. brown and blue . . . 20 25
909 – 60c. brown, blue and green 30 30
910 – 1f. indigo, bistre and blue 40 40
DESIGNS—VERT: 20c. "St. Nicholas" (after Louis Brea); 30c. "St. Benedict" (after Simone Martini); 60c. Subiaco Abbey. HORIZ: 1f. Old St. Nicholas' Church (on site of present cathedral).

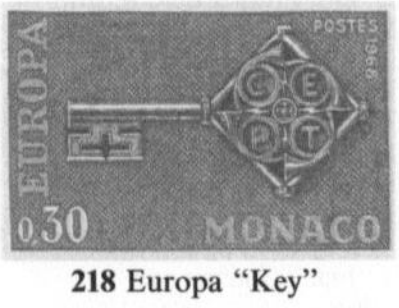

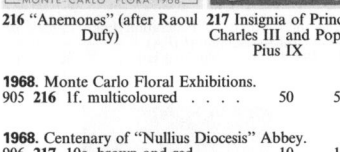

218 Europa "Key"

1968. Europa.
911 **218** 30c. red and orange . . . 40 25
912 60c. blue and red 70 60
913 1f. brown and green . . . 70 85

219 First Locomotive on Monaco Line, 1868

1968. Centenary of Nice–Monaco Railway.
914 **219** 20c. black, blue and purple 30 30
915 – 30c. black, blue and olive 50 50
916 – 60c. black, blue and ochre 70 70
917 – 70c. black, violet & brown 1·25 1·00
918 – 1f. black, blue and red . . 2·40 1·60
919 – 2f.30 blue, black and red . 3·25 2·75
DESIGNS: 30c. Class 220-C steam locomotive, 1898; 60c. Class 230-C steam locomotive, 1910; 70c. Class 231-F steam locomotive, 1925; 1f. Class 241-A steam locomotive, 1932; 2f.30, Class BB 25200 electric locomotive, 1968.

220 Chateaubriand and Combourg Castle

1968. Birth Centenary of Chateaubriand (novelist).
920 **220** 10c. plum, green & myrtle 10 10
921 – 20c. violet, purple and blue 10 10
922 – 25c. brown, violet and blue 10 10
923 – 30c. violet, choc & brn . . 20 20
924 – 60c. brown, green and red 30 20
925 – 2f.30 brown, mauve & bl 85 1·00
Scenes from Chateaubriand's novels: 20c. "Le Genie du Christianisme"; 25c. "Rene"; 30c. "Le Dernier Abencerage"; 60c. "Les Martyrs"; 2f.30, "Atala".

221 Law Courts, Paris, and statues–"La France et la Fidelite"

1968. Birth Centenary of J. F. Bosio (Monegasque sculptor).
926 **221** 20c. brown and purple . . 10 10
927 – 25c. brown and red . . . 10 10
928 – 30c. blue and green . . . 20 10
929 – 60c. green and myrtle . . 40 20
930 – 2f.30 black and slate . . . 70 75
DESIGNS—VERT (26 × 36 mm): 25c. "Henry IV as a Child"; 30c. "J. F. Bosio" (lithograph); 60c. "Louis XIV". HORIZ (as Type **221**): 2f.30, "Napoleon I, Louis XVIII and Charles X".

222 W.H.O. Emblem

1968. 20th Anniv of W.H.O.
931 **222** 60c. multicoloured 30 25

1968. Paintings. "Princes and Princesses of Monaco". As T **213**. Multicoloured.
932 1f. "Prince Charles II" (Mimault) 40 35
933 2f.30 "Princess Jeanne Grimaldi" (Mimault) . . . 70 85

223 The Hungarian March

1969. Death Centenary of Hector Berlioz (composer).
934 **223** 10c. brown, violet and green (postage) 10 10
935 – 20c. brown, olive & mauve 10 10
936 – 25c. brown, blue & mauve 10 10
937 – 30c. black, green and blue 10 20
938 – 40c. red, black and slate 10 20
939 – 50c. brown, slate & purple 20 25
940 – 70c. brown, slate and green 30 25
941 – 1f. black, mauve & brown 30 35
942 – 1f.15 black, blue & turq 50 45

943 – 2f. black, blue & grn (air) 90 90
DESIGNS—HORIZ: 20c. Mephistopheles appears to Faust; 25c. Auerbach's tavern; 30c. Sylphs' ballet; 40c. Minuet of the goblins; 50c. Marguerite's bedroom; 70c. "Forests and caverns"; 1f. The journey to Hell; 1f.15, Heaven; All scenes from Berlioz's "The Damnation of Faust". VERT: 2f. Bust of Berlioz.

224 "St. Elisabeth of Hungary"

1969. Monaco Red Cross.
944 **224** 3f. blue, brown and red 1·10 1·25

225 "Napoleon I" (P. Delaroche)

1969. Birth Bicentenary of Napoleon Bonaparte.
945 **225** 3f. multicoloured . . . . 1·10 1·10

226 Colonnade

1969. Europa.

946	**226**	40c. red and purple . . .	40	30
947		70c. blue, brown and black	60	45
948		1f. ochre, brown and blue	90	65

1969. Precancelled. As T **177**. No date.

949	22c. brown, blue and black	30	30
949a	26c. violet, blue and black	40	25
949b	30c. multicoloured	50	35
950	35c. multicoloured	40	35
950a	45c. multicoloured	60	55
951	70c. black and blue	60	55
951a	90c. green, blue and black	1·10	70

227 "Head of Woman" (Da Vinci)

228 Marine Fauna, King Alfonso XIII of Spain and Prince Albert I of Monaco

1969. 450th Death Anniv of Leonardo da Vinci.

952	**227**	30c. brown	10	10
953	–	40c. red and brown . . .	20	10
954	–	70c. green	30	20
955	–	80c. sepia	40	20
956	–	1f.15 brown	60	40
957	–	3f. brown	1·40	90

DRAWINGS: 40c. Self-portrait; 70c. "Head of an Old Man"; 80c. "Head of St. Madeleine"; 1f.15, "Man's Head"; 3f. "The Condottiere".

1969. Paintings. "Princes and Princesses of Monaco". As T **213**. Multicoloured.

958	1f. "Prince Honore II" (Champaigne)	30	50
959	3f. "Princess Louise-Hippolyte" (Champaigne)	90	1·00

1969. 50th Anniv of Int Commission for Scientific Exploration of the Mediterranean, Madrid.
960 **228** 40c. blue and black . . . 20 20

229 I.L.O. Emblem

1969. 50th Anniv of I.L.O.
961 **229** 40c. multicoloured 20 25

230 Aerial View of Monaco and T.V. Camera

1969. 10th International Television Festival.
962 **230** 40c. purple, lake and blue 20 20

231 J.C.C. Emblem

1969. 25th Anniv of Junior Chamber of Commerce.
963 **231** 40c. violet, bistre and blue 20 25

232 Alphonse Daudet and Scenes from "Lettres"

1969. Centenary of Daudet's "Lettres de Mon Moulin".

964	**232**	30c. lake, violet and green	10	10
965	–	40c. green, brown and blue	20	20
966	–	70c. multicoloured	30	30
967	–	80c. violet, brown & green	40	30
968	–	1f.15 brown, orange & bl	50	50

DESIGNS (Scenes from the book): 40c. "Installation" (Daudet writing); 70c. "Mule, Goat and Wolf"; 80c. "Gaucher's Elixir" and "The Three Low Masses"; 1f.15, Daudet drinking, "The Old Man" and "The Country Sub-Prefect".

233 Conference Building, Albert I and Rainier III

1970. Interparliamentary Union's Spring Meeting, Monaco.
969 **233** 40c. black, red and purple 20 20

234 Baby Common Seal

1970. Protection of Baby Seals.
970 **234** 40c. drab, blue and purple 40 50

235 Japanese Print

236 Dobermann

1970. Expo 70.

971	**235**	20c. brown, green and red	10	10
972	–	30c. brown, buff and green	20	20
973	–	40c. bistre and violet . .	20	20
974	–	70c. grey and red	50	60
975	–	1f.15 red, green & purple	60	75

DESIGNS—VERT: 30c. Manchurian Cranes (birds); 40c. Shinto temple gateway. HORIZ: 70c. Cherry blossom; 1f.15, Monaco Palace and Osaka Castle.

1970. International Dog Show, Monte Carlo.
976 **236** 40c. black and brown . . 80 85

237 Apollo

1970. 20th Anniv of World Federation for Protection of Animals.

977	**237**	30c. black, red and blue	20	25
978	–	40c. brown, blue and green	40	30
979	–	50c. brown, ochre and blue	60	50
980	–	80c. brown, blue and green	1·10	90
981	–	1f. brown, bistre and slate	1·60	1·90
982	–	1f.15 brown, green & blue	2·25	2·10

DESIGNS—HORIZ: 40c. Basque ponies; 50c. Common seal. VERT: 80c. Chamois; 1f. White-tailed sea eagles; 1f.15, European otter.

238 "St. Louis" (King of France)

1970. Monaco Red Cross.
983 **238** 3f. green, brown and slate 1·10 1·60
See also Nos. 1022, 1041, 1114, 1189 and 1270.

239 "Roses and Anemones" (Van Gogh)

1970. Monte Carlo Flower Show.
984 **239** 3f. multicoloured . . . . 1·50 2·00
See also Nos. 1042 and 1073.

240 Moon Plaque, Presidents Kennedy and Nixon

1970. 1st Man on the Moon (1969). Multicoloured.

985	40c. Type **240**	40	40
986	80c. Astronauts on Moon . .	60	55

241 New U.P.U. Building and Monument

242 "Flaming Sun"

1970. New U.P.U. Headquarters Building.
987 **241** 40c. brown, black & green 20 20

1970. Europa.

988	**242**	40c. purple	30	25
989		80c. green	1·10	80
990		1f. blue	1·60	1·25

243 Camargue Horse

1970. Horses.

991	**243**	10c. slate, olive and blue (postage)	10	10
992	–	20c. brown, olive and blue	20	20
993	–	30c. brown, green and blue	50	30
994	–	40c. grey, brown and slate	70	55
995	–	50c. brown, olive and blue	1·10	80
996	–	70c. brown, orange & grn	2·00	1·25
997	–	85c. blue, green and olive	2·00	1·75
998	–	1f.15 black, green & blue	2·10	2·10
999	–	3f. multicoloured (air) . .	1·50	1·75

HORSES—HORIZ: 20c. Anglo-Arab; 30c. French saddle-horse; 40c. Lippizaner; 50c. Trotter; 70c. English thoroughbred; 85c. Arab; 1f.15, Barbary. DIAMOND (50 × 50 mm): 3f. Rock-drawings of horses in Lascaux grotto.

244 Dumas, D'Artagnan and the Three Musketeers

1970. Death Centenary of Alexandre Dumas (pere) (author).
1000 **244** 30c. slate, brown and blue 20 20

245 Henri Rougier and Voisin "Boxkite"

1970. 60th Anniv of First Mediterranean Flight.
1001 **245** 40c. brown, blue and slate 20 20

246 De Lamartine and scene from "Meditations Poetiques"

1970. 150th Anniv of "Meditations Poetiques" by Alphonse de Lamartine (writer).
1002 **246** 80c. brown, blue & turq 30 30

247 Beethoven

1970. Birth Bicentenary of Beethoven.
1003 **247** 1f.30 brown and red . . 1·60 1·10

1970. 50th Death Anniv of Modigliani. Vert Painting as T **213**. Multicoloured.
1004 3f. "Portrait of Dedie" . . . 2·00 2·00

1970. Paintings. "Princes and Princesses of Monaco". As T **213**.

1005	1f. red and black	30	45
1006	3f. multicoloured	90	1·25

PORTRAITS: 1f. "Prince Louis I" (F. de Troy); 3f. "Princess Charlotte de Gramont" (S. Bourdon).

248 Cocker Spaniel **249** Razorbill

1971. International Dog Show, Monte Carlo.
1007 **248** 50c. multicoloured . . . 2·00 1·50
See also Nos. 1036, 1082, 1119, 1218 and 1239.

1971. Campaign Against Pollution of the Sea.
1008 **249** 50c. indigo and blue . . 40 45

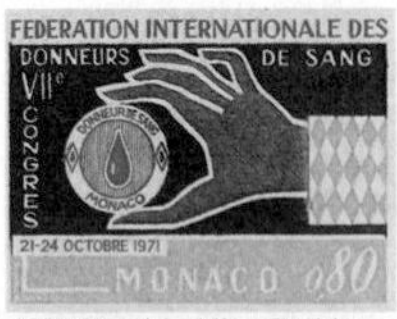

250 Hand holding Emblem

1971. 7th Int Blood Donors Federation Congress.
1009 **250** 80c. red, violet and grey 40 45

251 Sextant, Scroll and Underwater Scene

1971. 50th Anniv of Int Hydrographic Bureau.
1010 **251** 80c. brown, green & slate 40 45

252 Detail of Michelangelo Painting ("The Arts")

1971. 25th Anniv of UNESCO.
1011 **252** 30c. brown, blue & violet 10 20
1012 – 50c. blue and brown . . 20 20
1013 – 80c. brown and green . . 30 30
1014 – 1f.30 green 50 50
DESIGNS—VERT: 50c. Alchemist and dish aerial ("Sciences"); 1f.30, Prince Pierre of Monaco (National UNESCO Commission). HORIZ: 80c. Ancient scribe, book and T.V. screen ("Culture").

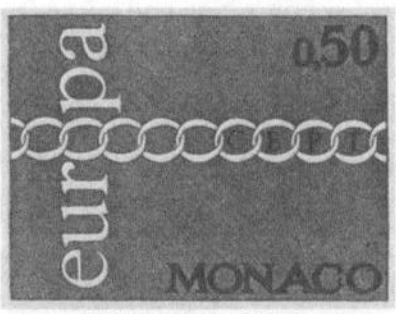

253 Europa Chain

1971. Europa.
1015 **253** 50c. red 70 45
1016 80c. blue . . . . 1·25 80
1017 1f.30 green . . . . . . 2·10 1·50

254 Old Bridge, Sospel

1971. Protection of Historic Monuments.
1018 **254** 50c. brown, blue & green 20 20
1019 – 80c. brown, green & grey 30 25
1020 – 1f.30 red, green & brown 50 50
1021 – 3f. slate, blue and olive 1·25 1·10
DESIGNS—HORIZ: 80c. Roquebrune Chateau; 1f.30, Grimaldi Chateau, Cagnes-sur-Mer. VERT: 3f. Roman "Trophy of the Alps", La Turbie.

1971. Monaco Red Cross. As T **238**.
1022 3f. brown, olive and green 1·25 1·40
DESIGN: 3f. St. Vincent de Paul.

1972. Paintings. "Princes and Princesses of Monaco". As T **213**. Multicoloured.
1023 1f. "Prince Antoine I" (Rigaud) 40 45
1024 3f. "Princess Marie de Lorraine" (18th-century French School) . . . . . 1·25 1·40

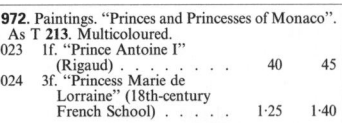

255 La Fontaine and Animal Fables (350th)

1972. Birth Anniversaries (1971).
1025 **255** 50c. brown, emer & grn 40 30
1026 – 1f.30 purple, black & red 65 60
DESIGN: 1f.30, Baudelaire, nudes and cats (150th).

256 Saint-Saens and scene from Opera, "Samson and Delilah"

1972. 50th Death Anniv (1971) of Camile Saint-Saens.
1027 **256** 90c. brown and sepia . . 40 35

257 Battle Scene

1972. 400th Anniv (1971) of Battle of Lepanto.
1028 **257** 1f. blue, brown and red 40 35

258 "Christ before Pilate" (engraving by Durer)

1972. 500th Birth Anniv (1971) of Albrecht Durer.
1029 **258** 2f. black and brown . . 1·10 1·25

259 "The Cradle" (B. Morisot)

1972. 25th Anniv (1971) of UNICEF.
1030 **259** 2f. multicoloured . . . . 1·10 1·10

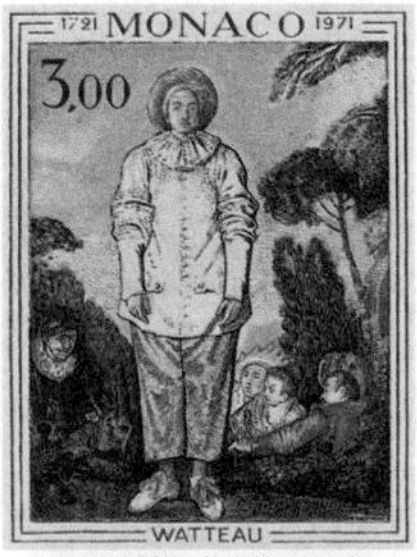

260 "Gilles" (Watteau)

1972. 250th Death Anniv (1971) of Watteau.
1031 **260** 3f. multicoloured . . . . 1·60 1·60

261 Santa Claus

1972. Christmas (1971).
1032 **261** 30c. red, blue and brown 10 20
1033 50c. red, green & orange 20 20
1034 90c. red, blue and brown 45 30

262 Class 743 Steam Locomotive, Italy, and TGV 001 Turbotrain, France

1972. 50th Anniv of International Railway Union.
1035 **262** 50c. purple, lilac and red 70 60

1972. Int Dog Show, Monte Carlo. As T **248**.
1036 60c. multicoloured . . . . . 1·60 1·60
DESIGN: 60c. Great Dane.

263 "Pollution Kills"

1972. Anti-pollution Campaign.
1037 **263** 90c. brown, green & black 40 35

264 Ski-jumping

1972. Winter Olympic Games, Sapporo, Japan.
1038 **264** 90c. black, red and green 55 50

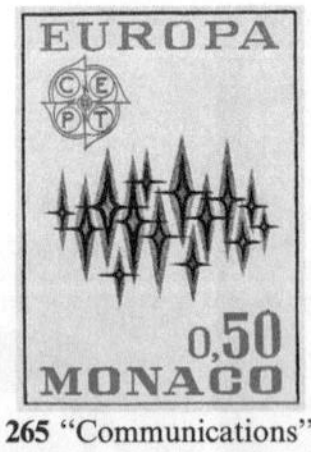

265 "Communications"

1972. Europa.
1039 **265** 50c. blue and orange . . 80 60
1040 90c. blue and green . . . 1·60 1·50

1972. Monaco Red Cross. As T **238**.
1041 3f. brown and purple . . . 1·25 1·40
DESIGN: 3f. St. Francis of Assisi.

1972. Monte Carlo Flower Show. As T **239**.
1042 3f. multicoloured . . . . . 2·40 2·00
DESIGN: 3f. "Vase of Flowers" (Cezanne).

266 "SS. Giovanni e Paolo" (detail, Canaletto)

1972. UNESCO "Save Venice" Campaign.
1043 **266** 30c. red 20 25
1044 – 60c. violet 30 30
1045 – 2f. blue . . . . 1·25 1·40
DESIGNS—27 × 48 mm: 60c. "S. Pietro di Castello" (F. Guradi). As Type **266**: 2f. "Piazzetta S. Marco" (B. Bellotto).

267 Dressage

1972. Olympic Games, Munich. Equestrian Events.
1046 **267** 60c. brown, blue and lake 40 55
1047 – 90c. lake, brown and blue . . . . 80 1·00
1048 – 1f.10 blue, lake & brown 1·25 1·50
1049 – 1f.40 brown, lake & blue 2·10 2·40
DESIGNS: 90c. Cross country; 1f.10, Show jumping (wall); 1f.40, Show jumping (parallel bars).

268 Escoffier and Birthplace

1972. 125th Birth Anniv of Auguste Escoffier (master chef).
1050 **268** 45c. black and brown . . 20 25

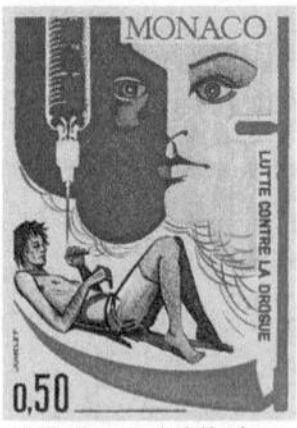

269 Drug Addiction **270** Globe, Birds and Animals

1972. Campaign Against Drugs.
1051 **269** 50c. red, brown & orange 30 25
1052 90c. green, brown & blue 40 45
See also Nos. 1088/91 and 1280/1.

1972. 17th Int Congress of Zoology, Monaco.
1053 **270** 30c. green, brown and red 10 10
1054 – 50c. brown, purple and red 20 20
1055 – 90c. blue, brown and red 40 30
DESIGNS—HORIZ: 50c. VERT: 90c. Similar symbolic design.

271 Bouquet

272 "The Nativity" and Child's face

1972. Monte Carlo Flower Show, 1973 (1st issue). Multicoloured.
1056 30c. Lilies in vase 40 30
1057 50c. Type **271** 70 45
1058 90c. Flowers in vase . . . . 1·25 90
See also Nos. 1073, 1105/7, 1143/4, 1225/6, 1244, 1282/3 and 1316/17.

1972. Christmas.
1059 **272** 30c. grey, blue and purple 10 10
1060 50c. red, purple & brown 20 10
1061 90c. violet, plum & pur 40 30

273 Louis Bleriot and Bleriot XI (Birth cent)

1972. Birth Anniversaries.
1062 **273** 30c. blue and brown . . 20 10
1063 – 50c. blue, turq & new blue 60 60
1064 – 90c. brown and buff . . 80 55
DESIGNS AND ANNIVERSARIES: 50c. Amundsen and polar scene (birth centenary); 90c. Pasteur and laboratory scene (150th birth anniv).

274 "Gethsemane"

1972. Protection of Historical Monuments. Frescoes by J. Canavesio, Chapel of Notre-Dame des Fontaines, La Brigue.
1065 **274** 30c. red 10 10
1066 – 50c. grey 20 25
1067 – 90c. green 40 40
1068 – 1f.40 red 60 55
1069 – 2f. purple . . . . 1·10 80
DESIGNS: 50c. "Christ Outraged"; 90c. "Ascent to Calvary"; 1f.40, "The Resurrection"; 2f. "The Crucifixion".

1972. Paintings. "Princes and Princesses of Monaco". As T **213**. Multicoloured.
1070 1f. "Prince Jacques 1" (N. Largilliere) 40 45
1071 3f. "Princess Louise-Hippolyte" (J. B. Vanloo) 1·25 1·50

275

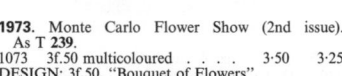

1973. 25th Anniv of Monaco Red Cross. Sheet 100 × 130 mm.
MS1072 **275** 5f. red . . . . . . 13·00 10·50

1973. Monte Carlo Flower Show (2nd issue). As T **239**.
1073 3f.50 multicoloured . . . . 3·50 3·25
DESIGN: 3f.50, "Bouquet of Flowers".

276 Europa "Posthorn"

1973. Europa.
1074 **276** 50c. orange . . . . . . 2·75 1·25
1075 90c. green . . . . 4·25 2·50

277 Moliere and Characters from "Le Malade Imaginaire"

1973. 300th Death Anniv of Moliere.
1076 **277** 20c. red, brown and blue 35 30

278 Colette, Cat and Books

1973. Birth Anniversaries.
1077 **278** 30c. black, blue and red 70 45
1078 – 45c. multicoloured . . . 1·75 1·25
1079 – 50c. lilac, purple and blue 35 25
1080 – 90c. multicoloured . . . 40 50
DESIGNS AND ANNIVERSARIES—HORIZ: 30c., Type **278** (nature writer, birth cent); 45c. J.-H. Fabre and insects (entomologists, 150th birth anniv); 90c. Sir George Cayley and his "convertiplane" (aviation pioneer, birth bicent). VERT: 50c. Blaise Pascal (philosopher and writer, 350th birth anniv).

279 E. Ducretet, "Les Invalides" and Eiffel Tower

1973. 75th Anniv of Eugene Ducretet's First Hertzian Radio Link.
1081 **279** 30c. purple and brown 20 25

1973. International Dog Show, Monte Carlo. As T **248**. Inscr "1973". Multicoloured.
1082 45c. Alsatian . . . . 7·25 4·25

280 C. Peguy and Chartres Cathedral

1973. Birth Bicentenary of Charles Peguy (writer).
1083 **280** 50c. brown, mauve & grey 30 35

281 Telecommunications Equipment

1973. 5th World Telecommunications Day.
1084 **281** 60c. violet, blue & brown 30 30

282 Stage Characters

1973. 5th World Amateur Theatre Festival.
1085 **282** 60c. lilac, blue and red 30 35

283 Ellis and Rugby Tackle

1973. 150th Anniv of Founding of Rugby Football by William Webb Ellis.
1086 **283** 90c. red, lake and brown 50 50

284 St. Theresa

1973. Birth Centenary of St. Theresa of Lisieux.
1087 **284** 1f.40 multicoloured . . . 60 55

285 Drug Addiction

1973. Campaign Against Drugs.
1088 **285** 50c. red, green and blue 20 25
1089 – 50c. multicoloured . . . 20 25
1090 **285** 90c. violet, green and red 40 45
1091 – 90c. multicoloured . . . 50 50
DESIGN: Nos. 1089, 1091, Children, syringes and addicts.

286 "Institution of the Creche" (Giotto)

1973. 750th Anniv of St. Francis of Assisi Creche.
1092 **286** 30c. purple (postage) . . 30 30
1093 – 45c. red 60 55
1094 – 50c. brown 70 70
1095 – 1f. green . . . . 1·60 1·25
1096 – 2f. brown . . . . 3·00 2·75
1097 – 3f. blue (air) . . . . . . 1·75 1·60
DESIGN—HORIZ: 45c. "The Nativity" (School of F. Lippi); 50c. "The Birth of Jesus Christ" (Giotto). VERT: 1f. "The Nativity" (15th-century miniature); 2f. "The Birth of Jesus" (Fra Angelico); 3f. "The Nativity" (Flemish school).

287 Country Picnic

1973. 50th Anniv of National Committee for Monegasque Traditions.
1098 **287** 10c. blue, green & brown 10 10
1099 – 20c. violet, blue and green 10 10
1100 – 30c. sepia, brown & green 20 25
1101 – 45c. red, violet and purple 40 35
1102 – 50c. black, red and brown 50 40
1103 – 60c. red, violet and blue 50 60
1104 – 1f. violet, blue and brown . . . . 95 1·10
DESIGNS—VERT: 20c. Maypole dance. HORIZ: 30c. "U Bradi" (local dance); 45c. St. Jean fire-dance; 50c. Blessing the Christmas loaf; 60c. Blessing the sea, Festival of St. Devote; 1f. Corpus Christi procession.

1973. Monte Carlo Flower Show, 1974. As T **271**. Multicoloured.
1105 45c. Roses and Strelitzia . . 80 55
1106 60c. Mimosa and myosotis 1·25 90
1107 1f. "Vase of Flowers" (Odilon Redon) . . . . . 2·00 1·60

1973. Paintings. "Princes and Princesses of Monaco". As T **213**. Multicoloured.
1108 2f. "Charlotte Grimaldi" (in day dress, P. Gobert) . . 1·40 1·40
1109 2f. "Charlotte Grimaldi" (in evening dress, P. Gobert) 1·40 1·40

288 Prince Rainier

1974. 25th Anniv of Prince Rainer's Accession. Sheet 100 × 130 mm.
MS1110 **288** 10f. black . . . . . 5·50 5·50

289 U.P.U. Emblem and Symbolic Heads

1974. Centenary of Universal Postal Union.
1111 **289** 50c. purple and brown 30 25
1112 – 70c. multicoloured . . . 40 30
1113 – 1f.10 multicoloured . . . 70 55
DESIGNS: 70c. Hands holding letters; 1f.10, "Countries of the World" (famous buildings).

1974. Monaco Red Cross. As T **238**.
1114 3f. blue, green and purple 1·40 1·25
DESIGN: 3f. St. Bernard of Menthon.

290 Farman, Farman F.60 Goliath and Farman H.F.III

1974. Birth Centenary of Henry Farman (aviation pioneer).
1115 **290** 30c. brown, purple & blue 10 10

291 Marconi, Circuit Plan and Destroyer

1974. Birth Centenary of Guglielmo Marconi (radio pioneer).
1116 **291** 40c. red, deep blue & blue 20 10

292 Duchesne and "Penicillium glaucum"

1974. Birth Centenary of Ernest Duchesne (microbiologist).
1117 **292** 45c. black, blue & purple 30 20

293 Forest and Engine

1974. 60th Death Anniv of Fernand Forest (motor engineer and inventor).
1118 **293** 50c. purple, red and black 30 25

1974. International Dog Show, Monte Carlo. As T **248**, inscr "1974".
1119 60c. multicoloured . . . . . 2·75 2·00
DESIGN: 60c. Schnauzer.

294 Ronsard and Characters from "Sonnet to Helene"

1974. 450th Birth Anniv of Pierre de Ronsard (poet).
1120 **294** 70c. brown and red . . . 40 45

295 Sir Winston Churchill (after bust by O. Nemon)

297 "The King of Rome" (Bosio)

296 Interpol Emblem, and Views of Monaco and Vienna

1974. Birth Centenary of Sir Winston Churchill.
1121 **295** 1f. brown and grey . . . 55 45

1974. 60th Anniv of 1st International Police Judiciary Congress and 50th Anniv of International Criminal Police Organization (Interpol).
1122 **296** 2f. blue, brown and green . . . . 1·10 90

1974. Europa. Sculptures by J. F. Bosio.
1123 **297** 45c. green and brown . . 1·00 75
1124 – 1f.10 bistre and brown 1·75 1·40
MS1125 170 × 140 mm. Nos. 1123/5 × 5 . . . . 18·00 17·00
DESIGN: 1f.10, "Madame Elizabeth".

298 "The Box" (A. Renoir)

1974. "The Impressionists". Multicoloured.
1126 1f. Type **298** . . . . 1·40 1·40
1127 1f. "The Dance Class" (E. Degas) . . . . 1·40 1·40
1128 2f. "Impression-Sunrise" (C. Monet) (horiz) . . . . 2·75 2·75
1129 2f. "Entrance to Voisins Village" (C. Pissarro) (horiz) . . . . 2·75 2·75
1130 2f. "The Hanged Man's House" (P. Cezanne) (horiz) . . . . 2·75 2·75
1131 2f. "Floods at Port Marly" (A. Sisley) (horiz) . . . . 2·75 2·75

299 Tigers and Trainer

1974. 1st International Circus Festival, Monaco.
1132 **299** 2c. brown, green and blue 10 10
1133 – 3c. brown and purple . . 10 10
1134 – 5c. blue, brown and red 10 10
1135 – 45c. brown, black and red 40 35
1136 – 70c. multicoloured . . . 60 45
1137 – 1f.10 brown, green and red . . . . 1·40 75
1138 – 5f. green, blue and brown . . . . 4·00 3·25
DESIGNS—VERT: 3c. Performing horse; 45c. Equestrian act; 1f.10, Acrobats; 5f. Trapeze act. HORIZ: 5c. Performing elephants; 70c. Clowns.

300 Honore II on Medal

1974. 350th Anniv of Monegasque Numismatic Art.
1139 **300** 60c. green and red . . . 40 35

301 Marine Flora and Fauna

1974. 24th Congress of the International Commission for the Scientific Exploration of the Mediterranean. Multicoloured.
1140 45c. Type **301** 80 60
1141 70c. Sea-bed flora and fauna 1·40 90
1142 1f.10 Sea-bed flora and fauna (different) . . . . 2·00 1·40
Nos. 1141/2 are larger, size 52 × 31 mm.

1974. Monte Carlo Flower Show. As T **271**. Multicoloured.
1143 70c. Honeysuckle and violets 70 60
1144 1f.10 Iris and chrysanthemums . . . . 1·00 1·00

302 Prince Rainier III (F. Messina)

303

1974.
1145 **302** 60c. green (postage) . . 70 30
1146 80c. red 80 45
1147 80c. green 40 10
1148 1f. brown . . . . . . 2·00 85
1149 1f. red 50 20
1149a 1f. green 40 20
1149b 1f.10 green 40 20
1150 1f.20 violet . . . . . . 4·25 2·00
1150a 1f.20 red 60 20
1150b 1f.20 green 70 20
1151 1f.25 blue . . . . . . 1·00 85
1151a 1f.30 red 70 25
1152 1f.40 red 80 20
1152a 1f.50 black 80 60
1153 1f.60 grey 80 50
1153a 1f.70 blue 90 60
1153b 1f.80 blue . . . . . . 1·40 1·40
1154 2f. mauve . . . . . . 1·50 1·50
1154a 2f.10 brown . . . . . . 1·40 75
1155 2f.30 violet . . . . . . 1·75 1·25
1156 2f.50 black . . . . . . 1·75 1·40
1157 9f. violet . . . . . . 5·00 3·25
1158 **303** 10f. violet (air) . . . . 6·00 2·50
1159 15f. red . . . . 9·00 5·50
1160 20f. blue . . . . 11·00 6·00

304 Coastline, Monte Carlo

305 "Haagocereus chosicensis"

1974.
1161 **304** 25c. blue, green & brown 1·50 45
1162 – 25c. brown, green & blue 30 20
1163 – 50c. brown and blue . . 1·50 45
1164 **304** 65c. blue, brown & green 30 25
1165 – 70c. multicoloured . . . 40 40
1166 **304** 1f.10 brown, green & bl 1·75 65
1167 – 1f.10 black, brown & bl 60 70
1168 – 1f.30 brown, green & bl 60 40
1169 – 1f.40 green, grey & brn 2·00 1·00
1170 – 1f.50 green, blue & black 1·00 90
1171 – 1f.70 brown, green & bl 3·00 2·00
1172 – 1f.80 brown, green & bl 1·10 85
1173 – 2f.30 brown, grey & blue 1·75 1·40
1174 – 3f. brown, grey and green . . . . 4·75 2·00
1175 – 5f.50 brown, green & blue . . . . 6·25 4·25
1176 – 6f.50 brown, blue & grn 3·00 2·40
DESIGNS—VERT: 50c. Palace clock tower; 70c. Botanical gardens; 1f.30, Monaco Cathedral; 1f.40, 1f.50, Prince Albert I statue and Museum; 3f. Fort Antoine. HORIZ: 25c. (1162), 1f.70, "All Saints" Tower; 1f.10 (1167), Palais de Justice; 1f.80, 5f.50, La Condamine; 2f.30, North Galleries of Palace; 6f.50, Aerial view of hotels and harbour.

1975. Plants. Multicoloured.
1180 10c. Type **305** 10 10
1181 20c. "Matucana madisoniarum" 20 20
1182 30c. "Parodia scopaioides" 40 25
1183 85c. "Mediolobivia arachnacantha" . . . . . 1·50 80
1184 1f.90 "Matucana yanganucensis" . . . . . 2·75 2·10
1185 4f. "Echinocereus marksianus" . . . . . . 5·25 3·75

306 "Portrait of a Sailor" (P. Florence)

308 "Prologue"

307 "St. Bernardin de Sienne"

1975. Europa.
1186 **306** 80c. purple . . . . . . 1·10 60
1187 – 1f.20 blue . . . . . . 1·60 80
MS1188 170 × 130 mm. Nos. 1186/7 × 5 . . . . 18·00 17·00
DESIGN: 1f.20, "St. Devote" (Ludovic Brea).

1975. Monaco Red Cross.
1189 **307** 4f. blue and purple . . . 1·90 1·75

1975. Centenary of "Carmen" (opera by Georges Bizet).
1190 **308** 30c. violet, brown & blk 10 10
1191 – 60c. grey, green and red 20 10
1192 – 80c. green, brown & blk 50 35
1193 – 1f.40 purple, brn & ochre 80 70
DESIGNS—HORIZ: 60c. Lilla Pastia's tavern; 80c. "The Smuggler's Den"; 1f.40, "Confrontation at Seville".

309 Saint-Simon

310 Dr. Albert Schweitzer

1975. 300th Birth Anniv of Louis de Saint-Simon (writer).
1194 **309** 40c. blue 30 25

1975. Birth Centenary of Dr. Schweitzer (Nobel Peace Prize Winner).
1195 **310** 60c. red and brown . . . 50 35

311 "Stamp" and Calligraphy

1975. "Arphila 75" International Stamp Exhibition, Paris.
1196 **311** 80c. brown and orange 50 45

312 Seagull and Sunrise

1975. International Exposition, Okinawa.
1197 **312** 85c. blue, green & orange 60 50

313 Pike smashing Crab

1975. Anti-cancer Campaign.
1198 **313** 1f. multicoloured 60 50

314 Christ with Crown of Thorns

1975. Holy Year.
1199 **314** 1f.15 black, brn & pur 85 60

315 Villa Sauber, Monte Carlo

1975. European Architectural Heritage Year.
1200 **315** 1f.20 green, brown & bl 80 60

316 Woman's Head and Globe

1975. International Women's Year.
1201 **316** 1f.20 multicoloured . . . 80 60

317 Rolls-Royce "Silver Ghost" (1907)

1975. History of the Motor Car.
1202 **317** 5c. blue, green and brown 10 10
1203 – 10c. indigo and blue . . 10 10
1204 – 20c. blue, ultram & black 20 10
1205 – 30c. purple and mauve 40 20
1206 – 50c. blue, purple & mauve 70 50
1207 – 60c. red and green . . . 1·00 70
1208 – 80c. indigo and blue . . 1·75 1·10
1209 – 85c. brown, orange & grn . . . . 2·00 1·50
1210 – 1f.20 blue, red and green 3·00 2·40
1211 – 1f.40 green and blue . . 4·25 2·75
1212 – 5f.50 blue, emerald and green . . . . 9·50 7·00
DESIGNS: 10c. Hispano-Suiza "H.6B" (1926); 20c. Isotta Fraschini "8A" (1928); 30c. Cord "L.29"; 50c. Voisin "V12" (1930); 60c. Duesenberg "SJ" (1933); 80c. Bugatti "57 C" (1938); 85c. Delahaye "135 M" (1940); 1f.20, Cisitalia "Pininfarina" (1945); 1f.40, Mercedes-Benz "300 SL" (1955); 5f.50, Lamborghini "Countach" (1974).

1975. Paintings. "Princes and Princesses of Monaco". As T **213**. Multicoloured.
1213 2f. "Prince Honore III" . . 1·25 85
1214 4f. "Princess Catherine de Brignole" . . . . 2·50 2·40

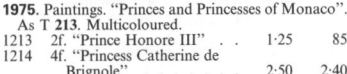

318 Dog behind Bars

1975. 125th Birth Anniv of Gen. J. P. Delmas de Grammont (author of Animal Protection Code).
1215 **318** 60c. black and brown . . 80 80
1216 – 80c. black and brown . . 1·10 85
1217 – 1f.20 green and purple 1·90 1·50
DESIGNS—VERT: 80c. Cat chased up tree. HORIZ: 1f.20, Horse being ill-treated.

1975. International Dog Show, Monte Carlo. As T **248**, but inscr "1975". Multicoloured.
1218 60c. black and purple . . . 3·50 2·75
DESIGN: 60c. French poodle.

319 Maurice Ravel

1975. Birth Centenaries of Musicians.
1219 **319** 60c. brown and purple 70 55
1220 – 1f.20 black and purple 1·50 1·25
DESIGN: 1f.20, Johann Strauss (the younger).

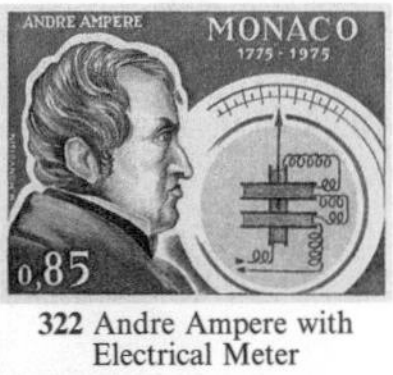

320 Circus Clown **322** Andre Ampere with Electrical Meter

321 Monaco Florin Coin, 1640

1975. 2nd International Circus Festival.
1221 **320** 80c. multicoloured . . . 80 55

1975. Monaco Numismatics.
1222 **321** 80c. brown and blue . . 50 50
See also Nos. 1275, 1320 and 1448.

1975. Birth Centenary of Andre Ampere (physicist).
1223 **322** 85c. indigo and blue . . 50 50

323 "Lamentations for the Dead Christ"

1975. 500th Birth Anniv of Michelangelo.
1224 **323** 1f.40 olive and black . . 80 80

1975. Monte Carlo Flower Show (1976). As T **271**. Multicoloured.
1225 60c. Bouquet of wild flowers 80 55
1226 80c. Ikebana flower arrangement . . . . . . 1·40 90

1975. Precancelled. Surch.
1227 42c. on 26c. violet, blue and black (No. 949a) . . . . 1·60 1·40
1228 48c. on 30c. multicoloured (No. 949b) . . . . 1·90 1·90
1229 70c. on 45c. multicoloured (No. 950a) . . . . 3·25 2·75
1230 1f.35 on 90c. green, blue and black (No. 951a) . . 4·25 3·75

325 Prince Pierre de Monaco

1976. 25th Anniv of Literary Council of Monaco.
1231 **325** 10c. black 10 10
1232 – 20c. blue and red 20 20
1233 – 25c. blue and red 20 20
1234 – 30c. brown 20 30
1235 – 50c. blue, red and purple 40 30
1236 – 60c. brown, grn & lt brn 50 35
1237 – 80c. purple and blue . . 80 75
1238 – 1f.20 violet, blue & mve 1·60 1·10
COUNCIL MEMBERS—HORIZ: 20c. A. Maurois and Colette; 25c. Jean and Jerome Tharaud; 30c. E. Henriot, M. Pagnol and G. Duhamel; 50c. Ph. Heriat, J. Supervielle and L. Pierard; 60c. R. Dorgeles, M. Achard and G. Bauer; 80c. F. Hellens, A. Billy and Mgr. Grente; 1f.20, J. Giono, L. Pasteur Vallery-Radot and M. Garcon.

326 Dachshunds

1976. International Dog Show, Monte Carlo.
1239 **326** 60c. multicoloured . . . 4·00 3·25

327 Bridge Table and Monte Carlo Coast

1976. 5th Bridge Olympiad, Monte Carlo.
1240 **327** 60c. brown, green and red 50 40

328 Alexander Graham Bell and Early Telephone

1976. Telephone Centenary.
1241 **328** 80c. brown, light brown and grey 50 30

329 Federation Emblem on Globe

1976. 50th Anniv of International Philatelic Federation.
1242 **329** 1f.20 red, blue and green 70 55

330 U.S.A. 2c. Stamp, 1926

1976. Bicent of American Revolution.
1243 **330** 1f.70 black and purple 80 55

331 "The Fritillaries" (Van Gogh)

1976. Monte Carlo Flower Show.
1244 **331** 3f. multicoloured . . . . 7·00 5·00

332 Diving **333** Decorative Plate

1976. Olympic Games, Montreal.
1245 **332** 60c. brown and blue . . 30 30
1246 – 80c. blue, brown & green 40 35
1247 – 85c. blue, green & brown 50 40
1248 – 1f.20 brown, green & bl 70 60
1249 – 1f.70 brown, blue & grn 1·00 1·00
MS1250 150 × 145 mm. Nos. 1245/9 4·00 4·00
DESIGNS—VERT: 80c. Gymnastics; 85c. Hammer-throwing. HORIZ: 1f.20, Rowing; 1f.70, Boxing.

1976. Europa. Monegasque Ceramics. Multicoloured.
1251 80c. Type **333** 70 70
1252 1f.20 Grape-harvester (statuette) . . . . 1·25 1·10
MS1253 170 × 140 mm. Nos. 1251/2 × 5 . . . . 17·00 17·00

334 Palace Clock Tower **335** "St. Louise de Marillac" (altar painting)

1976. Precancelled.
1254 **334** 50c. red 50 45
1255 52c. orange 30 20
1256 54c. green 40 20
1257 60c. green 50 55
1258 62c. mauve 40 40
1259 68c. yellow 50 45
1260 90c. violet 80 80
1261 95c. red 80 65
1262 1f.05 brown 80 60
1263 1f.60 blue . . . . 1·40 1·25
1264 1f.70 turquoise . . . . . 1·40 1·00
1265 1f.85 brown . . . . . . 1·40 1·25

1976. Monaco Red Cross.
1270 **335** 4f. black, purple & green 2·00 1·90

1976. Paintings. "Princes and Princesses of Monaco". As T **213**.
1271 2f. purple . . . . 1·60 1·50
1272 4f. multicoloured . . . . . 3·00 2·10
DESIGNS: 2f. "Prince Honore IV"; 4f. "Princess Louise d'Aumont-Mazarin".

336 St. Vincent-de-Paul **337** Marie de Rabutin Chantal

1976. Centenary of St. Vincent-de-Paul Conference, Monaco.
1273 **336** 60c. black, brown & blue 35 25

1976. 350th Birth Anniv of Marquise de Sevigne (writer).
1274 **337** 80c. black, violet and red 40 30

338 Monaco 2g. "Honore II" Coin, 1640

1976. Monaco Numismatics.
1275 **338** 80c. blue and green . . . 50 40

339 Richard Byrd, "Josephine Ford", Airship "Norge" and Roald Amundsen

1976. 50th Anniv of First Flights over North Pole.
1276 **339** 85c. black, blue and green . . . . 1·25 1·10

340 Gulliver and Lilliputians

1976. 250th Anniv of Jonathan Swift's "Gulliver's Travels".
1277 **340** 1f.20 multicoloured . . . 60 45

341 Girl's Head and Christmas Decorations

1976. Christmas.
1278 **341** 60c. multicoloured . . . 40 25
1279 1f.20 green, orge & pur 60 40

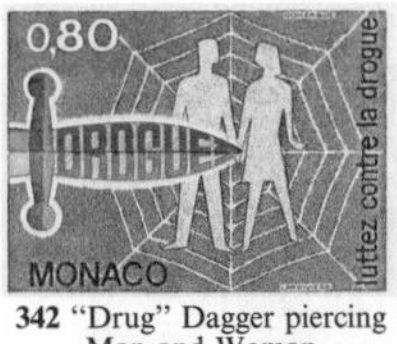

342 "Drug" Dagger piercing Man and Woman **343** Circus Clown

1976. Campaign against Drug Abuse.
1280 **342** 80c. blue, orge & bronze 50 30
1281 1f.20 lilac, purple & brn 70 50

1976. Monte Carlo Flower Show (1977). As T **271**. Multicoloured.
1282 80c. Flower arrangement . . 1·00 75
1283 1f. Bouquet of flowers . . . 1·50 1·25

1976. 3rd International Circus Festival, Monte Carlo.
1284 **343** 1f. multicoloured . . . . 1·40 1·00

344 Schooner "Hirondelle I"

1977. 75th Anniv of Publication of "Career of a Navigator" by Prince Albert I (1st issue). Illustrations by L. Tinayre.
1285 **344** 10c. brown, blue & turq 10 10
1286 – 20c. black, brown & lake 10 20
1287 – 30c. green, blue & orange 20 25
1288 – 80c. black, blue and red 40 40
1289 – 1f. black and brown . . 60 50
1290 – 1f.25 olive, green & violet 80 75
1291 – 1f.40 brown, olive & grn 1·25 1·25
1292 – 1f.90 blue, lt blue & red 2·25 1·60
1293 – 2f.50 brown, blue and turquoise . . . . . 3·25 2·75
DESIGNS—VERT: 20c. Prince Albert I; 1f. Helmsman; 1f.90, Bringing in the trawl. HORIZ: 30c. Crew-members; 80c. "Hirondelle" in a gale; 1f.25, Securing the lifeboat; 1f.40, Shrimp fishing; 2f.50, Capture of an oceanic sunfish.
See also Nos. 1305/13.

345 Pyrenean Sheep and Mountain Dogs

1977. International Dog Show, Monte Carlo.
1294 **345** 80c. multicoloured . . . 3·75 2·75

346 "Maternity" (M. Cassatt)

1977. World Association of the "Friends of Children".
1295 **346** 80c. deep brown, brown and black 95 70

347 Archers

1977. 10th International Archery Championships.
1296 **347** 1f.10 black, brown & bl 70 50

348 Charles Lindbergh and "Spirit of St. Louis"

1977. 50th Anniv of Lindbergh's Transatlantic Flight.
1297 **348** 1f.90 light blue, blue and brown . . . . 1·40 1·10

349 "Harbour, Deauville"

1977. Birth Centenary of Raoul Dufy (painter).
1298 **349** 2f. multicoloured . . . . 3·00 2·50

350 "Portrait of a Young Girl" **351** "L'Oreillon" Tower

1977. 400th Birth Anniv of Peter Paul Rubens (painter).
1299 **350** 80c. orange, brown & blk 50 45
1300 – 1f. red 85 60
1301 – 1f.40 orange and red . . 1·75 1·25
DESIGNS: 1f. "Duke of Buckingham"; 1f.40, "Portrait of a Child".

1977. Europa. Views.
1302 **351** 1f. brown and blue . . . 80 60
1303 – 1f.40 blue, brown and bistre . . . . 1·25 1·10
MS1304 169 × 130 mm. Nos. 1302/3 × 5 . . . . 18·00 18·00
DESIGN: 1f.40, St. Michael's Church, Menton.

1977. 75th Anniv of Publication of "Career of a Navigator" by Prince Albert I (2nd issue). Illustrations by L. Tinayre. As T **344**.
1305 10c. black and blue 10 10
1306 20c. blue 10 15
1307 30c. blue, light blue and green 20 25
1308 80c. brown, black and green 40 35
1309 1f. grey and green 50 50
1310 1f.25 black, brown and lilac 80 75
1311 1f.40 purple, blue and brown . . . . 1·25 1·25
1312 1f.90 black, blue and light blue . . . . 2·10 1·75
1313 3f. blue, brown and green 3·00 2·75
DESIGNS—HORIZ: 10c. "Princess Alice" (steam yacht) at Kiel; 20c. Ship's laboratory; 30c. "Princess Alice" in ice floes; 1f. Polar scene; 1f.25, Bridge of "Princess Alice" during snowstorm; 1f.40, Arctic camp; 1f.90, Ship's steam launch in floating ice; 3f. "Princess Alice" passing iceberg. VERT: 80c. Crewmen in Arctic dress.

352 Santa Claus & Sledge **353** Face, Poppy and Syringe

1977. Christmas.
1314 **352** 80c. red, green and blue 40 30
1315 1f.40 multicoloured . . . 60 40

1977. Monte Carlo Flower Show. As T **271**. Mult.
1316 80c. Snapdragons and campanula 80 70
1317 1f. Ikebana . . . . 1·25 1·00

1977. Campaign Against Drug Abuse.
1318 **353** 1f. black, red and violet 50 40

354 Clown and Flags

1977. 4th International Festival of Circus, Monaco.
1319 **354** 1f. multicoloured . . . . 1·40 1·10

355 Gold Coin of Honore II

1977. Monaco Numismatics.
1320 **355** 80c. brown and red . . . 50 45

356 Mediterranean divided by Industry

1977. Protection of the Mediterranean Environment.
1321 **356** 1f. black, green and blue 60 50

357 Dr. Guglielminetti and Road Tarrers

1977. 75th Anniv of First Experiments at Road Tarring in Monaco.
1322 **357** 1f.10 black, bistre and brown 60 45

358 F.M.L.T. Badge and Monte Carlo

1977. 50th Anniv of Monaco Lawn Tennis Federation.
1323 **358** 1f. blue, red and brown 1·00 50

359 Wimbledon and First Championships

1977. Centenary of Wimbledon Lawn Tennis Championships.
1324 **359** 1f.40 grey, green & brown . . . . 1·10 95

1977. Paintings. "Princes and Princesses of Monaco". As T **213**. Multicoloured.
1325 6f. "Prince Honore V" . . . 4·00 2·75

360 St. Jean Bosco

1977. Monaco Red Cross. Monegasque Art.
1326 **360** 4f. green, brown and blue . . . . 1·90 1·75

1978. Precancelled. Surch.
1327 **334** 58c. on 54c. green . . . 50 45
1328 73c. on 68c. yellow . . . 70 60
1329 1f.15 on 1f.05 brown . . 1·00 95
1330 2f. on 1f.85 brown . . . 1·75 1·75

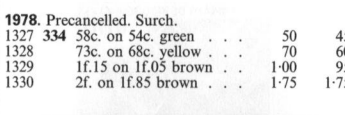

362 Aerial Shipwreck from "L'Ile Mysterieuse"

1978. 150th Birth Anniv of Jules Verne.
1331 **362** 5c. brown, red and olive 10 10
1332 – 25c. turquoise, blue & red 10 10
1333 – 30c. blue, brown & lt blue 20 10
1334 – 80c. black, green & orge 30 30
1335 – 1f. brown, lake and blue 60 50
1336 – 1f.40 bistre, brown and green 80 70
1337 – 1f.70 brown, light blue and blue . . . . . . 1·10 1·25
1338 – 5f.50 violet and blue . . 2·75 2·75
DESIGNS: 25c. The abandoned ship from "L'Ile Mysterieuse"; 30c. The secret of the island from "L'Ile Mysterieuse"; 80c. "Robur the Conqueror"; 1f. "Master Zacharius"; 1f.40, "The Castle in the Carpathians"; 1f.70, "The Children of Captain Grant"; 5f.50, Jules Verne and allegories.

363 Aerial View of Congress Centre

1978. Inauguration of Monaco Congress Centre.
1339 **363** 1f. brown, blue and green 40 40
1340 – 1f.40 blue, brown & grn 60 50
DESIGN: 1f.40, View of Congress Centre from sea.

364 Footballers and Globe

1978. World Cup Football Championship, Argentina.
1341 **364** 1f. blue, slate and green 60 55

365 Antonio Vivaldi **366** "Ramoge" (research vessel) and Grimaldi Palace

1978. 300th Birth Anniv of Antonio Vivaldi (composer).
1342 **365** 1f. brown and red . . . 70 70

1978. Environment Protection. "RAMOGE" Agreement.
1343 **366** 80c. multicoloured . . . 40 35
1344 – 1f. red, blue and green 60 40
DESIGN—HORIZ (48 × 27 mm): 1f. Map of coastline between St. Raphael and Genes.

367 Monaco Cathedral

1978. Europa. Monaco Views.
1345 **367** 1f. green, brown and blue 70 60
1346 – 1f.40 brown, green & bl 1·40 1·00
MS1347 170 × 143 mm. Nos. 1345/6 × 5 . . . . 18·00 18·00
DESIGN: 1f.40, View of Monaco from the east.

368 Monaco Congress Centre

1978. Precancelled.
1348 **368** 61c. orange 30 25
1349 64c. green 30 25
1350 68c. blue 30 25
1351 78c. purple 40 40
1352 83c. violet 40 40
1353 88c. orange 40 40
1354 1f.25 brown 70 60
1355 1f.30 red 70 60
1356 1f.40 green 70 60
1357 2f.10 blue . . . . 1·00 1·10
1358 2f.25 orange . . . . . 1·00 1·10
1359 2f.35 mauve . . . . . . 1·10 95

369 "Cinderella"

1978. 350th Birth Anniv of Charles Perrault (writer).
1360 **369** 5c. red, olive and violet 10 10
1361 – 25c. black, brown & mve 10 10
1362 – 30c. green, lake & brown 20 10
1363 – 80c. multicoloured . . . 40 30
1364 – 1f. red, brown and olive 60 55
1365 – 1f.40 mauve, ultramarine and blue 80 65
1366 – 1f.70 green, blue & grey 1·00 85
1367 – 1f.90 multicoloured . . . 1·40 1·10
1368 – 2f.50 blue, orange & grn 1·60 1·50
DESIGNS: 25c. "Puss in Boots"; 30c. "The Sleeping Beauty"; 80c. "Donkey's Skin"; 1f. "Little Red Riding Hood"; 1f.40, "Bluebeard"; 1f.70, "Tom Thumb"; 1f.90, "Riquet with a Tuft"; 2f.50, "The Fairies".

370 "The Sunflowers" (Van Gogh) **372** Girl with Letter

371 Afghan Hound

1978. Monte Carlo Flower Show (1979) and 125th Birth Anniv of Vincent Van Gogh. Multicoloured.
1369 1f. Type **370** . . . . . . 2·00 1·75
1370 1f.70 "The Iris" (Van Gogh) 3·00 1·90

1978. International Dog Show, Monte Carlo. Multicoloured.
1371 1f. Type **371** . . . . 2·75 1·90
1372 1f.20 Borzoi . . . . 3·25 2·50

1978. Christmas.
1373 **372** 1f. brown, blue and red 50 40

373 Catherine and William Booth

1978. Centenary of Salvation Army.
1374 **373** 1f.70 multicoloured . . . 90 85

374 Juggling Seals **376**

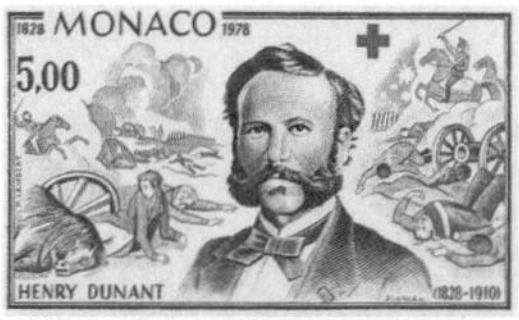

375

1978. 5th International Circus Festival, Monaco.
1375 **374** 80c. orange, black & blue 40 45
1376 – 1f. multicoloured 60 55
1377 – 1f.40 brown, mauve and bistre 90 90
1378 – 1f.90 blue, lilac and mauve . . . . 1·60 1·60
1379 – 2f.40 multicoloured . . . 2·50 1·90
DESIGNS—HORIZ: 1f.40, Horseback acrobatics; 1f.90, Musical monkeys; 2f.40, Trapeze. VERT: 1f. Lion tamer.

1978. Paintings. "Princes and Princesses of Monaco". As T **213**. Multicoloured.
1380 2f. "Prince Florestan I" (G. Dauphin) . . . . . . 1·60 1·50
1381 4f. "Princess Caroline Gilbert de la Metz" (Marie Verroust) . . . . 3·00 2·50

1978. 150th Anniv of Henri Dunant (founder of Red Cross). Sheet 100 × 130 mm.
MS1382 **375** 5f. chocolate, crimson and red . . . . 4·25 4·25

1979. 21st Birthday of Prince Albert. Sheet 80 × 105 mm.
MS1383 **376** 10f. green and brown 8·00 8·00

377 "Jongleur de Notre-Dame" (Massenet)

1979. Centenary of "Salle Garnier" (Opera House) (1st issue).
1384 **377** 1f. blue, orange & mauve 40 35
1385 – 1f.20 violet, black & turq 60 45
1386 – 1f.50 maroon, grn & turq 70 75
1387 – 1f.70 multicoloured . . . 1·25 1·40
1388 – 2f.10 turquoise and violet . . . . 1·75 1·75
1389 – 3f. multicoloured . . . . 2·50 2·40
DESIGNS—HORIZ: 1f.20, "Hans the Flute Player" (L. Ganne); 1f.50, "Don Quixote" (J. Massenet); 2f.10, "The Child and the Sorcerer" (M. Ravel); 3f. Charles Garnier (architect) and south facade of Opera House. VERT: 1f.70, "L'Aiglon" (A. Honegger and J. Ibert).
See also Nos. 1399/1404.

378 Flower, Bird and Butterfly

1979. International Year of the Child. Children's Paintings.
1390 **378** 50c. pink, green and black 25 25
1391 – 1f. slate, green and orange 40 40
1392 – 1f.20 slate, orange & mve 60 60
1393 – 1f.50 yellow, brown & bl 1·00 1·00
1394 – 1f.70 multicoloured . . . 1·25 1·25
DESIGNS: 1f. Horse and Child; 1f.20, "The Gift of Love"; 1f.50, "Peace in the World"; 1f.70, "Down with Pollution".

379 Armed Foot Messenger

1979. Europa.
1395 **379** 1f.20 brown, green & bl 60 45
1396 – 1f.50 brown, turq & bl 70 45
1397 – 1f.70 brown, green & bl 80 75
MS1398 129 × 149 mm. Nos. 1395/7, each × 2 . . . . 9·00 9·00
DESIGNS: 1f.50, 18th-cent felucca; 1f.70, Arrival of first train at Monaco.

380 "Instrumental Music" (G. Boulanger) (detail of Opera House interior)

1979. Centenary of "Salle Garnier" (Opera House) (2nd issue).
1399 – 1f. brown, orange & turq 50 40
1400 – 1f.20 multicoloured . . . 60 50
1401 – 1f.50 multicoloured . . . 1·00 80
1402 – 1f.70 blue, brown and red . . . . 1·40 1·25
1403 – 2f.10 red, violet & black 1·75 1·75
1404 **380** 3f. green, brown and light green . . . . . 2·75 2·50
DESIGNS (as Type **377**)—HORIZ: 1f. "Les Biches" (F. Poulenc); 1f.20, "The Sailors" (G. Auric); 1f.70, "Gaiete Parisienne" (J. Offenbach). VERT: 1f.50, "La Spectre de la Rose" (C. M. Weber) (after poster by Jean Cocteau); 2f.10, "Salome" (R. Strauss).

1979. Paintings. "Princes and Princesses of Monaco". As T **213**. Multicoloured.
1405 3f. "Prince Charles III" (B. Biard) . . . . 1·60 1·40
1406 4f. "Antoinette de Merode" 2·40 1·60

381 St. Pierre Claver **382** "Princess Grace" Orchid

1979. Monaco Red Cross.
1407 **381** 5f. multicoloured . . . . 2·25 2·25

1979. Monte Carlo Flora 1980.
1408 **382** 1f. multicoloured . . . . 1·75 1·40

383 "Princess Grace" Rose **384** Clown balancing on Ball

1979. Monte Carlo Flower Show.
1409 **383** 1f.20 multicoloured . . . 1·60 1·40

1979. 6th International Circus Festival.
1410 **384** 1f.20 multicoloured . . . 70 80

385 Sir Rowland Hill and Penny Black **386** Albert Einstein

1979. Death Centenary of Sir Rowland Hill.
1411 **385** 1f.70 brown, blue & blk 60 55

1979. Birth Centenary of Albert Einstein (physicist).
1412 **386** 1f.70 brown, grey and red 70 55

387 St. Patrick's Cathedral

1979. Centenary of St. Patrick's Cathedral, New York.
1413 **387** 2f.10 black, blue & brn 90 70

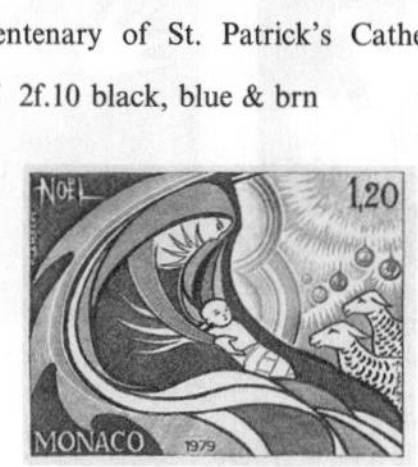

388 Nativity Scene

1979. Christmas.
1414 **388** 1f.20 blue, orange & mve 50 55

389 Early Racing Cars

1979. 50th Anniv of Grand Prix Motor Racing.
1415 **389** 1f. multicoloured 70 50

390 Arms of Charles V and Monaco

1979. 450th Anniv of Visit of Emperor Charles V.
1416 **390** 1f.50 brown, blue & blk 60 50

391 Setter and Pointer

1979. International Dog Show, Monte Carlo.
1417 **391** 1f.20 multicoloured . . . 3·00 2·50

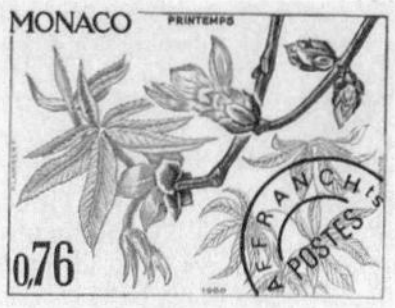

392 Spring

1980. Precancels. The Seasons.
1418 **392** 76c. brown and green . . 30 20
1419 88c. olive, emerald & grn 30 20
1420 – 99c. green and brown . . 50 30
1421 – 1f.14 green, emer & brn 30 30
1422 – 1f.60 brown, grey and deep brown 80 60
1423 – 1f.84 lake, grey & brown 80 60
1424 – 2f.65 brown, lt blue & bl 1·40 85
1425 – 3f.05 brown, bl & slate 1·40 85
DESIGNS: 99c., 1f.14, Summer; 1f.60, 1f.84, Autumn; 2f.65, 3f.05, Winter.

394 Paul P. Harris (founder) and View of Chicago

1980. 75th Anniv of Rotary International.
1434 **394** 1f.80 olive, blue & turq 80 65

395 Gymnastics

1980. Olympic Games, Moscow and Lake Placid.
1435 **395** 1f.10 blue, brown & grey 30 25
1436 – 1f.30 red, brown & blue 40 30
1437 – 1f.60 red, blue & brown 50 40
1438 – 1f.80 brown, bis & grn 60 50
1439 – 2f.30 grey, violet & mve 90 75
1440 – 4f. green, blue and brown . . . . 1·40 1·25
DESIGNS: 1f.30, Handball; 1f.60, Pistol-shooting; 1f.80, Volleyball; 2f.30, Ice hockey; 4f. Skiing.

396 Colette (novelist)

1980. Europa. Each black, green and red.
1441 1f.30 Type **396** 40 30
1442 1f.80 Marcel Pagnol (writer) 50 45
MS1443 171 × 143 mm. Nos. 1441/2, each × 5 . . . . 4·75 4·75

397 "La Source"

1980. Birth Bicentenary of Jean Ingres (artist).
1444 **397** 4f. multicoloured . . . . 5·00 3·75

398 Montaigne

399 Guillaume Apollinaire (after G. Pieret)

1980. 400th Anniv of Publication of Montaigne's "Essays".
1445 **398** 1f.30 black, red and blue 55 40

1980. Birth Centenary of Guillaume Apollinaire (poet).
1446 **399** 1f.10 brown 55 40

400 Congress Centre

1980. Kiwanis International European Convention.
1447 **400** 1f.30 black, blue and red 55 40

401 Honore II Silver Ecu, 1649

1980. Numismatics.
1448 **401** 1f.50 black and blue . . 60 55

402 Lhassa Apso and Shih Tzu

1980. International Dog Show, Monte Carlo.
1449 **402** 1f.30 multicoloured . . . 3·50 2·75

403 "The Princess and the Pea"

1980. 175th Birth Anniv of Hans Christian Andersen.
1450 **403** 70c. sepia, red and brown 30 25
1451 – 1f.30 blue, turq & red . . 40 45
1452 – 1f.50 black, blue & turq 70 65
1453 – 1f.60 red, black & brown 80 80
1454 – 1f.80 yellow, brn & turq 1·00 1·00
1455 – 2f.30 brown, pur & vio 1·40 1·25
DESIGNS: 1f.30, "The Little Mermaid"; 1f.50, "The Chimneysweep and Shepherdess"; 1f.60, "The Brave Little Lead Soldier"; 1f.80, "The Little Match Girl"; 2f.30, "The Nightingale".

404 "The Road" (M. Vlaminck)

1980. 75th Anniv of 1905 Autumn Art Exhibition. Multicoloured.
1456 2f. Type **404** . . . . 1·50 1·25
1457 3f. "Woman at Balustrade" (Van Dongen) . . . . . 2·50 1·25
1458 4f. "The Reader" (Henri Matisse) . . . . 3·00 3·00
1459 5f. "Three Figures in a Meadow" (A. Derain) . . 4·50 3·75

1980. Paintings. "Princes and Princesses of Monaco". As T **213**. Multicoloured.
1460 4f. "Prince Albert I" (L. Bonnat) . . . . . . 2·00 1·75
1461 4f. "Princess Marie Alice Heine" (L. Maeterlinck) 2·00 1·75

405 "Sunbirds"

1980. Monaco Red Cross.
1462 **405** 6f. red, bistre and brown 2·50 2·50

406 "MONACO" balanced on Tightrope

1980. 7th International Circus Festival, Monaco.
1463 **406** 1f.30 red, turquoise & blue . . . . 1·40 85

407 Children and Nativity

1980. Christmas.
1464 **407** 1f.10 blue, carmine and red 45 40
1465 2f.30 violet, orange and pink 95 60

1980. Monte Carlo Flower Show, 1981. As T **383**. Multicoloured.
1466 1f.30 "Princess Stephanie" rose 80 60
1467 1f.80 Ikebana . . . . 1·50 1·00

408 "Alcyonium"

409 Fish with Hand for Tail

1980. Marine Fauna. Multicoloured.
1468 5c. "Spirographis spallanzanli" 10 10
1469 10c. "Anemonia sulcata" . . 10 10
1470 15c. "Leptopsammia pruvoit" 10 10
1471 20c. "Pteroides" 10 20
1472 30c. "Paramuricea clavata" (horiz) 30 20
1473 40c. Type **408** 30 20
1474 50c. "Corallium rubrum" . . 40 30
1475 60c. Trunculus murex ("Calliactis parasitica") (horiz) 70 65
1476 70c. "Cerianthus membranaceus" (horiz) 90 80
1477 1f. "Actinia equina" (horiz) 1·00 80
1478 2f. "Protula" (horiz) . . . . 2·00 1·10

1981. "Respect the Sea".
1479 **409** 1f.20 multicoloured . . . 70 55

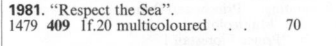

410 Prince Rainier and Princess Grace

1981. Royal Silver Wedding.
1480 **410** 1f.20 black and green . . 1·00 75
1481 1f.40 black and red . . . 1·40 1·25
1482 1f.70 black and green . . 1·60 1·40
1483 1f.80 black and brown 2·00 1·60
1484 2f. black and blue . . . 3·25 1·90

411 Mozart (after Lorenz Vogel)

412 Palm Cross

1981. 225th Birth Anniv of Wolfgang Amadeus Mozart (composer).
1485 **411** 2f. brown, dp brown & bl . . . . 1·25 85
1486 – 2f.50 blue, brn & dp brn 1·75 1·40
1487 – 3f.50 dp brown, bl & brn 2·75 1·75
DESIGNS—HORIZ: 2f.50, "Mozart at 7 with his Father and Sister" (engraving by Delafoose after drawing by Carmontelle); 3f.50 "Mozart directing Requiem two Days before his Death" (painting by Baude).

1981. Europa. Multicoloured.
1488 **412** 1f.40 green, brown & red 50 40
1489 – 2f. multicoloured 60 55
MS1490 171 × 143 mm. Nos. 1488/9, each × 5 . . . .
DESIGN: 2f. Children carrying palm crosses.

413 Paris Football Stadium, Cup and Footballer

1981. 25th Anniv of European Football Cup.
1491 **413** 2f. black and blue . . . 95 70

414 I.Y.D.P. Emblem and Girl in Wheelchair

1981. International Year of Disabled Persons.
1492 **414** 1f.40 blue and green . . 70 55

415 Palace flying Old Flag, National Flag and Monte Carlo

1981. Centenary of National Flag.
1493 **415** 2f. red, blue and brown 90 65

416 Oceanographic Institute, Paris and Oceanographic Museum, Monaco

1981. 75th Anniv of Oceanographic Institute.
1494 **416** 1f.20 blue, black & brn 60 60

417 Bureau Building and "Faddey Bellingshausen" (hydrographic research ship)

1981. 50th Anniv of Int Hydrographic Bureau.
1495 **417** 2f.50 sepia, brown and light brown . . . . . 1·40 1·25

418 Rough Collies and Shetland Sheepdogs

1981. International Dog Show, Monte Carlo.
1496 **418** 1f.40 multicoloured . . . 3·50 3·25

419 Rainier III and Prince Albert

421 Arctic Scene and Map

1981. (a) 23 × 28 mm.
1497 **419** 1f.40 green (postage) . . 70 20
1498 1f.60 red 95 15
1499 1f.60 green 50 20
1500 1f.70 green 80 25
1501 1f.80 red 60 40
1502 1f.80 green 70 20
1503 1f.90 green . . . . . . 1·40 50
1504 2f. red . . . . 1·25 40
1505 2f. green 85 25
1506 2f.10 red 90 25
1507 2f.20 red 80 40
1508 2f.30 blue . . . . . . 2·75 2·40
1509 2f.50 brown . . . . . 1·00 60
1510 2f.60 blue . . . . . . 1·90 1·75
1511 2f.80 blue . . . . . . 1·75 1·50
1512 3f. blue . . . . . . 1·75 1·25
1513 3f.20 blue . . . . . . 1·75 1·75
1514 3f.40 blue . . . . . . 2·75 1·60
1515 3f.60 blue . . . . . . 1·75 1·25
1516 4f. brown . . . . . . 1·40 75
1517 5f.50 black . . . . . 1·90 1·40
1518 10f. purple . . . . . 2·75 1·10
1519 15f. green . . . . . . 6·50 1·75
1520 20f. blue . . . . . . 6·50 2·50

(b) 36 × 27 mm.
1521 – 5f. violet (air) . . . . . . 1·60 75
1522 – 10f. red . . . . 3·75 1·50
1523 – 15f. green . . . . 5·00 1·60
1524 – 20f. blue . . . . 6·00 3·00
1525 – 30f. brown . . . . 8·00 4·00
DESIGN: Nos. 1521/5, Double portrait and monograms.

1981. 1st International Congress on Discovery and History of Northern Polar Regions, Rome.
1530 **421** 1f.50 multicoloured . . . 1·25 95

1981. Paintings. "Princes and Princesses of Monaco". Vert designs as T **213**. Multicoloured.
1531 3f. "Prince Louis II" (P.-A. de Laszlo) . . . . . . 1·60 1·00
1532 5f. "Princess Charlotte" (P.-A. de Laszlo) . . . . . . 3·25 1·90

422 Hercules fighting the Nemean Lion

1981. Monaco Red Cross. The Twelve Labours of Hercules (1st series).
1533 **422** 2f.50+50c. green, brown and red . . . . 1·00 1·25
1534 – 3f.50+50c. blue, green and red . . . . 1·25 1·25
DESIGN: 3f.50, Slaying the Hydra of Lerna.
See also Nos. 1584/5, 1631/2, 1699/1700, 1761/2 and 1794/5.

423 Ettore Bugatti (racing car designer) (Cent)

424 Eglantines and Morning Glory

1981. Birth Anniversaries.
1535 **423** 1f. indigo, blue and red 80 50
1536 – 2f. black, blue and brown 80 75
1537 – 2f.50 brown, black and red 1·10 80
1538 – 4f. multicoloured 2·50 2·40
1539 – 4f. multicoloured 2·50 2·40
DESIGNS: No. 1536, George Bernard Shaw (dramatist, 125th anniv); 1537, Fernand Leger (painter, centenary). LARGER: (37 × 48 mm): 1538, Pablo Picasso (self-portrait) (centenary); 1539, Rembrandt (self-portrait) (375th anniv).

1981. Monte Carlo Flower Show (1982). Mult.
1540 1f.40 Type **424** 1·00 75
1541 2f. "Ikebana" (painting by Ikenobo) 1·75 1·40

425 "Catherine Deneuve"

426 Tiger, Clown, Acrobat and Elephants

1981. 1st International Rose Show, Monte Carlo.
1542 **425** 1f.80 multicoloured 2·50 1·90

1981. 8th International Circus Festival, Monaco.
1543 **426** 1f.40 violet, mauve & blk 1·90 1·50

427 Praying Children and Nativity

1981. Christmas.
1544 **427** 1f.20 blue, mauve & brn 50 50

428 "Lancia-Stratos" Rally Car

1981. 50th Monte Carlo Rally (1982).
1545 **428** 1f. blue, red & turquoise 90 80

429 Spring

1981. Seasons of the Persimmon Tree. Sheet 143 × 100 mm containing T **429** and similar horiz designs.
MS1546 1f. green, yellow and blue (T **429**); 2f. green and blue (Summer); 3f. red, brown and yellow (Autumn); 4f. brown and red (Winter) 6·75 6·75

430 "Hoya bella"

431 Spring

1981. Plants in Exotic Garden. Multicoloured.
1547 1f.40 Type **430** 2·50 1·40
1548 1f.60 "Bolivicereus samaipatanus" 2·00 1·25
1549 1f.80 "Trichocereus grandiflorus" (horiz) 2·50 1·50
1550 2f. "Argyroderma roseum" 1·25 40
1551 2f.30 "Euphorbia milii" 2·00 1·75
1552 2f.60 "Echinocereus fitchii" (horiz) 2·00 1·75
1553 2f.90 "Rebutia heliosa" (horiz) 2·00 1·90
1554 4f.10 "Echinopsis multiplex cristata" (horiz) 3·00 2·50

1982. Precancels. The Seasons of the Peach Tree.
1555 **431** 97c. mauve and green 30 20
1556 – 1f.25 green, orge & mve 50 30
1557 – 2f.03 brown 80 60
1558 – 3f.36 brown and blue 1·40 90
DESIGNS: 1f.25, Summer; 2f.03, Autumn; 3f.36, Winter.

432 Common Nutcracker

433 Capture of Monaco Fortress, 1297

1982. Birds from Mercantour National Park.
1559 **432** 60c. black, brown & grn 60 70
1560 – 70c. black and mauve 70 70
1561 – 80c. red, black & orange 80 80
1562 – 90c. black, red and blue 1·40 1·25
1563 – 1f.40 brown, black & red 2·40 1·75
1564 – 1f.60 brown, black & blue 2·75 2·10
DESIGNS—VERT: 70c. Black grouse; 80c. Rock partridge; 1f.60, Golden eagle. HORIZ: 90c. Wallcreeper; 1f.40, Rock ptarmigan.

1982. Europa.
1565 **433** 1f.60 blue, brown and red 50 40
1566 – 2f.30 blue, brown and red 70 45
MS1567 173 × 143 mm. Nos. 1565/6, each × 5 6·50 6·50
DESIGN: 2f.30, Signing the Treaty of Peronne, 1641.

434 Old Quarter

1982. Fontvieille.
1568 **434** 1f.40 blue, brown & grn 60 40
1569 – 1f.60 light brown, brown and red 70 60
1570 – 2f.30 purple 1·25 80
DESIGNS: 1f.60, Land reclamation; 2f.30, Urban development.

435 Stadium

1982. Fontvieille Sports Stadium (1st series).
1571 **435** 2f.30 green, brown & blue 1·00 80
See also No. 1616.

436 Arms of Paris

1982. "Philexfrance" International Stamp Exhibition, Paris.
1572 **436** 1f.40 red, grey and deep red 70 60

437 Old English Sheepdog

1982. International Dog Show, Monte Carlo. Multicoloured.
1573 60c. Type **437** 2·00 1·50
1574 1f. Briard 2·50 1·90

438 Monaco Cathedral and Arms

1982. Creation of Archbishopric of Monaco (1981).
1575 **438** 1f.60 black, blue and red 60 60

439 St. Francis of Assisi

440 Dr. Robert Koch

1982. 800th Birth Anniv of St. Francis of Assisi.
1576 **439** 1f.40 grey and light grey 70 65

1982. Centenary of Discovery of Tubercle Bacillus.
1577 **440** 1f.40 purple and lilac 70 70

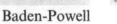

441 Lord Baden-Powell

443 St. Hubert (18th-century medallion)

442 Running for Ball

1982. 125th Birth Anniv of Lord Baden-Powell (founder of Boy Scout Movement).
1578 **441** 1f.60 brown and black 1·00 90

1982. World Cup Football Championship, Spain. Sheet 143 × 120 mm containing T **442** and similar square designs, each brown, blue and green.
MS1579 1f. Type **442**; 2f. Kicking ball; 3f. Heading ball; 4f. Goalkeeper 6·60 6·50

1982. 29th Meeting of International Hunting Council, Monte Carlo.
1580 **443** 1f.60 multicoloured 90 75

444 Books, Reader and Globe

1982. International Bibliophile Association General Assembly, Monte Carlo.
1581 **444** 1f.60 blue, purple & red 60 55

445 "Casino, 1870"

1982. Monaco in the "Belle Epoque" (1st series). Paintings by Hubert Clerissi. Multicoloured.
1582 3f. Type **445** 1·25 1·10
1583 5f. "Porte d'Honneur, Royal Palace, 1893" 2·50 1·60
See also Nos. 1629/30, 1701/2, 1763/4, 1801/2, 1851/2, 1889/90 and 1965/6.

1982. Monaco Red Cross. The Twelve Labours of Hercules (2nd series). As T **422**.
1584 2f.50+50c. green, red and bright red 1·25 1·40
1585 3f.50+50c. brown, blue and red 1·40 1·50
DESIGNS: 2f.50, Capturing the Erymanthine Boar; 3f.50, Shooting the Stymphalian Birds.

446 Nicolo Paganini (violinist and composer, bicent)

447 Vase of Flowers

1982. Birth Anniversaries.
1586 **446** 1f.60 brown and purple 90 60
1587 – 1f.80 red, mauve & brn 1·25 80
1588 – 2f.60 green and red 1·40 1·25
1589 – 4f. multicoloured 2·75 2·40
1590 – 4f. multicoloured 2·75 2·40
DESIGNS—VERT: No. 1587, Anna Pavlova (ballerina, centenary); 1588, Igor Stravinsky (composer, centenary). HORIZ (47 × 36 mm): 1589, "In a Boat" (Edouard Manet, 150th anniv); 1590, "The Black Fish" (Georges Braque, centenary).

1982. Monte Carlo Flower Show (1983). Mult.
1591 1f.60 Type **447** 1·40 90
1592 2f.60 Ikebana arrangement 1·75 1·50

448 Bowl of Flowers

449 The Three Kings

1982.
1593 **448** 1f.60 multicoloured 1·40 90

1982. Christmas.
1594 **449** 1f.60 green, blue & orge 50 35
1595 – 1f.80 green, blue & orge 60 35
1596 – 2f.60 green, blue & orge 90 50
MS1597 143 × 105 mm. Nos. 1594/6 2·50 2·50
DESIGNS: 1f.80, The Holy Family; 2f.60, Shepherds and angels.

450 Prince Albert I and Polar Scene

1982. Centenary of First International Polar Year.
1598 **450** 1f.60 brown, green & bl 1·75 1·40

451 Viking Longships off Greenland

1982. Millenary of Discovery of Greenland by Erik the Red.
1599 **451** 1f.60 blue, brown & blk 1·75 1·40

452 Julius Caesar in the Port of Monaco ("Aeneid", Book VI)

1982. 2000th Death Anniv of Virgil (poet).
1600 **452** 1f.80 deep blue, blue and brown . . . . 1·75 1·40

453 Spring **454** Tourism

1983. Precancels. The Seasons of the Apple Tree.
1601 **453** 1f.05 purple, green and yellow 40 50
1602 – 1f.35 light green, deep green and turquoise . . . 50 55
1603 – 2f.19 red, brown & grey 1·00 1·10
1604 – 3f.63 yellow and brown 1·60 1·50
DESIGNS: 1f.35, Summer; 2f.19, Autumn; 3f.63, Winter.

1983. 50th Anniv of Exotic Garden. Mult.
1605 1f.80 Type **454** 90 85
1606 2f. Cactus plants (botanical collections) . . . . 1·25 80
1607 2f.30 Cactus plants (international flower shows) . . . . 1·40 1·40
1608 2f.60 Observatory grotto (horiz) . . . . 1·75 1·50
1609 3f.30 Museum of Prehistoric Anthropology (horiz) . . 2·25 2·00

455 Alaskan Malamute **456** Princess Grace

1983. International Dog Show, Monte Carlo.
1610 **455** 1f.80 multicoloured . . . 4·50 3·75

1983. Princess Grace Commemoration. Sheet 105 × 143 mm.
MS1611 **456** 10f. black . . . . . 7·00 7·00

457 St. Charles Borromee and Church

1983. Centenary of St. Charles Church, Monte Carlo.
1612 **457** 2f.60 deep blue, blue and green 95 80

458 Montgolfier Balloon, 1783 **459** Franciscan College

1983. Europa.
1613 **458** 1f.80 blue, brown & grey 50 35
1614 – 2f.60 grey, blue & brown 70 60
MS1615 170 × 143 mm. Nos. 1613/14, each × 5 . . . . 7·25 7·25
DESIGN: 2f.60, Space shuttle.

1983. Centenary of Franciscan College, Monte Carlo.
1616 **459** 2f. grey, brown and red 70 60

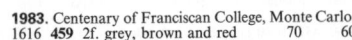

460 Stadium

1983. Fontvieille Sports Stadium (2nd series).
1617 **460** 2f. green, blue and brown 70 55

461 Early and Modern Cars

1983. Centenary of Petrol-driven Motor Car.
1618 **461** 2f.90 blue, brown & green . . . . 2·00 1·40

462 Blue Whale

1983. International Commission for the Protection of Whales.
1619 **462** 3f.30 blue, light blue and grey . . . . 2·75 2·50

463 Dish Aerial, Pigeon, W.C.Y. Emblem and Satellite

1983. World Communications Year.
1620 **463** 4f. lilac and mauve . . . 1·25 1·10

464 Smoking Moor **466** Circus Performers

465 Johannes Brahms (composer)

1983. Nineteenth Century Automata from the Galea Collection. Multicoloured.
1621 50c. Type **464** 20 20
1622 60c. Clown with diabolo . . 20 20
1623 70c. Smoking monkey . . . 20 20
1624 80c. Peasant with pig . . . 40 40
1625 90c. Buffalo Bill smoking 50 45
1626 1f. Snake charmer 50 45
1627 1f.50 Pianist 80 60
1628 2f. Young girl powdering herself . . . . 1·25 1·00

1983. Monaco in the "Belle Epoque" (2nd series). As T **445**. Multicoloured.
1629 3f. "The Beach, 1902" . . . 2·00 1·60
1630 5f. "Cafe de Paris, 1905" . . 3·25 2·75

1983. Monaco Red Cross. The Twelve Labours of Hercules (3rd series). As T **422**.
1631 2f.50+50c. brn, bl & red . . 1·25 1·00
1632 3f.50+50c. violet, mve & red 1·40 1·25
DESIGNS: 2f.50, Capturing the Hind of Ceryneia; 3f.50, Cleaning the Augean stables.

1983. Birth Anniversaries.
1633 **465** 3f. deep brown, brown and green . . . . . 1·00 80
1634 – 3f. black, brown and red 1·00 80
1635 – 4f. multicoloured . . . . 2·25 1·90
1636 – 4f. multicoloured . . . . 2·25 1·90

DESIGNS—HORIZ: No. 1633, Type **465** (150th anniv); 1634, Giacomo Puccini (composer) and scene from "Madame Butterfly" (125th anniv). VERT (37 × 48 mm): 1635, "Portrait of a Young Man" (Raphael (artist), 500th anniv); 1636, "Cottin Passage" (Utrillo (artist), centenary).

1983. 9th International Circus Festival, Monaco.
1637 **466** 2f. blue, red and green 1·40 1·25

467 Bouquet **468** Provencale Creche

1983. Monte Carlo Flower Show (1984). Mult.
1638 1f.60 Type **467** . . . . . . 1·00 70
1639 2f.60 Arrangement of poppies . . . . 1·50 1·10

1983. Christmas.
1640 **468** 2f. multicoloured . . . . 1·10 70

469 Nobel Literature Prize Medal

1983. 150th Birth Anniv of Alfred Nobel (inventor of dynamite and founder of Nobel Prizes).
1641 **469** 2f. black, grey and red 90 80

470 O. F. Ozanam (founder) and Paris Headquarters

1983. 150th Anniv of Society of St. Vincent de Paul.
1642 **470** 1f.80 violet and purple 70 50

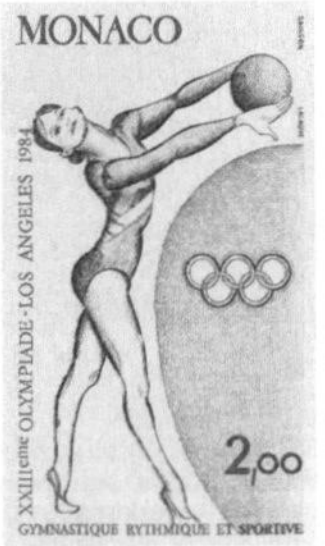

471 "Tazerka" (oil rig) **473** Gymnast will Ball

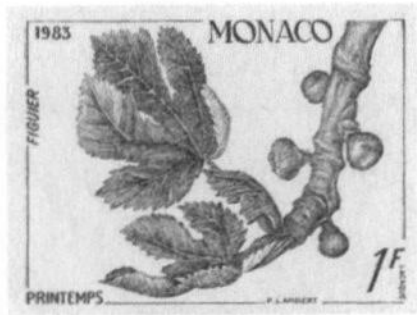

472 Spring

1983. Oil Industry.
1643 **471** 5f. blue, brown & turq 1·75 1·25

1983. Seasons of the Fig. Sheet 143 × 100 mm containing T **472** and similar horiz designs.
MS1644 1f. green (Type **472**); 2f. green, yellow and red (Summer); 3f. green and (Autumn); 4f. green and red (Winter) . . . . . . 6·75 65

1984. Olympic Games, Los Angeles. Sheet 161 × 143 mm containing T **473** and similar vert designs, each brown, slate and red.
MS1645 2f. Type **473**; 3f. Gymnast with clubs; 4f. Gymnast with ribbon; 5f. Gymnast with hoop 6·25 6·25

474 Skater and Stadium

1984. Winter Olympic Games, Sarajevo.
1646 **474** 2f. blue, green and turquoise 70 55
1647 – 4f. blue, violet and purple . . . . 1·40 1·00
DESIGN: 4f. Skater and snowflake.

475 Bridge

1984. Europa. 25th Anniv of European Post and Telecommunications Conference.
1648 **475** 2f. blue 70 50
1649 3f. green . . . . 1·10 95
MS1650 143 × 170 mm. Nos. 1648/9, each × 4 . . . . 6·25 6·25

476 Balkan Fritillary **478** Sanctuary and Statue of Virgin

477 Auvergne Pointer

1984. Butterflies and Moths in Mercantour National Park. Multicoloured.
1651 1f.60 Type **476** . . . . . 1·00 1·00
1652 2f. "Zygaena vesubiana" . . 1·50 1·10
1653 2f.80 False mnestra ringlet 1·60 1·40
1654 3f. Small apollo (horiz) . . 1·90 1·60
1655 3f.60 Southern swallowtail (horiz) . . . . 2·75 1·90

1984. International Dog Show, Monte Carlo.
1656 **477** 1f.60 multicoloured . . . 2·50 1·75

1984. Our Lady of Laghet Sanctuary.
1657 **478** 2f. blue, brown and green 70 45

479 Piccard's Stratosphere Balloon "F.N.R.S." **481** Place de la Visitation

480 Concert

1984. Birth Centenary of Auguste Piccard (physicist).
1658 **479** 2f.80 black, green & blue 80 55
1659 – 4f. blue, green & turq . . 1·25 80
DESIGN: 4f. Bathyscaphe.

1984. 25th Anniv of Palace Concerts.
1660 **480** 3f.60 blue and deep blue 1·25 80

1984. Bygone Monaco (1st series). Paintings by Hubert Clerissi.
1661 **481** 5c. brown 10 10
1662 – 10c. red 10 10
1663 – 15c. violet 10 10
1664 – 20c. blue 10 10
1665 – 30c. blue 10 10
1666 – 40c. green 40 20
1667 – 50c. red 10 10
1668 – 60c. blue 10 10
1669 – 70c. orange 50 35
1670 – 80c. green 20 20
1671 – 90c. mauve 30 25
1672 – 1f. blue 30 20
1673 – 2f. black 60 40
1674 – 3f. red . . . . 1·75 80
1675 – 4f. blue . . . . 1·40 75
1676 – 5f. green . . . . 1·40 75
1677 – 6f. green . . . . 2·10 1·10
DESIGNS: 10c. Town Hall; 15c. Rue Basse; 20c. Place Saint-Nicolas; 30c. Quai du Commerce; 40c. Rue des Iris; 50c. Ships in harbour; 60c. St. Charles's Church; 70c. Religious procession; 80c. Olive tree overlooking harbour; 90c. Quayside; 1f. Palace Square; 2f. Fishing boats in harbour; 3f. Bandstand; 4f. Railway station; 5f. Mail coach; 6f. Monte Carlo Opera House.
See also Nos. 2015/27.

482 Spring

1984. Precancels. The Seasons of the Quince.
1678 **482** 1f.14 red and green . . . 40 50
1679 – 1f.47 deep green & green 60 55
1680 – 2f.38 olive, turquoise and green . . . . 1·00 1·00
1681 – 3f.95 green . . . . . . 1·75 1·50
DESIGNS: 1f.47, Summer; 2f.38, Autumn; 3f.95, Winter.

483 Shepherd **485** Bowl of Mixed Flowers

484 Gargantua and Cattle

1984. Christmas. Crib Figures from Provence. Multicoloured.
1682 70c. Type **483** 30 20
1683 1f. Blind man 40 30
1684 1f.70 Happy man 70 50
1685 2f. Spinner 80 70
1686 2f.10 Angel playing trumpet 90 1·10
1687 2f.40 Garlic seller . . . . . 1·10 1·25
1688 3f. Drummer . . . . 1·25 1·25
1689 3f.70 Knife grinder . . . . 1·50 1·25
1690 4f. Elderly couple . . . . . 1·90 1·60

1984. 450th Anniv of First Edition of "Gargantua" by Francois Rabelais.
1691 **484** 2f. black, red and brown 70 50
1692 – 2f. black, red and blue 70 50
1693 – 4f. green . . . . 1·40 1·25
DESIGNS—As T **484**: No. 1692, Panurge's sheep. 36 × 48 mm: 1693, Francois Rabelais.

1984. Monte Carlo Flower Show (1985). Mult.
1694 2f.10 Type **485** . . . . . . 1·00 80
1695 3f. Ikebana arrangement . . 1·60 1·10

486 Television Lights and Emblem

1984. 25th Int Television Festival, Monte Carlo.
1696 **486** 2f.10 blue, grey and mauve 70 55
1697 – 3f. grey, blue and red . . 1·00 80
DESIGN: 3f. "Golden Nymph" (Grand Prix).

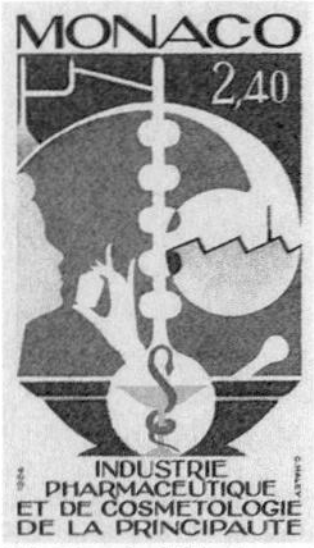

487 Chemical Equipment **488** Clown

1984. Pharmaceutical and Cosmetics Industry.
1698 **487** 2f.40 blue, deep blue and green 80 50

1984. Monaco Red Cross. The Twelve Labours of Hercules (4th series). As T **422**.
1699 3f.+50c. brown, light brown and red . . . . 1·00 1·25
1700 4f.+50c. green, brown and red . . . . 1·40 1·50
DESIGNS: 3f. Killing the Cretan bull; 4f. Capturing the Mares of Diomedes.

1984. Monaco in the "Belle Epoque" (3rd series). Paintings by Hubert Clerissi. As T **445**. Mult.
1701 4f. "Grimaldi Street, 1908" (vert) . . . . 2·25 1·90
1702 5f. "Railway Station, 1910" (vert) . . . . 3·50 2·75

489 "Woman with Chinese Vase"

1984. 150th Birth Anniv of Edgar Degas (artist).
1704 **489** 6f. multicoloured . . . . 3·50 2·50

490 Spring

1985. Precancels. Seasons of the Cherry.
1705 **490** 1f.22 olive, green and blue 40 50
1706 – 1f.57 red, green and yellow 60 55
1707 – 2f.55 orange and brown 1·10 1·10
1708 – 4f.23 purple, green and blue . . . . 1·75 1·60
DESIGNS: 1f.57, Summer; 2f.55, Autumn; 4f.23, Winter.

491 First Stamp

1985. Centenary of First Monaco Stamps.
1709 **491** 1f.70 green 60 40
1710 2f.10 red 70 20
1711 3f. blue . . . . 1·25 65

493 "Berardia subacaulis" **495** Nadia Boulanger (composer)

494 Spring

1985. Flowers in Mercantour National Park. Mult.
1724 1f.70 Type **493** 60 45
1725 2f.10 "Saxifraga florulenta" (vert) 70 55
1726 2f.40 "Fritillaria moggridgei" (vert) . . . . 1·00 75
1727 3f. "Sempervivum allionii" (vert) . . . . 1·25 1·10
1728 3f.60 "Silene cordifolia" (vert) . . . . 1·60 1·25
1729 4f. "Primula allionii" . . . 1·95 1·60

1985. Seasons of the Japanese Medlar. Sheet 144 × 100 mm containing T **494** and similar horiz designs.
MS1730 1f. olive and deep olive (Type **494**); 2f. olive, yellow and deep olive (Summer); 3f. olive and deep olive (Autumn); 4f. orange, yellow and olive (Winter) . . . 6·75 6·75

1985. 25th Anniv of First Musical Composition Competition.
1731 **495** 1f.70 brown 70 50
1732 – 2f.10 blue 90 90
DESIGN: 2f.10, Georges Auric (composer).

496 Stadium and Runners

1985. Inauguration of Louis II Stadium, Fontvieille, and Athletics and Swimming Championships.
1733 **496** 1f.70 brown, red and violet 50 40
1734 – 2f.10 blue, brown and green 85 50
DESIGN: 2f.10, Stadium and swimmers.

497 Prince Antoine I

1985. Europa.
1735 **497** 2f.10 blue 70 50
1736 – 3f. red 90 85
MS1737 170 × 143 mm. Nos. 1735/6, each × 5 . . . . 9·25 9·25
DESIGN: 3f. John-Baptiste Lully (composer).

498 Museum, "Hirondelle I" (schooner) and "Denise" (midget submarine)

1985. 75th Anniv of Oceanographic Museum.
1738 **498** 2f.10 black, green and blue 70 65

499 Boxer

1985. International Dog Show, Monte Carlo.
1739 **499** 2f.10 multicoloured . . . 1·90 1·50

500 Scientific Motifs

1985. 25th Anniv of Scientific Centre.
1740 **500** 3f. blue, black and violet 1·00 70

501 Children and Hands holding Seedling and Emblem

1985. International Youth Year.
1741 **501** 3f. brown, green and light brown . . . . . 1·00 70

502 Regal Angelfish **503** Catamaran

1985. Fishes in Oceanographic Museum Aquarium (1st series). Multicoloured.
1742 1f.80 Type **502** 90 80
1743 1f.90 Type **502** . . . . . . 1·50 80
1744 2f.20 Powder blue surgeonfish 90 75
1745 3f.20 Red-tailed butterflyfish 1·25 1·25
1746 3f.40 As No. 1745 . . . . . 2·75 1·90
1747 3f.90 Clown triggerfish . . . 1·90 1·75
1748 7f. Fishes in aquarium (36 × 48 mm) . . . . . . 3·25 2·75
See also Nos. 1857/62.

1985. Monaco–New York Sailing Race. Sheet 143 × 105 mm containing T **503** and similar vert designs. Each black, blue and turquoise.
MS1749 4f. Type **503**; 4f. Single hull yacht; 4f. Trimaran . . . . . 5·00 5·00

504 Rome Buildings and Emblem

1985. "Italia '85" International Stamp Exhibition, Rome.
1750 **504** 4f. black, green and red 1·25 85

505 Clown **506** Decorations

1985. 11th International Circus Festival, Monaco.
1751 **505** 1f.80 multicoloured . . . 1·25 85

1985. Christmas.
1752 **506** 2f.20 multicoloured . . . 80 45

507 Ship and Marine Life
508 Arrangement of Roses, Tulips and Jonquil

1985. Fish Processing Industry.
1753 **507** 2f.20 blue, turquoise and brown 70 45

1985. Monte Carlo Flower Show (1986). Mult.
1754 2f.20 Type **508** 90 80
1755 3f.20 Arrangement of chrysanthemums and heather . . . . 1·50 1·40

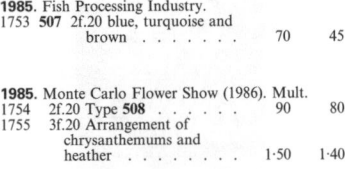

509 Globe and Satellite

1985. European Telecommunications Satellite Organization.
1756 **509** 3f. black, blue and violet 1·00 1·00

510 Sacha Guitry (actor, centenary)

1985. Birth Anniversaries.
1757 **510** 3f. orange and brown . . 1·00 95
1758 – 4f. blue, brown and mauve . . . . 1·25 1·10
1759 – 5f. turquoise, blue and grey . . . . 1·50 1·25
1760 – 6f. blue, brown and black . . . . 1·90 1·50
DESIGNS: 4f. Wilhelm and Jacob Grimm (folklorists, bicentenaries); 5f. Frederic Chopin and Robert Schumann (composers, 175th annivs); 6f. Johann Sebastian Bach and Georg Friedrich Handel (composers, 300th annivs).

1985. Monaco Red Cross. The Twelve Labours of Hercules (5th series). As T **422**.
1761 3f.+70c. green, deep red and red . . . . 1·00 90
1762 4f.+80c. brown, blue & red 1·25 1·25
DESIGNS: 3f. The Cattle of Geryon; 4f. The Girdle of Hippolyte.

1985. Monaco in the "Belle Epoque" (4th series). As T **445**, showing paintings by Hubert Clerissi. Multicoloured.
1763 4f. "Port of Monaco, 1912" 2·00 1·25
1764 6f. "Avenue de la Gare 1920" . . . . 2·50 2·00

511 Prince Charles III
512 Spring

1985. Centenary of First Monaco Stamps (2nd issue). Sheet 142 × 71 mm containing T **511** and similar vert designs. Each blue and black.
MS1765 5f. Type **511**; 5f. Prince Albert I; 5f. Prince Louis II; 5f. Prince Rainier III . . . . . . 6·25 6·25

1986. Precancels. Seasons of the Hazel Tree.
1766 **512** 1f.28 brown, green & bl 40 50
1767 – 1f.65 green, brown & yell 60 55
1768 – 2f.67 grey, brown and deep brown . . . . 1·00 1·10
1769 – 4f.44 green and brown 1·60 1·60
DESIGNS: 1f.65, Summer; 2f.67, Autumn; 4f.44, Winter.

513 Ancient Monaco

1986. 10th Anniv of "Annales Monegasques" (historical review).
1770 **513** 2f.20 grey, blue and brown 70 45

514 Scotch Terriers

1986. International Dog Show, Monte Carlo.
1771 **514** 1f.80 multicoloured . . . 3·00 2·10

515 Mouflon

1986. Mammals in Mercantour National Park. Multicoloured.
1772 2f.20 Type **515** 80 40
1773 2f.50 Ibex 90 60
1774 3f.20 Chamois . . . . . . 1·25 1·00
1775 3f.90 Alpine marmot (vert) 1·90 1·25
1776 5f. Arctic hare (vert) . . . . 2·25 1·75
1777 7f.20 Stoat (vert) . . . . . 2·75 2·25

516 Research Vessel "Ramoge"

1986. Europa. Each green, blue and red.
1778 2f.20 Type **516** 70 50
1779 3f.20 Underwater nature reserve, Larvotto beach 1·10 75
MS1780 171 × 144 mm. Nos. 1778/79, each × 5 . . . . 10·00 10·00

517 Prince Albert I and National Council Building

1986. Anniversaries and Events.
1781 **517** 2f.50 brown and green 80 80
1782 – 3f.20 brown, red and black . . . . 1·40 1·25
1783 – 3f.90 purple and red . . 1·75 1·75
1784 – 5f. green, red and blue 1·60 1·50
DESIGNS—HORIZ: 2f.50, Type **517** (75th anniv of First Constitution); 3f.20, Serge Diaghilev and dancers (creation of new Monte Carlo ballet company); 3f.90, Henri Rougier and Turcat-Mery car (75th Anniv of first Monte Carlo Rally). VERT: 5f. Flags and Statue of Liberty (centenary).

518 Chicago and Flags

1986. "Ameripex '86" International Stamp Exhibition, Chicago.
1785 **518** 5f. black, red and blue 1·60 1·10

519 Player and Mayan Figure

1986. World Cup Football Championship, Mexico. Sheet 100 × 143 mm containing T **519** and similar vert design. Each black, red and blue.
MS1786 5f. Type **519**; 7f. Goalkeeper and Mayan figures 5·75 5·75

520 Comet, Telescopes and 1532 Chart by Apian

1986. Appearance of Halley's Comet.
1787 **520** 10f. blue, brown & green 3·00 2·50

521 Monte Carlo and Congress Centre

1986. 30th International Insurance Congress.
1788 **521** 3f.20 blue, brown & grn 1·00 80

522 Christmas Tree Branch and Holly
523 Clown's Face and Elephant on Ball

1986. Christmas. Multicoloured.
1789 1f.80 Type **522** 60 25
1790 2f.50 Christmas tree branch and poinsettia 80 40

1986. 12th International Circus Festival, Monaco.
1791 **523** 2f.20 multicoloured . . . 1·10 95

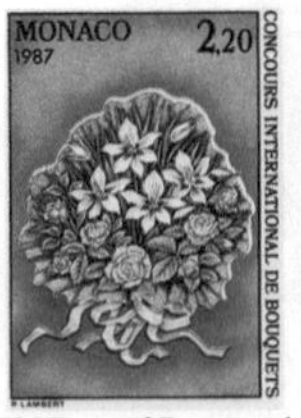
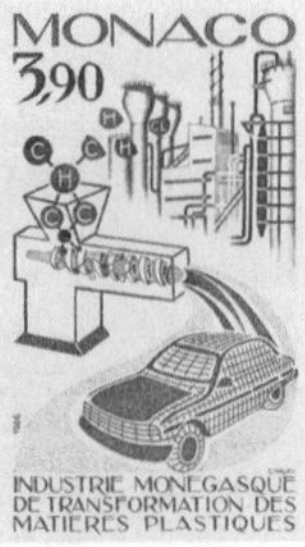

524 Posy of Roses and Acidanthera
525 Making Plastic Mouldings for Car Bodies

1986. Monte Carlo Flower Show (1987). Mult.
1792 2f.20 Type **524** . . . . . . 1·00 65
1793 3f.90 Lilies and beech in vase . . . . 1·60 1·50

1986. Monaco Red Cross. The Twelve Labours of Hercules (6th series). As T **422**.
1794 3f.+70c. green, yell & red 1·25 1·25
1795 4f.+80c. blue, brown & red 1·40 1·50
DESIGNS: 3f. The Golden Apples of the Hesperides; 4f. Capturing Cerberus.

1986. Plastics Industry.
1796 **525** 3f.90 turquoise, red and grey . . . . 1·25 80

526 Scenes from "Le Cid" (Pierre Corneille)

1986. Anniversaries.
1797 **526** 4f. deep brown & brown 1·25 1·00
1798 – 5f. brown and blue . . . 1·50 1·10
DESIGNS: 4f. Type **526** (350th anniv of first performance); 5f. Franz Liszt (composer) and bible (175th birth anniv).

527 Horace de Saussure, Mont Blanc and Climbers

1986. Bicentenary of First Ascent of Mont Blanc by Dr. Paccard and Jacques Balmat.
1799 **527** 5f.80 blue, red and black 1·75 1·50

528 "The Olympic Diver" (Emma de Sigaldi)

1986. 25th Anniv of Unveiling of "The Olympic Diver" (statue).
1800 **528** 6f. multicoloured . . . . 1·75 1·40

1986. Monaco in the "Belle Epoque" (5th series). Paintings by Hubert Clerissi. As T **445**. Mult.
1801 6f. "Bandstand and Casino, 1920" (vert) . . . . . . 2·50 1·90
1802 7f. "Avenue du Beau Rivage, 1925" (vert) . . . 4·25 3·25

1986. Seasons of the Strawberry Tree. Sheet 143 × 100 mm containing T **529** and similar horiz designs.
MS1803 3f. red and olive (T **529**); 4f. olive, lake and red (Summer); 5f. lake, olive and brown-red (Autumn); 6f. olive and red (Winter) . . . . 8·25 8·25

530 Spring

1987. Precancels. Seasons of the Chestnut.
1804 **530** 1f.31 green, yellow & brn 40 35
1805 – 1f.69 green and brown 60 45
1806 – 2f.74 brown, yellow & bl 1·00 85
1807 – 4f.56 brown, grn & grey 1·60 1·40
DESIGNS: 1f.69, Summer; 2f.74, Autumn; 4f.56, Winter.

531 Golden Hunter

1987. Insects in Mercantour National Park. Multicoloured.
1808 1f. Type **531** 40 35
1809 1f.90 Golden wasp (vert) . . 70 65
1810 2f. Green tiger beetle . . . 90 90
1811 2f.20 Brown aeshna (vert) 1·25 80
1812 3f. Leaf beetle . . . . . . 1·75 1·50
1813 3f.40 Grasshopper (vert) . . 2·50 1·90

532 St. Devote Church

1987. Centenary of St. Devote Parish Church.
1814 **532** 1f.90 brown 70 45

533 Dogs

1987. International Dog Show, Monte Carlo.
1815 **533** 1f.90 grey, black & brn 1·40 1·00
1816 – 2f.70 black and green . . 2·00 1·75
DESIGN: 2f.70, Poodle.

534 Stamp Album

1987. Stamp Day.
1817 **534** 2f.20 red, purple and mauve 70 45

535 Louis II Stadium, Fontvieille **536** Cathedral

1987. Europa. Each blue, green and red.
1818 2f.20 Type **535** 70 55
1819 3f.40 Crown Prince Albert Olympic swimming pool 1·25 85
MS1820 143 × 71 mm. Nos. 1818/19, each × 5 . . . . 10·50 10·50

1987. Centenary of Monaco Diocese.
1821 **536** 2f.50 green 70 50

537 Spring

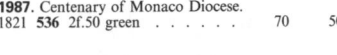

1987. Seasons of the Vine. Sheet 142 × 100 mm containing T **537** and similar horiz designs.
MS1822 3f. green and brown (Type **537**); 4f. green and brown (Summer); 5f. violet, brown and green (Autumn); 6f. orange-brown (Winter) . . . . 8·75 8·75

538 Lawn Tennis

1987. 2nd European Small States Games, Monaco.
1823 **538** 3f. black, red and purple 1·50 1·40
1824 – 5f. blue and black . . . 1·90 1·60
DESIGN: 5f. Sailing dinghies and windsurfer.

539 "Red Curly Tail" (Alexander Calder)

1987. "Monte Carlo Sculpture 1987" Exhibition.
1825 **539** 3f.70 multicoloured . . . 1·50 95

540 Prince Rainier III **542** Festival Poster (J. Ramel)

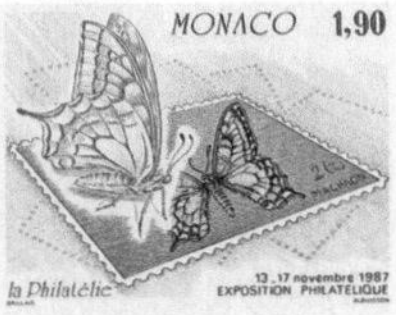

541 Swallowtail on Stamp

1987. 50th Anniv of Monaco Stamp Issuing Office.
1826 **540** 4f. blue . . . . 1·25 1·25
1827 – 4f. red . . . . 1·25 1·25
1828 – 8f. black . . . . 2·75 2·75
DESIGNS: No. 1827, Prince Louis II. (47 × 37 mm): 1828, Villa Miraflores.

1987. International Stamp Exhibition.
1829 **541** 1f.90 deep green and green 60 40
1830 2f.20 purple and red . . 70 45
1831 2f.50 purple and mauve 80 55
1832 3f.40 deep blue and blue 1·25 75

1987. 13th International Circus Festival, Monaco (1988).
1833 **542** 2f.20 multicoloured . . . 1·40 95

543 Christmas Scenes

1987. Christmas.
1834 **543** 2f.20 red 85 45

544 Strawberry Plants and Campanulas in Bowl

1987. Monte Carlo Flower Show (1988). Mult.
1835 2f.20 Type **544** 80 60
1836 3f.40 Ikebana arrangement of water lilies and dog roses (horiz) . . . . . . 1·40 1·10

545 Obverse and Reverse of Honore V 5f. Silver Coin

1987. 150th Anniv of Revival of Monaco Coinage.
1837 **545** 2f.50 black and red . . . 80 55

546 Graph, Factory, Electron Microscope and Printed Circuit

1987. Electro-Mechanical Industry.
1838 **546** 2f.50 blue, green and red 95 65

547 St. Devote

1987. Monaco Red Cross. St. Devote, Patron Saint of Monaco (1st series). Multicoloured.
1839 4f. Type **547** . . . . 1·25 80
1840 5f. St. Devote and her nurse 1·50 1·10
See also Nos. 1898/9, 1956/7, 1980/1, 2062/3 and 2101/2.

1987. 50th Anniv of Monaco Stamp Issuing Office (2nd issue). Sheet 140 × 70 mm containing T **540** and other designs. Each purple.
MS1841 4f. Type **540**; 4f. As No. 1827; 8f. As No. 1828 . . 6·00 6·00

548 Oceanographic Museum and I.A.E.A. Headquarters, Vienna

1987. 25th Anniv of International Marine Radioactivity Laboratory, Monaco.
1842 **548** 5f. black, brown and blue . . . . 1·50 1·25

549 Jouvet

1987. Birth Centenary of Louis Jouvet (actor).
1843 **549** 3f. black . . . . 1·00 95

550 River Crossing

1987. Bicentenary of First Edition of "Paul and Virginia" by Bernardin de Saint-Pierre.
1844 **550** 3f. green, orange and blue . . . . 1·00 85

551 Marc Chagall (painter)

1987. Anniversaries.
1845 **551** 4f. black and red . . . . 1·25 1·10
1846 – 4f. purple, red and brown . . . . 1·25 1·10
1847 – 4f. red, blue and brown 1·25 1·10
1848 – 4f. green, brown & purple . . . . 1·25 1·10
1849 – 5f. blue, brown and green . . . . 1·60 1·25
1850 – 5f. brown, green and blue . . . . 1·60 1·25
DESIGNS: No. 1845, Type **551** (birth centenary); 1846, Chapel of Ronchamp and Charles Edouard Jeanneret (Le Corbusier) (architect, birth centenary); 1847, Sir Isaac Newton (mathematician) and diagram (300th anniv of publication of "Principia Mathematica"); 1848, Key and Samuel Morse (inventor, 150th Anniv of Morse telegraph); 1849, Wolfgang Amadeus Mozart and scene from "Don Juan" (opera, bicentenary of composition); 1850, Hector Berlioz (composer) and scene from "Mass for the Dead" (150th anniv of composition).

1987. Monaco in the "Belle Epoque" (6th series). As T **445** showing paintings by Hubert Clerissi. Multicoloured.
1851 6f. "Main Ramp to Palace Square, 1925" (vert) . . . 2·50 1·60
1852 7f. "Monte Carlo Railway Station, 1925" (vert) . . . 3·25 2·75

552 Coat of Arms **553** Spanish Hogfish

1987.
1853 **552** 2f. multicoloured 65 35
1854 2f.20 multicoloured . . . 65 30

1988. Fishes in Oceanographic Museum Aquarium (2nd series). Multicoloured.
1857 2f. Type **553** 80 65
1858 2f.20 Copper-banded butterflyfish . . . . . . 1·10 50
1859 2f.50 Harlequin filefish . . . 1·40 95
1860 3f. Blue boxfish . . . . . . 1·40 75
1861 3f.70 Lionfish . . . . 2·10 1·60
1862 7f. Moon wrasse (horiz) . . 3·00 1·75

554 Spring **556** Dachshunds

555 Cross-country Skiing

1988. Precancels. Seasons of the Pear Tree. Multicoloured.
1863 1f.36 Type **554** 40 50
1864 1f.75 Summer 60 65
1865 2f.83 Autumn . . . . 1·10 1·10
1866 4f.72 Winter . . . . 1·60 1·60
See also Nos. 1952/5.

1988. Winter Olympic Games, Calgary. Sheet 143 × 93 mm containing T **555** and similar horiz design. Each black, lilac and blue.
MS1867 4f. Type **555**; 6f. Shooting 11·00 11·00

1988. European Dachshunds Show, Monte Carlo.
1868 **556** 3f. multicoloured . . . . 1·75 1·60

557 Children of different Races around Globe

1988. 25th Anniv of World Association of Friends of Children.
1869 **557** 5f. green, brown and blue . . . . 1·60 1·60

558 Satellite Camera above Man with World as Brain **560** Jean Monnet (statesman)

559 Coxless Four

1988. Europa. Transport and Communications. Each black, brown and red.
1870 2f.20 Type **558** . . . . . . 1·10 70
1871 3f.60 Atlantique high speed mail train and aircraft propeller . . . . 1·75 1·40
MS1872 170 × 143 mm. Nos. 1870/1, each × 5 . . . . 13·50 13·50

1988. Centenary of Monaco Nautical Society (formerly Regatta Society).
1873 **559** 2f. blue, green and red 80 55

1988. Birth Centenaries.
1874 **560** 2f. black, brown and blue . . . . 1·75 1·25
1875 – 2f. black and blue . . . 1·75 1·25
DESIGN: No. 1875, Maurice Chevalier (entertainer).

561 "Leccinum rotundifoliae"

1988. Fungi in Mercantour National Park. Multicoloured.
1876 2f. Type **561** 70 60
1877 2f.20 Crimson wax cap . . . 90 60
1878 2f.50 "Pholiota flammans" . . 1·00 1·25
1879 2f.70 "Lactarius lignyotus" . . 1·25 1·40
1880 3f. Goaty smell (vert) . . . 1·40 1·60
1881 7f. "Russula olivacea" (vert) 2·75 3·25

562 Nansen

563 Church and "Miraculous Virgin"

1988. Centenary of First Crossing of Greenland by Fridtjof Nansen (Norwegian explorer).
1882 **562** 4f. violet . . . . 1·75 1·40

1988. Restoration of Sanctuary of Our Lady of Laghet.
1883 **563** 5f. multicoloured . . . . 1·50 1·25

564 Anniversary Emblem

1988. 40th Anniv of W.H.O.
1884 **564** 6f. red and blue . . . . 1·75 1·40

565 Anniversary Emblem

1988. 125th Anniv of Red Cross.
1885 **565** 6f. red, grey and black 1·75 1·25

566 Congress Centre

1988. 10th Anniv of Monte Carlo Congress Centre.
1886 **566** 2f. green 70 75
1887 – 3f. red . . . . 90 1·10
DESIGN: 3f. Auditorium.

567 Tennis

1988. Olympic Games, Seoul. New Women's Disciplines. Sheet 143 × 100 mm containing T **567** and similar horiz designs. Each brown, black and blue.
MS1888 2f. Type **567**; 3f. Table tennis; 5f. "470" dinghy; 7f. Cycling . . . . 9·00 9·00

1988. Monaco in the "Belle Epoque" (7th series). Paintings by Hubert Clerissi. As T **445**. Mult.
1889 6f. "Steam packet in Monte Carlo Harbour, 1910" . . 2·50 1·90
1890 7f. "Place de la Gare, 1910" 2·75 2·50

568 Festival Poster (J. Ramel)

569 Star Decoration

1988. 14th International Circus Festival, Monaco (1989).
1891 **568** 2f. multicoloured . . . . 1·00 55

1988. Christmas.
1892 **569** 2f. multicoloured 80 60

570 Arrangement of Fuchsias, Irises, Roses and Petunias

571 Models

1988. Monte Carlo Flower Show (1989).
1893 **570** 3f. multicoloured . . . . 1·40 85

1988. Ready-to-Wear Clothing Industry.
1894 **571** 3f. green, orange & black 90 75

572 Lord Byron (bicentenary)

1988. Writers' Birth Anniversaries.
1895 **572** 3f. black, brown and blue 90 80
1896 – 3f. purple and blue . . . 90 80
DESIGN: No. 1896, Pierre de Marivaux (300th anniv).

573 Spring

1988. Seasons of the Olive Tree. Sheet 143 × 100 mm containing T **573** and similar horiz designs.
MS1897 3f. deep olive, yellow and olive (Type **573**); 4f. deep olive and olive (Summer); 5f. deep olive and olive (Autumn); 6f. deep olive and olive (Winter) . . . . 11·00 11·00

1988. Monaco Red Cross. St. Devote, Patron Saint of Monaco (2nd series). As T **547**. Multicoloured.
1898 4f. Roman governor Barbarus arriving at Corsica . . . . 1·25 80
1899 5f. St. Devote at the Roman senator Eutychius's house 1·90 1·25

574 "Le Nain and his Brothers" (Antoine Le Nain)

1988. Artists' Birth Anniversaries.
1900 **574** 5f. brown, olive and red 1·90 1·40
1901 – 5f. black, green and blue 1·90 1·40
DESIGNS: No. 1900, Type **574** (400th anniv): 1901, "The Great Archaeologists" (bronze statue, Giorgio de Chirico) (centenary).

575 Sorcerer

1989. Rock Carvings in Mercantour National Park. Multicoloured.
1902 2f. Type **575** 65 45
1903 2f.20 Oxen in yoke 75 55
1904 3f. Hunting implements . . 1·00 85
1905 3f.60 Tribal chief . . . . . 1·40 1·10
1906 4f. Puppet (vert) . . . . . 1·60 1·25
1907 5f. Jesus Christ (vert) . . . 2·00 1·40

576 Rue des Spelugues

577 Prince Rainier

1989. Old Monaco (1st series). Multicoloured.
1908 2f. Type **576** 60 45
1909 2f.20 Place Saint Nicolas . . 70 55
See also Nos. 1969/70 and 2090/1.

1989.
1910 **577** 2f. blue and azure . . . 70 20
1911 2f.10 blue and azure . . 70 25
1912 2f.20 brown and pink . . 90 30
1913 2f.20 blue and azure . . 70 20
1914 2f.30 brown and pink . . 80 30
1915 2f.40 blue and azure . . 70 25
1916 2f.50 brown and pink . . 80 30
1917 2f.70 blue 70 65
1918 2f.80 brown and pink . . 85 35
1919 3f. brown and pink . . . 85 25
1920 3f.20 blue and cobalt . . 1·10 75
1922 3f.40 blue and cobalt . . 1·40 95
1923 3f.60 blue and cobalt . . 1·60 1·25
1924 3f.70 blue and cobalt . . 1·10 70
1925 3f.80 purple and lilac . . 1·50 50
1926 3f.80 blue and cobalt . . 95 45
1927 4f. purple and lilac . . 1·00 95
1930 5f. brown and pink . . . 1·50 65
1932 10f. deep green and green . . . . 2·25 90
1934 15f. blue and grey . . . 3·75 1·25
1936 20f. red and pink . . . 4·50 1·75
1938 25f. black and grey . . . 6·00 2·10
1940 40f. brown and pink . . 8·00 4·25
See also Nos. 2388/90.

578 Yorkshire Terrier

1989. International Dog Show, Monte Carlo.
1941 **578** 2f.20 multicoloured . . . 90 65

579 Magician, Dove and Cards

1989. 5th Grand Prix of Magic, Monte Carlo.
1942 **579** 2f.20 black, blue and red 90 55

580 Nuns and Monks around "Our Lady of Misericorde"

1989. 350th Anniv of Archiconfrerie de la Misericorde.
1943 **580** 3f. brown, black and red 90 60

581 Charlie Chaplin (actor) and Film Scenes

1989. Birth Centenaries.
1944 – 3f. green, blue and mauve . . . . 1·00 95
1945 **581** 4f. purple, green and red 1·50 1·25
DESIGN: 3f. Jean Cocteau (writer and painter), scene from "The Double-headed Eagle" and frescoes in Villefrance-sur-Mer chapel.

582 Spring

1989. Seasons of the Pomegranate. Sheet 144 × 100 mm containing T **582** and similar horiz designs.
MS1946 3f. red, green and (Type **582**); 4f. brown, green and red (Summer); 5f. green, red and brown (Autumn); 6f. brown and green (Winter) . . . . 8·00 8·00

583 Boys playing Marbles

1989. Europa. Children's Games. Each mauve, brown and grey.
1947 2f.20 Type **583** 70 60
1948 3f.60 Girls skipping . . . . 1·10 1·00
MS1949 171 × 143 mm. Nos. 1947/8, each × 5 . . . . 10·50 10·50

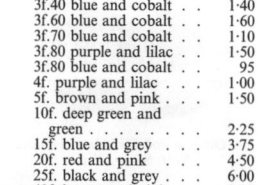

584 Prince Rainier

1989. 40th Anniv of Reign of Prince Rainier. Sheet 100 × 130 mm.
MS1950 **584** 20f. lilac . . . . . 8·25 8·25

585 "Lliberty"

1989. "Philexfrance 89" International Stamp Exhibition, Paris. Sheet 143 × 105 mm containing T **585** and similar vert designs.
MS1951 5f. blue (Type **585**); 5f. black ("Equality"); 5f. red ("Fraternity") . . . . 5·75 5·75

1989. Precancels. As Nos. 1863/6 but values changed. Multicoloured.
1952 1f.39 Type **554** 40 50
1953 1f.79 Summer 60 65
1954 2f.90 Autumn . . . . 1·40 1·10
1955 4f.84 Winter . . . . 1·90 1·60

1989. Monaco Red Cross. St. Devote, Patron Saint of Monaco (3rd series). As T **547**. Multicoloured.
1956 4f. St. Devote beside the dying Eutychius . . . . . 1·25 85
1957 5f. Barbarus condemns St. Devote to torture for refusing to make a sacrifice to the gods . . . 1·60 1·10

586 "Artist's Mother" (Philibert Florence)

1989. Artists' 150th Birth Anniversaries.
1958 **586** 4f. brown . . . . 1·60 1·40
1959 – 6f. multicoloured . . . . 2·00 1·60
1960 – 8f. multicoloured . . . . 2·75 2·00
DESIGNS—HORIZ: 6f. "Molesey Regatta" (Alfred Sisley). VERT: 8f. "Farmyard at Auvers" (Paul Cezanne).

587 Poinsettia, Christmas Roses and Holly

1989. Christmas.
1961 **587** 2f. multicoloured . . . . 1·60 70

588 Map and Emblem

1989. Centenary of Interparliamentary Union.
1962 **588** 4f. black, green and red 1·50 80

589 Princess Grace (founder)

1989. 25th Anniv of Princess Grace Foundation. Sheet 133 × 104 mm containing T **589** and similar vert design. Each blue.
MS1963 5f. Type **589**; 5f. Princess Caroline (Foundation president) 7·00 7·00

590 Monaco Palace, White House, Washington, and Emblem

1989. 20th U.P.U. Congress, Washington D.C.
1964 **590** 6f. blue, brown and black . . . . 1·60 1·25

1989. Monaco in the "Belle Epoque" (8th series). Paintings by Hubert Clerissi. As T **445**. Mult.
1965 7f. "Barque in Monte Carlo Harbour, 1915" (vert) . . 2·50 1·90
1966 8f. "Gaming Tables, Casino, 1915" (vert) . . . . . . 2·75 2·50

591 World Map

1989. 10th Anniv of Monaco Aide et Presence (welfare organization).
1967 **591** 2f.20 brown and red . . 1·50 1·10

592 Clown and Horses **593** Phalaenopsis "Princess Grace"

1989. 15th International Circus Festival, Monte Carlo.
1968 **592** 2f.20 multicoloured . . . 1·60 1·40

1990. Old Monaco (2nd series). Paintings by Claude Rosticher. As T **576**. Multicoloured.
1969 2f.10 La Rampe Major . . 70 45
1970 2f.30 Town Hall Courtyard 80 50

1990. International Garden and Greenery Exposition, Osaka, Japan. Multicoloured.
1971 2f. Type **593** 75 55
1972 3f. Iris "Grace Patricia" . . 1·00 70
1973 3f. "Paphiopedilum" "Prince Rainier III" . . . . . . 1·00 75
1974 4f. "Cattleya" "Principessa Grace" . . . . 1·40 80
1975 5f. Rose "Caroline of Monaco" . . . . 2·25 1·50

594 Bearded Collie

1990. International Dog Show, Monte Carlo.
1976 **594** 2f.30 multicoloured . . . 1·25 1·00

595 Noghes and Racing Car

1990. Birth Centenary of Antony Noghes (founder of Monaco Grand Prix and Monte Carlo Rally).
1977 **595** 3f. red, lilac and black 1·10 75

596 Cyclist and Lancia Rally Car

1990. Centenary of Automobile Club of Monaco (founded as Cycling Racing Club).
1978 **596** 4f. blue, brown & purple 1·50 1·25

597 Telephone, Satellite and Dish Aerial

1990. 125th Anniv of I.T.U.
1979 **597** 4f. lilac, mauve and blue 1·25 1·25

1990. Monaco Red Cross. St. Devote, Patron Saint of Monaco (4th series). As T **547**. Multicoloured.
1980 4f. St. Devote being flogged 1·25 1·00
1981 5f. Placing body of St. Devote in fishing boat 1·75 1·25

598 Sir Rowland Hill and Penny Black

1990. 150th Anniv of Penny Black.
1982 **598** 5f. blue and black . . . 2·00 1·50

599 "Post Office, Place de la Mairie"

1990. Europa. Post Office Buildings. Paintings by Hubert Clerissi. Multicoloured.
1983 2f.30 Type **599** 70 50
1984 3f.70 "Post Office, Avenue d'Ostende" . . . . 1·25 85
MS1985 170 × 145 mm. Nos. 1983/4, each × 4 . . . . 9·50 9·50

600 Ball, Player and Trophy

1990. World Cup Football Championship, Italy. Sheet 142 × 100 mm containing T **600** and similar horiz designs.
MS1986 5f. green, black and red; (Type **600**); 5f. black, red and green (Players); 5f. black and green (Pitch, ball and map of Italy); 5f. red, green and black (Pitch, players and stadium) . . 11·00 11·00

601 Anatase

1990. Minerals in Mercantour National Park. Mult.
1987 2f.10 Type **601** 60 35
1988 2f.30 Albite 70 45
1989 3f.20 Rutile . . . . 1·00 85
1990 3f.80 Chlorite . . . . 1·40 85
1991 4f. Brookite (vert) . . . . . 1·75 1·40
1992 6f. Quartz (vert) . . . . . 2·50 1·90

602 Powerboat **603** Pierrot writing (mechanical toy)

1990. World Offshore Powerboat Racing Championship.
1993 **602** 2f.30 brown, red & blue 90 60

1990. Philatelic Round Table.
1994 **603** 3f. blue . . . . 1·00 60

604 Christian Samuel Hahnemann (founding of homeopathy)

1990. Bicentenaries.
1995 **604** 3f. purple, green & black 1·00 75
1996 – 5f. chestnut, brown & bl 1·75 1·25
DESIGN: 5f. Jean-Francois Champollion (Egyptologist) and hieroglyphics (birth bicentenary).

605 Monaco Heliport, Fontvieille

1990. 30th International Civil Airports Association Congress, Monte Carlo.
1997 **605** 3f. black, red and brown 90 50
1998 – 5f. black, blue and brown . . . . 1·75 1·25
DESIGN: 5f. Aerospatiale Ecureuil helicopters over Monte Carlo Congress Centre.

606 Petanque Player **608** Miller on Donkey

607 Spring

1990. 26th World Petanque Championship.
1999 **606** 6f. blue, brown & orange 2·00 1·25

1990. Precancels. Seasons of the Plum Tree. Multicoloured.
2000 1f.46 Type **607** 45 35
2001 1f.89 Summer 65 45
2002 3f.06 Autumn . . . . 1·25 85
2003 5f.10 Winter . . . . 1·90 1·40

1990. Christmas. Crib figures from Provence. Multicoloured.
2004 2f.30 Type **608** 80 40
2005 3f.20 Woman carrying faggots . . . . 1·00 70
2006 3f.80 Baker . . . . 1·40 95
See also Nos. 2052/4, 2097/9, 2146/8 and 2191/3.

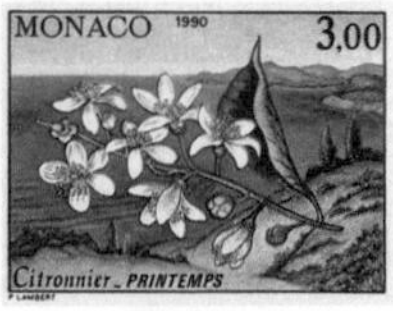

609 Spring

1990. Seasons of the Lemon Tree. Sheet 143 × 100 mm containing T **609** and similar horiz designs. Multicoloured.
MS2007 3f. Type **609**; 4f. Summer; 5f. Autumn; 6f. Winter . . . . 7·50 7·50

610 Pyotr Ilich Tchaikovsky (composer)
611 Clown playing Concertina

1990. 150th Birth Anniversaries.
2008 **610** 5f. blue and green . . . 1·75 1·10
2009 – 5f. bistre and blue . . . 1·75 1·10
2010 – 7f. multicoloured . . . . 3·50 3·00
DESIGNS—As T **610**: No. 2009, "Cathedral" (Auguste Rodin, sculptor). 48 × 37 mm: "The Magpie" (Claude Monet, painter).

1991. 16th International Circus Festival, Monte Carlo.
2011 **611** 2f.30 multicoloured . . . 95 75
See also No. 2069.

1991. Bygone Monaco (2nd series). Paintings by Hubert Clerissi. As T **481**.
2015 20c. purple 10 10
2017 40c. green 10 10
2018 50c. red 10 10
2019 60c. blue 20 10
2020 70c. green 20 10
2021 80c. blue 20 20
2022 90c. lilac 20 20
2023 1f. blue 30 20
2024 2f. red 50 25
2025 3f. black 80 30
2027 7f. grey and black . . . . . 1·60 80
DESIGNS: 20c. Rock of Monaco and Fontvieille; 40c. Place du Casino; 50c. Place de la Cremaillere and railway station; 60c. National Council building; 70c. Palace and Rampe Major; 80c. Avenue du Beau Rivage; 90c. Fishing boats, Fontvieille; 1f. Place d'Armes; 2f. Marche de la Condamine; 3f. Yacht; 7f. Oceanographic Museum.

612 Abdim's Stork
613 Phytoplankton

1991. International Symposium on Bird Migration. Multicoloured.
2029 2f. Type **612** 70 55
2030 3f. Broad-tailed hummingbirds 90 80
2031 4f. Garganeys . . . . . . 1·40 1·10
2032 5f. Eastern broad-billed roller . . . . 1·75 1·50
2033 6f. European bee eaters . . 2·25 1·90

1991. Oceanographic Museum (1st series).
2034 **613** 2f.10 multicoloured . . . 95 55
See also Nos. 2095/6.

614 Schnauzer

1991. International Dog Show, Monte Carlo.
2035 **614** 2f.50 multicoloured . . . 1·25 85

615 Cyclamen, Lily-of-the-Valley and Pine Twig in Fir-cone
616 Corals

1991. Monte Carlo Flower Show.
2036 **615** 3f. multicoloured . . . . 1·10 65

1991. "Joys of the Sea" Exhibition. Multicoloured.
2037 2f.20 Type **616** 85 65
2038 2f.40 Coral necklace 95 75

617 Control Room, "Eutelsat" Satellite and Globe

1991. Europa. Europe in Space. Each blue, black and green.
2039 2f.30 Type **617** 85 50
2040 3f.20 Computer terminal, "Inmarsat" satellite, research ship transmitting signal and man with receiving equipment . . . 1·10 70
MS2041 143 × 171 mm. Nos. 2039/40, each × 5 . . . . 9·50 9·50

618 Cross-country Skiers and Statue of Skiers by Emma de Sigaldi

1991. 1992 Olympic Games. (a) Winter Olympics, Albertville.
2042 **618** 3f. green, blue and olive 1·00 1·10
2043 – 4f. green, blue and olive 1·40 1·40

(b) Olympic Games, Barcelona.
2044 – 3f. green, lt brown & brown . . . . 1·00 1·25
2045 – 5f. black, brown and green 1·50 1·75
DESIGNS: No. 2043, Right-hand part of statue and cross-country skiers; 2044, Track, relay runners and left part of statue of relay runners by Emma de Sigaldi; 2045, Right part of statue, view of Barcelona and track.

619 Head of "David" (Michelangelo), Computer Image and Artist at Work
620 Prince Pierre, Open Book and Lyre

1991. 25th International Contemporary Art Prize.
2046 **619** 4f. green, dp green & lilac . . . . 1·40 95

1991. 25th Anniv of Prince Pierre Foundation.
2047 **620** 5f. black, blue and brown . . . . 1·50 1·25

621 Tortoises

1991. Endangered Species. Hermann's Tortoise. Multicoloured.
2048 1f.25 Type **621** 85 70
2049 1f.25 Head of tortoise . . . 85 70
2050 1f.25 Tortoise in grass . . . 85 70
2051 1f.25 Tortoise emerging from among plants . . . 85 70

1991. Christmas. As T **608** showing crib figures from Provence. Multicoloured.
2052 2f.50 Consul 80 35
2053 3f.50 Arlesian woman . . . 1·25 85
2054 4f. Mayor . . . . 1·50 1·10

622 Norway Spruce

1991. Conifers in Mercantour National Park. Multicoloured.
2055 2f.50 Type **622** 85 30
2056 3f.50 Silver fir . . . . . . 1·25 65
2057 4f. "Pinus uncinata" . . . . 1·25 80
2058 5f. Scots pine (vert) . . . . 1·50 1·00
2059 6f. Arolla pine . . . . . . 1·75 1·25
2060 7f. European larch (vert) . . 2·00 1·50

623 Spring

1991. Seasons of the Orange Tree. Sheet 142 × 101 mm containing T **623** and similar horiz designs.
MS2061 3f. orange, green and brown (Type **623**); 4d. green and brown (Summer); 5f. green, orange and brown (Autumn); 6f. green and olive-brown (Winter) . . . . . 7·50 7·50

1991. Monaco Red Cross. St. Devote, Patron Saint of Monaco (5th series). As T **547**. Multicoloured.
2062 4f.50 Fishing boat carrying body caught in storm . . 1·50 80
2063 5f.50 Dove guiding boatman to port of Monaco . . . 1·75 1·10

624 "Portrait of Claude Monet"

1991. 150th Birth Anniv of Auguste Renoir (painter).
2064 **624** 5f. multicoloured . . . . 1·60 1·25

625 Prince Honore II of Monaco

1991. 350th Anniv of Treaty of Peronne (giving French recognition of sovereignty of Monaco). Paintings by Philippe de Champagne. Mult.
2065 6f. Type **625** . . . . . . 2·10 1·60
2066 7f. King Louis XIII of France . . . . 2·50 1·75

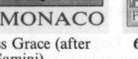

626 Princess Grace (after R. Samini)
627 1891 Stamp Design

1991. 10th Anniv of Princess Grace Theatre.
2067 **626** 8f. multicoloured . . . . 3·25 2·40

1991. Centenary of Prince Albert Stamps. Sheet 114 × 72 mm.
MS2068 **627** 10f. red; 10f. green; 10f. lilac . . . . 9·50 9·50

1992. 16th International Circus Festival, Monte Carlo. As No. 2011 but value and dates changed.
2069 **611** 2f.50 multicoloured . . . 95 75
The 1991 Festival was cancelled.

628 Two-man Bobsleighs

1992. Winter Olympic Games, Albertville (7f.), and Summer Games, Barcelona (8f.).
2070 **628** 7f. blue, turquoise & blk 2·10 1·40
2071 – 8f. purple, blue and green . . . . 2·50 1·50
DESIGN: 8f. Football.

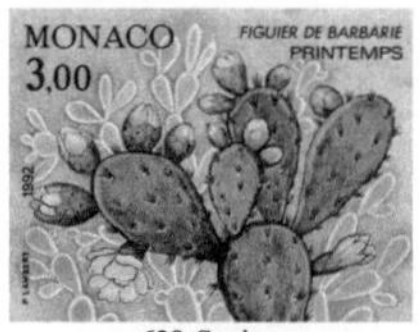

629 Spring

1992. Exotic Gardens. Seasons of the Prickly Pear. Sheet 142 × 100 mm containing T **629** and similar horiz designs. Multicoloured.
MS2072 3f. Type **629**; 4f. Summer; 5f. Autumn; 6f. Winter . . . . 8·00 8·00

630 Spring

1992. Precancels. Seasons of the Walnut Tree. Mult.
2073 1f.60 Type **630** 50 60
2074 2f.08 Summer 60 70
2075 2f.98 Autumn . . . . 1·10 1·10
2076 5f.28 Winter . . . . 1·75 1·75

631 Golden Labrador

1992. International Dog Show, Monte Carlo.
2077 **631** 2f.20 multicoloured . . . 1·25 80

632 Racing along Seafront

1992. 50th Monaco Grand Prix.
2078 **632** 2f.50 black, purple & bl 85 55

633 Mixed Bouquet

1992. 25th Monte Carlo Flower Show.
2079 **633** 3f.40 multicoloured . . . 1·40 85

634 Ford Sierra Rally Car

1992. 60th Monte Carlo Car Rally.
2080 **634** 4f. black, green and red 1·50 1·10

635 Rough-toothed Dolphin (*Steno bredanensis*)

1992. Mediterranean Dolphins. Sheet 142 × 100 mm containing T **635** and similar horiz designs. Multicoloured.
MS2081 4f. Type **635** 5f. Common dolphin (*Delphinus delphis*); 6f. Bottle-nosed dolphin (*Tursiops truncates*); 7f. Striped dolphin (*Stenella coeruleoalba*) . . . . 10·00 10·00

636 "Pinta" off Palos

1992. Europa. 500th Anniv of Discovery of America by Columbus. Multicoloured.
2082 2f.50 Type **636** 80 65
2083 3f.40 "Santa Maria" in the Antilles . . . . 1·40 1·10
2084 4f. "Nina" off Lisbon . . . 1·50 1·25
MS2085 140 × 170 mm. Nos. 2082/4, each × 2 . . . . 7·50 7·50

637 Produce

1992. "Ameriflora" Horticultural Show, Columbus, Ohio. Multicoloured.
2086 4f. Type **637** . . . . 1·25 95
2087 5f. Vase of mixed flowers . . 1·60 1·50

638 Prince Rainier I and Fleet (detail of fresco by E. Charpentier, Spinola Palace, Genoa)

1992. Columbus Exhibition, Genoa (6f.), and "Expo '92" World's Fair, Seville (7f.).
2088 **638** 6f. brown, red and blue 2·00 1·40
2089 – 7f. brown, red and blue 2·10 1·60
DESIGN: 7f. Monaco pavilion.

1992. Old Monaco (3rd series). Paintings by Claude Rosticher. As T **576**. Multicoloured.
2090 2f.20 La Porte Neuve (horiz) 75 25
2091 2f.50 La Placette Bosio (horiz) 85 25

639 "Christopher Columbus"

1992. "Genova '92" International Thematic Stamp Exhibition. Roses. Multicoloured.
2092 3f. Type **639** . . . . 1·25 1·00
2093 4f. "Prince of Monaco" . . 1·40 1·10

640 Lammergeier

1992.
2094 **640** 2f.20 orange, blk & grn 85 80

1992. Oceanographic Museum (2nd series). As T **613**. Multicoloured.
2095 2f.20 "Ceratium ranipes" . . 85 60
2096 2f.50 "Ceratium hexacanthum" 95 70

1992. Christmas. As T **608** showing crib figures from Provence. Multicoloured.
2097 2f.50 Basket-maker 85 30
2098 3f.40 Fishwife . . . . . . 1·25 65
2099 5f. Rural constable . . . . 1·75 1·40

641 "Seabus" (projected tourist submarine)

1992.
2100 **641** 4f. blue, red and brown 1·40 1·25

642 Burning Boat Ceremony, St. Devote's Eve

1992. Monaco Red Cross. St. Devote, Patron Saint of Monaco (6th series).
2101 **642** 6f. red, blue and brown 1·75 1·10
2102 – 8f. purple, orange and red . . . . 2·40 1·60
DESIGN: 8f. Procession of reliquary, St. Devote's Day.

643 Athletes, Sorbonne University and Coubertin

1992. Centenary of Pierre de Coubertin's Proposal for Revival of Olympic Games.
2103 **643** 10f. blue . . . . 3·00 1·90

644 Baux de Provence and St. Catherine's Chapel

1992. Titles of Princes of Monaco. Marquis of Baux de Provence.
2104 **644** 15f. multicoloured . . . 4·25 2·75

645 1856 40c. Sardinian Stamp **646** Clown and Tiger

1992. Stamp Museum. Sheet 115 × 72 mm containing T **645** and similar vert design.
MS2105 10f. red and black (Type **645**); 10f. green and black (1860 1c. French stamp) . . . 7·00 7·00

1993. 17th Int Circus Festival, Monte Carlo.
2106 **646** 2f.50 multicoloured . . . 85 55

647 Short-toed Eagles

1993. Birds of Prey in Mercantour National Park.
2107 **647** 2f. chestnut, brown and orange 65 50
2108 – 3f. indigo, orange & blue 1·10 65
2109 – 4f. brown, ochre and blue . . . . 1·25 1·10
2110 – 5f. brown, chestnut and green . . . . 1·60 1·40
2111 – 6f. brown, mauve & grn 1·90 1·60
DESIGNS—HORIZ: 3f. Peregrine falcon. VERT: 4f. Eagle owl; 5f. Western honey buzzard; 6f. Tengmalm's owl.

648 Fin Wale (*Balaenoptera physalus*)

1993. Mediterranean Whales. Sheet 143 × 100 mm containing T **648** and similar horiz designs. Multicoloured.
MS2112 4f. Type **648**; 5f. Minke whale (*Balaenoptera acutorostrata*); 6f. Sperm whale (Physeter catodon); 7f. Cuvier's beaked whale (Ziphius cavirostris) 9·50 9·50

649 Spring

1993. Seasons of the Almond. Sheet 142 × 100 mm containing T **649** and similar horiz designs. Multicoloured.
MS2113 5f. Type **649**; 5f. Summer; 5f. Autumn; 5f. Winter . . . . 8·25 8·25

650 Mixed Bouquet **652** Fire Fighting and Rescue

651 Pennants, Auditorium and Masks

1993. Monte Carlo Flower Show.
2114 **650** 3f.40 multicoloured . . . 1·10 75

1993. 10th International Amateur Theatre Festival.
2115 **651** 4f.20 multicoloured . . . 1·40 75

1993. World Civil Protection Day.
2116 **652** 6f. black, red and green 1·90 1·40

653 Newfoundland

1993. International Dog Show, Monte Carlo.
2117 **653** 2f.20 multicoloured . . . 90 70

654 Golfer

1993. 10th Monte Carlo Open Golf Tournament.
2118 **654** 2f.20 multicoloured . . . 70 65

655 Princess Grace **656** Mirror and Candelabra

1993. 10th Death Anniv (1992) of Princess Grace.
2119 **655** 5f. blue . . . . 1·50 1·25

1993. 10th Antiques Biennale.
2120 **656** 7f. multicoloured . . . . 2·10 1·40

657 "Echinopsis multiplex" **658** Monte Carlo Ballets

1993. Cacti.
2121 **657** 2f.50 green, purple & yell 70 60
2122 – 2f.50 green and purple 70 60
2123 – 2f.50 green, purple & yell 70 60
2124 – 2f.50 green and yellow 70 60
DESIGNS: No. 2122, "Zygocactus truncatus"; 2123, "Echinocereus procumbens"; 2124, "Euphorbia virosa".
See also Nos. 2154/66.

1993. Europa. Contemporary Art.
2125 **658** 2f.50 black, brn & pink 70 50
2126 – 4f.20 grey and brown . . 1·25 95
MS2127 143 × 172 mm. Nos. 2125/6, each × 3 . . . . 6·75 6·75
DESIGN: 4f.20, "Evolution" (sculpture, Emma de Sigaldi).

659 **660** State Arms and Olympic Rings

1993. Admission to United Nations Organization. Sheet 115 × 72 mm.
MS2128 10f. blue (T **659**); 10f. brown (T **577**); 10f. red and brown (state arms) . . . . 9·50 9·50

1993. 110th International Olympic Committee Session, Monaco.
2129 **660** 2f.80 red, brown & blue 80 85
2130 – 2f.80 blue, lt blue & red 80 85
2131 – 2f.80 brown, blue & red 80 85
2132 – 2f.80 blue, lt blue & red 80 85
2133 – 2f.80 brown, blue & red 80 85
2134 – 2f.80 blue, lt blue & red 80 85
2135 – 2f.80 brown, blue & red 80 85
2136 **660** 2f.80 blue, lt blue & red 80 85
2137 – 4f.50 multicoloured . . . 1·25 1·40
2138 – 4f.50 black, yellow & bl 1·25 1·40
2139 – 4f.50 red, yellow & blue 1·25 1·40
2140 – 4f.50 black, yellow & bl 1·25 1·40
2141 – 4f.50 red, yellow & blue 1·25 1·40
2142 – 4f.50 black, yellow & bl 1·25 1·40
2143 – 4f.50 red, yellow & blue 1·25 1·40
2144 – 4f.50 red, yellow & blue 1·25 1·40
DESIGNS: 2130, Bobsleighing; 2131, Skiing; 2132, Yachting; 2133, Rowing; 2134, Swimming; 2135, Cycling; 2136, 2144, Commemorative inscription; 2138, Gymnastics (rings exercise); 2139, Judo; 2140, Fencing; 2141, Hurdling; 2142, Archery; 2143, Weightlifting.

661 Examining 1891 1c. Stamp

1993. Centenary of Monaco Philatelic Union.
2145 **661** 2f.40 multicoloured . . . 70 45

1993. Christmas. Crib figures from Provence. As T **608**. Multicoloured.
2146 2f.80 Donkey 80 35
2147 3f.70 Shepherd holding lamb 1·00 90
2148 4f.40 Ox lying down in barn 1·25 1·25

662 Grieg, Music and Trolls

1993. 150th Birth Anniv of Edvard Grieg (composer).
2149 **662** 4f. blue . . . . 1·60 1·10

663 Abstract Lithograph

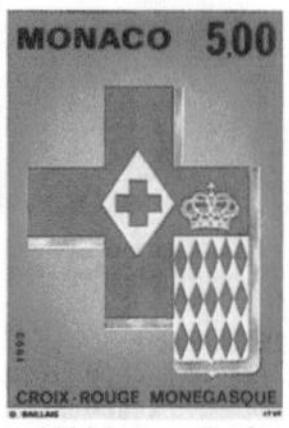

664 Monaco Red Cross Emblem

1993. Birth Centenary of Joan Miro (painter and sculptor).
2150 **663** 5f. multicoloured . . . . 1·60 1·40

1993. Monaco Red Cross.
2151 **664** 5f. red, yellow and black 1·40 1·10
2152 – 6f. red and black . . . . 1·90 1·60
DESIGN: 6f. Crosses inscribed with fundamental principles of the International Red Cross.

665 "St. Joseph the Carpenter"

1993. 400th Birth Anniv of Georges de la Tour (painter).
2153 **665** 6f. multicoloured . . . . 1·75 1·40

1994. Cacti. As Nos. 2121/4 but values changed and additional designs.
2153a – 10c. green, orange and red 10 10
2154 **657** 20c. green, purple and yellow 10 10
2155 – 30c. green and purple 10 10
2156 – 40c. green and yellow 10 10
2157 – 50c. green, red and olive 10 10
2158 – 60c. green, red and yellow 20 25
2159 – 70c. green, red and blue 20 25
2160 – 80c. green, orange and red 20 25
2162 – 1f. green, brown and yellow 25 25
2164 – 2f. green, red and yellow 50 45
2165 – 2f.70 green, red and yellow 70 50
2166 – 4f. green, purple and yellow . . . . 1·00 60
2166a – 4f. green, red and yellow 80 70
2167 – 5f. green, mauve and brown . . . . 1·25 85
2167a – 6f. brown, green and red . . . . 1·50 1·25
2167b – 7f. green, brown and red . . . . 1·90 1·50
DESIGNS: 10c. "Bromelia brevifolia"; 30c. "Zygocactus truncatus"; 40c. "Euphorbia virosa"; 50c. "Selenicereus grandiflorus"; 60c. "Opuntia basilaris"; 70c. "Aloe plicatilis"; 80c. "Opuntia hybride"; 1f. "Stapelia flavirostris"; 2f. "Aporocactus flagelliformis"; 2f.70, "Opuntia dejecta"; 4f. (2166), "Echinocereus procumbens"; 4f. (2166a), "Echinocereus blanckii"; 5f. "Cereus peruvianus"; 6f. "Euphorbia milii; 7f. "Stapelia variegata.

666 Festival Poster

667 Artist/Poet

668

1994. 18th Int Circus Festival, Monte Carlo.
2168 **666** 2f.80 multicoloured . . . 95 70

1994. Mechanical Toys.
2169 **667** 2f.80 blue 70 75
2170 – 2f.80 red 70 75
2171 – 2f.80 purple 70 75
2172 – 2f.80 green 70 75
DESIGNS: No. 2170, Bust of Japanese woman; 2171, Shepherdess with sheep; 2172, Young Parisienne.

1994. Mediterranean Whales and Dolphins. Sheet 143 × 100 mm containing horiz designs as T **648**. Multicoloured.
MS2173 4f. Killer whale (*Orcimus orca*); 5f. Risso's dolphin (*Grampus griseus*); 6f. False killer whale (*Pseudorca crassidens*); 7f. Long-finned pilot whale (*Globicephala melas*) . . . . . 8·50 8·50

1994. Winter Olympic Games, Lillehammer, Norway. Sheet 123 × 80 mm containing T **668** and similar horiz design. Each blue and red.
MS2174 10f. Type **668**; 10f. Bobsleighing . . . . 7·50 7·50

669 King Charles Spaniels

1994. International Dog Show, Monte Carlo.
2175 **669** 2f.40 multicoloured . . . 95 45

670 Couple, Leaves and Pollution

671 Iris

1994. Monaco Committee of Anti-tuberculosis and Respiratory Diseases Campaign.
2176 **670** 2f.40+60c. mult 85 75

1994. Monte Carlo Flower Show.
2177 **671** 4f.40 multicoloured . . . 1·40 85

672 Levitation Trick

1994. 10th Monte Carlo Magic Grand Prix.
2178 **672** 5f. blue, black and red 1·50 95

673 Ingredients and Dining Table overlooking Harbour

1994. 35th Anniv of Brotherhood of Cordon d'Or French Chefs.
2179 **673** 6f. multicoloured . . . . 1·75 1·25

674 Isfjord, Prince Albert I, Map of Spitzbergen and "Princess Alice II"

1994. Europa. Discoveries made by Prince Albert I. Each black, blue and red.
2180 2f.80 Type **674** 85 70
2181 4f.50 Oceanographic Museum, Grimaldi's spookfish and "Eryoneicus alberti" (crustacean) . . . . . . 1·40 1·10
MS2182 155 × 130 mm. Nos. 2180/1, each × 3 . . . . 7·50 7·50

675 Olympic Flag and Sorbonne University

676 Dolphins through Porthole

1994. Centenary of International Olympic Committee.
2183 **675** 3f. multicoloured 95 75

1994. Economic Institute of the Rights of the Sea Conference, Monaco.
2184 **676** 6f. multicoloured . . . . 1·75 1·50

677 Family around Tree of Hearts

678 Footballer's Legs and Ball

1994. International Year of the Family.
2185 **677** 7f. green, orange and blue . . . . 1·90 1·50

1994. World Cup Football Championship, U.S.A.
2186 **678** 8f. red and black . . . . 2·25 1·50

679 Athletes and Villa Miraflores

1994. Inauguration of New Seat of International Amateur Athletics Federation.
2187 **679** 8f. blue, purple and bistre . . . . 2·10 2·00

680 De Dion Bouton, 1903

1994. Vintage Car Collection of Prince Rainier III.
2188 **680** 2f.80 black, brown and mauve 85 80

681 Emblem and Monte Carlo

682 Emblem and Korean Scene

1994. 1st Association of Postage Stamp Catalogue Editors and Philatelic Publications Grand Prix.
2189 **681** 3f. multicoloured 95 55

1994. 21st Universal Postal Union Congress, Seoul.
2190 **682** 4f.40 black, blue and red 1·40 85

1994. Christmas. As T **608** showing crib figures from Provence. Multicoloured.
2191 2f.80 Virgin Mary 70 60
2192 4f.50 Baby Jesus . . . . . 1·25 85
2193 6f. Joseph . . . . 1·60 1·10

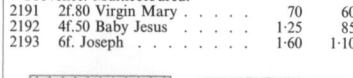

683 Prince Albert I

684 Three Ages of Voltaire (writer, 300th anniv)

1994. Inaug of Stamp and Coin Museum (1st issue). Coins.
2194 **683** 3f. stone, brown and red 85 65
2195 – 4f. grey, brown and red 1·25 95
2196 – 7f. stone, brown and red 1·90 1·50
MS2197 115 × 73 mm. 10f. × 3, As Nos. 2194/6 . . . . 9·75 9·75
DESIGNS: 4f. Arms of House of Grimaldi; 7f. Prince Rainier III.
See also Nos. **MS**2225; 2265/7 and 2283/**MS**6.

1994. Birth Anniversaries.
2198 **684** 5f. green . . . . 1·50 1·10
2199 – 6f. brown and purple . . 1·75 1·40
DESIGN—HORIZ: 6f. Sarah Bernhardt (actress, 150th anniv).

685 Heliport and Helicopter

1994. 50th Anniv of International Civil Aviation Organization.
2200 **685** 5f. green, black and blue 1·40 1·00
2201 – 7f. brown, black and red 1·90 1·60
DESIGN: 7f. Harbour and helicopter.

686 Spring

1994. 1st European Stamp Salon, Flower Gardens, Paris. Seasons of the Apricot. Sheet 142 × 100 mm containing T **686** and similar horiz designs. Multicoloured.
MS2202 6f. Type **686**; 7f. Summer; 8f. Autumn; 9f. Winter . . . . 9·75 9·75

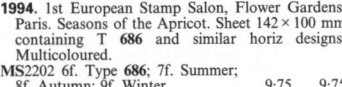

687 Blood Vessels on Woman (anti-cancer)

1994. Monaco Red Cross. Health Campaigns.
2203 **687** 6f. blue, black and red 1·60 1·10
2204 – 8f. green, black and red 2·10 1·60
DESIGN: 8f. Tree and woman (anti-AIDS).

688 Robinson Crusoe and Friday

1994. Anniversaries. Multicoloured.
2205 7f. Type **688** (275th anniv of publication of "Robinson Crusoe" by Daniel Defoe) 2·10 1·50
2206 9f. "The Snake Charmer" (150th birth anniv of Henri Rousseau, painter) 2·50 1·75

689 Clown playing Trombone **690** Crown Prince Albert

1995. 19th Int Circus Festival, Monte Carlo.
2207 **689** 2f.80 multicoloured . . . 70 65

1995. 35th Television Festival, Monte Carlo.
2208 **690** 8f. brown . . . . 2·00 2·00

691 Fontvieille

1995. European Nature Conservation Year.
2209 **691** 2f.40 multicoloured . . . 60 45

692 American Cocker Spaniel

1995. International Dog Show, Monte Carlo.
2210 **692** 4f. multicoloured . . . . 1·00 1·00

693 Parrot Tulips

1995. Monte Carlo Flower Show.
2211 **693** 5f. multicoloured . . . . 1·50 1·00

694 "Acer palmatum"

1995. European Bonsai Congress.
2212 **694** 6f. multicoloured . . . . 1·50 85

695 Alfred Nobel (founder of Nobel Prizes) and Dove

1995. Europa. Peace and Freedom. Multicoloured.
2213 2f.80 Type **695** 75 70
2214 5f. Roses, broken chain and watchtower . . . . 1·40 1·00

696 Emblem of Monagasque Disabled Children Association

1995. Int Special Olympics, New Haven, U.S.A.
2215 **696** 3f. multicoloured 75 55

697 Emblem

1995. Rotary International Convention, Nice.
2216 **697** 4f. blue . . . . 1·10 1·00

699 Jean Giono **701** Princess Caroline (President)

700 Saint Hubert (patron saint of hunting)

1995. Writers' Birth Centenaries.
2218 **699** 5f. lilac, brown and green . . . . 1·40 90
2219 – 6f. brown, violet and green . . . . 1·50 1·10
DESIGN: 6f. Marcel Pagnol.

1995. General Assembly of International Council for Hunting and Conservation of Game.
2220 **700** 6f. blue . . . . 1·50 1·40

1995. World Association of Friends of Children General Assembly, Monaco.
2221 **701** 7f. blue . . . . 1·60 1·40

702 Athletes and Medal

1995. International Amateur Athletics Federation Grand Prix, Monaco.
2222 **702** 7f. mauve, purple and grey . . . . 1·75 1·40

703 "Trophee des Alpes" (Hubert Clerissi)

1995. 2000th Anniv of Emperor Augustus Monument, La Turbie.
2223 **703** 8f. multicoloured . . . . 1·90 1·75

704 Prince Pierre (after Philip Laszlo de Lombos) **706** St. Antony (wooden statue)

705 1974 60c. Honore II Stamp

1995. Birth Centenary of Prince Pierre of Monaco.
2224 **704** 10f. purple . . . . . . 2·50 1·75

1995. Inauguration of Stamp and Coin Museum (2nd issue). Sheet 135 × 89 mm containing T **705** and similar designs.
MS2225 10f. red, brown and blue (T **706**); 10f. blue and brown (entrance of museum) (*vert*); 10f. blue (1051 30f. first museum stamp) . . . . 9·50 9·50

1995. 800th Birth Anniv of St. Antony of Padua.
2226 **706** 2f.80 multicoloured . . . 65 55

707 United Nations Charter and Peacekeeping Soldiers

1995. 50th Anniv of U.N.O.
2227 **707** 2f.50 multicoloured . . . 65 55
2228 – 2f.50 multicoloured . . . 65 55
2229 – 2f.50 multicoloured . . . 65 55
2230 – 2f.50 blue, black and brown 65 55
2231 – 3f. black, brown and blue 75 75
2232 – 3f. multicoloured 75 75
2233 – 3f. multicoloured 75 75
2234 – 3f. multicoloured 75 75
MS2235 112 × 151 mm. 3f. As No. 2227; 3f. As No. 2228; 3f. As No. 2229; 3f. As No. 2230; 4f.50, As No. 2231; 4f.50, As No. 2232; 4f.50, As No. 2233; 4f.50, As No. 2234 . . . . 11·00 11·00

DESIGNS: No. 2228, Wheat ears, boy and arid ground; 2229, Children from different nationalities; 2230, Head of Colossus, Abu Simbel Temple; 2231, United Nations meeting; 2232, Growing crops and hand holding seeds; 2233, Figures and alphabetic characters; 2234, Lute and UNESCO head-quarters, Paris.
Nos. 2228 and 2232 commemorate the F.A.O., Nos. 2229 and 2233 International Year of Tolerance, Nos. 2230 and 2234 UNESCO.

708 Rose "Grace de Monaco" **709** Balthazar

1995. Flowers. Multicoloured.
2236 3f. Type **708** 65 50
2237 3f. Fuchsia "Lakeland Princess" 65 50
2238 3f. Carnation "Centenaire de Monte-Carlo" 65 50
2239 3f. Fuchsia "Grace" 65 50
2240 3f. Rose "Princesse de Monaco" 65 50
2241 3f. Alstroemeria "Gracia" 65 50
2242 3f. Lily "Princess Gracia" 65 50
2243 3f. Carnation "Princesse Caroline" 65 50
2244 3f. Rose "Stephanie de Monaco" 65 50
2245 3f. Carnation "Prince Albert" 65 50
2246 3f. Sweet pea "Grace de Monaco" 65 50
2247 3f. Gerbera "Gracia" . . . 65 50

1995. Christmas. Crib Figures from Provence of the Three Wise Men. Multicoloured.
2248 3f. Type **709** 75 55
2249 5f. Gaspard . . . . 1·25 75
2250 6f. Melchior . . . . 1·50 1·10

710 Tree, Bird, Seahorse and Association Emblem

1995. 20th Anniv of Monaco Association for Nature Protection.
2251 **710** 4f. green, black and red 90 70

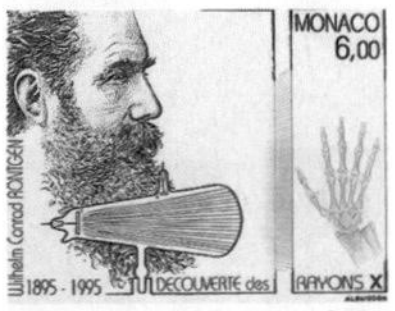

711 Rontgen and X-Ray of Hand

1995. Centenary of Discovery of X-Rays by Wilhelm Rontgen.
2252 **711** 6f. black, yellow and green . . . . 1·40 75

712 First Screening to Paying Public, Paris, December 1895

1995. Centenary of Motion Pictures.
2253 **712** 7f. blue . . . . 1·60 85

713 Allegory of Anti-leprosy Campaign

1995. Monaco Red Cross. Multicoloured.
2254 7f. Type **713** . . . . 1·75 1·40
2255 8f. Doctors Prakash and Mandakini Amte (anti-leprosy campaign in India) . . . . 1·90 1·75

714 First Car with Tyres

1995. Centenary of Invention of Inflatable Tyres.
2256 **714** 8f. purple and claret . . 1·90 1·40

715 "Spring"

1995. 550th Birth Anniv of Sandro Botticelli (artist).
2257 **715** 15f. blue . . . . 3·75 3·50

716 Poster

718 Rhododendron

717 Illusion

1996. 20th International Circus Festival, Monte Carlo.
2258 **716** 2f.40 multicoloured . . . 70 55

1996. Magic Festival, Monte Carlo.
2259 **717** 2f.80 black 85 55

1996. Monte Carlo Flower Show.
2260 **718** 3f. multicoloured 85 55

719 Wire-haired Fox Terrier

1996. International Dog Show, Monte Carlo.
2261 **719** 4f. multicoloured . . . . 1·25 95

720 "Chapel" (Hubert Clerissi)

1996. 300th Anniv of Chapel of Our Lady of Mercy.
2262 **720** 6f. multicoloured . . . . 1·75 1·60

721 Prince Albert I of Monaco (½-size illustration)

1996. Centenary of Oceanographic Expeditions. Multicoloured.
2263 3f. Type **721** 85 55
2264 4f.50 King Carlos I of Portugal . . . . 1·40 85

722 Prince Rainier III (after F. Messina)

723 Princess Grace

1996. Inauguration of Stamp and Coin Museum (2nd issue). 1974 Prince Rainier design.
2265 **722** 10f. violet . . . . 2·00 1·40
2266 15f. brown . . . . . . 3·25 1·75
2267 20f. blue . . . . . . 4·00 2·40

1996. Europa. Famous Women.
2268 **723** 3f. brown and red . . . 85 60

724 Fishes, Sea and Coastline

1996. 20th Anniv of Ramoge Agreement on Environmental Protection of Mediterranean.
2269 **724** 3f. multicoloured 85 60

725 Saint Nicolas (detail of altarpiece by Louis Brea)

1996. 20th Anniv of Annales Monegasques (historical review). Sheet 180 × 100 mm containing T **725**. and similar vert designs. Each brown.
MS2270 3f. Type **725**; 3f. hector Berlioz (composer); 4f. Guillaume Apollinaire (poet and art critic); 4f. Niccolo Machiavelli (statesman); 5f. Jean-Baptiste Bosio (painter); 5f. Sidonie Colette (writer); 6f. Francois-Joseph Bosio (sculptor); 6f. Michel Eyqem de Montaigne (writer and philosopher) . . . 11·50 11·50

726 Chinese Acrobatics Group in Monaco

1996. Monaco–Chinese Diplomatic Relations. Sheet 100 × 60 mm containing T **726** and similar horiz design. Multicoloured.
MS2271 5f. Type **726**; 5f. Fuling Tomg, Peking . . . . 3·50 3·50

727 Code and Monaco

728 Throwing the Javelin

1996. Introduction of International Dialling Code "377".
2272 **727** 3f. blue 85 60
2273 3f.80 red . . . . 1·10 85

1996. Olympic Games, Atlanta. Multicoloured.
2274 3f. Type **728** 85 80
2275 3f. Baseball 85 80
2276 4f.50 Running . . . . . . 1·40 1·40
2277 4f.50 Cycling . . . . 1·40 1·40

729 Children of Different Races with Balloon

730 Angel and Star

1996. 50th Anniv of UNICEF.
2278 **729** 3f. brown, blue and lilac 85 70

1996. Christmas. Multicoloured.
2279 3f. Type **730** 85 60
2280 6f. Angels heralding . . . . 1·50 1·25

731 Planet and Neptune, God of the Sea (after Roman mosaic, Sousse)

1996. Anniversaries.
2281 **731** 4f. red, blue and black 1·00 95
2282 – 5f. blue and red . . . . 1·25 1·10
DESIGNS—4f. Type **731** (150th anniv of discovery of planet Neptune by Johann Galle); 5f. Rene Descartes (after Franz Hals) (philosopher and scientist, 400th birth anniv).

732 Coins and Press

1996. Inauguaration of Stamp and Coin Museum (3rd issue).
2283 **732** 5f. brown and blue . . . 1·25 1·40
2284 – 5f. brown and purple . . 1·25 1·40
2285 – 10f. blue and brown . . 3·00 2·75
MS2286 130 × 80 mm. Nos. 2283/5 6·50 6·50
DESIGNS—As T **733**: 5f. Stamp press and engraver. 48 × 37 mm: 10f. Museum entrance.

733 Camille Corot (bicentenary)

1996. Artists' Birth Anniversaries. Self-portraits. Multicoloured.
2287 6f. Type **733** . . . . 1·50 1·40
2288 7f. Francisco Goya (250th anniv) . . . . 1·75 1·75

734 Allegory

1996. Monaco Red Cross. Anti-tuberculosis Campaign. Multicoloured.
2289 7f. Type **734** . . . . 1·75 1·25
2290 8f. Camille Guerin and Albert Calmette (developers of vaccine) . . 2·00 1·40

735 Spring

1996. Seasons of the Blackberry. Sheet 143 × 100 mm containing T **735** and similar horiz designs. Multicoloured.
MS2291 4f. Type **735**; 5f. Summer; 6f. Autumn; 7f. Winter . . . . 7·50 7·50

736 "Gloria" (cadet barque), Club, Motorboat and "Tuiga" (royal yacht)

1996. Monaco Yacht Club.
2292 **736** 3f. multicoloured 80 65

737 Seal of Prince Rainier III

738 Clown

1996. 700th Anniv of Grimaldi Dynasty (1st issue).
2293 **737** 2f.70 red, brown and blue 80 55
See also Nos. 2302/14 and 2326/38.

1996. 21st International Circus Festival, Monte Carlo (1997).
2294 **738** 3f. multicoloured 80 55

739 Old and New Racing and Rally Cars

1996. Motor Sport.
2295 **739** 3f. multicoloured 80 55

740 Pictures, Engraving Tools and "Stamps"

1996. 60th Anniv of Stamp Issuing Office (2296) and "Monaco 97" International Stamp Exhibition, Monte Carlo (2297). Each brown, mauve and blue.
2296 3f. Type **740** 80 55
2297 3f. Stamp, magnifying glass and letters 80 55
Nos. 2296/7 were issued together, se-tenant, forming a composite design featuring the Grand Staircase of the Prince's Palace.

741 Double Red Camellia

1996. Monte Carlo Flower Show (1997).
2298 **741** 3f.80 multicoloured . . . 1·00 70

742 Afghan Hound

1996. International Dog Show, Monte Carlo.
2299 **742** 4f.40 multicoloured . . . 1·40 1·25

743 Award

744 Giant Bellflower and Carob Pods and Leaves

1996. 37th Television Festival, Monte Carlo (1997).
2300 **743** 4f.90 multicoloured . . . 1·25 1·10

1996.
2301 **744** 5f. multicoloured . . . . 1·40 1·10

745 Rainier I, Battle of Zerikzee, Arms of his wife Andriola Grillo and Chateau de Cagnes

1997. 700th Anniv of Grimaldi Dynasty (2nd issue). The Seigneurs. Multicoloured.
2302 1f. Type **745** 35 35
2303 1f. Seal of Charles I, Battle of Crecy, Chateau de Roquebrune and Rocher fortifications 35 35
2304 1f. Siege of Rocher by Boccanegra, seal of Rainier II, arms of his two wives Ilaria del Caretto and Isabelle Asinari, Vatican and Papal Palace, Avignon . . 35 35
2305 2f. Defeat of combined fleets of Venice and Florence and Jean I on horseback and with his wife Pomelline Fregoso 55 60
2306 2f. Claudine, acclamation by crowd of her husband Lambert, seals of Lambert and his father Nicolas and strengthening of Monaco Castle 55 60
2307 7f. Statue of Francois Grimaldi disguised as Franciscan monk and clashes between Ghibellines and Guelphs at Genoa . . . . 1·90 1·75
2308 7f. Honore I flanked by Pope Paul III and Duke of Savoy and Battle of Lepanto . . . . 1·90 1·75
2309 7f. Charles II, flags of Genoa and Savoy and attack on Rocher by Capt. Cartier . . . . . . 1·90 1·75
2310 7f. Hercule I, flags of Savoy, Nice and Provence, assassination of Hercule and acclamation of his infant son Honore II . . 1·90 1·75
2311 9f. Catalan aiding Doge of Venice in war against Aragon, exercising "Right of the Sea" and entrusting education of his heiress Claudine to his wife Pomelline . . . . 2·75 2·75
2312 9f. Jean II with his wife Antoinette of Savoy, retable in Chapel of St. Nicholas and assassination of Jean by his brother Lucien . . . . 2·75 2·75
2313 9f. Lucien and siege of Monaco by Genoa . . . 2·75 2·75
2314 9f. Seal of Augustin, Treaty of Tordesillas, visit by King Charles V and Augustin as bishop with his nephew and heir Honore . . . . 2·75 2·75
MS2315 **737** 150 × 80 mm. 2 × 2f.70 red; 2 × 2f.70 brown; 2 × 2f.70 blue; 2 × 2f.70 red, brown and blue . . . . 7·50 7·50

746 Tennis Match and Players

1997. Centenary of Monaco Tennis Championships.
2316 **746** 4f.60 multicoloured . . . 1·25 95

747 Prince Rainier, Trophy and Stamp and Coin Museum

1997. Award to Prince Rainier of International Philately Grand Prix (made to "Person who has Contributed Most to Philately") by Association of Catalogue Editors.
2317 **747** 4f.60 multicoloured . . . 1·25 1·10

748 Images of St.Devote (patron saint)

749 Syringe and Drug Addicts

1997. Europa. Tales and Legends.
2318 **748** 3f. orange and brown . . 80 70
2319 – 3f. blue 80 70
DESIGN: No. 2319, Hercules.

1997. Monaco Red Cross. Anti-drugs Campaign.
2320 **749** 7f. black, blue and red 2·00 1·40

750 First Stamps of United States and Monaco 1996 15f. Stamp

1997. "Pacific 97" International Stamp Exhibiton, San Francisco. 150th Anniv of First United States Stamps.
2321 **750** 4f.90 multicoloured . . . 1·40 1·10

751 Winter and Summer Uniforms, 1997

1997. The Palace Guard. Multicoloured.
2322 3f. Type **751** 80 65
2323 3f.50 Uniforms of 1750, 1815, 1818, 1830 and 1853 1·00 70
2324 5f.20 Uniforms of 1865, 1870, 1904, 1916 and 1935 1·40 1·10

1997. Victory of Marcelo M. Rios at Monaco Tennis Championships. No. 2316 optd **M. RIOS.**
2325 **746** 4f.60 multicoloured . . . 1·40 1·25

1997. 700th Anniv of Grimaldi Dynasty (3rd issue). The Princes. As T **745**. Multicoloured.
2326 1f. Honore II 35 35
2327 1f. Louis I 35 35
2328 1f. Antoine I 35 35
2329 2f. Jacques I 65 65
2330 7f. Charles III . . . . . . 1·90 1·90
2331 7f. Albert I . . . . 1·90 1·90
2332 7f. Louis II . . . . 1·90 1·90
2333 7f. Rainier III . . . . . . 1·90 1·90
2334 9f. Louise-Hippolyte . . . . 2·50 2·50
2335 9f. Honore IV (wrongly inscr "Honore III") . . . 2·50 2·50
2336 9f. Honore III (wrongly inscr "Honore IV") . . . 2·50 2·50
2337 9f. Honore V . . . . 2·50 2·50
2338 9f. Florestan I . . . . . . 2·50 2·50

753 Club Badge, Ball as Globe and Stadium

1997. Monaco, Football Champion of France, 1996–97.
2339 **753** 3f. multicoloured 80 75

754 Magic Wand, Hands and Stars

1997. 13th Magic Grand Prix, Monte Carlo.
2340 **754** 4f.40 black and gold . . 1·25 1·10

755 "Francois Grimaldi" (Ernando Venanzi)

1997. Paintings. Multicoloured.
2341 8f. Type **755** . . . . 2·10 1·75
2342 9f. "St. Peter and St. Paul" (Peter Paul Rubens) . . . 2·25 2·25

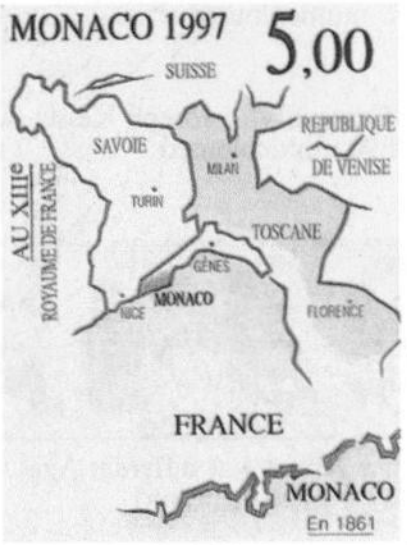

756 Monaco in 13th Century and 1861

1997. 700th Anniv of Grimaldi Dynasty (4th issue). Geographical Evolution of Monaco. Sheet 120 × 145 mm containing T **756** and similar vert designs. Multicoloured.
MS2343 5f. Type **756**; 5f. Monaco from 15th–19th centuries; 5f. Left half of Monaco; 5f. Right half of Monaco . . . . 7·00 7·00
The bottom two stamps of the miniature sheet form a composite design of present-day Monaco with a map showing dates at which the territory was expanded.

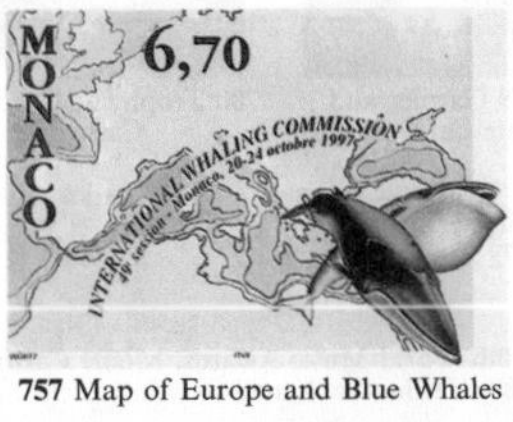

757 Map of Europe and Blue Whales

1997. 49th Session of International Whaling Commission, Monaco.
2344 **757** 6f.70 multicoloured . . . 1·40 1·25

1997. Election of 1995 Botticelli Stamp as Most Beautiful Stamp in the World. Sheet 115 × 100 mm.
MS2345 **715** 15f. blue . . . . . 5·25 5·25

758 Princess Charlotte

1997. 20th Death Anniv of Princess Charlotte.
2346 **758** 3f.80 brown . . . . . . 1·00 1·00

759 Dancer of Russian Ballet and Kremlin, Moscow

761 Diamond-Man (Ribeiro)

760 Trees in Monaco

1997. "Moskva 97" International Stamp Exhbition, Moscow.
2347 **759** 5f. multicoloured . . . . 1·25 1·25

1997. 10th Anniv of Marcel Korenlein Arboretum.
2348 **760** 9f. multicoloured . . . . 2·50 2·25

1997. Winning Entries in Schoolchildren's Drawing Competition.
2349 **761** 4f. multicoloured . . . . 1·00 90
2350 – 4f.50 blue, ultramarine and red . . . . 1·25 1·00
DESIGN—HORIZ: 4f.50, Flying diamonds (Testa).

762 Four-man Bobsleighing, Speed and Figure Skating and Ice Hockey

1997. Winter Olympic Games, Nagano, Japan (1998). Multicoloured.
2351 4f.90 Type **762** . . . . . . 1·40 1·40
2352 4f.90 Alpine skiing, biathlon, two-man bobsleighing and ski-jumping . . . . 1·40 1·40
Nos. 2351/2 were issued together, se-tenant, forming a composite design.

763 Albert I (statue) ($\frac{1}{2}$-size illustration)

1997. 150th Birth Anniv of Prince Albert I (1st issue).
2353 **763** 8f. multicoloured . . . . 2·10 2·10
See also No. 2368.

764 Clown and Horse

765 Pink Campanula and Carob Plant

1997. 22nd International Circus Festival, Monte Carlo (1998).
2354 **764** 3f. multicoloured 80 75

1997. Monte Carlo Flower Show (1998).
2355 **765** 4f.40 multicoloured . . . 1·25 1·10

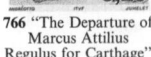

766 "The Departure of Marcus Attilius Regulus for Carthage"

768 Baseball Hat, Television Controller, Ballet Shoe and Football Boot

767 Pope Innocent IV

1997. 250th Birth Anniv of Louis David (painter).
2356 **766** 5f.20 green and red . . . 1·40 1·25

1997. 750th Anniv of Creation of Parish of Monaco by Papal Bull.
2357 **767** 7f.50 brown and blue . . 1·90 1·85

1998. 38th Television Festival.
2358 **768** 4f.50 multicoloured . . . 1·10 1·00

769 Past and Present Presidents

1998. 50th Anniv of Monaco Red Cross.
2359 **769** 5f. brown and red . . . 1·40 1·40

770 Boxer and Dobermann

1998. International Dog Show, Monte Carlo.
2360 **770** 2f.70 multicoloured . . . 80 70

771 White Doves and Laurel Wreath

1998. 30th Meeting of Academy of Peace and International Security.
2361 **771** 3f. green and blue . . . 80 70

772 Ballet Dancer, Piano Keys, Music Score and Violin

1998. 15th Spring Arts Festival.
2362 **772** 4f. multicoloured . . . . 1·00 65

773 Pierre and Marie Curie

1998. Centenary of Discovery of Radium.
2363 **773** 6f. blue and mauve . . . 1·60 1·50

774 Caravel and Globe

1998. "Expo '98" World's Fair, Lisbon. International Year of the Ocean.
2364 **774** 2f.70 multicoloured . . . 80 75

775 St. Devote (stained glass window, Palace Chapel) (½-size illustration)

1998. Europa (1st issue). National Festivals.
2365 **775** 3f. multicoloured 80 70
See also No. 2372.

776 Monte Carlo

777 Kessel

1998. Junior Chamber of Commerce European Conference, Monte Carlo.
2366 **776** 3f. multicoloured 80 75

1998. Birth Centenary of Joseph Kessel (writer).
2367 **777** 3f.90 multicoloured . . . 1·00 1·00

778 Prince Albert I at different Ages (½-size illustration)

1998. 150th Birth Anniv of Prince Albert I (2nd issue).
2368 **778** 7f. brown . . . . 1·75 1·60

779 Garnier and Monte Carlo Casino

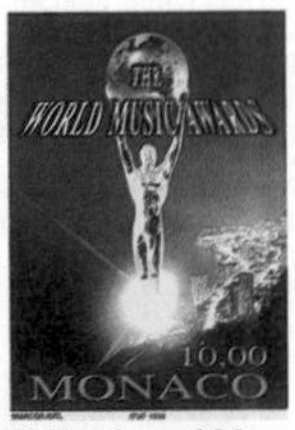

780 Trophy and Monte Carlo

1998. Death Centenary of Charles Garnier (architect).
2369 **779** 10f. multicoloured . . . 2·75 2·25

1998. 10th World Music Awards, Monte Carlo.
2370 **780** 10f. multicoloured . . . 2·75 2·50

781 Racing Cars

1998. 1st Formula 3000 Grand Prix, Monte Carlo.
2371 **781** 3f. red and black 85 45

782 Prince Rainier III, Prince Albert and Royal Palace (½-size illustration)

1998. Europa (2nd issue). National Festivals.
2372 **782** 3f. multicoloured 85 70

783 Porcelain Teapot and Figure of Francois Grimaldi

1998. Fine Arts. Multicoloured.
2373 8f. Type **783** . . . . 2·00 1·90
2374 9f. Fine-bound books and illustration . . . . 2·25 1·40

784 Player on Map of France

1998. World Cup Football Championship, France.
2375 **784** 15f. multicoloured . . . 4·25 4·00

785 Modern and Old Motor Cars and Ferrari

1998. Birth Centenary of Enzio Ferrari (motor manufacturer).
2376 **785** 7f. multicoloured . . . . 1·90 1·75

786 Gershwin, Trumpeter, Dancers and Opening Bars of "Rhapsody in Blue"

1998. Birth Cent of George Gershwin (composer).
2377 **786** 7f.50 ultramarine, blue and black . . . . . . 1·90 1·75

787 Int Marine Pollution College and Marine Environment Laboratory

1998. Int Marine Pollution Conference, Monaco.
2378 **787** 4f.50 multicoloured . . . 1·40 1·10

788 Venue

1998. Post Europ (successor to C.E.P.T.) Plenary Assembly, Monaco.
2379 **788** 5f. multicoloured . . . . 1·40 1·10

789 Belem Tower, Lisbon, and Palace, Monaco

1998. "Expo '98" World's Fair and Stamp Exhibition, Lisbon.
2380 **789** 6f.70 multicoloured . . . 1·75 1·75

790 Sportsmen

1998. 30th Anniv of International Association against Violence in Sport.
2381 **790** 4f.20 multicoloured . . . 1·10 1·00

791 Magician

1998. "Magic Stars" Magic Festival, Monte Carlo.
2382 **791** 3f.50 gold and red . . . 90 90

792 Statue and Vatican Colonnade

1998. 400th Birth Anniv of Giovanni Lorenzo Bernini (architect and sculptor).
2383 **792** 11f.50 blue and brown 3·00 3·25

793 Milan Cathedral

794 Christmas Tree Decoration

1998. "Italia 98" Int Stamp Exhibition, Milan.
2384 **793** 4f.90 green and red . . . 1·25 1·25

1998. Christmas. Multicoloured.
2385 3f. Type **794** 80 65
2386 6f.70 "The Nativity" (detail of icon) (horiz) . . . . . 1·75 1·75
MS2387 86×95 mm. 15f. "Virgin and Child" (detail of icon) (36×49 mm) . . . . 5·25 5·25

1998. As Nos. 1910 etc but no value expressed.
2388 **577** (2f.70) turquoise & blue 60 25
2389 (3f.) red and pink . . . 60 25
2390 (3f.80) blue and cobalt 80 40

795 Lion

1998. 23rd International Circus Festival, Monte Carlo (1999).
2391 **795** 2f.70 multicoloured . . . 70 55

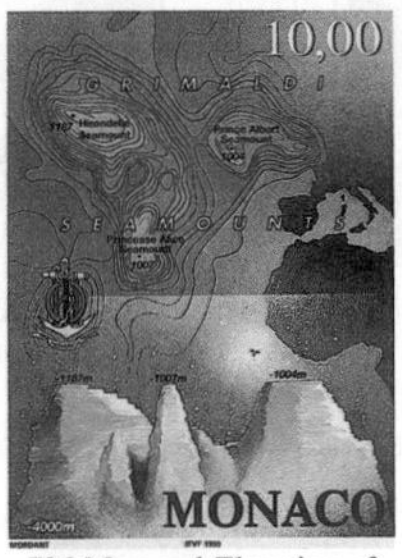

796 Map and Elevation of Seamounts

1998. Grimaldi Seamounts.
2392 **796** 10f. multicoloured . . . 2·50 2·00

797 Prince's Arms and Monogram

1998. 50th Anniv (1999) of Accession of Prince Rainier III (1st issue). Sheet 100×130 mm.
MS2393 **797** 25f. gold and red . . 6·25 6·25
See also No. **MS**2417.

798 1860 Cover and Stamp and Coin Museum

1999. "Monaco 99" International Stamp Exhibition.
2394 **798** 3f. multicoloured 80 50
MS2395 160×111 mm. No. 2394 ×4 . . . . 3·50 3·50

799 Festival Poster

1999. 39th Television Festival.
2396 **799** 3f.80 multicoloured . . . 1·00 60

800 Cocker Spaniel and American Cocker

1999. International Dog Show, Fontvieille.
2397 **800** 4f. multicoloured . . . . 1·00 65

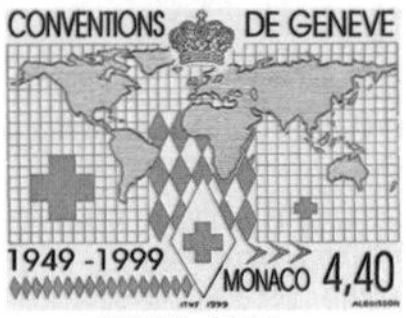

801 World Map

1999. 50th Anniv of Geneva Conventions.
2398 **801** 4f.40 red, brown and black . . . . 1·10 60

802 Arrangement of Flowers named after Grimaldi Family Members

1999. Monte Carlo Flower Show.
2399 **802** 4f.50 multicoloured . . . 1·10 60

803 Children and Heart

1999. 20th Anniv of Monaco Aid and Presence.
2400 **803** 6f.70 multicoloured . . . 1·75 1·00
No. 2400 is also denominated in euros.

804 Palace and Centre

1999. 20th Anniv of Congress Centre Auditorium.
2401 **804** 2f.70 multicoloured . . . 70 50

DENOMINATION. From No. 2402 Monaco stamps are denominated both in francs and in euros. As no cash for the latter was in circulation until 2002, the catalogue continues to use the franc value.

805 Globe and Piano Keys

1999. 10th Piano Masters, Monte Carlo.
2402 **805** 4f.60 multicoloured . . . 1·25 65

806 Rose "Jubile du Prince de Monaco"

808 Olympic Rings and Trophy

807 Williams's Bugatti (winner of first race) and Michael Schumacher's Car (winner of 1999 race)

1999. Flowers. Multicoloured.
2403 4f.90 Type **806** . . . . . . 1·25 70
2404 6f. Rose "Prince de Monaco", rose "Grimaldi" and orchid "Prince Rainier III" . . . 1·50 85

1999. 70th Anniv of Monaco Motor Racing Grand Prix.
2405 **807** 3f. multicoloured 85 50

1999. 3rd Association of Postage Stamp Catalogue Editors and Philatelic Publications Grand Prix.
2406 **808** 4f.40 multicoloured . . . 1·10 75

809 Riders jumping over Monte Carlo (½-size illustration)

1999. 5th International Show Jumping Competition, Monte Carlo.
2407 **809** 5f.20 red, black and blue 1·40 95

810 Footballer, Runner and Palace (½-size illustration)

1999. 75th Anniv of Monaco Sports Association. Multicoloured.
2408 7f. Type **810** . . . . 1·75 1·10
2409 7f. Boxer, footballer, harbour, runner and handballer . . . . 1·75 1·10

811 Architect's Drawing of Forum

1999. Construction of Grimaldi Forum (congress and exhibition centre).
2410 **811** 3f. multicoloured 80 50

812 Facade and Construction

1999. Centenary of Laying of First Stone of Oceanographic Museum.
2411 **812** 5f. multicoloured . . . . 1·25 1·10

813 Eiffel Tower on Map of France, 1849 20c. "Ceres" Stamp and Emblem

814 Casino and Rock

1999. "Philexfrance 99" International Stamp Exhibition, Paris (1st issue). 150th Anniv of First French Stamps.
2412 **813** 2f.70 multicoloured . . . 70 55
See also No. 2423.

1999. Europa. Parks and Gardens. Multicoloured.
2413 3f. Type **814** 70 60
2414 3f. Fontvieille (48×27 mm) 70 60

815 Fontvieille in 1949, Line Graph and Underground Station in 1999 (½-size illustration)

1999. 50 Years of the Economy. Multicoloured.
2415 5f. Type **815** (second sector) 1·25 1·10
2416 5f. Le Larvotto in 1949, line graph and Grimaldi Forum in 1999 (third sector) . . . . 1·25 1·10

816 Definitive Stamps, 2950—89 (½-size illustration)

1999. 50th Anniv of Accession of Prince Rainier III (2nd issue). Two sheets, 100×130 mm (a) or 119×145 mm (b).
MS2417 Two sheets. (a) 20f. blue and gold (as Type **584** but with monogram superimposed); (b) 30f. multicoloured (Type **816**) . . . 12·50 12·50

817 Honore de Balzac

818 Emblem and Chinese Drawing

1999. Writers' Birth Bicentenaries.
2418 **817** 4f.50 blue and scarlet . . 1·10 70
2419 – 5f.20 brown, blue and red . . . . 1·25 85
DESIGN: 5f.20, Sophie Rostopchine, Comtesse de Segur.

1999. 125th Anniv of Universal Postal Union.
2420 **818** 3f. blue, red and yellow 70 55

819 Iris "Rainier III" and Rose "Rainier III"

821 Emblem and Monaco 1885 and French 1878 Stamps

820 Anniversary Emblem

1999. Flowers.
2421 **819** 4f. multicoloured 90 75

1999. 50th Anniv of Monaco's Admission to United Nations Educational, Scientific and Educational Organization.
2422 **820** 4f.20 multicoloured . . . 1·00 80

1999. "Philexfrance 99" International Stamp Exhibition, Paris (2nd issue).
2423 **821** 7f. black, blue and mauve . . . . 1·60 1·50

822 Athletes

1999. 10th Sportel (sport and television) Congress, Fontvieille.
2424 **822** 10f. multicoloured . . . 2·25 2·00

823 Maltese Cross, Knights and Valletta

1999. 900th Anniv of Sovereign Military Order of Malta and 25th Anniv of National Association of the Order.
2425 **823** 11f.50 red, brown and blue . . . . 2·50 2·50

824 1999 Postcard of Monaco, 1989 Definitive Design and Obverse of Jubilee Coin

1999. Postcard, Coin and Stamp Exhibition, Fontvieille (1st issue).
2426 **824** 3f. multicoloured 70 55
See also No. 2429.

1999. "Magic Stars" Magic Festival, Monte Carlo. As No. 2382 but face value and date changed.
2427 **791** 4f.50 gold and red . . . 1·10 90

825 Fontvielle Project, Stage 2

1999. Achievements and Projects. Sheet 150 × 100 mm containing T **825** and similar multicoloured designs.
MS2428 4f. Type **825**; 9f. New harbour mole; 9f. Grimaldi Forum (congress centre); 19f. Underground train, harbour and station (76 × 36 mm) . . . . . 10·50 10·50

826 1949 Postcard of Monaco, Reverse of Jubilee Coin and 1950 Definitive

1999. Postcard, Coin and Stamp Exhibition, Fontvieille (2nd issue).
2429 **826** 6f.50 multicoloured . . . 1·60 1·40

827 Pierrot juggling "2000"

828 "Madonna and Child" (Simone Cantarini)

1999. 24th International Circus Festival, Monte Carlo (2000).
2430 **827** 2f.70 multicoloured . . . 65 55

1999. Christmas.
2431 **828** 3f. multicoloured 75 55

829 Blessing and Holy Door, St. Peter's Cathedral, Rome

1999. Holy Year 2000.
2432 **829** 3f.50 multicoloured . . . 80 65

830 Mixed Arrangement

831 Emblem

1999. 33rd Monte Carlo Flower Show.
2433 **830** 4f.50 multicoloured . . . 1·10 90

1999. "Monaco 2000" International Stamp Exhibitions.
2434 **831** 3f. multicoloured 75 55

832 Bust of Napoleon (Antonio Canova)

833 Festival Emblem

2000. 30th Anniv of Napoleonic Museum.
2435 **832** 4f.20 multicoloured . . . 1·00 80

2000. 40th Television Festival, Monte Carlo.
2436 **833** 4f.90 multicoloured . . . 1·10 95

834 St. Peter and St. James the Major

2000. The Twelve Apostles. Multicoloured.
2437 **834** 4f. blue, orange and gold 80 75
2438 – 5f. red and gold . . . . 1·00 95
2439 – 6f. violet and gold . . . 1·25 1·10
2440 – 7f. brown and gold . . . 1·50 1·40
2441 – 8f. green and gold . . . 1·75 1·50
2442 – 9f. red, orange and gold 1·90 1·75
DESIGNS: 5f. St. John and St. Andrew; 6f. St. Philip and St. Bartholomew; 7f. St. Matthew and St. Thomas; 8f. St. James the Minor and St. Jude; 9f. St. Simon and St. Mathias.

835 Golden Labrador and Golden Retriever

2000. International Dog Show, Monte Carlo.
2443 **835** 6f.50 multicoloured . . . 1·60 1·40

836 Man's Head, Drawings and Key (Adami)

2000. Monaco and the Sea. Multicoloured.
2444 6f.55 Type **836** . . . . . . 1·50 1·40
2445 6f.55 "Monaco" above sea (Arman) . . . . 1·50 1·40
2446 6f.55 Abstract designs (Cane) . . . . 1·50 1·40
2447 6f.55 Hand touching sun in sky (Folon) . . . . . . 1·50 1·40
2448 6f.55 Angel sleeping and boats (Fuchs) . . . . . . 1·50 1·40
2449 6f.55 Harbour (E. de Sigaldi) . . . . 1·50 1·40
2450 6f.55 Views of harbour on silhouettes of yachts (Sosno) . . . . 1·50 1·40
2451 6f.55 Waves and floating ball (Verkade) . . . . . 1·50 1·40

837 Olympic Rings on Globe and Flags

2000. Olympic Games, Sydney, Australia.
2452 **837** 7f. multicoloured . . . . 1·50 1·40

838 "Building Europe"

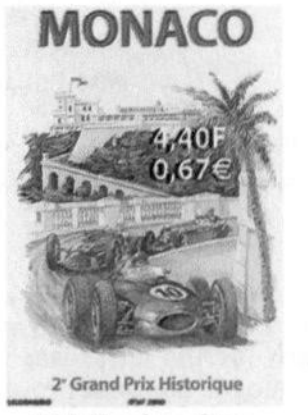

839 Racing Cars

2000. Europa. Multicoloured.
2453 3f. Type **838** 75 70
2454 3f. Map of Europe and Post Europ member countries' flags (56 × 37 mm) 75 70

2000. 2nd Historic Vehicles Grand Prix.
2455 **839** 4f.40 multicoloured . . . 90 80

840 Monaco Pavilion and Emblem

2000. "EXPO 2000" World's Fair, Hanover.
2456 **840** 5f. multicoloured . . . . 1·00 95

841 Sts. Mark, Matthew, John and Luke

2000. The Four Evangelists.
2457 **841** 20f. black, flesh and green . . . . 4·25 4·25

842 St. Stephen and Emblem

843 Golfer

2000. "WIPA 2000" International Stamp Exhibition, Vienna.
2458 **842** 4f.50 black, blue and red 90 85

2000. Pro-celebrity Golf Tournament, Monte Carlo.
2459 **843** 4f.40 multicoloured . . . 90 85

844 Fencing

2000. Olympic Games, Sydney. Multicoloured.
2460 2f.70 Type **844** 65 35
2461 4f.50 Rowing 90 55

845 Humber Beeston and Woman with Parasol, 1911

2000. Motor Cars and Fashion. Motor cars from the Royal Collection. Multicoloured.
2462 3f. Type **845** 65 45
2463 6f.70 Jaguar 4-cylinder and woman, 1947 . . . . . . 1·50 85
2464 10f. Rolls Royce Silver Cloud and woman wearing swing coat, 1956 2·00 1·25
2465 15f. Lamborghini Countach and woman wearing large hat, 1986 . . . . 3·25 1·60

846 Entrance to Museum

847 Open Hands and Emblem

2000. Philatelic Rarities Exhibition (1999), Stamp and Coin Museum, Monte Carlo.
2466 **846** 3f.50 multicoloured . . . 75 65

2000. Monaco Red Cross.
2467 **847** 10f. multicoloured . . . 2·10 1·90

848 Magnifying Glass, Stamps and Exhibition Hall

849 Magician

2000. "WORLD STAMP USA" International Exhibition, Anaheim, California.
2468 **848** 4f.40 multicoloured . . . 95 55

2000. "Magic Stars" Magic Festival, Monte Carlo.
2469 **849** 4f.60 multicoloured . . . 95 55

850 Da Vinci's "Man" and Mathematical Symbols

2000. World Mathematics Year.
2470 **850** 6f.50 brown . . . . . . 1·40 65

851 Right-hand Section of Screen

2000. Holy Year. Restoration of Altar Screen, Monaco Cathedral. Sheet 120 × 100 mm containing T **851** and similar design.
MS2471 10f. Type **851**; 20f. Left-hand and central sections (53 × 52 mm) . . . . 6·75 6·75

852 Shark and Museum Facade

2000. Opening of New Aquarium, Oceanographical Museum.
2472 **852** 3f. multicoloured 65 35

853 Cathedral and Statue of Bear

2000. "ESPANA 2000" International Stamp Exhibition, Madrid.
2473 **853** 3f.80 multicoloured . . . 85 45

854 Fishes and Corals

2000. 5th International Congress on Aquaria (5f.) and 25th Anniv of Monaco Nature Protection Association (9f.). Multicoloured.
2474 5f. Type **854** . . . . 1·10 55
2475 9f. Starfish, water plant and fish . . . . 1·90 95

855 Museum Facade and Plants

2000. 50th Anniv of Observatory Cave and 40th Anniv of Anthropological Museum.
2476 **855** 5f.20 purple, green and brown . . . . 1·00 55

856 Fresco, Oceanography Museum (½-size illustration)

2000. International Aquariological Congress.
2477 **856** 7f. multicoloured . . . . 1·50 65

857 18th-century Crib

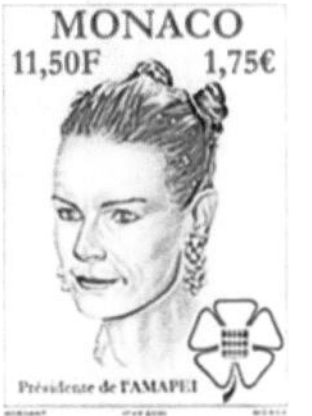

858 Princess Stephanie (President)

2000. Christmas.
2478 **857** 3f. multicoloured 65 25

2000. Motor Cars and Fashion. Motor cars from the Royal Collection. As T **845**. Multicoloured.
2479 5f. Ferrari Formula 1 racing car and woman in racing clothes, 1989 . . . . . . 1·10 55
2480 6f. Fiat 600 "Jolly" and woman wearing swimming costume, 1955 . . . . . 1·25 65
2481 8f. Citroen C4F "Autochenille" and woman wearing coat and hat, 1929 . . . . 1·75 85

2000. Association for Help and Protection of Disabled Children (A.M.A.P.E.I.).
2482 **858** 11f.50 blue and red . . . 2·40 1·10

859 Exhibition Poster

2000. "Monaco 2000" Stamp Exhibition. Sheet 150 × 90 mm containing two examples of T **859**.
MS2483 20f. × 2 multicoloured 4·50 4·50

860 Warrior kneeling

861 Museum Building

2000. Terracotta Warrior Exhibition, Grimaldi Forum (2001).
2484 **860** 2f.70 black and red . . . 65 25

2000. 50th Anniv of Postal Museum.
2485 **861** 3f. multicoloured 65 25

862 Arms

863 Iris "Princess Caroline of Monaco"

2000. Self-adhesive.
2486 **862** (3f.) black and red . . . 65 25

2000. 34th Monte Carlo Flower Show.
2487 **863** 3f.80 multicoloured . . . 85 35

864 Sardinian 1851 5c., 20c. and 40c. Stamps

2000. 150th Anniv (2001) of First Sardinian Stamp.
2488 **864** 6f.50 blue, red and black 1·40 65

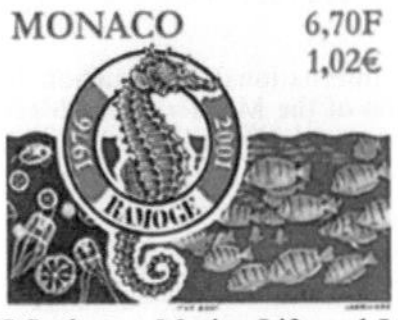

865 Seahorse, Marine Life and Life Belt

2000. 25th Anniv (2001) of the Ramoge Agreement on Environmental Protection of Mediterranean.
2489 **865** 6f.70 multicoloured . . . 1·50 65

866 Breitling Orbiter and 1984 2f.80 Stamp

867 Clown with Seal balancing Ball

2000. 1st Non-Stop Balloon Circumnavigation of Globe (1999). Award to Bertrand Picard of International Philately Grand Prix by Association of Catalogue Editors.
2490 **866** 9f. multicoloured . . . . 1·90 95

2000. 25th International Circus Festival, Monte Carlo (2001). Different poster designs by artist named. Multicoloured (except No. 2492).
2491 2f.70 Type **867** 65 35
2492 6f. Clown playing guitar (Hodge) (black, red and blue) . . . . 1·25 65
2493 6f. Clown resting head (Knie) . . . . 1·25 65
2494 6f. Tiger and circus tent (P. Merot) . . . . 1·25 65
2495 6f. Lions, horses and trapeze artists (Poulet) . . . . . . 1·25 65
2496 6f. Monkey and circus tents (T. Mordant) . . . . . . 1·25 65

868 Player kicking Ball

2000. Monaco, Football Champion of France, 1999–2000.
2497 **868** 4f.50 multicoloured . . . 1·00 45

869 Sea Mammals and Mediterranean Sea

2000. Mediterranean Sea Marine Mammals Sanctuary.
2498 **869** 5f.20 multicoloured . . . 1·10 55

870 Nativity Scene (½-size illustration)

2000. Christmas.
2499 **870** 10f. multicoloured . . . 2·00 1·10

871 Poster

873 Flower Arrangement

872 Leonberger and Newfoundland Dogs

2001. 41st Television Festival, Monte Carlo.
2500 **871** 3f.50 multicoloured . . . 70 50

2001. International Dog Show, Monte Carlo.
2501 **872** 6f.50 multicoloured . . . 1·25 95

2001. Flower Show, Genoa.
2502 **873** 6f.70 multicoloured . . . 1·25 95

874 Monaco Palace

875 Princess Caroline and Portrait of Prince Pierre of Monaco (founder)

2001. Europa. Water Resources. Multicoloured.
2503 3f. Type **874** 60 45
2504 3f. Undercover washing area 60 45

2001. 50th Anniv of Literary Council of Monaco.
2505 **875** 2f.70 black, brown and green 50 25

876 Malraux

877 Town Hall

2001. Birth Centenary of Andre Malraux (writer).
2506 **876** 10f. black and red . . . 1·90 1·40

2001. "BELGICA 2001" International Stamp Exhibition, Brussels.
2507 **877** 4f. blue and red 75 60

878 Coins, Stamp and Book

879 Princess Grace and Ballet Dancer

2001. Postcard, Coin and Stamp Exhibition, Fontvielle.
2508 **878** 2f.70 multicoloured . . . 50 40

2001. 25th Anniv of Princess Grace Dance Academy.
2509 **879** 4f.40 multicoloured . . . 85 65

880 Model

2001. Naval Museum, Fontvielle.
2510 **880** 4f.50 multicoloured . . . 85 65

881 Petanque Balls

2001. World Petanque Championships.
2511 **881** 5f. multicoloured 75 70

882 Fireplace, Throne Room

2001. Royal Palace (1st series). Multicoloured.
2512 3f. Type **882** 60 40
2513 4f.50 Blue Room 85 65
2514 6f.70 York Chamber . . . . 1·25 95
2515 15f. Throne room ceiling fresco . . . . 3·00 2·25
See also Nos. 2541/3.

883 Littre and Diderot

2001. 250th Anniv of *Encyclopaedia or Critical Dictionary of Sciences, Arts and Trades* (Denis Diderot) and Birth Bicentenary of Emile Littre (compiler of *Dictionary of the French Language*).
2516 **883** 4f.20 black, blue and green 80 60

884 Medal and Steam Yacht

2001. 30th Anniv of Prince Albert Oceanography Prize.
2517 **884** 9f. blue . . . . 1·75 1·25

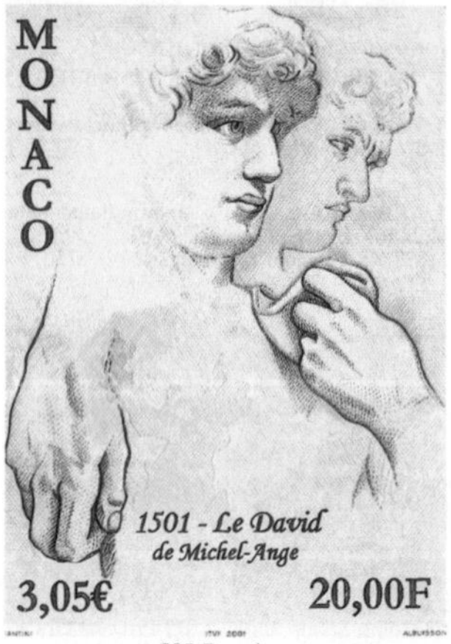

885 Drawings

2001. 500th Anniv of David (sculpture, Michaelangelo).
2518 **885** 20f. multicoloured . . . 3·75 3·00

886 Alfred Nobel (prize fund founder)

888 Virgin and Child

887 Prince Rainer, Prince Albert, Map, Satellite, Ship, and Submarine

2001. Centenary of the Nobel Prize. Multicoloured.
2519 5f. Type **886** 95 70
2520 8f. Henri Dunant (founder of Red Cross and winner of Peace Prize, 1901) . . 1·50 1·10
2521 11f.50 Enrico Fermi (physicist and winner of Physics Prize, 1938) . . . 2·25 1·75

2001. 36th International Commission for Scientific Exploration of the Mediterranean Meeting.
2522 **887** 3f. multicoloured 60 45

2001. Christmas.
2523 **888** 3f. multicoloured 60 45

889 Garden Tiger Moth (*Artica caja*)

890 Lion and Ringmaster

2002. Flora and Fauna.
2524 **889** 1c. black, red and sepia 10 10
2525 – 2c. multicoloured 10 10
2526 – 5c. multicoloured 10 10
2527 – 10c. black, green and yellow 15 10
2528 – 20c. red, yellow and black 25 20
2529 – 41c. multicoloured . . . 65 45
2530 – 50c. multicoloured . . . 60 45
2531 – €1 multicoloured . . . 1·25 1·00
2532 – €2 multicoloured . . . 2·50 2·00
2533 – €5 brown, green and black . . . . 6·25 4·75
2534 – €10 green, red and black . . . . 12·50 9·50
DESIGNS—VERT: 5c. Blue trumpet vine (*Thunbergia grandiflora*); 41c. *Helix aspera*; 50c. Foxy charaxes (*Charaxes jasius*); €2 Red thorn apple (*Datura sanguinea*); €5 Crested tit (*Parus crisatus*). HORIZ: 2c. *Luria lurida*; 10c. Great tit (*Parus major*); 20c. Common barberfish (*Anthias anthias*); €1 Zoned mitre (*Mitra zonata*); €10 Common snipefish (*Macroramphosus scolopax*).

2002. 26th International Circus Festival, Monte Carlo.
2540 **890** 41c. multicoloured . . . 50 40

891 Crystal Gallery

2002. Royal Palace (2nd series). Multicoloured.
2541 41c. Type **891** 50 40
2542 46c. Throne room (horiz) 60 45
2543 58c. Landscape painting in Crystal Gallery (horiz) . . 75 60

892 Rocking Horse of Flowers

2002. 35th Monte Carlo Flower Show.
2544 **892** 53c. multicoloured . . . 65 50

893 Old and Modern Rally Cars

2002. Motoring Events in Monaco. Sheet 124×95 mm, containing T **893** and similar vert design. Multicoloured.
MS2545 €1.07, Type **893** (70th Monte Carlo car rally); €1.22, Old racing car (Historic Vehicles third Grand Prix) and modern Formula 1 racing car (60th Monaco Grand Prix) . . . . . 3·25 2·40

894 Skiers, Ice Skater and Ice Hockey Player

2002. Winter Olympic Games, Salt Lake City, U.S.A. Multicoloured.
2546 23c. Type **894** 35 25
2547 23c. Bobsleigh, luge and skiers (face value, emblem and country inscription at right) 35 25
Nos. 2446/7 were issued together, se-tenant, forming a composite design.

895 Exhibition Cases and Prince Albert I

2002. Anniversaries. Multicoloured.
2548 64c. Type **895** (centenary of Prehistoric Anthropology Museum) 90 65
2549 67c. Title page, Prince Albert I and ship (centenary of publication of "La Carriere d'un Navigateur" (memoirs) by Prince Albert I) 95 70

896 Mazarin (painting, Phillippe de Champaigne)

2002. 400th Birth Anniv of Jules Mazarin (cardinal to Louis XIV).
2550 **896** 69c. multicoloured . . . 1·00 75

897 Bust of Napoleon Bonaparte and Medal

2002. Bicentenary of Legion d'Honneur.
2551 **897** 70c. multicoloured . . . 1·00 75

898 Whales and Dolphins

2002. 1st Meeting of Signatories to Agreement on the Conservation of Cetaceans of the Black Sea, Mediterranean Sea and Contiguous Atlantic Area (ACCOBAMS), Monaco.
2552 **898** 75c. multicoloured . . . 1·80 80

899 Da Vinci

2002. 550th Birth Anniv of Leonardo da Vinci (artist).
2553 **899** 76c. multicoloured . . . 1·10 80

900 St. Bernard and Bouvier

2002. International Dog Show, Monte Carlo.
2554 **900** 99c. multicoloured . . . 1·40 1·00

901 Police Officers and Badge

2002. Centenary of Police Force.
2555 **901** 53c. multicoloured . . . 75 55

902 Map of Europe and Flag

2002. 25th Anniv of European Academy of Postal Studies.
2556 **902** 58c. multicoloured . . . 85 60

903 Circus and Globe

904 Emblem

2002. Europa. Circus. Multicoloured.
2557 46c. Type **903** 65 45
2558 46c. "JOURS DE CIRQUE" and performers 65 45

2002. 20th International Swimming Competition.
2559 **904** 64c. multicoloured . . . 95 65

905 Tarmac Roads

2002. Centenary of First Tarmac Roads.
2560 **905** 41c. red, black and brown 60 45

906 Exhibition Hall and Displays

907 Emblem

2002. "Monacophil 2002" International Stamp Exhibition.
2561 **906** 46c. green, violet and red 65 45

2002. 42nd Television Festival, Monte Carlo.
2562 **907** 70c. multicoloured . . . 1·00 75

908 Footballers and Globe

2002. World Cup Football Championship, Japan and South Korea.
2563 **908** 75c. green, blue and red 1·10 80

909 Obverse of 1, 2 and 5 cent Coins and Reverse

2002. Coins.
2564 **909** 46c. copper, red and black 65 45
2565 – 46c. gold, red and black 65 45
2566 – €1.50 multicoloured . . 2·10 1·50
2567 – €1.50 multicoloured . . 2·10 1·50
DESIGNS: Type **909**; 46c. Obverse of 10, 20 and 50 cent coins and reverse; €1.50, Obverse and reverse of 1 euro coin; €1.50, Obverse and reverse of 2 euro coin.

910 Debussy, Pelleas and Melisande

2002. Centenary of First Performance of Claude Debussy's Opera "Pelleas and Melisande".
2568 **910** 69c. green, blue and red 1·00 75

911 Saint Devote, Boat and Dove

2002. Monaco Red Cross.
2569 **911** €1.02 red, greenish blue and black . . . . . . 1·50 1·10

912 Aerial View of Monaco

2002. International Year of Mountains.
2570 **912** €1.37 multicoloured . . 2·00 1·50

913 Hugo

914 Dumas

2002. Birth Bicentenary of Victor Hugo (writer). Each blue, brown and red.
2571 50c. Type **913** 70 50
2572 57c. Scenes from his books 80 60
Nos. 2571/2 were issued together, se-tenant, forming a composite design.

2002. Birth Bicentenary of Alexandre Dumas (writer). Multicoloured.
2573 61c. Type **914** 90 65
2574 61c. Scenes from his books 90 65
Nos. 2573/4 were issued together, se-tenant, forming a composite design.

915 Princess Grace

916 Star-shaped Flower

2002. 26th Publication of "Annales Monegasques" (archives).
2575 **915** €1.75 multicoloured . . 2·50 1·80

2002. Christmas.
2576 **916** 50c. multicoloured . . . 70 50

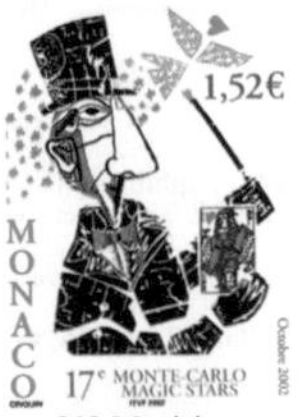

917 Frame from Film and Melies

918 Magician

2002. Centenary of "Le Voyage dans la Lune" (film by Georges Melies).
2577 **917** 76c. multicoloured . . . 1·10 80

2002. "Magic Stars" Magic Festival, Monte Carlo.
2578 **918** €1.52 multicoloured . . 2·20 1·60

919 1949 Mercedes 220A Cabriolet

2002. Motor Cars from the Royal Collection. Multicoloured.
2579 46c. Type **919** 65 45
2580 69c. 1956 Rolls Royce Silver Cloud . . . . 1·75 75
2581 €1.40 1974 Citroen DS 21 2·00 1·50

920 Spring

2002. Royal Palace (3rd series). Frescoes. Sheet 120 × 100 mm containing T **920** and similar horiz designs showing the Four Seasons. Multicoloured.
MS2582 50c. Type **920**; €1 Summer; €1.50, Autumn; €2 Winter 7·00 5·25

921 Footballer and Golden Ball

923 Flower Arrangement

922 Exhibition Poster

2002. Award of International Philatelic Grand Prix to Luis Figo (footballer and 2001 Golden Ball winner). Centenary of Real Madrid Football Club.
2583 **921** 91c. multicoloured . . . 1·80 30

2002. "MonacoPhil 2002" Stamp Exhibition (2nd issue). Sheet 120 × 82 mm, containing T **922** and similar vert design. Multicoloured. Imperf.
MS2584 €3 Type **922**; €3 Exhibition emblem . . . . . . 8·50 6·50

2002. 36th Monte Carlo Flower Show.
2585 **923** 67c. multicoloured . . . 95 70

924 Princesses Caroline and Stephanie (presidents)

2002. 40th Anniv of "Association Mondiale des Amis de l'Enfance" (children's society).
2586 **924** €1.25 multicoloured . . 1·80 1·30

925 St. George (statue)

926 Prince Louis II, Flag, Arch and Building

2002. 1700th Anniv of St. George's Martyrdom.
2587 **925** 53c. multicoloured . . . 75 55

2002. Bicentenary of Saint-Cyr Imperial Military School.
2588 **926** 61c. multicoloured . . . 90 65

927 Clown

928 Crossed Pennants and Part of Yacht and Crew

2003. 27th International Circus Festival, Monte Carlo.
2589 **927** 59c. multicoloured . . . 80 60

2003. 50th Anniv of Monaco Yacht Club.
2590 **928** 46c. multicoloured . . . 60 45

929 Children

2003. 15th Premiere Rampe (children's circus) Festival.
2591 **929** €2.82 multicoloured . . 3·75 2·75

930 Team Members pushing Bobsleigh

2003. 10th World Bobsleigh Pushing Championship.
2592 **930** 80c. multicoloured . . . 1·00 75

931 Dove, Globe and Prince Albert I

932 Leaves, Spectator, Tennis Court and Player

2003. Centenary of Monaco International Peace Institute.
2593 **931** €1.19 multicoloured . . 1·60 1·20

2003. Tennis Masters Championship, Monte Carlo.
2594 **932** €1.30 multicoloured . . 1·75 1·30

933 Rough Collie

2003. International Dog Show, Monte Carlo.
2595 **933** 79c. multicoloured . . . 1·00 75

934 Anniversary Emblem

2003. 40th Anniv of Monaco Junior Chamber of Commerce.
2596 **934** 41c. multicoloured . . . 55 40

935 Club Grounds

2003. 75th Anniv of Monte Carlo Country Club.
2597 **935** 46c. multicoloured . . . 60 45

936 Prince Albert I, Sextant, Maps and Emblem (½-size illustration)

2003. Centenary of First General Bathymetric Chart of the Oceans. Multicoloured.
2598 €1.25 Type **936** . . . . . 1·60 1·20
2599 €1.25, Buildings and maps 1·60 1·20
Nos. 2598/9 were issued together, se-tenant, forming a composite design.

937 Girl on Diving Board (Jean-Gabriel Domergue)

938 Castle, Coin and Ship

2003. Europa. Poster Art. Multicoloured.
2600 50c. Type **937** 65 50
2601 50c. Monte-Carlo (Alphonse Mucha) 65 50

2003. Postcard Coin and Stamp Exhibition, Fontvielle.
2602 **938** 45c. multicoloured . . . 60 45

939 Face

940 Bronze Statuette

2003. 43rd International Television Festival.
2603 **939** 90c. multicoloured . . . 1·20 90

2003. 15th Biannual Antique Dealers Meeting.
2604 **940** €1.80 multicoloured . . 2·40 1·80

941 Roald Amundsen and Polar Scene

2003. Centenaries. Multicoloured.
2605 90c. Type **941** (1st crossing of North Pole) . . . . . 1·20 90
2606 €1.80 Wright brothers and *Kitty Hawk* (1st powered flight) . . . . 2·40 1·80

942 Hector Berlioz

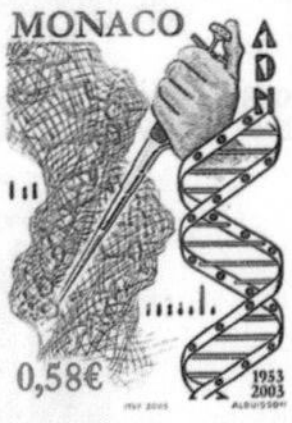
944 Hand holding Pipette and DNA Double Helix (50th anniv of discovery)

943 Woman's Head (Francois Boucher) (300th anniv)

2003. Composers Birth Anniversaries.
2607 **942** 75c. black and red . . . 1·00 75
2608 – €1.60 blue, sepia and red . . . . 2·10 1·60
DESIGNS—VERT: Type **942** (bicentenary). HORIZ: €1.60 Aram Khatchaturian (centenary).

2003. Artists' Birth Anniversaries.
2609 **943** €1.30 multicoloured . . 1·75 1·30
2610 – €3 mauve and black . . 4·00 3·00
2611 – €3.60 brown and black 4·75 3·50
DESIGNS: €1.30, Type **943**; €3 Vincent Van Gogh (150th anniv); €3.60, Girolamo Francesco Maria Mazzola (Le Parmigianino) (500th anniv).

2003. Scientific Anniversaries.
2612 **944** 58c. black, blue and red 80 50
2613 – €1.11 chestnut, blue and red . . . . 1·40 1·10
DESIGNS: Type **944**; Alexander Fleming (75th anniv of discovery of penicillin).

945 Nostradamus

946 Magician

2003. 500th Birth Anniv of Michel de Nostre-Dame (Nostradamus) (astrologer).
2614 **945** 70c. multicoloured . . . 40 30

2003. "Magic Stars" Magic Festival, Monte Carlo.
2615 **946** 75c. multicoloured . . . 1·00 75

947 Marie and Pierre Curie

2003. Centenary of Award of Nobel Prize for Physics to Antoine Henri Becquerel and Pierre and Marie Curie.
2616 **947** €1.20 multicoloured . . 1·60 1·20

948 St. Devote kneeling before Cross

950 Star-shaped Flower

949 Edmund Hilary and Mount Everest

2003. 1700th (2004) Anniv of Arrival of St. Devote (patron saint) in Monaco (1st series). Each blue, black and red.
2617 45c. Type **948** 60 45
2618 45c. St. Devote facing Barbarus 60 45
2619 45c. Boat carrying St. Devote's body 60 45
2620 45c. St. Devote (statue) . . 60 45
See also No. 2626/30.

2003. 50th Anniv of First Ascent of Mount Everest.
2621 **949** €1 multicoloured . . . 1·30 1·00

2003. Christmas.
2622 **950** 50c. multicoloured . . . 65 50

951 Lion and Lion Tamer

952 Exhibition Poster

2003. MonacoPhil 2004 Stamp Exhibition (December 2004).
2623 **951** 50c. multicoloured . . . 65 50

2003. 28th International Circus Festival (January 2004), Monte Carlo.
2624 **952** 70c. multicoloured . . . 95 70

953 Tram and Buildings

2004. Centenary of Beausoleil Municipality.
2625 **953** 75c. multicoloured . . . 1·00 75

954 St. Devote kneeling before Alta

955 Princesses Grace and Caroline

2004. 1700th Anniv of St. Devote's Arrival (2nd series).
2626 **954** 50c. red and brown . . . 65 50
2627 – 75c. orange and brown (horiz) . . . . 1·00 75
2628 – 90c. brown and deep brown (horiz) . . . . 1·20 90
2629 – €1 brown and deep brown . . . . 1·30 1·00
2630 – €4 purple and brown (horiz) . . . . 5·75 4·25
DESIGNS: 75c. Before Barbarus; 90c. Martyrdom; €1 Boat carrying St. Devote's body; €4 Arrival in Monaco.

2004. 40th Anniv of Princess Grace Foundation.
2640 **955** 50c. multicoloured . . . 65 50

956 *Hyla meridionalis*

2004. Amphibians.
2641 **956** 75c. green, yellow and black . . . . 1·00 75
2642 – €4.50 green, blue and black . . . . 6·00 4·50
DESIGN: Type **956**; €4.50, *Lacerte viridis*.

957 Princess Grace and Shamrock Leaf

2004. 20th Anniv of Princess Grace Irish Library.
2643 **957** €1.11 green and brown 1·50 1·10

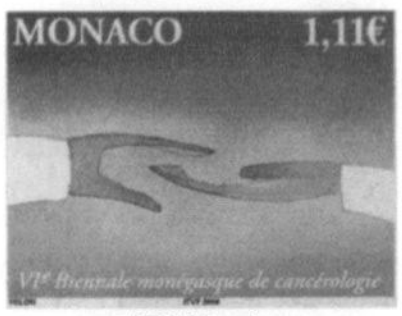
958 Hands

2004. 6th Biennial Oncological Meeting.
2644 **958** €1.11 multicoloured . . 1·50 1·10

959 Princess Grace (statue) (Daphne du Barry)

960 Garden

2004.
2645 **959** €1.45 multicoloured . . 2·00 1·50

2004. 20th Anniv of Princess Grace Rose Garden.
2646 **960** €1.90 multicoloured . . 2·50 1·90

961 Mask, Musical Instruments, Dancer and Actor

2004. Spring Arts Festival.
2647 **961** €1 brown, scarlet and green . . . . 1·40 1·00

962 Cathedral Facade, Choirboy and Emblem

963 Flower Arrangement

2004. Centenary of Cathedral Choir.
2648 **962** 45c. multicoloured . . . 60 45

2004. 37th Monte Carlo Flower Show.
2649 **963** 58c. multicoloured . . . 80 60

964 Cavalier King Charles Spaniels

2004. International Dog Show, Monte Carlo.
2650 **964** 90c. multicoloured . . . 1·20 90

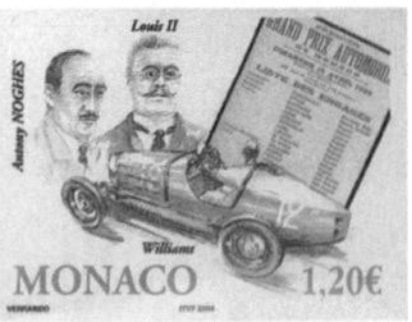
965 Antony Noghes, King Louis II and Bugatti 35B Race Car driven by William Grover-Williams

2004. 75th Anniv of First Monaco Motor Racing Grand Prix.
2651 **965** €1.20 multicoloured . . 1·60 1·20

966 Hands enclosing Children

2004. Monaco International School.
2652 **966** 50c. multicoloured . . . 70 50

967 Athens Stadium (1896) and Modern Runners (½-size illustration)

2004. Olympic Games, Athens. Multicoloured.
2653 45c. Type **967** 60 45
2654 45c. Classical Greek runners and Athens stadium (2004) 60 45
Nos. 2653/4 were issued together, se-tenant, forming a composite design.

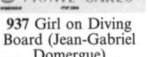

968 Women wearing Swimsuits ("What Joy to Live the Summer in Monte Carlo") (poster, 1948)

969 Medal

2004. Europa. Holidays. Multicoloured.
2655 50c. Type **968** 70 50
2656 50c. Frontier sign ("The border of your dreams") (poster, 1951) 70 50

2004. 50th Anniv of Order of Grimaldi (medal).
2657 **969** 90c. multicoloured . . . 1·20 90

970 Napoleon, Crown Prince Honore-Gabriel and Prince Joseph (officers in Napoleon's army)

2004. Bicentenary of Coronation of Emperor Napoleon I. Multicoloured.
2658 58c. Type **970** 80 60
2659 75c. Eagle and bees (imperial insignia) (horiz) 1·10 80
2660 €1.90 Stephanie de Beauharnais (Napoleon's niece and adopted daughter) . . . . 2·60 1·90
2661 €2.40 Napoleon I wearing coronation robes . . . . 3·25 2·40

971 George Balanchine (choreographer) and Serge Diaghilev (ballet impresario)

2004. First Production of Russian Ballet in Monaco.
2662 **971** €1.60 multicoloured . . 2·20 1·60

972 Eye enclosing Globe

2004. 44th International Television Festival.
2663 **972** €1.80 multicoloured . . 2·50 1·90

973 Frederic Mistral

2004. Centenary of Frederic Mistral's Nobel Prize for Literature.
2664 **973** 45c. vermilion, brown and green 60 45

974 Bird holding Envelope and Globe

2004. 23rd UPU Conference, Bucharest.
2665 **974** 50c. multicoloured . . . 70 50

975 Chinese Landscape and Marco Polo

2004. 750th Birth Anniv of Marco Polo (traveller).
2666 **975** 50c. multicoloured . . . 70 70

976 Stamps and Park

2004. Salon de Timbre International Stamp Exhibition, Paris.
2667 **976** 75c. brown, green and vermilion . . . . . . 1·00 75

977 Scenes from the Stories

2004. 300th Anniv of French Translation of "One Thousand and One Nights" (collection of stories).
2668 **977** €1 indigo . . . . . . 1·40 1·00

978 Hotel Complex

2004. 75th Anniv of Monte Carlo Beach Hotel.
2669 **978** 45c. multicoloured . . . 60 45

979 Anniversary Emblem

2004. Centenary of FIFA (Federation Internationale de Football Association).
2670 **979** €1.60 multicoloured . . 2·20 1·60

980 Female Magician

2004. "Magic Stars" Magic Festival.
2671 **980** 45c. multicoloured . . . 60 45

981 Cacti and Presents

982 Princess Grace

2004. Christmas.
2672 **981** 50c. multicoloured . . . 70 50

2004. 75th Birth Anniv of Princess Grace (**MS**2673a). MonacoPhil 2004 (**MS**2673b). Two sheets, each 141 × 75 mm containing T **982** and similar vert designs. Each ultramarine and green.
MS2673 (a) 75c. Type **982**; €1.75 Wearing tiara; €3.50 Wearing earrings. (b) As No. **MS**2673a but with colours reversed. Imperf
Set of 2 sheets . . . . 9·00 9·00

983 Monte Carlo and Emblem

2004. Monaco's Accession to the Council of Europe.
2674 **983** 50c. blue and vermilion 70 50

984 Equestrian Performer

2004. 29th International Circus Festival (January 2005), Monte Carlo.
2675 **984** 70c. multicoloured . . . 95 70

985 Stadium Building, Pool and Court

986 Prince Rainier III

2004. 20th Anniv of Louis II Stadium, Monte Carlo.
2676 **985** 50c. ultramarine, brown and vermilion 70 50

2004. Monaco Prince's Palace. Each salmon, deep green and green.
2677 50c. Type **986** 70 50
2678 50c. Palace facade (60 × 27 mm) 70 50
2679 50c. Prince Albert 70 50
Nos. 2677/9 were issued together, se-tenant, forming a composite design.

987 Entrance

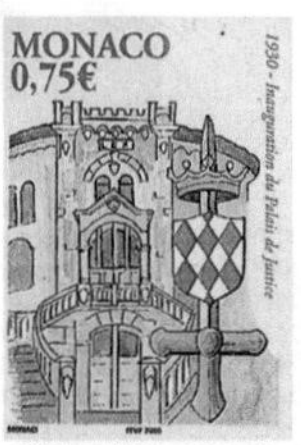

988 Building Facade

2004. 70th Anniv of Foundation of Monaco Hall of Residence, Cité University, Paris.
2680 **987** 58c. brown, black and vermilion 80 60

2004. 75th Anniv of Law Courts.
2681 **988** 75c. multicoloured . . . 1·00 75

989 Artistic and Cultural Symbols

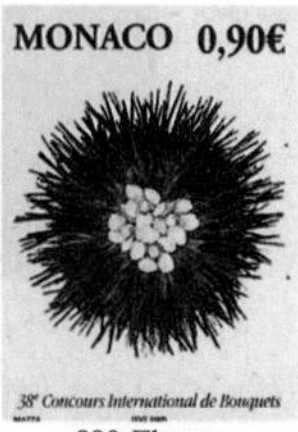

990 Flower Arrangement

2004. 25th Anniv of "Alliance Francaise" (French language and culture promotion organization).
2682 **989** 75c. multicoloured . . . 1·00 75

2004. 38th Monte Carlo Flower Show (2005).
2683 **990** 90c. multicoloured . . . 1·20 90

991 Luigi Valentino Brugnatelli (inventor)

2004. Bicentenary of Electroplating.
2684 **991** €1 brown and black . . 1·40 1·00

992 Goalkeeper's Hands holding Ball

2004. 75th Anniv of First Football World Cup Championship. Multicoloured.
2685 €1 Type **992** . . . . 1·40 1·00
2686 €1 Players' legs and ball . . 1·40 1·00

993 Jean-Paul Sartre

2004. Birth Centenary of Jean-Paul Sartre (writer).
2687 **993** €1.11 multicoloured . . 1·50 1·10

994 Johan Edvard Lundstrom (Swedish inventor)

2004. 150th Anniv of Safety Matches.
2688 **994** €1.20 multicoloured . . 1·60 1·20

995 Don Quixote and Sancho Panza

2004. 400th Anniv of "Don Quixote de la Mancha" (novel by Miguel de Cervantes Saavedra).
2689 **995** €1.20 black, brown and vermilion . . . . . . 1·60 1·20

996 Leo Ferre

2004. Leo Ferre (songwriter, singer and poet) Commemoration.

2690	**996**	€1.40 multicoloured . .	1·90	1·40

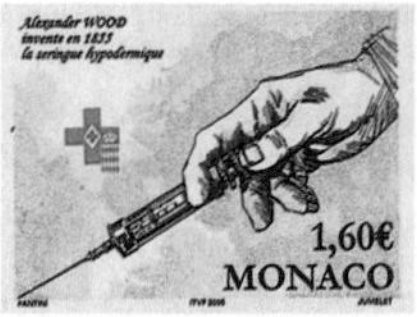

997 Hand holding Hypodermic

2004. 150th Anniv of Invention of Hypodermic Syringe by Alexander Wood.

2691	**997**	€1.60 purple, black and vermilion	2·20	1·60

998 Frank Libby

2004. 25th Death Anniv of Frank Willard Libby (inventor of Carbon 14 dating and winner of Nobel Prize for Chemistry, 1960).

2692	**998**	€1.80 multicoloured . .	2·50	1·90

999 Emblem and Founder Members (Rotary Club, Chicago)

2005. Centenary of Rotary International (charitable organization). Multicoloured.

2693		55c. Type **999**	75	55
2694		70c. Emblem and "100 ans" (vert)	95	70

1000 Artist and Castle

2005. 50th Anniv of Fine Arts Committee Exhibition.

2695	**1000**	48c. multicoloured . . .	65	50

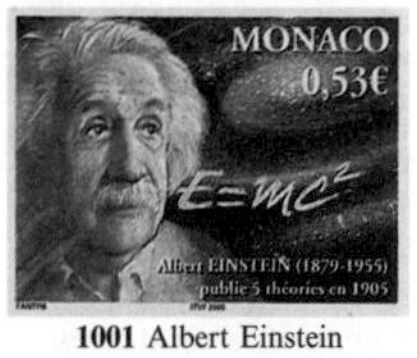

1001 Albert Einstein

2005. Centenary of Publication of Five Papers by Albert Einstein.

2696	**1001**	53c. multicoloured . . .	70	55

1002 Emblem

2005. Granting of University Diploma to Bosio Pavilion Fine Arts School.

2697	**1002**	64c. vermilion and black	85	65

1003 Dachshund

2005. International Dog Show, Monte Carlo.

2698	**1003**	82c. multicoloured . . .	1·10	80

POSTAGE DUE STAMPS

D 3 D 4 D 18

1906.

D 29a	**D 3**	1c. green	30	45
D 30		5c. green	40	55
D 31a		10c. red	30	55
D 32		10c. brown	£350	£110
D 33		15c. purple on cream	1·75	1·40
D113		20c. bistre on buff . .	30	30
D 34		30c. blue	30	55
D114		40c. mauve	30	30
D 35		50c. brown on buff . .	3·00	3·25
D115		50c. green	30	30
D116		60c. black	30	50
D117		60c. mauve	15·00	19·00
D118		1f. purple on cream . .	25	25
D119		2f. red	60	1·00
D120		3f. red	60	1·00
D121		5f. blue	60	75

1910.

D36	**D 4**	1c. olive	20	40
D37		10c. lilac	30	40
D38		30c. bistre	£150	£150

1919. Surch.

D39	**D 4**	20c. on 10c. lilac	3·00	4·50
D40		40c. on 30c. bistre . . .	3·00	5·50

1925.

D106	**D 18**	1c. olive	30	35
D107		10c. violet	20	45
D108		30c. bistre	30	55
D109		60c. red	45	65
D110		1f. blue	60·00	55·00
D111		2f. red	70·00	75·00

1925. Surch **1 franc a percevoir.**

D112	**D 3**	1f. on 50c. brown on buff	60	70

D 64 D 65

1946.

D327	**D 64**	10c. black	10	10
D328		30c. violet	10	10
D329		50c. blue	10	10
D330		1f. green	20	20
D331		2f. brown	20	25
D332		3f. mauve	20	25
D333		4f. red	30	35
D334	**D 65**	5f. brown	30	25
D335		10f. blue	50	30
D336		20f. turquoise	50	55
D337		50f. red and mauve . .	40·00	48·00
D338		100f. red and green . .	7·50	8·00

D 99 Buddicom Locomotive, 1843

1953.

D478	–	1f. red and green . . .	10	10
D479	–	1f. green and red . . .	10	10
D480	–	2f. turquoise and blue	10	10
D481	–	2f. blue and turquoise	10	10
D482	**D 99**	3f. lake and green . .	10	10
D483	–	3f. green and lake . .	10	10
D484	–	4f. slate and brown . .	25	25
D485	–	4f. brown and slate . .	25	25
D486	–	5f. violet and blue . .	45	45
D487	–	5f. blue and violet . .	45	45
D488	–	10f. indigo and blue . .	5·00	6·50
D489	–	10f. blue and indigo . .	5·00	6·50
D490	–	20f. violet and blue . .	2·00	3·00
D491	–	20f. blue and violet . .	2·00	3·00
D492	–	50f. brown and red . .	5·00	7·50
D493	–	50f. red and brown . .	5·00	7·50
D494	–	100f. green and purple	8·50	12·00
D495	–	100f. purple and green	8·50	12·00

TRIANGULAR DESIGNS: Nos. D478, Pigeons released from mobile loft; D479, Sikorsky S-51 helicopter; D480, Brig; D481, "United States" (liner); D483, Streamlined steam locomotive; D484, Santos-Dumont's monoplane No. 20 Demoiselle; D485, De Havilland Comet 1 airliner; D486, Old motor car; D487, "Sabre" racing-car; D488, Leonardo da Vinci's flying machine; D489, Postal rocket; D490, Mail balloon, Paris, 1870; D491, Airship "Graf Zeppelin"; D492, Postilion; D493, Motor cycle messenger; D494, Mail coach; D495, Railway mail van.

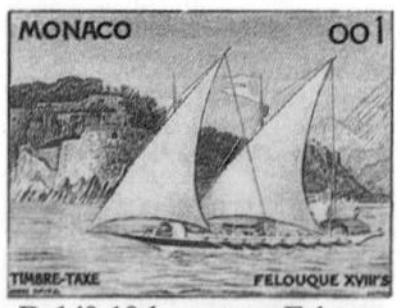

D 140 18th-century Felucca

1960.

D698	**D 140**	1c. brown, green & bl	55	55
D699	–	2c. sepia, blue & grn	10	10
D700	–	5c. purple, blk & turq	10	10
D701	–	10c. black, green & bl	10	10
D702	–	20c. purple, grn & bl	1·25	1·25
D703	–	30c. brown, bl & grn	80	80
D704	–	50c. blue, brn & myrtle	1·25	1·50
D705	–	1f. brown, myrtle & bl	1·75	1·75

DESIGNS: 2c. Paddle-steamer "La Palmaria"; 5c. Arrival of first railway train at Monaco; 10c. 15th–16th-century armed messenger; 20c. 18th-century postman; 30c. "Charles III" (paddle-steamer); 50c. 17th-century courier; 1f. Mail coach (19th-century).

D 393 Prince's Seal **D 492** Coat of Arms

1980.

D1426	**D 393**	5c. red and brown	10	10
D1427		10c. orange and red	10	10
D1428		15c. violet and red	10	10
D1429		20c. green and red	10	10
D1430		30c. blue and red . .	20	20
D1431		40c. bistre and red	20	20
D1432		50c. violet and red	30	30
D1433		1f. grey and blue . .	65	65
D1434		2f. brown and black	80	75
D1435		3f. red and green . .	1·25	1·00
D1436		4f. green and red . .	1·75	1·50
D1437		5f. brown and mauve	2·10	1·60

1985.

D1712	**D 492**	5c. multicoloured . .	10	10
D1713		10c. multicoloured	10	10
D1714		15c. multicoloured	10	10
D1715		20c. multicoloured	10	10
D1716		30c. multicoloured	10	10
D1717		40c. multicoloured	10	20
D1718		50c. multicoloured	10	20
D1719		1f. multicoloured . .	30	45
D1720		2f. multicoloured . .	60	65
D1721		3f. multicoloured . .	1·00	1·25
D1722		4f. multicoloured . .	1·25	1·40
D1723		5f. multicoloured . .	1·75	2·00

MONGOLIA Pt. 10

A republic in Central Asia between China and Russia, independent since 1921.

1924. 100 cents = 1 dollar (Chinese).
1926. 100 mung = 1 tugrik.

1 Eldev-Otchir Symbol **2** Soyombo Symbol

1924. Inscr in black.

1	**1**	1c. brown, pink and grey on bistre	4·00	4·00
2		2c. brown, blue and red on brown	5·00	3·50
3		5c. grey, red and yellow . . .	25·00	20·00
4		10c. blue and brown on blue	9·00	7·00
5		20c. grey, blue and white on blue	18·00	10·00
6		50c. red and orange on pink	30·00	18·00
7		$1 bistre, red and white on yellow	45·00	28·00

Stamps vary in size according to the face value.

1926. Fiscal stamps as T **2** optd **POSTAGE** in frame in English and Mongolian.

8	**2**	1c. blue	10·00	10·00
9		2c. buff	10·00	10·00
10		5c. purple	14·00	12·00
11		10c. green	18·00	15·00
12		20c. brown	20·00	17·00
13		50c. brown and yellow . . .	£175	£160
14		$1 brown and pink	£400	£325
15		$5 red and olive	£600	

Stamps vary in size according to the face value.

4 State Emblem: Soyombo Symbol **5** State Emblem: Soyombo Symbol

1926. New Currency.

16	**4**	5m. black and lilac	4·50	4·50
17		20m. black and blue	4·00	4·00

1926.

18	**5**	1m. black and yellow	1·40	80
19		2m. black and brown	1·60	90
20		5m. black and lilac (A) . . .	2·50	1·40
28		5m. black and lilac (B) . . .	13·00	9·50
21		10m. black and blue	1·60	1·10
30		20m. black and blue	14·00	8·00
22		25m. black and green . . .	4·00	1·75
23		40m. black and yellow . . .	5·75	2·00
24		50m. black and brown . . .	7·00	3·25
25		1t. black, green and brown	18·00	6·50
26		3t. black, yellow and red . .	38·00	30·00
27		5t. black, red and purple . .	60·00	48·00

In (A) the Mongolian numerals are in the upper and in (B) in the lower value tablets.

These stamps vary in size according to the face value.

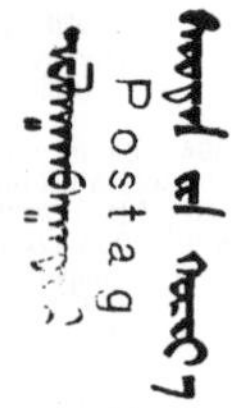

(6) (7)

1930. Surch as T **6**.

32	**5**	10m. on 1m. black & yellow	25·00	25·00
33		20m. on 2m. black & brown	35·00	30·00
34		25m. on 40m. black & yellow	40·00	35·00

1931. Optd with T **7**.

35	**2**	1c. blue	17·00	8·00
36		2c. buff	18·00	6·00
37		5c. purple	25·00	6·00
38		10c. green	20·00	6·00
39		20c. brown	32·00	8·50
40		50c. brown and yellow . . .	—	—
41		$1 brown and pink	—	—

1931. Surch **Postage** and value in **menge**.

43	**2**	5m. on 5c. purple	25·00	8·00
44		10m. on 10c. green	38·00	20·00
45		20m. on 20c. brown	50·00	25·00

9 Govt Building, Ulan Bator **11** Sukhe Bator

12 Lake and Mountain Scenery

1932.

46	–	1m. brown	1·75	1·00
47	–	2m. red	1·75	1·00
48	–	5m. blue	50	30
49	**9**	10m. green	50	30
50	–	15m. brown	50	30
51	–	20m. red	50	30
52	–	25m. violet	75	30
53	**11**	40m. black	75	40
54	–	50m. blue	50	30
55	**12**	1t. green	90	50
56	–	3t. violet	2·00	1·25
57	–	5t. brown	12·00	7·50
58	–	10t. blue	20·00	13·00

DESIGNS—As Type **9**: 1m. Weavers; 5m. Machinist. As Type **11**: 2m. Telegraphist; 15m. Revolutionary soldier carrying flag; 20m. Mongols learning Latin alphabet; 25m. Soldier; 50m. Sukhe Bator's monument. As Type **12**: 3t. Sheep-shearing; 5t. Camel caravan; 10t. Lassoing wild horses (after painting by Sampilon).

13 Mongol Man

14 Camel Caravan

1943. Network background in similar colour to stamps.

59	**13**	5m. green	3·50	3·50
60	–	10m. blue	6·00	3·75
61	–	15m. red	7·00	5·00
62	**14**	20m. brown	11·00	9·00
63	–	25m. brown	11·00	11·00
64	–	30m. red	12·00	12·00
65	–	45m. purple	17·00	17·00
66	–	60m. green	28·00	28·00

DESIGNS—VERT: 10m. Mongol woman; 15m. Soldier; 30m. Arms of the Republic; 45m. Portrait of Sukhe Bator, dated 1894–1923. HORIZ: 25m. Secondary school; 60m. Pastoral scene.

15 Marshal Kharloin Choibalsan

17 Victory Medal

16 Choibalsan and Sukhe Bator

1945. 50th Birthday of Choibalsan.

67	**15**	1t. black	9·00	8·00

1946. 25th Anniv of Independence. As T **16**/**17**.

68	–	30m. bistre	4·50	3·50
69	**16**	50m. purple	5·50	4·00
70	–	60m. brown	5·50	5·50
71	–	60m. black	8·00	5·50
72	**17**	80m. brown	7·50	7·50
73	–	1t. blue	11·00	12·00
74	–	2t. brown	14·00	16·00

DESIGNS—VERT: ($21\frac{1}{2} \times 32$ mm): 30m. Choibalsan, aged four. As Type **17**: 60m. (No. 71), Choibalsan when young man; 1t. 25th Anniversary Medal; 2t. Sukhe Bator. HORIZ: As Type **16**: 60m. (No. 70), Choibalsan University.

17a Flags of Communist Bloc

1951. Struggle for Peace.

75	**17a**	1t. multicoloured	7·50	7·50

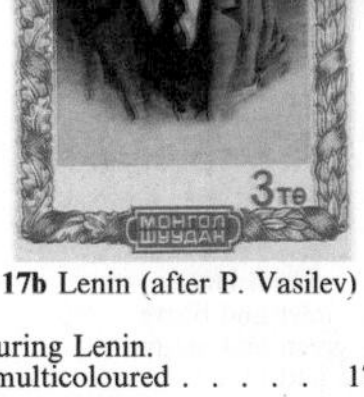

17b Lenin (after P. Vasilev)

1951. Honouring Lenin.

76	**17b**	3t. multicoloured	17·00	17·00

18 State Shop

19 Sukhe Bator

1951. 30th Anniv of Independence.

77	–	15m. green on azure	3·25	3·25
78	**18**	20m. orange	3·25	3·25
79	–	20m. multicoloured	3·75	3·75
80	–	25m. blue on azure	3·75	3·75
81	–	30m. multicoloured	4·25	4·25
82	–	40m. violet on pink	4·50	4·50
83	–	50m. brown on azure	9·00	9·00
84	–	60m. black on pink	8·00	8·00
85	**19**	2t. brown	15·00	15·00

DESIGNS—HORIZ: (As Type **18**): 15m. Alti Hotel; 40m. State Theatre, Ulan Bator; 50m. Pedagogical Institute. $55\frac{1}{2} \times 26$ mm: 25m. Choibalsan University. VERT: (As Type **19**): 20m. (No. 79); 30m. Arms and flag; 60m. Sukhe Bator Monument.

20 Schoolchildren

1952. Culture.

86	–	5m. brown on pink	2·00	1·75
87	**20**	10m. blue on pink	2·50	2·50

DESIGN: 5m. New houses.

21 Choibalsan in National Costume

22 Choibalsan and Farm Worker

1953. 1st Death Anniv of Marshal Choibalsan. As T **21**/**22**.

88	**21**	15m. blue	2·50	2·75
89	**22**	15m. green	2·50	2·75
90	**21**	20m. green	5·00	6·00
91	**22**	20m. sepia	2·50	2·50
92	–	20m. blue	2·50	2·50
93	–	30m. sepia	3·25	3·25
94	–	50m. brown	3·25	3·25
95	–	1t. red	4·00	4·00
96	–	1t. purple	4·00	4·00
97	–	2t. red	4·00	4·00
98	–	3t. purple	5·00	5·00
99	–	5t. red	19·00	19·00

DESIGNS: As Type **21**: 1t. (96); 2t. Choibalsan in uniform. 33×48 mm: 3, 5t. Busts of Choibalsan and Sukhe Bator. 33×46 mm: 50m., 1t. (95), Choibalsan and young pioneer. 48×33 mm: 20m. (92); 30m. Choibalsan and factory hand.

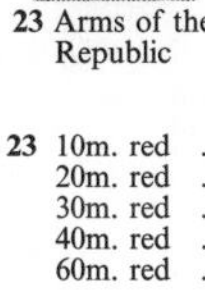

23 Arms of the Republic

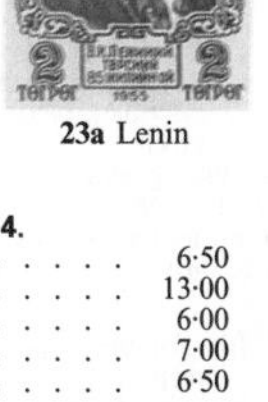

23a Lenin

1954.

100	**23**	10m. red	6·50	4·00
101		20m. red	13·00	5·00
102		30m. red	6·00	4·50
103		40m. red	7·00	4·50
104		60m. red	6·50	4·50

1955. 85th Birth Anniv of Lenin.

105	**23a**	2t. blue	3·75	2·00

23b Flags of the Communist Bloc

24 Sukhe Bator and Choibalsan

1955. Struggle for Peace.

106	**23b**	60m. multicoloured	1·25	65

1955.

107	**24**	30m. green	30	20
108	–	30m. blue	50	20
109	–	30m. red	40	20
110	–	40m. purple	1·00	40
111	–	50m. brown	1·00	45
112	–	1t. multicoloured	2·75	1·25

DESIGNS—HORIZ: 30m. blue, Lake Khobsogol; 50m. Choibalsan University. VERT: 30m. red, Lenin Statue, Ulan Bator; 40m. Sukhe Bator and dog; 1t. Arms and flag of the Republic.

24a Steam Train linking Ulan Bator and Moscow

25 Arms of the Republic

1956. Mongol–Soviet Friendship. Multicoloured.

113	1t. Type **24a**	25·00	13·00
114	2t. Flags of Mongolia and Russia	4·50	2·75

1956.

115	**25**	20m. brown	50	30
116		30m. brown	65	35
117		40m. blue	80	45
118		60m. green	1·00	65
119		1t. red	1·60	80

26 Hunter and Golden Eagle

27 Arms

27a Wrestlers

1956. 35th Anniv of Independence.

120	**26**	30m. brown	25·00	21·00
121	**27**	30m. blue	5·00	4·00
122	**27a**	60m. green	15·00	15·00
123	–	60m. orange	15·00	15·00

DESIGN: As Type **26**: 60m. (No. 123), Children. Also inscr "xxxv".

28

29

1958. With or without gum.

124	**28**	20m. red	1·50	1·00

1958. 13th Mongol People's Revolutionary Party Congress. With or without gum.

125	**29**	30m. red and salmon	3·00	2·25

1958. As T **27a** but without "xxxv". With or without gum.

126	50m. brown on pink	5·00	3·75

30 Dove and Globe

1958. 4th Congress of International Women's Federation, Vienna. With or without gum.

127	**30**	60m. blue	3·25	2·00

31 Ibex

32 Yak

1958. Mongolian Animals. As T **31**/**2**.

128	–	30m. pale blue	6·50	2·10
129	–	30m. turquoise	4·50	2·10
130	**31**	30m. green	3·00	1·50
131		30m. turquoise	3·00	1·00
132	**32**	60m. bistre	3·50	2·00
133		60m. orange	3·50	1·25
134	–	1t. blue	5·00	2·50
135	–	1t. light blue	4·00	1·75
136	–	1t. red	5·00	3·25
137	–	1t. red	4·00	2·00

DESIGNS—VERT: 30m. (Nos. 128/9), Dalmatian pelicans. HORIZ: 1t. (Nos. 134/5), Yak, facing right; 1t. (Nos. 136/7), Bactrian camels.

33 Goat

34 "Tulaga"

1958. Mongolian Animals.

138	**33**	5m. sepia and yellow	15	10
139	–	10m. sepia and green	20	10
140	–	15m. sepia and lilac	35	10
141	–	20m. sepia and blue	35	10
142	–	25m. sepia and red	40	10
143	–	30m. purple and mauve	50	10
144	**33**	40m. green	50	10
145	–	50m. brown and salmon	60	20
146	–	60m. blue	80	20
147	–	1t. bistre and yellow	1·75	50

ANIMALS: 10, 30m. Ram; 15, 60m. Stallion; 20, 50m. Bull; 25m., 1t. Bactrian camel.

1959.

148	**34**	1t. multicoloured	3·25	1·10

35 Taming a Wild Horse

1959. Mongolian Sports. Centres and inscriptions multicoloured: frame colours given below.

149	**35**	5m. yellow and orange	20	10
150	–	10m. purple	20	10
151	–	15m. yellow and green	20	10
152	–	20m. lake and red	25	10
153	–	25m. blue	40	15
154	–	30m. yellow, green & turq	55	15
155	–	70m. red and yellow	70	30
156	–	80m. purple	1·10	60

DESIGNS: 10m. Wrestlers; 15m. Introducing young rider; 20m. Archer; 25m. Galloping horseman; 30m. Archery contest; 70m. Hunting a wild horse; 80m. Proclaiming a champion.

36 Child Musician

1959. Mongolian Youth Festival (1st issue).

157	**36**	5m. purple and blue	20	10
158	–	10m. brown and green	25	10
159	–	20m. green and purple	25	10
160	–	25m. blue and green	50	25
161	–	40m. violet and myrtle	95	40

DESIGNS—VERT: 10m. Young wrestlers; 20m. Youth on horse; 25m. Artists in national costume. HORIZ: 40m. Festival parade.

37 Festival Badge

38 Kalmuck Script

1959. Mongolian Youth Festival (2nd issue).

162	**37**	30m. purple and blue	30	20

1959. Mongolists' Congress. Designs as T **38** incorporating "MONGOL" in various scripts.

163	–	30m. multicoloured	5·00	5·00
164	–	40m. red, blue and yellow	5·00	5·00
165	**38**	50m. multicoloured	7·00	7·00
166	–	60m. red, blue and yellow	11·00	11·00
167	–	1t. yellow, turquoise & orge	14·00	14·00

SCRIPTS (29½ × 42½ mm): 30m. Stylized Ulghur; 40m. Soyombo; 60m. Square (Pagspa). (21½ × 31 mm): 1t. Cyrillic.

39 Military Monument

40 Herdswoman and Lamb

1959. 20th Anniv of Battle of Khalka River.

168	–	40m. red, brown and yellow	55	15
169	**39**	50m. multicoloured	55	15

DESIGN: 40m. Mounted horseman with flag (emblem), inscr "AUGUST 1959 HALHIN GOL".

1959. 2nd Meeting of Rural Economy Co-operatives.

170	**40**	30m. green	3·50	3·50

41 Sable

1959. Mongolian Fauna.

171	**41**	5m. purple, yellow and blue	15	10
172	–	10m. multicoloured	55	10
173	–	15m. black, green and red	45	10
174	–	20m. purple, blue and red	55	15
175	–	30m. myrtle, purple & grn	50	15
176	–	50m. black, blue and green	1·10	30
177	–	1t. black, green and red	1·75	40

ANIMALS—HORIZ: (58 × 21 mm): 10m. Common pheasants; 20m. European otter; 50m. Saiga; 1t. Siberian musk deer. As Type **41**: 15m. Muskrat; 30m. Argali.

42 "Lunik 3" in Flight

44 "Flower" Emblem

43 Motherhood Badge

1959. Launching of "Lunik 3" Rocket.

178	**42**	30m. yellow and violet	65	25
179	–	50m. red, green and blue	80	35

DESIGN—HORIZ: 50m. Trajectory of "Lunik 3" around the Moon.

1960. International Women's Day.

180	**43**	40m. bistre and blue	40	15
181	**44**	50m. yellow, green and blue	70	20

45 Lenin

46 Larkspur

1960. 90th Birth Anniv of Lenin.

182	**45**	40m. red	40	15
183		50m. violet	60	30

1960. Flowers.

184	**46**	5m. blue, green and bistre	10	10
185	–	10m. red, green and orange	10	10
186	–	15m. violet, green and bistre	10	10
187	–	20m. yellow, green and olive	15	10
188	–	30m. violet, green & emer	15	10
189	–	40m. orange, green & violet	35	15
190	–	50m. violet, green and blue	45	20
191	–	1t. mauve, green & lt green	80	40

FLOWERS: 10m. Tulip; 15m. Jacob's ladder; 20m. Asiatic globe flower; 30m. Clustered bellflower; 40m. Grass of Parnassus; 50m. Meadow cranesbill; 1t. "Begonia vansiana".

47 Horse-jumping

1960. Olympic Games. Inscr "ROMA 1960" or "ROMA MCMLX". Centres in greenish grey.

192	**47**	5m. red, black & turquoise	10	10
193	–	10m. violet and yellow	10	10
194	–	15m. turquoise, black & red	10	10
195	–	20m. red and blue	10	10
196	–	30m. ochre, black and green	10	10
197	–	50m. blue and turquoise	15	10
198	–	70m. green, black and violet	25	20
199	–	1t. mauve and green	35	25

DESIGNS—DIAMOND SHAPED: 10m. Running; 20m. Wrestling; 50m. Gymnastics; 1t. Throwing the discus. As Type **47**: 15m. Diving; 30m. Hurdling; 70m. High-jumping.

48

1960. Red Cross.

200	**48**	20m. red, yellow and blue	70	25

49 Newspapers

1960. 40th Anniv of Mongolian Newspaper "Unen" ("Truth").

201	**49**	20m. buff, green and red	15	10
202		30m. red, yellow and green	20	15

50 Hoopoe

1961. Mongolian Songbirds.

203	–	5m. mauve, black and green	75	10
204	**50**	10m. red, black and green	85	10
205	–	15m. yellow, black & green	1·00	10
206	–	20m. green, black and bistre	1·25	15
207	–	50m. blue, black and red	1·75	30
208	–	70m. yellow, black & mauve	2·00	50
209	–	1t. mauve, orange and black	2·40	70

BIRDS: As Type **50**: 15m. Golden oriole; 20m. Black-billed capercaillie. Inverted triangulars: 5m. Rose-coloured starling; 50m. Eastern broad-billed roller; 70m. Tibetan sandgrouse; 1t. Mandarin.

51 Foundry Worker

52 Patrice Lumumba

1961. 15th Anniv of World Federation of Trade Unions.

210	**51**	30m. red and black	15	10
211	–	50m. red and violet	20	10

DESIGN—HORIZ: 50m. Hemispheres.

1961. Patrice Lumumba (Congolese politician) Commemoration.

212	**52**	30m. brown	1·50	1·00
213		50m. purple	2·00	1·25

53 Bridge

54 Yuri Gagarin with Capsule

1961. 40th Anniv of Independence (1st issue). Mongolian Modernization.

214	**53**	5m. green	10	10
215	–	10m. blue	10	10
216	–	15m. red	10	10
217	–	20m. brown	10	10
218	–	30m. blue	15	15
219	–	50m. green	25	15
220	–	1t. violet	50	30

DESIGNS: 10m. Shoe-maker; 15m. Store at Ulan Bator; 30m. Government Building, Ulan Bator; 50m. Machinist; 1t. Ancient and modern houses. (59 × 20½ mm): 20m. Choibalsan University.

See also Nos. 225/**MS**32a, 233/**MS**241c, **MS**241d, 242/8 and 249/56.

1961. World's First Manned Space Flight. Mult.

221	20m. Type **54**	15	10
222	30m. Gagarin and globe (horiz)	30	10
223	50m. Gagarin in capsule making parachute descent	30	20
224	1t. Globe and Gagarin (horiz)	50	35

55 Postman with Reindeer

1961. 40th Anniv of Independence (2nd issue). Mongolian Postal Service.

225	**55**	5m. red, brown and blue (postage)	15	10
226	–	15m. violet, brown & bistre	30	10
227	–	20m. blue, black and green	20	10
228	–	25m. violet, bistre and green	30	15
229	–	30m. green, black & lav	5·00	1·25
MS229a		115 × 90 mm. 5, 10, 15 and 50m. in designs of Nos. 226/9 but new colours	7·00	5·50
230	–	10m. orange, black and green (air)	35	10
231	–	50m. black, pink and green	1·00	25
232	–	1t. multicoloured	1·10	35
MS232a		115 × 90 mm. 20, 25, 30m., 1t. in designs of Nos. 225, 230/2 but new colours	3·50	3·50

DESIGNS: Postman with—10m. Horses; 15m. Camels; 20m. Yaks; 25m. "Sukhe Bator" (lake steamer); 30m. Diesel mail train; 50m. Ilyushin Il-14M mail plane over map; 1t. Postal emblem.

56 Rams

1961. 40th Anniv of Independence (3rd issue). Animal Husbandry.

233	**56**	5m. black, red and blue	10	10
234	–	10m. black, green & purple	10	10
235	–	15m. black, red and green	10	10
236	–	20m. sepia, blue and brown	10	10
237	–	25m. black, yellow & green	15	10
238	–	30m. black, red and violet	15	10
239	–	40m. black, green and red	25	15
240	–	50m. black, brown and blue	30	25
241	–	1t. black, violet and olive	55	40
MS241a		105 × 150 mm. 5, 15 and 40m. in designs of Nos. 241, 237 and 234 but new colours	50	50
MS241b		105 × 150 mm. 25, 50m. and 1t. in designs of Nos. 236, 239 and 240, but new colours	50	50
MS241c		105 × 150 mm. 25, 50m. and 1t. in designs of Nos. 235, 239 and 233 but new colours	50	50

DESIGNS: 10m. Oxen; 15m. Camels; 20m. Pigs and poultry; 25m. Angora goats; 30m. Mongolian horses; 40m. Ewes; 50m. Cows; 1t. Combine-harvester.

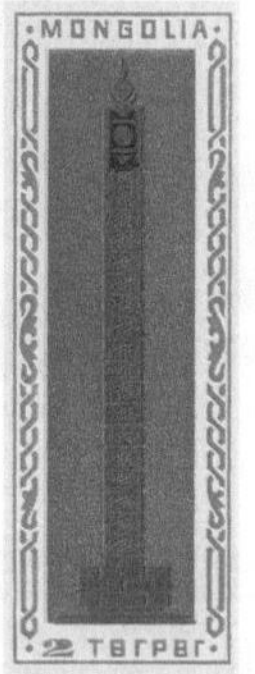

56a

1961. 40th Anniv of Independence (4th issue). Sheet 118 × 128 mm. Imperf.

MS241d	2t. gold, red and blue (pair separated by label)	1·00	1·00

57 Children Wrestling

1961. 40th Anniv of Independence (5th issue). Mongolian Sports.

242	**57**	5m. multicoloured	10	10
243	–	10m. sepia, red and green	10	10
244	–	15m. purple blue and yellow	10	10
245	–	20m. red, black and green	1·10	30
246	–	30m. purple, green & lav	15	10
247	–	50m. indigo, orange & blue	30	20
248	–	1t. purple, blue and grey	35	20

DESIGNS: 10m. Horse-riding; 15m. Children on camel and pony; 20m. Falconry; 30m. Skiing; 50m. Archery; 1t. Dancing.

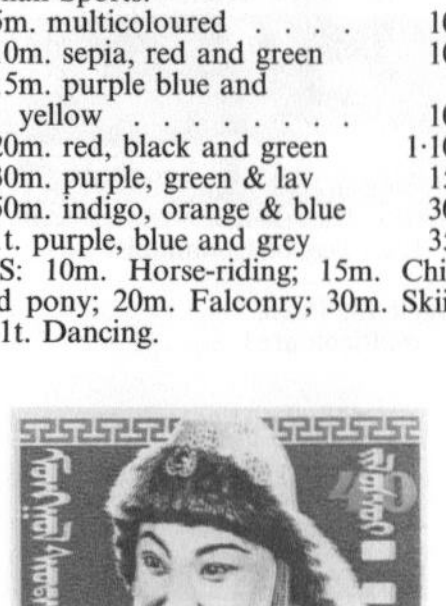

58 Young Mongol

1961. 40th Anniv of Independence (6th issue). Mongolian Culture.

249	**58**	5m. purple and green	10	10
250	–	10m. blue and red	10	10
251	–	15m. brown and blue	10	10
252	–	20m. green and violet	15	10
253	–	30m. red and blue	20	15
254	–	50m. violet and bistre	40	20
255	–	70m. green and mauve	45	25
256	–	1t. red and blue	65	60

DESIGNS—HORIZ: 10m. Mongol chief; 70m. Orchestra; 1t. Gymnast. VERT: 15m. Sukhe Bator Monument; 20m. Young singer; 30m. Young dancer; 50m. Dombra-player.

59 Mongol Arms

60 Congress Emblem

1961. Arms multicoloured; inscr in blue; background colours given.

257	**59**	5m. salmon	10	10
258		10m. lilac	10	10
259		15m. brown	10	10
260		20m. turquoise	10	10
261		30m. ochre	10	10
262		50m. mauve	15	10
263		70m. olive	20	10
264		1t. orange	30	15

1961. 5th World Federation of Trade Unions Congress, Moscow.

265	**60**	30m. red, yellow and blue	15	10
266		50m. red, yellow and sepia	20	10

61 Dove, Map and Globe

1962. Admission of Mongolia to U.N.O.

267	**61**	10m. multicoloured	10	10
268	–	30m. multicoloured	15	10
269	–	50m. multicoloured	20	15
270	–	60m. multicoloured	30	20
271	–	70m. multicoloured	35	30

DESIGNS: 30m. U.N. Emblem and Mongol Arms; 50m. U.N. and Mongol flags; 60m. U.N. Headquarters and Mongolian Parliament building; 70m. U.N. and Mongol flags, and Assembly.

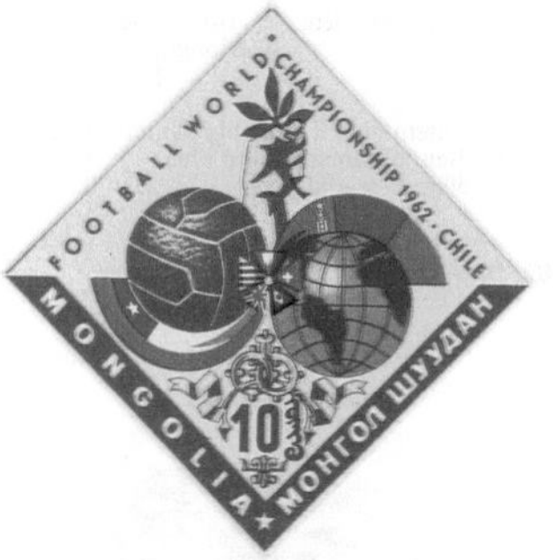

62 Football, Globe and Flags

1962. World Cup Football Championship, Chile. Multicoloured.

272		10m. Type **62**	10	10
273		30m. Footballers, globe and ball	10	10
274		50m. Footballers playing in stadium	20	15
275		60m. Goalkeeper saving goal	25	20
276		70m. Stadium	50	30

63 D. Natsagdorj

64 Torch and Handclasp

1962. 3rd Congress of Mongolian Writers.

277	**63**	30m. brown	15	10
278		50m. green	20	10

1962. Afro-Asian People's Solidarity.

279	**64**	20m. multicoloured	15	10
280		30m. multicoloured	20	10

65 Flags of Mongolia and U.S.S.R.

67 Victory Banner

1962. Mongol–Soviet Friendship.

281	**65**	30m. multicoloured	15	10
282		50m. multicoloured	20	10

1962. Malaria Eradication. Nos. 184/91 optd with Campaign emblem and **LUTTE CONTRE LE PALUDISME**.

283	**46**	5m.	20	20
284	–	10m.	20	20
285	–	15m.	20	20
286	–	20m.	20	20
287	–	30m.	30	30
288	–	40m.	30	30
289	–	50m.	50	50
290	–	1t.	80	80

1962. 800th Birth Anniv of Genghis Khan.

291	**67**	20m. multicoloured	5·50	5·50
292	–	30m. multicoloured	5·50	5·50
293	–	50m. black, brown and red	12·00	12·00
294	–	60m. buff, blue and brown	12·00	12·00

DESIGNS: 30m. Engraved lacquer tablets; 50m. Obelisk; 60m. Genghis Khan.

68 Eurasian Perch

1962. Fishes. Multicoloured.

295		5m. Type **68**	10	10
296		10m. Burbot	20	10
297		15m. Arctic grayling	30	10
298		20m. Short-spined seascorpion	40	15
299		30m. Estuarine zander	60	20
300		50m. Siberian sturgeon	95	30
301		70m. Waleck's dace	1·25	45
302		1t.50 Yellow-winged bullhead	2·25	70

69 Sukhe Bator

1963. 70th Birth Anniv of Sukhe Bator.

303	**69**	30m. blue	15	10
304		60m. lake	20	10

70 Dog "Laika" and "Sputnik 2"

1963. Space Flights. Multicoloured.

305		5m. Type **70**	10	10
306		15m. Rocket blasting off	15	10
307		25m. "Lunik 2" (1959)	15	10
308		70m. Nikolaev and Popovich	30	25
309		1t. Rocket "Mars" (1962)	40	35

SIZES: As Type **70**: 70m., 1t. VERT: (21 × 70 mm): 15m., 25m.

71 Children packing Red Cross Parcels

1963. Red Cross Centenary Multicoloured.

310		20m. Type **71**	10	10
311		30m. Blood transfusion	15	10
312		50m. Doctor treating child	20	15
313		60m. Ambulance at street accident	25	15
314		1t.30 Centenary emblem	40	20

72 Karl Marx

73 Woman

1963. 145th Birth Anniv of Karl Marx.

315	**72**	30m. blue	15	10
316		60m. lake	20	10

1963. 5th World Congress of Democratic Women, Moscow.

317	**73**	30m. multicoloured	15	10

74 Peacock

1963. Mongolian Butterflies. Multicoloured.

318		5m. Type **74**	30	10
319		10m. Brimstone	35	10
320		15m. Small tortoiseshell	35	15
321		20m. Apollo	55	20
322		30m. Swallowtail	85	25
323		60m. Damon blue	1·25	50
324		1t. Poplar admiral	1·75	65

75 Globe and Scales of Justice

1963. 15th Anniv of Declaration of Human Rights.

325	**75**	30m. red, blue and brown	15	20
326		60m. black, blue and yellow	25	10

76 Shaggy Ink Cap

1964. Fungi. Multicoloured.

327		5m. Type **76**	25	10
328		10m. Woolly milk cap	35	10
329		15m. Field mushroom	45	15
330		20m. Milk-white russula	50	20
331		30m. Granulated boletus	75	30
332		50m. "Lactarius scrobiculatus"	1·00	45
333		70m. Saffron milk cap	1·40	65
334		1t. Variegated boletus	1·90	85

77 Lenin when a Young Man

77a Cross-country Skier

1964. 60th Anniv of London Bolshevik (Communist) Party.

335	**77**	30m. red and brown	45	10
336		50m. ultramarine and blue	50	10

1964. 9th Winter Olympic Games, Innsbruck. Sheet 86 × 72 mm.

MS336a	**77a**	4t. black	1·00	1·00

78 Gymnastics

1964. Olympic Games, Tokyo. Multicoloured.

337		5m. Type **78**	10	10
338		10m. Throwing the javelin	10	10
339		15m. Wrestling	10	10
340		20m. Running	10	10
341		30m. Horse-jumping	10	10
342		50m. High-diving	20	15
343		60m. Cycling	25	20
344		1t. Emblem of Tokyo Games	40	30
MS344a		87 × 77 mm. 4t. black, green and red (Wrestlers–Horiz 38 × 28 mm)	1·00	1·00

79 Congress Emblem

1964. 4th Mongolian Women's Congress.

345	**79**	30m. multicoloured	20	10

80 "Lunik 1"

1964. Space Research. Multicoloured.

346		5m. Type **80**	10	10
347		10m. "Vostoks 1 and 2"	10	10
348		15m. "Tiros" (vert)	10	10
349		20m. "Cosmos" (vert)	10	10
350		30m. "Mars Probe" (vert)	10	10
351		60m. "Luna 4" (vert)	20	15
352		80m. "Echo 2"	30	20
353		1t. Radio telescope	35	25

81 Horseman and Flag

1964. 40th Anniv of Mongolian Constitution.

354	**81**	25m. multicoloured	20	10
355		50m. multicoloured	30	10

81a Austrian and Mongolian stamps encircling Globe

1965. "WPIA" Stamp Exhibition, Vienna. Sheet 90 × 130 mm.

MS355a	81a	4t. red	1·00	1·00

82 Marine Exploration

1965. International Quiet Sun Year. Multicoloured.

356	5m. Type **82** (postage)	40	10
357	10m. Weather balloon	15	10
358	60m. Northern Lights	60	20
359	80m. Geomagnetic emblems	70	25
360	1t. Globe and I.Q.S.Y. emblem	1·10	50
361	15m. Weather satellite (air)	40	10
362	20m. Antarctic exploration	3·00	55
363	30m. Space exploration	55	15

83 Horses Grazing

1965. Mongolian Horses. Multicoloured.

364	5m. Type **83**	15	10
365	10m. Hunting with golden eagles	50	20
366	15m. Breaking-in wild horse	20	10
367	20m. Horses racing	20	10
368	30m. Horses jumping	25	10
369	60m. Hunting wolves	30	25
370	80m. Milking a mare	40	30
371	1t. Mare and colt	70	40

84 Farm Girl with Lambs

1965. 40th Anniv of Mongolian Youth Movement.

372	**84**	5m. orange, bistre and green	10	10
373	–	10m. bistre, blue and red	10	10
374	–	20m. ochre, red and violet	20	15
375	–	30m. lilac, brown and green	30	20
376	–	50m. orange, buff and blue	55	35

DESIGNS: 10m. Young drummers; 20m. Children around campfire; 30m. Young wrestlers; 50m. Emblem.

85 Chinese Perch

1965. Mongolian Fishes. Multicoloured.

377	5m. Type **85**	25	10
378	10m. Lenok	25	10
379	15m. Siberian sturgeon	30	15
380	20m. Taimen	45	15
381	30m. Banded catfish	75	20
382	60m. Amur catfish	1·10	20
383	80m. Northern pike	1·25	40
384	1t. Eurasian perch	1·75	60

86 Marx and Lenin

87 I.T.U. Emblem and Symbols

1965. Organization of Socialist Countries' Postal Administrations Conference, Peking.

385	**86**	10m. black and red	15	10

1965. Air. I.T.U. Centenary.

386	**87**	30m. blue and bistre	15	10
387		50m. red, bistre and blue	20	10
MS387a		86 × 130 mm. 4t. blue, black and gold (Communications satellite, 38 × 51mm)	1·00	1·00

88 Sable

1966. Mongolian Fur Industry.

388	**88**	5m. purple, black & yellow	10	10
389	–	10m. brown, black and grey	10	10
390	–	15m. brown, black and blue	35	10
391	–	20m. multicoloured	20	10
392	–	30m. brown, black & mauve	25	10
393	–	60m. brown, black & green	40	25
394	–	80m. multicoloured	60	40
395	–	1t. blue, black and olive	1·40	50

DESIGNS (Fur animals): HORIZ: 10m. Red fox; 30m. Pallas's cat; 60m. Beech marten. VERT: 15m. European otter; 20m. Cheetah; 80m. Stoat; 1t. Woman in fur coat.

89 W.H.O. Building

1966. Inauguration of W.H.O. Headquarters, Geneva.

396	**89**	30m. blue, gold and green	15	10
397		50m. blue, gold and red	25	10

90 Footballers

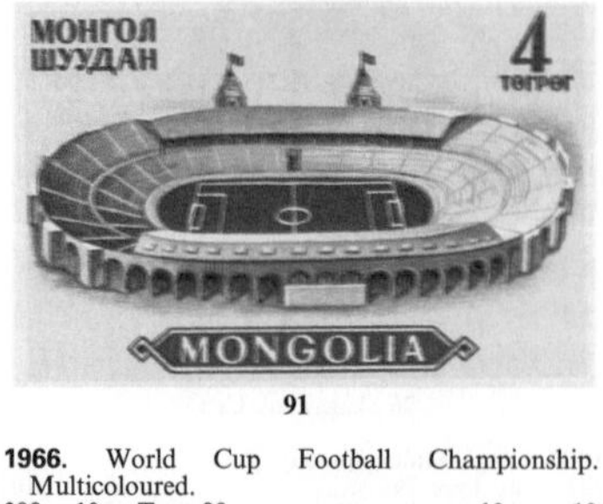

91

1966. World Cup Football Championship. Multicoloured.

398	10m. Type **90**	10	10
399	30m. Footballers (different)	10	10
400	60m. Goalkeeper saving goal	15	15
401	80m. Footballers (different)	30	20
402	1t. World Cup flag	50	35
MS403	**91** 4t. brown and grey	1·00	1·00

92 Sukhe Bator and Parliament Buildings, Ulan Bator

1966. 15th Mongolian Communist Party Congress.

404	**92**	30m. multicoloured	20	10

93 Wrestling

95 State Emblem

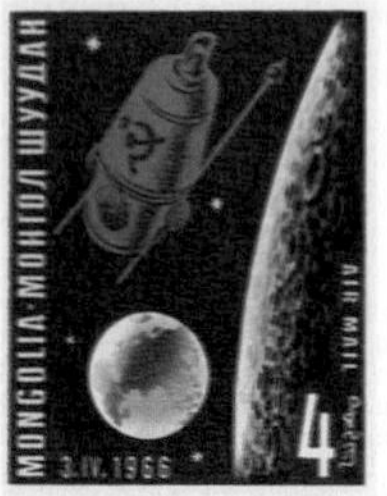

94 "Luna 10", Globe and Moon

1966. World Wrestling Championships, Toledo (Spain). Similar wrestling designs.

405	**93**	10m. black, mauve & purple	10	10
406	–	30m. black, mauve and grey	10	15
407	–	60m. black, mauve & brown	20	15
408	–	80m. black, mauve and lilac	30	20
409	–	1t. black, mauve & turq	40	20

1966. Air. "Luna 10" Commemoration. Sheet 84 × 130 mm.

MS410	**94**	4t. multicoloured	2·40	2·40

1966. 45th Anniv of Independence. Mult.

411	30m. Type **95**	1·25	50
412	50m. Sukhe Bator, emblems of agriculture and industry (horiz)	2·75	75

96 "Physochlaena physaloides"

1966. Flowers. Multicoloured.

413	5m. Type **96**	10	10
414	10m. Onion	15	10
415	15m. Red lily	20	10
416	20m. "Thermopsis lanceolata"	25	10
417	30m. "Amygdalus mongolica"	40	20
418	60m. Bluebeard	50	30
419	80m. "Piptanthus mongolicus"	60	40
420	1t. "Iris bungei"	85	55

1966. 60th Birth Anniv of D. Natsagdorj. Nos. 277/8 optd **1906 1966.**

420a	**63**	30m. brown	6·50	6·50
420b		50m. green	6·50	6·50

97 Child with Dove

1966. Children's Day. Multicoloured.

421	10m. Type **97**	10	10
422	15m. Children with reindeer (horiz)	10	10
423	20m. Boys wrestling	10	10
424	30m. Boy riding horse (horiz)	20	10
425	60m. Children on camel	30	15
426	80m. Shepherd boy with sheep (horiz)	35	15
427	1t. Boy archer	70	40

98 "Proton 1"

1966. Space Satellites. Multicoloured.

428	5m. "Vostok 2" (vert)	10	10
429	10m. Type **98**	10	10
430	15m. "Telstar 1" (vert)	10	10
431	20m. "Molniya 1" (vert)	10	10
432	30m. "Syncom 3" (vert)	10	10
433	60m. "Luna 9" (vert)	20	15
434	80m. "Luna 12" (vert)	30	20
435	1t. Mars and photographs taken by "Mariner 4"	35	25

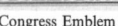

99 Tarbosaurus

1966. Prehistoric Animals. Multicoloured.

436	5m. Type **99**	20	10
437	10m. Talararus	20	10
438	15m. Protoceratops	30	15
439	20m. Indricotherium	30	15
440	30m. Saurolophus	50	20
441	60m. Mastodon	75	30
442	80m. Mongolotherium	90	45
443	1t. Mammuthus	1·00	70

100 Congress Emblem

101 Sukhe Bator and Mongolian and Soviet Soldiers

1967. 9th International Students' Union Congress.

444	**100**	30m. ultramarine and blue	15	10
445		50m. blue and pink	25	15

1967. 50th Anniv of October Revolution.

446	**101**	40m. multicoloured	25	20
447	–	60m. multicoloured	35	25

DESIGN: 60m. Lenin, and soldiers with sword.

102 Vietnamese Mother and Child

1967. Help for Vietnam.

448	**102**	30m.+20m. brown, red and blue	20	10
449		50m.+30m. brown, blue and red	30	15

103 Figure Skating

1967. Winter Olympic Games, Grenoble. Mult.

450	5m. Type **103**	10	10
451	10m. Speed skating	10	10
452	15m. Ice hockey	10	10
453	20m. Skijumping	15	10
454	30m. Bob sleighing	15	10

455	60m. Figure skating (pairs)	30	25
456	80m. Downhill skiing	40	30
MS457	92×92 mm. 4t. Figure skating (different)	1·00	1·00

104 Bactrian Camel and Calf

1968. Young Animals. Multicoloured.

458	5m. Type **104**	15	10
459	10m. Yak	15	10
460	15m. Lamb	20	10
461	20m. Foal	30	10
462	30m. Calf	30	10
463	60m. Bison	40	15
464	80m. Roe deer	55	30
465	1t. Reindeer	80	40

105 Prickly Rose

ЛЭХБ
20 ЖИЛ
WHO
(106)

1968. Mongolian Berries.

466 **105**	5m. ultramarine on blue	15	10
467 –	10m. brown on buff	15	10
468 –	15m. emerald on green	20	10
469 –	20m. red on cream	20	10
470 –	30m. red on pink	25	10
471 –	60m. brown on orange	45	20
472 –	80m. turquoise on blue	60	25
473 –	1t. red on cream	80	40

DESIGNS: 10m. Blackcurrant; 15m. Gooseberry; 20m. Crab-apple; 30m. Strawberry; 60m. Redcurrant; 80m. Cowberry; 1t. Sea buckthorn.

1968. 20th Anniv of World Health Organization. Nos. 396/7 optd with T **106**.

474 **89**	30m. blue, gold and green	2·50	2·50
475	50m. blue, gold and red	2·50	2·50

107 Human Rights Emblem

1968. Human Rights Year.

476 **107**	30m. green and blue	15	10

108 "Das Kapital"

1968. 150th Birth Anniv of Karl Marx. Mult.

477	30m. Type **108**	15	10
478	50m. Karl Marx	25	15

109 "Portrait of Artist Sharab" (A. Sangatzohyo)

1968. Mongolian Paintings. Multicoloured.

479	5m. Type **109**	15	10
480	10m. "On Remote Roads" (A. Sangatzohyo)	20	10
481	15m. "Camel Calf" (B. Avarzad)	30	10
482	20m. "The Milk" (B. Avarzad)	40	15
483	30m. "The Bowman" (B. Gombosuren)	55	30
484	80m. "Girl Sitting on a Yak" (A. Sangatzohyo)	95	55
485	1t.40 "Cagan Dara Ekke" (Janaivajara)	1·90	1·00
MS486	120×86 mm. 4t. "Meeting" (A. Sangatzohyo) (horiz)	4·25	4·25

110 Volleyball

1968. Olympic Games, Mexico. Multicoloured.

487	5m. Type **110**	10	10
488	10m. Wrestling	10	10
489	15m. Cycling	10	10
490	20m. Throwing the javelin	10	10
491	30m. Football	10	10
492	60m. Running	20	15
493	80m. Gymnastics	30	20
494	1t. Weightlifting	35	25
MS495	92×92 mm. 4t. Horse-jumping	1·00	1·00

111 Hammer and Spade

112 Gorky

1968. 7th Anniv of Darkhan Town.

496 **111**	50m. orange and blue	15	10

1968. Birth Centenary of Maksim Gorky (writer).

497 **112**	60m. ochre and blue	15	10

113 "Madonna and Child" (Boltraffio)

1968. 20th Anniv (1966) of UNESCO. Paintings by European Masters in National Gallery, Budapest. Multicoloured.

498	5m. Type **113**	20	10
499	10m. "St. Roch healed by an angel" (Moretto of Brescia)	25	10
500	15m. "Madonna and Child with St. Anne" (Macchietti)	35	10
501	20m. "St. John on Patmos" (Cano)	45	15
502	30m. "Young lady with viola da gamba" (Kupetzky)	50	15
503	80m. "Study of a head" (Amerling)	80	50
504	1t.40 "The death of Adonis" (Furini)	1·60	75
MS505	80×120 mm. 4t. "Portrait of a Lady" (Renoir)	4·25	4·25

114 Paavo Nurmi (running)

1969. Olympic Games' Gold-medal Winners. Multicoloured.

506	5m. Type **114**	10	10
507	10m. Jesse Owens (running)	10	10
508	15m. F. Blankers-Koen (hurdling)	10	10
509	20m. Laszlo Papp (boxing)	10	10
510	30m. Wilma Rudolph (running)	10	10
511	60m. Boris Sahlin (gymnastics)	20	10
512	80m. D. Schollander (swimming)	25	15
513	1t. A. Nakayama (ring exercises)	35	25

115 Bayit Costume (woman)

1969. Mongolian Costumes. Multicoloured.

515	5m. Type **115**	10	10
516	10m. Torgut (man)	15	10
517	15m. Sakhchin (woman)	20	10
518	20m. Khalka (woman)	30	10
519	30m. Daringanga (woman)	35	15
520	60m. Mingat (woman)	50	20
521	80m. Khalka (man)	65	25
522	1t. Barga (woman)	1·10	40

116 Emblem and Helicopter Rescue

1969. 30th Anniv of Mongolian Red Cross.

523 **116**	30m. red and blue	60	20
524 –	50m. red and violet	50	25

DESIGN: 50m. Shepherd and ambulance.

117 Yellow Lion's-foot

1969. Landscapes and Flowers. Multicoloured.

525	5m. Type **117**	15	10
526	10m. Variegated pink	15	10
527	15m. Superb pink	25	10
528	20m. Meadow cranesbill	25	10
529	30m. Mongolian pink	45	15
530	60m. Asiatic globe flower	50	15
531	80m. Long-lipped larkspur	70	30
532	1t. Saxaul	85	40

118 "Bullfight" (O. Tsewegdjaw)

1969. 10th Anniv of Co-operative Movement. Paintings in National Gallery, Ulan Bator. Mult.

533	5m. Type **118**	10	10
534	10m. "Colts Fighting" (O. Tsewegdjaw)	10	10
535	15m. "Horse-herd" (A. Sengetsohyo)	20	10
536	20m. "Camel Caravan" (D. Damdinsuren)	20	10
537	30m. "On the Steppe" (N. Tsultem)	35	15
538	60m. "Milking Mares" (O. Tsewegdjaw)	40	15
539	80m. "Off to School" (B. Avarzad)	50	30
540	1t. "After Work" (G. Odon)	80	40
MS541	121×85 mm. 4t. "Horse-herd" (D. Damdinsuren) (60×40 mm)	2·75	2·75

119 Astronaut and Module on Moon

1969. Air. First Man on the Moon. Sheet 86×121 mm.

MS542 **119**	4t. multicoloured	2·50	2·50

120 Army Crest

БНМАУ-ыг
тунхагласны
45
жилийн ой
1969—XI—26
(121)

1969. 30th Anniv of Battle of Khalka River.

543 **120**	50m. multicoloured	15	10

1969. 45th Anniv of Mongolian People's Republic. Nos. 411/12 optd with T **121**.

544 **95**	30m. multicoloured	3·75	3·75
545 –	50m. multicoloured	5·25	5·25

122 "Sputnik 3"

1969. Exploration of Space. Multicoloured.

546	5m. Type **122**	10	10
547	10m. "Vostok 1"	10	10
548	15m. "Mercury 7"	10	10
549	20m. Space-walk from "Voskhod 2"	10	10
550	30m. "Apollo 8" in Moon orbit	15	10
551	60m. Space-walk from "Soyuz 5"	30	20
552	80m. "Apollo 12" and Moon landing	40	30
MS553	108×77 mm. 4t. "Apollo 12"	1·00	1·00

123 Wolf

1970. Wild Animals. Multicoloured.

554	5m. Type **123**	20	10
555	10m. Brown bear	40	10
556	15m. Lynx	50	10
557	20m. Wild boar	50	10
558	30m. Elk	55	20
559	60m. Bobak marmot	65	20
560	80m. Argali	75	35
561	1t. "Hun Hunter and Hound" (tapestry)	90	50

124 "Lenin Centenary" (silk panel, Cerenhuu)

1970. Birth Centenary of Lenin. Multicoloured.

562	20m. Type **124**	15	10
563	50m. "Mongolians meeting Lenin" (Sangatzohyo) (horiz)	20	10
564	1t. "Lenin" (Mazhig)	35	15

125 "Fairy Tale" Pavilion

1970. "EXPO 70" World Trade Fair, Osaka, Japan. Multicoloured.

565	1t.50 Type **125**	50	45
MS566	111 × 81 mm. 4t. Matsushita Pavilion and "Time Capsule" (51 × 38 mm)	3·50	3·50

126 Footballers

1970. World Cup Football Championship, Mexico.

567	**126**	10m. multicoloured	10	10
568	–	20m. multicoloured	10	10
569	–	30m. multicoloured	10	10
570	–	50m. multicoloured	10	10
571	–	60m. multicoloured	15	10
572	–	1t. multicoloured	30	20
573	–	1t.30 multicoloured	35	25
MS574		122 × 95 mm 4t. multicoloured (50 × 37 mm)	1·00	1·00

DESIGNS: Nos. 568/**MS**574, Different football scenes.

127 Common Buzzard

1970. Birds of Prey. Multicoloured.

575	10m. Type **127**	75	15
576	20m. Tawny owls	1·00	15
577	30m. Northern goshawk	1·25	20
578	50m. White-tailed sea eagle	1·90	30
579	60m. Peregrine falcon	1·90	60
580	1t. Common kestrels	2·10	65
581	1t.30 Black kite	2·50	80

128 Soviet Memorial, Berlin-Treptow

1970. 25th Anniv of Victory in Second World War.

582	**128**	60m. multicoloured	15	10

129 Mongol Archery

1970. Mongolian Traditional Life. Multicoloured.

583	10m. Type **129**	30	15
584	20m. Bodg-gegeen's Palace, Ulan Bator	30	15
585	30m. Mongol horsemen	30	20
586	40m. "The White Goddess-Mother"	30	25
587	50m. Girl in National costume	65	45
588	60m. "Lion's Head" (statue)	75	45
589	70m. Dancer's mask	85	65
590	80m. Gateway, Bogd-gegeen's Palace	1·00	1·00

130 Frogmen boarding "Apollo 13"

1970. Safe Return of "Apollo 13" Spacecraft. Sheet 110 × 80 mm.

MS591	**130**	4t. multicoloured	1·00	1·00

131 I.E.Y. and U.N. Emblems with Flag

1970. International Education Year.

592	**131**	60m. multicoloured	35	15

132 Horseman, "50" and Sunrise

1970. 50th Anniv of National Press.

593	**132**	30m. multicoloured	25	10

133 "Vostok 3" and "4"

1971. Space Research. Multicoloured.

594	10m. Type **133**	10	10
595	20m. Space-walk from "Voskhod 2"	10	10
596	30m. "Gemini 6" and "7"	10	10
597	50m. Docking of "Soyuz 4" and "5"	10	10
598	60m. "Soyuz 6", "7" and "8"	15	10
599	80m. "Apollo 11" and lunar module	20	15
600	1t. "Apollo 13" damaged	25	20
601	1t.30 "Luna 16"	30	25
MS602	120 × 90 mm. 4t. Satellite communications station, Ulan Bator	2·10	2·10

No. 594 is incorrectly inscribed "Vostok 2-3". The date refers to flight of "Vostoks 3" and "4".

134 Sukhe Bator addressing Meeting

1971. 50th Anniv of Revolutionary Party. Mult.

603	30m. Type **134**	10	10
604	60m. Horseman with flag	15	10
605	90m. Sukhe Bator with Lenin	25	15
606	1t.20 Mongolians with banner	40	25

135 "Lunokhod 1"

1971. Exploration of the Moon. Sheet 114 × 95 mm containing T **135** and similar vert design. Multicoloured.

MS607	2t. × 2 (a) Type **135**; (b) "Apollo 14" module on Moon	1·90	1·90

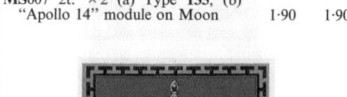

136 Tsam Mask

1971. Mongol Tsam Masks.

608	**136**	10m. multicoloured	15	10
609	–	20m. multicoloured	25	10
610	–	30m. multicoloured	30	10
611	–	50m. multicoloured	35	15
612	–	60m. multicoloured	45	20
613	–	1t. multicoloured	80	30
614	–	1t.30 multicoloured	1·00	50

DESIGNS: Nos. 609/14, Different dance masks.

137 Banner and Party Emblems

1971. 16th Revolutionary Party Congress.

615	**137**	60m. multicoloured	15	10

138 Steam Locomotive

1971. "50 Years of Transport Development". Multicoloured.

616	20m. Type **138**	70	10
617	30m. Diesel locomotive	70	10
618	40m. Russian "Urals" lorry	65	15
619	50m. Russian "Moskovich 412" car	75	15
620	60m. Polikarpov Po-2 biplane	90	25
621	80m. Antonov An-24B airliner	1·10	40
622	1t. Lake steamer "Sukhe Bator"	2·00	70

139 Soldier

1971. 50th Anniv of People's Army and Police. Multicoloured.

623	60m. Type **139**	10	10
624	1t.50 Policeman and child	40	15

140 Emblem and Red Flag

1971. 50th Anniv of Revolutionary Youth Organization.

625	**140**	60m. multicoloured	20	10

141 Mongolian Flag and Year Emblem

1971. Racial Equality Year.

626	**141**	60m. multicoloured	15	10

142 "The Old Man and the Tiger"

1971. Mongolian Folk Tales. Multicoloured.

627	10m. Type **142**	20	10
628	20m. "The Boy Giant-killer"	20	10
629	30m. Cat and mice	20	10
630	50m. Mongolians riding on eagle	25	10
631	60m. Girl on horseback ("The Wise Bride")	40	15
632	80m. King and courtiers with donkey	55	20
633	1t. Couple kneeling before empty throne ("Story of the Throne")	80	25
634	1t.30 "The Wise Bird"	95	40

143 Yaks

1971. Livestock Breeding. Multicoloured.

635	20m. Type **143**	20	10
636	30m. Bactrian camels	20	10
637	40m. Sheep	25	10
638	50m. Goats	40	10
639	60m. Cattle	50	20
640	80m. Horses	60	25
641	1t. Pony	95	45

144 Cross-country Skiing

1972. Winter Olympic Games, Sapporo, Japan. Multicoloured.

642	10m. Type **144**	10	10
643	20m. Bobsleighing	10	10
644	30m. Figure skating	10	10
645	50m. Slalom skiing	10	10
646	60m. Speed skating	15	10
647	80m. Downhill skiing	20	15
648	1t. Ice hockey	25	15
649	1t.30 Pairs figure skating	30	20
MS650	110 × 90 mm. 4t. Ski jumping (50 × 38 mm)	1·00	1·00

145 "Horse-breaking" (A. Sengatzohyo)

1972. Paintings by Contemporary Artists from the National Gallery, Ulan Bator. Multicoloured.

651	10m. Type **145**	15	10
652	20m. "Black Camel" (A. Sengatzohyo)	20	10
653	30m. "Jousting" (A. Sengatzohyo)	25	10
654	50m. "Wrestling Match" (A. Sengatzohyo)	30	10
655	60m. "Waterfall" (A. Sengatzohyo)	40	10
656	80m. "Old Musician" (U. Yadamsuren)	50	20
657	1t. "Young Musician" (U. Yadamsuren)	60	25
658	1t.30 "Ancient Prophet" (B. Avarzad)	85	40

146 "Apollo 16"

1972. Air. "Co-operation in Space Exploration". Sheet 111 × 90 mm.

MS659	**146** 4t. multicoloured	2·75	2·75

147 "Calosoma fischeri" (ground beetle)

1972. Beetles. Multicoloured.

660	10m. Type **147**	20	10
661	20m. "Mylabris mongolica" (blister beetle)	25	10
662	30m. "Sternoplax zichyi" (mealworm beetle)	30	10
663	50m. "Rhaebus komarovi" (snout weevil)	40	15
664	60m. "Meloe centripubens" (oil beetle)	55	15
665	80m. "Eodorcadion mongolicum" (longhorn beetle)	75	25
666	1t. "Platyope maongolica" (mealworm beetle)	90	30
667	1t.30 "Lixus nigrolineatus" (weevil)	1·40	50

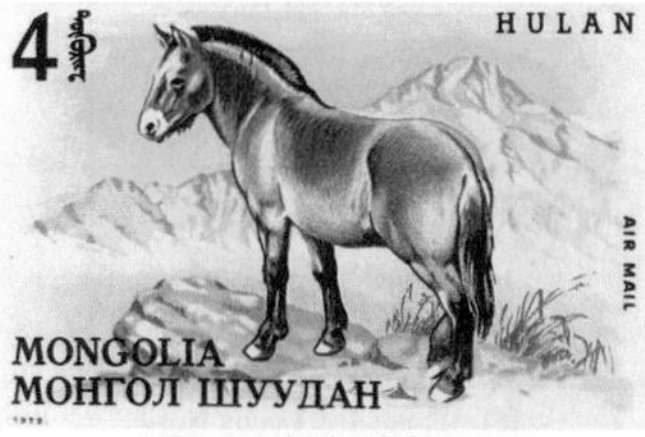

148 Przewalski's Wild Horse

1972. Air. Centenary of Discovery of Wild Horse Species by Nikolai Przewalski. Sheet 115 × 90 mm.

MS668	**148** 4t. multicoloured	7·00	6·00

149 Satellite and Dish Aerial ("Telecommunications")

1972. Air. National Achievements. Multicoloured.

669	20m. Type **149**	10	10
670	30m. Horse-herd ("Livestock Breeding")	20	10
671	40m. Diesel train and Tupolev Tu-144 jetliner ("Transport")	95	10
672	50m. Corncob and farm ("Agriculture")	25	15
673	60m. Ambulance and hospital ("Public Health")	60	15
674	80m. Actors ("Culture")	60	20
675	1t. Factory ("Industry")	65	30

150 Globe, Flag and Dish Aerial

1972. Air. World Telecommunications Day.

676	**150**	60m. multicoloured	25	15

151 Running

1972. Olympic Games, Munich. Multicoloured.

677	10m. Type **151**	10	10
678	15m. Boxing	10	10
679	20m. Judo	10	10
680	25m. High jumping	10	10
681	30m. Rifle-shooting	10	10
682	60m. Wrestling	20	15
683	80m. Weightlifting	25	20
684	1t. Mongolian flag and Olympic emblems	35	25
MS685	90 × 110 mm. 4t. Archery (vert)	1·00	1·00

152 E.C.A.F.E. Emblem

1972. 25th Anniv of E.C.A.F.E.

686	**152**	60m. blue, gold and red	20	10

153 Mongolian Racerunner

1972. Reptiles. Multicoloured.

687	10m. Type **153**	20	10
688	15m. Radde's toad	25	10
689	20m. Halys viper	35	10
690	25m. Toad-headed agama	40	15
691	30m. Asiatic grass frog	55	15
692	60m. Plate-tailed geckol	70	25
693	80m. Steppe ribbon snake	85	35
694	1t. Mongolian agama	1·25	55

154 "Technical Knowledge"

1972. 30th Anniv of Mongolian State University. Multicoloured.

695	50m. Type **154**	15	10
696	60m. University building	20	10

155 "Madonna and Child with St. John the Baptist and a Holy Woman" (Bellini)

1972. Air. UNESCO "Save Venice" Campaign. Paintings. Multicoloured.

697	10m. Type **155**	15	10
698	20m. "The Transfiguration" (Bellini) (vert)	20	10
699	30m. "Blessed Virgin with the Child" (Bellini) (vert)	25	10
700	50m. "Presentation of the Christ in the Temple" (Bellini)	40	15
701	60m. "St. George" (Bellini) (vert)	50	20
702	80m. "Departure of Ursula" (detail, Carpaccio) (vert)	65	35
703	1t. "Departure of Ursula" (different detail, Carpaccio)	85	45
MS704	90 × 111 mm. 3t.+1t. As No. 703	4·00	4·00

156 Manlay-Bator Damdinsuren

157 Spassky Tower, Moscow Kremlin

1972. National Heroes. Multicoloured.

705	10m. Type **156**	10	10
706	20m. Ard Ayus in chains (horiz)	20	10
707	50m. Hatan-Bator Magsarzhav	30	15
708	60m. Has-Bator on the march (horiz)	40	20
709	1t. Sukhe Bator	70	30

1972. 50th Anniv of U.S.S.R.

710	**157**	60m. multicoloured	25	15

158 Snake and "Mars 1"

1972. Air. Animal Signs of the Mongolian Calendar and Progress in Space Exploration. Multicoloured.

711	60m. Type **158**	70	25
712	60m. Horse and "Apollo 8" (square)	70	25
713	60m. Sheep and "Electron 2" (square)	70	25
714	60m. Monkey and "Explorer 6"	70	25
715	60m. Dragon and "Mariner 2"	70	25
716	60m. Pig and "Cosmos 110" (square)	70	25
717	60m. Dog and "Ariel 2" (square)	70	25
718	60m. Cockerel and "Venus 1"	70	25
719	60m. Hare and "Soyuz 5"	70	25
720	60m. Tiger and "Gemini 7" (square)	70	25
721	60m. Ox and "Venus 4" (square)	70	25
722	60m. Rat and "Apollo 15" lunar rover	70	25

The square designs are size 40 × 40 mm.

159 Swimming Gold Medal (Mark Spitz, U.S.A.)

1972. Gold Medal Winners, Munich Olympic Games. Multicoloured.

723	5m. Type **159**	10	10
724	10m. High jumping (Ulrike Meyfarth, West Germany)	10	10
725	20m. Gymnastics (Savao Kato, Japan)	10	10
726	30m. Show jumping (Andras Balczo, Hungary)	10	10
727	60m. Running (Lasse Viren, Finland)	25	15
728	80m. Swimming (Shane Gould, Australia)	35	20
729	1t. Putting the shot (Anatoli Bondarchuk, U.S.S.R.)	40	25
MS730	111 × 91 mm. 4t. Wrestling silver medal (Khorloo Baianmunk, Mongolia)	1·00	1·00

160 Monkey on Cycle

1973. Mongolian Circus (1st series). Mult.

731	5m. Type **160**	10	10
732	10m. Seal with ball	15	10
733	15m. Bear on mono-wheel	20	10
734	20m. Acrobat on camel	25	10
735	30m. Acrobat on horse	40	10
736	50m. Clown playing flute	50	20
737	60m. Contortionist	60	25
738	1t. New Circus Hall, Ulan Bator	80	40

See also Nos. 824/30.

161 Mounted Postman

162 Sukhe Bator receiving Traditional Gifts

1973.

739	**161**	50m. brown (postage)	60	10
740	–	60m. green	2·50	15
741	–	1t. purple	1·00	20
742	–	1t.50 blue (air)	1·75	25

DESIGNS: 60m. Diesel train; 1t. Mail truck; 1t.50, Antonov An-24 airliner.

1973. 80th Birth Anniv of Sukhe Bator. Mult.

743	10m. Type **162**	10	10
744	20m. Holding reception	10	10
745	50m. Leading army	20	10
746	60m. Addressing council	25	10
747	1t. Giving audience (horiz)	45	20

163 W.M.O. Emblem and Meteorological Symbols

1973. Air. Centenary of World Meteorological Organization.

748 **163** 60m. multicoloured . . . 30 10

164 "Copernicus" (anon)

1973. 500th Birth Anniv of Nicholas Copernicus (astronomer). Multicoloured.

749	50m. Type **164**	15	10
750	60m. "Copernicus in his Observatory" (J. Matejko) (55 × 35 mm)	25	10
751	1t. "Copernicus" (Jan Matejko)	35	15
MS752	151 × 115 mm. As Nos. 749/51 but face values 1, 2 and 1t. respectively	1·90	1·90

165 "Tulaga" Stamp of 1959

1973. "IBRA 73" International Stamp Exhibition, Munich. Sheet 81 × 116 mm.

MS753 **165** 4t. multicoloured . . 2·25 2·25

Нэгдлийн Холбооны IV Их
Хурал 1973—6—11
(166)

1973. 4th Agricultural Co-operative Congress, Ulan Bator. No. 538 optd with T **166**.

754 60m. multicoloured . . . . .

167 Marx and Lenin

1973. 9th Organization of Socialist States Postal Ministers Congress, Ulan Bator.

755 **167** 60m. multicoloured . . . 30 10

168 Russian Stamp and Emblems

1973. Air. Council for Mutual Economic Aid Posts and Telecommunications Conference, Ulan Bator. Multicoloured.

756	30m. Type **168**	1·25	30
757	30m. Mongolia	45	20
758	30m. Bulgaria	45	20
759	30m. Hungary	45	20
760	30m. Czechoslovakia	45	20
761	30m. German Democratic Republic	45	20
762	30m. Cuba	45	20
763	30m. Rumania	45	20
764	30m. Poland	1·25	30

169 Common Shelduck

1973. Aquatic Birds. Multicoloured.

765	5m. Type **169**	50	10
766	10m. Black-throated diver . .	70	10
767	15m. Bar-headed geese . . .	1·10	15
768	30m. Great crested grebe . .	1·50	25
769	50m. Mallard	2·00	50
770	60m. Mute swan	2·40	50
771	1t. Greater scaups	2·75	70

170 Siberian Weasel

1973. Small Fur Animals. Multicoloured.

772	5m. Type **170**	20	10
773	10m. Siberian chipmunk . .	20	10
774	15m. Siberian flying squirrel	20	10
775	20m. Eurasian badger	25	15
776	30m. Eurasian red squirrel . .	35	15
777	60m. Wolverine	70	30
778	80m. American mink	85	45
779	1t. Arctic hare	1·25	60

171 Launching "Soyuz" Spacecraft

1973. Air. "Apollo" and "Soyuz" Space Programmes. Multicoloured.

780	5m. Type **171**	10	10
781	10m. "Apollo 8"	10	10
782	15m. "Soyuz 4" and "5" linked	10	10
783	20m. "Apollo 11" module on Moon	10	10
784	30m. "Apollo 14" after splashdown	10	10
785	50m. Triple flight by "Soyuz 6", "7" and "8"	20	15
786	60m. "Apollo 16" lunar rover	25	15
787	1t. "Lunokhod 1"	40	30
MS788	110 × 91 mm. 4t. Proposed "Soyuz" and "Apollo" link-up	1·00	1·00

172 Global Emblem

1973. 15th Anniv of Review "Problems of Peace and Socialism".

789 **172** 60m. red, gold and blue 25 10

173 Alpine Aster

1973. Mongolian Flowers. Multicoloured.

790	5m. Type **173**	10	10
791	10m. Mongolian catchfly . .	20	10
792	15m. "Rosa davurica" . . .	25	10
793	20m. Mongolian dandelion	30	15
794	30m. "Rhododendron dahuricum"	45	25
795	50m. "Clematis tangutica" . .	55	40
796	60m. Siberian primrose . . .	65	45
797	1t. Pasque flower	85	75

174 Poplar Admiral

1974. Butterflies and Moths. Multicoloured.

798	5m. Type **174**	30	10
799	10m. Hebe tiger moth . . .	35	10
800	15m. Purple tiger moth . . .	40	10
801	20m. Rosy underwing	55	10
802	30m. "Isoceras kaszabi" (moth)	70	15
803	50m. Spurge hawk moth . .	1·00	30
804	60m. Garden tiger moth . .	1·10	40
805	1t. Clouded buff	1·50	50

175 "Hebe Namshil" (L. Merdorsh)

1974. Mongolian Opera and Drama. Multicoloured.

806	15m. Type **175**	15	10
807	20m. "Sive Hiagt" (D. Luvsansharav) (horiz)	15	10
808	25m. "Edre" (D. Namdag)	20	10
809	30m. "The Three Khans of Sara-gol" (horiz)	25	15
810	60m. "Amarsana" (B. Damdinsuren)	40	20
811	80m. "Edre" (different scene)	55	25
812	1t. "Edre" (different scene)	85	55

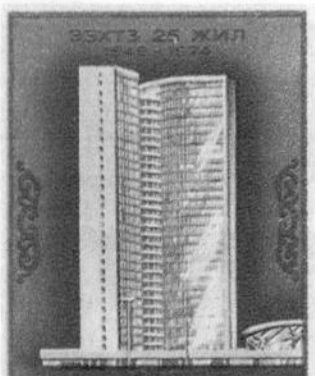

176 Comecon Headquarters, Moscow

1974. Air. 25th Anniv of Communist Council for Mutual Economic Aid ("Comecon").

813 **176** 60m. multicoloured . . . 30 20

177 Government Building and Sukhe Bator Monument, Ulan Bator

1974. 50th Anniv of Renaming of Capital as Ulan Bator.

814 **177** 60m. multicoloured . . . 20 10

178 Mongolian 10c. Stamp of 1924

1974. Air. 50th Anniv of First Mongolian Stamps. Sheet 130 × 85 mm.

MS815 **178** 4t. multicoloured . . 3·00 3·00

179 Mounted Courier

1974. Air. Centenary of U.P.U (1st issue). Multicoloured.

816	50m. Type **179**	1·50	40
817	50m. Reindeer mail sledge . .	1·50	40
818	50m. Mail coach	1·50	40
819	50m. Balloon post	2·00	40
820	50m. Lake steamer "Sukhe Bator" and Polikarpov Po-2 biplane	2·25	40
821	50m. Diesel train and P.O. truck	2·25	40
822	50m. Rocket in orbit	1·50	40
MS823	100 × 90 mm. 4t. "UPU" over globe (24 × 45 mm) . . .	14·00	14·00

See also 883/**MS**890.

180 Performing Horses

1974. Mongolian Circus (2nd series). Multicoloured.

824	10m. Type **180** (postage) . .	10	10
825	20m. Juggler (vert)	15	10
826	30m. Elephant on ball (vert)	20	10
827	40m. Performing yak	30	15
828	60m. Acrobats (vert)	45	20
829	80m. Trick cyclist (vert) . . .	60	25
830	1t. Contortionist (vert) (air)	70	35

181 "Training a Young Horse"

1974. International Children's Day. Drawings by Lhamsurem. Multicoloured.

831	10m. Type **181**	10	10
832	20m. "Boy with Calf" . . .	15	10

833	30m. "Riding untamed Horse"	20	10
834	40m. "Boy with Foal"	25	10
835	60m. "Girl dancing with Doves"	30	15
836	80m. "Wrestling"	35	25
837	1t. "Hobby-horse Dance"	60	30

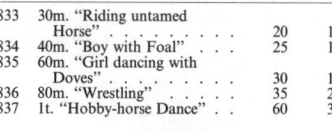

182 Archer on Foot

1974. "Nadam" Sports Festival. Multicoloured.

838	10m. Type **182**	10	10
839	20m. "Kazlodanie" (Kazakh mounted game)	15	10
840	30m. Mounted archer	20	10
841	40m. Horse-racing	25	10
842	60m. Bucking horse-riding	30	15
843	80m. Capturing wild horse	35	25
844	1t. Wrestling	60	30

183 Giant Panda

1974. Bears. Multicoloured.

845	10m. Brown bear	25	10
846	20m. Type **183**	25	10
847	30m. Giant Panda	45	15
848	40m. Brown bear	45	20
849	60m. Sloth bear	70	30
850	80m. Asiatic black bear	80	50
851	1t. Brown bear	1·50	65

184 Red Deer

1974. Games Reserves. Fauna. Multicoloured.

852	10m. Type **184**	15	10
853	20m. Eurasian beaver	30	10
854	30m. Leopard	40	15
855	40m. Herring gull	85	35
856	60m. Roe deer	80	30
857	80m. Argali	85	35
858	1t. Siberian musk deer	1·25	55

185 Detail of Buddhist Temple, Palace of Bogdo Gegen

1974. Mongolian Architecture. Multicoloured.

859	10m. Type **185**	10	10
860	15m. Buddhist temple (now museum)	10	10
861	30m. "Charity" Temple, Ulan Bator	20	10
862	50m. Yurt (tent)	30	20
863	80m. Arbour in court-yard	50	30

186 Spassky Tower, Moscow, and Sukhe Bator Statue, Ulan Bator

187 Proclamation of the Republic

1974. Brezhnev's Visit to Mongolia.

864	**186** 60m. multicoloured	30	10

1974. 50th Anniv of Mongolian People's Republic. Multicoloured.

865	60m. Type **187**	30	10
866	60m. "First Constitution" (embroidery)	30	10
867	60m. Mongolian flag	30	10

188 Gold Decanter

1974. Goldsmiths' Treasures of the 19th Century. Multicoloured.

868	10m. Type **188**	15	10
869	20m. Silver jug	20	10
870	30m. Night lamp	25	10
871	40m. Tea jug	35	20
872	60m. Candelabra	45	20
873	80m. Teapot	60	30
874	1t. Silver bowl on stand	80	40

189 Northern Lapwing

1974. Protection of Water and Nature Conservation. Multicoloured.

875	10m. Type **189** (postage)	40	10
876	20m. Lenok (fish)	45	10
877	30m. Marsh marigolds	40	15
878	40m. Dalmatian pelican	80	25
879	60m. Eurasian perch	75	25
880	80m. Sable	75	25
881	1t. Hydrologist with jar of water (air)	80	30
MS882	83×117 mm. 4t. Wild roses (60×60 mm)	3·25	3·25

190 U.S. Mail Coach

1974. Centenary of U.P.U. Multicoloured.

883	10m. Type **190**	15	10
884	20m. French postal cart	20	10
885	30m. Changing horses, Russian mail and passenger carriage	35	15
886	40m. Swedish postal coach with caterpillar tracks	45	20
887	50m. First Hungarian mail van	50	25
888	60m. German Daimler-Benz mail van and trailer	65	40
889	1t. Mongolian postal courier	95	55
MS890	111×90 mm. 4t. UPU emblem	6·25	6·25

191 Red Flag

193 Mongolian Woman

192 "Zygophyllum xanthoxylon" ($\frac{1}{2}$-size illustration)

1975. 30th Anniv of Victory.

891	**191** 60m. multicoloured	30	10

1975. 12th International Botanical Conference. Rare Medicinal Plants. Multicoloured.

892	10m. Type **192**	20	10
893	20m. "Incarvillea potaninii"	30	10
894	30m. "Lancea tibetica"	45	15
895	40m. "Jurinea mongolica"	45	20
896	50m. "Saussurea involucrata"	55	20
897	60m. "Allium mongolicum"	65	30
898	1t. "Adonis mongolica"	1·25	40

1975. International Women's Year.

899	**193** 60m. multicoloured	30	10

194 "Soyuz" on Launch-pad

1975. Air. Joint Soviet–American Space Project. Multicoloured.

900	10m. Type **194**	20	10
901	20m. Launch of "Apollo"	15	10
902	30m. "Apollo" and "Soyuz" spacecraft	30	10
903	40m. Docking manoeuvre	35	20
904	50m. Spacecraft docked together	50	20
905	60m. "Soyuz" in orbit	60	30
906	1t. "Apollo" and "Soyuz" spacecraft and communications satellite	95	40
MS907	102×83 mm. 4t. "Soyuz" and "Apollo" crewmen	3·00	3·00

195 Child and Lamb

1975. International Children's Day. Multicoloured.

908	10m. Type **195**	10	10
909	20m. Child riding horse	20	10
910	30m. Child with calf	20	10
911	40m. Child and "orphan camel"	25	15
912	50m. "The Obedient Yak"	30	20
913	60m. Child riding on swan	35	25
914	1t. Two children singing	55	40

See also Nos. 979/85.

196 Pioneers tending Tree

Тээвэр—50
1975—7—15.

(197)

1975. 50th Anniv of Mongolian Pioneer Organization. Multicoloured.

915	50m. Type **196**	20	10
916	60m. Children's study circle	30	10
917	1t. New emblem of Mongolian pioneers	40	20

1975. 50th Anniv of Public Transport. Nos. 616/22 optd with T **197**.

918	**138** 20m. multicoloured	2·50	2·50
919	– 30m. multicoloured	2·50	2·50
920	– 40m. multicoloured	1·90	1·90
921	– 50m. multicoloured	1·90	1·90
922	– 60m. multicoloured	2·50	2·50
923	– 80m. multicoloured	3·00	3·00
924	– 1t. multicoloured	3·75	3·75

198 Argali

1975. Air. South Asia Tourist Year.

925	**198** 1t.50 multicoloured	90	40

199 Golden Eagle attacking Red Fox

1975. Hunting Scenes. Multicoloured.

926	10m. Type **199**	50	10
927	20m. Lynx-hunting (vert)	45	10
928	30m. Hunter stalking bobak marmots	50	15
929	40m. Hunter riding on reindeer (vert)	60	20
930	50m. Shooting wild boar	60	25
931	60m. Wolf in trap (vert)	75	35
932	1t. Hunters with brown bear	1·00	50

200 Haite's Bullhead

1975. Fishes. Multicoloured.

933	10m. Type **200**	25	10
934	20m. Flat-headed asp	40	10
935	30m. Altai osman	45	15
936	40m. Tench	55	20
937	50m. Hump-backed whitefish	80	25
938	60m. Mongolian redfin	95	30
939	1t. Goldfish	1·60	60

201 "Morin Hur" (musical instrument)

1975. Mongolian Handicrafts. Multicoloured.

940	10m. Type **201**	10	10
941	20m. Saddle	15	10
942	30m. Headdress	20	10
943	40m. Boots	30	15
944	50m. Cap	40	15
945	60m. Pipe and tobacco pouch	45	20
946	1t. Fur hat	75	30

202 Revolutionary with Banner

1975. 70th Anniv of 1905 Russian Revolution.

947 **202**	60m. multicoloured . . .	25	10

203 "Taming a Wild Horse"

1975. Mongolian Paintings. Multicoloured.

948	10m. Type **203**	10	10
949	20m. "Camel Caravan" (horiz)	25	10
950	30m. "Man playing Lute" . .	35	10
951	40m. "Woman adjusting Headdress" (horiz)	40	15
952	50m. "Woman in ceremonial Costume"	40	25
953	60m. "Woman fetching Water"	50	30
954	1t. "Woman playing Yaga" (musical instrument) . . .	75	40
MS955	110 × 90 mm. 4t. "Warrior on horse-back"	3·00	2·75

204 Ski Jumping

1975. Winter Olympic Games, Innsbruck. Multicoloured.

956	10m. Type **204**	10	10
957	20m. Ice hockey	10	10
958	30m. Slalom skiing	10	10
959	40m. Bobsleighing	15	10
960	50m. Rifle shooting (biathlon)	20	10
961	60m. Speed skating	20	15
962	1t. Figure skating	35	25
MS963	110 × 70 mm. 4t. Skier carrying torch	1·00	1·00

205 "House of Young Technicians"

1975. Public Buildings.

964 **205**	50m. blue	40	10
965 –	60m. green	50	15
966 –	1t. brown	70	25

DESIGNS: 60m. Hotel, Ulan Bator; 1t. "Museum of the Revolution".

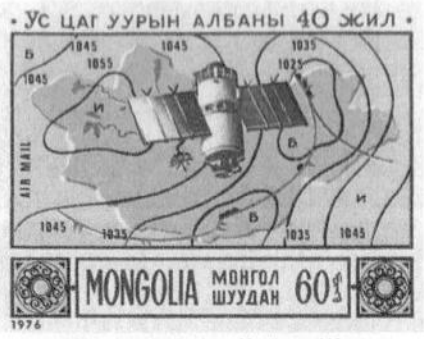

206 "Molniya" Satellite

1976. Air. 40th Anniv of Mongolian Meteorological Office.

967 **206**	60m. blue and yellow . .	40	15

207 Mongolian Girl **208** "The Wise Musician" (Sharav)

1976. Air. 30th Anniv of United Nations Educational, Scientific and Cultural Organization. Sheet 100 × 86 mm.

MS968 **207**	4t. multicoloured . .	3·25	3·00

1976. Air "Interphil 76" International Stamp Exhibition, Philadelphia. Sheet 97 × 70 mm.

MS969 **208**	4t. multicoloured . .	2·75	2·50

209 "National Economy" Star

1976. 17th Mongolian People's Revolutionary Party Congress, Ulan Bator.

970 **209**	60m. multicoloured . . .	30	10

210 Archery

1976. Olympic Games, Montreal. Multicoloured.

971	10m. Type **210**	10	10
972	20m. Judo	10	10
973	30m. Boxing	10	10
974	40m. Gymnastics	15	10
975	60m. Weightlifting	20	15
976	80m. High jumping	25	20
977	1t. Rifle shooting	35	25
MS978	105 × 78 mm. 4t. Wrestling	1·00	1·00

1976. Int Children's Day. As T **195**. Mult.

979	10m. Gobi Desert landscape	15	10
980	20m. Horse-taming	20	10
981	30m. Horse-riding	25	10
982	40m. Pioneers' camp	35	10
983	60m. Young musician	50	20
984	80m. Children's party	70	25
985	1t. Mongolian wrestling . . .	90	30

211 Cavalry Charge

1976. 55th Anniv of Revolution. Multicoloured.

986	60m. Type **211** (postage) . .	40	10
987	60m. Man and emblem (vert)	40	10
988	60m. "Industry and Agriculture" (air)	40	10

212 "Sukhe Bator" Star

1976. Mongolian Orders and Awards. Sheet 116 × 77 mm.

MS989 **212**	4t. multicoloured . .	1·00	1·00

213 Osprey

1976. Protected Birds. Multicoloured.

990	10m. Type **213**	1·50	40
991	20m. Griffon vulture	1·00	20
992	30m. Lammergeier	1·40	25
993	40m. Marsh harrier	1·75	25
994	60m. Cinerous vulture . . .	2·00	40
995	80m. Golden eagle	2·50	45
996	1t. Tawny eagle	2·75	55

214 "Rider on Wild Horse"

1976. Paintings by O. Tsewegdjaw. Multicoloured.

997	10m. Type **214**	15	10
998	20m. "The First Nadam" (game on horse-back) (horiz)	20	10
999	30m. "Harbour on Khobsogol Lake" (horiz)	55	15
1000	40m. "Awakening the Steppe" (horiz)	45	20
1001	80m. "Wrestling" (horiz) . .	60	25
1002	1t. "The Descent" (yak hauling timber)	1·10	50

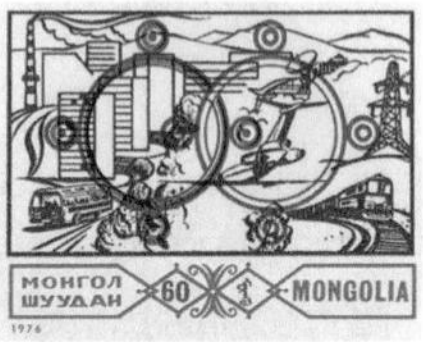

215 "Industrial Development"

1976. Mongolian–Soviet Friendship.

1003 **215**	60m. multicoloured . . .	1·25	20

216 John Naber of U.S.A. (Swimming) **217** Tablet on Tortoise

1976. Olympic Games, Montreal. Gold Medal Winners. Multicoloured.

1004	10m. Type **216**(postage) . .	10	10
1005	20m. Nadia Comaneci of Rumania (gymnastics) . .	10	10
1006	30m. Kornelia Ender of East Germany (swimming)	10	10
1007	40m. Mitsuo Tsukahara of Japan (gymnastics) . . .	15	10
1008	60m. Gregor Braun of West Germany (cycling)	20	15
1009	80m. Lasse Viren of Finland (running)	25	20
1010	1t. Nikolai Andrianov of U.S.S.R. (gymnastics) . .	35	25
MS1011	103 × 78 mm. 4t. Zeveg Oidov of Mongolia (wrestling) (air)	1·00	1·00

1976. Archaeology.

1012 **217**	50m. brown and blue . .	80	15
1013 –	60m. black and green . .	1·10	15

DESIGN: 60m. 6th-century stele.

218 R-1 Biplane

1976. Aircraft. Multicoloured.

1014	10m. Type **218**	20	10
1015	20m. Polikarpov R-5 biplane	30	10
1016	30m. Kalinin K-5 monoplane	40	10
1017	40m. Polikarpov Po-2 biplane	45	15
1018	60m. Polikarpov I-16 jet fighter	60	25
1019	80m. Yakovlev Ya-6 Air 6 monoplane	75	35
1020	1t. Junkers F-13 monoplane	95	40

219 Dancers in Folk Costume

1977. Mongolian Folk Dances. Multicoloured.

1021	10m. Type **219**	25	10
1022	20m. Dancing girls in 13th-century costume . .	35	10
1023	30m. West Mongolian dance	45	10
1024	40m. "Ekachi" dance . . .	50	15
1025	60m. "Bielge" ("Trunk") dance	80	20
1026	80m. "Hodak" dance . . .	95	30
1027	1t. "Dojarka" dance	1·10	45

220 Gravitational Effects on "Pioneer"

1977. 250th Death Anniv of Sir Isaac Newton (mathematician). Multicoloured.

1028	60m. Type **220** (postage) . .	25	15
1029	60m. Apple tree (25 × 32 mm)	25	15
1030	60m. Planetary motion and sextant	25	15
1031	60m. Sir Isaac Newton (25 × 32 mm)	25	15
1032	60m. Spectrum of light . . .	25	15
1033	60m. Attraction of Earth . .	25	15
1034	60m. Laws of motion of celestial bodies (25 × 32 mm)	25	15
1035	60m. Space-walking (air) . .	25	15
1036	60m. "Pioneer 10" and Jupiter	25	15

221 Natsagdorj, Mongolian Scenes and Extract from poem "Mother" (½-size illustration)

1977. Natsagdorj (poet) Commem. Mult.

1037	60m. Type **221**	40	25
1038	60m. Border stone, landscape and extract from poem "My Homeland"	40	25

222 Horse Race

1977. Horses. Multicoloured.

1039	10m. Type **222**	25	10
1040	20m. Girl on white horse . .	30	10
1041	30m. Rangeman on brown horse	40	10
1042	40m. Tethered horses . . .	55	20
1043	60m. White mare with foal	70	20

1044 80m. Brown horse with shepherd . . . . 1·00 30
1045 1t. White horse . . . . . . 1·25 45

223 "Mongolemys elegans"

1977. Prehistoric Animals. Multicoloured.
1046 10m. Type **223** 30 10
1047 20m. "Embolotherium ergiliense" 45 10
1048 30m. "Psittacosaurus mongoliensis" 55 15
1049 40m. Enthelodon 70 20
1050 60m. "Spirocerus kiakhtensis" . . . . . . 1·00 25
1051 80m. Hipparion . . . . . . 1·40 40
1052 1t. "Bos primigenius" . . . 1·60 55

224 Netherlands 5c. Stamp, 1852, and Mongolian $1 Fiscal Stamp, 1926

1977. "Amphilx 77" International Stamp Exhibition, Amsterdam. Sheet 100 × 76 mm.
MS1053 **224** 4t. multicoloured . . 1·00 1·00

225 Child feeding Lambs

1977. Children's Day and 1st Balloon Flight in Mongolia. Multicoloured.
1054 10m.+5m. Type **225**(postage) 30 15
1055 20m.+5m. Boy playing flute and girl dancing 45 15
1056 30m.+5m. Girl chasing butterflies 55 20
1057 40m.+5m. Girl with ribbon 60 25
1058 60m.+5m. Girl with flowers 70 40
1059 80m.+5m. Girl with bucket 90 50
1060 1t.+5m. Boy going to school 1·25 60
MS1061 83 × 72 mm. 4t.+50m. Children in balloon (air) . . . 5·50 5·00

226 Industrial Plant and Transport

1977. Erdenet (New Town).
1062 **226** 60m. multicoloured . . . 1·25 20

227 Trade Unions Emblem

1977. Air. 11th Mongolian Trade Unions Congress.
1063 **227** 60m. multicoloured . . . 1·00 15

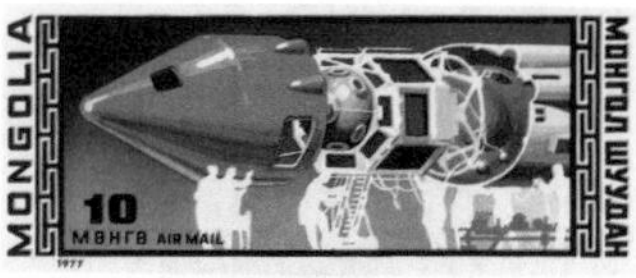

228 Mounting Bell-shaped Gear on Rocket (⅔-size illustration)

1977. Air. 11th Anniv of "Intercosmos" Co-operation. Multicoloured.
1064 10m. Type **228** 10 10
1065 20m. Launch of "Intercosmos 3" 10 10
1066 30m. Research ship "Kosmonavt Yury Gargarin" 40 15
1067 40m. Observation of lunar eclipse 15 10
1068 60m. Earth station's multiple antennae 15 15
1069 80m. Magnetosphere examination, Van Allen Zone 20 20
1070 1t. Meteorological satellites 30 25
MS1071 126 × 90 mm. 4t. Satellite linked to "Intercosmos" countries on globe (58 × 36 mm) . . . . 1·00 1·00

229 Fire-fighters' Bucket Chain

1977. Mongolian Fire-fighting Services. Multicoloured.
1072 10m. Type **229** 10 10
1073 20m. Horse-drawn hand pump 10 10
1074 30m. Horse-drawn steam pump 10 10
1075 40m. Fighting forest fire . . 15 10
1076 60m. Mobile foam extinguisher 20 15
1077 80m. Modern fire engine . . 25 20
1078 1t. Mil Mi-8 helicopter spraying fire 35 25

230 "Molniya" Satellite and Dish Aerial on TV Screen

1977. 40th Anniv of Technical Institute.
1079 **230** 60m. blue, black and grey 30 10

231 Black-veined White

1977. Butterflies and Moths. Multicoloured.
1080 10m. Type **231** 20 10
1081 20m. Lappet moth 35 10
1082 30m. Lesser clouded yellow 50 20
1083 40m. Dark tussock moth . . 70 20
1084 60m. Lackey moth . . . . 1·00 25
1085 80m. Clouded buff . . . . 1·40 35
1086 1t. Scarce copper . . . . . 1·60 50

232 Lenin Museum

1977. Inauguration of Lenin Museum, Ulan Bator.
1087 **232** 60m. multicoloured . . . 40 20

233 Cruiser "Aurora" and Soviet Flag

1977. 60th Anniv of Russian Revolution. Mult.
1088 50m. Type **233** 60 15
1089 60m. Dove and globe (horiz) 50 15
1090 1t.50 Freedom banner around the globe (horiz) 75 35

234 Giant Pandas

1977. Giant Pandas. Multicoloured.
1091 10m. Eating bamboo shoot (vert) 20 10
1092 20m. Type **234** 35 10
1093 30m. Female and cub in washtub (vert) 45 15
1094 40m. Male and cub with bamboo shoot 60 20
1095 60m. Female and cub (vert) 80 30
1096 80m. Family (horiz) . . . . 1·40 50
1097 1t. Male on hind legs (vert) 1·60 65

235 "Helene Fourment and her Chiildren"

1977. 400th Birth Anniv of Peter Paul Rubens (artist). Sheet 78 × 104 mm.
MS1098 **235** 4t. multicoloured . . 3·25 3·25

236 Montgolfier Brothers' Balloon

1977. Air. Airships and Balloons. Multicoloured.
1099 20m. Type **236** 10 10
1100 30m. Airship "Graf Zeppelin" over North Pole 10 10
1101 40m. Airship "Osoaviakhim" over the Arctic 20 10
1102 50m. Soviet Airship "Sever" 30 15
1103 60m. Aereon 340 airship . . 40 20
1104 80m. Nestrenko's planned airship 45 20
1105 1t.20 "Flying Crane" airship 70 35
MS1106 104 × 75 mm. 4t. Russian Zeppelin stamp of 1931 and statue of Sukhe Bator (46 × 31 mm) 2·00 2·00

237 Ferrari "312-T2"

1978. Racing Cars. Multicoloured.
1107 20m. Type **237** 25 10
1108 30m. Ford McLaren "M-23" 30 10
1109 40m. Soviet experimental car 40 20
1110 50m. Japanese Mazda . . . 50 20
1111 60m. Porsche "936-Turbo" 60 25
1112 80m. Model of Soviet car 65 25
1113 1t.20 American rocket car "Blue Flame" 95 40

238 Variegated Boletus (½-size illustration)

1978. Mushrooms. Multicoloured.
1114 20m. Type **238** 50 15
1115 30m. The charcoal burner 75 20
1116 40m. Red cap 80 25
1117 50m. Brown birch bolete . . 1·00 30
1118 60m. Yellow swamp russula 1·25 35
1119 80m. "Lactarius resimus" 1·50 50
1120 1t.20 "Flammula spumosa" 2·00 75

239 Aleksandr Mozhaisky and his Monoplane, 1884

1978. Air. History of Aviation. Multicoloured.
1121 20m. Type **239** 10 10
1122 30m. Henri Farman and Farman H.F.III biplane 10 10
1123 40m. Geoffrey de Havilland and De Havilland FE-1 biplane 20 10
1124 50m. Charles Lindbergh and "Spirit of St. Louis" . . . 30 15
1125 60m. Shagdarsuren, Demberel, biplane and glider 40 20
1126 80m. Chkalov, Baidukov, Belyakov and Tupolev ANT-25 airliner 45 25
1127 1t.20 A. N. Tupolev and Tupolev Tu-154 jetliner 70 35
MS1128 110 × 75 mm. 4t. Wright Brothers and Wright Flyer III 2·00 2·00

240 Footballers and View of Rio de Janeiro

1978. World Cup Football Championship, Argentina. Multicoloured.
1129 20m. Type **240**(postage) . . 10 10
1130 30m. Footballers and Old Town Tower, Berne . . . 10 10
1131 40m. Footballers and Stockholm Town Hall . . 15 10
1132 50m. Footballers and University of Chile . . . 20 10
1133 60m. Footballers, Houses of Parliament and Tower of London 30 15
1134 80m. Footballers and Theatre Degolladeo of Guadalajara, Mexico . . 35 15
1135 1t.20 Footballers and Munich Town Hall . . . 45 25
MS1136 105 × 70 mm. 4t. Footballers (44 × 38 mm) (air) 1·50 1·50

241 Mongolian Youth and Girl

1978. Mongolian Youth Congress, Ulan Bator.
1137 **241** 60m. multicoloured . . . 35 15

242 Eurasian Beaver and 1954 Canadian Beaver Stamp

1978. "CAPEX '78". International Stamp Exhibition, Toronto. Multicoloured.
1138 20m. Type **242**(postage) . . 20 10
1139 30m. Tibetan sandgrouse and Canada S.G. 620 . . 50 35

1140 40m. Black-throated diver and Canada S.G. 495 . . 65 40
1141 50m. Argali and Canada S.G. 449 . . . . 70 15
1142 60m. Brown bear and Canada S.G. 447 . . . . 80 15
1143 80m. Elk and Canada S.G. 448 . . . . 90 25
1144 1t.20 Herring gull and Canada S.G. 474 . . . . 1·90 75
MS1145 100 × 80 mm. 4t. Mongolian 1969 stamp and Canadian 1971 stamp depicting paintings (58 × 36 mm) (air) . . . . . . 3·75 3·75

243 Marx, Engels and Lenin

1978. 20th Anniv of Review "Problems of Peace and Socialism".
1146 **243** 60m. red, gold and black 35 15

244 Map of Cuba, Liner, Tupolev Tu-134 Jetliner and Emblem (½-size illustration)

1978. Air. 11th World Youth Festival, Havana.
1147 **244** 1t. multicoloured 90 20

245 "Open-air Repose"

1978. 20th Anniv of Philatelic Co-operation between Mongolia and Hungary. Paintings by P. Angalan. Multicoloured.
1148 1t.50 Type **245** 40 40
1149 1t.50 "Winter Night" . . . 40 40
1150 1t.50 "Saddling" 40 40

246 A. Gubarev, V. Remek and Exhibition Emblem

1978. Air. "PRAGA 1978" International Stamp Exhibition, Prague. Sheet 103 × 88 mm.
MS1151 **246** 4t. multicoloured . . 1·00 1·00

247 Butterfly Dog

1978. Dogs. Multicoloured.
1152 10m. Type **247** 20 10
1153 20m. Black Mongolian sheepdog 25 10
1154 30m. Puli (Hungarian sheepdog) 35 15
1155 40m. St. Bernard 40 20
1156 50m. German shepherd dog 55 25
1157 60m. Mongolian watchdog 65 25
1158 70m. Semoyedic spitz . . . 75 35
1159 80m. Laika (space dog) . . 90 35
1160 1t.20 Black and white poodles and cocker spaniel . . . . 1·10 55

248 Open Book showing Scenes from Mongolian Literary Works

1978. 50th Anniv of Mongolian Writers' Association.
1161 **248** 60m. blue and red . . . 35 15

249 "Dressed Maja" (Goya, 150th death anniv)

1978. Painters' Anniversaries.
1162 **249** 1t.50 multicoloured . . . 1·25 1·25
1163 – 1t.50 multicoloured . . . 1·25 1·25
1164 – 1t.50 multicoloured . . . 1·25 1·25
MS1165 105 × 132 mm. 4t. black and stone . . . . 3·00 3·00
DESIGNS: As T **249**—No. 1163, "Ta Matete" (Gauguin, 75th death Anniv); 1164, "Bridge at Arles" (Van Gogh, 125th birth anniv). 49 × 49 mm—4t. "Melancoly" (Durer, 450th death anniv).

250 Young Bactrian Camel

1978. Bactrian Camels. Multicoloured.
1166 20m. Camel with Foal . . . 25 15
1167 30m. Type **250** 30 15
1168 40m. Two camels 45 20
1169 50m. Woman leading loaded camel 55 25
1170 60m. Camel in winter coat 70 30
1171 80m. Camel-drawn water waggon 90 45
1172 1t.20 Camel racing . . . . 1·25 60

251 Flags of COMECON Countries

1979. 30th Anniv of Council of Mutual Economic Assistance.
1173 **251** 60m. multicoloured . . . 35 15

252 Children riding Camel

1979. International Year of the Child. Multicoloured.
1174 10m.+5m. Type **252** 20 15
1175 30m.+5m. Children feeding chickens 30 15
1176 50m.+5m. Children with deer 45 15
1177 60m.+5m. Children picking flowers 55 20
1178 70m.+5m. Children watering tree 65 25
1179 80m.+5m. Young scientists 75 35
1180 1t.+5m. Making music and dancing . . . . 1·00 50
MS1181 78 × 99 mm. 4t.+50m. Girl on horse . . . . 3·75 3·50
See also No. **MS**1449.

253 Silver Tabby

1978. Domestic Cats. Multicoloured.
1182 10m. Type **253** 20 10
1183 30m. White Persian 35 15
1184 50m. Red Persian 55 15
1185 60m. Blue-cream Persian . . 70 20
1186 70m. Siamese 80 30
1187 80m. Smoke Persian 90 35
1188 1t. Birman . . . . 1·25 50

254 "Potaninia mongolica"

1979. Flowers. Multicoloured.
1189 10m. Type **254** 20 10
1190 30m. "Sophora alopecuroides" 30 10
1191 50m. "Halimodendron halodendron" 35 15
1192 60m. "Myosotis asiatica" . . 50 20
1193 70m. "Scabiosa comosa" . . 50 30
1194 80m. "Leucanthemum sibiricum" 60 30
1195 1t. "Leontopodium ochroleucum" 80 45

255 Finland v. Czechoslovakia

1979. World Ice Hockey Championships, Moscow. Multicoloured.
1196 10m. Type **255** 10 10
1197 30m. West Germany v. Sweden 10 10
1198 50m. U.S.A. v. Canada . . 15 10
1199 60m. Russia v. Sweden . . . 15 10
1200 70m. Canada v. Russia . . 20 15
1201 80m. Swedish goalkeeper . . 20 15
1202 1t. Czechoslovakia v. Russia 30 20

256 Lambs (Sanzhid)

1979. Agriculture Paintings. Multicoloured.
1203 10m. Type **256** 10 10
1204 30m. "Milking camels" (Budbazar) 20 10
1205 50m. "Aircraft bringing help" (Radnabazar) . . . 40 15
1206 60m. "Herdsmen" (Budbazar) 40 15
1207 70m. "Milkmaids" "Nanzadsguren) (vert) . . 55 30
1208 80m. "Summer Evening" (Sanzhid) 75 40
1209 1t. "Country Landscape" (Tserendondog) 90 50
MS1210 86 × 70 mm. 4t. "After Rain" (Khaidav) . . . . . . 3·50 3·50

257 First Mongolian and Bulgarian Stamps

1979. Death Centenary of Sir Rowland Hill, and "Philaserdica 79" International Stamp Exn, Sofia. Each black, grey and brown.
1211 1t. Type **257** . . . . 1·50 1·00
1212 1t. American mail coach . . 1·50 1·00
1213 1t. Travelling post office, London–Birmingham railway . . . . 2·00 1·25
1214 1t. Paddle-steamer "Hindoostan" . . . . . 1·75 1·00

258 Stephenson's "Rocket"

1979. Development of Railways. Multicoloured.
1215 10m. Type **258** 30 10
1216 20m. Locomotive "Adler", 1835, Germany 35 10
1217 30m. Steam locomotive, 1860, U.S.A. 45 10
1218 40m. Class KB4 steam locomotive, 1931, Mongolia 55 15
1219 50m. Class Er steam locomotive, 1936, Mongolia 60 20
1220 60m. Diesel train, 1970, Mongolia 70 25
1221 70m. "Hikari" express train, 1963, Japan 90 30
1222 80m. Monorail aerotrain "Orleans", France 95 40
1223 1t.20 Experimental jet train "Rapidity", Russia . . . 1·10 50

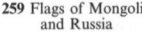

259 Flags of Mongolia and Russia

262 East German Flag, Berlin Buildings and "Soyuz 31"

260 Pallas's Cat

1979. 40th Anniv of Battle of Khalka River.
1224 **259** 60m. gold, red and yellow 30 20
1225 – 60m. red, yellow and blue 30 20
DESIGN: No. 1225, Ribbons, badge and military scene.

1979. Wild Cats. Multicoloured.
1226 10m. Type **260** 15 10
1227 30m. Lynx 30 15
1228 50m. Tiger 55 25
1229 60m. Snow leopard 65 25
1230 70m. Leopard 75 35
1231 80m. Cheetah 80 35
1232 1t. Lion . . . . 1·25 50

1979. 30th Anniv of German Democratic Republic (East Germany).
1234 **262** 60m. multicoloured . . . 35 10

263 Demoiselle Crane

1979. Air. Protected Birds. Multicoloured.

1235	10m. Type **263**	40	25
1236	30m. Barred warbler	60	25
1237	50m. Ruddy shelduck	70	35
1238	60m. Azure-winged magpie	85	50
1239	70m. Goldfinch	85	50
1240	80m. Great tit	95	65
1241	1t. Golden oriole	1·40	75

264 "Venus 5" and "6"

1979. Air. Space Research. Multicoloured.

1242	10m. Type **264**	10	10
1243	30m. "Mariner 5"	10	10
1244	50m. "Mars 3"	15	10
1245	60m. "Viking 1" and "2"	15	10
1246	70m. "Luna 1", "2" and "3"	20	15
1247	80m. "Lunokhod 2"	20	15
1248	1t. "Apollo 15" Moon-rover	30	20
MS1249	83 × 77 mm. 4t. Armstrong and Aldrin on Moon	1·00	75

265 Cross-country Skiing

1980. Winter Olympic Games, Lake Placid. Multicoloured.

1250	20m. Type **265**	10	10
1251	30m. Biathlon	10	10
1252	40m. Ice hockey	15	10
1253	50m. Ski jumping	15	10
1254	60m. Slalom	20	15
1255	80m. Speed skating	20	15
1256	1t.20 Four-man bobsleigh	30	20
MS1257	90 × 105 mm. 4t. Ice skating	1·00	1·00

266 "Andrena scita" (mining bee)

1980. Air. Wasps and Bees. Multicoloured.

1258	20m. Type **266**	10	10
1259	30m. "Paravespula germanica" (wasp)	10	10
1260	40m. "Perilampus ruficornis" (parasitic wasp)	20	10
1261	50m. Buff-tailed bumble bee	30	15
1262	60m. Honey bee	40	20
1263	80m. "Stilbum cyanurum" (cuckoo wasp)	45	25
1264	1t.20 "Parnopes grandior" (cuckoo wasp)	70	35

1980. "London 1980" International Stamp Exhibition. Sheet 95 × 64 mm.

MS1265	**117** 4t. multicoloured	1·00	1·00

267 Weightlifting

1980. Olympic Games, Moscow. Multicoloured.

1266	20m. Type **267**	10	10
1267	30m. Archery	10	10
1268	40m. Gymnastics	15	10
1269	50m. Running	15	10
1270	60m. Boxing	20	15
1271	80m. Judo	20	15
1272	1t.20 Cycling	30	20
MS1273	91 × 84 mm. 4t. Wrestling	1·00	1·00

268 Zlin Z-526 AFs Akrobat Special

1980. Air. World Acrobatic Championship, Oshkosh, Wisconsin. Multicoloured.

1274	20m. Type **268**	10	10
1275	30m. Socata RF-6B Sportsman (inscr "RS-180")	15	10
1276	40m. Grumman A-1 Yankee	20	10
1277	50m. MJ-2 Tempete	30	15
1278	60m. Pitts S-2A biplane (inscr "Pits")	35	20
1279	80m. Hirth Acrostar	45	25
1280	1t.20 Yakovlev Yak-50	65	35
MS1281	89 × 68 mm. 4t. Yakolev Yak-52 (49 × 42 mm)	2·00	2·00

269 Swimming

1980. Olympic Medal Winners. Multicoloured.

1282	20m. Type **269**(postage)	10	10
1283	30m. Fencing	10	10
1284	50m. Judo	10	10
1285	60m. Athletics	15	10
1286	80m. Boxing	20	10
1287	1t. Weightlifting	25	15
1288	1t.20 Kayak-canoe	30	20
MS1289	112 × 95 mm. 4t. Wrestling (silver medal, J. Davaazhav of Mongolia) (air)	1·00	1·50

270 Sukhe Bator

271 Gubarev

1980. Mongolian Politicians.

1290	**270** 60m. brown	15	10
1291	– 60m. blue	15	10
1292	– 60m. turquoise	15	10
1293	– 60m. bronze	15	10
1294	– 60m. green	15	10
1295	– 60m. red	15	10
1296	– 60m. brown	15	10

DESIGNS—VERT: No. 1291, Marshal Choibalsan; 1292, Yu. Tsedenbal aged 13; 1293, Tsedenbal as soldier, 1941; 1294, Pres. Tsedenbal in 1979; 1295, Tsedenbal with children. HORIZ: No. 1296, Tsedenbal and President Brezhnev of Russia.

See also **MS**1522.

1980. "Intercosmos" Space Programme. Multicoloured.

1297	40m. Type **271**	10	10
1298	40m. Czechoslovak stamp showing Gubarev and Remek	10	10
1299	40m. P. Klimuk	10	10
1300	40m. Polish stamp showing M. Hermaszewski	10	10
1301	40m. V. Bykovsky	10	10
1302	40m. East German stamp showing S. Jahn	10	10
1303	40m. N. Rukavishnikov	10	10
1304	40m. Bulgarian stamp showing G. Ivanov	10	10
1305	40m. V. Kubasov	10	10
1306	40m. Hungarian stamp showing Kubasov and B. Farkas	10	10

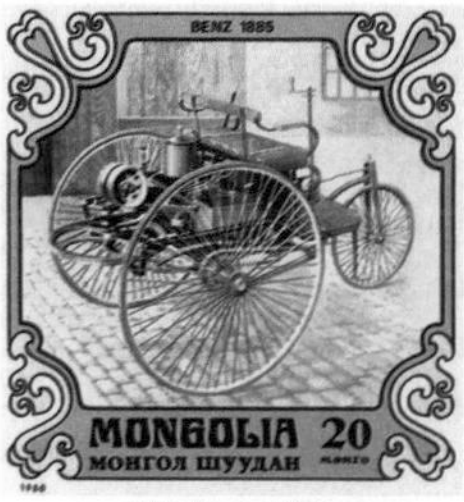

272 Benz, 1885

1980. Classic Cars. Multicoloured.

1307	20m. Type **272**	25	10
1308	30m. "President" Czechoslovakia, 1897	30	10
1309	40m. Armstrong Siddeley, 1904	35	25
1310	50m. Russo-Balt, 1909	45	20
1311	60m. Packard, 1909	50	20
1312	80m. Lancia, 1911	70	30
1313	1t.60 "Marne" taxi, 1914	1·60	60
MS1314	70 × 90 mm. 4t. "NAMI-1", Russia, 1927	4·25	4·25

273 Adelie Penguin

274 Kepler

1980. Antarctic Exploration. Multicoloured.

1315	20m. Type **273**	1·25	20
1316	30m. Blue whales	70	15
1317	40m. Wandering albatross and Jacques Cousteau's ship "Calypso" and bathysphere	1·90	40
1318	50m. Weddell seals and mobile research station	90	20
1319	60m. Emperor penguins	2·75	45
1320	70m. Great skuas	3·25	60
1321	80m. Killer whales	1·75	50
1322	1t.20 Adelie penguins, research station, Ilyushin Il-18B airplane and tracked vehicle	5·00	1·00
MS1323	90 × 120 mm. 4t. Map of Antarctica during carbon age (*circular*, 43 mm diameter)	6·25	5·00

1980. Air. 350th Death Anniv of Johannes Kepler (astronomer). Sheet 98 × 78 mm.

MS1324	**274** 4t. black and yellow	1·00	1·00

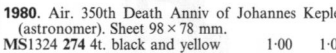

275 "Yurta Picture"

1980. 50th Anniv of Gombosuren (painter). Sheet 80 × 98 mm containing T **275** and similar horiz design. Multicoloured.

MS1325	2t. Type **275**; 2t. "Old-time Market"	1·00	1·00

276 "The Shepherd speaking the Truth"

1980. Nursery Tales. Multicoloured.

1326	20m. Type **276**	10	10
1327	30m. Children under umbrella and rainbow ("Above them the Sky is always clear")	10	10
1328	40m. Children on sledge and skis ("Winter's Joys")	10	10
1329	50m. Girl watching boy playing flute ("Little Musicians")	15	10
1330	60m. Boys giving girl leaves ("Happy Birthday")	15	10
1331	80m. Children with flowers and briefcase ("First Schoolday")	20	15
1332	1t.20 Girls dancing ("May Day")	35	25
MS1333	79 × 89 mm. Children and squirrels ("The Wonder-working Squirrels")	1·00	1·00

277 Soldier

1981. 60th Anniv of Mongolian People's Army.

1334	**277** 60m. multicoloured	40	15

278 Economy Emblems within Party Initials

1981. 60th Anniv of Mongolian Revolutionary People's Party.

1335	**278** 60m. gold, red and black	30	15

279 Motocross

1981. Motor Cycle Sports. Multicoloured.

1336	10m. Type **279**	10	10
1337	20m. Tour racing	10	10
1338	30m. Ice racing	10	10
1339	40m. Road racing	15	10
1340	50m. Motocross (different)	15	10
1341	60m. Road racing (different)	20	10
1342	70m. Speedway	20	10
1343	80m. Sidecar racing	25	15
1344	1t.20 Road racing (different)	40	20

280 Cosmonauts entering Space Capsule

1981. Soviet–Mongolian Space Flight. Mult.

1345	20m. Type **280**	10	10
1346	30m. Rocket and designer S. P. Korolev	10	10
1347	40m. "Vostok 1" and Yuri Gagarin	10	10
1348	50m. "Soyuz"–"Salyut" space station	15	10
1349	60m. Spectral photography	15	10

1350	80m. Crystal and space station	20	15
1351	1t.20 Space complex, Moscow Kremlin and Sukhe Bator statue, Ulan Bator	35	25
MS1352	70×80 mm. 4t. Cosmonauts Dzhanibekov and Gurragchaa (31×42 mm) . . .	1·00	1·00

281 Ulan Bator Buildings and 1961 Mongolian Stamp

1981. Stamp Exhibitions.

1353	**281**	1t. multicoloured	2·25	1·00
1354	–	1t. multicoloured	1·75	80
1355	–	1t. black, blue and magenta	1·75	80
1356	–	1t. multicoloured	2·25	1·00

DESIGNS: No. 1353, Type **281** (Mongolian stamp exhibition); 1354, Wurttemberg stamps of 1947 and 1949 and view of Old Stuttgart ("Naposta '81" exhibition); 1355, Parliament building and sculpture, Vienna, and Austrian stamp of 1933 ("WIPA 1981" exhibition); 1356, Japanese stamp of 1964, cherry blossom and girls in Japanese costume ("Japex '81" exhibition, Tokyo).

282 Star and Industrial and Agricultural Scenes

1981. 18th Mongolian Revolutionary People's Party Congress.

1357	**282**	60m. multicoloured . . .	30	10

283 Sukhe Bator Statue, Ulan Bator

1981. 60th Anniv of Mongolian Revolutionary People's Party (2nd issue). Sheet 70×90 mm.

MS1358	**283** 4t. multicoloured . .	1·00	1·00

284 Sheep Farming

1981. "Results of the People's Economy". Multicoloured.

1359	20m. Type **284**	10	10
1360	30m. Transport	1·25	15
1361	40m. Telecommunications	60	15
1362	50m. Public health service	20	10
1363	60m. Agriculture	30	10
1364	80m. Electrical industry . .	35	15
1365	1t.20 Housing	50	20

285 UN Emblem

287 Arms of Mongolia and Russia

286 Pharaonic Ship (15th century B.C.)

1981. 20th Anniv of United Nations Membership. Sheet 70×90 mm.

MS1366	**285** 4t. multicoloured . .	1·00	1·00

1981. Sailing Ships. Multicoloured.

1367	10m. Type **286**	15	10
1368	20m. Mediterranean sailing ship (9th century)	20	10
1369	40m. Hanse kogge (12th century) (vert)	30	10
1370	50m. Venetian felucca (13th century) (vert)	40	15
1371	60m. Columbus's "Santa Maria" (vert)	45	25
1372	80m. Cook's H.M.S. "Endeavour" (vert) . . .	50	30
1373	1t. "Poltava" (Russian ship of the line) (vert)	70	35
1374	1t.20 American schooner (19th century) (vert) . . .	80	40

1981. Soviet–Mongolian Friendship Pact.

1375	**287**	60m. red, blue and gold	35	10

288 "Hendrickje in Bed"

1981. 375th Birth Anniv of Rembrandt (artist). Multicoloured.

1376	20m. "Flora"	20	10
1377	30m. Type **288**	25	15
1378	40m. "Young Woman with Earrings"	45	20
1379	50m. "Young girl in the Window"	50	25
1380	60m. "Hendrickje like Flora"	60	30
1381	80m. "Saskia with Red Flower"	80	35
1382	1t.20 "The Holy Family with Drape" (detail) . . .	1·10	45
MS1383	68×85 mm. 4t. "Self-portrait with Saskia"	3·75	3·75

289 Billy Goat (pawn)

1981. Mongolian Chess Pieces. Multicoloured.

1384	20m. Type **289**	20	10
1385	40m. Horse-drawn cart (rook)	30	15
1386	50m. Camel (bishop)	40	20
1387	60m. Horse (knight)	60	25
1388	80m. Lion (queen)	75	30
1389	1t.20 Man with dog (king)	1·10	40
MS1390	90×70 mm. 4t. Chess game (illustration of Mongolian folk tale)	2·50	2·50

290 White-tailed Sea Eagle and German 1m. "Zeppelin" Stamp

1981. Air. 50th Anniv of "Graf Zeppelin" Polar Flight. Multicoloured.

1391	20m. Type **290**	75	25
1392	30m. Arctic fox and German 2m. "Zeppelin" stamp . .	40	15
1393	40m. Walrus and German 4m. "Zeppelin" stamp . .	50	15
1394	50m. Polar bear and Russian 30k. "Zeppelin" stamp	60	15
1395	60m. Snowy owl and Russian 35k. "Zeppelin" stamp	1·90	70
1396	80m. Atlantic puffin and Russian 1r. "Zeppelin" stamp	2·25	90
1397	1t.20 Northern sealion and Russian 2r. "Zeppelin" stamp	1·50	30
MS1398	93×77 mm. 4t. *Graf Zeppelin* and Russian ice-breaker *Malygin* (36×51 mm)	5·00	4·00

291 Circus Camel and Circus Building, Ulan Bator

1981. Mongolian Sport and Art. Multicoloured.

1399	10m. Type **291**	10	10
1400	20m. Horsemen and stadium (National holiday cavalcade)	15	10
1401	40m. Wrestling and Ulan Bator stadium	25	15
1402	50m. Archers and stadium	35	20
1403	60m. Folk singer-dancer and House of Culture	45	20
1404	80m. Girl playing jatga (folk instrument) and Ulan Bator Drama Theatre . .	60	30
1405	1t. Ballet dancers and Opera House	90	40
1406	1t.20 Exhibition Hall and statue of man on bucking horse	1·10	65

292 Mozart and scene from "The Magic Flute"

1981. Composers. Multicoloured.

1407	20m. Type **292**	15	10
1408	30m. Beethoven and scene from "Fidelio"	20	10
1409	40m. Bartok and scene from "The Miraculous Mandarin"	20	10
1410	50m. Verdi and scene from "Aida"	30	15
1411	60m. Tchaikovsky and scene from "The Sleeping Beauty"	35	15
1412	80m. Dvorak and score of "New World" symphony	45	25
1413	1t.20 Chopin, piano, score and quill pens	60	30

293 "Mongolian Women in Everyday Life" (detail, Davaakhuu)

294 Gorbatko

1981. International Decade for Women. Mult.

1414	20m. Type **293**	25	10
1415	30m. "Mongolian Women in Everyday Life" (different detail)	35	15
1416	40m. "National Day" (detail, Khishigbaiar) . .	40	20
1417	50m. "National Day" (detail) (different)	50	25
1418	60m. "National Day" (detail) (different)	60	35
1419	80m. "Ribbon Weaver" (Ts. Baidi)	85	40
1420	1t.20 "Expectant Mother" (Senghesokhio)	1·25	65

1981. "Intercosmos" Space Programme. Mult.

1422	50m. Type **294**	15	10
1423	50m. Vietnam stamp showing Gorbatko and Pham Tuan	15	10
1424	50m. Romanenko	15	10
1425	50m. Cuban stamp showing Tamayo	15	10
1426	50m. Dzhanibekov	15	10
1427	50m. Mongolian stamp showing Dzhanibekov and Gurrugchaa	15	10
1428	50m. Popov	15	10
1429	50m. Rumanian stamp showing "Salyut" space station and "Soyuz" space ship	15	10

295 Karl von Drais Bicycle, 1816

1982. History of the Bicycle. Multicoloured.

1430	10m. Type **295**	10	10
1431	20m. Macmillan bicycle, 1838	10	10
1432	40m. First American pedal bicycle by Pierre Lallament, 1866	15	10
1433	50m. First European pedal bicycle by Ernest Michaux	20	10
1434	60m. "Kangaroo" bicycle, 1877	20	10
1435	80m. Coventry Rotary Tandem, 1870s	30	10
1436	1t. Chain-driven bicycle, 1878	35	15
1437	1t.20 Modern bicycle . . .	40	20
MS1438	95×90 mm. 4t. Modern road racers (43×43 mm) . . .	1·50	1·50

296 Footballers (Brazil, 1950)

1982. World Cup Football Championship, Spain. Multicoloured.

1439	10m. Type **296**(postage) . .	10	10
1440	20m. Switzerland, 1954 . .	10	10
1441	40m. Sweden, 1958	15	10
1442	50m. Chile, 1962	20	10
1443	60m. England, 1966	20	10
1444	80m. Mexico, 1970	30	10
1445	1t. West Germany, 1974 . .	35	15
1446	1t.20 Argentina, 1978 . . .	40	20
MS1447	90×70 mm. 4t. Spain, 1982 (air) (44×44 mm)	1·50	1·50

297 Trade Union Emblem and Economic Symbols

299 Dimitrov

298 Children with Deer

1982. 12th Mongolian Trade Unions Congress.

1448	**297**	60m. multicoloured . . .	1·00	30

1982. "Philefrance 82" International Stamp Exhibition, Paris. Sheet 105×68 mm.

MS1449	**298** 4t. multicoloured . .	1·00	1·00

For 50m.+5m. as Type **298** but larger, see No. 1176.

1982. Birth Centenary of Georgi Dimitrov (Bulgarian statesman).
1450 **299** 60m. black, grey and gold 35 10

300 Chicks

1982. Young Animals. Multicoloured.
1451 10m. Type **300** 10 10
1452 20m. Colt 10 10
1453 30m. Lamb 15 10
1454 40m. Roe deer fawn 20 10
1455 50m. Bactrian camel 20 10
1456 60m. Kid 25 10
1457 70m. Calf 30 15
1458 1t.20 Wild piglet 40 20

301 Coal-fired Industry

1982. Coal Mining.
1459 **301** 60m. multicoloured . . . 35 10

302 Emblem **304** Revsomol Emblem within "Flower"

303 Siberian Pine

1982. 18th Revsomol Youth Congress.
1460 **302** 60m. multicoloured . . . 35 10

1982. Trees. Multicoloured.
1461 20m. Type **303** 10 10
1462 30m. Siberian fir 10 10
1463 40m. Poplar 20 10
1464 50m. Siberian larch 20 10
1465 60m. Scots pine 25 10
1466 80m. Birch 30 15
1467 1t.20 Spruce 50 25

1982. 60th Anniv of Revsomol Youth Organization.
1468 **304** 60m. multicoloured . . . 35 10

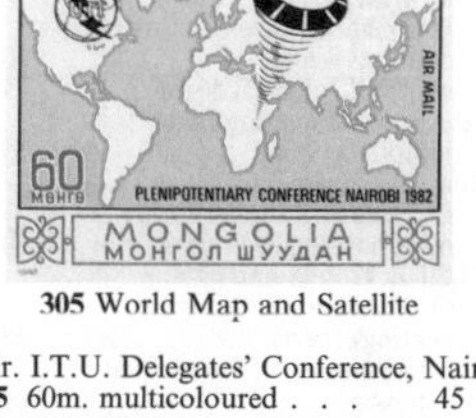

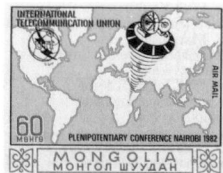

305 World Map and Satellite

1982. Air. I.T.U. Delegates' Conference, Nairobi.
1469 **305** 60m. multicoloured . . . 45 15

306 Japanese "Iseki-6500" Tractor

1982. Tractors. Multicoloured.
1470 10m. Type **306** 10 10
1471 20m. West German "Deutz-DX230" 10 10
1472 40m. British "Bonser" . . . 15 10
1473 50m. American "International-884" . . . 20 10
1474 60m. French Renault "TX 145-14" 20 10
1475 80m. Russian "Belarus-611" 25 10
1476 1t. Russian "K-7100" . . . 30 15
1477 1t.20 Russian "DT-75" . . 40 20

307 Hump-backed Whitefish and Lake Hevsgel

1982. Landscapes and Animals. Multicoloured.
1478 20m. Type **307** 50 15
1479 30m. Zavkhan Highlands and sheep 30 10
1480 40m. Lake Hovd and Eurasian beaver 40 10
1481 50m. Lake Uvs and horses 50 15
1482 60m. Bajankhongor Steppe and goitred gazelle . . . 60 20
1483 80m. Bajan-Elgii Highlands and rider with golden eagle 65 20
1484 1t.20 Gobi Desert and bactrian camels . . . . . 1·00 50

308 "Sputnik 1"

1982. Air. Second U.N. Conference on the Exploration and Peaceful Uses of Outer Space. Multicoloured.
1485 60m. Type **308** 15 10
1486 60m. "Sputnik 2" and Laika (first dog in space) . . . 15 10
1487 60m. "Vostok 1" and Yuri Gagarin (first man in space) 15 10
1488 60m. "Venera 8" 15 10
1489 60m. "Vostok 6" and V. Tereshkova (first woman in space) 15 10
1490 60m. Aleksei Leonov and space walker 15 10
1491 60m. Neil Armstrong and astronaut on Moon's surface 15 10
1492 60m. V. Dzhanibekov, Jean-Loup Chretien and "Soyuz T-6" 15 10
MS1493 88 × 70 mm. 4t. "Soyuz" and "Salyut" coupling (49 × 33 mm) . . . . 1·00 1·00

309 Montgolfier Brothers' Balloon, 1783

1982. Air. Bicentenary of Manned Flight. Mult.
1494 20m. Type **309** 10 10
1495 30m. Jean-Pierre Blanchard and John Jeffries crossing the channel, 1785 . . . . 15 10
1496 40m. Charles Green's flight to Germany in balloon "Royal Vauxhall", 1836 20 10
1497 50m. Salomon Andree's North Pole flight in balloon "Ornen", 1897 . . 25 10
1498 60m. First Gordon Bennett balloon race, Paris, 1906 30 15
1499 80m. First stratosphere flight by Auguste Piccard in balloon "F.N.R.S.", Switzerland, 1931 . . . . 40 20
1500 1t.20 Stratosphere balloon USSR-VR-62 flight, 1933 55 25
MS1501 78 × 98 mm. 4t. First Mongolian balloon flight, 1977 2·00 2·00

310 Sorcerer tells Mickey Mouse to clean up Quarters

1983. Drawings from "The Sorcerer's Apprentice" (section of Walt Disney's film "Fantasia"). Mult.
1502 25m. Type **310** 20 10
1503 35m. Mickey notices Sorcerer has left his cap behind 30 15
1504 45m. Mickey puts cap on and commands broom to fetch water 35 20
1505 55m. Broom carrying water 40 25
1506 65m. Mickey sleeps while broom continues to fetch water, flooding the room 50 30
1507 75m. Mickey uses axe on broom to try to stop it . . 55 35
1508 85m. Each splinter becomes a broom which continues to fetch water 65 40
1509 1t.40 Mickey, clinging to Sorcerer's Book of Spells, caught in whirlpool . . . 1·00 55
1510 2t. Mickey handing cap back to Sorcerer . . . . 1·40 75
MS1511 127 × 102 mm. 7t. Mickey dreaming himself to be Master of the Universe . . . . 5·00 4·50

311 Foal with Mother

1983. "The Foal and the Hare" (folk tale). Mult.
1512 10m. Type **311** 10 10
1513 20m. Foal wanders off alone 15 10
1514 30m. Foal finds sack 25 15
1515 40m. Foal unties sack . . . 30 15
1516 50m. Wolf jumps out of sack 40 20
1517 60m. Hare appears as wolf is about to eat foal . . . 45 25
1518 70m. Hare tricks wolf into re-entering sack 50 30
1519 80m. Hare ties up sack with wolf inside 60 35
1520 1t.20 Hare and foal look for foal's mother 90 50
MS1521 121 × 94 mm. 7t. Boy with foal (58 × 58 mm). Imperf . . . 5·00 4·50

311a Tank Monument, Ulan Bator

1983. Air. 40th Anniv of Formation of "Revolutionary Mongolia" Tank Regiment of Soviet Army. Sheet 110 x 75 mm.
MS1522 **311*a*** 4t. multicoloured

1983. 90th Birth Anniv of Sukhe Bator. Sheet 65 × 72 mm containing designs as T **270** but smaller, 25 × 32 mm.
MS1523 **270** 4t. purple . . . . . 1·00 1·00

312 Antonov An-24B Aircraft

1983. Tourism. Multicoloured.
1524 20m. Type **312** 20 10
1525 30m. Skin tent 10 10
1526 40m. Roe deer 15 10
1527 50m. Argali 25 10
1528 60m. Imperial eagle 85 40
1529 80m. Khan Museum, Ulan Bator 40 20
1530 1t.20 Sukhe Bator statue, Ulan Bator 55 25

313 Rose

1983. Flowers. Multicoloured.
1531 20m. Type **313** 10 10
1532 30m. Dahlia 15 10
1533 40m. Marigold 20 10
1534 50m. Narcissus 25 10
1535 60m. Viola 30 10
1536 80m. Tulip 40 15
1537 1t.20 Sunflower 50 25

314 Border Guard

1983. 50th Anniv of Border Guards.
1538 **314** 60m. multicoloured . . . 40 10

315 Boy riding Buffalo

1983. "Brasiliana 83" International Stamp Exhibition, Rio de Janeiro. Sheet 135 × 88 mm.
MS1539 **325** 4t. multicoloured . . 1·00 1·00

316 Karl Marx

1983. Death Centenary of Karl Marx.
1540 **316** 60m. red, gold and blue 35 10

317 Agriculture

1983. 18th Communist Party Congress Five Year Plan. Multicoloured.

1541	10m. Type **317**	10	10
1542	20m. Power industry	10	10
1543	30m. Textile industry	10	10
1544	40m. Science in industry and agriculture	15	10
1545	60m. Improvement of living standards	20	10
1546	80m. Communications	2·00	50
1547	1t. Children (education)	40	20

318 Young Inventors

1983. Children's Year. Multicoloured.

1548	10m. Type **318**	15	10
1549	20m. In school	25	10
1550	30m. Archery	40	15
1551	40m. Shepherdess playing flute	50	20
1552	50m. Girl with deer	65	30
1553	70m. Collecting rocks and mushrooms	2·25	50
1554	1t.20 Girl playing lute and boy singing	1·25	60

319 Skating

1983. 10th Anniv of Children's Fund. Mult.

1555	20m. Type **319**	10	10
1556	30m. Shepherds	10	10
1557	40m. Tree-planting	15	10
1558	50m. Playing by the sea	20	10
1559	60m. Carrying water	25	15
1560	80m. Folk dancing	30	20
1561	1t.20 Ballet	55	25
MS1562	93 × 110 mm. 4t. Christmas	1·50	1·00

320 Pallas's Pika

1983. Small Mammals. Multicoloured.

1563	20m. Type **320**	35	20
1564	30m. Long-eared jerboa	45	25
1565	40m. Eurasian red squirrel	55	30
1566	50m. Daurian hedgehog	65	40
1567	60m. Harvest mouse	80	45
1568	80m. Eurasian water shrew	1·25	70
1569	1t.20 Siberian chipmunk	1·75	95

321 "Sistine Madonna"

1983. 500th Birth Anniv of Raphael (artist). Sheet 102 × 138 mm.

MS1570	**321** 4t. multicoloured	2·00	2·00

322 Bobsleighing

1984. Winter Olympic Games, Sarajevo. Mult.

1571	20m. Type **322**	10	10
1572	30m. Cross-country skiing	10	10
1573	40m. Ice hockey	10	10
1574	50m. Speed skating	15	10
1575	60m. Ski jumping	15	10
1576	80m. Ice dancing	20	15
1577	1t.20 Biathlon (horiz)	35	25
MS1578	133 × 105 mm. 4t. Ski jumping (horiz)	1·00	1·00

323 Mail Van

1984. World Communications Year. Multicoloured.

1579	10m. Type **323**	10	10
1580	20m. Earth receiving station	10	10
1581	40m. Airliner	40	15
1582	50m. Central Post Office, Ulan Bator	25	10
1583	1t. Transmitter	40	15
1584	1t.20 Diesel train	3·50	1·25
MS1585	90 × 110 mm. 4t. Aerials (41 × 22 mm)	1·75	1·75

324 "Ausipex 84" Emblem and Tupolev Tu-154

1984. "Espana 84", Madrid and "Ausipex 84", Melbourne, International Stamp Exhibitions. Sheet 104 × 90 mm.

MS1586	**324** 4t. multicoloured	2·00	2·00

325 Cycling

326 Flag, Rocket and Coastal Scene

1984. Olympic Games, Los Angeles. Multicoloured.

1587	20m. Gymnastics (horiz)	10	10
1588	30m. Type **325**	10	10
1589	40m. Weightlifting	10	10
1590	50m. Judo	10	10
1591	60m. Archery	15	10
1592	80m. Boxing	20	15
1593	1t.20 High jumping (horiz)	35	25
MS1594	105 × 85 mm. 4t. Wrestling (horiz)	1·00	1·00

1984. 25th Anniv of Cuban Revolution.

1595	**326** 60m. multicoloured	25	10

327 1924 1c. Stamp

1984. 60th Anniv of Mongolian Stamps. Sheet 90 × 110 mm.

MS1596	**327** 4t. multicoloured	1·50	1·50

328 Douglas DC-10

329 Speaker, Radio and Transmitter

1984. Air. Civil Aviation. Multicoloured.

1597	20m. Type **328**	10	10
1598	30m. Airbus Industrie A300B2	20	10
1599	40m. Concorde supersonic jetliner	25	10
1600	50m. Boeing 747-200	30	15
1601	60m. Ilyushin Il-62M	30	20
1602	80m. Tupolev Tu-154	50	25
1603	1t.20 Ilyushin Il-86	60	35
MS1604	110 × 90 mm. 4t. Yakovlev Yak-42	2·00	2·00

1984. 50th Anniv of Mongolian Broadcasting.

1605	**329** 60m. multicoloured	60	20

330 Silver and Gold Coins

1984. 60th Anniv of State Bank.

1606	**330** 60m. multicoloured	25	10

331 Donshy Mask

333 Sukhe Bator Statue

332 Golden Harp

1984. Traditional Masks. Multicoloured.

1607	20m. Type **331**	10	10
1608	30m. Zamandi	25	10
1609	40m. Ulaan-Yadam	30	10
1610	50m. Lkham	45	15
1611	60m. Damdinchoizhoo	55	20
1612	80m. Ochirvaan	75	25
1613	1t.20 Namsrai	1·25	40
MS1614	90 × 110 mm. 4t. Ulaanzhamsran	3·50	3·50

1984. Scenes from Walt Disney's "Mickey and the Beanstalk" (cartoon film). Multicoloured.

1615	25m. Type **332**	20	10
1616	35m. Mickey holding box of magic beans	30	15
1617	45m. Mickey about to eat bean	40	20
1618	55m. Mickey looking for magic bean	50	25
1619	65m. Goofy, Mickey and Donald at top of beanstalk	55	30
1620	75m. Giant holding Mickey	60	35
1621	85m. Giant threatening Mickey	80	40
1622	140m. Goofy, Mickey and Donald cutting down beanstalk	1·40	65
1623	2t. Goofy and Donald rescuing golden harp	1·60	75
MS1624	126 × 101 mm. 7t. Mickey, Goofy, Donald and giant plants (50 × 37 mm)	5·50	4·50

1984. 60th Anniv of Ulan Bator City.

1625	**333** 60m. multicoloured	60	20

334 Arms, Flag and Landscape

335 Rider carrying Flag

1984. 60th Anniv of Mongolian People's Republic.

1626	**334** 60m. multicoloured	60	20

1984. 60th Anniv of Mongolian People's Revolutionary Party.

1627	**335** 60m. multicoloured	35	10

336 Collie

1984. Dogs. Multicoloured.

1628	20m. Type **336**	10	10
1629	30m. German shepherd	25	10
1630	40m. Papillon	35	10
1631	50m. Cocker spaniel	50	15
1632	60m. Terrier puppy (diamond-shaped)	60	20
1633	80m. Dalmatians (diamond-shaped)	75	25
1634	1t.20 Mongolian shepherd	1·25	40

337 Gaetan Boucher (speed skating)

1984. Winter Olympic Gold Medal Winners. Multicoloured.

1635	20m. Type **337**	10	10
1636	30m. Eirik Kvalfoss (biathlon)	10	10
1637	40m. Marja-Liisa Hamalainen (cross-country skiing)	10	10
1638	50m. Max Julen (slalom)	15	10
1639	60m. Jens Weissflog (ski jumping) (vert)	15	10
1640	80m. W. Hoppe and D. Schauerhammer (two-man bobsleigh) (vert)	20	15
1641	1t.20 J. Valova and O. Vassiliev (pairs figure skating) (vert)	35	25
MS1642	110 × 90 mm. 4t. Russia (ice hockey)	1·00	1·00

338 Four Animals and Tree

1984. "The Four Friendly Animals" (fairy tale). Multicoloured.

1643	10m. Type **338**	15	10
1644	20m. Animals discussing who was the oldest	20	10
1645	30m. Monkey and elephant beside tree	20	10
1646	40m. Elephant as calf and young tree	25	10
1647	50m. Monkey and young tree	40	15
1648	60m. Hare and young tree	50	20
1649	70m. Dove and sapling	55	20
1650	80m. Animals around mature tree	70	30
1651	1t.20 Animals supporting each other so that dove could reach fruit	95	40
MS1652	103 × 84 mm. 4t. Dove passing fruit to other animals (vert)	3·75	3·75

339 Fawn

1984. Red Deer. Multicoloured.

1653	50m. Type **339**	40	20
1654	50m. Stag	40	20
1655	50m. Adults and fawn by river	40	20
1656	50m. Doe in woodland	40	20

340 Flag and Pioneers 342 Black Stork

341 Shar Tarlan

1985. 60th Anniv of Mongolian Pioneer Organization.

1657	**340** 60m. multicoloured	40	15

1985. Cattle. Multicoloured.

1658	20m. Type **341**	10	10
1659	30m. Bor khalium	20	10
1660	40m. Sarlag	30	10
1661	50m. Dornod talin bukh	45	15
1662	60m. Char tarlan	55	20
1663	80m. Nutgiin uulderiin unee	65	20
1664	1t.20 Tsagaan tolgoit	1·10	35
MS1665	90 × 110 mm. 4t. Girl with calf (vert)	3·25	3·25

1985. Birds. Multicoloured.

1666	20m. Type **342**	30	45
1667	30m. White-tailed sea eagle	40	45
1668	40m. Great white crane	55	45
1669	50m. Heude's parrotbill	85	90
1670	60m. Hooded crane	1·00	90
1671	80m. Japanese white-naped crane	1·25	1·25
1672	1t.20 Rough-legged buzzard	2·10	2·25
MS1673	125 × 70 mm. 4t. Brandt's cormorant (*Phalacrocorax penicillatus*) (47 × 39 mm)	4·00	4·00

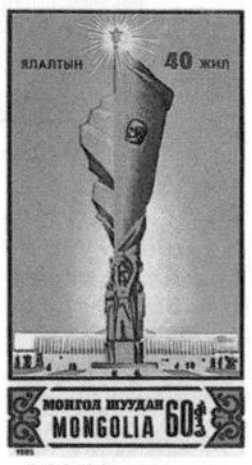

343 Footballers 344 Monument

1985. World Junior Football Championship, U.S.S.R.

1674	**343** 20m. multicoloured	10	10
1675	– 30m. multicoloured	10	10
1676	– 40m. multicoloured	15	10
1677	– 50m. multicoloured	20	10
1678	– 60m. multicoloured	25	10
1679	– 80m. multicoloured	30	15
1680	– 1t.20 multicoloured	50	25
MS1681	110 × 90 mm. 4t. multicoloured (horiz)	1·00	1·00

DESIGNS: 30m. to 4t., Different footballing scenes.

1985. 40th Anniv of Victory in Europe.

1682	**344** 60m. multicoloured	30	10

345 Snow Leopards

1985. The Snow Leopard. Multicoloured.

1683	50m. Type **345**	40	20
1684	50m. Leopard	40	20
1685	50m. Leopard on cliff ledge	40	20
1686	50m. Mother and cubs	40	20

346 Moscow Kremlin and Girls of Different Races 347 Monument

1985. 12th World Youth and Students' Festival, Moscow.

1687	**346** 60m. multicoloured	30	10

1985. 40th Anniv of Victory in Asia.

1688	**347** 60m. multicoloured	35	10

348 "Rosa dahurica"

1985. Plants. Multicoloured.

1689	20m. Type **348**	10	10
1690	30m. False chamomile	20	10
1691	40m. Dandelion	30	10
1692	50m. "Saxzitraga nirculus"	45	15
1693	60m. Cowberry	55	20
1694	80m. "Sanguisorba officinalis"	65	20
1695	1t.20 "Plantago major"	1·10	35
MS1696	90 × 110 mm. 4t. Sea buckthorn (*Hippophae rhamnoides*) (wrongly inscr "Hippopae thamnoides")	3·25	3·25

See also Nos. 1719/25.

349 Camel

1985. The Bactrian Camel. Multicoloured.

1697	50m. Type **349**	40	20
1698	50m. Adults and calf	40	20
1699	50m. Calf	40	20
1700	50m. Adult	40	20

350 "Soyuz" Spacecraft

1985. Space. Multicoloured.

1701	20m. Type **350**	10	10
1702	30m. "Kosmos" satellite	10	10
1703	40m. "Venera-9" satellite	10	10
1704	50m. "Salyut" space station	15	10
1705	60m. "Luna-9" landing vehicle	15	10
1706	80m. "Soyuz" rocket on transporter	1·10	50
1707	1t.20 Dish aerial receiving transmission from "Soyuz"	30	15
MS1708	110 × 90 mm. 4t. Cosmonauts on space walk	1·00	1·00

351 Horseman

1985. "Italia '85" International Stamp Exhibition, Rome. Sheet 110 × 90 mm.

MS1709	**351** 4t. multicoloured	1·00	1·00

352 U.N. and Mongolian Flags and U.N. Headquarters, New York 354 Congress Emblem

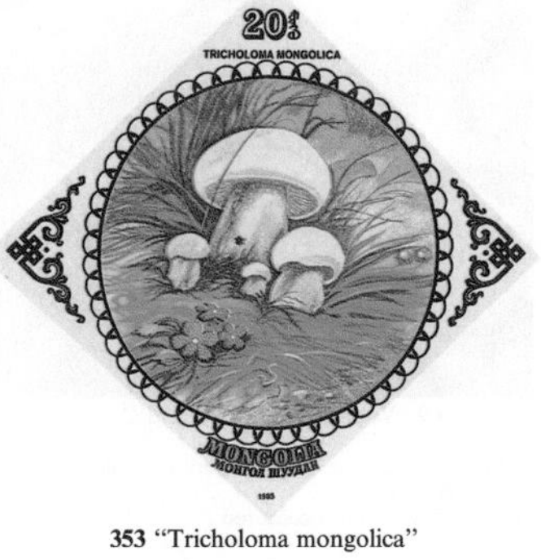

353 "Tricholoma mongolica"

1985. 40th Anniv of U.N.O.

1710	**352** 60m. multicoloured	30	10

1985. Fungi. Multicoloured.

1711	20m. Type **353**	20	10
1712	30m. Chanterelle	25	10
1713	40m. Honey fungus	30	10
1714	50m. Caesar's mushroom	55	15
1715	70m. Chestnut mushroom	80	20
1716	80m. Red-staining mushroom	90	25
1717	1t.20 Cep	1·40	35

1986. 19th Mongolian Revolutionary People's Party Congress.

1718	**354** 60m. multicoloured	25	10

1986. Plants. As T **348**. Multicoloured.

1719	20m. "Valeriana officinalis"	10	10
1720	30m. "Hyoscymus niger"	20	10
1721	40m. "Ephedra sinica"	30	10
1722	50m. "Thymus gobica"	45	15
1723	60m. "Paeonia anomalia"	55	20
1724	80m. "Achilea millefolium"	65	25
1725	1t.20 "Rhododendron adamsii"	1·10	35

355 Scene from Play

1986. 80th Birth Anniv of D. Natsagdorj (writer).

1726	**355** 60m. multicoloured	25	10

356 Thalmann 357 Man wearing Patterned Robe

1986. Birth Centenary of Ernst Thalmann (German politician).

1727	**356** 60m. multicoloured	25	10

1986. Costumes. Multicoloured.

1728	60m. Type **357**	25	10
1729	60m. Man in blue robe and fur-lined hat with car flaps	25	10
1730	60m. Woman in black and yellow dress and bolero	25	10
1731	60m. Woman in pink dress patterned with stars	25	10
1732	60m. Man in cream robe with fur cuffs	25	10
1733	60m. Man in brown robe and mauve and yellow tunic	25	10
1734	60m. Woman in blue dress with black, yellow and red overtunic	25	10

358 Footballers

1986. World Cup Football Championship, Mexico.

1735	**358** 20m. multicoloured	10	10
1736	– 30m. multicoloured	10	10
1737	– 40m. multicoloured	10	10
1738	– 50m. multicoloured	15	10
1739	– 60m. multicoloured	15	10
1740	– 80m. multicoloured	20	15
1741	– 1t.20 multicoloured	35	25
MS1742	110 × 90 mm. 4t. multicoloured (horiz)	1·00	1·00

DESIGNS: 30m. to 4t., Different footballing scenes.

359 Mink

1986. Mink. Multicoloured.

1743	60m. Type **359**	45	15
1744	60m. Mink on rock	45	15
1745	60m. Mink on snow-covered branch	45	15
1746	60m. Two mink	45	15

See also Nos. 1771/4, 1800/3, 1804/7, 1840/3 and 1844/7.

360 "Neptis coenobita"

361 Sukhe Bator Statue

1986. Butterflies and Moths. Multicoloured.
1747 20m. Type **360** 10 10
1748 30m. "Colias tycha" 15 10
1749 40m. "Leptidea amurensis" 20 10
1750 50m. "Oeneis tarpenledevi" 30 15
1751 60m. "Mesoacidalia charlotta" 40 20
1752 80m. Eyed hawk moth . . . 45 25
1753 1t.20 Large tiger moth . . . 75 40

1986. 65th Anniv of Independence.
1754 **361** 60m. multicoloured . . . 25 10

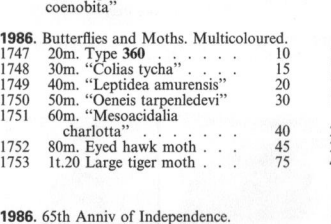

362 Yak and Goats Act

1986. Circus. Multicoloured.
1755 20m. Type **362** 10 10
1756 30m. Acrobat 10 10
1757 40m. Yak act 15 10
1758 50m. Acrobats (vert) 20 10
1759 60m. High wire act (vert) . . 25 15
1760 80m. Fire juggler on camel (vert) 30 15
1761 1t.20 Acrobats on camel-drawn cart (vert) 50 25

363 Morin Khuur

364 Flag and Emblem

1986. Musical Instruments. Multicoloured.
1762 20m. Type **363** 10 10
1763 30m. Bishguur (wind instrument) 20 10
1764 40m. Ever buree (wind) . . 30 10
1765 50m. Shudarga (string) . . . 45 15
1766 60m. Khiil (string) 55 20
1767 80m. Janchir (string) (horiz) 65 25
1768 1t.20 Jatga (string) (horiz) 1·10 35

1986. International Peace Year.
1770 **364** 10m. multicoloured . . . 50 20

1986. Przewalski's Horse. As T **359**. Mult.
1771 50m. Horses grazing on sparsely grassed plain . . 45 15
1772 50m. Horses grazing on grassy plain 45 15
1773 50m. Adults with foal . . . 45 15
1774 50m. Horses in snow . . . 45 15

365 Temple

1986. Ancient Buildings. Multicoloured.
1775 60m. Type **365** 60 20
1776 60m. Temple with light green roof and white doors 60 20
1777 60m. Temple with porch . . 60 20
1778 60m. White building with three porches 60 20

366 Redhead ("Aythya americana")

1986. Birds. Multicoloured.
1779 60m. Type **366** 85 55
1780 60m. Ruffed grouse ("Bonasa umbellus") . . 85 55
1781 60m. Tundra swan ("Olor columbianus") 85 55
1782 60m. Water pipit ("Anthus spinoletta") 85 55

367 Alfa Romeo "RL Sport", 1922

1986. Cars. Multicoloured.
1783 20m. Type **367** 10 10
1784 30m. Stutz "Bearcat", 1912 15 10
1785 40m. Mercedes "Simplex", 1902 . . . . 20 10
1786 50m. Tatra "11", 1923 . . . 25 10
1787 60m. Ford Model "T", 1908 30 15
1788 80m. Vauxhall, 1905 . . . . 40 20
1789 1t.20 Russo-Balt "K", 1913 60 30
MS1790 110 × 90 mm. 4t. As No. 1789 . . . . 2·00 2·00

368 Wilhelm Steinitz and Curt von Bardeleben Game, 1895

1986. World Chess Champions. Multicoloured.
1791 20m. Type **368** 10 10
1792 30m. Emanuel Lasker and Harry Pilsberi game, 1895 15 10
1793 40m. Alexander Alekhine and Richard Retti game, 1925 . . . . 20 10
1794 50m. Mikhail Botvinnik and Capablanca game, 1938 25 10
1795 60m. Anatoly Karpov and Wolfgang Untsiker game, 1975 . . . . 30 15
1796 80m. Nona Gaprindashvili and Lasarevich game, 1961 . . . . 40 20
1797 1t.20 Maia Chirburdanidze and Irina Levitina game, 1984 . . . . 60 30
MS1798 110 × 100 mm. 4t. Players around International Chess Federation emblem . . . . . 2·00 2·00

369 "Vega 2" Spacecraft and Comet

1986. Appearance of Halley's Comet. Sheet 110 × 90 mm.
MS1799 **369** 4t. multicoloured . . 1·00 1·00

1986. Saiga Antelope. As T **359**. Multicoloured.
1800 60m. Male 45 15
1801 60m. Female with calf . . . 45 15
1802 60m. Male and female . . . 45 15
1803 60m. Male and female in snow 45 15

1986. Pelicans. As T **359**. Multicoloured.
1804 60m. Dalmatian pelican ("Pelecanus crispus") . . 1·10 55
1805 60m. Dalmatian pelican preening . . . . 1·10 55
1806 60m. Eastern white pelican ("Pelecanus onocrotalus") 1·10 55
1807 60m. Eastern white pelicans in flight . . . . 1·10 55

370 Siamese Fighting Fish

1987. Aquarium Fishes. Multicoloured.
1808 20m. Type **370** 10 10
1809 30m. Goldfish 15 10
1810 40m. Glowlight rasbora . . 25 10
1811 50m. Acara 35 10
1812 60m. Platy 40 15
1813 80m. Green swordtail . . . 55 20
1814 1t.20 Freshwater angelfish (vert) 95 30
MS1815 111 × 91 mm. 4t. Sail-finned tetra (*Crenuchus spilurus*) (53 × 32 mm) . . . . 3·00 3·00

371 Lassoing Horse

1987. Traditional Equestrian Sports. Mult.
1816 20m. Type **371** 10 10
1817 30m. Breaking horse 15 10
1818 40m. Mounted archer . . . 20 10
1819 50m. Race 25 10
1820 60m. Horseman snatching flag from ground 35 15
1821 80m. Tug of war 40 20
1822 1t.20 Racing wolf 70 25

372 Grey-headed Woodpecker

373 Butterfly Hunting

1987. Woodpeckers. Multicoloured.
1823 20m. Type **372** 30 20
1824 30m. Wryneck 45 25
1825 40m. Great spotted woodpecker 75 25
1826 50m. White-backed woodpecker . . . . . . 1·10 35
1827 60m. Lesser spotted woodpecker . . . . . . 1·25 35
1828 80m. Black woodpecker . . 1·75 50
1829 1t.20 Three-toed woodpecker . . . . . . 3·25 85
MS1830 85 × 105 mm. 4t. Pryer's woodpecker (*Saphopipo noguchi*) 3·00 3·00

1987. Children's Activities. Multicoloured.
1831 20m. Type **373** 10 10
1832 30m. Feeding calves 10 10
1833 40m. Drawing on ground in chalk 15 10
1834 50m. Football 20 10
1835 60m. Go-carting 25 15
1836 80m. Growing vegetables . . 30 15
1837 1t.20 Playing string instrument 45 25

374 Industry and Agriculture

1987. 13th Congress and 60th Anniv of Mongolian Trade Union.
1838 **374** 60m. multicoloured . . . 1·00 30

375 Women in Traditional Costume

376 Flags of Member Countries

1987. 40th Anniv of Mongol–Soviet Friendship.
1839 **375** 60m. multicoloured . . . 40 10

1987. Argali. As T **359**. Multicoloured.
1840 60m. On grassy rock (full face) 45 15
1841 60m. On rock (three-quarter face) 45 15
1842 60m. Family 45 15
1843 60m. Close-up of head and upper body 45 15

1987. Swans. As T **359**. Multicoloured.
1844 60m. Mute Swan ("Cygnus olor") in water 85 55
1845 60m. Mute swan on land . . 85 55
1846 60m. Tundra swan ("Cygnus bewickii") 85 55
1847 60m. Tundra swan, ("Cygnus gunus") and mute swan 85 55

1987. 25th Anniv of Membership of Council for Mutual Economic Aid.
1848 **376** 60m. multicoloured . . . 35 10

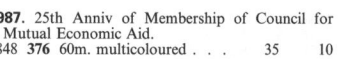

377 Sea Buckthorn

378 Couple in Traditional Costume

1987. Fruits. Multicoloured.
1849 20m. Type **377** 10 10
1850 30m. Blackcurrants 10 10
1851 40m. Redcurrants 15 10
1852 50m. Redcurrants 20 10
1853 60m. Raspberries 25 15
1854 80m. "Padus asiatica" . . . 30 15
1855 1t.20 Strawberries 45 25
MS1856 90 × 110 mm. 4t. Child with apple (29 × 51 mm) . . . . . 1·50 1·50

1987. Folk Art. Multicoloured.
1857 20m. Type **378** 10 10
1858 30m. Gold-inlaid baton and pouch 15 10
1859 40m. Gold and jewelled ornaments 20 10
1860 50m. Bag and dish 30 10
1861 60m. Earrings 35 15
1862 80m. Pipe, pouch and bottle 45 20
1863 1t.20 Decorative headdress 65 25

379 Dancer

1987. Dances.
1864 **379** 20m. multicoloured . . . 10 10
1865 – 30m. multicoloured . . . 15 10
1866 – 40m. multicoloured . . . 20 10
1867 – 50m. multicoloured . . . 30 10
1868 – 60m. multicoloured . . . 35 15
1869 – 80m. multicoloured . . . 45 20
1870 – 1t.20 multicoloured . . . 65 25
DESIGNS: 30m. to 1t.20, Different dances.

380 Lute Player

381 Scottish Fold

1987. Hafnia 87 International Stamp Exhibition, Copenhagen. Sheet 90 × 114 mm.
MS1871 **380** 4t. multicoloured . . 1·50 1·50

1987. Cats. Multicoloured.
1872 20m. Type **381** 10 10
1873 30m. Grey 15 10
1874 40m. Oriental 20 10
1875 50m. Abyssinian (horiz) . . 30 10
1876 60m. Manx (horiz) 35 15
1877 80m. Black shorthair (horiz) 45 20
1878 1t.20 Spotted (horiz) 65 25
MS1879 91 × 111 mm. 4t. Tabby shorthair . . . . 1·50 1·50

382 Mil Mi-V12

1987. Helicopters. Multicoloured.
1880 20m. Type **382** 10 10
1881 30m. Westland WG-30 . . . 15 10
1882 40m. Bell 206L LongRanger II 20 10
1883 50m. Kawasaki-Hughes 369HS 25 10
1884 60m. Kamov Ka-32 . . . . 30 10
1885 80m. Mil Mi-17 . . . . . 35 15
1886 1t.20 Mil Mi-10K 60 25

383 City Scene

384 Kremlin, Lenin and Revolutionaries

1987. 19th Mongolian People's Revolutionary Party Congress. Multicoloured.
1887 60m. Type **383** 25 10
1888 60m. Clothing and mining industries . . . . 1·00 25
1889 60m. Agriculture 25 10
1890 60m. Family 25 10
1891 60m. Workers, factories and fields 25 10
1892 60m. Building construction 25 10
1893 60m. Scientist 25 10

1987. 70th Anniv of Russian October Revolution.
1894 **384** 60m. multicoloured . . . 35 10

385 Seven with One Blow

1987. Walt Disney Cartoons. Multicoloured (a) "The Brave Little Tailor" (Grimm Brothers).
1895 25m. Type **385** 10 10
1896 35m. Brought before the King 20 10
1897 45m. Rewards for bravery 25 10
1898 55m. Fight between Mickey and the giant 30 15
1899 2t. Happy ending . . . . . 1·00 50
MS1900 126 × 102 mm. 7t. Mickey victorious . . . . 3·00 3·00

(b) "The Celebrated Jumping Frog of Calaveras County" (Mark Twain).
1901 65m. "He'd bet on anything" 30 15
1902 75m. "He never done nothing but ... learn that frog to jump" 45 20
1903 85m. "What might it be that you've got in that box?" 50 25
1904 1t. "40 He got the frog out and filled him full of quail shot" 80 40
MS1905 12 × 102 mm. 7t. "He set the frog down and took after that feller" . . . . 3·00 3·00

386 Head

1987. The Red Fox. Multicoloured.
1906 60m. Type **386** 45 15
1907 60m. Vixen and cubs . . . 45 15
1908 60m. Stalking 45 15
1909 60m. In the snow 45 15

387 "Mir" Space Station

1987. Intercosmos XX. Sheet 118 × 97 mm.
MS1910 **387** 4t. multicoloured . . 1·00 1·00

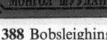

388 Bobsleighing

389 Sukhe Bator

1988. Air. Winter Olympic Games, Calgary. Mult.
1911 20m. Type **388** 10 10
1912 30m. Ski jumping 10 10
1913 40m. Skiing 15 10
1914 50m. Biathlon 20 10
1915 60m. Speed skating 25 10
1916 80m. Figure skating 30 15
1917 1t.20 Ice hockey 50 25
MS1918 91 × 110 mm. 4t. Cross-country skiing . . . . 1·40 1·40

1988. 95th Birth Anniv of Sukhe Bator.
1919 **389** 60m. multicoloured . . . 40 10

390 "Invitation"

1988. Roses. Multicoloured.
1920 20m. Type **390** 10 10
1921 30m. "Meilland" 10 10
1922 40m. "Pascali" 15 10
1923 50m. "Tropicana" 20 10
1924 60m. "Wendy Cussons" . . 25 10
1925 80m. "Rosa sp. " (wrongly inscr "Blue Moon") . . . 30 15
1926 1t.20 "Diorama" 50 25
MS1927 97 × 117 mm. 4t. Red rose 1·40 1·40

391 "Ukhaant Ekhner"

1988. Puppets. Multicoloured.
1928 20m. Type **391** 10 10
1929 30m. "Altan Everte Mungun Turuut" 10 10
1930 40m. "Aduuchyn Khuu" . . 15 10
1931 50m. "Suulenkhuu" 20 10
1932 60m. "Khonchyn Khuu" . . 25 10
1933 80m. "Argat Byatskhan Baatar" 30 15
1934 1t.20 "Botgochyn Khuu" . . 50 25

392 "Tatra 11" Car, 1923

1988. "Praga 88" International Stamp Exhibition, Prague. Sheet 110 × 90 mm.
MS1935 **392** 4t. multicoloured . .

393 Judo

394 Marx

1988. Olympic Games, Seoul. Multicoloured.
1936 20m. Type **393** 10 10
1937 30m. Archery 10 10
1938 40m. Weightlifting 15 10
1939 50m. Gymnastics 20 10
1940 60m. Cycling 25 10
1941 80m. Running 30 15
1942 1t.20 Wrestling 50 25
MS1943 90 × 110 mm. 4t. Boxing 1·40 1·40

1988. 170th Birth Anniv of Karl Marx.
1944 **394** 60m. multicoloured . . . 50 20

395 Couple and Congress Banner

396 "Kosmos"

1988. 19th Revsomol Youth Congress.
1945 **395** 60m. multicoloured . . . 1·00 30

1988. Spacecraft and Satellites. Multicoloured.
1946 20m. Type **396** 10 10
1947 30m. "Meteor" 10 10
1948 40m. "Salyut"–"Soyuz" space complex 10 10
1949 50m. "Prognoz-6" 15 10
1950 60m. "Molniya-1" 15 10
1951 80m. "Soyuz" 20 15
1952 1t.20 "Vostok" 35 20
MS1953 96 × 115 mm. 4t. Satellite scanning areas of Earth . . . 3·00 3·00

397 Buddha

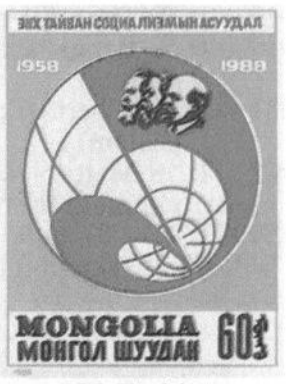

398 Emblem

1988. Religious Sculptures.
1954 **397** 20m. multicoloured . . . 10 10
1955 – 30m. multicoloured . . . 10 10
1956 – 40m. multicoloured . . . 20 10
1957 – 50m. multicoloured . . . 25 10
1958 – 60m. multicoloured . . . 30 10
1959 – 70m. multicoloured . . . 35 10
1960 – 80m. multicoloured . . . 40 15
1961 – 1t.20 multicoloured . . . 65 25
DESIGNS: 30m. to 1t.20, Different buddhas.

1988. 30th Anniv of Problems of "Peace and Socialism" (magazine).
1962 **398** 60m. multicoloured . . . 50 10

399 Eagle

1988. White-tailed Sea Eagle. Multicoloured.
1963 60m. Type **399** 90 60
1964 60m. Eagle on fallen branch and eagle landing 90 60
1965 60m. Eagle on rock 90 60
1966 60m. Eagle (horiz) 90 60

400 Ass

1988. Asiatic Wild Ass. Multicoloured.
1967 60m. Type **400** 40 15
1968 60m. Head of ass 40 15
1969 60m. Two adults 40 15
1970 60m. Mare and foal 40 15

401 Athlete

403 U.S.S.R. (ice hockey)

402 "Mongolian Camp" (H. Jargalsuren)

1988. Traditional Sports. Multicoloured.
1971 10m. Type **401** 10 10
1972 20m. Horseman 15 10
1973 30m. Archery 20 10
1974 40m. Wrestling 25 10
1975 50m. Archery (different) . . 35 15
1976 70m. Horsemen (national holiday cavalcade) 60 30
1977 1t.20 Horsemen, wrestlers and archers 95 45

1988. Childrens' Fund. Sheet 115 × 95 mm.
MS1978 **402** 4t. multicoloured . . 1·00 1·00

1988. Winter Olympic Games Gold Medal Winners. Multicoloured.
1979 1t.50 Type **403** 30 10
1980 1t.50 Bonnie Blair (speed skating) 30 10
1981 1t.50 Alberto Tomba (slalom) 30 10
1982 1t.50 Matti Nykanen (ski jumping) (horiz) 30 10
MS1983 110 × 87 mm. 4t. Katarina Witt (figure skating) (horiz) . . 1·00 1·00

404 Brown Goat

1988. Goats. Multicoloured.
1984 20m. Type **404** 10 10
1985 30m. Black goat 10 10
1986 40m. White long-haired goats 15 10
1987 50m. Black long-haired goat 20 10
1988 60m. White goat 25 10
1989 80m. Black short-haired goat 30 15
1990 1t.20 Nanny and kid . . . 50 25
MS1991 95 × 116 mm. 4t. Head of goat (vert) . . . . 1·40 1·40

405 Emblem

1989. 60th Anniv of Mongolian Writers' Association.
1992 **405** 60m. multicoloured . . . 40 10

406 Beaver gnawing Trees

1989. Eurasian Beaver. Multicoloured.
1993 60m. Type **406** 40 15
1994 60m. Beaver with young . . 40 15
1995 60m. Beavers beside tree stump and in water . . . 40 15
1996 60m. Beaver rolling log . . 40 15

407 Dancers

1989. Ballet.
1997 **407** 20m. multicoloured . . . 10 10
1998 – 30m. multicoloured . . . 10 10
1999 – 40m. multicoloured (vert) 15 10
2000 – 50m. multicoloured . . . 20 10
2001 – 60m. multicoloured . . . 25 10
2002 – 80m. multicoloured (vert) 30 15
2003 – 1t.20 multicoloured (vert) 50 25
DESIGNS: 30m. to 1t.20, Different dancing scenes.

408 "Ursus pruinosis"

1989. Bears. Multicoloured.
2004 20m. Type **408** 10 10
2005 30m. Brown bear 20 10
2006 40m. Asiatic black bear . . 30 15
2007 50m. Polar bear 40 20
2008 60m. Brown bear 55 25
2009 80m. Giant panda 70 35
2010 1t.20 Brown bear . . . . . 1·10 55
MS2011 110 × 90 mm. 4t. Giant panda (different) . . . . . . 3·00 3·00

409 "Soyuz" Spacecraft

1989. Space. Multicoloured.
2012 20m. Type **409** 10 10
2013 30m. "Apollo"–"Soyuz" link 15 10
2014 40m. "Columbia" space shuttle (vert) 20 10
2015 50m. "Hermes" spacecraft 30 15
2016 60m. "Nippon" spacecraft (vert) 45 20
2017 80m. "Energy" rocket (vert) 65 30
2018 1t.20 "Buran" space shuttle (vert) 95 45
MS2019 110 × 88 mm. 4t. German "Sanger" project . . . . . . 2·50 2·50

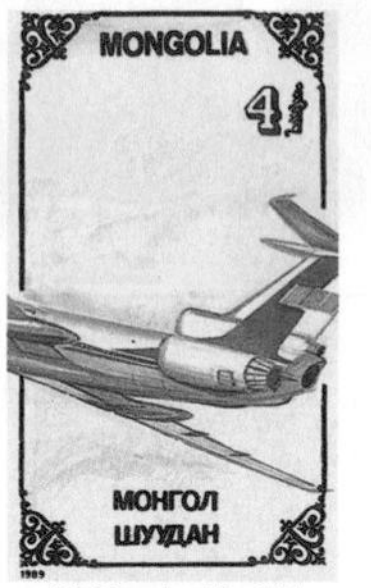

410 Tupolev Tu-154

1989. "Philexfrance 89", Paris (1st issue). and "Bulgaria '89", Sofia, International Stamp Exhibitions. Sheet 90 × 110 mm.
MS2020 **410** 4t. multicoloured . . 2·00 2·00
See also **MS**2034.

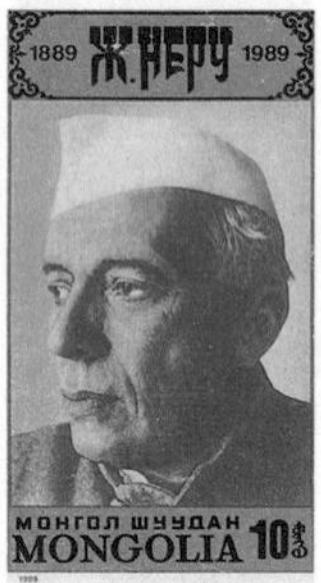

411 Nehru

412 "Opuntia microdasys"

1989. Birth Centenary of Jawaharial Nehru (Indian statesman).
2021 **411** 10m. multicoloured . . . 50 15

1989. Cacti. Multicoloured.
2022 20m. Type **412** 10 10
2023 30m. "Echinopsis multipiex" 10 10
2024 40m. "Rebutia tephracanthus" 15 10
2025 50m. "Brasilicactus haselbergii" 20 10
2026 60m. "Gymnocalycium mihanovichii" 25 10
2027 80m. "C. strausii" 30 15
2028 1t.20 "Horridocactus tuberisvicatus" 50 25
MS2029 90 × 110 mm. 4t. *Astrophytum ornatum* . . . . . 1·40 1·40

1989. 800th Anniv of Coronation of Genghis Khan. Nos. 291/4 optd **CHINGGIS KHAN CROWNATION 1189**.
2030 **67** 20m. multicoloured . . . 2·75 2·75
2031 – 30m. multicoloured . . . 4·25 4·25
2032 – 50m. black, brown and red . . . . 6·50 6·50
2033 – 60m. buff, blue and brown . . . . 8·50 8·50

414 Concorde

1989. "Philexfrance 89" International Stamp Exhibition, Paris (2nd issue). Sheet 130 × 55 mm containing T **414** and similar horiz designs. Multicoloured.
MS2034 20m. Type **414**; 60m. French TGV express train; 1t.20, Sukhe Bator statue . . . . . 4·50 4·50

415 Citroen "BX"

1989. Motor Cars. Multicoloured.
2035 20m. Type **415** 10 10
2036 30m. Volvo "760 GLF" . . 10 10
2037 40m. Honda "Civic" 60 25
2038 50m. Volga 20 10
2039 60m. Ford "Granada" . . . 25 10
2040 80m. Baz "21099" 30 15
2041 1t.20 Mercedes "190" . . . 50 20
MS2042 110 × 90 mm. 4t. As No. 2038 . . . . 1·50 1·50

416 Monument

417 Florence Griffith-Joyner (running)

1989. 50th Anniv of Battle of Khalka River.
2043 **416** 60m. multicoloured . . . 55 15

1989. Olympic Games Medal Winners. Mult.
2044 60m. Type **417** (wrongly inscr "Joyner-Griffith") 25 10
2045 60m. Stefano Cerioni (fencing) 25 10
2046 60m. Gintautas Umaras (cycling) 25 10
2047 60m. Kristin Otto (swimming) 25 10
MS2048 90 × 110 mm. 4t. N. Enkhbat (boxing) . . . . . 1·00 1·00

418 "Malchin Zaluus" (N. Sandagsuren)

1989. 30th Anniv of Co-operative Movement. Paintings. Multicoloured.
2049 20m. Type **418** 10 10
2050 30m. "Tsaatny Tukhai Dursamkh" (N. Sandagsuren) (vert) 20 10
2051 40m. "Uul Shig Tushigtei" (D. Amgalan) 30 15
2052 50m. "Goviin Egshig" (D. Amgalan) 40 20
2053 60m. "Tsagaan Sar" (Ts. Dagvanyam) 55 25
2054 80m. "Tumen Aduuny Bayar" (M. Butemkh) (vert) 65 30
2055 1t.20 "Bilcheer Deer" (N. Tsultem) . . . . . 1·10 50
MS2056 110 × 90 mm. 4t. "Naadam" (detail, Ts. Dagvanyam) . . . . 4·00 4·00

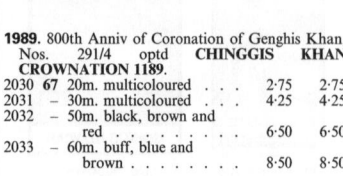

419 Four-man Bobsleighing

420 Victory Medal

1989. Ice Sports. Multicoloured.
2057 20m. Type **419** 10 10
2058 30m. Luge 10 10
2059 40m. Figure skating 15 10
2060 50m. Two-man bobsleighing 20 10
2061 60m. Ice dancing 25 10
2062 80m. Speed skating 30 15
2063 1t.20 Ice speedway 50 25
MS2064 90 × 110 mm. 4t. Ice hockey 1·40 1·40

1989. Orders. Designs showing different badges and medals. Multicoloured, background colour given.
2065 **420** 60m. blue 25 10
2066 – 60m. orange 25 10
2067 – 60m. mauve 25 10
2068 – 60m. violet 25 10
2069 – 60m. green 25 10
2070 – 60m. blue 25 10
2071 – 60m. red 25 10

1989. "World Stamp Expo 89" International Stamp Exhibition, Washington D.C. No. **MS**2034 optd **WORLD STAMP EXPO'89, WASHINGTON DC, WASHINGTON DC** and logo on the margin.
MS2072 130 × 55 mm. 20m. multicoloured; 60m. multicoloured; 1t.20, multicoloured . . . . 4·50 4·50

422 Chu Lha

423 Sukhe Bator Statue

1989. Buddhas. Multicoloured.
2073 20m. Damdin Sandub . . . 10 10
2074 30m. Pagwa Lama 20 10
2075 40m. Type **422** 30 15
2076 50m. Agwanglobsan 40 20
2077 60m. Dorje Dags Dan . . . 55 25
2078 80m. Wangchikdorje 65 30
2079 1t.20 Buddha . . . . 1·10 50
MS2080 74 × 89 mm. 4t. Migjid Jang-Rasek . . . . 3·00 3·00

1990. New Year.
2081 **423** 10m. multicoloured . . . 75 35

424 Newspapers and City

425 Emblem

1990. 70th Anniv of "Khuvisgalt Khevlel" (newspaper).
2082 **424** 60m. multicoloured . . . 65 30

1990. 20th Mongolian People's Revolutionary Party Congress.
2083 **425** 60m. multicoloured . . . 50 25

426 Male Character

1990. "Mandukhai the Wise" (film).
2084 **426** 20m. multicoloured . . . 20 10
2085 – 30m. multicoloured . . . 30 15
2086 – 40m. multicoloured . . . 45 20
2087 – 50m. multicoloured . . . 55 30
2088 – 60m. multicoloured . . . 75 35
2089 – 80m. multicoloured . . . 90 45
2090 – 1t.20 multicoloured . . . 1·25 65
MS2091 83 × 105 mm. 4t. multicoloured (vert) . . . . . 4·00 40
DESIGNS: 30m. to 4t., Different characters from the film.

427 Trophy and Players

1990. World Cup Football Championship, Italy.
2092 **427** 20m. multicoloured . . . 10 10
2093 – 30m. multicoloured . . . 10 10

2094	– 40m. multicoloured . . .	10	10
2095	– 50m. multicoloured . . .	15	10
2096	– 60m. multicoloured . . .	15	10
2097	– 80m. multicoloured . . .	20	10
2098	– 1t.20 multicoloured . . .	35	20
MS2099	89 × 110 mm. 4t. multicoloured (Trophy) (vert)	1·00	1·00

DESIGNS: 30m. to 4t., Trophy and different players.

428 Lenin

1990. 120th Birth Anniv of Lenin.

2100	**428** 60m. black, red and gold	65	30

429 Mother with Fawn

1990. Siberian Musk Deer. Multicoloured.

2101	60m. Type **429**	65	30
2102	60m. Deer in wood	65	30
2103	60m. Deer on river bank . .	65	30
2104	60m. Deer in winter landscape	65	30

430 Clock Tower, Houses of Parliament, London

1990. "Stamp World London '90" International Stamp Exhibition (1st issue) Sheet 91 × 105 mm.

MS2105	**430** 4t. multicoloured . .	2·00	2·00

See also Nos. **MS**2107 and 2191/**MS**2200.

1990. 800th Anniv (1989) of Coronation of Genghis Khan (2nd issue). Sheet 116 × 142 mm.

MS2106	**431** 7t. multicoloured . .	3·00	3·00

431 Genghis Khan

1990. "Stamp World London '90" International Stamp Exhibition (2nd issue). No. **MS**2106 optd with Penny Black and **Stamp World London 90** in margin.

MS2107	**431** 7t. multicoloured . .	3·00	2·00

433 Russian Victory Medal

434 Crane

1990. 45th Anniv of End of Second World War.

2108	**433** 60m. multicoloured . . .	65	30

1990. The Japanese White-naped Crane. Mult.

2109	60m. Type **434**	70	70
2110	60m. Crane feeding (horiz)	70	70
2111	60m. Cranes flying (horiz)	70	70
2112	60m. Crane on river bank	70	70

435 Fin Whale

1990. Marine Mammals. Multicoloured.

2113	20m. Type **435**	15	10
2114	30m. Humpback whale . .	30	15
2115	40m. Narwhal	40	20
2116	50m. Risso's dolphin . . .	50	25
2117	60m. Bottle-nosed dolphin	60	30
2118	80m. Atlantic white-sided dolphin	85	40
2119	1t.20 Bowhead whale . . .	1·10	55
MS2120	90 × 110 mm. 4t. Dall's porpoise (vert)	3·50	3·50

436 Weapons and Black Standard

437 Panda

1990. 750th Anniv of "Secret History of the Mongols" (book). Multicoloured.

2121	10m. Type **436**	10	10
2122	10m. Weapons and white standard	10	10
2123	40m. Brazier (17½ × 22 mm)	40	20
2124	60m. Genghis Khan (17½ × 22 mm)	60	30
2125	60m. Horses galloping . . .	60	30
2126	60m. Tartar camp	60	30
2127	80m. Men kneeling to ruler	75	35
2128	80m. Court	75	35

1990. The Giant Panda. Multicoloured.

2129	10m. Type **437**	15	10
2130	20m. Panda eating bamboo	25	10
2131	30m. Adult eating bamboo, and cub	40	20
2132	40m. Panda on tree branch (horiz)	45	25
2133	50m. Adult and cub resting (horiz)	55	25
2134	60m. Panda and mountains (horiz)	75	35
2135	80m. Adult and cub playing (horiz)	85	45
2136	1t.20 Panda on snow-covered river bank (horiz)	1·60	80
MS2137	94 × 114 mm. 4t. Panda holding bamboo shoots (vert)	4·25	4·25

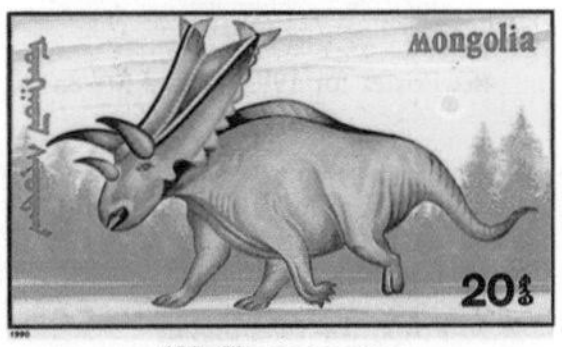

438 Chasmosaurus

1990. Prehistoric Animals. Multicoloured.

2138	20m. Type **438**	15	10
2139	30m. Stegosaurus	25	10
2140	40m. Probactrosaurus . . .	35	15
2141	50m. Opisthocoelicaudia . .	55	25
2142	60m. Iguanodon (vert) . . .	65	30
2143	80m. Tarbosaurus	90	45
2144	1t.20 Mamenchisaurus (after Mark Hallett) (60 × 22 mm)	1·10	55
MS2145	110 × 90 mm. 4t. Allosaurus attacking herd of Brachiosaurus (after John Gurche)	3·50	3·50

439 Lighthouse, Alexandria, Egypt

440 Kea

1990. Seven Wonders of the World. Mult.

2146	20m. Type **439**	15	10
2147	30m. Pyramids of Egypt (horiz)	25	10
2148	40m. Statue of Zeus, Olympia	35	20
2149	50m. Colossus of Rhodes	55	25
2150	60m. Mausoleum, Halicarnassus	65	35
2151	80m. Temple of Artemis, Ephesus (horiz)	90	45
2152	1t.20 Hanging Gardens of Babylon	1·10	55
MS2153	89 × 110 mm. 4t. Map and pyramids	3·50	3·50

1990. Parrots. Multicoloured.

2154	20m. Type **440**	20	20
2155	30m. Hyacinth macaw . . .	35	35
2156	40m. Australian king parrot	50	50
2157	50m. Grey parrot	65	65
2158	60m. Kakapo	75	75
2159	80m. Alexandrine parakeet	1·10	1·10
2160	1t.20 Scarlet macaw	1·25	1·25
MS2161	84 × 104 mm. 4t. Electus parrot	3·00	3·00

441 Purple Tiger Moth

1990. Moths and Butterflies. Multicoloured.

2162	20m. Type **441**	15	10
2163	30m. Viennese emperor moth	25	10
2164	40m. Comma	40	20
2165	50m. Magpie moth	50	25
2166	60m. Chequered moth . . .	60	30
2167	80m. Swallowtail	85	45
2168	1t.20 Orange-tip		
MS2169	90 × 110 mm. 4t. Striped hawk moth (vert). Perf or imperf	3·50	1·75

442 Jetsons in Flying Saucer

1991. The Jetsons (cartoon characters). Mult.

2170	20m. Type **442**	10	10
2171	25m. Family walking on planet, and dragon (horiz)	15	10
2172	30m. Jane, George, Elroy and dog Astro	20	10
2173	40m. George, Judy, Elroy and Astro crossing river	25	10
2174	50m. Flying in saucer (horiz)	30	15
2175	60m. Jetsons and Cosmo Spacely (horiz)	35	20
2176	70m. George and Elroy flying with jetpacks . . .	45	20
2177	80m. Elroy (horiz)	50	25
2178	1t.20 Judy and Astro watching Elroy doing acrobatics on tree	75	40
MS2179	Two sheets, each 102 × 127 mm. (a) 7t. Elroy with hands in pocket; (b) 7t. Elroy jumping	6·00	6·00

443 Dino and Bam-Bam meeting Mongolian Boy with Camel

1991. The Flintstones (cartoon characters). Mult.

2180	25m. Type **443**	10	10
2181	35m. Bam-Bam and Dino posing with boy (vert) . .	15	10
2182	45m. Mongolian mother greeting Betty Rubble, Wilma Flintstone and children	20	10
2183	55m. Barney Rubble and Fred riding dinosaurs . .	25	10
2184	65m. Flintstones and Rubbles by river	30	15
2185	75m. Bam-Bam and Dino racing boy on camel . . .	40	20
2186	85m. Fred, Barney and Bam-Bam with Mongolian boy	55	25
2187	1t.40 Flintstones and Rubbles in car	90	45
2188	2t. Fred and Barney taking refreshments with Mongolian	1·40	70
MS2189	Two sheets, each 126 × 101 mm. (a) 7t. Wilma, Betty and Bam-Bam; (b) 7t. Bam-Bam and Pebbles riding Dino . . .	6·00	6·00

444 Party Emblem

445 Black-capped Chickadee

1991. 70th Anniv of Mongolian People's Revolutionary Party.

2190	**444** 60m. multicoloured . . .	50	25

1991. "Stamp World London 90" International Stamp Exhibition. Multicoloured.

2191	25m. Type **445**	15	15
2192	35m. Common cardinal . .	20	20
2193	45m. Crested shelduck . . .	30	30
2194	55m. Mountain bluebird . .	35	35
2195	65m. Northern oriole . . .	45	45
2196	75m. Bluethroat (horiz) . .	50	50
2197	85m. Eastern bluebird . . .	65	65
2198	1t.40 Great reed warbler . .	1·25	1·25
2199	2t. Golden eagle	1·60	1·60
MS2200	Two sheets. (a) 94 × 76 mm. 7t. Ring-necked pheasant (*horiz*); (b) 76 x 94 mm. 7t. Great scaup	6·00	6·00

446 Black Grouse

1991. Birds. Multicoloured.

2201	20m. Type **446**	25	25
2202	30m. Common shelduck . .	35	35
2203	40m. Common pheasant . .	45	45
2204	50m. Long-tailed duck . . .	60	60
2205	60m. Hazel grouse	65	65
2206	80m. Red-breasted merganser	1·00	1·00
2207	1t.20 Goldeneye	1·75	1·75
MS2208	96 × 115 mm. 4t. Green-winged teal (*Anas crecca*) (vert)	4·00	4·00

447 Emblem

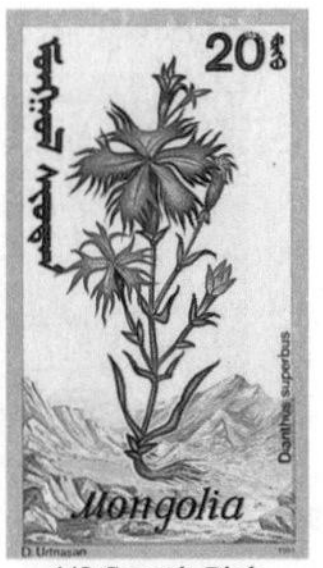

448 Superb Pink

1991. 70th Anniv of Mongolian People's Army.

2209 **447**	60m. multicoloured . . .	50	25

1991. Flowers. Multicoloured.

2210	20m. Type **448**	15	10
2211	30m. "Gentiana pneumonanthe" (wrongly inscr "puenmonanthe")	25	10
2212	40m. Dandelion	40	20
2213	50m. Siberian iris	55	25
2214	60m. Turk's-cap lily	65	30
2215	80m. "Aster amellus" . . .	90	45
2216	1t.20 Thistle	1·25	60
MS2217	95 × 115 mm. 4t. Bellflower (*Campanula persicifolia*) . . .	3·50	3·50

449 Stag Beetle

1991. Beetles. Multicoloured.

2218	20m. Type **449**	15	10
2219	30m. "Chelorrhina polyphemus"	25	10
2220	40m. "Coptolabrus coelestis"	40	20
2221	50m. "Epepeotes togatus"	55	25
2222	60m. Tiger beetle	65	30
2223	80m. "Macrodontia cervicornis"	90	45
2224	1t.20 Hercules beetle	1·25	60
MS2225	95 × 115 mm. 4t. *Cercopis sanguinolenta* (vert)	3·50	3·50

450 Defend

1991. Buddhas. Multicoloured.

2226	20m. Type **450**	15	10
2227	30m. Badmasanhava	25	10
2228	40m. Avalokitecvara	35	15
2229	50m. Buddha	50	25
2230	60m. Mintugwa	60	30
2231	80m. Shyamatara	70	35
2232	1t.20 Samvara	1·10	55
MS2233	95 × 116 mm. 4t. Lamidhatara	3·00	3·00

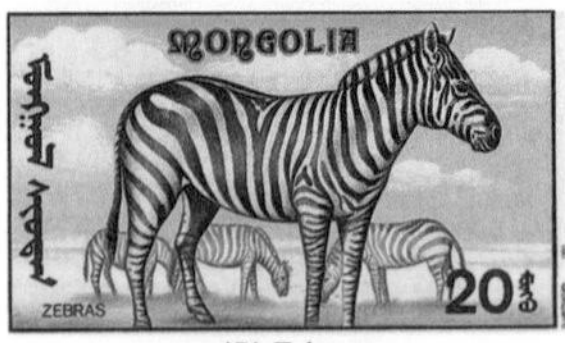

451 Zebras

1991. African Wildlife. Multicoloured.

2234	20m. Type **451**	15	10
2235	30m. Cheetah (wrongly inscr "Cheetan")	25	10
2236	40m. Black rhinoceros . . .	40	20
2237	50m. Giraffe (vert)	55	25
2238	60m. Gorilla	65	35
2239	80m. Elephants	90	45
2240	1t.20 Lion (vert)	1·25	60
MS2241	95 × 116 mm. 4t. Gazelle (vert)	3·50	3·50

452 Communications

1991. Meiso Mizuhara Stamp Exhibition, Ulan Bator.

2242 **452**	1t.20 multicoloured . . .	2·00	60

453 Scotch Bonnet

1991. Fungi. Multicoloured.

2243	20m. Type **453**	15	10
2244	30m. Oak mushroom . . .	20	10
2245	40m. "Hygrophorus marzuelus"	30	15
2246	50m. Chanterelle	40	20
2247	60m. Field mushroom . . .	55	25
2248	80m. Bronze boletus	70	35
2249	1t.20 Caesar's mushroom . .	1·25	60
2250	2t. "Tricholoma terreum"	2·10	1·00
MS2251	95 × 80 mm. 4t. *Mitrophora hybrida* (31 × 39 mm)	4·50	4·50

454 Emblem

1991. 70th Anniv of Revolution. Sheet 84 × 109 mm.

MS2252 **454**	4t. multicoloured . .	1·00	1·00

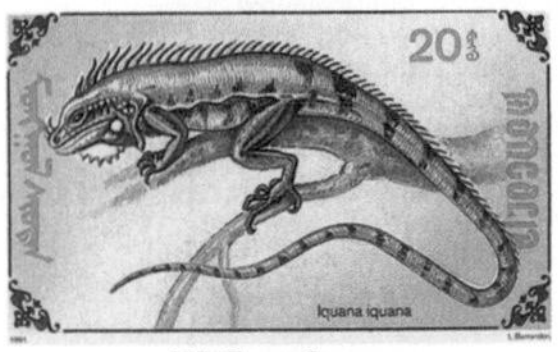

455 Green Iguana

1991. Reptiles. Multicoloured.

2253	20m. Type **455**	15	10
2254	30m. Flying gecko	30	15
2255	40m. Frilled lizard	40	20
2256	50m. Common cape lizard	55	25
2257	60m. Common basilisk . . .	65	30
2258	80m. Common tegu	90	45
2259	1t.20 Marine iguana	1·50	50
MS2260	75 × 96 mm. 4t. Bengal monitor lizard (Varanus bengalensis) (32 × 54 mm) . . .	3·75	3·75

456 Warrior

1991. Masked Costumes. Multicoloured.

2261	35m. Type **456**	20	10
2262	45m. Mask with fangs . . .	30	15
2263	55m. Bull mask	40	20
2264	65m. Dragon mask	55	25
2265	85m. Mask with beak . . .	65	30
2266	1t.40 Old man	1·25	60
2267	2t. Gold mask with earrings	1·50	75
MS2268	90 × 110 mm. 4t. Lion mask	4·00	4·00

457 German Shepherd

1991. Dogs. Multicoloured.

2269	20m. Type **457**	15	10
2270	30m. Dachshund (vert) . . .	30	15
2271	40m. Yorkshire terrier (vert)	40	20
2272	50m. Standard poodle . . .	50	25
2273	60m. Springer spaniel . . .	70	35
2274	80m. Norfolk terrier	90	45
2275	1t.20 Keeshund	1·50	75
MS2276	110 × 90 mm. 4t. Herding dog (54 × 32 mm)	3·75	3·75

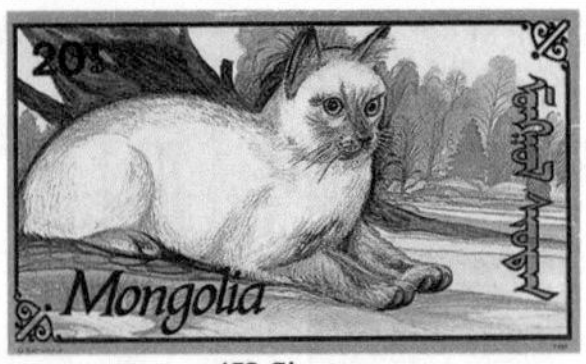

458 Siamese

1991. Cats. Multicoloured.

2277	20m. Type **458**	15	10
2278	30m. Black and white longhaired (vert)	30	15
2279	40m. Ginger red	40	20
2280	50m. Tabby (vert)	50	30
2281	60m. Red and white (vert)	70	35
2282	80m. Maine coon (vert) . .	90	45
2283	1t.20 Blue-eyed white persian (vert)	1·50	65
MS2284	101 × 91 mm. 4t. Tortoiseshell and white	3·75	3·75

459 Pagoda

460 "Zegris fausti"

1991. "Phila Nippon '91" International Stamp Exhibition, Tokyo. Multicoloured.

2285	1t. Type **459**	30	10
2286	2t. Japanese woman	55	25
2287	3t. Mongolian woman . . .	85	40
2288	4t. Temple	1·40	65

(b) No. **MS**2233 optd **PHILA NIPPON'91** and logos in the margin.

MS2288a	95 × 115 mm. 4t. multicoloured	1·60	1·00

1991. Butterflies and Flowers. Multicoloured.

2289	20m. Type **460**	10	10
2290	25m. Yellow roses	15	10
2291	30m. Apollo	20	10
2292	40m. Purple tiger moth . .	25	10
2293	50m. "Pseudochazara regeli"	30	15
2294	60m. "Colotis fausta" . . .	35	15
2295	70m. Red rose	40	20
2296	80m. Margueritas	50	25
2297	1t.20 Lily	75	35

1991. "Expo '90" International Garden and Greenery Exhibition, Osaka. Nos. 2289/97 optd **EXPO '90** and symbol.

2298	20m. multicoloured	10	10
2299	25m. multicoloured	15	10
2300	30m. multicoloured	20	10
2301	40m. multicoloured	25	10
2302	50m. multicoloured	30	15
2303	60m. multicoloured	35	15
2304	70m. multicoloured	40	20
2305	80m. multicoloured	50	25
2306	1t.20 multicoloured	75	35

(b) Two sheets, each 94 × 77 mm, containing horiz design as T **460**. Multicoloured.

MS2307	Two sheets. (a) 7t. Cactus; (b) 7t. Butterfly	9·00	9·00

462 Poster for 1985 Digital Stereo Re-issue

1991. 50th Anniv (1990) of Original Release of Walt Disney's "Fantasia" (cartoon film). Mult.

2308	1t.70 Type **462**	15	10
2309	2t. 1940 poster for original release	20	10
2310	2t.30 Poster for 1982 digital re-issue	25	10
2311	2t.60 Poster for 1981 stereo re-issue	35	15
2312	4t.20 Poster for 1969 "Psychedelic Sixties" release	60	30
2313	10t. 1941 poster for original release	1·50	75
2314	15t. Mlle. Upanova (sketch by Campbell Grant) . . .	2·00	90
2315	16t. Mickey as the Sorcerer's Apprentice (original sketch)	2·40	1·25
MS2316	Four sheets, each 127 × 102 mm. (a) 30t. "Russian Dance" (50 × 37 mm); (b) 30t. Stravinsky's "Rite of Spring" (48 × 35 mm); (c) 30t."The Sorcerer's Apprentice"; (d) 30t. "Chinese Dance" (50 × 36 mm)	15·00	15·00

463 Speed Skating

1992. Winter Olympic Games, Albertville. Mult.

2317	60m. Type **463**	10	10
2318	80m. Ski jumping	10	10
2319	1t. Ice hockey	15	10
2320	1t.20 Ice skating	15	10
2321	1t.50 Biathlon (horiz) . . .	15	10
2322	2t. Skiing (horiz)	20	15
2323	2t.40 Two-man bobsleigh (horiz)	25	15
MS2324	90 × 110 mm. 8t. Four-man bobsleigh (32 × 54 mm)	1·00	1·00

464 Zeppelin

1992. 75th Death Anniv of Count Ferdinand von Zeppelin (airship pioneer). Sheet 78 × 102 mm.

MS2325 **464**	16t. multicoloured	2·00	2·00

465 Elk

1992. The Elk. Multicoloured.

2326	3t. Type **465**	70	30
2327	3t. Female with young (horiz)	70	30
2328	3t. Adult male (horiz) . . .	70	30
2329	3t. Female	70	30

466 Steam Locomotive, Darjeeling–Himalaya Railway, India

1992. Multicoloured. (a) Railways of the World.

2330	3t. Type **466**	70	25
2331	3t. The "Royal Scot", Great Britain	70	25
2332	6t. Steam train on bridge over River Kwai, Burma–Siam Railway	1·60	60
2333	6t. Baltic steam locomotive No. 767, Burma	1·60	60
2334	8t. Baldwin steam locomotive, Thailand . .	2·10	70
2335	8t. Western Railways steam locomotive, Pakistan . . .	2·10	70

2336 16t. Class P36 locomotive, Russia . . . . 4·50 1·50
2337 16t. Shanghai–Peking express, China . . . . . 4·50 1·50
MS2338 Two sheets, each 112 × 83 mm. (a) 30t. "Hikari" express train, Japan (56 × 41 mm); (b) 30t. TGV express train, France (56 × 41 mm) . . . . 9·00 9·00

(b) "Orient Express". Black and gold (**MS**2347a) or multicoloured (others).
2339 3t. 1931 advertising poster 70 25
2340 3t. 1928 advertising poster 70 25
2341 6t. Dawn departure . . . . 1·60 60
2342 6t. The "Golden Arrow" leaving Victoria Station, London . . . . 1·60 60
2343 8t. Standing in station, Yugoslavia . . . . 2·10 70
2344 8t. Train passing through mountainous landcape, early 1900s . . . . 2·10 70
2345 16t. "Fleche d'Or" approaching Etaples . . . 4·50 1·50
2346 16t. Arrival in Istanbul . . 4·50 1·50
MS2347 Two sheets, each 113 × 84 mm. (a) 30t. Crowded railway platform; (b) 30t. Pullman Car Company arms; 30t. Compagnie Internationale des Wogons-Lits et des Grands Express Europeens arms . . . 11·00 11·00

467 Columbus

468 Black-billed Magpie

1992. 500th Anniv of Discovery of America by Columbus (1st issue). World Columbian Stamp "Expo '92", Chicago and "Genova '92" International Thematic Stamp Exhibition. Sheet 100 x 70 mm containing T **467** and similar vert design. Multicoloured.
MS2348 30t. Type **467**; 30t. *Santa Maria* . . . . 5·50 5·50
See also Nos. 2370/**MS**2377.

1992. Multicoloured. (a) Birds.
2349 3t. Type **468** 40 20
2350 3t. Northern eagle owl . . . 40 20
2351 6t. Relict gull (horiz) . . . 80 40
2352 6t. Redstart (horiz) 80 40
2353 8t. Demoiselle crane . . . . 1·10 55
2354 8t. Black stork (horiz) . . . 1·10 55
2355 16t. Rough-legged buzzard 2·25 1·10
2356 16t. Golden eagle (horiz) . . 2·25 1·10
MS2357 Two sheets, each 115 × 90 mm. (a) 30t. Mallards swimming and in flight (50 × 37); (b) 30t. Red-breasted goose (50 × 37 mm) . . . . 8·00 8·00

(b) Butterflies and Moths.
2358 3t. Scarce swallowtail (horiz) 40 20
2359 3t. Small tortoiseshell . . . 40 20
2360 6t. "Thyria jacobaeae" (value at right) (horiz) . . 80 40
2361 6t. Peacock (value at left) (horiz) 80 40
2362 8t. Camberwell beauty (value at left) (horiz) . . . 1·10 55
2363 8t. Red admiral (value at right) (horiz) . . . . 1·10 55
2364 16t. "Hyporhaia audica" (horiz) . . . . 2·25 1·10
2365 16t. Large tortoiseshell (flying over river) (horiz) 2·25 1·10
MS2366 Two sheets. (a) 114 × 90 mm. 30t. Swallowtail (50 × 37 mm); (b) 113 × 90 mm. 30t. Purple tiger moth (50 × 37 mm) . . . . 8·00 8·00

469 Bugler

1992. Celebrities and Events. Five sheets containing T **469** and similar horiz designs. Multicoloured.
MS2367 Five sheets (a) 120 × 80 mm. 30t. Mother Teresa of Calcutta (winner of Nobel Peace Prize, 1979); (b) 120 × 80 mm. 30t. Pope John Paul II celebrating Mass; (c) 115 × 89 mm. 30t. President Punsalmaagiyn Ochirbat of Mongolia and President George Bush of U.S.A.; (d) 120 × 80 mm. 30t. Type **469** (17th World Scout Jamboree, Korea (1991)); (e) 120 × 80 mm. 30t. Type **469** (18th World Scout Jamboree, Netherlands (1995)) . . . . . 16·00 16·00

470 Genghis Khan

471 Gold Medal

1992. 830th Birth Anniv of Genghis Khan. Sheet 100 × 120 mm.
MS2368 **470** 16t. multicoloured 5·00 5·00

1992. Olympic Games, Barcelona (1st issue), "Granada '92" International Thematic Stamp Exhibition and "Expo '92" World's Fair, Seville. Sheet 100 × 70 mm containing T **471** and similar vert design. Multicoloured.
MS2369 30t. Type **471**; 30t. Olympic torch . . . . 9·00 9·00
See also Nos. 2379/**MS**2388.

472 Fleet

1992. 500th Anniv of Discovery of America by Columbus (2nd issue). Multicoloured.
2370 3t. Type **472** 15 10
2371 7t. Amerindians' canoe approaching "Santa Maria" 25 10
2372 10t. "Pinta" 35 15
2373 16t. "Santa Maria" in open sea (vert) 55 25
2374 30t. "Santa Maria" passing coastline . . . . 1·10 50
2375 40t. Dolphins and "Santa Maria" . . . . 1·50 75
2376 50t. "Nina" . . . . 1·90 90
MS2377 Two sheets, each 94 × 115 mm. (a) 80t. Christopher Columbus (37 × 49 mm); (b) 80t. *Santa Maria* (37 × 49 mm) . . 7·50 7·50

1992. Mongolian Stamp Exhibition, Taiwan. No. **MS**1449 optd **MONGOLIAN STAMP EXHIBTION 1992 – TAIWAN** in margin.
MS2378 105 × 68 mm. **298** 4t. multicoloured . . . . 3·00 3·00

474 Long Jumping

1992. Olympic Games, Barcelona. Multicoloured.
2379 3t. Type **474** 10 10
2380 6t. Gymnastics (pommel exercise) 10 10
2381 8t. Boxing 10 10
2382 16t. Wrestling 10 10
2383 20t. Archery (vert) 10 10
2384 30t. Cycling 10 10
2385 40t. Show jumping 15 10
2386 50t. High jumping 20 10
2387 60t. Weightlifting 20 10
MS2388 Two sheets, each 100 × 82 mm. (a) 80t. Throwing the javelin (38 × 26 mm); (b) 80t. Judo (38 × 26 mm) . . . . . . 1·00 1·00

1993. Birth Centenary of Sukhe Bator. No. **MS**1523 optd **1893 – 1993** in the margin.
MS2389 65 × 72 mm. **270** 4t. purple 3·00 3·00

Eight designs, each 200t. and embossed on both gold and silver foil and accompanied by matching miniature sheets, were issued in 1993 in limited printings, depicting animals, sports or transport.

476 Black Grouse

1993. Birds. Multicoloured.
2390 3t. Type **476** 10 10
2391 8t. Moorhen 30 15
2392 10t. Golden-crowned kinglet 40 20
2393 16t. River kingfisher 60 30
2394 30t. Red-throated diver . . 1·10 50
2395 40t. Grey heron . . . . . . 1·50 75
2396 50t. Hoopoe . . . . 1·90 90
2397 60t. Blue-throated niltava 2·25 1·10
MS2398 Two sheets, each 115 × 90 mm. (a) 80t. Great crested grebe (*Podiceps cristatus*) (45 × 35 mm); (b) 80t. Griffon vulture (*Gyps fulvus*) (48 × 35 mm) 7·00 7·00

477 Orange-tip

1993. Butterflies and Moths. Multicoloured.
2399 3t. Type **477** 10 10
2400 8t. Peacock 30 15
2401 10t. High brown fritillary . . 40 20
2402 16t. "Limenitis reducta" . . 60 30
2403 30t. Common burnet . . . 1·10 50
2404 40t. Common blue . . . . 1·50 75
2405 50t. Apollo . . . . 1·90 90
2406 60t. Great peacock . . . . 2·25 1·10
MS2407 Two sheets, each 115 × 90 mm. (a) 80t. Poplar admiral (*Limenitis populi*) (49 × 37 mm); (b) 80t. Scarce copper (Heodes virgaureae) (49 × 37 mm) . . . . 7·00 7·00

1993. No. 1221 surch **XXX 15Ter**.
2408 15t. on 70m. multicoloured 2·75 1·00

479 Nicolas Copernicus (astronomer)

1993. "Polska'93" International Stamp Exhibition, Poznan. Multicoloured.
2409 30t. Type **479** (520th birth anniv) . . . . 2·00 90
2410 30t. Frederic Chopin (composer) . . . . 2·00 90
2411 30t. Pope John Paul II . . . 2·00 90
MS2412 Two sheets, each 98 × 122 mm. (a) 80t. Type **479**; (b) 80t. As No. 2411 . . . . . . 11·00 11·00

1993. No. 263 surch **8-Ter**.
2413 8t. on 70m. multicoloured 40 20

481 Sun Yat-sen (Chinese statesman)

1993. "Taipei '93" International Stamp Exhibition. Two sheets each containing vert design as T **481**. Multicoloured.
MS2414 Two sheets, each 100 × 124 mm. (a) 80t. Type **481**; (b) 80t. Genghis Khan (portrait as in Type **431**) . . . . 1·25 75

482 Hologram of Airship

1993. Airship Flight over Ulan Bator.
2415 **482** 80t. multicoloured . . . 1·00 50

483 Buddha

1993. "Bangkok 1993" International Stamp Exhibition. Multicoloured.
2416 50t. Buddha on throne . . . 55 25
2417 100t. Buddha (different) . . 1·10 50
2418 150t. Type **483** . . . . . . 1·60 80
2419 200t. Multi-armed Buddha 2·25 1·10
MS2420 90 × 125 mm. 300t. Buddha with right hand raised . . . . 3·00 3·00

484 Clouds, Mountains and Dog

1994. New Year. Year of the Dog. Multicoloured.
2421 60t. Type **484** 45 20
2422 60t. Dog reclining between mountains and waves (horiz) 45 20

485 Uruguay (1930, 1950)

1994. World Cup Football Championship, U.S.A. Previous Winners. Multicoloured.
2423 150t. Type **485** 30 15
2424 150t. Italy (1934) 30 15
2425 150t. German Federal Republic (1954) 30 15
2426 150t. Brazil (1958) 30 15
2427 150t. Argentina (1978, 1986) 30 15
2428 200t. Italy (1938) 40 20
2429 200t. Brazil (1962) 40 20
2430 200t. German Federal Republic (1974) 40 20
2431 250t. Brazil (1970) 50 25
2432 250t. Italy (1982) 50 25
2433 250t. German Federal Republic (1990) 50 25
MS2434 Five sheets. (a) 167 × 120 mm. Nos. 2427 and 2431/3; (b) 118 × 93 mm. Nos. 2423 and 2427; (c) 118 × 93 mm. Nos. 2424, 2428 and 2432; (d) 118 × 93 mm. Nos. 2425, 2430 and 2433; (e) 118 × 93 mm. Nos. 2426, 2429 and 2431 . . 16·00 16·00

486 Boeing 727

1994. Air. "Hong Kong '94" International Stamp Exhibition. Sheet 96 × 69 mm.
MS2435 **486** 600t. multicoloured 4·00 2·00

487 Pres. Punsalmaagin Ochirbat

1994. 1st Direct Presidential Election. Sheet 86 × 91 mm.
MS2436 **487** 150t. multicoloured 90 50

488 Biathlon

1994. Winter Olympic Games, Lillehammer, Norway. Multicoloured.

2437 50t. Type **488** 30 15
2438 60t. Two-man bobsleigh . . 35 15
2439 80t. Skiing 45 20
2440 100t. Ski jumping 60 30
2441 120t. Ice skating 70 35
2442 200t. Speed skating . . . . 1·25 60
MS2443 100 × 125 mm. 400t. Ice hockey . . . . 3·75 3·75

489 Dalai Lama

1994. Award of Nobel Peace Prize to Dalai Lama. Sheet 85 × 104 mm.

MS2444 **489** 400t. multicoloured 5·00 5·00

490 Lammergeier

1994. Wildlife. Multicoloured.

2445 60t. Type **490** 45 20
2446 60t. Grey-headed woodpecker on tree trunk 45 20
2447 60t. Japanese white-naped cranes 45 20
2448 60t. Western marsh harrier 45 20
2449 60t. Golden oriole on branch 45 20
2450 60t. Bank swallows 45 20
2451 60t. Montagu's harrier perched on rock 45 20
2452 60t. Pallid harriers in flight 45 20
2453 60t. Squirrel on branch . . 45 20
2454 60t. Dragonfly 45 20
2455 60t. Black stork 45 20
2456 60t. Northern pintail . . . 45 20
2457 60t. Spotted nutcracker standing on rock 45 20
2458 60t. Marmot 45 20
2459 60t. Ladybird on flower . . 45 20
2460 60t. Clutch of eggs in ground nest 45 20
2461 60t. Grasshopper 45 20
2462 60t. Butterfly 45 20

Nos. 2445/62 were issued together, se-tenant, forming a composite design.

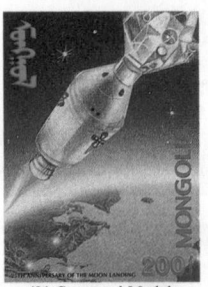

491 Command Module **492** Flowers

1994. 25th Anniv of First Manned Moon Landing. Multicoloured.

2463 200t. Type **491** 65 30
2464 200t. Earth, astronaut in chair and shuttle wing . . 65 30
2465 200t. Shuttle approaching Earth 65 30
2466 200t. Astronaut on Moon 65 30
MS2467 105 × 130 mm. Nos. 2463/6 2·40 1·25

1994.

2468 **492** 10t. green and black . . 10 10
2469 – 18t. purple and black . . 10 10
2470 – 22t. blue and black . . . 15 10
2471 – 44t. purple and black . . 25 10

DESIGNS: 18, 44t. Argali; 22t. Airplane.

493 Korean Empire 1884 5m. Stamp

1994. "Philakorea 1994" International Stamp Exhibition, Seoul. Multicoloured.

2472 600t. Type **493** . . . . . . 2·25 1·00
2473 600t. Mongolia 1924 1c. stamp . . . . 2·25 1·00
2474 600t. Mongolia 1966 Children's Day 15 m. stamp (47 × 34 mm) . . . 2·25 1·00
2475 600t. South Korea 1993 New Year 110 w. stamp (47 × 34 mm) . . . . . . 2·25 1·00
MS2476 94 × 76 mm. 600t. Korean man in traditional dress (34 × 47 mm) . . . . 2·50 2·50

494 Butterfly

1994. "Singpex '94" National Stamp Exhibtion, Singapore. Year of the Dog. Multicoloured.

2477 300t. Type **494** . . . . . . 1·00 50
MS2478 105 × 78 mm. 400t. Dog 3·50 3·50

495 1924 20c. Stamp

1994. 70th Anniv of First Mongolian Stamp. Sheet 91 × 111 mm.

MS2479 **495** 400t. multicoloured 3·50 3·50

496 Mammoth

1994. Prehistoric Animals. Multicoloured.

2480 60t. Type **496** 35 15
2481 80t. Stegosaurus 50 25
2482 100t. Talararus (horiz) . . . 75 35
2483 120t. Gorythosaurus (horiz) 90 45
2484 200t. Tyrannosaurus (horiz) 1·50 75
MS2485 124 × 99 mm. 400t. Triceratops (horiz) . . . . . . 3·75 2·00

497 National Flags

1994. Mongolia–Japan Friendship and Co-operation.

2486 **497** 20t. multicoloured . . . 15 10

498 Boar and Mountains

1995. New Year. Year of the Pig. Multicoloured.

2487 200t. Type **498** 65 30
2488 200t. Boar reclining amongst clouds (vert) 65 30

499 Dancer

1995. Tsam Religious Mask Dance.

2489 **499** 20t. multicoloured . . . 10 10
2490 – 50t. multicoloured . . . 20 10
2491 – 60t. multicoloured . . . 30 15
2492 – 100t. multicoloured . . . 50 25
2493 – 120t. multicoloured . . . 60 30
2494 – 150t. multicoloured . . . 65 30
2495 – 200t. multicoloured . . . 95 40
MS2496 92 × 133 mm. 400t. multicoloured . . . . 3·00 3·00

DESIGNS: 50t. to 400t. Different masked characters.

500 Saiga

1995. The Saiga. Multicoloured.

2497 40t. Type **500** 20 10
2498 50t. Male and female . . . 30 15
2499 70t. Male running 45 20
2500 200t. Head and neck of male . . . . 1·00 50

501 Garden Tiger Moth

1995. "Hong Kong '95" Stamp and Collecting Fair. Sheet 104 × 100 mm containing T **501** and similar square design plus two labels. Multicoloured.

MS2501 200t. Type **501**; 200t. Dandelion and anemone . . . 4·00 4·00

502 Yellow Oranda

1995. Goldfish. Multicoloured.

2502 20t. Type **502** 20 10
2503 50t. Red and white veil-tailed wen-yu 35 15
2504 60t. Brown oranda red-head 45 20
2505 100t. Pearl-scaled 80 30
2506 120t. Red lion-head . . . . 1·00 45
2507 150t. Brown oranda . . . . 1·40 55
2508 200t. Red and white oranda with narial . . . . . . 1·90 75
MS2509 136 × 110 mm. 400t. Red and white goldfish (49 × 37 mm) 3·25 3·25

See also No. **MS**2510.

1995. "Singapore '95" International Stamp Exhibition. As No. **MS**2509 but with exhibition embelm in the margin.

MS2510 136 × 110 mm. 400t. multicoloured . . . . 3·25 3·25

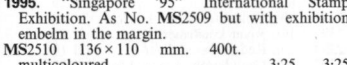

503 Bishop

1995. X-Men (comic strip). Designs showing characters. Multicoloured.

2511 30t. Type **503** 10 10
2512 50t. Beast 15 10
2513 60t. Rogue 25 10
2514 70t. Gambit 30 15
2515 80t. Cyclops 40 20
2516 100t. Storm 50 25
2517 200t. Professor X 95 45
2518 250t. Wolverine . . . . . . 1·25 60
MS2519 168 × 171 mm. 250t. Wolverine (horiz); 250t. Magneto (horiz) . . . . 3·50 3·50

504 Trygve Lie (1946—52)

1995. 50th Anniv of United Nations Organization. Sheet 125 × 115 mm containing T **504** and similar vert designs showing Secretaries-General and various views of the New York Headquarters complex. Multicoloured.

MS2520 60t. Type **504**; 60t. Dag Hammarskjold (1953–61); 60t. U. Thant (1961–71); 60t. Kurt Waldheim (1972–81); 60t. Javier Perez de Cuellar (1982–91); 60t. Boutros Boutros Ghali (from 1992) . . . . 4·00 4·00

505 Presley

1995. 60th Birth Anniv of Elvis Presley (entertainer). Multicoloured.

2521 60t. Type **505** 30 15
2522 80t. Wearing cap 35 15
2523 100t. Holding microphone 45 20
2524 120t. Wearing blue and white striped T-shirt . . . 60 30
2525 150t. With guitar and microphone 70 35
2526 200t. On motor bike with girl 85 40
2527 250t. On surfboard . . . . 1·10 50
2528 300t. Pointing with left hand 1·50 70
2529 350t. Playing guitar and girl clapping . . . . 1·90 85
MS2530 Two sheets. (a) 139 × 91 mm. 400t. Playing guitar; (b) 139 × 94 mm. 400t. Wearing army uniform with Priscilla Presley . . . . 12·00 12·00

Nos. 2521/9 were issued together, se-tenant, forming a composite design.

See also No. **MS**2543.

506 Monroe smiling

1995. 70th Birth Anniv (1996) of Marilyn Monroe (actress). Multicoloured.
2531 60t. Type **506** 30 15
2532 80t. Wearing white dress . . 35 15
2533 100t. Pouting 45 20
2534 120t. With naval officer and cello player 60 30
2535 150t. Wearing off-the-shoulder blouse 70 35
2536 200t. Using telephone and wearing magenta dress . . 85 40
2537 250t. Man kissing Monroe's shoulder . . . . 1·10 50
2538 300t. With white fur collar 1·50 70
2539 350t. With Clark Gable . . 1·90 85
MS2540 Two sheets. (a) 139 × 90 mm. 300t. Wearing black lace dress; (b) 137 × 106 mm. 300t. Lying on tiger skin rug . . . . 7·50 7·50
Nos. 2531/9 were issued together, se-tenant, forming a composite design.
Seel also No. **MS**2544.

507 Rat sitting between Mountains

1996. New Year. Year of the Rat. Multicoloured.
2541 150t. Type **507** 70 35
2542 200t. Rat crouching between mountains and waves (horiz) 85 40

1996. 70th Birth Anniv of Marilyn Monroe (actress) (2nd issue). Two sheets containing vert designs as T **506**.
MS2544 Two sheets. (a) 100 × 136 mm. 200t. Close-up of Monroe; (b) 146 × 112 mm. 300t. Close-up of Monroe and in scene from *Niagara* . . . . 6·50 6·50

1996. Mongolian–Chinese Friendship. Sheet 97 × 133 mm containing T **508** and similar vert designs. Multicoloured.
MS2545 65t. Type **508**; 65t. Temple of Heaven, Peking; 65t. Migjed Jang-Rasek; 65t. The Great Wall of China . . . . 7·25 7·25

1996. "China '96" International Stamp Exhibition, Peking. As No. **MS**2545 but with each stamp additionally bearing either the exhibition emblem or a mascot holding the emblem.
MS2546 65t. × 4 multicoloured 7·25 7·25

509 Mongolian 1924 2c. Stamp

510 Cycling

1996. "Capex '96" International Stamp Exhibition, Toronto. Sheet 116 × 90 mm containing T **509** and similar design. Multicoloured.
MS2547 350t. Type **509**; 400t. Canadian 1851 3d. stamp (36 × 26 mm) . . . . 7·00 7·00

1996. Olympic Games, Atlanta, U.S.A. Mult.
2548 30t. Type **510** 10 10
2549 60t. Shooting 10 10
2550 80t. Weightlifting 15 10
2551 100t. Boxing 20 10
2552 120t. Archery (vert) 25 10
2553 150t. Rhythmic gymnastics (vert) 30 15
2554 200t. Hurdling (vert) 40 20
2555 350t. Show jumping 70 35
2556 400t. Wrestling 80 40
MS2557 Two sheets, each 130 × 93 mm. (a) 500t. Basketball (37 × 53 mm); (b) 600t. Judo (51 × 39 *mm*) . . . . 5·00 5·00
MS2558 Two sheets. As No. **MS**2557 but additionally inscr in top margin " Centenary International Olympic Games 1896—1996" . . . . 5·00 5·00

(512a)

1996. Phila Seoul '96 International Stamp Exhibition. Nos. 2472/5 optd with T **512a** for the exhibition.
2560 600t. 1884 Korean Empire 5m. Stamp . . . . 1·10 55
2561 600t. 1924 Mongolia 1c. stamp . . . . 1·10 55
2562 600t. 1966 Mongolia Children's Day stamp (47 × 34 mm) . . . . . . 1·10 55
2563 600t. 1993 South Korea New Year stamp (47 × 34 mm) . . . . . . 1·10 55
MS2564 95 × 77 mm. 600t. Korean man wearing traditional dress 1·10 1·10

515 Girl and Mongolian Flag

1996. 50th Anniv of United Nations Children's Fund. Two sheets containing T **515** and similar vert designs.
MS2567 (a) 220 × 80 mm. 250t. × 6, Type **515**; Dutch girl; Japanese girl; German girl in traditional dress; Chinese girls dancing; Two American girls. (b) 107 × 83 mm. 700t. Mongolian boy . . . . . 3·50 3·30

250₮ **(516)**

250₮ [redacted] **(517)**

1996. No. 543 surch as T **516** and No. 2043 surch as T **517**.
2568 250t. on 50m. multicoloured **(516)** . . . .
2569 250t. on 60m. multicoloured **(517)** . . . .

518 Ox

1997. New Year. "Year of the Ox". Multicoloured.
2570 300t. Type **518** 60 30
2571 350t. Ox (horiz) 80 40

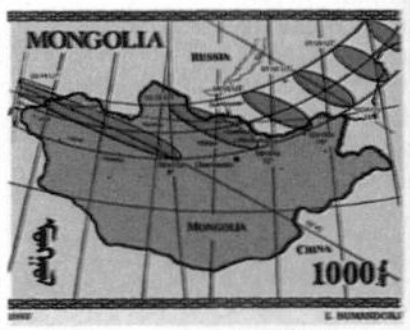

519 Map showing Path of Eclipse

521 Painting and Oil Lamp

520 Deng Xiaoping (Chinese leader) and Queen Elizabeth

1997. Total Eclipse of the Sun, 9 March 1997. Sheet 83 × 115 mm.
MS2572 **519** 1000t. multicoloured 3·00 3·00

1997. Return of Hong Kong to China. Multicoloured.
2573 200t. Type **520** 60 30
2574 250t. Tung Chee-hwa (head of government) and Jiang Zemin (Chinese president) 80 40

1997. Memorial for Victims of Political Oppression.
2575 **521** 150t. black 45 25

522 Adelie Penguin

1997. 25th Anniv of Greenpeace (ecological organization). Multicoloured.
2576 200t. Type **522** 45 25
2577 400t. Six Adelie penguins . . 80 40
2578 500t. Two Adelie penguins 95 45
2579 800t. Colony of Emperor penguins . . . . 1·60 80
MS2580 Two sheets. (a) 120 × 85 mm. 1000t. *Greenpeace* (ship) amongst icebergs. (b) 183 × 116 mm. Nos. 2576/9 and **MS**2580a . . . . 2·75 2·75

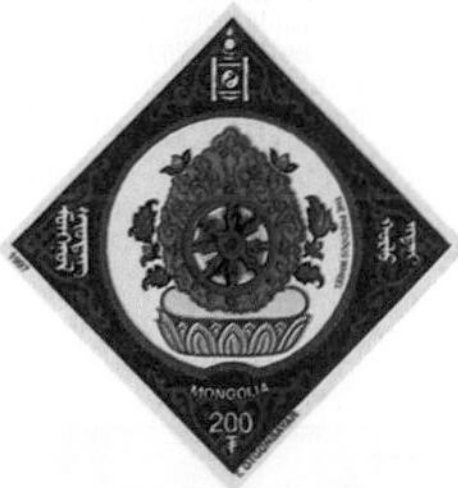

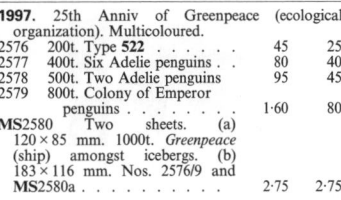

523 Dharma Wheel

1997. Religious Symbols. Multicoloured.
2581 200t. Type **523** 55 25
2582 200t. Precious Jewels . . . 55 25
2583 200t. Precious Minister . . . 55 25
2584 200t. Precious Queen . . . 55 25
2585 200t. Precious Elephant . . 55 25
2586 200t. Precious Horse 55 25
2587 200t. Precious General . . . 55 25

524 1961 15m. Stamp (Damdiny Sukhbaatar Monument)

526 *Dendrobium cunninghamii* and Adonis blue

525 Electric Locomotive LV-80

1997. MOCKBA '97 International Stamp Exhibition. Sheet 115 × 80 mm.
MS2588 **524** 1000t. multicoloured 2·75 2·75

1997. Trains. Multicoloured.
2589 20t. Type **525** 10 10
2590 40t. Japanese high-speed electric train 10 10
2591 120t. Diesel locomotive BL-80 . . . . 10 10
2592 200t. Steam locomotive . . 15 10
2593 300t. FDP steam locomotive *Lass* 30 15
2594 350t. 0-6-0 tank locomotive *Arima* 45 25
2595 400t. Diesel locomotive 216 25 15
2596 500t. Diesel locomotive T6-106 . . . . 40 40
2597 600t. Monorail *Europa* . . . 70 35
MS2598 Two sheets. (a) 133 × 112 mm. 800t. Eurostar locomotive (57 × 44 mm). (b) 137 × 112 mm. 800t. R. and G. Stephenson's locomotive *Rocket* (57 × 44 mm) . . . . . 2·00 2·00

1997. Orchids and Butterflies. Multicoloured.
2599 100t. Type **526** 15 10
2600 150t. Brown hairstreak and *Oncidium ampliatum* . . . 15 10
2601 200t. *Maxillaria triloris* and large skipper 20 10
2602 250t. *Calypso bulbosa* and orange tip 30 15
2603 300t. Painted lady and *Catasetum pileatum* . . . 30 15
2604 350t. Purple hairstreak and *Epidedrum fimbratum* . . 35 15
2605 400t. Red admiral and *Celeistes rosea* 40 20
2606 450t. Small copper and *Pontheiva maculate* . . . 50 25
2607 500t. Small tortoiseshell and *Cypripeium calceolus* . . . 60 30
MS2608 Two sheets, each 150 × 113 mm. (a) 800t. Red admiral and *Macranthum*. (b) Adonis blue and *Guttatum* . . 2·00 2·00

527 Princess Diana as Child

1997. Diana, Princess of Wales Commemoration. Six sheets containing T **527** and similar vert designs. Multicoloured.
MS2609 Six sheets. (a) 149 × 193 mm. 50t. Type **527**; 100t. Wearing high-necked blouse; 150t. As teenager; 200t. Wearing drop earrings and evening gown; 250t. Wearing tiara; 300t. Wearing pink outfit and pearl necklace; 350t. Wearing white outfit with gold frogging; 400t. Wearing black sweater; 450t. Wearing halter-necked dress. (b) 149 × 193 mm. 50t. As young girl; 100t. Wearing checked coat; 150t. As bride; 200t. With Princes William and Harry; 250t. Wearing red dress and tiara; 300t. Wearing black high-necked blouse; 350t. Wearing white blouse; 400t. Wearing pearl necklace and earrings; 450t. Wearing black outfit and pearl necklace. (c) 125 × 90 mm. 1000t. Wearing pink outfit. (d) 125 × 90 mm. 1000t. Wearing white dress. (e) 125 × 90 mm. 1000t. Holding baby Prince Harry. (f) 125 × 90 mm. 1000t. Wearing tiara Set of 6 sheets . . . . . 3·00 3·00

528 Soldier

1997. Soldiers of Chingis Khan. Multicoloured.
2610 100t. Type **528** 15 10
2611 150t. Riding galloping horse 30 15
2612 200t. Wearing winged helmet, armour and sword 35 20
2613 250t. Riding horse and holding flag 55 25
2614 300t. Wearing armour and holding two swords . . . 65 30
2615 350t. Archer 65 30
2616 400t. Wearing mailed visor and carrying spear and shield 90 45
2617 600t. Riding horse and leading cheetah . . . . . 1·40 70
MS2618 175 × 110 mm. 600t. Three riders; 600t. Two foot soldiers with cheetahs; 1000t. Riders carrying standards (65 × 60 mm) . . . . 5·00 5·00

529 Chingis Khan

1997. Khans of the Mongolian Empire. Multicoloured.
2619 1000t. Type **529** . . . . . . 2·00 1·00
2620 1000t. Ogodei . . . . 2·00 1·00
2621 1000t. Guyuk . . . . 2·00 1·00
2622 1000t. Mongke . . . . . . 2·00 1·00
2623 1000t. Kubilai (Hubilai) . . 2·00 1·00
MS2624 Four sheets, each 95 × 131 mm. (a) As Type **529** (22 × 32 mm). (b) As No. 2620 (22 × 32 mm). (c) As Nos. 2621/2 (22 × 32 mm). (d) As No. 2623 (22 × 32 mm). Set of 4 sheets 10·00 10·00

530 National Emblem **531** Crouching Tiger

1998. National Symbols. Multicoloured.

2625 300t. Type **530** 65 30
2626 300t. Flag (horiz) 65 30

1998. New Year. "Year of the Tiger". Multicoloured.

2627 150t. Type **531** 30 15
2628 200t. Tiger facing right . . . 35 20
2629 300t. Two tigers (triangle inverted) 65 30

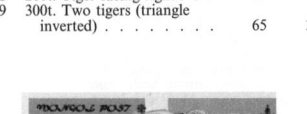

532 Speed Skating

1998. Winter Olympic Games, Nagano. Multicoloured.

2630 100t.+20t. Type **532** 15 10
2631 200t.+20t. Ski jump 35 20
2632 300t.+30t. Skateboard . . . 65 30
2633 600t.+60t. Skiing . . . . . 1·40 70

533 Three Yaks

1998. The Mongolian Yak. Multicoloured.

2634 20t. Type **533** 10 10
2635 30t. White yak 10 10
2636 50t. Yurt, cart and black yak 10 10
2637 100t. White-faced yak with horns 15 10
2638 150t. Mother and calf . . . 30 15
2639 200t. Tethered yak and milking buckets 35 20
2640 300t. Large grey yak with horns (53 × 39 mm) . . . 65 30
2641 400t. Brown yak with raised tail (53 × 39 mm) 90 45
MS2642 95 × 126 mm. 800t. Yak carrying children and furniture (60 × 47 mm) . . . . 1·75 1·75

534 Players and Competition Emblem

1998. World Cup Football Championship, France. Sheet 121 × 88 mm.

MS2643 **534** 1000t. multicoloured 2·00 2·00

535 Natsagyn Bagabandi

1998. President Natsagyn Bagabandi. Sheet 70 × 107 mm.

MS2644 **535** 1000t. multicoloured 2·00 2·00

536 *Lebistes reticulates*

1998. Fish. Multicoloured.

2645 20t. Type **536** 10 10
2646 30t. Inscr "Goldfish" . . . 10 10
2647 50t. *Balistes conspcillum* . . 10 10
2648 100t. Inscr "Goldfish" . . . 15 10
2649 150t. *Synchirops splendidus* 30 15
2650 200t. Inscr "C. auratus" . . 35 20
2651 300t. *Xiphophorus helleri* . . 65 30
2652 400t. *Pygoplites diacanthus* 90 45
2653 600t. *Chaetodon auriga* . . . 1·40 70
MS2654 Two sheets, each 141 × 86 mm. (a) 800t. Fish (105 × 49 mm). (b) 800t. Fish (different) (105 × 49 mm). Set of 2 sheets . . . . 3·50 3·50

537 Bear

1998. Gobi Bear (*Ursus arctos gobiensis*). Multicoloured.

2655 100t. Type **537** 15 10
2656 150t. Facing left 30 15
2657 200t. Two bears 35 20
2658 250t. Mother and cubs . . . 55 25
MS2659 Two sheets, each 111 × 70 mm. (a) 100t. Type **537**; 200t. No. 2657. (b) 150t. No. 2656; 250t. No. 2658 . . . . 1·50 1·50

538 Brown Cat (inscr "Red Persian")

1998. Cats. Multicoloured.

2660 50t. Type **538** 10 10
2661 100t. Blue shorthair (inscr "Man Cat") 15 10
2662 150t. Smoke Persian 30 15
2663 200t. Cream Persian (inscr "Long hairedwhite Persian") 35 20
2664 250t. Two silver tabbies . . 55 25
2665 300t. Two Siamese 65 30
MS2666 106 × 73 mm. 1000t. Two kittens and basket . . . . . . 2·00 2·00

539 Jerry Garcia

1998. American Musicians. Multicoloured.

2667 100t. Type **539** 15 10
2668 200t. Jerry Garcia wearing grey T-shirt 35 20
2669 200t. Bob Marley 35 20
2670 200t. Carlos Santana . . . 35 20
MS2671 Five sheets (a) 127 × 165 mm *Grateful Dead*. 50t. Bear as cyclist; 100t. Bear as footballer; 150t. Bear as basketball player; 200t. Bear as golfer; 250t. Bear as baseball player; 300t. Bear as skater; 350t. Bear as ice hockey player; 400t. Bear as American footballer; 450t. Bear as skier. (b) 127 × 165 mm. *Jerry Garcia*. 50t. Wearing blue T-shirt; 100t. Wearing jacket; 150t. Wearing dark T-shirt, shorter hair; 200t. Microphone, wearing black T-shirt; 250t. Wearing brown T-shirt; 300t. Wearing dark T-shirt; 350t. Wearing grey T-shirt; 400t. Wearing orange T-shirt; 450t. Wearing black T-shirt. (c) 152 × 102 mm. Jerry Garcia wearing blue T-shirt (51 × 77 mm). (d) 102 × 152 mm. 1000t. Jerry Garcia wearing orange T-shirt (51 × 77 mm). (e) 152 × 102 mm. 1000t. Bob Marley (51 × 77 mm). Set of 5 sheets 14·00 14·00

540 Building **542** T. Namnansuren

541 Three Stooges

1998. Communications and Transport. Multicoloured background colour given.

2672 100t. Type **540** (brown) . . 15 10
2673 100t. Computer screen (ultramarine) 15 10
2674 100t. Car (green) 15 10
2675 100t. Locomotive (mauve) 15 10
2676 100t. Airplane (violet) . . . 15 10
2677 200t. As No. 2672 (ultramarine) 35 20
2678 200t. As No. 2673 (green) 35 20
2679 200t. As No. 2674 (mauve) 35 20
2680 200t. As No. 2675 (violet) 35 20
2681 200t. As No. 2676 (brown) 35 20
2682 200t. As No. 2672 (green) 35 20
2683 200t. As No. 2673 (mauve) 35 20
2684 200t. As No. 2674 (violet) 35 20
2685 200t. As No. 2675 (brown) 35 20
2686 200t. As No. 2676 (ultramarine) 35 20
2687 400t. As No. 2672 (mauve) 90 45
2688 400t. As No. 2673 (violet) 90 45
2689 400t. As No. 2674 (brown) 90 45
2690 400t. As No. 2675 (ultramarine) 90 45
2691 400t. As No. 2676 (green) 90 45
2692 400t. As No. 2672 (violet) 90 45
2693 400t. As No. 2673 (brown) 90 45
2694 400t. As No. 2674 (ultramarine) 90 45
2695 400t. As No. 2675 (green) 90 45
2696 400t. As No. 2676 (mauve) 90 45

1998. "The Three Stooges" (comedy series starring Moe Howard, Larry Fine and Curly Howard). T **541** and similar multicoloured designs.

MS2697 Six sheets (a) 177 × 143 mm. 50t. Type **541**; 100t. With mandolin, saw and guitar; 150t. Curly with head in trouser press; 200t. Curly using shower head as microphone; 250t. Curly with head in wooden vice; 300t. Curly having dental treatment with percussion drill; 350t. Curly having dental treatment with pliers; 400t. Stuffing turkey; 450t. Curly with head in door jamb. (b) 177 × 143 mm. 50t. With pistols and cigars; 100t. Wearing pith helmets; 150t. Curly holding dynamite; 200t. As golfers; 250t. With right hands above heads; 300t. Curly holding bird; 350t. Holding bouquets; 400t. Pulling Moe's ears; 450t. Dressing Curly. (c) 176 × 130 mm. 50t. Wearing civil war uniforms; 100t. As foreign legionnaires; 150t. With two women; 200t. With horse; 250t. Wearing military uniforms, Curly holding candle; 300t. With anti-aircraft gun; 350t. With laughing general; 400t. With British soldier; 450t. Curly with straw beard. (d) 140 × 89 mm. 800t. Curly with head in trouser press (42 × 60 mm). (e) 90 × 137 mm. 800t. Wearing pith helmets (51 × 42 mm). (f) 101 × 127 mm. 800t. Playing football (60 × 51 mm). Set of 6 sheets . . . . 14·00 14·00

1998. Prime Ministers. Multicoloured.

2698/715 200t. × 18, Type **542**; Badamdorj; D. Chagdarjav; D. Bodoo; S. Damdinbazar; B. Tserendorj; A. Amar; Ts. Jigjidjav; P. Genden; Kh. Ghoibalsan; Yu. Tsedenbal; J. Batmunkh; D. Sodnom; Sh. Gungaadorj; D. Byambasuren; P. Jasrai; M. Enkhsaikhan; Ts. Elbegdorj . . . . . . 6·25 3·50

543 Conch Shell **545** D. Damien

544 People of Many Races and Rainbow

1998. Buddhist Symbols. Multicoloured.

2716 200t. Type **543** 35 20
2717 200t. Precious umbrella . . 35 20
2718 200t. Victory banner 35 20
2719 200t. Golden fish 35 20
2720 200t. Dharma wheel 35 20
2721 200t. Auspicious drawing . . 35 20
2722 200t. Lotus flower 35 20
2723 200t. Treasure vase 35 20

1998. 50th Anniv of Declaration of Human Rights.

2724 **544** 450t. multicoloured . . . 90 45

1998. National Wrestling Champions. Sheet 170 × 120 mm containing T **545** and similar diamond shaped designs. Multicoloured.

MS2725 200t. × 7, Type **545**; B. Batsuury; J. Munkhbat; H. Bakanmunkh; B. Tubdendorj; D. Tserentogtokh; B. Bat-Erdre 2·40 2·40

The stamps and margin of No. **MS**2725 form a composite design of bird and animals.

546 *Mercury 6* Space Capsule and Earth

1998. John Glenn's Return to Space. Two sheets, each 125 × 170 mm containing T **546** and similar vert designs. Multicoloured.

MS2726 (a) 50t. Type **546**; 100t. NASA emblem and earth; 150t. *Friendship-7* mission emblem and earth; 150t. Rocket lift off; 200t. John Glenn as young man; 250t. Capsule floating in sea; 250t. Capsule; 450t. Moon; 450t. Nebula and star. (b) 50t. NASA emblem and earth; 100t. John Glenn wearing space suit; 150t. *Discovery-7* mission emblem and earth; 150t. Shuttle space craft; 200t. John Glenn as older man; 250t. *Discovery-7* landing; 250t. Space craft, shuttle and moon's surface; 450t. Super nova and moon's surface; 450t. NASA 40th anniversary emblem and moon's surface . . . . 7·25 7·25

MONG-TSEU (MENGTSZ) Pt. 17

An Indo-Chinese P.O. in Yunnan province, China, closed in 1922.

1903. 100 centimes = 1 franc.
1919. 100 cents = 1 piastre.

Stamps of Indo-China surcharged.

1903. "Tablet" key-type surch **MONGTZE** and value in Chinese.

1 D 1c. black and red on buff . . 5·75 8·75
2 2c. brown and blue on buff 3·50 5·50
3 4c. brown and blue on grey 5·75 8·25
4 5c. green and red . . . . . 3·75 4·75
5 10c. red and blue . . . . . 5·75 11·00
6 15c. grey and red . . . . . 9·25 11·00
7 20c. red and blue on green 11·00 17·00
8 25c. blue and red . . . . . 10·50 11·50
9 25c. black and red on pink £500 £500
10 30c. brown & blue on drab 8·25 16·00
11 40c. red and blue on yellow 60·00 65·00
12 50c. red and blue on pink £275 £275
13 50c. brown and red on blue £100 £100
14 75c. brown and red on orge £120 £100
15 1f. green and red £120 £100
16 5f. mauve and blue on lilac £120 £100

1906. Surch **Mong-Tseu** and value in Chinese.

17	8	1c. green	80	3·50
18		2c. purple on yellow	90	3·75
19		4c. mauve on blue	75	3·75
20		5c. green	1·25	4·25
21		10c. pink	1·25	5·00
22		15c. brown on blue	1·40	5·00
23		20c. red on green	4·75	5·75
24		25c. blue	6·00	6·25
25		30c. brown on cream	8·00	11·00
26		35c. black on yellow	6·25	7·75
27		40c. black on grey	2·00	10·00
28		50c. brown	11·50	20·00
29	D	75c. brown & red on orange	45·00	45·00
30	8	1f. green	16·00	20·00
31		2f. brown on yellow	48·00	50·00
32	D	5f. mauve and blue on lilac	£100	£110
34	8	10f. red on green	90·00	90·00

1908. Surch **MONGTSEU** and value in Chinese.

35	10	1c. black and brown	1·10	80
36		2c. black and brown	1·40	95
37		4c. black and blue	1·90	1·90
38		5c. black and green	1·90	80
39		10c. black and red	1·75	2·75
40		15c. black and violet	2·75	3·25
41	11	20c. black and violet	4·00	5·25
42		25c. black and blue	3·75	7·75
43		30c. black and brown	4·00	4·75
44		35c. black and green	5·00	4·75
45		40c. black and brown	3·50	4·50
46		50c. black and red	5·00	5·50
47	12	75c. black and orange	9·25	12·50
48	–	1f. black and red	13·50	12·00
49	–	2f. black and green	15·00	18·00
50	–	5f. black and blue	£100	£110
51	–	10f. black and violet	£100	£110

1919. Nos. 35/51 further surch in figures and words.

52	10	2/5 c. on 1c. black and brown	1·25	3·00
53		4/5 c. on 2c. black and brown	1·25	3·00
54		1 3/5 c. on 4c. black and blue	1·75	2·75
55		2c. on 5c. black and green	2·00	3·00
56		4c. on 10c. black and red	3·00	3·25
57		6c. on 15c. black and violet	2·50	3·25
58	11	8c. on 20c. black and violet	5·00	5·00
59		10c. on 25c. black and blue	4·25	4·00
60		12c. on 30c. black & brown	3·50	4·00
61		14c. on 35c. black & green	3·00	3·75
62		16c. on 40c. black & brown	3·00	4·00
63		20c. on 50c. black and red	3·50	4·00
64	12	30c. on 75c. black & orange	4·00	4·75
65	–	40c. on 1f. black and red	7·50	9·50
66	–	80c. on 2f. black and green	6·00	6·50
67	–	2p. on 5f. black and blue	£120	£120
68	–	4p. on 10f. black and violet	18·00	26·00

MONTENEGRO Pt. 3

Formerly a monarchy on the Adriatic Sea, now part of Yugoslavia. In Italian and German occupation during 1939–45 war.

1874. 100 novcic = 1 florin.
1902. 100 heller = 1 krone.
1907. 100 para = 1 krone (1910 = 1 perper).

1 Prince Nicholas

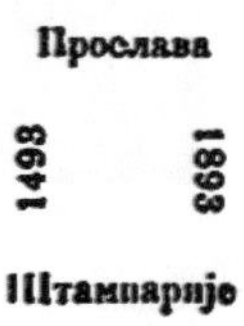

(2)

1874.

45	1	1n. blue	40	45
38		2n. yellow	2·00	2·00
51		2n. green	20	15
39		3n. green	50	50
52		3n. red	20	15
40		5n. red	50	50
53		5n. orange	45	20
19		7n. mauve	35·00	30·00
41		7n. pink	50	50
54		7n. grey	35	45
42		10n. blue	50	50
55		10n. purple	30	45
56		15n. brown	30	45
46		20n. brown	25	25
7		25n. purple	£250	£275
44		25n. brown	50	2·75
57		25n. blue	30	45
47		30n. brown	40	45
48		50n. blue	40	45
49		1f. green	1·25	2·75
50		2f. red	1·25	4·00

1893. 400th Anniv of Introduction of Printing into Montenegro. Optd with T **2**.

81	1	2n. yellow	24·00	2·75
82		3n. green	1·50	1·50
83		5n. red	1·25	1·25
84		7n. pink	1·00	1·00
86		10n. blue	1·75	1·75
87		15n. bistre	1·50	1·50
89		25n. brown	1·90	1·90

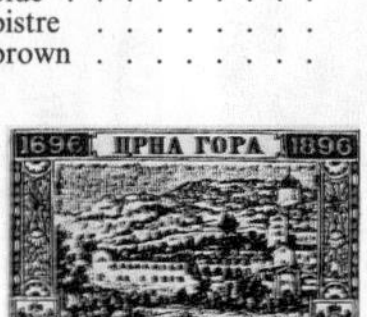

3 Monastery near Cetinje, Royal Mausoleum

1896. Bicentenary of Petrovich Niegush Dynasty.

90	3	1n. brown and blue	30	1·00
91		2n. yellow and purple	30	1·00
92		3n. green and brown	30	1·00
93		5n. brown and green	30	1·00
94		10n. blue and yellow	30	1·00
95		15n. green and blue	30	1·00
96		20n. blue and green	40	1·25
97		25n. yellow and blue	40	1·25
98		30n. brown and purple	45	1·25
99		50n. blue and red	50	1·50
100		1f. blue and pink	90	1·75
101		2f. black and brown	1·00	1·50

4

(5)

7

1902.

102	4	1h. blue	30	30
103		2h. mauve	30	30
104		5h. green	30	20
105		10h. red	30	30
106		25h. blue	30	50
107		50h. green	40	50
108		1k. brown	35	35
109		2k. brown	50	50
110		5k. brown	75	1·50

1905. Granting of Constitution. Optd with T **5**.

111	4	1h. blue	15	20
112		2h. mauve	15	20
113		5h. green	15	20
114		10h. red	50	50
124a		25h. blue	15	25
125a		50h. green	15	25
126a		1k. brown	15	25
127a		2k. brown	15	25
119		5k. orange	75	2·50

1907. New Currency.

129	7	1pa. yellow	15	20
130		2pa. black	15	20
131		5pa. green	1·00	10
132		10pa. red	1·50	10
133		15pa. blue	20	15
134		20pa. orange	20	20
135		25pa. blue	20	1·25
136		35pa. brown	25	15
137		50pa. lilac	45	35
138		1k. red	45	60
139		2k. green	45	60
140		5k. red	90	2·00

9 King Nicholas when a Youth

10 King Nicholas and Queen Milena

11 Prince Nicholas

12 Nicholas I

1910. Proclamation of Kingdom and 50th Anniv of Reign of Prince Nicholas.

141	9	1pa. black	35	15
142	10	2pa. purple	35	15
143	–	5pa. green	30	15
144	–	10pa. red	30	15
145	–	15pa. blue	30	15
146	10	20pa. olive	65	15
147	–	25pa. blue	65	15
148	–	35pa. brown	85	85
149	–	50pa. violet	65	35
150	–	1per. lake	65	35
151	–	2per. green	85	50
152	11	5per. blue	1·25	1·00

DESIGNS: As Type **9**: 5, 10, 25, 35pa. Nicholas I in 1910; 15pa. Nicholas I in 1878; 50pa., 1, 2per. Nicholas I in 1890.

1913.

153	12	1pa. orange	15	15
154		2pa. purple	15	15
155		5pa. green	15	15
156		10pa. red	15	15
157		15pa. blue	20	20
158		20pa. brown	20	20
159		25pa. blue	20	20
160		35pa. red	50	50
161		50pa. blue	25	25
162		1per. brown	25	25
163		2per. purple	65	65
164		5per. green	65	65

ITALIAN OCCUPATION

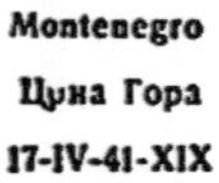

(1)

(2)

1941. Stamps of Yugoslavia optd with T **1**. (a) Postage. On Nos. 414, etc.

1	99	25p. black	30	65
2		1d. green	30	65
3		1d.50 red	30	65
4		2d. mauve	30	65
5		3d. brown	30	65
6		4d. blue	30	65
7		5d. blue	1·50	4·75
8		5d.50 violet	1·50	4·75
9		6d. blue	1·50	4·75
10		8d. brown	1·75	5·50
11		12d. violet	1·50	4·75
12		16d. purple	1·50	4·75
13		20d. blue	90·00	£140
14		30d. pink	40·00	65·00

(b) Air. On Nos. 360/7.

15	80	50p. brown	8·00	6·00
16	–	1d. green	2·00	5·00
17	–	2d. blue	2·00	5·50
18	–	2d.50 red	3·00	6·00
19	80	5d. violet	22·00	45·00
20	–	10d. red	22·00	45·00
21	–	20d. green	22·00	50·00
22	–	30d. blue	22·00	48·00

1941. Stamps of Italy optd with T **2**. (a) On Postage stamps of 1929.

28	98	5c. brown	15	50
29	–	10c. brown	15	50
30	–	15c. green	15	50
31	99	20c. red	15	50
32	–	25c. green	15	50
33	103	30c. brown	15	50
34		50c. violet	15	50
35	–	75c. red	15	50
36	–	1l.25 blue	15	50

(b) On Air stamp of 1930.

37	110	50c. brown	15	50

1942. Nos. 416 etc of Yugoslavia optd **Governatorato del Montenegro Valore LIRE**.

43	99	1d. green	75	1·40
44		1d.50 red	25·00	30·00
45		3d. brown	75	1·40
46		4d. blue	75	1·40
47		5d.50 violet	75	1·40
48		6d. blue	75	1·40
49		8d. brown	75	1·40
50		12d. violet	75	1·40
51		16d. purple	75	1·40

1942. Air. Nos. 360/7 of Yugoslavia optd **Governatorato del Montenegro Valore in Lire**.

52	80	0.50l. brown	2·50	3·50
53	–	1l. green	2·50	3·50
54	–	2l. blue	2·50	3·50
55	–	2.50l. red	2·50	3·50
56	80	5l. violet	2·50	3·50
57	–	10l. brown	2·50	3·50
58	–	20l. green	65·00	£100
59	–	30l. blue	20·00	32·00

4 Prince Bishop Peter Njegos and View

1943. National Poem Commemoratives. Each stamp has fragment of poetry inscr at back.

60	4	5c. violet	25	75
61	–	10c. green	25	75
62	–	15c. brown	25	75
63	–	20c. orange	25	75
64	–	25c. green	25	75
65	–	50c. mauve	25	75
66	–	1l.25 blue	25	75
67	–	2l. green	1·00	2·00
68	–	5l. red on buff	2·50	6·00
69	–	20l. purple on grey	5·00	13·00

DESIGNS—HORIZ: 10c. Meadow near Mt. Lovcen; 15c. Country Chapel; 20c. Chiefs Meeting; 25, 50c. Folk Dancing; 1l.25, Taking the Oath; 2l. Moslem wedding procession; 5l. Watch over wounded standard-bearer. VERT: 20l. Portrait of Prince Bishop Peter Njegos.

5 Cetinje

1943. Air. With Junkers G31 airplane (2, 20l.) or Fokker F.VIIa/3m airplane (others).

70	5	50c. brown	35	1·25
71	–	1l. blue	35	1·25
72	–	2l. mauve	35	1·25
73	–	5l. green	70	2·50
74	–	10l. purple on buff	4·00	9·00
75	–	20l. blue on pink	6·25	16·00

DESIGNS—HORIZ: 1l. Coastline; 2l. Budva; 5l. Mt. Lovcen; 10l. Lake of Scutari. VERT: 20l. Mt. Durmitor.

GERMAN OCCUPATION

1943. Nos. 419/20 of Yugoslavia surch **Deutsche Militaer-Verwaltung Montenegro** and new value in lire.

76	99	50c. on 3d. brown	3·00	24·00
77		1l. on 3d. brown	3·00	24·00
78		1l.50 on 3d. brown	3·00	24·00
79		2l. on 3d. brown	4·50	45·00
80		4l. on 3d. brown	4·50	45·00
81		5l. on 4d. blue	5·00	45·00
82		8l. on 4d. blue	9·75	90·00
83		10l. on 4d. blue	14·00	£150
84		20l. on 4d. blue	30·00	£325

1943. Appointment of National Administrative Committee. Optd **Nationaler Verwaltungsausschuss 10.XI.1943**. (a) Postage. On Nos. 64/8.

85		25c. green	5·75	£190
86		50c. mauve	5·75	£190
87		1l.25 blue	5·75	£190
88		2l. green	5·75	£190
89		5l. red on buff	£160	£2250

(b) Air. On Nos. 70/4.

90	5	50c. brown	9·50	£190
91		1l. blue	9·50	£190
92		2l. mauve	9·50	£190
93		5l. green	9·50	£190
94		10l. purple on buff	£2000	£16000

1944. Refugees Fund. Surch **Flüchtlingshilfe Montenegro** and new value in German currency. (a) On Nos. 419/20 of Yugoslavia.

95	99	0.15+0.85Rm. on 3d.	7·75	£170
96		0.15+0.85Rm. on 4d.	7·75	£170

(b) On Nos. 46/9.

97	–	0.15+0.85Rm. on 25c.	7·75	£170
98	–	0.15+1.35Rm. on 50c.	7·75	£170
99	–	0.25+1.75Rm. on 1l.25	7·75	£170
100	–	0.25+1.75Rm. on 2l.	7·75	£170

(c) Air. On Nos. A52/4.

101	5	0.15+0.85Rm. on 50c.	7·75	£180
102	–	0.25+1.25Rm. on 1l.	7·75	£180
103	–	0.50+1.50Rm. on 2l.	7·75	£180

1944. Red Cross. Surch **+Crveni krst Montenegro** and new value in German currency. (a) On Nos. 419/20 of Yugoslavia.

104	99	0.50+2.50Rm. on 3d.	6·50	£170
105		0.50+2.50Rm. on 4d.	6·50	£170

(b) On Nos. 64/5.

106	–	0.15+0.85Rm. on 25c.	6·50	£170
107	–	0.15+1.35Rm. on 50c.	6·50	£170

(c) Air. On Nos. 70/2.

108	5	0.25+1.75Rm. on 50c.	6·50	£170
109	–	0.25+2.75Rm. on 1l.	6·50	£170
110	–	0.50+2Rm. on 2l.	6·50	£170

ACKNOWLEDGEMENT OF RECEIPT STAMPS

A 3

A 4

1895.

A90	A 3	10n. blue and red	85	1·00

1902.

A111	A 4	25h. orange and red	75	75

1905. Optd with T **5**.

A120	A 4	25h. orange and red	60	60

1907. As T **7**, but letters "A" and "R" in top corners.

A141	7	25p. olive	50	65

1913. As T **12**, but letters "A" and "R" in top corners.

A169	12	25p. olive	40	70

POSTAGE DUE STAMPS

D 3

D 4

D 8

1894.

D90	D 3	1n. red	2·25	1·40
D91		2n. green	50	20
D92		3n. orange	50	20
D93		5n. green	50	20
D94		10n. purple	50	30
D95		20n. blue	50	30
D96		30n. green	50	30
D97		50n. pale green	50	30

1902.

D111	D 4	5h. orange	20	20
D112		10h. green	30	30
D113		25h. purple	30	30
D114		50h. green	30	30
D115		1k. grey	35	35

1905. Optd with T **5**.

D120	D 4	5h. orange	35	50
D121		10h. olive	50	1·00
D122		25h. purple	35	50
D123		50h. green	35	50
D124		1k. pale green	50	75

1907.

D141	D 8	5p. brown	25	35
D142		10p. violet	25	35
D143		25p. red	25	35
D144		50p. green	25	35

1913. As T **12** but inscr "HOPTOMAPKA" at top.

D165	5p. grey	75	75
D166	10p. lilac	50	50
D167	25p. blue	50	50
D168	50p. red	65	65

ITALIAN OCCUPATION

1941. Postage Due stamps of Yugoslavia optd **Montenegro Upha 17-IV-41-XIX**.

D23	D 56	50p. violet	50	1·00
D24		1d. mauve	50	1·00
D25		2d. blue	50	1·00
D26		5d. orange	30·00	50·00
D27		10d. brown	3·00	6·00

1942. Postage Due stamps of Italy optd **UPHATOPA**.

D38	D 141	10c. blue	15	1·25
D39		20c. red	15	1·25
D40		30c. orange	15	1·25
D41		50c. violet	15	1·25
D42		1l. orange	25	1·25

MONTSERRAT Pt. 1

One of the Leeward Is., Br. W. Indies. Used general issues for Leeward Is. concurrently with Montserrat stamps until 1 July 1956, when Leeward Is. stamps were withdrawn.

1876. 12 pence = 1 shilling;
20 shillings = 1 pound.
1951. 100 cents = 1 West Indian dollar.

1876. Stamps of Antigua as T **1** optd **MONTSERRAT**.

8c	1d. red	17·00	14·00
2	6d. green	70·00	42·00

3

1880.

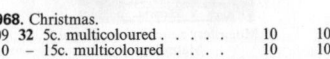

7	3	½d. green	1·00	8·50
9		2½d. brown	£225	65·00
10		2½d. blue	23·00	21·00
5		4d. blue	1·50	40·00
12		4d. mauve	5·50	3·00

4 Device of the Colony

5

1903.

24a	4	½d. green	1·00	1·25
15		1d. grey and red	75	40
26a		2d. grey and brown	2·25	1·25
17		2½d. grey and blue	1·50	1·75
28a		3d. orange and purple	9·50	2·50
29a		6d. purple and olive	11·00	5·50
30		1s. green and purple	11·00	7·00
21		2s. green and orange	25·00	17·00
22		2s.6d. green and black	20·00	40·00
33	5	5s. black and red	95·00	£110

1908.

36	4	1d. red	1·40	30
38		2d. grey	1·75	15·00
39		2½d. blue	2·25	3·50
40		3d. purple on yellow	1·00	18·00
43		6d. purple	6·50	50·00
44		1s. black on green	8·50	45·00
45		2s. purple and blue on blue	32·00	55·00
46		2s.6d. black and red on blue	32·00	70·00
47	5	5s. red and green on yellow	50·00	70·00

1914. As T **5**, but portrait of King George V.

48	5s. red and green on yellow	65·00	90·00

8

10 Plymouth

1916.

63	8	½d. brown	15	5·50
64		½d. green	30	30
50		1d. red	1·25	75
65		1d. violet	30	60
67		1½d. yellow	1·75	9·50
68		1½d. red	30	4·00
69		1½d. brown	2·25	50
70		2d. grey	50	2·00
71a		2½d. blue	60	90
72		2½d. yellow	1·25	19·00
74		3d. purple on yellow	1·10	4·75
73		3d. blue	60	16·00
75		4d. black and red on yellow	75	12·00
76		5d. purple and olive	3·75	10·00
77		6d. purple	3·00	7·50
78		1s. black on green	3·00	7·00
79		2s. purple and blue on blue	7·00	16·00
80		2s.6d. black and red on blue	12·00	50·00
81		3s. green and violet	12·00	19·00
82		4s. black and red	15·00	38·00
83		5s. green and red on yellow	27·00	45·00

1917. Optd **WAR STAMP**.

60	8	½d. green	10	1·50
62		1½d. black and orange	10	30

1932. 300th Anniv of Settlement of Montserrat.

84	10	½d. green	75	8·50
85		1d. red	75	5·50
86		1½d. brown	1·25	2·50
87		2d. grey	1·50	16·00
88		2½d. blue	1·25	15·00
89		3d. orange	1·50	18·00
90		6d. violet	2·25	29·00
91		1s. olive	12·00	40·00
92		2s.6d. purple	48·00	70·00
93		5s. brown	£100	£160

1935. Silver Jubilee. As T **14a** of Kenya, Uganda and Tanganyika.

94	1d. blue and red	85	3·25
95	1½d. blue and grey	1·50	2·75
96	2½d. brown and blue	2·25	3·25
97	1s. grey and purple	3·00	14·00

1937. Coronation. As T **14b** of Kenya, Uganda and Tanganyika.

98	1d. red	30	1·50
99	1½d. brown	40	40
100	2½d. blue	40	1·50

11 Carr's Bay

1938. King George VI.

101a	11	½d. green	15	20
102a	–	1d. red	50	30
103a	–	1½d. purple	50	50
104a	–	2d. orange	1·50	70
105a	–	2½d. blue	50	30
106a	11	3d. brown	2·00	40
107a	–	6d. violet	2·50	60
108a	11	1s. red	2·25	30
109a	–	2s.6d. blue	17·00	2·50
110a	11	5s. red	21·00	3·00
111	–	10s. blue	13·00	19·00
112	11	£1 black	13·00	27·00

DESIGNS: 1d., 1½d., 2½d. Sea Island cotton; 2d., 6d., 2s.6d., 10s. Botanic station.

1946. Victory. As T **60** of Jamaica.

113	1½d. purple	10	10
114	3d. brown	10	10

1949. Silver Wedding. As T **61/2** of Jamaica.

115	2½d. blue	10	10
116	5s. red	4·75	9·00

1949. U.P.U. As T **63/6** of Jamaica.

117	2½d. blue	15	1·25
118	3d. brown	1·75	60
119	6d. purple	30	50
120	1s. purple	30	60

1951. Inauguration of B.W.I. University College. As T **15a/b** of Leeward Islands.

121	3c. black and purple	20	1·25
122	12c. black and violet	20	1·25

14 Government House

1951.

123	14	1c. black	10	2·00
124	–	2c. green	15	70
125	–	3c. brown	30	70
126	–	4c. red	30	1·00
127	–	5c. violet	30	70
128	–	6c. brown	30	30
129	–	8c. blue	1·25	20
130	–	12c. blue and brown	50	30
131	–	24c. red and green	1·25	30
132	–	60c. black and red	7·00	3·75
133	–	$1.20 green and blue	7·00	6·00
134	–	$2.40 black and green	8·50	13·00
135	–	$4.80 black and purple	17·00	17·00

DESIGNS: 2c., $1.20, Sea Island cotton: cultivation; 3c. Map; 4c., 24c. Picking tomatoes; 5c., 12c. St. Anthony's Church; 6c., $4.80, Badge; 8c., 60c. Sea Island cotton: ginning; $2.40, Government House (portrait on right).

1953. Coronation. As T **71** of Jamaica.

136	2c. black and green	60	40

1953. As 1951 but portrait of Queen Elizabeth II.

136a	½c. violet (As 3c.) (I)	50	10
136b	½c. violet (II)	80	10
137	1c. black	10	10
138	2c. green	15	10
139	3c. brown (I)	50	10
139a	3c. brown (II)	80	2·00
140	4c. red	30	20
141	5c. violet	30	75
142	6c. brown (I)	30	10
142a	6c. brown (II)	55	15
143	8c. blue	1·00	10
144	12c. blue and brown	1·50	10
145	24c. red and green	1·50	20
145a	48c. olive and purple (As 2c.)	12·00	2·75
146	60c. black and red	8·00	2·25
147	$1.20 green and blue	15·00	7·00
148	$2.40 black and green	13·00	13·00
149	$4.80 black and purple (I)	5·00	10·00
149a	$4.80 black and purple (II)	16·00	7·50

I. Inscr "Presidency". II. Inscr "Colony".

18a Federation Map

1958. Inauguration of British Caribbean Federation.

150	18a	3c. green	55	20
151		6c. blue	75	60
152		12c. red	90	15

1963. Freedom from Hunger. As T **97** of Malta.

153	12c. violet	30	15

1963. Cent of Red Cross. As T **94** of Jamaica.

154	4c. red and black	15	20
155	12c. red and blue	35	50

20 Shakespeare and Memorial Theatre, Stratford-upon-Avon

1964. 400th Birth Anniv of Shakespeare.

156	20	12c. blue	10	10

1965. Cent of I.T.U. As T **71a** of Mauritius.

158	4c. red and violet	15	10
159	48c. green and red	30	20

21 Pineapple

1965. Multicoloured.

160	1c. Type **21**	10	10
161	2c. Avocado	10	10
162	3c. Soursop	10	10
163	4c. Pepper	10	10
164	5c. Mango	10	10
165	6c. Tomato	10	10
166	8c. Guava	10	10
167	10c. Ochro	10	10
168	12c. Lime	15	40
169	20c. Orange	30	10
170	24c. Banana	20	10
171	42c. Onion	75	60
172	48c. Cabbage	2·00	75
173	60c. Pawpaw	3·00	1·10
174	$1.20 Pumpkin	2·00	5·00
175	$2.40 Sweet potato	6·00	8·50
176	$4.80 Egg plant	6·00	11·00

1965. I.C.Y. As T **71b** of Mauritius.

177	2c. purple and turquoise	10	20
178	12c. green and lavender	25	10

1966. Churchill Commem. As T **71c** of Mauritius.

179	1c. blue	10	1·25
180	2c. green	10	10
181	24c. brown	50	10
182	42c. violet	60	60

23 Queen Elizabeth II and Duke of Edinburgh

1966. Royal Visit.

183	23	14c. black and blue	75	15
184		24c. black and mauve	1·25	15

24 W.H.O. Building

1966. Inauguration of W.H.O. Headquarters, Geneva.

185	24	12c. black, green and blue	15	25
186		60c. black, pur & ochre	35	75

1966. 20th Anniv of UNESCO. As T **72/4** of Mauritius.

187	4c. multicoloured	10	10
188	60c. yellow, violet and olive	35	10
189	$1.80 black, purple and orange	1·40	70

25 Sailing Dinghies

1967. International Tourist Year. Multicoloured.

190	5c. Type **25**	15	10
191	15c. Waterfall near Chance Mountain (vert)	20	10
192	16c. Fishing, skin diving and swimming	25	70
193	24c. Playing golf	1·60	45

1968. Nos. 168, 170, 172, 174/6 surch.

194	15c. on 12c. Lime	20	15
195	25c. on 24c. Banana	25	15
196	50c. on 48c. Cabbage	45	15
197	$1 on $1.20 Pumpkin	80	40
198	$2.50 on $2.40 Sweet potato	1·00	4·25
199	$5 on $4.80 Egg plant	1·10	4·25

27 Sprinting

1968. Olympic Games, Mexico.

200	27	15c. mauve, green and gold	10	10
201	–	25c. blue, orange and gold	15	10
202	–	50c. green, red and gold	25	10
203	–	$1 multicoloured	35	30

DESIGNS—HORIZ: 25c. Weightlifting; 50c. Gymnastics. VERT: $1 Sprinting and Aztec pillars.

31 Alexander Hamilton

1968. Human Rights Year. Multicoloured.

204	5c. Type **31**	10	10
205	15c. Albert T. Marryshow	10	10
206	25c. William Wilberforce	10	10
207	50c. Dag Hammarskjold	10	10
208	$1 Dr. Martin Luther King	25	30

32 "The Two Trinities" (Murillo)

34 Map showing CARIFTA Countries

1968. Christmas.

209	32	5c. multicoloured	10	10
210	–	15c. multicoloured	10	10

211	32 25c. multicoloured	10	10
212	– 50c. multicoloured	25	20

DESIGN: 15, 50c. "The Adoration of the Kings" (detail, Botticelli).

1969. 1st Anniv of CARIFTA (Caribbean Free Trade Area). Multicoloured.

223	15c. Type **34**	10	10
224	20c. Type **34**	10	10
225	35c. "Strength in Unity" (horiz)	10	20
226	50c. As 35c. (horiz)	15	20

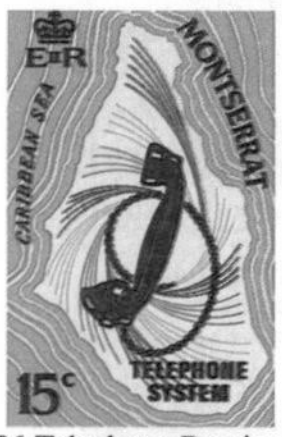

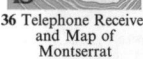

36 Telephone Receiver and Map of Montserrat

41 King Caspar before the Virgin and Child (detail) (Norman 16th-cent stained glass window)

40 Dolphin (fish)

1969. Development Projects. Multicoloured.

227	15c. Type **36**	10	10
228	25c. School symbols and map	10	10
229	50c. Hawker Siddeley H.S.748 aircraft and map	15	20
230	$1 Electricity pylon and map	25	75

1969. Game Fish. Multicoloured.

231	5c. Type **40**	35	10
232	15c. Atlantic sailfish	50	10
233	25c. Blackfin tuna	60	10
234	40c. Spanish mackerel	80	55

1969. Christmas. Paintings multicoloured; frame colours given.

235	**41** 15c. black, gold and violet	10	10
236	25c. black and red	10	10
237	– 50c. black, blue and orange	15	15

DESIGN—HORIZ: 50c. "Nativity" (Leonard Limosin).

43 "Red Cross Sale"

1970. Centenary of British Red Cross. Mult.

238	3c. Type **43**	10	25
239	4c. School for deaf children	10	25
240	15c. Transport services for disabled	10	20
241	20c. Workshop	10	60

44 Red-footed Booby

1970. Birds. Multicoloured.

242	1c. Type **44**	10	10
243	2c. American kestrel (vert)	15	15
244	3c. Magnificent frigate bird (vert)	15	15
245	4c. Great egret (vert)	1·00	15
299a	5c. Brown pelican (vert)	60	55
247	10c. Bananaquit (vert)	40	10
248	15c. Smooth-billed ani	30	15
249	20c. Red-billed tropic bird	35	15
250	25c. Montserrat oriole	50	50
251	50c. Green-throated carib (vert)	5·00	1·50
252	$1 Antillean crested hummingbird	6·50	1·00
253	$2.50 Little blue heron (vert)	5·50	12·00
254	$5 Purple-throated carib	7·50	16·00
254c	$10 Forest thrush	15·00	15·00

45 "Madonna and Child with Animals" (Brueghel the Elder, after Durer)

1970. Christmas. Multicoloured.

255	5c. Type **45**	10	10
256	15c. "The Adoration of the Shepherds" (Domenichino)	10	10
257	20c. Type **45**	10	10
258	$1 As 15c.	35	1·50

46 War Memorial

1970. Tourism. Multicoloured.

259	5c. Type **46**	10	10
260	15c. Plymouth from Fort St. George	10	10
261	25c. Carr's Bay	15	15
262	50c. Golf Fairway	1·00	2·25
MS263	135 × 109 mm. Nos. 259/62	2·50	2·25

47 Girl Guide and Badge

48 "Descent from the Cross" (Van Hemessen)

1970. Diamond Jubilee of Montserrat Girl Guides. Multicoloured.

264	10c. Type **47**	10	10
265	15c. Brownie and badge	10	10
266	25c. As 15c.	15	15
267	40c. Type **47**	20	80

1971. Easter. Multicoloured.

268	5c. Type **48**	10	10
269	15c. "Noli me tangere" (Orcagna)	10	10
270	20c. Type **48**	10	10
271	40c. As 15c.	15	85

49 D.F.C. and D.F.M. in Searchlights

50 "The Nativity with Saints" (Romanino)

1971. Golden Jubilee of Commonwealth Ex-Services League. Multicoloured.

272	10c. Type **49**	10	10
273	20c. M.C., M.M. and jungle patrol	15	10
274	40c. D.S.C., D.S.M. and submarine action	15	15
275	$1 V.C. and soldier attacking bunker	30	70

1971. Christmas. Multicoloured.

276	5c. Type **50**	10	10
277	15c. "Choir of Angels" (Simon Marmion)	10	10
278	20c. Type **50**	10	10
279	$1 As 15c.	35	40

51 Piper Apache

1971. 14th Anniv of Inauguration of L.I.A.T. (Leeward Islands Air Transport). Multicoloured.

280	5c. Type **51**	10	10
281	10c. Beech 50 Twin Bonanza	15	15
282	15c. De Havilland Heron	30	15
283	20c. Britten Norman Islander	35	15
284	40c. De Havilland Twin Otter 100	50	45
285	75c. Hawker Siddeley H.S.748	1·40	2·25
MS286	203 × 102 mm. Nos. 280/5	7·00	13·00

52 "Chapel of Christ in Gethsemane", Coventry Cathedral

1972. Easter. Multicoloured.

287	5c. Type **52**	10	10
288	10c. "The Agony in the Garden" (Bellini)	10	10
289	20c. Type **52**	10	10
290	75c. As 10c.	35	85

53 Lizard

54 "Madonna of the Chair" (Raphael)

1972. Reptiles. Multicoloured.

291	15c. Type **53**	15	10
292	20c. Mountain chicken (frog)	20	10
293	40c. Iguana (horiz)	35	20
294	$1 Tortoise (horiz)	1·00	1·00

1972. Christmas. Multicoloured.

303	10c. Type **54**	10	10
304	35c. "Virgin and Child with Cherub" (Fungai)	15	10
305	50c. "Madonna of the Magnificat" (Botticelli)	20	30
306	$1 "Virgin and Child with St. John and an Angel" (Botticelli)	30	65

55 Lime, Tomatoes and Pawpaw

1972. Royal Silver Wedding. Multicoloured, background colour given.

307	**55** 35c. pink	10	10
308	$1 blue	20	20

56 "Passiflora herbertiana"

58 "Virgin and Child" (School of Gerard David)

57 Montserrat Monastery, Spain

1973. Easter. Passion-flowers. Multicoloured.

309	20c. Type **56**	20	10
310	35c. "P. vitifolia"	25	10
311	75c. "P. amabilis"	35	75
312	$1 "P. alata-caerulea"	50	80

1973. 480th Anniv of Columbus's Discovery of Montserrat. Multicoloured.

313	10c. Type **57**	15	10
314	35c. Columbus sighting Montserrat	30	15
315	60c. "Santa Maria" off Montserrat	70	60
316	$1 Island badge and map of voyage	80	70
MS317	126 × 134 mm. Nos. 313/16	9·00	13·00

1973. Christmas. Multicoloured.

318	20c. Type **58**	15	10
319	35c. "The Holy Family with St. John" (Jordaens)	20	10
320	50c. "Virgin and Child" (Bellini)	25	30
321	90c. "Virgin and Child with Flowers" (Dolci)	50	70

58a Princess Anne and Captain Mark Phillips

1973. Royal Wedding. Multicoloured, background colour given.

322	**58a** 35c. green	10	10
323	$1 blue	20	20

59 Steel Band

1974. 25th Anniv of University of West Indies. Multicoloured.

324	20c. Type **59**	15	10
325	35c. Masqueraders (vert)	15	10
326	60c. Student weaving (vert)	25	45
327	$1 University Centre, Montserrat	30	55
MS328	130 × 89 mm. Nos. 324/7	1·75	6·00

60 Hands with Letters

1974. Centenary of U.P.U.

329	**60** 1c. multicoloured	10	10
330	– 2c. red, orange and black	10	10
331	**60** 3c. multicoloured	10	10
332	– 5c. orange, red and black	10	10
333	**60** 50c. multicoloured	20	20
334	– $1 blue, green and black	40	65

DESIGN: 2, 5c., $1 Figures from U.P.U. Monument.

1974. Various stamps surch.

335	2c. on $1 mult (No. 252)	30	2·50
336	5c. on 50c. mult (No. 333)	30	60
337	10c. on 60c. mult (No. 326)	65	1·75
338	20c. on $1 mult (No. 252)	30	2·25
339	35c. on $1 blue, green and black (No. 334)	40	1·25

62 Churchill and Houses of Parliament

1974. Birth Cent of Sir Winston Churchill. Mult.

340 35c. Type **62** 15 10
341 70c. Churchill and Blenheim Palace 20 20
MS342 81 × 85 mm. Nos. 340/1 50 70

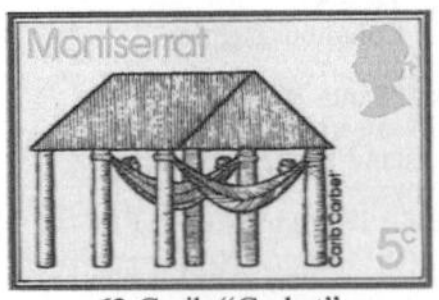

63 Carib "Carbet"

1975. Carib Artefacts. Self-adhesive or ordinary gum.

343 **63** 5c. brown, yellow and black 10 10
344 – 20c. black, brown & yellow 10 10
345 – 35c. black, yellow & brown 15 10
346 – 70c. yellow, brown & black 45 40

DESIGNS: 20c. "Caracoli"; 35c. Club or mace; 70c. Carib canoe.

64 One-Bitt Coin

1975. Local Coinage, 1785–1801.

351 **64** 5c. black, blue and silver 10 10
352 – 10c. black, pink and silver 15 10
353 – 35c. black, green and silver 20 15
354 – $2 black, red and silver 70 1·50
MS355 142 × 142 mm. Nos. 351/4 1·25 2·75

DESIGNS: 10c. Eighth dollar; 35c. Quarter dollar; $2 One dollar.

65 1d. and 6d. Stamps of 1876

1976. Centenary of First Montserrat Postage Stamp.

356 **65** 5c. red, green and black 15 10
357 – 10c. yellow, red and black 20 10
358 – 40c. multicoloured 40 40
359 – 55c. mauve, green and black 50 50
360 – 70c. multicoloured 60 70
361 – $1.10 green, blue and black 80 1·00
MS362 170 × 159 mm. Nos. 356/61 2·50 5·50

DESIGNS: 10c. G.P.O. and bisected 1d. stamp; 40c. Bisects on cover; 55c. G.B. 6d. used in Montserrat and local 6d. of 1876; 70c. Stamps for 2½d. rate, 1876; $1.10, Packet boat "Antelope" and 6d. stamp.

66 "The Trinity"

69 Mary and Joseph

68 White Frangipani

1976. Easter. Paintings by Orcagna. Multicoloured.

363 15c. Type **66** 10 10
364 40c. "The Resurrection" 15 15
365 55c. "The Ascension" 15 15
366 $1.10 "Pentecost" 30 40
MS367 160 × 142 mm. Nos. 363/6 1·25 2·25

1976. Nos. 244, 246 and 247 surch.

368 2c. on 5c. multicoloured 10 1·25
369 30c. on 10c. multicoloured 30 30
370 45c. on 3c. multicoloured 40 50

1976. Flowering Trees. Multicoloured.

371 1c. Type **68** 10 10
372 2c. Cannon-ball tree 10 10
373 3c. Lignum vitae 10 10
374 5c. Malay apple 15 10
375 10c. Jacaranda 30 10
376 15c. Orchid tree 50 10
377 20c. Manjak 30 10
378 25c. Tamarind 60 75
379 40c. Flame of the forest 30 30
380 55c. Pink cassia 40 40
381 70c. Long john 40 30
382 $1 Saman 50 80
383 $2.50 Immortelle 75 1·50
384 $5 Yellow poui 1·10 2·25
385 $10 Flamboyant 1·50 4·25

1976. Christmas. Multicoloured.

386 5c. Type **69** 10 10
387 20c. The Shepherds 10 10
388 55c. Mary and Jesus 15 15
389 $1.10 The Magi 30 50
MS390 95 × 135 mm. Nos. 386/9 60 2·25

70 Hudson River Review, 1976

1976. Bicent of American Revolution. Mult.

391 15c. Type **70** 65 20
392 40c. "Raleigh" (American frigate), 1777* 1·00 40
393 75c. H.M.S. "Druid" (frigate), 1777* 1·00 40
394 $1.25 Hudson River Review (different detail) 1·40 60
MS395 95 × 145 mm. Nos. 391/4 3·25 2·75

*The date is wrongly given on the stamps as "1776".

Nos. 391 and 394 and 392/3 respectively were issued in se-tenant pairs, each pair forming a composite design.

71 The Crowning

1977. Silver Jubilee. Multicoloured.

396 30c. Royal Visit, 1966 10 10
397 45c. Cannons firing salute 15 10
398 $1 Type **71** 25 50

72 "Ipomoea alba"

75 The Stable at Bethlehem

73 Princess Anne laying Foundation Stone of Glendon Hospital

1977. Flowers of the Night. Multicoloured.

399 15c. Type **72** 15 10
400 40c. "Epiphyllum hookeri" (horiz) 25 30
401 55c. "Cereus hexagonus" (horiz) 25 30
402 $1.50 "Cestrum nocturnum" 60 1·40
MS403 126 × 130 mm. Nos. 399/402 1·25 3·50

1977. Development. Multicoloured.

404 20c. Type **73** 30 10
405 40c. "Statesman" (freighter) in Plymouth Port 35 15
406 55c. Glendon Hospital 35 20
407 $1.50 Jetty at Plymouth Port 1·00 1·50
MS408 146 × 105 mm. Nos. 404/7 1·75 3·00

1977. Royal Visit. Nos. 380/1 and 383 surch **$1.00 SILVER JUBILEE 1977 ROYAL VISIT TO THE CARIBBEAN.**

409 $1 on 55c. Pink cassia 25 45
410 $1 on 70c. Long john 25 45
411 $1 on $2.50 Immortelle 25 45

1977. Christmas. Multicoloured.

412 5c. Type **75** 10 10
413 40c. The Three Kings 10 10
414 55c. Three Ships 15 10
415 $2 Three Angels 40 2·00
MS416 119 × 115 mm. Nos. 412/15 1·00 2·25

76 Four-eyed Butterflyfish

1978. Fish. Multicoloured.

417 30c. Type **76** 55 10
418 40c. French angelfish 60 15
419 55c. Blue tang 70 15
420 $1.50 Queen triggerfish 1·10 1·25
MS421 152 × 102 mm. Nos. 417/20 3·50 3·00

77 St. Paul's Cathedral

1978. 25th Anniv of Coronation. Multicoloured.

422 40c. Type **77** 10 10
423 55c. Chichester Cathedral 10 10
424 $1 Lincoln Cathedral 20 25
425 $2.50 Llandaff Cathedral 40 50
MS426 130 × 102 mm. Nos. 422/5 70 1·25

78 "Alpinia speciosa"

79 Private, 21st (Royal North British Fusiliers), 1786

1978. Flowers. Multicoloured.

427 40c. Type **78** 20 10
428 55c. "Allamanda cathartica" 20 15
429 $1 "Petrea volubilis" 35 45
430 $2 "Hippeastrum puniceum" 55 80

1978. Military Uniforms (1st series). British Infantry Regiments. Multicoloured.

431 30c. Type **79** 15 15
432 40c. Corporal, 86th (Royal County Down), 1831 20 15
433 55c. Sergeant, 14th (Buckinghamshire), 1837 25 15
434 $1.50 Officer, 55th (Westmorland), 1784 50 80
MS435 140 × 89 mm. Nos. 431/4 1·25 2·75

See also Nos. 441/5.

80 Cub Scouts

1979. 50th Anniv of Boy Scout Movement on Montserrat. Multicoloured.

436 40c. Type **80** 20 10
437 55c. Scouts with signalling equipment 20 15
438 $1.25 Camp fire (vert) 35 60
439 $2 Oath ceremony (vert) 45 1·00
MS440 120 × 110 mm. Nos. 436/9 1·25 2·25

1979. Military Uniforms (2nd series). As T **79**. Multicoloured.

441 30c. Private, 60th (Royal American), 1783 15 15
442 40c. Private, 1st West India, 1819 20 15
443 55c. Officer, 5th (Northumberland), 1819 20 15
444 $2.50 Officer, 93rd (Sutherland Highlanders), 1830 60 1·25
MS445 139 × 89 mm. Nos. 441/4 1·25 2·50

81 Child reaching out to Adult

1979. International Year of the Child.

446 **81** $2 black, brown and flesh 50 55
MS447 85 × 99 mm. No. 446 50 1·10

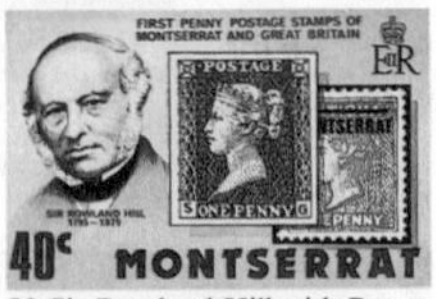

82 Sir Rowland Hill with Penny Black and Montserrat 1876 1d. Stamp

1979. Death Cent of Sir Rowland Hill and Cent of U.P.U. Membership. Multicoloured.

448 40c. Type **82** 20 10
449 55c. U.P.U. emblem and notice announcing Leeward Islands entry into Union 20 15
450 $1 1883 letter following U.P.U. membership 30 50
451 $2 Great Britain Post Office Regulations Notice and Sir Rowland Hill 40 1·50
MS452 135 × 154 mm. Nos. 448/51 1·00 2·25

83 Plume Worm

1979. Marine Life. Multicoloured.

453 40c. Type **83** 30 15
454 55c. Sea fans 40 20
455 $2 Sponge and coral 1·00 2·50

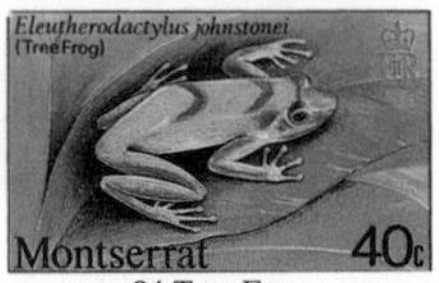

84 Tree Frog

1980. Reptiles and Amphibians. Mult.

456 40c. Type **84** 15 15
457 55c. Tree lizard 15 15
458 $1 Crapaud 30 50
459 $2 Wood slave 50 1·00

85 "Marquess of Salisbury" and 1838 Handstamps

1980. "London 1980" Int Stamp Exhibition. Mult.

460 40c. Type **85** 20 15
461 55c. Hawker Siddeley H.S.748 aircraft and 1976 55c. definitive 25 25
462 $1.20 "La Plata" (liner) and 1903 5s. stamp 30 45
463 $1.20 "Lady Hawkins" (packet steamer) and 1932 Tercentenary 5s. commemorative 30 45
464 $1.20 "Avon I" (paddle-steamer) and Penny Red stamp with "A 08" postmark 30 45
465 $1.20 Aeronca Champion 17 airplane and 1953 $1.20 definitive 30 45
MS466 115 × 110 mm. Nos. 460/5 1·25 2·50

1980. 75th Anniv of Rotary International. No. 383 optd **75th Anniversary of Rotary International**.
467 $2.50 Immortelle 55 85

87 Greek, French and U.S.A. Flags

1980. Olympic Games, Moscow. Multicoloured.
468 40c. Type **87** 20 60
469 55c. Union, Swedish and Belgian flags 20 60
470 70c. French, Dutch and U.S.A. flags 25 75
471 $1 German, Union and Finnish flags 30 75
472 $1.50 Australian, Italian and Japanese flags . . . . . . 35 1·00
473 $2 Mexican, West German and Canadian flags . . . . 40 1·00
474 $2.50 "The Discus Thrower" (sculpture, Miron) . . . . 40 1·10
MS475 150 × 100 mm. Nos. 468/74 1·50 3·50

1980. Nos. 371, 373, 376 and 379 surch.
476 5c. on 3c. Lignum vitae . . . 10 10
477 35c. on 1c. Type **68** 15 15
478 35c. on 3c. Lignum vitae . . . 15 15
479 35c. on 15c. Orchid tree . . . 15 15
480 55c. on 40c. Flame of the forest 15 15
481 $5 on 40c. Flame of the forest . . . . 60 2·00

89 "Lady Nelson", 1928

1980. Mail Packet Boats (1st series). Mult.
482 40c. Type **89** 30 15
483 55c. "Chignecto", 1913 . . . 30 15
484 $1 "Solent II", 1878 . . . . 50 65
485 $2 "Dee", 1841 . . . . . . 70 1·25
See also Nos. 615/19.

90 "Heliconius charithonia"

91 Atlantic Spadefish

1981. Butterflies. Multicoloured.
486 50c. Type **90** 50 40
487 65c. "Pyrgus oileus" 60 45
488 $1.50 "Phoebis agarithe" . . 70 85
489 $2.50 "Danaus plexippus" . . 1·00 1·10

1981. Fishes. Multicoloured.
555 5c. Type **91** 20 10
556 10c. Hogfish and neon goby . . 25 10
492 15c. Creole wrasse 80 30
493 20c. Three-spotted damselfish . 70 10
559 25c. Sergeant major 35 20
560 35c. Fin-spot wrasse 45 30
496 45c. Schoolmaster 80 40
497 55c. Striped parrotfish . . . 1·10 45
498 65c. Bigeye 80 60
564 75c. French grunt 75 55
565 $1 Rock beauty 85 65
501 $2 Blue chromis . . . . . . 1·50 1·10
502 $3 Royal gramma ("Fairy basslet") and blueheads . . 1·50 1·75
503 $5 Cherub angelfish . . . . 1·50 2·75
504 $7.50 Long-jawed squirrelfish 2·00 4·75
570 $10 Caribbean long-nosed butterflyfish . . . . 2·00 6·00

92 Fort St. George

1981. Montserrat National Trust. Multicoloured.
506 50c. Type **92** 25 20
507 65c. Bird sanctuary, Fox's Bay 45 35
508 $1.50 Museum 50 65
509 $2.50 Bransby Point Battery, c. 1780 . . . . . 60 1·10

1981. Royal Wedding. Royal Yachts. As T **26/27** of Kiribati. Multicoloured.
510 90c. "Charlotte" 25 25
511 90c. Prince Charles and Lady Diana Spencer 85 85
512 $3 "Portsmouth" 60 60
513 $3 As No. 511 . . . . . . 1·50 1·50
514 $4 "Britannia" 75 75
515 $4 As No. 511 . . . . . . 1·75 1·75
MS516 120 × 109 mm. $5 As No. 511 . . . . 1·00 1·00

93 H.M.S. "Dorsetshire" and Fairey Firefly Seaplane

1981. 50th Anniv of Montserrat Airmail Service. Multicoloured.
519 50c. Type **93** 30 30
520 65c. Beech 50 Twin Bonanza 40 30
521 $1.50 De Havilland Dragon Rapide "Lord Shaftesbury" 60 1·50
522 $2.50 Hawker Siddeley H.S.748 and maps of Montserrat and Antigua 80 2·75

94 Methodist Church, Bethel

95 Rubiaceae ("Rondeletia buxifolia")

1981. Christmas. Churches. Multicoloured.
523 50c. Type **94** 15 15
524 65c. St. George's Anglican Church, Harris 15 15
525 $1.50 St. Peter's Anglican Church, St. Peter's 30 60
526 $2.50 St. Patrick's R.C. Church, Plymouth . . . . 50 1·00
MS527 176 × 120 mm. Nos. 523/6 1·40 3·00

1982. Plant Life. Multicoloured.
528 50c. Type **95** 20 30
529 65c. Boraginaceae ("Heliotropium ternatum") (horiz) 25 40
530 $1.50 Simarubaceae ("Picramnia pentandra") 50 85
531 $2.50 Ebenaceae ("Diospyrus revoluta") (horiz) . . . . 70 1·25

96 Plymouth

1982. 350th Anniv of Settlement of Montserrat by Sir Thomas Warner.
532 **96** 40c. green 20 30
533 55c. red 20 35
534 65c. brown 25 50
535 75c. grey 25 60
536 85c. blue 25 75
537 95c. orange 25 80
538 $1 violet 25 80
539 $1.50 olive . . . . 30 1·25
540 $2 claret . . . . 35 1·50
541 $2.50 brown . . . . 40 1·50
The design of Nos. 532/41 is based on the 1932 Tercentenary set.

97 Catherine of Aragon, Princess of Wales, 1501

98 Local Scout

1982. 21st Birthday of Princess of Wales. Mult.
542 75c. Type **97** 15 15
543 $1 Coat of Arms of Catherine of Aragon . . . 15 15
544 $5 Diana, Princess of Wales 80 1·25

1982. 75th Anniv of Boy Scout Movement. Mult.
545 $1.50 Type **98** 50 50
546 $2.20 Lord Baden-Powell . . 60 75

99 Annunciation

1982. Christmas. Multicoloured.
547 35c. Type **99** 15 15
548 75c. Shepherds' Vision . . . 25 35
549 $1.50 The Stable 45 85
550 $2.50 Flight into Egypt . . . 55 1·10

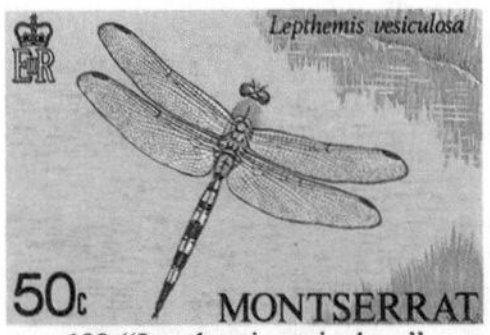

100 "Lepthemis vesiculosa"

1983. Dragonflies. Multicoloured.
551 50c. Type **100** 55 20
552 65c. "Orthemis ferruginea" 65 25
553 $1.50 "Triacanthagyna trifida" . . . . 1·25 1·50
554 $2.50 "Erythrodiplax umbrata" . . . . 1·75 3·00

101 Blue-headed Hummingbird

102 Montserrat Emblem

1983. Hummingbirds. Multicoloured.
571 35c. Type **101** . . . . . . 1·50 35
572 75c. Green-throated carib . . 1·75 85
573 $2 Antilean crested hummingbird . . . . . . 2·75 2·75
574 $3 Purple-throated carib . . 3·00 3·75

1983.
575 **102** $12 blue and red . . . . 3·50 5·00
576 $30 red and blue . . . . 6·50 12·00

1983. Various stamps surch. (a) Nos. 491, 494, 498/9 and 501.
577 40c. on 25c. Sergeant major (No. 494) 30 35
578 70c. on 10c. Hogfish and neon goby (No. 491) . . . 45 50
579 90c. on 65c. Bigeye (No. 498) 55 70
580 $1.15 on 75c. French grunt (No. 499) 65 80
581 $1.50 on $2 Blue chromis (No. 501) . . . . 85 1·00

(b) Nos. 512/15.
582 70c. on $3 "Portsmouth" . . 50 1·00
583 70c. on $3 Prince Charles and Lady Diana Spencer . . . 1·50 2·75
584 $1.15 on $4 "Britannia" . . 65 1·50
585 $1.15 on $4 As No. 583 . . . 1·75 3·25

104 Montgolfier Balloon, 1783

106 Statue of Discus Thrower

105 Boys dressed as Clowns

1983. Bicentenary of Manned Flight. Mult.
586 35c. Type **104** 15 15
587 75c. De Havilland Twin Otter 200/300 (horiz) 25 30
588 $1.50 Lockheed Vega V (horiz) 40 75
589 $2 Beardmore airship R.34 (horiz) . . . . 60 1·25
MS590 109 × 145 mm. Nos. 586/9 1·25 2·75

1983. Christmas. Carnival. Multicoloured.
591 55c. Type **105** 10 10
592 90c. Girls dressed as silver star bursts 15 20
593 $1.15 Flower girls 20 35
594 $2 Masqueraders 35 80

1984. Olympic Games, Los Angeles. Mult.
595 90c. Type **106** 30 35
596 $1 Olympic torch 35 45
597 $1.25 Los Angeles Olympic stadium 40 50
598 $2.50 Olympic and American flags . . . . 65 1·00
MS599 110 × 110 mm. Nos. 595/8 1·50 2·25

107 Cattle Egret

1984. Birds of Montserrat. Multicoloured.
600 5c. Type **107** 30 50
601 10c. Carib grackle 30 50
602 15c. Moorhen ("Common Gallinule") 30 50
603 20c. Brown booby 40 50
604 25c. Black-whiskered vireo 40 50
605 40c. Scaly-breasted thrasher 60 60
606 55c. Laughing gull 75 30
607 70c. Glossy ibis 90 50
608 90c. Green-backed heron ("Green Heron") . . . . . 1·00 60
609 $1 Belted kingfisher (vert) . . 1·25 70
610 $1.15 Bananaquit (vert) . . . 1·50 1·40
611 $3 American kestrel ("Sparrow Hawk") (vert) 3·25 5·50
612 $5 Forest thrush (vert) . . . 4·50 7·50
613 $7.50 Black-crowned night heron (vert) . . . . 5·00 13·00
614 $10 Bridled quail dove (vert) 5·50 13·00

1984. Mail Packet Boats (2nd series). As T **89**. Multicoloured.
615 55c. "Tagus II", 1907 . . . . 20 40
616 90c. "Cobequid", 1913 . . . 30 50
617 $1.15 "Lady Drake", 1942 40 70
618 $2 "Factor", 1948 . . . . . 60 1·75
MS619 152 × 100 mm. Nos. 615/18 1·50 5·00
No. **MS**619 also commemorates the 250th anniversary of "Lloyd's List" (newspaper).

108 Hermit Crab and West Indian Top Shell

1984. Marine Life. Multicoloured.
620 90c. Type **108** . . . . 1·50 1·00
621 $1.15 Rough file shell . . . . 1·75 1·40
622 $1.50 True tulip . . . . . . 2·50 3·25
623 $2.50 Queen or pink conch 3·25 5·00

109 "Bull Man"

1984. Christmas. Carnival Costumes. Mult.
624 55c. Type **109** 50 25
625 $1.15 Masquerader Captain 1·50 1·25
626 $1.50 "Fantasy" Carnival Queen . . . . 1·75 2·50
627 $2.30 "Ebony and Ivory" Carnival Queen . . . . . 2·50 4·25

110 Mango

111 "Oncidium urophyllum"

1985. National Emblems. Multicoloured.
628 $1.15 Type **110** 30 60
629 $1.50 Lobster claw . . . . . 40 1·00
630 $3 Montserrat oriole . . . . 60 2·75

1985. Orchids of Montserrat. Multicoloured.

631	90c. Type **111**	40	55
632	$1.15 "Epidendrum difforme"	40	80
633	$1.50 "Epidendrum ciliare"	45	1·25
634	$2.50 "Brassavola cucullata"	55	2·75
MS635	120 × 140 mm. Nos. 631/4	3·75	6·50

112 Queen Elizabeth the Queen Mother

115 Black-throated Blue Warbler

113 Cotton Plants

1985. Life and Times of Queen Elizabeth the Queen Mother. Various vertical portraits.

636	**112** 55c. multicoloured	25	45
637	– 55c. multicoloured	25	45
638	– 90c. multicoloured	25	55
639	– 90c. multicoloured	25	55
640	– $1.15 multicoloured . . .	25	60
641	– $1.15 multicoloured . . .	25	60
642	– $1.50 multicoloured . . .	30	70
643	– $1.50 multicoloured . . .	30	70
MS644	85 × 113 mm. $2 multicoloured; $2 multicoloured	65	1·90

Each value was issued in pairs showing a floral pattern across the bottom of the portraits which stops short of the left-hand edge on the first stamp and of the right-hand edge on the second.

1985. Montserrat Sea Island Cotton Industry. Multicoloured.

645	90c. Type **113**	25	45
646	$1 Operator at carding machine	25	50
647	$1.15 Threading loom . . .	25	65
648	$2.50 Weaving with hand loom	50	2·75
MS649	148 × 103 mm. Nos. 645/8	3·00	3·75

1985. Royal Visit. Nos. 514/15, 543, 587/8 and 640/1 optd **CARIBBEAN ROYAL VISIT 1985** or surch also.

650	75c. multicoloured (No. 587)	3·00	2·50
651	$1 multicoloured (No. 543)	4·50	3·50
652	$1.15 multicoloured (No. 640)	4·25	6·50
653	$1.15 multicoloured (No. 641)	4·25	6·50
654	$1.50 multicoloured (No. 588)	7·00	7·00
655	$1.60 on $4 mult (No. 514)	2·00	4·25
656	$1.60 on $4 mult (No. 515)	17·00	22·00

No. 656 shows a new face value only, "CARIBBEAN ROYAL VISIT 1985" being omitted from the surcharge.

1985. Leaders of the World. Birth Bicentenary of John J. Audubon (ornithologist). Designs showing original paintings. Multicoloured.

657	15c. Type **115**	15	40
658	15c. Palm warbler	15	40
659	30c. Bobolink	15	40
660	30c. Lark sparrow	15	40
661	55c. Chipping sparrow . . .	20	40
662	55c. Northern oriole	20	40
663	$2.50 American goldfinch . .	40	1·40
664	$2.50 Blue grosbeak	40	1·40

116 Herald Angel appearing to Goatherds

1985. Christmas. Designs showing Caribbean Nativity. Multicoloured.

665	70c. Type **116**	15	15
666	$1.15 Three Wise Men following Star	25	40
667	$1.50 Carol singing around War Memorial, Plymouth	30	85
668	$2.30 Praying to "Our Lady of Montserrat", Church of Our Lady, St. Patrick's Village	45	2·00

117 Lord Baden-Powell

1986. 50th Anniv of Montserrat Girl Guide Movement. Multicoloured.

669	20c. Type **117**	15	60
670	20c. Girl Guide saluting . . .	15	60
671	75c. Lady Baden-Powell . . .	25	75
672	75c. Guide assisting in old people's home	25	75
673	90c. Lord and Lady Baden-Powell	30	75
674	90c. Guides serving meal in old people's home	30	75
675	$1.15 Girl Guides of 1936 . .	40	80
676	$1.15 Two guides saluting . .	40	80

117a Queen Elizabeth II

1986. 60th Birthday of Queen Elizabeth II. Multicoloured.

677	10c. Type **117a**	10	10
678	$1.50 Princess Elizabeth in 1928	25	50
679	$3 In Antigua, 1977	40	1·25
680	$6 In Canberra, 1982 (vert)	65	2·25
MS681	85 × 115 mm. $8 Queen with bouquet	3·25	5·50

118 King Harold and Halley's Comet, 1066 (from Bayeux Tapestry)

1986. Appearance of Halley's Comet. Mult.

682	35c. Type **118**	20	25
683	50c. Comet of 1301 (from Giotto's "Adoration of the Magi")	25	30
684	70c. Edmond Halley and Comet of 1531	25	40
685	$1 Comets of 1066 and 1910	25	40
686	$1.15 Comet of 1910	30	50
687	$1.50 E.S.A. "Giotto" spacecraft and Comet . . .	30	80
688	$2.30 U.S. space telescope and Comet	40	1·75
689	$4 Computer reconstruction of 1910 Comet	50	3·25
MS690	Two sheets, each 140 × 115 mm. (a) 40c. Type **118**; $1.75, As No. 683; $2 As No. 684; $3 As No. 685. (b) 55c. As No. 686; 60c. As No. 687; 80c. As No. 688; $5 As No. 689 Set of 2 sheets	2·75	9·00

118a Prince Andrew

1986. Royal Wedding (1st issue). Multicoloured.

691	70c. Type **118a**	25	40
692	70c. Miss Sarah Ferguson . .	25	40
693	$2 Prince Andrew wearing stetson (horiz)	40	90
694	$2 Miss Sarah Ferguson on skiing holiday (horiz) . . .	40	90
MS695	115 × 85 mm. $10 Duke and Duchess of York on Palace balcony after wedding (horiz)	3·00	4·75

See also Nos. 705/8.

119 "Antelope" being attacked by "L'Atalante"

1986. Mail Packet Sailing Ships. Mult.

696	90c. Type **119**	2·00	1·50
697	$1.15 "Montagu" (1810) . .	2·25	2·00
698	$1.50 "Little Catherine" being pursued by "L'Etoile" (1813)	2·75	2·75
699	$2.30 "Hinchingbrook I" (1813)	3·50	5·00
MS700	165 × 123 mm. Nos. 696/9	10·00	11·00

120 Radio Montserrat Building, Dagenham

1986. Communications. Multicoloured.

701	70c. Type **120**	1·00	70
702	$1.15 Radio Gem dish aerial, Plymouth	1·00	1·50
703	$1.50 Radio Antilles studio, O'Garro's	1·75	2·25
704	$2.30 Cable and Wireless building, Plymouth	2·25	4·25

1986. Royal Wedding (2nd issue). Nos. 691/4 optd **Congratulations to T.R.H. The Duke & Duchess of York.**

705	70c. Prince Andrew	70	1·25
706	70c. Miss Sarah Ferguson . .	70	1·25
707	$2 Prince Andrew wearing stetson (horiz)	1·25	1·75
708	$2 Miss Sarah Ferguson on skiing holiday (horiz) . . .	1·25	1·75

121a Statue of Liberty

123 Christmas Rose

122 Sailing and Windsurfing

1986. Centenary of Statue of Liberty. Vert views of Statue as T **121a** in separate miniature sheets. Multicoloured.

MS709	Three sheets, each 85 × 115 mm. $3; $4.50; $5 Set of 3 sheets	3·75	9·00

1986. Tourism. Multicoloured.

710	70c. Type **122**	40	70
711	$1.15 Golf	70	1·50
712	$1.50 Plymouth market . . .	70	2·00
713	$2.30 Air Recording Studios	80	3·00

1986. Christmas. Flowering Shrubs. Mult.

714	70c. Type **123**	70	40
715	$1.15 Candle flower	95	85
716	$1.50 Christmas tree kalanchoe	1·50	1·50
717	$2.30 Snow on the mountain	2·00	4·50
MS718	150 × 110 mm. Nos. 714/17	7·50	8·00

124 Tiger Shark

1987. Sharks. Multicoloured.

719	40c. Type **124**	1·50	55
720	90c. Lemon shark	2·50	1·50
721	$1.15 Great white shark . . .	2·75	2·00
722	$3.50 Whale shark	5·50	8·00
MS723	150 × 102 mm. Nos. 719/22	12·00	14·00

1987. Nos. 601, 603, 607/8 and 611 surch.

724	5c. on 70c. Glossy ibis . . .	50	2·25
725	$1 on 20c. Brown booby . .	1·75	1·00
726	$1.15 on 10c. Carib grackle	2·00	1·40
727	$1.50 on 90c. Green-backed heron	2·25	2·50
728	$2.30 on $3 American kestrel (vert)	3·25	7·50

1987. "Capex '87" International Stamp Exhibition, Toronto. No. **MS**690 optd with **CAPEX 87** logo.

MS729	Two sheets. As No. **MS**690 Set of 2 sheets	4·00	10·00

No. **MS**729 also carries an overprint commemorating the exhibition on the lower sheet margins.

127 "Phoebis trite"

128 "Oncidium variegatum"

1987. Butterflies. Multicoloured.

730	90c. Type **127**	2·00	1·10
731	$1.15 "Biblis hyperia" . . .	2·50	1·60
732	$1.50 "Polygonus leo" . . .	3·00	2·50
733	$2.50 "Hypolimnas misippus"	4·50	6·50

1987. Christmas. Orchids. Multicoloured.

734	90c. Type **128**	60	45
735	$1.15 "Vanilla planifolia" (horiz)	85	55
736	$1.50 "Gongora quinquenervis"	1·10	1·10
737	$3.50 "Brassavola nodosa" (horiz)	2·00	5·00
MS738	100 × 75 mm. $5 "Oncidium lanceanum" (horiz)	10·00	12·00

1987. Royal Ruby Wedding. Nos. 601, 604/5 and 608 surch **40th Wedding Anniversary HM Queen Elizabeth II HRH Duke of Edinburgh. November 1987.** and value.

739B	5c. on 90c. Green-backed heron	30	40
740B	$1.15 on 10c. Carib grackle	1·00	1·00
741B	$2.30 on 25c. Black-whiskered vireo	1·75	2·25
742B	$5 on 40c. Scaly-breasted thrasher	3·50	5·00

130 Free-tailed Bat

131 Magnificent Frigate Bird

1988. Bats. Multicoloured.

743	55c. Type **130**	80	40
744	90c. "Chiroderma improvisum" (fruit bat) . .	1·25	90
745	$1.15 Fisherman bat	1·60	1·50
746	$2.30 "Brachyphylla cavernarum" (fruit bat) . .	3·00	5·50
MS747	133 × 110 mm. $2.50 Funnel-eared bat	6·50	8·00

1988. Easter. Birds. Multicoloured.

748	90c. Type **131**	60	45
749	$1.15 Caribbean elaenia . . .	80	75
750	$1.50 Glossy ibis	1·00	1·50
751	$3.50 Purple-throated carib	2·00	4·00
MS752	100 × 75 mm. $5 Brown pelican	2·50	3·50

132 Discus throwing

1988. Olympic Games, Seoul. Multicoloured.

753	90c. Type **132**	70	50
754	$1.15 High jumping	80	55
755	$3.50 Athletics	2·00	3·25
MS756	103 × 77 mm. $5 Rowing	3·00	3·00

133 Golden Tulip

1988. Sea Shells. Multicoloured.

757	5c. Type **133**	30	50
758	10c. Little knobbed scallop	40	50
759	15c. Sozoni's cone	40	50
760	20c. Globular coral shell	50	50
761	25c. American or common sundial	50	50
762	40c. King helmet	60	50
763	55c. Channelled turban	80	50
764	70c. True tulip	1·00	75
765	90c. Music volute	1·25	75
766	$1 Flame auger	1·40	80
767	$1.15 Rooster-tail conch	1·50	90
768	$1.50 Queen or pink conch	1·60	1·40
769	$3 Teramachi's slit shell	2·50	4·25
770	$5 Common or Florida crown conch	3·50	6·50
771	$7.50 Beau's murex	4·50	11·00
772	$10 Atlantic trumpet triton	5·50	11·00

134 University Crest

1988. 40th Anniv of University of West Indies.

773	**134** $5 multicoloured	2·40	3·50

1988. Princess Alexandra's Visit. Nos. 763, 766 and 769/70 surch **HRH PRINCESS ALEXANDRA'S VISIT NOVEMBER 1988** and new value.

774	40c. on 55c. Channelled turban	45	45
775	90c. on $1 Flame auger	70	80
776	$1.15 on $3 Teramachi's slit shell	85	95
777	$1.50 on $5 Common or Florida crown conch	1·10	1·50

136 Spotted Sandpiper

1988. Christmas. Sea Birds. Multicoloured.

778	90c. Type **136**	70	55
779	$1.15 Ruddy turnstone	85	70
780	$3.50 Red-footed booby	2·00	3·75
MS781	105 × 79 mm. $5 Audubon's shearwater	2·75	4·00

137 Handicapped Children in Classroom

1988. 125th Anniv of International Red Cross.

782	**137** $3.50 multicoloured	1·50	2·25

138 Drum Major in Ceremonial Uniform

1989. 75th Anniv (1986) of Montserrat Defence Force. Uniforms. Multicoloured.

783	90c. Type **138**	70	50
784	$1.15 Field training uniform	85	75
785	$1.50 Cadet in ceremonial uniform	1·25	1·75
786	$3.50 Gazetted Police Officer in ceremonial uniform	2·50	3·75
MS787	102 × 76 mm. $5 Island Girl Guide Commissioner and brownie	3·50	4·25

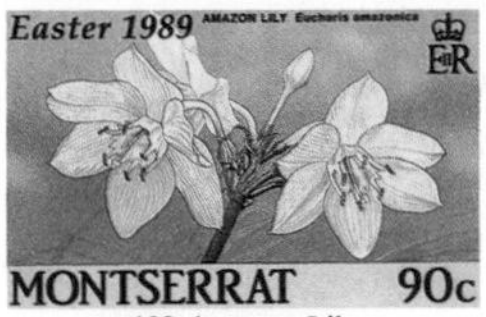

139 Amazon Lily

1989. Easter. Lilies. Multicoloured.

788	90c. Type **139**	50	50
789	$1.15 Salmon blood lily (vert)	70	70
790	$1.50 Amaryllis (vert)	85	1·25
791	$3.50 Amaryllis (vert)	1·90	3·00
MS792	103 × 77 mm. $5 Resurrection lily (vert)	4·25	6·50

140 "Morning Prince" (schooner), 1942

1989. Shipbuilding in Montserrat. Mult.

793	90c. Type **140**	1·00	60
794	$1.15 "Western Sun" (inter-island freighter)	1·50	1·10
795	$1.50 "Kim G" (inter-island freighter) under construction	1·75	2·25
796	$3.50 "Romaris" (inter-island ferry), c. 1942	3·00	5·00

141 The Scarecrow

1989. 50th Anniv of "The Wizard of Oz" (film). Multicoloured.

797	90c. Type **141**	40	45
798	$1.15 The Lion	55	60
799	$1.50 The Tin Man	70	85
800	$3.50 Dorothy	1·60	2·50
MS801	113 × 84 mm. $5 Characters from film (horiz)	2·40	3·75

1989. Hurricane Hugo Relief Fund. Nos. 795/6 surch **Hurricane Hugo Relief Surcharge $2.50**.

802	$1.50+$2.50 "Kim G" (inter-island freighter under construction)	2·75	4·00
803	$3.50+$2.50 "Romaris" (inter-island ferry), c. 1942	3·00	5·00

143 "Apollo 11" above Lunar Surface

1989. 20th Anniv of First Manned Landing on Moon. Multicoloured.

804	90c. Type **143**	35	40
805	$1.15 Astronaut alighting from lunar module "Eagle"	45	50
806	$1.50 "Eagle" and astronaut conducting experiment	60	80
807	$3.50 Opening "Apollo 11" hatch after splashdown	1·40	2·50
MS808	101 × 76 mm. $5 Astronaut on Moon	4·75	6·00

144 "Yamato" (Japanese battleship)

1990. World War II Capital Ships. Multicoloured.

809	70c. Type **144**	2·75	70
810	$1.15 U.S.S. "Arizona" at Pearl Harbor	3·25	95
811	$1.50 "Bismarck" (German battleship) in action	4·00	2·75
812	$3.50 H.M.S. "Hood" (battle cruiser)	6·00	9·00
MS813	118 × 90 mm. $5 "Bismarck" and map of North Atlantic	12·00	12·00

145 The Empty Tomb

1990. Easter. Stained glass windows from St. Michael's Parish Church, Bray, Berkshire. Multicoloured.

814	$1.15 Type **145**	2·00	2·25
815	$1.50 The Ascension	2·00	2·25
816	$3.50 The Risen Christ with Disciples	2·75	3·25
MS817	65 × 103 mm. $5 The Crucifixion	4·50	6·00

1990. "Stamp World London '90" International Stamp Exhibition. Nos. 460/4 surch **Stamp World London 90**, emblem and value.

818	70c. on 40c. Type **85**	60	60
819	90c. on 55c. Hawker Siddeley H.S.748 aircraft and 1976 55c. definitive	80	80
820	$1 on $1.20 "La Plata" (liner) and 1903 5s. stamp	90	90
821	$1.15 on $1.20 "Lady Hawkins" (packet steamer) and 1932 Tercentenary 5s. commemorative	1·10	1·10
822	$1.50 on $1.20 "Avon I" (paddle-steamer) and Penny Red stamp with "A 08" postmark	1·50	2·00

147 General Office, Montserrat and 1884 ½d. Stamp

1990. 150th Anniv of the Penny Black. Mult.

823	90c. Type **147**	65	65
824	$1.15 Sorting letters and Montserrat 1d. stamp of 1876 (vert)	85	90
825	$1.50 Posting letters and Penny Black (vert)	1·25	1·75
826	$3.50 Postman delivering letters and 1840 Twopence Blue	3·00	4·50
MS827	102 × 75 mm. $5 Montserrat soldier's letter of 1836 and Penny Black	8·50	10·00

148 Montserrat v. Antigua Match

1990. World Cup Football Championship, Italy. Multicoloured.

828	90c. Type **148**	65	55
829	$1.15 U.S.A. v. Trinidad match	85	75
830	$1.50 Montserrat team	1·25	1·50
831	$3.50 West Germany v. Wales match	2·25	3·50
MS832	77 × 101 mm. $5 World Cup trophy (vert)	6·00	7·50

149 Spinner Dolphin

1990. Dolphins. Multicoloured.

833	90c. Type **149**	1·50	85
834	$1.15 Common dolphin	1·75	1·25
835	$1.50 Striped dolphin	2·50	2·50
836	$3.50 Atlantic spotted dolphin	3·75	5·00
MS837	103 × 76 mm. $5 Atlantic white-sided dolphin	8·50	9·50

150 Spotted Goatfish

1991. Tropical Fishes. Multicoloured.

838	90c. Type **150**	1·50	95
839	$1.15 Cushion star	1·75	1·25
840	$1.50 Rock beauty	2·50	2·75
841	$3.50 French grunt	3·75	5·50
MS842	103 × 76 mm. $5 Buffalo trunkfish	5·50	7·00

1991. Nos. 760/1, 768 and 771 surch.

843	5c. on 20c. Globular coral shell	65	1·75
844	5c. on 25c. American or common sundial	65	1·75
845	$1.15 on $1.50 Queen or pink conch	2·75	3·25
846	$1.15 on $7.50 Beau's murex	2·75	3·25

152 Duck

1991. Domestic Birds. Multicoloured.

847	90c. Type **152**	60	60
848	$1.15 Hen and chicks	80	90
849	$1.50 Red junglefowl ("Rooster")	1·10	1·50
850	$3.50 Helmeted guineafowl	2·40	3·50

153 "Panaeolus antillarum"

1991. Fungi.

851	**153** 90c. grey	1·25	1·00
852	– $1.15 red	1·50	1·25
853	– $1.50 brown	2·25	2·25
854	– $2 purple	2·50	3·25
855	– $3.50 blue	3·75	5·00

DESIGNS: $1.15, "Cantharellus cinnabarinus"; $1.50, "Gymnopilus chrysopellus"; $2 "Psilocybe cubensis"; $3.50, "Leptonia caeruleocapitata".

154 Red Water Lily

155 Tree Frog

1991. Lilies. Multicoloured.

856	90c. Type **154**	65	65
857	$1.15 Shell ginger	75	85
858	$1.50 Early day lily	1·00	1·60
859	$3.50 Anthurium	2·50	3·75

1991. Frogs and Toad. Multicoloured.

860	$1.15 Type **155**	3·25	1·25
861	$2 Crapaud toad	4·50	4·50
862	$3.50 Mountain chicken (frog)	7·50	8·00
MS863	110 × 110 mm. $5 Tree frog, crapaud toad and mountain chicken (76½ × 44 mm)	11·00	12·00

156 Black British Shorthair Cat

1991. Cats. Multicoloured.

864	90c. Type **156**	1·50	90
865	$1.15 Seal point Siamese	1·75	1·10
866	$1.50 Silver tabby Persian	2·25	2·25
867	$2.50 Birman temple cat	3·00	3·75
868	$3.50 Egyptain mau	4·00	5·00

157 Navigational Instruments

1992. 500th Anniv of Discovery of America by Columbus. Multicoloured.

869 $1.50 Type **157** . . . . . . 1·25 1·50
870 $1.50 Columbus and coat of arms . . . . 1·25 1·50
871 $1.50 Landfall on the Bahamas . . . . 1·25 1·50
872 $1.50 Petitioning Queen Isabella . . . . 1·25 1·50
873 $1.50 Tropical birds . . . . 1·25 1·50
874 $1.50 Tropical fruits . . . . 1·25 1·50
875 $3 Ships of Columbus (81 × 26 mm) . . . . . . 1·75 2·00

158 Runner with Olympic Flame

1992. Olympic Games, Barcelona. Multicoloured.

876 $1 Type **158** 90 60
877 $1.15 Montserrat, Olympic and Spanish flags . . . . 1·25 90
878 $2.30 Olympic flame on map of Montserrat . . . . . . 2·25 2·75
879 $3.60 Olympic events . . . . 2·75 4·25

159 Tyrannosaurus

1992. Death Centenary of Sir Richard Owen (zoologist). Multicoloured.

880 $1 Type **159** . . . . 2·00 1·25
881 $1.15 Diplodocus . . . . . 2·25 1·40
882 $1.50 Apatosaurus . . . . . 2·75 2·75
883 $3.45 Dimetrodon . . . . . 5·50 8·00
MS884 114 × 84 mm. $4.60, Sir Richard Owen and dinosaur bone (vert) . . . . 8·50 10·00

160 Male Montserrat Oriole

1992. Montserrat Oriole. Multicoloured.

885 $1 Type **160** . . . . 1·10 1·10
886 $1.15 Male and female orioles 1·40 1·40
887 $1.50 Female oriole with chicks . . . . 1·75 2·00
888 $3.60 Map of Montserrat and male oriole . . . . 3·50 5·00

161 "Psophus stridulus" (grasshopper)

1992. Insects. Multicoloured.

889 5c. Type **161** 30 40
890 10c. "Gryllus campestris" (field cricket) 35 40
891 15c. "Lepthemis vesiculosa" (dragonfly) 40 40
892 20c. "Orthemis ferruginea" (red skimmer) 45 45
893 25c. "Gerris lacustris" (pond skater) 45 45
894 40c. "Byctiscus betulae" (leaf weevil) 60 50
895 55c. "Atta texana" (leaf-cutter ants) 60 40
896 70c. "Polistes fuscatus" (paper wasp) 70 60
897 90c. "Sparmopolius fulvus" (bee fly) 80 60
898 $1 "Chrysopa carnea" (lace wing) . . . . 1·25 65
899 $1.15 "Phoebis philea" (butterfly) . . . . 2·00 90
900 $1.50 "Cynthia cardui" (butterfly) . . . . 2·25 1·75
901 $3 "Utetheisa bella" (moth) 3·00 4·25
902 $5 "Alucita pentadactyla" (moth) . . . . 4·25 6·00
903 $7.50 "Anartia jatropha" (butterfly) . . . . 5·50 8·50
904 $10 "Heliconius melpomene" (butterfly) . . . . 5·50 8·50

162 Adoration of the Magi

1992. Christmas. Multicoloured.

905 $1.15 Type **162** . . . . . . 2·00 75
906 $4.60 Appearance of angel to shepherds . . . . 4·50 6·50

163 $1 Coin and $20 Banknote

164 Columbus meeting Amerindians

1993. East Caribbean Currency. Multicoloured.

907 $1 Type **163** 90 70
908 $1.15 10c. and 25c. coins with $10 banknote . . . . . . 1·25 85
909 $1.50 5c. coin and $5 banknote . . . . 1·75 2·00
910 $3.60 1c. and 2c. coins with $1 banknote . . . . 4·00 6·00

1993. Organization of East Caribbean States. 500th Anniv of Discovery of America by Columbus. Multicoloured.

911 $1 Type **164** . . . . 1·10 90
912 $2 Ships approaching island 2·00 2·75

165 Queen Elizabeth II on Montserrat with Chief Minister W. H. Bramble, 1966

1993. 40th Anniv of Coronation. Multicoloured.

913 $1.15 Type **165** . . . . . . 1·50 75
914 $4.60 Queen Elizabeth II in State Coach, 1953 . . . . 4·50 5·50

1993. 500th Anniv of Discovery of Montserrat. As Nos. 869/75, some with new values, each showing "500th ANNIVERSARY DISCOVERY OF MONTSERRAT" at foot and with additional historical inscr across the centre.

915 $1.15 mult (As Type **157**) . . 1·75 2·00
916 $1.15 multicoloured (As No. 870) . . . . 1·75 2·00
917 $1.15 multicoloured (As No. 871) . . . . 1·75 2·00
918 $1.50 multicoloured (As No. 872) . . . . 2·00 2·25
919 $1.50 multicoloured (As No. 873) . . . . 2·00 2·25
920 $1.50 multicoloured (As No. 874) . . . . 2·00 2·25
921 $3.45 multicoloured (As No. 875) . . . . 2·75 3·50

Additional inscriptions: No. 915, "PRE-COLUMBUS CARIB NAME OF ISLAND ALLIOUGANA"; 916, "COLUMBUS NAMED ISLAND SANTA MARIA DE MONTSERRATE"; 917, "COLUMBUS SAILED ALONG COASTLINE 11th NOV. 1493"; 918, "ISLAND OCCUPIED BY FRENCH BRIEFLY IN 1667"; 919, "ISLAND DECLARED ENGLISH BY TREATY OF BREDA 1667"; 920, "AFRICAN SLAVES BROUGHT IN DURING 1600's"; 921, "IRISH CATHOLICS FROM ST. KITTS AND VIRGINIA SETTLED ON ISLAND BETWEEN 1628–1634".

166 Boeing Sentry, 1993

1993. 75th Anniv of Royal Air Force. Mult.

922 15c. Type **166** 45 20
923 55c. Vickers Valiant B Mk 1, 1962 . . . . 65 40
924 $1.15 Handley Page Hastings C Mk 2, 1958 . . . . . . 1·25 75
925 $3 Lockheed Ventura, 1943 2·50 4·25
MS926 117 × 78 mm. $1.50 Felixstowe F5, 1921; $1.50 Armstrong Whitworth Atlas, 1934; $1.50 Fairey Gordon, 1935; $1.50 Boulton & Paul Overstrand, 1936 . . . . 4·50 6·00

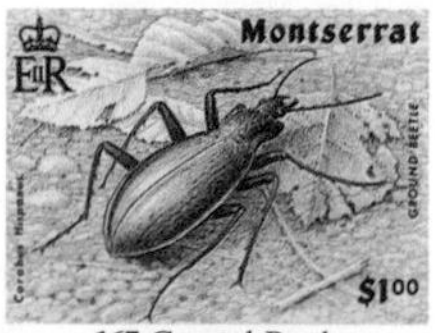

167 Ground Beetle

1994. Beetles. Multicoloured.

927 $1 Type **167** 65 65
928 $1.15 Click beetle 80 80
929 $1.50 Harlequin beetle . . . 1·25 1·50
930 $3.45 Leaf beetle . . . . . . 3·00 4·50
MS931 68 × 85 mm. $4.50 Scarab beetle . . . . 3·50 4·00

168 "Gossypium barbadense"

1994. Flowers. Multicoloured.

932 90c. Type **168** . . . . 1·25 80
933 $1.15 "Hibiscus sabdariffa" 1·50 1·00
934 $1.50 "Hibiscus esculentus" 1·75 1·75
935 $3.50 "Hibiscus rosa-sinensis" 3·75 6·00

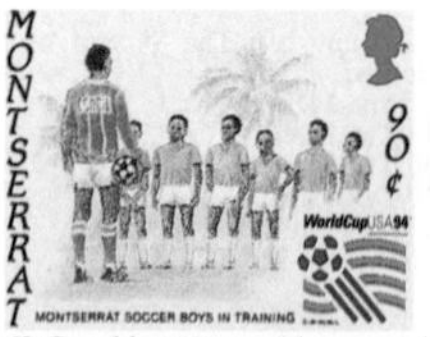

169 Coaching Young Players and Logo

1994. World Cup Football Championship, U.S.A. Multicoloured.

936 90c. Type **169** . . . . 1·90 2·25
937 $1 United States scoring against England, 1950 . . 1·90 2·25
938 $1.15 Rose Bowl stadium, Los Angeles, and trophy 1·90 2·25
939 $3.45 German players celebrating with trophy, 1990 . . . . 3·00 3·50
MS940 114 × 85 mm. $2 Jules Rimet (founder) and Jules Rimet Trophy; $2 Bobby Moore (England) holding trophy, 1966; $2 Lew Jaschin (U.S.S.R.); $2 Sepp Herberger (Germany) and German players celebrating, 1990 7·00 9·00

170 Elasmosaurus

1994. Aquatic Dinosaurs. Multicoloured.

941 $1 Type **170** . . . . 2·25 2·25
942 $1.15 Plesiosaurus . . . . . 2·25 2·25
943 $1.50 Nothosaurus . . . . . 2·75 2·75
944 $3.45 Mosasaurus . . . . . 3·50 4·25

1994. Space Anniversaries. Nos. 804/7 variously surch or optd, each including **Space Anniversaries**.

945 40c. on 90c. Type **143** . . . 1·50 80
946 $1.15 Astronaut alighting from lunar module "Eagle" 2·25 1·50
947 $1.50 "Eagle" and astronaut conducting experiment . . 2·75 2·75
948 $2.30 on $3.50 Opening "Apollo 11" hatch after splashdown . . . . 4·25 6·00

Surcharges and overprints: No. 945, **Juri Gagarin First man in space April 12, 1961**; 946, **First Joint US Soviet Mission July 15, 1975**; 947 **25th Anniversary First Moon Landing Apollo XI – July 20, 1994**; 948, **Columbia First Space Shuttle April 12, 1981.**

172 1969 Festival Logo

1994. 25th Anniv of Woodstock Music Festival. Multicoloured.

949 $1.15 Type **172** . . . . . . 1·00 1·00
950 $1.50 1994 anniversary festival logo . . . . 1·25 1·25

173 Sea Fan

1995. Marine Life. Multicoloured.

951 $1 Type **173** 60 50
952 $1.15 Sea lily 70 60
953 $1.50 Sea pen . . . . 90 1·00
954 $3.45 Sea fern . . . . 2·00 3·00
MS955 88 × 96 mm. $4.50 Sea rose 3·00 4·00

174 Marilyn Monroe

1995. Centenary of Cinema. Portraits of Marilyn Monroe (film star). Multicoloured.

956 $1.15 Type **174** . . . . . . 90 1·00
957 $1.15 Puckering lips . . . . 90 1·00
958 $1.15 Laughing in brown evening dress and earrings 90 1·00
959 $1.15 Wearing red earrings 90 1·00
960 $1.15 In brown dress without earrings . . . . 90 1·00
961 $1.15 With white boa . . . . 90 1·00
962 $1.15 In red dress . . . . . 90 1·00
963 $1.15 Wearing white jumper 90 1·00
964 $1.15 Looking over left shoulder . . . . 90 1·00
MS965 102 × 132 mm. $6 With Elvis Presley (50 × 56 mm) . . . . . 4·50 5·50

175 Jesse Owens (U.S.A.)

177 Ears of Wheat ("Food")

176 Atmospheric Sounding Experiments using V2 Rockets

1995. 5th International Amateur Athletic Federation Games, Göteborg. Sheet 181 × 103 mm, containing T **175** and similar vert designs.
MS966 $1.50 black and pink (Type **175**); $1.50 black and orange (Eric Lemming (Sweden)); $1.50 black and yellow (Rudolf Harbig (Germany)); $1.50 black and green (young Montserrat athletes) . . . . 4·50 6·00

1995. 50th Anniv of End of Second World War. Scientific Achievements. Multicoloured.
967 $1.15 Type **176** . . . . . . 80 1·00
968 $1.15 American space shuttle "Challenger" . . . . . . 80 1·00
969 $1.15 Nuclear experiment, Chicago, 1942 . . . . . . 80 1·00
970 $1.15 Calder Hall Atomic Power Station, 1956 . . . 80 1·00
971 $1.50 Radar-equipped Ju 88G 7a nightfighter . . . . . . 1·25 1·50
972 $1.50 Boeing E6 A.W.A.C.S. aircraft . . . . 1·25 1·50
973 $1.50 Gloster G.41 Meteor Mk III jet fighter . . . . 1·25 1·50
974 $1.50 Concorde (airliner) . . 1·25 1·50

1995. 50th Anniv of United Nations. Multicoloured.
975 $1.15 Type **177** 90 75
976 $1.50 Open book ("Education") . . . . . . 1·25 1·00
977 $2.30 P.T. class ("Health") 1·75 2·25
978 $3 Dove ("Peace") . . . . . 2·25 3·50
MS979 105×75 mm. $6 Scales ("Justice") . . . . 3·75 6·00

178 Headquarters Building

1995. 25th Anniv of Montserrat National Trust. Multicoloured.
980 $1.15 Type **178** 80 75
981 $1.50 17th-century cannon, Bransby Point . . . . . . 1·25 1·00
982 $2.30 Impression of Galways Sugar Mill (vert) . . . . . 2·25 2·50
983 $3 Great Alps Falls (vert) . . 4·00 5·00

1995. 25th Anniv of Air Recording Studios. No. 713 surch **air 25TH ANNIVERSARY 1970 - 1995.**
984 $2.30+$5 Air Recording Studios . . . . 4·25 5·50
The $5 premium on No. 984 was for relief following a volcanic eruption.

180 Bull Shark

1996. Scavengers of the Sea. Multicoloured.
985 $1 Type **180** 80 70
986 $1.15 Sea mouse 90 80
987 $1.50 Bristleworm . . . . . 1·25 1·50
988 $3.45 Prawn "Xiphocaris" . . 2·50 3·50
MS989 69×95 mm. $4.50 Man of war fish . . . . 3·00 4·00

181 Marconi and Radio Equipment, 1901

1996. Centenary of Radio. Multicoloured.
990 $1.15 Type **181** 90 80
991 $1.50 Marconi's steam yacht "Elettra" . . . . 1·25 1·00
992 $2.30 Receiving first Transatlantic radio message, Newfoundland, 1901 . . . . 1·75 2·25
993 $3 Imperial Airways airplane at Croydon Airport, 1920 2·25 3·50
MS994 74×105 mm. $4.50 Radio telescope, Jodrell Bank . . . . 3·00 4·00

182 Paul Masson (France) (Cycling)

1996. Olympic Games, Atlanta. Gold Medal Winners of 1896. Multicoloured.
995 $1.15 Type **182** 80 80
996 $1.50 Robert Garrett (U.S.A.) (Discus) . . . . . 1·00 1·00
997 $2.30 Spyridon Louis (Greece) (Marathon) . . . 1·50 1·75
998 $3 John Boland (Great Britain) (Tennis) . . . . . 2·00 3·25

183 James Dean

1996. James Dean (film star) Commemoration. Multicoloured.
999 $1.15 Type **183** 80 95
1000 $1.15 Wearing stetson facing right 80 95
1001 $1.15 Wearing blue sweater 80 95
1002 $1.15 Wearing black sweater 80 95
1003 $1.15 Full face portrait wearing stetson 80 95
1004 $1.15 Wearing fawn jacket 80 95
1005 $1.15 Wearing red wind-cheater 80 95
1006 $1.15 Smoking a cigarette 80 95
1007 $1.15 In open-necked shirt and green jumper 80 95
MS1008 169×133 mm. $6 As No. 1000 (51×57 mm) . . . . 4·50 6·00

184 Leprechaun

185 Blue and Green Teddybears

1996. Mythical Creatures. Multicoloured.
1009 5c. Type **184** 10 30
1010 10c. Pegasus 10 30
1011 15c. Griffin 15 30
1012 20c. Unicorn 20 30
1013 25c. Gnomes 25 30
1014 40c. Mermaid 40 40
1015 55c. Cockatrice 50 40
1016 70c. Fairy 65 40
1017 90c. Goblin 80 50
1018 $1 Faun 90 55
1019 $1.15 Dragon . . . . 1·00 65
1020 $1.50 Giant . . . . 1·25 85
1021 $3 Elves . . . . 2·00 2·50
1022 $5 Centaur . . . . 3·25 3·75
1023 $7.50 Phoenix . . . . . . 4·75 6·00
1024 $10 Erin . . . . 5·50 6·50

1996. Jerry Garcia and the Grateful Dead (rock group) Commemoration. Multicoloured.
1025 $1.15 Type **185** . . . . . . 1·00 1·00
1026 $1.15 Green and yellow teddybears . . . . 1·00 1·00
1027 $1.15 Brown and pink teddybears . . . . 1·00 1·00
1028 $6 Jerry Garcia (37×50 mm) . . . . . . 5·50 5·50
Nos. 1025/7 were printed together, se-tenant, forming a composite design.

186 Turkey Vulture

1997. Scavengers of the Sky. Multicoloured.
1029 $1 Type **186** 75 70
1030 $1.15 American crow . . . 90 70
1031 $1.50 Great skua . . . . . 1·25 1·50
1032 $3.45 Black-legged kittiwake ("Kittiwake") . . . . . . 2·25 3·75
MS1033 74×95 mm. $4.50 King vulture . . . . 3·00 4·00

1997. "HONG KONG '97" International Stamp Exhibition. Nos. 1025/7 optd **HONG KONG '97.**
1034 $1.15 Type **185** . . . . . . 70 1·00
1035 $1.15 Green and yellow teddybears . . . . 70 1·00
1036 $1.15 Brown and pink teddybears . . . . 70 1·00

1997. "PACIFIC '97" International Stamp Exhibition, San Francisco. Nos. 999/1007 optd **PACIFIC 97 World Philatelic Exhibition San Francisco, California 29 May - 8 June.**
1037 $1.15 Type **183** 80 95
1038 $1.15 Wearing stetson facing right 80 95
1039 $1.15 Wearing blue sweater 80 95
1040 $1.15 Wearing black sweater 80 95
1041 $1.15 Full-face portrait wearing stetson 80 95
1042 $1.15 Wearing fawn jacket 80 95
1043 $1.15 Wearing red wind-cheater 80 95
1044 $1.15 Smoking a cigarette 80 95
1045 $1.15 In open-necked shirt and green jumper 80 95

189 Heavy Ash Eruption over Plymouth, 1995

1997. Eruption of Soufriere Volcano. Mult.
1046 $1.50 Type **189** . . . . . . 1·10 1·25
1047 $1.50 Burning rock flow entering sea . . . . . . 1·10 1·25
1048 $1.50 Double venting at Castle Peak . . . . . . 1·10 1·25
1049 $1.50 Mangrove cuckoo . . . 1·10 1·25
1050 $1.50 Lava flow at night, 1996 . . . . 1·10 1·25
1051 $1.50 Antillean crested hummingbird . . . . . . 1·10 1·25
1052 $1.50 Ash cloud over Plymouth . . . . 1·10 1·25
1053 $1.50 Lava spine, 1996 . . . 1·10 1·25
1054 $1.50 Burning rock flows forming new land . . . . 1·10 1·25

190 Elvis Presley

1997. Rock Legends. Multicoloured.
1055 $1.15 Type **190** . . . . . . 1·50 1·40
1056 $1.15 Jimi Hendrix . . . . 1·50 1·40
1057 $1.15 Jerry Garcia . . . . . 1·50 1·40
1058 $1.15 Janis Joplin . . . . . 1·50 1·40

191 Untitled Painting by Frama

1997. Frama Exhibition at Guggenheim Museum, New York.
1059 **191** $1.50 multicoloured . . 1·00 1·25

1997. No. 1028 surch **$1.50.**
1060 $1.50 on $6 Jerry Garcia (37×50 mm) . . . . . . 1·00 1·25

193 Prickly Pear

194 Eva and Juan Peron (Argentine politicians)

1998. Medicinal Plants. Multicoloured.
1061 $1 Type **193** 65 50
1062 $1.15 Pomme coolie 70 55
1063 $1.50 Aloe 85 90
1064 $3.45 Bird pepper . . . . . 1·75 2·50

1998. Famous People of the 20th Century. Mult.
1065 $1.15 Type **194** . . . . . . 1·00 1·10
1066 $1.15 Pablo Picasso (painter) 1·00 1·10
1067 $1.15 Wernher von Braun (space scientist) . . . . . 1·00 1·10
1068 $1.15 David Ben Gurion (Israeli statesman) . . . . 1·00 1·10
1069 $1.15 Jean Henri Dunant (founder of Red Cross) 1·00 1·10
1070 $1.15 Dwight Eisenhower (President of U.S.A.) . . 1·00 1·10
1071 $1.15 Mahatma Gandhi (leader of Indian Independence movement) 1·00 1·10
1072 $1.15 King Leopold III and Queen Astrid of Belgium 1·00 1·10
1073 $1.15 Grand Duchess Charlotte and Prince Felix of Luxembourg . . . . . 1·00 1·10
1074 $1.50 Charles Augustus Lindbergh (pioneer aviator) . . . . 1·00 1·10
1075 $1.50 Mao Tse-tung (Chinese communist leader) . . . . 1·00 1·10
1076 $1.50 Earl Mountbatten (last Viceroy of India) . . 1·00 1·10
1077 $1.50 Konrad Adenauer (German statesman) . . . 1·00 1·10
1078 $1.50 Anne Frank (Holocaust victim) . . . . 1·00 1·10
1079 $1.50 Queen Wilhelmina of the Netherlands . . . . . 1·00 1·10
1080 $1.50 King George VI of Great Britain . . . . . . 1·00 1·10
1081 $1.50 King Christian X of Denmark . . . . 1·00 1·10
1082 $1.50 King Haakon VII and Crown Prince Olav of Norway . . . . 1·00 1·10
1083 $1.50 King Alfonso XIII of Spain . . . . 1·00 1·10
1084 $1.50 King Gustavus V of Sweden . . . . 1·00 1·10
MS1085 115×63 mm. $3 John F. Kennedy (Resident of U.S.A.) (50×32 mm) . . . . 1·75 2·50

195 Jerry Garcia

1998. Rock Music Legends. Multicoloured. (a) Jerry Garcia.
1086 $1.15 In long-sleeved blue shirt . . . . 90 1·10
1087 $1.15 With drum kit in background . . . . . . 90 1·10
1088 $1.15 Type **195** . . . . . . 90 1·10
1089 $1.15 Wearing long-sleeved black t-shirt . . . . . . 90 1·10
1090 $1.15 Close-up with left hand in foreground . . . 90 1·10
1091 $1.15 With purple and black background . . . . . . 90 1·10
1092 $1.15 Holding microphone 90 1·10
1093 $1.15 In short-sleeved blue t-shirt . . . . 90 1·10
1094 $1.15 In sunglasses with cymbal in background . . 90 1·10

(b) Bob Marley. Predominant colour for each design given.
1095 $1.15 Pointing (green) . . . 90 1·10
1096 $1.15 Wearing neck chain (green) . . . . 90 1·10
1097 $1.15 Singing into microphone (green) . . . 90 1·10
1098 $1.15 Singing with eyes closed (yellow) . . . . . 90 1·10
1099 $1.15 Facing audience (yellow) . . . . 90 1·10
1100 $1.15 In striped t-shirt with fingers on chin (red) . . . 90 1·10
1101 $1.15 In Rastafarian hat (red) . . . . 90 1·10
1102 $1.15 In striped t-shirt with hand closed (red) . . . . 90 1·10
MS1103 152×101 mm. $5 Jerry Garcia (50×75 mm) . . . . . 2·75 3·50

196 Ash Eruption from Soufriere Hills Volcano

1998. Total Eclipse of the Sun. Multicoloured.
1104 $1.15 Type **196** . . . . . . 1·75 1·50
1105 $1.15 Volcano emitting black cloud . . . . 1·75 1·50
1106 $1.15 Village below volcano 1·75 1·50
1107 $1.15 Lava flow and wrecked house . . . . . 1·75 1·50
MS1108 152×102 mm. $6 Solar eclipse (vert) . . . . 6·00 6·50

197 Princess Diana on Wedding Day, 1981

1998. Diana, Princess of Wales Commemoration. Multicoloured.

1109	$1.15 Type **197**	1·50	70
1110	$1.50 Accepting bouquet from children	1·75	1·10
1111	$3 At Royal Ascot	3·00	4·00
MS1112	133 × 100 mm. $6 Diana and "Princess of Wales" rose (50 × 37 mm)	5·50	5·50

1998. 19th World Scout Jamboree, Chile. Nos. 669/72 optd **19th WORLD JAMBOREE MONDIAL CHILE 1999** and emblem.

1113	20c. Type **117**	30	40
1114	20c. Girl Guide saluting	30	40
1115	75c. Lady Baden-Powell	70	1·00
1116	75c. Guide assisting in old people's home	70	1·00

199 Jerry Garcia

1999. Jerry Garcia (rock musician) Commem. Mult.

1117	$1.15 Type **199**	90	1·00
1118	$1.15 In front of drum kit (violet background)	90	1·00
1119	$1.15 Singing into microphone	90	1·00
1120	$1.15 Playing guitar, facing right (vert)	90	1·00
1121	$1.15 Singing with eyes closed (vert)	90	1·00
1122	$1.15 Singing in white spotlight (vert)	90	1·00
1123	$1.15 In front of drum kit (green background)	90	1·00
1124	$1.15 In long-sleeved black shirt	90	1·00
1125	$1.15 In red shirt	90	1·00
1126	$1.15 In short-sleeved black t-shirt (without frame) (vert)	90	1·00
1127	$1.15 In blue t-shirt (oval frame) (vert)	90	1·00
1128	$1.15 In short-sleeved black t-shirt (oval frame) (vert)	90	1·00
MS1129	Two sheets. (a) 115 × 153 mm. $6 Jerry Garcia in concert (50 × 75 mm). (b) 153 × 115 mm. $6 Singing into microphone (75 × 50 mm) Set of 2 sheets	7·00	8·00

1999. "iBRA '99" International Stamp Exhibition, Nuremberg. Nos. 975/6 optd **iBRA INTERNATIONALE BRIEFMARKEN WELTAUSSTELLUNG NURNBERG 27.4.-4.5.99.**

1130	$1.15 Type **177**	1·50	1·50
1131	$1.50 Open book ("Education")	1·75	2·25

201 Mango

1999. Tropical Caribbean Fruits. Multicoloured.

1132	$1.15 Type **201**	75	70
1133	$1.50 Breadfruit	90	85
1134	$2.30 Papaya	1·40	1·60
1135	$3 Lime	1·75	2·25
1136	$6 Akee	3·50	5·00
MS1137	134 × 95 mm. Nos. 1132/6	8·50	10·00

202 Yorkshire Terrier

1999. Dogs. Each black.

1138	70c. Type **202**	1·10	65
1139	$1 Welsh corgi	1·25	75
1140	$1.15 King Charles spaniel	1·40	85
1141	$1.50 Poodle	1·50	1·25
1142	$3 Beagle	2·75	4·00
MS1143	133 × 95 mm. Nos. 1138/42	8·00	8·50

203 Pupil's Equipment and World Map

1999. World Teachers' Day. Multicoloured.

1144	$1 Type **203**	1·25	70
1145	$1.15 Teacher and class	1·25	80
1146	$1.50 Emblems of vocational training	1·50	1·25
1147	$5 Scientific equipment	5·00	6·50

204 Great Hammerhead Shark

1999. Endangered Species. Great Hammerhead Shark. Multicoloured.

1148	50c. Type **204**	50	60
1149	50c. Two hammerhead sharks among fish	50	60
1150	50c. Two hammerhead sharks on sea-bed	50	60
1151	50c. Three hammerhead sharks	50	60

205 Flowers

2000. New Millennium.

1152	**205**	$1.50 multicoloured	1·50	1·50

206 Alfred Valentine

2000. West Indies Cricket Tour and 100th Test Match at Lord's. Multicoloured.

1153	$1 Type **206**	1·50	60
1154	$5 George Headley batting	3·00	4·00
MS1155	119 × 101 mm. $6 Lord's Cricket Ground (horiz)	5·50	6·00

207 Spitfire Squadron taking-off

2000. "The Stamp Show 2000" International Stamp Exhibition, London. 60th Anniv of Battle of Britain. Multicoloured.

1156	70c. Type **207**	1·00	50
1157	$1.15 Overhauling Hurricane Mk I	1·25	65
1158	$1.50 Hurricane MK I attacking	1·50	1·25
1159	$5 Flt. Lt. Frank Howell's Spitfire Mk IA	3·50	5·00
MS1160	110 × 87 mm. $6 Hawker Hurricane	4·50	5·50

208 Statue of Liberty and Carnival Scene

2000. New Millennium. Landmarks. Each including carnival scene. Multicoloured.

1161	90c. Type **208**	75	50
1162	$1.15 Great Wall of China	95	60
1163	$1.50 Eiffel Tower	1·25	1·25
1164	$3.50 Millennium Dome	2·50	3·50

209 Queen Elizabeth the Queen Mother and W.H. Bramble Airport

2000. Queen Elizabeth the Queen Mother's 100th Birthday. Each showing different portrait. Mult.

1165	70c. Type **209**	85	40
1166	$1.15 Government House	1·25	65
1167	$3 Court House	2·50	2·75
1168	$6 War Memorial Clock Tower	4·50	5·50
MS1169	120 × 75 mm. Nos. 1165/8	8·00	9·00

210 Three Wise Men following Star **211** Golden Swallow

2000. Christmas. Multicoloured.

1170	$1 Type **210**	1·00	55
1171	$1.15 Cavalla Hill Methodist Church	1·10	65
1172	$1.50 Shepherds with flocks	1·25	85
1173	$3 Mary and Joseph arriving at Bethlehem	2·25	2·75
MS1174	105 × 75 mm. $6 As $3	4·50	5·50

2001. Caribbean Birds. Multicoloured.

1175	$1 Type **211**	1·25	65
1176	$1.15 Crested quail dove (horiz)	1·40	75
1177	$1.50 Red-legged thrush (horiz)	1·50	1·10
1178	$5 Fernandina's flicker	4·25	5·50
MS1179	95 × 68 mm. $8 St. Vincent amazon (horiz)	7·00	8·00

212 Edward Stanley Gibbons, Charles J. Phillips and 391 Strand Shop

2001. Famous Stamp Personalities. Multicoloured.

1180	$1 Type **212**	1·10	60
1181	$1.15 John Lister and Montserrat stamps	1·25	70
1182	$1.50 Theodore Champion and French postilion	1·40	1·10
1183	$3 Thomas De La Rue and De La Rue's stand at Great Exhibition, 1851	2·75	3·50
MS1184	95 × 68 mm. $8 Sir Rowland Hill and Bruce Castle	5·50	6·50

213 Princess Elizabeth at International Horse Show, 1950

2001. Queen Elizabeth II's 75th Birthday. Mult.

1185	90c. Type **213**	90	55
1186	$1.15 Queen Elizabeth II, 1986	1·10	70
1187	$1.50 Queen Elizabeth II, 1967	1·25	1·25
1188	$5 Queen Elizabeth, 1976	4·00	4·75
MS1189	90 × 68 mm. $6 Queen Elizabeth, 2000	7·00	7·50

214 Look Out Village

2001. Reconstruction. Multicoloured.

1190	70c. Type **214**	70	50
1191	$1 St. John's Hospital	90	65
1192	$1.15 Tropical Mansions Suites Hotel	1·00	70
1193	$1.50 Montserrat Secondary School	1·25	1·10
1194	$3 Golden Years Care Home	2·75	3·50

215 West Indian Cherry

2001. Caribbean Fruits. Multicoloured.

1195	5c. Type **215**	10	10
1196	10c. Mammee apple	10	10
1197	15c. Lime	10	10
1198	20c. Grapefruit	10	15
1199	25c. Orange	10	15
1200	40c. Passion fruit	15	20
1201	55c. Banana	20	25
1202	70c. Pawpaw	30	35
1203	90c. Pomegranate	35	40
1204	$1 Guava	40	45
1205	$1.15 Mango	45	50
1206	$1.50 Sugar apple	60	65
1207	$3 Cashew	1·20	1·30
1208	$5 Soursop	2·00	2·10
1209	$7.50 Watermelon	3·00	3·25
1210	$10 Pineapple	4·00	4·25

216 Common Long-tail Skipper (butterfly)

2001. Caribbean Butterflies. Multicoloured.

1211	$1 Type **216**	90	60
1212	$1.15 Straight-line sulphur	1·00	70
1213	$1.50 Giant hairstreak	1·25	1·10
1214	$3 Monarch	2·00	2·75
MS1215	115 × 115 mm. $10 Painted Lady	7·00	8·00

The overall design of No. **MS**1215 is butterfly-shaped

217 Alpine Skiing

2002. Winter Olympic Games, Salt Lake City. Mult.

1216	$3 Type **217**	2·25	2·50
1217	$5 Four man bobsleigh	3·25	3·75

218 Sergeant Major (fish)

2002. Fishes of the Caribbean. Multicoloured.

1218	$1 Type **218**	90	55
1219	$1.15 Mutton snapper	1·00	60
1220	$1.50 Lantern bass	1·25	1·00
1221	$5 Shy Hamlet	4·75	5·50
MS1222	102 × 70 mm. $8 Queen angelfish	7·00	7·50

2002. Queen Elizabeth the Queen Mother Commemoration. Nos. 1165/8 optd **Life and Death of Her Majesty Queen Elizabeth The Queen Mother 1900 2002.**

1223	70c. Type **209**	70	40
1224	$1.15 Government House	1·00	60
1225	$3 Court House	2·75	2·75
1226	$6 War Memorial Clock Tower	4·75	5·50

220 *Allamanda cathartica*

2002. Wild Flowers. Multicoloured.
1227 70c. Type **220** 30 35
1228 $1.15 *Lantana camara* . . . 45 50
1229 $1.50 *Leonotis nepetifolia* . . 60 65
1230 $5 *Plumeria rubra* . . . . . 2·00 2·25
MS1231 105 × 75 mm. $8 *Alpinia purpurata* . . . . 3·25 3·50

221 Queen Elizabeth II wearing Imperial State Crown and Coronation Robes

223 Prince William

222 *Wright Flyer II* (blue)

2003. 50th Anniv of Coronation. Two sheets containing vert designs as T **221**. Multicoloured.
MS1232 153 × 85 mm. $3 Type **221**; $3 St. Edward's Crown; $3 Queen wearing diadem and blue sash . . . 3·75 4·00
MS1233 105 × 75 mm. $6 Queen wearing Imperial State Crown and Coronation robes . . . . . . 2·40 2·50

2003. Centenary of Powered Flight. Multicoloured.
MS1234 116 × 125 mm. $2 Type **222**; $2 Wright *Flyer II* (brown); $2 Orville and Wilbur Wright; $2 Wright *Flyer I* . . . . 2·40 2·50
MS1235 106 × 76 mm. $6 Wright *Flyer II* . . . . 2·40 2·50

2003. 21st Birthday of Prince William of Wales. Different portraits. Multicoloured.
MS1236 155 × 85 mm. $3 Type **223**; $3 Prince William (frame incomplete at bottom left); $3 Prince William (frame complete at bottom left) . . . . 3·75 4·00
MS1237 106 × 76 mm. $6 Prince William . . . . 2·40 2·50

224 Piping Frog

2003. Animals of the Caribbean. Multicoloured.
MS1238 145 × 90 mm. $1.50 Type **224**; $1.50 Land hermit crab; $1.50 Spix's pinche; $1.50 Dwarf Ggecko; $1.50 Green sea turtle; $1.50 Small Indian mongoose . . 3·75 9·00
MS1239 92 × 66 mm. $6 Sally lightfoot crab . . . . 2·40 2·50

225 *Lactarius trivialis*

2003. Mushrooms of the World. Multicoloured.
MS1240 145 × 90 mm. $1.50 Type **225**; $1.50 *Gomphidius roseus*; $1.50 *Lycoperdon pyriforme*; $1.50 *Hygrophorus coccineus*; $1.50 *Russula xerampelina*; $1.50 *Gomphus floccosus* . . . . 3·75 4·00
MS1241 92 × 66 mm. $6 *Amanita muscaria* . . . . 2·40 2·50

226 Belted Kingfisher

2003. Birds of the Caribbean. Multicoloured.
1242 90c. Type **226** 35 35
1243 $1.15 Yellow warbler . . . 45 50
1244 $1.50 Hooded warbler . . . 60 65
1245 $5 Cedar waxwing . . . . 2·00 2·10
MS1246 145 × 90 mm. $1.50 Roseate spoonbill; $1.50 Laughing gull; $1.50 White-tailed tropic bird; $1.50 Bare-eyed thrush; $1.50 Glittering-throated emerald; $1.50 Carib grackle ("Lesser Antillean Grackle") . . . . 3·75 4·00
MS1247 92 × 68 mm. $6 Bananaquit 2·40 2·50

227 Olympic Poster, Los Angeles, 1932

2004. Olympic Games, Athens. Multicoloured.
1248 90c. Type **227** 35 40
1249 $1.15 Olympic pin, Munich, 1972 . . . . 45 50
1250 $1.50 Olympic poster, Montreal, 1976 . . . . . 60 65
1251 $5 Greek art depicting Pankration (horiz) . . . . 2·00 2·10

228 Singapura

2004. Cats. Multicoloured.
1252 $1.15 Type **228** 45 50
1253 $1.50 Burmese 60 65
1254 $2 Abyssinian 80 85
1255 $5 Norwegian . . . . . . 2·00 2·10
MS1256 92 × 68 mm. $6 Russian blue . . . . 2·40 2·50

229 Lace Wing

2004. Butterflies. Multicoloured.
MS1257 125 × 88 mm. $2.30 Type **229**; $2.30 Swallowtail; $2.30 Shoemaker; $2.30 White peacock 3·50 3·75
MS1258 70 × 96 mm. $6 Flashing astraptes . . . . 2·40 2·50

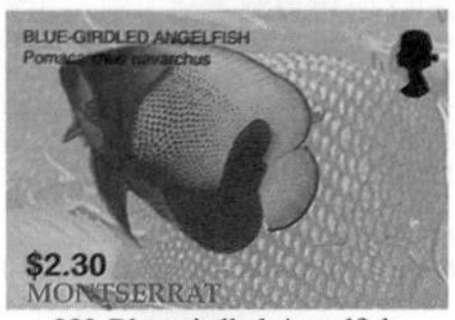

230 Blue-girdled Angelfish

2004. Fish. Multicoloured.
MS1259 122 × 93 mm. $2.30 Type **230**; $2.30 Regal angelfish; $2.30 Emperor angelfish; $2.30 Blotch-eye soldierfish . . . . . 3·50 3·75
MS1260 70 × 96 mm. $6 Banded butterflyfish . . . . 2·40 2·50

231 Austerity Steam Locomotive

2004. Bicentenary of Steam Locomotives. Multicoloured.
MS1261 159 × 120 mm. $1.50 Type **231**; $1.50 Deli Vasut No. 109.109; $1.50 Class 424 No. 424.247/287; $1.50 L1646; $1.50 No. 324.1564; $1.50 Class 204 . . . . 3·50 3·75
MS1262 119 × 159 mm. $2 375.562 Old Class TV; $2 Class Va 7111; $2 Class 424 No. 424.009; $2 Class III No. 269 . . . . 3·25 3·50
MS1263 92 × 106 mm. $6 Class QR1 No. 3038 . . . . 2·40 2·50

232 AIDS Ribbon

2004. World AIDS Day. Sheet 123 × 95 mm.
MS1264 **232** $3 × 4 multicoloured 4·75 5·00

233 National Football Team

2004. Centenary of FIFA (Federation Internationale de Football Association).
1265 **233** $6 multicoloured . . . . 2·40 2·50

234 Start of Air Assault

2004. 60th Anniv of D-Day Landings. Multicoloured.
1266 $1.15 Type **234** 45 50
1267 $1.50 Soldiers landing on Normandy beaches . . . 60 65
1268 $2 Field Marshall Montgomery 80 85
1269 $5 HMS *Belfast* . . . . . . 2·00 2·10

OFFICIAL STAMPS

1976. Various stamps, some already surch, optd **O.H.M.S.**
O1 5c. multicoloured (No. 246) † 65
O2 10c. multicoloured (No. 247) † 75
O3 30c. on 10c. mult (No. 369) † 1·50
O4 45c. on 3c. mult (No. 370) . . † 2·00
O5 $5 multicoloured (No. 254) † £100
O6 $10 multicoloured (No. 254a) † £550

These stamps were issued for use on mail from the Montserrat Philatelic Bureau. They were not sold to the public, either unused or used.

1976. Nos. 372, 374/82, 384/5 and 476 optd **O.H.M.S.** or surch also.
O17 5c. Malay apple . . . . . . † 10
O28 5c. on 3c. Lignum vitae . . † 20
O18 10c. Jacaranda . . . . . . † 10
O19 15c. Orchid tree . . . . . . † 10
O20 20c. Manjak . . . . † 10
O21 25c. Tamarind . . . . . . † 15
O33 30c. on 15c. Orchid tree . . † 30
O34 35c. on 2c. Cannon-ball tree † 30
O35 40c. Flame of the forest . . † 40
O22 55c. Pink cassia . . . . . † 35
O23 70c. Long john . . . . . . † 45
O24 $1 Saman . . . . † 60
O39 $2.50 on 40c. Flame of the forest . . . . † 2·00
O25 $5 Yellow poui . . . . . . † 1·50
O16 $10 Flamboyant . . . . . . † 3·75

1981. Nos. 490/4, 496, 498, 500, 502/3 and 505 optd **O.H.M.S.**
O42 5c. Type **91** 10 10
O43 10c. Hogfish and neon goby 10 10
O44 15c. Creole wrasse 10 10
O45 20c. Three-spotted damselfish 15 15
O46 25c. Sergeant major 15 15
O47 45c. Schoolmaster 25 20
O48 65c. Bigeye 35 30
O49 $1 Rock beauty 65 65
O50 $3 Royal gramma ("Fairy basslet") and blueheads . . 1·50 1·75
O51 $5 Cherub angelfish . . . . 2·00 2·25
O52 $10 Caribbean long-nosed butterflyfish . . . . 3·00 2·25

1983. Nos. 510/15 surch **O.H.M.S.** and value.
O53 45c. on 90c. "Charlotte" . . 20 30
O54 45c. on 90c. Prince Charles and Lady Diana Spencer 60 1·00
O55 75c. on $3 "Portsmouth" . . 25 35
O56 75c. on $3 Prince Charles and Lady Diana Spencer 90 1·40
O57 $1 on $4 "Britannia" 35 50
O58 $1 on $4 Prince Charles and Lady Diana Spencer . . . 1·00 1·50

1983. Nos. 542/4 surch **O.H.M.S.**
O59 70c. on 75c. Type **97** . . . 60 40
O60 $1 Coat of Arms of Catherine of Aragon . . . 70 50
O61 $1.50 on $5 Diana, Princess of Wales . . . . 1·00 80

1985. Nos. 600/12 and 614 optd **O H M S.**
O62 5c. Type **107** . . . . 1·25 1·00
O63 10c. Carib grackle . . . . . 1·25 1·00
O64 15c. Moorhen . . . . 1·50 1·00
O65 20c. Brown booby . . . . . 1·50 70
O66 25c. Black-whiskered vireo 1·50 70
O67 40c. Scaly-breasted thrasher 2·00 70
O68 55c. Laughing gull . . . . . 2·25 70
O69 70c. Glossy ibis . . . . . . 2·50 90
O70 90c. Green-backed heron . . 2·75 90
O71 $1 Belted kingfisher . . . . 2·75 90
O72 $1.15 Bananaquit . . . . . 3·00 90
O73 $3 American kestrel . . . . 4·50 2·50
O74 $5 Forest thrush . . . . . . 5·50 2·50
O75 $10 Bridled quail dove . . . 7·00 2·50

1989. Nos. 757/70 and 772 optd **O H M S.**
O76 5c. Type **133** 40 60
O77 10c. Little knobbed scallop 40 60
O78 15c. Sozoni's cone 50 60
O79 20c. Globular coral shell . . 55 50
O80 25c. American or common sundial 55 50
O81 40c. King helmet 60 55
O82 55c. Channelled turban . . . 70 50
O83 70c. True tulip shell 90 75
O84 90c. Music volute . . . . . 1·00 90
O85 $1 Flame auger . . . . . . 1·00 80
O86 $1.15 Rooster-tail conch . . 1·25 85
O87 $1.50 Queen or pink conch 1·40 1·40
O88 $3 Teramachi's slit shell . . 2·00 2·50
O89 $5 Common or Florida crown conch . . . . . . 3·25 3·25
O90 $10 Atlantic trumpet triton 5·50 5·50

1989. Nos. 578 and 580/1 surch **OHMS.**
O91 70c. on 10c. Hogfish and neon goby . . . . 2·00 1·75
O92 $1.15 on 75c. French grunt 2·50 1·75
O93 $1.50 on $2 Blue chromis . . 2·75 3·00

1992. Nos. 838/41, 847/50, 856/9 surch or optd **OHMS.**
O 94 70c. on 90c. Type **150** . . 1·40 1·40
O 95 70c. on 90c. Type **152** . . 1·40 1·40
O 96 70c. on 90c. Type **154** . . 1·40 1·40
O 97 70c. on $3.50 French grunt 1·40 1·40
O 98 $1 on $3.50 Helmeted guineafowl . . . . 1·50 1·50
O 99 $1 on $3.50 Anthurium . . 1·50 1·50
O100 $1.15 Cushion star . . . . 1·50 1·50
O101 $1.15 Hen and chicks . . . 1·50 1·50
O102 $1.15 Shell ginger . . . . . 1·50 1·50
O103 $1.50 Rock beauty . . . . 1·60 1·60
O104 $1.50 Red junglefowl . . . 1·60 1·60
O105 $1.50 Early day lily . . . 1·60 1·60

1993. Nos. 889/902 and 904 optd **OHMS.**
O106 5c. Type **161** 60 80
O107 10c. "Gryllus campestris" (field cricket) 60 80
O108 15c. "Lepthemis vesiculosa" (dragonfly) 70 80
O109 20c. "Orthemis ferruginea" (red skimmer) 70 60
O110 25c. "Gerris lacustris" (pond skater) 70 60
O111 40c. "Byctiscus betulae" (leaf weevil) 85 40
O112 55c. "Atta texana" (leaf-cutter ants) 90 40
O113 70c. "Polistes fuscatus" (paper wasp) . . . . . . 1·00 70
O114 90c. "Sparmopolius fulvus" (bee fly) . . . . 1·10 70
O115 $1 "Chrysopa carnea" (lace wing) . . . . 1·25 70
O116 $1.15 "Phoebis philea" (butterfly) . . . . 2·00 1·50
O117 $1.50 "Cynthia cardui" (butterfly) . . . . 2·25 2·25
O118 $3 "Utetheisa bella" (moth) 3·00 3·50
O119 $5 "Alucita pentadactyla" (moth) . . . . 3·75 4·25
O120 $10 "Heliconius melpomene" (butterfly) 6·00 6·50

1997. Nos. 1009/22 and 1024 optd **O.H.M.S.**

O121	5c. Type **184**	15	50
O122	10c. Pegasus	25	50
O123	15c. Griffin	35	50
O124	20c. Unicorn	35	50
O125	25c. Gnomes	35	50
O126	40c. Mermaid	50	50
O127	55c. Cockatrice	60	50
O128	70c. Fairy	70	55
O129	90c. Goblin	90	60
O130	$1 Faun	1·00	60
O131	$1.15 Dragon	1·25	65
O132	$1.50 Giant	1·40	85
O133	$3 Elves	2·50	2·75
O134	$5 Centaur	4·00	4·25
O135	$10 Erin	6·00	6·50

2002. Nos. 1195/1208 and 1210 optd **OHMS**.

O137	5c. Type **215**	10	10
O138	10c. Mammee apple	10	10
O139	15c. Lime	10	10
O140	20c. Grapefruit	10	15
O141	25c. Orange	10	15
O142	40c. Passion fruit	15	20
O143	55c. Banana	20	25
O144	70c. Pawpaw	30	35
O145	90c. Pomegranate	35	40
O146	$1 Guava	40	45
O147	$1.15 Mango	45	50
O148	$1.50 Sugar apple	60	65
O149	$3 Cashew	1·20	1·30
O150	$5 Soursop	2·00	2·10
O151	$10 Pineapple	4·00	4·25

MOROCCO Pt. 13

An independent kingdom, established in 1956, comprising the former French and Spanish International Zones.

A. NORTHERN ZONE

100 centimes = 1 peseta.

1 Sultan of Morocco

2 Polytechnic

1956.

1	**1**	10c. brown	10	10
2	–	15c. brown	10	10
3	**2**	25c. violet	10	10
4	–	50c. green	25	25
5	**1**	80c. green	90	90
6	–	2p. lilac	7·50	7·50
7	**2**	3p. blue	15·00	15·00
8	–	10p. green	31·00	31·00

DESIGNS—HORIZ: 15c., 2p. Villa Sanjurjo harbour. VERT: 50c., 10p. Cultural Delegation building, Tetuan.

3 Lockheed Super Constellation over Lau Dam

1956. Air.

9	**3**	25c. purple	20	15
10	–	1p.40 mauve	90	60
11	**3**	3p.40 red	1·90	1·50
12	–	4p.80 purple	3·50	2·50

DESIGN: 1p.40, 4p.80, Lockheed Super Constellation over Rio Nekor Bridge.

1957. 1st Anniv of Independence. As T **7** but with Spanish inscriptions and currency.

13	80c. green	65	50
14	1p.50 olive	1·90	1·40
15	3p. red	4·25	3·25

1957. As T **5** but with Spanish inscriptions and currency.

16	30c. indigo and blue	10	10
17	70c. purple and brown	20	10
18	80c. purple	1·60	40
19	1p.50 lake and green	50	15
20	3p. green	75	50
21	7p. red	5·25	1·50

1957. Investiture of Prince Moulay el Hassan. As T **9** but with Spanish inscriptions and currency.

22	80c. blue	65	25
23	1p.50 green	1·60	80
24	3p. red	4·75	2·50

1957. Nos. 17 and 19 surch.

25	15c. on 70c. purple and brown	75	75
26	1p.20 on 1p.50 lake and green	1·40	1·40

1957. 30th Anniv of Coronation of Sultan Sidi Mohammed ben Yusuf. As T **10** but with Spanish inscription and currency.

27	1p.20 green and black	65	50
28	1p.80 red and black	90	75
29	3p. violet and black	1·60	1·50

B. SOUTHERN ZONE

100 centimes = 1 franc.

5 Sultan of Morocco

6 Classroom

1956.

30	**5**	5f. indigo and blue	20	10
31		10f. sepia and brown	15	10
32		15f. lake and green	25	10
33		25f. purple	1·10	10
34		30f. green	1·90	10
35		50f. red	3·00	15
36		70f. brown and sepia	4·25	60

1956. Education Campaign.

37	–	10f. violet and purple	1·90	1·25
38	–	15f. lake and red	2·40	1·50
39	**6**	20f. green and turquoise	2·50	2·50
40	–	30f. red and lake	4·50	2·75
41	–	50f. blue and indigo	7·50	5·00

DESIGNS: 10f. Peasants reading book; 15f. Two girls reading; 30f. Child reading to old man; 50f. Child teaching parents the alphabet.

7 Sultan of Morocco

8 Emblem over Casablanca

1957. 1st Anniv of Independence.

42	**7**	15f. green	1·60	1·25
43		25f. olive	2·25	1·25
44		30f. red	4·00	1·90

1957. Air. International Fair, Casablanca.

45	**8**	15f. green and red	1·25	1·00
46		25f. turquoise	2·25	1·40
47		30f. brown	2·75	1·75

9 Crown Prince Moulay el Hassan

10 King Mohammed V

1957. Investiture of Crown Prince Moulay el Hassan.

48	**9**	15f. blue	1·50	95
49		25f. green	1·75	1·25
50		30f. red	2·75	1·60

1957. 30th Anniv of Coronation of King Mohammed V.

51	**10**	15f. green and black	95	50
52		25f. red and black	1·50	1·00
53		30f. violet and black	1·60	1·10

C. ISSUES FOR THE WHOLE OF MOROCCO

1958. 100 centimes = 1 franc.
1962. 100 francs = 1 dirham.

11 Moroccan Pavilion

1958. Brussels International Exhibition.

54	**11**	15f. turquoise	25	20
55		25f. red	25	25
56		30f. blue	35	30

12 King Mohammed V and UNESCO Headquarters, Paris

1958. Inauguration of UNESCO Headquarters Building, Paris.

57	**12**	15f. green	25	20
58		25f. lake	25	25
59		30f. blue	35	30

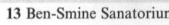

13 Ben-Smine Sanatorium

14 King Mohammed V on Horseback

1959. "National Aid".

60	**13**	50f. bistre, green and red	70	35

1959. King Mohammed V's 50th Birthday.

61	**14**	15f. lake	65	30
62		25f. blue	95	35
63		45f. green	1·10	45

15 Princess Lalla Amina

16

1959. Children's Week.

64	**15**	15f. blue	25	20
65		25f. green	30	25
66		45f. purple	60	30

1960. Meeting of U.N. African Economic Commission, Tangier.

67	**16**	45f. green, brown and violet	1·10	50

(17)

18 Arab Refugees

1960. Adulterated Cooking Oil Victims Relief Fund. Surch as T **17**.

68	**5**	5f.+10f. indigo and blue	35	30
69		10f.+10f. sepia and brown	70	45
70		15f.+10f. lake and green	1·25	95
71		25f.+15f. purple	1·40	1·10
72		30f.+20f. green	2·25	2·00

1960. World Refugee Year.

73	**18**	15f. black, green and ochre	25	20
74	–	45f. green and black	65	35

DESIGNS: 45f. "Uprooted tree" and Arab refugees.

19 Marrakesh

20 Lantern

1960. 900th Anniv of Marrakesh.

75	**19**	100f. green, brown and blue	1·40	95

1960. 1100th Anniv of Karaouiyne University.

76	**20**	15f. purple	60	50
77	–	25f. blue	65	55
78	–	30f. brown	1·25	60
79	–	35f. black	1·60	80
80	–	45f. green	2·25	1·40

DESIGNS: 25f. Fountain; 30f. Minaret; 35f. Frescoes; 45f. Courtyard.

21 Arab League Centre and King Mohammed V

1960. Inauguration of Arab League Centre, Cairo.

81	**21**	15f. black and green	20	20

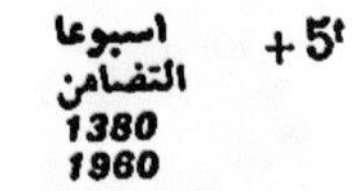

(22)

23 Wrestling

1960. Solidarity Fund. Nos. 458/9 (Mahakma, Casablanca) of French Morocco surch as T **22**.

82	**106**	15f.+3f. on 18f. myrtle	55	55
83		+5f. on 20f. lake	80	80

1960. Olympic Games.

84	**23**	5f. purple, green and violet	10	10
85	–	10f. chocolate, blue & brown	15	10
86	–	15f. brown, blue and green	20	15
87	–	20f. purple, blue and bistre	25	20
88	–	30f. brown, violet and red	30	25
89	–	40f. brown, blue and violet	60	25
90	–	45f. blue, green and purple	75	35
91	–	70f. black, blue and brown	1·40	45

DESIGNS: 10f. Gymnastics; 15f. Cycling; 20f. Weightlifting; 30f. Running; 40f. Boxing; 45f. Sailing; 70f. Fencing.

24 Runner

25 Post Office and Letters

1961. 3rd Pan-Arab Games, Casablanca.

92	**24**	20f. green	20	15
93		30f. lake	65	20
94		50f. blue	75	60

1961. African Postal and Telecommunications Conference, Tangier.

95	**25**	20f. purple and mauve	35	30
96	–	30f. turquoise and green	45	35
97	–	90f. ultramarine and blue	85	60

DESIGNS—VERT: 30f. Telephone operator. HORIZ: 90f. Sud Aviation Caravelle mail plane over Tangier.

26 King Mohammed V and African Map

27 Lumumba and Congo Map

1962. 1st Anniv of African Charter of Casablanca.

98	**26**	20f. purple and buff	20	20
99		30f. indigo and blue	25	25

1962. Patrice Lumumba Commemoration.

100	**27**	20f. black and bistre	20	20
101		30f. black and brown	30	25

28 King Hassan II

29 "Pupils of the Nation"

1962. Air.

102	**28**	90f. black	75	15
103		1d. red	90	15
104		2d. blue	1·10	45
105		3d. green	2·25	1·10
106		5d. violet	4·50	1·60

1962. Children's Education.
107 **29** 20f. blue, red and green . . 35 25
108 30f. sepia, brown and green 40 35
109 90f. blue, purple and green 90 50

1962. Arab League Week. As T **76** of Libya.
110 20f. brown 20 15

30 King Hassan II

31 Scout with Banner

1962.
111 **30** 1f. olive 10 10
112 2f. violet 10 10
113 5f. sepia 10 10
114 10f. brown 10 10
115 15f. turquoise 15 10
116 20f. purple (18 × 22 mm) 20 10
116a 20f. purple (17½ × 23½ mm) 30 10
116b 25f. red 20 10
117 30f. green 25 10
117a 35f. slate 65 10
117b 40f. blue 65 10
118 50f. purple 80 10
118a 60f. purple . . . . 1·10 10
119 70f. blue . . . . 1·25 10
120 80f. lake . . . . 2·10 15

1962. 5th Arab Scout Jamboree, Rabat.
121 **31** 20f. purple and blue . . . 20 15

32 Campaign Emblem and Swamp

33 Aquarium, Brown Trout and Fish

1962. Malaria Eradication Campaign.
122 **32** 20f. blue and green 20 15
123 – 50f. lake and green 35 25
DESIGN—VERT: 50f. Sword piercing mosquito.

1962. Casablanca Aquarium. Multicoloured.
124 20f. Type **33** 85 25
125 30f. Aquarium and Mediterranean moray . . . 90 25

34 Mounted Postman and 1912 Sherifian Stamp

فيضانات
1
9
6
3
20 + 5
(35)

1962. First National Philatelic Exhibition, Rabat, and Stamp Day.
126 **34** 20f. green and brown . . . 75 35
127 – 30f. black and red 90 40
128 – 50f. bistre and blue . . . . 1·25 50
DESIGNS: 30f. Postman and circular postmark; 50f. Sultan Hassan I and octagonal postmark. (Both stamps commemorate 70th anniv of Sherifian post.)

1963. Flood Relief Fund. Surch as T **35**.
129 **5** 20+5f. on 5f. indigo & bl . . 90 85
130 30+10f. on 50f. red . . . . 1·00 85

36 King Moulay Ismail

37 Ibn Batota (voyager)

1963. 300th Anniv of Meknes.
131 **36** 20f. sepia 25 20

1963. "Famous Men of Maghreb".
132 **37** 20f. purple 45 20
133 – 20f. black 45 20
134 – 20f. myrtle 25 25
134a **37** 40f. blue 30 10
PORTRAITS: No. 133, Ibn Khaldoun (historian); 134, Al Idrissi (geographer).

38 Sugar Beet and Refinery

39 Isis (bas relief)

1963. Freedom from Hunger.
135 **38** 20f. black, brown and green 25 20
136 – 50f. black, brown and blue 65 35
DESIGN—VERT: 50f. Fisherman and tuna.

1963. Nubian Monuments Preservation.
137 – 20f. black and grey 20 15
138 **39** 30f. violet 25 25
139 – 50f. purple 60 35
DESIGNS—HORIZ: 20f. Heads of Colossi, Abu Simbel; 50f. Philae Temple.

40 Agadir before Earthquake

1963. Reconstruction of Agadir.
140 **40** 20f. red and blue 35 35
141 30f. red and blue 45 35
142 – 50f. red and blue 80 40
DESIGNS: 30f. is optd with large red cross and date of earthquake, 29th February, 1960; 50f. Reconstructed Agadir.

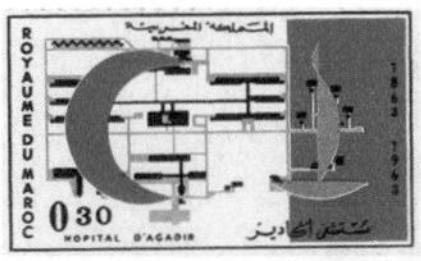
41 Plan of new Agadir Hospital

42 Emblems of Morocco and Rabat

1963. Centenary of International Red Cross.
143 **41** 30f. multicoloured 50 20

1963. Opening of Parliament.
144 **42** 20f. multicoloured 45 20

43 Hands breaking Chain

44 National Flag

1963. 15th Anniv of Declaration of Human Rights.
145 **43** 20f. brown, sepia and green 45 20

1963. Evacuation of Foreign Troops from Morocco.
146 **44** 20f. red, green and black 25 25

45 "Moulay Abdurrahman" (after Delacroix)

1964. 3rd Anniv of King Hassan's Coronation.
147 **45** 1d. multicoloured . . . . 2·75 1·90

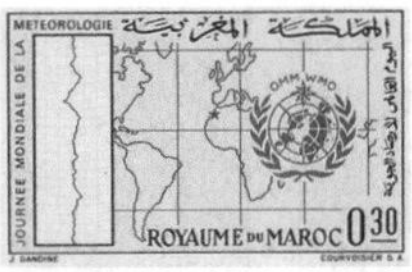
46 Map, Chart and W.M.O. Emblem

1964. World Meteorological Day. Multicoloured.
148 20f. African weather map (vert) (postage) 25 20
149 30f. Type **46** 40 35
150 90f. Globe and weather vane (vert) (air) 90 45

47 Fair Entrance

1964. Air. 20th Anniv of Casablanca Int Fair.
151 **47** 1d. red, drab and blue . . 95 60

48 Moroccan Pavilion at Fair

1964. Air. New York World's Fair.
152 **48** 1d. multicoloured . . . . 1·25 65

49 Children Playing in the Sun

50 Olympic Torch

1964. Postal Employees' Holiday Settlements.
153 **49** 20f. multicoloured 25 20
154 – 30f. multicoloured 35 25
DESIGN: 30f. Boy, girl and holiday settlement.

1964. Olympic Games, Tokyo.
155 **50** 20f. green, violet and red 25 25
156 30f. purple, blue and green 35 30
157 50f. red, blue and green . . 75 35

51 Lighthouse and Sultan Mohamed ben Abdurrahman (founder)

52 Tangier Iris

1964. Centenary of Cape Spartel Lighthouse.
158 **51** 25f. multicoloured 55 45

1965. Flowers. Multicoloured.
159 25f. Type **52** . . . . 1·00 45
160 40f. Gladiolus (vert) . . . . 1·25 55
161 60f. Caper (horiz) . . . . . 1·90 1·40

53 Return of King Mohammed

54 Early Telegraph Receiver

1965. 10th Anniv of Return of King Mohammed V from Exile.
162 **53** 25f. green 50 20

1965. Centenary of I.T.U. Multicoloured.
163 25f. Type **54** 20 20
164 40f. "TIROS" weather satellite 35 30

55 I.C.Y. Emblem

59 Corn

1965. International Co-operation Year.
165 **55** 25f. black and green . . . 25 20
166 60f. lake 40 35

1965. Sea Shells. As T **52**. Mult, background colours given.
167 25f. violet 55 25
168 25f. blue 55 25
169 25f. yellow 55 25
SEASHELLS: No. 167, Knobbed triton ("Charonia nodifera"); 168, Smooth callista ("Pitaria chione"); 169, "Cymbium tritonis".

1965. Shellfish. As T **52**. Multicoloured.
170 25f. Helmet crab 70 50
171 40f. Mantis shrimp . . . . . 1·60 95
172 1d. Royal prawn (horiz) . . . 2·25 1·40

1965. Orchids. As T **52**. Multicoloured.
173 25f. "Ophrys speculum" (vert) 60 45
174 40f. "Ophrys fusca" (vert) . . 95 50
175 60f. "Ophrys tenthredinifera" (horiz) . . . . 1·75 1·25

1966. Agricultural Products (1st issue).
176 **59** 25f. black and ochre . . . 20 15
See also Nos. 188/9 and 211.

60 Flag, Map and Dove

1966. 10th Anniv of Independence.
177 **60** 25f. red and green 20 15

61 King Hassan II and Crown

1966. 5th Anniv of King Hassan's Coronation.
178 **61** 25f. blue, green and red . . 20 15

62 Cross-country Runner

1966. 53rd "Cross des Nations" (Cross-country Race).
179 **62** 25f. green 20 15

63 W.H.O. Building

1966. Inaug of W.H.O. Headquarters, Geneva.
180 **63** 25f. black and purple . . . 20 15
181 – 40f. black and blue 25 20
DESIGN: 40f. W.H.O. Building (different view).

64 King Hassan and Parachutist

65 Brooch

1966. 10th Anniv of Royal Armed Forces.
182 **64** 25f. black and gold 60 25
183 – 40f. black and gold 60 25
DESIGN: 40f. Crown Prince Hassan kissing hand of King Mohammed.

1966. Palestine Week. As No. 110 but inscr "SEMAINE DE LA PALESTINE" at foot and dated "1966".
184 25f. blue 20 15

1966. Red Cross Seminar. Moroccan Jewellery. Multicoloured.
185 25f.+5f. Type **65** 90 45
186 40f.+10f. Pendant . . . . . 1·25 55
See also Nos. 203/4, 246/7, 274/5, 287/8, 303/4, 324/5, 370/1, 397/8, 414/15, 450/1 and 493.

66 Rameses II, Abu Simbel

67 Class XDd Diesel Train

1966. Air. 20th Anniv of UNESCO.
187 **66** 1d. red and yellow . . . . 1·25 75

1966. Agricultural Products (2nd and 3rd issue). As T **59**.
188 40f. multicoloured 25 10
189 60f. multicoloured 35 20
DESIGNS—VERT: 40f. Citrus fruits. HORIZ: 60f. Olives.

1966. Moroccan Transport. Multicoloured.
190 25f. Type **67** (postage) . . . 1·50 60
191 40f. Liner "Maroc" 80 40
192 1d. Tourist coach 95 60
193 3d. Sud Aviation Caravelle of Royal Air Maroc (48 × 27½ mm) (air) . . . . 4·50 1·90

68 Twaite Shad

1967. Fishes. Multicoloured.
194 25f. Type **68** . . . . 1·10 25
195 40f. Plain bonito . . . . . . 1·40 30
196 1d. Bluefish . . . . 3·00 1·40

69 Hilton Hotel, Ancient Ruin and Map

1967. Opening of Hilton Hotel, Rabat.
197 **69** 25f. black and blue 20 15
198 1d. purple and blue 50 20

70 Ait Aadel Dam

1967. Inauguration of Ait Aadel Dam.
199 **70** 25f. grey, blue and green 25 15
200 40f. bistre and blue 65 20

71 Moroccan Scene and Lions Emblem

1967. 50th Anniv of Lions International.
201 **71** 40f. blue and gold 50 20
202 1d. green and gold . . . . 1·00 25

1967. Moroccan Red Cross. As T **65**. Mult.
203 60f.+5f. Necklace 95 95
204 1d.+10f. Two bracelets . . . 1·90 1·90

72 Three Hands and Pickaxe

73 I.T.Y. Emblem

1967. Communal Development Campaign.
205 **72** 25f. green 20 15

1967. International Tourist Year.
206 **73** 1d. blue and cobalt 80 35

74 Arrow and Map

75 Horse-jumping

1967. Mediterranean Games, Tunis.
207 **74** 25f. multicoloured 25 20
208 40f. multicoloured 30 20

1967. International Horse Show.
209 **75** 40f. multicoloured 30 20
210 1d. multicoloured 75 35

1967. Agricultural Products (4th issue). As T **59**.
211 40f. mult (Cotton plant) . . . 65 15

76 Human Rights Emblem

77 Msouffa Woman

1968. Human Rights Year.
212 **76** 25f. slate 20 20
213 1d. lake 35 25

1968. Moroccan Costumes. Multicoloured.
214 10f. Ait Moussa or Ali . . . 65 25
215 15f. Ait Mouhad 90 30
216 25f. Barquemaster of Rabat-Sale . . . . 1·00 35
217 25f. Townsman . . . . . . 1·90 75
218 40f. Townswoman . . . . . 1·10 45
219 60f. Royal Mokhazni . . . . 1·50 60
220 1d. Type **77** . . . . 1·50 95
221 1d. Riff . . . . 1·50 95
222 1d. Zemmour woman . . . . 1·90 1·25
223 1d. Meknassa . . . . 1·90 60

78 King Hassan

79 Red Crescent Nurse and Child

1968.
224 **78** 1f. multicoloured 10 10
225 2f. multicoloured 10 10
226 5f. multicoloured 10 10
227 10f. multicoloured 10 10
228 15f. multicoloured 10 10
229 20f. multicoloured 10 10
230 25f. multicoloured 15 10
231 30f. multicoloured 15 10
232 35f. multicoloured 45 10
233 40f. multicoloured 45 10
234 50f. multicoloured 50 10
235 60f. multicoloured 50 10
236 70f. multicoloured . . . . 4·00 90
237 75f. multicoloured . . . . 1·00 15
238 80f. multicoloured 70 20
239 – 90f. multicoloured . . . . 1·40 20
240 – 1d. multicoloured . . . . 2·00 20
241 – 2d. multicoloured . . . . 2·50 35
242 – 3d. multicoloured . . . . 5·00 80
243 – 5d. multicoloured . . . . 8·75 2·50
Nos. 239/43 bear a similar portrait of King Hassan, but are larger, 26½ × 40½ mm.

1968. 20th Anniv of W.H.O.
244 **79** 25f. brown, red and blue 20 10
245 40f. brown, red and slate 25 15

1968. Red Crescent. Moroccan Jewellery. As T **65**. Multicoloured.
246 25f. Pendant brooch 80 40
247 40f. Bracelet . . . . 1·25 50

80 Rotary Emblem, Conference Building and Map

1968. Rotary Int District Conf, Casablanca.
248 **80** 40f. gold, blue and green 65 20
249 1d. gold, ultramarine and blue 75 30

81 Belt Pattern

82 Princess Lalla Meryem

1968. "The Belts of Fez". Designs showing ornamental patterns.
250 **81** 25f. multicoloured . . . . 1·90 70
251 – 40f. multicoloured . . . . 2·25 1·25
252 – 60f. multicoloured . . . . 3·50 1·75
253 – 1d. multicoloured . . . . 6·00 3·25

1968. World Children's Day. Multicoloured.
254 25f. Type **82** 25 20
255 40f. Princess Lalla Asmaa . . 65 25
256 1d. Crown Prince Sidi Mohammed . . . . 1·10 55

83 Wrestling

1968. Olympic Games, Mexico. Multicoloured.
257 15f. Type **83** 15 15
258 20f. Basketball 15 15
259 25f. Cycling 50 15
260 40f. Boxing 60 15
261 60f. Running 75 15
262 1d. Football . . . . 1·25 45

84 Silver Crown

85 Costumes of Zagora, South Morocco

1968. Ancient Moroccan Coins.
263 **84** 20f. silver and purple . . . 55 20
264 – 25f. gold and purple . . . 80 25
265 – 40f. silver and green . . . 1·40 65
266 – 60f. gold and red . . . . . 1·60 65
COINS: 25f. Gold dinar; 40f. Silver dirham; 60f. Gold piece.
See also Nos. 270/1.

1969. Traditional Women's Costumes. Mult.
267 15f. Type **85** (postage) . . . 1·25 75
268 25f. Ait Adidou costumes . . 1·90 1·10
269 1d. Ait Ouaouzguit costumes (air) . . . . 2·50 1·25

1969. 8th Anniv of Coronation of Hassan II. As T **84** (silver coins).
270 1d. silver and blue . . . . . 4·25 1·60
271 5d. silver and violet . . . . 10·00 6·00
COINS: 1d. One dirham coin of King Mohammed V; 5d. One dirham coin of King Hassan II.

86 Hands "reading" Braille on Map

1969. Protection of the Blind Week.
272 **86** 25f.+10f. multicoloured . . 45 15

87 "Actor"

89 King Hassan II

1969. World Theatre Day.
273 **87** 1d. multicoloured 45 25

1969. 50th Anniv of League of Red Cross Societies. Moroccan Jewellery as T **65**. Mult.
274 25f.+5f. Bracelets 90 45
275 40f.+10f. Pendant . . . . . 1·25 55

1969. King Hassan's 40th Birthday.
276 **89** 1d. multicoloured . . . . 1·25 35

مؤتمر القمة الاسلامى
الرباط ١٥ رجب 1389
(**90**)

91 Mahatma Gandhi

1969. Islamic Summit Conf, Rabat (1st issue). No. 240 optd with T **90**.
278 1d. multicoloured . . . . . 5·00 4·00

1969. Birth Centenary of Mahatma Gandhi.
279 **91** 40f. brown and lavender 60 15

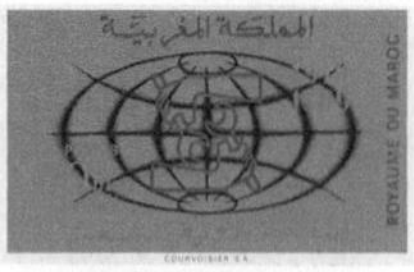
92 I.L.O. Emblem

1969. 50th Anniv of I.L.O.
280 **92** 50f. multicoloured 50 20

93 King Hassan on Horseback

1969. Islamic Summit Conference, Rabat (2nd issue).
281 **93** 1d. multicoloured . . . . 1·10 35

94 "Spahi Horseman" (Haram al Glaoui)

1970. Moroccan Art.
282 **94** 1d. multicoloured . . . . 1·10 30

1970. Flood Victims Relief Fund. Nos. 227/8 surch.
283 **78** 10f.+25f. multicoloured . . 3·50 3·50
284 15f.+25f. multicoloured . . 3·50 3·50

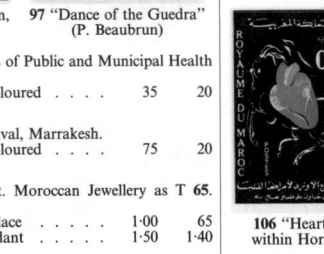

96 Drainage System, Fez **97** "Dance of the Guedra" (P. Beaubrun)

1970. 50th Congress of Public and Municipal Health Officials, Rabat.
285 **96** 60f. multicoloured 35 20

1970. Folklore Festival, Marrakesh.
286 **97** 40f. multicoloured 75 20

1970. Red Crescent. Moroccan Jewellery as T **65**. Multicoloured.
287 25f.+5f. Necklace . . . . . 1·00 65
288 50f.+10t. Pendant . . . . . 1·50 1·40

1970. Population Census. No. 189 surch **1970 0,25** and Arabic inscr.
290 25f. on 60f. multicoloured . . 50 10

99 Dish Aerial, Souk el Arba des Sehoul Communications Station **100** Ruddy Shelduck

1970. 17th Anniv of Revolution.
291 **99** 1d. multicoloured 80 35

1970. Nature Protection. Wild Birds. Mult.
292 25f. Type **100** 75 45
293 40f. Houbara bustard . . . . 1·75 65

101 I.E.Y. Emblem and Moroccan with Book

1970. International Education Year.
294 **101** 60f. multicoloured 65 20

102 Symbols of U.N.

1970. 25th Anniv of U.N.O.
295 **102** 50f. multicoloured 55 15

103 League Emblem, Map and Laurel

1970. 25th Anniv of Arab League.
296 **103** 50f. multicoloured 50 15

104 Olive Grove and Extraction Plant

1970. World Olive-oil Production Year.
297 **104** 50f. black, brown & green 55 15

105 Es Sounna Mosque

1971. Restoration of Es Sounna Mosque, Rabat.
298 **105** 60f. multicoloured 60 15

106 "Heart" within Horse **107** King Hassan II and Dam

1971. European and North African Heart Week.
299 **106** 50f. multicoloured 50 20

1971. 10th Anniv of King Hassan's Accession.
300 **107** 25f. multicoloured 45 10

108 Palestine on Globe

1971. Palestine Week.
302 **108** 25f.+10f. multicoloured 25 20

1971. Red Crescent, Moroccan Jewellery. As T **65**. Multicoloured.
303 25f.+5f. "Arrow-head" brooch 75 50
304 40f.+10f. Square pendant . . 1·10 90

109 Hands holding Peace Dove

1971. Racial Equality Year.
305 **109** 50f. multicoloured 50 15

110 Musical Instrument

1971. Protection of the Blind Week.
306 **110** 40f.+10f. multicoloured 60 20

111 Children at Play **112** Shah Mohammed Reza Pahlavi of Iran

1971. International Children's Day.
307 **111** 40f. multicoloured 45 15

1971. 2,500th Anniv of Persian Empire.
308 **112** 1d. multicoloured 70 30

113 Aerial View of Mausoleum

1971. Mausoleum of Mohammed V. Multicoloured.
309 25f. Type **113** 15 15
310 50f. Tomb of Mohammed V 20 20
311 1d. Interior of Mausoleum (vert) 80 50

114 Football and Emblem

1971. Mediterranean Games, Izmir, Turkey. Mult.
312 40f. Type **114** 55 15
313 60f. Athlete and emblem . . 70 20

115 A.P.U. Emblem

1971. 25th Anniv of Founding of Arab Postal Union at Sofar Conference.
314 **115** 25f. red, blue & light blue 15 10

116 Sun and Landscape

1971. 50th Anniv of Sherifian Phosphates Office.
315 **116** 70f. multicoloured 55 20

117 Torch and Book Year Emblem **118** Lottery Symbol

1972. International Book Year.
316 **117** 1d. multicoloured 65 25

1972. Creation of National Lottery.
317 **118** 25f. gold, black and brown 15 10

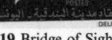

119 Bridge of Sighs **120** Mizmar (double-horned flute)

1972. UNESCO "Save Venice" Campaign. Multicoloured.
318 25f. Type **119** 15 15
319 50f. St. Mark's Basilica (horiz) 20 15
320 1d. Lion of St. Marks (horiz) 65 20

1972. Protection of the Blind Week.
321 **120** 25f.+10f. multicoloured 60 20

121 Bridge and Motorway

1972. 2nd African Highways Conference, Rabat.
322 **121** 75f. multicoloured 75 20

122 Moroccan Stamp of 1969, and Postmark

1972. Stamp Day.
323 **122** 1d. multicoloured 65 20

1972. Red Crescent. Moroccan Jewellery. As T **65**. Multicoloured.
324 25f.+5f. Jewelled bangles . . 75 75
325 70f.+10f. Filigree pendant . . 1·10 1·10

123 "Betrothal of Imilchil" (Tayeb Lahlou) **124** Dove on African Map

1972. Folklore Festival, Marrakesh.
326 **123** 60f. multicoloured 90 35

1972. 9th Organization of African Unity Summit Conference, Rabat.
327 **124** 25f. multicoloured 15 15

125 Polluted Beach

1972. U.N. Environmental Conservation Conf, Stockholm.
328 **125** 50f. multicoloured 50 20

126 Running **127** "Sonchus pinnatifidus"

1972. Olympic Games, Munich.
329 **126** 25f. red, pink and black 15 15
330 – 50f. violet, lilac and black 20 15
331 – 75f. green, yellow & black 60 20
332 – 1d. blue, lt blue & black 75 25
DESIGNS: 50f. Wrestling; 75f. Football; 1d. Cycling.

1972. Moroccan Flowers (1st series). Mult.
333 25f. Type **127** 45 15
334 40f. "Amberboa crupinoides" 55 15
See also Nos. 375/6.

128 Sand Gazelle **129** Rabat Carpet

1972. Nature Protection. Fauna. Multicoloured.
335 25f. Type **128** 75 25
336 40f. Barbary sheep . . . . . 1·00 60

1972. Moroccan Carpets (1st series). Mult.
337 50f. Type **129** . . . . 1·00 35
338 75f. Rabat carpet with "star-shaped" centre . . . . . . 1·50 50
See also Nos. 380/1, 406/7, 433/4, 485/7 and 513.

130 Mother and Child with U.N. Emblem

132 Global Weather Map

131 "Postman" and "Stamp"

1972. International Children's Day.
339 **130** 75f. blue, yellow and green 35 30

1973. Stamp Day.
340 **131** 25f. multicoloured 15 10

1973. Centenary of W.M.O.
341 **132** 70f. multicoloured 70 20

133 King Hassan and Arms

1973.
342 **133** 1f. multicoloured 10 10
343 2f. multicoloured 10 10
344 5f. multicoloured . . . 10 10
345 10f. multicoloured . . . 10 10
346 15f. multicoloured . . . 10 10
347 20f. multicoloured . . . 10 10
348 25f. multicoloured . . . 10 10
349 30f. multicoloured . . . 15 10
350 35f. multicoloured . . . 15 10
351 40f. multicoloured . . . 5·00 70
352 50f. multicoloured . . . 50 10
353 60f. multicoloured . . . 60 15
354 70f. multicoloured . . . 25 15
355 75f. multicoloured . . . 30 15
356 80f. multicoloured . . . 60 20
357 90f. multicoloured . . . 75 15
358 1d. multicoloured . . . 2·00 20
359 2d. multicoloured . . . 4·25 55
360 3d. multicoloured . . . 6·25 1·25
361 5d. multicoloured (brown background) . . . . . 4·25 1·25
361a 5d. multicoloured (pink background) . . . . . 4·00 90

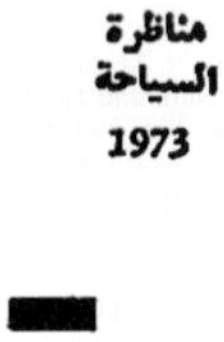

(134)

1973. Nat Tourist Conf. Nos. 324/5 surch with T **134**.
362 **65** 25f. on 5f. multicoloured 2·50 2·50
363 70f. on 10f. multicoloured 2·50 2·50
On No. 363 the Arabic text is arranged in one line.

135 Tambours

1973. Protection of the Blind Week.
364 **135** 70f.+10f. multicoloured 75 55

136 Kaaba, Mecca, and Mosque, Rabat

1973. Prophet Mohammed's Birthday.
365 **136** 25f. multicoloured 15 10

137 Roses and M'Gouna

1973. M'Gouna Rose Festival.
366 **137** 25f. multicoloured 45 10

138 Handclasp and Torch

139 Folk-dancers

1973. 10th Anniv of Organization of African Unity.
367 **138** 70f. multicoloured 30 15

1973. Folklore Festival, Marrakesh. Multicoloured.
368 50f. Type **139** 50 15
369 1d. Folk-musicians 75 25

1973. Red Crescent. Moroccan Jewellery. As T **65**. Multicoloured.
370 25f.+5f. Locket . . . . . . 1·00 50
371 70f.+10f. Bracelet inlaid with pearls . . . . 1·10 60

140 Solar System

141 Microscope

1973. 500th Birth Anniv of Nicholas Copernicus.
372 **140** 70f. multicoloured 60 20

1973. 25th Anniv of W.H.O.
373 **141** 70f. multicoloured 55 20

142 Interpol Emblem and Fingerprint

1973. 50th Anniv of International Criminal Police Organization (Interpol).
374 **142** 70f. multicoloured 30 25

1973. Moroccan Flowers (2nd series). As T **127**. Multicoloured.
375 25f. "Chrysanthemum carinatum" (horiz) 75 35
376 1d. "Amberboa muricata" . . 1·25 55

143 Striped Hyena

1973. Nature Protection. Multicoloured.
377 25f. Type **143** 95 40
378 50f. Eleonora's falcon (vert) 3·00 1·00

144 Map and Arrows

1973. Meeting of Maghreb Committee for Co-ordination of Posts and Telecommunications, Tunis.
379 **144** 25f. multicoloured 15 10

1973. Moroccan Carpets (2nd series). As T **129**. Multicoloured.
380 25f. Carpet from the High Atlas . . . . 1·00 25
381 70f. Tazenakht carpet . . . . 1·50 50

145 Golf Club and Ball

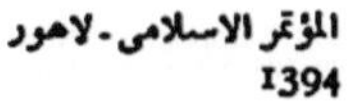

(146)

1974. International "Hassan II Trophy" Golf Grand Prix, Rabat.
382 **145** 70f. multicoloured . . . . 1·25 60

1974. Islamic Summit Conference, Lahore, Pakistan. No. 281 optd with T **146**.
383 1d. multicoloured . . . . . 2·75 1·60

147 Human Rights Emblem

148 Vanadinite

1974. 25th Anniv (1973) of Declaration of Human Rights.
384 **147** 70f. multicoloured 50 20

1974. Moroccan Mineral Sources. Multicoloured.
385 25f. Type **148** 95 50
386 70f. Erythrine . . . . 1·90 1·00

149 Marrakesh Minaret

150 U.P.U. Emblem and Congress Dates

1974. 173rd District of Rotary International Annual Conference, Marrakesh.
387 **149** 70f. multicoloured 70 20

1974. Centenary of U.P.U.
388 **150** 25f. black, red and green 15 10
389 – 1d. multicoloured 70 25
DESIGN—HORIZ: 1d. Commemorative scroll.

151 Drummers and Dancers

1974. 15th Folklore Festival, Marrakesh. Mult.
390 25f. Type **151** 35 15
391 70f. Juggler with woman . . 1·25 30

152 Environmental Emblem and Scenes

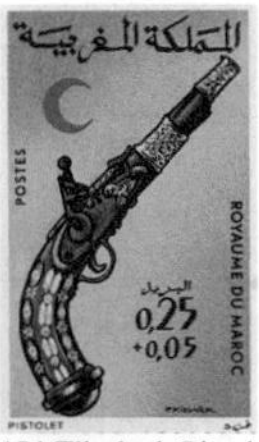

154 Flintlock Pistol

1974. World Environmental Day.
392 **152** 25f. multicoloured 20 15

1974. Red Crescent. Moroccan Firearms. Mult.
397 25f.+5f. Type **154** 75 75
398 70f.+10f. Gunpowder box . . 1·10 1·10

155 Stamps, Postmark and Magnifying Glass

(156)

1974. Stamp Day.
399 **155** 70f. multicoloured 60 20

1974. No. D393 surch with T **156**.
400 1d. on 5f. orange, green & blk . . . . 1·90 1·25

157 World Cup Trophy

158 Erbab (two-string fiddle)

1974. World Cup Football Championship, West Germany.
401 **157** 1d. multicoloured 85 65

1974. Blind Week.
402 **158** 70f.+10f. multicoloured 1·00 50
See also No. 423.

160 Double-spurred Francolin

162 Jasmine

1974. Moroccan Animals. Multicoloured.
404 25f. Type **160** 55 30
405 70f. Leopard (horiz) 95 40

1974. Moroccan Carpets (3rd series). As T **129**. Multicoloured.
406 25f. Zemmour carpet 65 10
407 1d. Beni M'Guild carpet . . 1·25 50

1975. Flowers (1st series). Multicoloured.
408 25f. Type **162** 50 10
409 35f. Orange lilies 60 10
410 70f. Poppies 85 35
411 90f. Carnations . . . . . . 1·10 50
See also Nos. 417/20.

163 Aragonite

165 "The Water-carrier" (Feu Taieb-Lalou)

1975. Minerals. Multicoloured.
412 50f. Type **163** 75 40
413 1d. Agate . . . . 1·50 75
See also Nos. 543 and 563/4.

1975. Red Crescent. Moroccan Jewellery. As T **65**. Multicoloured.
414 25f.+5f. Pendant 75 75
415 70f.+10f. Earring . . . . . . 1·10 1·00

1975. "Moroccan Painters".
416 **165** 1d. multicoloured . . . . 1·10 30

1975. Flowers (2nd series). As T **162**. Mult.
417 10f. Daisies 10 10
418 50f. Pelargoniums 60 10
419 60f. Orange blossom 75 30
420 1d. Pansies . . . . 1·10 60

166 Collector with Stamp Album

167 Dancer with Rifle

1975. Stamp Day.
421 **166** 40f. multicoloured 20 10

1975. 16th Nat Folklore Festival, Marrakesh.
422 **167** 1d. multicoloured 65 30

1975. Blind Week. As T **158**. Multicoloured.
423 1d. Mandolin 85 25

168 "Animals in Forest" (child's drawing)

1975. Children's Week.
424 **168** 25f. multicoloured 15 10

169 Games Emblem and Athletes

1975. 7th Mediterranean Games, Algiers.
425 **169** 40f. multicoloured 45 10

170 Waldrapp

1975. Fauna. Multicoloured.
426 40f. Type **170** . . . . 2·50 50
427 1d. Caracal (vert) . . . . . 1·50 75
See also Nos. 470/1.

1975. "Green March" (1st issue). Nos. 370/1 optd **1975** and Arabic inscr.
428 25f. (+ 5f.) multicoloured . . 2·50 2·50
429 70f. (+ 10f.) multicoloured . . 2·50 2·50
The premiums on the stamps are obliterated.

172 King Mohammed V greeting Crowd

1975. 20th Anniv of Independence. Mult.
430 40f. Type **172** 15 10
431 1d. King Hassan (vert) . . . 75 45
432 1d. King Hassan V wearing fez (vert) 75 45

1975. Moroccan Carpets (4th series). As T **129**. Multicoloured.
433 25f. Ouled Besseba carpet . . 60 35
434 1d. Ait Ouaouzguid carpet 90 45
See also Nos. 485/7 and 513.

173 Marchers crossing Desert

174 Fez Coin of 1883/4

1975. "Green March" (2nd issue).
435 **173** 40f. multicoloured 15 10

1976. Moroccan Coins (1st series). Multicoloured.
436 5f. Type **174** 10 10
437 15f. Rabat silver coin 1774/5 10 10
438 35f. Sabta coin, 13/14th centuries 75 35
439 40f. Type **174** 50 10
440 50f. As No. 437 . . . . . . 75 35
441 65f. As No. 438 . . . . . . 75 50
442 1d. Sabta coin, 12/13th centuries . . . . 1·10 60
See also Nos. 458/67a.
For Nos. 439/40 in smaller size, see Nos. 520/b.

175 Interior of Mosque

1976. Millennium of Ibn Zaidoun Mosque. Mult.
443 40f. Type **175** 15 10
444 65f. Interior archways (vert) 50 15

176 Moroccan Family

1976. Family Planning.
445 **176** 40f. multicoloured 15 10

177 Bou Anania College, Fez

1976. Moroccan Architecture.
446 **177** 1d. multicoloured 70 20

178 Temple Sculpture

1976. Borobudur Temple Preservation Campaign. Multicoloured.
447 40f. Type **178** 15 15
448 1d. View of Temple 60 20

179 Dome of the Rock, Jerusalem

1976. 6th Anniv of Islamic Conference.
449 **179** 1d. multicoloured 70 20

1976. Red Crescent. Moroccan Jewellery. As T **65**. Multicoloured.
450 40f. Jewelled purse 15 10
451 1d. Jewelled pectoral 65 25

180 George Washington, King Hassan I, Statue of Liberty and Mausoleum of Mohammed V

181 Wrestling

1976. Bicentenary of American Revolution. Mult.
452 40f. Flags of U.S.A. and Morocco (horiz) 45 15
453 1d. Type **180** 65 25

1976. Olympic Games, Montreal. Multicoloured.
454 35f. Type **181** 10 10
455 40f. Cycling 15 10
456 50f. Boxing 50 15
457 1d. Running 70 25

1976. Moroccan Coins (2nd series). As T **174**. Multicoloured.
458 5f. Medieval silver mohur 10 10
459 10f. Gold mohur 10 10
460 15f. Gold coin 10 10
461 20f. Gold coin (different) . . 10 10
461a 25f. As No. 437 . . . . . . 1·25 50
462 30f. As No. 459 . . . . . . 35 10
463 35f. Silver dinar 45 10
464 60f. As No. 458 . . . . . . 50 15
465 70f. Copper coin 80 15
466 75f. As No. 463 . . . . . . 50 15
466a 80f. As No. 460 . . . . . . 2·50 75
467 2d. As No. 465 . . . . . . 60 35
467a 3d. As No. 461 . . . . . . 3·75 1·25

182 Early and Modern Telephones with Dish Aerial

1976. Telephone Centenary.
468 **182** 1d. multicoloured 70 25

183 Gold Medallion

1976. Blind Week.
469 **183** 50f. multicoloured 50 10

1976. Birds. As T **170**. Multicoloured.
470 40f. Dark chanting goshawk (vert) . . . . 2·25 75
471 1d. Purple swamphen (vert) 3·50 1·40

185 King Hassan, Emblems and Map

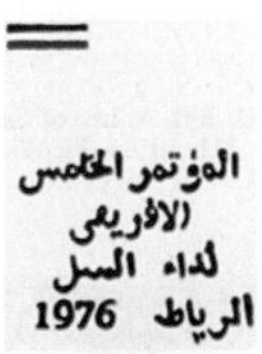
(186)

1976. 1st Anniv of "Green March".
472 **185** 40f. multicoloured 45 10

1976. Fifth African Tuberculosis Conference. Nos. 414/15 optd with T **186**.
473 25f. multicoloured . . . . . 1·90 1·90
474 70f. multicoloured . . . . . 2·25 2·25

187 Globe and Peace Dove

188 African Nations Cup

1976. Conference of Non-Aligned Countries, Colombo.
475 **187** 1d. red, black and blue 30 20

1976. African Nations Football Championship.
476 **188** 1d. multicoloured 65 20

189 Letters encircling Globe

1977. Stamp Day.
477 **189** 40f. multicoloured 40 10

190 "Aeonium arboreum"

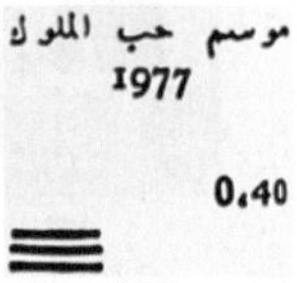

(192)

191 Ornamental Candle Lamps

1977. Flowers. Multicoloured.
478 40f. Type **190** 30 10
479 50f. "Malope trifida" (24 × 38 mm) 95 30
480 1d. "Hesperolaburnum platyclarpum" . . . . 1·10 30

1977. Procession of the Candles, Sale.
481 **191** 40f. multicoloured 45 10

1977. Cherry Festival. No. D394 surch with T **192**.
482 40f. on 10f. Cherries 75 30

193 Map and Emblem

1977. 5th Congress. Organization of Arab Towns.
483 **193** 50f. multicoloured 15 10

194 A.P.U. Emblem

1977. 25th Anniv of Arab Postal Union.
484 **194** 1d. multicoloured 60 20

1977. Moroccan Carpets (5th series). As T **129**. Multicoloured.
486 40f. Ait Haddou carpet . . . 40 20
487 1d. Henbel rug, Sale 95 30

195 Zither

196 Mohammed Ali Jinnah

1977. Blind Week.
488 **195** 1d. multicoloured 85 25

1977. Birth Centenary of Mohammed Ali Jinnah.
489 **196** 70f. multicoloured 50 20

197 Marcher with Flag

1977. 2nd Anniv of "Green March".
490 **197** 1d. multicoloured 60 20

198 Assembly Hall

1977. Opening of House of Representatives.
491 **198** 1d. multicoloured 65 20

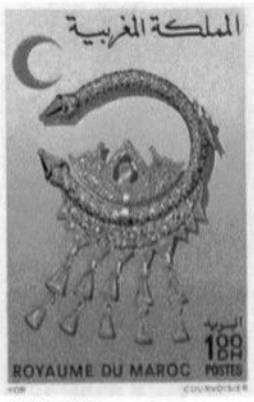
199 Silver Brooch

200 Bowl with Funnel

1977. Red Crescent.
493 **199** 1d. multicoloured . . . . 1·25 60

1978. Moroccan Copperware. Multicoloured.
494 40f. Type **200** 35 10
495 1d. Bowl with cover 70 20

201 Development Emblem

202 Decorative Pot with Lid

1978. Sahara Development. Multicoloured.
496 40f. Type **201** 35 10
497 1d. Fishes in net and camels at oasis (horiz) 60 20

1978. Blind Week. Multicoloured.
498 1d. Type **202** 90 30
499 1d. Decorative jar 90 30

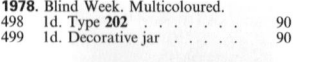

203 Map and Red Cross within Red Crescent

1978. 10th Conference of Arab Red Crescent and Red Cross Societies.
500 **203** 1d. red and black 65 20

204 View of Fez

205 Dome of the Rock

1978. Rotary International Meeting, Fez.
501 **204** 1d. multicoloured 65 20

1978. Palestine Welfare.
502 **205** 5f. multicoloured 10 10
503 10f. multicoloured 10 10

206 Flautist and Folk Dancers

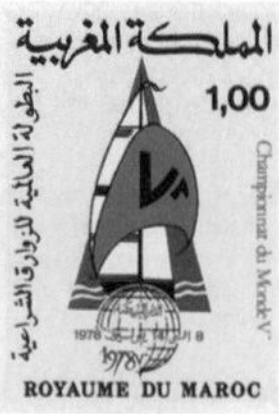
208 Yacht

207 Sugar Field and Crushing Plant

1978. National Folklore Festival, Marrakesh.
504 **206** 1d. multicoloured 55 20

1978. Sugar Industry.
505 **207** 40f. multicoloured 15 10

1978. World Sailing Championships.
506 **208** 1d. multicoloured 60 20

209 Tree, Tent and Scout Emblem

211 Human Rights Emblem

210 Moulay Idriss

1978. Pan-Arab Scout Festival, Rabat.
507 **209** 40f. multicoloured 15 10

1978. Moulay Idriss Great Festival.
508 **210** 40f. multicoloured 15 10

1978. 30th Anniv of Declaration of Human Rights.
509 **211** 1d. multicoloured 65 20

212 Houses in Agadir

214 Decorated Pot

213 Player, Football and Cup

1979. Southern Moroccan Architecture (1st series). Multicoloured.
510 40f. Type **212** 15 10
511 1d. Old fort at Marrakesh . . 60 15
See also Nos. 536 and 562.

1979. Mohammed V Football Cup.
512 **213** 40f. multicoloured 15 10

1979. Moroccan Carpets (6th series). As T **129**. Multicoloured.
513 40f. Marmoucha carpet . . . 40 15

1979. Blind Week.
514 **214** 1d. multicoloured 65 20

215 "Procession from a Mosque"

216 Coffee Pot and Heater

1979. Paintings by Mohamed Ben Ali Rbati. Mult.
515 40f. Type **215** 15 10
516 1d. "Religious Ceremony in a Mosque" (horiz) 55 20

1979. Red Cresent. Brassware. Multicoloured.
517 40f. Engraved circular boxes 25 15
518 1d. Type **216** 85 30

217 Costumed Girls

218 Curved Dagger in Jewelled Sheath

1979. National Folklore Festival, Marrakesh.
519 **217** 40f. multicoloured 15 10

1979. Moroccan Coins. As T **174**, but smaller, $17\frac{1}{2} \times 22\frac{1}{2}$ mm.
520 40f. multicoloured 10 10
520b 50f. multicoloured 10 10

1979. Ancient Weapons.
521 **218** 1d. black and yellow . . . 75 20

219 King Hassan II

221 King Hassan II

220 Festival Emblem

1979. King Hassan's 50th Birthday.
522 **219** 1d. multicoloured 70 20

1979. 4th Arab Youth Festival, Rabat.
523 **220** 1d. multicoloured 70 20

1979. "25th Anniv of Revolution of King and People".
524 **221** 1d. multicoloured 30 20

222 World Map superimposed on Open Book

1979. 50th Anniv of Int Bureau of Education.
525 **222** 1d. brown and yellow . . 60 20

223 Pilgrims in Wuquf, Arafat

1979. Pilgrimage to Mecca.
526 **223** 1d. multicoloured 70 20

استرجاع اقليم وادى الذهب
1979_8_14
(224)

1979. Recovery of Oued Eddahab Province. Design as No. 497, with face value amended (40f.), optd with T **224**.
527 40f. multicoloured 15 10
528 1d. multicoloured 65 20

225 Centaurium

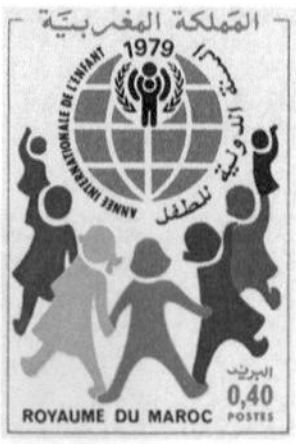
226 Children around Globe

1979. Flowers. Multicoloured.
529 40f. Type **225** 15 10
530 1d. "Leucanthemum catanance" 55 20

1979. International Year of the Child.
531 **226** 40f. multicoloured 60 25

227 European Otter

228 Traffic Signs

1979. Wildlife. Multicoloured.
532 40f. Type **227** 50 15
533 1d. Moussier's redstart . . . 1·60 50

1980. Road Safety. Multicoloured.
534 40f. Type **228** 15 10
535 1d. Children at crossing . . . 30 20

229 Fortress

1980. South Moroccan Architecture (2nd series).
536 **229** 1d. multicoloured 55 20

230 Copper Bowl with Lid

231 Pot

1980. Red Crescent. Multicoloured.
537 50f. Type **230** 50 15
538 70f. Copper kettle and brazier 60 20

1980. Blind Week.
539 **231** 40f. multicoloured 15 10

232 Mechanized Sorting Office, Rabat

1980. Stamp Day.
540 **232** 40f. multicoloured 15 10

233 World Map and Rotary Emblem

234 Leather Bag and Cloth

1980. 75th Anniv of Rotary International.
541 **233** 1d. multicoloured 55 20

1980. 4th Textile and Leather Exhibition, Casablanca.
542 **234** 1d. multicoloured 55 20

1980. Minerals (2nd series). As T **163**. Mult.
543 40f. Gypsum 85 10

235 Peregrine Falcon

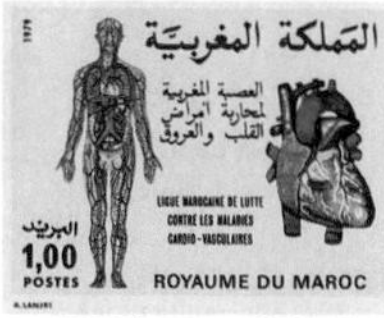

236 Diagram of Blood Circulation and Heart

1980. Hunting with Falcon.
544 **235** 40f. multicoloured . . . . 1·25 65

1980. Campaign against Cardiovascular Diseases.
545 **236** 1d. multicoloured 65 20

237 Decade Emblem and Human Figures

238 Harnessed Horse

1980. Decade for Women.
546 **237** 40f. mauve and blue . . . 15 10
547 – 1d. multicoloured 55 20
DESIGN: 1d. Decade and United Nations emblems.

1980. Ornamental Harnesses. Multicoloured.
548 40f. Harnessed horse (different) 15 10
549 1d. Type **238** 75 20

239 Satellite orbiting Earth and Dish Aerial

241 Conference Emblem

240 Light Bulb and Fuel Can

1980. World Meteorological Day.
550 **239** 40f. multicoloured 15 10

1980. Energy Conservation. Multicoloured.
551 40f. Type **240** 15 10
552 1d. Hand holding petrol pump 55 20

1980. World Tourism Conference, Manila.
553 **241** 40f. multicoloured 15 10

242 Tree bridging Straits of Gibraltar

1980. European–African Liaison over the Straits of Gibraltar.
554 **242** 1d. multicoloured 60 20

243 Flame and Marchers

1980. 5th Anniv of "The Green March".
555 **243** 1d. multicoloured 60 20

244 Holy Kaaba, Mecca

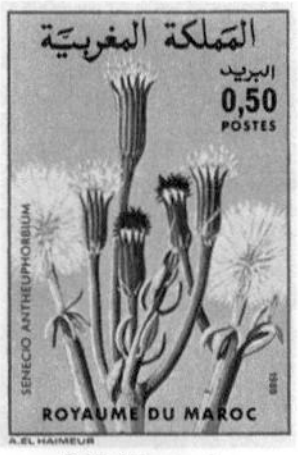

245 "Senecio antheuphorbium"

1980. 1400th Anniv of Hegira. Multicoloured.
556 40f. Type **244** 15 10
557 1d. Mosque, Mecca 60 20

1980. Flowers. Multicoloured.
558 40f. Type **245** 60 10
559 1d. "Periploca laevigata" . . 1·25 50

246 Painting by Aherdan

247 Nejjarine Fountain, Fez

1980. Paintings.
560 – 40f. bistre and brown . . 15 10
561 **246** 1d. multicoloured 60 20
DESIGN: 40f. Composition of bird and feathers.

1981. Moroccan Architecture (3rd series).
562 **247** 40f. multicoloured 10 10

1981. Minerals (3rd series). Vert designs as T **163**. Multicoloured.
563 40f. Onyx 95 35
564 1d. Malachite-azurite . . . . 1·60 75

248 King Hassan II

1981. 25th Anniv of Independence. Mult.
565 60f. Type **248** 35 10
566 60f. Map, flags, broken chains and "25" 35 10
567 60f. King Mohammed V. . . 35 10

249 King Hassan II

1981. 20th Anniv of King Hassan's Coronation.
568 **249** 1d.30 multicoloured . . . 50 25

250 "Source" (Jillali Gharbaoul)

1981. Moroccan Painting.
569 **250** 1d.30 multicoloured . . . 75 25

251 "Anagalis monelli"

252 King Hassan as Major General

1981. Flowers. Multicoloured.
570 40f. Type **251** 20 10
571 70f. "Bubonium intricatum" 40 15

1981. 25th Anniv of Moroccan Armed Forces.
572 **252** 60f. lilac, gold and green 35 10
573 – 60f. multicoloured 35 10
574 – 60f. lilac, gold and green 35 10
DESIGNS: No. 573, Army badge; 574, King Mohammed V (founder).

253 Caduceus (Telecommunications and Health)

254 Plate with Pattern

1981. World Telecommunications Day.
575 **253** 1d.30 multicoloured . . . 70 20

1981. Blind Week. Multicoloured.
576 50f. Type **254** 10 10
577 1d.30 Plate with ship pattern 60 20

255 Musicians and Dancers

256 "Seboula" Dagger

1981. 22nd National Folklore Festival, Marrakesh.
578 **255** 1d.30 multicoloured . . . 85 25

1981. Ancient Weapons.
579 **256** 1d.30 multicoloured . . . 75 20

257 Pestle and Mortar

258 Hands holding I.Y.D.P. Emblem

1981. Red Crescent. Moroccan Copperware. Mult.
580 60f. Type **257** 25 15
581 1d.30 Tripod brazier 80 25

1981. International Year of Disabled People.
582 **258** 60f. multicoloured 35 10

259 "Iphiclides feisthamelii Lotteri"

260 King Hassan and Marchers

1981. Butterflies (1st series). Multicoloured.
583 60f. Type **259** 50 25
584 1d.30 "Zerynthina rumina africana" . . . . 1·25 60
See also Nos. 609/10.

1981. 6th Anniv of "Green March".
585 **260** 1d.30 multicoloured . . . 70 20

261 Town Buildings and Congress Emblem

1981. 10th International Twinned Towns Congress, Casablanca.
586 **261** 1d.30 multicoloured . . . 20 20

262 Dome of the Rock

264 Terminal Building and Runway

1981. Palestinian Solidarity Day.
587 **262** 60f. multicoloured 35 10

1981. 12th Arab Summit Conference, Fez. Nos. 502/3 surch **1981 0,40**.
588 **205** 40f. on 5f. multicoloured 4·00 4·00
588a 40f. on 10f. multicoloured . . . . 2·75 2·75

1981. 1st Anniv of Mohammed V Airport.
589 **264** 1d.30 multicoloured . . . 70 20

265 Al Massira Dam

266 King Hassan II

1981. Al Massira Dam.
590 **265** 60f. multicoloured 35 10

1981.

591	266	5f. red, blue and gold . .	10	10
592		10f. red, yellow and gold	10	10
593		15f. red, green and gold	10	10
594		20f. red, pink and gold	10	10
595		25f. red, lilac and gold	10	10
596		30f. blue, lt blue & gold	10	10
597		35f. blue, yellow and gold	10	10
598		40f. blue, green and gold	10	10
599		50f. blue, pink and gold	10	10
600		60f. blue, lilac and gold	10	10
601		65f. blue, lilac and gold	10	10
602		70f. violet, yellow and gold	10	10
603		75f. violet, green and gold	15	15
604		80f. violet, pink and gold	15	15
605		90f. violet, lilac and gold	15	15
605a		1d.25 red, mauve & gold	20	15
605b		4d. brown, yell & gold	1·10	55

See also Nos. 624/9, 718/22, 759/61, 866, 895/6 and 930.

267 Horse Jumping

1981. Equestrian Sports.
606 **267** 1d.30 multicoloured . . . 1·25 25

268 Ait Quaquzguit

1982. Carpets (1st series). Multicoloured.
607 50f. Type **268** 10 10
608 1d.30 Ouled Besseba 60 30
See also Nos. 653/4.

1982. Butterflies and Moths (2nd series). As T **259**. Multicoloured.
609 60f. "Celerio oken lineata" 70 25
610 1d.30 "Mesoacidalia aglaja lyauteyi" . . . . 1·50 55

269 Tree and Emblem

270 Jug

1982. World Forestry Day.
611 **269** 40f. multicoloured 10 10

1982. Blind Week.
612 **270** 1d. multicoloured 50 25

271 Dancers

272 Candlestick

1982. Popular Art.
613 **271** 1d.40 multicoloured . . . 60 35

1982. Red Crescent.
614 **272** 1d.40 multicoloured . . . 60 35

273 Painting by M. Mezian

274 Buildings and People on Graph

1982. Moroccan Painting.
615 **273** 1d.40 multicoloured . . . 60 35

1982. Population and Housing Census.
616 **274** 60f. multicoloured 15 15

275 Dr. Koch, Lungs and Apparatus

276 I.T.U. Emblem

1982. Centenary of Discovery of Tubercle Bacillus.
617 **275** 1d.40 multicoloured . . . 75 35

1982. I.T.U. Delegates' Conference, Nairobi.
618 **276** 1d.40 multicoloured . . . 60 35

277 Wheat, Globe, Sea and F.A.O. Emblem

1982. World Food Day.
619 **277** 60f. multicoloured 15 15

278 Class XDd Diesel Locomotive (1956) and Route Map

1982. Unity Railway.
620 **278** 1d.40 multicoloured . . . 1·25 70

279 A.P.U. Emblem

1982. 30th Anniv of Arab Postal Union.
621 **279** 1d.40 multicoloured . . . 40 15

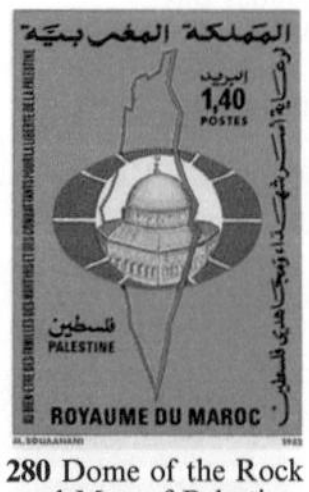
280 Dome of the Rock and Map of Palestine

281 Red Coral

1982. Palestinian Solidarity.
622 **280** 1d.40 multicoloured . . . 40 15

1982. Red Coral of Al Hoceima.
623 **281** 1d.40 multicoloured . . . 70 25

1983. Size 25 × 32 mm but inscribed "1982".

624	266	1d. red, blue and gold . .	25	10
625		1d.40 brown, lt brown & gold	35	10
626		2d. red, green and gold	45	15
627		3d. brown, yellow and gold	65	25
628		5d. brown, green and gold	1·40	50
629		10d. brown, orange and gold	2·75	90

282 Moroccan Stamps

283 King Hassan II

1983. Stamp Day.
630 **282** 1d.40 multicoloured . . . 60 20

1983.

631	283	1d.40 multicoloured . . .	25	20
632		2d. multicoloured	35	30
633		3d. multicoloured	80	50
634		5d. multicoloured	1·40	45
635		10d. multicoloured . . .	2·75	1·10

284 Decorated Pot

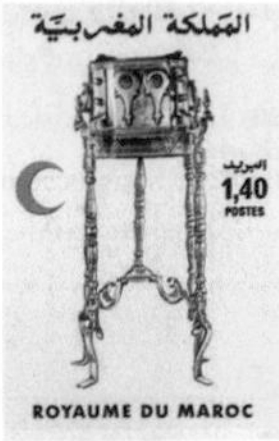
286 Ornamental Stand

285 Musicians

1983. Blind Week.
636 **284** 1d.40 multicoloured . . . 60 20

1983. Popular Arts.
637 **285** 1d.40 multicoloured . . . 75 20

1983. Red Crescent.
638 **286** 1d.40 multicoloured . . . 75 20

287 Commission Emblem

1983. 25th Anniv of Economic Commission for Africa.
639 **287** 1d.40 multicoloured . . . 55 20

288 "Tecoma sp."

290 Games Emblem and Stylized Sports

289 King Hassan II, Map and Sultan of Morocco

1983. Flowers. Multicoloured.
640 60c. Type **288** 10 10
641 1d.40 "Strelitzia sp." 75 20

1983. 30th Anniv of Revolution.
642 **289** 80c. multicoloured 20 20

1983. 9th Mediterranean Games, Casablanca.
644 **290** 80c. blue, silver and gold 20 20
645 – 1d. multicoloured 20 20
646 – 2d. multicoloured 60 30
DESIGNS—VERT: 1d. Games emblem. HORIZ: 2d. Stylized runner.

291 Ploughing

1983. Touiza.
648 **291** 80c. multicoloured 20 20

292 Symbol of "Green March"

293 Palestinian formed from Map and Globe

1983. 8th Anniv of "Green March".
649 **292** 80f. multicoloured 20 15

1983. Palestinian Welfare.
650 **293** 80f. multicoloured 20 15

294 Ouzoud Waterfall

295 Children's Emblem

1983. Ouzoud Waterfall.
651 **294** 80f. multicoloured 20 15

1983. Children's Day. Multicoloured.
652 **295** 2d. multicoloured 70 30

1983. Carpets (2nd series). As T **268**. Mult.
653 60f. Zemmouri 10 10
654 1d.40 Zemmouri (different) 55 20

296 Transport and W.C.Y. Emblem

1983. World Communications Year.
655 **296** 2d. multicoloured . . . . 1·75 70

297 Views of Jerusalem and Fez

1984. Twinned Towns.
656 **297** 2d. multicoloured 95 20

298 Fennec Fox

1984. Animals. Multicoloured.
657 80f. Type **298** 30 25
658 2d. Lesser Egyptian jerboa 60 35

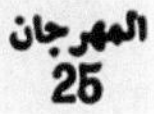

299 Map of League Members and Emblem (300)

1984. 39th Anniv of League of Arab States.
659 **299** 2d. multicoloured 70 20

1984. 25th National Folklore Festival, Marrakesh. No. 578 optd with T **300**.
660 **255** 1d.30 multicoloured . . . 75 15

301 "Metha viridis" **303** Lidded Container

302 Decorated Bowl

1984. Flowers. Multicoloured.
661 80f. Type **301** 20 15
662 2d. Aloe 75 30

1984. Blind Week.
663 **302** 80f. multicoloured 20 15

1984. Red Crescent.
664 **303** 2d. multicoloured 75 30

304 Sports Pictograms **305** Dove carrying Children

1984. Olympic Games, Los Angeles.
665 **304** 2d. multicoloured 75 30

1984. International Child Victims' Day.
666 **305** 2d. multicoloured 70 30

306 U.P.U. Emblem and Ribbons **307** Hands holding Ears of Wheat

1984. Universal Postal Union Day.
667 **306** 2d. multicoloured 40 30

1984. World Food Day.
668 **307** 80f. multicoloured 20 15

308 Stylized Bird, Airplane and Emblem **309** Inscribed Scroll

1984. 40th Anniv of I.C.A.O.
669 **308** 2d. multicoloured 40 30

1984. 9th Anniv of "Green March".
670 **309** 80f. multicoloured 20 15

311 Flag and Dome of the Rock **312** Emblem and People

1984. Palestinian Welfare.
672 **311** 2d. multicoloured 60 25

1984. 36th Anniv of Human Rights Declaration.
673 **312** 2d. multicoloured 60 25

313 Aidi **314** Weighing Baby

1984. Dogs. Multicoloured.
674 80f. Type **313** 50 10
675 2d. Sloughi . . . . 1·10 25

1985. Infant Survival Campaign.
676 **314** 80f. multicoloured 15 10

315 Children playing in Garden **316** Sherifian Mail Postal Cancellation, 1892

1985. 1st Moroccan S.O.S. Children's Village.
677 **315** 2d. multicoloured 60 25

1985. Stamp Day.
678 **316** 2d. grey, pink and black 60 25
See also Nos. 698/9, 715/16, 757/8, 778/9, 796/7, 818/19, 841/2, 877/8, 910/11 and 924/5.

317 Emblem, Birds, Landscape and Fish **318** Musicians

1985. World Environment Day.
680 **317** 80f. multicoloured 20 10

1985. National Folklore Festival, Marrakesh.
681 **318** 2d. multicoloured 75 25

319 Decorated Plate **320** Bougainvillea

1985. Blind Week.
682 **319** 80f. multicoloured 15 10

1985. Flowers. Multicoloured.
683 80f. Type **320** 60 10
684 2d. "Hibiscus rosasinensis" 1·25 50

321 Woman in Headdress **323** Map and Emblem

322 Musicians and Dancers

1985. Red Crescent.
685 **321** 2d. multicoloured . . . . 1·25 50

1985. National Folklore Festival, Marrakesh.
686 **322** 2d. multicoloured 95 25

1985. 6th Pan-Arab Games.
687 **323** 2d. multicoloured 95 25

324 Emblem on Globe **325** Emblem

1985. 40th Anniv of U.N.O.
688 **324** 2d. multicoloured 60 25

1986. International Youth Year.
689 **325** 2d. multicoloured 60 25

326 Medal **327** Clasped Hands around Flag

1985. 10th Anniv of "Green March".
690 **326** 2d. multicoloured 60 25

1985. Palestinian Welfare.
691 **327** 2d. multicoloured 60 25

328 "Euphydryas desfontainii" **329** Arms

1985. Butterflies (1st series). Multicoloured.
692 80f. Type **328** 45 30
693 2d. "Colotis evagore" . . . . 1·40 90
See also Nos. 713/14.

1986. 25th Anniv of King Hassan's Coronation. Multicoloured.
694 80f. Type **329** 15 10
695 2d. King Hassan II (horiz) 60 25

330 Emblem **331** Vase

1986. 26th International Military Medicine Congress.
697 **330** 2d. multicoloured 60 25

1986. Stamp Day. As T **316**.
698 80f. orange and black 15 10
699 2d. green and black 60 25
DESIGNS: 80f. Sherifian postal seal of Maghzen-Safi; 2d. Sherifian postal seal of Maghzen-Safi (different).

1986. Blind Week.
700 **331** 1d. multicoloured 15 10

332 Footballer and Emblem

1986. World Cup Football Championship, Mexico. Multicoloured.
701 1d. Type **332** 50 10
702 2d. Cup, pictogram of footballer and emblem . . 1·00 25

333 Copper Coffee Pot **334** "Warionia saharae"

1986. Red Crescent.
703 **333** 2d. multicoloured . . . . 1·25 50

1986. Flowers. Multicoloured.
704 1d. Type **334** 60 10
705 2d. "Mandragora autumnalis" . . . . 1·25 50

335 Emblem **336** Dove and Olive Branch

1986. 18th Parachute Championships.
706 **335** 2d. multicoloured 90 25

1986. International Peace Year.
707 **336** 2d. multicoloured 60 25

337 Horsemen **338** Book

1986. Horse Week.
708 **337** 1d. light brown, pink and brown 60 10

1986. 11th Anniv of "Green March".
709 **338** 1d. multicoloured 15 10

339 Stylized People and Wheat

340 Marrakesh

1986. Fight against Hunger.
710 **339** 2d. multicoloured 60 25

1986. Aga Khan Architecture Prize.
711 **340** 2d. multicoloured 60 25

341 Hands holding Wheat

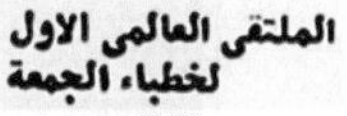

(342)

1986. "1,000,000 Hectares of Grain".
712 **341** 1d. multicoloured 15 10

1986. Butterflies (2nd series). As T **328**. Mult.
713 1d. "Elphinstonia charlonia" 65 35
714 2d. "Anthocharis belia" . . . 90 85

1987. Stamp Day. As T **316**.
715 1d. blue and black 15 10
716 2d. red and black 60 25
DESIGNS: 1d. Circular postal cancellation of Tetouan; 2d. Octagonal postal cancellation of Tetouan.

1987. Air. 1st World Reunion of Friday Preachers. Optd with T **342**.
717 **283** 2d. multicoloured 90 60

1987. Size 25 × 32 mm but inscr "1986".
718 **266** 1d.60 red, brown and gold 25 20
719 2d.50 red, grey and gold 60 25
720 6d.50 red, brown and gold 1·50 35
721 7d. red, brown and gold 1·75 45
722 8d.50 red, lilac and gold 2·00 50

343 Sidi Muhammad ben Yusuf addressing Crowd

1987. 40th Anniv of Tangier Conference. Each blue, silver and black.
723 1d. Type **343** 15 10
724 1d. King Hassan II making speech 15 10

344 Copper Lamp

345 Woman with Baby and Packet of Salt being emptied into Beaker

1987. Red Crescent.
726 **344** 2d. multicoloured 60 25

1987. UNICEF Child Survival Campaign.
727 **345** 1d. multicoloured 15 10

346 Decorated Pottery Jug

347 "Zygophyllum fontanesii"

1987. Blind Week.
728 **346** 1d. multicoloured 15 10

1987. Flowers. Multicoloured.
729 1d. Type **347** 15 10
730 2d. "Otanthus maritimus" . . 60 25

348 Arabesque from Door, Dar Batha Palace, Fez

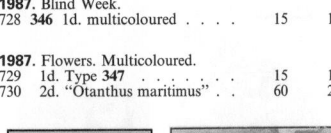

349 Map and King Hassan giving Blood

1987. Bicentenary of Diplomatic Relations with United States of America.
731 **348** 1d. blue, red and black 15 10

1987. Blood Transfusion Service.
732 **349** 2d. multicoloured 95 25

350 Woman from Melhfa

351 Emblem and Irrigated Field

1987. Sahara Costumes. Multicoloured.
733 1d. Type **350** 15 10
734 2d. Man from Derraa 60 25

1987. 13th International Irrigation and Drainage Congress.
735 **351** 1d. multicoloured 15 10

352 Baby on Hand and Syringe

353 Azurite

1987. United Nations Children's Fund Child Survival Campaign.
736 **352** 1d. multicoloured 15 10

1987. Mineral Industries Congress, Marrakesh. Multicoloured.
737 1d. Type **353** 50 10
738 2d. Wulfenite . . . . 1·00 50

354 "12" on Scroll

1987. 12th Anniv of "Green March".
739 **354** 1d. multicoloured 15 10

355 Activities

356 Desert Sparrow

1987. Armed Forces Social Services Month.
740 **355** 1d. multicoloured 15 10

1987. Birds. Multicoloured.
741 1d. Type **356** . . . . 1·10 45
742 2d. Barbary partridge . . . . 2·00 95

357 1912 25m. Stamp and Postmark

1987. 75th Anniv of Moroccan Stamps.
743 **357** 3d. mauve, black and green 80 40

358 "Cetiosaurus mogrebiensis"

1988. Dinosaur of Tilougguite.
744 **358** 2d. multicoloured . . . . 1·40 50

359 King Mohammed V

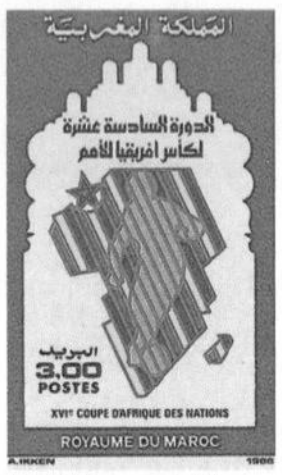

360 Map and Player in Arabesque Frame

1988. International Conf on King Mohammed V, Rabat.
745 **359** 2d. multicoloured 60 25

1988. 16th African Nations Cup Football Competition.
746 **360** 3d. multicoloured 75 40

361 Boy with Horse

1988. Horse Week.
747 **361** 3d. multicoloured . . . . 1·50 60

362 Pottery Flask

363 Anniversary Emblem

1988. Blind Week.
748 **362** 3d. multicoloured 75 35

1988. 125th Anniv of Red Cross.
749 **363** 3d. black, red and pink 75 35

364 "Citrullus colocynthis"

365 Breastfeeding Baby

1988. Flowers. Multicoloured.
750 3d.60 Type **364** 90 45
751 3d.60 "Calotropis procera" 90 45

1988. UNICEF Child Survival Campaign.
752 **365** 3d. multicoloured 95 35

366 Olympic Medals and Rings

367 Greater Bustard

1988. Olympic Games, Seoul.
753 **366** 2d. multicoloured 30 25

1988. Birds. Multicoloured.
754 3d.60 Type **367** . . . . . . 1·90 80
755 3d.60 Greater flamingo . . . 1·90 80

368 "13" on Scroll

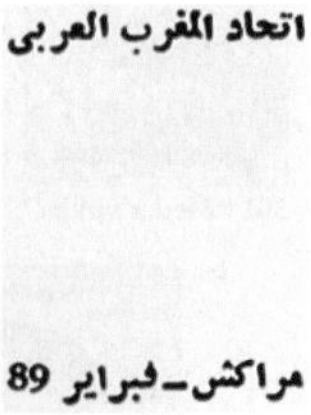

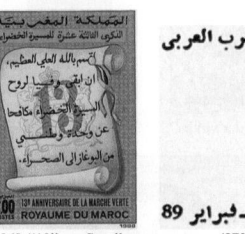

(370)

369 Housing of the Ksours and Csbaha

1988. 13th Anniv of "Green March".
756 **368** 2d. multicoloured 60 25

1988. Stamp Day. As T **316**.
757 3d. brown and black 95 35
758 3d. violet and black 95 35
DESIGNS: No. 757, Octagonal postal cancellation of Maghzen el Jadida; 758, Circular postal cancel-lation of Maghzen el Jadida.

1988. Size 25 × 32 mm but inscr "1988".
759 **266** 1d.20 blue, lilac and gold 15 10
760 3d.60 red and gold . . . 75 20
761 5d.20 brown, bis & gold 1·25 30

1989. Architecture.
762 **369** 2d. multicoloured 60 25

1989. Union of Arab Maghreb. No. 631 optd with T **370**.
763 **283** 1d.40 multicoloured . . . 50 15

371 King and Bishop with Chess Symbols

1989. 25th Anniv of Royal Moroccan Chess Federation.
764 **371** 2d. multicoloured 85 25

372 Copper Vase

373 Ceramic Vase

1989. Red Crescent.
765 **372** 2d. multicoloured 60 25

1989. Blind Week.
766 **373** 2d. multicoloured 60 25

374 King Hassan

375 "Cerinthe major"

1989. 60th Birthday of King Hassan II. Mult.
767 2d. Type **374** 75 25
768 2d. King Hassan in robes . . 75 25

1989. Flowers. Multicoloured.
770 2d. Type **375** 75 25
771 2d. "Narcissus papyraceus" 75 25

376 Telephone Handset linking Landmarks

1989. World Telecommunications Day.
772 **376** 2d. multicoloured 60 25

377 Gender Symbols forming Globe, Woman and Eggs

1989. 1st World Fertility and Sterility Congress.
773 **377** 2d. multicoloured 75 25

378 Desert Wheatear

1989. Birds. Multicoloured.
774 2d. Type **378** 50 50
775 3d. Shore lark . . . . 1·75 75

379 House of Representatives

1989. Centenary of Interparliamentary Union.
776 **379** 2d. multicoloured 60 25

380 Scroll

1989. 14th Anniv of "Green March".
777 **380** 3d. multicoloured 70 35

1990. Stamp Day. As T **316**.
778 2d. orange and black 60 20
779 3d. green and black 70 35
DESIGNS: 2d. Round postal cancellation of Casablanca; 3d. Octagonal postal cancellation of Casablanca.

381 Flags forming Map

1990. 1st Anniv of Union of Arab Maghreb.
780 **381** 2d. multicoloured 65 20

382 Oil Press

1990. 3rd World Olive Year. Multicoloured.
782 2d. Type **382** 60 15
783 3d. King Hassan and olives 85 25

383 Decorated Pot

1990. Blind Week.
784 **383** 2d. multicoloured 55 15

384 Silver Teapot

1990. Red Crescent.
785 **384** 2d. multicoloured 60 15

385 Arabic Script and Open Book

386 Turtle Dove

1990. International Literacy Year.
786 **385** 3d. green, yellow and black 80 25

1990. Birds. Multicoloured.
787 2d. Type **386** . . . . 1·10 35
788 3d. Hoopoe (horiz) . . . . . 1·90 65

387 "15" on Scroll

388 "35", Sun's Rays and Flag

1990. 15th Anniv of "Green March".
789 **387** 3d. multicoloured 80 25

1990. 35th Anniv of Independence.
790 **388** 3d. multicoloured 80 25

389 Dam

1990.
791 **389** 3d. multicoloured 80 25

390 Emblem

392 Projects and Emblem

391 Morse Code Apparatus

1990. 10th Anniv of Royal Academy of Morocco.
792 **390** 3d. multicoloured 85 25

1990. 20th Anniv of National Postal Museum. Multicoloured.
793 2d. Type **391** 60 15
794 3d. Horse-drawn mail wagon, 1913 . . . . 85 25

1991. Stamp Day. As T **316**.
796 2d. red and black 60 15
797 3d. blue and black 85 25
DESIGNS: 2d. Round postal cancellation of Rabat; 3d. Octagonal postal cancellation of Rabat.

1991. 40th Anniv of United Nations Development Programme.
798 **392** 3d. turquoise, yellow & blk 85 25

393 King Hassan

394 Mining

1991. 30th Anniv of Enthronement of King Hassan II. Multicoloured.
799 3d. Type **393** 85 25
800 3d. King Hassan in robes . . 85 25

1991. 70th Anniv of Mineral Exploitation by Sherifian Phosphates Office.
802 **394** 3d. multicoloured 85 25

395 Kettle on Stand

396 Lantern

1991. Blind Week.
803 **395** 3d. multicoloured 85 25

1991. Red Crescent.
804 **396** 3d. multicoloured 85 25

397 "Cynara humilis"

398 Man

1991. Flowers. Multicoloured.
805 3d. Type **397** 85 25
806 3d. "Pyrus mamorensis" . . 85 25

1991. Ouarzazate Costumes. Multicoloured.
807 3d. Type **398** 85 20
808 3d. Woman 85 20

1991. Inscribed "1991".
809 **266** 1d.35 red, green and gold 20 10

399 Road

400 Members' Flags and Map

1991. 19th World Roads Congress, Marrakesh.
810 **399** 3d. multicoloured 85 20

1991. 4th Ordinary Session of Arab Maghreb Union Presidential Council, Casablanca.
811 **400** 3d. multicoloured 85 20

401 "16" on Scroll

402 White Stork

1991. 16th Anniv of "Green March".
812 **401** 3d. multicoloured 85 20

1991. Birds. Multicoloured.
813 3d. Type **402** . . . . 1·50 50
814 3d. European bee eater . . . 1·50 50

403 Figures and Blood Splash

405 Zebra and Map of Africa

404 Emblem

1991. World AIDS Day.
815 **403** 3d. multicoloured 85 20

1991. 20th Anniv of Islamic Conf Organization.
816 **404** 3d. multicoloured 85 20

1991. African Tourism Year.
817 **405** 3d. multicoloured 85 20

1992. Stamp Day. As T **316**.
818 3d. green and black 85 20
819 3d. violet and black 85 20
DESIGNS: No. 818, Circular postal cancellation of Essaouira; No. 819, Octagonal postal cancellation of Essaouira.

406 Satellites around Earth

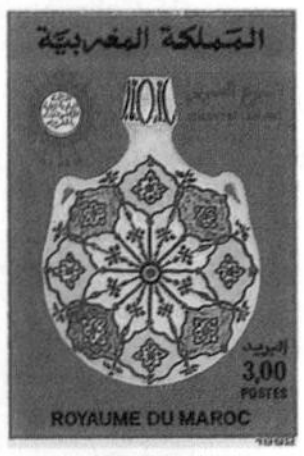
407 Bottle

1992. International Space Year.
820 **406** 3d. multicoloured 85 20

1992. Blind Week.
821 **407** 3d. multicoloured 85 20

408 Brass Jug

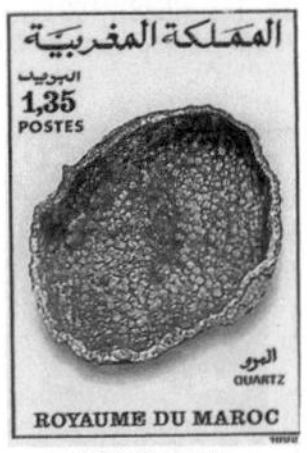

409 Quartz

1992. Red Crescent.
822 **408** 3d. multicoloured 85 50

1992. Minerals. Multicoloured.
823 1d.35 Type **409** 45 10
824 3d.40 Calcite . . . . 1·10 60

410 Woman

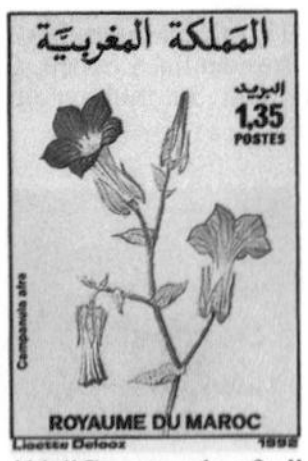

411 "Campanula afra"

1992. Tata Costumes. Multicoloured.
825 1d.35 Type **410** 20 10
826 3d.40 Man . . . . 1·10 60

1992. Flowers. Multicoloured.
827 1d.35 Type **411** 20 10
828 3d.40 "Thymus broussonetii" 1·10 60

412 Olympic Rings and Torch

414 La Koutoubia, La Giralda (cathedral bell-tower) and Exhibition Emblem

413 Map of Africa and Methods of Transport and Communication

1992. Olympic Games, Barcelona.
829 **412** 3d.40 multicoloured . . . 1·10 20

1992. Decade of Transport and Communications in Africa.
830 **413** 3d.40 multicoloured . . . 3·00 1·00

1992. "Expo '92" World's Fair, Seville.
831 **414** 3d.40 multicoloured . . . 1·10 50

415 Columbus's Fleet and Route Map

1992. 500th Anniv of Discovery of America by Columbus.
832 **415** 3d.40 multicoloured . . . 1·25 50

416 Pin-tailed Sandgrouse

1992. Birds. Multicoloured.
833 3d. Type **416** . . . . 1·10 40
834 3d. Griffon vulture ("Gyps fulvus") (vert) . . . . . . 1·10 40

417 "17" on Scroll

1992. 17th Anniv of "Green March".
835 **417** 3d.40 multicoloured . . . 1·10 20

418 Postal Messenger, Route Map and Cancellations

1992. Centenary of Sherifian Post. Multicoloured.
836 1d.35 Type **418** 20 10
837 3d.40 Postal cancellation, "100" on scroll and Sultan Mulay al-Hassan . . . . . 1·10 50

419 Conference Emblem

1992. International Nutrition Conference, Rome.
839 **419** 3d.40 multicoloured . . . 1·10 50

420 Douglas DC-9 Airliners on Runway

422 Satellite orbiting Earth

421 Dishes

1992. Al Massira Airport, Agadir.
840 **420** 3d.40 multicoloured . . . 1·10 20

1993. Stamp Day. As T **316**.
841 1d.70 green and black . . . 25 10
842 3d.80 orange and black . . . 1·10 50
DESIGNS: 1d.70, Round postal cancellation of Tangier; 3d.80, Octagonal postal cancellation of Tangier.

1993. Blind Week.
843 **421** 4d.40 multicoloured . . . 1·25 25

1993. World Meteorological Day.
844 **422** 4d.40 multicoloured . . . 1·25 25

423 Kettle on Stand

424 Emblem

1993. Red Crescent.
845 **423** 4d.40 multicoloured . . . 1·25 25

1993. World Telecommunications Day.
846 **424** 4d.40 multicoloured . . . 60 25

425 Woman extracting Argan Oil

426 Prince Sidi Mohammed

1993. Argan Oil. Multicoloured.
847 1d.70 Type **425** 25 10
848 4d.80 Branch and fruit of argan tree 70 30

1993. 30th Birthday of Prince Sidi Mohammed.
849 **426** 4d.80 multicoloured . . . 70 30

427 King Hassan and Mosque

428 Canopy, Sceptres, Flag and "40" on Sun

1993. Inauguration of King Hassan II Mosque.
850 **427** 4d.80 multicoloured . . . 70 30

1993. 40th Anniv of Revolution.
851 **428** 4d.80 multicoloured . . . 70 30

429 Post Box and Globe

430 Emblem

1993. World Post Day.
852 **429** 4d.80 multicoloured . . . 70 30

1993. Islamic Summer University.
853 **430** 4d.80 multicoloured . . . 70 30

431 "18" on Scroll

433 Flags, Scroll and "50"

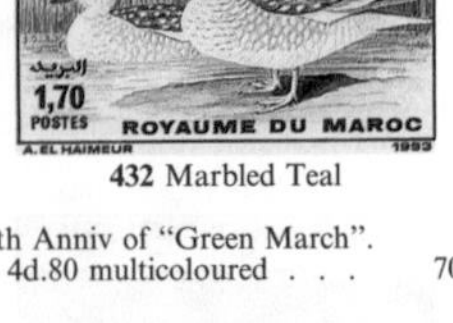

432 Marbled Teal

1993. 18th Anniv of "Green March".
854 **431** 4d.80 multicoloured . . . 70 30

1993. Waterfowl. Multicoloured.
855 1d.70 Type **432** 25 10
856 4d.80 Red-knobbed coot . . 70 30

1994. 50th Anniv of Istaqlal (Independence) Party.
857 **433** 4d.80 multicoloured . . . 70 30

434 House

435 Decorated Vase

1994. Signing of Uruguay Round Final Act of General Agreement on Tariffs and Trade, Marrakesh.
858 **434** 1d.70 multicoloured . . . 25 10
859 – 4d.80 multicoloured . . . 70 30
DESIGN: 4d.80, Mosque.

1994. Blind Week.
861 **435** 4d.80 multicoloured . . . 70 30

436 Copper Vessel

437 Couple

1994. Red Crescent.
862 **436** 4d.80 multicoloured . . . 70 30

1994. National Congress on Children's Rights. Children's Drawings. Multicoloured.
863 1d.70 Type **437** 25 10
864 4d.80 Couple under sun . . . 70 30

438 Ball, Moroccan and U.S.A. Flags, Pictogram and Trophy

1994. World Cup Football Championship, U.S.A.
865 **438** 4d.80 multicoloured . . . 70 30

1994. Size 25 × 32 mm but inscr "1994".
866 **266** 1d.70 red, blue and gold 25 10

439 King Hassan II and Arms

1994. 65th Birthday of King Hassan II. Mult.
867 1d.70 Type **439** 25 10
868 4d.80 King Hassan II (vert) 70 30

440 "100" and Rings

441 Saint-Exupery, Route Map and Biplane

1994. Centenary of International Olympic Committee.
869 **440** 4d.80 multicoloured . . . 70 30

1994. 50th Death Anniv of Antoine de Saint-Exupery (writer and pilot).
870 **441** 4d.80 multicoloured . . . 70 30

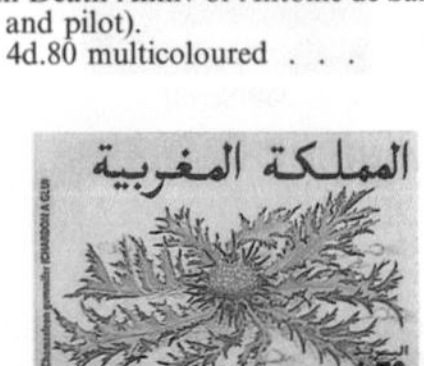

442 "Chamaeleon gummifer"

1994. Flowers. Multicoloured.
871 1d.70 Type **442** 25 10
872 4d.80 "Pancratium maritimum" (vert) 70 30

443 Slender-billed Curlew

1994. Birds. Multicoloured.
873 1d.70 Type **443** 25 10
874 4d.80 Audouin's gull 70 30

444 Scroll and March **445** Decorated Vase

1994. 19th Anniv of "Green March". Mult.
875 1d.70 Type **444** 25 10
876 4d.80 Marchers and Moroccan coastline 70 30

1994. Stamp Day. As T **316**.
877 1d.70 blue and black 25 10
878 4d.80 red and black 70 30
DESIGNS: 1d.70, Round postal cancellation of Marrakesh; 4d.80, Octagonal postal cancellation of Marrakesh.

1995. Blind Week.
879 **445** 4d.80 multicoloured . . . 70 30

446 Anniversary Emblem **447** Copper Vessel

1995. 50th Anniv of League of Arab States.
880 **446** 4d.80 multicoloured . . . 70 30

1995. Red Crescent.
881 **447** 4d.80 multicoloured . . . 70 30

448 "Malva hispanica" **449** European Roller

1995. Flowers. Multicoloured.
882 2d. Type **448** 30 10
883 4d.80 "Phlomis crinita" . . . 70 30

1995. Birds. Multicoloured.
884 1d.70 Type **449** 25 10
885 4d.80 Eurasian goldfinch . . 70 30

450 Anniversary Emblem, Building and Map

1995. 50th Anniv of F.A.O.
886 **450** 4d.80 multicoloured . . . 70 30

451 "50" and Flags

1995. 50th Anniv of U.N.O. Multicoloured.
887 1d.70 Type **451** 25 10
888 4d.80 U.N. emblem, doves and map 70 30

452 "20" on Scroll **453** "40", National Flag and Crown

1995. 20th Anniv of "Green March". Mult.
889 1d.70 Type **452** 25 10
890 4d.80 National flag, book and medal 70 30

1995. 40th Anniv of Independence.
891 **453** 4d.80 multicoloured . . . 70 30

1995. Stamp Day. As T **316**.
893 1d.70 bistre and black . . . 25 10
894 4d.80 lilac and black 70 30
DESIGNS: 1d.70, Round postal cancellation of Meknes; 4d.80, Octagonal cancellation of Meknes.

1996. Size 25 × 32 mm but inscr "1996".
895 **266** 5d.50 brown, red and gold 80 35
896 20d. brown, blue and gold 2·75 1·10

454 National Arms **455** Decorated Vase

1996. 35th Anniv of Enthronement of King Hassan II. Multicoloured.
897 2d. Type **454** 30 15
898 5d.50 King Hassan II 80 35

1996.
900 **455** 5d.50 multicoloured . . . 80 35

456 Leather Flask **457** "Cleonia lusitanica"

1996.
901 **456** 5d.50 multicoloured . . . 80 35

1996. Flowers. Multicoloured.
902 2d. Type **457** 30 15
903 5d.50 "Tulipa sylvestris" . . 80 35

458 King Hassan II wearing Military Uniform **459** Emblem and Runners

1996. 40th Anniv of Royal Armed Forces. Mult.
904 2d. Type **458** 30 15
905 5d.50 King Hassan II and globe 80 35

1996. Centenary of Modern Olympic Games. Olympic Games, Atlanta, U.S.A.
906 **459** 5d.50 multicoloured . . . 70 30

460 Osprey **461** "21" on Scroll

1996. Birds. Multicoloured.
907 2d. Type **460** 25 10
908 5d.50 Little egret 70 30

1996. 21st Anniv of "Green March".
909 **461** 5d.50 multicoloured . . . 70 30

1996. Stamp Day. As T **316**.
910 2d. orange and black 25 10
911 5d.50 green and black . . . 70 30
DESIGNS: 2d. Round postal cancellation of Maghzen-Fes; 5d.50, Octagonal postal cancellation of Maghzen-Fes.

462 Rainbow and Emblem

1996. 50th Anniv of UNICEF.
912 **462** 5d.50 multicoloured . . . 70 30

463 Terracotta Vessel

1997.
913 **463** 5d.50 multicoloured . . . 70 30

464 Lupin **465** King Mohammed V

1997. Flowers. Multicoloured.
914 2d. Type **464** 25 10
915 5d.50 Milk thistle 70 30

1997. 50th Anniv of Tangier Talks (determining future status of Tangier).
916 2d. Type **465** 25 10
917 2d. King Hassan II 25 10

466 Map in Open Book and Quill **468** Copper Door Knocker

467 Ibn Battuta and Globe

1997. World Book Day.
918 **466** 5d.50 multicoloured . . . 70 30

1997. International Conference on Ibn Battuta (explorer).
919 **467** 5d.50 multicoloured . . . 70 30

1997.
920 **468** 5d.50 multicoloured . . . 70 30

469 Demoiselle Crane **470** "22" on Scroll

1997. Birds. Multicoloured.
921 2d. Type **469** 25 10
922 5d.50 Blue tit 70 30

1997. 22nd Anniv of "Green March".
923 **470** 5d.50 multicoloured . . . 70 30

1997. Stamp Day. As T **316**.
924 2d. blue and black 25 10
925 5d.50 red and black 70 30
DESIGNS: 2d. Round postal cancellation of Maghzen-Larache; 5d.50, Octagonal postal cancellation of Maghzen-Larache.

471 Flask

1998. Moroccan Pottery.
926 **471** 6d. multicoloured 75 30

472 "Rhus pentaphylla" **473** Route Map and Emblem

1998. Plants. Multicoloured.
927 2d.30 Type **472** 30 15
928 6d. "Orchis papilionacea" . . 75 30

1998. 26th International Road Haulage Union Congress, Marrakesh.
929 **473** 6d. multicoloured 75 30

1998. Size 25 × 32 mm but inscr "1998".
930 **266** 2d.30 red, green and gold 30 15

474 Sconce **475** Players and Ball

1998. Moroccan Copperware.
931 **474** 6d. multicoloured 75 30

1998. World Cup Football Championship, France.
932 **475** 6d. multicoloured 75 30

476 Emblem, Rainbow, World Map and Hands

1998. International Year of the Ocean.
933 **476** 6d. multicoloured 75 30

477 King Mohammed V and King Hassan II

1998. 45th Anniv of Revolution.
934 **477** 6d. multicoloured 75 30

478 Globe and Letter

479 Nightingale

1998. World Stamp Day.
935 **478** 6d. multicoloured 75 30

1998. Birds. Multicoloured.
936 2d.30 Type **479** 30 15
937 6d. Ostrich 75 30

480 Scroll

481 Arabic Script

1998. 23rd Anniv of "Green March".
938 **480** 6d. multicoloured 75 30

1998. 40th Anniv of Code of Civil Liberties.
939 **481** 6d. multicoloured 75 30

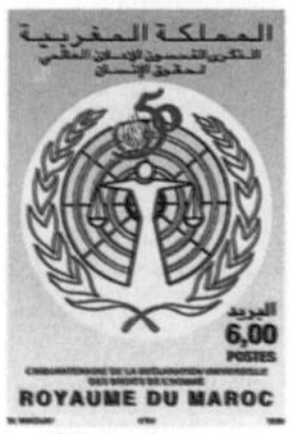

482 Anniversary Emblem

483 Mask and Globe

1998. 50th Anniv of Universal Declaration of Human Rights.
940 **482** 6d. multicoloured 75 30

1999. World Theatre Day.
941 **483** 6d. multicoloured 75 30

484 *Eryngium triquetrum*

1999. Flowers. Multicoloured.
942 2d.30 Type **484** 30 15
943 6d. Mistletoe 75 30

485 Bab Mansour Laalej

1999.
944 **485** 6d. multicoloured 75 30

486 King Hassan II on Throne

1999. 70th Birthday of King Hassan II. Mult.
945 2d.30 Type **486** 30 15
946 6d. King Hassan wearing robes 75 30

487 Necklace

1999. Moroccan Jewellery.
948 **487** 6d. multicoloured 75 30

488 Hands holding Globe and Water falling on Tree

489 Emblem

1999. World Environment Day.
949 **488** 6d. multicoloured 75 30

1999. 125th Anniv of Universal Postal Union.
950 **489** 6d. multicoloured 75 30

490 Obverse and Reverse of Medal

1999. F.A.O. Agriculture Medal.
951 **490** 6d. multicoloured 75 30

491 Stylized People

1999. Solidarity Week.
952 **491** 6d. blue, yellow and black 75 30

492 "24" on Scroll

1999. 24th Anniv of "Green March".
953 **492** 6d. multicoloured 75 30

493 Zebra Seabream

1999. Fishes. Multicoloured.
954 2d.30 Type **493** 30 15
955 6d. Opah 75 30

494 Stork on Nest (A. Slaoui)

1999. "Year of Morocco in France". Paintings. Multicoloured.
956 6d. Type **494** 75 30
957 6d. Women sitting on mat (Afif Bennani) 75 30
958 6d. Guitar (Abdelkader Rhorbal) 75 30
959 6d. View of harbour (A. Slaoui) 75 30

495 Players and Globe

2000. African Nations' Cup Football Championship.
960 **495** 6d. multicoloured 75 30

496 Globe and "2000"

2000. New Year.
961 **496** 6d. multicoloured 75 30

497 Beach and Calendar

2000. 40th Anniv of the Reconstruction of Agadir.
962 **497** 6d.50 multicoloured . . . 80 35

498 Emblem and Building

2000. 25th Anniv of Islamic Development Bank.
963 **498** 6d.50 multicoloured . . . 80 35

499 Stylized People

2000. National Disabled Persons Day.
964 **499** 6d.50 multicoloured . . . 80 35

500*Jasione montana*

2000. Flowers. Multicoloured.
965 2d.50 Type **500** 30 10
966 6d.60 *Pistorica breviflora* . . 80 30

501 Emblem

2000. 50th Anniv of World Meteorological Organization.
967 **501** 6d.50 multicoloured . . . 80 30

502 People dancing

2000. National Festival of Popular Arts, Marrakesh.
968 **502** 6d.50 multicoloured . . . 80 30

503 Open Book and White Dove

2000. International Year of Culture and Peace.
969 **503** 6d.50 multicoloured . . . 80 30

(504)

505 King Mohammed VI

2000. Air. International Conference on Hassan II. No. 631 optd with T **504**.
970 6d.50 on 1d.40 multicoloured 80 30

2000. 1st Anniv of Enthronement of King Mohammed VI. Multicoloured.
971 2d.50 Type **505** 30 10
972 6d.50 King Mohammed VI 80 30

506 Ruins, Volubis and Performers

2000. Mediterranean Song and Dance Festival.
974 **506** 6d.50 multicoloured . . . 80 30

507 Emblem and Olympic Torch

508 Emblem, House and Children

2000. Olympic Games, Sydney.
975 **507** 6d.50 multicoloured . . . 80 30

2000. 50th Anniv of S.O.S. Children's Villages.
976 **508** 6d.50 multicoloured . . . 80 30

509 Quill, Globe and Emblem

511 "25" on Scroll

510 Emblem

2000. International Teachers' Day.
977 **509** 6d.50 multicoloured . . . 80 30

2000. King Mohammed VI Solidarity Foundation.
978 **510** 6d.50 blue, yellow and black 80 30

2000. 25th Anniv of "Green March". Mult.
979 2d.50 Type **511** 30 10
980 6d.50 "25" and text 80 30

512 St. Exupery and Plane

513 "45" and National Flag

2000. Birth Centenary of Antonie de Saint.-Exupery (author).
981 **512** 6d.50 multicoloured . . . 80 30

2000. 45th Anniv of Independence.
982 **513** 6d.50 multicoloured . . . 80 30

514 Mediterranean Cardinalfish (*Apogon imberbis*)

2000. Fishes. Multicoloured.
983 2d.50 Type **514** 30 10
984 6d.50 Cadenat's rockfish (*Scorpaena loppei*) 80 30

515 El Bab el Gharbi

2001.
985 **515** 6d.50 multicoloured . . . 80 30

516 Hands holding Globe

517 King Mohammed VI enclosed in Droplet of Water

2001. International Water Day.
986 **516** 6d.50 multicoloured . . . 80 30

2001. 45th Anniv of Armed Forces. Multicoloured.
987 2d.50 Type **517** 30 10
988 6d.50 King Mohammed VI (different) 80 30

518 Spurge (*Euphorbia rigida*)

519 Koekelberg Basilica, Brussels

2001. Flowers. Multicoloured.
989 2d.50 Type **518** 30 10
990 6d.50 Horned poppy (*Glaucium flavum*) 80 30

2001. Religious Buildings.
991 2d.50 Type **519** 30 10
992 6d.50 Hassan II Mosque, Casablanca 80 30
Stamps of a similar design were issued by Belgium.

520 Globe and Dove

521 King Mohammed VI

2001. National Diplomacy Day.
993 **520** 6d.50 multicoloured . . . 80 30

2001. 2nd Anniv of Enthronement of King Mohammed VI. Multicoloured.
994 2d.50 Type **521** 30 10
995 6d. Smiling facing left 70 30
996 6d.50 Wearing decorated tie (crown upper left) 80 30
997 10d. King Mohammed VI (horiz) . . . . 1·20 50

522 Black-bellied Angler

523 Postal Seal, Kasir el Kabir (*Lophus budegassa*)

2001. Marine Life. Multicoloured.
998 2d.50 Type **522** 30 10
999 6d.50 Monk seal (*Monachus monachus*) (horiz) 80 10

2001. Stamp Day.
1000 **523** 2d.50 bistre and black 30 10
1001 – 6d.50 lilac and black . . 80 10
DESIGN: 6d.50 Octagonal seal.

524 Hands holding Globe

525 Palm Trees

2001. 7th Conference Session of Signatory States to United Nations Framework Convention on Climatic Change, Marrakech.
1002 **524** 6d.50 multicoloured . . 80 30

2001. World Day to Combat Desertification.
1003 **525** 6d.50 multicoloured . . 80 30

526 Flags and Marchers

2001. 26th Anniv of "Green March".
1004 **526** 6d.50 multicoloured . . 80 30

527 King Mohammed VI and Children

2001. King Mohammed VI Solidarity Foundation.
1005 **527** 6d.50 multicoloured . . 80 30
1006 – 6d.50 ultramarine, lemon and black (28 × 28 mm) 80 30
DESIGN: As No. 978 but inscr "2001".

528 Wallace Fountain, Paris

529 Hands holding Globe

2001. Moroccan—French Cultural Heritage. Fountains. Multicoloured.
1007 2d.50 Type **528** 30 10
1008 6d.50 Nejjarine fountain, Fez 80 30
Stamps of the same design were issued by France.

2001. United Nations Year of Dialogue among Civilizations.
1009 **529** 6d.50 multicoloured . . 80 30

530 Bab Chellah, Rabat

2002.
1010 **530** 6d.50 multicoloured . . 80 30

531 Globe and Woman

532 Cedar Tree

2002. International Women's Day.
1011 **531** 6d.50 multicoloured . . 80 30

2002.
1012 **532** 6d.50 multicoloured . . 60 30

533 Baby and Elderly Couple

2002. Second World Assembly on Aging.
1013 **533** 6d.50 multicoloured . . 80 30

534 Emblem

535 *Linaria bipartite*

2002. United Nations Special Session for Children (September 2001).
1014 **534** 6d.50 multicoloured . . 80 30

2002. Flowers. Multicoloured.
1015 2d.50 Type **535** 30 10
1016 6d.50 *Verbascum pseudocreticum* 80 30

536 Emblem and Map

2002. International Union of Telecommunications Conference, Marrakech. Multicoloured.
1017 6d.50 Type **536** 80 30
MS1018 120 × 90 mm. 10d. As No. 1017 but with design enlarged. Imperf . . . . 1·20 1·20

537 Mohamed Dorra, Father and Protestors

2002. Al Aqsa Intifada.
1019 **537** 6d.50 multicoloured . . 80 30

538 Oasis

2002. International Year of EcoTourism.
1020 **538** 6d.50 multicoloured . . 80 30

539 Map and Marchers

540 King Mohammed VI

2002. 27th Anniv of "Green March".
1021 **539** 6d.50 multicoloured . . 80 30

2002. King Mohammed VI Solidarity Foundation.
1022 **540** 6d.50 multicoloured . . 80 30
1023 – 6d.50 lemon and ultramarine (28 × 28 mm) 80 30
DESIGN: No. 1023 As No. 978 but inscr "2002".

541 Sultan Moulay Hassan and City

2002. 110th Anniv of Maghzen Post. Multicoloured.
1024 2d.50 Type **541** 30 10
1025 6d.50 Sultan Moulay Hassan and tall building 80 30

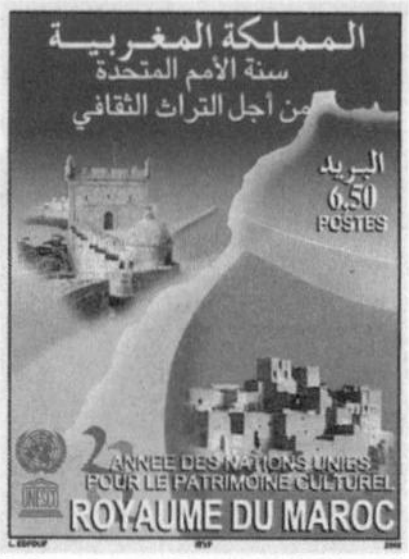

542 Fortresses, Dune and Coastline

2002. International Year of Cultural Heritage.
1026 **542** 6d.50 nmulticoloured . . 80 30

543 Allis Shad (*Alosa alosa*)

2002. Fish. Multicoloured.
1027 2d.50 Type **543** 30 10
1028 6d.50 *Epinephelus marginatus* 80 30

545 Bab El Okla, Tetouan

2003.
1032 **545** 6d.50 multicoloured . . 80 30

546 Le Sapin Forest

2003.
1033 **546** 6d.50 multicoloured . . 80 30

547 Child and Fountain

548 *Limonium sinuatum*

2003. International Year of Freshwater.
1034 **547** 6d.50 multicoloured . . 80 30

2003. Flora. Multicoloured.
1035 2d.50 Type **548** 30 10
1036 6d.50 *Echinops spinosus* . . 80 30

549 King Mohammed VI

2003.
1037 **549** 70f. multicoloured . . . 10 10
1038 80f. multicoloured . . . 10 10
1039 5d. multicoloured . . . 30 10
1040 20d. multicoloured . . . 2·40 1·00

550 Courtyard

2003. Millenary of Grand Mosque, Sale.
1060 **550** 6d.50 multicoloured . . 80 30

551 Stylized Figures and Globe

2003. World Youth Congress, Morocco.
1061 **551** 6d.50 multicoloured . . 80 30

552 Kings Mohammed V, Hassan II and Mohammed VI

2003. 50th Anniv of Revolution of King and People.
1062 **552** 6d.50 multicoloured . . 80 30

553 King Mohammed VI

2003. 40th Birthday of King Mohammed VI. Multicoloured.
1063 2d.50 Type **553** 30 10
1064 6d.50 Wearing traditional dress 80 30
MS1065 121 × 90 mm. Nos. 1063/4 1·10 1·10

2003. As T **521**. Self-adhesive.
1066 2d.50 As No. 994 . . . . . 30 10
1067 6d.50 As No. 1008 . . . . 80 30

554 *Sparisoma cretense*

2003. Fish. Multicoloured.
1068 2d.50 Type **554** 30 10
1069 6d. *Anthias anthias* 75 25

555 Satellites circling Globe

2003. World Post Day.
1070 **555** 6d.50 multicoloured . . 80 30

556 King Mohammed VI and Sick Child

2003. King Mohammed VI Solidarity Foundation.
1071 **556** 6d.50 multicoloured . . 80 30
1072 – 6d.50 lemon and ultramarine (28 × 28 mm) 80 30
DESIGN: No. 1072 As No. 978 but inscr "2003".

557 "28" and Marchers

2003. 28th Anniv of "Green March".
1073 **557** 6d.50 multicoloured . . 80 30

558 City and Cultural Symbols

2003. Rabat—Arab Cultural Capital, 2003.
1074 **558** 6d.50 multicoloured . . 80 30

559 School Children examining Stamps

2003. Philately in Schools.
1075 **559** 6d.50 multicoloured . . 80 30

560 Sun, Child writing and Clouds

2003. United Nations Decade for Literacy.
1076 **560** 6d.50 multicoloured . . 80 30

561 Chinese and Moroccan Flags as Clasped Hands

2003. 45th Anniv of Morocco—China Diplomatic Relations.
1077 **561** 6d.50 multicoloured . . 80 30

562 Ship and D'Ibn Battutah

2004. 700th Birth Anniv of D'Ibn Battutah (traveller).
1078 **562** 6d.50 multicoloured . . 80 30

563 Bab Agnaou, Marrakech

2004.
1079 **563** 6d.50 multicoloured . . 80 30

564 *Linaria gharbensis*

566 Trophy

565 Equestrian, Globe and Emblem

2004. Flowers. Multicoloured.
1080 2d.50 Type **564** 30 10
1081 6d.50 *Nigella damascene* . . 80 30

2004. 16th World Military Equestrian Championship, Temara, Morocco.
1082 **565** 6d.50 multicoloured . . 80 30

2004. 20th Anniv of Hassan II Tennis Grand Prix.
1083 **566** 6d.50 multicoloured . . 80 30

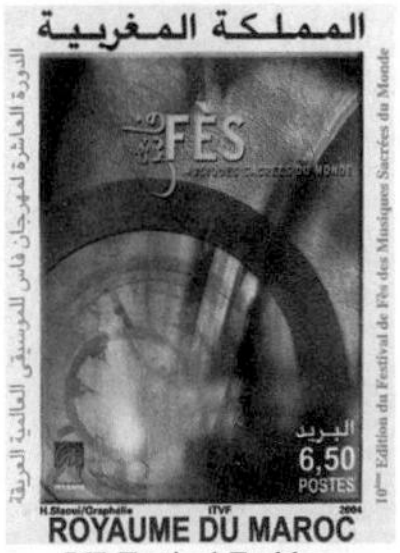

567 Festival Emblem

2004. 10th World Festival of Sacred Music.

1084	567	6d.50 multicoloured . .	80	30

568 Woman wearing Kaftan

570 Emblem

569 Tazoudasaurus Naimi

2004. Traditional Costume.

1085	568	6d.50 multicoloured . .	80	30

2004. Tazoudasaurus Naimi (dinosaur, newly discovered at Tazouda).

1086	569	6d.50 multicoloured . .	80	30

2004. 30th International Military History Congress, Rabat.

1087	570	6d.50 multicoloured . .		

571 King Mohammed VI

572 Dove holding Olive Branch and Globe

2004. 5th Anniv of Enthronement of King Mohammed VI.

1088		2d.50 Type 571	30	10
1089		6d. Seated	80	30

2004. International Peace Day.

1090	572	6d. multicoloured . . .	75	25

573 King Mohammed VI and Sick Woman

2004. King Mohammed VI Solidarity Foundation.

1091	573	6d.50 multicoloured . .	80	30
1092	–	6d.50 lemon and deep ultramarine (28 × 28 mm)	80	30

DESIGN: No. 1092 As No. 978 but inscr "2004".

574 "29" and Marchers

576 Child Holding Globe and Dove

575 Swordfish (*Xiphias gladius*)

2004. 29th Anniv of "Green March".

1093	574	6d. multicoloured . . .	75	25

2004. Marine Fauna. Multicoloured.

1094	2d.50 Type 575	30	10
1095	6d.50 Octopus (*Octopus vulgaris*)	80	30

2004. International Day of the Child.

1096	576	6d.50 multicoloured . .	80	30

POSTAGE DUE STAMPS

D 53

1965.

D162	D 53	5f. green	3·00	1·25
D163		10f. brown	50	25
D164		20f. red	50	25
D165		30f. sepia	1·25	50

D 153 Peaches

D 544 Strawberries

1974.

D393	–	5f. orange, grn & blk	10	10
D394	–	10f. green, red & blk	10	10
D395	–	20f. green and black	50	10
D396	D 153	30f. orge, grn & blk	60	35
D397	–	40f. green and black	15	10
D398	–	60f. orge, grn & blk	20	15
D399	–	80f. orge, grn & blk	50	20
D399a	–	1d. multicoloured	20	15
D400	–	1d.20 multicoloured	50	15
D401	–	1d.60 multicoloured	60	20
D402	–	2d. multicoloured	55	25
D403	–	5d. multicoloured	65	30

DESIGNS: 60f., 1d.60, Peaches. VERT: 5f. Oranges; 10f., 1d.20, Cherries; 20f. Raisins; 40f. Grapes; 80f. Oranges; 1, 5d. Apples; 2d. Strawberries.

2003. Multicoloured.

D1029	1d.50 Type D 544	10	10
D1030	2d. Cherries	25	10
D1031	5d. Apples	60	15

MOROCCO AGENCIES Pt. 1

Stamps used at British postal agencies in Morocco, N. Africa, the last of which closed on 30 April 1957.

I. GIBRALTAR ISSUES OVERPRINTED.

For use at all British Post Offices in Morocco.

All British P.O.s in Morocco were under the control of the Gibraltar P.O. until 1907 when control was assumed by H.M. Postmaster-General.

1898. Stamps of Gibraltar (Queen Victoria) optd **Morocco Agencies.**

9	7	5c. green	50	1·00
10		10c. red	2·25	30
11		20c. olive	7·00	70
3		20c. olive and brown	8·50	1·75
4		25c. blue	4·00	60
5		40c. brown	6·00	3·25
14		50c. lilac	9·50	3·50
7		1p. brown and blue	18·00	27·00
8		2p. black and red	22·00	27·00

1903. Stamps of Gibraltar (King Edward VII) optd **Morocco Agencies.**

24	8	5c. light green and green . .	9·50	3·00
18		10c. purple on red	9·00	40
26		20c. green and red	5·50	30·00
20		25c. purple and black on blue	8·00	30
28		50c. purple and violet	7·50	45·00
29		1p. black and red	29·00	80·00
30		2p. black and blue	16·00	35·00

II. BRITISH CURRENCY.

On sale at British P.O.s throughout Morocco, including Tangier, until 1937.

PRICES. Our prices for used stamps with these overprints are for examples used in Morocco. These stamps could also be used in the United Kingdom, with official sanction, from the summer of 1950 onwards, and with U.K. postmarks are worth about 50 per cent less.

Stamps of Great Britain optd **MOROCCO AGENCIES.**

1907. King Edward VII.

31	83	½d. green	2·25	8·50
32		1d. red	9·50	5·50
33	–	2d. green and red	10·00	5·50
34	–	4d. green and brown	3·75	4·00
35	–	4d. orange	12·00	12·00
36	–	6d. purple	16·00	19·00
37	–	1s. green and red	26·00	17·00
38	–	2s.6d. purple	80·00	£120

1914. King George V.

55	105	½d. green	2·00	50
43	104	1d. red	85	20
44	105	1½d. brown	3·25	12·00
45	106	2d. orange	4·00	60
58	104	2½d. blue	2·25	5·00
46	106	3d. violet	1·25	35
47		4d. green	3·25	1·25
60b	107	6d. purple	1·00	60
49	108	1s. brown	5·50	1·25
53	109	2s.6d. brown	38·00	25·00
74		5s. red	23·00	£100

1935. Silver Jubilee.

62	123	½d. green	1·25	6·50
63		1d. red	1·25	6·50
64		1½d. brown	2·25	10·00
65		2½d. blue	2·50	2·50

1935. King George V.

66	119	1d. red	3·25	14·00
67	118	1½d. brown	3·25	17·00
68	120	2d. orange	1·25	8·00
69	119	2½d. blue	1·75	4·25
70	120	3d. violet	50	30
71		4d. green	50	30
72	122	1s. brown	80	3·50

1936. King Edward VIII.

75	124	1d. red	10	30
76		2½d. blue	10	15

In 1937 unoverprinted Great Britain stamps replaced overprinted **MOROCCO AGENCIES** issues as stocks became exhausted. In 1949 overprinted issues reappeared and were in use at Tetuan (Spanish Zone), the only remaining British P.O. apart from that at Tangier.

1949. King George VI.

77	128	½d. green	1·75	7·00
94		½d. orange	2·00	1·00
78		1d. red	2·75	9·00
95		1d. blue	2·00	1·40
79		1½d. brown	2·75	8·50
96		1½d. green	2·00	2·75
80		2d. orange	3·00	9·00
97		2d. brown	2·25	4·00
81		2½d. blue	3·25	10·00
98		2½d. red	2·00	4·25
82		3d. violet	1·50	1·75
83	129	4d. green	50	1·25
84		5d. brown	3·00	15·00
85		6d. purple	1·50	1·50
86	130	7d. green	50	16·00
87		8d. red	3·00	6·50
88		9d. olive	50	11·00
89		10d. blue	50	6·50
90		11d. plum	70	7·50
91		1s. brown	2·75	6·00
92	131	2s.6d. green	16·00	35·00
93		5s. red	28·00	60·00

1951. Pictorials.

99	147	2s.6d. green	13·00	21·00
100	–	5s. red (No. 510)	13·00	23·00

1952. Queen Elizabeth II.

101	154	½d. orange	10	10
102		1d. blue	15	1·75
103		1½d. green	15	20
104		2d. brown	20	2·00
105	155	2½d. red	15	1·25
106		4d. blue	1·25	3·50
107	156	5d. brown	65	60
108		6d. purple	85	3·50
109	158	8d. mauve	70	70
110	159	1s. bistre	70	60

III. SPANISH CURRENCY.

Stamps surcharged in Spanish currency were sold at British P.O.s throughout Morocco until the establishment of the French Zone and the Tangier International Zone, when their use was confined to the Spanish Zone.

Stamps of Great Britain surch **MOROCCO AGENCIES** and value in Spanish currency.

1907. King Edward VII.

112	83	5c. on ½d. green	8·00	20
113		10c. on 1d. red	12·00	10
114a	–	15c. on 1½d. purple and green	3·00	20
115	–	20c. on 2d. green and red	2·75	20
116a	83	25c. on 2½d. blue	1·75	20
117	–	40c. on 4d. green & brown	1·25	3·00
118a	–	40c. on 4d. orange . . .	1·00	60
119a	–	50c. on 5d. purple and blue	2·00	3·25
120a	–	1p. on 10d. purple and red	22·00	12·00
121	–	3p. on 2s.6d. purple . . .	21·00	25·00
122	–	6p. on 5s. red	35·00	45·00
123	–	12p. on 10s. blue	75·00	75·00

1912. King George V.

126	101	5c. on ½d. green	3·00	20
127	102	10c. on 1d. red	1·00	10

1914. King George V.

128	105	3c. on ½d. green	1·25	4·50
129		5c. on ½d. green	75	10
130	104	10c. on 1d. red	1·50	10
131	105	15c. on 1½d. brown . . .	1·00	10
132	106	20c. on 2d. orange . . .	1·00	25
133	104	25c. on 2½d. blue	1·75	25
148	106	40c. on 4d. green	2·50	2·50
135	108	1p. on 10d. blue	3·50	7·00
142	109	3p. on 2s.6d. brown . . .	23·00	75·00
136		6p. on 5s. red	29·00	48·00
138		12p. on 10s. blue	£100	£170

1935. Silver Jubilee.

149	123	5c. on ½d. green	1·00	1·00
150		10c. on 1d. red	2·75	2·25
151		15c. on 1½d. brown . . .	5·50	18·00
152		25c. on 2½d. blue	3·50	2·25

1935. King George V.

153	118	5c. on ½d. green	1·00	19·00
154	119	10c. on 1d. red	2·50	9·50
155	118	15c. on 1½d. brown . . .	6·00	3·25
156	120	20c. on 2d. orange . . .	50	25
157	119	25c. on 2½d. blue	1·25	4·50
158	120	40c. on 4d. green	50	3·00
159	122	1p. on 10d. blue	6·00	30

1936. King Edward VIII.

160	124	5c. on ½d. green	10	10
161		10c. on 1d. red	50	2·00
162		15c. on 1½d. brown . . .	10	15
163		25c. on 2½d. blue	10	10

1937. Coronation.

164	126	15c. on 1½d. brown . . .	70	70

1937. King George VI.

165	128	5c. on ½d. green	1·25	30
182		5c. on ½d. orange	2·00	4·50
166		10c. on 1d. red	1·00	10
183		10c. on 1d. blue	3·25	7·50
167		15c. on 1½d. brown . . .	1·25	25
184		15c. on 1½d. green	1·75	17·00
168		25c. on 2½d. blue	2·00	1·25
185		25c. on 2½d. red	1·75	9·50
169	129	40c. on 4d. green	30·00	13·00
186		40c. on 4d. blue	60	10·00
170	130	70c. on 7d. green	1·75	14·00
171		1p. on 10d. blue	2·25	3·50

1940. Stamp Centenary.

172	134	5c. on ½d. green	30	2·75
173		10c. on 1d. red	3·75	2·50
174		15c. on 1½d. brown . . .	70	2·50
175		25c. on 2½d. blue	80	1·00

1948. Silver Wedding.

176	137	25c. on 2½d. blue	1·00	30
177	138	45p. on £1 blue	17·00	22·00

1948. Olympic Games.

178	139	25c. on 2½d. blue	50	1·25
179	140	30c. on 3d. violet	50	1·25
180	–	60c. on 6d. purple	50	1·25
181	–	1p.20 on 1s. brown . . .	60	1·25

1954. Queen Elizabeth II.

189	154	5c. on ½d. orange	15	2·75
188		10c. on 1d. blue	50	1·00
190	155	40c. on 4d. blue	70	1·75

IV. FRENCH CURRENCY.

Stamps surch in French currency were sold at British P.O.s in the French Zone.

Stamps of Great Britain surch **MOROCCO AGENCIES** and value in French currency.

1917. King George V.
191 **105** 3c. on ½d. green . . . . . 1·00 2·50
192 5c. on ½d. green 40 20
203 **104** 10c. on 1d. red . . . . . 30 2·00
194 **105** 15c. on 1½d. brown . . . 2·50 20
205 **104** 25c. on 2½d. blue . . . . 1·50 50
206 **106** 40c. on 4d. green 60 80
207 **107** 50c. on 5d. brown . . . . 1·50 10
198 **108** 75c. on 9d. green . . . . 1·00 75
209 90c. on 9d. green . . . . 16·00 7·50
210 1f. on 10d. blue . . . . . 1·00 10
211 1f.50 on 1s. brown . . . 10·00 2·25
200 **109** 3f. on 2s.6d. brown . . . 7·50 1·50
226 6f. on 5s. red . . . . . . 6·00 21·00

1935. Silver Jubilee.
212 **123** 5c. on ½d. green 15 15
213 10c. on 1d. red . . . . . 2·75 50
214 15c. on 1½d. brown . . . 35 50
215 25c. on 2½d. blue 30 25

1935. King George V.
216 **118** 5c. on ½d. green . . . . . 50 5·00
217 **119** 10c. on 1d. red 35 30
218 **118** 15c. on 1½d. brown . . . 4·75 5·50
219 **119** 25c. on 2½d. blue 30 15
220 **120** 40c. on 4d. green 30 15
221 **121** 50c. on 5d. brown 30 15
222 **122** 90c. on 9d. olive . . . . 35 1·75
223 1f. on 10d. blue 30 30
224 1f.50 on 1s. brown . . . 75 3·25

1936. King Edward VIII.
227 **124** 5c. on ½d. green 10 15
228 15c. on 1½d. brown . . . 10 15

1937. Coronation.
229 **126** 15c. on 1½d. brown . . . 30 20

1937. King George VI.
230 **128** 5c. on ½d. green . . . . . 2·25 2·50

V. TANGIER INTERNATIONAL ZONE.

This Zone was established in 1924 and the first specially overprinted stamps issued in 1927.

PRICES. Our note re U.K. usage (at beginning of Section II) also applies to **TANGIER** optd stamps.

Stamps of Great Britain optd **TANGIER**.

1927. King George V.
231 **105** ½d. green . . . . 3·00 20
232 **104** 1d. red . . . . 3·25 25
233 **105** 1½d. brown . . . . 6·00 3·75
234 **106** 2d. orange . . . . 3·25 20

1934. King George V.
235 **118** ½d. green . . . . 1·25 1·60
236 **119** 1d. red . . . . 4·25 2·50
237 **118** 1½d. brown 50 20

1935. Silver Jubilee optd **TANGIER TANGIER**.
238 **123** ½d. green . . . . 1·25 5·00
239 1d. red . . . . 14·00 15·00
240 1½d. brown . . . . 1·25 1·00

1936. King Edward VIII.
241 **124** ½d. green 10 20
242 1d. red 10 10
243 1½d. brown 15 10

1937. Coronation optd **TANGIER TANGIER**.
244 **126** 1½d. brown 50 50

1937. King George VI.
245 **128** ½d. green . . . . 2·50 1·50
280 ½d. orange . . . . 85 1·50
246 1d. red . . . . 7·00 1·50
281 1d. blue . . . . 1·00 3·00
247 1½d. brown . . . . 2·50 25
282 1½d. green . . . . 1·00 14·00
261 2d. orange . . . . 5·00 6·00
283 2d. brown . . . . 1·00 2·50
262 2½d. blue . . . . 1·75 6·00
284 2½d. red . . . . 1·00 5·50
263 3d. violet . . . . 70 1·25
264 **129** 4d. green . . . . 11·00 10·00
285 4d. blue . . . . 3·00 3·00
265 5d. brown . . . . 3·75 20·00
266 6d. purple 70 30
267 **130** 7d. green . . . . 1·25 13·00
268 8d. red . . . . 3·75 11·00
269 9d. olive . . . . 1·25 12·00
270 10d. blue . . . . 1·25 13·00
271 11d. plum . . . . 1·50 11·00
272 1s. brown . . . . 1·25 2·75
273 **131** 2s.6d. green . . . . . . 4·50 12·00
274 5s. red . . . . 13·00 38·00
275 – 10s. blue (No. 478a) . . . 45·00 £100

1940. Stamp Centenary.
248 **134** ½d. green . . . . 30 4·75
249 1d. red 45 50
250 1½d. brown . . . . 2·00 5·00

1946. Victory.
253 **135** 2½d. blue 65 65
254 – 3d. violet . . . . 65 2·00

1948. Silver Wedding.
255 **137** 2½d. blue 50 15
256 **138** £1 blue . . . . 20·00 25·00

1948. Olympic Games.
257 **139** 2½d. blue . . . . 1·00 2·00
258 **140** 3d. violet . . . . 1·00 2·00
259 – 6d. purple . . . . 1·00 2·00
260 – 1s. brown . . . . 1·00 1·25

1949. U.P.U.
276 **143** 2½d. blue . . . . 70 2·75
277 **144** 3d. violet . . . . 70 1·75
278 – 6d. purple . . . . 70 1·25
279 – 1s. brown . . . . 70 3·25

1951. Pictorial stamps.
286 **147** 2s.6d. green . . . . . . 9·50 5·00
287 – 5s. red (No. 510) . . . . 15·00 17·00
288 – 10s. blue (No. 511) . . . 20·00 17·00

1952. Queen Elizabeth II.
313 **154** ½d. orange 10 30
314 1d. blue 20 40
291 1½d. green 10 30
292 2d. brown 20 80
293 **155** 2½d. red . . . . 10 1·00
294 3d. lilac . . . . 20 1·25
320 4d. blue . . . . 65 2·00
296 **157** 5d. brown . . . . 60 1·00
297 6d. purple 45 15
298 7d. green . . . . 80 2·75
299 **158** 8d. mauve . . . . 60 1·50
300 9d. olive . . . . 1·40 75
301 10d. blue . . . . 1·40 2·75
302 11d. purple . . . . 1·40 3·25
303 **159** 1s. brown 50 70
304 1s.3d. green . . . . . . 65 4·25
305 1s.6d. blue . . . . 1·00 1·75

1953. Coronation.
306 **161** 2½d. red 40 50
307 – 4d. blue . . . . 1·00 50
308 **163** 1s.3d. green . . . . . . 1·00 1·25
309 – 1s.6d. blue . . . . 1·00 1·25

1955. Pictorials.
310 **166** 2s.6d. brown . . . . . . 3·50 9·00
311 – 5s. red . . . . 4·50 16·00
312 – 10s. blue . . . . 16·00 21·00

1957. Cent of British Post Office in Tangier. Queen Elizabeth II stamps optd **1857-1957 TANGIER**.
323 **154** ½d. orange 10 10
324 1d. blue 10 10
325 1½d. green 10 10
326 2d. brown 10 10
327 **155** 2½d. red . . . . 15 1·25
328 3d. lilac 15 40
329 4d. blue 30 20
330 **157** 5d. brown 30 35
331 6d. purple 30 35
332 7d. green 30 35
333 **158** 8d. mauve . . . . 30 1·00
334 9d. olive 30 30
335 10d. blue 30 30
336 11d. plum 30 30
337 **159** 1s. bistre 30 30
338 1s.3d. green . . . . . . 45 4·75
339 1s.6d. blue . . . . 50 1·60
340 **166** 2s.6d. brown . . . . . . 2·00 3·75
341 – 5s. red (No. 596a) . . . . 2·75 6·00
342 – 10s. blue (No. 597a) . . . 3·75 7·50

MORVI Pt. 1

A state of India, Bombay district. Now uses Indian stamps.

12 pies = 1 anna.

1 Maharaja Lakhdirji

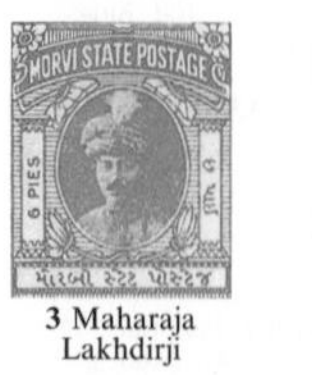

3 Maharaja Lakhdirji

1931.
8 **1** 3p. red . . . . 4·00 11·00
9b 6p. green . . . . 4·50 11·00
5 ½a. blue . . . . 2·75 14·00
6 1a. brown . . . . 3·25 24·00
10 1a. blue . . . . 3·75 11·00
7 2a. brown . . . . 4·00 35·00
11 2a. violet . . . . 10·00 32·00

1934.
16 **3** 3p. red . . . . 1·50 3·50
17 6p. green . . . . 90 2·75
14 1a. brown . . . . 1·10 11·00
19 2a. violet . . . . 2·50 17·00

MOSUL Pt. 1

Stamps used by Indian forces in Mesopotamia (now Iraq) at the close of the 1914–18 war.

12 pies = 1 anna; 16 annas = 1 rupee.

1919. Turkish Fiscal stamps surch **POSTAGE I.E.F. 'D'** and value in annas.
1 ½a. on 1pi. green and red . . . 2·25 1·90
2 1a. on 20pa. black on red . . . 1·40 1·75
4 2½a. on 1pi. mauve and yellow 1·50 1·50
5 3a. on 20pa. green . . . . . . 1·60 4·00
6 3a. on 20pa. green and orange 38·00 55·00
7 4a. on 1pi. violet . . . . . . 3·00 3·50
8 8a. on 10pa. red . . . . 4·00 5·00

MOZAMBIQUE Pt. 9; Pt. 13; Pt. 1

Former Overseas Province of Portugal in East Africa, granted independence in 1975. The Republic of Mozambique joined the Commonwealth on 12 November 1995.

1876. 1000 reis = 1 milreis.
1913. 100 centavos = 1 escudo.
1980. 100 centavos = 1 metical.

1876. "Crown" key-type inscr "MOCAMBIQUE".
1 P 5r. black . . . . 1·30 75
11 10r. yellow . . . . 6·25 3·50
19 10r. green . . . . 1·00 70
3 20r. bistre . . . . 1·30 65
20 20r. red £1100 £600
4a 25r. red 50 50
21 25r. lilac . . . . 3·50 1·40
14 40r. blue . . . . 22·00 9·25
22 40r. buff . . . . 3·00 2·75
6 50r. green . . . . £250 90·00
23 50r. blue 75 65
7 100r. lilac . . . . 1·30 70
8 200r. orange . . . . 5·25 3·75
9 300r. brown . . . . 3·00 1·90

1886. "Embossed" key-type inscr "PROVINCIA DE MOCAMBIQUE".
30 Q 5r. black . . . . 1·30 75
32 10r. green . . . . 1·30 75
34 20r. red . . . . 1·30 75
48 25r. lilac . . . . 11·00 5·25
37 40r. brown . . . . 1·70 1·20
38 50r. blue . . . . 2·10 75
40 100r. brown . . . . 2·10 75
42 200r. violet . . . . 3·75 2·30
43 300r. orange . . . . 5·00 3·25

1893. No. 37 surch **PROVISORIO 5 5**.
53 Q 5 on 40r. brown . . . . . . £140 95·00

1894. "Figures" key-type inscr "MOCAMBIQUE".
56 R 5r. orange 55 45
57 10r. mauve 55 45
58 15r. brown 70 55
59 20r. lilac 75 70
65 25r. green 55 30
60 50r. blue . . . . 3·50 70
67 75r. pink . . . . 1·60 1·30
61 80r. green . . . . 3·50 1·60
62 100r. brown on buff . . . . 1·80 1·50
68 150r. red on pink . . . . . 12·50 4·50
64 200r. blue on blue . . . . 3·75 3·25
69 300r. blue on brown . . . . 6·25 3·50

1895. "Embossed" key-type of Mozambique optd **1195 CENTENARIO ANTONINO 1895**.
71 Q 5r. black . . . . 7·75 5·75
72 10r. green . . . . 11·00 7·00
73 20r. red . . . . 12·50 7·75
74 25r. purple . . . . 12·50 7·75
75 40r. brown . . . . 12·50 10·50
76 50r. blue . . . . 12·50 10·50
77 100r. brown . . . . 12·50 10·50
78 200r. lilac . . . . 25·00 18·00
79 300r. orange . . . . 31·00 19·00

1897. No. 69 surch **50 reis**.
82 R 50r. on 300r. blue on brown £180 £190

1898. Nos. 34 and 37 surch **MOCAMBIQUE** and value.
84 Q 2½r. on 20r. red . . . . . . 21·00 17·00
85 5r. on 40r. brown . . . . . 28·00 21·00

1898. "King Carlos" key type inscr "MOCAMBIQUE". Name and value in red (500r.) or black (others).
86 S 2½r. grey 35 15
87 5r. red 35 20
88 10r. green 35 20
89 15r. brown . . . . 3·50 2·10
138 15r. green . . . . 1·30 90
90 20r. lilac 90 50
91 25r. green . . . . 1·00 50
139 25r. red . . . . 1·30 40
92 50r. blue . . . . 1·20 60
140 50r. brown . . . . 2·50 1·70
141 65r. blue . . . . 7·75 5·75
93 75r. pink . . . . 4·50 2·10
142 75r. purple . . . . 2·50 1·70
94 80r. mauve . . . . 4·50 2·10
95 100r. blue on blue . . . . 2·30 1·50
143 115r. brown on pink . . . 7·75 4·50
144 130r. brown on yellow . . . 7·75 4·75
96 150r. brown on yellow . . . 2·30 2·50
97 200r. purple on pink . . . . 2·20 1·50
98 300r. blue on pink . . . . 4·75 2·50
145 400r. blue on cream . . . . 11·50 8·75
99 500r. black on blue . . . . 10·00 5·25
100 700r. mauve on yellow . . . 17·00 7·50

1902. Various types surch.
146 S 50r. on 65r. blue . . . . . 3·25 2·50
101 R 65r. on 10r. mauve . . . . 2·50 2·30
102 65r. on 15r. brown . . . . 2·50 2·30
105 Q 65r. on 20r. red . . . . . 3·25 1·70
106 R 65r. on 20r. lilac . . . . 2·50 2·30
108 Q 65r. on 40r. brown . . . . 3·75 1·90
110 65r. on 200r. violet . . . . 3·25 1·70
111 V 115r. on 2½r. brown . . . . 2·50 2·30
113 Q 115r. on 5r. black . . . . 1·40 1·20
114 R 115r. on 5r. orange . . . . 2·50 2·30
115 115r. on 25r. green . . . . 2·50 2·30
117 Q 115r. on 50r. blue . . . . 1·40 1·20
120 130r. on 25r. mauve . . . . 1·90 1·20
121 R 130r. on 75r. red . . . . . 2·50 2·30
122 130r. on 100r. brn on buff 5·50 5·25
123 130r. on 150r. red on pink 2·50 2·30
124 130r. on 200r. blue on bl 5·00 4·75
126 Q 130r. on 300r. orange . . . 2·20 1·40
128 400r. on 10r. green . . . . 4·25 3·50
129 R 400r. on 50r. blue . . . . 1·50 1·20
130 400r. on 80r. green . . . . 1·50 1·40
132 Q 400r. on 100r. brown . . . 33·00 23·00
133 R 400r. on 300r. bl on brn . . 1·50 1·20

1902. "King Carlos" key-type of Mozambique optd **PROVISORIO**.
134 S 15r. brown . . . . 1·90 1·00
135 25r. green . . . . 1·90 1·00
136 50r. blue . . . . 3·75 2·20
137 75r. pink . . . . 5·50 3·00

1911. "King Carlos" key-type of Mozambique optd **REPUBLICA**.
147 S 2½r. grey 30 20
148 5r. orange 30 20
149 10r. green . . . . 1·00 60
150 15r. green 25 15
151 20r. lilac . . . . 1·00 25
152 25r. red 20 15
153 50r. brown 35 25
154 75r. purple 70 60
155 100r. blue on blue 70 60
156 115r. brown on pink . . . 1·00 60
157 130r. brown on yellow . . . 1·00 60
158 200r. purple on pink . . . . 2·00 1·00
159 400r. blue on yellow . . . . 2·00 1·00
160 500r. black on blue . . . . 2·00 1·30
161 700r. mauve on yellow . . . 2·00 1·30

1912. "King Manoel" key-type inscr "MOCAMBIQUE" with opt **REPUBLICA**.
162 T 2½r. lilac 25 15
163 5r. black 25 20
164 10r. green 25 20
165 20r. red 75 50
166 25r. brown 25 20
167 50r. blue 60 35
168 75r. brown 60 35
169 100r. brown on green . . . 60 35
170 200r. green on orange . . . 1·70 85
171 300r. black on blue . . . . 1·10 85
172 500r. brown and green . . 3·50 1·70

1913. Surch **REPUBLICA MOCAMBIQUE** and value on "Vasco da Gama" issues. (a) Portuguese Colonies.
173 ¼c. on 2½r. green 90 65
174 ½c. on 5r. red 90 65
175 1c. on 10r. purple 90 65
176 2½c. on 25r. green 90 65
177 5c. on 50r. blue . . . . . . 1·00 70
178 7½c. on 75r. brown . . . . . 1·70 95
179 10c. on 100r. brown . . . . 1·20 95
180 15c. on 150r. brown . . . . 1·20 1·10

(b) Macao.
181 ¼c. on ½a. green . . . . . . 1·30 1·10
182 ½c. on 1a. red . . . . 1·30 1·10
183 1c. on 2a. purple . . . . . 1·30 1·10
184 2½c. on 4a. green . . . . . 1·30 1·10
185 5c. on 8a. blue . . . . . . 3·50 2·50
186 7½c. on 12a. brown . . . . . 1·90 1·80
187 10c. on 16a. brown . . . . 1·50 1·10
188 15c. on 24a. brown . . . . 1·50 1·10

(c) Timor.
189 ¼c. on ½a. green . . . . . . 1·40 1·10
190 ½c. on 1a. red . . . . 1·40 1·10
191 1c. on 2a. purple . . . . . 1·40 1·10
192 2½c. on 4a. green . . . . . 1·40 1·10
193 5c. on 8a. blue . . . . . . 2·10 1·50
194 7½c. on 12a. brown . . . . . 2·10 1·50
195 10c. on 16a. brown . . . . 1·30 85
196 15c. on 24a. brown . . . . 1·30 85

1914. "Ceres" key-type inscr "MOCAMBIQUE".

197	U	¼c. green	25	20
198		½c. black	25	20
199		1c. green	25	25
200		1½c. brown	25	20
201		2c. red	25	20
270		2c. grey	20	20
202		2½c. violet	25	20
255		3c. orange	20	20
256		4c. pink	20	20
257		4½c. grey	20	20
203		5c. blue	25	20
275		6c. mauve	20	20
259		7c. blue	20	20
260		7½c. brown	20	15
278		8c. grey	20	15
279		10c. red	20	15
280		12c. brown	20	20
281		12c. green	20	20
283		15c. purple	20	15
284		20c. green	40	35
285		24c. blue	25	20
286		25c. brown	30	25
209		30c. brown on green	1·90	1·20
287		30c. green	30	20
295		30c. lilac on pink	1·30	1·10
210		40c. brown on pink	2·10	1·30
288		40c. turquoise	70	25
211		50c. orange on orange	3·50	2·50
289		50c. mauve	40	25
297		60c. brown on pink	1·40	1·10
290		60c. blue	75	40
291		60c. pink	1·20	70
298		80c. brown on blue	1·20	90
293		80c. red	95	40
299		1e. green on blue	2·00	1·30
264		1e. pink	1·20	75
301		1e. blue	1·20	85
300		2e. mauve on pink	1·70	90
302		2e. purple	95	55
303		5e. brown	8·75	5·50
304		10e. pink	13·00	5·25
305		20e. green	39·00	16·00

1915. Provisional issues of 1902 optd **REPUBLICA**.

226	S	50r. blue (No. 136)	75	65
227		50r. on 65r. blue	75	65
213		75r. pink (No. 137)	1·70	1·20
228	V	115r. on 2½r. brown	75	65
216	Q	115r. on 5r. black	45·00	32·00
229	R	115r. on 5r. orange	1·20	95
230		115r. on 25r. green	1·20	95
231		130r. on 75r. red	1·20	95
220		130r. on 100r. brown on buff	1·20	95
232		130r. on 150r. red on pink	1·20	95
233		130r. on 200r. blue on bl	1·20	95
223		400r. on 50r. blue	1·50	1·20
224		400r. on 80r. green	1·50	1·20
225		400r. on 300r. blue on brn	1·50	1·20

1918. Charity Tax stamp surch **2½ CENTAVOS**. Roul or perf.

248	C 16	2½c. on 5c. red	75	65

1920. Charity Tax stamps surch. (a) **CORREIOS** and value in figures.

306	C 15	1c. on 1c. green	70	55
307	C 16	1½c. on 5c. red	70	55

(b) **SEIS CENTAVOS**.

308	C 16	6c. on 5c. red	75	65

1921. "Ceres" stamps of 1913 surch.

309	U	10c. on ½c. black	1·60	1·00
310		30c. on 1½c. brown	1·60	1·00
316		50c. on 4c. pink	1·30	65
311		60c. on 2½c. violet	2·30	1·30
328		70c. on 2e. purple	75	40
329		1e.40 on 2e. purple	95	40

1922. "Ceres" key-type of Lourenco Marques surch.

312	U	10c. on ½c. black	1·60	1·10
314		30c. on 1½c. brown	1·60	1·10

1922. Charity Tax stamp surch **2$00**.

315	C 16	$2 on 5c. red	1·40	65

1924. 4th Death Centenary of Vasco da Gama. "Ceres" key-type of Mozambique optd **Vasco da Gama 1924**.

317	U	80c. pink	1·30	65

1925. Nos. 129 and 130 surch **Republica 40 C.**

318	R	40c. on 400r. on 50r.	90	50
319		40c. on 400r. on 80r.	90	50

1929. "Due" key-type inscr "MOCAMBIQUE" optd **CORREIOS**.

320	W	50c. lilac	1·20	90

23 Mousinho de Albuquerque

25 "Portugal" and Camoens' "The Lusiads"

1930. Albuquerque's Victories Commemorative. Vignette in grey.

321	23	50c. lake and red (Macontene)	8·75	8·75
322		50c. orge & red (Mujenga)	8·75	8·75
323		50c. mve & brn (Coolela)	8·75	8·75
324		50c. grey and green (Chaimite)	8·75	8·75
325		50c. bl & ind (Ibrahimo)	8·75	8·75
326		50c. blue and black (Mucuto-muno)	8·75	8·75
327		50c. vio & lilac (Naguema)	8·75	8·75

The above were for compulsory use throughout Mozambique in place of ordinary postage stamps on certain days in 1930 and 1931. They are not listed among the Charity Tax stamps as the revenue was not applied to any charitable fund.

1938. Value in red (1, 15c., 1e.40) or black (others).

330	25	1c. brown	10	10
331		5c. brown	15	10
332		10c. purple	15	10
333		15c. black	15	10
334		20c. grey	15	10
335		30c. green	15	10
336		35c. green	5·75	2·30
337		40c. red	15	10
338		45c. blue	25	20
339		50c. brown	25	10
340		60c. green	35	20
341		70c. brown	35	20
342		80c. green	35	20
343		85c. red	1·00	60
344		1e. purple	70	20
345		1e.40 blue	8·00	2·10
346		1e.75 blue	5·25	2·00
347		2e. lilac	1·80	80
348		5e. green	3·00	80
349		10e. brown	6·50	1·60
350		20e. orange	35·00	4·25

1938. As 1938 issue of Macao. Name and value in black.

351	54	1c. green (postage)	15	15
352		5c. brown	15	15
353		10c. red	15	15
354		15c. purple	15	15
355		20c. grey	15	15
356	–	30c. purple	15	15
357	–	35c. green	30	15
358	–	40c. brown	30	15
359	–	50c. mauve	30	15
360	–	60c. black	30	15
361	–	70c. violet	30	15
362	–	80c. orange	30	15
363	–	1e. red	65	30
364	–	1e.75 blue	2·30	50
365	–	2e. red	2·30	60
366	–	5e. green	4·50	90
367	–	10e. blue	10·50	1·30
368	–	20e. brown	27·00	2·50
369	56	10c. red (air)	35	35
370		20c. violet	35	35
371		50c. orange	45	35
372		1e. blue	45	35
373		2e. red	75	35
374		3e. green	1·60	35
375		5e. brown	2·75	60
376		9e. red	5·00	1·00
377		10e. mauve	8·75	1·90

DESIGNS: 30 to 50c. Mousinho de Albuquerque; 60c. to 1e. Dam; 1e.75 to 5e. Henry the Navigator; 10, 20e. Afonso de Albuquerque.

1938. No. 338 surch **40 centavos**.

378	25	40c. on 45c. blue	4·00	2·50

26a Route of President's Tour

27 New Cathedral, Lourenco Marques

1938. President Carmona's 2nd Colonial Tour.

379	26a	80c. violet on mauve	3·00	2·00
380		1e.75 blue on blue	10·00	4·00
381		3e. green on green	17·00	6·25
382		20e. brown on cream	90·00	36·00

1944. 400th Anniv of Lourenco Marques.

383	27	50c. brown	1·30	50
384	–	50c. green	1·30	50
385	–	1e.75 blue	5·75	1·70
386a	–	20e. black	16·00	1·60

DESIGNS—HORIZ: 1e.75, Lourenco Marques Central Railway Station; 20e. Town Hall, Lourenco Marques.

See also No. 405.

1946. Nos. 354, 364 and 375 surch.

387		10c. on 15c. purple (postage)	1·00	45
388		60c. on 1e.75 blue	1·70	50
389		3e. on 5e. brown (air)	15·00	10·00

1947. No. 386a surch.

390		2e. on 20e. black	2·75	80

30 Lockheed L.18 Lodestar

1946. Air. Values in black.

391	30	1e.20 red	3·00	1·00
392		1e.60 blue	3·00	1·10
393		1e.70 purple	5·00	1·50
394		2e.90 brown	8·00	3·00
395		3e. green	8·75	3·00

1947. Air. Optd **Taxe percue**. Values in red (50c.) or black (others).

397	30	50c. black	1·30	55
398		1e. pink	1·30	55
399		3e. green	2·20	70
400		4e.50 green	3·75	1·20
401		5e. red	5·25	1·30
402		10e. blue	15·00	3·50
403		20e. violet	39·00	9·50
404		50e. orange	80·00	24·00

1948. As T **27** but without commemorative inscr.

405		4e.50 red	3·25	70

31 Antonio Enes

33 Lourenco Marques

1948. Birth Centenary of Antonio Enes.

406	31	50c. black and cream	95	45
407		5e. purple and cream	2·10	1·40

1948.

408	–	5c. brown	40	15
409	–	10c. purple	40	15
410	–	20c. brown	40	15
411	–	30c. purple	40	15
412	–	40c. green	50	15
413	33	50c. grey	50	15
414	–	60c. purple	50	15
415	33	80c. violet	50	15
416	–	1e. red	75	25
417	–	1e.20 grey	85	25
418	–	1e.50 violet	1·10	30
419	–	1e.75 blue	1·70	40
420	–	2e. brown	1·50	30
421	–	2e.50 blue	5·25	25
422	–	3e. green	2·50	25
423	–	3e.50 green	3·25	25
424	–	5e. green	3·25	25
425	–	10e. brown	8·25	35
426	–	15e. red	19·00	1·90
427	–	20e. orange	29·00	3·25

DESIGNS—VERT: 5, 30c. Gogogo Peak; 20, 40c. Zumbo River; 60c., 3e.50, Nhanhangare Waterfall. HORIZ: 10c., 1e.20, Railway bridge over River Zambesi at Sena; 1, 5e. Gathering coconuts; 1e.50, 2e. River Pungue at Beira; 1e.75, 3e. Polana beach, Lourenco Marques; 2e.50, 10e. Bird's eye view of Lourenco Marques; 15, 20e. Malema River.

1949. Honouring the Statue of Our Lady of Fatima. As T **62** of Macao.

428		50c. blue	3·25	1·00
429		1e.20 mauve	7·00	2·10
430		4e.50 green	25·00	7·00
431		20e. brown	55·00	10·50

35 Aircraft and Globe

36 Clown Triggerfish

1949. Air.

432	35	50c. brown	65	20
433		1e.20 violet	1·30	40
434		4e.50 blue	2·75	65
435		5e. green	10·00	85
436		20e. brown	14·50	4·25

1949. 75th Anniv of U.P.U. As T **64** of Macao.

437		4e.50 blue	3·25	1·00

1950. Holy Year. As Nos. 425/6 of Macao.

438		1e.50 orange	85	40
439		3e. blue	1·20	60

1951. Fishes. Multicoloured.

440		5c. Type **36**	35	10
441		10c. Thread-finned butterflyfish	20	10
442		15c. Racoon butterflyfish	80	30
443		20c. Lionfish	25	10
444		30c. Pearl puffer	25	10
445		40c. Golden filefish	20	10
446		50c. Spot-cheeked surgeonfish	20	10
447		1e. Pennant coralfish (vert)	30	10
448		1e.50 Seagrass wrasse	30	10
449		2e. Sombre sweetlips	30	10
450		2e.50 Blue-striped snapper	90	15
451		3e. Convict tang	90	15
452		3e.50 Starry triggerfish	1·10	10
453		4e. Cornetfish	1·10	25
454		4e.50 Vagabond butterflyfish	2·40	25
455		5e. Sail-backed mailcheek	2·40	10
456		6e. Dusky batfish (vert)	2·40	10
457		8e. Moorish idol (vert)	4·00	35
458		9e. Triangulate boxfish	4·00	30
459		10e. Eastern flying gurnard	10·50	1·50
460		15e. Red-toothed triggerfish	60·00	12·50
461		20e. Picasso triggerfish	31·00	4·50
462		30e. Long-horned cowfish	37·00	6·25
463		50e. Spotted cowfish	46·00	11·50

1951. Termination of Holy Year. As T **69** of Macao.

464		5e. red and orange	2·40	1·00

37 Victor Cordon (colonist)

39 Liner and Lockheed Constellation Airliner

1951. Birth Centenary of Cordon.

465	37	1e. brown and light brown	2·40	40
466		5e. black and blue	12·00	1·10

1952. 1st Tropical Medicine Congress, Lisbon. As T **71** of Macao.

467		3e. orange and blue	1·50	50

DESIGN: 3e. Miguela Bombarda Hospital.

1952. 4th African Tourist Congress.

468	39	1e.50 multicoloured	85	45

40 Missionary

41 Citrus Butterfly

1953. Missionary Art Exhibition.

469	40	10c. red and lilac	15	10
470		1e. red and green	85	20
471		5e. black and blue	2·30	60

1953. Butterflies and Moths. Multicoloured.

472		10c. Type **41**	10	10
473		15c. "Amphicallia thelwalli"	10	10
474		20c. Forest queen	10	10
475		30c. Western scarlet	10	10
476		40c. Black-barred red-tip	10	10
477		50c. Mocker swallowtail	10	10
478		80c. "Nudaurelia hersilia dido"	15	10
479		1e. African moon moth	15	10
480		1e.50 Large striped swallowtail	20	10
481		2e. "Athletes ethica"	5·00	35
482		2e.30 African monarch	4·00	35
483		2e.50 Green swallowtail	9·00	35
484		3e. "Arniocera ericata"	1·10	15
485		4e. Apollo moth	45	10
486		4e.50 Peach moth	65	10
487		5e. "Metarctica lateritia"	65	10
488		6e. "Xanthospilopteryx mozambica"	75	20
489		7e.50 White bear	4·00	35
490		10e. Flame-coloured charaxes	7·00	1·20
491		20e. Fervid tiger moth	13·50	1·20

42 Stamps

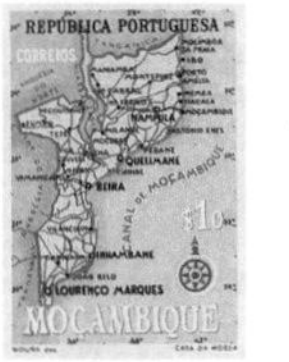

43 Map of Mozambique

1953. Philatelic Exhibition, Lourenco Marques.

492	42	1e. multicoloured	1·30	35
493		3e. multicoloured	5·00	90

1953. Portuguese Postage Stamp Centenary. As T **75** of Macao.

494		50c. multicoloured	80	50

1954. 4th Centenary of Sao Paulo. As T **76** of Macao.

495		3e.50 multicoloured	40	20

1954. Multicoloured map; Mozambique territory in colours given.
496 **43** 10c. lilac 10 10
497 20c. yellow 10 10
498 50c. blue 10 10
499 1e. yellow 20 10
500 2e.30 white 55 40
501 4e. orange 65 30
502 10e. green . . . . 1·70 20
503 20e. brown . . . . 3·00 40

44 Arms of Beira

45 Mousinho de Albuquerque

1954. 1st Philatelic Exhibition, Manica and Sofala.
504 **44** 1e.50 multicoloured 40 20
505 3e.50 multicoloured 90 40

1955. Birth Centenary of M. de Albuquerque.
506 **45** 2e. brown and grey 55 30
507 – 2e.50 multicoloured . . . . 1·10 50
DESIGN: 2e.50, Equestrian statue of Albuquerque.

46 Arms and Inhabitants

47 Beira

1956. Visit of President to Mozambique. Multicoloured. Background in colours given.
508 **46** 1e. cream 40 15
509 2e.50 blue 85 40

1957. 50th Anniv of Beira.
510 **47** 2e.50 multicoloured 80 40

1958. 6th International Congress of Tropical Medicine. As T **79** of Macao.
511 1e.50 multicoloured . . . . . 1·70 90
DESIGN: 1e.50, "Strophanthus grandiflorus" (plant).

1958. Brussels International Exn. As T **78** of Macao.
512 3e.50 multicoloured 30 20

48 Caravel

49 "Arts and Crafts"

1960. 500th Death Anniv of Prince Henry the Navigator.
513 **48** 5e. multicoloured 65 20

1960. 10th Anniv of African Technical Co-operation Commission.
514 **49** 3e. multicoloured 50 30

50 Arms of Lourenco Marques

51 Fokker F.27 Friendship and De Havilland D.H.89 Dragon Rapide over Route Map

1961. Arms. Multicoloured.
515 5c. Type **50** 10 10
516 15c. Chibuto 10 10
517 20c. Nampula 10 10
518 30c. Inhambane 10 10
519 50c. Mozambique (city) . . . 10 10
520 1e. Matola 25 10
521 1e.50 Quelimane 25 10
522 2e. Mocuba 40 10
523 2e.50 Antonio Enes . . . . . 1·30 10
524 3e. Cabral 50 15
525 4e. Manica 50 15
526 4e.50 Pery 50 15
527 5e. St. Tiago de Tete 50 15
528 7e.50 Porto Amelia . . . . . 1·10 30
529 10e. Chinde . . . . 1·60 40
530 20e. Joao Belo . . . . 3·75 65
531 50e. Beira . . . . 7·75 1·50

1962. Sports. As T **82** of Macao. Multicoloured.
532 50c. Water-skiing 10 10
533 1e. Wrestling 90 20
534 1e.50 Gymnastics 40 15
535 2e.50 Hockey 35 15
536 4e.50 Netball . . . . 1·00 40
537 15e. Outboard speedboat racing . . . . 1·90 1·10

1962. Malaria Eradication. Mosquito design as T **83** of Macao. Multicoloured.
538 2e.50 "Anopheles funestus" 95 35

1962. 25th Anniv of D.E.T.A. (Mozambique Airline).
539 **51** 3e. multicoloured 60 20

52 Lourenco Marques in 1887 and 1962

53 Oil Refinery, Sonarep

1962. 75th Anniv of Lourenco Marques.
540 **52** 1e. multicoloured 45 20

1962. Air. Multicoloured.
541 1e.50 Type **53** 65 20
542 2e. Salazar Academy 55 20
543 3e.50 Aerial view of Lourenco Marques Port . . 55 20
544 4e.50 Salazar Barrage 55 20
545 5e. Trigo de Morais Bridge and Dam 55 20
546 20e. Marcelo Caetano Bridge and Dam . . . . 2·40 70
Each design includes an airplane in flight.

54 Arms of Mozambique and Statue of Vasco da Gama

55 Nef, 1430

1963. Bicentenary of City of Mozambique.
547 **54** 3e. multicoloured 45 20

1963. 10th Anniv of T.A.P. Airline. As T **52** of Portuguese Guinea.
548 2e.50 multicoloured 40 20

1963. Evolution of Sailing Ships. Multicoloured.
549 10c. Type **55** 10 10
550 20c. Caravel, 1436 (vert) . . 10 10
551 30c. Lateen-rigged caravel, 1460 (vert) 10 10
552 50c. Vasco da Gama's ship "Sao Gabriel", 1497 (vert) 10 10
553 1e. Don Manuel's nau, 1498 (vert) 40 10
554 1e.50 Galleon, 1530 (vert) . . 40 10
555 2e. Nau "Flor de la Mer", 1511 (vert) 40 10
556 2e.50 Caravel "Redonda", 1519 . . . . 40 10
557 3e.50 Nau, 1520 (vert) . . . 50 10
558 4e. Portuguese Indies galley, 1521 . . . . 60 15
559 4e.50 Galleon "Santa Tereza", 1639 (vert) . . . 60 15
560 5e. Nau "N. Senhora da Conceicao", 1716 (vert) . . 15·00 25
561 6e. Warship "N. Senhora do Bom Sucesso", 1764 . . 75 25
562 7e.50 Bomb launch, 1788 . . 1·10 30
563 8e. Naval brigantine "Lebre", 1793 . . . . 1·10 30
564 10e. Corvette "Andorinha", 1799 . . . . 1·10 30
565 12e.50 Naval schooner "Maria Teresa", 1820 . . . 1·20 65
566 15e. Warship "Vasco da Gama", 1841 . . . . . . 1·90 65
567 20e. Sail frigate "Don Fernando II e Gloria", 1843 (vert) . . . . 2·50 75
568 30e. Cadet barque "Sagres I", 1924 (vert) . . . . 4·00 1·50

1964. Centenary of National Overseas Bank. As T **84** of Macao but view of Bank building, Lourenco Marques.
569 1e.50 multicoloured 40 10

56 Pres. Tomas

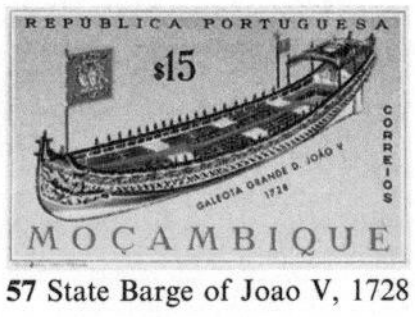

57 State Barge of Joao V, 1728

1964. Presidential Visit.
570 **56** 2e.50 multicoloured 40 10

1964. Portuguese Marine, 18th and 19th Centuries. Multicoloured.
571 15c. Type **57** 10 10
572 35c. State barge of Jose I, 1753 . . . . 10 10
573 1e. Barge of Alfandega, 1768 35 10
574 1e.50 Oarsman of 1780 (vert) 45 20
575 2e.50 State barge "Pinto da Fonseca", 1780 . . . . . 25 10
576 5e. State barge of Carlota Joaquina, 1790 . . . . . 45 20
577 9e. Don Miguel's state barge, 1831 . . . . 1·20 70

1965. I.T.U. Centenary. As T **85** of Macao.
578 1e. multicoloured 40 20

1966. 40th Anniv of Portuguese National Revolution. As T **86** of Macao, but showing different building. Multicoloured.
579 1e. Beira railway station and Antonio Enes Academy . . 30 20

58 Arquebusier, 1560

59 Luis de Camoens (poet)

1967. Portuguese Military Uniforms. Mult.
580 20c. Type **58** 10 10
581 30c. Arquebusier, 1640 . . . 10 10
582 40c. Infantryman, 1777 . . . 10 10
583 50c. Infantry officer, 1777 . . 10 10
584 80c. Drummer, 1777 . . . . 40 15
585 1e. Infantry sergeant, 1777 40 10
586 2e. Infantry major, 1784 . . 45 10
587 2e.50 Colonial officer, 1788 45 15
588 3e. Infantryman, 1789 . . . 45 15
589 5e. Colonial bugler, 1801 . . 1·00 30
590 10e. Colonial officer, 1807 . . 1·10 45
591 15e. Infantryman, 1817 . . . 1·90 1·20

1967. Centenary of Military Naval Association. As T **88** of Macao. Multicoloured.
592 3e. A. Coutinho and paddle-gunboat "Tete" 20 15
593 10e. J. Roby and paddle-gunboat "Granada" . . . 1·00 40

1967. 50th Anniv of Fatima Apparitions. As T **89** of Macao.
594 50c. "Golden Crown" . . . 20 15

1968. 500th Birth Anniv of Pedro Cabral (explorer). As T **90** of Macao.
595 1e. Erecting the Cross at Porto Sequro (horiz) . . . 15 10
596 1e.50 First mission service in Brazil (horiz) 35 10
597 3e. Church of Grace, Santarem 65 30

1969. Birth Centenary of Admiral Gago Coutinho. As T **91** of Macao.
598 70c. Admiral Gago Coutinho Airport, Lourenco Marques (horiz) 25 10

1969. 400th Anniv of Camoens' Visit to Mozambique. Multicoloured.
599 15c. Type **59** 10 10
600 50c. Nau of 1553 (horiz) . . 15 10
601 1e.50 Map of Mozambique, 1554 . . . . 25 15
602 2e.50 Chapel of Our Lady of Baluarte (horiz) 35 20
603 5e. Part of the "Lusiad" (poem) 50 35

1969. 500th Birth Anniv of Vasco da Gama (explorer). As T **92** of Macao. Multicoloured.
604 1e. Route map of Da Gama's Voyage to India (horiz) . . 20 10

1969. Centenary of Overseas Administrative Reforms. As T **93** of Macao.
605 1e.50 multicoloured 25 10

1969. 500th Birth Anniv of King Manoel I. As T **95** of Macao. Multicoloured.
606 80c. Illuminated arms (horiz) 20 10

1970. Birth Centenary of Marshal Carmona. As T **96** of Macao. Multicoloured.
607 5e. Portrait in ceremonial dress 35 20

60 Fossilized Fern

1971. Rocks, Minerals and Fossils. Mult.
608 15c. Type **60** 10 10
609 50c. "Lytodiscoides conduciensis" (fossilized snail) 10 10
610 1e. Stibnite 15 10
611 1e.50 Pink beryl 20 10
612 2e. Endothiodon and fossil skeleton 25 10
613 3e. Tantalocolumbite 35 10
614 3e.50 Verdelite 60 15
615 4e. Zircon 65 25
616 10e. Petrified tree-stump . . . 2·20 60

1972. 400th Anniv of Camoens' "The Lusiads" (epic poem). As T **98** of Macao. Multicoloured.
617 4e. Mozambique Island in 16th century 40 20

1972. Olympic Games, Munich. As T **99** of Macao. Multicoloured.
618 3e. Hurdling and swimming 25 20

1972. 50th Anniv of 1st Flight, Lisbon–Rio de Janeiro. As T **100** of Macao. Multicoloured.
619 1e. Fairey IIID seaplane "Santa Cruz" at Recife . . 15 10

61 Racing Dinghies

1973. World Championships for "Vauriens" Class Yachts, Lourenco Marques.
620 **61** 1e. multicoloured 15 10
621 – 1e.50 multicoloured 15 10
622 – 3e. multicoloured 40 20
DESIGNS: Nos. 621/2 similar to Type **61**.

1973. Centenary of I.M.O./W.M.O. As T **102** of Macao.
623 2e. multicoloured 30 20

62 Dish Aerials

1974. Inauguration of Satellite Communications Station Network.
624 **62** 50c. multicoloured 20 10

63 Bird with "Flag" Wings

1975. Implementation of Lusaka Agreement.
625 **63** 1e. multicoloured 10 10
626 1e.50 multicoloured 15 10
627 2e. multicoloured 25 10
628 3e.50 multicoloured 35 25
629 6e. multicoloured 80 30

1975. Independence. Optd **INDEPENDENCIA 25 JUN 75**.
631 **43** 10c. multicoloured (postage) 50 50
632 – 40c. mult (No. 476) 10 10
633 **62** 50c. multicoloured 20 15
634 **61** 1e. multicoloured 30 25
635 – 1e.50 mult (No. 621) . . . 85 75
636 – 2e. multicoloured (No. 623) 2·40 2·40
637 – 2e.50 mult (No. 535) 35 30
638 – 3e. multicoloured (No. 618) 40 35
639 – 3e. multicoloured (No. 622) 45 40
640 – 3e.50 mult (No. 614) . . . 2·40 2·40
641 – 4e.50 mult (No. 536) . . . 2·75 1·50
642 – 7e.50 mult (No. 489) . . . 80 30
643 – 10e. mult (No. 616) . . . . 1·40 35
644 – 15e. mult (No. 537) . . . . 1·75 1·50
645 **43** 20e. multicoloured . . . . 4·75 4·25
646 – 3e.50 multicoloured (No. 543) (air) 35 25
647 – 4e.50 mult (No. 544) 40 25
648 – 5e. multicoloured (No. 545) 1·25 50
649 – 20e. mult (No. 546) . . . . 2·00 4·25

66 Workers, Farmers and Children

67 Farm Worker

1975. "Vigilance, Unity, Work". Multicoloured.

650	20c. Type **66**	10	10
651	30c. Type **66**	10	10
652	50c. Type **66**	10	10
653	2e.50 Type **66**	15	10
654	4e.50 Armed family, workers and dancers	25	15
655	5e. As No. 654	35	15
656	10e. As No. 654	95	30
657	50e. As No. 654	4·25	2·10

1976. Women's Day.

659 **67**	1e. black and green	10	10
660 –	1e.50 black and brown	10	10
661 –	2e.50 black and blue	15	10
662 –	10e. black and red	90	40

DESIGNS: 1e.50, Teaching; 2e.50, Nurse; 10e. Mother.

1976. Pres. Kaunda's First Visit to Mozambique. Optd **PRESIDENTE KENNETH KAUNDA PREMEIRA VISITA 20/4/1976.**

663 **63**	2e. multicoloured	15	10
664	3e.50 multicoloured	25	15
665	6e. multicoloured	50	30

69 Arrival of President Machel

70 Mozambique Stamp of 1876 and Emblem

1976. 1st Anniv of Independence. Mult.

666	50c. Type **69**	10	10
667	1e. Proclamation ceremony	10	10
668	2e.50 Signing ceremony	15	10
669	7e.50 Soldiers on parade	40	20
670	20e. Independence flame	1·50	1·10

1976. Stamp Centenary.

671 **70**	1e.50 multicoloured	10	10
672	6e. multicoloured	30	20

1976. "FACIM" Industrial Fair. Optd **FACIM 1976.**

673 **66**	2e.50 multicoloured	30	15

72 Weapons and Flag

73 Thick-tailed Bush baby

1976. Army Day.

674 **72**	3e. multicoloured	20	10

1977. Animals. Multicoloured.

675	50c. Type **73**	15	10
676	1e. Ratel (horiz)	15	10
677	1e.50 Temminck's ground pangolin	20	10
678	2e. Steenbok (horiz)	20	10
679	2e.50 Diademed monkey	25	10
680	3e. Hunting dog (horiz)	25	10
681	4e. Cheetah (horiz)	35	10
682	5e. Spotted hyena	50	15
683	7e.50 Warthog (horiz)	1·00	25
684	8e. Hippopotamus (horiz)	1·10	30
685	10e. White rhinoceros (horiz)	1·10	30
686	15e. Sable antelope	1·60	65

74 Congress Emblem

75 "Women" (child's drawing)

1977. 3rd Frelimo Congress, Maputo. Mult.

687	3e. Type **74**	15	10
688	3e.50 Macheje Monument (site of 2nd Congress) (34 × 24 mm)	20	10
689	20e. Maputo Monument (23 × 34 mm)	1·40	50

1977. Mozambique Women's Day.

690 **75**	5e. multicoloured	25	10
691	15e. multicoloured	65	25

76 Labourer and Farmer

77 Crowd with Arms and Crops

1977. Labour Day.

692 **76**	5e. multicoloured	25	10

1977. 2nd Anniv of Independence.

693 **77**	50c. multicoloured	10	10
694	1e.50 multicoloured	10	10
695	3e. multicoloured	15	10
696	15e. multicoloured	60	25

78 "Encephalartos ferox"

79 "Chariesthes bella"

1978. Stamp Day. Nature Protection. Mult.

697	1e. Type **78**	10	10
698	10e. Nyala	50	20

1978. Beetles. Multicoloured.

699	50c. Type **79**	10	10
700	1e. "Tragocephalus variegata"	10	10
701	1e.50 "Monochamus leuconotus"	10	10
702	3e. "Prosopocera lactator"	25	10
703	5e. "Dinocephalus ornatus"	40	10
704	10e. "Tragiscoschema nigroscriptus"	60	20

80 Violet-crested Turaco

81 Mother and Child

1978. Birds. Multicoloured.

705	50c. Type **80**	35	15
706	1e. Lilac-breasted roller	45	15
707	1e.50 Red-headed weaver	45	15
708	2e.50 Violet starling	50	25
709	3e. Peter's twin-spot	1·00	35
710	15e. European bee eater	2·50	70

1978. Global Eradication of Smallpox.

711 **81**	15e. multicoloured	45	25

82 "Crinum delagoense"

83 First Stamps of Mozambique and Canada

1978. Flowers. Multicoloured.

712	50c. Type **82**	10	10
713	1e. "Gloriosa superba"	10	10
714	1e.50 "Eulophia speciosa"	10	10
715	3e. "Erithrina humeana"	15	10
716	5e. "Astripomoea malvacea"	80	15
717	10e. "Kigelia africana"	1·00	60

1978. "CAPEX '78" International Stamp Exhibition, Toronto.

718 **83**	15e. multicoloured	45	25

84 Mozambique Flag

85 Boy with Books

1978. 3rd Anniv of Independence. Multicoloured.

719	1e. Type **84**	10	10
720	1e.50 Coat of Arms	10	10
721	7e.50 People and Constitution	25	15
722	10e. Band and National Anthem	30	20

1978. 11th World Youth Festival, Havana. Mult.

724	2e.50 Type **85**	10	10
725	3e. Soldiers	15	10
726	7e.50 Harvesting wheat	25	20

86 Czechoslovakian 50h. Stamp, 1919

1978. "PRAGA '78" International Stamp Exhibition.

727 **86**	15e. blue, ochre and red	45	30

87 Football

1978. Stamp Day. Sports. Multicoloured.

729	50c. Type **87**	10	10
730	1e.50 Putting the shot	10	10
731	3e. Hurdling	15	10
732	7e.50 Basketball	35	20
733	12e.50 Swimming	45	35
734	25e. Roller-skate hockey	1·25	60

88 U.P.U. Emblem and Dove

1979. Membership of U.P.U.

735 **88**	20e. multicoloured	1·00	45

89 Eduardo Mondlane

1979. 10th Death Anniv of Eduardo Mondlane (founder of FRELIMO). Multicoloured.

736	1e. Soldier handing gourd to woman	10	10
737	3e. FRELIMO soldiers	15	10
738	7e.50 Children learning to write	30	20
739	12e.50 Type **89**	40	30

90 Shaded Silver

91 I.Y.C. Emblem

1979. Domestic Cats. Multicoloured.

740	50c. Type **90**	10	10
741	1e.50 Manx cat	10	10
742	2e.50 British blue	15	10
743	3e. Turkish cat	20	10
744	12e.50 Long-haired tabby	85	55
745	20e. African wild cat	1·50	90

1979. Obligatory Tax. International Year of the Child.

746 **91**	50c. red	15	10

92 Wrestling

1979. Olympic Games, Moscow (1980). Mult.

747	1e. Type **92**	10	10
748	2e. Running	10	10
749	3e. Horse jumping	15	10
750	5e. Canoeing	15	10
751	10e. High jump	30	20
752	15e. Archery	50	40

93 Flowers

1979. International Year of the Child. Mult.

754	50c. Type **93**	10	10
755	1e.50 Dancers	10	10
756	3e. In the city	15	10
757	5e. Working in the country	15	10
758	7e.50 Houses	25	15
759	12e.50 Transport	1·50	50

94 Flight from Colonialism

1979. 4th Anniv of Independence. Multicoloured.

760	50c. Type **94**	10	10
761	2e. Eduardo Mondlane (founder of FRELIMO)	10	10
762	3e. Armed struggle, death of Mondlane	15	10
763	7e.50 Final fight for liberation	25	15
764	15e. President Samora Machel proclaims victory	45	35

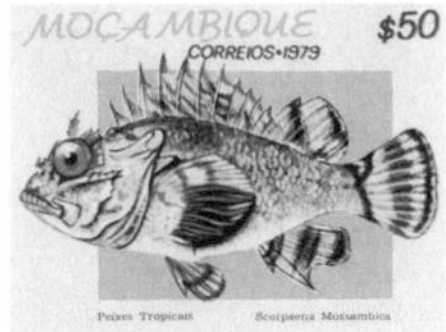

95 Golden Scorpionfish

1979. Tropical Fish. Multicoloured.

766	50c. Type **95**	10	10
767	1e.50 Golden trevally	15	10
768	2e.50 Brick goby	20	10
769	3e. Clown surgeonfish	25	15
770	10e. Lace goby	60	25
771	12e.50 Yellow-edged lyretail	95	40

96 Quartz

1979. Minerals. Multicoloured.
772 1e. Type **96** 10 10
773 1e.50 Beryl 10 10
774 2e.50 Magnetite 15 10
775 5e. Tourmaline 30 10
776 10e. Euxenite 60 20
777 20e. Fluorite . . . . 1·40 45

97 Soldier handing out Guns

1979. 15th Anniv of Fight for Independence.
778 **97** 5e. multicoloured 25 15

98 Locomotive No. 1, 1914

1979. Early Locomotives. Multicoloured.
779 50c. Type **98** 15 10
780 1e.50 Gaza Railway locomotive No. 1, 1898 . . 20 10
781 3e. Cape Government Railway 1st Class locomotive, 1878 . . . . . 45 10
782 7e.50 Delagoa Bay Railway locomotive No. 9, 1892 . . 75 20
783 12e.50 Locomotive No. 41, 1896 . . . . 1·25 30
784 15e. Trans Zambesia Railway Class D steam locomotive 1·40 35

99 Dalmatian

1979. Dogs. Multicoloured.
785 50c. Basenji (vert) 10 10
786 1e.50 Type **99** 15 10
787 3e. Boxer 15 10
788 7e.50 Blue gascon pointer . . 35 15
789 12e.50 English cocker spaniel 85 25
790 15e. Pointer . . . . 1·25 30

100 "Papilio nireus"

1979. Stamp Day. Butterflies. Multicoloured.
791 1e. Type **100** 10 10
792 1e.50 "Amauris ochlea" . . . 10 10
793 2e.50 "Pinacopterix eriphia" 15 10
794 5e. "Junonia hierta" 35 10
795 10e. "Nephronia argia" . . . 1·00 20
796 20e. "Catacroptera cloanthe" 2·10 90

101 "Dermacentor circumguttatus cunhasilvai" and African Elephant

1980. Ticks. Multicoloured.
797 50c. Type **101** 20 10
798 1e.50 "Dermacentor rhinocerinos" and black rhinoceros 30 10
799 2e.50 "Amblyomma hebraeum" and giraffe . . 40 15
800 3e. "Amblyomma pomposum" and eland . . 50 15
801 5e. "Amblyomma theilerae" and cow 60 15
802 7e.50 "Amblyomma eburneum" and African buffalo 85 30

102 Ford "Hercules" Bus, 1950

1980. Road Transport. Multicoloured.
803 50c. Type **102** 10 10
804 1e.50 Scania "Marco-Polo" bus, 1978 . . . . 10 10
805 3e. Bussing Nag Bus, 1936 15 10
806 5e. Ikarus articulated bus, 1978 . . . . 20 10
807 7e.50 Ford Taxi, 1929 . . . 40 15
808 12e.50 Fiat "131" Taxi, 1978 80 20

103 Soldier and Map of Southern Africa

1980. Zimbabwe Independence.
809 **103** 10e. blue and brown . . . 40 15

104 Marx, Engels and Lenin

1980. International Workers' Day.
810 **104** 10e. multicoloured 40 15

105 "Market" (Moises Simbine)

1980. "London 1980" International Stamp Exhibition. Multicoloured.
811 50c. "Heads" (Malangatana) 10 10
812 1e.50 Type **105** 10 10
813 3e. "Heads with Helmets" (Malangatana) 15 10
814 5e. "Women with Goods" (Machiana) 20 10
815 7e.50 "Crowd with Masks" (Malangatana) 25 15
816 12e.50 "Man and Woman with Spear" (Mankeu) . . 50 25

106 Telephone

1980. World Telecommunications Day.
817 **106** 15e. multicoloured 60 25

107 Mueda Massacre **108** Crowd waving Tools

1980. 20th Anniv of Mueda Massacre.
818 **107** 15e. green, brown and red 60 25

1980. 5th Anniv of Independence.
819 – 1e. black and red 10 10
820 **108** 2e. multicoloured 10 10
821 – 3e. multicoloured 15 10
822 – 4e. multicoloured 20 10
823 – 5e. black, yellow and red 20 10
824 – 10e. multicoloured 40 15
DESIGNS—As T **108**: 1e. Crowd, doctor tending patient, soldier and workers tilling land; 3e. Crowd with flags and tools; 4e. Stylized figures raising right hand; 5e. Hand grasping flags, book and plants; 10e. Figures carrying banners each with year date. 55 × 37 mm: 30e. Soldiers.

109 Gymnastics

1980. Olympic Games, Moscow. Multicoloured.
826 50c. Type **109** 10 10
827 1e.50 Football 10 10
828 2e.50 Running 10 10
829 3e. Volleyball 20 10
830 10e. Cycling 40 15
831 12e.50 Boxing 45 20

110 Narina's Trogon

1980. Birds. Multicoloured.
832 1m. Type **110** 35 10
833 1m.50 South African crowned crane 40 10
834 2m.50 Red-necked spurfowl 45 10
835 5m. Ostrich 85 20
836 7m.50 Spur-winged goose . . 1·00 25
837 12m.50 African fish eagle . . 1·40 35

111 Family and Census Officer

1980. First General Census.
838 **111** 3m.50 multicoloured . . . 25 10

112 Animals fleeing from Fire

1980. Campaign against Bush Fires.
839 **112** 3m.50 multicoloured . . . 25 10

113 Common Harp

1980. Stamp Day. Shells. Multicoloured.
840 1m. Type **113** 10 10
841 1m.50 Arthritic spider conch 15 10
842 2m.50 Venus comb murex . . 20 10
843 5m. Clear sundial 40 15
844 7m.50 Ramose murex 50 20
845 12m.50 Diana conch . . . . 1·10 35

114 Pres. Machel, Electricity Pylons, Aircraft and Lorry

1981. "Decade for Victory over Underdevelopment".
846 **114** 3m.50 blue and red . . . 2·00 75
847 – 7m.50 brown and green 25 15
848 – 12m.50 mauve and blue 50 30
DESIGNS: 7m.50, Pres. Machel and armed forces on parade; 12m.50, Pres. Machel and classroom scenes.

115 Footballer and *Athletic de Bilbao* Stadium

1981. World Cup Football Championship, Spain (1982). Multicoloured.
849 1m. Type **115** 10 10
850 1m.50 Valencia, C.F. 10 10
851 2m.50 Oviedo C.F. 10 10
852 5m. R. Betis Balompie . . . 20 10
853 7m.50 Real Zaragoza 25 15
854 12m.50 R.C.D. Espanol . . . 50 25

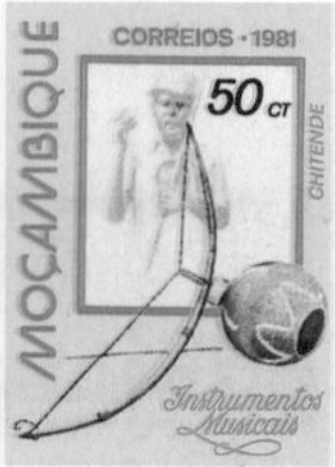

116 Giraffe **117** Chitende

1981. Protected Animals. Multicoloured.
856 50c. Type **116** 10 10
857 1m.50 Topi 10 10
858 2m.50 Aardvark 10 10
859 3m. African python 10 10
860 5m. Loggerhead turtle . . . 20 15
861 10m. Marabou stork . . . . 1·10 45
862 12m.50 Saddle-bill stork . . . 1·40 55
863 15m. Kori bustard . . . . . 1·90 65

1981. Musical Instruments. Multicoloured.
864 50c. Type **117** 10 10
865 2m. Pankwe (horiz) 10 10
866 2m.50 Kanyembe 10 10
867 7m. Nyanga (horiz) 30 20
868 10m. Likuti and M'Petheni (horiz) 70 25

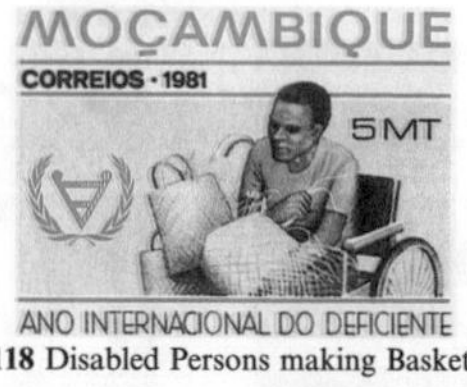

118 Disabled Persons making Baskets

1981. International Year of Disabled People.
869 **118** 5m. multicoloured 25 15

119 De Havilland Dragon Rapide

1981. Air. Mozambique Aviation History. Mult.

870	50c. Type **119**	10	10
871	1m.50 Junkers Ju 52/3m	10	10
872	3m. Lockheed Super Electra	20	15
873	7m.50 De Havilland Dove	35	30
874	10m. Douglas DC-3	50	35
875	12m.50 Fokker Friendship	75	50

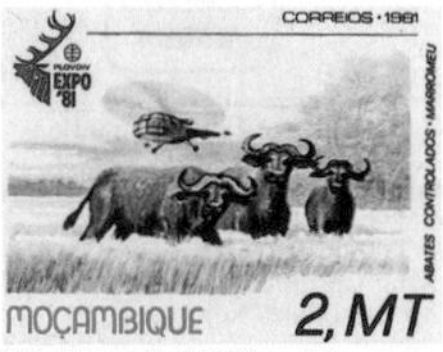

120 Controlled Killing, Marromeu

1981. World Hunting Exhibition, Plovdiv. Mult.

876	2m. Type **120**	30	15
877	5m. Traditional hunting Cheringoma	20	15
878	6m. Tourist hunting, Save	40	30
879	7m.60 Marksmanship, Gorongosa	40	20
880	12m.50 African elephants, Gorongosa	1·50	60
881	20m. Trap, Cabo Delgado	80	50

121 50 Centavos Coin

122 Sunflower

1981. 1st Anniv of New Currency. Mult.

883	50c. Type **121**	10	10
884	1m. One metical coin	10	10
885	2m.50 Two meticals 50 coin	10	10
886	5m. Five meticals coin	20	15
887	10m. Ten meticals coin	50	25
888	20m. Twenty meticals coin	1·40	55·00

1981. Agricultural Resources.

890	**122** 50c. orange and red	10	10
891	– 1m. black and red	10	10
892	– 1m.50 blue and red	10	10
893	– 2m.50 yellow and red	10	10
894	– 3m.50 green and red	15	10
895	– 4m.50 grey and red	15	10
896	– 10m. blue and red	40	15
897	– 12m.50 brown and red	50	20
898	– 15m. brown and red	60	25
899	– 25m. green and red	1·40	40
900	– 40m. orange and red	2·00	60
901	– 60m. brown and red	2·75	1·00

DESIGNS: 1m. Cotton; 1m.50, Sisal; 2m.50, Cashew; 3m.50, Tea; 4m.50, Sugar cane; 10m. Castor oil; 12m.50, Coconut; 15m. Tobacco; 25m. Rice; 40m. Maize; 60m. Groundnut.

123 Archaeological Excavation, Manyikeni

1981. Archaeological Excavation. Mult.

902	1m. Type **123**	10	10
903	1m.50 Hand-axe (Massingir Dam)	10	10
904	2m.50 Ninth century bowl (Chibuene)	10	10
905	7m.50 Ninth century pot (Chibuene)	30	20
906	12m.50 Gold beads (Manyikeni)	50	30
907	20m. Gong (Manyikeni)	80	50

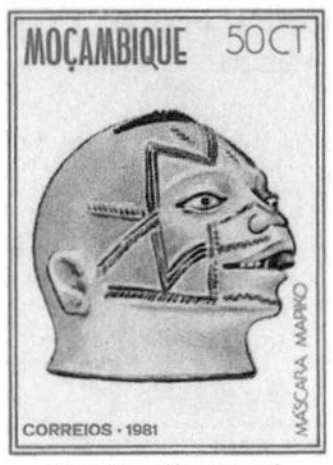

124 Mapiko Mask

1981. Sculptures. Multicoloured.

908	50c. Type **124**	10	10
909	1m. Woman who suffers	10	10
910	2m.50 Woman with a child	10	10
911	3m.50 The man who makes fire	15	10
912	5m. Chietane	20	15
913	12m.50 Chietane (different)	70	30

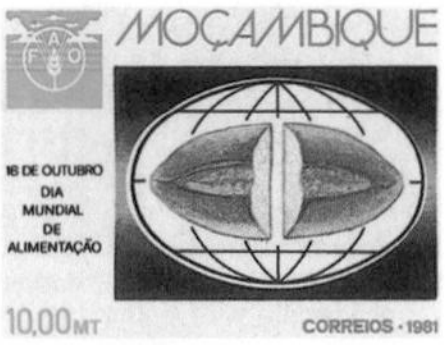

125 Broken Loaf on Globe

1981. World Food Day.

914	**125** 10m. multicoloured	45	25

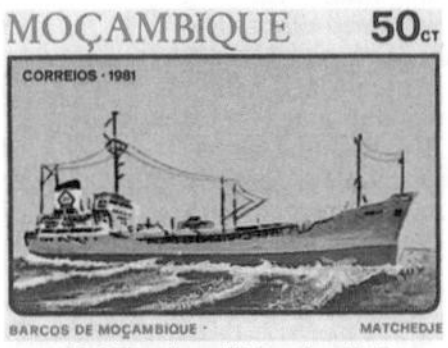

126 Tanker "Matchedje"

1981. Mozambique Ships. Multicoloured.

915	50c. Type **126**	15	15
916	1m.50 Tug "Macuti"	15	15
917	3m. Trawler "Vega 7"	25	15
918	5m. Freighter "Linde"	35	25
919	7m.50 Freighter "Pemba"	55	30
920	12m.50 Dredger "Rovuma"	95	55

127 "Portunus pelagicus"

1981. Crustaceans. Multicoloured.

921	50c. Type **127**	10	10
922	1m.50 "Scylla serrata"	10	10
923	3m. "Penacus indicus"	15	10
924	7m.50 "Palinurus delagoae"	35	20
925	12m.50 "Lysiosquilla maculata"	55	35
926	15m. "Panulirus ornatus"	80	45

128 "Hypoxis multiceps"

129 Telex Tape, Telephone and Globe

1981. Flowers. Multicoloured.

927	1m. Type **128**	10	10
928	1m.50 "Pelargonium luridun"	10	10
929	2m.50 "Caralluma melanathera"	10	10
930	7m.50 "Ansellia gigantea"	35	20
931	12m.50 "Stapelia leendertsiae"	60	35
932	25m. "Adenium multiflorum"	1·50	70

1982. 1st Anniv of Mozambique Post and Telecommunications. Multicoloured.

933	6m. Type **129**	35	20
934	15m. Winged envelope and envelope forming railway wagon	3·00	1·50

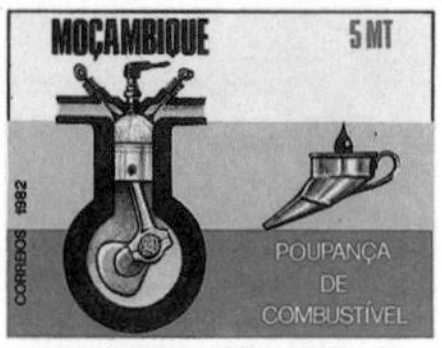

130 Diagram of Petrol Engine

1982. Fuel Saving. Multicoloured.

935	5m. Type **130**	30	15
936	7m.50 Speeding car	45	25
937	10m. Loaded truck	60	35

131 Sea-snake

1982. Reptiles. Multicoloured.

938	50c. Type **131**	20	10
939	1m.50 "Naja mossambica mossambica"	10	10
940	3m. "Thelotornis capensis mossambica"	20	15
941	6m. "Dendroaspis polylepis polylepis"	35	25
942	15m. "Dispholidus typus"	80	50
943	20m. "Bitis arietans arietans"	1·50	75

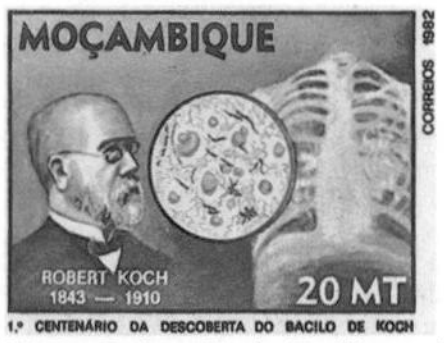

132 Dr. Robert Koch, Bacillus and X-Ray

1982. Centenary of Discovery of Tubercle Bacillus.

944	**132** 20m. multicoloured	1·75	1·00

133 Telephone Line

134 Player with Ball

1982. International Telecommunications Union. Plenipotentiary Conference.

945	**133** 20m. multicoloured	1·00	75

1982. World Cup Football Championship, Spain. Multicoloured.

946	1m.50 Type **134**	10	10
947	3m.50 Player heading ball	25	15
948	7m. Two players fighting for ball	40	20
949	10m. Player receiving ball	60	30
950	20m. Goalkeeper	1·25	1·00

135 Political Rally

137 "Vangueria infausta"

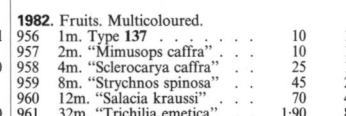

1982. 25th Anniv of FRELIMO. Multicoloured.

953	4m. Type **135**	25	15
954	8m. Agriculture	45	25
955	12m. Marching workers	70	35

1982. Fruits. Multicoloured.

956	1m. Type **137**	10	10
957	2m. "Mimusops caffra"	10	10
958	4m. "Sclerocarya caffra"	25	15
959	8m. "Strychnos spinosa"	45	25
960	12m. "Salacia kraussi"	70	40
961	32m. "Trichilia emetica"	1·90	85

138 "Sputnik I"

1982. 25th Anniv of First Artificial Satellite. Multicoloured.

962	1m. Type **138**	10	10
963	2m. First manned space flight	10	10
964	4m. First walk in space	25	15
965	8m. First manned flight to the Moon	45	25
966	16m. "Soyuz"–"Apollo" mission	1·25	70
967	20m. "Intercosmos" rocket	1·50	70

139 Vigilantes

1982. People's Surveillance Day.

968	**139** 4m. multicoloured	25	15

140 Caique

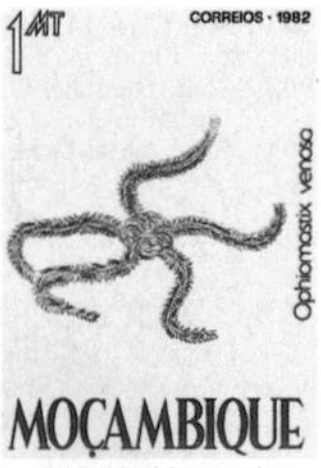

141 "Ophiomostix venosa"

1982. Traditional Boats. Multicoloured.

969	1m. Type **140**	10	10
970	2m. Machua	15	10
971	4m. Calaua (horiz)	30	15
972	8m. Chitatarro (horiz)	60	25
973	12m. Cangaia (horiz)	80	35
974	16m. Chata (horiz)	1·75	60

1982. Starfishes and Sea Urchins. Multicoloured.

975	1m. Type **141**	10	10
976	2m. "Protoreaster lincki"	10	10
977	4m. "Tropiometra carinata"	15	10
978	8m. "Holothuria scabra"	35	20
979	12m. "Prionocidaris baculosa"	60	35
980	16m. "Colobocentrotus atnatus"	80	40

142 Soldiers defending Mozambique

1983. 4th Frelimo Party Congress. Multicoloured.

981	4m. Type **142**	15	10
982	8m. Crowd waving voting papers	30	20
983	16m. Agriculture, industry and education	65	40

143 "Codium duthierae"

1983. Seaweeds. Multicoloured.

984	1m. Type **143**	10	10
985	2m. "Halimeda cunata"	10	10
986	4m. "Dictyota liturata"	15	10
987	8m. "Endorachne binghamiae"	40	20
988	12m. "Laurencia flexuosa"	60	30
989	20m. "Acrosorium sp."	1·25	55

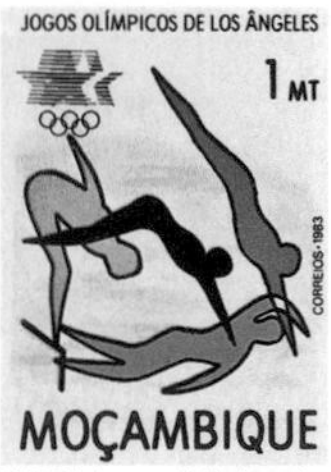

144 Diving and Swimming

1983. Olympic Games, Los Angeles (1st issue). Multicoloured.

990	1m. Type **144**	10	10
991	2m. Boxing	10	10
992	4m. Basketball	20	10
993	8m. Handball	35	20
994	12m. Volleyball	55	30
995	16m. Running	65	40
996	20m. Yachting	1·25	65

See also Nos. 1029/34.

145 Mallet Type Locomotive

1983. Steam Locomotives. Multicoloured.

998	1m. Type **145**	10	10
999	2m. Baldwin, 1915–45	20	10
1000	4m. Class 141-148, 1950	40	15
1001	8m. Baldwin, 1926	75	25
1002	16m. Henschel Garratt type, 1956	1·40	50
1003	32m. Natal Government Class H, 1899–1903	3·00	1·00

146 O.A.U. Emblem

1983. 20th Anniv of Organization of African Unity.

1004	**146**	4m. multicoloured	20	15

147 Four-toed Elephant-shrew

150 "Communications"

148 Aiding Flood Victims

1983. Mozambique Mammals. Multicoloured.

1005	1m. Type **147**	10	10
1006	2m. Four-striped grass mouse	15	10
1007	4m. Vincent's bush squirrel	25	15
1008	8m. Hottentot mole-rat	50	25
1009	12m. Natal red hare	75	40
1010	16m. Straw-coloured fruit bat	1·25	75

1983. 2nd Anniv of Mozambique Red Cross. Multicoloured.

1011	4m. Type **148**	20	10
1012	8m. Red Cross lorry	40	20
1013	16m. First aid demonstration	75	40
1014	32m. Agricultural worker performing first aid	1·90	75

1983. World Communications Year.

1016	**150**	8m. multicoloured	1·50	75

151 Line Fishing

1983. Fishery Resources. Multicoloured.

1017	50c. Type **151**	10	10
1018	2m. Chifonho (basket trap)	10	10
1019	4m. Spear fishing	25	15
1020	8m. Gamboa (fence trap)	40	25
1021	16m. Mono (basket trap)	1·50	40
1022	20m. Lema (basket trap)	1·60	55

152 Kudu Horn

153 Swimming

1983. Stamp Day. Multicoloured.

1023	50c. Type **152**	10	10
1024	1m. Drum communication	10	10
1025	4m. Postal runners	20	15
1026	8m. Mail canoe	40	40
1027	16m. Mail van	75	40
1028	20m. Steam mail train	3·25	1·50

1984. Olympic Games, Los Angeles (2nd issue). Multicoloured.

1029	50c. Type **153**	10	10
1030	4m. Football	20	10
1031	8m. Hurdling	35	20
1032	16m. Basketball	90	50
1033	32m. Handball	1·90	80
1034	60m. Boxing	3·00	1·75

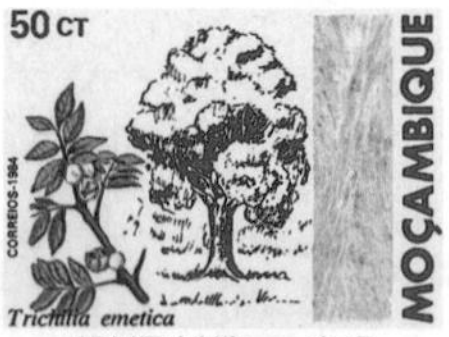

154 "Trichilia emetica"

1984. Indigenous Trees. Multicoloured.

1035	50c. Type **154**	10	10
1036	2m. "Brachystegia spiciformis"	10	10
1037	4m. "Androstachys johnsonii"	20	10
1038	8m. "Pterocarpus angolensis"	35	20
1039	16m. "Milletia stuhlmannii"	80	40
1040	50m. "Dalbergia melanoxylon"	2·75	1·75

155 Dove with Olive Sprig

1984. Nkomati South Africa–Mozambique Non-aggression Pact.

1041	**155**	4m. multicoloured	25	10

156 State Arms

1984. Emblems of the Republic. Multicoloured.

1042	4m. Type **156**	20	10
1043	8m. State Flag	40	20

157 Makway Dance

1984. "Lubrapex '84" Portuguese–Brazilian Stamp Exhibition, Lisbon. Traditional Mozambican dances. Multicoloured.

1044	4m. Type **157**	20	10
1045	8m. Mapiko dance	40	20
1046	16m. Wadjaba dance	1·40	50

158 Nampula Museum and Statuette of Woman with Water Jug

1984. Museums. Multicoloured.

1047	50c. Type **158**	10	10
1048	4m. Natural History Museum and secretary bird	35	10
1049	8m. Revolution Museum and soldier carrying wounded comrade	35	20
1050	16m. Colonial History Museum and cannon	65	40
1051	20m. National Numismatic Museum and coins	1·25	65
1052	30m. St. Paul's Palace and antique chair	1·50	95

159 Imber's Tetra

1984. Fishes. Multicoloured.

1053	50c. Type **159**	10	10
1054	4m. Purple labeo	25	10
1055	12m. Brown squeaker	75	35
1056	16m. Blue-finned notho	95	55
1057	40m. Slender serrate barb	2·50	1·40
1058	60m. Barred minnow	3·75	1·90

160 Badge and Laurels

162 Knife and Club

161 Rural Landscape and Emblem

1984. International Fair, Maputo.

1059	**160**	16m. multicoloured	70	50

1984. 20th Anniv of African Development Bank.

1060	**161**	4m. multicoloured	30	10

1984. Traditional Weapons. Multicoloured.

1061	50c. Type **162**	10	10
1062	4m. Axes	20	10
1063	8m. Spear and shield	35	15
1064	16m. Bow and arrow	75	35
1065	32m. Rifle	1·90	95
1066	50m. Assegai and arrow	2·75	1·90

163 Workers and Emblem

1984. 1st Anniv of Organization of Mozambican Workers.

1067	**163**	4m. multicoloured	20	10

164 Barue 1902 Postmark

1984. Stamp Day. Postmarks. Multicoloured.

1068	4m. Type **164**	15	10
1069	8m. Zumbo postmark and King Carlos 15r. Mozambique "key type" stamp	35	20
1070	12m. Mozambique Company postmark and 1935 airmail stamp	55	30
1071	16m. Macequece postmark and 1937 2e. Mozambique Company stamp	70	40

165 Keeper and Hive

166 Shot-putter and Emblem

1985. Bee-keeping. Multicoloured.

1072	4m. Type **165**	15	10
1073	8m. Worker bee	45	20
1074	16m. Drone	1·25	40
1075	20m. Queen bee	1·75	60

1985. "Olymphilex 85" Olympic Stamps Exhibition, Lausanne.

1076	**166**	16m. blue, black and red	75	35

167 Forecasting Equipment and Desert

1985. World Meteorology Day.

1077	**167**	4m. multicoloured	35	10

168 Map

1985. 5th Anniv of Southern African Development Co-ordination Conference. Multicoloured.

1078	4m. Type **168**	15	10
1079	8m. Map and pylon	45	20
1080	16m. Industry and transport	2·50	1·25
1081	32m. Member states' flags	1·90	95

169 Battle of Mujenga, 1896

1985. 10th Anniv of Independence. Mult.

1082	1m. Type **169**	10	10
1083	4m. Attack on Barue by Macombe, 1917	25	10

1084	8m. Attack on Massangano, 1868	55	20
1085	16m. Battle of Marracuene, 1895, and Gungunhana	1·50	50

170 U.N. Building, New York and Flag

1985. 40th Anniv of U.N.O.

1086	**170** 16m. multicoloured	80	50

171 Mathacuzana

1985. Traditional Games and Sports. Multicoloured.

1087	50c. Type **171**	10	10
1088	4m. Mudzobo	20	10
1089	8m. Muravarava (board game)	40	20
1090	16m. N'tshuwa	90	50

172 "Rana angolensis"

1985. Frogs and Toads. Multicoloured.

1091	50c. Type **172**	10	10
1092	1m. "Hyperolius pictus"	10	10
1093	4m. "Ptychadena porosissima"	15	10
1094	8m. "Afrixalus formasinii"	50	20
1095	16m. "Bufo regularis"	95	50
1096	32m. "Hyperolius marmoratus"	2·40	95

174 "Aloe ferox"

176 Comet and "Giotto" Space Probe

175 Mozambique Company 1918 10c. Stamp

1985. Medicinal Plants. Multicoloured.

1099	50c. Type **174**	10	10
1100	1m. "Boophone disticha"	10	10
1101	3m.50 "Gloriosa superba"	15	10
1102	4m. "Cotyledon orbiculata"	15	10
1103	8m. "Homeria breyniana"	55	20
1104	50m. "Haemanthus coccineus"	3·75	1·90

1985. Stamp Day. Multicoloured.

1105	1m. Type **175**	1·25	75
1106	4m. Nyassa Co. 1911 25r. stamp	15	10
1107	8m. Mozambique Co. 1918 ½c. stamp	50	20
1108	16m. Nyassa Co. 1924 1c. Postage Due stamp	1·25	50

1986. Appearance of Halley's Comet.

1109	**176** 4m. blue and light blue	20	10
1110	– 8m. violet and light violet	50	20
1111	– 16m. multicoloured	95	50
1112	– 30m. multicoloured	2·00	95

DESIGNS: 8m. Comet orbits; 16m. Small and large telescopes, comet and space probe; 30m. Comet, stars and globe.

177 Vicente

1986. World Cup Football Championship, Mexico. Multicoloured.

1113	3m. Type **177**	15	10
1114	4m. Coluna	20	10
1115	8m. Costa Pereira	40	20
1116	12m. Hilario	65	35
1117	16m. Matateu	95	50
1118	50m. Eusebio	3·25	1·90

178 Dove and Emblem

179 "Amanita muscaria"

1986. International Peace Year.

1119	**178** 16m. multicoloured	85	45

1986. Fungi. Multicoloured.

1120	4m. Type **179**	50	20
1121	8m. "Lactarius deliciosus"	95	30
1122	16m. "Amanita phaloides"	2·00	65
1123	30m. "Tricholoma nudum"	4·25	1·25

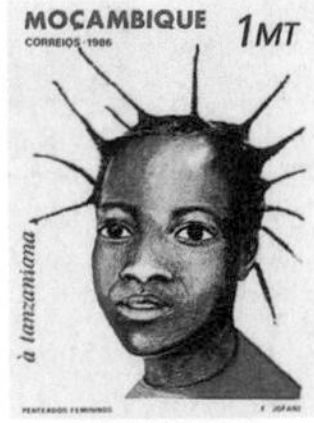

181 Spiky Style

1986. Women's Hairstyles. Multicoloured.

1125	1m. Type **181**	10	10
1126	4m. Beaded plaits	25	10
1127	8m. Plaited tightly to head	50	20
1128	16m. Plaited tightly to head with ponytail	1·25	55

182 Dugong

1986. Marine Mammals. Multicoloured.

1129	1m. Type **182**	10	10
1130	8m. Common dolphin	35	20
1131	16m. "Neobalena marginata"	1·25	85
1132	50f. Fin whale	4·25	2·75

183 Children Studying

1986. 1st Anniv of Continuadores Youth Organization.

1133	**183** 4m. multicoloured	30	15

184 50m. Notes

1986. Savings. Multicoloured.

1134	4m. Type **184**	25	10
1135	8m. 100m. notes	50	20
1136	16m. 500m. notes	1·40	50
1137	30m. 1000m. notes	2·75	1·25

185 Quelimane Post Office

1986. Stamp Day. Post Offices. Multicoloured.

1138	3m. Type **185**	20	10
1139	4m. Maputo	30	10
1140	8m. Beira	65	20
1141	16m. Nampula	1·40	50

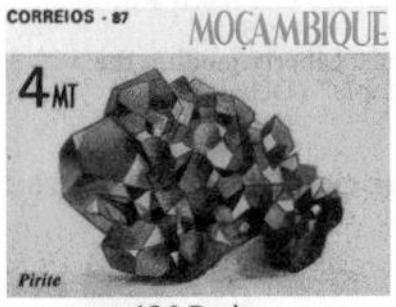

186 Pyrite

1987. Minerals. Multicoloured.

1142	4m. Type **186**	30	10
1143	8m. Emerald	60	20
1144	12m. Agate	85	40
1145	16m. Malachite	1·40	50
1146	30m. Garnet	2·50	1·25
1147	50m. Amethyst	4·25	2·00

187 Crowd beneath Flag

1987. 10th Anniv of Mozambique Liberation Front.

1148	**187** 4m. multicoloured	30	15

188 Little Libombos Dam

1987.

1149	**188** 16m. multicoloured	1·40	60

189 Children being Vaccinated

1987. World Health Day. Vaccination Campaign.

1150	**189** 50m. multicoloured	1·90	1·50

190 Common Grenadier

191 Football

1987. Birds. Multicoloured.

1151	3m. Type **190**	25	15
1152	4m. Woodland kingfisher	30	20
1153	8m. White-fronted bee eater	65	40
1154	12m. Lesser seedcracker	1·10	60
1155	16m. African broad-billed roller	1·25	90
1156	30m. Neergaard's sunbird	2·50	1·60

1987. Olympic Games, Seoul (1988) (1st issue). Multicoloured.

1157	12m.50 Type **191**	10	10
1158	25m. Running	20	10
1159	50m. Handball	40	20
1160	75m. Chess	1·25	30
1161	100m. Basketball	1·25	35
1162	200m. Swimming	2·00	65

See also Nos. 1176/81.

193 Work on Loom

1987. Weaving. Multicoloured.

1164	20m. Type **193**	15	10
1165	40m. Triangle and diamond design	40	10
1166	80m. "Eye" design	70	20
1167	200m. Red carpet	2·00	60

194 Piper "Navajo"

1987. Air. History of Aviation in Mozambique. Multicoloured.

1168	20m. Type **194**	15	10
1169	40m. De Havilland Hornet moth	25	10
1170	80m. Boeing 737	50	20
1171	120m. Beechcraft King Air	75	20
1172	160m. Piper Aztec	1·00	35
1173	320m. Douglas DC-10	2·00	75

195 Early Plan

1987. Centenary of Maputo as City.

1174	**195** 20m. multicoloured	20	15

1987. No. 895 surch **4,00 MT.**

1175	4m. on 4m.50 grey and red	15	10

197 Javelin throwing

198 "Boophane disticha"

1988. Olympic Games, Seoul (2nd issue). Mult.

1176	10m. Type **197**	10	10
1177	20m. Baseball	10	10
1178	40m. Boxing	10	10
1179	80m. Hockey	40	10
1180	100m. Gymnastics	50	15
1181	400m. Cycling	1·50	75

1988. Flowers. Multicoloured.

1182	10m. "Heamanthus nelsonii"	10	10
1183	20m. "Crinum polyphyllum"	15	10

1184	40m. Type **198**	15	10
1185	80m. "Cyrtanthus contractus"	35	10
1186	100m. "Nerine angustifolia"	50	15
1187	400m. "Cyrtanthus galpinnii"	2·00	75

199 Man refusing Cigarette

1988. 40th Anniv of W.H.O. Anti-smoking Campaign.

1188 **199**	20m. multicoloured	20	10

201 Mat

1988. Basketry. Multicoloured.

1190	20m. Type **201**	10	10
1191	25m. Basket with lid	10	10
1192	80m. Basket with handle	20	10
1193	100m. Fan	30	10
1194	400m. Dish	1·50	1·00
1195	500m. Conical basket	1·90	1·40

203 Percheron

1988. Horses. Multicoloured.

1197	20m. Type **203**	15	10
1198	40m. Arab	20	10
1199	80m. Pure blood	40	10
1200	100m. Pony	50	15

204 Machel

1988. 2nd Death Anniv of Samora Machel (President 1975–86).

1201 **204**	20m. multicoloured	15	10

205 Inhambane

1988. Ports. Multicoloured.

1202	20m. Type **205**	15	10
1203	50m. Quelimane (vert)	40	10
1204	75m. Pemba	50	10
1205	100m. Beira	55	20
1206	250m. Nacali (vert)	1·10	50
1207	500m. Maputo	2·75	1·25

206 Mobile Post Office

1988. Stamp Day. Multicoloured.

1208	20m. Type **206**	10	10
1209	40m. Posting box (vert)	15	10

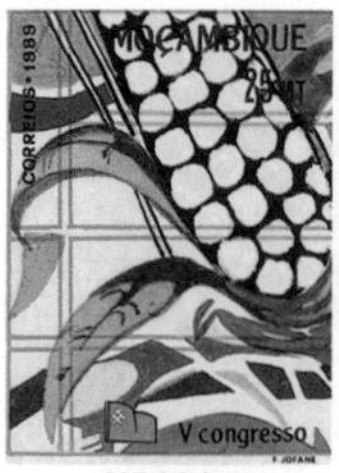

207 Maize **208** Mondlane

1989. 5th FRELIMO Congress. Multicoloured.

1210	25m. Type **207**	10	10
1211	50m. Hoe	10	10
1212	75m. Abstract	10	10
1213	100m. Cogwheels	20	10
1214	250m. Right-half of cogwheel	50	25

Nos. 1210/14 were printed together, se-tenant, forming a composite design.

1989. 20th Anniv of Assassination of Pres. Mondlane.

1215 **208**	25m. black, gold and red	15	10

209 "Storming the Bastille" (Thevenin)

1989. Bicentenary of French Revolution. Mult.

1216	100m. Type **209**	25	10
1217	250m. "Liberty guiding the People" (Delacroix)	60	35

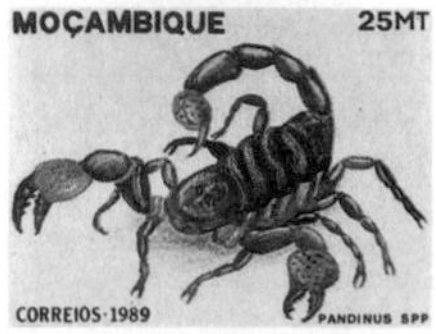

210 "Pandinus sp."

1989. Venomous Animals. Multicoloured.

1219	25m. Type **210**	10	10
1220	50m. Egyptian cobra	10	10
1221	75m. "Bombus sp." (bee)	15	10
1222	100m. "Paraphysa sp." (spider)	25	10
1223	250m. Marble cone	90	40
1224	500m. Lionfish	1·90	70

211 "Acropora pulchra"

1989. Corals. Multicoloured.

1225	25m. Type **211**	10	10
1226	50m. "Eunicella papilosa"	15	10
1227	100m. "Dendrophyla migrantus"	30	10
1228	250m. "Favia fragum"	50	35

212 Footballers **213** Macuti Lighthouse

1989. World Cup Football Championship, Italy (1990). Designs showing various footballing scenes.

1229 **212**	30m. multicoloured	10	10
1230	– 60m. multicoloured	15	10
1231	– 125m. multicoloured	30	10
1232	– 200m. multicoloured	50	25
1233	– 250m. multicoloured	65	35
1234	– 500m. multicoloured	1·50	70

1989. Lighthouses. Multicoloured.

1235	30m. Type **213**	15	10
1236	60m. Pinda	15	10
1237	125m. Cape Delgado	30	10
1238	200m. Goa Island	60	25
1239	250m. Caldeira Point	80	35
1240	500m. Vilhena	1·50	70

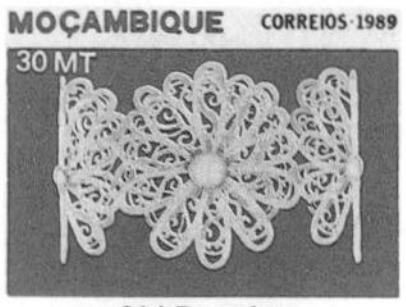

214 Bracelet

1989. Silver Filigree Work.

1241 **214**	30m. grey, red and black	10	10
1242	– 60m. grey, blue and black	15	10
1243	– 125m. grey, red and black	25	10
1244	– 200m. grey, blue & black	40	25
1245	– 250m. grey, purple & blk	55	35
1246	– 500m. grey, green & blk	1·25	70

DESIGNS: 60m. Flower belt; 125m. Necklace; 200m. Casket; 250m. Spoons; 500m. Butterfly.

215 Flag and Soldiers **216** Rain Gauge

1989. 25th Anniv of Fight for Independence.

1247 **215**	30m. multicoloured	15	10

1989. Meteorological Instruments. Multicoloured.

1248	30m. Type **216**	10	10
1249	60m. Radar graph	15	10
1250	125m. Sheltered measuring instruments	30	10
1251	200m. Computer terminal	55	25

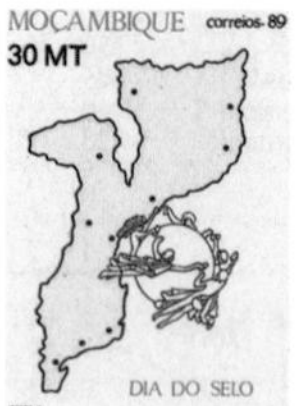

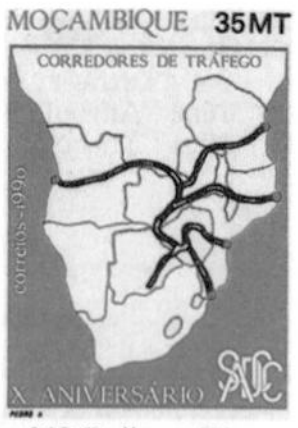

218 Map and U.P.U. Emblem **219** Railway Map

1989. Stamp Day.

1253 **218**	30m. multicoloured	15	10
1254	– 60m. black, green and red	15	10

DESIGN: 60m. Map and Mozambique postal emblem.

1990. 10th Anniv of Southern Africa Development Co-ordination Conference.

1255 **219**	35m. multicoloured	1·00	50

220 Cloth and Woman wearing Dress

1990. Traditional Dresses. Designs showing women wearing different dresses and details of cloth used.

1256 **220**	42m. multicoloured	10	10
1257	– 90m. multicoloured	15	10
1258	– 150m. multicoloured	20	10
1259	– 200m. multicoloured	25	15
1260	– 400m. multicoloured	55	40
1261	– 500m. multicoloured	65	50

221 Sena Fortress, Sofala

1990. Fortresses.

1262 **221**	45m. blue and black	10	10
1263	– 90m. blue and black	15	10
1264	– 150m. multicoloured	20	10
1265	– 200m. multicoloured	30	15
1266	– 400m. red and black	55	40
1267	– 500m. red and black	70	40

DESIGNS: 90m. Sto. Antonio, Ibo Island; 150m. S. Sebastiao, Mozambique Island; 200m. S. Caetano, Sofala; 400m. Our Lady of Conception, Maputo; 500m. S. Luis, Tete.

223 Obverse and Reverse of 50m. Coin

1990. 15th Anniv of Bank of Mozambique.

1269 **223**	100m. multicoloured	20	10

224 Statue of Eduardo Mondlane (founder of FRELIMO)

1990. 15th Anniv of Independence. Mult.

1270	42m.50 Type **224**	10	10
1271	150m. Statue of Samora Machel (President, 1975–86)	25	15

225 White Rhinoceros

1990. Endangered Animals. Multicoloured.

1272	42m.50 Type **225**	15	10
1273	100m. Dugong	20	10
1274	150m. African elephant	35	15
1275	200m. Cheetah	40	15
1276	400m. Spotted-necked otter	70	40
1277	500m. Hawksbill turtle	85	50

226 "Dichrostachys cinerea" **227** Pillar Box waving to Kurika

1990. Environmental Protection. Plants. Mult.

1278	42m.50 Type **226**	10	10
1279	100m. Forest fire	20	10
1280	150m. Horsetail tree	25	10
1281	200m. Mangrove	30	15
1282	400m. "Estrato herbaceo" (grass)	65	40
1283	500m. Pod mahogany	80	50

1990. Kurika (post mascot) at Work. Mult.

1284	42m.50 Type **227**	15	10
1285	42m.50 Hand cancelling envelopes	15	10
1286	42m.50 Leaping across hurdles	15	10
1287	42m.50 Delivering post to chicken	15	10

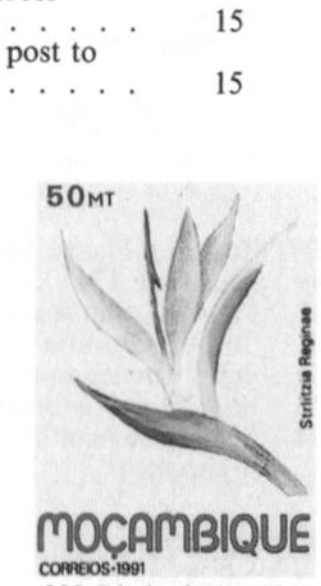

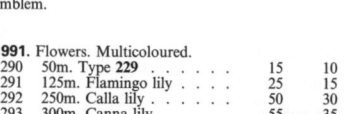

228 "10" and Posts Emblem **229** Bird-of-Paradise Flower

1991. 10th Anniv of National Posts and Telecommunications Enterprises, Mozambique.

1288 **228**	50m. blue, red and black	15	10
1289	– 50m. brown, green & black	15	10

DESIGN: No. 1289, "10" and telecommunications emblem.

1991. Flowers. Multicoloured.

1290	50m. Type **229**	15	10
1291	125m. Flamingo lily	25	15
1292	250m. Calla lily	50	30
1293	300m. Canna lily	55	35

230 Two Hartebeest

231 Mpompine

1991. Lichtenstein's Hartebeest. Multicoloured.

1294	50m. Type **230**	15	10
1295	100m. Alert hartebeest . . .	20	10
1296	250m. Hartebeest grazing . .	1·50	70
1297	500m. Mother feeding young	2·10	1·40

1991. Maputo Drinking Fountains. Mult.

1298	50m. Type **231**	10	10
1299	125m. Chinhambanine . . .	15	10
1300	250m. S. Pedro-Zaza . . .	25	10
1301	300m. Xipamanine	35	15

232 Painting by Samate

233 Diving

1991. Paintings by Mozambican Artists. Mult.

1302	180m. Type **232**	15	10
1303	250m. Malangatana Ngwenya	20	15
1304	560m. Malangatana Ngwenya (different) . . .	40	30

1991. Olympic Games, Barcelona (1992). Mult.

1305	10m. Type **233**	10	10
1306	50m. Roller hockey	15	10
1307	100m. Tennis	20	10
1308	200m. Table tennis	30	10
1309	500m. Running	50	20
1310	1000m. Badminton	1·10	40

234 Proposed Boundaries in 1890 Treaty

236 Skipping

1991. Centenary of Settling of Mozambique Borders. Multicoloured.

1311	600m. Type **234**	50	25
1312	800m. Frontiers settled in English–Portuguese 1891 treaty	75	35

1991. Stamp Day. Children's Games. Mult.

1314	40m. Type **236**	10	10
1315	150m. Spinning top	10	10
1316	400m. Marbles	20	10
1317	900m. Hopscotch	45	20

237 "Christ"

238 "Rhisophora mucronata"

1992. Stained Glass Windows. Multicoloured.

1318	40m. Type **237**	10	10
1319	150m. "Faith"	10	10
1320	400m. "IC XC"	20	10
1321	900m. Window in three sections	45	20

1992. Marine Flowers. Multicoloured.

1322	300m. Type **238**	15	10
1323	600m. "Cymodocea ciliata"	30	15
1324	1000m. "Sophora inhambanensis"	85	25

239 Spears

240 Amethyst Sunbird

1992. "Lubrapex 92" Brazilian–Portuguese Stamp Exhibition, Lisbon. Weapons. Multicoloured.

1325	100m. Type **239**	10	10
1326	300m. Tridents	15	10
1327	500m. Axe	25	10
1328	1000m. Dagger	85	25

1992. Birds. Multicoloured.

1329	150m. Type **240**	30	30
1330	200m. Mosque swallow . .	30	30
1331	300m. Red-capped robin chat	45	30
1332	400m. Lesser blue-eared glossy starling	60	30
1333	500m. Grey-headed bush shrike	1·50	30
1334	800m. African golden oriole	2·25	70

241 Emblem

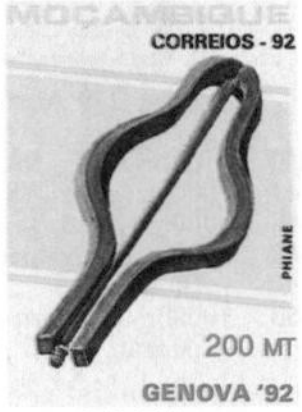

242 Phiane

1992. 30th Anniv of Eduardo Mondlane University.

1335	**241** 150m. green and brown	10	10

1992. "Genova '92" International Thematic Stamp Exn. Musical Instruments. Multicoloured.

1336	200m. Type **242**	10	10
1337	300m. Xirupe (rattle) . . .	15	10
1338	500m. Ngulula (drum) . . .	25	10
1339	1500m. Malimba (drum) . .	75	35

243 Children Eating

244 Parachutist

1992. International Nutrition Conference, Rome.

1341	**243** 450m. multicoloured . .	20	10

1992. Parachuting. Multicoloured.

1342	50m. Type **244**	10	10
1343	400m. Parachutist and buildings	20	10
1344	500m. Airplane dropping parachutists	25	10
1345	1500m. Parachutist (different)	1·10	1·10

1992. No. 890 surch **50MT**.

1346	**122** 50m. on 50c. orge & red	10	10

246 Order of Peace and Friendship

1993. Mozambique Decorations. Multicoloured.

1347	400m. Type **246**	20	10
1348	800m. Bagamoyo Medal . .	40	20
1349	1000m. Order of Eduardo Mondlane	50	25
1350	1500m. Veteran of the Struggle for National Liberation Medal	70	35

247 Tree Stumps and Girl carrying Wood

1993. Pollution. Multicoloured.

1351	200m. Type **247**	10	10
1352	750m. Chimneys smoking	35	15
1353	1000m. Tanker sinking . . .	50	25
1354	1500m. Car exhaust fumes	70	35

248 Lion (Gorongosa Park, Sofala)

1993. National Parks. Multicoloured.

1355	200m. Type **248**	10	10
1356	800m. Giraffes (Banhine Park, Gaza)	40	20
1357	1000m. Dugongs (Bazoruto Park, Inhambane)	50	25
1358	1500m. Ostriches (Zinave Park, Inhambane)	1·75	75

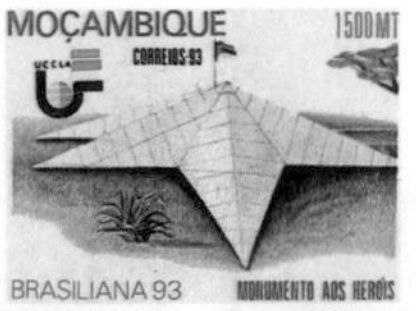

249 Heroes Monument, Maputo

1993. "Brasiliana 93" International Stamp Exhibition, Rio de Janeiro.

1359	**249** 1500m. multicoloured . .	55	25

250 Conference Emblem

251 "Cycas cercinalis"

1993. National Culture Conference, Maputo.

1360	**250** 200m. multicoloured . .	10	10

1993. Forest Plants. Multicoloured.

1361	200m. Type **251**	10	10
1362	250m. "Cycas revoluta" . .	10	10
1363	900m. "Encephalartos ferox"	25	10
1364	2000m. "Equisetum ramosissimum"	50	25

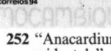

252 "Anacardium occidentale"

254 Mozambique Rough-scaled Sand Lizard

1994. Medicinal Plants. Multicoloured.

1365	200m. Type **252**	10	10
1366	250m. "Sclerocarya caffra"	10	10
1367	900m. "Annona senegalensis"	25	10
1368	2000m. "Crinum delagoense"	50	25

1994. Various stamps surch.

1369	50m. on 7m.50 mult (No. 905)	10	10
1370	50m. on 7m.50 mult (No. 924)	10	10
1371	50m. on 7m.50 mult (No. 930)	10	10
1372	100m. on 10m. blue and red (No. 896)	10	10
1373	100m. on 12m.50 mult (No. 931)	10	10
1374	200m. on 12m.50 brown and red (No. 897)	10	10
1375	250m. on 12m.50 mult (No. 925)	10	10

1994. "Philakorea 1994" International Stamp Exhibition, Seoul. Reptiles. Multicoloured.

1376	300m. Type **254**	10	10
1377	500m. Olive loggerhead turtle	10	10
1378	2000m. Northern coppery snake	40	20
1379	3500m. Marshall's chameleon	75	35

255 Crop-spraying

1994. 50th Anniv of I.C.A.O. Multicoloured.

1381	300m. Type **255**	10	10
1382	500m. Airport	10	10
1383	2000m. Air transport . . .	40	20
1384	3500m. Aircraft maintenance	75	35

256 Bean Plant

257 Queue of Voters

1994. "Lubrapex'94" Portuguese–Brazilian Stamp Exhibition. World Food Day.

1385	**256** 2000m. multicoloured . .	40	20

1994. 1st Multiparty Elections.

1386	**257** 900m. multicoloured . .	20	10

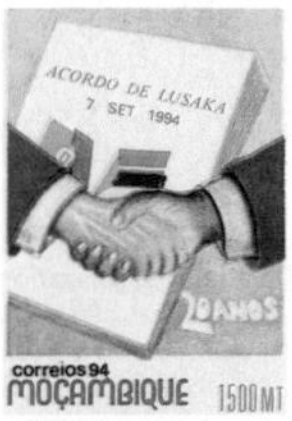

258 Document and Handshake

259 Couple using Drugs

1994. 20th Anniv of Lusaka Accord (establishing independence).

1387	**258** 1500m. multicoloured . .	30	15

1994. Anti-drugs Campaign. Multicoloured.

1388	500m. Type **259**	10	10
1389	1000m. Couple, syringe, cigarette and skeleton . .	20	10
1390	2000m. Addict	40	20
1391	5000m. Sniffer dog capturing man with drugs	1·00	50

260 Basket

261 Dress and Cloak

1995. Baskets and Bags. Multicoloured.

1392	250m. Type **260**	10	10
1393	300m. Bag with two handles	10	10
1394	1200m. Circular bag with one handle	20	10
1395	5000m. Bag with flap . . .	85	40

1995. Women's Costumes. Multicoloured.

1396	250m. Type **261**	10	10
1397	300m. Blouse and calf-length skirt	10	10
1398	1200m. Blouse and ankle-length skirt	20	10
1399	5000m. Strapless top and skirt	85	40

262 State Arms

263 Bushbaby

1995. Investiture (1994) of President Joaquim Chissano. Multicoloured.

1400	900m. Type **262**	15	10
1401	2500m. National flag . . .	45	20
1402	5000m. Pres. Chissano . . .	85	40

Nos. 1400/2 were issued together, se-tenant, the commemorative inscription at the foot extending across the strip.

1995. Mammals. Multicoloured.
1403 500m. Type **263** 10 10
1404 2000m. Greater kudu (horiz) 25 10
1405 3000m. Bush pig (horiz) . . 40 20
1406 5000m. Bushbuck 65 30

1995. Various stamps surch.
1407 250m. on 12m.50 multicoloured (No. 931) 10 10
1408 300m. on 10m. blue and red (No. 896) 10 10
1409 500m. on 12m.50 multicoloured (No. 925) 10 10
1410 900m. on 12e.50 multicoloured (No. 771) 10 10
1411 1000m. on 12m.50 multicoloured (No. 837) 15 10
1412 1500m. on 16m. multicoloured (No. 1064) 20 10
1413 2000m. on 16m. multicoloured (No. 995) 25 10
1414 2500m. on 12m. multicoloured (No. 880) 35 15

265 Family carrying Foodstuffs

266 Emblem

1995. 50th Anniv of F.A.O.
1415 **265** 5000m. multicoloured . . 65 30

1995. 50th Anniv of United Nations Organization.
1416 **266** 5000m. blue and black 65 30

267 Child wearing Blue Cloak

1995. 20th Anniv of UNICEF in Mozambique.
1417 **267** 5000m. multicoloured . . 60 65

268 Player scoring Goal

1996. Football. Multicoloured.
1418 1000m. Type **268** 25 15
1419 2000m. Goalkeeper holding ball 40 25
1420 4000m. Referee admonishing players 60 70
1421 6000m. Two players tackling for ball 75 75

269 Mask

270 "Mae Africa" (De Malangatana)

1996. Local Masks.
1422 **269** 1000m. multicoloured . . 10 15
1423 – 2000m. multicoloured . . 20 25
1424 – 4000m. multicoloured . . 40 45
1425 – 6000m. multicoloured . . 60 65
DESIGNS: 2000 to 6000m. Different masks.

1996. 15th Anniv of Mozambique Red Cross.
1426 **270** 5000m. multicoloured . . 50 55

271 African Elephant

272 Mine Field

1996. Wild Animals. Multicoloured.
1427 1000m. Type **271** 65 30
1428 2000m. White rhinoceros . . 85 55
1429 4000m. Leopard 90 90
1430 6000m. Pel's fishing owl . . 1·75 1·50

1996. Land Mine Clearance Campaign. Mult.
1431 2000m. Type **272** 30 25
1432 6000m. Warning sign . . . 75 65
1433 8000m. Soldier with mine detector 90 90
1434 10000m. Soldier lifting mine 1·25 1·25

273 City Street

274 5r. Stamp of 1876 and Magnifying Glass

1996. "Keeping the City Clean".
1435 **273** 2000m. multicoloured . . 30 25

1996. 120th Anniv of Mozambique Stamps.
1436 **274** 2000m. multicoloured . . 30 25

275 Mitumbui

1997. Local Boats. Multicoloured.
1437 2000m. Type **275** 20 25
1438 6000m. Muterere 60 65
1439 8000m. Lancha 80 85
1440 10000m. Dhow . . . . . . 1·00 1·10

275a Anhinga

1997. 1st AICEP (Association of Post Office and Telecommunications Operators of Portuguese Speaking Territories) Philatelic Conference, Sao Tome. Sheet 70 × 91 mm.
MS1440a **275a** 5000m. multicoloured 25 30

276 Village Scene

1997. International Children's Day.
1441 **276** 2000m. multicoloured . . 30 25

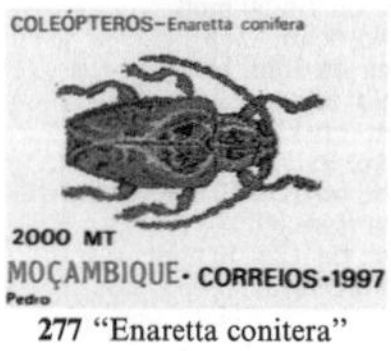

277 "Enaretta conitera"

1997. Beetles. Multicoloured.
1442 2000m. Type **277** 30 25
1443 6000m. "Zographus hieroglyphicus 70 65
1444 8000m. "Tragiscoschema bertolonii" 90 90
1445 10000m. "Tragocephala ducalis" . . . . 1·25 1·25
MS1446 97 × 105 mm. Nos. 1442/5 2·50 2·75

No. MS1446 also commemorates the "LUBRAPEX 97" International Stamp Exhibition, Brazil.

278 Yellow-billed Stork

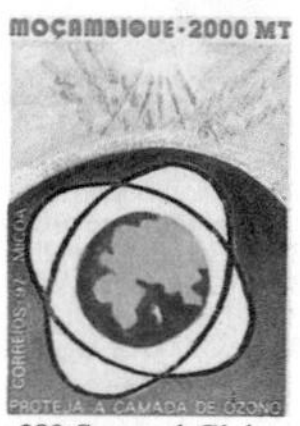

280 Sun and Globe

279 Abstract Patterns

1997. Aquatic Birds. Multicoloured.
1447 2000m. Type **278** 50 25
1448 4000m. Black-winged stilt 70 45
1449 8000m. Long-toed stint (horiz) . . . . 1·25 1·10
1450 10000m. Eastern white pelican . . . . 1·40 1·40

1997. Centenary of Joao Ferreira dos Santos Group.
1451 **279** 2000m. multicoloured . . 30 25

1997. Protection of Ozone Layer.
1452 **280** 2000m. multicoloured . . 30 25

284 Coelacanth

1998. "EXPO '98" International Stamp Exhibition, Lisbon.
1463 **284** 2000m. multicoloured . . 55 25

285 Woman with Food Products

1998. Food Production.
1464 **285** 2000m. multicoloured . . 30 25

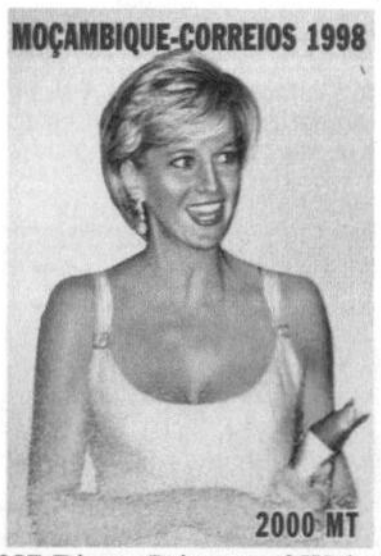

287 Diana, Princess of Wales

1998. Diana, Princess of Wales Commemoration (1st issue). T **287** and similar vert designs. Multicoloured.
MS1473 135 × 189 mm. 2000m. Type **287**; 2000m. Wearing tiara and white dress; 2000m. Wearing black V-neck dress; 2000m. Wearing blue sleeveless dress and choker; 2000m. With Indian woman and baby; 2000m. Wearing black halter-neck dress; 2000m. In RNLI uniform; 2000m. Wearing red dress; 2000m. Wearing Red Cross badge and protective vest 85 90
MS1474 135 × 189 mm. 5000m. Wearing red and white hat and pearl necklace; 5000m.Wearing pink check hat and dress; 5000m. Wearing red hat and red patterned dress; 5000m. Wearing blue hat and white jacket with blue edging; 5000m. Wearing red and black hat and red and white check jacket; 5000m. Wearing dark blue and white hat and white jacket with dark blue edging; 5000m. Wearing white and grey hat and white dress; 5000m. Turquoise and white hat and dress; 5000m. Wearing blue hat and blue jacket with flower brooch . . . . 2·20 2·30
MS1475 135 × 190 mm. 8000m. Wearing cream embroidered dress and bolero; 8000m. Wearing black dress and choker; 8000m. Wearing red dress; 8000m. Wearing red dress (different); 8000m. Wearing beige embroidered dress and bolero; 8000m. Wearing white dress and choker; 8000m. Wearing pale blue dress and pearl necklace; 8000m. Wearing dark blue dress; 8000m. Wearing white lace dress and carrying clutch bag . . . 3·25 3·50
MS1476 Two sheets, each 130 × 100 mm. (a) 30000m. Wearing mauve dress (41 × 59 mm). (b) 30000m. With African child (41 × 59 mm). Set of 2 sheets . . . . 3·00 3·25
See also Nos. **MS**1506, **MS**1507, **MS**1593 and **MS**1594.

296 Lucy (Lucille Ball) wearing Dark Brown Hat and Coat

297 Diana, Princess of Wales

1999. Scenes from *I Love Lucy* (American TV comedy series). Two sheets containing T **296** and similar multicoloured design.
MS1505 (a) 88 × 121 mm. 35000m. Type **296**; (b) 121 × 88 mm. 35000m. Lucy as ballet dancer 3·50 3·75

1999. Diana, Princess of Wales Commemoration (2nd issue). T **297** and similar vert designs. Stamp colours shown.
MS1506 165 × 170 mm. 6500m. Type **297** (violet and black); 6500m. In profile, looking left (brown and black); 6500m. Wearing jacket and pearl necklace (chestnut and black); 6500m. Wearing round-collared dress (olive and black); 6500m. Wearing hat with feathers (lilac and black); 6500m. Wearing white blouse with pointed collar, looking to left (brown and black) . . . . . 1·80 1·90
MS1507 165 × 170 mm. 6500m. Wearing large white collar (lilac and black); 6500m. Wearing hat (lilac and black); 6500m. Wearing white (brown and black); 6500m. Wearing dress with narrow straps (brown and black); 6500m. Wearing patterned blouse (violet and black); 6500m. In profile, with bouquet of flowers (olive and black) . . . . 1·50 1·60

298 Joe Besser, Larry and Moe with Frying Pan

1999. Scenes from "The Three Stooges" (American TV comedy series). T **298** and similar horiz designs. Multicoloured.

MS1508 174 × 140 mm. 5000m. Type **298**; 5000m. Shemp wearing trilby; 5000m. Moe and Larry putting pan on Joe Besser's head; 5000m. Moe with pipe; 5000m. Larry and Moe pouring drinks on Curly's head; 5000m. Larry wearing straw hat; 5000m. Joe Besser and Larry pulling Moe's tooth; 5000m. Curly wearing mauve shirt; 5000m. Shemp, Larry and Moe behind green sofa . . 2·20 2·30

MS1509 Two sheets, each 140 × 89 mm. (a) 35000m. Larry wearing pink shirt. (b) 35000m. Larry holding shovel . . . . . 3·50 3·75

299 AE-AC "Blue Tiger", Germany

1999. Trains. Multicoloured.

1510 2000m. Type **299** 10 15

1511 2500m. DB 218 locomotive, Germany 15 20

1512 3000m. Mt. Pilatus incline railway car, Switzerland 1·20 1·30

1513 3500m. Berlin underground railway train, Germany 1·80 1·90

MS1514 162 × 219 mm. 2500m. DB V200 locomotive, Germany; 2500m. Union Pacific locomotive, USA; 2500m. Class 613 locomotive, Germany; 2500m. Canadian Pacific 4242 locomotive, Canada; 2500m. *Duchess of Hamilton* steam locomotive, Great Britain; 2500m. Pacific Delhi locomotive, India; 2500m. ISA locomotive, South Africa; 2500m. DR VT 18-16-07 locomotive, Germany; 2500m. DB-DE locomotive, Australia . . . . 1·20 1·30

MS1515 162 × 219 mm. 3000m. DB 218 locomotive, Germany; 3000m. QJ Class 2-10-2 steam locomotive, China; 3000m. 232 232.9 locomotive, Germany; 3000m. *Flying Scotsman* steam locomotive, Great Britain; 3000m. WR 360 CH locomotive, Germany; 3000m. Henschel 2-8-2 steam locomotive; 3000m. Santa Fe 39C locomotive (EUA); 3000m. Steam locomotive heading "Balkan Express", Greece; 3000m. DB 218 locomotive, Germany 1·20 1·30

MS1516 Two sheets, each 81 × 106 mm. (a) 25000m. German 2-8-2 steam locomotive. (b) 25000m. German DMU Talento Talbot Alamao locomotive . . 2·50 2·60

300 Betty Boop astride Motorcycle

1999. Betty Boop (cartoon character). T **300** and similar vert designs. Multicoloured.

MS1517 132 × 178 mm. 3500m. Type **300**; 3500m. Riding motorcycle, wearing purple top; 3500m. Wearing cap and light brown patterned top; 3500m. Astride motorcycle, wearing cap and jeans; 3500m. Looking through handlebars, wearing blue jacket and cap; 3500m. Riding motorcycle, wearing "Biker Betty" top; 3500m. With gasoline can, hitching lift; 3500m. Astride motorcycle, wearing bandana; 3500m. Astride motorcycle, wearing red jacket . . . . . . 1·80 1·90

MS1518 Two sheets, each 140 × 89 mm. (a) 35000m. Astride motorcycle, wearing red jacket. (b) 35000m. Sat beside motorcycle, with gasoline can . . . . . . 1·80 1·90

301 Chartreux

303 *Palla usher*

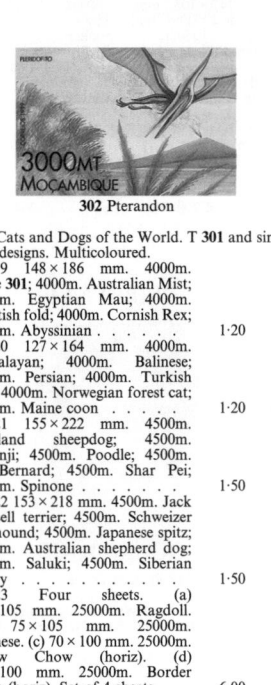

302 Pterandon

2000. Cats and Dogs of the World. T **301** and similar vert designs. Multicoloured.

MS1519 148 × 186 mm. 4000m. Type **301**; 4000m. Australian Mist; 4000m. Egyptian Mau; 4000m. Scottish fold; 4000m. Cornish Rex; 4000m. Abyssinian . . . . . . 1·20 1·30

MS1520 127 × 164 mm. 4000m. Himalayan; 4000m. Balinese; 4000m. Persian; 4000m. Turkish van; 4000m. Norwegian forest cat; 4000m. Maine coon . . . . . 1·20 1·30

MS1521 155 × 222 mm. 4500m. Shetland sheepdog; 4500m. Basenji; 4500m. Poodle; 4500m. St. Bernard; 4500m. Shar Pei; 4500m. Spinone . . . . 1·50 1·60

MS1522 153 × 218 mm. 4500m. Jack Russell terrier; 4500m. Schweizer laufhound; 4500m. Japanese spitz; 4500m. Australian shepherd dog; 4500m. Saluki; 4500m. Siberian husky . . . . 1·50 1·60

MS1523 Four sheets. (a) 75 × 105 mm. 25000m. Ragdoll. (b) 75 × 105 mm. 25000m. Siamese. (c) 70 × 100 mm. 25000m. Chow Chow (horiz). (d) 70 × 100 mm. 25000m. Border collie (horiz). Set of 4 sheets 6·00 6·00

2000. Dinosaurs. T **303** and similar horiz designs. Multicoloured.

MS1524 139 × 116 mm. 3000m. Type **302**; 3000m. Bothriospondylus; 3000m. Iguanodon (head); 3000m. Stegosaurus; 3000m. Nodosaurus; 3000m. Elaphrosaurus and Iguanodon (body); 3000m. Petrolacosaurus; 3000m. Procompsognathus; 3000m. Dimetrodon . . . . 1·40 1·50

MS1525 139 × 116 mm. 3000m. Plesiosaurus; 3000m. Ceresiosaurus; 3000m. Cryptoclidus; 3000m. Placochelys; 3000m. Plotosaurus; 3000m. Ictiosaurus; 3000m. Platecarpus; 3000m. Archelon; 3000m. Mosasaur . . . . 1·40 1·50

MS1526 Two sheets, each 110 × 85 mm. (a) 20000m. Tyrannosaurus rex. (b) 20000m. Honodus. Set of 2 sheets . . . 2·00 2·10

2000. Butterflies of the World. Multicoloured.

1527 2000m. Type **303** 10 10

1528 2500m. *Euschemon rafflesia* 15 20

1529 3000m. *Buttus philenor* . . . 20 25

1530 3000m. *Hypolimnas bolina* 20 25

1531 3500m. *Lycorea cleobaea* . . 20 25

1532 4000m. *Dynastor napoleon* 40 25

1533 4500m. *Callimorpha dominula* 25 30

1534 5000m. *Pereute leucodrosime* 25 30

MS1535 95 × 100 mm. 4500m. *Tisiphone abeone*; 4500m. *Pseudacraea boisduvali*; 4500m. *Mylothris chloris*; 4500m. *Papilio glaucus*; 4500m. *Mimacraea marshalli*; 4500m. *Gonepteryx Cleopatra* . . . . 1·20 1·30

MS1536 95 × 100 mm. 4500m. *Palla ussheri*; 4500m. *Hypolimnas salmacis*; 4500m. *Pereute leucodrosime*; 4500m. *Anteos clorinde*; 4500m. *Colias eurytheme*; 4500m. *Hebomoia glaucippe* . . 1·20 1·30

MS1537 95 × 100 mm. 4500m. *Thauria aliris*; 4500m. *Catocala ilia*; 4500m. *Colotis danae*; 4500m. *Agrias Claudia*; 4500m. *Euploe core*; 4500m. *Scoptes alphaeus* (all horiz) . . . . 1·20 1·30

MS1538 95 × 100 mm. 4500m. *Phoebis philea*; 4500m. *Anteos clorinde*; 4500m. *Arhopala amantes*; 4500m. *Mesene phareus*; 4500m. *Euploea mulciber*; 4500m. *Heliconius ricini* (all horiz) . . 1·20 1·30

MS1539 141 × 112 mm. 4500m. *Euphaedra neophorn*; 4500m. *Catopsilia florella*; 4500m. *Charaxes bohemani*; 4500m. *Junonia orithya*; 4500m. *Colotis danae*; 4500m. *Eurytela dryope* 1·20 1·30

MS1540 141 × 112 mm. 4500m. *Papilio demodocus*; 4500m. *Kallimoides rumia*; 4500m. *Danaus chrysippus*; 4500m. *Palla ussheri*; 4500m. *Hypolimnas salmacis*; 4500m. *Zinina otis* . . . . . . 1·20 1·30

MS1541 Six sheets. (a) 85 × 110 mm. 20000m. *Papilio glaucus*. (b) 85 × 110 mm. 20000m. *Delias mysis* (horiz). (c) 85 × 110 mm. 20000m. *Mylothris cloris* (horiz). (d) 20000m. *Loxura atymnus* (horiz). (e) 70 × 100 mm. 20000m. *Hemiolaus coeculus* (horiz). (f) 73 × 103 mm. 20000m. *Euxanthe wakefieldii* (horiz). Set of 6 sheets 6·00 6·25

304 Male and Female Blue Wildebeest

2000. Endangered Species. Blue Wildebeest. Multicoloured.

1542 6500m. Type **304** 30 35

1543 6500m. Female and calf . . 30 35

1544 6500m. Lion catching blue wildebeest 30 35

1545 6500m. Blue wildebeest . . 30 35

305 *Leptailerus several*

2000. Wild Cats of the World. T **305** and similar multicoloured designs.

MS1546 134 × 200 mm. 3000m. Type **305**; 3000m. *Panthera onca*; 3000m. *Panthera tigris corbetti*; 3000m. *Puma concolor*; 3000m. *Panthera leo persica*; 3000m. *Felis pardina*; 3000m. *Lepardus pardalia*; 3000m. *Acinonyx jubatus*; 3000m. *Felis wrangeli* . . . . 1·30 1·40

MS1547 134 × 200 mm. 3000m. *Felis silvestris grampia*; 3000m. *Felis ourata*; 3000m. *Panthera tigris tigris*; 3000m. *Panthera uncial*; 3000m. *Felis caracal*; 3000m. *Panthera pardus*; 3000m. *Panthera tigris amoyensis*; 3000m. *Panthera once*; 3000m. *Neofelis nabuluso* 1·30 1·40

MS1548 Two sheets. (a) 25000m.85 × 110 mm. *Panthera tigris altaica*. (b) 110 × 85 mm. 25000m. *Panthera tigris* (horiz). Set of 2 sheets . . . . 2·50 2·60

306 *Laetiocottleya*

2000. Exotic Flowers. Multicoloured.

MS1549 137 × 105 mm. 3000m. Type **306**; 3000m. *Papaver orientale* and *Nomada* (wasp); 3000m. *Anemone blanda*; 3000m. *Ipoema alba* and hawkmoth; 3000m. *Phalaenopsis luma* and *Delta unguiculata* (wasp); 3000m. *Iris ensata* and Colorado beetle; 3000m. *Bomarea caldasil* and *Coenagrion puella* (dragonfly); 3000m. Rosa "Raubritter" and *Bombus hortorum* (bumble bee); 3000m. *Iris x daylily hybrid* and fly 1·20 1·30

MS1550 137 × 105 mm. 3000m. *Lilium auratum* and *Tragocephala variegate* (beetle); 3000m. *Oncidim macianthum* and beetle; 3000m. *Dendrobium* and *Agelia petali* (beetle); 3000m. *Cobaea scandens*; 3000m. *Paphiopedium gilda* and *Cotalpa linegera scarabaedae*; 3000m. *Papaver nudicaule* and *Delta unduiculate* (wasp); 3000m. *Colocasia esculenta*; 3000m. *Carinatum tricolor* and butterfly; 3000m. *Phalaenopsis* and locust 1·20 1·30

MS1551 125 × 103 mm. 3500m. *Euanthe sanderiana* and *Teirataenia surinama* (grasshopper); 3500m. *Torenia fourleri*; 3500m. Pansies and *Papilio polyxenes* caterpillar; 3500m. *Gladiolus* "Preludio"; 3500m. *Dendrobium primulinum* and beetle; 3500m. *Clematis* "Lasurstern" and carrion beetle; 3500m. *Helianthus annuus* and beetle; 3500m. *Jacinto Grana* (all vert) . . . . 1·60 1·70

MS1552 Four sheets, each 100 × 70 mm. (a) 20000m. *Viola × wittrockiana* (pansies). (b) 20000m. *Nelimbo nucifera*. (c) 20000m. *Gerbera jamesoni*. (d) 20000m. Daffodils and anemones. Set of 4 sheets . . . . 4·00 4·25

311 Cycling

2000. Sports and Chess. T **311** and similar horiz designs. Multicoloured.

MS1562 140 × 115 mm. 6500m. Type **311**; 6500m. Volleyball; 6500m. Boxing; 6500m. Weightlifting; 6500m. Fencing; 6500m. Judo . . . . 1·80 1·90

MS1563 140 × 115 mm. 9000m. Six chess pieces, including red queen and elephant carrying palanquin; 9000m. Six pieces, including ivory bishop and grey bishop; 9000m. Five knights; 9000m. Six rooks, including red elephant and sailing ship; 9000m. Six pawns; 9000m. Six pawns, including soldiers, flute player and spearholder . . . . 2·75 2·75

MS1564 140 × 115 mm. 9500m. Paul Morphy; 9500m. Mikhail Botvinnik; 9500m. Emanuel Lasker; 9500m. Wilhelm Steinitz; 9500m. Jose Raul Capablanca; 9500m. Howard Staunton . . . 2·75 2·75

MS1565 140 × 115 mm. 12500m. Cricket (batsmen and bowler); 12500m. Cricket (four batsmen and fielder); 12500m. Polo players on horseback and elephant polo; 12500m. Four galloping polo players; 12500m. Golf (two men); 12500m. Man and woman playing golf . . . . 3·50 3·75

MS1566 140 × 115 mm. 14000m. Two tennis players (woman with headband serving at right); 14000m. Table tennis (two men); 14000m. Table tennis (man with pink shirt and woman); 14000m. Three tennis players (two men at left); 14000m. Tennis players (man with cap at left); 14000m. Table tennis (man with red shirt and woman) . . . . 3·60 3·75

MS1567 Two sheets, each 110 × 87 mm. (a) 35000m. Garry Kasparov (chess champion) (50 × 35 mm). (b) 35000m. Table tennis (50 × 35 mm). Set of 2 sheets 3·75 4·00

312 Threadfin Butterflyfish

2001. Marine Life. T **312** and similar horiz designs. Multicoloured.

MS1568 162 × 177 mm. 4550m. Type **312**; 4550m. Common clownfish; 4550m. Regal tang; 4550m. Regal angelfish; 4550m. Copperbanded butterflyfish; 4550m. Blue-girdled angelfish; 4550m. Sharpnosed pufferfish; 4550m. Humbug damselfish; 4550m. Tailbar lionfish; 4550m. Forcepsfish; 4550m. Powder blue surgeonfish; 4550m. Moorish idol 2·00 2·10

MS1569 155 × 117 mm. 9500m. Oceanic whitetip shark; 9500m. Grey reef shark; 9500m. Tiger shark; 9500m. Silky shark; 9500m. Basking shark; 9500m. Epaulette shark . . . . 2·75 3·00

MS1570 117 × 131 mm. 9500m. Sperm whale; 9500m. Giant squid; 9500m. Killer whale; 9500m. Great hite shark; 9500m. Manta ray; 9500m. Octopus . . . . 2·75 3·00

MS1571 117 × 131 mm. 9500m. Blue whale; 9500m. Dolphinfish; 9500m. Hammerhead shark; 9500m. Whale shark; 9500m. Leatherback turtle; 9500m. Porkfish . . . . 2·75 3·00

MS1572 Five sheets, each 85 × 57 mm. (a) 35000m. Wimple fish. (b) 35000m. Queen angelfish. (c) 35000m. *Phryniehthys wedli*. (d) 35000m. Bull shark. (e) 35000m. Spotted trunkfish. Set of 5 sheets 9·00 9·25

313 Luis Figo

2001. European Football Championship, Belgium and The Netherlands (2000). T **313** and similar square designs. Multicoloured.

MS1573 131 × 99 mm. 10000m. Type **313**; 10000m. Fernando Couto; 10000m. Luis Figo diving at ball; 10000m. Sergio Conceicao; 10000m. Nuno Gomes; 10000m. Rui Costa . . . . 3·00 3·25

MS1574 131 × 99 mm. 17000m. Nicolas Anelka; 17000m. Didier Deschamps; 17000m. Emmanuel Petit; 17000m. Thierry Henry; 17000m. Marcel Desailly; 17000m. Zinedine Zidane . . . . 5·25 5·50

314 Domenico Fivaranti (swimming)

2001. Olympic Games, Sydney (2000). T **314** and similar square designs. Multicoloured.

MS1575 131 × 135 mm. 8500m. Type **314**; 8500m. Stacy Dragila (pole vault); 8500m. Pieter van den Hoogenband (swimming); 8500m. David O'Connor (three day eventing); 8500m. Venus Williams (tennis); 8500m. Maurice Greene (athletics); 8500m. Joy Fawcett (football); 8500m. Marion Jones (athletics); 8500m. Patricio Ormazabal and Jeff Agoos (football) . . . . 3·75 4·00

MS1576 131 × 135 mm. 10000m. Agnes Kovacs (swimming); 10000m. Youlia Rasksina (gymnastics); 10000m. Kong Linghui and Lui Guoliang (table tennis); 10000m. Nicolas Gill; 10000m. Anky van Grunsven (dressage); 10000m. Brian Olsen; 10000m. Wang Nan (table tennis); 10000m. Megan Quann (swimming); 10000m. Venus Williams (tennis) . . . . . . 6·25 6·50

MS1577 131 × 99 mm. 17000m. Vince Carter (basketball); 17000m. Blaine Wilson (gymnastics); 17000m. Steve Keir (handball); 17000m. Wen Xiao Wang and Chris Xu (table tennis); 17000m. Venus and Serena Williams (tennis); 17000m. Gu Jun and Ge Fei (table tennis) . . . . . . 5·25 5·50

MS1578 131 × 99 mm. 20000m. Clara Hughes (cycling); 20000m. Martina Hingis (tennis); 20000m. Otilla Badescu (table tennis); 20000m. Isabel Fernandez (judo); 20000m. Coralie Simmons (water polo). 20000m. Mia Hamm (football) . . . . 6·00 6·25

MS1579 131 × 99 mm. 28000m. Patrick Rafter (tennis); 28000m. Tadahiro Nomura (judo); 28000m. Seiko Iseki (table tennis); 28000m. Michael Dodge (cycling); 28000m. Ann Dow (water polo); 28000m. David Beckham (football) . . 8·25 8·50

MS1580 Six sheets, each 95 × 98 mm. (a) 50000m. Andre Agassi (tennis). (b) 50000m.Chang Jun Gao and Michelle Do (table tennis). (c) 50000m. Kong Linghui (table tennis). (d) 50000m. Michelle Do (table tennis); (e) 100000m. Michelle Do. (f) 100000m. Serena Williams (tennis). (g) 100000m. Christophe Legout and Damien Eldi (table tennis). Set of 6 sheets 12·00 12·50

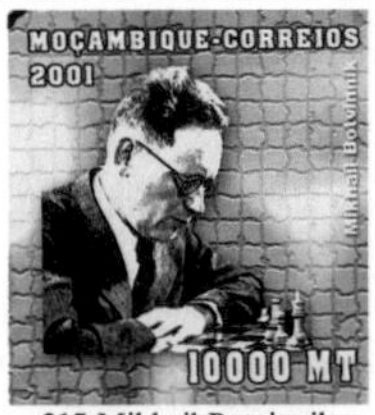

315 Mikhail Botvinnik

2001. Chess Players. Multicoloured.

MS1581 131 × 135 mm. 10000m. Type **315**; 10000m. Garry Kasparov; 10000m. Wilhelm Steinitz; 10000m. Emanuel Lasker; 10000m. Paul Morphy; 10000m. Anatoly Karpov; 10000m. Tigran Petrossian; 10000m. Mikhail Tal; 10000m. Jose Raul Capablanca 4·00 4·25

MS1582 131 × 135 mm. 10000m. Judith Polgar (wearing maroon jumper); 10000m. Xie Jun; 10000m. Zsuza Polgar; 10000m. Nana Ioseliani; 10000m. Alisa Galliamova; 10000m. Judith Polgar (with head in hands); 10000m. Judith Polgar (wearing blouse); 10000m. Monica Calzetta; 10000m. Anjelina Belakovskaia 4·00 4·25

MS1583 Two sheets, each 96 × 100 mm. (a) 100000m. Garry Kasparov. (b) 100000m. Judith Polgar. Set of 2 sheets . . . . 5·00 5·25

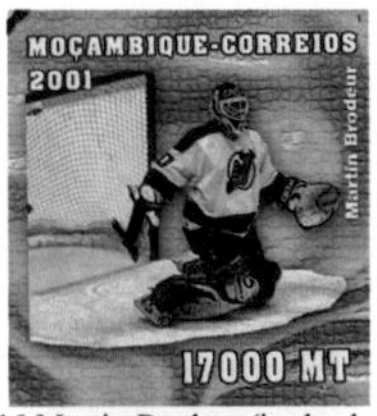

316 Martin Brodeur (ice hockey goalkeeper)

2001. Winter Olympic Games, Salt Lake City (2002) (1st issue). T **316** and similar square designs. Multicoloured.

MS1584 131 × 99 mm. 17000m. Type **316**; 17000m. Svetlana Vysokova (speed skating); 17000m. Ray Bourque and Patrik Elias (ice hockey); 17000m. Rachel Belliveau (cross-country skiing); 17000m. Scott Gomez and Janne Laukkanen (ice hockey); 17000m. Sonja Nef (skiing) . . . . . . 5·25 5·00

MS1585 131 × 99 mm. 20000m. Rusty Smith (speed skating); 20000m. Sandra Schmirler (curling); Totmianina and Marinin (ice skating); 20000m. Brigitte Obermoser (skiing); 20000m. Roman Turek (ice hockey); 20000m. Jennifer Heil (skiing) 5·00 5·25

MS1586 131 × 99 mm. 28000m. Kovarikova and Novotny (skating); 28000m. Li Song (speed skating); 28000m. Armin Zoeggeler (bobsleigh); 28000m. Michael von Gruenigen (skiing); 28000m. Tami Bradley (skiing); 28000m. Chris Drury, Turner Stevenson and Greg de Vries (ice hockey) . . . . 8·00 8·25

MS1587 Three sheets, each 95 × 98 mm. (a) 50000m. Armin Zoggeler (toboggan). (b) 75000m. Tommy Salo. (c) 100000m. Jayne Torvill and Christopher Dean (ice dancing) Set of 3 sheets . . . 10·00 10·50

See also 1588/9.

317 Skier

2002. Winter Olympic Games, Salt Lake City, U.S.A. (2nd issue). Multicoloured.

1588	10000m. Type **317**	50	55
1589	17000m. Skier upside down (vert)	85	90

318 Dhow

2002. Ships. Multicoloured.

MS1590 147 × 105 mm. 13500m. Type **318**; 13500m. Junk; 13500m. Galleon; 13500m. Schooner; 13500m. Full-rigged ship; 13500m. Barque . . . . 4·00 4·25

MS1591 147 × 105 mm. 13500m. Viking Longboat; 13500m. Canoe; 13500m. Gondola; 13500m. Fishing boat; 13500m. Light boat; 13500m. Tug . . . . 4·00 4·25

MS1592 Two sheets. (a) 79 × 60 mm. 40000m. Aircraft carrier; (b) 60 × 80 mm. 40000m. Figurehead (vert). Set of 2 sheets . . . . . 4·00 4·25

319 Princess Diana

2002. Diana, Princess of Wales Commemoration (3rd issue). T **319** and similar vert designs. Multicoloured.

MS1593 Three sheets each 132 × 135 mm. (a) 28000m. Type **319**; 28000m. Wearing feathered hat; 28000m. Wearing pearl necklace; 28000m. Wearing wide brimmed hat. (b) 28000m. Wearing blue top; 28000m. Wearing white top; 28000m. Looking right; 28000m. Holding bouquet. (c) 28000m. Wearing pink outfit; 28000m. Wearing black with drop earrings; 28000m. Looking straight ahead; 28000m. Wearing black and white outfit. Set of 3 sheets . . . . 12·00 12·50

MS1594 Three sheets each 81 × 112 mm. (a) 50000m. Wearing hat and wrap. (b) 50000m. With hand on chin; (c) 50000m. Wearing large stud earrings. Set of 3 sheets . . . . 7·50 8·00

320 Americo Vespucio

2002. 500th Anniv (2001) of Amerigo Vespucci's Third Voyage. T **320** and similar multicoloured designs.

MS1595 157 × 117 mm. 30000m. Type **320**; 30000m. Green parrot; 30000m. Homes on stilts and ship 4·50 4·75

MS1596 55 × 76 mm. 50000m. Outline of Brazil and ship's course 2·50 2·75

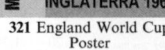

321 England World Cup Poster

322 Horse

2002. World Cup Football Championship, Japan and South Korea. T **321** and similar multicoloured designs.

MS1597 Two sheets each 153 × 175 mm. (a) 28000m. Type **321**; 28000m. Italian player; 28000m. Danish player (red strip); 28000m. Colombian player; 28000m. Munhak stadium (55 × 41 mm). (b) 28000m. Brazilian player; 28000m. Swedish poster; 28000m. Nigerian player; 28000m. Danish player (white strip); 28000m. Gwangju stadium (55 × 41 mm). Set of 2 sheets 12·00 12·50

MS1598 Two sheets. (a) 53 × 73 mm. 50000m. Pele (Brazilian player). (b) 73 × 53 mm. 50000m. Max Morlock (German player). Set of 2 sheets . . . . 5·00 5·25

2002. Chinese New Year ("Year of the Horse"). T **322** and similar multicoloured designs.

MS1599 68 × 58 mm. 11000m. Type **322**; 11000m. Purple and red horse; 11000m. Purple horse; 11000m. Orange and red horse 2·20 2·30

MS1600 100 × 70 mm. 11000m. Horse cantering (27 × 41 mm) 55 60

323 Mount Binga, Mozambique

2002. International Year of Mountains. T **323** and similar horiz designs. Multicoloured.

1601	17000m. Type **323**	85	90
1602	17000m. Mount Namuli, Mozambique	85	90

MS1603 160 × 98 mm. 17000m. Mount Kenya, Kenya; 17000m. Mount Cook, New Zealand; 17000m. Mount Ararat, Turkey; 17000m. Mount Paine, Chile; 17000m. Mount Everest, Nepal; 17000m. Mount Kilimanjaro, Tanzania . . . . 5·00 5·25

MS1604 72 × 51 mm. 50000m. Mount Zugspitze, Germany . . 2·50 3·00

324 *Papilio demoleus*

2002. Butterflies. Multicoloured.

1605	5000m. Type **324**	25	30
1606	10000m. *Euschemon rafflesia*	50	55
1607	17000m. *Liphyra brassolis*	85	90
1608	28000m. *Mimacraea marshalli*	1·40	1·50

MS1609 Two sheets each 112 × 155 mm. (a) 10000m. *Parides coon*; 10000m. *Delias mysis*; 10000m. *Troides brookiana*; 10000m. *Syrmatia dorilas*; 10000m. *Danis danis*; 10000m. *Lycaena dispar*; 10000m. *Mesene phareus*; 10000m. *Kallima inachus*; 10000m. *Morpho rhetenor*. (b) 10000m. *Eurema brigitta*; 10000m. *Loxura atymunus*; 10000m. *Arhopala amantes*; 10000m. *Junonia coenia*; 10000m. *Eurides isabella*; 10000m. *Heliconius ricini*; 10000m. *Zipaetis xcylax* (scylax); 10000m. *Cepheuptychia cephus*; 10000m. *Philaethria dido*. Set of 2 sheets . . . . 9·00 9·25

MS1610 Two sheets each 106 × 81 mm. (a) 50000m. *Papilio cresphontes*. (b) 50000m. *Ornithoptera alexandrae*. Set of 2 sheets . . . . 5·00 5·25

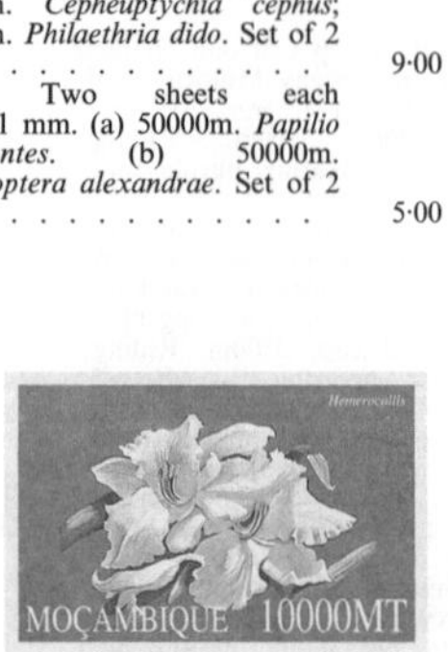

325 *Hemerocallis*

2002. Flowers. T **325** and similar multicoloured designs.

MS1611 Three sheets. (a) 150 × 117 mm. 10000m. Type **325**; 10000m. *Nazcissys* (Narcissus); 10000m. Hybrid tea; 10000m. Cayenne capers; 10000m. *Araceae*; 10000m. *Hymenocallis narcissiflora*; 10000m. *Hymenocallis*; 10000m. *Tulipa*; 10000m. *Lachenalia aloides* and *meconopsis poppies*. (b) 150 × 117 mm. 10000m. Narcissus; 10000m. L. *Bulbiferum var croceum*; 10000m. *Iris purpureobractea* and butterfly; 10000m. *Neomarica caerulea*; 10000m. *Peonia lactiflora*, *Primula chungensis* and *Viola cornuta*; 10000m. *Cayenne caper* and beetle; 10000m. *Iris purpureobractea*; 10000m. *Tuberous begonia cultivar*; 10000m. Oriental hybrid lily. (c) 108 × 160 mm. 10000m. *Viola jeannie*; 10000m. Sunflower; 10000m. *Momo botan*; 10000m. *Scho,buzgkia* orchid; 10000m. Dahlia hybrid; 10000m. *Sparaxis elegans harlequin*; 10000m. Dianthus; 10000m. *Tulipa saxatilis* and *camassia leichtlinii*; 10000m. Hybrid ("Hibrid"). Set of 3 sheets 13·00 13·50

326 *Tachymarptis melba*

2002. Birds. Multicoloured.

1612	5000m. Type **326**	25	30
1613	5000m. *Falco tinnunculus* . .	25	30
1614	10000m. *Ardea cinerea* . . .	50	55
1615	10000m. *Pitta angolensis* . .	50	55
1616	17000m. *Corythaeola cristata*	85	90
1617	28000m. *Butastur rufipennis*	1·40	1·50

MS1618 Two sheets each 116 × 116 mm. (a) 17000m. *Coracias garrulous*; 17000m. *Estrilda astrild*; 17000m. *Upupa epops*; 17000m. *Merops apiaster*; 17000m. *Ploceus Cucullatus*; 17000m. *Clamator glandarius*. (b) 17000m. *Psittacus erithacus*; 17000m. *Ficedula hypoleuca*; 17000m. *Tchagra senegala*; 17000m. *Oriolus oriolus*; 17000m. *Luscinia megarhynchos*; 17000m. *Halcyon malimbica* . Set of 12 sheets . . . . 10·00 10·50

MS1619 Four sheets. (a) 83 × 108 mm. 50000m. *Sitrix varia*. (b) 83 × 108 mm. 50000m. *Falco subbuteo*. (c) 83 × 108 mm. 50000m. *Butorides striatus*. (d) 108 × 83 mm 50000m. *Actophilornis Africana* (*africanus*) (horiz). Set of 4 sheets . . . . 10·00 10·50

The stamps in No. **MS**1618a/b were printed together, se-tenant, with the backgrounds forming composite designs.

327 *Creagrus furcatus*

2002. Sea Birds. Multicoloured.

1620	5000m. Type **327**	25	30
1621	10000m. *Larosterna inca* . .	50	55
1622	17000m. *Pelecanus crispus*	85	90
1623	28000m. *Morus bassanus* . .	1·20	1·50

MS1624 110 × 162 mm. 10000m. *Phaethon aethereus*; 10000m. *Catharacta Maccormicki*; 10000m. *Diomedea bulleri*; 10000m. *Puffinus iherminieri*; 10000m. *Oceanities oceanicus*; 10000m. *Pterodroma hasitata*; 10000m. *Fregata magnificens*; 10000m. *Sula nebouxii*; 10000m. *Uria aagle* 4·50 4·75

MS1625 Two sheets. (a) 98 × 68 mm. 50000m. *Spheniscus demersus*. (b) 97 × 68 mm. 50000m. *Rynchops niger* (horiz). Set of 2 sheets . . 5·00 5·25

The stamps in No. **MS**1624 were printed together, se-tenant, with the background forming a composite design.

328 Maine Coon Cat

2002. Cats. Multicoloured.

MS1626 118 × 91 mm. 17000m. Type **328**; 17000m. Cornish Rex; 17000m. La Perm (Red Tabby); 17000m. Sphynx; 17000m. Siamese; 17000m. Persian . . . 4·25 4·25

MS1627 66 × 96 mm. 50000m. Chestnut (Oriental Longhair) 2·50 2·75

2002. Dogs. As T **328**. Multicoloured.

MS1628 118 × 91 mm. 17000m. Labrador; 17000m. Bulldog; 17000m. Cocker spaniel; 17000m. Golden retriever; 17000m. Boxer; 17000m. Bloodhound . . . . 5·00 5·25

MS1629 66 × 96 mm. 40000m. Basset hound . . . . 2·00 2·10

2002. Horses. As T **328**. Multicoloured.

MS1630 118 × 91 mm. 17000m. Hanoverian; 17000m. Haflinger; 17000m. Nonius; 17000m. Belgian Heavy Draughts; 17000m. Australian-bred Arab; 17000m. Thoroughbred . . . . 5·00 5·25

MS1631 96 × 66 mm. 50000m. Two Don horses . . . . 2·50 2·75

329 Protosaurus

2002. Prehistoric Animals. Multicoloured.

1632	5000m. Type **329**	25	30
1633	10000m. Psittacosaurus . .	50	55
1634	17000m. Torosaurus	85	90
1635	28000m. Triceratops	1·40	1·50

MS1636 Two sheets each 180 × 135 mm. (a) 10000m. Diplodocus; 10000m. Pterosaurs; 10000m. Young diplodocus; 10000m. Afrovenator; 10000m. Parasarolophus; 10000m. Ramphorincus; 10000m. Lambeosaur; 10000m. Euoplocephalus; 10000m. Cynodont. (b) 10000m. Brachiosaur; 10000m. Monoclonius; 10000m. Homalocephale; 10000m. Pterodactyl; 10000m. Deinonychus; 10000m. Archaeopteryx; 10000m. Cretaceous landscape; 10000m. Hypsilophodon; 10000m. Lystrosaur. Set of 2 sheets . . 9·00 9·25

MS1637 Two sheets. (a) 100 × 68 mm. 50000m. Baryonyx. (b) 100 × 70 mm. 50000m. Styracosaurus (vert). Set of 2 sheets . . . . 5·00 5·25

The stamps in No. **MS**1636a/b were each printed together, se-tenant, plus labels, with the backgrounds forming composite designs.

330 *Heraclides cresphontes*

2002. Woodland Fauna and Flora. Multicoloured.

MS1638 Two sheets each 153 × 115 mm. (a) 10000m. Type **330**; 10000m. *Tyto alba*; 10000m. *Drocopus pileatus*; 10000m. *Archilochus colobris* (colubris) (Ruby-throated Hummingbird) and *Cypripedium parviflorum*; 10000m. *Vulpes vulpes*; 10000m. *Odocoileus virginianus*; 10000m. *Enallagma* sp.; 10000m. *Amanita muscaria*; 10000m. *Tamiasciurus hudsonicus*. (b) 10000m. *Pandion haliaetus*; 10000m. Flying squirrel; 10000m. Fox squirrel; 10000m. *Agelaius phoeniceus*; 10000m. *Papilio polyxenes*; 10000m. *Didelphus viginiana*; 10000m. *Hyla crucifer*; 10000m. Two *Odocoileus virginianus*; 10000m. *Procyon lotor* Set of 2 sheets . . . . 9·00 9·25

The stamps in No. **MS**1638a/b were each printed together, se-tenant, with the backgrounds forming composite designs.

331 Scout Badge

2002. World Scout Congress. T **331** and similar multicoloured designs.

MS1639 109 × 99 mm. 28000m. Type **331**; 28000m. 19th Jamboree badge; 28000m. Tiger mascot; 28000m. 20th Jamboree logo 5·50 5·75

MS1640 111 × 82 mm. 28000m. Scout (vert) . . . . 1·40 1·50

332 African Elephant

2002. Endangered Animals. African Elephant. Multicoloured.

1641	1900m. Type **332**	10	10
1642	1900m. Elephants at waterhole	10	10
1643	1900m. Elephant in swamp	10	10
1644	1900m. Elephant with calf	10	10

MS1645 145 × 170 mm. Nos. 1641/4 plus four stamp-sized labels, each picturing Prince Bernhard or elephants 40 45

333 Lord Baden Powell

2002. World Scout Jamboree (2003). T **333** and similar vert designs showing Lord Baden Powell and plants or butterflies. Multicoloured.

MS1646 Two sheets each 133 × 101 mm. (a) 17000m. Type **333**; 17000m. *Morpho Aega*; 17000m. *Prepona meander*; 17000m. *Charaxes bernardus*; 17000m. *Hypolimnas salmacis*; 17000m. *Morpho rhetenor*. (b) 17000m. Four mushrooms; 17000m. Two pink and white flowers; 17000m. Three orange mushrooms; 17000m. Five purple and red flowers; 17000m. Three brownish white mushrooms; 17000m. Two striped-petal flowers 10·00 10·50

MS1647 98 × 100 mm. 88000m. Lord Baden Powell with arms crossed 4·25 4·50

2002. Aviation. Sheet 96 × 100 mm containing vert designs as T **333**. Multicoloured.

MS1648 22000m. Antoine de Saint-Exupery; 22000m. Charles Lindberg and *Spirit of St. Louis*; 22000m. Charles Lindberg and light aircraft; 22000m. Concorde 2·30 2·40

2002. Cinematic Personalities. Sheet 97 × 101 mm containing vert designs as T **333**. Multicoloured.

MS1649 25000m. Charlie Chaplin; 25000m. Frank Sinatra; 25000m. Alfred Hitchcock; 25000m. Walt Disney . . . . 2·50 2·60

2002. John Audubon (ornithologist) Commemoration. Vert designs as T **333**. Multicoloured.

MS1650 97 × 101 mm. 33000m. John Audubon; 33000m. *Aix sponsa*; 33000m. *Toxostoma rufum* ("Toxastoma montanum") and *Ixoreus naevius*; 33000m. *Loxia Leucoptera* . . . . 3·25 3·50

MS1651 Two sheets each 97 × 101 mm. (a) 11000m. *Quiscalus quiscula*. (b) 11000m. *Columba leucocephala* ("Patagioenas leucocephala"). Set of 2 sheets 60 65

2002. 40th Death Anniv of Marilyn Monroe. Vert designs as T **333**.

MS1652 Two sheets each 133 × 101 mm. (a) 17000m. Looking at camera; 17000m.Wearing drop earrings; 17000m. Laughing; 17000m. Wearing choker; 17000m. Looking over shoulder; 17000m. Looking surprised. (b) 17000m. Wearing sleeveless top; 17000m. Looking over shoulder (different); 17000m. Beckoning with finger; 17000m. Wearing fur stole and drop earrings; 17000m. With arms folded; 17000m. Smiling with long hair. Set of 2 sheets . . . . . 10·00 10·50

MS1653 Two sheets each 97 × 100 mm. (a) 88000m. Wearing crochet top. (b) 88000m. Wearing red top with pearls. Set of 2 sheets 4·50 4·75

2002. Visits of Pope John Paul II. Vert designs as T **333**. Multicolored.

MS1654 133 × 100 mm. 15000m. Pope John Paul II waving; 15000m. Wearing red robe; 15000m. Carrying Pastoral staff; 15000m. Wearing mitre; 15000m. Sitting in chair; 15000m. Looking left . . . . 4·75 5·00

MS1655 97 × 100 mm. 20000m. Princess Diana wearing poppy; 20000m. Princess Diana carrying bouquet; 20000m. The Pope looking down; 20000m. The Pope looking up . . . . 4·00 4·25

MS1656 Two sheets each 97 × 100 mm. (a) 88000m. Pope John Paul II. (b) 110000m. Mother Teresa. Set of 2 sheets . . . . 5·00 5·25

2002. Egyptian Pharaohs. Vert designs as T **333**. Multicoloured.

MS1657 Two sheets each 133 × 100 mm. (a) 15000m. Seti I; 15000m. Djedefre; 15000m. Smenkhkare; 15000m. Seti II; 15000m. Senusret III; 15000m. Tutankhamun. (b) 17000m. Netjenkhet Djoser; 17000m. Death mask of Tutankhamun (front); 17000m. Neferefre; 17000m. Amenhotep III; 17000m. Pepi I; 17000m. Amenmesses. Set of 2 sheets . . . . 7·25 7·50

MS1658 Three sheets each 98 × 100 mm. (a) 20000m. Amenhotep II; 20000m. Merenptah; 20000m. Amenophis IV; 20000m. Tuthmosis (stone). (b) 20000m. Nefertiti (profile); 20000m. Cleopatra VII; 20000m. Nefertari (facing left); 20000m. Nefertiti (front). (c) 20000m. Nefertari (facing right); 20000m. Death mask of Tutankhamun (from angle); 20000m. Tuthmosis (black and gold); Nefertiti (from angle). Set of 3 sheets . . . . 11·00 11·50

MS1659 Two sheets each 97 × 101 mm. (a) 110000m. Nefertiti. (b) 110000m. Tutankhamun. Set of 3 sheets 10·00 10·50

2002. Nobel Prize Winners. Vert designs as T **333**. Multicoloured.
MS1660 Two sheets each 133 × 100 mm. (a) 15000m. Henri ("Hemri") Dunant; 15000m. Theodore Roosevelt; 15000m. Albert Einstein; 15000m. Ernest Hemingway; 15000m. Thomas Nast; 15000m. Albert Camus. (b) 17000m. Albert Einstein with hands clasped; 17000m. Dalai Lama; 17000m. Winston Churchill; 17000m. Hideki Yukawa; 17000m. Albert Schweitzer; 17000m. Linus Pauling 8·25 8·25
Although included in the set, Thomas Nast was not the recipient of a Nobel Prize.

2002. Robert Stephenson Commemoration. Vert designs as T **333**. Multicoloured.
MS1661 97 × 100 mm. 25000m. Robert Stephenson (black); 25000m. Early U.S steam locomotive; 25000m. Great Western Railway steam locomotive; 25000m. Early steam locomotive 5·00 55
MS1662 Two sheets each 97 × 101 mm. (a) 110000m. Robert Stephenson (sepia). (b) 110000m. Robert Stephenson (green). Set of 2 stamps 2·75 2·50

2002. Explorers. Vert designs as T **333**. Multicoloured.
MS1663 97 × 101 mm. 22000m. Vasco de Gama; 22000m. Ferdinand Magellan; 22000m. Christopher Columbus; 22000m. Amerigo Vespucci 1·10 1·20
MS1664 97 × 101 mm. 110000m. Vasco de Gama 5·50 5·75

2002. Charles Darwin and Alexander Fleming Commemorations. Sheet 97 × 100 mm containing vert designs as T **333**. Multicoloured.
MS1665 33000m. Charles Darwin and Byronosaurus; 33000m. Alexander Fleming and *Tricholoma terreum*; 33000m. Alexander Fleming and *Boletus edulis*; 33000m. Charles Darwin and Irratator 6·00 6·25

2002. Composers. Vert designs as T **333**. Multicoloured.
MS1666 97 × 101 mm. 5000m. Antonio Vivaldi; 5000m. Franz Liszt; 5000m. Ludwig van Beethoven; 5000m. Wolfgang Mozart 1·00 1·25
MS1667 97 × 101 mm. 88000m. Wolfgang Mozart at piano 2·20 2·30

2002. 25th Death Anniv of Elvis Presley (entertainer). Vert designs as T **333**. Multicoloured.
MS1668 133 × 101 mm. 15000m. Wearing jacket and tie; 15000m. Looking down in cable-knit sweater; 15000m. Wearing white shirt; 15000m. Wearing square checked shirt; 15000m. Reclining in cable-knit sweater; 15000m. Wearing hat 4·50 4·75
MS1669 97 × 100 mm. 110000m. Wearing blue jacket 5·50 5·75

2002. Personalities. Vert designs as T **333**. Multicoloured.
MS1670 Three sheets each 97 × 100 mm. (a) 20000m. Che Guevara; 20000m. Pope John Paul II; 20000m. Martin Luther King; 20000m. Mao Zedung. (b) 22000m. Dalai Lama; 22000m. Mother Teresa; 22000m. Pope John Paul II waving; 22000m. Mahatma Gandhi. (c) 33000m. Albert Schweitzer; 33000m. Claude Bernard; 33000m. Henri Dunant; 33000m. Raoul Follerau. Set of 3 sheets 10·00 10·50

2002. Formula 1 Motor Sport. Sheet 97 × 100 mm containing vert designs as T **333**. Multicoloured.
MS1671 20000m. Ayrton Senna; 20000m. Modern Formula 1 racing car; 20000m. Early Formula 1 racing car; 20000m. Juan Manuel Fangio 4·00 4·25

2002. Birth Centenary of Victor Hugo (author). Sheet 97 × 101 mm containing vert design as T **333**. Multicoloured.
MS1672 88000m. Victor Hugo 4·25 4·50

2002. John F. Kennedy (President. of U.S.A. 1961–3) Commemoration. Sheet 97 × 101 mm. Vert design as T **333**. Multicoloured.
MS1673 88000m. John F. Kennedy 4·25 4·50

2002. Political Leaders. Sheet 97 × 100 mm containing vert designs as T **333**. Multicoloured.
MS1674 25000m. Winston Churchill; 25000m. John F. Kennedy; 25000m. Konrad Adenauer; 25000m. Charles de Gaulle 5·00 5·25

2002. Haroun Tazieff (French vulcanologist and geologist) Commemoration. Sheet 97 × 100 mm containing vert designs as T **333**. Multicoloured.
MS1675 25000m. Scipionyx and erupting volcano; 25000m. Beipiaosaurus and erupting volcano; 25000m. Haroun Tazieff wearing radiation suit and vanadinite rock; 25000m. Haroun Tazieff and adamite rock 5·00 5·25

2002. Astronauts and Concorde. Vert designs as T **333**. Multicoloured.
MS1676 133 × 101 mm. 17000m. Michael Collins; 17000m. Concorde taking off to right; 17000m. John Glenn ("Genn"); 17000m. Concorde flying left; 17000m. Neil Armstrong; 17000m. Concorde taking off to left 4·75 5·00
MS1677 97 × 101 mm. 88000m. John Glenn 4·25 4·50

2002. 180th Birth Anniv of Louis Pasteur (French Chemist). Sheet 97 × 101mm containing vert designs as T **333**, each showing Louis Pasteur with a different breed of dog. Multicoloured.
MS1678 25000m. Husky; 25000m. Weimaraner; 25000m. Wolfhound; 25000m. Springer spaniel 5·00 5·25

2002. 5th Death Anniv of Diana, Princess of Wales. Vert designs as T **333**. Multicoloured.
MS1679 133 × 100 mm. 15000m. Diana and Pope John Paul II; 15000m. Wearing white halter-neck top; 15000m. Wearing red hat and spotted top; 15000m. Holding award; 15000m. Wearing deep purple dress; 15000m. Wearing blue dress and choker 4·75 5·00
MS1680 97 × 101 mm. 88000m. Wearing tiara 4·25 4·50

334 Ferdinand von Zeppelin

2002. Ferdinand von Zeppelin (inventor) Commemoration. Multicoloured.
MS1681 Two sheets each 173 × 120 mm. (a) 28000m. Type **334**; 28000m. LZ 2 airship (1905); 28000m. LZ 10 airship (1911); 28000m. LZ 1 airship (1900). (b) 28000m. LZ 1 airship over water; 28000m. LZ 2 airship over water; 28000m. LZ 10 airship over field of sheep; 28000m. Ferdinand von Zeppelin holding binoculars. Set of 2 sheets 10·00 10·50
MS1682 Two sheets. (a) 106 × 70 mm. 50000m. Ferdinand von Zeppelin wearing shirt and tie (vert). (b) 70 × 106 mm. 50000m. Ferdinand von Zeppelin wearing army uniform (vert). Set of 2 sheets 5·00 5·25

335 Mercedes (1906)

2002. Vintage Cars (1st series). Racing Cars. Multicoloured.
MS1683 Two sheets each 172 × 146 mm. (a) 13000m. Type **335**; 13000m. Morgan (1951); 13000m. Sunbeam (1912); 13000m. Sunbeam (1922); 13000m. Sunbeam Tiger (1925); 13000m. Austin 100 HP (1908). (b) 13000m. Bentley (1912); 13000m. Delage Grand Prix (1914); 13000m. Healey Silverstone (1949); 13000m. Duesenberg (1922); 13000m. Delage 1500cc Grand Prix; 13000m. Ferrari 375 F1 (1961). Set of 2 sheets 8·25 8·50
MS1684 Two sheets. (a) 100 × 70 mm. 40000m. Marmon Wasp (1911). (b) 70 × 100 mm. 40000m. Alfa Romeo (1931). Set of 2 sheets 8·00 8·25

336 Austin (1908)

2002. Vintage Cars (2nd series). Multicoloured.
MS1685 Two sheets each 165 × 102 mm. (a) 17000m. Type 336; 17000m. Studebaker Coupe (1937): 17000m. Type 40GP Bugatti (1930); 17000m. FordModel A Roadster (1931); 17000m. Alfa Romeo 2900B (1937); 17000m. Cord 812 (1937). (b) 17000m. Type 57 Bugatti Alalanta Coupe (1937); 17000m. Tucker Torpedo (1948); 17000m. Honda S 800M (1966); 17000m. Cisitalia 202 GT (1946): 17000m. Chevy Impala (1958); 17000m. Cadillac LaSalle Convertible (1934). Set of 2 sheets 10·00 10·50
MS1686 Two sheets each 92 × 60 mm. (a) 50000m. Mercedes Benz SSK (1928). (b) 50000m. Plymouth Fury (1957) Set of 2 sheets 4·75 5·00

337 Western Railway of France

2002. Trains. Multicoloured.
MS1687 Three sheets each 161 × 114 mm. (a) 17000m. Type **337**; 17000m. Netherlands State Railway (bridge); 17000m. Great Indian Peninsula Railway; 17000m. Paris Orleans Railway; 17000m. Madras and Southern Mahratta Railway of India; 17000m. Netherlands State Railway. (b) 17000m. Great Southern Railway of Spain; 17000m. Shantung Railway of China; 17000m. Shanghai—Nanking Railway of China; 17000m. Austrian State Railway; 17000m. Victorian Government Railways of Australia; 17000m. London and Northwestern Railways. (c) 17000m. London, Midland and Scottish Railway; 17000m. Great Northern Railway of Ireland; 17000m. Southern Railway of England; 17000m. Great Northern Railway of USA; 17000m. Chicago, Milwaukee, St. Paul and Pacific Railroad; 17000m. London and Northeastern Railway. Set of 3 sheets 12·00 12·50
MS1688 Two sheets each 98 × 67 mm. (a) 50000m. New York Central Lines (vert). (b) 50000m. London, Brighton and South Coast Railway (vert). Set of 2 sheets 4·75 5·00

CHARITY TAX STAMPS

The notes under this heading in Portugal also apply here.

C 15 Arms of Portugal and Mozambique and Allegorical Figures

C 16 Prow of Galley of Discoveries and Symbols of Declaration of War

1916. War Tax Fund. Imperf, roul or perf.

C234	C **15**	1c. green	95	50
C235	C **16**	5c. red	95	50

C 18 "Charity"

C 22 Society's Emblem

1920. 280th Anniv of Restoration of Portugal. Wounded Soldiers and Social Assistance Funds.

C309	C **18**	¼c. green	1·60	1·60
C310		½c. black	1·60	1·60
C311		1c. brown	1·60	1·60
C312		2c. brown	1·60	1·60
C313		3c. lilac	1·70	1·70
C314		4c. green	1·70	1·70
C315	–	5c. green	2·00	1·80
C316	–	6c. blue	2·00	1·80
C317	–	7½c. brown	2·00	1·80
C318	–	8c. yellow	2·00	1·80
C319	–	10c. lilac	2·00	1·80
C320	–	12c. pink	2·00	1·80
C321	–	18c. red	2·00	1·80
C322	–	24c. brown	2·75	2·10
C323	–	30c. green	2·75	2·10
C324	–	40c. red	2·75	2·10
C325	–	50c. yellow	2·75	2·10
C326	–	1e. blue	2·75	2·10

DESIGNS: 5c. to 12c. Wounded soldier and nurse; 18c. to 1e. Family scene.

1925. Marquis de Pombal stamps of Portugal, but inscr "MOCAMBIQUE".

C327	C **73**	15c. brown	40	25
C328	–	15c. brown	40	30
C329	C **75**	15c. brown	40	25

1925. Red Cross. Surch **50 CENTAVOS**.

C330	C **22**	50c. yellow and grey	95	80

1926. Surch **CORREIOS** and value.

C337	C **22**	5c. yellow and red	1·30	1·20
C338		10c. yellow and green	1·30	1·20
C339		20c. yellow and grey	1·50	1·40
C340		30c. yellow and blue	1·50	1·40
C331		40c. yellow and grey	2·10	1·50
C341		40c. yellow and violet	1·50	1·40
C332		50c. yellow and grey	2·10	1·50
C342		50c. yellow and red	1·80	1·60
C333		60c. yellow and grey	2·10	1·50
C343		60c. yellow and brown	1·80	1·60
C334		80c. yellow and grey	2·10	1·50
C344		80c. yellow and blue	1·80	1·60
C335		1e. yellow and grey	2·10	1·50
C345		1e. yellow and green	1·80	1·60
C336		2e. yellow and grey	2·20	2·10
C346		2e. yellow and brown	2·20	2·00

C 25

1928. Surch **CORREIOS** and value in black, as in Type **C 25**.

C347	C **25**	5c. yellow and green	2·50	2·40
C348		10c. yellow and blue	2·50	2·40
C349		20c. yellow and black	2·50	2·40
C350		30c. yellow and red	2·50	2·40
C351		40c. yellow and purple	2·50	2·40
C352		50c. yellow and red	2·50	2·40
C353		60c. yellow and brown	2·50	2·40
C354		80c. yellow and brown	2·50	2·40
C355		1e. yellow and grey	2·50	2·40
C356		2e. yellow and red	2·50	2·40

C 27

C 29 Pelican

C **28** "Charity"

1929. Value in black.

C357	C **27**	40c. purple and blue	2·75	2·50
C358		40c. violet and red	2·75	2·50
C359		40c. violet and green	2·75	2·50
C360		40c. red and brown	2·75	2·50
C361		(No value) red & green	2·75	2·50
C362		40c. blue and orange	4·25	4·00
C363		40c. blue and brown	2·75	2·50
C364		40c. purple and green	2·75	2·50
C365		40c. black and yellow	4·25	4·00
C366		40c. black and brown	4·25	4·00

1942.

C383	C **28**	50c. pink and black	8·75	2·30

1943. Inscr "Colonia de Mocambique". Value in black.

C390	C **29**	50c. red	9·75	1·30
C389		50c. blue	9·75	1·30
C386		50c. violet	9·75	1·30
C387		50c. brown	9·75	1·30
C393		50c. green	6·25	1·30

1952. Inscr "Provincia de Mocambique". Value in black.

C514	C **29**	30c. yellow	85	65
C515		50c. orange	85	65
C469		50c. green	90	65
C470		50c. brown	90	65

1957. No. C470 surch **$30**.

C511	C **29**	30c. on 50c. brown	65	35

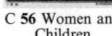

C **56** Women and Children

C **58** Telegraph Poles and Map

1963.

C569	C **56**	30c. black, green & red	35	25
C570		50c. black, bistre & red	35	25
C571		50c. black, pink & red	35	25
C572		50c. black, green & red	35	25
C573		50c. black, blue & red	35	25
C574		50c. black, buff & red	35	25
C575		50c. black, grey & red	35	25
C576		50c. black, yell & red	25	15
C577		1e. grey, black and red	1·10	45
C578		1e. black, buff and red	30	20
C578a		1e. black, mauve & red	30	20

1965. Mozambique Telecommunications Improvement.

C579	C **58**	30c. black, pink & vio	20	15
C580	–	50c. black, brown & blue	20	15
C581	–	1e. black, orange & green	25	20

DESIGN—19½ × 36 mm: 50c., 1e. Telegraph linesman.

A 2e.50 in Type C **58** was also issued for compulsory use on telegrams.

NEWSPAPER STAMPS

1893. "Embossed" key-type of Mozambique surch.

(a) **JORNAES 2½ 2½.**

N53	Q	2½r. on 40r. brown	42·00	23·00

(b) **JORNAES 2½ REIS.**

N54	Q	2½r. on 40r. brown	£170	£120
N57		5r. on 40r. brown	85·00	50·00

1893. "Newspaper" key-type inscribed "MOCAMBIQUE".

N58	V	2½r. brown	60	45

POSTAGE DUE STAMPS

1904. "Due" key-type inscr "MOCAMBIQUE".

D146	W	5r. green	25	25
D147		10r. grey	25	25
D148		20r. brown	35	35
D149		30r. orange	75	45
D150		50r. brown	75	45
D151		60r. brown	2·75	1·70
D152		100r. mauve	2·75	1·70
D153		130r. blue	1·70	1·30
D154		200r. red	2·30	1·30
D155		500r. violet	3·00	1·50

1911. "Due" key-type of Mozambique optd **REPUBLICA**.

D162	W	5r. green	25	20
D163		10r. grey	45	20
D164		20r. brown	45	20
D165		30r. orange	45	20
D166		50r. brown	50	30
D167		60r. brown	70	35
D168		100r. mauve	90	50
D169		130r. blue	1·00	70
D170		200r. red	1·30	1·10
D171		500r. lilac	1·80	1·30

1917. "Due" key-type of Mozambique, but currency changed.

D246	W	½c. green	35	30
D247		1c. grey	35	30
D248		2c. brown	35	30
D249		3c. orange	35	30
D250		5c. brown	35	30
D251		6c. brown	35	30
D252		10c. mauve	35	30
D253		13c. blue	70	55
D254		20c. red	70	55
D255		50c. lilac	70	55

1918. Charity Tax stamps optd **PORTEADO**.

D256	C **15**	1c. green	1·20	90
D257	C **16**	5c. red	1·20	90

1922. "Ceres" key-type of Lourenco Marques (½, 1½c.) and of Mozambique (1, 2½, 4c.) surch **PORTEADO** and value and bar.

D316	U	5c. on ½c. black	1·20	85
D318		6c. on 1c. green	1·20	85
D317		10c. on 1½c. brown	1·20	85
D319		20c. on 2½c. violet	1·20	85
D320		50c. on 4c. pink	1·20	85

1924. "Ceres" key-type of Mozambique surch **Porteado** and value.

D321	U	20c. on 30c. green	75	55
D323		50c. on 60c. blue	1·20	90

1925. Marquis de Pombal charity tax designs as Nos. C327/9, optd **MULTA**.

D327	C **73**	30c. brown	30	30
D328	–	30c. brown	30	30
D329	C **75**	30c. brown	30	30

1952. As Type D **70** of Macao, but inscr "MOCAMBIQUE".

D468		10c. multicoloured	15	15
D469		30c. multicoloured	15	15
D470		50c. multicoloured	20	15
D471		1e. multicoloured	25	20
D472		2e. multicoloured	25	20
D473		5e. multicoloured	65	40

MOZAMBIQUE COMPANY Pt. 9

The Mozambique Company was responsible from 1891 until 1942 for the administration of Manica and Sofala territory in Portuguese East Africa. Now part of Mozambique.

1899. 1000 reis = 1 milreis.
1913. 100 centavos = 1 escudo.

1892. "Embossed" key-type inscr "PROVINCIA DE MOCAMBIQUE" optd **COMPA. DE MOCAMBIQUE**.

10	Q	5r. black	70	40
2		10r. green	75	60
3		20r. red	95	60
4		25r. mauve	75	60
5		40r. brown	75	60
6		50r. blue	1·00	70
7		100r. brown	1·00	70
8		200r. violet	1·30	1·00
9		300r. orange	1·30	65

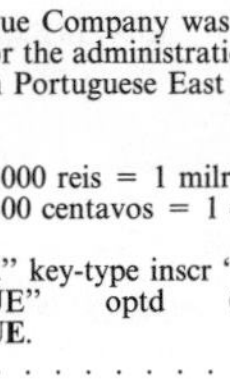

2

1895. Value in black or red (500, 1000r.).

33	**2**	2½r. yellow	30	25
114		2½r. grey	1·00	60
17		5r. orange	30	25
36		10r. mauve	45	30
115		10r. green	75	55
39		15r. brown	45	30
116		15r. green	1·00	60
20		20r. lilac	30	25
45		25r. green	45	30
117		25r. red	1·00	60
46		50r. blue	45	30
118		50r. brown	1·10	75
109		65r. blue	60	50
48		75r. red	45	30
119		75r. mauve	2·10	95
50		80r. green	45	30
52		100r. brown on buff	1·20	70
120		100r. blue on blue	2·10	1·50
110		115r. pink on pink	1·70	1·30
121		115r. brown on pink	2·75	1·90
111		130r. green on pink	1·70	1·30
122		130r. brown on yellow	3·00	1·90
54		150r. orange on pink	1·20	70
55		200r. blue on blue	95	90
123		200r. lilac on pink	3·00	2·00
56		300r. blue on brown	1·20	90
112		400r. black on blue	1·70	1·30
124		400r. blue on yellow	3·75	3·25
58		500r. black	1·20	90
125		500r. black on blue	3·75	3·25
126		700r. mauve on buff	3·75	3·50
59		1000r. mauve	1·30	90

1895. Surch **PROVISORIO 25**.

77	**2**	25 on 80r. green	21·00	24·00

1895. No. 6 optd **PROVISORIO**.

78	Q	50r. blue	4·25	3·50

1898. Vasco da Gama. Optd **1498 Centenario da India 1898**.

80	**2**	2½r. yellow	1·20	95
81		5r. orange	1·60	1·20
82		10r. mauve	1·60	1·20
84		15r. brown	3·00	1·90
86		20r. lilac	3·00	1·90
87		25r. green	3·00	1·90
99		50r. blue	2·10	1·70
89		75r. red	5·50	3·50
91		80r. green	3·75	2·75
101		100r. brown on buff	4·25	3·50
102		150r. orange on pink	4·25	3·50
94		200r. blue on blue	6·25	4·25
104		300r. blue on brown	7·50	5·25

1899. Surch **25 PROVISORIO**.

105	**2**	25 on 75r. red	3·25	2·75

1900. Surch **25 Reis** and bar.

106	**2**	25r. on 5r. orange	2·75	1·50

1900. Perforated through centre and surch **50 REIS**.

108	**2**	50r. on half of 20r. lilac	1·20	95

1911. Optd **REPUBLICA**.

145	**2**	2½r. grey	40	35
147		5r. orange	40	35
148		10r. green	40	35
150		15r. green	25	20
151		20r. lilac	40	35
153		25r. red	40	35
155		50r. brown	40	35
156		75r. mauve	40	35
157		100r. blue on blue	40	35
159		115r. brown on pink	75	55
160		130r. brown on yellow	75	55
161		200r. lilac on pink	75	55
162		400r. blue on yellow	75	55
163		500r. black on blue	75	55
164		700r. mauve on yellow	1·20	70

1916. Surch **REPUBLICA** and value in figures.

166	**2**	¼c. on 2½r. grey	25	20
168		½c. on 5r. orange	25	20
170		1c. on 10r. green	30	30
173		1½c. on 15r. green	30	30
175		2c. on 20r. lilac	30	30
178		2½c. on 25r. red	30	30
180		5c. on 50r. brown	30	30
181		7½c. on 75r. mauve	70	45
182		10c. on 100r. blue on blue	60	30
183		11½c. on 115r. brown on pink	1·40	65
184		13c. on 130r. brown on yell	1·40	65
185		20c. on 200r. lilac on pink	1·50	60
186		40c. on 400r. blue on yellow	1·50	60
187		50c. on 500r. black on blue	1·70	75
188		70c. on 700r. mauve on yell	1·70	90

1917. Red Cross Fund. Stamps of 1911 (optd **REPUBLICA**) optd with red cross and **31.7.17**.

189	**2**	2½r. grey	5·50	4·50
190		10r. green	5·50	4·50
191		20r. lilac	6·75	5·50
192		50r. brown	21·00	15·00
193		75r. mauve	48·00	44·00
194		100r. blue on blue	55·00	55·00
195		700r. mauve on yellow	75·00	75·00

1918. Stamps of 1911 (optd **REPUBLICA**) surch with new value.

196	**2**	¼c. on 700r. mauve on yellow	1·50	1·30
197		2½c. on 500r. black on blue	1·50	1·30
198		5c. on 400r. blue on yellow	1·50	1·30

14 Native Village

15 Ivory

1918.

199	**14**	¼c. green and brown	15	15
233		¼c. black and green	25	25
200	**15**	½c. black	15	15
201	–	1c. black and green	15	15
202	–	1½c. green and black	15	15
203	–	2c. black and red	15	15
235	–	2c. black and grey	25	25
204	–	2½c. black and lilac	15	15
236	–	3c. black and orange	35	30
205	–	4c. brown and green	15	15
237	–	4c. black and red	35	30
227	**14**	4½c. black and grey	20	15
206	–	5c. black and blue	25	15
207	–	6c. blue and purple	30	25
238	–	6c. black and mauve	40	30
228	–	7c. black and blue	75	25
208	–	7½c. green and orange	35	30
239	–	8c. black and lilac	75	60
210	–	10c. black and red	45	30
229	–	12c. black and brown	65	45
241	–	12c. black and green	65	45
242	–	15c. black and red	60	55
212	–	20c. black and green	20	15
213	–	30c. black and brown	40	30
244	–	30c. black and green	75	65
214	–	40c. black and green	30	20
246	–	40c. black and blue	1·00	75
215	–	50c. black and orange	40	30
247	–	50c. black and mauve	1·20	1·00
230	–	60c. brown and red	75	50
231	–	80c. brown and blue	1·75	80
248	–	80c. black and red	1·20	1·00
216	–	1e. black and green	70	50
249	–	1e. black and blue	1·20	1·00
232	–	2e. violet and red	2·25	80
250	–	2e. black and lilac	3·00	1·30

DESIGNS—HORIZ: 1, 3c. Maize field; 2c. Sugar factory; 5c., 2e. Beira; 20c. Law Court; 40c. Mangrove swamp. VERT: 1½c. India-rubber; 2½c. River Buzi; 4c. Tobacco bushes; 6c. Coffee bushes; 7, 15c. Steam train, Amatongas Forest; 7½c. Orange tree; 8, 12c. Cotton plants; 10, 80c. Sisal plantation; 30c. Coconut palm; 50, 60c. Cattle breeding; 1e. Mozambique Co's Arms.

1920. Pictorial issue surch in words.

217		½c. on 30c. (No. 213)	3·50	3·25
218		½c. on 1e. (No. 216)	3·50	3·25
219		1½c. on 2½c. (No. 204)	2·30	1·40
220		1½c. on 5c. (No. 206)	2·30	1·40
221		2c. on 2½c. (No. 204)	2·30	1·40
222		4c. on 20c. (No. 212)	2·75	2·20
223		4c. on 40c. (No. 214)	2·75	2·20
224		6c. on 8c. (No. 239)	3·75	2·20
225		6c. on 50c. (No. 215)	3·75	2·20

33

36 Tea

1925.

251	**33**	24c. black and blue	1·60	1·20
252	–	25c. blue and brown	1·60	1·20
253	**33**	85c. black and red	1·30	90
254	–	1e.40 black and blue	1·30	90
255	–	5e. blue and brown	2·00	75
256	**36**	10e. black and red	3·50	1·00
257	–	20e. black and green	4·25	1·50

DESIGNS—VERT: 25c., 1e.40, Beira; 5e. Tapping rubber. HORIZ: 20e. River Zambesi.

38 Ivory

1931.

258	**38**	45c. blue	2·50	1·40
259	–	70c. brown	1·30	90

DESIGN—VERT: 70c. Gold mining.

40 Zambesi Bridge

1935. Opening of River Zambesi Railway Bridge at Sena.

260	**40**	1e. black and blue	3·00	2·00

41 Armstrong-Whitworth Atalanta Airliner over Beira

1935. Inauguration of Blantyre–Beira–Salisbury Air Route.

261	**41**	5c. black and blue	75	50
262		10c. black and red	75	50
263		15c. black and red	75	50
264		20c. black and green	75	50
265		30c. black and green	75	50
266		40c. black and blue	1·00	65
267		45c. black and blue	1·00	65
268		50c. black and purple	1·00	65
269		60c. brown and red	1·70	1·00
270		80c. black and red	1·70	1·00

42 Armstrong-Whitworth Atalanta Airliner over Beira

1935. Air.

271	**42**	5c. black and blue	20	20
272		10c. black and red	20	20
273		15c. black and red	20	20

274		20c. black and green	20	20
275		30c. black and green	20	20
276		40c. black and green	20	20
277		45c. black and blue	20	20
278		50c. black and purple	20	20
279		60c. brown and red	20	20
280		80c. black and red	20	20
281		1e. black and blue	20	20
282		2e. black and lilac	50	45
283		5e. blue and brown	85	70
284		10e. black and red	1·10	85
285		20e. black and green	2·20	1·10

43 Coastal Dhow

46 Palms at Beira

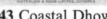

45 Crocodile

1937.

286	–	1c. lilac and green	20	20
287	–	5c. green and blue	20	20
288	43	10c. blue and red	20	20
289	–	15c. black and red	20	20
290	–	20c. blue and green	25	20
291	–	30c. blue and green	25	20
292	–	40c. black and blue	25	20
293	–	45c. brown and blue	25	20
294	45	50c. green and violet	25	20
295	–	60c. blue and red	25	20
296	–	70c. green and brown	25	20
297	–	80c. green and red	35	25
298	–	85c. black and red	35	30
299	–	1e. black and blue	35	30
300	46	1e.40 green and blue	75	30
301	–	2e. brown and lilac	1·20	35
302	–	5e. blue and brown	75	35
303	–	10e. black and red	1·20	60
304	–	20e. purple and green	1·90	1·10

DESIGNS—VERT: 21 × 29 mm—1c. Giraffe; 20c. Common zebra; 70c. Native woman. 23 × 31 mm—10e. Old Portuguese gate, Sena; 20e. Arms. HORIZ: 29 × 21 mm—5c. Native huts; 15c. S. Caetano fortress, Sofala; 60c. Leopard; 80c. Hippopotami. 37 × 22 mm—5e. Railway bridge over River Zambesi. TRIANGULAR: 30c. Python; 40c. White rhinoceros; 45c. Lion; 85c. Vasco da Gama's flagship "Sao Gabriel"; 1e. Native in dugout canoe; 2e. Greater kudu.

1939. President Carmona's Colonial Tour. Optd **28-VII-1939 Visita Presidencial**.

305	–	30c. (No. 291)	1·20	90
306	–	40c. (No. 292)	1·20	90
307	–	45c. (No. 293)	1·20	90
308	45	50c. green and violet	1·20	90
309	–	85c. (No. 298)	1·20	90
310	–	1e. (No. 299)	2·10	1·10
311	–	2e. (No. 301)	2·50	2·00

49 King Afonso Henriques

51 "Don John IV" after Alberto de Souza

1940. 800th Anniv of Portuguese Independence.

312	49	1e.75 light blue and blue	1·90	90

1940. Tercentenary of Restoration of Independence.

313	51	40c. black and blue	50	35
314		50c. green and violet	50	35
315		60c. blue and red	50	35
316		70c. green and brown	50	35
317		80c. green and red	50	35
318		1e. black and blue	50	35

CHARITY TAX STAMPS

The notes under this heading in Portugal also apply here.

1932. No. 236 surch **Assistencia Publica 2 Ctvos. 2.**

C260		2c. on 3c. black and orange	1·50	1·10

C 41 "Charity"

C 50

1934.

C261	C 41	2c. black and mauve	1·60	1·10

1940.

C313	C 50	2c. blue and black	8·00	5·25

C 52

1941.

C319	C 52	2c. red and black	8·00	5·25

NEWSPAPER STAMPS

1894. "Newspaper" key-type inscr "MOCAMBIQUE" optd **COMPA. DE MOCAMBIQUE.**

N15	V	2½r. brown	75	60

POSTAGE DUE STAMPS

D 9

D 32

1906.

D114	D 9	5r. green	50	40
D115		10r. grey	50	40
D116		20r. brown	50	40
D117		30r. orange	80	60
D118		50r. brown	80	60
D119		60r. brown	3·50	3·50
D120		100r. mauve	1·10	1·00
D121		130r. blue	7·00	3·75
D122		200r. red	1·80	1·30
D123		500r. lilac	3·00	2·40

1911. Optd **REPUBLICA**.

D166	D 9	5r. green	25	25
D167		10r. grey	30	30
D168		20r. brown	30	30
D169		30r. orange	30	30
D170		50r. brown	30	30
D171		60r. brown	60	45
D172		100r. mauve	60	45
D173		130r. blue	1·30	1·20
D174		200r. red	1·60	1·30
D175		500r. lilac	1·90	1·60

1916. Currency changed.

D189	D 9	½c. green	25	25
D190		1c. grey	25	25
D191		2c. brown	25	25
D192		3c. orange	25	25
D193		5c. brown	25	25
D194		6c. brown	40	40
D195		10c. mauve	70	70
D196		13c. blue	1·30	1·30
D197		20c. red	1·30	1·30
D198		50c. lilac	2·00	2·00

1919.

D217	D 32	½c. green	10	10
D218		1c. black	10	10
D219		2c. brown	10	10
D220		3c. orange	10	10
D221		5c. brown	15	10
D222		6c. brown	20	20
D223		10c. red	20	20
D224		13c. blue	25	25
D225		20c. red	25	20
D226		50c. grey	30	30

MUSCAT — Pt. 1

Independent Sultanate in Eastern Arabia with Indian and, subsequently, British postal administration.

12 pies = 1 anna; 16 annas = 1 rupee.

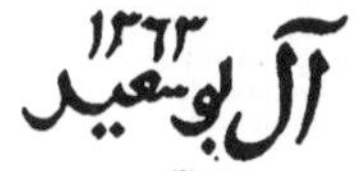

(2)

1944. Bicentenary of Al-Busaid Dynasty. Stamps of India (King George VI) optd as T **2**.

1	100a	3p. slate	30	6·50
2		½a. mauve	30	6·50
3		9p. green	30	6·50
4		1a. red	30	6·50
5	101	1½a. plum	30	6·50
6		2a. red	60	6·50
7		3a. violet	1·00	6·50
8		3½a. blue	1·00	6·50
9	102	4a. brown	1·00	6·50
10		6a. green	1·25	6·50
11		8a. violet	1·25	6·50
12		12a. red	1·25	6·50
13	–	14a. purple (No. 277)	4·00	10·00
14	93	1r. slate and brown	1·50	11·00
15		2r. purple and brown	3·00	17·00

OFFICIAL STAMPS

1944. Bicentenary of Al-Busaid Dynasty. Official stamps of India optd as T **2**.

O 1	O 20	3p. slate	50	12·00
O 2		½a. purple	50	12·00
O 3		9p. green	50	12·00
O 4		1a. red	50	12·00
O 5		1½a. violet	50	12·00
O 6		2a. orange	70	12·00
O 7		2½a. violet	4·00	12·00
O 8		4a. brown	2·00	12·00
O 9		8a. violet	4·00	14·00
O10	93	1r. slate and brown (No. O138)	2·50	22·00

For later issues see **BRITISH POSTAL AGENCIES IN EASTERN ARABIA**.

MUSCAT AND OMAN — Pt. 19

Independent Sultanate in Eastern Arabia. The title of the Sultanate was changed in 1971 to Oman.

1966. 64 baizas = 1 rupee.
1970. 1000 baizas = 1 rial saidi.

12 Sultan's Crest

14 Nakhal Fort

1966.

94	12	3b. purple	15	15
95		5b. brown	15	15
96		10b. brown	15	15
97	A	15b. black and violet	55	15
98		20b. black and blue	75	15
99		25b. black and orange	1·20	40
100	14	30b. mauve and blue	1·50	40
101	B	50b. green and brown	1·90	90
102	C	1r. blue and orange	3·75	90
103	D	2r. brown and green	7·00	2·75
104	E	5r. violet and red	15·00	9·25
105	F	10r. red and violet	31·00	19·00

DESIGNS—VERT: 21½ × 25½ mm: A, Crest and Muscat harbour. HORIZ (as Type **14**): B, Samail Fort; C, Sohar Fort; D, Nizwa Fort; E, Matrah Fort; F, Mirani Fort.

15 Mina el Fahal

1969. 1st Oil Shipment (July 1967). Multicoloured.

106		20b. Type **15**	2·30	55
107		25b. Storage tanks	3·00	75
108		40b. Desert oil-rig	4·50	1·20
109		1r. Aerial view from "Gemini 4"	11·50	2·50

1970. Designs as issue of 1966, but inscribed in new currency.

110	12	5b. purple	45	10
111		10b. brown	75	15
112		20b. brown	90	15
113	A	25b. black and violet	1·70	25
114		30b. black and blue	1·80	40
115		40b. black and orange	2·30	45
116	14	50b. mauve and blue	3·50	55
117	B	75b. green and brown	4·50	1·20
118	C	100b. blue and orange	5·75	1·20
119	D	¼r. brown and green	11·00	3·50
120	E	½r. violet and red	15·00	6·75
121	F	1r. red and violet	27·00	14·00

For later issues see **OMAN**.

MYANMAR — Pt. 21

Formerly known as Burma.

100 pyas = 1 kyat.

81 Fountain, National Assembly Park (½-size illustration)

1990. State Law and Order Restoration Council.

312	81	1k. multicoloured	1·10	70

1990. As Nos. 258/61 of Burma but inscr "UNION OF MYANMAR".

313		15p. deep green and green	15	15
314		20p. black, brown and blue	00	00
315		50p. violet and brown	50	25
316		1k. violet, mauve and black	1·00	70

82 Map and Emblem

83 Nawata Ruby

1990. 40th Anniv of United Nations Development Programme.

322	82	2k. blue, yellow and black	2·20	1·40

1991. Gem Emporium.

323	83	50p. multicoloured	1·00	70

84 "Grandfather giving Sword to Grandson" (statuette, Nan Win)

85 Emblem

1992. 44th Anniv of Independence. Multicoloured.

324		50p. Warrior defending personification of Myanmar and map (poster, Khin Thein)	50	45
325		2k. Type **84**	2·30	1·70

1992. National Sports Festival.

326	85	50p. multicoloured	60	45

86 Campaign Emblem

87 Fish, Water Droplet and Leaf

1992. Anti-AIDS Campaign.

327	86	50p. red	50	45

1992. International Nutrition Conference, Rome.

328	87	50p. multicoloured	35	15
329		1k. multicoloured	60	45
330		3k. multicoloured	1·70	1·30
331		5k. multicoloured	3·00	2·20

88 Statue

89 Hintha (legendary bird)

1993. National Convention for Drafting of New Constitution.

332	88	50p. multicoloured	25	15
333		3k. multicoloured	1·70	1·30

1993. Statuettes. Multicoloured.

334		5k. Type **89**	2·75	2·30
335		10k. Lawkanat	5·75	4·75

90 Horseman aiming Spear at Target

1993. Festival of Traditional Equestrian Sports, Sittwe.
336 **90** 3k. multicoloured . . . . 1·70 1·30

91 Tree, Globe and Figures

92 Association Emblem

1994. World Environment Day.
337 **91** 4k. multicoloured . . . . 2·30 1·70

1994. 1st Anniv of Union Solidarity and Development Association.
338 **92** 3k. multicoloured . . . . 1·50 1·10

93 City and Emblem

1995. 50th Anniv of Armed Forces Day.
339 **93** 50p. multicoloured 45 45

94 Cross through Poppy Head

95 Camera and Film

1995. International Day against Drug Abuse.
340 **94** 2k. multicoloured . . . . 1·60 1·20

1995. 60th Anniv of Myanmar Film Industry.
341 **95** 50p. multicoloured 45 45

96 Figures around Emblem

97 Convocation Hall

1995. 50th Anniv of United Nations Organization.
342 **96** 4k. multicoloured . . . . 3·00 3·00

1995. 60th Anniv of Yangon University.
343 **97** 50p. multicoloured 45 45
344 2k. multicoloured . . . . 1·50 1·50

98 Punt

1996. Visit Myanmar Year. Multicoloured.
345 50p. Type **98** 35 35
346 4k. Karaweik Hall . . . . . 2·75 2·75
347 5k. Mandalay Palace . . . . 3·50 3·50

99 Four-man Canoe

1996. International Letter Writing Week. "Unity equals Success". Multicoloured.
348 2k. Type **99** . . . . 1·40 1·40
349 5k. Human pyramid holding flag aloft (vert) . . . . . 3·50 3·50

100 Breastfeeding

101 Emblem and Map of Myanmar

1996. 50th Anniv of UNICEF. Multicoloured.
350 1k. Type **100** 70 70
351 2k. Nurse inoculating child 1·40 1·40
352 4k. Children outside school 2·75 2·75

1997. 30th Anniv of Association of South-East Asian Nations.
353 **101** 1k. multicoloured 85 85
354 2k. multicoloured . . . . 1·70 1·70

102 Throne

103 Xylophone

1998. 50th Anniv of Independence.
355 **102** 2k. multicoloured . . . . 1·60 1·60

1998. Musical Instruments. Multicoloured.
356 5k. Type **103** . . . . 4·00 4·00
357 10k. Mon brass gongs . . . 7·75 7·75
358 20k. Rakhine auspicious drum . . . . 13·00 13·00
359 30k. Myanmar harp . . . . 19·00 19·00
360 50k. Shan pot drum . . . . 31·00 31·00
361 100k. Kachin brass gong . . 44·00 44·00

104 Emblem

105 Dove and U.P.U. Emblem

1999. Asian and Pacific Decade of Disabled Persons. Seventh Far East and South Pacific Region Disabled Games.
365 **104** 2k. multicoloured . . . . 1·70 1·70
366 5k. multicoloured . . . . 3·50 3·50

1999. 125th Anniv of Universal Postal Union.
367 **105** 2k. multicoloured . . . . 1·50 1·50
368 5k. multicoloured . . . . 3·25 3·25

106 People linking Hands around Map of Myanmar

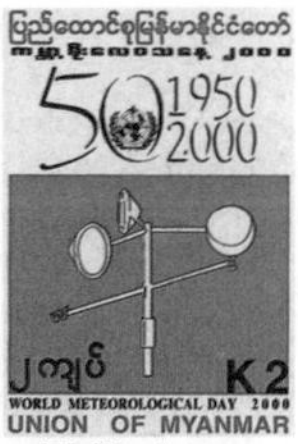

107 Weathervane

2000. 52nd Anniv of Independence.
369 **106** 2k. multicoloured . . . . 1·50 1·50

2000. World Meteorological Day. 50th Anniv of World Meteorological Organization.
370 **107** 2k. black and blue . . . 1·70 1·70
371 – 5k. multicoloured . . . . 4·00 4·00
372 – 10k. multicoloured . . . 7·50 7·50
DESIGNS—HORIZ: 5k. Emblem and globe; 10k. Emblem and symbols for rain and sunshine.

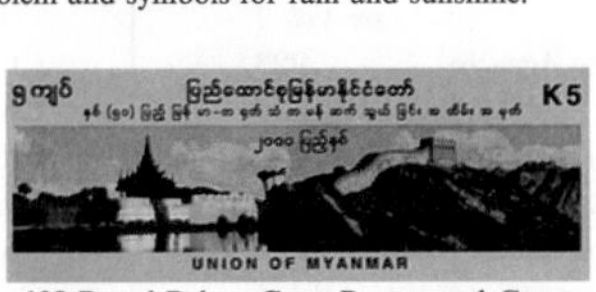

108 Royal Palace Gate, Burma and Great Wall of China (½-size illustration)

2000. 50th Anniv of Burma–China Relations.
373 **108** 5k. multicoloured . . . . 4·00 4·00

109 Burning Poppy Heads and Needles

2000. Anti-drugs Campaign.
374 **109** 2k. multicoloured . . . . 1·50 1·50

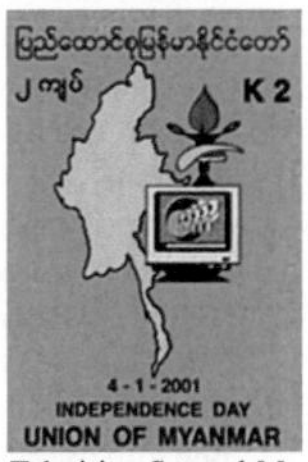

110 Television Set and Map of Myanmar

2001. 53rd Anniv of Independence.
375 **110** 2k. multicoloured . . . . 1·50 1·50

111 National Flag and Globe

2002. 54th Anniv of Independence. Multicoloured.
376 2k. Type **111** 50 50
377 30k. As No. 376 but inscriptions and face value in English . . . . 8·25 8·25

112 Flag and Statue

2003. 55th Anniv of Independence. Multicoloured.
378 2k. Type **112** 50 50
379 30k. As No. 378 but inscriptions and face value in English . . . . 8·25 8·25

113 Black Orchid

2004. Flora. Multicoloured.
380 30k. Type **113** . . . . 5·25 5·25
381 30k. Mango . . . . 5·25 5·25

INDEX

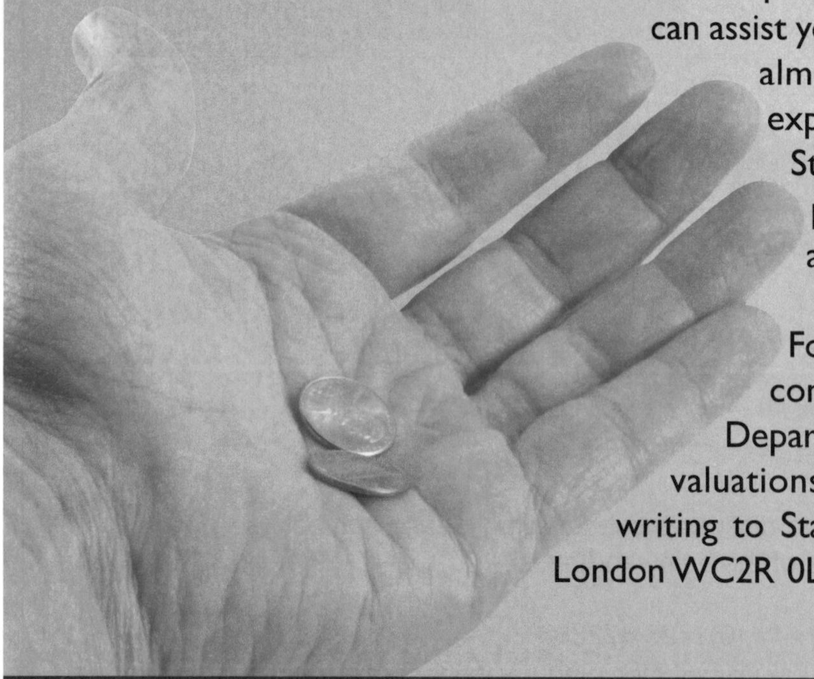

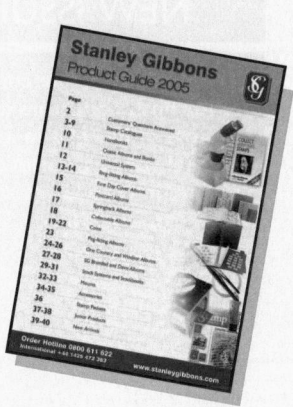

COLLECT

STAMPS OF THE WORLD

Priority order form
Four easy ways to order

Phone:
020 7836 8444
Overseas: +44 (0)20 7836 8444

Fax:
020 7557 4499
Overseas: +44 (0)20 7557 4499

Email:
stampsales@stanleygibbons.com

Post:
Stamp Mail Order Department
Stanley Gibbons Ltd, 399 Strand
London, WC2R 0LX, England

Customer details

Account Number____________________

Name____________________

Address____________________

____________________ Postcode__________

Country____________________ Email __________

Tel no ____________________ Fax no __________

Payment details

Registered Postage & Packing £3.60

I enclose my cheque/postal order for £............ in full payment. Please make cheques/postal orders payable to Stanley Gibbons Ltd. Cheques must be in £ sterling and drawn on a UK bank

Please debit my credit card for £............. in full payment. I have completed the Credit Card section below.

Card Number

☐☐☐☐☐☐☐☐☐☐☐☐☐☐☐☐

Start Date (Switch & Amex) ☐☐☐☐

Expiry Date ☐☐☐☐

Issue No (switch) ☐☐

Signature____________________ Date ____________________

COLLECT

STAMPS OF THE WORLD

Condition (mint/UM/used)	Country	SG No.	Description	Price	Office use only

POSTAGE & PACKAGING	£3.60
GRAND TOTAL	£

Please complete payment, name and address details overleaf